BECKETT®

Football
Card Price Guide
Number 14

Edited by

DR. JAMES BECKETT & DAN HITT
with the Price Guide staff of
BECKETT FOOTBALL CARD MONTHLY

Beckett Publications • Dallas, Texas

BECKETT is a registered trademark of

BECKETT PUBLICATIONS
DALLAS, TEXAS

Manufactured in the United States of America
First Printing
ISBN 1-887432-29-9

Beckett Football Card Price Guide
Table of Contents

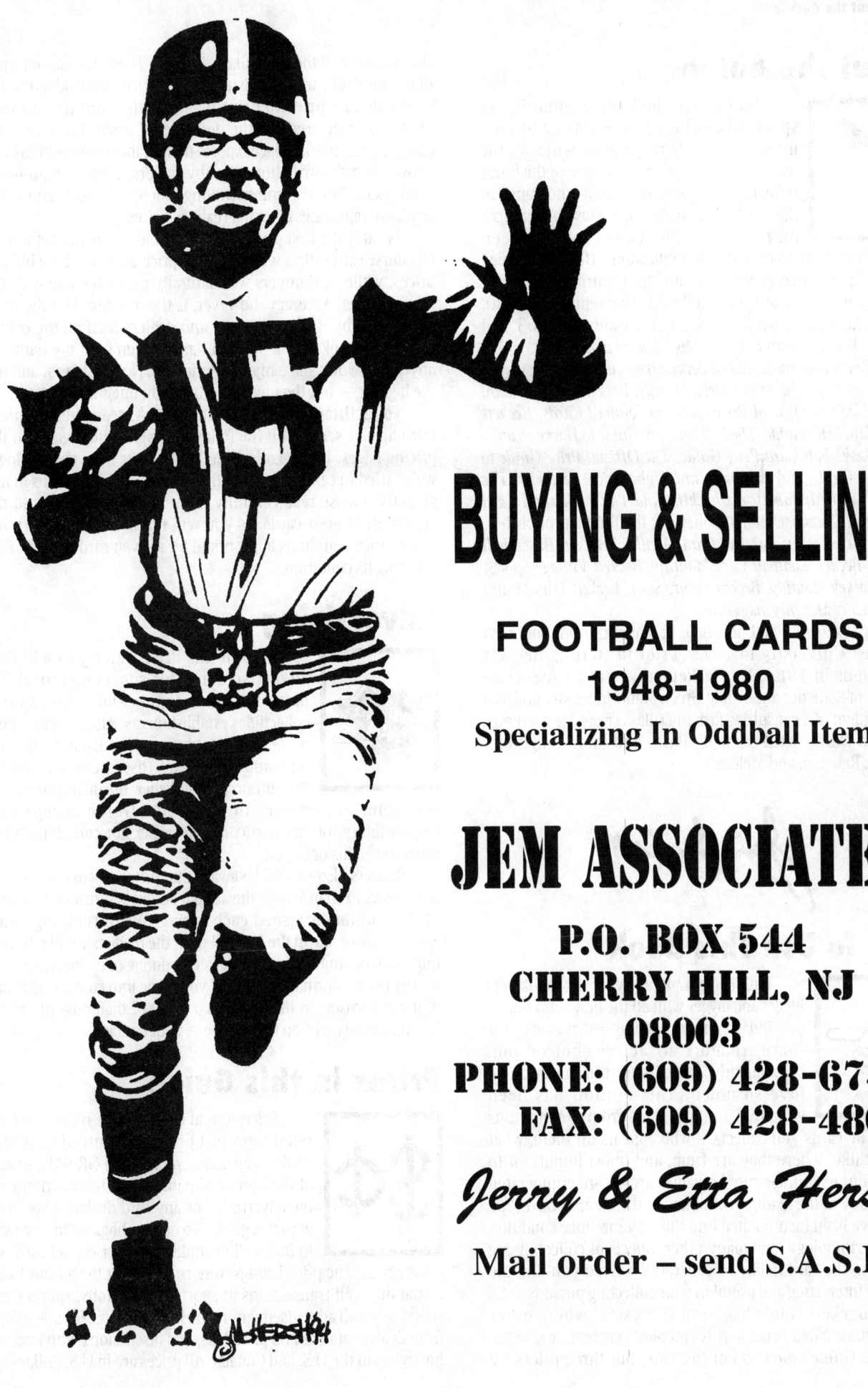

About the Author

Jim Beckett, the leading authority on sport card values in the United States, maintains a wide range of activities in the world of sports. He possesses one of the finest collections of sports cards and autographs in the world, has made numerous appearances on radio and television, and has been frequently cited in many national publications. He was awarded the first "Special Achievement Award" for Contributions to the Hobby by the National Sports Collectors Convention in 1980, the "Jock-Jaspersen Award" for Hobby Dedication in 1983, and the "Buck Barker, Spirit of the Hobby" Award in 1991.

Dr. Beckett is the author of *Beckett Baseball Card Price Guide, The Official Price Guide to Baseball Cards, Beckett Football Card Price Guide, The Official Price Guide to Football Cards, Beckett Hockey Card Price Guide, The Official Price Guide to Hockey Cards, Beckett Basketball Card Price Guide, The Official Price Guide to Basketball Cards,* and *Baseball Card Alphabetical Checklist The Football Card Alphabetical Checklist and The Basketball Card Alphabetical Checklist.* In addition, he is the founder, publisher, and editor of *Beckett Baseball Card Monthly, Beckett Basketball Monthly, Beckett Football Card Monthly, Beckett Vintage Sports, Beckett Hockey Monthly, Beckett Future Stars, Beckett Tribute,* and *Beckett Racing Monthly* magazines.

Jim Beckett received his Ph.D. in Statistics from Southern Methodist University in 1975. Prior to starting Beckett Publications in 1984, Dr. Beckett served as an Associate Professor of Statistics at Bowling Green State University and as a Vice President of a consulting firm in Dallas, Texas. He currently resides in Dallas with his wife, Patti, and their daughters, Christina, Rebecca, and Melissa.

Jim Beckett

How To Use This Book

Isn't it great? Every year this book gets bigger and bigger with all the new sets coming out. But even more exciting is that every year there are more attractive choices and, subsequently, more interest in the cards we love so much. This edition has been enhanced and expanded from the previous edition. The cards you collect — who appears on them, what they look like, where they are from, and (most important to most of you) what their current values are — are enumerated within. Many of the features contained in the other *Beckett Price Guides* have been incorporated into this volume since condition grading, terminology, and many other aspects of collecting are common to the card hobby in general. We hope you find the book both interesting and useful in your collecting pursuits.

The Beckett Guide has been successful where other attempts have failed because it is complete, current, and valid. This Price Guide contains not just one, but three prices by condition for all the football cards listed. These account for most of the football cards in existence. The prices were added to the card lists just prior to printing and reflect not the author's opinions or desires but the going retail prices for each card, based on the marketplace (sports memorabilia conventions and shows, sports card shops, hobby papers, current mail-order catalogs, on-line computer trading, auction results, and other firsthand reportings of actual realized prices).

What is the best price guide available on the market today? Of course card sellers will prefer the price guide with the highest prices, while card buyers will naturally prefer the one with the lowest prices. Accuracy, however, is the true test. Use the price guide used by more collectors and dealers than all the others combined. Look for the Beckett name. I won't put my name on anything I won't stake my reputation on. Not the lowest and not the highest — but the most accurate, with integrity.

To facilitate your use of this book, read the complete introductory section on the following pages before going to the pricing pages. Every collectible field has its own terminology; we've tried to capture most of these terms and definitions in our glossary. Please read carefully the section on grading and the condition of your cards, as you will not be able to determine which price column is appropriate for a given card without first knowing its condition.

Advertising

Within this Price Guide you will find advertisements for sports memorabilia material, mail order, and retail sports collectibles establishments. All advertisements were accepted in good faith based on the reputation of the advertiser; however, neither the author, the publisher, the distributors, nor the other advertisers in this Price Guide accept any responsibility for any particular advertiser not complying with the terms of his or her ad.

Readers also should be aware that prices in advertisements are subject to change over the annual period before a new edition of this volume is issued each spring. When replying to an advertisement late in the football year, the reader should take this into account, and contact the dealer by phone or in writing for up-to-date price information. Should you come into contact with any of the advertisers in this guide as a result of their advertisement herein, please mention this source as your contact.

Prices in this Guide

Prices found in this guide reflect current retail rates just prior to the printing of this book. They do not reflect the FOR SALE prices of the author, the publisher, the distributors, the advertisers, or any card dealers associated with this guide. No one is obligated in any way to buy, sell or trade his or her cards based on these prices. The price listings were compiled by the author from actual buy/sell transactions at sports conventions, sports card shops, buy/sell advertisements in the hobby papers, for sale prices from dealer catalogs and price lists, and discussions with leading hobbyists in the U.S. and Canada. All prices are in U.S. dollars.

Acknowledgments

A great deal of diligence, hard work, and dedicated effort went into this year's volume. The high standards to which we hold ourselves, however, could not have been met without the expert input and generous amount of time contributed by many people. Our sincere thanks are extended to each and every one of you.

A complete list of these invaluable contributors appears after the Price Guide section.

Introduction

Welcome to the exciting world of sports card collecting, one of America's most popular avocations. You have made a good choice in buying this book, since it will open up to you the entire panorama of this field in the simplest, most concise way.

The growth of *Beckett Baseball Card Monthly, Beckett Basketball Monthly, Beckett Football Card Monthly, Beckett Hockey Monthly, Beckett Future Stars* and *Beckett Racing Monthly* is an indication of the unprecedented popularity of sports cards. Founded in 1984 by Dr. James Beckett, the author of this Price Guide, *Beckett Baseball Card Monthly* contains the most extensive and accepted monthly Price Guide, collectible glossy superstar covers, colorful feature articles, "Hot List," Convention Calendar, tips for beginners, "Readers Write" letters to and responses from the editor, information on errors and varieties, autograph collecting tips and profiles of the sport's Hottest stars. Published every month, *BBCM* is the hobby's largest paid circulation periodical. The other five magazines were built on the success of *BBCM*.

So collecting sports cards — while still pursued as a hobby with youthful exuberance by kids in the neighborhood — has also taken on the trappings of an industry, with thousands of full- and part-time card dealers, as well as vendors of supplies, clubs and conventions. In fact, each year since 1980 thousands of hobbyists have assembled for a National Sports Collectors Convention, at which hundreds of dealers have displayed their wares, seminars have been conducted, autographs penned by sports notables, and millions of cards changed hands. The Beckett Guide is the best annual guide available to the exciting world of football cards. Read it and use it. May your enjoyment and your card collection increase in the coming months and years.

How to Collect

Each collection is personal and reflects the individuality of its owner. There are no set rules on how to collect cards. Since card collecting is a hobby or leisure pastime, what you collect, how much you collect, and how much time and money you spend collecting are entirely up to you. The funds you have available for collecting and your own personal taste should determine how you collect. The information and ideas presented here are intended to help you get the most enjoyment from this hobby.

It is impossible to collect every card ever produced. Therefore, beginners as well as intermediate and advanced collectors usually specialize in some way. One of the reasons this hobby is popular is that individual collectors can define and tailor their collecting methods to match their own tastes. To give you some ideas of the various approaches to collecting, we will list some of the more popular areas of specialization.

Many collectors select complete sets from particular years. For example, they may concentrate on assembling complete sets from all the years since their birth or since they became avid sports fans. They may try to collect a card for every player during that specified period of time. Many others wish to acquire only certain players. Usually such players are the superstars of the sport, but occasionally collectors will specialize in all the cards of players who attended a particular college or came from a certain town. Some collectors are only interested in the first cards or Rookie Cards of certain players.

Another fun way to collect cards is by team. Most fans have a favorite NFL or College team, and it is natural for that loyalty to be translated into a desire for cards of the players on that favorite team. For most of the recent years, team sets (all the cards from a given team for that year) are readily available at a reasonable price. The Beckett Football Card Alphabetical Checklist will open up this field to the collector.

Obtaining Cards

Several avenues are open to card collectors. Cards still can be purchased in the traditional way: by the pack at the local discount, grocery or convenience stores. But there are also thousands of card shops across the country that specialize in selling cards individually or by the pack, box, or set. Another alternative is the thousands of card shows held each month around the country, which feature anywhere from five to 800 tables of sports cards and memorabilia for sale.

For many years, it has been possible to purchase complete sets of cards through mail-order advertisers found in traditional sports media publications, such as *The Sporting News, Football Digest, Street & Smith* yearbooks, and others. These sets also are advertised in the card collecting periodicals. Many collectors will begin by subscribing to at least one of the hobby periodicals, all with good up-to-date information. In fact, subscription offers can be found in the advertising section of this book.

Most serious card collectors obtain old (and new) cards from one or more of several main sources: (1) trading or buying from other collectors or dealers; (2) responding to sale or auction ads in the hobby publications; (3) buying at a local hobby store; and/or (4) attending sports collectibles shows or conventions.

We advise that you try all four methods since each has its own distinct advantages: (1) trading is a great way to make new friends; (2) hobby periodicals help you keep up with what's going on in the hobby (including when and where the conventions are happening); (3) stores provide the opportunity to enjoy personalized service and consider a great diversity of material in a relaxed sports-oriented atmosphere; and (4) shows allow you to choose from multiple dealers and thousands of cards under one roof in a competitive situation.

Preserving Your Cards

Cards are fragile. They must be handled properly in order to retain their value. Careless handling can easily result in creased or bent cards. It is, however, not recommended that tweezers or tongs be used to pick up your cards since such utensils might mar or indent card surfaces and thus reduce those cards' conditions and values. In general, your cards should be handled directly as little as possible. This is sometimes easier to say than to do.

Although there are still many who use custom boxes, storage trays, or even shoe boxes, plastic sheets are the preferred method of many collectors for storing cards. A collection stored in plastic pages in a three-ring album allows you to view your collection at any time without the need to touch the card itself. Cards can also be kept in single holders (of various types and thickness) designed for the enjoyment of each card individually. For a large collection, some collectors may use a combination of the above methods. When purchasing plastic sheets for your cards, be sure that you find the pocket size that fits the cards snugly. Don't put your 1951 Bowman in a sheet designed to fit 1981 Topps.

Most hobby and collectibles shops and virtually all collectors' conventions will have these plastic pages available in quantity for the various sizes offered, or you can purchase them directly from the advertisers in this book. Also, remember that pocket size isn't the only factor to consider when looking for plastic sheets. Other factors such as safety, economy, appearance, availability, or personal preference also may indicate which types of sheets a collector may want to buy.

Damp, sunny and/or hot conditions — no, this is not a weather forecast — are three elements to avoid in extremes if you are interested in preserving your collection. Too much (or too little) humidity can cause gradual deterioration of a card. Direct, bright sun (or fluorescent light) over time will bleach out the color of a card. Extreme heat accelerates the decomposition of the card. On the other hand, many cards have lasted more than 50 years without much scientific intervention. So be cautious, even if the above factors typically present a problem only when present in the extreme. It never hurts to be prudent.

Collecting vs. Investing

Collecting individual players and collecting complete sets are both popular vehicles for investment and speculation. Most investors and speculators stock up on complete sets or on quantities of players they think have good investment potential.

There is obviously no guarantee in this book, or anywhere else for that matter, that cards will outperform the stock market or other investment alternatives in the future. After all, football cards do not pay quarterly dividends and cards cannot be sold at their "current values" as easily as stocks or bonds.

Nevertheless, investors have noticed a favorable long-term trend in the past performance of sports collectibles, and certain cards and sets have outperformed just about any other investment in some years. Many hobbyists maintain that the best investment is and always will be the building of a collection, which traditionally has held up better than outright speculation.

Some of the obvious questions are: Which cards? When to buy? When to sell? The best investment you can make is in your own education. The more you know about your collection and the hobby, the more informed the decisions you will be able to make. We're not selling investment tips. We're selling information about the current value of football cards. It's up to you to use that information to your best advantage.

Terminology

Each hobby has its own language to describe its area of interest. The terminology traditionally used for trading cards is derived from the American Card Catalog, published in 1960 by Nostalgia Press. That catalog, written by Jefferson Burdick (who is called the "Father of Card Collecting" for his pioneering work), uses letter and number designations for each separate set of cards. The letter used in the ACC designation refers to the generic type of card. While both sport and non-sport issues are classified in the ACC, we shall confine ourselves to the sport issues. The following list defines the letters and their meanings as used by the American Card Catalog, as applied to football cards:

(none) or N - 19th Century U.S. Tobacco
F - Food Inserts
H - Advertising
M - Periodicals
N - 19th Century U.S. Tobacco
PC - Postcards
R - Recent Candy and Gum Cards, 1930 to Present
UO - Gas and Oil Inserts
V - Canadian Candy
W - Exhibits, Strip Cards, Team Cards

Following the letter prefix and an optional hyphen are one-, two-, or three-digit numbers, R(-)999. These typically represent the company or entity issuing the cards. In several cases, the ACC number is extended by an additional hyphen and another one- or two-digit numerical suffix. For example, the 1957 Topps regular-series football card issue carries an ACC designation of R415-5. The "R" indicates a Candy or Gum card produced since 1930. The "415" is the ACC designation for the 1957 regular issue (Topps fifth football set).

Like other traditional methods of identification, this system provides order to the process of cataloging cards; however, most serious collectors learn the ACC designation of the popular sets by repetition and familiarity, rather than by attempting to "figure out" what they might or should be. From 1948 forward, collectors and dealers commonly refer to all sets by their year, maker, type of issue, and any other distinguishing characteristic. For example, such a characteristic could be an unusual issue or one of several regular issues put out by a specific maker in a single year. Regional issues are usually referred to by year, maker, and sometimes by title or theme of the set.

Glossary/Legend

Our glossary defines terms frequently used in the card collecting hobby. Many of these terms are also common to other types of sports memorabilia collecting. Some terms may have

several meanings depending on use and context.

ACC - Acronym for American Card Catalog.

ACETATE - A transparent plastic.

AFC - American Football Conference.

AFL - American Football League.

AS - All-Star.

ATG - All Time Great card.

AU(TO) - An autographed card.

BRICK - A group or "lot" or cards, usually 50 or more having common characteristics, that is intended to be bought, sold, or traded as a unit.

C - Center.

CB - Cornerback.

CFL - Canadian Football League.

CL - Checklist card. A card that lists in order the cards and players in the set or series. Older checklist cards in Mint condition that have not been checked off are very desirable and command large premiums.

CO - Coach card.

COLLECTOR ISSUE - A set produced for the sake of the card itself, with no product or service sponsor. It derives its name from the fact that most of these sets are produced for sale directly to the hobby market.

COMBINATION CARD - A single card depicting two or more players (not including team cards).

COMMON CARD - The typical card of any set; it has no premium value accruing from subject matter, numerical scarcity, popular demand, or anomaly.

CONVENTION - A large gathering of dealers and collectors at a single location for the purpose of buying, selling, and sometimes trading sports memorabilia items. Conventions are open to the public and sometimes also feature autograph guests, door prizes, films, contests, etc. More commonly called "shows."

COR - Corrected card. A version of an error card that was fixed by the manufacturer.

DB - Defensive back.

DIE-CUT - A card with its stock partially cut. In some cases, after removal or appropriate folding, the remaining part of the card can be made to stand up.

DISC - A circular-shaped card.

DISPLAY SHEET - A clear, plastic page that is punched for insertion into a binder (with standard three-ring spacing) containing pockets for displaying cards. Many different styles of sheets exist with pockets of varying sizes to hold the many differing card formats. The vast majority of current cards measure 2 1/2 by 3 1/2 inches and fit in nine-pocket sheets.

DP - Double Print. A card that was printed in approximately double the quantity compared to other cards in the same series, or draft pick card.

DT - Defensive tackle or Dream Team.

DUFEX - A method of card manufacturing technology patented by Pinnacle Brands, Inc. It involves a refractive quality to a card with a foil coating.

EMBOSSED - A raised surface; features of a card that are projected from a flat background.

ERR - Error card. A card with erroneous information, spelling, or depiction on either side of the card. Most errors are never corrected by the producing card company.

ETCHED - Impressions within the surface of a card.

EXHIBIT - The generic name given to thick stock, postcard-size cards with single-color, obverse pictures. The name is derived from the Exhibit Supply Co. of Chicago, the principal manufacturer of this type of card. These are also known as Arcade cards since they were found in many arcades.

FB - Fullback.

FDP - First (round) draft pick.

FG - Field goal.

FOIL - A special type of sticker with a metallic-looking surface.

FULL-BLEED - A borderless card; a card containing a photo that encompasses the entire card.

FULL SHEET - A complete sheet of cards that has not been cut into individual cards by the manufacturer. Also called an uncut sheet.

G - Guard.

GLOSS - A card with luster; a shiny finish as in a card with UV coating.

HIGH NUMBER - The cards in the last series of number, in a year in which such higher-numbered cards were printed or distributed in significantly lesser amount than the lower-numbered cards. The high-number designation refers to a scarcity of the high-numbered cards.

HL - Highlight card, for example from the 1978 Topps subset.

HOF - Hall of Fame, or Hall of Famer (also abbreviated HOFer).

HOLOGRAM - A three-dimensional photographic image.

HOR - Horizontal pose on a card as opposed to the standard vertical orientation found on most cards.

IA - In Action card. A special type of card depicting a player in an action photo, such as the 1982 Topps cards.

IL - Inside linebacker.

INSERT - A card of a different type, e.g., a poster, or any other sports collectible contained and sold in the same package along with a card or cards of a major set.

INTERACTIVE - A concept that involves collector participation.

K - Kicker.

KARAT - A unit of measure for the fineness of gold; i.e. 24K.

KP - Kid Picture card.

LAYERING - The separation or peeling of one or more layers of the card stock, usually at the corner of the card. Also see the Condition Guide.

LB - Linebacker.

LID - A circular-shaped card (possibly with tab) that forms the top of the container for the product being promoted.

LL - League leader card. A card depicting the leader or leaders in a specific statistical category from the previous season. Not to be confused with team leader (TL).

LOGO - NFLPA logo on card.

MAJOR SET - A set produced by a national manufacturer of cards, containing a large number of cards. Usually 100 or more different cards comprise a major set.

MEM - Memorial.

METALLIC - A glossy design that enhances card features.

MINI - A small card or stamp (specifically the 1969 Topps Four-in-One football inserts or the 1987 Topps mini football set issued for the United Kingdom).

MVP - Most Valuable Player.

NFLPA - National Football League Players Association.

NO LOGO - No NFLPA logo on card.

NO TR - No trade reference on card.

NPO - No position.

NT - Nose tackle.

OFF - Officials cards.

O-ROY - Offensive Rookie of the Year.

OT - Offensive tackle.

P - Punter.

P1 - First Printing.

P2 - Second Printing.

PACKS - A means with which cards are issued in terms of pack type (wax, cello, foil, rack, etc.) and channels of distribution (hobby, retail, etc.).

PANEL - An extended card that is composed of multiple individual cards.

PARALLEL - A card that is similar in design to its counterpart from a basic set, but offers a distinguishing quality.

PB - Pro Bowl.

PLATINUM - A metallic element used in the process of creating a glossy card.

POY - Player of the Year.

PREMIUM - A card, sometimes on photographic stock, that is purchased or obtained in conjunction with (or redeemed for) another card or product. This term applies mainly to older products, as newer cards distributed in this manner are generally lumped together as peripheral sets.

PREMIUM CARDS - A class of products introduced recently, intended to have higher quality card stock and photography than regular cards, but more limited production and higher cost. Defining what is and isn't a premium card is somewhat subjective.

PRISMATIC/PRISM - A glossy or bright design that refracts or disperses light.

PROMOTIONAL SET - A set, usually containing a small number of cards, issued by a national card producer and distributed in limited quantities or to a select group of people, such as major show attendees or dealers with wholesale accounts. Presumably, the purpose of a promo set is to stir up demand for an upcoming set. Also called a preview, prototype or test set.

QB - Quarterback.

RARE - A card or series of cards of very limited availability. Unfortunately, "rare" is a subjective term sometimes used indiscriminately. Using the strict definitions, rare cards are harder to obtain than scarce cards.

RB - Record Breaker card or running back.

RC - Rookie Card. A player's first appearance on a regular issue card from one of the major card companies. Each company has only one regular issue set per season, and that is the widely available traditional set. With a few exceptions, each player has only one RC in any given set. A Rookie Card cannot be an All-Star, Highlight, In Action, league leader, Super Action or team leader card. It can, however, be a coach card or draft pick card.

REDEMPTION - A program established by manufacturers that allows collectors to mail in a special card (usually a random insert) in return for special cards, sets or other prizes not available through conventional channels.

REFRACTORS - A card that features a design element which enhances (distorts) its color/appearance through deflecting light.

REGIONAL - A card issued and distributed only in a limited geographical area of the country. The producer may or may not be a major, national producer of trading cards. The key is whether the set was distributed nationally in any form or not.

REPLICA - An identical copy or reproduction.

RET - Retired.

REV NEG - Reversed or flopped photo side of the card. This is a major type of error card, but only some are corrected.

ROY - Rookie of the Year.

S - Safety.

SB - Super Bowl.

SCARCE - A card or series of cards of limited availability. This subjective term is sometimes used indiscriminately to promote or hype value. Using strict definitions, scarce cards are easier to obtain than rare cards.

SEMI-HIGH - A card from the next-to-last series of a sequentially issued set. It has more value than an average card and generally less value than a high number. A card is not called a semi-high unless its next-to-last series has an additional premium attached to it.

SERIES - The entire set of cards issued by a particular producer in a particular year, e.g., the 1978 Topps series. Also, within a particular set, series can refer to a group of (consecutively numbered) cards printed at the same time, e.g., the first series of the 1948 Leaf set (#1 through #49).

SET - One each of an entire run of cards of the same type, produced by a particular manufacturer during a single season. In other words, if you have a complete set of 1975 Topps football cards, then you have every card from #1 up to and including #528; i.e., all the different cards that were produced.

SHEEN - Brightness or luster emitted by a card.

SKIP-NUMBERED - A set that has many unissued card numbers between the lowest number in the set and the highest number in the set, e.g., the 1949 Leaf football set contains 49 cards skip-numbered from number 1-144. A major set in which a few numbers were not printed is not considered to be skip-numbered.

SP - Single or Short Print. A card which was printed in lesser quantity compared to the other cards in the same series (also see DP). This term only can be used in a relative sense and in reference to one particular set. For instance, the 1989 Pro Set Pete Rozelle SP is less common than the other cards in that set, but it isn't necessarily scarcer than regular cards of any other set.

SPECIAL CARD - A card that portrays something other than a single player or team; for example, the 1990 Fleer Joe Montana/Jerry Rice Super Bowl MVPs card #397.

SR - Super Rookie.

STAMP - Adhesive-backed papers depicting a player. The stamp may be individual or in a sheet of many stamps. Moisture must be applied to the adhesive in order for the stamp to be attached to another surface.

STAR CARD - A card that portrays a player of some repute, usually determined by his ability, but sometimes referring to sheer popularity.

STICKER - A card-like item with a removable layer that can be affixed to another surface. Example: 1983 Topps inserts.

STOCK - The cardboard or paper on which the card is printed.

SUPERIMPOSED - To be affixed on top of something, i.e., a

player photo over a solid background.

SUPERSTAR CARD - A card that portrays a superstar, e.g., a Hall of Fame member or a player whose current performance may eventually warrant serious Hall of Fame consideration.

TAB - A card portion set off from the rest of the card, usually with perforations, that may be removed without damaging the central character or event depicted by the card.

TC - Team card or team checklist card.

TEAM CARD - A card that depicts an entire team.

THREE-DIMENSIONAL (3D) - A visual image that provides an illusion of depth and perspective.

TL - Team leader card or Top Leader.

TOPICAL - a subset or group of cards that have a common theme, i.e., MVP award winners.

TR - Trade reference on card.

TRANSPARENT - Clear, see through.

TRIMMED - A card cut down from its original size. Trimmed cards are undesirable to most collectors, and are therefore less valuable than otherwise identical, untrimmed cards. Also see the Condition Guide.

UER - Uncorrected error card.

USFL - United States Football League.

UV - Ultraviolet, a glossy coating used in producing cards.

VAR - Variation card. One of two or more cards from the same series, with the same card number (or player with identical pose, if the series is unnumbered) differing from one another in some aspect, from the printing, stock or other feature of the card. This is often caused when the manufacturer of the cards notices an error in a particular card, corrects the error and then resumes the print run. In this case there will be two versions or variations of the same card. Sometimes one of the variations is relatively scarce. Variations also can result from accidental or deliberate design changes, information updates, photo substitutions, etc.

VERT - Vertical pose on a card.

WFL - World Football League.

WLAF - World League of American Football.

WR - Wide receiver.

XRC - Extended Rookie Card. A player's first appearance on a card, but issued in a set that was not distributed nationally nor in packs. In football sets, this term generally refers to the 1984 and 1985 Topps USFL sets.

Understanding Card Values

Determining Value

Why are some cards more valuable than others? Obviously, the economic laws of supply and demand are applicable to card collecting just as they are to any other field where a commodity is bought, sold or traded in a free, unregulated market.

Supply (the number of cards available on the market) is less than the total number of cards originally produced since attrition diminishes that original quantity. Each year a percentage of cards is typically thrown away, destroyed or otherwise lost to collectors. This percentage is much, much smaller today than it was in the past because more and more people have become increasingly aware of the value of their cards.

For those who collect only Mint condition cards, the supply of older cards can be quite small indeed. Until recently, collectors were not so conscious of the need to preserve the condition of their cards. For this reason, it is difficult to know exactly how many 1962 Topps are currently available, Mint or otherwise. It is generally accepted that there are fewer 1962 Topps available than 1972, 1982 or 1992 Topps cards. If demand were equal for each of these sets, the law of supply and demand would increase the price for the least available sets.

Demand, however, is never equal for all sets, so price correlations can be complicated. The demand for a card is influenced by many factors. These include: (1) the age of the card; (2) the number of cards printed; (3) the player(s) portrayed on the card; (4) the attractiveness and popularity of the set; and (5) the physical condition of the card.

In general, (1) the older the card, (2) the fewer the number of the cards printed, (3) the more famous, popular and talented the player, (4) the more attractive and popular the set, and (5) the better the condition of the card, the higher the value of the card will be. There are exceptions to all but one of these factors: the condition of the card. Given two cards similar in all respects except condition, the one in the best condition will always be valued higher.

While those guidelines help to establish the value of a card, the countless exceptions and peculiarities make any simple, direct mathematical formula to determine card values impossible.

Regional Variation

Since the market varies from region to region, card prices of local players may be higher. This is known as a regional premium. How significant the premium is — and if there is any premium at all — depends on the local popularity of the team and the player.

The largest regional premiums usually do not apply to superstars, who often are so well known nationwide that the prices of their key cards are too high for local dealers to realize a premium.

Lesser stars often command the strongest premiums. Their popularity is concentrated in their home region, creating local demand that greatly exceeds overall demand.

Regional premiums can apply to popular retired players and sometimes can be found in the areas where the players grew up or starred in college.

A regional discount is the converse of a regional premium. Regional discounts occur when a player has been so popular in his region for so long that local collectors and dealers have accumulated quantities of his cards. The abundant supply may make the cards available in that area at the lowest prices anywhere.

Set Prices

A somewhat paradoxical situation exists in the price of a complete set vs. the combined cost of the individual cards in the set. In nearly every case, the sum of the prices for the individual cards is higher than the cost for the complete set. This is prevalent especially in the cards of the past few years. The reasons for this apparent anomaly stem from the habits of collectors and

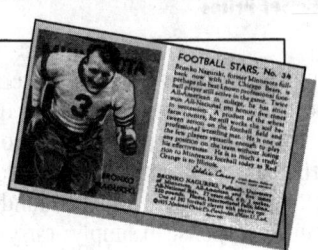

from the carrying costs to dealers. Today, each card in a set normally is produced in the same quantity as all others in its set.

Many collectors pick up only stars, superstars and particular teams. As a result, the dealer is left with a shortage of certain player cards and an abundance of others. He therefore incurs an expense in simply "carrying" these less desirable cards in stock. On the other hand, if he sells a complete set, he gets rid of large numbers of cards at one time. For this reason, he generally is willing to receive less money for a complete set. By doing this, he recovers all of his costs and also makes a profit.

Set prices do not include rare card varieties, unless specifically stated. Of course, the prices for sets do include one example of each type for the given set, but this is the least expensive variety.

Scarce Series

Scarce series occur because cards issued before 1973 were made available to the public each year in several series of finite numbers of cards, rather than all cards of the set being available for purchase at one time. At some point during the season, interest in current year cards waned. Consequently, the manufacturers produced smaller numbers of these later-series cards. Nearly all nationwide issues from post-World War II manufacturers (1948 to 1972) exhibit these series variations.

In the past, Topps, for example, may have issued series consisting of many different numbers of cards, including 55, 66, 80, 88, 110 and others. However, after 1968, the sheet size generally has been 132. Despite Topps' standardization of the sheet size, the company double-printed one sheet in 1983.

We are always looking for information or photographs of printing sheets of cards for research. Each year, we try to update the hobby's knowledge of distribution anomalies. Please let us know at the address in this book if you have first-hand knowledge that would be helpful in this pursuit.

Grading Your Cards

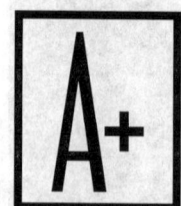

Each hobby has its own grading terminology — stamps, coins, comic books, record collecting, etc. Collectors of sports cards are no exception. The one invariable criterion for determining the value of a card is its condition: the better the condition of the card, the more valuable it is. Condition grading, however, is subjective. Individual card dealers and collectors differ in the strictness of their grading, but the stated condition of a card should be determined without regard to whether it is being bought or sold.

No allowance is made for age. A 1952 card is judged by the same standards as a 1992 card. But there are specific sets and cards that are condition sensitive because of their border color, consistently poor centering, etc. Such cards and sets sometimes command premiums above the listed percentages in Mint condition.

Centering

Current centering terminology uses numbers representing the percentage of border on either side of the main design. Obviously, centering is diminished in importance for borderless cards such as Stadium Club.

Slightly Off-Center (60/40): A slightly off-center card is one that upon close inspection is found to have one border bigger than the opposite border. This degree once was offensive to only purists, but now some hobbyists try to avoid cards that are anything other than perfectly centered.

Off-Center (70/30): An off-center card has one border that is noticeably more than twice as wide as the opposite border.

Badly Off-Center (80/20 or worse): A badly off-center card has virtually no border on one side of the card.

Miscut: A miscut card actually shows part of the adjacent card in its larger border and consequently a corresponding amount of its card is cut off.

Corner Wear

Corner wear is the most scrutinized grading criteria in the hobby. These are the major categories of corner wear:

Corner with a slight touch of wear: The corner still is sharp, but there is a slight touch of wear showing. On a dark-bordered card, this shows as a dot of white.

Fuzzy corner: The corner still comes to a point, but the point has just begun to fray. A slightly "dinged" corner is considered the same as a fuzzy corner.

Slightly rounded corner: The fraying of the corner has increased to where there is only a hint of a point. Mild layering may be evident. A "dinged" corner is considered the same as a slightly rounded corner.

Rounded corner: The point is completely gone. Some layering is noticeable.

Badly rounded corner: The corner is completely round and rough. Severe layering is evident.

Creases

A third common defect is the crease. The degree of creasing in a card is difficult to show in a drawing or picture. On giving the specific condition of an expensive card for sale, the seller should note any creases additionally. Creases can be categorized as to severity according to the following scale.

Light Crease: A light crease is a crease that is barely noticeable upon close inspection. In fact, when cards are in plastic sheets or holders, a light crease may not be seen (until the card is taken out of the holder). A light crease on the front is much more serious than a light crease on the card back only.

Medium Crease: A medium crease is noticeable when held and studied at arm's length by the naked eye, but does not overly detract from the appearance of the card. It is an obvious crease, but not one that breaks the picture surface of the card.

Heavy Crease: A heavy crease is one that has torn or broken through the card's picture surface, e.g., puts a tear in the photo surface.

Alterations

Deceptive Trimming: This occurs when someone alters the card in order (1) to shave off edge wear, (2) to improve the sharpness of the corners, or (3) to improve centering — obviously their objective is to falsely increase the perceived value of the card to an unsuspecting buyer. The shrinkage

Centering

Well-centered

Slightly Off-centered

Off-centered

Badly Off-centered

Miscut

Corner Wear

The partial cards shown at right have been photographed at 300%. This was done in order to magnify each card's corner wear to such a degree that differences could be shown on a printed page.

This 1985 Topps Fred Quillan card has a fuzzy corner. Notice the extremely slight fraying on the corner.

This 1985 Topps Fred Smerlas card has a slightly rounded corner. Notice that there is no longer a sharp corner but heavy wear.

This 1985 Topps Daryl Turner card has a rounded corner evident by the lack of a sharp point and heavy wear on both edges.

This 1985 Topps Kim Bokamper card displays a badly rounded corner. Notice a large portion of missing cardboard accompanied by heavy wear and excessive fraying.

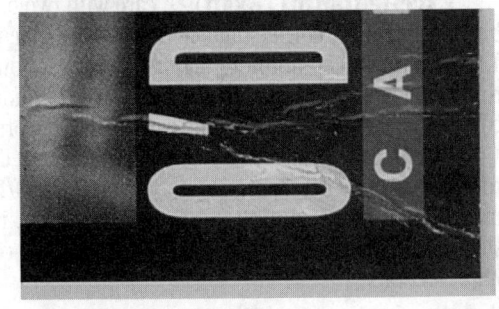

This 1985 Topps Neil O'Donaghue card displays creases of varying degrees. Light creases (left side of the card) may not break the card's surface, while heavy creases (right side) will.

usually is evident only if the trimmed card is compared to an adjacent full-sized card or if the trimmed card is itself measured.

Obvious Trimming: Obvious trimming is noticeable and unfortunate. It is usually performed by non-collectors who give no thought to the present or future value of their cards.

Deceptively Retouched Borders: This occurs when the borders (especially on those cards with dark borders) are touched up on the edges and corners with magic marker or crayons of appropriate color in order to make the card appear to be Mint.

Categorization of Defects

Miscellaneous Flaws

The following are common minor flaws that, depending on severity, lower a card's condition by one to four grades and often render it no better than Excellent-Mint: bubbles (lumps in surface), gum and wax stains, diamond cutting (slanted borders), notching, off-centered backs, paper wrinkles, scratched-off cartoons or puzzles on back, rubber band marks, scratches, surface impressions and warping.

The following are common serious flaws that, depending on severity, lower a card's condition at least four grades and often render it no better than Good: chemical or sun fading, erasure marks, mildew, miscutting (severe off-centering), holes, bleached or retouched borders, tape marks, tears, trimming, water or coffee stains and writing.

Condition Guide

Grades

Mint (Mt) - A card with no flaws or wear. The card has four perfect corners, 60/40 or better centering from top to bottom and from left to right, original gloss, smooth edges and original color borders. A Mint card does not have print spots, color or focus imperfections.

Near Mint-Mint (NrMt-Mt) - A card with one minor flaw. Any one of the following would lower a Mint card to Near Mint-Mint: one corner with a slight touch of wear, barely noticeable print spots, color or focus imperfections. The card must have 60/40 or better centering in both directions, original gloss, smooth edges and original color borders.

Near Mint (NrMt) - A card with one minor flaw. Any one of the following would lower a Mint card to Near Mint: one fuzzy corner or two to four corners with slight touches of wear, 70/30 to 60/40 centering, slightly rough edges, minor print spots, color or focus imperfections. The card must have original gloss and original color borders.

Excellent-Mint (ExMt) - A card with two or three fuzzy, but not rounded, corners and centering no worse than 80/20. The card may have no more than two of the following: slightly rough edges, very slightly discolored borders, minor print spots, color or focus imperfections. The card must have original gloss.

Excellent (Ex) - A card with four fuzzy but definitely not rounded corners and centering no worse than 80/20. The card may have a small amount of original gloss lost, rough edges, slightly discolored borders and minor print spots, color or focus imperfections.

Very Good (Vg) - A card that has been handled but not abused: slightly rounded corners with slight layering, slight notching on edges, a significant amount of gloss lost from the surface but no scuffing and moderate discoloration of borders. The card may have a few light creases.

Good (G), **Fair (F)**, **Poor (P)** - A well-worn, mishandled or abused card: badly rounded and layered corners, scuffing, most or all original gloss missing, seriously discolored borders, moderate or heavy creases, and one or more serious flaws. The grade of Good, Fair or Poor depends on the severity of wear and flaws. Good, Fair and Poor cards generally are used only as fillers.

The most widely used grades are defined above. Obviously, many cards will not perfectly fit one of the definitions.

Therefore, categories between the major grades known as in-between grades are used, such as Good to Very Good (G-Vg), Very Good to Excellent (VgEx), and Excellent-Mint to Near Mint (ExMt-NrMt). Such grades indicate a card with all qualities of the lower category but with at least a few qualities of the higher category.

The Beckett Guide lists each card and set in three grades, with the middle grade valued at about 40-45% of the top grade, and the bottom grade valued at about 10-15% of the top grade.

The value of cards that fall between the listed columns can also be calculated using a percentage of the top grade. For example, a card that falls between the top and middle grades (Ex, ExMt or NrMt in most cases) will generally be valued at anywhere from 50% to 90% of the top grade.

Similarly, a card that falls between the middle and bottom grades (G-Vg, Vg or VgEx in most cases) will generally be valued at anywhere from 20% to 40% of the top grade.

There are also cases where cards are in better condition than the top grade or worse than the bottom grade. Cards that grade worse than the lowest grade are generally valued at 5-10% of the top grade.

When a card exceeds the top grade by one — such as NrMt-Mt when the top grade is NrMt, or Mint when the top grade is NrMt-Mt — a premium of up to 50% is possible, with 10-20% the usual norm.

When a card exceeds the top grade by two — such as Mint when the top grade is NrMt, or NrMt-Mt when the top grade is ExMt — a premium of 25-50% is the usual norm. But certain condition sensitive cards or sets, particularly those from the pre-war era, can bring premiums of up to 100% or even more.

Unopened packs, boxes and factory-collated sets are considered Mint in their unknown (and presumed perfect) state. Once opened, however, each card can be graded (and valued) in its own right by taking into account any defects that may be present in spite of the fact that the card has never been handled.

Selling Your Cards

Just about every collector sells cards or will sell cards eventually. Someday you may be interested in selling your duplicates or maybe even your whole collection. You may sell to other collectors, friends or dealers. You may even sell cards you purchased from a certain dealer back to that same dealer. In any event, it helps to know some of the mechanics of the typical transaction between buyer and seller.

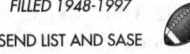

Dealers will buy cards in order to resell them to other collectors who are interested in the cards. Dealers will always pay a higher percentage for items that (in their opinion) can be resold quickly, and a much lower percentage for those items that are perceived as having low demand and hence are slow moving. In either case, dealers must buy at a price that allows for the expense of doing business and a margin for profit.

If you have cards for sale, the best advice we can give is that you get several offers for your cards — either from card shops or at a card show — and take the best offer, all things considered. Note, the "best" offer may not be the one for the highest amount. And remember, if a dealer really wants your cards, he won't let you get away without making his best competitive offer. Another alternative is to place your cards in an auction as one or several lots.

Many people think nothing of going into a department store and paying $15 for an item of clothing for which the store paid $5. But if you were selling your $15 card to a dealer and he offered you $5 for it, you might think his mark-up unreasonable. To complete the analogy: most department stores (and card dealers) that consistently pay $10 for $15 items eventually go out of business. An exception is when the dealer has lined up a willing buyer for the item(s) you are attempting to sell, or if the cards are so Hot that it's likely he'll have to hold the cards for only a short period of time.

In those cases, an offer of up to 75 percent of book value still will allow the dealer to make a reasonable profit considering the short time he will need to hold the merchandise. In general, however, most cards and collections will bring offers in the range of 25 to 50 percent of retail price. Also consider that most material from the past five to 10 years is plentiful. If that's what you're selling, don't be surprised if your best offer is well below that range.

Interesting Notes

The first card numerically of an issue is the single card most likely to obtain excessive wear. Consequently, you typically will find the price on the #1 card (in NrMt or Mint condition) somewhat higher than might otherwise be the case. Similarly, but to a lesser extent (because normally the less important, reverse side of the card is the one exposed), the last card numerically in an issue also is prone to abnormal wear. This extra wear and tear occurs because the first and last cards are exposed to the elements (human element included) more than any other cards. They are generally end cards in any brick formations, rubber bandings, stackings on wet surfaces, and like activities.

Sports cards have no intrinsic value. The value of a card, like the value of other collectibles, can be determined only by you and your enjoyment in viewing and possessing these cardboard treasures.

Remember, the buyer ultimately determines the price of each card. You are the determining price factor because you have the ability to say "No" to the price of any card by not exchanging your hard-earned money for a given card. When the cost of a trading card exceeds the enjoyment you will receive from it, your answer should be "No." We assess and report the prices. You set them!

We are always interested in receiving the price input of collectors and dealers from around the country. We happily credit major contributors. We welcome your opinions, since your contributions assist us in ensuring a better guide each year. If you would like to join our survey list for the next editions of this book and others authored by Dr. Beckett, please send your name and address to Dr. James Beckett, 15850 Dallas Parkway, Dallas, Texas 75248.

History of Football Cards

Until the 1930s, the only set devoted exclusively to football players was the Mayo N302 set. The first bubblegum issue dedicated entirely to football players did not appear until the National Chicle issue of 1935. Before this, athletes from several sports were pictured in the multi-sport Goudey Sport Kings issue of 1933. In that set, football was represented by three legends whose fame has not diminished through the years: Red Grange, Knute Rockne and Jim Thorpe.

But it was not until 1948, and the post-war bubblegum boom, that the next football issues appeared. Bowman and Leaf Gum companies both issued football card sets in that year. From this point on, football cards have been issued annually by one company or another up to the present time, with Topps being the only major card producer until 1989, when Pro Set and Score debuted and sparked a football card boom.

Football cards depicting players from the Canadian Football League (CFL) did not appear until Parkhurst issued a 100-card set in 1952. Four years later, Parkhurst issued another CFL set with 50 small cards this time. Topps began issuing CFL sets in 1958 and continued annually until 1965, although from 1961 to 1965 these cards were printed in Canada by O-Pee-Chee. Post Cereal issued two CFL sets in 1962 and 1963; these cards formed the backs of boxes of Post Cereals distributed in Canada. The O-Pee-Chee company, which has maintained a working relationship with the Topps Gum Company, issued four CFL sets in the years 1968, 1970, 1971, and 1972. Since 1981, the JOGO Novelties Company has been producing a number of CFL sets depicting past and present players.

Returning to American football issues, Bowman resumed its football cards (by then with full-color fronts) from 1950 to 1955. The company twice increased the size of its card during that period. Bowman was unopposed during most of the early 1950s as the sole producer of cards featuring pro football players.

Topps issued its first football card set in 1950 with a group of very small, felt-back cards. In 1951 Topps issued what is referred to as the "Magic Football Card" set. This set of 75 has a scratch-off section on the back which answers a football quiz. Topps did not issue another football set until 1955 when its All-American Football set paid tribute to past college football greats. In January of 1956, Topps Gum Company (of Brooklyn) purchased the Bowman Company (of Philadelphia).

After the purchase, Topps issued sets of National Football League (NFL) players up until 1963. The 1961 Topps football set also included American Football League (AFL) players in the high number series (133-198). Topps sets from 1964 to 1967 contained AFL players only. From 1968 to the present, Topps has issued a major set of football cards each year.

Get All The Runs, Hits and Errors --

EVERY MONTH!

Subscribe to *Beckett Baseball Card Monthly* today!

Why wait 'til spring training for another great Price Guide? With a subscription to *Beckett Baseball Card Monthly*, you'll get the hobby's most accurate baseball card Price Guide <u>every</u> <u>month</u>!

Plus get great inside info about new product releases, superstar player coverage, off-season news and answers to all your collecting questions too!

When the AFL was founded in 1960, Fleer produced a 132-card set of AFL players and coaches. In 1961, Fleer issued a 220-card set (even larger than the Topps issue of that year) featuring players from both the NFL and AFL. Apparently, for that one year, Topps and Fleer tested a reciprocal arrangement, trading the card printing rights to each other's contracted players. The 1962 and 1963 Fleer sets feature only AFL players. Both sets are relatively small at 88 cards each.

Post Cereal issued a 200-card set of National League football players in 1962 which contains numerous scarcities, namely those players appearing on unpopular varieties of Post Cereal. From 1964 to 1967, the Philadelphia Gum company issued four 198-card NFL player sets.

In 1984 and 1985, Topps produced a set for the now defunct United States Football League, in addition to its annual NFL set. The 1984 set in particular is quite scarce, due to both low distribution and the high demand for the extended Rookie Cards of current NFL superstars Jim Kelly and Reggie White, among others.

In 1986, the McDonald's Restaurants generated the most excitement in football cards in many years. McDonald's created a nationwide football card promotion in which customers could receive a card or two per food purchase, upon request. However, the cards distributed were only of the local team, or of the "McDonald's All-Stars" for areas not near NFL cities. Also, each set was produced with four possible color tabs: blue, black, gold, and green. The tab color distributed depended on the week of the promotion. In general, cards with blue tabs are the scarcest, although for some teams the cards with black tabs are the hardest to find. The tabs were intended to be scratched off and removed by customers to be redeemed for food and other prizes, but among collectors, cards with scratched or removed tabs are categorized as having a major defect, and therefore are valued considerably less.

The entire set, including four color tabs for all 29 subsets, totals over 2800 different cards. The hoopla over the McDonald's cards fell off precipitiously after 1988, as collector interest shifted to the new 1989 Score and Pro Set issues.

The popularity of football cards has continued to grow since 1986. Topps introduced "Super Rookie" cards in 1987. Card companies other than Topps noticed the burgeoning interest in football cards, resulting in the two landmark 1989 football sets: a 330-card Score issue, and a 440-card Pro Set release. Score later produced a self-contained 110-card supplemental set, while Pro Set printed 100 Series II cards and a 21-card "Final Update" set. Topps, Pro Set and Score all improved card quality and increased the size of their sets for 1990. That season also marked Fleer's return to football cards and Action Packed's first major set.

In 1991, Pacific, Pro Line, Upper Deck and Wild Card joined a market that is now at least as competitive as the baseball card market. And the premium card trend that began in baseball cards spilled over to the gridiron in the form of Fleer Ultra, Pro Set Platinum, Score Pinnacle, and Topps Stadium Club sets.

The year 1992 brought even more growth with the debuts of All World, Collectors Edge, GameDay, Playoff, Pro Set Power, SkyBox Impact and SkyBox Primetime.

The football card market stabilized somewhat in 1993 thanks to an agreement between the long-feuding NFL licensing bodies, NFL Properties and the NFL Players Association. Also helping the stabilization was the emergence of several promising rookies, including Drew Bledsoe, Jerome Bettis and Rick Mirer. Limited production became the industry buzzword in sports cards, and football was no exception. The result was the success of three new product lines: 1993 Playoff Contenders, 1993 Select and 1993 SP.

The year 1994 brought furthur stabilization and limited production. Pro Set and Wild Card dropped out, while no new card companies joined the ranks. However, several new NFL sets were added to the mix by existing manufacturers: Classic NFL Experience, Collector's Choice, Excalibur, Finest and Sportflics. The new trend centered around multi-level parallel sets and interactive game inserts with parallel prizes. Another strong rookie crop and reported production cut backs contributed to strong football card sales throughout 1994.

The football card market continued to grow in 1995 and 1996. Many new sets were released by the major manufacturers and a few new players entered the hobby. Companies continued to push the limits of printing technology with issues printed on plastic, leather, cloth and various metals. There are more choices than ever before for the football card collector - most like it that way.

Additional Reading

 Each year Beckett Publications produces comprehensive annual price guides for each of the four major sports: *Beckett Baseball Card Price Guide*, *Beckett Football Card Price Guide*, *Beckett Basketball Card Price Guide*, and *Beckett Hockey Card Price Guide*. The aim of these annual guides is to provide information and accurate pricing on a wide array of sports cards, ranging from main issues by the major card manufacturers to various regional, promotional, and food issues. Also alphabetical checklists, such as *Beckett Football Card Alphabetical Checklist #1*, are published to assist the collector in identifying all the cards of any particular player. The seasoned collector will find these tools valuable sources of information that will enable him to pursue his hobby interests.

In addition, abridged editions of the Beckett Price Guides have been published for each of the four major sports as part of the House of Collectible series: *The Official Price Guide to Baseball Cards*, *The Official Price Guide to Football Cards*, *The Official Price Guide to Basketball Cards*, and *The Official Price Guide to Hockey Cards*. Published in a convenient mass-market paperback format, these price guides provide information and accurate pricing on all the main issues by the major card manufacturers.

LOOK FOR THESE 1997 BECKETT HOBBY TITLES AT A CARD SHOP OR BOOKSTORE NEAR YOU!

- *Beckett Baseball Card Price Guide No. 19 – April 1997*

- *Beckett Racing Price Guide and Alphabetical Checklist No. 2 – June 1997*

 *Beckett Basketball Card Alphabetical Checklist No. 1 – July 1997*

- *Beckett Almanac of Baseball Cards and Collectibles No. 2 – July 1997*

1st Edition! • *Beckett Football Card Alphabetical Checklist No. 1 – August 1997*

- *Beckett Football Card Price Guide No.14 – September 1997*

- *Beckett Hockey Card Price Guide and Alphabetical Checklist No. 7 – October 1997*

- *Beckett Basketball Card Price Guide No. 6 – November 1997*

1994 A1 Masters of the Grill

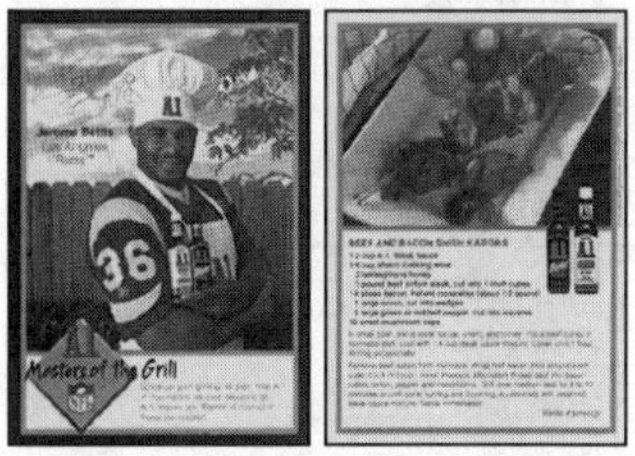

Sponsored by A.1. Steak Sauce, this 28-card standard-size set is actually a recipe card set. Inside gold and black borders, the fronts display a football player wearing his team's jersey, an apron, a hat with A.1. on it, and holding either A.1. steak sauce or barbeque utensils. The player's facsimile autograph appears in one of the upper corners, with player's name and team name immediately below. The backs present a picture of a prepared dish as well as recipe instructions for its preparing the food. The cards are unnumbered and checklisted below in alphabetical order.

	MINT	NRMT	EXC
COMPLETE SET (28)	15.00	6.75	1.85
COMMON CARD (1-28)	.40	.18	.05
☐ 1 Harris Barton	.50	.23	.06
☐ 2 Jerome Bettis	1.50	.70	.19
☐ 3 Ray Childress	.50	.23	.06
☐ 4 Eugene Chung	.40	.18	.05
☐ 5 Jamie Dukes	.40	.18	.05
☐ 6 Steve Emtman	.40	.18	.05
☐ 7 Burt Grossman	.40	.18	.05
☐ 8 Ken Harvey	.50	.23	.06
☐ 9 Courtney Hall	.40	.18	.05
☐ 10 Chris Hinton	.40	.18	.05
☐ 11 Kent Hull	.40	.18	.05
☐ 12 Keith Jackson	.75	.35	.09
☐ 13 Rickey Jackson	.50	.23	.06
☐ 14 Cortez Kennedy	.75	.35	.09
☐ 15 Tim Krumrie	.40	.18	.05
☐ 16 Jeff Lageman	.40	.18	.05
☐ 17 Greg Lloyd	1.00	.45	.12
☐ 18 Howie Long	1.00	.45	.12
☐ 19 Hardy Nickerson	.50	.23	.06
☐ 20 Bart Oates	.40	.18	.05
☐ 21 Ken Ruettgers	.40	.18	.05
☐ 22 Dan Saleaumua	.40	.18	.05
☐ 23 Alonzo Spellman	.50	.23	.06
☐ 24 Eric Swann	.75	.35	.09
☐ 25 Pat Swilling	.50	.23	.06
☐ 26 Tommy Vardell	.40	.18	.05
☐ 27 Erik Williams	.50	.23	.06
☐ 28 Gary Zimmerman	.40	.18	.05

1989 Action Packed Prototypes

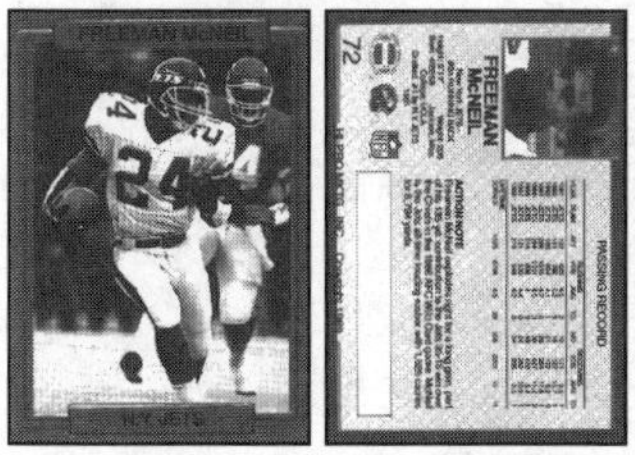

These two prototype cards were issued before the 1989 Test issue was released to show the style of Action Packed cards. The cards were folded by hand when they were made, which is why there is no seam on the back of the card as is typical of other Action Packed cards. The standard-size cards feature on the fronts embossed color photos bordered in gold. The horizontally oriented backs have a mugshot, biography, statistics, and an "Action Note" in the form of a caption to the action shot on the front. The primary stylistic difference between these prototype cards and the test set issued later that year is the location of the card number.

	MINT	NRMT	EXC
COMPLETE SET (2)	50.00	22.00	6.25
COMMON CARD	20.00	9.00	2.50
☐ 72 Freeman McNeil	20.00	9.00	2.50
☐ 101 Phil Simms	30.00	13.50	3.70

1989 Action Packed Test

The 1989 Action Packed Football Test set contains 30 standard-size cards. The cards have rounded corners and gold borders. The fronts have "raised" color action shots, and the horizontally-oriented backs feature mug shots and complete stats. The set, which includes ten players each from the Chicago Bears, New York Giants, and Washington Redskins, was packaged in six-card poly packs. These cards were not packaged very well; many cards come creased or bent out of packs, and a typical box will yield quite a few duplicates. Although this is considered to be a limited test issue, the test apparently was successful as there were reports that more than 4300 cases were produced of these cards. Factory sets packaged in small

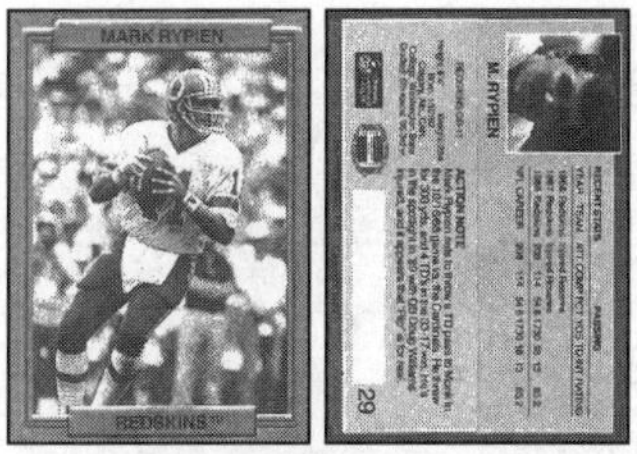

dull-gold colored boxes were also available on a limited basis. The cards are copyrighted by Hi-Pro Marketing of Northbrook, Illinois and the packs are labeled "Action Packed." On the card back of number 6 Dan Hampton it lists his uniform number as 95 which is actually Richard Dent's number; Hampton wears 99 for the Bears. The cards are numbered in alphabetical order within teams, Chicago Bears (1-10), New York Giants (11-20), and Washington Redskins (21-30). Since this set was a test issue, the cards of Dave Meggett and Mark Rypien are not considered true Rookie Cards.

	MINT	NRMT	EXC
COMPLETE SET (30)	18.00	8.00	2.20
COMMON CARD (1-30)	.50	.23	.06
☐ 1 Neal Anderson	.75	.35	.09
☐ 2 Trace Armstrong	.50	.23	.06
☐ 3 Kevin Butler	.50	.23	.06
☐ 4 Richard Dent	.75	.35	.09
☐ 5 Dennis Gentry	.50	.23	.06
☐ 6 Dan Hampton UER	.75	.35	.09
(Wrong uniform			
number on back)			
☐ 7 Jay Hilgenberg	.50	.23	.06
☐ 8 Thomas Sanders	.50	.23	.06
☐ 9 Mike Singletary	1.00	.45	.12
☐ 10 Mike Tomczak	1.00	.45	.12
☐ 11 Raul Allegre	.50	.23	.06
☐ 12 Ottis Anderson	.75	.35	.09
☐ 13 Mark Bavaro	.75	.35	.09
☐ 14 Terry Kinard	.50	.23	.06
☐ 15 Lionel Manuel	.50	.23	.06
☐ 16 Leonard Marshall	.75	.35	.09
☐ 17 Dave Meggett	1.00	.45	.12
☐ 18 Joe Morris	.75	.35	.09
☐ 19 Phil Simms	1.50	.70	.19
☐ 20 Lawrence Taylor	1.00	.45	.12
☐ 21 Kelvin Bryant	.50	.23	.06
☐ 22 Darrell Green	.75	.35	.09
☐ 23 Dexter Manley	.50	.23	.06
☐ 24 Charles Mann	.50	.23	.06
☐ 25 Wilber Marshall	.50	.23	.06
☐ 26 Art Monk	1.00	.45	.12
☐ 27 Jamie Morris	.50	.23	.06
☐ 28 Tracy Rocker	.50	.23	.06
☐ 29 Mark Rypien UER	.75	.35	.09
(Born 10/2/52,			
should be 10/2/62)			
☐ 30 Ricky Sanders	.75	.35	.09

1990 Action Packed

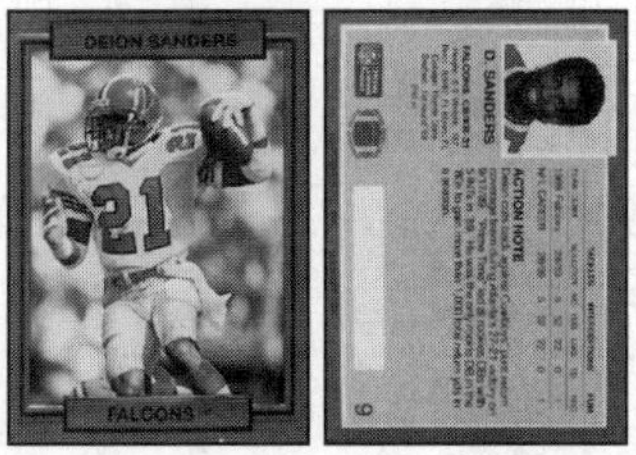

This 280-card standard-size set was issued in two skip-numbered series. The cards are the same style as previous year's "test" issue. The set is organized numerically in alphabetical order within team and teams themselves are in alphabetical order by city. For cards numbered 3, 26, 193 and 222, the action note on the card back does not correspond with the picture on the front. Later in the year Action Packed released these cards in the form of pre-packed ten-card complete team sets. The only Rookie Card of any note is Ken Harvey. A special Braille-backed card of Jim Plunkett was released in both 281-card factory sets and as a random insert in wax packs.

	MINT	NRMT	EXC
COMPLETE SET (280)	20.00	9.00	2.50
COMPLETE FACT.SET (281)	25.00	11.00	3.10
COMMON CARD (1-280)	.15	.07	.02
☐ 1 Aundray Bruce UER	.15	.07	.02
(Andre on back)			
☐ 2 Scott Case	.15	.07	.02
☐ 3 Tony Casillas	.15	.07	.02
☐ 4 Shawn Collins	.15	.07	.02
☐ 5 Marcus Cotton	.15	.07	.02
☐ 6 Bill Fralic	.15	.07	.02
☐ 7 Tim Green	.15	.07	.02
☐ 8 Chris Miller	.50	.23	.06
☐ 9 Deion Sanders	1.50	.70	.19
☐ 10 John Settle	.15	.07	.02
☐ 11 Cornelius Bennett	.25	.11	.03
☐ 12 Shane Conlan	.15	.07	.02
☐ 13 Kent Hull	.15	.07	.02
☐ 14 Jim Kelly	.50	.23	.06
☐ 15 Mark Kelso	.15	.07	.02
☐ 16 Scott Norwood	.15	.07	.02
☐ 17 Andre Reed	.50	.23	.06
☐ 18 Fred Smerlas	.15	.07	.02
☐ 19 Bruce Smith	.50	.23	.06
☐ 20 Thurman Thomas	1.00	.45	.12
☐ 21 Neal Anderson UER	.25	.11	.03
(Action note begins"Neil ...")			
☐ 22 Kevin Butler	.15	.07	.02
☐ 23 Richard Dent	.25	.11	.03
☐ 24 Dennis Gentry	.15	.07	.02
☐ 25 Dan Hampton	.25	.11	.03
☐ 26 Jay Hilgenberg	.15	.07	.02
☐ 27 Steve McMichael	.25	.11	.03
☐ 28 Brad Muster	.15	.07	.02
☐ 29 Mike Singletary	.25	.11	.03
☐ 30 Mike Tomczak	.25	.11	.03
☐ 31 James Brooks	.25	.11	.03
☐ 32 Rickey Dixon	.15	.07	.02
☐ 33 Boomer Esiason	.25	.11	.03
☐ 34 David Fulcher	.15	.07	.02
☐ 35 Rodney Holman	.15	.07	.02
☐ 36 Tim Krumrie	.15	.07	.02
☐ 37 Tim McGee	.15	.07	.02
☐ 38 Anthony Munoz UER	.25	.11	.03
(Action note says he's			
blocking Howie Long,			
but jersey begins			
with a nine)			
☐ 39 Reggie Williams	.15	.07	.02
☐ 40 Ickey Woods	.15	.07	.02
☐ 41 Thane Gash	.15	.07	.02
☐ 42 Mike Johnson	.15	.07	.02
☐ 43 Bernie Kosar	.25	.11	.03
☐ 44 Reggie Langhorne	.15	.07	.02
☐ 45 Clay Matthews	.25	.11	.03
☐ 46 Eric Metcalf	.50	.23	.06
☐ 47 Frank Minnifield	.15	.07	.02
☐ 48 Ozzie Newsome	.25	.11	.03
☐ 49 Webster Slaughter	.25	.11	.03
☐ 50 Felix Wright	.15	.07	.02
☐ 51 Troy Aikman	3.00	1.35	.35
☐ 52 James Dixon	.15	.07	.02
☐ 53 Michael Irvin	.50	.23	.06
☐ 54 Jim Jeffcoat	.15	.07	.02
☐ 55 Ed Too Tall Jones	.25	.11	.03
☐ 56 Eugene Lockhart	.15	.07	.02
☐ 57 Danny Noonan	.15	.07	.02
☐ 58 Paul Palmer	.15	.07	.02
☐ 59 Everson Walls	.15	.07	.02
☐ 60 Steve Walsh	.25	.11	.03
☐ 61 Steve Atwater	.15	.07	.02
☐ 62 Tyrone Braxton	.15	.07	.02
☐ 63 John Elway	1.50	.70	.19
☐ 64 Bobby Humphrey	.15	.07	.02
☐ 65 Mark Jackson	.15	.07	.02
☐ 66 Vance Johnson	.15	.07	.02
☐ 67 Greg Kragen	.15	.07	.02
☐ 68 Karl Mecklenburg	.15	.07	.02
☐ 69 Dennis Smith	.25	.11	.03
☐ 70 David Treadwell	.15	.07	.02
☐ 71 Jim Arnold	.15	.07	.02
☐ 72 Jerry Ball	.15	.07	.02
☐ 73 Bennie Blades	.15	.07	.02
☐ 74 Mel Gray	.25	.11	.03
☐ 75 Richard Johnson	.15	.07	.02
☐ 76 Eddie Murray	.15	.07	.02
☐ 77 Rodney Peete UER	.25	.11	.03
(On back, squeaker			
misspelled as squeeker)			
☐ 78 Barry Sanders	3.00	1.35	.35
☐ 79 Chris Spielman	.50	.23	.06
☐ 80 Walter Stanley	.15	.07	.02
☐ 81 Dave Brown	.15	.07	.02
☐ 82 Brent Fullwood	.15	.07	.02
☐ 83 Tim Harris	.15	.07	.02
☐ 84 Johnny Holland	.15	.07	.02
☐ 85 Don Majkowski	.15	.07	.02
☐ 86 Tony Mandarich	.15	.07	.02
☐ 87 Mark Murphy	.15	.07	.02
☐ 88 Brian Noble UER	.15	.07	.02
(Fumble recovery stats			
show 9 instead of 7)			
☐ 89 Ken Ruettgers	.15	.07	.02
☐ 90 Sterling Sharpe UER	.50	.23	.06
(Born Glenville, Ga.,			
should be Chicago)			
☐ 91 Ray Childress	.15	.07	.02
☐ 92 Ernest Givins	.25	.11	.03
☐ 93 Alonzo Highsmith	.15	.07	.02
☐ 94 Drew Hill	.15	.07	.02
☐ 95 Bruce Matthews	.25	.11	.03
☐ 96 Bubba McDowell	.15	.07	.02
☐ 97 Warren Moon	.50	.23	.06
☐ 98 Mike Munchak	.15	.07	.02
☐ 99 Allen Pinkett	.15	.07	.02
☐ 100 Mike Rozier	.15	.07	.02
☐ 101 Albert Bentley	.15	.07	.02
☐ 102 Duane Bickett	.15	.07	.02
☐ 103 Bill Brooks	.15	.07	.02
☐ 104 Chris Chandler	.50	.23	.06
☐ 105 Ray Donaldson	.15	.07	.02
☐ 106 Chris Hinton	.15	.07	.02
☐ 107 Andre Rison	.50	.23	.06
☐ 108 Keith Taylor	.15	.07	.02
☐ 109 Clarence Verdin	.15	.07	.02
☐ 110 Fredd Young	.15	.07	.02
☐ 111 Deron Cherry	.15	.07	.02
☐ 112 Steve DeBerg	.15	.07	.02
☐ 113 Dino Hackett	.15	.07	.02
☐ 114 Albert Lewis	.15	.07	.02
☐ 115 Nick Lowery	.15	.07	.02
☐ 116 Christian Okoye	.15	.07	.02
☐ 117 Stephone Paige	.15	.07	.02
☐ 118 Kevin Ross	.15	.07	.02
☐ 119 Derrick Thomas	.50	.23	.06
☐ 120 Mike Webster	.25	.11	.03
☐ 121 Marcus Allen	.50	.23	.06
☐ 122 Eddie Anderson	.15	.07	.02
☐ 123 Steve Beuerlein	.25	.11	.03
☐ 124 Tim Brown	.50	.23	.06
☐ 125 Mervyn Fernandez	.15	.07	.02
☐ 126 Willie Gault	.25	.11	.03
☐ 127 Bob Golic	.15	.07	.02
☐ 128 Bo Jackson UER	.50	.23	.06
(Final column in stats			
has LG, should be TD)			
☐ 129 Howie Long	.25	.11	.03
☐ 130 Greg Townsend	.15	.07	.02
☐ 131 Flipper Anderson	.15	.07	.02
☐ 132 Greg Bell	.15	.07	.02
☐ 133 Robert Delpino	.15	.07	.02
☐ 134 Henry Ellard	.25	.11	.03
☐ 135 Jim Everett	.25	.11	.03
☐ 136 Jerry Gray	.15	.07	.02
☐ 137 Kevin Greene	.50	.23	.06
☐ 138 Tom Newberry	.15	.07	.02
☐ 139 Jackie Slater	.15	.07	.02
☐ 140 Doug Smith	.15	.07	.02
☐ 141 Mark Clayton	.25	.11	.03
☐ 142 Jeff Cross	.15	.07	.02
☐ 143 Mark Duper	.25	.11	.03
☐ 144 Ferrell Edmunds	.15	.07	.02
☐ 145 Jim C.Jensen	.15	.07	.02
☐ 146 Dan Marino	3.00	1.35	.35
☐ 147 John Offerdahl	.15	.07	.02
☐ 148 Louis Oliver	.15	.07	.02
☐ 149 Reggie Roby	.15	.07	.02
☐ 150 Sammie Smith	.15	.07	.02
☐ 151 Joey Browner	.15	.07	.02
☐ 152 Anthony Carter	.25	.11	.03
☐ 153 Chris Doleman	.15	.07	.02
☐ 154 Steve Jordan	.15	.07	.02
☐ 155 Carl Lee	.15	.07	.02
☐ 156 Randall McDaniel	.15	.07	.02
☐ 157 Keith Millard	.15	.07	.02
☐ 158 Herschel Walker	.25	.11	.03
☐ 159 Wade Wilson	.25	.11	.03
☐ 160 Gary Zimmerman	.15	.07	.02
☐ 161 Hart Lee Dykes	.15	.07	.02
☐ 162 Irving Fryar	.50	.23	.06
☐ 163 Steve Grogan	.25	.11	.03
☐ 164 Maurice Hurst	.15	.07	.02
☐ 165 Fred Marion	.15	.07	.02
☐ 166 Stanley Morgan	.15	.07	.02
☐ 167 Robert Perryman	.15	.07	.02
☐ 168 John Stephens UER	.15	.07	.02
(Taking handoff from			
Eason, not Grogan)			
☐ 169 Andre Tippett	.15	.07	.02
☐ 170 Brent Williams	.15	.07	.02
☐ 171 John Fourcade	.15	.07	.02
☐ 172 Bobby Hebert	.15	.07	.02
☐ 173 Dalton Hilliard	.15	.07	.02
☐ 174 Rickey Jackson	.25	.11	.03
☐ 175 Vaughan Johnson	.15	.07	.02
☐ 176 Eric Martin	.15	.07	.02
☐ 177 Robert Massey	.15	.07	.02
☐ 178 Rueben Mayes UER	.15	.07	.02
(Final column in stats			
has LG, should be TD)			
☐ 179 Sam Mills	.25	.11	.03
☐ 180 Pat Swilling	.25	.11	.03
☐ 181 Ottis Anderson	.25	.11	.03
☐ 182 Carl Banks	.15	.07	.02
☐ 183 Mark Bavaro	.15	.07	.02
☐ 184 Mark Collins	.15	.07	.02
☐ 185 Leonard Marshall	.15	.07	.02
☐ 186 Dave Meggett	.25	.11	.03
☐ 187 Gary Reasons	.15	.07	.02
☐ 188 Phil Simms	.50	.23	.06
☐ 189 Lawrence Taylor	.50	.23	.06
☐ 190 Odessa Turner	.15	.07	.02
☐ 191 Kyle Clifton	.15	.07	.02
☐ 192 James Hasty	.15	.07	.02
☐ 193 Johnny Hector	.15	.07	.02
☐ 194 Jeff Lageman	.15	.07	.02
☐ 195 Pat Leahy	.15	.07	.02
☐ 196 Erik McMillan	.15	.07	.02
☐ 197 Ken O'Brien	.15	.07	.02
☐ 198 Mickey Shuler	.15	.07	.02
☐ 199 Al Toon	.25	.11	.03
☐ 200 Jo Jo Townsell	.15	.07	.02
☐ 201 Eric Allen UER	.15	.07	.02
(Card has 24 passes de-			
fended, Eagles say 25)			
☐ 202 Jerome Brown	.15	.07	.02
☐ 203 Keith Byars UER	.15	.07	.02

(LG column shows TD's, not longest run)			
204 Cris Carter	.50	.23	.06
205 Wes Hopkins	.15	.07	.02
(Photo from 1985 season)			
206 Keith Jackson UER	.25	.11	.03
(Born AK, should be AR)			
207 Seth Joyner	.25	.11	.03
(Photo not from an Eagle home game)			
208 Mike Quick	.15	.07	.02
(Photo is from a pre-1985 game)			
209 Andre Waters	.15	.07	.02
210 Reggie White	.50	.23	.06
211 Rich Camarillo	.15	.07	.02
212 Roy Green	.15	.07	.02
213 Ken Harvey	.50	.23	.06
214 Gary Hogeboom	.15	.07	.02
215 Tim McDonald	.15	.07	.02
216 Stump Mitchell	.15	.07	.02
217 Luis Sharpe	.15	.07	.02
218 Vai Sikahema	.15	.07	.02
219 J.T. Smith	.15	.07	.02
220 Ron Wolfley	.15	.07	.02
221 Gary Anderson K	.15	.07	.02
222 Bubby Brister UER	.15	.07	.02
(Stats say 0 TD passes in 1989, should be 9)			
223 Merril Hoge	.15	.07	.02
224 Tunch Ilkin	.15	.07	.02
225 Louis Lipps	.25	.11	.03
226 David Little	.15	.07	.02
227 Greg Lloyd	.50	.23	.06
228 Dwayne Woodruff	.15	.07	.02
229 Rod Woodson	.50	.23	.06
(AJR patch is from 1988 season, not 1989)			
230 Tim Worley	.15	.07	.02
231 Marion Butts	.25	.11	.03
232 Gill Byrd	.15	.07	.02
233 Burt Grossman	.15	.07	.02
234 Jim McMahon	.25	.11	.03
235 Anthony Miller UER	.50	.23	.06
(Text says 76 catches, stats say 75)			
236 Leslie O'Neal UER	.25	.11	.03
(Born AK, should be AR)			
237 Gary Plummer	.15	.07	.02
238 Billy Ray Smith	.15	.07	.02
(Action note begins,"Bily Ray ...")			
239 Tim Spencer	.15	.07	.02
240 Lee Williams	.15	.07	.02
241 Mike Cofer	.15	.07	.02
242 Roger Craig	.25	.11	.03
243 Charles Haley	.25	.11	.03
244 Ronnie Lott	.25	.11	.03
245 Guy McIntyre	.15	.07	.02
246 Joe Montana	3.00	1.35	.35
247 Tom Rathman	.15	.07	.02
248 Jerry Rice	2.50	1.10	.30
249 John Taylor	.50	.23	.06
250 Michael Walter	.15	.07	.02
251 Brian Blades	.25	.11	.03
252 Jacob Green	.15	.07	.02
253 Dave Krieg	.25	.11	.03
254 Steve Largent	.50	.23	.06
255 Joe Nash	.15	.07	.02
256 Rufus Porter	.15	.07	.02
257 Eugene Robinson	.15	.07	.02
258 Paul Skansi	.15	.07	.02
259 Curt Warner UER	.15	.07	.02
(Yards and attempts are reversed in text)			
260 John L. Williams	.15	.07	.02
261 Mark Carrier WR	.50	.23	.06
262 Reuben Davis	.15	.07	.02
263 Harry Hamilton	.15	.07	.02
264 Bruce Hill	.15	.07	.02
265 Donald Igwebuike	.15	.07	.02
266 Eugene Marve	.15	.07	.02
267 Kevin Murphy	.15	.07	.02
268 Mark Robinson	.15	.07	.02
269 Lars Tate	.15	.07	.02
270 Vinny Testaverde	.25	.11	.03
271 Gary Clark	.50	.23	.06
272 Monte Coleman	.15	.07	.02
273 Darrell Green	.25	.11	.03
274 Charles Mann UER	.15	.07	.02
(CA is not alphabetized on back)			
275 Wilber Marshall	.15	.07	.02
276 Art Monk	.25	.11	.03
277 Gerald Riggs	.15	.07	.02
278 Mark Rypien	.25	.11	.03
279 Ricky Sanders	.15	.07	.02
280 Alvin Walton	.15	.07	.02
NNO Jim Plunkett BR	4.00	1.80	.50
(Braille on card back)			

1990 Action Packed Rookie Update

This 84-card standard-size set was issued to feature most of the rookies who made an impact in the 1990 season that Action Packed did not issue in their regular set. The first 64 cards in the set are 1990 rookies while the last 20 cards are either players who were traded

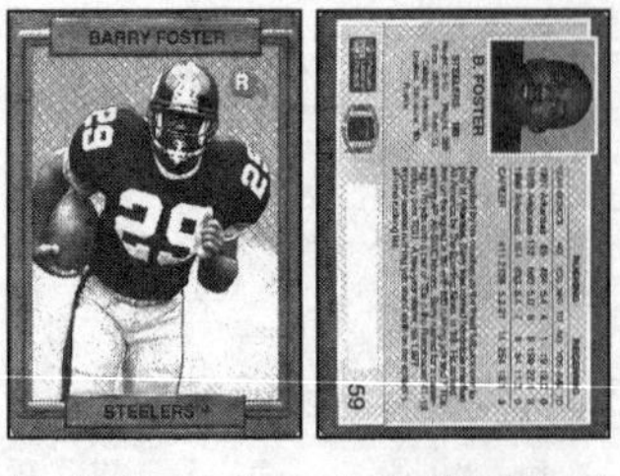

during the off-season or players such as Randall Cunningham who were not included in the regular set. Rookie Cards include Fred Barnett, Reggie Cobb, Barry Foster, Jeff George, Eric Green, Rodney Hampton, Johnny Johnson, Cortez Kennedy, Scott Mitchell, Rob Moore, Junior Seau, Shannon Sharpe, Emmitt Smith, Chris Warren and Calvin Williams. The set was released through both the Action Packed dealer network and via traditional retail outlets and was available both in wax packs and as collated factory sets.

	MINT	NRMT	EXC
COMPLETE SET (84)	30.00	13.50	3.70
COMPLETE FACT.SET (84)	30.00	13.50	3.70
COMMON CARD (1-84)	.15	.07	.02

1 Jeff George	2.50	1.10	.30
2 Richmond Webb	.15	.07	.02
3 James Williams	.15	.07	.02
4 Tony Bennett	.25	.11	.03
5 Darrell Thompson	.15	.07	.02
6 Steve Broussard	.15	.07	.02
7 Rodney Hampton	3.00	1.35	.35
8 Rob Moore	1.25	.55	.16
9 Alton Montgomery	.15	.07	.02
10 LeRoy Butler	.50	.23	.06
11 Anthony Johnson	.50	.23	.06
12 Scott Mitchell	3.00	1.35	.35
13 Mike Fox	.15	.07	.02
14 Robert Blackmon	.15	.07	.02
15 Blair Thomas	.15	.07	.02
16 Tony Stargell	.15	.07	.02
17 Peter Tom Willis	.15	.07	.02
18 Harold Green	.25	.11	.03
19 Bernard Clark	.15	.07	.02
20 Aaron Wallace	.15	.07	.02
21 Dennis Brown	.15	.07	.02
22 Johnny Johnson	.25	.11	.03
23 Chris Calloway	.15	.07	.02
24 Walter Wilson	.15	.07	.02
25 Dexter Carter	.15	.07	.02
26 Percy Snow	.15	.07	.02
27 Johnny Bailey	.15	.07	.02
28 Mike Bellamy	.15	.07	.02
29 Ben Smith	.15	.07	.02
30 Mark Carrier DB UER	.50	.23	.06
(stats say 54 yards in '89, text has 58)			
31 James Francis	.15	.07	.02
32 Lamar Lathon	.25	.11	.03
33 Bern Brostek	.15	.07	.02
34 Emmitt Smith UER	20.00	9.00	2.50
(Career yardage on back is 4232, should be 3928)			
35 Andre Collins UER	.15	.07	.02
(born '86, should be '66)			
36 Alexander Wright	.15	.07	.02
37 Fred Barnett	1.25	.55	.16
38 Junior Seau	4.00	1.80	.50
39 Cortez Kennedy	.50	.23	.06
40 Terry Wooden	.15	.07	.02
41 Eric Davis	.25	.11	.03
42 Fred Washington	.15	.07	.02
43 Reggie Cobb	.15	.07	.02
44 Andre Ware	.25	.11	.03
45 Anthony Smith	.15	.07	.02
46 Shannon Sharpe	5.00	2.20	.60
47 Harlon Barnett	.15	.07	.02
48 Greg McMurtry	.15	.07	.02
49 Stacey Simmons	.15	.07	.02
50 Calvin Williams	.25	.11	.03
51 Anthony Thompson	.15	.07	.02
52 Ricky Proehl	.25	.11	.03
53 Tony Jones	.25	.11	.03
54 Ray Agnew	.15	.07	.02
55 Tommy Hodson	.15	.07	.02
56 Ron Cox	.15	.07	.02
57 Leroy Hoard	.50	.23	.06
58 Eric Green UER	.25	.11	.03
(Back photo reversed)			
59 Barry Foster	.25	.11	.03
60 Keith McCants	.15	.07	.02
61 Oliver Barnett	.15	.07	.02
62 Chris Warren	4.00	1.80	.50
63 Pat Terrell	.15	.07	.02
64 Renaldo Turnbull	.15	.07	.02
65 Chris Chandler	.50	.23	.06
66 Everson Walls	.15	.07	.02
67 Alonzo Highsmith	.15	.07	.02
68 Gary Anderson RB	.15	.07	.02
69 Fred Smerlas	.15	.07	.02
70 Jim McMahon	.25	.11	.03
71 Curt Warner	.15	.07	.02
72 Stanley Morgan	.15	.07	.02
73 Dave Waymer	.15	.07	.02
74 Billy Joe Tolliver	.15	.07	.02
75 Tony Eason	.15	.07	.02
76 Max Montoya	.15	.07	.02
77 Greg Bell	.15	.07	.02
78 Dennis McKinnon	.15	.07	.02
79 Raymond Clayborn	.15	.07	.02
80 Broderick Thomas	.15	.07	.02
81 Timm Rosenbach	.15	.07	.02
82 Tim McKyer	.15	.07	.02
83 Andre Rison	.50	.23	.06
84 Randall Cunningham	.25	.11	.03

1991 Action Packed

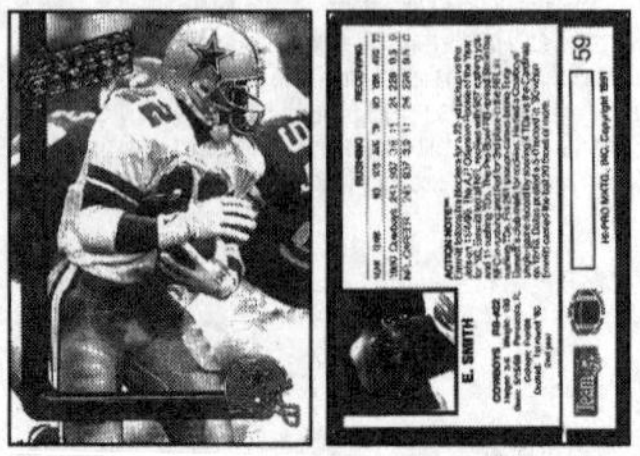

This 280-card, standard-size set features action photos on the front that are framed in gold along the left side and on the bottom of the card. The cards feature sharp photography on the front while the backs feature biographical information, a portrait shot of the player, stats from the last five seasons and career highlights. There is also a small space on the bottom for the player's signature. The cards are arranged by team. Complete factory sets also included an exclusive subset of 8 Braille cards; card numbers 281-288 which feature the category leaders of the AFC and NFC. They have the same front design as the regular issue, but different borderless embossed color player photos and horizontally oriented backs written in Braille. Two logo cards and an unnumbered checklist card complete the set. There are no key Rookie Cards in this set. Two prototype cards were issued as well and priced below. Each contains the word "prototype" stamped on the card back and neither is considered part of the complete set.

	MINT	NRMT	EXC
COMPLETE SET (280)	25.00	11.00	3.10
COMPLETE FACT.SET (291)	30.00	13.50	3.70
COMMON CARD (1-280)	.10	.05	.01

1 Steve Broussard	.10	.05	.01
2 Scott Case	.10	.05	.01
3 Brian Jordan	.20	.09	.03
4 Darion Conner	.10	.05	.01
5 Tim Green	.10	.05	.01
6 Chris Miller	.20	.09	.03
7 Andre Rison	.20	.09	.03
8 Mike Rozier	.10	.05	.01
9 Deion Sanders	1.25	.55	.16
10 Jessie Tuggle	.10	.05	.01
11 Leonard Smith	.10	.05	.01
12 Shane Conlan	.10	.05	.01
13 Kent Hull	.10	.05	.01
14 Keith McKeller	.10	.05	.01
15 James Lofton	.20	.09	.03
16 Andre Reed	.20	.09	.03
17 Bruce Smith	.50	.23	.06
18 Darryl Talley	.10	.05	.01
19 Steve Tasker	.20	.09	.03
20 Thurman Thomas	.50	.23	.06
21 Neal Anderson	.20	.09	.03
22 Trace Armstrong	.10	.05	.01
23 Mark Bortz	.10	.05	.01
24 Mark Carrier DB	.20	.09	.03
25 Wendell Davis	.10	.05	.01
26 Richard Dent	.20	.09	.03
27 Jim Harbaugh	.50	.23	.06
28 Jay Hilgenberg	.10	.05	.01
29 Brad Muster	.10	.05	.01
30 Mike Singletary	.20	.09	.03
31 Harold Green	.10	.05	.01
32 James Brooks	.10	.05	.01
33 Eddie Brown	.10	.05	.01
34 Boomer Esiason	.20	.09	.03
35 James Francis	.10	.05	.01
36 David Fulcher	.10	.05	.01
37 Rodney Holman	.10	.05	.01
38 Tim McGee	.10	.05	.01
39 Anthony Munoz	.20	.09	.03
40 Ickey Woods	.10	.05	.01
41 Rob Burnett	.10	.05	.01
42 Thane Gash	.10	.05	.01
43 Mike Johnson	.10	.05	.01
44 Brian Brennan	.10	.05	.01
45 Reggie Langhorne	.10	.05	.01
46 Kevin Mack	.10	.05	.01
47 Clay Matthews	.20	.09	.03
48 Eric Metcalf	.20	.09	.03
49 Anthony Pleasant	.10	.05	.01
50 Ozzie Newsome	.20	.09	.03
51 Troy Aikman	2.00	.90	.25
52 Issiac Holt	.10	.05	.01
53 Michael Irvin	.50	.23	.06
54 Jimmie Jones	.10	.05	.01
55 Eugene Lockhart	.10	.05	.01
56 Kelvin Martin	.10	.05	.01
57 Ken Norton Jr.	.50	.23	.06
58 Jay Novacek	.50	.23	.06
59 Emmitt Smith	4.00	1.80	.50
60 Daniel Stubbs	.10	.05	.01
61 Steve Atwater	.10	.05	.01
62 Michael Brooks	.10	.05	.01
63 John Elway	1.50	.70	.19
64 Simon Fletcher	.10	.05	.01
65 Bobby Humphrey	.10	.05	.01
66 Mark Jackson	.10	.05	.01
67 Vance Johnson	.10	.05	.01
68 Karl Mecklenburg	.10	.05	.01
69 Dennis Smith	.10	.05	.01
70 Greg Kragen UER	.10	.05	.01
(NT, not DT)			
71 Jerry Ball	.10	.05	.01
72 Lomas Brown	.10	.05	.01
73 Robert Clark	.10	.05	.01
74 Michael Cofer	.10	.05	.01
75 Mel Gray	.10	.05	.01
76 Richard Johnson	.10	.05	.01
77 Rodney Peete	.20	.09	.03
78 Barry Sanders	2.00	.90	.25
79 Chris Spielman	.20	.09	.03
80 Andre Ware	.20	.09	.03
81 Matt Brock	.10	.05	.01
82 LeRoy Butler	.20	.09	.03
83 Tim Harris	.10	.05	.01
84 Perry Kemp	.10	.05	.01
85 Don Majkowski	.10	.05	.01
86 Mark Murphy	.10	.05	.01
87 Brian Noble	.10	.05	.01
88 Sterling Sharpe	.50	.23	.06
89 Darrell Thompson	.10	.05	.01
90 Ed West	.10	.05	.01
91 Ray Childress	.10	.05	.01
92 Ernest Givins	.20	.09	.03
93 Drew Hill	.10	.05	.01
94 Haywood Jeffires	.20	.09	.03
95 Richard Johnson	.10	.05	.01
96 Sean Jones	.20	.09	.03
97 Bruce Matthews	.10	.05	.01
98 Warren Moon	.50	.23	.06
99 Mike Munchak	.10	.05	.01
100 Lorenzo White	.10	.05	.01
101 Albert Bentley	.10	.05	.01
102 Duane Bickett	.10	.05	.01
103 Bill Brooks	.10	.05	.01
104 Jeff George	.50	.23	.06
105 Jon Hand	.10	.05	.01
106 Jeff Herrod	.10	.05	.01
107 Jessie Hester	.10	.05	.01
108 Mike Prior UER	.10	.05	.01
(Did not play in '86)			
109 Rohn Stark	.10	.05	.01
110 Clarence Verdin	.10	.05	.01
111 Steve DeBerg	.10	.05	.01
112 Dan Saleaumua UER	.10	.05	.01
(NT, not DT)			
113 Albert Lewis	.10	.05	.01
114 Nick Lowery	.10	.05	.01
115 Christian Okoye	.10	.05	.01
116 Stephone Paige	.10	.05	.01
117 Kevin Ross	.10	.05	.01
118 Dino Hackett	.10	.05	.01
119 Derrick Thomas UER	.50	.23	.06
(Drafted in '89, not '90)			
120 Barry Word UER	.10	.05	.01
(Bio says 1105 yards, stats say 1015)			
121 Marcus Allen	.50	.23	.06
122 Mervyn Fernandez UER	.10	.05	.01
(Drafted by Raiders)			
123 Willie Gault	.10	.05	.01
124 Bo Jackson	.20	.09	.03
125 Terry McDaniel	.10	.05	.01
126 Don Mosebar	.10	.05	.01
127 Jay Schroeder	.10	.05	.01
128 Greg Townsend UER	.10	.05	.01
(B in DeBerg not in caps)			
129 Aaron Wallace	.10	.05	.01
130 Steve Wisniewski	.10	.05	.01
131 Flipper Anderson	.10	.05	.01
132 Henry Ellard	.20	.09	.03
133 Jim Everett	.20	.09	.03
134 Cleveland Gary	.10	.05	.01
135 Jerry Gray	.10	.05	.01
136 Kevin Greene	.50	.23	.06
137 Buford McGee	.10	.05	.01
138 Vince Newsome	.10	.05	.01
139 Jackie Slater	.10	.05	.01
140 Frank Stams	.10	.05	.01
141 Jeff Cross	.10	.05	.01
142 Mark Duper	.20	.09	.03
143 Ferrell Edmunds	.10	.05	.01
144 Dan Marino	3.00	1.35	.35
145 Louis Oliver	.10	.05	.01
146 John Offerdahl	.10	.05	.01
147 Tony Paige	.10	.05	.01
148 Sammie Smith	.10	.05	.01
149 Richmond Webb	.10	.05	.01
150 Jarvis Williams	.10	.05	.01
151 Joey Browner	.10	.05	.01

	MINT	NRMT	EXC
☐ 152 Anthony Carter	.20	.09	.03
☐ 153 Chris Doleman	.10	.05	.01
☐ 154 Hassan Jones	.10	.05	.01
☐ 155 Steve Jordan	.10	.05	.01
☐ 156 Carl Lee	.10	.05	.01
☐ 157 Randall McDaniel	.10	.05	.01
☐ 158 Mike Merriweather	.10	.05	.01
☐ 159 Herschel Walker	.20	.09	.03
☐ 160 Wade Wilson	.20	.09	.03
☐ 161 Ray Agnew	.10	.05	.01
☐ 162 Bruce Armstrong	.10	.05	.01
☐ 163 Marv Cook	.10	.05	.01
☐ 164 Hart Lee Dykes	.10	.05	.01
☐ 165 Irving Fryar	.20	.09	.03
☐ 166 Tommy Hodson	.10	.05	.01
☐ 167 Ronnie Lippett	.10	.05	.01
☐ 168 Fred Marion	.10	.05	.01
☐ 169 John Stephens	.10	.05	.01
☐ 170 Brent Williams	.10	.05	.01
☐ 171A Morten Andersen ERR (Back photo has white emblem, should be black)	.10	.05	.01
☐ 171B Morten Andersen COR	.10	.05	.01
☐ 172A Gene Atkins ERR (Back photo has white emblem, should be black)	.10	.05	.01
☐ 172B Gene Atkins COR	.10	.05	.01
☐ 173A Craig Heyward ERR (Back photo has white emblem, should be black)	.20	.09	.03
☐ 173B Craig Heyward COR	.20	.09	.03
☐ 174A Rickey Jackson ERR (Back photo has white emblem, should be black)	.10	.05	.01
☐ 174B Rickey Jackson COR	.10	.05	.01
☐ 175A Vaughan Johnson ERR (Back photo has white emblem, should be black)	.10	.05	.01
☐ 175B Vaughan Johnson COR	.10	.05	.01
☐ 176A Eric Martin ERR (Back photo has white emblem, should be black)	.10	.05	.01
☐ 176B Eric Martin COR	.10	.05	.01
☐ 177A Rueben Mayes ERR (Back photo has white emblem, should be black; would have been fifth season, not sixth)	.10	.05	.01
☐ 177B Rueben Mayes COR	.10	.05	.01
☐ 178A Pat Swilling ERR (Back photo has white emblem, should be black)	.20	.09	.03
☐ 178B Pat Swilling COR	.20	.09	.03
☐ 179A Renaldo Turnbull ERR (Back photo has white emblem, should be black)	.20	.09	.03
☐ 179B Renaldo Turnbull COR	.20	.09	.03
☐ 180A Steve Walsh ERR (Back photo has white emblem, should be black)	.10	.05	.01
☐ 180B Steve Walsh COR	.10	.05	.01
☐ 181 Ottis Anderson	.20	.09	.03
☐ 182 Rodney Hampton	.50	.23	.06
☐ 183 Jeff Hostetler	.50	.23	.06
☐ 184 Pepper Johnson	.10	.05	.01
☐ 185 Sean Landeta	.10	.05	.01
☐ 186 Dave Meggett	.20	.09	.03
☐ 187 Bart Oates	.10	.05	.01
☐ 188 Phil Simms	.50	.23	.06
☐ 189 Lawrence Taylor	.50	.23	.06
☐ 190 Reyna Thompson	.10	.05	.01
☐ 191 Brad Baxter	.10	.05	.01
☐ 192 Dennis Byrd	.10	.05	.01
☐ 193 Kyle Clifton	.10	.05	.01
☐ 194 James Hasty	.10	.05	.01
☐ 195 Pat Leahy	.10	.05	.01
☐ 196 Erik McMillan	.10	.05	.01
☐ 197 Rob Moore	.50	.23	.06
☐ 198 Ken O'Brien	.10	.05	.01
☐ 199 Mark Boyer	.10	.05	.01
☐ 200 Al Toon	.20	.09	.03
☐ 201 Fred Barnett	.50	.23	.06
☐ 202 Jerome Brown	.10	.05	.01
☐ 203 Keith Byars	.10	.05	.01
☐ 204 Randall Cunningham	.20	.09	.03
☐ 205 Wes Hopkins	.10	.05	.01
☐ 206 Keith Jackson	.20	.09	.03
☐ 207 Seth Joyner	.20	.09	.03
☐ 208 Heath Sherman	.10	.05	.01
☐ 209 Reggie White	.50	.23	.06
☐ 210 Calvin Williams	.20	.09	.03
☐ 211 Roy Green	.10	.05	.01
☐ 212 Ken Harvey UER (Tackling Rodney Hampton, not Howard Cross)	.20	.09	.03
☐ 213 Luis Sharpe	.10	.05	.01
☐ 214 Ernie Jones	.10	.05	.01
☐ 215 Tim McDonald	.10	.05	.01
☐ 216 Freddie Joe Nunn	.10	.05	.01
☐ 217 Ricky Proehl	.10	.05	.01
☐ 218 Timm Rosenbach	.10	.05	.01
☐ 219 Anthony Thompson	.10	.05	.01
☐ 220 Lonnie Young	.10	.05	.01
☐ 221 Gary Anderson K	.10	.05	.01
☐ 222 Bubby Brister	.10	.05	.01
☐ 223 Eric Green	.10	.05	.01
☐ 224 Merril Hoge	.10	.05	.01
☐ 225 Carnell Lake	.10	.05	.01
☐ 226 Louis Lipps	.10	.05	.01
☐ 227 David Little	.10	.05	.01
☐ 228 Greg Lloyd	.50	.23	.06
☐ 229 Gerald Williams	.10	.05	.01
☐ 230 Rod Woodson	.50	.23	.06
☐ 231 Marion Butts	.10	.05	.01
☐ 232 Gill Byrd	.10	.05	.01
☐ 233 Burt Grossman	.10	.05	.01
☐ 234 Courtney Hall	.10	.05	.01
☐ 235 Ronnie Harmon	.10	.05	.01
☐ 236 Anthony Miller	.20	.09	.03
☐ 237 Leslie O'Neal	.20	.09	.03
☐ 238 Junior Seau	.75	.35	.09
☐ 239 Billy Joe Tolliver	.10	.05	.01
☐ 240 Lee Williams	.10	.05	.01
☐ 241 Dexter Carter	.10	.05	.01
☐ 242 Kevin Fagan	.10	.05	.01
☐ 243 Charles Haley	.20	.09	.03
☐ 244 Brent Jones	.50	.23	.06
☐ 245 Ronnie Lott	.20	.09	.03
☐ 246 Guy McIntyre	.10	.05	.01
☐ 247 Joe Montana	2.00	.90	.25
☐ 248 Jerry Rice	2.00	.90	.25
☐ 249 John Taylor	.20	.09	.03
☐ 250 Roger Craig	.20	.09	.03
☐ 251 Brian Blades	.20	.09	.03
☐ 252 Derrick Fenner	.10	.05	.01
☐ 253 Nesby Glasgow UER ('91 was his 13th season, not 12th)	.10	.05	.01
☐ 254 Jacob Green	.10	.05	.01
☐ 255 Tommy Kane	.10	.05	.01
☐ 256 Dave Krieg	.20	.09	.03
☐ 257 Rufus Porter	.10	.05	.01
☐ 258 Eugene Robinson	.10	.05	.01
☐ 259 Cortez Kennedy	.50	.23	.06
☐ 260 John L. Williams	.10	.05	.01
☐ 261 Gary Anderson RB	.10	.05	.01
☐ 262 Mark Carrier WR	.50	.23	.06
☐ 263 Steve Christie	.10	.05	.01
☐ 264 Reggie Cobb	.10	.05	.01
☐ 265 Paul Gruber	.10	.05	.01
☐ 266 Wayne Haddix	.10	.05	.01
☐ 267 Bruce Hill	.10	.05	.01
☐ 268 Keith McCants	.10	.05	.01
☐ 269 Vinny Testaverde	.20	.09	.03
☐ 270 Broderick Thomas	.10	.05	.01
☐ 271 Earnest Byner	.10	.05	.01
☐ 272 Gary Clark	.50	.23	.06
☐ 273 Darrell Green	.10	.05	.01
☐ 274 Jim Lachey	.10	.05	.01
☐ 275 Chip Lohmiller	.10	.05	.01
☐ 276 Charles Mann	.10	.05	.01
☐ 277 Wilber Marshall	.10	.05	.01
☐ 278 Art Monk	.20	.09	.03
☐ 279 Mark Rypien	.20	.09	.03
☐ 280 Alvin Walton	.10	.05	.01
☐ 281 Randall Cunningham BR NFC Passing Leader	.35	.16	.04
☐ 282 Warren Moon BR AFC Passing Leader	.50	.23	.06
☐ 283 Barry Sanders BR NFC Rushing Leader	2.00	.90	.25
☐ 284 Thurman Thomas BR AFC Rushing Leader	.50	.23	.06
☐ 285 Jerry Rice BR NFC Receiving Leader	2.00	.90	.25
☐ 286 Haywood Jeffires BR AFC Receiving Leader	.35	.16	.04
☐ 287 Charles Haley BR NFC Sack Leader	.35	.16	.04
☐ 288 Derrick Thomas BR AFC Sack Leader	.35	.16	.04
☐ 289 NFC Logo Card	.20	.09	.03
☐ 290 AFC Logo Card	.20	.09	.03
☐ P1 Randall Cunningham Prototype	4.00	1.80	.50
☐ P2 Emmitt Smith Rookie prototype	10.00	4.50	1.25
☐ NNO Checklist Card (Double fold)	.40	.18	.05

1991 Action Packed 24K Gold

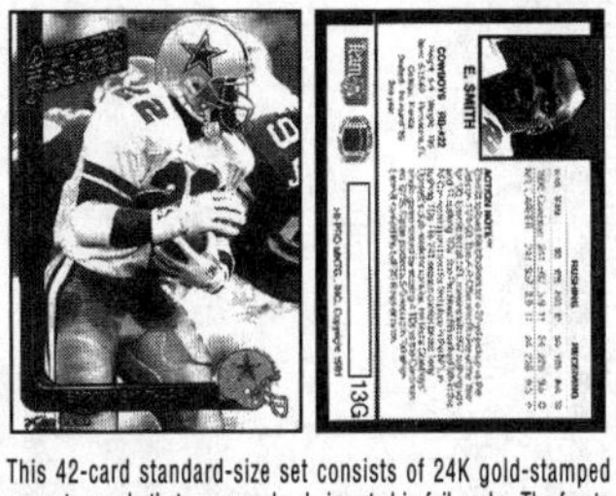

This 42-card standard-size set consists of 24K gold-stamped superstar cards that were randomly inserted in foil packs. The fronts of these cards feature borderless embossed color player photos, with gold indicia bordered in black. The team logo appears in the lower right corner. In a horizontal format, the gold-bordered backs have color head shots, biographical information, statistics, and an "Action Note" in the form of a caption to the action shot on the card front. The cards are numbered on the back. The set numbering follows an alphabetical team order. Also distributed was an 18K version of Randall Cunningham; only 23 were produced.

	MINT	NRMT	EXC
COMPLETE SET (42)	900.00	400.00	110.00
COMMON CARD (1G-42G)	12.00	5.50	1.50
☐ 1G Andre Rison	30.00	13.50	3.70
☐ 2G Deion Sanders	50.00	22.00	6.25
☐ 3G Andre Reed	30.00	13.50	3.70
☐ 4G Bruce Smith	30.00	13.50	3.70
☐ 5G Thurman Thomas	30.00	13.50	3.70
☐ 6G Neal Anderson	20.00	9.00	2.50
☐ 7G Mark Carrier DB	20.00	9.00	2.50
☐ 8G Mike Singletary	20.00	9.00	2.50
☐ 9G Boomer Esiason	20.00	9.00	2.50
☐ 10G James Francis	12.00	5.50	1.50
☐ 11G Anthony Munoz	30.00	13.50	3.70
☐ 12G Troy Aikman	90.00	40.00	11.00
☐ 13G Emmitt Smith	150.00	70.00	19.00
☐ 14G John Elway	60.00	27.00	7.50
☐ 15G Bobby Humphrey	12.00	5.50	1.50
☐ 16G Barry Sanders	90.00	40.00	11.00
☐ 17G Don Majkowski	12.00	5.50	1.50
☐ 18G Sterling Sharpe	30.00	13.50	3.70
☐ 19G Warren Moon	30.00	13.50	3.70
☐ 20G Jeff George	30.00	13.50	3.70
☐ 21G Christian Okoye	20.00	9.00	2.50
☐ 22G Derrick Thomas	30.00	13.50	3.70
☐ 23G Barry Word	12.00	5.50	1.50
☐ 24G Marcus Allen	30.00	13.50	3.70
☐ 25G Bo Jackson	30.00	13.50	3.70
☐ 26G Jim Everett	20.00	9.00	2.50
☐ 27G Cleveland Gary	12.00	5.50	1.50
☐ 28G Dan Marino	150.00	70.00	19.00
☐ 29G Herschel Walker	20.00	9.00	2.50
☐ 30G Ottis Anderson	20.00	9.00	2.50
☐ 31G Rodney Hampton	30.00	13.50	3.70
☐ 32G Dave Meggett	20.00	9.00	2.50
☐ 33G Marion Butts	20.00	9.00	2.50
☐ 34G Randall Cunningham	20.00	9.00	2.50
☐ 35G Reggie White	30.00	13.50	3.70
☐ 36G Jerry Rice	90.00	40.00	11.00
☐ 37G Eric Green	20.00	9.00	2.50
☐ 38G Charles Haley	20.00	9.00	2.50
☐ 39G Ronnie Lott	20.00	9.00	2.50
☐ 40G Joe Montana	90.00	40.00	11.00
☐ 41G Vinny Testaverde	20.00	9.00	2.50
☐ 42G Gary Clark	30.00	13.50	3.70
☐ NNO Randall Cunningham 18K Gold Card	400.00	180.00	50.00

1991 Action Packed Rookie Update

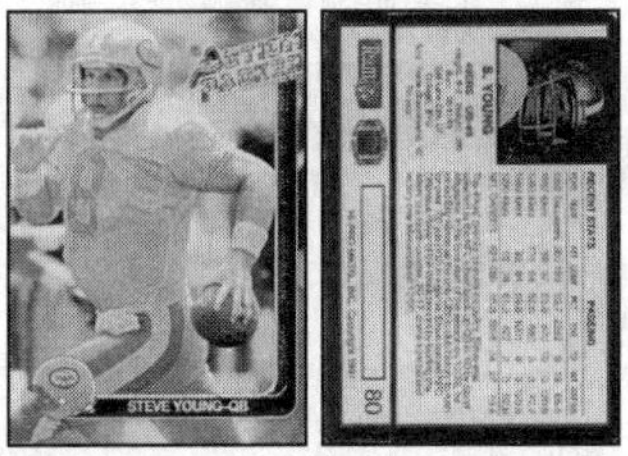

This 84-card standard-size set contains 74 Rookie Cards (including 26 first round draft picks) plus ten traded and update cards. The front design consists of embossed color player photos. Designated rookies have an embossed red helmet with a white "R". The gold indicia and logo are bordered in red instead of black as on the regular set. In red print, the horizontally oriented backs have the player's college regular season and career statistics. An Emmitt Smith rookie prototype card was included as a bonus with each case of 1991 Action Packed Rookie Update foil or sets ordered. Rookie Cards in this set include Bryan Cox, Ricky Ervins, Brett Favre, Alvin Harper, Randal Hill, Herman Moore, Russell Maryland, Eric Pegram, Mike Pritchard, Leonard Russell, Ricky Watters, and Harvey Williams.

	MINT	NRMT	EXC
COMPLETE SET (84)	15.00	6.75	1.85
COMPLETE FACT.SET (84)	16.00	7.25	2.00
COMMON CARD (1-84)	.10	.05	.01
☐ 1 Herman Moore	4.00	1.80	.50
☐ 2 Eric Turner	.20	.09	.03
☐ 3 Mike Croel	.10	.05	.01
☐ 4 Alfred Williams	.10	.05	.01
☐ 5 Stanley Richard	.10	.05	.01
☐ 6 Russell Maryland	.40	.18	.05
☐ 7 Pat Harlow	.10	.05	.01
☐ 8 Alvin Harper	.40	.18	.05
☐ 9 Mike Pritchard	.20	.09	.03
☐ 10 Leonard Russell	.40	.18	.05
☐ 11 Jarrod Bunch	.10	.05	.01
☐ 12 Dan McGwire	.10	.05	.01
☐ 13 Bobby Wilson	.10	.05	.01
☐ 14 Vinnie Clark	.10	.05	.01
☐ 15 Kelvin Pritchett	.20	.09	.03
☐ 16 Harvey Williams	.40	.18	.05
☐ 17 Stan Thomas	.10	.05	.01
☐ 18 Todd Marinovich	.10	.05	.01
☐ 19 Antone Davis	.10	.05	.01
☐ 20 Greg Lewis	.10	.05	.01
☐ 21 Brett Favre	10.00	4.50	1.25
☐ 22 Wesley Carroll	.10	.05	.01
☐ 23 Ed McCaffrey	.20	.09	.03
☐ 24 Reggie Barrett	.10	.05	.01
☐ 25 Chris Zorich	.40	.18	.05
☐ 26 Kenny Walker	.10	.05	.01
☐ 27 Aaron Craver	.10	.05	.01
☐ 28 Browning Nagle	.10	.05	.01
☐ 29 Nick Bell	.10	.05	.01
☐ 30 Anthony Morgan	.10	.05	.01
☐ 31 Jesse Campbell	.10	.05	.01
☐ 32 Eric Bieniemy	.10	.05	.01
☐ 33 Ricky Ervins UER (Totals don't add up)	.20	.09	.03
☐ 34 Kanavis McGhee	.10	.05	.01
☐ 35 Shawn Moore	.10	.05	.01
☐ 36 Todd Lyght	.10	.05	.01
☐ 37 Eric Swann	.40	.18	.05
☐ 38 Henry Jones	.20	.09	.03
☐ 39 Ted Washington	.10	.05	.01
☐ 40 Charles McRae	.10	.05	.01
☐ 41 Randal Hill	.20	.09	.03
☐ 42 Huey Richardson	.10	.05	.01
☐ 43 Roman Phifer	.10	.05	.01
☐ 44 Ricky Watters	3.00	1.35	.35
☐ 45 Esera Tuaolo	.10	.05	.01
☐ 46 Michael Jackson	.40	.18	.05
☐ 47 Shawn Jefferson	.20	.09	.03
☐ 48 Tim Barnett	.10	.05	.01
☐ 49 Chuck Webb	.10	.05	.01
☐ 50 Moe Gardner	.10	.05	.01
☐ 51 Mo Lewis	.20	.09	.03
☐ 52 Mike Dumas	.10	.05	.01
☐ 53 Jon Vaughn	.10	.05	.01
☐ 54 Jerome Henderson	.10	.05	.01
☐ 55 Harry Colon	.10	.05	.01
☐ 56 David Daniels	.10	.05	.01
☐ 57 Phil Hansen	.10	.05	.01
☐ 58 Ernie Mills	.20	.09	.03
☐ 59 John Kasay	.20	.09	.03
☐ 60 Darren Lewis	.10	.05	.01
☐ 61 James Joseph	.10	.05	.01
☐ 62 Robert Wilson	.10	.05	.01
☐ 63 Lawrence Dawsey	.20	.09	.03
☐ 64 Mike Jones	.10	.05	.01
☐ 65 Dave McCloughan	.10	.05	.01
☐ 66 Erric Pegram	.40	.18	.05
☐ 67 Aeneas Williams	.40	.18	.05
☐ 68 Reggie Johnson	.10	.05	.01
☐ 69 Todd Scott	.10	.05	.01
☐ 70 James Jones	.10	.05	.01
☐ 71 Lamar Rogers	.10	.05	.01
☐ 72 Darryll Lewis	.20	.09	.03
☐ 73 Bryan Cox	.40	.18	.05
☐ 74 Leroy Thompson	.10	.05	.01
☐ 75 Mark Higgs	.10	.05	.01
☐ 76 John Friesz	.40	.18	.05
☐ 77 Tim McKyer	.10	.05	.01
☐ 78 Roger Craig	.20	.09	.03
☐ 79 Ronnie Lott	.20	.09	.03
☐ 80 Steve Young	1.25	.55	.16
☐ 81 Percy Snow	.10	.05	.01
☐ 82 Cornelius Bennett	.20	.09	.03
☐ 83 Johnny Johnson	.10	.05	.01
☐ 84 Blair Thomas	.10	.05	.01

1991 Action Packed Rookie Update 24K Gold

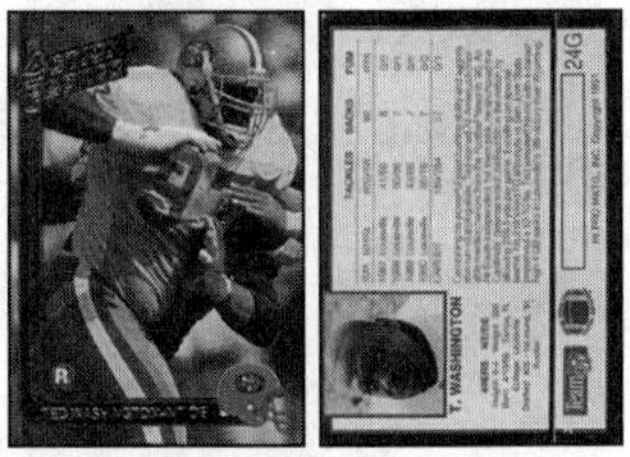

This 26-card standard-size set was issued in honor of the first round draft picks. These special cards are identified by "24K" stamped on the card front, and they were randomly inserted in 1991 Rookie Update foil packs. Like the other Rookie Update cards, the fronts have borderless embossed color player photos, with gold indicia and logo bordered in red. In a horizontal format, the backs have the player's collegiate regular season and career statistics in red print. The set numbering order is according to NFL draft order.

	MINT	NRMT	EXC
COMPLETE SET (26)	450.00	200.00	55.00
COMMON CARD (1G-26G)	15.00	6.75	1.85
☐ 1G Russell Maryland	20.00	9.00	2.50
☐ 2G Eric Turner	30.00	13.50	3.70
☐ 3G Mike Croel	15.00	6.75	1.85
☐ 4G Todd Lyght	15.00	6.75	1.85
☐ 5G Eric Swann	30.00	13.50	3.70
☐ 6G Charles McRae	15.00	6.75	1.85

	MINT	NRMT	EXC
☐ 7G Antone Davis	15.00	6.75	1.85
☐ 8G Stanley Richard	20.00	9.00	2.50
☐ 9G Herman Moore	50.00	22.00	6.25
☐ 10G Pat Harlow	15.00	6.75	1.85
☐ 11G Alvin Harper	30.00	13.50	3.70
☐ 12G Mike Pritchard	30.00	13.50	3.70
☐ 13G Leonard Russell	30.00	13.50	3.70
☐ 14G Huey Richardson	15.00	6.75	1.85
☐ 15G Dan McGwire	20.00	9.00	2.50
☐ 16G Bobby Wilson	15.00	6.75	1.85
☐ 17G Alfred Williams	15.00	6.75	1.85
☐ 18G Vinnie Clark	15.00	6.75	1.85
☐ 19G Kelvin Pritchett	20.00	9.00	2.50
☐ 20G Harvey Williams	30.00	13.50	3.70
☐ 21G Stan Thomas	15.00	6.75	1.85
☐ 22G Randal Hill	15.00	6.75	1.85
☐ 23G Todd Marinovich	20.00	9.00	2.50
☐ 24G Ted Washington	15.00	6.75	1.85
☐ 25G Henry Jones	15.00	6.75	1.85
☐ 26G Jarrod Bunch	15.00	6.75	1.85

1991 Action Packed NFLPA Awards

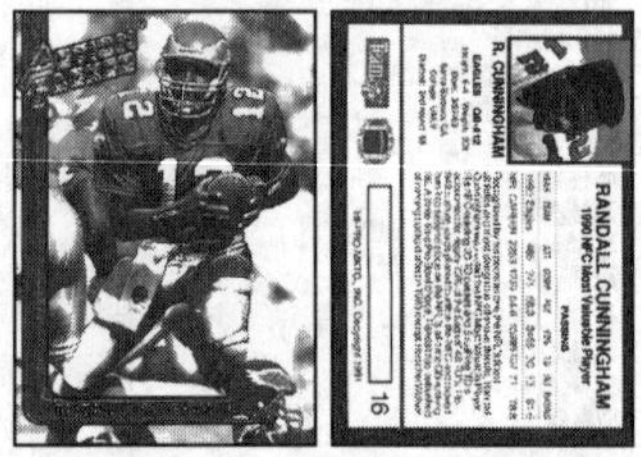

This 16-card standard-size set was produced by Action Packed to honor the athletes who earned various awards in the 1990 NFL season. There were 5,000 sets issued each in their own attractive solid black box; these boxes were individually numbered on the back. The box has the inscription NFLPA/MDA Awards Dinner March 12, 1991 on it. The cards are in the 1991 Action Packed design with a raised, 3-D like photo on the front and a hockey-stick like frame going down the left side of the card and on the bottom identifying the player. The card backs feature a portrait of the player along with biographical information and statistical information where applicable. The cards feature the now-traditional Action Packed rounded corners.

	MINT	NRMT	EXC
COMPLETE SET (16)	50.00	22.00	6.25
COMMON CARD (1-16)	3.00	1.35	.35
☐ 1 Jim Lachey NFC Offensive Lineman	3.00	1.35	.35
☐ 2 Anthony Munoz AFC Offensive Lineman	4.00	1.80	.50
☐ 3 Bruce Smith AFC Defensive Lineman	5.00	2.20	.60
☐ 4 Reggie White NFC Defensive Lineman	8.00	3.60	1.00
☐ 5 Charles Haley NFC Linebacker	4.00	1.80	.50
☐ 6 Derrick Thomas AFC Linebacker	5.00	2.20	.60
☐ 7 Albert Lewis AFC Defensive Back	3.00	1.35	.35
☐ 8 Mark Carrier DB NFC Defensive Back	4.00	1.80	.50
☐ 9 Reyna Thompson NFC Special Teams	3.00	1.35	.35
☐ 10 Steve Tasker AFC Special Teams	4.00	1.80	.50
☐ 11 James Francis AFC Defensive Rookie	3.00	1.35	.35
☐ 12 Mark Carrier DB NFC Defensive Rookie	4.00	1.80	.50
☐ 13 Johnny Johnson NFC Offensive Rookie	3.00	1.35	.35
☐ 14 Eric Green AFC Offensive Rookie	4.00	1.80	.50
☐ 15 Warren Moon AFC MVP	5.00	2.20	.60
☐ 16 Randall Cunningham NFC MVP	4.00	1.80	.50

1991 Action Packed Whizzer White Award

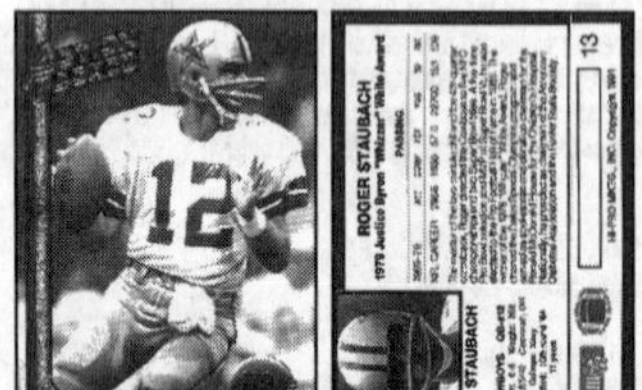

At the silver anniversary NFLPA/Mackey Awards banquet in Chicago (June 23, 1991), Action Packed presented this 25-card commemorative standard-size set in honor of the 25 winners of the Justice Byron "Whizzer" White Humanitarian Award from 1967-91. Reportedly 3,500 sets were distributed at the dinner and another 5,000 numbered boxed sets were produced for sale into the hobby. The front design features a color embossed action photo, with indicia in silver and the award year inscribed on a silver helmet. The backs have a color head shot, biographical information, career statistics, and a tribute to the player's professional career and community contributions. The card numbering follows chronologically the order in which the award was won, 1967 through 1991, inclusive.

	MINT	NRMT	EXC
COMPLETE SET (25)	60.00	27.00	7.50
COMMON CARD (1-25)	2.00	.90	.25
☐ 1 Bart Starr	8.00	3.60	1.00
☐ 2 Willie Davis	3.00	1.35	.35
☐ 3 Ed Meador	2.00	.90	.25
☐ 4 Gale Sayers	8.00	3.60	1.00
☐ 5 Kermit Alexander	2.00	.90	.25
☐ 6 Ray May	2.00	.90	.25
☐ 7 Andy Russell	2.00	.90	.25
☐ 8 Floyd Little	3.00	1.35	.35
☐ 9 Rocky Bleier	4.00	1.80	.50
☐ 10 Jim Hart	2.00	.90	.25
☐ 11 Lyle Alzado	3.00	1.35	.35
☐ 12 Archie Manning	3.00	1.35	.35
☐ 13 Roger Staubach	15.00	6.75	1.85
☐ 14 Gene Upshaw	3.00	1.35	.35
☐ 15 Ken Houston	3.00	1.35	.35
☐ 16 Franco Harris	6.00	2.70	.75
☐ 17 Doug Dieken	2.00	.90	.25
☐ 18 Rolf Benirschke	2.00	.90	.25
☐ 19 Reggie Williams	2.00	.90	.25
☐ 20 Nat Moore	2.00	.90	.25
☐ 21 George Martin	2.00	.90	.25
☐ 22 Deron Cherry	2.00	.90	.25
☐ 23 Mike Singletary	4.00	1.80	.50
☐ 24 Ozzie Newsome	3.00	1.35	.35
☐ 25 Mike Kenn	2.00	.90	.25

1992 Action Packed Prototypes

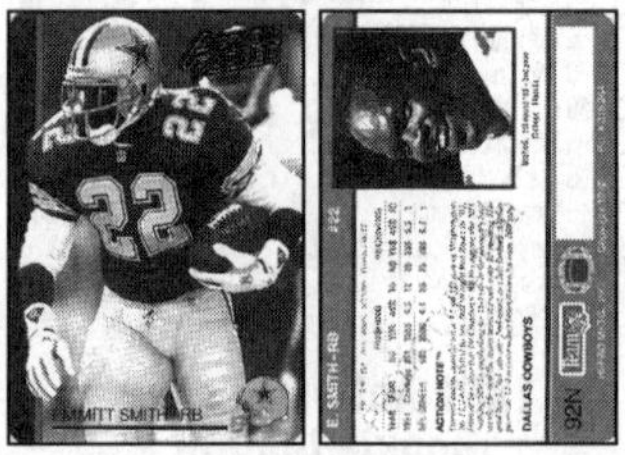

The 1992 Action Packed Prototype set contains three standard-size cards. The card design is very similar to the 1992 Action Packed regular issue cards. The cards were first distributed at the Super Bowl Show in Minneapolis in January, 1992. The cards are overstamped "Prototype" on the back. The Barry Sanders card seems to be a little more difficult to find than the other two cards.

	MINT	NRMT	EXC
COMPLETE SET (3)	20.00	9.00	2.50
COMMON CARD	3.00	1.35	.35
☐ 92A Thurman Thomas	3.00	1.35	.35
☐ 92N Emmitt Smith	12.00	5.50	1.50
☐ 92P Barry Sanders	6.00	2.70	.75

1992 Action Packed

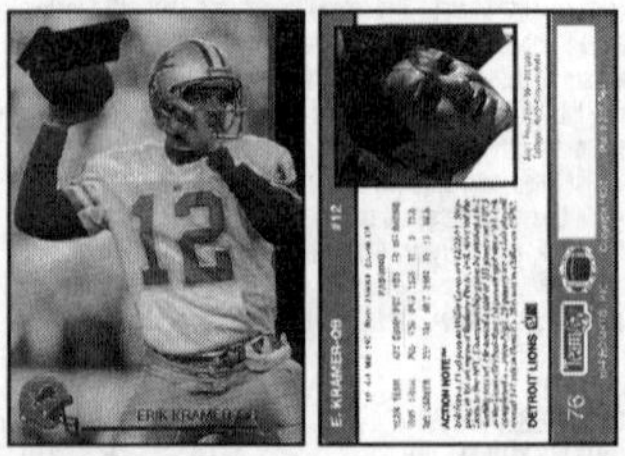

The 1992 Action Packed football set contains 280 standard-size cards. Cards were issued six per pack. The fronts feature borderless embossed color player photos, accented by either gold and aqua (NFC) or gold and red (AFC) border stripes running down either the left or right side of the card face. The team helmet appears in the lower left or right corner, with the player's name and position printed at the card bottom. The horizontally oriented backs carry biography, player profile, a color head shot, and an "Action Note" in the form of an extended caption to the photo on the front. The cards are numbered on the back and checklisted below alphabetically according to teams. There are no key Rookie Cards in this set. To show support for their injured teammate, a special "thumbs up" logo with Mike Utley's number 60 was placed on the back of all Detroit Lions' cards. The factory set closes with a Braille subset (281-288) and Logo cards (289-290). The inside lid of the factory set box has the set checklist printed on it. The eight Braille cards, available in foil packs as well as factory sets, feature category leaders by division. Action Packed also made 26 18K solid gold Tiffany-designed cards of Action Packed Player of the Year Barry Sanders. Certificates for a chance to win these cards were randomly inserted in the regular series foil packs. Action Packed also produced a 288-card "Mint" parallel version of the regular set. The Mint cards were pacakged seperately in boxes of twenty-four six-card packs.

	MINT	NRMT	EXC
COMPLETE SET (280)	35.00	16.00	4.40
COMPLETE FACT.SET (292)	50.00	22.00	6.25
COMMON CARD (1-280)	.15	.07	.02
☐ 1 Steve Broussard	.15	.07	.02
☐ 2 Michael Haynes	.25	.11	.03
☐ 3 Tim McKyer	.15	.07	.02
☐ 4 Chris Miller	.25	.11	.03
☐ 5 Andre Rison	.25	.11	.03
☐ 6 Jessie Tuggle	.15	.07	.02
☐ 7 Mike Pritchard	.15	.07	.02
☐ 8 Moe Gardner	.15	.07	.02
☐ 9 Brian Jordan	.25	.11	.03
☐ 10 Mike Kenn and Chris Hinton	.15	.07	.02
☐ 11 Steve Tasker	.25	.11	.03
☐ 12 Cornelius Bennett	.25	.11	.03
☐ 13 Shane Conlan	.15	.07	.02
☐ 14 Darryl Talley	.15	.07	.02
☐ 15 Thurman Thomas	.50	.23	.06
☐ 16 James Lofton	.25	.11	.03
☐ 17 Don Beebe	.15	.07	.02
☐ 18 Jim Ritcher	.15	.07	.02
☐ 19 Keith McKeller	.15	.07	.02
☐ 20 Nate Odomes	.15	.07	.02
☐ 21 Mark Carrier DB	.15	.07	.02
☐ 22 Wendell Davis	.15	.07	.02
☐ 23 Richard Dent	.25	.11	.03
☐ 24 Jim Harbaugh	.50	.23	.06
☐ 25 Jay Hilgenberg	.15	.07	.02
☐ 26 Steve McMichael	.25	.11	.03
☐ 27 Tom Waddle	.15	.07	.02
☐ 28 Neal Anderson	.15	.07	.02
☐ 29 Brad Muster	.15	.07	.02
☐ 30 Shaun Gayle	.15	.07	.02
☐ 31 Jim Breech	.15	.07	.02
☐ 32 James Brooks	.15	.07	.02
☐ 33 James Francis	.15	.07	.02
☐ 34 David Fulcher	.15	.07	.02
☐ 35 Harold Green	.15	.07	.02
☐ 36 Rodney Holman	.15	.07	.02
☐ 37 Anthony Munoz	.25	.11	.03
☐ 38 Tim Krumrie	.15	.07	.02
☐ 39 Tim McGee	.15	.07	.02
☐ 40 Eddie Brown	.15	.07	.02
☐ 41 Kevin Mack	.15	.07	.02
☐ 42 James Jones	.15	.07	.02
☐ 43 Vince Newsome	.15	.07	.02
☐ 44 Ed King	.15	.07	.02
☐ 45 Eric Metcalf	.25	.11	.03
☐ 46 Leroy Hoard	.25	.11	.03
☐ 47 Stephen Braggs	.15	.07	.02
☐ 48 Clay Matthews	.25	.11	.03
☐ 49 David Brandon	.15	.07	.02
☐ 50 Rob Burnett	.15	.07	.02
☐ 51 Larry Brown DB	.15	.07	.02
☐ 52 Alvin Harper	.25	.11	.03
☐ 53 Michael Irvin	.50	.23	.06
☐ 54 Ken Norton Jr.	.50	.23	.06
☐ 55 Jay Novacek	.25	.11	.03
☐ 56 Emmitt Smith	5.00	2.20	.60
☐ 57 Tony Tolbert	.15	.07	.02
☐ 58 Nate Newton	.25	.11	.03
☐ 59 Steve Beuerlein	.15	.07	.02
☐ 60 Tony Casillas	.15	.07	.02
☐ 61 Steve Atwater	.15	.07	.02
☐ 62 Mike Croel	.15	.07	.02
☐ 63 Gaston Green	.15	.07	.02
☐ 64 Mark Jackson	.15	.07	.02
☐ 65 Greg Kragen	.15	.07	.02
☐ 66 Karl Mecklenburg	.15	.07	.02
☐ 67 Dennis Smith	.15	.07	.02
☐ 68 Steve Sewell	.15	.07	.02
☐ 69 John Elway	2.00	.90	.25
☐ 70 Simon Fletcher	.15	.07	.02
☐ 71 Mel Gray	.15	.07	.02
☐ 72 Barry Sanders	3.00	1.35	.35
☐ 73 Jerry Ball	.15	.07	.02
☐ 74 Bennie Blades	.15	.07	.02
☐ 75 Lomas Brown	.15	.07	.02
☐ 76 Erik Kramer	.25	.11	.03
☐ 77 Chris Spielman	.25	.11	.03
☐ 78 Ray Crockett	.15	.07	.02
☐ 79 Willie Green	.15	.07	.02
☐ 80 Rodney Peete	.25	.11	.03
☐ 81 Sterling Sharpe	.50	.23	.06
☐ 82 Tony Bennett	.15	.07	.02
☐ 83 Chuck Cecil	.15	.07	.02
☐ 84 Perry Kemp	.15	.07	.02
☐ 85 Brian Noble	.15	.07	.02
☐ 86 Darrell Thompson	.15	.07	.02
☐ 87 Mike Tomczak	.15	.07	.02
☐ 88 Vince Workman	.15	.07	.02
☐ 89 Esera Tuaolo	.15	.07	.02
☐ 90 Mark Murphy	.15	.07	.02
☐ 91 William Fuller	.25	.11	.03
☐ 92 Ernest Givins	.25	.11	.03
☐ 93 Drew Hill	.15	.07	.02
☐ 94 Al Smith	.15	.07	.02
☐ 95 Ray Childress	.15	.07	.02
☐ 96 Haywood Jeffires	.25	.11	.03
☐ 97 Cris Dishman	.15	.07	.02
☐ 98 Warren Moon	.50	.23	.06
☐ 99 Lamar Lathon	.15	.07	.02
☐ 100 Mike Munchak and Bruce Matthews	.15	.07	.02
☐ 101 Bill Brooks	.15	.07	.02
☐ 102 Duane Bickett	.15	.07	.02
☐ 103 Eugene Daniel	.15	.07	.02
☐ 104 Jeff Herrod	.15	.07	.02
☐ 105 Jessie Hester	.15	.07	.02
☐ 106 Donnell Thompson	.15	.07	.02
☐ 107 Anthony Johnson	.25	.11	.03
☐ 108 Jon Hand	.15	.07	.02
☐ 109 Rohn Stark	.15	.07	.02
☐ 110 Clarence Verdin	.15	.07	.02
☐ 111 Derrick Thomas	.50	.23	.06
☐ 112 Steve DeBerg	.15	.07	.02
☐ 113 Deron Cherry	.15	.07	.02
☐ 114 Chris Martin	.15	.07	.02
☐ 115 Christian Okoye	.15	.07	.02
☐ 116 Dan Saleaumua	.15	.07	.02
☐ 117 Neil Smith	.50	.23	.06
☐ 118 Barry Word	.15	.07	.02
☐ 119 Tim Barnett	.15	.07	.02
☐ 120 Albert Lewis	.15	.07	.02
☐ 121 Ronnie Lott	.25	.11	.03
☐ 122 Marcus Allen	.50	.23	.06
☐ 123 Todd Marinovich	.15	.07	.02
☐ 124 Nick Bell	.15	.07	.02
☐ 125 Tim Brown	.50	.23	.06
☐ 126 Ethan Horton	.15	.07	.02
☐ 127 Greg Townsend	.15	.07	.02
☐ 128 Jeff Gossett and Jeff Jaeger	.15	.07	.02
☐ 129 Scott Davis	.15	.07	.02
☐ 130 Steve Wisniewski and Don Mosebar	.15	.07	.02
☐ 131 Kevin Greene	.50	.23	.06
☐ 132 Roman Phifer	.15	.07	.02
☐ 133 Tony Zendejas	.15	.07	.02
☐ 134 Pat Terrell	.15	.07	.02
☐ 135 Flipper Anderson	.15	.07	.02
☐ 136 Robert Delpino	.15	.07	.02
☐ 137 Jim Everett	.25	.11	.03
☐ 138 Larry Kelm	.15	.07	.02
☐ 139 Todd Lyght	.15	.07	.02
☐ 140 Henry Ellard	.25	.11	.03
☐ 141 Mark Clayton	.25	.11	.03
☐ 142 Jeff Cross	.15	.07	.02
☐ 143 Mark Duper	.15	.07	.02
☐ 144 John Offerdahl	.15	.07	.02
☐ 145 Louis Oliver	.15	.07	.02
☐ 146 Pete Stoyanovich	.15	.07	.02
☐ 147 Richmond Webb	.15	.07	.02
☐ 148 Mark Higgs	.15	.07	.02
☐ 149 Tony Paige	.15	.07	.02
☐ 150 Bryan Cox	.25	.11	.03
☐ 151 Anthony Carter	.25	.11	.03
☐ 152 Cris Carter	.50	.23	.06
☐ 153 Rich Gannon	.15	.07	.02
☐ 154 Steve Jordan	.15	.07	.02
☐ 155 Mike Merriweather	.15	.07	.02
☐ 156 Henry Thomas	.15	.07	.02
☐ 157 Herschel Walker	.25	.11	.03
☐ 158 Randall McDaniel	.15	.07	.02
☐ 159 Terry Allen	1.25	.55	.16
☐ 160 Joey Browner	.15	.07	.02
☐ 161 Leonard Russell	.25	.11	.03
☐ 162 Bruce Armstrong	.15	.07	.02
☐ 163 Vincent Brown	.15	.07	.02
☐ 164 Hugh Millen	.15	.07	.02
☐ 165 Andre Tippett	.15	.07	.02
☐ 166 Jon Vaughn	.15	.07	.02
☐ 167 Pat Harlow	.15	.07	.02
☐ 168 Marv Cook	.15	.07	.02
☐ 169 Irving Fryar	.25	.11	.03
☐ 170 Maurice Hurst	.15	.07	.02
☐ 171 Pat Swilling	.25	.11	.03
☐ 172 Vince Buck	.15	.07	.02
☐ 173 Rickey Jackson	.15	.07	.02
☐ 174 Sam Mills	.15	.07	.02
☐ 175 Bobby Hebert	.15	.07	.02
☐ 176 Vaughan Johnson	.15	.07	.02
☐ 177 Floyd Turner	.15	.07	.02
☐ 178 Fred McAfee	.15	.07	.02
☐ 179 Morten Andersen	.15	.07	.02
☐ 180 Eric Martin	.15	.07	.02
☐ 181 Rodney Hampton	.50	.23	.06
☐ 182 Pepper Johnson	.15	.07	.02
☐ 183 Leonard Marshall	.15	.07	.02
☐ 184 Stephen Baker	.15	.07	.02
☐ 185 Mark Ingram	.15	.07	.02
☐ 186 Dave Meggett	.25	.11	.03
☐ 187 Bart Oates	.15	.07	.02
☐ 188 Mark Collins	.15	.07	.02
☐ 189 Myron Guyton	.15	.07	.02
☐ 190 Jeff Hostetler	.25	.11	.03
☐ 191 Jeff Lageman	.15	.07	.02
☐ 192 Brad Baxter	.15	.07	.02
☐ 193 Mo Lewis	.15	.07	.02
☐ 194 Chris Burkett	.15	.07	.02
☐ 195 James Hasty	.15	.07	.02
☐ 196 Rob Moore	.25	.11	.03

☐ 197 Kyle Clifton	.15	.07	.02
☐ 198 Terance Mathis	.25	.11	.03
☐ 199 Marvin Washington	.15	.07	.02
☐ 200 Lonnie Young	.15	.07	.02
☐ 201 Reggie White	.50	.23	.06
☐ 202 Eric Allen	.15	.07	.02
☐ 203 Fred Barnett	.25	.11	.03
☐ 204 Keith Byars	.15	.07	.02
☐ 205 Seth Joyner	.25	.11	.03
☐ 206 Clyde Simmons	.15	.07	.02
☐ 207 Jerome Brown	.15	.07	.02
☐ 208 Wes Hopkins	.15	.07	.02
☐ 209 Keith Jackson	.25	.11	.03
☐ 210 Calvin Williams	.25	.11	.03
☐ 211 Aeneas Williams	.25	.11	.03
☐ 212 Ken Harvey	.15	.07	.02
☐ 213 Ernie Jones	.15	.07	.02
☐ 214 Freddie Joe Nunn	.15	.07	.02
☐ 215 Rich Camarillo	.15	.07	.02
☐ 216 Johnny Johnson	.15	.07	.02
☐ 217 Tim McDonald	.15	.07	.02
☐ 218 Eric Swann	.25	.11	.03
☐ 219 Eric Hill	.15	.07	.02
☐ 220 Anthony Thompson	.15	.07	.02
☐ 221 Hardy Nickerson	.50	.23	.06
☐ 222 Barry Foster	.25	.11	.03
☐ 223 Louis Lipps	.15	.07	.02
☐ 224 Greg Lloyd	.50	.23	.06
☐ 225 Neil O'Donnell	.50	.23	.06
☐ 226 Jerrol Williams	.15	.07	.02
☐ 227 Eric Green	.15	.07	.02
☐ 228 Rod Woodson	.50	.23	.06
☐ 229 Carnell Lake	.15	.07	.02
☐ 230 Dwight Stone	.15	.07	.02
☐ 231 Marion Butts	.15	.07	.02
☐ 232 John Friesz	.25	.11	.03
☐ 233 Burt Grossman	.15	.07	.02
☐ 234 Ronnie Harmon	.15	.07	.02
☐ 235 Gill Byrd	.15	.07	.02
☐ 236 Rod Bernstine	.15	.07	.02
☐ 237 Courtney Hall	.15	.07	.02
☐ 238 Nate Lewis	.15	.07	.02
☐ 239 Joe Phillips	.15	.07	.02
☐ 240 Henry Rolling	.15	.07	.02
☐ 241 Keith Henderson	.15	.07	.02
☐ 242 Guy McIntyre	.15	.07	.02
☐ 243 Bill Romanowski	.15	.07	.02
☐ 244 Don Griffin	.15	.07	.02
☐ 245 Dexter Carter	.15	.07	.02
☐ 246 Charles Haley	.25	.11	.03
☐ 247 Brent Jones	.25	.11	.03
☐ 248 John Taylor	.25	.11	.03
☐ 249 Steve Young	2.00	.90	.25
☐ 250 Larry Roberts	.15	.07	.02
☐ 251 Brian Blades	.25	.11	.03
☐ 252 Jacob Green	.15	.07	.02
☐ 253 John Kasay	.15	.07	.02
☐ 254 Cortez Kennedy	.25	.11	.03
☐ 255 Rufus Porter	.15	.07	.02
☐ 256 John L. Williams	.15	.07	.02
☐ 257 Tommy Kane	.15	.07	.02
☐ 258 Eugene Robinson	.15	.07	.02
☐ 259 Terry Wooden	.15	.07	.02
☐ 260 Chris Warren	.50	.23	.06
☐ 261 Lawrence Dawsey	.15	.07	.02
☐ 262 Mark Carrier WR	.25	.11	.03
☐ 263 Keith McCants	.15	.07	.02
☐ 264 Jesse Solomon	.15	.07	.02
☐ 265 Vinny Testaverde	.25	.11	.03
☐ 266 Ricky Reynolds	.15	.07	.02
☐ 267 Broderick Thomas	.15	.07	.02
☐ 268 Gary Anderson RB	.15	.07	.02
☐ 269 Reggie Cobb	.15	.07	.02
☐ 270 Tony Covington	.15	.07	.02
☐ 271 Darrell Green	.15	.07	.02
☐ 272 Charles Mann	.15	.07	.02
☐ 273 Wilber Marshall	.15	.07	.02
☐ 274 Gary Clark	.50	.23	.06
☐ 275 Chip Lohmiller	.15	.07	.02
☐ 276 Earnest Byner	.15	.07	.02
☐ 277 Jim Lachey	.15	.07	.02
☐ 278 Art Monk	.25	.11	.03
☐ 279 Mark Rypien	.15	.07	.02
☐ 280 Mark Schlereth	.15	.07	.02
☐ 281 Mark Rypien BR NFC Passing Yardage Leader	.50	.23	.06
☐ 282 Warren Moon BR AFC Passing Yardage Leader	.50	.23	.06
☐ 283 Emmitt Smith BR NFC Rushing Leader	4.00	1.80	.50
☐ 284 Thurman Thomas BR AFC Rushing Leader	.50	.23	.06
☐ 285 Michael Irvin BR NFC Receiving Leader	.50	.23	.06
☐ 286 Haywood Jeffires BR AFC Receiving Leader	.50	.23	.06
☐ 287 Pat Swilling BR NFC Sack Leader	.50	.23	.06
☐ 288 Ronnie Lott BR AFC Interception Leader	.50	.23	.06
☐ 289 NFC Logo (Only available in factory sets)	.25	.11	.03
☐ 290 AFC Logo (Only available in factory sets)	.25	.11	.03
☐ 43G Barry Sanders 24K GOLD	15.00	6.75	1.85
☐ 44G Barry Sanders 24K GOLD	15.00	6.75	1.85
☐ NNO Barry Sanders (18K version)	500.00	220.00	60.00

1992 Action Packed Mint Parallel

Action Packed produced this 288-card "Mint" version of the regular set pacaged seperately. Production was limited to 500 individually numbered "Mint" versions of each player card. Twenty-four six-card packs were packaged in a gold, velour-lined box, and purchase of an even-numbered box and an odd-numbered box guaranteed receipt of the complete 288-card set. Sets were initially offered for sale on July 7, 1992 at a special reception during the 13th Annual National Sports Card Convention in Atlanta, Georgia. Collectors who placed an order on that day received a free Barry Sanders prototype card. The player's image on the front is embossed and accented by 24K gold leaf. The card edges are black.

	MINT	NRMT	EXC
COMPLETE SET (288)	2500.00	1100.00	300.00
COMMON CARD (1-288)	20.00	9.00	2.50

*MINT CARDS: 75X TO 125X BASIC CARDS

1992 Action Packed 24K Gold

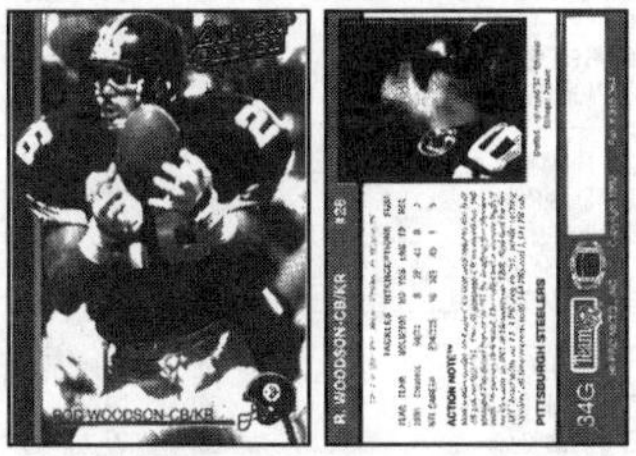

This 42-card standard-size set consists of 24K gold-stamped cards that were randomly inserted in foil packs. Barry Sanders (card number 13G) autographed 1,000 of his cards. The set numbering follows alphabetical order of team names. The fronts feature borderless embossed color player photos with gold indicia. The horizontally oriented backs have a mugshot, biography, statistics, and an "Action Note" in the form of a caption to the action shot on the front. The style of the cards is very similar to that of the 1992 Action Packed regular issue cards.

	MINT	NRMT	EXC
COMPLETE SET (42)	900.00	400.00	110.00
COMMON CARD (1G-42G)	15.00	6.75	1.85
☐ 1G Michael Haynes	25.00	11.00	3.10
☐ 2G Chris Miller	25.00	11.00	3.10
☐ 3G Andre Rison	35.00	16.00	4.40
☐ 4G Cornelius Bennett	25.00	11.00	3.10
☐ 5G James Lofton	25.00	11.00	3.10
☐ 6G Thurman Thomas	35.00	16.00	4.40
☐ 7G Neal Anderson	15.00	6.75	1.85
☐ 8G Michael Irvin	35.00	16.00	4.40
☐ 9G Emmitt Smith	160.00	70.00	20.00
☐ 10G Mike Croel	15.00	6.75	1.85
☐ 11G John Elway	60.00	27.00	7.50
☐ 12G Gaston Green	15.00	6.75	1.85
☐ 13G Barry Sanders	90.00	40.00	11.00
☐ 14G Sterling Sharpe	35.00	16.00	4.40
☐ 15G Ernest Givins	15.00	6.75	1.85
☐ 16G Drew Hill	15.00	6.75	1.85
☐ 17G Haywood Jeffires	25.00	11.00	3.10
☐ 18G Warren Moon	35.00	16.00	4.40
☐ 19G Christian Okoye	15.00	6.75	1.85
☐ 20G Derrick Thomas	35.00	16.00	4.40
☐ 21G Ronnie Lott	25.00	11.00	3.10
☐ 22G Todd Marinovich	15.00	6.75	1.85
☐ 23G Henry Ellard	25.00	11.00	3.10
☐ 24G Mark Clayton	25.00	11.00	3.10
☐ 25G Herschel Walker	25.00	11.00	3.10
☐ 26G Irving Fryar	25.00	11.00	3.10
☐ 27G Leonard Russell	25.00	11.00	3.10
☐ 28G Pat Swilling	25.00	11.00	3.10
☐ 29G Rodney Hampton	35.00	16.00	4.40
☐ 30G Rob Moore	25.00	11.00	3.10
☐ 31G Seth Joyner	15.00	6.75	1.85
☐ 32G Reggie White	35.00	16.00	4.40
☐ 33G Eric Green	25.00	11.00	3.10
☐ 34G Rod Woodson	35.00	16.00	4.40
☐ 35G Marion Butts	15.00	6.75	1.85
☐ 36G Charles Haley	25.00	11.00	3.10
☐ 37G John Taylor	25.00	11.00	3.10
☐ 38G Steve Young	60.00	27.00	7.50
☐ 39G Earnest Byner	15.00	6.75	1.85
☐ 40G Gary Clark	35.00	16.00	4.40
☐ 41G Art Monk	25.00	11.00	3.10
☐ 42G Mark Rypien	15.00	6.75	1.85
☐ 13GAU Barry Sanders AUTO Signed 24K Gold Card	375.00	170.00	47.50

1992 Action Packed Rookie Update

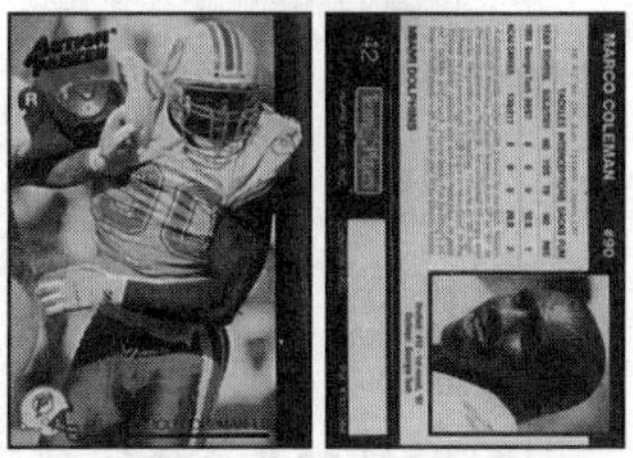

This 84-card standard-size set features 25 first round draft choices pictured in their NFL uniforms and some of the league's outstanding veteran players. Cards were issued in six-card packs. Action Packed guaranteed one 1st round draft pick in each seven-card foil pack. The foil packs also included randomly inserted 24K gold cards of the quarterbacks and 1st round draft choices as well as a special "Neon Deion Sanders" card featuring neon fluorescent orange and numbered "84N". No factory sets were made. The fronts feature full-bleed embossed color player photos that are edged on one side by black and gold foil stripes. The player's name and position are gold-foil stamped at the bottom alongside a representation of the team helmet. The horizontal backs display a color head shot, biography, statistics, and career summary. A black stripe at the bottom carries the card number and an autograph slot. Players aligned with both NFL Properties and the NFL Players Association appear together in this set. Rookie Cards in this set include Edgar Bennett, Terrell Buckley, Marco Coleman,Quentin Coryatt, Steve Emtman, Sean Gilbert, Johnny Mitchell and Carl Pickens. Action Packed also produced a 24K Gold "Mint" rookie/update set. The 24K gold "Mint" cards were sold in seperately issued six-card packs, with seven packs to a box. Each of the 250 "Mint" cards of each player were individually numbered (1/250, 2/250, etc.).

	MINT	NRMT	EXC
COMPLETE SET (84)	15.00	6.75	1.85
COMMON CARD (1-84)	.15	.07	.02
☐ 1 Steve Emtman	.15	.07	.02
☐ 2 Quentin Coryatt	.50	.23	.06
☐ 3 Sean Gilbert	.50	.23	.06
☐ 4 John Fina	.15	.07	.02
☐ 5 Alonzo Spellman	.25	.11	.03
☐ 6 Amp Lee	.15	.07	.02
☐ 7 Robert Porcher	.15	.07	.02
☐ 8 Jason Hanson	.25	.11	.03
☐ 9 Ty Detmer	1.00	.45	.12
☐ 10 Ray Roberts	.15	.07	.02
☐ 11 Bob Whitfield	.15	.07	.02
☐ 12 Greg Skrepenak	.15	.07	.02
☐ 13 Vaughn Dunbar	.15	.07	.02
☐ 14 Siran Stacy	.15	.07	.02
☐ 15 Mark D'Onofrio	.15	.07	.02
☐ 16 Tony Sacca	.15	.07	.02
☐ 17 Dana Hall	.25	.11	.03
☐ 18 Courtney Hawkins	.25	.11	.03
☐ 19 Shane Collins	.15	.07	.02
☐ 20 Tony Smith	.15	.07	.02
☐ 21 Rod Smith	.15	.07	.02
☐ 22 Troy Auzenne	.15	.07	.02
☐ 23 David Klingler	.25	.11	.03
☐ 24 Darryl Williams	.15	.07	.02
☐ 25 Carl Pickens	5.00	2.20	.60
☐ 26 Ricardo McDonald	.15	.07	.02
☐ 27 Tommy Vardell	.25	.11	.03
☐ 28 Kevin Smith	.50	.23	.06
☐ 29 Rodney Culver	.15	.07	.02
☐ 30 Jimmy Smith	.50	.23	.06
☐ 31 Robert Jones	.15	.07	.02
☐ 32 Tommy Maddox	.15	.07	.02
☐ 33 Shane Dronett	.15	.07	.02
☐ 34 Terrell Buckley	.15	.07	.02
☐ 35 Santana Dotson	.50	.23	.06
☐ 36 Edgar Bennett	2.50	1.10	.30
☐ 37 Ashley Ambrose	.25	.11	.03
☐ 38 Dale Carter	.50	.23	.06
☐ 39 Chester McGlockton	.50	.23	.06
☐ 40 Steve Israel	.15	.07	.02
☐ 41 Marc Boutte	.15	.07	.02
☐ 42 Marco Coleman	.25	.11	.03
☐ 43 Troy Vincent	.25	.11	.03
☐ 44 Mark Wheeler	.15	.07	.02
☐ 45 Darren Perry	.15	.07	.02
☐ 46 Eugene Chung	.15	.07	.02
☐ 47 Derek Brown TE	.15	.07	.02
☐ 48 Phillippi Sparks	.15	.07	.02
☐ 49 Johnny Mitchell	.15	.07	.02
☐ 50 Kurt Barber	.15	.07	.02
☐ 51 Leon Searcy	.25	.11	.03
☐ 52 Chris Mims	.25	.11	.03
☐ 53 Keith Jackson	.25	.11	.03
☐ 54 Charles Haley	.25	.11	.03
☐ 55 Dave Krieg	.25	.11	.03
☐ 56 Dan McGwire	.15	.07	.02
☐ 57 Phil Simms	.25	.11	.03
☐ 58 Bobby Humphrey	.15	.07	.02
☐ 59 Jerry Rice	2.50	1.10	.30
☐ 60 Joe Montana	2.50	1.10	.30
☐ 61 Junior Seau	.50	.23	.06
☐ 62 Leslie O'Neal	.25	.11	.03
☐ 63 Anthony Miller	.25	.11	.03
☐ 64 Timm Rosenbach	.15	.07	.02
☐ 65 Herschel Walker	.25	.11	.03
☐ 66 Randal Hill	.15	.07	.02
☐ 67 Randall Cunningham	.25	.11	.03
☐ 68 Al Toon	.25	.11	.03
☐ 69 Browning Nagle	.15	.07	.02
☐ 70 Lawrence Taylor	.50	.23	.06
☐ 71 Dan Marino	4.00	1.80	.50
☐ 72 Eric Dickerson	.25	.11	.03
☐ 73 Harvey Williams	.50	.23	.06
☐ 74 Jeff George	.50	.23	.06
☐ 75 Russell Maryland	.25	.11	.03
☐ 76 Troy Aikman	2.50	1.10	.30
☐ 77 Michael Dean Perry	.25	.11	.03
☐ 78 Bernie Kosar	.25	.11	.03
☐ 79 Boomer Esiason	.25	.11	.03
☐ 80 Mike Singletary	.25	.11	.03
☐ 81 Bruce Smith	.50	.23	.06
☐ 82 Andre Reed	.25	.11	.03
☐ 83 Jim Kelly	.50	.23	.06
☐ 84 Deion Sanders	1.50	.70	.19
☐ 84N Deion Sanders Neon orange card	15.00	6.75	1.85

1992 Action Packed Rookie Update Mint Parallel

Action Packed produced this 24K Gold Mint Parallel set to its 1992 Rookie/Update release. The Mint cards were seperately released in six-card packs, with seven packs to a box. Each box was numbered 1 through 500, and the purchase of an even-numbered and an odd-numbered box produced a complete set of cards. Moreover, each card was individually numbered of 250 (1/250, 2/250, etc.).

	MINT	NRMT	EXC
COMPLETE SET (84)	1500.00	700.00	190.00
COMMON CARD (1-84)	30.00	13.50	3.70

*MINT CARDS: 100X TO 200X BASIC CARDS

1992 Action Packed Rookie Update 24K Gold

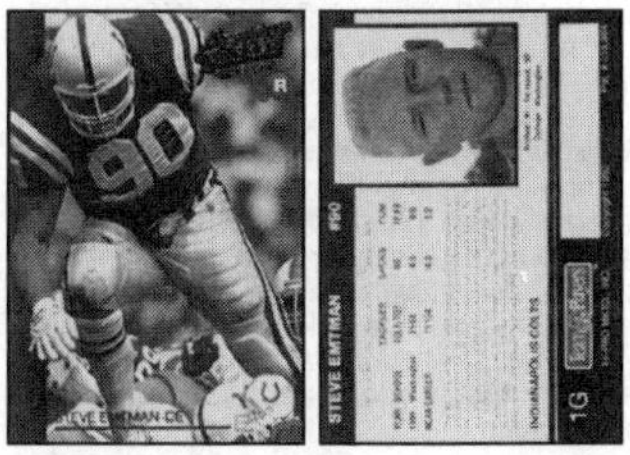

The players selected by Action Packed for this 35-card 24K Gold set include eight NFL quarterbacks (26-33) and first round draft picks in the regular Rookie/Update set. These rounded-corner cards were randomly inserted into packs and have a similar design to the basic cards. The words, "24 KARAT GOLD" are on front.

	MINT	NRMT	EXC
COMPLETE SET (35)	700.00	325.00	90.00
COMMON CARD (1G-35G)	15.00	6.75	1.85
☐ 1G Steve Emtman	25.00	11.00	3.10
☐ 2G Quentin Coryatt	30.00	13.50	3.70
☐ 3G Sean Gilbert	25.00	11.00	3.10
☐ 4G Terrell Buckley	25.00	11.00	3.10
☐ 5G David Klingler	30.00	13.50	3.70
☐ 6G Troy Vincent	30.00	13.50	3.70
☐ 7G Tommy Vardell	25.00	11.00	3.10
☐ 8G Leon Searcy	25.00	11.00	3.10
☐ 9G Marco Coleman	25.00	11.00	3.10
☐ 10G Eugene Chung	15.00	6.75	1.85
☐ 11G Derek Brown TE	25.00	11.00	3.10
☐ 12G Johnny Mitchell	30.00	13.50	3.70
☐ 13G Chester McGlockton	30.00	13.50	3.70
☐ 14G Kevin Smith	30.00	13.50	3.70
☐ 15G Dana Hall	25.00	11.00	3.10
☐ 16G Tony Smith	15.00	6.75	1.85
☐ 17G Dale Carter	25.00	11.00	3.10
☐ 18G Vaughn Dunbar	25.00	11.00	3.10
☐ 19G Alonzo Spellman	30.00	13.50	3.70
☐ 20G Chris Mims	30.00	13.50	3.70
☐ 21G Robert Jones	25.00	11.00	3.10
☐ 22G Tommy Maddox	25.00	11.00	3.10
☐ 23G Robert Porcher	25.00	11.00	3.10
☐ 24G John Fina	15.00	6.75	1.85
☐ 25G Darryl Williams	15.00	6.75	1.85
☐ 26G Jim Kelly	30.00	13.50	3.70
☐ 27G Randall Cunningham	25.00	11.00	3.10
☐ 28G Dan Marino	125.00	55.00	15.50
☐ 29G Troy Aikman	90.00	40.00	11.00
☐ 30G Boomer Esiason	25.00	11.00	3.10
☐ 31G Bernie Kosar	25.00	11.00	3.10
☐ 32G Jeff George	30.00	13.50	3.70
☐ 33G Phil Simms	25.00	11.00	3.10
☐ 34G Ray Roberts	15.00	6.75	1.85
☐ 35G Bob Whitfield	15.00	6.75	1.85

1992 Action Packed Mackey Award

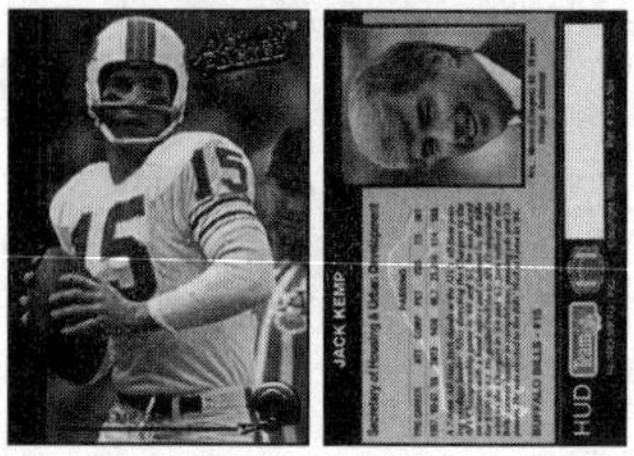

Only 2,000 numbered sets of these three 24K gold standard-size cards were produced for the attendees at the 1992 NFLPA Mackey Awards Banquet.

	MINT	NRMT	EXC
COMPLETE SET (3)	100.00	45.00	12.50
COMMON CARD	20.00	9.00	2.50
☐ 92W Reggie White	30.00	13.50	3.70
☐ HOF John Mackey	20.00	9.00	2.50
☐ HUD Jack Kemp	50.00	22.00	6.25

1992 Action Packed NFLPA/MDA Award 24K

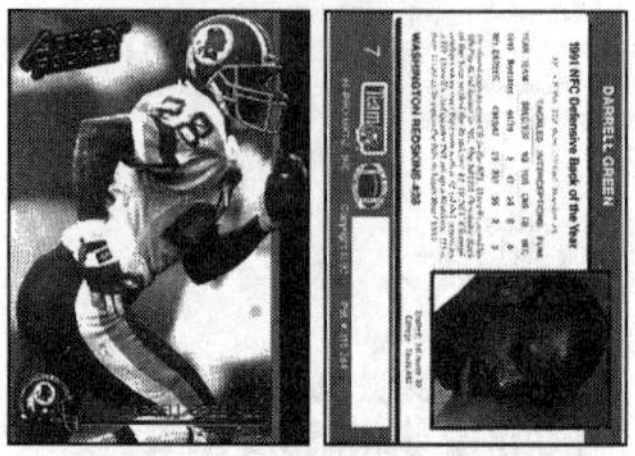

This 16-card, 24K gold standard-size set was produced by Action Packed to honor NFL Players of the Year for the 1991 season. Cards come packed in an attractive black box imprinted on front with NFLPA/MDA Awards Dinner, March 5, 1992. Only 1,000 sets were produced, and banquet attendees each received a set stamped "Banquet Edition." Card fronts feature a raised-print player photo and team helmet. The Action Packed logo appears in the upper left corner of red cards (AFC) and in the upper right on blue cards (NFC). Players' names appear at the lower right or left of each card offsetting the logo. Handsomely designed with 24K gold borders and lettering, horizontally designed backs feature biographical and statistical information and a head shot of each player within a 24K gold box. Featuring the traditional rounded corners, cards are numbered in the lower left corner.

	MINT	NRMT	EXC
COMPLETE SET (16)	250.00	110.00	31.00
COMMON CARD (1-16)	10.00	4.50	1.25
☐ 1 Steve Wisniewski	10.00	4.50	1.25
☐ 2 Jim Lachey	10.00	4.50	1.25
☐ 3 Reggie White	30.00	13.50	3.70
☐ 4 William Fuller	10.00	4.50	1.25
☐ 5 Derrick Thomas	20.00	9.00	2.50
☐ 6 Pat Swilling	10.00	4.50	1.25
☐ 7 Darrell Green	10.00	4.50	1.25
☐ 8 Ronnie Lott	15.00	6.75	1.85
☐ 9 Steve Tasker	10.00	4.50	1.25
☐ 10 Mel Gray	10.00	4.50	1.25
☐ 11 Aeneas Williams	10.00	4.50	1.25
☐ 12 Mike Croel	10.00	4.50	1.25
☐ 13 Leonard Russell	15.00	6.75	1.85
☐ 14 Lawrence Dawsey	15.00	6.75	1.85
☐ 15 Barry Sanders	75.00	34.00	9.50
☐ 16 Thurman Thomas	40.00	18.00	5.00

1993 Action Packed Troy Aikman Promos

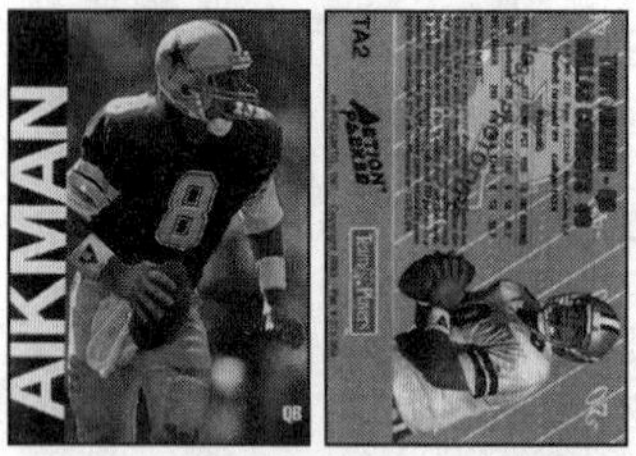

This two-card standard-size set honors Cowboys' quarterback, Troy Aikman. The fronts feature borderless embossed color player photos, accented by a gold border stripe running down either the right or left side of the card face. The stripe is printed with the player's name in large white block letters. The horizontal backs display a color cut-out image from the waist up of Aikman against a green football field background. The player's name and team name are printed in red above biographical information, statistics, and career highlights. Sponsor logos appear in the green margin at the bottom. The phrase "1993 Prototype" are printed in gray across the text. The cards were produced on a prototype sheet which included eleven different Aikmans, TA1 through TA11; however only TA2 and TA3 were formally released.

	MINT	NRMT	EXC
COMPLETE SET (2)	50.00	22.00	6.25
COMMON CARD (TA2-TA3)	25.00	11.00	3.10
☐ TA2 Troy Aikman (Running with ball)	25.00	11.00	3.10
☐ TA3 Troy Aikman (Pitching the ball)	25.00	11.00	3.10

1993 Action Packed Emmitt Smith Promos

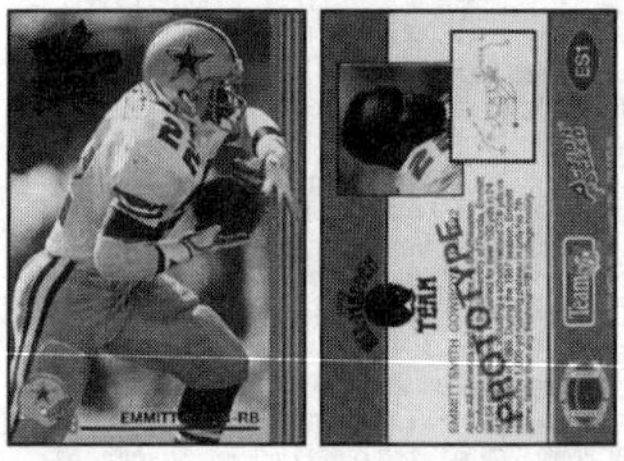

This five-card standard-size set was issued to promote the 1993 Action Packed All-Madden Team set. The fronts feature borderless embossed color player photos, accented by gold and aqua border stripes running down the right side of the card face. The All-Madden Team logo appears in the upper left corner, with the team helmet, player's name, and position printed at the card bottom. Between aqua border stripes, the horizontal backs carry player profile, a color headshot, and a diagram of a football play. The word "Prototype" is printed across the text. Two of these cards (ES1 and ES4) were given out at the 1993 Super Bowl Card Show. The ES5 card was a give-away to members of the Tuff Stuff Buyers Club.

	MINT	NRMT	EXC
COMPLETE SET (5)	35.00	16.00	4.40
COMMON CARD (ES1-ES5)	5.00	2.20	.60
☐ ES1 Emmitt Smith (Receiving handoff from quarterback; side view)	5.00	2.20	.60
☐ ES2 Emmitt Smith	10.00	4.50	1.25
☐ ES3 Emmitt Smith	10.00	4.50	1.25
☐ ES4 Emmitt Smith (Cutting to right to elude tackler; ball cradled in left arm)	5.00	2.20	.60
☐ ES5 Emmitt Smith (Running to right; ball in left arm)	8.00	3.60	1.00

1993 Action Packed Prototypes

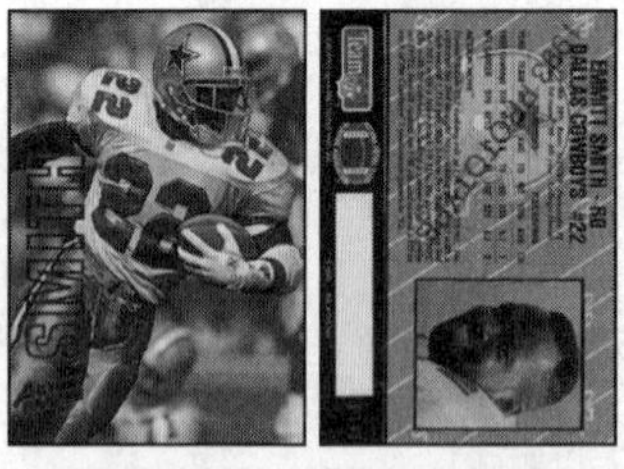

These six standard-size cards were issued to show the design of the 1993 Action Packed regular series. The fronts feature the traditional full-bleed embossed color player photos. The player's last name is printed vertically in gold-foil block lettering running down one of the sides. On a green football field design, the horizontal backs carry biography, 1992 season and career statistics, and an "Action Note". The disclaimer "1993 Prototype" is printed diagonally across the back. A black stripe edged by gold foil has an autograph space and the card number.

	MINT	NRMT	EXC
COMPLETE SET (6)	35.00	16.00	4.40
COMMON CARD (FB1-FB6)	4.00	1.80	.50
☐ FB1 Emmitt Smith	12.00	5.50	1.50
☐ FB2 Thurman Thomas	5.00	2.20	.60
☐ FB3 Steve Young	6.00	2.70	.75
☐ FB4 Barry Sanders	7.00	3.10	.85
☐ FB5 Barry Foster	4.00	1.80	.50
☐ FB6 Warren Moon	5.00	2.20	.60

1993 Action Packed

The 1993 Action Packed football set consists of 222 standard-size cards. The full-bleed color action photos on the fronts have the player's name etched in a two-tone gold foil strip running down the

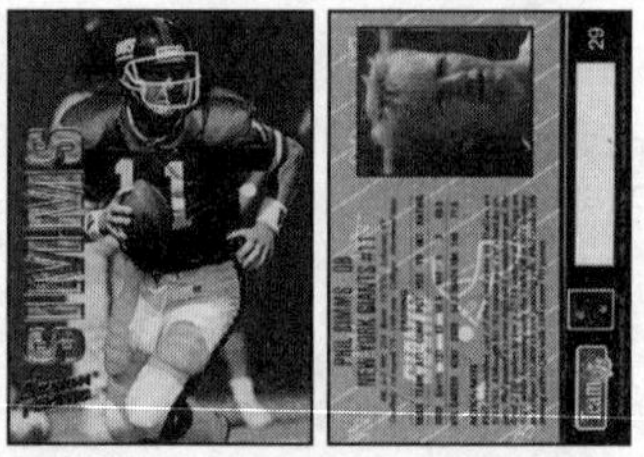

side. The backs have a playing field with the team helmet in the center and player information, statistics, an Action Note, and a head shot. A 60-card Rookie Update series begins at card number 163, where the first series leaves off. It features players selected in the early rounds of the NFL draft wearing their NFL uniforms. The fronts feature an embossed color player cut-out against a full-bleed background that consists of a tilted colored panel bordered on two sides by foil. Depending on the round the player was drafted, the foil varies from gold (first round, 163-192); to silver (second round, 193-210); to bronze (third round, 211-215). Players drafted after the third round have their panels bordered in a non-foil sky blue color (cards 217-222). The horizontal backs carry a color close-up photo, '92 college season and NCAA career statistics, biography and college career highlights. Rookie Cards include Jerome Bettis, Drew Bledsoe, Vincent Brisby, Reggie Brooks, Mark Brunell, Curtis Conway, Garrison Hearst, Qadry Ismail, Terry Kirby, O.J. McDuffie, Natrone Means, Rick Mirer, Glyn Milburn, Dana Stubblefield and Kevin Williams.

	MINT	NRMT	EXC
COMPLETE SET (222)	75.00	34.00	9.50
COMPLETE SERIES 1 (162)	45.00	20.00	5.50
COMPLETE SERIES 2 (60)	30.00	13.50	3.70
COMMON CARD (1-222)	.20	.09	.03
☐ 1 Michael Haynes	.30	.14	.04
☐ 2 Chris Miller	.30	.14	.04
☐ 3 Andre Rison	.30	.14	.04
☐ 4 Jim Kelly	.60	.25	.07
☐ 5 Andre Reed	.30	.14	.04
☐ 6 Thurman Thomas	.60	.25	.07
☐ 7 Jim Harbaugh	.60	.25	.07
☐ 8 Harold Green	.20	.09	.03
☐ 9 David Klingler	.20	.09	.03
☐ 10 Bernie Kosar	.30	.14	.04
☐ 11 Troy Aikman	3.00	1.35	.35
☐ 12 Michael Irvin	.60	.25	.07
☐ 13 Emmitt Smith	5.00	2.20	.60
☐ 14 John Elway	2.00	.90	.25
☐ 15 Barry Sanders	3.00	1.35	.35
☐ 16 Brett Favre	5.00	2.20	.60
☐ 17 Sterling Sharpe	.60	.25	.07
☐ 18 Ernest Givins	.30	.14	.04
☐ 19 Haywood Jeffires	.30	.14	.04
☐ 20 Warren Moon	.60	.25	.07
☐ 21 Lorenzo White	.20	.09	.03
☐ 22 Jeff George	.60	.25	.07
☐ 23 Joe Montana	3.00	1.35	.35
☐ 24 Jim Everett	.30	.14	.04
☐ 25 Cleveland Gary	.20	.09	.03
☐ 26 Dan Marino	5.00	2.20	.60
☐ 27 Terry Allen	.60	.25	.07
☐ 28 Rodney Hampton	.60	.25	.07
☐ 29 Phil Simms	.30	.14	.04
☐ 30 Fred Barnett	.30	.14	.04
☐ 31 Randall Cunningham	.30	.14	.04
☐ 32 Gary Clark	.30	.14	.04
☐ 33 Barry Foster	.30	.14	.04
☐ 34 Neil O'Donnell	.60	.25	.07
☐ 35 Stan Humphries	.60	.25	.07
☐ 36 Anthony Miller	.30	.14	.04
☐ 37 Jerry Rice	3.00	1.35	.35
☐ 38 Ricky Watters	.60	.25	.07
☐ 39 Steve Young	2.00	.90	.25
☐ 40 Chris Warren	.30	.14	.04
☐ 41 Reggie Cobb	.20	.09	.03
☐ 42 Mark Rypien	.20	.09	.03
☐ 43 Deion Sanders	2.00	.90	.25
☐ 44 Henry Jones	.20	.09	.03
☐ 45 Bruce Smith	.60	.25	.07
☐ 46 Richard Dent	.30	.14	.04
☐ 47 Tommy Vardell	.20	.09	.03
☐ 48 Charles Haley	.30	.14	.04
☐ 49 Ken Norton Jr.	.30	.14	.04
☐ 50 Jay Novacek	.30	.14	.04
☐ 51 Simon Fletcher	.20	.09	.03
☐ 52 Pat Swilling	.20	.09	.03
☐ 53 Tony Bennett	.20	.09	.03
☐ 54 Reggie White	.60	.25	.07
☐ 55 Ray Childress	.20	.09	.03
☐ 56 Quentin Coryatt	.30	.14	.04
☐ 57 Steve Emtman	.20	.09	.03
☐ 58 Derrick Thomas	.60	.25	.07
☐ 59 James Lofton	.30	.14	.04
☐ 60 Marco Coleman	.20	.09	.03
☐ 61 Bryan Cox	.20	.09	.03
☐ 62 Troy Vincent	.20	.09	.03
☐ 63 Chris Doleman	.20	.09	.03
☐ 64 Audray McMillian	.20	.09	.03
☐ 65 Vaughn Dunbar	.20	.09	.03
☐ 66 Rickey Jackson	.20	.09	.03
☐ 67 Lawrence Taylor	.60	.25	.07
☐ 68 Ronnie Lott	.30	.14	.04
☐ 69 Rob Moore	.30	.14	.04
☐ 70 Browning Nagle	.20	.09	.03
☐ 71 Eric Allen	.20	.09	.03
☐ 72 Tim Harris	.20	.09	.03
☐ 73 Clyde Simmons	.20	.09	.03
☐ 74 Steve Beuerlein	.20	.09	.03
☐ 75 Randal Hill	.20	.09	.03
☐ 76 Darren Perry	.20	.09	.03
☐ 77 Rod Woodson	.60	.25	.07
☐ 78 Marion Butts	.20	.09	.03
☐ 79 Chris Mims	.20	.09	.03
☐ 80 Junior Seau	.60	.25	.07
☐ 81 Cortez Kennedy	.30	.14	.04
☐ 82 Santana Dotson	.30	.14	.04
☐ 83 Earnest Byner	.20	.09	.03
☐ 84 Charles Mann	.20	.09	.03
☐ 85 Pierce Holt	.20	.09	.03
☐ 86 Mike Pritchard	.30	.14	.04
☐ 87 Cornelius Bennett	.30	.14	.04
☐ 88 Neal Anderson	.20	.09	.03
☐ 89 Carl Pickens	2.00	.90	.25
☐ 90 Eric Metcalf	.30	.14	.04
☐ 91 Michael Dean Perry	.30	.14	.04
☐ 92 Alvin Harper	.30	.14	.04
☐ 93 Robert Jones	.20	.09	.03
☐ 94 Steve Atwater	.20	.09	.03
☐ 95 Rod Bernstine	.20	.09	.03
☐ 96 Herman Moore	2.00	.90	.25
☐ 97 Chris Spielman	.30	.14	.04
☐ 98 Terrell Buckley	.20	.09	.03
☐ 99 Dale Carter	.20	.09	.03
☐ 100 Terry McDaniel	.20	.09	.03
☐ 101 Tim Brown	.60	.25	.07
☐ 102 Gaston Green	.20	.09	.03
☐ 103 Howie Long	.30	.14	.04
☐ 104 Todd Marinovich	.20	.09	.03
☐ 105 Anthony Smith	.20	.09	.03
☐ 106 Flipper Anderson	.20	.09	.03
☐ 107 Henry Ellard	.30	.14	.04
☐ 108 Mark Higgs	.20	.09	.03
☐ 109 Keith Jackson	.30	.14	.04
☐ 110 Irving Fryar	.30	.14	.04
☐ 111 Cris Carter	.60	.25	.07
☐ 112 Leonard Russell	.30	.14	.04
☐ 113 Wayne Martin	.20	.09	.03
☐ 114 Mark Jackson	.20	.09	.03
☐ 115 Dave Meggett	.20	.09	.03
☐ 116 Brad Baxter	.20	.09	.03
☐ 117 Boomer Esiason	.30	.14	.04
☐ 118 Johnny Johnson	.20	.09	.03
☐ 119 Seth Joyner	.20	.09	.03
☐ 120 Kevin Greene	.60	.25	.07
☐ 121 Greg Lloyd	.60	.25	.07
☐ 122 Brent Jones	.30	.14	.04
☐ 123 Amp Lee	.20	.09	.03
☐ 124 Tim McDonald	.20	.09	.03
☐ 125 Darrell Green	.20	.09	.03
☐ 126 Art Monk	.30	.14	.04
☐ 127 Tony Smith	.20	.09	.03
☐ 128 Bill Brooks	.20	.09	.03
☐ 129 Kenneth Davis	.20	.09	.03
☐ 130 Donnell Woolford	.20	.09	.03
☐ 131 Derrick Fenner	.20	.09	.03
☐ 132 Michael Jackson	.30	.14	.04
☐ 133 Mark Clayton	.20	.09	.03
☐ 134 Al Smith	.20	.09	.03
☐ 135 Curtis Duncan	.20	.09	.03
☐ 136 Rodney Culver	.20	.09	.03
☐ 137 Harvey Williams	.30	.14	.04
☐ 138 Neil Smith	.60	.25	.07
☐ 139 Marcus Allen	.60	.25	.07
☐ 140 Eric Dickerson	.30	.14	.04
☐ 141 Sean Gilbert	.30	.14	.04
☐ 142 Shane Conlan	.20	.09	.03
☐ 143 Todd Scott	.20	.09	.03
☐ 144 Vincent Brown	.20	.09	.03
☐ 145 Andre Tippett	.20	.09	.03
☐ 146 Jon Vaughn	.20	.09	.03
☐ 147 Marv Cook	.20	.09	.03
☐ 148 Morten Andersen	.20	.09	.03
☐ 149 Sam Mills	.20	.09	.03
☐ 150 Mark Collins	.20	.09	.03
☐ 151 Heath Sherman	.20	.09	.03
☐ 152 Johnny Bailey	.20	.09	.03
☐ 153 Eric Green	.20	.09	.03
☐ 154 Ronnie Harmon	.20	.09	.03
☐ 155 Gill Byrd	.20	.09	.03
☐ 156 Leslie O'Neal	.30	.14	.04
☐ 157 Rufus Porter	.20	.09	.03
☐ 158 Eugene Robinson	.20	.09	.03
☐ 159 Broderick Thomas	.20	.09	.03
☐ 160 Lawrence Dawsey	.20	.09	.03
☐ 161 Anthony Munoz	.30	.14	.04
☐ 162 Wilber Marshall	.20	.09	.03
☐ 163 Drew Bledsoe	8.00	3.60	1.00
☐ 164 Rick Mirer	3.50	1.55	.45
☐ 165 Garrison Hearst	3.50	1.55	.45
☐ 166 Marvin Jones	.20	.09	.03
☐ 167 John Copeland	.30	.14	.04
☐ 168 Eric Curry	.20	.09	.03
☐ 169 Curtis Conway	2.50	1.10	.30
☐ 170 William Roaf	.30	.14	.04
☐ 171 Lincoln Kennedy	.20	.09	.03
☐ 172 Jerome Bettis	4.00	1.80	.50

	MINT	NRMT	EXC
☐ 173 Dan Williams	.20	.09	.03
☐ 174 Patrick Bates	.20	.09	.03
☐ 175 Brad Hopkins	.20	.09	.03
☐ 176 Steve Everitt	.20	.09	.03
☐ 177 Wayne Simmons UER (College touchdowns and yards are in wrong columns)	.20	.09	.03
☐ 178 Tom Carter	.30	.14	.04
☐ 179 Ernest Dye	.20	.09	.03
☐ 180 Lester Holmes	.20	.09	.03
☐ 181 Irv Smith	.20	.09	.03
☐ 182 Robert Smith	2.50	1.10	.30
☐ 183 Darrien Gordon	.20	.09	.03
☐ 184 Deon Figures	.30	.14	.04
☐ 185 Leonard Renfro	.20	.09	.03
☐ 186 O.J. McDuffie	2.50	1.10	.30
☐ 187 Dana Stubblefield	.60	.25	.07
☐ 188 Todd Kelly	.20	.09	.03
☐ 189 Thomas Smith	.30	.14	.04
☐ 190 George Teague	.30	.14	.04
☐ 191 Wilber Marshall	.20	.09	.03
☐ 192 Reggie White	.60	.25	.07
☐ 193 Carlton Gray	.20	.09	.03
☐ 194 Chris Slade	.30	.14	.04
☐ 195 Ben Coleman	.20	.09	.03
☐ 196 Ryan McNeil	.20	.09	.03
☐ 197 Demetrius DuBose	.20	.09	.03
☐ 198 Coleman Rudolph	.20	.09	.03
☐ 199 Tony McGee	.30	.14	.04
☐ 200 Troy Drayton	.30	.14	.04
☐ 201 Natrone Means	3.50	1.55	.45
☐ 202 Glyn Milburn	.60	.25	.07
☐ 203 Chad Brown	.30	.14	.04
☐ 204 Reggie Brooks	.30	.14	.04
☐ 205 Kevin Williams	.75	.35	.09
☐ 206 Micheal Barrow	.20	.09	.03
☐ 207 Roosevelt Potts	.20	.09	.03
☐ 208 Victor Bailey	.20	.09	.03
☐ 209 Qadry Ismail	.60	.25	.07
☐ 210 Vincent Brisby	.60	.25	.07
☐ 211 Billy Joe Hobert	1.25	.55	.16
☐ 212 Lamar Thomas	.20	.09	.03
☐ 213 Jason Elam	.20	.09	.03
☐ 214 Andre Hastings	.60	.25	.07
☐ 215 Terry Kirby	1.00	.45	.12
☐ 216 Joe Montana	3.00	1.35	.35
☐ 217 Derrick Lassic	.20	.09	.03
☐ 218 Mark Brunell	8.00	3.60	1.00
☐ 219 Vaughn Hebron	.20	.09	.03
☐ 220 Troy Brown	.20	.09	.03
☐ 221 Derek Brown RB	.20	.09	.03
☐ 222 Raghib Ismail	.30	.14	.04

1993 Action Packed 24K Gold

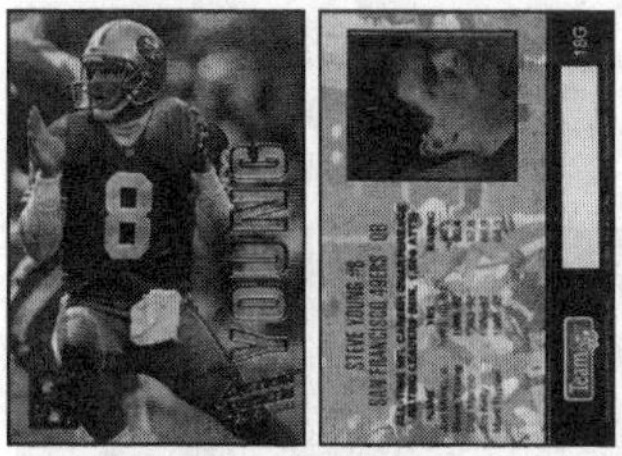

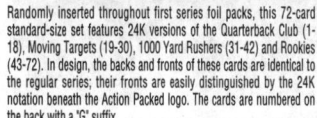

Randomly inserted throughout first series foil packs, this 72-card standard-size set features 24K versions of the Quarterback Club (1-18), Moving Targets (19-30), 1000 Yard Rushers (31-42) and Rookies (43-72). In design, the backs and fronts of these cards are identical to the regular series; their fronts are easily distinguished by the 24K notation beneath the Action Packed logo. The cards are numbered on the back with a "G" suffix.

	MINT	NRMT	EXC
COMPLETE SET (72)	2000.00	900.00	250.00
COMPLETE SERIES 1 (42)	1200.00	550.00	150.00
COMPLETE SERIES 2 (30)	800.00	350.00	100.00
COMMON CARD (1G-72G)	15.00	6.75	1.85
☐ 1G Troy Aikman	70.00	32.00	8.75
☐ 2G Randall Cunningham	25.00	11.00	3.10
☐ 3G John Elway	60.00	27.00	7.50
☐ 4G Jim Everett	25.00	11.00	3.10
☐ 5G Brett Favre	125.00	55.00	15.50
☐ 6G Jim Harbaugh	35.00	16.00	4.40
☐ 7G Jeff Hostetler	25.00	11.00	3.10
☐ 8G Jim Kelly	35.00	16.00	4.40
☐ 9G David Klingler	25.00	11.00	3.10
☐ 10G Bernie Kosar	25.00	11.00	3.10
☐ 11G Dan Marino	125.00	55.00	15.50
☐ 12G Chris Miller	25.00	11.00	3.10
☐ 13G Boomer Esiason	25.00	11.00	3.10
☐ 14G Warren Moon	35.00	16.00	4.40
☐ 15G Neil O'Donnell	35.00	16.00	4.40
☐ 16G Mark Rypien	25.00	11.00	3.10
☐ 17G Phil Simms	25.00	11.00	3.10
☐ 18G Steve Young	60.00	27.00	7.50
☐ 19G Fred Barnett	25.00	11.00	3.10
☐ 20G Gary Clark	25.00	11.00	3.10
☐ 21G Mark Clayton	25.00	11.00	3.10
☐ 22G Ernest Givins	25.00	11.00	3.10
☐ 23G Michael Haynes	15.00	6.75	1.85
☐ 24G Michael Irvin	35.00	16.00	4.40
☐ 25G Haywood Jeffires	15.00	6.75	1.85
☐ 26G Anthony Miller	25.00	11.00	3.10
☐ 27G Andre Reed	35.00	16.00	4.40
☐ 28G Jerry Rice	70.00	32.00	8.75
☐ 29G Andre Rison	35.00	16.00	4.40
☐ 30G Sterling Sharpe	35.00	16.00	4.40
☐ 31G Terry Allen	35.00	16.00	4.40
☐ 32G Reggie Cobb	15.00	6.75	1.85
☐ 33G Barry Foster	25.00	11.00	3.10
☐ 34G Cleveland Gary	15.00	6.75	1.85
☐ 35G Harold Green	15.00	6.75	1.85
☐ 36G Rodney Hampton	35.00	16.00	4.40
☐ 37G Barry Sanders	70.00	32.00	8.75
☐ 38G Emmitt Smith	125.00	55.00	15.50
☐ 39G Thurman Thomas	35.00	16.00	4.40
☐ 40G Chris Warren	35.00	16.00	4.40
☐ 41G Ricky Watters	35.00	16.00	4.40
☐ 42G Lorenzo White	15.00	6.75	1.85
☐ 43G Drew Bledsoe	80.00	36.00	10.00
☐ 44G Rick Mirer	40.00	18.00	5.00
☐ 45G Garrison Hearst	40.00	18.00	5.00
☐ 46G Marvin Jones	15.00	6.75	1.85
☐ 47G John Copeland	25.00	11.00	3.10
☐ 48G Eric Curry	25.00	11.00	3.10
☐ 49G Curtis Conway	35.00	16.00	4.40
☐ 50G Willie Roaf	25.00	11.00	3.10
☐ 51G Lincoln Kennedy	15.00	6.75	1.85
☐ 52G Jerome Bettis	50.00	22.00	6.25
☐ 53G Dan Williams	15.00	6.75	1.85
☐ 54G Patrick Bates	15.00	6.75	1.85
☐ 55G Brad Hopkins	15.00	6.75	1.85
☐ 56G Steve Everitt	25.00	11.00	3.10
☐ 57G Wayne Simmons	25.00	11.00	3.10
☐ 58G Tom Carter	25.00	11.00	3.10
☐ 59G Ernest Dye	15.00	6.75	1.85
☐ 60G Lester Holmes	15.00	6.75	1.85
☐ 61G Irv Smith	25.00	11.00	3.10
☐ 62G Robert Smith	35.00	16.00	4.40
☐ 63G Darrien Gordon	15.00	6.75	1.85
☐ 64G Deon Figures	25.00	11.00	3.10
☐ 65G Leonard Renfro	15.00	6.75	1.85
☐ 66G O.J. McDuffie	35.00	16.00	4.40
☐ 67G Dana Stubblefield	25.00	11.00	3.10
☐ 68G Todd Kelly	15.00	6.75	1.85
☐ 69G Thomas Smith	25.00	11.00	3.10
☐ 70G George Teague	25.00	11.00	3.10
☐ 71G Wilber Marshall	15.00	6.75	1.85
☐ 72G Reggie White	35.00	16.00	4.40

1993 Action Packed Moving Targets

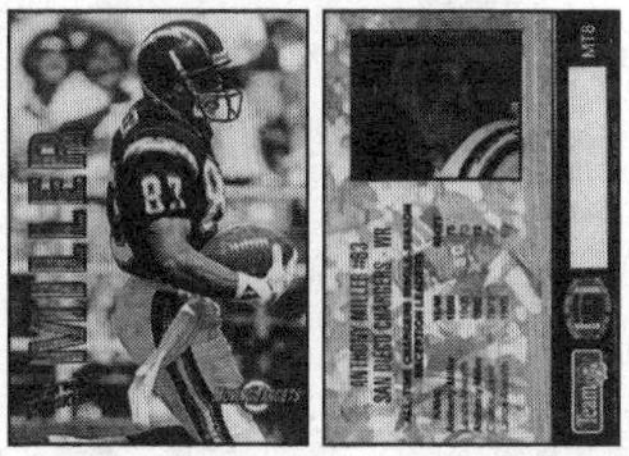

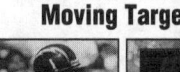

This 12-card standard-size set was randomly inserted in first series packs. The full-bleed embossed player photos on the fronts have the player's name printed in gold foil running down the left edge. The "Moving Targets" logo appears in the lower right corner. On a background consisting of an oil painting of a football scene depicting the position featured, the backs show a color head shot and charts highlighting the player's accomplishment. A black stripe carrying an autograph slot and the card number (with a "MT" prefix) round out the back.

	MINT	NRMT	EXC
COMPLETE SET (12)	10.00	4.50	1.25
COMMON CARD (MT1-MT12)	.50	.23	.06
☐ MT1 Fred Barnett	.75	.35	.09
☐ MT2 Gary Clark	.75	.35	.09
☐ MT3 Mark Clayton	.75	.35	.09
☐ MT4 Ernest Givins	.75	.35	.09
☐ MT5 Michael Haynes	.50	.23	.06
☐ MT6 Michael Irvin	1.25	.55	.16
☐ MT7 Haywood Jeffires	.50	.23	.06
☐ MT8 Anthony Miller	.75	.35	.09
☐ MT9 Andre Reed	1.25	.55	.16
☐ MT10 Jerry Rice	4.00	1.80	.50
☐ MT11 Andre Rison	1.25	.55	.16
☐ MT12 Sterling Sharpe	1.25	.55	.16

1993 Action Packed QB Club

This 18-card set was randomly inserted in first series packs. The Quarterback Club cards were also done in braille; these cards have a "B" prefix after the number, and some were donated to over 400 schools for the blind. Finally, certificates for Mint versions (which are totally 24K gold leaf) of these cards were randomly packed in hobby boxes. Five hundred of each card were produced and individually numbered. They typically carry a 50-100 times premium. The regular cards are numbered on the back with a "QB" prefix. Complete sheets were also available as a pack redemption offer. The uncut sheets are worth the same as the complete sets.

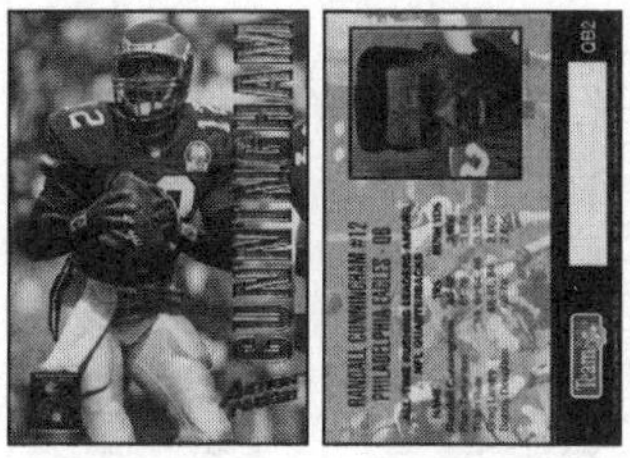

	MINT	NRMT	EXC
COMPLETE SET (18)	18.00	8.00	2.20
COMMON CARD (QB1-QB18)	.50	.23	.06
☐ QB1 Troy Aikman	4.00	1.80	.50
☐ QB2 Randall Cunningham	.75	.35	.09
☐ QB3 John Elway	3.00	1.35	.35
☐ QB4 Jim Everett	.50	.23	.06
☐ QB5 Brett Favre	6.00	2.70	.75
☐ QB6 Jim Harbaugh	1.25	.55	.16
☐ QB7 Jeff Hostetler	.75	.35	.09
☐ QB8 Jim Kelly	1.25	.55	.16
☐ QB9 David Klingler	.50	.23	.06
☐ QB10 Bernie Kosar	.50	.23	.06
☐ QB11 Dan Marino	6.00	2.70	.75
☐ QB12 Chris Miller	.50	.23	.06
☐ QB13 Boomer Esiason	.75	.35	.09
☐ QB14 Warren Moon	1.25	.55	.16
☐ QB15 Neil O'Donnell	1.25	.55	.16
☐ QB16 Mark Rypien	.50	.23	.06
☐ QB17 Phil Simms	.75	.35	.09
☐ QB18 Steve Young	3.00	1.35	.35

1993 Action Packed QB Club Braille

A parallel set of the Quarterback Club cards were produced with a braille cardback. These cards carry a "B" suffix after the card number and were randomly inserted in packs. A number of the cards were donated to over 400 schools for the blind.

	MINT	NRMT	EXC
COMPLETE SET (18)	50.00	22.00	6.25
COMMON CARD (QB1B-QB18B)	1.50	.70	.09

*BRAILLE VERSIONS: 2X to 3X BASIC CARDS

1993 Action Packed QB Club Mint

The Action Packed Quarterback Club cards were produced in a 24K gold Mint version. Certificates for these Mint cards (which are fully 24K gold leaf) were randomly packed in hobby boxes. Five hundred of each card was produced and individually numbered.

	MINT	NRMT	EXC
COMPLETE SET (18)	1500.00	700.00	190.00
COMMON CARD (QB1-QB18)	50.00	22.00	6.25

MINT CARDS: 50X TO 100X BASIC CARDS

1993 Action Packed Rookie Update Previews

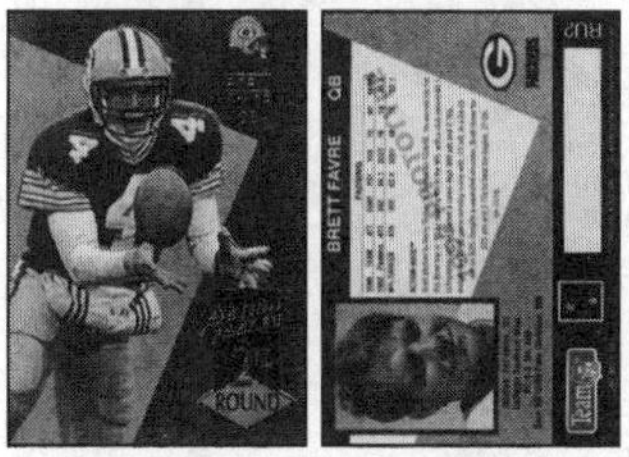

These three standard-size cards preview the design of the 1993 Action Packed Rookies set. Card numbers 1-3 represent quarterbacks taken in the first three rounds of various NFL drafts. The fronts feature a color player cut-out against a full-bleed background that consists of a tilted colored panel bordered on two sides by foil. Depending on the round the player was drafted, the foil varies from gold (first round) to silver (second round) and then to bronze (third round). The horizontal backs carry a color close-up photo, '92 and career passing statistics, biography, and an "Action Note" that describes the game situation portrayed by the front picture before summarizing the player's performance. The set was issued as a special chiptopper in first series hobby boxes. The cards are numbered on the back with an "RU" prefix.

	MINT	NRMT	EXC
COMPLETE SET (3)	5.00	2.20	.60
COMMON CARD (RU1-RU3)	1.00	.45	.12
☐ RU1 Troy Aikman	2.00	.90	.25
☐ RU2 Brett Favre	2.50	1.10	.30
☐ RU3 Neil O'Donnell	1.00	.45	.12

1993 Action Packed Rushers

Featuring outstanding running backs, this 12-card set was randomly inserted in first series packs. The fronts display full-bleed, embossed

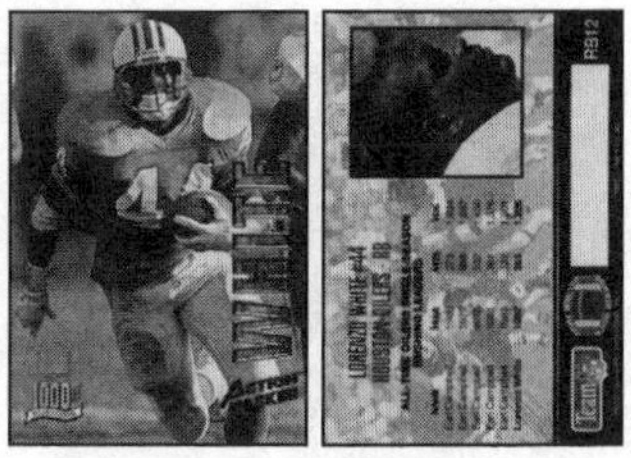

color action player photos, with a special "1000 Yard Rushers" logo in one of the lower corners. The player's last name is gold-foil stamped in block lettering and runs parallel to the side of the card. On a background consisting of an oil painting of a runner breaking through the line, the horizontal backs carry a color head shot and statistics on all-time single-season rushing leaders for the player's team. A black stripe at the bottom with a white slot for autograph rounds out the back. The cards are numbered on the back with an "RB" prefix.

	MINT	NRMT	EXC
COMPLETE SET (12)	15.00	6.75	1.85
COMMON CARD (RB1-RB12)	.50	.23	.06
☐ RB1 Terry Allen	1.25	.55	.16
☐ RB2 Reggie Cobb	.50	.23	.06
☐ RB3 Barry Foster	.75	.35	.09
☐ RB4 Cleveland Gary	.50	.23	.06
☐ RB5 Harold Green	.50	.23	.06
☐ RB6 Rodney Hampton	1.25	.55	.16
☐ RB7 Barry Sanders	4.00	1.80	.50
☐ RB8 Emmitt Smith	6.00	2.70	.75
☐ RB9 Thurman Thomas	1.25	.55	.16
☐ RB10 Chris Warren	1.25	.55	.16
☐ RB11 Ricky Watters	1.25	.55	.16
☐ RB12 Lorenzo White	.50	.23	.06

1993 Action Packed NFLPA Awards

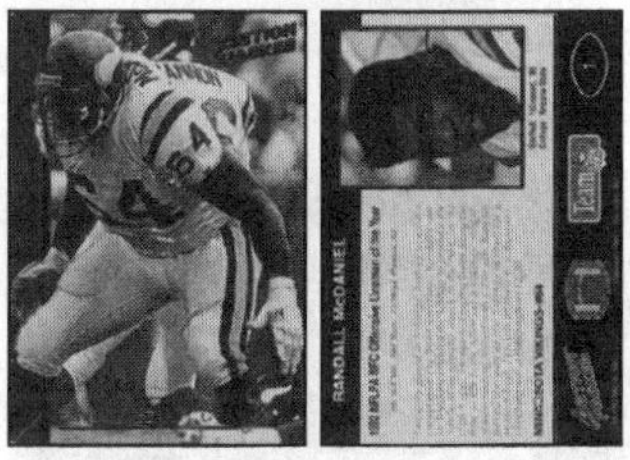

Held on March 4, 1993 in Washington, D.C., and sponsored by Action Packed, the 20th annual NFLPA banquet honored outstanding professional football players from the 1992 season. The set was produced to benefit the District of Columbia's Special Olympics. Reportedly less than 2,000 sets were produced. This 17-card standard-size set features the players selected as the best at their position by their peers and was issued in a special black box. The fronts feature an embossed action player photo overlapping a black-bordered gold stripe. The backs have a player photo and the award recipient's statistics.

	MINT	NRMT	EXC
COMPLETE SET (17)	75.00	34.00	9.50
COMMON CARD (1-17)	4.00	1.80	.50
☐ 1 Randall McDaniel	4.00	1.80	.50
☐ 2 Bruce Matthews	4.00	1.80	.50
☐ 3 Richmond Webb	4.00	1.80	.50
☐ 4 Cortez Kennedy	5.00	2.20	.60
☐ 5 Clyde Simmons	4.00	1.80	.50
☐ 6 Wilber Marshall	4.00	1.80	.50
☐ 7 Junior Seau	8.00	3.60	1.00
☐ 8 Henry Jones	4.00	1.80	.50
☐ 9 Audray McMillian	4.00	1.80	.50
☐ 10 Mel Gray	4.00	1.80	.50
☐ 11 Steve Tasker	4.00	1.80	.50
☐ 12 Marco Coleman	4.00	1.80	.50
☐ 13 Santana Dotson	4.00	1.80	.50
☐ 14 Vaughn Dunbar	4.00	1.80	.50
☐ 15 Carl Pickens	8.00	3.60	1.00
☐ 16 Barry Foster	4.00	1.80	.50
☐ 17 Steve Young	15.00	6.75	1.85

1994 Action Packed Prototypes

The 1994 Action Packed Prototype set consists of 12 standard-size cards with rounded corners. An 11-card set (without Barry Foster) was distributed in a black cardboard display frame which held three cards horizontally down the middle and four cards vertically on either side. The display frame is packaged with a black cardboard sleeve with the gold-stamped Action Packed logo and lettering. The prototypes were made available to dealers. The cards were also given out at the Super Bowl XXVIII card show. The set includes: one regular issue 1994 Action Packed card; one "Quarterback Challenge" subset card; one "Catching the Fire" subset card that honors NFL's best receivers; and one "Warp Speed" subset card featuring the fastest running backs. Also included in the set are one "Rookie Update" card, two "The Golden Domers Class of '93" subset cards featuring Notre

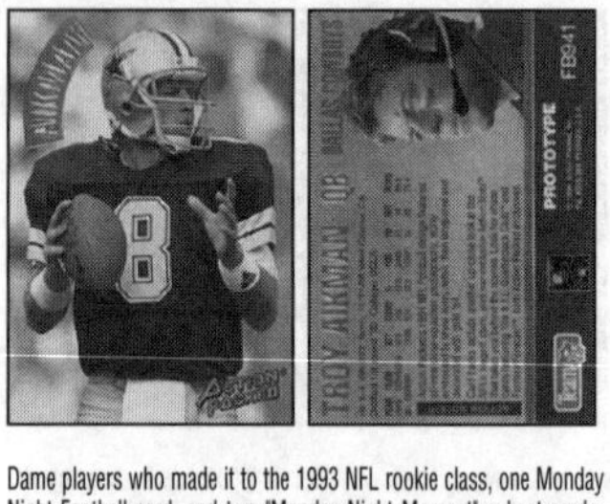

Dame players who made it to the 1993 NFL rookie class, one Monday Night Football card, and two "Monday Night Moment" subset cards. Each card carries its number and the word "Prototype" on the back.

	MINT	NRMT	EXC
COMPLETE SET (12)	50.00	22.00	6.25
COMMON CARD	2.50	1.10	.30
FB941 Troy Aikman 1994 Action Packed	6.00	2.70	.75
FB942 Jeff Hostetler Quarterback Challenge	2.50	1.10	.30
FB943 Emmitt Smith Warp Speed	10.00	4.50	1.25
FB944 Jerry Rice Catching Fire	6.00	2.70	.75
FB945 Barry Foster Fantasy Forecast	2.50	1.10	.30
RU941 Drew Bledsoe Rookie Update	8.00	3.60	1.00
RU942 Derrick Lassic Rookie Update	2.50	1.10	.30
RU943 Rick Mirer (Golden Domers)	3.00	1.35	.35
RU944 Jerome Bettis (Golden Domers)	4.00	1.80	.50
MNF941 Steve Young Sept. 12, 1994 S.F. at Cleveland Monday Night Football	5.00	2.20	.60
MNF942 Steve Young Monday Night Moment	5.00	2.20	.60
MNF943 Barry Foster Monday Night Moment	2.50	1.10	.30

1994 Action Packed

The 1994 Action Packed football set contains 198 standard-size cards. The cards were issued in two series of 120 and 78. The fronts feature borderless embossed color action player photos with the player's last name burnished in gold. On a metallic foil background, the horizontal backs carry a player head shot along with his 1993 stats and an "Action Note". The 120th card has a special twist. It is a Troy Aikman Back-To-Back Super Bowl card with Troy on the front holding up a number 1 of his first Super Bowl and on the back holding two fingers up to signify his second win. There are 12 Braille cards in this set. The cards are numbered on the back and checklisted below according to teams. Second series cards include rookies and traded players, Quarterback Club (172-184) and Golden Domers (193-198). Rookie Cards include Derrick Alexander, Mario Bates, Isaac Bruce, Lake Dawson, Trent Dilfer, Bert Emanuel, Marshall Faulk, William Floyd, Gus Frerotte, Greg Hill, Charles Johnson, Byron Bam Morris, Errict Rhett, Darnay Scott and Heath Shuler.

	MINT	NRMT	EXC
COMPLETE SET (198)	60.00	27.00	7.50
COMPLETE SERIES 1 (120)	40.00	18.00	5.00
COMPLETE SERIES 2 (78)	30.00	13.50	3.70
COMMON CARD (1-198)	.20	.09	.03

*BRAILLE VERSIONS: 1X to 2X BASIC CARDS
*GOLD SIGNATURES: 2X to 3X BASIC CARDS

1 Michael Haynes	.30	.14	.04
2 Andre Rison	.30	.14	.04
3 Mike Pritchard	.20	.09	.03
4 Erric Pegram	.20	.09	.03
5 Deion Sanders	1.50	.70	.19
6 Jim Kelly	.50	.23	.06
7 Andre Reed	.30	.14	.04
8 Thurman Thomas	.50	.23	.06
9 Bruce Smith	.50	.23	.06
10 Cornelius Bennett	.30	.14	.04
11 Nate Odomes	.20	.09	.03
12 Richard Dent	.30	.14	.04
13 Donnell Woolford	.20	.09	.03
14 Harold Green	.20	.09	.03
15 David Klingler	.20	.09	.03
16 Eric Metcalf	.30	.14	.04
17 Michael Dean Perry	.30	.14	.04
18 Michael Jackson	.30	.14	.04
19 Vinny Testaverde	.30	.14	.04
20 Troy Aikman	3.00	1.35	.35
21 Michael Irvin	.50	.23	.06
22 Emmitt Smith	5.00	2.20	.60
23 Jay Novacek	.30	.14	.04
24 Alvin Harper	.30	.14	.04
25 Charles Haley	.30	.14	.04
26 John Elway	2.00	.90	.25
27 Shannon Sharpe	.30	.14	.04
28 Rod Bernstine	.20	.09	.03
29 Simon Fletcher	.20	.09	.03
30 Barry Sanders	3.00	1.35	.35
31 Herman Moore	1.25	.55	.16
32 Pat Swilling	.20	.09	.03
33 Chris Spielman	.30	.14	.04
34 Brett Favre	5.00	2.20	.60
35 Sterling Sharpe UER (Photo on back is Shannon Sharpe)	.50	.23	.06
36 Reggie White	.50	.23	.06
37 Jackie Harris	.20	.09	.03
38 Tony Bennett	.20	.09	.03
39 LeRoy Butler	.20	.09	.03
40 Warren Moon	.50	.23	.06
41 Ernest Givins	.30	.14	.04
42 Haywood Jeffires	.30	.14	.04
43 Webster Slaughter	.20	.09	.03
44 Ray Childress	.20	.09	.03
45 Gary Brown	.20	.09	.03
46 Jeff George	.50	.23	.06
47 Roosevelt Potts	.20	.09	.03
48 Quentin Coryatt	.20	.09	.03
49 Joe Montana	3.00	1.35	.35
50 Derrick Thomas	.50	.23	.06
51 Neil Smith	.50	.23	.06
52 Marcus Allen	.50	.23	.06
53 Willie Davis	.30	.14	.04
54 Jerome Bettis	1.50	.70	.19
55 Sean Gilbert	.20	.09	.03
56 Chris Miller	.20	.09	.03
57 Jeff Hostetler	.30	.14	.04
58 Tim Brown	.50	.23	.06
59 Anthony Smith	.20	.09	.03
60 Greg Townsend	.20	.09	.03
61 Terry McDaniel	.20	.09	.03
62 Dan Marino	5.00	2.20	.60
63 Irving Fryar	.30	.14	.04
64 Keith Jackson	.20	.09	.03
65 Terry Kirby	.50	.23	.06
66 Bryan Cox	.20	.09	.03
67 Chris Doleman	.20	.09	.03
68 Cris Carter	.50	.23	.06
69 John Randle	.20	.09	.03
70 Drew Bledsoe	3.00	1.35	.35
71 Ben Coates	.50	.23	.06
72 Vincent Brisby	.50	.23	.06
73 Rickey Jackson	.20	.09	.03
74 Eric Martin	.20	.09	.03
75 Renaldo Turnbull	.20	.09	.03
76 Rodney Hampton	.50	.23	.06
77 Mike Sherrard	.20	.09	.03
78 Phil Simms	.30	.14	.04
79 Keith Hamilton	.20	.09	.03
80 Rob Moore	.30	.14	.04
81 Brad Baxter	.20	.09	.03
82 Boomer Esiason	.30	.14	.04
83 Johnny Johnson	.20	.09	.03
84 Ronnie Lott	.30	.14	.04
85 Randall Cunningham	.30	.14	.04
86 Herschel Walker	.30	.14	.04
87 Eric Allen	.20	.09	.03
88 Clyde Simmons	.20	.09	.03
89 Seth Joyner	.20	.09	.03
90 Calvin Williams	.30	.14	.04
91 Garrison Hearst	1.25	.55	.16
92 Steve Beuerlein	.20	.09	.03
93 Ricky Proehl	.20	.09	.03
94 Ronald Moore	.20	.09	.03
95 Barry Foster	.20	.09	.03
96 Neil O'Donnell	.50	.23	.06
97 Eric Green	.20	.09	.03
98 Rod Woodson	.50	.23	.06
99 Greg Lloyd	.50	.23	.06
100 Kevin Greene	.50	.23	.06
101 Stan Humphries	.50	.23	.06
102 Anthony Miller	.30	.14	.04
103 Junior Seau	.50	.23	.06
104 Leslie O'Neal	.20	.09	.03
105 Ronnie Harmon	.20	.09	.03
106 Jerry Rice	3.00	1.35	.35
107 Ricky Watters	.50	.23	.06
108 Steve Young	2.00	.90	.25
109 Brent Jones	.30	.14	.04
110 John Taylor	.30	.14	.04
111 Rick Mirer	.50	.23	.06
112 Chris Warren	.30	.14	.04
113 Cortez Kennedy	.30	.14	.04
114 Brian Blades	.30	.14	.04
115 Eugene Robinson	.20	.09	.03
116 Reggie Cobb	.20	.09	.03
117 Hardy Nickerson	.30	.14	.04
118 Reggie Brooks	.30	.14	.04
119 Darrell Green	.20	.09	.03
120 Troy Aikman Back to Back	3.00	1.35	.35
121 Dan Wilkinson	.30	.14	.04
122 Marshall Faulk	6.00	2.70	.75
123 Heath Shuler	2.00	.90	.25
124 Willie McGinest	.50	.23	.06
125 Trev Alberts	.30	.14	.04
126 Trent Dilfer	1.50	.70	.19
127 Bryant Young	1.00	.45	.12
128 Sam Adams	.30	.14	.04
129 Antonio Langham	.30	.14	.04
130 Jamir Miller	.20	.09	.03
131 John Thierry	.20	.09	.03
132 Aaron Glenn	.30	.14	.04
133 Joe Johnson	.20	.09	.03
134 Bernard Williams	.20	.09	.03
135 Wayne Gandy	.20	.09	.03
136 Charles Johnson	1.00	.45	.12
137 Dewayne Washington	.30	.14	.04
138 Todd Steussie	.30	.14	.04
139 Tim Bowens	.30	.14	.04
140 Johnnie Morton	1.00	.45	.12
141 Rob Fredrickson	.30	.14	.04
142 Shante Carver	.20	.09	.03
143 Thomas Lewis	.30	.14	.04
144 Greg Hill	1.25	.55	.16
145 Henry Ford	.20	.09	.03
146 Jeff Burris	.30	.14	.04
147 William Floyd	2.00	.90	.25
148 Derrick Alexander WR	.50	.23	.06
149 Darnay Scott	3.50	1.55	.45
150 Isaac Bruce	6.00	2.70	.75
151 Errict Rhett	2.50	1.10	.30
152 Kevin Lee	.20	.09	.03
153 Chuck Levy	.20	.09	.03
154 David Palmer	.30	.14	.04
155 Ryan Yarborough	.20	.09	.03
156 Charlie Garner	.30	.14	.04
157 Mario Bates	1.00	.45	.12
158 Bert Emanuel	2.00	.90	.25
159 Bucky Brooks	.20	.09	.03
160 Donnell Bennett	.20	.09	.03
161 Tydus Winans	.20	.09	.03
162 Andre Coleman	.20	.09	.03
163 Calvin Jones	.20	.09	.03
164 LeShon Johnson	.30	.14	.04
165 Doug Brien	.20	.09	.03
166 Byron Bam Morris	.50	.23	.06
167 Lake Dawson	1.25	.55	.16
168 Perry Klein	.20	.09	.03
169 Doug Nussmeier	.20	.09	.03
170 Lamont Warren	.20	.09	.03
171 Gus Frerotte	4.00	1.80	.50
172 Troy Aikman QC	1.50	.70	.19
173 Randall Cunningham QC	.20	.09	.03
174 John Elway QC	1.00	.45	.12
175 Jim Everett QC	.20	.09	.03
176 Drew Bledsoe QC	1.50	.70	.19
177 Jim Kelly QC	.30	.14	.04
178 Dan Marino QC	2.50	1.10	.30
179 Chris Miller QC	.20	.09	.03
180 Warren Moon QC	.30	.14	.04
181 Rick Mirer QC	.50	.23	.06
182 Jeff Hostetler QC	.20	.09	.03
183 Brett Favre QC	2.50	1.10	.30
184 Steve Young QC	1.00	.45	.12
185 Anthony Miller	.30	.14	.04
186 Michael Haynes	.30	.14	.04
187 Mike Pritchard	.20	.09	.03
188 Jeff George	.50	.23	.06
189 Lewis Tillman	.20	.09	.03
190 Ken Norton	.30	.14	.04
191 Erik Kramer	.30	.14	.04
192 Richard Dent	.30	.14	.04
193 Rick Mirer GD	.50	.23	.06
194 Jerome Bettis GD	.75	.35	.09
195 Reggie Brooks GD	.20	.09	.03
196 Tom Carter GD	.20	.09	.03
197 Irv Smith GD	.20	.09	.03
198 Rocket Ismail GD	.30	.14	.04

1994 Action Packed 24K Gold

Randomly inserted in foil packs, this 42-card standard-size set features 24K versions of the Quarterback Club (1-20), Catching Fire (21-30), and Warp Speed (31-42) inserts. In design, these cards are identical to their regular issue counterparts, except for the gold on the fronts. The cards are numbered on the back with a "G" prefix.

	MINT	NRMT	EXC
COMPLETE SET (55)	1800.00	800.00	220.00
COMP.SERIES 1 (42)	1400.00	650.00	180.00
COMP.SERIES 2 (13)	400.00	180.00	50.00
COMMON CARD (G1-G55)	15.00	6.75	1.85

G1 Troy Aikman	70.00	32.00	8.75
G2 Randall Cunningham	15.00	6.75	1.85
G3 John Elway	55.00	25.00	7.00
G4 Boomer Esiason	25.00	11.00	3.10
G5 Jim Everett	15.00	6.75	1.85
G6 Brett Favre	100.00	45.00	12.50
G7 Jerry Rice	70.00	32.00	8.75
G8 Jeff Hostetler	25.00	11.00	3.10
G9 Jim Kelly	30.00	13.50	3.70
G10 David Klingler	15.00	6.75	1.85
G11 Bernie Kosar	25.00	11.00	3.10
G12 Dan Marino	100.00	45.00	12.50
G13 Chris Miller	15.00	6.75	1.85
G14 Warren Moon	30.00	13.50	3.70
G15 Neil O'Donnell	30.00	13.50	3.70
G16 Michael Irvin	30.00	13.50	3.70
G17 Phil Simms	25.00	11.00	3.10
G18 Steve Young	55.00	25.00	7.00
G19 Rick Mirer	30.00	13.50	3.70
G20 Drew Bledsoe	70.00	32.00	8.75
G21 Jerry Rice	70.00	32.00	8.75
G22 Sterling Sharpe	30.00	13.50	3.70
G23 Michael Irvin	30.00	13.50	3.70
G24 Andre Rison	30.00	13.50	3.70
G25 Anthony Miller	25.00	11.00	3.10
G26 Tim Brown	30.00	13.50	3.70
G27 Andre Reed	25.00	11.00	3.10
G28 Herman Moore	40.00	18.00	5.00
G29 Irving Fryar	25.00	11.00	3.10
G30 Shannon Sharpe	25.00	11.00	3.10
G31 Emmitt Smith	100.00	45.00	12.50
G32 Barry Sanders	70.00	32.00	8.75
G33 Thurman Thomas	30.00	13.50	3.70
G34 Jerome Bettis	40.00	18.00	5.00
G35 Barry Foster	15.00	6.75	1.85
G36 Ricky Watters	30.00	13.50	3.70
G37 Rodney Hampton	30.00	13.50	3.70
G38 Chris Warren	30.00	13.50	3.70
G39 Erric Pegram	25.00	11.00	3.10
G40 Reggie Brooks	15.00	6.75	1.85
G41 Marcus Allen	30.00	13.50	3.70
G42 Ronald Moore	15.00	6.75	1.85
G43 Troy Aikman QC	60.00	27.00	7.50
G44 Randall Cunningham QC	15.00	6.75	1.85
G45 John Elway QC	50.00	22.00	6.25
G46 Jim Everett QC	15.00	6.75	1.85
G47 Drew Bledsoe QC	60.00	27.00	7.50
G48 Jim Kelly QC	30.00	13.50	3.70
G49 Dan Marino QC	80.00	36.00	10.00
G50 Chris Miller QC	15.00	6.75	1.85
G51 Warren Moon QC	30.00	13.50	3.70
G52 Rick Mirer QC	30.00	13.50	3.70
G53 Jeff Hostetler QC	25.00	11.00	3.10
G54 Brett Favre QC	80.00	36.00	10.00
G55 Steve Young QC	50.00	22.00	6.25

1994 Action Packed Catching Fire

This 10-card standard-size set highlights the hottest receivers in the NFL. The fronts feature embossed color action photos of the player catching a pass while surrounded by metallic foil flames. The backs carry another player shot and a player profile. The cards are numbered on the back with an "R" prefix.

	MINT	NRMT	EXC
COMPLETE SET (10)	10.00	4.50	1.25
COMMON CARD (R1-R10)	.50	.23	.06
R1 Jerry Rice	5.00	2.20	.60
R2 Sterling Sharpe	.75	.35	.09
R3 Michael Irvin	1.25	.55	.16
R4 Andre Rison	1.25	.55	.16
R5 Anthony Miller	.75	.35	.09
R6 Tim Brown	1.25	.55	.16
R7 Andre Reed	.75	.35	.09
R8 Herman Moore	2.50	1.10	.30
R9 Irving Fryar	.50	.23	.06
R10 Shannon Sharpe	.75	.35	.09

1994 Action Packed Fantasy Forecast

This 42-card set provides a scouting report on 42 of the top football players. The cards measure the standard size (2 1/2" by 3 1/2"). The fronts feature embossed color action player photos, with a football in a corner that is covered with heat sensitive ink. When you touch the football, it reveals what number you should draft the player if you were fielding a fantasy football team.

	MINT	NRMT	EXC
COMPLETE SET (42)	16.00	7.25	2.00
COMMON CARD (FF1-FF42)	.30	.14	.04
☐ FF1 Rodney Hampton	.50	.23	.06
☐ FF2 Steve Young	1.50	.70	.19
☐ FF3 Michael Irvin	.75	.35	.09
☐ FF4 Emmitt Smith	4.00	1.80	.50
☐ FF5 Troy Aikman	2.00	.90	.25
☐ FF6 Jerry Rice	2.00	.90	.25
☐ FF7 Brett Favre	4.00	1.80	.50
☐ FF8 Jerome Bettis	1.00	.45	.12
☐ FF9 Reggie Brooks	.30	.14	.04
☐ FF10 John Elway	1.50	.70	.19
☐ FF11 Jim Kelly	.75	.35	.09
☐ FF12 Dan Marino	4.00	1.80	.50
☐ FF13 Randall Cunningham	.50	.23	.06
☐ FF14 Sterling Sharpe	.50	.23	.06
☐ FF15 Chris Warren	.75	.35	.09
☐ FF16 Andre Rison	.75	.35	.09
☐ FF17 Mike Pritchard	.30	.14	.04
☐ FF18 Barry Sanders	2.00	.90	.25
☐ FF19 Marcus Allen	.75	.35	.09
☐ FF20 Thurman Thomas	.75	.35	.09
☐ FF21 Erric Pegram	.50	.23	.06
☐ FF22 Barry Foster	.30	.14	.04
☐ FF23 Anthony Miller	.50	.23	.06
☐ FF24 Shannon Sharpe	.50	.23	.06
☐ FF25 Tim Brown	.75	.35	.09
☐ FF26 Ricky Watters	.75	.35	.09
☐ FF27 Ernest Givins	.30	.14	.04
☐ FF28 Cris Carter	.75	.35	.09
☐ FF29 Willie Davis	.30	.14	.04
☐ FF30 Warren Moon	.75	.35	.09
☐ FF31 Joe Montana	2.00	.90	.25
☐ FF32 Herman Moore	1.00	.45	.12
☐ FF33 Terry Kirby	.30	.14	.04
☐ FF34 Eric Green	.30	.14	.04
☐ FF35 Michael Jackson	.50	.23	.06
☐ FF36 Johnny Johnson	.30	.14	.04
☐ FF37 Calvin Williams	.30	.14	.04
☐ FF38 Michael Haynes	.50	.23	.06
☐ FF39 Irving Fryar	.50	.23	.06
☐ FF40 Gary Brown	.30	.14	.04
☐ FF41 Jeff Hostetler	.50	.23	.06
☐ FF42 Keith Jackson	.30	.14	.04

1994 Action Packed Quarterback Challenge

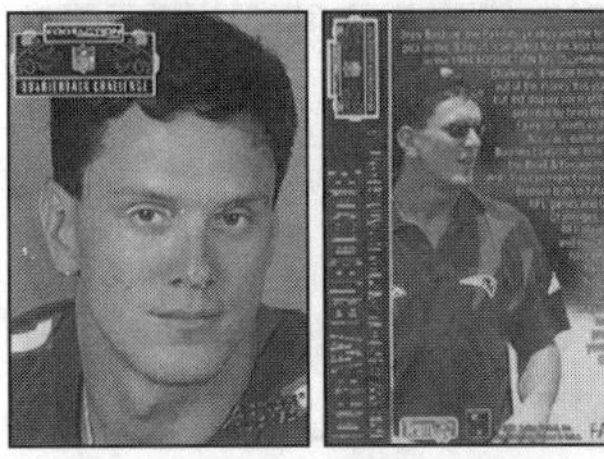

Inserted one per special retail pack through Foot Action stores, this set of 12 quarterbacks features card fronts that are silver embossed with an outline of the player's face. The backs contain photos from the Quarterback Challenge competition and a brief write-up.

	MINT	NRMT	EXC
COMPLETE SET (12)	16.00	7.25	2.00
COMMON CARD (FA1-FA12)	.50	.23	.06
☐ FA1 Steve Young	2.00	.90	.25
☐ FA2 John Elway	2.00	.90	.25
☐ FA3 Troy Aikman	2.50	1.10	.30
☐ FA4 Randall Cunningham	.50	.23	.06
☐ FA5 Warren Moon	1.00	.45	.12
☐ FA6 Brett Favre	4.00	1.80	.50
☐ FA7 Rick Mirer	1.50	.70	.19
☐ FA8 Drew Bledsoe	2.50	1.10	.30
☐ FA9 Boomer Esiason	1.00	.45	.12
☐ FA10 Jeff Hostetler	.50	.23	.06
☐ FA11 Jim Kelly	1.50	.70	.19
☐ FA12 Dan Marino	4.00	1.80	.50

1994 Action Packed Quarterback Club

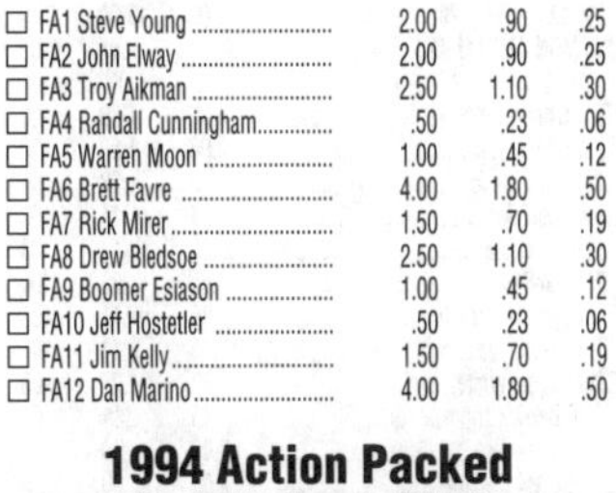

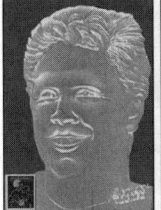

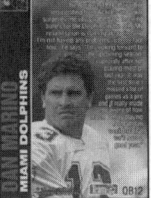

These cards were randomly inserted into packs and measure the standard-size. The fronts feature a silver foil player headshot, while the backs carry another color player action photo.

	MINT	NRMT	EXC
COMPLETE SET (20)	16.00	7.25	2.00
COMMON CARD (QB1-QB20)	.60	.25	.07
☐ QB1 Troy Aikman	3.00	1.35	.35
☐ QB2 Randall Cunningham	.60	.25	.07
☐ QB3 John Elway	2.00	.90	.25
☐ QB4 Boomer Esiason	1.00	.45	.12
☐ QB5 Jim Everett	.60	.25	.07
☐ QB6 Brett Favre	5.00	2.20	.60
☐ QB7 Jerry Rice	3.00	1.35	.35
☐ QB8 Jeff Hostetler	.60	.25	.07
☐ QB9 Jim Kelly	1.50	.70	.19
☐ QB10 David Klingler	.60	.25	.07
☐ QB11 Bernie Kosar	.60	.25	.07
☐ QB12 Dan Marino	5.00	2.20	.60
☐ QB13 Chris Miller	.60	.25	.07
☐ QB14 Warren Moon	1.00	.45	.12
☐ QB15 Neil O'Donnell	1.00	.45	.12
☐ QB16 Michael Irvin	1.50	.70	.19
☐ QB17 Phil Simms	1.00	.45	.12
☐ QB18 Steve Young	2.00	.90	.25
☐ QB19 Rick Mirer	1.50	.70	.19
☐ QB20 Drew Bledsoe	3.00	1.35	.35

1994 Action Packed Warp Speed

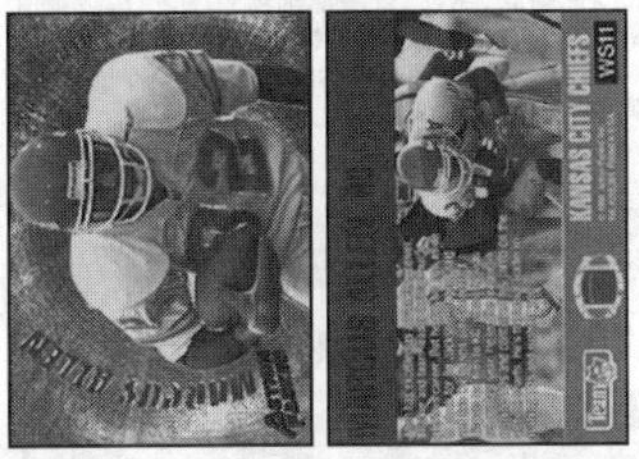

This 12-card standard-size set showcases the fastest running backs in the NFL. The horizontal fronts feature embossed color player action photos with a colored foil design made to give the feel of a time tunnel vortex. The player's name and words "Warp Speed" in gold lettering surround the player. The horizontal backs carry another player action shot and behind-the-scene stories that capture the essence of the speed game.

	MINT	NRMT	EXC
COMPLETE SET (12)	15.00	6.75	1.85
COMMON CARD (WS1-WS12)	.60	.25	.07
☐ WS1 Emmitt Smith	8.00	3.60	1.00
☐ WS2 Barry Sanders	4.00	1.80	.50
☐ WS3 Thurman Thomas	1.25	.55	.16
☐ WS4 Jerome Bettis	1.25	.55	.16
☐ WS5 Barry Foster	.60	.25	.07
☐ WS6 Ricky Watters	1.25	.55	.16
☐ WS7 Rodney Hampton	1.25	.55	.16
☐ WS8 Chris Warren	1.25	.55	.16
☐ WS9 Erric Pegram	.60	.25	.07
☐ WS10 Reggie Brooks	.60	.25	.07
☐ WS11 Marcus Allen	1.25	.55	.16
☐ WS12 Ronald Moore	.60	.25	.07

1994 Action Packed Badge of Honor Pins

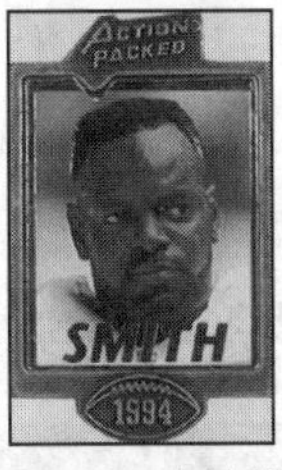

This set of 25 pins measures approximately 1 1/2" by 1". The pins came in packs of four inside a cardboard holder. The back of the holder contained a checklist for the set. Each box contained three packs of 4-pins along with one of five different black pin "albums" to house five of the pins. On a bronze background, the fronts feature color player portraits with a gold border. The player's last name appears in gold lettering at the bottom. The Action Packed logo is above the picture, while the year 1994 inside a football icon is below. The backs carry the copyrights "1994 Action Packed" and "1994 NFL/NFL QB Club." The pins are unnumbered and checklisted below in alphabetical order. A 24K Gold parallel version of each pin was also produced and randomly inserted in packs.

	MINT	NRMT	EXC
COMPLETE SET (25)	35.00	16.00	4.40
COMMON PIN (1-25)	.75	.35	.09
*24K GOLD PINS: 10X TO 20X			
☐ 1 Troy Aikman	3.00	1.35	.35
☐ 2 Drew Bledsoe	3.00	1.35	.35
☐ 3 Bubby Brister	.75	.35	.09
☐ 4 Randall Cunningham	1.00	.45	.12
☐ 5 John Elway	2.50	1.10	.30
☐ 6 Boomer Esiason	1.00	.45	.12
☐ 7 Jim Everett	.75	.35	.09
☐ 8 Brett Favre	5.00	2.20	.60
☐ 9 Jim Harbaugh	1.50	.70	.19
☐ 10 Jeff Hostetler	.75	.35	.09
☐ 11 Michael Irvin	1.50	.70	.19
☐ 12 Jim Kelly	1.50	.70	.19
☐ 13 David Klingler	.75	.35	.09
☐ 14 Bernie Kosar	.75	.35	.09
☐ 15 Dan Marino	5.00	2.20	.60
☐ 16 Chris Miller	.75	.35	.09
☐ 17 Rick Mirer	1.50	.70	.19
☐ 18 Warren Moon	1.00	.45	.12
☐ 19 Neil O'Donnell	1.00	.45	.12
☐ 20 Jerry Rice	3.00	1.35	.35
☐ 21 Mark Rypien	.75	.35	.09
☐ 22 Barry Sanders	3.00	1.35	.35
☐ 23 Phil Simms	1.00	.45	.12
☐ 24 Emmitt Smith	5.00	2.20	.60
☐ 25 Steve Young	2.50	1.10	.30

1994 Action Packed Mammoth

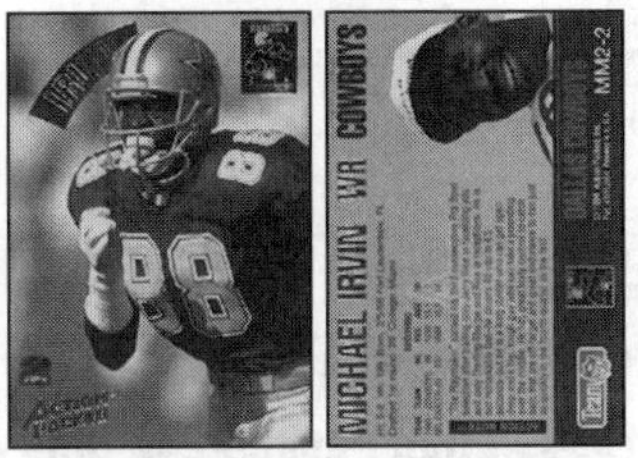

Large versions of the basic cards, this 25-card set spotlights some of the NFL's top names. The cards were offered to dealers by Action Packed. Twenty-five thousand of each card were produced and they are individually numbered. Card MM25 was not issued. These cards measure 7 1/2" by 10 1/2". Three prototype cards and three series 2 cards were produced as well and priced below. We've assigned card numbers to the six and none is considered part of the complete set. The two 24K Gold prototypes were randomly inserted in 28-count Mammoth sets sold to hobby dealers.

	MINT	NRMT	EXC
COMPLETE SET (25)	100.00	45.00	12.50
COMMON CARD (MM1-MM26)	3.00	1.35	.35
☐ MM1 Troy Aikman	8.00	3.60	1.00
☐ MM2 Drew Bledsoe	8.00	3.60	1.00
☐ MM3 Barry Sanders	8.00	3.60	1.00
☐ MM4 Chris Miller	3.00	1.35	.35
☐ MM5 Randall Cunningham	3.00	1.35	.35
☐ MM6 John Elway	6.00	2.70	.75
☐ MM7 Boomer Esiason	4.00	1.80	.50
☐ MM8 Jim Everett	3.00	1.35	.35
☐ MM9 Brett Favre	14.00	6.25	1.75
☐ MM10 Jim Harbaugh	4.00	1.80	.50
☐ MM11 Jeff Hostetler	3.00	1.35	.35
☐ MM12 Michael Irvin	4.00	1.80	.50
☐ MM13 Jim Kelly			
☐ MM14 David Klingler	3.00	1.35	.35
☐ MM15 Bernie Kosar	3.00	1.35	.35
☐ MM16 Dan Marino	14.00	6.25	1.75
☐ MM17 Rick Mirer			
☐ MM18 Warren Moon	4.00	1.80	.50
☐ MM19 Neil O'Donnell	4.00	1.80	.50
☐ MM20 Jerry Rice	8.00	3.60	1.00
☐ MM21 Mark Rypien	3.00	1.35	.35
☐ MM22 Phil Simms	4.00	1.80	.50
☐ MM23 Emmitt Smith	14.00	6.25	1.75
☐ MM24 Steve Young	6.00	2.70	.75
☐ MM26 Bubby Brister	3.00	1.35	.35
☐ 2MM1 Troy Aikman Series 2 card numbered MM1-2	8.00	3.60	1.00
☐ 2MM2 Michael Irvin Series 2 card numbered MM2-2	5.00	2.20	.60
☐ 2MM6 Emmitt Smith Series 2 card numbered MM6-2	15.00	6.75	1.85
☐ P1 Troy Aikman Prototype Numbered MMP	10.00	4.50	1.25
☐ P2 Emmitt Smith Prototype 24K Gold Numbered MMP1G reportedly 2500 made	50.00	22.00	6.25
☐ P3 Troy Aikman Prototype 24K Gold Numbered MMP2G reportedly 1000 made	30.00	13.50	3.70

1994 Action Packed CoaStars

Issued in six-card shrink-wrapped retail sheets, these 25 coaster cards have rounded corners and measure 3 1/4" by 3 1/4". The front of each features a borderless player action shot that is full color within

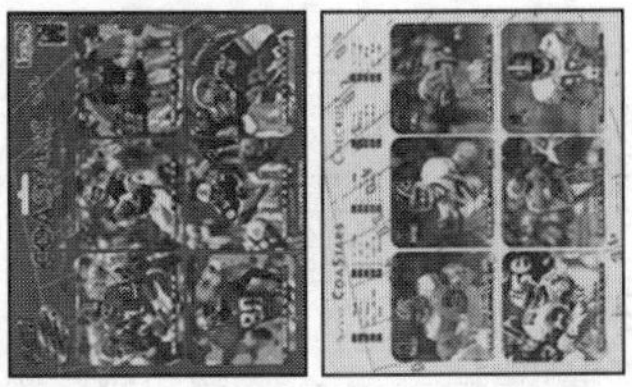

the 2 3/4" diameter central circle, and black-and-white outside. The player's name and position appear in an arc at the upper right. The player's '93 home statistics are shown in a red stripe at the bottom. The back features a borderless color player action shot, with the player's name and '93 away statistics appearing near the bottom. The coasters are numbered on the front.

	MINT	NRMT	EXC
COMPLETE SET (25)	20.00	9.00	2.50
COMMON CARD (1-25)	.30	.14	.04
☐ 1 Troy Aikman	2.00	.90	.25
☐ 2 Drew Bledsoe	2.00	.90	.25
☐ 3 Bubby Brister	.30	.14	.04
☐ 4 Randall Cunningham	.40	.18	.05
☐ 5 John Elway	1.50	.70	.19
☐ 6 Boomer Esiason	.40	.18	.05
☐ 7 Jim Everett	.30	.14	.04
☐ 8 Brett Favre	4.00	1.80	.50
☐ 9 Jim Harbaugh	.50	.23	.06
☐ 10 Jeff Hostetler	.40	.18	.05
☐ 11 Michael Irvin	.50	.23	.06
☐ 12 Jim Kelly	.50	.23	.06
☐ 13 David Klingler	.30	.14	.04
☐ 14 Bernie Kosar	.30	.14	.04
☐ 15 Dan Marino	4.00	1.80	.50
☐ 16 Rick Mirer	.75	.35	.09
☐ 17 Chris Miller	.40	.18	.05
☐ 18 Warren Moon	.50	.23	.06
☐ 19 Neil O'Donnell	.50	.23	.06
☐ 20 Jerry Rice	2.00	.90	.25
☐ 21 Mark Rypien	.40	.18	.05
☐ 22 Barry Sanders	2.00	.90	.25
☐ 23 Phil Simms	.40	.18	.05
☐ 24 Emmitt Smith	4.00	1.80	.50
☐ 25 Steve Young	1.50	.70	.19

1995 Action Packed Promos

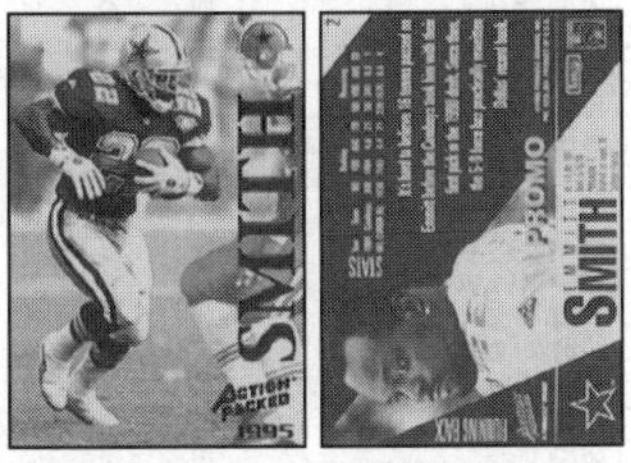

Wrapped in a cello pack, this 4-card standard-size was issued to preview the design of the 1995 Action Packed series. The set features two regular cards, one "Armed Forces" card, and an ad card. The cards are identical to their regular issue counterparts, except for the word "Promo" stamped in yellow block lettering on their backs.

	MINT	NRMT	EXC
COMPLETE SET (4)	8.00	3.60	1.00
COMMON CARD	.50	.23	.06
☐ 1 Jerry Rice	2.50	1.10	.30
☐ 2 Emmitt Smith	4.00	1.80	.50
☐ AF4 Steve Young Armed Forces card	2.00	.90	.25
☐ NNO Action Packed Ad Card	.50	.23	.06

1995 Action Packed

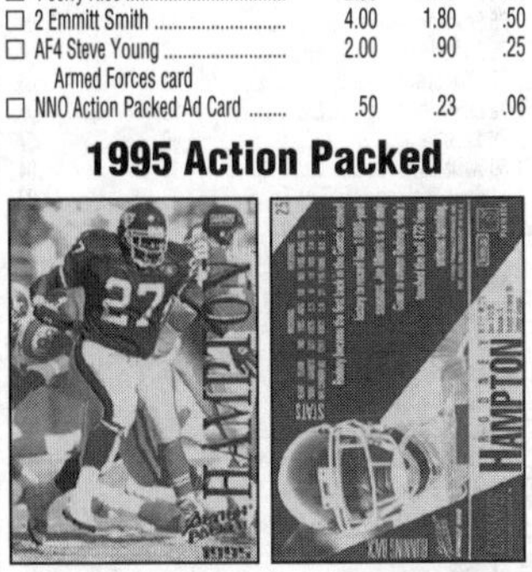

This 126-card standard size set is the first Action Packed set issued by Pinnacle Brands. The fronts display full-bleed, embossed color action photos, with the team's helmet, player's name and the words "Action Packed 1995" on the right side. The horizontal backs feature season and career statistics, a player photo as well as biographical information. Rookie Cards include Ki-Jana Carter, Kerry Collins, Joey Galloway, Steve McNair, Rashaan Salaam, J.J. Stokes, Michael Westbrook and Tyrone Wheatley.

	MINT	NRMT	EXC
COMPLETE SET (126)	30.00	13.50	3.70
COMMON CARD (1-126)	.20	.09	.03

☐ 1 Jerry Rice	2.00	.90	.25
☐ 2 Emmitt Smith	4.00	1.80	.50
☐ 3 Drew Bledsoe	2.00	.90	.25
☐ 4 Ben Coates	.30	.14	.04
☐ 5 Jim Everett	.20	.09	.03
☐ 6 Warren Moon	.30	.14	.04
☐ 7 Herman Moore	1.00	.45	.12
☐ 8 Deion Sanders	1.25	.55	.16
☐ 9 Rick Mirer	.60	.25	.07
☐ 10 Natrone Means	.60	.25	.07
☐ 11 Jeff Blake	2.50	1.10	.30
☐ 12 William Floyd	.60	.25	.07
☐ 13 Steve Young	1.50	.70	.19
☐ 14 John Elway	1.50	.70	.19
☐ 15 Brett Favre	4.00	1.80	.50
☐ 16 Marshall Faulk	1.00	.45	.12
☐ 17 Heath Shuler	.60	.25	.07
☐ 18 Ricky Watters	.60	.25	.07
☐ 19 Michael Haynes	.30	.14	.04
☐ 20 Troy Aikman	2.00	.90	.25
☐ 21 Dan Marino	4.00	1.80	.50
☐ 22 Byron Bam Morris	.30	.14	.04
☐ 23 Marcus Allen	.60	.25	.07
☐ 24 Carl Pickens	.60	.25	.07
☐ 25 Rodney Hampton	.30	.14	.04
☐ 26 Dave Brown	.30	.14	.04
☐ 27 Jerome Bettis	.75	.35	.09
☐ 28 Jim Kelly	.60	.25	.07
☐ 29 Andre Reed	.30	.14	.04
☐ 30 Michael Irvin	.60	.25	.07
☐ 31 Barry Sanders	2.00	.90	.25
☐ 32 Chris Warren	.30	.14	.04
☐ 33 Jeff Hostetler	.30	.14	.04
☐ 34 Alvin Harper	.20	.09	.03
☐ 35 Rob Moore	.20	.09	.03
☐ 36 Steve McNair	6.00	2.70	.75
☐ 37 Rashaan Salaam	2.50	1.10	.30
☐ 38 Joey Galloway	4.00	1.80	.50
☐ 39 J.J. Stokes	2.00	.90	.25
☐ 40 Michael Westbrook	2.50	1.10	.30
☐ 41 Kerry Collins	7.00	3.10	.85
☐ 42 Ki-Jana Carter	2.00	.90	.25
☐ 43 Boomer Esiason	.30	.14	.04
☐ 44 Chris Spielman	.30	.14	.04
☐ 45 Vinny Testaverde	.30	.14	.04
☐ 46 Kevin Williams WR	.30	.14	.04
☐ 47 Ronnie Harmon	.20	.09	.03
☐ 48 Fred Barnett	.30	.14	.04
☐ 49 Harvey Williams	.20	.09	.03
☐ 50 Reggie White	.60	.25	.07
☐ 51 Brent Jones	.20	.09	.03
☐ 52 Henry Ellard	.30	.14	.04
☐ 53 Cris Carter	.60	.25	.07
☐ 54 Leroy Hoard	.20	.09	.03
☐ 55 Trent Dilfer	.60	.25	.07
☐ 56 Raymont Harris	.20	.09	.03
☐ 57 Garrison Hearst	.60	.25	.07
☐ 58 Lewis Tillman	.20	.09	.03
☐ 59 Mark Brunell	2.00	.90	.25
☐ 60 Bruce Smith	.60	.25	.07
☐ 61 Lake Dawson	.30	.14	.04
☐ 62 Bert Emanuel	.60	.25	.07
☐ 63 Eric Green	.20	.09	.03
☐ 64 Barry Foster	.30	.14	.04
☐ 65 Jeff Graham	.20	.09	.03
☐ 66 Curtis Conway	.60	.25	.07
☐ 67 Herschel Walker	.30	.14	.04
☐ 68 Edgar Bennett	.30	.14	.04
☐ 69 Mario Bates	.60	.25	.07
☐ 70 Irving Fryar	.30	.14	.04
☐ 71 Gary Brown	.20	.09	.03
☐ 72 Cortez Kennedy	.30	.14	.04
☐ 73 John Taylor	.20	.09	.03
☐ 74 Jeff George	.30	.14	.04
☐ 75 Shannon Sharpe	.30	.14	.04
☐ 76 Andre Rison	.30	.14	.04
☐ 77 Mike Sherrard	.20	.09	.03
☐ 78 Errict Rhett	.60	.25	.07
☐ 79 Junior Seau	.60	.25	.07
☐ 80 Willie Davis	.30	.14	.04
☐ 81 Craig Erickson	.20	.09	.03
☐ 82 Torrance Small	.20	.09	.03
☐ 83 Randall Cunningham	.30	.14	.04
☐ 84 Robert Brooks	.60	.25	.07
☐ 85 Terance Mathis	.30	.14	.04
☐ 86 Rod Woodson	.30	.14	.04
☐ 87 Anthony Miller	.30	.14	.04
☐ 88 Stan Humphries	.30	.14	.04
☐ 89 Chris Miller	.20	.09	.03
☐ 90 Steve Beuerlein	.20	.09	.03
☐ 91 Steve Bono	.30	.14	.04
☐ 92 Frank Reich	.20	.09	.03
☐ 93 Cory Fleming	.20	.09	.03
☐ 94 Isaac Bruce	1.00	.45	.12
☐ 95 Dave Meggett	.20	.09	.03
☐ 96 Jackie Harris	.20	.09	.03
☐ 97 J.J. Birden	.20	.09	.03
☐ 98 Flipper Anderson	.20	.09	.03
☐ 99 Johnnie Morton	.30	.14	.04
☐ 100 Michael Timpson	.20	.09	.03
☐ 101 Derek Brown RB	.20	.09	.03
☐ 102 Ricky Ervins	.20	.09	.03
☐ 103 Derrick Alexander DE	.20	.09	.03
☐ 104 Dave Barr	.20	.09	.03
☐ 105 Tony Boselli	.30	.14	.04
☐ 106 Kyle Brady	.60	.25	.07
☐ 107 Mark Bruener	.30	.14	.04
☐ 108 Kevin Carter	.60	.25	.07
☐ 109 Neil O'Donnell	.30	.14	.04
☐ 110 Derrick Alexander WR	.60	.25	.07
☐ 111 Charlie Garner	.30	.14	.04
☐ 112 Darnay Scott	.60	.25	.07
☐ 113 Scott Mitchell	.30	.14	.04
☐ 114 Charles Johnson	.30	.14	.04
☐ 115 Greg Hill	.30	.14	.04
☐ 116 Ty Law	.30	.14	.04
☐ 117 Frank Sanders	2.00	.90	.25
☐ 118 James O.Stewart	.60	.25	.07
☐ 119 James A.Stewart	.20	.09	.03
☐ 120 Kordell Stewart	6.00	2.70	.75
☐ 121 Rob Johnson	.20	.09	.03
☐ 122 John Walsh	.20	.09	.03
☐ 123 Stoney Case	.20	.09	.03
☐ 124 Tyrone Wheatley	1.25	.55	.16
☐ 125 Sherman Williams	.20	.09	.03
☐ 126 Ray Zellars	.30	.14	.04

1995 Action Packed Quick Silver

This 126 card parallel was randomly inserted into packs at a rate of one in six and is differentiated by a silver foil background on the front of the card. Card backs also contain the "Quick Silver" title ghosted in the background.

	MINT	NRMT	EXC
COMPLETE SET (126)	400.00	180.00	50.00
COMMON CARD (1-126)	1.00	.45	.12

*VETERAN STARS: 3X TO 6X BASIC CARDS
*YOUNG STARS: 2.5X TO 5X BASIC CARDS
*RCs STARS: 2X TO 4X BASIC CARDS

1995 Action Packed 24K Gold

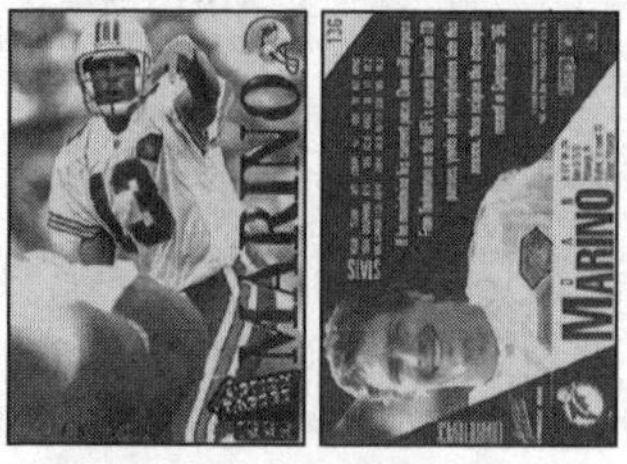

This 42 card standard-size set was randomly inserted into packs. The cards are similar in design to the basic issue. The player's name, Action Packed logo and the "24 Kt Gold" logo are imprinted in gold. The cards are numbered with a "G" suffix.

	MINT	NRMT	EXC
COMPLETE SET (21)	600.00	275.00	75.00
COMMON CARD (1G-21G)	10.00	4.50	1.25
☐ 1G Jerry Rice	40.00	18.00	5.00
☐ 2G Emmitt Smith	80.00	36.00	10.00
☐ 3G Drew Bledsoe	40.00	18.00	5.00
☐ 4G Warren Moon	10.00	4.50	1.25
☐ 5G Deion Sanders	25.00	11.00	3.10
☐ 6G Natrone Means	10.00	4.50	1.25
☐ 7G Steve Young	30.00	13.50	3.70
☐ 8G John Elway UER	35.00	16.00	4.40
Last year is shown as 994			
☐ 9G Brett Favre	80.00	36.00	10.00
☐ 10G Marshall Faulk	20.00	9.00	2.50
☐ 11G Heath Shuler	15.00	6.75	1.85
☐ 12G Troy Aikman	40.00	18.00	5.00
☐ 13G Dan Marino	80.00	36.00	10.00
☐ 14G Jerome Bettis	15.00	6.75	1.85
☐ 15G Jim Kelly	15.00	6.75	1.85
☐ 16G Michael Irvin	15.00	6.75	1.85
☐ 17G Barry Sanders	40.00	18.00	5.00
☐ 18G Steve McNair	40.00	18.00	5.00
☐ 19G Rashaan Salaam	20.00	9.00	2.50
☐ 20G Kerry Collins	50.00	22.00	6.25
☐ 21G Ki-Jana Carter	10.00	4.50	1.25

1995 Action Packed Armed Forces

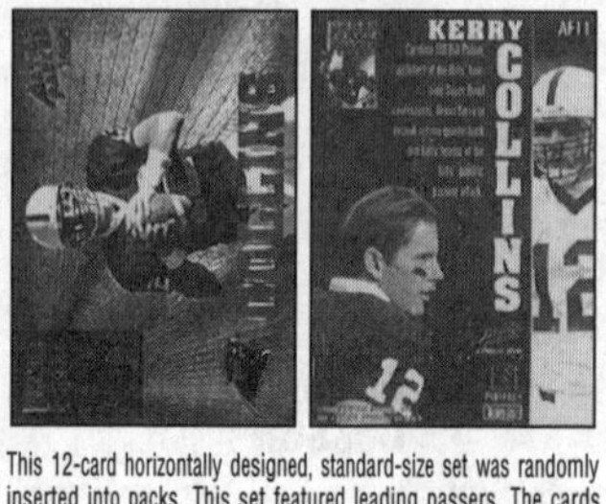

This 12-card horizontally designed, standard-size set was randomly inserted into packs. This set featured leading passers. The cards feature a full-bleed, embossed color-action photo against a gold metallic background. In addition, other card features include an "Armed Forces" logo with a quarterback icon. The backs have two photos of the player. One is a full-color profile shot in the lower left corner and the other is a small action shot on the right side. The player's name is written in large white letters against a black background and there is a short profile as well. The cards are numbered with an "AF" prefix. Braille parallel versions of each card were also randomly inserted.

	MINT	NRMT	EXC
COMPLETE SET (12)	90.00	40.00	11.00
COMMON CARD (AF1-AF12)	4.00	1.80	.50
☐ AF1 Drew Bledsoe	10.00	4.50	1.25
☐ AF2 Dan Marino	20.00	9.00	2.50
☐ AF3 Troy Aikman	10.00	4.50	1.25
☐ AF4 Steve Young	8.00	3.60	1.00
☐ AF5 Brett Favre	20.00	9.00	2.50
☐ AF6 Heath Shuler	5.00	2.20	.60
☐ AF7 Dave Brown	4.00	1.80	.50
☐ AF8 Jeff Blake	5.00	2.20	.60
☐ AF9 John Elway	8.00	3.60	1.00
☐ AF10 Rick Mirer	5.00	2.20	.60
☐ AF11 Kerry Collins	12.00	5.50	1.50
☐ AF12 Steve McNair	10.00	4.50	1.25

1995 Action Packed Armed Forces Braille

These Braille parallels to the 1995 Action Packed Armed Forces cards were randomly inserted in packs. Each features a Braille cardback and was slightly more difficult to pull from packs than its base counterpart.

	MINT	NRMT	EXC
COMPLETE BRAILLE SET (12)	125.00	55.00	15.50
COMMON CARD (AF1-AF12)	5.00	2.20	.60

*BRAILLES: .75X TO 1.25X BASIC CARDS

1995 Action Packed G-Force

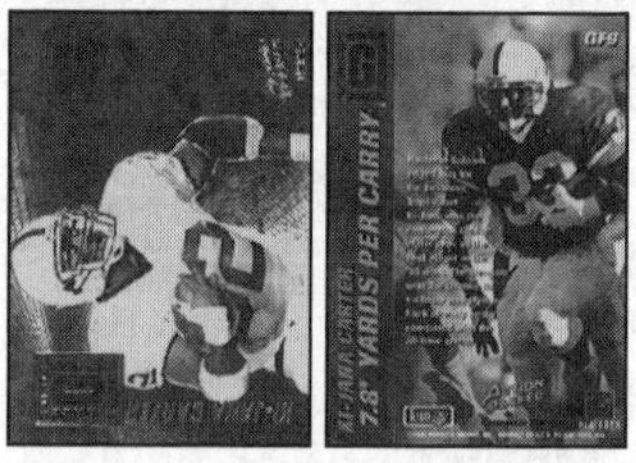

This horizontal 12 card standard-size set was randomly inserted into packs. This set features leading running backs. The full-bleed fronts contain two photos. One photo is a full-color action embossed shot while the other is a ghosted head photo. The words "Ground Force" are located in the upper left corner. Running horizontally up the left side of the back, are the player's name and his 1994 yards per carry average. The rest of the card back contains a player photo and information about his running ability.

	MINT	NRMT	EXC
COMPLETE SET (12)	60.00	27.00	7.50
COMMON CARD (GF1-GF12)	4.00	1.80	.50
☐ GF1 Emmitt Smith	15.00	6.75	1.85
☐ GF2 Barry Sanders	8.00	3.60	1.00
☐ GF3 Marshall Faulk	6.00	2.70	.75
☐ GF4 Natrone Means	5.00	2.20	.60
☐ GF5 Chris Warren	5.00	2.20	.60
☐ GF6 Jerome Bettis	5.00	2.20	.60
☐ GF7 Errict Rhett	5.00	2.20	.60
☐ GF8 Byron Bam Morris	4.00	1.80	.50
☐ GF9 Ki-Jana Carter	5.00	2.20	.60
☐ GF10 Mario Bates	4.00	1.80	.50
☐ GF11 Ricky Watters	5.00	2.20	.60
☐ GF12 Tyrone Wheatley	4.00	1.80	.50

1995 Action Packed Rocket Men

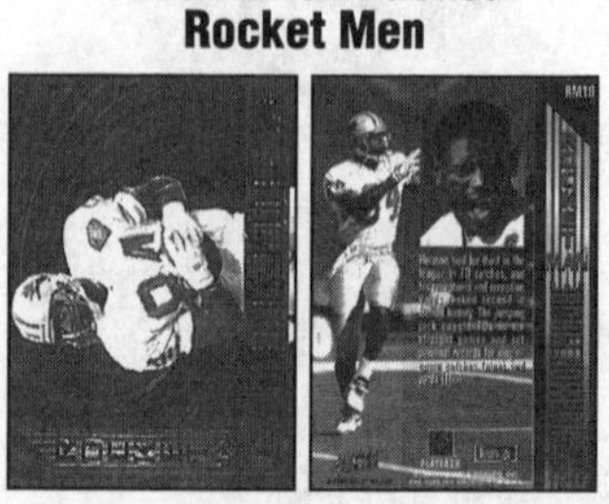

This horizontal 18 card standard-size set was randomly inserted at approximately one in 12 jumbo packs. The full-bleed fronts contain one photo with a "swirl" in the background. The words "Rocket Man" are located on the left side of the card. Running horizontally on the bottom of the card is the player's name. The rest of the card back contains two player photos and information.

	MINT	NRMT	EXC
COMPLETE SET (18)	150.00	70.00	19.00
COMMON CARD (RM1-RM18)	4.00	1.80	.50
☐ RM1 Marshall Faulk	6.00	2.70	.75
☐ RM2 Emmitt Smith	20.00	9.00	2.50
☐ RM3 Barry Sanders	10.00	4.50	1.25
☐ RM4 Natrone Means	5.00	2.20	.60
☐ RM5 Errict Rhett	5.00	2.20	.60
☐ RM6 Ki-Jana Carter	4.00	1.80	.50
☐ RM7 Tyrone Wheatley	4.00	1.80	.50
☐ RM8 Drew Bledsoe	10.00	4.50	1.25
☐ RM9 Dan Marino	20.00	9.00	2.50
☐ RM10 Steve Young	8.00	3.60	1.00
☐ RM11 Troy Aikman	10.00	4.50	1.25
☐ RM12 Brett Favre	20.00	9.00	2.50
☐ RM13 Kerry Collins	12.00	5.50	1.50
☐ RM14 Steve McNair	10.00	4.50	1.25
☐ RM15 Heath Shuler	5.00	2.20	.60
☐ RM16 Jerry Rice	10.00	4.50	1.25
☐ RM17 Michael Irvin	5.00	2.20	.60
☐ RM18 Herman Moore	6.00	2.70	.75

1996 Action Packed Promos

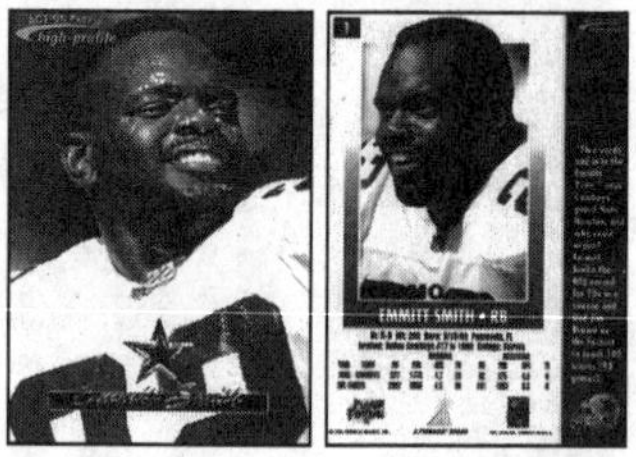

This three-card set was issued to preview the 1996 Action Packed series. The cards are identical to their regular issue counterparts, except for the word "Promo" printed in black on the card back.

	MINT	NRMT	EXC
COMPLETE SET (4)	25.00	11.00	3.10
COMMON CARD	1.00	.45	.12
☐ 1 Emmitt Smith	4.00	1.80	.50
☐ 3 Jerry Rice	15.00	6.75	1.65
Studs Card			
☐ 16 Steve Young	2.00	.90	.25
☐ 105 Neil O'Donnell	1.00	.45	.12

1996 Action Packed

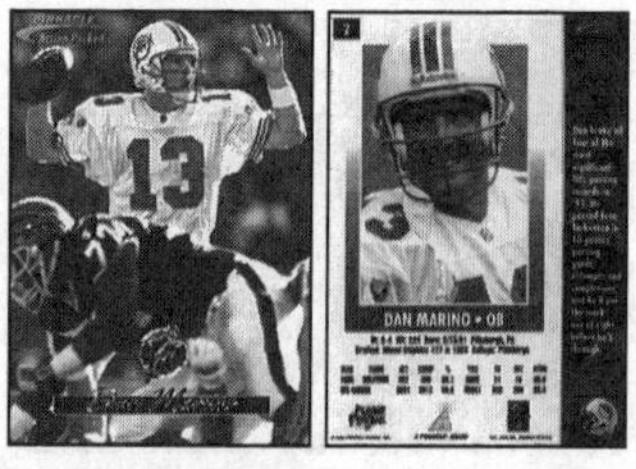

The 1996 Action Packed set was issued by Pinnacle in one series totalling 126 standard-size cards. The set was issued in three different pack forms. Retail and Hobby packs each contained five cards per pack while the magazine packs contained four cards per pack. For the first time, these cards had square corners instead of the traditional round corners. Cards numbered 115-126 are a subset titled "Eyeing the Storm". There are no Rookie Cards in this set.

	MINT	NRMT	EXC
COMPLETE SET (126)	30.00	13.50	3.70
COMMON CARD (1-126)	.15	.07	.02
☐ 1 Emmitt Smith	4.00	1.80	.50
☐ 2 Dan Marino	4.00	1.80	.50
☐ 3 Isaac Bruce	.50	.23	.06
☐ 4 Eric Zeier	.25	.11	.03
☐ 5 Ben Coates	.25	.11	.03
☐ 6 Jim Kelly	.50	.23	.06
☐ 7 Rodney Hampton	.25	.11	.03
☐ 8 Greg Lloyd	.25	.11	.03
☐ 9 Reggie White	.50	.23	.06
☐ 10 Derrick Thomas	.25	.11	.03
☐ 11 Jerry Rice	2.00	.90	.25
☐ 12 Drew Bledsoe	2.00	.90	.25
☐ 13 Cris Carter	.50	.23	.06
☐ 14 Troy Aikman	2.00	.90	.25
☐ 15 Steve McNair	2.00	.90	.25
☐ 16 Steve Young	1.50	.70	.19
☐ 17 Ricky Watters	.25	.11	.03
☐ 18 Brett Favre	4.00	1.80	.50
☐ 19 Michael Westbrook	.50	.23	.06
☐ 20 Charles Haley	.25	.11	.03
☐ 21 Heath Shuler	.50	.23	.06
☐ 22 Tim Brown	.25	.11	.03
☐ 23 Kerry Collins	2.50	1.10	.30
☐ 24 Hugh Douglas	.15	.07	.02
☐ 25 Marcus Allen	.50	.23	.06
☐ 26 Steve Bono	.25	.11	.03
☐ 27 Curtis Martin	3.00	1.35	.35
☐ 28 Wayne Chrebet	.25	.11	.03
☐ 29 Dave Brown	.25	.11	.03
☐ 30 James O.Stewart	.50	.23	.06

☐ 31 Chris Sanders	.25	.11	.03
☐ 32 Deion Sanders	1.25	.55	.16
☐ 33 Rodney Thomas	.15	.07	.02
☐ 34 Rashaan Salaam	.50	.23	.06
☐ 35 Curtis Conway	.50	.23	.06
☐ 36 Harvey Williams	.15	.07	.02
☐ 37 William Floyd	.25	.11	.03
☐ 38 Carl Pickens	.50	.23	.06
☐ 39 Herman Moore	.50	.23	.06
☐ 40 Stan Humphries	.25	.11	.03
☐ 41 Orlando Thomas	.15	.07	.02
☐ 42 Bert Emanuel	.25	.11	.03
☐ 43 Yancey Thigpen	.25	.11	.03
☐ 44 Darick Holmes	.25	.11	.03
☐ 45 Mario Bates	.25	.11	.03
☐ 46 Greg Hill	.25	.11	.03
☐ 47 Errict Rhett	.25	.11	.03
☐ 48 Erik Kramer	.15	.07	.02
☐ 49 Garrison Hearst	.25	.11	.03
☐ 50 Jim Everett	.15	.07	.02
☐ 51 Barry Sanders	2.00	.90	.25
☐ 52 Eric Metcalf	.25	.11	.03
☐ 53 Marshall Faulk	.50	.23	.06
☐ 54 Junior Seau	.50	.23	.06
☐ 55 Bruce Smith	.50	.23	.06
☐ 56 Kordell Stewart	2.50	1.10	.30
☐ 57 Edgar Bennett	.25	.11	.03
☐ 58 Joey Galloway	1.00	.45	.12
☐ 59 Jeff Hostetler	.25	.11	.03
☐ 60 Frank Sanders	.25	.11	.03
☐ 61 John Elway	1.50	.70	.19
☐ 62 Tyrone Wheatley	.25	.11	.03
☐ 63 Jeff George	.25	.11	.03
☐ 64 Ken Norton, Jr.	.25	.11	.03
☐ 65 Bryan Cox	.15	.07	.02
☐ 66 Bryce Paup	.25	.11	.03
☐ 67 Larry Centers	.25	.11	.03
☐ 68 Bernie Parmalee	.15	.07	.02
☐ 69 Jeff Graham	.15	.07	.02
☐ 70 Rick Mirer	.25	.11	.03
☐ 71 Chris Warren	.25	.11	.03
☐ 72 Charlie Garner	.15	.07	.02
☐ 73 Robert Brooks	.50	.23	.06
☐ 74 Jim Harbaugh	.25	.11	.03
☐ 75 Tamarick Vanover	.50	.23	.06
☐ 76 Napoleon Kaufman	.25	.11	.03
☐ 77 Warren Moon	.25	.11	.03
☐ 78 Vincent Brisby	.15	.07	.02
☐ 79 Ki-Jana Carter	.25	.11	.03
☐ 80 Michael Irvin	.50	.23	.06
☐ 81 Trent Dilfer	.25	.11	.03
☐ 82 Byron Bam Morris	.25	.11	.03
☐ 83 Mark Brunell	2.00	.90	.25
☐ 84 Jeff Blake	.50	.23	.06
☐ 85 Kevin Williams	.15	.07	.02
☐ 86 Rod Woodson	.25	.11	.03
☐ 87 Andre Reed	.25	.11	.03
☐ 88 Erric Pegram	.25	.11	.03
☐ 89 Anthony Miller	.25	.11	.03
☐ 90 Gus Frerotte	.50	.23	.06
☐ 91 Quinn Early	.15	.07	.02
☐ 92 Daryl Johnston	.25	.11	.03
☐ 93 Tony Martin	.25	.11	.03
☐ 94 Terrell Davis	3.00	1.35	.35
☐ 95 Brent Jones	.15	.07	.02
☐ 96 Mark Chmura	.25	.11	.03
☐ 97 Kyle Brady	.25	.11	.03
☐ 98 J.J. Stokes	.50	.23	.06
☐ 99 Rodney Peete	.15	.07	.02
☐ 100 Natrone Means	.50	.23	.06
☐ 101 Sherman Williams	.15	.07	.02
☐ 102 Brian Blades	.25	.11	.03
☐ 103 Brett Perriman	.25	.11	.03
☐ 104 Antonio Freeman	1.00	.45	.12
☐ 105 Neil O'Donnell	.25	.11	.03
☐ 106 Craig Heyward	.15	.07	.02
☐ 107 Derek Loville	.15	.07	.02
☐ 108 Jay Novacek	.25	.11	.03
☐ 109 Scott Mitchell	.25	.11	.03
☐ 110 Bill Brooks	.15	.07	.02
☐ 111 Shannon Sharpe	.25	.11	.03
☐ 112 Jake Reed	.25	.11	.03
☐ 113 Derrick Moore	.15	.07	.02
☐ 114 Steve Atwater	.15	.07	.02
☐ 115 Darren Woodson ETS	.25	.11	.03
☐ 116 Junior Seau ETS	.25	.11	.03
☐ 117 Quentin Coryatt ETS	.15	.07	.02
☐ 118 Bruce Smith ETS	.50	.23	.06
☐ 119 Rod Woodson ETS	.25	.11	.03
☐ 120 Charles Haley ETS	.25	.11	.03
☐ 121 Derrick Thomas ETS	.25	.11	.03
☐ 122 Ken Norton, Jr. ETS	.15	.07	.02
☐ 123 Steve Atwater ETS	.15	.07	.02
☐ 124 Greg Lloyd ETS	.25	.11	.03
☐ 125 Reggie White ETS	.50	.23	.06
☐ 126 Bryan Cox ETS	.15	.07	.02

1996 Action Packed 24K Gold

Randomly inserted in packs at a rate of one in 72 Retail and Hobby packs, this 14-card insert set features leading NFL players. These cards have the words "24 Karat" printed in the lower right corner.

	MINT	NRMT	EXC
COMPLETE SET (14)	600.00	275.00	75.00
COMMON CARD (1-14)	20.00	9.00	2.50

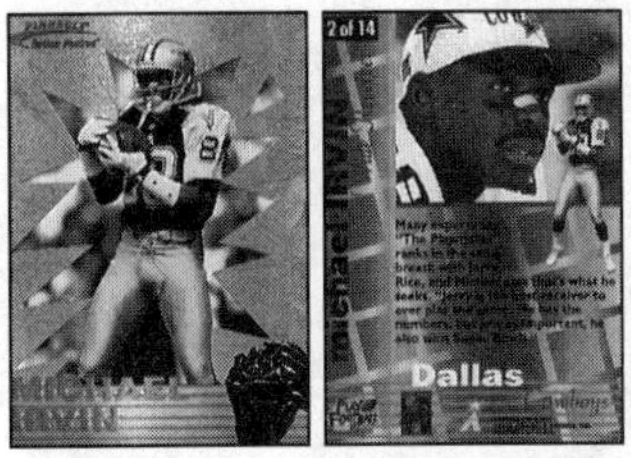

☐ 1 Brett Favre	80.00	36.00	10.00
☐ 2 Michael Irvin	20.00	9.00	2.50
☐ 3 Drew Bledsoe	50.00	22.00	6.25
☐ 4 Jerry Rice	50.00	22.00	6.25
☐ 5 Troy Aikman	50.00	22.00	6.25
☐ 6 Dan Marino	80.00	36.00	10.00
☐ 7 Errict Rhett	35.00	16.00	4.40
☐ 8 Curtis Martin	60.00	27.00	7.50
☐ 9 Steve Young	35.00	16.00	4.40
☐ 10 Barry Sanders	50.00	22.00	6.25
☐ 11 Marshall Faulk	40.00	18.00	5.00
☐ 12 Isaac Bruce	35.00	16.00	4.40
☐ 13 John Elway	40.00	18.00	5.00
☐ 14 Emmitt Smith	80.00	36.00	10.00

1996 Action Packed Artist's Proofs

This 126-card standard-size set is a parallel to the regular Action Packed set. These cards were inserted one in 24 Hobby and Retail packs and one in 30 Magazine packs. The cards have the words "Artist's Proof" printed on the front.

	MINT	NRMT	EXC
COMP.AP SET (126)	1250.00	550.00	160.00
COMMON CARD (1-126)	4.00	1.80	.50

*AP STARS: 15X TO 30X BASIC CARDS
*AP YOUNG STARS: 10X TO 20X BASIC CARDS

1996 Action Packed Ball Hog

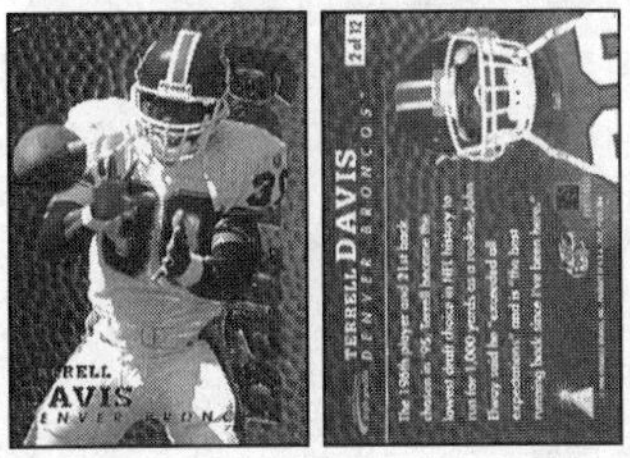

Randomly inserted in packs at a rate of one in 23 regular packs and one in 29 magazine packs, this 12-card insert set uses embossed leather-like technology on the front of the card. These cards feature the player's portrait against a football-like background.

	MINT	NRMT	EXC
COMPLETE SET (12)	100.00	45.00	12.50
COMMON CARD (1-12)	4.00	1.80	.50
☐ 1 Carl Pickens	4.00	1.80	.50
☐ 2 Terrell Davis	15.00	6.75	1.85
☐ 3 Jerry Rice	12.00	5.50	1.50
☐ 4 Barry Sanders	12.00	5.50	1.50
☐ 5 Marshall Faulk	8.00	3.60	1.00
☐ 6 Isaac Bruce	8.00	3.60	1.00
☐ 7 Michael Irvin	8.00	3.60	1.00
☐ 8 Cris Carter	4.00	1.80	.50
☐ 9 Rashaan Salaam	6.00	2.70	.75
☐ 10 Herman Moore	8.00	3.60	1.00
☐ 11 Chris Warren	6.00	2.70	.75
☐ 12 Emmitt Smith	25.00	11.00	3.10

1996 Action Packed Jumbo Inserts

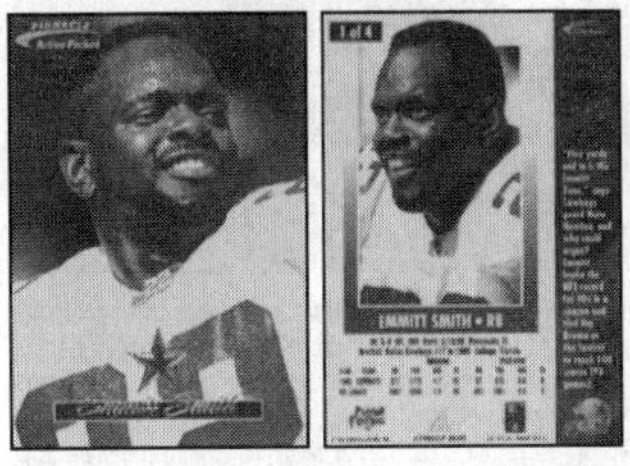

These oversized cards were parallel to the regular issue cards, other than in size and numbering. They were inserted one per box in special retail packaging as a chiptopper insert.

	MINT	NRMT	EXC
COMPLETE SET (4)	20.00	9.00	2.50
COMMON CARD (1-4)	4.00	1.80	.50
☐ 1 Emmitt Smith	6.00	2.70	.75
☐ 2 Drew Bledsoe	4.00	1.80	.50
☐ 3 Troy Aikman	4.00	1.80	.50
☐ 4 Brett Favre	6.00	2.70	.75

1996 Action Packed Longest Yard

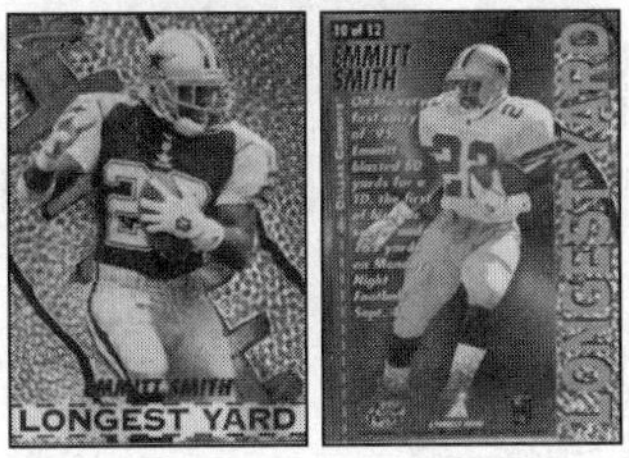

Randomly inserted in packs at a rate of one in 24 magazine packs, this 12-card insert set features leading players.

	MINT	NRMT	EXC
COMPLETE SET (12)	200.00	90.00	25.00
COMMON CARD (1-12)	6.00	2.70	.75
☐ 1 Brett Favre/R. Brooks	50.00	22.00	6.25
☐ 2 Tamarick Vanover	10.00	4.50	1.25
☐ 3 Joey Galloway	12.00	5.50	1.50
☐ 4 Kerry Collins	25.00	11.00	3.10
☐ 5 Jeff Blake	10.00	4.50	1.25
☐ 6 Jerry Rice	25.00	11.00	3.10
☐ 7 Barry Sanders	25.00	11.00	3.10
☐ 8 Rodney Thomas	6.00	2.70	.75
☐ 9 Herman Moore	8.00	3.60	1.00
☐ 10 Emmitt Smith	50.00	22.00	6.25
☐ 11 Terrell Davis	25.00	11.00	3.10
☐ 12 Cris Carter	6.00	2.70	.75

1996 Action Packed Sculptor's Proof Redemption

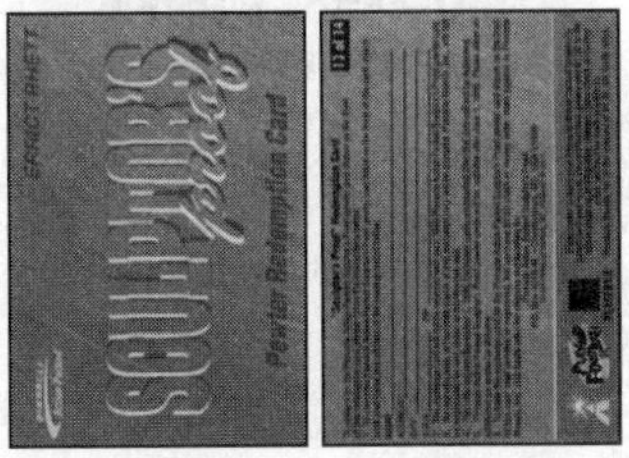

Randomly inserted in packs at a rate of one in 192 Hobby and Retail packs and one in 288 Magazine packs, these cards were part of a redemption program. Out of the packs, a collector would acquire a redemption card that would be mailed in, with a $2.50 postage fee, for a pewter metal version of the card. The redemption offer expired on November 1, 1996. We've listed prices below for the pewter cards.

	MINT	NRMT	EXC
COMPLETE SET (14)	1000.00	450.00	125.00
COMMON CARD (1-14)	30.00	13.50	3.70
☐ 1 Dan Marino	140.00	65.00	17.50
☐ 2 Deion Sanders	40.00	18.00	5.00
☐ 3 Joey Galloway	40.00	18.00	5.00
☐ 4 Brett Favre	140.00	65.00	17.50
☐ 5 Barry Sanders	70.00	32.00	8.75
☐ 6 Michael Irvin	30.00	13.50	3.70
☐ 7 Drew Bledsoe	70.00	32.00	8.75
☐ 8 Emmitt Smith	140.00	65.00	17.50
☐ 9 Curtis Martin	80.00	36.00	10.00
☐ 10 Steve Young	40.00	18.00	5.00
☐ 11 John Elway	50.00	22.00	6.25
☐ 12 Jerry Rice	70.00	32.00	8.75
☐ 13 Errict Rhett	35.00	16.00	4.40
☐ 14 Troy Aikman	70.00	32.00	8.75

1996 Action Packed Studs

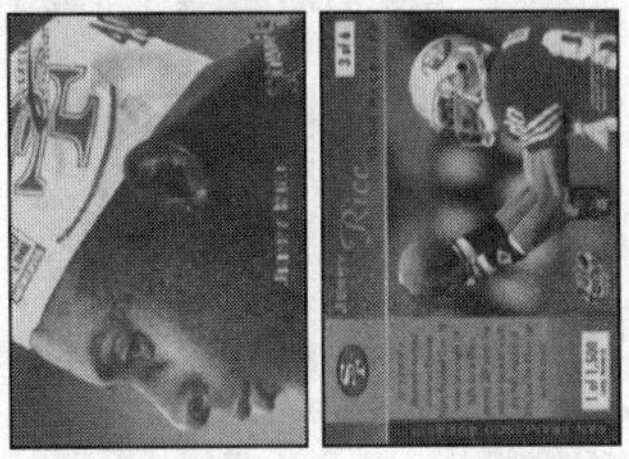

Randomly inserted in packs at a rate of one in 161 Hobby and Retail packs, this six-card insert set features NFL players sporting their diamond stud earrings. These cards are numbered out of 1500 sets produced and each contains a genuine diamond chip.

	MINT	NRMT	EXC
COMPLETE SET (6)	500.00	220.00	60.00
COMMON CARD (1-6)	40.00	18.00	5.00
COMP.24K GOLD SET (6)	700.00	325.00	90.00

24K STUDS: .75X TO 1.5X BASIC CARDS

☐ 1 Emmitt Smith	200.00	90.00	25.00
☐ 2 Deion Sanders	90.00	40.00	11.00
☐ 3 Jerry Rice	100.00	45.00	12.50
☐ 4 Michael Irvin	35.00	16.00	4.40
☐ 5 Kordell Stewart	100.00	45.00	12.50
☐ 6 Ricky Watters	40.00	18.00	5.00

1997 Action Packed

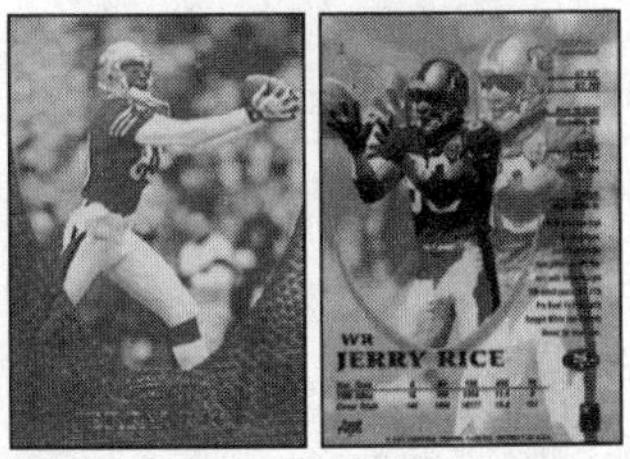

The 1997 Action Packed set was issued in one series totaling 125 cards and was distributed in five card packs with a suggested retail price of $2.99. The fronts feature embossed color action player photos on a pebble-grained pigskin background. The backs carry another player photo with a faded background version of it and career statistics. Three promo cards were produced to promote the set.

	MINT	NRMT	EXC
COMPLETE SET (125)	45.00	20.00	5.50
COMMON CARD (1-125)	.15	.07	.02
☐ 1 Jerry Rice	2.50	1.10	.30
☐ 2 Troy Aikman	2.50	1.10	.30
☐ 3 Ricky Watters	.25	.11	.03
☐ 4 Dan Marino	5.00	2.20	.60
☐ 5 Emmitt Smith	5.00	2.20	.60
☐ 6 Warren Moon	.25	.11	.03
☐ 7 Rashaan Salaam	.50	.23	.06
☐ 8 Drew Bledsoe	2.50	1.10	.30
☐ 9 Eddie George	3.00	1.35	.35
☐ 10 John Elway	2.00	.90	.25
☐ 11 Robert Brooks	.50	.23	.06
☐ 12 Scott Mitchell	.25	.11	.03
☐ 13 Isaac Bruce	.50	.23	.06
☐ 14 Marshall Faulk	.50	.23	.06
☐ 15 Steve Bono	.15	.07	.02
☐ 16 Barry Sanders	2.50	1.10	.30
☐ 17 Brett Favre	5.00	2.20	.60
☐ 18 Curtis Martin	2.50	1.10	.30
☐ 19 Keyshawn Johnson	1.00	.45	.12
☐ 20 Dave Brown	.25	.11	.03
☐ 21 Frank Sanders	.25	.11	.03
☐ 22 Gus Frerotte	.50	.23	.06
☐ 23 Eric Metcalf	.25	.11	.03
☐ 24 Thurman Thomas	.50	.23	.06
☐ 25 Steve Young	1.50	.70	.19
☐ 26 Alvin Harper	.15	.07	.02
☐ 27 Mark Brunell	2.50	1.10	.30
☐ 28 Kordell Stewart	2.00	.90	.25
☐ 29 Terry Glenn	2.50	1.10	.30
☐ 30 Junior Seau	.50	.23	.06
☐ 31 Karim Abdul-Jabbar	1.50	.70	.19
☐ 32 Jeff Hostetler	.25	.11	.03
☐ 33 Rodney Hampton	.25	.11	.03
☐ 34 Irving Fryar	.25	.11	.03
☐ 35 Cris Carter	.50	.23	.06
☐ 36 James O.Stewart	.50	.23	.06
☐ 37 Marcus Allen	.50	.23	.06
☐ 38 Napoleon Kaufman	.25	.11	.03
☐ 39 Shannon Sharpe	.25	.11	.03
☐ 40 LeShon Johnson	.15	.07	.02
☐ 41 Tony Banks	.75	.35	.09
☐ 42 Lawrence Phillips	.25	.11	.03
☐ 43 Kerry Collins	2.00	.90	.25
☐ 44 Curtis Conway	.50	.23	.06
☐ 45 Jim Harbaugh	.25	.11	.03
☐ 46 Garrison Hearst	.25	.11	.03
☐ 47 Trent Dilfer	.25	.11	.03
☐ 48 Terance Mathis	.15	.07	.02
☐ 49 Jerome Bettis	.50	.23	.06
☐ 50 Chris Sanders	.25	.11	.03
☐ 51 Deion Sanders	1.25	.55	.16
☐ 52 Herman Moore	.50	.23	.06
☐ 53 Elvis Grbac	.25	.11	.03
☐ 54 O.J. McDuffie	.25	.11	.03
☐ 55 Ben Coates	.25	.11	.03
☐ 56 Jim Kelly	.50	.23	.06
☐ 57 J.J. Stokes	.25	.11	.03
☐ 58 Terrell Davis	2.50	1.10	.30
☐ 59 Stan Humphries	.25	.11	.03
☐ 60 Carl Pickens	.50	.23	.06
☐ 61 Neil O'Donnell	.25	.11	.03
☐ 62 Edgar Bennett	.25	.11	.03
☐ 63 Yancey Thigpen	.25	.11	.03
☐ 64 Bert Emanuel	.25	.11	.03
☐ 65 Amani Toomer	.25	.11	.03
☐ 66 Jeff Blake	.50	.23	.06
☐ 67 Eddie Kennison	1.25	.55	.16
☐ 68 Jason Dunn	.25	.11	.03
☐ 69 Rob Moore	.15	.07	.02

☐ 70 Andre Rison	.25	.11	.03
☐ 71 Vinny Testaverde	.25	.11	.03
☐ 72 Henry Ellard	.25	.11	.03
☐ 73 Dale Carter	.15	.07	.02
☐ 74 Tony Martin	.25	.11	.03
☐ 75 Jim Everett	.15	.07	.02
☐ 76 Joey Galloway	.75	.35	.09
☐ 77 Mike Alstott	.50	.23	.06
☐ 78 Kevin Hardy	.25	.11	.03
☐ 79 Jake Reed	.25	.11	.03
☐ 80 Tim Brown	.25	.11	.03
☐ 81 Sean Dawkins	.15	.07	.02
☐ 82 Bobby Engram	.25	.11	.03
☐ 83 Michael Irvin	.50	.23	.06
☐ 84 Rickey Dudley	.25	.11	.03
☐ 85 Chris Chandler	.25	.11	.03
☐ 86 Keith Jackson	.15	.07	.02
☐ 87 Muhsin Muhammad	.75	.35	.09
☐ 88 Tamarick Vanover	.25	.11	.03
☐ 89 Chris Warren	.25	.11	.03
☐ 90 Johnnie Morton	.25	.11	.03
☐ 91 Terry Allen	.25	.11	.03
☐ 92 Stanley Pritchett	.15	.07	.02
☐ 93 Charles Johnson	.25	.11	.03
☐ 94 Chris T. Jones	.50	.23	.06
☐ 95 Winslow Oliver	.15	.07	.02
☐ 96 Anthony Miller	.25	.11	.03
☐ 97 Tyrone Wheatley	.25	.11	.03
☐ 98 Robert Smith	.25	.11	.03
☐ 99 Eric Moulds	.50	.23	.06
☐ 100 Hardy Nickerson	.15	.07	.02
☐ 101 Derrick Alexander WR	.25	.11	.03
☐ 102 Michael Haynes	.25	.11	.03
☐ 103 Jamal Anderson	.25	.11	.03
☐ 104 Marvin Harrison	1.00	.45	.12
☐ 105 Antonio Freeman	.75	.35	.09
☐ 106 Dorsey Levens	.25	.11	.03
☐ 107 Natrone Means	.50	.23	.06
☐ 108 Keenan McCardell	.25	.11	.03
☐ 109 Mark Chmura	.25	.11	.03
☐ 110 Darren Woodson	.25	.11	.03
☐ 111 Brett Favre DD	2.50	1.10	.30
☐ 112 Emmitt Smith DD	2.50	1.10	.30
☐ 113 Junior Seau DD	.25	.11	.03
☐ 114 Jerry Rice DD	1.25	.55	.16
☐ 115 Barry Sanders DD	1.25	.55	.16
☐ 116 Bruce Smith DD	.50	.23	.06
☐ 117 Troy Aikman DD	1.25	.55	.16
☐ 118 Bryan Cox DD	.15	.07	.02
☐ 119 Zach Thomas DD	.25	.11	.03
☐ 120 Reggie White DD	.50	.23	.06
☐ 121 Ben Coates DD	.25	.11	.03
☐ 122 Jerome Bettis DD	.25	.11	.03
☐ 123 Michael Irvin DD	.25	.11	.03
☐ 124 Quentin Coryatt DD	.15	.07	.02
☐ 125 Checklist Card	.15	.07	.02
☐ P4 Jerry Rice Promo Studs Card	4.00	1.80	.50
☐ P28 Kordell Stewart Promo	1.50	.70	.19
☐ P45 Jim Harbaugh Promo	.50	.23	.06

1997 Action Packed 24K Gold

Randomly inserted in hobby packs at a rate of one in 71, this 15-card set features color player photos of some of the league's premier players. Card fronts feature Action Packed's Prime Frost printing technology with 24K Gold foil highlights. Magazine packs (4-card packs) also contained the inserts at a rate of 1:89.

	MINT	NRMT	EXC
COMPLETE SET (15)	500.00	220.00	60.00
COMMON CARD (1-15)	15.00	6.75	1.85
☐ 1 Brett Favre	80.00	36.00	10.00
☐ 2 Steve Young	30.00	13.50	3.70
☐ 3 Terrell Davis	40.00	18.00	5.00
☐ 4 Barry Sanders	40.00	18.00	5.00
☐ 5 Isaac Bruce	20.00	9.00	2.50
☐ 6 Deion Sanders	25.00	11.00	3.10
☐ 7 Dan Marino	80.00	36.00	10.00
☐ 8 Jim Harbaugh	15.00	6.75	1.85
☐ 9 Jerry Rice	40.00	18.00	5.00
☐ 10 John Elway	35.00	16.00	4.40
☐ 11 Herman Moore	20.00	9.00	2.50
☐ 12 Troy Aikman	40.00	18.00	5.00
☐ 13 Emmitt Smith	80.00	36.00	10.00
☐ 14 Drew Bledsoe	40.00	18.00	5.00
☐ 15 Eddie George	50.00	22.00	6.25

1997 Action Packed Crash Course

Randomly inserted in hobby packs at a rate of one in 23, this 18-card set features color player photos of some of the league's toughest superstars and is printed on rainbow holographic foil. Magazine packs (4-card packs) also contained the cards at a rate of 1:29.

	MINT	NRMT	EXC
COMPLETE SET (18)	200.00	90.00	25.00
COMMON CARD (1-18)	5.00	2.20	.60
☐ 1 Dan Marino	35.00	16.00	4.40
☐ 2 Troy Aikman	20.00	9.00	2.50
☐ 3 Barry Sanders	20.00	9.00	2.50
☐ 4 Emmitt Smith	35.00	16.00	4.40

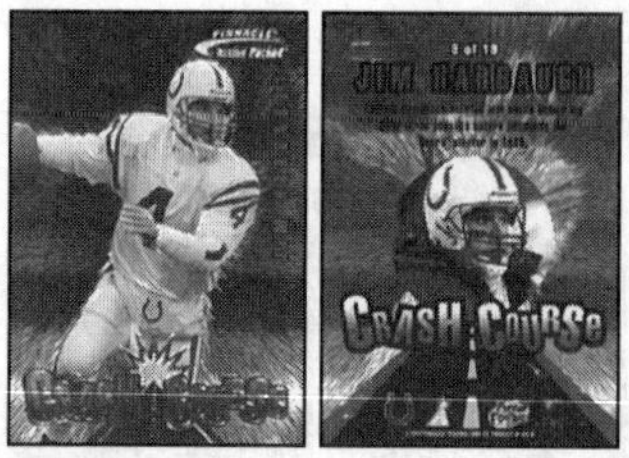

☐ 5 Brett Favre	35.00	16.00	4.40
☐ 6 John Elway	15.00	6.75	1.85
☐ 7 Keyshawn Johnson	10.00	4.50	1.25
☐ 8 Jim Harbaugh	8.00	3.60	1.00
☐ 9 Kerry Collins	15.00	6.75	1.85
☐ 10 Karim Abdul-Jabbar	12.00	5.50	1.50
☐ 11 Eddie Kennison	10.00	4.50	1.25
☐ 12 Curtis Martin	20.00	9.00	2.50
☐ 13 Tony Banks	8.00	3.60	1.00
☐ 14 Dorsey Levens	5.00	2.20	.60
☐ 15 Jerome Bettis	8.00	3.60	1.00
☐ 16 Drew Bledsoe	20.00	9.00	2.50
☐ 17 Marvin Harrison	10.00	4.50	1.25
☐ 18 Jerry Rice	20.00	9.00	2.50

1997 Action Packed First Impressions

Randomly inserted in hobby packs at a rate of one in 12 and in retail packs at a rate of one in 15, this 125-card set is a parallel version of the base set. Each card features silver foil printing highlights on the card fronts.

	MINT	NRMT	EXC
COMPLETE SET (125)	500.00	220.00	60.00
COMMON CARD (1-125)	2.00	.90	.25

*VETERAN STARS: 4X TO 10X BASIC CARDS
*YOUNG STARS: 3X TO 8X BASIC CARDS

1997 Action Packed Gold Impressions

Randomly inserted in hobby packs at a rate of one in 35 and in retail packs at a rate of one in 44, this 125-card set is a parallel version of the silver foil First Impressions. These cards feature gold foil stamping instead of silver.

	MINT	NRMT	EXC
COMPLETE SET (125)	1500.00	700.00	190.00
COMMON CARD (1-125)	5.00	2.20	.60

*VETERAN STARS: 12X TO 25X BASIC CARDS
*YOUNG STARS: 10X TO 20X BASIC CARDS

1997 Action Packed Studs

Randomly inserted in hobby packs at a rate of one in 167, this nine-card set features NFL superstars who wear diamond stud earrings. Only 1500 sets were produced and each card is sequentially numbered with each including a genuine diamond chip. Magazine packs (4-card packs) also contained the cards at a rate of 1:209.

	MINT	NRMT	EXC
COMPLETE SET (9)	700.00	325.00	90.00
COMMON CARD (1-9)	30.00	13.50	3.70
☐ 1 Deion Sanders	50.00	22.00	6.25
☐ 2 Barry Sanders	100.00	45.00	12.50
☐ 3 Eddie George	120.00	55.00	15.00
☐ 4 Jerry Rice	100.00	45.00	12.50
☐ 5 Kordell Stewart	70.00	32.00	8.75
☐ 6 Emmitt Smith	200.00	90.00	25.00
☐ 7 Terrell Davis	80.00	36.00	10.00
☐ 8 Keyshawn Johnson	40.00	18.00	5.00
☐ 9 Robert Smith	30.00	13.50	3.70

1990 Action Packed All-Madden

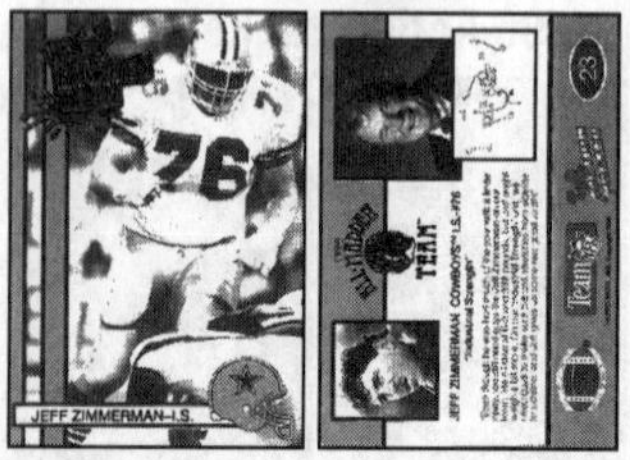

This 58-card standard-size set honors the members of the annual team selected by CBS analyst John Madden. The set was released both in 6-card packs as well as in a factory set. This set features a borderless design on the front and an action shot of the player and a brief description on the back about what qualifies the player to be on the All-Madden Team. The back also features a portrait shot of the player and a portrait shot of John Madden as well. The set also has some of the features standard in Action Packed sets, rounded corners, and the All-Madden Team logo in embossed, raised letters as well as the players' photos being raised. The Neal Anderson prototype (12A) is not included in the complete set as it was passed out to dealers prior to the mass distribution of the set. The Anderson prototype was also available as a special magazine insert in SCD.

	MINT	NRMT	EXC
COMPLETE SET (58)	20.00	9.00	2.50
COMMON CARD (1-58)	.25	.11	.03
☐ 1 Joe Montana	2.50	1.10	.30
☐ 2 Jerry Rice	2.00	.90	.25
☐ 3 Charles Haley	.50	.23	.06
☐ 4 Steve Wisniewski	.35	.16	.04
☐ 5 Dave Meggett	.35	.16	.04
☐ 6 Ottis Anderson	.35	.16	.04
☐ 7 Nate Newton	.35	.16	.04
☐ 8 Warren Moon	.50	.23	.06
☐ 9 Emmitt Smith	4.00	1.80	.50
☐ 10 Jackie Slater	.25	.11	.03
☐ 11 Pepper Johnson	.25	.11	.03
☐ 12 Lawrence Taylor	.50	.23	.06
☐ 13 Sterling Sharpe	.75	.35	.09
☐ 14 Sean Landeta	.25	.11	.03
☐ 15 Richard Dent (tackling Jim Kelly)	.35	.16	.04
☐ 16 Neal Anderson	.35	.16	.04
☐ 17 Bruce Matthews	.35	.16	.04
☐ 18 Matt Millen	.35	.16	.04
☐ 19 Reggie White	.60	.25	.07
☐ 20 Greg Townsend	.35	.16	.04
☐ 21 Troy Aikman	2.00	.90	.25
☐ 22 Don Mosebar	.25	.11	.03
☐ 23 Jeff Zimmerman	.25	.11	.03
☐ 24 Rod Woodson	.60	.25	.07
☐ 25 Keith Byars	.35	.16	.04
☐ 26 Randall Cunningham	.35	.16	.04
☐ 27 Reyna Thompson	.25	.11	.03
☐ 28 Marcus Allen	.50	.23	.06
☐ 29 Gary Clark	.50	.23	.06
☐ 30 Anthony Carter	.35	.16	.04
☐ 31 Bubba Paris	.25	.11	.03
☐ 32 Ronnie Lott	.35	.16	.04
☐ 33 Erik Howard	.25	.11	.03
☐ 34 Ernest Givins	.35	.16	.04
☐ 35 Mike Munchak	.25	.11	.03
☐ 36 Jim Lachey	.25	.11	.03
☐ 37 Merril Hoge UER (Back photo reversed)	.25	.11	.03
☐ 38 Darrell Green	.35	.16	.04
☐ 39 Pierce Holt	.25	.11	.03
☐ 40 Jerome Brown	.35	.16	.04
☐ 41 William Perry UER (Back photo reversed)	.35	.16	.04
☐ 42 Michael Carter	.25	.11	.03
☐ 43 Keith Jackson	.35	.16	.04
☐ 44 Kevin Fagan	.25	.11	.03
☐ 45 Mark Carrier DB	.50	.23	.06
☐ 46 Fred Barnett	.50	.23	.06
☐ 47 Barry Sanders	2.00	.90	.25
☐ 48 Pat Swilling and Rickey Jackson	.35	.16	.04
☐ 49 Sam Mills and Vaughan Johnson	.25	.11	.03
☐ 50 Jacob Green	.25	.11	.03
☐ 51 Stan Brock	.25	.11	.03
☐ 52 Dan Hampton	.35	.16	.04
☐ 53 Brian Noble	.25	.11	.03
☐ 54 John Elliott	.25	.11	.03
☐ 55 Matt Bahr	.25	.11	.03
☐ 56 Bill Parcells CO	.35	.16	.04
☐ 57 Art Shell CO	.35	.16	.04
☐ 58 All-Madden Team Trophy	.25	.11	.03
☐ P12 Neal Anderson (Prototype)	2.00	.90	.25

1991 Action Packed All-Madden

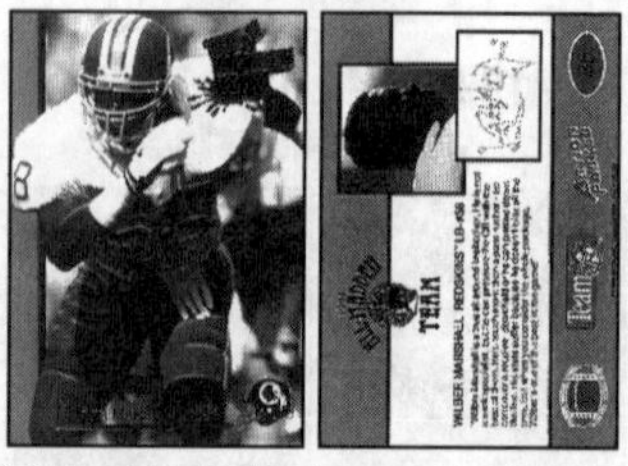

In its second year, this 52-card standard-size set honors the selections to the All-Madden Team. The fronts feature borderless embossed color player photos, accented by gold and aqua border stripes running down either the left or right side of the card face. The All-Madden Team logo appears in the upper left corner, with the team helmet, player's name, and position printed at the card bottom. Between aqua border stripes, the horizontally oriented backs carry player profile, a color head shot, and a diagram of a football play. The cards are numbered on the back. The cards were issued in foil packs as well as in factory sets. Each of the cards in the set was also available in a randomly inserted 24K Gold parallel version.

	MINT	NRMT	EXC
COMPLETE SET (52)	15.00	6.75	1.85
COMMON CARD (1-52)	.25	.11	.03
☐ 1 Mark Rypien	.35	.16	.04
☐ 2 Erik Kramer	.35	.16	.04
☐ 3 Jim McMahon	.35	.16	.04
☐ 4 Jesse Sapolu	.25	.11	.03
☐ 5 Jay Hilgenberg	.25	.11	.03
☐ 6 Howard Ballard	.25	.11	.03
☐ 7 Lomas Brown	.25	.11	.03
☐ 8 John Elliott	.25	.11	.03
☐ 9 Joe Jacoby	.25	.11	.03
☐ 10 Jim Lachey	.25	.11	.03
☐ 11 Anthony Munoz	.35	.16	.04
☐ 12 Nate Newton	.35	.16	.04
☐ 13 Will Wolford	.25	.11	.03
☐ 14 Jerry Ball	.25	.11	.03
☐ 15 Jerome Brown	.35	.16	.04
☐ 16 William Perry	.35	.16	.04
☐ 17 Charles Mann	.25	.11	.03
☐ 18 Clyde Simmons	.35	.16	.04
☐ 19 Reggie White	.50	.23	.06
☐ 20 Eric Allen	.25	.11	.03
☐ 21 Darrell Green	.25	.11	.03
☐ 22 Bennie Blades	.25	.11	.03
☐ 23 Chuck Cecil	.25	.11	.03
☐ 24 Rickey Dixon	.25	.11	.03
☐ 25 David Fulcher	.25	.11	.03
☐ 26 Ronnie Lott	.50	.23	.06
☐ 27 Emmitt Smith	4.00	1.80	.50
☐ 28 Neal Anderson	.35	.16	.04
☐ 29 Robert Delpino	.25	.11	.03
☐ 30 Barry Sanders	2.00	.90	.25
☐ 31 Thurman Thomas	.75	.35	.09
☐ 32 Cornelius Bennett	.35	.16	.04
☐ 33 Rickey Jackson	.35	.16	.04
☐ 34 Seth Joyner	.35	.16	.04
☐ 35 Wilber Marshall	.25	.11	.03
☐ 36 Clay Matthews	.35	.16	.04
☐ 37 Chris Spielman	.35	.16	.04
☐ 38 Pat Swilling	.35	.16	.04
☐ 39 Fred Barnett	.50	.23	.06
☐ 40 Gary Clark	.50	.23	.06
☐ 41 Michael Irvin	.75	.35	.09
☐ 42 Art Monk	.50	.23	.06
☐ 43 Jerry Rice	2.00	.90	.25
☐ 44 John Taylor	.35	.16	.04
☐ 45 Tom Waddle	.25	.11	.03
☐ 46 Kevin Butler	.25	.11	.03
☐ 47 Bill Bates	.35	.16	.04
☐ 48 Greg Manusky	.25	.11	.03
☐ 49 Elvis Patterson	.25	.11	.03
☐ 50 Steve Tasker	.35	.16	.04
☐ 51 John Daly (Golfer)	1.00	.45	.12
☐ 52 All-Madden Team Trophy	.25	.11	.03

1991 Action Packed All-Madden 24K Gold

Each of the cards in the regular set was available in a 24K Gold parallel version. The Gold cards were randomly inserted in packs and feature the typical Action Packed 24K Gold foil stamp.

	MINT	NRMT	EXC
COMPLETE SET (52)	1000.00	450.00	125.00
COMMON CARD (1-52)	10.00	4.50	1.25

*24K GOLD CARDS: 30X TO 60X

1992 Action Packed All-Madden

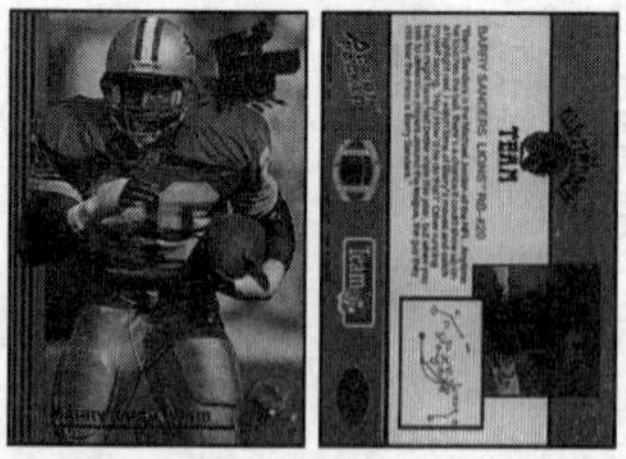

For the third consecutive year, Action Packed has issued a 55-card standard-size set to honor the toughest players in the game as picked by sportscaster John Madden. For hobby dealers only, Action Packed inserted two prototype cards of upcoming products in each display box of All-Madden Team foil packs. Moreover, 24K Gold leaf versions of each card were randomly inserted in foil packs. The cards measure the standard size. The fronts display full-bleed embossed color player photos that are edged on one side by turquoise and variegated gold foil stripes. The player's name and position are gold-foil stamped at the bottom alongside a representation of the team helmet. The horizontal backs display a color head shot, player profile in the form of a quote by Madden, and a play diagram. The card number appears in a turquoise stripe at the bottom.

	MINT	NRMT	EXC
COMPLETE SET (55)	15.00	6.75	1.85
COMMON CARD (1-55)	.25	.11	.03
☐ 1 Emmitt Smith	4.00	1.80	.50
☐ 2 Reggie White	.50	.23	.06
☐ 3 Deion Sanders	1.25	.55	.16
☐ 4 Wilber Marshall	.25	.11	.03

	MINT	NRMT	EXC
☐ 5 Barry Sanders	2.00	.90	.25
☐ 6 Derrick Thomas	.35	.16	.04
☐ 7 Troy Aikman	2.00	.90	.25
☐ 8 Eric Allen	.25	.11	.03
☐ 9 Cris Carter	.50	.23	.06
☐ 10 Jerry Rice	2.00	.90	.25
☐ 11 Rickey Jackson	.25	.11	.03
☐ 12 Bubba McDowell	.25	.11	.03
☐ 13 Jack Del Rio	.25	.11	.03
☐ 14 Nate Newton	.35	.16	.04
☐ 15 John Elliott	.25	.11	.03
☐ 16 Fred Barnett	.35	.16	.04
☐ 17 Mike Singletary	.35	.16	.04
☐ 18 Lawrence Taylor	.35	.16	.04
☐ 19 Bruce Matthews	.25	.11	.03
☐ 20 Pat Swilling	.35	.16	.04
☐ 21 Charles Haley	.35	.16	.04
☐ 22 Andre Rison	.50	.23	.06
☐ 23 Seth Joyner	.35	.16	.04
☐ 24 Steve Young	1.50	.70	.19
☐ 25 Gary Clark	.35	.16	.04
☐ 26 Jerry Ball	.25	.11	.03
☐ 27 Michael Irvin	.50	.23	.06
☐ 28 Haywood Jeffires	.35	.16	.04
☐ 29 Kevin Ross	.25	.11	.03
☐ 30 Chris Doleman	.35	.16	.04
☐ 31 Vai Sikahema	.25	.11	.03
☐ 32 Ricky Watters	.35	.16	.04
☐ 33 Henry Thomas	.25	.11	.03
☐ 34 Mike Kenn	.25	.11	.03
☐ 35 Erik Williams	.35	.16	.04
☐ 36 Neil Smith	.35	.16	.04
☐ 37 Mark Schlereth	.25	.11	.03
☐ 38 Steve Wallace	.25	.11	.03
☐ 39 Randall McDaniel	.25	.11	.03
☐ 40 Kurt Gouveia	.25	.11	.03
☐ 41 Al Noga	.25	.11	.03
☐ 42 Tom Rathman	.25	.11	.03
☐ 43 Harris Barton	.25	.11	.03
☐ 44 Mel Gray	.35	.16	.04
☐ 45 Keith Byars	.25	.11	.03
☐ 46 Todd Scott	.25	.11	.03
☐ 47 Brent Jones	.35	.16	.04
☐ 48 Audray McMillian	.25	.11	.03
☐ 49 Ray Childress	.35	.16	.04
☐ 50 Dennis Smith	.25	.11	.03
☐ 51 Mark McMillian	.25	.11	.03
☐ 52 Sean Gilbert	.35	.16	.04
☐ 53 Pierce Holt	.25	.11	.03
☐ 54 Daryl Johnston	.35	.16	.04
☐ 55 Madden Cruiser (Bus)	.25	.11	.03

1992 Action Packed All-Madden 24K Gold

Action Packed produced these 24K Gold stamped versions of each base card. They were randomly inserted in 1992 All-Madden Team foil packs.

	MINT	NRMT	EXC
COMPLETE SET (55)	1000.00	450.00	125.00
COMMON CARD (1-55)	10.00	4.50	1.25

*24K GOLDS: 30X TO 60X BASIC CARDS

1993 Action Packed All-Madden

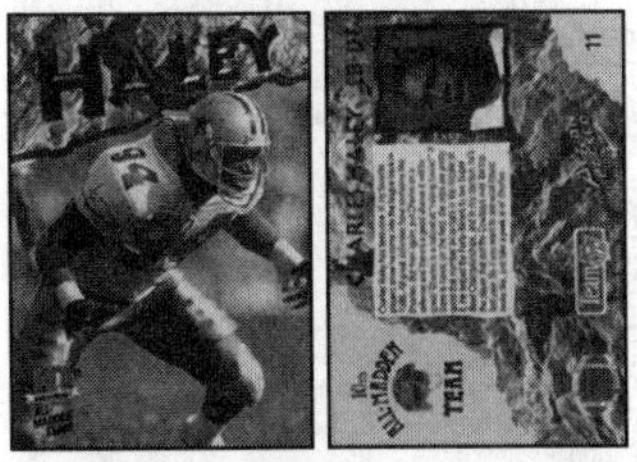

This 42-card standard-size set marks the fourth consecutive year Action Packed honored the toughest players in the game as picked by sportscaster John Madden, and commemorated the 10th anniversary of his All-Madden Team by featuring his all-time favorites from the last 10 years. Action Packed produced 1,000 numbered cases and distributed them only through hobby distributors and dealers. Every case contained a certificate for an uncut sheet of the set autographed by John Madden. Also, 24K gold versions of some of the set were randomly inserted in packs. The fronts feature embossed color player action shots that are borderless, except at the top, where an irregular gray lithic margin set off by a wavy black line carries the player's name in embossed gold foil. The 10th Anniversary logo rests at the lower left. On a background of a mountainous rocky slope, the horizontal back carries a color player head shot toward the upper right. The player's career highlights appear in a white rectangle to the left of the photo. His name and position appear in gold foil across the top. A Troy Aikman prototype card was produced as well and priced below. It is not considered part of the set.

	MINT	NRMT	EXC
COMPLETE SET (42)	15.00	6.75	1.85
COMMON CARD (1-42)	.20	.09	.03
☐ 1 Troy Aikman	1.50	.70	.19
☐ 2 Bill Bates	.30	.14	.04
☐ 3 Mark Bavaro	.20	.09	.03
☐ 4 Jim Burt	.20	.09	.03
☐ 5 Gary Clark	.30	.14	.04
☐ 6 Richard Dent	.30	.14	.04
☐ 7 Gary Fencik	.20	.09	.03
☐ 8 Darrell Green	.20	.09	.03
☐ 9 Roy Green	.30	.14	.04
☐ 10 Russ Grimm	.20	.09	.03
☐ 11 Charles Haley	.30	.14	.04
☐ 12 Dan Hampton	.30	.14	.04
☐ 13 Lester Hayes	.20	.09	.03
☐ 14 Mike Haynes	.20	.09	.03
☐ 15 Jay Hilgenberg	.20	.09	.03
☐ 16 Michael Irvin	.40	.18	.05
☐ 17 Joe Jacoby	.20	.09	.03
☐ 18 Steve Largent	.40	.18	.05
☐ 19 Howie Long	.30	.14	.04
☐ 20 Ronnie Lott	.30	.14	.04
☐ 21 Dan Marino	3.00	1.35	.35
☐ 22 Jim McMahon	.30	.14	.04
☐ 23 Matt Millen	.20	.09	.03
☐ 24 Art Monk	.30	.14	.04
☐ 25 Joe Montana	1.50	.70	.19
☐ 26 Anthony Munoz	.30	.14	.04
☐ 27 Nate Newton	.30	.14	.04
☐ 28 Walter Payton	1.00	.45	.12
☐ 29 William Perry	.30	.14	.04
☐ 30 Jack Reynolds	.20	.09	.03
☐ 31 Jerry Rice	1.50	.70	.19
☐ 32 Barry Sanders	1.50	.70	.19
☐ 33 Sterling Sharpe	.30	.14	.04
☐ 34 Mike Singletary	.30	.14	.04
☐ 35 Jackie Slater	.20	.09	.03
☐ 36 Emmitt Smith	3.00	1.35	.35
☐ 37 Pat Summerall	.30	.14	.04
☐ 38 Lawrence Taylor	.40	.18	.05
☐ 39 Jeff Van Note	.20	.09	.03
☐ 40 Reggie White	.40	.18	.05
☐ 41 Otis Wilson	.20	.09	.03
☐ 42 Jack Youngblood	.20	.09	.03
☐ P1 Troy Aikman Prototype	6.00	2.70	.75

1993 Action Packed All-Madden 24K Gold

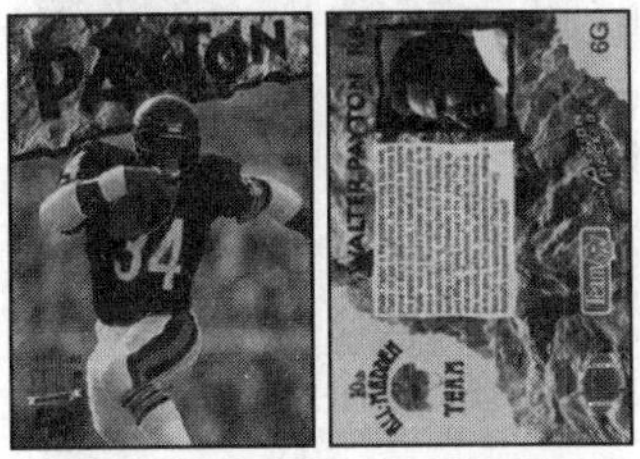

These twelve 24K gold standard-size cards were randomly inserted in packs of 1993 Action Packed 10th Anniversary All-Madden Team. Except for the richer tone of the 24K gold foil and the words "24 Kt. Gold" stamped on the front in gold foil, the design is identical to the regular 10th Anniversary All-Madden cards. The cards are numbered on the back with a "G" suffix.

	MINT	NRMT	EXC
COMPLETE SET (12)	450.00	200.00	55.00
COMMON CARD (1-12)	20.00	9.00	2.50
☐ 1G Troy Aikman	50.00	22.00	6.25
☐ 2G Michael Irvin	25.00	11.00	3.10
☐ 3G Ronnie Lott	20.00	9.00	2.50
☐ 4G Dan Marino	90.00	40.00	11.00
☐ 5G Joe Montana	50.00	22.00	6.25
☐ 6G Walter Payton	40.00	18.00	5.00
☐ 7G Jerry Rice	50.00	22.00	6.25
☐ 8G Barry Sanders	50.00	22.00	6.25
☐ 9G Sterling Sharpe	20.00	9.00	2.50
☐ 10G Emmitt Smith	90.00	40.00	11.00
☐ 11G Lawrence Taylor	20.00	9.00	2.50
☐ 12G Reggie White	25.00	11.00	3.10

1994 Action Packed All-Madden

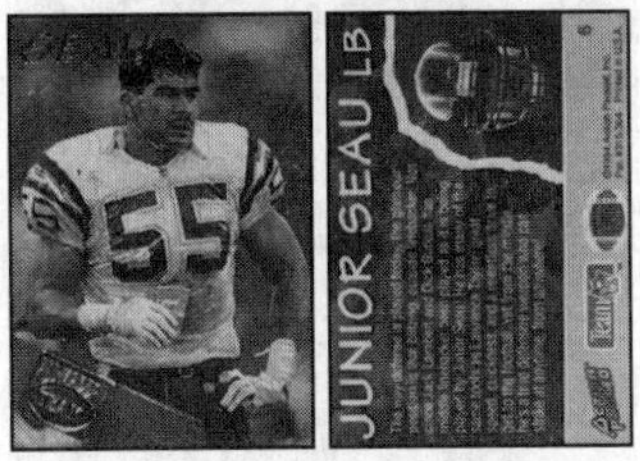

In this 41-card standard-size set, Action Packed presented the 10th Annual All Madden team. Each card has a 24K version; these gold cards were seeded approximately one per box. In addition to the regular players, each pack included a "Smash Mouth" scratch-and-win game card with various Sony TV models and All-Madden 24K cards as prizes. Also, non-winning cards were redeemable for one 11th Annual All-Madden Team Prototype card. The contest ran through June 30, 1995. The embossed fronts feature a borderless design that incorporates the band-aid logo. The backs feature Madden's comments on the player and a color headshot of Madden.

	MINT	NRMT	EXC
COMPLETE SET (41)	15.00	6.75	1.85
COMMON CARD (1-41)	.20	.09	.03
☐ 1 Emmitt Smith	2.50	1.10	.30
☐ 2 Jerome Bettis	.40	.18	.05
☐ 3 Steve Young	.75	.35	.09
☐ 4 Jerry Rice	1.25	.55	.16
☐ 5 Richard Dent	.30	.14	.04
☐ 6 Junior Seau	.40	.18	.05
☐ 7 Harris Barton	.20	.09	.03
☐ 8 Steve Wallace	.20	.09	.03
☐ 9 Keith Byars	.20	.09	.03
☐ 10 Michael Irvin	.40	.18	.05
☐ 11 Joe Montana	1.25	.55	.16
☐ 12 Jesse Sapolu	.20	.09	.03
☐ 13 Rickey Jackson	.20	.09	.03
☐ 14 Ronnie Lott	.30	.14	.04
☐ 15 Donnell Woolford	.20	.09	.03
☐ 16 Reggie White	.40	.18	.05
☐ 17 John Taylor	.30	.14	.04
☐ 18 Bruce Matthews	.20	.09	.03
☐ 19 Ronald Moore	.20	.09	.03
☐ 20 Bill Bates	.30	.14	.04
☐ 21 Steve Hendrickson	.20	.09	.03
☐ 22 Eric Allen	.20	.09	.03
☐ 23 Monte Coleman	.20	.09	.03
☐ 24 Mark Collins	.20	.09	.03
☐ 25 Barry Sanders	1.25	.55	.16
☐ 26 Erik Williams	.30	.14	.04
☐ 27 Phil Simms	.30	.14	.04
☐ 28 Chris Zorich	.30	.14	.04
☐ 29 Troy Aikman	1.25	.55	.16
☐ 30 Charles Haley	.30	.14	.04
☐ 31 Darrell Green	.30	.14	.04
☐ 32 Sean Gilbert	.30	.14	.04
☐ 33 Kevin Gogan	.20	.09	.03
☐ 34 Rodney Hampton	.30	.14	.04
☐ 35 Chris Doleman	.20	.09	.03
☐ 36 Nate Newton	.30	.14	.04
☐ 37 Jackie Slater	.20	.09	.03
☐ 38 Ricky Watters	.40	.18	.05
☐ 39 LeRoy Butler	.20	.09	.03
☐ 40 Gary Clark	.30	.14	.04
☐ 41 Sterling Sharpe	.30	.14	.04

1994 Action Packed All-Madden 24K Gold

Each card in the 1994 Action Packed 10th Annual All-Madden series had a 24K version; these gold cards were seeded approximately one per box. The embossed fronts feature a borderless design that incorporates the band-aid logo. The words "24 Kt. Gold" are stamped on the front to distinguish these cards from their regular series counterparts. The backs feature Madden's comments on the player and a color headshot.

	MINT	NRMT	EXC
COMPLETE SET (41)	1000.00	450.00	125.00
COMMON CARD (1G-41G)	15.00	6.75	1.85
☐ 1G Emmitt Smith	150.00	70.00	19.00
☐ 2G Jerome Bettis	35.00	16.00	4.40
☐ 3G Steve Young	65.00	29.00	8.00
☐ 4G Jerry Rice	75.00	34.00	9.50
☐ 5G Richard Dent	20.00	9.00	2.50
☐ 6G Junior Seau	35.00	16.00	4.40
☐ 7G Harris Barton	15.00	6.75	1.85
☐ 8G Steve Wallace	15.00	6.75	1.85
☐ 9G Keith Byars	15.00	6.75	1.85
☐ 10G Michael Irvin	35.00	16.00	4.40
☐ 11G Joe Montana	75.00	34.00	9.50
☐ 12G Jesse Sapolu	15.00	6.75	1.85
☐ 13G Rickey Jackson	15.00	6.75	1.85
☐ 14G Ronnie Lott	20.00	9.00	2.50
☐ 15G Donnell Woolford	15.00	6.75	1.85
☐ 16G Reggie White	35.00	16.00	4.40
☐ 17G John Taylor	20.00	9.00	2.50
☐ 18G Bruce Matthews	15.00	6.75	1.85
☐ 19G Ronald Moore	15.00	6.75	1.85
☐ 20G Bill Bates	20.00	9.00	2.50
☐ 21G Steve Hendrickson	15.00	6.75	1.85
☐ 22G Eric Allen	15.00	6.75	1.85
☐ 23G Monte Coleman	15.00	6.75	1.85
☐ 24G Mark Collins	15.00	6.75	1.85
☐ 25G Barry Sanders	75.00	34.00	9.50
☐ 26G Erik Williams	20.00	9.00	2.50
☐ 27G Phil Simms	20.00	9.00	2.50
☐ 28G Chris Zorich	20.00	9.00	2.50
☐ 29G Troy Aikman	75.00	34.00	9.50
☐ 30G Charles Haley	20.00	9.00	2.50
☐ 31G Darrell Green	15.00	6.75	1.85
☐ 32G Sean Gilbert	20.00	9.00	2.50
☐ 33G Kevin Gogan	15.00	6.75	1.85
☐ 34G Rodney Hampton	20.00	9.00	2.50
☐ 35G Chris Doleman	15.00	6.75	1.85
☐ 36G Nate Newton	20.00	9.00	2.50
☐ 37G Jackie Slater	15.00	6.75	1.85
☐ 38G Ricky Watters	35.00	16.00	4.40
☐ 39G LeRoy Butler	15.00	6.75	1.85
☐ 40G Gary Clark	20.00	9.00	2.50
☐ 41G Sterling Sharpe	20.00	9.00	2.50

1993 Action Packed Monday Night Football Prototypes

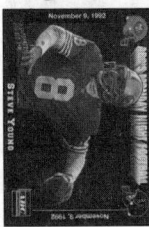

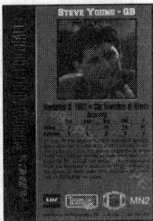

These six standard-size cards were issued to show the design of the 1993 Action Packed ABC Monday Night Football series. On a gold-foil background with black borders, the horizontal fronts feature cut-out embossed color player photos. The set title "ABC's Monday Night Football" is printed across the top between two helmets representing the teams that played. The cards highlight two of the 1992 season's best games. The date of the game is given in each side border, while the player's name is printed in the bottom black border. On the back, a gold foil border stripe carrying the words "ABC's Monday Night Football" edges the left side of the card. The rest of the back consists of a rose-colored panel that displays a color head shot, the scoring broken down by quarter, a summary of the player's performance, and various logos. The disclaimer "1993 Prototype" is printed diagonally across the back.

	MINT	NRMT	EXC
COMPLETE SET (6)	40.00	18.00	5.00
COMMON CARD (MN1-MN6)	6.00	2.70	.75
☐ MN1 Barry Sanders	10.00	4.50	1.25
☐ MN2 Steve Young	8.00	3.60	1.00
☐ MN3 Emmitt Smith	15.00	6.75	1.85
☐ MN4 Thurman Thomas	7.00	3.10	.85
☐ MN5 Barry Foster	6.00	2.70	.75
☐ MN6 Warren Moon	7.00	3.10	.85

1993 Action Packed Monday Night Football

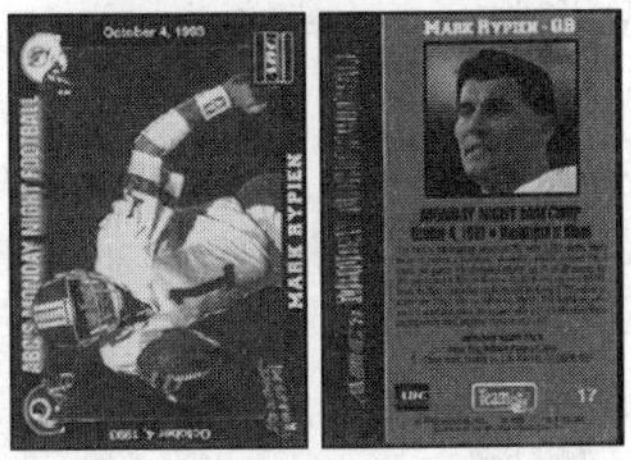

Previewing the top players and match-ups for the 1993 games, this 81-card standard-size set consists of cards for each game of the 1993 Monday Night Football schedule. In addition to featuring the top players in the games, the set also includes a card for each of the three ABC Monday Night Football announcers and a card with all three announcers together. On a gold-foil background with black borders, the horizontal fronts feature cut-out embossed color player photos. The set title "ABC's Monday Night Football" is printed across the top between two helmets representing the teams that played. The date of the game is given in each side border, while the player's name is printed in the bottom black border. On the back, a gold foil border stripe carrying the words "ABC's Monday Night Football" edges the left side of the card. The rest of the back consists of a rose-colored panel that displays a color head shot, the date of the upcoming game, and a game preview focusing on that player's performances versus the future opponent. Also a special "Monday Night Fact" highlights a record set during a Monday Night Football matchup by a player who shares the position of the player on the card. The card numbering was done chronologically. Moreover, 250 individually numbered gold Mint cards of each card were produced, and winning certificates for these were randomly inserted in the foil packs. Certificates entitling the collector to an all-expense paid trip to the Pro Bowl were also randomly inserted in the packs. A limited number of 24K Gold foil stamped versions of all the cards were randomly inserted throughout the foil packs. Finally, Chiptopper preview cards were packed two per hobby box.

	MINT	NRMT	EXC
COMPLETE SET (81)	15.00	6.75	1.85
COMMON CARD (1-81)	.15	.07	.02
☐ 1 Michael Irvin	.40	.18	.05
☐ 2 Charles Haley	.25	.11	.03
☐ 3 Art Monk	.25	.11	.03
☐ 4 Earnest Byner	.15	.07	.02
☐ 5 Tom Rathman	.15	.07	.02
☐ 6 John Taylor	.25	.11	.03
☐ 7 Bernie Kosar	.15	.07	.02
☐ 8 Clay Matthews	.25	.11	.03
☐ 9 Simon Fletcher	.15	.07	.02
☐ 10 John Elway	1.00	.45	.12
☐ 11 Joe Montana	1.50	.70	.19

☐ 12 Derrick Thomas	.40	.18	.05
☐ 13 Rod Woodson	.40	.18	.05
☐ 14 Gary Anderson K	.15	.07	.02
☐ 15 Chris Miller	.25	.11	.03
☐ 16 Andre Rison	.40	.18	.05
☐ 17 Mark Rypien	.15	.07	.02
☐ 18 Charles Mann	.15	.07	.02
☐ 19 John Offerdahl	.15	.07	.02
☐ 20 Pete Stoyanovich	.15	.07	.02
☐ 21 Warren Moon	.40	.18	.05
☐ 22 Lorenzo White	.25	.11	.03
☐ 23 Haywood Jeffires	.15	.07	.02
☐ 24 Andre Reed	.40	.18	.05
☐ 25 Darryl Talley	.15	.07	.02
☐ 26 Tim Brown	.40	.18	.05
☐ 27 Howie Long	.25	.11	.03
☐ 28 Steve Atwater	.15	.07	.02
☐ 29 Karl Mecklenburg	.15	.07	.02
☐ 30 Chris Doleman	.25	.11	.03
☐ 31 Terry Allen	.40	.18	.05
☐ 32 Richard Dent	.25	.11	.03
☐ 33 Neal Anderson	.15	.07	.02
☐ 34 Darrell Green	.15	.07	.02
☐ 35 Chip Lohmiller	.15	.07	.02
☐ 36 Jim Kelly	.40	.18	.05
☐ 37 Cornelius Bennett	.25	.11	.03
☐ 38 Brett Favre	3.00	1.35	.35
☐ 39 Sterling Sharpe	.25	.11	.03
☐ 40 Reggie White	.40	.18	.05
☐ 41 Neil Smith	.40	.18	.05
☐ 42 Nick Lowery	.15	.07	.02
☐ 43 Thurman Thomas	.40	.18	.05
☐ 44 Bruce Smith	.40	.18	.05
☐ 45 Barry Foster	.15	.07	.02
☐ 46 Neil O'Donnell	.40	.18	.05
☐ 47 Rickey Jackson	.15	.07	.02
☐ 48 Morten Andersen	.15	.07	.02
☐ 49 Brent Jones	.25	.11	.03
☐ 50 Ricky Watters	.40	.18	.05
☐ 51 Leslie O'Neal	.25	.11	.03
☐ 52 Marion Butts	.15	.07	.02
☐ 53 Anthony Miller	.25	.11	.03
☐ 54 Jeff George	.40	.18	.05
☐ 55 Steve Emtman	.15	.07	.02
☐ 56 Herschel Walker	.25	.11	.03
☐ 57 Randall Cunningham	.25	.11	.03
☐ 58 Clyde Simmons	.15	.07	.02
☐ 59 Emmitt Smith	3.00	1.35	.35
☐ 60 Ken Norton Jr.	.25	.11	.03
☐ 61 Troy Aikman	1.50	.70	.19
☐ 62 Eric Green	.15	.07	.02
☐ 63 Greg Lloyd	.40	.18	.05
☐ 64 Bryan Cox	.15	.07	.02
☐ 65 Mark Higgs	.15	.07	.02
☐ 66 Phil Simms	.25	.11	.03
☐ 67 Lawrence Taylor	.40	.18	.05
☐ 68 Rodney Hampton	.25	.11	.03
☐ 69 Wayne Martin	.25	.11	.03
☐ 70 Vaughn Dunbar	.15	.07	.02
☐ 71 Keith Jackson	.25	.11	.03
☐ 72 Dan Marino	3.00	1.35	.35
☐ 73 Junior Seau	.40	.18	.05
☐ 74 Stan Humphries	.25	.11	.03
☐ 75 Fred Barnett	.25	.11	.03
☐ 76 Seth Joyner	.25	.11	.03
☐ 77 Steve Young	1.00	.45	.12
☐ 78 Jerry Rice	1.50	.70	.19
☐ 79 Dan Dierdorf ANN	.25	.11	.03
☐ 80 Frank Gifford ANN	.40	.18	.05
☐ 81 Al Michaels ANN	.25	.11	.03
☐ HW1 Hank Williams Jr.	.25	.11	.03

1993 Action Packed Monday Night Football Mint Parallel

Action Packed produced 250 individually numbered gold Mint versions of each base brand card. Winning certificates for each Mint card were randomly inserted in foil packs. The cards are easily distinguishable by the complete gold leaf cardfront.

	MINT	NRMT	EXC
COMPLETE SET (81)	1500.00	700.00	190.00
COMMON CARD (1-81)	30.00	13.50	3.70

MINT CARDS: 100X TO 200X BASIC CARDS

1993 Action Packed Monday Night Football 24K Gold

A limited number of 24K Gold parallels of each card were randomly inserted throughout the run of foil packs. Each card carries the now traditional 24K Gold foil stamp.

	MINT	NRMT	EXC
COMPLETE SET (81)	800.00	350.00	100.00
COMMON CARD (1-81)	15.00	6.75	1.85

24K GOLDS: 50X TO 100X BASIC CARDS

1994 Action Packed Monday Night Football

Issued in a silver cardboard box, these 71 standard-size cards have rounded corners and feature embossed color action player photos on their silver foil-bordered fronts (except the announcer cards 61-71 are borderless). These cards are sequenced in the order of their planned Monday Night matchup. The horizontal back carries at its lower right a

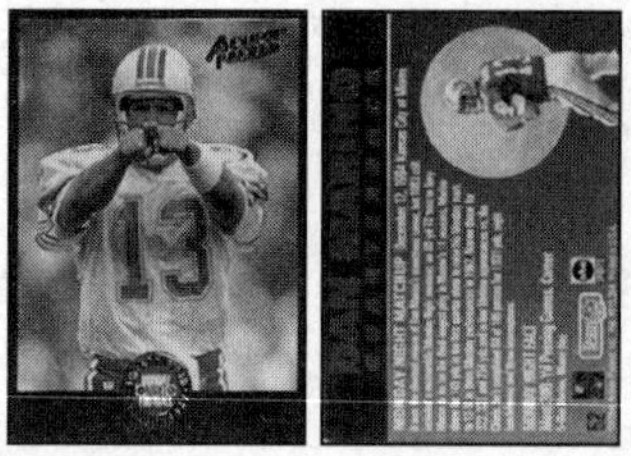

color action player cutout silhouetted against the full moon. The player's name and position appear within the silver-foil margin at the top. The back also carries a Monday Night matchup that gives a sneak preview of the game, as well as a Monday Night Fact.

	MINT	NRMT	EXC
COMPLETE SET (71)	15.00	6.75	1.85
COMMON CARD (1-71)	.15	.07	.02
☐ 1 Jeff Hostetler	.25	.11	.03
☐ 2 Terry McDaniel	.15	.07	.02
☐ 3 Steve Young	1.00	.45	.12
☐ 4 Jerry Rice	1.25	.55	.16
☐ 5 Donnell Woolford	.15	.07	.02
☐ 6 Eric Allen	.15	.07	.02
☐ 7 Herschel Walker	.25	.11	.03
☐ 8 Barry Sanders	1.25	.55	.16
☐ 9 Herman Moore	.35	.16	.04
☐ 10 Emmitt Smith	2.50	1.10	.30
☐ 11 Michael Irvin	.35	.16	.04
☐ 12 John Elway	1.00	.45	.12
☐ 13 Jim Kelly	.35	.16	.04
☐ 14 Andre Reed	.25	.11	.03
☐ 15 Gary Brown	.15	.07	.02
☐ 16 Ernest Givins	.25	.11	.03
☐ 17 Barry Foster	.35	.16	.04
☐ 18 Rod Woodson	.35	.16	.04
☐ 19 Warren Moon	.35	.16	.04
☐ 20 Cris Carter	.35	.16	.04
☐ 21 Rodney Hampton	.35	.16	.04
☐ 22 Derrick Thomas	.35	.16	.04
☐ 23 Marcus Allen	.35	.16	.04
☐ 24 Shannon Sharpe	.25	.11	.03
☐ 25 Cody Carlson	.15	.07	.02
☐ 26 Haywood Jeffires	.25	.11	.03
☐ 27 Randall Cunningham	.25	.11	.03
☐ 28 Calvin Williams	.25	.11	.03
☐ 29 Brett Favre	2.50	1.10	.30
☐ 30 Sterling Sharpe	.35	.16	.04
☐ 31 Chris Zorich	.25	.11	.03
☐ 32 Dante Jones	.15	.07	.02
☐ 33 Mike Sherrard	.15	.07	.02
☐ 34 Keith Hamilton	.15	.07	.02
☐ 35 Charles Haley	.25	.11	.03
☐ 36 Thurman Thomas	.35	.16	.04
☐ 37 Bruce Smith	.35	.16	.04
☐ 38 Greg Lloyd	.35	.16	.04
☐ 39 Michael Brooks	.15	.07	.02
☐ 40 Jumbo Elliott	.15	.07	.02
☐ 41 Ray Childress	.15	.07	.02
☐ 42 Bruce Matthews	.15	.07	.02
☐ 43 Ricky Watters	.35	.16	.04
☐ 44 Brent Jones	.25	.11	.03
☐ 45 Morten Andersen	.15	.07	.02
☐ 46 Tim Brown	.35	.16	.04
☐ 47 Anthony Smith	.25	.11	.03
☐ 48 Natrone Means	.35	.16	.04
☐ 49 Rickey Jackson	.15	.07	.02
☐ 50 Joe Montana	1.25	.55	.16
☐ 51 Neil Smith	.35	.16	.04
☐ 52 Dan Marino	2.50	1.10	.30
☐ 53 Keith Jackson	.15	.07	.02
☐ 54 Troy Aikman	1.25	.55	.16
☐ 55 Jay Novacek	.35	.16	.04
☐ 56 Junior Seau	.35	.16	.04
☐ 57 John Taylor	.25	.11	.03
☐ 58 Tim McDonald	.15	.07	.02
☐ 59 John Randle	.15	.07	.02
☐ 60 Henry Thomas	.15	.07	.02
☐ 61 Prime Time Players ANN Don Meredith Howard Cosell Frank Gifford	.35	.16	.04
☐ 62 The Don and Howard Show ANN Howard Cosell Don Meredith	.50	.23	.06
☐ 63 The Entertainers ANN Don Meredith Howard Cosell Frank Gifford	.35	.16	.04
☐ 64 Howard Cosell ANN	.35	.16	.04
☐ 65 Monday Night Madness Don Meredith ANN Howard Cosell ANN Frank Gifford ANN	.35	.16	.04
☐ 66 Keith Jackson ANN	.15	.07	.02
☐ 67 Don Meredith ANN	.35	.16	.04
☐ 68 Howard Cosell ANN	.35	.16	.04
☐ 69 Chris Hinton Donning a Dierdorf (mask)	.15	.07	.02
☐ 70 Brent Musburger ANN	.15	.07	.02
☐ 71 Lynn Swann ANN	.25	.11	.03

1994 Action Packed Monday Night Football Silver

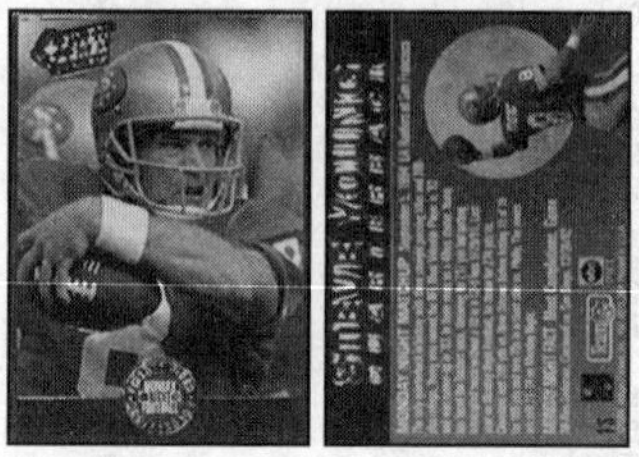

This 12-card standard-size set was randomly inserted in packs. Other than Howard Cosell, all the players featured play offense. In addition to these cards, 25 certificates for a sterling silver card of Dallas Cowboy stars Troy Aikman, Michael Irvin and Emmitt Smith were included in packs.

	MINT	NRMT	EXC
COMPLETE SET (12)	500.00	220.00	60.00
COMMON CARD (1S-12S)	15.00	6.75	1.85
☐ 1S Steve Young	40.00	18.00	5.00
☐ 2S Jerry Rice	50.00	22.00	6.25
☐ 3S Barry Sanders	50.00	22.00	6.25
☐ 4S Emmitt Smith	100.00	45.00	12.50
☐ 5S John Elway	40.00	18.00	5.00
☐ 6S Jim Kelly	20.00	9.00	2.50
☐ 7S Warren Moon	15.00	6.75	1.85
☐ 8S Randall Cunningham	15.00	6.75	1.85
☐ 9S Brett Favre	50.00	22.00	6.25
☐ 10S Dan Marino	100.00	45.00	12.50
☐ 11S Troy Aikman	50.00	22.00	6.25
☐ 12S Howard Cosell ANN Speaking of Sports	25.00	11.00	3.10

1995 Action Packed Monday Night Football Promos

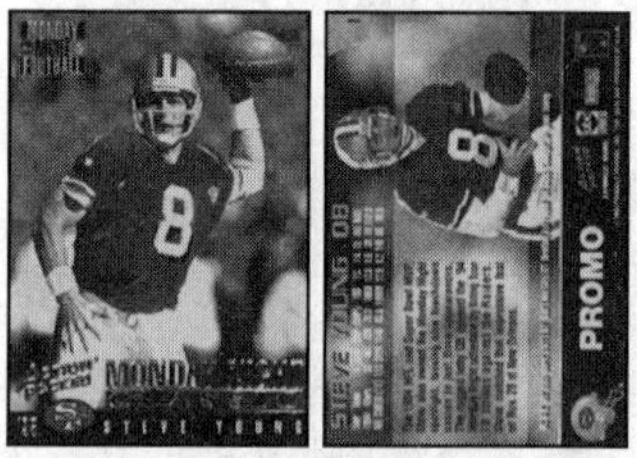

Wrapped in a cello pack, this 4-card standard-size was issued to preview the design of the 1995 Action Packed ABC MNF series. The set features two regular cards, one "Night Flights" insert card, and an ad card. The cards are identical to their regular issue counterparts, except for the word "Promo" stamped in yellow block lettering on their backs.

	MINT	NRMT	EXC
COMPLETE SET (4)	25.00	11.00	3.10
COMMON CARD	.50	.23	.06
☐ 1 Steve Young	2.50	1.10	.30
☐ 3A Troy Aikman	3.00	1.35	.35
☐ 3B Drew Bledsoe Night Flights card	3.00	1.35	.35
☐ NNO NMFB Ad Card	.50	.23	.06

1995 Action Packed Monday Night Football

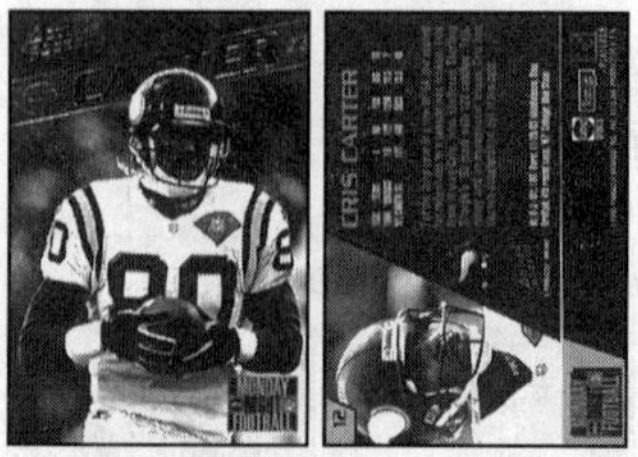

This 126-card standard size set was issued by Pinnacle Brands. The fronts display full-bleed, embossed color action photos, with the player's name and team logo "slanted" across the top. The Monday Night Football logo is located in the lower right hand side of the card. The horizontal backs feature season and career statistics, a player photo as well as biographical information. A parallel set was also inserted called Highlights. Rookie Cards include Ki-Jana Carter, Kerry Collins, Joey Galloway, Steve McNair, Rashaan Salaam, Kordell Stewart, J.J. Stokes and Michael Westbrook in the subset "The Night is Young".

	MINT	NRMT	EXC
COMPLETE SET (126)	22.00	10.00	2.70
COMMON CARD (1-126)	.10	.05	.01
☐ 1 Jerry Rice	1.50	.70	.19
☐ 2 Barry Sanders	1.50	.70	.19
☐ 3 Troy Aikman	1.50	.70	.19
☐ 4 Jerome Bettis	.25	.11	.03
☐ 5 Tim Brown	.25	.11	.03
☐ 6 Marcus Allen	.25	.11	.03
☐ 7 Jeff Blake	3.00	1.35	.35
☐ 8 Rodney Hampton	.25	.11	.03
☐ 9 Reggie White	.25	.11	.03
☐ 10 Warren Moon	.25	.11	.03
☐ 11 William Floyd	.20	.09	.03
☐ 12 Cris Carter	.25	.11	.03
☐ 13 Stan Humphries	.20	.09	.03
☐ 14 Herschel Walker	.20	.09	.03
☐ 15 Dave Brown	.20	.09	.03
☐ 16 Jim Everett	.10	.05	.01
☐ 17 Mario Bates	.20	.09	.03
☐ 18 Terance Mathis	.10	.05	.01
☐ 19 Chris Spielman	.10	.05	.01
☐ 20 Neil O'Donnell	.25	.11	.03
☐ 21 Anthony Miller	.20	.09	.03
☐ 22 Steve Bono	.20	.09	.03
☐ 23 Henry Ellard	.10	.05	.01
☐ 24 Dave Meggett	.10	.05	.01
☐ 25 Flipper Anderson	.10	.05	.01
☐ 26 Rocket Ismail	.20	.09	.03
☐ 27 Leroy Hoard	.10	.05	.01
☐ 28 Steve Young	1.25	.55	.16
☐ 29 Marshall Faulk	1.50	.70	.19
☐ 30 Dan Marino	3.00	1.35	.35
☐ 31 Errict Rhett	1.25	.55	.16
☐ 32 Michael Irvin	.25	.11	.03
☐ 33 Byron Bam Morris	.10	.05	.01
☐ 34 Heath Shuler	.75	.35	.09
☐ 35 Jim Kelly	.25	.11	.03
☐ 36 Deion Sanders	.75	.35	.09
☐ 37 Jeff Hostetler	.20	.09	.03
☐ 38 Jeff George	.25	.11	.03
☐ 39 Alvin Harper	.20	.09	.03
☐ 40 Barry Foster	.10	.05	.01
☐ 41 Craig Erickson	.10	.05	.01
☐ 42 Vinny Testaverde	.20	.09	.03
☐ 43 Andre Reed	.20	.09	.03
☐ 44 Eric Green	.10	.05	.01
☐ 45 Bruce Smith	.25	.11	.03
☐ 46 Frank Reich	.10	.05	.01
☐ 47 Shannon Sharpe	.20	.09	.03
☐ 48 Chris Miller	.10	.05	.01
☐ 49 Darnay Scott	.60	.25	.07
☐ 50 Eric Metcalf	.25	.11	.03
☐ 51 Mike Sherrard	.10	.05	.01
☐ 52 Lorenzo White	.10	.05	.01
☐ 53 Scott Mitchell	.25	.11	.03
☐ 54 Jay Novacek	.20	.09	.03
☐ 55 Emmitt Smith	3.00	1.35	.35
☐ 56 Drew Bledsoe	1.25	.55	.16
☐ 57 Natrone Means	.25	.11	.03
☐ 58 John Elway	.60	.25	.07
☐ 59 Herman Moore	.50	.23	.06
☐ 60 Brett Favre	3.00	1.35	.35
☐ 61 Ricky Watters	.25	.11	.03
☐ 62 Andre Rison	.20	.09	.03
☐ 63 Junior Seau	.25	.11	.03
☐ 64 Randall Cunningham	.20	.09	.03
☐ 65 Chris Warren	.25	.11	.03
☐ 66 Garrison Hearst	.50	.23	.06
☐ 67 Ben Coates	.25	.11	.03
☐ 68 Rick Mirer	.25	.11	.03
☐ 69 Johnny Mitchell	.10	.05	.01
☐ 70 Trent Dilfer	.25	.11	.03
☐ 71 Carl Pickens	.25	.11	.03
☐ 72 Craig Heyward	.10	.05	.01
☐ 73 Greg Lloyd	.25	.11	.03
☐ 74 Boomer Esiason	.20	.09	.03
☐ 75 Greg Hill	.20	.09	.03
☐ 76 Lewis Tillman	.10	.05	.01
☐ 77 Willie Davis	.10	.05	.01
☐ 78 Brent Jones	.10	.05	.01
☐ 79 Michael Haynes	.10	.05	.01
☐ 80 Daryl Johnston	.20	.09	.03
☐ 81 Steve Beuerlein	.20	.09	.03
☐ 82 Ki-Jana Carter NY	1.00	.45	.12
☐ 83 Steve McNair NY	3.50	1.55	.45
☐ 84 Michael Westbrook NY	1.50	.70	.19
☐ 85 Kerry Collins NY	4.00	1.80	.50
☐ 86 Joey Galloway NY	2.50	1.10	.30
☐ 87 Kyle Brady NY	.20	.09	.03
☐ 88 J.J. Stokes NY	1.00	.45	.12
☐ 89 Tyrone Wheatley NY	.50	.23	.06
☐ 90 Rashaan Salaam NY	1.50	.70	.19
☐ 91 Napoleon Kaufman NY	.50	.23	.06
☐ 92 Frank Sanders NY	.50	.23	.06
☐ 93 Stoney Case NY	.10	.05	.01
☐ 94 Todd Collins NY	.20	.09	.03
☐ 95 James O.Stewart NY	.25	.11	.03
☐ 96 Kordell Stewart NY	4.00	1.80	.50
☐ 97 Joe Aska NY	.20	.09	.03
☐ 98 Terrell Fletcher NY	.25	.11	.03
☐ 99 Rob Johnson NY	.10	.05	.01
☐ 100 Steve Young C	.50	.23	.06
☐ 101 Jerry Rice C	.60	.25	.07
☐ 102 Emmitt Smith C	1.25	.55	.16
☐ 103 Barry Sanders C	.60	.25	.07
☐ 104 Marshall Faulk C	.60	.25	.07
☐ 105 Drew Bledsoe C	.50	.23	.06

	MINT	NRMT	EXC
☐ 106 Dan Marino C	1.25	.55	.16
☐ 107 Troy Aikman C	.60	.25	.07
☐ 108 John Elway C	.35	.16	.04
☐ 109 Brett Favre C	.60	.25	.07
☐ 110 Michael Irvin C	.25	.11	.03
☐ 111 Heath Shuler C	.40	.18	.05
☐ 112 Warren Moon C	.25	.11	.03
☐ 113 Chris Warren C	.25	.11	.03
☐ 114 Natrone Means C	.25	.11	.03
☐ 115 Errict Rhett C	.50	.23	.06
☐ 116 Byron Bam Morris C	.10	.05	.01
☐ 117 Randall Cunningham C	.10	.05	.01
☐ 118 Jim Kelly C	.25	.11	.03
☐ 119 Jeff Hostetler C	.20	.09	.03
☐ 120 Barry Foster C	.10	.05	.01
☐ 121 Jim Everett C	.20	.09	.03
☐ 122 Neil O'Donnell C	.25	.11	.03
☐ 123 Jerome Bettis C	.25	.11	.03
☐ 124 Ricky Watters C	.25	.11	.03
☐ 125 Joe Montana C	.75	.35	.09
☐ 126 Rodney Hampton C	.25	.11	.03

1995 Action Packed Monday Night Football Highlights

This 126 card parallel set was randomly inserted into packs at a rate of one in six. The background on the front of the card has silver foil and the card name "Highlights" is located diagonally in gold on the back.

	MINT	NRMT	EXC
COMP.HIGHLIGHTS SET (126)	200.00	90.00	25.00
COMMON HIGHLIGHTS	.60	.25	.07
HIGHLIGHTS VET.STARS: 5X TO 8X			
HIGHLIGHTS YOUNG STARS: 3X TO 6X			
HIGHLIGHTS RCs: 2X TO 5X			

1995 Action Packed Monday Night Football 24K Gold Team

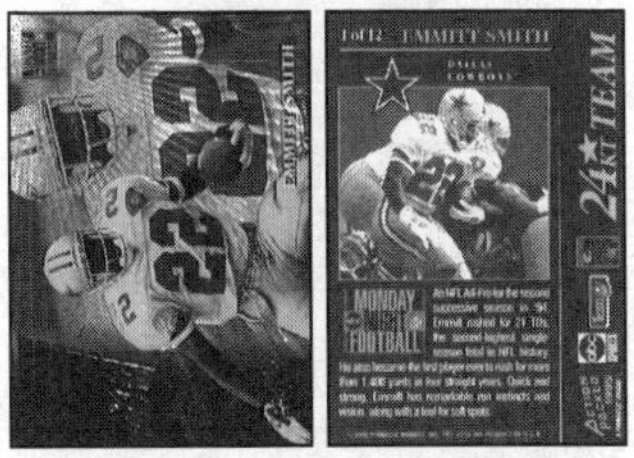

This horizontal 12 card set was randomly inserted at a rate of one in 72 packs. The fronts feature two shots of the player, one being the basic photo and the other using the same image enlarged in the background. The cards are printed on rainbow holographic foil with a "24KT Team" logo running vertically along the left side of the card, the player's name written horizontally along the lower right hand side and the Action Packed 24KT Gold logo on the lower left side. The backs have a single photo running vertically with statistical information about the player.

	MINT	NRMT	EXC
COMPLETE SET (12)	450.00	200.00	55.00
COMMON CARD (1-12)	20.00	9.00	2.50
☐ 1 Emmitt Smith	75.00	34.00	9.50
☐ 2 Barry Sanders	40.00	18.00	5.00
☐ 3 Marshall Faulk	25.00	11.00	3.10
☐ 4 Dan Marino	75.00	34.00	9.50
☐ 5 Steve Young	30.00	13.50	3.70
☐ 6 Drew Bledsoe	40.00	18.00	5.00
☐ 7 Troy Aikman	40.00	18.00	5.00
☐ 8 John Elway	30.00	13.50	3.70
☐ 9 Brett Favre	75.00	34.00	9.50
☐ 10 Ki-Jana Carter	20.00	9.00	2.50
☐ 11 Steve McNair	45.00	20.00	5.50
☐ 12 Kerry Collins	45.00	20.00	5.50

1995 Action Packed Monday Night Football Night Flight

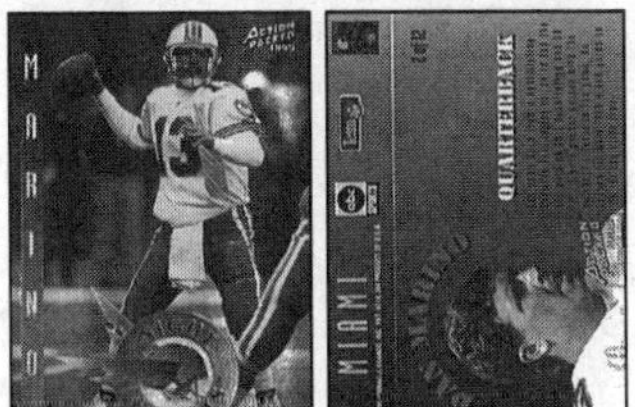

This 12 card set was randomly inserted into packs at a rate of one in 48. It features 12 members of the NFL Quarterback Club with a rainbow holographic background. The card fronts are vertical with the player's name running along the left side of the card and the "Night Flights" logo in the bottom center. The card backs are horizontal with the player's photo on the left side and his name running over the photo. A brief summary of the player is listed on the right side.

	MINT	NRMT	EXC
COMPLETE SET (12)	90.00	40.00	11.00
COMMON CARD (1-12)	4.00	1.80	.50
☐ 1 Steve Young	10.00	4.50	1.25
☐ 2 Dan Marino	20.00	9.00	2.50
☐ 3 Drew Bledsoe	10.00	4.50	1.25
☐ 4 Troy Aikman	10.00	4.50	1.25
☐ 5 John Elway	8.00	3.60	1.00
☐ 6 Brett Favre	20.00	9.00	2.50
☐ 7 Heath Shuler	6.00	2.70	.75
☐ 8 Dave Brown	4.00	1.80	.50
☐ 9 Steve McNair	12.00	5.50	1.50
☐ 10 Kerry Collins	12.00	5.50	1.50
☐ 11 Warren Moon	6.00	2.70	.75
☐ 12 Jeff Hostetler	4.00	1.80	.50

1995 Action Packed Monday Night Football Reverse Angle

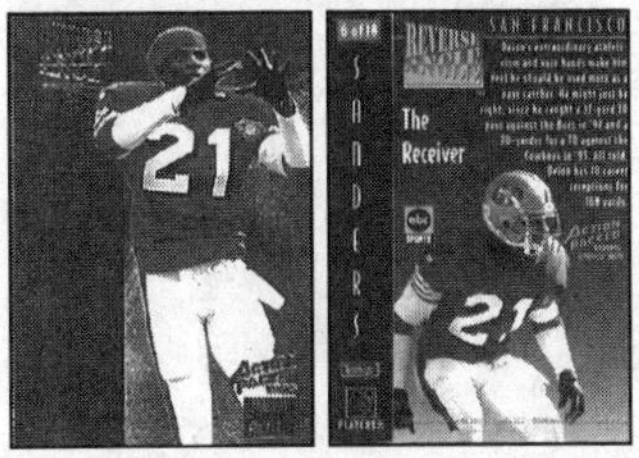

This 18 card set was randomly inserted into hobby packs at a rate of one in 24. The set focuses on top stars making unusual plays. The card fronts show the player on the right side of the card, with the "Reverse Angle" logo located in the top left corner and the player's name running vertically along the same side. The card backs are very similar to the fronts with the name running vertically on the left side, the shot of the player located at the bottom and information on the player above the photo. Reportedly, fewer than 1500 sets were made.

	MINT	NRMT	EXC
COMPLETE SET (18)	60.00	27.00	7.50
COMMON CARD (1-18)	3.00	1.35	.35
☐ 1 Emmitt Smith	16.00	7.25	2.00
☐ 2 Barry Sanders	8.00	3.60	1.00
☐ 3 Steve Young	6.00	2.70	.75
☐ 4 Marshall Faulk	4.00	1.80	.50
☐ 5 Randall Cunningham	3.00	1.35	.35
☐ 6 Deion Sanders	5.00	2.20	.60
☐ 7 John Elway	6.00	2.70	.75
☐ 8 Brett Favre	16.00	7.25	2.00
☐ 9 William Floyd	3.00	1.35	.35
☐ 10 Ricky Watters	4.00	1.80	.50
☐ 11 Ben Coates	3.00	1.35	.35
☐ 12 Rod Woodson	3.00	1.35	.35
☐ 13 Marcus Allen	4.00	1.80	.50
☐ 14 Eric Metcalf	4.00	1.80	.50
☐ 15 Keith Byars	3.00	1.35	.35
☐ 16 Jerry Rice	8.00	3.60	1.00
☐ 17 Alvin Harper	3.00	1.35	.35
☐ 18 Eric Green	3.00	1.35	.35

1995 Action Packed Rookies/Stars

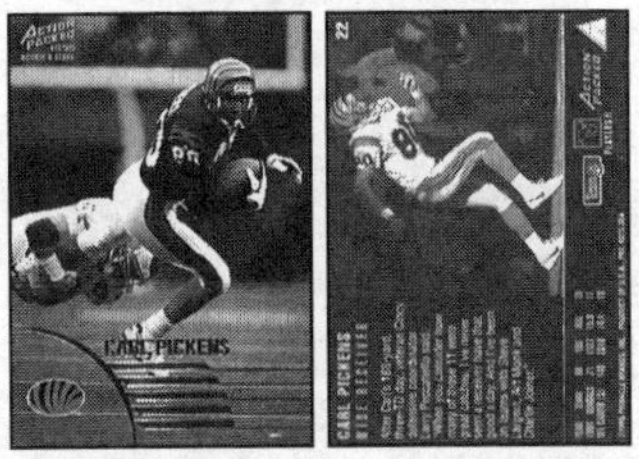

This 105-card standard size set was issued by Pinnacle Brands. The fronts display full-bleed, embossed color action photos, with the player's name and team logo running along the bottom of the card. The Action Packed Rookies and Stars logo is located in the top left hand corner. The horizontal backs feature season and career statistics, a player photo as well as biographical information. A parallel set called Stargazers was also inserted into packs. Rookie Cards include Ki-Jana Carter, Kerry Collins, Joey Galloway, Curtis Martin, Steve McNair, Rashaan Salaam, Kordell Stewert, J.J. Stokes and Michael Westbrook.

	MINT	NRMT	EXC
COMPLETE SET (105)	22.00	10.00	2.70
COMMON CARD (1-105)	.08	.04	.01
☐ 1 Steve Young	1.25	.55	.16
☐ 2 Steve Bono	.12	.05	.01
☐ 3 Natrone Means	.25	.11	.03
☐ 4 Steve Beuerlein	.08	.04	.01
☐ 5 Neil O'Donnell	.12	.05	.01
☐ 6 Marshall Faulk	.75	.35	.09
☐ 7 Ricky Watters	.25	.11	.03
☐ 8 Gary Brown	.08	.04	.01
☐ 9 Jeff Hostetler	.12	.05	.01
☐ 10 Robert Brooks	.25	.11	.03
☐ 11 Johnny Mitchell	.08	.04	.01
☐ 12 Barry Sanders	1.50	.70	.19
☐ 13 Dave Brown	.12	.05	.01
☐ 14 John Elway	1.25	.55	.16
☐ 15 Garrison Hearst	.25	.11	.03
☐ 16 Jim Everett	.08	.04	.01
☐ 17 Michael Irvin	.25	.11	.03
☐ 18 Dan Marino	3.00	1.35	.35
☐ 19 Jeff George	.12	.05	.01
☐ 20 Ben Coates	.12	.05	.01
☐ 21 Charles Johnson	.12	.05	.01
☐ 22 Carl Pickens	.25	.11	.03
☐ 23 Deion Sanders	1.00	.45	.12
☐ 24 Errict Rhett	.25	.11	.03
☐ 25 Steve Walsh	.08	.04	.01
☐ 26 Bruce Smith	.25	.11	.03
☐ 27 Andre Rison	.12	.05	.01
☐ 28 Warren Moon	.12	.05	.01
☐ 29 Terry Allen	.12	.05	.01
☐ 30 Desmond Howard	.12	.05	.01
☐ 31 Shannon Sharpe	.12	.05	.01
☐ 32 Dave Krieg	.08	.04	.01
☐ 33 Byron Bam Morris	.12	.05	.01
☐ 34 Rodney Hampton	.12	.05	.01
☐ 35 Scott Mitchell	.12	.05	.01
☐ 36 Alvin Harper	.08	.04	.01
☐ 37 Robert Smith	.25	.11	.03
☐ 38 Troy Aikman	1.50	.70	.19
☐ 39 William Floyd	.25	.11	.03
☐ 40 Randall Cunningham	.12	.05	.01
☐ 41 Mario Bates	.25	.11	.03
☐ 42 Reggie White	.25	.11	.03
☐ 43 Chris Chandler	.12	.05	.01
☐ 44 Erik Kramer	.08	.04	.01
☐ 45 Emmitt Smith	3.00	1.35	.35
☐ 46 Irving Fryar	.12	.05	.01
☐ 47 Jeff Blake	1.50	.70	.19
☐ 48 Drew Bledsoe	1.50	.70	.19
☐ 49 Anthony Miller	.12	.05	.01
☐ 50 Marcus Allen	.25	.11	.03
☐ 51 Leroy Hoard	.08	.04	.01
☐ 52 Stan Humphries	.12	.05	.01
☐ 53 Eric Green	.08	.04	.01
☐ 54 Herschel Walker	.12	.05	.01
☐ 55 Junior Seau	.25	.11	.03
☐ 56 Terance Mathis	.12	.05	.01
☐ 57 Boomer Esiason	.12	.05	.01
☐ 58 Lorenzo White	.08	.04	.01
☐ 59 Tim Brown	.25	.11	.03
☐ 60 Brett Favre	3.00	1.35	.35
☐ 61 Craig Erickson	.08	.04	.01
☐ 62 Rod Woodson	.12	.05	.01
☐ 63 Frank Reich	.08	.04	.01
☐ 64 Cris Carter	.25	.11	.03
☐ 65 Jerry Rice	1.50	.70	.19
☐ 66 Greg Hill	.12	.05	.01
☐ 67 Andre Reed	.12	.05	.01
☐ 68 Trent Dilfer	.25	.11	.03
☐ 69 Eric Metcalf	.12	.05	.01
☐ 70 Jim Kelly	.25	.11	.03
☐ 71 Herman Moore	.75	.35	.09
☐ 72 Vinny Testaverde	.12	.05	.01
☐ 73 Jeff Graham	.08	.04	.01
☐ 74 Edgar Bennett	.12	.05	.01
☐ 75 Jerome Bettis	.50	.23	.06
☐ 76 Heath Shuler	.25	.11	.03
☐ 77 Chris Warren	.12	.05	.01
☐ 78 Reggie Brooks	.12	.05	.01
☐ 79 Rick Mirer	.25	.11	.03
☐ 80 Chris Miller	.08	.04	.01
☐ 81 Napoleon Kaufman	1.00	.45	.12
☐ 82 Christian Fauria	.08	.04	.01
☐ 83 Todd Collins	.25	.11	.03
☐ 84 J.J. Stokes	1.00	.45	.12
☐ 85 Mark Bruener	.12	.05	.01
☐ 86 Frank Sanders	1.00	.45	.12
☐ 87 Chad May	.08	.04	.01
☐ 88 Kordell Stewart	3.50	1.55	.45
☐ 89 Ki-Jana Carter	1.00	.45	.12
☐ 90 Curtis Martin	5.00	2.20	.60
☐ 91 Sherman Williams	.08	.04	.01
☐ 92 Terrell Davis	4.00	1.80	.50
☐ 93 Chris Sanders	1.50	.70	.19
☐ 94 Kyle Brady	.25	.11	.03
☐ 95 Tyrone Wheatley	.50	.23	.06
☐ 96 Rodney Thomas	.25	.11	.03
☐ 97 James O.Stewart	.25	.11	.03
☐ 98 Kerry Collins	4.00	1.80	.50
☐ 99 Rashaan Salaam	1.50	.70	.19
☐ 100 Stoney Case	.08	.04	.01
☐ 101 Steve McNair	3.50	1.55	.45
☐ 102 Joey Galloway	2.50	1.10	.30
☐ 103 Michael Westbrook	1.50	.70	.19
☐ 104 Eric Zeier	.25	.11	.03
☐ 105 Ray Zellars	.12	.05	.01

1995 Action Packed Rookies/Stars Stargazers

This 105 card parallel set was randomly inserted into packs at a rate of one in six. The background of the card fronts contain silver foil and the backs have the card name "Stargazers" in gold to differentiate them from the basic card.

	MINT	NRMT	EXC
COMPLETE SET (105)	500.00	220.00	60.00
COMMON CARD (1-105)	1.00	.45	.12
*VETERAN STARS: 7X TO 14X BASIC CARDS			
*YOUNG STARS: 5X TO 10X BASIC CARDS			
*RCs: 4X TO 8X BASIC CARDS			

1995 Action Packed Rookies/Stars 24K Gold Team

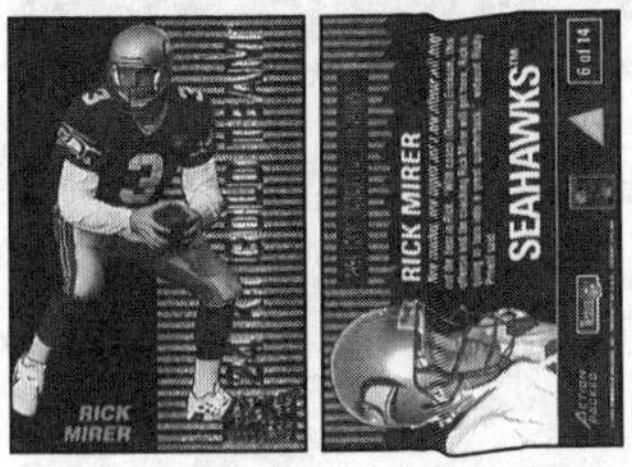

This 14 card set was randomly inserted into packs at a rate of one in 72 packs. The card fronts feature a shot of the player with the player's name and the "24KT Gold Team" phrase listed vertically along the right hand side of the card. The fronts utilize a "prime frost" technology along the right hand side with a black background on the left. The card backs are horizontal with a player shot and brief commentary.

	MINT	NRMT	EXC
COMPLETE SET (14)	600.00	275.00	75.00
COMMON CARD (1-14)	25.00	11.00	3.10
☐ 1 Steve Young	35.00	16.00	4.40
☐ 2 Brett Favre	80.00	36.00	10.00
☐ 3 Rashaan Salaam	30.00	13.50	3.70
☐ 4 Tyrone Wheatley	25.00	11.00	3.10
☐ 5 Marshall Faulk	30.00	13.50	3.70
☐ 6 Rick Mirer	30.00	13.50	3.70
☐ 7 Troy Aikman	50.00	22.00	6.25
☐ 8 John Elway	40.00	18.00	5.00
☐ 9 Dan Marino	80.00	36.00	10.00
☐ 10 Barry Sanders	50.00	22.00	6.25
☐ 11 Jerry Rice	50.00	22.00	6.25
☐ 12 Emmitt Smith	80.00	36.00	10.00
☐ 13 Michael Irvin	30.00	13.50	3.70
☐ 14 Drew Bledsoe	50.00	22.00	6.25

1995 Action Packed Rookies/Stars Bustout

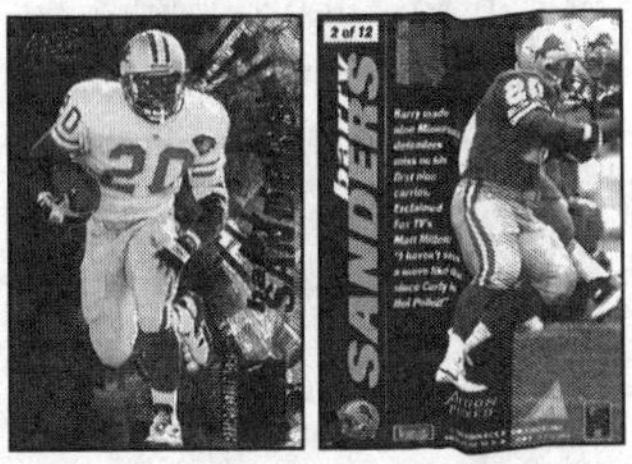

This 12 card set was randomly inserted into jumbo packs only. The fronts feature a silver foil etched design in the background with a shot of the player over it. The player's name is listed vertically along the right side of the card with the "Bustout '95" logo under it. The card backs feature a player shot, brief commentary and the player's name and team logo on the left side of the card.

	MINT	NRMT	EXC
COMPLETE SET (12)	50.00	22.00	6.25
COMMON CARD (1-12)	4.00	1.80	.50
☐ 1 Marshall Faulk	6.00	2.70	.75
☐ 2 Barry Sanders	8.00	3.60	1.00
☐ 3 Emmitt Smith	15.00	6.75	1.85
☐ 4 Natrone Means	5.00	2.20	.60
☐ 5 Errict Rhett	5.00	2.20	.60
☐ 6 Byron Bam Morris	4.00	1.80	.50
☐ 7 Terry Allen	5.00	2.20	.60
☐ 8 Rodney Hampton	4.00	1.80	.50
☐ 9 Ricky Watters	5.00	2.20	.60
☐ 10 Chris Warren	4.00	1.80	.50
☐ 11 Jerome Bettis	5.00	2.20	.60
☐ 12 Gary Brown	4.00	1.80	.50

1995 Action Packed Rookies/Stars Closing Seconds

This 12 card set was randomly inserted into hobby packs only at a rate of one in 36. The fronts have two photos of the player, one in the foreground and the other shadowed behind it. The fronts are printed with rainbow holographic foil and have the player's name in the top left corner with the "Closing Seconds" logo running horizontally along the bottom. The vertical backs feature a shot of the player with his name, position and team located directly underneath along with a short commentary running to the left of the player.

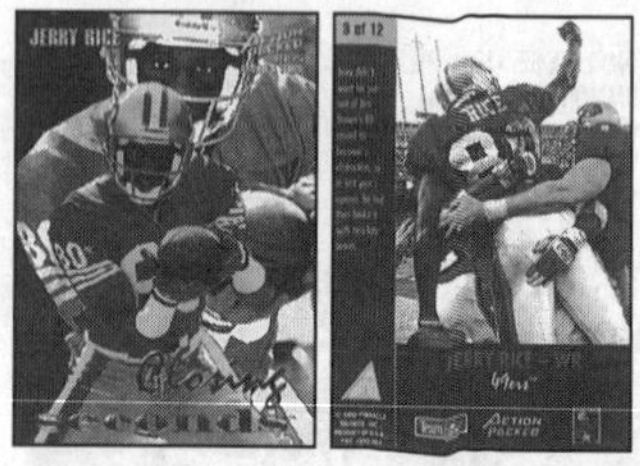

	MINT	NRMT	EXC
COMPLETE SET (12)	130.00	57.50	16.00
COMMON CARD (1-12)	5.00	2.20	.60
□ 1 Dan Marino	25.00	11.00	3.10
□ 2 Steve Young	10.00	4.50	1.25
□ 3 Jerry Rice	12.00	5.50	1.50
□ 4 Emmitt Smith	25.00	11.00	3.10
□ 5 Barry Sanders	12.00	5.50	1.50
□ 6 Brett Favre	25.00	11.00	3.10
□ 7 Drew Bledsoe	12.00	5.50	1.50
□ 8 Troy Aikman	12.00	5.50	1.50
□ 9 John Elway	10.00	4.50	1.25
□ 10 Dave Brown	5.00	2.20	.60
□ 11 Warren Moon	6.00	2.70	.75
□ 12 Jim Kelly	6.00	2.70	.75

1995 Action Packed Rookies/Stars Instant Impressions

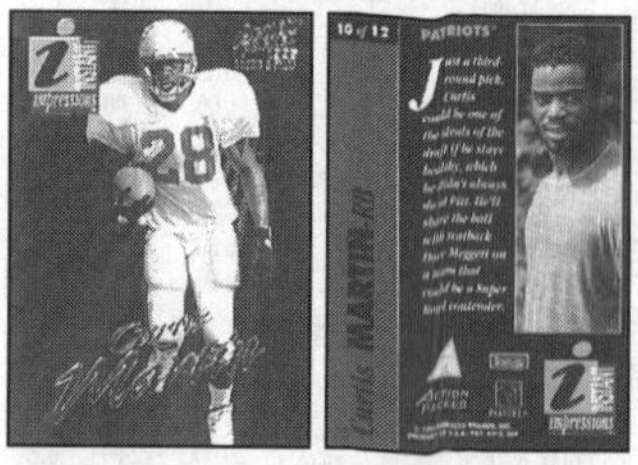

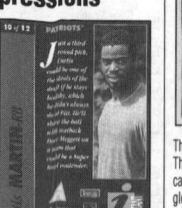

This 12 card set was randomly inserted into packs at a rate of one in 24. The cards utilize a silver "micro-etched" technology. The fronts contain a player shot with his name written in script along the bottom of the card and the "Instant Impressions" logo located in the upper left hand corner. The horizontal backs feature a shot of the player along the right side of the card with a brief commentary located to the left. The player's name runs vertically along the left side of the card on a red background.

	MINT	NRMT	EXC
COMPLETE SET (12)	100.00	45.00	12.50
COMMON CARD (1-12)	5.00	2.20	.60
□ 1 Ki-Jana Carter	6.00	2.70	.75
□ 2 Steve McNair	14.00	6.25	1.75
□ 3 Kerry Collins	16.00	7.25	2.00
□ 4 Michael Westbrook	8.00	3.60	1.00
□ 5 Joey Galloway	10.00	4.50	1.25
□ 6 J.J. Stokes	6.00	2.70	.75
□ 7 Rashaan Salaam	8.00	3.60	1.00
□ 8 Tyrone Wheatley	6.00	2.70	.75
□ 9 Eric Zeier	6.00	2.70	.75
□ 10 Curtis Martin	18.00	8.00	2.20
□ 11 Napoleon Kaufman	6.00	2.70	.75
□ 12 Kyle Brady	5.00	2.20	.60

1991 All World Troy Aikman Promos

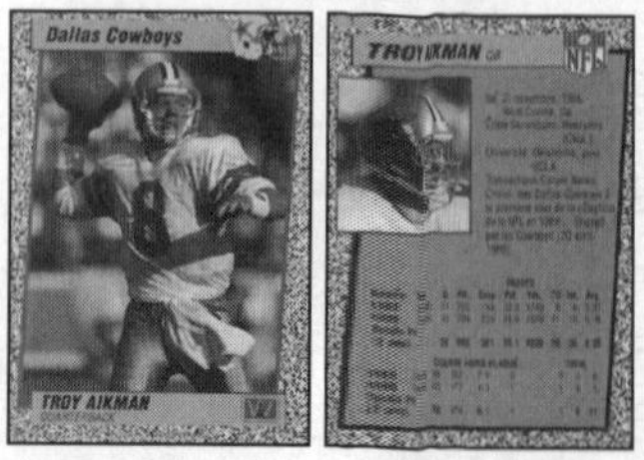

This set consists of six standard-size cards. The cards feature the same color action photo of Aikman, with his arm cocked behind his head ready to pass. On the first three cards, the top of the photo is oval-shaped and framed by yellow stripes. The space above the oval as well as the stripe at the bottom carrying player information are purple. The outer border is green. Inside green borders, the horizontal back has a color close-up photo, biography (there were French, Spanish, and English versions), and statistics. On the second three cards listed below, the player photo is tilted slightly to the right and framed by a thin green border. Yellow stripes above and below the picture carry information, and the outer border is black-and-white speckled. The backs have a similar design and display a close-up color head shot and biographical and statistical information on a pastel green panel. All versions use the same color action photo, but differ in that the photo is cropped differently on the green-border cards compared to the speckled-border cards. All cards are numbered on the back as number 1.

	MINT	NRMT	EXC
COMPLETE SET (6)	10.00	4.50	1.25
COMMON CARD (1A-1F)	2.00	.90	.25
□ 1A Troy Aikman (Green border; English bio)	2.00	.90	.25
□ 1B Troy Aikman (Green border; French bio)	2.00	.90	.25
□ 1C Troy Aikman (Green border; Spanish bio)	2.00	.90	.25
□ 1D Troy Aikman (Speckled border; English bio)	2.00	.90	.25
□ 1E Troy Aikman (Speckled border; French bio)	2.00	.90	.25
□ 1F Troy Aikman (Speckled border; Spanish bio)	2.00	.90	.25

1992 All World

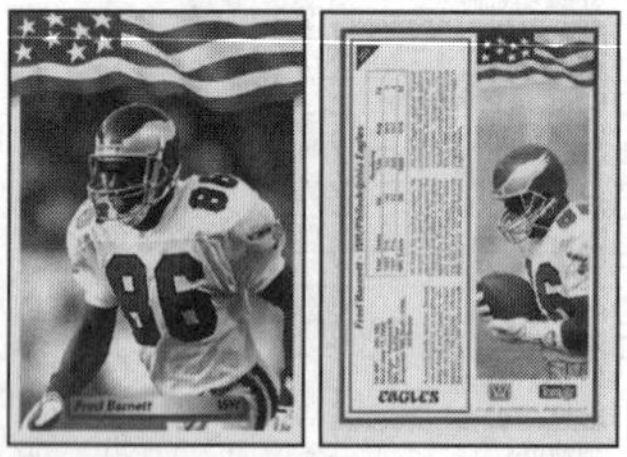

The 1992 All World NFL football set contains 300 standard-size cards. The production run was reported to be 8,000 foil cases. There are 12 cards per foil pack and 26 per rack pack. The front design features glossy color player photos, bordered on top by a full-bleed American flag and by white on the remaining three sides. Ten rookies and ten "Legends in the Making" cards, embossed with gold-foil stars, were randomly inserted in the foil packs. Likewise, autographed cards by Joe Namath (1,000), Jim Brown (1,000), and Desmond Howard (2,500) were inserted in both foil and rack packs. Although the player's name is not printed on the front, his autograph and number do appear. A special double-fold card (TR1) of the three autographed cards was inserted only in the rack packs. It is distinguished from the regular issue triple cards by foil-stamping. The regular card backs have a second color player photo, with player information (biography and player profile) in a horizontally oriented box alongside the picture. Topical subsets featured include Legends in the Making (1-10) and Greats of the Game (266-300). Rookie Cards include Edgar Bennett, Steve Bono, Terrell Buckley, Dale Carter, Marco Coleman, Quentin Coryatt, Vaughn Dunbar, Steve Emtman, Desmond Howard (AW had exclusive rights), Carl Pickens, and Tommy Vardell. A Desmond Howard promo card was released and is priced below.

	MINT	NRMT	EXC
COMPLETE SET (300)	16.00	7.25	2.00
COMMON CARD (1-300)	.05	.02	.01
□ 1 Emmitt Smith LM	1.00	.45	.12
□ 2 Thurman Thomas LM	.10	.05	.01
□ 3 Deion Sanders LM	.25	.11	.03
□ 4 Randall Cunningham LM	.10	.05	.01
□ 5 Michael Irvin LM	.10	.05	.01
□ 6 Bruce Smith LM	.10	.05	.01
□ 7 Jeff George LM	.10	.05	.01
□ 8 Derrick Thomas LM	.10	.05	.01
□ 9 Andre Rison LM	.15	.07	.02
□ 10 Troy Aikman LM	.50	.23	.06
□ 11 Quentin Coryatt	.25	.11	.03
□ 12 Carl Pickens	2.00	.90	.25
□ 13 Steve Emtman	.10	.05	.01
□ 14 Derek Brown TE	.10	.05	.01
□ 15 Desmond Howard	.40	.18	.05
□ 16 Troy Vincent	.15	.07	.02
□ 17 David Klingler	.10	.05	.01
□ 18 Vaughn Dunbar	.05	.02	.01
□ 19 Terrell Buckley	.10	.05	.01
□ 20 Jimmy Smith	.10	.05	.01
□ 21 Marquez Pope	.05	.02	.01
□ 22 Kurt Barber	.05	.02	.01
□ 23 Robert Harris	.05	.02	.01
□ 24 Tony Sacca	.05	.02	.01
□ 25 Alonzo Spellman	.15	.07	.02
□ 26 Shane Collins	.05	.02	.01
□ 27 Chris Mims	.15	.07	.02
□ 28 Siran Stacy	.05	.02	.01
□ 29 Edgar Bennett	.60	.25	.07
□ 30 Sean Gilbert	.15	.07	.02
□ 31 Eugene Chung	.05	.02	.01
□ 32 Levon Kirkland	.05	.02	.01
□ 33 Chuck Smith	.05	.02	.01
□ 34 Chester McGlockton	.15	.07	.02
□ 35 Ashley Ambrose	.10	.05	.01
□ 36 Phillippi Sparks	.05	.02	.01
□ 37 Darryl Williams	.10	.05	.01
□ 38 Tracy Scroggins	.10	.05	.01
□ 39 Mike Gaddis	.05	.02	.01
□ 40 Tony Brooks	.05	.02	.01
□ 41 Steve Israel	.05	.02	.01
□ 42 Patrick Rowe	.05	.02	.01
□ 43 Shane Dronett	.05	.02	.01
□ 44 Mike Pawlawski	.05	.02	.01
□ 45 Dale Carter	.15	.07	.02
□ 46 Tyji Armstrong	.05	.02	.01
□ 47 Kevin Smith	.15	.07	.02
□ 48 Courtney Hawkins	.10	.05	.01
□ 49 Marco Coleman	.10	.05	.01
□ 50 Tommy Vardell	.10	.05	.01
□ 51 Ray Ethridge	.05	.02	.01
□ 52 Robert Porcher	.10	.05	.01
□ 53 Todd Collins	.05	.02	.01
□ 54 Robert Jones	.10	.05	.01
□ 55 Tommy Maddox	.10	.05	.01
□ 56 Dana Hall	.10	.05	.01
□ 57 Leon Searcy	.10	.05	.01
□ 58 Robert Brooks	1.50	.70	.19
□ 59 Darren Woodson	.15	.07	.02
□ 60 Jeremy Lincoln	.05	.02	.01
□ 61 Sean Jones	.10	.05	.01
□ 62 Howie Long	.10	.05	.01
□ 63 Rich Gannon	.05	.02	.01
□ 64 Keith Byars	.05	.02	.01
□ 65 John Taylor	.10	.05	.01
□ 66 Burt Grossman	.05	.02	.01
□ 67 Chris Hinton	.05	.02	.01
□ 68 Brad Muster	.05	.02	.01
□ 69 Cris Dishman	.05	.02	.01
□ 70 Russell Maryland	.10	.05	.01
□ 71 Harvey Williams	.15	.07	.02
□ 72 Broderick Thomas	.05	.02	.01
□ 73 Louis Lipps	.05	.02	.01
□ 74 Erik Kramer	.05	.02	.01
□ 75 David Fulcher	.05	.02	.01
□ 76 Andre Tippett	.05	.02	.01
□ 77 Timm Rosenbach	.05	.02	.01
□ 78 Mark Rypien	.10	.05	.01
□ 79 James Lofton	.10	.05	.01
□ 80 Dan Saleaumua	.05	.02	.01
□ 81 John L. Williams	.05	.02	.01
□ 82 Kevin Fagan	.05	.02	.01
□ 83 Flipper Anderson	.05	.02	.01
□ 84 Michael Dean Perry	.10	.05	.01
□ 85 Mark Higgs	.05	.02	.01
□ 86 Pat Swilling	.10	.05	.01
□ 87 Pierce Holt	.05	.02	.01
□ 88 John Elway	.75	.35	.09
□ 89 Bill Brooks	.10	.05	.01
□ 90 Rob Moore	.10	.05	.01
□ 91 Junior Seau	.30	.14	.04
□ 92 Wendell Davis	.05	.02	.01
□ 93 Brian Noble	.05	.02	.01
□ 94 Ernest Givins	.10	.05	.01
□ 95 Phil Simms	.10	.05	.01
□ 96 Eric Dickerson	.15	.07	.02
□ 97 Bennie Blades	.05	.02	.01
□ 98 Gary Anderson RB	.05	.02	.01
□ 99 Erric Pegram	.15	.07	.02
□ 100 Hart Lee Dykes	.05	.02	.01
□ 101 Charles Haley	.10	.05	.01
□ 102 Bruce Smith	.15	.07	.02
□ 103 Nick Lowery	.05	.02	.01
□ 104 Webster Slaughter	.05	.02	.01
□ 105 Ray Childress	.10	.05	.01
□ 106 Gene Atkins	.05	.02	.01
□ 107 Bruce Armstrong	.05	.02	.01
□ 108 Anthony Miller	.15	.07	.02
□ 109 Eric Thomas	.05	.02	.01
□ 110 Greg Townsend	.05	.02	.01
□ 111 Anthony Carter	.10	.05	.01
□ 112 James Hasty	.05	.02	.01
□ 113 Chris Miller	.05	.02	.01
□ 114 Sammie Smith	.05	.02	.01
□ 115 Bubby Brister	.10	.05	.01
□ 116 Mark Clayton	.10	.05	.01
□ 117 Richard Johnson	.05	.02	.01
□ 118 Bernie Kosar	.10	.05	.01
□ 119 Lionel Washington	.05	.02	.01
□ 120 Gary Clark	.10	.05	.01
□ 121 Anthony Munoz	.15	.07	.02
□ 122 Brent Jones	.10	.05	.01
□ 123 Thurman Thomas	.15	.07	.02
□ 124 Lee Williams	.05	.02	.01
□ 125 Jessie Hester	.05	.02	.01
□ 126 Andre Ware	.10	.05	.01
□ 127 Patrick Hunter	.05	.02	.01
□ 128 Erik Howard	.05	.02	.01
□ 129 Keith Jackson	.10	.05	.01
□ 130 Troy Aikman	1.00	.45	.12
□ 131 Mike Singletary	.10	.05	.01
□ 132 Carnell Lake	.10	.05	.01
□ 133 Jeff Hostetler	.10	.05	.01
□ 134 Alonzo Highsmith	.05	.02	.01
□ 135 Vaughan Johnson	.05	.02	.01
□ 136 Louis Oliver	.05	.02	.01
□ 137 Mel Gray	.10	.05	.01
□ 138 Al Toon	.10	.05	.01
□ 139 Bubba McDowell	.05	.02	.01
□ 140 Ronnie Lott	.10	.05	.01
□ 141 Deion Sanders	.50	.23	.06
□ 142 Jim Harbaugh	.15	.07	.02
□ 143 Gary Zimmerman	.05	.02	.01
□ 144 Ernie Jones	.05	.02	.01
□ 145 Cortez Kennedy	.10	.05	.01
□ 146 Jeff Cross	.05	.02	.01
□ 147 Floyd Turner UER (Bio says he was drafted in 4th round)	.05	.02	.01
□ 148 Mike Tomczak	.10	.05	.01
□ 149 Lorenzo White	.05	.02	.01
□ 150 Mark Carrier DB	.05	.02	.01
□ 151 John Stephens	.05	.02	.01
□ 152 Jerry Rice	1.00	.45	.12
□ 153 Jim Kelly	.15	.07	.02
□ 154 Al Smith	.05	.02	.01
□ 155 Duane Bickett	.05	.02	.01
□ 156 Brett Perriman	.15	.07	.02
□ 157 Boomer Esiason	.10	.05	.01
□ 158 Neil Smith	.15	.07	.02
□ 159 Eddie Anderson	.05	.02	.01
□ 160 Browning Nagle	.05	.02	.01
□ 161 John Friesz	.10	.05	.01
□ 162 Robert Delpino	.05	.02	.01
□ 163 Darren Lewis	.05	.02	.01
□ 164 Roger Craig	.10	.05	.01
□ 165 Keith McCants	.05	.02	.01
□ 166 Stephone Paige	.05	.02	.01
□ 167 Steve Broussard	.05	.02	.01
□ 168 Gaston Green	.05	.02	.01
□ 169 Ethan Horton	.05	.02	.01
□ 170 Lewis Billups	.05	.02	.01
□ 171 Mike Merriweather	.05	.02	.01
□ 172 Randall Cunningham	.10	.05	.01
□ 173 Leonard Marshall	.05	.02	.01
□ 174 Jay Novacek	.15	.07	.02
□ 175 Irving Fryar	.10	.05	.01
□ 176 Randal Hill	.05	.02	.01
□ 177 Keith Henderson	.05	.02	.01
□ 178 Brad Baxter	.05	.02	.01
□ 179 William Fuller	.10	.05	.01
□ 180 Leslie O'Neal	.10	.05	.01
□ 181 Steve Smith	.05	.02	.01
□ 182 Joe Montana UER (Born 1956, not 1965)	1.00	.45	.12
□ 183 Eric Green	.10	.05	.01
□ 184 Rodney Peete	.10	.05	.01
□ 185 Lawrence Dawsey	.10	.05	.01
□ 186 Brian Mitchell	.10	.05	.01
□ 187 Rickey Jackson	.05	.02	.01
□ 188 Christian Okoye	.10	.05	.01
□ 189 David Wyman	.05	.02	.01
□ 190 Jessie Tuggle	.05	.02	.01
□ 191 Ronnie Harmon	.10	.05	.01
□ 192 Andre Reed	.15	.07	.02
□ 193 Chris Doleman	.10	.05	.01
□ 194 Leroy Hoard	.05	.02	.01
□ 195 Mark Ingram	.05	.02	.01
□ 196 Willie Gault	.05	.02	.01
□ 197 Eugene Lockhart	.05	.02	.01
□ 198 Jim Everett	.10	.05	.01
□ 199 Doug Smith	.05	.02	.01
□ 200 Clarence Verdin	.05	.02	.01
□ 201 Steve Bono	.75	.35	.09
□ 202 Mark Vlasic	.05	.02	.01
□ 203 Fred Barnett	.10	.05	.01
□ 204 Henry Thomas	.05	.02	.01
□ 205 Shaun Gayle	.05	.02	.01
□ 206 Rod Bernstine	.05	.02	.01
□ 207 Harold Green	.10	.05	.01
□ 208 Dan McGwire	.05	.02	.01
□ 209 Marv Cook	.05	.02	.01
□ 210 Emmitt Smith	2.00	.90	.25
□ 211 Merril Hoge	.05	.02	.01
□ 212 Darion Conner	.05	.02	.01
□ 213 Mike Sherrard	.10	.05	.01
□ 214 Jeff George	.10	.05	.01
□ 215 Craig Heyward	.05	.02	.01
□ 216 Henry Ellard	.10	.05	.01
□ 217 Lawrence Taylor	.15	.07	.02
□ 218 Jerry Ball	.05	.02	.01
□ 219 Tom Rathman	.05	.02	.01
□ 220 Warren Moon	.15	.07	.02
□ 221 Ricky Proehl	.05	.02	.01
□ 222 Sterling Sharpe	.15	.07	.02
□ 223 Earnest Byner	.05	.02	.01
□ 224 Jay Schroeder	.05	.02	.01
□ 225 Vance Johnson	.05	.02	.01
□ 226 Cornelius Bennett	.10	.05	.01
□ 227 Ken O'Brien	.05	.02	.01
□ 228 Ferrell Edmunds	.05	.02	.01
□ 229 Eric Allen	.05	.02	.01
□ 230 Derrick Thomas	.15	.07	.02
□ 231 Cris Carter	.15	.07	.02
□ 232 Jon Vaughn	.05	.02	.01
□ 233 Eric Metcalf	.15	.07	.02
□ 234 William Perry	.10	.05	.01
□ 235 Vinny Testaverde	.10	.05	.01
□ 236 Chip Banks	.05	.02	.01
□ 237 Brian Blades	.10	.05	.01
□ 238 Calvin Williams	.05	.02	.01
□ 239 Andre Rison	.15	.07	.02
□ 240 Neil O'Donnell	.10	.05	.01
□ 241 Michael Irvin	.10	.05	.01
□ 242 Gary Plummer	.05	.02	.01
□ 243 Nick Bell	.05	.02	.01
□ 244 Ray Crockett	.05	.02	.01

☐ 245 Sam Mills	.05	.02	.01
☐ 246 Haywood Jeffires	.05	.02	.01
☐ 247 Steve Young	.75	.35	.09
☐ 248 Martin Bayless	.05	.02	.01
☐ 249 Dan Marino	2.00	.90	.25
☐ 250 Carl Banks	.05	.02	.01
☐ 251 Keith McKeller	.05	.02	.01
☐ 252 Aaron Wallace	.05	.02	.01
☐ 253 Lamar Lathon	.05	.02	.01
☐ 254 Derrick Fenner	.05	.02	.01
☐ 255 Vai Sikahema	.05	.02	.01
☐ 256 Keith Sims	.05	.02	.01
☐ 257 Rohn Stark	.05	.02	.01
☐ 258 Reggie Roby	.05	.02	.01
☐ 259 Tony Zendejas	.05	.02	.01
☐ 260 Harris Barton	.05	.02	.01
☐ 261 Checklist 1-100	.05	.02	.01
☐ 262 Checklist 101-200	.05	.02	.01
☐ 263 Checklist 201-300	.05	.02	.01
☐ 264 Rookies Checklist	.05	.02	.01
☐ 265 Greats Checklist	.05	.02	.01
☐ 266 Joe Namath GG	.15	.07	.02
☐ 267 Joe Namath GG	.15	.07	.02
☐ 268 Joe Namath GG	.15	.07	.02
☐ 269 Joe Namath GG	.15	.07	.02
☐ 270 Joe Namath GG	.15	.07	.02
☐ 271 Jim Brown GG	.15	.07	.02
☐ 272 Jim Brown GG	.15	.07	.02
☐ 273 Jim Brown GG	.15	.07	.02
☐ 274 Jim Brown GG	.15	.07	.02
☐ 275 Jim Brown GG	.15	.07	.02
☐ 276 Vince Lombardi GG	.05	.02	.01
☐ 277 Jim Thorpe GG	.05	.02	.01
☐ 278 Tom Fears GG	.05	.02	.01
☐ 279 John Henry Johnson GG	.05	.02	.01
☐ 280 Gale Sayers GG	.10	.05	.01
☐ 281 Willie Brown GG	.05	.02	.01
☐ 282 Doak Walker GG	.05	.02	.01
☐ 283 Dick Lane GG	.05	.02	.01
☐ 284 Otto Graham GG	.10	.05	.01
☐ 285 Hugh McElhenny GG	.05	.02	.01
☐ 286 Roger Staubach GG	.10	.05	.01
☐ 287 Steve Largent GG	.15	.07	.02
☐ 288 Otis Taylor GG	.05	.02	.01
☐ 289 Sam Huff GG	.05	.02	.01
☐ 290 Harold Carmichael GG	.05	.02	.01
☐ 291 Steve Van Buren GG	.05	.02	.01
☐ 292 Gino Marchetti GG	.05	.02	.01
☐ 293 Tony Dorsett GG	.05	.02	.01
☐ 294 Leo Nomellini GG	.05	.02	.01
☐ 295 Jack Lambert GG	.05	.02	.01
☐ 296 Joe Theismann GG	.05	.02	.01
☐ 297 Bobby Layne GG	.05	.02	.01
☐ 298 John Stallworth GG	.05	.02	.01
☐ 299 Paul Hornung GG	.05	.02	.01
☐ 300 Don Maynard GG	.05	.02	.01
☐ A1 Desmond Howard AU (Certified autograph)	50.00	22.00	6.25
☐ A2 Jim Brown AU (Certified autograph)	100.00	45.00	12.50
☐ A3 Joe Namath AU (Certified autograph)	125.00	55.00	15.50
☐ P1 Desmond Howard Promo Numbered P	1.50	.70	.19
☐ TRI Desmond Howard Jim Brown Joe Namath (Triplefolder)	3.00	1.35	.35

1992 All World Greats/Rookies

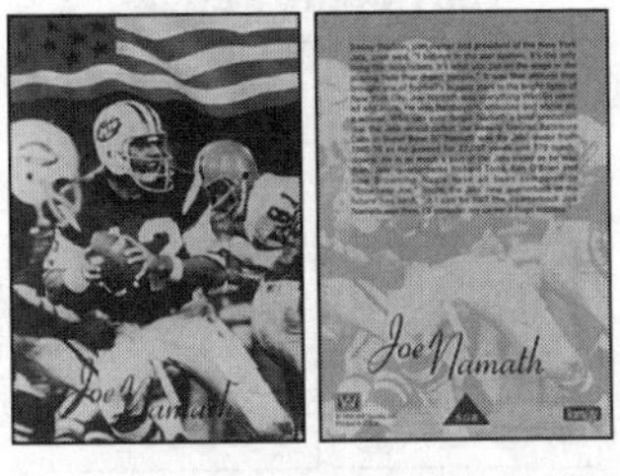

One of these 20 standard-size cards was inserted into every 1992 All World rack pack. The fronts display borderless color or black-and-white player photos, with the U.S. flag blazing across the top. Those cards of current players are color. Those of older players are black-and-white. The first ten have gold foil-embossed stars on the flag and the player's name is gold foil-embossed in script across the bottom of the card. The second ten have the same design but have silver embossing instead. The backs carry a full-bleed ghosted photo of the player with biography printed over the picture. The player's name appears at the bottom in black script that is similar to that on the front. Reportedly, 60,000 of each card were produced. The cards are numbered with an "SG" prefix.

	MINT	NRMT	EXC
COMPLETE SET (20)	10.00	4.50	1.25
COMMON GREATS (SG1-SG10)	.60	.25	.07
COMMON ROOKIES (SG11-SG20)	.30	.14	.04

☐ SG1 Troy Aikman	3.00	1.35	.35
☐ SG2 Thurman Thomas	1.00	.45	.12
☐ SG3 Andre Rison	.60	.25	.07
☐ SG4 Emmitt Smith	5.00	2.20	.60
☐ SG5 Derrick Thomas	.75	.35	.09
☐ SG6 Joe Namath	.60	.25	.07
☐ SG7 Jim Brown	.60	.25	.07
☐ SG8 Roger Staubach	.60	.25	.07
☐ SG9 Gale Sayers	.60	.25	.07
☐ SG10 Jim Thorpe	.60	.25	.07
☐ SG11 Quentin Coryatt	.75	.35	.09
☐ SG12 Carl Pickens	3.00	1.35	.35
☐ SG13 Steve Emtman	.30	.14	.04
☐ SG14 Derek Brown TE	.30	.14	.04
☐ SG15 Desmond Howard	.60	.25	.07
☐ SG16 Troy Vincent	.30	.14	.04
☐ SG17 David Klinger	.60	.25	.07
☐ SG18 Vaughn Dunbar	.30	.14	.04
☐ SG19 Terrell Buckley	.30	.14	.04
☐ SG20 Jimmy Smith	.30	.14	.04

1992 All World Legends/Rookies

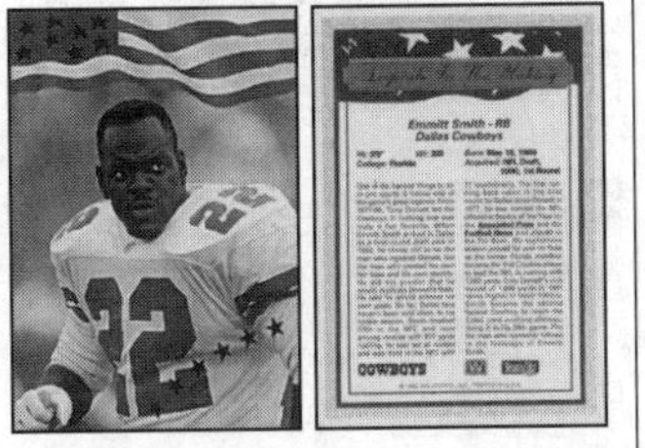

Randomly inserted in the foil packs, this insert set consists of ten Legends in the Making cards (1-10) and ten Rookie (11-20) cards. The cards measure the standard size. All the fronts display borderless color player photos, with gold foil stars on the U.S. flag draped across the top of the card. Also a row of gold foil stars appears in the shape of a crescent at the lower right corner of the picture. The top of the backs of the Legends cards feature a gold plaque with the words "Legends in the Making" superimposed on navy blue with white stars of the American flag. On the other hand, the Rookie cards have a red circular "92 Rookie" logo superimposed on red and white stripes of the American flag. Beneath these decorative elements, both backs present biographical information and, in a two-column format, career summary. Reportedly, 5000 of each card were produced. The cards were numbered with an "L" prefix.

	MINT	NRMT	EXC
COMPLETE SET (20)	35.00	16.00	4.40
COMMON LEGENDS (L1-L10)	1.00	.45	.12
COMMON ROOKIES (L11-L20)	1.00	.45	.12

☐ L1 Emmitt Smith	12.00	5.50	1.50
☐ L2 Thurman Thomas	2.00	.90	.25
☐ L3 Deion Sanders	4.00	1.80	.50
☐ L4 Randall Cunningham	1.00	.45	.12
☐ L5 Michael Irvin	2.00	.90	.25
☐ L6 Bruce Smith	2.00	.90	.25
☐ L7 Jeff George	2.00	.90	.25
☐ L8 Derrick Thomas	2.00	.90	.25
☐ L9 Andre Rison	2.00	.90	.25
☐ L10 Troy Aikman	6.00	2.70	.75
☐ L11 Quentin Coryatt	1.50	.70	.19
☐ L12 Carl Pickens	5.00	2.20	.60
☐ L13 Steve Emtman	1.00	.45	.12
☐ L14 Derek Brown TE	1.00	.45	.12
☐ L15 Desmond Howard	2.00	.90	.25
☐ L16 Troy Vincent	1.00	.45	.12
☐ L17 David Klinger	1.50	.70	.19
☐ L18 Vaughn Dunbar	1.00	.45	.12
☐ L19 Terrell Buckley	1.00	.45	.12
☐ L20 Jimmy Smith	1.00	.45	.12

1966 American Oil All-Pro

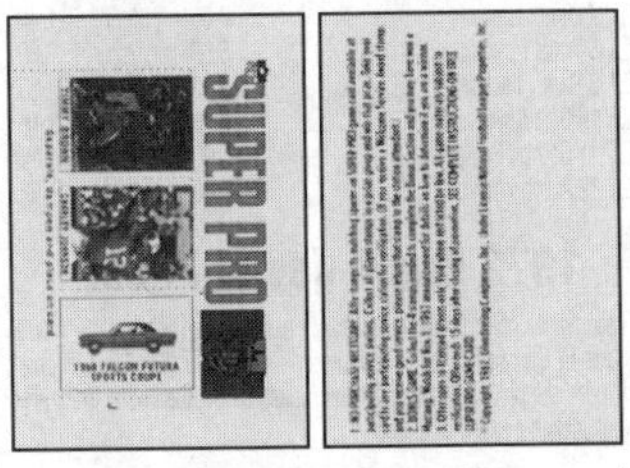

The 1966 American Oil All-Pro set featured 20 stamps, each measuring approximately 15/16" by 1 1/8". To participate in the contest, the consumer needed to acquire an 8 1/2" by 11" collection sheet from a participating American Oil dealer. This sheet is horizontally oriented and presents rules governing the contest as well as 20 slots in which to paste the stamps. The 20 slots are arranged in five rows in the shape of an inverted triangle (6, 5, 4, 3, and 2 stamps per row as one moves from top to bottom) with the prizes listed to the left of each row. The consumer also received envelopes from participating dealers that contained small sheets of three perforated player stamps each. These stamps feature crude color head shots with the players' wearing their helmets. After separating the stamps, the consumer was instructed to paste them on the matching squares of the collection sheet. If all the stamps in a particular prize group row were collected, the consumer won that particular prize. Top prize for all six stamps in the top group was a 1967 Ford Mustang. The other prizes were 250.00, 25.00, 5.00, and 1.00 for five-, four-, three-, and two-stamp prize groups respectively. Prizes were to be redeemed within 15 days after the closing of the promotion, but no later than March 1, 1967 in any event. Complete three stamp panels carry a 50 percent premium. The stamps are blank backed and unnumbered, and they have been checklisted below alphabetically. Wayne Walker and Tommy Nobis were required to win 1.00; Herb Adderley and Dave Parks and Lenny Moore were required to win 5.00; John Unitas and Dave Jones, Mick Tingelhoff, and Alex Karras were required to win 25.00; Dick Butkus and Charley Johnson, Gary Ballman, Frank Ryan, and Willie Davis were required to win 250.00; and Gary Collins and Tucker Frederickson, Pete Retzlaff, Sam Huff, Gale Sayers, and Bob Lilly were required to win the 1967 Mustang. The winner cards indicated below are not priced (and not considered necessary for a complete set) since each was the particular scarce card that made that specific prize a serious challenge.

	NRMT	VG-E	GOOD
COMPLETE SET (15)	350.00	160.00	45.00
COMMON CARD (1-20)	15.00	6.75	1.85

☐ 1 Herb Adderley (Winner 5.00)			
☐ 2 Gary Ballman	15.00	6.75	1.85
☐ 3 Dick Butkus (Winner 250.00)			
☐ 4 Gary Collins (Winner Car)			
☐ 5 Willie Davis	25.00	11.00	3.10
☐ 6 Tucker Frederickson	15.00	6.75	1.85
☐ 7 Sam Huff	30.00	13.50	3.70
☐ 8 Charlie Johnson	15.00	6.75	1.85
☐ 9 Deacon Jones	30.00	13.50	3.70
☐ 10 Alex Karras	25.00	11.00	3.10
☐ 11 Bob Lilly	35.00	16.00	4.40
☐ 12 Lenny Moore	35.00	16.00	4.40
☐ 13 Tommy Nobis	20.00	9.00	2.50
☐ 14 Dave Parks	15.00	6.75	1.85
☐ 15 Pete Retzlaff	15.00	6.75	1.85
☐ 16 Frank Ryan	15.00	6.75	1.85
☐ 17 Gale Sayers	50.00	22.00	6.25
☐ 18 Mick Tingelhoff	15.00	6.75	1.85
☐ 19 Johnny Unitas (Winner 25.00)			
☐ 20 Wayne Walker (Winner 1.00)			
☐ NNO Saver Sheet	25.00	11.00	3.10

1968 American Oil Mr. and Mrs.

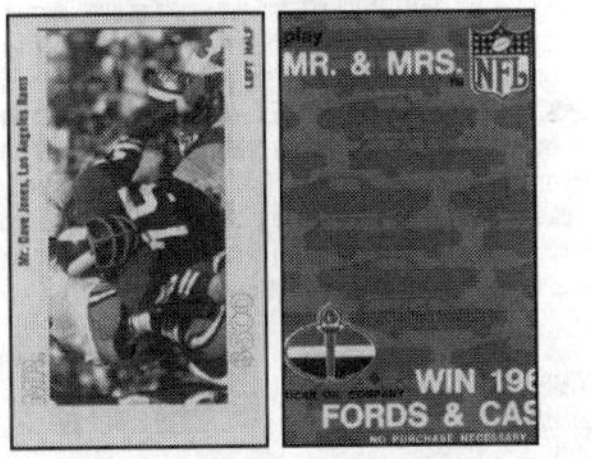

This 32-card set was produced by Glendinning Companies and distributed by the American Oil Company. The cards measure approximately 2 1/8" by 3 7/16". The set is made up of 16 player cards and 16 wife/family cards that were originally connected by perforation in pairs. The cards were distributed as pieces of the "Mr. and Mrs. NFL" game. If a matched pair (i.e. a player card and his wife/family card) were obtained, the holder was an instant winner of either a 1969 Ford (choice of Mustang Mach I or Country Squire), 500.00, 100.00, 10.00, 5.00, 1.00, or 50 cents. The cards are most frequently found as detached halves. The horizontally oriented fronts feature action color player photos or color family photos featuring the wife. On the player card, the player's name is printed above the picture. On the wife card, the woman's married name (i.e. Mrs. Bobby Mitchell) and a caption defining the activity shown are above the picture. Each card is bordered in a different color and the prize corresponding to that card is printed in the border. The backs of the cards vary. In each pair that were originally connected, the wife card back features contest rules in a blue box on a red background with darker red car silhouettes. The player card back carries the game title (Mr. and Mrs. NFL), the American Oil Company logo, and the words "Win 1969 Fords and Cash" on the same background. In addition, attached to each pair at either end and forming a 12" strip, two more cardlike pieces contained further information and a game piece for predicting the 1969 Super Bowl scores. The smaller of the two (approximately 1 7/8" by 2 1/8") is printed with the NFL players and the corresponding prizes. The larger of the two (2 1/8" by 3 1/4") is the game piece for the second part of the contest with blanks for recording a score prediction for one NFL and one AFL team. This piece was mailed in to Super Bowl Scoreboard in New York. Each correct entry would share equally in the 100,000.00 Super Bowl Scoreboard cash prize. The cards are checklisted below alphabetically. The prize corresponding to each married couple is listed under the tougher of the pair. Prices listed are for single cards. Complete two-card panels are valued at approximately double the value of the individual cards. There are 16 tougher pieces that were the cards needed to win prizes. These 16 are not considered necessary for a complete set.

	NRMT-MT	EXC	G-VG
COMPLETE SET (16)	110.00	50.00	14.00
COMMON PLAYER (1-32)	8.00	3.60	1.00
COMMON WIFE (1-32)	4.00	1.80	.50

☐ 1 Kermit Alexander (Winner 100.00)			
☐ 2 Mrs. Kermit Alexander Jogging with Family	4.00	1.80	.50
☐ 3 Jim Bakken	8.00	3.60	1.00
☐ 4 Mrs. Jim Bakken (Winner 1.00)			
☐ 5 Gary Collins (Winner 500.00)			
☐ 6 Mrs. Gary Collins Enjoying the Outdoors	4.00	1.80	.50
☐ 7 Jim Grabowski (Winner 1969 Ford)			
☐ 8 Mrs. Jim Grabowski At the Fireside	4.00	1.80	.50
☐ 9 Earl Gros (Winner 1.00)			
☐ 10 Mrs. Earl Gros At the Park	4.00	1.80	.50
☐ 11 Deacon Jones	20.00	9.00	2.50
☐ 12 Mrs. Deacon Jones (Winner 500.00)			
☐ 13 Billy Lothridge (Winner 10.00)			
☐ 14 Mrs. Billy Lothridge And Baby Daughter	4.00	1.80	.50
☐ 15 Tom Matte	10.00	4.50	1.25
☐ 16 Mrs. Tom Matte (Winner 50 cents)			
☐ 17 Bobby Mitchell (Winner 5.00)			
☐ 18 Mrs. Bobby Mitchell At a Backyard Barbecue	4.00	1.80	.50
☐ 19 Joe Morrison	10.00	4.50	1.25
☐ 20 Mrs. Joe Morrison (Winner 1969 Ford)			
☐ 21 Dave Osborn	8.00	3.60	1.00
☐ 22 Mrs. Dave Osborn (Winner 5.00)			
☐ 23 Dan Reeves (Winner 50 cents)			
☐ 24 Mrs. Dan Reeves Enjoying the Children	4.00	1.80	.50
☐ 25 Gale Sayers	30.00	13.50	3.70
☐ 26 Mrs. Gale Sayers (Winner 100.00)			
☐ 27 Norm Snead (Winner 1.00)			
☐ 28 Mrs. Norm Snead On the Family Boat	4.00	1.80	.50
☐ 29 Steve Stonebreaker	8.00	3.60	1.00
☐ 30 Mrs. Steve Stonebreaker (Winner 10.00)			
☐ 31 Wayne Walker (Winner 50 cents)			
☐ 32 Mrs. Wayne Walker At a Family Picnic	4.00	1.80	.50

1962 American Tract Society

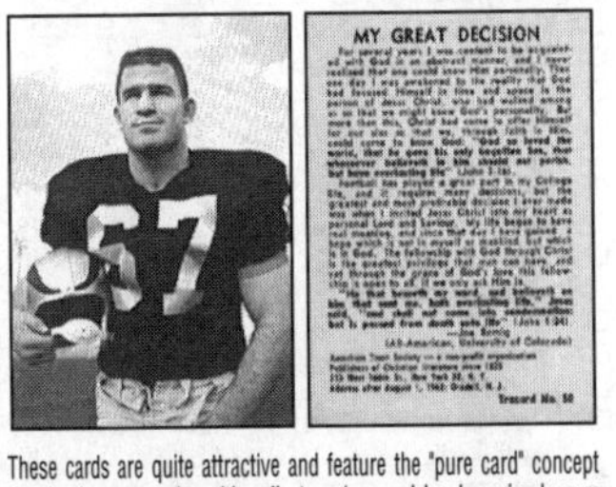

These cards are quite attractive and feature the "pure card" concept that is always popular with collectors (no card borders simply pure photo on front). The cards are numbered on the back and are skip-numbered below due to the fact that these singles are part of a much larger (sport and non-sport) set. The issue features Christian ballplayers giving first-person testimonies on the cardbacks describing how Jesus has changed their lives. These cards are often referred to as "Tracards." Each measures approximately 2 3/4" X 3 1/2". Many of the baseball subjects contain variations. No known variations exist for the football cards.

	NRMT	VG-E	GOOD
COMPLETE SET (2)	14.00	6.25	1.75
COMMON CARD (1-2)	6.00	2.70	.75

☐ 21 Donn Moomaw	6.00	2.70	.75
☐ 50 Joe Romig	8.00	3.60	1.00

1988 Athletes in Action *

The set features six Texas Rangers (1-6) and six Dallas Cowboys (7-12). The cards are standard size, 2 1/2" by 3 1/2". The fronts display color action player photos bordered in white. The words "Athletes in Action" are printed in black across the lower edge of the picture. The backs carry a player quote, a salvation message, and the player's favorite Scripture.

Doug Cosbie - Dallas Cowboys - #11 of 12

"Good news and bad news. I was drafted by the Cowboys in 1975. This was good news, but I was one of 100 rookies and free agents that year. That was bad news. The good news is that I've played 10 summer in the NFL. The bad news is the conflict of time away from my family. There's only one deity I've found that is all good news. And that is Jesus Christ."

For you to have your good news in your life you need a personal relationship with Jesus Christ. God has a special plan for our lives, but due to the way we are (our nature), we are separated from God. God wants us to have a way to reach God through our own efforts to be God. Christ died for our sins and is the only way to God. "But God demonstrates his own love toward us, in that while we were yet sinners, Christ died for us." (Romans 5:8). "Jesus said to him, 'I am the way, and the truth and the life; no one comes to the Father, but through me'" (John 14:6). We must individually receive Christ as Savior and Lord through faith. "For to grant you have been saved through faith; and that not of yourselves, it is the gift of God; not as a result of works, that no one should boast" (Ephesians 2:8,9). Trust Christ and receive a personal relationship with him, pray the following prayer: "Lord Jesus, I need you. Thank you for dying on the cross for my sins. I open the door of my life and receive you as my Savior and Lord. Thank you for forgiving my sins and giving me eternal life. Take control of my life. Make me the kind of person you want me to be." If this is the attitude of your heart, God will share your life forward plan for your life.

Emmitt Newspaper Item #11: "To all who received him, to those that believed on his name, he gave the right to become children of God."

	MINT	NRMT	EXC
COMPLETE SET (12)	8.00	3.60	1.00
COMMON CARD (1-12)	.50	.23	.06
☐ 1 Pete O'Brien	.50	.23	.06
☐ 2 Scott Fletcher	.50	.23	.06
☐ 3 Oddibe McDowell	.50	.23	.06
☐ 4 Steve Buechele	.50	.23	.06
☐ 5 Jerry Browne	.50	.23	.06
☐ 6 Larry Parrish	.50	.23	.06
☐ 7 Tom Landry CO	2.50	1.10	.30
☐ 8 Steve Pelluer	.75	.35	.09
☐ 9 Gordon Banks	.50	.23	.06
☐ 10 Bill Bates	1.00	.45	.12
☐ 11 Doug Cosbie	.50	.23	.06
☐ 12 Herschel Walker	1.25	.55	.16

1990 Bandits Smokey

This 25-card standard-size set features the Fresno Bandits, a semi-professional football team. The fronts display black-and-white posed player photos inside white borders. Red and black designs edge the picture. The Smokey the Bear logo appears in the upper left corner, while the team logo is printed in the lower right. The backs carry biography, a black-and-white photo picturing the player with Smokey, and a safety slogan. The cards are unnumbered and checklisted below in alphabetical order.

	MINT	EXC	G-VG
COMPLETE SET (25)	25.00	11.00	3.10
COMMON CARD (1-25)	1.25	.55	.16
☐ 1 Allan Blades	1.25	.55	.16
☐ 2 Corey Clark	1.25	.55	.16
☐ 3 Darryl Duke	1.25	.55	.16
☐ 4 Heikoti Fakava	1.25	.55	.16
☐ 5 Charles Frazier	1.25	.55	.16
☐ 6 Chris Geile	1.25	.55	.16
☐ 7 Mike Henson	1.25	.55	.16
☐ 8 James Hickey	1.25	.55	.16
☐ 9 Anthony Howard	1.25	.55	.16
☐ 10 Derrick Jinks	1.25	.55	.16
☐ 11 Anthony Jones	1.25	.55	.16
☐ 12 Marvin Jones	1.25	.55	.16
☐ 13 Mike Jones	1.25	.55	.16
☐ 14 Steve Loop	1.25	.55	.16
☐ 15 Thomas Ireland	1.25	.55	.16
☐ 16 Jay Lynch	1.25	.55	.16
☐ 17 Sheldon Martin	1.25	.55	.16
☐ 18 Chuckie McCutchen	1.25	.55	.16
☐ 19 Lance Oberparleiter	1.25	.55	.16
☐ 20 Darrell Rosette	1.25	.55	.16
☐ 21 Fred Sims	1.25	.55	.16
☐ 22 Bryan Turner	1.25	.55	.16
☐ 23 Jim Woods CO	1.25	.55	.16
☐ 24 Rick Zumwalt	1.50	.70	.19
☐ 25 Coaching Staff	1.25	.55	.16

1959 Bazooka

The 1959 Bazooka football cards made up the back of the Bazooka Bubble Gum boxes of that year. The cards are blank backed and measure approximately 2 13/16" by 4 15/16". Comparable to the

Bazooka baseball cards of that year, they are relatively difficult to obtain and fairly attractive considering they form part of the box. The cards are unnumbered but have been numbered alphabetically in the checklist below for your convenience. The cards marked with SP in the checklist below are apparently printed in shorter supply and are more difficult to find. The catalog number for this set is R414-15A. The value of complete intact boxes would be 50 percent greater than the prices listed below.

	NRMT	VG-E	GOOD
COMPLETE SET (18)	5500.00	2500.00	700.00
COMMON CARD (1-18)	175.00	80.00	22.00
☐ 1 Alan Ameche	225.00	100.00	28.00
☐ 2 Don Arnett	175.00	80.00	22.00
☐ 3 Jim Brown	600.00	275.00	75.00
☐ 4 Rick Casares	200.00	90.00	25.00
☐ 5A Charley Conerly SP ERR (Baltimore Colts)	500.00	220.00	60.00
☐ 5B Charley Conerly SP COR (New York Giants)	350.00	160.00	45.00
☐ 6 Howard Ferguson	175.00	80.00	22.00
☐ 7 Frank Gifford	400.00	180.00	50.00
☐ 8 Lou Groza SP	500.00	220.00	60.00
☐ 9 Bobby Layne	300.00	135.00	38.00
☐ 10 Eddie LeBaron	225.00	100.00	28.00
☐ 11 Woodley Lewis	175.00	80.00	22.00
☐ 12 Ollie Matson	250.00	110.00	31.00
☐ 13 Joe Perry	250.00	110.00	31.00
☐ 14 Pete Retzlaff	175.00	80.00	22.00
☐ 15 Tobin Rote	200.00	90.00	25.00
☐ 16 Y.A. Tittle	300.00	135.00	38.00
☐ 17 Tom Tracy SP	350.00	160.00	45.00
☐ 18 Johnny Unitas	500.00	220.00	60.00

1971 Bazooka

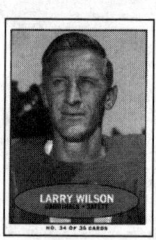

LARRY WILSON

The 1971 Bazooka football cards were issued as twelve panels of three on the backs of Bazooka Bubble Gum boxes. Consequently, cards are seen in panels of three or as individual cards which have been cut from panels of three. The individual cards measure approximately 1 15/16" by 2 5/8" and the panels of three measure 2 5/8" by 5 7/8". The 36 individual blank-backed cards are numbered on the card front. The checklist below presents prices for the individual cards. Complete panels are worth 25 percent more than the sum of the individual players making up the panel; complete boxes are worth approximately 50 percent more (i.e., an additional 25 percent premium) than the sum of the three players on the box. With regard to cut single cards, the mid-panel players (2, 5, 8, ...) seem to be somewhat easier to find in nice shape.

	NRMT-MT	EXC	G-VG
COMPLETE SET (36)	225.00	100.00	28.00
COMMON CARD (1-36)	3.00	1.35	.35
☐ 1 Joe Namath	35.00	16.00	4.40
☐ 2 Larry Brown	5.00	2.20	.60
☐ 3 Bobby Bell	5.00	2.20	.60
☐ 4 Dick Butkus	18.00	8.00	2.20
☐ 5 Charlie Sanders	4.00	1.80	.50
☐ 6 Chuck Howley	5.00	2.20	.60
☐ 7 Gale Gillingham	3.00	1.35	.35
☐ 8 Leroy Kelly	6.00	2.70	.75
☐ 9 Floyd Little	5.00	2.20	.60
☐ 10 Dan Abramowicz	4.00	1.80	.50
☐ 11 Sonny Jurgensen	12.00	5.50	1.50
☐ 12 Andy Russell	4.00	1.80	.50
☐ 13 Tommy Nobis	5.00	2.20	.60
☐ 14 O.J. Simpson	20.00	9.00	2.50
☐ 15 Tom Woodeshick	3.00	1.35	.35
☐ 16 Roman Gabriel	5.00	2.20	.60
☐ 17 Claude Humphrey	3.00	1.35	.35
☐ 18 Merlin Olsen	9.00	4.00	1.10
☐ 19 Daryle Lamonica	5.00	2.20	.60
☐ 20 Fred Cox	3.00	1.35	.35
☐ 21 Bart Starr	20.00	9.00	2.50
☐ 22 John Brodie	9.00	4.00	1.10
☐ 23 Jim Nance	3.00	1.35	.35
☐ 24 Gary Garrison	3.00	1.35	.35
☐ 25 Fran Tarkenton	16.00	7.25	2.00
☐ 26 Johnny Robinson	4.00	1.80	.50
☐ 27 Gale Sayers	20.00	9.00	2.50
☐ 28 Johnny Unitas	25.00	11.00	3.10
☐ 29 Jerry LeVias	3.00	1.35	.35
☐ 30 Virgil Carter	3.00	1.35	.35
☐ 31 Bill Nelsen	3.00	1.35	.35
☐ 32 Dave Osborn	3.00	1.35	.35
☐ 33 Matt Snell	3.00	1.35	.35
☐ 34 Larry Wilson	5.00	2.20	.60
☐ 35 Bob Griese	18.00	8.00	2.20
☐ 36 Lance Alworth	10.00	4.50	1.25

1972 Bazooka Official Signals

A children's guide to TV football.

This 12-card set was issued on the bottom of Bazooka Bubble Gum boxes. The box bottom measures approximately 6 1/4" by 2 7/8". The bottoms are numbered in the upper left corner and the text appears between cartoon characters on the sides of the bottom. The material is entitled "A children's guide to TV football," having been extracted from the book Football Lingo. Cards 1-8 provide definitions of numerous terms associated with football. Card number 9 lists the six different officials and describes their responsibilities. Cards 10-12 picture the officials' signals and explain their meanings. The value of complete intact boxes would be 50 percent greater than the prices listed below.

	NRMT-MT	EXC	G-VG
COMPLETE SET (12)	100.00	45.00	12.50
COMMON PANEL (1-12)	9.00	4.00	1.10
☐ 1 Football Lingo Automatic through Bread and Butter Play	9.00	4.00	1.10
☐ 2 Football Lingo Broken-Field Runner through Dive	9.00	4.00	1.10
☐ 3 Football Lingo Double-Coverage through Interference	9.00	4.00	1.10
☐ 4 Football Lingo Game Plan through Lateral Pass	9.00	4.00	1.10
☐ 5 Football Lingo Interception through Man-to-Man Coverage	9.00	4.00	1.10
☐ 6 Football Lingo Killing the Clock through Punt	9.00	4.00	1.10
☐ 7 Football Lingo Belly Series through Quick Whistle	9.00	4.00	1.10
☐ 8 Football Lingo Prevent Defense through Primary Receiver	9.00	4.00	1.10
☐ 9 Officials' Duties Referee through Line Judge	9.00	4.00	1.10
☐ 10 Officials' Duties	9.00	4.00	1.10
☐ 11 Officials' Signals	9.00	4.00	1.10
☐ 12 Officials' Signals	9.00	4.00	1.10

1971 Bears Team Issue

These twelve black and white photos were released as a set by the Chicago Bears in 1971. Each measures approximately 4 1/2" by 7" and includes the player's name and team name below the photo. They are blankbacked and unnumbered.

	NRMT-MT	EXC	G-VG
COMPLETE SET (12)	100.00	45.00	12.50
COMMON CARD (1-12)	5.00	2.20	.60
☐ 1 Doug Buffone	5.00	2.20	.60
☐ 2 Dick Butkus	25.00	11.00	3.10
☐ 3 Rich Coady	5.00	2.20	.60
☐ 4 Jack Concannon	8.00	3.60	1.00
☐ 5 Bobby Douglass	10.00	4.50	1.25
☐ 6 Dick Gordon	8.00	3.60	1.00
☐ 7 Jim Grabowski	8.00	3.60	1.00
☐ 8 Willie Holman	5.00	2.20	.60
☐ 9 Randy Jackson	5.00	2.20	.60
☐ 10 Gale Sayers	25.00	11.00	3.10
☐ 11 George Seals	5.00	2.20	.60
☐ 12 Aaron Thomas	8.00	3.60	1.00

1972 Bears Jewel Foods

These twelve color photos are thought to have been released by Jewel Foods in Chicago. Each measures approximately 7" by 8 3/4" and includes the player's name and team name below the photo. They are blankbacked and unnumbered.

	NRMT-MT	EXC	G-VG
COMPLETE SET (12)	125.00	55.00	15.50
COMMON CARD (1-12)	10.00	4.50	1.25
☐ 1 Doug Buffone	12.00	5.50	1.50
☐ 2 Dick Butkus	40.00	18.00	5.00
☐ 3 Bobby Douglass UER name misspelled Douglas	15.00	6.75	1.85
☐ 4 George Farmer	10.00	4.50	1.25
☐ 5 Carl Garrett	12.00	5.50	1.50
☐ 6 Jimmy Gunn	10.00	4.50	1.25

☐ 7 Jim Harrison	10.00	4.50	1.25
☐ 8 Willie Holman	10.00	4.50	1.25
☐ 9 Mac Percival	10.00	4.50	1.25
☐ 10 Jim Seymour	10.00	4.50	1.25
☐ 11 Don Shy	10.00	4.50	1.25
☐ 12 Cecil Turner	10.00	4.50	1.25

1976 Bears Coke Discs

The cards in this 22-player disc set are unnumbered so they are listed below alphabetically. All players in the set are members of the Chicago Bears suggesting that these cards were issued as part of a local Chicago Coca-Cola promotion. The discs measure approximately 3 3/8" in diameter but with the hang tab intact the whole card is 5 1/4" long. There are two versions of the Doug Plank disc (green and yellow) and two versions of Clemons (yellow and orange); both of these variations were printed in the same quantities as all the other cards in the set and hence are not that difficult to find. The discs were produced by Mike Schechter Associates (MSA). These cards are frequently found with their hang tabs intact and hence they are priced that way in the list below. The back of each disc contains the phrase, "Coke adds life to ... halftime fun." The set price below includes all the variation cards. The set is also noteworthy in that it contains another card (albeit round) of Walter Payton in 1976, the same year as his Topps Rookie Card.

	NRMT-MT	EXC	G-VG
COMPLETE SET (24)	45.00	20.00	5.50
COMMON CARD (1-22)	1.25	.55	.16
SEMISTARS	1.50	.70	.19
☐ 1 Lionel Antoine	1.25	.55	.16
☐ 2 Bob Avellini	2.00	.90	.25
☐ 3 Waymond Bryant	1.50	.70	.19
☐ 4 Doug Buffone	2.00	.90	.25
☐ 5 Wally Chambers	2.00	.90	.25
☐ 6A Craig Clemons (Yellow border)	1.25	.55	.16
☐ 6B Craig Clemons (Orange border)	1.25	.55	.16
☐ 7 Allan Ellis	1.25	.55	.16
☐ 8 Roland Harper	1.50	.70	.19
☐ 9 Mike Hartenstine	1.25	.55	.16
☐ 10 Noah Jackson	1.50	.70	.19
☐ 11 Virgil Livers	1.25	.55	.16
☐ 12 Jim Osborne	1.25	.55	.16
☐ 13 Bob Parsons	1.25	.55	.16
☐ 14 Walter Payton	30.00	13.50	3.70
☐ 15 Dan Peiffer	1.25	.55	.16
☐ 16A Doug Plank (Yellow border)	2.00	.90	.25
☐ 16B Doug Plank (Green border)	2.00	.90	.25
☐ 17 Bo Rather	1.50	.70	.19
☐ 18 Don Rives	1.25	.55	.16
☐ 19 Jeff Sevy	1.25	.55	.16
☐ 20 Ron Shanklin	1.50	.70	.19
☐ 21 Revie Sorey	1.50	.70	.19
☐ 22 Roger Stillwell	1.25	.55	.16

1981 Bears Police

CHICAGO BEARS TIPS

82 - Alan Page

The 1981 Chicago Bears police set contains 24 unnumbered cards. The cards measure approximately 2 5/8" by 4 1/8". Although uniform numbers appear on the fronts of the cards, they have been listed alphabetically in the checklist below. The set is sponsored by the Kiwanis Club, the local law enforcement agency and the Chicago Bears. Appearing on the backs along with a Chicago Bears helmet are "Chicago Bears Tips". The card backs have blue print with orange accent. The Kiwanis logo and Chicago Bears helmet appear on the fronts of the cards.

	MINT	NRMT	EXC
COMPLETE SET (24)	20.00	9.00	2.50
COMMON CARD (1-24)	.50	.23	.06
☐ 1 Ted Albrecht	.50	.23	.06
☐ 2 Neill Armstrong CO	.75	.35	.09
☐ 3 Brian Baschnagel	.75	.35	.09

☐ 4 Gary Campbell	.50	.23	.06
☐ 5 Robin Earl	.50	.23	.06
☐ 6 Allan Ellis	.50	.23	.06
☐ 7 Vince Evans	1.50	.70	.19
☐ 8 Gary Fencik	1.00	.45	.12
☐ 9 Dan Hampton	4.00	1.80	.50
☐ 10 Roland Harper	.75	.35	.09
☐ 11 Mike Hartenstine	.50	.23	.06
☐ 12 Tom Hicks	.50	.23	.06
☐ 13 Noah Jackson	.75	.35	.09
☐ 14 Dennis Lick	.50	.23	.06
☐ 15 Jerry Muckensturm	.50	.23	.06
☐ 16 Dan Neal	.50	.23	.06
☐ 17 Jim Osborne	.50	.23	.06
☐ 18 Alan Page	4.00	1.80	.50
☐ 19 Walter Payton	12.00	5.50	1.50
☐ 20 Doug Plank	.75	.35	.09
☐ 21 Terry Schmidt	.50	.23	.06
☐ 22 James Scott	.50	.23	.06
☐ 23 Revie Sorey	.75	.35	.09
☐ 24 Rickey Watts	.50	.23	.06

1994 Bears 75th Anniversary Sheets

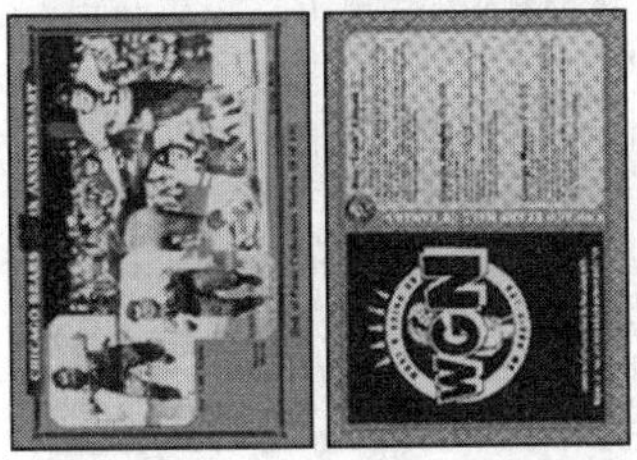

Throughout the 1994 season, these ten 10 3/4" by 7 5/8" Hall of Fame Collector Series sheets were inserted in Game Day programs sold at Soldier's Field. Commemorating the 75th anniversary of the NFL and the Chicago Bears, the sheets were inserted one per program and could be removed by tearing the perforation. On a light blue card face, the fronts feature a montage of sepia-tone action player photos of Chicago Bear Hall of Famers. The backs feature a WGN AM radio 720 advertisement on the left half and player information on the right half. The sheets are numbered on the front "(X of 10)" and listed in chronological order.

	MINT	NRMT	EXC
COMPLETE SET (10)	50.00	22.00	6.25
COMMON CARD (1-10)	3.00	1.35	.35
☐ 1 George Halas OWN/CO (Vs. Eagles; 8/5/94)	5.00	2.20	.60
☐ 2 Doug Atkins George Connor George Blanda (Vs. Giants; 8/27/94)	3.00	1.35	.35
☐ 3 Walter Payton (Vs. Bucs; 9/4/94)	8.00	3.60	1.00
☐ 4 Dan Fortmann Mike Ditka Paddy Driscoll (Vs. Vikings; 9/18/94)	5.00	2.20	.60
☐ 5 Dick Butkus (Vs. Bills; 10/2/94)	8.00	3.60	1.00
☐ 6 Bill George Red Grange Ed Healey (Vs. Saints; 10/9/94)	5.00	2.20	.60
☐ 7 Gale Sayers (Vs. Packers; 10/31/94)	8.00	3.60	1.00
☐ 8 Bill Hewitt Stan Jones Sid Luckman (Vs. Lions; 11/20/94)	4.00	1.80	.50
☐ 9 Roy(Link) Lyman George Musso George McAfee (Vs. Rams; 12/18/94)	3.00	1.35	.35
☐ 10 Bronko Nagurski Bulldog Turner Joe Stydahar George Trafton (Vs. Patriots; 12/24/94)	4.00	1.80	.50

1994 Bears Toyota

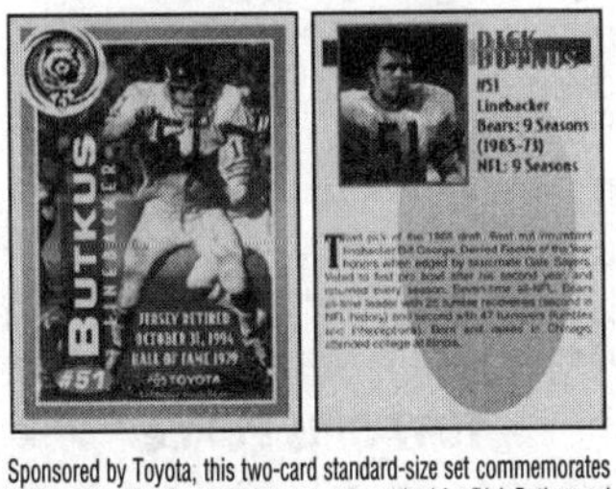

Sponsored by Toyota, this two-card standard-size set commemorates October 31, 1994, the day the jerseys were retired for Dick Butkus and Gale Sayers, two Chicago Bear Hall of Famers. The fronts display color action player photos inside white and orange borders. The team's 75th anniversary logo, player information, and the sponsor logo are overprinted on the picture. The backs carry a color closeup photo, career summary, and career highlights. The cards are unnumbered and checklisted below in alphabetical order.

	MINT	NRMT	EXC
COMPLETE SET (2)	15.00	6.75	1.85
COMMON CARD (1-2)	7.50	3.40	.95
☐ 1 Dick Butkus	7.50	3.40	.95
☐ 2 Gale Sayers	7.50	3.40	.95

1995 Bears Program Sheets

These eight sheets measure approximately 8" by 10" and appeared in regular-season issues of the Bears' GameDay program. The set features large action photos of various individuals involved in the Chicago Bears Super Bowl XX championship. The sheets are listed below in chronological order.

	MINT	NRMT	EXC
COMPLETE SET (8)	40.00	18.00	5.00
COMMON CARD	4.00	1.80	.50
☐ 1 Mike Ditka 9/3/95 vs Vikings	5.00	2.20	.60
☐ 2 Walter Payton 9/11/95 vs Packers	8.00	3.60	1.00
☐ 3 Jim McMahon 10/8/95 vs Panthers	5.00	2.20	.60
☐ 4 Mike Singletary Gary Fencik 10/22/95 vs Oilers	6.00	2.70	.75
☐ 5 Richard Dent 11/5/95 vs Steelers	5.00	2.20	.60
☐ 6 William Perry 11/19/95 vs Lions	5.00	2.20	.60
☐ 7 Otis Wilson 12/17/95 vs Buccaneers	4.00	1.80	.50
☐ 8 Wilber Marshall 12/24/95 vs Eagles	4.00	1.80	.50

1995 Bears Super Bowl XX 10th Anniversary Kemper

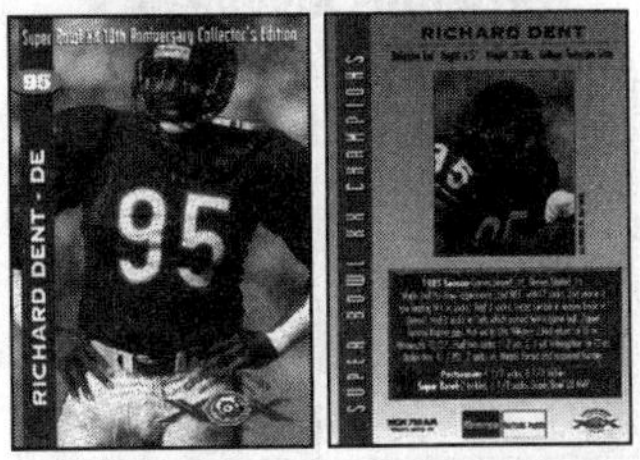

The Chicago Bears, in conjunction with Kemper Mutual Funds, produced this 20-card set commemorating the 10th anniversary of the Chicago Bears winning Super Bowl XX. The fronts feature color action player photos from that championship team with the player's name, position, and jersey number in a vertical blue strip on the left. The backs display a small player portrait with the player's name, biographical information, and 1985 season and postseason highlights. The cards are unnumbered and checklisted below in alphabetical order.

	MINT	NRMT	EXC
COMPLETE SET (20)	18.00	8.00	2.20
COMMON CARD (1-20)	.75	.35	.09
☐ 1 Mark Bortz	.75	.35	.09
☐ 2 Kevin Butler	.75	.35	.09
☐ 3 Jim Covert	.75	.35	.09
☐ 4 Richard Dent	1.25	.55	.16
☐ 5 Dave Duerson	.75	.35	.09
☐ 6 Gary Fencik	.75	.35	.09
☐ 7 Willie Gault	1.25	.55	.16
☐ 8 Dan Hampton	1.25	.55	.16
☐ 9 Jay Hilgenberg	.75	.35	.09
☐ 10 Wilber Marshall	1.25	.55	.16
☐ 11 Dennis McKinnon	.75	.35	.09
☐ 12 Jim McMahon	1.50	.70	.19
☐ 13 Steve McMichael	.75	.35	.09
☐ 14 Walter Payton	3.00	1.35	.35
☐ 15 William Perry	1.25	.55	.16
☐ 16 Mike Singletary	1.50	.70	.19
☐ 17 Matt Suhey	.75	.35	.09
☐ 18 Tom Thayer	.75	.35	.09
☐ 19 Keith Van Horne	.75	.35	.09
☐ 20 Otis Wilson	.75	.35	.09

1995 Bears Super Bowl XX Montgomery Ward Cards/Coins

The Chicago Bears, in conjunction with Montgomery Ward Stores, produced this 8-card and 8-coin set commemorating the 10th anniversary of the Chicago Bears winning Super Bowl XX. The card fronts feature color action player photos from that championship team with the player's name and position in a diagonal blue and orange strip. The backs display the complete 8-card checklist and individual

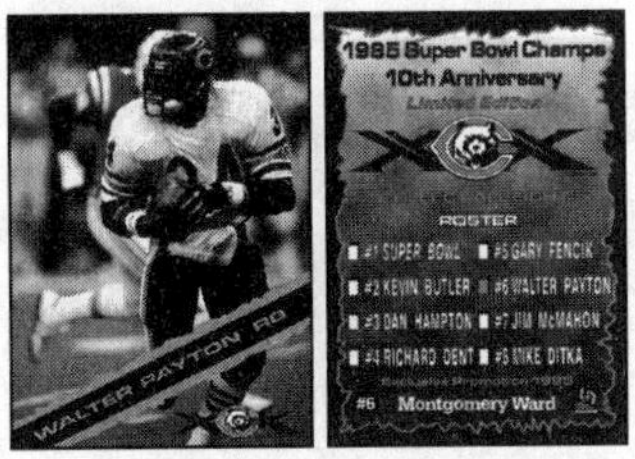

card numbers. We've listed the cards below using a "CA" prefix. The coin fronts feature a player from the championship team with the player's name and jersey number. The backs display the Bears Super Bowl XX logo. The coins are unnumbered but have been listed below alphabetically using a "CO" prefix. A cardboard holder was produced to house the set that featured all the players included in the set.

	MINT	NRMT	EXC
COMP.CARD/COIN SET (16)	20.00	9.00	2.50
COMPLETE CARD SET (8)	10.00	4.50	1.25
COMPLETE COIN SET (8)	10.00	4.50	1.25
COMMON CARD (CA1-CA8)	1.00	.45	.12
COMMON COIN (CO1-CO8)	1.00	.45	.12
☐ CA1 Mike Ditka CO '85 Super Bowl	1.50	.70	.19
☐ CA2 Kevin Butler	1.00	.45	.12
☐ CA3 Dan Hampton	1.00	.45	.12
☐ CA4 Richard Dent	1.25	.55	.16
☐ CA5 Gary Fencik	1.00	.45	.12
☐ CA6 Walter Payton	1.00	.45	.12
☐ CA7 Jim McMahon	1.25	.55	.16
☐ CA8 Mike Ditka	1.50	.70	.19
☐ CO1 Kevin Butler	1.00	.45	.12
☐ CO2 Richard Dent	1.25	.55	.16
☐ CO3 Mike Ditka CO	1.50	.70	.19
☐ CO4 Gary Fencik	1.00	.45	.12
☐ CO5 Dan Hampton	1.00	.45	.12
☐ CO6 Jim McMahon	1.25	.55	.16
☐ CO7 Walter Payton	2.00	.90	.25
☐ CO8 Super Bowl Trophy	1.00	.45	.12
☐ NNO Set Display Holder Mike Ditka Jim McMahon Richard Dent Walter Payton Gary Fencik William Perry Dan Hampton	1.00	.45	.12

1996 Bears Illinois State Lottery

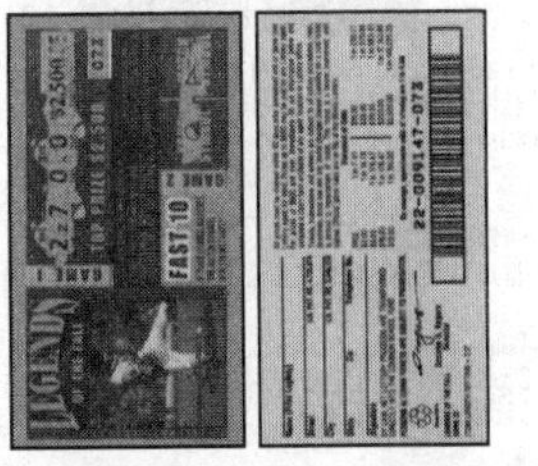

These "cards" were actually issued as Illinois State Lottery tickets. It is common to find them stratched since the potential lottery prize far outweighed the value of the ticket unscratched. Each includes a small color photo of the player along with the rules for the contest.

	MINT	NRMT	EXC
COMPLETE SET (5)	3.00	1.35	.35
COMMON CARD (1-5)	.25	.11	.03
☐ 1 Richard Dent	.50	.23	.06
☐ 2 Mike Ditka	1.00	.45	.12
☐ 3 Dan Hampton	.50	.23	.06
☐ 4 William Perry	.25	.11	.03
☐ 5 Gale Sayers	1.00	.45	.12

1968 Bengals Team Issue

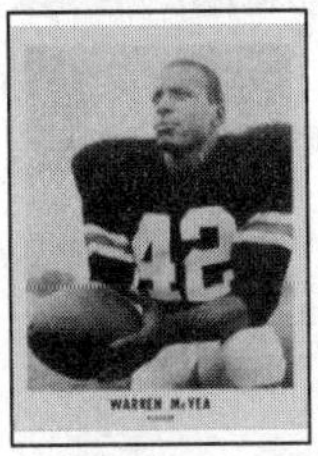

The Cincinnati Bengals issued and distributed this set of player photos. Each measures approximately 8 1/2" by 11" and features a black and white photo. The player's name and position appear in the bottom border below the photo.

	NRMT-MT	EXC	G-VG
COMPLETE SET (7)	40.00	18.00	5.00
COMMON CARD (1-7)	5.00	2.20	.60
☐ 1 Frank Buncom	5.00	2.20	.60
☐ 2 Sherrill Headrick	5.00	2.20	.60
☐ 3 Warren McVea	5.00	2.20	.60
☐ 4 Fletcher Smith	5.00	2.20	.60
☐ 5 John Stofa	8.00	3.60	1.00
☐ 6 Dewey Warren	5.00	2.20	.60
☐ 7 Ernie Wright	8.00	3.60	1.00

1969 Bengals Tresler Comet

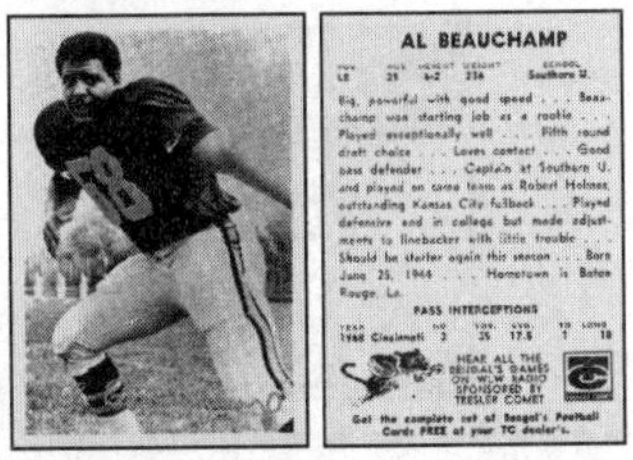

The 1969 Tresler Comet set contains 20 cards featuring Cincinnati Bengals only. The cards measure 2 1/2" by 3 1/2". The set is quite attractive in its sepia and orange color front with a facsimile autograph of the player portrayed. The cards are unnumbered but have been listed below in alphabetical order for convenience. The card of Bob Johnson (not alphabetized below) is much scarcer than the other cards, although some collectors and dealers consider Howard Fest, Harry Gunner, and Warren McVea to be somewhat more difficult to find as well. The backs contain biographical and statistical data of the player and the Tresler Comet logo. An offer to obtain a free set of these cards at a Tresler Comet (gasoline) dealer is stated at the bottom on the back.

	NRMT-MT	EXC	G-VG
COMPLETE SET (20)	300.00	135.00	38.00
COMMON CARD (1-20)	6.00	2.70	.75
☐ 1 Al Beauchamp	6.00	2.70	.75
☐ 2 Bill Bergey	12.00	5.50	1.50
☐ 3 Royce Berry	8.00	3.60	1.00
☐ 4 Paul Brown CO	30.00	13.50	3.70
☐ 5 Frank Buncom	6.00	2.70	.75
☐ 6 Greg Cook	12.00	5.50	1.50
☐ 7 Howard Fest SP	20.00	9.00	2.50
☐ 8 Harry Gunner SP	20.00	9.00	2.50
☐ 9 Bobby Hunt	6.00	2.70	.75
☐ 10 Bob Johnson SP	100.00	45.00	12.50
☐ 11 Charley King	6.00	2.70	.75
☐ 12 Dale Livingston	6.00	2.70	.75
☐ 13 Warren McVea SP	20.00	9.00	2.50
☐ 14 Bill Peterson	6.00	2.70	.75
☐ 15 Jess Phillips	6.00	2.70	.75
☐ 16 Andy Rice	6.00	2.70	.75
☐ 17 Bill Staley	6.00	2.70	.75
☐ 18 Bob Trumpy	15.00	6.75	1.85
☐ 19 Ernie Wright	8.00	3.60	1.00
☐ 20 Sam Wyche	20.00	9.00	2.50

1960 Bills Team Issue

Issued by the team, this set of 40 black-and-white (approximately) 5" by 7" pictures was given to each 1960 Bills season ticketholder. The photos are unnumbered and checklisted below in alphabetical order. The photos are frequently found personally autographed.

	NRMT	VG-E	GOOD
COMPLETE SET (40)	200.00	90.00	25.00
COMMON CARD (1-40)	5.00	2.20	.60
☐ 1 Bill Atkins	7.00	3.10	.85
☐ 2 Bob Barrett	5.00	2.20	.60
☐ 3 Phil Blazer	5.00	2.20	.60
☐ 4 Bob Brodhead	5.00	2.20	.60
☐ 5 Dick Brubacher	5.00	2.20	.60
☐ 6 Bernie Buzyniski	5.00	2.20	.60
☐ 7 Wray Carlton	10.00	4.50	1.25
☐ 8 Don Chelf	5.00	2.20	.60
☐ 9 Monte Crockett	7.00	3.10	.85
☐ 10 Bob Dove	5.00	2.20	.60
☐ 11 Elbert Dubenion	12.00	5.50	1.50
☐ 12 Fred Ford	5.00	2.20	.60
☐ 13 Dick Gallagher	5.00	2.20	.60
☐ 14 Darrell Harper	5.00	2.20	.60
☐ 15 Harvey Johnson	7.00	3.10	.85
☐ 16 John Johnson	5.00	2.20	.60
☐ 17 Billy Kinard	5.00	2.20	.60
☐ 18 Joe Kulbacki	5.00	2.20	.60
☐ 19 John Laraway	5.00	2.20	.60
☐ 20 Richie Lucas	12.00	5.50	1.50
☐ 21 Archie Matsos	10.00	4.50	1.25
☐ 22 Rich McCabe	10.00	4.50	1.25
☐ 23 Dan McGrew	7.00	3.10	.85
☐ 24 Chuck McMurtry	5.00	2.20	.60
☐ 25 Ed Meyer	5.00	2.20	.60
☐ 26 Ed Muelhaupt	5.00	2.20	.60
☐ 27 Tom O'Connell	5.00	2.20	.60
☐ 28 Harold Olson	5.00	2.20	.60
☐ 29 Buster Ramsey CO	5.00	2.20	.60
☐ 30 Floyd Reid	5.00	2.20	.60

☐ 31 Tom Rychlec	7.00	3.10	.85
☐ 32 Joe Schaffer	5.00	2.20	.60
☐ 33 John Scott	5.00	2.20	.60
☐ 34 Bob Sedlock	5.00	2.20	.60
☐ 35 Carl Smith	5.00	2.20	.60
☐ 36 Jim Sorey	5.00	2.20	.60
☐ 37 Lavern Torczon	7.00	3.10	.85
☐ 38 Jim Wagstaff	5.00	2.20	.60
☐ 39 Ralph Wilson OWN	10.00	4.50	1.25
☐ 40 Mack Yoho	7.00	3.10	.85

1963 Bills Jones Dairy

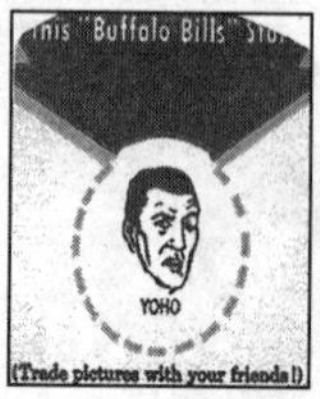

This set of 40 crude drawings features members of the Buffalo Bills. These "cards" are actually cardboard cut from the side of the milk cartons. These circular cards measure approximately 1" in diameter and are frequently found miscut, i.e., off-centered. The catalog designation for this set is F118-1. This unnumbered set is listed alphabetically below for convenience.

	NRMT	VG-E	GOOD
COMPLETE SET (40)	1400.00	650.00	180.00
COMMON CARD (1-40)	25.00	11.00	3.10
☐ 1 Ray Abruzzese	25.00	11.00	3.10
☐ 2 Art Baker	25.00	11.00	3.10
☐ 3 Stew Barber	30.00	13.50	3.70
☐ 4 Glenn Bass	30.00	13.50	3.70
☐ 5 Dave Behrman	30.00	13.50	3.70
☐ 6 Al Bemiller	25.00	11.00	3.10
☐ 7 Wray Carlton	35.00	16.00	4.40
☐ 8 Carl Charon	25.00	11.00	3.10
☐ 9 Monte Crockett	30.00	13.50	3.70
☐ 10 Wayne Crow	25.00	11.00	3.10
☐ 11 Tom Day	30.00	13.50	3.70
☐ 12 Elbert Dubenion	40.00	18.00	5.00
☐ 13 Jim Dunaway	30.00	13.50	3.70
☐ 14 Booker Edgerson	25.00	11.00	3.10
☐ 15 Cookie Gilchrist	40.00	18.00	5.00
☐ 16 Dick Hudson	30.00	13.50	3.70
☐ 17 Frank Jackunas	25.00	11.00	3.10
☐ 18 Harry Jacobs	30.00	13.50	3.70
☐ 19 Jack Kemp	350.00	160.00	45.00
☐ 20 Roger Kochman	25.00	11.00	3.10
☐ 21 Daryle Lamonica	75.00	34.00	9.50
☐ 22 Charley Leo	25.00	11.00	3.10
☐ 23 Marv Matuszak	30.00	13.50	3.70
☐ 24 Bill Miller	25.00	11.00	3.10
☐ 25 Leroy Moore	25.00	11.00	3.10
☐ 26 Harold Olson	25.00	11.00	3.10
☐ 27 Herb Paterra	25.00	11.00	3.10
☐ 28 Ken Rice	25.00	11.00	3.10
☐ 29 Henry Rivera	25.00	11.00	3.10
☐ 30 Ed Rutkowski	30.00	13.50	3.70
☐ 31 George Saimes	35.00	16.00	4.40
☐ 32 Tom Sestak	35.00	16.00	4.40
☐ 33 Billy Shaw	35.00	16.00	4.40
☐ 34 Mike Stratton	35.00	16.00	4.40
☐ 35 Gene Sykes	25.00	11.00	3.10
☐ 36 John Tracey	30.00	13.50	3.70
☐ 37 Ernie Warlick	30.00	13.50	3.70
☐ 38 Willie West	35.00	16.00	4.40
☐ 39 Mack Yoho	30.00	13.50	3.70
☐ 40 Sid Youngelman	30.00	13.50	3.70

1965 Bills Matchbooks

The 1965 Buffalo Bills set contains at least 3 different matchbooks. Any additions to the checklist below would be greatly appreciated.

	NRMT	VG-E	GOOD
COMPLETE SET (3)	50.00	22.00	6.25
COMMON MATCHBOOK (1-3)	15.00	6.75	1.85
☐ 1 Elbert Dubenion	25.00	11.00	3.10
☐ 2 Billy Shaw	15.00	6.75	1.85
☐ 3 Tom Sestak	20.00	9.00	2.50

1965 Bills Super Duper Markets

Super Duper Food Markets offered these black-and-white approximately 8 1/2" by 11" Buffalo Bills player photos to shoppers during the fall of 1965. The photos were a weekly giveaway during the football season by Super Duper markets in western New York. The photos are unnumbered and checklisted below in alphabetical order.

	NRMT	VG-E	GOOD
COMPLETE SET (10)	175.00	80.00	22.00
COMMON CARD (1-10)	6.00	2.70	.75
☐ 1 Glenn Bass	6.00	2.70	.75
☐ 2 Elbert Dubenion	12.50	5.50	1.55

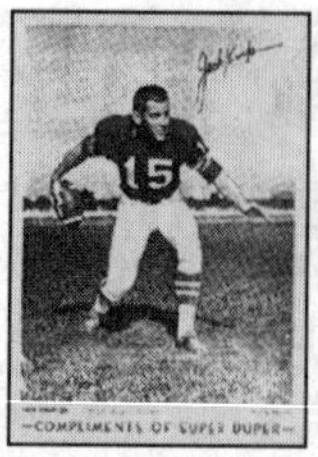

☐ 3 Billy Joe	10.00	4.50	1.25
☐ 4 Jack Kemp	90.00	40.00	11.00
☐ 5 Daryle Lamonica	25.00	11.00	3.10
☐ 6 Tom Sestak	6.00	2.70	.75
☐ 7 Billy Shaw	7.50	3.40	.95
☐ 8 Mike Stratton	6.00	2.70	.75
☐ 9 Ernie Warlick	6.00	2.70	.75
☐ 10 Team Photo	30.00	13.50	3.70

1965 Bills Volpe Tumblers

These Bills artist's renderings were part of a plastic cup tumbler produced in 1965. The noted sports artist Volpe created the artwork which includes an action scene and a player portrait. The "cards" are unnumbered, each measures approximately 5" by 8 1/2" and is curved in the shape required to fit inside a plastic cup. Any additions to this list are welcomed.

	NRMT	VG-E	GOOD
COMPLETE SET (7)	200.00	90.00	25.00
COMMON CARD	30.00	13.50	3.70
☐ 1 Glenn Bass	30.00	13.50	3.70
☐ 2 Butch Byrd	35.00	16.00	4.40
☐ 3 Wray Carlton	35.00	16.00	4.40
☐ 4 Tom Day	30.00	13.50	3.70
☐ 5 Billy Joe	35.00	16.00	4.40
☐ 6 Lou Saban	35.00	16.00	4.40
☐ 7 Billy Shaw	30.00	13.50	3.70

1966 Bills Matchbooks

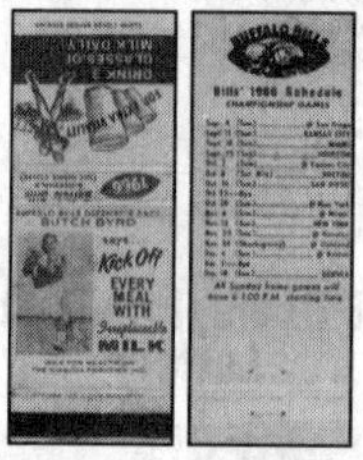

The 1966 Bills Matchbook set contains at least 3 different matchbooks. Any additions to the checklist below would be greatly appreciated.

	NRMT	VG-E	GOOD
COMPLETE SET (3)	125.00	55.00	15.50
COMMON MATCHBOOK (1-3)	15.00	6.75	1.85
☐ 1 Butch Byrd	15.00	6.75	1.85
☐ 2 Jack Kemp	100.00	45.00	12.50
☐ 3 Mike Stratton	15.00	6.75	1.85

1967 Bills Jones-Rich Milk

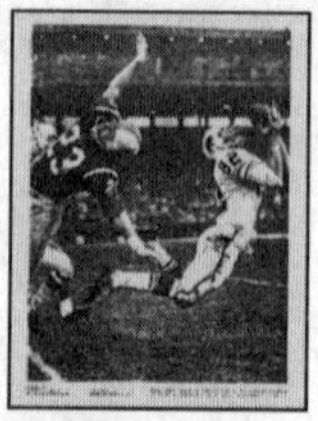

Through a special mail-in offer, Jones-Rich Milk Co. offered this set of six Buffalo Bills' highlight action photos from the 1965 and 1966 seasons. These black-and-white photos measure approximately 8 1/2" by 11".

	NRMT	VG-E	GOOD
COMPLETE SET (6)	100.00	45.00	12.50
COMMON CARD (1-6)	15.00	6.75	1.85
☐ 1 George Butch Byrd	20.00	9.00	2.50
☐ 2 Wray Carlton	20.00	9.00	2.50
☐ 3 Hagood Clarke	15.00	6.75	1.85
☐ 4 Paul Costa	18.00	8.00	2.20
☐ 5 Jim Dunaway	18.00	8.00	2.20
☐ 6 Jack Spikes	20.00	9.00	2.50

1967 Bills Matchbooks

The 1967 Buffalo Bills matchbook set contains at least 4 matchbooks. Any additions to the checklist below would be greatly appreciated.

	NRMT	VG-E	GOOD
COMPLETE SET (4)	60.00	27.00	7.50
COMMON MATCHBOOK (1-4)	15.00	6.75	1.85
☐ 1 Bobby Burnett	15.00	6.75	1.85
☐ 2 Butch Byrd	20.00	9.00	2.50
☐ 3 Roland McDole	15.00	6.75	1.85
☐ 4 Ed Rutkowski	15.00	6.75	1.85

1974 Bills Team Issue

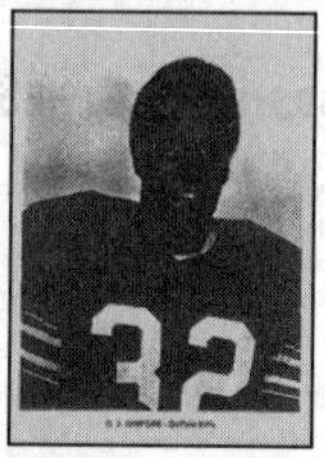

Measuring approximately 8 1/2" by 11", this set of 12 team-issued Buffalo Bills color player photos was sold at the concession stands in Rich Stadium in Buffalo during the 1974 season.

	NRMT-MT	EXC	G-VG
COMPLETE SET (12)	85.00	38.00	10.50
COMMON CARD (1-12)	4.00	1.80	.50
☐ 1 Jim Braxton	6.00	2.70	.75
☐ 2 Bob Chandler	10.00	4.50	1.25
☐ 3 Jim Cheyunski	6.00	2.70	.75
☐ 4 Earl Edwards	4.00	1.80	.50
☐ 5 Joe Ferguson	12.00	5.50	1.50
☐ 6 Dave Foley	4.00	1.80	.50
☐ 7 Robert James	4.00	1.80	.50
☐ 8 Reggie McKenzie	8.00	3.60	1.00
☐ 9 Jerry Patton	4.00	1.80	.50
☐ 10 Walt Patulski	6.00	2.70	.75
☐ 11 John Skorupan	6.00	2.70	.75
☐ 12 O.J. Simpson	25.00	11.00	3.10

1976 Bills McDonald's

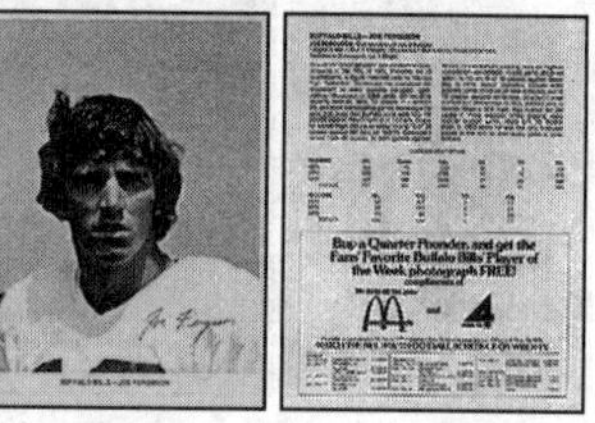

This set of three photos was sponsored by McDonald's in conjunction with WBEN-TV. These "Player of the Week" photos were given away free with the purchase of a Quarter Pounder at participating McDonald's restaurants of Western New York. The offer was valid while supplies lasted but ended Nov. 28, 1976. Each photo measures approximately 8" by 10" and features a posed color close-up photo bordered in white. The player's name and team name are printed in black in the bottom white border, and his facsimile autograph is inscribed across the photo toward the lower right corner. The top portion of the back has biographical information, career summary, and career statistics (except the McKenzie back omits statistics). Inside a rectangle, the bottom portion describes the promotion and presents the 1976-77 football schedule on WBEN-TV. The photos are unnumbered and are checklisted below alphabetically.

	NRMT-MT	EXC	G-VG
COMPLETE SET (3)	25.00	11.00	3.10
COMMON CARD (1-3)	7.00	3.10	.85
☐ 1 Bob Chandler	9.00	4.00	1.10
☐ 2 Joe Ferguson	12.00	5.50	1.50
☐ 3 Reggie McKenzie	7.00	3.10	.85

1979 Bills Bell's Market

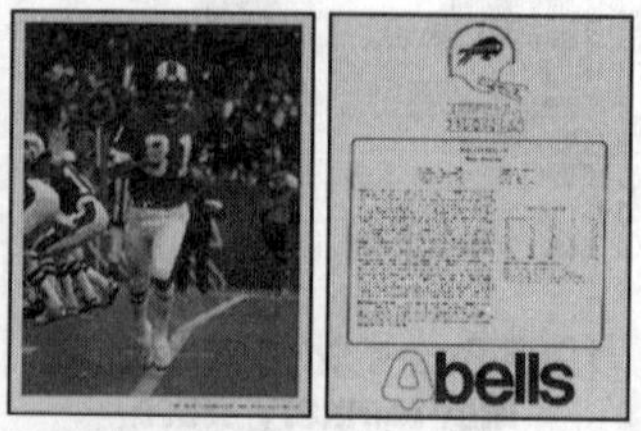

The 1979 Bell's Market Buffalo Bills set contains 11 photos which were issued one per week, with purchase, at Bell's Markets during the football season. The cards measure approximately 7 5/8" by 10" and were printed on thin stock. The Bills' logo as well as the Bell's Markets logo appears on the back along with information and statistics about the players. The cards show the player portrayed in action in full color. The photos are unnumbered and are listed below in alphabetical order by name.

	NRMT-MT	EXC	G-VG
COMPLETE SET (11)	40.00	18.00	5.00
COMMON CARD (1-11)	3.00	1.35	.35
☐ 1 Curtis Brown	3.00	1.35	.35
☐ 2 Bob Chandler	6.00	2.70	.75
☐ 3 Joe DeLamielleure	4.00	1.80	.50
☐ 4 Joe Ferguson	9.00	4.00	1.10
☐ 5 Reuben Gant	4.00	1.80	.50
☐ 6 Dee Hardison	3.00	1.35	.35
☐ 7 Frank Lewis	4.00	1.80	.50
☐ 8 Reggie McKenzie	4.00	1.80	.50
☐ 9 Terry Miller	4.00	1.80	.50
☐ 10 Shane Nelson	3.00	1.35	.35
☐ 11 Lucius Sanford	3.00	1.35	.35

1980 Bills Bell's Market

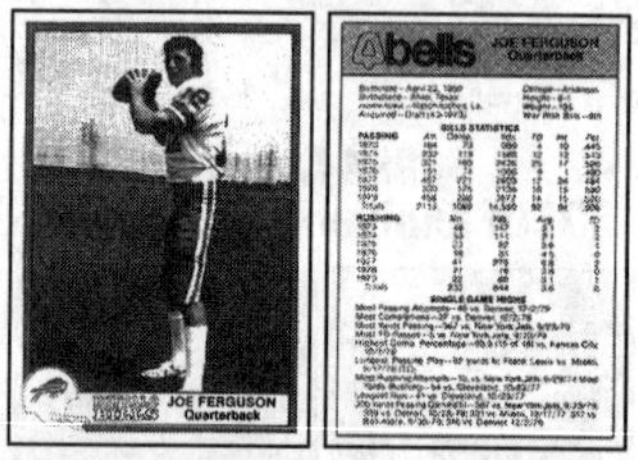

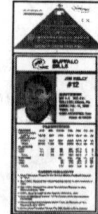

The 1980 Bell's Market Buffalo Bills cards were available in ten strips of two (connected together by a perforation) or singly as 20 individual cards. The individual cards measure approximately 2 1/2" by 3 1/2". The cards are in full color and contain a red frame line on the front. The back features blue printing listing player biographies, statistics and the Bell's Markets logo. The prices below are for the individual cards. The value of a connected pair is approximately the sum of the two individual cards listed below. The pairings were as follows: 1-2, 3-4, 5-6, 7-8, 9-10, 11-12, 13-14, 15-16, 17-18, and 19-20.

	MINT	NRMT	EXC
COMPLETE SET (20)	10.00	4.50	1.25
COMMON CARD (1-20)	.50	.23	.06
☐ 1 Curtis Brown	.50	.23	.06
☐ 2 Shane Nelson	.50	.23	.06
☐ 3 Jerry Butler	.75	.35	.09
☐ 4 Joe Ferguson	1.50	.70	.19
☐ 5 Joe Cribbs	1.00	.45	.12
☐ 6 Reggie McKenzie	.75	.35	.09
☐ 7 Joe Devlin	.75	.35	.09
☐ 8 Ken Jones	.50	.23	.06
☐ 9 Steve Freeman	.50	.23	.06
☐ 10 Mike Kadish	.50	.23	.06
☐ 11 Jim Haslett	.50	.23	.06
☐ 12 Isiah Robertson	.75	.35	.09
☐ 13 Frank Lewis	.75	.35	.09
☐ 14 Jeff Nixon	.50	.23	.06
☐ 15 Nick Mike-Mayer	.50	.23	.06
☐ 16 Jim Ritcher	.75	.35	.09
☐ 17 Charles Romes	.50	.23	.06
☐ 18 Fred Smerlas	1.00	.45	.12
☐ 19 Ben Williams	.50	.23	.06
☐ 20 Roland Hooks	.50	.23	.06

1986 Bills Sealtest

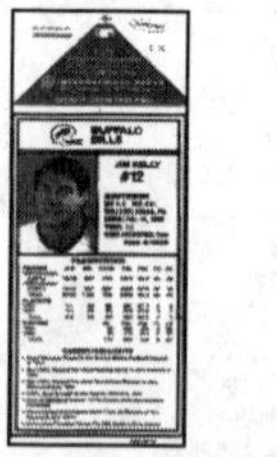

These panels were issued on the sides of half-gallon Sealtest milk cartons. The Freeman and Marve panels were issued on the sides of vitamin D cartons, and the Kelly and Romes panels appeared on two percent lowfat cartons. The panels measure approximately 3 5/8" by 7 5/8" and feature a black and white head shot of the player, biographical information, statistics, and career highlights, all in black lettering. The panels are unnumbered and listed below in alphabetical order.

	MINT	NRMT	EXC
COMPLETE SET (6)	30.00	13.50	3.70
COMMON CARD (1-6)	1.25	.55	.16
☐ 1 Greg Bell SP	5.00	2.20	.60
☐ 2 Jerry Butler SP	5.00	2.20	.60
☐ 3 Steve Freeman	1.25	.55	.16
☐ 4 Jim Kelly	20.00	9.00	2.50
☐ 5 Eugene Marve	1.25	.55	.16
☐ 6 Charles Romes	1.25	.55	.16

1987 Bills Police

This eight-card set of Buffalo Bills is numbered on the back. The card backs are printed in gray and black ink on white card stock. Cards

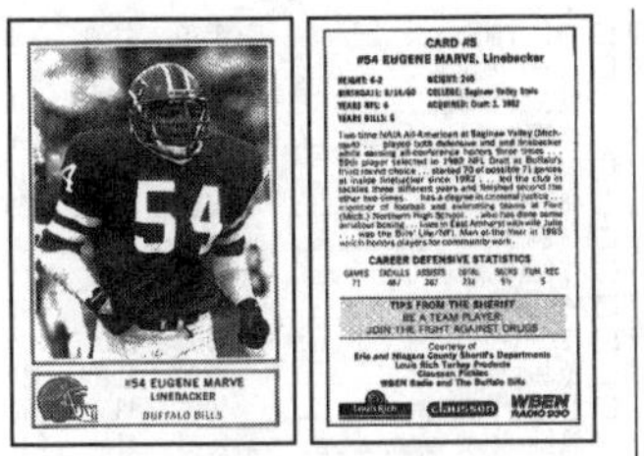

measure approximately 2 5/8" by 4 1/8". The set was sponsored by the Buffalo Bills, Erie and Niagara County Sheriff's Departments, Louis Rich Turkey Products, Claussen Pickles, and WBEN Radio. Uniform numbers are printed on the card front along with the player's name and position. The photos in the set were taken by Robert L. Smith, the Bills' official team photographer.

	MINT	NRMT	EXC
COMPLETE SET (8)	12.00	5.50	1.50
COMMON CARD (1-8)	.75	.35	.09
☐ 1 Marv Levy CO	1.00	.45	.12
☐ 2 Bruce Smith	2.50	1.10	.30
☐ 3 Joe Devlin	.75	.35	.09
☐ 4 Jim Kelly	5.00	2.20	.60
☐ 5 Eugene Marve	.75	.35	.09
☐ 6 Andre Reed	2.50	1.10	.30
☐ 7 Pete Metzelaars	1.00	.45	.12
☐ 8 John Kidd	.75	.35	.09

1988 Bills Police

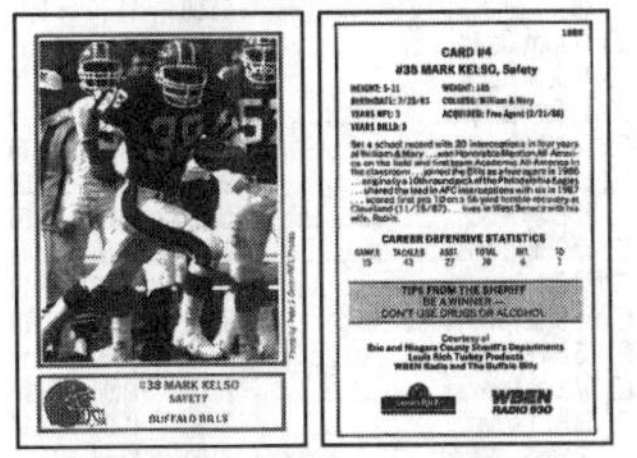

This eight-card set of Buffalo Bills is numbered in the upper right corner of each reverse. Cards measure approximately 2 5/8" by 4 1/8". The set was sponsored by the Buffalo Bills, Erie and Niagara County Sheriff's Departments, Louis Rich Turkey Products, and WBEN Radio. Uniform numbers are printed on the card front along with the player's name and position. The photos in the set were taken by several photographers, each of whom is credited on the lower right front beside the respective photo.

	MINT	NRMT	EXC
COMPLETE SET (8)	6.00	2.70	.75
COMMON CARD (1-8)	.75	.35	.09
☐ 1 Steve Tasker	1.25	.55	.16
☐ 2 Cornelius Bennett	2.00	.90	.25
☐ 3 Shane Conlan	1.00	.45	.12
☐ 4 Mark Kelso	.75	.35	.09
☐ 5 Will Wolford	.75	.35	.09
☐ 6 Chris Burkett	.75	.35	.09
☐ 7 Kent Hull	1.00	.45	.12
☐ 8 Art Still	.75	.35	.09

1989 Bills Police

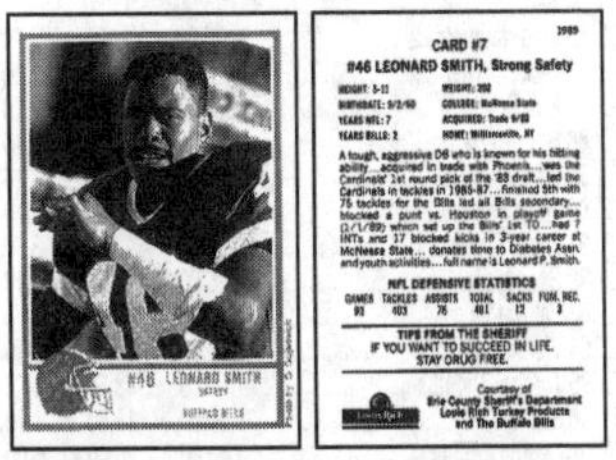

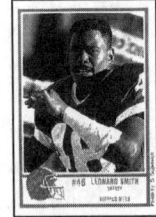

This eight-card set of Buffalo Bills is numbered in the upper right corner of each reverse. Cards measure approximately 2 1/2" by 3 1/2". The set was sponsored by the Buffalo Bills, Erie County Sheriff's Department, Louis Rich Turkey Products, and WBEN Radio. Uniform numbers are printed on the card front along with the player's name and position. The photos in the set were taken by several photographers, each of whom is credited on the lower right front beside the respective photo.

	MINT	NRMT	EXC
COMPLETE SET (8)	8.00	3.60	1.00
COMMON CARD (1-8)	.60	.25	.07
☐ 1 Leon Seals	.75	.35	.09
☐ 2 Thurman Thomas	5.00	2.20	.60
☐ 3 Jim Ritcher	.75	.35	.09
☐ 4 Scott Norwood	.60	.25	.07
☐ 5 Darryl Talley	1.25	.55	.16
☐ 6 Nate Odomes	.75	.35	.09
☐ 7 Leonard Smith	.60	.25	.07
☐ 8 Ray Bentley	.75	.35	.09

1990 Bills Police

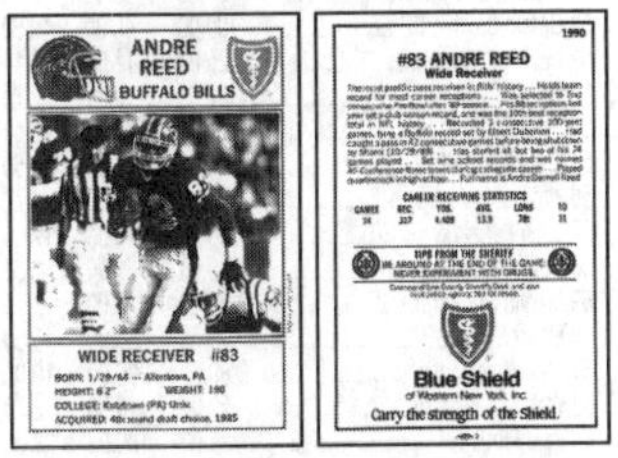

This eight-card set was sponsored by Blue Shield of Western New York, and its company logo graces both sides of the card. The oversized cards measure approximately 4" by 6". The color action player photos on the fronts have red borders on a white card face. The Bills' helmet and player identification appear above the picture, while biography is given below the picture. In black print, the back has career summary, statistics, and 'Tips from the Sheriff' in the form of anti-drug and alcohol messages. The cards are unnumbered and checklisted below in alphabetical order.

	MINT	NRMT	EXC
COMPLETE SET (8)	10.00	4.50	1.25
COMMON CARD (1-8)	.60	.25	.07
☐ 1 Carlton Bailey	.75	.35	.09
☐ 2 Kirby Jackson	.60	.25	.07
☐ 3 Jim Kelly	5.00	2.20	.60
☐ 4 James Lofton	1.50	.70	.19
☐ 5 Keith McKeller	.75	.35	.09
☐ 6 Mark Pike	.60	.25	.07
☐ 7 Andre Reed	2.00	.90	.25
☐ 8 Jeff Wright	.75	.35	.09

1991 Bills Police

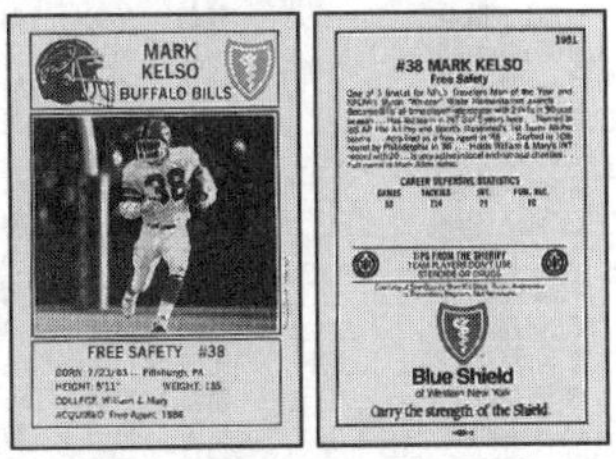

This eight-card Police standard-size set was sponsored by Blue Shield of Western New York. The cards are printed on white card stock. The top portion of the front features the player's name centered above the team name, with the team helmet and Blue Shield logo on either side. The center features an action player photo while biographical information is printed below. The three-sectioned front is separated by red borders. The backs have player profile, career statistics, and safety tips sponsored by the Erie County Sheriff's Department. The cards are unnumbered and checklisted below alphabetically.

	MINT	NRMT	EXC
COMPLETE SET (8)	6.00	2.70	.75
COMMON CARD (1-8)	.75	.35	.09
☐ 1 Howard Ballard	.75	.35	.09
☐ 2 Don Beebe	1.25	.55	.16
☐ 3 John Davis	.75	.35	.09
☐ 4 Kenneth Davis	1.25	.55	.16
☐ 5 Mark Kelso	.75	.35	.09
☐ 6 Frank Reich	1.50	.70	.19
☐ 7 Butch Rolle	.75	.35	.09
☐ 8 J.D. Williams	.75	.35	.09

1992 Bills Police

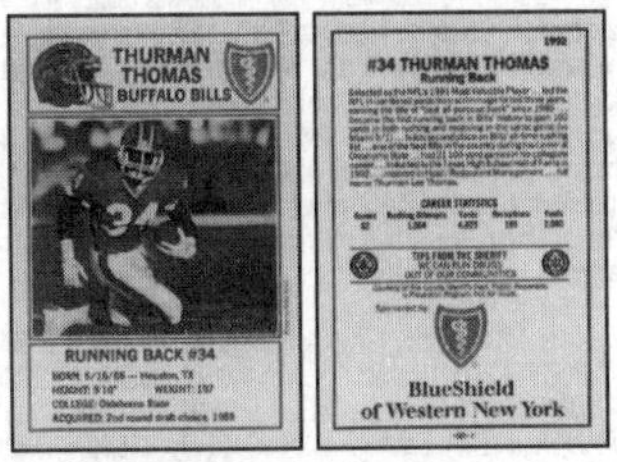

This seven-card set was sponsored by Blue Shield of Western New York. The oversized cards measure approximately 4" by 6" and are printed on white card stock. The top portion of the front features the player's name centered above the team name, with the team helmet and Blue Shield logo on either side. The center features an action color player photo while biographical information is printed below. The three-section front is separated by red borders. The backs have player profile, career statistics, and safety tips sponsored by the Erie County Sheriff's Department. The cards are unnumbered and checklisted below alphabetically.

	MINT	NRMT	EXC
COMPLETE SET (7)	6.00	2.70	.75
COMMON CARD (1-7)	.60	.25	.07
☐ 1 Carlton Bailey	.75	.35	.09
☐ 2 Steve Christie	.75	.35	.09
☐ 3 Shane Conlan	.75	.35	.09
☐ 4 Phil Hansen	.75	.35	.09
☐ 5 Henry Jones	1.00	.45	.12
☐ 6 Chris Mohr	.60	.25	.07
☐ 7 Thurman Thomas	2.50	1.10	.30

1994 Bills Police

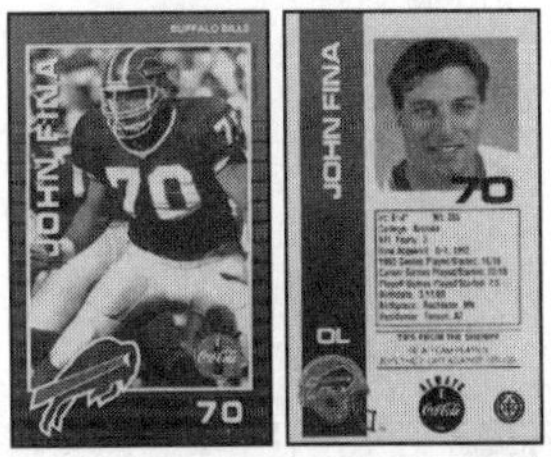

Sponsored by Coca-Cola and the Sheriff's office in Erie County, this six-card set measures approximately 3" by 5". The fronts feature color action shots framed by a white inner border and an outer border that shades from red to purple as one moves down the card. This outer border is accented by horizontal black lines that become thicker toward the bottom of the card. Alongside a gray stripe carrying the player's name, position, and team helmet, the backs show a black-and-white head shot, biography, and 'Tips from the Sheriff.' The cards are unnumbered and checklisted below in alphabetical order.

	MINT	NRMT	EXC
COMPLETE SET (6)	5.00	2.20	.60
COMMON CARD (1-6)	.75	.35	.09
☐ 1 Bill Brooks	1.00	.45	.12
☐ 2 Kenneth Davis	1.00	.45	.12
☐ 3 John Fina	.75	.35	.09
☐ 4 Phil Hansen	.75	.35	.09
☐ 5 Pete Metzelaars	1.00	.45	.12
☐ 6 Marvcus Patton	.75	.35	.09

1995 Bills Police

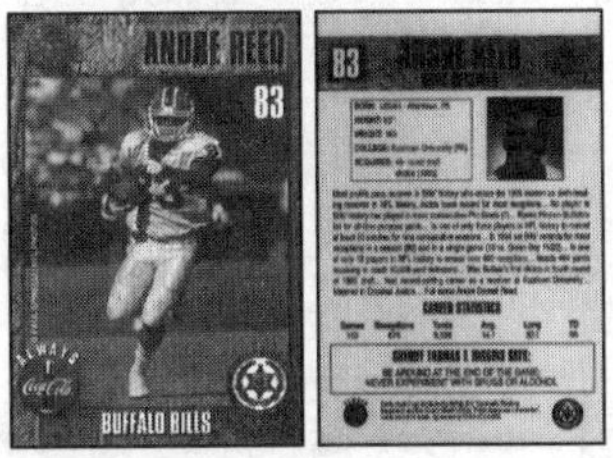

This six-card set of the Buffalo Bills was sponsored by Coca-Cola and the Erie County Office of Sheriff. The cards measure approximately 4" by 6" and feature a color action player photo set on a colorful stone-look background. The backs carry player information and a safety tip. The cards are unnumbered and checklisted below in alphabetical order.

	MINT	NRMT	EXC
COMPLETE SET (6)	6.00	2.70	.75
COMMON CARD	.75	.35	.09
☐ 1 Jeff Burris	1.00	.45	.12
☐ 2 Joe Ferguson All-Time Great	1.00	.45	.12
☐ 3 Kent Hull	.75	.35	.09
☐ 4 Adam Lingner	.75	.35	.09
☐ 5 Glenn Parker	.75	.35	.09
☐ 6 Andre Reed	2.00	.90	.25

1996 Bills Police

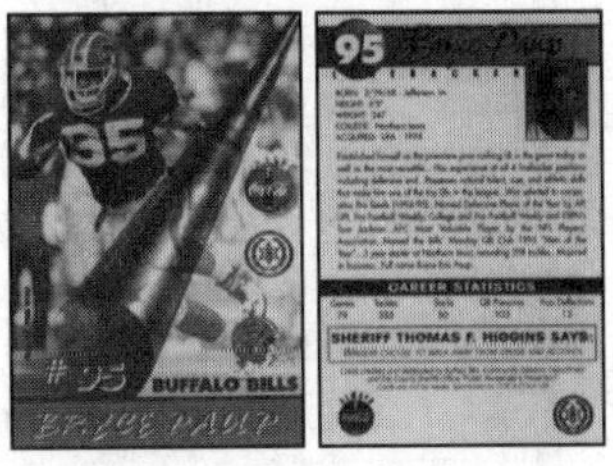

This five-card set of the Buffalo Bills was sponsored by Coca-Cola and the Erie County Sheriff's Officef. The cards measure approximately 4" by 6" and feature a color action player photo with the sponsor logos on the cardfront. The cards are unnumbered but have been checklisted below according to the player's jersey number which is prominently displayed.

	MINT	NRMT	EXC
COMPLETE SET (5)	4.00	1.80	.50
COMMON CARD	.75	.35	.09
☐ 24 Kurt Schulz	.75	.35	.09
☐ 55 Mark Maddox	.75	.35	.09
☐ 79 Ruben Brown	1.25	.55	.16
☐ 94 Mark Pike	.75	.35	.09
☐ 95 Bryce Paup	1.25	.55	.16

1993 Bleachers Troy Aikman Promos

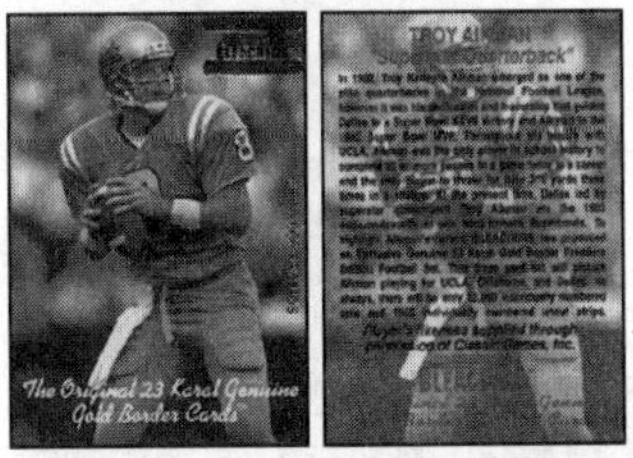

Issued to herald the release of the three-card 23K Gold Border Troy Aikman set, these standard-size promo cards feature a borderless color photo of Aikman in his UCLA uniform. The Bleachers logo at the upper right is highlighted by gold-foil bars above and below. The words "1 of 10,000 Promos" appears vertically in gold foil near the right edge. The back carries Aikman's career highlights over a ghosted black-and-white version of the front photo. The cards are unnumbered. A special version of this promo was produced by Bleachers for both 1993 Comicfest and Tri-Star's 1994 Houston card show with the show's title printed in 23K gold lettering on the cardfront.

	MINT	NRMT	EXC
COMPLETE SET (3)	3.00	1.35	.35
COMMON CARD (1-3)	1.00	.45	.12
☐ 1 Troy Aikman UCLA	1.00	.45	.12
☐ 2 Troy Aikman UCLA (Comicfest '93)	1.00	.45	.12
☐ 3 Troy Aikman UCLA (Houston '94)	1.00	.45	.12

1993 Bleachers 23K Troy Aikman

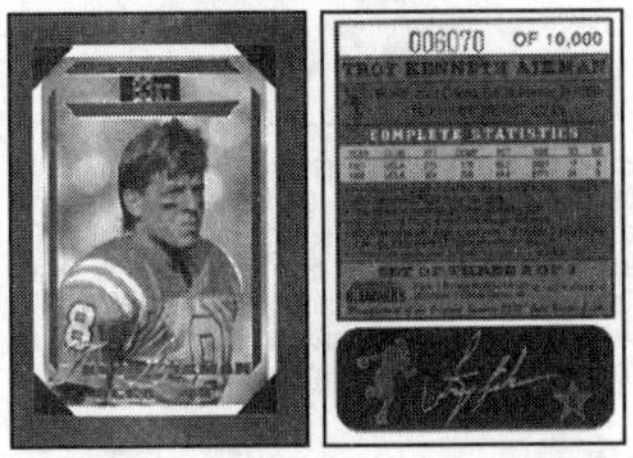

These three standard-size cards feature on their fronts color photos of Aikman with wide gold outer borders, and colored and gold-foil inner borders. Aikman's name, team, and position are stamped in gold foil near the bottom. The back carries at the top the set's production number out of a total of 10,000 produced. Below are Aikman's name, biography, and stats and highlights for the team Aikman is pictured playing for on the front. A facsimile Aikman autograph appears in gold foil at the bottom. The cards are numbered on the back as "X of 3". A promo card was also distributed that features Aikman in a Cowboys uniform.

	MINT	NRMT	EXC
COMPLETE SET (3)	18.00	8.00	2.20
COMMON CARD (1-3)	6.00	2.70	.75
☐ 1 Troy Aikman (Oklahoma)	6.00	2.70	.75
☐ 2 Troy Aikman (UCLA)	6.00	2.70	.75
☐ 3 Troy Aikman (Cowboys)	6.00	2.70	.75
☐ P1 Troy Aikman Promo (Cowboys)	6.00	2.70	.75

1994 Bleachers 23K Troy Aikman

Bleachers again prodcued a 23 Karat Gold card of Tryo Aikman in 1994. The gold card was issued in a blue box along with a more traditional appearing card. The 2-card set was limited to 10,000 produced.

	MINT	NRMT	EXC
COMPLETE SET (2)	10.00	4.50	1.25
COMMON CARD (1-2)	5.00	2.20	.60

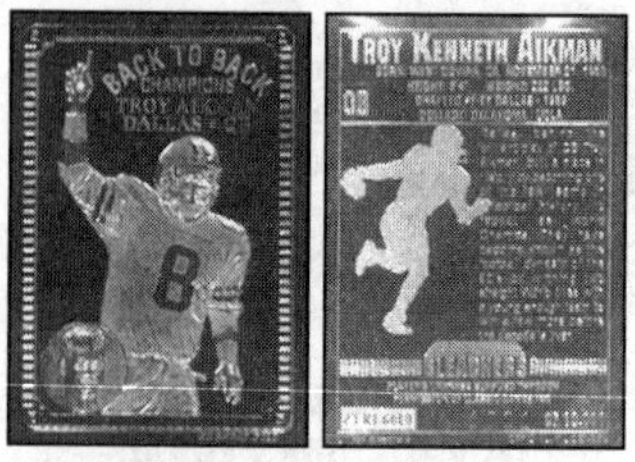

□ 1 Troy Aikman Gold (gold foil card)	5.00	2.20	.60
□ 2 Troy Aikman Blue (standard cardboard)	5.00	2.20	.60

1995 Bleachers 23K Emmitt Smith

Issued in a cello-wrapped cardboard sleeve, these four standard-size cards capture Emmitt Smith during his high school, collegiate, and pro career. The fronts of the regular-issue cards feature color player photos inside a 23K gold outer border and a black-and-white inner border. The back carries at the top the set's production number (of 10,000). Below are biography, statistics, a color head shot, and gold-foil on black autographs and images at the bottom. The promo card has a full-bleed color player photo on its front, and an advertisement and career summary on its back. Each set included a certificate of authenticity. A Promo card was produced to promote the set and is priced below.

	MINT	NRMT	EXC
COMPLETE SET (3)	24.00	11.00	3.00
COMMON CARD (1-3)	8.00	3.60	1.00
□ 1 Emmitt Smith Escambia High School	8.00	3.60	1.00
□ 2 Emmitt Smith Florida Gators	8.00	3.60	1.00
□ 3 Emmitt Smith	8.00	3.60	1.00
□ NNO Emmitt Smith Promo Escambia High School	3.00	1.35	.35

1983 Blitz Team Issue USFL

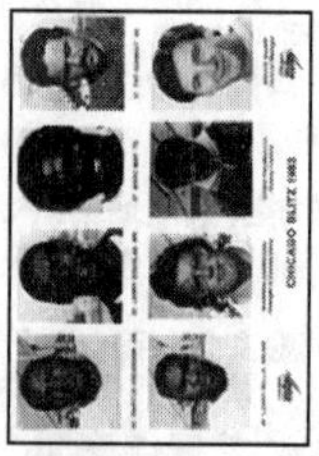

Each of these sheets measures approximately 10" by 8" and features two rows with four players per row. The first sheet presents the coaching staff, while the other seven sheets feature players. The individual photos measure 2 1/4" by 2 1/2" and have white borders. The photos are head-and-shoulders shots, with player information immediately below. A title between two team logos running across the bottom of the sheets completes them. The sheets are unnumbered.

	MINT	NRMT	EXC
COMPLETE SET (7)	40.00	18.00	5.00
COMMON PANEL (1-7)	5.00	2.20	.60
□ 1 Coaching Staff	10.00	4.50	1.25
George Allen			
Joe Haering			
Paul Lanham			
John Payne			
John Teerlink			
Dick Walker			
Charlie Waller			
Ray Wietecha			
□ 2 Luther Bradley	7.50	3.40	.95
Eddie Brown			
Virgil Livers			
Frank Minnifield			
Lance Shields			
Don Schwartz			
Maurice Tyler			
Ted Walton			
□ 3 Mack Boatner	5.00	2.20	.60
Frank Collins			
Frank Corral			
Doug Cozen			
Doug Dennison			
John Roveto			
Jim Stone			
Tim Wrightman			
□ 4 Robert Barnes	5.00	2.20	.60
Bruce Branch			
Nick Eyre			
Tim Norman			
Wally Pesuit			
Mark Stevenson			
Rob Taylor T			
Steve Tobin			
□ 5 Junior Ah You	5.00	2.20	.60
Mark Buben			
Bob Cobb			
Joe Ehrmann			
Kit Lathrop			
Karl Lorch			
Troy Thomas			
□ 6 Jim Fahnhorst	5.00	2.20	.60
Joe Federspiel			
Doak Field			
Bruce Gheesling			
Andy Melontree			
Ed Smith			
Stan White			
Kari Yli-Renko			
□ 7 Marcus Anderson	5.00	2.20	.60
Larry Douglas			
Marc May			
Pat Schmidt			
Lenny Willis			
Warren Anderson CO			
Chris Pagnucco CO			
Bruce Allen GM			

1948 Bowman

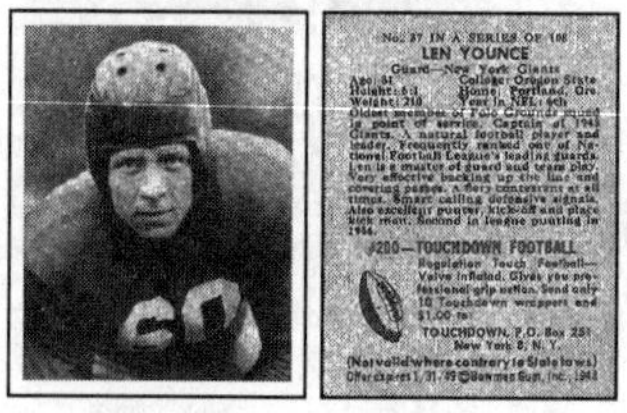

The 1948 Bowman set is considered the first football set of the modern era. The set consists of 108 cards measuring 2 1/16" by 2 1/2". Cards were issued in one-card penny packs. The entire front is comprised of a black and white photo. The backs contain a write-up and an offer for a football. The cards were printed in three sheets; the third sheet (containing all the card numbers divisible by three, i.e., 3, 6, 9, 12, 15, etc.) being printed in much lesser quantities. Hence, cards with numbers divisible by three are substantially more valuable than the other cards in the set. The second sheet (numbers 2, 5, 8, 11, 14, etc.) is also regarded as slightly tougher to obtain than the first sheet (numbers 1, 4, 7, 10, 13, etc.) which contains the most plentiful cards. An album with which to house the set was produced. Key Rookie Cards in this set are Sammy Baugh, Charley Conerly, Sid Luckman, Johnny Lujack, Pete Pihos, Bulldog Turner, Steve Van Buren, and Bob Waterfield.

	NRMT	VG-E	GOOD
COMPLETE SET (108)	6000.00	2700.00	750.00
COMMON CARD (1-108)	20.00	9.00	2.50
SECOND SERIES 2/5/8/	22.00	10.00	2.70
THIRD SERIES 3/6/9/	100.00	45.00	12.50
WRAPPER (1-CENT)	200.00	90.00	25.00
□ 1 Joe Tereshinski	140.00	35.00	11.00
□ 2 Larry Olsonoski	22.00	10.00	2.70
□ 3 John Lujack SP	325.00	145.00	40.00
□ 4 Ray Poole	20.00	9.00	2.50
□ 5 Bill DeCorrevont	22.00	10.00	2.70
□ 6 Paul Briggs SP	100.00	45.00	12.50
□ 7 Steve Van Buren	150.00	70.00	19.00
□ 8 Kenny Washington	50.00	22.00	6.25
□ 9 Nolan Luhn SP	100.00	45.00	12.50
□ 10 Chris Iversen	20.00	9.00	2.50
□ 11 Jack Wiley	22.00	10.00	2.70
□ 12 Charley Conerly SP	325.00	145.00	40.00
□ 13 Hugh Taylor	25.00	11.00	3.10
□ 14 Frank Seno	22.00	10.00	2.70
□ 15 Gil Bouley SP	100.00	45.00	12.50
□ 16 Tommy Thompson	35.00	16.00	4.40
□ 17 Charley Trippi	100.00	45.00	12.50
□ 18 Vince Banonis SP	100.00	45.00	12.50
□ 19 Art Faircloth	20.00	9.00	2.50
□ 20 Clyde Goodnight	22.00	10.00	2.70
□ 21 Bill Chipley SP	100.00	45.00	12.50
□ 22 Sammy Baugh	450.00	200.00	55.00
□ 23 Don Kindt	22.00	10.00	2.70
□ 24 John Koniszewski SP	100.00	45.00	12.50
□ 25 Pat McHugh	20.00	9.00	2.50
□ 26 Bob Waterfield	200.00	90.00	25.00
□ 27 Tony Compagno SP	100.00	45.00	12.50
□ 28 Paul Governali	25.00	11.00	3.10
□ 29 Pat Harder	50.00	22.00	6.25
□ 30 Vic Lindskog SP	100.00	45.00	12.50
□ 31 Salvatore Rosato	20.00	9.00	2.50
□ 32 John Mastrangelo	22.00	10.00	2.70
□ 33 Fred Gehrke SP	100.00	45.00	12.50
□ 34 Bosh Pritchard	20.00	9.00	2.50
□ 35 Mike Micka	22.00	10.00	2.70
□ 36 Bulldog Turner SP	275.00	125.00	34.00
□ 37 Len Younce	20.00	9.00	2.50
□ 38 Pat West	22.00	10.00	2.70
□ 39 Russ Thomas SP	100.00	45.00	12.50
□ 40 James Peebles	20.00	9.00	2.50
□ 41 Bob Skoglund	22.00	10.00	2.70
□ 42 Walt Stickle SP	100.00	45.00	12.50
□ 43 Whitey Wistert	25.00	11.00	3.10
□ 44 Paul Christman	45.00	20.00	5.50
□ 45 Jay Rhodemyre SP	100.00	45.00	12.50
□ 46 Tony Minisi	20.00	9.00	2.50
□ 47 Bob Mann	22.00	10.00	2.70
□ 48 Mal Kutner SP	110.00	50.00	14.00
□ 49 Dick Poillon	20.00	9.00	2.50
□ 50 Charles Cherundolo	22.00	10.00	2.70
□ 51 Gerald Cowhig SP	100.00	45.00	12.50
□ 52 Neill Armstrong	25.00	11.00	3.10
□ 53 Frank Maznicki	22.00	10.00	2.70
□ 54 John Sanchez SP	100.00	45.00	12.50
□ 55 Frank Reagan	20.00	9.00	2.50
□ 56 Jim Hardy	22.00	10.00	2.70
□ 57 John Badaczewski SP	100.00	45.00	12.50
□ 58 Robert Nussbaumer	20.00	9.00	2.50
□ 59 Marvin Pregulman	22.00	10.00	2.70
□ 60 Elbert Nickel SP	120.00	55.00	15.00
□ 61 Alex Wojciechowicz	80.00	36.00	10.00
□ 62 Walt Schlinkman	22.00	10.00	2.70
□ 63 Pete Pihos SP	225.00	100.00	28.00
□ 64 Joseph Sulaitis	20.00	9.00	2.50
□ 65 Mike Holovak	45.00	20.00	5.50
□ 66 Cecil Souders SP	100.00	45.00	12.50
□ 67 Paul McKee	20.00	9.00	2.50
□ 68 Bill Moore	22.00	10.00	2.70
□ 69 Frank Minini SP	100.00	45.00	12.50
□ 70 Jack Ferrante	20.00	9.00	2.50
□ 71 Les Horvath	50.00	22.00	6.25
□ 72 Ted Fritsch Sr. SP	110.00	50.00	14.00
□ 73 Tex Coulter	25.00	11.00	3.10
□ 74 Boley Dancewicz	22.00	10.00	2.70
□ 75 Dante Mangani SP	100.00	45.00	12.50
□ 76 James Hefti	20.00	9.00	2.50
□ 77 Paul Sarringhaus	22.00	10.00	2.70
□ 78 Joe Scott SP	100.00	45.00	12.50
□ 79 Bucko Kilroy	25.00	11.00	3.10
□ 80 Bill Dudley	100.00	45.00	12.50
□ 81 Marshall Goldberg SP	110.00	50.00	14.00
□ 82 John Cannady	20.00	9.00	2.50
□ 83 Perry Moss	22.00	10.00	2.70
□ 84 Harold Crisler SP	110.00	50.00	14.00
□ 85 Bill Gray	20.00	9.00	2.50
□ 86 John Clement	22.00	10.00	2.70
□ 87 Dan Sandifer SP	100.00	45.00	12.50
□ 88 Ben Kish	20.00	9.00	2.50
□ 89 Herbert Banta	22.00	10.00	2.70
□ 90 Bill Garnaas SP	100.00	45.00	12.50
□ 91 Jim White	20.00	9.00	2.50
□ 92 Frank Barzilauskas	22.00	10.00	2.70
□ 93 Vic Sears SP	100.00	45.00	12.50
□ 94 John Adams	20.00	9.00	2.50
□ 95 George McAfee	90.00	40.00	11.00
□ 96 Ralph Heywood SP	100.00	45.00	12.50
□ 97 Joe Muha	20.00	9.00	2.50
□ 98 Fred Enke	22.00	10.00	2.70
□ 99 Harry Gilmer SP	150.00	70.00	19.00
□ 100 Bill Miklich	20.00	9.00	2.50
□ 101 Joe Gottlieb	22.00	10.00	2.70
□ 102 Bud Angsman SP	110.00	50.00	14.00
□ 103 Tom Farmer	20.00	9.00	2.50
□ 104 Bruce Smith	50.00	22.00	6.25
□ 105 Bob Cifers SP	100.00	45.00	12.50
□ 106 Ernie Steele	20.00	9.00	2.50
□ 107 Sid Luckman	225.00	100.00	28.00
□ 108 Buford Ray SP	350.00	90.00	28.00

1950 Bowman

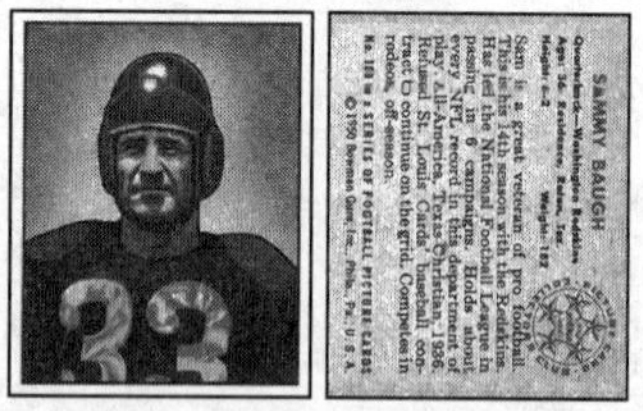

After a one year hiatus, Bowman issued its first color football set for 1950. The set comprises 144 cards measuring 2 1/16" by 2 1/2". Cards were issued in six-card nickel packs with two pieces of gum. The fronts contain a black and white photo that was colored in. The card backs, which contain a write-up, feature black printing except for the player's name and the logo for the "5-Star Bowman Picture Card Collectors Club" which are both in red. The set features the Rookie Cards of Tony Canadeo, Glenn Davis, Tom Fears, Otto Graham, Lou Groza, Elroy Hirsch, Dante Lavelli, Marion Motley, Joe Perry, and Y.A. Tittle. With a few exceptions the set numbering is arranged so that trios of players from the same team are numbered together in sequence.

	NRMT	VG-E	GOOD
COMPLETE SET (144)	4000.00	1800.00	500.00
COMMON CARD (1-144)	25.00	11.00	3.10
WRAPPER (5-CENT)	125.00	55.00	15.50
□ 1 Doak Walker	180.00	45.00	14.50
□ 2 John Greene	25.00	11.00	3.10
□ 3 Bob Nowasky	25.00	11.00	3.10
□ 4 Jonathan Jenkins	25.00	11.00	3.10
□ 5 Y.A. Tittle	250.00	110.00	31.00
□ 6 Lou Groza	150.00	70.00	19.00
□ 7 Alex Agase	30.00	13.50	3.70
□ 8 Mac Speedie	45.00	20.00	5.50
□ 9 Tony Canadeo	80.00	36.00	10.00
□ 10 Larry Craig	25.00	11.00	3.10
□ 11 Ted Fritsch Sr.	30.00	13.50	3.70
□ 12 Joe Golding	25.00	11.00	3.10
□ 13 Martin Ruby	30.00	13.50	3.70
□ 14 George Taliaferro	30.00	13.50	3.70
□ 15 Tank Younger	45.00	20.00	5.50
□ 16 Glenn Army Davis	110.00	50.00	14.00
□ 17 Bob Waterfield	80.00	36.00	10.00
□ 18 Val Jansante	25.00	11.00	3.10
□ 19 Joe Geri	25.00	11.00	3.10
□ 20 Jerry Nuzum	25.00	11.00	3.10
□ 21 Elmer Bud Angsman	30.00	13.50	3.70
□ 22 Billy Dewell	25.00	11.00	3.10
□ 23 Steve Van Buren	65.00	29.00	8.00
□ 24 Cliff Patton	25.00	11.00	3.10
□ 25 Bosh Pritchard	25.00	11.00	3.10
□ 26 John Lujack	65.00	29.00	8.00
□ 27 Sid Luckman	90.00	40.00	11.00
□ 28 Bulldog Turner	50.00	22.00	6.25
□ 29 Bill Dudley	50.00	22.00	6.25
□ 30 Hugh Taylor	30.00	13.50	3.70
□ 31 George Thomas	25.00	11.00	3.10
□ 32 Ray Poole	25.00	11.00	3.10
□ 33 Travis Tidwell	25.00	11.00	3.10
□ 34 Gail Bruce	25.00	11.00	3.10
□ 35 Joe Perry	150.00	70.00	19.00
□ 36 Frankie Albert	35.00	16.00	4.40
□ 37 Bobby Layne	200.00	90.00	25.00
□ 38 Leon Hart	35.00	16.00	4.40
□ 39 Bob Hoernschemeyer	30.00	13.50	3.70
□ 40 Dick Barwegan	25.00	11.00	3.10
□ 41 Adrian Burk	30.00	13.50	3.70
□ 42 Barry French	25.00	11.00	3.10
□ 43 Marion Motley	175.00	80.00	22.00
□ 44 Jim Martin	30.00	13.50	3.70
□ 45 Otto Graham	450.00	200.00	55.00
□ 46 Al Baldwin	25.00	11.00	3.10
□ 47 Larry Coutre	25.00	11.00	3.10
□ 48 John Rauch	25.00	11.00	3.10
□ 49 Sam Tamburo	25.00	11.00	3.10
□ 50 Mike Swistowicz	25.00	11.00	3.10
□ 51 Tom Fears	90.00	40.00	11.00
□ 52 Elroy Hirsch	150.00	70.00	19.00
□ 53 Dick Huffman	25.00	11.00	3.10
□ 54 Bob Gage	25.00	11.00	3.10
□ 55 Buddy Tinsley	30.00	13.50	3.70
□ 56 Bill Blackburn	25.00	11.00	3.10
□ 57 John Cochran	25.00	11.00	3.10
□ 58 Bill Fischer	25.00	11.00	3.10
□ 59 Whitey Wistert	30.00	13.50	3.70
□ 60 Clyde Scott	25.00	11.00	3.10
□ 61 Walter Barnes	25.00	11.00	3.10
□ 62 Bob Perina	25.00	11.00	3.10
□ 63 Bill Wightkin	25.00	11.00	3.10
□ 64 Bob Goode	25.00	11.00	3.10
□ 65 Al Demao	25.00	11.00	3.10
□ 66 Harry Gilmer	30.00	13.50	3.70
□ 67 Bill Austin	25.00	11.00	3.10
□ 68 Joe Scott	25.00	11.00	3.10
□ 69 Tex Coulter	30.00	13.50	3.70
□ 70 Paul Salata	25.00	11.00	3.10
□ 71 Emil Sitko	25.00	11.00	3.10
□ 72 Bill Johnson	25.00	11.00	3.10
□ 73 Don Doll	25.00	11.00	3.10
□ 74 Dan Sandifer	25.00	11.00	3.10
□ 75 John Panelli	25.00	11.00	3.10
□ 76 Bill Leonard	25.00	11.00	3.10
□ 77 Bob Kelly	25.00	11.00	3.10
□ 78 Dante Lavelli	90.00	40.00	11.00
□ 79 Tony Adamle	30.00	13.50	3.70
□ 80 Dick Wildung	25.00	11.00	3.10
□ 81 Tobin Rote	40.00	18.00	5.00
□ 82 Paul Burris	25.00	11.00	3.10
□ 83 Lowell Tew	25.00	11.00	3.10
□ 84 Barney Poole	25.00	11.00	3.10
□ 85 Fred Naumetz	25.00	11.00	3.10
□ 86 Dick Hoerner	25.00	11.00	3.10
□ 87 Bob Reinhard	25.00	11.00	3.10
□ 88 Howard Hartley	25.00	11.00	3.10
□ 89 Darrell Hogan	25.00	11.00	3.10
□ 90 Jerry Shipkey	25.00	11.00	3.10
□ 91 Frank Tripucka	30.00	13.50	3.70
□ 92 Garrard Ramsey	25.00	11.00	3.10
□ 93 Pat Harder	30.00	13.50	3.70
□ 94 Vic Sears	25.00	11.00	3.10
□ 95 Tommy Thompson	30.00	13.50	3.70
□ 96 Bucko Kilroy	30.00	13.50	3.70
□ 97 George Connor	40.00	18.00	5.00
□ 98 Fred Morrison	25.00	11.00	3.10
□ 99 Jim Keane	25.00	11.00	3.10
□ 100 Sammy Baugh	225.00	100.00	28.00
□ 101 Harry Ulinski	25.00	11.00	3.10
□ 102 Frank Spaniel	25.00	11.00	3.10
□ 103 Charley Conerly	70.00	32.00	8.75
□ 104 Dick Hensley	25.00	11.00	3.10
□ 105 Eddie Price	25.00	11.00	3.10
□ 106 Ed Carr	25.00	11.00	3.10
□ 107 Leo Nomellini	65.00	29.00	8.00
□ 108 Verl Lillywhite	25.00	11.00	3.10
□ 109 Wallace Triplett	25.00	11.00	3.10
□ 110 Joe Watson	25.00	11.00	3.10
□ 111 Cloyce Box	30.00	13.50	3.70
□ 112 Billy Stone	25.00	11.00	3.10
□ 113 Earl Murray	25.00	11.00	3.10
□ 114 Chet Mutryn	30.00	13.50	3.70

	NRMT	VG-E	GOOD
☐ 115 Ken Carpenter	30.00	13.50	3.70
☐ 116 Lou Rymkus	30.00	13.50	3.70
☐ 117 Dub Jones	30.00	13.50	3.70
☐ 118 Clayton Tonnemaker	25.00	11.00	3.10
☐ 119 Walt Schlinkman	25.00	11.00	3.10
☐ 120 Billy Grimes	25.00	11.00	3.10
☐ 121 George Ratterman	30.00	13.50	3.70
☐ 122 Bob Mann	25.00	11.00	3.10
☐ 123 Buddy Young	45.00	20.00	5.50
☐ 124 Jack Zilly	25.00	11.00	3.10
☐ 125 Tom Kalmanir	25.00	11.00	3.10
☐ 126 Frank Sinkovitz	30.00	13.50	3.70
☐ 127 Elbert Nickel	30.00	13.50	3.70
☐ 128 Jim Finks	50.00	22.00	6.25
☐ 129 Charley Trippi	50.00	22.00	6.25
☐ 130 Tom Wham	25.00	11.00	3.10
☐ 131 Ventan Yablonski	25.00	11.00	3.10
☐ 132 Chuck Bednarik	90.00	40.00	11.00
☐ 133 Joe Muha	25.00	11.00	3.10
☐ 134 Pete Pihos	50.00	22.00	6.25
☐ 135 Washington Serini	25.00	11.00	3.10
☐ 136 George Gulyanics	25.00	11.00	3.10
☐ 137 Ken Kavanaugh	30.00	13.50	3.70
☐ 138 Howie Livingston	25.00	11.00	3.10
☐ 139 Joe Tereshinski	25.00	11.00	3.10
☐ 140 Jim White	25.00	11.00	3.10
☐ 141 Gene Roberts	25.00	11.00	3.10
☐ 142 Bill Swiacki	30.00	13.50	3.70
☐ 143 Norm Standlee	25.00	11.00	3.10
☐ 144 Knox Ramsey	80.00	20.00	6.50

1951 Bowman

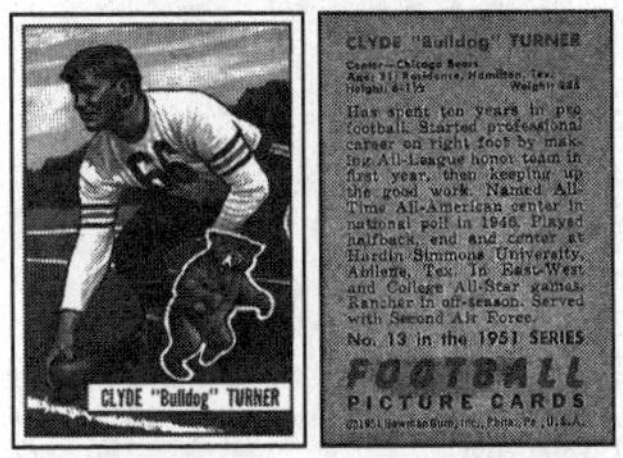

The 1951 Bowman set of 144 numbered cards witnessed an increase in card size from previous Bowman football sets. Cards were issued in six-card nickel packs and one-card penny packs. The cards were enlarged from the previous year to 2 1/16" by 3 1/8". The set is very similar in format to the baseball card set of that year. The fronts feature black and white photos that were colored in. The player's name is in a bar toward the bottom that runs from the right border toward the middle of the photo. A team logo or mascot is on top of the bar. The card backs are printed in maroon and blue on gray card stock and contain a write-up. The set features the Rookie Cards of Tom Landry, Emlen Tunnell, and Norm Van Brocklin. The Bill Walsh in this set went to Notre Dame and is not the Bill Walsh who coached the San Francisco 49ers in the 1980s. The set numbering is arranged so that two, three, or four players from the same team are together.

	NRMT	VG-E	GOOD
COMPLETE SET (144)	3400.00	1500.00	425.00
COMMON CARD (1-144)	20.00	9.00	2.50
WRAPPER (1-CENT)	150.00	70.00	19.00
WRAPPER (5-CENT)	200.00	90.00	25.00

	NRMT	VG-E	GOOD
☐ 1 Weldon Humble	70.00	17.50	5.50
☐ 2 Otto Graham	160.00	70.00	20.00
☐ 3 Mac Speedie	25.00	11.00	3.10
☐ 4 Norm Van Brocklin	250.00	110.00	31.00
☐ 5 Woodley Lewis	25.00	11.00	3.10
☐ 6 Tom Fears	45.00	20.00	5.50
☐ 7 George Musacco	20.00	9.00	2.50
☐ 8 George Taliaferro	25.00	11.00	3.10
☐ 9 Barney Poole	20.00	9.00	2.50
☐ 10 Steve Van Buren	60.00	27.00	7.50
☐ 11 Whitey Wistert	25.00	11.00	3.10
☐ 12 Chuck Bednarik	80.00	36.00	10.00
☐ 13 Bulldog Turner	45.00	20.00	5.50
☐ 14 Bob Williams	20.00	9.00	2.50
☐ 15 John Lujack	60.00	27.00	7.50
☐ 16 Roy Rebel Steiner	20.00	9.00	2.50
☐ 17 Jug Girard	25.00	11.00	3.10
☐ 18 Bill Neal	20.00	9.00	2.50
☐ 19 Travis Tidwell	20.00	9.00	2.50
☐ 20 Tom Landry	500.00	220.00	60.00
☐ 21 Arnie Weinmeister	50.00	22.00	6.25
☐ 22 Joe Geri	20.00	9.00	2.50
☐ 23 Bill Walsh	25.00	11.00	3.10
☐ 24 Fran Rogel	20.00	9.00	2.50
☐ 25 Doak Walker	55.00	25.00	7.00
☐ 26 Leon Hart	25.00	11.00	3.10
☐ 27 Thurman McGraw	20.00	9.00	2.50
☐ 28 Buster Ramsey	20.00	9.00	2.50
☐ 29 Frank Tripucka	25.00	11.00	3.10
☐ 30 Don Paul	20.00	9.00	2.50
☐ 31 Alex Loyd	20.00	9.00	2.50
☐ 32 Y.A. Tittle	135.00	60.00	17.00
☐ 33 Verl Lillywhite	20.00	9.00	2.50
☐ 34 Sammy Baugh	175.00	80.00	22.00
☐ 35 Chuck Drazenovich	20.00	9.00	2.50
☐ 36 Bob Goode	20.00	9.00	2.50
☐ 37 Horace Gillom	20.00	9.00	2.50
☐ 38 Lou Rymkus	25.00	11.00	3.10
☐ 39 Ken Carpenter	20.00	9.00	2.50
☐ 40 Bob Waterfield	70.00	32.00	8.75
☐ 41 Vitamin Smith	25.00	11.00	3.10
☐ 42 Glenn Army Davis	40.00	18.00	5.00
☐ 43 Dan Edwards	20.00	9.00	2.50
☐ 44 John Rauch	20.00	9.00	2.50
☐ 45 Zollie Toth	20.00	9.00	2.50
☐ 46 Pete Pihos	40.00	18.00	5.00
☐ 47 Russ Craft	20.00	9.00	2.50
☐ 48 Walter Barnes	20.00	9.00	2.50
☐ 49 Fred Morrison	20.00	9.00	2.50
☐ 50 Ray Bray	20.00	9.00	2.50
☐ 51 Ed Sprinkle	25.00	11.00	3.10
☐ 52 Floyd Reid	20.00	9.00	2.50
☐ 53 Billy Grimes	20.00	9.00	2.50
☐ 54 Ted Fritsch Sr.	25.00	11.00	3.10
☐ 55 Al DeRogatis	25.00	11.00	3.10
☐ 56 Charley Conerly	60.00	27.00	7.50
☐ 57 Jon Baker	20.00	9.00	2.50
☐ 58 Tom McWilliams	20.00	9.00	2.50
☐ 59 Jerry Shipkey	20.00	9.00	2.50
☐ 60 Lynn Chandnois	25.00	11.00	3.10
☐ 61 Don Doll	20.00	9.00	2.50
☐ 62 Lou Creekmur	45.00	20.00	5.50
☐ 63 Bob Hoernschemeyer	25.00	11.00	3.10
☐ 64 Tom Wham	20.00	9.00	2.50
☐ 65 Bill Fischer	20.00	9.00	2.50
☐ 66 Robert Nussbaumer	20.00	9.00	2.50
☐ 67 Gordy Soltau	20.00	9.00	2.50
☐ 68 Visco Grgich	20.00	9.00	2.50
☐ 69 John Strzykalski	20.00	9.00	2.50
☐ 70 Pete Stout	20.00	9.00	2.50
☐ 71 Paul Lipscomb	20.00	9.00	2.50
☐ 72 Harry Gilmer	25.00	11.00	3.10
☐ 73 Dante Lavelli	45.00	20.00	5.50
☐ 74 Dub Jones	25.00	11.00	3.10
☐ 75 Lou Groza	70.00	32.00	8.75
☐ 76 Elroy Hirsch	70.00	32.00	8.75
☐ 77 Tom Kalmanir	20.00	9.00	2.50
☐ 78 Jack Zilly	20.00	9.00	2.50
☐ 79 Bruce Alford	20.00	9.00	2.50
☐ 80 Art Weiner	20.00	9.00	2.50
☐ 81 Brad Ecklund	20.00	9.00	2.50
☐ 82 Bosh Pritchard	20.00	9.00	2.50
☐ 83 John Green	20.00	9.00	2.50
☐ 84 Ebert Van Buren	20.00	9.00	2.50
☐ 85 Julie Rykovich	20.00	9.00	2.50
☐ 86 Fred Davis	20.00	9.00	2.50
☐ 87 John Hoffman	20.00	9.00	2.50
☐ 88 Tobin Rote	25.00	11.00	3.10
☐ 89 Paul Burris	20.00	9.00	2.50
☐ 90 Tony Canadeo	40.00	18.00	5.00
☐ 91 Emlen Tunnell	100.00	45.00	12.50
☐ 92 Otto Schnellbacher	20.00	9.00	2.50
☐ 93 Ray Poole	20.00	9.00	2.50
☐ 94 Darrell Hogan	20.00	9.00	2.50
☐ 95 Frank Sinkovitz	20.00	9.00	2.50
☐ 96 Ernie Stautner	70.00	32.00	8.75
☐ 97 Elmer Bud Angsman	20.00	9.00	2.50
☐ 98 Jack Jennings	20.00	9.00	2.50
☐ 99 Jerry Groom	20.00	9.00	2.50
☐ 100 John Prchlik	20.00	9.00	2.50
☐ 101 J. Robert Smith	20.00	9.00	2.50
☐ 102 Bobby Layne	135.00	60.00	17.00
☐ 103 Frankie Albert	25.00	11.00	3.10
☐ 104 Gail Bruce	20.00	9.00	2.50
☐ 105 Joe Perry	65.00	29.00	8.00
☐ 106 Leon Heath	20.00	9.00	2.50
☐ 107 Ed Quirk	20.00	9.00	2.50
☐ 108 Hugh Taylor	25.00	11.00	3.10
☐ 109 Marion Motley	75.00	34.00	9.50
☐ 110 Tony Adamle	20.00	9.00	2.50
☐ 111 Alex Agase	25.00	11.00	3.10
☐ 112 Tank Younger	25.00	11.00	3.10
☐ 113 Bob Boyd	20.00	9.00	2.50
☐ 114 Jerry Williams	20.00	9.00	2.50
☐ 115 Joe Golding	20.00	9.00	2.50
☐ 116 Sherman Howard	20.00	9.00	2.50
☐ 117 John Wozniak	20.00	9.00	2.50
☐ 118 Frank Reagan	20.00	9.00	2.50
☐ 119 Vic Sears	20.00	9.00	2.50
☐ 120 Clyde Scott	20.00	9.00	2.50
☐ 121 George Gulyanics	20.00	9.00	2.50
☐ 122 Bill Wightkin	20.00	9.00	2.50
☐ 123 Chuck Hunsinger	20.00	9.00	2.50
☐ 124 Jack Cloud	20.00	9.00	2.50
☐ 125 Abner Wimberly	20.00	9.00	2.50
☐ 126 Dick Wildung	20.00	9.00	2.50
☐ 127 Eddie Price	20.00	9.00	2.50
☐ 128 Joe Scott	20.00	9.00	2.50
☐ 129 Jerry Nuzum	20.00	9.00	2.50
☐ 130 Jim Finks	35.00	16.00	4.40
☐ 131 Bob Gage	20.00	9.00	2.50
☐ 132 Bill Swiacki	25.00	11.00	3.10
☐ 133 Joe Watson	20.00	9.00	2.50
☐ 134 Ollie Cline	20.00	9.00	2.50
☐ 135 Jack Lininger	20.00	9.00	2.50
☐ 136 Fran Polsfoot	20.00	9.00	2.50
☐ 137 Charley Trippi	40.00	18.00	5.00
☐ 138 Ventan Yablonski	20.00	9.00	2.50
☐ 139 Emil Sitko	20.00	9.00	2.50
☐ 140 Leo Nomellini	55.00	25.00	7.00
☐ 141 Norm Standlee	20.00	9.00	2.50
☐ 142 Eddie Saenz	20.00	9.00	2.50
☐ 143 Al Demao	20.00	9.00	2.50
☐ 144 Bill Dudley	90.00	22.00	7.25

1952 Bowman Large

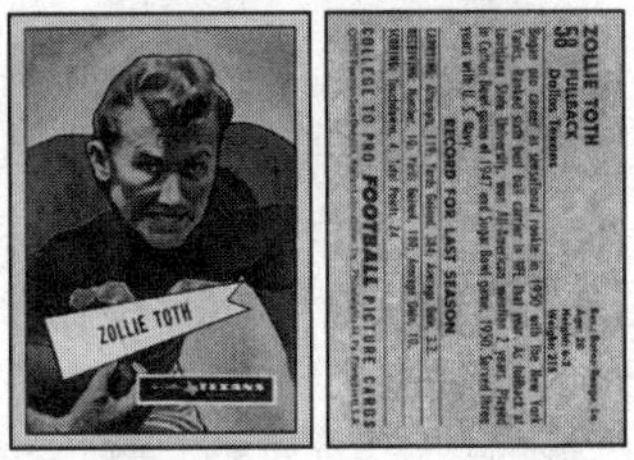

One of two different sized sets produced by Bowman in 1952, the large version measures 2 1/2" by 3 3/4". Cards were issued in five-card, five-cent packs. The 144-card issue is identical to the smaller version in every respect except size. Either horizontal or vertical fronts contain a player portrait, a white banner with the player's name and a bar containing the team name and logo. Horizontal backs have a small write-up, previous year's stats and biographical information. Certain numbers were systematically printed in lesser quantities due to the fact that Bowman apparently could not fit each 72-card series on their respective sheets. The affected cards are those which are divisible by nine (i.e. 9, 18, 27 etc.) and those which are numbered one more than those divisible by nine (i.e. 10, 19, 28 etc.). These short-print cards are marked in the checklist below by SP. The set features NFL veterans and college players that entered the pro ranks in '52. The set features the Rookie Cards of Paul Brown, Jack Christiansen, Art Donovan, Frank Gifford, George Halas, Yale Lary, Gino Marchetti, Ollie Matson, Hugh McElhenny, and Andy Robustelli. The last card in the set, No. 144 Jim Lansford, is among the toughest football cards to acquire. It is generally accepted among hobbyists that the card was located at the bottom right corner of the production sheet and was subject to much abuse including numerous poor cuts. The problem was such that many copies never made it out of the factory as they were discarded. This card is also indicated below by SP.

	NRMT	VG-E	GOOD
COMPLETE SET (144)	12500.00	5600.00	1600.00
COMMON CARD (1-72)	35.00	16.00	4.40
COMMON CARD (73-144)	40.00	18.00	5.00
WRAPPER (5-CENT)	75.00	34.00	9.50

	NRMT	VG-E	GOOD
☐ 1 Norm Van Brocklin	425.00	105.00	34.00
☐ 2 Otto Graham	300.00	135.00	38.00
☐ 3 Doak Walker	70.00	32.00	8.75
☐ 4 Steve Owen CO	60.00	27.00	7.50
☐ 5 Frankie Albert	45.00	20.00	5.50
☐ 6 Laurie Niemi	35.00	16.00	4.40
☐ 7 Chuck Hunsinger	35.00	16.00	4.40
☐ 8 Ed Modzelewski	45.00	20.00	5.50
☐ 9 Joe Spencer SP	70.00	32.00	8.75
☐ 10 Chuck Bednarik SP	175.00	80.00	22.00
☐ 11 Barney Poole	35.00	16.00	4.40
☐ 12 Charley Trippi	60.00	27.00	7.50
☐ 13 Tom Fears	60.00	27.00	7.50
☐ 14 Paul Brown CO	225.00	100.00	28.00
☐ 15 Leon Hart	45.00	20.00	5.50
☐ 16 Frank Gifford	450.00	200.00	55.00
☐ 17 Y.A. Tittle	150.00	70.00	19.00
☐ 18 Charlie Justice SP	160.00	70.00	20.00
☐ 19 George Connor SP	120.00	55.00	15.00
☐ 20 Lynn Chandnois	45.00	20.00	5.50
☐ 21 Billy Howton	45.00	20.00	5.50
☐ 22 Kenneth Snyder	35.00	16.00	4.40
☐ 23 Gino Marchetti	175.00	80.00	22.00
☐ 24 John Karras	35.00	16.00	4.40
☐ 25 Tank Younger	45.00	20.00	5.50
☐ 26 Tommy Thompson	35.00	16.00	4.40
☐ 27 Bob Miller SP	300.00	135.00	38.00
☐ 28 Kyle Rote SP	150.00	70.00	19.00
☐ 29 Hugh McElhenny	200.00	90.00	25.00
☐ 30 Sammy Baugh	350.00	160.00	45.00
☐ 31 Jim Dooley	45.00	20.00	5.50
☐ 32 Ray Mathews	35.00	16.00	4.40
☐ 33 Fred Cone	35.00	16.00	4.40
☐ 34 Al Pollard	35.00	16.00	4.40
☐ 35 Brad Ecklund	35.00	16.00	4.40
☐ 36 John Lee Hancock SP	325.00	145.00	40.00
☐ 37 Elroy Hirsch SP	150.00	70.00	19.00
☐ 38 Keever Jankovich	35.00	16.00	4.40
☐ 39 Emlen Tunnell	60.00	27.00	7.50
☐ 40 Steve Dowden	35.00	16.00	4.40
☐ 41 Claude Hipps	35.00	16.00	4.40
☐ 42 Norm Standlee	35.00	16.00	4.40
☐ 43 Dick Todd CO	35.00	16.00	4.40
☐ 44 Babe Parilli	45.00	20.00	5.50
☐ 45 Steve Van Buren SP	225.00	100.00	28.00
☐ 46 Art Donovan SP	350.00	160.00	45.00
☐ 47 Bill Fischer	35.00	16.00	4.40
☐ 48 George Halas CO	275.00	125.00	34.00
☐ 49 Jerrell Price	35.00	16.00	4.40
☐ 50 John Sandusky	35.00	16.00	4.40
☐ 51 Ray Beck	35.00	16.00	4.40
☐ 52 Jim Martin	45.00	20.00	5.50
☐ 53 Joe Bach CO UER (Misspelled Back)	35.00	16.00	4.40
☐ 54 Glen Christian SP	70.00	32.00	8.75
☐ 55 Andy Davis SP	70.00	32.00	8.75
☐ 56 Tobin Rote	45.00	20.00	5.50
☐ 57 Wayne Millner CO	60.00	27.00	7.50
☐ 58 Zollie Toth	35.00	16.00	4.40
☐ 59 Jack Jennings	35.00	16.00	4.40
☐ 60 Bill McColl	35.00	16.00	4.40
☐ 61 Les Richter	45.00	20.00	5.50
☐ 62 Walt Michaels	45.00	20.00	5.50
☐ 63 Charley Conerly SP	500.00	220.00	60.00
☐ 64 Howard Hartley SP	70.00	32.00	8.75
☐ 65 Jerome Smith	35.00	16.00	4.40
☐ 66 James Clark	35.00	16.00	4.40
☐ 67 Dick Logan	35.00	16.00	4.40
☐ 68 Wayne Robinson	35.00	16.00	4.40
☐ 69 James Hammond	35.00	16.00	4.40
☐ 70 Gene Schroeder	35.00	16.00	4.40
☐ 71 Tex Coulter	45.00	20.00	5.50
☐ 72 John Schweder SP	500.00	220.00	60.00
☐ 73 Vitamin Smith SP	125.00	55.00	15.50
☐ 74 Joe Campanella	40.00	18.00	5.00
☐ 75 Joe Kuharich CO	50.00	22.00	6.25
☐ 76 Herman Clark	40.00	18.00	5.00
☐ 77 Dan Edwards	40.00	18.00	5.00
☐ 78 Bobby Layne	225.00	100.00	28.00
☐ 79 Bob Hoernschemeyer	50.00	22.00	6.25
☐ 80 John Carr Blount	40.00	18.00	5.00
☐ 81 John Kastan SP	125.00	55.00	15.50
☐ 82 Harry Minarik SP	140.00	65.00	17.50
☐ 83 Joe Perry	80.00	36.00	10.00
☐ 84 Ray(Buddy) Parker CO	50.00	22.00	6.25
☐ 85 Andy Robustelli	175.00	80.00	22.00
☐ 86 Dub Jones	50.00	22.00	6.25
☐ 87 Mal Cook	40.00	18.00	5.00
☐ 88 Billy Stone	40.00	18.00	5.00
☐ 89 George Taliaferro	40.00	18.00	5.00
☐ 90 Thomas Johnson SP	125.00	55.00	15.50
☐ 91 Leon Heath SP	100.00	45.00	12.50
☐ 92 Pete Pihos	70.00	32.00	8.75
☐ 93 Fred Benners	40.00	18.00	5.00
☐ 94 George Tarasovic	40.00	18.00	5.00
☐ 95 Lawr. (Buck) Shaw CO	40.00	18.00	5.00
☐ 96 Bill Wightkin	40.00	18.00	5.00
☐ 97 John Wozniak	40.00	18.00	5.00
☐ 98 Bobby Dillon	50.00	22.00	6.25
☐ 99 Joe Stydahar CO SP	550.00	250.00	70.00
☐ 100 Dick Alban SP	125.00	55.00	15.50
☐ 101 Arnie Weinmeister	60.00	27.00	7.50
☐ 102 Robert Joe Cross	40.00	18.00	5.00
☐ 103 Don Paul	40.00	18.00	5.00
☐ 104 Buddy Young	50.00	22.00	6.25
☐ 105 Lou Groza	90.00	40.00	11.00
☐ 106 Ray Pelfrey	40.00	18.00	5.00
☐ 107 Maurice Nipp	40.00	18.00	5.00
☐ 108 Hubert Johnston SP	600.00	275.00	75.00
☐ 109 Volney Quinlan SP	100.00	45.00	12.50
☐ 110 Jack Simmons	40.00	18.00	5.00
☐ 111 George Ratterman	50.00	22.00	6.25
☐ 112 John Badaczewski	40.00	18.00	5.00
☐ 113 Bill Reichardt	40.00	18.00	5.00
☐ 114 Art Weiner	40.00	18.00	5.00
☐ 115 Keith Flowers	40.00	18.00	5.00
☐ 116 Russ Craft	40.00	18.00	5.00
☐ 117 Jim O'Donahue SP	125.00	55.00	15.50
☐ 118 Darrell Hogan SP	100.00	45.00	12.50
☐ 119 Frank Ziegler	40.00	18.00	5.00
☐ 120 Deacon Dan Towler	50.00	22.00	6.25
☐ 121 Fred Williams	40.00	18.00	5.00
☐ 122 Jimmy Phelan CO	40.00	18.00	5.00
☐ 123 Eddie Price	40.00	18.00	5.00
☐ 124 Chet Ostrowski	40.00	18.00	5.00
☐ 125 Leo Nomellini	75.00	34.00	9.50
☐ 126 Steve Romanik SP	300.00	135.00	38.00
☐ 127 Ollie Matson SP	275.00	125.00	34.00
☐ 128 Dante Lavelli	75.00	34.00	9.50
☐ 129 Jack Christiansen	150.00	70.00	19.00
☐ 130 Dom Moselle	40.00	18.00	5.00
☐ 131 John Rapacz	40.00	18.00	5.00
☐ 132 Chuck Ortmann UER (Avg. gain 9.4, should be 4.8)	40.00	18.00	5.00
☐ 133 Bob Williams	40.00	18.00	5.00
☐ 134 Chuck Ulrich	40.00	18.00	5.00
☐ 135 Gene Ronzani CO SP	600.00	275.00	75.00
☐ 136 Bert Rechichar SP	100.00	45.00	12.50
☐ 137 Bob Waterfield	120.00	55.00	15.00
☐ 138 Bobby Walston	50.00	22.00	6.25
☐ 139 Jerry Shipkey	40.00	18.00	5.00
☐ 140 Yale Lary	150.00	70.00	19.00
☐ 141 Gordy Soltau	40.00	18.00	5.00
☐ 142 Tom Landry	600.00	275.00	75.00
☐ 143 John Papit	40.00	18.00	5.00
☐ 144 Jim Lansford SP	3000.00	750.00	240.00

1952 Bowman Small

One of two different sized sets issued by Bowman in 1952, this 144-card set is identical in every respect to the large version except for the smaller size of 2 1/16" by 3 1/8". Cards were issued in one-card penny packs. The fronts are either horizontal or vertical and feature a player protrait, a white banner with the player's name and a bar containing the team name and logo. All backs are horizontal and contain a brief write-up, previous year's stats and a bio. The set features NFL veterans and college players that entered the pro ranks in '52. The set features the Rookie Cards of Paul Brown, Jack Christiansen, Art Donovan, Frank Gifford, George Halas, Yale Lary, Gino Marchetti, Ollie Matson, Hugh McElhenny, and Andy Robustelli.

	NRMT	VG-E	GOOD
COMPLETE SET (144)	5000.00	2200.00	600.00
COMMON CARD (1-72)	25.00	11.00	3.10
COMMON CARD (73-144)	30.00	13.50	3.70
WRAPPER (1-CENT)	50.00	22.00	6.25

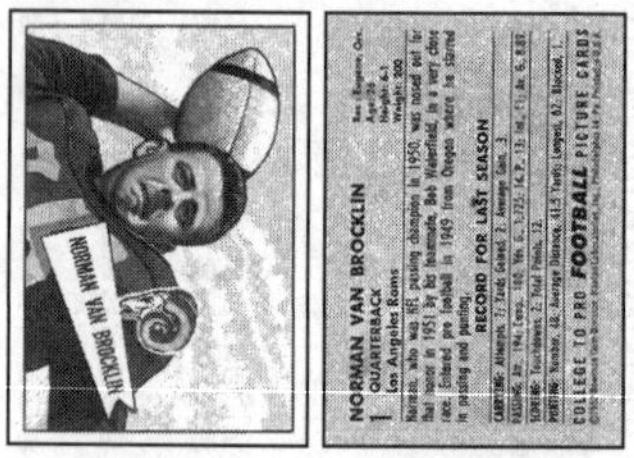

	NRMT	VG-E	GOOD
☐ 1 Norm Van Brocklin	225.00	55.00	18.00
☐ 2 Otto Graham	150.00	70.00	19.00
☐ 3 Doak Walker	45.00	20.00	5.50
☐ 4 Steve Owen CO	45.00	20.00	5.50
☐ 5 Frankie Albert	30.00	13.50	3.70
☐ 6 Laurie Niemi	25.00	11.00	3.10
☐ 7 Chuck Hunsinger	25.00	11.00	3.10
☐ 8 Ed Modzelewski	30.00	13.50	3.70
☐ 9 Joe Spencer	25.00	11.00	3.10
☐ 10 Chuck Bednarik	65.00	29.00	8.00
☐ 11 Barney Poole	25.00	11.00	3.10
☐ 12 Charley Trippi	40.00	18.00	5.00
☐ 13 Tom Fears	45.00	20.00	5.50
☐ 14 Paul Brown CO	130.00	57.50	16.00
☐ 15 Leon Hart	30.00	13.50	3.70
☐ 16 Frank Gifford	400.00	180.00	50.00
☐ 17 Y.A. Tittle	100.00	45.00	12.50
☐ 18 Charlie Justice	45.00	20.00	5.50
☐ 19 George Connor	35.00	16.00	4.40
☐ 20 Lynn Chandnois	25.00	11.00	3.10
☐ 21 Billy Howton	40.00	18.00	5.00
☐ 22 Kenneth Snyder	25.00	11.00	3.10
☐ 23 Gino Marchetti	110.00	50.00	14.00
☐ 24 John Karras	25.00	11.00	3.10
☐ 25 Tank Younger	30.00	13.50	3.70
☐ 26 Tommy Thompson	25.00	11.00	3.10
☐ 27 Bob Miller	25.00	11.00	3.10
☐ 28 Kyle Rote	50.00	22.00	6.25
☐ 29 Hugh McElhenny	150.00	70.00	19.00
☐ 30 Sammy Baugh	225.00	100.00	28.00
☐ 31 Jim Dooley	30.00	13.50	3.70
☐ 32 Ray Mathews	25.00	11.00	3.10
☐ 33 Fred Cone	25.00	11.00	3.10
☐ 34 Al Pollard	25.00	11.00	3.10
☐ 35 Brad Ecklund	25.00	11.00	3.10
☐ 36 John Lee Hancock	25.00	11.00	3.10
☐ 37 Elroy Hirsch	50.00	22.00	6.25
☐ 38 Keever Jankovich	25.00	11.00	3.10
☐ 39 Emlen Tunnell	40.00	18.00	5.00
☐ 40 Steve Dowden	25.00	11.00	3.10
☐ 41 Claude Hipps	25.00	11.00	3.10
☐ 42 Norm Standlee	25.00	11.00	3.10
☐ 43 Dick Todd CO	25.00	11.00	3.10
☐ 44 Babe Parilli	30.00	13.50	3.70
☐ 45 Steve Van Buren	50.00	22.00	6.25
☐ 46 Art Donovan	175.00	80.00	22.00
☐ 47 Bill Fischer	25.00	11.00	3.10
☐ 48 George Halas CO	160.00	70.00	20.00
☐ 49 Jerrell Price	25.00	11.00	3.10
☐ 50 John Sandusky	25.00	11.00	3.10
☐ 51 Ray Beck	25.00	11.00	3.10
☐ 52 Jim Martin	30.00	13.50	3.70
☐ 53 Joe Bach CO UER (Misspelled Back)	25.00	11.00	3.10
☐ 54 Glen Christian	25.00	11.00	3.10
☐ 55 Andy Davis	25.00	11.00	3.10
☐ 56 Tobin Rote	30.00	13.50	3.70
☐ 57 Wayne Millner CO	45.00	20.00	5.50
☐ 58 Zollie Toth	25.00	11.00	3.10
☐ 59 Jack Jennings	25.00	11.00	3.10
☐ 60 Bill McColl	25.00	11.00	3.10
☐ 61 Les Richter	30.00	13.50	3.70
☐ 62 Walt Michaels	30.00	13.50	3.70
☐ 63 Charley Conerly	50.00	22.00	6.25
☐ 64 Howard Hartley	25.00	11.00	3.10
☐ 65 Jerome Smith	25.00	11.00	3.10
☐ 66 James Clark	25.00	11.00	3.10
☐ 67 Dick Logan	25.00	11.00	3.10
☐ 68 Wayne Robinson	25.00	11.00	3.10
☐ 69 James Hammond	25.00	11.00	3.10
☐ 70 Gene Schroeder	25.00	11.00	3.10
☐ 71 Tex Coulter	30.00	13.50	3.70
☐ 72 John Schweder	25.00	11.00	3.10
☐ 73 Vitamin Smith	35.00	16.00	4.40
☐ 74 Joe Campanella	30.00	13.50	3.70
☐ 75 Joe Kuharich CO	35.00	16.00	4.40
☐ 76 Herman Clark	30.00	13.50	3.70
☐ 77 Dan Edwards	30.00	13.50	3.70
☐ 78 Bobby Layne	125.00	55.00	15.50
☐ 79 Bob Hoernschemeyer	35.00	16.00	4.40
☐ 80 John Carr Blount	30.00	13.50	3.70
☐ 81 John Kastan	30.00	13.50	3.70
☐ 82 Harry Minarik	30.00	13.50	3.70
☐ 83 Joe Perry	60.00	27.00	7.50
☐ 84 Ray(Buddy) Parker CO	35.00	16.00	4.40
☐ 85 Andy Robustelli	110.00	50.00	14.00
☐ 86 Dub Jones	35.00	16.00	4.40
☐ 87 Mal Cook	30.00	13.50	3.70
☐ 88 Billy Stone	30.00	13.50	3.70
☐ 89 George Taliaferro	30.00	13.50	3.70
☐ 90 Thomas Johnson	30.00	13.50	3.70
☐ 91 Leon Heath	30.00	13.50	3.70
☐ 92 Pete Pihos	45.00	20.00	5.50
☐ 93 Fred Benners	30.00	13.50	3.70
☐ 94 George Tarasovic	30.00	13.50	3.70
☐ 95 Lawr. (Buck) Shaw CO	30.00	13.50	3.70
☐ 96 Bill Wightkin	30.00	13.50	3.70
☐ 97 John Wozniak	30.00	13.50	3.70
☐ 98 Bobby Dillon	35.00	16.00	4.40
☐ 99 Joe Stydahar CO	45.00	20.00	5.50
☐ 100 Dick Alban	30.00	13.50	3.70
☐ 101 Arnie Weinmeister	40.00	18.00	5.00
☐ 102 Robert Joe Cross	30.00	13.50	3.70
☐ 103 Don Paul	30.00	13.50	3.70
☐ 104 Buddy Young	35.00	16.00	4.40
☐ 105 Lou Groza	50.00	22.00	6.25
☐ 106 Ray Pelfrey	30.00	13.50	3.70
☐ 107 Maurice Nipp	30.00	13.50	3.70
☐ 108 Hubert Johnston	30.00	13.50	3.70
☐ 109 Volney Quinlan	30.00	13.50	3.70
☐ 110 Jack Simmons	30.00	13.50	3.70
☐ 111 George Ratterman	35.00	16.00	4.40
☐ 112 John Badaczewski	30.00	13.50	3.70
☐ 113 Bill Reichardt	30.00	13.50	3.70
☐ 114 Art Weiner	30.00	13.50	3.70
☐ 115 Keith Flowers	30.00	13.50	3.70
☐ 116 Russ Craft	30.00	13.50	3.70
☐ 117 Jim O'Donahue	30.00	13.50	3.70
☐ 118 Darrell Hogan	30.00	13.50	3.70
☐ 119 Frank Ziegler	30.00	13.50	3.70
☐ 120 Deacon Dan Towler	35.00	16.00	4.40
☐ 121 Fred Williams	30.00	13.50	3.70
☐ 122 Jimmy Phelan CO	30.00	13.50	3.70
☐ 123 Eddie Price	30.00	13.50	3.70
☐ 124 Chet Ostrowski	30.00	13.50	3.70
☐ 125 Leo Nomellini	55.00	25.00	7.00
☐ 126 Steve Romanik	30.00	13.50	3.70
☐ 127 Ollie Matson	125.00	55.00	15.50
☐ 128 Dante Lavelli	50.00	22.00	6.25
☐ 129 Jack Christiansen	80.00	36.00	10.00
☐ 130 Dom Moselle	30.00	13.50	3.70
☐ 131 John Rapacz	30.00	13.50	3.70
☐ 132 Chuck Ortmann UER (Avg. gain 9.4, should be 4.8)	30.00	13.50	3.70
☐ 133 Bob Williams	30.00	13.50	3.70
☐ 134 Chuck Ulrich	30.00	13.50	3.70
☐ 135 Gene Ronzani CO	30.00	13.50	3.70
☐ 136 Bert Rechichar	35.00	16.00	4.40
☐ 137 Bob Waterfield	65.00	29.00	8.00
☐ 138 Bobby Walston	35.00	16.00	4.40
☐ 139 Jerry Shipkey	30.00	13.50	3.70
☐ 140 Yale Lary	80.00	36.00	10.00
☐ 141 Gordy Soltau	30.00	13.50	3.70
☐ 142 Tom Landry	350.00	160.00	45.00
☐ 143 John Papit	30.00	13.50	3.70
☐ 144 Jim Lansford	150.00	38.00	12.00

1953 Bowman

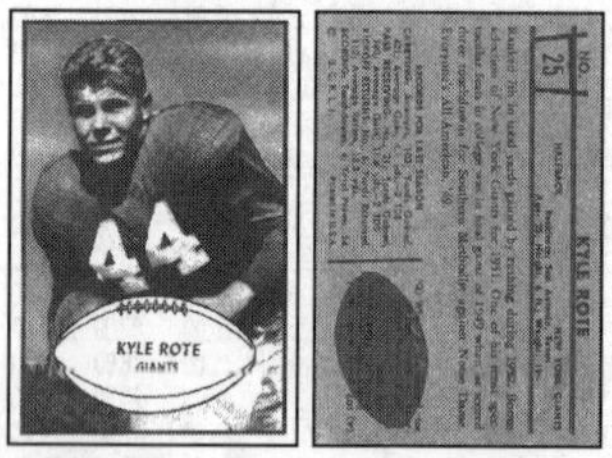

The 1953 Bowman set of 96 cards measures approximately 2 1/2" by 3 3/4". Cards were issued in five-card, five-cent packs. The set is somewhat smaller in number than would be thought since Bowman was the only major producer of football cards during this year. The fronts feature a player portrait with a football that contains player and team names. Horizontal backs contain a brief write-up, previous year's stats, a bio and a quiz. There are 24 cards marked SP in the checklist below which are considered in shorter supply than the other cards in the set. The Bill Walsh in this set went to Notre Dame and is not the Bill Walsh who coached the San Francisco 49ers in the 1980s. The most notable Rookie Card in this set is Eddie LeBaron.

	NRMT	VG-E	GOOD
COMPLETE SET (96)	3200.00	1450.00	400.00
COMMON CARD (1-96)	30.00	13.50	3.70
WRAPPER (5-CENT)	175.00	80.00	22.00

	NRMT	VG-E	GOOD
☐ 1 Eddie LeBaron	120.00	30.00	9.50
☐ 2 John Dottley	30.00	13.50	3.70
☐ 3 Babe Parilli	35.00	16.00	4.40
☐ 4 Bucko Kilroy	35.00	16.00	4.40
☐ 5 Joe Tereshinski	30.00	13.50	3.70
☐ 6 Doak Walker	50.00	22.00	6.25
☐ 7 Fran Polsfoot	30.00	13.50	3.70
☐ 8 Sisto Averno	30.00	13.50	3.70
☐ 9 Marion Motley	75.00	34.00	9.50
☐ 10 Pat Brady	30.00	13.50	3.70
☐ 11 Norm Van Brocklin	90.00	40.00	11.00
☐ 12 Bill McColl	30.00	13.50	3.70
☐ 13 Jerry Groom	30.00	13.50	3.70
☐ 14 Al Pollard	30.00	13.50	3.70
☐ 15 Dante Lavelli	45.00	20.00	5.50
☐ 16 Eddie Price	30.00	13.50	3.70
☐ 17 Charley Trippi	45.00	20.00	5.50
☐ 18 Elbert Nickel	35.00	16.00	4.40
☐ 19 George Taliaferro	30.00	13.50	3.70
☐ 20 Charley Conerly	60.00	27.00	7.50
☐ 21 Bobby Layne	110.00	50.00	14.00
☐ 22 Elroy Hirsch	65.00	29.00	8.00
☐ 23 Jim Finks	40.00	18.00	5.00
☐ 24 Chuck Bednarik	70.00	32.00	8.75
☐ 25 Kyle Rote	40.00	18.00	5.00
☐ 26 Otto Graham	140.00	65.00	17.50
☐ 27 Harry Gilmer	35.00	16.00	4.40
☐ 28 Tobin Rote	35.00	16.00	4.40
☐ 29 Billy Stone	30.00	13.50	3.70
☐ 30 Buddy Young	35.00	16.00	4.40
☐ 31 Leon Hart	35.00	16.00	4.40
☐ 32 Hugh McElhenny	60.00	27.00	7.50
☐ 33 Dale Samuels	30.00	13.50	3.70
☐ 34 Lou Creekmur	45.00	20.00	5.50
☐ 35 Tom Catlin	30.00	13.50	3.70
☐ 36 Tom Fears	45.00	20.00	5.50
☐ 37 George Connor	40.00	18.00	5.00
☐ 38 Bill Walsh	30.00	13.50	3.70
☐ 39 Leo Sanford SP	40.00	18.00	5.00
☐ 40 Horace Gillom	30.00	13.50	3.70
☐ 41 John Schweder SP	40.00	18.00	5.00
☐ 42 Tom O'Connell	30.00	13.50	3.70
☐ 43 Frank Gifford SP	400.00	180.00	50.00
☐ 44 Frank Continetti SP	40.00	18.00	5.00
☐ 45 John Olszewski SP	40.00	18.00	5.00
☐ 46 Dub Jones	35.00	16.00	4.40
☐ 47 Don Paul SP	40.00	18.00	5.00
☐ 48 Gerald Weatherly	30.00	13.50	3.70
☐ 49 Fred Bruney SP	40.00	18.00	5.00
☐ 50 Jack Scarbath	30.00	13.50	3.70
☐ 51 John Karras	30.00	13.50	3.70
☐ 52 Al Conway	30.00	13.50	3.70
☐ 53 Emlen Tunnell SP	100.00	45.00	12.50
☐ 54 Gern Nagler SP	40.00	18.00	5.00
☐ 55 Kenneth Snyder SP	40.00	18.00	5.00
☐ 56 Y.A. Tittle	100.00	45.00	12.50
☐ 57 John Rapacz SP	40.00	18.00	5.00
☐ 58 Harley Sewell SP	40.00	18.00	5.00
☐ 59 Don Bingham	30.00	13.50	3.70
☐ 60 Darrell Hogan	30.00	13.50	3.70
☐ 61 Tony Curcillo	30.00	13.50	3.70
☐ 62 Ray Renfro SP	50.00	22.00	6.25
☐ 63 Leon Heath	30.00	13.50	3.70
☐ 64 Tex Coulter SP	40.00	18.00	5.00
☐ 65 Dewayne Douglas	30.00	13.50	3.70
☐ 66 J. Robert Smith SP	40.00	18.00	5.00
☐ 67 Bob McChesney SP	40.00	18.00	5.00
☐ 68 Dick Alban SP	40.00	18.00	5.00
☐ 69 Andy Kozar	30.00	13.50	3.70
☐ 70 Merwin Hodel SP	40.00	18.00	5.00
☐ 71 Thurman McGraw	30.00	13.50	3.70
☐ 72 Cliff Anderson	30.00	13.50	3.70
☐ 73 Pete Pihos	45.00	20.00	5.50
☐ 74 Julie Rykovich	30.00	13.50	3.70
☐ 75 John Kreamcheck SP	40.00	18.00	5.00
☐ 76 Lynn Chandnois	35.00	16.00	4.40
☐ 77 Cloyce Box SP	40.00	18.00	5.00
☐ 78 Ray Mathews	30.00	13.50	3.70
☐ 79 Bobby Walston	35.00	16.00	4.40
☐ 80 Jim Dooley	30.00	13.50	3.70
☐ 81 Pat Harder SP	40.00	18.00	5.00
☐ 82 Jerry Shipkey	30.00	13.50	3.70
☐ 83 Bobby Thomason	30.00	13.50	3.70
☐ 84 Hugh Taylor	35.00	16.00	4.40
☐ 85 George Ratterman	35.00	16.00	4.40
☐ 86 Don Stonesifer	30.00	13.50	3.70
☐ 87 John Williams SP	40.00	18.00	5.00
☐ 88 Leo Nomellini	50.00	22.00	6.25
☐ 89 Frank Ziegler	30.00	13.50	3.70
☐ 90 Don Paul UER (19th in punt returns, should be 9th) Chicago Cardinals	30.00	13.50	3.70
☐ 91 Tom Dublinski	30.00	13.50	3.70
☐ 92 Ken Carpenter	30.00	13.50	3.70
☐ 93 Ted Marchibroda	40.00	18.00	5.00
☐ 94 Chuck Drazenovich	30.00	13.50	3.70
☐ 95 Lou Groza SP	100.00	45.00	12.50
☐ 96 William Cross SP	90.00	22.00	7.25

1954 Bowman

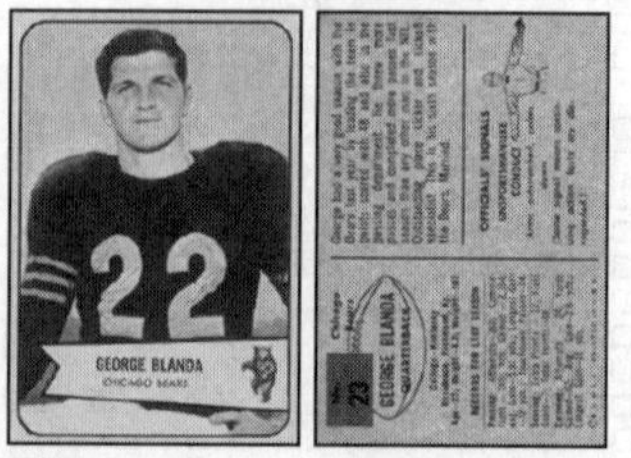

Measuring 2 1/2" by 3 3/4", the 1954 set consists of 128 cards. Cards were issued in seven-card five-cent packs and one-card penny packs. Toward the bottom of the photo is a white banner that contains the player's name, team name and mascot. The card backs feature the player's name in black print inside a red outline of a football. The player's statistical information from the previous season and a quiz are also on back. The "Whizzer" White in the set (125) is not Byron White, the Supreme Court Justice, but Wilford White. Wilford is the father of former Dallas Cowboys quarterback Danny White. The Bill Walsh in this set went to Notre Dame and is not the Bill Walsh who coached the San Francisco 49ers in the 1980s. The mid-series, cards 65-96, is very tough to find in relationship to other series. Rookie Cards in this set include Doug Atkins and George Blanda.

	NRMT	VG-E	GOOD
COMPLETE SET (128)	1700.00	750.00	210.00
COMMON CARD (1-64)	5.00	2.20	.60
COMMON CARD SP (65-96)	25.00	11.00	3.10
COMMON CARD (97-128)	5.00	2.20	.60
WRAPPER (1-CENT)	15.00	6.75	1.85
WRAPPER (5-CENT)	30.00	13.50	3.70

	NRMT	VG-E	GOOD
☐ 1 Ray Mathews	30.00	7.50	2.40
☐ 2 John Huzvar	5.00	2.20	.60
☐ 3 Jack Scarbath	5.00	2.20	.60
☐ 4 Doug Atkins	45.00	20.00	5.50
☐ 5 Bill Stits	5.00	2.20	.60
☐ 6 Joe Perry	30.00	13.50	3.70
☐ 7 Kyle Rote	16.00	7.25	2.00
☐ 8 Norm Van Brocklin	45.00	20.00	5.50
☐ 9 Pete Pihos	20.00	9.00	2.50
☐ 10 Babe Parilli	8.00	3.60	1.00
☐ 11 Zeke Bratkowski	25.00	11.00	3.10
☐ 12 Ollie Matson	25.00	11.00	3.10
☐ 13 Pat Brady	5.00	2.20	.60
☐ 14 Fred Enke	5.00	2.20	.60
☐ 15 Harry Ulinski	5.00	2.20	.60
☐ 16 Bob Garrett	5.00	2.20	.60
☐ 17 Bill Bowman	5.00	2.20	.60
☐ 18 Leo Rucka	5.00	2.20	.60
☐ 19 John Cannady	5.00	2.20	.60
☐ 20 Tom Fears	20.00	9.00	2.50
☐ 21 Norm Willey	5.00	2.20	.60
☐ 22 Floyd Reid	5.00	2.20	.60
☐ 23 George Blanda	160.00	70.00	20.00
☐ 24 Don Doheney	5.00	2.20	.60
☐ 25 John Schweder	5.00	2.20	.60
☐ 26 Bert Rechichar	5.00	2.20	.60
☐ 27 Harry Dowda	5.00	2.20	.60
☐ 28 John Sandusky	5.00	2.20	.60
☐ 29 Les Bingaman	8.00	3.60	1.00
☐ 30 Joe Arenas	5.00	2.20	.60
☐ 31 Ray Wietecha	5.00	2.20	.60
☐ 32 Elroy Hirsch	30.00	13.50	3.70
☐ 33 Harold Giancanelli	5.00	2.20	.60
☐ 34 Billy Howton	8.00	3.60	1.00
☐ 35 Fred Morrison	5.00	2.20	.60
☐ 36 Bobby Cavazos	5.00	2.20	.60
☐ 37 Darrell Hogan	5.00	2.20	.60
☐ 38 Buddy Young	8.00	3.60	1.00
☐ 39 Charlie Justice	18.00	8.00	2.20
☐ 40 Otto Graham	75.00	34.00	9.50
☐ 41 Doak Walker	25.00	11.00	3.10
☐ 42 Y.A. Tittle	60.00	27.00	7.50
☐ 43 Buford Long	5.00	2.20	.60
☐ 44 Volney Quinlan	5.00	2.20	.60
☐ 45 Bobby Thomason	5.00	2.20	.60
☐ 46 Fred Cone	5.00	2.20	.60
☐ 47 Gerald Weatherly	5.00	2.20	.60
☐ 48 Don Stonesifer	5.00	2.20	.60
☐ 49 Lynn Chandnois	5.00	2.20	.60
☐ 50 George Taliaferro	5.00	2.20	.60
☐ 51 Dick Alban	5.00	2.20	.60
☐ 52 Lou Groza	30.00	13.50	3.70
☐ 53 Bobby Layne	60.00	27.00	7.50
☐ 54 Hugh McElhenny	30.00	13.50	3.70
☐ 55 Frank Gifford UER (Avg. gain 7.83, should be 3.1)	110.00	50.00	14.00
☐ 56 Leon McLaughlin	5.00	2.20	.60
☐ 57 Chuck Bednarik	35.00	16.00	4.40
☐ 58 Art Hunter	5.00	2.20	.60
☐ 59 Bill McColl	5.00	2.20	.60
☐ 60 Charley Trippi	20.00	9.00	2.50
☐ 61 Jim Finks	18.00	8.00	2.20
☐ 62 Bill Lange	5.00	2.20	.60
☐ 63 Laurie Niemi	5.00	2.20	.60
☐ 64 Ray Renfro	8.00	3.60	1.00
☐ 65 Dick Chapman	25.00	11.00	3.10
☐ 66 Bob Hantla	25.00	11.00	3.10
☐ 67 Ralph Starkey	25.00	11.00	3.10
☐ 68 Don Paul	25.00	11.00	3.10
☐ 69 Kenneth Snyder	25.00	11.00	3.10
☐ 70 Tobin Rote	25.00	11.00	3.10
☐ 71 Art DeCarlo	25.00	11.00	3.10
☐ 72 Tom Keane	25.00	11.00	3.10
☐ 73 Hugh Taylor	25.00	11.00	3.10
☐ 74 Warren Lahr	25.00	11.00	3.10
☐ 75 Jim Neal	25.00	11.00	3.10
☐ 76 Leo Nomellini	60.00	27.00	7.50
☐ 77 Dick Yelvington	25.00	11.00	3.10
☐ 78 Les Richter	25.00	11.00	3.10
☐ 79 Bucko Kilroy	25.00	11.00	3.10
☐ 80 John Martinkovic	25.00	11.00	3.10
☐ 81 Dale Dodrill	25.00	11.00	3.10
☐ 82 Ken Jackson	25.00	11.00	3.10
☐ 83 Paul Lipscomb	25.00	11.00	3.10
☐ 84 John Bauer	25.00	11.00	3.10
☐ 85 Lou Creekmur	45.00	20.00	5.50
☐ 86 Eddie Price	25.00	11.00	3.10
☐ 87 Kenneth Farragut	25.00	11.00	3.10
☐ 88 Dave Hanner	25.00	11.00	3.10
☐ 89 Don Boll	25.00	11.00	3.10

90 Chet Hanulak	25.00	11.00	3.10
91 Thurman McGraw	25.00	11.00	3.10
92 Don Heinrich	25.00	11.00	3.10
93 Dan McKown	25.00	11.00	3.10
94 Bob Fleck	25.00	11.00	3.10
95 Jerry Hilgenberg	25.00	11.00	3.10
96 Bill Walsh	25.00	11.00	3.10
97A Tom Finnin ERR	60.00	27.00	7.50
97B Tom Finnan COR	8.00	3.60	1.00
98 Paul Barry	5.00	2.20	.60
99 Chick Jagade	5.00	2.20	.60
100 Jack Christiansen	20.00	9.00	2.50
101 Gordy Soltau	5.00	2.20	.60
102 Emlen Tunnell	20.00	9.00	2.50
103 Stan West	5.00	2.20	.60
104 Jerry Williams	5.00	2.20	.60
105 Veryl Switzer	5.00	2.20	.60
106 Billy Stone	5.00	2.20	.60
107 Jerry Watford	5.00	2.20	.60
108 Elbert Nickel	8.00	3.60	1.00
109 Ed Sharkey	5.00	2.20	.60
110 Steve Meilinger	5.00	2.20	.60
111 Dante Lavelli	20.00	9.00	2.50
112 Leon Hart	8.00	3.60	1.00
113 Charley Conerly	30.00	13.50	3.70
114 Richard Lemmon	5.00	2.20	.60
115 Al Carmichael	5.00	2.20	.60
116 George Connor	20.00	9.00	2.50
117 John Olszewski	5.00	2.20	.60
118 Ernie Stautner	20.00	9.00	2.50
119 Ray Smith	5.00	2.20	.60
120 Neil Worden	5.00	2.20	.60
121 Jim Dooley	5.00	2.20	.60
122 Arnold Galiffa	5.00	2.20	.60
123 Kline Gilbert	5.00	2.20	.60
124 Bob Hoernschemeyer	8.00	3.60	1.00
125 Wilford Whizzer White	14.00	6.25	1.75
126 Art Spinney	5.00	2.20	.60
127 Joe Koch	5.00	2.20	.60
128 John Lattner	80.00	20.00	6.50

1955 Bowman

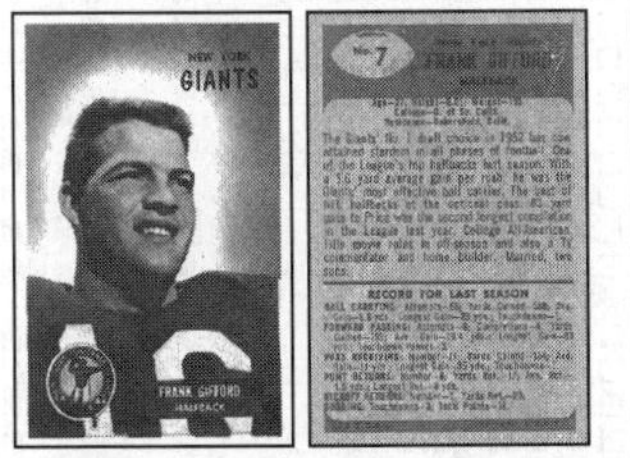

The 1955 Bowman set of 160 cards was Bowman's last sports issue before the company was purchased by Topps in January of 1956. Cards were issued in seven-card, five-cent packs and one-card penny packs. The cards measure approximately 2 1/2" by 3 3/4". The fronts contain player photos with player name and team logo at the bottom. The team name appears at the top. Card backs are printed in red and blue on gray card stock. Information includes, a write-up and previous year's stats. On the bottom of most of the card backs is a play diagram. Cards 65-160 are slightly more difficult to obtain. The notable Rookie Cards in this set are Alan Ameche, Len Ford, Frank Gatski, John Henry Johnson, Mike McCormack, Jim Ringo, Bob St. Clair, and Pat Summerall.

	NRMT	VG-E	GOOD
COMPLETE SET (160)	1600.00	700.00	200.00
COMMON CARD (1-64)	5.00	2.20	.60
COMMON CARD (65-160)	7.00	3.10	.85
WRAPPER (1-CENT)	200.00	90.00	25.00
WRAPPER (5-CENT)	75.00	34.00	9.50

1 Doak Walker	55.00	14.00	4.40
2 Mike McCormack	30.00	13.50	3.70
3 John Olszewski	5.00	2.20	.60
4 Dorne Dibble	5.00	2.20	.60
5 Lindon Crow	5.00	2.20	.60
6 Hugh Taylor UER (First word in bio should be Bones)	8.00	3.60	1.00
7 Frank Gifford	70.00	32.00	8.75
8 Alan Ameche	35.00	16.00	4.40
9 Don Stonesifer	5.00	2.20	.60
10 Pete Pihos	16.00	7.25	2.00
11 Bill Austin	5.00	2.20	.60
12 Dick Alban	5.00	2.20	.60
13 Bobby Walston	8.00	3.60	1.00
14 Len Ford	35.00	16.00	4.40
15 Jug Girard	5.00	2.20	.60
16 Charley Conerly	25.00	11.00	3.10
17 Volney Peters	5.00	2.20	.60
18 Max Boydston	5.00	2.20	.60
19 Leon Hart	8.00	3.60	1.00
20 Bert Rechichar	5.00	2.20	.60
21 Lee Riley	5.00	2.20	.60
22 Johnny Carson	5.00	2.20	.60
23 Harry Thompson	5.00	2.20	.60
24 Ray Wietecha	5.00	2.20	.60
25 Ollie Matson	25.00	11.00	3.10
26 Eddie LeBaron	12.00	5.50	1.50
27 Jack Simmons	5.00	2.20	.60
28 Jack Christiansen	16.00	7.25	2.00
29 Bucko Kilroy	8.00	3.60	1.00
30 Tom Keane	5.00	2.20	.60
31 Dave Leggett	5.00	2.20	.60
32 Norm Van Brocklin	35.00	16.00	4.40
33 Harlon Hill	8.00	3.60	1.00
34 Robert Haner	5.00	2.20	.60
35 Veryl Switzer	5.00	2.20	.60
36 Dick Stanfel	8.00	3.60	1.00
37 Lou Groza	25.00	11.00	3.10
38 Tank Younger	8.00	3.60	1.00
39 Dick Flanagan	5.00	2.20	.60
40 Jim Dooley	5.00	2.20	.60
41 Ray Collins	5.00	2.20	.60
42 John Henry Johnson	35.00	16.00	4.40
43 Tom Fears	16.00	7.25	2.00
44 Joe Perry	30.00	13.50	3.70
45 Gene Brito	5.00	2.20	.60
46 Bill Johnson	5.00	2.20	.60
47 Deacon Dan Towler	8.00	3.60	1.00
48 Dick Moegle	8.00	3.60	1.00
49 Kline Gilbert	5.00	2.20	.60
50 Les Gobel	5.00	2.20	.60
51 Ray Krouse	5.00	2.20	.60
52 Pat Summerall	60.00	27.00	7.50
53 Ed Brown	8.00	3.60	1.00
54 Lynn Chandnois	5.00	2.20	.60
55 Joe Heap	5.00	2.20	.60
56 John Hoffman	5.00	2.20	.60
57 Howard Ferguson	5.00	2.20	.60
58 Bobby Watkins	5.00	2.20	.60
59 Charlie Ane	5.00	2.20	.60
60 Ken MacAfee	8.00	3.60	1.00
61 Ralph Guglielmi	8.00	3.60	1.00
62 George Blanda	65.00	29.00	8.00
63 Kenneth Snyder	5.00	2.20	.60
64 Chet Ostrowski	5.00	2.20	.60
65 Buddy Young	10.00	4.50	1.25
66 Gordy Soltau	7.00	3.10	.85
67 Eddie Bell	7.00	3.10	.85
68 Ben Agajanian	10.00	4.50	1.25
69 Tom Dahms	7.00	3.10	.85
70 Jim Ringo	45.00	20.00	5.50
71 Bobby Layne	70.00	32.00	8.75
72 Y.A. Tittle	60.00	27.00	7.50
73 Bob Gaona	7.00	3.10	.85
74 Tobin Rote	10.00	4.50	1.25
75 Hugh McElhenny	30.00	13.50	3.70
76 John Kreamcheck	7.00	3.10	.85
77 Al Dorow	10.00	4.50	1.25
78 Bill Wade	12.00	5.50	1.50
79 Dale Dodrill	7.00	3.10	.85
80 Chuck Drazenovich	7.00	3.10	.85
81 Billy Wilson	10.00	4.50	1.25
82 Les Richter	10.00	4.50	1.25
83 Pat Brady	7.00	3.10	.85
84 Bob Hoernschemeyer	10.00	4.50	1.25
85 Joe Arenas	7.00	3.10	.85
86 Len Szafaryn UER (Listed as Ben on front)	7.00	3.10	.85
87 Rick Casares	18.00	8.00	2.20
88 Leon McLaughlin	7.00	3.10	.85
89 Charley Toogood	7.00	3.10	.85
90 Tom Bettis	7.00	3.10	.85
91 John Sandusky	7.00	3.10	.85
92 Bill Wightkin	7.00	3.10	.85
93 Darrell Brewster	7.00	3.10	.85
94 Marion Campbell	10.00	4.50	1.25
95 Floyd Reid	7.00	3.10	.85
96 Chick Jagade	7.00	3.10	.85
97 George Taliaferro	7.00	3.10	.85
98 Carlton Massey	7.00	3.10	.85
99 Fran Rogel	7.00	3.10	.85
100 Alex Sandusky	7.00	3.10	.85
101 Bob St. Clair	35.00	16.00	4.40
102 Al Carmichael	7.00	3.10	.85
103 Carl Taseff	7.00	3.10	.85
104 Leo Nomellini	20.00	9.00	2.50
105 Tom Scott	7.00	3.10	.85
106 Ted Marchibroda	15.00	6.75	1.85
107 Art Spinney	7.00	3.10	.85
108 Wayne Robinson	7.00	3.10	.85
109 Jim Ricca	7.00	3.10	.85
110 Lou Ferry	7.00	3.10	.85
111 Roger Zatkoff	7.00	3.10	.85
112 Lou Creekmur	16.00	7.25	2.00
113 Kenny Konz	7.00	3.10	.85
114 Doug Eggers	7.00	3.10	.85
115 Bobby Thomason	7.00	3.10	.85
116 Bill McPeak	7.00	3.10	.85
117 William Brown	7.00	3.10	.85
118 Royce Womble	7.00	3.10	.85
119 Frank Gatski	30.00	13.50	3.70
120 Jim Finks	15.00	6.75	1.85
121 Andy Robustelli	20.00	9.00	2.50
122 Bobby Dillon	7.00	3.10	.85
123 Leo Sanford	7.00	3.10	.85
124 Elbert Nickel	10.00	4.50	1.25
125 Wayne Hansen	7.00	3.10	.85
126 Buck Lansford	7.00	3.10	.85
127 Gern Nagler	7.00	3.10	.85
128 Jim Salsbury	7.00	3.10	.85
129 Dale Atkeson	7.00	3.10	.85
130 John Schweder	7.00	3.10	.85
131 Dave Hanner	7.00	3.10	.85
132 Eddie Price	7.00	3.10	.85
133 Vic Janowicz	25.00	11.00	3.10
134 Ernie Stautner	20.00	9.00	2.50
135 James Parmer	7.00	3.10	.85
136 Emlen Tunnell UER (Misspelled Tunnel on card front)	20.00	9.00	2.50
137 Kyle Rote UER (Longest gain 1.8 yards, should be 18 yards)	15.00	6.75	1.85
138 Norm Willey	7.00	3.10	.85
139 Charley Trippi	20.00	9.00	2.50
140 Billy Howton	10.00	4.50	1.25
141 Bobby Clatterbuck	7.00	3.10	.85
142 Bob Boyd	7.00	3.10	.85
143 Bob Toneff	7.00	3.10	.85
144 Jerry Helluin	7.00	3.10	.85
145 Adrian Burk	7.00	3.10	.85
146 Walt Michaels	10.00	4.50	1.25
147 Zollie Toth	7.00	3.10	.85
148 Frank Varrichione	7.00	3.10	.85
149 Dick Bielski	7.00	3.10	.85
150 George Ratterman	10.00	4.50	1.25
151 Mike Jarmoluk	7.00	3.10	.85
152 Tom Landry	180.00	80.00	22.00
153 Ray Renfro	10.00	4.50	1.25
154 Zeke Bratkowski	10.00	4.50	1.25
155 Jerry Norton	7.00	3.10	.85
156 Maurice Bassett	7.00	3.10	.85
157 Volney Quinlan	7.00	3.10	.85
158 Chuck Bednarik	30.00	13.50	3.70
159 Don Colo	7.00	3.10	.85
160 L.G. Dupre	35.00	8.75	2.80

1991 Bowman

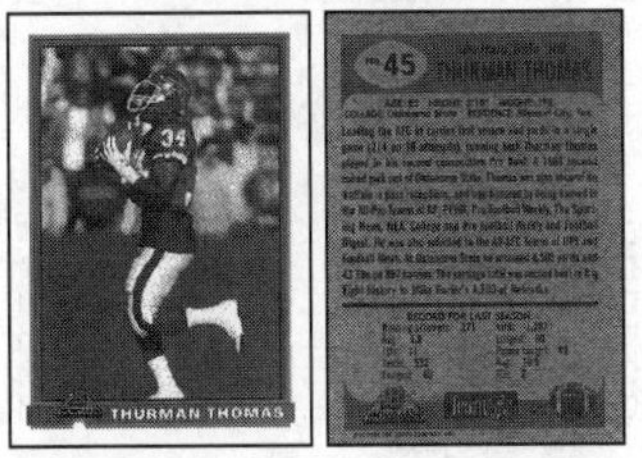

Resurrected by Topps after a 36 year hiatus, Bowman returned to the football card playing field with a 561-card standard-size set. The cards retain some of the qualities from early Bowman products. The fronts feature color player photos with the player's name and Bowman logo at the bottom. As far as layout, the backs resemble those of the 1950s. They are printed in black and green on gray and have a write-up, bio and stats from the previous season. The cards are checklisted below alphabetically according to teams. Subsets include Rookie Superstars (1-11), League Leaders (273-283) and Road to Super Bowl XXV (547-557). Rookie Cards include Alvin Harper, Randal Hill, Derek Loville, Herman Moore, Mike Pritchard, Ricky Watters, and Harvey Williams.

	MINT	NRMT	EXC
COMPLETE SET (561)	12.00	5.50	1.50
COMPLETE FACT.SET (561)	14.00	6.25	1.75
COMMON CARD (1-561)	.04	.02	.01

1 Jeff George RS	.25	.11	.03
2 Richmond Webb RS	.04	.02	.01
3 Emmitt Smith RS	1.00	.45	.12
4 Mark Carrier DB RS UER (Chambers was rookie in '73, not '74)	.04	.02	.01
5 Steve Christie RS	.04	.02	.01
6 Keith Sims RS	.04	.02	.01
7 Rob Moore RS UER (Yards misspelled as yarders on back)	.25	.11	.03
8 Johnny Johnson RS	.04	.02	.01
9 Eric Green RS	.04	.02	.01
10 Ben Smith RS	.04	.02	.01
11 Tory Epps RS	.04	.02	.01
12 Andre Rison	.10	.05	.01
13 Shawn Collins	.04	.02	.01
14 Chris Hinton	.04	.02	.01
15 Deion Sanders UER (Bio says he played for Georgia, College listed should be Florida State)	.60	.25	.07
16 Darion Conner	.04	.02	.01
17 Michael Haynes	.25	.11	.03
18 Chris Miller	.10	.05	.01
19 Jessie Tuggle	.04	.02	.01
20 Scott Fulhage	.04	.02	.01
21 Bill Fralic	.04	.02	.01
22 Floyd Dixon	.04	.02	.01
23 Oliver Barnett	.04	.02	.01
24 Mike Rozier	.04	.02	.01
25 Tory Epps	.04	.02	.01
26 Tim Green	.04	.02	.01
27 Steve Broussard	.04	.02	.01
28 Bruce Pickens	.04	.02	.01
29 Mike Pritchard	.25	.11	.03
30 Andre Reed	.10	.05	.01
31 Darryl Talley	.04	.02	.01
32 Nate Odomes	.04	.02	.01
33 Jamie Mueller	.04	.02	.01
34 Leon Seals	.04	.02	.01
35 Keith McKeller	.04	.02	.01
36 Al Edwards	.04	.02	.01
37 Butch Rolle	.04	.02	.01
38 Jeff Wright	.04	.02	.01
39 Will Wolford	.04	.02	.01
40 James Williams	.04	.02	.01
41 Kent Hull	.04	.02	.01
42 James Lofton	.10	.05	.01
43 Frank Reich	.10	.05	.01
44 Bruce Smith	.25	.11	.03
45 Thurman Thomas	.25	.11	.03
46 Leonard Smith	.04	.02	.01
47 Shane Conlan	.04	.02	.01
48 Steve Tasker	.10	.05	.01
49 Ray Bentley	.04	.02	.01
50 Cornelius Bennett	.10	.05	.01
51 Stan Thomas	.04	.02	.01
52 Shaun Gayle	.04	.02	.01
53 Wendell Davis	.04	.02	.01
54 James Thornton	.04	.02	.01
55 Mark Carrier DB	.10	.05	.01
56 Richard Dent	.10	.05	.01
57 Ron Morris	.04	.02	.01
58 Mike Singletary	.10	.05	.01
59 Jay Hilgenberg	.04	.02	.01
60 Donnell Woolford	.04	.02	.01
61 Jim Covert	.04	.02	.01
62 Jim Harbaugh	.25	.11	.03
63 Neal Anderson	.10	.05	.01
64 Brad Muster	.04	.02	.01
65 Kevin Butler	.04	.02	.01
66 Trace Armstrong UER (Bio says 80 tackles in '90, stats say 82)	.04	.02	.01
67 Ron Cox	.04	.02	.01
68 Peter Tom Willis	.04	.02	.01
69 Johnny Bailey	.04	.02	.01
70 Mark Bortz UER (Bio has 6th round, but was 8th round)	.04	.02	.01
71 Chris Zorich	.25	.11	.03
72 Lamar Rogers	.04	.02	.01
73 David Grant UER (Listed as DE, but should be NT)	.04	.02	.01
74 Lewis Billups	.04	.02	.01
75 Harold Green	.10	.05	.01
76 Ickey Woods	.04	.02	.01
77 Eddie Brown	.04	.02	.01
78 David Fulcher	.04	.02	.01
79 Anthony Munoz	.10	.05	.01
80 Carl Zander	.04	.02	.01
81 Rodney Holman	.04	.02	.01
82 James Brooks	.10	.05	.01
83 Tim McGee	.04	.02	.01
84 Boomer Esiason	.10	.05	.01
85 Leon White	.04	.02	.01
86 James Francis UER (Ron is CB, card says he's LB)	.04	.02	.01
87 Mitchell Price	.04	.02	.01
88 Ed King	.04	.02	.01
89 Eric Turner	.10	.05	.01
90 Rob Burnett	.04	.02	.01
91 Leroy Hoard	.10	.05	.01
92 Kevin Mack UER (Height 6-2, should be 6-0)	.04	.02	.01
93 Thane Gash UER (Comma omitted after name in bio)	.04	.02	.01
94 Gregg Rakoczy	.04	.02	.01
95 Clay Matthews	.10	.05	.01
96 Eric Metcalf	.10	.05	.01
97 Stephen Braggs	.04	.02	.01
98 Frank Minnifield	.04	.02	.01
99 Reggie Langhorne	.04	.02	.01
100 Mike Johnson	.04	.02	.01
101 Brian Brennan	.04	.02	.01
102 Anthony Pleasant	.04	.02	.01
103 Godfrey Myles UER (Vertical misspelled as verticle)	.04	.02	.01
104 Russell Maryland	.25	.11	.03
105 James Washington	.04	.02	.01
106 Nate Newton	.10	.05	.01
107 Jimmie Jones	.04	.02	.01
108 Jay Novacek	.25	.11	.03
109 Alexander Wright	.04	.02	.01
110 Jack Del Rio	.04	.02	.01
111 Jim Jeffcoat	.04	.02	.01
112 Mike Saxon	.04	.02	.01
113 Troy Aikman	1.00	.45	.12
114 Issiac Holt	.04	.02	.01
115 Ken Norton	.25	.11	.03
116 Kelvin Martin	.04	.02	.01
117 Emmitt Smith	2.00	.90	.25
118 Ken Willis	.04	.02	.01
119 Daniel Stubbs	.04	.02	.01
120 Michael Irvin	.25	.11	.03
121 Danny Noonan	.04	.02	.01
122 Alvin Harper UER	.25	.11	.03

(Drafted in first round, not second)			
☐ 123 Reggie Johnson	.04	.02	.01
☐ 124 Vance Johnson	.04	.02	.01
☐ 125 Steve Atwater	.04	.02	.01
☐ 126 Greg Kragen	.04	.02	.01
☐ 127 John Elway	.75	.35	.09
☐ 128 Simon Fletcher	.04	.02	.01
☐ 129 Wymon Henderson	.04	.02	.01
☐ 130 Ricky Nattiel	.04	.02	.01
☐ 131 Shannon Sharpe	.50	.23	.06
☐ 132 Ron Holmes	.04	.02	.01
☐ 133 Karl Mecklenburg	.04	.02	.01
☐ 134 Bobby Humphrey	.04	.02	.01
☐ 135 Clarence Kay	.04	.02	.01
☐ 136 Dennis Smith	.04	.02	.01
☐ 137 Jim Juriga	.04	.02	.01
☐ 138 Melvin Bratton	.04	.02	.01
☐ 139 Mark Jackson UER	.04	.02	.01
(Apostrophe placed in front of longest)			
☐ 140 Michael Brooks	.04	.02	.01
☐ 141 Alton Montgomery	.04	.02	.01
☐ 142 Mike Croel	.04	.02	.01
☐ 143 Mel Gray	.10	.05	.01
☐ 144 Michael Cofer	.04	.02	.01
☐ 145 Jeff Campbell	.04	.02	.01
☐ 146 Dan Owens	.04	.02	.01
☐ 147 Robert Clark UER	.04	.02	.01
(Drafted in '87, not '89)			
☐ 148 Jim Arnold	.04	.02	.01
☐ 149 William White	.04	.02	.01
☐ 150 Rodney Peete	.10	.05	.01
☐ 151 Jerry Ball	.04	.02	.01
☐ 152 Bennie Blades	.04	.02	.01
☐ 153 Barry Sanders UER	1.00	.45	.12
(Drafted in '89, not '88)			
☐ 154 Andre Ware	.10	.05	.01
☐ 155 Lomas Brown	.04	.02	.01
☐ 156 Chris Spielman	.10	.05	.01
☐ 157 Kelvin Pritchett	.10	.05	.01
☐ 158 Herman Moore	2.00	.90	.25
☐ 159 Chris Jacke	.04	.02	.01
☐ 160 Tony Mandarich	.04	.02	.01
☐ 161 Perry Kemp	.04	.02	.01
☐ 162 Johnny Holland	.04	.02	.01
☐ 163 Mark Lee	.04	.02	.01
☐ 164 Anthony Dilweg	.04	.02	.01
☐ 165 Scott Stephen	.04	.02	.01
☐ 166 Ed West	.04	.02	.01
☐ 167 Mark Murphy	.04	.02	.01
☐ 168 Darrell Thompson	.04	.02	.01
☐ 169 James Campen	.04	.02	.01
☐ 170 Jeff Query	.04	.02	.01
☐ 171 Brian Noble	.04	.02	.01
☐ 172 Sterling Sharpe UER	.25	.11	.03
(Card says he gained 3314 yards in 1990)			
☐ 173 Robert Brown	.04	.02	.01
☐ 174 Tim Harris	.04	.02	.01
☐ 175 LeRoy Butler	.10	.05	.01
☐ 176 Don Majkowski	.04	.02	.01
☐ 177 Vinnie Clark	.04	.02	.01
☐ 178 Esera Tuaolo	.04	.02	.01
☐ 179 Lorenzo White UER	.04	.02	.01
(Bio says 3rd year, actually 4th year)			
☐ 180 Warren Moon	.25	.11	.03
☐ 181 Sean Jones	.10	.05	.01
☐ 182 Curtis Duncan	.04	.02	.01
☐ 183 Al Smith	.04	.02	.01
☐ 184 Richard Johnson	.04	.02	.01
☐ 185 Tony Jones	.10	.05	.01
☐ 186 Bubba McDowell	.04	.02	.01
☐ 187 Bruce Matthews	.10	.05	.01
☐ 188 Ray Childress	.04	.02	.01
☐ 189 Haywood Jeffires	.10	.05	.01
☐ 190 Ernest Givins	.10	.05	.01
☐ 191 Mike Munchak	.04	.02	.01
☐ 192 Greg Montgomery	.04	.02	.01
☐ 193 Cody Carlson	.04	.02	.01
☐ 194 Johnny Meads	.04	.02	.01
☐ 195 Drew Hill UER	.04	.02	.01
(Age listed as 24, should be 34)			
☐ 196 Mike Dumas	.04	.02	.01
☐ 197 Darryll Lewis	.10	.05	.01
☐ 198 Rohn Stark	.04	.02	.01
☐ 199 Clarence Verdin UER	.04	.02	.01
(Played 2 seasons in USFL, not one)			
☐ 200 Mike Prior	.04	.02	.01
☐ 201 Eugene Daniel	.04	.02	.01
☐ 202 Dean Biasucci	.04	.02	.01
☐ 203 Jeff Herrod	.04	.02	.01
☐ 204 Keith Taylor	.04	.02	.01
☐ 205 Jon Hand	.04	.02	.01
☐ 206 Pat Beach	.04	.02	.01
☐ 207 Duane Bickett	.04	.02	.01
☐ 208 Jessie Hester UER	.04	.02	.01
(Bio confuses Hester's NFL history)			
☐ 209 Chip Banks	.04	.02	.01
☐ 210 Ray Donaldson	.04	.02	.01
☐ 211 Bill Brooks	.04	.02	.01
☐ 212 Jeff George	.25	.11	.03
☐ 213 Tony Siragusa	.04	.02	.01
☐ 214 Albert Bentley	.04	.02	.01
☐ 215 Joe Valerio	.04	.02	.01
☐ 216 Chris Martin	.04	.02	.01
☐ 217 Christian Okoye	.04	.02	.01
☐ 218 Stephone Paige	.04	.02	.01
☐ 219 Percy Snow	.04	.02	.01
☐ 220 David Szott	.04	.02	.01
☐ 221 Derrick Thomas	.25	.11	.03
☐ 222 Todd McNair	.04	.02	.01
☐ 223 Albert Lewis	.04	.02	.01
☐ 224 Neil Smith	.25	.11	.03
☐ 225 Barry Word	.04	.02	.01
☐ 226 Robb Thomas	.04	.02	.01
☐ 227 John Alt	.04	.02	.01
☐ 228 Jonathan Hayes	.04	.02	.01
☐ 229 Kevin Ross	.04	.02	.01
☐ 230 Nick Lowery	.04	.02	.01
☐ 231 Tim Grunhard	.04	.02	.01
☐ 232 Dan Saleaumua	.04	.02	.01
☐ 233 Steve DeBerg	.04	.02	.01
☐ 234 Harvey Williams	.25	.11	.03
☐ 235 Nick Bell UER	.04	.02	.01
(Lives in Nevada, not California)			
☐ 236 Mervyn Fernandez UER	.04	.02	.01
(Drafted in '83, not FA '87 as on card)			
☐ 237 Howie Long	.10	.05	.01
☐ 238 Marcus Allen	.25	.11	.03
☐ 239 Eddie Anderson	.04	.02	.01
☐ 240 Ethan Horton	.04	.02	.01
☐ 241 Lionel Washington	.04	.02	.01
☐ 242 Steve Wisniewski UER	.04	.02	.01
(Drafted, should be traded to)			
☐ 243 Bo Jackson UER	.25	.11	.03
(Drafted by Raiders, should say drafted by Tampa Bay in '86)			
☐ 244 Greg Townsend	.04	.02	.01
☐ 245 Jeff Jaeger	.04	.02	.01
☐ 246 Aaron Wallace	.04	.02	.01
☐ 247 Garry Lewis	.04	.02	.01
☐ 248 Steve Smith	.04	.02	.01
☐ 249 Willie Gault UER	.04	.02	.01
('90 stats 839 yards, should be 985)			
☐ 250 Scott Davis	.04	.02	.01
☐ 251 Jay Schroeder	.04	.02	.01
☐ 252 Don Mosebar	.04	.02	.01
☐ 253 Todd Marinovich	.04	.02	.01
☐ 254 Irv Pankey	.04	.02	.01
☐ 255 Flipper Anderson	.04	.02	.01
☐ 256 Tom Newberry	.04	.02	.01
☐ 257 Kevin Greene	.25	.11	.03
☐ 258 Mike Wilcher	.04	.02	.01
☐ 259 Bern Brostek	.04	.02	.01
☐ 260 Buford McGee	.04	.02	.01
☐ 261 Cleveland Gary	.04	.02	.01
☐ 262 Jackie Slater	.04	.02	.01
☐ 263 Henry Ellard	.10	.05	.01
☐ 264 Alvin Wright	.04	.02	.01
☐ 265 Darryl Henley	.04	.02	.01
☐ 266 Damone Johnson	.04	.02	.01
☐ 267 Frank Stams	.04	.02	.01
☐ 268 Jerry Gray	.04	.02	.01
☐ 269 Jim Everett	.10	.05	.01
☐ 270 Pat Terrell	.04	.02	.01
☐ 271 Todd Lyght	.04	.02	.01
☐ 272 Aaron Cox	.04	.02	.01
☐ 273 Barry Sanders LL	.50	.23	.06
Rushing Leader			
☐ 274 Jerry Rice LL	.50	.23	.06
Receiving Leader			
☐ 275 Derrick Thomas LL	.25	.11	.03
Sack Leader			
☐ 276 Mark Carrier DB LL	.10	.05	.01
Interception Leader			
☐ 277 Warren Moon LL	.25	.11	.03
Passing Yardage Leader			
☐ 278 Randall Cunningham LL	.10	.05	.01
Rushing Average Leader			
☐ 279 Nick Lowery LL	.04	.02	.01
Scoring Leader			
☐ 280 Clarence Verdin LL	.04	.02	.01
Punt Return Leader			
☐ 281 Thurman Thomas LL	.25	.11	.03
Yards From Scrimmage Leader			
☐ 282 Mike Horan LL	.04	.02	.01
Punting Average Leader			
☐ 283 Flipper Anderson LL	.04	.02	.01
Receiving Average Leader			
☐ 284 John Offerdahl	.04	.02	.01
☐ 285 Dan Marino UER	1.50	.70	.19
(2637 yards gained, should be 3563)			
☐ 286 Mark Clayton	.10	.05	.01
☐ 287 Tony Paige	.04	.02	.01
☐ 288 Keith Sims	.04	.02	.01
☐ 289 Jeff Cross	.04	.02	.01
☐ 290 Pete Stoyanovich	.04	.02	.01
☐ 291 Ferrell Edmunds	.04	.02	.01
☐ 292 Reggie Roby	.04	.02	.01
☐ 293 Louis Oliver	.04	.02	.01
☐ 294 Jarvis Williams	.04	.02	.01
☐ 295 Sammie Smith	.04	.02	.01
☐ 296 Richmond Webb	.04	.02	.01
☐ 297 J.B. Brown	.04	.02	.01
☐ 298 Jim C.Jensen	.04	.02	.01
☐ 299 Mark Duper	.10	.05	.01
☐ 300 David Griggs	.04	.02	.01
☐ 301 Randal Hill	.10	.05	.01
☐ 302 Aaron Craver	.04	.02	.01
(See also 320)			
☐ 303 Keith Millard	.04	.02	.01
☐ 304 Steve Jordan	.04	.02	.01
☐ 305 Anthony Carter	.10	.05	.01
☐ 306 Mike Merriweather	.04	.02	.01
☐ 307 Audray McMillian UER	.04	.02	.01
(Front Audray, back Audrey)			
☐ 308 Randall McDaniel	.04	.02	.01
☐ 309 Gary Zimmerman	.04	.02	.01
☐ 310 Carl Lee	.04	.02	.01
☐ 311 Reggie Rutland	.04	.02	.01
☐ 312 Hassan Jones	.04	.02	.01
☐ 313 Kirk Lowdermilk UER	.04	.02	.01
(Reversed negative)			
☐ 314 Herschel Walker	.10	.05	.01
☐ 315 Chris Doleman	.04	.02	.01
☐ 316 Joey Browner	.04	.02	.01
☐ 317 Wade Wilson	.10	.05	.01
☐ 318 Henry Thomas	.04	.02	.01
☐ 319 Rich Gannon	.04	.02	.01
☐ 320 Al Noga UER	.04	.02	.01
(Numbered incorrectly as 302 on card)			
☐ 321 Pat Harlow	.04	.02	.01
☐ 322 Bruce Armstrong	.04	.02	.01
☐ 323 Maurice Hurst	.04	.02	.01
☐ 324 Brent Williams	.04	.02	.01
☐ 325 Chris Singleton	.04	.02	.01
☐ 326 Jason Staurovsky	.04	.02	.01
☐ 327 Marvin Allen	.04	.02	.01
☐ 328 Hart Lee Dykes	.04	.02	.01
☐ 329 Johnny Rembert	.04	.02	.01
☐ 330 Andre Tippett	.04	.02	.01
☐ 331 Greg McMurtry	.04	.02	.01
☐ 332 John Stephens	.04	.02	.01
☐ 333 Ray Agnew	.04	.02	.01
☐ 334 Tommy Hodson	.04	.02	.01
☐ 335 Ronnie Lippett	.04	.02	.01
☐ 336 Marv Cook	.04	.02	.01
☐ 337 Tommy Barnhardt	.04	.02	.01
☐ 338 Dalton Hilliard	.04	.02	.01
☐ 339 Sam Mills	.04	.02	.01
☐ 340 Morten Andersen	.04	.02	.01
☐ 341 Stan Brock	.04	.02	.01
☐ 342 Brett Maxie	.04	.02	.01
☐ 343 Steve Walsh	.04	.02	.01
☐ 344 Vaughan Johnson	.04	.02	.01
☐ 345 Rickey Jackson	.04	.02	.01
☐ 346 Renaldo Turnbull	.04	.02	.01
☐ 347 Joel Hilgenberg	.04	.02	.01
☐ 348 Toi Cook	.04	.02	.01
☐ 349 Robert Massey	.04	.02	.01
☐ 350 Pat Swilling	.10	.05	.01
☐ 351 Eric Martin	.04	.02	.01
☐ 352 Rueben Mayes UER	.04	.02	.01
(Bio says 2nd round, should be 3rd)			
☐ 353 Vince Buck	.04	.02	.01
☐ 354 Brett Perriman	.25	.11	.03
☐ 355 Wesley Carroll	.04	.02	.01
☐ 356 Jarrod Bunch	.04	.02	.01
☐ 357 Pepper Johnson	.04	.02	.01
☐ 358 Dave Meggett	.10	.05	.01
☐ 359 Mark Collins	.04	.02	.01
☐ 360 Sean Landeta	.04	.02	.01
☐ 361 Maurice Carthon	.04	.02	.01
☐ 362 Mike Fox UER	.04	.02	.01
(Listed as DE, should say DT)			
☐ 363 Jeff Hostetler	.10	.05	.01
☐ 364 Phil Simms	.10	.05	.01
☐ 365 Leonard Marshall	.04	.02	.01
☐ 366 Gary Reasons	.04	.02	.01
☐ 367 Rodney Hampton	.25	.11	.03
☐ 368 Greg Jackson	.04	.02	.01
☐ 369 Jumbo Elliott	.04	.02	.01
☐ 370 Bob Kratch	.04	.02	.01
☐ 371 Lawrence Taylor	.25	.11	.03
☐ 372 Erik Howard	.04	.02	.01
☐ 373 Carl Banks	.04	.02	.01
☐ 374 Stephen Baker	.04	.02	.01
☐ 375 Mark Ingram	.10	.05	.01
☐ 376 Browning Nagle	.04	.02	.01
☐ 377 Jeff Lageman	.04	.02	.01
☐ 378 Ken O'Brien	.04	.02	.01
☐ 379 Al Toon	.10	.05	.01
☐ 380 Joe Prokop	.04	.02	.01
☐ 381 Tony Stargell	.04	.02	.01
☐ 382 Blair Thomas	.04	.02	.01
☐ 383 Erik McMillan	.04	.02	.01
☐ 384 Dennis Byrd	.04	.02	.01
☐ 385 Freeman McNeil	.04	.02	.01
☐ 386 Brad Baxter	.04	.02	.01
☐ 387 Mark Boyer	.04	.02	.01
☐ 388 Terance Mathis	.10	.05	.01
☐ 389 Jim Sweeney	.04	.02	.01
☐ 390 Kyle Clifton	.04	.02	.01
☐ 391 Pat Leahy	.04	.02	.01
☐ 392 Rob Moore	.25	.11	.03
☐ 393 James Hasty	.04	.02	.01
☐ 394 Blaise Bryant	.04	.02	.01
☐ 395A Jesse Campbell ERR	1.00	.45	.12
(Photo actually Dan McGwire; see 509)			
☐ 395B Jesse Campbell COR	.04	.02	.01
☐ 396 Keith Jackson	.10	.05	.01
☐ 397 Jerome Brown	.04	.02	.01
☐ 398 Keith Byars	.04	.02	.01
☐ 399 Seth Joyner	.10	.05	.01
☐ 400 Mike Bellamy	.04	.02	.01
☐ 401 Fred Barnett	.25	.11	.03
☐ 402 Reggie Singletary	.04	.02	.01
☐ 403 Reggie White	.25	.11	.03
☐ 404 Randall Cunningham	.10	.05	.01
☐ 405 Byron Evans	.04	.02	.01
☐ 406 Wes Hopkins	.04	.02	.01
☐ 407 Ben Smith	.04	.02	.01
☐ 408 Roger Ruzek	.04	.02	.01
☐ 409 Eric Allen UER	.04	.02	.01
(Comparative misspelled as comparate)			
☐ 410 Anthony Toney UER	.04	.02	.01
(Heath Sherman was rookie in '89, not '90)			
☐ 411 Clyde Simmons	.04	.02	.01
☐ 412 Andre Waters	.04	.02	.01
☐ 413 Calvin Williams	.10	.05	.01
☐ 414 Eric Swann	.25	.11	.03
☐ 415 Eric Hill	.04	.02	.01
☐ 416 Tim McDonald	.04	.02	.01
☐ 417 Luis Sharpe	.04	.02	.01
☐ 418 Ernie Jones UER	.04	.02	.01
(Photo actually Steve Jordan)			
☐ 419 Ken Harvey	.10	.05	.01
☐ 420 Ricky Proehl	.04	.02	.01
☐ 421 Johnny Johnson	.04	.02	.01
☐ 422 Anthony Bell	.04	.02	.01
☐ 423 Timm Rosenbach	.04	.02	.01
☐ 424 Rich Camarillo	.04	.02	.01
☐ 425 Walter Reeves	.04	.02	.01
☐ 426 Freddie Joe Nunn	.04	.02	.01
☐ 427 Anthony Thompson UER	.04	.02	.01
(40 touchdowns, sic)			
☐ 428 Bill Lewis	.04	.02	.01
☐ 429 Jim Wahler	.04	.02	.01
☐ 430 Cedric Mack	.04	.02	.01
☐ 431 Michael Jones	.04	.02	.01
☐ 432 Ernie Mills	.10	.05	.01
☐ 433 Tim Worley	.04	.02	.01
☐ 434 Greg Lloyd	.25	.11	.03
☐ 435 Dermontti Dawson	.04	.02	.01
☐ 436 Louis Lipps	.04	.02	.01
☐ 437 Eric Green	.04	.02	.01
☐ 438 Donald Evans	.04	.02	.01
☐ 439 D.J. Johnson	.04	.02	.01
☐ 440 Tunch Ilkin	.04	.02	.01
☐ 441 Bubby Brister	.04	.02	.01
☐ 442 Chris Calloway	.04	.02	.01
☐ 443 David Little	.04	.02	.01
☐ 444 Thomas Everett	.04	.02	.01
☐ 445 Carnell Lake	.04	.02	.01
☐ 446 Rod Woodson	.25	.11	.03
☐ 447 Gary Anderson K	.04	.02	.01
☐ 448 Merril Hoge	.04	.02	.01
☐ 449 Gerald Williams	.04	.02	.01
☐ 450 Eric Moten	.04	.02	.01
☐ 451 Marion Butts	.10	.05	.01
☐ 452 Leslie O'Neal	.10	.05	.01
☐ 453 Ronnie Harmon	.04	.02	.01
☐ 454 Gill Byrd	.04	.02	.01
☐ 455 Junior Seau	.40	.18	.05
☐ 456 Nate Lewis	.04	.02	.01
☐ 457 Leo Goeas	.04	.02	.01
☐ 458 Burt Grossman	.04	.02	.01
☐ 459 Courtney Hall	.04	.02	.01
☐ 460 Anthony Miller	.10	.05	.01
☐ 461 Gary Plummer	.04	.02	.01
☐ 462 Billy Joe Tolliver	.04	.02	.01
☐ 463 Lee Williams	.04	.02	.01
☐ 464 Arthur Cox	.04	.02	.01
☐ 465 John Kidd UER	.04	.02	.01
(Stron gleg, sic)			
☐ 466 Frank Cornish	.04	.02	.01
☐ 467 John Carney	.04	.02	.01
☐ 468 Eric Bieniemy	.04	.02	.01
☐ 469 Don Griffin	.04	.02	.01
☐ 470 Jerry Rice	1.00	.45	.12
☐ 471 Keith DeLong	.04	.02	.01
☐ 472 John Taylor	.10	.05	.01
☐ 473 Brent Jones	.25	.11	.03
☐ 474 Pierce Holt	.04	.02	.01
☐ 475 Kevin Fagan	.04	.02	.01
☐ 476 Bill Romanowski	.04	.02	.01
☐ 477 Dexter Carter	.04	.02	.01
☐ 478 Guy McIntyre	.04	.02	.01
☐ 479 Joe Montana	1.00	.45	.12

☐ 480 Charles Haley	.10	.05	.01
☐ 481 Mike Cofer	.04	.02	.01
☐ 482 Jesse Sapolu	.04	.02	.01
☐ 483 Eric Davis	.04	.02	.01
☐ 484 Mike Sherrard	.04	.02	.01
☐ 485 Steve Young	.75	.35	.09
☐ 486 Darryl Pollard	.04	.02	.01
☐ 487 Tom Rathman	.04	.02	.01
☐ 488 Michael Carter	.04	.02	.01
☐ 489 Ricky Watters	1.50	.70	.19
☐ 490 John Johnson	.04	.02	.01
☐ 491 Eugene Robinson	.04	.02	.01
☐ 492 Andy Heck	.04	.02	.01
☐ 493 John L. Williams	.04	.02	.01
☐ 494 Norm Johnson	.04	.02	.01
☐ 495 David Wyman	.04	.02	.01
☐ 496 Derrick Fenner UER (Drafted in '88, should be '89)	.04	.02	.01
☐ 497 Rick Donnelly	.04	.02	.01
☐ 498 Tony Woods	.04	.02	.01
☐ 499 Derek Loville UER (Ahmad Rashad is misspelled Ahmed)	.04	.02	.01
☐ 500 Dave Krieg	.10	.05	.01
☐ 501 Joe Nash	.04	.02	.01
☐ 502 Brian Blades	.10	.05	.01
☐ 503 Cortez Kennedy	.25	.11	.03
☐ 504 Jeff Bryant	.04	.02	.01
☐ 505 Tommy Kane	.04	.02	.01
☐ 506 Travis McNeal	.04	.02	.01
☐ 507 Terry Wooden	.04	.02	.01
☐ 508 Chris Warren	.40	.18	.05
☐ 509A Dan McGwire ERR (Photo actually Jesse Campbell; see 395)	.04	.02	.01
☐ 509B Dan McGwire COR	.04	.02	.01
☐ 510 Mark Robinson	.04	.02	.01
☐ 511 Ron Hall	.04	.02	.01
☐ 512 Paul Gruber	.04	.02	.01
☐ 513 Harry Hamilton	.04	.02	.01
☐ 514 Keith McCants	.04	.02	.01
☐ 515 Reggie Cobb	.04	.02	.01
☐ 516 Steve Christie UER (Listed as Californian, should be Canadian)	.04	.02	.01
☐ 517 Broderick Thomas	.04	.02	.01
☐ 518 Mark Carrier WR	.25	.11	.03
☐ 519 Vinny Testaverde	.10	.05	.01
☐ 520 Ricky Reynolds	.04	.02	.01
☐ 521 Jesse Anderson	.04	.02	.01
☐ 522 Reuben Davis	.04	.02	.01
☐ 523 Wayne Haddix	.04	.02	.01
☐ 524 Gary Anderson RB UER (Photo actually Don Mosebar)	.04	.02	.01
☐ 525 Bruce Hill	.04	.02	.01
☐ 526 Kevin Murphy	.04	.02	.01
☐ 527 Lawrence Dawsey	.10	.05	.01
☐ 528 Ricky Ervins	.10	.05	.01
☐ 529 Charles Mann	.04	.02	.01
☐ 530 Jim Lachey	.04	.02	.01
☐ 531 Mark Rypien UER (No stat for percentage; 2,0703 yards, sic)	.10	.05	.01
☐ 532 Darrell Green	.04	.02	.01
☐ 533 Stan Humphries	.25	.11	.03
☐ 534 Jeff Bostic UER (Age listed as 32 in stats and 33 in bio)	.04	.02	.01
☐ 535 Earnest Byner	.04	.02	.01
☐ 536 Art Monk UER (Bio says 718 receptions, should be 730)	.10	.05	.01
☐ 537 Don Warren	.04	.02	.01
☐ 538 Darryl Grant	.04	.02	.01
☐ 539 Wilber Marshall	.04	.02	.01
☐ 540 Kurt Gouveia	.04	.02	.01
☐ 541 Markus Koch	.04	.02	.01
☐ 542 Andre Collins	.04	.02	.01
☐ 543 Chip Lohmiller	.04	.02	.01
☐ 544 Alvin Walton	.04	.02	.01
☐ 545 Gary Clark	.25	.11	.03
☐ 546 Ricky Sanders	.04	.02	.01
☐ 547 Redskins vs. Eagles (Gary Clark)	.04	.02	.01
☐ 548 Bengals vs. Oilers (Cody Carlson)	.04	.02	.01
☐ 549 Dolphins vs. Chiefs (Mark Clayton)	.04	.02	.01
☐ 550 Bears vs. Saints UER (Neal Anderson; Name misspelled Andersen on back)	.04	.02	.01
☐ 551 Bills vs. Dolphins (Thurman Thomas)	.10	.05	.01
☐ 552 49ers vs. Redskins (Line play)	.04	.02	.01
☐ 553 Giants vs. Bears (Ottis Anderson)	.04	.02	.01
☐ 554 Raiders vs. Bengals (Bo Jackson)	.10	.05	.01
☐ 555 AFC Championship (Andre Reed)	.04	.02	.01
☐ 556 NFC Championship (Jeff Hostetler)	.04	.02	.01
☐ 557 Super Bowl XXV (Ottis Anderson)	.04	.02	.01
☐ 558 Checklist 1-140	.04	.02	.01
☐ 559 Checklist 141-280	.04	.02	.01
☐ 560 Checklist 281-420 UER (301 Randall Hill)	.04	.02	.01
☐ 561 Checklist 421-561 UER	.04	.02	.01

1992 Bowman

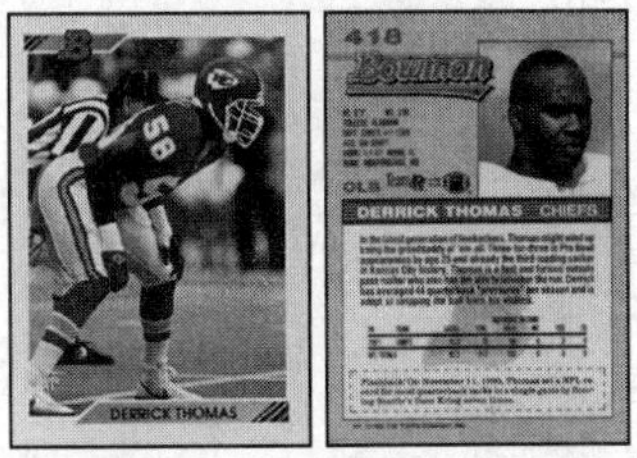

The 1992 Bowman football set consists of 573 standard-size glossy cards that were issued 14 per foil pack. The set includes 45 foil cards that are broken into three subsets: 28 Team Leader (TL) cards, 12 Playoff Star (PS) cards and five cards highlighting the longest plays (LP) of the 1991 season (field goal, run, reception, kick return, and punt). The foil cards were issued one per pack and include a number of short-prints which are designated by SP in the checklist below. The standard card front features color action player photos with white borders. The player's name is at the bottom and the Bowman logo is at the top. The foil cards are similar except for gold foil borders. Card backs have a small color photo, highlights and statistics. There is also a flashback section that highlights a memorable moment in that player's career. Rookie Cards include Steve Bono and Jackie Harris.

	MINT	NRMT	EXC
COMPLETE SET (573)	175.00	80.00	22.00
COMMON CARD (1-573)	.25	.11	.03
☐ 1 Reggie White	1.00	.45	.12
☐ 2 Johnny Meads	.25	.11	.03
☐ 3 Chip Lohmiller	.25	.11	.03
☐ 4 James Lofton	.50	.23	.06
☐ 5 Ray Horton	.25	.11	.03
☐ 6 Rich Moran	.25	.11	.03
☐ 7 Howard Cross	.25	.11	.03
☐ 8 Mike Horan	.25	.11	.03
☐ 9 Erik Kramer	.50	.23	.06
☐ 10 Steve Wisniewski	.25	.11	.03
☐ 11 Michael Haynes	.50	.23	.06
☐ 12 Donald Evans	.25	.11	.03
☐ 13 Michael Irvin FOIL	1.50	.70	.19
☐ 14 Gary Zimmerman	.25	.11	.03
☐ 15 John Friesz	.50	.23	.06
☐ 16 Mark Carrier WR	1.00	.45	.12
☐ 17 Mark Duper	.25	.11	.03
☐ 18 James Thornton	.25	.11	.03
☐ 19 Jon Hand	.25	.11	.03
☐ 20 Sterling Sharpe	1.00	.45	.12
☐ 21 Jacob Green	.25	.11	.03
☐ 22 Wesley Carroll	.25	.11	.03
☐ 23 Clay Matthews	.50	.23	.06
☐ 24 Kevin Greene	1.00	.45	.12
☐ 25 Brad Baxter	.25	.11	.03
☐ 26 Don Griffin	.25	.11	.03
☐ 27 Robert Delpino FOIL SP	1.50	.70	.19
☐ 28 Lee Johnson	.25	.11	.03
☐ 29 Jim Wahler	.25	.11	.03
☐ 30 Leonard Russell	.50	.23	.06
☐ 31 Eric Moore	.25	.11	.03
☐ 32 Dino Hackett	.25	.11	.03
☐ 33 Simon Fletcher	.25	.11	.03
☐ 34 Al Edwards	.25	.11	.03
☐ 35 Brad Edwards	.25	.11	.03
☐ 36 James Joseph	.25	.11	.03
☐ 37 Rodney Peete	.50	.23	.06
☐ 38 Ricky Reynolds	.25	.11	.03
☐ 39 Eddie Anderson	.25	.11	.03
☐ 40 Ken Clarke	.25	.11	.03
☐ 41 Tony Bennett FOIL	.60	.25	.07
☐ 42 Larry Brown DB	.25	.11	.03
☐ 43 Ray Childress	.25	.11	.03
☐ 44 Mike Kenn	.25	.11	.03
☐ 45 Vestee Jackson	.25	.11	.03
☐ 46 Neil O'Donnell	1.00	.45	.12
☐ 47 Bill Brooks	.25	.11	.03
☐ 48 Kevin Butler	.25	.11	.03
☐ 49 Joe Phillips	.25	.11	.03
☐ 50 Cortez Kennedy	.50	.23	.06
☐ 51 Rickey Jackson	.25	.11	.03
☐ 52 Vinnie Clark	.25	.11	.03
☐ 53 Michael Jackson	.50	.23	.06
☐ 54 Ernie Jones	.25	.11	.03
☐ 55 Tom Newberry	.25	.11	.03
☐ 56 Pat Harlow	.25	.11	.03
☐ 57 Craig Taylor	.25	.11	.03
☐ 58 Joe Prokop	.25	.11	.03
☐ 59 Warren Moon FOIL SP	2.00	.90	.25
☐ 60 Jeff Lageman	.25	.11	.03
☐ 61 Neil Smith	.50	.23	.06
☐ 62 Jim Jeffcoat	.25	.11	.03
☐ 63 Bill Fralic	.25	.11	.03
☐ 64 Mark Schlereth	.25	.11	.03
☐ 65 Keith Byars	.25	.11	.03
☐ 66 Jeff Hostetler	.50	.23	.06
☐ 67 Joey Browner	.25	.11	.03
☐ 68 Bobby Hebert FOIL SP	1.50	.70	.19
☐ 69 Keith Sims	.25	.11	.03
☐ 70 Warren Moon	1.00	.45	.12
☐ 71 Pio Sagapolutele	.25	.11	.03
☐ 72 Cornelius Bennett	.50	.23	.06
☐ 73 Greg Davis	.25	.11	.03
☐ 74 Ronnie Harmon	.25	.11	.03
☐ 75 Ron Hall	.25	.11	.03
☐ 76 Howie Long	.50	.23	.06
☐ 77 Greg Lewis	.25	.11	.03
☐ 78 Carnell Lake	.25	.11	.03
☐ 79 Ray Crockett	.25	.11	.03
☐ 80 Tom Waddle	.25	.11	.03
☐ 81 Vincent Brown	.25	.11	.03
☐ 82 Bill Brooks FOIL	.60	.25	.07
☐ 83 John L. Williams	.25	.11	.03
☐ 84 Floyd Turner	.25	.11	.03
☐ 85 Scott Radecic	.25	.11	.03
☐ 86 Anthony Munoz	.50	.23	.06
☐ 87 Lonnie Young	.25	.11	.03
☐ 88 Dexter Carter	.25	.11	.03
☐ 89 Tony Zendejas	.25	.11	.03
☐ 90 Tim Jorden	.25	.11	.03
☐ 91 LeRoy Butler	.25	.11	.03
☐ 92 Richard Brown	.25	.11	.03
☐ 93 Erric Pegram	.50	.23	.06
☐ 94 Sean Landeta	.25	.11	.03
☐ 95 Clyde Simmons	.25	.11	.03
☐ 96 Martin Mayhew	.25	.11	.03
☐ 97 Jarvis Williams	.25	.11	.03
☐ 98 Barry Word	.25	.11	.03
☐ 99 John Taylor FOIL	.60	.25	.07
☐ 100 Emmitt Smith	18.00	8.00	2.20
☐ 101 Leon Seals	.25	.11	.03
☐ 102 Marion Butts	.25	.11	.03
☐ 103 Mike Merriweather	.25	.11	.03
☐ 104 Ernest Givins	.50	.23	.06
☐ 105 Wymon Henderson	.25	.11	.03
☐ 106 Robert Wilson	.25	.11	.03
☐ 107 Bobby Hebert	.25	.11	.03
☐ 108 Terry McDaniel	.25	.11	.03
☐ 109 Jerry Ball	.25	.11	.03
☐ 110 John Taylor	.50	.23	.06
☐ 111 Rob Moore	.50	.23	.06
☐ 112 Thurman Thomas FOIL	1.50	.70	.19
☐ 113 Checklist 1-115	.25	.11	.03
☐ 114 Brian Blades	.50	.23	.06
☐ 115 Larry Kelm	.25	.11	.03
☐ 116 James Francis	.25	.11	.03
☐ 117 Rod Woodson	1.00	.45	.12
☐ 118 Trace Armstrong	.25	.11	.03
☐ 119 Eugene Daniel	.25	.11	.03
☐ 120 Andre Tippett	.25	.11	.03
☐ 121 Chris Jacke	.25	.11	.03
☐ 122 Jessie Tuggle	.25	.11	.03
☐ 123 Chris Chandler	.50	.23	.06
☐ 124 Tim Johnson	.25	.11	.03
☐ 125 Mark Collins	.25	.11	.03
☐ 126 Aeneas Williams FOIL SP	1.50	.70	.19
☐ 127 James Jones	.25	.11	.03
☐ 128 George Jamison	.25	.11	.03
☐ 129 Deron Cherry	.25	.11	.03
☐ 130 Mark Clayton	.50	.23	.06
☐ 131 Keith DeLong	.25	.11	.03
☐ 132 Marcus Allen	1.00	.45	.12
☐ 133 Joe Walter	.25	.11	.03
☐ 134 Reggie Rutland	.25	.11	.03
☐ 135 Kent Hull	.25	.11	.03
☐ 136 Jeff Feagles	.25	.11	.03
☐ 137 Ronnie Lott FOIL SP	2.00	.90	.25
☐ 138 Henry Rolling	.25	.11	.03
☐ 139 Gary Anderson RB	.25	.11	.03
☐ 140 Morten Andersen	.25	.11	.03
☐ 141 Cris Dishman	.25	.11	.03
☐ 142 David Treadwell	.25	.11	.03
☐ 143 Kevin Gogan	.25	.11	.03
☐ 144 James Hasty	.25	.11	.03
☐ 145 Robert Delpino	.25	.11	.03
☐ 146 Patrick Hunter	.25	.11	.03
☐ 147 Gary Anderson K	.25	.11	.03
☐ 148 Chip Banks	.25	.11	.03
☐ 149 Dan Fike	.25	.11	.03
☐ 150 Chris Miller	.50	.23	.06
☐ 151 Hugh Millen	.25	.11	.03
☐ 152 Courtney Hall	.25	.11	.03
☐ 153 Gary Clark	.50	.23	.06
☐ 154 Michael Brooks	.25	.11	.03
☐ 155 Jay Hilgenberg	.25	.11	.03
☐ 156 Tim McDonald	.25	.11	.03
☐ 157 Andre Tippett FOIL	.60	.25	.07
☐ 158 Doug Riesenberg	.25	.11	.03
☐ 159 Bill Maas	.25	.11	.03
☐ 160 Fred Barnett	.50	.23	.06
☐ 161 Pierce Holt	.25	.11	.03
☐ 162 Brian Noble	.25	.11	.03
☐ 163 Harold Green	.25	.11	.03
☐ 164 Joel Hilgenberg	.25	.11	.03
☐ 165 Mervyn Fernandez	.25	.11	.03
☐ 166 John Offerdahl	.25	.11	.03
☐ 167 Shane Conlan	.25	.11	.03
☐ 168 Mark Higgs FOIL SP	1.50	.70	.19
☐ 169 Bubba McDowell	.25	.11	.03
☐ 170 Barry Sanders	10.00	4.50	1.25
☐ 171 Larry Roberts	.25	.11	.03
☐ 172 Herschel Walker	.50	.23	.06
☐ 173 Steve McMichael	.50	.23	.06
☐ 174 Kelly Stouffer	.25	.11	.03
☐ 175 Louis Lipps	.25	.11	.03
☐ 176 Jim Everett	.50	.23	.06
☐ 177 Tony Tolbert	.25	.11	.03
☐ 178 Mike Baab	.25	.11	.03
☐ 179 Eric Swann	.50	.23	.06
☐ 180 Emmitt Smith FOIL SP	60.00	27.00	7.50
☐ 181 Tim Brown	1.00	.45	.12
☐ 182 Dennis Smith	.25	.11	.03
☐ 183 Moe Gardner	.25	.11	.03
☐ 184 Derrick Walker	.25	.11	.03
☐ 185 Reyna Thompson	.25	.11	.03
☐ 186 Esera Tuaolo	.25	.11	.03
☐ 187 Jeff Wright	.25	.11	.03
☐ 188 Mark Rypien	.25	.11	.03
☐ 189 Quinn Early	.50	.23	.06
☐ 190 Christian Okoye	.25	.11	.03
☐ 191 Keith Jackson	.50	.23	.06
☐ 192 Doug Smith	.25	.11	.03
☐ 193 John Elway FOIL	8.00	3.60	1.00
☐ 194 Reggie Cobb	.25	.11	.03
☐ 195 Reggie Roby	.25	.11	.03
☐ 196 Clarence Verdin	.25	.11	.03
☐ 197 Jim Breech	.25	.11	.03
☐ 198 Jim Sweeney	.25	.11	.03
☐ 199 Marv Cook	.25	.11	.03
☐ 200 Ronnie Lott	.50	.23	.06
☐ 201 Mel Gray	.50	.23	.06
☐ 202 Maury Buford	.25	.11	.03
☐ 203 Lorenzo Lynch	.25	.11	.03
☐ 204 Jesse Sapolu	.25	.11	.03
☐ 205 Steve Jordan	.25	.11	.03
☐ 206 Don Majkowski	.25	.11	.03
☐ 207 Flipper Anderson	.25	.11	.03
☐ 208 Ed King	.25	.11	.03
☐ 209 Tony Woods	.25	.11	.03
☐ 210 Ron Heller	.25	.11	.03
☐ 211 Greg Kragen	.25	.11	.03
☐ 212 Scott Case	.25	.11	.03
☐ 213 Tommy Barnhardt	.25	.11	.03
☐ 214 Charles Mann	.25	.11	.03
☐ 215 David Griggs	.25	.11	.03
☐ 216 Kenneth Davis FOIL SP	1.50	.70	.19
☐ 217 Lamar Lathon	.25	.11	.03
☐ 218 Nate Odomes	.25	.11	.03
☐ 219 Vinny Testaverde	.50	.23	.06
☐ 220 Rod Bernstine	.25	.11	.03
☐ 221 Barry Sanders FOIL	16.00	7.25	2.00
☐ 222 Carlton Haselrig	.25	.11	.03
☐ 223 Steve Beuerlein	.25	.11	.03
☐ 224 John Alt	.25	.11	.03
☐ 225 Pepper Johnson	.25	.11	.03
☐ 226 Checklist 116-230	.25	.11	.03
☐ 227 Irv Eatman	.25	.11	.03
☐ 228 Greg Townsend	.25	.11	.03
☐ 229 Mark Jackson	.25	.11	.03
☐ 230 Robert Blackmon	.25	.11	.03
☐ 231 Terry Allen	3.00	1.35	.35
☐ 232 Bennie Blades	.25	.11	.03
☐ 233 Sam Mills FOIL	1.50	.70	.19
☐ 234 Richmond Webb	.25	.11	.03
☐ 235 Richard Dent	.50	.23	.06
☐ 236 Alonzo Mitz	.25	.11	.03
☐ 237 Steve Young	6.00	2.70	.75
☐ 238 Pat Swilling	.50	.23	.06
☐ 239 James Campen	.25	.11	.03
☐ 240 Earnest Byner	.25	.11	.03
☐ 241 Pat Terrell	.25	.11	.03
☐ 242 Carwell Gardner	.25	.11	.03
☐ 243 Charles McRae	.25	.11	.03
☐ 244 Vince Newsome	.25	.11	.03
☐ 245 Eric Hill	.25	.11	.03
☐ 246 Steve Young FOIL	8.00	3.60	1.00
☐ 247 Nate Lewis	.25	.11	.03
☐ 248 William Fuller	.50	.23	.06
☐ 249 Andre Waters	.25	.11	.03
☐ 250 Dean Biasucci	.25	.11	.03
☐ 251 Andre Rison	.50	.23	.06
☐ 252 Brent Williams	.25	.11	.03
☐ 253 Todd McNair	.25	.11	.03
☐ 254 Jeff Davidson	.25	.11	.03
☐ 255 Art Monk	.50	.23	.06
☐ 256 Kirk Lowdermilk	.25	.11	.03
☐ 257 Bob Golic	.25	.11	.03
☐ 258 Michael Irvin	1.00	.45	.12
☐ 259 Eric Green	.25	.11	.03
☐ 260 David Fulcher FOIL	.60	.25	.07
☐ 261 Damone Johnson	.25	.11	.03
☐ 262 Marc Spindler	.25	.11	.03
☐ 263 Alfred Williams	.25	.11	.03
☐ 264 Donnie Elder	.25	.11	.03
☐ 265 Keith McKeller	.25	.11	.03
☐ 266 Steve Bono	2.50	1.10	.30
☐ 267 Jumbo Elliott	.25	.11	.03
☐ 268 Randy Hilliard	.25	.11	.03
☐ 269 Rufus Porter	.25	.11	.03
☐ 270 Neal Anderson	.25	.11	.03
☐ 271 Dalton Hilliard	.25	.11	.03
☐ 272 Michael Zordich	.25	.11	.03
☐ 273 Cornelius Bennett FOIL	.60	.25	.07

□ 274 Louie Aguiar	.25	.11	.03
□ 275 Aaron Craver	.25	.11	.03
□ 276 Tony Bennett	.25	.11	.03
□ 277 Terry Wooden	.25	.11	.03
□ 278 Mike Munchak	.25	.11	.03
□ 279 Chris Hinton	.25	.11	.03
□ 280 John Elway	6.00	2.70	.75
□ 281 Randall McDaniel	.25	.11	.03
□ 282 Brad Baxter FOIL	.60	.25	.07
□ 283 Wes Hopkins	.25	.11	.03
□ 284 Scott Davis	.25	.11	.03
□ 285 Mark Tuinei	.25	.11	.03
□ 286 Broderick Thompson	.25	.11	.03
□ 287 Henry Ellard	.50	.23	.06
□ 288 Adrian Cooper	.25	.11	.03
□ 289 Don Warren	.25	.11	.03
□ 290 Rodney Hampton	1.00	.45	.12
□ 291 Kevin Ross	.25	.11	.03
□ 292 Mark Carrier DB	.25	.11	.03
□ 293 Ian Beckles	.25	.11	.03
□ 294 Gene Atkins	.25	.11	.03
□ 295 Mark Rypien FOIL	.60	.25	.07
□ 296 Eric Metcalf	.50	.23	.06
□ 297 Howard Ballard	.25	.11	.03
□ 298 Nate Newton	.50	.23	.06
□ 299 Dan Owens	.25	.11	.03
□ 300 Tim McGee	.25	.11	.03
□ 301 Greg McMurtry	.25	.11	.03
□ 302 Walter Reeves	.25	.11	.03
□ 303 Jeff Herrod	.25	.11	.03
□ 304 Darren Comeaux	.25	.11	.03
□ 305 Pete Stoyanovich	.25	.11	.03
□ 306 Johnny Holland	.25	.11	.03
□ 307 Jay Novacek	.50	.23	.06
□ 308 Steve Broussard	.25	.11	.03
□ 309 Darrell Green	.25	.11	.03
□ 310 Sam Mills	.25	.11	.03
□ 311 Tim Barnett	.25	.11	.03
□ 312 Steve Atwater	.25	.11	.03
□ 313 Tom Waddle FOIL	.60	.25	.07
□ 314 Felix Wright	.25	.11	.03
□ 315 Sean Jones	.50	.23	.06
□ 316 Jim Harbaugh	1.00	.45	.12
□ 317 Eric Allen	.25	.11	.03
□ 318 Don Mosebar	.25	.11	.03
□ 319 Rob Taylor	.25	.11	.03
□ 320 Terance Mathis	.50	.23	.06
□ 321 Leroy Hoard	.50	.23	.06
□ 322 Kenneth Davis	.25	.11	.03
□ 323 Guy McIntyre	.25	.11	.03
□ 324 Deron Cherry FOIL	.60	.25	.07
□ 325 Tunch Ilkin	.25	.11	.03
□ 326 Willie Green	.25	.11	.03
□ 327 Darryl Henley	.25	.11	.03
□ 328 Shawn Jefferson	.25	.11	.03
□ 329 Greg Jackson	.25	.11	.03
□ 330 John Roper	.25	.11	.03
□ 331 Bill Lewis	.25	.11	.03
□ 332 Rodney Holman	.25	.11	.03
□ 333 Bruce Armstrong	.25	.11	.03
□ 334 Robb Thomas	.25	.11	.03
□ 335 Alvin Harper	.50	.23	.06
□ 336 Brian Jordan	.50	.23	.06
□ 337 Morten Andersen FOIL	.60	.25	.07
□ 338 Dermontti Dawson	.25	.11	.03
□ 339 Checklist 231-345	.25	.11	.03
□ 340 Louis Oliver	.25	.11	.03
□ 341 Paul McJulien	.25	.11	.03
□ 342 Karl Mecklenburg	.25	.11	.03
□ 343 Lawrence Dawsey	.50	.23	.06
□ 344 Kyle Clifton	.25	.11	.03
□ 345 Jeff Bostic	.25	.11	.03
□ 346 Cris Carter	1.00	.45	.12
□ 347 Al Smith	.25	.11	.03
□ 348 Mark Kelso	.25	.11	.03
□ 349 Art Monk FOIL	1.50	.70	.19
□ 350 Michael Carter	.25	.11	.03
□ 351 Ethan Horton	.25	.11	.03
□ 352 Andy Heck	.25	.11	.03
□ 353 Gill Fenerty	.25	.11	.03
□ 354 David Brandon	.25	.11	.03
□ 355 Anthony Johnson	1.00	.45	.12
□ 356 Mike Golic	.25	.11	.03
□ 357 Ferrell Edmunds	.25	.11	.03
□ 358 Dennis Gibson	.25	.11	.03
□ 359 Gill Byrd	.25	.11	.03
□ 360 Todd Lyght	.25	.11	.03
□ 361 Jayice Pearson	.25	.11	.03
□ 362 John Rade	.25	.11	.03
□ 363 Keith Van Horne	.25	.11	.03
□ 364 John Kasay	.25	.11	.03
□ 365 Broderick Thomas FOIL SP	1.50	.70	.19
□ 366 Ken Harvey	.25	.11	.03
□ 367 Rich Gannon	.25	.11	.03
□ 368 Darrell Thompson	.25	.11	.03
□ 369 Jon Vaughn	.25	.11	.03
□ 370 Jesse Solomon	.25	.11	.03
□ 371 Erik McMillan	.25	.11	.03
□ 372 Bruce Matthews	.25	.11	.03
□ 373 Wilber Marshall	.25	.11	.03
□ 374 Brian Blades FOIL SP	1.50	.70	.19
□ 375 Vance Johnson	.25	.11	.03
□ 376 Eddie Brown	.25	.11	.03
□ 377 Don Beebe	.25	.11	.03
□ 378 Brent Jones	.50	.23	.06
□ 379 Matt Bahr	.25	.11	.03
□ 380 Dwight Stone	.25	.11	.03
□ 381 Tony Casillas	.25	.11	.03
□ 382 Jay Schroeder	.25	.11	.03
□ 383 Byron Evans	.25	.11	.03
□ 384 Dan Saleaumua	.25	.11	.03
□ 385 Wendell Davis	.25	.11	.03
□ 386 Ron Holmes	.25	.11	.03
□ 387 George Thomas	.25	.11	.03
□ 388 Ray Berry	.25	.11	.03
□ 389 Eric Martin	.25	.11	.03
□ 390 Kevin Mack	.25	.11	.03
□ 391 Natu Tuatagaloa	.25	.11	.03
□ 392 Bill Romanowski	.25	.11	.03
□ 393 Nick Bell FOIL SP	1.50	.70	.19
□ 394 Grant Feasel	.25	.11	.03
□ 395 Eugene Lockhart	.25	.11	.03
□ 396 Lorenzo White	.25	.11	.03
□ 397 Mike Farr	.25	.11	.03
□ 398 Eric Bieniemy	.25	.11	.03
□ 399 Kevin Murphy	.25	.11	.03
□ 400 Luis Sharpe	.25	.11	.03
□ 401 Jessie Tuggle FOIL SP	1.50	.70	.19
□ 402 Cleveland Gary	.25	.11	.03
□ 403 Tony Mandarich	.25	.11	.03
□ 404 Bryan Cox	.50	.23	.06
□ 405 Marvin Washington	.25	.11	.03
□ 406 Fred Stokes	.25	.11	.03
□ 407 Duane Bickett	.25	.11	.03
□ 408 Leonard Marshall	.25	.11	.03
□ 409 Barry Foster	.50	.23	.06
□ 410 Thurman Thomas	1.00	.45	.12
□ 411 Willie Gault	.50	.23	.06
□ 412 Vinson Smith	.25	.11	.03
□ 413 Mark Bortz	.25	.11	.03
□ 414 Johnny Johnson	.25	.11	.03
□ 415 Rodney Hampton FOIL	1.50	.70	.19
□ 416 Steve Wallace	.25	.11	.03
□ 417 Fuad Reveiz	.25	.11	.03
□ 418 Derrick Thomas	.50	.23	.06
□ 419 Jackie Harris	1.00	.45	.12
□ 420 Derek Russell	.25	.11	.03
□ 421 David Grant	.25	.11	.03
□ 422 Tommy Kane	.25	.11	.03
□ 423 Stan Brock	.25	.11	.03
□ 424 Haywood Jeffires	.50	.23	.06
□ 425 Broderick Thomas	.25	.11	.03
□ 426 John Kidd	.25	.11	.03
□ 427 Shawn McCarthy FOIL	.60	.25	.07
□ 428 Jim Arnold	.25	.11	.03
□ 429 Scott Fulhage	.25	.11	.03
□ 430 Jackie Slater	.25	.11	.03
□ 431 Scott Galbraith	.25	.11	.03
□ 432 Roger Ruzek	.25	.11	.03
□ 433 Irving Fryar	.50	.23	.06
□ 434A Derrick Thomas FOIL ERR (Misnumbered 494)	1.50	.70	.19
□ 434B Derrick Thomas FOIL COR (Numbered 434)	1.50	.70	.19
□ 435 D.J. Johnson	.25	.11	.03
□ 436 Jim C.Jensen	.25	.11	.03
□ 437 James Washington	.25	.11	.03
□ 438 Phil Hansen	.25	.11	.03
□ 439 Rohn Stark	.25	.11	.03
□ 440 Jarrod Bunch	.25	.11	.03
□ 441 Todd Marinovich	.25	.11	.03
□ 442 Brett Perriman	1.00	.45	.12
□ 443 Eugene Robinson	.25	.11	.03
□ 444 Robert Massey	.25	.11	.03
□ 445 Nick Lowery	.25	.11	.03
□ 446 Rickey Dixon	.25	.11	.03
□ 447 Jim Lachey	.25	.11	.03
□ 448 Johnny Hector FOIL	.60	.25	.07
□ 449 Gary Plummer	.25	.11	.03
□ 450 Robert Brown	.25	.11	.03
□ 451 Gaston Green	.25	.11	.03
□ 452 Checklist 346-459	.25	.11	.03
□ 453 Darion Conner	.25	.11	.03
□ 454 Mike Cofer	.25	.11	.03
□ 455 Craig Heyward	.50	.23	.06
□ 456 Anthony Carter	.50	.23	.06
□ 457 Pat Coleman	.25	.11	.03
□ 458 Jeff Bryant	.25	.11	.03
□ 459 Mark Gunn	.25	.11	.03
□ 460 Stan Thomas	.25	.11	.03
□ 461 Simon Fletcher FOIL SP	1.50	.70	.19
□ 462 Ray Agnew	.25	.11	.03
□ 463 Jessie Hester	.25	.11	.03
□ 464 Rob Burnett	.25	.11	.03
□ 465 Mike Croel	.25	.11	.03
□ 466 Mike Pitts	.25	.11	.03
□ 467 Darryl Talley	.25	.11	.03
□ 468 Rich Camarillo	.25	.11	.03
□ 469 Reggie White FOIL	1.50	.70	.19
□ 470 Nick Bell	.25	.11	.03
□ 471 Tracy Hayworth	.25	.11	.03
□ 472 Eric Thomas	.25	.11	.03
□ 473 Paul Gruber	.25	.11	.03
□ 474 David Richards	.25	.11	.03
□ 475 T.J. Turner	.25	.11	.03
□ 476 Mark Ingram	.25	.11	.03
□ 477 Tim Grunhard	.25	.11	.03
□ 478 Marion Butts FOIL	.60	.25	.07
□ 479 Tom Rathman	.25	.11	.03
□ 480 Brian Mitchell	.50	.23	.06
□ 481 Bryce Paup	1.00	.45	.12
□ 482 Mike Pritchard	.50	.23	.06
□ 483 Ken Norton Jr.	.50	.23	.06
□ 484 Roman Phifer	.25	.11	.03
□ 485 Greg Lloyd	1.00	.45	.12
□ 486 Brett Maxie	.25	.11	.03
□ 487 Richard Dent FOIL SP	1.50	.70	.19
□ 488 Curtis Duncan	.25	.11	.03
□ 489 Chris Burkett	.25	.11	.03
□ 490 Travis McNeal	.25	.11	.03
□ 491 Carl Lee	.25	.11	.03
□ 492 Clarence Kay	.25	.11	.03
□ 493 Tom Thayer	.25	.11	.03
□ 494 Erik Kramer FOIL SP (See also 434A)	2.00	.90	.25
□ 495 Perry Kemp	.25	.11	.03
□ 496 Jeff Jaeger	.25	.11	.03
□ 497 Eric Sanders	.25	.11	.03
□ 498 Burt Grossman	.25	.11	.03
□ 499 Ben Smith	.25	.11	.03
□ 500 Keith McCants	.25	.11	.03
□ 501 John Stephens	.25	.11	.03
□ 502 John Rienstra	.25	.11	.03
□ 503 Jim Ritcher	.25	.11	.03
□ 504 Harris Barton	.25	.11	.03
□ 505 Andre Rison FOIL SP	2.00	.90	.25
□ 506 Chris Martin	.25	.11	.03
□ 507 Freddie Joe Nunn	.25	.11	.03
□ 508 Mark Higgs	.25	.11	.03
□ 509 Norm Johnson	.25	.11	.03
□ 510 Stephen Baker	.25	.11	.03
□ 511 Ricky Sanders	.25	.11	.03
□ 512 Ray Donaldson	.25	.11	.03
□ 513 David Fulcher	.25	.11	.03
□ 514 Gerald Williams	.25	.11	.03
□ 515 Toi Cook	.25	.11	.03
□ 516 Chris Warren	2.00	.90	.25
□ 517 Jeff Gossett	.25	.11	.03
□ 518 Ken Lanier	.25	.11	.03
□ 519 Haywood Jeffires FOIL SP	2.00	.90	.25
□ 520 Kevin Glover	.25	.11	.03
□ 521 Mo Lewis	.25	.11	.03
□ 522 Bern Brostek	.25	.11	.03
□ 523 Bo Orlando	.25	.11	.03
□ 524 Mike Saxon	.25	.11	.03
□ 525 Seth Joyner	.50	.23	.06
□ 526 John Carney	.25	.11	.03
□ 527 Jeff Cross	.25	.11	.03
□ 528 Gary Anderson K FOIL SP	1.50	.70	.19
□ 529 Chuck Cecil	.25	.11	.03
□ 530 Tim Green	.25	.11	.03
□ 531 Kevin Porter	.25	.11	.03
□ 532 Chris Spielman	.50	.23	.06
□ 533 Willie Drewrey	.25	.11	.03
□ 534 Chris Singleton UER (Card has wrong score for Super Bowl XX)	.25	.11	.03
□ 535 Matt Stover	.25	.11	.03
□ 536 Andre Collins	.25	.11	.03
□ 537 Erik Howard	.25	.11	.03
□ 538 Steve Tasker	.50	.23	.06
□ 539 Anthony Thompson	.25	.11	.03
□ 540 Charles Haley	.50	.23	.06
□ 541 Mike Merriweather FOIL	.60	.25	.07
□ 542 Henry Thomas	.25	.11	.03
□ 543 Scott Stephen	.25	.11	.03
□ 544 Bruce Kozerski	.25	.11	.03
□ 545 Tim McKyer	.25	.11	.03
□ 546 Chris Doleman	.25	.11	.03
□ 547 Riki Ellison	.25	.11	.03
□ 548 Mike Prior	.25	.11	.03
□ 549 Dwayne Harper	.25	.11	.03
□ 550 Bubby Brister	.25	.11	.03
□ 551 Dave Meggett	.50	.23	.06
□ 552 Greg Montgomery	.25	.11	.03
□ 553 Kevin Mack FOIL	.60	.25	.07
□ 554 Mark Stepnoski	.50	.23	.06
□ 555 Kenny Walker	.25	.11	.03
□ 556 Eric Moten	.25	.11	.03
□ 557 Michael Stewart	.25	.11	.03
□ 558 Calvin Williams	.50	.23	.06
□ 559 Johnny Hector	.25	.11	.03
□ 560 Tony Paige	.25	.11	.03
□ 561 Tim Newton	.25	.11	.03
□ 562 Brad Muster	.25	.11	.03
□ 563 Aeneas Williams	.50	.23	.06
□ 564 Herman Moore	8.00	3.60	1.00
□ 565 Checklist 460-573	.25	.11	.03
□ 566 Jerome Henderson	.25	.11	.03
□ 567 Danny Copeland	.25	.11	.03
□ 568 Alexander Wright FOIL	.60	.25	.07
□ 569 Tim Harris	.25	.11	.03
□ 570 Jonathan Hayes	.25	.11	.03
□ 571 Tony Jones	.25	.11	.03
□ 572 Carlton Bailey	.50	.23	.06
□ 573 Vaughan Johnson	.25	.11	.03

1993 Bowman

The 423 standard-size cards comprising the 1993 Bowman set feature full-bleed photos. The player's name is at the bottom with the Bowman logo in one upper corner. The backs are horizontal and have a small player photo with various stats. Several cards are bordered in prismatic foil. These cards are not subset cards like the previous year, but are the basic cards for several star players. Each foil pack contained one foil card and each jumbo pack contained two foil cards.

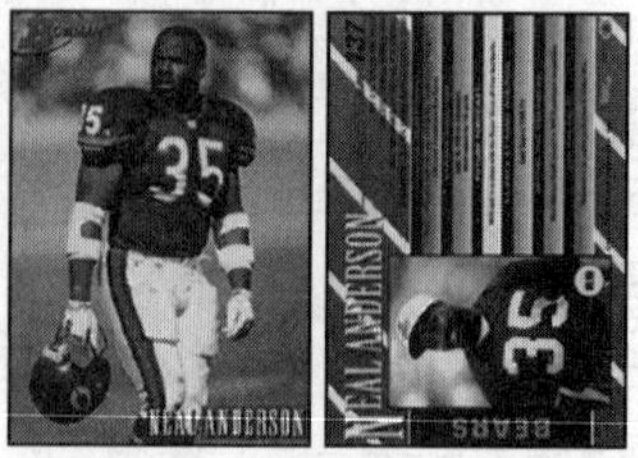

A solid Rookie Card crop includes Jerome Bettis, Drew Bledsoe, Vincent Brisby, Reggie Brooks, Mark Brunell, Curtis Conway, Troy Drayton, Garrison Hearst, Qadry Ismail, O.J. McDuffie, Natrone Means, Rick Mirer, Robert Smith, Dana Stubblefield and Kevin Williams.

	MINT	NRMT	EXC
COMPLETE SET (423)	70.00	32.00	8.75
COMMON CARD (1-423)	.15	.07	.02
□ 1 Troy Aikman FOIL	4.00	1.80	.50
□ 2 John Parrella	.15	.07	.02
□ 3 Dana Stubblefield	.50	.23	.06
□ 4 Mark Higgs	.15	.07	.02
□ 5 Tom Carter	.30	.14	.04
□ 6 Nate Lewis	.15	.07	.02
□ 7 Vaughn Hebron	.15	.07	.02
□ 8 Ernest Givins	.30	.14	.04
□ 9 Vince Buck	.15	.07	.02
□ 10 Levon Kirkland	.15	.07	.02
□ 11 J.J. Birden	.15	.07	.02
□ 12 Steve Jordan	.15	.07	.02
□ 13 Simon Fletcher	.15	.07	.02
□ 14 Willie Green	.15	.07	.02
□ 15 Pepper Johnson	.15	.07	.02
□ 16 Roger Harper	.15	.07	.02
□ 17 Rob Moore	.30	.14	.04
□ 18 David Lang	.15	.07	.02
□ 19 David Klingler	.15	.07	.02
□ 20 Garrison Hearst FOIL	4.00	1.80	.50
□ 21 Anthony Johnson	.30	.14	.04
□ 22 Eric Curry FOIL	.15	.07	.02
□ 23 Nolan Harrison	.15	.07	.02
□ 24 Earl Dotson	.15	.07	.02
□ 25 Leonard Russell	.30	.14	.04
□ 26 Doug Riesenberg	.15	.07	.02
□ 27 Dwayne Harper	.15	.07	.02
□ 28 Richard Dent	.30	.14	.04
□ 29 Victor Bailey	.15	.07	.02
□ 30 Junior Seau	.50	.23	.06
□ 31 Steve Tasker	.30	.14	.04
□ 32 Kurt Gouveia	.15	.07	.02
□ 33 Renaldo Turnbull UER (Listed as wide receiver)	.15	.07	.02
□ 34 Dale Carter	.15	.07	.02
□ 35 Russell Maryland	.15	.07	.02
□ 36 Dana Hall	.15	.07	.02
□ 37 Marco Coleman	.15	.07	.02
□ 38 Greg Montgomery	.15	.07	.02
□ 39 Deon Figures	.30	.14	.04
□ 40 Troy Drayton	.30	.14	.04
□ 41 Eric Metcalf	.30	.14	.04
□ 42 Michael Husted	.15	.07	.02
□ 43 Harry Newsome	.15	.07	.02
□ 44 Kelvin Pritchett	.15	.07	.02
□ 45 Andre Ricon FOIL	.50	.23	.06
□ 46 John Copeland	.30	.14	.04
□ 47 Greg Biekert	.15	.07	.02
□ 48 Johnny Johnson	.15	.07	.02
□ 49 Chuck Cecil	.15	.07	.02
□ 50 Rick Mirer FOIL	4.00	1.80	.50
□ 51 Rod Bernstine	.15	.07	.02
□ 52 Steve McMichael	.30	.14	.04
□ 53 Roosevelt Potts	.15	.07	.02
□ 54 Mike Sherrard	.15	.07	.02
□ 55 Terrell Buckley	.15	.07	.02
□ 56 Eugene Chung	.15	.07	.02
□ 57 Kimble Anders	.50	.23	.06
□ 58 Daryl Johnston	.50	.23	.06
□ 59 Harris Barton	.15	.07	.02
□ 60 Thurman Thomas FOIL	.50	.23	.06
□ 61 Eric Martin	.15	.07	.02
□ 62 Reggie Brooks FOIL	.40	.18	.05
□ 63 Eric Bieniemy	.15	.07	.02
□ 64 John Offerdahl	.15	.07	.02
□ 65 Wilber Marshall	.15	.07	.02
□ 66 Mark Carrier WR	.30	.14	.04
□ 67 Merril Hoge	.15	.07	.02
□ 68 Cris Carter	.50	.23	.06
□ 69 Marty Thompson	.15	.07	.02
□ 70 Randall Cunningham FOIL	.40	.18	.05
□ 71 Winston Moss	.15	.07	.02
□ 72 Doug Pelfrey	.15	.07	.02
□ 73 Jackie Slater	.15	.07	.02
□ 74 Pierce Holt	.15	.07	.02
□ 75 Hardy Nickerson	.30	.14	.04
□ 76 Chris Burkett	.15	.07	.02
□ 77 Michael Brandon	.15	.07	.02
□ 78 Tom Waddle	.15	.07	.02
□ 79 Walter Reeves	.15	.07	.02
□ 80 Lawrence Taylor FOIL	.50	.23	.06
□ 81 Wayne Simmons	.15	.07	.02

☐ 82 Brent Williams	.15	.07	.02
☐ 83 Shannon Sharpe	.50	.23	.06
☐ 84 Robert Blackmon	.15	.07	.02
☐ 85 Keith Jackson	.30	.14	.04
☐ 86 A.J. Johnson	.15	.07	.02
☐ 87 Ryan McNeil	.15	.07	.02
☐ 88 Michael Dean Perry	.30	.14	.04
☐ 89 Russell Copeland	.30	.14	.04
☐ 90 Sam Mills	.15	.07	.02
☐ 91 Courtney Hall	.15	.07	.02
☐ 92 Gino Torretta	.30	.14	.04
☐ 93 Artie Smith	.15	.07	.02
☐ 94 David Whitmore	.15	.07	.02
☐ 95 Charles Haley	.30	.14	.04
☐ 96 Rod Woodson	.50	.23	.06
☐ 97 Lorenzo White	.15	.07	.02
☐ 98 Tom Scott	.15	.07	.02
☐ 99 Tyji Armstrong	.15	.07	.02
☐ 100 Boomer Esiason	.30	.14	.04
☐ 101 Rocket Ismail FOIL	.40	.18	.05
☐ 102 Mark Carrier DB	.15	.07	.02
☐ 103 Broderick Thompson	.15	.07	.02
☐ 104 Bob Whitfield	.15	.07	.02
☐ 105 Ben Coleman	.15	.07	.02
☐ 106 Jon Vaughn	.15	.07	.02
☐ 107 Marcus Buckley	.15	.07	.02
☐ 108 Cleveland Gary	.15	.07	.02
☐ 109 Ashley Ambrose	.15	.07	.02
☐ 110 Reggie White FOIL	.50	.23	.06
☐ 111 Arthur Marshall	.15	.07	.02
☐ 112 Greg McMurtry	.15	.07	.02
☐ 113 Mike Johnson	.15	.07	.02
☐ 114 Tim McGee	.15	.07	.02
☐ 115 John Carney	.15	.07	.02
☐ 116 Neil Smith	.50	.23	.06
☐ 117 Mark Stepnoski	.15	.07	.02
☐ 118 Don Beebe	.15	.07	.02
☐ 119 Scott Mitchell	.50	.23	.06
☐ 120 Randall McDaniel	.15	.07	.02
☐ 121 Chidi Ahanotu	.15	.07	.02
☐ 122 Ray Childress	.15	.07	.02
☐ 123 Tony McGee	.30	.14	.04
☐ 124 Marc Boutte	.15	.07	.02
☐ 125 Ronnie Lott	.30	.14	.04
☐ 126 Jason Elam	.15	.07	.02
☐ 127 Martin Harrison	.15	.07	.02
☐ 128 Leonard Renfro	.15	.07	.02
☐ 129 Jessie Armstead	.15	.07	.02
☐ 130 Quentin Coryatt	.30	.14	.04
☐ 131 Luis Sharpe	.15	.07	.02
☐ 132 Bill Maas	.15	.07	.02
☐ 133 Jesse Solomon	.15	.07	.02
☐ 134 Kevin Greene	.50	.23	.06
☐ 135 Derek Brown RB	.30	.14	.04
☐ 136 Greg Townsend	.15	.07	.02
☐ 137 Neal Anderson	.15	.07	.02
☐ 138 John L. Williams	.15	.07	.02
☐ 139 Vincent Brisby	.50	.23	.06
☐ 140 Barry Sanders FOIL	4.00	1.80	.50
☐ 141 Charles Mann	.15	.07	.02
☐ 142 Ken Norton	.30	.14	.04
☐ 143 Eric Moten	.15	.07	.02
☐ 144 John Alt	.15	.07	.02
☐ 145 Dan Footman	.15	.07	.02
☐ 146 Bill Brooks	.15	.07	.02
☐ 147 James Thornton	.15	.07	.02
☐ 148 Martin Mayhew	.15	.07	.02
☐ 149 Andy Harmon	.30	.14	.04
☐ 150 Dan Marino FOIL	7.00	3.10	.85
☐ 151 Micheal Barrow	.15	.07	.02
☐ 152 Flipper Anderson	.15	.07	.02
☐ 153 Jackie Harris	.15	.07	.02
☐ 154 Todd Kelly	.15	.07	.02
☐ 155 Dan Williams	.15	.07	.02
☐ 156 Harold Green	.15	.07	.02
☐ 157 David Treadwell	.15	.07	.02
☐ 158 Chris Doleman	.15	.07	.02
☐ 159 Eric Hill	.15	.07	.02
☐ 160 Lincoln Kennedy	.15	.07	.02
☐ 161 Devon McDonald	.15	.07	.02
☐ 162 Natrone Means	5.00	2.20	.60
☐ 163 Rick Hamilton	.15	.07	.02
☐ 164 Kelvin Martin	.15	.07	.02
☐ 165 Jeff Hostetler	.30	.14	.04
☐ 166 Mark Brunell	15.00	6.75	1.85
☐ 167 Tim Barnett	.15	.07	.02
☐ 168 Ray Crockett	.15	.07	.02
☐ 169 William Perry	.30	.14	.04
☐ 170 Michael Irvin	.50	.23	.06
☐ 171 Marvin Washington	.15	.07	.02
☐ 172 Irving Fryar	.30	.14	.04
☐ 173 Scott Sisson	.15	.07	.02
☐ 174 Gary Anderson K	.15	.07	.02
☐ 175 Bruce Smith	.50	.23	.06
☐ 176 Clyde Simmons	.15	.07	.02
☐ 177 Russell White	.30	.14	.04
☐ 178 Irv Smith	.15	.07	.02
☐ 179 Mark Wheeler	.15	.07	.02
☐ 180 Warren Moon	.50	.23	.06
☐ 181 Del Speer	.15	.07	.02
☐ 182 Henry Thomas	.15	.07	.02
☐ 183 Keith Kartz	.15	.07	.02
☐ 184 Ricky Ervins	.15	.07	.02
☐ 185 Phil Simms	.30	.14	.04
☐ 186 Tim Brown	.50	.23	.06
☐ 187 Willis Peguese	.15	.07	.02
☐ 188 Rich Moran	.15	.07	.02
☐ 189 Robert Jones	.15	.07	.02
☐ 190 Craig Heyward	.30	.14	.04
☐ 191 Ricky Watters	.50	.23	.06
☐ 192 Stan Humphries	.50	.23	.06
☐ 193 Larry Webster	.15	.07	.02
☐ 194 Brad Baxter	.15	.07	.02
☐ 195 Randal Hill	.15	.07	.02
☐ 196 Robert Porcher	.15	.07	.02
☐ 197 Patrick Robinson	.15	.07	.02
☐ 198 Ferrell Edmunds	.15	.07	.02
☐ 199 Melvin Jenkins	.15	.07	.02
☐ 200 Joe Montana FOIL	4.00	1.80	.50
☐ 201 Marv Cook	.15	.07	.02
☐ 202 Henry Ellard	.30	.14	.04
☐ 203 Calvin Williams	.30	.14	.04
☐ 204 Craig Erickson	.30	.14	.04
☐ 205 Steve Atwater	.15	.07	.02
☐ 206 Najee Mustafaa	.15	.07	.02
☐ 207 Darryl Talley	.15	.07	.02
☐ 208 Jarrod Bunch	.15	.07	.02
☐ 209 Tim McDonald	.15	.07	.02
☐ 210 Patrick Bates	.15	.07	.02
☐ 211 Sean Jones	.15	.07	.02
☐ 212 Leslie O'Neal	.30	.14	.04
☐ 213 Mike Golic	.15	.07	.02
☐ 214 Mark Clayton	.15	.07	.02
☐ 215 Leonard Marshall	.15	.07	.02
☐ 216 Curtis Conway	3.00	1.35	.35
☐ 217 Andre Hastings	.50	.23	.06
☐ 218 Barry Word	.15	.07	.02
☐ 219 Will Wolford	.15	.07	.02
☐ 220 Desmond Howard	.30	.14	.04
☐ 221 Rickey Jackson	.15	.07	.02
☐ 222 Alvin Harper	.30	.14	.04
☐ 223 William White	.15	.07	.02
☐ 224 Steve Broussard	.15	.07	.02
☐ 225 Aeneas Williams	.15	.07	.02
☐ 226 Michael Brooks	.15	.07	.02
☐ 227 Reggie Cobb	.15	.07	.02
☐ 228 Derrick Walker	.15	.07	.02
☐ 229 Marcus Allen	.50	.23	.06
☐ 230 Jerry Ball	.15	.07	.02
☐ 231 J.B. Brown	.15	.07	.02
☐ 232 Terry McDaniel	.15	.07	.02
☐ 233 LeRoy Butler	.15	.07	.02
☐ 234 Kyle Clifton	.15	.07	.02
☐ 235 Henry Jones	.15	.07	.02
☐ 236 Shane Conlan	.15	.07	.02
☐ 237 Michael Bates	.15	.07	.02
☐ 238 Vincent Brown	.15	.07	.02
☐ 239 William Fuller	.15	.07	.02
☐ 240 Ricardo McDonald	.15	.07	.02
☐ 241 Gary Zimmerman	.15	.07	.02
☐ 242 Fred Barnett	.30	.14	.04
☐ 243 Elvis Grbac	5.00	2.20	.60
☐ 244 Myron Baker	.15	.07	.02
☐ 245 Steve Emtman	.15	.07	.02
☐ 246 Mike Compton	.15	.07	.02
☐ 247 Mark Jackson	.15	.07	.02
☐ 248 Santo Stephens	.15	.07	.02
☐ 249 Tommie Agee	.15	.07	.02
☐ 250 Broderick Thomas	.15	.07	.02
☐ 251 Fred Baxter	.15	.07	.02
☐ 252 Andre Collins	.15	.07	.02
☐ 253 Ernest Dye	.15	.07	.02
☐ 254 Raylee Johnson	.15	.07	.02
☐ 255 Rickey Dixon	.15	.07	.02
☐ 256 Ron Heller	.15	.07	.02
☐ 257 Joel Steed	.15	.07	.02
☐ 258 Everett Lindsay	.15	.07	.02
☐ 259 Tony Smith	.15	.07	.02
☐ 260 Sterling Sharpe UER	.50	.23	.06
(Edgar Bennett is pictured on front)			
☐ 261 Tommy Vardell	.15	.07	.02
☐ 262 Morten Andersen	.15	.07	.02
☐ 263 Eddie Robinson	.15	.07	.02
☐ 264 Jerome Bettis	7.00	3.10	.85
☐ 265 Alonzo Spellman	.15	.07	.02
☐ 266 Harvey Williams	.30	.14	.04
☐ 267 Jason Belser	.15	.07	.02
☐ 268 Derek Russell	.15	.07	.02
☐ 269 Derrick Lassic	.15	.07	.02
☐ 270 Steve Young FOIL	3.00	1.35	.35
☐ 271 Adrian Murrell	3.00	1.35	.35
☐ 272 Lewis Tillman	.15	.07	.02
☐ 273 O.J. McDuffie	3.00	1.35	.35
☐ 274 Marty Carter	.15	.07	.02
☐ 275 Ray Seals	.15	.07	.02
☐ 276 Earnest Byner	.15	.07	.02
☐ 277 Marion Butts	.15	.07	.02
☐ 278 Chris Spielman	.30	.14	.04
☐ 279 Carl Pickens	2.00	.90	.25
☐ 280 Drew Bledsoe FOIL	15.00	6.75	1.85
☐ 281 Mark Kelso	.15	.07	.02
☐ 282 Eugene Robinson	.15	.07	.02
☐ 283 Eric Allen	.15	.07	.02
☐ 284 Ethan Horton	.15	.07	.02
☐ 285 Greg Lloyd	.50	.23	.06
☐ 286 Anthony Carter	.30	.14	.04
☐ 287 Edgar Bennett	.50	.23	.06
☐ 288 Bobby Hebert	.15	.07	.02
☐ 289 Haywood Jeffires	.30	.14	.04
☐ 290 Glyn Milburn	.50	.23	.06
☐ 291 Bernie Kosar	.30	.14	.04
☐ 292 Jumbo Elliott	.15	.07	.02
☐ 293 Jessie Hester	.15	.07	.02
☐ 294 Brent Jones	.30	.14	.04
☐ 295 Carl Banks	.15	.07	.02
☐ 296 Brian Washington	.15	.07	.02
☐ 297 Steve Beuerlein	.15	.07	.02
☐ 298 John Lynch	.15	.07	.02
☐ 299 Troy Vincent	.15	.07	.02
☐ 300 Emmitt Smith FOIL	7.00	3.10	.85
☐ 301 Chris Zorich	.15	.07	.02
☐ 302 Wade Wilson	.15	.07	.02
☐ 303 Darrien Gordon	.15	.07	.02
☐ 304 Fred Stokes	.15	.07	.02
☐ 305 Nick Lowery	.15	.07	.02
☐ 306 Rodney Peete	.15	.07	.02
☐ 307 Chris Warren	.30	.14	.04
☐ 308 Herschel Walker	.30	.14	.04
☐ 309 Aundray Bruce	.15	.07	.02
☐ 310 Barry Foster FOIL	.40	.18	.05
☐ 311 George Teague	.30	.14	.04
☐ 312 Darryl Williams	.15	.07	.02
☐ 313 Thomas Smith	.30	.14	.04
☐ 314 Dennis Brown	.15	.07	.02
☐ 315 Marvin Jones FOIL	.40	.18	.05
☐ 316 Andre Tippett	.15	.07	.02
☐ 317 Demetrius DuBose	.15	.07	.02
☐ 318 Kirk Lowdermilk	.15	.07	.02
☐ 319 Shane Dronett	.15	.07	.02
☐ 320 Terry Kirby	1.00	.45	.12
☐ 321 Qadry Ismail	.50	.23	.06
☐ 322 Lorenzo Lynch	.15	.07	.02
☐ 323 Willie Drewrey	.15	.07	.02
☐ 324 Jessie Tuggle	.15	.07	.02
☐ 325 Leroy Hoard	.30	.14	.04
☐ 326 Mark Collins	.15	.07	.02
☐ 327 Darrell Green	.15	.07	.02
☐ 328 Anthony Miller	.30	.14	.04
☐ 329 Brad Muster	.15	.07	.02
☐ 330 Jim Kelly FOIL	.50	.23	.06
☐ 331 Sean Gilbert	.30	.14	.04
☐ 332 Tim McKyer	.15	.07	.02
☐ 333 Scott Mersereau	.15	.07	.02
☐ 334 Willie Davis	.50	.23	.06
☐ 335 Brett Favre FOIL	7.00	3.10	.85
☐ 336 Kevin Gogan	.15	.07	.02
☐ 337 Jim Harbaugh	.50	.23	.06
☐ 338 James Trapp	.15	.07	.02
☐ 339 Pete Stoyanovich	.15	.07	.02
☐ 340 Jerry Rice FOIL	4.00	1.80	.50
☐ 341 Gary Anderson RB	.15	.07	.02
☐ 342 Carlton Gray	.15	.07	.02
☐ 343 Dermontti Dawson	.15	.07	.02
☐ 344 Ray Buchanan	.15	.07	.02
☐ 345 Derrick Fenner	.15	.07	.02
☐ 346 Dennis Smith	.15	.07	.02
☐ 347 Todd Rucci	.15	.07	.02
☐ 348 Seth Joyner	.15	.07	.02
☐ 349 Jim McMahon	.15	.07	.02
☐ 350 Rodney Hampton	.50	.23	.06
☐ 351 Al Smith	.15	.07	.02
☐ 352 Steve Everitt	.15	.07	.02
☐ 353 Vinnie Clark	.15	.07	.02
☐ 354 Eric Swann	.30	.14	.04
☐ 355 Brian Mitchell	.30	.14	.04
☐ 356 Will Shields	.15	.07	.02
☐ 357 Cornelius Bennett	.30	.14	.04
☐ 358 Darrin Smith	.30	.14	.04
☐ 359 Chris Mims	.15	.07	.02
☐ 360 Blair Thomas	.15	.07	.02
☐ 361 Dennis Gibson	.15	.07	.02
☐ 362 Santana Dotson	.30	.14	.04
☐ 363 Mark Ingram	.15	.07	.02
☐ 364 Don Mosebar	.15	.07	.02
☐ 365 Ty Detmer	.50	.23	.06
☐ 366 Bob Christian	.15	.07	.02
☐ 367 Adrian Hardy	.15	.07	.02
☐ 368 Vaughan Johnson	.15	.07	.02
☐ 369 Jim Everett	.30	.14	.04
☐ 370 Ricky Sanders	.15	.07	.02
☐ 371 Jonathan Hayes	.15	.07	.02
☐ 372 Bruce Matthews	.15	.07	.02
☐ 373 Darren Drozdov	.15	.07	.02
☐ 374 Scott Brumfield	.15	.07	.02
☐ 375 Cortez Kennedy	.30	.14	.04
☐ 376 Tim Harris	.15	.07	.02
☐ 377 Neil O'Donnell	.50	.23	.06
☐ 378 Robert Smith	3.00	1.35	.35
☐ 379 Mike Caldwell	.15	.07	.02
☐ 380 Burt Grossman	.15	.07	.02
☐ 381 Corey Miller	.15	.07	.02
☐ 382 Kevin Williams FOIL	1.25	.55	.16
☐ 383 Ken Harvey	.15	.07	.02
☐ 384 Greg Robinson	.15	.07	.02
☐ 385 Harold Alexander	.15	.07	.02
☐ 386 Andre Reed	.30	.14	.04
☐ 387 Reggie Langhorne	.15	.07	.02
☐ 388 Courtney Hawkins	.15	.07	.02
☐ 389 James Hasty	.15	.07	.02
☐ 390 Pat Swilling	.15	.07	.02
☐ 391 Chris Slade	.30	.14	.04
☐ 392 Keith Byars	.15	.07	.02
☐ 393 Dalton Hilliard	.15	.07	.02
☐ 394 David Williams	.15	.07	.02
☐ 395 Terry Obee	.15	.07	.02
☐ 396 Heath Sherman	.15	.07	.02
☐ 397 John Taylor	.30	.14	.04
☐ 398 Irv Eatman	.15	.07	.02
☐ 399 Johnny Holland	.15	.07	.02
☐ 400 John Elway FOIL	3.00	1.35	.35
☐ 401 Clay Matthews	.30	.14	.04
☐ 402 Dave Meggett	.15	.07	.02
☐ 403 Eric Green	.15	.07	.02
☐ 404 Bryan Cox	.15	.07	.02
☐ 405 Jay Novacek	.30	.14	.04
☐ 406 Kenneth Davis	.15	.07	.02
☐ 407 Lamar Thomas	.15	.07	.02
☐ 408 Lance Gunn	.15	.07	.02
☐ 409 Audray McMillian	.15	.07	.02
☐ 410 Derrick Thomas FOIL	.50	.23	.06
☐ 411 Rufus Porter	.15	.07	.02
☐ 412 Coleman Rudolph	.15	.07	.02
☐ 413 Mark Rypien	.15	.07	.02
☐ 414 Duane Bickett	.15	.07	.02
☐ 415 Chris Singleton	.15	.07	.02
☐ 416 Mitch Lyons	.15	.07	.02
☐ 417 Bill Fralic	.15	.07	.02
☐ 418 Gary Plummer	.15	.07	.02
☐ 419 Ricky Proehl	.15	.07	.02
☐ 420 Howie Long	.30	.14	.04
☐ 421 Willie Roaf FOIL	.50	.23	.06
☐ 422 Checklist 1-212	.15	.07	.02
☐ 423 Checklist 213-423	.15	.07	.02

1994 Bowman

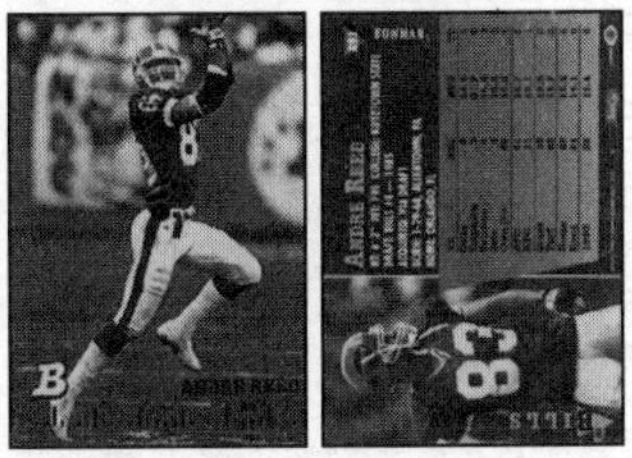

The 1994 Bowman set consists of 390 standard-size cards. The fronts feature borderless color action player photos. The player's name appears in gold foil letters in the lower right corner. The horizontal backs carry a color player close-up on the left, his name, biography and statistics on the right. The set includes a 30-card foil subset (215-244, one per pack) of rookies. Rookie Cards include Mario Bates, Isaac Bruce, Lake Dawson, Trent Dilfer, Bert Emanuel, William Floyd, Marshall Faulk, Gus Frerotte, Charles Johnson, Errict Rhett, Darnay Scott and Heath Shuler.

	MINT	NRMT	EXC
COMPLETE SET (390)	75.00	34.00	9.50
COMMON CARD (1-390)	.15	.07	.02
☐ 1 Dan Wilkinson	.25	.11	.03
☐ 2 Marshall Faulk	6.00	2.70	.75
☐ 3 Heath Shuler	2.00	.90	.25
☐ 4 Willie McGinest	.40	.18	.05
☐ 5 Trent Dilfer	1.50	.70	.19
☐ 6 Brent Jones	.25	.11	.03
☐ 7 Sam Adams	.25	.11	.03
☐ 8 Randy Baldwin	.15	.07	.02
☐ 9 Jamir Miller	.15	.07	.02
☐ 10 John Thierry	.15	.07	.02
☐ 11 Aaron Glenn	.25	.11	.03
☐ 12 Joe Johnson	.15	.07	.02
☐ 13 Bernard Williams	.15	.07	.02
☐ 14 Wayne Gandy	.15	.07	.02
☐ 15 Aaron Taylor	.15	.07	.02
☐ 16 Charles Johnson	1.00	.45	.12
☐ 17 Dewayne Washington	.25	.11	.03
☐ 18 Bernie Kosar	.25	.11	.03
☐ 19 Johnnie Morton	1.00	.45	.12
☐ 20 Rob Fredrickson	.25	.11	.03
☐ 21 Shante Carver	.15	.07	.02
☐ 22 Thomas Lewis	.25	.11	.03
☐ 23 Greg Hill	1.25	.55	.16
☐ 24 Cris Dishman	.15	.07	.02
☐ 25 Jeff Burris	.25	.11	.03
☐ 26 Isaac Davis	.15	.07	.02
☐ 27 Bert Emanuel	2.00	.90	.25
☐ 28 Allen Aldridge	.15	.07	.02
☐ 29 Kevin Lee	.15	.07	.02
☐ 30 Chris Brantley	.15	.07	.02
☐ 31 Rich Braham	.15	.07	.02
☐ 32 Ricky Watters	.40	.18	.05
☐ 33 Quentin Coryatt	.15	.07	.02
☐ 34 Hardy Nickerson	.25	.11	.03
☐ 35 Johnny Johnson	.15	.07	.02
☐ 36 Ken Harvey	.15	.07	.02
☐ 37 Chris Zorich	.15	.07	.02
☐ 38 Chris Warren	.25	.11	.03
☐ 39 David Palmer	.25	.11	.03
☐ 40 Chris Miller	.15	.07	.02
☐ 41 Ken Ruettgers	.15	.07	.02
☐ 42 Joe Panos	.15	.07	.02
☐ 43 Mario Bates	1.00	.45	.12
☐ 44 Harry Colon	.15	.07	.02
☐ 45 Barry Foster	.15	.07	.02
☐ 46 Steve Tasker	.25	.11	.03
☐ 47 Richmond Webb	.15	.07	.02

☐ 48 James Folston	.15	.07	.02
☐ 49 Erik Williams	.15	.07	.02
☐ 50 Rodney Hampton	.40	.18	.05
☐ 51 Derek Russell	.15	.07	.02
☐ 52 Greg Montgomery	.15	.07	.02
☐ 53 Anthony Phillips	.15	.07	.02
☐ 54 Andre Coleman	.15	.07	.02
☐ 55 Gary Brown	.15	.07	.02
☐ 56 Neil Smith	.40	.18	.05
☐ 57 Myron Baker	.15	.07	.02
☐ 58 Sean Dawkins	1.00	.45	.12
☐ 59 Marvin Washington	.15	.07	.02
☐ 60 Steve Beuerlein	.15	.07	.02
☐ 61 Brenston Buckner	.15	.07	.02
☐ 62 William Gaines	.15	.07	.02
☐ 63 LeShon Johnson	.25	.11	.03
☐ 64 Errict Rhett	2.50	1.10	.30
☐ 65 Jim Everett	.25	.11	.03
☐ 66 Desmond Howard	.25	.11	.03
☐ 67 Jack Del Rio	.15	.07	.02
☐ 68 Isaac Bruce	6.00	2.70	.75
☐ 69 Van Malone	.15	.07	.02
☐ 70 Jim Kelly	.40	.18	.05
☐ 71 Leon Lett	.15	.07	.02
☐ 72 Greg Robinson	.15	.07	.02
☐ 73 Ryan Yarborough	.15	.07	.02
☐ 74 Terry Wooden	.15	.07	.02
☐ 75 Eric Allen	.15	.07	.02
☐ 76 Ernest Givins	.25	.11	.03
☐ 77 Marcus Spears	.15	.07	.02
☐ 78 Thomas Randolph	.15	.07	.02
☐ 79 Willie Clark	.15	.07	.02
☐ 80 John Elway	2.00	.90	.25
☐ 81 Aubrey Beavers	.15	.07	.02
☐ 82 Jeff Cothran	.15	.07	.02
☐ 83 Norm Johnson	.15	.07	.02
☐ 84 Donnell Bennett	.15	.07	.02
☐ 85 Phillippi Sparks	.15	.07	.02
☐ 86 Scott Mitchell	.40	.18	.05
☐ 87 Bucky Brooks	.15	.07	.02
☐ 88 Courtney Hawkins	.15	.07	.02
☐ 89 Kevin Greene	.40	.18	.05
☐ 90 Doug Nussmeier	.15	.07	.02
☐ 91 Floyd Turner	.15	.07	.02
☐ 92 Anthony Newman	.15	.07	.02
☐ 93 Vinny Testaverde	.25	.11	.03
☐ 94 Ronnie Lott	.25	.11	.03
☐ 95 Troy Aikman	3.00	1.35	.35
☐ 96 John Taylor	.25	.11	.03
☐ 97 Henry Ellard	.25	.11	.03
☐ 98 Carl Lee	.15	.07	.02
☐ 99 Terry McDaniel	.15	.07	.02
☐ 100 Joe Montana	3.00	1.35	.35
☐ 101 David Klingler	.15	.07	.02
☐ 102 Bruce Walker	.15	.07	.02
☐ 103 Rick Cunningham	.15	.07	.02
☐ 104 Robert Delpino	.15	.07	.02
☐ 105 Mark Ingram	.15	.07	.02
☐ 106 Leslie O'Neal	.15	.07	.02
☐ 107 Darrell Thompson	.15	.07	.02
☐ 108 Dave Meggett	.15	.07	.02
☐ 109 Chris Gardocki	.15	.07	.02
☐ 110 Andre Rison	.25	.11	.03
☐ 111 Kelvin Martin	.15	.07	.02
☐ 112 Marcus Robertson	.15	.07	.02
☐ 113 Jason Gildon	.15	.07	.02
☐ 114 Mel Gray	.15	.07	.02
☐ 115 Tommy Vardell	.15	.07	.02
☐ 116 Dexter Carter	.15	.07	.02
☐ 117 Scottie Graham	.25	.11	.03
☐ 118 Horace Copeland	.15	.07	.02
☐ 119 Cornelius Bennett	.25	.11	.03
☐ 120 Chris Maumalanga	.15	.07	.02
☐ 121 Mo Lewis	.15	.07	.02
☐ 122 Toby Wright	.15	.07	.02
☐ 123 George Hegamin	.15	.07	.02
☐ 124 Chip Lohmiller	.15	.07	.02
☐ 125 Calvin Jones	.15	.07	.02
☐ 126 Steve Shine	.15	.07	.02
☐ 127 Chuck Levy	.15	.07	.02
☐ 128 Sam Mills	.15	.07	.02
☐ 129 Terance Mathis	.25	.11	.03
☐ 130 Randall Cunningham	.25	.11	.03
☐ 131 John Fina	.15	.07	.02
☐ 132 Reggie White	.40	.18	.05
☐ 133 Tom Waddle	.15	.07	.02
☐ 134 Chris Calloway	.15	.07	.02
☐ 135 Kevin Mawae	.15	.07	.02
☐ 136 Lake Dawson	1.25	.55	.16
☐ 137 Alai Kalaniuhalu	.15	.07	.02
☐ 138 Tom Nalen	.15	.07	.02
☐ 139 Cody Carlson	.15	.07	.02
☐ 140 Dan Marino	5.00	2.20	.60
☐ 141 Harris Barton	.15	.07	.02
☐ 142 Don Mosebar	.15	.07	.02
☐ 143 Romeo Bandison	.15	.07	.02
☐ 144 Bruce Smith	.40	.18	.05
☐ 145 Warren Moon	.40	.18	.05
☐ 146 David Lutz	.15	.07	.02
☐ 147 Dermontti Dawson	.15	.07	.02
☐ 148 Ricky Proehl	.15	.07	.02
☐ 149 Lou Benfatti	.15	.07	.02
☐ 150 Craig Erickson	.15	.07	.02
☐ 151 Sean Gilbert	.15	.07	.02
☐ 152 Zefross Moss	.15	.07	.02
☐ 153 Darnay Scott	3.50	1.55	.45
☐ 154 Courtney Hall	.15	.07	.02
☐ 155 Brian Mitchell	.15	.07	.02
☐ 156 Joe Burch UER	.15	.07	.02
☐ 157 Terry Mickens	.15	.07	.02
☐ 158 Jay Novacek	.25	.11	.03
☐ 159 Chris Gedney	.15	.07	.02
☐ 160 Bruce Matthews	.15	.07	.02
☐ 161 Mario Perry	.15	.07	.02
☐ 162 Vince Buck	.15	.07	.02
☐ 163 Michael Bates	.15	.07	.02
☐ 164 Willie Davis	.25	.11	.03
☐ 165 Mike Pritchard	.15	.07	.02
☐ 166 Doug Riesenberg	.15	.07	.02
☐ 167 Herschel Walker	.25	.11	.03
☐ 168 Tim Ruddy	.15	.07	.02
☐ 169 William Floyd	2.00	.90	.25
☐ 170 John Randle	.15	.07	.02
☐ 171 Winston Moss	.15	.07	.02
☐ 172 Thurman Thomas	.40	.18	.05
☐ 173 Eric England	.15	.07	.02
☐ 174 Vincent Brisby	.40	.18	.05
☐ 175 Greg Lloyd	.40	.18	.05
☐ 176 Paul Gruber	.15	.07	.02
☐ 177 Brad Ottis	.15	.07	.02
☐ 178 George Teague	.15	.07	.02
☐ 179 Willie Jackson	1.00	.45	.12
☐ 180 Barry Sanders	3.00	1.35	.35
☐ 181 Brian Washington	.15	.07	.02
☐ 182 Michael Jackson	.25	.11	.03
☐ 183 Jason Mathews	.15	.07	.02
☐ 184 Chester McGlockton	.15	.07	.02
☐ 185 Tydus Winans	.15	.07	.02
☐ 186 Michael Haynes	.25	.11	.03
☐ 187 Erik Kramer	.25	.11	.03
☐ 188 Chris Doleman	.15	.07	.02
☐ 189 Haywood Jeffires	.25	.11	.03
☐ 190 Larry Whigham	.15	.07	.02
☐ 191 Shawn Jefferson	.15	.07	.02
☐ 192 Pete Stoyanovich	.15	.07	.02
☐ 193 Rod Bernstine	.15	.07	.02
☐ 194 William Thomas	.15	.07	.02
☐ 195 Marcus Allen	.40	.18	.05
☐ 196 Dave Brown	.25	.11	.03
☐ 197 Harold Bishop	.15	.07	.02
☐ 198 Lorenzo Lynch	.15	.07	.02
☐ 199 Dwight Stone	.15	.07	.02
☐ 200 Jerry Rice	3.00	1.35	.35
☐ 201 Rocket Ismail	.25	.11	.03
☐ 202 LeRoy Butler	.15	.07	.02
☐ 203 Glenn Parker	.15	.07	.02
☐ 204 Bruce Armstrong	.15	.07	.02
☐ 205 Shane Conlan	.15	.07	.02
☐ 206 Russell Maryland	.15	.07	.02
☐ 207 Herman Moore	1.25	.55	.16
☐ 208 Eric Martin	.15	.07	.02
☐ 209 John Friesz	.25	.11	.03
☐ 210 Boomer Esiason	.25	.11	.03
☐ 211 Jim Harbaugh	.40	.18	.05
☐ 212 Harold Green	.15	.07	.02
☐ 213 Perry Klein	.15	.07	.02
☐ 214 Eric Metcalf	.25	.11	.03
☐ 215 Steve Everitt	.15	.07	.02
☐ 216 Victor Bailey	.15	.07	.02
☐ 217 Lincoln Kennedy	.15	.07	.02
☐ 218 Glyn Milburn	.25	.11	.03
☐ 219 John Copeland	.15	.07	.02
☐ 220 Drew Bledsoe	3.00	1.35	.35
☐ 221 Kevin Williams	.25	.11	.03
☐ 222 Roosevelt Potts	.15	.07	.02
☐ 223 Troy Drayton	.15	.07	.02
☐ 224 Terry Kirby	.40	.18	.05
☐ 225 Ronald Moore	.15	.07	.02
☐ 226 Tyrone Hughes	.25	.11	.03
☐ 227 Wayne Simmons	.15	.07	.02
☐ 228 Tony McGee	.15	.07	.02
☐ 229 Derek Brown RB	.15	.07	.02
☐ 230 Jason Elam	.15	.07	.02
☐ 231 Qadry Ismail	.40	.18	.05
☐ 232 O.J. McDuffie	.40	.18	.05
☐ 233 Mike Caldwell	.15	.07	.02
☐ 234 Reggie Brooks	.25	.11	.03
☐ 235 Rick Mirer	.40	.18	.05
☐ 236 Steve Tovar	.15	.07	.02
☐ 237 Patrick Robinson	.15	.07	.02
☐ 238 Tom Carter	.15	.07	.02
☐ 239 Ben Coates	.40	.18	.05
☐ 240 Jerome Bettis	1.50	.70	.19
☐ 241 Garrison Hearst	1.25	.55	.16
☐ 242 Natrone Means	1.25	.55	.16
☐ 243 Dana Stubblefield	.40	.18	.05
☐ 244 Willie Roaf	.15	.07	.02
☐ 245 Cortez Kennedy	.25	.11	.03
☐ 246 Todd Steussie	.25	.11	.03
☐ 247 Pat Coleman	.15	.07	.02
☐ 248 David Wyman	.15	.07	.02
☐ 249 Jeremy Lincoln	.15	.07	.02
☐ 250 Carlester Crumpler	.15	.07	.02
☐ 251 Dale Carter	.15	.07	.02
☐ 252 Corey Raymond	.15	.07	.02
☐ 253 Bryan Cox	.15	.07	.02
☐ 254 Charlie Garner	.25	.11	.03
☐ 255 Jeff Hostetler	.25	.11	.03
☐ 256 Shane Bonham	.15	.07	.02
☐ 257 Thomas Everett	.15	.07	.02
☐ 258 John Jackson	.15	.07	.02
☐ 259 Terry Irving	.15	.07	.02
☐ 260 Corey Sawyer	.15	.07	.02
☐ 261 Rob Waldrop	.15	.07	.02
☐ 262 Curtis Conway	.40	.18	.05
☐ 263 Winfred Tubbs	.25	.11	.03
☐ 264 Sean Jones	.15	.07	.02
☐ 265 James Washington	.15	.07	.02
☐ 266 Lonnie Johnson	.15	.07	.02
☐ 267 Rob Moore	.25	.11	.03
☐ 268 Flipper Anderson	.15	.07	.02
☐ 269 Jon Hand	.15	.07	.02
☐ 270 Joe Patton	.15	.07	.02
☐ 271 Howard Ballard	.15	.07	.02
☐ 272 Fernando Smith	.15	.07	.02
☐ 273 Jessie Tuggle	.15	.07	.02
☐ 274 John Alt	.15	.07	.02
☐ 275 Corey Miller	.15	.07	.02
☐ 276 Gus Frerotte	4.00	1.80	.50
☐ 277 Jeff Cross	.15	.07	.02
☐ 278 Kevin Smith	.15	.07	.02
☐ 279 Corey Louchiey	.15	.07	.02
☐ 280 Micheal Barrow	.15	.07	.02
☐ 281 Jim Flanigan	.25	.11	.03
☐ 282 Calvin Williams	.25	.11	.03
☐ 283 Jeff Jaeger	.15	.07	.02
☐ 284 John Reece	.15	.07	.02
☐ 285 Jason Hanson	.15	.07	.02
☐ 286 Kurt Haws	.15	.07	.02
☐ 287 Eric Davis	.15	.07	.02
☐ 288 Maurice Hurst	.15	.07	.02
☐ 289 Kirk Lowdermilk	.15	.07	.02
☐ 290 Rod Woodson	.40	.18	.05
☐ 291 Andre Reed	.25	.11	.03
☐ 292 Vince Workman	.15	.07	.02
☐ 293 Wayne Martin	.15	.07	.02
☐ 294 Keith Lyle	.15	.07	.02
☐ 295 Brett Favre	5.00	2.20	.60
☐ 296 Doug Brien	.15	.07	.02
☐ 297 Junior Seau	.40	.18	.05
☐ 298 Randall McDaniel	.15	.07	.02
☐ 299 Johnny Mitchell	.15	.07	.02
☐ 300 Emmitt Smith	5.00	2.20	.60
☐ 301 Michael Brooks	.15	.07	.02
☐ 302 Steve Jackson	.15	.07	.02
☐ 303 Jeff George	.40	.18	.05
☐ 304 Irving Fryar	.25	.11	.03
☐ 305 Derrick Thomas	.40	.18	.05
☐ 306 Dante Jones	.15	.07	.02
☐ 307 Darrell Green	.15	.07	.02
☐ 308 Mark Bavaro	.15	.07	.02
☐ 309 Eugene Robinson	.15	.07	.02
☐ 310 Shannon Sharpe	.25	.11	.03
☐ 311 Michael Timpson	.15	.07	.02
☐ 312 Kevin Mitchell	.15	.07	.02
☐ 313 Stevon Moore	.15	.07	.02
☐ 314 Eric Swann	.25	.11	.03
☐ 315 James Bostic	.15	.07	.02
☐ 316 Robert Brooks	.75	.35	.09
☐ 317 Pete Pierson	.15	.07	.02
☐ 318 Jim Sweeney	.15	.07	.02
☐ 319 Anthony Smith	.15	.07	.02
☐ 320 Rohn Stark	.15	.07	.02
☐ 321 Gary Anderson K	.15	.07	.02
☐ 322 Robert Porcher	.15	.07	.02
☐ 323 Darryl Talley	.15	.07	.02
☐ 324 Stan Humphries	.40	.18	.05
☐ 325 Shelly Hammonds	.15	.07	.02
☐ 326 Jim McMahon	.15	.07	.02
☐ 327 Lamont Warren	.15	.07	.02
☐ 328 Chris Penn	.15	.07	.02
☐ 329 Tony Woods	.15	.07	.02
☐ 330 Raymont Harris	.15	.07	.02
☐ 331 Mitch Davis	.15	.07	.02
☐ 332 Michael Irvin	.40	.18	.05
☐ 333 Kent Graham	.25	.11	.03
☐ 334 Brian Blades	.25	.11	.03
☐ 335 Lomas Brown	.15	.07	.02
☐ 336 Willie Drewrey	.15	.07	.02
☐ 337 Russell Freeman	.15	.07	.02
☐ 338 Eric Zomalt	.15	.07	.02
☐ 339 Santana Dotson	.25	.11	.03
☐ 340 Sterling Sharpe	.25	.11	.03
☐ 341 Ray Crittenden	.15	.07	.02
☐ 342 Perry Carter	.15	.07	.02
☐ 343 Austin Robbins	.15	.07	.02
☐ 344 Mike Wells	.15	.07	.02
☐ 345 Toddrick McIntosh	.15	.07	.02
☐ 346 Mark Carrier WR	.25	.11	.03
☐ 347 Eugene Daniel	.15	.07	.02
☐ 348 Tre Johnson	.15	.07	.02
☐ 349 D.J. Johnson	.15	.07	.02
☐ 350 Steve Young	2.00	.90	.25
☐ 351 Jim Pyne	.15	.07	.02
☐ 352 Jocelyn Borgella	.15	.07	.02
☐ 353 Pat Carter	.15	.07	.02
☐ 354 Sam Rogers	.15	.07	.02
☐ 355 Jason Sehorn	.15	.07	.02
☐ 356 Darren Carrington	.15	.07	.02
☐ 357 Lamar Smith	.15	.07	.02
☐ 358 James Burton	.15	.07	.02
☐ 359 Darrin Smith	.15	.07	.02
☐ 360 Marco Coleman	.15	.07	.02
☐ 361 Webster Slaughter	.15	.07	.02
☐ 362 Lewis Tillman	.15	.07	.02
☐ 363 David Alexander	.15	.07	.02
☐ 364 Bradford Banta	.15	.07	.02
☐ 365 Erric Pegram	.15	.07	.02
☐ 366 Mike Fox	.15	.07	.02
☐ 367 Jeff Lageman	.15	.07	.02
☐ 368 Kurt Gouveia	.15	.07	.02
☐ 369 Tim Brown	.40	.18	.05
☐ 370 Seth Joyner	.15	.07	.02
☐ 371 Irv Eatman	.15	.07	.02
☐ 372 Dorsey Levens	2.00	.90	.25
☐ 373 Anthony Pleasant	.15	.07	.02
☐ 374 Henry Jones	.15	.07	.02
☐ 375 Cris Carter	.40	.18	.05
☐ 376 Morten Andersen	.15	.07	.02
☐ 377 Neil O'Donnell	.40	.18	.05
☐ 378 Tyronne Drakeford	.15	.07	.02
☐ 379 John Carney	.15	.07	.02
☐ 380 Vincent Brown	.15	.07	.02
☐ 381 J.J. Birden	.15	.07	.02
☐ 382 Chris Spielman	.25	.11	.03
☐ 383 Mark Bortz	.15	.07	.02
☐ 384 Ray Childress	.15	.07	.02
☐ 385 Carlton Bailey	.15	.07	.02
☐ 386 Charles Haley	.25	.11	.03
☐ 387 Shane Dronett	.15	.07	.02
☐ 388 Jon Vaughn	.15	.07	.02
☐ 389 Checklist 1-195	.15	.07	.02
☐ 390 Checklist 196-390	.15	.07	.02

1995 Bowman

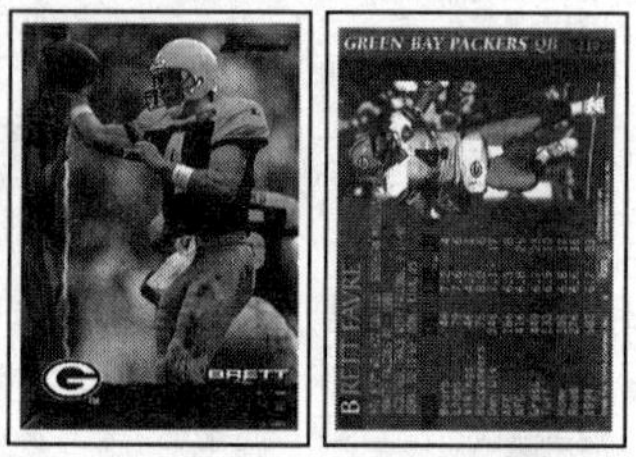

This 357-card standard size set was issued by Topps. The fronts display a player photo on the right hand side with a "reverse shot" of the same photo on the left side. The player's name is listed along the bottom right side of the card and the Bowman logo is at the top of the card in red foil. The horizontal backs feature 1994 statistics and biographical information for veteran players as well as a picture of the player. The backs for rookie cards contain biographical information and lists briefly the player's college resume, skills and an "up close" section. There are no photos on the back of the rookie cards. Parallel sets of the expansion team cards and rookie draft picks were included. The expansion team parallel had extra gold foil while the draft pick parallel had a "First Round" stamp on the front. Rookie Cards in this set include Jeff Blake, Ki-Jana Carter, Kerry Collins, Joey Galloway, Napoleon Kaufman, Steve McNair, Curtis Martin, Rashan Salaam, Chris Sanders, Kordell Stewart, J.J. Stokes, Rodney Thomas, Tamarick Vanover and Michael Westbrook.

	MINT	NRMT	EXC
COMPLETE SET (357)	90.00	40.00	11.00
COMMON CARD (1-357)	.10	.05	.01
☐ 1 Ki-Jana Carter	1.50	.70	.19
☐ 2 Tony Boselli	.20	.09	.03
☐ 3 Steve McNair	7.00	3.10	.85
☐ 4 Michael Westbrook	2.00	.90	.25
☐ 5 Kerry Collins	8.00	3.60	1.00
☐ 6 Kevin Carter	.40	.18	.05
☐ 7 Mike Mamula	.20	.09	.03
☐ 8 Joey Galloway	3.00	1.35	.35
☐ 9 Kyle Brady	.40	.18	.05
☐ 10 J.J. Stokes	1.50	.70	.19
☐ 11 Derrick Alexander DE	.10	.05	.01
☐ 12 Warren Sapp	.20	.09	.03
☐ 13 Mark Fields	.10	.05	.01
☐ 14 Ruben Brown	.10	.05	.01
☐ 15 Ellis Johnson	.10	.05	.01
☐ 16 Hugh Douglas	.20	.09	.03
☐ 17 Mike Pelton	.10	.05	.01
☐ 18 Napoleon Kaufman	1.50	.70	.19
☐ 19 James O.Stewart	.40	.18	.05
☐ 20 Luther Elliss	.10	.05	.01
☐ 21 Rashaan Salaam	2.00	.90	.25
☐ 22 Tyrone Poole	.20	.09	.03
☐ 23 Ty Law	.20	.09	.03
☐ 24 Korey Stringer	.10	.05	.01
☐ 25 Billy Milner	.10	.05	.01
☐ 26 Devin Bush	.10	.05	.01
☐ 27 Mark Bruener	.20	.09	.03
☐ 28 Derrick Brooks	.10	.05	.01
☐ 29 Blake Brockermeyer	.10	.05	.01
☐ 30 Alundis Brice	.10	.05	.01
☐ 31 Trezelle Jenkins	.10	.05	.01
☐ 32 Craig Newsome	.10	.05	.01
☐ 33 Fred Barnett	.20	.09	.03
☐ 34 Ray Childress	.10	.05	.01
☐ 35 Chris Miller	.10	.05	.01
☐ 36 Charles Haley	.20	.09	.03
☐ 37 Ray Crittenden	.10	.05	.01
☐ 38 Gus Frerotte	.75	.35	.09
☐ 39 Jeff George	.20	.09	.03
☐ 40 Dan Marino	3.00	1.35	.35

☐ 41 Shawn Lee	.10	.05	.01
☐ 42 Herman Moore	.75	.35	.09
☐ 43 Chris Calloway	.10	.05	.01
☐ 44 Jeff Graham	.10	.05	.01
☐ 45 Ray Buchanan	.10	.05	.01
☐ 46 Doug Pelfrey	.10	.05	.01
☐ 47 Lake Dawson	.20	.09	.03
☐ 48 Glenn Parker	.10	.05	.01
☐ 49 Terry McDaniel	.10	.05	.01
☐ 50 Rod Woodson	.20	.09	.03
☐ 51 Santana Dotson	.10	.05	.01
☐ 52 Anthony Miller	.20	.09	.03
☐ 53 Bo Orlando	.10	.05	.01
☐ 54 David Palmer	.20	.09	.03
☐ 55 William Floyd	.40	.18	.05
☐ 56 Edgar Bennett	.20	.09	.03
☐ 57 Jeff Blake	2.00	.90	.25
☐ 58 Anthony Pleasant	.10	.05	.01
☐ 59 Quinn Early	.20	.09	.03
☐ 60 Bobby Houston	.10	.05	.01
☐ 61 Terrell Fletcher	.10	.05	.01
☐ 62 Gary Brown	.10	.05	.01
☐ 63 Dwayne Sabb	.10	.05	.01
☐ 64 Roman Phifer	.10	.05	.01
☐ 65 Sherman Williams	.10	.05	.01
☐ 66 Roosevelt Potts	.10	.05	.01
☐ 67 Darnay Scott	.40	.18	.05
☐ 68 Charlie Garner	.20	.09	.03
☐ 69 Bert Emanuel	.40	.18	.05
☐ 70 Herschel Walker	.20	.09	.03
☐ 71 Lorenzo Styles	.10	.05	.01
☐ 72 Andre Coleman	.10	.05	.01
☐ 73 Tyronne Drakeford	.10	.05	.01
☐ 74 Jay Novacek	.20	.09	.03
☐ 75 Raymont Harris	.10	.05	.01
☐ 76 Tamarick Vanover	2.00	.90	.25
☐ 77 Tom Carter	.10	.05	.01
☐ 78 Eric Green	.10	.05	.01
☐ 79 Patrick Hunter	.10	.05	.01
☐ 80 Jeff Hostetler	.20	.09	.03
☐ 81 Robert Blackmon	.10	.05	.01
☐ 82 Anthony Cook	.10	.05	.01
☐ 83 Craig Erickson	.10	.05	.01
☐ 84 Glyn Milburn	.10	.05	.01
☐ 85 Greg Lloyd	.20	.09	.03
☐ 86 Brent Jones	.10	.05	.01
☐ 87 Barrett Brooks	.10	.05	.01
☐ 88 Alvin Harper	.10	.05	.01
☐ 89 Sean Jones	.10	.05	.01
☐ 90 Cris Carter	.40	.18	.05
☐ 91 Russell Copeland	.10	.05	.01
☐ 92 Frank Sanders	1.50	.70	.19
☐ 93 Mo Lewis	.10	.05	.01
☐ 94 Michael Haynes	.20	.09	.03
☐ 95 Andre Rison	.20	.09	.03
☐ 96 Jesse James	.10	.05	.01
☐ 97 Stan Humphries	.20	.09	.03
☐ 98 James Hasty	.10	.05	.01
☐ 99 Ricardo McDonald	.10	.05	.01
☐ 100 Jerry Rice	1.50	.70	.19
☐ 101 Chris Hudson	.10	.05	.01
☐ 102 Dave Meggett	.10	.05	.01
☐ 103 Brian Mitchell	.10	.05	.01
☐ 104 Mike Johnson	.10	.05	.01
☐ 105 Kordell Stewart	7.00	3.10	.85
☐ 106 Michael Brooks	.10	.05	.01
☐ 107 Steve Walsh	.10	.05	.01
☐ 108 Eric Metcalf	.20	.09	.03
☐ 109 Ricky Watters	.40	.18	.05
☐ 110 Brett Favre	3.00	1.35	.35
☐ 111 Aubrey Beavers	.10	.05	.01
☐ 112 Brian Williams	.10	.05	.01
☐ 113 Eugene Robinson	.10	.05	.01
☐ 114 Matt O'Dwyer	.10	.05	.01
☐ 115 Micheal Barrow	.10	.05	.01
☐ 116 Rocket Ismail	.20	.09	.03
☐ 117 Scott Gragg	.10	.05	.01
☐ 118 Leon Lett	.10	.05	.01
☐ 119 Reggie Roby	.10	.05	.01
☐ 120 Marshall Faulk	.75	.35	.09
☐ 121 Jack Jackson	.10	.05	.01
☐ 122 Keith Byars	.10	.05	.01
☐ 123 Eric Hill	.10	.05	.01
☐ 124 Todd Sauerbrun	.10	.05	.01
☐ 125 Dexter Carter	.10	.05	.01
☐ 126 Vinny Testaverde	.20	.09	.03
☐ 127 Shane Conlan	.10	.05	.01
☐ 128 Terrance Shaw	.10	.05	.01
☐ 129 Willie Roaf	.10	.05	.01
☐ 130 Jim Kelly	.40	.18	.05
☐ 131 Neil O'Donnell	.20	.09	.03
☐ 132 Ray McElroy	.10	.05	.01
☐ 133 Ed McDaniel	.10	.05	.01
☐ 134 Brian Gelzheiser	.20	.09	.03
☐ 135 Marcus Allen	.40	.18	.05
☐ 136 Carl Pickens	.40	.18	.05
☐ 137 Mike Verstegen	.10	.05	.01
☐ 138 Chris Mims	.10	.05	.01
☐ 139 Darryl Pounds	.10	.05	.01
☐ 140 Emmitt Smith	3.00	1.35	.35
☐ 141 Mike Frederick	.10	.05	.01
☐ 142 Henry Ellard	.20	.09	.03
☐ 143 Willie McGinest	.20	.09	.03
☐ 144 Michael Roan	.10	.05	.01
☐ 145 Chris Spielman	.20	.09	.03
☐ 146 Darryl Talley	.10	.05	.01
☐ 147 Randall Cunningham	.20	.09	.03
☐ 148 Andrew Greene	.10	.05	.01
☐ 149 George Teague	.10	.05	.01
☐ 150 Tyrone Hughes	.20	.09	.03
☐ 151 Ron Davis	.10	.05	.01
☐ 152 Stevon Moore	.10	.05	.01
☐ 153 Merton Hanks	.10	.05	.01
☐ 154 Darren Perry	.10	.05	.01
☐ 155 Dave Brown	.20	.09	.03
☐ 156 Mike Morton	.10	.05	.01
☐ 157 Seth Joyner	.10	.05	.01
☐ 158 Bryan Cox	.10	.05	.01
☐ 159 Corey Fuller	.10	.05	.01
☐ 160 John Elway	1.25	.55	.16
☐ 161 Dewayne Washington	.20	.09	.03
☐ 162 Chris Warren	.20	.09	.03
☐ 163 Jeff Kopp	.10	.05	.01
☐ 164 Sean Dawkins	.20	.09	.03
☐ 165 Mark Carrier DB	.10	.05	.01
☐ 166 Andre Hastings	.20	.09	.03
☐ 167 Derek West	.10	.05	.01
☐ 168 Glenn Montgomery	.10	.05	.01
☐ 169 Trent Dilfer	.40	.18	.05
☐ 170 Rob Johnson	.10	.05	.01
☐ 171 Todd Scott	.10	.05	.01
☐ 172 Charles Johnson	.20	.09	.03
☐ 173 Kez McCorvey	.10	.05	.01
☐ 174 Rob Fredrickson	.10	.05	.01
☐ 175 Corey Sawyer	.10	.05	.01
☐ 176 Brett Perriman	.20	.09	.03
☐ 177 Ken Dilger	.20	.09	.03
☐ 178 Dana Stubblefield	.40	.18	.05
☐ 179 Eric Allen	.10	.05	.01
☐ 180 Drew Bledsoe	1.50	.70	.19
☐ 181 Tyrone Davis	.10	.05	.01
☐ 182 Reggie Brooks	.20	.09	.03
☐ 183 Dale Carter	.20	.09	.03
☐ 184 William Henderson	.10	.05	.01
☐ 185 Reggie White	.40	.18	.05
☐ 186 Lorenzo White	.10	.05	.01
☐ 187 Leslie O'Neal	.20	.09	.03
☐ 188 Stoney Case	.10	.05	.01
☐ 189 Jeff Burris	.10	.05	.01
☐ 190 Leroy Hoard	.10	.05	.01
☐ 191 Thomas Randolph	.10	.05	.01
☐ 192 Rodney Thomas	.40	.18	.05
☐ 193 Quentin Coryatt	.20	.09	.03
☐ 194 Terry Wooden	.10	.05	.01
☐ 195 David Sloan	.20	.09	.03
☐ 196 Bernie Parmalee	.20	.09	.03
☐ 197 Zack Crockett	.10	.05	.01
☐ 198 Troy Aikman	1.50	.70	.19
☐ 199 Bruce Smith	.40	.18	.05
☐ 200 Eric Zeier	.40	.18	.05
☐ 201 Anthony Smith	.10	.05	.01
☐ 202 Jake Reed	.20	.09	.03
☐ 203 Hardy Nickerson	.10	.05	.01
☐ 204 Patrick Riley	.10	.05	.01
☐ 205 Bruce Matthews	.10	.05	.01
☐ 206 Larry Centers	.20	.09	.03
☐ 207 Troy Drayton	.10	.05	.01
☐ 208 John Burrough	.10	.05	.01
☐ 209 Jason Elam	.10	.05	.01
☐ 210 Donnell Woolford	.10	.05	.01
☐ 211 Sam Shade	.10	.05	.01
☐ 212 Kevin Greene	.20	.09	.03
☐ 213 Ronald Moore	.10	.05	.01
☐ 214 Shane Hannah	.10	.05	.01
☐ 215 Jim Everett	.10	.05	.01
☐ 216 Scott Mitchell	.20	.09	.03
☐ 217 Antonio Freeman	3.00	1.35	.35
☐ 218 Tony McGee	.10	.05	.01
☐ 219 Clay Matthews	.20	.09	.03
☐ 220 Neil Smith	.20	.09	.03
☐ 221 Mark Williams FOIL	.40	.18	.05
☐ 222 Derrick Graham FOIL	.40	.18	.05
☐ 223 Mike Hollis FOIL	.40	.18	.05
☐ 224 Darion Conner FOIL	.40	.18	.05
☐ 225 Steve Beuerlein FOIL	.40	.18	.05
☐ 226 Rod Smith DB FOIL	.40	.18	.05
☐ 227 James Williams FOIL	.40	.18	.05
☐ 228 Bob Christian FOIL	.40	.18	.05
☐ 229 Jeff Lageman FOIL	.40	.18	.05
☐ 230 Frank Reich FOIL	.40	.18	.05
☐ 231 Harry Colon FOIL	.40	.18	.05
☐ 232 Carlton Bailey FOIL	.40	.18	.05
☐ 233 Mickey Washington FOIL	.40	.18	.05
☐ 234 Shawn Bouwens FOIL	.40	.18	.05
☐ 235 Don Beebe FOIL	.40	.18	.05
☐ 236 Kelvin Pritchett FOIL	.40	.18	.05
☐ 237 Tommy Barnhardt FOIL	.40	.18	.05
☐ 238 Mike Dumas FOIL	.40	.18	.05
☐ 239 Brett Maxie FOIL	.40	.18	.05
☐ 240 Desmond Howard FOIL	.40	.18	.05
☐ 241 Sam Mills FOIL	.40	.18	.05
☐ 242 Keith Goganious FOIL	.40	.18	.05
☐ 243 Bubba McDowell FOIL	.40	.18	.05
☐ 244 Vinnie Clark FOIL	.40	.18	.05
☐ 245 Lamar Lathon FOIL	.40	.18	.05
☐ 246 Bryan Barker FOIL	.40	.18	.05
☐ 247 Darren Carrington FOIL	.40	.18	.05
☐ 248 Jay Barker	.10	.05	.01
☐ 249 Eric Davis	.10	.05	.01
☐ 250 Heath Shuler	.40	.18	.05
☐ 251 Donta Jones	.10	.05	.01
☐ 252 LeRoy Butler	.10	.05	.01
☐ 253 Michael Zordich	.10	.05	.01
☐ 254 Cortez Kennedy	.20	.09	.03
☐ 255 Brian DeMarco	.20	.09	.03
☐ 256 Randal Hill	.10	.05	.01
☐ 257 Michael Irvin	.40	.18	.05
☐ 258 Natrone Means	.40	.18	.05
☐ 259 Linc Harden	.10	.05	.01
☐ 260 Jerome Bettis	.60	.25	.07
☐ 261 Tony Bennett	.10	.05	.01
☐ 262 Dameian Jeffries	.10	.05	.01
☐ 263 Cornelius Bennett	.20	.09	.03
☐ 264 Chris Zorich	.10	.05	.01
☐ 265 Bobby Taylor	.20	.09	.03
☐ 266 Terrell Buckley	.10	.05	.01
☐ 267 Troy Dumas	.10	.05	.01
☐ 268 Rodney Hampton	.20	.09	.03
☐ 269 Steve Everitt	.10	.05	.01
☐ 270 Mel Gray	.10	.05	.01
☐ 271 Antonio Armstrong	.10	.05	.01
☐ 272 Jim Harbaugh	.20	.09	.03
☐ 273 Gary Clark	.10	.05	.01
☐ 274 Tau Pupua	.10	.05	.01
☐ 275 Warren Moon	.20	.09	.03
☐ 276 Corey Croom	.10	.05	.01
☐ 277 Tony Berti	.10	.05	.01
☐ 278 Shannon Sharpe	.20	.09	.03
☐ 279 Boomer Esiason	.20	.09	.03
☐ 280 Aeneas Williams	.10	.05	.01
☐ 281 Lethon Flowers	.10	.05	.01
☐ 282 Derek Brown TE	.10	.05	.01
☐ 283 Charlie Williams	.10	.05	.01
☐ 284 Dan Wilkinson	.20	.09	.03
☐ 285 Mike Sherrard	.10	.05	.01
☐ 286 Evan Pilgrim	.10	.05	.01
☐ 287 Kimble Anders	.20	.09	.03
☐ 288 Greg Jefferson	.10	.05	.01
☐ 289 Ken Norton	.20	.09	.03
☐ 290 Terance Mathis	.20	.09	.03
☐ 291 Torey Hunter	.10	.05	.01
☐ 292 Ken Harvey	.10	.05	.01
☐ 293 Irving Fryar	.20	.09	.03
☐ 294 Michael Reed	.10	.05	.01
☐ 295 Andre Reed	.20	.09	.03
☐ 296 Vencie Glenn	.10	.05	.01
☐ 297 Corey Swinson	.10	.05	.01
☐ 298 Harvey Williams	.10	.05	.01
☐ 299 Willie Davis	.20	.09	.03
☐ 300 Barry Sanders	1.50	.70	.19
☐ 301 Curtis Martin	8.00	3.60	1.00
☐ 302 Johnny Mitchell	.10	.05	.01
☐ 303 Daryl Johnston	.20	.09	.03
☐ 304 Lorenzo Lynch	.10	.05	.01
☐ 305 Christian Fauria	.10	.05	.01
☐ 306 Sean Gilbert	.20	.09	.03
☐ 307 Ray Zellars	.20	.09	.03
☐ 308 William Strong	.10	.05	.01
☐ 309 Jack Del Rio	.10	.05	.01
☐ 310 Junior Seau	.40	.18	.05
☐ 311 Justin Armour	.10	.05	.01
☐ 312 Eric Bjornson	.20	.09	.03
☐ 313 Vincent Brown	.10	.05	.01
☐ 314 Darius Holland	.10	.05	.01
☐ 315 Chad May	.10	.05	.01
☐ 316 Simon Fletcher	.10	.05	.01
☐ 317 Roell Preston	.10	.05	.01
☐ 318 John Thierry	.10	.05	.01
☐ 319 Orlando Thomas	.10	.05	.01
☐ 320 Zach Wiegert	.10	.05	.01
☐ 321 Derrick Alexander WR	.40	.18	.05
☐ 322 Chris Cowart	.10	.05	.01
☐ 323 Chris Sanders	2.00	.90	.25
☐ 324 Robert Brooks	.40	.18	.05
☐ 325 Todd Collins	.40	.18	.05
☐ 326 Ken Irvin	.10	.05	.01
☐ 327 Eric Pegram	.20	.09	.03
☐ 328 Damien Covington	.10	.05	.01
☐ 329 Brendan Stai	.10	.05	.01
☐ 330 James A.Stewart	.10	.05	.01
☐ 331 Jessie Tuggle	.10	.05	.01
☐ 332 Marco Coleman	.10	.05	.01
☐ 333 Steve Young	1.25	.55	.16
☐ 334 Greg Hill	.20	.09	.03
☐ 335 Darryl Williams	.10	.05	.01
☐ 336 Calvin Williams	.20	.09	.03
☐ 337 Cris Dishman	.10	.05	.01
☐ 338 Anthony Morgan	.10	.05	.01
☐ 339 Renaldo Turnbull	.10	.05	.01
☐ 340 Rick Mirer	.40	.18	.05
☐ 341 Tim Brown	.40	.18	.05
☐ 342 Dennis Gibson	.10	.05	.01
☐ 343 Brad Baxter	.10	.05	.01
☐ 344 Henry Jones	.10	.05	.01
☐ 345 Johnny Bailey	.10	.05	.01
☐ 346 Rocket Ismail	.20	.09	.03
☐ 347 Richmond Webb	.10	.05	.01
☐ 348 Robert Jones	.10	.05	.01
☐ 349 Garrison Hearst	.40	.18	.05
☐ 350 Errict Rhett	.40	.18	.05
☐ 351 Steve Atwater	.10	.05	.01
☐ 352 Joe Cain	.10	.05	.01
☐ 353 Ben Coates	.20	.09	.03
☐ 354 Aaron Glenn	.10	.05	.01
☐ 355 Antonio Langham	.10	.05	.01
☐ 356 Eugene Daniel	.10	.05	.01
☐ 357 Tim Bowens	.10	.05	.01

1995 Bowman Expansion Team Gold

Each of the 27-expansion team foil cards (card #'s 221-247) included in the regular Bowman set were produced in a Gold foil parallel. The Gold cards were randomly inserted in packs at the rate of 1:12.

	MINT	NRMT	EXC
COMPLETE SET (27)	20.00	9.00	2.50
COMMON CARD (221-247)	.80	.35	.10

EXPANSION GOLDS: 1X TO 2X BASIC CARDS

1995 Bowman First Rounders

Topps produced 22-parallel cards stamped "First Round" for its 1995 Bowman issue. The cards were randomly inserted in packs at the rate of 1:12. Card #17 was not issued.

	MINT	NRMT	EXC
COMPLETE SET (22)	30.00	13.50	3.70
COMMON CARD (1-23)	.25	.11	.03

*FIRST ROUND STAMPED: 1X TO 2X BASIC CARDS

1995 Bowman's Best

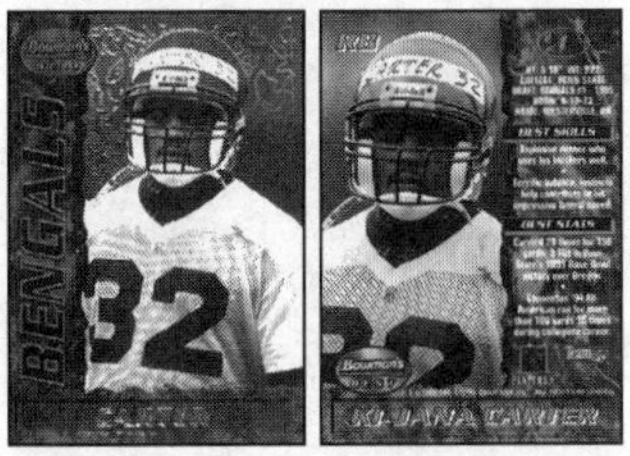

This 180 card set was issued by Topps and broken down into two subsets: Bowman's Best Black for veterans (V1-V90) and Bowman's Best Blue for rookies (R1-R90). The fronts utilize Finest technology with the player's name across the bottom and the team name listed vertically on the left side of the card. Card backs use the same photo as the fronts with biological information and player skill and statistical summaries. Rookie Cards in this set include Mark Bruener, Ki-Jana Carter, Kerry Collins, Joey Galloway, Darrick Holmes, Napoleon Kaufman, Steve McNair, Curtis Martin, Chris Sanders, Frank Sanders, Rashaan Salaam, Kordell Stewart, Tamarick Vanover and Michael Westbrook

	MINT	NRMT	EXC
COMPLETE SET (180)	100.00	45.00	12.50
COMMON BLUE CARD (R1-R90)	.30	.14	.04
COMMON BLACK CARD (V1-V90)	.30	.14	.04

☐ R1 Ki-Jana Carter	3.00	1.35	.35
☐ R2 Tony Boselli	.50	.23	.06
☐ R3 Steve McNair	10.00	4.50	1.25
☐ R4 Michael Westbrook	4.00	1.80	.50
☐ R5 Kerry Collins	12.00	5.50	1.50
☐ R6 Kevin Carter	1.00	.45	.12
☐ R7 Mike Mamula	.50	.23	.06
☐ R8 Joey Galloway	6.00	2.70	.75
☐ R9 Kyle Brady	1.00	.45	.12
☐ R10 Ray McElroy	.30	.14	.04
☐ R11 Derrick Alexander DE	.30	.14	.04
☐ R12 Warren Sapp	.50	.23	.06
☐ R13 Mark Fields	.30	.14	.04
☐ R14 Ruben Brown	.30	.14	.04
☐ R15 Ellis Johnson	.30	.14	.04
☐ R16 Hugh Douglas	.50	.23	.06
☐ R17 Alundis Brice	.30	.14	.04
☐ R18 Napoleon Kaufman	3.00	1.35	.35
☐ R19 James O.Stewart	.50	.23	.06
☐ R20 Luther Elliss	.30	.14	.04
☐ R21 Rashaan Salaam	4.00	1.80	.50
☐ R22 Tyrone Poole	.50	.23	.06
☐ R23 Ty Law	.50	.23	.06
☐ R24 Korey Stringer	.30	.14	.04
☐ R25 Billy Milner	.30	.14	.04
☐ R26 Roell Preston	.30	.14	.04
☐ R27 Mark Bruener	.50	.23	.06
☐ R28 Derrick Brooks	.30	.14	.04
☐ R29 Blake Brockermeyer	.30	.14	.04
☐ R30 Mike Frederick	.30	.14	.04
☐ R31 Trezelle Jenkins	.30	.14	.04
☐ R32 Craig Newsome	.30	.14	.04
☐ R33 Matt O'Dwyer	.30	.14	.04
☐ R34 Terrance Shaw	.30	.14	.04
☐ R35 Anthony Cook	.30	.14	.04
☐ R36 Darick Holmes	2.00	.90	.25
☐ R37 Cory Raymer	.30	.14	.04
☐ R38 Zach Wiegert	.30	.14	.04
☐ R39 Sam Shade	.30	.14	.04
☐ R40 Brian DeMarco	.50	.23	.06
☐ R41 Ron Davis	.30	.14	.04
☐ R42 Orlando Thomas	.30	.14	.04
☐ R43 Derek West	.30	.14	.04
☐ R44 Ray Zellars	.50	.23	.06
☐ R45 Todd Collins	1.00	.45	.12
☐ R46 Linc Harden	.30	.14	.04
☐ R47 Frank Sanders	3.00	1.35	.35

☐ R48 Ken Dilger	.50	.23	.06
☐ R49 Barrett Robbins	.30	.14	.04
☐ R50 Bobby Taylor	.50	.23	.06
☐ R51 Terrell Fletcher	.30	.14	.04
☐ R52 Jack Jackson	.30	.14	.04
☐ R53 Jeff Kopp	.30	.14	.04
☐ R54 Brendan Stai	.30	.14	.04
☐ R55 Corey Fuller	.30	.14	.04
☐ R56 Todd Sauerbrun	.30	.14	.04
☐ R57 Dameian Jeffries	.30	.14	.04
☐ R58 Troy Dumas	.30	.14	.04
☐ R59 Charlie Williams	.30	.14	.04
☐ R60 Kordell Stewart	10.00	4.50	1.25
☐ R61 Jay Barker	.30	.14	.04
☐ R62 Jesse James	.30	.14	.04
☐ R63 Shane Hannah	.30	.14	.04
☐ R64 Rob Johnson	.30	.14	.04
☐ R65 Darius Holland	.30	.14	.04
☐ R66 William Henderson	.30	.14	.04
☐ R67 Chris Sanders	4.00	1.80	.50
☐ R68 Darryl Pounds	.30	.14	.04
☐ R69 Melvin Tuten	.30	.14	.04
☐ R70 David Sloan	.50	.23	.06
☐ R71 Chris Hudson	.30	.14	.04
☐ R72 William Strong	.30	.14	.04
☐ R73 Brian Williams	.30	.14	.04
☐ R74 Curtis Martin	12.00	5.50	1.50
☐ R75 Mike Verstegen	.30	.14	.04
☐ R76 Justin Armour	.30	.14	.04
☐ R77 Lorenzo Styles	.30	.14	.04
☐ R78 Oliver Gibson	.30	.14	.04
☐ R79 Zack Crockett	.30	.14	.04
☐ R80 Tau Pupua	.30	.14	.04
☐ R81 Tamarick Vanover	4.00	1.80	.50
☐ R82 Steve McLaughlin	.30	.14	.04
☐ R83 Sean Harris	.30	.14	.04
☐ R84 Eric Zeier	1.00	.45	.12
☐ R85 Rodney Young	.30	.14	.04
☐ R86 Chad May	.30	.14	.04
☐ R87 Evan Pilgrim	.30	.14	.04
☐ R88 James A.Stewart	.30	.14	.04
☐ R89 Torey Hunter	.30	.14	.04
☐ R90 Antonio Freeman	6.00	2.70	.75
☐ V1 Rob Moore	.30	.14	.04
☐ V2 Craig Heyward	.50	.23	.06
☐ V3 Jim Kelly	1.00	.45	.12
☐ V4 John Kasay	.30	.14	.04
☐ V5 Jeff Graham	.30	.14	.04
☐ V6 Jeff Blake	4.00	1.80	.50
☐ V7 Antonio Langham	.30	.14	.04
☐ V8 Troy Aikman	6.00	2.70	.75
☐ V9 Simon Fletcher	.30	.14	.04
☐ V10 Barry Sanders	6.00	2.70	.75
☐ V11 Edgar Bennett	.50	.23	.06
☐ V12 Ray Childress	.30	.14	.04
☐ V13 Ray Buchanan	.30	.14	.04
☐ V14 Desmond Howard	.50	.23	.06
☐ V15 Dale Carter	.50	.23	.06
☐ V16 Troy Vincent	.30	.14	.04
☐ V17 David Palmer	.50	.23	.06
☐ V18 Ben Coates	.50	.23	.06
☐ V19 Derek Brown TE	.30	.14	.04
☐ V20 Dave Brown	.50	.23	.06
☐ V21 Mo Lewis	.30	.14	.04
☐ V22 Harvey Williams	.30	.14	.04
☐ V23 Randall Cunningham	.50	.23	.06
☐ V24 Kevin Greene	.50	.23	.06
☐ V25 Junior Seau	1.00	.45	.12
☐ V26 Merton Hanks	.30	.14	.04
☐ V27 Cortez Kennedy	.50	.23	.06
☐ V28 Troy Drayton	.30	.14	.04
☐ V29 Hardy Nickerson	.30	.14	.04
☐ V30 Brian Mitchell	.30	.14	.04
☐ V31 Raymont Harris	.30	.14	.04
☐ V32 Keith Goganious	.30	.14	.04
☐ V33 Andre Reed	.50	.23	.06
☐ V34 Terance Mathis	.50	.23	.06
☐ V35 Garrison Hearst	1.00	.45	.12
☐ V36 Glyn Milburn	.30	.14	.04
☐ V37 Emmitt Smith	10.00	4.50	1.25
☐ V38 Vinny Testaverde	.50	.23	.06
☐ V39 Darnay Scott	4.00	1.80	.50
☐ V40 Mickey Washington	.30	.14	.04
☐ V41 Craig Erickson	.30	.14	.04
☐ V42 Chris Chandler	.50	.23	.06
☐ V43 Brett Favre	10.00	4.50	1.25
☐ V44 Scott Mitchell	.50	.23	.06
☐ V45 Chris Slade	.50	.23	.06
☐ V46 Warren Moon	.50	.23	.06
☐ V47 Dan Marino	10.00	4.50	1.25
☐ V48 Greg Hill	.50	.23	.06
☐ V49 Rocket Ismail	.50	.23	.06
☐ V50 Bobby Houston	.30	.14	.04
☐ V51 Rodney Hampton	.50	.23	.06
☐ V52 Jim Everett	.30	.14	.04
☐ V53 Rick Mirer	1.00	.45	.12
☐ V54 Steve Young	5.00	2.20	.60
☐ V55 Dennis Gibson	.30	.14	.04
☐ V56 Rod Woodson	.50	.23	.06
☐ V57 Calvin Williams	.50	.23	.06
☐ V58 Tom Carter	.30	.14	.04
☐ V59 Trent Dilfer	1.00	.45	.12
☐ V60 Shane Conlan	.30	.14	.04
☐ V61 Cornelius Bennett	.50	.23	.06
☐ V62 Eric Metcalf	.50	.23	.06
☐ V63 Frank Reich	.30	.14	.04
☐ V64 Eric Hill	.30	.14	.04
☐ V65 Erik Kramer	.30	.14	.04
☐ V66 Michael Irvin	1.00	.45	.12
☐ V67 Tony McGee	.30	.14	.04
☐ V68 Andre Rison	.50	.23	.06
☐ V69 Shannon Sharpe	.50	.23	.06
☐ V70 Quentin Coryatt	.50	.23	.06
☐ V71 Robert Brooks	1.00	.45	.12
☐ V72 Steve Beuerlein	.30	.14	.04
☐ V73 Herman Moore	3.50	1.55	.45
☐ V74 Jack Del Rio	.30	.14	.04
☐ V75 Dave Meggett	.30	.14	.04
☐ V76 Pete Stoyanovich	.30	.14	.04
☐ V77 Neil Smith	.50	.23	.06
☐ V78 Corey Miller	.30	.14	.04
☐ V79 Tim Brown	1.00	.45	.12
☐ V80 Tyrone Hughes	.50	.23	.06
☐ V81 Boomer Esiason	.50	.23	.06
☐ V82 Natrone Means	1.00	.45	.12
☐ V83 Chris Warren	.50	.23	.06
☐ V84 Byron Bam Morris	.50	.23	.06
☐ V85 Jerry Rice	6.00	2.70	.75
☐ V86 Michael Zordich	.30	.14	.04
☐ V87 Errict Rhett	1.00	.45	.12
☐ V88 Henry Ellard	.50	.23	.06
☐ V89 Chris Miller	.30	.14	.04
☐ V90 John Elway	5.00	2.20	.60

1995 Bowman's Best Refractors

This 180 card set is a parallel of the basic set utilizing Topps refractor technology. These cards were inserted at a rate of one in six packs.

	MINT	NRMT	EXC
COMPLETE SET (180)	1250.00	550.00	160.00
COMMON CARD	3.00	1.35	.35
*STARS : 5X TO 10X BASIC CARDS			
*YOUNG STARS : 4X TO 8X BASIC CARDS			
*RCs : 3.5X TO 7X BASIC CARDS			
☐ R3 Steve McNair	70.00	32.00	8.75
☐ R5 Kerry Collins	75.00	34.00	9.50
☐ R60 Kordell Stewart	70.00	32.00	8.75
☐ R74 Curtis Martin	75.00	34.00	9.50
☐ V8 Troy Aikman	60.00	27.00	7.50
☐ V10 Barry Sanders	60.00	27.00	7.50
☐ V37 Emmitt Smith	100.00	45.00	12.50
☐ V43 Brett Favre	100.00	45.00	12.50
☐ V47 Dan Marino	100.00	45.00	12.50
☐ V54 Steve Young	40.00	18.00	5.00
☐ V85 Jerry Rice	60.00	27.00	7.50

1995 Bowman's Best Mirror Images Draft Picks

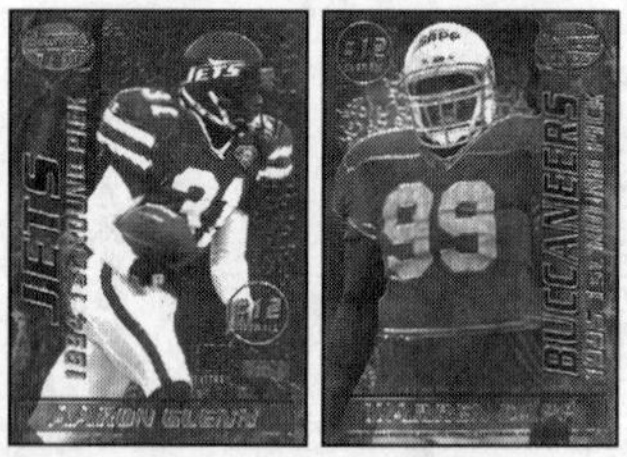

This 15-card set was randomly inserted into packs at a ratio of 1:2. The cards feature the top 15 draft picks from 1994 and 1995 "back-to-back." Each card is numbered according to the player's draft position. Cards were also available as Refractor parallels inserted at a rate of one in 18 packs.

	MINT	NRMT	EXC
COMPLETE SET (15)	35.00	16.00	4.40
COMMON CARD (1-15)	1.25	.55	.16
☐ 1 Ki-Jana Carter	2.00	.90	.25
Dan Wilkinson			
☐ 2 Marshall Faulk	3.00	1.35	.35
Tony Boselli			
☐ 3 Steve McNair	8.00	3.60	1.00
Heath Shuler			
☐ 4 Michael Westbrook	4.00	1.80	.50
Willie McGinest			
☐ 5 Kerry Collins	10.00	4.50	1.25
Trev Alberts			
☐ 6 Trent Dilfer	2.00	.90	.25
Kevin Carter			
☐ 7 Bryant Young	2.00	.90	.25
Mike Mamula			
☐ 8 Joey Galloway	6.00	2.70	.75
Sam Adams			
☐ 9 Antonio Langham	1.25	.55	.16
Kyle Brady			
☐ 10 J.J.Stokes	3.00	1.35	.35
Jamir Miller			
☐ 11 John Thierry	2.00	.90	.25
Derrick Alexander DE			
☐ 12 Aaron Glenn	1.25	.55	.16
Warren Sapp			
☐ 13 Joe Johnson	1.25	.55	.16
Mark Fields			
☐ 14 Bernard Williams	1.25	.55	.16
Ruben Brown			
☐ 15 Wayne Gandy	1.25	.55	.16
Ellis Johnson			

1996 Bowman's Best

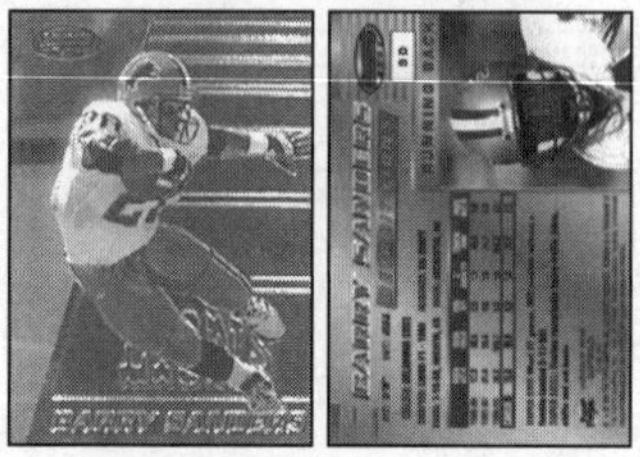

The 1996 Bowman's Best set was issued in one series totalling 180 cards. The six-card packs retail for $5.00 each. The fronts of the 135 veterans' cards feature color action player photos in a gold design. The cards for the 45 draft picks display color action player photos in a silver design. The backs carry player information and statistics.

	MINT	NRMT	EXC
COMPLETE SET (180)	100.00	45.00	12.50
COMMON CARD (1-180)	.30	.14	.04
☐ 1 Emmitt Smith	8.00	3.60	1.00
☐ 2 Kordell Stewart	4.00	1.80	.50
☐ 3 Mark Chmura	.50	.23	.06
☐ 4 Sean Dawkins	.30	.14	.04
☐ 5 Steve Young	3.00	1.35	.35
☐ 6 Tamarick Vanover	1.00	.45	.12
☐ 7 Scott Mitchell	.50	.23	.06
☐ 8 Aaron Hayden	.30	.14	.04
☐ 9 William Thomas	.30	.14	.04
☐ 10 Dan Marino	8.00	3.60	1.00
☐ 11 Curtis Conway	1.00	.45	.12
☐ 12 Steve Atwater	.30	.14	.04
☐ 13 Derrick Brooks	.30	.14	.04
☐ 14 Rick Mirer	.50	.23	.06
☐ 15 Mark Brunell	4.00	1.80	.50
☐ 16 Garrison Hearst	.50	.23	.06
☐ 17 Eric Turner	.30	.14	.04
☐ 18 Mark Carrier	.30	.14	.04
☐ 19 Darnay Scott	.50	.23	.06
☐ 20 Steve McNair	3.00	1.35	.35
☐ 21 Jim Everett	.30	.14	.04
☐ 22 Wayne Chrebet	.50	.23	.06
☐ 23 Ben Coates	.50	.23	.06
☐ 24 Harvey Williams	.30	.14	.04
☐ 25 Michael Westbrook	1.00	.45	.12
☐ 26 Kevin Carter	.50	.23	.06
☐ 27 Dave Brown	.50	.23	.06
☐ 28 Jake Reed	.50	.23	.06
☐ 29 Thurman Thomas	1.00	.45	.12
☐ 30 Jeff George	.50	.23	.06
☐ 31 Carnell Lake	.30	.14	.04
☐ 32 J.J. Stokes	1.00	.45	.12
☐ 33 Jay Novacek	.50	.23	.06
☐ 34 Brett Perriman	.50	.23	.06
☐ 35 Robert Brooks	1.00	.45	.12
☐ 36 Neil Smith	.50	.23	.06
☐ 37 Chris Zorich	.30	.14	.04
☐ 38 Micheal Barrow	.30	.14	.04
☐ 39 Quentin Coryatt	.30	.14	.04
☐ 40 Kerry Collins	4.00	1.80	.50
☐ 41 Aeneas Williams	.30	.14	.04
☐ 42 James O.Stewart	.50	.23	.06
☐ 43 Warren Moon	.50	.23	.06
☐ 44 Willie McGinest	.30	.14	.04
☐ 45 Rodney Hampton	.50	.23	.06
☐ 46 Jeff Hostetler	.50	.23	.06
☐ 47 Darrell Green	.30	.14	.04
☐ 48 Warren Sapp	.30	.14	.04
☐ 49 Troy Drayton	.30	.14	.04
☐ 50 Junior Seau	1.00	.45	.12
☐ 51 Mike Mamula	.30	.14	.04
☐ 52 Antonio Langham	.30	.14	.04
☐ 53 Eric Metcalf	.50	.23	.06
☐ 54 Adrian Murrell	.50	.23	.06
☐ 55 Joey Galloway	2.00	.90	.25
☐ 56 Anthony Miller	.50	.23	.06
☐ 57 Carl Pickens	1.00	.45	.12
☐ 58 Bruce Smith	1.00	.45	.12
☐ 59 Merton Hanks	.30	.14	.04
☐ 60 Troy Aikman	4.00	1.80	.50
☐ 61 Erik Kramer	.30	.14	.04
☐ 62 Tyrone Poole	.30	.14	.04
☐ 63 Michael Jackson	.50	.23	.06
☐ 64 Rob Moore	.30	.14	.04
☐ 65 Marcus Allen	1.00	.45	.12
☐ 66 Orlando Thomas	.30	.14	.04
☐ 67 Dave Meggett	.30	.14	.04
☐ 68 Trent Dilfer	.50	.23	.06
☐ 69 Herman Moore	1.00	.45	.12
☐ 70 Brett Favre	8.00	3.60	1.00
☐ 71 Blaine Bishop	.30	.14	.04
☐ 72 Eric Allen	.30	.14	.04
☐ 73 Bernie Parmalee	.30	.14	.04
☐ 74 Kyle Brady	.50	.23	.06
☐ 75 Terry McDaniel	.30	.14	.04
☐ 76 Rodney Peete	.30	.14	.04
☐ 77 Yancey Thigpen	.50	.23	.06
☐ 78 Stan Humphries	.50	.23	.06
☐ 79 Craig Heyward	.30	.14	.04
☐ 80 Rashaan Salaam	1.00	.45	.12
☐ 81 Shannon Sharpe	.50	.23	.06
☐ 82 Jim Harbaugh	.50	.23	.06
☐ 83 Vinnie Clark	.30	.14	.04
☐ 84 Steve Bono	.50	.23	.06
☐ 85 Drew Bledsoe	4.00	1.80	.50
☐ 86 Ken Norton	.50	.23	.06
☐ 87 Brian Mitchell	.30	.14	.04
☐ 88 Hardy Nickerson	.30	.14	.04
☐ 89 Todd Lyght	.30	.14	.04
☐ 90 Barry Sanders	4.00	1.80	.50
☐ 91 Robert Blackmon	.30	.14	.04
☐ 92 Larry Centers	.50	.23	.06
☐ 93 Jim Kelly	1.00	.45	.12
☐ 94 Lamar Lathon	.30	.14	.04
☐ 95 Cris Carter	1.00	.45	.12
☐ 96 Hugh Douglas	.30	.14	.04
☐ 97 Michael Strahan	.30	.14	.04
☐ 98 Lee Woodall	.30	.14	.04
☐ 99 Michael Irvin	1.00	.45	.12
☐ 100 Marshall Faulk	1.00	.45	.12
☐ 101 Terance Mathis	.30	.14	.04
☐ 102 Eric Zeier	.50	.23	.06
☐ 103 Marty Carter	.30	.14	.04
☐ 104 Steve Tovar	.30	.14	.04
☐ 105 Isaac Bruce	1.00	.45	.12
☐ 106 Tony Martin	.50	.23	.06
☐ 107 Dale Carter	.30	.14	.04
☐ 108 Terry Kirby	.50	.23	.06
☐ 109 Tyrone Hughes	.30	.14	.04
☐ 110 Bryce Paup	.50	.23	.06
☐ 111 Errict Rhett	.50	.23	.06
☐ 112 Ricky Watters	.50	.23	.06
☐ 113 Chris Chandler	.50	.23	.06
☐ 114 Edgar Bennett	.50	.23	.06
☐ 115 John Elway	3.00	1.35	.35
☐ 116 Sam Mills	.50	.23	.06
☐ 117 Seth Joyner	.30	.14	.04
☐ 118 Jeff Lageman	.30	.14	.04
☐ 119 Chris Calloway	.30	.14	.04
☐ 120 Curtis Martin	5.00	2.20	.60
☐ 121 Ken Harvey	.30	.14	.04
☐ 122 Eugene Daniel	.30	.14	.04
☐ 123 Tim Brown	.50	.23	.06
☐ 124 Mo Lewis	.30	.14	.04
☐ 125 Jeff Blake	1.00	.45	.12
☐ 126 Jessie Tuggle	.30	.14	.04
☐ 127 Vinny Testaverde	.50	.23	.06
☐ 128 Chris Warren	.50	.23	.06
☐ 129 Terrell Davis	5.00	2.20	.60
☐ 130 Greg Lloyd	.50	.23	.06
☐ 131 Deion Sanders	2.00	.90	.25
☐ 132 Derrick Thomas	.50	.23	.06
☐ 133 Darryll Lewis	.30	.14	.04
UER back Daryl Lewis			
☐ 134 Reggie White	1.00	.45	.12
☐ 135 Jerry Rice	4.00	1.80	.50
☐ 136 Tony Banks	2.50	1.10	.30
☐ 137 Derrick Mayes	2.00	.90	.25
☐ 138 Leeland McElroy	1.50	.70	.19
☐ 139 Bryan Still	.30	.14	.04
☐ 140 Tim Biakabutuka	2.00	.90	.25
☐ 141 Rickey Dudley	1.50	.70	.19
☐ 142 Tory James	.30	.14	.04
☐ 143 Lawyer Milloy	.30	.14	.04
☐ 144 Mike Ulufale	.30	.14	.04
☐ 145 Bobby Engram	2.00	.90	.25
☐ 146 Willie Anderson	.30	.14	.04
☐ 147 Terrell Owens	4.00	1.80	.50
☐ 148 Jonathan Ogden	.30	.14	.04
☐ 149 Darrius Johnson	.30	.14	.04
☐ 150 Kevin Hardy	1.25	.55	.16
☐ 151 Simeon Rice	1.25	.55	.16
☐ 152 Alex Molden	.30	.14	.04
☐ 153 Cedric Jones	.50	.23	.06
☐ 154 Duane Clemons	.30	.14	.04
☐ 155 Karim Abdul-Jabbar	6.00	2.70	.75
☐ 156 Dedric Mathis	.30	.14	.04
☐ 157 John Michels	.30	.14	.04
☐ 158 Winslow Oliver	.30	.14	.04
☐ 159 Stepfret Williams	.30	.14	.04
☐ 160 Eddie Kennison	3.00	1.35	.35
☐ 161 Marcus Coleman	.30	.14	.04
☐ 162 Tedy Bruschi	.30	.14	.04
☐ 163 Detron Smith	.30	.14	.04
☐ 164 Ray Lewis	.30	.14	.04
☐ 165 Marvin Harrison	3.00	1.35	.35
☐ 166 Je'rod Cherry	.30	.14	.04
☐ 167 Jerris McPhail	.30	.14	.04
☐ 168 Eric Moulds	2.00	.90	.25
☐ 169 Walt Harris	.30	.14	.04
☐ 170 Eddie George	10.00	4.50	1.25
☐ 171 Jermaine Lewis	.30	.14	.04
☐ 172 Jeff Lewis	.50	.23	.06
☐ 173 Ray Mickens	.30	.14	.04
☐ 174 Amani Toomer	1.25	.55	.16
☐ 175 Zach Thomas	2.50	1.10	.30
☐ 176 Lawrence Phillips	2.00	.90	.25
☐ 177 John Mobley	.30	.14	.04

☐ 178 Anthony Dorsett	.30	.14	.04
☐ 179 DeRon Jenkins	.30	.14	.04
☐ 180 Keyshawn Johnson	3.00	1.35	.35

1996 Bowman's Best Atomic Refractors

Randomly inserted in hobby packs at a rate of one in 48, and retail packs at a ratio of 1:80, this 180-card parallel set was printed with a checker board type Refractor pattern.

	MINT	NRMT	EXC
COMP.ATOMIC REF.SET (180)	3000.00	1350.00	375.00
COMMON CARD (1-180)	8.00	3.60	1.00

*ATOMIC REF.STARS: 15X TO 30X BASE CARDS
*ATOMIC REF.YOUNG STARS: 12.5X TO 25X BASE CARDS
*ATOMIC REF.RCs: 10X TO 20X BASE CARDS

☐ 1 Emmitt Smith	250.00	110.00	31.00
☐ 2 Kordell Stewart	100.00	45.00	12.50
☐ 5 Steve Young	90.00	40.00	11.00
☐ 10 Dan Marino	250.00	110.00	31.00
☐ 15 Mark Brunell	125.00	55.00	15.50
☐ 20 Steve McNair	80.00	36.00	10.00
☐ 40 Kerry Collins	100.00	45.00	12.50
☐ 60 Troy Aikman	125.00	55.00	15.50
☐ 70 Brett Favre	250.00	110.00	31.00
☐ 85 Drew Bledsoe	125.00	55.00	15.50
☐ 90 Barry Sanders	125.00	55.00	15.50
☐ 115 John Elway	100.00	45.00	12.50
☐ 120 Curtis Martin	100.00	45.00	12.50
☐ 129 Terrell Davis	100.00	45.00	12.50
☐ 131 Deion Sanders	80.00	36.00	10.00
☐ 135 Jerry Rice	125.00	55.00	15.50
☐ 136 Tony Banks	50.00	22.00	6.25
☐ 147 Terrell Owens	80.00	36.00	10.00
☐ 155 Karim Abdul-Jabbar	100.00	45.00	12.50
☐ 160 Eddie Kennison	60.00	27.00	7.50
☐ 165 Marvin Harrison	60.00	27.00	7.50
☐ 170 Eddie George	160.00	70.00	20.00
☐ 175 Zach Thomas	50.00	22.00	6.25
☐ 180 Keyshawn Johnson	60.00	27.00	7.50

1996 Bowman's Best Refractors

Randomly inserted in hobby packs at a rate of 1:12, and retail packs at a rate of 1:20, this 180-card set is a parallel to the base issue and virtually identical in design. The difference can be seen in the rainbow "Refractor" background of the cards.

	MINT	NRMT	EXC
COMP.REF.SET (180)	1250.00	550.00	160.00
COMMON CARD (1-180)	3.00	1.35	.35

*REF.STARS: 6X TO 12X BASE CARDS
*REF.YOUNG STARS: 5X TO 10X BASE CARDS
*REF.RCs: 4X TO 8X BASE CARDS ....

☐ 1 Emmitt Smith	80.00	36.00	10.00
☐ 2 Kordell Stewart	40.00	18.00	5.00
☐ 5 Steve Young	35.00	16.00	4.40
☐ 10 Dan Marino	80.00	36.00	10.00
☐ 15 Mark Brunell	50.00	22.00	6.25
☐ 20 Steve McNair	35.00	16.00	4.40
☐ 40 Kerry Collins	40.00	18.00	5.00
☐ 60 Troy Aikman	50.00	22.00	6.25
☐ 70 Brett Favre	80.00	36.00	10.00
☐ 85 Drew Bledsoe	50.00	22.00	6.25
☐ 90 Barry Sanders	50.00	22.00	6.25
☐ 115 John Elway	40.00	18.00	5.00
☐ 120 Curtis Martin	40.00	18.00	5.00
☐ 129 Terrell Davis	40.00	18.00	5.00
☐ 131 Deion Sanders	30.00	13.50	3.70
☐ 135 Jerry Rice	50.00	22.00	6.25
☐ 147 Terrell Owens	35.00	16.00	4.40
☐ 155 Karim Abdul-Jabbar	40.00	18.00	5.00
☐ 160 Eddie Kennison	30.00	13.50	3.70
☐ 165 Marvin Harrison	30.00	13.50	3.70
☐ 170 Eddie George	70.00	32.00	8.75
☐ 180 Keyshawn Johnson	30.00	13.50	3.70

1996 Bowman's Best Bets

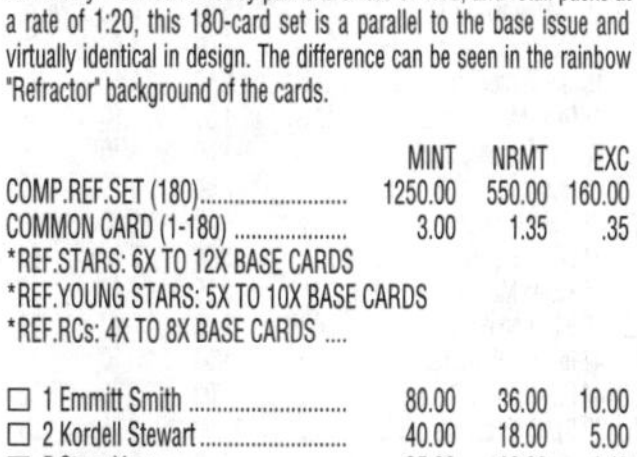

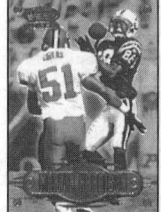

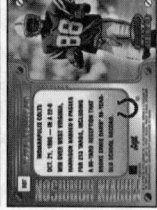

Randomly inserted in hobby packs at a rate of 1:12, and retail at 1:20 packs, this nine-card set features borderless color action player photos of nine 1996 NFL rookies and was printed using Topps' chromium technology. Parallel Refractor (1:48 odds hobby, 1:80 packs retail) and Atomic Refractor (1:96 odds hobby, 1:160 retail) cards were also produced.

	MINT	NRMT	EXC
COMPLETE SET (9)	40.00	18.00	5.00
COMMON CARD (1-9)	2.50	1.10	.30

*ATOMIC REFRACTORS:2X TO 5X BASE CARDS
*REFRACTORS: 1X TO 2.5X BASE CARDS

☐ 1 Keyshawn Johnson	6.00	2.70	.75
☐ 2 Lawrence Phillips	4.00	1.80	.50
☐ 3 Tim Biakabutuka	4.00	1.80	.50
☐ 4 Eddie George	20.00	9.00	2.50
☐ 5 John Mobley	2.50	1.10	.30
☐ 6 Eddie Kennison	6.00	2.70	.75
☐ 7 Marvin Harrison	6.00	2.70	.75
☐ 8 Amani Toomer	4.00	1.80	.50
☐ 9 Bobby Engram	2.50	1.10	.30

1996 Bowman's Best Cuts

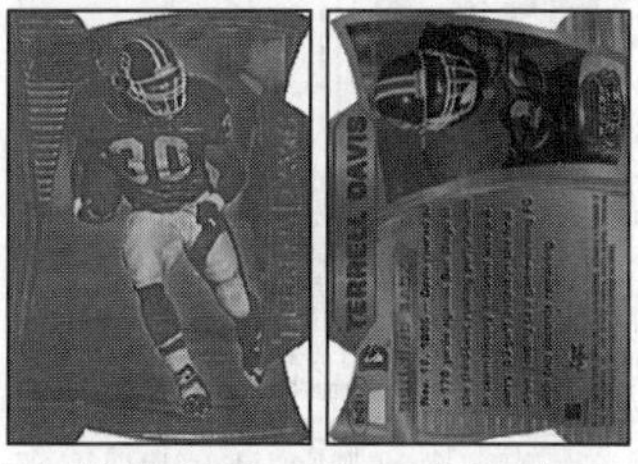

Randomly inserted in hobby packs at a rate of 1:24, and 1:40 retail, this 15-card set features color action player photos of NFL stars and was printed on a die cut chromium foil card stock. Parallel Refractor (1:48 odds hobby, 1:96 retail) and Atomic Refractor (1:96 odds hobby, 1:160 retail) cards were also produced.

	MINT	NRMT	EXC
COMPLETE SET (15)	200.00	90.00	25.00
COMMON CARD (1-15)	5.00	2.20	.60

*ATOMIC REFRACTORS: 1.5X TO 4X BASIC CARDS
*REFRACTORS: .75X TO 2X BASE CARDS

☐ 1 Dan Marino	30.00	13.50	3.70
☐ 2 Emmitt Smith	30.00	13.50	3.70
☐ 3 Rashaan Salaam	5.00	2.20	.60
☐ 4 Herman Moore	8.00	3.60	1.00
☐ 5 Brett Favre	30.00	13.50	3.70
☐ 6 Marshall Faulk	5.00	2.20	.60
☐ 7 John Elway	12.00	5.50	1.50
☐ 8 Curtis Martin	18.00	8.00	2.20
☐ 9 Deion Sanders	10.00	4.50	1.25
☐ 10 Jerry Rice	15.00	6.75	1.85
☐ 11 Terrell Davis	18.00	8.00	2.20
☐ 12 Kerry Collins	16.00	7.25	2.00
☐ 13 Steve Young	12.00	5.50	1.50
☐ 14 Troy Aikman	15.00	6.75	1.85
☐ 15 Barry Sanders	15.00	6.75	1.85

1996 Bowman's Best Mirror Image

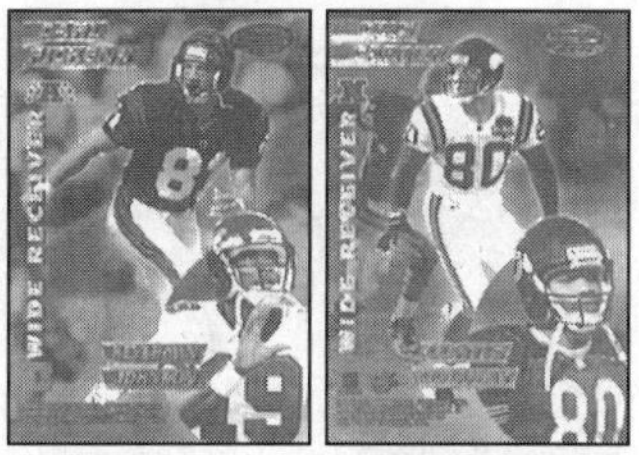

Randomly inserted in hobby packs at a rate of 1:48, and 1:80 retail, this nine-card set features double-sided cards with color photos of four top players from the same position. One side displays an AFC veteran alongside an AFC young star. The opposite side shows an NFC veteran next to an NFC young star. Parallel Refractor (1:96 odds hobby, 1:160 retail) and Atomic Refractor (1:192 odds hobby, 1:320 retail) cards were also produced.

	MINT	NRMT	EXC
COMPLETE SET (9)	150.00	70.00	19.00
COMMON CARD (1-9)	10.00	4.50	1.25

*ATOMIC REFRACTORS: 2X TO 4X BASE CARDS
*REFRACTORS: 1X TO 2X BASE CARDS

☐ 1 Steve Young	50.00	22.00	6.25
Kerry Collins			
Dan Marino			
Mark Brunell			
☐ 2 Brett Favre	50.00	22.00	6.25
Elvis Grbac			
John Elway			
Drew Bledsoe			
☐ 3 Troy Aikman	25.00	11.00	3.10
Gus Frerotte			
Jim Harbaugh			
Jeff Blake			
☐ 4 Emmitt Smith	40.00	18.00	5.00
Errict Rhett			
Chris Warren			
Curtis Martin			
☐ 5 Barry Sanders	25.00	11.00	3.10
Rashaan Salaam			
Thurman Thomas			
Terrell Davis			
☐ 6 Rodney Hampton	10.00	4.50	1.25
Lawrence Phillips			
Marcus Allen			
Marshall Faulk			
☐ 7 Jerry Rice	25.00	11.00	3.10
Isaac Bruce			
Tim Brown			
Joey Galloway			
☐ 8 Cris Carter	15.00	6.75	1.85
Curtis Conway			
Carl Pickens			
Keyshawn Johnson			
☐ 9 Robert Brooks	15.00	6.75	1.85
Michael Westbrook			
Anthony Miller			
O.J. McDuffie			

1950 Bread for Health

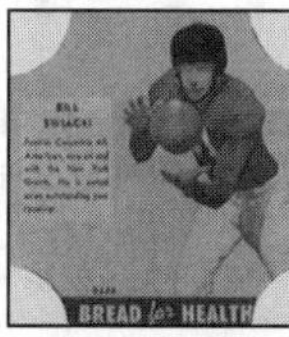

The 1950 Bread for Health football card (actually bread end labels) set contains 32 bread-end labels of players in the National Football League. The cards (actually paper thin labels) measure approximately 2 3/4" by 2 3/4". These labels are not usually found in top condition due to the difficulty in removing them from the bread package. While all the bakeries who issued this set are not presently known, Fisher's Bread in the New Jersey, New York and Pennsylvania area and NBC Bread in the Michigan area are two of the bakeries that have been confirmed to date. As with many of the bread label sets of the early 1950's, an album to house the set was probably issued. Each label contains the B.E.B. copyright found on so many of the labels of this period. Labels which contain "Bread for Energy" at the bottom are not a part of the set but part of a series of movie, western and sport stars issued during the same approximate time period. The catalog designation for this set is D290-15. The cards are unnumbered but are arranged alphabetically below for convenience.

	NRMT	VG-E	GOOD
COMPLETE SET (32)	9000.00	4000.00	1100.00
COMMON CARD (1-32)	150.00	70.00	19.00

☐ 1 Frankie Albert	175.00	80.00	22.00
☐ 2 Elmer Bud Angsman	150.00	70.00	19.00
☐ 3 Dick Barwegan	150.00	70.00	19.00
☐ 4 Sammy Baugh	800.00	350.00	100.00
☐ 5 Charley Conerly	350.00	160.00	45.00
☐ 6 Glenn Davis	250.00	110.00	31.00
☐ 7 Don Doll	150.00	70.00	19.00
☐ 8 Tom Fears	275.00	125.00	34.00
☐ 9 Harry Gilmer	175.00	80.00	22.00
☐ 10 Otto Graham	750.00	350.00	95.00
☐ 11 Pat Harder	225.00	100.00	28.00
☐ 12 Bobby Layne	600.00	275.00	75.00
☐ 13 Sid Luckman	500.00	220.00	60.00
☐ 14 Johnny Lujack	350.00	160.00	45.00
☐ 15 John Panelli	150.00	70.00	19.00
☐ 16 Barney Poole	150.00	70.00	19.00
☐ 17 George Ratterman	175.00	80.00	22.00
☐ 18 Tobin Rote	200.00	90.00	25.00
☐ 19 Jack Russell	150.00	70.00	19.00
☐ 20 Lou Rymkus	175.00	80.00	22.00
☐ 21 Joe Sigiagio	150.00	70.00	19.00
☐ 22 Mac Speedie	225.00	100.00	28.00
☐ 23 Bill Swiacki	175.00	80.00	22.00
☐ 24 Tommy Thompson	200.00	90.00	25.00
☐ 25 Y.A. Tittle	600.00	275.00	75.00
☐ 26 Clayton Tonnemaker	150.00	70.00	19.00
☐ 27 Charley Trippi	275.00	125.00	34.00
☐ 28 Bulldog Turner	300.00	135.00	38.00
☐ 29 Steve Van Buren	350.00	160.00	45.00
☐ 30 Bill Walsh	175.00	80.00	22.00
☐ 31 Bob Waterfield	450.00	200.00	55.00
☐ 32 Jim White	150.00	70.00	19.00

1992 Breyers Bookmarks

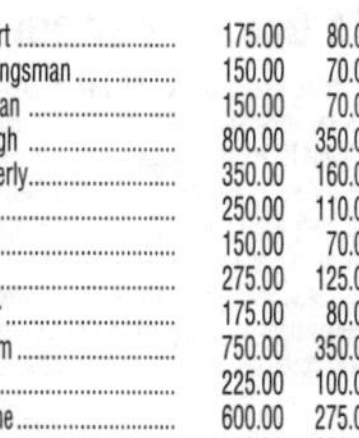

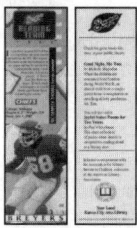

This 66-card set (of bookmarks) was produced by Breyers to promote reading in the home cities of eleven NFL teams. The bookmarks measure approximately 2" by 8". The fronts feature a cut-out player photo superimposed on a yellow background decorated with open books. A lighter yellow panel above the player contains a player profile and a biography. The player's name appears in a black stripe that borders the panel. The Breyers logo and the words "Reading Team" appear on an electronic billboard design. The backs list book selections found at the library, the American Library Association logo, and the sponsor logo. The cards are numbered on the front and are arranged in team order.

	MINT	NRMT	EXC
COMPLETE SET (66)	150.00	70.00	19.00
COMMON CARD (1-66)	2.00	.90	.25

☐ 1 Greg Townsend	2.00	.90	.25
☐ 2 Steve Wisniewski	2.00	.90	.25
☐ 3 Art Shell CO	2.50	1.10	.30
☐ 4 Jeff Jaeger	2.00	.90	.25
☐ 5 Lisa O'Day (Cheerleader)	2.00	.90	.25
☐ 6 Los Angeles Raiders Helmet and SB trophies	2.00	.90	.25
☐ 7 Jerry Rice	12.00	5.50	1.50
☐ 8 Don Griffin	2.00	.90	.25
☐ 9 John Taylor	2.50	1.10	.30
☐ 10 Joe Montana	16.00	7.25	2.00
☐ 11 Michael Walter	2.00	.90	.25
☐ 12 San Francisco 49ers Helmet	2.00	.90	.25
☐ 13 Junior Seau	4.00	1.80	.50
☐ 14 John Friesz	2.50	1.10	.30
☐ 15 Ronnie Harmon	2.50	1.10	.30
☐ 16 Marion Butts	2.50	1.10	.30
☐ 17 Gill Byrd	2.00	.90	.25
☐ 18 San Diego Chargers Helmet	2.00	.90	.25
☐ 19 Kelly Stouffer	2.00	.90	.25
☐ 20 John Kasay	2.00	.90	.25
☐ 21 Andy Heck	2.00	.90	.25
☐ 22 Jacob Green	2.00	.90	.25
☐ 23 Eugene Robinson	2.00	.90	.25
☐ 24 Seattle Seahawks Helmet	2.00	.90	.25
☐ 25 Pat Swilling	2.50	1.10	.30
☐ 26 Vaughan Johnson	2.00	.90	.25
☐ 27 Bobby Hebert	2.50	1.10	.30
☐ 28 Floyd Turner	2.00	.90	.25
☐ 29 Rickey Jackson	2.00	.90	.25
☐ 30 New Orleans Saints Helmet	2.00	.90	.25
☐ 31 Harvey Williams	2.50	1.10	.30
☐ 32 Derrick Thomas	4.00	1.80	.50
☐ 33 Bill Maas	2.00	.90	.25
☐ 34 Tim Grunhard	2.00	.90	.25
☐ 35 Jonathan Hayes	2.00	.90	.25
☐ 36 Kansas City Chiefs Mascot	2.00	.90	.25
☐ 37 Rich Gannon	2.50	1.10	.30
☐ 38 Tim Irwin	2.00	.90	.25
☐ 39 Audray McMillian	2.50	1.10	.30
☐ 40 Gary Zimmerman	2.00	.90	.25
☐ 41 Hassan Jones	2.00	.90	.25
☐ 42 Minnesota Vikings Helmet	2.00	.90	.25
☐ 43 Eric Green	2.50	1.10	.30
☐ 44 Louis Lipps	2.00	.90	.25
☐ 45 Rod Woodson	2.50	1.10	.30
☐ 46 Merril Hoge	2.00	.90	.25
☐ 47 Gary Anderson RB	2.00	.90	.25
☐ 48 Pittsburgh Steelers 60-Season Emblem	2.00	.90	.25
☐ 49 Anthony Johnson	2.00	.90	.25
☐ 50 Bill Brooks	2.50	1.10	.30
☐ 51 Jeff Herrod	2.00	.90	.25
☐ 52 Mike Prior	2.00	.90	.25
☐ 53 Jeff George	4.00	1.80	.50
☐ 54 Indianapolis Colts Ted Marchibroda CO	2.00	.90	.25
☐ 55 Troy Aikman	12.00	5.50	1.50
☐ 56 Jay Novacek	2.50	1.10	.30
☐ 57 Emmitt Smith	20.00	9.00	2.50
☐ 58 Michael Irvin	5.00	2.20	.60
☐ 59 Dorie Braddy (Cheerleader)	2.00	.90	.25
☐ 60 Dallas Cowboys Super Bowl trophy	2.00	.90	.25
☐ 61 Clay Matthews	2.50	1.10	.30
☐ 62 Tommy Vardell	2.50	1.10	.30
☐ 63 Eric Turner	2.50	1.10	.30
☐ 64 Mike Johnson	2.00	.90	.25
☐ 65 James Jones	2.50	1.10	.30
☐ 66 Cleveland Browns Helmet	2.00	.90	.25

1990 British Petroleum

This 36-card standard-size set was issued two cards at a time by British Petroleum gas stations throughout California in association with Talent Network Inc. of Skokie, Illinois. There were five winning player cards issued in the following quantities. Andre Tippett: 5.00 - 990 cards, Freeman McNeil: 10.00 - 325 cards, Clay Matthews: 100.00 - 18 cards, Tim Harris: 1,000.00 - three cards, and Deion Sanders 10,000.00 - one card. These winning cards are not valued as collectibles in the checklist below as they were more valuable as prize winners. The set has multiple players numbered 1, 3, 6, 8, and 10, and we have arranged each group of same-numbered cards into alphabetical order. Each game piece was two NFL football cards inside a cardboard frame, with full-color head shots in uniform of the player. Cards are frequently found in less than Mint condition due to the fact

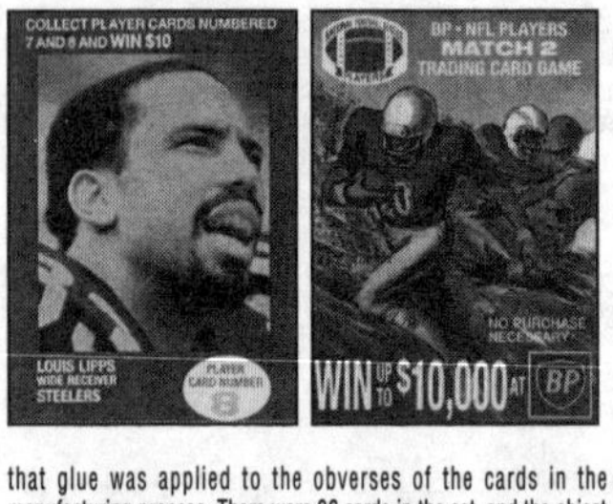

that glue was applied to the obverses of the cards in the manufacturing process. There were 36 cards in the set, and the object of the game was to collect two adjacent numbers, 1-2, 3-4, 5-6, 7-8, or 9-10. One number was easy to get, but the other was difficult. The game redemptions expired in October 1991. Each card was produced in two different card back variations: black with contest rules and advertising design.

	MINT	NRMT	EXC
COMPLETE SET (36)	40.00	18.00	5.00
COMMON CARD	.50	.23	.06
☐ 1A John Elway	4.00	1.80	.50
☐ 1B Boomer Esiason	.75	.35	.09
☐ 1C Jim Everett	.75	.35	.09
☐ 1D Bernie Kosar	.75	.35	.09
☐ 1E Karl Mecklenburg	.50	.23	.06
☐ 1F Bruce Smith	.75	.35	.09
☐ 2 Deion Sanders (Winning card)			
☐ 3A Roger Craig	.75	.35	.09
☐ 3B Randall Cunningham	.75	.35	.09
☐ 3C Keith Jackson	.75	.35	.09
☐ 3D Dan Marino	10.00	4.50	1.25
☐ 3E Freddie Joe Nunn	.50	.23	.06
☐ 3F Jerry Rice	5.00	2.20	.60
☐ 3G Vinny Testaverde	.75	.35	.09
☐ 3H John L. Williams	.50	.23	.06
☐ 4 Tim Harris (Winning card)			
☐ 5 Clay Matthews (Winning card)			
☐ 6A Neal Anderson	.50	.23	.06
☐ 6B Duane Bickett	.50	.23	.06
☐ 6C Ronnie Lott	.75	.35	.09
☐ 6D Anthony Munoz	.75	.35	.09
☐ 6E Christian Okoye	.50	.23	.06
☐ 6F Barry Sanders	5.00	2.20	.60
☐ 7 Freeman McNeil (Winning card)			
☐ 8A Cornelius Bennett	.75	.35	.09
☐ 8B Anthony Carter	.75	.35	.09
☐ 8C Jim Kelly	1.50	.70	.19
☐ 8D Louis Lipps	.50	.23	.06
☐ 8E Phil Simms	.75	.35	.09
☐ 8F Billy Ray Smith	.50	.23	.06
☐ 8G Lawrence Taylor	.75	.35	.09
☐ 9 Andre Tippett (Winning card)			
☐ 10A Bo Jackson	.75	.35	.09
☐ 10B Howie Long	.75	.35	.09
☐ 10C Don Majkowski	.50	.23	.06
☐ 10D Art Monk	.75	.35	.09
☐ 10E Warren Moon	.75	.35	.09
☐ 10F Mike Singletary	.75	.35	.09
☐ 10G Al Toon	.75	.35	.09
☐ 10H Herschel Walker	.75	.35	.09
☐ 10I Reggie White	1.50	.70	.19

1967-68 Broncos Team Issue

The Broncos issued several series of player photos in the late 1960s through early 1970s with many invariably being released in multiple years. The format is the same for most of the sets with only subtle differences in the type (size and style) and information contained below the photo. Each of the photos in this group are black-and-white measuring approximately 5" by 7" and are blankbacked and unnumbered. The line of text contains the following from left to right: player name, position (completely spelled out), height, weight, and team name. We've included what is thought to be the year of issue. The 1967 photos were printed with both upper and lower case lettering, while the 1968 issue was done in all caps. We've listed the only known photos in the set.

	NRMT	VG-E	GOOD
COMPLETE SET (4)	15.00	6.75	1.85
COMMON CARD (1-4)	4.00	1.80	.50
☐ 1 Carl Cunningham 67	4.00	1.80	.50
☐ 2 Al Denson 67	5.00	2.20	.60
☐ 3 Wallace Dickey 68	4.00	1.80	.50
☐ 4 Charlie Greer 68	4.00	1.80	.50

1969 Broncos Team Issue

The Broncos issued several series of player photos in the 1960s and 1970s with many invariably being released in multiple years. The format is the same for most of the sets with only subtle differences in the type (size and style) and information contained below the photo. Each of these black-and-white photos measures approximately 5" by 7" and is blankbacked and unnumbered. The line of text for the 1969 issue contains the following from left to right: player name (in all caps), position (spelled out in all caps), height, weight, and team name (in all caps). We've listed the only known photos in the set.

	NRMT-MT	EXC	G-VG
COMPLETE SET (16)	50.00	22.00	6.25
COMMON CARD (1-16)	3.00	1.35	.35
☐ 1 Tom Beer	4.00	1.80	.50
☐ 2 Phil Brady	3.00	1.35	.35
☐ 3 Sam Brunelli	4.00	1.80	.50
☐ 4 George Burrell	3.00	1.35	.35
☐ 5 Grady Cavness	4.00	1.80	.50
☐ 6 Ken Criter	3.00	1.35	.35
☐ 7 Al Denson	4.00	1.80	.50
☐ 8 John Embree	3.00	1.35	.35
☐ 9 Walter Highsmith	3.00	1.35	.35
☐ 10 Gus Hollomon	3.00	1.35	.35
☐ 11 Pete Liske	5.00	2.20	.60
☐ 12 Rex Mirich	3.00	1.35	.35
☐ 13 Tom Oberg	3.00	1.35	.35
☐ 14 Frank Richter	3.00	1.35	.35
☐ 15 Paul Smith	4.00	1.80	.50
☐ 16 Bob Young	3.00	1.35	.35

1970 Broncos Team Issue

The Broncos issued several series of player photos in the 1960s and 1970s with many invariably being released in multiple years. The format is the same for most of the sets with only subtle differences in the type (size and style) and information contained below the photo. Each of these black-and-white photos measures approximately 5" by 7" and is blankbacked and unnumbered. The line of text for the 1970 issue contains the following from left to right: player name (in upper and lower case), position (initials), and team name (in upper and lower case). We've listed the only known photos in the set.

	NRMT-MT	EXC	G-VG
COMPLETE SET (11)	30.00	13.50	3.70
COMMON CARD (1-11)	3.00	1.35	.35
☐ 1 Bob Anderson	4.00	1.80	.50
☐ 2 Dave Costa	4.00	1.80	.50
☐ 3 Ken Criter	3.00	1.35	.35
☐ 4 Mike Current	3.00	1.35	.35
☐ 5 Fred Forsberg	3.00	1.35	.35
☐ 6 Charles Greer	3.00	1.35	.35
☐ 7 Larry Kaminski	3.00	1.35	.35
☐ 8 Fran Lynch	3.00	1.35	.35
☐ 9 Mike Schnitker	3.00	1.35	.35
☐ 10 Paul Smith	3.00	1.35	.35
☐ 11 Dave Washington	3.00	1.35	.35

1971 Broncos Team Issue

The Broncos issued several series of player photos in the 1960s and 1970s with many invariably being released in multiple years. The format is the same for most of the sets with only subtle differences in the type (size and style) and information contained below the photo. Each of these black-and-white photos measures approximately 5" by 7" and is blankbacked and unnumbered. The line of text for the 1971 issue contains the following from left to right: player name (in upper and lower case), height, weight, position (initials), and team name (in upper and lower case). We've listed the only known photos in the set.

	NRMT-MT	EXC	G-VG
COMPLETE SET (6)	18.00	8.00	2.20
COMMON CARD (1-6)	3.00	1.35	.35
☐ 1 Jack Gehrke	3.00	1.35	.35
☐ 2 Dwight Harrison	3.00	1.35	.35
☐ 3 Randy Montgomery	3.00	1.35	.35
☐ 4 Steve Ramsey	4.00	1.80	.50
☐ 5 Roger Shoals	3.00	1.35	.35
☐ 6 Olen Underwood	3.00	1.35	.35

1972-73 Broncos Team Issue

The Broncos issued several series of player photos in the 1960s and 1970s with many invariably being released in multiple years. The format is the same for most of the sets with only subtle differences in the type (size and style) and information contained below the photo. Each of these black-and-white photos measures approximately 5" by 7" and is blankbacked and unnumbered. The line of text for the 1972-73 issue contains the following from left to right: player name (in all caps), position (initials), and team name (in all caps). We've listed the only known photos in the set.

	NRMT-MT	EXC	G-VG
COMPLETE SET (16)	50.00	22.00	6.25
COMMON CARD (1-16)	3.00	1.35	.35
☐ 1 Carter Campbell 72	3.00	1.35	.35
☐ 2 Barney Chavous 73	5.00	2.20	.60
☐ 3 Mike Current 73	4.00	1.80	.50
☐ 4 Joe Dawkins 73	4.00	1.80	.50
☐ 5 Cornell Gordon 72	3.00	1.35	.35
☐ 6 John Grant 73	3.00	1.35	.35
☐ 7 Larron Jackson 72 position "GUARD" spelled out	3.00	1.35	.35
☐ 8 Larron Jackson 73 position initial "G" only	3.00	1.35	.35
☐ 9 Calvin Jones 73	3.00	1.35	.35
☐ 10 Larry Kaminski 73	3.00	1.35	.35
☐ 11 Bill Laskey 73	3.00	1.35	.35
☐ 12 Tommy Lyons 72	3.00	1.35	.35
☐ 13 Tom Lyons 73	3.00	1.35	.35
☐ 14 Randy Montgomery 73	3.00	1.35	.35
☐ 15 Jerry Simmons 72 all capital letters used	4.00	1.80	.50
☐ 16 Jerry Simmons 72 upper and lower case letters used	4.00	1.80	.50

1980 Broncos Stamps Police

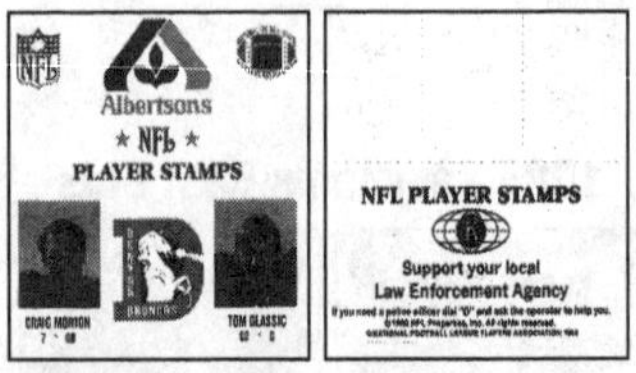

The 1980 Denver Broncos set are not cards but stamps each measuring approximately 3" by 3". Each stamp actually contains three smaller stamps, two player stamps and the Denver Broncos logo stamp. The set is co-sponsored by Albertson's, the Kiwanis Club, and the local law enforcement agency. A different stamp pair was given away each week for nine weeks by Albertson's food stores in the Denver Metro area. The set is unnumbered, although player uniform numbers appear on each small stamp. The set has been listed below in alphabetical order based on the player stamp on the left side. The back of each pair states "Support your local Law Enforcement Agency" and gives instructions on how to reach the police by phone. The backs of the stamps contain 1980 NFL and NFL Player's Association copyright dates. There was also a poster (to hold the stamps) issued which originally was priced at 99 cents. It was a color action picture of four Broncos tackling a Chargers running back measuring approximately 21" by 29"; the poster is much more difficult to find now than the set of stamps.

	MINT	NRMT	EXC
COMPLETE SET (9)	8.00	3.60	1.00
COMMON PAIR (1-9)	.75	.35	.09
☐ 1 Barney Chavous and Rubin Carter	1.00	.45	.12
☐ 2 Bernard Jackson and Haven Moses	1.00	.45	.12
☐ 3 Tom Jackson and Riley Odoms	2.00	.90	.25
☐ 4 Brison Manor and Steve Foley	.75	.35	.09
☐ 5 Claudie Minor and Randy Gradishar	1.00	.45	.12
☐ 6 Craig Morton and Tom Glassic	1.50	.70	.19
☐ 7 Jim Turner and Bob Swenson	1.00	.45	.12
☐ 8 Rick Upchurch and Bill Thompson	1.50	.70	.19
☐ 9 Louis Wright and Joe Rizzo	.75	.35	.09

1982 Broncos Police

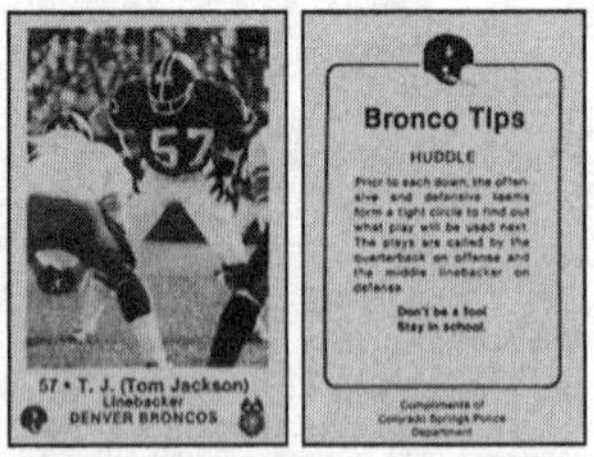

The 1982 Denver Broncos set contains 15 unnumbered cards. The cards measure approximately 2 5/8" by 4 1/8". The uniform numbers, which appear on the fronts of the cards, are used in the checklist below. The set was sponsored by the Colorado Springs Police Department and features "Broncos Tips" and the Broncos helmet logo on the back. Card backs feature black print on white card stock. The fronts contain both the Denver helmet logo and the logo of the Colorado Springs Police Department. The cards of Barney Chavous and Randy Gradishar are supposedly harder to find than the other cards in the set, with Chavous considered the more difficult of the two. In addition Riley Odoms and Dave Preston seem to be harder to find.

	MINT	NRMT	EXC
COMPLETE SET (15)	140.00	65.00	17.50
COMMON CARD	2.00	.90	.25
☐ 7 Craig Morton	10.00	4.50	1.25
☐ 11 Luke Prestridge	2.00	.90	.25
☐ 20 Louis Wright	4.00	1.80	.50
☐ 24 Rick Parros	2.00	.90	.25
☐ 36 Bill Thompson	4.00	1.80	.50
☐ 41 Rob Lytle	2.00	.90	.25
☐ 46 Dave Preston SP	6.00	2.70	.75
☐ 51 Bob Swenson	2.00	.90	.25
☐ 53 Randy Gradishar SP	50.00	22.00	6.25
☐ 57 Tom Jackson	10.00	4.50	1.25
☐ 60 Paul Howard	2.00	.90	.25
☐ 68 Rubin Carter	2.00	.90	.25
☐ 79 Barney Chavous SP	50.00	22.00	6.25
☐ 80 Rick Upchurch	6.00	2.70	.75
☐ 88 Riley Odoms SP	10.00	4.50	1.25

1984 Broncos KOA

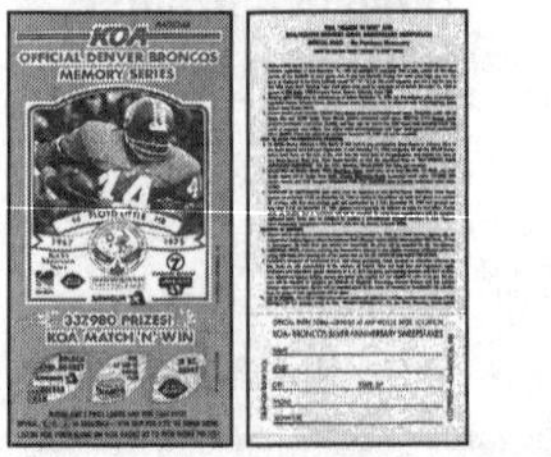

These cards were issued as part of a KOA "Match 'N Win" and KOA/Denver Broncos Silver Anniversary Sweepstakes. They were distributed at any participating Dairy Queen or Safeway in the Metro Denver area between September 17 and November 11, 1984. The cards measure approximately 2" by 4", with a tab at the bottom (measuring 1 1/8" in length). The front has a black and white photo of the player from the waist up. Above the photo the card reads "KOA Official Denver Broncos Memory Series" in blue print with white outlining. The lower portion of the photo is covered over by three items: 1) player number, name, and position; 2) a logo of the original American Football League and the sponsor's name or logo (Rocky Mountain News, Kodak, Dairy Queen, Wood Bros. Homes, KMGH-TV-7 Denver, Safeway, and Armour). The picture and these items are enframed by a color border on a color background. There were three each of eight different color schemes used. The tab portion of the card has three silver footballs that were to be scratched off with a coin. The back lists the rules governing the sweepstakes. There are four players marked as SP in the checklist below who are supposedly tougher to find than the others; they are Bobby Anderson, Randy Gradishar, Floyd Little, and Claudie Minor. The cards are unnumbered but are listed below in uniform number order. The prices listed refer to unscratched cards.

	MINT	NRMT	EXC
COMPLETE SET (24)	80.00	36.00	10.00
COMMON CARD (1-24)	1.50	.70	.19
☐ 7 Craig Morton	4.00	1.80	.50
☐ 11 Bob Anderson SP	10.00	4.50	1.25
☐ 12 Charlie Johnson	4.00	1.80	.50
☐ 15 Jim Turner	2.50	1.10	.30
☐ 21 Gene Mingo	1.50	.70	.19
☐ 22 Fran Lynch	1.50	.70	.19
☐ 23 Goose Gonsoulin	2.50	1.10	.30
☐ 24 Otis Armstrong	4.00	1.80	.50
☐ 24 Willie Brown	5.00	2.20	.60
☐ 25 Haven Moses	2.50	1.10	.30
☐ 36 Bill Thompson	2.50	1.10	.30
☐ 42 Bill Van Heusen	1.50	.70	.19
☐ 44 Floyd Little SP	20.00	9.00	2.50
☐ 53 Randy Gradishar SP	15.00	6.75	1.85
☐ 71 Claudie Minor SP	6.00	2.70	.75
☐ 72 Sam Brunelli	1.50	.70	.19
☐ 74 Mike Current	1.50	.70	.19
☐ 75 Eldon Danenhauer	1.50	.70	.19
☐ 78 Marv Montgomery	1.50	.70	.19
☐ 81 Billy Masters	1.50	.70	.19
☐ 82 Bob Scarpitto	1.50	.70	.19
☐ 87 Lionel Taylor	2.50	1.10	.30
☐ 87 Rich Jackson	1.50	.70	.19
☐ 88 Riley Odoms	2.50	1.10	.30

1987 Broncos Orange Crush

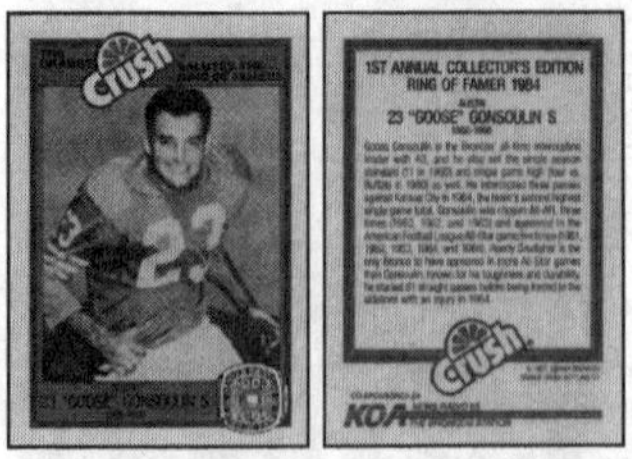

This nine-card set of Denver Broncos' ex-players was sponsored by Orange Crush and KOA Radio. The cards are standard size, 2 1/2" by 3 1/2", and feature black and white photos inside a blue and orange frame. The set is a salute to the "Ring of Famers," Denver's best players in its history as a franchise. Card backs (written in black, orange, and blue on white card stock) feature a capsule biography and indicate the year of induction into the Ring of Fame. Reportedly 1.35 million cards were distributed over a three-week period at participating 7-Eleven and Albertsons stores in Denver and surrounding areas.

	MINT	NRMT	EXC
COMPLETE SET (9)	4.00	1.80	.50
COMMON CARD (1-9)	.50	.23	.06
☐ 1 Bill Thompson	.60	.25	.07
☐ 2 Lionel Taylor	.60	.25	.07
☐ 3 Goose Gonsoulin	.50	.23	.06
☐ 4 Paul Smith	.50	.23	.06

□ 5 Rich Jackson	.50	.23	.06
□ 6 Charlie Johnson	.60	.25	.07
□ 7 Floyd Little	1.00	.45	.12
□ 8 Frank Tripucka	.60	.25	.07
□ 9 Gerald Phipps (Owner 1960-1981)	.50	.23	.06

1986 Brownell Heisman

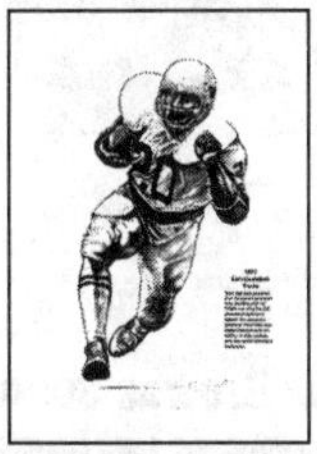

This large-sized black and white set features drawings of past Heisman Trophy winners by Art Brownell. The set (first 50-cards) was originally available as part of a promotion. They are unnumbered and blank backed so they have been assigned numbers below in chronological order according to when each player won the Heisman Trophy. Since Archie Griffin of Ohio State won the Heisman in both 1974 and 1975 there is only one card for him. The Vinny Testaverde and Tim Brown cards were produced at a later date. The cards measure approximately 7 15/16" by 10".

	MINT	NRMT	EXC
COMPLETE SET (52)	300.00	135.00	38.00
COMMON CARD (1-52)	4.00	1.80	.50
□ 1 Jay Berwanger	5.00	2.20	.60
□ 2 Larry Kelley	4.00	1.80	.50
□ 3 Clint Frank	4.00	1.80	.50
□ 4 Davey O'Brien	5.00	2.20	.60
□ 5 Nile Kinnick	10.00	4.50	1.25
□ 6 Tom Harmon	5.00	2.20	.60
□ 7 Bruce Smith	4.00	1.80	.50
□ 8 Frank Sinkwich	4.00	1.80	.50
□ 9 Angelo Bertelli	5.00	2.20	.60
□ 10 Les Horvath	5.00	2.20	.60
□ 11 Doc Blanchard	8.00	3.60	1.00
□ 12 Glenn Davis	8.00	3.60	1.00
□ 13 Johnny Lujack	15.00	6.75	1.85
□ 14 Doak Walker	10.00	4.50	1.25
□ 15 Leon Hart	5.00	2.20	.60
□ 16 Vic Janowicz	8.00	3.60	1.00
□ 17 Dick Kazmaier	4.00	1.80	.50
□ 18 Bill Vessels	4.00	1.80	.50
□ 19 John Lattner	8.00	3.60	1.00
□ 20 Alan Ameche	5.00	2.20	.60
□ 21 Howard Cassady	4.00	1.80	.50
□ 22 Paul Hornung	15.00	6.75	1.85
□ 23 John David Crow	4.00	1.80	.50
□ 24 Pete Dawkins	5.00	2.20	.60
□ 25 Billy Cannon	5.00	2.20	.60
□ 26 Joe Bellino	4.00	1.80	.50
□ 27 Ernie Davis	30.00	13.50	3.70
□ 28 Terry Baker	4.00	1.80	.50
□ 29 Roger Staubach	25.00	11.00	3.10
□ 30 John Huarte	5.00	2.20	.60
□ 31 Mike Garrett	4.00	1.80	.50
□ 32 Steve Spurrier	15.00	6.75	1.85
□ 33 Gary Beban	4.00	1.80	.50
□ 34 O.J. Simpson	12.50	5.50	1.55
□ 35 Steve Owens	4.00	1.80	.50
□ 36 Jim Plunkett	8.00	3.60	1.00
□ 37 Pat Sullivan	5.00	2.20	.60
□ 38 Johnny Rodgers	4.00	1.80	.50
□ 39 John Cappelletti	4.00	1.80	.50
□ 40 Archie Griffin	8.00	3.60	1.00
□ 41 Tony Dorsett	15.00	6.75	1.85
□ 42 Earl Campbell	15.00	6.75	1.85
□ 43 Billy Sims	4.00	1.80	.50
□ 44 Charles White	4.00	1.80	.50
□ 45 George Rogers	4.00	1.80	.50
□ 46 Marcus Allen	8.00	3.60	1.00
□ 47 Herschel Walker	8.00	3.60	1.00
□ 48 Mike Rozier	4.00	1.80	.50
□ 49 Doug Flutie	8.00	3.60	1.00
□ 50 Bo Jackson	6.00	2.70	.75
□ 51 Vinny Testaverde	15.00	6.75	1.85
□ 52 Tim Brown	15.00	6.75	1.85

1946 Browns Sears

These eight cards measure approximately 2 1/2" by 4". They were issued by Sears and Roebuck and feature players from the debut season of the Cleveland Browns. The cards were printed on heavy white paper stock and include a black and white photo of the featured player on the front with a team schedule on back. Cardfronts also included a message to follow the Browns and shop at Sears Stores. Several very early cards of Hall of Famers are included in this set. We have checklisted this set in alphabetical order.

	EX	VG	GOOD
COMPLETE SET (8)	550.00	250.00	70.00
COMMON CARD (1-8)	50.00	22.00	6.25
□ 1 Ernie Blandin	50.00	22.00	6.25
□ 2 Jim Daniell	50.00	22.00	6.25
□ 3 Fred Evans	50.00	22.00	6.25
□ 4 Frank Gatski	60.00	27.00	7.50
□ 5 Otto Graham	200.00	90.00	25.00
□ 6 Dante Lavelli	75.00	34.00	9.50
□ 7 Mel Maceau	50.00	22.00	6.25
□ 8 George Young	50.00	22.00	6.25

1950 Browns Team Issue

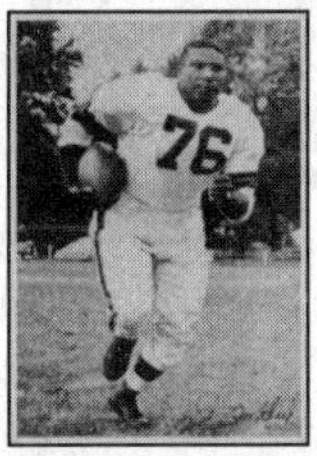

This set of team-issued photos measures approximately 6 1/8" by 9" and was printed on thin paper stock. The fronts feature black-and-white posed action shots framed by white borders. The set is similar to the 1951 issue, but the player's facsimile autograph appears very near the bottom border. The cardbacks are blank. The photos are unnumbered and checklisted below in alphabetical order. There are five known photos in the set. Any additions to this listing are appreciated.

	NRMT	VG-E	GOOD
COMPLETE SET (5)	125.00	55.00	15.50
COMMON CARD (1-5)	20.00	9.00	2.50
□ 1 Frank Gatski	30.00	13.50	3.70
□ 2 Tommy James	20.00	9.00	2.50
□ 3 Dom Moselle	20.00	9.00	2.50
□ 4 Marion Motley	50.00	22.00	6.25
□ 5 Derrell F. Palmer	20.00	9.00	2.50

1951 Browns Team Issue

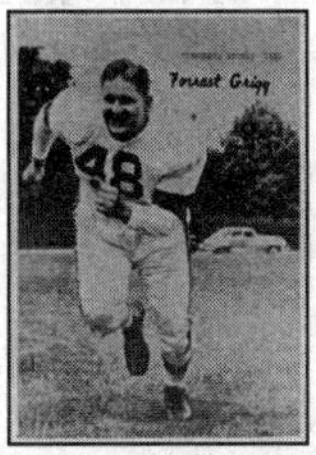

This set of team-issued photos measures approximately 6 1/2" by 9" and features black and white posed action shots framed by white borders. The set was distributed in an attractive off-white envelope with orange and brown trim titled "Cleveland Browns Photographs". The set is similar to the 1950 issue, but the player's name appears in script close to the photo. The backs are blank. The cards are unnumbered and checklisted below in alphabetical order.

	NRMT	VG-E	GOOD
COMPLETE SET (25)	450.00	200.00	55.00
COMMON CARD (1-25)	10.00	4.50	1.25
□ 1 Tony Adamle	7.50	3.40	.95
□ 2 Alex Agase	7.50	3.40	.95
□ 3 Rex Bumgardner	10.00	4.50	1.25
□ 4 Emerson Cole	10.00	4.50	1.25
□ 5 Len Ford	25.00	11.00	3.10
□ 6 Frank Gatski	25.00	11.00	3.10
□ 7 Horace Gillom	10.00	4.50	1.25
□ 8 Ken Gorgal	10.00	4.50	1.25
□ 9 Otto Graham	75.00	34.00	9.50
□ 10 Forrest Grigg	10.00	4.50	1.25
□ 11 Lou Groza	50.00	22.00	6.25
□ 12 Hal Herring	10.00	4.50	1.25
□ 13 Lin Houston	10.00	4.50	1.25
□ 14 Weldon Humble	10.00	4.50	1.25
□ 15 Tommy James	10.00	4.50	1.25
□ 16 Dub Jones	15.00	6.75	1.85
□ 17 Warren Lahr	10.00	4.50	1.25
□ 18 Dante Lavelli	40.00	18.00	5.00
□ 19 Cliff Lewis	10.00	4.50	1.25
□ 20 Marion Motley	50.00	22.00	6.25
□ 21 Lou Rymkus	7.50	3.40	.95
□ 22 Mac Speedie	18.00	8.00	2.20
□ 23 Tommy Thompson	15.00	6.75	1.85
□ 24 Bill Willis	25.00	11.00	3.10
□ 25 George Young	15.00	6.75	1.85

1953 Browns Team Issue

The Cleveland Browns issued and distributed this 12-card set of player photos. Each measures approximately 8 1/2" by 10 1/4" and features a black and white photo. The player's name and position appear in a small white box near the photo.

	NRMT	VG-E	GOOD
COMPLETE SET (12)	400.00	180.00	50.00
COMMON CARD (1-12)	15.00	6.75	1.85
□ 1 Len Ford	30.00	13.50	3.70
□ 2 Frank Gatski	30.00	13.50	3.70
□ 3 Abe Gibron	25.00	11.00	3.10
□ 4 Ken Gorgal	15.00	6.75	1.85
□ 5 Otto Graham	100.00	45.00	12.50
□ 6 Lou Groza	60.00	27.00	7.50
□ 7 Harry Jagade	15.00	6.75	1.85
□ 8 Dub Jones	25.00	11.00	3.10
□ 9 Dante Lavelli	50.00	22.00	6.25
□ 10 Ray Renfro	25.00	11.00	3.10
□ 11 Tommy Thompson	20.00	9.00	2.50
□ 12 Bill Willis	30.00	13.50	3.70

1954-55 Browns Team Issue

This set consists of twenty 8 1/2" by 10" posed player photos, with white borders and blank backs. Most of the photos are poses shot from the waist up; a few (Colo, Ford, and Lahr) picture the player in an action pose. The player's name and position are printed in the bottom white border. The photos are unnumbered and checklisted below in alphabetical order.

	NRMT	VG-E	GOOD
COMPLETE SET (20)	175.00	80.00	22.00
COMMON CARD (1-20)	6.00	2.70	.75
□ 1 Maurice Bassett	6.00	2.70	.75
□ 2 Harold Bradley	6.00	2.70	.75
□ 3 Darrell(Pete) Brewster	6.00	2.70	.75
□ 4 Don Colo	6.00	2.70	.75
□ 5 Len Ford	15.00	6.75	1.85
□ 6 Bob Gain	8.00	3.60	1.00
□ 7 Frank Gatski	15.00	6.75	1.85
□ 8 Abe Gibron	8.00	3.60	1.00
□ 9 Tommy James	6.00	2.70	.75
□ 10 Dub Jones	10.00	4.50	1.25
□ 11 Kenny Konz	6.00	2.70	.75
□ 12 Warren Lahr	6.00	2.70	.75
□ 13 Dante Lavelli	20.00	9.00	2.50
□ 14 Carlton Massey	6.00	2.70	.75
□ 15 Mike McCormack	15.00	6.75	1.85
□ 16 Walt Michaels	8.00	3.60	1.00
□ 17 Chuck Noll	30.00	13.50	3.70
□ 18 Don Paul	6.00	2.70	.75
□ 19 Ray Renfro	10.00	4.50	1.25
□ 20 George Ratterman	8.00	3.60	1.00

1955 Browns Carling Beer

This set of ten black and white posed action shots was sponsored by Carling Black Label Beer and features members of the Cleveland Browns. The pictures measure approximately 8 1/2" by 11 1/2" and have white borders. The sponsor's name and the team name appear below the picture in black lettering. The cards are unnumbered and the backs are blank. The serial number in the lower right corner on the fronts lists "DBL 54". The photos were shot against a background of an open field with trees.

	NRMT	VG-E	GOOD
COMPLETE SET (10)	300.00	135.00	38.00
COMMON CARD (1-10)	15.00	6.75	1.85
□ 1 Darrell(Pete) Brewster	15.00	6.75	1.85
□ 2 Tom Catlin	15.00	6.75	1.85
□ 3 Len Ford	30.00	13.50	3.70
□ 4 Otto Graham	75.00	34.00	9.50
□ 5 Lou Groza	50.00	22.00	6.25
□ 6 Kenny Konz	15.00	6.75	1.85
□ 7 Dante Lavelli	40.00	18.00	5.00
□ 8 Mike McCormack	35.00	16.00	4.40
□ 9 Fred Morrison	15.00	6.75	1.85
□ 10 Chuck Noll	75.00	34.00	9.50

1955 Browns Color Postcards

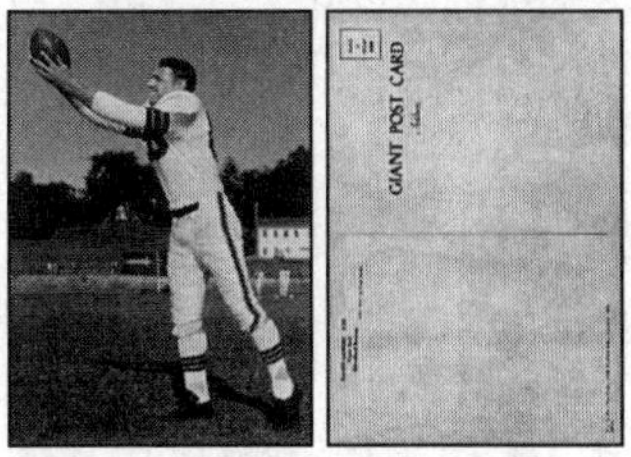

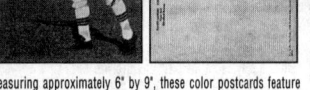

Measuring approximately 6" by 9", these color postcards feature Cleveland Browns players. The cards have rounded corners.

	NRMT	VG-E	GOOD
COMPLETE SET (6)	150.00	70.00	19.00
COMMON CARD (1-6)	15.00	6.75	1.85
□ 1 Maurice Bassett	15.00	6.75	1.85
□ 2 Don Colo	15.00	6.75	1.85
□ 3 Frank Gatski	30.00	13.50	3.70
□ 4 Lou Groza	50.00	22.00	6.25
□ 5 Dante Lavelli	40.00	18.00	5.00
□ 6 George Ratterman	20.00	9.00	2.50

1959 Browns Carling Beer

This set of nine black and white posed action shots was sponsored by Carling Black Label Beer and features members of the Cleveland

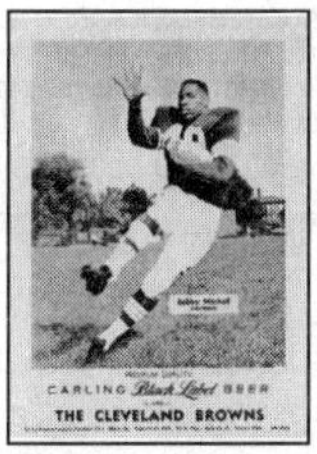

Browns. The pictures measure approximately 8 1/2" by 11 1/2" and have white borders. The sponsor's name and the team name appear below the picture in black lettering. The backs are typically blank, but are sometimes found with a rubber-stamped identification that reads "Henry M. Barr Studios, Berea, Ohio BE4-1330." The pictures are numbered in the lower right corner on the fronts, with the exception of Jim Brown's picture. The photos were shot against a background of an open field with trees. The set is dated by the fact that Billy Howton's last year with Cleveland was 1959. This set was illegally reprinted in the late 1980's; the reprints are on thinner paper and typically show the Henry M. Barr stamp on the back. In fact the Jimmy Brown photo is apparently only available in the reprint set.

	NRMT	VG-E	GOOD
COMPLETE SET (9)	150.00	70.00	19.00
COMMON CARD (302A-302K)	12.00	5.50	1.50
□ 302A Leroy Bolden	12.00	5.50	1.50
□ 302B Vince Costello	12.00	5.50	1.50
□ 302C Galen Fiss	12.00	5.50	1.50
□ 302E Lou Groza	35.00	16.00	4.40
□ 302F Walt Michaels	15.00	6.75	1.85
□ 302G Bobby Mitchell	35.00	16.00	4.40
□ 302J Bob Gain	12.00	5.50	1.50
□ 302K Bill Howton	15.00	6.75	1.85
□ NNO Jim Brown DP	12.00	5.50	1.50

1961 Browns Carling Beer

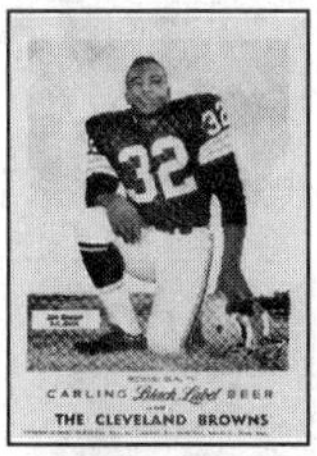

This set of ten black and white posed action shots was sponsored by Carling Black Label Beer and features members of the Cleveland Browns. The pictures measure approximately 8 1/2" by 11 1/2" and have white borders. The sponsor's name and the team name appear below the picture in black lettering. The banks are blank. The pictures are numbered in the lower right corner on the fronts. The set is dated by the fact that Jim Houston's first year was 1960 and Bobby Mitchell and Milt Plum's last year with the Browns was 1961.

	NRMT	VG-E	GOOD
COMPLETE SET (10)	225.00	100.00	28.00
COMMON CARD (439A-439L)	12.00	5.50	1.50
□ 439A Milt Plum	20.00	9.00	2.50
□ 439B Mike McCormack	25.00	11.00	3.10
□ 439C Bob Gain	12.00	5.50	1.50
□ 439D John Morrow	12.00	5.50	1.50
□ 439E Jim Brown	100.00	45.00	12.50
□ 439F Bobby Mitchell	30.00	13.50	3.70
□ 439G Bobby Franklin	12.00	5.50	1.50
□ 439H Jim Ray Smith	12.00	5.50	1.50
□ 439K Jim Houston	15.00	6.75	1.85
□ 439L Ray Renfro	15.00	6.75	1.85

1961 Browns National City Bank

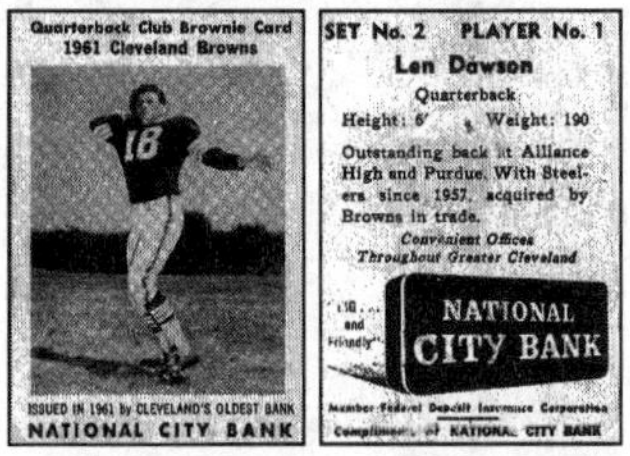

The 1961 National City Bank Cleveland Browns football card set contains 36 brown and white cards each measuring approximately 2 1/2" by 3 9/16". The cards were issued in sheets of six cards, with each sheet of six given a set number and each individual card within the sheet given a player number. In the checklist below the cards have been numbered consecutively from one to 36. On the actual card, set number one will appear on cards 1 through 6, set number two on cards 7 through 12, etc. The front of the card states that the card is a "Quarterback Club Brownie Card". The backs of the cards contain the

card number, a short biography and an ad for the National City Bank. Cards still in their uncut (sheet of six) state are valued at 50 percent higher than the prices listed below. Len Dawson's card predates his 1963 Fleer Rookie Card by two years.

	NRMT	VG-E	GOOD
COMPLETE SET (36)	2200.00	1000.00	275.00
COMMON CARD (1-36)	35.00	16.00	4.40
☐ 1 Mike McCormack	75.00	34.00	9.50
☐ 2 Jim Brown	600.00	275.00	75.00
☐ 3 Leon Clarke	35.00	16.00	4.40
☐ 4 Walt Michaels	40.00	18.00	5.00
☐ 5 Jim Ray Smith	35.00	16.00	4.40
☐ 6 Quarterback Club Membership Card	225.00	100.00	28.00
☐ 7 Len Dawson	250.00	110.00	31.00
☐ 8 John Morrow	35.00	16.00	4.40
☐ 9 Bernie Parrish	40.00	18.00	5.00
☐ 10 Floyd Peters	40.00	18.00	5.00
☐ 11 Paul Wiggin	40.00	18.00	5.00
☐ 12 John Wooten	40.00	18.00	5.00
☐ 13 Ray Renfro	40.00	18.00	5.00
☐ 14 Galen Fiss	35.00	16.00	4.40
☐ 15 Dave Lloyd	35.00	16.00	4.40
☐ 16 Dick Schafrath	40.00	18.00	5.00
☐ 17 Ross Fichtner	35.00	16.00	4.40
☐ 18 Gern Nagler	35.00	16.00	4.40
☐ 19 Rich Kreitling	35.00	16.00	4.40
☐ 20 Duane Putnam	35.00	16.00	4.40
☐ 21 Vince Costello	35.00	16.00	4.40
☐ 22 Jim Shofner	40.00	18.00	5.00
☐ 23 Sam Baker	40.00	18.00	5.00
☐ 24 Bob Gain	40.00	18.00	5.00
☐ 25 Lou Groza	100.00	45.00	12.50
☐ 26 Don Fleming	50.00	22.00	6.25
☐ 27 Tom Watkins	35.00	16.00	4.40
☐ 28 Jim Houston	40.00	18.00	5.00
☐ 29 Larry Stephens	35.00	16.00	4.40
☐ 30 Bobby Mitchell	100.00	45.00	12.50
☐ 31 Bobby Franklin	35.00	16.00	4.40
☐ 32 Charley Ferguson	35.00	16.00	4.40
☐ 33 Johnny Brewer	35.00	16.00	4.40
☐ 34 Bob Crespino	35.00	16.00	4.40
☐ 35 Milt Plum	50.00	22.00	6.25
☐ 36 Preston Powell	35.00	16.00	4.40

1961 Browns Team Issue

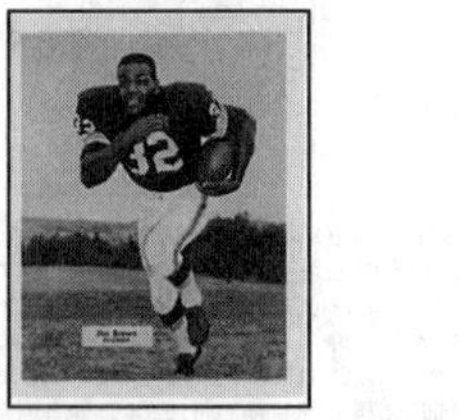

These 20 large photo cards are an unnumbered, blank-backed, team issue set of black and white photographs of the Cleveland Browns measuring approximately 8 1/2" by 10 1/2". The set features posed action shots of players whose name and position appear in a white reverse-out block burned into the bottom of each picture. The cards are listed below alphabetically.

	NRMT	VG-E	GOOD
COMPLETE SET (20)	175.00	80.00	22.00
COMMON CARD (1-20)	5.00	2.20	.60
☐ 1 Jim Brown	75.00	34.00	9.50
☐ 2 Galen Fiss	5.00	2.20	.60
☐ 3 Don Fleming	10.00	4.50	1.25
☐ 4 Bobby Franklin	5.00	2.20	.60
☐ 5 Bob Gain	6.00	2.70	.75
☐ 6 Jim Houston	6.00	2.70	.75
☐ 7 Rich Kreitling	5.00	2.20	.60
☐ 8 Dave Lloyd	5.00	2.20	.60
☐ 9 Mike McCormack	12.00	5.50	1.50
☐ 10 Bobby Mitchell	20.00	9.00	2.50
☐ 11 John Morrow	5.00	2.20	.60
☐ 12 Bernie Parrish	6.00	2.70	.75
☐ 13 Milt Plum	10.00	4.50	1.25
☐ 14 Ray Renfro	6.00	2.70	.75
☐ 15 Dick Schafrath	6.00	2.70	.75
☐ 16 Jim Shofner	6.00	2.70	.75
☐ 17 Jim Ray Smith	5.00	2.20	.60
☐ 18 Tom Watkins	5.00	2.20	.60
☐ 19 Paul Wiggin	6.00	2.70	.75
☐ 20 John Wooten	6.00	2.70	.75

1963 Browns Team Issue

These large photo cards measure approximately 7 1/2" by 9 1/2" are feature a black-and-white player photo on blankbacked glossy paper stock. Each includes the player's name, position (initials) and team name in the bottom border. The photos are unnumbered and checklisted below in alphabetical order.

	NRMT	VG-E	GOOD
COMPLETE SET (26)	150.00	70.00	19.00
COMMON CARD (1-26)	5.00	2.20	.60
☐ 1 Johnny Brewer	5.00	2.20	.60
☐ 2 Monte Clark	8.00	3.60	1.00
☐ 3 Gary Collins	15.00	6.75	1.85
☐ 4 Vince Costello	6.00	2.70	.75
☐ 5 Bob Crespino	5.00	2.20	.60
☐ 6 Ross Fichtner	5.00	2.20	.60
☐ 7 Galen Fiss	6.00	2.70	.75
☐ 8 Bob Gain	6.00	2.70	.75
☐ 9 Bill Glass	8.00	3.60	1.00
☐ 10 Ernie Green	12.00	5.50	1.50
☐ 11 Lou Groza	20.00	9.00	2.50
☐ 12 Gene Hickerson	12.00	5.50	1.50
☐ 13 Jim Houston	6.00	2.70	.75
☐ 14 Tom Hutchinson	5.00	2.20	.60
☐ 15 Rich Kreitling	5.00	2.20	.60
☐ 16 Mike Lucci	8.00	3.60	1.00
☐ 17 John Morrow	5.00	2.20	.60
☐ 18 Jim Ninowski	6.00	2.70	.75
☐ 19 Frank Parker	5.00	2.20	.60
☐ 20 Bernie Parrish	6.00	2.70	.75
☐ 21 Ray Renfro	6.00	2.70	.75
☐ 22 Dick Schafrath	6.00	2.70	.75
☐ 23 Jim Shofner	6.00	2.70	.75
☐ 24 Ken Webb	5.00	2.20	.60
☐ 25 Paul Wiggin	6.00	2.70	.75
☐ 26 John Wooten	6.00	2.70	.75

1965 Browns Volpe Tumblers

These Browns artist's renderings were part of a plastic cup tumbler produced in 1965. The noted sports artist Volpe created the artwork which includes an action scene and a player portrait. The "cards" are unnumbered, each measures approximately 5" by 8 1/2" and is curved in the shape required to fit inside a plastic cup. Any additions to this list are welcomed.

	NRMT	VG-E	GOOD
COMPLETE SET (6)	300.00	135.00	38.00
COMMON CARD (1-6)	30.00	13.50	3.70
☐ 1 Jim Brown	125.00	55.00	15.50
☐ 2 Blanton Collier CO	40.00	18.00	5.00
☐ 3 Gary Collins	30.00	13.50	3.70
☐ 4 Lou Groza	60.00	27.00	7.50
☐ 5 Jim Houston	30.00	13.50	3.70
☐ 6 Frank Ryan	40.00	18.00	5.00

1968 Browns Team Issue

(From Mossier at Philly show) The Cleveland Browns issued and distributed this set of player photos. Each measures approximately 8" by 10" and features a black and white photo. The player's name and position appear in the bottom border below the photo. Any additions to this list are appreciated.

	NRMT-MT	EXC	G-VG
COMPLETE SET (11)	80.00	36.00	10.00
COMMON CARD (1-11)	4.00	1.80	.50
☐ 1 Don Cockroft	6.00	2.70	.75
☐ 2 Gary Collins	7.50	3.40	.95
☐ 3 Ernie Green	6.00	2.70	.75
☐ 4 Gene Hickerson	6.00	2.70	.75
☐ 5 Ernie Kellerman	4.00	1.80	.50
☐ 6 Leroy Kelly	20.00	9.00	2.50
☐ 7 Milt Morin	4.00	1.80	.50
☐ 8 Frank Ryan	6.00	2.70	.75
☐ 9 Marvin Upshaw	4.00	1.80	.50
☐ 10 Paul Warfield	20.00	9.00	2.50
☐ 11 Coaching Staff	12.00	5.50	1.50

1985 Browns Coke/Mr. Hero

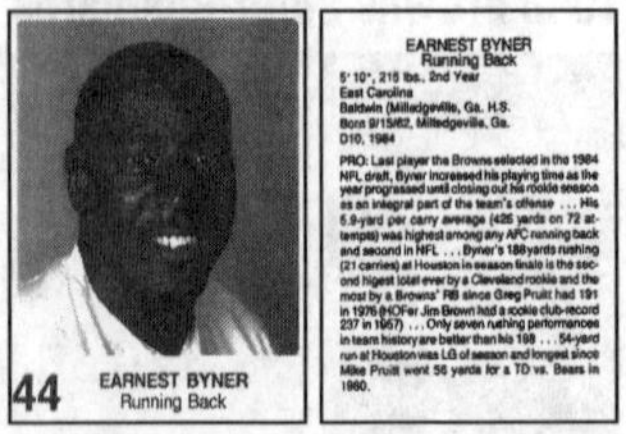

This 48-card set was issued as six sheets of eight cards each featuring players on the Cleveland Browns. Each card measures approximately 2 3/4" by 3 1/4". Each sheet was numbered; the sheet number is given after each player in the checklist below. The cards are otherwise unnumbered except for uniform number as they are listed below. The bottom of each sheet had coupons for discounts on food and drink from the sponsors.

	MINT	NRMT	EXC
COMPLETE SET (48)	25.00	11.00	3.10
COMMON CARD	.50	.23	.06
☐ 7 Jeff Gossett 4	.75	.35	.09
☐ 9 Matt Bahr 1	.75	.35	.09
☐ 16 Paul McDonald 4	.75	.35	.09
☐ 18 Gary Danielson 5	.75	.35	.09
☐ 19 Bernie Kosar 6	2.50	1.10	.30
☐ 20 Don Rogers 4	.75	.35	.09
☐ 22 Felix Wright 2	.75	.35	.09
☐ 26 Greg Allen 3	.50	.23	.06
☐ 27 Al Gross 2	.50	.23	.06
☐ 29 Hanford Dixon 5	.75	.35	.09
☐ 30 Boyce Green 1	.50	.23	.06
☐ 31 Frank Minnifield 1	.75	.35	.09
☐ 34 Kevin Mack 3	1.25	.55	.16
☐ 37 Chris Rockins 1	.50	.23	.06
☐ 38 Johnny Davis 5	.50	.23	.06
☐ 44 Earnest Byner 2	1.50	.70	.19
☐ 47 Larry Braziel 4	.50	.23	.06
☐ 50 Tom Cousineau 6	.75	.35	.09
☐ 51 Eddie Johnson 2	.50	.23	.06
☐ 55 Curtis Weathers 1	.50	.23	.06
☐ 56 Chip Banks 6	.75	.35	.09
☐ 57 Clay Matthews 5	1.50	.70	.19
☐ 58 Scott Nicolas 1	.50	.23	.06
☐ 61 Mike Baab 4	.75	.35	.09
☐ 62 George Lilja 5	.50	.23	.06
☐ 63 Cody Risien 6	.75	.35	.09
☐ 65 Mark Krerowicz 3	.50	.23	.06
☐ 68 Robert Jackson 4	.50	.23	.06
☐ 69 Dan Fike 2	.50	.23	.06
☐ 72 Dave Puzzuoli 1	.50	.23	.06
☐ 74 Paul Farren 2	.50	.23	.06
☐ 77 Rickey Bolden 3	.50	.23	.06
☐ 78 Carl Hairston 2	.75	.35	.09
☐ 79 Bob Golic 6	.75	.35	.09
☐ 80 Willis Adams 2	.50	.23	.06
☐ 81 Harry Holt 3	.50	.23	.06
☐ 82 Ozzie Newsome 3	2.50	1.10	.30
☐ 83 Fred Banks 3	.50	.23	.06
☐ 84 Glen Young 1	.50	.23	.06
☐ 85 Clarence Weathers 6	.50	.23	.06
☐ 86 Brian Brennan 5	.75	.35	.09
☐ 87 Travis Tucker 6	.50	.23	.06
☐ 88 Reggie Langhorne 5	.75	.35	.09
☐ 89 John Jefferson 4	1.00	.45	.12
☐ 91 Sam Clancy 4	.75	.35	.09
☐ 96 Reggie Camp 5	.50	.23	.06
☐ 99 Keith Baldwin 6	.50	.23	.06
☐ NNO Action Photo 3 (Clay Matthews tackling Eric Dickerson)	1.50	.70	.19

1987 Browns Louis Rich

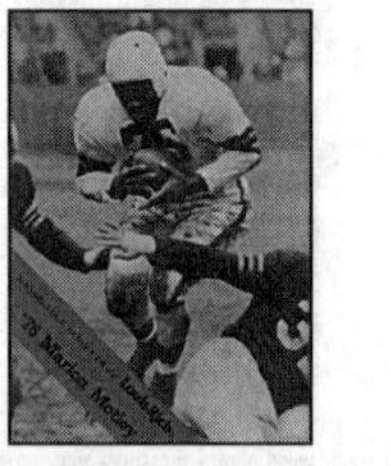

This five-card set was originally produced as a food product insert for Louis Rich products. Apparently, the promotion was canceled, and collectors were known to have acquired these cards directly from the Cleveland office of Oscar Mayer, which produces the Louis Rich brand. On card number 4 below, the player was unidentified as a question mark, and it is rumored that this was intended to be part of a contest in the promotion. Both Dante Lavelli and Dub Jones wore number 86. Jones wore uniform number 86 in his earlier years with the Browns, in 1952 he began to wear number 40. Also that same year Lavelli changed from wearing number 56 to number 86, Jones' former uniform number. The plastic helmet dates the photo as after 1952 since the Browns changed to this type of helmet in 1952. Therefore, Dante Lavelli appears to be the correct identification. The oversized cards measure approximately 5" by 7 1/8" and are printed on heavy white card stock. The fronts feature full-bleed sepia-toned player photos. An orange diagonal cuts across the lower left corner and carries the set title ("Memorable Moments by Louis Rich"), uniform number, and player's name. The backs are blank. The cards are unnumbered and checklisted below in alphabetical order.

	MINT	NRMT	EXC
COMPLETE SET (5)	50.00	22.00	6.25
COMMON CARD (1-5)	7.50	3.40	.95
☐ 1 Jim Brown Bobby Mitchell	20.00	9.00	2.50
☐ 2 Otto Graham	15.00	6.75	1.85
☐ 3 Lou Groza	10.00	4.50	1.25
☐ 4 Dante Lavelli (Question Mark)	7.50	3.40	.95
☐ 5 Marion Motley	10.00	4.50	1.25

1987 Browns Team Issue

The Cleveland Browns issued this set of black and white player photos. Each card measures roughly 5" by 7" and includes the player's jersey number, name, position initials, and team name below the photo. The cards are blankbacked and unnumbered.

	MINT	NRMT	EXC
COMPLETE SET (9)	40.00	18.00	5.00
COMMON CARD (1-9)	5.00	2.20	.60
☐ 1 Mike Baab	5.00	2.20	.60
☐ 2 Earnest Byner	9.00	4.00	1.10
☐ 3 Reggie Camp	5.00	2.20	.60
☐ 4 Bob Golic	5.00	2.20	.60

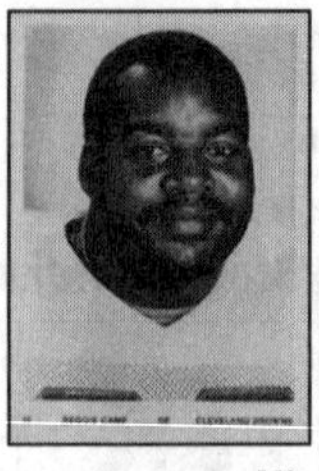

☐ 5 Al Gross	5.00	2.20	.60
☐ 6 Mike Junkin	5.00	2.20	.60
☐ 7 Reggie Langhorne	7.50	3.40	.95
☐ 8 Gerald McNeil	5.00	2.20	.60
☐ 9 Frank Minnifield	7.50	3.40	.95

1992 Browns Sunoco

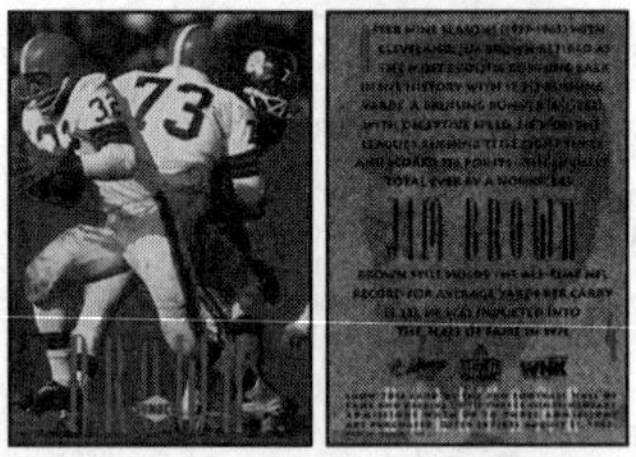

Featuring Cleveland Browns' Hall of Famers, this 24-card set was produced by NFL Properties for an Ohio-area promotion sponsored by Sunoco. Two AM radio stations, WMMS 100.7 and WHK 14.20, cosponsored the set. The cards were available in cello packs that contained a cover card, a player card, and an official sweepstakes entry blank. Some packs contained autograph cards of featured players who were still living. The grand prize offered to the winner was a trip for two to the Super Bowl in Pasadena, California. One player card shown at the Pro Football Hall of Fame would entitle the holder to receive up to three complimentary admissions when up to three admissions were purchased. The offer expired August 31, 1993. The fronts of the cover cards have the words "The Cleveland Browns' Collection" printed in black near the top. A Browns helmet is near the center with the player's name printed below it. The words "Hall of Famer Limited Edition" are printed at the bottom with the Sunoco logo. The backs are simple showing only the Pro Football Hall of Fame logo and sponsors' logos. The player cards exhibit a mix of color and black-and-white full-bleed photos with the player's last name printed in oversized orange letters at the bottom. The Sunoco logo is superimposed on the player's name. The backs are sandstone-textured in varying pastel shades and display a ghosted picture of the player. A career summary and the year the player was inducted into the Hall of Fame are overprinted in black. The player cards are numbered on the back. The cover cards are unnumbered but are checklisted below as they appear in the set and assigned corresponding card numbers with a "C" suffix. There was also an album produced for this set.

	MINT	NRMT	EXC
COMPLETE SET (24)	15.00	6.75	1.85
COMMON CARD (1-12)	.75	.35	.09
COMMON COVER CARD (1-12C)	.25	.11	.03
☐ 1 Otto Graham (Player card)	2.00	.90	.25
☐ 1C Otto Graham (Cover card)	.25	.11	.03
☐ 2 Paul Brown CO (Player card)	1.50	.70	.19
☐ 2C Paul Brown CO (Cover card)	.25	.11	.03
☐ 3 Marion Motley (Player card)	1.50	.70	.19
☐ 3C Marion Motley (Cover card)	.25	.11	.03
☐ 4 Jim Brown (Player card)	4.00	1.80	.50
☐ 4C Jim Brown (Cover card)	.50	.23	.06
☐ 5 Lou Groza (Player card)	1.50	.70	.19
☐ 5C Lou Groza (Cover card)	.25	.11	.03
☐ 6 Dante Lavelli (Player card)	1.25	.55	.16
☐ 6C Dante Lavelli (Cover card)	.25	.11	.03
☐ 7 Len Ford (Player card)	.75	.35	.09
☐ 7C Len Ford (Cover card)	.25	.11	.03
☐ 8 Bill Willis (Player card)	.75	.35	.09
☐ 8C Bill Willis (Cover card)	.25	.11	.03
☐ 9 Bobby Mitchell (Player card)	1.25	.55	.16
☐ 9C Bobby Mitchell (Cover card)	.25	.11	.03
☐ 10 Paul Warfield (Player card)	1.50	.70	.19

☐ 10C Paul Warfield (Cover card)	.25	.11	.03
☐ 11 Mike McCormack (Player card)	.75	.35	.09
☐ 11C Mike McCormack (Cover card)	.25	.11	.03
☐ 12 Frank Gatski (Player card)	.75	.35	.09
☐ 12C Frank Gatski (Cover card)	.25	.11	.03

1980 Buccaneers Police

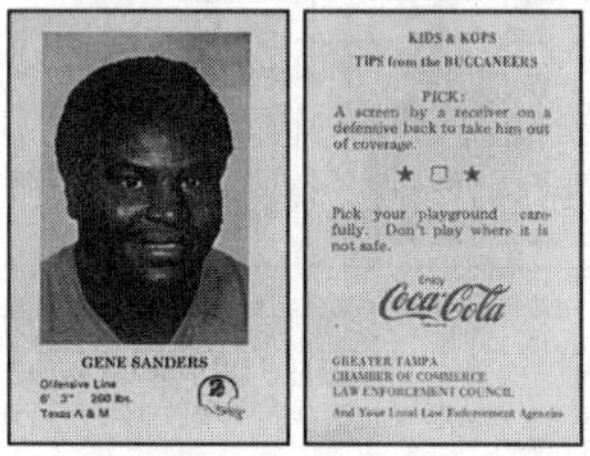

This set is complete at 56 cards measuring approximately 2 5/8" by 4 1/8". Since there are no numbers on the cards, the set has been listed in alphabetical order by player. In addition to player cards, an assortment of coaches, mascots, and Swash-Buc-Lers (cheerleaders) are included. The set was sponsored by the Greater Tampa Chamber of Commerce Law Enforcement Council, the local law enforcement agencies, and Coca-Cola. Tips from the Buccaneers are written on the backs. The fronts contain the Tampa Bay helmet logo. Cards are also available with a tougher Paradyne (Corporation) cardback sponsorship.

	MINT	NRMT	EXC
COMPLETE SET (56)	135.00	60.00	17.00
COMMON CARD (1-56)	2.50	1.10	.30
*PARADYNE CARDS: 2X TO 3X BASIC CARDS			
☐ 1 Ricky Bell	7.00	3.10	.85
☐ 2 Rick Berns	3.50	1.55	.45
☐ 3 Tom Blanchard	2.50	1.10	.30
☐ 4 Scot Brantley	2.50	1.10	.30
☐ 5 Aaron Brown	2.50	1.10	.30
☐ 6 Cedric Brown	2.50	1.10	.30
☐ 7 Mark Cotney	2.50	1.10	.30
☐ 8 Randy Crowder	2.50	1.10	.30
☐ 9 Gary Davis	2.50	1.10	.30
☐ 10 Johnny Davis	3.50	1.55	.45
☐ 11 Tony Davis	2.50	1.10	.30
☐ 12 Jerry Eckwood	5.00	2.20	.60
☐ 13 Chuck Fusina	3.50	1.55	.45
☐ 14 Jimmie Giles	5.00	2.20	.60
☐ 15 Isaac Hagins	2.50	1.10	.30
☐ 16 Charley Hannah	2.50	1.10	.30
☐ 17 Andy Hawkins	2.50	1.10	.30
☐ 18 Kevin House	5.00	2.20	.60
☐ 19 Cecil Johnson	2.50	1.10	.30
☐ 20 Gordon Jones	3.50	1.55	.45
☐ 21 Curtis Jordan	2.50	1.10	.30
☐ 22 Bill Kollar	2.50	1.10	.30
☐ 23 Jim Leonard	2.50	1.10	.30
☐ 24 David Lewis	3.50	1.55	.45
☐ 25 Reggie Lewis	2.50	1.10	.30
☐ 26 David Logan	3.50	1.55	.45
☐ 27 Larry Mucker	2.50	1.10	.30
☐ 28 Jim O'Bradovich	3.50	1.55	.45
☐ 29 Mike Rae	2.50	1.10	.30
☐ 30 Dave Reavis	2.50	1.10	.30
☐ 31 Danny Reece	2.50	1.10	.30
☐ 32 Greg Roberts	2.50	1.10	.30
☐ 33 Gene Sanders	2.50	1.10	.30
☐ 34 Dewey Selmon	5.00	2.20	.60
☐ 35 Lee Roy Selmon	15.00	6.75	1.85
☐ 36 Ray Snell	2.50	1.10	.30
☐ 37 Dave Stalls	2.50	1.10	.30
☐ 38 Norris Thomas	2.50	1.10	.30
☐ 39 Mike Washington	2.50	1.10	.30
☐ 40 Doug Williams	8.00	3.60	1.00
☐ 41 Steve Wilson	2.50	1.10	.30
☐ 42 Richard Wood	3.50	1.55	.45
☐ 43 George Yarno	2.50	1.10	.30
☐ 44 Garo Yepremian	5.00	2.20	.60
☐ 45 Logo Card	2.50	1.10	.30
☐ 46 Team Photo	5.00	2.20	.60
☐ 47 Hugh Culverhouse OWN	3.50	1.55	.45
☐ 48 John McKay CO	3.50	1.55	.45
☐ 49 Mascot Capt. Crush	2.50	1.10	.30
☐ 50 Cheerleaders: Swash-Buc-Lers	3.50	1.55	.45
☐ 51 Swash-Buc-Lers (Buzz)	3.50	1.55	.45
☐ 52 Swash-Buc-Lers (Check with me)	3.50	1.55	.45
☐ 53 Swash-Buc-Lers (Gap Two)	3.50	1.55	.45
☐ 54 Swash-Buc-Lers (Gas)	3.50	1.55	.45
☐ 55 Swash-Buc-Lers (Pass Protection)	3.50	1.55	.45
☐ 56 Swash-Buc-Lers (Post Pattern)	3.50	1.55	.45

1982 Buccaneers Shell

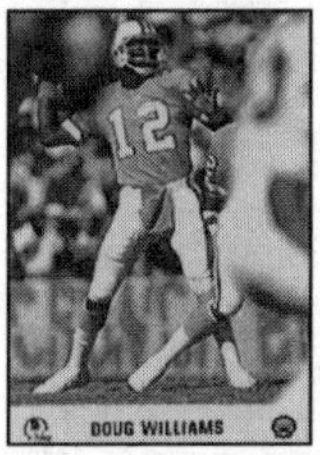

Sponsored by Shell Oil Co., these 32 paper-thin blank-backed cards measure approximately 1 1/2" by 2 1/2" and feature color action player photos. The photos are borderless, except at the bottom, where the player's name, his team's helmet, and the Shell logo appear in a white margin. The cards are unnumbered and checklisted below in alphabetical order.

	MINT	NRMT	EXC
COMPLETE SET (32)	25.00	11.00	3.10
COMMON CARD (1-32)	.60	.25	.07
☐ 1 Theo Bell	1.00	.45	.12
☐ 2 Scot Brantley	.75	.35	.09
☐ 3 Cedric Brown	.60	.25	.07
☐ 4 Bill Capece	.60	.25	.07
☐ 5 Neal Colzie	1.00	.45	.12
☐ 6 Mark Cotney	.60	.25	.07
☐ 7 Hugh Culverhouse OWN	1.00	.45	.12
☐ 8 Jeff Davis	.75	.35	.09
☐ 9 Jerry Eckwood	1.00	.45	.12
☐ 10 Sean Farrell	.75	.35	.09
☐ 11 Jimmie Giles	1.00	.45	.12
☐ 12 Hugh Green	1.25	.55	.16
☐ 13 Charley Hannah	.60	.25	.07
☐ 14 Andy Hawkins	.60	.25	.07
☐ 15 John Holt	.60	.25	.07
☐ 16 Kevin House	1.00	.45	.12
☐ 17 Cecil Johnson	.60	.25	.07
☐ 18 Gordon Jones	.75	.35	.09
☐ 19 David Logan	.75	.35	.09
☐ 20 John McKay CO	1.50	.70	.19
☐ 21 James Owens	1.00	.45	.12
☐ 22 Greg Roberts	.60	.25	.07
☐ 23 Gene Sanders	.60	.25	.07
☐ 24 Lee Roy Selmon	4.00	1.80	.50
☐ 25 Ray Snell	.60	.25	.07
☐ 26 Larry Swider	.60	.25	.07
☐ 27 Norris Thomas	.60	.25	.07
☐ 28 Mike Washington	.60	.25	.07
☐ 29 James Wilder	1.00	.45	.12
☐ 30 Doug Williams	2.00	.90	.25
☐ 31 Steve Wilson	.60	.25	.07
☐ 32 Richard Wood	1.00	.45	.12

1984 Buccaneers Police

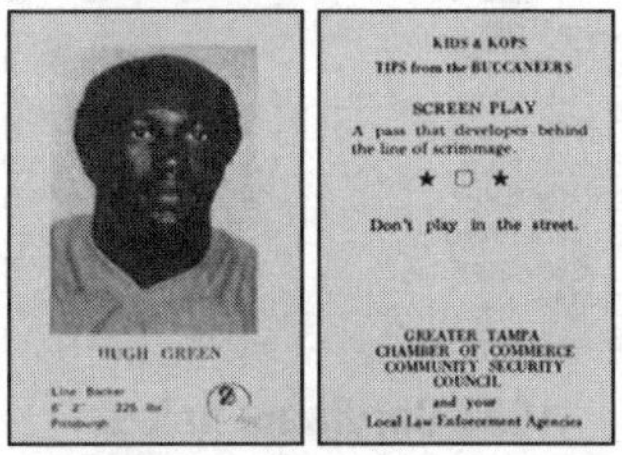

This unnumbered 56-card set features the Tampa Bay Buccaneers players, cheerleaders, and other personnel. Cards measure approximately 2 5/8" by 4 1/8". Backs are printed in red ink on thin white card stock and feature "Kids and Kops Tips from the Buccaneers". Cards were sponsored by the Greater Tampa Chamber of Commerce Community Security Council, Coca Cola, and the local law enforcement agencies. In action (IA) cards were issued as an additional card for three players. The cards are essentially ordered below alphabetically according to the player's name with the exception of the non-player cards who are listed first.

	MINT	NRMT	EXC
COMPLETE SET (56)	60.00	27.00	7.50
COMMON CARD (1-56)	1.00	.45	.12
☐ 1 Swash-Buc-Lers	2.00	.90	.25
☐ 2 Hugh Culverhouse OWN	1.50	.70	.19
☐ 3 John McKay (25 Years as Head Coach)	1.50	.70	.19
☐ 4 John McKay CO	1.50	.70	.19
☐ 5 Defensive Action	1.50	.70	.19
☐ 6 Fred Acorn	1.00	.45	.12
☐ 7 Obed Ariri	1.00	.45	.12
☐ 8 Adger Armstrong	1.00	.45	.12
☐ 9 Jerry Bell	1.00	.45	.12
☐ 10 Theo Bell	2.00	.90	.25
☐ 11 Byron Braggs	1.00	.45	.12
☐ 12 Scot Brantley	1.00	.45	.12
☐ 13 Cedric Brown	1.00	.45	.12
☐ 14 Keith Browner	1.50	.70	.19
☐ 15 John Cannon	1.00	.45	.12
☐ 16 Jay Carroll	1.00	.45	.12
☐ 17 Gerald Carter	1.00	.45	.12
☐ 18 Melvin Carver	1.00	.45	.12
☐ 19 Jeremiah Castille	1.50	.70	.19
☐ 20 Mark Cotney	1.00	.45	.12
☐ 21 Steve Courson	1.50	.70	.19
☐ 22 Jeff Davis	1.00	.45	.12
☐ 23 Steve DeBerg	4.00	1.80	.50
☐ 24 Sean Farrell	1.50	.70	.19
☐ 25 Frank Garcia	1.00	.45	.12
☐ 26 Jimmie Giles	2.00	.90	.25
☐ 27 Hugh Green	2.50	1.10	.30
☐ 28 Hugh Green IA	1.50	.70	.19
☐ 29 Randy Grimes	1.00	.45	.12
☐ 30 Ron Heller	2.00	.90	.25
☐ 31 John Holt	1.00	.45	.12
☐ 32 Kevin House	2.00	.90	.25
☐ 33 Noah Jackson	1.50	.70	.19
☐ 34 Cecil Johnson	1.00	.45	.12
☐ 35 Ken Kaplan	1.00	.45	.12
☐ 36 Blair Kiel	2.00	.90	.25
☐ 37 David Logan	1.50	.70	.19
☐ 38 Brison Manor	1.00	.45	.12
☐ 39 Michael Morton	1.00	.45	.12
☐ 40 James Owens	1.00	.45	.12
☐ 41 Beasley Reece	1.50	.70	.19
☐ 42 Gene Sanders	1.00	.45	.12
☐ 43 Lee Roy Selmon	6.00	2.70	.75
☐ 44 Lee Roy Selmon IA	4.00	1.80	.50
☐ 45 Danny Spradlin	1.00	.45	.12
☐ 46 Kelly Thomas	1.00	.45	.12
☐ 47 Norris Thomas	1.00	.45	.12
☐ 48 Jack Thompson	2.00	.90	.25
☐ 49 Perry Tuttle	1.00	.45	.12
☐ 50 Chris Washington	1.00	.45	.12
☐ 51 Mike Washington	1.00	.45	.12
☐ 52 James Wilder	2.00	.90	.25
☐ 53 James Wilder IA	1.00	.45	.12
☐ 54 Steve Wilson	1.00	.45	.12
☐ 55 Mark White	1.00	.45	.12
☐ 56 Richard Wood	2.00	.90	.25

1989 Buccaneers Police

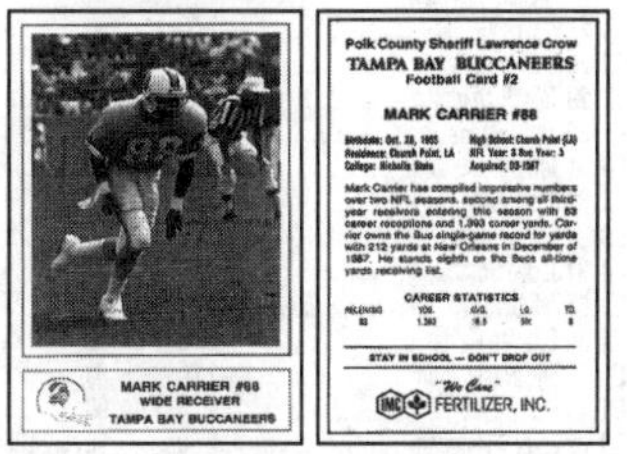

This ten-card set measures 2 5/8" by 4 1/8" and features members of the Tampa Bay Buccaneers. The fronts of the cards feature an action color shot along with the identification of the player and his position and uniform number. The back of the card features biographical information, some text, one line of career statistics, and the card number. This set was sponsored by IMC Fertilizer, Inc. and the Polk County Law Enforcement Office.

	MINT	NRMT	EXC
COMPLETE SET (10)	18.00	8.00	2.20
COMMON CARD (1-10)	1.50	.70	.19
☐ 1 Vinny Testaverde	5.00	2.20	.60
☐ 2 Mark Carrier WR	4.00	1.80	.50
☐ 3 Randy Grimes	1.50	.70	.19
☐ 4 Paul Gruber	2.50	1.10	.30
☐ 5 Ron Hall	2.00	.90	.25
☐ 6 William Howard	1.50	.70	.19
☐ 7 Curt Jarvis	1.50	.70	.19
☐ 8 Ervin Randle	1.50	.70	.19
☐ 9 Ricky Reynolds	2.00	.90	.25
☐ 10 Rob Taylor	1.50	.70	.19

1976 Buckmans Discs

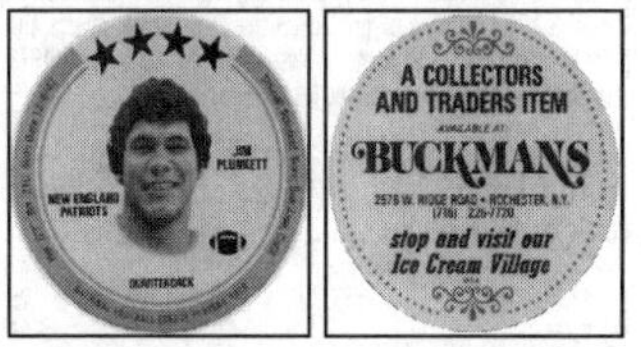

The 1976 Buckmans football disc set of 20 is unnumbered and features star players from the National Football League. The circular cards measure approximately 3 3/8" in diameter. The players' pictures are in black and white with a colored arc serving as the disc border. Four stars complete the border. The backs contain the address of the Buckmans ice cream outlet in Rochester, New York. The MSA marking, signifying Michael Schechter Associates, is also contained on the reverse. Since the set is unnumbered, the cards are ordered below alphabetically by player's name.

	NRMT-MT	EXC	G-VG
COMPLETE SET (20)	45.00	20.00	5.50
COMMON CARD (1-20)	.75	.35	.09
☐ 1 Otis Armstrong	1.00	.45	.12
☐ 2 Steve Bartkowski	1.50	.70	.19
☐ 3 Terry Bradshaw	10.00	4.50	1.25
☐ 4 Doug Buffone	.75	.35	.09
☐ 5 Wally Chambers	.75	.35	.09
☐ 6 Chuck Foreman	1.00	.45	.12
☐ 7 Roman Gabriel	1.25	.55	.16
☐ 8 Mel Gray	1.00	.45	.12
☐ 9 Franco Harris	7.50	3.40	.95
☐ 10 James Harris	1.00	.45	.12
☐ 11 Jim Hart	1.00	.45	.12
☐ 12 Gary Huff	.75	.35	.09
☐ 13 Billy Kilmer	1.00	.45	.12
☐ 14 Terry Metcalf	1.00	.45	.12
☐ 15 Jim Otis	.75	.35	.09
☐ 16 Jim Plunkett	1.25	.55	.16
☐ 17 Greg Pruitt	1.00	.45	.12
☐ 18 Roger Staubach	12.00	5.50	1.50
☐ 19 Jan Stenerud	1.50	.70	.19
☐ 20 Roger Wehrli	.75	.35	.09

1960 Cardinals Mayrose Franks

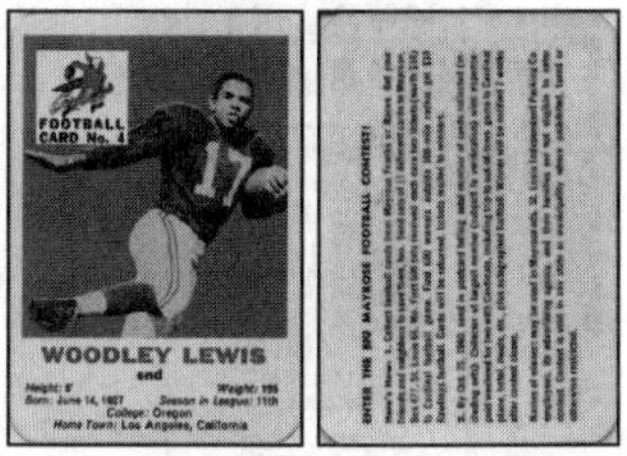

The Mayrose Franks set of 11 cards features players on the St. Louis (Football) Cardinals. The cards are plastic coated (they were intended as inserts in hot dog and bacon packages) with slightly rounded corners and are numbered. The cards measure approximately 2 1/2" by 3 1/2". The fronts, with a black and white photograph of the player and a red background, contain the card number, player statistics and the Cardinal's logo. The backs contain a description of the Big Mayrose Football Contest.

	NRMT	VG-E	GOOD
COMPLETE SET (11)	90.00	40.00	11.00
COMMON CARD (1-11)	7.50	3.40	.95
☐ 1 Don Gillis	7.50	3.40	.95
☐ 2 Frank Fuller	7.50	3.40	.95
☐ 3 George Izo	7.50	3.40	.95
☐ 4 Woodley Lewis	7.50	3.40	.95
☐ 5 King Hill	10.00	4.50	1.25
☐ 6 John David Crow	15.00	6.75	1.85
☐ 7 Bill Stacy	7.50	3.40	.95
☐ 8 Ted Bates	7.50	3.40	.95
☐ 9 Mike McGee	7.50	3.40	.95
☐ 10 Bobby Joe Conrad	10.00	4.50	1.25
☐ 11 Ken Panfil	7.50	3.40	.95

1961 Cardinals Jay Publishing

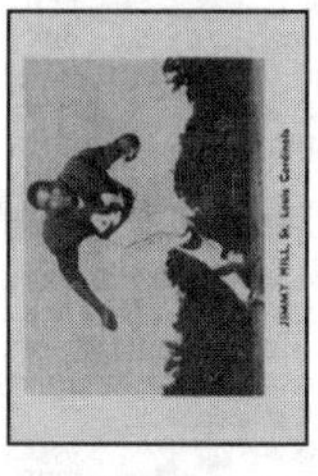

This 12-card set features (approximately) 5" by 7" black-and-white player photos. The pictures show players in traditional poses with the quarterback preparing to throw, the runner heading downfield, and the defensive player ready for the tackle. These cards were packaged 12 to a packet and originally sold for 25 cents. The backs are blank. The cards are unnumbered and checklisted below in alphabetical order.

	NRMT	VG-E	GOOD
COMPLETE SET (12)	60.00	27.00	7.50
COMMON CARD (1-12)	5.00	2.20	.60
☐ 1 Joe Childress	5.00	2.20	.60
☐ 2 Sam Etcheverry	7.50	3.40	.95
☐ 3 Ed Henke	5.00	2.20	.60
☐ 4 Jimmy Hill	5.00	2.20	.60
☐ 5 Bill Koman	5.00	2.20	.60
☐ 6 Roland McDole	5.00	2.20	.60
☐ 7 Mike McGee	5.00	2.20	.60
☐ 8 Dale Meinert	5.00	2.20	.60
☐ 9 Jerry Norton	5.00	2.20	.60
☐ 10 Sonny Randle	7.50	3.40	.95
☐ 11 Joe Robb	5.00	2.20	.60
☐ 12 Billy Stacy	5.00	2.20	.60

1962-63 Cardinals Team Issue

The Cardinals issued these photos likely over a period of years. Each measures approximately 5" by 7" and features a black and white player photo along with player information below the photo. The photos we've listed as 1962 contain only the player's name, positon and team name. While, the 1963 photos also include the player's height and weight. They are unnumbered and blankbacked and listed below alphabetically.

	NRMT	VG-E	GOOD
COMPLETE SET (9)	40.00	18.00	5.00
COMMON CARD (1-9)	5.00	2.20	.60
☐ 1 Taz Anderson 63	5.00	2.20	.60
☐ 2 Garland Boyette 62	7.50	3.40	.95
☐ 3 Don Brumm 63	5.00	2.20	.60
☐ 4 Bill Koman 62	5.00	2.20	.60
☐ 5 Ernie McMillan 63	7.50	3.40	.95
☐ 6 Luke Owens 63	5.00	2.20	.60
☐ 7 Bob Reynolds 63	5.00	2.20	.60
☐ 8 Joe Robb 63	5.00	2.20	.60
☐ 9 Bill Triplett 62	5.00	2.20	.60

1965 Cardinals Big Red Biographies

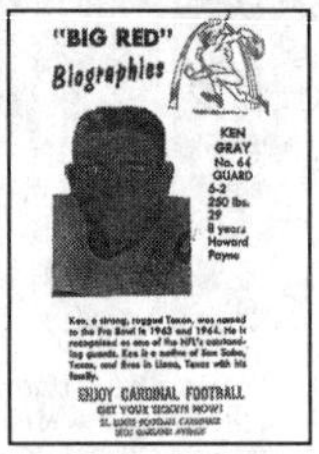

This set was featured during the 1965 football season as the side panels of half-gallon milk cartons from Adams Dairy in St. Louis. When cut, the cards measure approximately 3 1/16" by 5 9/16". The printing on the cards is in purple and orange. All cards feature members of the St. Louis Cardinals. The catalog designation for this set is F112. The list below contains those cards known at this time; any additions to the list would be most welcome. The cards have blank backs as is the case with most milk carton issues. Complete milk cartons would be valued at double the prices listed below.

	NRMT	VG-E	GOOD
COMPLETE SET (17)	1000.00	450.00	125.00
COMMON CARD (1-17)	60.00	27.00	7.50
☐ 1 Monk Bailey	60.00	27.00	7.50
☐ 2 Jim Bakken	100.00	45.00	12.50
☐ 3 Jim Burson	60.00	27.00	7.50
☐ 4 Willis Crenshaw	60.00	27.00	7.50
☐ 5 Bob DeMarco	60.00	27.00	7.50
☐ 6 Pat Fischer	100.00	45.00	12.50
☐ 7 Billy Gambrell	60.00	27.00	7.50
☐ 8 Irv Goode	60.00	27.00	7.50
☐ 9 Ken Gray	75.00	34.00	9.50
☐ 10 Mike Melinkovich	60.00	27.00	7.50
☐ 11 Bob Reynolds	60.00	27.00	7.50
☐ 12 Marion Rushing	60.00	27.00	7.50
☐ 13 Carl Silvestri	60.00	27.00	7.50
☐ 14 Dave Simmons	60.00	27.00	7.50
☐ 15 Jackie Smith	150.00	70.00	19.00
☐ 16 Bill(Thunder) Thornton	60.00	27.00	7.50
☐ 17 Herschel Turner	60.00	27.00	7.50

1965 Cardinals Team Issue

This 10-card set of the St. Louis Cardinals measures approximately 7 3/8" by 9 3/8" and features black-and-white player photos in a white border. The player's name, position and team are printed in the wide bottom margin. The backs are blank. The cards are unnumbered and checklisted below in alphabetical order.

	NRMT	VG-E	GOOD
COMPLETE SET (10)	40.00	18.00	5.00
COMMON CARD	4.00	1.80	.50
☐ 1 Don Brumm	4.00	1.80	.50
☐ 2 Bobby Joe Conrad	5.00	2.20	.60
☐ 3 Bob DeMarco	4.00	1.80	.50
☐ 4 Charley Johnson	6.00	2.70	.75
☐ 5 Ernie McMillan	5.00	2.20	.60
☐ 6 Dale Meinert	4.00	1.80	.50
☐ 7 Luke Owens	4.00	1.80	.50
☐ 8 Sonny Randle	4.00	1.80	.50
☐ 9 Joe Robb	4.00	1.80	.50
☐ 10 Jerry Stovall	5.00	2.20	.60

1972 Cardinals Team Issue

The Cardinals issued these photos likely over a period of years. Each measures approximately 5" by 7" and features a black and white player photo along with the player's name, positon, height, weight, and team name below the photo. The team name varies slightly, either "St. Louis Cardinals" or "St. Louis Football Cardinals." The type size and style used also varies slightly from photo to photo. They are unnumbered and blankbacked and listed below alphabetically.

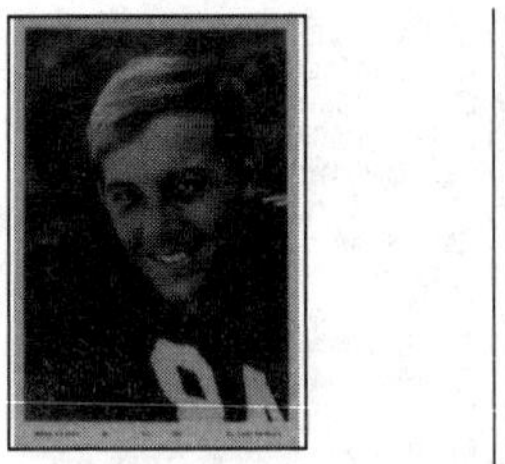

	NRMT-MT	EXC	G-VG
COMPLETE SET (42)	100.00	45.00	12.50
COMMON CARD (1-42)	2.00	.90	.25
☐ 1 Jeff Allen	2.00	.90	.25
☐ 2 Donny Anderson	4.00	1.80	.50
☐ 3 Tom Banks	2.00	.90	.25
☐ 4 Craig Baynham	2.00	.90	.25
☐ 5 Chuck Beatty	2.00	.90	.25
☐ 6 Tom Beckman	2.00	.90	.25
☐ 7 Dave Bradley	2.00	.90	.25
☐ 8 Don Brumm	2.00	.90	.25
☐ 9 Leon Burns	2.00	.90	.25
☐ 10 Steve Conley	2.00	.90	.25
☐ 11 Gary Cuozzo	3.00	1.35	.35
☐ 12 Miller Farr	3.00	1.35	.35
☐ 13 Walker Gillette	2.00	.90	.25
☐ 14 Dale Hackbart	2.00	.90	.25
☐ 15 Jim Hargrove	2.00	.90	.25
☐ 16 Leo Hayden	2.00	.90	.25
☐ 17 Fred Heron	2.00	.90	.25
☐ 18 Bob Holloway CO	2.00	.90	.25
☐ 19 Chuck Hutchison	2.00	.90	.25
☐ 20 Fred Hyatt	2.00	.90	.25
☐ 21 Martin Imhof	2.00	.90	.25
☐ 22 Jim McFarland	2.00	.90	.25
☐ 23 Mike McGill	2.00	.90	.25
☐ 24 Ernie McMillan	3.00	1.35	.35
☐ 25 Terry Miller	2.00	.90	.25
☐ 26 Bobby Moore (Ahmad Rashaad)	15.00	6.75	1.85
☐ 27 Wayne Mulligan	2.00	.90	.25
☐ 28 Ara Person	2.00	.90	.25
☐ 29 John Richardson	2.00	.90	.25
☐ 30 Jamie Rivers	2.00	.90	.25
☐ 31 Johnny Roland	3.00	1.35	.35
☐ 32 Bob Rowe	3.00	1.35	.35
☐ 33 Roy Shivers	2.00	.90	.25
☐ 34 Jackie Smith	7.50	3.40	.95
☐ 35 Jeff Staggs	2.00	.90	.25
☐ 36 Tim Van Galder	2.00	.90	.25
☐ 37 Eric Washington	2.00	.90	.25
☐ 38 Bob Wicks	2.00	.90	.25
☐ 39 Larry Willingham	2.00	.90	.25
☐ 40 Larry Wilson	7.50	3.40	.95
☐ 41 Steve Wright T	2.00	.90	.25
☐ 42 Ron Yankowski	3.00	1.35	.35

1976 Cardinals Team Issue

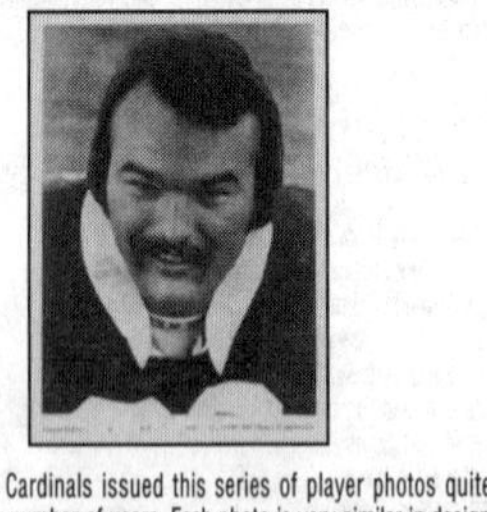

The St. Louis Cardinals issued this series of player photos quite possibly over a number of years. Each photo is very similar in design and is only differentiated by the size and type style of the print. The unnumbered black and white photos measure approximately 5 1/8" by 7" and all, except John Zook, include the player's name, position, height and weight below the photo and "St. Louis Football Cardinals." The team name printed on the cards varies in size and print type from photo to photo. We've included them all as a 1976 release since all players performed for that year's team.

	NRMT-MT	EXC	G-VG
COMPLETE SET (40)	100.00	45.00	12.50
COMMON CARD (1-40)	2.00	.90	.25
☐ 1 Mark Arneson	2.00	.90	.25
☐ 2 Jim Bakken	3.00	1.35	.35
☐ 3 Al Beauchamp	2.00	.90	.25
☐ 4 Bob Bell	2.00	.90	.25
☐ 5 Tom Brahaney	2.00	.90	.25
☐ 6 Leo Brooks	2.00	.90	.25
☐ 7 J.V. Cain	2.00	.90	.25
☐ 8 Don Coryell CO	6.00	2.70	.75
☐ 9 Dwayne Crump	2.00	.90	.25
☐ 10 Charlie Davis	2.00	.90	.25
☐ 11 Mike Dawson	2.00	.90	.25
☐ 12 Dan Dierdorf	7.50	3.40	.95
☐ 13 Conrad Dobler	5.00	2.20	.60
☐ 14 Bill Donckers	2.00	.90	.25
☐ 15 Clarence Duren	2.00	.90	.25
☐ 16 Roger Finnie	2.00	.90	.25
☐ 17 Carl Gersbach	2.00	.90	.25
☐ 18 Mel Gray	4.00	1.80	.50
☐ 19 Gary Hammond	2.00	.90	.25
☐ 20 Ike Harris	3.00	1.35	.35
☐ 21 Jim Hart	6.00	2.70	.75
☐ 22 Steve Jones	2.00	.90	.25
☐ 23 Terry Joyce	2.00	.90	.25
☐ 24 Tim Kearney	2.00	.90	.25
☐ 25 Jerry Latin	2.00	.90	.25
☐ 26 Mike McGraw	2.00	.90	.25
☐ 27 Terry Metcalf	5.00	2.20	.60
☐ 28 Wayne Morris	2.00	.90	.25
☐ 29 Steve Neils	2.00	.90	.25
☐ 30 Brad Oates	2.00	.90	.25
☐ 31 Steve Okoniewski	2.00	.90	.25
☐ 32 Ken Reaves	3.00	1.35	.35
☐ 33 Mike Sensibaugh	2.00	.90	.25
☐ 34 Jeff Severson	2.00	.90	.25
☐ 35 Larry Stallings	4.00	1.80	.50
☐ 36 Norm Thompson	2.00	.90	.25
☐ 37 Pat Tilley	3.00	1.35	.35
☐ 38 Roger Wehrli	4.00	1.80	.50
☐ 39 Bob Young	3.00	1.35	.35
☐ 40 John Zook	2.00	.90	.25

1980 Cardinals Police

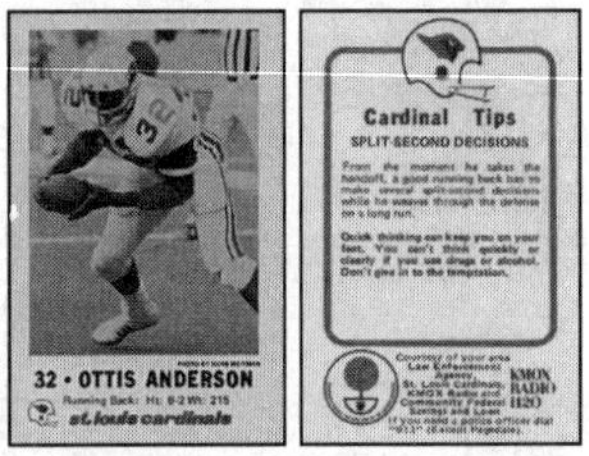

The 15-card 1980 St. Louis Cardinals set was sponsored by the local law enforcement agency, the St. Louis Cardinals, KMOX Radio (which broadcasts the Cardinals' games), and Community Federal Savings and Loan: the last three of which have their logos on the backs of the cards. The cards measure approximately 2 5/8" by 4 1/8". The set is unnumbered but has been listed by player uniform number in the checklist below. The backs present "Cardinal Tips" and information on how to contact a police officer by telephone. Card backs feature black print with red trim on white card stock. Ottis Anderson appears in his Rookie Card year.

	MINT	NRMT	EXC
COMPLETE SET (15)	15.00	6.75	1.85
COMMON CARD	.75	.35	.09
☐ 17 Jim Hart	2.00	.90	.25
☐ 22 Roger Wehrli	1.50	.70	.19
☐ 24 Wayne Morris	.75	.35	.09
☐ 32 Ottis Anderson	2.50	1.10	.30
☐ 33 Theotis Brown	.75	.35	.09
☐ 37 Ken Green	.75	.35	.09
☐ 55 Eric Williams	.75	.35	.09
☐ 56 Tim Kearney	.75	.35	.09
☐ 59 Calvin Favron	.75	.35	.09
☐ 68 Terry Stieve	.75	.35	.09
☐ 72 Dan Dierdorf	3.00	1.35	.35
☐ 73 Mike Dawson	.75	.35	.09
☐ 82 Bob Pollard	.75	.35	.09
☐ 83 Pat Tilley	1.25	.55	.16
☐ 85 Mel Gray	1.50	.70	.19

1988 Cardinals Holsum

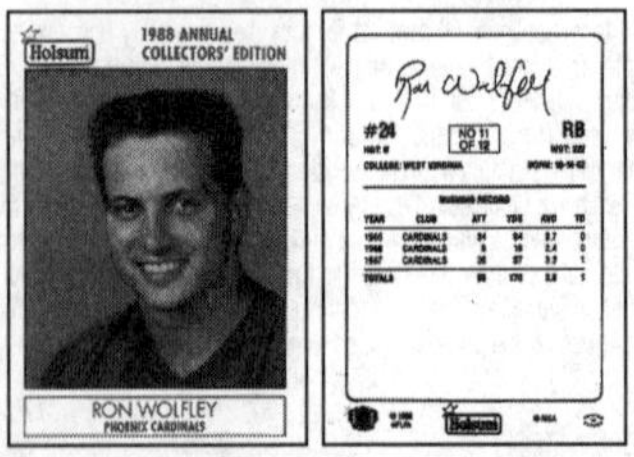

This 12-card standard-size full-color set features players of the St. Louis Cardinals; cards were available only in Holsum Bread packages. The set was co-produced by Mike Schechter Associates on behalf of the NFL Players Association. Card fronts have a color photo within a green border and the backs are printed in black ink on white card stock.

	MINT	NRMT	EXC
COMPLETE SET (12)	45.00	20.00	5.50
COMMON CARD (1-12)	4.00	1.80	.50
☐ 1 Roy Green	6.00	2.70	.75
☐ 2 Stump Mitchell	5.00	2.20	.60
☐ 3 J.T. Smith	5.00	2.20	.60
☐ 4 E.J. Junior	5.00	2.20	.60
☐ 5 Cedric Mack	4.00	1.80	.50
☐ 6 Curtis Greer	4.00	1.80	.50
☐ 7 Lonnie Young	4.00	1.80	.50
☐ 8 David Galloway	4.00	1.80	.50
☐ 9 Luis Sharpe	5.00	2.20	.60
☐ 10 Leonard Smith	4.00	1.80	.50
☐ 11 Ron Wolfley	4.00	1.80	.50
☐ 12 Earl Ferrell	4.00	1.80	.50

1989 Cardinals Holsum

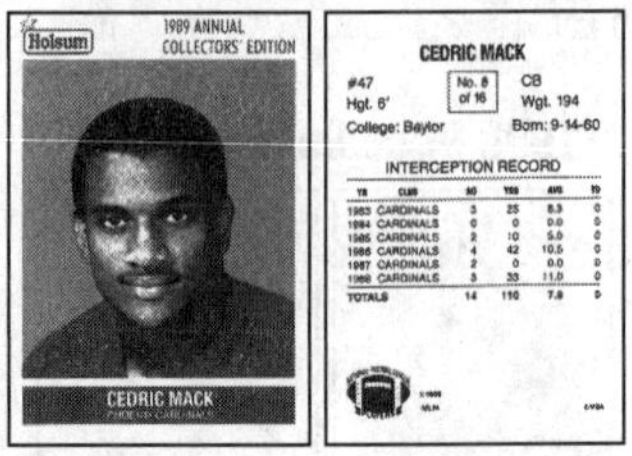

The 1989 Holsum Phoenix Cardinals set features 16 standard-size cards. The set was co-produced by Mike Schechter Associates on behalf of the NFL Players Association. The fronts have helmetless color mug shots; the vertically oriented backs have bios, stats, and card numbers.

	MINT	NRMT	EXC
COMPLETE SET (16)	8.00	3.60	1.00
COMMON CARD (1-16)	.40	.18	.05
☐ 1 Roy Green	1.00	.45	.12
☐ 2 J.T. Smith	.75	.35	.09
☐ 3 Neil Lomax	1.00	.45	.12
☐ 4 Stump Mitchell	.75	.35	.09
☐ 5 Vai Sikahema	.75	.35	.09
☐ 6 Lonnie Young	.40	.18	.05
☐ 7 Robert Awalt	.50	.23	.06
☐ 8 Cedric Mack	.40	.18	.05
☐ 9 Earl Ferrell	.40	.18	.05
☐ 10 Ron Wolfley	.40	.18	.05
☐ 11 Bob Clasby	.40	.18	.05
☐ 12 Luis Sharpe	.50	.23	.06
☐ 13 Steve Alvord	.40	.18	.05
☐ 14 David Galloway	.40	.18	.05
☐ 15 Freddie Joe Nunn	.50	.23	.06
☐ 16 Niko Noga	.40	.18	.05

1989 Cardinals Police

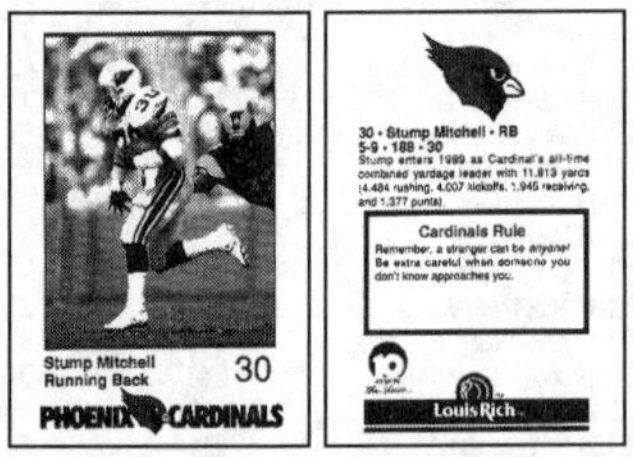

The 1989 Police Phoenix Cardinals set contains 15 cards measuring approximately 2 5/8" by 4 3/16". The fronts have white borders and color action photos; the vertically oriented backs have brief bios, career highlights, and safety messages. The set features members of the Phoenix Cardinals. The set was also sponsored by Louis Rich Meats and KTSP-TV. The cards are unnumbered except for uniform number which is prominently displayed on both sides of the card. Two cards were given out every two weeks during the season. It has been reported that 1.6 million cards were produced; 100,000 of each player. Derek Kennard's card was supposedly withdrawn at some time during the promotion after he was arrested. Reportedly, Freddie Joe Nunn was also planned for inclusion in this set but was withdrawn as well.

	MINT	NRMT	EXC
COMPLETE SET (15)	20.00	9.00	2.50
COMMON CARD	.75	.35	.09
☐ 5 Gary Hogeboom	1.00	.45	.12
☐ 24 Ron Wolfley	.75	.35	.09
☐ 30 Stump Mitchell	1.00	.45	.12
☐ 31 Earl Ferrell	.75	.35	.09
☐ 36 Vai Sikahema	1.00	.45	.12
☐ 43 Lonnie Young	.75	.35	.09
☐ 46 Tim McDonald	1.50	.70	.19
☐ 65 David Galloway	.75	.35	.09
☐ 67 Luis Sharpe	1.00	.45	.12
☐ 70 Derek Kennard SP	8.00	3.60	1.00
☐ 79 Bob Clasby	.75	.35	.09
☐ 80 Robert Awalt	.75	.35	.09
☐ 81 Roy Green	1.50	.70	.19
☐ 84 J.T. Smith	1.25	.55	.16
☐ 85 Jay Novacek	4.00	1.80	.50

1990 Cardinals Police

This 16-card police set was sponsored by Louis Rich Meats and KTSP-TV. The cards measure approximately 2 5/8" by 4 1/4". The color action player photos on the fronts have maroon borders, with player information below the pictures in the bottom border. The team and NFL logos overlay the upper corners of the pictures. The backs have biography, a "Cardinal Rule" in the form of a safety tip, and

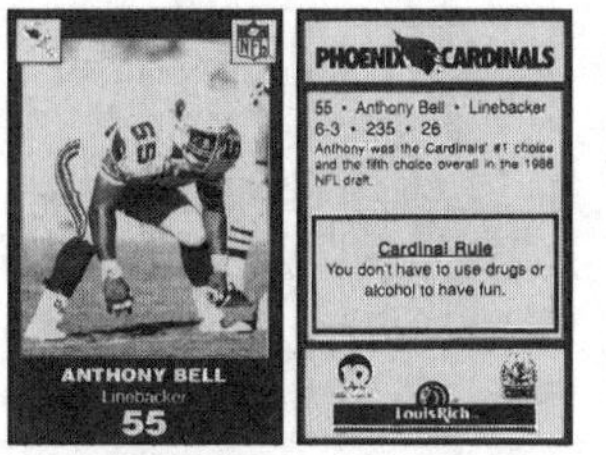

sponsor logos. The cards are unnumbered (except for the prominent display of the player's uniform number) and checklisted below in alphabetical order.

	MINT	NRMT	EXC
COMPLETE SET (16)	8.00	3.60	1.00
COMMON CARD (1-16)	.30	.14	.04
☐ 1 Anthony Bell	.50	.23	.06
☐ 2 Joe Bugel CO	.50	.23	.06
☐ 3 Rich Camarillo	.30	.14	.04
☐ 4 Roy Green	1.00	.45	.12
☐ 5 Ken Harvey	1.00	.45	.12
☐ 6 Eric Hill	1.25	.55	.16
☐ 7 Tim McDonald	.75	.35	.09
☐ 8 Tootie Robbins	.30	.14	.04
☐ 9 Timm Rosenbach	.75	.35	.09
☐ 10 Luis Sharpe	.50	.23	.06
☐ 11 Vai Sikahema	.50	.23	.06
☐ 12 J.T. Smith	.75	.35	.09
☐ 13 Lance Smith	.30	.14	.04
☐ 14 Jim Wahler	.30	.14	.04
☐ 15 Ron Wolfley	.30	.14	.04
☐ 16 Lonnie Young	.30	.14	.04

1992 Cardinals Police

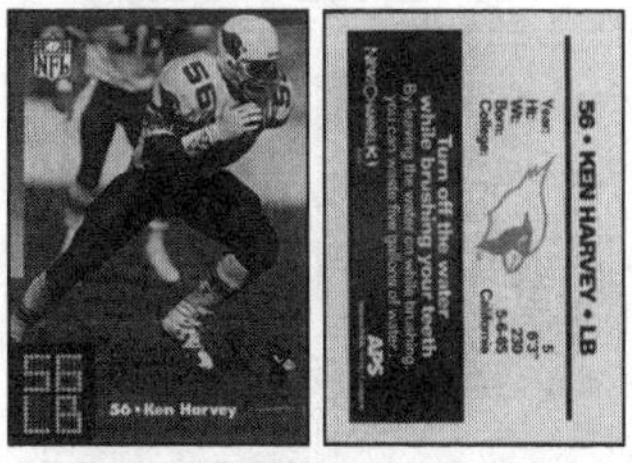

Sponsored by KTVK-TV (Channel 3) and the Arizona Public Service Co., this 16-card set measures the standard-size. The fronts display color player photos bordered above and partially on the left by stripes that fade from red to yellow. In the lower left corner, an electronic scoreboard gives the player's jersey number and position. Beneath the team name and logo, the player's name and jersey number are printed between two red stripes toward the bottom of the card. The horizontal backs present biographical information and, on a red panel, recycling and conservation tips. The cards are unnumbered and checklisted below in alphabetical order.

	MINT	NRMT	EXC
COMPLETE SET (16)	10.00	4.50	1.25
COMMON CARD (1-16)	.50	.23	.06
☐ 1 Joe Bugel CO	.50	.23	.06
☐ 2 Rich Camarillo	.50	.23	.06
☐ 3 Ed Cunningham	.50	.23	.06
☐ 4 Greg Davis	.50	.23	.06
☐ 5 Ken Harvey	1.00	.45	.12
☐ 6 Randal Hill	.75	.35	.09
☐ 7 Ernie Jones	.75	.35	.09
☐ 8 Mike Jones	.50	.23	.06
☐ 9 Tim McDonald	1.00	.45	.12
☐ 10 Freddie Joe Nunn	.50	.23	.06
☐ 11 Ricky Proehl	.75	.35	.09
☐ 12 Timm Rosenbach	.50	.23	.06
☐ 13 Tony Sacca	.75	.35	.09
☐ 14 Lance Smith	.50	.23	.06
☐ 15 Eric Swann	1.50	.70	.19
☐ 16 Aeneas Williams	1.00	.45	.12

1994 Cardinals Police

The cards are unnumbered, but listed below alphabetically. They feature a color player photo surrounded by a maroon and orange border. The set is thought to be complete at four cards.

	MINT	NRMT	EXC
COMPLETE SET (4)	10.00	4.50	1.25
COMMON CARD (1-4)	2.50	1.10	.30
☐ 1 Greg Davis	2.50	1.10	.30
☐ 2 Anthony Edwards	2.50	1.10	.30
☐ 3 Terry Hoage	2.50	1.10	.30
☐ 4 Aeneas Williams	3.50	1.55	.45

1989 CBS Television Announcers

This ten-card set (with cards measuring approximately 2 3/4" by 3 7/8") features those members of the 1989 CBS Football Announcing

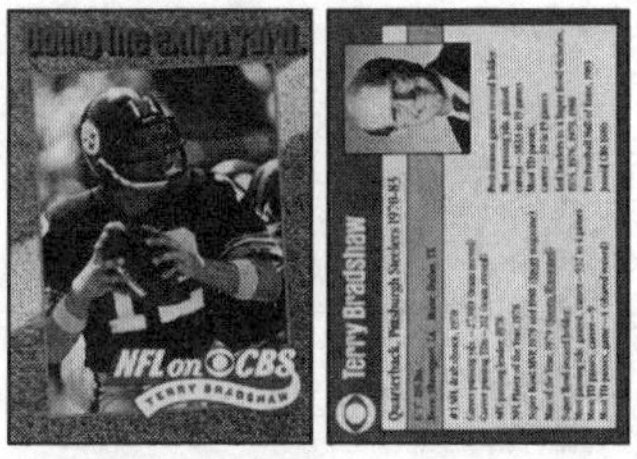

team who had been involved in professional football. The front of the card features a color action shot from the person's professional career bordered in orange and superimposed over a green football field with a white yard stripe. The words "Going the extra yard" appear in red block lettering at the card top, while the words "NFL on CBS" appear in the lower right corner. The backs are horizontally oriented and have a black and white studio portrait head shot of the announcer. Biography and career highlights are bordered in red. It has been reported that 500 sets were distributed to various CBS outlets and publication sources. The set was split into two series of five announcers each and are unnumbered.

	MINT	NRMT	EXC
COMPLETE SET (10)	250.00	110.00	31.00
COMMON CARD (1-10)	10.00	4.50	1.25
☐ 1 Terry Bradshaw	50.00	22.00	6.25
☐ 2 Dick Butkus	40.00	18.00	5.00
☐ 3 Irv Cross	10.00	4.50	1.25
☐ 4 Dan Fouts	25.00	11.00	3.10
☐ 5 Pat Summerall	20.00	9.00	2.50
☐ 6 Gary Fencik	10.00	4.50	1.25
☐ 7 Dan Jiggetts	10.00	4.50	1.25
☐ 8 John Madden	40.00	18.00	5.00
☐ 9 Ken Stabler	40.00	18.00	5.00
☐ 10 Hank Stram	15.00	6.75	1.85

1968 Champion Corn Flakes

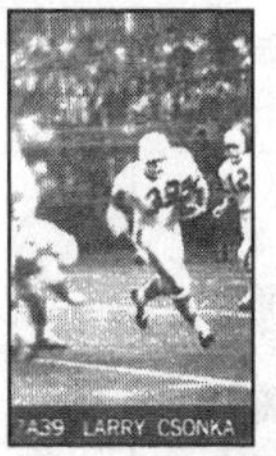

These cards were issued on backs of Champion Corn Flakes around 1968. There are thought to be 22-cards released. Each card measures approximately 2 1/16" by 3 3/16 and is blank backed. Cardfronts feature a color action player photo surrounded by a thin black border on three sides and player name and number at the bottom within a thick black border. Any additional information on the checklist below would be appreciated.

	NRMT-MT	EXC	G-VG
COMPLETE SET (10)	350.00	160.00	45.00
COMMON CARD (1-10)	25.00	11.00	3.10
☐ 6N20 Lem Barney	40.00	18.00	5.00
☐ 7A39 Larry Csonka Bob Griese in background	75.00	34.00	9.50
☐ 7N33 Jim Grabowski	30.00	13.50	3.70
☐ 7N66 Ray Nitschke	50.00	22.00	6.25
☐ 8N18 Roman Gabriel	30.00	13.50	3.70
☐ 9N30 Bill Brown RB	25.00	11.00	3.10
☐ 10N17 Billy Kilmer	30.00	13.50	3.70
☐ 10N31 Jim Taylor	50.00	22.00	6.25
☐ 11N45 Homer Jones	25.00	11.00	3.10
☐ 12N16 Norm Snead	30.00	13.50	3.70

1961 Chargers Golden Tulip

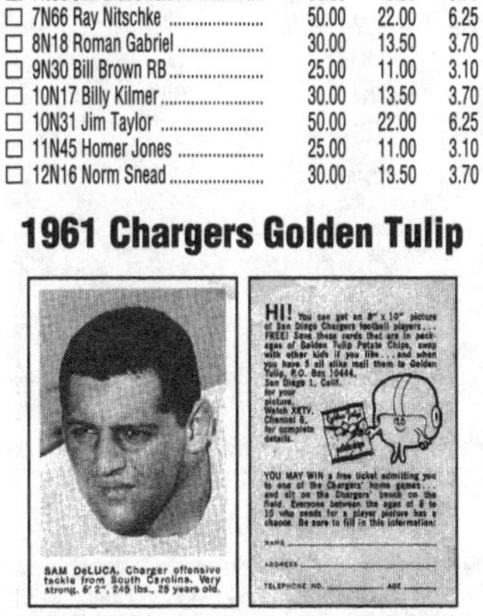

The 1961 Golden Tulip Chips football card set contains 22 black and white cards featuring San Diego (Los Angeles in 1960) Chargers AFL players. The cards measure approximately 2" by 3". The fronts contain the player's name, a short biography, and vital statistics. The backs, which are the same for all cards, contain an ad for XETV television, a premium offer for (approximately) 8" by 10" photos and an ad for a free ticket contest. The cards are unnumbered but have been numbered in alphabetical order in the checklist below for your convenience. The catalog designation for this set is F395.

	NRMT	VG-E	GOOD
COMPLETE SET (22)	1400.00	650.00	180.00
COMMON CARD (1-22)	35.00	16.00	4.40
☐ 1 Ron Botchan	35.00	16.00	4.40
☐ 2 Howard Clark	35.00	16.00	4.40
☐ 3 Fred Cole	35.00	16.00	4.40
☐ 4 Sam DeLuca	35.00	16.00	4.40
☐ 5 Orlando Ferrante	35.00	16.00	4.40
☐ 6 Charlie Flowers	35.00	16.00	4.40
☐ 7 Dick Harris	40.00	18.00	5.00
☐ 8 Emil Karas	35.00	16.00	4.40
☐ 9 Jack Kemp	700.00	325.00	90.00
☐ 10 Dave Kocourek	40.00	18.00	5.00
☐ 11 Bob Laraba	35.00	16.00	4.40
☐ 12 Paul Lowe	60.00	27.00	7.50
☐ 13 Paul Maguire	60.00	27.00	7.50
☐ 14 Charley McNeil	40.00	18.00	5.00
☐ 15 Ron Mix	125.00	55.00	15.50
☐ 16 Ron Nery	35.00	16.00	4.40
☐ 17 Don Norton	35.00	16.00	4.40
☐ 18 Volney Peters	35.00	16.00	4.40
☐ 19 Don Rogers	35.00	16.00	4.40
☐ 20 Maury Schleicher	35.00	16.00	4.40
☐ 21 Ernie Wright	40.00	18.00	5.00
☐ 22 Bob Zeman	35.00	16.00	4.40

1962 Chargers Team Issue

The Chargers likely released these photos over a number of seasons. Each measures approximately 8" by 10" and includes a black and white photo on the cardfront with a blankback. The player's name appears below the photo and to the left with the team name oriented to the right. As is common with many team issued photos, the text style and size varies slightly from photo to photo. The checklist is thought to be incomplete; any additions to this list are appreciated.

	NRMT	VG-E	GOOD
COMPLETE SET (12)	60.00	27.00	7.50
COMMON CARD (1-12)	5.00	2.20	.60
☐ 1 Chuck Allen	7.50	3.40	.95
☐ 2 Frank Buncom	5.00	2.20	.60
☐ 3 Reg Carolan	5.00	2.20	.60
☐ 4 Bert Coan	6.00	2.70	.75
☐ 5 Earl Faison	6.00	2.70	.75
☐ 6 Claude Gibson	5.00	2.20	.60
☐ 7 Bill Hudson Richard Hudson	5.00	2.20	.60
☐ 8 Emil Karas	5.00	2.20	.60
☐ 9 Tommy Minter	5.00	2.20	.60
☐ 10 Bob Mitinger	5.00	2.20	.60
☐ 11 Ron Mix	10.00	4.50	1.25
☐ 12 Jerry Robinson	5.00	2.20	.60

1962 Chargers Union Oil

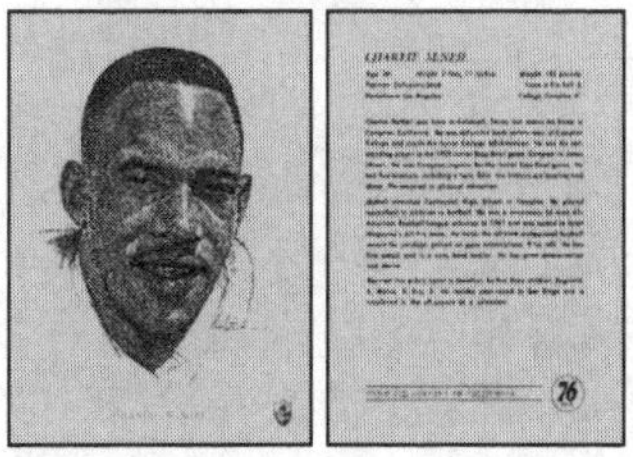

The set was sponsored by Union 76. All players featured in the set are members of the San Diego Chargers. They are derived from sketches by the artist, Patrick. The cards are black and white, approximately 6" by 8" with player biography and Union Oil logo on backs. The catalog designation for the set is UO35-2. The cards were reportedly issued with an album with 24 spaces for the photos. The key cards in this set are quarterback Jack Kemp, who would later gain fame as a politician, as well as cards issued during the rookie season of future Hall of Famer Lance Alworth and star quarterback John Hadl.

	NRMT	VG-E	GOOD
COMPLETE SET (14)	550.00	250.00	70.00
COMMON CARD (1-14)	12.00	5.50	1.50
☐ 1 Chuck Allen	15.00	6.75	1.85
☐ 2 Lance Alworth	125.00	55.00	15.50
☐ 3 John Hadl	40.00	18.00	5.00
☐ 4 Dick Harris	15.00	6.75	1.85
☐ 5 Bill Hudson	12.00	5.50	1.50
☐ 6 Jack Kemp	250.00	110.00	31.00
☐ 7 Dave Kocourek	15.00	6.75	1.85
☐ 8 Ernie Ladd	35.00	16.00	4.40
☐ 9 Keith Lincoln	25.00	11.00	3.10
☐ 10 Paul Lowe	25.00	11.00	3.10
☐ 11 Charley McNeil	15.00	6.75	1.85
☐ 12 Ron Mix	35.00	16.00	4.40
☐ 13 Ron Nery	12.00	5.50	1.50
☐ 14 Team Photo	30.00	13.50	3.70

1963 Chargers Team Issue

The Chargers likely released these photos over a number of seasons. Each measures approximately 8" by 10" and includes a black and white photo on the cardfront with a blankback. The player's name appears below the photo and to the left, while the team name appears centered below the picture. The text style and size varies slightly from photo to photo and the checklist is thought to be incomplete. Any additions to this list are appreciated.

	NRMT	VG-E	GOOD
COMPLETE SET (9)	50.00	22.00	6.25
COMMON CARD (1-9)	5.00	2.20	.60
☐ 1 George Blair	5.00	2.20	.60
☐ 2 Sam DeLuca	5.00	2.20	.60
☐ 3 Dave Kocourek	6.00	2.70	.75
☐ 4 Keith Lincoln	8.00	3.60	1.00
☐ 5 Paul Lowe	8.00	3.60	1.00
☐ 6 Don Norton	5.00	2.20	.60
☐ 7 Don Rogers	5.00	2.20	.60
☐ 8 Bob Lane	5.00	2.20	.60
☐ 9 Bob Petrich	5.00	2.20	.60

1966 Chargers Team Issue

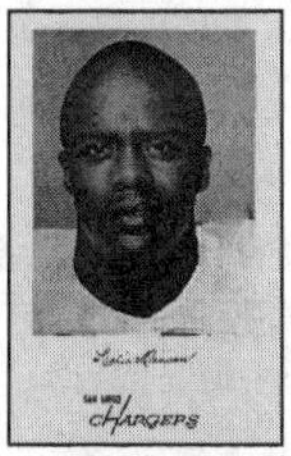

This team issue set, with cards measuring approximately 5 1/2" by 8 1/2", features black and white close-up player photos on off-white linen weave paper. The player's facsimile autograph is centered beneath each picture above the team name. The photo of George Gross has biographical information on the back. The other pictures have blank backs. Because the set is unnumbered, players and coaches are listed alphabetically.

	NRMT	VG-E	GOOD
COMPLETE SET (50)	250.00	110.00	31.00
COMMON CARD (1-50)	4.00	1.80	.50
☐ 1 Chuck Allen	5.00	2.20	.60
☐ 2 Jim Allison	4.00	1.80	.50
☐ 3 Lance Alworth	35.00	16.00	4.40
☐ 4 Tom Bass	4.00	1.80	.50
☐ 5 Joe Beauchamp	4.00	1.80	.50
☐ 6 Frank Buncom	5.00	2.20	.60
☐ 7 Richard Degen	4.00	1.80	.50
☐ 8 Steve DeLong	5.00	2.20	.60
☐ 9 Les(Speedy) Duncan	5.00	2.20	.60
☐ 10 John Farris	4.00	1.80	.50
☐ 11 Gene Foster	4.00	1.80	.50
☐ 12 Willie Frazier	5.00	2.20	.60
☐ 13 Gary Garrison	5.00	2.20	.60
☐ 14 Sid Gillman CO	12.00	5.50	1.50
☐ 15 Kenny Graham	4.00	1.80	.50
☐ 16 George Gross	4.00	1.80	.50
☐ 17 Sam Gruneisen	4.00	1.80	.50
☐ 18 Walt Hackett CO	4.00	1.80	.50
☐ 19 John Hadl	16.00	7.25	2.00
☐ 20 Dick Harris	5.00	2.20	.60
☐ 21 Dan Henning	10.00	4.50	1.25
☐ 22 Bob Horton	4.00	1.80	.50
☐ 23 Harry Johnston CO	4.00	1.80	.50
☐ 24 Howard Kindig	4.00	1.80	.50
☐ 25 Keith Lincoln	7.50	3.40	.95
☐ 26 Paul Lowe	7.50	3.40	.95
☐ 27 Jacque MacKinnon	4.00	1.80	.50
☐ 28 Joe Madro CO	4.00	1.80	.50
☐ 29 Ed Mitchell	4.00	1.80	.50
☐ 30 Bob Mitinger	4.00	1.80	.50
☐ 31 Ron Mix	15.00	6.75	1.85
☐ 32 Fred Moore	4.00	1.80	.50
☐ 33 Don Norton	4.00	1.80	.50
☐ 34 Terry Owens	5.00	2.20	.60
☐ 35 Bob Petrich	4.00	1.80	.50
☐ 36 Dave Plump	4.00	1.80	.50
☐ 37 Rick Redman	4.00	1.80	.50
☐ 38 Houston Ridge	4.00	1.80	.50
☐ 39 Pat Shea	4.00	1.80	.50
☐ 40 Walt Sweeney	5.00	2.20	.60
☐ 41 Sammy Taylor	4.00	1.80	.50
☐ 42 Steve Tensi	5.00	2.20	.60
☐ 43 Herb Travenio	4.00	1.80	.50
☐ 44 John Travis	4.00	1.80	.50
☐ 45 Dick Van Raaphorst	4.00	1.80	.50
☐ 46 Charlie Waller CO	4.00	1.80	.50
☐ 47 Bud Whitehead	4.00	1.80	.50
☐ 48 Nat Whitmyer	4.00	1.80	.50
☐ 49 Ernie Wright	5.00	2.20	.60
☐ 50 Bob Zeman	4.00	1.80	.50

1976 Chargers Dean's Photo

This 10-card set was sponsored by Dean's Photo Service and features nine San Diego Chargers' players. The cards were released on an uncut perforated sheet with each card measuring approximately 5" by 8." The player photos are black and white, but the team helmet is printed in color. The cards are blank backed and unnumbered.

	NRMT-MT	EXC	G-VG
COMPLETE SET (10)	40.00	18.00	5.00
COMMON CARD	3.00	1.35	.35

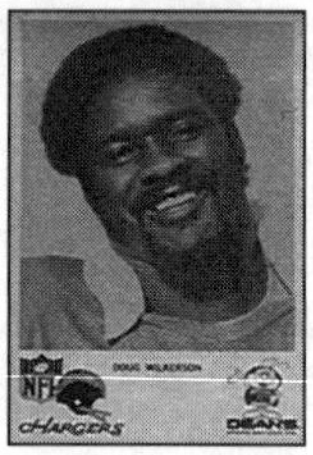

	MINT	NRMT	EXC
☐ 1 Pat Currin	3.00	1.35	.35
☐ 2 Chris Fletcher	3.00	1.35	.35
☐ 3 Dan Fouts	12.00	5.50	1.50
☐ 4 Gary Garrison	4.00	1.80	.50
☐ 5 Louie Kelcher	4.00	1.80	.50
☐ 6 Joe Washington	4.00	1.80	.50
☐ 7 Russ Washington	3.00	1.35	.35
☐ 8 Doug Wilkerson	3.00	1.35	.35
☐ 9 Don Woods	3.00	1.35	.35
☐ 10 Schedule Card	3.00	1.35	.35
Dean's coupons attached			

1981 Chargers Police

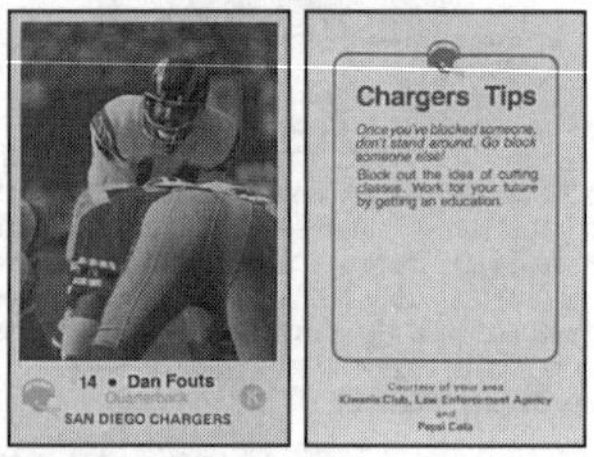

The 1981 San Diego Chargers set contains 24 unnumbered cards of 22 subjects. The cards measure approximately 2 5/8" by 4 1/8". The cards are listed in the checklist below by the uniform number which appears on the fronts of the cards. The set is sponsored by the Kiwanis Club, the local law enforcement agency, and Pepsi-Cola. A Chargers helmet logo and "Chargers Tips" appear on the card backs. The card backs have black print with blue trim on white card stock. The Kiwanis and Chargers helmet logos appear on the fronts. Fouts and Winslow each exist with two different safety tips on the backs; the variations are distinguished below by the first few words of the safety tip. The complete set price below includes the variation cards.

	MINT	NRMT	EXC
COMPLETE SET (24)	70.00	32.00	8.75
COMMON CARD	1.25	.55	.16
☐ 6 Rolf Benirschke	2.00	.90	.25
☐ 14A Dan Fouts (After a team ...)	15.00	6.75	1.85
☐ 14B Dan Fouts (Once you've ...)	7.50	3.40	.95
☐ 18 Charlie Joiner	5.00	2.20	.60
☐ 25 John Cappelletti	2.00	.90	.25
☐ 28 Willie Buchanon	1.50	.70	.19
☐ 29 Mike Williams	1.25	.55	.16
☐ 43 Bob Gregor	1.25	.55	.16
☐ 44 Pete Shaw	1.25	.55	.16
☐ 46 Chuck Muncie	2.00	.90	.25
☐ 51 Woodrow Lowe	1.50	.70	.19
☐ 57 Linden King	1.25	.55	.16
☐ 59 Cliff Thrift	1.25	.55	.16
☐ 62 Don Macek	1.25	.55	.16
☐ 63 Doug Wilkerson	1.25	.55	.16
☐ 66 Billy Shields	1.25	.55	.16
☐ 67 Ed White	1.50	.70	.19
☐ 68 Leroy Jones	1.25	.55	.16
☐ 70 Russ Washington	1.25	.55	.16
☐ 74 Louie Kelcher	1.50	.70	.19
☐ 79 Gary Johnson	1.50	.70	.19
☐ 80A Kellen Winslow (Go all out ...)	15.00	6.75	1.85
☐ 80B Kellen Winslow (The length of ...)	7.50	3.40	.95
☐ NNO Don Coryell CO	2.00	.90	.25

1982 Chargers Police

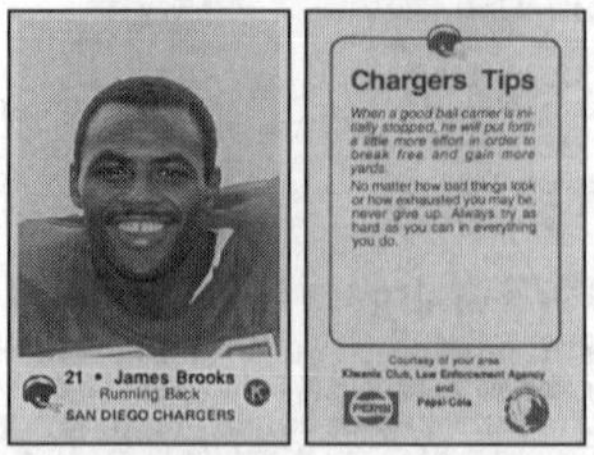

The 1982 San Diego Chargers Police set contains 16 unnumbered cards. The cards measure approximately 2 5/8" by 4 1/8". Although uniform numbers appear on the fronts of the cards, the set has been listed below in alphabetical order. The set is sponsored by the Kiwanis Club, the local law enforcement agency, and Pepsi-Cola. Chargers Tips, in addition to the helmet logo of the Chargers, the Pepsi-Cola logo and a police logo appear on the backs. Card backs have black printing with blue accent on white backs. The Kiwanis logo and Chargers helmet appear on the fronts of the cards.

	MINT	NRMT	EXC
COMPLETE SET (16)	40.00	18.00	5.00
COMMON CARD (1-16)	2.00	.90	.25
☐ 1 Rolf Benirschke	2.50	1.10	.30
☐ 2 James Brooks	4.00	1.80	.50
☐ 3 Wes Chandler	4.00	1.80	.50
☐ 4 Dan Fouts	8.00	3.60	1.00
☐ 5 Tim Fox	2.50	1.10	.30
☐ 6 Gary Johnson	2.50	1.10	.30
☐ 7 Charlie Joiner	6.00	2.70	.75
☐ 8 Louie Kelcher	2.50	1.10	.30
☐ 9 Linden King	2.00	.90	.25
☐ 10 Bruce Laird	2.00	.90	.25
☐ 11 David Lewis	2.00	.90	.25
☐ 12 Don Macek	2.00	.90	.25
☐ 13 Billy Shields	2.00	.90	.25
☐ 14 Eric Sievers	2.00	.90	.25
☐ 15 Russ Washington	2.00	.90	.25
☐ 16 Kellen Winslow	8.00	3.60	1.00

1985 Chargers Kodak

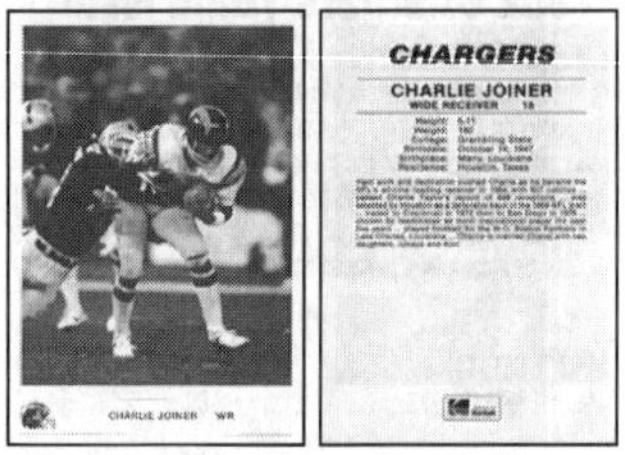

This 20-card set was sponsored by Kodak and measures approximately 5 1/2" by 8 1/2". The fronts have white borders and action color photos. The player's name, position, and a Chargers helmet icon appear below the picture. The backs have biographical information. The set is listed below in alphabetical order by player's name.

	MINT	NRMT	EXC
COMPLETE SET (20)	50.00	22.00	6.25
COMMON CARD (1-20)	2.00	.90	.25
☐ 1 Carlos Bradley	2.00	.90	.25
☐ 2 Gill Byrd	3.00	1.35	.35
☐ 3 Wes Chandler	5.00	2.20	.60
☐ 4 Sam Claphan	3.00	1.35	.35
☐ 5 Chuck Ehin	2.00	.90	.25
☐ 6 Mike Green	2.00	.90	.25
☐ 7 Pete Holohan	2.50	1.10	.30
☐ 8 Lionel James	2.50	1.10	.30
☐ 9 Charlie Joiner	10.00	4.50	1.25
☐ 10 Woodrow Lowe	2.00	.90	.25
☐ 11 Don Macek	3.00	1.35	.35
☐ 12 Dennis McKnight	2.00	.90	.25
☐ 13 Miles McPherson	2.00	.90	.25
☐ 14 Derrie Nelson	2.00	.90	.25
☐ 15 Vince Osby	2.00	.90	.25
☐ 16 Fred Robinson	3.00	1.35	.35
☐ 17 Billy Ray Smith	2.50	1.10	.30
☐ 18 Lucious Smith	3.00	1.35	.35
☐ 19 Danny Walters	2.00	.90	.25
☐ 20 Ed White	2.50	1.10	.30

1986 Chargers Kodak

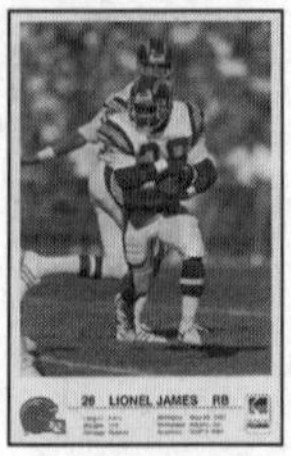

This set of 48-photos featuring the San Diego Chargers was sponsored by Kodak and measures approximately 5 1/2" by 8 1/2". The fronts feature color action photos with white borders. Biographical information is given below the photo between the Chargers' helmet on the left and the Kodak logo on the right. The backs are blank. The photos are unnumbered and checklisted below in alphabetical order.

	MINT	NRMT	EXC
COMPLETE SET (48)	100.00	45.00	12.50
COMMON CARD (1-48)	1.50	.70	.19
☐ 1 Curtis Adams	1.50	.70	.19
☐ 2 Gary Anderson RB	4.00	1.80	.50
☐ 3 Jesse Bendross	1.50	.70	.19
☐ 4 Rolf Benirschke	3.00	1.35	.35
☐ 5 Carlos Bradley	3.00	1.35	.35
☐ 6 Gill Byrd	3.00	1.35	.35
☐ 7 Wes Chandler	3.00	1.35	.35
☐ 8 Sam Claphan	1.50	.70	.19
☐ 9 Don Coryell CO	3.00	1.35	.35
☐ 10 Jeffery Dale	1.50	.70	.19
☐ 11 Wayne Davis	1.50	.70	.19
☐ 12 Jerry Doerger	1.50	.70	.19
☐ 13 Chuck Ehin	3.00	1.35	.35
☐ 14 Chris Faulkner	1.50	.70	.19
☐ 15 Mark Fellows	1.50	.70	.19
☐ 16 Dan Fouts	12.00	5.50	1.50
☐ 17 Mike Green	3.00	1.35	.35
☐ 18 Mike Guendling	1.50	.70	.19
☐ 19 John Hendy	1.50	.70	.19
☐ 20 Mark Herrmann	1.50	.70	.19
☐ 21 Pete Holohan	3.00	1.35	.35
☐ 22 Lionel James	3.00	1.35	.35
☐ 23 Trumaine Johnson	1.50	.70	.19
☐ 24 Charlie Joiner	3.00	1.35	.35
☐ 25 David King	1.50	.70	.19
☐ 26 Linden King	1.50	.70	.19
☐ 27 Gary Kowalski	3.00	1.35	.35
☐ 28 Jim Lachey	4.00	1.80	.50
☐ 29 Woodrow Lowe	3.00	1.35	.35
☐ 30 Don Macek	1.50	.70	.19
☐ 31 Buford McGee	1.50	.70	.19
☐ 32 Dennis McKnight	1.50	.70	.19
☐ 33 Ralf Mojsiejenko	1.50	.70	.19
☐ 34 Derrie Nelson	3.00	1.35	.35
☐ 35 Ron O'Bard	1.50	.70	.19
☐ 36 Fred Robinson	1.50	.70	.19
☐ 37 Eric Sievers	1.50	.70	.19
☐ 38 Tony Simmons	1.50	.70	.19
☐ 39 Billy Ray Smith	3.00	1.35	.35
☐ 40 Lucious Smith	1.50	.70	.19
☐ 41 Alex G. Spanos PRES	1.50	.70	.19
☐ 42 Tim Spencer	3.00	1.35	.35
☐ 43 Bob Thomas	3.00	1.35	.35
☐ 44 Rich Umphrey	1.50	.70	.19
☐ 45 Danny Walters	3.00	1.35	.35
☐ 46 Ed White	3.00	1.35	.35
☐ 47 Lee Williams	3.00	1.35	.35
☐ 48 Earl Wilson	1.50	.70	.19

1987 Chargers Junior Coke Tickets

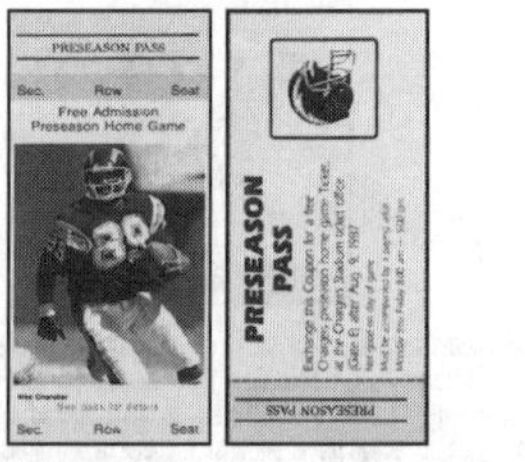

This 11" by 8 1/2" perforated sheet features two rows of six coupons each. The coupons resemble tickets, with each coupon measuring approximately 1 7/8" by 4 1/4". They were given to members of the Coca-Cola Junior Chargers club. Edged below by a mustard stripe, a powder blue strip at the top carries the coupon's subtitle. The large middle panel of the ticket carries a color action player photo with white borders and the player's name immediately below. Another powder blue stripe at the bottom of the coupon reads "Sec. Row Seat" in imitation of an actual ticket. The horizontal backs vary in their content, consisting of either a membership card, season schedule, Coca-Cola Junior Chargers club, preseason pass, or various coupons to attractions in the San Diego area. The coupons are unnumbered and are listed below in alphabetical order by subject.

	MINT	NRMT	EXC
COMPLETE SET (12)	20.00	9.00	2.50
COMMON CARD (1-12)	1.00	.45	.12
☐ 1 Gary Anderson RB	2.00	.90	.25
☐ 2 Rolf Benirschke	1.50	.70	.19
☐ 3 Wes Chandler	2.00	.90	.25
☐ 4 Jeffery Dale	1.00	.45	.12
☐ 5 Dan Fouts	4.00	1.80	.50
☐ 6 Pete Holohan	1.00	.45	.12
☐ 7 Lionel James	1.50	.70	.19
☐ 8 Don Macek	1.00	.45	.12
☐ 9 Dennis McKnight	1.00	.45	.12
☐ 10 Al Saunders CO	1.00	.45	.12
☐ 11 Billy Ray Smith	1.50	.70	.19
☐ 12 Kellen Winslow	4.00	1.80	.50

1987 Chargers Police

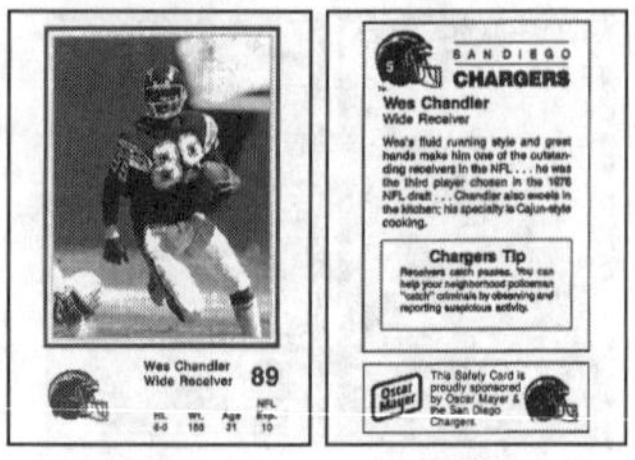

The 1987 San Diego Chargers Police set contains 21 numbered cards. The cards measure approximately 2 5/8" by 4 1/8". Uniform numbers appear on the fronts of the cards. The set is sponsored by the San Diego Chargers, Oscar Mayer, and local law enforcement agencies. The Chargers helmet logo, "Chargers Tips," and the Oscar Mayer logo appear on the backs. Card backs have black printing on white backs. The Chargers helmet along with height, weight, age, and experience statistics appear on the fronts of the cards. Card 13 was never issued apparently for superstitious reasons. Cards 3 (Benirschke released) and 17 (Walters arrested) were distributed in lesser quantities and hence are a little tougher to find, especially Benirschke. Chip Banks (22) was the player substituted in the set for Rolf Benirschke.

	MINT	NRMT	EXC
COMPLETE SET (21)	25.00	11.00	3.10
COMMON CARD (1-22)	.75	.35	.09
☐ 1 Alex Spanos OWN	.75	.35	.09
☐ 2 Gary Anderson RB	1.50	.70	.19
☐ 3 Rolf Benirschke SP	6.00	2.70	.75
☐ 4 Gill Byrd	.75	.35	.09
☐ 5 Wes Chandler	1.50	.70	.19
☐ 6 Sam Claphan	.75	.35	.09
☐ 7 Jeffery Dale	.75	.35	.09
☐ 8 Pete Holohan	.75	.35	.09
☐ 9 Lionel James	.75	.35	.09
☐ 10 Jim Lachey	.75	.35	.09
☐ 11 Woodrow Lowe	.75	.35	.09
☐ 12 Don Macek	.75	.35	.09
☐ 14 Dan Fouts	4.00	1.80	.50
☐ 15 Eric Sievers	.75	.35	.09
☐ 16 Billy Ray Smith	.75	.35	.09
☐ 17 Danny Walters SP	5.00	2.20	.60
☐ 18 Lee Williams	.75	.35	.09
☐ 19 Kellen Winslow	3.00	1.35	.35
☐ 20 Al Saunders CO	.75	.35	.09
☐ 21 Dennis McKnight	.75	.35	.09
☐ 22 Chip Banks	.75	.35	.09

1987 Chargers Smokey

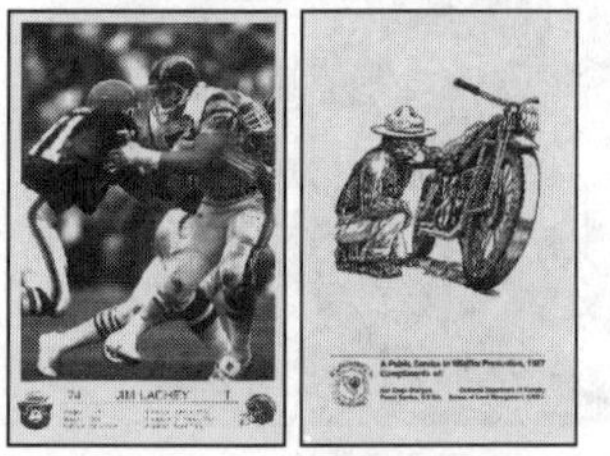

This 48-card set features players of the San Diego Chargers in a set sponsored by the California Forestry Department. The cards measure approximately 5 1/2" by 8 1/2"; card fronts show a full-color action photo of the player. Card backs have a forestry safety tip cartoon with Smokey the Bear. Cards are unnumbered but are ordered below in alphabetical order according to the subject's last name. Cards of Donald Brown, Mike Douglas, and Fred Robinson were withdrawn after they were cut from the team and the card of Don Coryell was withdrawn after he was replaced as head coach.

	MINT	NRMT	EXC
COMPLETE SET (48)	100.00	45.00	12.50
COMMON CARD (1-48)	1.25	.55	.16
COMMON SP (6/10/13/37)	7.50	3.40	.95
☐ 1 Curtis Adams	1.25	.55	.16
☐ 2 Ty Allert	1.25	.55	.16
☐ 3 Gary Anderson RB	3.00	1.35	.35
☐ 4 Rolf Benirschke	2.00	.90	.25
☐ 5 Thomas Benson	2.00	.90	.25
☐ 6 Donald Brown SP	7.50	3.40	.95
☐ 7 Gill Byrd	2.00	.90	.25
☐ 8 Wes Chandler	3.50	1.55	.45
☐ 9 Sam Claphan	1.25	.55	.16
☐ 10 Don Coryell CO SP	7.50	3.40	.95
☐ 11 Jeffery Dale	1.25	.55	.16
☐ 12 Wayne Davis	1.25	.55	.16
☐ 13 Mike Douglass SP	7.50	3.40	.95
☐ 14 Chuck Ehin	1.25	.55	.16
☐ 15 James Fitzpatrick	1.25	.55	.16
☐ 16 Tom Flick	1.25	.55	.16
☐ 17 Dan Fouts	10.00	4.50	1.25
☐ 18 Dee Hardison	1.25	.55	.16
☐ 19 Andy Hawkins	1.25	.55	.16
☐ 20 John Hendy	1.25	.55	.16
☐ 21 Mark Herrmann	2.00	.90	.25
☐ 22 Pete Holohan	2.00	.90	.25
☐ 23 Lionel James	2.00	.90	.25
☐ 24 Trumaine Johnson	1.25	.55	.16
☐ 25 Charlie Joiner	6.00	2.70	.75
☐ 26 Gary Kowalski	1.25	.55	.16
☐ 27 Jim Lachey	2.00	.90	.25
☐ 28 Jim Leonard	1.25	.55	.16
☐ 29 Woodrow Lowe	1.25	.55	.16
☐ 30 Don Macek	1.25	.55	.16
☐ 31 Buford McGee	1.25	.55	.16
☐ 32 Dennis McKnight	1.25	.55	.16
☐ 33 Ralf Mojsiejenko	1.25	.55	.16
☐ 34 Derrie Nelson	1.25	.55	.16
☐ 35 Leslie O'Neal	4.00	1.80	.50
☐ 36 Gary Plummer	2.00	.90	.25

☐ 37 Fred Robinson SP	7.50	3.40	.95
☐ 38 Eric Sievers	1.25	.55	.16
☐ 39 Billy Ray Smith	2.00	.90	.25
☐ 40 Tim Spencer	2.00	.90	.25
☐ 41 Kenny Taylor	1.25	.55	.16
☐ 42 Terry Unrein	1.25	.55	.16
☐ 43 Jeff Walker	1.25	.55	.16
☐ 44 Danny Walters	1.25	.55	.16
☐ 45 Lee Williams	2.00	.90	.25
☐ 46 Earl Wilson	1.25	.55	.16
☐ 47 Kellen Winslow	7.50	3.40	.95
☐ 48 Kevin Wyatt	1.25	.55	.16

1988 Chargers Police

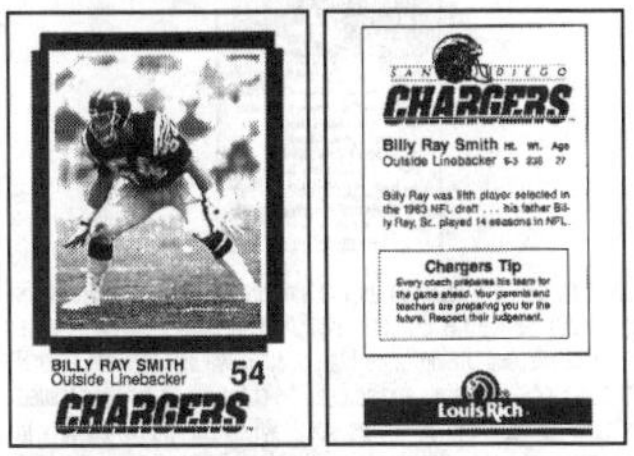

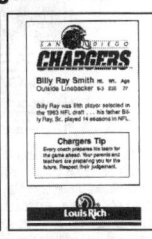

The 1988 Police San Diego Chargers set contains 12 cards each measuring approximately 2 5/8" by 4". The fronts are white and navy blue with color photos, and the backs feature career highlights and safety tips.

	MINT	NRMT	EXC
COMPLETE SET (12)	10.00	4.50	1.25
COMMON CARD (1-12)	.50	.23	.06
☐ 1 Gary Anderson RB	1.00	.45	.12
☐ 2 Rod Bernstine	1.25	.55	.16
☐ 3 Gill Byrd	.75	.35	.09
☐ 4 Vencie Glenn	.75	.35	.09
☐ 5 Lionel James	.75	.35	.09
☐ 6 Babe Laufenberg	.75	.35	.09
☐ 7 Don Macek	.50	.23	.06
☐ 8 Mark Malone	.75	.35	.09
☐ 9 Dennis McKnight	.50	.23	.06
☐ 10 Anthony Miller	4.00	1.80	.50
☐ 11 Billy Ray Smith	.75	.35	.09
☐ 12 Lee Williams	.75	.35	.09

1988 Chargers Smokey

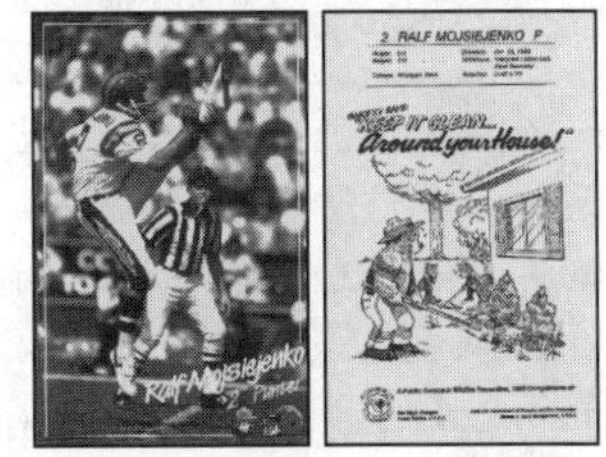

This 52-card set features players of the San Diego Chargers in a set sponsored by the California Forestry Department. The cards measure approximately 5" by 8"; card fronts show a full-color action photo of the player. Card backs have a forestry safety tip cartoon with Smokey Bear. Cards are unnumbered but are ordered below in numerical order according to the subject's uniform number as listed on the card's front and back. There is a variation on the Spanos card, which was originally issued indicating he bought the Chargers in 1987 and was quickly corrected to 1984. There are 35 cards which are easier to obtain as they were available all year and 18 cards (marked below by SP) who are more difficult to find as their cards were withdrawn after they were cut from the team, retired, traded, or put on injured reserve. The set is considered complete with only one Spanos card.

	MINT	NRMT	EXC
COMPLETE SET (52)	50.00	22.00	6.25
COMMON CARD	.50	.23	.06
☐ 2 Ralf Mojsiejenko	.50	.23	.06
☐ 9 Mark Herrmann SP	2.00	.90	.25
☐ 10 Vince Abbott	.50	.23	.06
☐ 13 Mark Vlasic	.75	.35	.09
☐ 14 Dan Fouts	4.00	1.80	.50
☐ 20 Barry Redden	.50	.23	.06
☐ 22 Gill Byrd	.75	.35	.09
☐ 23 Danny Walters SP	2.00	.90	.25
☐ 25 Vencie Glenn	.50	.23	.06
☐ 26 Lionel James	.75	.35	.09
☐ 27 Daniel Hunter SP	2.00	.90	.25
☐ 34 Elvis Patterson	.50	.23	.06
☐ 36 Mike Davis SP	2.00	.90	.25
☐ 40 Gary Anderson RB	1.00	.45	.12
☐ 42 Curtis Adams	.50	.23	.06
☐ 43 Tim Spencer	.75	.35	.09
☐ 44 Martin Bayless	.50	.23	.06
☐ 50 Gary Plummer	.75	.35	.09
☐ 52 Jeff Jackson	.50	.23	.06
☐ 54 Billy Ray Smith	.75	.35	.09
☐ 55 Steve Busick SP	2.00	.90	.25
☐ 56 Chip Banks SP	2.00	.90	.25
☐ 57 Thomas Benson SP	2.00	.90	.25
☐ 58 David Brandon	.50	.23	.06
☐ 60 Dennis McKnight	.50	.23	.06
☐ 61 Ken Dallafior	.50	.23	.06
☐ 62 Don Macek	.50	.23	.06
☐ 68 Gary Kowalski	.50	.23	.06
☐ 69 Les Miller	.50	.23	.06
☐ 70 James Fitzpatrick	.50	.23	.06
☐ 71 Mike Charles	.50	.23	.06
☐ 72 Karl Wilson	.50	.23	.06
☐ 74 Jim Lachey SP	3.00	1.35	.35
☐ 75 Joe Phillips	.75	.35	.09
☐ 76 Broderick Thompson	.50	.23	.06
☐ 77 Sam Claphan SP	2.00	.90	.25
☐ 78 Chuck Ehin SP	2.00	.90	.25
☐ 79 Curtis Rouse SP	2.00	.90	.25
☐ 80 Kellen Winslow	4.00	1.80	.50
☐ 81 Timmie Ware SP	2.00	.90	.25
☐ 82 Rod Bernstine	1.00	.45	.12
☐ 85 Eric Sievers	.50	.23	.06
☐ 86 Jamie Holland	.50	.23	.06
☐ 88 Pete Holohan SP	2.00	.90	.25
☐ 89 Wes Chandler SP	4.00	1.80	.50
☐ 92 Dee Hardison SP	2.00	.90	.25
☐ 94 Randy Kirk	.50	.23	.06
☐ 96 Keith Baldwin SP	2.00	.90	.25
☐ 98 Terry Unrein SP	2.00	.90	.25
☐ 99 Lee Williams	.75	.35	.09
☐ NNO Al Saunders CO	.50	.23	.06
☐ NNO Alex G. Spanos ERR SP Chairman of the Board (Purchased team 1987)	5.00	2.20	.60
☐ NNO Alex G. Spanos COR Chairman of the Board (Purchased team 1984)	.75	.35	.09

1989 Chargers Junior Ralph's Tickets

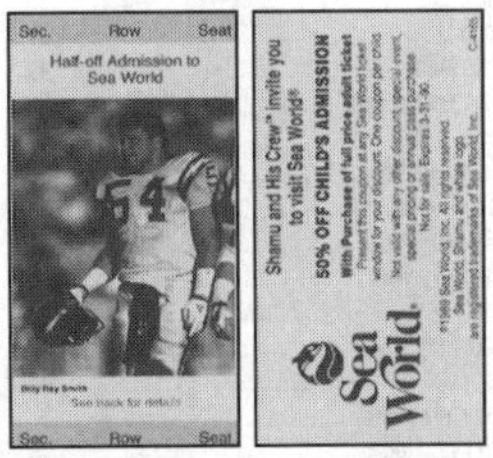

This perforated sheet features two rows of six cards each. If the cards were separated, they would measure 1 7/8" by 3 5/8". The color action player photos are bordered in white. A bonus gift is listed at the top of each card and the player's name printed below the photo. The set was sponsored by Ralph's and XTRA. The backs contain information about the bonus gift or discount available to the ticket holder. The coupons are unnumbered and are listed below in alphabetical order by subject.

	MINT	NRMT	EXC
COMPLETE SET (12)	10.00	4.50	1.25
COMMON CARD (1-12)	.50	.23	.06
☐ 1 Gary Anderson RB	1.00	.45	.12
☐ 2 Gill Byrd	.75	.35	.09
☐ 3 Quinn Early	2.00	.90	.25
☐ 4 Vencie Glenn	.75	.35	.09
☐ 5 Jamie Holland	.50	.23	.06
☐ 6 Don Macek	.50	.23	.06
☐ 7 Dennis McKnight	.50	.23	.06
☐ 8 Anthony Miller	4.00	1.80	.50
☐ 9 Ralf Mojsiejenko	.50	.23	.06
☐ 10 Leslie O'Neal	1.50	.70	.19
☐ 11 Billy Ray Smith	.75	.35	.09
☐ 12 Lee Williams	.75	.35	.09

1989 Chargers Police

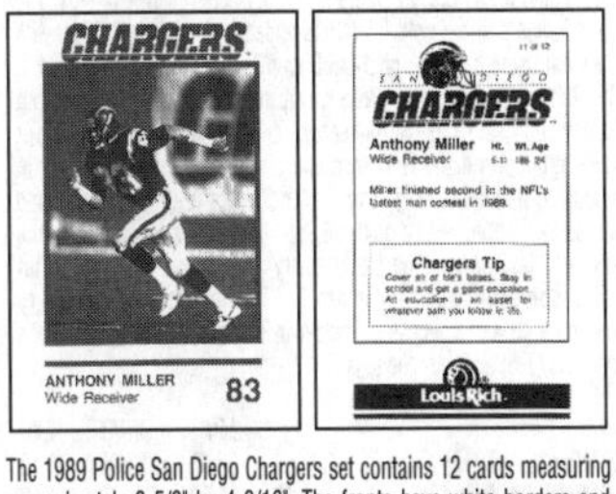

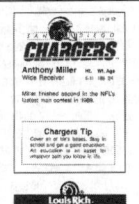

The 1989 Police San Diego Chargers set contains 12 cards measuring approximately 2 5/8" by 4 3/16". The fronts have white borders and color action photos; the vertically oriented backs have brief bios, career highlights, and safety messages. The set was sponsored by Louis Rich Co. The set was given away in two six-card panels; the first group at the Chargers' October 22nd home game and the other at the November 5th game. The cards are numbered on the back.

	MINT	NRMT	EXC
COMPLETE SET (12)	10.00	4.50	1.25
COMMON CARD (1-12)	.50	.23	.06
☐ 1 Tim Spencer	.75	.35	.09
☐ 2 Vencie Glenn	.75	.35	.09
☐ 3 Gill Byrd	.75	.35	.09
☐ 4 Jim McMahon	1.25	.55	.16
☐ 5 David Richards	.50	.23	.06
☐ 6 Don Macek	.50	.23	.06
☐ 7 Billy Ray Smith	.75	.35	.09
☐ 8 Gary Plummer	.75	.35	.09
☐ 9 Lee Williams	.75	.35	.09
☐ 10 Leslie O'Neal	1.00	.45	.12
☐ 11 Anthony Miller	2.50	1.10	.30
☐ 12 Broderick Thompson	.50	.23	.06

1989 Chargers Smokey

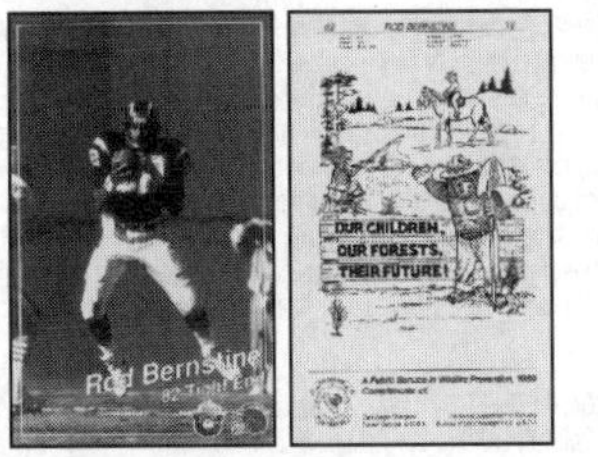

This 48-card set is very similar in style to the Smokey Chargers set of the previous year. This set gives the 1989 date on the bottom of every reverse. Cards are unnumbered except for uniform number which appears on the card front and back. The cards are ordered below by uniform number. The cards measure approximately 5" by 8". Each card back shows a different fire safety cartoon.

	MINT	NRMT	EXC
COMPLETE SET (48)	50.00	22.00	6.25
COMMON CARD	1.00	.45	.12
☐ 2 Ralf Mojsiejenko	1.00	.45	.12
☐ 6 Steve DeLine	1.00	.45	.12
☐ 10 Vince Abbott	1.00	.45	.12
☐ 13 Mark Vlasic	1.00	.45	.12
☐ 16 Mark Malone	1.00	.45	.12
☐ 20 Barry Redden	1.00	.45	.12
☐ 22 Gill Byrd	1.00	.45	.12
☐ 23 Roy Bennett	1.00	.45	.12
☐ 25 Vencie Glenn	1.00	.45	.12
☐ 26 Lionel James	1.00	.45	.12
☐ 30 Sam Seale	1.00	.45	.12
☐ 31 Leonard Coleman	1.00	.45	.12
☐ 34 Elvis Patterson	1.00	.45	.12
☐ 40 Gary Anderson RB	1.25	.55	.16
☐ 42 Curtis Adams	1.00	.45	.12
☐ 43 Tim Spencer	1.00	.45	.12
☐ 44 Martin Bayless	1.00	.45	.12
☐ 48 Pat Miller	1.00	.45	.12
☐ 50 Gary Plummer	1.00	.45	.12
☐ 51 Cedric Figaro	1.00	.45	.12
☐ 52 Jeff Jackson	1.00	.45	.12
☐ 53 Chuck Faucette	1.00	.45	.12
☐ 54 Billy Ray Smith	1.00	.45	.12
☐ 57 Keith Browner	1.00	.45	.12
☐ 58 David Brandon	1.00	.45	.12
☐ 59 Ken Woodard	1.00	.45	.12
☐ 60 Dennis McKnight	1.00	.45	.12
☐ 61 Ken Dallafior	1.00	.45	.12
☐ 65 David Richards	1.00	.45	.12
☐ 66 Dan Rosado	1.00	.45	.12
☐ 69 Les Miller	1.00	.45	.12
☐ 70 James Fitzpatrick	1.00	.45	.12
☐ 71 Mike Charles	1.00	.45	.12
☐ 72 Karl Wilson	1.00	.45	.12
☐ 73 Darrick Brilz	1.00	.45	.12
☐ 75 Joe Phillips	1.00	.45	.12
☐ 76 Broderick Thompson	1.00	.45	.12
☐ 82 Rod Bernstine	1.50	.70	.19
☐ 83 Anthony Miller	5.00	2.20	.60
☐ 86 Jamie Holland	1.00	.45	.12
☐ 87 Quinn Early	1.25	.55	.16
☐ 88 Arthur Cox	1.00	.45	.12
☐ 89 Darren Flutie	1.50	.70	.19
☐ 91 Leslie O'Neal	2.00	.90	.25
☐ 93 Tyrone Keys	1.00	.45	.12
☐ 95 Joe Campbell	1.00	.45	.12
☐ 97 George Hinkle	1.00	.45	.12
☐ 99 Lee Williams	1.00	.45	.12

1990 Chargers Police

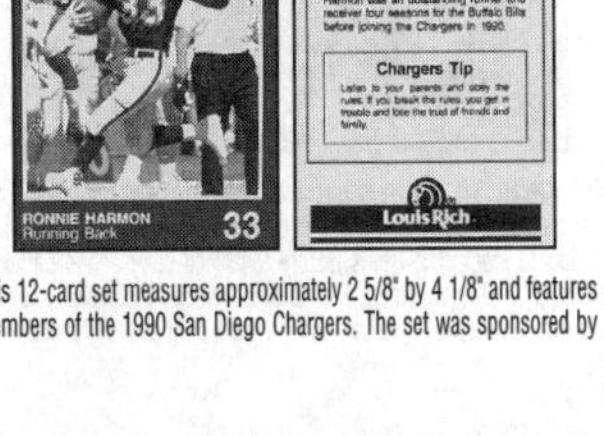

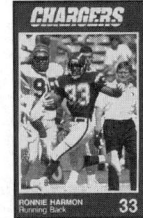

This 12-card set measures approximately 2 5/8" by 4 1/8" and features members of the 1990 San Diego Chargers. The set was sponsored by Louis Rich Meats. The card fronts have full-color photos framed by solid blue borders while the backs have brief biographies of the players and limited personal information. There is also a safety tip on the back of the card. The set was issued in two six-card panels or sheets (but is also found as individual cards). The cards are numbered on the back.

	MINT	NRMT	EXC
COMPLETE SET (12)	8.00	3.60	1.00
COMMON CARD (1-12)	.50	.23	.06
☐ 1 Martin Bayless	.50	.23	.06
☐ 2 Marion Butts	.75	.35	.09
☐ 3 Gill Byrd	.50	.23	.06
☐ 4 Burt Grossman	.50	.23	.06
☐ 5 Ronnie Harmon	.75	.35	.09
☐ 6 Anthony Miller	2.00	.90	.25
☐ 7 Leslie O'Neal	1.00	.45	.12
☐ 8 Joe Phillips	.50	.23	.06
☐ 9 Gary Plummer	.75	.35	.09
☐ 10 Billy Ray Smith	.50	.23	.06
☐ 11 Billy Joe Tolliver	.75	.35	.09
☐ 12 Lee Williams	.75	.35	.09

1990 Chargers Smokey

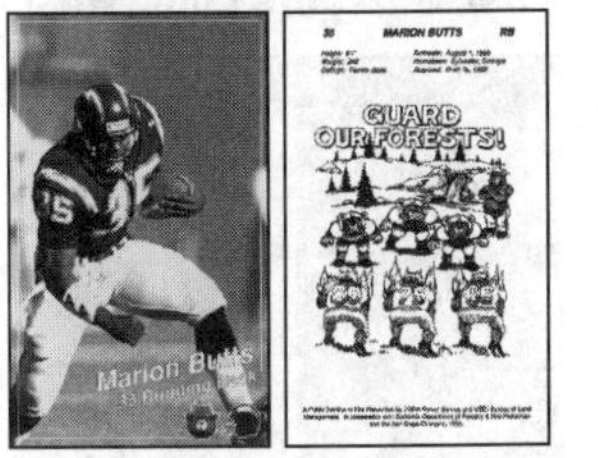

This attractive 36-card set was distributed in the San Diego area and features members of the Chargers. The cards measure approximately 5" by 8" and are very similar in style to previous Chargers Smokey issues. Since the cards are unnumbered except for uniform number, they are ordered below in that manner. The cardbacks contain a fire safety cartoon and very brief biographical information.

	MINT	NRMT	EXC
COMPLETE SET (36)	40.00	18.00	5.00
COMMON CARD	1.00	.45	.12
☐ 11 Billy Joe Tolliver	1.25	.55	.16
☐ 13 Mark Vlasic	1.25	.55	.16
☐ 15 David Archer	2.00	.90	.25
☐ 20 Darrin Nelson	1.00	.45	.12
☐ 22 Gill Byrd	1.25	.55	.16
☐ 24 Lester Lyles	1.00	.45	.12
☐ 25 Vencie Glenn	1.25	.55	.16
☐ 30 Sam Seale	1.00	.45	.12
☐ 31 Craig McEwen	1.00	.45	.12
☐ 35 Marion Butts	1.25	.55	.16
☐ 43 Tim Spencer	1.25	.55	.16
☐ 44 Martin Bayless	1.00	.45	.12
☐ 46 Joe Caravello	1.00	.45	.12
☐ 50 Gary Plummer	1.25	.55	.16
☐ 51 Cedric Figaro	1.00	.45	.12
☐ 53 Courtney Hall	1.00	.45	.12
☐ 54 Billy Ray Smith	1.25	.55	.16
☐ 58 David Brandon	1.00	.45	.12
☐ 59 Ken Woodard	1.00	.45	.12
☐ 60 Dennis McKnight	1.00	.45	.12
☐ 65 David Richards	1.00	.45	.12
☐ 69 Les Miller	1.00	.45	.12
☐ 75 Joe Phillips	1.25	.55	.16
☐ 76 Broderick Thompson	1.00	.45	.12
☐ 78 Joel Patten	1.00	.45	.12
☐ 79 Joey Howard	1.00	.45	.12
☐ 80 Wayne Walker	1.00	.45	.12
☐ 82 Rod Bernstine	1.25	.55	.16
☐ 83 Anthony Miller	4.00	1.80	.50
☐ 85 Andy Parker	1.00	.45	.12
☐ 87 Quinn Early	1.50	.70	.19
☐ 88 Arthur Cox	1.00	.45	.12
☐ 91 Leslie O'Neal	1.50	.70	.19
☐ 92 Burt Grossman	1.25	.55	.16
☐ 97 George Hinkle	1.00	.45	.12
☐ 99 Lee Williams	1.25	.55	.16

1991 Chargers Vons

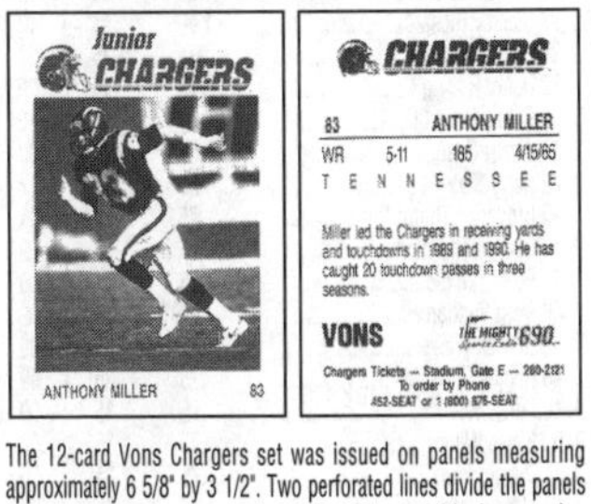

The 12-card Vons Chargers set was issued on panels measuring approximately 6 5/8" by 3 1/2". Two perforated lines divide the panels into three sections: a standard size (2 1/2" by 3 1/2") player card, a

1991 Junior Charger Official Membership Card, and a Sea World of California discount coupon. The player cards have color action player photos on the fronts, with yellow borders on a white card face. A Charger helmet and the words "Junior Chargers" appear at the top of the card. In a horizontal format with dark blue print, the back has biography, career highlights, and sponsors' logos. The cards are unnumbered and checklisted below in alphabetical order.

	MINT	NRMT	EXC
COMPLETE SET (12)	10.00	4.50	1.25
COMMON CARD (1-12)	.50	.23	.06
☐ 1 Rod Bernstine	.75	.35	.09
☐ 2 Gill Byrd	.75	.35	.09
☐ 3 Burt Grossman	.75	.35	.09
☐ 4 Ronnie Harmon	.75	.35	.09
☐ 5 Anthony Miller	1.50	.70	.19
☐ 6 Leslie O'Neal	1.00	.45	.12
☐ 7 Gary Plummer	.75	.35	.09
☐ 8 Junior Seau	2.00	.90	.25
☐ 9 Billy Ray Smith	.75	.35	.09
☐ 10 Broderick Thompson	.50	.23	.06
☐ 11 Billy Joe Tolliver	.75	.35	.09
☐ 12 Lee Williams	.75	.35	.09

1992 Chargers Louis Rich

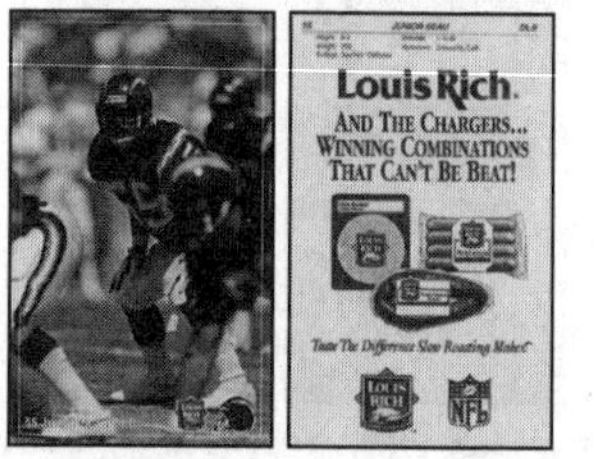

Sponsored by Louis Rich, this 52-card oversized set measures approximately 5" by 8". The fronts feature full-bleed glossy color action photos that are framed by a thin white line. The player's jersey number, name, and position appear at the lower left corner, while the sponsor logo and a replica of the team helmet are printed in the lower right corner. In addition to biographical information, the backs are dominated by a large advertisement for Louis Rich products. The cards are unnumbered and checklisted below in alphabetical order.

	MINT	NRMT	EXC
COMPLETE SET (52)	40.00	18.00	5.00
COMMON CARD (1-52)	.75	.35	.09
☐ 1 Sam Anno	.75	.35	.09
☐ 2 Johnnie Barnes	.75	.35	.09
☐ 3 Rod Bernstine	1.00	.45	.12
☐ 4 Eric Bieniemy	1.00	.45	.12
☐ 5 Anthony Blaylock	.75	.35	.09
☐ 6 Brian Brennan	.75	.35	.09
☐ 7 Marion Butts	1.00	.45	.12
☐ 8 Gill Byrd	1.00	.45	.12
☐ 9 John Carney	1.00	.45	.12
☐ 10 Darren Carrington	.75	.35	.09
☐ 11 Robert Claborne	1.00	.45	.12
☐ 12 Floyd Fields	.75	.35	.09
☐ 13 Donald Frank	.75	.35	.09
☐ 14 Bob Gagliano	.75	.35	.09
☐ 15 Leo Goeas	.75	.35	.09
☐ 16 Burt Grossman	.75	.35	.09
☐ 17 Courtney Hall	1.00	.45	.12
☐ 18 Delton Hall	.75	.35	.09
☐ 19 Ronnie Harmon	1.00	.45	.12
☐ 20 Steve Hendrickson	.75	.35	.09
☐ 21 Stan Humphries	2.00	.90	.25
☐ 22 Shawn Jefferson	1.00	.45	.12
☐ 23 John Kidd	.75	.35	.09
☐ 24 Shawn Lee	.75	.35	.09
☐ 25 Nate Lewis	1.00	.45	.12
☐ 26 Eugene Marve	.75	.35	.09
☐ 27 Deems May	.75	.35	.09
☐ 28 Anthony Miller	1.50	.70	.19
☐ 29 Chris Mims	1.25	.55	.16
☐ 30 Eric Moten	.75	.35	.09
☐ 31 Kevin Murphy	.75	.35	.09
☐ 32 Pat O'Hara	.75	.35	.09
☐ 33 Leslie O'Neal	1.25	.55	.16
☐ 34 Gary Plummer	1.00	.45	.12
☐ 35 Marquez Pope	.75	.35	.09
☐ 36 Alfred Pupunu	1.00	.45	.12
☐ 37 Stanley Richard	1.00	.45	.12
☐ 38 David Richards	.75	.35	.09
☐ 39 Henry Rolling	.75	.35	.09
☐ 40 Bobby Ross CO	1.25	.55	.16
☐ 41 Junior Seau	2.50	1.10	.30
☐ 42 Harry Swayne	1.00	.45	.12
☐ 43 Broderick Thompson	.75	.35	.09
☐ 44 George Thornton	.75	.35	.09
☐ 45 Peter Tuipulotu	.75	.35	.09
☐ 46 Sean Vanhorse	.75	.35	.09
☐ 47 Derrick Walker	.75	.35	.09
☐ 48 Reggie E. White	.75	.35	.09
☐ 49 Curtis Whitley	.75	.35	.09
☐ 50 Blaise Winter	.75	.35	.09
☐ 51 Duane Young	.75	.35	.09
☐ 52 Mike Zandofsky	.75	.35	.09

1993 Chargers Police

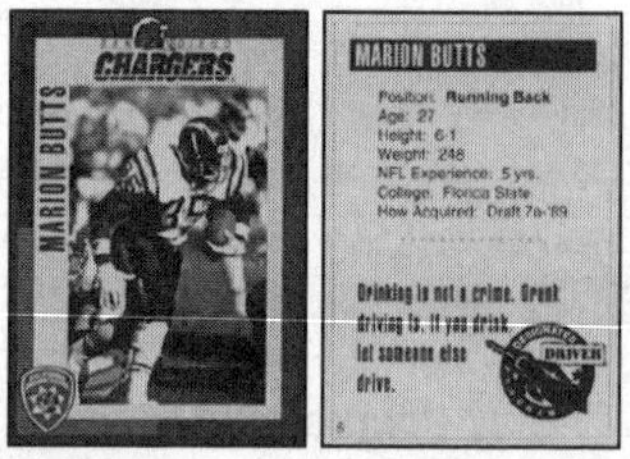

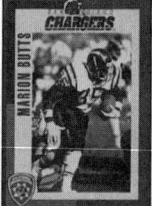

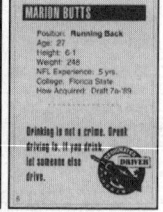

These 32 standard-size cards of the San Diego Chargers feature color player action shots on their blue- and yellow-bordered fronts. The player's name appears in vertical blue lettering within the inner yellow border on the left. The California Highway Patrol (CHP) shield logo appears at the lower left. The white back is framed by a thin blue line and carries the player's name at the top, followed below by position and biography. A safety message at the bottom from the CHP's "Designated Driver" campaign cautions against driving while intoxicated. Natrone Means is featured during his Rookie season.

	MINT	NRMT	EXC
COMPLETE SET (32)	12.00	5.50	1.50
COMMON CARD (1-32)	.25	.11	.03
☐ 1 Darrien Gordon	.40	.18	.05
☐ 2 Natrone Means	2.50	1.10	.30
☐ 3 John Friesz	.40	.18	.05
☐ 4 Stan Humphries	1.25	.55	.16
☐ 5 Anthony Miller	1.25	.55	.16
☐ 6 Marion Butts	.75	.35	.09
☐ 7 Ronnie Harmon	.75	.35	.09
☐ 8 Stanley Richard	.40	.18	.05
☐ 9 Leslie O'Neal	.75	.35	.09
☐ 10 Harry Swayne	.25	.11	.03
☐ 11 Junior Seau	1.50	.70	.19
☐ 12 Courtney Hall	.40	.18	.05
☐ 13 Gary Plummer	.40	.18	.05
☐ 14 Eric Moten	.25	.11	.03
☐ 15 Chris Mims	.75	.35	.09
☐ 16 Burt Grossman	.40	.18	.05
☐ 17 Blaise Winter	.25	.11	.03
☐ 18 Donald Frank	.25	.11	.03
☐ 19 Sean Vanhorse	.25	.11	.03
☐ 20 John Carney	.25	.11	.03
☐ 21 Floyd Fields	.25	.11	.03
☐ 22 Gill Byrd	.40	.18	.05
☐ 23 Shawn Jefferson	.40	.18	.05
☐ 24 Shawn Lee	.25	.11	.03
☐ 25 Alfred Pupunu	.40	.18	.05
☐ 26 Marquez Pope	.25	.11	.03
☐ 27 Darren Carrington	.25	.11	.03
☐ 28 Duane Young	.25	.11	.03
☐ 29 Derrick Walker	.25	.11	.03
☐ 30 Deems May	.25	.11	.03
☐ 31 Nate Lewis	.40	.18	.05
☐ 32 Bobby Ross CO Clarence Tuck (CHP Chief)	.75	.35	.09

1994 Chargers Castrol Promos

This six-card promo set was cosponsored by Castrol and Pepboys. The cards measure approximately 5" by 8" and are printed on white cardboard stock. The fronts feature full-bleed color action photos, except at the bottom where a white stripe carries the player's name, uniform number, and sponsor logos. In blue print over a ghosted NFL emblem, the backs show biography and sponsor advertisements.

	MINT	NRMT	EXC
COMPLETE SET (6)	6.00	2.70	.75
COMMON CARD (1-6)	.60	.25	.07
☐ 1 Courtney Hall	.60	.25	.07
☐ 2 Ronnie Harmon	.60	.25	.07
☐ 3 Stan Humphries	1.00	.45	.12
☐ 4 Natrone Means	2.00	.90	.25
☐ 5 Leslie O'Neal	.75	.35	.09
☐ 6 Junior Seau	1.25	.55	.16

1994 Chargers Castrol

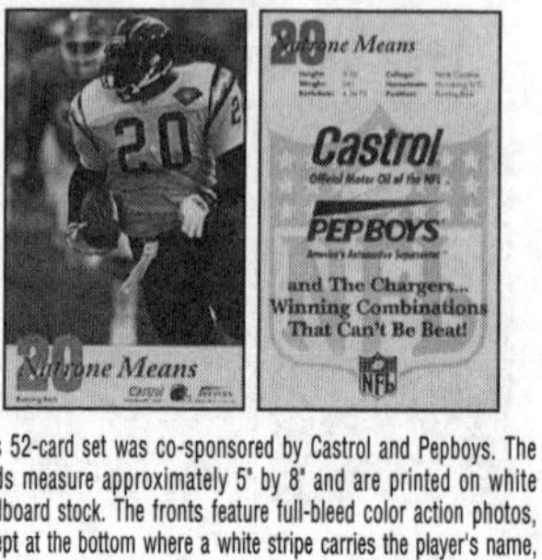

This 52-card set was co-sponsored by Castrol and Pepboys. The cards measure approximately 5" by 8" and are printed on white cardboard stock. The fronts feature full-bleed color action photos, except at the bottom where a white stripe carries the player's name, uniform number, and sponsor logos. In blue print over a ghosted NFL emblem, the backs show biography and sponsor advertisements. The cards are unnumbered and checklisted below in alphabetical order.

	MINT	NRMT	EXC
COMPLETE SET (52)	40.00	18.00	5.00
COMMON CARD (1-52)	.75	.35	.09
☐ 1 Johnnie Barnes	.75	.35	.09
☐ 2 Eric Bieniemy	1.00	.45	.12
☐ 3 David Binn	.75	.35	.09
☐ 4 Stan Brock	.75	.35	.09
☐ 5 Jeff Brohm	.75	.35	.09
☐ 6 Lewis Bush	.75	.35	.09
☐ 7 John Carney	1.00	.45	.12
☐ 8 Darren Carrington	.75	.35	.09
☐ 9 Eric Castle	.75	.35	.09
☐ 10 Willie Clark	1.00	.45	.12
☐ 11 Joe Cocozzo	.75	.35	.09
☐ 12 Andre Coleman	1.00	.45	.12
☐ 13 Rodney Culver	1.00	.45	.12
☐ 14 Isaac Davis	.75	.35	.09
☐ 15 Reuben Davis	.75	.35	.09
☐ 16 Greg Engel	.75	.35	.09
☐ 17 Dennis Gilbert	.75	.35	.09
☐ 18 Gale Gilbert	.75	.35	.09
☐ 19 Darrien Gordon	1.00	.45	.12
☐ 20 David Griggs	.75	.35	.09
☐ 21 Courtney Hall	.75	.35	.09
☐ 22 Ronnie Harmon	1.00	.45	.12
☐ 23 Dwayne Harper	.75	.35	.09
☐ 24 Rodney Harrison	.75	.35	.09
☐ 25 Steve Hendrickson	.75	.35	.09
☐ 26 Stan Humphries	2.00	.90	.25
☐ 27 Shawn Jefferson	1.25	.55	.16
☐ 28 Raylee Johnson	.75	.35	.09
☐ 29 Eric Jonassen	.75	.35	.09
☐ 30 Aaron Laing	.75	.35	.09
☐ 31 Shawn Lee	.75	.35	.09
☐ 32 Deems May	.75	.35	.09
☐ 33 Natrone Means	3.00	1.35	.35
☐ 34 Joe Milinichik	.75	.35	.09
☐ 35 Doug Miller	.75	.35	.09
☐ 36 Chris Mims	1.00	.45	.12
☐ 37 Shannon Mitchell	.75	.35	.09
☐ 38 Leslie O'Neal	1.25	.55	.16
☐ 39 Vaughn Parker	.75	.35	.09
☐ 40 John Parrella	.75	.35	.09
☐ 41 Alfred Pupunu	1.00	.45	.12
☐ 42 Stanley Richard	1.00	.45	.12
☐ 43 Junior Seau	3.00	1.35	.35
☐ 44 Mark Seay	1.50	.70	.19
☐ 45 Harry Swayne	.75	.35	.09
☐ 46 Cornell Thomas	.75	.35	.09
☐ 47 Sean Van Horse	.75	.35	.09
☐ 48 Bryan Wagner	.75	.35	.09
☐ 49 Reggie E. White	.75	.35	.09
☐ 50 Curtis Whitley	.75	.35	.09
☐ 51 Duane Young	.75	.35	.09
☐ 52 Lonnie Young	.75	.35	.09

1994 Chargers Pro Mags/Pro Tags

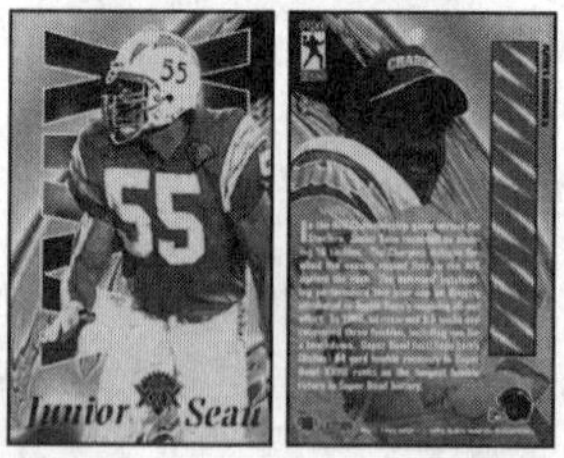

Issued in a black cardboard box and featuring the San Diego Chargers, this set consists of six Pro Mags and six Pro Tags, both with rounded corners and measuring 2 1/8" by 3 3/8". Each box is individually numbered out of 750. On a team color-coded background, the magnet fronts display borderless color action player photos. The player's name in big gold-foil letters appears along the left side, with the team name below. A gold-foil Super Bowl XXIX logo is printed in the lower right corner. On a computerized team color-coded background, the tag fronts feature a color action player cutout superimposed on the Roman numerals XXIX printed vertically in oversized block lettering. The player's name is gold foil-stamped across the bottom, with a gold-foil Super Bowl XXIX logo between the first and last name. The backs carry a color closeup photo, an autograph strip, and player profile. The magnets and tags are unnumbered and checklisted below in alphabetical order, first the magnets (1-6) and then the tags (7-12).

	MINT	NRMT	EXC
COMPLETE SET (12)	25.00	11.00	3.10
COMMON CARD (1-12)	1.50	.70	.19
☐ 1 Stan Humphries	2.50	1.10	.30
☐ 2 Tony Martin	2.00	.90	.25
☐ 3 Natrone Means	3.00	1.35	.35
☐ 4 Leslie O'Neal	1.50	.70	.19
☐ 5 Junior Seau	3.00	1.35	.35
☐ 6 Mark Seay	1.50	.70	.19
☐ 7 Stan Humphries	2.50	1.10	.30
☐ 8 Tony Martin	2.00	.90	.25
☐ 9 Natrone Means	3.00	1.35	.35
☐ 10 Leslie O'Neal	1.50	.70	.19
☐ 11 Junior Seau	3.00	1.35	.35
☐ 12 Mark Seay	1.50	.70	.19

1964-69 Chiefs Fairmont Dairy

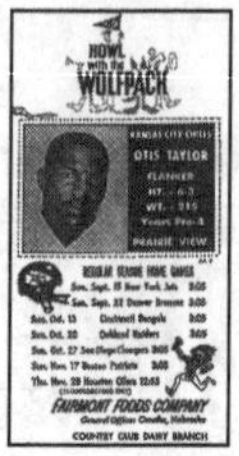

These cards were featured as the side panels of half-gallon milk cartons in the Kansas City area by Fairmont Dairy. The cards were apparently issued during more than one season as there are several styles with different sizes and colors. The cards may have been issued as early as 1964 and as late as 1969. When cut, the cards vary in measurement from approximately 3 3/8" by 2 3/8" to 3 1/2" by 1 1/2." The printing on the cards is either in black or red depending apparently on the year of issue. The fronts feature close-up player photos with the player's team, name, position, jersey number, and biographical information appearing to the right. All cards feature members of the Kansas City Chiefs. The catalog designation for this set is F120. This list below are those known at this time. The cards have blank backs as is the case with most milk carton issues. Complete milk cartons would be valued at double the prices listed below. The set is thought to contain 22-cards. Additions to the list are welcomed.

	NRMT	VG-E	GOOD
COMPLETE SET (19)	2000.00	900.00	250.00
COMMON CARD	75.00	34.00	9.50
☐ 1 Fred Arbanas (Red printing)	100.00	45.00	12.50
☐ 2 Bobby Bell (Red printing)	200.00	90.00	25.00
☐ 3 Buck Buchanan (Black print)	200.00	90.00	25.00
☐ 4 Chris Burford (Red printing)	100.00	45.00	12.50
☐ 5 Len Dawson (Red printing)	300.00	135.00	38.00
☐ 6 Dave Grayson (Red printing)	75.00	34.00	9.50
☐ 7 Abner Haynes (Red printing)	125.00	55.00	15.50
☐ 8 Sherrill Headrick (Red printing)	100.00	45.00	12.50
☐ 9 Bobby Hunt (Red printing)	75.00	34.00	9.50
☐ 10 Frank Jackson (Red printing)	75.00	34.00	9.50
☐ 11 Curtis McClinton (Red printing)	100.00	45.00	12.50
☐ 12 Bobby Ply (Red printing)	75.00	34.00	9.50
☐ 13 Al Reynolds (Red printing)	75.00	34.00	9.50
☐ 14 Johnny Robinson (Red printing)	125.00	55.00	15.50
☐ 15 Noland Smith	75.00	34.00	9.50
☐ 16 Smokey Stover (Red printing)	75.00	34.00	9.50
☐ 17 Otis Taylor	150.00	70.00	19.00
☐ 18 Jim Tyrer (Red printing)	100.00	45.00	12.50
☐ 19 Jerrel Wilson (Red Printing)	75.00	34.00	9.50

1969 Chiefs Kroger

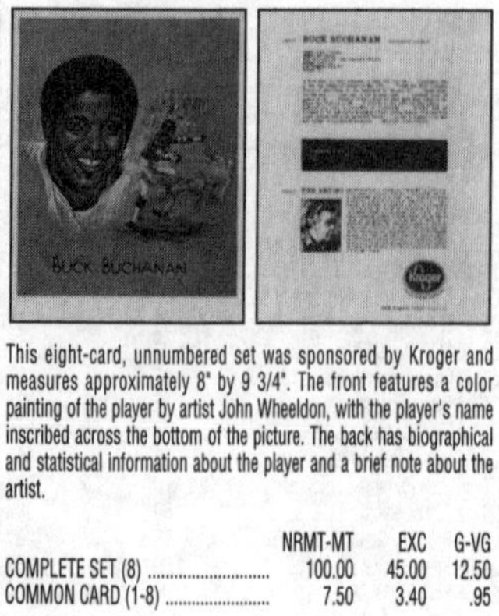

This eight-card, unnumbered set was sponsored by Kroger and measures approximately 8" by 9 3/4". The front features a color painting of the player by artist John Wheeldon, with the player's name inscribed across the bottom of the picture. The back has biographical and statistical information about the player and a brief note about the artist.

	NRMT-MT	EXC	G-VG
COMPLETE SET (8)	100.00	45.00	12.50
COMMON CARD (1-8)	7.50	3.40	.95

☐ 1 Buck Buchanan	15.00	6.75	1.85
☐ 2 Len Dawson	25.00	11.00	3.10
☐ 3 Mike Garrett	10.00	4.50	1.25
☐ 4 Willie Lanier	20.00	9.00	2.50
☐ 5 Jerry Mays	7.50	3.40	.95
☐ 6 Johnny Robinson	10.00	4.50	1.25
☐ 7 Jan Stenerud	15.00	6.75	1.85
☐ 8 Jim Tyrer	7.50	3.40	.95

1971 Chiefs Team Issue

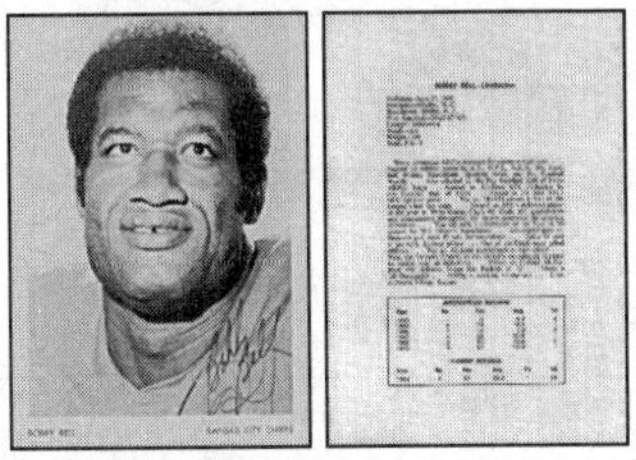

This set of ten photos is a team-issued set. Each photo measures approximately 7" by 10" and features a black-and-white head shot bordered in white. The player's name and team name are printed in the lower white border, while the player's facsimile autograph is inscribed across the picture. The backs carry biography and career summary; some of the backs also have statistics. The photos are unnumbered and checklisted below in alphabetical order.

	NRMT-MT	EXC	G-VG
COMPLETE SET (10)	60.00	27.00	7.50
COMMON CARD (1-10)	5.00	2.20	.60
☐ 1 Bobby Bell	12.00	5.50	1.50
☐ 2 Wendell Hayes	6.00	2.70	.75
☐ 3 Ed Lothamer	5.00	2.20	.60
☐ 4 Jim Lynch	6.00	2.70	.75
☐ 5 Jack Rudnay	6.00	2.70	.75
☐ 6 Sid Smith	5.00	2.20	.60
☐ 7 Bob Stein	5.00	2.20	.60
☐ 8 Jan Stenerud	12.00	5.50	1.50
☐ 9 Otis Taylor	10.00	4.50	1.25
☐ 10 Jim Tyrer	6.00	2.70	.75

1973-74 Chiefs Team Issue

This 18-card set of the Kansas City Chiefs measures approximately 5" by 7" and features black-and-white player photos with a white border. The backs are blank. The cards are unnumbered and checklisted below in alpabetical order.

	NRMT-MT	EXC	G-VG
COMPLETE SET (18)	50.00	22.00	6.25
COMMON CARD	3.00	1.35	.35
☐ 1 Bob Briggs	3.00	1.35	.35
☐ 2 Larry Brunson	3.00	1.35	.35
☐ 3 Gary Butler	3.00	1.35	.35
☐ 4 Dean Carlson	3.00	1.35	.35
☐ 5 Tom Condon	3.00	1.35	.35
☐ 6 George Daney	3.00	1.35	.35
☐ 7 Andy Hamilton	3.00	1.35	.35
☐ 8 Dave Hill	3.00	1.35	.35
☐ 9 Jim Kearney	4.00	1.80	.50
☐ 10 Mike Livingston	4.00	1.80	.50
☐ 11 Jim Marsalis	4.00	1.80	.50
☐ 12 Barry Pearson	4.00	1.80	.50
☐ 13 Francis Peay	3.00	1.35	.35
☐ 14 Kerry Reardon	3.00	1.35	.35
☐ 15 Mike Sensibaugh	4.00	1.80	.50
☐ 16 Bill Thomas	3.00	1.35	.35
☐ 17 Marvin Upshaw	4.00	1.80	.50
☐ 18 Clyde Werner	3.00	1.35	.35

1979 Chiefs Police

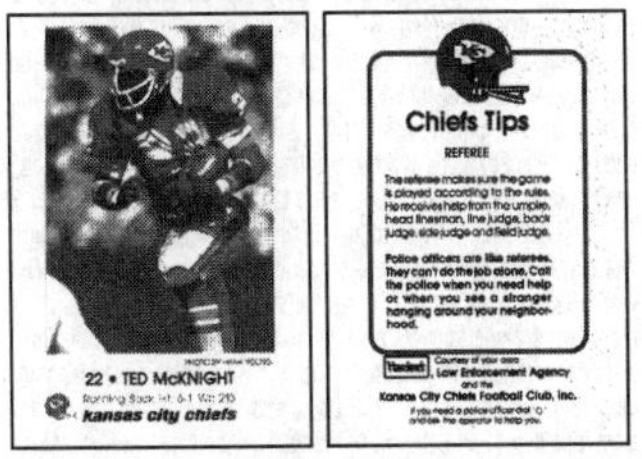

The 1979 Kansas City Chiefs Police set consists of ten cards co-sponsored by Hardee's Restaurants and the Kansas City (Missouri) Police Department, in addition to the Chiefs' football club. The cards measure approximately 2 5/8" by 4 1/8". The card backs discuss a football term and related legal/safety issue in a section entitled "Chief's Tips". The set is unnumbered but the player's uniform number appears on the front of the cards; the cards are numbered and ordered below by uniform number. The Chiefs' helmet logo is found on both the fronts and backs of the cards.

	NRMT-MT	EXC	G-VG
COMPLETE SET (10)	15.00	6.75	1.85
COMMON CARD	1.25	.55	.16
☐ 1 Bob Grupp	1.25	.55	.16
☐ 4 Steve Fuller	1.50	.70	.19
☐ 22 Ted McKnight	1.25	.55	.16
☐ 24 Gary Green	1.50	.70	.19
☐ 26 Gary Barbaro	2.00	.90	.25
☐ 32 Tony Reed	1.50	.70	.19
☐ 58 Jack Rudnay	1.25	.55	.16
☐ 67 Art Still	2.00	.90	.25
☐ 73 Bob Simmons	1.25	.55	.16
☐ NNO Marv Levy CO	3.00	1.35	.35

1980 Chiefs Police

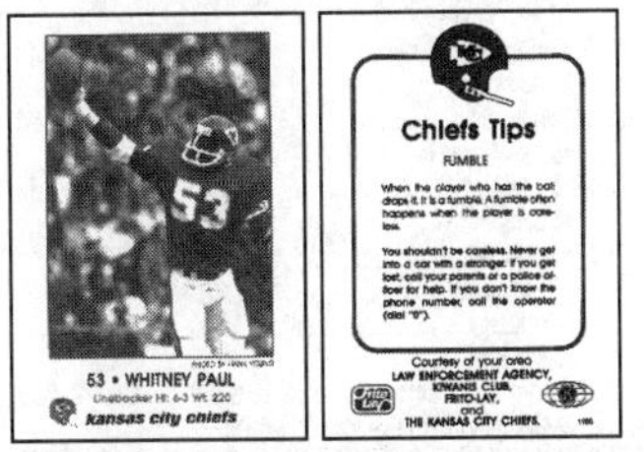

The unnumbered, ten-card, 1980 Kansas City Chiefs Police set has been listed by the player's uniform number in the checklist below. The cards measure approximately 2 5/8" by 4 1/8". The Stenerud card was supposedly distributed on a limited basis and is thus more difficult to obtain. In addition to the Chiefs and the local law enforcement agencies, the set is sponsored by the Kiwanis Club and Frito-Lay, whose logos appear on the backs of the cards. The 1980 date can be found on the back of the cards as can "Chiefs Tips".

	MINT	NRMT	EXC
COMPLETE SET (10)	10.00	4.50	1.25
COMMON CARD	1.00	.45	.12
☐ 1 Bob Grupp	1.00	.45	.12
☐ 3 Jan Stenerud SP	4.00	1.80	.50
☐ 32 Tony Reed	1.25	.55	.16
☐ 53 Whitney Paul	1.00	.45	.12
☐ 59 Gary Spani	1.00	.45	.12
☐ 67 Art Still	1.50	.70	.19
☐ 86 J.T. Smith	1.50	.70	.19
☐ 99 Mike Bell	1.00	.45	.12
☐ NNO Defensive Team	1.50	.70	.19
☐ NNO Offensive Team	1.50	.70	.19

1981 Chiefs Police

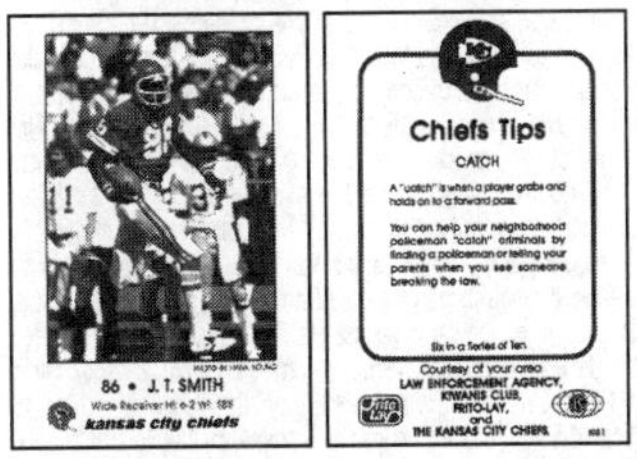

The 1981 Kansas City Chiefs Police set consists of ten cards, some of which have more than one player pictured. The cards are numbered on the back as well as prominently displaying the player's uniform number on the fronts of the cards. The cards measure approximately 2 5/8" by 4 1/8". The set is sponsored by the area law enforcement agency, the Kiwanis Club, Frito-Lay, and the Kansas City Chiefs. The Kiwanis Club and Frito-Lay logos, in addition to the Chiefs helmet logo, appear on the backs of the cards. Also "Chiefs Tips" are featured on the card backs. The card backs have black print with red accent on white card stock.

	MINT	NRMT	EXC
COMPLETE SET (10)	4.00	1.80	.50
COMMON CARD (1-10)	.40	.18	.05
☐ 1 Warpaint and Carla (Mascots)	.40	.18	.05
☐ 2 Art Still	.75	.35	.09
☐ 3 Steve Fuller and Jack Rudnay	.50	.23	.06
☐ 4 Gary Green	.50	.23	.06
☐ 5 Tom Condon and Marv Levy CO	.75	.35	.09
☐ 6 J.T. Smith	.75	.35	.09
☐ 7 Gary Spani and Whitney Paul	.40	.18	.05
☐ 8 Nick Lowery and Steve Fuller	.75	.35	.09
☐ 9 Gary Barbaro	.50	.23	.06
☐ 10 Henry Marshall	.40	.18	.05

1982 Chiefs Police

The 1982 Kansas City Chiefs Police set features ten numbered (on back) cards, some of which portray more than one player. The cards measure approximately 2 5/8" by 4 1/8". The backs deviate somewhat from a standard police set in that a cartoon is utilized to drive home the sage "Chiefs Tips". This set is sponsored by the local law enforcement agency, Frito-Lay, and the Kiwanis Club. The backs contain a 1982 date and logos of the Kiwanis, Frito-Lay, and the

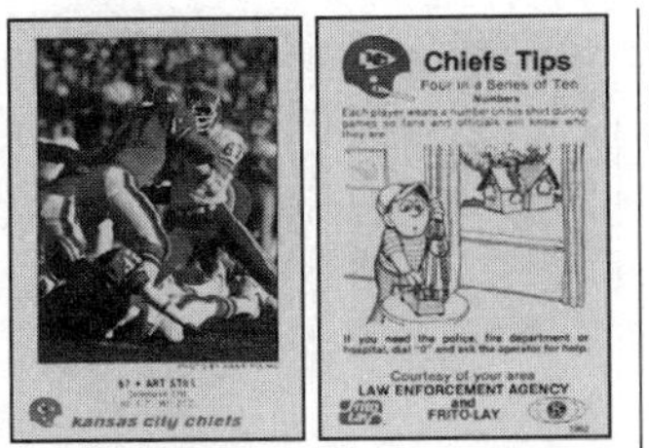

Chiefs. Card backs have black print with red accent on white card stock. Each player's uniform number is given on the front of the card.

	MINT	NRMT	EXC
COMPLETE SET (10)	5.00	2.20	.60
COMMON CARD (1-10)	.50	.23	.06
☐ 1 Bill Kenney and Jack Rudnay	.60	.25	.07
☐ 2 Steve Fuller and Nick Lowery	1.00	.45	.12
☐ 3 Matt Herkenhoff	.50	.23	.06
☐ 4 Art Still	.75	.35	.09
☐ 5 Gary Spani	.50	.23	.06
☐ 6 James Hadnot	.60	.25	.07
☐ 7 Mike Bell	.60	.25	.07
☐ 8 Carol Canfield (Chiefette)	.50	.23	.06
☐ 9 Gary Green	.60	.25	.07
☐ 10 Joe Delaney	1.00	.45	.12

1983 Chiefs Police

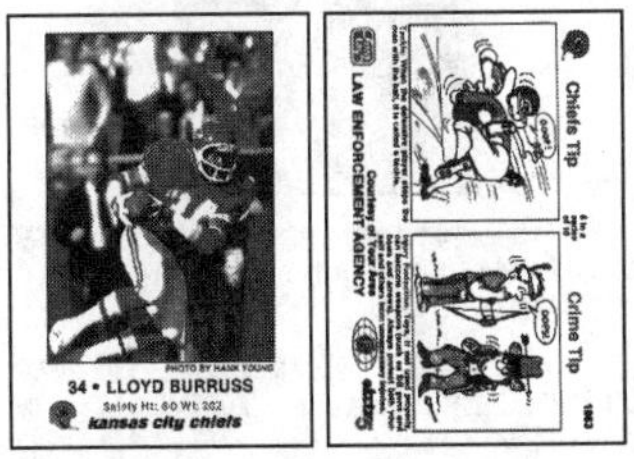

The 1983 Kansas City Chiefs set contains ten numbered cards. The cards measure approximately 2 5/8" by 4 1/8". Sponsored by Frito-Lay, the local law enforcement agency, the Kiwanis Club, and KCTV-5, the set features cartoon "Chiefs Tips" and Crime Tips on the backs. A 1983 date plus logos of the Chiefs, Frito-Lay, the Kiwanis, and KCTV-5 also appear on the backs. Uniform numbers are given on the front of the player's card.

	MINT	NRMT	EXC
COMPLETE SET (10)	5.00	2.20	.60
COMMON CARD (1-10)	.50	.23	.06
☐ 1 John Mackovic CO	1.00	.45	.12
☐ 2 Tom Condon	.50	.23	.06
☐ 3 Gary Spani	.50	.23	.06
☐ 4 Carlos Carson	.75	.35	.09
☐ 5 Brad Budde	.60	.25	.07
☐ 6 Lloyd Burruss	.50	.23	.06
☐ 7 Gary Green	.60	.25	.07
☐ 8 Mike Bell	.60	.25	.07
☐ 9 Nick Lowery	1.00	.45	.12
☐ 10 Sandi Byrd (Chiefette)	.50	.23	.06

1984 Chiefs Police

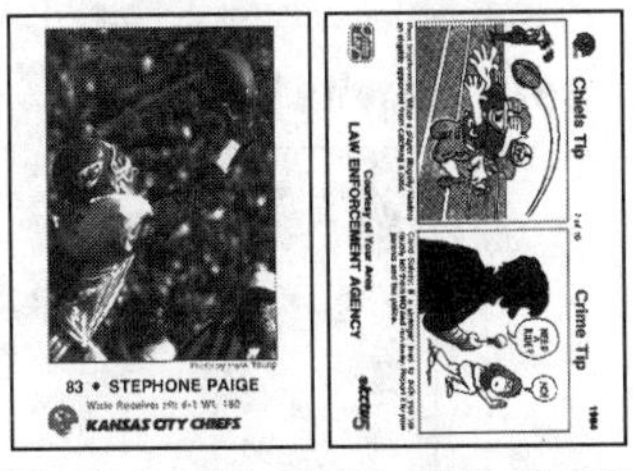

This numbered (on back) ten-card set features the Kansas City Chiefs. Backs contain a "Chiefs Tip" and a "Crime Tip," each with an accompanying cartoon. Cards measure approximately 2 5/8" by 4 1/8". Cards were also sponsored by Frito-Lay and KCTV.

	MINT	NRMT	EXC
COMPLETE SET (10)	5.00	2.20	.60
COMMON CARD (1-10)	.50	.23	.06
☐ 1 John Mackovic CO	.75	.35	.09
☐ 2 Deron Cherry	1.00	.45	.12
☐ 3 Bill Kenney	.60	.25	.07
☐ 4 Henry Marshall	.50	.23	.06
☐ 5 Nick Lowery	.75	.35	.09
☐ 6 Theotis Brown	.60	.25	.07
☐ 7 Stephone Paige	1.25	.55	.16
☐ 8 Gary Spani and Art Still	.75	.35	.09
☐ 9 Albert Lewis	1.00	.45	.12
☐ 10 Carlos Carson	.75	.35	.09

1985 Chiefs Police

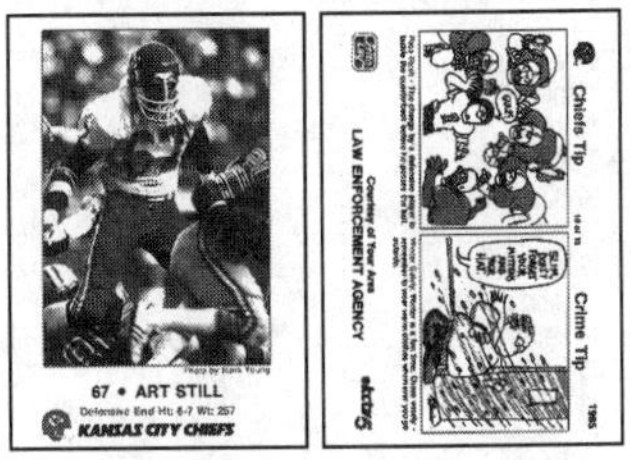

This ten-card set features the Kansas City Chiefs. Cards in the set measure approximately 2 5/8" by 4 1/8". The card back gives the card number and the year of issue; printing is in black and red on white card stock. The set was sponsored by Frito-Lay, KCTV-5, and area law enforcement agencies. Two cartoons are featured on the back of each card picturing a Chiefs Tip and a Crime Tip.

	MINT	NRMT	EXC
COMPLETE SET (10)	5.00	2.20	.60
COMMON CARD (1-10)	.50	.23	.06
☐ 1 John Mackovic CO	.75	.35	.09
☐ 2 Herman Heard	.60	.25	.07
☐ 3 Bill Kenney	.75	.35	.09
☐ 4 Deron Cherry and Lloyd Burruss	1.00	.45	.12
☐ 5 Jim Arnold	.50	.23	.06
☐ 6 Kevin Ross	.60	.25	.07
☐ 7 David Lutz	.50	.23	.06
☐ 8 Chiefettes Cheerleaders	.50	.23	.06
☐ 9 Bill Maas	.75	.35	.09
☐ 10 Art Still	.75	.35	.09

1986 Chiefs Police

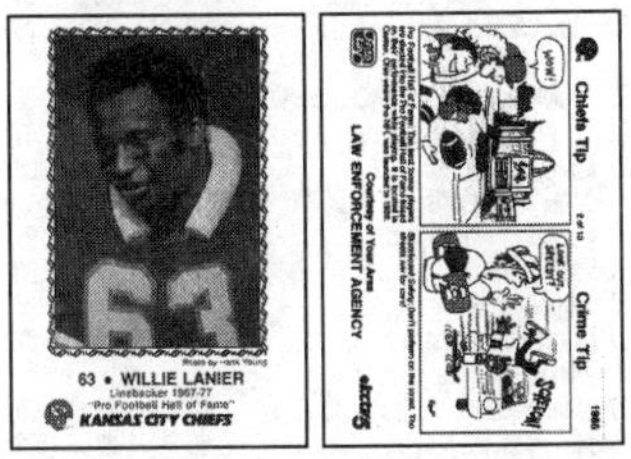

This ten-card set features the Kansas City Chiefs. Cards in the set measure approximately 2 5/8" by 4 1/8" and the card back gives the card number and the year of issue. Printing is in black and red on white card stock. The set was sponsored by Frito-Lay, KCTV-5, and area law enforcement agencies. Two cartoons are featured on the back of each card picturing a "Chiefs Tip" and a "Crime Tip".

	MINT	NRMT	EXC
COMPLETE SET (10)	6.00	2.70	.75
COMMON CARD (1-10)	.50	.23	.06
☐ 1 John Mackovic CO	.75	.35	.09
☐ 2 Willie Lanier (Hall of Fame)	1.50	.70	.19
☐ 3 Stephone Paige	1.00	.45	.12
☐ 4 Brad Budde	.50	.23	.06
☐ 5 Nick Lowery	.75	.35	.09
☐ 6 Scott Radecic	.50	.23	.06
☐ 7 Mike Pruitt	.60	.25	.07
☐ 8 Albert Lewis	1.00	.45	.12
☐ 9 Todd Blackledge	.75	.35	.09
☐ 10 Deron Cherry	1.00	.45	.12

1987 Chiefs Louis Rich

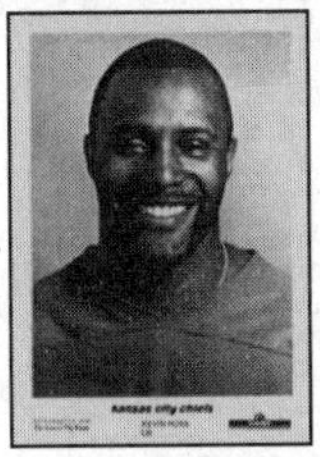

The Kansas City Chiefs issued this set sponsored by Louis Rich and The Kansas City Star. The cards are blankbacked, unnumbered, measure approximately 5" by 7", and contain black and white player photos. The cards can be distinguished from other Chiefs Louis Rich issues by the team name appearing in all lower case letters below the player photo. There are 16-known cards in the set. Any additions to this checklist would be appreciated.

	MINT	NRMT	EXC
COMPLETE SET (16)	20.00	9.00	2.50
COMMON CARD (1-16)	1.00	.45	.12
☐ 1 John Alt	1.50	.70	.19
☐ 2 Carlos Carson	1.50	.70	.19
☐ 3 Deron Cherry	2.00	.90	.25
☐ 4 Sherman Cocroft	1.00	.45	.12
☐ 5 Irv Eatman	1.00	.45	.12
☐ 6 Frank Gansz	1.00	.45	.12
☐ 7 Dino Hackett	1.50	.70	.19
☐ 8 Jonathan Hayes	1.00	.45	.12
☐ 9 Bill Kenney	1.50	.70	.19
☐ 10 Albert Lewis	2.00	.90	.25
☐ 11 Nick Lowery	1.50	.70	.19
☐ 12 Bill Maas	1.00	.45	.12
☐ 13 Christian Okoye	2.00	.90	.25
☐ 14 Stephone Paige	2.00	.90	.25
☐ 15 Paul Palmer	1.00	.45	.12
☐ 16 Kevin Ross	1.50	.70	.19

1987 Chiefs Police

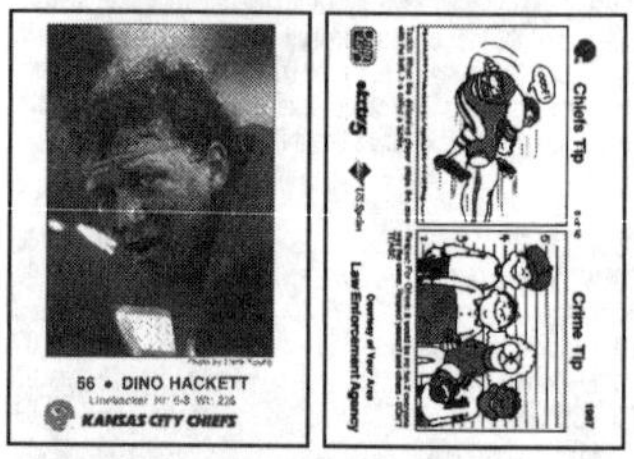

This ten-card set features the Kansas City Chiefs. Cards in the set measure approximately 2 5/8" by 4 1/8". The card back gives the card number and the year of issue; printing is in black and red on white card stock. The set was sponsored by Frito-Lay, US Sprint, KCTV-5, and area law enforcement agencies. Two cartoons are featured on the back of each card picturing a "Chiefs Tip" and a "Crime Tip". Reportedly more than 4.5 million cards were given out by over 275 different police departments.

	MINT	NRMT	EXC
COMPLETE SET (10)	4.00	1.80	.50
COMMON CARD (1-10)	.40	.18	.05
☐ 1 Frank Gansz CO	.50	.23	.06
☐ 2 Tim Cofield	.40	.18	.05
☐ 3 Deron Cherry and Albert Lewis	.75	.35	.09
☐ 4 Chiefs Cheerleaders	.50	.23	.06
☐ 5 Jeff Smith	.50	.23	.06
☐ 6 Rick Donnalley	.40	.18	.05
☐ 7 Lloyd Burruss and Kevin Ross	.60	.25	.07
☐ 8 Dino Hackett	.50	.23	.06
☐ 9 Bill Maas	.50	.23	.06
☐ 10 Carlos Carson	.60	.25	.07

1988 Chiefs Police

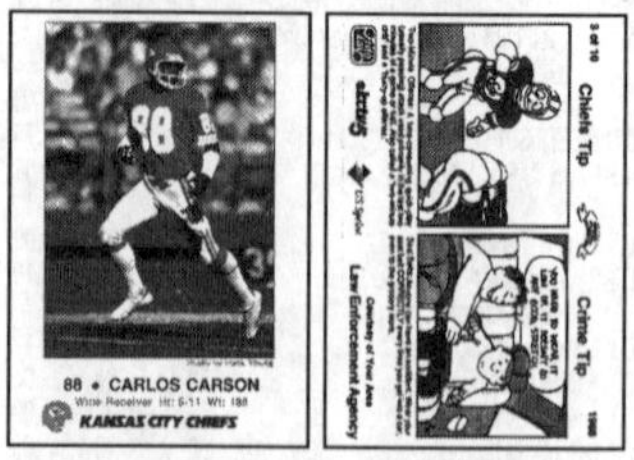

The 1988 Police Kansas City Chiefs set contains ten numbered cards each measuring approximately 2 5/8" by 4 1/8". There are nine player cards and one coach card. The backs have one "Chiefs Tip" and one "Crime Tip."

	MINT	NRMT	EXC
COMPLETE SET (10)	5.00	2.20	.60
COMMON CARD (1-10)	.50	.23	.06
☐ 1 Frank Gansz CO	.60	.25	.07
☐ 2 Bill Kenney	.75	.35	.09
☐ 3 Carlos Carson	.60	.25	.07
☐ 4 Paul Palmer	.60	.25	.07
☐ 5 Christian Okoye	1.25	.55	.16
☐ 6 Mark Adickes	.50	.23	.06
☐ 7 Bill Maas	.60	.25	.07
☐ 8 Albert Lewis	.75	.35	.09
☐ 9 Deron Cherry	.75	.35	.09
☐ 10 Stephone Paige	.75	.35	.09

1989 Chiefs Police

The 1989 Police Kansas City Chiefs set contains ten cards measuring approximately 2 5/8" by 4 1/8". The fronts have white borders and color action photos; the horizontally-oriented backs have safety tips. The set was sponsored by Western Auto and KCTV Channel 5. These cards were printed on very thin stock.

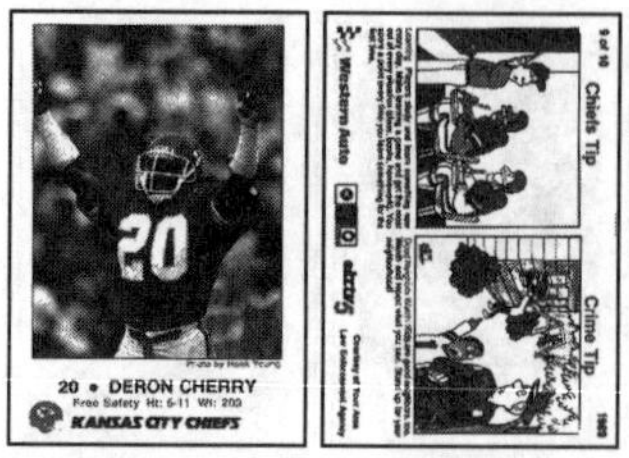

	MINT	NRMT	EXC
COMPLETE SET (10)	5.00	2.20	.60
COMMON CARD (1-10)	.50	.23	.06
☐ 1 Marty Schottenheimer CO	.75	.35	.09
☐ 2 Irv Eatman	.50	.23	.06
☐ 3 Kevin Ross	.60	.25	.07
☐ 4 Bill Maas	.60	.25	.07
☐ 5 Chiefs Cheerleaders	.60	.25	.07
☐ 6 Carlos Carson	.60	.25	.07
☐ 7 Steve DeBerg	1.00	.45	.12
☐ 8 Jonathan Hayes	.60	.25	.07
☐ 9 Deron Cherry	.75	.35	.09
☐ 10 Dino Hackett	.60	.25	.07

1969 Chiquita Team Logo Stickers

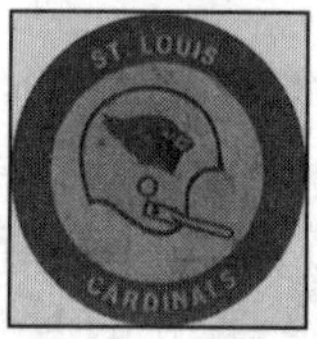

In 1969, Chiquita produced team logo stickers for the 26 Pro Football teams. We have sequenced these unnumbered sticker cards in alphabetical order.

	NRMT-MT	EXC	G-VG
COMPLETE SET (26)	300.00	135.00	38.00
COMMON STICKER (1-26)	10.00	4.50	1.25
☐ 1 Atlanta Falcons	10.00	4.50	1.25
☐ 2 Baltimore Colts	12.50	5.50	1.55
☐ 3 Boston Patriots	10.00	4.50	1.25
☐ 4 Buffalo Bills	12.50	5.50	1.55
☐ 5 Chicago Bears	12.50	5.50	1.55
☐ 6 Cincinnati Bengals	10.00	4.50	1.25
☐ 7 Cleveland Browns	15.00	6.75	1.85
☐ 8 Dallas Cowboys	15.00	6.75	1.85
☐ 9 Denver Broncos	12.50	5.50	1.55
☐ 10 Detroit Lions	10.00	4.50	1.25
☐ 11 Green Bay Packers	15.00	6.75	1.85
☐ 12 Houston Oilers	10.00	4.50	1.25
☐ 13 Kansas City Chiefs	10.00	4.50	1.25
☐ 14 Los Angeles Rams	10.00	4.50	1.25
☐ 15 Miami Dolphins	15.00	6.75	1.85
☐ 16 Minnesota Vikings	12.50	5.50	1.55
☐ 17 New Orleans Saints	10.00	4.50	1.25
☐ 18 New York Giants	12.50	5.50	1.55
☐ 19 New York Jets	12.50	5.50	1.55
☐ 20 Oakland Raiders	15.00	6.75	1.85
☐ 21 Philadelphia Eagles	10.00	4.50	1.25
☐ 22 Pittsburgh Steelers	15.00	6.75	1.85
☐ 23 San Diego Chargers	10.00	4.50	1.25
☐ 24 San Francisco 49ers	12.50	5.50	1.55
☐ 25 St. Louis Cardinals	10.00	4.50	1.25
☐ 26 Washington Redskins	12.50	5.50	1.55

1972 Chiquita NFL Slides

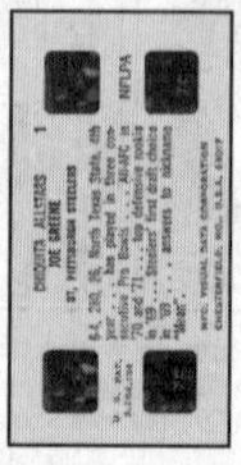

This set consists of 13 slides and a yellow plastic viewer for viewing the slides. Each slide measures approximately 3 9/16" by 1 3/4" and features two players (one on each side); each of the 26 NFL teams is represented by one player. Each side has a player summary on its middle portion, with two small color action slides at each end stacked one above the other. When the slide is placed in the viewer, the two bottom slides, which are identical, reveal the first player. Flipping the slide over reveals the other player biography and enables one to view the other two slides, which show the second player. The text on the cards is printed in either black or blue ink. Each side of the slides is numbered as listed below. The set is considered complete without the yellow viewer.

	NRMT-MT	EXC	G-VG
COMPLETE SET (13)	350.00	160.00	45.00
COMMON PAIR	20.00	9.00	2.50
☐ 1 Joe Greene / 2 Bob Lilly	70.00	32.00	8.75
☐ 3 Bill Bergey / 4 Gary Collins	25.00	11.00	3.10
☐ 5 Walt Sweeney / 6 Bubba Smith	25.00	11.00	3.10
☐ 7 Larry Wilson / 8 Fred Carr	25.00	11.00	3.10
☐ 9 Mac Percival / 10 John Brodie	25.00	11.00	3.10
☐ 11 Lem Barney / 12 Ron Yary	25.00	11.00	3.10
☐ 13 Curt Knight / 14 Alvin Haymond	20.00	9.00	2.50
☐ 15 Floyd Little / 16 Gerry Philbin	25.00	11.00	3.10
☐ 17 Jim Mitchell / 18 Paul Costa	20.00	9.00	2.50
☐ 19 Jake Kupp / 20 Ben Hawkins	20.00	9.00	2.50
☐ 21 Johnny Robinson / 22 George Webster	20.00	9.00	2.50
☐ 23 Mercury Morris / 24 Willie Brown	40.00	18.00	5.00
☐ 25 Ron Johnson / 26 Jon Morris	20.00	9.00	2.50
☐ NNO Yellow Viewer	40.00	18.00	5.00

1992 Chris Martin Dog Tags

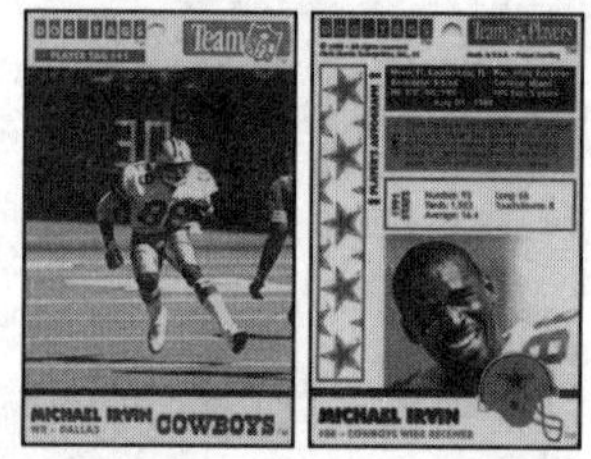

Produced by Chris Martin Enterprises, Inc., this boxed set consists of 81 dog tags. Made of durable plastic, each tag measures approximately 2 1/8" by 3 3/8" and, with its rounded corners, resembles a credit card. All the tags are bordered on each end by white stripes, and in the top stripe, a hole was bore through so that it could be worn on a chain. The team tags are horizontally oriented and display a picture of the team's stadium on their fronts. The backs present a variety of information, including individual career record holders and pictures of the team's uniform, logo, and helmet. The regular player tags have a color action player photo on their fronts. The backs have biography, 1991 season summary, 1991 statistics, color head shot, and autograph slot. The rookie tags are identical to the regular player tags, except that their top border stripe is gold foil; they are distinguished in the checklist below by an R prefix which is not present on the cards themselves. The set subdivides into three groups: team tags (1-28), regular player tags (29-76), and rookie tags (R1-R5). The cards are numbered on both sides. Tag number 42 (Emmitt Smith) was also issued as a promo, stamped "PROMO TAG" on its back. Also produced was a Chris Martin dog tag that was personally autographed.

	MINT	NRMT	EXC
COMPLETE SET (81)	80.00	36.00	10.00
COMMON TEAM (1-28)	.50	.23	.06
COMMON CARD (29-76)	.75	.35	.09
COMMON ROOKIE (R1-R5)	1.00	.45	.12
☐ 1 Atlanta Falcons	.50	.23	.06
☐ 2 Buffalo Bills	.50	.23	.06
☐ 3 Chicago Bears	.50	.23	.06
☐ 4 Cincinnati Bengals	.50	.23	.06
☐ 5 Cleveland Browns	.50	.23	.06
☐ 6 Dallas Cowboys	.75	.35	.09
☐ 7 Denver Broncos	.50	.23	.06
☐ 8 Detroit Lions	.50	.23	.06
☐ 9 Green Bay Packers	.50	.23	.06
☐ 10 Houston Oilers	.50	.23	.06
☐ 11 Indianapolis Colts	.50	.23	.06
☐ 12 Kansas City Chiefs	.50	.23	.06
☐ 13 Los Angeles Raiders	.75	.35	.09
☐ 14 Los Angeles Rams	.50	.23	.06
☐ 15 Miami Dolphins	.75	.35	.09
☐ 16 Minnesota Vikings	.50	.23	.06
☐ 17 New England Patriots	.50	.23	.06
☐ 18 New Orleans Saints	.50	.23	.06
☐ 19 New York Giants	.50	.23	.06
☐ 20 New York Jets	.50	.23	.06
☐ 21 Philadelphia Eagles	.50	.23	.06
☐ 22 Phoenix Cardinals	.50	.23	.06
☐ 23 Pittsburgh Steelers	.50	.23	.06
☐ 24 San Diego Chargers	.50	.23	.06
☐ 25 San Francisco 49ers	.50	.23	.06
☐ 26 Seattle Seahawks	.50	.23	.06
☐ 27 Tampa Bay Buccaneers	.50	.23	.06
☐ 28 Washington Redskins	.50	.23	.06
☐ 29 Chris Martin	.75	.35	.09
☐ 30 Dan Marino	8.00	3.60	1.00
☐ 31 Chris Miller	1.00	.45	.12
☐ 32 Deion Sanders	3.00	1.35	.35
☐ 33 Jim Kelly	1.50	.70	.19
☐ 34 Thurman Thomas	2.00	.90	.25
☐ 35 Jim Harbaugh	1.25	.55	.16
☐ 36 Mike Singletary	1.00	.45	.12
☐ 37 Boomer Esiason	1.00	.45	.12
☐ 38 Anthony Munoz	1.25	.55	.16
☐ 39 Bernie Kosar	1.00	.45	.12
☐ 40 Troy Aikman	5.00	2.20	.60
☐ 41 Michael Irvin	2.00	.90	.25
☐ 42 Emmitt Smith	8.00	3.60	1.00
☐ 43 John Elway	4.00	1.80	.50
☐ 44 Rodney Peete	1.00	.45	.12
☐ 45 Sterling Sharpe	1.25	.55	.16
☐ 46 Haywood Jeffires	1.00	.45	.12
☐ 47 Warren Moon	1.50	.70	.19
☐ 48 Jeff George	1.50	.70	.19
☐ 49 Christian Okoye	1.00	.45	.12
☐ 50 Derrick Thomas	1.50	.70	.19
☐ 51 Howie Long	1.00	.45	.12
☐ 52 Ronnie Lott	1.00	.45	.12
☐ 53 Jim Everett	1.00	.45	.12
☐ 54 Mark Clayton	1.00	.45	.12
☐ 55 Anthony Carter	1.00	.45	.12
☐ 56 Chris Doleman	1.00	.45	.12
☐ 57 Andre Tippett	.75	.35	.09
☐ 58 Pat Swilling	1.00	.45	.12
☐ 59 Jeff Hostetler	1.00	.45	.12
☐ 60 Lawrence Taylor	1.50	.70	.19
☐ 61 Rob Moore	1.00	.45	.12
☐ 62 Ken O'Brien	.75	.35	.09
☐ 63 Keith Byars	.75	.35	.09
☐ 64 Randall Cunningham	1.00	.45	.12
☐ 65 Johnny Johnson	.50	.23	.06
☐ 66 Timm Rosenbach	.75	.35	.09
☐ 67 Bubby Brister	1.00	.45	.12
☐ 68 John Friesz	1.00	.45	.12
☐ 69 Jerry Rice	5.00	2.20	.60
☐ 70 Steve Young	4.00	1.80	.50
☐ 71 Dan McGwire	.75	.35	.09
☐ 72 Broderick Thomas	.75	.35	.09
☐ 73 Vinny Testaverde	1.00	.45	.12
☐ 74 Gary Clark	1.00	.45	.12
☐ 75 Mark Rypien	1.00	.45	.12
☐ 76 Neil Smith	1.25	.55	.16
☐ P1 Chris Martin Promo	2.00	.90	.25
☐ P2 Emmitt Smith Promo	8.00	3.60	1.00
☐ R1 Dale Carter	1.00	.45	.12
☐ R2 Steve Emtman	1.00	.45	.12
☐ R3 David Klingler	1.00	.45	.12
☐ R4 Tommy Maddox	1.00	.45	.12
☐ R5 Vaughn Dunbar	1.00	.45	.12
☐ 29AU Chris Martin AUTO signed card	10.00	4.50	1.25

1993 Chris Martin Dog Tags

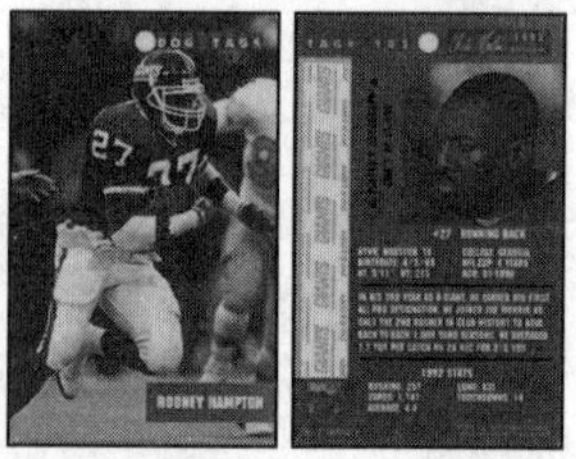

Produced by Chris Martin Enterprises, Inc., this set of "Dog Tags Plus" consists of 110 individual player tags and 28 team tags. Two tags, numbers 48 and 138, were not produced. The dog tags were originally distributed in random assortments but later as complete team sets. The only two teams not included in the team set packaging were the Atlanta Falcons and the Los Angeles Raiders. There were also 25,000 sequentially numbered Joe Montana limited edition bonus tags. The collector could obtain one of these Montana tags through a mail-in offer for 5.00 and three proofs of purchase. Reportedly 50,000 of each tag were produced, with each one sequentially numbered. Autographed tags were randomly inserted throughout the cases. The players with randomly-inserted autograph tags were Dale Carter, Chris Martin, Emmitt Smith, and Harvey Williams. Also collectors could enter a contest to win a seven-point diamond tag and a 14K gold bead chain. Made of durable plastic, each tag measures approximately 2 1/8" by 3 3/8" and, with its rounded corners, resembles a credit card. The player tags show a full-bleed action photo on their fronts. The year "1993" and the word "Plus" are gold foil stamped at the top, while the player's name appears on a short bar toward the bottom. On a team color-coded background, the backs have a color close-up photo, biography, player profile, 1992 stats, and an autograph slot. After team logo tags (1-28), the set is arranged alphabetically within teams.

	MINT	NRMT	EXC
COMPLETE SET (138)	125.00	55.00	15.50
COMMON TEAM (1-28)	.50	.23	.06
COMMON CARD (29-140)	.75	.35	.09
☐ 1 Atlanta Falcons	.50	.23	.06
☐ 2 Buffalo Bills	.50	.23	.06
☐ 3 Chicago Bears	.50	.23	.06
☐ 4 Cincinnati Bengals	.50	.23	.06
☐ 5 Cleveland Browns	.50	.23	.06
☐ 6 Dallas Cowboys	.75	.35	.09
☐ 7 Denver Broncos	.50	.23	.06

☐ 8 Detroit Lions	.50	.23	.06
☐ 9 Green Bay Packers	.50	.23	.06
☐ 10 Houston Oilers	.50	.23	.06
☐ 11 Indianapolis Colts	.50	.23	.06
☐ 12 Kansas City Chiefs	.50	.23	.06
☐ 13 Los Angeles Raiders	.75	.35	.09
☐ 14 Los Angeles Rams	.50	.23	.06
☐ 15 Miami Dolphins	.75	.35	.09
☐ 16 Minnesota Vikings	.50	.23	.06
☐ 17 New England Patriots	.50	.23	.06
☐ 18 New Orleans Saints	.50	.23	.06
☐ 19 New York Giants	.50	.23	.06
☐ 20 New York Jets	.50	.23	.06
☐ 21 Philadelphia Eagles	.50	.23	.06
☐ 22 Phoenix Cardinals	.50	.23	.06
☐ 23 Pittsburgh Steelers	.50	.23	.06
☐ 24 San Diego Chargers	.50	.23	.06
☐ 25 San Francisco 49ers	.50	.23	.06
☐ 26 Seattle Seahawks	.50	.23	.06
☐ 27 Tampa Bay Buccaneers	.50	.23	.06
☐ 28 Washington Redskins	.50	.23	.06
☐ 29 Steve Broussard	.75	.35	.09
☐ 30 Chris Miller	.75	.35	.09
☐ 31 Andre Rison	1.50	.70	.19
☐ 32 Deion Sanders	2.50	1.10	.30
☐ 33 Cornelius Bennett	1.00	.45	.12
☐ 34 Jim Kelly	1.50	.70	.19
☐ 35 Bruce Smith	1.50	.70	.19
☐ 36 Thurman Thomas	1.50	.70	.19
☐ 37 Neal Anderson	.75	.35	.09
☐ 38 Mark Carrier DB	.75	.35	.09
☐ 39 Jim Harbaugh	1.50	.70	.19
☐ 40 Alonzo Spellman	.75	.35	.09
☐ 41 David Fulcher	.75	.35	.09
☐ 42 Harold Green	.75	.35	.09
☐ 43 David Klingler	.75	.35	.09
☐ 44 Carl Pickens	3.50	1.55	.45
☐ 45 Bernie Kosar	.75	.35	.09
☐ 46 Clay Matthews	1.00	.45	.12
☐ 47 Eric Metcalf	1.00	.45	.12
☐ 49 Troy Aikman	4.00	1.80	.50
☐ 50 Michael Irvin	1.50	.70	.19
☐ 51 Russell Maryland	1.00	.45	.12
☐ 52 Emmitt Smith	7.00	3.10	.85
☐ 53 Steve Atwater	.75	.35	.09
☐ 54 John Elway	3.00	1.35	.35
☐ 55 Tommy Maddox	.75	.35	.09
☐ 56 Shannon Sharpe	1.50	.70	.19
☐ 57 Herman Moore	1.50	.70	.19
☐ 58 Rodney Peete	1.00	.45	.12
☐ 59 Barry Sanders	4.00	1.80	.50
☐ 60 Andre Ware	1.00	.45	.12
☐ 61 Terrell Buckley	.75	.35	.09
☐ 62 Brett Favre	7.00	3.10	.85
☐ 63 Sterling Sharpe	1.00	.45	.12
☐ 64 Reggie White	1.50	.70	.19
☐ 65 Ray Childress	1.00	.45	.12
☐ 66 Haywood Jeffires	1.00	.45	.12
☐ 67 Warren Moon	1.50	.70	.19
☐ 68 Lorenzo White	.75	.35	.09
☐ 69 Duane Bickett	.75	.35	.09
☐ 70 Quentin Coryatt	1.00	.45	.12
☐ 71 Steve Emtman	.75	.35	.09
☐ 72 Jeff George	1.50	.70	.19
☐ 73 Dale Carter	1.00	.45	.12
☐ 74 Neil Smith	1.00	.45	.12
☐ 75 Derrick Thomas	1.50	.70	.19
☐ 76 Harvey Williams	1.00	.45	.12
☐ 77 Eric Dickerson	1.00	.45	.12
☐ 78 Howie Long	1.00	.45	.12
☐ 79 Todd Marinovich	.75	.35	.09
☐ 80 Alexander Wright	.75	.35	.09
☐ 81 Flipper Anderson	.75	.35	.09
☐ 82 Jim Everett	.75	.35	.09
☐ 83 Cleveland Gary	.75	.35	.09
☐ 84 Chris Martin	.75	.35	.09
☐ 85 Irving Fryar	1.00	.45	.12
☐ 86 Keith Jackson	1.00	.45	.12
☐ 87 Dan Marino	7.00	3.10	.85
☐ 88 Louis Oliver	.75	.35	.09
☐ 89 Terry Allen	1.50	.70	.19
☐ 90 Anthony Carter	1.00	.45	.12
☐ 91 Chris Doleman	1.00	.45	.12
☐ 92 Rich Gannon	.75	.35	.09
☐ 93 Eugene Chung	.75	.35	.09
☐ 94 Marv Cook	.75	.35	.09
☐ 95 Leonard Russell	1.00	.45	.12
☐ 96 Andre Tippett	.75	.35	.09
☐ 97 Morten Andersen	.75	.35	.09
☐ 98 Vaughn Dunbar	.75	.35	.09
☐ 99 Rickey Jackson	.75	.35	.09
☐ 100 Sam Mills	.75	.35	.09
☐ 101 Derek Brown TE	.75	.35	.09
☐ 102 Lawrence Taylor	1.50	.70	.19
☐ 103 Rodney Hampton	1.00	.45	.12
☐ 104 Phil Simms	1.00	.45	.12
☐ 105 Johnny Mitchell	1.00	.45	.12
☐ 106 Rob Moore	1.00	.45	.12
☐ 107 Blair Thomas	.75	.35	.09
☐ 108 Browning Nagle	.75	.35	.09
☐ 109 Eric Allen	.75	.35	.09
☐ 110 Fred Barnett	1.00	.45	.12
☐ 111 Randall Cunningham	1.00	.45	.12
☐ 112 Herschel Walker	1.00	.45	.12
☐ 113 Chris Chandler	1.00	.45	.12
☐ 114 Randal Hill	.75	.35	.09
☐ 115 Ricky Proehl	.75	.35	.09
☐ 116 Eric Swann	1.00	.45	.12
☐ 117 Barry Foster	1.00	.45	.12
☐ 118 Eric Green	.75	.35	.09
☐ 119 Neil O'Donnell	1.00	.45	.12
☐ 120 Rod Woodson	1.00	.45	.12
☐ 121 Marion Butts	1.00	.45	.12
☐ 122 Stan Humphries	1.00	.45	.12
☐ 123 Anthony Miller	1.00	.45	.12
☐ 124 Junior Seau	1.50	.70	.19
☐ 125 Amp Lee	.75	.35	.09
☐ 126 Jerry Rice	4.00	1.80	.50
☐ 127 Ricky Watters	1.50	.70	.19
☐ 128 Steve Young	3.00	1.35	.35
☐ 129 Brian Blades	1.00	.45	.12
☐ 130 Cortez Kennedy	1.00	.45	.12
☐ 131 Dan McGwire	.75	.35	.09
☐ 132 John L. Williams	.75	.35	.09
☐ 133 Reggie Cobb	.75	.35	.09
☐ 134 Steve DeBerg	1.00	.45	.12
☐ 135 Keith McCants	.75	.35	.09
☐ 136 Broderick Thomas	.75	.35	.09
☐ 137 Earnest Byner	.75	.35	.09
☐ 139 Mark Rypien	.75	.35	.09
☐ 140 Ricky Sanders	.75	.35	.09
☐ B1 Joe Montana Bonus numbered of 25,000	5.00	2.20	.60
☐ P1 Chris Martin Promo	.50	.23	.06

1994 Chris Martin Pro Mags

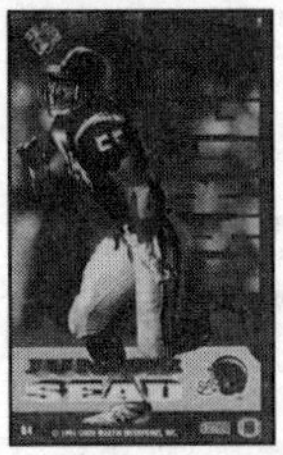

These magnets measure approximately 2 1/8" by 3 3/8" and have rounded corners. They were sold in five-magnet packs that included a free team magnet, measuring 2 1/8" by 3/4" and a checklist of all 140 players. Collectors could receive a special Warren Moon magnet by mailing in a redemption card that was included in every pack, three proofs of purchase, and 6.00. The fronts display borderless color action player photos. The player's last name in big letters appears along the right side. His first name in team color-coded letters is printed on the bottom, with the team logo next to it. There was a parallel set issued for Super Bowl XXIX, this set is valued at the same price as the regular set. The magnets are numbered on the front, grouped alphabetically within teams, and checklisted below according to teams. The team magnets are unnumbered and are checklisted below in alphabetical order with a "T" prefix. Troy Aikman and Chris Martin promo magnets were produced and are listed below. An oversized Warren Moon artist's rendering magnet was randomly inserted in boxes.

	MINT	NRMT	EXC
COMPLETE SET (168)	125.00	55.00	15.50
COMMON CARD (1-140)	.60	.25	.07
COMMON TEAM (T1-T28)	.35	.16	.04

☐ 1 Rod Bernstine	.60	.25	.07
☐ 2 John Elway	2.50	1.10	.30
☐ 3 Glyn Milburn	1.00	.45	.12
☐ 4 Shannon Sharpe	1.00	.45	.12
☐ 5 Dennis Smith	.60	.25	.07
☐ 6 Cody Carlson	.60	.25	.07
☐ 7 Ernest Givins	1.00	.45	.12
☐ 8 Haywood Jeffires	1.00	.45	.12
☐ 9 Bruce Matthews	.60	.25	.07
☐ 10 Webster Slaughter	.60	.25	.07
☐ 11 O.J. McDuffie	1.00	.45	.12
☐ 12 Keith Byars	.60	.25	.07
☐ 13 Bryan Cox	.60	.25	.07
☐ 14 Irving Fryar	1.00	.45	.12
☐ 15 Dan Marino	5.00	2.20	.60
☐ 16 Barry Foster	.60	.25	.07
☐ 17 Kevin Greene	1.50	.70	.19
☐ 18 Greg Lloyd	1.50	.70	.19
☐ 19 Neil O'Donnell	1.00	.45	.12
☐ 20 Rod Woodson	1.50	.70	.19
☐ 21 Steve Beuerlein	.60	.25	.07
☐ 22 Chuck Cecil	.60	.25	.07
☐ 23 Randal Hill	.60	.25	.07
☐ 24 Ricky Proehl	.60	.25	.07
☐ 25 Eric Swann	1.00	.45	.12
☐ 26 Troy Aikman	3.00	1.35	.35
☐ 27 Emmitt Smith	5.00	2.20	.60
☐ 28 Michael Irvin	1.50	.70	.19
☐ 29 Russell Maryland	1.00	.45	.12
☐ 30 Jay Novacek	1.00	.45	.12
☐ 31 Jerome Bettis	2.00	.90	.25
☐ 32 Sean Gilbert	.60	.25	.07
☐ 33 Todd Lyght	.60	.25	.07
☐ 34 Chris Martin	.60	.25	.07
☐ 35 Roman Phifer	.60	.25	.07
☐ 36 Neal Anderson	.60	.25	.07
☐ 37 Quinn Early	.60	.25	.07
☐ 38 Rickey Jackson	.60	.25	.07
☐ 39 Sam Mills	.60	.25	.07
☐ 40 Willie Roaf	.60	.25	.07
☐ 41 Cornelius Bennett	1.00	.45	.12
☐ 42 Jim Kelly	1.50	.70	.19
☐ 43 Kenneth Davis	.60	.25	.07
☐ 44 Darryl Talley	.60	.25	.07
☐ 45 Andre Reed	1.00	.45	.12
☐ 46 Cris Carter	1.50	.70	.19
☐ 47 Warren Moon	1.50	.70	.19
☐ 48 Terry Allen	1.00	.45	.12
☐ 49 Qadry Ismail	1.00	.45	.12
☐ 50 Robert Smith	1.50	.70	.19
☐ 51 Erric Pegram	1.00	.45	.12
☐ 52 Andre Rison	1.50	.70	.19
☐ 53 Deion Sanders	2.00	.90	.25
☐ 54 Jessie Tuggle	.60	.25	.07
☐ 55 Jeff George	1.50	.70	.19
☐ 56 Brian Blades	1.00	.45	.12
☐ 57 Rick Mirer	1.50	.70	.19
☐ 58 Cortez Kennedy	1.00	.45	.12
☐ 59 Chris Warren	1.50	.70	.19
☐ 60 Eugene Robinson	.60	.25	.07
☐ 61 Reggie Brooks	.60	.25	.07
☐ 62 Ricky Ervins	.60	.25	.07
☐ 63 Brian Mitchell	.60	.25	.07
☐ 64 Ricky Sanders	.60	.25	.07
☐ 65 Sterling Palmer	.60	.25	.07
☐ 66 Tim Brown	1.50	.70	.19
☐ 67 Jeff Hostetler	1.00	.45	.12
☐ 68 Rocket Ismail	1.00	.45	.12
☐ 69 Terry McDaniel	.60	.25	.07
☐ 70 James Jett	.60	.25	.07
☐ 71 Sterling Sharpe	1.00	.45	.12
☐ 72 Brett Favre	5.00	2.20	.60
☐ 73 Reggie White	1.50	.70	.19
☐ 74 Terrell Buckley	.60	.25	.07
☐ 75 Edgar Bennett	1.50	.70	.19
☐ 76 Jerry Rice	3.00	1.35	.35
☐ 77 Steve Young	2.50	1.10	.30
☐ 78 Ricky Watters	1.50	.70	.19
☐ 79 Dana Stubblefield	1.50	.70	.19
☐ 80 John Taylor	1.00	.45	.12
☐ 81 Ronnie Harmon	1.00	.45	.12
☐ 82 Stan Humphries	1.00	.45	.12
☐ 83 Natrone Means	1.50	.70	.19
☐ 84 Junior Seau	1.50	.70	.19
☐ 85 Eric Bieniemy	.60	.25	.07
☐ 86 Dean Biasucci	.60	.25	.07
☐ 87 Jim Harbaugh	1.50	.70	.19
☐ 88 Roosevelt Potts	.60	.25	.07
☐ 89 Scott Radecic	.60	.25	.07
☐ 90 Rohn Stark	.60	.25	.07
☐ 91 Eric Metcalf	1.00	.45	.12
☐ 92 Michael Dean Perry	1.00	.45	.12
☐ 93 Vinny Testaverde	1.00	.45	.12
☐ 94 Mark Carrier WR	.60	.25	.07
☐ 95 Michael Jackson	1.00	.45	.12
☐ 96 Marcus Allen	1.50	.70	.19
☐ 97 Dale Carter	.60	.25	.07
☐ 98 Neil Smith	1.00	.45	.12
☐ 99 J.J. Birden	.60	.25	.07
☐ 100 Willie Davis	1.00	.45	.12
☐ 101 Rodney Hampton	1.00	.45	.12
☐ 102 Mark Jackson	.60	.25	.07
☐ 103 Dave Meggett	.60	.25	.07
☐ 104 Jumbo Elliott	.60	.25	.07
☐ 105 Kenyon Rasheed	.60	.25	.07
☐ 106 Boomer Esiason	1.00	.45	.12
☐ 107 Johnny Johnson	.60	.25	.07
☐ 108 Johnny Mitchell	.60	.25	.07
☐ 109 Brad Baxter	.60	.25	.07
☐ 110 Ronnie Lott	1.00	.45	.12
☐ 111 Derrick Fenner	.60	.25	.07
☐ 112 David Klingler	.60	.25	.07
☐ 113 Bruce Pickens	.60	.25	.07
☐ 114 Harold Green	.60	.25	.07
☐ 115 Jeff Query	.60	.25	.07
☐ 116 Leonard Russell	.60	.25	.07
☐ 117 Drew Bledsoe	3.00	1.35	.35
☐ 118 Marv Cook	.60	.25	.07
☐ 119 Vincent Brisby	1.50	.70	.19
☐ 120 Vincent Brown	.60	.25	.07
☐ 121 Trace Armstrong	.60	.25	.07
☐ 122 Curtis Conway	1.50	.70	.19
☐ 123 Dante Jones	.60	.25	.07
☐ 124 Tim Worley	.60	.25	.07
☐ 125 Chris Zorich	1.00	.45	.12
☐ 126 Ronald Moore	.60	.25	.07
☐ 127 Barry Sanders	3.00	1.35	.35
☐ 128 Pat Swilling	1.00	.45	.12
☐ 129 Brett Perriman	1.00	.45	.12
☐ 130 Chris Spielman	1.00	.45	.12
☐ 131 Keith Byars	.60	.25	.07
☐ 132 Fred Barnett	1.00	.45	.12
☐ 133 Randall Cunningham	1.00	.45	.12
☐ 134 Herschel Walker	1.00	.45	.12
☐ 135 Bubby Brister	.60	.25	.07
☐ 136 Craig Erickson	.60	.25	.07
☐ 137 Hardy Nickerson	1.00	.45	.12
☐ 138 Demetrius DuBose	.60	.25	.07
☐ 139 Dan Stryzinski	.60	.25	.07
☐ 140 Charles Wilson	.60	.25	.07
☐ T1 Arizona Cardinals	.35	.16	.04
☐ T2 Atlanta Falcons	.35	.16	.04
☐ T3 Buffalo Bills	.50	.23	.06
☐ T4 Chicago Bears	.50	.23	.06
☐ T5 Cincinnati Bengals	.35	.16	.04
☐ T6 Cleveland Browns	.50	.23	.06
☐ T7 Dallas Cowboys	.50	.23	.06
☐ T8 Denver Broncos	.50	.23	.06
☐ T9 Detroit Lions	.35	.16	.04
☐ T10 Green Bay Packers	.50	.23	.06
☐ T11 Houston Oilers	.35	.16	.04
☐ T12 Indianapolis Colts	.35	.16	.04
☐ T13 Kansas City Chiefs	.50	.23	.06
☐ T14 Los Angeles Raiders	.50	.23	.06
☐ T15 Los Angeles Rams	.35	.16	.04
☐ T16 Miami Dolphins	.50	.23	.06
☐ T17 Minnesota Vikings	.50	.23	.06
☐ T18 New England Patriots	.35	.16	.04
☐ T19 New Orleans Saints	.35	.16	.04
☐ T20 New York Giants	.50	.23	.06
☐ T21 New York Jets	.50	.23	.06
☐ T22 Philadelphia Eagles	.35	.16	.04
☐ T23 Pittsburgh Steelers	.50	.23	.06
☐ T24 San Diego Chargers	.35	.16	.04
☐ T25 San Francisco 49ers	.50	.23	.06
☐ T26 Seattle Seahawks	.35	.16	.04
☐ T27 Tampa Bay Buccaneers	.35	.16	.04
☐ T28 Washington Redskins	.50	.23	.06
☐ P1 Chris Martin Promo	2.00	.90	.25
☐ P2 Troy Aikman Promo	4.00	1.80	.50
☐ NNO Warren Moon 3 3/4" by 7" Bonus Magnet	10.00	4.50	1.25

1994 Chris Martin Pro Tags

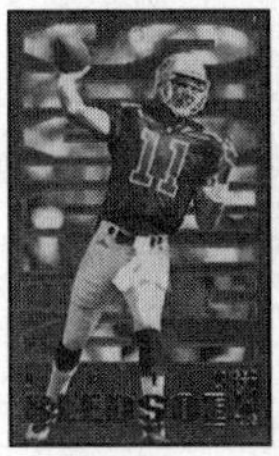

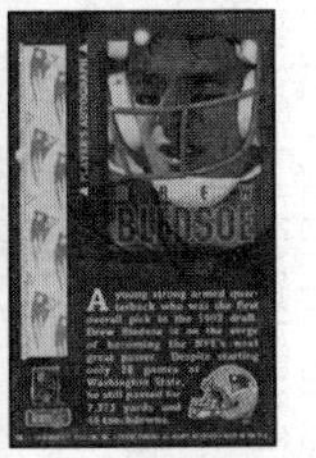

This set of 168 Pro Tags marks the third consecutive year that Chris Martin Enterprises, Inc. has issued this line of sports collectibles. This first two sets were called Dog Tags. Measuring approximately 2 1/8" by 3 3/8", the plastic tags were sold six to a blister pack. A checklist card (printed on glossy paper) and a free team tag were included in each blister pack. Pro tags autographed by Jerome Bettis, J.J. Birden, Dale Carter, Keith Cash, Willie Davis, Sean Gilbert, Todd Lyght, Chris Martin, Roman Phifer, and Neil Smith were randomly seeded in packs. The set included an offer to receive 6 AFC or 6 NFC Super Rookie Pro Tags at 10.99 and 3 Proofs-of-Purchase for each set, or all 12 Pro Tags for 15.99 and 5 Proofs-of-Purchase. A parallel set was issued for Super Bowl XXIX, this set is valued the same as the regular issue. On a team color-coded background, the fronts feature a color player cutout superposed on the team name printed vertically in oversized block lettering. The player's name is gold foil-stamped across the bottom. The backs carry color closeup photo, autograph strip, and player profile. The Pro Tags are grouped alphabetically within teams and checklisted below alphabetically according to teams.

	MINT	NRMT	EXC
COMPLETE SET (168)	125.00	55.00	15.50
COMMON CARD (1-168)	.60	.25	.07

☐ 1 Steve Beuerlein	.60	.25	.07
☐ 2 Chuck Cecil	.60	.25	.07
☐ 3 Randal Hill	.60	.25	.07
☐ 4 Garrison Hearst	.60	.25	.07
☐ 5 Ricky Proehl	.60	.25	.07
☐ 6 Eric Swann	1.00	.45	.12
☐ 7 Jeff George	1.25	.55	.16
☐ 8 Drew Hill	.60	.25	.07
☐ 9 Erric Pegram	1.00	.45	.12
☐ 10 Andre Rison	1.25	.55	.16
☐ 11 Deion Sanders	1.50	.70	.19
☐ 12 Jessie Tuggle	.60	.25	.07
☐ 13 Cornelius Bennett	1.00	.45	.12
☐ 14 Kenneth Davis	.60	.25	.07
☐ 15 Jim Kelly	1.25	.55	.16
☐ 16 Andre Reed	1.00	.45	.12
☐ 17 Darryl Talley	.60	.25	.07
☐ 18 Steve Tasker	1.00	.45	.12
☐ 19 Trace Armstrong	.60	.25	.07
☐ 20 Curtis Conway	1.25	.55	.16
☐ 21 Dante Jones	.60	.25	.07
☐ 22 Donnell Woolford	.60	.25	.07
☐ 23 Tim Worley	.60	.25	.07
☐ 24 Chris Zorich	1.00	.45	.12
☐ 25 Derrick Fenner	.60	.25	.07
☐ 26 Harold Green	.60	.25	.07
☐ 27 David Klingler	.60	.25	.07
☐ 28 Tony McGee	.60	.25	.07
☐ 29 Carl Pickens	1.25	.55	.16
☐ 30 Jeff Query	.60	.25	.07
☐ 31 Mark Carrier WR	1.00	.45	.12
☐ 32 Michael Jackson	1.00	.45	.12
☐ 33 Eric Metcalf	1.00	.45	.12
☐ 34 Michael Dean Perry	1.00	.45	.12
☐ 35 Vinny Testaverde	1.00	.45	.12

☐ 36 Tommy Vardell	.60	.25	.07
☐ 37 Troy Aikman	3.00	1.35	.35
☐ 38 Alvin Harper	.60	.25	.07
☐ 39 Michael Irvin	1.25	.55	.16
☐ 40 Russell Maryland	1.00	.45	.12
☐ 41 Jay Novacek	1.25	.55	.16
☐ 42 Emmitt Smith	5.00	2.20	.60
☐ 43 Rod Bernstine	.60	.25	.07
☐ 44 Mike Croel	.60	.25	.07
☐ 45 John Elway	2.50	1.10	.30
☐ 46 Glyn Milburn	1.25	.55	.16
☐ 47 Shannon Sharpe	1.25	.55	.16
☐ 48 Dennis Smith	.60	.25	.07
☐ 49 Jason Hanson	.60	.25	.07
☐ 50 Herman Moore	1.25	.55	.16
☐ 51 Brett Perriman	1.00	.45	.12
☐ 52 Barry Sanders	3.00	1.35	.35
☐ 53 Chris Spielman	1.00	.45	.12
☐ 54 Pat Swilling	1.00	.45	.12
☐ 55 Edgar Bennett	1.00	.45	.12
☐ 56 Terrell Buckley	.60	.25	.07
☐ 57 Brett Favre	5.00	2.20	.60
☐ 58 Chris Jacke	.60	.25	.07
☐ 59 Sterling Sharpe	1.00	.45	.12
☐ 60 Reggie White	1.25	.55	.16
☐ 61 Gary Brown	.60	.25	.07
☐ 62 Cody Carlson	.60	.25	.07
☐ 63 Ernest Givins	.60	.25	.07
☐ 64 Haywood Jeffires	1.00	.45	.12
☐ 65 Bruce Matthews	.60	.25	.07
☐ 66 Webster Slaughter	.60	.25	.07
☐ 67 Jason Belser	.60	.25	.07
☐ 68 Roosevelt Potts	.60	.25	.07
☐ 69 Rodney Culver	.60	.25	.07
☐ 70 Jim Harbaugh	1.25	.55	.16
☐ 71 Scott Radecic	.60	.25	.07
☐ 72 Kerry Cash	.60	.25	.07
☐ 73 Marcus Allen	1.25	.55	.16
☐ 74 J.J. Birden	.60	.25	.07
☐ 75 Dale Carter	.60	.25	.07
☐ 76 Keith Cash	.60	.25	.07
☐ 77 Willie Davis	1.00	.45	.12
☐ 78 Neil Smith	1.25	.55	.16
☐ 79 Eddie Anderson	.60	.25	.07
☐ 80 Tim Brown	1.25	.55	.16
☐ 81 Jeff Hostetler	1.00	.45	.12
☐ 82 Rocket Ismail	1.00	.45	.12
☐ 83 James Jett	.60	.25	.07
☐ 84 Terry McDaniel	.60	.25	.07
☐ 85 Flipper Anderson	.60	.25	.07
☐ 86 Jerome Bettis	1.50	.70	.19
☐ 87 Troy Drayton	1.00	.45	.12
☐ 88 Sean Gilbert	.60	.25	.07
☐ 89 Todd Lyght	.60	.25	.07
☐ 90 Chris Martin	.60	.25	.07
☐ 91 Keith Byars	.60	.25	.07
☐ 92 Bryan Cox	.60	.25	.07
☐ 93 Irving Fryar	1.00	.45	.12
☐ 94 Terry Kirby	1.00	.45	.12
☐ 95 Dan Marino	5.00	2.20	.60
☐ 96 O.J. McDuffie	1.25	.55	.16
☐ 97 Terry Allen	1.25	.55	.16
☐ 98 Cris Carter	1.25	.55	.16
☐ 99 Qadry Ismail	1.00	.45	.12
☐ 100 Randall McDaniel	.60	.25	.07
☐ 101 Warren Moon	1.25	.55	.16
☐ 102 Robert Smith	1.25	.55	.16
☐ 103 Drew Bledsoe	3.00	1.35	.35
☐ 104 Vincent Brisby	1.00	.45	.12
☐ 105 Vincent Brown	.60	.25	.07
☐ 106 Marv Cook	.60	.25	.07
☐ 107 Leonard Russell	.60	.25	.07
☐ 108 Reyna Thompson	.60	.25	.07
☐ 109 Morten Andersen	.60	.25	.07
☐ 110 Quinn Early	.60	.25	.07
☐ 111 Tyrone Hughes	.60	.25	.07
☐ 112 Sam Mills	.60	.25	.07
☐ 113 Willie Roaf	.60	.25	.07
☐ 114 Renaldo Turnbull	.60	.25	.07
☐ 115 Stephen Baker	.60	.25	.07
☐ 116 John Elliott	.60	.25	.07
☐ 117 Rodney Hampton	1.25	.55	.16
☐ 118 Mark Jackson	.60	.25	.07
☐ 119 Dave Meggett	.60	.25	.07
☐ 120 Kenyon Rasheed	.60	.25	.07
☐ 121 Brad Baxter	.60	.25	.07
☐ 122 Boomer Esiason	1.00	.45	.12
☐ 123 Johnny Johnson	.60	.25	.07
☐ 124 Ronnie Lott	1.00	.45	.12
☐ 125 Johnny Mitchell	.60	.25	.07
☐ 126 Rob Moore	1.00	.45	.12
☐ 127 Fred Barnett	1.00	.45	.12
☐ 128 Mark Bavaro	.60	.25	.07
☐ 129 Bubby Brister	.60	.25	.07
☐ 130 Randall Cunningham	1.00	.45	.12
☐ 131 Tim Harris	.60	.25	.07
☐ 132 Herschel Walker	1.00	.45	.12
☐ 133 Gary Anderson K	.60	.25	.07
☐ 134 Barry Foster	.60	.25	.07
☐ 135 Kevin Greene	1.00	.45	.12
☐ 136 Greg Lloyd	1.25	.55	.16
☐ 137 Neil O'Donnell	1.25	.55	.16
☐ 138 Rod Woodson	1.25	.55	.16
☐ 139 Eric Bieniemy	.60	.25	.07
☐ 140 Ronnie Harmon	1.00	.45	.12
☐ 141 Stan Humphries	1.00	.45	.12
☐ 142 Natrone Means	1.25	.55	.16
☐ 143 Leslie O'Neal	1.00	.45	.12
☐ 144 Junior Seau	1.25	.55	.16
☐ 145 Tim McDonald	.60	.25	.07
☐ 146 Jerry Rice	3.00	1.35	.35
☐ 147 Dana Stubblefield	1.00	.45	.12
☐ 148 John Taylor	1.00	.45	.12
☐ 149 Ricky Watters UER (Card misnumbered 147)	1.25	.55	.16
☐ 150 Steve Young	2.50	1.10	.30
☐ 151 Brian Blades	1.00	.45	.12
☐ 152 Cortez Kennedy	1.00	.45	.12
☐ 153 Rick Mirer	1.25	.55	.16
☐ 154 Rufus Porter	.60	.25	.07
☐ 155 Eugene Robinson	.60	.25	.07
☐ 156 Chris Warren	1.00	.45	.12
☐ 157 Santana Dotson	1.00	.45	.12
☐ 158 Craig Erickson	.60	.25	.07
☐ 159 Hardy Nickerson	1.00	.45	.12
☐ 160 Dan Stryzinski	.60	.25	.07
☐ 161 Charles Wilson	.60	.25	.07
☐ 162 Thomas Everett	.60	.25	.07
☐ 163 Reggie Brooks	.60	.25	.07
☐ 164 Darrell Green	.60	.25	.07
☐ 165 Ricky Ervins	.60	.25	.07
☐ 166 John Friesz	1.00	.45	.12
☐ 167 Brian Mitchell	1.00	.45	.12
☐ 168 Sterling Palmer	.60	.25	.07

1995 Chris Martin Pro Mags

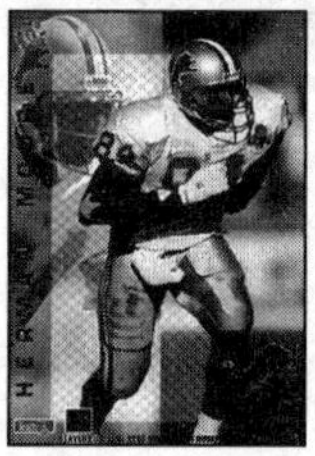

Sold in packs of five and produced by Chris Martin Enterprises, this 150-magnet set features borderless color player photos with rounded corners. The magnets, measuring approximately 2 1/8" by 3 3/8," are grouped alphabetically within teams and checklisted below according to team. Some packs also contained a random assortment of insert magnets.

	MINT	NRMT	EXC
COMPLETE SET (150)	125.00	55.00	15.50
COMMON CARD (1-150)	.60	.25	.07
☐ 1 Larry Centers	.60	.25	.07
☐ 2 Garrison Hearst	1.50	.70	.19
☐ 3 Seth Joyner	.60	.25	.07
☐ 4 Ronald Moore	.60	.25	.07
☐ 5 Eric Swann	1.00	.45	.12
☐ 6 Chris Doleman	.60	.25	.07
☐ 7 Jeff George	1.25	.55	.16
☐ 8 Craig Heyward	1.00	.45	.12
☐ 9 Terance Mathis	1.00	.45	.12
☐ 10 Jessie Tuggle	.60	.25	.07
☐ 11 Cornelius Bennett	1.00	.45	.12
☐ 12 Jim Kelly	1.25	.55	.16
☐ 13 Andre Reed	1.00	.45	.12
☐ 14 Bruce Smith	1.25	.55	.16
☐ 15 Darryl Talley	.60	.25	.07
☐ 16 Trace Armstrong	.60	.25	.07
☐ 17 Dante Jones	.60	.25	.07
☐ 18 Steve Walsh	1.00	.45	.12
☐ 19 Donnell Woolford	.60	.25	.07
☐ 20 Tim Worley	.60	.25	.07
☐ 21 Jeff Blake	4.00	1.80	.50
☐ 22 Harold Green	.60	.25	.07
☐ 23 Carl Pickens	1.50	.70	.19
☐ 24 Darnay Scott	1.25	.55	.16
☐ 25 Dan Wilkinson	.60	.25	.07
☐ 26 Derrick Alexander WR	1.00	.45	.12
☐ 27 Leroy Hoard	.60	.25	.07
☐ 28 Antonio Langham	.60	.25	.07
☐ 29 Vinny Testaverde	1.00	.45	.12
☐ 30 Eric Turner	1.00	.45	.12
☐ 31 Troy Aikman	3.00	1.35	.35
☐ 32 Michael Irvin	1.25	.55	.16
☐ 33 Daryl Johnston	1.00	.45	.12
☐ 34 Russell Maryland	1.00	.45	.12
☐ 35 Emmitt Smith	5.00	2.20	.60
☐ 36 Rod Bernstine	.60	.25	.07
☐ 37 John Elway	2.50	1.10	.30
☐ 38 Glyn Milburn	1.00	.45	.12
☐ 39 Anthony Miller	1.00	.45	.12
☐ 40 Shannon Sharpe	1.25	.55	.16
☐ 41 Scott Mitchell	1.25	.55	.16
☐ 42 Herman Moore	1.50	.70	.19
☐ 43 Brett Perriman	1.00	.45	.12
☐ 44 Barry Sanders	3.00	1.35	.35
☐ 45 Chris Spielman	1.00	.45	.12
☐ 46 Edgar Bennett	1.25	.55	.16
☐ 47 Robert Brooks	1.25	.55	.16
☐ 48 Brett Favre	5.00	2.20	.60
☐ 49 Sean Jones	1.00	.45	.12
☐ 50 Reggie White	1.25	.55	.16
☐ 51 Gary Brown	.60	.25	.07
☐ 52 Cody Carlson	.60	.25	.07
☐ 53 Ernest Givins	.60	.25	.07
☐ 54 Haywood Jeffires	.60	.25	.07
☐ 55 Bruce Matthews	.60	.25	.07
☐ 56 Quentin Coryatt	1.00	.45	.12
☐ 57 Steve Emtman	.60	.25	.07
☐ 58 Marshall Faulk	1.50	.70	.19
☐ 59 Jim Harbaugh	1.25	.55	.16
☐ 60 Roosevelt Potts	.60	.25	.07
☐ 61 Marcus Allen	1.25	.55	.16
☐ 62 Steve Bono	1.25	.55	.16
☐ 63 Willie Davis	1.00	.45	.12
☐ 64 Lake Dawson	.60	.25	.07
☐ 65 Neil Smith	1.25	.55	.16
☐ 66 Tim Brown	1.25	.55	.16
☐ 67 Jeff Hostetler	1.00	.45	.12
☐ 68 Rocket Ismail	1.00	.45	.12
☐ 69 James Jett	.60	.25	.07
☐ 70 Harvey Williams	1.00	.45	.12
☐ 71 Jerome Bettis	1.25	.55	.16
☐ 72 Troy Drayton	1.00	.45	.12
☐ 73 Wayne Gandy	.60	.25	.07
☐ 74 Sean Gilbert	1.00	.45	.12
☐ 75 Todd Lyght	.60	.25	.07
☐ 76 Tim Bowens	1.00	.45	.12
☐ 77 Bryan Cox	.60	.25	.07
☐ 78 Irving Fryar	1.00	.45	.12
☐ 79 Dan Marino	5.00	2.20	.60
☐ 80 Bernie Parmalee	.60	.25	.07
☐ 81 Terry Allen	1.25	.55	.16
☐ 82 Cris Carter	1.25	.55	.16
☐ 83 Qadry Ismail	1.00	.45	.12
☐ 84 Warren Moon	1.25	.55	.16
☐ 85 John Randle	1.00	.45	.12
☐ 86 Bruce Armstrong	.60	.25	.07
☐ 87 Drew Bledsoe	3.00	1.35	.35
☐ 88 Vincent Brisby	1.00	.45	.12
☐ 89 Marion Butts	.60	.25	.07
☐ 90 Ben Coates	1.00	.45	.12
☐ 91 Morten Andersen	.60	.25	.07
☐ 92 Quinn Early	.60	.25	.07
☐ 93 Jim Everett	.60	.25	.07
☐ 94 Tyrone Hughes	.60	.25	.07
☐ 95 Renaldo Turnbull	.60	.25	.07
☐ 96 Michael Brooks	.60	.25	.07
☐ 97 Dave Brown	.60	.25	.07
☐ 98 Jumbo Elliott	.60	.25	.07
☐ 99 Rodney Hampton	1.00	.45	.12
☐ 100 Mike Sherrard	.60	.25	.07
☐ 101 Boomer Esiason	1.00	.45	.12
☐ 102 Johnny Johnson	.60	.25	.07
☐ 103 Nick Lowery	.60	.25	.07
☐ 104 Johnny Mitchell	.60	.25	.07
☐ 105 Aaron Glenn	1.00	.45	.12
☐ 106 Fred Barnett	1.00	.45	.12
☐ 107 Bubby Brister	.60	.25	.07
☐ 108 Randall Cunningham	.60	.25	.07
☐ 109 Charlie Garner	1.00	.45	.12
☐ 110 Calvin Williams	1.00	.45	.12
☐ 111 Byron Bam Morris	1.00	.45	.12
☐ 112 Barry Foster	.60	.25	.07
☐ 113 Kevin Greene	1.25	.55	.16
☐ 114 Neil O'Donnell	1.25	.55	.16
☐ 115 Rod Woodson	1.25	.55	.16
☐ 116 Ronnie Harmon	1.00	.45	.12
☐ 117 Stan Humphries	1.25	.55	.16
☐ 118 Tony Martin	1.00	.45	.12
☐ 119 Natrone Means	1.25	.55	.16
☐ 120 Junior Seau	1.25	.55	.16
☐ 121 William Floyd	1.00	.45	.12
☐ 122 Jerry Rice	3.00	1.35	.35
☐ 123 Deion Sanders	2.00	.90	.25
☐ 124 Dana Stubblefield	1.00	.45	.12
☐ 125 Steve Young	2.50	1.10	.30
☐ 126 Brian Blades	1.00	.45	.12
☐ 127 Cortez Kennedy	1.00	.45	.12
☐ 128 Rick Mirer	1.25	.55	.16
☐ 129 Eugene Robinson	.60	.25	.07
☐ 130 Chris Warren	1.25	.55	.16
☐ 131 Trent Dilfer	1.25	.55	.16
☐ 132 Santana Dotson	.60	.25	.07
☐ 133 Craig Erickson	1.00	.45	.12
☐ 134 Thomas Everett	.60	.25	.07
☐ 135 Errict Rhett	1.50	.70	.19
☐ 136 Reggie Brooks	.60	.25	.07
☐ 137 Ricky Ervins	.60	.25	.07
☐ 138 Darrell Green	.60	.25	.07
☐ 139 Brian Mitchell	1.00	.45	.12
☐ 140 Heath Shuler	1.50	.70	.19
☐ 141 Sam Mills	1.00	.45	.12
☐ 142 Tim McKyer	.60	.25	.07
☐ 143 Mark Carrier WR	1.00	.45	.12
☐ 144 Derrick Lassic	.60	.25	.07
☐ 145 Andre Ware	.60	.25	.07
☐ 146 Steve Beuerlein	1.00	.45	.12
☐ 147 Cedric Tillman	1.00	.45	.12
☐ 148 Reggie Cobb	.60	.25	.07
☐ 149 Eugene Chung	.60	.25	.07
☐ 150 Desmond Howard	1.00	.45	.12
☐ NNO Steve Young MVP Super Bowl XXIX MVP Promo	3.00	1.35	.35

1995 Chris Martin Pro Mags In The Zone

This 12-card In The Zone set features borderless color action player photos on a flexible magnet. The magnets were randomly inserted in packs of 1995 Pro Mags at the rate of 1:3 packs.

	MINT	NRMT	EXC
COMPLETE SET (12)	15.00	6.75	1.85
COMMON CARD (1-12)	.75	.35	.09
☐ 1 Troy Aikman	2.50	1.10	.30
☐ 2 Drew Bledsoe	2.50	1.10	.30
☐ 3 John Elway	2.00	.90	.25
☐ 4 Brett Favre	4.00	1.80	.50
☐ 5 Jeff Hostetler	.75	.35	.09
☐ 6 Stan Humphries	1.00	.45	.12
☐ 7 Dan Marino	4.00	1.80	.50
☐ 8 Jim Kelly	1.25	.55	.16
☐ 9 Warren Moon	1.25	.55	.16
☐ 10 Neil O'Donnell	1.00	.45	.12
☐ 11 Rick Mirer	1.25	.55	.16
☐ 12 Steve Young	2.00	.90	.25

1995 Chris Martin Pro Mags Classics

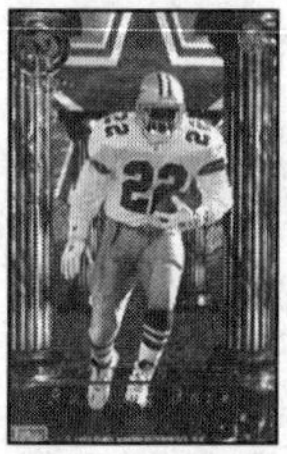

This 12-card set was produced by Chris Martin Enterprises and features color action player photos over a background of columns with the team logo on a flexible magnet. The magnets were randomly inserted in packs of 1995 Pro Mags at the average rate of one per three packs.

	MINT	NRMT	EXC
COMPLETE SET (12)	15.00	6.75	1.85
COMMON CARD (CL1-CL12)	.75	.35	.09
☐ CL1 Barry Sanders	2.50	1.10	.30
☐ CL2 Deion Sanders	2.00	.90	.25
☐ CL3 Dan Marino	4.00	1.80	.50
☐ CL4 Drew Bledsoe	2.50	1.10	.30
☐ CL5 Marcus Allen	1.00	.45	.12
☐ CL6 Jerome Bettis	.75	.35	.09
☐ CL7 John Elway	2.00	.90	.25
☐ CL8 Jerry Rice	2.50	1.10	.30
☐ CL9 Emmitt Smith	4.00	1.80	.50
☐ CL10 Steve Young	2.00	.90	.25
☐ CL11 Marshall Faulk	1.25	.55	.16
☐ CL12 Troy Aikman	2.50	1.10	.30

1995 Chris Martin Pro Mags Rookies

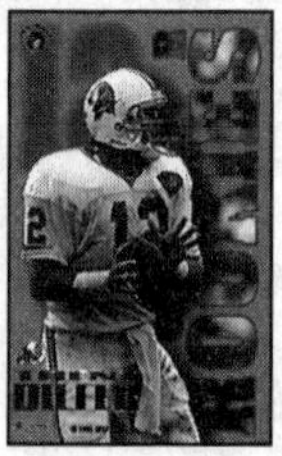

This 12-magnet set features top rookies from the 1994 NFL Draft. Each measures approximately 2-1/8" by 3-3/8" and includes a color player photo with the player's name printed in gold foil near the bottom of the card.

	MINT	NRMT	EXC
COMPLETE SET (12)	12.00	5.50	1.50
COMMON CARD (1-12)	.75	.35	.09
☐ 1 Trent Dilfer	1.25	.55	.16
☐ 2 Heath Shuler	1.50	.70	.19
☐ 3 John Thierry	.75	.35	.09
☐ 4 Wayne Gandy	.75	.35	.09
☐ 5 Errict Rhett	1.25	.55	.16
☐ 6 David Palmer	1.00	.45	.12
☐ 7 Andre Coleman	.75	.35	.09
☐ 8 Lake Dawson	1.00	.45	.12
☐ 9 Marshall Faulk	1.50	.70	.19
☐ 10 Dan Wilkinson	.75	.35	.09
☐ 11 Greg Hill	1.00	.45	.12
☐ 12 Willie McGinest	1.00	.45	.12

1995 Chris Martin Pro Mags Superhero Jumbos

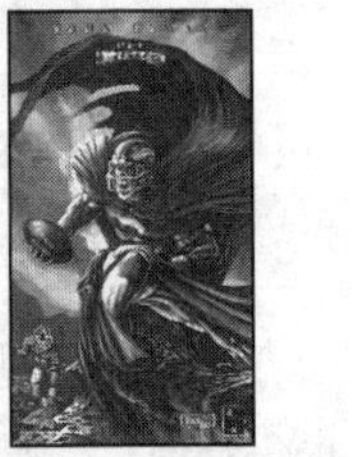

These three jumbo Pro Magnets were released one per box, as well as via mail order for $6 each directly from Chris Martin Enterprises, Inc. The offer could be found in packs of the 1995 Pro Magnets product. The jumbos feature an artist's rendering of the player, measure approximately 3-3/4" by 7" and have rounded corners.

	MINT	NRMT	EXC
COMPLETE SET (3)	20.00	9.00	2.50
COMMON CARD	6.00	2.70	.75
☐ 1 Jerome Bettis	6.00	2.70	.75
☐ 2 John Elway	8.00	3.60	1.00
☐ 3 Warren Moon	6.00	2.70	.75

1995 Chris Martin Pro Mags Teams

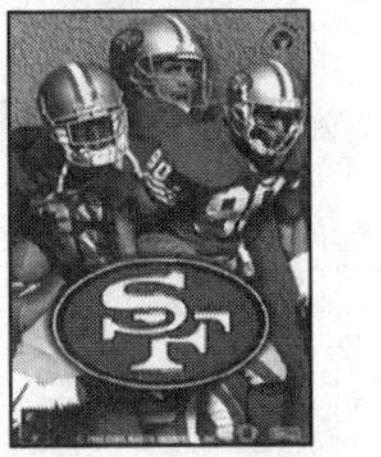

This set of magnets was released as a 5-card promotional set. Each unnumbered magnet features color photos of three top players from one team along with an embossed team logo.

	MINT	NRMT	EXC
COMPLETE SET (5)	20.00	9.00	2.50
COMMON CARD (1-5)	3.00	1.35	.35
☐ 1 Chargers	3.00	1.35	.35
Junior Seau			
Stan Humphries			
Natrone Means			
☐ 2 Cowboys	6.00	2.70	.75
Michael Irvin			
Troy Aikman			
Emmitt Smith			
☐ 3 Dolphins	6.00	2.70	.75
Dan Marino			
O.J. McDuffie			
Bernie Parmalee			
☐ 4 49ers	5.00	2.20	.60
Ricky Watters			
Steve Young			
Jerry Rice			
☐ 5 Steelers	3.00	1.35	.35
Barry Foster			
Neil O'Donnell			
Rod Woodson			

1995 Chris Martin Pro Stamps

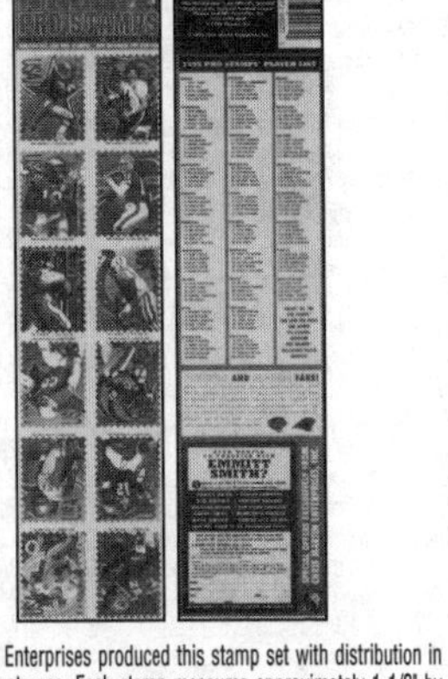

Chris Martin Enterprises produced this stamp set with distribution in sheets of 12 stamps. Each stamp measures approximately 1 1/2" by 2." The first 140-stamps were included as part of the 12-stamp sheets with four stamps being double-printed.

	MINT	NRMT	EXC
COMPLETE SET (140)	40.00	18.00	5.00
COMMON CARD (1-140)	.25	.11	.03
☐ 1 Steve Young DP	.50	.23	.06
☐ 2 Jerry Rice	1.00	.45	.12
☐ 3 Deion Sanders	.75	.35	.09
☐ 4 Dana Stubblefield	.25	.11	.03
☐ 5 William Floyd	.40	.18	.05
☐ 6 Troy Aikman DP	.75	.35	.09
☐ 7 Michael Irvin	.60	.25	.07
☐ 8 Emmitt Smith DP	1.50	.70	.19
☐ 9 Russell Maryland	.25	.11	.03
☐ 10 Daryl Johnston	.40	.18	.05
☐ 11 Dan Marino DP	1.50	.70	.19
☐ 12 Bernie Parmalee	.25	.11	.03
☐ 13 Tim Bowens	.25	.11	.03
☐ 14 Irving Fryar	.40	.18	.05
☐ 15 Bryan Cox	.25	.11	.03
☐ 16 Drew Bledsoe	1.00	.45	.12
☐ 17 Bruce Armstrong	.25	.11	.03
☐ 18 Vincent Brisby	.25	.11	.03
☐ 19 Marion Butts	.25	.11	.03
☐ 20 Ben Coates	.40	.18	.05
☐ 21 Dave Brown	.25	.11	.03
☐ 22 Michael Brooks	.25	.11	.03
☐ 23 Jumbo Elliott	.25	.11	.03
☐ 24 Rodney Hampton	.40	.18	.05
☐ 25 Mike Sherrard	.25	.11	.03
☐ 26 Jeff Hostetler	.25	.11	.03
☐ 27 Tim Brown	.60	.25	.07
☐ 28 Rocket Ismail	.25	.11	.03
☐ 29 James Jett	.25	.11	.03
☐ 30 Harvey Williams	.25	.11	.03
☐ 31 Heath Shuler	.60	.25	.07
☐ 32 Reggie Brooks	.25	.11	.03
☐ 33 Ricky Ervins	.25	.11	.03
☐ 34 Darrell Green UER	.25	.11	.03
Darryl on front			
☐ 35 Brian Mitchell	.25	.11	.03
☐ 36 Trace Armstrong	.25	.11	.03
☐ 37 Dante Jones	.25	.11	.03
☐ 38 Steve Walsh	.25	.11	.03
☐ 39 Donnell Woolford	.25	.11	.03
☐ 40 Tim Worley	.25	.11	.03
☐ 41 Boomer Esiason	.40	.18	.05
☐ 42 Aaron Glenn	.25	.11	.03
☐ 43 Johnny Johnson	.25	.11	.03
☐ 44 Nick Lowery	.25	.11	.03
☐ 45 Johnny Mitchell	.25	.11	.03
☐ 46 Neil O'Donnell	.40	.18	.05
☐ 47 Barry Foster	.25	.11	.03
☐ 48 Byron Bam Morris	.25	.11	.03
☐ 49 Rod Woodson	.40	.18	.05
☐ 50 Kevin Greene	.40	.18	.05
☐ 51 Randall Cunningham	.25	.11	.03
☐ 52 Bubby Brister	.25	.11	.03
☐ 53 Fred Barnett	.25	.11	.03
☐ 54 Charlie Garner	.25	.11	.03
☐ 55 Calvin Williams	.25	.11	.03
☐ 56 Brett Favre	2.00	.90	.25
☐ 57 Reggie White	.60	.25	.07
☐ 58 Edgar Bennett	.25	.11	.03
☐ 59 Robert Brooks	.60	.25	.07
☐ 60 Sean Jones	.25	.11	.03
☐ 61 Ronnie Harmon	.25	.11	.03
☐ 62 Stan Humphries	.40	.18	.05
☐ 63 Natrone Means	.60	.25	.07
☐ 64 Tony Martin	.60	.25	.07
☐ 65 Junior Seau	.60	.25	.07
☐ 66 John Elway	.75	.35	.09
☐ 67 Glyn Milburn	.25	.11	.03
☐ 68 Rod Bernstine	.25	.11	.03
☐ 69 Anthony Miller	.40	.18	.05
☐ 70 Shannon Sharpe	.60	.25	.07
☐ 71 Barry Sanders	1.00	.45	.12
☐ 72 Scott Mitchell	.40	.18	.05
☐ 73 Herman Moore	.60	.25	.07
☐ 74 Brett Perriman	.40	.18	.05
☐ 75 Chris Spielman	.40	.18	.05
☐ 76 Marcus Allen	.60	.25	.07
☐ 77 Steve Bono	.40	.18	.05
☐ 78 Willie Davis	.40	.18	.05
☐ 79 Lake Dawson	.25	.11	.03
☐ 80 Neil Smith	.40	.18	.05
☐ 81 Vinny Testaverde	.60	.25	.07
☐ 82 Eric Turner	.25	.11	.03
☐ 83 Antonio Langham	.25	.11	.03
☐ 84 Leroy Hoard	.25	.11	.03
☐ 85 Derrick Alexander WR	.40	.18	.05
☐ 86 Jim Kelly	.60	.25	.07
☐ 87 Cornelius Bennett	.40	.18	.05
☐ 88 Andre Reed	.25	.11	.03
☐ 89 Bruce Smith	.60	.25	.07
☐ 90 Darryl Talley	.25	.11	.03
☐ 91 Warren Moon	.60	.25	.07
☐ 92 Qadry Ismail	.25	.11	.03
☐ 93 Terry Allen	.60	.25	.07
☐ 94 Cris Carter	.60	.25	.07
☐ 95 John Randle	.25	.11	.03
☐ 96 Jeff George	.60	.25	.07
☐ 97 Chris Doleman	.25	.11	.03
☐ 98 Craig Heyward	.40	.18	.05
☐ 99 Terance Mathis	.40	.18	.05
☐ 100 Jessie Tuggle	.25	.11	.03
☐ 101 Jerome Bettis	.60	.25	.07
☐ 102 Sean Gilbert	.25	.11	.03
☐ 103 Troy Drayton	.25	.11	.03
☐ 104 Wayne Gandy	.25	.11	.03
☐ 105 Todd Lyght	.25	.11	.03
☐ 106 Jeff Blake	.75	.35	.09
☐ 107 Harold Green	.25	.11	.03
☐ 108 Carl Pickens	.60	.25	.07
☐ 109 Dan Wilkinson	.25	.11	.03
☐ 110 Darnay Scott	.40	.18	.05
☐ 111 Cody Carlson	.25	.11	.03
☐ 112 Gary Brown	.25	.11	.03
☐ 113 Ernest Givins	.25	.11	.03
☐ 114 Haywood Jeffires	.25	.11	.03
☐ 115 Bruce Matthews	.25	.11	.03
☐ 116 Jim Everett	.25	.11	.03
☐ 117 Morten Andersen	.25	.11	.03
☐ 118 Quinn Early	.25	.11	.03
☐ 119 Tyrone Hughes	.25	.11	.03
☐ 120 Renaldo Turnbull	.25	.11	.03
☐ 121 Larry Centers	.40	.18	.05
☐ 122 Garrison Hearst	.60	.25	.07
☐ 123 Seth Joyner	.25	.11	.03
☐ 124 Ronald Moore	.25	.11	.03
☐ 125 Eric Swann	.25	.11	.03
☐ 126 Rick Mirer	.60	.25	.07
☐ 127 Chris Warren	.40	.18	.05
☐ 128 Brian Blades	.25	.11	.03
☐ 129 Cortez Kennedy	.25	.11	.03
☐ 130 Eugene Robinson	.25	.11	.03
☐ 131 Marshall Faulk	.60	.25	.07
☐ 132 Quentin Coryatt	.25	.11	.03
☐ 133 Jim Harbaugh	.60	.25	.07
☐ 134 Roosevelt Potts	.25	.11	.03
☐ 135 Steve Emtman	.25	.11	.03
☐ 136 Trent Dilfer	.40	.18	.05
☐ 137 Santana Dotson	.25	.11	.03
☐ 138 Errict Rhett	.60	.25	.07
☐ 139 Thomas Everett	.25	.11	.03
☐ 140 Craig Erickson	.25	.11	.03

1996 Chris Martin Die-Cut Magnets

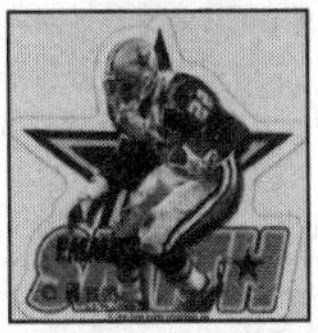

Chris Martin Enterprises produced these fifteen Die-Cut Magnets packaged one per cello pack. Each measures roughly 3 1/2" by 3 1/2." The magnets are unnumbered and listed below alphabetically.

	MINT	NRMT	EXC
COMPLETE SET (15)	40.00	18.00	5.00
COMMON CARD (1-15)	2.00	.90	.25
☐ 1 Troy Aikman	3.50	1.55	.45
☐ 2 Marcus Allen	2.50	1.10	.30
☐ 3 Drew Bledsoe	3.50	1.55	.45
☐ 4 John Elway	3.00	1.35	.35
☐ 5 Marshall Faulk	2.50	1.10	.30
☐ 6 Brett Favre	6.00	2.70	.75
☐ 7 Jeff Hostetler	2.00	.90	.25
☐ 8 Dan Marino	6.00	2.70	.75
☐ 9 Jerry Rice	3.50	1.55	.45
☐ 10 Rashaan Salaam	2.00	.90	.25
☐ 11 Barry Sanders	3.50	1.55	.45
☐ 12 Deion Sanders	3.00	1.35	.35
☐ 13 Emmitt Smith	6.00	2.70	.75
☐ 14 Kordell Stewart	2.00	.90	.25
☐ 15 Steve Young	3.00	1.35	.35

1996 Chris Martin Pro Mags

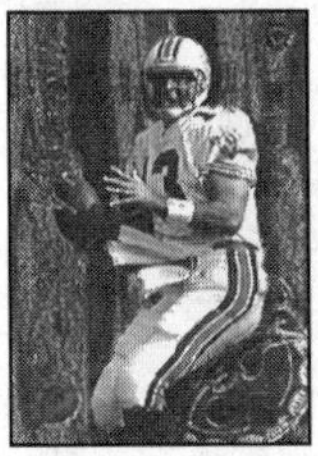

Chris Martin Enterprises issued this set through five-magnet packs with 24-packs per box. Each magnet featured a borderless color player photo with rounded corners. The magnets, measuring approximately 2 1/8" by 3 3/8," are grouped alphabetically within teams below. Some hobby packs contained randomly inserted Draft Day Future Stars magnets, while retail packs had randomly inserted Destination All-Pro magnets.

	MINT	NRMT	EXC
COMPLETE SET (100)	100.00	45.00	12.50
COMMON CARD (1-100)	.60	.25	.07
☐ 1 Troy Aikman	.60	.25	.07
☐ 2 Michael Irvin	.60	.25	.07
☐ 3 Emmitt Smith	.60	.25	.07
☐ 4 Deion Sanders	.60	.25	.07
☐ 5 Jay Novacek	1.00	.45	.12
☐ 6 Jerry Rice	.60	.25	.07
☐ 7 Steve Young	2.00	.90	.25
☐ 8 J.J. Stokes	.60	.25	.07
☐ 9 William Floyd	1.00	.45	.12
☐ 10 Merton Hanks	.60	.25	.07
☐ 11 Greg Lloyd	.60	.25	.07
☐ 12 Rod Woodson	.60	.25	.07
☐ 13 Kordell Stewart	2.50	1.10	.30
☐ 14 Yancey Thigpen	1.25	.55	.16
☐ 15 Charles Johnson	.60	.25	.07
☐ 16 Richmond Webb	.60	.25	.07
☐ 17 Eric Green	.60	.25	.07
☐ 18 Bernie Parmalee	.60	.25	.07
☐ 19 Dan Marino	5.00	2.20	.60
☐ 20 O.J. McDuffie	1.00	.45	.12
☐ 21 Brett Favre	5.00	2.20	.60
☐ 22 Reggie White	1.25	.55	.16
☐ 23 Robert Brooks	1.25	.55	.16
☐ 24 Edgar Bennett	1.00	.45	.12
☐ 25 Marcus Allen	1.25	.55	.16
☐ 26 Tamarick Vanover	1.00	.45	.12
☐ 27 Lake Dawson	.60	.25	.07
☐ 28 Neil Smith	1.00	.45	.12
☐ 29 Steve Bono	1.00	.45	.12
☐ 30 Harvey Williams	.60	.25	.07
☐ 31 Tim Brown	1.25	.55	.16
☐ 32 Jeff Hostetler	.60	.25	.07
☐ 33 Drew Bledsoe	3.00	1.35	.35
☐ 34 Vincent Brisby	.60	.25	.07
☐ 35 Curtis Martin	2.50	1.10	.30
☐ 36 Rashaan Salaam	1.25	.55	.16
☐ 37 Erik Kramer	.60	.25	.07
☐ 38 Curtis Conway	.60	.25	.07
☐ 39 Kerry Collins	2.50	1.10	.30
☐ 40 Sam Mills	.60	.25	.07
☐ 41 Mark Carrier	.60	.25	.07
☐ 42 Dave Brown	.60	.25	.07
☐ 43 Rodney Hampton	1.00	.45	.12
☐ 44 Tyrone Wheatley	1.00	.45	.12
☐ 45 Vinny Testaverde	1.00	.45	.12
☐ 46 Andre Rison	1.25	.55	.16
☐ 47 Eric Turner	.60	.25	.07
☐ 48 Michael Jackson	1.00	.45	.12
☐ 49 Mark Brunell	3.00	1.35	.35
☐ 50 Jeff Lageman	.60	.25	.07
☐ 51 Roman Phifer	.60	.25	.07
☐ 52 Isaac Bruce	1.25	.55	.16
☐ 53 Rodney Peete	.60	.25	.07
☐ 54 Ricky Watters	1.25	.55	.16
☐ 55 Calvin Williams	.60	.25	.07
☐ 56 Warren Moon	1.25	.55	.16
☐ 57 Cris Carter	1.25	.55	.16
☐ 58 David Palmer	.60	.25	.07
☐ 59 Scott Mitchell	1.00	.45	.12
☐ 60 Barry Sanders	3.00	1.35	.35
☐ 61 Herman Moore	1.25	.55	.16
☐ 62 Brett Perriman	1.00	.45	.12
☐ 63 Jim Kelly	1.25	.55	.16
☐ 64 Bruce Smith	1.25	.55	.16
☐ 65 Bryce Paup	1.25	.55	.16
☐ 66 Junior Seau	1.25	.55	.16
☐ 67 Stan Humphries	1.00	.45	.12
☐ 68 Andre Coleman	.60	.25	.07
☐ 69 Tony Martin	1.25	.55	.16
☐ 70 Terry Allen	1.25	.55	.16
☐ 71 Heath Shuler	1.25	.55	.16
☐ 72 John Elway	2.50	1.10	.30
☐ 73 Terrell Davis	3.00	1.35	.35
☐ 74 Mike Pritchard	.60	.25	.07
☐ 75 Neil O'Donnell	1.00	.45	.12
☐ 76 Kyle Brady	.60	.25	.07
☐ 77 Jim Harbaugh	1.25	.55	.16
☐ 78 Marshall Faulk	1.25	.55	.16
☐ 79 Zack Crockett	1.00	.45	.12
☐ 80 Quentin Coryatt	.60	.25	.07
☐ 81 Jeff George	1.25	.55	.16
☐ 82 Morten Andersen	.60	.25	.07
☐ 83 Eric Metcalf	1.00	.45	.12
☐ 84 Joey Galloway	1.25	.55	.16
☐ 85 Rick Mirer	1.25	.55	.16
☐ 86 Chris Warren	1.00	.45	.12
☐ 87 Ray Zellars	.60	.25	.07
☐ 88 Eric Allen	.60	.25	.07
☐ 89 Jim Everett	.60	.25	.07
☐ 90 Jeff Blake	1.50	.70	.19
☐ 91 Carl Pickens	1.25	.55	.16
☐ 92 Ki-Jana Carter	1.00	.45	.12
☐ 93 Larry Centers	1.00	.45	.12
☐ 94 Garrison Hearst	1.25	.55	.16
☐ 95 Trent Dilfer	1.25	.55	.16
☐ 96 Errict Rhett	.60	.25	.07
☐ 97 Hardy Nickerson	.60	.25	.07
☐ 98 Alvin Harper	.60	.25	.07
☐ 99 Steve McNair	2.00	.90	.25
☐ 100 Haywood Jeffires	.60	.25	.07

1996 Chris Martin Pro Mags Destination All-Pro

These magnets were randomly inserted in 1996 Chris Martin Enterprises Pro Mags retail packs. The odds of pulling one of the inserts was 1:4 packs.

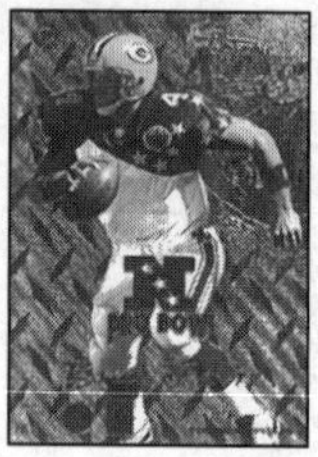

	MINT	NRMT	EXC
COMPLETE SET (6)	25.00	11.00	3.10
COMMON CARD (PB1-PB6)	2.50	1.10	.30
☐ PB1 Jim Harbaugh	3.00	1.35	.35
☐ PB2 Curtis Martin	4.00	1.80	.50
☐ PB3 Yancey Thigpen	2.50	1.10	.30
☐ PB4 Brett Favre	8.00	3.60	1.00
☐ PB5 Jerry Rice	5.00	2.20	.60
☐ PB6 Barry Sanders	5.00	2.20	.60

1996 Chris Martin Pro Mags Draft Day Future Stars

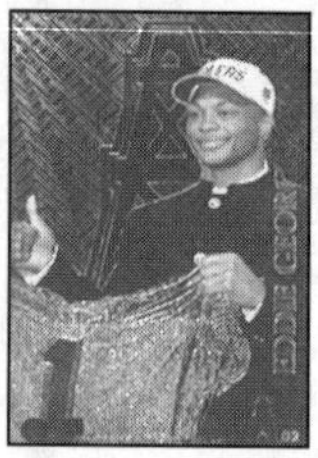

These magnets were randomly inserted in 1996 Chris Martin Enterprises Pro Mags hobby packs. The odds of pulling one of the inserts was 1:4 packs.

	MINT	NRMT	EXC
COMPLETE SET (6)	20.00	9.00	2.50
COMMON CARD (1-6)	2.00	.90	.25
☐ 1 Kevin Hardy	2.00	.90	.25
☐ 2 Eddie George	8.00	3.60	1.00
☐ 3 Keyshawn Johnson	3.00	1.35	.35
☐ 4 Tim Biakabutuka	4.00	1.80	.50
☐ 5 Lawrence Phillips	3.00	1.35	.35
☐ 6 Alex Molden	2.00	.90	.25

1996 Chris Martin Pro Mags 12

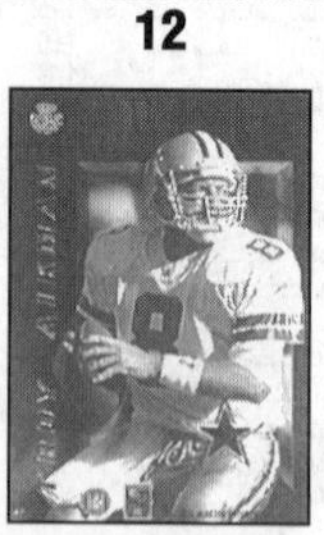

Produced by Chris Martin Enterprises, these 12-magnets contain a player photo against a metallic foil background. They were issued one per cello pack and measure approximately 3 1/2" by 2 1/4."

	MINT	NRMT	EXC
COMPLETE SET (12)	25.00	11.00	3.10
COMMON CARD (1-12)	1.50	.70	.19
☐ 1 Tim Brown	2.00	.90	.25
☐ 2 John Elway	2.50	1.10	.30
☐ 3 Marshall Faulk	2.00	.90	.25
☐ 4 Dan Marino	5.00	2.20	.60
☐ 5 Curtis Martin	3.00	1.35	.35
☐ 6 Rashaan Salaam	2.00	.90	.25
☐ 7 Barry Sanders	3.00	1.35	.35
☐ 8 Emmitt Smith	5.00	2.20	.60
☐ 9 Neil Smith	1.50	.70	.19
☐ 10 Reggie White	2.00	.90	.25
☐ 11 Rod Woodson	1.50	.70	.19
☐ 12 Steve Young	2.50	1.10	.30

1996 Chris Martin Pro Stamps

Chris Martin Enterprises released two different Pro Stamps sets in 1996. This set was sold in 12-stamp packages. They were essentially a re-make of the 1995 issue with the same stamp design and many of the same player photos. Some new players, however, were added for 1996 as were stamps for the two expansion teams. Each stamp measures approximately 1 1/2" by 2." Unlike the team set stamps, these are numbered in gold foil above the player's name.

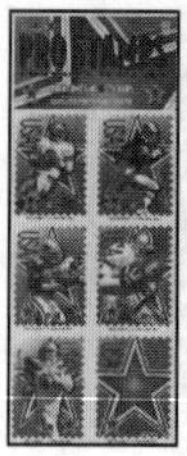

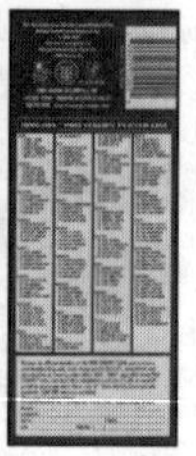

	MINT	NRMT	EXC
COMPLETE SET (144)	35.00	16.00	4.40
COMMON STAMP (1-144)	.25	.11	.03
☐ 1 Steve Young	.75	.35	.09
☐ 2 Jerry Rice	1.00	.45	.12
☐ 3 Merton Hanks	.25	.11	.03
☐ 4 J.J.Stokes	.40	.18	.05
☐ 5 William Floyd	.40	.18	.05
☐ 6 Troy Aikman	1.00	.45	.12
☐ 7 Michael Irvin	.50	.23	.06
☐ 8 Emmitt Smith	2.00	.90	.25
☐ 9 Deion Sanders	.60	.25	.07
☐ 10 Daryl Johnston	.40	.18	.05
☐ 11 Dan Marino	2.00	.90	.25
☐ 12 Bernie Parmalee	.25	.11	.03
☐ 13 O.J. McDuffie	.40	.18	.05
☐ 14 Richmond Webb	.25	.11	.03
☐ 15 Eric Green	.25	.11	.03
☐ 16 Drew Bledsoe	1.00	.45	.12
☐ 17 Bruce Armstrong	.25	.11	.03
☐ 18 Dave Meggett	.25	.11	.03
☐ 19 Curtis Martin	1.00	.45	.12
☐ 20 Ben Coates	.40	.18	.05
☐ 21 Dave Brown	.25	.11	.03
☐ 22 Michael Brooks	.25	.11	.03
☐ 23 Tyrone Wheatley	.40	.18	.05
☐ 24 Rodney Hampton	.40	.18	.05
☐ 25 Jeff Hostetler	.25	.11	.03
☐ 26 Tim Brown	.50	.23	.06
☐ 27 Rocket Ismail	.40	.18	.05
☐ 28 James Jett	.25	.11	.03
☐ 29 Harvey Williams	.40	.18	.05
☐ 30 Heath Shuler	.50	.23	.06
☐ 31 Michael Westbrook	.50	.23	.06
☐ 32 Terry Allen	.50	.23	.06
☐ 33 Darrell Green	.40	.18	.05
☐ 34 Brian Mitchell	.25	.11	.03
☐ 35 Rashaan Salaam	.50	.23	.06
☐ 36 Erik Kramer UER 37	.25	.11	.03
☐ 37 Donnell Woolford	.25	.11	.03
☐ 38 Alonzo Spellman	.25	.11	.03
☐ 39 Kyle Brady	.40	.18	.05
☐ 40 Aaron Glenn	.25	.11	.03
☐ 41 Adrian Murrell	.40	.18	.05
☐ 42 Nick Lowery	.25	.11	.03
☐ 43 Charles Johnson	.40	.18	.05
☐ 44 Kordell Stewart	1.00	.45	.12
☐ 45 Yancey Thigpen	.40	.18	.05
☐ 46 Rod Woodson	.40	.18	.05
☐ 47 Greg Lloyd	.50	.23	.06
☐ 48 Randall Cunningham	.40	.18	.05
☐ 49 Rodney Peete	.25	.11	.03
☐ 50 Ricky Watters	.50	.23	.06
☐ 51 Charlie Garner	.25	.11	.03
☐ 52 Calvin Williams	.25	.11	.03
☐ 53 Brett Favre	2.00	.90	.25
☐ 54 Reggie White	.50	.23	.06
☐ 55 Edgar Bennett	.40	.18	.05
☐ 56 Robert Brooks	.50	.23	.06
☐ 57 Sean Jones	.25	.11	.03
☐ 58 Ronnie Harmon	.25	.11	.03
☐ 59 Stan Humphries	.40	.18	.05
☐ 60 Andre Coleman	.25	.11	.03
☐ 61 Tony Martin	.40	.18	.05
☐ 62 Junior Seau	.50	.23	.06
☐ 63 John Elway	.75	.35	.09
☐ 64 Mike Pritchard	.25	.11	.03
☐ 65 Terrell Davis	1.00	.45	.12
☐ 66 Anthony Miller	.40	.18	.05
☐ 67 Shannon Sharpe	.50	.23	.06
☐ 68 Barry Sanders	1.00	.45	.12
☐ 69 Scott Mitchell	.40	.18	.05
☐ 70 Herman Moore	.50	.23	.06
☐ 71 Brett Perriman	.40	.18	.05
☐ 72 Johnnie Morton	.40	.18	.05
☐ 73 Marcus Allen	.50	.23	.06
☐ 74 Steve Bono	.40	.18	.05
☐ 75 Tamarick Vanover	.25	.11	.03
☐ 76 Lake Dawson	.25	.11	.03
☐ 77 Neil Smith	.25	.11	.03
☐ 78 Vinny Testaverde	.40	.18	.05
☐ 79 Eric Turner	.25	.11	.03
☐ 80 Michael Jackson	.40	.18	.05
☐ 81 Leroy Hoard	.25	.11	.03
☐ 82 Andre Rison	.50	.23	.06
☐ 83 Jim Kelly	.50	.23	.06
☐ 84 Carwell Gardner	.25	.11	.03
☐ 85 Andre Reed	.40	.18	.05
☐ 86 Bruce Smith	.50	.23	.06
☐ 87 Bryce Paup	.40	.18	.05
☐ 88 Warren Moon	.50	.23	.06
☐ 89 Qadry Ismail	.40	.18	.05
☐ 90 Robert Smith	.40	.18	.05
☐ 91 Cris Carter	.50	.23	.06
☐ 92 David Palmer	.25	.11	.03
☐ 93 Jeff George	.50	.23	.06
☐ 94 Morten Andersen	.25	.11	.03
☐ 95 Craig Heyward	.25	.11	.03
☐ 96 Eric Metcalf	.40	.18	.05
☐ 97 Jessie Tuggle	.25	.11	.03
☐ 98 Roman Phifer	.25	.11	.03
☐ 99 Todd Lyght	.25	.11	.03
☐ 100 Troy Drayton	.25	.11	.03
☐ 101 Isaac Bruce	.50	.23	.06
☐ 102 Sean Gilbert	.25	.11	.03
☐ 103 Jeff Blake	.60	.25	.07
☐ 104 Harold Green	.25	.11	.03
☐ 105 Carl Pickens	.50	.23	.06
☐ 106 Dan Wilkinson	.25	.11	.03
☐ 107 Ki-Jana Carter	.40	.18	.05
☐ 108 Steve McNair	.75	.35	.09
☐ 109 Gary Brown	.25	.11	.03
☐ 110 Haywood Jeffires	.25	.11	.03
☐ 111 Bruce Matthews	.25	.11	.03
☐ 112 Jim Everett	.25	.11	.03
☐ 113 Mario Bates	.25	.11	.03
☐ 114 Ray Zellars	.25	.11	.03
☐ 115 Tyrone Hughes	.25	.11	.03
☐ 116 Eric Allen	.25	.11	.03
☐ 117 Larry Centers	.40	.18	.05
☐ 118 Garrison Hearst	.50	.23	.06
☐ 119 Aeneas Williams	.25	.11	.03
☐ 120 Rob Moore	.25	.11	.03
☐ 121 Neil O'Donnell	.40	.18	.05
☐ 122 Rick Mirer	.25	.11	.03
☐ 123 Chris Warren	.40	.18	.05
☐ 124 Eric Swann	.25	.11	.03
☐ 125 Cortez Kennedy	.25	.11	.03
☐ 126 Joey Galloway	.50	.23	.06
☐ 127 Marshall Faulk	.50	.23	.06
☐ 128 Quentin Coryatt	.25	.11	.03
☐ 129 Jim Harbaugh	.50	.23	.06
☐ 130 Trev Alberts	.25	.11	.03
☐ 131 Zack Crockett	.25	.11	.03
☐ 132 Trent Dilfer	.40	.18	.05
☐ 133 Hardy Nickerson	.25	.11	.03
☐ 134 Errict Rhett	.50	.23	.06
☐ 135 Alvin Harper	.25	.11	.03
☐ 136 Sam Mills	.25	.11	.03
☐ 137 Tyrone Poole	.40	.18	.05
☐ 138 Kerry Collins	1.00	.45	.12
☐ 139 Bob Christian	.25	.11	.03
☐ 140 Randy Baldwin	.25	.11	.03
☐ 141 Steve Beuerlein	.25	.11	.03
☐ 142 Mark Brunell	1.00	.45	.12
☐ 143 Tony Boselli	.40	.18	.05
☐ 144 Jeff Lageman	.25	.11	.03

1996 Chris Martin Pro Stamps Team Sets

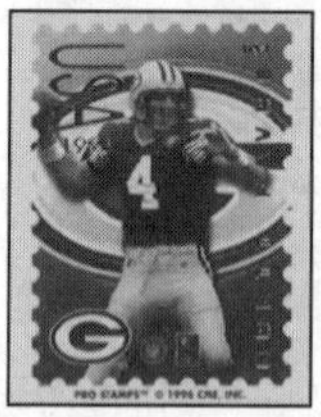

Chris Martin Enterprises released a second version of some of its Pro Stamps from 1996. This set was sold as four different 6-stamp team sets. Five player stamps and one team logo stamp was included in each pack. They were essentially a re-make of the 1995 issue with the same stamp design and many of the same player photos. Some new players, however, were added for 1996 as were stamps for the two expansion teams. Each stamp measures approximately 1 1/2" by 2." These team set stamps are unnumbered, but have been assigned numbers below according to the alphabetical player list by team. The team logos were added to the end of the player listings.

	MINT	NRMT	EXC
COMPLETE SET (24)	15.00	6.75	1.85
COMMON STAMP	.35	.16	.04
☐ CP1 Randy Baldwin	.35	.16	.04
☐ CP2 Bob Christian	.35	.16	.04
☐ CP3 Kerry Collins	1.25	.55	.16
☐ CP4 Sam Mills	.35	.16	.04
☐ CP5 Tyrone Poole	.35	.16	.04
☐ CP6 Panthers Logo	.50	.23	.06
☐ DC1 Troy Aikman	1.25	.55	.16
☐ DC2 Michael Irvin	.50	.23	.06
☐ DC3 Daryl Johnston	.50	.23	.06
☐ DC4 Deion Sanders	1.00	.45	.12
☐ DC5 Emmitt Smith	2.50	1.10	.30
☐ DC6 Cowboys Logo	.50	.23	.06
☐ JJ1 Steve Beuerlein	.35	.16	.04
☐ JJ2 Tony Boselli	.50	.23	.06
☐ JJ3 Mark Brunell	1.25	.55	.16
☐ JJ4 Desmond Howard	.35	.16	.04
☐ JJ5 Jeff Lageman	.35	.16	.04
☐ JJ6 Jaguars Logo	.35	.16	.04
☐ SF1 William Floyd	.50	.23	.06
☐ SF2 Merton Hanks	.35	.16	.04
☐ SF3 Jerry Rice	1.25	.55	.16
☐ SF4 Dana Stubblefield	.50	.23	.06
☐ SF5 Steve Young	1.00	.45	.12
☐ SF6 49ers Logo	.50	.23	.06

1970 Clark Volpe

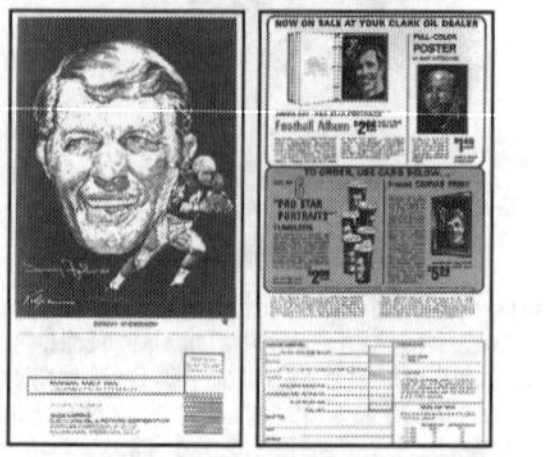

This 66-card set is actually a collection of team sets. Each team subset contains between six and nine cards. These unnumbered cards are listed below alphabetically by player within team as follows: Chicago Bears (1-8), Cincinnati Bengals (9-14), Cleveland Browns (15-21), Detroit Lions (22-30), Green Bay Packers (31-39), Kansas City Chiefs (40-48), Minnesota Vikings (49-57), St. Louis Cardinals (58-66). The cards measure approximately 7 1/2" by 9 15/16" (or 7 1/2" by 14" with mail-in tab intact). The back of the (top) drawing portion describes the mail-in offers for tumblers, posters, etc. The bottom tab is a business-reply mail-in card addressed to Clark Oil and Refining Corporation to the attention of Alex Karras. The artist for these drawings was Nicholas Volpe. The cards are typically found with tabs intact and hence they are priced that way below.

	NRMT-MT	EXC	G-VG
COMPLETE SET (66)	400.00	180.00	50.00
COMMON CARD (1-66)	4.00	1.80	.50
☐ 1 Ron Bull	4.00	1.80	.50
☐ 2 Dick Butkus	25.00	11.00	3.10
☐ 3 Lee Roy Caffey	4.00	1.80	.50
☐ 4 Bobby Douglass	5.00	2.20	.60
☐ 5 Dick Gordon	4.00	1.80	.50
☐ 6 Bennie McRae	4.00	1.80	.50
☐ 7 Ed O'Bradovich	4.00	1.80	.50
☐ 8 George Seals	4.00	1.80	.50
☐ 9 Bill Bergey	6.00	2.70	.75
☐ 10 Jess Phillips	4.00	1.80	.50
☐ 11 Mike Reid	7.50	3.40	.95
☐ 12 Paul Robinson	5.00	2.20	.60
☐ 13 Bob Trumpy	7.50	3.40	.95
☐ 14 Sam Wyche	10.00	4.50	1.25
☐ 15 Erich Barnes	4.00	1.80	.50
☐ 16 Gary Collins	5.00	2.20	.60
☐ 17 Gene Hickerson	4.00	1.80	.50
☐ 18 Jim Houston	4.00	1.80	.50
☐ 19 Leroy Kelly	12.00	5.50	1.50
☐ 20 Ernie Kellerman	4.00	1.80	.50
☐ 21 Bill Nelsen	5.00	2.20	.60
☐ 22 Lem Barney	10.00	4.50	1.25
☐ 23 Mel Farr	5.00	2.20	.60
☐ 24 Larry Hand	4.00	1.80	.50
☐ 25 Alex Karras	12.00	5.50	1.50
☐ 26 Mike Lucci	5.00	2.20	.60
☐ 27 Bill Munson	5.00	2.20	.60
☐ 28 Charlie Sanders	5.00	2.20	.60
☐ 29 Tom Vaughn	4.00	1.80	.50
☐ 30 Wayne Walker	5.00	2.20	.60
☐ 31 Lionel Aldridge	4.00	1.80	.50
☐ 32 Donny Anderson	5.00	2.20	.60
☐ 33 Ken Bowman	4.00	1.80	.50
☐ 34 Carroll Dale	5.00	2.20	.60
☐ 35 Jim Grabowski	5.00	2.20	.60
☐ 36 Ray Nitschke	15.00	6.75	1.85
☐ 37 Dave Robinson	5.00	2.20	.60
☐ 38 Travis Williams	5.00	2.20	.60
☐ 39 Willie Wood	10.00	4.50	1.25
☐ 40 Fred Arbanas	4.00	1.80	.50
☐ 41 Bobby Bell	10.00	4.50	1.25
☐ 42 Aaron Brown	4.00	1.80	.50
☐ 43 Buck Buchanan	10.00	4.50	1.25
☐ 44 Len Dawson	20.00	9.00	2.50
☐ 45 Jim Marsalis	4.00	1.80	.50
☐ 46 Jerry Mays	4.00	1.80	.50
☐ 47 Johnny Robinson	5.00	2.20	.60
☐ 48 Jim Tyrer	5.00	2.20	.60
☐ 49 Bill Brown	5.00	2.20	.60
☐ 50 Fred Cox	4.00	1.80	.50
☐ 51 Gary Cuozzo	5.00	2.20	.60
☐ 52 Carl Eller	10.00	4.50	1.25
☐ 53 Jim Marshall	10.00	4.50	1.25
☐ 54 Dave Osborn	5.00	2.20	.60
☐ 55 Alan Page	15.00	6.75	1.85
☐ 56 Mick Tingelhoff	6.00	2.70	.75
☐ 57 Gene Washington	5.00	2.20	.60
☐ 58 Pete Beathard	5.00	2.20	.60
☐ 59 John Gilliam	5.00	2.20	.60
☐ 60 Jim Hart	7.50	3.40	.95
☐ 61 Johnny Roland	5.00	2.20	.60
☐ 62 Jackie Smith	10.00	4.50	1.25
☐ 63 Larry Stallings	4.00	1.80	.50
☐ 64 Roger Wehrli	5.00	2.20	.60
☐ 65 Dave Williams	4.00	1.80	.50
☐ 66 Larry Wilson	10.00	4.50	1.25

1992 Classic NFL Game

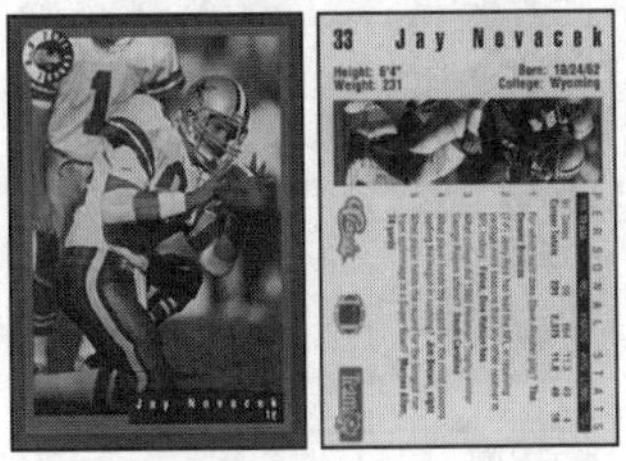

The 1992 Classic NFL Game football set consists of 60 standard-size cards, a travel game board, player piece and die, rules, and scoreboard. Apparently cards number 13 and 51 were never issued. The game board included with each 60-card blister pack featured a football field and a list of plays at each end with the outcome of each play determining by a roll of the die. The board is folded in half and measures approximately 15 1/2" by 6" after unfolding. The rules for the game are printed on the backs of the Andre Ware and Cris Dishman cards. The cards measure the standard size. The fronts feature color player photos with a dusty rose inner border and a dark blue outer border. The player's name and position appear in a black bar at the lower right corner. The horizontal backs are white and carry a second color player photo, a "personal bio" feature, and five trivia questions with answers.

	MINT	NRMT	EXC
COMPLETE SET (60)	6.00	2.70	.75
COMMON CARD (1-60)	.10	.05	.01
☐ 1 Steve Atwater	.10	.05	.01
☐ 2 Louis Oliver	.10	.05	.01
☐ 3 Ronnie Lott	.15	.07	.02
☐ 4 Reggie White	.25	.11	.03
☐ 5 Cortez Kennedy	.15	.07	.02
☐ 6 Derrick Thomas	.25	.11	.03
☐ 7 Pat Swilling	.15	.07	.02
☐ 8 Cornelius Bennett	.15	.07	.02
☐ 9 Mark Rypien	.15	.07	.02
☐ 10 Todd Marinovich	.10	.05	.01
☐ 11 Steve Young	.60	.25	.07
☐ 12 Warren Moon	.25	.11	.03
☐ 14 Hugh Millen	.10	.05	.01
☐ 15 John Friesz	.15	.07	.02
☐ 16 John Elway	.60	.25	.07
☐ 17 Chris Miller	.15	.07	.02
☐ 18 Jim Everett	.15	.07	.02
☐ 19 Emmitt Smith	1.50	.70	.19
☐ 20 Johnny Johnson	.10	.05	.01
☐ 21 Thurman Thomas	.25	.11	.03
☐ 22 Leonard Russell	.15	.07	.02
☐ 23 Rodney Hampton	.25	.11	.03
☐ 24 Marion Butts	.15	.07	.02
☐ 25 Neal Anderson	.15	.07	.02
☐ 26 Barry Sanders	.75	.35	.09
☐ 27 Dexter Carter	.10	.05	.01
☐ 28 Gaston Green	.10	.05	.01
☐ 29 Barry Word	.10	.05	.01
☐ 30 Eric Bieniemy	.10	.05	.01
☐ 31 Nick Bell	.10	.05	.01
☐ 32 Reggie Cobb	.10	.05	.01
☐ 33 Jay Novacek	.25	.11	.03
☐ 34 Keith Jackson	.15	.07	.02
☐ 35 Eric Green	.15	.07	.02
☐ 36 Lawrence Dawsey	.15	.07	.02
☐ 37 Mike Pritchard	.10	.05	.01
☐ 38 Michael Haynes	.15	.07	.02
☐ 39 James Lofton	.15	.07	.02
☐ 40 Art Monk	.15	.07	.02
☐ 41 Herman Moore	.40	.18	.05
☐ 42 Andre Rison	.25	.11	.03
☐ 43 Wendell Davis	.10	.05	.01
☐ 44 Sterling Sharpe	.15	.07	.02
☐ 45 Fred Barnett	.15	.07	.02
☐ 46 Rob Moore	.15	.07	.02
☐ 47 Gary Clark	.15	.07	.02
☐ 48 Wesley Carroll	.10	.05	.01
☐ 49 Michael Irvin	.25	.11	.03
☐ 50 John Taylor	.15	.07	.02
☐ 52 Ray Bentley	.10	.05	.01
☐ 53 Eric Swann	.15	.07	.02
☐ 54 Amp Lee	.15	.07	.02
☐ 55 Darryl Williams	.10	.05	.01
☐ 56 Wilber Marshall	.10	.05	.01
☐ 57 Siran Stacy	.10	.05	.01
☐ 58 Chip Lohmiller	.10	.05	.01
☐ 59 Rodney Culver	.15	.07	.02
☐ 60 Tommy Vardell	.15	.07	.02
☐ NNO Cris Dishman (Rules on back)	.10	.05	.01
☐ NNO Andre Ware (Rules on back)	.15	.07	.02

1993 Classic TONX

These 150 tonx (or player caps) were sold in a clear plastic bag; the attached paper display tag advertises that 123 players and 27 quarterbacks from all NFL teams are featured in the set. Each tonx measures approximately 1 5/8" in diameter and features a full-bleed color action player photo. The Classic logo at the bottom rounds out the front. The backs have a black background bisected by a purple stripe carrying the player's name. The tonx number, the team helmet, and logos fill out the back.

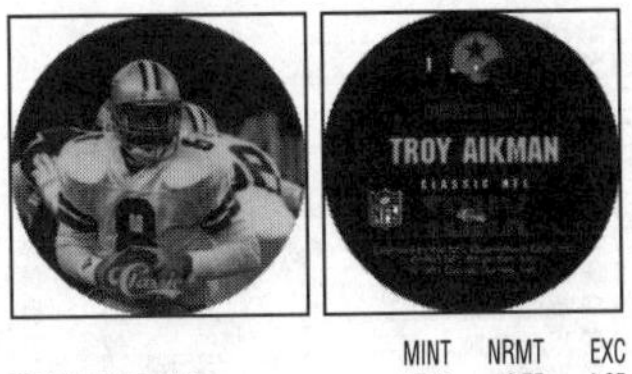

	MINT	NRMT	EXC
COMPLETE SET (150)	15.00	6.75	1.85
COMMON CARD (1-150)	.05	.02	.01
☐ 1 Troy Aikman	.75	.35	.09
☐ 2 Eric Allen	.05	.02	.01
☐ 3 Terry Allen	.20	.09	.03
☐ 4 Morten Andersen	.05	.02	.01
☐ 5 Neal Anderson	.05	.02	.01
☐ 6 Flipper Anderson	.05	.02	.01
☐ 7 Steve Atwater	.05	.02	.01
☐ 8 Carl Banks	.05	.02	.01
☐ 9 Patrick Bates	.05	.02	.01
☐ 10 Cornelius Bennett	.10	.05	.01
☐ 11 Rod Bernstine	.05	.02	.01
☐ 12 Jerome Bettis	.75	.35	.09
☐ 13 Steve Beuerlein	.05	.02	.01
☐ 14 Bennie Blades	.05	.02	.01
☐ 15 Brian Blades	.10	.05	.01
☐ 16 Drew Bledsoe	1.00	.45	.12
☐ 17 Tim Brown	.20	.09	.03
☐ 18 Terrell Buckley	.05	.02	.01
☐ 19 Marion Butts	.10	.05	.01
☐ 20 Mark Carrier DB	.05	.02	.01
☐ 21 Anthony Carter	.10	.05	.01
☐ 22 Cris Carter	.20	.09	.03
☐ 23 Dale Carter	.10	.05	.01
☐ 24 Ray Childress	.10	.05	.01
☐ 25 Gary Clark	.10	.05	.01
☐ 26 Reggie Cobb	.05	.02	.01
☐ 27 Marco Coleman	.05	.02	.01
☐ 28 Curtis Conway	.20	.09	.03
☐ 29 John Copeland	.10	.05	.01
☐ 30 Quentin Coryatt	.20	.09	.03
☐ 31 Randall Cunningham	.10	.05	.01
☐ 32 Eric Curry	.10	.05	.01
☐ 33 Lawrence Dawsey	.05	.02	.01
☐ 34 Chris Doleman	.10	.05	.01
☐ 35 Vaughn Dunbar	.05	.02	.01
☐ 36 Henry Ellard	.10	.05	.01
☐ 37 John Elway	.60	.25	.07
☐ 38 Steve Emtman	.05	.02	.01
☐ 39 Ricky Ervins	.05	.02	.01
☐ 40 Jim Everett	.05	.02	.01
☐ 41 Brett Favre	1.50	.70	.19
☐ 42 Barry Foster	.10	.05	.01
☐ 43 Cleveland Gary	.05	.02	.01
☐ 44 Jeff George	.20	.09	.03
☐ 45 Sean Gilbert	.10	.05	.01
☐ 46 Ernest Givins	.05	.02	.01
☐ 47 Harold Green	.05	.02	.01
☐ 48 Kevin Greene	.20	.09	.03
☐ 49 Paul Gruber	.05	.02	.01
☐ 50 Charles Haley	.10	.05	.01
☐ 51 Rodney Hampton	.20	.09	.03
☐ 52 Jim Harbaugh	.20	.09	.03
☐ 53 Ronnie Harmon	.05	.02	.01
☐ 54 Michael Haynes	.10	.05	.01
☐ 55 Garrison Hearst	.60	.25	.07
☐ 56 Randal Hill	.05	.02	.01
☐ 57 Merril Hoge	.05	.02	.01
☐ 58 Pierce Holt	.05	.02	.01
☐ 59 Jeff Hostetler	.10	.05	.01
☐ 60 Stan Humphries	.10	.05	.01
☐ 61 Michael Irvin	.20	.09	.03
☐ 62 Keith Jackson	.10	.05	.01
☐ 63 Rickey Jackson	.05	.02	.01
☐ 64 Haywood Jeffires	.05	.02	.01
☐ 65 Pepper Johnson	.05	.02	.01
☐ 66 Brent Jones	.10	.05	.01
☐ 67 Marvin Jones	.05	.02	.01
☐ 68 Seth Joyner	.10	.05	.01
☐ 69 Jim Kelly	.20	.09	.03
☐ 70 Cortez Kennedy	.10	.05	.01
☐ 71 David Klingler	.05	.02	.01
☐ 72 Bernie Kosar	.10	.05	.01
☐ 73 Reggie Langhorne	.05	.02	.01
☐ 74 Mo Lewis	.05	.02	.01
☐ 75 Howie Long	.20	.09	.03
☐ 76 Ronnie Lott	.10	.05	.01
☐ 77 Charles Mann	.05	.02	.01
☐ 78 Dan Marino	1.50	.70	.19
☐ 79 Todd Marinovich	.05	.02	.01
☐ 80 Eric Martin	.05	.02	.01
☐ 81 Clay Matthews	.10	.05	.01
☐ 82 Ed McCaffrey	.05	.02	.01
☐ 83 O.J. McDuffie	.40	.18	.05
☐ 84 Steve McMichael	.05	.02	.01
☐ 85 Audray McMillian	.05	.02	.01
☐ 86 Greg McMurtry	.05	.02	.01
☐ 87 Karl Mecklenburg	.05	.02	.01
☐ 88 Dave Meggett	.05	.02	.01
☐ 89 Eric Metcalf	.10	.05	.01
☐ 90 Anthony Miller	.10	.05	.01
☐ 91 Chris Miller	.05	.02	.01
☐ 92 Sam Mills	.05	.02	.01
☐ 93 Rick Mirer	.20	.09	.03
☐ 94 Johnny Mitchell	.05	.02	.01
☐ 95 Art Monk	.10	.05	.01
☐ 96 Joe Montana	.75	.35	.09
☐ 97 Warren Moon	.20	.09	.03
☐ 98 Rob Moore	.10	.05	.01
☐ 99 Brad Muster	.05	.02	.01
☐ 100 Browning Nagle	.05	.02	.01
☐ 101 Ken Norton Jr.	.10	.05	.01
☐ 102 Jay Novacek	.20	.09	.03
☐ 103 Neil O'Donnell	.20	.09	.03
☐ 104 Leslie O'Neal	.10	.05	.01
☐ 105 Louis Oliver	.05	.02	.01
☐ 106 Rodney Peete	.10	.05	.01
☐ 107 Michael Dean Perry	.10	.05	.01
☐ 108 Carl Pickens	.20	.09	.03
☐ 109 Ricky Proehl	.05	.02	.01
☐ 110 Andre Reed	.20	.09	.03
☐ 111 Jerry Rice	.75	.35	.09
☐ 112 Andre Rison	.20	.09	.03
☐ 113 Leonard Russell	.10	.05	.01
☐ 114 Mark Rypien	.05	.02	.01
☐ 115 Barry Sanders	.75	.35	.09
☐ 116 Deion Sanders	.50	.23	.06
☐ 117 Junior Seau	.20	.09	.03
☐ 118 Shannon Sharpe	.20	.09	.03
☐ 119 Sterling Sharpe	.10	.05	.01
☐ 120 Clyde Simmons	.05	.02	.01
☐ 121 Wayne Simmons	.05	.02	.01
☐ 122 Phil Simms	.10	.05	.01
☐ 123 Bruce Smith	.20	.09	.03
☐ 124 Emmitt Smith	1.50	.70	.19
☐ 126 Alonzo Spellman	.05	.02	.01
☐ 127 Pat Swilling	.10	.05	.01
☐ 128 John Taylor	.10	.05	.01
☐ 129 Lawrence Taylor	.20	.09	.03
☐ 130 Broderick Thomas	.05	.02	.01
☐ 131 Derrick Thomas	.20	.09	.03
☐ 132 Thurman Thomas	.20	.09	.03
☐ 133 Andre Tippett	.05	.02	.01
☐ 134 Jessie Tuggle	.05	.02	.01
☐ 135 Tommy Vardell	.05	.02	.01
☐ 136 Jon Vaughn	.05	.02	.01
☐ 137 Clarence Verdin	.05	.02	.01
☐ 138 Herschel Walker	.10	.05	.01
☐ 139 Andre Ware	.05	.02	.01
☐ 140 Chris Warren	.10	.05	.01
☐ 141 Ricky Watters	.20	.09	.03
☐ 142 Lorenzo White	.05	.02	.01
☐ 143 Reggie White	.20	.09	.03
☐ 144 Alfred Williams	.05	.02	.01
☐ 145 Calvin Williams	.10	.05	.01
☐ 146 Harvey Williams	.10	.05	.01
☐ 147 John L. Williams	.05	.02	.01
☐ 148 Rod Woodson	.20	.09	.03
☐ 149 Barry Word	.05	.02	.01
☐ 150 Steve Young	.60	.25	.07

1995 Classic Draft Day Jaguars

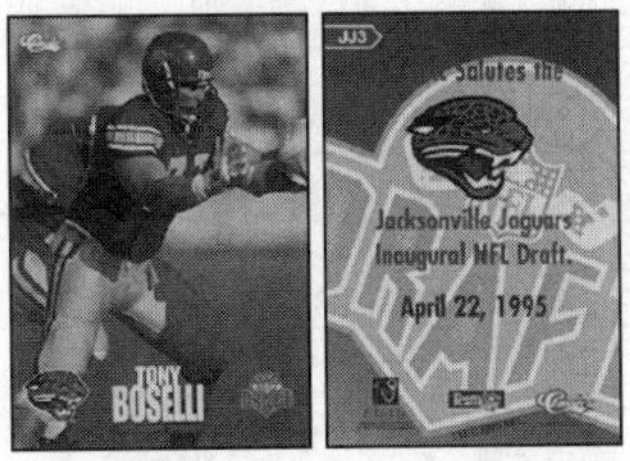

This 5-card standard-size set was issued on April 22 to salute the Jacksonville Jaguars' inaugural NFL Draft. The cards were given to individuals attending the Jaguars' reception. The fronts display color action player photos, with the team logo, player's name and position, and a 1995 NFL Draft emblem across the bottom. On a background consisting of an enlarged version of the 1995 NFL Draft emblem, the back carries the team logo and a salutation.

	MINT	NRMT	EXC
COMPLETE SET (5)	20.00	9.00	2.50
COMMON CARD (JJ1-JJ5)	2.00	.90	.25
☐ JJ1 Kerry Collins	7.50	3.40	.95
☐ JJ2 Steve McNair	6.00	2.70	.75
☐ JJ3 Tony Boselli	3.00	1.35	.35
☐ JJ4 Kevin Carter	2.00	.90	.25
☐ JJ5 Ki-Jana Carter	4.00	1.80	.50

1996 Classic SP Autographs

This eight-card set was offered as a mail-in order from Score Board Inc. (Classic) and Scott Paper Company. Each card was personally autographed by the player featured on the front and is accompanied by a Score Board certificate of authenticity. The cards were initially offered for $7.95 each with two UPCs or $10.95 without UPC labels. Complete could be had for $54.95 with eight UPCs or $64.95 without. Although the cards contain the 1995 date on the copyright line, they were first offered in early 1996.

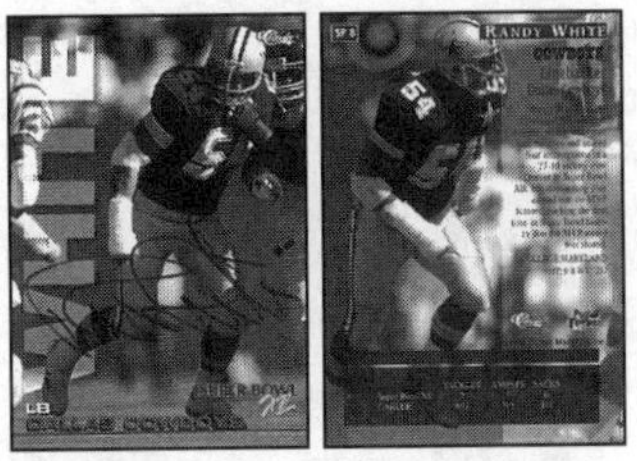

	MINT	NRMT	EXC
COMPLETE SET (8)	100.00	45.00	12.50
COMMON CARD (SP1-SP8)	12.00	5.50	1.50
☐ SP1 Kyle Brady	12.00	5.50	1.50
☐ SP2 Kerry Collins	20.00	9.00	2.50
☐ SP3 Ron Jaworski	12.00	5.50	1.50
☐ SP4 Napoleon Kaufman	12.00	5.50	1.50
☐ SP5 Jim Kiick	12.00	5.50	1.50
☐ SP6 Steve McNair	15.00	6.75	1.85
☐ SP7 Jim Plunkett	12.00	5.50	1.50
☐ SP8 Randy White	15.00	6.75	1.85

1994 Classic NFL Experience Promos

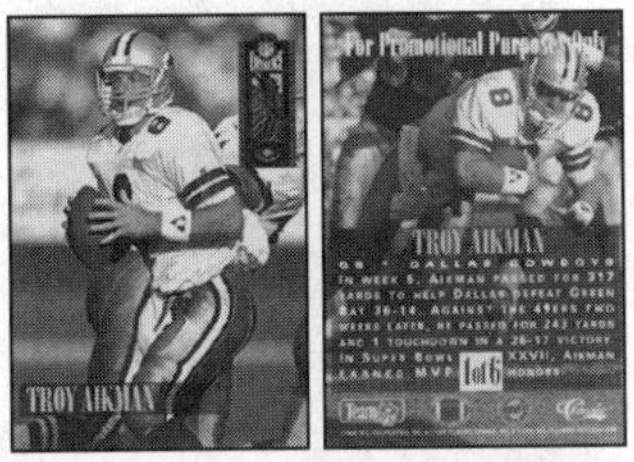

Classic released this set to preview the design of the 1994 Classic NFL Experience series. The cards feature full-bleed color action shots on the front with the player's name appearing at the bottom. The back clearly states "For Promotional Purposes Only" at the top with the card number (of 6) at the bottom. The Aikman card features a typical Classic NFL Experience card back, while the other five contain an ad for the 1994 Super Bowl Card Show V convention in Atlanta.

	MINT	NRMT	EXC
COMPLETE SET (6)	20.00	9.00	2.50
COMMON CARD (1-6)	1.50	.70	.19
☐ 1 Troy Aikman	5.00	2.20	.60
☐ 2 Jerry Rice	5.00	2.20	.60
☐ 3 Emmitt Smith	8.00	3.60	1.00
☐ 4 Derrick Thomas	1.50	.70	.19
☐ 5 Thurman Thomas	2.00	.90	.25
☐ 6 Rod Woodson	1.50	.70	.19

1994 Classic NFL Experience

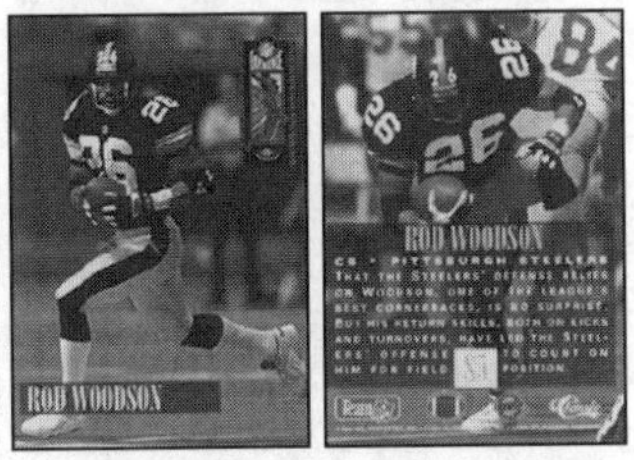

These 100 standard-size cards were released by Classic Games in celebration of Super Bowl XXVIII. Classic produced 1,500 sequentially numbered cases that were offered to hobby dealers only. Cards from the 10-card 1994 Classic NFL Experience LPs and 1,994 Troy Aikman Super Bowl XXVII MVP cards were randomly inserted in the eight-card foil packs. The fronts feature full-bleed color action player photos, with the player's name displayed on a ghosted dark stripe near the bottom. The NFL Experience logo overlays the picture at one of the upper corners. The backs carry a second full-bleed action photo, with game highlights summarized on a ghosted panel toward the bottom. The cards are numbered on the back, checklisted alphabetically according to teams, and arranged alphabetically within teams. There are no key Rookie Cards in this set.

	MINT	NRMT	EXC
COMPLETE SET (100)	10.00	4.50	1.25
COMMON CARD (1-100)	.05	.02	.01
☐ 1 Checklist 1	.05	.02	.01
☐ 2 Checklist 2	.05	.02	.01
☐ 3 Bobby Hebert	.05	.02	.01
☐ 4 Erric Pegram	.05	.02	.01
☐ 5 Andre Rison	.10	.05	.01
☐ 6 Deion Sanders	.60	.25	.07
☐ 7 Cornelius Bennett	.10	.05	.01
☐ 8 Jim Kelly	.20	.09	.03
☐ 9 Andre Reed	.10	.05	.01
☐ 10 Bruce Smith	.20	.09	.03
☐ 11 Thurman Thomas	.20	.09	.03
☐ 12 Curtis Conway	.20	.09	.03
☐ 13 Jim Harbaugh	.20	.09	.03
☐ 14 John Copeland	.05	.02	.01

☐ 15 David Klingler	.05	.02	.01
☐ 16 Carl Pickens	.50	.23	.06
☐ 17 Eric Metcalf	.10	.05	.01
☐ 18 Vinny Testaverde	.10	.05	.01
☐ 19 Eric Turner	.05	.02	.01
☐ 20 Tommy Vardell	.05	.02	.01
☐ 21 Troy Aikman	1.00	.45	.12
☐ 22 Michael Irvin	.20	.09	.03
☐ 23 Emmitt Smith	2.00	.90	.25
☐ 24 Kevin Williams WR	.10	.05	.01
☐ 25 John Elway	.75	.35	.09
☐ 26 Glyn Milburn	.10	.05	.01
☐ 27 Shannon Sharpe	.10	.05	.01
☐ 28 Herman Moore	.50	.23	.06
☐ 29 Rodney Peete	.05	.02	.01
☐ 30 Barry Sanders	1.00	.45	.12
☐ 31 Pat Swilling	.05	.02	.01
☐ 32 Brett Favre	2.00	.90	.25
☐ 33 Sterling Sharpe	.10	.05	.01
☐ 34 Reggie White	.20	.09	.03
☐ 35 Haywood Jeffires	.10	.05	.01
☐ 36 Warren Moon	.20	.09	.03
☐ 37 Webster Slaughter	.05	.02	.01
☐ 38 Lorenzo White	.05	.02	.01
☐ 39 Quentin Coryatt	.05	.02	.01
☐ 40 Jeff George	.20	.09	.03
☐ 41 Roosevelt Potts	.05	.02	.01
☐ 42 Marcus Allen	.20	.09	.03
☐ 43 Joe Montana	1.00	.45	.12
☐ 44 Neil Smith	.10	.05	.01
☐ 45 Derrick Thomas	.20	.09	.03
☐ 46 Tim Brown	.20	.09	.03
☐ 47 Jeff Hostetler	.10	.05	.01
☐ 48 Rocket Ismail	.10	.05	.01
☐ 49 Anthony Smith	.05	.02	.01
☐ 50 Jerome Bettis	.60	.25	.07
☐ 51 Jim Everett	.10	.05	.01
☐ 52 T.J. Rubley	.05	.02	.01
☐ 53 Keith Jackson	.05	.02	.01
☐ 54 Terry Kirby	.20	.09	.03
☐ 55 Dan Marino	2.00	.90	.25
☐ 56 O.J. McDuffie	.20	.09	.03
☐ 57 Scott Mitchell	.20	.09	.03
☐ 58 Cris Carter	.20	.09	.03
☐ 59 Chris Doleman	.05	.02	.01
☐ 60 Robert Smith	.20	.09	.03
☐ 61 Drew Bledsoe	1.25	.55	.16
☐ 62 Vincent Brisby	.05	.02	.01
☐ 63 Derek Brown RB	.05	.02	.01
☐ 64 Willie Roaf	.05	.02	.01
☐ 65 Irv Smith	.05	.02	.01
☐ 66 Renaldo Turnbull	.05	.02	.01
☐ 67 Rodney Hampton	.10	.05	.01
☐ 68 Phil Simms	.10	.05	.01
☐ 69 Lawrence Taylor	.20	.09	.03
☐ 70 Boomer Esiason	.10	.05	.01
☐ 71 Marvin Jones	.05	.02	.01
☐ 72 Ronnie Lott	.10	.05	.01
☐ 73 Johnny Mitchell	.05	.02	.01
☐ 74 Rob Moore	.10	.05	.01
☐ 75 Victor Bailey	.05	.02	.01
☐ 76 Randall Cunningham	.10	.05	.01
☐ 77 Ken O'Brien	.05	.02	.01
☐ 78 Steve Beuerlein	.05	.02	.01
☐ 79 Garrison Hearst	.50	.23	.06
☐ 80 Ronald Moore	.05	.02	.01
☐ 81 Ricky Proehl	.05	.02	.01
☐ 82 Deon Figures	.05	.02	.01
☐ 83 Barry Foster	.05	.02	.01
☐ 84 Neil O'Donnell	.10	.05	.01
☐ 85 Rod Woodson	.10	.05	.01
☐ 86 Natrone Means	.50	.23	.06
☐ 87 Anthony Miller	.10	.05	.01
☐ 88 Junior Seau	.20	.09	.03
☐ 89 Jerry Rice	1.00	.45	.12
☐ 90 Ricky Watters	.20	.09	.03
☐ 91 Steve Young	.75	.35	.09
☐ 92 Brian Blades	.10	.05	.01
☐ 93 Cortez Kennedy	.10	.05	.01
☐ 94 Rick Mirer	.20	.09	.03
☐ 95 Reggie Cobb	.05	.02	.01
☐ 96 Eric Curry	.05	.02	.01
☐ 97 Craig Erickson	.05	.02	.01
☐ 98 Reggie Brooks	.10	.05	.01
☐ 99 Desmond Howard	.10	.05	.01
☐ 100 Mark Rypien	.05	.02	.01
☐ SP1 Troy Aikman	40.00	18.00	5.00

1994 Classic NFL Experience LPs

Randomly inserted in 1994 Classic NFL Experience packs, these ten standard-size cards feature 1993 first-year players. Card fronts feature color action player photos with fading blue borders on the left and above the photo. Reportedly only 2,400 of each card were produced. Each card includes an embossed gold-foil Super Bowl XXVIII logo with "1 of 2,400" printed on it. The cards are numbered on the back with an "LP" prefix. The set is sequenced in alphabetical order.

	MINT	NRMT	EXC
COMPLETE SET (10)	90.00	40.00	11.00
COMMON CARD (LP1-LP10)	4.00	1.80	.50

☐ LP1 Jerome Bettis	12.00	5.50	1.50
☐ LP2 Drew Bledsoe	25.00	11.00	3.10

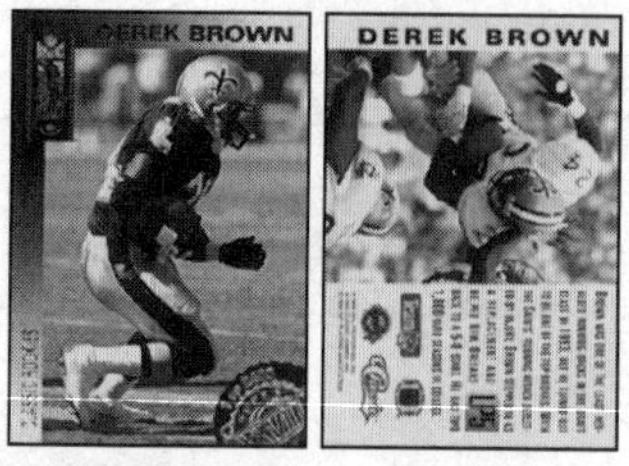

☐ LP3 Reggie Brooks	4.00	1.80	.50
☐ LP4 Garrison Hearst	8.00	3.60	1.00
☐ LP5 Derek Brown RB	4.00	1.80	.50
☐ LP6 Terry Kirby	6.00	2.70	.75
☐ LP7 Natrone Means	8.00	3.60	1.00
☐ LP8 Glyn Milburn	4.00	1.80	.50
☐ LP9 Rick Mirer	8.00	3.60	1.00
☐ LP10 Robert Smith	6.00	2.70	.75

1995 Classic NFL Experience

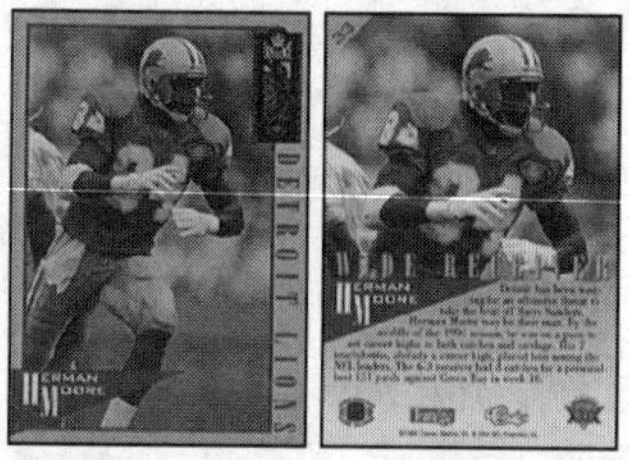

This 110-card standard-size set features color player action shots with team color-coded borders. The backs carry a second action shot, accompanied by highlighting of the player's achievements from the first 10 weeks of the 1994 season. This set also includes a Miami Dolphins commemorative card featuring legendary head coach Don Shula and quarterback Dan Marino (on average of one per box), and 1,995 sequentially numbered "Emmitt Zone" insert cards. Gold cards were inserted one per hobby pack. The cards are grouped alphabetically within teams and checklisted below alphabetically according to teams. The only key Rookie Card in this set is Jeff Blake. There was an Emmitt Smith Preview card issued for the set one per box in 1994 Classic Images. It is priced along with the Images release.

	MINT	NRMT	EXC
COMPLETE SET (110)	10.00	4.50	1.25
COMMON CARD (1-110)	.05	.02	.01

☐ 1 Seth Joyner	.05	.02	.01
☐ 2 Clyde Simmons	.05	.02	.01
☐ 3 Ronald Moore	.05	.02	.01
☐ 4 Andre Rison	.10	.05	.01
☐ 5 Bert Emanuel	.20	.09	.03
☐ 6 Jeff George	.10	.05	.01
☐ 7 Terance Mathis	.10	.05	.01
☐ 8 Jim Kelly	.20	.09	.03
☐ 9 Thurman Thomas	.20	.09	.03
☐ 10 Andre Reed	.10	.05	.01
☐ 11 Bruce Smith	.20	.09	.03
☐ 12 Cornelius Bennett	.10	.05	.01
☐ 13 Steve Walsh	.05	.02	.01
☐ 14 Lewis Tillman	.05	.02	.01
☐ 15 Chris Zorich	.05	.02	.01
☐ 16 Jeff Blake	1.25	.55	.16
☐ 17 Darnay Scott	.20	.09	.03
☐ 18 Dan Wilkinson	.10	.05	.01
☐ 19 Eric Metcalf	.10	.05	.01
☐ 20 Antonio Langham	.05	.02	.01
☐ 21 Pepper Johnson	.05	.02	.01
☐ 22 Eric Turner	.05	.02	.01
☐ 23 Leroy Hoard	.05	.02	.01
☐ 24 Vinny Testaverde	.10	.05	.01
☐ 25 Troy Aikman	.75	.35	.09
☐ 26 Emmitt Smith	1.50	.70	.19
☐ 27 Michael Irvin	.20	.09	.03
☐ 28 Alvin Harper	.05	.02	.01
☐ 29 Charles Haley	.10	.05	.01
☐ 30 John Elway	.60	.25	.07
☐ 31 Leonard Russell	.05	.02	.01
☐ 32 Shannon Sharpe	.10	.05	.01
☐ 33 Herman Moore	.40	.18	.05
☐ 34 Barry Sanders	.75	.35	.09
☐ 35 Brett Favre	1.50	.70	.19
☐ 36 Sterling Sharpe	.10	.05	.01
☐ 37 Reggie White	.20	.09	.03
☐ 38 Gary Brown	.05	.02	.01
☐ 39 Haywood Jeffires	.05	.02	.01
☐ 40 Quentin Coryatt	.10	.05	.01
☐ 41 Marshall Faulk	.40	.18	.05
☐ 42 Tony Bennett	.05	.02	.01
☐ 43 Joe Montana	.75	.35	.09
☐ 44 Marcus Allen	.20	.09	.03
☐ 45 Derrick Thomas	.10	.05	.01
☐ 46 Neil Smith	.10	.05	.01
☐ 47 Tim Brown	.20	.09	.03
☐ 48 Jeff Hostetler	.10	.05	.01
☐ 49 Terry McDaniel	.05	.02	.01
☐ 50 Jerome Bettis	.30	.14	.04
☐ 51 Sean Gilbert	.10	.05	.01
☐ 52 Dan Marino	1.50	.70	.19
☐ 53 Irving Fryar	.10	.05	.01
☐ 54 Keith Jackson	.05	.02	.01
☐ 55 Bernie Parmalee	.10	.05	.01
☐ 56 Tim Bowens	.05	.02	.01
☐ 57 Cris Carter	.20	.09	.03
☐ 58 Terry Allen	.10	.05	.01
☐ 59 Warren Moon	.10	.05	.01
☐ 60 John Randle	.05	.02	.01
☐ 61 Jake Reed	.10	.05	.01
☐ 62 Drew Bledsoe	.75	.35	.09
☐ 63 Marion Butts	.05	.02	.01
☐ 64 Ben Coates	.10	.05	.01
☐ 65 Derek Brown RB	.05	.02	.01
☐ 66 Jim Everett	.05	.02	.01
☐ 67 Michael Haynes	.10	.05	.01
☐ 68 Darion Conner	.05	.02	.01
☐ 69 Rodney Hampton	.10	.05	.01
☐ 70 Dave Meggett	.05	.02	.01
☐ 71 Boomer Esiason	.10	.05	.01
☐ 72 Johnny Johnson	.05	.02	.01
☐ 73 Ronnie Lott	.10	.05	.01
☐ 74 Rob Moore	.05	.02	.01
☐ 75 Mo Lewis	.05	.02	.01
☐ 76 Randall Cunningham	.10	.05	.01
☐ 77 Herschel Walker	.10	.05	.01
☐ 78 Charlie Garner	.10	.05	.01
☐ 79 Calvin Williams	.10	.05	.01
☐ 80 Fred Barnett	.10	.05	.01
☐ 81 William Fuller	.05	.02	.01
☐ 82 Eric Allen	.05	.02	.01
☐ 83 Barry Foster	.10	.05	.01
☐ 84 Neil O'Donnell	.10	.05	.01
☐ 85 Rod Woodson	.10	.05	.01
☐ 86 Kevin Greene	.10	.05	.01
☐ 87 Byron Bam Morris	.10	.05	.01
☐ 88 Darren Perry	.05	.02	.01
☐ 89 Greg Lloyd	.10	.05	.01
☐ 90 Steve Young	.60	.25	.07
☐ 91 Ricky Watters	.20	.09	.03
☐ 92 Jerry Rice	.75	.35	.09
☐ 93 Ken Norton Jr.	.10	.05	.01
☐ 94 Deion Sanders	.50	.23	.06
☐ 95 Stan Humphries	.10	.05	.01
☐ 96 Natrone Means	.20	.09	.03
☐ 97 Junior Seau	.20	.09	.03
☐ 98 Leslie O'Neal	.10	.05	.01
☐ 99 Chris Mims	.05	.02	.01
☐ 100 Rick Mirer	.20	.09	.03
☐ 101 Chris Warren	.10	.05	.01
☐ 102 Brian Blades	.10	.05	.01
☐ 103 Trent Dilfer	.20	.09	.03
☐ 104 Errict Rhett	.20	.09	.03
☐ 105 Heath Shuler	.20	.09	.03
☐ 106 Henry Ellard	.10	.05	.01
☐ 107 Ken Harvey	.05	.02	.01
☐ 108 Gus Frerotte	.40	.18	.05
☐ 109 Checklist 1	.10	.05	.01
☐ 110 Checklist 2	.10	.05	.01
☐ EZ1 Emmitt Smith Zone/1995	80.00	36.00	10.00
☐ GC1 Dan Marino Don Shula Play Card Super Bowl pack insert	2.00	.90	.25
☐ GC2 Dan Marino Don Shula VIP Card Super Bowl pack insert	5.00	2.20	.60
☐ MD1 Dan Marino Don Shula Dolphins Commemorative regular pack insert	4.00	1.80	.50
☐ PC1 Marshall Faulk Promo Throwbacks card	2.00	.90	.25

1995 Classic NFL Experience Gold

This 110-card standard-size set was issued as a parallel to the regular Classic NFL Experience issue. They were issued one per hobby pack. The only difference between these cards and the regular cards is that the player's name is framed in gold foil.

	MINT	NRMT	EXC
COMPLETE SET (110)	40.00	18.00	5.00
COMMON CARD (1-110)	.25	.11	.03

*VETERAN STARS: 1.5X to 3X BASIC CARDS
*YOUNG STARS: 1.25X to 2.5X BASIC CARDS

1995 Classic NFL Experience Rookies

Inserted on average of 1:6 packs, this insert set honors ten rookies of 1994. Vertically designed, the fronts have an action photo with a gold-foil stamped and embossed Super Bowl XXIX logo. The backs have a player photo with career highlights. The cards are numbered with an "R" prefix.

	MINT	NRMT	EXC
COMPLETE SET (10)	14.00	6.25	1.75
COMMON CARD (R1-R10)	1.00	.45	.12

☐ R1 Marshall Faulk	4.00	1.80	.50
☐ R2 Bert Emanuel	1.50	.70	.19

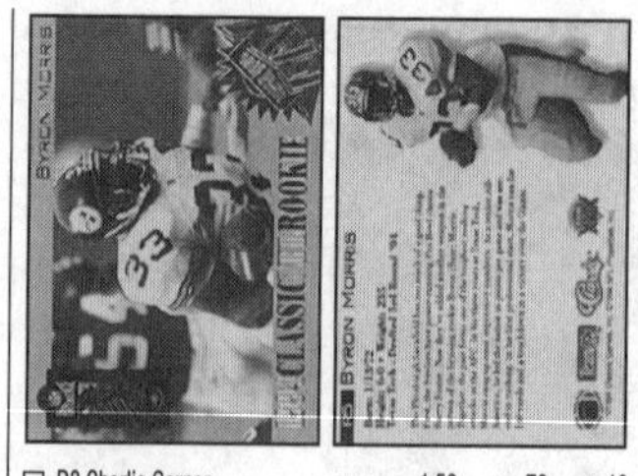

☐ R3 Charlie Garner	1.50	.70	.19
☐ R4 Errict Rhett	1.50	.70	.19
☐ R5 Byron Bam Morris	1.50	.70	.19
☐ R6 Heath Shuler	1.50	.70	.19
☐ R7 Trent Dilfer	1.50	.70	.19
☐ R8 Darnay Scott	2.50	1.10	.30
☐ R9 Tim Bowens	1.00	.45	.12
☐ R10 Antonio Langham	1.00	.45	.12

1995 Classic NFL Experience Super Bowl Game

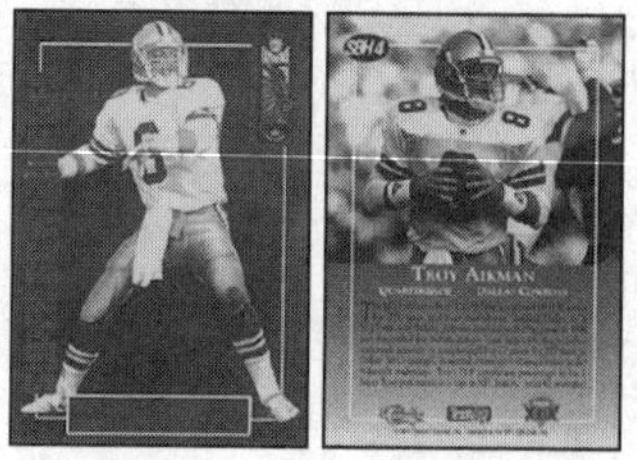

This 20-card standard-size set was issued one per special jumbo pack. The set consists of ten stars from each conference. If the card number corresponded to the last digit of the conference representative's score in the 1995 Super Bowl, the collector redeemed the card for a prize. The contest expired on March 6, 1995.

	MINT	NRMT	EXC
COMPLETE SET (20)	25.00	11.00	3.10
COMMON CARD	.50	.23	.06

☐ A0 Marshall Faulk	1.00	.45	.12
☐ A1 Natrone Means	.75	.35	.09
☐ A2 Thurman Thomas	.75	.35	.09
☐ A3 Joe Montana	2.00	.90	.25
☐ A4 John Elway	1.50	.70	.19
☐ A5 Rick Mirer	.75	.35	.09
☐ A6 Drew Bledsoe WIN Exp	2.50	1.10	.30
☐ A7 Dan Marino	3.50	1.55	.45
☐ A8 Jim Kelly	.75	.35	.09
☐ A9 Marcus Allen	.75	.35	.09
☐ N0 Troy Aikman	2.00	.90	.25
☐ N1 Steve Young	1.50	.70	.19
☐ N2 Jerome Bettis	.75	.35	.09
☐ N3 Barry Sanders	2.00	.90	.25
☐ N4 Randall Cunningham	.50	.23	.06
☐ N5 Andre Rison	.50	.23	.06
☐ N6 Jerry Rice	2.00	.90	.25
☐ N7 Emmitt Smith	3.50	1.55	.45
☐ N8 Michael Irvin	.75	.35	.09
☐ N9 Sterling Sharpe WIN Exp	.75	.35	.09

1995 Classic NFL Experience Super Bowl Inserts

This 5-card set was sold on Home Shopping Network with the regular 1994 NFL Experience set. It was made exclusively for them. The fronts feature color player action shots with the player's name and a Super Bowl XXX highlight at the bottom in a red stripe. The backs carry another color player action shot with the player's name, position, and team name below it along with a brief biography of the player.

	MINT	NRMT	EXC
COMPLETE SET (5)	12.00	5.50	1.50
COMMON CARD (SBF1-SBF5)	2.00	.90	.25

☐ SBF1 Jerry Rice	4.00	1.80	.50
☐ SBF2 Ricky Watters	2.00	.90	.25
☐ SBF3 Natrone Means	2.00	.90	.25
☐ SBF4 Steve Young	3.00	1.35	.35
☐ SBF5 Steve Young	3.00	1.35	.35

1995 Classic NFL Experience Throwbacks

Inserted on average of two per box, these standard-size cards are printed on parchment paper to look and feel like an old-time card. The set commemorates the NFL's 75th anniversary by picturing one player from each team in his "Throwbacks" uniform. The photo on front has a white border and a "Throwbacks" logo at the bottom. The backs carry a brief history of each NFL franchise along with the reason the team chose that particular uniform. The set is arranged in alphabetical order by teams. The cards are numbered with a "T" prefix.

	MINT	NRMT	EXC
COMPLETE SET (28)	120.00	55.00	15.00
COMMON CARD (T1-T28)	2.00	.90	.25

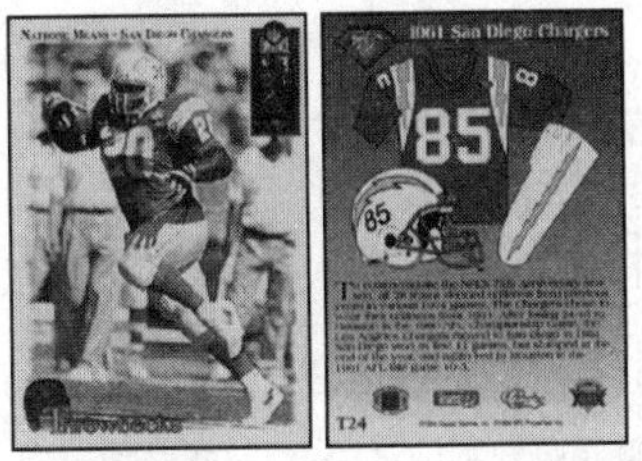

□ T1 Seth Joyner	2.00	.90	.25
□ T2 Andre Rison	2.00	.90	.25
□ T3 Thurman Thomas	5.00	2.20	.60
□ T4 Lewis Tillman	2.00	.90	.25
□ T5 Dan Wilkinson	2.00	.90	.25
□ T6 Eric Metcalf	5.00	2.20	.60
□ T7 Emmitt Smith	20.00	9.00	2.50
□ T8 John Elway	8.00	3.60	1.00
□ T9 Barry Sanders	10.00	4.50	1.25
□ T10 Reggie White	5.00	2.20	.60
□ T11 Haywood Jeffires	2.00	.90	.25
□ T12 Marshall Faulk	5.00	2.20	.60
□ T13 Joe Montana	10.00	4.50	1.25
□ T14 Jeff Hostetler	2.00	.90	.25
□ T15 Jerome Bettis	5.00	2.20	.60
□ T16 Dan Marino	20.00	9.00	2.50
□ T17 Warren Moon	5.00	2.20	.60
□ T18 Drew Bledsoe	10.00	4.50	1.25
□ T19 Jim Everett	2.00	.90	.25
□ T20 Dave Meggett	2.00	.90	.25
□ T21 Ronnie Lott	5.00	2.20	.60
□ T22 Randall Cunningham	3.00	1.35	.35
□ T23 Rod Woodson	5.00	2.20	.60
□ T24 Natrone Means	5.00	2.20	.60
□ T25 Rick Mirer	5.00	2.20	.60
□ T26 Steve Young	8.00	3.60	1.00
□ T27 Trent Dilfer	3.00	1.35	.35
□ T28 Henry Ellard	2.00	.90	.25

1996 Classic NFL Experience

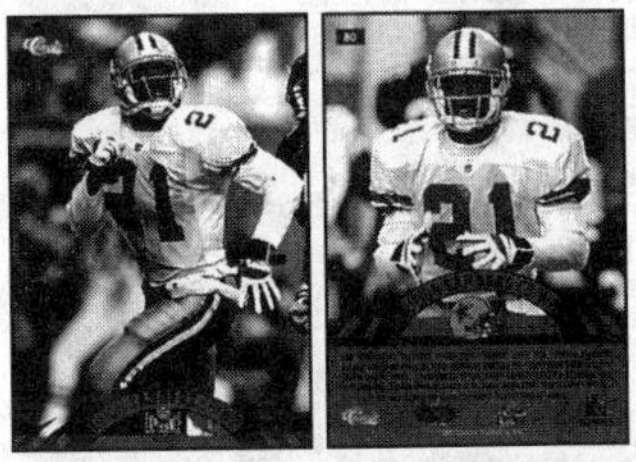

This 125 card standard-size set was issued in 10 card packs, with 24 cards in a box and 16 boxes in a case. There were also factory sets issued with Emmitt Smith featured on the front, and was released as part of a retail package that included 12-packs of 1996 NFL Experience as well. There are no key Rookie Cards in this set. Special Super Bowl packs were issued with special parallel versions of these cards. An Emmitt Smith Sculpted Promo card (#XXX) was produced to preview the set. We've included it below in the price listings.

	MINT	NRMT	EXC
COMPLETE SET (125)	12.00	5.50	1.50
COMP.FACT SET (130)	20.00	9.00	2.50
COMMON CARD (1-125)	.05	.02	.01
□ 1 Emmitt Smith	1.50	.70	.19
□ 2 Jerry Rice	.75	.35	.09
□ 3 Carl Pickens	.20	.09	.03
□ 4 Curtis Conway	.20	.09	.03
□ 5 Isaac Bruce	.20	.09	.03
□ 6 Marshall Faulk	.20	.09	.03
□ 7 Errict Rhett	.10	.05	.01
□ 8 Troy Aikman	.75	.35	.09
□ 9 Jeff Hostetler	.10	.05	.01
□ 10 Dan Marino	1.50	.70	.19
□ 11 Barry Sanders	.75	.35	.09
□ 12 Drew Bledsoe	.75	.35	.09
□ 13 Ricky Watters	.10	.05	.01
□ 14 Natrone Means	.20	.09	.03
□ 15 Chris Warren	.10	.05	.01
□ 16 Jim Kelly	.20	.09	.03
□ 17 Jeff George	.10	.05	.01
□ 18 Garrison Hearst	.10	.05	.01
□ 19 Brett Favre	1.50	.70	.19
□ 20 John Elway	.60	.25	.07
□ 21 Robert Smith	.10	.05	.01
□ 22 Steve Bono	.10	.05	.01
□ 23 Byron Bam Morris	.10	.05	.01
□ 24 Jim Everett	.05	.02	.01
□ 25 Steve Young	.60	.25	.07
□ 26 Rodney Hampton	.10	.05	.01
□ 27 Terry Allen	.10	.05	.01
□ 28 Chris Chandler	.10	.05	.01
□ 29 Mark Carrier WR	.10	.05	.01
□ 30 Desmond Howard	.10	.05	.01
□ 31 Erik Kramer	.05	.02	.01
□ 32 Irving Fryar	.10	.05	.01
□ 33 Jeff Blake	.20	.09	.03
□ 34 Vinny Testaverde	.10	.05	.01
□ 35 Stan Humphries	.10	.05	.01
□ 36 Tim Brown	.10	.05	.01
□ 37 Trent Dilfer	.10	.05	.01
□ 38 Jim Harbaugh	.10	.05	.01
□ 39 Warren Moon	.10	.05	.01
□ 40 Ben Coates	.10	.05	.01
□ 41 Boomer Esiason	.10	.05	.01
□ 42 Rodney Peete	.05	.02	.01
□ 43 Gus Frerotte	.20	.09	.03
□ 44 Jerome Bettis	.20	.09	.03
□ 45 Dave Brown	.10	.05	.01
□ 46 William Floyd	.20	.09	.03
□ 47 Andre Rison	.10	.05	.01
□ 48 Robert Brooks	.20	.09	.03
□ 49 Marcus Allen	.20	.09	.03
□ 50 Rick Mirer	.10	.05	.01
□ 51 Alvin Harper	.05	.02	.01
□ 52 Chris Miller	.05	.02	.01
□ 53 Eric Metcalf	.10	.05	.01
□ 54 Dave Krieg	.05	.02	.01
□ 55 Darnay Scott	.10	.05	.01
□ 56 Cris Carter	.20	.09	.03
□ 57 Lake Dawson	.10	.05	.01
□ 58 Haywood Jeffires	.05	.02	.01
□ 59 Herman Moore	.20	.09	.03
□ 60 Michael Irvin	.20	.09	.03
□ 61 Anthony Miller	.10	.05	.01
□ 62 Troy Vincent	.05	.02	.01
□ 63 Jake Reed	.10	.05	.01
□ 64 Michael Haynes	.10	.05	.01
□ 65 Scott Mitchell	.10	.05	.01
□ 66 Roman Phifer	.05	.02	.01
□ 67 Harvey Williams	.05	.02	.01
□ 68 Darren Perry	.05	.02	.01
□ 69 Brian Mitchell	.05	.02	.01
□ 70 Derek Loville	.05	.02	.01
□ 71 Junior Seau	.20	.09	.03
□ 72 Bruce Smith	.20	.09	.03
□ 73 Willie Davis	.10	.05	.01
□ 74 Charles Haley	.10	.05	.01
□ 75 Mike Sherrard	.05	.02	.01
□ 76 Pat Swilling	.05	.02	.01
□ 77 Yancey Thigpen	.10	.05	.01
□ 78 Bryce Paup	.10	.05	.01
□ 79 Eric Green	.05	.02	.01
□ 80 Deion Sanders	.40	.18	.05
□ 81 Mario Bates	.10	.05	.01
□ 82 John Randle	.05	.02	.01
□ 83 Charlie Garner	.05	.02	.01
□ 84 Chris Doleman	.05	.02	.01
□ 85 Robert Porcher	.05	.02	.01
□ 86 Rob Moore	.05	.02	.01
□ 87 Anthony Pleasant	.05	.02	.01
□ 88 Bryan Cox	.05	.02	.01
□ 89 Greg Hill	.10	.05	.01
□ 90 Reggie White	.20	.09	.03
□ 91 Shannon Sharpe	.10	.05	.01
□ 92 Leroy Hoard	.05	.02	.01
□ 93 John Copeland	.05	.02	.01
□ 94 Tony Martin	.10	.05	.01
□ 95 Greg Lloyd	.10	.05	.01
□ 96 Tony Bennett	.05	.02	.01
□ 97 Alonzo Spellman	.05	.02	.01
□ 98 Wayne Martin	.05	.02	.01
□ 99 Craig Heyward	.05	.02	.01
□ 100 Leslie O'Neal	.05	.02	.01
□ 101 Andy Harmon	.05	.02	.01
□ 102 Edgar Bennett	.10	.05	.01
□ 103 Derrick Moore	.05	.02	.01
□ 104 Terrell Davis	1.00	.45	.12
□ 105 Kerry Collins	.75	.35	.09
□ 106 Rodney Thomas	.05	.02	.01
□ 107 Mark Brunell	.75	.35	.09
□ 108 Curtis Martin	1.00	.45	.12
□ 109 Tyrone Wheatley	.10	.05	.01
□ 110 Rashaan Salaam	.20	.09	.03
□ 111 Kevin Carter	.10	.05	.01
□ 112 Joey Galloway	.30	.14	.04
□ 113 Mike Mamula	.05	.02	.01
□ 114 Kyle Brady	.10	.05	.01
□ 115 James O.Stewart	.10	.05	.01
□ 116 Michael Westbrook	.20	.09	.03
□ 117 J.J. Stokes	.20	.09	.03
□ 118 Wayne Chrebet	.10	.05	.01
□ 119 Warren Sapp	.05	.02	.01
□ 120 Hugh Douglas	.05	.02	.01
□ 121 Jim Flanigan	.05	.02	.01
□ 122 Chester McGlockton	.05	.02	.01
□ 123 Shawn Lee	.05	.02	.01
□ 124 Emmitt Smith CL	.30	.14	.04
□ 125 Kerry Collins CL	.20	.09	.03
□ P1 Emmitt Smith Promo Sculpted card, #XXX	2.00	.90	.25

1996 Classic NFL Experience Printer's Proofs

This 125-card standard-size set is a parallel to the regular Classic NFL Experience set. These cards are numbered as 1 of 499 on the front. They were inserted one in every 20 packs.

	MINT	NRMT	EXC
COMPLETE SET (125)	250.00	110.00	31.00
COMMON CARD (1-125)	.75	.35	.09

*VETERAN STARS: 12X TO 25X BASIC CARDS
*YOUNG STARS: 10X TO 20X BASIC CARDS

1996 Classic NFL Experience Super Bowl Gold

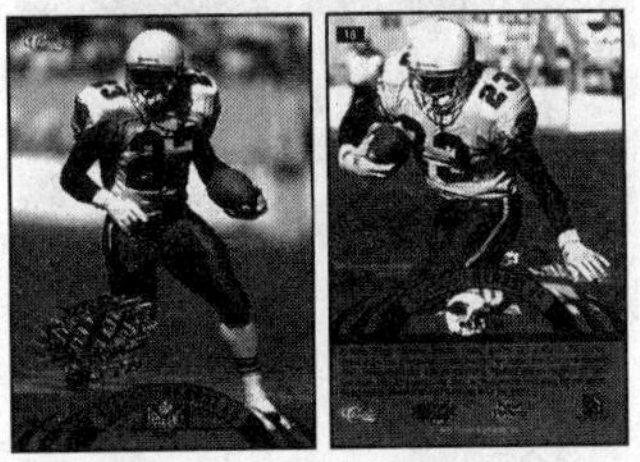

This 125 standard-size Gold parallel set was issued in special NFL Experience Super Bowl packs. The cards have a gold foil Super Bowl XXX stamp and were numbered of 799 made.

	MINT	NRMT	EXC
COMPLETE GOLD SET (125)	125.00	55.00	15.50
COMMON GOLD CARD (1-125)	.40	.18	.05

*GOLD VETERAN STARS: 5X TO 10X BASIC CARDS
*GOLD YOUNG STARS/RCs: 3.5X TO 7X BASIC CARDS

1996 Classic NFL Experience Class of 1995

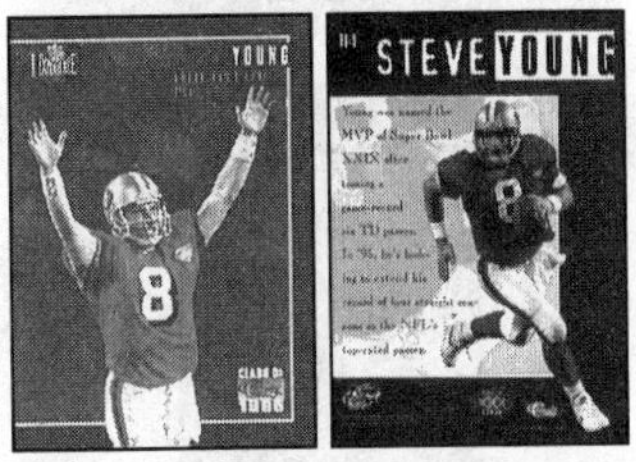

As a special factory set insert, these five cards were included. These standard-size cards feature various award winners and have the player's portrait against a silver background. The cards are numbered with a "FI" prefix on the back.

	MINT	NRMT	EXC
COMPLETE SET (5)	10.00	4.50	1.25
COMMON CARD (FI1-FI5)	1.25	.55	.16
□ FI1 Steve Young	2.00	.90	.25
□ FI2 Emmitt Smith	4.00	1.80	.50
□ FI3 Deion Sanders	1.50	.70	.19
□ FI4 Rashaan Salaam	1.25	.55	.16
□ FI5 Kerry Collins	2.50	1.10	.30

1996 Classic NFL Experience Emmitt Zone

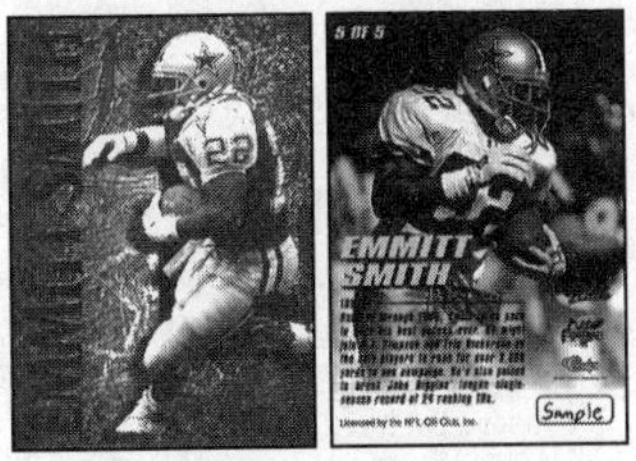

Randomly inserted into packs, this five-card standard-size set features highlights from Emmitt Smith's career. The set breaks down his career into year by year breakdown. The name "Emmitt Smith" is printed down the left side of the front while Emmitt has a picture on the right. The words "Emmitt Zone" are printed in the lower right hand corner. The cards are numbered as "X" of 5 . A special "Emmitt Zone" phone card was issued as well. That card was inserted one every 375 Super Bowl packs and had a calling value of $5.

	MINT	NRMT	EXC
COMPLETE SET (5)	300.00	135.00	38.00
COMMON CARD (1-5)	60.00	27.00	7.50
□ 1 Emmitt Smith 1990-91 ROY	60.00	27.00	7.50
□ 2 Emmitt Smith 1992 NFL Leading Rusher	60.00	27.00	7.50
□ 3 Emmitt Smith 1993 3rd NFL Rushing Title	60.00	27.00	7.50
□ 4 Emmitt Smith 1994 Leader in League Touchdowns	60.00	27.00	7.50
□ 5 Emmitt Smith 1995 Best Season Ever	60.00	27.00	7.50

1996 Classic NFL Experience Super Bowl Die Cut Promos

This 10-card promo set was given away at the NFL Experience 1996 Super Bowl Card Show in Tempe, Arizona. The cards feature players that are represented on the Classic NFL Experience Super Bowl Die

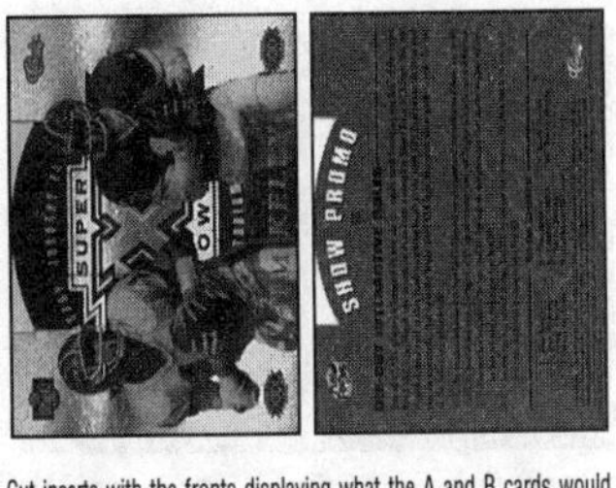

Cut inserts with the fronts displaying what the A and B cards would look like if matched. The backs carry the interactive rules to claim a prize with the Super Bowl Die Cut contest cards. Various prize levels could be attained depending on which group of cards the collector had acquired. Both the show Promos and Die Cut contest cards could be combined to win advanced prizes from Classic.

	MINT	NRMT	EXC
COMPLETE SET (10)	40.00	18.00	5.00
COMMON CARD (1C-10C)	1.50	.70	.19
□ 1C Jim Kelly	2.00	.90	.25
□ 2C Dan Marino	10.00	4.50	1.25
□ 3C Greg Lloyd	1.50	.70	.19
□ 4C Marcus Allen	2.00	.90	.25
□ 5C Tim Brown	2.00	.90	.25
□ 6C Emmitt Smith	10.00	4.50	1.25
□ 7C Steve Young	4.00	1.80	.50
□ 8C Rashaan Salaam	2.00	.90	.25
□ 9C Brett Favre	10.00	4.50	1.25
□ 10C Isaac Bruce	3.00	1.35	.35

1996 Classic NFL Experience Super Bowl Die Cut Contest

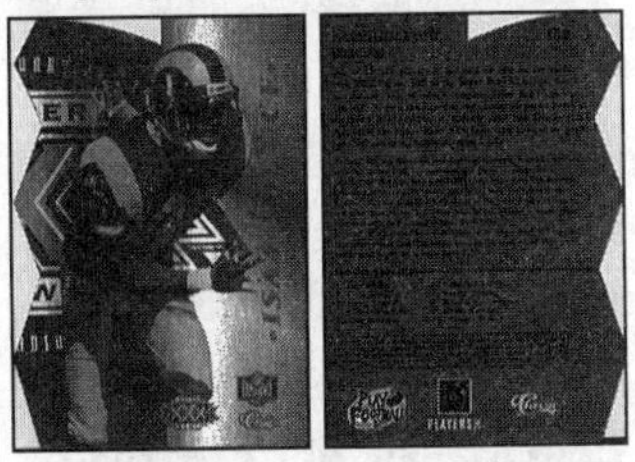

This 20-card set consists of ten players with each featured on two die-cut cards which fit together to form the Super Bowl XXX logo. The cards are numbered 1A-10A and 1B-10B with the A's having the left side of the Super Bowl logo as a background and the B's the right. The Die Cuts were randomly inserted in the Card Show version of 1996 Classic NFL Experience at the rate of 1:12 packs. Two die-cut cards forming the Super Bowl XXX logo and a show promo card could be redeemed for one of four levels of prizes. The fronts display a color action player photo with the player's name in the gold side border. The backs carry the rules and how to redeem the cards for a prize.

	MINT	NRMT	EXC
COMPLETE SET (20)	150.00	70.00	19.00
COMMON CARD (1A-10B)	3.00	1.35	.35
□ 1A Jim Kelly	5.00	2.20	.60
□ 1B Jim Kelly	5.00	2.20	.60
□ 2A Dan Marino	18.00	8.00	2.20
□ 2B Dan Marino	18.00	8.00	2.20
□ 3A Greg Lloyd	3.00	1.35	.35
□ 3B Greg Lloyd	3.00	1.35	.35
□ 4A Marcus Allen	5.00	2.20	.60
□ 4B Marcus Allen	5.00	2.20	.60
□ 5A Tim Brown	5.00	2.20	.60
□ 5B Tim Brown	5.00	2.20	.60
□ 6A Emmitt Smith	18.00	8.00	2.20
□ 6B Emmitt Smith	18.00	8.00	2.20
□ 7A Steve Young	8.00	3.60	1.00
□ 7B Steve Young	8.00	3.60	1.00
□ 8A Rashaan Salaam	5.00	2.20	.60
□ 8B Rashaan Salaam	5.00	2.20	.60
□ 9A Brett Favre	18.00	8.00	2.20
□ 9B Brett Favre	18.00	8.00	2.20
□ 10A Isaac Bruce	5.00	2.20	.60
□ 10B Isaac Bruce	5.00	2.20	.60

1996 Classic NFL Experience Super Bowl Game

These 20 standard-size cards were inserted approximately one every four packs. The cards were winners based on the "box pool" concept in which numbers from each row and column corresponds to the last digit in each team's score. All collectors who sent in winning cards were eligible for the grand prize of a trip for 2 to New Orleans for Super Bowl XXX1. The deadline for mailing in the contest cards were March 8, 1996.

	MINT	NRMT	EXC
COMPLETE SET (20)	40.00	18.00	5.00
COMMON CARD	.75	.35	.09
□ A0 Drew Bledsoe	3.00	1.35	.35
□ A1 John Elway	2.00	.90	.25

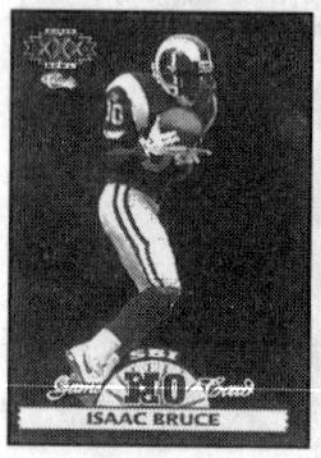

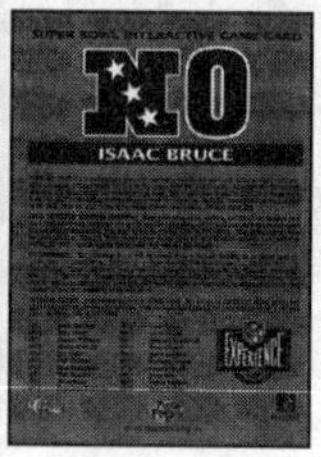

☐ A2 Harvey Williams	.75	.35	.09
☐ A3 Marshall Faulk	1.25	.55	.16
☐ A4 Jim Kelly	1.25	.55	.16
☐ A5 Carl Pickens	1.25	.55	.16
☐ A6 Stan Humphries	.75	.35	.09
☐ A7 Dan Marino	6.00	2.70	.75
☐ A8 Steve Bono	.75	.35	.09
☐ A9 Napoleon Kaufman	.75	.35	.09
☐ N0 Isaac Bruce	1.25	.55	.16
☐ N1 Steve Young	2.00	.90	.25
☐ N2 Michael Westbrook	1.25	.55	.16
☐ N3 Troy Aikman	3.00	1.35	.35
☐ N4 Barry Sanders	3.00	1.35	.35
☐ N5 Rashaan Salaam	1.25	.55	.16
☐ N6 Emmitt Smith	6.00	2.70	.75
☐ N7 Jerry Rice	3.00	1.35	.35
☐ N8 Deion Sanders	1.50	.70	.19
☐ N9 Kerry Collins	3.00	1.35	.35

1996 Classic NFL Experience Super Bowl Game Redemption

This five-card prize set was a redemption set for Game cards at the Super Bowl Game Show in Phoenix, Arizona. They have a "SBR" prefix on the cards.

	MINT	NRMT	EXC
COMPLETE SET (5)	20.00	9.00	2.50
COMMON CARD (SBR1-SBR5)	2.00	.90	.25
☐ SBR1 Jay Novacek	3.00	1.35	.35
☐ SBR2 Yancey Thigpen	3.00	1.35	.35
☐ SBR3 Emmitt Smith	10.00	4.50	1.25
☐ SBR4 Byron Bam Morris	2.00	.90	.25
☐ SBR5 Troy Aikman	5.00	2.20	.60

1996 Classic NFL Experience Sculpted

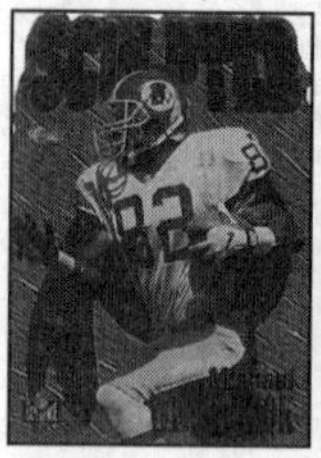
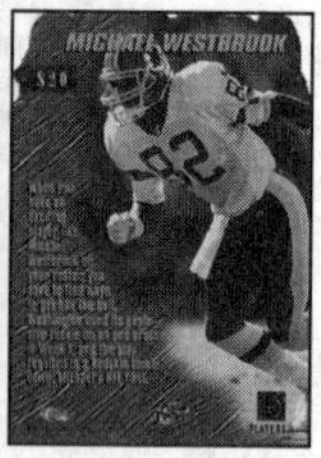

These cards were inserted approximately one every 15 hobby packs. They feature a die cut pattern with the player's picture against a gold background which features the team's logo. The cards are numbered with an "S" prefix.

	MINT	NRMT	EXC
COMPLETE SET (20)	150.00	70.00	19.00
COMMON CARD (S1-S20)	2.50	1.10	.30
☐ S1 Kerry Collins	10.00	4.50	1.25
☐ S2 Jeff Blake	4.00	1.80	.50
☐ S3 Vinny Testaverde	2.50	1.10	.30
☐ S4 Emmitt Smith	18.00	8.00	2.20
☐ S5 Troy Aikman	10.00	4.50	1.25
☐ S6 Deion Sanders	6.00	2.70	.75
☐ S7 John Elway	8.00	3.60	1.00
☐ S8 Barry Sanders	10.00	4.50	1.25
☐ S9 Brett Favre	18.00	8.00	2.20
☐ S10 Marshall Faulk	4.00	1.80	.50
☐ S11 Steve Bono	2.50	1.10	.30
☐ S12 Dan Marino	18.00	8.00	2.20
☐ S13 Robert Smith	2.50	1.10	.30
☐ S14 Drew Bledsoe	10.00	4.50	1.25
☐ S15 Natrone Means	4.00	1.80	.50
☐ S16 Steve Young	8.00	3.60	1.00
☐ S17 Jerry Rice	10.00	4.50	1.25
☐ S18 Isaac Bruce	4.00	1.80	.50
☐ S19 Errict Rhett	4.00	1.80	.50
☐ S20 Michael Westbrook	4.00	1.80	.50

1996 Classic NFL Experience X

These 10 standard-size cards feature leading NFL players. The cards were randomly inserted into hobby packs at a rate of one in 70. The cards have the words "Genuine Silver" in the upper left corner and the letter "X" in red in the lower right. The backs have the sequential number in the lower right. The cards are numbered with an "X" prefix.

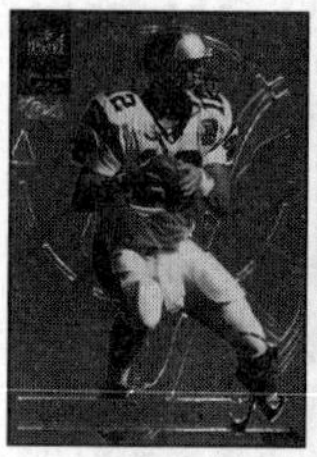
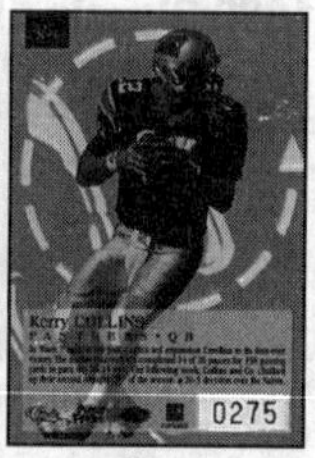

	MINT	NRMT	EXC
COMPLETE SET (10)	300.00	135.00	38.00
COMMON CARD (X1-X10)	20.00	9.00	2.50
☐ X1 Kerry Collins	35.00	16.00	4.40
☐ X2 Rashaan Salaam	20.00	9.00	2.50
☐ X3 Michael Westbrook	20.00	9.00	2.50
☐ X4 Terrell Davis	35.00	16.00	4.40
☐ X5 Joey Galloway	25.00	11.00	3.10
☐ X6 Deion Sanders	25.00	11.00	3.10
☐ X7 Steve Young	30.00	13.50	3.70
☐ X8 Dan Marino	60.00	27.00	7.50
☐ X9 Drew Bledsoe	35.00	16.00	4.40
☐ X10 Emmitt Smith	60.00	27.00	7.50

1995 Cleo Quarterback Club Valentines

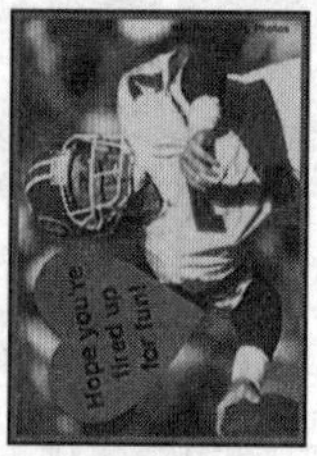

These blank-backed red-bordered valentine cards came in 38-card boxes of Cleo Valentines and feature color action photos of eight NFL quarterbacks. The valentines are printed on thin white card stock and measure approximately 2 1/2" by 3 1/2". They came in 4-card perforated sheets, with two rows of two cards each. The back of the box features three bonus cards that are identical to three of the cards inside. We've included those in the complete set price below. Non-mailable envelopes were included in the boxes. The cards are unnumbered and checklisted below in alphabetical order.

	MINT	NRMT	EXC
COMPLETE SET (11)	3.00	1.35	.35
COMMON CARD (1-8)	.15	.07	.02
☐ 1A Troy Aikman Valentine	.40	.18	.05
☐ 1B Troy Aikman box bottom card	.50	.23	.06
☐ 2 John Elway	.30	.14	.04
☐ 3A Brett Favre Valentine	.60	.25	.07
☐ 3B Brett Favre box bottom card	.75	.35	.09
☐ 4 Jim Kelly	.15	.07	.02
☐ 5 Dan Marino	.60	.25	.07
☐ 6A Warren Moon Valentine	.15	.07	.02
☐ 6B Warren Moon box bottom card	.25	.11	.03
☐ 7 Phil Simms	.15	.07	.02
☐ 8 Steve Young	.30	.14	.04

1996 Cleo Quarterback Club Valentines

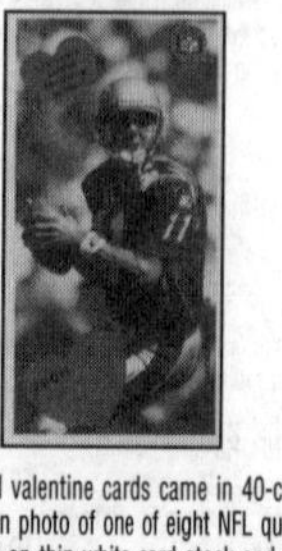

These white-bordered valentine cards came in 40-card boxes with featuring a color action photo of one of eight NFL quarterbacks. The valentines are printed on thin white card stock and each measures approximately 2 1/2" by 5" except Marcus Allen measures 3 3/4" by 5". The back of the box features two bonus cards that are identical to two of the cards inside. We've included those in the complete set price. The cards are unnumbered and checklisted below in alphabetical order.

	MINT	NRMT	EXC
COMPLETE SET (10)	2.50	1.10	.30
COMMON CARD (1-8)	.15	.07	.02
☐ 1 Troy Aikman	.40	.18	.05
☐ 2 Marcus Allen	.15	.07	.02
☐ 3 Drew Bledsoe	.40	.18	.05
☐ 4 John Elway	.30	.14	.04
☐ 5 Jim Kelly	.25	.11	.03
☐ 6A Junior Seau Valentine	.15	.07	.02
☐ 6B Junior Seau box bottom card	.25	.11	.03
☐ 7A Emmitt Smith Valentine	.60	.25	.07
☐ 7B Emmitt Smith box bottom card	.75	.35	.09
☐ 8 Steve Young	.30	.14	.04

1964 Coke Caps All-Stars AFL

These AFL All-Star caps were issued in AFL cities (and a few other cities as well) along with the local team caps as part of the Go with the Pros promotion. The AFL team Cap Saver sheets had separate sections in which to affix the local team's player caps, the AFL team logos, and the All-Stars' caps. The caps measure approximately 1 1/8" in diameter and have the drink logo and a football on the outside, while the inside has the player's face printed in black, with text surrounding the face. The consumer could turn in his completed saver sheet to receive various prizes. The caps are unnumbered, but have been alphabetically listed below. These caps were also produced for 1964 on Sprite bottles. Sprite caps typically carry a slight premium (1.5-2 times) over the value of the Coke version.

	NRMT	VG-E	GOOD
COMPLETE SET (44)	175.00	80.00	22.00
COMMON CAP (1-44)	3.00	1.35	.35
☐ 1 Tommy Addison	3.00	1.35	.35
☐ 2 Dalva Allen	3.00	1.35	.35
☐ 3 Lance Alworth	15.00	6.75	1.85
☐ 4 Houston Antwine	3.00	1.35	.35
☐ 5 Fred Arbanas	3.00	1.35	.35
☐ 6 Tony Banfield	3.00	1.35	.35
☐ 7 Stew Barber	3.00	1.35	.35
☐ 8 George Blair	3.00	1.35	.35
☐ 9 Mel Branch	3.00	1.35	.35
☐ 10 Nick Buoniconti	7.50	3.40	.95
☐ 11 Doug Cline	3.00	1.35	.35
☐ 12 Eldon Danenhauer	3.00	1.35	.35
☐ 13 Clem Daniels	4.00	1.80	.50
☐ 14 Larry Eisenhauer	3.00	1.35	.35
☐ 15 Earl Faison	3.00	1.35	.35
☐ 16 Cookie Gilchrist	5.00	2.20	.60
☐ 17 Freddy Glick	3.00	1.35	.35
☐ 18 Larry Grantham	4.00	1.80	.50
☐ 19 Ron Hall	3.00	1.35	.35
☐ 20 Charlie Hennigan	4.00	1.80	.50
☐ 21 E.J. Holub	4.00	1.80	.50
☐ 22 Ed Husmann	3.00	1.35	.35
☐ 23 Jack Kemp	25.00	11.00	3.10
☐ 24 Dave Kocourek	3.00	1.35	.35
☐ 25 Keith Lincoln	4.00	1.80	.50
☐ 26 Charles Long	3.00	1.35	.35
☐ 27 Paul Lowe	4.00	1.80	.50
☐ 28 Archie Matsos	3.00	1.35	.35
☐ 29 Jerry Mays	4.00	1.80	.50
☐ 30 Ron Mix	6.00	2.70	.75
☐ 31 Tom Morrow	3.00	1.35	.35
☐ 32 Billy Neighbors	4.00	1.80	.50
☐ 33 Jim Otto	7.50	3.40	.95
☐ 34 Art Powell	4.00	1.80	.50
☐ 35 Johnny Robinson	4.00	1.80	.50
☐ 36 Tobin Rote	4.00	1.80	.50
☐ 37 Bob Schmidt	3.00	1.35	.35
☐ 38 Tom Sestak	3.00	1.35	.35
☐ 39 Billy Shaw	3.00	1.35	.35
☐ 40 Bob Talamini	3.00	1.35	.35
☐ 41 Lionel Taylor	4.00	1.80	.50
☐ 42 Jim Tyrer	4.00	1.80	.50
☐ 43 Dick Westmoreland	3.00	1.35	.35
☐ 44 Fred Williamson	6.00	2.70	.75

1964 Coke Caps All-Stars NFL

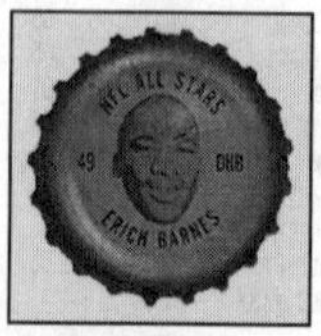

These NFL All-Star caps were issued in NFL cities (and a few other cities as well) along with the local team caps as part of the Go with the Pros promotion. The NFL team Cap Saver sheets had separate sections in which to affix the local team's player caps, the NFL team logos, and the All-Stars' caps. The caps measure approximately 1 1/8" in diameter and have the drink logo and a football on the outside, while the inside has the player's face printed in black, with text surrounding the face. The consumer could turn in his completed saver sheet to receive various prizes. The caps are unnumbered, but have been alphabetically listed below. These caps were also produced for 1964 on Sprite bottles. Sprite caps typically carry a slight premium (1.5-2 times) over the value of the Coke version.

	NRMT	VG-E	GOOD
COMPLETE SET (44)	175.00	80.00	22.00
COMMON CAP (1-44)	2.50	1.10	.30
☐ 1 Doug Atkins	6.00	2.70	.75
☐ 2 Terry Barr	2.50	1.10	.30
☐ 3 Jim Brown	25.00	11.00	3.10
☐ 4 Roger Brown	4.00	1.80	.50
☐ 5 Roosevelt Brown	5.00	2.20	.60
☐ 6 Timmy Brown	4.00	1.80	.50
☐ 7 Bobby Joe Conrad	4.00	1.80	.50
☐ 8 Willie Davis	6.00	2.70	.75
☐ 9 Bob DeMarco	2.50	1.10	.30
☐ 10 Darrell Dess	2.50	1.10	.30
☐ 11 Mike Ditka	15.00	6.75	1.85
☐ 12 Bill Forester	2.50	1.10	.30
☐ 13 Joe Fortunato	2.50	1.10	.30
☐ 14 Bill George	6.00	2.70	.75
☐ 15 Ken Gray	2.50	1.10	.30
☐ 16 Forrest Gregg	6.00	2.70	.75
☐ 17 Roosevelt Grier	5.00	2.20	.60
☐ 18 Hank Jordan	6.00	2.70	.75
☐ 19 Jim Katcavage	4.00	1.80	.50
☐ 20 Jerry Kramer	5.00	2.20	.60
☐ 21 Ron Kramer	2.50	1.10	.30
☐ 22 Dick Lane	6.00	2.70	.75
☐ 23 Dick Lynch	2.50	1.10	.30
☐ 24 Gino Marchetti	6.00	2.70	.75
☐ 25 Tommy Mason	4.00	1.80	.50
☐ 26 Ed Meador	2.50	1.10	.30
☐ 27 Bobby Mitchell	6.00	2.70	.75
☐ 28 Larry Morris	2.50	1.10	.30
☐ 29 Merlin Olsen	6.00	2.70	.75
☐ 30 Jim Parker	5.00	2.20	.60
☐ 31 Jim Patton	4.00	1.80	.50
☐ 32 Myron Pottios	2.50	1.10	.30
☐ 33 Jim Ringo	5.00	2.20	.60
☐ 34 Dick Schafrath	2.50	1.10	.30
☐ 35 Joe Schmidt	6.00	2.70	.75
☐ 36 Del Shofner	4.00	1.80	.50
☐ 37 Bob St. Clair	5.00	2.20	.60
☐ 38 Jim Taylor	8.00	3.60	1.00
☐ 39 Roosevelt Taylor	4.00	1.80	.50
☐ 40 Y.A. Tittle	10.00	4.50	1.25
☐ 41 Johnny Unitas	15.00	6.75	1.85
☐ 42 Larry Wilson	6.00	2.70	.75
☐ 43 Willie Wood	6.00	2.70	.75
☐ 44 Abe Woodson	4.00	1.80	.50

1964 Coke Caps Browns

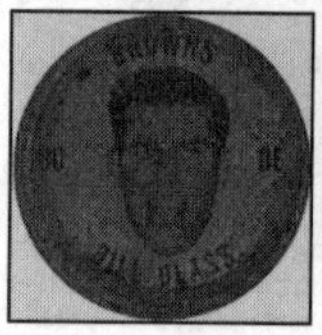

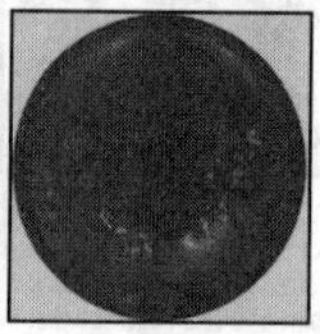

These Browns caps were issued in the Cleveland area along with the NFL All-Stars caps as part of the 1964 Go with the Pros promotion. The NFL team Cap Saver sheets had separate sections in which to affix both the local team's caps, the NFL team logos, and the All-Stars' caps. The caps measure approximately 1 1/8" in diameter and have the drink logo and a football on the outside, while the inside has the player's face printed in black, with text surrounding the face. The consumer could turn in his completed saver sheet (before the expiration date of Nov. 21, 1964) to receive various prizes. The caps are unnumbered, but have been arranged alphabetically below. These caps were also produced for Sprite bottles. Sprite caps typically carry a slight premium (1.5-2 times) over the value of the Coke version.

	NRMT	VG-E	GOOD
COMPLETE SET (35)	140.00	65.00	17.50
COMMON CAP (1-35)	3.00	1.35	.35
☐ 1 Walter Beach	3.00	1.35	.35
☐ 2 Larry Benz	3.00	1.35	.35
☐ 3 Johnny Brewer	3.00	1.35	.35
☐ 4 Jim Brown	30.00	13.50	3.70
☐ 5 John Brown	3.00	1.35	.35
☐ 6 Monte Clark	4.00	1.80	.50
☐ 7 Gary Collins	4.00	1.80	.50
☐ 8 Vince Costello	4.00	1.80	.50
☐ 9 Ross Fichtner	3.00	1.35	.35
☐ 10 Galen Fiss	3.00	1.35	.35
☐ 11 Bobby Franklin	3.00	1.35	.35
☐ 12 Bob Gain	3.00	1.35	.35
☐ 13 Bill Glass	4.00	1.80	.50
☐ 14 Ernie Green	3.00	1.35	.35
☐ 15 Lou Groza	10.00	4.50	1.25
☐ 16 Gene Hickerson	3.00	1.35	.35
☐ 17 Jim Houston	3.00	1.35	.35
☐ 18 Tom Hutchinson	3.00	1.35	.35
☐ 19 Jim Kanicki	3.00	1.35	.35
☐ 20 Mike Lucci	4.00	1.80	.50
☐ 21 Dick Modzelewski	4.00	1.80	.50
☐ 22 John Morrow	3.00	1.35	.35
☐ 23 Jim Ninowski	4.00	1.80	.50
☐ 24 Frank Parker	3.00	1.35	.35
☐ 25 Bernie Parrish	4.00	1.80	.50
☐ 26 Frank Ryan	5.00	2.20	.60
☐ 27 Charlie Scales	3.00	1.35	.35

☐ 28 Dick Schafrath	4.00	1.80	.50
☐ 29 Roger Shoals	3.00	1.35	.35
☐ 30 Jim Shorter	3.00	1.35	.35
☐ 31 Billy Truax	4.00	1.80	.50
☐ 32 Paul Warfield	15.00	6.75	1.85
☐ 33 Ken Webb	3.00	1.35	.35
☐ 34 Paul Wiggin	3.00	1.35	.35
☐ 35 John Wooten	4.00	1.80	.50
☐ NNO Browns Saver Sheet	30.00	13.50	3.70
Frank Ryan pictured			

1964 Coke Caps Chargers

These Chargers caps were issued in the San Diego area along with the AFL All-Stars caps as part of the 1964 Go with the Pros promotion. The AFL team Cap Saver sheets had separate sections in which to affix both the local team's caps, the AFL team logos, and the All-Stars' caps. The caps measure approximately 1 1/8" in diameter and have the drink logo and a football on the outside, while the inside has the player's face printed in black, with text surrounding the face. The consumer could turn in his completed saver sheet (before the expiration date of Nov. 21, 1964) to receive various prizes. The caps are unnumbered, but have been arranged alphabetically below. These caps were also produced for Sprite bottles. Sprite caps typically carry a slight premium (1.5-2 times) over the value of the Coke version.

	NRMT	VG-E	GOOD
COMPLETE SET (35)	110.00	50.00	14.00
COMMON CAP (1-35)	3.00	1.35	.35
☐ 1 Chuck Allen	4.00	1.80	.50
☐ 2 Lance Alworth	20.00	9.00	2.50
☐ 3 George Blair	3.00	1.35	.35
☐ 4 Frank Buncom	3.00	1.35	.35
☐ 5 Earl Faison	4.00	1.80	.50
☐ 6 Kenny Graham	3.00	1.35	.35
☐ 7 George Gross	3.00	1.35	.35
☐ 8 Sam Gruneisen	3.00	1.35	.35
☐ 9 John Hadl	10.00	4.50	1.25
☐ 10 Dick Harris	4.00	1.80	.50
☐ 11 Bob Jackson	3.00	1.35	.35
☐ 12 Emil Karas	3.00	1.35	.35
☐ 13 Dave Kocourek	3.00	1.35	.35
☐ 14 Ernie Ladd	10.00	4.50	1.25
☐ 15 Bob Lane	3.00	1.35	.35
☐ 16 Keith Lincoln	6.00	2.70	.75
☐ 17 Paul Lowe	6.00	2.70	.75
☐ 18 Jacque MacKinnon	3.00	1.35	.35
☐ 19 Gerry McDougall	3.00	1.35	.35
☐ 20 Charley McNeil	4.00	1.80	.50
☐ 21 Bob Mitinger	3.00	1.35	.35
☐ 22 Ron Mix	10.00	4.50	1.25
☐ 23 Don Norton	3.00	1.35	.35
☐ 24 Ernie Park	3.00	1.35	.35
☐ 25 Bob Petrich	3.00	1.35	.35
☐ 26 Jerry Robinson	3.00	1.35	.35
☐ 27 Don Rogers	3.00	1.35	.35
☐ 28 Tobin Rote	4.00	1.80	.50
☐ 29 Henry Schmidt	3.00	1.35	.35
☐ 30 Pat Shea	3.00	1.35	.35
☐ 31 Walt Sweeney	4.00	1.80	.50
☐ 32 Jim Warren	3.00	1.35	.35
☐ 33 Dick Westmoreland	3.00	1.35	.35
☐ 34 Bud Whitehead	3.00	1.35	.35
☐ 35 Ernie Wright	4.00	1.80	.50
☐ NNO Chargers Saver Sheet	30.00	13.50	3.70

1964 Coke Caps Lions

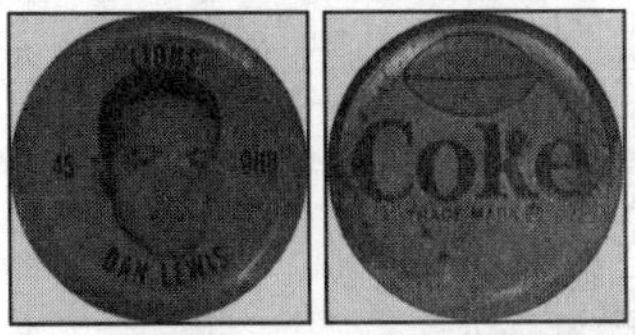

These Lions caps were issued in the Detroit area along with the NFL All-Stars caps as part of the 1964 Go with the Pros promotion. The NFL team Cap Saver sheets had separate sections in which to affix both the local team's caps, the NFL team logos, and the All-Stars' caps. The caps measure approximately 1 1/8" in diameter and have the drink logo and a football on the outside, while the inside has the player's face printed in black, with text surrounding the face. The consumer could turn in his completed saver sheet (before the expiration date of Nov. 21, 1964) to receive various prizes. The caps are unnumbered, but have been arranged alphabetically below. These caps were also produced for Sprite bottles. Sprite caps typically carry a slight premium (1.5-2 times) over the value of the Coke version.

	NRMT	VG-E	GOOD
COMPLETE SET (35)	110.00	50.00	14.00
COMMON CAP (1-35)	3.00	1.35	.35
☐ 1 Terry Barr	3.00	1.35	.35
☐ 2 Carl Brettschneider	3.00	1.35	.35
☐ 3 Roger Brown	4.00	1.80	.50
☐ 4 Mike Bundra	3.00	1.35	.35
☐ 5 Ernie Clark	3.00	1.35	.35
☐ 6 Gail Cogdill	4.00	1.80	.50
☐ 7 Larry Ferguson	3.00	1.35	.35
☐ 8 Dennis Gaubatz	3.00	1.35	.35
☐ 9 Jim Gibbons	4.00	1.80	.50
☐ 10 John Gonzaga	3.00	1.35	.35
☐ 11 John Gordy	3.00	1.35	.35
☐ 12 Tom Hall	3.00	1.35	.35
☐ 13 Alex Karras	10.00	4.50	1.25
☐ 14 Dick Lane	8.00	3.60	1.00
☐ 15 Dan LaRose	3.00	1.35	.35
☐ 16 Yale Lary	8.00	3.60	1.00
☐ 17 Dick LeBeau	4.00	1.80	.50
☐ 18 Dan Lewis	3.00	1.35	.35
☐ 19 Gary Lowe	3.00	1.35	.35
☐ 20 Bruce Maher	3.00	1.35	.35
☐ 21 Darris McCord	3.00	1.35	.35
☐ 22 Max Messner	3.00	1.35	.35
☐ 23 Earl Morrall	6.00	2.70	.75
☐ 24 Nick Pietrosante	4.00	1.80	.50
☐ 25 Milt Plum	4.00	1.80	.50
☐ 26 Daryl Sanders	3.00	1.35	.35
☐ 27 Joe Schmidt	10.00	4.50	1.25
☐ 28 Bob Scholtz	3.00	1.35	.35
☐ 29 J.D. Smith	4.00	1.80	.50
☐ 30 Pat Studstill	4.00	1.80	.50
☐ 31 Larry Vargo	3.00	1.35	.35
☐ 32 Wayne Walker	4.00	1.80	.50
☐ 33 Tom Watkins	3.00	1.35	.35
☐ 34 Bob Whitlow	3.00	1.35	.35
☐ 35 Sam Williams	3.00	1.35	.35
☐ NNO Lions Saver Sheet	30.00	13.50	3.70

1964 Coke Caps Rams

These Rams caps were issued in the Los Angeles area along with the NFL All-Stars caps as part of the 1964 Go with the Pros promotion. The NFL team Cap Saver sheets had separate sections in which to affix both the local team's caps, the NFL team logos, and the All-Stars' caps. The caps measure approximately 1 1/8" in diameter and have the drink logo and a football on the outside, while the inside has the player's face printed in black, with text surrounding the face. The consumer could turn in his completed saver sheet (before the expiration date of Nov. 21, 1964) to receive various prizes. The caps are unnumbered, but have been arranged alphabetically below. These caps were also produced for Sprite bottles. Sprite caps typically carry a slight premium (1.5-2 times) over the value of the Coke version.

	NRMT	VG-E	GOOD
COMPLETE SET (35)	110.00	50.00	14.00
COMMON CAP (1-35)	3.00	1.35	.35
☐ 1 Jon Arnett	4.00	1.80	.50
☐ 2 Pervis Atkins	3.00	1.35	.35
☐ 3 Terry Baker	4.00	1.80	.50
☐ 4 Dick Bass	4.00	1.80	.50
☐ 5 Charley Britt	3.00	1.35	.35
☐ 6 Willie Brown	4.00	1.80	.50
☐ 7 Joe Carollo	3.00	1.35	.35
☐ 8 Don Chuy	3.00	1.35	.35
☐ 9 Charlie Cowan	3.00	1.35	.35
☐ 10 Lindon Crow	3.00	1.35	.35
☐ 11 Carroll Dale	4.00	1.80	.50
☐ 12 Roman Gabriel	6.00	2.70	.75
☐ 13 Roosevelt Grier	6.00	2.70	.75
☐ 14 Mike Henry	3.00	1.35	.35
☐ 15 Art Hunter	3.00	1.35	.35
☐ 16 Ken Iman	3.00	1.35	.35
☐ 17 Deacon Jones	10.00	4.50	1.25
☐ 18 Cliff Livingston	3.00	1.35	.35
☐ 19 Lamar Lundy	4.00	1.80	.50
☐ 20 Marlin McKeever	3.00	1.35	.35
☐ 21 Ed Meador	4.00	1.80	.50
☐ 22 Bill Munson	4.00	1.80	.50
☐ 23 Merlin Olsen	10.00	4.50	1.25
☐ 24 Jack Pardee	5.00	2.20	.60
☐ 25 Art Perkins	3.00	1.35	.35
☐ 26 Jim Phillips	4.00	1.80	.50
☐ 27 Roger Pillath	3.00	1.35	.35
☐ 28 Mel Profit	3.00	1.35	.35
☐ 29 Joe Scibelli	3.00	1.35	.35
☐ 30 Carver Shannon	3.00	1.35	.35
☐ 31 Bobby Smith	3.00	1.35	.35
☐ 32 Bill Swain	3.00	1.35	.35
☐ 33 Frank Varrichione	3.00	1.35	.35
☐ 34 Danny Villanueva	3.00	1.35	.35
☐ 35 Nat Whitmyer	3.00	1.35	.35
☐ NNO Rams Saver Sheet	30.00	13.50	3.70

1964 Coke Caps Redskins

These Redskins caps were issued in the Washington D.C. area along with the NFL All-Stars caps as part of the 1964 Go with the Pros promotion. The NFL team Cap Saver sheets had separate sections in which to affix both the local team's caps, the NFL team logos, and the All-Stars' caps. The caps measure approximately 1 1/8" in diameter and have the drink logo and a football on the outside, while the inside has the player's face printed in black, with text surrounding the face. The consumer could turn in his completed saver sheet (before the expiration date of Nov. 21, 1964) to receive various prizes. The caps are unnumbered, but have been arranged alphabetically below. These caps were also produced for Sprite bottles. Sprite caps typically carry a slight premium (1.5-2 times) over the value of the Coke version.

	NRMT	VG-E	GOOD
COMPLETE SET (32)	90.00	40.00	11.00
COMMON CAP (1-32)	3.00	1.35	.35
☐ 1 Bill Barnes	3.00	1.35	.35
☐ 2 Don Bosseler	3.00	1.35	.35
☐ 3 Rod Breedlove	3.00	1.35	.35
☐ 4 Frank Budd	3.00	1.35	.35
☐ 5 Henry Butsko	3.00	1.35	.35
☐ 6 Jimmy Carr	3.00	1.35	.35
☐ 7 Angelo Coia	3.00	1.35	.35
☐ 8 Fred Dugan	3.00	1.35	.35
☐ 9 Fred Hageman	3.00	1.35	.35
☐ 10 Sam Huff	10.00	4.50	1.25
☐ 11 Sonny Jurgensen	10.00	4.50	1.25
☐ 12 Carl Kammerer	3.00	1.35	.35
☐ 13 Gordon Kelley	3.00	1.35	.35
☐ 14 Bob Khayat	3.00	1.35	.35
☐ 15 Paul Krause	5.00	2.20	.60
☐ 16 J.W. Lockett	3.00	1.35	.35
☐ 17 Riley Mattson	3.00	1.35	.35
☐ 18 Bobby Mitchell	8.00	3.60	1.00
☐ 19 John Nisby	3.00	1.35	.35
☐ 20 Fran O'Brien	3.00	1.35	.35
☐ 21 John Paluck	3.00	1.35	.35
☐ 22 Jack Pardee	5.00	2.20	.60
☐ 23 Vince Promuto	3.00	1.35	.35
☐ 24 Pat Richter	4.00	1.80	.50
☐ 25 Johnny Sample	4.00	1.80	.50
☐ 26 Lonnie Sanders	3.00	1.35	.35
☐ 27 Dick Shiner	4.00	1.80	.50
☐ 28 Ron Snidow	3.00	1.35	.35
☐ 29 Jim Steffen	3.00	1.35	.35
☐ 30 Charley Taylor	10.00	4.50	1.25
☐ 31 Tom Tracy	4.00	1.80	.50
☐ 32 Fred Williams	3.00	1.35	.35

1964 Coke Caps Steelers

These Steelers caps were issued in the Pittsburgh area along with the NFL All-Stars caps as part of the 1964 Go with the Pros promotion. The NFL team Cap Saver sheets had separate sections in which to affix both the local team's caps, the NFL team logos, and the All-Stars' caps. The caps measure approximately 1 1/8" in diameter and have the drink logo and a football on the outside, while the inside has the player's face printed in black, with text surrounding the face. The consumer could turn in his completed saver sheet (before the expiration date of Nov. 21, 1964) to receive various prizes. The caps are unnumbered, but have been arranged alphabetically below. These caps were also produced for Sprite bottles. Sprite caps typically carry a slight premium (1.5-2 times) over the value of the Coke version. The listing below is partial; any additions would be appreciated

	NRMT	VG-E	GOOD
COMPLETE SET (34)	100.00	45.00	12.50
COMMON CAP (1-34)	3.00	1.35	.35
☐ 1 Art Anderson	3.00	1.35	.35
☐ 2 Frank Atkinson	3.00	1.35	.35
☐ 3 Gary Ballman	4.00	1.80	.50
☐ 4 John Baker	4.00	1.80	.50
☐ 5 Charley Bradshaw	4.00	1.80	.50
☐ 6 Jim Bradshaw	3.00	1.35	.35
☐ 7 Ed Brown	4.00	1.80	.50
☐ 8 John Burrell	3.00	1.35	.35
☐ 9 Preston Carpenter	5.00	2.20	.60
☐ 10 Lou Cordileone	3.00	1.35	.35
☐ 11 Willie Daniel	3.00	1.35	.35
☐ 12 Dick Haley	3.00	1.35	.35
☐ 13 Bob Harrison	3.00	1.35	.35
☐ 14 Dick Hoak	5.00	2.20	.60
☐ 15 Dan James	3.00	1.35	.35
☐ 16 Tom Jenkins	3.00	1.35	.35
☐ 17 John Henry Johnson	8.00	3.60	1.00
☐ 18 Jim Kelly	3.00	1.35	.35
☐ 19 Brady Keys	3.00	1.35	.35
☐ 20 Joe Krupa	3.00	1.35	.35
☐ 21 Ray Lemek	3.00	1.35	.35
☐ 22 Paul Martha	4.00	1.80	.50
☐ 23 Lou Michaels	4.00	1.80	.50
☐ 24 Bill Nelsen	5.00	2.20	.60
☐ 25 Terry Nofsinger	3.00	1.35	.35
☐ 26 Clarence Peaks	4.00	1.80	.50
☐ 27 Myron Pottios	4.00	1.80	.50
☐ 28 John Reger	4.00	1.80	.50
☐ 29 Mike Sandusky	3.00	1.35	.35
☐ 30 Theron Sapp	3.00	1.35	.35
☐ 31 Bob Schmitz	3.00	1.35	.35
☐ 32 Ron Stehouwer	3.00	1.35	.35
☐ 33 Clendon Thomas	4.00	1.80	.50
☐ 34 Joe Womack	3.00	1.35	.35

1964 Coke Caps Team Emblems NFL

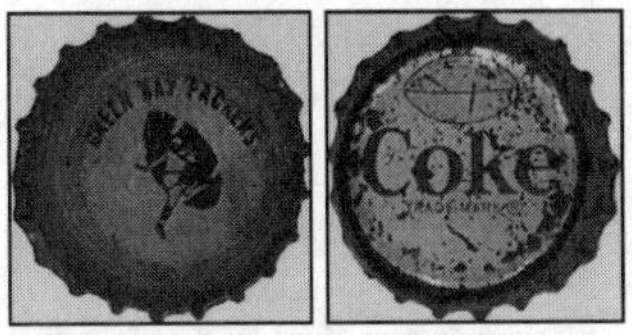

Each 1964 Coke Caps saver sheet had a section for collecting caps featuring the team emblem for all fourteen NFL teams. The caps are unnumbered and checklisted below in alphabetical order. These "Coke" caps were also available on Sprite bottles. Sprite caps typically carry a 1.5X-2X premium over the Coke version.

	NRMT	VG-E	GOOD
COMPLETE SET (14)	60.00	27.00	7.50
COMMON TEAM (1-14)	5.00	2.20	.60
☐ 1 Baltimore Colts	5.00	2.20	.60
☐ 2 Chicago Bears	5.00	2.20	.60
☐ 3 Cleveland Browns	5.00	2.20	.60
☐ 4 Dallas Cowboys	6.00	2.70	.75
☐ 5 Detroit Lions	5.00	2.20	.60
☐ 6 Green Bay Packers	6.00	2.70	.75
☐ 7 Los Angeles Rams	5.00	2.20	.60
☐ 8 Minnesota Vikings	5.00	2.20	.60
☐ 9 New York Giants	5.00	2.20	.60
☐ 10 Philadelphia Eagles	5.00	2.20	.60
☐ 11 Pittsburgh Steelers	5.00	2.20	.60
☐ 12 San Francisco 49ers	5.00	2.20	.60
☐ 13 St. Louis Cardinals	5.00	2.20	.60
☐ 14 Washington Redskins	6.00	2.70	.75

1965 Coke Caps All-Stars AFL

These NFL All-Star caps were issued in NFL cities (and a few other cities as well) along with the local team caps as part of the Go with the Pros promotion. The NFL team Cap Saver sheets had separate sections in which to affix both the local team's caps and the All-Stars' caps. The caps measure approximately 1 1/8" in diameter and have the drink logo and a football on the outside, while the inside has the player's face printed in black, with text surrounding the face. The consumer could turn in his completed saver sheet to receive various prizes. The caps are numbered with a "C" prefix. These caps were also produced for 1965 on other Coca-Cola products: TAB, Fanta and Sprite. The other drink caps typically carry a slight premium (1.5-2 times) over the value of the Coke version.

	NRMT	VG-E	GOOD
COMPLETE SET (34)	150.00	70.00	19.00
COMMON CAP (C37-C70)	2.50	1.10	.30
☐ C37 Jerry Mays	2.50	1.10	.30
☐ C38 Cookie Gilchrist	3.50	1.55	.45
☐ C39 Lionel Taylor	3.00	1.35	.35
☐ C40 Goose Gonsoulin	3.50	1.55	.45
☐ C41 Gino Cappelletti	3.50	1.55	.45
☐ C42 Nick Buoniconti	5.00	2.20	.60
☐ C43 Larry Eisenhauer	2.50	1.10	.30
☐ C44 Babe Parilli	3.50	1.55	.45
☐ C45 Jack Kemp	25.00	11.00	3.10
☐ C46 Billy Shaw	2.50	1.10	.30
☐ C47 Scott Appleton	2.50	1.10	.30
☐ C48 Matt Snell	3.50	1.55	.45
☐ C49 Charlie Hennigan	3.50	1.55	.45
☐ C50 Tom Flores	5.00	2.20	.60
☐ C51 Clem Daniels	3.50	1.55	.45
☐ C52 George Blanda	12.50	5.50	1.55
☐ C53 Art Powell	3.50	1.55	.45
☐ C54 Jim Otto	7.50	3.40	.95
☐ C55 Larry Grantham	2.50	1.10	.30
☐ C56 Don Maynard	10.00	4.50	1.25
☐ C57 Gerry Philbin	2.50	1.10	.30
☐ C58 E.J. Holub	2.50	1.10	.30
☐ C59 Chris Burford	2.50	1.10	.30
☐ C60 Ron Mix	6.00	2.70	.75
☐ C61 Ernie Ladd	7.50	3.40	.95
☐ C62 Fred Arbanas	2.50	1.10	.30
☐ C63 Tom Sestak	2.50	1.10	.30
☐ C64 Elbert Dubenion	3.50	1.55	.45
☐ C65 Mike Stratton	2.50	1.10	.30
☐ C66 Willie Brown	7.50	3.40	.95
☐ C67 Sid Blanks	2.50	1.10	.30
☐ C68 Len Dawson	10.00	4.50	1.25
☐ C69 Lance Alworth	10.00	4.50	1.25
☐ C70 Keith Lincoln	3.50	1.55	.45

1965 Coke Caps All-Stars NFL

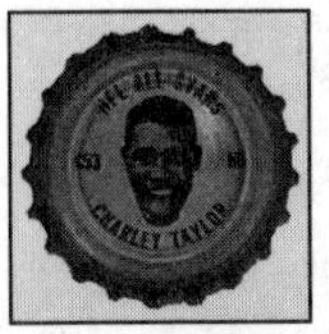

These NFL All-Star caps were issued in NFL cities (and a few other cities as well) along with the local team caps as part of the Go with the Pros promotion. The NFL team Cap Saver sheets had separate sections in which to affix both the local team's caps and the All-Stars' caps. The caps measure approximately 1 1/8" in diameter and have the drink logo and a football on the outside, while the inside has the player's face printed in black, with text surrounding the face. The consumer could turn in his completed saver sheet to receive various prizes. The caps are numbered with a "C" prefix. These caps were also produced for 1965 on other Coca-Cola products: TAB, Fanta and Sprite. The other drink caps typically carry a slight premium (1.5-2 times) over the value of the Coke version.

	NRMT	VG-E	GOOD
COMPLETE SET (34)	135.00	60.00	17.00
COMMON CAP (C37-C70)	2.50	1.10	.30
☐ C37 Sonny Jurgensen	7.00	3.10	.85
☐ C38 Fran Tarkenton	10.00	4.50	1.25
☐ C39 Frank Ryan	3.50	1.55	.45
☐ C40 Johnny Unitas	12.00	5.50	1.50

☐ C41 Tommy Mason	3.50	1.55	.45
☐ C42 Mel Renfro	5.00	2.20	.60
☐ C43 Ed Meador	2.50	1.10	.30
☐ C44 Paul Krause	4.00	1.80	.50
☐ C45 Irv Cross	3.50	1.55	.45
☐ C46 Bill Brown	3.50	1.55	.45
☐ C47 Joe Fortunato	2.50	1.10	.30
☐ C48 Jim Taylor	7.50	3.40	.95
☐ C49 John Henry Johnson	6.00	2.70	.75
☐ C50 Pat Fischer	2.50	1.10	.30
☐ C51 Bob Boyd	2.50	1.10	.30
☐ C52 Terry Barr	2.50	1.10	.30
☐ C53 Charley Taylor	6.00	2.70	.75
☐ C54 Paul Warfield	7.50	3.40	.95
☐ C55 Pete Retzlaff	3.50	1.55	.45
☐ C56 Maxie Baughan	2.50	1.10	.30
☐ C57 Matt Hazeltine	2.50	1.10	.30
☐ C58 Ken Gray	2.50	1.10	.30
☐ C59 Ray Nitschke	7.50	3.40	.95
☐ C60 Myron Pottios	2.50	1.10	.30
☐ C61 Charlie Krueger	2.50	1.10	.30
☐ C62 Deacon Jones	6.00	2.70	.75
☐ C63 Bob Lilly	10.00	4.50	1.25
☐ C64 Merlin Olsen	6.00	2.70	.75
☐ C65 Jim Parker	5.00	2.20	.60
☐ C66 Roosevelt Brown	5.00	2.20	.60
☐ C67 Jim Gibbons	2.50	1.10	.30
☐ C68 Mike Ditka	12.00	5.50	1.50
☐ C69 Willie Davis	6.00	2.70	.75
☐ C70 Aaron Thomas	2.50	1.10	.30

1965 Coke Caps Bills

This set of 35 Coke caps was issued on bottled soft drinks specifically for Western New York and featured Buffalo Bills players. The caps were issued along with their own Saver Sheet. The caps measure approximately 1 1/8" in diameter and have the drink logo and a football on the outside, while the inside has the player's face printed in black, with text surrounding the face. The consumer could turn in his completed saver sheet to receive various prizes. The caps are numbered with a "B" prefix. These caps were also produced for 1965 on other Coca-Cola products: TAB, Fanta and Sprite. The other drink caps typically carry a slight premium (1.5-2 times) over the value of the Coke version.

	NRMT	VG-E	GOOD
COMPLETE SET (35)	125.00	55.00	15.50
COMMON CAP (B1-B35)	3.00	1.35	.35
☐ B1 Ray Abruzzese	3.00	1.35	.35
☐ B2 Joe Auer	3.00	1.35	.35
☐ B3 Stew Barber	3.00	1.35	.35
☐ B4 Glenn Bass	3.00	1.35	.35
☐ B5 Dave Behrman	3.00	1.35	.35
☐ B6 Al Bemiller	3.00	1.35	.35
☐ B7 George Butch Byrd	4.00	1.80	.50
☐ B8 Wray Carlton	4.00	1.80	.50
☐ B9 Hagood Clarke	3.00	1.35	.35
☐ B10 Jack Kemp	30.00	13.50	3.70
☐ B11 Oliver Dobbins	3.00	1.35	.35
☐ B12 Elbert Dubenion	4.00	1.80	.50
☐ B13 Jim Dunaway	3.00	1.35	.35
☐ B14 Booker Edgerson	3.00	1.35	.35
☐ B15 George Flint	3.00	1.35	.35
☐ B16 Pete Gogolak	4.00	1.80	.50
☐ B17 Dick Hudson	4.00	1.80	.50
☐ B18 Harry Jacobs	3.00	1.35	.35
☐ B19 Tom Keating	3.00	1.35	.35
☐ B20 Tom Day	3.00	1.35	.35
☐ B21 Daryle Lamonica	10.00	4.50	1.25
☐ B22 Paul Maguire	6.00	2.70	.75
☐ B23 Roland McDole	3.00	1.35	.35
☐ B24 Dudley Meredith	3.00	1.35	.35
☐ B25 Joe O'Donnell	3.00	1.35	.35
☐ B26 Willie Ross	3.00	1.35	.35
☐ B27 Ed Rutkowski	3.00	1.35	.35
☐ B28 George Saimes	4.00	1.80	.50
☐ B29 Tom Sestak	4.00	1.80	.50
☐ B30 Billy Shaw	4.00	1.80	.50
☐ B31 Bob Lee Smith	3.00	1.35	.35
☐ B32 Mike Stratton	4.00	1.80	.50
☐ B33 Gene Sykes	3.00	1.35	.35
☐ B34 John Tracey	3.00	1.35	.35
☐ B35 Ernie Warlick	3.00	1.35	.35
☐ NNO Bills Saver Sheet	30.00	13.50	3.70

1965 Coke Caps Eagles

These Eagles caps were issued in the Philadelphia area along with the NFL All-Stars caps as part of the Go with the Pros promotion. The NFL team Cap Saver sheets had separate sections in which to affix both the local team's caps and the All-Stars' caps. The caps measure approximately 1 1/8" in diameter and have the drink logo and a football on the outside, while the inside has the player's face printed in black, with text surrounding the face. The consumer could turn in his completed saver sheet to receive various prizes. The caps are numbered with a "C" prefix. These caps were also produced for 1965 on other Coca-Cola products: TAB, Fanta and Sprite. The other drink caps typically carry a slight premium (1.5-2 times) over the value of the Coke version. The checklist below is partial, any additions would be welcome.

	NRMT	VG-E	GOOD
COMPLETE SET (36)	100.00	45.00	12.50
COMMON CAP (C1-C36)	3.00	1.35	.35
☐ C1 Norm Snead	5.00	2.20	.60
☐ C2 Al Nelson	3.00	1.35	.35
☐ C3 Jim Skaggs	3.00	1.35	.35
☐ C4 Glenn Glass	3.00	1.35	.35
☐ C5 Pete Retzlaff	3.00	1.35	.35
☐ C6 Bill Mack	3.00	1.35	.35
☐ C7 Ray Rissmiller	3.00	1.35	.35
☐ C8 Lynn Hoyem	3.00	1.35	.35
☐ C9 King Hill	4.00	1.80	.50
☐ C10 Timmy Brown	5.00	2.20	.60
☐ C11 Ollie Matson	10.00	4.50	1.25
☐ C12 Dave Lloyd	4.00	1.80	.50
☐ C13 Jim Ringo	7.00	3.10	.85
☐ C15 Riley Gunnels	3.00	1.35	.35
☐ C16 Claude Crabb	3.00	1.35	.35
☐ C17 Earl Gros	4.00	1.80	.50
☐ C18 Fred Hill	3.00	1.35	.35
☐ C19 Don Hultz	3.00	1.35	.35
☐ C20 Ray Poage	3.00	1.35	.35
☐ C21 Irv Cross	5.00	2.20	.60
☐ C22 Mike Morgan	3.00	1.35	.35
☐ C23 Maxie Baughan	4.00	1.80	.50
☐ C24 Ed Blaine	3.00	1.35	.35
☐ C25 Jack Concannon	4.00	1.80	.50
☐ C26 Sam Baker	3.00	1.35	.35
☐ C27 Tom Woodeshick	4.00	1.80	.50
☐ C29 John Meyers	3.00	1.35	.35
☐ C30 Nate Ramsey	3.00	1.35	.35
☐ C31 George Tarasovic	3.00	1.35	.35
☐ C32 Bob Brown T	5.00	2.20	.60
☐ C33 Willie Brown	3.00	1.35	.35
☐ C34 Ron Goodwin	3.00	1.35	.35
☐ C35 Dave Graham	3.00	1.35	.35
☐ C36 Team Logo	3.00	1.35	.35

1965 Coke Caps Giants

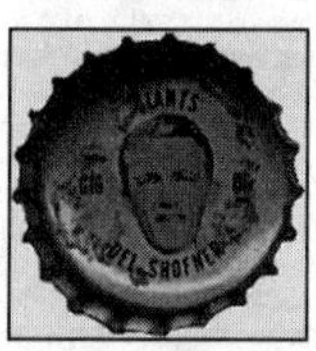

This set of 35 Coke caps was issued on bottled soft drinks specifically for the New York City area and featured Giants players. The caps were issued along with their own Saver Sheet. The caps measure approximately 1 1/8" in diameter and have the drink logo and a football on the outside, while the inside has the player's face printed in black, with text surrounding the face. The consumer could turn in his completed saver sheet to receive various prizes. The caps are numbered with a "G" prefix. These caps were also produced for 1965 on other Coca-Cola products: TAB, Fanta and Sprite. The other drink caps typically carry a slight premium (1.5-2 times) over the value of the Coke version.

	NRMT	VG-E	GOOD
COMPLETE SET (35)	110.00	50.00	14.00
COMMON CAP (G1-G35)	3.00	1.35	.35
☐ G1 Joe Morrison	3.00	1.35	.35
☐ G2 Dick Lynch	4.00	1.80	.50
☐ G3 Andy Stynchula	3.00	1.35	.35
☐ G4 Clarence Childs	3.00	1.35	.35
☐ G5 Aaron Thomas	4.00	1.80	.50
☐ G6 Mickey Walker	3.00	1.35	.35
☐ G7 Bill Winter	3.00	1.35	.35
☐ G8 Bookie Bolin	3.00	1.35	.35
☐ G9 Tom Scott	3.00	1.35	.35
☐ G10 John Lovetere	3.00	1.35	.35
☐ G11 Jim Patton	4.00	1.80	.50
☐ G12 Darrell Dess	3.00	1.35	.35
☐ G13 Dick James	3.00	1.35	.35
☐ G14 Jerry Hillebrand	3.00	1.35	.35
☐ G15 Dick Pesonen	3.00	1.35	.35
☐ G16 Del Shofner	4.00	1.80	.50
☐ G17 Erich Barnes	4.00	1.80	.50
☐ G18 Roosevelt Brown	6.00	2.70	.75
☐ G19 Greg Larson	3.00	1.35	.35
☐ G20 Jim Katcavage	4.00	1.80	.50
☐ G21 Frank Lasky	3.00	1.35	.35
☐ G22 Lou Slaby	3.00	1.35	.35
☐ G23 Jim Moran	3.00	1.35	.35
☐ G24 Roger Anderson	3.00	1.35	.35
☐ G25 Steve Thurlow	3.00	1.35	.35
☐ G26 Ernie Wheelwright	3.00	1.35	.35
☐ G27 Gary Wood	4.00	1.80	.50
☐ G28 Tony Dimidio	3.00	1.35	.35
☐ G29 John Contoulis	3.00	1.35	.35
☐ G30 Tucker Frederickson	4.00	1.80	.50
☐ G31 Bob Timberlake	3.00	1.35	.35
☐ G32 Chuck Mercein	4.00	1.80	.50
☐ G33 Ernie Koy	4.00	1.80	.50
☐ G34 Tom Costello	3.00	1.35	.35
☐ G35 Homer Jones	4.00	1.80	.50
☐ NNO Giants Saver Sheet	30.00	13.50	3.70

1965 Coke Caps Jets

This set of 35 Coke caps was issued on bottled soft drinks specifically for the New York City area and featured Giants players. The caps were issued along with their own Saver Sheet. The caps measure approximately 1 1/8" in diameter and have the drink logo and a

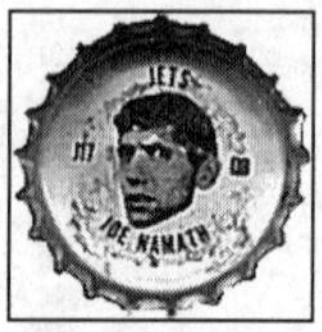

football on the outside, while the inside has the player's face printed in black, with text surrounding the face. The consumer could turn in his completed saver sheet to receive various prizes. The caps are numbered with a "J" prefix. These caps were also produced for 1965 on other Coca-Cola products: TAB, Fanta and Sprite. The other drink caps typically carry a slight premium (1.5-2 times) over the value of the Coke version.

	NRMT	VG-E	GOOD
COMPLETE SET (35)	175.00	80.00	22.00
COMMON CAP (J1-J35)	3.00	1.35	.35
☐ J1 Don Maynard	10.00	4.50	1.25
☐ J2 George Sauer Jr.	6.00	2.70	.75
☐ J3 Cosmo Iacavazzi	3.00	1.35	.35
☐ J4 Jim O'Mahoney	3.00	1.35	.35
☐ J5 Matt Snell	6.00	2.70	.75
☐ J6 Clyde Washington	3.00	1.35	.35
☐ J7 Jim Turner	4.00	1.80	.50
☐ J8 Mike Taliaferro	3.00	1.35	.35
☐ J9 Marshall Starks	3.00	1.35	.35
☐ J10 Mark Smolinski	3.00	1.35	.35
☐ J11 Bob Schweickert	3.00	1.35	.35
☐ J12 Paul Rochester	3.00	1.35	.35
☐ J13 Sherman Plunkett	4.00	1.80	.50
☐ J14 Gerry Philbin	4.00	1.80	.50
☐ J15 Pete Perreault	3.00	1.35	.35
☐ J16 Dainard Paulson	3.00	1.35	.35
☐ J17 Joe Namath	60.00	27.00	7.50
☐ J18 Winston Hill	4.00	1.80	.50
☐ J19 Dee Mackey	3.00	1.35	.35
☐ J20 Curley Johnson	3.00	1.35	.35
☐ J21 Mike Hudock	3.00	1.35	.35
☐ J22 John Huarte	6.00	2.70	.75
☐ J23 Gordy Holz	3.00	1.35	.35
☐ J24 Gene Heeter	4.00	1.80	.50
☐ J25 Larry Grantham	4.00	1.80	.50
☐ J26 Dan Ficca	3.00	1.35	.35
☐ J27 Sam DeLuca	3.00	1.35	.35
☐ J28 Bill Baird	3.00	1.35	.35
☐ J29 Ralph Baker	3.00	1.35	.35
☐ J30 Wahoo McDaniel	10.00	4.50	1.25
☐ J31 Jim Evans	3.00	1.35	.35
☐ J32 Dave Herman	3.00	1.35	.35
☐ J33 John Schmitt	3.00	1.35	.35
☐ J34 Jim Harris	3.00	1.35	.35
☐ J35 Bake Turner	4.00	1.80	.50
☐ NNO Jets Saver Sheet	30.00	13.50	3.70

1965 Coke Caps Lions

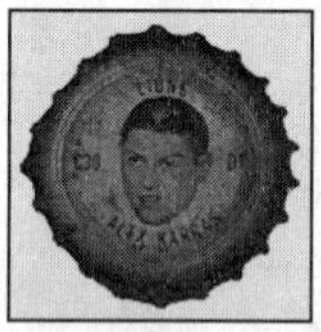

These Lions caps were issued in the Detroit area along with the NFL All-Stars caps as part of the Go with the Pros promotion. The NFL team Cap Saver sheets had separate sections in which to affix both the local team's caps and the All-Stars' caps. The caps measure approximately 1 1/8" in diameter and have the drink logo and a football on the outside, while the inside has the player's face printed in black, with text surrounding the face. The consumer could turn in his completed saver sheet to receive various prizes. The caps are numbered with a "C" prefix. These caps were also produced for 1965 on other Coca-Cola products: TAB, Fanta and Sprite. The other drink caps typically carry a slight premium (1.5-2 times) over the value of the Coke version.

	NRMT	VG-E	GOOD
COMPLETE SET (36)	110.00	50.00	14.00
COMMON CAP (C1-C36)	3.00	1.35	.35
☐ C1 Pat Studstill	4.00	1.80	.50
☐ C2 Bob Whitlow	3.00	1.35	.35
☐ C3 Wayne Walker	4.00	1.80	.50
☐ C4 Tom Watkins	3.00	1.35	.35
☐ C5 Jim Simon	3.00	1.35	.35
☐ C6 Sam Williams	3.00	1.35	.35
☐ C7 Terry Barr	3.00	1.35	.35
☐ C8 Jerry Rush	3.00	1.35	.35
☐ C9 Roger Brown	4.00	1.80	.50
☐ C10 Tom Nowatzke	4.00	1.80	.50
☐ C11 Dick Lane	8.00	3.60	1.00
☐ C12 Dick Compton	3.00	1.35	.35
☐ C13 Yale Lary	8.00	3.60	1.00
☐ C14 Dick Lebeau	4.00	1.80	.50
☐ C15 Dan Lewis	4.00	1.80	.50
☐ C16 Wally Hilgenberg	4.00	1.80	.50
☐ C17 Bruce Maher	3.00	1.35	.35
☐ C18 Darris McCord	3.00	1.35	.35
☐ C19 Hugh McInnis	3.00	1.35	.35
☐ C20 Ernie Clark	3.00	1.35	.35
☐ C21 Gail Cogdill	4.00	1.80	.50
☐ C22 Wayne Rasmussen	3.00	1.35	.35
☐ C23 Joe Don Looney	10.00	4.50	1.25
☐ C24 Jim Gibbons	4.00	1.80	.50
☐ C25 John Gonzaga	3.00	1.35	.35
☐ C26 John Gordy	3.00	1.35	.35
☐ C27 Bobby Thompson DB	3.00	1.35	.35
☐ C28 J.D. Smith	4.00	1.80	.50
☐ C29 Earl Morrall	5.00	2.20	.60
☐ C30 Alex Karras	10.00	4.50	1.25
☐ C31 Nick Pietrosante	4.00	1.80	.50
☐ C32 Milt Plum	4.00	1.80	.50
☐ C33 Daryl Sanders	3.00	1.35	.35
☐ C34 Joe Schmidt	10.00	4.50	1.25
☐ C35 Bob Scholtz	3.00	1.35	.35
☐ C36 Team Logo	3.00	1.35	.35
☐ NNO Lions Saver Sheet	30.00	13.50	3.70

1965 Coke Caps National NFL

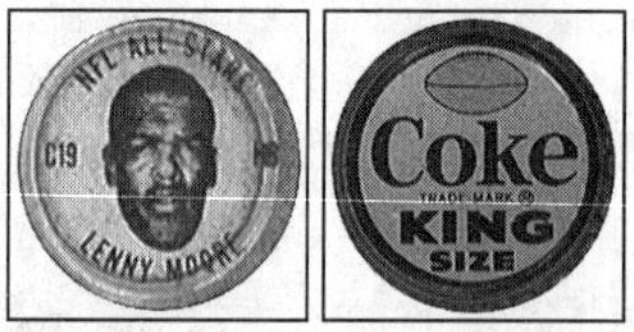

This set of 70 Coke caps was issued on bottled soft drinks primarily in cities without an NFL team. The caps were issued along with their own Saver Sheet. Each measures approximately 1 1/8" in diameter and has the drink logo and a football on the outside, while the inside has the player's face printed in brown or red, with text surrounding the face. An "NFL ALL STARS" title appears above the player's photo. The consumer could turn in his completed saver sheet to receive various prizes. The caps are numbered with a "C" prefix. These caps were also produced for 1965 on other Coca-Cola products: TAB, Fanta and Sprite. The other drink caps typically carry a slight premium (1.5-2 times) over the value of the Coke version.

	NRMT	VG-E	GOOD
COMPLETE SET (70)	225.00	100.00	28.00
COMMON CAP (C1-C70)	3.00	1.35	.35
☐ C1 Herb Adderley	5.00	2.20	.60
☐ C2 Yale Lary	5.00	2.20	.60
☐ C3 Dick LeBeau	3.00	1.35	.35
☐ C4 Bill Brown	4.00	1.80	.50
☐ C5 Jim Taylor	7.50	3.40	.95
☐ C6 Joe Fortunato	3.00	1.35	.35
☐ C7 Bob Boyd DB	3.00	1.35	.35
☐ C8 Terry Barr	3.00	1.35	.35
☐ C9 Dick Szymanski	3.00	1.35	.35
☐ C10 Mick Tingelhoff	4.00	1.80	.50
☐ C11 Wayne Walker	3.00	1.35	.35
☐ C12 Matt Hazeltine	3.00	1.35	.35
☐ C13 Ray Nitschke	7.50	3.40	.95
☐ C14 Grady Alderman	3.00	1.35	.35
☐ C15 Charlie Krueger	3.00	1.35	.35
☐ C16 Tommy Mason	3.00	1.35	.35
☐ C17 Willie Wood	5.00	2.20	.60
☐ C18 John Unitas	12.00	5.50	1.50
☐ C19 Lenny Moore	6.00	2.70	.75
☐ C20 Fran Tarkenton	10.00	4.50	1.25
☐ C21 Deacon Jones	6.00	2.70	.75
☐ C22 Bob Vogel	3.00	1.35	.35
☐ C23 John Gordy	3.00	1.35	.35
☐ C24 Jim Parker	5.00	2.20	.60
☐ C25 Jim Gibbons	3.00	1.35	.35
☐ C26 Merlin Olsen	6.00	2.70	.75
☐ C27 Forrest Gregg	5.00	2.20	.60
☐ C28 Roger Brown	3.00	1.35	.35
☐ C29 Dave Parks	3.00	1.35	.35
☐ C30 Raymond Berry	6.00	2.70	.75
☐ C31 Mike Ditka	12.00	5.50	1.50
☐ C32 Gino Marchetti	6.00	2.70	.75
☐ C33 Willie Davis	5.00	2.20	.60
☐ C34 Ed Meador	3.00	1.35	.35
☐ C35 Browns Logo	3.00	1.35	.35
☐ C36 Colts Logo	3.00	1.35	.35
☐ C37 Sam Baker	3.00	1.35	.35
☐ C38 Irv Cross	4.00	1.80	.50
☐ C39 Maxie Baughan	3.00	1.35	.35
☐ C40 Vince Promuto	3.00	1.35	.35
☐ C41 Paul Krause	3.00	1.35	.35
☐ C42 Charley Taylor	6.00	2.70	.75
☐ C43 John Paluck	3.00	1.35	.35
☐ C44 Paul Warfield	7.50	3.40	.95
☐ C45 Dick Modzelewski	3.00	1.35	.35
☐ C46 Myron Pottios	3.00	1.35	.35
☐ C47 Erich Barnes	3.00	1.35	.35
☐ C48 Bill Koman	3.00	1.35	.35
☐ C49 John Thomas	3.00	1.35	.35
☐ C50 Gary Ballman	3.00	1.35	.35
☐ C51 Sam Huff	6.00	2.70	.75
☐ C52 Ken Gray	3.00	1.35	.35
☐ C53 Roosevelt Brown	5.00	2.20	.60
☐ C54 Bobby Joe Conrad	3.00	1.35	.35
☐ C55 Pat Fischer	3.00	1.35	.35
☐ C56 Irv Goode	3.00	1.35	.35

☐ C57 Floyd Peters	3.00	1.35	.35
☐ C58 Charlie Johnson	4.00	1.80	.50
☐ C59 John Henry Johnson	6.00	2.70	.75
☐ C60 Charles Bradshaw	3.00	1.35	.35
☐ C61 Jim Ringo	5.00	2.20	.60
☐ C62 Pete Retzlaff	4.00	1.80	.50
☐ C63 Sonny Jurgensen	7.00	3.10	.85
☐ C64 Don Meredith	12.00	5.50	1.50
☐ C65 Bob Lilly	10.00	4.50	1.25
☐ C66 Bill Glass	3.00	1.35	.35
☐ C67 Dick Schafrath	3.00	1.35	.35
☐ C68 Mel Renfro	6.00	2.70	.75
☐ C69 Jim Houston	3.00	1.35	.35
☐ C70 Frank Ryan	4.00	1.80	.50

1965 Coke Caps Packers

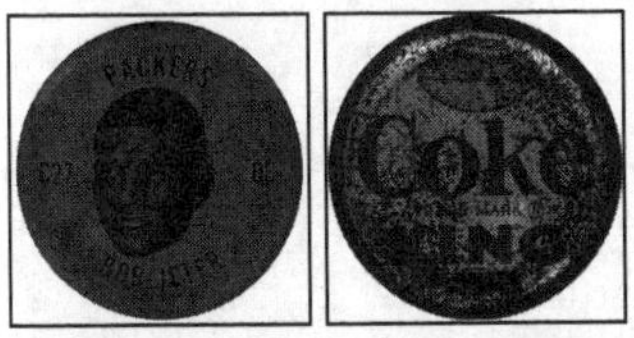

These Packers caps were issued in the Green Bay/Milwaukee area along with the NFL All-Stars caps as part of the Go with the Pros promotion. The NFL team Cap Saver sheets had separate sections in which to affix both the local team's caps and the All-Stars' caps. The caps measure approximately 1 1/8" in diameter and have the drink logo and a football on the outside, while the inside has the player's face printed in black, with text surrounding the face. The consumer could turn in his completed saver sheet to receive various prizes. The caps are numbered with a "C" prefix. These caps were also produced for 1965 on other Coca-Cola products: TAB, Fanta and Sprite. The other drink caps typically carry a slight premium (1.5-2 times) over the value of the Coke version.

	NRMT	VG-E	GOOD
COMPLETE SET (36)	160.00	70.00	20.00
COMMON CAP (C1-C36)	3.00	1.35	.35
☐ C1 Herb Adderley	6.00	2.70	.75
☐ C2 Lionel Aldridge	3.00	1.35	.35
☐ C3 Hank Gremminger	3.00	1.35	.35
☐ C4 Willie Davis	6.00	2.70	.75
☐ C5 Boyd Dowler	4.00	1.80	.50
☐ C6 Marv Fleming	4.00	1.80	.50
☐ C7 Ken Bowman	4.00	1.80	.50
☐ C8 Tom Brown	3.00	1.35	.35
☐ C9 Doug Hart	4.00	1.80	.50
☐ C10 Steve Wright	3.00	1.35	.35
☐ C11 Dennis Claridge	3.00	1.35	.35
☐ C12 Dave Hanner	4.00	1.80	.50
☐ C13 Tommy Crutcher	3.00	1.35	.35
☐ C14 Fred Thurston	4.00	1.80	.50
☐ C15 Elijah Pitts	4.00	1.80	.50
☐ C16 Lloyd Voss	3.00	1.35	.35
☐ C17 Lee Roy Caffey	4.00	1.80	.50
☐ C18 Dave Robinson	4.00	1.80	.50
☐ C19 Bart Starr	15.00	6.75	1.85
☐ C20 Ray Nitschke	10.00	4.50	1.25
☐ C21 Max McGee	4.00	1.80	.50
☐ C22 Don Chandler	4.00	1.80	.50
☐ C23 Norman Masters	3.00	1.35	.35
☐ C24 Ron Kostelnik	3.00	1.35	.35
☐ C25 Carroll Dale	4.00	1.80	.50
☐ C26 Hank Jordan	6.00	2.70	.75
☐ C27 Bob Jeter	3.00	1.35	.35
☐ C28 Bob Skoronski	3.00	1.35	.35
☐ C29 Jerry Kramer	5.00	2.20	.60
☐ C30 Willie Wood	5.00	2.20	.60
☐ C31 Paul Hornung	15.00	6.75	1.85
☐ C32 Forrest Gregg	6.00	2.70	.75
☐ C33 Zeke Bratkowski	4.00	1.80	.50
☐ C34 Tom Moore	4.00	1.80	.50
☐ C35 Jim Taylor	10.00	4.50	1.25
☐ C36 Team Logo	3.00	1.35	.35
☐ NNO Packers Saver Sheet	30.00	13.50	3.70

1965 Coke Caps Patriots

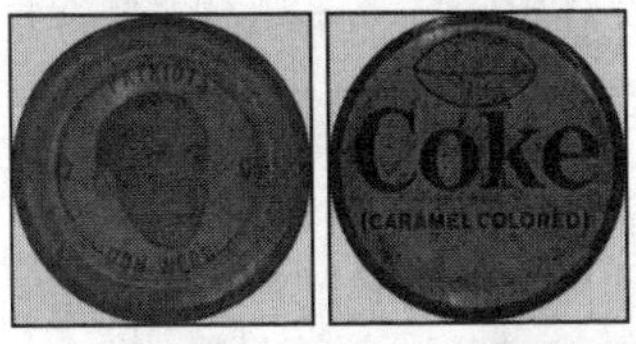

These Patriots caps were issued in the Boston area along with the AFL All-Stars caps as part of the Go with the Pros promotion. The AFL team Cap Saver sheets had separate sections in which to affix both the local team's caps and the All-Stars' caps. The caps measure approximately 1 1/8" in diameter and have the drink logo and a football on the outside, while the inside has the player's face printed in black, with text surrounding the face. The consumer could turn in his completed saver sheet to receive various prizes. The caps are numbered with a "C" prefix. These caps were also produced for 1965 on other Coca-Cola products: TAB, Fanta and Sprite. The other drink caps typically carry a slight premium (1.5-2 times) over the value of the Coke version.

	NRMT	VG-E	GOOD
COMPLETE SET (36)	100.00	45.00	12.50
COMMON CAP (C1-C36)	3.00	1.35	.35
☐ C1 Jon Morris	4.00	1.80	.50
☐ C2 Don Webb	3.00	1.35	.35
☐ C3 Charles Long	4.00	1.80	.50
☐ C4 Tony Romeo	3.00	1.35	.35
☐ C5 Bob Dee	3.00	1.35	.35
☐ C6 Tommy Addison	4.00	1.80	.50
☐ C7 Bob Yates	3.00	1.35	.35
☐ C8 Ron Hall	3.00	1.35	.35
☐ C9 Billy Neighbors	4.00	1.80	.50
☐ C10 Jack Rudolph	3.00	1.35	.35
☐ C11 Don Oakes	3.00	1.35	.35
☐ C12 Tom Yewcic	3.00	1.35	.35
☐ C13 Ron Burton	4.00	1.80	.50
☐ C14 Jim Colclough	3.00	1.35	.35
☐ C15 Larry Garron	4.00	1.80	.50
☐ C16 Dave Watson	3.00	1.35	.35
☐ C17 Art Graham	4.00	1.80	.50
☐ C18 Babe Parilli	6.00	2.70	.75
☐ C19 Jim Hunt	3.00	1.35	.35
☐ C20 Don McKinnon	3.00	1.35	.35
☐ C21 Houston Antwine	3.00	1.35	.35
☐ C22 Nick Buoniconti	10.00	4.50	1.25
☐ C23 Ross O'Hanley	3.00	1.35	.35
☐ C24 Gino Cappelletti	6.00	2.70	.75
☐ C25 Chuck Shonta	3.00	1.35	.35
☐ C26 Dick Felt	3.00	1.35	.35
☐ C27 Mike Dukes	3.00	1.35	.35
☐ C28 Larry Eisenhauer	3.00	1.35	.35
☐ C29 Bob Schmidt	3.00	1.35	.35
☐ C30 Len St. Jean	3.00	1.35	.35
☐ C31 J.D. Garrett	3.00	1.35	.35
☐ C32 Jim Whalen	3.00	1.35	.35
☐ C33 Jim Nance	5.00	2.20	.60
☐ C34 Eddie Wilson	3.00	1.35	.35
☐ C35 Lonnie Farmer	3.00	1.35	.35
☐ C36 Boston Patriots Logo	3.00	1.35	.35
☐ NNO Patriots Saver Sheet	30.00	13.50	3.70

1965 Coke Caps Redskins

These Redskins caps were issued in the Washington D.C. area along with the NFL All-Stars caps as part of the Go with the Pros promotion. The NFL team Cap Saver sheets had separate sections in which to affix both the local team's caps and the All-Stars' caps. The caps measure approximately 1 1/8" in diameter and have the drink logo and a football on the outside, while the inside has the player's face printed in black, with text surrounding the face. The consumer could turn in his completed saver sheet to receive various prizes. The caps are numbered with a "C" prefix. These caps were also produced for 1965 on other Coca-Cola products: TAB, Fanta and Sprite. The other drink caps typically carry a slight premium (1.5-2 times) over the value of the Coke version.

	NRMT	VG-E	GOOD
COMPLETE SET (36)	110.00	50.00	14.00
COMMON CAP (C1-C36)	3.00	1.35	.35
☐ C1 Jim Carr	3.00	1.35	.35
☐ C2 Fred Mazurek	3.00	1.35	.35
☐ C3 Lonnie Sanders	3.00	1.35	.35
☐ C4 Jim Steffen	3.00	1.35	.35
☐ C5 John Nisby	3.00	1.35	.35
☐ C6 George Izo	4.00	1.80	.50
☐ C7 Vince Promuto	3.00	1.35	.35
☐ C8 Johnny Sample	4.00	1.80	.50
☐ C9 Pat Richter	4.00	1.80	.50
☐ C10 Preston Carpenter	3.00	1.35	.35
☐ C11 Sam Huff	10.00	4.50	1.25
☐ C12 Pervis Atkins	3.00	1.35	.35
☐ C13 Steve Barnett	3.00	1.35	.35
☐ C14 Len Hauss	4.00	1.80	.50
☐ C15 Bill Anderson	3.00	1.35	.35
☐ C16 John Reger	3.00	1.35	.35
☐ C17 George Seals	3.00	1.35	.35
☐ C18 J.W. Lockett	3.00	1.35	.35
☐ C19 Tom Walters	3.00	1.35	.35
☐ C20 Joe Rutgens	3.00	1.35	.35
☐ C21 John Paluck	3.00	1.35	.35
☐ C22 Fran O'Brien	3.00	1.35	.35
☐ C23 Joe Rutgens	3.00	1.35	.35
☐ C24 Rod Breedlove	3.00	1.35	.35
☐ C25 Bob Pellegrini	3.00	1.35	.35
☐ C26 Bob Jencks	3.00	1.35	.35
☐ C27 Joe Hernandez	3.00	1.35	.35
☐ C28 Sonny Jurgensen	10.00	4.50	1.25
☐ C29 Bob Toneff	3.00	1.35	.35
☐ C30 Charley Taylor	10.00	4.50	1.25
☐ C31 Bob Shiner	3.00	1.35	.35
☐ C32 Bobby Williams	3.00	1.35	.35
☐ C33 Angelo Coia	3.00	1.35	.35
☐ C34 Ron Snidow	3.00	1.35	.35
☐ C35 Paul Krause	5.00	2.20	.60
☐ C36 Team Logo	3.00	1.35	.35
☐ NNO Redskins Saver Sheet	30.00	13.50	3.70

1966 Coke Caps All-Stars AFL

These AFL All-Star caps were issued in AFL cities (and a few other cities as well) along with the local team caps as part of the Score with the Pros promotion. The local team cap saver sheets had separate sections in which to affix both the local team's caps and the All-Stars' caps. The caps measure approximately 1 1/8" in diameter and have

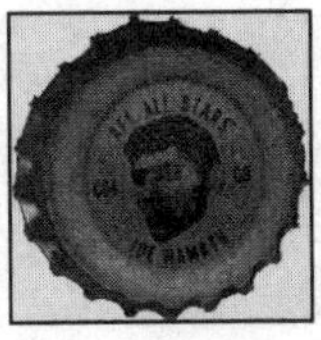

the drink logo and a football on the outside, while the inside has the player's face printed in black, with text surrounding the face. The consumer could turn in his completed saver sheet to receive various prizes. The caps are numbered with a "C" prefix. These caps were also produced for 1966 on other Coca-Cola products: Tab, Fanta, Fresca and Sprite. The other drink caps typically carry a slight premium of 1.5X to 2X the value of the Coke version.

	NRMT	VG-E	GOOD
COMPLETE SET (34)	125.00	55.00	15.50
COMMON CAP (C37-C70)	2.00	.90	.25
☐ C37 Babe Parilli	3.00	1.35	.35
☐ C38 Mike Stratton	2.00	.90	.25
☐ C39 Jack Kemp	25.00	11.00	3.10
☐ C40 Len Dawson	7.50	3.40	.95
☐ C41 Fred Arbanas	2.00	.90	.25
☐ C42 Bobby Bell	5.00	2.20	.60
☐ C43 Willie Brown	5.00	2.20	.60
☐ C44 Buck Buchanan	5.00	2.20	.60
☐ C45 Frank Buncom	2.00	.90	.25
☐ C46 Nick Buoniconti	4.00	1.80	.50
☐ C47 Gino Cappelletti	3.00	1.35	.35
☐ C48 Eldon Danenhauer	2.00	.90	.25
☐ C49 Clem Daniels	3.00	1.35	.35
☐ C50 Les Speedy Duncan	3.00	1.35	.35
☐ C51 Willie Frazier	2.00	.90	.25
☐ C52 Cookie Gilchrist	3.00	1.35	.35
☐ C53 Dave Grayson	2.00	.90	.25
☐ C54 John Hadl	4.00	1.80	.50
☐ C55 Wayne Hawkins	2.00	.90	.25
☐ C56 Sherrill Headrick	2.00	.90	.25
☐ C57 Charlie Hennigan	3.00	1.35	.35
☐ C58 E.J. Holub	2.00	.90	.25
☐ C59 Curley Johnson	2.00	.90	.25
☐ C60 Keith Lincoln	3.00	1.35	.35
☐ C61 Paul Lowe	3.00	1.35	.35
☐ C62 Don Maynard	6.00	2.70	.75
☐ C63 Jon Morris	2.00	.90	.25
☐ C64 Joe Namath	30.00	13.50	3.70
☐ C65 Jim Otto	5.00	2.20	.60
☐ C66 Dainard Paulson	2.00	.90	.25
☐ C67 Art Powell	3.00	1.35	.35
☐ C68 Walt Sweeney	3.00	1.35	.35
☐ C69 Bob Talamini	2.00	.90	.25
☐ C70 Lance Alworth UER (Name misspelled Alsworth)	7.50	3.40	.95

1966 Coke Caps All-Stars NFL

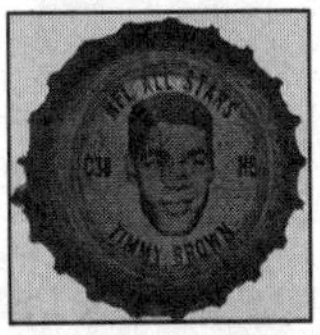

These NFL All-Star caps were issued in NFL cities (and a few other cities as well) along with the local team caps as part of the Score with the Pros promotion. The local team cap saver sheets had separate sections in which to affix both the local team's caps and the All-Stars' caps. The caps measure approximately 1 1/8" in diameter and have the drink logo and a football on the outside, while the inside has the player's face printed in black, with text surrounding the face. The consumer could turn in his completed saver sheet to receive various prizes. The caps are numbered with a "C" prefix. These caps were also produced for 1966 on other Coca-Cola products: Tab, Fanta, Fresca and Sprite. The other drink caps typically carry a slight premium of 1.5X to 2X the value of the Coke version.

	NRMT	VG-E	GOOD
COMPLETE SET (34)	125.00	55.00	15.50
COMMON CAP (C37-C70)	2.00	.90	.25
☐ C37 Frank Ryan	3.00	1.35	.35
☐ C38 Timmy Brown	3.00	1.35	.35
☐ C39 Tucker Frederickson	2.00	.90	.25
☐ C40 Cornell Green	3.00	1.35	.35
☐ C41 Bob Hayes	6.00	2.70	.75
☐ C42 Charley Taylor	5.00	2.20	.60
☐ C43 Pete Retzlaff	3.00	1.35	.35
☐ C44 Jim Ringo	5.00	2.20	.60
☐ C45 John Wooten	2.00	.90	.25
☐ C46 Dave Meinert	2.00	.90	.25
☐ C47 Bob Lilly	7.50	3.40	.95
☐ C48 Sam Silas	2.00	.90	.25
☐ C49 Roosevelt Brown	5.00	2.20	.60
☐ C50 Gary Ballman	2.00	.90	.25
☐ C51 Gary Collins	2.00	.90	.25
☐ C52 Sonny Randle	2.00	.90	.25
☐ C53 Charlie Johnson	3.00	1.35	.35
☐ C54 Herb Adderley	5.00	2.20	.60
☐ C55 Doug Atkins	5.00	2.20	.60
☐ C56 Roger Brown	2.00	.90	.25
☐ C57 Dick Butkus	15.00	6.75	1.85
☐ C58 Willie Davis	5.00	2.20	.60
☐ C59 Tommy McDonald	3.00	1.35	.35
☐ C60 Alex Karras	6.00	2.70	.75
☐ C61 John Mackey	5.00	2.20	.60
☐ C62 Ed Meador	2.00	.90	.25
☐ C63 Merlin Olsen	6.00	2.70	.75
☐ C64 Dave Parks	2.00	.90	.25
☐ C65 Gale Sayers	15.00	6.75	1.85
☐ C66 Fran Tarkenton	10.00	4.50	1.25
☐ C67 Mick Tingelhoff	2.00	.90	.25
☐ C68 Ken Willard	2.00	.90	.25
☐ C69 Willie Wood	5.00	2.20	.60
☐ C70 Bill Brown	3.00	1.35	.35

1966 Coke Caps Bills

As part of an advertising promotion, Coca-Cola issued 21 sets of bottle caps, covering the 14 NFL cities, the six AFL cities, and a separate National set for cities not reached by the leagues. These Bills caps were issued in the Western New York area along with the AFL All-Stars caps as part of the Score with the Pros promotion. The AFL team Cap Saver sheets had separate sections in which to affix both the local team's caps and the All-Stars' caps. The caps measure approximately 1 1/8" in diameter and have the drink logo and a football on the outside, while the inside has the player's face printed in black, with text surrounding the face. The consumer could turn in his completed saver sheet to receive various prizes. The caps are numbered with a "B" prefix. These caps were also produced for 1966 on other Coca-Cola products: Tab, Fanta, Fresca and Sprite. The other drink caps typically carry a slight premium of 1.5X to 2X the value of the Coke version.

	NRMT	VG-E	GOOD
COMPLETE SET (36)	135.00	60.00	17.00
COMMON CAP (B1-B36)	2.50	1.10	.30
☐ B1 Bill Laskey	2.50	1.10	.30
☐ B2 Marty Schottenheimer	12.00	5.50	1.50
☐ B3 Stew Barber	3.50	1.55	.45
☐ B4 Glenn Bass	2.50	1.10	.30
☐ B5 Remi Prudhomme	2.50	1.10	.30
☐ B6 Al Bemiller	2.50	1.10	.30
☐ B7 George Butch Byrd	3.50	1.55	.45
☐ B8 Wray Carlton	3.50	1.55	.45
☐ B9 Hagood Clarke	2.50	1.10	.30
☐ B10 Jack Kemp	30.00	13.50	3.70
☐ B11 Charley Warner	2.50	1.10	.30
☐ B12 Elbert Dubenion	3.50	1.55	.45
☐ B13 Jim Dunaway	3.50	1.55	.45
☐ B14 Booker Edgerson	3.50	1.55	.45
☐ B15 Paul Costa	2.50	1.10	.30
☐ B16 Henry Schmidt	2.50	1.10	.30
☐ B17 Dick Hudson	2.50	1.10	.30
☐ B18 Harry Jacobs	3.50	1.55	.45
☐ B19 Tom Janik	2.50	1.10	.30
☐ B20 Tom Day	3.50	1.55	.45
☐ B21 Daryle Lamonica	7.50	3.40	.95
☐ B22 Paul Maguire	6.00	2.70	.75
☐ B23 Roland McDole	2.50	1.10	.30
☐ B24 Dudley Meredith	2.50	1.10	.30
☐ B25 Joe O'Donnell	2.50	1.10	.30
☐ B26 Charley Ferguson	2.50	1.10	.30
☐ B27 Ed Rutkowski	2.50	1.10	.30
☐ B28 George Saimes	3.50	1.55	.45
☐ B29 Tom Sestak	3.50	1.55	.45
☐ B30 Billy Shaw	2.50	1.10	.30
☐ B31 Bob Lee Smith	2.50	1.10	.30
☐ B32 Mike Stratton	3.50	1.55	.45
☐ B33 Gene Sykes	2.50	1.10	.30
☐ B34 John Tracey	2.50	1.10	.30
☐ B35 Ernie Warlick	2.50	1.10	.30
☐ B36 Bills Logo	2.50	1.10	.30
☐ NNO Bills Saver Sheet	30.00	13.50	3.70

1966 Coke Caps Broncos

As part of an advertising promotion, Coca-Cola issued 21 sets of bottle caps, covering the 14 NFL cities, the six AFL cities, and a separate National set for cities not reached by the leagues. These Broncos caps were issued in the Denver area along with the AFL All-Stars caps as part of the Score with the Pros promotion. The AFL team Cap Saver sheets had separate sections in which to affix both the local team's caps and the All-Stars' caps. The caps measure approximately 1 1/8" in diameter and have the drink logo and a football on the outside, while the inside has the player's face printed in black, with text surrounding the face. The consumer could turn in his completed saver sheet to receive various prizes. The caps are numbered with a "C" prefix. These caps were also produced for 1966 on other Coca-Cola products: Tab, Fanta, Fresca and Sprite. The other drink caps typically carry a slight premium of 1.5X to 2X the value of the Coke version.

	NRMT	VG-E	GOOD
COMPLETE SET (36)	110.00	50.00	14.00
COMMON CAP (C1-C36)	3.00	1.35	.35
☐ C1 Fred Forsberg	3.00	1.35	.35
☐ C2 Willie Brown DB	10.00	4.50	1.25
☐ C3 Bob Scarpitto	4.00	1.80	.50
☐ C4 Butch Davis	3.00	1.35	.35
☐ C5 Al Denson	3.00	1.35	.35
☐ C6 Ron Sbranti	3.00	1.35	.35

☐ C7 John Bramlett	3.00	1.35	.35
☐ C8 Mickey Slaughter	4.00	1.80	.50
☐ C9 Lionel Taylor	5.00	2.20	.60
☐ C10 Jerry Sturm	3.00	1.35	.35
☐ C11 Jerry Hopkins	3.00	1.35	.35
☐ C12 Charlie Mitchell	3.00	1.35	.35
☐ C13 Ray Jacobs	3.00	1.35	.35
☐ C14 Lonnie Wright	3.00	1.35	.35
☐ C15 Goldie Sellers	3.00	1.35	.35
☐ C16 Ray Kubala	3.00	1.35	.35
☐ C17 John Griffin	3.00	1.35	.35
☐ C18 Bob Breitenstein	3.00	1.35	.35
☐ C19 Eldon Danenhauer	3.00	1.35	.35
☐ C20 Wendell Hayes	4.00	1.80	.50
☐ C21 Max Leetzow	3.00	1.35	.35
☐ C22 Nemiah Wilson	4.00	1.80	.50
☐ C23 Jim Thibert	3.00	1.35	.35
☐ C24 Gerry Bussell	3.00	1.35	.35
☐ C25 Bob McCullough	3.00	1.35	.35
☐ C26 Jim McMillin	3.00	1.35	.35
☐ C27 Abner Haynes	6.00	2.70	.75
☐ C28 Darrell Lester	3.00	1.35	.35
☐ C29 Cookie Gilchrist	6.00	2.70	.75
☐ C30 John McCormick	4.00	1.80	.50
☐ C31 Lee Bernet	3.00	1.35	.35
☐ C32 Goose Gonsoulin	5.00	2.20	.60
☐ C33 Scotty Glacken	3.00	1.35	.35
☐ C34 Bob Hadrick	3.00	1.35	.35
☐ C35 Archie Matsos	4.00	1.80	.50
☐ C36 Broncos Logo	3.00	1.35	.35

1966 Coke Caps Browns

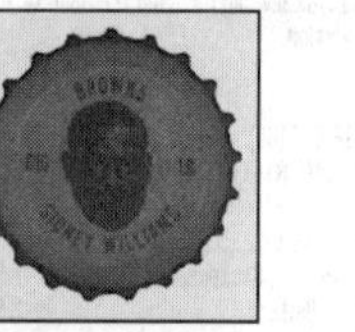

As part of an advertising promotion, Coca-Cola issued 21 sets of bottle caps, covering the 14 NFL cities, the six AFL cities, and a separate National set for cities not reached by the leagues. These Browns caps were issued in the Cleveland area along with the NFL All-Stars caps as part of the Score with the Pros promotion. The NFL team Cap Saver sheets had separate sections in which to affix both the local team's caps and the All-Stars' caps. The caps measure approximately 1 1/8" in diameter and have the drink logo and a football on the outside, while the inside has the player's face printed in black, with text surrounding the face. The consumer could turn in his completed saver sheet to receive various prizes. The caps are numbered with a "C" prefix. These caps were also produced for 1966 on other Coca-Cola products: Tab, Fanta, Fresca and Sprite. The other drink caps typically carry a slight premium of 1.5X to 2X the value of the Coke version.

	NRMT	VG-E	GOOD
COMPLETE SET (36)	100.00	45.00	12.50
COMMON CAP (C1-C36)	2.50	1.10	.30
☐ C1 Jim Ninowski	3.50	1.55	.45
☐ C2 Leroy Kelly	8.00	3.60	1.00
☐ C3 Lou Groza	8.00	3.60	1.00
☐ C4 Gary Collins	3.50	1.55	.45
☐ C5 Bill Glass	3.50	1.55	.45
☐ C6 Dale Lindsey	2.50	1.10	.30
☐ C7 Galen Fiss	2.50	1.10	.30
☐ C8 Ross Fichtner	2.50	1.10	.30
☐ C9 John Wooten	2.50	1.10	.30
☐ C10 Clifton McNeil	2.50	1.10	.30
☐ C11 Paul Wiggin	2.50	1.10	.30
☐ C12 Gene Hickerson	3.50	1.55	.45
☐ C13 Ernie Green	2.50	1.10	.30
☐ C14 Mike Howell	2.50	1.10	.30
☐ C15 Dick Schafrath	2.50	1.10	.30
☐ C16 Sidney Williams	2.50	1.10	.30
☐ C17 Frank Ryan	3.50	1.55	.45
☐ C18 Bernie Parrish	3.50	1.55	.45
☐ C19 Vince Costello	2.50	1.10	.30
☐ C20 John Brown OT	2.50	1.10	.30
☐ C21 Monte Clark	2.50	1.10	.30
☐ C22 Walter Roberts	2.50	1.10	.30
☐ C23 Johnny Brewer	2.50	1.10	.30
☐ C24 Walter Beach	2.50	1.10	.30
☐ C25 Dick Modzelewski	2.50	1.10	.30
☐ C26 Gary Lane	2.50	1.10	.30
☐ C27 Jim Houston	2.50	1.10	.30
☐ C28 Milt Morin	2.50	1.10	.30
☐ C29 Erich Barnes	2.50	1.10	.30
☐ C30 Tom Hutchinson	2.50	1.10	.30
☐ C31 John Morrow	2.50	1.10	.30
☐ C32 Jim Kanicki	2.50	1.10	.30
☐ C33 Paul Warfield	8.00	3.60	1.00
☐ C34 Jim Garcia	2.50	1.10	.30
☐ C35 Walter Johnson	2.50	1.10	.30
☐ C36 Browns Logo	2.50	1.10	.30
☐ NNO Browns Saver Sheet	30.00	13.50	3.70

1966 Coke Caps Cardinals

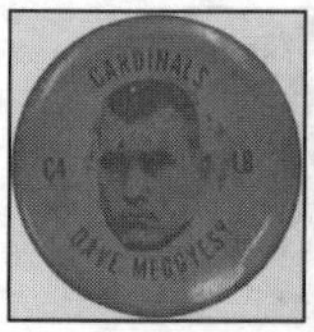

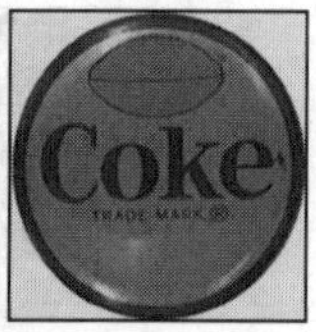

As part of an advertising promotion, Coca-Cola issued 21 sets of bottle caps, covering the 14 NFL cities, the six AFL cities, and a separate National set for cities not reached by the leagues. These Cardinals caps were issued in the St. Louis area along with the NFL All-Stars caps as part of the Score with the Pros promotion. The NFL team Cap Saver sheets had separate sections in which to affix both the local team's caps and the All-Stars' caps. The caps measure approximately 1 1/8" in diameter and have the drink logo and a football on the outside, while the inside has the player's face printed in black, with text surrounding the face. The consumer could turn in his completed saver sheet to receive various prizes. The caps are numbered with a "C" prefix. These caps were also produced for 1966 on other Coca-Cola products: Tab, Fanta, Fresca and Sprite. The other drink caps typically carry a slight premium of 1.5X to 2X the value of the Coke version.

	NRMT	VG-E	GOOD
COMPLETE SET (36)	90.00	40.00	11.00
COMMON CAP (C1-C36)	2.50	1.10	.30
☐ C1 Pat Fischer	3.50	1.55	.45
☐ C2 Sonny Randle	2.50	1.10	.30
☐ C3 Joe Childress	2.50	1.10	.30
☐ C4 Dave Meggysey UER (Name misspelled Meggyesy)	5.00	2.20	.60
☐ C5 Joe Robb	2.50	1.10	.30
☐ C6 Jerry Stovall	3.50	1.55	.45
☐ C7 Ernie McMillan	3.50	1.55	.45
☐ C8 Dale Meinert	2.50	1.10	.30
☐ C9 Irv Goode	2.50	1.10	.30
☐ C10 Bob DeMarco	2.50	1.10	.30
☐ C11 Mal Hammack	2.50	1.10	.30
☐ C12 Jim Bakken	3.50	1.55	.45
☐ C13 Bill Thornton	2.50	1.10	.30
☐ C14 Buddy Humphrey	2.50	1.10	.30
☐ C15 Bill Koman	2.50	1.10	.30
☐ C16 Larry Wilson	7.50	3.40	.95
☐ C17 Charles Walker	2.50	1.10	.30
☐ C18 Prentice Gautt	3.50	1.55	.45
☐ C19 Charlie Johnson UER (Name misspelled Charley)	3.50	1.55	.45
☐ C20 Ken Gray	2.50	1.10	.30
☐ C21 Dave Simmons	2.50	1.10	.30
☐ C22 Sam Silas	2.50	1.10	.30
☐ C23 Larry Stallings	2.50	1.10	.30
☐ C24 Don Brumm	2.50	1.10	.30
☐ C25 Bobby Joe Conrad	3.50	1.55	.45
☐ C26 Bill Triplett	2.50	1.10	.30
☐ C27 Luke Owens	2.50	1.10	.30
☐ C28 Jackie Smith	7.50	3.40	.95
☐ C29 Bob Reynolds	2.50	1.10	.30
☐ C30 Abe Woodson	3.50	1.55	.45
☐ C31 Jim Burson	2.50	1.10	.30
☐ C32 Willis Crenshaw	2.50	1.10	.30
☐ C33 Billy Gambrell	2.50	1.10	.30
☐ C34 Ray Ogden	2.50	1.10	.30
☐ C35 Herschel Turner	2.50	1.10	.30
☐ C36 Cardinals Logo	2.50	1.10	.30
☐ NNO Cardinals Saver Sheet	30.00	13.50	3.70

1966 Coke Caps Chiefs

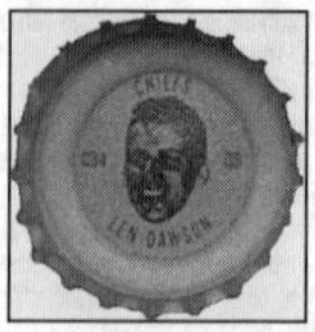

As part of an advertising promotion, Coca-Cola issued 21 sets of bottle caps, covering the 14 NFL cities, the six AFL cities, and a separate National set for cities not reached by the leagues. These Chiefs caps were issued in the Kansas City area along with the AFL All-Stars caps as part of the Score with the Pros promotion. The AFL team Cap Saver sheets had separate sections in which to affix both the local team's caps and the All-Stars' caps. The caps measure approximately 1 1/8" in diameter and have the drink logo and a football on the outside, while the inside has the player's face printed in black, with text surrounding the face. The consumer could turn in his completed saver sheet to receive various prizes. The caps are numbered with a "C" prefix. These caps were also produced for 1966 on other Coca-Cola products: Tab, Fanta, Fresca and Sprite. The other drink caps typically carry a slight premium of 1.5X to 2X the value of the Coke version.

	NRMT	VG-E	GOOD
COMPLETE SET (36)	110.00	50.00	14.00
COMMON CAP (1-36)	2.50	1.10	.30
☐ C1 E.J. Holub	3.50	1.55	.45
☐ C2 Al Reynolds	2.50	1.10	.30
☐ C3 Buck Buchanan	7.50	3.40	.95
☐ C4 Curt Merz SP	7.50	3.40	.95
☐ C5 Dave Hill	2.50	1.10	.30
☐ C6 Bobby Hunt	2.50	1.10	.30
☐ C7 Jerry Mays	3.50	1.55	.45
☐ C8 Jon Gilliam	2.50	1.10	.30
☐ C9 Walt Corey	2.50	1.10	.30
☐ C10 Solomon Brannan	2.50	1.10	.30
☐ C11 Aaron Brown	2.50	1.10	.30
☐ C12 Bert Coan	2.50	1.10	.30
☐ C13 Ed Budde	2.50	1.10	.30
☐ C14 Tommy Brooker	2.50	1.10	.30
☐ C15 Bobby Bell	7.50	3.40	.95
☐ C16 Smokey Stover	2.50	1.10	.30
☐ C17 Curtis McClinton	3.50	1.55	.45
☐ C18 Jerrel Wilson	3.50	1.55	.45
☐ C19 Ron Burton	3.50	1.55	.45
☐ C20 Mike Garrett	5.00	2.20	.60
☐ C21 Jim Tyrer	3.50	1.55	.45
☐ C22 Johnny Robinson	3.50	1.55	.45
☐ C23 Bobby Ply	2.50	1.10	.30
☐ C24 Frank Pitts	2.50	1.10	.30
☐ C25 Ed Lothamer	2.50	1.10	.30
☐ C26 Sherrill Headrick	3.50	1.55	.45
☐ C27 Fred Williamson	6.00	2.70	.75
☐ C28 Chris Burford	3.50	1.55	.45
☐ C29 Willie Mitchell	2.50	1.10	.30
☐ C30 Otis Taylor	6.00	2.70	.75
☐ C31 Fred Arbanas	2.50	1.10	.30
☐ C32 Hatch Rosdahl	2.50	1.10	.30
☐ C33 Reg Carolan	2.50	1.10	.30
☐ C34 Len Dawson	12.00	5.50	1.50
☐ C35 Pete Beathard	3.50	1.55	.45
☐ C36 Chiefs Logo	2.50	1.10	.30
☐ NNO Chiefs Saver Sheet	30.00	13.50	3.70

1966 Coke Caps Colts

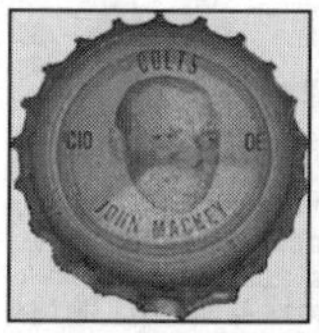

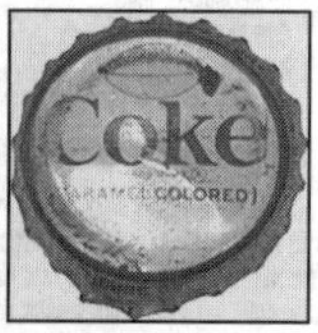

As part of an advertising promotion, Coca-Cola issued 21 sets of bottle caps, covering the 14 NFL cities, the six AFL cities, and a separate National set for cities not reached by the leagues. These Colts caps were issued in the Baltimore area along with the NFL All-Stars caps as part of the Score with the Pros promotion. The NFL team Cap Saver sheets had separate sections in which to affix both the local team's caps and the All-Stars' caps. The caps measure approximately 1 1/8" in diameter and have the drink logo and a football on the outside, while the inside has the player's face printed in black, with text surrounding the face. The consumer could turn in his completed saver sheet to receive various prizes. The caps are numbered with a "C" prefix. These caps were also produced for 1966 on other Coca-Cola products: Tab, Fanta, Fresca and Sprite. The other drink caps typically carry a slight premium of 1.5X to 2X the value of the Coke version.

	NRMT	VG-E	GOOD
COMPLETE SET (36)	110.00	50.00	14.00
COMMON CAP (1-36)	2.50	1.10	.30
☐ C1 Ted Davis	2.50	1.10	.30
☐ C2 Bob Boyd	2.50	1.10	.30
☐ C3 Lenny Moore	10.00	4.50	1.25
☐ C4 Jackie Burkett	2.50	1.10	.30
☐ C5 Jimmy Orr	3.50	1.55	.45
☐ C6 Andy Stynchula	2.50	1.10	.30
☐ C7 Mike Curtis	6.00	2.70	.75
☐ C8 Jerry Logan	2.50	1.10	.30
☐ C9 Steve Stonebreaker	2.50	1.10	.30
☐ C10 John Mackey	8.00	3.60	1.00
☐ C11 Dennis Gaubatz	2.50	1.10	.30
☐ C12 Don Shinnick	2.50	1.10	.30
☐ C13 Dick Szymanski	2.50	1.10	.30
☐ C14 Ordell Braase	2.50	1.10	.30
☐ C15 Lenny Lyles	2.50	1.10	.30
☐ C16 Rick Kestner	2.50	1.10	.30
☐ C17 Dan Sullivan	2.50	1.10	.30
☐ C18 Lou Michaels	3.50	1.55	.45
☐ C19 Gary Cuozzo	3.50	1.55	.45
☐ C20 Butch Wilson	2.50	1.10	.30
☐ C21 Willie Richardson	3.50	1.55	.45
☐ C22 Jim Welch	2.50	1.10	.30
☐ C23 Tony Lorick	2.50	1.10	.30
☐ C24 Billy Ray Smith	3.50	1.55	.45
☐ C25 Fred Miller	2.50	1.10	.30
☐ C26 Tom Matte	5.00	2.20	.60
☐ C27 Johnny Unitas	15.00	6.75	1.85
☐ C28 Glenn Ressler	2.50	1.10	.30
☐ C29 Alvin Haymond	3.50	1.55	.45
☐ C30 Jim Parker	6.00	2.70	.75
☐ C31 Butch Allison	2.50	1.10	.30
☐ C32 Bob Vogel	2.50	1.10	.30
☐ C33 Jerry Hill	2.50	1.10	.30
☐ C34 Raymond Berry	10.00	4.50	1.25
☐ C35 Sam Ball	2.50	1.10	.30
☐ C36 Colts Team Logo	2.50	1.10	.30
☐ NNO Colts Saver Sheet	30.00	13.50	3.70

1966 Coke Caps Cowboys

As part of an advertising promotion, Coca-Cola issued 21 sets of bottle caps, covering the 14 NFL cities, the six AFL cities, and a separate National set for cities not reached by the leagues. These Cowboys caps were issued in the Dallas area along with the NFL All-Stars caps as part of the Score with the Pros promotion. The NFL team Cap Saver sheets had separate sections in which to affix both the local team's caps and the All-Stars' caps. The caps measure approximately 1 1/8" in diameter and have the drink logo and a football on the outside, while the inside has the player's face printed in black, with text surrounding the face. The consumer could turn in his completed saver sheet to receive various prizes. The caps are numbered with a "C" prefix. These caps were also produced for 1966 on other Coca-Cola products: Tab, Fanta, Fresca and Sprite. The other drink caps typically carry a slight premium of 1.5X to 2X the value of the Coke version.

	NRMT	VG-E	GOOD
COMPLETE SET (36)	150.00	70.00	19.00
COMMON CAP (C1-C36)	2.50	1.10	.30
☐ C1 Mike Connelly	2.50	1.10	.30
☐ C2 Tony Liscio	2.50	1.10	.30
☐ C3 Jethro Pugh	3.50	1.55	.45
☐ C4 Larry Stephens	2.50	1.10	.30
☐ C5 Jim Colvin	2.50	1.10	.30
☐ C6 Malcolm Walker	2.50	1.10	.30
☐ C7 Danny Villanueva	2.50	1.10	.30
☐ C8 Frank Clarke	3.50	1.55	.45
☐ C9 Don Meredith	15.00	6.75	1.85
☐ C10 George Andrie	3.50	1.55	.45
☐ C11 Mel Renfro	7.50	3.40	.95
☐ C12 Pettis Norman	3.50	1.55	.45
☐ C13 Buddy Dial	3.50	1.55	.45
☐ C14 Pete Gent	3.50	1.55	.45
☐ C15 Jerry Rhome	5.00	2.20	.60
☐ C16 Bob Hayes	12.00	5.50	1.50
☐ C17 Mike Gaechter	2.50	1.10	.30
☐ C18 Joe Bob Isbell	2.50	1.10	.30
☐ C19 Harold Hays	2.50	1.10	.30
☐ C20 Craig Morton	6.00	2.70	.75
☐ C21 Jake Kupp	2.50	1.10	.30
☐ C22 Cornell Green	3.50	1.55	.45
☐ C23 Dan Reeves	15.00	6.75	1.85
☐ C24 Leon Donohue	2.50	1.10	.30
☐ C25 Dave Manders	2.50	1.10	.30
☐ C26 Warren Livingston	2.50	1.10	.30
☐ C27 Bob Lilly	10.00	4.50	1.25
☐ C28 Chuck Howley	6.00	2.70	.75
☐ C29 Don Bishop	3.50	1.55	.45
☐ C30 Don Perkins	3.50	1.55	.45
☐ C31 Jim Boeke	2.50	1.10	.30
☐ C32 Dave Edwards	3.50	1.55	.45
☐ C33 Lee Roy Jordan	6.00	2.70	.75
☐ C34 Obert Logan	2.50	1.10	.30
☐ C35 Ralph Neely	3.50	1.55	.45
☐ C36 Cowboys Logo	2.50	1.10	.30
☐ NNO Cowboys Saver Sheet	30.00	13.50	3.70

1966 Coke Caps Eagles

As part of an advertising promotion, Coca-Cola issued 21 sets of bottle caps, covering the 14 NFL cities, the six AFL cities, and a separate National set for cities not reached by the leagues. These Eagles caps were issued in the Philadelphia area along with the NFL All-Stars caps as part of the Score with the Pros promotion. The NFL team Cap Saver sheets had separate sections in which to affix both the local team's caps and the All-Stars' caps. The caps measure approximately 1 1/8" in diameter and have the drink logo and a football on the outside, while the inside has the player's face printed in black, with text surrounding the face. The consumer could turn in his completed saver sheet to receive various prizes. The caps are numbered with a "C" prefix. These caps were also produced for 1966 on other Coca-Cola products: Tab, Fanta, Fresca and Sprite. The other drink caps typically carry a slight premium of 1.5X to 2X the value of the Coke version.

	NRMT	VG-E	GOOD
COMPLETE SET (36)	90.00	40.00	11.00
COMMON CAP (C1-C36)	2.50	1.10	.30
☐ C1 Norm Snead	4.00	1.80	.50
☐ C2 Al Nelson	2.50	1.10	.30
☐ C3 Jim Skaggs	2.50	1.10	.30
☐ C4 Glenn Glass	2.50	1.10	.30
☐ C5 Pete Retzlaff	3.50	1.55	.45
☐ C6 John Osmond	2.50	1.10	.30
☐ C7 Ray Rissmiller	2.50	1.10	.30
☐ C8 Lynn Hoyem	2.50	1.10	.30
☐ C9 King Hill	3.50	1.55	.45
☐ C10 Timmy Brown	3.50	1.55	.45
☐ C11 Ollie Matson	7.50	3.40	.95
☐ C12 Dave Lloyd	3.50	1.55	.45
☐ C13 Jim Ringo	6.00	2.70	.75
☐ C14 Floyd Peters	3.50	1.55	.45
☐ C15 Gary Pettigrew	2.50	1.10	.30
☐ C16 Frank Molden	2.50	1.10	.30
☐ C17 Earl Gros	3.50	1.55	.45
☐ C18 Fred Hill	2.50	1.10	.30
☐ C19 Don Hultz	2.50	1.10	.30
☐ C20 Ray Poage	2.50	1.10	.30
☐ C21 Aaron Martin	2.50	1.10	.30
☐ C22 Mike Morgan	2.50	1.10	.30
☐ C23 Lane Howell	2.50	1.10	.30

☐ C24 Ed Blaine	2.50	1.10	.30
☐ C25 Jack Concannon	3.50	1.55	.45
☐ C26 Sam Baker	2.50	1.10	.30
☐ C27 Tom Woodeshick	3.50	1.55	.45
☐ C28 Joe Scarpati	2.50	1.10	.30
☐ C29 John Meyers	2.50	1.10	.30
☐ C30 Nate Ramsey	3.50	1.55	.45
☐ C31 Ben Hawkins	2.50	1.10	.30
☐ C32 Bob Brown T	3.50	1.55	.45
☐ C33 Willie Brown	2.50	1.10	.30
☐ C34 Ron Goodwin	2.50	1.10	.30
☐ C35 Randy Beisler	2.50	1.10	.30
☐ C36 Team Logo	2.50	1.10	.30
☐ NNO Eagles Saver Sheet	30.00	13.50	3.70

1966 Coke Caps Falcons

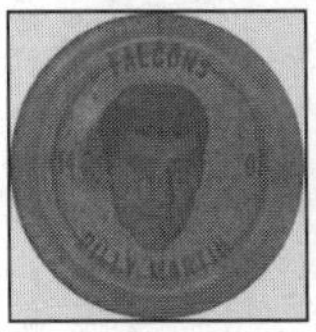
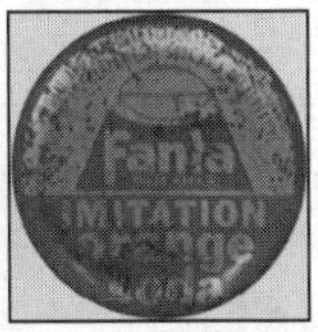

As part of an advertising promotion, Coca-Cola issued 21 sets of bottle caps, covering the 14 NFL cities, the six AFL cities, and a separate National set for cities not reached by the leagues. These Falcons caps were issued in the Atlanta area along with the NFL All-Stars caps as part of the Score with the Pros promotion. The NFL team Cap Saver sheets had separate sections in which to affix both the local team's caps and the All-Stars' caps. The caps measure approximately 1 1/8" in diameter and have the drink logo and a football on the outside, while the inside has the player's face printed in black, with text surrounding the face. The consumer could turn in his completed saver sheet to receive various prizes. The caps are numbered with a "C" prefix. These caps were also produced for 1966 on other Coca-Cola products: Tab, Fanta, Fresca and Sprite. The other drink caps typically carry a slight premium of 1.5X to 2X the value of the Coke version.

	NRMT	VG-E	GOOD
COMPLETE SET (36)	90.00	40.00	11.00
COMMON CAP (C1-C36)	2.50	1.10	.30
☐ C1 Tommy Nobis	8.00	3.60	1.00
☐ C2 Ernie Wheelwright	3.50	1.55	.45
☐ C3 Lee Calland	2.50	1.10	.30
☐ C4 Chuck Sieminski	2.50	1.10	.30
☐ C5 Dennis Claridge	3.50	1.55	.45
☐ C6 Ralph Heck	2.50	1.10	.30
☐ C7 Alex Hawkins	3.50	1.55	.45
☐ C8 Dan Grimm	3.50	1.55	.45
☐ C9 Marion Rushing	2.50	1.10	.30
☐ C10 Bobbie Johnson	2.50	1.10	.30
☐ C11 Bobby Franklin	2.50	1.10	.30
☐ C12 Bill McWatters	2.50	1.10	.30
☐ C13 Billy Lothridge	3.50	1.55	.45
☐ C14 Billy Martin	2.50	1.10	.30
☐ C15 Tom Wilson	2.50	1.10	.30
☐ C16 Dennis Murphy	2.50	1.10	.30
☐ C17 Randy Johnson	3.50	1.55	.45
☐ C18 Guy Reese	2.50	1.10	.30
☐ C19 Frank Marchlewski	2.50	1.10	.30
☐ C20 Don Talbert	2.50	1.10	.30
☐ C21 Errol Linden	2.50	1.10	.30
☐ C22 Dan Lewis	2.50	1.10	.30
☐ C23 Ed Cook	2.50	1.10	.30
☐ C24 Hugh McInnis	2.50	1.10	.30
☐ C25 Frank Lasky	2.50	1.10	.30
☐ C26 Bob Jencks	2.50	1.10	.30
☐ C27 Bill Jobko	2.50	1.10	.30
☐ C28 Nick Rassas	2.50	1.10	.30
☐ C29 Bob Riggle	2.50	1.10	.30
☐ C30 Ken Reaves	3.50	1.55	.45
☐ C31 Bob Sanders	2.50	1.10	.30
☐ C32 Steve Sloan	3.50	1.55	.45
☐ C33 Ron Smith	3.50	1.55	.45
☐ C34 Bob Whitlow	2.50	1.10	.30
☐ C35 Roger Anderson	2.50	1.10	.30
☐ C36 Falcons Logo	2.50	1.10	.30
☐ NNO Falcons Saver Sheet	30.00	13.50	3.70

1966 Coke Caps 49ers

As part of an advertising promotion, Coca-Cola issued 21 sets of bottle caps, covering the 14 NFL cities, the six AFL cities, and a separate National set for cities not reached by the leagues. These 49ers caps were issued in the San Francisco area along with the NFL All-Stars caps as part of the Score with the Pros promotion. The NFL team Cap Saver sheets had separate sections in which to affix both the local team's caps and the All-Stars' caps. The caps measure approximately 1 1/8" in diameter and have the drink logo and a football on the outside, while the inside has the player's face printed in black, with text surrounding the face. The consumer could turn in his completed saver sheet to receive various prizes. The caps are numbered with a "C" prefix. These caps were also produced for 1966 on other Coca-Cola products: Tab, Fanta, Fresca and Sprite. The other drink caps typically carry a slight premium of 1.5X to 2X the value of the Coke version.

	NRMT	VG-E	GOOD
COMPLETE SET (36)	100.00	45.00	12.50
COMMON CAP (C1-C36)	2.50	1.10	.30
☐ C1 Bernie Casey	3.50	1.55	.45
☐ C2 Bruce Bosley	3.50	1.55	.45
☐ C3 Kermit Alexander	3.50	1.55	.45
☐ C4 John Brodie	7.50	3.40	.95
☐ C5 Dave Parks	3.50	1.55	.45
☐ C6 Len Rohde	3.50	1.55	.45
☐ C7 Walter Rock	2.50	1.10	.30
☐ C8 George Mira	5.00	2.20	.60
☐ C9 Karl Rubke	2.50	1.10	.30
☐ C10 Ken Willard	3.50	1.55	.45
☐ C11 John David Crow UER (Name misspelled Crowe)	4.00	1.80	.50
☐ C12 George Donnelly	2.50	1.10	.30
☐ C13 Dave Wilcox	3.50	1.55	.45
☐ C14 Vern Burke	2.50	1.10	.30
☐ C15 Wayne Swinford	2.50	1.10	.30
☐ C16 Elbert Kimbrough	2.50	1.10	.30
☐ C17 Clark Miller	2.50	1.10	.30
☐ C18 Dave Kopay	3.50	1.55	.45
☐ C19 Joe Cerne	2.50	1.10	.30
☐ C20 Roland Lakes	2.50	1.10	.30
☐ C21 Charlie Krueger	3.50	1.55	.45
☐ C22 Billy Kilmer	5.00	2.20	.60
☐ C23 Jim Johnson	6.00	2.70	.75
☐ C24 Matt Hazeltine	3.50	1.55	.45
☐ C25 Mike Dowdle	2.50	1.10	.30
☐ C26 Jim Wilson	2.50	1.10	.30
☐ C27 Tommy Davis	3.50	1.55	.45
☐ C28 Jim Norton	2.50	1.10	.30
☐ C29 Jack Chapple	2.50	1.10	.30
☐ C30 Ed Beard	2.50	1.10	.30
☐ C31 John Thomas	2.50	1.10	.30
☐ C32 Monty Stickles	2.50	1.10	.30
☐ C33 Kay McFarland	2.50	1.10	.30
☐ C34 Gary Lewis	2.50	1.10	.30
☐ C35 Howard Mudd	2.50	1.10	.30
☐ C36 49ers Logo	2.50	1.10	.30
☐ NNO 49ers Saver Sheet	30.00	13.50	3.70

1966 Coke Caps Giants

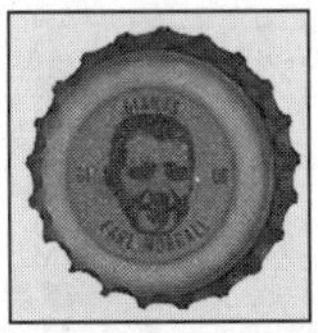

As part of an advertising promotion, Coca-Cola issued 21 sets of bottle caps, covering the 14 NFL cities, the six AFL cities, and a separate National set for cities not reached by the leagues. These Giants caps were issued in the New York City area along with the NFL All-Stars caps as part of the Score with the Pros promotion. The NFL team Cap Saver sheets had separate sections in which to affix both the local team's caps and the All-Stars' caps. The caps measure approximately 1 1/8" in diameter and have the drink logo and a football on the outside, while the inside has the player's face printed in black, with text surrounding the face. The consumer could turn in his completed saver sheet to receive various prizes. The caps are numbered with a "G" prefix. These caps were also produced for 1966 on other Coca-Cola products: Tab, Fanta, Fresca and Sprite. The other drink caps typically carry a slight premium of 1.5X to 2X the value of the Coke version.

	NRMT	VG-E	GOOD
COMPLETE SET (35)	100.00	45.00	12.50
COMMON CAP (G1-G35)	2.50	1.10	.30
☐ G1 Joe Morrison	3.50	1.55	.45
☐ G2 Dick Lynch	3.50	1.55	.45
☐ G3 Pete Case	3.50	1.55	.45
☐ G4 Clarence Childs	2.50	1.10	.30
☐ G5 Aaron Thomas	3.50	1.55	.45
☐ G6 Jim Carroll	2.50	1.10	.30
☐ G7 Henry Carr	3.50	1.55	.45
☐ G8 Bookie Bolin	2.50	1.10	.30
☐ G9 Roosevelt Davis	2.50	1.10	.30
☐ G10 John Lovetere	2.50	1.10	.30
☐ G11 Jim Patton	3.50	1.55	.45
☐ G12 Wendell Harris	2.50	1.10	.30
☐ G13 Roger LaLonde	2.50	1.10	.30
☐ G14 Jerry Hillebrand	2.50	1.10	.30
☐ G15 Spider Lockhart	3.50	1.55	.45
☐ G16 Del Shofner	3.50	1.55	.45
☐ G17 Earl Morrall	5.00	2.20	.60
☐ G18 Roosevelt Brown	5.00	2.20	.60
☐ G19 Greg Larson	3.50	1.55	.45
☐ G20 Jim Katcavage	3.50	1.55	.45
☐ G21 Smith Reed	2.50	1.10	.30
☐ G22 Lou Slaby	2.50	1.10	.30
☐ G23 Jim Moran	2.50	1.10	.30
☐ G24 Bill Swain	2.50	1.10	.30
☐ G25 Steve Thurlow	2.50	1.10	.30
☐ G26 Olen Underwood	2.50	1.10	.30
☐ G27 Gary Wood	3.50	1.55	.45
☐ G28 Larry Vargo	2.50	1.10	.30
☐ G29 Jim Prestel (Cap saver sheet reads Ed Prestel)	2.50	1.10	.30
☐ G30 Tucker Frederickson	3.50	1.55	.45
☐ G31 Bob Timberlake	2.50	1.10	.30
☐ G32 Chuck Mercein	4.00	1.80	.50
☐ G33 Ernie Koy	3.50	1.55	.45
☐ G34 Tom Costello	2.50	1.10	.30
☐ G35 Homer Jones	3.50	1.55	.45
☐ NNO Giants Saver Sheet	30.00	13.50	3.70

1966 Coke Caps Jets

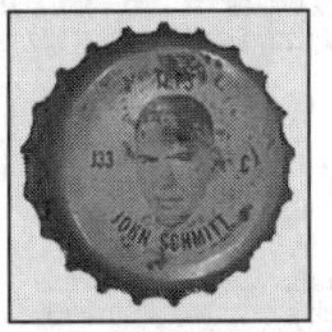

As part of an advertising promotion, Coca-Cola issued 21 sets of bottle caps, covering the 14 NFL cities, the six AFL cities, and a separate National set for cities not reached by the leagues. These Jets caps were issued in the New York City area along with the AFL All-Stars caps as part of the Score with the Pros promotion. The AFL team Cap Saver sheets had separate sections in which to affix both the local team's caps and the All-Stars' caps. The caps measure approximately 1 1/8" in diameter and have the drink logo and a football on the outside, while the inside has the player's face printed in black, with text surrounding the face. The consumer could turn in his completed saver sheet to receive various prizes. The caps are numbered with a "J" prefix. These caps were also produced for 1966 on other Coca-Cola products: Tab, Fanta, Fresca and Sprite. The other drink caps typically carry a slight premium of 1.5X to 2X the value of the Coke version.

	NRMT	VG-E	GOOD
COMPLETE SET (35)	140.00	65.00	17.50
COMMON CAP (J1-J35)	2.50	1.10	.30
☐ J1 Don Maynard	10.00	4.50	1.25
☐ J2 George Sauer Jr.	3.50	1.55	.45
☐ J3 Paul Crane	2.50	1.10	.30
☐ J4 Jim Colclough	2.50	1.10	.30
☐ J5 Matt Snell	6.00	2.70	.75
☐ J6 Sherman Lewis	5.00	2.20	.60
☐ J7 Jim Turner	3.50	1.55	.45
☐ J8 Mike Taliaferro	2.50	1.10	.30
☐ J9 Cornell Gordon	3.50	1.55	.45
☐ J10 Mark Smolinski	2.50	1.10	.30
☐ J11 Al Atkinson	3.50	1.55	.45
☐ J12 Paul Rochester	2.50	1.10	.30
☐ J13 Sherman Plunkett	2.50	1.10	.30
☐ J14 Gerry Philbin	3.50	1.55	.45
☐ J15 Pete Lammons	3.50	1.55	.45
☐ J16 Dainard Paulson	2.50	1.10	.30
☐ J17 Joe Namath	40.00	18.00	5.00
☐ J18 Winston Hill	3.50	1.55	.45
☐ J19 Dee Mackey	2.50	1.10	.30
☐ J20 Curley Johnson	2.50	1.10	.30
☐ J21 Verlon Biggs	3.50	1.55	.45
☐ J22 Bill Mathis	3.50	1.55	.45
☐ J23 Carl McAdams	2.50	1.10	.30
☐ J24 Bert Wilder	2.50	1.10	.30
☐ J25 Larry Grantham	3.50	1.55	.45
☐ J26 Bill Yearby	2.50	1.10	.30
☐ J27 Sam DeLuca	2.50	1.10	.30
☐ J28 Bill Baird	2.50	1.10	.30
☐ J29 Ralph Baker	3.50	1.55	.45
☐ J30 Ray Abruzzese	2.50	1.10	.30
☐ J31 Jim Hudson	2.50	1.10	.30
☐ J32 Dave Herman	3.50	1.55	.45
☐ J33 John Schmitt	2.50	1.10	.30
☐ J34 Jim Harris	2.50	1.10	.30
☐ J35 Bake Turner	3.50	1.55	.45
☐ NNO Jets Saver Sheet	30.00	13.50	3.70

1966 Coke Caps Lions

As part of an advertising promotion, Coca-Cola issued 21 sets of bottle caps, covering the 14 NFL cities, the six AFL cities, and a separate National set for cities not reached by the leagues. These Lions caps were issued in the Detroit area along with the NFL All-Stars caps as part of the Score with the Pros promotion. The NFL team Cap Saver sheets had separate sections in which to affix both the local team's caps and the All-Stars' caps. The caps measure approximately 1 1/8" in diameter and have the drink logo and a football on the outside, while the inside has the player's face printed in black, with text surrounding the face. The consumer could turn in his completed saver sheet to receive various prizes. The caps are numbered with a "C" prefix. These caps were also produced for 1966 on other Coca-Cola products: Tab, Fanta, Fresca and Sprite. The other drink caps typically carry a slight premium of 1.5X to 2X the value of the Coke version.

	NRMT	VG-E	GOOD
COMPLETE SET(36)	100.00	45.00	12.50
COMMON CAP (C1-C36)	2.50	1.10	.30
☐ C1 Pat Studstill	3.50	1.55	.45
☐ C2 Ed Flanagan	2.50	1.10	.30
☐ C3 Wayne Walker	3.50	1.55	.45
☐ C4 Tom Watkins	2.50	1.10	.30
☐ C5 Tommy Vaughn	2.50	1.10	.30
☐ C6 Jim Kearney	2.50	1.10	.30
☐ C7 Larry Hand	3.50	1.55	.45
☐ C8 Jerry Rush	2.50	1.10	.30
☐ C9 Roger Brown	3.50	1.55	.45
☐ C10 Tom Nowatzke	3.50	1.55	.45
☐ C11 John Henderson	2.50	1.10	.30
☐ C12 Tom Myers	2.50	1.10	.30
☐ C13 Ron Kramer	2.50	1.10	.30
☐ C14 Dick LeBeau	3.50	1.55	.45
☐ C15 Amos Marsh	3.50	1.55	.45
☐ C16 Wally Hilgenberg	3.50	1.55	.45
☐ C17 Bruce Maher	2.50	1.10	.30
☐ C18 Darris McCord	2.50	1.10	.30
☐ C19 Ted Karras	2.50	1.10	.30
☐ C20 Ernie Clark	2.50	1.10	.30
☐ C21 Gail Cogdill	3.50	1.55	.45
☐ C22 Wayne Rasmussen	2.50	1.10	.30
☐ C23 Joe Don Looney	8.00	3.60	1.00
☐ C24 Jim Gibbons	2.50	1.10	.30
☐ C25 John Gonzaga	2.50	1.10	.30
☐ C26 John Gordy	2.50	1.10	.30
☐ C27 Bobby Thompson	2.50	1.10	.30
☐ C28 J.D. Smith	2.50	1.10	.30
☐ C29 Roger Shoals	2.50	1.10	.30
☐ C30 Alex Karras	7.00	3.10	.85
☐ C31 Nick Pietrosante	3.50	1.55	.45
☐ C32 Milt Plum	4.00	1.80	.50
☐ C33 Daryl Sanders	2.50	1.10	.30
☐ C34 Mike Lucci	3.50	1.55	.45
☐ C35 George Izo	3.50	1.55	.45
☐ C36 Lions Logo	2.50	1.10	.30

1966 Coke Caps National NFL

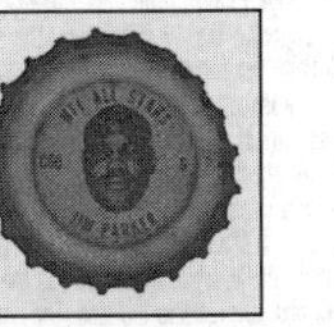

As part of an advertising promotion, Coca-Cola issued 21 sets of bottle caps, covering the 14 NFL cities, the six AFL cities, and a separate National set for cities not reached by the leagues. This National issue was released primarily in non-NFL cities as part of the Score with the Pros promotion. There was a separate Saver Sheet for the National set. The caps measure approximately 1 1/8" in diameter and have the drink logo and a football on the outside, while the inside has the player's face printed in black, with text surrounding the face. The consumer could turn in his completed saver sheet to receive various prizes. The caps are numbered with a "C" prefix. These caps were also produced for 1966 on other Coca-Cola products: Tab, Fanta, Fresca and Sprite. The other drink caps typically carry a slight premium of 1.5X to 2X the value of the Coke version.

	NRMT	VG-E	GOOD
COMPLETE SET (70)	225.00	100.00	28.00
COMMON CAP (C1-C70)	2.50	1.10	.30
☐ C1 Larry Wilson	5.00	2.20	.60
☐ C2 Frank Ryan	3.50	1.55	.45
☐ C3 Norm Snead	3.50	1.55	.45
☐ C4 Mel Renfro	5.00	2.20	.60
☐ C5 Timmy Brown	3.50	1.55	.45
☐ C6 Tucker Frederickson	2.50	1.10	.30
☐ C7 Jim Bakken	2.50	1.10	.30
☐ C8 Paul Krause	4.00	1.80	.50
☐ C9 Irv Cross	2.50	1.10	.30
☐ C10 Cornell Green	3.50	1.55	.45
☐ C11 Pat Fischer	2.50	1.10	.30
☐ C12 Bob Hayes	5.00	2.20	.60
☐ C13 Charley Taylor	5.00	2.20	.60
☐ C14 Pete Retzlaff	3.50	1.55	.45
☐ C15 Jim Ringo	5.00	2.20	.60
☐ C16 Maxie Baughan	2.50	1.10	.30
☐ C17 Chuck Howley	3.00	1.35	.35
☐ C18 John Wooten	2.50	1.10	.30
☐ C19 Bob DeMarco	2.50	1.10	.30
☐ C20 Dale Meinert	2.50	1.10	.30
☐ C21 Gene Hickerson	2.50	1.10	.30
☐ C22 George Andrie	2.50	1.10	.30
☐ C23 Joe Rutgens	2.50	1.10	.30
☐ C24 Bob Lilly	7.50	3.40	.95
☐ C25 Sam Silas	2.50	1.10	.30
☐ C26 Bob Brown OT	2.50	1.10	.30
☐ C27 Dick Schafrath	2.50	1.10	.30
☐ C28 Roosevelt Brown	5.00	2.20	.60
☐ C29 Jim Houston	2.50	1.10	.30
☐ C30 Paul Wiggin	2.50	1.10	.30
☐ C31 Gary Ballman	2.50	1.10	.30
☐ C32 Gary Collins	3.50	1.55	.45
☐ C33 Sonny Randle	2.50	1.10	.30
☐ C34 Charlie Johnson	3.50	1.55	.45
☐ C35 Browns Logo	2.50	1.10	.30
☐ C36 Packers Logo	2.50	1.10	.30
☐ C37 Herb Adderley	5.00	2.20	.60
☐ C38 Grady Alderman	2.50	1.10	.30
☐ C39 Doug Atkins	5.00	2.20	.60
☐ C40 Bruce Bosley UER (name spelled Bosely)	2.50	1.10	.30
☐ C41 John Brodie UER (name spelled Brody)	5.00	2.20	.60
☐ C42 Roger Brown	2.50	1.10	.30
☐ C43 Bill Brown	2.50	1.10	.30
☐ C44 Dick Butkus	15.00	6.75	1.85
☐ C45 Lee Roy Caffey	2.50	1.10	.30

☐ C46 John David Crow UER name spelled Crowe	3.50	1.55	.45
☐ C47 Willie Davis	5.00	2.20	.60
☐ C48 Mike Ditka	12.00	5.50	1.50
☐ C49 Joe Fortunato	2.50	1.10	.30
☐ C50 John Gordy	2.50	1.10	.30
☐ C51 Deacon Jones	5.00	2.20	.60
☐ C52 Alex Karras	7.50	3.40	.95
☐ C53 Dick LeBeau	2.50	1.10	.30
☐ C54 Jerry Logan	2.50	1.10	.30
☐ C55 John Mackey	5.00	2.20	.60
☐ C56 Ed Meador	2.50	1.10	.30
☐ C57 Tommy McDonald	3.50	1.55	.45
☐ C58 Merlin Olsen	7.50	3.40	.95
☐ C59 Jimmy Orr	3.50	1.55	.45
☐ C60 Jim Parker	5.00	2.20	.60
☐ C61 Dave Parks	2.50	1.10	.30
☐ C62 Walter Rock	2.50	1.10	.30
☐ C63 Gale Sayers	15.00	6.75	1.85
☐ C64 Pat Studstill	2.50	1.10	.30
☐ C65 Fran Tarkenton	12.00	5.50	1.50
☐ C66 Mick Tingelhoff	2.50	1.10	.30
☐ C67 Bob Vogel	2.50	1.10	.30
☐ C68 Wayne Walker	2.50	1.10	.30
☐ C69 Ken Willard	2.50	1.10	.30
☐ C70 Willie Wood	5.00	2.20	.60
☐ NNO National Saver Sheet	15.00	6.75	1.85

1966 Coke Caps Oilers

As part of an advertising promotion, Coca-Cola issued 21 sets of bottle caps, covering the 14 NFL cities, the six AFL cities, and a separate National set for cities not reached by the leagues. These Oilers caps were issued in the Houston area along with the AFL All-Stars caps as part of the Score with the Pros promotion. The AFL team Cap Saver sheets had separate sections in which to affix both the local team's caps and the All-Stars' caps. The caps measure approximately 1 1/8" in diameter and have the drink logo and a football on the outside, while the inside has the player's face printed in black, with text surrounding the face. The consumer could turn in his completed saver sheet to receive various prizes. The caps are numbered with a "C" prefix. These caps were also produced for 1966 on other Coca-Cola products: Tab, Fanta, Fresca and Sprite. The other drink caps typically carry a slight premium of 1.5X to 2X the value of the Coke version.

	NRMT	VG-E	GOOD
COMPLETE SET (36)	110.00	50.00	14.00
COMMON CAP (C1-C36)	2.50	1.10	.30
☐ C1 Scott Appleton	2.50	1.10	.30
☐ C2 George Allen	3.50	1.55	.45
☐ C3 Don Floyd	2.50	1.10	.30
☐ C4 Ronnie Caveness	2.50	1.10	.30
☐ C5 Jim Norton	2.50	1.10	.30
☐ C6 Jacky Lee	3.50	1.55	.45
☐ C7 George Blanda	15.00	6.75	1.85
☐ C8 Tony Banfield	3.50	1.55	.45
☐ C9 George Rice	2.50	1.10	.30
☐ C10 Charley Tolar	3.50	1.55	.45
☐ C11 Bobby Jancik	2.50	1.10	.30
☐ C12 Freddy Glick	2.50	1.10	.30
☐ C13 Ode Burrell	3.50	1.55	.45
☐ C14 Walt Suggs	3.50	1.55	.45
☐ C15 Bob McLeod	2.50	1.10	.30
☐ C16 Johnny Baker	2.50	1.10	.30
☐ C17 Danny Brabham	2.50	1.10	.30
☐ C18 Gary Cutsinger	3.50	1.55	.45
☐ C19 Doug Cline	2.50	1.10	.30
☐ C20 Hoyle Granger	3.50	1.55	.45
☐ C21 Bob Talamini	3.50	1.55	.45
☐ C22 Don Trull	3.50	1.55	.45
☐ C23 Charlie Hennigan	3.50	1.55	.45
☐ C24 Sid Blanks	3.50	1.55	.45
☐ C25 Pat Holmes	2.50	1.10	.30
☐ C26 John Frongillo	2.50	1.10	.30
☐ C27 John Wittenborn	2.50	1.10	.30
☐ C28 George Kinney	2.50	1.10	.30
☐ C29 Charles Frazier	2.50	1.10	.30
☐ C30 Ernie Ladd	10.00	4.50	1.25
☐ C31 W.K. Hicks	2.50	1.10	.30
☐ C32 Sonny Bishop	3.50	1.55	.45
☐ C33 Larry Elkins	3.50	1.55	.45
☐ C34 Glen Ray Hines	3.50	1.55	.45
☐ C35 Bobby Maples	3.50	1.55	.45
☐ C36 Oilers Logo	2.50	1.10	.30
☐ NNO Oilers Saver Sheet	30.00	13.50	3.70

1966 Coke Caps Packers

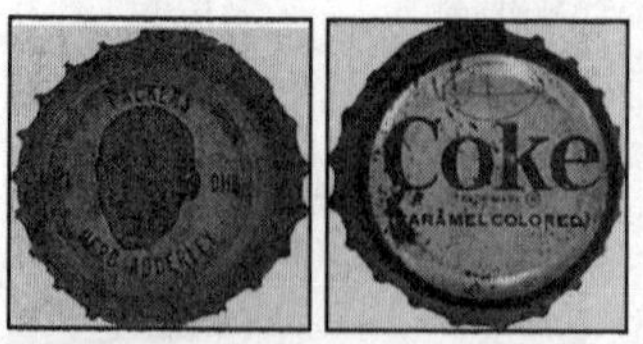

As part of an advertising promotion, Coca-Cola issued 21 sets of bottle caps, covering the 14 NFL cities, the six AFL cities, and a separate National set for cities not reached by the leagues. These Packers caps were issued in the Green Bay/Milwaukee area along with the NFL All-Stars caps as part of the Score with the Pros promotion. The NFL team Cap Saver sheets had separate sections in which to affix both the local team's caps and the All-Stars' caps. The caps measure approximately 1 1/8" in diameter and have the drink logo and a football on the outside, while the inside has the player's face printed in black, with text surrounding the face. The consumer could turn in his completed saver sheet to receive various prizes. The caps are numbered with a "C" prefix. These caps were also produced for 1966 on other Coca-Cola products: Tab, Fanta, Fresca and Sprite. The other drink caps typically carry a slight premium of 1.5X to 2X the value of the Coke version.

	NRMT	VG-E	GOOD
COMPLETE SET (31)	150.00	70.00	19.00
COMMON CAP (C1-C36)	2.50	1.10	.30
☐ C1 Herb Adderley	6.00	2.70	.75
☐ C2 Lionel Aldridge	3.50	1.55	.45
☐ C3 Bob Long	2.50	1.10	.30
☐ C4 Willie Davis	6.00	2.70	.75
☐ C5 Boyd Dowler	3.50	1.55	.45
☐ C6 Marv Fleming	3.50	1.55	.45
☐ C7 Ken Bowman	3.50	1.55	.45
☐ C8 Tom Brown	2.50	1.10	.30
☐ C9 Doug Hart	2.50	1.10	.30
☐ C10 Steve Wright	2.50	1.10	.30
☐ C11 Bill Anderson	2.50	1.10	.30
☐ C12 Bill Curry	3.50	1.55	.45
☐ C13 Tommy Crutcher	2.50	1.10	.30
☐ C14 Fred Thurston	3.50	1.55	.45
☐ C15 Elijah Pitts	3.50	1.55	.45
☐ C16 Lloyd Voss	2.50	1.10	.30
☐ C17 Lee Roy Caffey	3.50	1.55	.45
☐ C18 Dave Robinson	3.50	1.55	.45
☐ C19 Bart Starr	15.00	6.75	1.85
☐ C20 Ray Nitschke	10.00	4.50	1.25
☐ C21 Max McGee	3.50	1.55	.45
☐ C22 Don Chandler	2.50	1.10	.30
☐ C23 Rich Marshall	2.50	1.10	.30
☐ C24 Ron Kostelnik	2.50	1.10	.30
☐ C25 Carroll Dale	3.50	1.55	.45
☐ C26 Hank Jordan	6.00	2.70	.75
☐ C27 Bob Jeter	3.50	1.55	.45
☐ C28 Bob Skoronski	2.50	1.10	.30
☐ C29 Jerry Kramer	5.00	2.20	.60
☐ C30 Willie Wood	6.00	2.70	.75
☐ C31 Paul Hornung	15.00	6.75	1.85
☐ C32 Forrest Gregg	6.00	2.70	.75
☐ C33 Zeke Bratkowski	3.50	1.55	.45
☐ C34 Tom Moore	3.50	1.55	.45
☐ C35 Jim Taylor	10.00	4.50	1.25
☐ C36 Packers Team Emblem	2.50	1.10	.30
☐ NNO Packers Saver Sheet	30.00	13.50	3.70

1966 Coke Caps Patriots

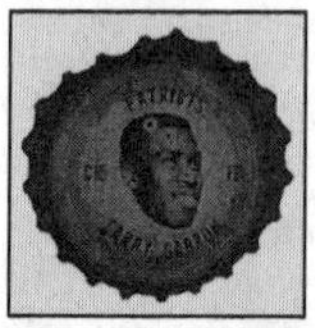

As part of an advertising promotion, Coca-Cola issued 21 sets of bottle caps, covering the 14 NFL cities, the six AFL cities, and a separate National set for cities not reached by the leagues. These Patriots caps were issued in the Boston area along with the AFL All-Stars caps as part of the Score with the Pros promotion. The AFL team Cap Saver sheets had separate sections in which to affix both the local team's caps and the All-Stars' caps. The caps measure approximately 1 1/8" in diameter and have the drink logo and a football on the outside, while the inside has the player's face printed in black, with text surrounding the face. The consumer could turn in his completed saver sheet to receive various prizes. The caps are numbered with a "C" prefix. These caps were also produced for 1966 on other Coca-Cola products: Tab, Fanta, Fresca and Sprite. The other drink caps typically carry a slight premium of 1.5X to 2X the value of the Coke version.

	NRMT	VG-E	GOOD
COMPLETE SET (36)	90.00	40.00	11.00
COMMON CAP (C1-C36)	2.50	1.10	.30
☐ C1 Jon Morris	3.50	1.55	.45
☐ C2 Don Webb	2.50	1.10	.30
☐ C3 Charles Long	2.50	1.10	.30
☐ C4 Tony Romeo	2.50	1.10	.30
☐ C5 Bob Dee	3.50	1.55	.45
☐ C6 Tommy Addison	3.50	1.55	.45
☐ C7 Tom Neville	3.50	1.55	.45
☐ C8 Ron Hall	2.50	1.10	.30
☐ C9 White Graves	2.50	1.10	.30
☐ C10 Ellis Johnson	2.50	1.10	.30
☐ C11 Don Oakes	2.50	1.10	.30
☐ C12 Tom Yewcic	2.50	1.10	.30
☐ C13 Tom Hennessey	2.50	1.10	.30
☐ C14 Jay Cunningham	2.50	1.10	.30
☐ C15 Larry Garron	3.50	1.55	.45
☐ C16 Justin Canale	2.50	1.10	.30
☐ C17 Art Graham	3.50	1.55	.45
☐ C18 Babe Parilli	3.50	1.55	.45
☐ C19 Jim Hunt	2.50	1.10	.30
☐ C20 Karl Singer	2.50	1.10	.30
☐ C21 Houston Antwine	3.50	1.55	.45
☐ C22 Nick Buoniconti	6.00	2.70	.75
☐ C23 John Huarte	5.00	2.20	.60
☐ C24 Gino Cappelletti	3.50	1.55	.45
☐ C25 Chuck Shonta	2.50	1.10	.30
☐ C26 Dick Felt	3.50	1.55	.45
☐ C27 Mike Dukes	2.50	1.10	.30
☐ C28 Larry Eisenhauer	3.50	1.55	.45
☐ C29 Jim Fraser	2.50	1.10	.30
☐ C30 Len St. Jean	2.50	1.10	.30
☐ C31 J.D. Garrett	2.50	1.10	.30
☐ C32 Jim Whalen	2.50	1.10	.30
☐ C33 Jim Nance	5.00	2.20	.60
☐ C34 Dick Arrington	2.50	1.10	.30
☐ C35 Lonnie Farmer	2.50	1.10	.30
☐ C36 Patriots Logo	2.50	1.10	.30
☐ NNO Patriots Saver Sheet	30.00	13.50	3.70

1966 Coke Caps Rams

As part of an advertising promotion, Coca-Cola issued 21 sets of bottle caps, covering the 14 NFL cities, the six AFL cities, and a separate National set for cities not reached by the leagues. These Rams caps were issued in the Los Angeles area along with the NFL All-Stars caps as part of the Score with the Pros promotion. The NFL team Cap Saver sheets had separate sections in which to affix both the local team's caps and the All-Stars' caps. The caps measure approximately 1 1/8" in diameter and have the drink logo and a football on the outside, while the inside has the player's face printed in black, with text surrounding the face. The consumer could turn in his completed saver sheet to receive various prizes. The caps are numbered with a "C" prefix. These caps were also produced for 1966 on other Coca-Cola products: Tab, Fanta, Fresca and Sprite. The other drink caps typically carry a slight premium of 1.5X to 2X the value of the Coke version.

	NRMT	VG-E	GOOD
COMPLETE SET (36)	110.00	50.00	14.00
COMMON CAP (C1-C36)	2.50	1.10	.30
☐ C1 Tom Mack	6.00	2.70	.75
☐ C2 Tom Moore	2.50	1.10	.30
☐ C3 Bill Munson	3.50	1.55	.45
☐ C4 Bill George	6.00	2.70	.75
☐ C5 Joe Carollo	2.50	1.10	.30
☐ C6 Dick Bass	3.50	1.55	.45
☐ C7 Ken Iman	2.50	1.10	.30
☐ C8 Charlie Cowan	2.50	1.10	.30
☐ C9 Terry Baker	5.00	2.20	.60
☐ C10 Don Chuy	2.50	1.10	.30
☐ C11 Jack Pardee	5.00	2.20	.60
☐ C12 Lamar Lundy	3.50	1.55	.45
☐ C13 Bill Anderson	2.50	1.10	.30
☐ C14 Roman Gabriel	6.00	2.70	.75
☐ C15 Roosevelt Grier	6.00	2.70	.75
☐ C16 Billy Truax	3.50	1.55	.45
☐ C17 Merlin Olsen	7.00	3.10	.85
☐ C18 Deacon Jones	6.00	2.70	.75
☐ C19 Joe Scibelli	2.50	1.10	.30
☐ C20 Marlin McKeever	2.50	1.10	.30
☐ C21 Doug Woodlief	2.50	1.10	.30
☐ C22 Chuck Lamson	2.50	1.10	.30
☐ C23 Dan Currie	2.50	1.10	.30
☐ C24 Maxie Baughan	3.50	1.55	.45
☐ C25 Bruce Gossett	3.50	1.55	.45
☐ C26 Les Josephson	3.50	1.55	.45
☐ C27 Ed Meador	3.50	1.55	.45
☐ C28 Anthony Guillory	2.50	1.10	.30
☐ C29 Irv Cross	3.50	1.55	.45
☐ C30 Tommy McDonald	3.50	1.55	.45
☐ C31 Bucky Pope	2.50	1.10	.30
☐ C32 Jack Snow	5.00	2.20	.60
☐ C33 Joe Wendryhoski	2.50	1.10	.30
☐ C34 Clancy Williams	2.50	1.10	.30
☐ C35 Ben Wilson	2.50	1.10	.30
☐ C36 Rams Logo	2.50	1.10	.30
☐ NNO Rams Saver Sheet	30.00	13.50	3.70

1966 Coke Caps Steelers

As part of an advertising promotion, Coca-Cola issued 21 sets of bottle caps, covering the 14 NFL cities, the six AFL cities, and a separate National set for cities not reached by the leagues. These Steelers caps were issued in the Pittsburgh area along with the NFL All-Stars caps as part of the Score with the Pros promotion. The NFL team Cap Saver sheets had separate sections in which to affix both the local team's caps and the All-Stars' caps. The caps measure approximately 1 1/8" in diameter and have the drink logo and a football on the outside, while the inside has the player's face printed in black, with text surrounding the face. The consumer could turn in his completed saver sheet to receive various prizes. The caps are numbered with a "C" prefix. These caps were also produced for 1966 on other Coca-Cola products: Tab, Fanta, Fresca and Sprite. The other drink caps typically carry a slight premium of 1.5X to 2X the value of the Coke version.

	NRMT	VG-E	GOOD
COMPLETE SET (36)	100.00	45.00	12.50
COMMON CAP (C1-C36)	2.50	1.10	.30
☐ C1 John Baker	2.50	1.10	.30
☐ C2 Mike Lind	3.50	1.55	.45
☐ C3 Ken Kortas	2.50	1.10	.30
☐ C4 Willie Daniel	2.50	1.10	.30
☐ C5 Roy Jefferson	3.50	1.55	.45
☐ C6 Bob Hohn	2.50	1.10	.30
☐ C7 Dan James	2.50	1.10	.30
☐ C8 Gary Ballman	3.50	1.55	.45
☐ C9 Brady Keys	2.50	1.10	.30
☐ C10 Charley Bradshaw	3.50	1.55	.45
☐ C11 Jim Bradshaw	2.50	1.10	.30
☐ C12 Jim Butler	3.50	1.55	.45
☐ C13 Paul Martha	5.00	2.20	.60
☐ C14 Mike Clark	2.50	1.10	.30
☐ C15 Ray Lemek	2.50	1.10	.30
☐ C16 Clarence Peaks	3.50	1.55	.45
☐ C17 Theron Sapp	2.50	1.10	.30
☐ C18 Ray Mansfield	3.50	1.55	.45
☐ C19 Chuck Hinton	2.50	1.10	.30
☐ C20 Bill Nelsen	3.50	1.55	.45
☐ C21 Rod Breedlove	2.50	1.10	.30
☐ C22 Frank Lambert	2.50	1.10	.30
☐ C23 Ben McGee	2.50	1.10	.30
☐ C24 Myron Pottios	3.50	1.55	.45
☐ C25 John Campbell	2.50	1.10	.30
☐ C26 Andy Russell	5.00	2.20	.60
☐ C27 Mike Sandusky	2.50	1.10	.30
☐ C28 Bob Schmitz	2.50	1.10	.30
☐ C29 Riley Gunnels	2.50	1.10	.30
☐ C30 Clendon Thomas	3.50	1.55	.45
☐ C31 Tommy Wade	2.50	1.10	.30
☐ C32 Dick Hoak	3.50	1.55	.45
☐ C33 Marv Woodson	2.50	1.10	.30
☐ C34 Bob Nichols	2.50	1.10	.30
☐ C35 John Henry Johnson	6.00	2.70	.75
☐ C36 Steelers Logo	2.50	1.10	.30
☐ NNO Steelers Saver Sheet	30.00	13.50	3.70

1966 Coke Caps Vikings

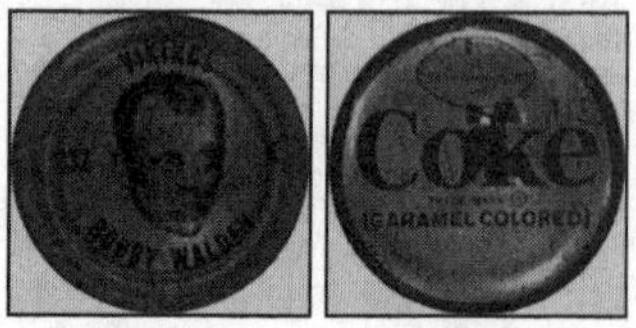

As part of an advertising promotion, Coca-Cola issued 21 sets of bottle caps, covering the 14 NFL cities, the six AFL cities, and a separate National set for cities not reached by the leagues. These Vikings caps were issued in the Minneapolis/St. Paul area along with the NFL All-Stars caps as part of the Score with the Pros promotion. The NFL team Cap Saver sheets had separate sections in which to affix both the local team's caps and the All-Stars' caps. The caps measure approximately 1 1/8" in diameter and have the drink logo and a football on the outside, while the inside has the player's face printed in black, with text surrounding the face. The consumer could turn in his completed saver sheet to receive various prizes. The caps are numbered with a "C" prefix. These caps were also produced for 1966 on other Coca-Cola products: Tab, Fanta, Fresca and Sprite. The other drink caps typically carry a slight premium of 1.5X to 2X the value of the Coke version. This is a partial checklist, and any additions would be appreciated.

	NRMT	VG-E	GOOD
COMPLETE SET (34)	100.00	45.00	12.50
COMMON CAP (C1-C36)	2.50	1.10	.30
☐ C1 Milt Sunde	3.50	1.55	.45
☐ C2 Don Hansen	2.50	1.10	.30
☐ C3 Jim Marshall	6.00	2.70	.75
☐ C4 Jerry Shay	2.50	1.10	.30
☐ C5 Ken Byers	2.50	1.10	.30
☐ C6 Rip Hawkins	2.50	1.10	.30
☐ C7 John Kirby	2.50	1.10	.30
☐ C8 Roy Winston	3.50	1.55	.45
☐ C9 Ron VanderKelen	3.50	1.55	.45
☐ C10 Jim Lindsey	2.50	1.10	.30
☐ C11 Paul Flatley	3.50	1.55	.45
☐ C12 Larry Bowie	2.50	1.10	.30
☐ C13 Grady Alderman	3.50	1.55	.45
☐ C14 Mick Tingelhoff	5.00	2.20	.60
☐ C15 Lonnie Warwick	3.50	1.55	.45
☐ C16 Fred Cox	3.50	1.55	.45
☐ C17 Bill Brown	3.50	1.55	.45
☐ C18 Ed Sharockman	3.50	1.55	.45
☐ C19 George Rose	2.50	1.10	.30
☐ C20 Paul Dickson	2.50	1.10	.30
☐ C21 Tommy Mason	3.50	1.55	.45
☐ C22 Carl Eller	6.00	2.70	.75
☐ C23 Jim Young	2.50	1.10	.30
☐ C24 Hal Bedsole	2.50	1.10	.30
☐ C25 Karl Kassulke	5.00	2.20	.60
☐ C26 Fran Tarkenton	10.00	4.50	1.25
☐ C27 Tom Hall	2.50	1.10	.30
☐ C28 Archie Sutton	2.50	1.10	.30
☐ C29 Jim Phillips	2.50	1.10	.30
☐ C30 Gary Larsen	2.50	1.10	.30
☐ C31 Phil King	2.50	1.10	.30
☐ C32 Bobby Walden	2.50	1.10	.30
☐ C33 Bob Berry	3.50	1.55	.45
☐ C36 Team Logo	2.50	1.10	.30
☐ NNO Vikings Saver Sheet	30.00	13.50	3.70

1971 Coke Caps Packers

This is a 22-player set of Coca-Cola bottle caps featuring members of the Green Bay Packers. They have the Coke logo and a football on the outside, while the inside has the player's face printed in black, with the player's name below the picture. The caps measure approximately

1 1/8" in diameter. A cap-saver sheet was also issued to aid in collecting the bottle caps, and the consumer could turn in his completed sheet to receive various prizes. The caps are unnumbered and therefore listed below alphabetically. The caps were also produced in a twist-off version which usually carries a premium.

	NRMT-MT	EXC	G-VG
COMPLETE SET (22)	50.00	22.00	6.25
COMMON CAP (1-22)	1.50	.70	.19
☐ 1 Ken Bowman	2.00	.90	.25
☐ 2 John Brockington	3.00	1.35	.35
☐ 3 Bob Brown DT	1.50	.70	.19
☐ 4 Fred Carr	2.00	.90	.25
☐ 5 Jim Carter	1.50	.70	.19
☐ 6 Carroll Dale	2.00	.90	.25
☐ 7 Ken Ellis	2.00	.90	.25
☐ 8 Gale Gillingham	2.00	.90	.25
☐ 9 Dave Hampton	1.50	.70	.19
☐ 10 Doug Hart	1.50	.70	.19
☐ 11 Jim Hill	1.50	.70	.19
☐ 12 Dick Himes	1.50	.70	.19
☐ 13 Scott Hunter	2.00	.90	.25
☐ 14 MacArthur Lane	3.00	1.35	.35
☐ 15 Bill Lueck	1.50	.70	.19
☐ 16 Al Matthews	1.50	.70	.19
☐ 17 Rich McGeorge	2.00	.90	.25
☐ 18 Ray Nitschke	7.50	3.40	.95
☐ 19 Francis Peay	1.50	.70	.19
☐ 20 Dave Robinson	2.50	1.10	.30
☐ 21 Alden Roche	1.50	.70	.19
☐ 22 Bart Starr	15.00	6.75	1.85

1981 Coke Caps

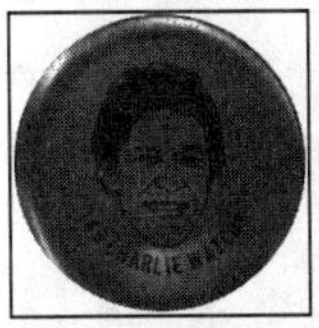
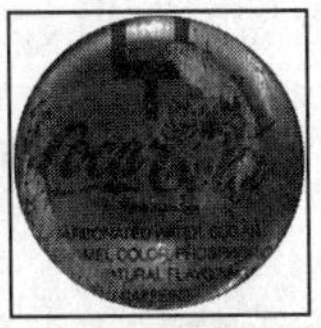

Although the same players are featured on each sheet, three different cap saver sheets were issued for this game. The game required the consumer to collect Coke or TAB bottle caps of certain players and attach them to the saver sheets. Each sheet measures approximately 6 3/8" by 9 1/8" and is divided into three 2 1/8" columns. The top of each column has a hole so that the offer could hang on a soft drink bottle. The first column has a picture of Joe Greene with the quote "Look for me and my friends under caps from Coke and TAB." If one finds all seven caps required to complete the yellow middle column, a cash prize of 1,000.00 is awarded. If one completes the five caps required by the third column on the front, the prize is one "Mean" Joe jersey. Finally, the first column on the back requires four caps in order to win a player T-shirt. Columns two and three on the back present official rules for the game. The more difficult caps to find were Steve Fuller, Gene Upshaw and Ed Jones. These three have not been priced below. The caps were issued as twist-off caps as well and have been checklisted below according to their skip-number.

	MINT	NRMT	EXC
COMPLETE SET (15)	35.00	16.00	4.40
COMMON CAP	1.50	.70	.19
☐ 1 Joe Greene	4.00	1.80	.50
☐ 3 Steve Grogan	2.00	.90	.25
☐ 6 Mike Siani	1.50	.70	.19
☐ 11 Dan Fouts	5.00	2.20	.60
☐ 12 Wesley Walker	2.00	.90	.25
☐ 23 Harold Carmichael	2.00	.90	.25
☐ 30 Greg Pruitt	2.00	.90	.25
☐ 38 Gene Upshaw SP			
☐ 47 Steve Fuller SP			
☐ 49 Walter Payton	10.00	4.50	1.25
☐ 53 Ed Too Tall Jones SP			
☐ 107 Benny Barnes	1.50	.70	.19
☐ 108 Billy Sims	3.00	1.35	.35
☐ 127 Robert Newhouse	1.50	.70	.19
☐ 146 Charlie Waters	2.00	.90	.25

1981 Coke

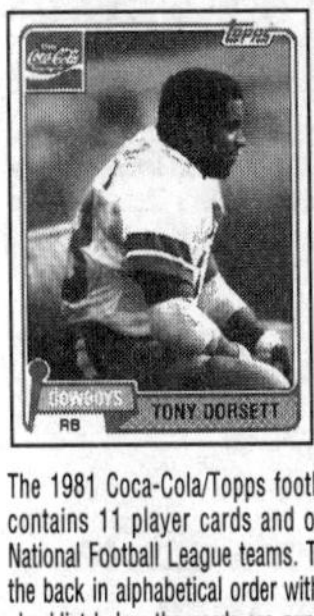

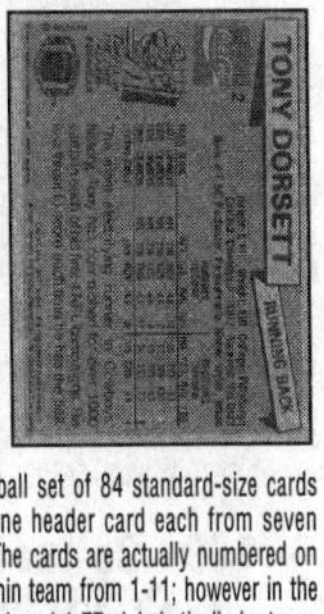

The 1981 Coca-Cola/Topps football set of 84 standard-size cards contains 11 player cards and one header card each from seven National Football League teams. The cards are actually numbered on the back in alphabetical order within team from 1-11; however in the checklist below the cards are numbered 1-77 alphabetically by team. The backs of the header cards carried an offer to receive one (of four) uncut sheet(s) of the 1981 Topps regular series. Similar in design to the Topps cards of that year, these cards contain the Coke logo on both the front and the back. The key cards in the set are Art Monk and Kellen Winslow, both appearing in their "Rookie" year for cards.

	MINT	NRMT	EXC
COMPLETE SET (84)	60.00	27.00	7.50
COMMON CARD (1-77)	.40	.18	.05
☐ 1 Raymond Butler	.40	.18	.05
☐ 2 Roger Carr	.60	.25	.07
☐ 3 Curtis Dickey	.60	.25	.07
☐ 4 Nesby Glasgow	.40	.18	.05
☐ 5 Bert Jones	.75	.35	.09
☐ 6 Bruce Laird	.40	.18	.05
☐ 7 Greg Landry	.60	.25	.07
☐ 8 Reese McCall	.40	.18	.05
☐ 9 Don McCauley	.40	.18	.05
☐ 10 Herb Orvis	.40	.18	.05
☐ 11 Ed Simonini	.40	.18	.05
☐ 12 Pat Donovan	.40	.18	.05
☐ 13 Tony Dorsett	5.00	2.20	.60
☐ 14 Billy Joe DuPree	.60	.25	.07
☐ 15 Tony Hill	.60	.25	.07
☐ 16 Ed Too Tall Jones	1.50	.70	.19
☐ 17 Harvey Martin	.60	.25	.07
☐ 18 Robert Newhouse	.40	.18	.05
☐ 19 Drew Pearson	.75	.35	.09
☐ 20 Charlie Waters	.60	.25	.07
☐ 21 Danny White	.75	.35	.09
☐ 22 Randy White	2.50	1.10	.30
☐ 23 Mike Barber	.40	.18	.05
☐ 24 Elvin Bethea	.40	.18	.05
☐ 25 Gregg Bingham	.40	.18	.05
☐ 26 Robert Brazile	.60	.25	.07
☐ 27 Ken Burrough	.40	.18	.05
☐ 28 Rob Carpenter	.40	.18	.05
☐ 29 Leon Gray	.40	.18	.05
☐ 30 Vernon Perry	.40	.18	.05
☐ 31 Mike Renfro	.40	.18	.05
☐ 32 Carl Roaches	.40	.18	.05
☐ 33 Morris Towns	.40	.18	.05
☐ 34 Harry Carson	.60	.25	.07
☐ 35 Mike Dennis	.40	.18	.05
☐ 36 Mike Friede	.40	.18	.05
☐ 37 Earnest Gray	.40	.18	.05
☐ 38 Dave Jennings	.40	.18	.05
☐ 39 Gary Jeter	.40	.18	.05
☐ 40 George Martin	.40	.18	.05
☐ 41 Roy Simmons	.40	.18	.05
☐ 42 Phil Simms	3.00	1.35	.35
☐ 43 Billy Taylor	.40	.18	.05
☐ 44 Brad Van Pelt	.40	.18	.05
☐ 45 Ottis Anderson	1.00	.45	.12
☐ 46 Rush Brown	.40	.18	.05
☐ 47 Theotis Brown	.40	.18	.05
☐ 48 Dan Dierdorf	.75	.35	.09
☐ 49 Mel Gray	.60	.25	.07
☐ 50 Ken Greene	.40	.18	.05
☐ 51 Jim Hart	.60	.25	.07
☐ 52 Doug Marsh	.40	.18	.05
☐ 53 Wayne Morris	.40	.18	.05
☐ 54 Pat Tilley	.40	.18	.05
☐ 55 Roger Wehrli	.40	.18	.05
☐ 56 Rolf Benirschke	.60	.25	.07
☐ 57 Fred Dean	.60	.25	.07
☐ 58 Dan Fouts	2.50	1.10	.30
☐ 59 John Jefferson	1.00	.45	.12
☐ 60 Gary Johnson	.40	.18	.05
☐ 61 Charlie Joiner	1.25	.55	.16
☐ 62 Louie Kelcher	.40	.18	.05
☐ 63 Chuck Muncie	.60	.25	.07
☐ 64 Doug Wilkerson	.40	.18	.05
☐ 65 Clarence Williams	.40	.18	.05
☐ 66 Kellen Winslow	4.00	1.80	.50
☐ 67 Coy Bacon	.40	.18	.05
☐ 68 Wilbur Jackson	.40	.18	.05
☐ 69 Karl Lorch	.40	.18	.05
☐ 70 Rich Milot	.40	.18	.05
☐ 71 Art Monk	8.00	3.60	1.00
☐ 72 Mark Moseley	.40	.18	.05
☐ 73 Mike Nelms	.40	.18	.05
☐ 74 Lemar Parrish	.40	.18	.05
☐ 75 Joe Theismann	1.50	.70	.19
☐ 76 Ricky Thompson	.40	.18	.05
☐ 77 Joe Washington	.60	.25	.07
☐ NNO Colts Header Card	.40	.18	.05
☐ NNO Cowboys Header Card	.40	.18	.05
☐ NNO Oilers Header Card	.40	.18	.05
☐ NNO Giants Header Card	.40	.18	.05
☐ NNO Cardinals Header Card	.40	.18	.05
☐ NNO Chargers Header Card	.40	.18	.05
☐ NNO Redskins Header Card	.40	.18	.05

1993 Coke Monsters of the Gridiron

Sponsored by Coca-Cola, this 30-card standard-size set was released as a complete set at Super Bowl Card Show V, January 27-30, 1994 in Atlanta. The set was available to the first 10,000 fans at the redemption booth in exchange for ten wrappers from any 1993 NFL-licensed trading card packs. The fronts feature borderless color studio shots of NFL players posed in their uniforms. The players are also dressed in horror costumes and made up to look like "monsters." Three of the cards (10, 19, and 20) feature fanciful color paintings of the players instead of photos. The white back carries the player's

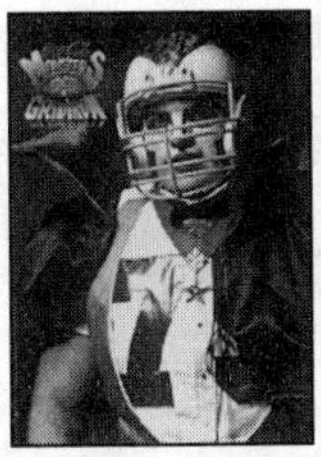
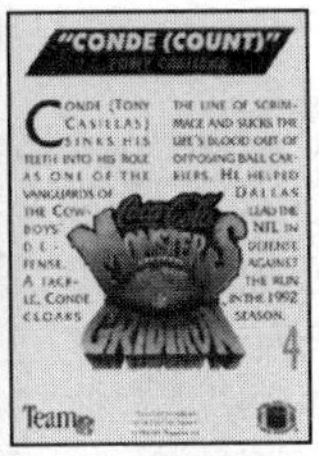

name and "monstrous" nickname at the top, followed below by career highlights. The cards are numbered on the back. Television ads featuring Randall Cunningham helped promote this set. The actual in-store promotion consisted of two randomly selected cards included in specially marked multi-packs of Coca-Cola Classic, diet Coke, Caffeine-free diet Coke, and Sprite. An "instant win" scratch-off game piece inside the same multi-packs could entitle the collector to win various prizes, including a gold foil edition of the entire set. Also collectors could obtain a random set of five cards by sending in a proof-of-purchase from any specially marked two-liter bottle. Reportedly more than 100 million collector cards were available nationwide. The promotion ran from Sept. 19 until Halloween, or while supplies lasted. Although the cards carry a 1994 copyright line date, they are considered a 1993 issue.

	MINT	NRMT	EXC
COMPLETE SET (30)	18.00	8.00	2.20
COMMON CARD (1-30)	.25	.11	.03
☐ 1 Title Card Checklist	.40	.18	.05
☐ 2 Cornelius Bennett Big Bear	.40	.18	.05
☐ 3 Terrell Buckley Tiger	.25	.11	.03
☐ 4 Tony Casillas Conde (Count)	.25	.11	.03
☐ 5 Reggie Cobb Crossbones	.25	.11	.03
☐ 6 Marco Coleman Cobra	.40	.18	.05
☐ 7 Shane Conlan Conlan The Barbarian	.25	.11	.03
☐ 8 Randall Cunningham Rocket Man	.75	.35	.09
☐ 9 Chris Doleman Dr. Doomsday	.40	.18	.05
☐ 10 Steve Emtman Beast-Man	.40	.18	.05
☐ 11 Harold Green Slime	.40	.18	.05
☐ 12 Michael Haynes Moonlight Flyer	.40	.18	.05
☐ 13 Garrison Hearst Hearse	2.00	.90	.25
☐ 14 Craig Heyward Iron Head	.40	.18	.05
☐ 15 Rickey Jackson The Jackal	.25	.11	.03
☐ 16 Joe Jacoby Frankenstein	.25	.11	.03
☐ 17 Sean Jones Ghost	.40	.18	.05
☐ 18 Cortez Kennedy Tez Rex	.75	.35	.09
☐ 19 Howie Long Howlin'	1.00	.45	.12
☐ 20 Ronnie Lott The Rattler	.75	.35	.09
☐ 21 Karl Mecklenburg Midnight Marauder	.25	.11	.03
☐ 22 Neil O'Donnell Knight Raider	.75	.35	.09
☐ 23 Tom Rathman Psycho	.40	.18	.05
☐ 24 Junior Seau Stealth	1.00	.45	.12
☐ 25 Emmitt Smith Lone Star Sheriff	8.00	3.60	1.00
☐ 26 Pat Swilling Chillin'	.40	.18	.05
☐ 27 Lawrence Taylor Six Gun	1.00	.45	.12
☐ 28 Derrick Thomas Attack Cat	1.00	.45	.12
☐ 29 Andre Tippett Andre The Terrible	.25	.11	.03
☐ 30 Eric Turner Bad Bone	.40	.18	.05

1994 Coke Monsters of the Gridiron

This 31-card set was sponsored by Coca-Cola and features color player photos dressed in horror costumes and made to look like monsters. The backs carry a head photo of the player with player information. The set was primarily distributed at the 1995 Super Bowl Card Show VI in Miami in exchange for 10 wrappers from any 1994 NFL card set.

	MINT	NRMT	EXC
COMPLETE SET (31)	25.00	11.00	3.10
COMMON CARD (1-30)	.35	.16	.04
☐ 1 Eric Swann	.75	.35	.09
☐ 2 Jessie Tuggle	.35	.16	.04
☐ 3 Cornelius Bennett	.50	.23	.06
☐ 4 Carolina Panthers Mascot	1.00	.45	.12
☐ 5 Chris Zorich	.50	.23	.06
☐ 6 Dan Wilkinson	.50	.23	.06
☐ 7 Eric Turner	.50	.23	.06
☐ 8 Emmitt Smith	10.00	4.50	1.25
☐ 9 Steve Atwater	.35	.16	.04
☐ 10 Pat Swilling	.50	.23	.06
☐ 11 Sean Jones	.50	.23	.06
☐ 12 Ray Childress	.35	.16	.04
☐ 13 Marshall Faulk	4.00	1.80	.50
☐ 14 Jacksonville Jaguars Mascot	1.00	.45	.12
☐ 15 Derrick Thomas	.75	.35	.09
☐ 16 Chester McGlockton	.50	.23	.06
☐ 17 Shane Conlan	.35	.16	.04
☐ 18 Marco Coleman	.35	.16	.04
☐ 19 John Randle	.35	.16	.04
☐ 20 Bruce Armstrong	.35	.16	.04
☐ 21 Renaldo Turnbull	.50	.23	.06
☐ 22 Jumbo Elliott	.35	.16	.04
☐ 23 Ronnie Lott	.75	.35	.09
☐ 24 Randall Cunningham	.75	.35	.09
☐ 25 Neil O'Donnell	1.00	.45	.12
☐ 26 Junior Seau	1.00	.45	.12
☐ 27 Tom Rathman	.35	.16	.04
☐ 28 Cortez Kennedy	.75	.35	.09
☐ 29 Hardy Nickerson	.50	.23	.06
☐ 30 Ken Harvey UER Name spelled Hen	.50	.23	.06
☐ NNO Title Card Checklist	.50	.23	.06

1994 Collector's Choice

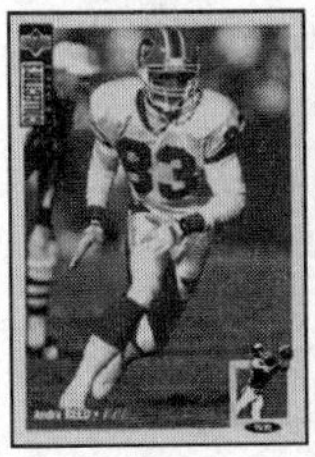
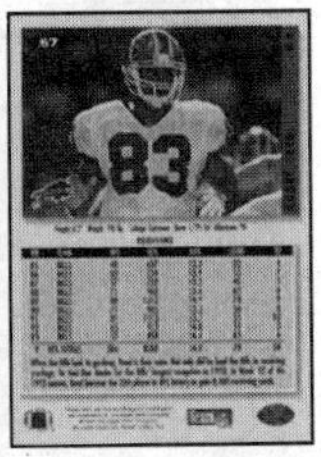

This standard-size 384-card set features color action player photos. Cards were issued in 12, 13 and 20-card packs. The set's title appears at the upper left while the player's name and team appear at the lower left. The player's position is at lower right. The white-bordered backs carry color action player photos with the player's name, position, biography, and NFL career statistics under the photo. One gold or silver parallel card was inserted per pack. Also issued was a 36-card Spanish promo set and a 260-card full Spanish set. Rookie Cards include Derrick Alexander, Marshall Faulk, William Floyd, Greg Hill, Charles Johnson, Errict Rhett, Darnay Scott and Heath Shuler. A Joe Montana Promo card was produced and priced below.

	MINT	NRMT	EXC
COMPLETE SET (384)	20.00	9.00	2.50
COMMON CARD (1-384)	.05	.02	.01
☐ 1 Antonio Langham	.10	.05	.01
☐ 2 Aaron Glenn	.10	.05	.01
☐ 3 Sam Adams	.10	.05	.01
☐ 4 Dewayne Washington	.10	.05	.01
☐ 5 Dan Wilkinson	.10	.05	.01
☐ 6 Bryant Young	.20	.09	.03
☐ 7 Aaron Taylor	.05	.02	.01
☐ 8 Willie McGinest	.10	.05	.01
☐ 9 Trev Alberts	.10	.05	.01
☐ 10 Jamir Miller	.05	.02	.01
☐ 11 John Thierry	.05	.02	.01
☐ 12 Heath Shuler	1.00	.45	.12
☐ 13 Trent Dilfer	.60	.25	.07
☐ 14 Marshall Faulk	3.00	1.35	.35
☐ 15 Greg Hill	.20	.09	.03
☐ 16 William Floyd	1.00	.45	.12
☐ 17 Chuck Levy	.05	.02	.01
☐ 18 Charlie Garner	.10	.05	.01
☐ 19 Mario Bates	.50	.23	.06
☐ 20 Donnell Bennett	.05	.02	.01
☐ 21 LeShon Johnson	.10	.05	.01
☐ 22 Calvin Jones	.05	.02	.01
☐ 23 Darnay Scott	2.00	.90	.25
☐ 24 Charles Johnson	.20	.09	.03
☐ 25 Johnnie Morton	.20	.09	.03
☐ 26 Shante Carver	.05	.02	.01
☐ 27 Derrick Alexander WR	.20	.09	.03
☐ 28 David Palmer	.10	.05	.01
☐ 29 Ryan Yarborough	.05	.02	.01
☐ 30 Errict Rhett	1.25	.55	.16
☐ 31 James Washington I93	.05	.02	.01
☐ 32 Sterling Sharpe I93	.05	.02	.01
☐ 33 Drew Bledsoe I93	.50	.23	.06
☐ 34 Eric Allen I93	.05	.02	.01
☐ 35 Jerome Bettis I93	.30	.14	.04
☐ 36 Joe Montana I93	.50	.23	.06
☐ 37 John Carney I93	.05	.02	.01
☐ 38 Emmitt Smith I93	1.00	.45	.12
☐ 39 Chris Warren I93	.20	.09	.03
☐ 40 Reggie Brooks I93	.05	.02	.01

□ 41 Gary Brown I93	.05	.02	.01
□ 42 Tim Brown I93	.20	.09	.03
□ 43 Erric Pegram I93	.05	.02	.01
□ 44 Ronald Moore I93	.05	.02	.01
□ 45 Jerry Rice I93	.50	.23	.06
□ 46 Ricky Watters TE	.20	.09	.03
□ 47 Joe Montana TE	.50	.23	.06
□ 48 Reggie Brooks TE	.05	.02	.01
□ 49 Rick Mirer TE	.20	.09	.03
□ 50 Rocket Ismail TE	.10	.05	.01
□ 51 Curtis Conway TE	.10	.05	.01
□ 52 Junior Seau TE	.20	.09	.03
□ 53 Mark Carrier DB TE	.05	.02	.01
□ 54 Ronnie Lott TE	.10	.05	.01
□ 55 Marcus Allen TE	.20	.09	.03
□ 56 Michael Irvin TE	.20	.09	.03
□ 57 Bennie Blades	.05	.02	.01
□ 58 Randal Hill	.05	.02	.01
□ 59 Brian Blades	.10	.05	.01
□ 60 Russell Maryland	.05	.02	.01
□ 61 Jim Kelly	.20	.09	.03
□ 62 Arthur Marshall	.05	.02	.01
□ 63 Webster Slaughter	.05	.02	.01
□ 64 Dave Krieg	.10	.05	.01
□ 65 Steve Jordan	.05	.02	.01
□ 66 Neil O'Donnell	.20	.09	.03
□ 67 Andre Reed	.10	.05	.01
□ 68 Mike Croel	.05	.02	.01
□ 69 Al Smith	.05	.02	.01
□ 70 Joe Montana	1.00	.45	.12
□ 71 Randall McDaniel	.05	.02	.01
□ 72 Greg Lloyd	.20	.09	.03
□ 73 Thomas Smith	.05	.02	.01
□ 74 Glyn Milburn	.10	.05	.01
□ 75 Lorenzo White	.05	.02	.01
□ 76 Neil Smith	.20	.09	.03
□ 77 John Randle	.05	.02	.01
□ 78 Rod Woodson	.20	.09	.03
□ 79 Russell Maryland	.05	.02	.01
□ 80 Rodney Peete	.05	.02	.01
□ 81 Jackie Harris	.05	.02	.01
□ 82 James Jett	.05	.02	.01
□ 83 Rodney Hampton	.20	.09	.03
□ 84 Bill Romanowski	.05	.02	.01
□ 85 Ken Norton Jr.	.10	.05	.01
□ 86 Barry Sanders	1.00	.45	.12
□ 87 Johnny Holland	.05	.02	.01
□ 88 Terry McDaniel	.05	.02	.01
□ 89 Greg Jackson	.05	.02	.01
□ 90 Dana Stubblefield	.20	.09	.03
□ 91 Jay Novacek	.10	.05	.01
□ 92 Chris Spielman	.10	.05	.01
□ 93 Ken Ruettgers	.05	.02	.01
□ 94 Greg Robinson	.05	.02	.01
□ 95 Mark Jackson	.05	.02	.01
□ 96 John Taylor	.10	.05	.01
□ 97 Roger Harper	.05	.02	.01
□ 98 Jerry Ball	.05	.02	.01
□ 99 Keith Byars	.05	.02	.01
□ 100 Morten Andersen	.05	.02	.01
□ 101 Eric Allen	.05	.02	.01
□ 102 Marion Butts	.05	.02	.01
□ 103 Michael Haynes	.10	.05	.01
□ 104 Rob Burnett	.05	.02	.01
□ 105 Marco Coleman	.05	.02	.01
□ 106 Derek Brown RB	.05	.02	.01
□ 107 Andy Harmon	.05	.02	.01
□ 108 Darren Carrington	.05	.02	.01
□ 109 Bobby Hebert	.05	.02	.01
□ 110 Mark Carrier WR	.10	.05	.01
□ 111 Bryan Cox	.05	.02	.01
□ 112 Toi Cook	.05	.02	.01
□ 113 Tim Harris	.05	.02	.01
□ 114 John Friesz	.10	.05	.01
□ 115 Neal Anderson	.05	.02	.01
□ 116 Jerome Bettis	.60	.25	.07
□ 117 Bruce Armstrong	.05	.02	.01
□ 118 Brad Baxter	.05	.02	.01
□ 119 Johnny Bailey	.05	.02	.01
□ 120 Brian Blades	.10	.05	.01
□ 121 Mark Carrier DB	.05	.02	.01
□ 122 Shane Conlan	.05	.02	.01
□ 123 Drew Bledsoe	1.00	.45	.12
□ 124 Chris Burkett	.05	.02	.01
□ 125 Steve Beuerlein	.05	.02	.01
□ 126 Ferrell Edmunds	.05	.02	.01
□ 127 Curtis Conway	.20	.09	.03
□ 128 Troy Drayton	.05	.02	.01
□ 129 Vincent Brown	.05	.02	.01
□ 130 Boomer Esiason	.10	.05	.01
□ 131 Larry Centers	.20	.09	.03
□ 132 Carlton Gray	.05	.02	.01
□ 133 Chris Miller	.05	.02	.01
□ 134 Eric Metcalf	.10	.05	.01
□ 135 Mark Higgs	.05	.02	.01
□ 136 Tyrone Hughes	.10	.05	.01
□ 137 Randall Cunningham	.10	.05	.01
□ 138 Ronnie Harmon	.05	.02	.01
□ 139 Andre Rison	.10	.05	.01
□ 140 Eric Turner	.05	.02	.01
□ 141 Terry Kirby	.20	.09	.03
□ 142 Eric Martin	.05	.02	.01
□ 143 Seth Joyner	.05	.02	.01
□ 144 Stan Humphries	.20	.09	.03
□ 145 Deion Sanders	.60	.25	.07
□ 146 Vinny Testaverde	.10	.05	.01
□ 147 Dan Marino	2.00	.90	.25
□ 148 Renaldo Turnbull	.05	.02	.01
□ 149 Herschel Walker	.10	.05	.01
□ 150 Anthony Miller	.10	.05	.01
□ 151 Richard Dent	.10	.05	.01
□ 152 Jim Everett	.10	.05	.01
□ 153 Ben Coates	.20	.09	.03
□ 154 Jeff Lageman	.05	.02	.01
□ 155 Garrison Hearst	.50	.23	.06
□ 156 Kelvin Martin	.05	.02	.01
□ 157 Dante Jones	.05	.02	.01
□ 158 Sean Gilbert	.05	.02	.01
□ 159 Leonard Russell	.05	.02	.01
□ 160 Ronnie Lott	.10	.05	.01
□ 161 Randal Hill	.05	.02	.01
□ 162 Rick Mirer	.20	.09	.03
□ 163 Alonzo Spellman	.05	.02	.01
□ 164 Todd Lyght	.05	.02	.01
□ 165 Chris Slade	.05	.02	.01
□ 166 Johnny Mitchell	.05	.02	.01
□ 167 Ronald Moore	.05	.02	.01
□ 168 Eugene Robinson	.05	.02	.01
□ 169 Chris Hinton	.05	.02	.01
□ 170 Dan Footman	.05	.02	.01
□ 171 Keith Jackson	.05	.02	.01
□ 172 Rickey Jackson	.05	.02	.01
□ 173 Heath Sherman	.05	.02	.01
□ 174 Chris Mims	.05	.02	.01
□ 175 Erric Pegram	.05	.02	.01
□ 176 Leroy Hoard	.05	.02	.01
□ 177 O.J. McDuffie	.20	.09	.03
□ 178 Wayne Martin	.05	.02	.01
□ 179 Clyde Simmons	.05	.02	.01
□ 180 Leslie O'Neal	.05	.02	.01
□ 181 Mike Pritchard	.05	.02	.01
□ 182 Michael Jackson	.10	.05	.01
□ 183 Scott Mitchell	.20	.09	.03
□ 184 Lorenzo Neal	.05	.02	.01
□ 185 William Thomas	.05	.02	.01
□ 186 Junior Seau UER (Career tackles 322, but add up to 451)	.20	.09	.03
□ 187 Chris Gedney	.05	.02	.01
□ 188 Tim Lester	.05	.02	.01
□ 189 Sam Gash	.05	.02	.01
□ 190 Johnny Johnson	.05	.02	.01
□ 191 Chuck Cecil	.05	.02	.01
□ 192 Cortez Kennedy	.10	.05	.01
□ 193 Jim Harbaugh	.20	.09	.03
□ 194 Roman Phifer	.05	.02	.01
□ 195 Pat Harlow	.05	.02	.01
□ 196 Rob Moore	.10	.05	.01
□ 197 Gary Clark	.10	.05	.01
□ 198 Jon Vaughn	.05	.02	.01
□ 199 Craig Heyward	.10	.05	.01
□ 200 Michael Stewart	.05	.02	.01
□ 201 Greg McMurtry	.05	.02	.01
□ 202 Brian Washington	.05	.02	.01
□ 203 Ken Harvey	.05	.02	.01
□ 204 Chris Warren	.10	.05	.01
□ 205 Bruce Smith	.20	.09	.03
□ 206 Tom Rouen	.05	.02	.01
□ 207 Cris Dishman	.05	.02	.01
□ 208 Keith Cash	.05	.02	.01
□ 209 Carlos Jenkins	.05	.02	.01
□ 210 Levon Kirkland	.05	.02	.01
□ 211 Pete Metzelaars	.05	.02	.01
□ 212 Shannon Sharpe	.10	.05	.01
□ 213 Cody Carlson	.05	.02	.01
□ 214 Derrick Thomas	.20	.09	.03
□ 215 Emmitt Smith	2.00	.90	.25
□ 216 Robert Porcher	.05	.02	.01
□ 217 Sterling Sharpe	.10	.05	.01
□ 218 Anthony Smith	.05	.02	.01
□ 219 Mike Sherrard	.05	.02	.01
□ 220 Tom Rathman	.05	.02	.01
□ 221 Nate Newton	.05	.02	.01
□ 222 Pat Swilling	.05	.02	.01
□ 223 George Teague	.05	.02	.01
□ 224 Greg Townsend	.05	.02	.01
□ 225 Eric Guliford	.05	.02	.01
□ 226 Leroy Thompson	.05	.02	.01
□ 227 Thurman Thomas	.20	.09	.03
□ 228 Dan Williams	.05	.02	.01
□ 229 Bubba McDowell	.05	.02	.01
□ 230 Tracy Simien	.05	.02	.01
□ 231 Scottie Graham	.10	.05	.01
□ 232 Eric Green	.05	.02	.01
□ 233 Phil Simms	.10	.05	.01
□ 234 Ricky Watters	.20	.09	.03
□ 235 Kevin Williams	.10	.05	.01
□ 236 Brett Perriman	.10	.05	.01
□ 237 Reggie White	.20	.09	.03
□ 238 Steve Wisniewski	.05	.02	.01
□ 239 Mark Collins	.05	.02	.01
□ 240 Steve Young	.75	.35	.09
□ 241 Steve Tovar	.05	.02	.01
□ 242 Jason Belser	.05	.02	.01
□ 243 Ray Seals	.05	.02	.01
□ 244 Earnest Byner	.05	.02	.01
□ 245 Ricky Proehl	.05	.02	.01
□ 246 Rich Miano	.05	.02	.01
□ 247 Alfred Williams	.05	.02	.01
□ 248 Ray Buchanan UER (Buchannan on front)	.05	.02	.01
□ 249 Hardy Nickerson	.10	.05	.01
□ 250 Brad Edwards	.05	.02	.01
□ 251 Jerrol Williams	.05	.02	.01
□ 252 Marvin Washington	.05	.02	.01
□ 253 Tony McGee	.05	.02	.01
□ 254 Jeff George	.20	.09	.03
□ 255 Ron Hall	.05	.02	.01
□ 256 Tim Johnson	.05	.02	.01
□ 257 Willie Roaf	.05	.02	.01
□ 258 Corwin Brown	.05	.02	.01
□ 259 Ricardo McDonald	.05	.02	.01
□ 260 Jeff Herrod	.05	.02	.01
□ 261 Demetrius DuBose	.05	.02	.01
□ 262 Ricky Sanders	.05	.02	.01
□ 263 John L. Williams	.05	.02	.01
□ 264 John Lynch	.05	.02	.01
□ 265 Lance Gunn	.05	.02	.01
□ 266 Jessie Hester	.05	.02	.01
□ 267 Mark Wheeler	.05	.02	.01
□ 268 Chip Lohmiller	.05	.02	.01
□ 269 Eric Swann	.10	.05	.01
□ 270 Byron Evans	.05	.02	.01
□ 271 Gary Plummer	.05	.02	.01
□ 272 Roger Duffy	.05	.02	.01
□ 273 Irv Smith	.05	.02	.01
□ 274 Todd Collins	.05	.02	.01
□ 275 Robert Blackmon	.05	.02	.01
□ 276 Reggie Roby	.05	.02	.01
□ 277 Russell Copeland	.05	.02	.01
□ 278 Simon Fletcher	.05	.02	.01
□ 279 Ernest Givins	.10	.05	.01
□ 280 Tim Barnett	.05	.02	.01
□ 281 Chris Doleman	.05	.02	.01
□ 282 Jeff Graham	.05	.02	.01
□ 283 Kenneth Davis	.05	.02	.01
□ 284 Vance Johnson	.05	.02	.01
□ 285 Haywood Jeffires	.10	.05	.01
□ 286 Todd McNair	.05	.02	.01
□ 287 Daryl Johnston	.10	.05	.01
□ 288 Ryan McNeil	.05	.02	.01
□ 289 Terrell Buckley	.05	.02	.01
□ 290 Ethan Horton	.05	.02	.01
□ 291 Corey Miller	.05	.02	.01
□ 292 Marc Logan	.05	.02	.01
□ 293 Lincoln Coleman	.05	.02	.01
□ 294 Derrick Moore	.05	.02	.01
□ 295 LeRoy Butler	.05	.02	.01
□ 296 Jeff Hostetler	.10	.05	.01
□ 297 Qadry Ismail	.20	.09	.03
□ 298 Andre Hastings	.10	.05	.01
□ 299 Henry Jones	.05	.02	.01
□ 300 John Elway	.75	.35	.09
□ 301 Warren Moon	.20	.09	.03
□ 302 Willie Davis	.10	.05	.01
□ 303 Vencie Glenn	.05	.02	.01
□ 304 Kevin Greene	.20	.09	.03
□ 305 Marcus Buckley	.05	.02	.01
□ 306 Tim McDonald	.05	.02	.01
□ 307 Michael Irvin	.20	.09	.03
□ 308 Herman Moore	.50	.23	.06
□ 309 Brett Favre	2.00	.90	.25
□ 310 Rocket Ismail	.10	.05	.01
□ 311 Jarrod Bunch	.05	.02	.01
□ 312 Don Beebe	.05	.02	.01
□ 313 Steve Atwater	.05	.02	.01
□ 314 Gary Brown	.05	.02	.01
□ 315 Marcus Allen	.20	.09	.03
□ 316 Terry Allen	.10	.05	.01
□ 317 Chad Brown	.05	.02	.01
□ 318 Cornelius Bennett	.10	.05	.01
□ 319 Rod Bernstine	.05	.02	.01
□ 320 Greg Montgomery	.05	.02	.01
□ 321 Kimble Anders	.10	.05	.01
□ 322 Charles Haley	.10	.05	.01
□ 323 Mel Gray	.05	.02	.01
□ 324 Edgar Bennett	.20	.09	.03
□ 325 Eddie Anderson	.05	.02	.01
□ 326 Derek Brown TE	.05	.02	.01
□ 327 Steve Bono	.10	.05	.01
□ 328 Alvin Harper	.10	.05	.01
□ 329 Willie Green	.05	.02	.01
□ 330 Robert Brooks	.40	.18	.05
□ 331 Patrick Bates	.05	.02	.01
□ 332 Anthony Carter	.10	.05	.01
□ 333 Barry Foster	.05	.02	.01
□ 334 Bill Brooks	.05	.02	.01
□ 335 Jason Elam	.05	.02	.01
□ 336 Ray Childress	.05	.02	.01
□ 337 J.J. Birden	.05	.02	.01
□ 338 Cris Carter	.20	.09	.03
□ 339 Deon Figures	.05	.02	.01
□ 340 Carlton Bailey	.05	.02	.01
□ 341 Brent Jones	.10	.05	.01
□ 342 Troy Aikman UER (Stats on back has 60 Int., should be 66)	1.00	.45	.12
□ 343 Rodney Holman	.05	.02	.01
□ 344 Tony Bennett	.05	.02	.01
□ 345 Tim Brown	.20	.09	.03
□ 346 Michael Brooks	.05	.02	.01
□ 347 Martin Harrison	.05	.02	.01
□ 348 Jerry Rice	1.00	.45	.12
□ 349 John Copeland	.05	.02	.01
□ 350 Kerry Cash	.05	.02	.01
□ 351 Reggie Cobb	.05	.02	.01
□ 352 Brian Mitchell	.05	.02	.01
□ 353 Derrick Fenner	.05	.02	.01
□ 354 Roosevelt Potts	.05	.02	.01
□ 355 Courtney Hawkins	.05	.02	.01
□ 356 Carl Banks	.05	.02	.01
□ 357 Harold Green	.05	.02	.01
□ 358 Steve Emtman	.05	.02	.01
□ 359 Santana Dotson	.10	.05	.01
□ 360 Reggie Brooks	.10	.05	.01
□ 361 Terry Obee	.05	.02	.01
□ 362 David Klingler	.05	.02	.01
□ 363 Quentin Coryatt	.05	.02	.01
□ 364 Craig Erickson	.05	.02	.01
□ 365 Desmond Howard	.10	.05	.01
□ 366 Carl Pickens	.50	.23	.06
□ 367 Lawrence Dawsey	.05	.02	.01
□ 368 Henry Ellard	.10	.05	.01
□ 369 Shaun Gayle	.05	.02	.01
□ 370 David Lang	.05	.02	.01
□ 371 Anthony Johnson	.10	.05	.01
□ 372 Darnell Walker	.05	.02	.01
□ 373 Pepper Johnson	.05	.02	.01
□ 374 Kurt Gouveia	.05	.02	.01
□ 375 Louis Oliver	.05	.02	.01
□ 376 Lincoln Kennedy	.05	.02	.01
□ 377 Anthony Pleasant	.05	.02	.01
□ 378 Irving Fryar	.10	.05	.01
□ 379 Carolina Panthers Expansion Team Card	.20	.09	.03
□ 380 Jacksonville Jaguars Expansion Team Card	.05	.02	.01
□ 381 Checklist UER Sterling Sharpe (Front has 193-288 and back has Sharp; should be Sharpe)	.10	.05	.01
□ 382 Dan Marino ART Checklist Card	.20	.09	.03
□ 383 Jerry Rice ART UER Checklist Card (Front has 289-384)	.20	.09	.03
□ 384 Joe Montana ART UER Checklist Card (Front has 1-96) Joe Montana	.20	.09	.03
□ P19 Joe Montana Promo	4.00	1.80	.50

1994 Collector's Choice Gold

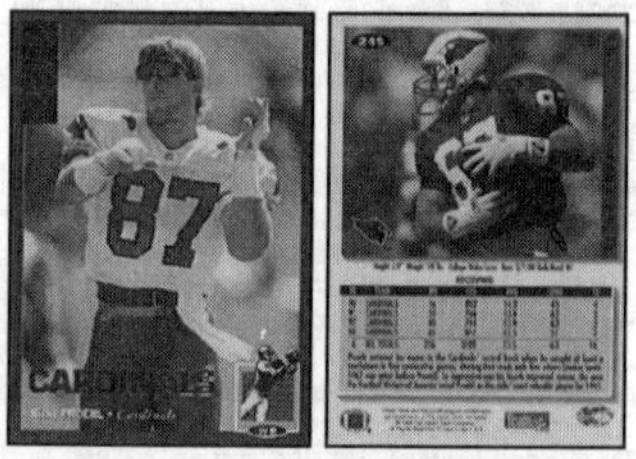

This 384 card standard-size set is a parallel to the regular set listings. These cards were inserted at a rate of one in 35 packs. These cards differ from the regular issue in that the borders are gold. In addition, the team name is printed in gold above the player's name.

	MINT	NRMT	EXC
COMPLETE SET (384)	1200.00	550.00	150.00
COMMON CARD (1-384)	2.00	.90	.25
*VETERAN STARS: 25X TO 40X BASIC CARDS			
*RCs: 10X TO 18X BASIC CARDS			

1994 Collector's Choice Silver

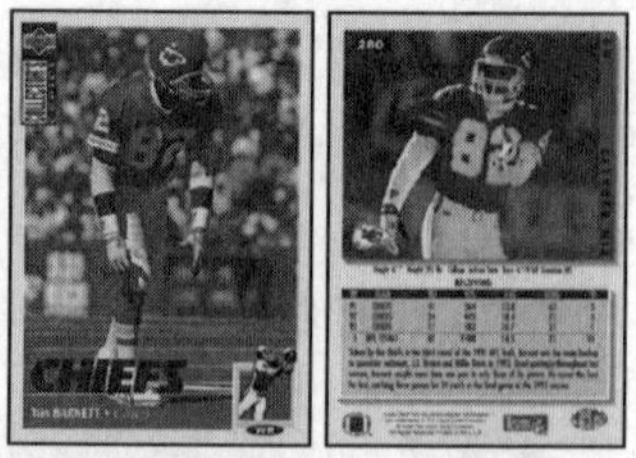

Inserted one per foil pack, two per special retail pack and three per jumbo pack, this standard-size 384-card parallel set features a similar design to the regular 1994 Upper Deck Collector's Choice issue. The difference being that the team's name appears in big silver foil letters above the player's name on the front.

	MINT	NRMT	EXC
COMPLETE SET (384)	80.00	36.00	10.00
COMMON CARD (1-384)	.20	.09	.03
*VETERAN STARS: 2X TO 4X BASIC CARDS			
*RCS: 1.5X TO 3X BASIC CARDS			

1994 Collector's Choice Crash the Game

Upper Deck produced the first release of Crash the Game in 1994. Each player was produced with two different colored foils on the card

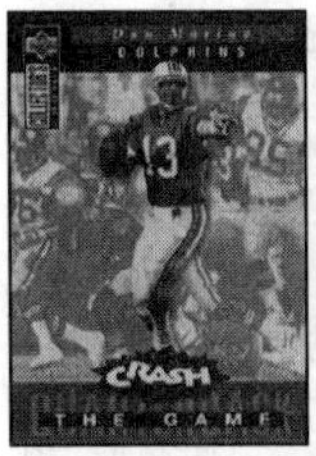

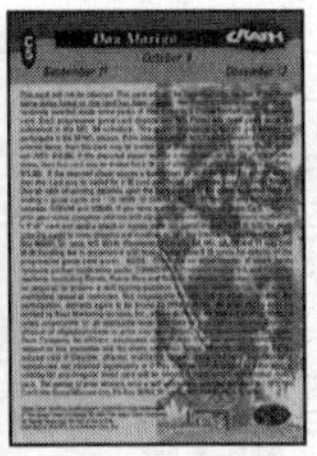

front (blue in hobby packs, green in retail packs). If the player featured scored or passed for a touchdown on one, two or three of the game dates included on the cardback, the card could be exchanged for a parallel prize card featuring bronze, silver, or gold foil. We've listed the cards below along with the prize level category, if any, that could be redeemed. The expiration date for the contest was April 30, 1995.

	MINT	NRMT	EXC
COMP.BLUE SET (30)	75.00	34.00	9.50
COMP.GREEN SET (30)	75.00	34.00	9.50
COMMON BLUE/GREEN (C1-C30)	1.00	.45	.12
COMP.BRONZE SET (30)	12.00	5.50	1.50
COMMON BRONZE FOIL (C1-C30)	.50	.23	.06
*BRONZE CARDS: .1X to .2X BASIC CARD			
COMP.SILVER SET (30)	16.00	7.25	2.00
COMMON SILVER FOIL (C1-C30)	.75	.35	.09
*SILVER CARDS: .15X to .3X BASIC CARD			
COMP.GOLD SET (30)	25.00	11.00	3.10
COMMON GOLD FOIL (C1-C30)	1.00	.45	.12
*GOLD CARDS: .25X to .5X BASIC CARD			
☐ C1B Steve Young WIN G	3.00	1.35	.35
☐ C1G Steve Young WIN G	4.00	1.80	.50
☐ C2B Troy Aikman WIN S	4.00	1.80	.50
☐ C2G Troy Aikman WIN B	4.00	1.80	.50
☐ C3B Rick Mirer WIN B	4.00	1.80	.50
☐ C3G Rick Mirer WIN B	1.50	.70	.19
☐ C4B Trent Dilfer WIN B	2.00	.90	.25
☐ C4G Trent Dilfer NO WIN	2.00	.90	.25
☐ C5B Dan Marino WIN G	8.00	3.60	1.00
☐ C5G Dan Marino WIN S	8.00	3.60	1.00
☐ C6B John Elway WIN S	3.00	1.35	.35
☐ C6G John Elway WIN S	3.00	1.35	.35
☐ C7B Heath Shuler WIN S	2.50	1.10	.30
☐ C7G Heath Shuler NO WIN	2.00	.90	.25
☐ C8B Joe Montana WIN G	4.00	1.80	.50
☐ C8G Joe Montana WIN S	3.50	1.55	.45
☐ C9B Drew Bledsoe WIN G UER	4.00	1.80	.50
☐ C9G Drew Bledsoe WIN G UER	4.00	1.80	.50
☐ C10B Warren Moon WIN S	1.50	.70	.19
☐ C10G Warren Moon WIN S	1.50	.70	.19
☐ C11B Marshall Faulk WIN B	4.00	1.80	.50
☐ C11G Marshall Faulk WIN S	4.00	1.80	.50
☐ C12B Thurman Thomas WIN B	1.50	.70	.19
☐ C12G Thurman Thomas WIN B	1.50	.70	.19
☐ C13B Barry Foster WIN B	1.00	.45	.12
☐ C13G Barry Foster WIN B	1.00	.45	.12
☐ C14B Gary Brown NO WIN	1.00	.45	.12
☐ C14G Gary Brown NO WIN	1.00	.45	.12
☐ C15B Emmitt Smith WIN G	8.00	3.60	1.00
☐ C15G Emmitt Smith WIN G	8.00	3.60	1.00
☐ C16B Barry Sanders WIN B	4.00	1.80	.50
☐ C16G Barry Sanders WIN B	4.00	1.80	.50
☐ C17B Rodney Hampton WIN B	1.50	.70	.19
☐ C17G Rodney Hampton WIN B	1.50	.70	.19
☐ C18B Jerome Bettis WIN B	2.50	1.10	.30
☐ C18G Jerome Bettis NO WIN	2.00	.90	.25
☐ C19B Ricky Watters WIN B	1.50	.70	.19
☐ C19G Ricky Watters NO WIN	1.50	.70	.19
☐ C20B Ronald Moore WIN B	1.50	.70	.19
☐ C20G Ronald Moore WIN B	1.50	.70	.19
☐ C21B Jerry Rice WIN G	4.00	1.80	.50
☐ C21G Jerry Rice NO WIN	3.00	1.35	.35
☐ C22B Andre Rison WIN G	1.50	.70	.19
☐ C22G Andre Rison WIN B	1.50	.70	.19
☐ C23B Michael Irvin NO WIN	1.50	.70	.19
☐ C23G Michael Irvin WIN S	1.50	.70	.19
☐ C24B Sterling Sharpe WIN S	1.50	.70	.19
☐ C24G Sterling Sharpe WIN B	1.50	.70	.19
☐ C25B Shannon Sharpe NO WIN	1.00	.45	.12
☐ C25G Shannon Sharpe NO WIN	1.00	.45	.12
☐ C26B Darnay Scott NO WIN	1.50	.70	.19
☐ C26G Darnay Scott WIN B	2.50	1.10	.30
☐ C27B Andre Reed WIN S	1.50	.70	.19
☐ C27G Andre Reed WIN B	1.50	.70	.19
☐ C28B Tim Brown NO WIN	1.50	.70	.19
☐ C28G Tim Brown WIN S	1.50	.70	.19
☐ C29B Charles Johnson WIN B	1.50	.70	.19
☐ C29G Charles Johnson NO WIN	1.00	.45	.12
☐ C30B Irving Fryar NO WIN	1.00	.45	.12
☐ C30G Irving Fryar NO WIN	1.00	.45	.12

1994 Collector's Choice Then and Now

This eight card set could be obtained by sending in a Then and Now exchange card. The theme of the set is portraying an active player with one from the same team from yesteryear. Horizontally designed, the fronts feature a color player photo superimposed over holographic background that contains the former player. The back contains a write-up about each player along with a small photo of both.

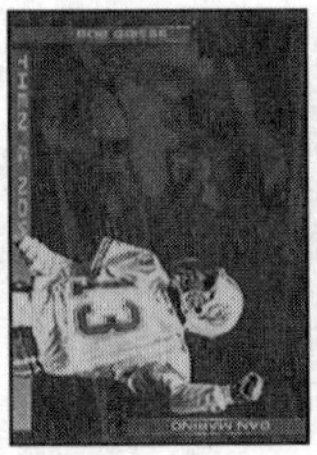

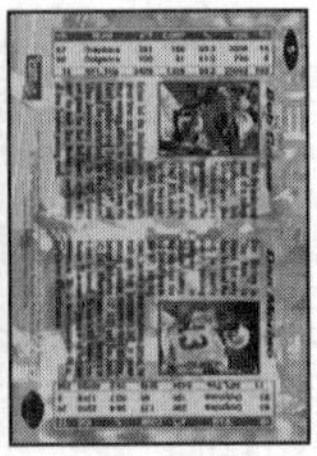

	MINT	NRMT	EXC
COMPLETE SET (8)	10.00	4.50	1.25
COMMON CARD (1-8)	.75	.35	.09
☐ 1 Eric Dickerson Jerome Bettis	1.00	.45	.12
☐ 2 Fred Biletnikoff Tim Brown	.75	.35	.09
☐ 3 Len Dawson Joe Montana	2.00	.90	.25
☐ 4 Joe Montana Steve Young	2.50	1.10	.30
☐ 5 Bob Griese Dan Marino	4.00	1.80	.50
☐ 6 Jim Zorn Rick Mirer	.75	.35	.09
☐ NNO Joe Montana Header Card	2.50	1.10	.30
☐ NNO Then/Now Exch. Card	.30	.14	.04

1994 Collector's Choice Spanish Promos

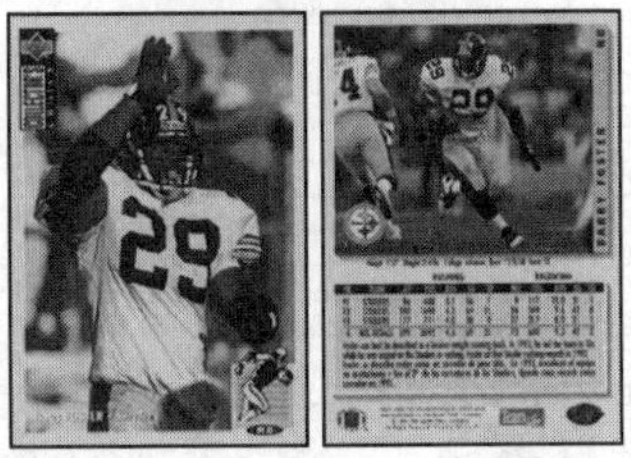

This 36-card standard-size set was issued to preview the Collector's Choice Spanish series. The cards are identical to their American counterparts, with the exception that the player profile on the backs have been shortened to create space for the Spanish translation. Also these cards are unnumbered; thus they are checklisted below alphabetically.

	MINT	NRMT	EXC
COMPLETE SET (36)	75.00	34.00	9.50
COMMON CARD	2.00	.90	.25
☐ 1 Troy Aikman	5.00	2.20	.60
☐ 2 Marcus Allen	3.00	1.35	.35
☐ 3 Terry Allen	2.50	1.10	.30
☐ 4 Kimble Anders	2.00	.90	.25
☐ 5 Eddie Anderson	2.00	.90	.25
☐ 6 Steve Atwater	2.00	.90	.25
☐ 7 Carlton Bailey	2.00	.90	.25
☐ 8 Patrick Bates	2.00	.90	.25
☐ 9 Don Beebe	2.00	.90	.25
☐ 10 Cornelius Bennett	2.00	.90	.25
☐ 11 Edgar Bennett	2.00	.90	.25
☐ 12 Tony Bennett	2.00	.90	.25
☐ 13 Rod Bernstine	2.00	.90	.25
☐ 14 J.J.Birden	2.00	.90	.25
☐ 15 Steve Bono	2.00	.90	.25
☐ 16 Bill Brooks	2.00	.90	.25
☐ 17 Michael Brooks	2.00	.90	.25
☐ 18 Robert Brooks	3.00	1.35	.35
☐ 19 Chad Brown	2.00	.90	.25
☐ 20 Derek Brown TE	2.00	.90	.25
☐ 21 Gary Brown	2.00	.90	.25
☐ 22 Tim Brown	3.00	1.35	.35
☐ 23 Anthony Carter	2.00	.90	.25
☐ 24 Cris Carter	3.00	1.35	.35
☐ 25 Ray Childress	2.00	.90	.25
☐ 26 Jason Elam	2.00	.90	.25
☐ 27 Deon Figures	2.00	.90	.25
☐ 28 Barry Foster	2.00	.90	.25
☐ 29 Mel Gray	2.00	.90	.25
☐ 30 Willie Green	2.00	.90	.25
☐ 31 Charles Haley	2.00	.90	.25
☐ 32 Alvin Harper	2.00	.90	.25
☐ 33 Martin Harrison	2.00	.90	.25
☐ 34 Rodney Holman	2.00	.90	.25
☐ 35 Brent Jones	2.00	.90	.25
☐ 36 Greg Montgomery	2.00	.90	.25

1994 Collector's Choice Spanish

Produced by Upper Deck for sale in Mexico, this 260-card set measures the standard size. The set starts with the subsets Rookie Class 1994 (1-30) and Images of 93 (31-45), followed by regular cards. The subsets feature full-bleed color action player photos, with

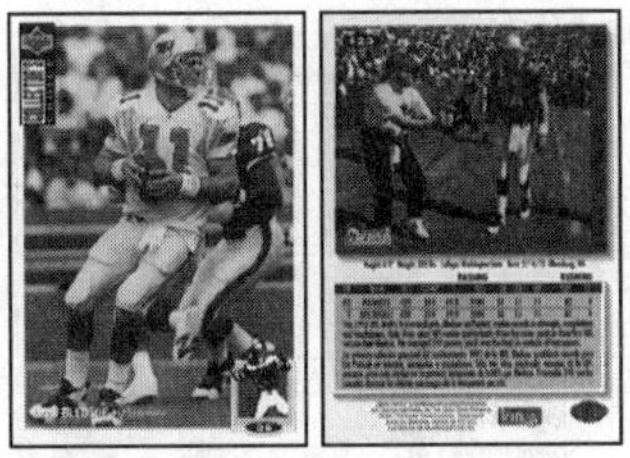

the player's name and the team name on the fronts. The backs carry another small color player photo, along with player profile in English and Spanish. The regular cards feature color action player photos with white borders on the fronts. The player's name appears on the bottom. The backs carry another color action player photo, with biography, statistics and profile, both in English and in Spanish.

	MINT	NRMT	EXC
COMPLETE SET (260)	50.00	22.00	6.25
COMMON CARD (1-260)	.20	.09	.03
☐ 1 Antonio Langham	.30	.14	.04
☐ 2 Aaron Glenn	.30	.14	.04
☐ 3 Sam Adams	.30	.14	.04
☐ 4 Dewayne Washington	.30	.14	.04
☐ 5 Dan Wilkinson	.30	.14	.04
☐ 6 Bryant Young	.40	.18	.05
☐ 7 Aaron Taylor	.20	.09	.03
☐ 8 Willie McGinest	.30	.14	.04
☐ 9 Trev Alberts	.30	.14	.04
☐ 10 Jamir Miller	.20	.09	.03
☐ 11 John Thierry	.20	.09	.03
☐ 12 Heath Shuler	2.00	.90	.25
☐ 13 Trent Dilfer	1.25	.55	.16
☐ 14 Marshall Faulk	6.00	2.70	.75
☐ 15 Greg Hill	.40	.18	.05
☐ 16 William Floyd	2.00	.90	.25
☐ 17 Chuck Levy	.20	.09	.03
☐ 18 Charlie Garner	.30	.14	.04
☐ 19 Mario Bates	1.00	.45	.12
☐ 20 Donnell Bennett	.20	.09	.03
☐ 21 LeShon Johnson	.30	.14	.04
☐ 22 Calvin Jones	.20	.09	.03
☐ 23 Darnay Scott	.40	.18	.05
☐ 24 Charles Johnson	.40	.18	.05
☐ 25 Johnnie Morton	.40	.18	.05
☐ 26 Shante Carver	.20	.09	.03
☐ 27 Derrick Alexander WR	.40	.18	.05
☐ 28 David Palmer	.30	.14	.04
☐ 29 Ryan Yarborough	.20	.09	.03
☐ 30 Errict Rhett	2.50	1.10	.30
☐ 31 James Washington I93	.20	.09	.03
☐ 32 Sterling Sharpe I93	.20	.09	.03
☐ 33 Drew Bledsoe I93	1.00	.45	.12
☐ 34 Eric Allen I93	.20	.09	.03
☐ 35 Jerome Bettis I93	.60	.25	.07
☐ 36 Joe Montana I93	.50	.23	.06
☐ 37 John Carney I93	.20	.09	.03
☐ 38 Emmitt Smith I93	2.00	.90	.25
☐ 39 Chris Warren I93	.40	.18	.05
☐ 40 Reggie Brooks I93	.20	.09	.03
☐ 41 Gary Brown I93	.20	.09	.03
☐ 42 Tim Brown I93	.30	.14	.04
☐ 43 Erric Pegram I93	.20	.09	.03
☐ 44 Ronald Moore I93	.20	.09	.03
☐ 45 Jerry Rice I93	.50	.23	.06
☐ 46 Don Beebe	.20	.09	.03
☐ 47 Steve Atwater	.20	.09	.03
☐ 48 Gary Brown	.20	.09	.03
☐ 49 Marcus Allen	.40	.18	.05
☐ 50 Terry Allen	.30	.14	.04
☐ 51 Chad Brown	.20	.09	.03
☐ 52 Cornelius Bennett	.30	.14	.04
☐ 53 Rod Bernstine	.20	.09	.03
☐ 54 Greg Montgomery	.20	.09	.03
☐ 55 Kimble Anders	.20	.09	.03
☐ 56 Charles Haley	.30	.14	.04
☐ 57 Mel Gray	.20	.09	.03
☐ 58 Edgar Bennett	.40	.18	.05
☐ 59 Eddie Anderson	.20	.09	.03
☐ 60 Derek Brown TE	.20	.09	.03
☐ 61 Jim Kelly	.40	.18	.05
☐ 62 Arthur Marshall	.20	.09	.03
☐ 63 Webster Slaughter	.20	.09	.03
☐ 64 Dave Krieg	.30	.14	.04
☐ 65 Steve Jordan	.20	.09	.03
☐ 66 Neil O'Donnell	.40	.18	.05
☐ 67 Andre Reed	.30	.14	.04
☐ 68 Mike Croel	.20	.09	.03
☐ 69 Al Smith	.20	.09	.03
☐ 70 Joe Montana	2.00	.90	.25
☐ 71 Randall McDaniel	.20	.09	.03
☐ 72 Greg Lloyd	.40	.18	.05
☐ 73 Thomas Smith	.20	.09	.03
☐ 74 Glyn Milburn	.30	.14	.04
☐ 75 Lorenzo White	.20	.09	.03
☐ 76 Neil Smith	.40	.18	.05
☐ 77 John Randle	.20	.09	.03
☐ 78 Rod Woodson	.40	.18	.05
☐ 79 Russell Maryland	.20	.09	.03
☐ 80 Rodney Peete	.20	.09	.03
☐ 81 Jackie Harris	.20	.09	.03
☐ 82 James Jett	.20	.09	.03
☐ 83 Rodney Hampton	.40	.18	.05
☐ 84 Bill Romanowski	.20	.09	.03
☐ 85 Ken Norton, Jr.	.30	.14	.04
☐ 86 Barry Sanders	2.00	.90	.25
☐ 87 Johnny Holland	.20	.09	.03
☐ 88 Terry McDaniel	.20	.09	.03
☐ 89 Greg Jackson	.20	.09	.03
☐ 90 Dana Stubblefield	.40	.18	.05
☐ 91 Jay Novacek	.30	.14	.04
☐ 92 Chris Spielman	.30	.14	.04
☐ 93 Ken Ruettgers	.20	.09	.03
☐ 94 Greg Robinson	.20	.09	.03
☐ 95 Mark Jackson	.20	.09	.03
☐ 96 John Taylor	.30	.14	.04
☐ 97 Roger Harper	.20	.09	.03
☐ 98 Jerry Ball	.20	.09	.03
☐ 99 Keith Byars	.20	.09	.03
☐ 100 Morten Andersen	.20	.09	.03
☐ 101 Eric Allen	.20	.09	.03
☐ 102 Marion Butts	.20	.09	.03
☐ 103 Michael Haynes	.30	.14	.04
☐ 104 Rob Burnett	.20	.09	.03
☐ 105 Marco Coleman	.20	.09	.03
☐ 106 Derek Brown RB	.20	.09	.03
☐ 107 Andy Harmon	.20	.09	.03
☐ 108 Darren Carrington	.20	.09	.03
☐ 109 Bobby Hebert	.20	.09	.03
☐ 110 Mark Carrier WR	.30	.14	.04
☐ 111 Bryan Cox	.20	.09	.03
☐ 112 Toi Cook	.20	.09	.03
☐ 113 Tim Harris	.20	.09	.03
☐ 114 John Friesz	.30	.14	.04
☐ 115 Neal Anderson	.20	.09	.03
☐ 116 Jerome Bettis	1.25	.55	.16
☐ 117 Bruce Armstrong	.20	.09	.03
☐ 118 Brad Baxter	.20	.09	.03
☐ 119 Johnny Bailey	.20	.09	.03
☐ 120 Brian Blades	.30	.14	.04
☐ 121 Mark Carrier DB UER listed as WR on back	.20	.09	.03
☐ 122 Shane Conlan	.20	.09	.03
☐ 123 Drew Bledsoe	2.00	.90	.25
☐ 124 Chris Burkett	.20	.09	.03
☐ 125 Steve Beuerlein	.20	.09	.03
☐ 126 Ferrell Edmunds	.20	.09	.03
☐ 127 Curtis Conway	.40	.18	.05
☐ 128 Troy Drayton	.20	.09	.03
☐ 129 Vincent Brown	.20	.09	.03
☐ 130 Boomer Esiason	.30	.14	.04
☐ 131 Larry Centers	.40	.18	.05
☐ 132 Carlton Gray	.20	.09	.03
☐ 133 Chris Miller	.20	.09	.03
☐ 134 Eric Metcalf	.30	.14	.04
☐ 135 Mark Higgs	.20	.09	.03
☐ 136 Tyrone Hughes	.30	.14	.04
☐ 137 Randall Cunningham	.30	.14	.04
☐ 138 Ronnie Harmon	.20	.09	.03
☐ 139 Andre Rison	.30	.14	.04
☐ 140 Eric Turner	.20	.09	.03
☐ 141 Terry Kirby	.40	.18	.05
☐ 142 Eric Martin	.20	.09	.03
☐ 143 Seth Joyner	.20	.09	.03
☐ 144 Stan Humphries	.40	.18	.05
☐ 145 Deion Sanders	1.25	.55	.16
☐ 146 Vinny Testaverde	.30	.14	.04
☐ 147 Dan Marino	4.00	1.80	.50
☐ 148 Renaldo Turnbull	.20	.09	.03
☐ 149 Herschel Walker	.30	.14	.04
☐ 150 Anthony Miller	.30	.14	.04
☐ 151 Richard Dent	.30	.14	.04
☐ 152 Jim Everett	.30	.14	.04
☐ 153 Ben Coates	.40	.18	.05
☐ 154 Jeff Lageman	.20	.09	.03
☐ 155 Garrison Hearst	1.00	.45	.12
☐ 156 Kelvin Martin	.20	.09	.03
☐ 157 Dante Jones	.20	.09	.03
☐ 158 Sean Gilbert	.20	.09	.03
☐ 159 Leonard Russell	.20	.09	.03
☐ 160 Ronnie Lott	.30	.14	.04
☐ 161 Randal Hill	.20	.09	.03
☐ 162 Rick Mirer	.40	.18	.05
☐ 163 Alonzo Spellman	.20	.09	.03
☐ 164 Todd Lyght	.20	.09	.03
☐ 165 Chris Slade	.20	.09	.03
☐ 166 Johnny Mitchell	.20	.09	.03
☐ 167 Ronald Moore	.20	.09	.03
☐ 168 Eugene Robinson	.20	.09	.03
☐ 169 John Copeland	.20	.09	.03
☐ 170 Kerry Cash	.20	.09	.03
☐ 171 Reggie Cobb	.20	.09	.03
☐ 172 Brian Mitchell	.20	.09	.03
☐ 173 Derrick Fenner	.20	.09	.03
☐ 174 Roosevelt Potts	.20	.09	.03
☐ 175 Courtney Hawkins	.20	.09	.03
☐ 176 Carl Banks	.20	.09	.03
☐ 177 Harold Green	.20	.09	.03
☐ 178 Steve Emtman	.20	.09	.03
☐ 179 Santana Dotson	.30	.14	.04
☐ 180 Reggie Brooks	.30	.14	.04
☐ 181 Terry Obee	.20	.09	.03
☐ 182 David Klingler	.20	.09	.03
☐ 183 Quentin Coryatt	.20	.09	.03
☐ 184 Craig Erickson	.20	.09	.03
☐ 185 Desmond Howard	.30	.14	.04

☐ 186 Carl Pickens	1.00	.45	.12
☐ 187 Lawrence Dawsey	.20	.09	.03
☐ 188 Henry Ellard	.20	.09	.03
☐ 189 Shaun Gayle	.20	.09	.03
☐ 190 David Lang	.20	.09	.03
☐ 191 Anthony Johnson	.30	.14	.04
☐ 192 Darnell Walker	.20	.09	.03
☐ 193 Pepper Johnson	.20	.09	.03
☐ 194 Kurt Gouveia	.20	.09	.03
☐ 195 Louis Oliver	.20	.09	.03
☐ 196 Lincoln Kennedy	.20	.09	.03
☐ 197 Anthony Pleasant	.20	.09	.03
☐ 198 Irving Fryar	.30	.14	.04
☐ 199 Steve Bono	.30	.14	.04
☐ 200 Alvin Harper	.30	.14	.04
☐ 201 Willie Green	.20	.09	.03
☐ 202 Robert Brooks	.75	.35	.09
☐ 203 Patrick Bates	.20	.09	.03
☐ 204 Anthony Carter	.30	.14	.04
☐ 205 Bruce Smith	.40	.18	.05
☐ 206 Tom Rouen	.20	.09	.03
☐ 207 Cris Dishman	.20	.09	.03
☐ 208 Keith Cash	.20	.09	.03
☐ 209 Carlos Jenkins	.20	.09	.03
☐ 210 Levon Kirkland	.20	.09	.03
☐ 211 Pete Metzelaars	.20	.09	.03
☐ 212 Shannon Sharpe	.30	.14	.04
☐ 213 Cody Carlson	.20	.09	.03
☐ 214 Derrick Thomas	.40	.18	.05
☐ 215 Emmitt Smith	4.00	1.80	.50
☐ 216 Robert Porcher	.20	.09	.03
☐ 217 Sterling Sharpe	.30	.14	.04
☐ 218 Anthony Smith	.20	.09	.03
☐ 219 Mike Sherrard	.20	.09	.03
☐ 220 Tom Rathman	.20	.09	.03
☐ 221 Nate Newton	.20	.09	.03
☐ 222 Pat Swilling	.20	.09	.03
☐ 223 George Teague	.20	.09	.03
☐ 224 Greg Townsend	.20	.09	.03
☐ 225 Eric Guliford	.20	.09	.03
☐ 226 Leroy Thompson	.20	.09	.03
☐ 227 Thurman Thomas	.40	.18	.05
☐ 228 Dan Williams	.20	.09	.03
☐ 229 Bubba McDowell	.20	.09	.03
☐ 230 Tracy Simien	.20	.09	.03
☐ 231 Scottie Graham	.30	.14	.04
☐ 232 Eric Green	.20	.09	.03
☐ 233 Phil Simms	.30	.14	.04
☐ 234 Ricky Watters	.40	.18	.05
☐ 235 Kevin Williams WR	.30	.14	.04
☐ 236 Brett Perriman	.30	.14	.04
☐ 237 Reggie White	.40	.18	.05
☐ 238 Steve Wisniewski	.20	.09	.03
☐ 239 Mark Collins	.20	.09	.03
☐ 240 Steve Young	1.50	.70	.19
☐ 241 Barry Foster	.20	.09	.03
☐ 242 Bill Brooks	.20	.09	.03
☐ 243 Jason Elam	.20	.09	.03
☐ 244 Ray Childress	.20	.09	.03
☐ 245 J.J. Birden	.20	.09	.03
☐ 246 Cris Carter	.40	.18	.05
☐ 247 Deon Figures	.20	.09	.03
☐ 248 Carlton Bailey	.20	.09	.03
☐ 249 Brent Jones	.30	.14	.04
☐ 250 Troy Aikman	2.00	.90	.25
☐ 251 Rodney Holman	.20	.09	.03
☐ 252 Tony Bennett	.20	.09	.03
☐ 253 Tim Brown	.40	.18	.05
☐ 254 Michael Brooks	.20	.09	.03
☐ 255 Martin Harrison	.20	.09	.03
☐ 256 Carolina Panthers Logo	.40	.18	.05
☐ 257 Jacksonville Jaguars Logo	.20	.09	.03
☐ 258 Dan Marino ART	.50	.23	.06
Checklist Card			
card #170 Kerry not Keith			
☐ 259 Jerry Rice ART	.50	.23	.06
Checklist Card			
☐ 260 Joe Montana ART UER	.50	.23	.06
Checklist Card			
several incorrect player listings			

1994-95 Collector's Choice Crash the Super Bowl XXIX

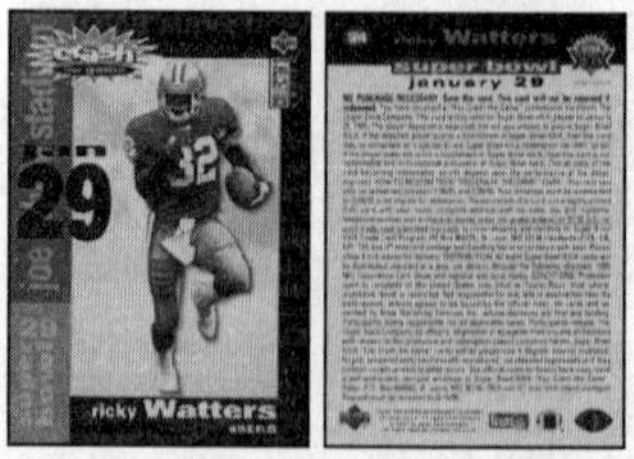

Upper Deck produced eight standard-size cards specifically for Super Bowl XXIX. These cards were available at the NFL Experience card show in Miami, in various hobby publications and through the nationally-syndicated "Sports Collector's Radio Network." The set features four players from the AFC champion San Diego Chargers (1-4) and four from the NFC San Francisco 49ers (5-8). If the player featured scored a touchdown in the Super Bowl, the card was redeemable for a special nine-card set. The redemption prize set featured the eight players in the set plus a Super Bowl "header" card. The redemption prize cards' text were rewritten to present a summary of that player's Super Bowl performance.

	MINT	NRMT	EXC
COMPLETE SET (9)	10.00	4.50	1.25
COMMON CARD (SB1-SB8)	.75	.35	.09
☐ 1 Steve Young WIN	2.50	1.10	.30
☐ 2 Jerry Rice WIN	3.00	1.35	.35
☐ 3 Brent Jones	.75	.35	.09
☐ 4 Ricky Watters WIN	1.00	.45	.12
☐ 5 Stan Humphries WIN	1.00	.45	.12
☐ 6 Natrone Means WIN	1.00	.45	.12
☐ 7 Ronnie Harmon	.75	.35	.09
☐ 8 Tony Martin WIN	1.00	.45	.12
☐ NNO Header Card	.75	.35	.09

1995 Collector's Choice

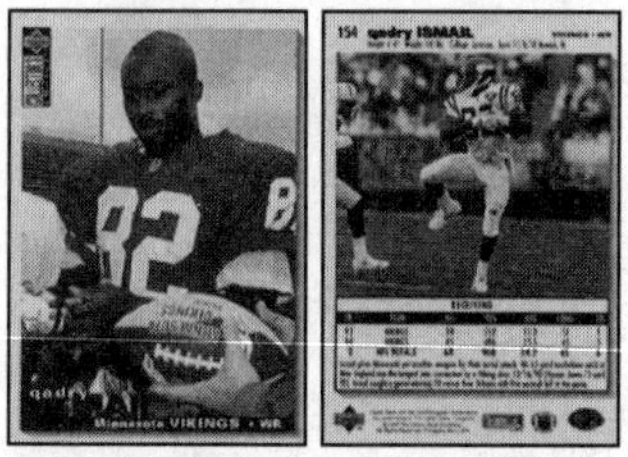

This 348-card standard-size set features color action player photos with white borders on the front. The player's name, position and team name are printed at the bottom of the card. On a white background, the backs carry another color player photo with yearly and career stats and, as space permits, a short biography. Subsets include 1995 Rookie Class (1-30, sequenced in draft order), Did You Know (31-50), Jacksonville Jaguars expansion selections (331-338) and Carolina Panthers picks (339-346). The 12-card packs had a suggested retail price of .99 cents. Each pack contained a Player's Club parallel insert card. Inserted one per hobby boxes was a Platinum Player's Club card. Hobby dealers ordering cases directly from Upper Deck received 30 silver Crash the Game cards for their first case ordered and 90 silver Crash the Game cards if they ordered two cases. Rookie Cards in this set include Ki-Jana Carter, Kerry Collins, Joey Galloway, Steve McNair, Rashaan Salaam, J.J.Stokes and Michael Westbrook. A Joe Montana Promo card was produced and priced below.

	MINT	NRMT	EXC
COMPLETE SET (348)	22.00	10.00	2.70
COMMON CARD (1-348)	.05	.02	.01
☐ 1 Ki-Jana Carter	1.00	.45	.12
☐ 2 Tony Boselli	.10	.05	.01
☐ 3 Steve McNair	2.50	1.10	.30
☐ 4 Michael Westbrook	1.25	.55	.16
☐ 5 Kerry Collins	3.00	1.35	.35
☐ 6 Kevin Carter	.20	.09	.03
☐ 7 Mike Mamula	.10	.05	.01
☐ 8 Joey Galloway	2.00	.90	.25
☐ 9 Kyle Brady	.20	.09	.03
☐ 10 J.J. Stokes	1.00	.45	.12
☐ 11 Derrick Alexander DE	.05	.02	.01
☐ 12 Warren Sapp	.10	.05	.01
☐ 13 Mark Fields	.05	.02	.01
☐ 14 Tyrone Wheatley	.50	.23	.06
☐ 15 Napoleon Kaufman	1.00	.45	.12
☐ 16 James O.Stewart	.10	.05	.01
☐ 17 Luther Elliss	.05	.02	.01
☐ 18 Rashaan Salaam	1.50	.70	.19
☐ 19 Ty Law	.10	.05	.01
☐ 20 Mark Bruener	.10	.05	.01
☐ 21 Derrick Brooks	.05	.02	.01
☐ 22 Christian Fauria	.05	.02	.01
☐ 23 Ray Zellars	.10	.05	.01
☐ 24 Todd Collins	.20	.09	.03
☐ 25 Sherman Williams	.05	.02	.01
☐ 26 Frank Sanders	.20	.09	.03
☐ 27 Rodney Thomas	.20	.09	.03
☐ 28 Rob Johnson	.05	.02	.01
☐ 29 Steve Stenstrom	.05	.02	.01
☐ 30 James A.Stewart	.05	.02	.01
☐ 31 Barry Sanders DYK	.50	.23	.06
☐ 32 Marshall Faulk DYK	.20	.09	.03
☐ 33 Darnay Scott DYK	.20	.09	.03
☐ 34 Joe Montana DYK	.50	.23	.06
☐ 35 Michael Irvin DYK	.10	.05	.01
☐ 36 Jerry Rice DYK	.50	.23	.06
☐ 37 Errict Rhett DYK	.20	.09	.03
☐ 38 Drew Bledsoe DYK	.50	.23	.06
☐ 39 Dan Marino DYK	1.00	.45	.12
☐ 40 Terance Mathis DYK	.05	.02	.01
☐ 41 Natrone Means DYK	.20	.09	.03
☐ 42 Tim Brown DYK	.10	.05	.01
☐ 43 Steve Young DYK	.40	.18	.05
☐ 44 Mel Gray DYK	.05	.02	.01
☐ 45 Jerome Bettis DYK	.20	.09	.03
☐ 46 Aeneas Williams DYK	.05	.02	.01
☐ 47 Charlie Garner DYK	.10	.05	.01
☐ 48 Deion Sanders DYK	.30	.14	.04
☐ 49 Ken Harvey DYK	.05	.02	.01
☐ 50 Emmitt Smith DYK	1.00	.45	.12
☐ 51 Andre Reed	.10	.05	.01
☐ 52 Sean Dawkins	.10	.05	.01
☐ 53 Irving Fryar	.10	.05	.01
☐ 54 Vincent Brisby	.05	.02	.01
☐ 55 Rob Moore	.05	.02	.01
☐ 56 Carl Pickens	.20	.09	.03
☐ 57 Vinny Testaverde	.10	.05	.01
☐ 58 Webster Slaughter	.05	.02	.01
☐ 59 Eric Green	.05	.02	.01
☐ 60 Anthony Miller	.10	.05	.01
☐ 61 Lake Dawson	.10	.05	.01
☐ 62 Tim Brown	.20	.09	.03
☐ 63 Stan Humphries	.10	.05	.01
☐ 64 Rick Mirer	.20	.09	.03
☐ 65 Gary Clark	.05	.02	.01
☐ 66 Troy Aikman	1.00	.45	.12
☐ 67 Mike Sherrard	.05	.02	.01
☐ 68 Fred Barnett	.10	.05	.01
☐ 69 Henry Ellard	.10	.05	.01
☐ 70 Terry Allen	.10	.05	.01
☐ 71 Jeff Graham	.05	.02	.01
☐ 72 Herman Moore	.50	.23	.06
☐ 73 Brett Favre	2.00	.90	.25
☐ 74 Trent Dilfer	.20	.09	.03
☐ 75 Derek Brown RB	.05	.02	.01
☐ 76 Andre Rison	.10	.05	.01
☐ 77 Flipper Anderson	.05	.02	.01
☐ 78 Jerry Rice UER	1.00	.45	.12
Career totals are all wrong			
☐ 79 Thurman Thomas	.20	.09	.03
☐ 80 Marshall Faulk	.50	.23	.06
☐ 81 O.J. McDuffie	.20	.09	.03
☐ 82 Ben Coates	.10	.05	.01
☐ 83 Johnny Mitchell	.05	.02	.01
☐ 84 Darnay Scott	.20	.09	.03
☐ 85 Derrick Alexander WR	.20	.09	.03
☐ 86 Micheal Barrow UER	.05	.02	.01
Name spelled Michael on both sides			
☐ 87 Charles Johnson	.10	.05	.01
☐ 88 John Elway	.75	.35	.09
☐ 89 Willie Davis	.10	.05	.01
☐ 90 James Jett	.10	.05	.01
☐ 91 Mark Seay	.10	.05	.01
☐ 92 Brian Blades	.10	.05	.01
☐ 93 Ricky Proehl	.05	.02	.01
☐ 94 Charles Haley	.10	.05	.01
☐ 95 Chris Calloway	.05	.02	.01
☐ 96 Calvin Williams	.10	.05	.01
☐ 97 Ethan Horton	.05	.02	.01
☐ 98 Cris Carter	.20	.09	.03
☐ 99 Curtis Conway	.20	.09	.03
☐ 100 Lomas Brown	.05	.02	.01
☐ 101 Edgar Bennett	.10	.05	.01
☐ 102 Craig Erickson	.05	.02	.01
☐ 103 Jim Everett	.05	.02	.01
☐ 104 Terance Mathis	.10	.05	.01
☐ 105 Wayne Gandy	.05	.02	.01
☐ 106 Brent Jones	.05	.02	.01
☐ 107 Bruce Smith	.20	.09	.03
☐ 108 Roosevelt Potts	.05	.02	.01
☐ 109 Dan Marino	2.00	.90	.25
☐ 110 Michael Timpson	.05	.02	.01
☐ 111 Boomer Esiason	.10	.05	.01
☐ 112 David Klingler	.10	.05	.01
☐ 113 Eric Metcalf	.10	.05	.01
☐ 114 Lorenzo White	.05	.02	.01
☐ 115 Neil O'Donnell	.10	.05	.01
☐ 116 Shannon Sharpe	.10	.05	.01
☐ 117 Joe Montana	1.00	.45	.12
☐ 118 Jeff Hostetler	.10	.05	.01
☐ 119 Ronnie Harmon	.05	.02	.01
☐ 120 Chris Warren	.10	.05	.01
☐ 121 Randal Hill	.05	.02	.01
☐ 122 Alvin Harper	.05	.02	.01
☐ 123 Dave Brown	.10	.05	.01
☐ 124 Randall Cunningham	.10	.05	.01
☐ 125 Heath Shuler	.20	.09	.03
☐ 126 Jake Reed	.10	.05	.01
☐ 127 Donnell Woolford	.05	.02	.01
☐ 128 Scott Mitchell	.10	.05	.01
☐ 129 Reggie White	.20	.09	.03
☐ 130 Lawrence Dawsey	.05	.02	.01
☐ 131 Michael Haynes	.10	.05	.01
☐ 132 Bert Emanuel	.20	.09	.03
☐ 133 Troy Drayton	.05	.02	.01
☐ 134 Merton Hanks	.05	.02	.01
☐ 135 Jim Kelly	.20	.09	.03
☐ 136 Tony Bennett	.05	.02	.01
☐ 137 Terry Kirby	.10	.05	.01
☐ 138 Drew Bledsoe	1.00	.45	.12
☐ 139 Johnny Johnson	.05	.02	.01
☐ 140 Dan Wilkinson	.10	.05	.01
☐ 141 Leroy Hoard	.05	.02	.01
☐ 142 Gary Brown	.05	.02	.01
☐ 143 Barry Foster	.10	.05	.01
☐ 144 Shane Dronett	.05	.02	.01
☐ 145 Marcus Allen	.20	.09	.03
☐ 146 Harvey Williams	.05	.02	.01
☐ 147 Tony Martin	.10	.05	.01
☐ 148 Rod Stephens	.05	.02	.01
☐ 149 Ronald Moore	.05	.02	.01
☐ 150 Michael Irvin	.20	.09	.03
☐ 151 Rodney Hampton	.10	.05	.01
☐ 152 Herschel Walker	.10	.05	.01
☐ 153 Reggie Brooks	.10	.05	.01
☐ 154 Qadry Ismail	.10	.05	.01
☐ 155 Chris Zorich	.05	.02	.01
☐ 156 Barry Sanders	1.00	.45	.12
☐ 157 Sean Jones	.05	.02	.01
☐ 158 Errict Rhett	.20	.09	.03
☐ 159 Tyrone Hughes	.10	.05	.01
☐ 160 Jeff George	.10	.05	.01
☐ 161 Chris Miller	.05	.02	.01
☐ 162 Steve Young	.75	.35	.09
☐ 163 Cornelius Bennett	.10	.05	.01
☐ 164 Trev Alberts	.05	.02	.01
☐ 165 J.B. Brown	.05	.02	.01
☐ 166 Marion Butts	.05	.02	.01
☐ 167 Aaron Glenn	.05	.02	.01
☐ 168 James Francis	.05	.02	.01
☐ 169 Eric Turner	.05	.02	.01
☐ 170 Darryll Lewis	.05	.02	.01
☐ 171 John L. Williams	.05	.02	.01
☐ 172 Simon Fletcher	.05	.02	.01
☐ 173 Neil Smith	.10	.05	.01
☐ 174 Chester McGlockton	.10	.05	.01
☐ 175 Natrone Means	.20	.09	.03
☐ 176 Michael Sinclair	.05	.02	.01
☐ 177 Larry Centers	.10	.05	.01
☐ 178 Daryl Johnston	.10	.05	.01
☐ 179 Dave Meggett	.05	.02	.01
☐ 180 Greg Jackson	.05	.02	.01
☐ 181 Ken Harvey	.05	.02	.01
☐ 182 Warren Moon	.10	.05	.01
☐ 183 Steve Walsh	.05	.02	.01
☐ 184 Chris Spielman	.10	.05	.01
☐ 185 Bryce Paup	.20	.09	.03
☐ 186 Courtney Hawkins	.05	.02	.01
☐ 187 Willie Roaf	.05	.02	.01
☐ 188 Chris Doleman	.05	.02	.01
☐ 189 Jerome Bettis	.30	.14	.04
☐ 190 Ricky Watters	.20	.09	.03
☐ 191 Henry Jones	.05	.02	.01
☐ 192 Quentin Coryatt	.10	.05	.01
☐ 193 Bryan Cox	.05	.02	.01
☐ 194 Kevin Turner	.05	.02	.01
☐ 195 Siupeli Malamala	.05	.02	.01
☐ 196 Louis Oliver	.05	.02	.01
☐ 197 Rob Burnett	.05	.02	.01
☐ 198 Cris Dishman	.05	.02	.01
☐ 199 Byron Bam Morris	.10	.05	.01
☐ 200 Ray Crockett	.05	.02	.01
☐ 201 Jon Vaughn	.05	.02	.01
☐ 202 Nolan Harrison	.05	.02	.01
☐ 203 Leslie O'Neal	.10	.05	.01
☐ 204 Sam Adams	.05	.02	.01
☐ 205 Eric Swann	.10	.05	.01
☐ 206 Jay Novacek	.10	.05	.01
☐ 207 Keith Hamilton	.05	.02	.01
☐ 208 Charlie Garner	.10	.05	.01
☐ 209 Tom Carter	.05	.02	.01
☐ 210 Henry Thomas	.05	.02	.01
☐ 211 Lewis Tillman	.05	.02	.01
☐ 212 Pat Swilling	.05	.02	.01
☐ 213 Terrell Buckley	.05	.02	.01
☐ 214 Hardy Nickerson	.05	.02	.01
☐ 215 Mario Bates	.20	.09	.03
☐ 216 D.J. Johnson	.05	.02	.01
☐ 217 Robert Young	.05	.02	.01
☐ 218 Dana Stubblefield	.20	.09	.03
☐ 219 Jeff Burris	.05	.02	.01
☐ 220 Floyd Turner	.05	.02	.01
☐ 221 Troy Vincent	.05	.02	.01
☐ 222 Willie McGinest	.10	.05	.01
☐ 223 James Hasty	.05	.02	.01
☐ 224 Jeff Blake	1.25	.55	.16
☐ 225 Stevon Moore	.05	.02	.01
☐ 226 Ernest Givins	.05	.02	.01
☐ 227 Greg Lloyd	.10	.05	.01
☐ 228 Steve Atwater	.10	.05	.01
☐ 229 Dale Carter	.10	.05	.01
☐ 230 Terry McDaniel	.05	.02	.01
☐ 231 John Carney	.05	.02	.01
☐ 232 Cortez Kennedy	.10	.05	.01
☐ 233 Clyde Simmons	.05	.02	.01
☐ 234 Emmitt Smith	2.00	.90	.25
☐ 235 Thomas Lewis	.10	.05	.01
☐ 236 William Fuller	.05	.02	.01
☐ 237 Ricky Ervins	.05	.02	.01
☐ 238 John Randle	.05	.02	.01
☐ 239 John Thierry	.05	.02	.01
☐ 240 Mel Gray	.05	.02	.01
☐ 241 George Teague	.05	.02	.01
☐ 242 Charles Wilson Bucs	.05	.02	.01
see '95 Coll.Choice			
Update #U170			
☐ 243 Joe Johnson	.05	.02	.01
☐ 244 Chuck Smith	.05	.02	.01
☐ 245 Sean Gilbert	.10	.05	.01
☐ 246 Bryant Young	.10	.05	.01
☐ 247 Bucky Brooks	.05	.02	.01
☐ 248 Ray Buchanan	.05	.02	.01
☐ 249 Tim Bowens	.05	.02	.01
☐ 250 Vincent Brown	.05	.02	.01
☐ 251 Marcus Turner	.05	.02	.01
☐ 252 Derrick Fenner	.05	.02	.01
☐ 253 Antonio Langham	.05	.02	.01
☐ 254 Cody Carlson	.05	.02	.01
☐ 255 Kevin Greene	.10	.05	.01
☐ 256 Leonard Russell	.05	.02	.01
☐ 257 Donnell Bennett	.05	.02	.01

☐ 258 Rocket Ismail	.10	.05	.01
☐ 259 Alfred Pupunu	.05	.02	.01
☐ 260 Eugene Robinson	.05	.02	.01
☐ 261 Seth Joyner	.05	.02	.01
☐ 262 Darren Woodson	.10	.05	.01
☐ 263 Phillippi Sparks	.05	.02	.01
☐ 264 Andy Harmon	.05	.02	.01
☐ 265 Brian Mitchell	.05	.02	.01
☐ 266 Fuad Reveiz	.05	.02	.01
☐ 267 Mark Carrier DB	.05	.02	.01
☐ 268 Johnnie Morton	.10	.05	.01
☐ 269 LeShon Johnson	.10	.05	.01
☐ 270 Eric Curry	.05	.02	.01
☐ 271 Quinn Early	.10	.05	.01
☐ 272 Elbert Shelley	.05	.02	.01
☐ 273 Roman Phifer	.05	.02	.01
☐ 274 Ken Norton Jr.	.10	.05	.01
☐ 275 Steve Tasker	.10	.05	.01
☐ 276 Jim Harbaugh	.10	.05	.01
☐ 277 Aubrey Beavers	.05	.02	.01
☐ 278 Chris Slade	.10	.05	.01
☐ 279 Mo Lewis	.05	.02	.01
☐ 280 Alfred Williams	.05	.02	.01
☐ 281 Michael Dean Perry UER misspelled Micheal	.05	.02	.01
☐ 282 Marcus Robertson	.05	.02	.01
☐ 283 Rod Woodson	.10	.05	.01
☐ 284 Glyn Milburn	.05	.02	.01
☐ 285 Greg Hill	.10	.05	.01
☐ 286 Rob Fredrickson	.05	.02	.01
☐ 287 Junior Seau	.20	.09	.03
☐ 288 Rick Tuten	.05	.02	.01
☐ 289 Aeneas Williams	.05	.02	.01
☐ 290 Darrin Smith	.05	.02	.01
☐ 291 John Booty	.05	.02	.01
☐ 292 Eric Allen	.05	.02	.01
☐ 293 Reggie Roby	.05	.02	.01
☐ 294 David Palmer	.10	.05	.01
☐ 295 Trace Armstrong	.05	.02	.01
☐ 296 Dave Krieg UER misspelled Kreig on front	.05	.02	.01
☐ 297 Robert Brooks	.20	.09	.03
☐ 298 Brad Culpepper	.05	.02	.01
☐ 299 Wayne Martin	.05	.02	.01
☐ 300 Craig Heyward	.10	.05	.01
☐ 301 Isaac Bruce	.50	.23	.06
☐ 302 Deion Sanders	.60	.25	.07
☐ 303 Matt Darby	.05	.02	.01
☐ 304 Kirk Lowdermilk	.05	.02	.01
☐ 305 Bernie Parmalee	.10	.05	.01
☐ 306 Leroy Thompson	.05	.02	.01
☐ 307 Ronnie Lott	.10	.05	.01
☐ 308 Steve Tovar	.05	.02	.01
☐ 309 Michael Jackson	.10	.05	.01
☐ 310 Al Smith	.05	.02	.01
☐ 311 Chad Brown	.10	.05	.01
☐ 312 Elijah Alexander	.05	.02	.01
☐ 313 Kimble Anders	.10	.05	.01
☐ 314 Anthony Smith	.05	.02	.01
☐ 315 Andre Coleman	.05	.02	.01
☐ 316 Terry Wooden	.05	.02	.01
☐ 317 Garrison Hearst	.20	.09	.03
☐ 318 Russell Maryland	.05	.02	.01
☐ 319 Michael Brooks	.05	.02	.01
☐ 320 Bernard Williams	.05	.02	.01
☐ 321 Andre Collins	.05	.02	.01
☐ 322 Dewayne Washington	.10	.05	.01
☐ 323 Raymont Harris	.05	.02	.01
☐ 324 Brett Perriman	.10	.05	.01
☐ 325 LeRoy Butler	.05	.02	.01
☐ 326 Santana Dotson	.05	.02	.01
☐ 327 Irv Smith	.05	.02	.01
☐ 328 Ron George	.05	.02	.01
☐ 329 Marquez Pope	.05	.02	.01
☐ 330 William Floyd	.20	.09	.03
☐ 331 Mickey Washington	.05	.02	.01
☐ 332 Keith Goganious	.05	.02	.01
☐ 333 Derek Brown TE	.05	.02	.01
☐ 334 Steve Beuerlein UER Name spelled Beuerlien on front	.05	.02	.01
☐ 335 Reggie Cobb	.05	.02	.01
☐ 336 Jeff Lageman	.05	.02	.01
☐ 337 Kelvin Martin	.05	.02	.01
☐ 338 Darren Carrington	.05	.02	.01
☐ 339 Mark Carrier WR	.10	.05	.01
☐ 340 Willie Green	.05	.02	.01
☐ 341 Frank Reich	.05	.02	.01
☐ 342 Don Beebe	.05	.02	.01
☐ 343 Lamar Lathon	.05	.02	.01
☐ 344 Tim McKyer	.05	.02	.01
☐ 345 Pete Metzelaars	.05	.02	.01
☐ 346 Vernon Turner	.05	.02	.01
☐ 347 Dan Marino Checklist 1-174	.25	.11	.03
☐ 348 Joe Montana Checklist 175-348	.20	.09	.03
☐ P1 Joe Montana Promo	1.50	.70	.19

1995 Collector's Choice Player's Club

This 348 card parallel set was randomly inserted into packs at a rate of one per pack. It features a silver "Player's Club" logo between a goal post in silver foil as well as having a silver border.

	MINT	NRMT	EXC
COMPLETE SET (348)	50.00	22.00	6.25
COMMON CARD (1-348)	.20	.09	.03
*VETERAN STARS: 1.25X TO 2.5X BASIC CARDS			
*YOUNG STARS: 1X TO 2X BASIC CARDS			
*RCs: 1X TO 2X BASIC CARDS			

1995 Collector's Choice Player's Club Platinum

This 348 card parallel set was randomly inserted into packs at a rate of one in 35 packs. It features a silver "Platinum Player's Club" logo between a goal post in silver foil as well as having a silver foil border.

	MINT	NRMT	EXC
COMPLETE SET (348)	800.00	350.00	100.00
COMMON CARD (1-348)	1.25	.55	.16
*VETERAN STARS: 15X TO 30X BASIC CARDS			
*YOUNG STARS: 10X TO 20X BASIC CARDS			
*RCs: 8X TO 16X BASIC CARDS			

1995 Collector's Choice Crash The Game

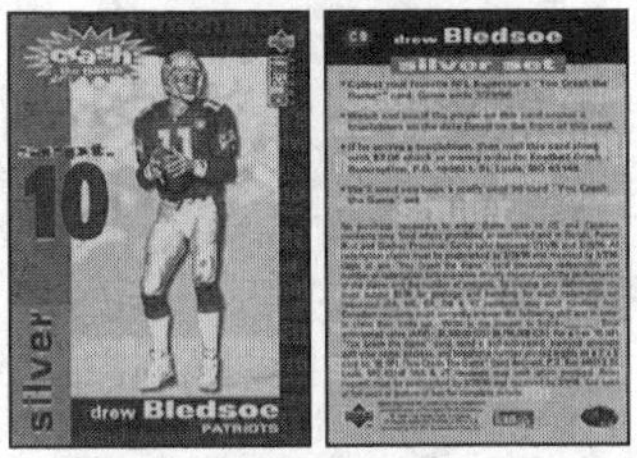

Thirty offensive players are included in this set. Each player has three different cards with different dates in foil layering on the front for a total of 90 cards. If the player scored or passed for a touchdown, the cards could be redeemed ($3 check or money order) for a special prize set. Each of the 90 cards were issued in Silver and Gold varieties. Silver cards were inserted one every five hobby packs, while the gold varieties were included one every 50 packs. The expiration date for the contest was February 29, 1996. The fronts feature posed player shots against a yellow background, surrounded by multi-colored borders. The backs contain contest information.

	MINT	NRMT	EXC
COMPLETE SILVER SET (90)	60.00	27.00	7.50
COMMON SILVER (C1A-C30C)	.40	.18	.05
COMPLETE GOLD SET (90)	600.00	275.00	75.00
*GOLD CARDS: 1.5X to 3X BASIC CARDS			
COMP.SILVER REDEMPT.(30)	8.00	3.60	1.00
*SILVER REDEMPT.CARDS: .25X TO .5X BASIC CARDS			
COMP.GOLD REDEMPT.(30)	40.00	18.00	5.00
*GOLD REDEMPT.CARDS: 1X TO 2X BASIC CARDS			

☐ C1A Dan Marino 9/10 W	2.50	1.10	.30
☐ C1B Dan Marino 10/8 W	2.50	1.10	.30
☐ C1C Dan Marino 11/20 W	2.50	1.10	.30
☐ C2A John Elway 9/3 L	1.00	.45	.12
☐ C2B John Elway 11/12 W	.75	.35	.09
☐ C2C John Elway 11/19 W	.75	.35	.09
☐ C3A Kerry Collins 10/1 W	1.50	.70	.19
☐ C3B Kerry Collins 10/29 W	1.50	.70	.19
☐ C3C Kerry Collins 11/12 W	1.50	.70	.19
☐ C4A Stan Humphries 9/3 W	.40	.18	.05
☐ C4B Stan Humphries 10/9 W	.40	.18	.05
☐ C4C Stan Humphries 11/5 W	.40	.18	.05
☐ C5A Steve Young 9/10 W	1.00	.45	.12
☐ C5B Steve Young 10/15 W	1.25	.55	.16
☐ C5C Steve Young 11/5 L	1.25	.55	.16
☐ C6A Brett Favre 9/17 W	2.50	1.10	.30
☐ C6B Brett Favre 9/24 W	1.25	.55	.16
☐ C6C Brett Favre 10/29 W	1.25	.55	.16
☐ C7A Troy Aikman 9/4 W	1.25	.55	.16
☐ C7B Troy Aikman 10/1 L	1.00	.45	.12
☐ C7C Troy Aikman 11/12 L	1.00	.45	.12
☐ C8A Warren Moon 9/3 W	.60	.25	.07
☐ C8B Warren Moon 10/8 W	.60	.25	.07
☐ C8C Warren Moon 11/23 W	.60	.25	.07
☐ C9A Drew Bledsoe 9/10 L	1.25	.55	.16
☐ C9B Drew Bledsoe 9/17 L	.75	.35	.09
☐ C9C Drew Bledsoe 10/23 W	1.00	.45	.12
☐ C10A Steve McNair 10/1 L	1.25	.55	.16
☐ C10B Steve McNair 10/29 L	1.25	.55	.16
☐ C10C Steve McNair 11/19 L	1.25	.55	.16
☐ C11A Chris Warren 10/22 W	.60	.25	.07
☐ C11B Chris Warren 11/12 W	.60	.25	.07
☐ C11C Chris Warren 11/26 L	.60	.25	.07
☐ C12A Natrone Means 10/1 W	.60	.25	.07
☐ C12B Natrone Means 10/9 W	.60	.25	.07
☐ C12C Natrone Means 11/27 L	.60	.25	.07
☐ C13A Thurman Thomas 9/17 W	.60	.25	.07
☐ C13B Thurman Thomas 10/22 L	.60	.25	.07
☐ C13C Thurman Thomas 12/3 L	.60	.25	.07
☐ C14A Barry Sanders 9/25 L	1.25	.55	.16
☐ C14B Barry Sanders 10/22 L	1.00	.45	.12
☐ C14C Barry Sanders 11/23 W	1.25	.55	.16
☐ C15A Emmitt Smith 9/10 W	2.50	1.10	.30
☐ C15B Emmitt Smith 10/29 W	2.50	1.10	.30
☐ C15C Emmitt Smith 11/19 W	2.50	1.10	.30
☐ C16A Jerome Bettis 9/10 L	.60	.25	.07
☐ C16B Jerome Bettis 10/22 L	.60	.25	.07
☐ C16C Jerome Bettis 11/19 L	.60	.25	.07
☐ C17A Ki-Jana Carter 9/10 L	.40	.18	.05
☐ C17B Ki-Jana Carter 10/1 L	.40	.18	.05
☐ C17C Ki-Jana Carter 11/12 L	.40	.18	.05
☐ C18A Napoleon Kaufman 10/8 L	.40	.18	.05
☐ C18B Napoleon Kaufman 11/5 L	.40	.18	.05
☐ C18C Napoleon Kaufman 12/3 L	.40	.18	.05
☐ C19A Marshall Faulk 9/3 L	.75	.35	.09
☐ C19B Marshall Faulk 10/1 W	1.00	.45	.12
☐ C19C Marshall Faulk 11/5 W	1.00	.45	.12
☐ C20A Errict Rhett 10/8 W	.60	.25	.07
☐ C20B Errict Rhett 10/22 W	.60	.25	.07
☐ C20C Errict Rhett 11/19 W	.60	.25	.07
☐ C21A Cris Carter 9/17 W	.60	.25	.07
☐ C21B Cris Carter 10/30 L	.60	.25	.07
☐ C21C Cris Carter 11/19 W	.60	.25	.07
☐ C22A Jerry Rice 9/3 W	1.25	.55	.16
☐ C22B Jerry Rice 10/1 W	1.25	.55	.16
☐ C22C Jerry Rice 11/26 W	1.25	.55	.16
☐ C23A Tim Brown 10/1 W	.60	.25	.07
☐ C23B Tim Brown 10/16 L	.60	.25	.07
☐ C23C Tim Brown 11/27 L	.60	.25	.07
☐ C24A Andre Reed 9/10 L	.40	.18	.05
☐ C24B Andre Reed 10/29 L	.40	.18	.05
☐ C24C Andre Reed 11/26 L	.40	.18	.05
☐ C25A Andre Rison 9/3 L	.40	.18	.05
☐ C25B Andre Rison 10/2 L	.40	.18	.05
☐ C25C Andre Rison 10/22 L	.40	.18	.05
☐ C26A Ben Coates 10/8 L	.40	.18	.05
☐ C26B Ben Coates 10/29 L	.40	.18	.05
☐ C26C Ben Coates 11/19 L	.40	.18	.05
☐ C27A Michael Irvin 9/17 W	.60	.25	.07
☐ C27B Michael Irvin 10/15 L	.60	.25	.07
☐ C27C Michael Irvin 11/6 W	.60	.25	.07
☐ C28B Terance Mathis 10/1 L	.40	.18	.05
☐ C28C Terance Mathis 10/12 L	.40	.18	.05
☐ C29A Michael Westbrook 9/24 L	.60	.25	.07
☐ C29B Michael Westbrook 10/22 L	.60	.25	.07
☐ C29C Michael Westbrook 11/19 W	.60	.25	.07
☐ C30A Herman Moore 9/10 W	.60	.25	.07
☐ C30B Herman Moore 10/15 W	.60	.25	.07
☐ C30C Herman Moore 11/12 L	.60	.25	.07

1995 Collector's Choice Dan Marino Chronicles

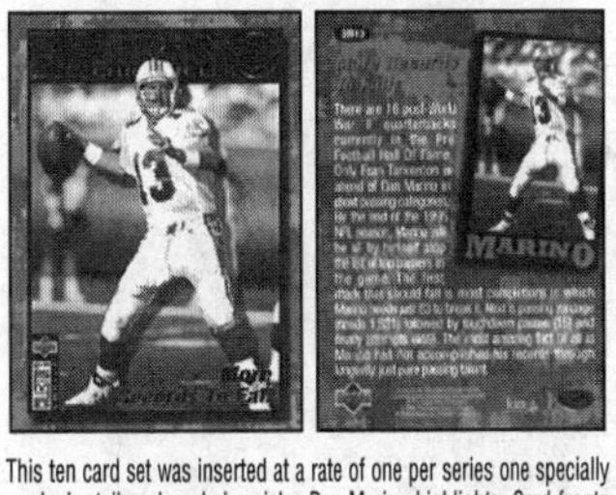

This ten card set was inserted at a rate of one per series one specially marked retail pack and chronicles Dan Marino highlights. Card fronts contain an aqua border with the title "Marino" in gold foil at the top of the card. The feat being highlighted on the card is also written in gold foil on the card fronts. Card backs contain a commentary on the highlight. Cards are numbered with a "DM" prefix.

	MINT	NRMT	EXC
COMPLETE SET (10)	12.00	5.50	1.50
COMMON CARD (DM1-DM10)	1.50	.70	.19

☐ DM1 Dan Marino Rookie of the Year	1.50	.70	.19
☐ DM2 Dan Marino 5000 Yards Passing	1.50	.70	.19
☐ DM3 Dan Marino 48 TD Passes	1.50	.70	.19
☐ DM4 Dan Marino Super Bowl XIX	1.50	.70	.19
☐ DM5 Dan Marino 30,000 Yards Passing	1.50	.70	.19
☐ DM6 Dan Marino 4000-Yard Season	1.50	.70	.19
☐ DM7 Dan Marino 40,000 Yards Passing	1.50	.70	.19
☐ DM8 Dan Marino Marino's Back	1.50	.70	.19
☐ DM9 Dan Marino 300th TD Pass	1.50	.70	.19
☐ DM10 Dan Marino More Records to Fall	1.50	.70	.19

1995 Collector's Choice Joe Montana Chronicles

This ten card set was inserted at a rate of one per series two specially marked retail pack and chronicles Joe Montana highlights. Card fronts contain a red border with the title "Montana" in gold foil at the top of the card. The feat being highlighted on the card is also written in gold foil on the card fronts. Card backs contain a commentary on the highlight. Cards are numbered with a "JM" prefix.

	MINT	NRMT	EXC
COMPLETE SET (10)	12.00	5.50	1.50
COMMON CARD (JM1-JM10)	1.50	.70	.19

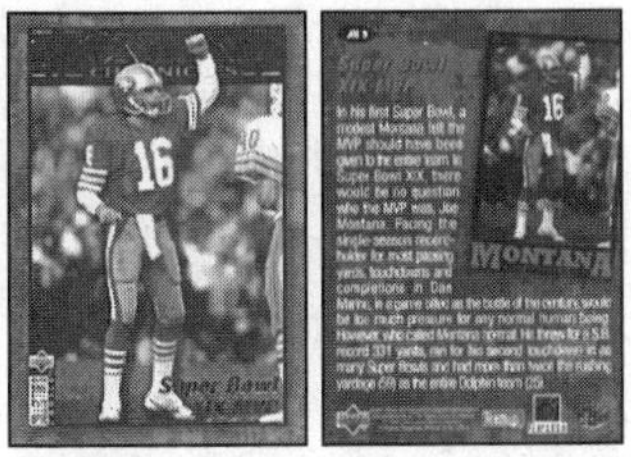

☐ JM1 Joe Montana The Catch	1.50	.70	.19
☐ JM2 Joe Montana Super Bowl XVI	1.50	.70	.19
☐ JM3 Joe Montana	1.50	.70	.19
☐ JM4 Joe Montana Super Bowl XIX	1.50	.70	.19
☐ JM5 Joe Montana	1.50	.70	.19
☐ JM6 Joe Montana	1.50	.70	.19
☐ JM7 Joe Montana Super Bowl XXIII	1.50	.70	.19
☐ JM8 Joe Montana Super Bowl XXIV	1.50	.70	.19
☐ JM9 Joe Montana Super Bowl XXIV MVP	1.50	.70	.19
☐ JM10 Joe Montana Back to Back Super Bowls	1.50	.70	.19

1995 Collector's Choice Update

This 225 card update set was produced late in the 1995 season and the format of the cards are identical to the regular Collector's Choice release. Subsets include Rookie Collection cards featuring first-year players, Expansion cards from Carolina and Jacksonville and The Key cards describing what NFL teams do to stop "key" players on each NFL team. Rookie Cards not included in the first issue include Terrell Davis, Curtis Martin, Kordell Stewart and Tamarick Vanover. Each card has a "U" prefix. Also, a parallel of the cards were randomly inserted in packs as Silver and Gold versions.

	MINT	NRMT	EXC
COMPLETE SET (225)	18.00	8.00	2.20
COMMON CARD (U1-U225)	.05	.02	.01

☐ U1 Roell Preston	.05	.02	.01
☐ U2 Lorenzo Styles	.05	.02	.01
☐ U3 Todd Collins	.20	.09	.03
☐ U4 Darick Holmes	.50	.23	.06
☐ U5 Justin Armour	.05	.02	.01
☐ U6 Tony Cline	.05	.02	.01
☐ U7 Tyrone Poole	.10	.05	.01
☐ U8 Kerry Collins	1.50	.70	.19
☐ U9 Sean Harris	.05	.02	.01
☐ U10 Steve Stenstrom	.05	.02	.01
☐ U11 Rashaan Salaam	.60	.25	.07
☐ U12 Ki-Jana Carter	.50	.23	.06
☐ U13 Craig Powell	.05	.02	.01
☐ U14 Eric Zeier	.20	.09	.03
☐ U15 Ernest Hunter	.05	.02	.01
☐ U16 Sherman Williams	.05	.02	.01
☐ U17 Terrell Davis	4.00	1.80	.50
☐ U18 Luther Elliss	.05	.02	.01
☐ U19 Craig Newsome	.05	.02	.01
☐ U20 Steve McNair	1.25	.55	.16
☐ U21 Chris Sanders	1.25	.55	.16
☐ U22 Rodney Thomas	.20	.09	.03
☐ U23 Ellis Johnson	.05	.02	.01
☐ U24 Ken Dilger	.10	.05	.01
☐ U25 Zack Crockett	.05	.02	.01
☐ U26 Tony Boselli	.10	.05	.01
☐ U27 Rob Johnson	.05	.02	.01
☐ U28 James O.Stewart	.10	.05	.01
☐ U29 Tamarick Vanover	1.25	.55	.16
☐ U30 Napoleon Kaufman	.20	.09	.03
☐ U31 Kevin Carter	.20	.09	.03
☐ U32 Steve McLaughlin	.05	.02	.01
☐ U33 Lovell Pinkney	.05	.02	.01
☐ U34 Pete Mitchell	.10	.05	.01
☐ U35 James A.Stewart	.05	.02	.01
☐ U36 Chad May	.05	.02	.01
☐ U37 Derrick Alexander DE	.05	.02	.01
☐ U38 Curtis Martin	4.00	1.80	.50
☐ U39 Will Moore	.05	.02	.01
☐ U40 Ty Law	.10	.05	.01
☐ U41 Ray Zellars	.10	.05	.01
☐ U42 Mark Fields	.05	.02	.01
☐ U43 Tyrone Wheatley	.20	.09	.03
☐ U44 Kyle Brady	.20	.09	.03
☐ U45 Mike Mamula	.10	.05	.01
☐ U46 Bobby Taylor	.10	.05	.01
☐ U47 Chris T.Jones	.20	.09	.03
☐ U48 Frank Sanders	.50	.23	.06
☐ U49 Stoney Case	.05	.02	.01
☐ U50 Mark Bruener	.10	.05	.01
☐ U51 Kordell Stewart	3.00	1.35	.35
☐ U52 Jimmy Oliver	.05	.02	.01
☐ U53 Terrance Shaw	.05	.02	.01
☐ U54 Terrell Fletcher	.05	.02	.01
☐ U55 J.J. Stokes	.50	.23	.06
☐ U56 Christian Fauria	.05	.02	.01
☐ U57 Joey Galloway	1.00	.45	.12

	MINT	NRMT	EXC
☐ U58 Warren Sapp	.10	.05	.01
☐ U59 Derrick Brooks	.05	.02	.01
☐ U60 Michael Westbrook	.60	.25	.07
☐ U61 Emmitt Smith K	1.00	.45	.12
☐ U62 Barry Sanders K	.50	.23	.06
☐ U63 Marshall Faulk K	.20	.09	.03
☐ U64 Troy Aikman K	.50	.23	.06
☐ U65 Steve Young K	.40	.18	.05
☐ U66 Junior Seau K	.20	.09	.03
☐ U67 John Elway K	.40	.18	.05
☐ U68 Dan Marino K	1.00	.45	.12
☐ U69 Drew Bledsoe K	.50	.23	.06
☐ U70 Errict Rhett K	.20	.09	.03
☐ U71 Natrone Means K	.20	.09	.03
☐ U72 Deion Sanders K	.30	.14	.04
☐ U73 Brett Favre K	1.00	.45	.12
☐ U74 Cris Carter K	.20	.09	.03
☐ U75 Ben Coates K	.10	.05	.01
☐ U76 Jerome Bettis K	.20	.09	.03
☐ U77 Reggie White K	.20	.09	.03
☐ U78 Stan Humphries K	.05	.02	.01
☐ U79 Michael Westbrook K	.40	.18	.05
☐ U80 Steve McNair K	.75	.35	.09
☐ U81 Kevin Greene K	.10	.05	.01
☐ U82 Joey Galloway K	.60	.25	.07
☐ U83 Napoleon Kaufman K	.10	.05	.01
☐ U84 Jerry Rice K	.50	.23	.06
☐ U85 Andre Rison K	.10	.05	.01
☐ U86 Eric Metcalf K	.10	.05	.01
☐ U87 Kerry Collins K	1.00	.45	.12
☐ U88 Chris Warren K	.10	.05	.01
☐ U89 Irving Fryar K	.10	.05	.01
☐ U90 Michael Irvin K	.20	.09	.03
☐ U91 Don Beebe	.05	.02	.01
☐ U92 Pete Metzelaars	.05	.02	.01
☐ U93 Mark Carrier	.05	.02	.01
☐ U94 Frank Reich	.05	.02	.01
☐ U95 Randy Baldwin	.05	.02	.01
☐ U96 Bob Christian	.05	.02	.01
☐ U97 John Kasay	.05	.02	.01
☐ U98 Lamar Lathon	.05	.02	.01
☐ U99 Sam Mills	.10	.05	.01
☐ U100 Carlton Bailey	.05	.02	.01
☐ U101 Darion Conner	.05	.02	.01
☐ U102 Blake Brockermeyer	.05	.02	.01
☐ U103 Gerald Williamss	.05	.02	.01
☐ U104 Willie Green	.05	.02	.01
☐ U105 Derrick Moore	.05	.02	.01
☐ U106 Desmond Howard	.10	.05	.01
☐ U107 Harry Colon	.05	.02	.01
☐ U108 Steve Beuerlein	.05	.02	.01
☐ U109 Reggie Cobb	.05	.02	.01
☐ U110 Jeff Lageman	.05	.02	.01
☐ U111 Mark Brunell UER	1.25	.55	.16
name spelled Brunnell on front			
☐ U112 Darren Carrington	.05	.02	.01
☐ U113 Brian DeMarco	.10	.05	.01
☐ U114 Ernest Givins	.05	.02	.01
☐ U115 Le'shai Maston	.05	.02	.01
☐ U116 Willie Jackson	.10	.05	.01
☐ U117 Keith Goganious	.05	.02	.01
☐ U118 Kelvin Pritchett	.05	.02	.01
☐ U119 Ryan Christopherson	.05	.02	.01
☐ U120 Bryan Schwartz	.05	.02	.01
☐ U121 Dave Krieg UER	.05	.02	.01
name spelled Kreig on front			
☐ U122 Darryl Talley	.05	.02	.01
☐ U123 Bryce Paup	.20	.09	.03
☐ U124 Anthony Johnson	.10	.05	.01
☐ U125 Eric Bieniemy	.05	.02	.01
☐ U126 Andre Rison	.10	.05	.01
☐ U127 Rodney Peete	.05	.02	.01
☐ U128 Aaron Craver	.05	.02	.01
☐ U129 Henry Thomas	.05	.02	.01
☐ U130 Antonio Freeman	1.50	.70	.19
☐ U131 Chris Chandler	.10	.05	.01
☐ U132 Craig Erickson	.05	.02	.01
☐ U133 Roell Preston	.05	.02	.01
☐ U134 Brian Washington	.05	.02	.01
☐ U135 Eric Green	.05	.02	.01
☐ U136 Broderick Thomas	.05	.02	.01
☐ U137 Dave Meggett	.05	.02	.01
☐ U138 Eric Allen	.05	.02	.01
☐ U139 Herschel Walker	.10	.05	.01
☐ U140 Dexter Carter	.05	.02	.01
☐ U141 Kerry Cash	.05	.02	.01
☐ U142 Kelvin Martin	.05	.02	.01
☐ U143 Erric Pegram	.10	.05	.01
☐ U144 Bo Orlando	.05	.02	.01
☐ U145 Ricky Ervins	.05	.02	.01
☐ U146 John Friesz	.10	.05	.01
☐ U147 Alexander Wright	.05	.02	.01
☐ U148 Alvin Harper	.05	.02	.01
☐ U149 Gus Frerotte	.50	.23	.06
☐ U150 Duval Love	.05	.02	.01
☐ U151 Eric Metcalf	.10	.05	.01
☐ U152 Ruben Brown	.05	.02	.01
☐ U153 Marty Carter	.05	.02	.01
☐ U154 James Joseph	.05	.02	.01
☐ U155 Hugh Douglas	.10	.05	.01
☐ U156 Wade Wilson	.05	.02	.01
☐ U157 Britt Hager	.05	.02	.01
☐ U158 Mark Schlereth	.05	.02	.01
☐ U159 Cory Schlesinger UER	.05	.02	.01
(name spelled Corey)			
☐ U160 Mark Ingram	.05	.02	.01
☐ U161 Mark Stepnoski	.05	.02	.01
☐ U162 Flipper Anderson	.05	.02	.01
☐ U163 Donta Jones	.05	.02	.01
☐ U164 James Hasty	.05	.02	.01
☐ U165 Gary Clark	.05	.02	.01
☐ U166 David Sloan	.10	.05	.01
☐ U167 Jeff Dellenbach	.05	.02	.01
☐ U168 Rufus Porter	.05	.02	.01
☐ U169 Mike Croel	.05	.02	.01
☐ U170 Charles Wilson Jets UER	.05	.02	.01
Card number 242			
see '95 Coll.Choice #242			
☐ U171 Pat Swilling	.05	.02	.01
☐ U172 Kurt Gouveia	.05	.02	.01
☐ U173 Norm Johnson	.05	.02	.01
☐ U174 Shaun Gayle	.05	.02	.01
☐ U175 Marquez Pope	.05	.02	.01
☐ U176 Tyronne Stowe	.05	.02	.01
☐ U177 Anthony Parker	.05	.02	.01
☐ U178 Kenneth Gant	.05	.02	.01
☐ U179 James Washington	.05	.02	.01
☐ U180 Rob Moore	.05	.02	.01
☐ U181 Alundis Brice	.05	.02	.01
☐ U182 Lamont Warren	.05	.02	.01
☐ U183 Michael Timpson	.05	.02	.01
☐ U184 Lorenzo White	.05	.02	.01
☐ U185 Charlie Williams	.05	.02	.01
☐ U186 Ed McCaffrey	.05	.02	.01
☐ U187 James Jones	.05	.02	.01
☐ U188 Derrick Fenner	.05	.02	.01
☐ U189 Mel Gray	.05	.02	.01
☐ U190 James Williams	.05	.02	.01
☐ U191 Jeff Criswell	.05	.02	.01
☐ U192 Randal Hill	.05	.02	.01
☐ U193 Terry Allen	.10	.05	.01
☐ U194 Joel Smeenge	.05	.02	.01
☐ U195 Ricky Watters	.20	.09	.03
☐ U196 Don Sasa	.05	.02	.01
☐ U197 Steve Bono	.10	.05	.01
☐ U198 Steve Broussard	.05	.02	.01
☐ U199 Carlos Jenkins	.05	.02	.01
☐ U200 Reggie Roby	.05	.02	.01
☐ U201 Stanley Richard	.05	.02	.01
☐ U202 Vince Workman	.05	.02	.01
☐ U203 Eric Guilford	.05	.02	.01
☐ U204 Lionel Washington	.05	.02	.01
☐ U205 Brian Williams	.05	.02	.01
☐ U206 Ronnie Lott	.10	.05	.01
☐ U207 Corey Harris	.05	.02	.01
☐ U208 Harlon Barnett	.05	.02	.01
☐ U209 Bubby Brister	.05	.02	.01
☐ U210 Darren Bennett	.10	.05	.01
☐ U211 Winston Moss	.05	.02	.01
☐ U212 Leonard Russell	.05	.02	.01
☐ U213 Ron Davis	.05	.02	.01
☐ U214 Curtis Whitley	.05	.02	.01
☐ U215 Webster Slaughter	.05	.02	.01
☐ U216 Korey Stringer	.05	.02	.01
☐ U217 Don Davey	.05	.02	.01
☐ U218 Mark Rypien	.05	.02	.01
☐ U219 Chad Cota	.05	.02	.01
☐ U220 Tim Ruddy	.05	.02	.01
☐ U221 Corey Fuller	.05	.02	.01
☐ U222 Mike Dumas	.05	.02	.01
☐ U223 Eddie Murray	.05	.02	.01
☐ U224 Checklist (U1-U114)	.50	.23	.06
Dan Marino			
☐ U225 Checklist (U115-U228)	.50	.23	.06
Dan Marino			
☐ P1 Michael Westbrook Promo	.75	.35	.09
Numbered CUS1			
☐ P2 Dan Marino Promo	1.00	.45	.12
Stick-um card, blankbacked			
☐ P3 Dan Marino Promo	.75	.35	.09
Michael Westbrook			
Tim Brown			
Stick-um card, blankbacked			

1995 Collector's Choice Update Gold

This 90 card set was randomly inserted into packs at a rate of one in 35 packs for the Rookie Collection subset and one in 52 packs for The Key subset. The cards are differentiated on the front with the card name in gold foil.

	MINT	NRMT	EXC
COMPLETE SET (90)	450.00	200.00	55.00
COMMON CARD (U1-U90)	1.50	.70	.19

*VETERAN STARS: 15X TO 30X BASIC CARDS
*YOUNG STARS/RCs: 10X TO 20X BASIC CARDS

1995 Collector's Choice Update Silver

This 90 card set was randomly inserted into packs at a rate of one in three packs for the Rookie Collection subset and one in five packs for The Key subset. The cards are differentiated on the front with the card name in silver foil.

	MINT	NRMT	EXC
COMPLETE SET (90)	50.00	22.00	6.25
COMMON CARD (U1-U90)	.15	.07	.02

*VETERAN STARS: 1.5X TO 3X BASIC CARDS
*YOUNG STARS/RCs: 1.25X TO 2.5X BASIC CARDS

1995 Collector's Choice Update Crash the Playoffs

This 18 card set was randomly inserted in packs at a rate of one in five for silver and one in 50 for gold. Each card contains five players representing the same position - either quarterback, running back or receiver. If any of the players pictured on the card threw or caught a touchdown pass, or rushed or returned a kick for a touchdown during the 1995 NFL Playoffs and Super Bowl XXX, the card was a winner. Winning cards could be redeemed for the Post Season Heroics set in either Gold foil or silver foil depending on which foil the winning Crash card featured.

	MINT	NRMT	EXC
COMPLETE SET (18)	20.00	9.00	2.50
COMMON CARD (CP1-CP18)	.50	.23	.06
☐ CP1 AFC East QB	3.00	1.35	.35
☐ CP2 AFC Central QB	1.25	.55	.16
☐ CP3 AFC West QB	1.00	.45	.12
☐ CP4 NFC East QB	1.50	.70	.19
☐ CP5 NFC Central QB	3.00	1.35	.35
☐ CP6 NFC West QB	1.50	.70	.19
☐ CP7 AFC East RB	2.50	1.10	.30
☐ CP8 AFC Central RB	.50	.23	.06
☐ CP9 AFC West RB	2.50	1.10	.30
☐ CP10 NFC East RB	.75	.35	.09
☐ CP11 NFC Central WR	.50	.23	.06
☐ CP12 NFC West RB	.50	.23	.06
☐ CP13 AFC East WR	.50	.23	.06
☐ CP14 AFC Central WR	.50	.23	.06
☐ CP15 AFC West WR	1.00	.45	.12
☐ CP16 NFC East WR	.75	.35	.09
☐ CP17 NFC Central RB	1.50	.70	.19
☐ CP18 NFC West WR	1.50	.70	.19

1995 Collector's Choice Update Crash the Playoffs Gold

This set is the Gold foil parallel to the 1995 Collector's Choice Update Crash the Playoffs insert. The cards were randomly inserted in packs and carry a gold, instead of silver, foil layering.

	MINT	NRMT	EXC
COMP.GOLD SET (18)	50.00	22.00	6.25
COMMON GOLD CARD (CP1-CP18) ..	1.50	.70	.19

*GOLD CARDS: 1.5X TO3 X BASIC CARDS

1995 Collector's Choice Update Post Season Heroics

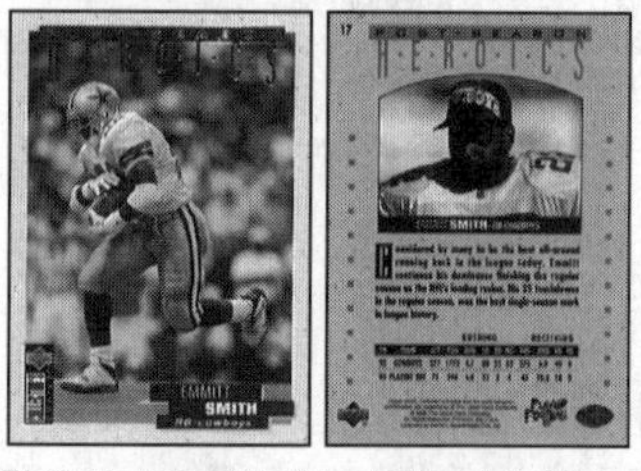

This 20 card set was available only by redeeming a winning Collectors Choice Update Crash the Playoffs silver or gold card. The cards are similar to regular Collector's Choice cards with the phrase "Post Season Heroics" written across the top of the card in either silver or gold foil. Card backs include regular season and playoff statistics.

	MINT	NRMT	EXC
COMPLETE SET (20)	12.00	5.50	1.50
COMMON CARD (1-20)	.30	.14	.04
☐ 1 Stan Humphries	.30	.14	.04
☐ 2 Natrone Means	.60	.25	.07
☐ 3 Tony Martin	.30	.14	.04
☐ 4 Neil O'Donnell	.60	.25	.07
☐ 5 Byron Bam Morris	.30	.14	.04
☐ 6 Charles Johnson	.30	.14	.04
☐ 7 Jim Harbaugh	.60	.25	.07
☐ 8 Darick Holmes	.30	.14	.04
☐ 9 Sean Dawkins	.30	.14	.04
☐ 10 Steve Young	1.50	.70	.19
☐ 11 Craig Heyward	.30	.14	.04
☐ 12 Jerry Rice	2.00	.90	.25
☐ 13 Brett Favre	4.00	1.80	.50
☐ 14 Edgar Bennett	.50	.23	.06
☐ 15 Robert Brooks	.60	.25	.07
☐ 16 Troy Aikman	2.00	.90	.25
☐ 17 Emmitt Smith	4.00	1.80	.50
☐ 18 Michael Irvin	.60	.25	.07
☐ 19 Byron Bam Morris	.30	.14	.04
☐ 20 Larry Brown	.30	.14	.04

1995 Collector's Choice Update Post Season Heroics Gold

This 20 card set was available only by redeeming a winning Collectors Choice Update Crash the Playoffs gold card. The cards are similar to regular Collector's Choice cards with the phrase "Post Season

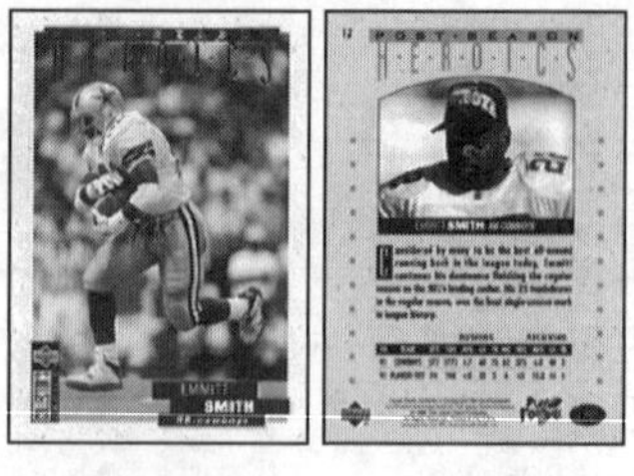

Heroics" written across the top of the card in gold foil. Card backs include regular season and playoff statistics.

	MINT	NRMT	EXC
COMP.GOLD SET (20)	40.00	18.00	5.00
COMMON GOLD CARD (1-20)	1.00	.45	.12
☐ 1 Stan Humphries	1.00	.45	.12
☐ 2 Natrone Means	2.00	.90	.25
☐ 3 Tony Martin	1.00	.45	.12
☐ 4 Neil O'Donnell	2.00	.90	.25
☐ 5 Byron Bam Morris	1.00	.45	.12
☐ 6 Charles Johnson	1.00	.45	.12
☐ 7 Jim Harbaugh	2.00	.90	.25
☐ 8 Darick Holmes	1.00	.45	.12
☐ 9 Sean Dawkins	1.00	.45	.12
☐ 10 Steve Young	4.50	2.00	.55
☐ 11 Craig Heyward	1.00	.45	.12
☐ 12 Jerry Rice	6.00	2.70	.75
☐ 13 Brett Favre	12.00	5.50	1.50
☐ 14 Edgar Bennett	1.50	.70	.19
☐ 15 Robert Brooks	2.00	.90	.25
☐ 16 Troy Aikman	6.00	2.70	.75
☐ 17 Emmitt Smith	12.00	5.50	1.50
☐ 18 Michael Irvin	2.00	.90	.25
☐ 19 Byron Bam Morris	1.00	.45	.12
☐ 20 Larry Brown	1.00	.45	.12

1995 Collector's Choice Update Stick-Ums

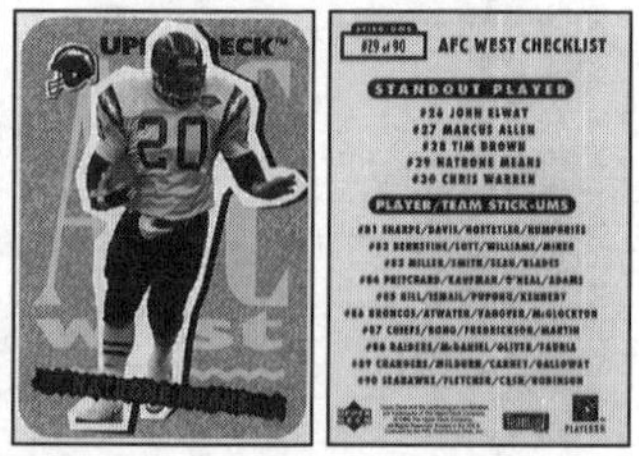

Randomly inserted in packs at a rate of one per pack, this 90-card set features a trading-card size sticker picturing the NFL's top stars. The Stick-Ums were available in three versions - one with four players on a card, one with three players and a team helmet and one with a larger photo of a star player. Stick-Ums Collector books were available through an on-pack offer for $2 and two Collector's Choice Update wrappers.

	MINT	NRMT	EXC
COMPLETE SET (90)	12.00	5.50	1.50
COMMON CARD (1-90)	.10	.05	.01
☐ 1 Jeff George	.25	.11	.03
☐ 2 Kerry Collins	.60	.25	.07
☐ 3 Jerome Bettis	.25	.11	.03
☐ 4 Mario Bates	.15	.07	.02
☐ 5 Steve Young	.40	.18	.05
☐ 6 Rashaan Salaam	.25	.11	.03
☐ 7 Barry Sanders	.50	.23	.06
☐ 8 Brett Favre	1.00	.45	.12
☐ 9 Warren Moon	.25	.11	.03
☐ 10 Errict Rhett	.15	.07	.02
☐ 11 Emmitt Smith	1.00	.45	.12
☐ 12 Rodney Hampton	.15	.07	.02
☐ 13 Ricky Watters	.25	.11	.03
☐ 14 Garrison Hearst	.25	.11	.03
☐ 15 Michael Westbrook	.25	.11	.03
☐ 16 Jim Kelly	.25	.11	.03
☐ 17 Marshall Faulk	.25	.11	.03
☐ 18 Dan Marino	1.00	.45	.12
☐ 19 Drew Bledsoe	.50	.23	.06
☐ 20 Kyle Brady	.15	.07	.02
☐ 21 Ki-Jana Carter	.15	.07	.02
☐ 22 Andre Rison	.15	.07	.02
☐ 23 Steve McNair	.50	.23	.06
☐ 24 James O.Stewart	.25	.11	.03
☐ 25 Byron Bam Morris	.15	.07	.02
☐ 26 John Elway	.40	.18	.05
☐ 27 Marcus Allen	.25	.11	.03
☐ 28 Tim Brown	.25	.11	.03
☐ 29 Natrone Means	.25	.11	.03
☐ 30 Chris Warren	.15	.07	.02
☐ 31 Terence Mathis	.15	.07	.02
Mark Carrier WR			
Chris Miller			
Jim Everett			
☐ 32 Bert Emanuel	.25	.11	.03

Pete Metzelaars
Isaac Bruce
Dana Stubblefield
□ 33 Chris Doleman .30 .14 .04
Frank Reich
Derek Brown RB
Jerry Rice
□ 34 Jesse Tuggle .30 .14 .04
Roman Phifer
Tyrone Hughes
Steve Young
□ 35 Sam Mills .10 .05 .01
Kevin Carter
Michael Haynes
Brent Jones
□ 36 Falcons Helmet .10 .05 .01
Eric Metcalf
Tyrone Poole
Lovell Pinkney
□ 37 Panthers Helmet .10 .05 .01
Morten Andersen UER
(Morton on front)
John Kasay
Troy Drayton
□ 38 Rams Helmet .30 .14 .04
Sean Gilbert
Mark Fields
J.J.Stokes
□ 39 Saints Helmet#Bob Christian .. .10 .05 .01
Willie Roaf
Ken Norton
□ 40 49ers Helmet .10 .05 .01
Craig Heyward
Renaldo Turnbull
William Floyd
□ 41 Raymont Harris .25 .11 .03
Herman Moore
Edgar Bennett
Cris Carter
□ 42 Jeff Graham .25 .11 .03
Henry Thomas
Reggie White
Trent Dilfer
□ 43 Curtis Conway .25 .11 .03
Scott Mitchell
Robert Smith
Alvin Harper
□ 44 Steve Walsh .10 .05 .01
Sean Jones
Qadry Ismail
Hardy Nickerson
□ 45 Bennie Blades .10 .05 .01
John Jurkovic
John Randle
Courtney Hawkins
□ 46 Bears Helmet .10 .05 .01
John Thierry
Luther Elliss
Leroy Butler
□ 47 Lions Helmet .25 .11 .03
Johnnie Morton
Robert Brooks
Jake Reed
□ 48 Packers Helmet .10 .05 .01
LeShon Johnson
Dewayne Washington
Jackie Harris
□ 49 Vikings Helmet .10 .05 .01
Donnell Woolford
James A.Stewart
Eric Curry
□ 50 Buccaneers Helmet .10 .05 .01
Mark Carrier DB
Chris Spielman
Warren Sapp
□ 51 Troy Aikman .30 .14 .04
Mike Sherrard
Fred Barnett
Dave Krieg
□ 52 Michael Irvin .15 .07 .02
Chris Calloway
Calvin Williams
Henry Ellard
□ 53 Sherman Williams .25 .11 .03
Dave Brown
Rob Moore
Heath Shuler
□ 54 Charles Haley .15 .07 .02
Randall Cunningham
Eric Swann
Ken Harvey
□ 55 Thomas Lewis .10 .05 .01
Charlie Garner
Clyde Simmons
Tom Carter
□ 56 Cowboys Helmet .15 .07 .02
Tyrone Wheatley
Bobby Taylor
Daryl Johnston
□ 57 Giants Helmet .10 .05 .01
Mike Croel
Byron Evans
Aeneas Williams
□ 58 Eagles Helmet .10 .05 .01
Mike Mamula
Larry Centers
Brian Mitchell
□ 59 Cardinals Helmet .25 .11 .03
Jay Novacek
Frank Sanders
Terry Allen
□ 60 Redskins Helmet .25 .11 .03
Deion Sanders
Herschel Walker
Sterling Palmer
□ 61 Henry Jones .10 .05 .01
Craig Erickson
Terry Kirby
Ben Coates
□ 62 Andre Reed .15 .07 .02
Flipper Anderson
Irving Fryar
Johnny Mitchell
□ 63 Russell Copeland .15 .07 .02
Sean Dawkins
Vincent Brisby
Boomer Esiason
□ 64 Bruce Smith .25 .11 .03
O.J.McDuffie
Willie McGinest
Ryan Yarborough
□ 65 Roosevelt Potts .75 .35 .09
Keith Byars
Curtis Martin
Brad Baxter
□ 66 Bills Helmet .10 .05 .01
Cornelius Bennett
Ray Buchanan
Marco Coleman
□ 67 Colts Helmet .10 .05 .01
Quentin Coryatt
Bryan Cox
Chris Slade
□ 68 Dolphins Helmet .10 .05 .01
Eric Green
Ty Law
Marvin Washington
□ 69 Patriots Helmet .10 .05 .01
Todd Collins
Vincent Brown
Ronald Moore
□ 70 Jets Helmet .10 .05 .01
Jeff Burris
Floyd Turner
Aaron Glenn
□ 71 Carl Pickens .25 .11 .03
Vinny Testaverde
Haywood Jeffires
Desmond Howard
□ 72 Darnay Scott .15 .07 .02
Eric Turner
Gary Brown
Neil O'Donnell
□ 73 David Klingler .15 .07 .02
Leroy Hoard
Tony Boselli
Charles Johnson
□ 74 Steve Tovar .10 .05 .01
Al Smith
Derek Brown TE
John L.Williams
□ 75 Lorenzo White .15 .07 .02
Rodney Thomas
Steve Beuerlein
Kevin Greene
□ 76 Bengals Helmet .30 .14 .04
Jeff Blake
Derrick Alexander WR
Ray Childress
□ 77 Browns Helmet .10 .05 .01
Eric Zeier
Mel Gray
Reggie Cobb
□ 78 Oilers Helmet .15 .07 .02
Todd McNair
Jeff Lageman
Greg Lloyd
□ 79 Jaguars Helmet .10 .05 .01
Dan Wilkinson
Rob Johnson
Rod Woodson
□ 80 Steelers Helmet .10 .05 .01
Eric Bieniemy
Antonio Langham
Mark Bruener
□ 81 Shannon Sharpe .25 .11 .03
Willie Davis
Jeff Hostetler
Stan Humphries
□ 82 Rod Bernstine .15 .07 .02
Ronnie Lott
Harvey Williams
Rick Mirer
□ 83 Anthony Miller .15 .07 .02
Neil Smith
Junior Seau
Brian Blades
□ 84 Mike Pritchard .15 .07 .02
Napoleon Kaufman
Leslie O'Neal
Sam Adams
□ 85 Greg Hill .15 .07 .02
Rocket Ismail
Alfred Pupunu
Cortez Kennedy
□ 86 Broncos Helmet .15 .07 .02
Steve Atwater
Tamarick Vanover
Chester McGlockton
□ 87 Chiefs Helmet .15 .07 .02
Steve Bono
Rob Fredrickson
Tony Martin
□ 88 Raiders Helmet .10 .05 .01
Terry McDaniel
Jimmy Oliver
Christian Fauria
□ 89 Chargers Helmet .30 .14 .04
Glen Milburn
John Carney
Joey Galloway
□ 90 Seahawks Helmet .10 .05 .01
Terrell Fletcher
Keith Cash
Eugene Robinson

1996 Collector's Choice

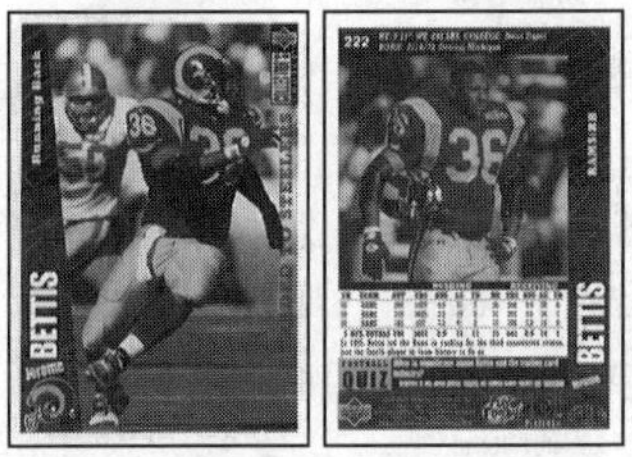

The 1996 Collector's Choice first series containted 375 standard-size cards. The 14-card hobby packs had a suggested retail price of $.99 each. A factory set was produced and sold with ten Stick-Ums inserts and ten Gold foil MVPs inserts. The set features the topical subsets: Rookie Class (1-45) and Season To Remember (46-79). This set has a slightly different design than previous Collector's Choice sets in that the player's name and position was printed either on the side or the bottom. Rookie Cards in this set include Karim Abdul-Jabbar, Tim Biakabutuka, Bobby Engram, Terry Glenn, Eddie George, Keyshawn Johnson and Lawrence Phillips. A Jerry Rice base brand and a Dan Marino unnumbered Promo Crash the Game card were produced to promote the set and are priced below.

	MINT	NRMT	EXC
COMPLETE SET (375)	25.00	11.00	3.10
COMP.FACT.SET (395)	30.00	13.50	3.70
COMMON CARD (1-375)	.05	.02	.01
COMP.MARINO CUT ABOVE (10)	15.00	6.75	1.85
COMMON MARINO ACA	1.50	.70	.19

□ 1 Keyshawn Johnson	1.00	.45	.12
□ 2 Kevin Hardy	.10	.05	.01
□ 3 Simeon Rice	.20	.09	.03
□ 4 Jonathan Ogden	.05	.02	.01
□ 5 Cedric Jones	.10	.05	.01
□ 6 Lawrence Phillips	.40	.18	.05
□ 7 Tim Biakabutuka	.50	.23	.06
□ 8 Terry Glenn	2.00	.90	.25
□ 9 Rickey Dudley	.20	.09	.03
□ 10 Regan Upshaw	.05	.02	.01
□ 11 Walt Harris	.05	.02	.01
□ 12 Eddie George	2.50	1.10	.30
□ 13 John Mobley	.05	.02	.01
□ 14 Duane Clemons	.05	.02	.01
□ 15 Marvin Harrison	1.00	.45	.12
□ 16 Daryl Gardener	.10	.05	.01
□ 17 Pete Kendall	.05	.02	.01
□ 18 Marcus Jones	.05	.02	.01
□ 19 Eric Moulds	.50	.23	.06
□ 20 Ray Lewis	.05	.02	.01
□ 21 Alex Van Dyke	.10	.05	.01
□ 22 Leeland McElroy	.20	.09	.03
□ 23 Mike Alstott	.40	.18	.05
□ 24 Lawyer Milloy	.05	.02	.01
□ 25 Marco Battaglia	.05	.02	.01
□ 26 Je'Rod Cherry	.05	.02	.01
□ 27 Israel Ifeanyi	.05	.02	.01
□ 28 Bobby Engram	.50	.23	.06
□ 29 Jason Dunn	.10	.05	.01
□ 30 Derrick Mayes	.50	.23	.06
□ 31 Stepfret Williams	.05	.02	.01
□ 32 Bobby Hoying	.20	.09	.03
□ 33 Karim Abdul-Jabbar	1.50	.70	.19
□ 34 Danny Kanell	.20	.09	.03
□ 35 Chris Darkins	.10	.05	.01
□ 36 Charlie Jones	.05	.02	.01
□ 37 Tedy Bruschi	.05	.02	.01
□ 38 Stanley Pritchett	.10	.05	.01
□ 39 Donnie Edwards	.05	.02	.01
□ 40 Jeff Lewis	.10	.05	.01
□ 41 Stephen Davis	.20	.09	.03
□ 42 Winslow Oliver	.05	.02	.01
□ 43 Mercury Hayes	.05	.02	.01
□ 44 Jon Runyan	.05	.02	.01
□ 45 Steve Taneyhill	.05	.02	.01
□ 46 Eric Metcalf SR	.10	.05	.01
□ 47 Bryce Paup SR	.10	.05	.01
□ 48 Kerry Collins SR	.40	.18	.05
□ 49 Rashaan Salaam SR	.20	.09	.03
□ 50 Carl Pickens SR	.20	.09	.03
□ 51 Emmitt Smith SR	.75	.35	.09
□ 52 Michael Irvin SR	.10	.05	.01
□ 53 Troy Aikman SR	.40	.18	.05
□ 54 Terrell Davis SR	.50	.23	.06
□ 55 John Elway SR	.30	.14	.04
□ 56 Herman Moore SR	.20	.09	.03
□ 57 Brett Favre SR	.75	.35	.09
□ 58 Rodney Thomas SR	.05	.02	.01
□ 59 Jim Harbaugh SR	.10	.05	.01
□ 60 Mark Brunell SR	.40	.18	.05
□ 61 Marcus Allen SR	.20	.09	.03
□ 62 Tamarick Vanover SR	.20	.09	.03
□ 63 Steve Bono SR	.05	.02	.01
□ 64 Dan Marino SR	.75	.35	.09
□ 65 Warren Moon SR	.05	.02	.01
□ 66 Curtis Martin SR	.50	.23	.06
□ 67 Tyrone Hughes SR	.05	.02	.01
□ 68 Rodney Hampton SR	.05	.02	.01
□ 69 Hugh Douglas SR	.05	.02	.01
□ 70 Tim Brown SR	.10	.05	.01
□ 71 Ricky Watters SR	.10	.05	.01
□ 72 Kordell Stewart SR	.40	.18	.05
□ 73 Andre Coleman SR	.05	.02	.01
□ 74 Jerry Rice SR	.40	.18	.05
□ 75 Joey Galloway SR	.20	.09	.03
□ 76 Isaac Bruce SR	.20	.09	.03
□ 77 Errict Rhett SR	.10	.05	.01
□ 78 Michael Westbrook SR	.20	.09	.03
□ 79 Brian Mitchell SR	.05	.02	.01
□ 80 Aeneas Williams	.05	.02	.01
□ 81 Andre Reed	.10	.05	.01
□ 82 Brett Maxie	.05	.02	.01
□ 83 Jim Flanigan	.05	.02	.01
□ 84 Jeff Blake	.20	.09	.03
□ 85 Mike Frederick	.05	.02	.01
□ 86 Michael Irvin	.20	.09	.03
□ 87 Aaron Craver	.05	.02	.01
□ 88 Barry Sanders	.75	.35	.09
□ 89 Travis Jervey	.05	.02	.01
□ 90 Chris Sanders	.10	.05	.01
□ 91 Marshall Faulk	.20	.09	.03
□ 92 Bryan Schwartz	.05	.02	.01
□ 93 Tamarick Vanover	.20	.09	.03
□ 94 Troy Vincent	.05	.02	.01
□ 95 Robert Smith	.10	.05	.01
□ 96 Drew Bledsoe	.75	.35	.09
□ 97 Quinn Early	.05	.02	.01
□ 98 Wayne Chrebet	.10	.05	.01
□ 99 Tim Brown	.10	.05	.01
□ 100 Charlie Garner	.05	.02	.01
□ 101 Yancey Thigpen	.10	.05	.01
□ 102 Isaac Bruce	.20	.09	.03
□ 103 Natrone Means	.20	.09	.03
□ 104 Jerry Rice	.75	.35	.09
□ 105 Chris Warren	.10	.05	.01
□ 106 Errict Rhett	.10	.05	.01
□ 107 Heath Shuler	.20	.09	.03
□ 108 Eric Swann	.10	.05	.01
□ 109 Jeff George	.10	.05	.01
□ 110 Steve Tasker	.05	.02	.01
□ 111 Sam Mills	.10	.05	.01
□ 112 Jeff Graham	.05	.02	.01
□ 113 Carl Pickens	.20	.09	.03
□ 114 Vinny Testaverde	.10	.05	.01
□ 115 Emmitt Smith	1.50	.70	.19
□ 116 John Elway	.60	.25	.07
□ 117 Henry Thomas	.05	.02	.01
□ 118 LeRoy Butler	.05	.02	.01
□ 119 Blaine Bishop	.05	.02	.01
□ 120 Floyd Turner	.05	.02	.01
□ 121 Jeff Lageman	.05	.02	.01
□ 122 Kimble Anders	.05	.02	.01
□ 123 Bryan Cox	.05	.02	.01
□ 124 Qadry Ismail	.10	.05	.01
□ 125 Ted Johnson	.05	.02	.01
□ 126 Wesley Walls	.10	.05	.01
□ 127 Rodney Hampton	.10	.05	.01
□ 128 Adrian Murrell	.10	.05	.01
□ 129 Daryl Hobbs	.05	.02	.01
□ 130 Ricky Watters	.10	.05	.01
□ 131 Carnell Lake	.05	.02	.01
□ 132 Toby Wright	.05	.02	.01
□ 133 Darren Bennett	.10	.05	.01
□ 134 J.J. Stokes	.20	.09	.03
□ 135 Eugene Robinson	.05	.02	.01
□ 136 Eric Curry	.05	.02	.01
□ 137 Tom Carter	.05	.02	.01
□ 138 Dave Krieg	.05	.02	.01
□ 139 Eric Metcalf	.10	.05	.01
□ 140 Bill Brooks	.05	.02	.01
□ 141 Pete Metzelaars	.05	.02	.01
□ 142 Kevin Butler	.05	.02	.01
□ 143 John Copeland	.05	.02	.01
□ 144 Keenan McCardell	.20	.09	.03
□ 145 Larry Brown	.05	.02	.01
□ 146 Jason Elam	.05	.02	.01
□ 147 Willie Clay	.05	.02	.01
□ 148 Robert Brooks	.20	.09	.03
□ 149 Chris Chandler	.10	.05	.01
□ 150 Quentin Coryatt	.05	.02	.01
□ 151 Pete Mitchell	.05	.02	.01

☐ 152 Martin Bayless	.05	.02	.01
☐ 153 Pete Stoyanovich	.05	.02	.01
☐ 154 Cris Carter	.20	.09	.03
☐ 155 Jimmy Hitchcock	.05	.02	.01
☐ 156 Mario Bates	.10	.05	.01
☐ 157 Mike Sherrard	.05	.02	.01
☐ 158 Boomer Esiason	.10	.05	.01
☐ 159 Chester McGlockton	.05	.02	.01
☐ 160 Bobby Taylor	.10	.05	.01
☐ 161 Kordell Stewart	.75	.35	.09
☐ 162 Kevin Carter	.10	.05	.01
☐ 163 Junior Seau	.20	.09	.03
☐ 164 Derek Loville	.05	.02	.01
☐ 165 Brian Blades	.10	.05	.01
☐ 166 Jackie Harris	.05	.02	.01
☐ 167 Michael Westbrook	.20	.09	.03
☐ 168 Rob Moore	.05	.02	.01
☐ 169 Jessie Tuggle	.05	.02	.01
☐ 170 Darick Holmes	.10	.05	.01
☐ 171 Tim McKyer	.05	.02	.01
☐ 172 Erik Kramer	.05	.02	.01
☐ 173 Harold Green	.05	.02	.01
☐ 174 Stevon Moore	.05	.02	.01
☐ 175 Deion Sanders	.40	.18	.05
☐ 176 Anthony Miller	.10	.05	.01
☐ 177 Herman Moore	.20	.09	.03
☐ 178 Brett Favre	1.50	.70	.19
☐ 179 Rodney Thomas	.05	.02	.01
☐ 180 Ken Dilger	.10	.05	.01
☐ 181 Mark Brunell	.75	.35	.09
☐ 182 Marcus Allen	.20	.09	.03
☐ 183 Dan Marino	1.50	.70	.19
☐ 184 John Randle	.05	.02	.01
☐ 185 Ben Coates	.10	.05	.01
☐ 186 Tyrone Hughes	.05	.02	.01
☐ 187 Dave Brown	.10	.05	.01
☐ 188 Johnny Mitchell	.05	.02	.01
☐ 189 Harvey Williams	.05	.02	.01
☐ 190 Andy Harmon	.05	.02	.01
☐ 191 Kevin Greene	.10	.05	.01
☐ 192 D'Marco Farr	.05	.02	.01
☐ 193 Andre Coleman	.05	.02	.01
☐ 194 Bryant Young	.10	.05	.01
☐ 195 Rick Mirer	.10	.05	.01
☐ 196 Horace Copeland	.05	.02	.01
☐ 197 Leslie Shepherd	.05	.02	.01
☐ 198 Jamir Miller	.05	.02	.01
☐ 199 Bert Emanuel	.10	.05	.01
☐ 200 Steve Christie	.05	.02	.01
☐ 201 Kerry Collins	.75	.35	.09
☐ 202 Rashaan Salaam	.20	.09	.03
☐ 203 Steve Tovar	.05	.02	.01
☐ 204 Michael Jackson	.10	.05	.01
☐ 205 Kevin Williams	.05	.02	.01
☐ 206 Glyn Milburn	.05	.02	.01
☐ 207 Johnnie Morton	.10	.05	.01
☐ 208 Antonio Freeman	.30	.14	.04
☐ 209 Cris Dishman	.05	.02	.01
☐ 210 Ellis Johnson	.05	.02	.01
☐ 211 Cedric Tillman	.05	.02	.01
☐ 212 Steve Bono	.10	.05	.01
☐ 213 Eric Green	.05	.02	.01
☐ 214 David Palmer	.10	.05	.01
☐ 215 Vincent Brisby	.05	.02	.01
☐ 216 Michael Haynes	.10	.05	.01
☐ 217 Chris Calloway	.05	.02	.01
☐ 218 Kyle Brady	.10	.05	.01
☐ 219 Terry McDaniel	.05	.02	.01
☐ 220 Calvin Williams	.20	.09	.03
☐ 221 Greg Lloyd	.10	.05	.01
☐ 222 Jerome Bettis	.20	.09	.03
☐ 223 Stan Humphries	.10	.05	.01
☐ 224 Lee Woodall	.05	.02	.01
☐ 225 Robert Blackmon	.05	.02	.01
☐ 226 Warren Sapp	.05	.02	.01
☐ 227 Brian Mitchell	.05	.02	.01
☐ 228 Garrison Hearst	.10	.05	.01
☐ 229 Terance Mathis	.05	.02	.01
☐ 230 Bryce Paup	.10	.05	.01
☐ 231 Derrick Moore	.05	.02	.01
☐ 232 Curtis Conway	.20	.09	.03
☐ 233 Darnay Scott	.10	.05	.01
☐ 234 Andre Rison	.10	.05	.01
☐ 235 Jay Novacek	.10	.05	.01
☐ 236 Terrell Davis	1.00	.45	.12
☐ 237 David Sloan	.10	.05	.01
☐ 238 Reggie White	.20	.09	.03
☐ 239 Todd McNair	.05	.02	.01
☐ 240 Ray Buchanan	.05	.02	.01
☐ 241 Steve Beuerlein	.05	.02	.01
☐ 242 Dan Saleaumua	.05	.02	.01
☐ 243 Bernie Parmalee	.05	.02	.01
☐ 244 Warren Moon	.10	.05	.01
☐ 245 Ty Law	.05	.02	.01
☐ 246 Torrance Small	.05	.02	.01
☐ 247 Phillippi Sparks	.05	.02	.01
☐ 248 Mo Lewis	.05	.02	.01
☐ 249 Jeff Hostetler	.10	.05	.01
☐ 250 Rodney Peete	.05	.02	.01
☐ 251 Byron Bam Morris	.10	.05	.01
☐ 252 Chris Miller	.05	.02	.01
☐ 253 Tony Martin	.10	.05	.01
☐ 254 Eric Davis	.05	.02	.01
☐ 255 Joey Galloway	.30	.14	.04
☐ 256 Derrick Brooks	.05	.02	.01
☐ 257 Ken Harvey	.05	.02	.01
☐ 258 Frank Sanders	.10	.05	.01
☐ 259 Morten Andersen	.05	.02	.01
☐ 260 Marlon Kerner	.05	.02	.01
☐ 261 Mark Carrier WR	.10	.05	.01
☐ 262 Mark Carrier DB	.05	.02	.01
☐ 263 Tony McGee	.05	.02	.01
☐ 264 Eric Zeier	.10	.05	.01
☐ 265 Darren Woodson	.10	.05	.01
☐ 266 Shannon Sharpe	.10	.05	.01
☐ 267 Brett Perriman	.10	.05	.01
☐ 268 Edgar Bennett	.10	.05	.01
☐ 269 Darryll Lewis	.05	.02	.01
☐ 270 Jim Harbaugh	.10	.05	.01
☐ 271 Desmond Howard	.10	.05	.01
☐ 272 Derrick Thomas	.10	.05	.01
☐ 273 Irving Fryar	.10	.05	.01
☐ 274 Jake Reed	.10	.05	.01
☐ 275 Curtis Martin	1.00	.45	.12
☐ 276 Eric Allen	.05	.02	.01
☐ 277 Thomas Lewis	.05	.02	.01
☐ 278 Hugh Douglas	.05	.02	.01
☐ 279 Pat Swilling	.05	.02	.01
☐ 280 William Thomas	.05	.02	.01
☐ 281 Norm Johnson	.05	.02	.01
☐ 282 Roman Phifer	.05	.02	.01
☐ 283 Chris Mims	.05	.02	.01
☐ 284 Steve Young	.60	.25	.07
☐ 285 Cortez Kennedy	.10	.05	.01
☐ 286 Trent Dilfer	.10	.05	.01
☐ 287 Terry Allen	.10	.05	.01
☐ 288 Clyde Simmons	.05	.02	.01
☐ 289 Craig Heyward	.05	.02	.01
☐ 290 Jim Kelly	.20	.09	.03
☐ 291 Tyrone Poole	.05	.02	.01
☐ 292 Chris Zorich	.05	.02	.01
☐ 293 Dan Wilkinson	.05	.02	.01
☐ 294 Antonio Langham	.05	.02	.01
☐ 295 Troy Aikman	.75	.35	.09
☐ 296 Steve Atwater	.05	.02	.01
☐ 297 Scott Mitchell	.10	.05	.01
☐ 298 Mark Chmura	.10	.05	.01
☐ 299 Steve McNair	.50	.23	.06
☐ 300 Tony Bennett	.05	.02	.01
☐ 301 Willie Jackson	.10	.05	.01
☐ 302 Neil Smith	.10	.05	.01
☐ 303 Terry Kirby	.10	.05	.01
☐ 304 Orlando Thomas	.05	.02	.01
☐ 305 Willie McGinest	.05	.02	.01
☐ 306 Wayne Martin	.05	.02	.01
☐ 307 Michael Brooks	.05	.02	.01
☐ 308 Marvin Washington	.05	.02	.01
☐ 309 Nolan Harrison	.05	.02	.01
☐ 310 William Fuller	.05	.02	.01
☐ 311 Willie Williams	.05	.02	.01
☐ 312 Troy Drayton	.05	.02	.01
☐ 313 Shawn Lee	.05	.02	.01
☐ 314 Ken Norton	.10	.05	.01
☐ 315 Terry Wooden	.05	.02	.01
☐ 316 Hardy Nickerson	.05	.02	.01
☐ 317 Gus Frerotte	.20	.09	.03
☐ 318 Oscar McBride	.05	.02	.01
☐ 319 Merton Hanks	.05	.02	.01
☐ 320 Justin Armour	.05	.02	.01
☐ 321 Willie Green	.05	.02	.01
☐ 322 Roger Jones	.05	.02	.01
☐ 323 Leroy Hoard	.05	.02	.01
☐ 324 Chris Boniol	.05	.02	.01
☐ 325 Jason Hanson	.05	.02	.01
☐ 326 Sean Jones	.05	.02	.01
☐ 327 Roosevelt Potts	.05	.02	.01
☐ 328 Greg Hill	.10	.05	.01
☐ 329 O.J. McDuffie	.10	.05	.01
☐ 330 Amp Lee	.05	.02	.01
☐ 331 Chris Slade	.05	.02	.01
☐ 332 Jim Everett	.05	.02	.01
☐ 333 Tyrone Wheatley	.10	.05	.01
☐ 334 Charles Wilson	.05	.02	.01
☐ 335 Napoleon Kaufman	.10	.05	.01
☐ 336 Fred Barnett	.10	.05	.01
☐ 337 Neil O'Donnell	.10	.05	.01
☐ 338 Sean Gilbert	.05	.02	.01
☐ 339 Aaron Hayden	.10	.05	.01
☐ 340 Brent Jones	.05	.02	.01
☐ 341 Christian Fauria	.05	.02	.01
☐ 342 Alvin Harper	.05	.02	.01
☐ 343 Henry Ellard	.10	.05	.01
☐ 344 Willie Davis	.10	.05	.01
☐ 345 Charles Haley	.10	.05	.01
☐ 346 Chris Jacke	.05	.02	.01
☐ 347 Allen Aldridge	.05	.02	.01
☐ 348 Jeff Herrod	.05	.02	.01
☐ 349 Rocket Ismail	.10	.05	.01
☐ 350 Leslie O'Neal	.05	.02	.01
☐ 351 Marquez Pope	.05	.02	.01
☐ 352 Brock Marion	.05	.02	.01
☐ 353 Ernie Mills	.05	.02	.01
☐ 354 Larry Centers	.10	.05	.01
☐ 355 Chris Doleman	.05	.02	.01
☐ 356 Bruce Smith	.20	.09	.03
☐ 357 John Kasay	.05	.02	.01
☐ 358 Donnell Woolford	.05	.02	.01
☐ 359 David Dunn	.05	.02	.01
☐ 360 Eric Turner	.05	.02	.01
☐ 361 Sherman Williams	.05	.02	.01
☐ 362 Chris Spielman	.10	.05	.01
☐ 363 Craig Newsome	.05	.02	.01
☐ 364 Sean Dawkins	.05	.02	.01
☐ 365 James O. Stewart	.10	.05	.01
☐ 366 Dale Carter	.05	.02	.01
☐ 367 Marco Coleman	.05	.02	.01
☐ 368 Dave Meggett	.05	.02	.01
☐ 369 Irv Smith	.05	.02	.01
☐ 370 Mike Mamula	.05	.02	.01
☐ 371 Erric Pegram	.10	.05	.01
☐ 372 Dana Stubblefield	.10	.05	.01
☐ 373 Terrance Shaw	.05	.02	.01
☐ 374 Jerry Rice CL	.25	.11	.03
☐ 375 Dan Marino CL	.40	.18	.05
☐ P1 Jerry Rice Promo Base brand card #801	1.00	.45	.12
☐ P2 Dan Marino Promo Crash the Game April 1	1.50	.70	.19

1996 Collector's Choice A Cut Above

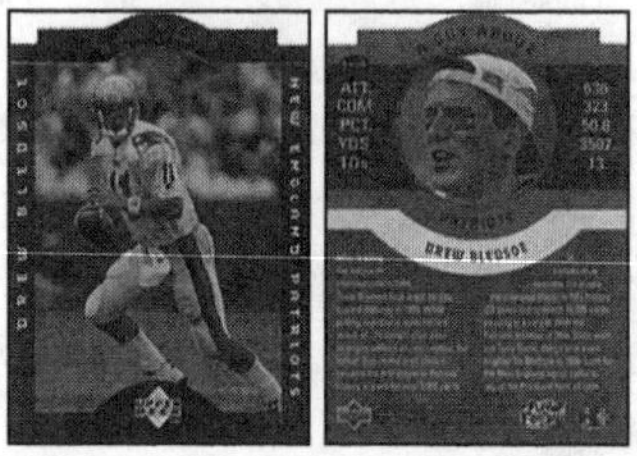

This 10-card set features color action player photos of top NFL stars on a die cut card. The backs carry a small circular head photo with player information and why this particular player was selected for the set. These cards were available one per special retail pack.

	MINT	NRMT	EXC
COMPLETE SET	12.00	5.50	1.50
COMMON CARD (1-10)	1.00	.45	.12
☐ 1 Troy Aikman	1.25	.55	.16
☐ 2 Tim Biakabutuka	1.00	.45	.12
☐ 3 Drew Bledsoe	1.25	.55	.16
☐ 4 Emmitt Smith	2.50	1.10	.30
☐ 5 Marshall Faulk	1.00	.45	.12
☐ 6 Brett Favre	2.50	1.10	.30
☐ 7 Keyshawn Johnson	1.00	.45	.12
☐ 8 Deion Sanders	1.50	.70	.19
☐ 9 Lawrence Phillips	1.00	.45	.12
☐ 10 Jerry Rice	1.25	.55	.16

1996 Collector's Choice Crash The Game

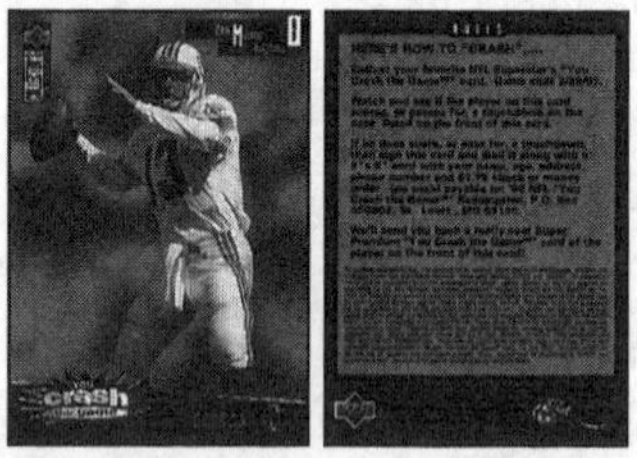

Randomly inserted in packs at a rate of one in five, this 90-card insert standard-size set was redeemable for a super premium quality card of the winning player. The redemption card will include Light F/X technology and feature a new photo of the player. If the card was a winner a collector could mail in the game card along with $1.75 and receive either a silver or a gold (depending on which game card they had) card. The gold cards were inserted one every 50 packs.

	MINT	NRMT	EXC
COMPLETE SET (90)	75.00	34.00	9.50
COMP.SHORT SET (30)	25.00	11.00	3.10
COMMON CARD (CG1-CG30)	.50	.23	.06
COMP.GOLD SET (90)	300.00	135.00	38.00
*GOLD CARDS: 2X TO 4X BASIC CARDS			
COMP.GOLD REDEMPT.(22)	225.00	100.00	28.00
*GOLD REDEMPTIONS: 5X TO 10X			
COMP.SILVER REDEMPT.(22)	75.00	34.00	9.50
*SILVER REDEMPTION CARDS: 1.5X TO 3X			
☐ CG1A Dan Marino 9/23 L	3.00	1.35	.35
☐ CG1B Dan Marino 10/27 W	3.00	1.35	.35
☐ CG1C Dan Marino 11/25 W	3.00	1.35	.35
☐ CG2A John Elway 10/6 W	1.25	.55	.16
☐ CG2B John Elway 10/27 W	1.25	.55	.16
☐ CG2C John Elway 12/24 W	1.25	.55	.16
☐ CG3A Jeff Blake 9/29 W	1.00	.45	.12
☐ CG3B Jeff Blake 10/20 W	1.00	.45	.12
☐ CG3C Jeff Blake 12/1 W	1.00	.45	.12
☐ CG4A Drew Bledsoe 9/22 W	1.50	.70	.19
☐ CG4B Drew Bledsoe 10/13 L	1.50	.70	.19
☐ CG4C Drew Bledsoe 12/1 W	1.50	.70	.19
☐ CG5A Steve Young 9/29 L	1.25	.55	.16
☐ CG5B Steve Young 10/14 L	1.25	.55	.16
☐ CG5C Steve Young 12/8 W	1.25	.55	.16
☐ CG6A Brett Favre 10/6 W	3.00	1.35	.35
☐ CG6B Brett Favre 11/3 W	3.00	1.35	.35
☐ CG6C Brett Favre 11/24 W	3.00	1.35	.35
☐ CG7A Jim Kelly 9/22 L	1.00	.45	.12
☐ CG7B Jim Kelly 10/27 W	1.00	.45	.12
☐ CG7C Jim Kelly 11/10 W	1.00	.45	.12
☐ CG8A Scott Mitchell 10/6 W	.50	.23	.06
☐ CG8B Scott Mitchell 10/27 W	.50	.23	.06
☐ CG8C Scott Mitchell 11/11 L	.50	.23	.06
☐ CG9A Jeff George 9/22 W	.50	.23	.06
☐ CG9B Jeff George 10/20 L	.50	.23	.06
☐ CG9C Jeff George 11/17 L	.50	.23	.06
☐ CG10A Erik Kramer 9/29 L	.50	.23	.06
☐ CG10B Erik Kramer 10/28 L	.50	.23	.06
☐ CG10C Erik Kramer 11/24 L	.50	.23	.06
☐ CG11A Jerry Rice 9/22 L	1.50	.70	.19
☐ CG11B Jerry Rice 10/27 L	1.50	.70	.19
☐ CG11C Jerry Rice 11/17 W	1.50	.70	.19
☐ CG12A Michael Irvin 9/30 L	1.00	.45	.12
☐ CG12B Michael Irvin 10/13 L	1.00	.45	.12
☐ CG12C Michael Irvin 11/10 L	1.00	.45	.12
☐ CG13A Joey Galloway 9/22 L	1.00	.45	.12
☐ CG13B Joey Galloway 10/27 L	1.00	.45	.12
☐ CG13C Joey Galloway 11/24 L	1.00	.45	.12
☐ CG14A Cris Carter 9/29 L	.75	.35	.09
☐ CG14B Cris Carter 11/3 W	.75	.35	.09
☐ CG14C Cris Carter 12/1 W	.75	.35	.09
☐ CG15A Carl Pickens 10/6 L	.75	.35	.09
☐ CG15B Carl Pickens 10/27 W	.75	.35	.09
☐ CG15C Carl Pickens 11/17 W	.75	.35	.09
☐ CG16A Herman Moore 9/22 L	1.00	.45	.12
☐ CG16B Herman Moore 10/13 W	1.00	.45	.12
☐ CG16C Herman Moore 11/28 L	1.00	.45	.12
☐ CG17A Isaac Bruce 10/13 L	1.00	.45	.12
☐ CG17B Isaac Bruce 11/10 W	1.00	.45	.12
☐ CG17C Isaac Bruce 11/24 W	1.00	.45	.12
☐ CG18A Tim Brown 9/22 W	.75	.35	.09
☐ CG18B Tim Brown 10/21L	.75	.35	.09
☐ CG18C Tim Brown 11/24 L	.75	.35	.09
☐ CG19A Keyshawn Johnson 10/6 L	1.00	.45	.12
☐ CG19B Keyshawn Johnson 11/10 L	1.00	.45	.12
☐ CG19C Keyshawn Johnson 12/1 W	1.00	.45	.12
☐ CG20A Terry Glenn 10/13 L	1.50	.70	.19
☐ CG20B Terry Glenn 11/10 W	1.50	.70	.19
☐ CG20C Terry Glenn 12/1 W	1.50	.70	.19
☐ CG21A Emmitt Smith 9/22 W	3.00	1.35	.35
☐ CG21B Emmitt Smith 11/3 W	3.00	1.35	.35
☐ CG21C Emmitt Smith 11/28 W	3.00	1.35	.35
☐ CG22A Edgar Bennett 10/6 L	.50	.23	.06
☐ CG22B Edgar Bennett 11/3 L	.50	.23	.06
☐ CG22C Edgar Bennett 11/18 L	.50	.23	.06
☐ CG23A Chris Warren 10/6 L	.75	.35	.09
☐ CG23B Chris Warren 10/27 W	.75	.35	.09
☐ CG23C Chris Warren 11/17 L	.75	.35	.09
☐ CG24A Marshall Faulk 9/23 L	1.00	.45	.12
☐ CG24B Marshall Faulk 11/3 L	1.00	.45	.12
☐ CG24C Marshall Faulk 11/24 L	1.00	.45	.12
☐ CG25A Curtis Martin 9/22 W	2.00	.90	.25
☐ CG25B Curtis Martin 10/20 W	2.00	.90	.25
☐ CG25C Curtis Martin 12/1 L	2.00	.90	.25
☐ CG26A Barry Sanders 9/29 L	1.50	.70	.19
☐ CG26B Barry Sanders 10/17 W	1.50	.70	.19
☐ CG26C Barry Sanders 11/17 W	1.50	.70	.19
☐ CG27A Rashaan Salaam 9/22 L	1.00	.45	.12
☐ CG27B Rashaan Salaam 10/28 W	1.00	.45	.12
☐ CG27C Rashaan Salaam 11/17 L	1.00	.45	.12
☐ CG28A Leeland McElroy 9/29 L	.50	.23	.06
☐ CG28B Leeland McElroy 10/27 L	.50	.23	.06
☐ CG28C Leeland McElroy 11/17 L	.50	.23	.06
☐ CG29A Tim Biakabutuka 9/22 L	1.00	.45	.12
☐ CG29B Tim Biakabutuka 10/13 L	1.00	.45	.12
☐ CG29C Tim Biakabutuka 11/3 L	1.00	.45	.12
☐ CG30A Lawrence Phillips 9/29 L	.75	.35	.09
☐ CG30B Lawrence Phillips 10/20 L	.75	.35	.09
☐ CG30C Lawrence Phillips 10/27 L	.75	.35	.09

1996 Collector's Choice Jumbos

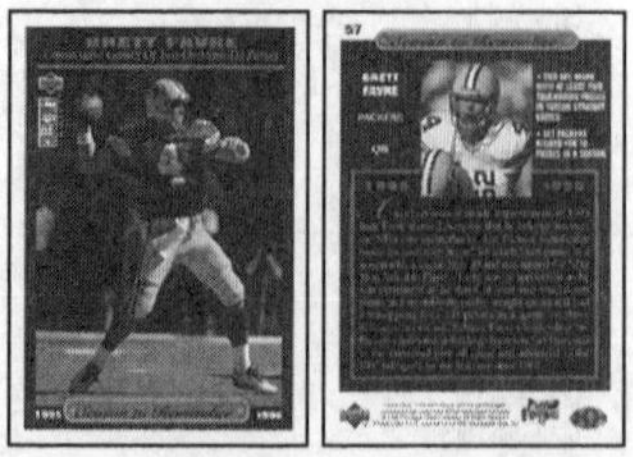

Cards from this nine-card set were inserted one per special retail blister pack that also included a complete team set and foil pack from 1996 Collector's Choice. The blister packs containing one of the oversized cards originally retailed for $4.97 each. Each card is an enlarged (3 1/2" by 5") version of that player's Season to Remember subset card from the regular 1996 Collector's Choice set. The card numbering is also the same.

	MINT	NRMT	EXC
COMPLETE SET (9)	30.00	13.50	3.70
COMMON CARD	2.00	.90	.25

☐ 48 Kerry Collins	3.00	1.35	.35
☐ 49 Rashaan Salaam	2.00	.90	.25
☐ 51 Emmitt Smith	5.00	2.20	.60
☐ 57 Brett Favre	5.00	2.20	.60
☐ 60 Mark Brunell	3.00	1.35	.35
☐ 64 Dan Marino	5.00	2.20	.60
☐ 70 Tim Brown	2.00	.90	.25
☐ 72 Kordell Stewart	3.00	1.35	.35
☐ 74 Jerry Rice	3.00	1.35	.35

1996 Collector's Choice Dan Marino A Cut Above

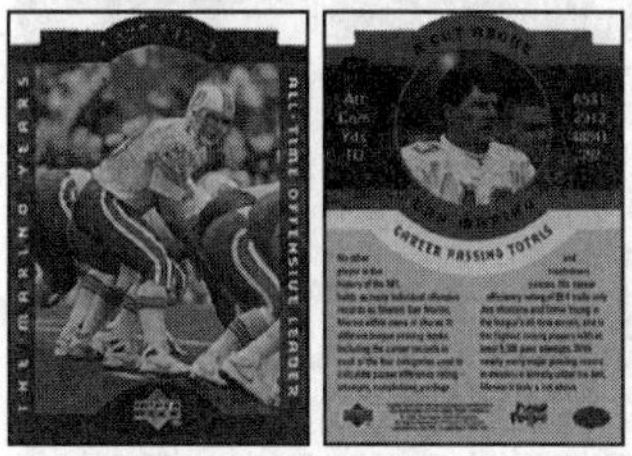

Inserted one per special Collector's Choice six-card retail pack, this 10-card set features color photos of various highlights from Dan Marino's career printed on a die cut card.

	MINT	NRMT	EXC
COMPLETE SET (10)	15.00	6.75	1.85
COMMON CARD (CA1-CA10)	1.50	.70	.19
☐ CA1 All-Time Offensive Leader	1.50	.70	.19
☐ CA2 Dream Season	1.50	.70	.19
☐ CA3 Pass Master	1.50	.70	.19
☐ CA4 True Visionary	1.50	.70	.19
☐ CA5 Tough Under Pressure	1.50	.70	.19
☐ CA6 Consummate Leader	1.50	.70	.19
☐ CA7 All-Time Passing Marks	1.50	.70	.19
☐ CA8 Pointing to the Hall	1.50	.70	.19
☐ CA9 Season-Opening Comeback	1.50	.70	.19
☐ CA10 Coming From Behind	1.50	.70	.19

1996 Collector's Choice MVPs

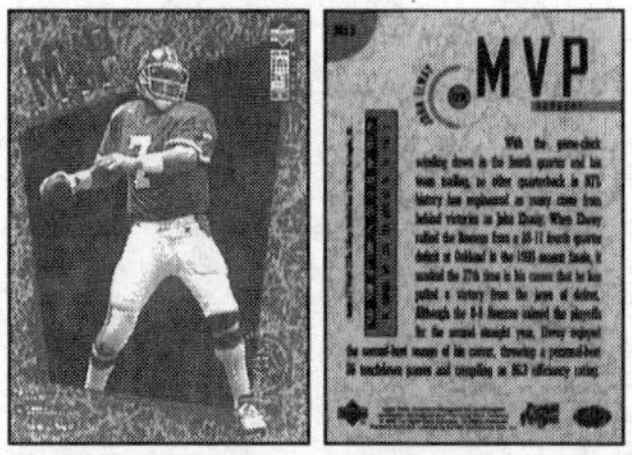

Inserted one per pack, this 45-card insert set highlights each NFL Team's MVP and co-MVP. There was also a gold version of these cards issued they were inserted one every 35 packs. The words MVP are in the upper left corner with the player's name in the lower left. The cards are numbered with a "M" prefix.

	MINT	NRMT	EXC
COMPLETE SET (45)	10.00	4.50	1.25
COMMON CARD (M1-M45)	.20	.09	.03
COMP.GOLD SET (45)	125.00	55.00	15.50
COMMON GOLD	2.00	.90	.25

*GOLD STARS: 5X TO 10X BASIC CARDS
*GOLD YOUNG STARS: 3X TO 6X BASIC CARDS

☐ M1 Larry Centers	.20	.09	.03
☐ M2 Jeff George	.20	.09	.03
☐ M3 Jim Kelly	.60	.25	.07
☐ M4 Bryce Paup	.40	.18	.05
☐ M5 Kerry Collins	1.00	.45	.12
☐ M6 Erik Kramer	.20	.09	.03
☐ M7 Rashaan Salaam	.60	.25	.07
☐ M8 Jeff Blake	.40	.18	.05
☐ M9 Carl Pickens	.40	.18	.05
☐ M10 Vinny Testaverde	.20	.09	.03
☐ M11 Michael Irvin	.60	.25	.07
☐ M12 Emmitt Smith	2.00	.90	.25
☐ M13 John Elway	.75	.35	.09
☐ M14 Terrell Davis	1.25	.55	.16
☐ M15 Herman Moore	.60	.25	.07
☐ M16 Barry Sanders	1.00	.45	.12
☐ M17 Brett Favre	2.00	.90	.25
☐ M18 Edgar Bennett	.20	.09	.03
☐ M19 Rodney Thomas	.40	.18	.05
☐ M20 Jim Harbaugh	.40	.18	.05
☐ M21 Marshall Faulk	.60	.25	.07
☐ M22 Mark Brunell	1.00	.45	.12
☐ M23 Steve Bono	.40	.18	.05
☐ M24 Marcus Allen	.60	.25	.07
☐ M25 Dan Marino	2.00	.90	.25
☐ M26 Bryan Cox	.20	.09	.03
☐ M27 Cris Carter	.40	.18	.05
☐ M28 Curtis Martin	1.25	.55	.16
☐ M29 Drew Bledsoe	1.00	.45	.12
☐ M30 Jim Everett	.20	.09	.03
☐ M31 Rodney Hampton	.40	.18	.05
☐ M32 Adrian Murrell	.20	.09	.03
☐ M33 Tim Brown	.40	.18	.05
☐ M34 Rodney Peete	.20	.09	.03
☐ M35 Ricky Watters	.40	.18	.05
☐ M36 Yancey Thigpen	.40	.18	.05
☐ M37 Greg Lloyd	.40	.18	.05
☐ M38 Isaac Bruce	.60	.25	.07
☐ M39 Tony Martin	.20	.09	.03
☐ M40 Junior Seau	.40	.18	.05
☐ M41 Steve Young	.75	.35	.09
☐ M42 Jerry Rice	1.00	.45	.12
☐ M43 Chris Warren	.40	.18	.05
☐ M44 Errict Rhett	.60	.25	.07
☐ M45 Brian Mitchell	.20	.09	.03

1996 Collector's Choice Stick-Ums

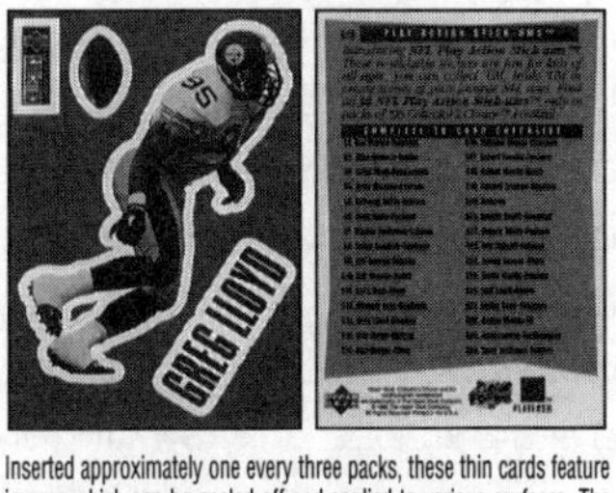

Inserted approximately one every three packs, these thin cards feature images which can be peeled off and applied to various surfaces. The player's picture is identified on the front. The back has a checklist of the set and the cards are numbered with an "S" prefix.

	MINT	NRMT	EXC
COMPLETE SET (30)	12.00	5.50	1.50
COMMON CARD (S1-S30)	.30	.14	.04
☐ S1 Dan Marino	2.00	.90	.25
☐ S2 Mike Mamula	.30	.14	.04
☐ S3 Errict Rhett	.50	.23	.06
☐ S4 Drew Bledsoe	1.00	.45	.12
☐ S5 Anthony Smith	.30	.14	.04
☐ S6 Brett Favre UER named spelled Farve	2.00	.90	.25
☐ S7 Morten Andersen	.30	.14	.04
☐ S8 Deion Sanders	.60	.25	.07
☐ S9 Jeff George	.30	.14	.04
☐ S10 Erik Kramer	.30	.14	.04
☐ S11 Jerry Rice	1.00	.45	.12
☐ S12 Michael Irvin	.60	.25	.07
☐ S13 Greg Lloyd	.50	.23	.06
☐ S14 Cris Carter	.50	.23	.06
☐ S15 Ken Norton	.30	.14	.04
☐ S16 Natrone Means	.60	.25	.07
☐ S17 Robert Brooks	.60	.25	.07
☐ S18 Bomb/Blitz	.30	.14	.04
☐ S19 Kordell Stewart	1.00	.45	.12
☐ S20 Referee	.30	.14	.04
☐ S21 Emmitt Smith	2.00	.90	.25
☐ S22 Reggie White	.60	.25	.07
☐ S23 Eric Metcalf	.50	.23	.06
☐ S24 Jesse Sapolu	.30	.14	.04
☐ S25 Curtis Martin	1.50	.70	.19
☐ S26 Neil Smith	.30	.14	.04
☐ S27 Junior Seau	.50	.23	.06
☐ S28 TD	.30	.14	.04
☐ S29 Yardmarkers	.30	.14	.04
☐ S30 Terry McDaniel	.30	.14	.04

1996 Collector's Choice Update

The 1996 Collector's Choice Update set was issued in one series totalling 200 cards. The 12-card packs retail for $.99 each. The set contains the topical subsets: Rookie Collection (1-60), Franchise Playmaker (61-90) and Regular cards (91-200).

	MINT	NRMT	EXC
COMPLETE SET (200)	15.00	6.75	1.85
COMMON CARD (U1-U200)	.05	.02	.01
☐ U1 Zach Thomas	.75	.35	.09
☐ U2 Simeon Rice	.20	.09	.03
☐ U3 Jonathan Ogden	.05	.02	.01
☐ U4 Eric Moulds	.20	.09	.03
☐ U5 Tim Biakabutuka	.20	.09	.03
☐ U6 Walt Harris	.05	.02	.01
☐ U7 Willie Anderson	.05	.02	.01
☐ U8 Ricky Whittle	.05	.02	.01
☐ U9 John Mobley	.05	.02	.01
☐ U10 Reggie Brown	.05	.02	.01
☐ U11 John Michels	.05	.02	.01
☐ U12 Eddie George	1.25	.55	.16
☐ U13 Marvin Harrison	.50	.23	.06
☐ U14 Kevin Hardy	.10	.05	.01
☐ U15 Kavika Pittman	.05	.02	.01
☐ U16 Daryl Gardener	.10	.05	.01
☐ U17 Duane Clemons	.05	.02	.01
☐ U18 Terry Glenn	1.00	.45	.12
☐ U19 Alex Molden	.05	.02	.01
☐ U20 Cedric Jones	.10	.05	.01
☐ U21 Keyshawn Johnson	.50	.23	.06
☐ U22 Rickey Dudley	.20	.09	.03
☐ U23 Jason Dunn	.10	.05	.01
☐ U24 Jamain Stephens	.05	.02	.01
☐ U25 Lawrence Phillips	.20	.09	.03
☐ U26 Bryan Still	.05	.02	.01
☐ U27 Israel Ifeanyi	.05	.02	.01
☐ U28 Pete Kendall	.05	.02	.01
☐ U29 Regan Upshaw	.05	.02	.01
☐ U30 Andre Johnson	.05	.02	.01
☐ U31 Leeland McElroy	.20	.09	.03
☐ U32 Ray Lewis	.05	.02	.01
☐ U33 Sean Moran	.05	.02	.01
☐ U34 Muhsin Muhammad	.75	.35	.09
☐ U35 Bobby Engram	.20	.09	.03
☐ U36 Marco Battaglia	.05	.02	.01
☐ U37 Stepfret Williams	.05	.02	.01
☐ U38 Jeff Lewis	.10	.05	.01
☐ U39 Derrick Mayes	.20	.09	.03
☐ U40 Reggie Tongue	.05	.02	.01
☐ U41 Tory James	.05	.02	.01
☐ U42 Tony Banks	.75	.35	.09
☐ U43 Tedy Bruschi	.05	.02	.01
☐ U44 Mike Alstott	.20	.09	.03
☐ U45 Anthony Dorsett	.05	.02	.01
☐ U46 Tony Brackens	.10	.05	.01
☐ U47 Bryant Mix	.05	.02	.01
☐ U48 Karim Abdul-Jabbar	.75	.35	.09
☐ U49 Moe Williams	.05	.02	.01
☐ U50 Lawyer Milloy	.05	.02	.01
☐ U51 Je'Rod Cherry	.05	.02	.01
☐ U52 Amani Toomer	.20	.09	.03
☐ U53 Alex Van Dyke	.10	.05	.01
☐ U54 Lance Johnstone	.05	.02	.01
☐ U55 Bobby Hoying	.20	.09	.03
☐ U56 Jon Witman	.10	.05	.01
☐ U57 Eddie Kennison	1.00	.45	.12
☐ U58 Brian Roche	.05	.02	.01
☐ U59 Terrell Owens	1.25	.55	.16
☐ U60 Stephen Davis	.20	.09	.03
☐ U61 Jeff George FP	.10	.05	.01
☐ U62 Darick Holmes FP	.10	.05	.01
☐ U63 Kerry Collins FP	.50	.23	.06
☐ U64 Rashaan Salaam FP	.20	.09	.03
☐ U65 Jeff Blake FP	.10	.05	.01
☐ U66 Emmitt Smith FP	1.00	.45	.12
☐ U67 Troy Aikman FP	.50	.23	.06
☐ U68 John Elway FP	.40	.18	.05
☐ U69 Terrell Davis FP	.60	.25	.07
☐ U70 Barry Sanders FP	.50	.23	.06
☐ U71 Herman Moore FP	.20	.09	.03
☐ U72 Brett Favre FP	1.00	.45	.12
☐ U73 Robert Brooks FP	.20	.09	.03
☐ U74 Steve McNair FP	.40	.18	.05
☐ U75 Marshall Faulk FP	.10	.05	.01
☐ U76 Marcus Allen FP	.20	.09	.03
☐ U77 Dan Marino FP	1.00	.45	.12
☐ U78 Warren Moon FP	.05	.02	.01
☐ U79 Drew Bledsoe FP	.50	.23	.06
☐ U80 Curtis Martin FP	.60	.25	.07
☐ U81 Mario Bates FP	.10	.05	.01
☐ U82 Tim Brown FP	.10	.05	.01
☐ U83 Charlie Garner FP	.05	.02	.01
☐ U84 Kordell Stewart FP	.50	.23	.06
☐ U85 Isaac Bruce FP	.20	.09	.03
☐ U86 Tony Martin FP	.05	.02	.01
☐ U87 Jerry Rice FP	.50	.23	.06
☐ U88 J.J. Stokes FP	.20	.09	.03
☐ U89 Joey Galloway FP	.20	.09	.03
☐ U90 Errict Rhett FP	.10	.05	.01
☐ U91 Mike Pritchard	.05	.02	.01
☐ U92 Jerome Bettis	.20	.09	.03
☐ U93 Winslow Oliver	.05	.02	.01
☐ U94 David Klingler	.05	.02	.01
☐ U95 Lawrence Dawsey	.05	.02	.01
☐ U96 Charlie Jones	.05	.02	.01
☐ U97 Dave Krieg	.05	.02	.01
☐ U98 Chris Spielman	.10	.05	.01
☐ U99 Stanley Pritchett	.10	.05	.01
☐ U100 Sean Gilbert	.05	.02	.01
☐ U101 Tommy Vardell	.05	.02	.01
☐ U102 DeRon Jenkins	.05	.02	.01
☐ U103 Larry Bowie	.05	.02	.01
☐ U104 Kyle Wachholtz	.05	.02	.01
☐ U105 Brady Smith	.05	.02	.01
☐ U106 Steve Walsh	.05	.02	.01
☐ U107 Wesley Walls	.10	.05	.01
☐ U108 Kevin Ross	.05	.02	.01
☐ U109 Willie Clay	.05	.02	.01
☐ U110 Olanda Truitt	.05	.02	.01
☐ U111 Calvin Williams	.05	.02	.01
☐ U112 Chris Doleman	.05	.02	.01
☐ U113 Irving Fryar	.10	.05	.01
☐ U114 Jimmy Spencer	.05	.02	.01
☐ U115 Reggie Barlow	.05	.02	.01
☐ U116 Reggie Brown	.05	.02	.01
☐ U117 Dixon Edwards	.05	.02	.01
☐ U118 Haywood Jeffires	.05	.02	.01
☐ U119 Santana Dotson	.05	.02	.01
☐ U120 Herschel Walker	.10	.05	.01
☐ U121 Darryl Williams	.05	.02	.01
☐ U122 Bryan Cox	.05	.02	.01
☐ U123 Lamar Thomas	.05	.02	.01
☐ U124 Hendrick Lusk	.05	.02	.01
☐ U125 Jahine Arnold	.05	.02	.01
☐ U126 Boomer Esiason	.10	.05	.01
☐ U127 Willie Davis	.10	.05	.01
☐ U128 Pete Stoyanovich	.05	.02	.01
☐ U129 Bill Romanowski	.05	.02	.01
☐ U130 Tim McKyer	.05	.02	.01
☐ U131 Patrick Sapp	.05	.02	.01
☐ U132 Natrone Means	.20	.09	.03
☐ U133 Quinn Early	.05	.02	.01
☐ U134 Leslie O'Neal	.05	.02	.01
☐ U135 Mark Seay	.05	.02	.01
☐ U136 Pete Metzelaars	.05	.02	.01
☐ U137 Jay Leeuwenburg UER name misspelled ...berg	.05	.02	.01
☐ U138 Buster Owens	.05	.02	.01
☐ U139 Todd McNair	.05	.02	.01
☐ U140 Eugene Robinson	.05	.02	.01
☐ U141 Sean Salisbury	.05	.02	.01
☐ U142 Eddie Robinson	.05	.02	.01
☐ U143 Jerris McPhail	.05	.02	.01
☐ U144 Ray Farmer	.05	.02	.01
☐ U145 Garrison Hearst	.10	.05	.01
☐ U146 Leonard Russell	.05	.02	.01
☐ U147 Roy Barker	.05	.02	.01
☐ U148 Larry Brown	.05	.02	.01
☐ U149 Webster Slaughter	.05	.02	.01
☐ U150 Roman Oben	.05	.02	.01
☐ U151 LeShon Johnson	.05	.02	.01
☐ U152 Patrick Bates	.05	.02	.01
☐ U153 Iheanyi Uwaezuoke UER Uwaezoke on back	.05	.02	.01
☐ U154 Scott Slutzker	.05	.02	.01
☐ U155 John Jurkovic	.05	.02	.01
☐ U156 Brian Milne	.05	.02	.01
☐ U157 Mike Sherrard	.05	.02	.01
☐ U158 Neil O'Donnell	.10	.05	.01
☐ U159 Roger Harper	.05	.02	.01
☐ U160 Desmond Howard	.10	.05	.01
☐ U161 Alfred Williams	.05	.02	.01
☐ U162 Ronnie Harmon	.05	.02	.01
☐ U163 Sammie Burroughs	.05	.02	.01
☐ U164 Keenan McCardell	.20	.09	.03
☐ U165 Shane Dronett	.05	.02	.01
☐ U166 Jeff Graham	.05	.02	.01
☐ U167 Bill Brooks	.05	.02	.01
☐ U168 Shawn Jefferson	.05	.02	.01
☐ U169 Detron Smith	.05	.02	.01
☐ U170 Danny Kanell	.20	.09	.03
☐ U171 Jevon Langford	.05	.02	.01
☐ U172 Russell Maryland	.05	.02	.01
☐ U173 Scott Milanovich	.05	.02	.01
☐ U174 Eric Davis	.05	.02	.01
☐ U175 Ernie Conwell	.05	.02	.01
☐ U176 Kurt Gouveia	.05	.02	.01
☐ U177 Andre Rison	.10	.05	.01
☐ U178 Harold Green	.05	.02	.01
☐ U179 Frank Reich	.05	.02	.01
☐ U180 Glyn Milburn	.05	.02	.01
☐ U181 Nilo Silvan	.05	.02	.01
☐ U182 Cornelius Bennett	.10	.05	.01
☐ U183 Freddie Solomon	.05	.02	.01
☐ U184 Pat Terrell	.05	.02	.01
☐ U185 Miles Macik	.05	.02	.01
☐ U186 Bo Orlando	.05	.02	.01
☐ U187 Kelvin Martin	.05	.02	.01
☐ U188 Todd Kinchen	.05	.02	.01
☐ U189 Reggie Brooks	.10	.05	.01
☐ U190 Steve Beuerlein UER name misspelled Beurlein	.05	.02	.01
☐ U191 Marco Coleman	.05	.02	.01
☐ U192 Johnny Johnson	.05	.02	.01
☐ U193 Dedric Mathis	.05	.02	.01
☐ U194 Leon Searcy	.05	.02	.01
☐ U195 Kevin Greene	.10	.05	.01
☐ U196 Daniel Stubbs	.05	.02	.01
☐ U197 Ray Mickens	.05	.02	.01
☐ U198 Devin Wyman	.05	.02	.01
☐ U199 Lorenzo Lynch	.05	.02	.01
☐ U200 Checklist Card Jerry Rice and Dan Marino ghosted images	.30	.14	.04

1996 Collector's Choice Update Record Breaking Trio

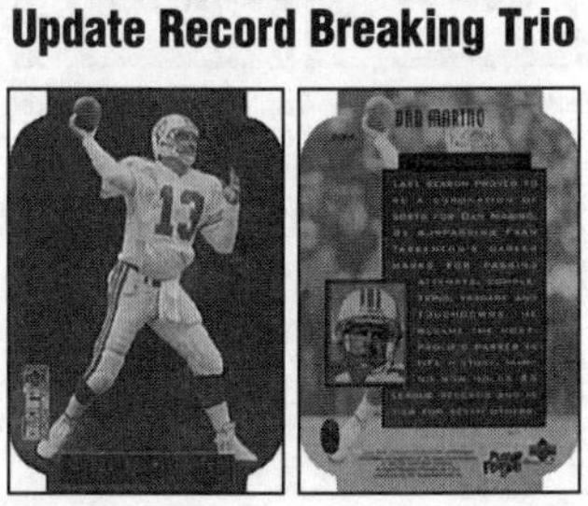

Randomly inserted in packs at the rate of one in 100, this four-card set features color player images of three record breaking players on sepia-colored crowd backgrounds and printed on Light F/X cards. The fourth card displays images of all three players.

	MINT	NRMT	EXC
COMPLETE SET (4)	80.00	36.00	10.00
COMMON CARD (1-4)	15.00	6.75	1.85
☐ 1 Joe Montana	15.00	6.75	1.85
☐ 2 Dan Marino	30.00	13.50	3.70
☐ 3 Jerry Rice	15.00	6.75	1.85
☐ 4 Joe Montana Dan Marino Jerry Rice	25.00	11.00	3.10

1996 Collector's Choice Update Stick-Ums

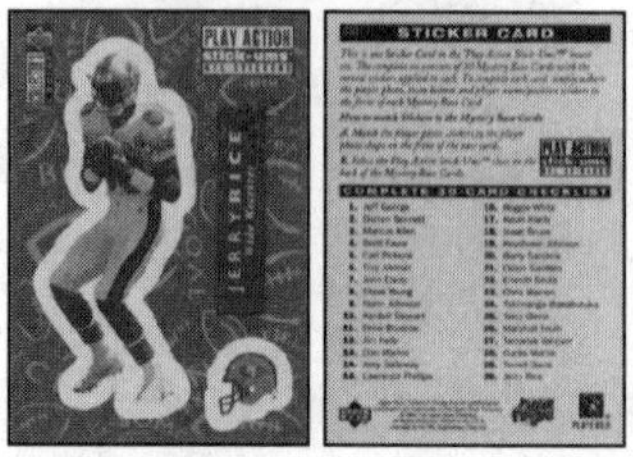

Randomly inserted in packs at a rate of one in four, this 30-card set features color player images on re-stickable stickers along with their team helmet and name and position printed in a re-stickable bar. The stickers from this set were made to stick on to their corresponding card in the Collector's Choice Update Stick-Ums Mystery Base Card set.

	MINT	NRMT	EXC
COMPLETE SET (30)	15.00	6.75	1.85
COMMON CARD (S1-S30)	.20	.09	.03
MYSTERY BASE CARDS: .25X TO .5X			
☐ S1 Jeff George	.20	.09	.03
☐ S2 Darren Bennett	.20	.09	.03
☐ S3 Marcus Allen	.40	.18	.05
☐ S4 Brett Favre	2.00	.90	.25
☐ S5 Carl Pickens	.20	.09	.03
☐ S6 Troy Aikman	1.00	.45	.12
☐ S7 John Elway	.75	.35	.09
☐ S8 Steve Young	.75	.35	.09
☐ S9 Norm Johnson	.20	.09	.03
☐ S10 Kordell Stewart	1.00	.45	.12
☐ S11 Drew Bledsoe	1.00	.45	.12
☐ S12 Jim Kelly	.40	.18	.05
☐ S13 Dan Marino	2.00	.90	.25
☐ S14 Joey Galloway	.60	.25	.07
☐ S15 Lawrence Phillips	.40	.18	.05
☐ S16 Reggie White	.40	.18	.05
☐ S17 Kevin Hardy	.20	.09	.03
☐ S18 Isaac Bruce	.40	.18	.05
☐ S19 Keyshawn Johnson	.50	.23	.06
☐ S20 Barry Sanders	1.00	.45	.12
☐ S21 Deion Sanders	.60	.25	.07
☐ S22 Emmitt Smith	2.00	.90	.25
☐ S23 Chris Warren	.20	.09	.03
☐ S24 Tim Biakabutuka	.40	.18	.05
☐ S25 Terry Glenn	1.00	.45	.12
☐ S26 Marshall Faulk	.40	.18	.05
☐ S27 Tamarick Vanover	.40	.18	.05
☐ S28 Curtis Martin	1.50	.70	.19
☐ S29 Terrell Davis	1.50	.70	.19
☐ S30 Jerry Rice	1.00	.45	.12

1996 Collector's Choice Update You Make The Play

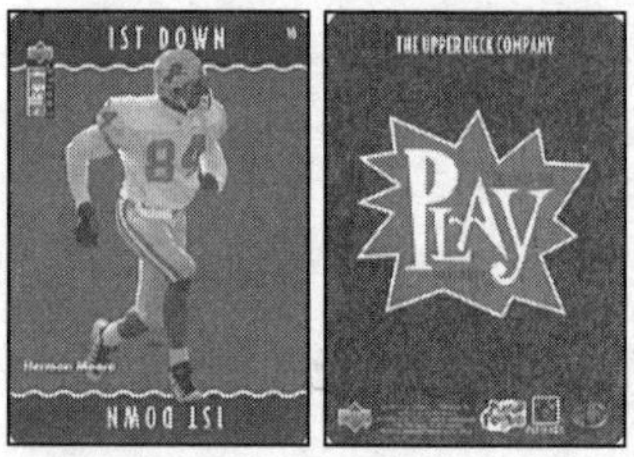

Randomly inserted one in every pack, this 90-card set features color player images on cards that are used in playing a game. Touchdowns, extra points and field goals are scored by drawing cards from stacks of Offensive and Kicking cards. Information cards with rules are inserted one in every five Collector's Choice Update packs. A set of 12 game cards could be obtained from a special mail-in offer.

	MINT	NRMT	EXC
COMPLETE SET (90)	20.00	9.00	2.50
COMMON CARD (Y1-Y90)	.15	.07	.02
☐ Y1 Norm Johnson Kick Good	.15	.07	.02
☐ Y2 Jerry Rice Touchdown	1.00	.45	.12
☐ Y3 Dan Marino 9 Yards	2.00	.90	.25
☐ Y4 Marshall Faulk 3 Yards	.50	.23	.06
☐ Y5 Neil Smith Sack - 5 Yards	.15	.07	.02
☐ Y6 Herman Moore 1st Down	.50	.23	.06
☐ Y7 Brett Favre 8 Yards	2.00	.90	.25
☐ Y8 Curtis Martin 5 Yards	1.25	.55	.16
☐ Y9 Reggie White Sack - 8 Yards	.50	.23	.06
☐ Y10 Cris Carter 12 Yards	.25	.11	.03
☐ Y11 Rick Tuten Kick Good	.15	.07	.02
☐ Y12 Steve Young 6 Yards	.75	.35	.09
☐ Y13 Barry Sanders 6 Yards	1.00	.45	.12
☐ Y14 Deion Sanders Interception	.60	.25	.07
☐ Y15 Isaac Bruce 11 Yards	.50	.23	.06
☐ Y16 Troy Aikman 6 Yards	1.00	.45	.12
☐ Y17 Emmitt Smith 7 Yards	2.00	.90	.25
☐ Y18 Junior Seau Fumble	.25	.11	.03
☐ Y19 Joey Galloway 17 Yards	.50	.23	.06
☐ Y20 Drew Bledsoe 4 Yards	1.00	.45	.12
☐ Y21 Jason Elam Kick No Good	.15	.07	.02
☐ Y22 Edgar Bennett 3 Yards	.15	.07	.02
☐ Y23 Greg Lloyd Fumble	.25	.11	.03
☐ Y24 Tamarick Vanover 13 Yards	.50	.23	.06
☐ Y25 John Elway 5 Yards	.75	.35	.09
☐ Y26 Larry Centers 4 Yards	.15	.07	.02
☐ Y27 Derrick Thomas Sack - 7 Yards	.25	.11	.03
☐ Y28 Michael Irvin 12 Yards	.50	.23	.06
☐ Y29 Jeff George 3 Yards	.25	.11	.03
☐ Y30 Thurman Thomas 3 Yards	.50	.23	.06
☐ Y31 Darren Bennett Kick Good	.15	.07	.02
☐ Y32 Ken Norton Fumble	.15	.07	.02
☐ Y33 Carl Pickens 14 Yards	.25	.11	.03
☐ Y34 Jeff Blake 10 Yards	.50	.23	.06
☐ Y35 Craig Heyward 3 Yards	.15	.07	.02
☐ Y36 Aeneas Williams No Gain	.15	.07	.02
☐ Y37 Terance Mathis 10 Yards	.15	.07	.02
☐ Y38 Jim Kelly 7 Yards	.50	.23	.06
☐ Y39 Marcus Allen 5 Yards	.50	.23	.06
☐ Y40 Tim McDonald 1 Yard	.15	.07	.02
☐ Y41 Jason Hanson Kick No Good	.15	.07	.02
☐ Y42 Scott Mitchell 4 Yards	.25	.11	.03
☐ Y43 Tim Brown 16 Yards	.25	.11	.03
☐ Y44 Kordell Stewart 3 Yards	1.00	.45	.12
☐ Y45 Eric Metcalf 4 Yards	.25	.11	.03
☐ Y46 Norm Johnson Kick Good	.15	.07	.02
☐ Y47 Jerry Rice 1st Down	1.00	.45	.12
☐ Y48 Dan Marino 1st Down	2.00	.90	.25
☐ Y49 Marshall Faulk 8 Yards	.50	.23	.06
☐ Y50 Neil Smith 2 Yards	.15	.07	.02
☐ Y51 Herman Moore 14 Yards	.50	.23	.06
☐ Y52 Brett Favre 1st Down	2.00	.90	.25
☐ Y53 Curtis Martin 6 Yards	1.25	.55	.16
☐ Y54 Reggie White 2 Yards	.50	.23	.06
☐ Y55 Cris Carter 1st Down	.25	.11	.03
☐ Y56 Rick Tuten Kick No Good	.15	.07	.02
☐ Y57 Steve Young 1st Down	.75	.35	.09
☐ Y58 Barry Sanders 4 Yards	1.00	.45	.12
☐ Y59 Deion Sanders 1 Yard	.60	.25	.07
☐ Y60 Isaac Bruce 1st Down	.50	.23	.06
☐ Y61 Troy Aikman 1st Down	1.00	.45	.12
☐ Y62 Emmitt Smith Touchdown	2.00	.90	.25
☐ Y63 Junior Seau -2 Yards	.25	.11	.03
☐ Y64 Joey Galloway 1st Down	.50	.23	.06
☐ Y65 Drew Bledsoe 1st Down	1.00	.45	.12
☐ Y66 Jason Elam Kick Good	.15	.07	.02
☐ Y67 Edgar Bennett 4 Yards	.15	.07	.02
☐ Y68 Greg Lloyd -4 Yards	.25	.11	.03
☐ Y69 Tamarick Vanover 15 Yards	.50	.23	.06
☐ Y70 John Elway 1st Down	.75	.35	.09
☐ Y71 Larry Centers 7 Yards	.15	.07	.02
☐ Y72 Derrick Thomas No Gain	.25	.11	.03
☐ Y73 Michael Irvin 1st Down	.50	.23	.06
☐ Y74 Jeff George 12 Yards	.25	.11	.03
☐ Y75 Thurman Thomas 5 Yards	.50	.23	.06
☐ Y76 Darren Bennett Kick No Good	.15	.07	.02
☐ Y77 Ken Norton -3 Yards	.15	.07	.02
☐ Y78 Carl Pickens 1st Down	.25	.11	.03
☐ Y79 Jeff Blake 1st Down	.50	.23	.06
☐ Y80 Craig Heyward 5 Yards	.15	.07	.02
☐ Y81 Aeneas Williams -3 Yards	.15	.07	.02
☐ Y82 Terance Mathis 14 Yards	.15	.07	.02
☐ Y83 Jim Kelly 1st Down	.50	.23	.06
☐ Y84 Marcus Allen 6 Yards	.50	.23	.06
☐ Y85 Tim McDonald No Gain	.15	.07	.02
☐ Y86 Jason Hanson Kick Good	.15	.07	.02
☐ Y87 Scott Mitchell 7 Yards	.25	.11	.03
☐ Y88 Tim Brown 1st Down	.25	.11	.03
☐ Y89 Kordell Stewart 7 Yards	1.00	.45	.12
☐ Y90 Eric Metcalf 7 Yards	.25	.11	.03

1992 Collector's Edge Prototypes

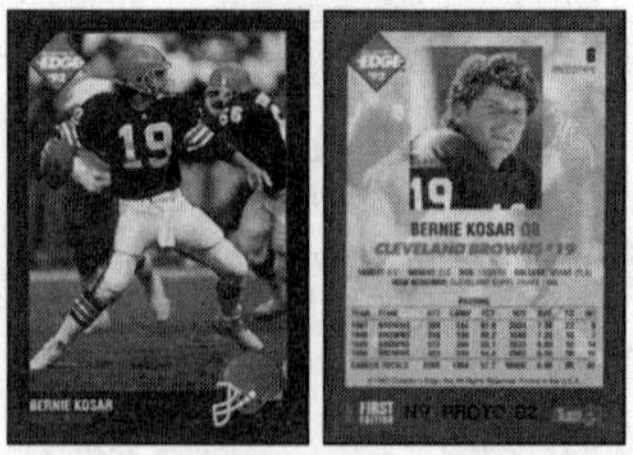

These six prototype cards were issued before the 1992 regular issue was released to show the design of Collector's Edge cards. The standard-size cards feature on the fronts color action photos bordered in black. The team helmet appears in the lower right corner. Inside a dark green border, the backs have a head shot, biography, and statistics against a ghosted reproduction of the front photo. The cards were issued in two different styles, with slightly sticky backs with a removable paper protective cover backing or with a non-sticky back. The paper-covered back versions are somewhat more difficult to find. The production figures were reportedly 8,000 for each card.

	MINT	NRMT	EXC
COMPLETE SET (6)	20.00	9.00	2.50
COMMON CARD (1-6)	1.50	.70	.19
☐ 1 Jim Kelly	2.00	.90	.25
☐ 2 Randall Cunningham	1.50	.70	.19
☐ 3 Warren Moon	2.00	.90	.25
☐ 4 John Elway	4.00	1.80	.50
☐ 5 Dan Marino	10.00	4.50	1.25
☐ 6 Bernie Kosar	1.50	.70	.19

1992 Collector's Edge

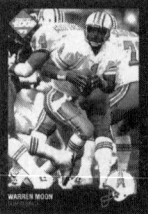

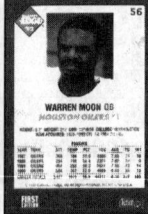

This 250-card standard-size set was issued in two series of 175 and 75 cards, respectively. Cards were issued six per pack. The cards are printed on plastic stock and production quantities were limited to 100,000 of each card; with every card individually numbered on the back. The fronts have color action photos bordered in black. The team helmet appears in the lower right corner. Inside a dark green border, the backs have a head shot, biography, and statistics against a ghosted reproduction of the front photo. The cards are checklisted below alphabetically according to teams. There are a few cards in the set which were apparently late additions as counterparts have been found with a large "X" on the cardfront. We've listed the X-out variation cards below, but they are not considered part of the complete set. It is thought card number 179 was also changed, but has not been confirmed. Rookie Cards include Edgar Bennett, Steve Bono, Robert Brooks, Terrell Buckley, Dale Carter, Marco Coleman, Quentin Coryatt, Steve Emtman, Chris Mims, Carl Pickens, Robert Porcher, Kevin Smith, Alonzo Spellman and Tommy Vardell. Two thousand five hundred cards autographed by John Elway and Ken O'Brien were randomly inserted in first series foil packs as well as factory sets. Randomly inserted in second series (Rookies) packs were 2,500 signed Ronnie Lott cards. Two Rookie/Update Prototype cards were produced as well and listed below.

	MINT	NRMT	EXC
COMPLETE SET (250)	40.00	18.00	5.00
COMPLETE SERIES 1 (175)	25.00	11.00	3.10
COMPLETE FACT.SER.1 (175)	30.00	13.50	3.70
COMPLETE SERIES 2 (75)	15.00	6.75	1.85
COMPLETE FACT.SER.2 (75)	20.00	9.00	2.50
COMMON CARD (1-250)	.10	.05	.01
☐ 1 Chris Miller	.20	.09	.03
☐ 2 Steve Broussard	.10	.05	.01
☐ 3 Mike Pritchard	.20	.09	.03
☐ 4 Tim Green	.10	.05	.01
☐ 5 Andre Rison	.20	.09	.03
☐ 6 Deion Sanders	2.00	.90	.25
☐ 7 Jim Kelly	.30	.14	.04
☐ 8 James Lofton	.20	.09	.03
☐ 9 Andre Reed	.20	.09	.03
☐ 10 Bruce Smith	.30	.14	.04
☐ 11 Thurman Thomas	.30	.14	.04
☐ 12 Cornelius Bennett	.20	.09	.03
☐ 13 Jim Harbaugh	.30	.14	.04
☐ 14 William Perry	.20	.09	.03
☐ 15 Mike Singletary	.20	.09	.03
☐ 16 Mark Carrier DB	.10	.05	.01
☐ 17 Kevin Butler	.10	.05	.01
☐ 18 Tom Waddle	.10	.05	.01
☐ 19 Boomer Esiason	.20	.09	.03
☐ 20 David Fulcher	.10	.05	.01
☐ 21 Anthony Munoz	.20	.09	.03
☐ 22 Tim McGee	.10	.05	.01
☐ 23 Harold Green	.10	.05	.01
☐ 24 Rickey Dixon	.10	.05	.01
☐ 25 Bernie Kosar	.20	.09	.03
☐ 26 Michael Dean Perry	.20	.09	.03
☐ 27 Mike Baab	.10	.05	.01
☐ 28 Brian Brennan	.10	.05	.01
☐ 29 Michael Jackson	.20	.09	.03
☐ 30 Eric Metcalf	.20	.09	.03
☐ 31 Troy Aikman	3.00	1.35	.35
☐ 32 Emmitt Smith	6.00	2.70	.75
☐ 33 Michael Irvin	.30	.14	.04
☐ 34 Jay Novacek	.20	.09	.03
☐ 35 Issiac Holt	.10	.05	.01
☐ 36 Ken Norton	.30	.14	.04
☐ 37 John Elway	2.00	.90	.25
☐ 38 Gaston Green	.10	.05	.01
☐ 39 Charles Dimry	.10	.05	.01
☐ 40 Vance Johnson	.10	.05	.01
☐ 41 Dennis Smith	.10	.05	.01
☐ 42 David Treadwell	.10	.05	.01
☐ 43 Michael Young	.10	.05	.01
☐ 44 Bennie Blades	.10	.05	.01
☐ 45 Mel Gray	.20	.09	.03
☐ 46 Andre Ware	.10	.05	.01
☐ 47 Rodney Peete	.20	.09	.03
☐ 48 Toby Caston	.10	.05	.01
☐ 49 Herman Moore	2.00	.90	.25
☐ 50 Brian Noble	.10	.05	.01
☐ 51 Sterling Sharpe	.30	.14	.04
☐ 52 Mike Tomczak	.10	.05	.01
☐ 53 Vinnie Clark	.10	.05	.01
☐ 54 Tony Mandarich	.10	.05	.01
☐ 55 Ed West	.10	.05	.01
☐ 56 Warren Moon	.30	.14	.04
☐ 57 Ray Childress	.10	.05	.01
☐ 58 Haywood Jeffires	.20	.09	.03
☐ 59 Al Smith	.10	.05	.01
☐ 60 Cris Dishman	.10	.05	.01

☐ 61 Ernest Givins	.20	.09	.03
☐ 62 Richard Johnson	.10	.05	.01
☐ 63 Eric Dickerson	.20	.09	.03
☐ 64 Jessie Hester	.10	.05	.01
☐ 65 Rohn Stark	.10	.05	.01
☐ 66 Clarence Verdin	.10	.05	.01
☐ 67 Dean Biasucci	.10	.05	.01
☐ 68 Duane Bickett	.10	.05	.01
☐ 69 Jeff George	.30	.14	.04
☐ 70 Christian Okoye	.10	.05	.01
☐ 71 Derrick Thomas	.30	.14	.04
☐ 72 Stephone Paige	.10	.05	.01
☐ 73 Dan Saleaumua	.10	.05	.01
☐ 74 Deron Cherry	.10	.05	.01
☐ 75 Kevin Ross	.10	.05	.01
☐ 76 Barry Word	.10	.05	.01
☐ 77 Ronnie Lott	.20	.09	.03
☐ 78 Greg Townsend	.10	.05	.01
☐ 79 Willie Gault	.20	.09	.03
☐ 80 Howie Long	.20	.09	.03
☐ 81 Winston Moss	.10	.05	.01
☐ 82 Steve Smith	.10	.05	.01
☐ 83 Jay Schroeder	.10	.05	.01
☐ 84 Jim Everett	.20	.09	.03
☐ 85 Flipper Anderson	.10	.05	.01
☐ 86 Henry Ellard	.20	.09	.03
☐ 87 Tony Zendejas	.10	.05	.01
☐ 88 Robert Delpino	.10	.05	.01
☐ 89 Pat Terrell	.10	.05	.01
☐ 90 Dan Marino	5.00	2.20	.60
☐ 91 Mark Clayton	.20	.09	.03
☐ 92 Jim C.Jensen	.10	.05	.01
☐ 93 Reggie Roby	.10	.05	.01
☐ 94 Sammie Smith	.10	.05	.01
☐ 95 Tony Martin	.30	.14	.04
☐ 96 Jeff Cross	.10	.05	.01
☐ 97 Anthony Carter	.20	.09	.03
☐ 98 Chris Doleman	.10	.05	.01
☐ 99 Wade Wilson	.20	.09	.03
☐ 100 Cris Carter	.30	.14	.04
☐ 101 Mike Merriweather	.10	.05	.01
☐ 102 Gary Zimmerman	.10	.05	.01
☐ 103 Chris Singleton	.10	.05	.01
☐ 104 Bruce Armstrong	.10	.05	.01
☐ 105 Marv Cook	.10	.05	.01
☐ 106 Andre Tippett	.10	.05	.01
☐ 107 Tommy Hodson	.10	.05	.01
☐ 108 Greg McMurtry	.10	.05	.01
☐ 109 Jon Vaughn	.10	.05	.01
☐ 110 Vaughan Johnson	.10	.05	.01
☐ 111 Craig Heyward	.20	.09	.03
☐ 112 Floyd Turner	.10	.05	.01
☐ 113 Pat Swilling	.20	.09	.03
☐ 114 Rickey Jackson	.10	.05	.01
☐ 115 Steve Walsh	.10	.05	.01
☐ 116 Phil Simms	.20	.09	.03
☐ 117 Carl Banks	.10	.05	.01
☐ 118 Mark Ingram	.10	.05	.01
☐ 119 Bart Oates	.10	.05	.01
☐ 120 Lawrence Taylor	.30	.14	.04
☐ 121 Jeff Hostetler	.20	.09	.03
☐ 122 Rob Moore	.20	.09	.03
☐ 123 Ken O'Brien	.10	.05	.01
☐ 124 Bill Pickel	.10	.05	.01
☐ 125 Irv Eatman	.10	.05	.01
☐ 126 Browning Nagle	.10	.05	.01
☐ 127 Al Toon	.20	.09	.03
☐ 128 Randall Cunningham	.20	.09	.03
☐ 129 Eric Allen	.10	.05	.01
☐ 130 Mike Golic	.10	.05	.01
☐ 131 Fred Barnett	.30	.14	.04
☐ 132 Keith Byars	.10	.05	.01
☐ 133 Calvin Williams	.20	.09	.03
☐ 134 Randal Hill	.10	.05	.01
☐ 135 Ricky Proehl	.10	.05	.01
☐ 136 Lance Smith	.10	.05	.01
☐ 137 Ernie Jones	.10	.05	.01
☐ 138 Timm Rosenbach	.10	.05	.01
☐ 139 Anthony Thompson	.10	.05	.01
☐ 140 Bubby Brister	.10	.05	.01
☐ 141 Merril Hoge	.10	.05	.01
☐ 142 Louis Lipps	.10	.05	.01
☐ 143 Eric Green	.10	.05	.01
☐ 144 Gary Anderson K	.10	.05	.01
☐ 145 Neil O'Donnell	.30	.14	.04
☐ 146 Rod Bernstine	.10	.05	.01
☐ 147 John Friesz	.20	.09	.03
☐ 148 Anthony Miller	.20	.09	.03
☐ 149 Junior Seau	.30	.14	.04
☐ 150 Leslie O'Neal	.20	.09	.03
☐ 151 Nate Lewis	.10	.05	.01
☐ 152 Steve Young	2.00	.90	.25
☐ 153 Kevin Fagan	.10	.05	.01
☐ 154 Charles Haley	.20	.09	.03
☐ 155 Tom Rathman	.10	.05	.01
☐ 156 Jerry Rice	3.00	1.35	.35
☐ 157 John Taylor	.20	.09	.03
☐ 158 Brian Blades	.20	.09	.03
☐ 159 Patrick Hunter	.10	.05	.01
☐ 160 Cortez Kennedy	.20	.09	.03
☐ 161 Vann McElroy	.10	.05	.01
☐ 162 Dan McGwire	.10	.05	.01
☐ 163 John L. Williams	.10	.05	.01
☐ 164 Gary Anderson RB	.10	.05	.01
☐ 165 Broderick Thomas	.10	.05	.01
☐ 166 Vinny Testaverde	.20	.09	.03
☐ 167 Lawrence Dawsey	.20	.09	.03
☐ 168 Paul Gruber	.10	.05	.01
☐ 169 Keith McCants	.10	.05	.01
☐ 170 Mark Rypien	.10	.05	.01
☐ 171 Gary Clark	.30	.14	.04
☐ 172 Earnest Byner	.10	.05	.01
☐ 173 Brian Mitchell	.20	.09	.03
☐ 174 Monte Coleman	.10	.05	.01
☐ 175 Joe Jacoby	.10	.05	.01
☐ 176 Tommy Vardell	.20	.09	.03
☐ 177 Troy Vincent	.20	.09	.03
☐ 178 Robert Jones	.10	.05	.01
☐ 179 Marc Boutte	.10	.05	.01
☐ 180 Marco Coleman	.20	.09	.03
☐ 181 Chris Mims	.20	.09	.03
☐ 182 Tony Casillas	.10	.05	.01
☐ 182X Ray Roberts Large X on front	10.00	4.50	1.25
☐ 183 Shane Dronett	.10	.05	.01
☐ 184 Sean Gilbert	.30	.14	.04
☐ 185 Siran Stacy	.10	.05	.01
☐ 186 Tommy Maddox	.10	.05	.01
☐ 187 Steve Israel	.10	.05	.01
☐ 188 Brad Muster	.10	.05	.01
☐ 188X Casey Weldon large X on front	10.00	4.50	1.25
☐ 189 Shane Collins	.10	.05	.01
☐ 190 Terrell Buckley	.10	.05	.01
☐ 191 Eugene Chung	.10	.05	.01
☐ 192 Leon Searcy	.20	.09	.03
☐ 193 Chuck Smith	.10	.05	.01
☐ 194 Patrick Rowe	.10	.05	.01
☐ 195 Bill Johnson	.10	.05	.01
☐ 196 Gerald Dixon	.10	.05	.01
☐ 197 Robert Porcher	.20	.09	.03
☐ 198 Tracy Scroggins	.10	.05	.01
☐ 199 Jason Hanson	.20	.09	.03
☐ 200 Corey Harris	.10	.05	.01
☐ 201 Eddie Robinson	.10	.05	.01
☐ 202 Steve Emtman	.10	.05	.01
☐ 203 Ashley Ambrose	.20	.09	.03
☐ 204 Greg Skrepenak	.10	.05	.01
☐ 205 Todd Collins	.10	.05	.01
☐ 206 Derek Brown TE	.10	.05	.01
☐ 207 Kurt Barber	.10	.05	.01
☐ 208 Tony Sacca	.10	.05	.01
☐ 209 Mark Wheeler	.10	.05	.01
☐ 210 Kevin Smith	.30	.14	.04
☐ 211 John Fina	.10	.05	.01
☐ 212 Johnny Mitchell	.10	.05	.01
☐ 213 Dale Carter	.30	.14	.04
☐ 214 Bob Spitulski	.10	.05	.01
☐ 215 Phillippi Sparks	.10	.05	.01
☐ 216 Levon Kirkland	.10	.05	.01
☐ 217 Mike Sherrard	.10	.05	.01
☐ 218 Marquez Pope	.10	.05	.01
☐ 219 Courtney Hawkins	.20	.09	.03
☐ 220 Tyji Armstrong	.10	.05	.01
☐ 221 Keith Jackson	.20	.09	.03
☐ 222 Clayton Holmes	.10	.05	.01
☐ 223 Quentin Coryatt	.30	.14	.04
☐ 224 Troy Auzenne	.10	.05	.01
☐ 225 David Klingler	.20	.09	.03
☐ 226 Darryl Williams	.10	.05	.01
☐ 227 Carl Pickens	3.00	1.35	.35
☐ 228 Jimmy Smith	.30	.14	.04
☐ 229 Chester McGlockton	.30	.14	.04
☐ 230 Robert Brooks	2.50	1.10	.30
☐ 231 Alonzo Spellman	.20	.09	.03
☐ 232 Darren Woodson	.30	.14	.04
☐ 233 Lewis Billups	.10	.05	.01
☐ 234 Edgar Bennett	1.50	.70	.19
☐ 235 Vaughn Dunbar	.10	.05	.01
☐ 236 Steve Bono	.50	.23	.06
☐ 237 Clarence Kay	.10	.05	.01
☐ 238 Chris Hinton	.10	.05	.01
☐ 239 Jimmie Jones	.10	.05	.01
☐ 240 Vai Sikahema	.10	.05	.01
☐ 241 Russell Maryland	.20	.09	.03
☐ 241X Bobby Humphrey large X on front	10.00	4.50	1.25
☐ 242 Neal Anderson	.10	.05	.01
☐ 242X Mark Bavaro large X on front	10.00	4.50	1.25
☐ 243 Charles Mann	.10	.05	.01
☐ 244 Hugh Millen	.10	.05	.01
☐ 245 Roger Craig	.20	.09	.03
☐ 246 Rich Gannon	.10	.05	.01
☐ 247 Ricky Ervins	.10	.05	.01
☐ 247X Marion Butts large X on front	10.00	4.50	1.25
☐ 248 Leonard Marshall	.10	.05	.01
☐ 249 Eric Dickerson	.20	.09	.03
☐ 250 Joe Montana	3.00	1.35	.35
☐ RU1 Terrell Buckley Prototype	4.00	1.80	.50
☐ RU2 Tommy Maddox Prototype	4.00	1.80	.50
☐ AU37 John Elway (2,500 signed)	80.00	36.00	10.00
☐ AU77 Ronnie Lott Bonus (2,500 signed)	30.00	13.50	3.70
☐ AU123 Ken O'Brien (2,500 signed)	20.00	9.00	2.50

1992 Collector's Edge Special

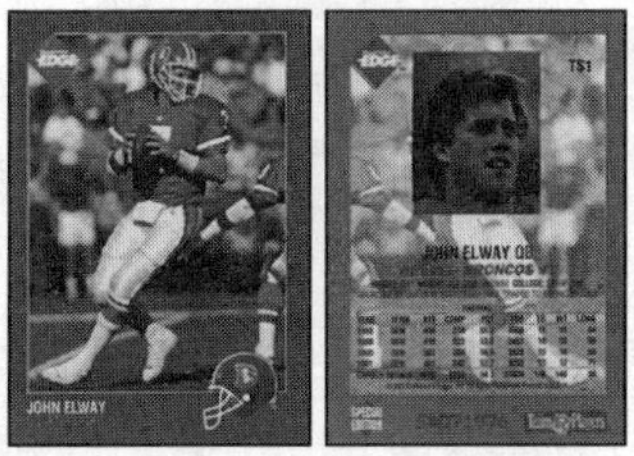

This four-card set was issued to promote the Tuff Stuff Buyer's Club. The Elway card was distributed in all copies of the November issue of Tuff Stuff. More than 250,000 cards were printed; only about 40,000 each of the remaining three cards were printed. One of these was given away with each paid membership in the Buyers Club. The Elway card was also printed with the designations "Proto 1," "Elway Foundation," and "John Elway Dealerships." The number of these additional cards is reportedly less than 50,000 and they are not included in the complete set price. The fronts of these standard-size promo cards have a color action player photo inside a gold frame and dark blue borders. The upper left corner of the picture is cut off. The player's name and position appear in the bottom border, and the team helmet is superimposed at the lower right corner of the picture. Within bright blue borders, the backs carry a color head shot, biography, and statistics on a ghosted version of the front photo. The cards are numbered on the back, and each has a serial number in the bottom border.

	MINT	NRMT	EXC
COMPLETE SET (4)	10.00	4.50	1.25
COMMON CARD (TS1-TS4)	2.00	.90	.25
☐ TS1 John Elway	2.00	.90	.25
☐ TS2 Ronnie Lott	4.00	1.80	.50
☐ TS3 Jim Everett	3.00	1.35	.35
☐ TS4 Bernie Kosar	3.00	1.35	.35
☐ PROT1 John Elway	8.00	3.60	1.00
☐ NNO Elway Foundation	25.00	11.00	3.10
☐ NNO Elway Dealerships	25.00	11.00	3.10

1993 Collector's Edge Prototypes

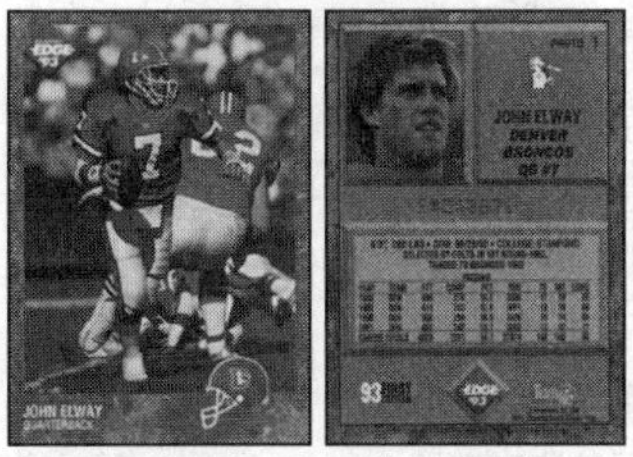

These six prototype cards were issued before the 1993 regular issue set was released to show the design of the 1993 Collector's Edge regular series. Forty thousand six-card sets were produced, with each card serial-numbered from 00001 to 40,000 on the backs. The standard-size cards feature color action photos with blue marbleized borders on their fronts. The team helmet appears in the lower right corner. Inside a green marbleized border, the backs have a head shot, biography, and statistics placed on a three-dimensional style gray granite panel. The cards are numbered on the back "Proto X." Also, 8 1/2" by 11" versions of these prototypes were packed in dealer cases. The oversized cards are unnumbered, and the production number is handwritten on the back in a gold-colored permanent marker. Otherwise, the cards are identical to their standard-size counterparts but are valued at two to three times the corresponding values listed below.

	MINT	NRMT	EXC
COMPLETE SET (6)	12.00	5.50	1.50
COMMON CARD (1-6)	1.50	.70	.19
☐ 1 John Elway	3.50	1.55	.45
☐ 2 Derrick Thomas	1.50	.70	.19
☐ 3 Randall Cunningham	1.50	.70	.19
☐ 4 Thurman Thomas	2.00	.90	.25
☐ 5 Warren Moon	1.50	.70	.19
☐ 6 Barry Sanders	5.00	2.20	.60

1993 Collector's Edge RU Prototypes

These five prototypes were issued to herald the design of the regular 1993 Collector's Edge Rookie/Update set. Each card carries a production number on its back. The standard-size cards feature on their fronts color player action shots framed by a thin red line and having blue marbleized borders. The backgrounds of the photos are slightly ghosted, making the image of the featured player stand out. The player's name and position, as well as the team helmet, rest at the bottom. The back has a gray lithic design with green marbleized borders. A color player head shot appears at the upper left. His name, team name and logo, position, and uniform number are shown alongside to the right. Biography and statistics appear below. The cards are numbered on the back with an "RU" prefix.

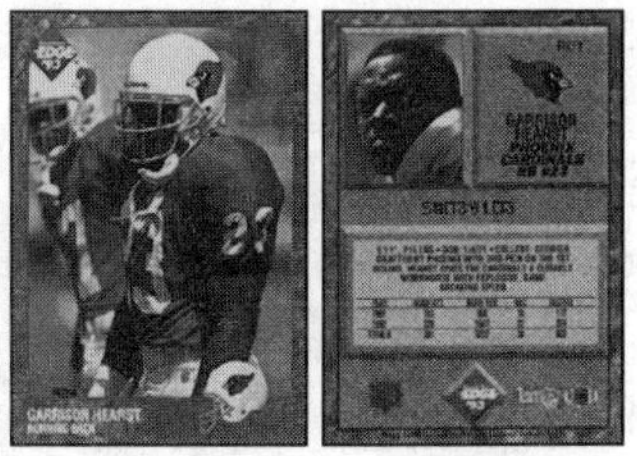

	MINT	NRMT	EXC
COMPLETE SET (5)	5.00	2.20	.60
COMMON CARD (RU1-RU5)	1.00	.45	.12
☐ RU1 Garrison Hearst	1.50	.70	.19
☐ RU2 Reggie White	1.50	.70	.19
☐ RU3 Boomer Esiason	1.00	.45	.12
☐ RU4 Rod Bernstine	1.00	.45	.12
☐ RU5 Dana Stubblefield	1.25	.55	.16

1993 Collector's Edge

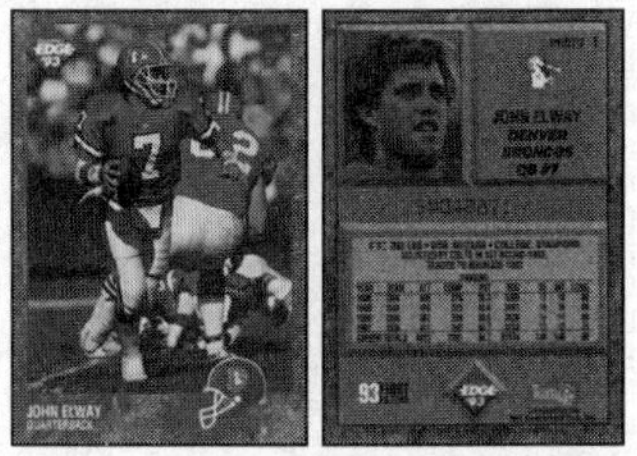

The 1993 Collector's Edge football set consists of 325 standard-size cards. The cards feature on their fronts color action shots with blue marbleized borders. The player's name and position appear at the lower left; the team helmet appears at the lower right. Inside a green marbleized border, the backs have a head shot, biography, and statistics placed on a gray, simulated three-dimensional granite panel. The production run was limited to 100,000 of each player, with each card serially numbered from 000001 to 100,000. In this year's issue, the cards were printed on heavier, 20-mil, thick plastic stock. Also this year's set added new Team Cards that depict whole-team portraits of the 28 NFL teams. The cards are numbered on the back and checklisted below according to teams. Cards 251-325 comprise the Rookie Update series. Randomly inserted in the foil packs was a factory redemption card that entitled the holder to redeem the card for a factory set, in which every card had the same serial number. The offer expired at noon on February 28, 1994. Two cards commemorating the newest expansion teams in the NFL, the Jacksonville Jaguars and the Carolina Panthers, were produced. The Panthers card, originally numbered 326, was issued very late in the pack production run. Only 4,000 of these cards were issued. The company then produced a second version of the Panthers card as well as a Jaguars card. These are numbered with an "M" prefix. The cards were available by mail and cost $3.95 with a production figure of 25,000. The purple marbleized fronts have a grey granite panel with a welcome to the new expansion team. The team logo appears in the lower right corner. Rookie Cards include Drew Bledsoe, Vincent Brisby, Reggie Brooks, Mark Brunell, Curtis Conway, Garrison Hearst, Billy Jo Hobert, Qadry Ismail, Glyn Milburn, Rick Mirer, Roosevelt Potts, Robert Smith and Dana Stubblefield.

	MINT	NRMT	EXC
COMPLETE SET (325)	20.00	9.00	2.50
COMPLETE SERIES 1 (250)	10.00	4.50	1.25
COMPLETE SERIES 2 (75)	10.00	4.50	1.25
COMMON CARD (1-325)	.05	.02	.01
COMPLETE CHECKLISTS (5)	2.00	.90	.25
☐ 1 Falcons Team Photo	.05	.02	.01
☐ 2 Michael Haynes	.10	.05	.01
☐ 3 Chris Miller	.10	.05	.01
☐ 4 Mike Pritchard	.10	.05	.01
☐ 5 Andre Rison	.10	.05	.01
☐ 6 Deion Sanders	.60	.25	.07
☐ 7 Chuck Smith	.05	.02	.01
☐ 8 Drew Hill	.05	.02	.01
☐ 9 Bobby Hebert	.05	.02	.01
☐ 10 Bills Team Photo	.05	.02	.01
☐ 11 Matt Darby	.05	.02	.01
☐ 12 John Fina	.05	.02	.01
☐ 13 Jim Kelly	.25	.11	.03
☐ 14 Marvcus Patton	.05	.02	.01
☐ 15 Andre Reed	.10	.05	.01
☐ 16 Thurman Thomas	.25	.11	.03
☐ 17 James Lofton	.10	.05	.01
☐ 18 Bruce Smith	.25	.11	.03
☐ 19 Bears Team Photo	.05	.02	.01
☐ 20 Neal Anderson	.05	.02	.01
☐ 21 Troy Auzenne	.05	.02	.01
☐ 22 Jim Harbaugh	.25	.11	.03
☐ 23 Alonzo Spellman	.05	.02	.01
☐ 24 Tom Waddle	.05	.02	.01
☐ 25 Darren Lewis	.05	.02	.01
☐ 26 Wendell Davis	.05	.02	.01
☐ 27 Will Furrer	.05	.02	.01
☐ 28 Bengals Team Photo	.05	.02	.01
☐ 29 David Klingler	.05	.02	.01
☐ 30 Ricardo McDonald	.05	.02	.01

☐ 31 Carl Pickens	.75	.35	.09
☐ 32 Harold Green	.05	.02	.01
☐ 33 Anthony Munoz	.10	.05	.01
☐ 34 Darryl Williams	.05	.02	.01
☐ 35 Browns Team Photo	.05	.02	.01
☐ 36 Michael Jackson	.10	.05	.01
☐ 37 Pio Sagapolutele	.05	.02	.01
☐ 38 Tommy Vardell	.05	.02	.01
☐ 39 Bernie Kosar	.10	.05	.01
☐ 40 Michael Dean Perry	.10	.05	.01
☐ 41 Bill Johnson	.05	.02	.01
☐ 42 Vinny Testaverde	.10	.05	.01
☐ 43 Cowboys Team Photo	.05	.02	.01
☐ 44 Troy Aikman	1.00	.45	.12
☐ 45 Alvin Harper	.10	.05	.01
☐ 46 Michael Irvin	.25	.11	.03
☐ 47 Russell Maryland	.05	.02	.01
☐ 48 Emmitt Smith	2.00	.90	.25
☐ 49 Kenneth Gant	.05	.02	.01
☐ 50 Jay Novacek	.10	.05	.01
☐ 51 Robert Jones	.05	.02	.01
☐ 52 Clayton Holmes	.05	.02	.01
☐ 53 Broncos Team Photo	.05	.02	.01
☐ 54 Mike Croel	.05	.02	.01
☐ 55 Shane Dronett	.05	.02	.01
☐ 56 Kenny Walker	.05	.02	.01
☐ 57 Tommy Maddox	.05	.02	.01
☐ 58 Dennis Smith	.05	.02	.01
☐ 59 John Elway	.75	.35	.09
☐ 60 Karl Mecklenburg	.05	.02	.01
☐ 61 Steve Atwater	.05	.02	.01
☐ 62 Vance Johnson	.05	.02	.01
☐ 63 Lions Team Photo	.05	.02	.01
☐ 64 Barry Sanders	1.00	.45	.12
☐ 65 Andre Ware	.05	.02	.01
☐ 66 Pat Swilling	.05	.02	.01
☐ 67 Jason Hanson	.05	.02	.01
☐ 68 Willie Green	.05	.02	.01
☐ 69 Herman Moore	.75	.35	.09
☐ 70 Rodney Peete	.05	.02	.01
☐ 71 Erik Kramer	.10	.05	.01
☐ 72 Robert Porcher	.05	.02	.01
☐ 73 Packers Team Photo	.05	.02	.01
☐ 74 Terrell Buckley	.05	.02	.01
☐ 75 Reggie White	.25	.11	.03
☐ 76 Brett Favre	2.00	.90	.25
☐ 77 Don Majkowski	.05	.02	.01
☐ 78 Edgar Bennett	.25	.11	.03
☐ 79 Ty Detmer	.25	.11	.03
☐ 80 Sanjay Beach	.05	.02	.01
☐ 81 Sterling Sharpe	.25	.11	.03
☐ 82 Oilers Team Photo	.05	.02	.01
☐ 83 Gary Brown	.05	.02	.01
☐ 84 Ernest Givins	.10	.05	.01
☐ 85 Haywood Jeffires	.10	.05	.01
☐ 86 Corey Harris	.05	.02	.01
☐ 87 Warren Moon	.25	.11	.03
☐ 88 Eddie Robinson	.05	.02	.01
☐ 89 Lorenzo White	.05	.02	.01
☐ 90 Bo Orlando	.05	.02	.01
☐ 91 Colts Team Photo	.05	.02	.01
☐ 92 Quentin Coryatt	.10	.05	.01
☐ 93 Steve Emtman	.05	.02	.01
☐ 94 Jeff George	.25	.11	.03
☐ 95 Jessie Hester	.05	.02	.01
☐ 96 Rohn Stark	.05	.02	.01
☐ 97 Ashley Ambrose	.05	.02	.01
☐ 98 John Baylor	.05	.02	.01
☐ 99 Chiefs Team Photo	.05	.02	.01
☐ 100 Tim Barnett	.05	.02	.01
☐ 101 Derrick Thomas	.25	.11	.03
☐ 102 Barry Word	.05	.02	.01
☐ 103 Dale Carter	.05	.02	.01
☐ 104 Jayice Pearson	.05	.02	.01
☐ 105 Tracy Simien	.05	.02	.01
☐ 106 Harvey Williams	.10	.05	.01
☐ 107 Dave Krieg	.10	.05	.01
☐ 108 Christian Okoye	.05	.02	.01
☐ 109 Joe Montana	1.00	.45	.12
☐ 110 Dolphins Team Photo	.05	.02	.01
☐ 111 J.B. Brown	.05	.02	.01
☐ 112 Marco Coleman	.05	.02	.01
☐ 113 Dan Marino	2.00	.90	.25
☐ 114 Mark Clayton	.05	.02	.01
☐ 115 Mark Higgs	.05	.02	.01
☐ 116 Bryan Cox	.05	.02	.01
☐ 117 Chuck Klingbeil	.05	.02	.01
☐ 118 Troy Vincent	.05	.02	.01
☐ 119 Keith Jackson	.10	.05	.01
☐ 120 Bruce Alexander	.05	.02	.01
☐ 121 Vikings Team Photo	.05	.02	.01
☐ 122 Terry Allen	.25	.11	.03
☐ 123 Rich Gannon	.05	.02	.01
☐ 124 Todd Scott	.05	.02	.01
☐ 125 Cris Carter	.25	.11	.03
☐ 126 Sean Salisbury	.05	.02	.01
☐ 127 Jack Del Rio	.05	.02	.01
☐ 128 Chris Doleman	.05	.02	.01
☐ 129 Anthony Carter	.10	.05	.01
☐ 130 Patriots Team Photo	.05	.02	.01
☐ 131 Eugene Chung	.05	.02	.01
☐ 132 Todd Collins	.05	.02	.01
☐ 133 Tommy Hodson	.05	.02	.01
☐ 134 Leonard Russell	.10	.05	.01
☐ 135 Jon Vaughn	.05	.02	.01

☐ 136 Andre Tippett	.05	.02	.01
☐ 137 Saints Team Photo	.05	.02	.01
☐ 138 Wesley Carroll	.05	.02	.01
☐ 139 Richard Cooper	.05	.02	.01
☐ 140 Vaughn Dunbar	.05	.02	.01
☐ 141 Fred McAfee	.05	.02	.01
☐ 142 Torrance Small	.05	.02	.01
☐ 143 Steve Walsh	.05	.02	.01
☐ 144 Vaughan Johnson	.05	.02	.01
☐ 145 Giants Team Photo	.05	.02	.01
☐ 146 Jarrod Bunch	.05	.02	.01
☐ 147 Phil Simms	.10	.05	.01
☐ 148 Carl Banks	.05	.02	.01
☐ 149 Lawrence Taylor	.25	.11	.03
☐ 150 Rodney Hampton	.25	.11	.03
☐ 151 Phillippi Sparks	.05	.02	.01
☐ 152 Derek Brown TE	.05	.02	.01
☐ 153 Jets Team Photo	.05	.02	.01
☐ 154 Boomer Esiason	.10	.05	.01
☐ 155 Johnny Mitchell	.05	.02	.01
☐ 156 Rob Moore	.10	.05	.01
☐ 157 Ronnie Lott	.10	.05	.01
☐ 158 Browning Nagle	.05	.02	.01
☐ 159 Johnny Johnson	.05	.02	.01
☐ 160 Dwayne White	.05	.02	.01
☐ 161 Blair Thomas	.05	.02	.01
☐ 162 Eagles Team Photo	.05	.02	.01
☐ 163 Randall Cunningham	.10	.05	.01
☐ 164 Fred Barnett	.10	.05	.01
☐ 165 Siran Stacy	.05	.02	.01
☐ 166 Keith Byars	.05	.02	.01
☐ 167 Calvin Williams	.10	.05	.01
☐ 168 Jeff Sydner	.05	.02	.01
☐ 169 Tommy Jeter	.05	.02	.01
☐ 170 Andre Waters	.05	.02	.01
☐ 171 Phoenix Team Photo	.05	.02	.01
☐ 172 Steve Beuerlein	.05	.02	.01
☐ 173 Randal Hill	.05	.02	.01
☐ 174 Timm Rosenbach	.05	.02	.01
☐ 175 Ed Cunningham	.05	.02	.01
☐ 176 Walter Reeves	.05	.02	.01
☐ 177 Michael Zordich	.05	.02	.01
☐ 178 Gary Clark	.10	.05	.01
☐ 179 Ken Harvey	.05	.02	.01
☐ 180 Steelers Team Photo	.05	.02	.01
☐ 181 Barry Foster	.10	.05	.01
☐ 182 Neil O'Donnell	.25	.11	.03
☐ 183 Leon Searcy	.05	.02	.01
☐ 184 Bubby Brister	.05	.02	.01
☐ 185 Merril Hoge	.05	.02	.01
☐ 186 Joel Steed	.05	.02	.01
☐ 187 Raiders Team Photo	.05	.02	.01
☐ 188 Nick Bell	.05	.02	.01
☐ 189 Eric Dickerson	.10	.05	.01
☐ 190 Nolan Harrison	.05	.02	.01
☐ 191 Todd Marinovich	.05	.02	.01
☐ 192 Greg Skrepenak	.05	.02	.01
☐ 193 Howie Long	.10	.05	.01
☐ 194 Jay Schroeder	.05	.02	.01
☐ 195 Chester McGlockton	.10	.05	.01
☐ 196 Rams Team Photo	.05	.02	.01
☐ 197 Jim Everett	.10	.05	.01
☐ 198 Sean Gilbert	.10	.05	.01
☐ 199 Steve Israel	.05	.02	.01
☐ 200 Marc Boutte	.05	.02	.01
☐ 201 Joe Milinichik	.05	.02	.01
☐ 202 Henry Ellard	.10	.05	.01
☐ 203 Jackie Slater	.05	.02	.01
☐ 204 Chargers Team Photo	.05	.02	.01
☐ 205 Eric Bieniemy	.05	.02	.01
☐ 206 Marion Butts	.05	.02	.01
☐ 207 Nate Lewis	.05	.02	.01
☐ 208 Junior Seau	.25	.11	.03
☐ 209 Steve Hendrickson	.05	.02	.01
☐ 210 Chris Mims	.05	.02	.01
☐ 211 Harry Swayne	.05	.02	.01
☐ 212 Marquez Pope	.05	.02	.01
☐ 213 Donald Frank	.05	.02	.01
☐ 214 Anthony Miller	.10	.05	.01
☐ 215 Seahawks Team Photo	.05	.02	.01
☐ 216 Cortez Kennedy	.10	.05	.01
☐ 217 Dan McGwire	.05	.02	.01
☐ 218 Kelly Stouffer	.05	.02	.01
☐ 219 Chris Warren	.10	.05	.01
☐ 220 Brian Blades	.10	.05	.01
☐ 221 Rod Stephens	.05	.02	.01
☐ 222 49ers Team Photo	.05	.02	.01
☐ 223 Jerry Rice	1.00	.45	.12
☐ 224 Ricky Watters	.25	.11	.03
☐ 225 Steve Young	.75	.35	.09
☐ 226 Tom Rathman	.05	.02	.01
☐ 227 Dana Hall	.05	.02	.01
☐ 228 Amp Lee	.05	.02	.01
☐ 229 Brian Bollinger	.05	.02	.01
☐ 230 Keith DeLong	.05	.02	.01
☐ 231 John Taylor	.10	.05	.01
☐ 232 Buccaneers Team Photo	.05	.02	.01
☐ 233 Tyji Armstrong	.05	.02	.01
☐ 234 Lawrence Dawsey	.05	.02	.01
☐ 235 Mark Wheeler	.05	.02	.01
☐ 236 Vince Workman	.05	.02	.01
☐ 237 Reggie Cobb	.05	.02	.01
☐ 238 Tony Mayberry	.05	.02	.01
☐ 239 Marty Carter	.05	.02	.01
☐ 240 Courtney Hawkins	.05	.02	.01

☐ 241 Ray Seals	.05	.02	.01
☐ 242 Mark Carrier WR	.10	.05	.01
☐ 243 Redskins Team Photo	.05	.02	.01
☐ 244 Mark Rypien	.05	.02	.01
☐ 245 Ricky Ervins	.05	.02	.01
☐ 246 Gerald Riggs	.05	.02	.01
☐ 247 Art Monk	.10	.05	.01
☐ 248 Mark Schlereth	.05	.02	.01
☐ 249 Monte Coleman	.05	.02	.01
☐ 250 Wilber Marshall	.05	.02	.01
☐ 251 Ben Coleman	.05	.02	.01
☐ 252 Curtis Conway	.75	.35	.09
☐ 253 Ernest Dye	.05	.02	.01
☐ 254 Todd Kelly	.05	.02	.01
☐ 255 Patrick Bates	.05	.02	.01
☐ 256 George Teague	.10	.05	.01
☐ 257 Mark Brunell	3.00	1.35	.35
☐ 258 Adrian Hardy	.05	.02	.01
☐ 259 Dana Stubblefield	.25	.11	.03
☐ 260 William Roaf	.10	.05	.01
☐ 261 Irv Smith	.05	.02	.01
☐ 262 Drew Bledsoe	3.00	1.35	.35
☐ 263 Dan Williams	.05	.02	.01
☐ 264 Jerry Ball	.05	.02	.01
☐ 265 Mark Clayton	.05	.02	.01
☐ 266 John Stephens	.05	.02	.01
☐ 267 Reggie White	.25	.11	.03
☐ 268 Jeff Hostetler	.10	.05	.01
☐ 269 Boomer Esiason	.10	.05	.01
☐ 270 Wade Wilson	.05	.02	.01
☐ 271 Steve Beuerlein	.05	.02	.01
☐ 272 Tim McDonald	.05	.02	.01
☐ 273 Craig Heyward	.10	.05	.01
☐ 274 Everson Walls	.05	.02	.01
☐ 275 Stan Humphries	.25	.11	.03
☐ 276 Carl Banks	.05	.02	.01
☐ 277 Brad Muster	.05	.02	.01
☐ 278 Tim Harris	.05	.02	.01
☐ 279 Gary Clark	.10	.05	.01
☐ 280 Joe Milinichik	.05	.02	.01
☐ 281 Leonard Marshall	.05	.02	.01
☐ 282 Joe Montana	1.00	.45	.12
☐ 283 Rod Bernstine	.05	.02	.01
☐ 284 Mark Carrier WR	.10	.05	.01
☐ 285 Michael Brooks	.05	.02	.01
☐ 286 Marvin Jones	.05	.02	.01
☐ 287 John Copeland	.10	.05	.01
☐ 288 Eric Curry	.05	.02	.01
☐ 289 Steve Everitt	.05	.02	.01
☐ 290 Tom Carter	.10	.05	.01
☐ 291 Deon Figures	.10	.05	.01
☐ 292A Leonard Renfro	.05	.02	.01
☐ 292B Leonard Renfro	.05	.02	.01
☐ 293 Thomas Smith	.10	.05	.01
☐ 294 Carlton Gray	.05	.02	.01
☐ 295 Demetrius DuBose	.05	.02	.01
☐ 296 Coleman Rudolph	.05	.02	.01
☐ 297 John Parrella	.05	.02	.01
☐ 298 Billy Joe Hobert	.25	.11	.03
☐ 299 Reggie Brooks	.10	.05	.01
☐ 300 Garrison Hearst	1.25	.55	.16
☐ 301 John Elway	.75	.35	.09
☐ 302 Brad Hopkins	.05	.02	.01
☐ 303 Darrien Gordon UER Card states he was drafted 12th instead of 22nd	.05	.02	.01
☐ 304 Robert Smith	.75	.35	.09
☐ 305 Chris Slade	.10	.05	.01
☐ 306 Ryan McNeil	.05	.02	.01
☐ 307 Micheal Barrow	.05	.02	.01
☐ 308 Roosevelt Potts	.05	.02	.01
☐ 309 Qadry Ismail	.25	.11	.03
☐ 310 Reggie Freeman	.05	.02	.01
☐ 311 Vincent Brisby	.25	.11	.03
☐ 312 Rick Mirer	1.25	.55	.16
☐ 313 Billy Joe Hobert	.40	.18	.05
☐ 314 Natrone Means	1.25	.55	.16
☐ 315 Gary Zimmerman	.05	.02	.01
☐ 316 Bobby Hebert	.05	.02	.01
☐ 317 Don Beebe	.05	.02	.01
☐ 318 Wilber Marshall	.05	.02	.01
☐ 319 Marcus Allen	.25	.11	.03
☐ 320 Ronnie Lott	.10	.05	.01
☐ 321 Ricky Sanders	.05	.02	.01
☐ 322 Charles Mann	.05	.02	.01
☐ 323 Simon Fletcher	.05	.02	.01
☐ 324 Johnny Johnson	.05	.02	.01
☐ 325 Gary Plummer	.05	.02	.01
☐ 326 Carolina Panthers Insert	35.00	16.00	4.40
☐ M326 Carolina Panthers Send Away	5.00	2.20	.60
☐ M327 Jacksonville Jaguars Send Away	5.00	2.20	.60
☐ PRO1 John Elway AU/3000	80.00	36.00	10.00
☐ NNO Factory Set Redemption Card (Expired)	1.00	.45	.12

1993 Collector's Edge Elway Prisms

Randomly inserted in 1993 Collector's Edge packs, these five standard-size cards feature blue-bordered prismatic foil fronts that carry color cut-outs of John Elway in action against a silver prismatic background. The Collector's Edge logo appears at the upper left, and a

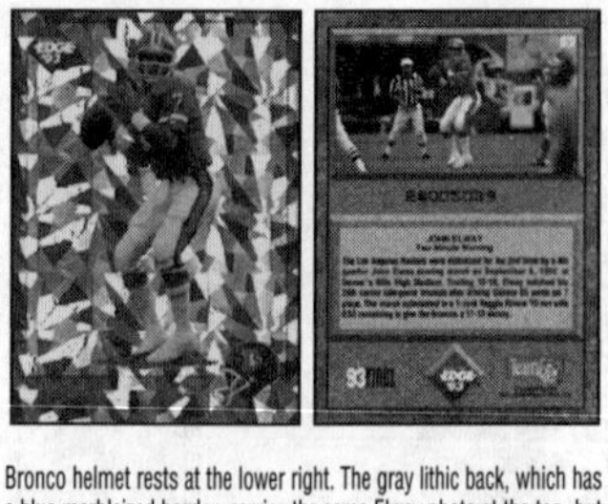

Bronco helmet rests at the lower right. The gray lithic back, which has a blue marbleized border, carries the same Elway photo at the top, but this time with its original on-field background. The production number appears below and, further below, career highlights. The cards are numbered on the back with an "E" prefix. There are two versions of each card. Tougher to find early packs contained cards with the serial number starting with "S" and cards found in packs released later had the serial number start with "E". A noted difference between the two versions are the prismatic backgrounds. Every collector who purchased All Star Collection Manager software direct from Taurus Technologies received a free Collector's Edge five-card John Elway (S-prefix) prism set. These cards have a blue (rather than silver) prismatic background on front. Just 500 sets were available through this offer. Titled the "Two Minute Warning" set, these standard-size cards highlight some of Elway's greatest two-minute marches.

	MINT	NRMT	EXC
COMPLETE E SET (5)	4.00	1.80	.50
COMMON ELWAY (E1-E5)	1.00	.45	.12
☐ E1 John Elway (Both arms outstretched)	1.00	.45	.12
☐ E2 John Elway (Passing, orange jersey)	1.00	.45	.12
☐ E3 John Elway (Running, orange jersey)	1.00	.45	.12
☐ E4 John Elway (Passing, white jersey)	1.00	.45	.12
☐ E5 John Elway (Running, white jersey)	1.00	.45	.12
☐ S1 John Elway (Both arms outstretched)	3.00	1.35	.35
☐ S2 John Elway (Passing, orange jersey)	3.00	1.35	.35
☐ S3 John Elway (Running, orange jersey)	3.00	1.35	.35
☐ S4 John Elway (Passing, white jersey)	3.00	1.35	.35
☐ S5 John Elway (Running, white jersey)	3.00	1.35	.35
☐ PRO1 John Elway AU/3000	75.00	34.00	9.50

1993 Collector's Edge Jumbos

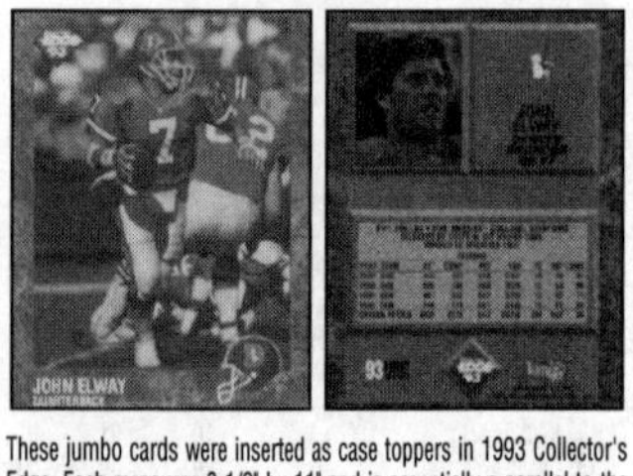

These jumbo cards were inserted as case toppers in 1993 Collector's Edge. Each measures 8 1/2" by 11" and is essentially a parallel to the respective regular issue card minus the card number. They are also individually numbered in gold ink on the cardback.

	MINT	NRMT	EXC
COMPLETE SET (6)	35.00	16.00	4.40
COMMON CARD (1-6)	4.00	1.80	.50
☐ 1 Randall Cunningham	4.00	1.80	.50
☐ 2 John Elway	8.00	3.60	1.00
☐ 3 Warren Moon	6.00	2.70	.75
☐ 4 Barry Sanders	10.00	4.50	1.25
☐ 5 Derrick Thomas	6.00	2.70	.75
☐ 6 Thurman Thomas	6.00	2.70	.75

1993 Collector's Edge Rookies FX

One of these 25 standard-size cards was inserted in each Rookie/Update foil pack. Each clear plastic card has its front textured with a diffraction grating and features a color action player shot within a wide maroon inner border. The player's name and position appear at the upper right in white lettering. The team helmet is printed at the lower right. The backs are blank, or rather, clear, allowing the reverse image of the front to show through. The cards are numbered on the front with an "F/X" prefix. Gold-colored background versions of these cards were also randomly inserted in packs. Two Prototype cards were produced as well and listed below. They are not considered part of the complete set.

	MINT	NRMT	EXC
COMPLETE SET (25)	16.00	7.25	2.00
COMMON CARD (1-25)	.30	.14	.04

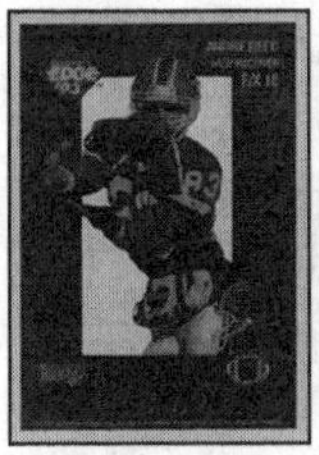
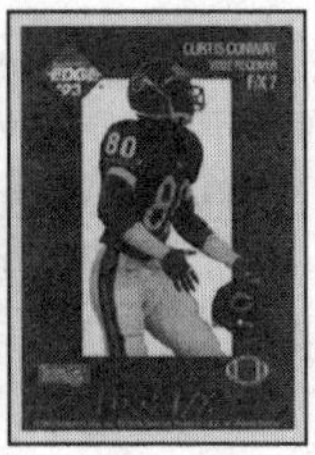

	MINT	NRMT	EXC
☐ 1 Garrison Hearst	1.25	.55	.16
☐ 2 Glyn Milburn	.75	.35	.09
☐ 3 Demetrius DuBose	.30	.14	.04
☐ 4 Joe Montana	2.50	1.10	.30
☐ 5 Thomas Smith	.50	.23	.06
☐ 6 Mark Clayton	.50	.23	.06
☐ 7 Curtis Conway	.75	.35	.09
☐ 8 Drew Bledsoe	2.50	1.10	.30
☐ 9 Todd Kelly	.30	.14	.04
☐ 10 Stan Humphries	.75	.35	.09
☐ 11 John Elway	1.50	.70	.19
☐ 12 Troy Aikman	2.50	1.10	.30
☐ 13 Marion Butts	.50	.23	.06
☐ 14 Alvin Harper	.50	.23	.06
☐ 15 Drew Hill	.30	.14	.04
☐ 16 Michael Irvin	.30	.14	.04
☐ 17 Warren Moon	.75	.35	.09
☐ 18 Andre Reed	.75	.35	.09
☐ 19 Andre Rison	.75	.35	.09
☐ 20 Emmitt Smith	4.00	1.80	.50
☐ 21 Thurman Thomas	.75	.35	.09
☐ 22 Ricky Watters	.75	.35	.09
☐ 23 Calvin Williams	.50	.23	.06
☐ 24 Steve Young	1.50	.70	.19
☐ 25 Howie Long	.50	.23	.06
☐ P1 Drew Bledsoe Prototype Gray checkered border	10.00	4.50	1.25
☐ P2 Drew Bledsoe Prototype Red border	10.00	4.50	1.25

1993 Collector's Edge Rookies FX Gold

This set is a parallel to the 1993 Collector's Edge Rookies FX issue. Each card carries a gold-colored background instead of the clear background of the regular issue.

	MINT	NRMT	EXC
COMPLETE GOLD SET (25)	150.00	70.00	19.00
COMMON GOLD CARD (1-25)	2.50	1.10	.30

*GOLD CARDS: 4X to 8X BASIC CARDS

1994 Collector's Edge Boss Rookies Update Promos

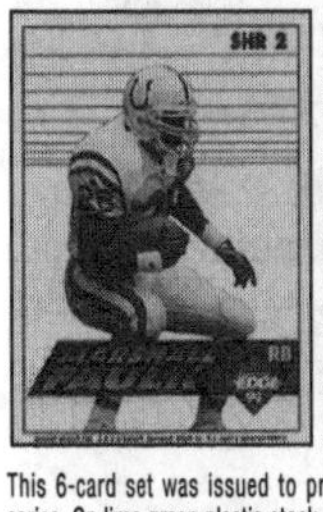
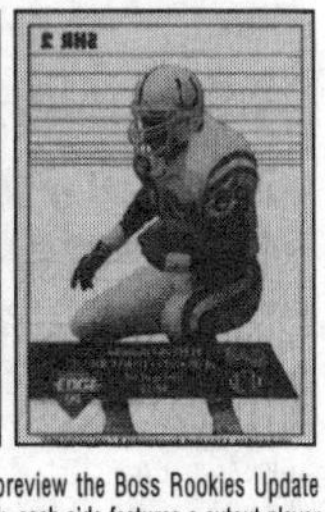

This 6-card set was issued to preview the Boss Rookies Update series. On lime green plastic stock, each side features a cutout player photo very similar the regular cards. Each card is numbered on the front with either a "P" or "SHR" prefix. Prices below reflect that of either card variation.

	MINT	NRMT	EXC
COMPLETE SET (6)	10.00	4.50	1.25
COMMON CARD (1-6)	.50	.23	.06

☐ 1 Trent Dilfer	1.00	.45	.12
☐ 2 Marshall Faulk	4.00	1.80	.50
☐ 3 Heath Shuler	2.00	.90	.25
☐ 4 Errict Rhett	3.00	1.35	.35
☐ 5 Johnnie Morton	.75	.35	.09
☐ 6 Charlie Garner	.50	.23	.06

1994 Collector's Edge

Consisting of 200 cards, this standard size set features full-bleed photos on front with the player's name and team logo at the bottom. The backs are horizontal and contain a small player photo and a stat box at the top that are ghosted over a photo of the player's home stadium. The cards are checklisted below alphabetically according to teams. There are no key Rookie Cards in this set. A Shannon Sharpe prototype card was produced and is listed below. It is not considered part of the complete set.

	MINT	NRMT	EXC
COMPLETE SET (200)	15.00	6.75	1.85
COMMON CARD (1-200)	.05	.02	.01

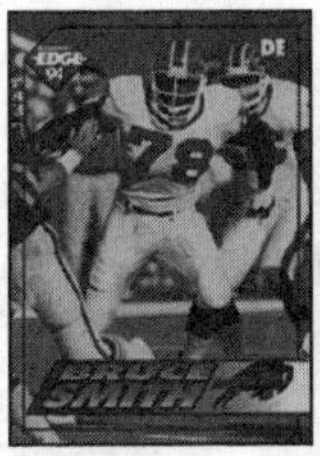
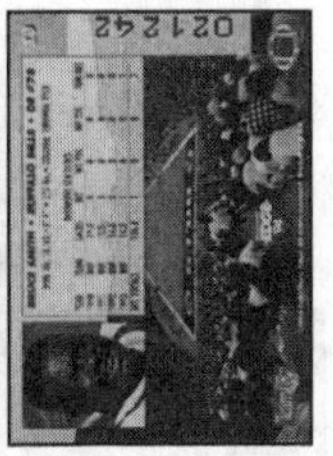

☐ 1 Mike Pritchard	.05	.02	.01
☐ 2 Erric Pegram	.05	.02	.01
☐ 3 Michael Haynes	.10	.05	.01
☐ 4 Bobby Hebert	.05	.02	.01
☐ 5 Deion Sanders	.60	.25	.07
☐ 6 Andre Rison	.10	.05	.01
☐ 7 Don Beebe	.05	.02	.01
☐ 8 Mark Kelso	.05	.02	.01
☐ 9 Darryl Talley	.05	.02	.01
☐ 10 Cornelius Bennett	.10	.05	.01
☐ 11 Jim Kelly	.20	.09	.03
☐ 12 Andre Reed	.10	.05	.01
☐ 13 Bruce Smith	.20	.09	.03
☐ 14 Thurman Thomas	.20	.09	.03
☐ 15 Craig Heyward	.10	.05	.01
☐ 16 Chris Zorich	.05	.02	.01
☐ 17 Alonzo Spellman	.05	.02	.01
☐ 18 Tom Waddle	.05	.02	.01
☐ 19 Neal Anderson	.05	.02	.01
☐ 20 Kevin Butler	.05	.02	.01
☐ 21 Curtis Conway	.20	.09	.03
☐ 22 Richard Dent	.10	.05	.01
☐ 23 Jim Harbaugh	.20	.09	.03
☐ 24 Derrick Fenner	.05	.02	.01
☐ 25 Harold Green	.05	.02	.01
☐ 26 David Klingler	.05	.02	.01
☐ 27 Daniel Stubbs	.05	.02	.01
☐ 28 Alfred Williams	.05	.02	.01
☐ 29 John Copeland	.05	.02	.01
☐ 30 Mark Carrier WR	.10	.05	.01
☐ 31 Michael Jackson	.10	.05	.01
☐ 32 Eric Metcalf	.10	.05	.01
☐ 33 Vinny Testaverde	.10	.05	.01
☐ 34 Tommy Vardell	.05	.02	.01
☐ 35 Alvin Harper	.10	.05	.01
☐ 36 Ken Norton Jr.	.10	.05	.01
☐ 37 Tony Casillas	.05	.02	.01
☐ 38 Leon Lett	.05	.02	.01
☐ 39 Jay Novacek	.10	.05	.01
☐ 40 Kevin Smith	.05	.02	.01
☐ 41 Troy Aikman	1.00	.45	.12
☐ 42 Michael Irvin	.20	.09	.03
☐ 43 Russell Maryland	.05	.02	.01
☐ 44 Emmitt Smith	2.00	.90	.25
☐ 45 Robert Delpino	.05	.02	.01
☐ 46 Simon Fletcher	.05	.02	.01
☐ 47 Greg Kragen	.05	.02	.01
☐ 48 Arthur Marshall	.05	.02	.01
☐ 49 Steve Atwater	.05	.02	.01
☐ 50 Rod Bernstine	.05	.02	.01
☐ 51 John Elway	.75	.35	.09
☐ 52 Glyn Milburn	.10	.05	.01
☐ 53 Shannon Sharpe	.10	.05	.01
☐ 54 Bennie Blades	.05	.02	.01
☐ 55 Mel Gray	.05	.02	.01
☐ 56 Herman Moore	.40	.18	.05
☐ 57 Pat Swilling	.05	.02	.01
☐ 58 Chris Spielman	.10	.05	.01
☐ 59 Rodney Peete	.05	.02	.01
☐ 60 Andre Ware	.05	.02	.01
☐ 61 Brett Perriman	.10	.05	.01
☐ 62 Erik Kramer	.10	.05	.01
☐ 63 Barry Sanders	1.00	.45	.12
☐ 64 Mark Clayton	.05	.02	.01
☐ 65 Chris Jacke	.05	.02	.01
☐ 66 Terrell Buckley	.05	.02	.01
☐ 67 Ty Detmer	.10	.05	.01
☐ 68 Sanjay Beach	.05	.02	.01
☐ 69 Brian Noble	.05	.02	.01
☐ 70 Edgar Bennett	.20	.09	.03
☐ 71 Brett Favre	2.00	.90	.25
☐ 72 Sterling Sharpe	.10	.05	.01
☐ 73 Reggie White	.20	.09	.03
☐ 74 Ernest Givins	.10	.05	.01
☐ 75 Al Del Greco	.05	.02	.01
☐ 76 Cris Dishman	.05	.02	.01
☐ 77 Curtis Duncan	.05	.02	.01
☐ 78 Webster Slaughter	.05	.02	.01
☐ 79 Spencer Tillman	.05	.02	.01
☐ 80 Warren Moon	.20	.09	.03
☐ 81 Wilber Marshall	.05	.02	.01
☐ 82 Haywood Jeffires	.10	.05	.01
☐ 83 Lorenzo White	.05	.02	.01
☐ 84 Gary Brown	.05	.02	.01
☐ 85 Reggie Langhorne	.05	.02	.01
☐ 86 Dean Biasucci	.05	.02	.01
☐ 87 Steve Emtman	.05	.02	.01
☐ 88 Jessie Hester	.05	.02	.01
☐ 89 Quentin Coryatt	.05	.02	.01
☐ 90 Roosevelt Potts	.05	.02	.01
☐ 91 Jeff George	.20	.09	.03
☐ 92 Nick Lowery	.05	.02	.01
☐ 93 Willie Davis	.10	.05	.01
☐ 94 Joe Montana	1.00	.45	.12
☐ 95 Neil Smith	.20	.09	.03
☐ 96 Marcus Allen	.20	.09	.03
☐ 97 Derrick Thomas	.20	.09	.03
☐ 98 Greg Townsend	.05	.02	.01
☐ 99 Willie Gault	.05	.02	.01
☐ 100 Ethan Horton	.05	.02	.01
☐ 101 Jeff Hostetler	.10	.05	.01
☐ 102 Tim Brown	.20	.09	.03
☐ 103 Rocket Ismail	.10	.05	.01
☐ 104 Shane Conlan	.05	.02	.01
☐ 105 Henry Ellard	.10	.05	.01
☐ 106 T.J. Rubley	.05	.02	.01
☐ 107 Sean Gilbert	.05	.02	.01
☐ 108 Troy Drayton	.05	.02	.01
☐ 109 Jerome Bettis	.50	.23	.06
☐ 110 Terry Kirby	.20	.09	.03
☐ 111 Mark Ingram	.05	.02	.01
☐ 112 John Offerdahl	.05	.02	.01
☐ 113 Louis Oliver	.05	.02	.01
☐ 114 Irving Fryar	.10	.05	.01
☐ 115 Dan Marino	2.00	.90	.25
☐ 116 Keith Jackson	.05	.02	.01
☐ 117 O.J. McDuffie	.20	.09	.03
☐ 118 Jim McMahon	.05	.02	.01
☐ 119 Sean Salisbury	.05	.02	.01
☐ 120 Randall McDaniel	.05	.02	.01
☐ 121 Jack Del Rio	.05	.02	.01
☐ 122 Cris Carter	.20	.09	.03
☐ 123 Chris Doleman	.05	.02	.01
☐ 124 John Randle	.05	.02	.01
☐ 125 Vincent Brisby	.20	.09	.03
☐ 126 Greg McMurtry	.05	.02	.01
☐ 127 Drew Bledsoe	1.00	.45	.12
☐ 128 Leonard Russell	.05	.02	.01
☐ 129 Michael Brooks	.05	.02	.01
☐ 130 Mark Jackson	.05	.02	.01
☐ 131 Pepper Johnson	.05	.02	.01
☐ 132 Doug Riesenberg	.05	.02	.01
☐ 133 Phil Simms	.10	.05	.01
☐ 134 Rodney Hampton	.20	.09	.03
☐ 135 Leonard Marshall	.05	.02	.01
☐ 136 Rob Moore	.10	.05	.01
☐ 137 Chris Burkett	.05	.02	.01
☐ 138 Boomer Esiason	.10	.05	.01
☐ 139 Johnny Johnson	.05	.02	.01
☐ 140 Ronnie Lott	.10	.05	.01
☐ 141 Brad Muster	.05	.02	.01
☐ 142 Renaldo Turnbull	.05	.02	.01
☐ 143 Willie Roaf	.05	.02	.01
☐ 144 Rickey Jackson	.05	.02	.01
☐ 145 Morten Andersen	.05	.02	.01
☐ 146 Vaughn Dunbar	.05	.02	.01
☐ 147 Wade Wilson	.05	.02	.01
☐ 148 Eric Martin	.05	.02	.01
☐ 149 Seth Joyner	.05	.02	.01
☐ 150 Calvin Williams	.10	.05	.01
☐ 151 Vai Sikahema	.05	.02	.01
☐ 152 Herschel Walker	.10	.05	.01
☐ 153 Eric Allen	.05	.02	.01
☐ 154 Fred Barnett	.10	.05	.01
☐ 155 Randall Cunningham	.10	.05	.01
☐ 156 Steve Beuerlein	.05	.02	.01
☐ 157 Gary Clark	.10	.05	.01
☐ 158 Anthony Edwards	.05	.02	.01
☐ 159 Randal Hill	.05	.02	.01
☐ 160 Freddie Joe Nunn	.05	.02	.01
☐ 161 Garrison Hearst	.40	.18	.05
☐ 162 Ricky Proehl	.05	.02	.01
☐ 163 Eric Green	.05	.02	.01
☐ 164 Levon Kirkland	.05	.02	.01
☐ 165 Joel Steed	.05	.02	.01
☐ 166 Deon Figures	.05	.02	.01
☐ 167 Leroy Thompson	.05	.02	.01
☐ 168 Barry Foster	.05	.02	.01
☐ 169 Neil O'Donnell	.20	.09	.03
☐ 170 Junior Seau	.20	.09	.03
☐ 171 Leslie O'Neal	.05	.02	.01
☐ 172 Stan Humphries	.20	.09	.03
☐ 173 Marion Butts	.05	.02	.01
☐ 174 Anthony Miller	.10	.05	.01
☐ 175 Natrone Means	.40	.18	.05
☐ 176 Odessa Turner	.05	.02	.01
☐ 177 Dana Stubblefield	.20	.09	.03
☐ 178 John Taylor	.10	.05	.01
☐ 179 Ricky Watters	.20	.09	.03
☐ 180 Steve Young	.75	.35	.09
☐ 181 Jerry Rice	1.00	.45	.12
☐ 182 Tom Rathman	.05	.02	.01
☐ 183 Brian Blades	.10	.05	.01
☐ 184 Patrick Hunter	.05	.02	.01
☐ 185 Rick Mirer	.20	.09	.03
☐ 186 Chris Warren	.10	.05	.01
☐ 187 Cortez Kennedy	.10	.05	.01
☐ 188 Reggie Cobb	.05	.02	.01
☐ 189 Craig Erickson	.05	.02	.01
☐ 190 Hardy Nickerson	.10	.05	.01
☐ 191 Lawrence Dawsey	.05	.02	.01
☐ 192 Broderick Thomas	.05	.02	.01
☐ 193 Ricky Sanders	.05	.02	.01
☐ 194 Carl Banks	.05	.02	.01
☐ 195 Ricky Ervins	.05	.02	.01
☐ 196 Darrell Green	.05	.02	.01
☐ 197 Mark Rypien	.05	.02	.01
☐ 198 Desmond Howard	.10	.05	.01
☐ 199 Art Monk	.10	.05	.01
☐ 200 Reggie Brooks	.10	.05	.01
☐ P1 Shannon Sharpe Prototype Numbered 53	1.00	.45	.12

1994 Collector's Edge Gold

This 200 card standard-size set is a parallel of the regular Collector's Edge issue. The cards are differentiated by having a Gold "First Day" logo on the front of the card. The backs are individually sequenced like the regular issue.

	MINT	NRMT	EXC
COMPLETE SET (200)	40.00	18.00	5.00
COMMON CARD (1-200)	.15	.07	.02

*GOLD CARDS: 1.25X TO 2X BASIC CARDS

1994 Collector's Edge Pop Warner

As part of a fund-raising effort for local Pop Warner teams around the country, Collector's Edge released The Pop Warner Commemorative Edition of 1994 Collector's Edge set. The cards were distributed through two channels: 1) Pop Warner football players and cheerleaders; and 2) select Edge retailers. Just 1,000 cases were produced; the suggested retail price for each pack was $5.00. Each seven-card pack included a gold-stamped card and also randomly-seeded Boss Squad game cards. Also a new 25-card updated Boss Rookie insert was foil-stamped and printed on Edge-glo card stock.

	MINT	NRMT	EXC
COMPLETE SET (200)	20.00	9.00	2.50
COMMON CARD (1-200)	.08	.04	.01

*PW CARDS: SAME PRICE AS BASIC CARDS

1994 Collector's Edge Pop Warner 22K Gold

This is a 200-card standard-size parallel to the Collector's Edge Pop Warner set. These cards feature not only the Pop Warner logo but a gold helmet icon on them. The words 22K are printed just under the helmet.

	MINT	NRMT	EXC
COMPLETE SET (200)	100.00	45.00	12.50
COMMON CARD (1-200)	.40	.18	.05

*PW 22K GOLDS: 2.5X TO 5X BASIC CARDS

1994 Collector's Edge Silver

This 200-card standard-size set is a parallel to the regular Collector's Edge issue. These cards have silver foil on the front. The backs, similar to all Collector's Edge issues, are sequentially numbered.

	MINT	NRMT	EXC
COMPLETE SET (200)	25.00	11.00	3.10
COMMON CARD (1-200)	.10	.05	.01

*SILVER CARDS: .75X TO 1.25X BASIC CARDS

1994 Collector's Edge Boss Rookies

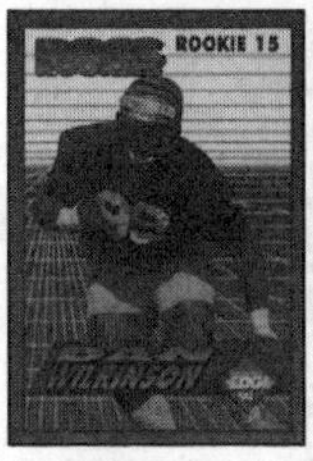
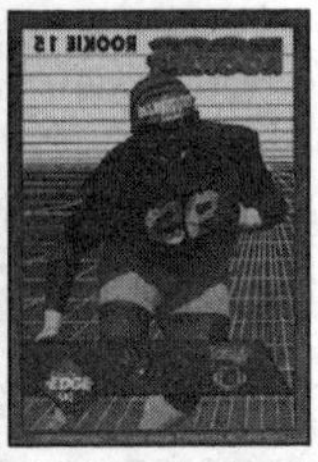

This 19-card standard-size set depicts NFL rookies in action shots wearing either their NFL or college uniforms. The cards were printed on transparent plastic and have the "Boss Rookies" logo at top right and the player's name at the bottom. Reportedly 25,000 numbered sets were produced, and each set sold originally for $49.95 with ten Edge foil wrappers.

	MINT	NRMT	EXC
COMPLETE SET (19)	16.00	7.25	2.00
COMMON CARD (1-19)	.30	.14	.04

☐ 1 Isaac Bruce	3.00	1.35	.35
☐ 2 Jeff Burris	.50	.23	.06
☐ 3 Shante Carver	.30	.14	.04
☐ 4 Lake Dawson	.30	.14	.04
☐ 5 Bert Emanuel	.75	.35	.09
☐ 6 William Floyd	.75	.35	.09
☐ 7 Wayne Gandy	.50	.23	.06
☐ 8 Aaron Glenn	.50	.23	.06
☐ 9 Chris Maumalanga	.30	.14	.04
☐ 10 David Palmer	.75	.35	.09
☐ 11 Errict Rhett	1.25	.55	.16
☐ 12 Heath Shuler	.75	.35	.09
☐ 13 Dewayne Washington	.75	.35	.09
☐ 14 Bryant Young	.75	.35	.09
☐ 15 Dan Wilkinson	.75	.35	.09
☐ 16 Rob Fredrickson	.75	.35	.09
☐ 17 Calvin Jones	.50	.23	.06
☐ 18 James Folston	.30	.14	.04
☐ 19 Marshall Faulk	3.00	1.35	.35

1994 Collector's Edge Boss Rookies Update

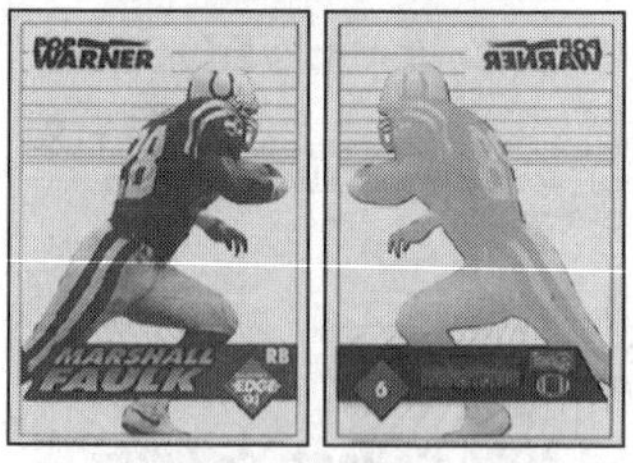

The base set version of the 1994 Collector's Edge Boss Rookies Update cards was made available via a mail order offer in complete set form. Two parallel versions were also produced; one with a Diamond logo and one printed on Green card stock.

	MINT	NRMT	EXC
COMPLETE FACT.SET (25)	40.00	18.00	5.00
COMMON CARD (1-25)	.75	.35	.09

	MINT	NRMT	EXC
☐ 1 Trent Dilfer	2.00	.90	.25
☐ 2 Jeff Burris	1.25	.55	.16
☐ 3 Shante Carver	.75	.35	.09
☐ 4 Lake Dawson	.75	.35	.09
☐ 5 Bert Emanuel	2.00	.90	.25
☐ 6 Marshall Faulk	6.00	2.70	.75
☐ 7 William Floyd	2.00	.90	.25
☐ 8 Charlie Garner	2.00	.90	.25
☐ 9 Rob Fredrickson	2.00	.90	.25
☐ 10 Wayne Gandy	1.25	.55	.16
☐ 11 Aaron Glenn	1.25	.55	.16
☐ 12 Greg Hill	2.00	.90	.25
☐ 13 Isaac Bruce	6.00	2.70	.75
☐ 14 Charles Johnson	2.00	.90	.25
☐ 15 Johnnie Morton	2.00	.90	.25
☐ 16 Calvin Jones	1.25	.55	.16
☐ 17 Tim Bowens	2.00	.90	.25
☐ 18 David Palmer	2.00	.90	.25
☐ 19 Errict Rhett	2.50	1.10	.30
☐ 20 Darnay Scott	3.50	1.55	.45
☐ 21 Heath Shuler	2.00	.90	.25
☐ 22 John Thierry	1.25	.55	.16
☐ 23 Bernard Williams	.75	.35	.09
☐ 24 Dan Wilkinson	2.00	.90	.25
☐ 25 Bryant Young	2.00	.90	.25

1994 Collector's Edge Boss Rookies Update Diamond

The Diamond parallel version of the 1994 Collector's Edge Boss Rookies Update set was made available via a mail redemption card randomly inserted into packs. The cards carry a silver refractive foil diamond shaped logo on the cardfronts.

	MINT	NRMT	EXC
COMPLETE DIAMOND SET (25)	100.00	45.00	12.50
COMMON CARD (1-25)	3.50	1.55	.45

*DIAMOND CARDS: 1.5X to 3X BASIC CARDS

	MINT	NRMT	EXC
☐ NNO Diamond Exch. Expired	1.50	.70	.19

1994 Collector's Edge Boss Rookies Update Green

The Green parallel version of the 1994 Collector's Edge Boss Rookies Update set was randomly inserted in Collector's Edge Pop Warner version packs. The cards were printed on a clear green plastic card stock.

	MINT	NRMT	EXC
COMPLETE GREEN SET (25)	30.00	13.50	3.70
COMMON CARD (1-25)	.50	.23	.06

*GREEN CARDS: .4X TO 8X BASIC CARDS

1994 Collector's Edge Boss Squad

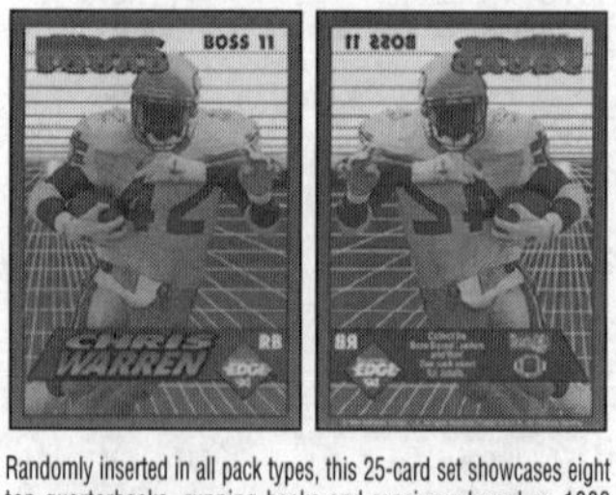

Randomly inserted in all pack types, this 25-card set showcases eight top quarterbacks, running backs and receivers based on 1993 performance. The plastic transparent cards contain an action photo on front. The player's name and position are at the bottom with the Boss Squad logo in silver at top left and the card number at top right.

	MINT	NRMT	EXC
COMPLETE SET (25)	18.00	8.00	2.20
COMMON CARD (1-25)	.30	.14	.04

	MINT	NRMT	EXC
☐ 1 John Elway W/2	1.50	.70	.19
☐ 2 Joe Montana	2.00	.90	.25
☐ 3 Vinny Testaverde	.30	.14	.04
☐ 4 Boomer Esiason	.30	.14	.04
☐ 5 Steve Young W/1	1.50	.70	.19
☐ 6 Troy Aikman	2.00	.90	.25
☐ 7 Phil Simms	.50	.23	.06
☐ 8 Bobby Hebert	.30	.14	.04
☐ 9 Thurman Thomas	.50	.23	.06
☐ 10 Leonard Russell	.30	.14	.04
☐ 11 Chris Warren W/2	.50	.23	.06
☐ 12 Gary Brown	.30	.14	.04
☐ 13 Emmitt Smith	4.00	1.80	.50
☐ 14 Jerome Bettis	1.00	.45	.12
☐ 15 Erric Pegram	.30	.14	.04
☐ 16 Barry Sanders W/1	2.00	.90	.25
☐ 17 Reggie Langhorne	.30	.14	.04
☐ 18 Anthony Miller	.30	.14	.04
☐ 19 Shannon Sharpe	.50	.23	.06
☐ 20 Tim Brown	.50	.23	.06
☐ 21 Sterling Sharpe W/2	.50	.23	.06
☐ 22 Jerry Rice W/1	2.00	.90	.25
☐ 23 Michael Irvin	.50	.23	.06
☐ 24 Andre Rison	.50	.23	.06
☐ 25 Checklist	.30	.14	.04

1994 Collector's Edge Boss Squad Bronze EQII

This parallel set to the 1994 Collector's Edge Boss Squad insert set was made available as a prize to winners of the EdgeQuest contest. Each card includes a bronze foil "Boss EQII" logo on the cardfront. Collectors were to spell the word "EdgeQuest" using letter cards pulled from 1994 Collector's Edge packs. The contest expired on March 31, 1995.

	MINT	NRMT	EXC
COMPLETE SET (25)	18.00	8.00	2.20
COMMON CARD (1-25)	.30	.14	.04

*BRONZE EQII: SAME PRICE AS BASIC CARDS

1994 Collector's Edge Boss Squad Silver

This parallel set to the 1994 Collector's Edge Boss Squad insert set was made available as a random insert in Pop Warner card packs. Each card includes a silver foil "Boss Squad" logo on the cardfront. A Gold Helmet parallel to this set was issued as a prize to the Pop Warner version of the Edgequest contest.

	MINT	NRMT	EXC
COMPLETE SILVER SET (25)	18.00	8.00	2.20
COMMON SILVER CARD (1-25)	.30	.14	.04

*SILVER CARDS: SAME PRICE AS BASIC CARDS

1994 Collector's Edge Boss Squad Silver/Gold Helmet

This parallel set to the 1994 Collector's Edge Boss Squad Silver insert set was made available as a prize to winners of the Pop Warner version of the EdgeQuest contest. Pop Warner EdgeQuest contest cards were printed on clear plastic card stock. Each Gold Helmet card includes the silver foil "Boss Squad" logo along with a gold foil helmet logo on the cardfront.

	MINT	NRMT	EXC
COMP.GOLD HELMET SET (25)	18.00	8.00	2.20
COMMON GOLD HEL.CARD (1-25)	.20	.14	.04

1994 Collector's Edge Boss Squad Promos

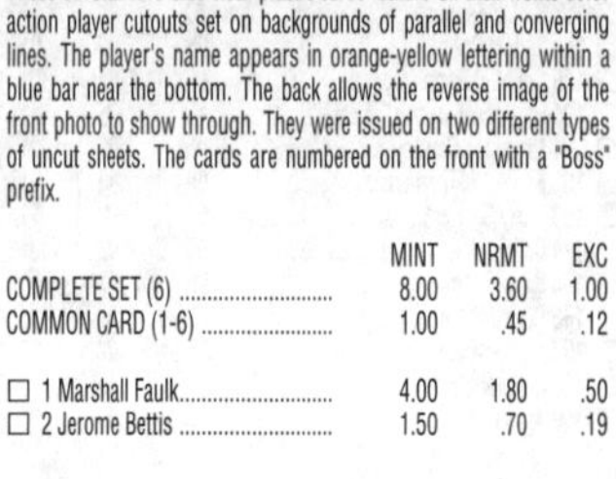

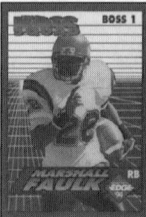

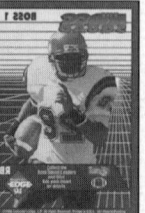

These six standard-size clear plastic cards feature on their fronts color action player cutouts set on backgrounds of parallel and converging lines. The player's name appears in orange-yellow lettering within a blue bar near the bottom. The back allows the reverse image of the front photo to show through. They were issued on two different types of uncut sheets. The cards are numbered on the front with a "Boss" prefix.

	MINT	NRMT	EXC
COMPLETE SET (6)	8.00	3.60	1.00
COMMON CARD (1-6)	1.00	.45	.12

	MINT	NRMT	EXC
☐ 1 Marshall Faulk	4.00	1.80	.50
☐ 2 Jerome Bettis	1.50	.70	.19
☐ 3 Erric Pegram	1.25	.55	.16
☐ 4 Sterling Sharpe	1.25	.55	.16
☐ 5 Shannon Sharpe	1.00	.45	.12
☐ 6 Leonard Russell	1.00	.45	.12

1994 Collector's Edge EdgeQuest

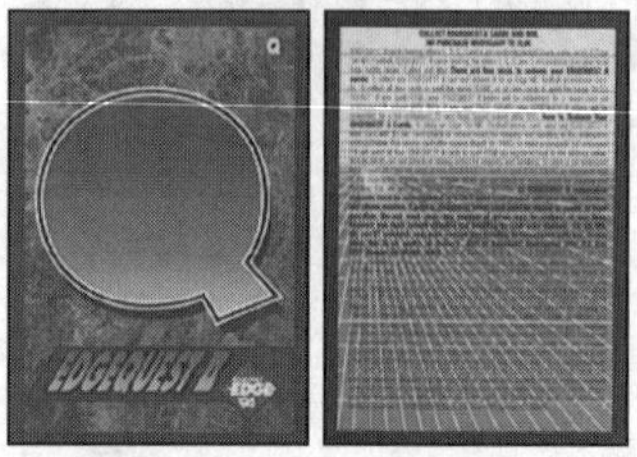

This nine-card standard-size set was issued both as a dealer premium and as an insert in packs. The letter Q was issued in shorter quantities in packs. The fronts have a large letter with the words "EdgeQuest II" underneath. The letter and title are rainbow colored against a green background. The backs have redemption information. These same cards with clear backgrounds were issued in Collector's Edge Pop Warner packs. The redemption deadline was March 31, 1995.

	MINT	NRMT	EXC
COMPLETE SET (9)	3.00	1.35	.35
COMM.PACK INSERT (A/B/D/U)	.40	.18	.05
COMM.BOX INSERT (E/G/O/S)	.40	.18	.05

*CLEAR CARDS: SAME PRICE

	MINT	NRMT	EXC
☐ 1 Letter A	.40	.18	.05
☐ 2 Letter B	.40	.18	.05
☐ 3 Letter D	.40	.18	.05
☐ 4 Letter E	.40	.18	.05
☐ 5 Letter G	.40	.18	.05
☐ 6 Letter O	.40	.18	.05
☐ 7 Letter Q SP Expired	1.00	.45	.12
☐ 8 Letter S	.40	.18	.05
☐ 9 Letter U	.40	.18	.05
☐ 10 Clear Star Wild Card	1.00	.45	.12

1994 Collector's Edge FX

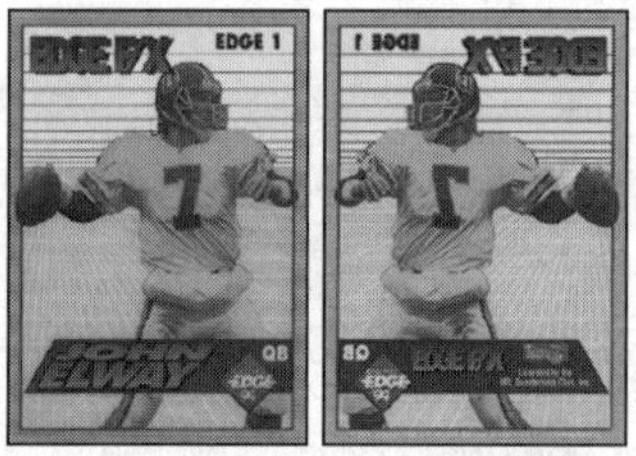

This seven-card standard-size set was randomly inserted into the various Collector's Edge packs. There are many parallel versions of these cards. The cards with gold shields were also found in Collector's Edge gold packs. Cards with white backs or silver shields were inserted in Collector's Edge retail jumbo packs. Cards featuring silver or gold backs are found in Collector's Edge silver packs. Cards with silver or gold lettering are found in Collector's Edge Pop Warner packs. Also, cards with red lettering were sent out as part of the EdgeQuest redemption program. The cards are transparent with the player's image and the words "Edge F/X" located in the upper left corner. The player is identified near the bottom of the card.

	MINT	NRMT	EXC
COMPLETE SET (7)	20.00	9.00	2.50
COMMON CARD (1-7)	2.00	.90	.25

	MINT	NRMT	EXC
☐ 1 John Elway	3.00	1.35	.35
☐ 2 Joe Montana	4.00	1.80	.50
☐ 3 Troy Aikman	4.00	1.80	.50
☐ 4 Emmitt Smith	8.00	3.60	1.00
☐ 5 Jerome Bettis	3.00	1.35	.35
☐ 6 Anthony Miller	2.00	.90	.25
☐ 7 Sterling Sharpe	2.50	1.10	.30

1994 Collector's Edge FX Gold Backs

This parallel of the 1994 Collector's Edge FX is distinguishable from the base due to its solid gold back on the card.

	MINT	NRMT	EXC
COMP.GOLD BACK SET (7)	70.00	32.00	8.75
COMMON GOLD BACK (1-7)	6.00	2.70	.75

*GOLD BACKS: 1.5X to 3X BASIC CARDS

1994 Collector's Edge FX Gold Letters

This parallel of the 1994 Collector's Edge FX is distinguishable from the base due to its use of gold lettering on the front on the card.

	MINT	NRMT	EXC
COMP.GOLD LETTERS SET (7)	40.00	18.00	5.00
COMMON GOLD LETTERS CARD (1-7)	4.00	1.80	.50

*GOLD LETTERS: 1X to 2X BASIC CARDS

1994 Collector's Edge FX Gold Shield

This parallel of the 1994 Collector's Edge FX is distinguishable from the base due to its use of gold within the FX shield on the front on the card.

	MINT	NRMT	EXC
COMP.GOLD SHIELD SET (7)	40.00	18.00	5.00
COMMON GOLD SHIELD (1-7)	4.00	1.80	.50

*GOLD SHIELDS: 1X to 2X BASIC CARDS

1994 Collector's Edge FX Red Letters

This parallel of the 1994 Collector's Edge FX is distinguishable from the base due to its use of red lettering on the front on the card.

	MINT	NRMT	EXC
COMP.RED LETTERS SET (7)	16.00	7.25	2.00
COMMON RED LETTERS (1-7)	1.50	.70	.19

*RED LETTERS: .35X to .7X BASIC CARDS

1994 Collector's Edge FX Silver Backs

This parallel of the 1994 Collector's Edge FX is distinguishable from the base due to its use of a solid silver back on the card.

	MINT	NRMT	EXC
COMP.SILVER BACKS SET (7)	10.00	4.50	1.25
COMMON SILVER BACK (1-7)	1.00	.45	.12

*SILVER BACKS: HALF VALUE OF BASIC CARDS

1994 Collector's Edge FX Silver Letters

This parallel of the 1994 Collector's Edge FX is distinguishable from the base due to its use of silver lettering on the front on the card.

	MINT	NRMT	EXC
COMP.SILVER LETTERS SET (7)	20.00	9.00	2.50
COMMON SILVER LETTERS (1-7)	2.00	.90	.25

*SILVER LETTERS: SAME PRICE AS BASIC CARDS

1994 Collector's Edge FX Silver Shield

This parallel of the 1994 Collector's Edge FX is distinguishable from the base due to its use of silver on the F/X shield on the front on the card.

	MINT	NRMT	EXC
COMPLETE SET (7)	175.00	80.00	22.00
COMMON CARD (1-7)	10.00	4.50	1.25

*SILVER SHIELDS: 2.5X to 5X BASIC CARDS

1994 Collector's Edge FX White Backs

This parallel of the 1994 Collector's Edge FX is distinguishable from the base due to its use of a solid white back on the card.

	MINT	NRMT	EXC
COMPLETE SET (7)	20.00	9.00	2.50
COMMON CARD (1-7)	2.00	.90	.25

*WHITE BACKS: SAME PRICE AS BASIC CARDS

1995 Collector's Edge

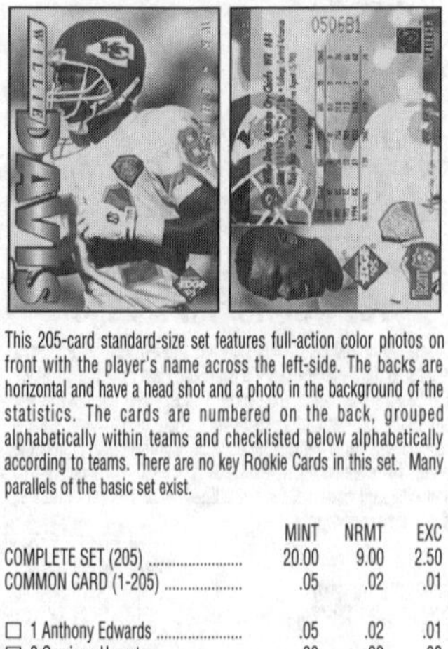

This 205-card standard-size set features full-action color photos on front with the player's name across the left-side. The backs are horizontal and have a head shot and a photo in the background of the statistics. The cards are numbered on the back, grouped alphabetically within teams and checklisted below alphabetically according to teams. There are no key Rookie Cards in this set. Many parallels of the basic set exist.

	MINT	NRMT	EXC
COMPLETE SET (205)	20.00	9.00	2.50
COMMON CARD (1-205)	.05	.02	.01

	MINT	NRMT	EXC
☐ 1 Anthony Edwards	.05	.02	.01
☐ 2 Garrison Hearst	.20	.09	.03
☐ 3 Seth Joyner	.05	.02	.01

☐ 4 Dave Krieg	.05	.02	.01
☐ 5 Chuck Levy	.05	.02	.01
☐ 6 Rob Moore	.05	.02	.01
☐ 7 J.J. Birden	.05	.02	.01
☐ 8 Jeff George	.10	.05	.01
☐ 9 Craig Heyward	.10	.05	.01
☐ 10 Norm Johnson	.05	.02	.01
☐ 11 Terance Mathis	.10	.05	.01
☐ 12 Eric Metcalf	.10	.05	.01
☐ 13 Chuck Smith	.05	.02	.01
☐ 14 Darryl Talley	.05	.02	.01
☐ 15 Cornelius Bennett	.10	.05	.01
☐ 16 Steve Christie	.05	.02	.01
☐ 17 Kenneth Davis	.05	.02	.01
☐ 18 Phil Hansen	.05	.02	.01
☐ 19 Jim Kelly	.20	.09	.03
☐ 20 Bryce Paup	.20	.09	.03
☐ 21 Andre Reed	.10	.05	.01
☐ 22 Bruce Smith	.20	.09	.03
☐ 23 Eric Ball	.05	.02	.01
☐ 24 Don Beebe	.05	.02	.01
☐ 25 Mark Carrier WR	.10	.05	.01
☐ 26 Tim McKyer	.05	.02	.01
☐ 27 Pete Metzelaars	.05	.02	.01
☐ 28 Sam Mills	.10	.05	.01
☐ 29 Jack Trudeau	.05	.02	.01
☐ 30 Mark Carrier DB	.05	.02	.01
☐ 31 Curtis Conway	.20	.09	.03
☐ 32 Erik Kramer	.05	.02	.01
☐ 33 Lewis Tillman	.05	.02	.01
☐ 34 Michael Timpson	.05	.02	.01
☐ 35 Steve Walsh	.05	.02	.01
☐ 36 Chris Zorich	.05	.02	.01
☐ 37 Jeff Blake	1.25	.55	.16
☐ 38 Harold Green	.05	.02	.01
☐ 39 David Klingler	.10	.05	.01
☐ 40 Carl Pickens	.20	.09	.03
☐ 41 Tom Waddle	.05	.02	.01
☐ 42 Dan Wilkinson	.10	.05	.01
☐ 43 Leroy Hoard	.05	.02	.01
☐ 44 Michael Jackson	.10	.05	.01
☐ 45 Antonio Langham	.05	.02	.01
☐ 46 Andre Rison	.10	.05	.01
☐ 47 Vinny Testaverde	.10	.05	.01
☐ 48 Eric Turner	.05	.02	.01
☐ 49 Tommy Vardell	.05	.02	.01
☐ 50 Troy Aikman	1.00	.45	.12
☐ 51 Charles Haley	.10	.05	.01
☐ 52 Michael Irvin	.20	.09	.03
☐ 53 Daryl Johnston	.10	.05	.01
☐ 54 Leon Lett	.05	.02	.01
☐ 55 Jay Novacek	.10	.05	.01
☐ 56 Emmitt Smith	2.00	.90	.25
☐ 57 Kevin Williams WR	.10	.05	.01
☐ 58 Steve Atwater	.05	.02	.01
☐ 59 John Elway	.75	.35	.09
☐ 60 Simon Fletcher	.05	.02	.01
☐ 61 Glyn Milburn	.05	.02	.01
☐ 62 Anthony Miller	.10	.05	.01
☐ 63 Leonard Russell	.05	.02	.01
☐ 64 Shannon Sharpe	.10	.05	.01
☐ 65 Scott Mitchell	.10	.05	.01
☐ 66 Herman Moore	.50	.23	.06
☐ 67 Johnnie Morton	.10	.05	.01
☐ 68 Brett Perriman	.10	.05	.01
☐ 69 Barry Sanders	1.00	.45	.12
☐ 70 Edgar Bennett	.10	.05	.01
☐ 71 Brett Favre	2.00	.90	.25
☐ 72 Mark Ingram	.05	.02	.01
☐ 73 Chris Jacke	.05	.02	.01
☐ 74 Guy McIntyre	.05	.02	.01
☐ 75 Reggie White	.20	.09	.03
☐ 76 Gary Brown	.05	.02	.01
☐ 77 Ernest Givins	.05	.02	.01
☐ 78 Mel Gray	.05	.02	.01
☐ 79 Haywood Jeffires	.05	.02	.01
☐ 80 Webster Slaughter	.05	.02	.01
☐ 81 Craig Erickson	.05	.02	.01
☐ 82 Marshall Faulk	.50	.23	.06
☐ 83 Jim Harbaugh	.10	.05	.01
☐ 84 Roosevelt Potts	.05	.02	.01
☐ 85 Floyd Turner	.05	.02	.01
☐ 86 Steve Beuerlein	.05	.02	.01
☐ 87 Reggie Cobb	.05	.02	.01
☐ 88 Jeff Lageman	.05	.02	.01
☐ 89 Mazio Royster	.05	.02	.01
☐ 90 Marcus Allen	.20	.09	.03
☐ 91 Steve Bono	.10	.05	.01
☐ 92 Willie Davis	.10	.05	.01
☐ 93 Lake Dawson	.10	.05	.01
☐ 94 Ronnie Lott	.10	.05	.01
☐ 95 Eric Martin	.05	.02	.01
☐ 96 Chris Penn	.05	.02	.01
☐ 97 Tim Brown	.20	.09	.03
☐ 98 Derrick Fenner	.05	.02	.01
☐ 99 Rob Fredrickson	.05	.02	.01
☐ 100 Nolan Harrison	.05	.02	.01
☐ 101 Jeff Hostetler	.10	.05	.01
☐ 102 Rocket Ismail	.10	.05	.01
☐ 103 James Jett	.10	.05	.01
☐ 104 Chester McGlockton	.10	.05	.01
☐ 105 Anthony Smith	.05	.02	.01
☐ 106 Harvey Williams	.05	.02	.01
☐ 107 Jerome Bettis	.30	.14	.04
☐ 108 Troy Drayton	.05	.02	.01
☐ 109 Chris Miller	.05	.02	.01
☐ 110 Robert Young	.05	.02	.01
☐ 111 Keith Byars	.05	.02	.01
☐ 112 Gary Clark	.05	.02	.01
☐ 113 Bryan Cox	.05	.02	.01
☐ 114 Jeff Cross	.05	.02	.01
☐ 115 Irving Fryar	.10	.05	.01
☐ 116 Randal Hill	.05	.02	.01
☐ 117 Terry Kirby	.10	.05	.01
☐ 118 Dan Marino	2.00	.90	.25
☐ 119 O.J. McDuffie	.20	.09	.03
☐ 120 Bernie Parmalee	.10	.05	.01
☐ 121 Terry Allen	.10	.05	.01
☐ 122 Cris Carter	.20	.09	.03
☐ 123 Qadry Ismail	.10	.05	.01
☐ 124 Warren Moon	.10	.05	.01
☐ 125 John Randle	.05	.02	.01
☐ 126 Jake Reed	.10	.05	.01
☐ 127 Fuad Reveiz	.05	.02	.01
☐ 128 Broderick Thomas	.05	.02	.01
☐ 129 Drew Bledsoe	1.00	.45	.12
☐ 130 Vincent Brisby	.05	.02	.01
☐ 131 Ben Coates	.10	.05	.01
☐ 132 Dave Meggett	.05	.02	.01
☐ 133 Chris Slade	.10	.05	.01
☐ 134 Leroy Thompson	.05	.02	.01
☐ 135 Eric Allen	.05	.02	.01
☐ 136 Mario Bates	.20	.09	.03
☐ 137 Quinn Early	.05	.02	.01
☐ 138 Jim Everett	.05	.02	.01
☐ 139 Michael Haynes	.10	.05	.01
☐ 140 Torrance Small	.05	.02	.01
☐ 141 Dave Brown	.10	.05	.01
☐ 142 Chris Calloway	.05	.02	.01
☐ 143 Keith Hamilton	.05	.02	.01
☐ 144 Rodney Hampton	.10	.05	.01
☐ 145 Mike Sherrard	.05	.02	.01
☐ 146 David Treadwell	.05	.02	.01
☐ 147 Herschel Walker	.10	.05	.01
☐ 148 Boomer Esiason	.10	.05	.01
☐ 149 Erik Howard	.05	.02	.01
☐ 150 Johnny Johnson	.05	.02	.01
☐ 151 Mo Lewis	.05	.02	.01
☐ 152 Johnny Mitchell	.05	.02	.01
☐ 153 Fred Barnett	.10	.05	.01
☐ 154 Randall Cunningham	.10	.05	.01
☐ 155 William Fuller	.05	.02	.01
☐ 156 Charlie Garner	.10	.05	.01
☐ 157 Greg Jackson	.05	.02	.01
☐ 158 Ricky Watters	.20	.09	.03
☐ 159 Calvin Williams	.10	.05	.01
☐ 160 Barry Foster	.10	.05	.01
☐ 161 Kevin Greene	.10	.05	.01
☐ 162 Greg Lloyd	.10	.05	.01
☐ 163 Byron Bam Morris	.10	.05	.01
☐ 164 Neil O'Donnell	.10	.05	.01
☐ 165 Erric Pegram	.10	.05	.01
☐ 166 John L. Williams	.05	.02	.01
☐ 167 Rod Woodson	.10	.05	.01
☐ 168 John Carney	.05	.02	.01
☐ 169 Stan Humphries	.10	.05	.01
☐ 170 Natrone Means	.20	.09	.03
☐ 171 Chris Mims	.05	.02	.01
☐ 172 Leslie O'Neal	.10	.05	.01
☐ 173 Alfred Pupunu	.05	.02	.01
☐ 174 Junior Seau	.20	.09	.03
☐ 175 Mark Seay	.10	.05	.01
☐ 176 William Floyd	.20	.09	.03
☐ 177 Jerry Rice	1.00	.45	.12
☐ 178 Deion Sanders	.60	.25	.07
☐ 179 Dana Stubblefield	.20	.09	.03
☐ 180 John Taylor	.05	.02	.01
☐ 181 Steve Young	.75	.35	.09
☐ 182 Bryant Young	.10	.05	.01
☐ 183 Brian Blades	.10	.05	.01
☐ 184 Cortez Kennedy	.10	.05	.01
☐ 185 Kelvin Martin	.05	.02	.01
☐ 186 Rick Mirer	.20	.09	.03
☐ 187 Ricky Proehl	.05	.02	.01
☐ 188 Michael Sinclair	.05	.02	.01
☐ 189 Chris Warren	.10	.05	.01
☐ 190 Trent Dilfer	.20	.09	.03
☐ 191 Alvin Harper	.05	.02	.01
☐ 192 Jackie Harris	.05	.02	.01
☐ 193 Hardy Nickerson	.05	.02	.01
☐ 194 Errict Rhett	.20	.09	.03
☐ 195 Reggie Roby	.05	.02	.01
☐ 196 Henry Ellard	.10	.05	.01
☐ 197 Ricky Ervins	.05	.02	.01
☐ 198 Darrell Green	.05	.02	.01
☐ 199 Brian Mitchell	.05	.02	.01
☐ 200 Heath Shuler	.20	.09	.03
☐ 201 Checklist	.05	.02	.01
☐ 202 Checklist	.05	.02	.01
☐ 203 Checklist	.05	.02	.01
☐ 204 Checklist	.05	.02	.01
☐ 205 Checklist	.05	.02	.01
☐ P1 Natrone Means Promo	.50	.23	.06

1995 Collector's Edge Black Label

This 205-card set is the Hobby edition of the Collector's Edge product and was issued in six card backs. Card fronts contain a full bleed photo with the player's last name in block letters at the bottom. The "Black Label" logo is located in the upper left corner. Card backs are horizontal with a head shot and an action shot in the background. Biographical and statistical information is also included.

	MINT	NRMT	EXC
COMPLETE SET (205)	20.00	9.00	2.50
COMMON CARD (1-205)	.05	.02	.01

*BLACK LABEL: SAME PRICE AS BASIC CARDS

1995 Collector's Edge Black Label Silver Die Cuts

This 205-card parallel set is differentiated from the basic card by having a die cut design at the top of the card. The "Black Label" logo is also in silver foil on the card fronts. Cards were randomly inserted in Black Label packs at a rate of one in 24.

	MINT	NRMT	EXC
COMPLETE SET (205)	350.00	160.00	45.00
COMMON CARD (1-205)	.75	.35	.09

*VETERAN STARS: 9X TO 16X BASIC CARDS
*YOUNG STARS: 6X TO 12X BASIC CARDS

1995 Collector's Edge Black Label 22K Gold

This 205-card parallel set is differentiated from the basic card by having the "Black Label" logo in gold foil as well as a gold foil "22K" logo on the card fronts. Cards were randomly inserted in Black Label packs.

	MINT	NRMT	EXC
COMPLETE SET (205)	2500.00	1100.00	300.00
COMMON CARD (1-205)	4.00	1.80	.50

*VETERAN STARS: 40X TO 80X BASIC CARDS
*YOUNG STARS: 35X TO 70X BASIC CARDS

1995 Collector's Edge Die Cuts

This 205 card parallel set is differentiated from the basic card by having a die cut design at the top of the card. Card fronts also contain the "Edge" logo in silver foil. Cards were randomly inserted in all pack types.

	MINT	NRMT	EXC
COMPLETE SET (205)	160.00	70.00	20.00
COMMON CARD (1-205)	.35	.16	.04

*VETERAN STARS: 4X TO 7X BASIC CARDS
*YOUNG STARS: 3X TO 5X BASIC CARDS

1995 Collector's Edge Gold Logo

This 205-card parallel set was randomly inserted into both hobby and retail packs. The cards are differentiated by having a gold foil "Edge" logo at the bottom right of the card, replacing the regular "Edge" logo.

	MINT	NRMT	EXC
COMPLETE SET (205)	20.00	9.00	2.50
COMMON CARD (1-205)	.05	.02	.01

*GOLD LOGOS: SAME PRICE AS BASIC CARDS

1995 Collector's Edge Nitro 22K

The 1995 Collector's Edge Nitro 22K inserts parallel the regular cards in number and player only, as they are significantly different in design than the regular cards. These parallels were available through insertion in 1995 Collector's Edge Nitro boxes, as well as a mail-in redemption.

	MINT	NRMT	EXC
COMPLETE SET (205)	600.00	275.00	75.00
COMMON CARD (1-205)	2.00	.90	.25

*NITRO 22K VETERANS: 20X TO 40X
*NITRO 22K YOUNG STARS: 15X TO 30X

1995 Collector's Edge 22K Gold

This 205-card parallel set is differentiated from the basic card by having a gold "22K" logo on the front. Cards were randomly inserted in Edge retail packs.

	MINT	NRMT	EXC
COMPLETE SET (205)	2500.00	1100.00	300.00
COMMON CARD (1-205)	4.00	1.80	.50

*VETERAN STARS: 50X TO 90X BASIC CARDS
*YOUNG STARS: 40X TO 75X BASIC CARDS

1995 Collector's Edge EdgeTech

This 37-card set was randomly inserted in regular, Black Label, and special retail packs. The card fronts have a circular green background with the player's name, position and team listed in the lower left hand corner. Card backs feature the card title "EdgeTech" as well as statistical information. There are several parallels of the set including a 22K gold set randomly inserted in retail packs, a Quantum set randomly inserted in Black Label packs, a Quantum die-cut set randomly inserted in Black Label packs and a Circular Prism set

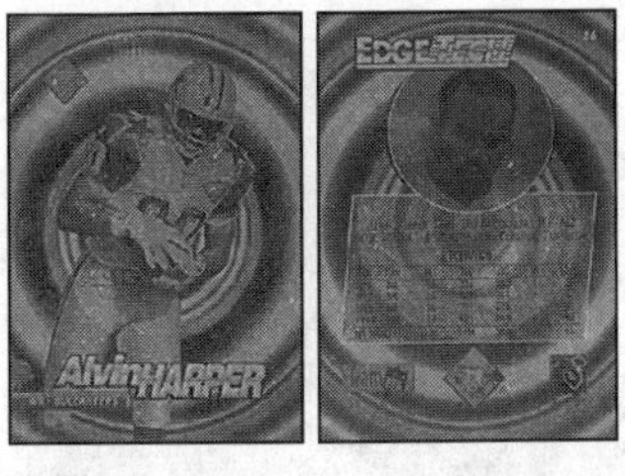

inserted one per special retail pack. The Quantum parallel differs from the regular card by having a lenticular front instead of the green background.

	MINT	NRMT	EXC
COMPLETE SET (37)	60.00	27.00	7.50
COMMON CARD (1-37)	1.25	.55	.16
*BLACK LABEL CARDS: HALF VALUE			
COMP.22K GOLD SET (37)	300.00	135.00	38.00
*22K GOLD CARDS: 2X TO 4X BASIC CARDS			
COMP.QUANTUM SET (37)	600.00	275.00	75.00
*QUANTUM CARDS: 4X TO 8X BASIC CARDS			
COMP.QUANTUM DIE CUT (37)	1000.00	450.00	125.00
*QUANTUM DIE CUTS: 7X TO 14X BASIC CARDS			
COMP.CIRCULAR PRISMS (37)	50.00	22.00	6.25
*CIRCULAR PRISMS: .4X TO .8X BASIC CARDS			

☐ 1 Dan Marino	10.00	4.50	1.25
☐ 2 Steve Young	4.00	1.80	.50
☐ 3 Rick Mirer	2.00	.90	.25
☐ 4 Emmitt Smith	10.00	4.50	1.25
☐ 5 John Elway	4.00	1.80	.50
☐ 6 Neil O'Donnell	2.00	.90	.25
☐ 7 Marshall Faulk	2.50	1.10	.30
☐ 8 Deion Sanders	3.00	1.35	.35
☐ 9 Terance Mathis	1.25	.55	.16
☐ 10 Kevin Greene	1.25	.55	.16
☐ 11 Ricky Watters	2.00	.90	.25
☐ 12 Tim Brown	2.00	.90	.25
☐ 13 Antonio Langham	1.25	.55	.16
☐ 14 Lake Dawson	1.25	.55	.16
☐ 15 Jay Novacek	2.00	.90	.25
☐ 16 Herman Moore	2.00	.90	.25
☐ 17 Mark Seay	1.25	.55	.16
☐ 18 Bernie Parmalee	1.25	.55	.16
☐ 19 Drew Bledsoe	5.00	2.20	.60
☐ 20 Troy Aikman	5.00	2.20	.60
☐ 21 Brett Favre	10.00	4.50	1.25
☐ 22 Jerry Rice	5.00	2.20	.60
☐ 23 Barry Sanders	5.00	2.20	.60
☐ 24 Heath Shuler	2.00	.90	.25
☐ 25 Errict Rhett	2.00	.90	.25
☐ 26 Cris Carter	2.00	.90	.25
☐ 27 Jerome Bettis	2.00	.90	.25
☐ 28 Reggie White	2.00	.90	.25
☐ 29 Chris Warren	2.00	.90	.25
☐ 30 Ben Coates	1.25	.55	.16
☐ 31 Bryant Young	1.25	.55	.16
☐ 32 Mel Gray	1.25	.55	.16
☐ 33 Darryl Talley	1.25	.55	.16
☐ 34 Mike Sherrard	1.25	.55	.16
☐ 35 William Floyd	2.00	.90	.25
☐ 36 Alvin Harper	2.00	.90	.25
☐ 37 Checklist (1-36)	1.25	.55	.16

1995 Collector's Edge Nitro Redemption

Collector's Edge released this set to collectors who accumulated XX points from the 1995 Nitro Game. Game pieces were randomly inserted into 1995 Edge packs. Collectors were encouraged to watch the NFL games featured on the game piece. If the featured players were declared game winners (based on NFL game stats), the collector could send in the game piece, along with the base brand card of the featured players and $4.95 postage, to receive a Nitro 22K gold foil parallel card. The collector also received 150 Nitro Redemption points that could then be accumulated and traded later for this Nitro Redemption set.

	MINT	NRMT	EXC
COMPLETE SET (25)	60.00	27.00	7.50
COMMON CARD (1-25)	1.25	.55	.16

☐ 1 Warren Moon	3.00	1.35	.35
☐ 2 Scott Mitchell	2.00	.90	.25
☐ 3 Jeff Blake	3.00	1.35	.35
☐ 4 Emmitt Smith	10.00	4.50	1.25
☐ 5 Barry Sanders	5.00	2.20	.60
☐ 6 Terance Mathis	1.25	.55	.16
☐ 7 Herman Moore	3.00	1.35	.35
☐ 8 Isaac Bruce	3.00	1.35	.35
☐ 9 Cris Carter	3.00	1.35	.35
☐ 10 Ben Coates	1.25	.55	.16
☐ 11 Shannon Sharpe	2.00	.90	.25
☐ 12 Jay Novacek	2.00	.90	.25
☐ 13 Norm Johnson	1.25	.55	.16
☐ 14 Morten Andersen	1.25	.55	.16
☐ 15 Fuad Reveiz	1.25	.55	.16
☐ 16 Bryce Paup	2.00	.90	.25
☐ 17 Jim Flanigan	1.25	.55	.16
☐ 18 Kevin Carter	1.25	.55	.16
☐ 19 Sam Mills	1.25	.55	.16

☐ 20 Willie McGinest	1.25	.55	.16
☐ 21 Orlando Thomas	1.25	.55	.16
☐ 22 Brett Favre	10.00	4.50	1.25
☐ 23 Dan Marino	10.00	4.50	1.25
☐ 24 Jerry Rice	5.00	2.20	.60
☐ 25 Larry Brown	1.25	.55	.16

1995 Collector's Edge Junior Seau Promos

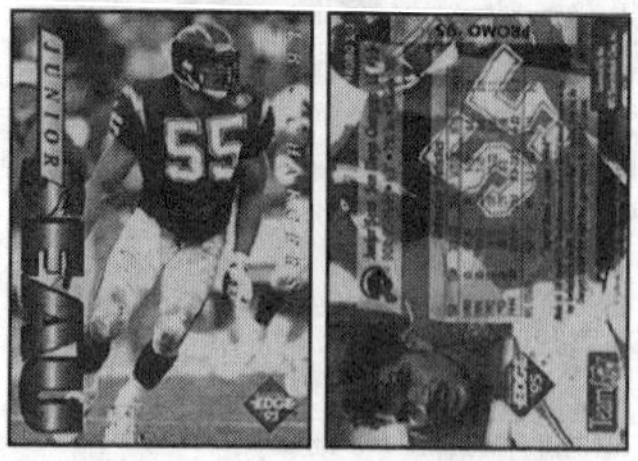

This 5-card standard-size set features the San Diego Chargers' All-Pro linebacker Junior Seau. Each card celebrates a different year in his 5-year career. The fronts feature full-bleed color action photos. His name is printed vertically along the left edge in team color-coded lettering. There were several versions produced of each card: blue foil "Promo" stamped, gold foil "Promo" stamped, non-foil base brand, Black Label foil stamped, blue foil stamped '95 National St.Louis," and blue foil stamped "Sack-A-Seau." There are no price differences for the various versions.

	MINT	NRMT	EXC
COMPLETE SET (5)	5.00	2.20	.60
COMMON CARD (1-5)	1.00	.45	.12
☐ 1 Rookie Season 1990	1.00	.45	.12
☐ 2 Second Season 1991	1.00	.45	.12
☐ 3 Third Season 1992	1.00	.45	.12
☐ 4 Fourth Season 1993	1.00	.45	.12
☐ 5 Super Bowl Season 1994	1.00	.45	.12

1995 Collector's Edge Rookies

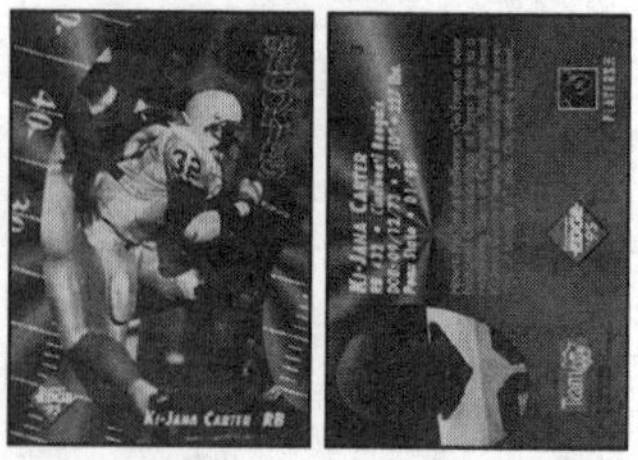

This 25 card set was randomly inserted in retail and Black Label packs. The card fronts show the top draft picks from 1995 in their college uniforms. The Black Label version differs from the regular by having the gold Black Label seal in the top left hand corner. Card backs contain biographical information and a short summary on the player.

	MINT	NRMT	EXC
COMPLETE SET (25)	40.00	18.00	5.00
COMMON CARD (1-25)	.60	.25	.07
COMP.22K GOLD SET (25)	125.00	55.00	15.50

*22K GOLD CARDS: 2X TO 3X BASIC CARDS
*BLACK LABEL CARDS: SAME VALUE

☐ 1 Derrick Alexander DE	.60	.25	.07
☐ 2 Tony Boselli	1.00	.45	.12
☐ 3 Ki-Jana Carter	2.00	.90	.25
☐ 4 Kevin Carter	1.00	.45	.12
☐ 5 Kerry Collins	6.00	2.70	.75
☐ 6 Steve McNair	5.00	2.20	.60
☐ 7 Billy Milner	.60	.25	.07
☐ 8 Rashaan Salaam	2.50	1.10	.30
☐ 9 Warren Sapp	1.00	.45	.12
☐ 10 James O.Stewart	1.00	.45	.12
☐ 11 J.J.Stokes	2.00	.90	.25
☐ 12 Bobby Taylor	1.00	.45	.12
☐ 13 Tyrone Wheatley UER	1.25	.55	.16
☐ 14 Derrick Brooks	.60	.25	.07
☐ 15 Reuben Brown	.60	.25	.07
☐ 16 Mark Bruener	1.00	.45	.12
☐ 17 Joey Galloway	4.00	1.80	.50
☐ 18 Napoleon Kaufman	2.00	.90	.25
☐ 19 Ty Law	1.00	.45	.12
☐ 20 Craig Newsome	1.00	.45	.12
☐ 21 Kordell Stewart	6.00	2.70	.75
☐ 22 Korey Stringer	.60	.25	.07
☐ 23 Zach Wiegert	.60	.25	.07
☐ 24 Michael Westbrook	2.50	1.10	.30
☐ 25 Checklist	.60	.25	.07

1995 Collector's Edge TimeWarp

These cards were randomly inserted in both regular and Black Label packs. Card fronts feature a shot of a current player matched up

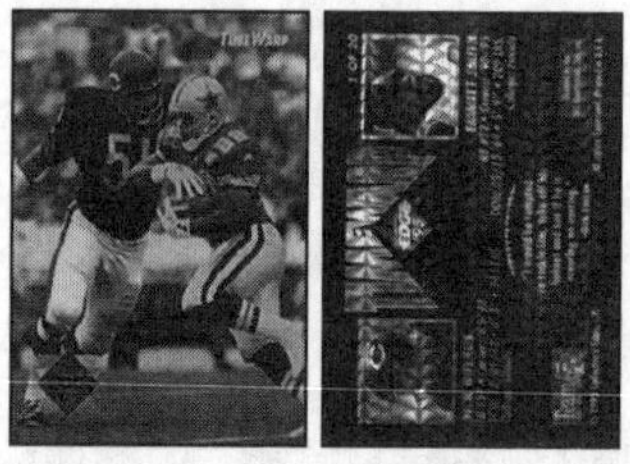

against a player from the past. The Black Label version differs by having the gold Black Label seal on the front of the card. Card backs have biographical information of both players and a commentary by Dick Butkus. Card backs also have a "prism" effect. Parallels of this set include a 22K gold set inserted in all pack types and a Prism set, where both the front and back of the card have prisms in the background.

	MINT	NRMT	EXC
COMPLETE SET (21)	350.00	160.00	45.00
COMMON CARD (1-20)	12.00	5.50	1.50
COMP.22K GOLD SET (21)	1200.00	550.00	150.00

*22K GOLDS: 1.25 TO 2X BASIC CARDS

COMPLETE PRISM SET (21)	500.00	220.00	60.00

*PRISM CARDS: .2X TO .6X BASIC CARDS
*BLACK LABEL VERSIONS:SAME VALUE

☐ 1 Emmitt Smith Dick Butkus	60.00	27.00	7.50
☐ 2 Troy Aikman Gino Marchetti	30.00	13.50	3.70
☐ 3 Natrone Means Ray Nitschke	12.00	5.50	1.50
☐ 4 Chris Zorich Steve Van Buren	12.00	5.50	1.50
☐ 5 Barry Sanders Deacon Jones	30.00	13.50	3.70
☐ 6 Kevin Greene Paul Hornung	16.00	7.25	2.00
☐ 7 Charles Haley Len Dawson	12.00	5.50	1.50
☐ 8 Marshall Faulk Willie Lanier	16.00	7.25	2.00
☐ 9 Ronnie Lott Gale Sayers	16.00	7.25	2.00
☐ 10 Cris Carter Jack Ham	12.00	5.50	1.50
☐ 11 Junior Seau Gale Sayers	16.00	7.25	2.00
☐ 12 Reggie White Otto Graham	16.00	7.25	2.00
☐ 13 Leslie O'Neal Y.A.Tittle	12.00	5.50	1.50
☐ 14 Drew Bledsoe Ted Hendricks	30.00	13.50	3.70
☐ 15 Heath Shuler Bob Lilly	16.00	7.25	2.00
☐ 16 Ricky Watters Daryl Lamonica	16.00	7.25	2.00
☐ 17 Marshall Faulk Dick Butkus	35.00	16.00	4.40
☐ 18 Deion Sanders Raymond Berry	20.00	9.00	2.50
☐ 19 Steve Young Jack Youngblood	20.00	9.00	2.50
☐ 20 Bruce Smith Sammy Baugh	16.00	7.25	2.00
☐ NNO Checklist	2.00	.90	.25
☐ TW1 Gale Sayers Junior Seau Dick Butkus Promo card	2.00	.90	.25

1995 Collector's Edge 12th Man Redemption

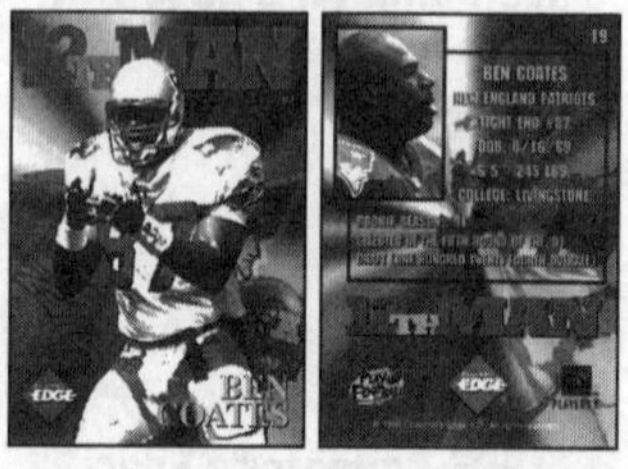

Collector's Edge produced this redemption card set for insertion in 1995 Black Label and retail version packs. The letter trade cards pulled from packs were to be assembled by collectors to form the words "12TH MAN." Collectors could trade single card letters to Collector's Edge for promo cards or complete letter sets for the 25-card 12th Man prize set listed below. Postage and handling was $19.95 for complete set redemption and the expiration date was March 1, 1996. Although the prize cards feature a 1996 date on the copyright line, the cards are considered part of the 1995 release.

	MINT	NRMT	EXC
COMPLETE PRIZE SET (25)	20.00	9.00	2.50
COMMON CARD (1-25)	.30	.14	.04
COMP.LETTERS SET (7)	.75	.35	.09
☐ 1 Dan Marino	3.00	1.35	.35
☐ 2 Jeff Blake	.75	.35	.09
☐ 3 Steve Bono	.50	.23	.06
☐ 4 Brett Favre	3.00	1.35	.35
☐ 5 Steve Young	1.25	.55	.16
☐ 6 Scott Mitchell	.50	.23	.06
☐ 7 Chris Warren	.50	.23	.06
☐ 8 Marshall Faulk	.75	.35	.09
☐ 9 Byron Bam Morris	.30	.14	.04
☐ 10 Emmitt Smith	3.00	1.35	.35
☐ 11 Barry Sanders	1.50	.70	.19
☐ 12 Rashaan Salaam	.75	.35	.09
☐ 13 Carl Pickens	2.00	.90	.25
☐ 14 Anthony Miller	.50	.23	.06
☐ 15 Tim Brown	2.00	.90	.25
☐ 16 Jerry Rice	1.50	.70	.19
☐ 17 Herman Moore	2.00	.90	.25
☐ 18 Isaac Bruce	2.00	.90	.25
☐ 19 Ben Coates	.50	.23	.06
☐ 20 Shannon Sharpe	2.00	.90	.25
☐ 21 Alfred Pupunu	.30	.14	.04
☐ 22 Jackie Harris	.30	.14	.04
☐ 23 Jay Novacek	.50	.23	.06
☐ 24 Brent Jones	.30	.14	.04
☐ 25 Checklist Card	.50	.23	.06

1995 Collector's Edge Instant Replay

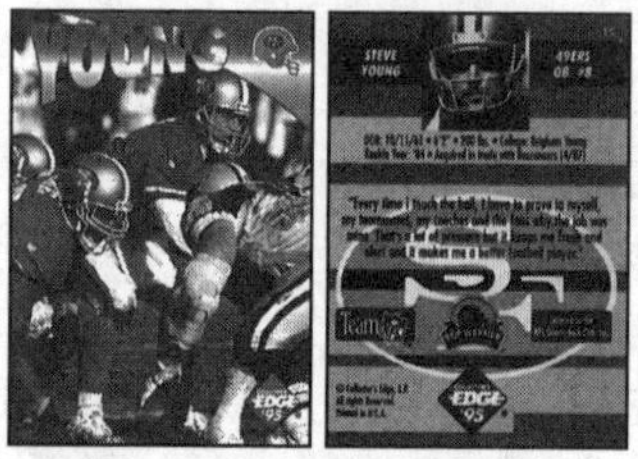

This 51 card set was produced late in the year by Collector's Edge and replaced last year's Pop Warner set. Card fronts contain a full shot of the player with the player's name and team helmet logo located at the top. The Collector's Edge '95 logo is located in the lower right hand corner. Card backs are vertical with a small headshot of the player at the top, biographical information under the shot and a brief commentary about the player. Rookies included in this set are Kerry Collins, Terrell Davis, Joey Galloway, Steve McNair, J.J. Stokes and Michael Westbrook. In addition to the basic set, there is a Prism parallel set. These cards were inserted approximately one in every 2 packs. There is also a Micro Mini set, which is an 8 card set of Black Label base cards. These cards were inserted at a rate of one in 14 packs. Each card contains 50 total "mini" cards with 25 on each side.

	MINT	NRMT	EXC
COMPLETE SET (51)	12.00	5.50	1.50
COMMON CARD (1-50)	.05	.02	.01
COMP.MICRO MINI SET (8)	5.00	2.20	.60

*PRISM RCs: 1X TO 2X BASIC CARDS

☐ 1 Jeff George	.10	.05	.01
☐ 2 Eric Metcalf	.10	.05	.01
☐ 3 Jim Kelly	.20	.09	.03
☐ 4 Jeff Blake	.75	.35	.09
☐ 5 Andre Rison	.10	.05	.01
☐ 6 Troy Aikman	1.00	.45	.12
☐ 7 Michael Irvin	.20	.09	.03
☐ 8 Emmitt Smith	2.00	.90	.25
☐ 9 John Elway	.75	.35	.09
☐ 10 Terrell Davis	3.00	1.35	.35
☐ 11 Herman Moore	.50	.23	.06
☐ 12 Barry Sanders	1.00	.45	.12
☐ 13 Brett Favre	2.00	.90	.25
☐ 14 Marshall Faulk	.50	.23	.06
☐ 15 Steve Beuerlein	.05	.02	.01
☐ 16 Steve Bono	.10	.05	.01
☐ 17 Tim Brown	.20	.09	.03
☐ 18 Jeff Hostetler	.10	.05	.01
☐ 19 Jerome Bettis	.20	.09	.03
☐ 20 Dan Marino	2.00	.90	.25
☐ 21 Cris Carter	.20	.09	.03
☐ 22 Drew Bledsoe	1.00	.45	.12
☐ 23 Ben Coates	.10	.05	.01
☐ 24 Randall Cunningham	.10	.05	.01
☐ 25 Terry Kirby	.10	.05	.01
☐ 26 Ricky Watters	.20	.09	.03
☐ 27 Kyle Brady	.20	.09	.03
☐ 28 Byron Bam Morris	.10	.05	.01
☐ 29 Neil O'Donnell	.10	.05	.01
☐ 30 Natrone Means	.20	.09	.03
☐ 31 Junior Seau	.20	.09	.03
☐ 32 William Floyd	.20	.09	.03
☐ 33 Jerry Rice	1.00	.45	.12
☐ 34 Deion Sanders	.60	.25	.07
☐ 35 Steve Young	.75	.35	.09
☐ 36 Rick Mirer	.20	.09	.03
☐ 37 Chris Warren	.10	.05	.01
☐ 38 Trent Dilfer	.20	.09	.03
☐ 39 Errict Rhett	.20	.09	.03
☐ 40 Heath Shuler	.20	.09	.03
☐ 41 Ki-Jana Carter	.20	.09	.03
☐ 42 Kerry Collins	2.50	1.10	.30
☐ 43 Steve McNair	2.00	.90	.25
☐ 44 Rashaan Salaam	.75	.35	.09
☐ 45 James O.Stewart	.10	.05	.01
☐ 46 J.J. Stokes	.60	.25	.07
☐ 47 Tyrone Wheatley	.40	.18	.05
☐ 48 Joey Galloway	1.00	.45	.12
☐ 49 Napoleon Kaufman	.60	.25	.07
☐ 50 Michael Westbrook	.75	.35	.09
☐ NNO Checklist Card	.05	.02	.01

1995 Collector's Edge Instant Replay Prisms

This 50 card parallel set to the base 1995 Collector's Edge Instant Replay series was issued at a ratio of 1:2 packs. The distinguishing characteristic of this card is it's prism appearance.

	MINT	NRMT	EXC
COMP.PRISM SET (50)	40.00	18.00	5.00
COMMON PRISM (1-50)	.20	.09	.03

*PRISM VETERAN STARS: 1.5X TO 3X BASIC CARDS
*PRISM YOUNG STARS: 1.25X TO 2X BASIC CARDS
*PRISM RCs: 1X TO 2X BASIC CARDS

1995 Collector's Edge Instant Replay EdgeTech Die Cuts

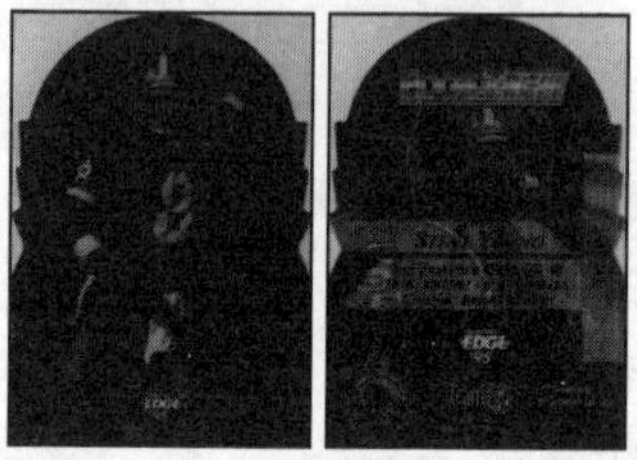

This 13 card set was randomly inserted at a rate of one in four regular retail packs and one per pack in special retail packs. The card fronts are die cut in the shape of a helmet at the top of the card with the player's name beneath the shot. The background of the fronts also resemble a football field. Card backs contain the "EdgeTech" logo at the top of the card, with a headshot of the player in a circle underneath it. Also listed are the player's name and biological information. In the background is a shot of the team helmet and a football field.

	MINT	NRMT	EXC
COMPLETE SET (13)	12.00	5.50	1.50
COMMON CARD (1-12)	.30	.14	.04
☐ 1 Troy Aikman	1.50	.70	.19
☐ 2 Drew Bledsoe	1.50	.70	.19
☐ 3 Tim Brown	.50	.23	.06
☐ 4 Ben Coates	.30	.14	.04
☐ 5 Marshall Faulk	.75	.35	.09
☐ 6 William Floyd	.30	.14	.04
☐ 7 Dan Marino	3.00	1.35	.35
☐ 8 Errict Rhett	.50	.23	.06
☐ 9 Deion Sanders	.75	.35	.09
☐ 10 Emmitt Smith	3.00	1.35	.35
☐ 11 Ricky Watters	.50	.23	.06
☐ 12 Steve Young	1.25	.55	.16
☐ NNO Checklist	.30	.14	.04

1995 Collector's Edge Instant Replay Quantum Motion

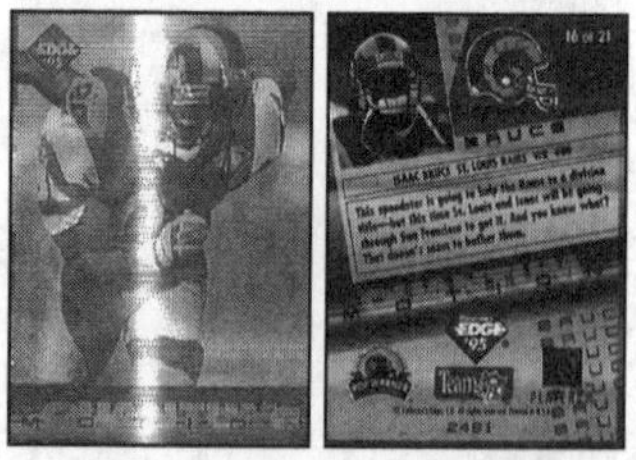

This complete 22 card set was available in packs through a couple of different ways. The first 10 cards plus the checklist were inserted in packs at a rate of one in 12 packs. The other 11 cards were available through a mail redemption, where an exchange card was available for each individual card. Cards 1-10 feature actual game footage on the front of the card and the player's name alternating with the words Quantum Motion. Card backs contain a small headshot in the top left hand corner with the team's logo located to the right. Under the shot is the player's name, team, position and number. A short commentary is also included. For cards 11-21, exchange cards were available. The exchange cards were gray/black on the top and bottom with the word Quantum written in white over a red background in the center of the card. The cards are numbered out of 21 on the front. Card backs contain lines to fill out to exchange the card for a Quantum card. The redeemed cards feature "double face" fronts that alternate

between two different action shots rather than actual game footage. Card backs are the same as the first ten cards.

	MINT	NRMT	EXC
COMPLETE SET (22)	55.00	25.00	7.00
COMPLETE SERIES 1 (11)	35.00	16.00	4.40
COMPLETE SERIES 2 (11)	20.00	9.00	2.50
COMMON CARD (1-21)	1.50	.70	.19
☐ 1 Troy Aikman	5.00	2.20	.60
☐ 2 Drew Bledsoe	5.00	2.20	.60
☐ 3 Marshall Faulk	2.50	1.10	.30
☐ 4 Michael Irvin	2.00	.90	.25
☐ 5 Dan Marino	10.00	4.50	1.25
☐ 6 Jerry Rice	5.00	2.20	.60
☐ 7 Rod Smith	1.50	.70	.19
☐ 8 Emmitt Smith	10.00	4.50	1.25
☐ 9 Michael Westbrook	2.50	1.10	.30
☐ 10 Steve Young	4.00	1.80	.50
☐ 11 Erik Kramer	1.50	.70	.19
☐ 12 Jeff Blake	2.50	1.10	.30
☐ 13 Eric Metcalf	2.00	.90	.25
☐ 14 Steve Bono	2.00	.90	.25
☐ 15 Carl Pickens	2.00	.90	.25
☐ 16 Isaac Bruce	2.50	1.10	.30
☐ 17 Erict Rhett	2.00	.90	.25
☐ 18 Kerry Collins	5.00	2.20	.60
☐ 19 Rashaan Salaam	2.50	1.10	.30
☐ 20 Gus Frerotte	2.00	.90	.25
☐ 21 Terry Kirby	1.50	.70	.19
☐ NNO Checklist	1.50	.70	.19

1995 Collector's Edge TimeWarp Jumbos

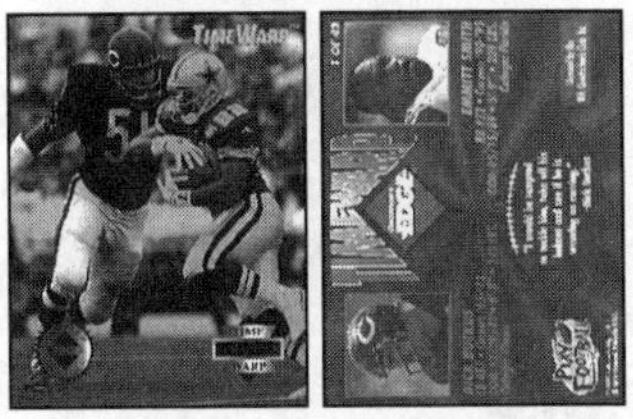

This 42-card set features borderless color player photos and measures approximately 8" by 10". The cards are similar to the regular issue 1995 Collector's Edge TimeWarp cards, except in jumbo format. Distributed to hobby dealers, 5000 of each card was produced with every card serial numbered. Signed versions of each of the cards were also available autographed by the Hall of Fame player featured. The cards were also made available through a 1996 Collector's Edge special retail pack redemption offer for $3.95 each with 12-wrappers of product.

	MINT	NRMT	EXC
COMPLETE SET (42)	500.00	220.00	60.00
COMMON CARD (1-42)	10.00	4.50	1.25
☐ 1 Dick Butkus	25.00	11.00	3.10
Emmitt Smith			
☐ 2 Dick Butkus	25.00	11.00	3.10
Emmitt Smith			
☐ 3 Gino Marchetti	18.00	8.00	2.20
Troy Aikman			
☐ 4 Gino Marchetti	18.00	8.00	2.20
Troy Aikman			
☐ 5 Ray Nitschke	12.00	5.50	1.50
Natrone Means			
☐ 6 Ray Nitschke	12.00	5.50	1.50
Natrone Means			
☐ 7 Steve Van Buren	10.00	4.50	1.25
Chris Zorich			
☐ 8 Steve Van Buren	10.00	4.50	1.25
Chris Zorich			
☐ 9 Deacon Jones	18.00	8.00	2.20
Barry Sanders			
☐ 10 Deacon Jones	18.00	8.00	2.20
Barry Sanders			
☐ 11 Paul Hornung	12.00	5.50	1.50
Kevin Greene			
☐ 12 Paul Hornung	12.00	5.50	1.50
Kevin Greene			
☐ 13 Len Dawson	10.00	4.50	1.25
Charles Haley			
☐ 14 Len Dawson	10.00	4.50	1.25
Charles Haley			
☐ 15 Willie Lanier	15.00	6.75	1.85
Marshall Faulk			
☐ 16 Willie Lanier	15.00	6.75	1.85
Marshall Faulk			
☐ 17 Gale Sayers	12.00	5.50	1.50
Ronnie Lott			
☐ 18 Gale Sayers	12.00	5.50	1.50
Ronnie Lott			
☐ 19 Jack Ham	10.00	4.50	1.25
Cris Carter			
☐ 20 Jack Ham	10.00	4.50	1.25
Cris Carter			
☐ 21 Gale Sayers	12.00	5.50	1.50
Junior Seau			
☐ 22 Gale Sayers	12.00	5.50	1.50
Junior Seau			
☐ 23 Otto Graham	12.00	5.50	1.50
Reggie White			
☐ 24 Otto Graham	12.00	5.50	1.50
Reggie White			
☐ 25 Y.A.Tittle	12.00	5.50	1.50
Leslie O'Neal			
☐ 26 Y.A.Tittle	12.00	5.50	1.50
Leslie O'Neal			
☐ 27 Daryle Lamonica	10.00	4.50	1.25
Ricky Watters			
☐ 28 Daryle Lamonica	10.00	4.50	1.25
Ricky Watters			
☐ 29 Dick Butkus	15.00	6.75	1.85
Marshall Faulk			
☐ 30 Dick Butkus	15.00	6.75	1.85
Marshall Faulk			
☐ 31 Raymond Berry	15.00	6.75	1.85
Deion Sanders			
☐ 32 Raymond Berry	15.00	6.75	1.85
Deion Sanders			
☐ 33 Jack Youngblood	15.00	6.75	1.85
Steve Young			
☐ 34 Jack Youngblood	15.00	6.75	1.85
Steve Young			
☐ 35 Sammy Baugh	12.00	5.50	1.50
Bruce Smith			
☐ 36 Sammy Baugh	12.00	5.50	1.50
Bruce Smith			
☐ 37 Ted Hendricks	25.00	11.00	3.10
Dan Marino			
☐ 38 Bob Lilly	25.00	11.00	3.10
Dan Marino			
☐ 39 Ted Hendricks	15.00	6.75	1.85
Drew Bledsoe			
☐ 40 Bob Lilly	12.00	5.50	1.50
Heath Shuler			
☐ 41 Dick Butkus	15.00	6.75	1.85
Jeff Blake			
☐ 42 Dick Butkus	15.00	6.75	1.85
Michael Westbrook			

1995 Collector's Edge TimeWarp Sunday Ticket

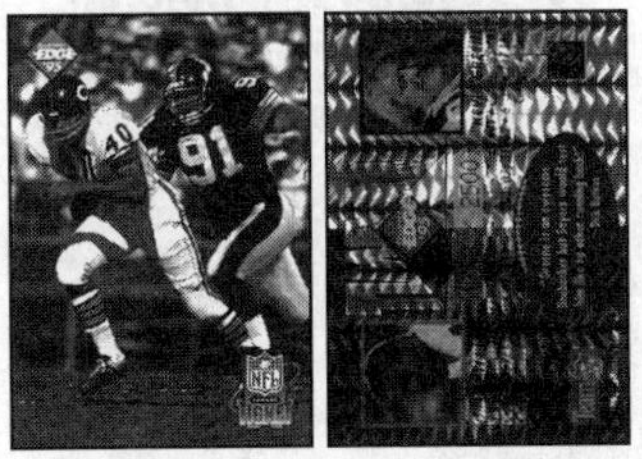

Collector's Edge originally released this set through a direct mail order offer at $19.95 per set. Each order also included a group of various free promo and preview cards. The five-card Sunday Ticket set features borderless color action player photos of a current player interacting with a previous player in a fictitious game. The backs carry information about both players on a metallic background with the serial number (of 2500 sets produced).

	MINT	NRMT	EXC
COMPLETE SET (5)	10.00	4.50	1.25
COMMON CARD (1-5)	1.25	.55	.16
☐ 1 Paul Hornung	1.25	.55	.16
Chris Zorich			
☐ 2 Gale Sayers	1.25	.55	.16
Kevin Greene			
☐ 3 Ted Hendricks	2.00	.90	.25
Ricky Watters			
☐ 4 Sammy Baugh	2.00	.90	.25
Bruce Smith			
☐ 5 Dick Butkus	3.50	1.55	.45
Marshall Faulk			

1996 Collector's Edge Promos

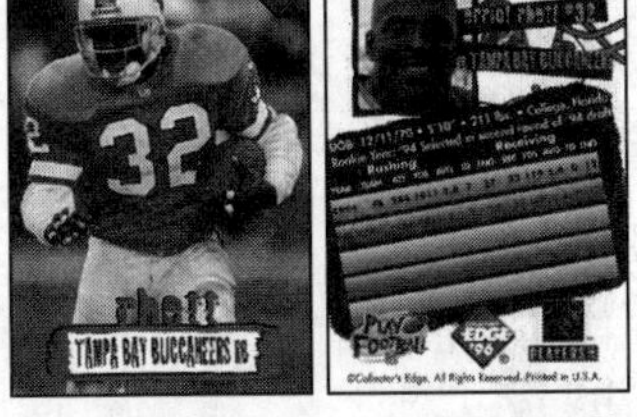

These four cards were issued to preview the 1996 Collector's Edge set. The three player cards are numbered on the back.

	MINT	NRMT	EXC
COMPLETE SET (4)	3.00	1.35	.35
COMMON CARD	.30	.14	.04
☐ P1 Errict Rhett	1.50	.70	.19
☐ P2 Junior Seau	1.00	.45	.12
☐ P3 Terry Kirby	.50	.23	.06
☐ NNO Cover Card	.30	.14	.04

1996 Collector's Edge

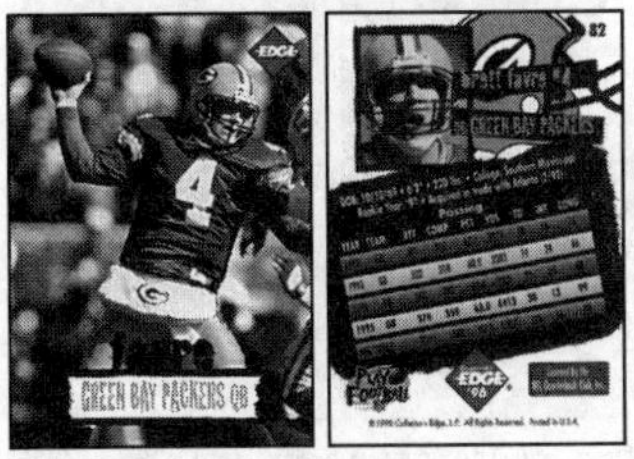

The 1996 Collector's Edge set was issued in one series totalling 240 cards. The cards were issued in six card packs with 10 packs per box and 24 boxes per case in retail, hobby, and special retail packaging. The cards are grouped alphabetically within teams and checklisted below alphabetically according to teams. Collector's Edge Cowboybilia packs also contained the base brand and insert cards with the same pack configuration. Draft Redemption cards were also randomly inserted into packs. When redeemed, a collector would receive a card of one of that teams' draft picks selected by the company. A special die cut Crucibles Eddie George promo card was produced, apparently for an insert set never released.

	MINT	NRMT	EXC
COMPLETE SET (250)	25.00	11.00	3.10
COMMON CARD (1-250)	.05	.02	.01
☐ 1 Larry Centers	.10	.05	.01
☐ 2 Garrison Hearst	.10	.05	.01
☐ 3 Dave Krieg	.05	.02	.01
☐ 4 Rob Moore	.05	.02	.01
☐ 5 Frank Sanders	.10	.05	.01
☐ 6 Eric Swann	.10	.05	.01
☐ 7 Morten Andersen	.05	.02	.01
☐ 8 Chris Doleman	.05	.02	.01
☐ 9 Bert Emanuel	.10	.05	.01
☐ 10 Jeff George	.10	.05	.01
☐ 11 Craig Heyward	.05	.02	.01
☐ 12 Terance Mathis	.05	.02	.01
☐ 13 Clay Matthews	.10	.05	.01
☐ 14 Eric Metcalf	.10	.05	.01
☐ 15 Bill Brooks	.05	.02	.01
☐ 16 Todd Collins	.10	.05	.01
☐ 17 Russell Copeland	.05	.02	.01
☐ 18 Jim Kelly	.20	.09	.03
☐ 19 Bryce Paup	.10	.05	.01
☐ 20 Andre Reed	.10	.05	.01
☐ 21 Bruce Smith	.20	.09	.03
☐ 22 Mark Carrier WR	.10	.05	.01
☐ 23 Kerry Collins	1.25	.55	.16
☐ 24 Willie Green	.05	.02	.01
☐ 25 Eric Guliford	.05	.02	.01
☐ 26 Brett Maxie	.05	.02	.01
☐ 27 Tim McKyer	.05	.02	.01
☐ 28 Derrick Moore	.05	.02	.01
☐ 29 Curtis Conway	.20	.09	.03
☐ 30 Jim Flanigan	.05	.02	.01
☐ 31 Jeff Graham	.05	.02	.01
☐ 32 Robert Green	.05	.02	.01
☐ 33 Erik Kramer	.05	.02	.01
☐ 34 Rashaan Salaam	.20	.09	.03
☐ 35 Alonzo Spellman	.05	.02	.01
☐ 36 Donnell Woolford	.05	.02	.01
☐ 37 Chris Zorich	.05	.02	.01
☐ 38 Eric Bieniemy	.05	.02	.01
☐ 39 Jeff Blake	.20	.09	.03
☐ 40 Ki-Jana Carter	.10	.05	.01
☐ 41 John Copeland	.05	.02	.01
☐ 42 Harold Green	.05	.02	.01
☐ 43 Tony McGee	.05	.02	.01
☐ 44 Carl Pickens	.20	.09	.03
☐ 45 Darnay Scott	.10	.05	.01
☐ 46 Bracey Walker	.05	.02	.01
☐ 47 Dan Wilkinson	.05	.02	.01
☐ 48 Rob Burnett	.05	.02	.01
☐ 49 Leroy Hoard	.05	.02	.01
☐ 50 Ernest Hunter	.05	.02	.01
☐ 51 Michael Jackson	.10	.05	.01
☐ 52 Stevon Moore	.05	.02	.01
☐ 53 Anthony Pleasant	.05	.02	.01
☐ 54 Andre Rison	.10	.05	.01
☐ 55 Vinny Testaverde	.10	.05	.01
☐ 56 Eric Zeier	.10	.05	.01
☐ 57 Troy Aikman	1.00	.45	.12
☐ 58 Bill Bates	.10	.05	.01
☐ 59 Shante Carver	.05	.02	.01
☐ 60 Michael Irvin	.20	.09	.03
☐ 61 Daryl Johnston	.10	.05	.01
☐ 62 Jay Novacek	.10	.05	.01
☐ 63 Deion Sanders	.60	.25	.07
☐ 64 Emmitt Smith	2.00	.90	.25
☐ 65 Sherman Williams	.05	.02	.01
☐ 66 Terrell Davis	1.50	.70	.19
☐ 67 John Elway	.75	.35	.09
☐ 68 Ed McCaffrey	.05	.02	.01
☐ 69 Glyn Milburn	.05	.02	.01
☐ 70 Anthony Miller	.10	.05	.01
☐ 71 Michael Dean Perry	.05	.02	.01
☐ 72 Shannon Sharpe	.10	.05	.01
☐ 73 Willie Clay	.05	.02	.01
☐ 74 Scott Mitchell	.10	.05	.01
☐ 75 Herman Moore	.20	.09	.03
☐ 76 Johnnie Morton	.10	.05	.01
☐ 77 Brett Perriman	.10	.05	.01
☐ 78 Barry Sanders	1.00	.45	.12
☐ 79 Tracy Scroggins	.05	.02	.01
☐ 80 Edgar Bennett	.10	.05	.01
☐ 81 Robert Brooks	.20	.09	.03
☐ 82 Brett Favre	2.00	.90	.25
☐ 83 Dorsey Levens	.10	.05	.01
☐ 84 Craig Newsome	.05	.02	.01
☐ 85 Wayne Simmons	.05	.02	.01
☐ 86 Reggie White	.20	.09	.03
☐ 87 Chris Chandler	.10	.05	.01
☐ 88 Anthony Cook	.05	.02	.01
☐ 89 Mel Gray	.05	.02	.01
☐ 90 Haywood Jeffires	.05	.02	.01
☐ 91 Darryll Lewis	.05	.02	.01
☐ 92 Steve McNair	1.00	.45	.12
☐ 93 Todd McNair	.05	.02	.01
☐ 94 Rodney Thomas	.05	.02	.01
☐ 95 Trev Alberts	.05	.02	.01
☐ 96 Tony Bennett	.05	.02	.01
☐ 97 Quentin Coryatt	.05	.02	.01
☐ 98 Sean Dawkins	.05	.02	.01
☐ 99 Ken Dilger	.10	.05	.01
☐ 100 Marshall Faulk	.20	.09	.03
☐ 101 Jim Harbaugh	.10	.05	.01
☐ 102 Ronald Humphrey	.05	.02	.01
☐ 103 Floyd Turner	.05	.02	.01
☐ 104 Steve Beuerlein	.05	.02	.01
☐ 105 Tony Boselli	.10	.05	.01
☐ 106 Mark Brunell	1.00	.45	.12
☐ 107 Willie Jackson	.10	.05	.01
☐ 108 Jeff Lageman	.05	.02	.01
☐ 109 James O. Stewart	.10	.05	.01
☐ 110 Cedric Tillman	.05	.02	.01
☐ 111 Marcus Allen	.20	.09	.03
☐ 112 Kimble Anders	.05	.02	.01
☐ 113 Steve Bono	.10	.05	.01
☐ 114 Dale Carter	.05	.02	.01
☐ 115 Willie Davis	.10	.05	.01
☐ 116 Lake Dawson	.10	.05	.01
☐ 117 Dan Saleaumua	.05	.02	.01
☐ 118 Neil Smith	.10	.05	.01
☐ 119 Derrick Thomas	.10	.05	.01
☐ 120 Tamarick Vanover	.20	.09	.03
☐ 121 Marco Coleman	.05	.02	.01
☐ 122 Bryan Cox	.05	.02	.01
☐ 123 Steve Emtman	.05	.02	.01
☐ 124 Irving Fryar	.10	.05	.01
☐ 125 Eric Green	.05	.02	.01
☐ 126 Terry Kirby	.10	.05	.01
☐ 127 Dan Marino	2.00	.90	.25
☐ 128 O.J. McDuffie	.10	.05	.01
☐ 129 Bernie Parmalee	.05	.02	.01
☐ 130 Troy Vincent	.05	.02	.01
☐ 131 Cris Carter	.20	.09	.03
☐ 132 Jack Del Rio	.05	.02	.01
☐ 133 Qadry Ismail	.10	.05	.01
☐ 134 Amp Lee	.05	.02	.01
☐ 135 Warren Moon	.10	.05	.01
☐ 136 John Randle	.05	.02	.01
☐ 137 Jake Reed	.10	.05	.01
☐ 138 Robert Smith	.10	.05	.01
☐ 139 Drew Bledsoe	1.00	.45	.12
☐ 140 Vincent Brisby	.05	.02	.01
☐ 141 Ben Coates	.10	.05	.01
☐ 142 Curtis Martin	1.50	.70	.19
☐ 143 Dave Meggett	.05	.02	.01
☐ 144 Will Moore	.05	.02	.01
☐ 145 Chris Slade	.05	.02	.01
☐ 146 Mario Bates	.10	.05	.01
☐ 147 Quinn Early	.05	.02	.01
☐ 148 Jim Everett	.05	.02	.01
☐ 149 Michael Haynes	.10	.05	.01
☐ 150 Tyrone Hughes	.05	.02	.01
☐ 151 Wayne Martin	.05	.02	.01
☐ 152 Renaldo Turnbull	.05	.02	.01
☐ 153 Dave Brown	.10	.05	.01
☐ 154 Chris Calloway	.05	.02	.01
☐ 155 Rodney Hampton	.10	.05	.01
☐ 156 Mike Sherrard	.05	.02	.01
☐ 157 Michael Strahan	.05	.02	.01
☐ 158 Herschel Walker	.10	.05	.01
☐ 159 Tyrone Wheatley	.10	.05	.01
☐ 160 Kyle Brady	.10	.05	.01
☐ 161 Wayne Chrebet	.10	.05	.01
☐ 162 Hugh Douglas	.05	.02	.01
☐ 163 Adrian Murrell	.10	.05	.01
☐ 164 Todd Scott	.05	.02	.01
☐ 165 Charles Wilson	.05	.02	.01
☐ 166 Tim Brown	.10	.05	.01
☐ 167 Aundray Bruce	.05	.02	.01
☐ 168 Andrew Glover	.05	.02	.01
☐ 169 Jeff Hostetler	.10	.05	.01
☐ 170 Napoleon Kaufman	.10	.05	.01
☐ 171 Terry McDaniel	.05	.02	.01
☐ 172 Chester McGlockton	.05	.02	.01
☐ 173 Pat Swilling	.05	.02	.01
☐ 174 Harvey Williams	.05	.02	.01

☐ 175 Fred Barnett	.10	.05	.01
☐ 176 Randall Cunningham	.10	.05	.01
☐ 177 William Fuller	.05	.02	.01
☐ 178 Charlie Garner	.05	.02	.01
☐ 179 Andy Harmon	.05	.02	.01
☐ 180 Rodney Peete	.05	.02	.01
☐ 181 Ricky Watters	.10	.05	.01
☐ 182 Calvin Williams	.20	.09	.03
☐ 183 Chad Brown	.10	.05	.01
☐ 184 Kevin Greene	.10	.05	.01
☐ 185 Greg Lloyd	.10	.05	.01
☐ 186 Byron Bam Morris	.10	.05	.01
☐ 187 Neil O'Donnell	.10	.05	.01
☐ 188 Erric Pegram	.10	.05	.01
☐ 189 Kordell Stewart	1.25	.55	.16
☐ 190 Yancey Thigpen	.10	.05	.01
☐ 191 Rod Woodson	.10	.05	.01
☐ 192 Darren Bennett	.10	.05	.01
☐ 193 Ronnie Harmon	.05	.02	.01
☐ 194 Stan Humphries	.10	.05	.01
☐ 195 Tony Martin	.10	.05	.01
☐ 196 Natrone Means	.20	.09	.03
☐ 197 Leslie O'Neal	.05	.02	.01
☐ 198 Junior Seau	.20	.09	.03
☐ 199 Mark Seay	.05	.02	.01
☐ 200 William Floyd	.10	.05	.01
☐ 201 Merton Hanks	.05	.02	.01
☐ 202 Brent Jones	.05	.02	.01
☐ 203 Derek Loville	.05	.02	.01
☐ 204 Ken Norton, Jr.	.10	.05	.01
☐ 205 Gary Plummer	.05	.02	.01
☐ 206 Jerry Rice	1.00	.45	.12
☐ 207 J.J. Stokes	.20	.09	.03
☐ 208 Dana Stubblefield	.10	.05	.01
☐ 209 John Taylor	.05	.02	.01
☐ 210 Bryant Young	.10	.05	.01
☐ 211 Steve Young	.75	.35	.09
☐ 212 Brian Blades	.10	.05	.01
☐ 213 Joey Galloway	.40	.18	.05
☐ 214 Carlton Gray	.05	.02	.01
☐ 215 Cortez Kennedy	.10	.05	.01
☐ 216 Rick Mirer	.10	.05	.01
☐ 217 Chris Warren	.10	.05	.01
☐ 218 Jerome Bettis	.20	.09	.03
☐ 219 Isaac Bruce	.20	.09	.03
☐ 220 Troy Drayton	.05	.02	.01
☐ 221 D'Marco Farr	.05	.02	.01
☐ 222 Sean Gilbert	.05	.02	.01
☐ 223 Chris Miller	.05	.02	.01
☐ 224 Roman Phifer	.05	.02	.01
☐ 225 Trent Dilfer	.10	.05	.01
☐ 226 Santana Dotson	.05	.02	.01
☐ 227 Alvin Harper	.05	.02	.01
☐ 228 Jackie Harris	.05	.02	.01
☐ 229 John Lynch	.05	.02	.01
☐ 230 Hardy Nickerson	.05	.02	.01
☐ 231 Errict Rhett	.10	.05	.01
☐ 232 Warren Sapp	.05	.02	.01
☐ 233 Terry Allen	.10	.05	.01
☐ 234 Henry Ellard	.10	.05	.01
☐ 235 Gus Frerotte	.20	.09	.03
☐ 236 Ken Harvey	.05	.02	.01
☐ 237 Brian Mitchell	.05	.02	.01
☐ 238 Heath Shuler	.20	.09	.03
☐ 239 James Washington	.05	.02	.01
☐ 240 Michael Westbrook	.20	.09	.03
☐ 241 Checklist	.05	.02	.01
☐ 242 Checklist	.05	.02	.01
☐ 243 Checklist	.05	.02	.01
☐ 244 Checklist	.05	.02	.01
☐ 245 Checklist	.05	.02	.01
☐ 246 Checklist	.05	.02	.01
☐ 247 Checklist	.05	.02	.01
☐ 248 Checklist	.05	.02	.01
☐ 249 Checklist	.05	.02	.01
☐ 250 Checklist	.05	.02	.01
☐ PR1 Eddie George Promo die cut Crucibles promo	3.00	1.35	.35

1996 Collector's Edge Die Cuts

This die cut parallel set was released by Collector's Edge in its special retail packs. The cards were distributed one per pack, featuring a pink colored front, and differ from the base brand only by the die cut design.

	MINT	NRMT	EXC
COMPLETE SET (240)	70.00	32.00	8.75
COMMON CARD (1-240)	.25	.11	.03

*VETERAN STARS: 2X TO 4X BASIC CARDS
*YOUNG STARS: 1.5X TO 3X BASIC CARDS
*RCs: 1.25X TO 2.5X BASIC CARDS ..

1996 Collector's Edge Holofoil

The 1996 Collector's Edge Holofoil is a 240-card parallel of the 1996 Collector's Edge regular version. These cards were issued one every 48 packs of retail, hobby or Cowboybilia.

	MINT	NRMT	EXC
COMPLETE SET (240)	550.00	250.00	70.00
COMMON CARD (1-240)	2.50	1.10	.30

*VETERAN STARS: 15X TO 30X BASIC CARDS
*YOUNG STARS: 12.5X TO 25X BASIC CARDS
*RCs: 10X TO 20X BASIC CARDS ......

1996 Collector's Edge Big Easy

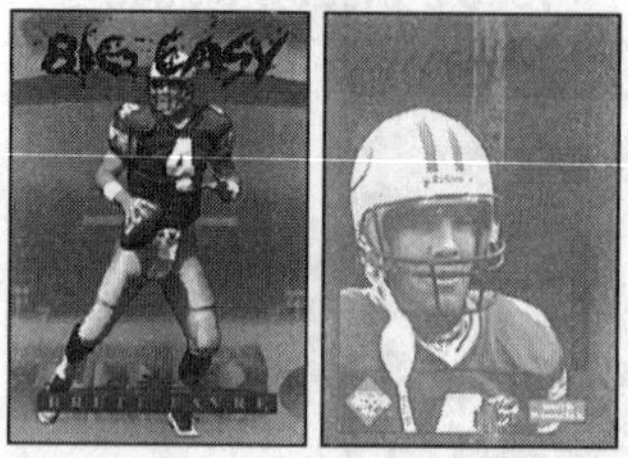

This set was distributed as a random insert in various 1996 Collector's Edge pack types. The cards feature metallized foil printing on the cardback with the Big Easy title on the cardfront with a mustard colored background. Each card was numbered of 2000 made and an unnumbered checklist card was produced as well. A gold foil parallel set was later released via mail order. Each was numbered of 3100 made.

	MINT	NRMT	EXC
COMPLETE SET (19)	200.00	90.00	25.00
COMMON CARD (1-18)	5.00	2.20	.60
☐ 1 Kerry Collins	16.00	7.25	2.00
☐ 2 Rashaan Salaam	8.00	3.60	1.00
☐ 3 Troy Aikman	16.00	7.25	2.00
☐ 4 Deion Sanders	10.00	4.50	1.25
☐ 5 Emmitt Smith	30.00	13.50	3.70
☐ 6 Terrell Davis	16.00	7.25	2.00
☐ 7 Barry Sanders	16.00	7.25	2.00
☐ 8 Brett Favre	30.00	13.50	3.70
☐ 9 Marshall Faulk	8.00	3.60	1.00
☐ 10 Tamarick Vanover	8.00	3.60	1.00
☐ 11 Dan Marino	30.00	13.50	3.70
☐ 12 Drew Bledsoe	16.00	7.25	2.00
☐ 13 Curtis Martin	16.00	7.25	2.00
☐ 14 J.J.Stokes	8.00	3.60	1.00
☐ 15 Joey Galloway	8.00	3.60	1.00
☐ 16 Isaac Bruce	8.00	3.60	1.00
☐ 17 Errict Rhett	5.00	2.20	.60
☐ 18 Carl Pickens	5.00	2.20	.60
☐ NNO Checklist Card	1.50	.70	.19

1996 Collector's Edge Cowboybilia Promos

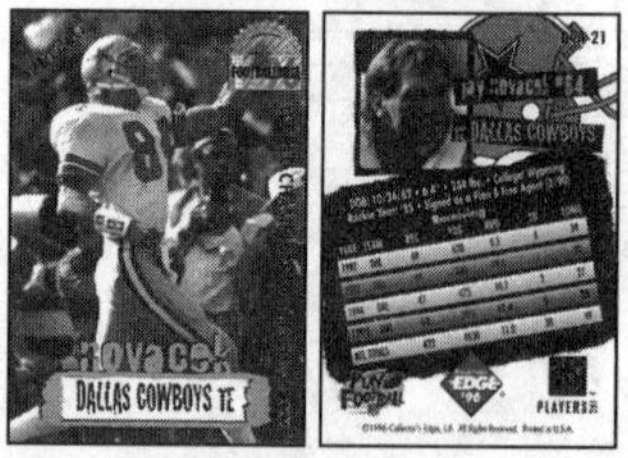

This 3 card set looks like the 1996 Cowboybilia series that was inserted into 1996 Collector's Edge Cowboybilia packs, with the difference being the fact that these cards are unsigned, and have "PROMO" stamped across the front of them.

	MINT	NRMT	EXC
COMPLETE SET (3)	5.00	2.20	.60
COMMON CARD (1-3)	1.50	.70	.19
☐ DCA20 Daryl Johnston	2.00	.90	.25
☐ DCA21 Jay Novacek	1.50	.70	.19
☐ DCA22 Charles Haley	1.50	.70	.19

1996 Collector's Edge Cowboybilia

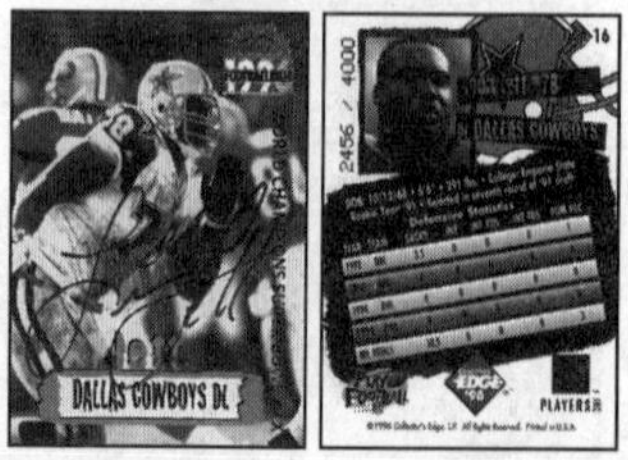

These 25 cards feature members of the Dallas Cowboys and were randomly inserted into Collector's Edge Cowboybilia packs. Each card was signed by the player, except for Troy Aikman and randomly inserted at the rate of 1:2.5 packs. The production number for each card is listed after the player's name. Every other pack contained an autographed Cowboys card or certificate for a signed Cowboys item. Other items included: Signed jerseys, helmets, photos, pennants and footballs. Also 24K Prism parallel cards of Emmitt Smith, Troy Aikman, Michael Irvin and Deion Sanders were inserted at a rate of approximately four per case (one per player per case). The Staubach/Pearson signed Hail Mary card was randomly inserted in 1 per 192 packs. The REAP program (Roever Educational Assistance Programs) was the charitable beneficiary of this issue.

	MINT	NRMT	EXC
COMPLETE SET (25)	750.00	350.00	95.00
COMMON CARD (DC1-DC25)	15.00	6.75	1.85
☐ DC1 Chris Boniol/4000	15.00	6.75	1.85
☐ DC2 John Jett/4000	15.00	6.75	1.85
☐ DC3 Sherman Williams/4000	15.00	6.75	1.85
☐ DC4 Chad Hennings/4000	20.00	9.00	2.50
☐ DC5 Larry Allen/4000	15.00	6.75	1.85
☐ DC6 Jason Garrett/4000	15.00	6.75	1.85
☐ DC7 Tony Tolbert/4000	15.00	6.75	1.85
☐ DC8 Kevin Williams/4000	20.00	9.00	2.50
☐ DC9 Mark Tuinei/4000	15.00	6.75	1.85
☐ DC10 Larry Brown/4000 MVP gold foil	15.00	6.75	1.85
☐ DC11 Kevin Smith/4000	20.00	9.00	2.50
☐ DC12 Darrin Smith/4000	15.00	6.75	1.85
☐ DC13 Robert Jones/4000	15.00	6.75	1.85
☐ DC14 Nate Newton/4000	20.00	9.00	2.50
☐ DC15 Darren Woodson/4000	20.00	9.00	2.50
☐ DC16 Leon Lett/4000	20.00	9.00	2.50
☐ DC17 Russell Maryland/4000	15.00	6.75	1.85
☐ DC18 Erik Williams/4000	15.00	6.75	1.85
☐ DC19 Bill Bates/4000	20.00	9.00	2.50
☐ DC20 Daryl Johnston/2300	30.00	13.50	3.70
☐ DC21 Jay Novacek/2300	30.00	13.50	3.70
☐ DC22 Charles Haley/2300	30.00	13.50	3.70
☐ DC23 Troy Aikman/600 all cards unsigned	70.00	32.00	8.75
☐ DC24 Michael Irvin/500	100.00	45.00	12.50
☐ DC25 Emmitt Smith/500	300.00	135.00	38.00
☐ NNO Roger Staubach Drew Pearson Hail Mary Pass numbered of 1000	175.00	80.00	22.00

1996 Collector's Edge Cowboybilia 24K Holofoil

These four cards are parallels to the player's 1995 Collector's Edge Holofoil card. To differentiate them, they were printed with a 24K logo. They were randomly inserted into 1996 Collector's Edge Cowboybilia packs at the rate of 1:48.

	MINT	NRMT	EXC
COMPLETE SET (4)	300.00	135.00	38.00
COMMON CARD	30.00	13.50	3.70
☐ CB57 Troy Aikman	75.00	34.00	9.50
☐ CB60 Michael Irvin	30.00	13.50	3.70
☐ CB63 Deion Sanders	50.00	22.00	6.25
☐ CB64 Emmitt Smith	150.00	70.00	19.00

1996 Collector's Edge Draft Day Redemption

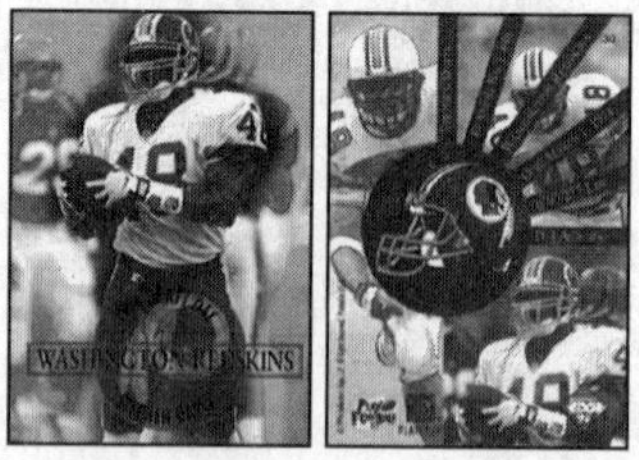

This 30-card set features color player photos of the Draft picks of the NFL teams. One of these player cards was received when the trade card for the appropriate team was redeemed. The redemption cards were randomly inserted in packs at the rate of one in eight. The trade cards expired 3/3/1997.

	MINT	NRMT	EXC
COMPLETE SET (30)	100.00	45.00	12.50
COMMON CARD (1-30)	2.00	.90	.25
TRADE CARDS	.10	.05	.01
☐ 1 Simeon Rice	2.00	.90	.25
☐ 2 Richard Huntley	2.00	.90	.25
☐ 3 Jonathan Ogden	2.00	.90	.25
☐ 4 Eric Moulds	4.00	1.80	.50
☐ 5 Tim Biakabutuka	4.00	1.80	.50
☐ 6 Walt Harris	2.00	.90	.25
☐ 7 Marco Battaglia	2.00	.90	.25
☐ 8 Stepfret Williams	2.00	.90	.25
☐ 9 John Mobley	2.00	.90	.25
☐ 10 Reggie Brown LB	2.00	.90	.25
☐ 11 Derrick Mayes	3.00	1.35	.35
☐ 12 Eddie George	8.00	3.60	1.00
☐ 13 Marvin Harrison	5.00	2.20	.60
☐ 14 Kevin Hardy	3.00	1.35	.35
☐ 15 Jerome Woods	2.00	.90	.25
☐ 16 Karim Abdul-Jabbar	6.00	2.70	.75
☐ 17 Duane Clemons	2.00	.90	.25
☐ 18 Terry Glenn	7.00	3.10	.85
☐ 19 Ricky Whittle	2.00	.90	.25
☐ 20 Amani Toomer	4.00	1.80	.50
☐ 21 Keyshawn Johnson	5.00	2.20	.60
☐ 22 Rickey Dudley	3.00	1.35	.35
☐ 23 Bobby Hoying	3.00	1.35	.35
☐ 24 Jahine Arnold	2.00	.90	.25
☐ 25 Tony Banks	5.00	2.20	.60
☐ 26 Bryan Still	2.00	.90	.25
☐ 27 Terrell Owens	5.00	2.20	.60
☐ 28 Reggie Brown RB	2.00	.90	.25
☐ 29 Mike Alstott	2.00	.90	.25
☐ 30 Stephen Davis	3.00	1.35	.35

1996 Collector's Edge Proteges

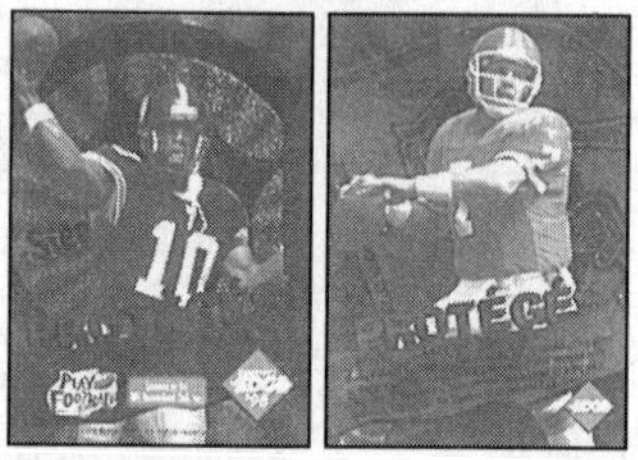

Randomly inserted (1:164 packs) in all Collector's Edge package types for 1996, these cards feature a top NFL veteran matched with a comparable younger player -- one on each side of the card. Each card is individually numbered and an unnumbered checklist card was produced as well.

	MINT	NRMT	EXC
COMPLETE SET (13)	200.00	90.00	25.00
COMMON CARD (1-12)	8.00	3.60	1.00
☐ 1 Eric Metcalf Joey Galloway	12.00	5.50	1.50
☐ 2 Herman Moore Michael Westbrook	12.00	5.50	1.50
☐ 3 Emmitt Smith Errict Rhett	30.00	13.50	3.70
☐ 4 Kordell Stewart John Elway	20.00	9.00	2.50
☐ 5 Terrell Davis Marshall Faulk	20.00	9.00	2.50
☐ 6 Rashaan Salaam Marcus Allen	12.00	5.50	1.50
☐ 7 Dan Marino Drew Bledsoe	30.00	13.50	3.70
☐ 8 Brett Favre Kerry Collins	30.00	13.50	3.70
☐ 9 Tim Brown Isaac Bruce	12.00	5.50	1.50
☐ 10 Cris Carter Chris Sanders	8.00	3.60	1.00
☐ 11 Curtis Martin Chris Warren	20.00	9.00	2.50
☐ 12 Tamarick Vanover Brian Mitchell	12.00	5.50	1.50
☐ NNO Checklist Card	2.00	.90	.25
☐ P1 Rashaan Salaam Promo Terry Kirby Promo	2.00	.90	.25

1996 Collector's Edge Quantum Motion

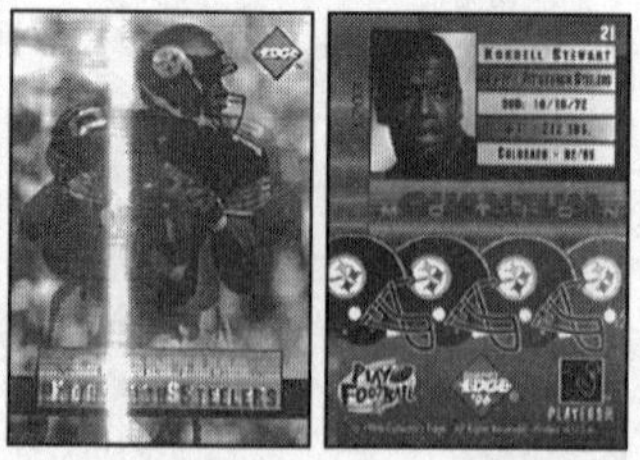

Randomly inserted at a rate of one in 36 in retail, hobby and Cowboybilia packs, this 24-card set changes images before your eyes using lenticular printing technology. They feature top NFL stars in both their current NFL uniform and their college uniform. This set is sequenced in alphabetical order.

	MINT	NRMT	EXC
COMPLETE SET (25)	325.00	145.00	40.00
COMMON CARD (1-24)	8.00	3.60	1.00
COMPLETE FOIL SET (24)	500.00	220.00	60.00
COMMON FOIL CARD (1-20)	12.00	5.50	1.50

*FOIL CARDS: .75X TO 1.5X BASIC CARDS

☐ 1 Troy Aikman	25.00	11.00	3.10
☐ 2 Marcus Allen	10.00	4.50	1.25
☐ 3 Drew Bledsoe	25.00	11.00	3.10
☐ 4 Tim Brown	8.00	3.60	1.00
☐ 5 Isaac Bruce	10.00	4.50	1.25
☐ 6 Mark Brunell	25.00	11.00	3.10
☐ 7 Kerry Collins	20.00	9.00	2.50
☐ 8 John Elway	18.00	8.00	2.20

☐ 9 Marshall Faulk	10.00	4.50	1.25
☐ 10 Brett Favre	40.00	18.00	5.00
☐ 11 Jeff George	8.00	3.60	1.00
☐ 12 Terry Kirby	8.00	3.60	1.00
☐ 13 Dan Marino	40.00	18.00	5.00
☐ 14 Natrone Means	8.00	3.60	1.00
☐ 15 Carl Pickens	8.00	3.60	1.00
☐ 16 Errict Rhett	8.00	3.60	1.00
☐ 17 Rashaan Salaam	10.00	4.50	1.25
☐ 18 Deion Sanders	15.00	6.75	1.85
☐ 19 Barry Sanders	25.00	11.00	3.10
☐ 20 Emmitt Smith	40.00	18.00	5.00
☐ 21 Kordell Stewart	20.00	9.00	2.50
☐ 22 Tamarick Vanover	10.00	4.50	1.25
☐ 23 Michael Westbrook	10.00	4.50	1.25
☐ 24 Steve Young	18.00	8.00	2.20
☐ QM1 Rashaan Salaam Promo	2.00	.90	.25
☐ NNO Checklist Card	2.00	.90	.25

1996 Collector's Edge Ripped

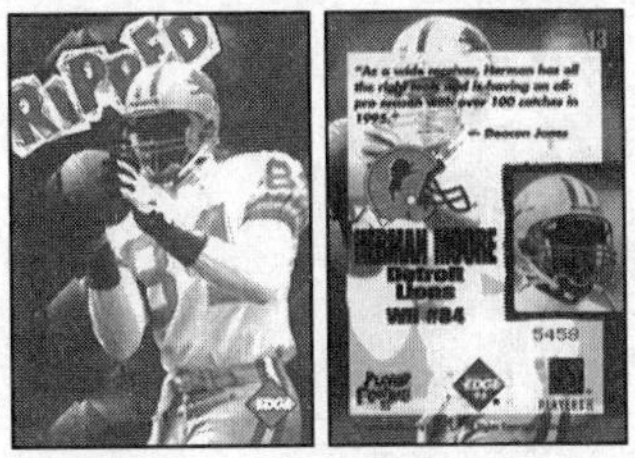

Randomly inserted in hobby, retail and Cowboybilia packs at a rate of one 12, this 19-card insert set (series one) features celebrities offering their commentary on NFL players. Cards numbered 1-18 with an unnumbered checklist (listed below) were available in 1996 Edge packs. A series two set (cards numbered 19-36) was released later in 1997 Collector's Edge Masters. A Jeff Blake Promo card was also produced and priced below. In addition, the series one set was produced and sold as a complete 18-card die cut set. Although the die cuts were produced in smaller numbers (500 of each card), they were released in full set form and thus are often available in larger group quantities.

	MINT	NRMT	EXC
COMP.SERIES 1 (19)	50.00	22.00	6.25
COMMON CARD (1-18)	.75	.35	.09
☐ 1 Jeff Blake	2.50	1.10	.30
☐ 2 Steve Bono	.75	.35	.09
☐ 3 Terrell Davis	6.00	2.70	.75
☐ 4 John Elway	4.00	1.80	.50
☐ 6 Brett Favre	10.00	4.50	1.25
☐ 8 Erik Kramer	.75	.35	.09
☐ 9 Dan Marino	10.00	4.50	1.25
☐ 10 Natrone Means	1.50	.70	.19
☐ 11 Eric Metcalf	1.50	.70	.19
☐ 12 Anthony Miller	.75	.35	.09
☐ 13 Herman Moore	1.50	.70	.19
☐ 14 Errict Rhett	1.50	.70	.19
☐ 15 Andre Rison	.75	.35	.09
☐ 17 Yancey Thigpen	2.50	1.10	.30
☐ 18 Michael Westbrook	2.50	1.10	.30
☐ CK1 Checklist Series 1	1.00	.45	.12
☐ R1 Jeff Blake Promo	2.00	.90	.25

1996 Collector's Edge Too Cool Rookies

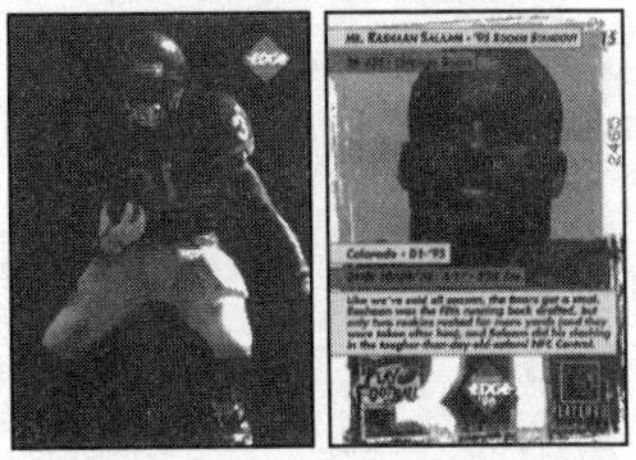

Randomly inserted in retail, hobby and Cowboybilia packs at a rate of one in eight, this 25-card set features some of the best rookies from the 1995 NFL season. The set is sequenced in alphabetical order. A Michael Westbrook Promo (#TC1) was produced and distributed with the base brand promos.

	MINT	NRMT	EXC
COMPLETE SET (25)	90.00	40.00	11.00
COMMON CARD (1-25)	2.50	1.10	.30
☐ 1 Tony Boselli	2.50	1.10	.30
☐ 2 Kyle Brady	2.50	1.10	.30
☐ 3 Ki-Jana Carter	4.00	1.80	.50
☐ 4 Kerry Collins	10.00	4.50	1.25
☐ 5 Todd Collins	4.00	1.80	.50
☐ 6 Terrell Davis	12.00	5.50	1.50
☐ 7 Hugh Douglas	2.50	1.10	.30
☐ 8 Joey Galloway	5.00	2.20	.60
☐ 9 Darius Holland	2.50	1.10	.30
☐ 10 Napoleon Kaufman	4.00	1.80	.50
☐ 11 Mike Mamula	2.50	1.10	.30
☐ 12 Curtis Martin	12.00	5.50	1.50
☐ 13 Steve McNair	8.00	3.60	1.00
☐ 14 Billy Milner	2.50	1.10	.30
☐ 15 Rashaan Salaam	4.00	1.80	.50
☐ 16 Frank Sanders	4.00	1.80	.50
☐ 17 Warren Sapp	2.50	1.10	.30
☐ 18 James O. Stewart	4.00	1.80	.50
☐ 19 J.J. Stokes	4.00	1.80	.50
☐ 20 Tamarick Vanover	4.00	1.80	.50
☐ 21 Michael Westbrook	4.00	1.80	.50
☐ 22 Tyrone Wheatley	4.00	1.80	.50
☐ 23 Kordell Stewart	10.00	4.50	1.25
☐ 24 Sherman Williams	2.50	1.10	.30
☐ 25 Eric Zeier	4.00	1.80	.50
☐ TC1 Michael Westbrook Promo	2.00	.90	.25

1996 Collector's Edge All-Stars

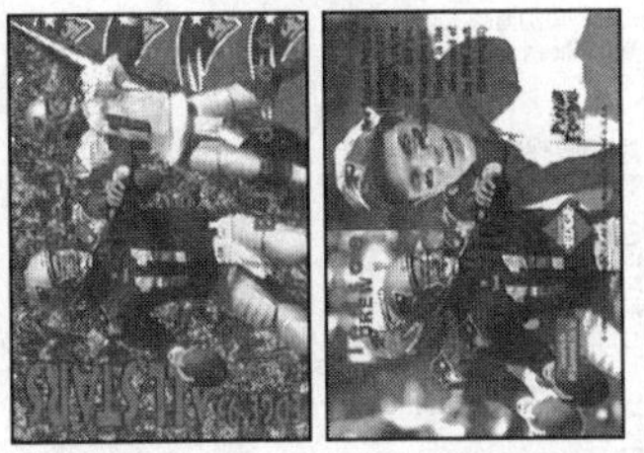

This set was released in late 1996, although the tag "Edge '95" appears on the cardfronts. Each is printed on the typical Edge plastic stock and features two color photos of the player on the front.

	MINT	NRMT	EXC
COMPLETE SET (13)	40.00	18.00	5.00
COMMON CARD (1-13)	2.00	.90	.25
☐ 1 Junior Seau	3.00	1.35	.35
☐ 2 Drew Bledsoe	6.00	2.70	.75
☐ 3 Marshall Faulk	3.00	1.35	.35
☐ 4 John Elway	5.00	2.20	.60
☐ 5 Jerry Rice	6.00	2.70	.75
☐ 6 Errict Rhett	2.00	.90	.25
☐ 7 Jerome Bettis	2.00	.90	.25
☐ 8 Deion Sanders	4.00	1.80	.50
☐ 9 Byron Bam Morris	2.00	.90	.25
☐ 10 Cris Carter	3.00	1.35	.35
☐ 11 Terrell Davis	6.00	2.70	.75
☐ 12 Terance Mathis	2.00	.90	.25
☐ 13 Checklist Card unnumbered	1.00	.45	.12

1996 Collector's Edge Advantage Promos

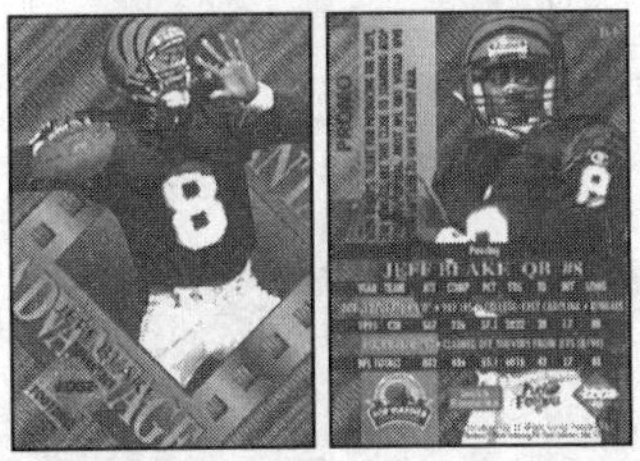

This four-card set was issued to preview the 1996 Collector's Edge Advantage series. The Promo set contains one card from each of three Advantage insert sets and one base set Promo. The fronts feature designs very similar to the regular release while the backs carry the word "Promo." The cards are all numbered 1 with a prefix and, therefore, checklisted below in alphabetical order.

	MINT	NRMT	EXC
COMPLETE SET (4)	6.00	2.70	.75
COMMON CARD	1.50	.70	.19
☐ 1 Jeff Blake Base Brand	1.50	.70	.19
☐ 2 Steve Bono Game Ball	2.00	.90	.25
☐ 3 Rashaan Salaam Crystal Cuts	1.50	.70	.19
☐ 4 Michael Westbrook Role Models	1.50	.70	.19

1996 Collector's Edge Advantage

The 1996 Collector's Edge Advantage set was issued in one series totalling 150 cards and features color player photos on front and back embossed gold foil stamped cards. The six-card packs retail for $2.69 each.

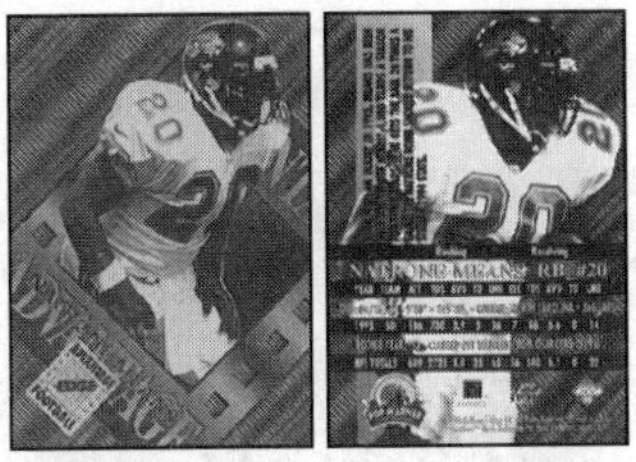

	MINT	NRMT	EXC
COMPLETE SET (150)	30.00	13.50	3.70
COMMON CARD (1-150)	.08	.04	.01
☐ 1 Drew Bledsoe	1.25	.55	.16
☐ 2 Chris Warren	.15	.07	.02
☐ 3 Eddie George	4.00	1.80	.50
☐ 4 Barry Sanders	1.25	.55	.16
☐ 5 Scott Mitchell	.15	.07	.02
☐ 6 Carl Pickens	.30	.14	.04
☐ 7 Tim Brown	.15	.07	.02
☐ 8 John Elway	1.00	.45	.12
☐ 9 Michael Westbrook	.30	.14	.04
☐ 10 Cris Carter	.30	.14	.04
☐ 11 Troy Aikman	1.25	.55	.16
☐ 12 Ben Coates	.15	.07	.02
☐ 13 Brett Favre	2.50	1.10	.30
☐ 14 Marshall Faulk	.30	.14	.04
☐ 15 Steve Young	1.00	.45	.12
☐ 16 Terrell Davis	2.00	.90	.25
☐ 17 Keyshawn Johnson	1.50	.70	.19
☐ 18 Mario Bates	.15	.07	.02
☐ 19 Steve McNair	1.25	.55	.16
☐ 20 Kerry Collins	1.50	.70	.19
☐ 21 Natrone Means	.30	.14	.04
☐ 22 Kordell Stewart	1.50	.70	.19
☐ 23 Jeff George	.15	.07	.02
☐ 24 Rick Mirer	.15	.07	.02
☐ 25 Herman Moore	.30	.14	.04
☐ 26 Rodney Peete	.08	.04	.01
☐ 27 Isaac Bruce	.30	.14	.04
☐ 28 Errict Rhett	.15	.07	.02
☐ 29 Jerry Rice	1.25	.55	.16
☐ 30 Rashaan Salaam	.30	.14	.04
☐ 31 Eric Metcalf	.15	.07	.02
☐ 32 Jim Kelly	.30	.14	.04
☐ 33 Jerome Bettis	.30	.14	.04
☐ 34 Deion Sanders	.75	.35	.09
☐ 35 J.J. Stokes	.30	.14	.04
☐ 36 Neil O'Donnell	.15	.07	.02
☐ 37 Marcus Allen	.30	.14	.04
☐ 38 Thurman Thomas	.30	.14	.04
☐ 39 Dan Marino	2.50	1.10	.30
☐ 40 Rickey Dudley	.30	.14	.04
☐ 41 Napoleon Kaufman	.15	.07	.02
☐ 42 Kyle Brady	.15	.07	.02
☐ 43 Emmitt Smith	2.50	1.10	.30
☐ 44 Tyrone Wheatley	.15	.07	.02
☐ 45 Jeff Blake	.30	.14	.04
☐ 46 Reggie White	.30	.14	.04
☐ 47 Joey Galloway	.60	.25	.07
☐ 48 Antonio Langham	.08	.04	.01
☐ 49 Craig Heyward	.08	.04	.01
☐ 50 Curtis Martin	2.00	.90	.25
☐ 51 Karim Abdul-Jabbar	2.50	1.10	.30
☐ 52 Antonio Freeman	.60	.25	.07
☐ 53 Ki-Jana Carter	.15	.07	.02
☐ 54 Willie Davis	.15	.07	.02
☐ 55 Jim Everett	.08	.04	.01
☐ 56 Gus Frerotte	.30	.14	.04
☐ 57 Daryl Gardener	.15	.07	.02
☐ 58 Charles Haley	.15	.07	.02
☐ 59 Michael Irvin	.30	.14	.04
☐ 60 Keith Jackson	.08	.04	.01
☐ 61 Cortez Kennedy	.15	.07	.02
☐ 62 Greg Lloyd	.15	.07	.02
☐ 63 Tony Martin	.15	.07	.02
☐ 64 Ken Norton Jr.	.15	.07	.02
☐ 65 Bobby Hoying	.30	.14	.04
☐ 66 Bryce Paup	.15	.07	.02
☐ 67 Jake Reed	.15	.07	.02
☐ 68 Frank Sanders	.15	.07	.02
☐ 69 Vinny Testaverde	.15	.07	.02
☐ 70 Regan Upshaw	.08	.04	.01
☐ 71 Tamarick Vanover	.30	.14	.04
☐ 72 Walt Harris	.08	.04	.01
☐ 73 John Randle	.08	.04	.01
☐ 74 Ricky Watters	.15	.07	.02
☐ 75 Terry Allen	.15	.07	.02
☐ 76 Edgar Bennett	.15	.07	.02
☐ 77 Larry Centers	.15	.07	.02
☐ 78 Chris Penn	.08	.04	.01
☐ 79 Bobby Engram	1.00	.45	.12
☐ 80 Irving Fryar	.15	.07	.02
☐ 81 Charlie Garner	.08	.04	.01
☐ 82 Rodney Hampton	.15	.07	.02
☐ 83 Michael Jackson	.15	.07	.02
☐ 84 O.J. McDuffie	.15	.07	.02
☐ 85 Shannon Sharpe	.15	.07	.02
☐ 86 Aaron Hayden	.08	.04	.01
☐ 87 Muhsin Muhammad	1.25	.55	.16
☐ 88 Rod Woodson	.15	.07	.02
☐ 89 Levon Kirkland	.08	.04	.01
☐ 90 Chad Brown	.15	.07	.02
☐ 91 Junior Seau	.30	.14	.04
☐ 92 Terry Kirby	.15	.07	.02
☐ 93 Zach Thomas	1.25	.55	.16
☐ 94 Harvey Williams	.08	.04	.01
☐ 95 Robert Brooks	.30	.14	.04
☐ 96 Darrell Green	.08	.04	.01
☐ 97 Chester McGlockton	.08	.04	.01
☐ 98 Neil Smith	.15	.07	.02
☐ 99 Eric Swann	.15	.07	.02
☐ 100 Mike Alstott	.50	.23	.06
☐ 101 Tim Biakabutuka	1.00	.45	.12
☐ 102 Mark Brunell	1.25	.55	.16
☐ 103 Chris Doleman	.08	.04	.01
☐ 104 Sean Gilbert	.08	.04	.01
☐ 105 Jim Harbaugh	.15	.07	.02
☐ 106 Chris T. Jones	.30	.14	.04
☐ 107 Tyrone Hughes	.08	.04	.01
☐ 108 Amani Toomer	.30	.14	.04
☐ 109 Larry Brown	.08	.04	.01
☐ 110 Kevin Greene	.15	.07	.02
☐ 111 John Mobley	.08	.04	.01
☐ 112 Danny Kanell	.30	.14	.04
☐ 113 Kevin Hardy	.15	.07	.02
☐ 114 Brett Perriman	.15	.07	.02
☐ 115 Simeon Rice	.30	.14	.04
☐ 116 Chris Sanders	.15	.07	.02
☐ 117 Dave Brown	.15	.07	.02
☐ 118 Bryan Cox	.08	.04	.01
☐ 119 Yancey Thigpen	.15	.07	.02
☐ 120 Terance Mathis	.08	.04	.01
☐ 121 Warren Moon	.15	.07	.02
☐ 122 Derrick Thomas	.15	.07	.02
☐ 123 Trent Dilfer	.15	.07	.02
☐ 124 Terry Glenn	3.00	1.35	.35
☐ 125 Jeff Hostetler	.15	.07	.02
☐ 126 Leeland McElroy	.30	.14	.04
☐ 127 Hardy Nickerson	.08	.04	.01
☐ 128 Steve Bono	.15	.07	.02
☐ 129 Stanley Pritchett	.15	.07	.02
☐ 130 Dana Stubblefield	.15	.07	.02
☐ 131 Andre Coleman	.08	.04	.01
☐ 132 Anthony Miller	.15	.07	.02
☐ 133 Stan Humphries	.15	.07	.02
☐ 134 Robert Smith	.15	.07	.02
☐ 135 Curtis Conway	.30	.14	.04
☐ 136 Darick Holmes	.15	.07	.02
☐ 137 Pat Swilling	.08	.04	.01
☐ 138 Andre Rison	.15	.07	.02
☐ 139 Erik Kramer	.08	.04	.01
☐ 140 Jason Dunn	.15	.07	.02
☐ 141 Torrance Small	.08	.04	.01
☐ 142 Cedric Jones	.15	.07	.02
☐ 143 Derek Loville	.08	.04	.01
☐ 144 Brian Mitchell	.08	.04	.01
☐ 145 Eric Moulds	1.00	.45	.12
☐ 146 James O.Stewart	.15	.07	.02
☐ 147 Bruce Smith	.30	.14	.04
☐ 148 Keenan McCardell	.30	.14	.04
☐ 149 Warren Sapp	.08	.04	.01
☐ 150 Marvin Harrison	1.50	.70	.19

1996 Collector's Edge Advantage Perfect Play Foils

Randomly inserted in packs at the rate of one in two, this 150-card set is a gold foil stamped parallel version of the regular set and features state of the art prism technology.

	MINT	NRMT	EXC
COMPLETE SET (150)	150.00	70.00	19.00
COMMON CARD (1-150)	.50	.23	.06
*VETERAN STARS: 3X TO 6X			
*YOUNG STARS: 2X TO 4X			
*RCs: 1.5X TO 3X			

1996 Collector's Edge Advantage Crystal Cuts

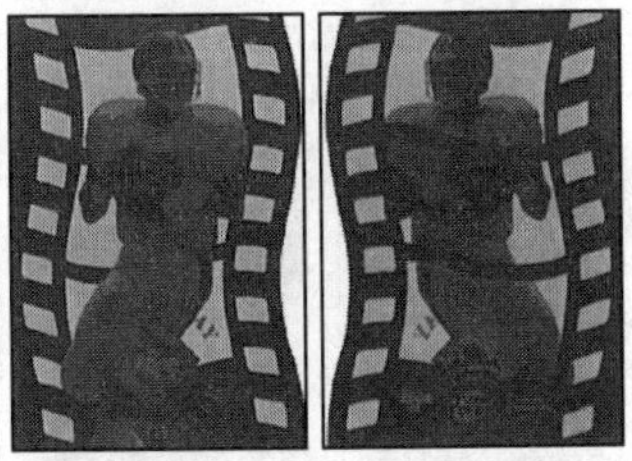

Randomly inserted in packs at a rate of one in eight, this 25-card set features a player photo against a background resembling a section of movie film. Each of the pack inserted cards are numbered of 5000 sets made. A silver foil parallel set was produced as well and distributed via mail order. Each silver card is numbered of 3100 made.

	MINT	NRMT	EXC
COMPLETE SET (25)	100.00	45.00	12.50
COMMON CARD (CC1-CC25)	2.00	.90	.25
☐ CC1 Barry Sanders	6.00	2.70	.75
☐ CC2 Eddie George	10.00	4.50	1.25
☐ CC3 Curtis Martin	8.00	3.60	1.00

☐ CC4 J.J. Stokes	3.00	1.35	.35
☐ CC5 Kyle Brady	2.00	.90	.25
☐ CC6 Chris Warren	2.00	.90	.25
☐ CC7 Jerry Rice	6.00	2.70	.75
☐ CC8 Ben Coates	2.00	.90	.25
☐ CC9 Terrell Davis	8.00	3.60	1.00
☐ CC10 Marcus Allen	3.00	1.35	.35
☐ CC11 John Elway	5.00	2.20	.60
☐ CC12 Joey Galloway	4.00	1.80	.50
☐ CC13 Dan Marino	12.00	5.50	1.50
☐ CC14 Napoleon Kaufman	2.00	.90	.25
☐ CC15 Emmitt Smith	12.00	5.50	1.50
☐ CC16 Eric Metcalf	2.00	.90	.25
☐ CC17 Kerry Collins	6.00	2.70	.75
☐ CC18 Troy Aikman	6.00	2.70	.75
☐ CC19 Rickey Dudley	2.00	.90	.25
☐ CC20 Steve McNair	5.00	2.20	.60
☐ CC21 Steve Young	4.00	1.80	.50
☐ CC22 Isaac Bruce	3.00	1.35	.35
☐ CC23 Kordell Stewart	6.00	2.70	.75
☐ CC24 LeShon Jonson	2.00	.90	.25
☐ CC25 Scott Mitchell	2.00	.90	.25

1996 Collector's Edge Advantage Video

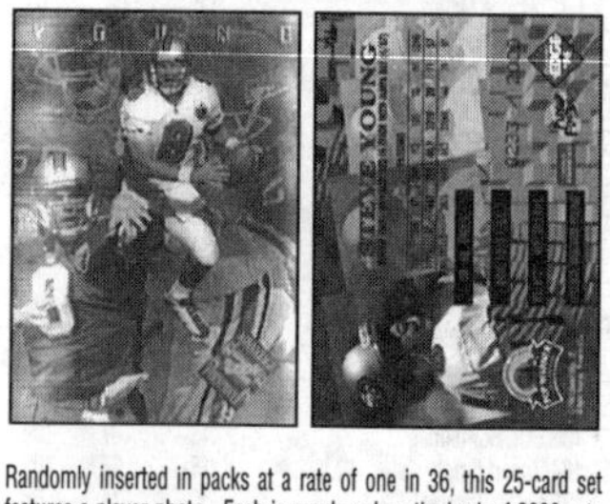

Randomly inserted in packs at a rate of one in 36, this 25-card set features a player photo . Each is numbered on the back of 2000 sets produced. A die cut parallel set was produced and released primarily through The Home Shopping television program and other mail order outlets. Reported only 300 of each die cut card was produced, except for Emmitt Smith, of which there were only 150 made.

	MINT	NRMT	EXC
COMPLETE SET (25)	200.00	90.00	25.00
COMMON CARD (V1-V25)	4.00	1.80	.50
☐ V1 Brett Favre	30.00	13.50	3.70
☐ V2 Keyshawn Johnson	8.00	3.60	1.00
☐ V3 Deion Sanders	10.00	4.50	1.25
☐ V4 Marcus Allen	6.00	2.70	.75
☐ V5 Rashaan Salaam	6.00	2.70	.75
☐ V6 Thurman Thomas	6.00	2.70	.75
☐ V7 Emmitt Smith	30.00	13.50	3.70
☐ V8 Isaac Bruce	6.00	2.70	.75
☐ V9 Michael Westbrook	6.00	2.70	.75
☐ V10 Cris Carter	4.00	1.80	.50
☐ V11 Marshall Faulk	6.00	2.70	.75
☐ V12 Jerry Rice	15.00	6.75	1.85
☐ V13 Tim Brown	4.00	1.80	.50
☐ V14 Steve Young	12.00	5.50	1.50
☐ V15 Eric Metcalf	4.00	1.80	.50
☐ V16 Chris Warren	4.00	1.80	.50
☐ V17 Drew Bledsoe	15.00	6.75	1.85
☐ V18 Barry Sanders	15.00	6.75	1.85
☐ V19 Herman Moore	6.00	2.70	.75
☐ V20 Rodney Peete	4.00	1.80	.50
☐ V21 Troy Aikman	15.00	6.75	1.85
☐ V22 Jerome Bettis	6.00	2.70	.75
☐ V23 Errict Rhett	6.00	2.70	.75
☐ V24 Dan Marino	30.00	13.50	3.70
☐ V25 Natrone Means	6.00	2.70	.75

1996 Collector's Edge Advantage Video Die Cuts

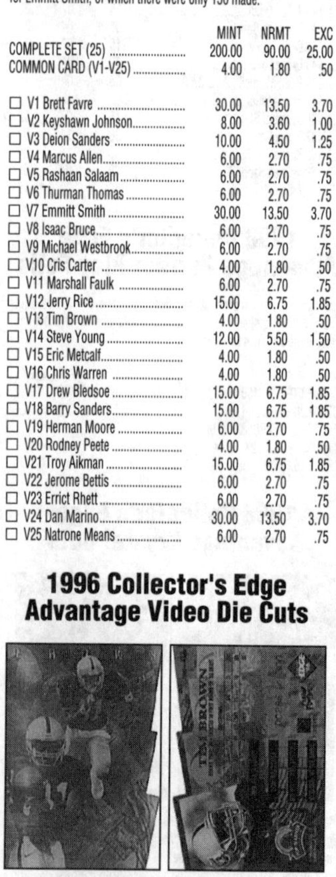

This die cut parallel set was produced and released primarily through The Home Shopping television program and other mail order outlets. Reported only 300 of each die cut card was produced, except for Emmitt Smith, of which there were only 150 made.

	MINT	NRMT	EXC
COMPLETE SET (25)	600.00	275.00	75.00
COMMON CARD (V1-V25)	15.00	6.75	1.85

DIE CUTS: 1.5X TO 3X BASE CARDS ..

1996 Collector's Edge Advantage Game Ball

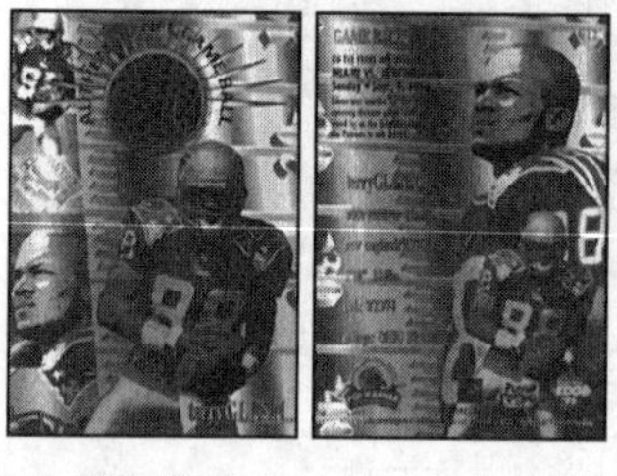

Randomly inserted in packs at a rate of one in 72, this 37-card set features a medallion cut from an authentic NFL game-used football, with highlights of the game in which the ball was used. A different game ball is paired with each color player photo.

	MINT	NRMT	EXC
COMPLETE SET (37)	1600.00	700.00	200.00
COMMON CARD (G1-G36)	20.00	9.00	2.50
☐ G1 Kordell Stewart	70.00	32.00	8.75
☐ G2 Emmitt Smith	150.00	70.00	19.00
☐ G3 Brett Favre	150.00	70.00	19.00
☐ G4 Steve Young	50.00	22.00	6.25
☐ G5 Barry Sanders	75.00	34.00	9.50
☐ G6 John Elway	55.00	25.00	7.00
☐ G7 Drew Bledsoe	60.00	27.00	7.50
☐ G8 Dan Marino	150.00	70.00	19.00
☐ G9 Keyshawn Johnson	35.00	16.00	4.40
☐ G10 Eddie George	90.00	40.00	11.00
☐ G11 Kevin Hardy	20.00	9.00	2.50
☐ G12 Terry Glenn	75.00	34.00	9.50
☐ G13 Michael Westbrook	35.00	16.00	4.40
☐ G14 Joey Galloway	35.00	16.00	4.40
☐ G15 John Mobley	20.00	9.00	2.50
☐ G16 Curtis Martin	75.00	34.00	9.50
☐ G17 Rashaan Salaam	35.00	16.00	4.40
☐ G18 J.J. Stokes	35.00	16.00	4.40
☐ G19 Kerry Collins	75.00	34.00	9.50
☐ G20 Deion Sanders	45.00	20.00	5.50
☐ G21 Shannon Sharpe	20.00	9.00	2.50
☐ G22 Terry Allen	25.00	11.00	3.10
☐ G23 Ricky Watters	25.00	11.00	3.10
☐ G24 Marshall Faulk	35.00	16.00	4.40
☐ G25 Tim Biakabutuka	35.00	16.00	4.40
☐ G26 Troy Aikman	60.00	27.00	7.50
☐ G27 Jerry Rice	75.00	34.00	9.50
☐ G28 Chris Warren	20.00	9.00	2.50
☐ G29 Jeff Blake	35.00	16.00	4.40
☐ G30 Carl Pickens	25.00	11.00	3.10
☐ G31 Isaac Bruce	35.00	16.00	4.40
☐ G32 Terrell Davis	75.00	34.00	9.50
☐ G33 Mark Brunell	75.00	34.00	9.50
☐ G34 Karim Abdul-Jabbar	60.00	27.00	7.50
☐ G35 Herman Moore	35.00	16.00	4.40
☐ G36 Cris Carter	25.00	11.00	3.10
☐ NNO Checklist Card	1.00	.45	.12

1996 Collector's Edge Advantage Role Models

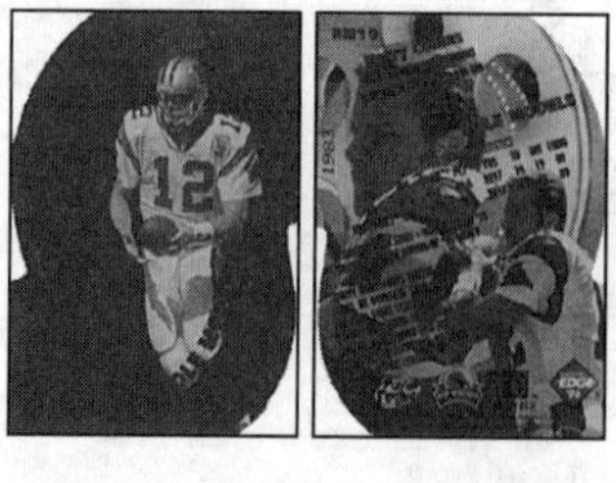

Randomly inserted in packs at a rate of one in 12, this 13-card set featues color player action photos on specially die cut, embossed, metalized cards.

	MINT	NRMT	EXC
COMPLETE SET (13)	60.00	27.00	7.50
COMMON CARD (RM1-RM12)	2.00	.90	.25
☐ RM1 John Elway	6.00	2.70	.75
☐ RM2 Dan Marino	15.00	6.75	1.85
☐ RM3 Jerry Rice	8.00	3.60	1.00
☐ RM4 Emmitt Smith	15.00	6.75	1.85
☐ RM5 Chris Warren	2.00	.90	.25
☐ RM6 Tim Brown	3.00	1.35	.35
☐ RM7 Jeff George	2.00	.90	.25
☐ RM8 Tyrone Wheatley	2.00	.90	.25
☐ RM9 Steve Bono	2.00	.90	.25
☐ RM10 Kerry Collins	8.00	3.60	1.00
☐ RM11 Jerome Bettis	3.00	1.35	.35
☐ RM12 Steve Beuerlein	2.00	.90	.25
☐ NNO Checklist Card	2.00	.90	.25

1996 Collector's Edge Advantage Super Bowl Game Ball

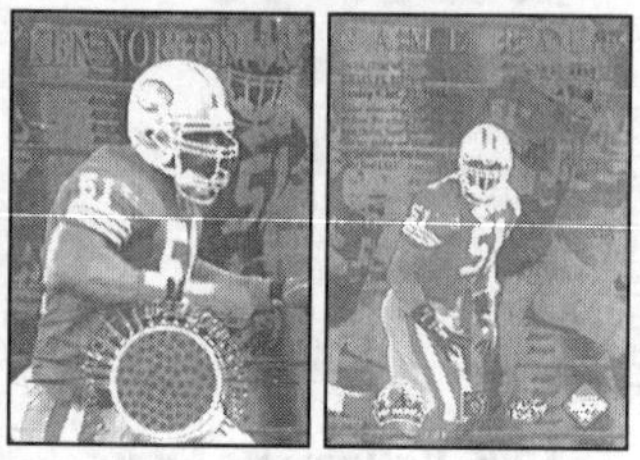

Randomly inserted in packs at a rate of one in 164, this 36-card set features a medallion cut from an authentic NFL Super Bowl game-used football with highlights of the Super Bowl game in which the ball was used. Different game balls are paired with each of the 36 color player photos.

	MINT	NRMT	EXC
COMPLETE SET (36)	2000.00	900.00	250.00
COMMON CARD (SB1-SB36)	25.00	11.00	3.10
☐ SB1 Emmitt Smith	300.00	135.00	38.00
☐ SB2 Troy Aikman	175.00	80.00	22.00
☐ SB3 Michael Irvin	60.00	27.00	7.50
☐ SB4 Deion Sanders	100.00	45.00	12.50
☐ SB5 John Elway	150.00	70.00	19.00
☐ SB6 Dan Marino	300.00	135.00	38.00
☐ SB7 Marcus Allen	90.00	40.00	11.00
☐ SB8 Kordell Stewart	175.00	80.00	22.00
☐ SB9 Steve Young	135.00	60.00	17.00
☐ SB10 Ricky Watters	25.00	11.00	3.10
☐ SB11 Jerry Rice	175.00	80.00	22.00
☐ SB12 Jim Kelly	90.00	40.00	11.00
☐ SB13 Thurman Thomas	60.00	27.00	7.50
☐ SB14 Bruce Smith	60.00	27.00	7.50
☐ SB15 Stan Humphries	35.00	16.00	4.40
☐ SB16 Junior Seau	35.00	16.00	4.40
☐ SB17 Natrone Means	35.00	16.00	4.40
☐ SB18 Neil O'Donnell	25.00	11.00	3.10
☐ SB19 Rod Woodson	25.00	11.00	3.10
☐ SB20 Andre Reed	35.00	16.00	4.40
☐ SB21 Jeff Hostetler	25.00	11.00	3.10
☐ SB22 Dave Meggett	25.00	11.00	3.10
☐ SB23 Greg Lloyd	25.00	11.00	3.10
☐ SB24 Kevin Greene	35.00	16.00	4.40
☐ SB25 Yancey Thigpen	35.00	16.00	4.40
☐ SB26 Charles Haley	25.00	11.00	3.10
☐ SB27 Byron Bam Morris	35.00	16.00	4.40
☐ SB28 Alvin Harper	25.00	11.00	3.10
☐ SB29 Ken Norton Jr.	25.00	11.00	3.10
☐ SB30 William Floyd	35.00	16.00	4.40
☐ SB31 Leslie O'Neal	25.00	11.00	3.10
☐ SB32 Jay Novacek	25.00	11.00	3.10
☐ SB33 Irving Fryar	25.00	11.00	3.10
☐ SB34 Leon Lett	25.00	11.00	3.10
☐ SB35 Tony Martin	25.00	11.00	3.10
☐ SB36 Mark Collins	25.00	11.00	3.10

1997 Collector's Edge Masters

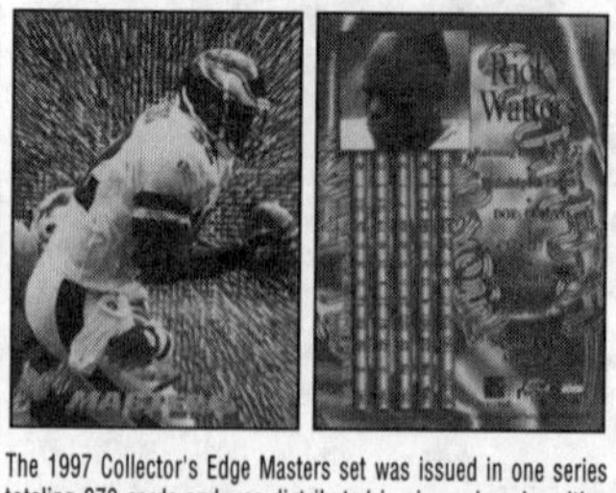

The 1997 Collector's Edge Masters set was issued in one series totaling 270 cards and was distributed in six-card packs with a suggested retail price of $3.49. The set contains color photos of 240 top players in the NFL printed on metalized card stock with silver texture or regular backgrounds and ultra-premium embossed fronts plus 30 team flag cards which were inserted randomly at the rate of one every three packs. A collector could send in the Flag Card for either Green Bay or New England plus one Flag Card for each opponent beaten by these teams during the regular and post-season (one Flag Card per game) and receive a foil stamped limited edition team set of the Packers or the Patriots. The card wrappers carried the rules and details for this limited offer.

	MINT	NRMT	EXC
COMPLETE SET (270)	50.00	22.00	6.25
COMP.PLAYER SET (240)	30.00	13.50	3.70
COMMON CARD (1-270)	.10	.05	.01
COMMON FLAG	1.00	.45	.12
☐ 1 Cardinals Flag	1.00	.45	.12
☐ 2 Larry Centers	.20	.09	.03
☐ 3 Rob Moore	.10	.05	.01
☐ 4 Frank Sanders	.20	.09	.03
☐ 5 Eric Swann	.20	.09	.03
☐ 6 Falcons Flag	1.00	.45	.12
☐ 7 Morten Andersen UER misspelled Morton	.10	.05	.01
☐ 8 Bert Emanuel	.20	.09	.03
☐ 9 Jeff George	.20	.09	.03
☐ 10 Craig Heyward	.10	.05	.01
☐ 11 Terance Mathis	.10	.05	.01
☐ 12 Clay Matthews	.20	.09	.03
☐ 13 Eric Metcalf	.20	.09	.03
☐ 14 Ravens Flag	1.00	.45	.12
☐ 15 Rob Burnett	.10	.05	.01
☐ 16 Leroy Hoard	.10	.05	.01
☐ 17 Ernest Hunter	.10	.05	.01
☐ 18 Michael Jackson	.20	.09	.03
☐ 19 Stevon Moore	.10	.05	.01
☐ 20 Anthony Pleasant	.10	.05	.01
☐ 21 Vinny Testaverde	.20	.09	.03
☐ 22 Eric Zeier	.20	.09	.03
☐ 23 Bills Flag	1.00	.45	.12
☐ 24 Todd Collins	.20	.09	.03
☐ 25 Russell Copeland	.10	.05	.01
☐ 26 Quinn Early	.10	.05	.01
☐ 27 Jim Kelly	.40	.18	.05
☐ 28 Bryce Paup	.10	.05	.01
☐ 29 Andre Reed	.20	.09	.03
☐ 30 Bruce Smith	.40	.18	.05
☐ 31 Panthers Flag	1.00	.45	.12
☐ 32 Steve Beuerlein	.10	.05	.01
☐ 33 Mark Carrier WR	.20	.09	.03
☐ 34 Kerry Collins	1.00	.45	.12
☐ 35 Willie Green	.10	.05	.01
☐ 36 Kevin Greene	.20	.09	.03
☐ 37 Eric Guliford	.10	.05	.01
☐ 38 Brett Maxie	.10	.05	.01
☐ 39 Tim McKyer	.10	.05	.01
☐ 40 Derrick Moore	.10	.05	.01
☐ 41 Bears Flag	1.00	.45	.12
☐ 42 Curtis Conway	.40	.18	.05
☐ 43 Bryan Cox	.10	.05	.01
☐ 44 Jim Flanigan	.10	.05	.01
☐ 45 Robert Green	.10	.05	.01
☐ 46 Erik Kramer	.10	.05	.01
☐ 47 Dave Krieg	.10	.05	.01
☐ 48 Rashaan Salaam	.40	.18	.05
☐ 49 Alonzo Spellman	.10	.05	.01
☐ 50 Donnell Woolford	.10	.05	.01
☐ 51 Chris Zorich	.10	.05	.01
☐ 52 Bengals Flag	1.00	.45	.12
☐ 53 Eric Bieniemy	.10	.05	.01
☐ 54 Jeff Blake	.40	.18	.05
☐ 55 Ki-Jana Carter	.20	.09	.03
☐ 56 John Copeland	.10	.05	.01
☐ 57 Garrison Hearst	.20	.09	.03
☐ 58 Tony McGee	.10	.05	.01
☐ 59 Carl Pickens	.40	.18	.05
☐ 60 Darnay Scott	.20	.09	.03
☐ 61 Bracey Walker	.10	.05	.01
☐ 62 Dan Wilkinson	.10	.05	.01
☐ 63 Cowboys Flag	1.00	.45	.12
☐ 64 Troy Aikman	1.25	.55	.16
☐ 65 Bill Bates	.20	.09	.03
☐ 66 Shante Carver	.10	.05	.01
☐ 67 Michael Irvin	.40	.18	.05
☐ 68 Daryl Johnston	.20	.09	.03
☐ 69 Jay Novacek	.20	.09	.03
☐ 70 Deion Sanders	.60	.25	.07
☐ 71 Emmitt Smith	2.50	1.10	.30
☐ 72 Herschel Walker	.20	.09	.03
☐ 73 Sherman Williams	.10	.05	.01
☐ 74 Broncos Flag	1.00	.45	.12
☐ 75 Terrell Davis	1.25	.55	.16
☐ 76 John Elway	1.00	.45	.12
☐ 77 Ed McCaffrey	.10	.05	.01
☐ 78 Anthony Miller	.20	.09	.03
☐ 79 Michael Dean Perry	.10	.05	.01
☐ 80 Shannon Sharpe	.20	.09	.03
☐ 81 Mike Sherrard	.10	.05	.01
☐ 82 Lions Flag	1.00	.45	.12
☐ 83 Scott Mitchell	.20	.09	.03
☐ 84 Glyn Milburn	.10	.05	.01
☐ 85 Herman Moore	.40	.18	.05
☐ 86 Johnnie Morton	.20	.09	.03
☐ 87 Brett Perriman	.20	.09	.03
☐ 88 Barry Sanders	1.25	.55	.16
☐ 89 Tracy Scroggins	.10	.05	.01
☐ 90 Packers Flag	1.00	.45	.12
☐ 91 Edgar Bennett	.20	.09	.03
☐ 92 Robert Brooks	.40	.18	.05
☐ 93 Santana Dotson	.10	.05	.01
☐ 94 Brett Favre	2.50	1.10	.30
☐ 95 Dorsey Levens	.20	.09	.03
☐ 96 Craig Newsome	.10	.05	.01
☐ 97 Wayne Simmons	.10	.05	.01
☐ 98 Reggie White	.40	.18	.05
☐ 99 Oilers Flag	1.00	.45	.12
☐ 100 Chris Chandler	.20	.09	.03
☐ 101 Anthony Cook	.10	.05	.01
☐ 102 Willie Davis	.20	.09	.03
☐ 103 Mel Gray	.10	.05	.01
☐ 104 Ronnie Harmon	.10	.05	.01
☐ 105 Darryll Lewis	.10	.05	.01
☐ 106 Steve McNair	.75	.35	.09
☐ 107 Todd McNair	.10	.05	.01
☐ 108 Rodney Thomas	.10	.05	.01
☐ 109 Colts Flag	1.00	.45	.12

☐ 110 Trev Alberts	.10	.05	.01
☐ 111 Tony Bennett	.10	.05	.01
☐ 112 Quentin Coryatt	.10	.05	.01
☐ 113 Sean Dawkins	.10	.05	.01
☐ 114 Ken Dilger	.20	.09	.03
☐ 115 Marshall Faulk	.40	.18	.05
☐ 116 Jim Harbaugh UER numbered 115 on back	.20	.09	.03
☐ 117 Ronald Humphrey	.10	.05	.01
☐ 118 Floyd Turner	.10	.05	.01
☐ 119 Jaguars Flag	1.00	.45	.12
☐ 120 Tony Boselli	.20	.09	.03
☐ 121 Mark Brunell	1.25	.55	.16
☐ 122 Willie Jackson	.20	.09	.03
☐ 123 Jeff Lageman	.10	.05	.01
☐ 124 Natrone Means	.40	.18	.05
☐ 125 Andre Rison	.20	.09	.03
☐ 126 James O.Stewart	.20	.09	.03
☐ 127 Cedric Tillman	.10	.05	.01
☐ 128 Chiefs Flag	1.00	.45	.12
☐ 129 Marcus Allen	.40	.18	.05
☐ 130 Kimble Anders	.10	.05	.01
☐ 131 Steve Bono	.10	.05	.01
☐ 132 Dale Carter	.10	.05	.01
☐ 133 Lake Dawson	.20	.09	.03
☐ 134 Dan Saleaumua	.10	.05	.01
☐ 135 Neil Smith	.20	.09	.03
☐ 136 Derrick Thomas	.20	.09	.03
☐ 137 Tamarick Vanover	.20	.09	.03
☐ 138 Dolphins Flag	1.00	.45	.12
☐ 139 Fred Barnett	.20	.09	.03
☐ 140 Steve Emtman	.10	.05	.01
☐ 141 Eric Green	.10	.05	.01
☐ 142 Dan Marino	2.50	1.10	.30
☐ 143 O.J. McDuffie	.20	.09	.03
☐ 144 Bernie Parmalee	.10	.05	.01
☐ 145 Vikings Flag	1.00	.45	.12
☐ 146 Cris Carter	.40	.18	.05
☐ 147 Jack Del Rio	.10	.05	.01
☐ 148 Qadry Ismail	.20	.09	.03
☐ 149 Amp Lee	.10	.05	.01
☐ 150 Warren Moon	.20	.09	.03
☐ 151 John Randle	.10	.05	.01
☐ 152 Jake Reed	.20	.09	.03
☐ 153 Robert Smith	.20	.09	.03
☐ 154 Patriots Flag	1.00	.45	.12
☐ 155 Drew Bledsoe	1.25	.55	.16
☐ 156 Vincent Brisby	.10	.05	.01
☐ 157 Willie Clay	.10	.05	.01
☐ 158 Ben Coates	.20	.09	.03
☐ 159 Curtis Martin	1.25	.55	.16
☐ 160 Dave Meggett	.10	.05	.01
☐ 161 Will Moore	.10	.05	.01
☐ 162 Chris Slade	.10	.05	.01
☐ 163 Saints Flag	1.00	.45	.12
☐ 164 Mario Bates	.20	.09	.03
☐ 165 Jim Everett	.10	.05	.01
☐ 166 Michael Haynes	.20	.09	.03
☐ 167 Tyrone Hughes	.10	.05	.01
☐ 168 Haywood Jeffires	.10	.05	.01
☐ 169 Wayne Martin	.10	.05	.01
☐ 170 Renaldo Turnbull	.10	.05	.01
☐ 171 Giants Flag	1.00	.45	.12
☐ 172 Dave Brown	.20	.09	.03
☐ 173 Chris Calloway	.10	.05	.01
☐ 174 Rodney Hampton see card 259	.20	.09	.03
☐ 175 Michael Strahan	.10	.05	.01
☐ 176 Tyrone Wheatley	.20	.09	.03
☐ 177 Jets Flag	1.00	.45	.12
☐ 178 Kyle Brady	.10	.05	.01
☐ 179 Wayne Chrebet	.10	.05	.01
☐ 180 Hugh Douglas	.10	.05	.01
☐ 181 Jeff Graham	.10	.05	.01
☐ 182 Adrian Murrell	.20	.09	.03
☐ 183 Neil O'Donnell	.20	.09	.03
☐ 184 Raiders Flag	1.00	.45	.12
☐ 185 Tim Brown	.20	.09	.03
☐ 186 Aundray Bruce	.10	.05	.01
☐ 187 Andrew Glover	.10	.05	.01
☐ 188 Jeff Hostetler	.20	.09	.03
☐ 189 Napoleon Kaufman	.20	.09	.03
☐ 190 Terry McDaniel	.10	.05	.01
☐ 191 Chester McGlockton	.10	.05	.01
☐ 192 Pat Swilling	.10	.05	.01
☐ 193 Harvey Williams	.10	.05	.01
☐ 194 Eagles Flag	1.00	.45	.12
☐ 195 Randall Cunningham	.20	.09	.03
☐ 196 Irving Fryar	.20	.09	.03
☐ 197 William Fuller	.10	.05	.01
☐ 198 Charlie Garner	.10	.05	.01
☐ 199 Andy Harmon	.10	.05	.01
☐ 200 Rodney Peete	.10	.05	.01
☐ 201 Mark Seay	.10	.05	.01
☐ 202 Troy Vincent	.10	.05	.01
☐ 203 Ricky Watters	.20	.09	.03
☐ 204 Calvin Williams	.10	.05	.01
☐ 205 Steelers Flag	1.00	.45	.12
☐ 206 Jerome Bettis	.40	.18	.05
☐ 207 Chad Brown	.20	.09	.03
☐ 208 Greg Lloyd	.20	.09	.03
☐ 209 Byron Bam Morris	.20	.09	.03
☐ 210 Erric Pegram	.10	.05	.01
☐ 211 Kordell Stewart	1.00	.45	.12
☐ 212 Yancey Thigpen	.20	.09	.03
☐ 213 Rod Woodson	.20	.09	.03
☐ 214 Chargers Flag	1.00	.45	.12
☐ 215 Darren Bennett	.10	.05	.01
☐ 216 Marco Coleman	.10	.05	.01
☐ 217 Stan Humphries	.20	.09	.03
☐ 218 Tony Martin	.20	.09	.03
☐ 219 Junior Seau	.40	.18	.05
☐ 220 49ers Flag	1.00	.45	.12
☐ 221 Chris Doleman	.10	.05	.01
☐ 222 William Floyd	.20	.09	.03
☐ 223 Merton Hanks	.10	.05	.01
☐ 224 Brent Jones	.10	.05	.01
☐ 225 Terry Kirby	.20	.09	.03
☐ 226 Derek Loville	.10	.05	.01
☐ 227 Ken Norton Jr.	.10	.05	.01
☐ 228 Gary Plummer	.10	.05	.01
☐ 229 Jerry Rice	1.25	.55	.16
☐ 230 J.J. Stokes	.20	.09	.03
☐ 231 Dana Stubblefield	.20	.09	.03
☐ 232 John Taylor	.10	.05	.01
☐ 233 Bryant Young	.20	.09	.03
☐ 234 Steve Young	1.00	.45	.12
☐ 235 Seahawks Flag	1.00	.45	.12
☐ 236 Brian Blades	.20	.09	.03
☐ 237 Joey Galloway	.50	.23	.06
☐ 238 Carlton Gray	.10	.05	.01
☐ 239 Cortez Kennedy	.20	.09	.03
☐ 240 Rick Mirer	.20	.09	.03
☐ 241 Chris Warren	.20	.09	.03
☐ 242 Rams Flag	1.00	.45	.12
☐ 243 Isaac Bruce	.40	.18	.05
☐ 244 Troy Drayton	.10	.05	.01
☐ 245 D'Marco Farr	.10	.05	.01
☐ 246 Harold Green	.10	.05	.01
☐ 247 Chris Miller	.10	.05	.01
☐ 248 Leslie O'Neal	.10	.05	.01
☐ 249 Roman Phifer	.10	.05	.01
☐ 250 Buccaneers Flag	1.00	.45	.12
☐ 251 Trent Dilfer	.20	.09	.03
☐ 252 Alvin Harper	.10	.05	.01
☐ 253 Jackie Harris	.10	.05	.01
☐ 254 John Lynch	.10	.05	.01
☐ 255 Hardy Nickerson	.10	.05	.01
☐ 256 Errict Rhett	.20	.09	.03
☐ 257 Warren Sapp	.10	.05	.01
☐ 258 Todd Scott	.10	.05	.01
☐ 259 Charles Wilson UER numbered 174 on back	.10	.05	.01
☐ 260 Redskins Flag	1.00	.45	.12
☐ 261 Terry Allen	.20	.09	.03
☐ 262 Bill Brooks	.10	.05	.01
☐ 263 Henry Ellard	.20	.09	.03
☐ 264 Gus Frerotte	.40	.18	.05
☐ 265 Sean Gilbert	.10	.05	.01
☐ 266 Ken Harvey	.10	.05	.01
☐ 267 Brian Mitchell	.10	.05	.01
☐ 268 Heath Shuler	.40	.18	.05
☐ 269 James Washington	.10	.05	.01
☐ 270 Michael Westbrook	.40	.18	.05

1997 Collector's Edge Masters Holofoil

This 270-card set is a parallel version of the 1997 Collector's Edge Masters base set and is similar in design. The set is distinguished by the holofoil card stock it is printed on.

	MINT	NRMT	EXC
COMPLETE SET (270)	50.00	22.00	6.25
COMMON CARD (1-270)	.10	.05	.01
*HOLOFOILS: SAME PRICE AS BASIC CARDS			

1997 Collector's Edge Masters Crucibles

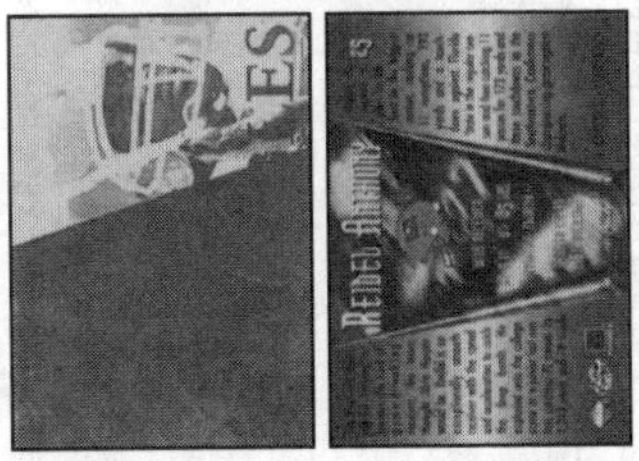

Randomly inserted in hobby packs only at a rate of one in six, this 25-card set features color photos of the top draft picks for the 1997 season. Only 3000 of each card were produced and are sequentially numbered.

	MINT	NRMT	EXC
COMPLETE SET (25)	70.00	32.00	8.75
COMMON CARD (1-25)	1.50	.70	.19
☐ 1 Jake Plummer	3.00	1.35	.35
☐ 2 Byron Hanspard	4.00	1.80	.50
☐ 3 Peter Boulware	2.00	.90	.25
☐ 4 Jay Graham	1.50	.70	.19
☐ 5 Antowain Smith	3.00	1.35	.35
☐ 6 Rae Carruth	4.00	1.80	.50
☐ 7 Darnell Autry	3.00	1.35	.35
☐ 8 Corey Dillon	4.00	1.80	.50
☐ 9 Bryant Westbrook	2.00	.90	.25
☐ 10 Joey Kent	2.00	.90	.25
☐ 11 Kevin Lockett	1.50	.70	.19
☐ 12 Pat Barnes	3.00	1.35	.35
☐ 13 Tony Gonzalez	3.00	1.35	.35
☐ 14 Yatil Green	5.00	2.20	.60
☐ 15 Danny Wuerffel	6.00	2.70	.75
☐ 16 Troy Davis	5.00	2.20	.60
☐ 17 Tiki Barber	3.00	1.35	.35
☐ 18 Ike Hilliard	5.00	2.20	.60
☐ 19 Leon Johnson	1.50	.70	.19
☐ 20 Darrell Russell	2.00	.90	.25
☐ 21 Jim Druckenmiller	6.00	2.70	.75
☐ 22 Shawn Springs	3.00	1.35	.35
☐ 23 Orlando Pace	2.50	1.10	.30
☐ 24 Warrick Dunn	8.00	3.60	1.00
☐ 25 Reidel Anthony	5.00	2.20	.60

1997 Collector's Edge Masters Night Games

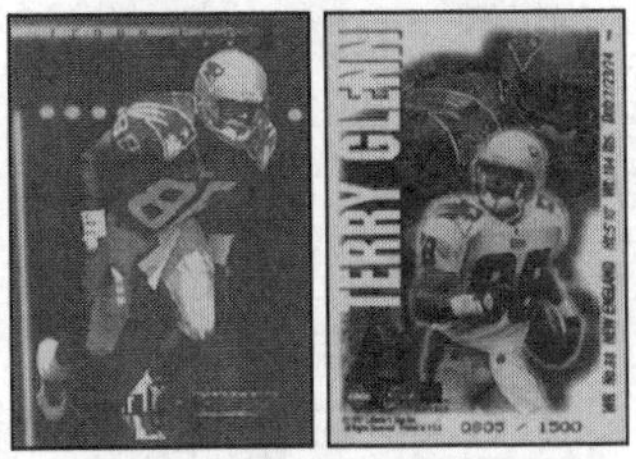

Randomly inserted in packs at a rate of one in 20, this 25-card set features embossed color photos of the hottest players with foil printing that fit together to form a spectacular background.

	MINT	NRMT	EXC
COMPLETE SET (25)	300.00	135.00	38.00
COMMON CARD (1-25)	5.00	2.20	.60
*PRISMS: 2X TO 4X			
☐ 1 Terry Glenn	20.00	9.00	2.50
☐ 2 Eddie George	25.00	11.00	3.10
☐ 3 Ricky Watters	5.00	2.20	.60
☐ 4 Barry Sanders	20.00	9.00	2.50
☐ 5 Curtis Martin	18.00	8.00	2.20
☐ 6 Brett Favre	35.00	16.00	4.40
☐ 7 Emmitt Smith	35.00	16.00	4.40
☐ 8 John Elway	15.00	6.75	1.85
☐ 9 Keyshawn Johnson	8.00	3.60	1.00
☐ 10 Kordell Stewart	15.00	6.75	1.85
☐ 11 Vinny Testaverde	5.00	2.20	.60
☐ 12 Kerry Collins	18.00	8.00	2.20
☐ 13 Terrell Davis	18.00	8.00	2.20
☐ 14 Karim Abdul-Jabbar	15.00	6.75	1.85
☐ 15 Drew Bledsoe	20.00	9.00	2.50
☐ 16 Antonio Freeman	8.00	3.60	1.00
☐ 17 Tony Banks	10.00	4.50	1.25
☐ 18 Jerry Rice	20.00	9.00	2.50
☐ 19 Mark Brunell	20.00	9.00	2.50
☐ 20 Mike Alstott	5.00	2.20	.60
☐ 21 Napoleon Kaufman	5.00	2.20	.60
☐ 22 Herman Moore	8.00	3.60	1.00
☐ 23 Terry Allen	5.00	2.20	.60
☐ 24 Jerome Bettis	8.00	3.60	1.00
☐ 25 Dorsey Levens	5.00	2.20	.60

1997 Collector's Edge Masters 1996 Rookies

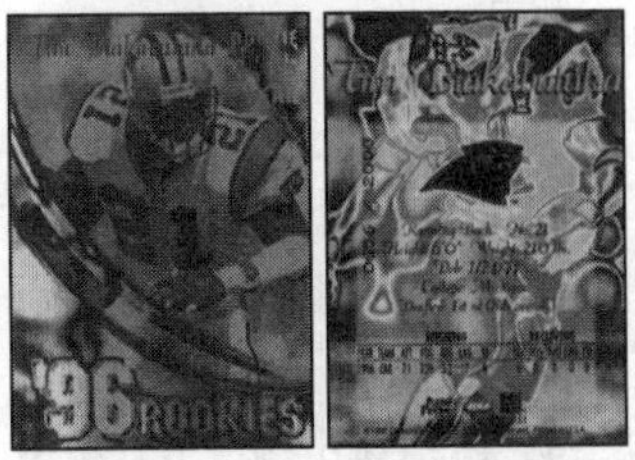

Randomly inserted in retail packs only at a rate of one in eight, this 25-card set features color player photos of the top rookies in their team uniforms from the 1996 season with '96 Rookie Year' foil stamped in gold. Only 2000 sets were made and each card is sequentially numbered.

	MINT	NRMT	EXC
COMPLETE SET (25)	60.00	27.00	7.50
COMMON CARD (1-25)	2.00	.90	.25
☐ 1 Simeon Rice	2.00	.90	.25
☐ 2 Jonathan Ogden	2.00	.90	.25
☐ 3 Eric Moulds	4.00	1.80	.50
☐ 4 Tim Biakabutuka	4.00	1.80	.50
☐ 5 Walt Harris	2.00	.90	.25
☐ 6 John Mobley	2.00	.90	.25
☐ 7 Stephen Davis	2.00	.90	.25
☐ 8 Derrick Mayes	3.00	1.35	.35
☐ 9 Eddie George	12.00	5.50	1.50
☐ 10 Marvin Harrison	5.00	2.20	.60
☐ 11 Kevin Hardy	3.00	1.35	.35
☐ 12 Jerome Woods	2.00	.90	.25
☐ 13 Karim Abdul-Jabbar	8.00	3.60	1.00
☐ 14 Duane Clemons	2.00	.90	.25
☐ 15 Terry Glenn	10.00	4.50	1.25
☐ 16 Ricky Whittle	2.00	.90	.25
☐ 17 Amani Toomer	4.00	1.80	.50
☐ 18 Keyshawn Johnson	5.00	2.20	.60
☐ 19 Rickey Dudley	3.00	1.35	.35
☐ 20 Bobby Hoying	4.00	1.80	.50
☐ 21 Tony Banks	4.00	1.80	.50
☐ 22 Bryan Still	2.00	.90	.25
☐ 23 Terrell Owens	6.00	2.70	.75
☐ 24 Reggie Brown RB	2.00	.90	.25
☐ 25 Mike Alstott	4.00	1.80	.50

1997 Collector's Edge Masters Nitro

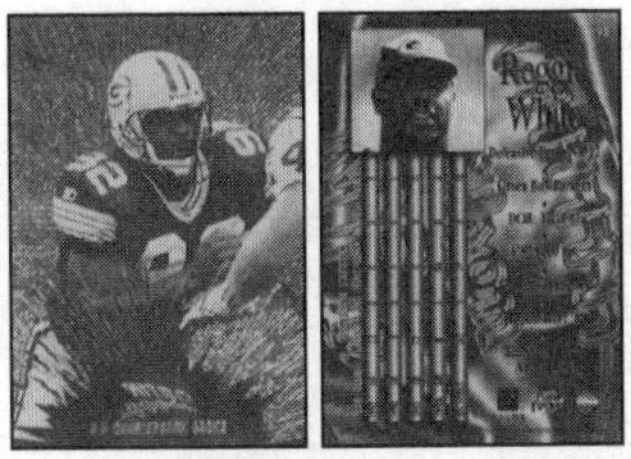

Each of these cards is essentially a parallel to its corresponding base Collector's Edge Masters card. The addition of a gold foil starburst logo was included at the bottom of the card front. They were randomly inserted in packs at a rate of one in eight.

	MINT	NRMT	EXC
COMPLETE SET (36)	80.00	36.00	10.00
COMMON CARD	1.00	.45	.12
☐ 2 Larry Centers	1.00	.45	.12
☐ 18 Michael Jackson	1.00	.45	.12
☐ 24 Todd Collins	1.50	.70	.19
☐ 30 Bruce Smith	2.00	.90	.25
☐ 34 Kerry Collins	4.00	1.80	.50
☐ 36 Kevin Greene	1.50	.70	.19
☐ 59 Carl Pickens	1.50	.70	.19
☐ 64 Troy Aikman	5.00	2.20	.60
☐ 71 Emmitt Smith	10.00	4.50	1.25
☐ 75 Terrell Davis	5.00	2.20	.60
☐ 76 John Elway	4.00	1.80	.50
☐ 85 Herman Moore	2.00	.90	.25
☐ 88 Barry Sanders	5.00	2.20	.60
☐ 94 Brett Favre	10.00	4.50	1.25
☐ 98 Reggie White	2.00	.90	.25
☐ 106 Steve McNair	3.00	1.35	.35
☐ 115 Jim Harbaugh	1.50	.70	.19
☐ 121 Mark Brunell	5.00	2.20	.60
☐ 136 Derrick Thomas	1.50	.70	.19
☐ 137 Tamarick Vanover	1.50	.70	.19
☐ 142 Dan Marino	10.00	4.50	1.25
☐ 155 Drew Bledsoe	5.00	2.20	.60
☐ 159 Curtis Martin	5.00	2.20	.60
☐ 167 Tyrone Hughes	1.00	.45	.12
☐ 189 Napoleon Kaufman	1.00	.45	.12
☐ 203 Ricky Watters	1.50	.70	.19
☐ 206 Jerome Bettis	2.00	.90	.25
☐ 207 Chad Brown	1.00	.45	.12
☐ 211 Kordell Stewart	4.00	1.80	.50
☐ 218 Tony Martin	1.00	.45	.12
☐ 229 Jerry Rice	5.00	2.20	.60
☐ 234 Steve Young	5.00	2.20	.60
☐ 237 Joey Galloway	2.50	1.10	.30
☐ 243 Isaac Bruce	2.00	.90	.25
☐ 261 Terry Allen	1.50	.70	.19
☐ 264 Gus Frerotte	2.00	.90	.25

1997 Collector's Edge Masters Playoff Game Ball

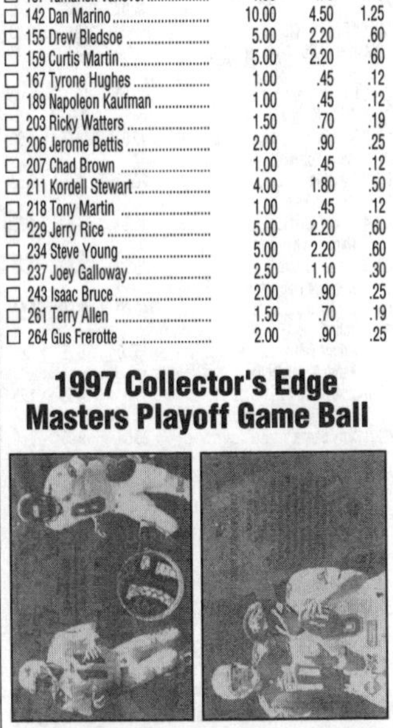

Randomly inserted in packs at a rate of one in 72, this 19-card set features color images of two rival players printed on metallic card stock with an embedded medallion struck from an authentic NFL football used by the rivals in the 1996 playoffs. The backs carry the game notes. A Gold Logo parallel version of the regular set with gold foil stamping limited to10 copies was also randomly inserted into packs.

	MINT	NRMT	EXC
COMPLETE SET (19)	1000.00	450.00	125.00
COMMON CARD (1-19)	20.00	9.00	2.50
☐ 1 Natrone Means	30.00	13.50	3.70
Thurman Thomas			
☐ 2 Tony Boselli	30.00	13.50	3.70
Bruce Smith			
☐ 3 Jerome Bettis	30.00	13.50	3.70
Marshall Faulk			
☐ 4 Kordell Stewart	50.00	22.00	6.25
Jim Harbaugh			
☐ 5 Natrone Means	50.00	22.00	6.25
Terrell Davis			
☐ 6 Mark Brunell	100.00	45.00	12.50
John Elway			
☐ 7 Curtis Martin	60.00	27.00	7.50
Jerome Bettis			
☐ 8 Drew Bledsoe	120.00	55.00	15.00
Mark Brunell			
☐ 9 Terry Glenn	60.00	27.00	7.50
Keenan McCardell			
☐ 10 Ricky Watters	20.00	9.00	2.50
Terry Kirby			
☐ 11 Kevin Greene	30.00	13.50	3.70
Reggie White			
☐ 12 Jerry Rice	70.00	32.00	8.75
Irving Fryar			
☐ 13 Dorsey Levens	20.00	9.00	2.50
Terry Kirby			
☐ 14 Brett Favre	120.00	55.00	15.00
Steve Young			
☐ 15 Andre Rison	70.00	32.00	8.75
Jerry Rice			
☐ 16 Reggie White	30.00	13.50	3.70
Ken Norton Jr.			
☐ 17 Kerry Collins	80.00	36.00	10.00
Troy Aikman			
☐ 18 Kerry Collins	125.00	55.00	15.50
Brett Favre			
☐ 19 Mark Carrier WR	30.00	13.50	3.70
Antonio Freeman			

1997 Collector's Edge Masters Radical Rivals

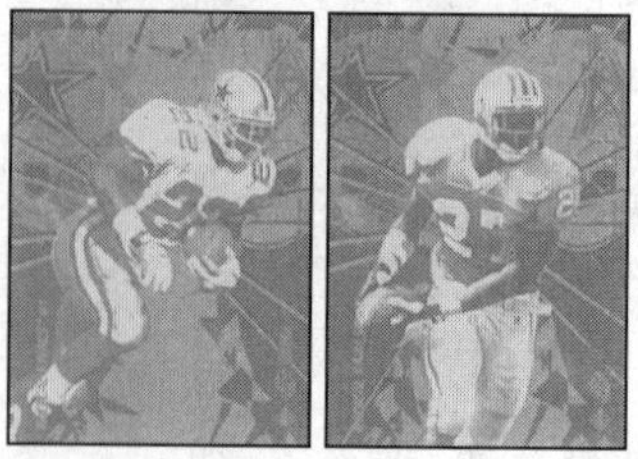

Randomly inserted in hobby packs only at the rate of one in 30, this 12-card set features color photos of two top NFL star rivals matched-up on a double thick metalized card. Only 1000 of each card were produced and are sequentially numbered.

	MINT	NRMT	EXC
COMPLETE SET (13)	250.00	110.00	31.00
COMMON CARD (1-12)	10.00	4.50	1.25
☐ 1 Emmitt Smith	40.00	18.00	5.00
Eddie George			
☐ 2 Brett Favre	40.00	18.00	5.00
Kerry Collins			
☐ 3 Jerry Rice	20.00	9.00	2.50
Antonio Freeman			
☐ 4 Ricky Watters	10.00	4.50	1.25
Napoleon Kaufman			
☐ 5 Herman Moore	10.00	4.50	1.25
Keyshawn Johnson			
☐ 6 Dan Marino	40.00	18.00	5.00
John Elway			
☐ 7 Jerome Bettis	15.00	6.75	1.85
Karim Abdul-Jabbar			
☐ 8 Isaac Bruce	10.00	4.50	1.25
Carl Pickens			
☐ 9 Barry Sanders	20.00	9.00	2.50
Terry Allen			
☐ 10 Terry Glenn	25.00	11.00	3.10
Joey Galloway			
☐ 11 Mark Brunell	20.00	9.00	2.50
Steve Young			
☐ 12 Terrell Davis	20.00	9.00	2.50
Curtis Martin			
☐ NNO Title Card CL	1.00	.45	.12

1997 Collector's Edge Masters Ripped

Randomly inserted in packs at a rate of one in 24, this 19-card set features 18 color player photos on cards 19-36 with the nineteenth card being an unnumbered checklist. This set was a completion of the 1996 Collector's Edge Ripped set, and the cards were numbered accordingly.

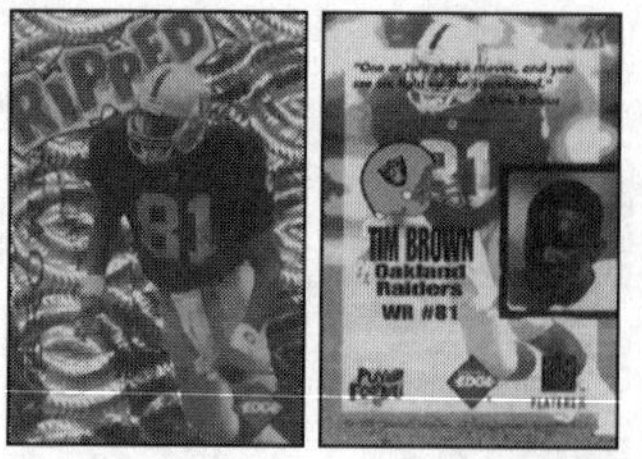

	MINT	NRMT	EXC
COMPLETE SET (19)	150.00	70.00	19.00
COMMON CARD (19-36)	2.50	1.10	.30
☐ 19 Troy Aikman	15.00	6.75	1.85
☐ 20 Drew Bledsoe	15.00	6.75	1.85
☐ 21 Tim Brown	2.50	1.10	.30
☐ 22 Mark Brunell	15.00	6.75	1.85
☐ 23 Cris Carter	2.50	1.10	.30
☐ 24 Kerry Collins	12.00	5.50	1.50
☐ 25 Barry Sanders	15.00	6.75	1.85
☐ 26 Eddie George	20.00	9.00	2.50
☐ 27 Karim Abdul-Jabbar	10.00	4.50	1.25
☐ 28 Curtis Martin	15.00	6.75	1.85
☐ 29 Carl Pickens	2.50	1.10	.30
☐ 30 Marshall Faulk	4.00	1.80	.50
☐ 31 Rashaan Salaam	4.00	1.80	.50
☐ 32 Deion Sanders	6.00	2.70	.75
☐ 33 Emmitt Smith	25.00	11.00	3.10
☐ 34 Herman Moore	4.00	1.80	.50
☐ 35 Ricky Watters	2.50	1.10	.30
☐ 36 Terry Allen	2.50	1.10	.30
☐ NNO Checklist Card	1.00	.45	.12

1997 Collector's Edge Masters Super Bowl Game Ball

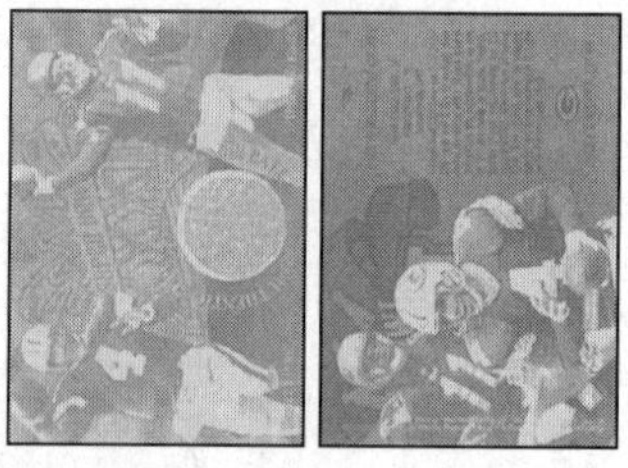

Randomly inserted in packs at a rate of one in 350, this six-card set features color photos printed on gold metallic stock with an embedded medallion struck from an authentic NFL football used by players in Super Bowl XXXI. Only 250 of each card was produced. There was also a Silver Logo set, inserted randomly in packs that is distinguished by its silver foil stamping. Only one of these sets exist, and it is not priced due to its rarity and therefor low trading activity.

	MINT	NRMT	EXC
COMPLETE SET (6)	550.00	250.00	70.00
COMMON CARD (1-6)	40.00	18.00	5.00
☐ 1 Brett Favre	250.00	110.00	31.00
Drew Bledsoe			
☐ 2 Dorsey Levens	100.00	45.00	12.50
Curtis Martin			
☐ 3 Desmond Howard	40.00	18.00	5.00
Dave Meggett			
☐ 4 Antonio Freeman	100.00	45.00	12.50
Terry Glenn			
☐ 5 Keith Jackson	40.00	18.00	5.00
Ben Coates			
☐ 6 Willie McGinest	60.00	27.00	7.50
Reggie White			

1996 Collector's Edge President's Reserve Promos

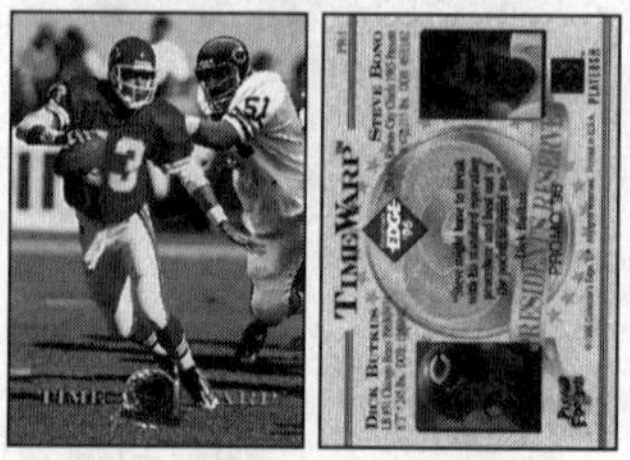

This six-card set was issued to preview the 1996 Collector's Edge President's Reserve series. The Promo set contains one card from each of the President's Reserve base and insert sets. The fronts feature color action player photos on various backgrounds while the backs carry player information and the word "Promo." The cards are virtually all numbered 1 and, therefore checklisted below in alphabetical order.

	MINT	NRMT	EXC
COMPLETE SET (6)	8.00	3.60	1.00
COMMON CARD	.50	.23	.06
☐ 1 Jeff Blake	2.00	.90	.25
Errict Rhett			
Running Mates			
☐ 2 Dick Butkus	3.00	1.35	.35
Steve Bono			
TimeWarp			
☐ 3 Philadelphia Eagles	.50	.23	.06
Candidates Rookie Redemption			
☐ 4 Rashaan Salaam	1.00	.45	.12
New Regime			
☐ 5 Junior Seau	.75	.35	.09
Base Brand			
☐ 6 Michael Westbrook	1.00	.45	.12
Air Force One			

1996 Collector's Edge President's Reserve

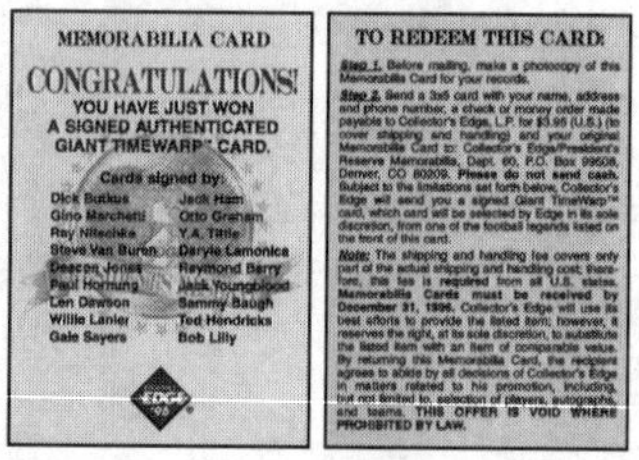

The 1996 Collector's Edge President's Reserve set was issued in two series of 200 cards, for a total of 400 cards. A collector could preorder a box (either series) from a dealer for $149.95. Card fronts have a clear plastic background with the card and player's name in gold foil. Card backs contain statistical and biographical information. The only rookie card of note in the set is Aaron Hayden.

	MINT	NRMT	EXC
COMPLETE SET (400)	70.00	32.00	8.75
COMPLETE SERIES 1 (200)	40.00	18.00	5.00
COMPLETE SERIES 2 (200)	30.00	13.50	3.70
COMMON CARD (1-400)	.15	.07	.02
☐ 1 Larry Centers	.25	.11	.03
☐ 2 Frank Sanders	.25	.11	.03
☐ 3 Clyde Simmons	.15	.07	.02
☐ 4 Eric Swann	.25	.11	.03
☐ 5 Morten Andersen	.15	.07	.02
☐ 6 Lester Archambeau	.15	.07	.02
☐ 7 J.J. Birden	.15	.07	.02
☐ 8 Bert Emanuel	.25	.11	.03
☐ 9 Jumpy Geathers	.15	.07	.02
☐ 10 Jeff George	.25	.11	.03
☐ 11 Craig Heyward	.15	.07	.02
☐ 12 Bill Brooks	.15	.07	.02
☐ 13 Steve Christie	.15	.07	.02
☐ 14 Todd Collins	.25	.11	.03
☐ 15 Darick Holmes	.25	.11	.03
☐ 16 Andre Reed	.25	.11	.03
☐ 17 Bryce Paup	.25	.11	.03
☐ 18 Bruce Smith	.50	.23	.06
☐ 19 Blake Brockermeyer	.15	.07	.02
☐ 20 Mark Carrier	.15	.07	.02
☐ 21 Kerry Collins	3.00	1.35	.35
☐ 22 Darion Conner	.15	.07	.02
☐ 23 Eric Guliford	.15	.07	.02
☐ 24 Lamar Lathon	.15	.07	.02
☐ 25 Derrick Moore	.15	.07	.02
☐ 26 Frank Reich	.15	.07	.02
☐ 27 Kevin Butler	.15	.07	.02
☐ 28 Tony Carter	.15	.07	.02
☐ 29 Curtis Conway	.50	.23	.06
☐ 30 Robert Green	.15	.07	.02
☐ 31 Jay Leeuwenburg	.15	.07	.02
☐ 32 Alonzo Spellman	.15	.07	.02
☐ 33 Chris Zorich	.15	.07	.02
☐ 34 Eric Bieniemy	.15	.07	.02
☐ 35 Jeff Blake	.50	.23	.06
☐ 36 Tony McGee	.15	.07	.02
☐ 37 Carl Pickens	.50	.23	.06
☐ 38 Rob Burnett	.15	.07	.02
☐ 39 Earnest Byner	.15	.07	.02
☐ 40 Michael Jackson	.25	.11	.03
☐ 41 Antonio Langham	.15	.07	.02
☐ 42 Anthony Pleasant	.15	.07	.02
☐ 43 Vinny Testaverde	.25	.11	.03
☐ 44 Troy Aikman	2.50	1.10	.30
☐ 45 Larry Allen	.15	.07	.02
☐ 46 Bill Bates	.25	.11	.03
☐ 47 Chris Boniol	.15	.07	.02
☐ 48 Charles Haley	.25	.11	.03
☐ 49 Michael Irvin	.50	.23	.06
☐ 50 Robert Jones	.15	.07	.02
☐ 51 Leon Lett	.15	.07	.02
☐ 52 Russell Maryland	.15	.07	.02
☐ 53 Nate Newton	.15	.07	.02
☐ 54 Deion Sanders	1.50	.70	.19
☐ 55 Sherman Williams	.15	.07	.02
☐ 56 Darren Woodson	.25	.11	.03
☐ 57 Aaron Craver	.15	.07	.02
☐ 58 Terrell Davis	4.00	1.80	.50
☐ 59 Jason Elam	.15	.07	.02
☐ 60 Simon Fletcher	.15	.07	.02
☐ 61 Anthony Miller	.25	.11	.03
☐ 62 Shannon Sharpe	.25	.11	.03
☐ 63 Tracy Scroggins	.15	.07	.02
☐ 64 Antonio London	.15	.07	.02
☐ 65 Scott Mitchell	.25	.11	.03
☐ 66 Johnnie Morton	.25	.11	.03
☐ 67 Barry Sanders	2.50	1.10	.30
☐ 68 Edgar Bennett	.25	.11	.03
☐ 69 Mark Chmura	.25	.11	.03
☐ 70 Brett Favre	5.00	2.20	.60
☐ 71 Mark Ingram	.15	.07	.02
☐ 72 Dorsey Levens	.25	.11	.03
☐ 73 Wayne Simmons	.15	.07	.02
☐ 74 Gary Brown	.15	.07	.02
☐ 75 Anthony Cook	.15	.07	.02
☐ 76 Al Del Greco	.15	.07	.02
☐ 77 Haywood Jeffires	.15	.07	.02
☐ 78 Steve McNair	2.00	.90	.25
☐ 79 Rodney Thomas	.15	.07	.02
☐ 80 Trev Alberts	.15	.07	.02
☐ 81 Quentin Coryatt	.15	.07	.02
☐ 82 Ken Dilger	.25	.11	.03
☐ 83 Jim Harbaugh	.25	.11	.03
☐ 84 Floyd Turner	.15	.07	.02
☐ 85 Lamont Warren	.15	.07	.02
☐ 86 Steve Beuerlein	.15	.07	.02
☐ 87 Mark Brunell	2.50	1.10	.30
☐ 88 Eugene Chung	.15	.07	.02
☐ 89 Jeff Lageman	.15	.07	.02
☐ 90 Willie Jackson	.25	.11	.03
☐ 91 Kimble Anders	.15	.07	.02
☐ 92 Steve Bono	.25	.11	.03
☐ 93 Derrick Thomas	.25	.11	.03
☐ 94 Willie Davis	.25	.11	.03
☐ 95 Greg Hill	.25	.11	.03
☐ 96 Neil Smith	.25	.11	.03
☐ 97 Tamarick Vanover	.50	.23	.06
☐ 98 James Hasty	.15	.07	.02
☐ 99 Gary Clark	.15	.07	.02
☐ 100 Marco Coleman	.15	.07	.02
☐ 101 Steve Emtman	.15	.07	.02
☐ 102 Irving Fryar	.25	.11	.03
☐ 103 Randal Hill	.15	.07	.02
☐ 104 Terry Kirby	.25	.11	.03
☐ 105 Dan Marino	5.00	2.20	.60
☐ 106 Cris Carter	.50	.23	.06
☐ 107 Jack Del Rio	.15	.07	.02
☐ 108 David Palmer	.25	.11	.03
☐ 109 Jake Reed	.25	.11	.03
☐ 110 Robert Smith	.25	.11	.03
☐ 111 Korey Stringer	.15	.07	.02
☐ 112 Orlando Thomas	.15	.07	.02
☐ 113 Drew Bledsoe	2.50	1.10	.30
☐ 114 Vincent Brisby	.15	.07	.02
☐ 115 Ted Johnson	.15	.07	.02
☐ 116 Curtis Martin	4.00	1.80	.50
☐ 117 Chris Slade	.15	.07	.02
☐ 118 Jim Dombrowski	.15	.07	.02
☐ 119 William Roaf	.15	.07	.02
☐ 120 Quinn Early	.15	.07	.02
☐ 121 Wesley Walls	.25	.11	.03
☐ 122 Wayne Martin	.15	.07	.02
☐ 123 Irv Smith	.15	.07	.02
☐ 124 Torrance Small	.15	.07	.02
☐ 125 Dave Brown	.25	.11	.03
☐ 126 Chris Calloway	.15	.07	.02
☐ 127 Jumbo Elliott	.15	.07	.02
☐ 128 Rodney Hampton	.25	.11	.03
☐ 129 Tyrone Wheatley	.25	.11	.03
☐ 130 Kyle Brady	.25	.11	.03
☐ 131 Hugh Douglas	.15	.07	.02
☐ 132 Todd Scott	.15	.07	.02
☐ 133 Adrian Murrell	.25	.11	.03
☐ 134 Wayne Chrebet	.25	.11	.03
☐ 135 Aundray Bruce	.15	.07	.02
☐ 136 Andrew Glover	.15	.07	.02
☐ 137 Daryl Hobbs	.15	.07	.02
☐ 138 Napoleon Kaufman	.25	.11	.03
☐ 139 Chester McGlockton	.15	.07	.02
☐ 140 Rob Fredrickson	.15	.07	.02
☐ 141 Guy McIntyre	.15	.07	.02
☐ 142 Bobby Taylor	.25	.11	.03
☐ 143 Fred Barnett	.25	.11	.03
☐ 144 William Fuller	.15	.07	.02
☐ 145 Rodney Peete	.15	.07	.02
☐ 146 Daniel Stubbs	.15	.07	.02
☐ 147 Charlie Garner	.15	.07	.02
☐ 148 Myron Bell	.15	.07	.02
☐ 149 Rod Woodson	.25	.11	.03
☐ 150 Charles Johnson	.25	.11	.03
☐ 151 Ernie Mills	.15	.07	.02
☐ 152 Levon Kirkland	.15	.07	.02
☐ 153 Carnell Lake	.15	.07	.02
☐ 154 Kevin Greene	.25	.11	.03
☐ 155 Neil O'Donnell	.25	.11	.03
☐ 156 Erric Pegram	.25	.11	.03
☐ 157 Ray Seals	.15	.07	.02
☐ 158 Willie Williams	.15	.07	.02
☐ 159 Kordell Stewart	3.00	1.35	.35
☐ 160 Yancey Thigpen	.25	.11	.03
☐ 161 Darren Bennett	.25	.11	.03
☐ 162 Andre Coleman	.15	.07	.02
☐ 163 Aaron Hayden	.50	.23	.06
☐ 164 Tony Martin	.25	.11	.03
☐ 165 Chris Mims	.15	.07	.02
☐ 166 Shawn Lee	.15	.07	.02

☐ 167 Junior Seau	.50	.23	.06
☐ 168 Merton Hanks	.15	.07	.02
☐ 169 Rickey Jackson	.15	.07	.02
☐ 170 Derek Loville	.15	.07	.02
☐ 171 Gary Plummer	.15	.07	.02
☐ 172 J.J. Stokes	.50	.23	.06
☐ 173 John Taylor	.15	.07	.02
☐ 174 Bryant Young	.25	.11	.03
☐ 175 Antonio Edwards	.15	.07	.02
☐ 176 Joey Galloway	1.00	.45	.12
☐ 177 Carlton Gray	.15	.07	.02
☐ 178 Rick Mirer	.25	.11	.03
☐ 179 Winston Moss	.15	.07	.02
☐ 180 Jerome Bettis	.50	.23	.06
☐ 181 Troy Drayton	.15	.07	.02
☐ 182 Wayne Gandy	.15	.07	.02
☐ 183 Sean Gilbert	.15	.07	.02
☐ 184 Jessie Hester	.15	.07	.02
☐ 185 Sean Landeta	.15	.07	.02
☐ 186 Roman Phifer	.15	.07	.02
☐ 187 Alberto White	.15	.07	.02
☐ 188 Santana Dotson	.15	.07	.02
☐ 189 Jerry Ellison	.15	.07	.02
☐ 190 Jackie Harris	.15	.07	.02
☐ 191 Courtney Hawkins	.15	.07	.02
☐ 192 Horace Copeland	.15	.07	.02
☐ 193 Hardy Nickerson	.15	.07	.02
☐ 194 Warren Sapp	.15	.07	.02
☐ 195 Terry Allen	.25	.11	.03
☐ 196 Henry Ellard	.25	.11	.03
☐ 197 Gus Frerotte	.50	.23	.06
☐ 198 John Gesek	.15	.07	.02
☐ 199 Jim Lachey	.15	.07	.02
☐ 200 Brian Mitchell	.15	.07	.02
☐ 201 Garrison Hearst	.25	.11	.03
☐ 202 Dave Krieg	.15	.07	.02
☐ 203 Rob Moore	.15	.07	.02
☐ 204 Aeneas Williams	.15	.07	.02
☐ 205 Chris Doleman	.15	.07	.02
☐ 206 Terance Mathis	.15	.07	.02
☐ 207 Clay Matthews	.25	.11	.03
☐ 208 Eric Metcalf	.25	.11	.03
☐ 209 Jessie Tuggle	.15	.07	.02
☐ 210 Cornelius Bennett	.25	.11	.03
☐ 211 Ruben Brown	.15	.07	.02
☐ 212 Russell Copeland	.15	.07	.02
☐ 213 Phil Hansen	.15	.07	.02
☐ 214 Jim Kelly	.50	.23	.06
☐ 215 Don Beebe	.15	.07	.02
☐ 216 Willie Green	.15	.07	.02
☐ 217 Howard Griffith	.15	.07	.02
☐ 218 John Kasay	.15	.07	.02
☐ 219 Brett Maxie	.15	.07	.02
☐ 220 Tim McKyer	.15	.07	.02
☐ 221 Sam Mills	.25	.11	.03
☐ 222 Jim Flanigan	.15	.07	.02
☐ 223 Jeff Graham	.15	.07	.02
☐ 224 Erik Kramer	.15	.07	.02
☐ 225 Rashaan Salaam	.50	.23	.06
☐ 226 Steve Walsh	.15	.07	.02
☐ 227 Donnell Woolford	.15	.07	.02
☐ 228 Ki-Jana Carter	.25	.11	.03
☐ 229 John Copeland	.15	.07	.02
☐ 230 Harold Green	.15	.07	.02
☐ 231 Doug Pelfrey	.15	.07	.02
☐ 232 Darnay Scott	.25	.11	.03
☐ 233 Bracey Walker	.15	.07	.02
☐ 234 Dan Wilkinson	.15	.07	.02
☐ 235 Leroy Hoard	.15	.07	.02
☐ 236 Ernest Hunter UER name spelled Earnest	.15	.07	.02
☐ 237 Keenan McCardell	.50	.23	.06
☐ 238 Stevon Moore	.15	.07	.02
☐ 239 Andre Rison	.25	.11	.03
☐ 240 Eric Zeier	.25	.11	.03
☐ 241 Larry Brown	.15	.07	.02
☐ 242 Shante Carver	.15	.07	.02
☐ 243 Chad Hennings	.25	.11	.03
☐ 244 John Jett	.15	.07	.02
☐ 245 Daryl Johnston	.25	.11	.03
☐ 246 Derek Kennard	.15	.07	.02
☐ 247 Brock Marion	.15	.07	.02
☐ 248 Jay Novacek	.25	.11	.03
☐ 249 Emmitt Smith	5.00	2.20	.60
☐ 250 Tony Tolbert	.15	.07	.02
☐ 251 Mark Tuinei	.15	.07	.02
☐ 252 Erik Williams	.15	.07	.02
☐ 253 Kevin Williams	.15	.07	.02
☐ 254 John Elway	2.00	.90	.25
☐ 255 Ed McCaffrey	.15	.07	.02
☐ 256 Glyn Milburn	.15	.07	.02
☐ 257 Michael Dean Perry	.15	.07	.02
☐ 258 Mike Pritchard	.15	.07	.02
☐ 259 Willie Clay	.15	.07	.02
☐ 260 Jason Hanson	.15	.07	.02
☐ 261 Herman Moore	.50	.23	.06
☐ 262 Brett Perriman	.25	.11	.03
☐ 263 Lomas Brown	.15	.07	.02
☐ 264 Chris Spielman	.25	.11	.03
☐ 265 Henry Thomas	.15	.07	.02
☐ 266 Robert Brooks	.50	.23	.06
☐ 267 Sean Jones	.15	.07	.02
☐ 268 John Jurkovic	.15	.07	.02
☐ 269 Anthony Morgan	.15	.07	.02
☐ 270 Craig Newsome	.15	.07	.02
☐ 271 Reggie White	.50	.23	.06
☐ 272 Chris Chandler	.25	.11	.03
☐ 273 Mel Gray	.15	.07	.02
☐ 274 Darryll Lewis	.15	.07	.02
☐ 275 Bruce Matthews	.15	.07	.02
☐ 276 Todd McNair	.15	.07	.02
☐ 277 Chris Sanders	.25	.11	.03
☐ 278 Mark Stepnoski	.15	.07	.02
☐ 279 Ashley Ambrose	.15	.07	.02
☐ 280 Tony Bennett	.15	.07	.02
☐ 281 Zack Crockett	.15	.07	.02
☐ 282 Sean Dawkins	.15	.07	.02
☐ 283 Marshall Faulk	.50	.23	.06
☐ 284 Ronald Humphrey	.15	.07	.02
☐ 285 Tony Siragusa	.15	.07	.02
☐ 286 Roosevelt Potts	.15	.07	.02
☐ 287 Bryan Barker	.15	.07	.02
☐ 288 Tony Boselli	.25	.11	.03
☐ 289 Keith Goganious	.15	.07	.02
☐ 290 Desmond Howard	.25	.11	.03
☐ 291 Don Davey	.15	.07	.02
☐ 292 Corey Mayfield	.15	.07	.02
☐ 293 James O. Stewart	.25	.11	.03
☐ 294 Cedric Tillman	.15	.07	.02
☐ 295 Marcus Allen	.50	.23	.06
☐ 296 Dale Carter	.15	.07	.02
☐ 297 Lake Dawson	.25	.11	.03
☐ 298 Darren Mickell	.15	.07	.02
☐ 299 Dan Saleaumua	.15	.07	.02
☐ 300 Webster Slaughter	.15	.07	.02
☐ 301 Derrick Thomas	.25	.11	.03
☐ 302 Bryan Cox	.15	.07	.02
☐ 303 Jeff Cross	.15	.07	.02
☐ 304 Eric Green	.15	.07	.02
☐ 305 O.J. McDuffie	.25	.11	.03
☐ 306 Bernie Parmalee	.15	.07	.02
☐ 307 Billy Milner	.15	.07	.02
☐ 308 Pete Stoyanovich	.15	.07	.02
☐ 309 Troy Vincent	.15	.07	.02
☐ 310 Qadry Ismail	.25	.11	.03
☐ 311 Amp Lee	.15	.07	.02
☐ 312 Warren Moon	.25	.11	.03
☐ 313 Scottie Graham	.15	.07	.02
☐ 314 John Randle	.15	.07	.02
☐ 315 Fuad Reveiz	.15	.07	.02
☐ 316 Broderick Thomas	.15	.07	.02
☐ 317 Ben Coates	.25	.11	.03
☐ 318 Willie McGinest	.15	.07	.02
☐ 319 Dave Meggett	.15	.07	.02
☐ 320 Will Moore	.15	.07	.02
☐ 321 Dave Wohlabaugh	.15	.07	.02
☐ 322 Mario Bates	.25	.11	.03
☐ 323 Jim Everett	.15	.07	.02
☐ 324 Tyrone Hughes	.15	.07	.02
☐ 325 Vaughn Dunbar	.15	.07	.02
☐ 326 Renaldo Turnbull	.15	.07	.02
☐ 327 Michael Haynes	.25	.11	.03
☐ 328 Mike Sherrard	.15	.07	.02
☐ 329 Michael Strahan	.15	.07	.02
☐ 330 Herschel Walker	.25	.11	.03
☐ 331 Charles Wilson	.15	.07	.02
☐ 332 Otis Smith	.15	.07	.02
☐ 333 Mo Lewis	.15	.07	.02
☐ 334 Marvin Washington	.15	.07	.02
☐ 335 Tim Brown	.25	.11	.03
☐ 336 Greg Skrepenak	.15	.07	.02
☐ 337 Kevin Gogan	.15	.07	.02
☐ 338 Jeff Hostetler	.25	.11	.03
☐ 339 Terry McDaniel	.15	.07	.02
☐ 340 Anthony Smith	.15	.07	.02
☐ 341 Pat Swilling	.15	.07	.02
☐ 342 Harvey Williams	.15	.07	.02
☐ 343 Tom Hutton	.15	.07	.02
☐ 344 Mike Mamula	.15	.07	.02
☐ 345 Randall Cunningham	.25	.11	.03
☐ 346 Ricky Watters	.25	.11	.03
☐ 347 Andy Harmon	.15	.07	.02
☐ 348 William Thomas	.15	.07	.02
☐ 349 Calvin Williams	.50	.23	.06
☐ 350 Mark Bruener	.15	.07	.02
☐ 351 Dermontti Dawson	.15	.07	.02
☐ 352 Greg Lloyd	.25	.11	.03
☐ 353 Norm Johnson	.15	.07	.02
☐ 354 Byron Bam Morris	.25	.11	.03
☐ 355 Thomas Newberry	.15	.07	.02
☐ 356 Darren Perry	.15	.07	.02
☐ 357 Rohn Stark	.15	.07	.02
☐ 358 Joel Steed	.15	.07	.02
☐ 359 Brendan Stai UER name spelled Brenden	.15	.07	.02
☐ 360 Justin Strzelczyk	.15	.07	.02
☐ 361 Leon Searcy	.15	.07	.02
☐ 362 Chad Brown	.25	.11	.03
☐ 363 John Carney	.15	.07	.02
☐ 364 Rodney Culver	.25	.11	.03
☐ 365 Ronnie Harmon	.15	.07	.02
☐ 366 Stan Humphries	.25	.11	.03
☐ 367 Leslie O'Neal	.15	.07	.02
☐ 368 Natrone Means	.50	.23	.06
☐ 369 Mark Seay	.15	.07	.02
☐ 370 William Floyd	.25	.11	.03
☐ 371 Brent Jones	.15	.07	.02
☐ 372 Tim McDonald	.15	.07	.02
☐ 373 Ken Norton, Jr.	.25	.11	.03
☐ 374 Jerry Rice	2.50	1.10	.30
☐ 375 Dana Stubblefield	.25	.11	.03
☐ 376 Steve Young	2.00	.90	.25
☐ 377 Brian Blades	.25	.11	.03
☐ 378 Cortez Kennedy	.25	.11	.03
☐ 379 Michael Sinclair	.15	.07	.02
☐ 380 Lamar Smith	.15	.07	.02
☐ 381 Chris Warren	.25	.11	.03
☐ 382 Johnny Bailey	.15	.07	.02
☐ 383 Isaac Bruce	.50	.23	.06
☐ 384 Kevin Carter	.25	.11	.03
☐ 385 Shane Conlan	.15	.07	.02
☐ 386 D'Marco Farr	.15	.07	.02
☐ 387 Todd Kinchen	.15	.07	.02
☐ 388 Chris Miller	.15	.07	.02
☐ 389 Lonnie Marts	.15	.07	.02
☐ 390 Trent Dilfer	.25	.11	.03
☐ 391 Alvin Harper	.15	.07	.02
☐ 392 John Lynch	.15	.07	.02
☐ 393 Errict Rhett	.25	.11	.03
☐ 394 Darnell Stephens	.15	.07	.02
☐ 395 Ken Harvey	.15	.07	.02
☐ 396 Eddie Murray	.15	.07	.02
☐ 397 Heath Shuler	.50	.23	.06
☐ 398 Matt Turk	.15	.07	.02
☐ 399 Michael Westbrook	.50	.23	.06
☐ 400 James Washington	.15	.07	.02

1996 Collector's Edge President's Reserve Air Force One

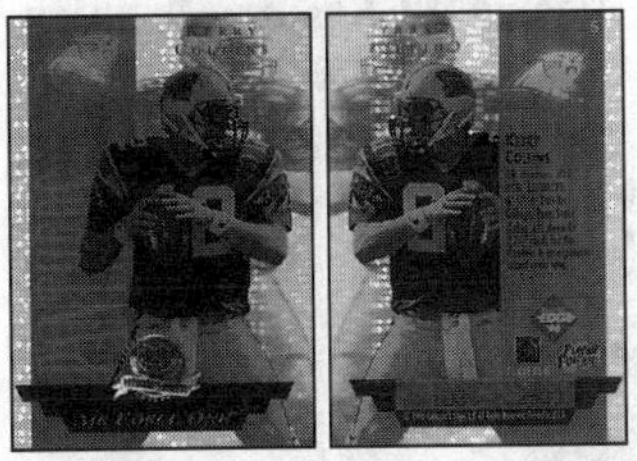

Randomly inserted in packs at a rate of one in 16, this 38-card set featured the most potent long ball threats in the game. Opalescent accents highlight both sides of these two-way-view plastic cards. Each card is individually numbered out of 2,500. Jumbo versions of these cards were issued as well (numbered of 1300). They were inserted one per box.

	MINT	NRMT	EXC
COMPLETE SET (38)	200.00	90.00	25.00
COMPLETE SERIES 1 (19)	100.00	45.00	12.50
COMPLETE SERIES 2 (19)	100.00	45.00	12.50
COMMON CARD (1-36)	2.00	.90	.25
*JUMBO CARDS: HALF VALUE			
☐ 1 Brett Favre	25.00	11.00	3.10
☐ 2 Neil O'Donnell	3.00	1.35	.35
☐ 3 Steve Young	10.00	4.50	1.25
☐ 4 Dan Marino	25.00	11.00	3.10
☐ 5 Kerry Collins	12.00	5.50	1.50
☐ 6 Scott Mitchell	2.00	.90	.25
☐ 7 Deion Sanders	8.00	3.60	1.00
☐ 8 Cris Carter	3.00	1.35	.35
☐ 9 Tim Brown	3.00	1.35	.35
☐ 10 Joey Galloway	6.00	2.70	.75
☐ 11 Robert Brooks	5.00	2.20	.60
☐ 12 Tony Martin	2.00	.90	.25
☐ 13 Michael Westbrook	5.00	2.20	.60
☐ 14 Eric Metcalf	3.00	1.35	.35
☐ 15 Vincent Brisby	2.00	.90	.25
☐ 16 Anthony Miller	2.00	.90	.25
☐ 17 J.J. Stokes	5.00	2.20	.60
☐ 18 Kordell Stewart	12.00	5.50	1.50
☐ 19 Troy Aikman	12.00	5.50	1.50
☐ 20 Drew Bledsoe	12.00	5.50	1.50
☐ 21 Jeff Blake	5.00	2.20	.60
☐ 22 John Elway	10.00	4.50	1.25
☐ 23 Jim Harbaugh	3.00	1.35	.35
☐ 24 Erik Kramer	2.00	.90	.25
☐ 25 Herman Moore	5.00	2.20	.60
☐ 26 Carl Pickens	3.00	1.35	.35
☐ 27 Michael Irvin	5.00	2.20	.60
☐ 28 Jerry Rice	12.00	5.50	1.50
☐ 29 Isaac Bruce	5.00	2.20	.60
☐ 30 Yancey Thigpen	5.00	2.20	.60
☐ 31 Brett Perriman	2.00	.90	.25
☐ 32 Ben Coates	3.00	1.35	.35
☐ 33 Jay Novacek	2.00	.90	.25
☐ 34 Tamarick Vanover	5.00	2.20	.60
☐ 35 Terrell Davis	15.00	6.75	1.85
☐ 36 Jeff Graham	2.00	.90	.25
☐ NNO Checklist (1-18)	.75	.35	.09
☐ NNO Checklist (19-36)	.75	.35	.09

1996 Collector's Edge President's Reserve Candidates Long Shots

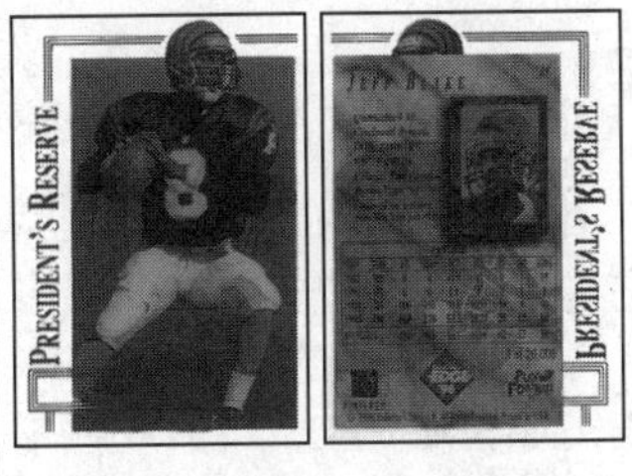

This set could be assembled via a mail redemption. Collector's Edge produced an exchange card for each team featuring that team's helmet logo and randomly inserted them into series one packs. The trade card could be sent-in (before the expiration date of 3/31/97) for another card featuring a "long shot" rookie from that team.

	MINT	NRMT	EXC
COMPLETE SET (30)	80.00	36.00	10.00
COMMON CARD (LS1-LS30)	2.50	1.10	.30
TRADE CARDS	.10	.05	.01
☐ LS1 Leeland McElroy	4.00	1.80	.50
☐ LS2 Richard Huntley	2.50	1.10	.30
☐ LS3 Ray Lewis	2.50	1.10	.30
☐ LS4 Sean Moran	2.50	1.10	.30
☐ LS5 Muhsin Muhammad	4.00	1.80	.50
☐ LS6 Bobby Engram	4.00	1.80	.50
☐ LS7 Marco Battaglia	2.50	1.10	.30
☐ LS8 Stepfret Williams	2.50	1.10	.30
☐ LS9 Jeff Lewis	2.50	1.10	.30
☐ LS10 Ryan Stewart	2.50	1.10	.30
☐ LS11 Derrick Mayes	4.00	1.80	.50
☐ LS12 Terry Killens	2.50	1.10	.30
☐ LS13 Scott Slutzker	2.50	1.10	.30
☐ LS14 Reggie Barlow	2.50	1.10	.30
☐ LS15 Joe Horn	2.50	1.10	.30
☐ LS16 Karim Abdul-Jabbar	6.00	2.70	.75
☐ LS17 Moe Williams	2.50	1.10	.30
☐ LS18 Kantroy Barber	2.50	1.10	.30
☐ LS19 Je'Rod Cherry	2.50	1.10	.30
☐ LS20 Amani Toomer	4.00	1.80	.50
☐ LS21 Alex Van Dyke	4.00	1.80	.50
☐ LS22 Tim Hall	2.50	1.10	.30
☐ LS23 Bobby Hoying	4.00	1.80	.50
☐ LS24 Jahine Arnold	2.50	1.10	.30
☐ LS25 Tony Banks	4.00	1.80	.50
☐ LS26 Freddie Bradley	2.50	1.10	.30
☐ LS27 Stephen Pitts	2.50	1.10	.30
☐ LS28 Reggie Brown RB	2.50	1.10	.30
☐ LS29 Mike Alstott	4.00	1.80	.50
☐ LS30 Stephen Davis	4.00	1.80	.50

1996 Collector's Edge President's Reserve Candidates Top Picks

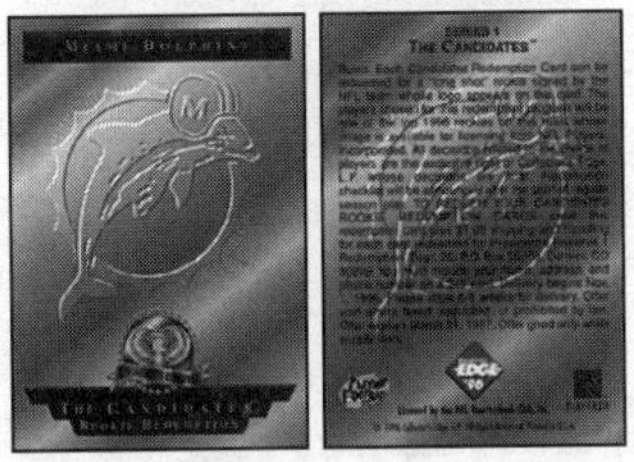

This set could be assembled via a mail redemption. Collector's Edge produced an exchange card for each team featuring that team's helmet logo and randomly inserted them into series two packs. The trade card could be sent-in (before the expiration date of 3/31/97) for another card featuring a "top early pick" of that team from the 1996 NFL Draft. Collector's Edge actually had eight of the trade cards ready when packaging began for the series two product and inserted those eight player's cards directly into packs instead of the helmet redemption card. We've noted those eight below.

	MINT	NRMT	EXC
COMPLETE SET (30)	100.00	45.00	12.50
COMMON CARD (1-30)	2.50	1.10	.30
TRADE CARDS	.10	.05	.01
☐ 1 Simeon Rice inserted in packs	2.50	1.10	.30
☐ 2 Shannon Brown	2.50	1.10	.30
☐ 3 Willie Anderson	2.50	1.10	.30
☐ 4 Tim Biakabutuka inserted in packs	4.00	1.80	.50
☐ 5 Eric Moulds	4.00	1.80	.50
☐ 6 Kavika Pittman	2.50	1.10	.30
☐ 7 Jonathan Ogden inserted in packs	2.50	1.10	.30
☐ 8 Reggie Brown LB	2.50	1.10	.30
☐ 9 John Mobley inserted in packs	2.50	1.10	.30
☐ 10 John Michels	2.50	1.10	.30
☐ 11 Walt Harris	2.50	1.10	.30
☐ 12 Eddie George inserted in packs	8.00	3.60	1.00
☐ 13 Marvin Harrison	5.00	2.20	.60
☐ 14 Kevin Hardy	4.00	1.80	.50

inserted in packs			
☐ 15 Jerome Woods	2.50	1.10	.30
☐ 16 Duane Clemons	2.50	1.10	.30
☐ 17 Daryl Gardener	2.50	1.10	.30
inserted in packs			
☐ 18 Terry Glenn	7.00	3.10	.85
☐ 19 Alex Molden	2.50	1.10	.30
☐ 20 Cedric Jones	2.50	1.10	.30
☐ 21 Rickey Dudley	4.00	1.80	.50
☐ 22 Keyshawn Johnson	5.00	2.20	.60
inserted in packs			
☐ 23 Jermane Mayberry	2.50	1.10	.30
☐ 24 Jamain Stephens	2.50	1.10	.30
☐ 25 Lawrence Phillips	4.00	1.80	.50
☐ 26 Bryan Still	2.50	1.10	.30
☐ 27 Israel Ifeanyi	2.50	1.10	.30
☐ 28 Pete Kendall	2.50	1.10	.30
☐ 29 Regan Upshaw	2.50	1.10	.30
☐ 30 Andre Johnson	2.50	1.10	.30

1996 Collector's Edge President's Reserve Honor Guard

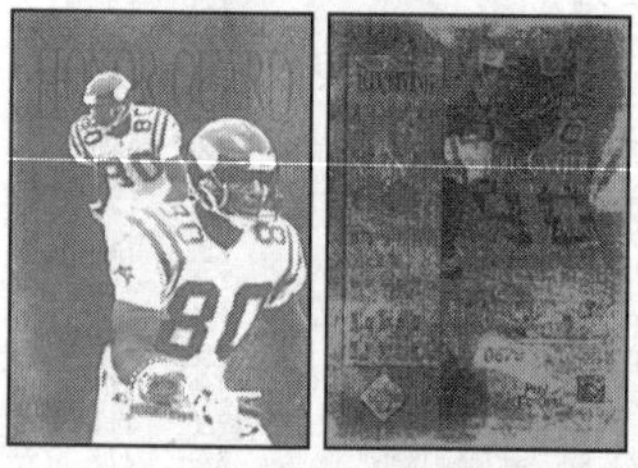

Collector's Edge released these cards as part of a President's Reserve wrapper redemption offer. The offer allowed the collector to send in 16-wrappers for a Jumbo Running Mates card or 64-wrappers for a Jumbo Running Mates Gold card. One Honor Guard card was mailed out with each redemption. The offer expired March 31, 1997. Each card is individually numbered of 1000.

	MINT	NRMT	EXC
COMPLETE SET (30)	75.00	34.00	9.50
COMMON CARD (HG1-HG30)	2.00	.90	.25
☐ HG1 Troy Aikman	5.00	2.20	.60
☐ HG2 Michael Irvin	3.00	1.35	.35
☐ HG3 Emmitt Smith	10.00	4.50	1.25
☐ HG4 Brett Favre	10.00	4.50	1.25
☐ HG5 Steve Young	4.00	1.80	.50
☐ HG6 Tim Brown	2.50	1.10	.30
☐ HG7 Errict Rhett	2.50	1.10	.30
☐ HG8 Curtis Martin	5.00	2.20	.60
☐ HG9 Carl Pickens	3.00	1.35	.35
☐ HG10 Herman Moore	3.00	1.35	.35
☐ HG11 Robert Brooks	3.00	1.35	.35
☐ HG12 Michael Westbrook	2.50	1.10	.30
☐ HG13 Leon Lett	2.00	.90	.25
☐ HG14 Russell Maryland	2.00	.90	.25
☐ HG15 Eric Swann	2.00	.90	.25
☐ HG16 John Elway	4.00	1.80	.50
☐ HG17 Barry Sanders	5.00	2.20	.60
☐ HG18 Dan Marino	10.00	4.50	1.25
☐ HG19 Drew Bledsoe	5.00	2.20	.60
☐ HG20 Jerry Rice	5.00	2.20	.60
☐ HG21 Deion Sanders	3.50	1.55	.45
☐ HG22 Rashaan Salaam	3.00	1.35	.35
☐ HG23 Marshall Faulk	2.50	1.10	.30
☐ HG24 Napoleon Kaufman	2.00	.90	.25
☐ HG25 Ki-Jana Carter	2.00	.90	.25
☐ HG26 Cris Carter	2.50	1.10	.30
☐ HG27 Joey Galloway	3.00	1.35	.35
☐ HG28 Eric Metcalf	2.50	1.10	.30
☐ HG29 Derrick Thomas	2.00	.90	.25
☐ HG30 Bruce Smith	2.00	.90	.25

1996 Collector's Edge President's Reserve New Regime

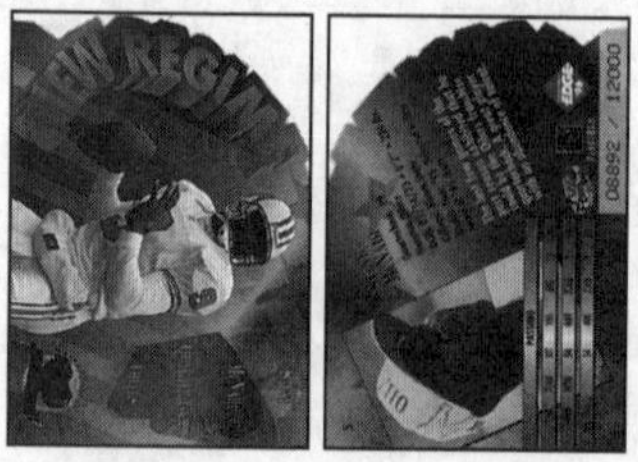

Randomly inserted in packs at a rate of one in five, this 26-card set highlights 1995's top rookies. These diecut cards are individually numbered out of 12,000.

	MINT	NRMT	EXC
COMPLETE SET (26)	50.00	22.00	6.25
COMPLETE SERIES 1 (13)	25.00	11.00	3.10
COMPLETE SERIES 2 (13)	25.00	11.00	3.10
COMMON CARD (1-24)	1.25	.55	.16
☐ 1 Tamarick Vanover	3.00	1.35	.35
☐ 2 Kerry Collins	7.00	3.10	.85
☐ 3 J.J. Stokes	3.00	1.35	.35
☐ 4 Napoleon Kaufman	2.00	.90	.25
☐ 5 Steve McNair	5.00	2.20	.60
☐ 6 Todd Collins	2.00	.90	.25
☐ 7 Frank Sanders	2.00	.90	.25
☐ 8 Warren Sapp	1.25	.55	.16
☐ 9 Tony Boselli	2.00	.90	.25
☐ 10 Curtis Martin	8.00	3.60	1.00
☐ 11 Ki-Jana Carter	3.00	1.35	.35
☐ 12 Zack Crockett	1.25	.55	.16
☐ 13 Joey Galloway	3.00	1.35	.35
☐ 14 Terrell Davis	8.00	3.60	1.00
☐ 15 Chris Sanders	2.00	.90	.25
☐ 16 Rashaan Salaam	3.00	1.35	.35
☐ 17 Michael Westbrook	3.00	1.35	.35
☐ 18 Hugh Douglas	1.25	.55	.16
☐ 19 Eric Zeier	2.00	.90	.25
☐ 20 Kordell Stewart	7.00	3.10	.85
☐ 21 Ted Johnson	1.25	.55	.16
☐ 22 Ken Dilger	2.00	.90	.25
☐ 23 Darick Holmes	2.00	.90	.25
☐ 24 Wayne Chrebet	2.00	.90	.25
☐ NNO Checklist (1-12)	1.25	.55	.16
☐ NNO Checklist (13-24)	1.25	.55	.16

1996 Collector's Edge President's Reserve Running Mates

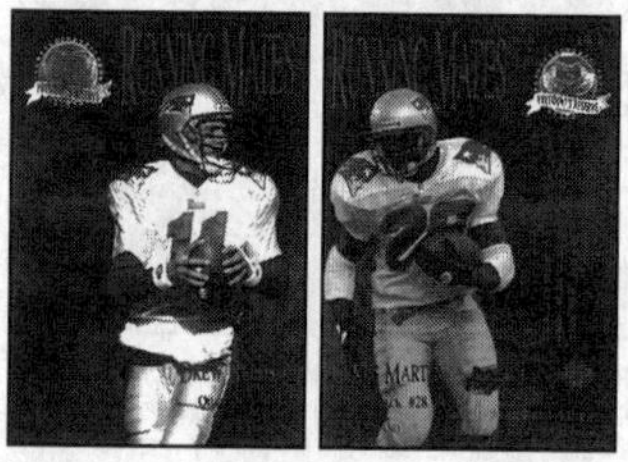

Randomly inserted in packs at a rate of one in 33, this 24-card set features teammates of quarterbacks and running backs on double-front cards made of sterling substrate. The cards are individually numbered out of 2,000 and have an "RM" prefix. Gold parallel versions of both series were inserted into packs as well. Reportedly, only 10 of each series one Gold cards were numbered and inserted into packs and 100 of each series two card inserted in Gold form. Jumbo versions of all 24-cards were also produced and released via a mail order wrapper redemption. The large cards measure approximately 8" by 10" and were individually numbered of 2000 for the silver version and 200 for the gold version. Each silver version card was available in exchange for 16 President's Reserve wrappers, with the gold cards exchanged for 64 wrappers. No postage fee was charged for the exchange.

	MINT	NRMT	EXC
COMPLETE SET (24)	600.00	275.00	75.00
COMPLETE SERIES 1 (12)	300.00	135.00	38.00
COMPLETE SERIES 2 (12)	300.00	135.00	38.00
COMMON CARD (1-24)	12.00	5.50	1.50
☐ 1 Emmitt Smith Troy Aikman	60.00	27.00	7.50
☐ 2 Marshall Faulk Jim Harbaugh	20.00	9.00	2.50
☐ 3 Terrell Davis John Elway	50.00	22.00	6.25
☐ 4 Stan Humphries Natrone Means	15.00	6.75	1.85
☐ 5 Rashaan Salaam Erik Kramer	18.00	8.00	2.20
☐ 6 Chris Miller Jerome Bettis	18.00	8.00	2.20
☐ 7 Errict Rhett Trent Dilfer	15.00	6.75	1.85
☐ 8 Jeff George Craig Heyward	12.00	5.50	1.50
☐ 9 Gus Frerotte Terry Allen	15.00	6.75	1.85
☐ 10 Curtis Martin Drew Bledsoe	60.00	27.00	7.50
☐ 11 Jeff Blake Ki-Jana Carter	15.00	6.75	1.85
☐ 12 Rick Mirer Chris Warren	15.00	6.75	1.85
☐ 13 Brett Favre Edgar Bennett	60.00	27.00	7.50
☐ 14 Neil O'Donnell Byron Bam Morris	15.00	6.75	1.85
☐ 15 Scott Mitchell Barry Sanders	40.00	18.00	5.00
☐ 16 Steve Young Derek Loville	30.00	13.50	3.70
☐ 17 Warren Moon Robert Smith	12.00	5.50	1.50
☐ 18 Heath Shuler Brian Mitchell	15.00	6.75	1.85
☐ 19 Rodney Peete Ricky Watters	15.00	6.75	1.85
☐ 20 Kerry Collins Derrick Moore	30.00	13.50	3.70
☐ 21 Dan Marino Terry Kirby	60.00	27.00	7.50
☐ 22 Steve Bono Marcus Allen	18.00	8.00	2.20
☐ 23 Jim Kelly Darick Holmes	18.00	8.00	2.20
☐ 24 Kordell Stewart Erric Pegram	40.00	18.00	5.00

1996 Collector's Edge President's Reserve Tanned Rested Ready

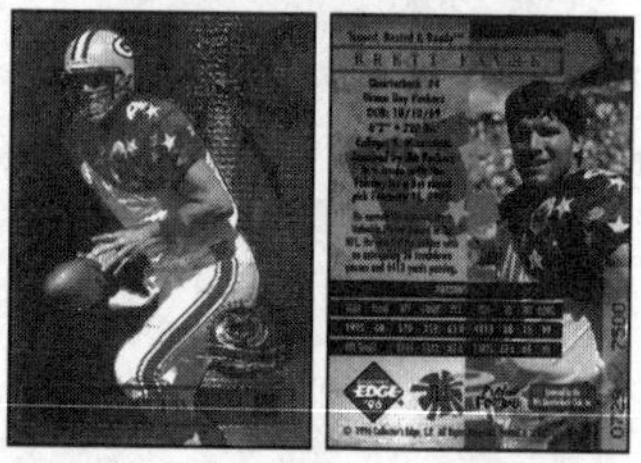

Randomly inserted in packs at a rate of one in eight, this 27-card set features NFL stars in action shots from the February 1996 Pro Bowl. The player's photos are showcased in front of a palm treee. The backs have necessary player information and are individually numbered out of 7,500. Cards 1-12 were issued in the first series and Cards 13-25 were included in second series packs.

	MINT	NRMT	EXC
COMPLETE SET (27)	110.00	50.00	14.00
COMPLETE SERIES 1 (13)	60.00	27.00	7.50
COMPLETE SERIES 2 (14)	50.00	22.00	6.25
COMMON CARD (1-25)	2.50	1.10	.30
☐ 1 Jeff Blake	5.00	2.20	.60
☐ 2 Warren Moon	4.00	1.80	.50
☐ 3 Brett Favre	16.00	7.25	2.00
☐ 4 Steve Young	6.00	2.70	.75
☐ 5 Emmitt Smith	16.00	7.25	2.00
☐ 6 Ricky Watters	4.00	1.80	.50
☐ 7 Michael Irvin	5.00	2.20	.60
☐ 8 Carl Pickens	4.00	1.80	.50
☐ 9 Tim Brown	5.00	2.20	.60
☐ 10 Anthony Miller	2.50	1.10	.30
☐ 11 Darren Bennett	2.50	1.10	.30
☐ 12 Yancey Thigpen	4.00	1.80	.50
☐ 13 Bryce Paup	2.50	1.10	.30
☐ 14 Jim Harbaugh	4.00	1.80	.50
☐ 15 Barry Sanders	8.00	3.60	1.00
☐ 16 Herman Moore	5.00	2.20	.60
☐ 17 Cris Carter	4.00	1.80	.50
☐ 18 Chris Warren	4.00	1.80	.50
☐ 19 Marshall Faulk	5.00	2.20	.60
☐ 20 Curtis Martin	12.00	5.50	1.50
☐ 21 Ben Coates	4.00	1.80	.50
☐ 22 Brent Jones	2.50	1.10	.30
☐ 23 Shannon Sharpe	2.50	1.10	.30
☐ 24 Brian Mitchell	2.50	1.10	.30
☐ 25 Ken Harvey	2.50	1.10	.30
☐ NNO Checklist (1-12)	1.00	.45	.12
☐ NNO Checklist (13-25)	1.00	.45	.12

1996 Collector's Edge President's Reserve TimeWarp

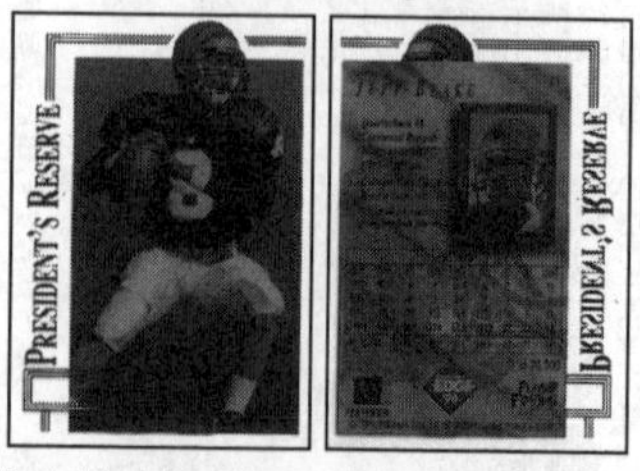

Randomly inserted in packs at a rate of one in 64, this 12-card insert standard-size set features two players per card. One of the players is still active, while the other is a retired superstar. The backs are individually numbered out of 2,000.

	MINT	NRMT	EXC
COMPLETE SET (12)	500.00	220.00	60.00
COMPLETE SERIES 1 (6)	250.00	110.00	31.00
COMPLETE SERIES 2 (6)	250.00	110.00	31.00
COMMON CARD (1-12)	15.00	6.75	1.85
☐ 1 Jack Kemp Greg Lloyd	25.00	11.00	3.10
☐ 2 Sonny Jurgensen Marshall Faulk	25.00	11.00	3.10
☐ 3 Fran Tarkenton Bryce Paup	15.00	6.75	1.85
☐ 4 Roger Staubach Emmitt Smith	90.00	40.00	11.00
☐ 5 Jack Lambert Curtis Martin	50.00	22.00	6.25
☐ 6 Jack Youngblood Brett Favre	90.00	40.00	11.00
☐ 7 Fran Tarkenton Reggie White	25.00	11.00	3.10
☐ 8 Art Donovan Steve Bono	15.00	6.75	1.85
☐ 9 Bobby Mitchell Troy Aikman	50.00	22.00	6.25
☐ 10 Larry Csonka Kordell Stewart	50.00	22.00	6.25
☐ 11 Dick Butkus Deion Sanders	30.00	13.50	3.70
☐ 12 Deacon Jones Dan Marino	90.00	40.00	11.00

1961 Colts Jay Publishing

This 12-card set features (approximately) 5" by 7" black-and-white player photos. The photos show players in traditional poses with the quarterback preparing to throw, the runner heading downfield, and the defenseman ready for the tackle. These cards were packaged 12 to a packet and originally sold for 25 cents. The backs are blank. The cards are unnumbered and checklisted below in alphabetical order.

	NRMT	VG-E	GOOD
COMPLETE SET (12)	100.00	45.00	12.50
COMMON CARD (1-12)	5.00	2.20	.60
☐ 1 Raymond Berry	12.00	5.50	1.50
☐ 2 Art Donovan	10.00	4.50	1.25
☐ 3 Weeb Ewbank CO	6.00	2.70	.75
☐ 4 Alex Hawkins	5.00	2.20	.60
☐ 5 Gino Marchetti	9.00	4.00	1.10
☐ 6 Lenny Moore	12.00	5.50	1.50
☐ 7 Jim Mutscheller	5.00	2.20	.60
☐ 8 Steve Myhra	5.00	2.20	.60
☐ 9 Jimmy Orr	6.00	2.70	.75
☐ 10 Jim Parker	8.00	3.60	1.00
☐ 11 Joe Perry	12.00	5.50	1.50
☐ 12 Johnny Unitas	25.00	11.00	3.10

1967 Colts Johnny Pro

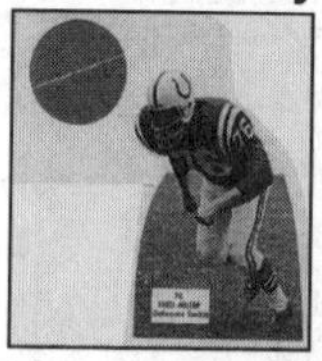

These 41 die-cut punchouts were issued (six or seven per page) in an album which itself measured approximately 11" by 14". Each punchout is approximately 4 1/8" tall and 2 7/8" wide at its base. A stand came with each punchout, and by inserting the punchout in it, the player stood upright. Each punchout consisted of a color player photo against a green grass background. The player's jersey number, name, and position are printed in a white box toward the bottom. The punchouts are unnumbered and checklisted below in alphabetical order.

	NRMT	VG-E	GOOD
COMPLETE SET (41)	800.00	350.00	100.00
COMMON CARD (1-41)	15.00	6.75	1.85
☐ 1 Sam Ball	15.00	6.75	1.85
☐ 2 Raymond Berry	50.00	22.00	6.25
☐ 3 Bob Boyd	15.00	6.75	1.85
☐ 4 Ordell Braase	15.00	6.75	1.85
☐ 5 Barry Brown	15.00	6.75	1.85
☐ 6 Bill Curry	25.00	11.00	3.10
☐ 7 Mike Curtis	25.00	11.00	3.10
☐ 8 Norman Davis	15.00	6.75	1.85
☐ 9 Jim Detwiler	15.00	6.75	1.85
☐ 10 Dennis Gaubatz	15.00	6.75	1.85
☐ 11 Alvin Haymond	15.00	6.75	1.85
☐ 12 Jerry Hill	15.00	6.75	1.85
☐ 13 Roy Hilton	15.00	6.75	1.85
☐ 14 David Lee	15.00	6.75	1.85
☐ 15 Jerry Logan	15.00	6.75	1.85
☐ 16 Tony Lorick	15.00	6.75	1.85
☐ 17 Lenny Lyles	15.00	6.75	1.85
☐ 18 John Mackey	40.00	18.00	5.00
☐ 19 Tom Matte	25.00	11.00	3.10
☐ 20 Lou Michaels	20.00	9.00	2.50
☐ 21 Fred Miller	15.00	6.75	1.85
☐ 22 Lenny Moore	50.00	22.00	6.25
☐ 23 Jimmy Orr	20.00	9.00	2.50
☐ 24 Jim Parker	30.00	13.50	3.70
☐ 25 Ray Perkins	25.00	11.00	3.10
☐ 26 Glenn Ressler	15.00	6.75	1.85
☐ 27 Willie Richardson	20.00	9.00	2.50
☐ 28 Don Shinnick	15.00	6.75	1.85
☐ 29 Billy Ray Smith	20.00	9.00	2.50
☐ 30 Bubba Smith	50.00	22.00	6.25
☐ 31 Charlie Stukes	15.00	6.75	1.85
☐ 32 Andy Stynchula	15.00	6.75	1.85

☐ 33 Dan Sullivan	15.00	6.75	1.85
☐ 34 Dick Szymanski	15.00	6.75	1.85
☐ 35 Johnny Unitas	80.00	36.00	10.00
☐ 36 Bob Vogel	15.00	6.75	1.85
☐ 37 Rick Volk	20.00	9.00	2.50
☐ 38 Bob Wade	15.00	6.75	1.85
☐ 39 Jim Ward	15.00	6.75	1.85
☐ 40 Jim Welch	15.00	6.75	1.85
☐ 41 Butch Wilson	15.00	6.75	1.85

1967 Colts Team Issue

These large photo cards were produced and distributed by the Baltimore Colts. Each photo measures approximately 7 5/8" by 10" and is black-and-white, blank backed, and printed on glossy heavy paper stock. The player's name appears in bold lettering below the photo with the team name and player's position, height, weight, and college below that. The cards are unnumbered and checklisted below in alphabetical order.

	NRMT	VG-E	GOOD
COMPLETE SET (41)	200.00	90.00	25.00
COMMON CARD (1-41)	3.00	1.35	.35
☐ 1 Bob Baldwin	3.00	1.35	.35
☐ 2 Sam Ball	3.00	1.35	.35
☐ 3 Raymond Berry	15.00	6.75	1.85
☐ 4 Bob Boyd	3.00	1.35	.35
☐ 5 Bill Curry	6.00	2.70	.75
☐ 6 Mike Curtis	6.00	2.70	.75
☐ 7 Norman Davis	3.00	1.35	.35
☐ 8 Jim Detwiler	3.00	1.35	.35
☐ 9 Dennis Gaubatz	3.00	1.35	.35
☐ 10 Alvin Haymond	3.00	1.35	.35
☐ 11 Jerry Hill	3.00	1.35	.35
☐ 12 Roy Hilton	3.00	1.35	.35
☐ 13 David Lee	3.00	1.35	.35
☐ 14 Jerry Logan	3.00	1.35	.35
☐ 15 Tony Lorick	4.00	1.80	.50
☐ 16 Lenny Lyles	3.00	1.35	.35
☐ 17 John Mackey	10.00	4.50	1.25
☐ 18 Tom Matte	4.00	1.80	.50
☐ 19 Dale Memmelaar	3.00	1.35	.35
☐ 20 Lou Michaels	4.00	1.80	.50
☐ 21 Fred Miller	3.00	1.35	.35
☐ 22 Lenny Moore	15.00	6.75	1.85
☐ 23 Jimmy Orr	4.00	1.80	.50
☐ 24 Jim Parker	8.00	3.60	1.00
☐ 25 Ray Perkins	6.00	2.70	.75
☐ 26 Glenn Ressler	3.00	1.35	.35
☐ 27 Willie Richardson	3.00	1.35	.35
☐ 28 Don Shinnick	3.00	1.35	.35
☐ 29 Don Shula CO	25.00	11.00	3.10
☐ 30 Billy Ray Smith	4.00	1.80	.50
☐ 31 Bubba Smith	15.00	6.75	1.85
☐ 32 Andy Stynchula	3.00	1.35	.35
☐ 33 Dan Sullivan	3.00	1.35	.35
☐ 34 Dick Szymanski	3.00	1.35	.35
☐ 35 Johnny Unitas	25.00	11.00	3.10
☐ 36 Bob Vogel	3.00	1.35	.35
☐ 37 Rick Volk	4.00	1.80	.50
☐ 38 Jim Ward	3.00	1.35	.35
☐ 39 Jim Welch	3.00	1.35	.35
☐ 40 Butch Wilson	3.00	1.35	.35
☐ 41 Coaching Staff Bill Arnsparger Don Shula Chuck Noll Dick Bielski John Sandusky Ed Rutledge Don McCafferty	6.00	2.70	.75

1971 Colts Jewel Foods

These six color photos are thought to have been released by Jewel Foods in Baltimore. Each measures approximately 7" by 8 3/4" and includes the player's name and team name below the photo. They are blankbacked and unnumbered.

	NRMT-MT	EXC	G-VG
COMPLETE SET (6)	50.00	22.00	6.25
COMMON CARD (1-6)	5.00	2.20	.60
☐ 1 Norm Bulaich	5.00	2.20	.60
☐ 2 Mike Curtis	5.00	2.20	.60
☐ 3 Ted Hendricks	15.00	6.75	1.85
☐ 4 Tom Matte	5.00	2.20	.60
☐ 5 Bubba Smith	10.00	4.50	1.25
☐ 6 Johnny Unitas	20.00	9.00	2.50

1972-74 Colts Team Issue

This set of photos was issued over a number of years by the Baltimore Colts. Many of the photos vary in terms of text size and fonts. Several players were issued with different pose variations. Each card typically features a black and white player photo with the player's name and team name below the picture. They measure approximately 8" by 10" and are blankbacked and unnumbered. Any additions to this list are welcomed.

	NRMT-MT	EXC	G-VG
COMPLETE SET (35)	100.00	45.00	12.50
COMMON CARD (1-35)	3.00	1.35	.35
☐ 1 Dick Amman	3.00	1.35	.35
☐ 2 John Andrews TE	3.00	1.35	.35
☐ 3 Jim Bailey	3.00	1.35	.35
☐ 4 Mike Barnes	3.00	1.35	.35
☐ 5 Raymond Chester	4.00	1.80	.50
☐ 6 Elmer Collett	3.00	1.35	.35
☐ 7 Mike Curtis	5.00	2.20	.60
☐ 8 Marty Domres	4.00	1.80	.50
☐ 9 Glenn Doughty	4.00	1.80	.50
☐ 10 Joe Ehrmann	4.00	1.80	.50
☐ 11 Hubert Ginn	3.00	1.35	.35
☐ 12 Sam Havrilak	3.00	1.35	.35
☐ 13 Brian Herosian	3.00	1.35	.35
☐ 14 Bert Jones	7.50	3.40	.95
☐ 15 Rex Kern	4.00	1.80	.50
☐ 16 Bruce Laird	3.00	1.35	.35
☐ 17 David Lee	3.00	1.35	.35
☐ 18 Don McCauley	4.00	1.80	.50
☐ 19 Ken Mendenhall	3.00	1.35	.35
☐ 20 Nelson Munsey	3.00	1.35	.35
☐ 21 Dan Neal	3.00	1.35	.35
☐ 22 Dennis Nelson	3.00	1.35	.35
☐ 23 Ray Oldham	3.00	1.35	.35
☐ 24 Bill Olds	3.00	1.35	.35
☐ 25 Gary Palmer	3.00	1.35	.35
☐ 26 T Pierantozzi	3.00	1.35	.35
☐ 27 Glenn Ressler	3.00	1.35	.35
☐ 28 Joe Schmiesing	3.00	1.35	.35
☐ 29 Howard Schnellenberger CO	6.00	2.70	.75
☐ 30 Ollie Smith	3.00	1.35	.35
☐ 31 Cotton Speyrer	4.00	1.80	.50
☐ 32 David Taylor T	3.00	1.35	.35
☐ 33 Rick Volk	4.00	1.80	.50
☐ 34 Stan White LB	4.00	1.80	.50
☐ 35 Bill Windauer	3.00	1.35	.35

1978 Colts Team Issue

This set of photos was issued by the Baltimore Colts. Each photo measures approximately 5" by 7". The fronts display player portrait photos with player name, postion, and team below the photo. The photos are blank backed, unnumbered and checklisted below in alphabetical order. This set was likely issued over a number of years by the team.

	NRMT-MT	EXC	G-VG
COMPLETE SET (36)	60.00	27.00	7.50
COMMON CARD (1-36)	2.00	.90	.25
☐ 1 Mack Alston	2.50	1.10	.30
☐ 2 Ron Baker	2.00	.90	.25
☐ 3 Mike Barnes	2.00	.90	.25
☐ 4 Tim Baylor	2.00	.90	.25
☐ 5 Lyle Blackwood	2.50	1.10	.30
☐ 6 Randy Burke	2.00	.90	.25
☐ 7 Fred Cook	2.50	1.10	.30
☐ 8 Glenn Doughty	2.50	1.10	.30
☐ 9 Joe Ehrmann	2.50	1.10	.30
☐ 10 Wade Griffin	2.00	.90	.25
☐ 11 Don Hardeman	2.00	.90	.25
☐ 12 Dwight Harrison	2.00	.90	.25
☐ 13 Ken Huff	2.00	.90	.25
☐ 14 Marshall Johnson	2.00	.90	.25
☐ 15 Bert Jones	7.50	3.40	.95
☐ 16 Bruce Laird	2.00	.90	.25
☐ 17 Roosevelt Leaks	3.00	1.35	.35
☐ 18 David Lee	2.00	.90	.25
☐ 19 Ron Lee	2.00	.90	.25
☐ 20 Toni Linhart	2.00	.90	.25
☐ 21 Derrel Luce	2.00	.90	.25
☐ 22 Reese McCall	2.00	.90	.25
☐ 23 Ken Mendenhall	2.00	.90	.25
☐ 24 Don Morrison	2.00	.90	.25
☐ 25 Lloyd Mumphord	2.00	.90	.25
☐ 26 Doug Nettles	2.00	.90	.25
☐ 27 Calvin O'Neal	2.00	.90	.25
☐ 28 Mike Ozdowski	2.00	.90	.25
☐ 29 Robert Pratt	2.00	.90	.25
☐ 30 Dave Rowe	2.50	1.10	.30
☐ 31 Sanders Shiver	2.00	.90	.25
☐ 32 Mike Siani	2.50	1.10	.30
☐ 33 Norm Thompson	2.50	1.10	.30
☐ 34 Bill Troup	2.00	.90	.25
☐ 35 Bob Van Duyne	2.00	.90	.25
☐ 36 Stan White	2.50	1.10	.30

1985 Colts Kroger

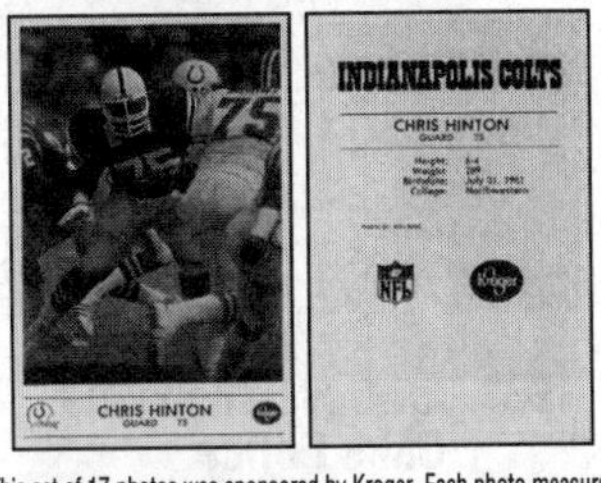

This set of 17 photos was sponsored by Kroger. Each photo measures approximately 5 1/2" by 8 1/2". The fronts display color action player photos with white borders. Player identification is given below the photo between the Colts' helmet on the left and the Kroger logo on the right. In navy blue print on a white background, the backs carry biographical information, the NFL logo, and the Kroger emblem. The photos are unnumbered and checklisted below in alphabetical order.

	MINT	NRMT	EXC
COMPLETE SET (17)	20.00	9.00	2.50
COMMON CARD (1-17)	1.00	.45	.12
☐ 1 Karl Baldischwiler	1.00	.45	.12
☐ 2 Pat Beach	1.50	.70	.19
☐ 3 Albert Bentley	2.00	.90	.25
☐ 4 Duane Bickett	2.50	1.10	.30
☐ 5 Matt Bouza	1.00	.45	.12
☐ 6 Nesby Glasgow	1.50	.70	.19
☐ 7 Chris Hinton	2.00	.90	.25
☐ 8 Lamonte Hunley	1.00	.45	.12
☐ 9 Barry Krauss	1.50	.70	.19
☐ 10 Orlando Lowry	1.00	.45	.12
☐ 11 Tate Randle	1.00	.45	.12
☐ 12 Tim Sherwin	1.00	.45	.12
☐ 13 Ron Solt	1.50	.70	.19
☐ 14 Rohn Stark	1.50	.70	.19
☐ 15 Ben Utt	1.00	.45	.12
☐ 16 Brad White	1.00	.45	.12
☐ 17 Anthony Young	1.50	.70	.19

1988 Colts Police

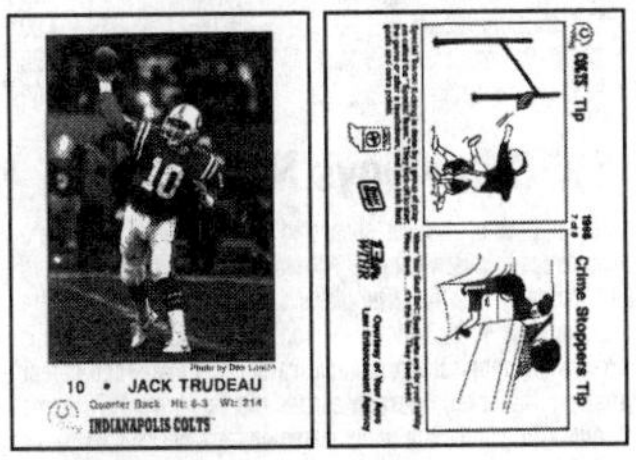

The 1988 Police Indianapolis Colts set contains eight numbered cards measuring approximately 2 5/8" by 4 1/8". There are seven player cards and one coach card. The backs have one "Colts Tip" and one "Crime Tip."

	MINT	NRMT	EXC
COMPLETE SET (8)	7.00	3.10	.85
COMMON CARD (1-8)	.75	.35	.09
☐ 1 Eric Dickerson	2.50	1.10	.30
☐ 2 Barry Krauss	1.00	.45	.12
☐ 3 Bill Brooks	1.25	.55	.16
☐ 4 Duane Bickett	1.00	.45	.12
☐ 5 Chris Hinton	1.00	.45	.12
☐ 6 Eugene Daniel	.75	.35	.09
☐ 7 Jack Trudeau	1.25	.55	.16
☐ 8 Ron Meyer CO	1.00	.45	.12

1989 Colts Police

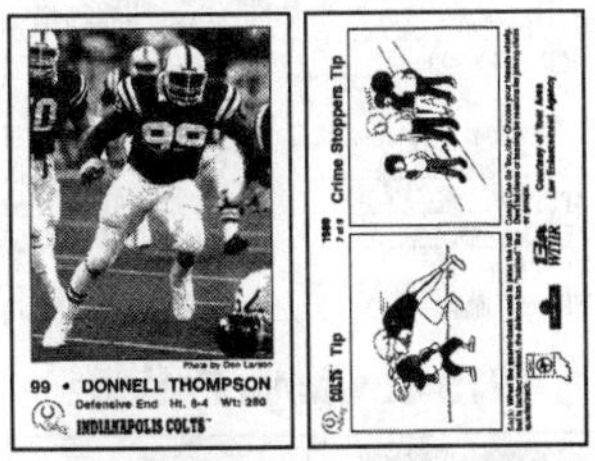

The 1989 Police Indianapolis Colts set contains nine numbered cards measuring approximately 2 5/8" by 4 1/8". The fronts have white borders and color action photos; the horizontally-oriented backs have safety tips. These cards were printed on very thin stock. The set was also sponsored by Louis Rich Co. and WTHR-TV-13. According to sources, at least 50,000 sets were given away. One card was given to young persons each week during the season.

	MINT	NRMT	EXC
COMPLETE SET (9)	7.00	3.10	.85
COMMON CARD (1-9)	.50	.23	.06
☐ 1 Colts Team Card	.60	.25	.07
☐ 2 Dean Biasucci	.60	.25	.07
☐ 3 Andre Rison	2.50	1.10	.30
☐ 4 Chris Chandler	1.00	.45	.12
☐ 5 O'Brien Alston	.60	.25	.07
☐ 6 Ray Donaldson	.50	.23	.06
☐ 7 Donnell Thompson	.60	.25	.07
☐ 8 Fredd Young	.60	.25	.07
☐ 9 Eric Dickerson	1.25	.55	.16

1990 Colts Police

This eight-card set features members of the 1990 Indianapolis Colts. The cards in the set measure approximately 2 5/8" by 4 1/8" and have full-color action shots of the featured players on the front along with safety and crime-prevention tips on the back. The set was sponsored by Region Central Indiana Crime Stoppers, Louis Rich, and Station 13 WTHR.

	MINT	NRMT	EXC
COMPLETE SET (8)	5.00	2.20	.60
COMMON CARD (1-8)	.60	.25	.07

☐ 1 Harvey Armstrong	.60	.25	.07
☐ 2 Pat Beach	.60	.25	.07
☐ 3 Albert Bentley	.75	.35	.09
☐ 4 Kevin Call	.60	.25	.07
☐ 5 Jeff George	3.00	1.35	.35
☐ 6 Mike Prior	.60	.25	.07
☐ 7 Rohn Stark	.75	.35	.09
☐ 8 Clarence Verdin	.75	.35	.09

1991 Colts Police

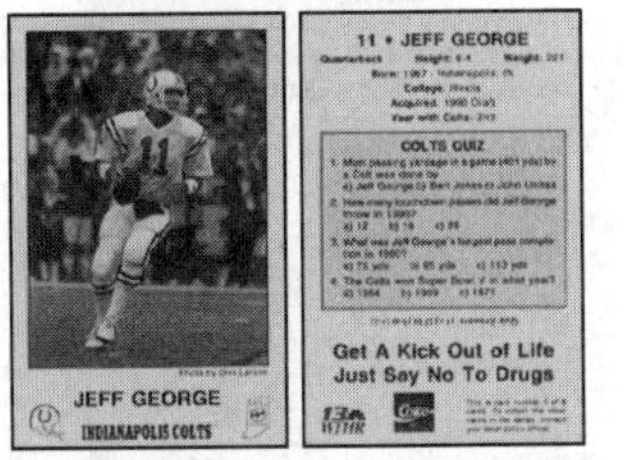

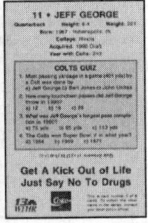

Sponsored by 13 WTHR and Coke, this eight-card measure 2 5/8" by 4 1/4". The fronts feature color action player photos inside white borders. The player's name, team name, and two logos occupy the lower white border. The backs carry biography, a Colts Quiz feature (with four questions and their answers), an anti-drug or alcohol message, and sponsor logos. The cards are numbered in the lower right corner; a message encourages the holder to contact his local police officer to collect the other cards in the set.

	MINT	NRMT	EXC
COMPLETE SET (8)	7.00	3.10	.85
COMMON CARD (1-8)	.75	.35	.09
☐ 1 Jeff George	2.50	1.10	.30
☐ 2 Jack Trudeau	1.00	.45	.12
☐ 3 Jeff Herrod	.75	.35	.09
☐ 4 Eric Dickerson	1.25	.55	.16
☐ 5 Bill Brooks	1.25	.55	.16
☐ 6 Jon Hand	1.00	.45	.12
☐ 7 Keith Taylor	.75	.35	.09
☐ 8 Randy Dixon	.75	.35	.09

1994 Costacos Brothers Postcards

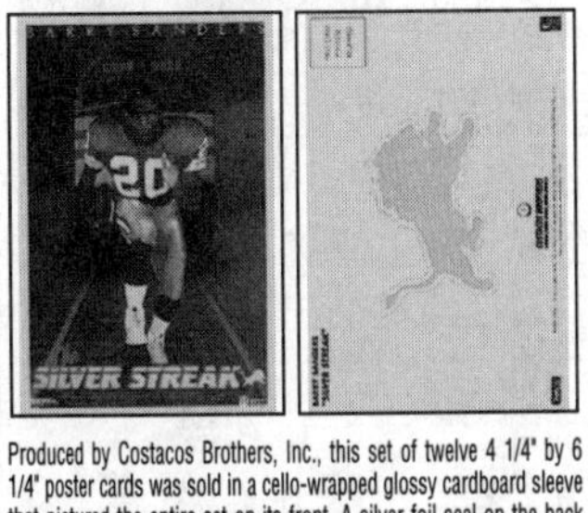

Produced by Costacos Brothers, Inc., this set of twelve 4 1/4" by 6 1/4" poster cards was sold in a cello-wrapped glossy cardboard sleeve that pictured the entire set on its front. A silver foil seal on the back carries the set serial number out of 25,000 produced. Inside white borders, the front pictures highlight in a unique style the player's nickname, reputation, or image. The horizontal backs have a postcard design, with a light gray team logo in the middle.

	MINT	NRMT	EXC
COMPLETE SET (12)	12.00	5.50	1.50
COMMON CARD (1-12)	.50	.23	.06
☐ 1 Troy Aikman Strong Arm of the Law	1.50	.70	.19
☐ 2 Barry Sanders The Silver Streak	1.50	.70	.19
☐ 3 Steve Young Run and Gun	1.25	.55	.16
☐ 4 Rick Mirer Natural Wonder	.75	.35	.09
☐ 5 John Elway The Rifleman	1.25	.55	.16
☐ 6 Dan Marino Tropical Storm	2.50	1.10	.30
☐ 7 Drew Bledsoe Patriot Games	1.50	.70	.19
☐ 8 Emmitt Smith Catch 22	2.50	1.10	.30
☐ 9 Warren Moon	.50	.23	.06

Moonshine			
☐ 10 Jerry Rice	1.50	.70	.19
Elite			
☐ 11 Michael Irvin	.60	.25	.07
Playmaker			
☐ 12 Jim Kelly	.60	.25	.07
Machine Gun Kelly			

1969 Cowboys Team Issue

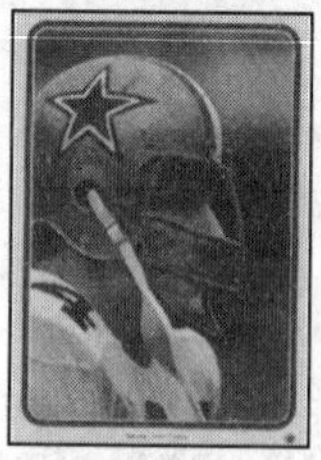

Measuring approximately 7" by 10", these five color action photos of Dallas Cowboys have rounded-corner black borders on thin white paper. The player's name and team are printed below the picture in the white margin. The backs are blank. The photos are unnumbered and checklisted below in alphabetical order.

	NRMT-MT	EXC	G-VG
COMPLETE SET (5)	40.00	18.00	5.00
COMMON CARD (1-5)	5.00	2.20	.60
☐ 1 Walt Garrison	7.50	3.40	.95
☐ 2 Lee Roy Jordan	10.00	4.50	1.25
☐ 3 Bob Lilly	12.00	5.50	1.50
☐ 4 Dave Manders	5.00	2.20	.60
☐ 5 Mel Renfro	10.00	4.50	1.25

1971 Cowboys Team Issue

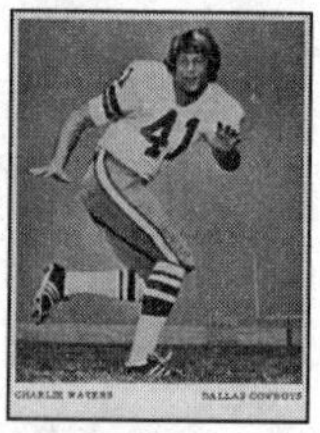

This team-issued 42-card set features black-and-white posed action player photos with white borders. Each photo measures approximately 5" by 6 1/2". A wider white border at the bottom contains the player's name and team. These cards are printed on thin card stock and have blank backs. The cards are unnumbered and checklisted below in alphabetical order.

	NRMT-MT	EXC	G-VG
COMPLETE SET (42)	225.00	100.00	28.00
COMMON CARD (1-42)	2.00	.90	.25
☐ 1 Herb Adderley	8.00	3.60	1.00
☐ 2 Lance Alworth	15.00	6.75	1.85
☐ 3 George Andrie	3.00	1.35	.35
☐ 4 Mike Clark	2.00	.90	.25
☐ 5 Larry Cole	3.00	1.35	.35
☐ 6 Mike Ditka	20.00	9.00	2.50
☐ 7 Dave Edwards	3.00	1.35	.35
☐ 8 John Fitzgerald	2.00	.90	.25
☐ 9 Toni Fritsch	2.00	.90	.25
☐ 10 Walt Garrison	4.00	1.80	.50
☐ 11 Cornell Green	4.00	1.80	.50
☐ 12 Bill Gregory	2.00	.90	.25
☐ 13 Cliff Harris	5.00	2.20	.60
☐ 14 Bob Hayes	10.00	4.50	1.25
☐ 15 Calvin Hill	6.00	2.70	.75
☐ 16 Chuck Howley	5.00	2.20	.60
☐ 17 Lee Roy Jordan	6.00	2.70	.75
☐ 18 Tom Landry	15.00	6.75	1.85
☐ 19 D.D. Lewis	3.00	1.35	.35
☐ 20 Bob Lilly	15.00	6.75	1.85
☐ 21 Tony Liscio	2.00	.90	.25
☐ 22 Dave Manders	2.00	.90	.25
☐ 23 Craig Morton	6.00	2.70	.75
☐ 24 Ralph Neely	3.00	1.35	.35
☐ 25 John Niland	3.00	1.35	.35
☐ 26 Jethro Pugh	3.00	1.35	.35
☐ 27 Dan Reeves	15.00	6.75	1.85
☐ 28 Mel Renfro	10.00	4.50	1.25
☐ 29 Gloster Richardson	2.00	.90	.25
☐ 30 Tody Smith	2.00	.90	.25
☐ 31 Roger Staubach	35.00	16.00	4.40
☐ 32 Don Talbert	2.00	.90	.25
☐ 33 Duane Thomas	6.00	2.70	.75
☐ 34 Isaac Thomas	2.00	.90	.25
☐ 35 Pat Toomay	3.00	1.35	.35
☐ 36 Billy Truax	3.00	1.35	.35
☐ 37 Rodney Wallace	2.00	.90	.25
☐ 38 Mark Washington	2.00	.90	.25
☐ 39 Charlie Waters	5.00	2.20	.60
☐ 40 Claxton Welch	2.00	.90	.25
☐ 41 Ron Widby	2.00	.90	.25
☐ 42 Rayfield Wright	3.00	1.35	.35

1972 Cowboys Team Issue

This 13-card set of the Dallas Cowboys measures approximately 4 1/4" by 5 1/2" and features black-and -white player photos in a white border with the player's name printed in the bottom margin. The backs are blank. The cards are unnumbered and checklisted below in alphabetical order.

	NRMT-MT	EXC	G-VG
COMPLETE SET (13)	75.00	34.00	9.50
COMMON CARD (1-13)	2.00	.90	.25
☐ 1 Herb Adderley	7.50	3.40	.95
☐ 2 Mike Ditka	15.00	6.75	1.85
☐ 3 Toni Fritsch	2.00	.90	.25
☐ 4 Walt Garrison	4.00	1.80	.50
☐ 5 Cornell Green	3.00	1.35	.35
☐ 6 Cliff Harris	5.00	2.20	.60
☐ 7 Bob Hayes	8.00	3.60	1.00
☐ 8 Calvin Hill	7.50	3.40	.95
☐ 9 Robert Newhouse	3.00	1.35	.35
☐ 10 Billy Parks	2.00	.90	.25
☐ 11 Mel Renfro	8.00	3.60	1.00
☐ 12 Dan Reeves	12.00	5.50	1.50
☐ 13 Charlie Waters	5.00	2.20	.60

1973 Cowboys McDonald's

This set of three photos was sponsored by McDonald's. Each photo measures approximately 8" by 10" and features a posed color close-up photo bordered in white. The player's name and team name are printed in black in the bottom white border. The top portion of the back has biographical information, career summary, and career statistics. The bottom portion carries the Cowboys 1973 game schedule. The photos are unnumbered and are checklisted below alphabetically.

	NRMT-MT	EXC	G-VG
COMPLETE SET (3)	65.00	29.00	8.00
COMMON CARD (1-3)	10.00	4.50	1.25
☐ 1 Walt Garrison	10.00	4.50	1.25
☐ 2 Calvin Hill	15.00	6.75	1.85
☐ 3 Roger Staubach	40.00	18.00	5.00

1979 Cowboys McDonald's

These cards were issued two per box on three different Happy Meal type boxes numbered "Super Box I" through "Super Box III." The individual cards, meant to be cut from the boxes, are unnumbered and blankbacked. We've listed prices for single cards, neatly cut from the box, below alphabetically according to the box on which the player appears. Complete Happy Meal Boxes carry a premium of 1.25X to 2X the prices listed below.

	NRMT-MT	EXC	G-VG
COMPLETE SET (6)	90.00	40.00	11.00
COMMON CARD (1-6)	10.00	4.50	1.25
☐ 1 Chuck Howley	10.00	4.50	1.25
☐ 2 Don Perkins	10.00	4.50	1.25
☐ 3 Bob Lilly	20.00	9.00	2.50
☐ 4 Don Meredith	20.00	9.00	2.50
☐ 5 Walt Garrison	10.00	4.50	1.25
☐ 6 Roger Staubach	30.00	13.50	3.70

1979 Cowboys Police

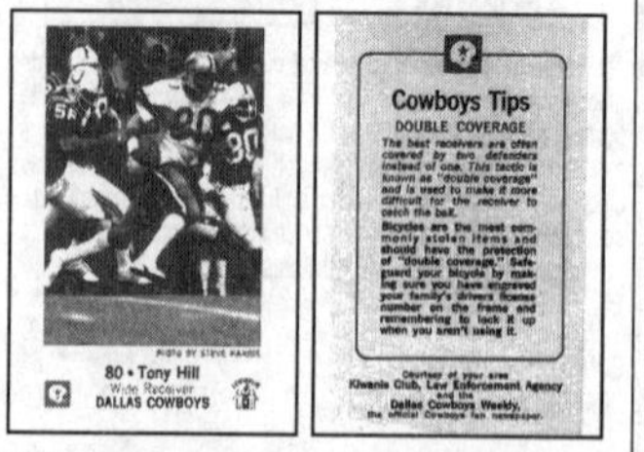

The 1979 Dallas Cowboy Police set consists of 15 cards sponsored by the Kiwanis Clubs, the Dallas Cowboys Weekly (the official fan newspaper), and the local law enforcement agency. The cards measure approximately 2 5/8" by 4 1/8". The cards are unnumbered but have been numbered in the checklist below by the player's uniform number which appears on the fronts of the cards. The backs contain "Cowboys Tips" which draw analogies between action on the football field and law abiding action in real life. D.D. Lewis replaced Thomas (Hollywood) Henderson midway through the season; hence, both of these cards are available in lesser quantities than the other cards in this set.

	NRMT-MT	EXC	G-VG
COMPLETE SET (15)	25.00	11.00	3.10
COMMON CARD	.60	.25	.07
☐ 12 Roger Staubach	7.00	3.10	.85
☐ 33 Tony Dorsett	5.00	2.20	.60
☐ 41 Charlie Waters	1.00	.45	.12
☐ 43 Cliff Harris	1.00	.45	.12
☐ 44 Robert Newhouse	.60	.25	.07
☐ 50 D.D. Lewis SP	3.00	1.35	.35
☐ 53 Bob Breunig	.60	.25	.07
☐ 54 Randy White	2.50	1.10	.30
☐ 56 Thomas Henderson SP	3.00	1.35	.35
☐ 67 Pat Donovan	.60	.25	.07
☐ 79 Harvey Martin	1.00	.45	.12
☐ 80 Tony Hill	1.00	.45	.12
☐ 88 Drew Pearson	1.25	.55	.16
☐ 89 Billy Joe DuPree	1.00	.45	.12
☐ NNO Tom Landry CO	4.00	1.80	.50

1980 Cowboys Police

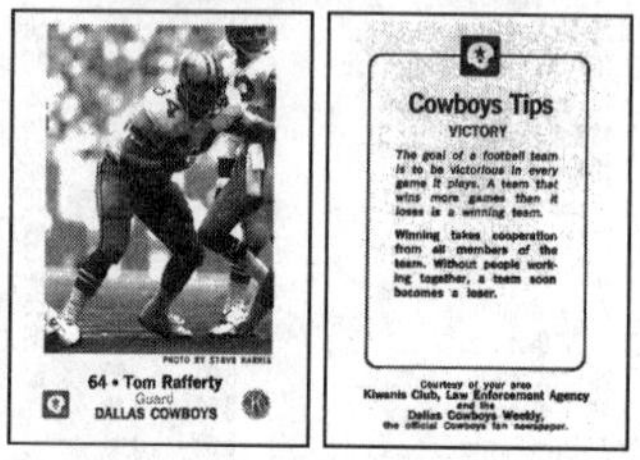

Quite similar to the 1979 set, the 1980 Dallas Cowboys police set is unnumbered other than the player's uniform number (as is listed in the checklist below). The cards in this 14-card set measure approximately 2 5/8" by 4 1/8". The sponsors are the same as those of the 1979 issue and the section entitled "Cowboys Tips" is contained on the back. The Kiwanis and Cowboys helmet logos appear on the fronts of the cards.

	MINT	NRMT	EXC
COMPLETE SET (14)	12.00	5.50	1.50
COMMON CARD	.60	.25	.07
☐ 1 Rafael Septien	1.00	.45	.12
☐ 11 Danny White	2.50	1.10	.30
☐ 25 Aaron Kyle	.60	.25	.07
☐ 26 Preston Pearson	1.50	.70	.19
☐ 31 Benny Barnes	1.00	.45	.12
☐ 35 Scott Laidlaw	.60	.25	.07
☐ 42 Randy Hughes	.60	.25	.07
☐ 62 John Fitzgerald	1.00	.45	.12
☐ 63 Larry Cole	1.00	.45	.12
☐ 64 Tom Rafferty	1.00	.45	.12
☐ 68 Herb Scott	.60	.25	.07
☐ 70 Rayfield Wright	1.00	.45	.12
☐ 78 John Dutton	1.00	.45	.12
☐ 87 Jay Saldi	1.00	.45	.12

1981 Cowboys Police

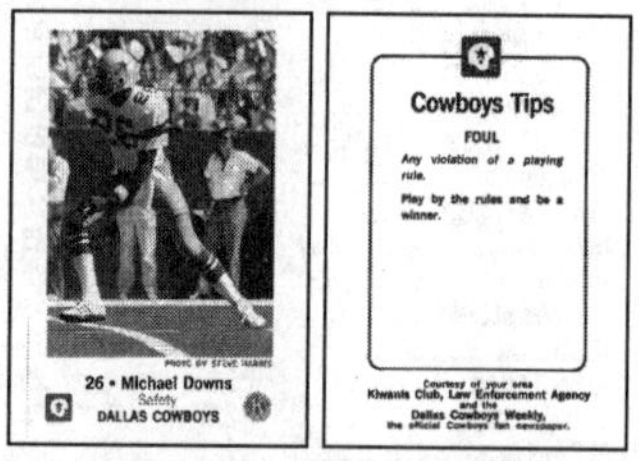

The 1981 Dallas Cowboys set of 14 cards is quite similar to sets of the previous two years. Since the cards are unnumbered, except for uniform number, the players have been listed by uniform number in the checklist below. The cards measure approximately 2 5/8" by 4 1/8". The set is sponsored by the Kiwanis Club, the local law enforcement agency, and the Dallas Cowboys Weekly. Appearing on the back along with a Cowboys helmet logo are "Cowboys Tips". A Kiwanis logo and Cowboys helmet logo appear on the front.

	MINT	NRMT	EXC
COMPLETE SET (14)	12.00	5.50	1.50
COMMON CARD	.60	.25	.07
☐ 18 Glenn Carano	1.00	.45	.12
☐ 20 Ron Springs	1.00	.45	.12
☐ 23 James Jones	.60	.25	.07
☐ 26 Michael Downs	1.00	.45	.12
☐ 32 Dennis Thurman	1.00	.45	.12
☐ 45 Steve Wilson	.60	.25	.07
☐ 51 Anthony Dickerson	.60	.25	.07
☐ 52 Robert Shaw	.60	.25	.07
☐ 58 Mike Hegman	1.00	.45	.12
☐ 59 Guy Brown	.60	.25	.07
☐ 61 Jim Cooper	.60	.25	.07
☐ 72 Ed Too Tall Jones	2.50	1.10	.30
☐ 84 Doug Cosbie	1.25	.55	.16
☐ 86 Butch Johnson	1.25	.55	.16

1981 Cowboys Thousand Oaks Police

This 14-card set was issued in Thousand Oaks, California, where the Cowboys conduct their summer pre-season workouts. These unnumbered cards measure approximately 2 5/8" by 4 1/8". Similar to other Cowboys sets, the distinguishing factors of this set are the Thousand Oaks Kiwanis Club and Thousand Oaks Police Department names printed on the backs in the place where other sets had the

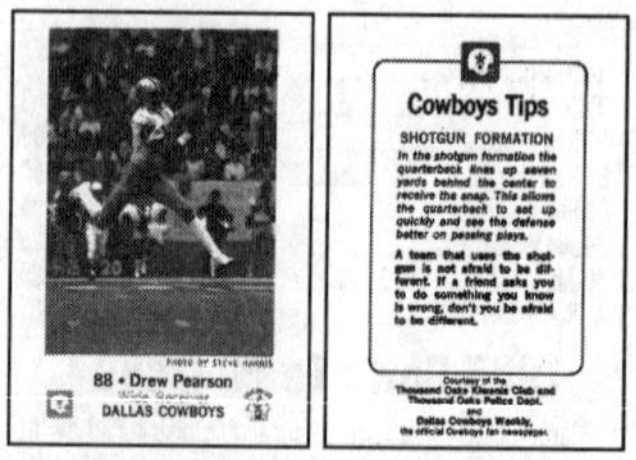

Kiwanis Club and law enforcement agency printed. The 14 players in this set are different from those in the regular set above. The cards are listed below by uniform number.

	MINT	NRMT	EXC
COMPLETE SET (14)	40.00	18.00	5.00
COMMON CARD	1.50	.70	.19
☐ 11 Danny White	3.50	1.55	.45
☐ 31 Benny Barnes	1.50	.70	.19
☐ 33 Tony Dorsett	7.50	3.40	.95
☐ 41 Charlie Waters	3.00	1.35	.35
☐ 42 Randy Hughes	1.50	.70	.19
☐ 44 Robert Newhouse	2.00	.90	.25
☐ 54 Randy White	5.00	2.20	.60
☐ 55 D.D. Lewis	1.50	.70	.19
☐ 78 John Dutton	1.50	.70	.19
☐ 79 Harvey Martin	2.50	1.10	.30
☐ 80 Tony Hill	2.50	1.10	.30
☐ 88 Drew Pearson	4.00	1.80	.50
☐ 89 Billy Joe DuPree	3.00	1.35	.35
☐ NNO Tom Landry CO	6.00	2.70	.75

1982 Cowboys Carrollton Park

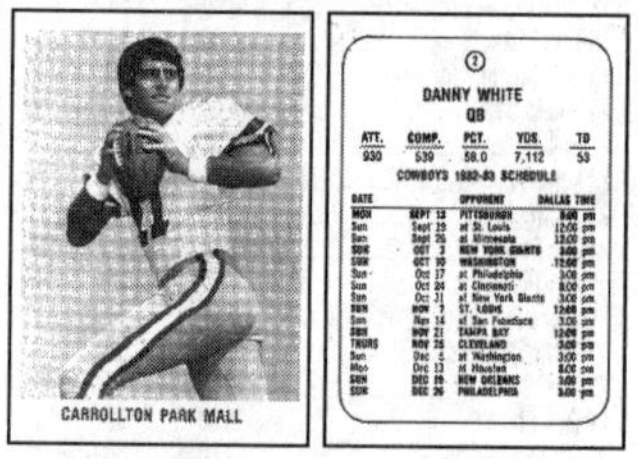

The 1982 Carrollton Park Mall Cowboys set contains six photo cards in black and white with the words "Carrollton Park Mall" in blue at the bottom of the card front. The cards measure approximately 3" by 4". The backs contain the 1982 Cowboys schedule and brief career statistics of the player portrayed. The cards are numbered on the back and the set is available as an uncut sheet with no difference in value.

	MINT	NRMT	EXC
COMPLETE SET (6)	7.00	3.10	.85
COMMON CARD (1-6)	.50	.23	.06
☐ 1 Roger Staubach	3.00	1.35	.35
☐ 2 Danny White	.75	.35	.09
☐ 3 Tony Dorsett	1.50	.70	.19
☐ 4 Randy White	1.00	.45	.12
☐ 5 Charlie Waters	.50	.23	.06
☐ 6 Billy Joe DuPree	.50	.23	.06

1983 Cowboys Police

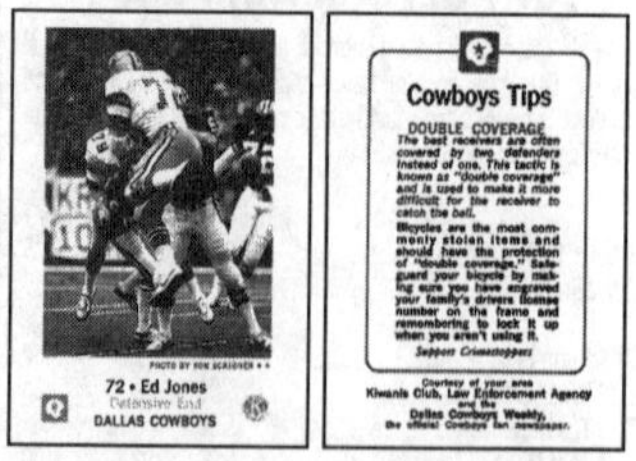

This unnumbered set of 28 cards was sponsored by the Kiwannis Club, Law Enforcement Agency, and the Dallas Cowboys Weekly. Cards are approximately 2 5/8" by 4 1/8" and have a white border around the photo on the front of the cards. The backs each contain a safety tip. Cards are listed in the checklist below in uniform number order. Four cheerleaders are included in the set and are so indicated by CHEER.

	MINT	NRMT	EXC
COMPLETE SET (28)	20.00	9.00	2.50
COMMON CARD	.50	.23	.06
☐ 1 Rafael Septien	.60	.25	.07
☐ 11 Danny White	1.50	.70	.19
☐ 20 Ron Springs	.60	.25	.07
☐ 24 Everson Walls	.60	.25	.07
☐ 26 Michael Downs	.50	.23	.06
☐ 30 Timmy Newsome	.50	.23	.06
☐ 32 Dennis Thurman	.60	.25	.07

	MINT	NRMT	EXC
☐ 33 Tony Dorsett	3.00	1.35	.35
☐ 47 Dextor Clinkscale	.50	.23	.06
☐ 53 Bob Breunig	.75	.35	.09
☐ 54 Randy White	3.00	1.35	.35
☐ 65 Kurt Petersen	.50	.23	.06
☐ 67 Pat Donovan	.50	.23	.06
☐ 70 Howard Richards	.50	.23	.06
☐ 72 Ed Too Tall Jones	2.50	1.10	.30
☐ 78 John Dutton	.60	.25	.07
☐ 79 Harvey Martin	1.25	.55	.16
☐ 80 Tony Hill	.75	.35	.09
☐ 83 Doug Donley	.50	.23	.06
☐ 84 Doug Cosbie	.60	.25	.07
☐ 86 Butch Johnson	.60	.25	.07
☐ 88 Drew Pearson	2.00	.90	.25
☐ 89 Billy Joe DuPree	.75	.35	.09
☐ NNO Tom Landry CO	2.50	1.10	.30
☐ NNO Melinda May CHEER	.50	.23	.06
☐ NNO Dana Presley CHEER	.50	.23	.06
☐ NNO Judy Trammell CHEER	.50	.23	.06
☐ NNO Toni Washington CHEER	.50	.23	.06

1985 Cowboys Frito Lay

The 1985 Cowboys Frito Lay set contains 41 photo cards. The cards measure approximately 4" by 5 1/2" and are printed on photographic quality paper stock. The white-bordered fronts display black-and-white player photos. The player's name, position, a brief biography, and team number appear on a wider lower border. The Frito Lay logo in the lower right corner rounds out the front. The backs are blank. The cards are unnumbered and checklisted below alphabetically. Roger Staubach is included in the set even though he retired in 1979.

	MINT	NRMT	EXC
COMPLETE SET (41)	75.00	34.00	9.50
COMMON CARD (1-41)	1.50	.70	.19
☐ 1 Vince Albritton	1.50	.70	.19
☐ 2 Brian Baldinger	1.50	.70	.19
☐ 3 Dextor Clinkscale	1.50	.70	.19
☐ 4 Jim Cooper	1.50	.70	.19
☐ 5 Fred Cornwell	1.50	.70	.19
☐ 6 Doug Cosbie	2.00	.90	.25
☐ 7 Steve DeOssie	1.50	.70	.19
☐ 8 John Dutton	2.00	.90	.25
☐ 9 Ricky Easmon	1.50	.70	.19
☐ 10 Ron Fellows	1.50	.70	.19
☐ 11 Leon Gonzalez	1.50	.70	.19
☐ 12 Gary Hogeboom	2.00	.90	.25
☐ 13 Jim Jeffcoat	3.00	1.35	.35
☐ 14 Ed Too Tall Jones	4.00	1.80	.50
☐ 15 James Jones	1.50	.70	.19
☐ 16 Crawford Ker	1.50	.70	.19
☐ 17 Robert Lavette	1.50	.70	.19
☐ 18 Eugene Lockhart	2.00	.90	.25
☐ 19 Timmy Newsome	1.50	.70	.19
☐ 20 Drew Pearson ACO	3.00	1.35	.35
☐ 21 Steve Pelluer	2.00	.90	.25
☐ 22 Jesse Penn	1.50	.70	.19
☐ 23 Kurt Petersen	1.50	.70	.19
☐ 24 Karl Powe	1.50	.70	.19
☐ 25 Phil Pozderac	1.50	.70	.19
☐ 26 Tom Rafferty	2.00	.90	.25
☐ 27 Mike Renfro	1.50	.70	.19
☐ 28 Howard Richards	1.50	.70	.19
☐ 29 Jeff Rohrer	1.50	.70	.19
☐ 30 Mike Saxon	1.50	.70	.19
☐ 31 Victor Scott	1.50	.70	.19
☐ 32 Rafael Septien	2.00	.90	.25
☐ 33 Don Smerek	1.50	.70	.19
☐ 34 Roger Staubach	12.00	5.50	1.50
☐ 35 Broderick Thompson	1.50	.70	.19
☐ 36 Dennis Thurman	2.00	.90	.25
☐ 37 Glen Titensor	1.50	.70	.19
☐ 38 Mark Tuinei	2.50	1.10	.30
☐ 39 Everson Walls	2.00	.90	.25
☐ 40 John Williams	1.50	.70	.19
☐ 41 Team Photo	3.00	1.35	.35

1993 Cowboys Taco Bell Cups

These cups were issued at Dallas area Taco Bell restaurants during the 1993 season. Each cup contains 2 players on each side, and caricatures the players featured.

	MINT	NRMT	EXC
COMPLETE SET	5.00	2.20	.60
COMMON CUP (1-2)	2.00	.90	.25
☐ 1 Bill Bates/Alvin Harper	2.00	.90	.25
☐ 2 Jay Novacek/Emmitt Smith	3.00	1.35	.35

1994 Cowboys Pro Line Live Kroger Stickers

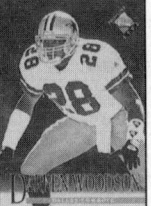 

Each vertical strip measures 2 1/2" by 12" and features three stickers. Each of the three stickers are roughly 3 5/8" in height; a white tab at the top of the strip carries the week the stickers were available and the price (99 cents). The fronts display the same design as the 1994 Pro Line series, with full-bleed color action photos. The backs of the strips, which peel off, contain two different $1.00 Fuji film coupons and an official entry form to enter a sweepstakes for a team poster. The strips are numbered below by weeks.

	MINT	NRMT	EXC
COMPLETE SET (7)	6.00	2.70	.75
COMMON CARD (1-7)	.50	.23	.06
☐ 1 Troy Aikman	1.50	.70	.19
Darren Woodson			
Erik Williams			
☐ 2 Emmitt Smith	2.50	1.10	.30
James Washington			
Mark Stepnoski			
☐ 3 Michael Irvin	.75	.35	.09
Kenneth Gant			
Tony Tolbert			
☐ 4 Daryl Johnston	.75	.35	.09
Kevin Williams WR			
Leon Lett			
☐ 5 Nate Newton	.50	.23	.06
Shante Carver			
Charles Haley			
☐ 6 Russell Maryland	.50	.23	.06
Mark Tuinei			
Kevin Smith			
☐ 7 Alvin Harper	.50	.23	.06
Willie Jackson			
Jay Novacek			

1995 Coyotes Arena

The Connecticut Coyotes released this set of 5-cards at their final home game of the 1995 Arena Football League season. The cardfronts feature a full bleed color photo while the unnumbered backs include player information. Reportedly, 5000 sets were produced.

	MINT	NRMT	EXC
COMPLETE SET (5)	8.00	3.60	1.00
COMMON CARD (1-5)	2.00	.90	.25
☐ 1 Rick Buffington CO	2.00	.90	.25
☐ 2 Mike Hold	2.00	.90	.25
☐ 3 Merv Mosley	2.00	.90	.25
☐ 4 Tyrone Thurman	2.00	.90	.25
☐ 5 Team Photo	2.00	.90	.25

1976 Crane Discs

The 1976 Crane football disc set of 30 cards contains a black and white photo of the player surrounded by a colored border. These circular cards measure 3 3/8" in diameter. The word Crane completes the circle of the border. The backs contain a Crane advertisement and the letters MSA, signifying Michael Schechter Associates. The set has benefited in recent years from the presence of Walter Payton in the set; Payton's 1976 Topps card is his Rookie Card and this Crane disc is one of the few other football cards or items of Payton from 1976. These discs were available as a mail-in offer but were not inserted in the Crane Potato Chip bags; consequently they are normally found in nice condition. There are 12 discs that were produced in shorter supply than the other 18; these are noted by SP in the checklist below. These extras found their way into the hobby when Crane sold their leftovers to a major midwestern dealer. Since the cards are unnumbered, they are ordered below alphabetically. The discs can also be found with the sponsor Saga Philadelphia School District on the cardback. The Saga discs are much more difficult to find and are priced in another part of this book.

	NRMT-MT	EXC	G-VG
COMPLETE SET (30)	18.00	8.00	2.20
COMMON CARD (1-30)	.25	.11	.03
☐ 1 Ken Anderson	.60	.25	.07
☐ 2 Otis Armstrong	.40	.18	.05

	MINT	NRMT	EXC
☐ 3 Steve Bartkowski	.40	.18	.05
☐ 4 Terry Bradshaw	2.50	1.10	.30
☐ 5 John Brockington SP	.35	.16	.04
☐ 6 Doug Buffone	.25	.11	.03
☐ 7 Wally Chambers	.25	.11	.03
☐ 8 Isaac Curtis SP	.50	.23	.06
☐ 9 Chuck Foreman	.40	.18	.05
☐ 10 Roman Gabriel SP	.50	.23	.06
☐ 11 Mel Gray	.40	.18	.05
☐ 12 Joe Greene	1.00	.45	.12
☐ 13 James Harris SP	.35	.16	.04
☐ 14 Jim Hart	.40	.18	.05
☐ 15 Billy Kilmer	.40	.18	.05
☐ 16 Greg Landry SP	.50	.23	.06
☐ 17 Ed Marinaro SP	.50	.23	.06
☐ 18 Lawrence McCutcheon SP	.50	.23	.06
☐ 19 Terry Metcalf	.40	.18	.05
☐ 20 Lydell Mitchell SP	.50	.23	.06
☐ 21 Jim Otis	.25	.11	.03
☐ 22 Alan Page	.60	.25	.07
☐ 23 Walter Payton SP	10.00	4.50	1.25
☐ 24 Greg Pruitt SP	.50	.23	.06
☐ 25 Charlie Sanders SP	.35	.16	.04
☐ 26 Ron Shanklin SP	.35	.16	.04
☐ 27 Roger Staubach	3.50	1.55	.45
☐ 28 Jan Stenerud	.40	.18	.05
☐ 29 Charley Taylor	.60	.25	.07
☐ 30 Roger Wehrli	.25	.11	.03

1986 DairyPak Cartons

This set of 24 numbered cards was issued as the side panel on half-gallon cartons of various brands of milk all over the country. Depending on the sponsoring milk company, the cards can be found in black, brown, red, green, dark blue, light blue, aqua, orange, purple, or lavender. The actual pictures of the players on the cards are in black and white. Each player's card also contains a facsimile autograph above or to the side of his head. The prices listed below are for cards cut from the carton. Complete carton prices are 50 percent greater than the prices listed below. The cards, when cut on the dotted line, measure approximately 3 1/4" by 4 7/16". The set was only licensed by the NFL Players Association and hence team logos are not shown, i.e., the players are pictured without helmets. The bottom of the panel details an offer to receive a 24" by 32" poster (featuring the card fronts of the 24 NFL Superstars featured in this set) for 1.95 and two proofs-of-purchase. The Lofton card was supposedly withdrawn at some time during the promotion; however there does not appear to be any drastic shortage of Lofton cards needed for complete sets.

	MINT	NRMT	EXC
COMPLETE SET (24)	75.00	34.00	9.50
COMMON CARD (1-24)	1.00	.45	.12
☐ 1 Joe Montana	20.00	9.00	2.50
☐ 2 Marcus Allen	3.00	1.35	.35
☐ 3 Art Monk	3.00	1.35	.35
☐ 4 Mike Quick	1.50	.70	.19
☐ 5 John Elway	12.50	5.50	1.55
☐ 6 Eric Hipple	1.00	.45	.12
☐ 7 Louis Lipps	1.50	.70	.19
☐ 8 Dan Fouts	3.00	1.35	.35
☐ 9 Phil Simms	2.00	.90	.25
☐ 10 Mike Rozier	1.00	.45	.12
☐ 11 Greg Bell	1.00	.45	.12
☐ 12 Ottis Anderson	2.00	.90	.25
☐ 13 Dave Krieg	2.00	.90	.25
☐ 14 Anthony Carter	2.00	.90	.25
☐ 15 Freeman McNeil	1.50	.70	.19
☐ 16 Doug Cosbie	1.00	.45	.12
☐ 17 James Lofton SP	4.00	1.80	.50
☐ 18 Dan Marino	25.00	11.00	3.10
☐ 19 James Wilder	1.00	.45	.12
☐ 20 Cris Collinsworth UER	1.50	.70	.19
(Name misspelled Chris)			
☐ 21 Eric Dickerson	3.00	1.35	.35
☐ 22 Walter Payton	10.00	4.50	1.25
☐ 23 Ozzie Newsome	2.00	.90	.25
☐ 24 Chris Hinton	1.00	.45	.12

1970 Dayton Daily News

Each of these 18 "bubble gum-less cards" are actually a cut-out from The Dayton Daily News newspaper. Each card measures approximately 3 1/2" by 4". The checklist below is incomplete, any additions to it would be appreciated.

	NRMT-MT	EXC	G-VG
COMPLETE SET (18)	50.00	22.00	6.25
COMMON CARD (1-18)	2.00	.90	.25
☐ 1 Herb Adderley	3.00	1.35	.35
☐ 2 Virgil Carter	2.00	.90	.25

	MINT	NRMT	EXC
☐ 3 Pete Case	2.00	.90	.25
☐ 4 Gary Cuozzo	2.00	.90	.25
☐ 5 Mike Curtis	2.50	1.10	.30
☐ 6 Ken Dyer	2.00	.90	.25
☐ 7 Walt Garrison	2.50	1.10	.30
☐ 8 Bob Hayes	4.00	1.80	.50
☐ 9 Bob Lilly	5.00	2.20	.60
☐ 10 John Mackey	4.00	1.80	.50
☐ 11 Bennie McRae	2.00	.90	.25
☐ 12 Earl Morrall	3.00	1.35	.35
☐ 13 Joe Morrison	2.50	1.10	.30
☐ 14 Craig Morton	3.00	1.35	.35
☐ 15 Jim O'Brien	2.00	.90	.25
☐ 16 Bart Starr	7.50	3.40	.95
☐ 17 Ken Willard	2.50	1.10	.30
☐ 18 Mike Wilson	2.00	.90	.25

1971-72 Dell

Measuring approximately 8 1/4" by 10 3/4", the 1971-72 Dell Pro Football Guide features a center insert that unfolds to display 48 color player photos that are framed by black and yellow border stripes. Each picture measures approximately 1 3/4" by 3" and is not perforated. The player's name and team name are printed beneath the picture. The backs have various color action shots that are framed by a black-and-white film type pattern. Biographies on the NFL stars featured on the insert are found throughout the guide. The uncut set still in the book brings up to a 25 percent premium over the complete set price. The pictures are unnumbered and checklisted below in alphabetical order.

	NRMT-MT	EXC	G-VG
COMPLETE SET (48)	100.00	45.00	12.50
COMMON CARD (1-48)	1.00	.45	.12
☐ 1 Dan Abramowicz	1.00	.45	.12
☐ 2 Herb Adderley	2.00	.90	.25
☐ 3 Lem Barney	2.00	.90	.25
☐ 4 Bobby Bell	2.00	.90	.25
☐ 5 George Blanda	3.50	1.55	.45
☐ 6 Terry Bradshaw	15.00	6.75	1.85
☐ 7 John Brodie	2.50	1.10	.30
☐ 8 Larry Brown	1.25	.55	.16
☐ 9 Dick Butkus	8.00	3.60	1.00
☐ 10 Fred Carr	1.00	.45	.12
☐ 11 Virgil Carter	1.00	.45	.12
☐ 12 Mike Curtis	1.25	.55	.16
☐ 13 Len Dawson	3.00	1.35	.35
☐ 14 Carl Eller	1.50	.70	.19
☐ 15 Mel Farr	1.00	.45	.12
☐ 16 Roman Gabriel	2.00	.90	.25
☐ 17 Gary Garrison	1.00	.45	.12
☐ 18 Dick Gordon	1.00	.45	.12
☐ 19 Bob Griese	6.00	2.70	.75
☐ 20 Bob Hayes	2.00	.90	.25
☐ 21 Rich Jackson	1.00	.45	.12
☐ 22 Charlie Johnson	1.25	.55	.16
☐ 23 Ron Johnson	1.00	.45	.12
☐ 24 Deacon Jones	2.00	.90	.25
☐ 25 Sonny Jurgensen	2.50	1.10	.30
☐ 26 Leroy Kelly	2.00	.90	.25
☐ 27 Daryle Lamonica	1.50	.70	.19
☐ 28 MacArthur Lane	1.00	.45	.12
☐ 29 Willie Lanier	2.00	.90	.25
☐ 30 Bob Lilly	3.00	1.35	.35
☐ 31 Floyd Little	1.25	.55	.16
☐ 32 Mike Lucci	1.00	.45	.12
☐ 33 Don Maynard	3.00	1.35	.35
☐ 34 Joe Namath	15.00	6.75	1.85
☐ 35 Tommy Nobis	2.00	.90	.25
☐ 36 Merlin Olsen	2.50	1.10	.30
☐ 37 Alan Page	2.50	1.10	.30
☐ 38 Gerry Philbin	1.00	.45	.12
☐ 39 Jim Plunkett	2.00	.90	.25
☐ 40 Tim Rossovich	1.00	.45	.12
☐ 41 Gale Sayers	8.00	3.60	1.00
☐ 42 Dennis Shaw	1.00	.45	.12
☐ 43 O.J. Simpson	12.00	5.50	1.50
☐ 44 Fran Tarkenton	6.00	2.70	.75
☐ 45 Johnny Unitas	10.00	4.50	1.25
☐ 46 Paul Warfield	3.50	1.55	.45
☐ 47 Gene Washington	1.25	.55	.16
☐ 48 Larry Wilson	2.00	.90	.25

1933 Diamond Matchbooks Silver

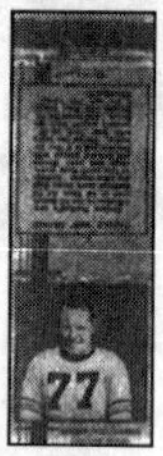

Diamond Match Co. produced their first football matchbook set in 1933. Each cover appears with both a pink or green background surrounded by a silver border, making a set with all variations complete at 190 covers. This set is thought to be the most difficult to complete. The covers measure approximately 1 1/2" by 4 1/2" (when completely folded out) and are priced below as unfolded with the matches removed. Complete covers with matches intact are valued at approximately 1 1/2 to 2 times the prices listed below. Although the covers are not numbered, we've assigned numbers alphabetically with the All-American Seal leading off.

	EX-MT	VG-E	GOOD
COMPLETE SET (95)	1600.00	700.00	200.00
COMMON MATCHBOOK (1-95)	12.00	5.50	1.50
☐ 1 All-American Board of Football Seal	15.00	6.75	1.85
☐ 2 Gene Alford	12.00	5.50	1.50
☐ 3 Marger Apsit	12.00	5.50	1.50
☐ 4 Red Badgro	25.00	11.00	3.10
☐ 5 Cliff Battles	30.00	13.50	3.70
☐ 6 Maury Bodenger	12.00	5.50	1.50
☐ 7 Jimmy Bowdoin	12.00	5.50	1.50
☐ 8 John Boylan	12.00	5.50	1.50
☐ 9 Hank Bruder	12.00	5.50	1.50
☐ 10 Carl Brumbaugh	15.00	6.75	1.85
☐ 11 Bill Buckler	12.00	5.50	1.50
☐ 12 Jerome Buckley	12.00	5.50	1.50
☐ 13 Dale Burnett	12.00	5.50	1.50
☐ 14 Ernie Caddel	15.00	6.75	1.85
☐ 15 Chris(Red) Cagle	15.00	6.75	1.85
☐ 16 Glen Campbell	12.00	5.50	1.50
☐ 17 John Cannella	12.00	5.50	1.50
☐ 18 Zuck Carlson	12.00	5.50	1.50
☐ 19 George Christensen	25.00	11.00	3.10
☐ 20 Stu Clancy	12.00	5.50	1.50
☐ 21 Paul(Rip) Collins	12.00	5.50	1.50
☐ 22 Jack Connell	12.00	5.50	1.50
☐ 23 George Corbett	12.00	5.50	1.50
☐ 24 Orien Crow	12.00	5.50	1.50
☐ 25 Ed Danowski	12.00	5.50	1.50
☐ 26 Sylvester(Red) Davis	12.00	5.50	1.50
☐ 27 Johnny Dell Isola	15.00	6.75	1.85
☐ 28 John Doehring	12.00	5.50	1.50
☐ 29 Turk Edwards	30.00	13.50	3.70
☐ 30 Earl Elser	12.00	5.50	1.50
☐ 31 Ox Emerson	15.00	6.75	1.85
☐ 32 Tiny Feather	12.00	5.50	1.50
☐ 33 Ray Flaherty	30.00	13.50	3.70
☐ 34 Ike Frankian	12.00	5.50	1.50
☐ 35 Red Grange	350.00	160.00	45.00
☐ 36 Len Grant	12.00	5.50	1.50
☐ 37 Ace Gutowsky	15.00	6.75	1.85
☐ 38 Mel Hein	30.00	13.50	3.70
☐ 39 Arnie Herber	25.00	11.00	3.10
☐ 40 Bill Hewitt	25.00	11.00	3.10
☐ 41 Herman Hickman	15.00	6.75	1.85
☐ 42 Clarke Hinkle	30.00	13.50	3.70
☐ 43 Cal Hubbard	25.00	11.00	3.10
☐ 44 George Hurley	12.00	5.50	1.50
☐ 45 Herman Hussey	12.00	5.50	1.50
☐ 46 Cecil(Tex) Irvin	12.00	5.50	1.50
☐ 47 Luke Johnsos	15.00	6.75	1.85
☐ 48 Bruce Jones	12.00	5.50	1.50
☐ 49 Potsy Jones	12.00	5.50	1.50
☐ 50 Thacker Kaye	12.00	5.50	1.50
☐ 51 Shipwreck Kelly	15.00	6.75	1.85
☐ 52 Joe Doc Kopcha	15.00	6.75	1.85
☐ 53 Joe Kurth	12.00	5.50	1.50
☐ 54 Milo Lubratevich	12.00	5.50	1.50
☐ 55 Father Lumpkin	15.00	6.75	1.85
☐ 56 Jim MacMurdo	12.00	5.50	1.50
☐ 57 Joe Maniaci	12.00	5.50	1.50
☐ 58 Jack McBride	12.00	5.50	1.50
☐ 59 Ookie Miller	12.00	5.50	1.50
☐ 60 Buster Mitchell	12.00	5.50	1.50
☐ 61 Keith Molesworth	15.00	6.75	1.85
☐ 62 Bob Monnett	12.00	5.50	1.50
☐ 63 Hap Moran	12.00	5.50	1.50
☐ 64 Bill Morgan	12.00	5.50	1.50
☐ 65 Maynard Morrison	12.00	5.50	1.50
☐ 66 Mathew Murray	12.00	5.50	1.50
☐ 67 Jim Musick	12.00	5.50	1.50
☐ 68 Bronko Nagurski	350.00	160.00	45.00
☐ 69 Dick Nesbitt	12.00	5.50	1.50
☐ 70 Harry Newman	15.00	6.75	1.85
☐ 71 Steve Owen	25.00	11.00	3.10
☐ 72 Bill(Red) Owen	12.00	5.50	1.50
☐ 73 Andy Pavlicovic	12.00	5.50	1.50
☐ 74 Bert Pearson	12.00	5.50	1.50
☐ 75 William Pendergast	12.00	5.50	1.50
☐ 76 Jerry Pepper	12.00	5.50	1.50
☐ 77 Stan Piawlock	12.00	5.50	1.50
☐ 78 Erny Pinckert	15.00	6.75	1.85
☐ 79 Glenn Presnell	12.00	5.50	1.50
☐ 80 Jess Quatse	12.00	5.50	1.50
☐ 81 Hank Reese	12.00	5.50	1.50
☐ 82 Dick Richards	12.00	5.50	1.50
☐ 83 Tony Sarausky	12.00	5.50	1.50
☐ 84 Elmer Schaake	12.00	5.50	1.50
☐ 85 John Schneller	12.00	5.50	1.50
☐ 86 Johnny Sisk	12.00	5.50	1.50
☐ 87 Mike Steponovich	12.00	5.50	1.50
☐ 88 Ken Strong	40.00	18.00	5.00
☐ 89 Charles Tackwell	12.00	5.50	1.50
☐ 90 Harry Thayer	15.00	6.75	1.85
☐ 91 Walt Uzdavinis	12.00	5.50	1.50
☐ 92 John Welch	12.00	5.50	1.50
☐ 93 William Whalen	12.00	5.50	1.50
☐ 94 Fay(Mule) Wilson	15.00	6.75	1.85
☐ 95 Frank(Babe) Wright	12.00	5.50	1.50

1934 Diamond Matchbooks

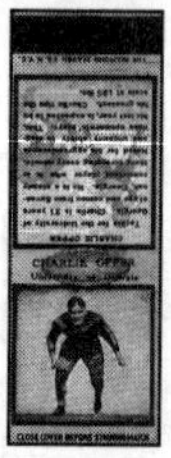

The 1934 Diamond Matchbook set is the first of many issues from the company printed with colorful borders. Four border colors were used for this set: blue, green, red, and tan. Many players appear with all four border color variations, while some only appear with one or two different border colors. It is thought that a complete checklist with all color variations is still unknown. There is no player position included nor picture frame border shown on the player photo. The text printing is in black ink and each cover measures approximately 1 1/2" by 4 1/2" when completely unfolded. The set is very similar in appearance to the 1935 issues, but can be distinguished by the single lined manufacturer's identification "The Diamond Match Co., N.Y.C." Complete covers with matches intact are valued at approximately 1 1/2 times the prices listed below. Although the covers are not numbered, we've assigned numbers alphabetically.

	EX-MT	VG-E	GOOD
COMPLETE SET (121)	1500.00	700.00	190.00
COMMON MATCHBOOK (1-121)	10.00	4.50	1.25
☐ 1 Arvo Antilla	10.00	4.50	1.25
☐ 2 Red Badgro	20.00	9.00	2.50
☐ 3 Norbert Bartell	10.00	4.50	1.25
☐ 4 Cliff Battles	35.00	16.00	4.40
☐ 5 Chuck Bennis	10.00	4.50	1.25
☐ 6 Jack Beynon	12.00	5.50	1.50
☐ 7 Maury Bodenger	10.00	4.50	1.25
☐ 8 John Bond	10.00	4.50	1.25
☐ 9 John Brown	10.00	4.50	1.25
☐ 10 Carl Brumbaugh	12.00	5.50	1.50
☐ 11 Dale Burnett	10.00	4.50	1.25
☐ 12 Ernie Caddel	12.00	5.50	1.50
☐ 13 Chris(Red) Cagle	12.00	5.50	1.50
☐ 14 Glen Campbell	10.00	4.50	1.25
☐ 15 John Cannella	10.00	4.50	1.25
☐ 16 Joe Carter	10.00	4.50	1.25
☐ 17 Les Caywood	10.00	4.50	1.25
☐ 18 George(Buck) Chapman	10.00	4.50	1.25
☐ 19 Frank Christensen	10.00	4.50	1.25
☐ 20 Stu Clancy	10.00	4.50	1.25
☐ 21 Algy Clark	10.00	4.50	1.25
☐ 22 Paul(Rip) Collins	10.00	4.50	1.25
☐ 23 Jack Connell	10.00	4.50	1.25
☐ 24 Orien Crow	10.00	4.50	1.25
☐ 25 Lone Star Dietz CO	10.00	4.50	1.25
☐ 26 John Doehring	10.00	4.50	1.25
☐ 27 Turk Edwards	25.00	11.00	3.10
☐ 28 Ox Emerson	12.00	5.50	1.50
☐ 29 Tiny Feather	10.00	4.50	1.25
☐ 30 Ray Flaherty	20.00	9.00	2.50
☐ 31 Frank Froschauer	10.00	4.50	1.25
☐ 32 Chuck Galbreath	10.00	4.50	1.25
☐ 33 Red Gragg	10.00	4.50	1.25
☐ 34 Red Grange	250.00	110.00	31.00
☐ 35 Cy Grant	10.00	4.50	1.25
☐ 36 Len Grant	10.00	4.50	1.25
☐ 37 Ross Grant	10.00	4.50	1.25
☐ 38 Jack Griffith	10.00	4.50	1.25
☐ 39 Ed Gryboski	10.00	4.50	1.25
☐ 40 Ace Gutowsky	12.00	5.50	1.50
☐ 41 Swede Hanson	12.00	5.50	1.50
☐ 42 Mel Hein	25.00	11.00	3.10
☐ 43 Warren Heller	10.00	4.50	1.25
☐ 44 Bill Hewitt	20.00	9.00	2.50
☐ 45 Cecil(Tex) Irvin	10.00	4.50	1.25
☐ 46 Frank Johnson	10.00	4.50	1.25
☐ 47 Jack Johnson	10.00	4.50	1.25
☐ 48 Bob Jones	10.00	4.50	1.25
☐ 49 Potsy Jones	10.00	4.50	1.25
☐ 50 Carl Jorgensen	10.00	4.50	1.25
☐ 51 John Karcis	10.00	4.50	1.25
☐ 52 Eddie Kawal	10.00	4.50	1.25
☐ 53 Shipwreck Kelly	12.00	5.50	1.50
☐ 54 George Kenneally	12.00	5.50	1.50
☐ 55 Walt Kiesling	20.00	9.00	2.50
☐ 56 Jack Knapper	10.00	4.50	1.25
☐ 57 Frank Knox	10.00	4.50	1.25
☐ 58 Joe Doc Kopcha	12.00	5.50	1.50
☐ 59 Joe Kresky	10.00	4.50	1.25
☐ 60 Joe Laws	10.00	4.50	1.25
☐ 61 Russ Lay	10.00	4.50	1.25
☐ 62 Biff Lee	10.00	4.50	1.25
☐ 63 Gil LeFebvre	10.00	4.50	1.25
☐ 64 Jim Leonard	10.00	4.50	1.25
☐ 65 Les Lindberg	10.00	4.50	1.25
☐ 66 John Lipski	10.00	4.50	1.25
☐ 67 Milo Lubratevich	10.00	4.50	1.25
☐ 68 Father Lumpkin	12.00	5.50	1.50
☐ 69 Jim MacMurdo	10.00	4.50	1.25
☐ 70 Ed Matesic	10.00	4.50	1.25
☐ 71 Dave McCollough	10.00	4.50	1.25
☐ 72 John McKnight	10.00	4.50	1.25
☐ 73 Johnny(Blood) McNally	35.00	16.00	4.40
☐ 74 Al Minot	10.00	4.50	1.25
☐ 75 Keith Molesworth	12.00	5.50	1.50
☐ 76 Jim Mooney	10.00	4.50	1.25
☐ 77 Leroy Moorehead	10.00	4.50	1.25
☐ 78 Bill Morgan	10.00	4.50	1.25
☐ 79 Bob Moser	10.00	4.50	1.25
☐ 80 Lee Mulleneaux	10.00	4.50	1.25
☐ 81 George Munday	10.00	4.50	1.25
☐ 82 George Musso	20.00	9.00	2.50
☐ 83 Harry Newman	12.00	5.50	1.50
☐ 84 Al Norgard	10.00	4.50	1.25
☐ 85 John(Cap) Oehler	10.00	4.50	1.25
☐ 86 Charlie Opper	10.00	4.50	1.25
☐ 87 Bill(Red) Owen	10.00	4.50	1.25
☐ 88 Steve Owen	20.00	9.00	2.50
☐ 89 Bert Pearson	10.00	4.50	1.25
☐ 90 Tom Perkinson	10.00	4.50	1.25
☐ 91 Mace Pike	10.00	4.50	1.25
☐ 92 Joe Pilconis	10.00	4.50	1.25
☐ 93 Lew Pope	10.00	4.50	1.25
☐ 94 Crain Portman	10.00	4.50	1.25
☐ 95 Glenn Presnell	12.00	5.50	1.50
☐ 96 Jess Quatse	10.00	4.50	1.25
☐ 97 Clare Randolph	10.00	4.50	1.25
☐ 98 Hank Reese	10.00	4.50	1.25
☐ 99 Paul Riblett	10.00	4.50	1.25
☐ 100 Dick Richards	10.00	4.50	1.25
☐ 101 Jack Roberts	10.00	4.50	1.25
☐ 102 John Rogers	10.00	4.50	1.25
☐ 103 Gene Ronzani	12.00	5.50	1.50
☐ 104 Bob Rowe	10.00	4.50	1.25
☐ 105 Big John Schueller	10.00	4.50	1.25
☐ 106 Adolph Schwammel	10.00	4.50	1.25
☐ 107 Earl(Red) Seick	10.00	4.50	1.25
☐ 108 Allen Shi	10.00	4.50	1.25
☐ 109 Ben Smith	10.00	4.50	1.25
☐ 110 Ken Strong	35.00	16.00	4.40
☐ 111 Elmer Taber	10.00	4.50	1.25
☐ 112 Charles Tackwell	10.00	4.50	1.25
☐ 113 Ray Tesser	10.00	4.50	1.25
☐ 114 John Thomason	10.00	4.50	1.25
☐ 115 Charlie Turbyville	10.00	4.50	1.25
☐ 116 Claude Urevig	10.00	4.50	1.25
☐ 117 John(Harp) Vaughan	10.00	4.50	1.25
☐ 118 Henry Wagnon	10.00	4.50	1.25
☐ 119 John West	10.00	4.50	1.25
☐ 120 Lee Woodruff	10.00	4.50	1.25
☐ 121 Jim Zyntell	10.00	4.50	1.25

1934 Diamond Matchbooks College Rivals

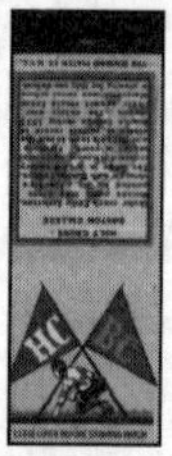

Diamond Match Co. produced this set issued in 1934. Each cover features a top college rivalry with a short write-up about the latest games between the two teams. The covers contain a single line manufacturer's identification "The Diamond Match Co. N.Y.C." This set is very similar to the 1935 issues, but can be distinguished by the last line of type in the text as indicated below. Each of the twelve unnumbered covers was produced with either a black or tan colored border. Some collectors attempt to assemble a complete 24-card set with all variations. Complete covers with matches intact are valued at approximately 1-1/2 times the prices listed below.

	EX-MT	VG-E	GOOD
COMPLETE SET (12)	90.00	40.00	11.00
COMMON MATCHBOOK (1-12)	8.00	3.60	1.00
☐ 1 Alabama vs. Fordham 1933	8.00	3.60	1.00
☐ 2 Army vs. Navy start to finish	10.00	4.50	1.25
☐ 3 Fordham vs. St. Mary's lose by a 13-6 score	8.00	3.60	1.00
☐ 4 Georgia vs. Georgia Tech Bulldog Alumni and followers	8.00	3.60	1.00
☐ 5 Holy Cross vs. Boston College in atoning for this one defeat	8.00	3.60	1.00
☐ 6 Lafayette vs. Lehigh victory for Lafayette	8.00	3.60	1.00
☐ 7 Michigan vs. Ohio State Champions	8.00	3.60	1.00
☐ 8 Notre Dame vs. Army leader of men, Knute Rockne	10.00	4.50	1.25
☐ 9 Penn vs. Cornell pass	8.00	3.60	1.00
☐ 10 USC vs. Notre Dame year	10.00	4.50	1.25
☐ 11 Yale vs. Harvard Harvard	8.00	3.60	1.00
☐ 12 Yale vs. Princeton scoring 27.	8.00	3.60	1.00

1935 Diamond Matchbooks

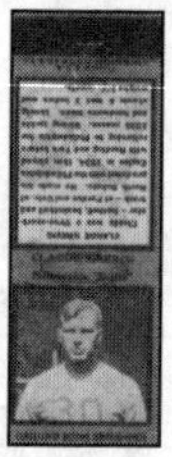

The 1935 Diamond Matchbook set is very similar in design to the 1934 set, but can be distinguished by the double lined manufacturer's identification "Made in U.S.A./The Diamond Match Co., N.Y.C." Only three border colors were used for this set: green, red, and tan and each player appears with only one border color. There is no player position included nor picture frame border shown on the player photo. The text printing is in black ink and each cover measures approximately 1 1/2" by 4 1/2" when completely unfolded. Complete covers with matches intact are valued at approximately 1 1/2 times the prices listed below. Although the covers are not numbered, we've assigned numbers alphabetically.

	EX-MT	VG-E	GOOD
COMPLETE SET (96)	1200.00	550.00	150.00
COMMON MATCHBOOK (1-96)	10.00	4.50	1.25
☐ 1 Alf Anderson	10.00	4.50	1.25
☐ 2 Alec Ashford	10.00	4.50	1.25
☐ 3 Gene Augusterfer	10.00	4.50	1.25
☐ 4 Red Badgro	20.00	9.00	2.50
☐ 5 Cliff Battles	30.00	13.50	3.70
☐ 6 Harry Benson	10.00	4.50	1.25
☐ 7 Tony Blazine	10.00	4.50	1.25
☐ 8 John Bond	10.00	4.50	1.25
☐ 9 Maurice (Mule) Bray	10.00	4.50	1.25
☐ 10 Dale Burnett	10.00	4.50	1.25
☐ 11 Charles(Cocky) Bush	10.00	4.50	1.25
☐ 12 Ernie Caddel	12.00	5.50	1.50
☐ 13 Zuck Carlson	10.00	4.50	1.25
☐ 14 Joe Carter	10.00	4.50	1.25
☐ 15 Cy Casper	10.00	4.50	1.25
☐ 16 Paul Causey	10.00	4.50	1.25
☐ 17 Frank Christensen	10.00	4.50	1.25
☐ 18 Stu Clancy	10.00	4.50	1.25
☐ 19 Dutch Clark	35.00	16.00	4.40
☐ 20 Paul(Rip) Collins	10.00	4.50	1.25
☐ 21 Dave Cook	10.00	4.50	1.25
☐ 22 Fred Crawford	10.00	4.50	1.25
☐ 23 Paul Cuba	10.00	4.50	1.25
☐ 24 Harry Ebding	10.00	4.50	1.25
☐ 25 Turk Edwards	25.00	11.00	3.10
☐ 26 Marvin(Swede) Ellstrom	10.00	4.50	1.25
☐ 27 Beattie Feathers	20.00	9.00	2.50
☐ 28 Ray Flaherty	20.00	9.00	2.50
☐ 29 John Gildea	10.00	4.50	1.25
☐ 30 Tom Graham	10.00	4.50	1.25
☐ 31 Len Grant	10.00	4.50	1.25
☐ 32 Maurice Green	10.00	4.50	1.25
☐ 33 Norman Greeney	10.00	4.50	1.25
☐ 34 Ace Gutowsky	12.00	5.50	1.50
☐ 35 Julius Hall	10.00	4.50	1.25
☐ 36 Swede Hanson	12.00	5.50	1.50
☐ 37 Charles Harold	10.00	4.50	1.25
☐ 38 Tom Haywood	10.00	4.50	1.25
☐ 39 Mel Hein	25.00	11.00	3.10
☐ 40 Bill Hewitt	20.00	9.00	2.50
☐ 41 Cecil(Tex) Irvin	10.00	4.50	1.25
☐ 42 Frank Johnson	10.00	4.50	1.25
☐ 43 Jack Johnson	10.00	4.50	1.25
☐ 44 Luke Johnsos	10.00	4.50	1.25
☐ 45 Potsy Jones	10.00	4.50	1.25
☐ 46 Carl Jorgensen	10.00	4.50	1.25
☐ 47 George Kenneally	10.00	4.50	1.25
☐ 48 Roger(Reds) Kirkman	10.00	4.50	1.25
☐ 49 Frank Knox	10.00	4.50	1.25

☐ 50 Joe Doc Kopcha	12.00	5.50	1.50
☐ 51 Rick Lackman	10.00	4.50	1.25
☐ 52 Jim Leonard	10.00	4.50	1.25
☐ 53 Joe(Hunk) Malkovich	10.00	4.50	1.25
☐ 54 Ed Manske	10.00	4.50	1.25
☐ 55 Bernie Masterson	12.00	5.50	1.50
☐ 56 James McMillen	10.00	4.50	1.25
☐ 57 Mike Mikulak	10.00	4.50	1.25
☐ 58 Ookie Miller	10.00	4.50	1.25
☐ 59 Milford(Dub) Miller	10.00	4.50	1.25
☐ 60 Al Minot	10.00	4.50	1.25
☐ 61 Buster Mitchell	10.00	4.50	1.25
☐ 62 Bill Morgan	10.00	4.50	1.25
☐ 63 George Musso	25.00	11.00	3.10
☐ 64 Harry Newman	12.00	5.50	1.50
☐ 65 Al Nichelini	10.00	4.50	1.25
☐ 66 Bill(Red) Owen	10.00	4.50	1.25
☐ 67 Steve Owen	20.00	9.00	2.50
☐ 68 Max Padlow	10.00	4.50	1.25
☐ 69 Hal Pangle	10.00	4.50	1.25
☐ 70 Melvin(Swede) Pittman	10.00	4.50	1.25
☐ 71 William(Red) Pollock	10.00	4.50	1.25
☐ 72 Glenn Presnell	12.00	5.50	1.50
☐ 73 George(Mousie) Rado	10.00	4.50	1.25
☐ 74 Clare Randolph	10.00	4.50	1.25
☐ 75 Hank Reese	10.00	4.50	1.25
☐ 76 Ray Richards	10.00	4.50	1.25
☐ 77 Doug Russell	10.00	4.50	1.25
☐ 78 Sandy Sandberg	10.00	4.50	1.25
☐ 79 Phil Sarboe	10.00	4.50	1.25
☐ 80 Big John Schneller	10.00	4.50	1.25
☐ 81 Michael Sebastian	10.00	4.50	1.25
☐ 82 Allen Shi	10.00	4.50	1.25
☐ 83 Johnny Sisk	12.00	5.50	1.50
☐ 84 James(Red) Stacy	10.00	4.50	1.25
☐ 85 Ed Storm	10.00	4.50	1.25
☐ 86 Ken Strong	35.00	16.00	4.40
☐ 87 Art Strutt	10.00	4.50	1.25
☐ 88 Frank Sullivan	10.00	4.50	1.25
☐ 89 Charles Treadaway	10.00	4.50	1.25
☐ 90 John Turley	10.00	4.50	1.25
☐ 91 Claude Urevig	10.00	4.50	1.25
☐ 92 Charles(Pug) Vaughan	10.00	4.50	1.25
☐ 93 Izzy Weinstock	10.00	4.50	1.25
☐ 94 Henry Wiesenbaugh	10.00	4.50	1.25
☐ 95 Joe Zeller	10.00	4.50	1.25
☐ 96 Vince Zizak	10.00	4.50	1.25

1935 Diamond Matchbooks College Rivals

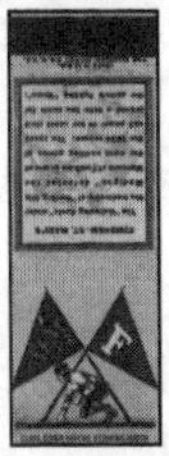

Diamond Match Co. produced this set issued in 1935. Each cover features a top college rivalry with a short write-up about the latest games between the two teams. The covers contain a double line manufacturer's identification "Made in U.S.A./The Diamond Match Co. N.Y.C." This set is very similar to the 1934 issue, but can be distinguished by the last line of type in the text as indicated below. Each of the twelve unnumbered covers was produced with three versions. The manufacturer's name can be found as a single line with both a black and a tan colored border: and the covers can be found in tan with a double lined manufacturer's name. Some collectors attempt to assemble a complete 36-book set with all variations. Complete matchbooks with matches intact are valued at approximately 1-1/2 times the prices listed below.

	EX-MT	VG-E	GOOD
COMPLETE SET (12)	90.00	40.00	11.00
COMMON MATCHBOOK (1-12)	8.00	3.60	1.00
☐ 1 Alabama vs. Fordham	8.00	3.60	1.00
once championship			
☐ 2 Army vs. Navy	10.00	4.50	1.25
over the Cadets since 1921			
☐ 3 Fordham vs. St. Mary's	8.00	3.60	1.00
the gamely fighting "Rams"			
☐ 4 Georgia vs. Georgia Tech	8.00	3.60	1.00
7-0 defeat.			
☐ 5 Holy Cross vs. Boston College	8.00	3.60	1.00
defeat.			
☐ 6 Lafayette vs. Lehigh	8.00	3.60	1.00
in a 13-7 victory for Lehigh.			
☐ 7 Michigan vs. Ohio State	8.00	3.60	1.00
tory for State.			
☐ 8 Notre Dame vs. Army	10.00	4.50	1.25
Cadets 12-6.			
☐ 9 Penn vs. Cornell	8.00	3.60	1.00
from start to finish.			
☐ 10 USC vs. Notre Dame	10.00	4.50	1.25
carries of Elmer Layden.			
☐ 11 Yale vs. Harvard	8.00	3.60	1.00
set back.			
☐ 12 Yale vs. Princeton	8.00	3.60	1.00
ed still led 7-0.			

1936 Diamond Matchbooks

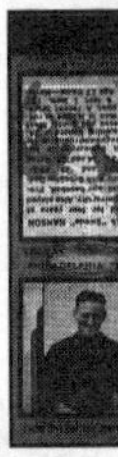

The Diamond Match Co. produced these matchbook covers featuring players of the Chicago Bears and Philadelphia Eagles. They measure approximately 1 1/2" by 4 1/2" (when completely folded out). We've listed below the players alphabetically by team with the Bears first. Each of the covers was produced with either black or brown ink on the text. Three border colors (green, red and tan) were used on the covers, but each player appears with only one border color in black ink and one border color in brown ink. The only exception is Ray Nolting who appears with two border colors with both black and brown ink versions. A picture frame design is included on the left and right sides of the player photo. Don Jackson's and all of the Bears' players' positions are included before the bio. Some collectors consider these two or more separate issues due to the variations and assemble "sets" with either the brown or black printing. Since no price differences are seen between variations and the text and photos are identical for each version, we've listed them together. With all variations, a total of 96-covers were produced. A few of the players are included in the 1937 set as well with only slight differences between the two issues. For those players, we've included the first or last lines of text to help identify the year. Complete covers with matches intact are valued at approximately 1 1/2 times the prices listed below.

	EX-MT	VG-E	GOOD
COMPLETE SET (47)	500.00	220.00	60.00
COMMON MATCHBOOK (1-47)	8.00	3.60	1.00
☐ 1 Carl Brumbaugh	10.00	4.50	1.25
☐ 2 Zuck Carlson	8.00	3.60	1.00
☐ 3 George Corbett	8.00	3.60	1.00
last line (Sigma Alpha Epsilon.)			
☐ 4 John Doehring	8.00	3.60	1.00
last line (is a bachelor.)			
☐ 5 Beattie Feathers	15.00	6.75	1.85
first line (...will be 28 years)			
☐ 6 Dan Fortmann	15.00	6.75	1.85
first line (...April 11, 1916, at)			
☐ 7 George Grosvenor	8.00	3.60	1.00
☐ 8 Bill Hewitt	15.00	6.75	1.85
☐ 9 Luke Johnsos	10.00	4.50	1.25
☐ 10 William Karr	8.00	3.60	1.00
first line (... in Ripley,)			
☐ 11 Eddie Kawal	8.00	3.60	1.00
☐ 12 Jack Manders	10.00	4.50	1.25
last line (200, Height 6 ft. 1 in.)			
☐ 13 Bernie Masterson	10.00	4.50	1.25
last line (Alpha Epsilon. Single.)			
☐ 14 Eddie Michaels	8.00	3.60	1.00
☐ 15 Ookie Miller	8.00	3.60	1.00
☐ 16 Keith Molesworth	10.00	4.50	1.25
last line (5 ft. 9 1/2 in. Weight 168.)			
☐ 17 George Musso	18.00	8.00	2.20
last line (Science degree. Is single.)			
☐ 18 Bronko Nagurski	200.00	90.00	25.00
☐ 19 Ray Nolting	8.00	3.60	1.00
first line (...three years for Cin-)			
☐ 20 Vernon Oech	8.00	3.60	1.00
☐ 21 William(Red) Pollock	8.00	3.60	1.00
☐ 22 Gene Ronzani	10.00	4.50	1.25
last line (is married.)			
☐ 23 Ted Rosequist	8.00	3.60	1.00
☐ 24 Johnny Sisk	10.00	4.50	1.25
☐ 25 Joe Stydahar	15.00	6.75	1.85
last line (Is single.)			
☐ 26 Frank Sullivan	8.00	3.60	1.00
first line (...Loyola U. (New)			
☐ 27 Russell Thompson	8.00	3.60	1.00
last line (Sigma Nu fraternity.)			
☐ 28 Milt Trost	8.00	3.60	1.00
last line (Is single.)			
☐ 29 Joe Zeller	8.00	3.60	1.00
last line (and is single. Sigma Nu.)			
☐ 30 Bill Brian	8.00	3.60	1.00
☐ 31 Art Buss	8.00	3.60	1.00
☐ 32 Joe Carter	8.00	3.60	1.00
☐ 33 Swede Hanson	10.00	4.50	1.25
☐ 34 Don Jackson	8.00	3.60	1.00
☐ 35 John Kusko	8.00	3.60	1.00
☐ 36 Jim Leonard	8.00	3.60	1.00
☐ 37 Jim MacMurdo	8.00	3.60	1.00
☐ 38 Ed Manske	8.00	3.60	1.00
☐ 39 Forrest McPherson	8.00	3.60	1.00
☐ 40 George Mulligan	8.00	3.60	1.00
☐ 41 Joe Pilconis	8.00	3.60	1.00
☐ 42 Hank Reese	8.00	3.60	1.00
☐ 43 Jim Russell	8.00	3.60	1.00
☐ 44 Dave Smukler	8.00	3.60	1.00
☐ 45 Pete Stevens	8.00	3.60	1.00
☐ 46 John Thomason	8.00	3.60	1.00
☐ 47 Vince Zizak	8.00	3.60	1.00

1937 Diamond Matchbooks

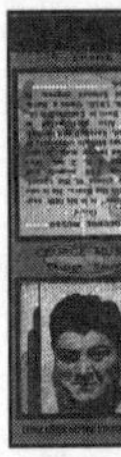

The Diamond Match Co. produced these matchbook covers featuring players of the Chicago Bears. They measure approximately 1 1/2" by 4 1/2" (when completely folded out). The covers look very similar to the 1936 set, but use a slightly smaller print type. Each of the 24-covers was produced with either black or brown ink on the text. Three border colors (green, red and tan) were used on the covers, with all three used for each of the brown ink varieties. Only one border color was used for each cover printed in black ink. Similar to the 1936 issue, a picture frame design is included on the left and right sides of the player photo. Some collectors consider these two separate issues due to the variations and assemble "sets" with either the brown or black printing. Since no price differences are seen between variations and the text and photos are identical for each version, we've listed them together. With all variations, a total of 96-covers were produced. Several of the players are included in the 1936 set as well with only slight differences between the two issues. For those players, we've included the first or last lines of text to help identify the year. Complete covers with matches intact are valued at approximately 1 1/2 times the prices listed below. Although the covers are not numbered, we've assigned numbers alphabetically.

	EX-MT	VG-E	GOOD
COMPLETE SET (24)	200.00	90.00	25.00
COMMON MATCHBOOK (1-24)	8.00	3.60	1.00
☐ 1 Frank Bausch	8.00	3.60	1.00
☐ 2 Delbert Bjork	8.00	3.60	1.00
☐ 3 William(Red) Conkright	8.00	3.60	1.00
☐ 4 George Corbett	8.00	3.60	1.00
last line (ion.)			
☐ 5 John Doehring	8.00	3.60	1.00
last line (baseball.)			
☐ 6 Beattie Feathers	15.00	6.75	1.85
first line (...turned 29 years)			
☐ 7 Dan Fortmann	15.00	6.75	1.85
first line (April 11, 1916, in)			
☐ 8 Sam Francis	8.00	3.60	1.00
☐ 9 Henry Hammond	8.00	3.60	1.00
☐ 10 William Karr	8.00	3.60	1.00
first line (in Ripley, W.)			
☐ 11 Jack Manders	10.00	4.50	1.25
last line (height 6 ft. 1 in.)			
☐ 12 Ed Manske	8.00	3.60	1.00
☐ 13 Bernie Masterson	10.00	4.50	1.25
last line (single.)			
☐ 14 Keith Molesworth	10.00	4.50	1.25
last line (9 1/2 in. Weight 168.)			
☐ 15 George Musso	18.00	8.00	2.20
last line (married.)			
☐ 16 Ray Nolting	8.00	3.60	1.00
first line (...three years for)			
☐ 17 Richard Plasman	8.00	3.60	1.00
☐ 18 Gene Ronzani	10.00	4.50	1.25
last line (married.)			
☐ 19 Joe Stydahar	15.00	6.75	1.85
last line (ing. Is single.)			
☐ 20 Frank Sullivan	8.00	3.60	1.00
first line (Loyola U. New)			
☐ 21 Russell Thompson	8.00	3.60	1.00
last line (year.)			
☐ 22 Milt Trost	8.00	3.60	1.00
last line (pounds. Is single.)			
☐ 23 George Wilson	10.00	4.50	1.25
☐ 24 Joe Zeller	8.00	3.60	1.00
last line (Nu.)			

1938 Diamond Matchbooks

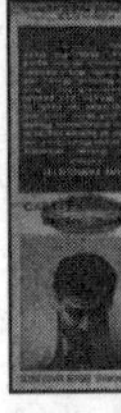

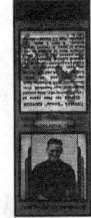

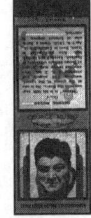

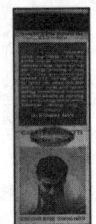

Diamond Match Co. again produced a matchcover set for 1938 featuring players from the Bears and Lions. They measure approximately 1 1/2" by 4 1/2" (when completely folded out). The overall border color is silver with the bio background color being red for the Bears (1-12) and blue for the Lions (13-24). We've assigned card numbers below alphabetically by the two teams included. There are no known variations. Complete covers with matches intact are valued at approximately 1 1/2 times the prices listed below.

	EX-MT	VG-E	GOOD
COMPLETE SET (24)	200.00	90.00	25.00
COMMON MATCHBOOK (1-24)	8.00	3.60	1.00
☐ 1 Delbert Bjork	8.00	3.60	1.00
☐ 2 Raymond Buivid	8.00	3.60	1.00
☐ 3 Gary Famiglietti	8.00	3.60	1.00
☐ 4 Dan Fortmann	15.00	6.75	1.85
☐ 5 Bert Johnson	8.00	3.60	1.00
☐ 6 Jack Manders	10.00	4.50	1.25
☐ 7 Joe Maniaci	10.00	4.50	1.25
☐ 8 Lester McDonald	8.00	3.60	1.00
☐ 9 Frank Sullivan	8.00	3.60	1.00
☐ 10 Robert Swisher	8.00	3.60	1.00
☐ 11 Russell Thompson	8.00	3.60	1.00
☐ 12 Gust Zarnas	8.00	3.60	1.00
☐ 13 Ernie Caddel	10.00	4.50	1.25
☐ 14 Lloyd Cardwell	8.00	3.60	1.00
☐ 15 Dutch Clark	30.00	13.50	3.70
☐ 16 Jack Johnson	8.00	3.60	1.00
☐ 17 Ed Klewicki	8.00	3.60	1.00
☐ 18 James McDonald	8.00	3.60	1.00
☐ 19 James(Monk) Moscrip	8.00	3.60	1.00
☐ 20 Maurice (Babe) Patt	8.00	3.60	1.00
☐ 21 Bob Reynolds	8.00	3.60	1.00
☐ 22 Kent Ryan	8.00	3.60	1.00
☐ 23 Fred Vanzo	8.00	3.60	1.00
☐ 24 Alex Wojciechowicz	25.00	11.00	3.10

1992 Diamond Stickers

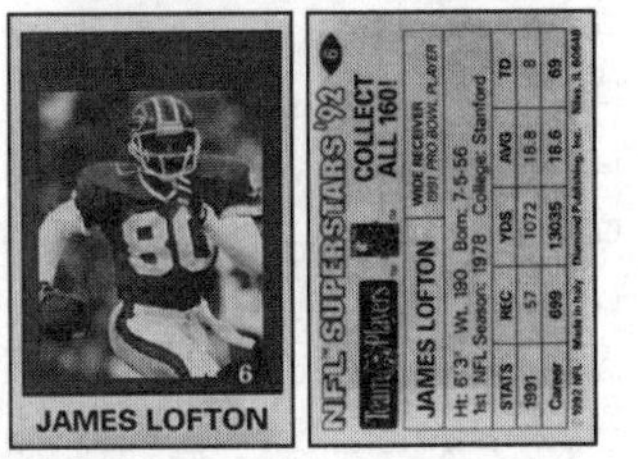

Produced by Diamond Publishing Inc., the first series of NFL Superstar stickers consists of 160 stickers, each measuring approximately 1 15/16" by 2 15/16". The stickers were sold in six-sticker packets and could be pasted in a 36-page sticker album. Eight hundred autographed stickers were randomly inserted throughout the packs; apparently, each of the featured stars (Mark Carrier, Cornelius Bennett, Chris Miller, and Rob Moore) signed 200 each. The fronts feature action color player photos framed by a team-color coded inner border and a white outer border. The team name appears in the team's accent color within the top border. The horizontally oriented backs are white with purple print and carry biographical and statistical information. The stickers are numbered on the back and checklisted alphabetically according to teams in the AFC and NFC.

	MINT	NRMT	EXC
COMPLETE SET (160)	20.00	9.00	2.50
COMMON CARD (1-160)	.10	.05	.01
☐ 1 Super Bowl XXVI logo	.10	.05	.01
(Top portion)			
☐ 2 Super Bowl XXVI logo	.10	.05	.01
(Bottom portion)			
☐ 3 Jim Kelly	.25	.11	.03
☐ 4 Thurman Thomas	.25	.11	.03
☐ 5 Andre Reed	.25	.11	.03
☐ 6 James Lofton	.20	.09	.03
☐ 7 Cornelius Bennett	.20	.09	.03
☐ 8 Boomer Esiason	.20	.09	.03
☐ 9 Harold Green	.10	.05	.01
☐ 10 Anthony Munoz	.25	.11	.03
☐ 11 Mitchell Price	.10	.05	.01
☐ 12 Lewis Billups	.10	.05	.01
☐ 13 Bernie Kosar	.20	.09	.03
☐ 14 Eric Metcalf	.25	.11	.03
☐ 15 Michael Dean Perry	.20	.09	.03
☐ 16 Van Waiters	.10	.05	.01
☐ 17 Brian Brennan	.10	.05	.01
☐ 18 John Elway	.75	.35	.09
☐ 19 Gaston Green	.10	.05	.01
☐ 20 Vance Johnson	.10	.05	.01
☐ 21 Dennis Smith	.10	.05	.01
☐ 22 Clarence Kay	.10	.05	.01
☐ 23 Warren Moon	.25	.11	.03
☐ 24 Haywood Jeffires	.20	.09	.03
☐ 25 Cris Dishman	.10	.05	.01
☐ 26 Bubba McDowell	.10	.05	.01
☐ 27 Ray Childress	.20	.09	.03
☐ 28 Eric Dickerson	.25	.11	.03
☐ 29 Jessie Hester	.10	.05	.01
☐ 30 Clarence Verdin	.10	.05	.01
☐ 31 Bill Brooks	.20	.09	.03
☐ 32 Albert Bentley	.10	.05	.01
☐ 33 Christian Okoye	.20	.09	.03
☐ 34 Derrick Thomas	.25	.11	.03
☐ 35 Dino Hackett	.10	.05	.01
☐ 36 Deron Cherry	.10	.05	.01
☐ 37 Bill Maas	.10	.05	.01
☐ 38 Todd Marinovich	.10	.05	.01
☐ 39 Roger Craig	.20	.09	.03
☐ 40 Greg Townsend	.10	.05	.01
☐ 41 Ronnie Lott	.20	.09	.03

☐ 42 Howie Long	.25	.11	.03
☐ 43 Dan Marino	2.00	.90	.25
☐ 44 Mark Clayton	.20	.09	.03
☐ 45 Sammie Smith	.10	.05	.01
☐ 46 Jim Jensen	.10	.05	.01
☐ 47 Reggie Roby	.10	.05	.01
☐ 48 Brent Williams	.10	.05	.01
☐ 49 Andre Tippett	.10	.05	.01
☐ 50 John Stephens	.10	.05	.01
☐ 51 Johnny Rembert	.10	.05	.01
☐ 52 Irving Fryar	.20	.09	.03
☐ 53 Ken O'Brien	.10	.05	.01
☐ 54 Al Toon	.20	.09	.03
☐ 55 Brad Baxter	.20	.09	.03
☐ 56 James Hasty	.10	.05	.01
☐ 57 Rob Moore	.20	.09	.03
☐ 58 Neil O'Donnell	.20	.09	.03
☐ 59 Bubby Brister	.20	.09	.03
☐ 60 Louis Lipps	.10	.05	.01
☐ 61 Merril Hoge	.10	.05	.01
☐ 62 Gary Anderson K	.10	.05	.01
☐ 63 John Friesz	.20	.09	.03
☐ 64 Junior Seau	.25	.11	.03
☐ 65 Leslie O'Neal	.10	.05	.01
☐ 66 Rod Bernstine	.10	.05	.01
☐ 67 Burt Grossman	.10	.05	.01
☐ 68 Brian Blades	.20	.09	.03
☐ 69 Cortez Kennedy	.20	.09	.03
☐ 70 David Wyman	.10	.05	.01
☐ 71 John L. Williams	.10	.05	.01
☐ 72 Robert Blackmon	.10	.05	.01
☐ 73 Checklist 33-48 Jim Kelly	.20	.09	.03
☐ 74 Checklist 49-64 Ronnie Lott	.10	.05	.01
☐ 75 Jerry Rice Andre Reed	.50	.23	.06
☐ 76 Jay Novacek Dennis Smith	.25	.11	.03
☐ 77 Mark Rypien Jim Kelly	.20	.09	.03
☐ 78 Pat Swilling Derrick Thomas	.20	.09	.03
☐ 79 Deion Sanders Cris Dishman	.25	.11	.03
☐ 80 Mel Gray Gaston Green	.10	.05	.01
☐ 81 Earnest Byner Christian Okoye	.10	.05	.01
☐ 82 Eric Allen Ronnie Lott	.10	.05	.01
☐ 83 Mike Singletary Junior Seau	.20	.09	.03
☐ 84 Andre Rison Haywood Jeffires	.25	.11	.03
☐ 85 Checklist 65-80 Steve Young	.30	.14	.04
☐ 86 Checklist 81-96 Pat Swilling	.10	.05	.01
☐ 87 Chris Miller	.20	.09	.03
☐ 88 Andre Rison	.25	.11	.03
☐ 89 Deion Sanders	.50	.23	.06
☐ 90 Michael Haynes	.10	.05	.01
☐ 91 Tim Green	.10	.05	.01
☐ 92 Jim Harbaugh	.25	.11	.03
☐ 93 Mark Carrier DB	.10	.05	.01
☐ 94 Mike Singletary	.20	.09	.03
☐ 95 William Perry	.20	.09	.03
☐ 96 Donnell Woolford	.10	.05	.01
☐ 97 Troy Aikman	1.00	.45	.12
☐ 98 Michael Irvin	.25	.11	.03
☐ 99 Russell Maryland	.10	.05	.01
☐ 100 Jay Novacek	.25	.11	.03
☐ 101 Ken Norton Jr.	.25	.11	.03
☐ 102 Mel Gray	.10	.05	.01
☐ 103 Bennie Blades	.10	.05	.01
☐ 104 Rodney Peete	.20	.09	.03
☐ 105 Brett Perriman	.25	.11	.03
☐ 106 William White	.10	.05	.01
☐ 107 Vai Sikahema	.10	.05	.01
☐ 108 Vince Workman	.10	.05	.01
☐ 109 Jeff Query	.10	.05	.01
☐ 110 Sterling Sharpe	.20	.09	.03
☐ 111 Tony Mandarich	.10	.05	.01
☐ 112 Jim Everett	.20	.09	.03
☐ 113 Flipper Anderson	.10	.05	.01
☐ 114 Robert Delpino	.10	.05	.01
☐ 115 Darryl Henley	.10	.05	.01
☐ 116 Henry Ellard	.20	.09	.03
☐ 117 Wade Wilson	.10	.05	.01
☐ 118 Anthony Carter	.20	.09	.03
☐ 119 Chris Doleman	.20	.09	.03
☐ 120 Cris Carter	.25	.11	.03
☐ 121 Henry Thomas	.10	.05	.01
☐ 122 Steve Walsh	.20	.09	.03
☐ 123 Pat Swilling	.20	.09	.03
☐ 124 Dalton Hilliard	.10	.05	.01
☐ 125 Floyd Turner	.10	.05	.01
☐ 126 Craig Heyward	.20	.09	.03
☐ 127 Jeff Hostetler	.20	.09	.03
☐ 128 Phil Simms	.20	.09	.03
☐ 129 Lawrence Taylor	.25	.11	.03
☐ 130 Mark Ingram	.10	.05	.01
☐ 131 Leonard Marshall	.10	.05	.01
☐ 132 Randall Cunningham	.20	.09	.03
☐ 133 Eric Allen	.10	.05	.01
☐ 134 Keith Byars	.10	.05	.01
☐ 135 Fred Barnett	.25	.11	.03
☐ 136 Wes Hopkins	.10	.05	.01
☐ 137 Ernie Jones	.10	.05	.01
☐ 138 Johnny Johnson	.10	.05	.01
☐ 139 Anthony Thompson	.10	.05	.01
☐ 140 Timm Rosenbach	.10	.05	.01
☐ 141 Randal Hill	.10	.05	.01
☐ 142 Steve Young	.75	.35	.09
☐ 143 Jerry Rice	1.00	.45	.12
☐ 144 Tom Rathman	.10	.05	.01
☐ 145 Charles Haley	.20	.09	.03
☐ 146 John Taylor	.20	.09	.03
☐ 147 Vinny Testaverde	.25	.11	.03
☐ 148 Gary Anderson RB	.10	.05	.01
☐ 149 Broderick Thomas	.10	.05	.01
☐ 150 Mark Carrier WR	.20	.09	.03
☐ 151 Ian Beckles	.10	.05	.01
☐ 152 Mark Rypien	.10	.05	.01
☐ 153 Earnest Byner	.10	.05	.01
☐ 154 Gary Clark	.25	.11	.03
☐ 155 Monte Coleman	.10	.05	.01
☐ 156 Ricky Ervins	.10	.05	.01
☐ 157 Earnest Byner	.10	.05	.01
☐ 158 Jim Kelly Fred Stokes Jumpy Geathers	.25	.11	.03
☐ 159 Checklist 129-144 Mark Rypien	.10	.05	.01
☐ 160 Mark Rypien	.20	.09	.03

1967 Dolphins Royal Castle

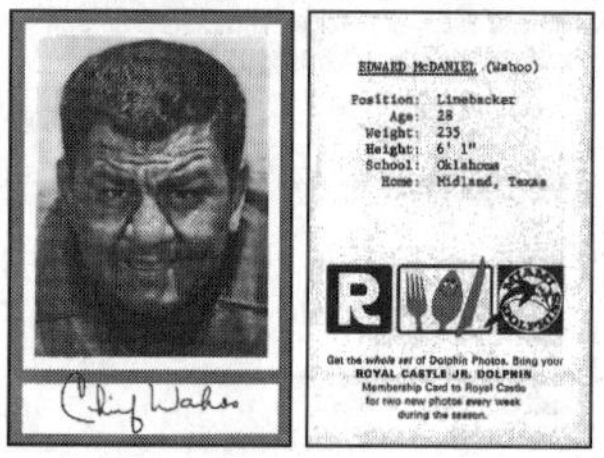

This 27-card set was issued by Royal Castle, a south Florida hamburger stand, at a rate of two new cards every week during the season. These unnumbered cards measure approximately 3" by 4 3/8". The front features a black and white (almost sepia-toned) posed photo of the player enframed by an orange border, with the player's signature below the photo. Biographical information is given on the back (including player's nickname where appropriate), along with the logos for the Miami Dolphins and Royal Castle. This set features a card of Bob Griese during his rookie season. There may be a 28th card: George Wilson Jr. There are 16 cards that are easier than the others; rather than calling these double prints, the other eleven cards are marked as SP's in the checklist below.

	NRMT	VG-E	GOOD
COMPLETE SET (27)	2500.00	1100.00	300.00
COMMON CARD (1-27)	30.00	13.50	3.70
COMMON CARD SP	100.00	45.00	12.50
☐ 1 Joe Auer SP	100.00	45.00	12.50
☐ 2 Tom Beier	30.00	13.50	3.70
☐ 3 Mel Branch	30.00	13.50	3.70
☐ 4 Jon Brittenum	35.00	16.00	4.40
☐ 5 George Chesser	30.00	13.50	3.70
☐ 6 Edward Cooke	30.00	13.50	3.70
☐ 7 Frank Emanuel SP	125.00	55.00	15.50
☐ 8 Tom Erlandson SP	100.00	45.00	12.50
☐ 9 Norm Evans SP	150.00	70.00	19.00
☐ 10 Bob Griese SP	750.00	350.00	95.00
☐ 11 Abner Haynes SP	200.00	90.00	25.00
☐ 12 Jerry Hopkins SP	100.00	45.00	12.50
☐ 13 Frank Jackson	30.00	13.50	3.70
☐ 14 Billy Joe	35.00	16.00	4.40
☐ 15 Wahoo McDaniel	135.00	60.00	17.00
☐ 16 Robert Neff	30.00	13.50	3.70
☐ 17 Billy Neighbors	35.00	16.00	4.40
☐ 18 Rick Norton	30.00	13.50	3.70
☐ 19 Bob Petrich	30.00	13.50	3.70
☐ 20 Jim Riley	30.00	13.50	3.70
☐ 21 John Stofa SP	150.00	70.00	19.00
☐ 22 Lavern Torczon	30.00	13.50	3.70
☐ 23 Howard Twilley	75.00	34.00	9.50
☐ 24 Jim Warren SP	100.00	45.00	12.50
☐ 25 Dick Westmoreland	30.00	13.50	3.70
☐ 26 Maxie Williams SP	150.00	70.00	19.00
☐ 27 George Wilson Sr. SP (Head Coach)	150.00	70.00	19.00

1970 Dolphins Team Issue

The Miami Dolphins likely issued this series of player photos over a two or three year period around 1970. The format is the same for each photo with only subtle differences in the type (size and style) and player position (some spelled out and others initials only). Each of these black-and-white photos measures approximately 5" by 7" and is blankbacked and unnumbered.

	NRMT-MT	EXC	G-VG
COMPLETE SET (12)	40.00	18.00	5.00
COMMON CARD (1-12)	3.00	1.35	.35
☐ 1 Dean Brown	3.00	1.35	.35
☐ 2 Frank Cornish	3.00	1.35	.35
☐ 3 Ted Davis	3.00	1.35	.35
☐ 4 Norm Evans	5.00	2.20	.60
☐ 5 Hubert Ginn	3.00	1.35	.35
☐ 6 Mike Kolen	3.00	1.35	.35
☐ 7 Bob Kuechenberg	5.00	2.20	.60
☐ 8 Stan Mitchell	3.00	1.35	.35
☐ 9 Lloyd Mumphord	4.00	1.80	.50
☐ 10 Dick Palmer	3.00	1.35	.35
☐ 11 Barry Pryor	3.00	1.35	.35
☐ 12 Bill Stanfill	4.00	1.80	.50

1974 Dolphins All-Pro Graphics

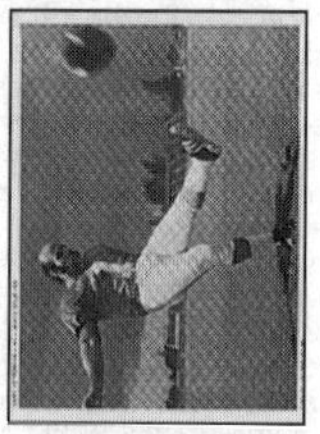

Each of these ten photos measures approximately 8 1/4" by 10 3/4". The fronts feature color action photos bordered in white. The player's name, position, and team name appear in the top border, while the copyright year (1974) and the manufacturer "All Pro Graphics, Inc." are printed in the bottom white border at the left. It is reported that several of these photos do not have the tagline in the lower left corner. The backs are blank. The photos are unnumbered and checklisted below in alphabetical order.

	NRMT-MT	EXC	G-VG
COMPLETE SET (10)	90.00	40.00	11.00
COMMON CARD (1-10)	6.00	2.70	.75
☐ 1 Dick Anderson	10.00	4.50	1.25
☐ 2 Nick Buoniconti	12.00	5.50	1.50
☐ 3 Larry Csonka	15.00	6.75	1.85
☐ 4 Manny Fernandez	6.00	2.70	.75
☐ 5 Bob Griese	20.00	9.00	2.50
☐ 6 Jim Kiick	10.00	4.50	1.25
☐ 7 Earl Morrall	12.00	5.50	1.50
☐ 8 Mercury Morris	10.00	4.50	1.25
☐ 9 Jake Scott	7.50	3.40	.95
☐ 10 Garo Yepremian	6.00	2.70	.75

1974 Dolphins Team Issue

The Miami Dolphins likely issued this series of player photos over a two or three year period around 1974. The format is the same for each photo with only subtle differences in the type size and style. The photos are similar to the 1970 release but feature a distinctly different type style. Each of these black-and-white photos measures approximately 5" by 7" and is blankbacked and unnumbered.

	NRMT-MT	EXC	G-VG
COMPLETE SET (19)	60.00	27.00	7.50
COMMON CARD (1-19)	3.00	1.35	.35
☐ 1 Charlie Babb	3.00	1.35	.35
☐ 2 Mel Baker	3.00	1.35	.35
☐ 3 Bruce Bannon	3.00	1.35	.35
☐ 4 Norm Evans	5.00	2.20	.60
☐ 5 Hubert Ginn	3.00	1.35	.35
☐ 6 Irv Goode	3.00	1.35	.35
☐ 7 Bob Heinz	3.00	1.35	.35
☐ 8 Curtis Johnson	3.00	1.35	.35
☐ 9 Bob Kuechenberg	4.00	1.80	.50
☐ 10 Nat Moore	6.00	2.70	.75
☐ 11 Wayne Moore	3.00	1.35	.35
☐ 12 Lloyd Mumphord	4.00	1.80	.50
☐ 13 Ed Newman	3.00	1.35	.35
☐ 14 Don Reese	3.00	1.35	.35
☐ 15 Bill Stanfill	4.00	1.80	.50
☐ 16 Henry Stuckey	3.00	1.35	.35
☐ 17 Doug Swift	4.00	1.80	.50
☐ 18 Jeris White	3.00	1.35	.35
☐ 19 Tom Wickert	3.00	1.35	.35

1980 Dolphins Police

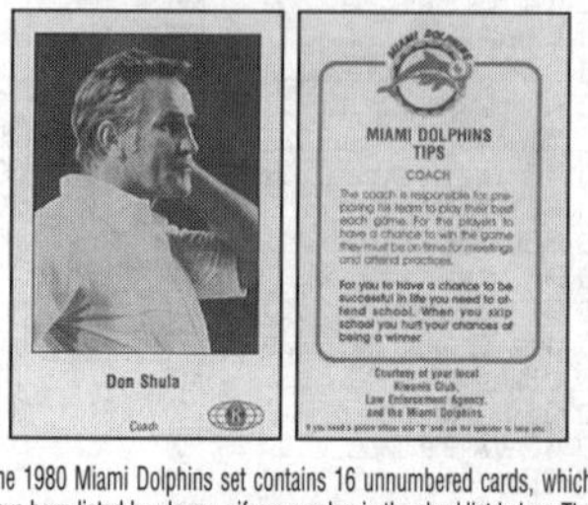

The 1980 Miami Dolphins set contains 16 unnumbered cards, which have been listed by player uniform number in the checklist below. The caros measure approximately 2 5/8" by 4 1/8". The set was sponsored by the Kiwanis Club, the local law enforcement agency, and the Miami Dolphins. The backs contain "Dolphins Tips" and the Miami Dolphins logo. The backs are printed in black with blue accent on white card stock. The fronts contain the Kiwanis logo, but not the Dolphins logo as in the following year. The card of Larry Little is reportedly more difficult to obtain than other cards in this set.

	MINT	NRMT	EXC
COMPLETE SET (16)	90.00	40.00	11.00
COMMON CARD	3.00	1.35	.35
☐ 5 Uwe Von Schamann	3.00	1.35	.35
☐ 10 Don Strock	6.00	2.70	.75
☐ 12 Bob Griese	15.00	6.75	1.85
☐ 22 Tony Nathan	6.00	2.70	.75
☐ 24 Delvin Williams	6.00	2.70	.75
☐ 25 Tim Foley	4.00	1.80	.50
☐ 50 Larry Gordon	3.00	1.35	.35
☐ 58 Kim Bokamper	3.00	1.35	.35
☐ 64 Ed Newman	3.00	1.35	.35
☐ 66 Larry Little SP	20.00	9.00	2.50
☐ 67 Bob Kuechenberg	6.00	2.70	.75
☐ 73 Bob Baumhower	4.00	1.80	.50
☐ 77 A.J. Duhe	6.00	2.70	.75
☐ 82 Duriel Harris	4.00	1.80	.50
☐ 89 Nat Moore	6.00	2.70	.75
☐ NNO Don Shula CO	15.00	6.75	1.85

1981 Dolphins Police

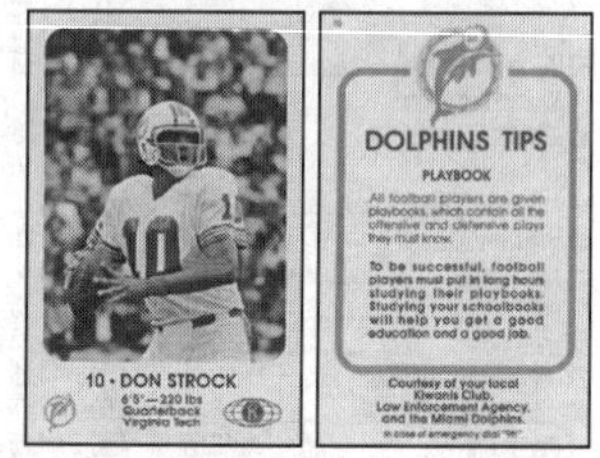

The 1981 Miami Dolphins police set consists of 16 numbered cards. The cards measure approximately 2 5/8" by 4 1/8". Player uniform numbers also appear on the fronts of the cards, as does a Kiwanis and blue Dolphins logo. The set is sponsored by the local Kiwanis Club, the local law enforcement agency, and the Dolphins. The backs feature the Dolphins logo and "Dolphins Tips". Card backs are printed in black with gold and blue accent on thin white card stock.

	MINT	NRMT	EXC
COMPLETE SET (16)	20.00	9.00	2.50
COMMON CARD (1-16)	1.00	.45	.12
☐ 1 Duriel Harris	1.50	.70	.19
☐ 2 Bob Kuechenberg	1.50	.70	.19
☐ 3 Don Bessillieu	1.00	.45	.12
☐ 4 Gerald Small	1.00	.45	.12
☐ 5 David Woodley	1.50	.70	.19
☐ 6 Don McNeal	1.00	.45	.12
☐ 7 Nat Moore	2.00	.90	.25
☐ 8 A.J. Duhe	1.50	.70	.19
☐ 9 Glenn Blackwood	1.00	.45	.12
☐ 10 Don Strock	2.00	.90	.25
☐ 11 Doug Betters	1.00	.45	.12
☐ 12 George Roberts	1.00	.45	.12
☐ 13 Bob Baumhower	1.50	.70	.19
☐ 14 Kim Bokamper	1.00	.45	.12
☐ 15 Tony Nathan	2.00	.90	.25
☐ 16 Don Shula CO	5.00	2.20	.60

1982 Dolphins Police

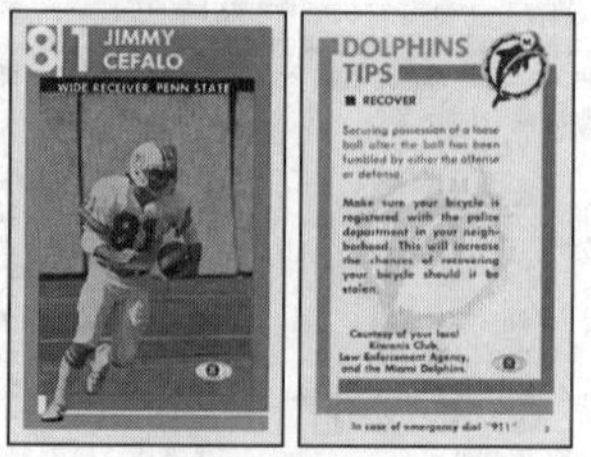

The 1982 Miami Dolphins set of 16 numbered cards is one of the most attractive of the police sets. The cards measure approximately 2 5/8" by 4 1/8". The orange and greenish-blue frame line on the front contains the player's number and name. The Kiwanis logo is also contained on the front. The backs are printed in black, orange, greenish-blue, and blue ink and feature "Dolphins Tips," the Dolphins logo, and the Kiwanis logo. The set is sponsored by the Kiwanis Club, the local law enforcement agency, and the Dolphins. Shula and Von Schamann are supposedly a little tougher to find than the other cards in the set.

	MINT	NRMT	EXC
COMPLETE SET (16)	30.00	13.50	3.70
COMMON CARD (1-16)	1.00	.45	.12
☐ 1 Don Shula CO SP	9.00	4.00	1.10
☐ 2 Uwe Von Schamann SP	4.00	1.80	.50
☐ 3 Jimmy Cefalo	1.50	.70	.19
☐ 4 Andra Franklin	1.50	.70	.19

	MINT	NRMT	EXC
☐ 5 Larry Gordon	1.00	.45	.12
☐ 6 Nat Moore	2.00	.90	.25
☐ 7 Bob Baumhower	1.50	.70	.19
☐ 8 A.J. Duhe	1.50	.70	.19
☐ 9 Tony Nathan	2.00	.90	.25
☐ 10 Glenn Blackwood	1.00	.45	.12
☐ 11 Don Strock	2.00	.90	.25
☐ 12 David Woodley	1.50	.70	.19
☐ 13 Kim Bokamper	1.00	.45	.12
☐ 14 Bob Kuechenberg	1.50	.70	.19
☐ 15 Duriel Harris	1.50	.70	.19
☐ 16 Fd Newman	1.00	.45	.12

1983 Dolphins Police

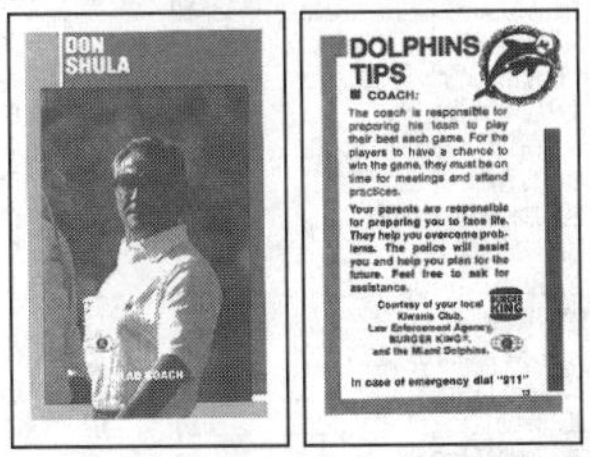

This numbered set of 16 cards features the Miami Dolphins. Cards measure approximately 2 5/8" by 4 1/8". The cards are numbered on the back in the bottom right corner. The cards look very similar to the 1982 Police Dolphins set. Card backs feature black print with orange and aquamarine accent on white card stock. The cards were sponsored by Kiwanis, Law Enforcement Agencies, Burger King, and the Miami Dolphins. The Burger King and Kiwanis logos both appear on the fronts of the cards.

	MINT	NRMT	EXC
COMPLETE SET (16)	12.00	5.50	1.50
COMMON CARD (1-16)	.60	.25	.07
☐ 1 Earnie Rhone	.60	.25	.07
☐ 2 Andra Franklin	.75	.35	.09
☐ 3 Eric Laakso	.60	.25	.07
☐ 4 Joe Rose	.60	.25	.07
☐ 5 David Woodley	1.00	.45	.12
☐ 6 Uwe Von Schamann	.60	.25	.07
☐ 7 Eddie Hill	.60	.25	.07
☐ 8 Bruce Hardy	.60	.25	.07
☐ 9 Woody Bennett	.60	.25	.07
☐ 10 Fulton Walker	.75	.35	.09
☐ 11 Lyle Blackwood	.60	.25	.07
☐ 12 A.J. Duhe	1.00	.45	.12
☐ 13 Bob Baumhower	.75	.35	.09
☐ 14 Duriel Harris	.75	.35	.09
☐ 15 Bob Brudzinski	.75	.35	.09
☐ 16 Don Shula CO	3.00	1.35	.35

1984 Dolphins Police

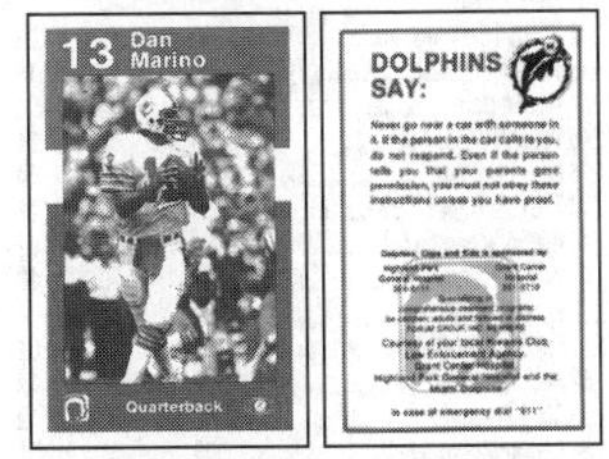

This unnumbered 17-card set features the Miami Dolphins. The Mark Clayton card was added to the set after the first sixteen cards had been distributed. Cards measure approximately 2 5/8" by 4 1/8". Cards are listed below alphabetically by player's name. The Dan Marino card is noteworthy in that it features Marino during his rookie year for cards.

	MINT	NRMT	EXC
COMPLETE SET (17)	30.00	13.50	3.70
COMMON CARD (1-17)	.50	.23	.06
☐ 1 Bob Baumhower	.75	.35	.09
☐ 2 Doug Betters	.75	.35	.09
☐ 3 Glenn Blackwood	.50	.23	.06
☐ 4 Kim Bokamper	.50	.23	.06
☐ 5 Dolfan Denny (Mascot)	.50	.23	.06
☐ 6 A.J. Duhe	.75	.35	.09
☐ 7 Mark Duper	2.00	.90	.25
☐ 8 Jim Jensen	.75	.35	.09
☐ 9 Dan Marino	25.00	11.00	3.10
☐ 10 Don McNeal	.50	.23	.06
☐ 11 Nat Moore	1.00	.45	.12
☐ 12 Tony Nathan	1.00	.45	.12
☐ 13 Ed Newman	.50	.23	.06
☐ 14 Don Shula CO	2.00	.90	.25
☐ 15 Dwight Stephenson	.75	.35	.09
☐ 16 Fulton Walker	.50	.23	.06
☐ 17 Mark Clayton SP	4.00	1.80	.50

1985 Dolphins Police

This 16-card set is numbered on the back. The card backs are printed in black ink on white card stock. Cards measure 2 5/8" by 4 1/8". The

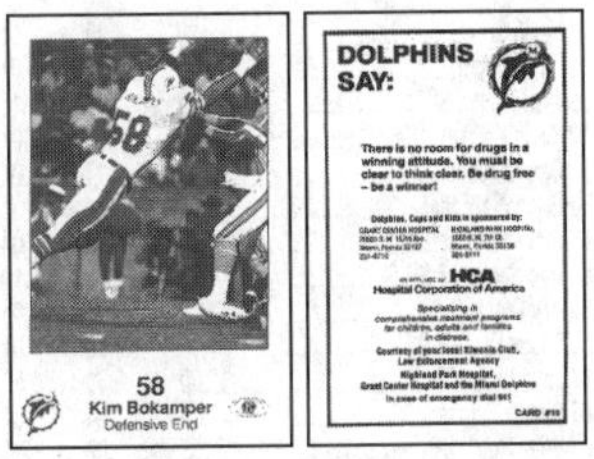

set was sponsored by Kiwanis, Hospital Corporation of America, the Dolphins, and area law enforcement agencies. Uniform numbers are printed on the card front above the player's name.

	MINT	NRMT	EXC
COMPLETE SET (16)	20.00	9.00	2.50
COMMON CARD (1-16)	.40	.18	.05
☐ 1 William Judson	.40	.18	.05
☐ 2 Fulton Walker	.50	.23	.06
☐ 3 Mark Clayton	1.50	.70	.19
☐ 4 Lyle Blackwood and Glenn Blackwood (Bruise Brothers)	.50	.23	.06
☐ 5 Dan Marino	12.00	5.50	1.50
☐ 6 Reggie Roby	.75	.35	.09
☐ 7 Doug Betters	.50	.23	.06
☐ 8 Jay Brophy	.40	.18	.05
☐ 9 Dolfan Denny (Mascot)	.40	.18	.05
☐ 10 Kim Bokamper	.40	.18	.05
☐ 11 Mark Duper	1.25	.55	.16
☐ 12 Nat Moore	.75	.35	.09
☐ 13 Mike Kozlowski	.40	.18	.05
☐ 14 Don Shula CO	1.50	.70	.19
☐ 15 Don McNeal	.40	.18	.05
☐ 16 Tony Nathan	.75	.35	.09

1986 Dolphins Police

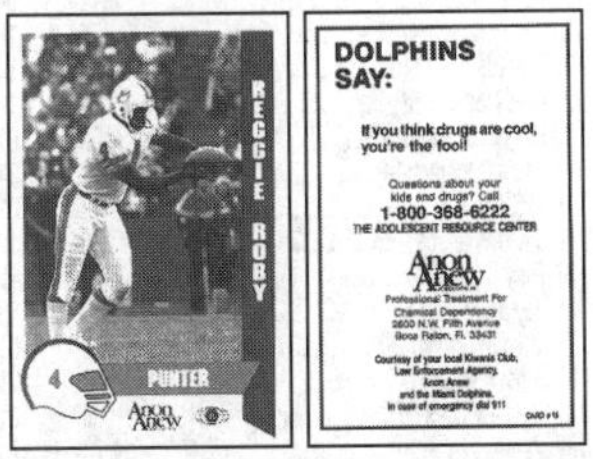

This 16-card set is numbered on the card backs, which are printed in black ink on white card stock. Cards measure approximately 2 5/8" by 4 1/8". The set was sponsored by Kiwanis, Anon Anew, the Dolphins, and area law enforcement agencies. Uniform numbers are printed on the front of the card.

	MINT	NRMT	EXC
COMPLETE SET (16)	15.00	6.75	1.85
COMMON CARD (1-16)	.40	.18	.05
☐ 1 Dwight Stephenson	.75	.35	.09
☐ 2 Bob Baumhower	.50	.23	.06
☐ 3 Dolfan Denny (Mascot)	.40	.18	.05
☐ 4 Don Shula CO	1.50	.70	.19
☐ 5 Dan Marino	8.00	3.60	1.00
☐ 6 Tony Nathan	.75	.35	.09
☐ 7 Mark Duper	1.25	.55	.16
☐ 8 John Offerdahl	1.00	.45	.12
☐ 9 Fuad Reveiz	.40	.18	.05
☐ 10 Hugh Green	.50	.23	.06
☐ 11 Lorenzo Hampton	.50	.23	.06
☐ 12 Mark Clayton	1.50	.70	.19
☐ 13 Nat Moore	.75	.35	.09
☐ 14 Bob Brudzinski	.40	.18	.05
☐ 15 Reggie Roby	.50	.23	.06
☐ 16 T.J. Turner	.50	.23	.06

1987 Dolphins Holsum

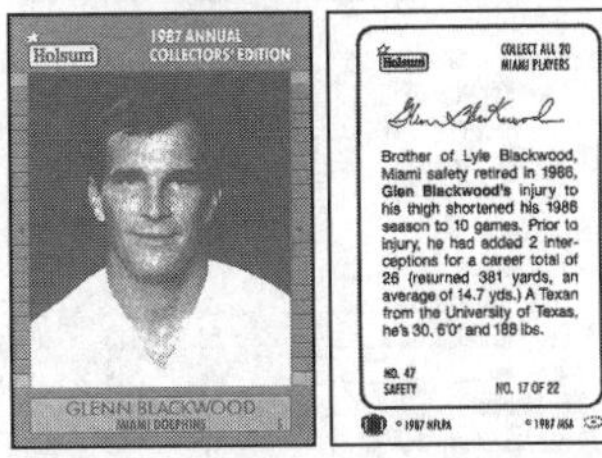

This 22-card set features players of the Miami Dolphins; cards were available only in Holsum Bread packages. The set was co-produced by Mike Schechter Associates on behalf of the NFL Players Association. The cards are standard size, 2 1/2" by 3 1/2", and are done in full color. Card fronts have a color photo within a green border and the backs are printed in black ink on white card stock. Cards are numbered on the back.

	MINT	NRMT	EXC
COMPLETE SET (22)	60.00	27.00	7.50
COMMON CARD (1-22)	2.00	.90	.25
☐ 1 Bob Baumhower	3.00	1.35	.35
☐ 2 Mark Brown	2.00	.90	.25
☐ 3 Mark Clayton	5.00	2.20	.60
☐ 4 Mark Duper	4.00	1.80	.50
☐ 5 Roy Foster	2.00	.90	.25
☐ 6 Hugh Green	3.00	1.35	.35
☐ 7 Lorenzo Hampton	2.00	.90	.25
☐ 8 William Judson	2.00	.90	.25
☐ 9 George Little	2.00	.90	.25
☐ 10 Dan Marino	35.00	16.00	4.40
☐ 11 Nat Moore	3.00	1.35	.35
☐ 12 Tony Nathan	3.00	1.35	.35
☐ 13 John Offerdahl	4.00	1.80	.50
☐ 14 James Pruitt	2.00	.90	.25
☐ 15 Fuad Reveiz	2.00	.90	.25
☐ 16 Dwight Stephenson	3.00	1.35	.35
☐ 17 Glenn Blackwood	2.00	.90	.25
☐ 18 Bruce Hardy	2.00	.90	.25
☐ 19 Reggie Roby	2.00	.90	.25
☐ 20 Bob Brudzinski	2.00	.90	.25
☐ 21 Ron Jaworski	3.00	1.35	.35
☐ 22 T.J. Turner	2.00	.90	.25

1987 Dolphins Police

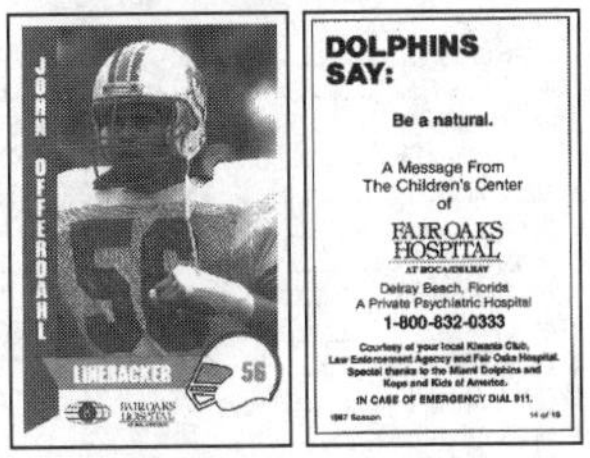

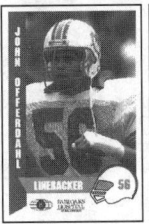

This 16-card set is numbered on the back and measures approximately 2 5/8" by 4 1/8". The set was sponsored by Kiwanis, Children's Center of Fair Oaks Hospital at Boca/Delray, the Dolphins, and area law enforcement agencies. Uniform numbers are printed on the front of the card. Reportedly approximately three million cards were produced for this promotion. The Dwight Stephenson card is considered more difficult to find than the other cards in the set.

	MINT	NRMT	EXC
COMPLETE SET (16)	20.00	9.00	2.50
COMMON CARD (1-16)	.60	.25	.07
☐ 1 Joe Robbie OWN	.75	.35	.09
☐ 2 Glenn Blackwood	.60	.25	.07
☐ 3 Mark Duper	1.25	.55	.16
☐ 4 Fuad Reveiz	.60	.25	.07
☐ 5 Dolfan Denny (Mascot)	.60	.25	.07
☐ 6 Dwight Stephenson SP	4.00	1.80	.50
☐ 7 Hugh Green	.75	.35	.09
☐ 8 Larry Csonka (All-Time Great)	2.50	1.10	.30
☐ 9 Bud Brown	.60	.25	.07
☐ 10 Don Shula CO	1.50	.70	.19
☐ 11 T.J. Turner	.60	.25	.07
☐ 12 Reggie Roby	.75	.35	.09
☐ 13 Dan Marino	10.00	4.50	1.25
☐ 14 John Offerdahl	1.00	.45	.12
☐ 15 Bruce Hardy	.60	.25	.07
☐ 16 Lorenzo Hampton	.75	.35	.09

1988 Dolphins Holsum

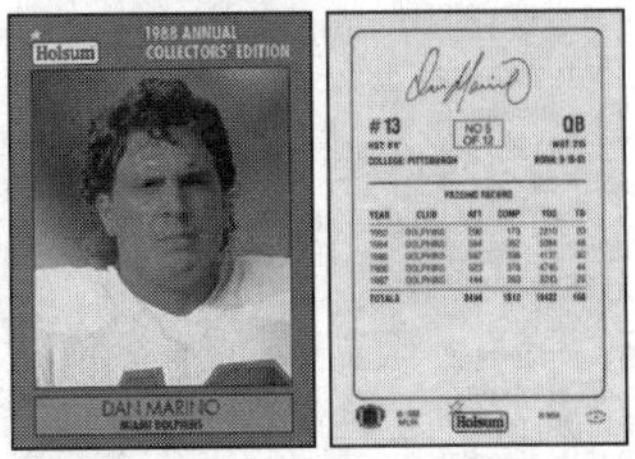

This 12-card set features players of the Miami Dolphins; cards were available only in Holsum Bread packages. The set was co-produced by Mike Schechter Associates on behalf of the NFL Players Association. The cards are standard size, 2 1/2" by 3 1/2", and are done in full color. Card fronts have a color photo within a green border and the backs are printed in black ink on white card stock. The cards are numbered on the back.

	MINT	NRMT	EXC
COMPLETE SET (12)	40.00	18.00	5.00
COMMON CARD (1-12)	1.50	.70	.19
☐ 1 Mark Clayton	3.00	1.35	.35
☐ 2 Dwight Stephenson	2.00	.90	.25
☐ 3 Mark Duper	2.50	1.10	.30
☐ 4 John Offerdahl	2.00	.90	.25
☐ 5 Dan Marino	25.00	11.00	3.10
☐ 6 T.J. Turner	1.50	.70	.19
☐ 7 Lorenzo Hampton	1.50	.70	.19
☐ 8 Bruce Hardy	1.50	.70	.19
☐ 9 Fuad Reveiz	1.50	.70	.19
☐ 10 Reggie Roby	2.00	.90	.25
☐ 11 William Judson	1.50	.70	.19
☐ 12 Bob Brudzinski	2.00	.90	.25

1995 Dolphins Chevron Pin Cards

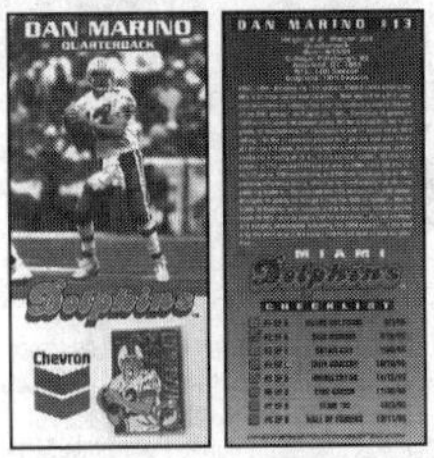

Chevron released these 8-cards as a promotion throughout the 1995 season. The cards themselves are unnumbered, but have been arranged below in accordance with the checklist printed on each cardback. A lapel pin was included with and attached to each card in the lower right hand corner. Each card measures approximately 3" by 5" and includes a color photo on front and text on back along with a checklist.

	MINT	NRMT	EXC
COMPLETE SET (8)	20.00	9.00	2.50
COMMON CARD (1-8)	2.00	.90	.25
☐ 1 Miami Dolphins	2.00	.90	.25
☐ 2 Dan Marino	10.00	4.50	1.25
☐ 3 Bryan Cox	2.00	.90	.25
☐ 4 Troy Vincent	2.00	.90	.25
☐ 5 Irving Fryar	3.00	1.35	.35
☐ 6 Eric Green	2.00	.90	.25
☐ 7 Team '95	3.00	1.35	.35
☐ 8 Hall of Famers	4.00	1.80	.50

1996 Dolphins Miami Subs Cards/Coins

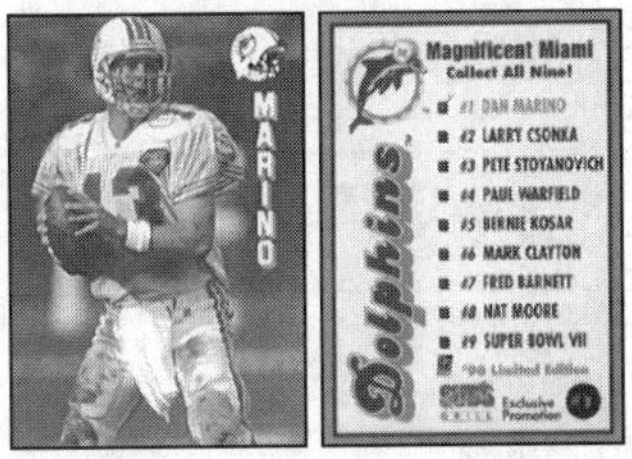

The Miami Dolphins, in conjunction with Miami Subs Restaurants, produced this 9-card and 9-coin set commemorating the 1972 Super Bowl VII team and the present Miami Dolphins. The card fronts feature color action player photos with the player's name printed diagonally on the right side on the card. The backs display the complete 9-card checklist and individual card numbers. We've listed the cards below using a "CA" prefix. The coin fronts feature a player likeness with the player's name and jersey number. The backs display the Dolphins team logo. The coins are unnumbered but have been listed below alphabetically using a "CO" prefix. A cardboard holder featuring Dan Marino, Bernie Kosar, Jimmy Johnson, Fred Barnett, and Mark Clayton was produced to house the set.

	MINT	NRMT	EXC
COMP.CARD/COIN SET (18)	20.00	9.00	2.50
COMPLETE CARD SET (9)	10.00	4.50	1.25
COMPLETE COIN SET (9)	10.00	4.50	1.25
COMMON CARD (CA1-CA9)	.75	.35	.09
COMMON COIN (CO1-CO9)	.75	.35	.09
☐ CA1 Dan Marino	5.00	2.20	.60
☐ CA2 Larry Csonka	1.50	.70	.19
☐ CA3 Pete Stoyanovich	.75	.35	.09
☐ CA4 Paul Warfield	1.50	.70	.19
☐ CA5 Bernie Kosar	.75	.35	.09
☐ CA6 Mark Clayton	.75	.35	.09
☐ CA7 Fred Barnett	.75	.35	.09
☐ CA8 Nat Moore	1.00	.45	.12
☐ CA9 Don Shula George Allen Super Bowl VII	2.00	.90	.25
☐ CO1 Fred Barnett	.75	.35	.09
☐ CO2 Mark Clayton	.75	.35	.09
☐ CO3 Larry Csonka	1.50	.70	.19
☐ CO4 Bernie Kosar	.75	.35	.09
☐ CO5 Dan Marino	5.00	2.20	.60
☐ CO6 Nat Moore	1.00	.45	.12
☐ CO7 Pete Stoyanovich	.75	.35	.09
☐ CO8 Paul Warfield	1.50	.70	.19
☐ CO9 Super Bowl VII Trophy gold coin	1.25	.55	.16
☐ NNO Display Holder Dan Marino Jimmy Johnson	1.50	.70	.19

Bernie Kosar
Mark Clayton
Fred Barnett
Pete Stoyanovich

1991 Domino's Quarterbacks

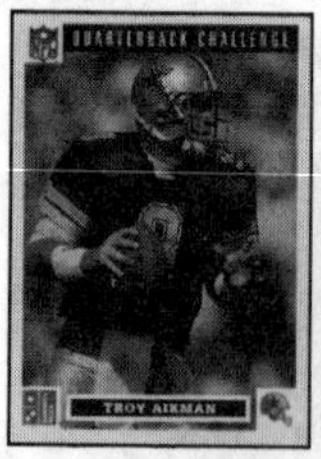

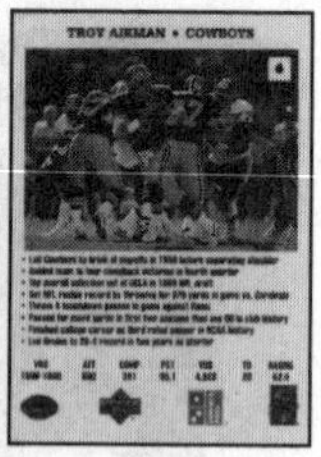

This 50-card NFL quarterback set was produced by Upper Deck and sponsored by Domino's Pizza in conjunction with Coca-Cola and NFL Properties. These standard-size cards were part of a national promotion that was kicked off during the August 3, 1991, "NBC Sportsworld" telecast of "NFL Quarterback Challenge". The cards were distributed through the 5,000 Domino's restaurants across the country. During August, or while supplies lasted, customers who ordered the Domino's Pizza NFL Kick-off Deal received two medium cheese pizzas, four cans of Coke, Diet Coke, or Coke Classic, and one free foil pack with four NFL Quarterback cards, all for 9.99. The front design has color action player photos bordered in white, with the words "Quarterback Challenge" inscribed across the top of the card in a black stripe. The Domino's logo, the player's name, and the team logo appear across the bottom of the card face. The backs picture smaller color action shots, statistics, and career highlights. The first 32 cards in the set were active quarterbacks arranged in alphabetical order by teams. Cards 33-46 feature retired quarterbacks in alphabetical order by player name and cards 47-49 depict quarterback duos from the same team but different eras.

	MINT	NRMT	EXC
COMPLETE SET (50)	6.00	2.70	.75
COMMON CARD (1-50)	.10	.05	.01
☐ 1 Chris Miller	.15	.07	.02
☐ 2 Jim Kelly	.25	.11	.03
☐ 3 Jim Harbaugh	.25	.11	.03
☐ 4 Boomer Esiason	.15	.07	.02
☐ 5 Bernie Kosar	.10	.05	.01
☐ 6 Troy Aikman	.75	.35	.09
☐ 7 John Elway	.60	.25	.07
☐ 8 Rodney Peete	.15	.07	.02
☐ 9 Andre Ware	.10	.05	.01
☐ 10 Anthony Dilweg	.10	.05	.01
☐ 11 Warren Moon	.25	.11	.03
☐ 12 Jeff George	.25	.11	.03
☐ 13 Jim Everett	.10	.05	.01
☐ 14 Jay Schroeder	.10	.05	.01
☐ 15 Wade Wilson	.10	.05	.01
☐ 16 Dan Marino	1.25	.55	.16
☐ 17 Phil Simms	.15	.07	.02
☐ 18 Jeff Hostetler	.10	.05	.01
☐ 19 Ken O'Brien	.10	.05	.01
☐ 20 Timm Rosenbach	.10	.05	.01
☐ 21 Bubby Brister	.10	.05	.01
☐ 22 Steve DeBerg	.15	.07	.02
☐ 23 Randall Cunningham	.10	.05	.01
☐ 24 Steve Walsh	.10	.05	.01
☐ 25 Billy Joe Tolliver	.10	.05	.01
☐ 26 Steve Young	.60	.25	.07
☐ 27 Dave Krieg	.10	.05	.01
☐ 28 Dan McGwire	.10	.05	.01
☐ 29 Vinny Testaverde	.15	.07	.02
☐ 30 Stan Humphries	.10	.05	.01
☐ 31 Mark Rypien	.10	.05	.01
☐ 32 Terry Bradshaw	.50	.23	.06
☐ 33 John Brodie	.15	.07	.02
☐ 34 Len Dawson	.15	.07	.02
☐ 35 Dan Fouts	.25	.11	.03
☐ 36 Otto Graham	.40	.18	.05
☐ 37 Bob Griese	.25	.11	.03
☐ 38 Sonny Jurgensen	.25	.11	.03
☐ 39 Daryle Lamonica	.15	.07	.02
☐ 40 Archie Manning	.15	.07	.02
☐ 41 Jim Plunkett	.15	.07	.02
☐ 42 Bart Starr	.40	.18	.05
☐ 43 Roger Staubach	.75	.35	.09
☐ 44 Joe Theismann	.25	.11	.03
☐ 45 Y.A. Tittle	.25	.11	.03
☐ 46 Johnny Unitas	.60	.25	.07
☐ 47 Cowboy Gunslingers Troy Aikman Roger Staubach	.75	.35	.09
☐ 48 Cajun Connection Bubby Brister Terry Bradshaw	.40	.18	.05
☐ 49 Dolphin Duo Dan Marino Bob Griese	1.00	.45	.12
☐ 50 Checklist Card	.10	.05	.01

1995 Donruss Red Zone

The 1995 Donruss Red Zone series consists of 336 cards. The standard-sized rounded-corner playing cards were distributed as part of a football game. The cards were available in both 80-card starter decks and 12-card booster packs. A Deluxe Double Deck Game Set was distributed as well that contained two 80-card decks and one 12-card pack. The red backs carry the game logo. The cards were unnumbered and are checklisted in alphabetical order within each team below. All cards were available in both issues, but some cards were printed in greater supply than others, and those are noted with the designation DP below. Conversely, there are cards that were produced in smaller quantities than the others, and those are listed with the designation SP below.

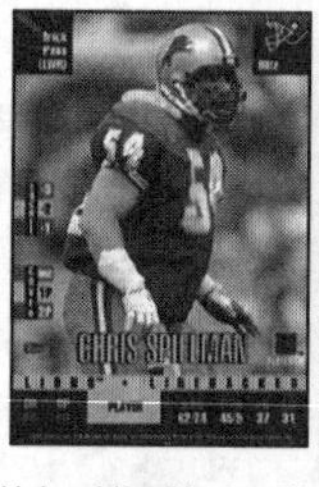

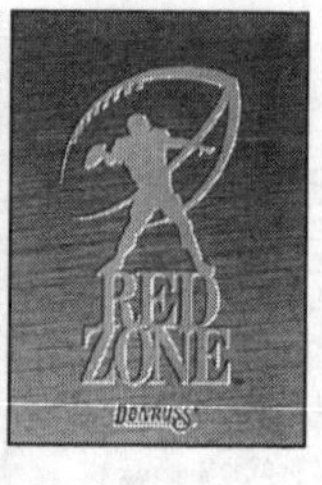

	MINT	NRMT	EXC
COMPLETE SET (336)	250.00	110.00	31.00
COMMON DP CARD (1-336)	.05	.02	.01
COMMON CARD (1-336)	.30	.14	.04
COMMON SP CARD (1-336)	1.50	.70	.19
☐ 1 Michael Bankston	.30	.14	.04
☐ 2 Larry Centers	.50	.23	.06
☐ 3 Ben Coleman DP	.05	.02	.01
☐ 4 Ed Cunningham DP	.05	.02	.01
☐ 5 Garrison Hearst	1.50	.70	.19
☐ 6 Eric Hill	.30	.14	.04
☐ 7 Lorenzo Lynch DP	.05	.02	.01
☐ 8 Clyde Simmons DP	.05	.02	.01
☐ 9 Eric Swann	.50	.23	.06
☐ 10 Aeneas Williams SP	1.50	.70	.19
☐ 11 Chris Doleman	.30	.14	.04
☐ 12 Bert Emanuel DP	.50	.23	.06
☐ 13 Roman Fortin DP	.05	.02	.01
☐ 14 Jeff George SP	3.00	1.35	.35
☐ 15 Craig Heyward DP	.10	.05	.01
☐ 16 D.J. Johnson SP	1.50	.70	.19
☐ 17 Terance Mathis SP	2.00	.90	.25
☐ 18 Clay Matthews DP	.05	.02	.01
☐ 19 Kevin Ross DP	.05	.02	.01
☐ 20 Jessie Tuggle DP	.05	.02	.01
☐ 21 Bob Whitfield SP	1.50	.70	.19
☐ 22 Cornelius Bennett SP	1.50	.70	.19
☐ 23 Russell Copeland DP	.30	.14	.04
☐ 24 John Fina SP	1.50	.70	.19
☐ 25 Carwell Gardner DP	.05	.02	.01
☐ 26 Henry Jones DP	.05	.02	.01
☐ 27 Jim Kelly SP	4.00	1.80	.50
☐ 28 Mark Maddox DP	.05	.02	.01
☐ 29 Glenn Parker	.30	.14	.04
☐ 30 Andre Reed SP	2.00	.90	.25
☐ 31 Bruce Smith SP	4.00	1.80	.50
☐ 32 Thomas Smith DP	.05	.02	.01
☐ 33 Joe Cain DP	.05	.02	.01
☐ 34 Mark Carrier DB	.50	.23	.06
☐ 35 Curtis Conway DP	.50	.23	.06
☐ 36 Albert Fontenot DP	.05	.02	.01
☐ 37 Jeff Graham DP	.10	.05	.01
☐ 38 Raymont Harris DP	.05	.02	.01
☐ 39 Andy Heck	.30	.14	.04
☐ 40 Erik Kramer DP	.10	.05	.01
☐ 41 Vinson Smith	.30	.14	.04
☐ 42 Lewis Tillman DP	.05	.02	.01
☐ 43 Steve Walsh	.30	.14	.04
☐ 44 James Williams DP	.05	.02	.01
☐ 45 Donnell Woolford SP	1.50	.70	.19
☐ 46 Mike Brim DP	.05	.02	.01
☐ 47 Tony McGee DP	.05	.02	.01
☐ 48 Carl Pickens	1.00	.45	.12
☐ 49 Keith Rucker DP	.05	.02	.01
☐ 50 Darnay Scott SP	3.00	1.35	.35
☐ 51 Dan Wilkinson DP	.10	.05	.01
☐ 52 Darryl Williams DP	.05	.02	.01
☐ 53 Derrick Alexander WR	.50	.23	.06
☐ 54 Carl Banks DP	.05	.02	.01
☐ 55 Rob Burnett SP	1.50	.70	.19
☐ 56 Earnest Byner	.30	.14	.04
☐ 57 Steve Everitt DP	.05	.02	.01
☐ 58 Leroy Hoard SP	1.50	.70	.19
☐ 59 Michael Jackson DP	.05	.02	.01
☐ 60 Pepper Johnson	.30	.14	.04
☐ 61 Tony Jones	.30	.14	.04
☐ 62 Antonio Langham	.30	.14	.04
☐ 63 Anthony Pleasant DP	.05	.02	.01
☐ 64 Vinny Testaverde DP	.10	.05	.01
☐ 65 Eric Turner SP	2.00	.90	.25
☐ 66 Tommy Vardell	.30	.14	.04
☐ 67 Troy Aikman SP	15.00	6.75	1.85
☐ 68 Larry Brown	.30	.14	.04
☐ 69 Dixon Edwards DP	.30	.14	.04
☐ 70 Charles Haley SP	2.00	.90	.25
☐ 71 Michael Irvin SP	3.00	1.35	.35
☐ 72 Daryl Johnston DP	.10	.05	.01
☐ 73 Leon Lett	.30	.14	.04
☐ 74 Nate Newton	.30	.14	.04
☐ 75 Jay Novacek SP	2.00	.90	.25
☐ 76 Darrin Smith	.30	.14	.04
☐ 77 Kevin Smith	.30	.14	.04
☐ 78 Tony Tolbert DP	.05	.02	.01
☐ 79 Mark Tuinei SP	1.50	.70	.19
☐ 80 Kevin Williams DP	.10	.05	.01
☐ 81 Darren Woodson	.30	.14	.04
☐ 82 Elijah Alexander	.30	.14	.04
☐ 83 Steve Atwater	.30	.14	.04
☐ 84 Rod Bernstine SP	1.50	.70	.19
☐ 85 Ray Crockett	.30	.14	.04
☐ 86 Shane Dronett DP	.05	.02	.01
☐ 87 John Elway SP	12.00	5.50	1.50
☐ 88 Simon Fletcher	.30	.14	.04
☐ 89 Brian Habib DP	.05	.02	.01
☐ 90 Glyn Milburn	.30	.14	.04
☐ 91 Anthony Miller SP	2.00	.90	.25
☐ 92 Mike Pritchard DP	.10	.05	.01
☐ 93 Shannon Sharpe	.50	.23	.06
☐ 94 Gary Zimmerman DP	.05	.02	.01
☐ 95 Bennie Blades	.30	.14	.04
☐ 96 Lomas Brown SP	1.50	.70	.19
☐ 97 Mike Johnson DP	.05	.02	.01
☐ 98 Robert Massey DP	.05	.02	.01
☐ 99 Scott Mitchell DP	.10	.05	.01
☐ 100 Herman Moore SP	5.00	2.20	.60
☐ 101 Brett Perriman	.50	.23	.06
☐ 102 Barry Sanders SP	15.00	6.75	1.85
☐ 103 Tracy Scroggins DP	.05	.02	.01
☐ 104 Chris Spielman	.30	.14	.04
☐ 105 Doug Widell SP	1.50	.70	.19
☐ 106 Edgar Bennett SP	2.50	1.10	.30
☐ 107 LeRoy Butler DP	.05	.02	.01
☐ 108 Harry Galbreath DP	.05	.02	.01
☐ 109 Sean Jones SP	1.50	.70	.19
☐ 110 George Koonce DP	.05	.02	.01
☐ 111 Anthony Morgan DP	.05	.02	.01
☐ 112 Ken Ruettgers DP	.05	.02	.01
☐ 113 Fred Strickland DP	.05	.02	.01
☐ 114 George Teague	.30	.14	.04
☐ 115 Reggie White SP	4.00	1.80	.50
☐ 116 Micheal Barrow	.30	.14	.04
☐ 117 Blaine Bishop DP	.05	.02	.01
☐ 118 Gary Brown	.30	.14	.04
☐ 119 Ray Childress	.30	.14	.04
☐ 120 Kenny Davidson SP	1.50	.70	.19
☐ 121 Cris Dishman SP	1.50	.70	.19
☐ 122 Brad Hopkins SP	1.50	.70	.19
☐ 123 Haywood Jeffires DP	.05	.02	.01
☐ 124 Eddie Robinson DP	.05	.02	.01
☐ 125 Al Smith DP	.05	.02	.01
☐ 126 David Williams SP	1.50	.70	.19
☐ 127 Tony Bennett SP	1.50	.70	.19
☐ 128 Ray Buchanan SP	1.50	.70	.19
☐ 129 Quentin Coryatt DP	.10	.05	.01
☐ 130 Eugene Daniel DP	.05	.02	.01
☐ 131 Sean Dawkins DP	.10	.05	.01
☐ 132 Marshall Faulk SP	6.00	2.70	.75
☐ 133 Jim Harbaugh	.50	.23	.06
☐ 134 Jeff Herrod DP	.05	.02	.01
☐ 135 Kirk Lowdermilk DP	.05	.02	.01
☐ 136 Tony Siragusa DP	.05	.02	.01
☐ 137 Floyd Turner DP	.05	.02	.01
☐ 138 Will Wolford SP	1.50	.70	.19
☐ 139 Marcus Allen	.50	.23	.06
☐ 140 Kimble Anders SP	2.00	.90	.25
☐ 141 Steve Bono DP	.30	.14	.04
☐ 142 Dale Carter DP	.05	.02	.01
☐ 143 Mark Collins DP	.05	.02	.01
☐ 144 Willie Davis	.50	.23	.06
☐ 145 Lake Dawson DP	.25	.11	.03
☐ 146 Tim Grunhard DP	.05	.02	.01
☐ 147 Greg Hill DP	.25	.11	.03
☐ 148 George Jamison DP	.05	.02	.01
☐ 149 Darren Mickell DP	.05	.02	.01
☐ 150 Will Shields DP	.05	.02	.01
☐ 151 Tracy Simien DP	.05	.02	.01
☐ 152 Neil Smith SP	2.00	.90	.25
☐ 153 Tim Bowens DP	.05	.02	.01
☐ 154 J.B. Brown DP	.05	.02	.01
☐ 155 Keith Byars	.30	.14	.04
☐ 156 Bryan Cox	.30	.14	.04
☐ 157 Jeff Cross	.30	.14	.04
☐ 158 Irving Fryar SP	2.00	.90	.25
☐ 159 Ron Heller	.30	.14	.04
☐ 160 Terry Kirby SP	2.00	.90	.25
☐ 161 Dan Marino SP	25.00	11.00	3.10
☐ 162 O.J. McDuffie	.50	.23	.06
☐ 163 Bernie Parmalee DP	.10	.05	.01
☐ 164 Chris Singleton DP	.05	.02	.01
☐ 165 Troy Vincent SP	1.50	.70	.19
☐ 166 Richmond Webb SP	1.50	.70	.19
☐ 167 Roy Barker DP	.05	.02	.01
☐ 168 Cris Carter DP	.25	.11	.03
☐ 169 Jack Del Rio SP	1.50	.70	.19
☐ 170 Chris Hinton DP	.05	.02	.01
☐ 171 Qadry Ismail	.50	.23	.06
☐ 172 Amp Lee	.30	.14	.04
☐ 173 Ed McDaniel	.30	.14	.04
☐ 174 Randall McDaniel DP	.05	.02	.01
☐ 175 Warren Moon SP	3.00	1.35	.35
☐ 176 John Randle SP	1.50	.70	.19
☐ 177 Jake Reed DP	.10	.05	.01
☐ 178 Robert Smith DP	.10	.05	.01
☐ 179 Todd Steussie DP	.05	.02	.01
☐ 180 Dewayne Washington DP	.05	.02	.01
☐ 181 Bruce Armstrong DP	.05	.02	.01
☐ 182 Drew Bledsoe	2.50	1.10	.30
☐ 183 Vincent Brisby DP	.05	.02	.01
☐ 184 Vincent Brown DP	.05	.02	.01
☐ 185 Ben Coates SP	3.00	1.35	.35
☐ 186 Sam Gash DP	.05	.02	.01
☐ 187 Myron Guyton DP	.05	.02	.01
☐ 188 Maurice Hurst SP	1.50	.70	.19
☐ 189 Mike Jones DP	.05	.02	.01
☐ 190 Bob Kratch DP	.05	.02	.01
☐ 191 Chris Slade SP	1.50	.70	.19
☐ 192 Derek Brown	.30	.14	.04
☐ 193 Vince Buck DP	.05	.02	.01
☐ 194 Jim Dombrowski DP	.05	.02	.01
☐ 195 Quinn Early DP	.10	.05	.01
☐ 196 Jim Everett	.50	.23	.06
☐ 197 Michael Haynes DP	.10	.05	.01
☐ 198 Wayne Martin SP	1.50	.70	.19
☐ 199 Lorenzo Neal DP	.05	.02	.01
☐ 200 William Roaf SP	1.50	.70	.19
☐ 201 Irv Smith DP	.05	.02	.01
☐ 202 Jimmy Spencer DP	.05	.02	.01
☐ 203 Winfred Tubbs DP	.05	.02	.01
☐ 204 Renaldo Turnbull SP	1.50	.70	.19
☐ 205 Michael Brooks DP	.05	.02	.01
☐ 206 Dave Brown DP	.10	.05	.01
☐ 207 Chris Calloway	.30	.14	.04
☐ 208 Jesse Campbell DP	.05	.02	.01
☐ 209 Jumbo Elliott DP	.05	.02	.01
☐ 210 Keith Hamilton DP	.05	.02	.01
☐ 211 Rodney Hampton DP	.20	.09	.03
☐ 212 Corey Miller DP	.05	.02	.01
☐ 213 Doug Riesenberg DP	.05	.02	.01
☐ 214 Mike Sherrard	.30	.14	.04
☐ 215 Phillippi Sparks	.30	.14	.04
☐ 216 Michael Strahan DP	.05	.02	.01
☐ 217 Richie Anderson DP	.05	.02	.01
☐ 218 Brad Baxter DP	.05	.02	.01
☐ 219 Tony Casillas DP	.05	.02	.01
☐ 220 Roger Duffy	.30	.14	.04
☐ 221 Boomer Esiason DP	.10	.05	.01
☐ 222 Aaron Glenn DP	.05	.02	.01
☐ 223 Bobby Houston DP	.05	.02	.01
☐ 224 Mo Lewis SP	1.50	.70	.19
☐ 225 Siupeli Malamala DP	.05	.02	.01
☐ 226 Johnny Mitchell DP	.05	.02	.01
☐ 227 Eddie Anderson DP	.05	.02	.01
☐ 228 Jerry Ball DP	.05	.02	.01
☐ 229 Greg Biekert	.30	.14	.04
☐ 230 Tim Brown SP	3.00	1.35	.35
☐ 231 Rob Fredrickson DP	.05	.02	.01
☐ 232 Nolan Harrison	.30	.14	.04
☐ 233 Jeff Hostetler DP	.10	.05	.01
☐ 234 Rocket Ismail SP	2.00	.90	.25
☐ 235 Terry McDaniel SP	1.50	.70	.19
☐ 236 Chester McGlockton SP	2.00	.90	.25
☐ 237 Don Mosebar	.30	.14	.04
☐ 238 Anthony Smith	.30	.14	.04
☐ 239 Harvey Williams DP	.10	.05	.01
☐ 240 Steve Wisniewski DP	.05	.02	.01
☐ 241 Fred Barnett	.50	.23	.06
☐ 242 Randall Cunningham	.30	.14	.04
☐ 243 William Fuller SP	1.50	.70	.19
☐ 244 Charlie Garner	.30	.14	.04
☐ 245 Vaughn Hebron DP	.05	.02	.01
☐ 246 Lester Holmes	.30	.14	.04
☐ 247 Greg Jackson SP	1.50	.70	.19
☐ 248 Bill Romanowski DP	.05	.02	.01
☐ 249 William Thomas SP	1.50	.70	.19
☐ 250 Bernard Williams	.30	.14	.04
☐ 251 Calvin Williams DP	.05	.02	.01
☐ 252 Michael Zordich SP	1.50	.70	.19
☐ 253 Chad Brown SP	1.50	.70	.19
☐ 254 Dermontti Dawson DP	.05	.02	.01
☐ 255 Kevin Greene SP	2.50	1.10	.30
☐ 256 Charles Johnson	.50	.23	.06
☐ 257 Carnell Lake	.30	.14	.04
☐ 258 Greg Lloyd SP	2.00	.90	.25
☐ 259 Neil O'Donnell DP	.30	.14	.04
☐ 260 Ray Seals DP	.05	.02	.01
☐ 261 Leon Searcy SP	1.50	.70	.19
☐ 262 Yancey Thigpen DP	1.50	.70	.19
☐ 263 John L. Williams DP	.05	.02	.01
☐ 264 Rod Woodson SP	2.00	.90	.25
☐ 265 Stan Brock	.30	.14	.04
☐ 266 Courtney Hall	.30	.14	.04
☐ 267 Ronnie Harmon	.30	.14	.04
☐ 268 Dwayne Harper DP	.05	.02	.01
☐ 269 Rodney Harrison DP	.05	.02	.01
☐ 270 Stan Humphries DP	.50	.23	.06
☐ 271 Shawn Jefferson	.30	.14	.04
☐ 272 Shawn Lee	.30	.14	.04
☐ 273 Tony Martin	.50	.23	.06
☐ 274 Natrone Means SP	3.00	1.35	.35
☐ 275 Chris Mims SP	1.50	.70	.19
☐ 276 Leslie O'Neal SP	2.00	.90	.25
☐ 277 Junior Seau SP	4.00	1.80	.50
☐ 278 Mark Seay DP	.10	.05	.01
☐ 279 Harry Swayne DP	.05	.02	.01
☐ 280 Eric Davis	.30	.14	.04
☐ 281 William Floyd	.50	.23	.06
☐ 282 Merton Hanks SP	1.50	.70	.19
☐ 283 Brent Jones	.50	.23	.06
☐ 284 Tim McDonald DP	.05	.02	.01
☐ 285 Ken Norton SP	1.50	.70	.19
☐ 286 Gary Plummer DP	.05	.02	.01

Card	MINT	NRMT	EXC
☐ 287 Jerry Rice SP	15.00	6.75	1.85
☐ 288 Dana Stubblefield SP	2.00	.90	.25
☐ 289 John Taylor SP	2.00	.90	.25
☐ 290 Bryant Young DP	.10	.05	.01
☐ 291 Steve Young SP	12.00	5.50	1.50
☐ 292 Steve Wallace SP	1.50	.70	.19
☐ 293 Sam Adams DP	.05	.02	.01
☐ 294 Robert Blackmon DP	.05	.02	.01
☐ 295 Jeff Blackshear DP	.05	.02	.01
☐ 296 Brian Blades	.50	.23	.06
☐ 297 Howard Ballard SP	1.50	.70	.19
☐ 298 Cortez Kennedy DP	.05	.02	.01
☐ 299 Rick Mirer	.50	.23	.06
☐ 300 Eugene Robinson DP	.05	.02	.01
☐ 301 Chris Warren SP	2.50	1.10	.30
☐ 302 Terry Wooden SP	1.50	.70	.19
☐ 303 Johnny Bailey	.30	.14	.04
☐ 304 Isaac Bruce DP	.75	.35	.09
☐ 305 Shane Conlan DP	.05	.02	.01
☐ 306 Troy Drayton DP	.05	.02	.01
☐ 307 Sean Gilbert DP	.05	.02	.01
☐ 308 Leo Goeas DP	.05	.02	.01
☐ 309 Jessie Hester	.30	.14	.04
☐ 310 Clarence Jones	.30	.14	.04
☐ 311 Todd Lyght	.30	.14	.04
☐ 312 Chris Miller DP	.10	.05	.01
☐ 313 Toby Wright DP	.05	.02	.01
☐ 314 Robert Young DP	.05	.02	.01
☐ 315 Eric Curry DP	.05	.02	.01
☐ 316 Trent Dilfer	.50	.23	.06
☐ 317 Thomas Everett DP	.05	.02	.01
☐ 318 Paul Gruber DP	.05	.02	.01
☐ 319 Jackie Harris DP	.05	.02	.01
☐ 320 Courtney Hawkins DP	.05	.02	.01
☐ 321 Lonnie Marts DP	.05	.02	.01
☐ 322 Tony Mayberry DP	.05	.02	.01
☐ 323 Martin Mayhew DP	.05	.02	.01
☐ 324 Hardy Nickerson DP	.05	.02	.01
☐ 325 Errict Rhett DP	.75	.35	.09
☐ 326 Reggie Brooks DP	.05	.02	.01
☐ 327 Tom Carter DP	.05	.02	.01
☐ 328 Henry Ellard SP	2.00	.90	.25
☐ 329 Darrell Green SP	1.50	.70	.19
☐ 330 Ken Harvey SP	1.50	.70	.19
☐ 331 James Jenkins DP	.05	.02	.01
☐ 332 Tim Johnson DP	.05	.02	.01
☐ 333 Jim Lachey	.30	.14	.04
☐ 334 Brian Mitchell	.30	.14	.04
☐ 335 Heath Shuler	1.25	.55	.16
☐ 336 Tony Woods DP	.05	.02	.01

1996 Donruss

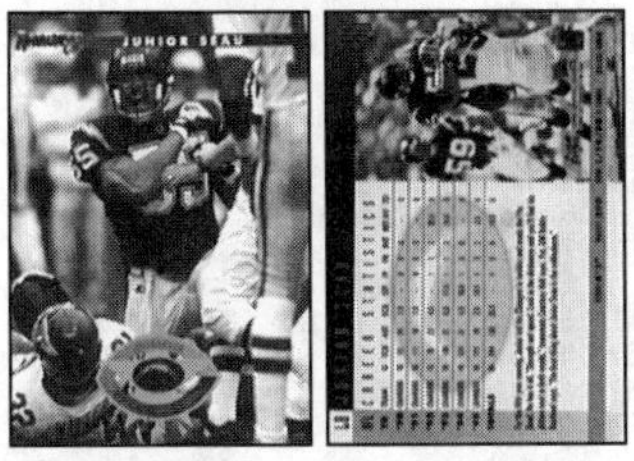

The 1996 Donruss set was issued in one series totalling 240 cards. The only subset included was Rookies (208-237). The fronts feature color action player photos. The backs carry a small player photo with biographical information and career statistics.

	MINT	NRMT	EXC
COMPLETE SET (240)	25.00	11.00	3.10
COMMON CARD (1-240)	.05	.02	.01
☐ 1 Barry Sanders	1.00	.45	.12
☐ 2 Flipper Anderson	.05	.02	.01
☐ 3 Ben Coates	.10	.05	.01
☐ 4 Rob Johnson	.05	.02	.01
☐ 5 Rodney Hampton	.10	.05	.01
☐ 6 Desmond Howard	.10	.05	.01
☐ 7 Craig Heyward	.05	.02	.01
☐ 8 Alvin Harper	.05	.02	.01
☐ 9 Todd Collins	.10	.05	.01
☐ 10 Ken Norton Jr.	.10	.05	.01
☐ 11 Stan Humphries	.10	.05	.01
☐ 12 Aeneas Williams	.05	.02	.01
☐ 13 Jeff Hostetler	.10	.05	.01
☐ 14 Frank Sanders	.10	.05	.01
☐ 15 J.J. Birden	.05	.02	.01
☐ 16 Bryce Paup	.10	.05	.01
☐ 17 Bill Brooks	.05	.02	.01
☐ 18 Kevin Williams	.05	.02	.01
☐ 19 Boomer Esiason	.10	.05	.01
☐ 20 O.J. McDuffie	.10	.05	.01
☐ 21 Eric Swann	.10	.05	.01
☐ 22 Neil Smith	.10	.05	.01
☐ 23 Charlie Garner	.05	.02	.01
☐ 24 Greg Lloyd	.10	.05	.01
☐ 25 Willie Jackson	.10	.05	.01
☐ 26 Shawn Jefferson	.05	.02	.01
☐ 27 Rodney Peete	.05	.02	.01
☐ 28 Michael Westbrook	.20	.09	.03
☐ 29 J.J. Stokes	.20	.09	.03
☐ 30 Troy Aikman	1.00	.45	.12
☐ 31 Sean Dawkins	.05	.02	.01
☐ 32 Larry Centers	.10	.05	.01
☐ 33 Herschel Walker	.10	.05	.01
☐ 34 Stoney Case	.05	.02	.01
☐ 35 Kevin Greene	.10	.05	.01
☐ 36 Quinn Early	.05	.02	.01
☐ 37 Fred Barnett	.10	.05	.01
☐ 38 Andre Coleman	.05	.02	.01
☐ 39 Mark Chmura	.10	.05	.01
☐ 40 Adrian Murrell	.10	.05	.01
☐ 41 Roosevelt Potts	.05	.02	.01
☐ 42 Jay Novacek	.10	.05	.01
☐ 43 Derrick Alexander WR	.10	.05	.01
☐ 44 Ken Dilger	.10	.05	.01
☐ 45 Rob Moore	.05	.02	.01
☐ 46 Cris Carter	.20	.09	.03
☐ 47 Jeff Blake	.20	.09	.03
☐ 48 Derek Loville	.05	.02	.01
☐ 49 Tyrone Wheatley	.10	.05	.01
☐ 50 Terrell Fletcher	.05	.02	.01
☐ 51 Sherman Williams	.05	.02	.01
☐ 52 Justin Armour	.05	.02	.01
☐ 53 Kordell Stewart	1.25	.55	.16
☐ 54 Tim Brown	.10	.05	.01
☐ 55 Kevin Carter	.10	.05	.01
☐ 56 Andre Rison	.10	.05	.01
☐ 57 James O.Stewart	.10	.05	.01
☐ 58 Brent Jones	.05	.02	.01
☐ 59 Erik Kramer	.05	.02	.01
☐ 60 Floyd Turner	.05	.02	.01
☐ 61 Ricky Watters	.10	.05	.01
☐ 62 Hardy Nickerson	.05	.02	.01
☐ 63 Aaron Craver	.05	.02	.01
☐ 64 Dave Krieg	.05	.02	.01
☐ 65 Warren Moon	.10	.05	.01
☐ 66 Wayne Chrebet	.10	.05	.01
☐ 67 Napoleon Kaufman	.10	.05	.01
☐ 68 Terance Mathis	.05	.02	.01
☐ 69 Chad May	.05	.02	.01
☐ 70 Andre Reed	.10	.05	.01
☐ 71 Reggie White	.20	.09	.03
☐ 72 Brett Favre	2.00	.90	.25
☐ 73 Chris Zorich	.05	.02	.01
☐ 74 Kerry Collins	1.25	.55	.16
☐ 75 Herman Moore	.20	.09	.03
☐ 76 Yancey Thigpen	.10	.05	.01
☐ 77 Glenn Foley	.05	.02	.01
☐ 78 Quentin Coryatt	.05	.02	.01
☐ 79 Terry Kirby	.10	.05	.01
☐ 80 Edgar Bennett	.10	.05	.01
☐ 81 Mark Brunell	1.00	.45	.12
☐ 82 Heath Shuler	.20	.09	.03
☐ 83 Gus Frerotte	.20	.09	.03
☐ 84 Deion Sanders	.60	.25	.07
☐ 85 Calvin Williams	.05	.02	.01
☐ 86 Junior Seau	.20	.09	.03
☐ 87 Jim Kelly	.20	.09	.03
☐ 88 Daryl Johnston	.10	.05	.01
☐ 89 Irving Fryar	.10	.05	.01
☐ 90 Brian Blades	.10	.05	.01
☐ 91 Willie Davis	.10	.05	.01
☐ 92 Jerome Bettis	.20	.09	.03
☐ 93 Marcus Allen	.20	.09	.03
☐ 94 Jeff Graham	.05	.02	.01
☐ 95 Rick Mirer	.10	.05	.01
☐ 96 Harvey Williams	.05	.02	.01
☐ 97 Steve Atwater	.05	.02	.01
☐ 98 Carl Pickens	.20	.09	.03
☐ 99 Darick Holmes	.10	.05	.01
☐ 100 Bruce Smith	.20	.09	.03
☐ 101 Vinny Testaverde	.10	.05	.01
☐ 102 Thurman Thomas	.20	.09	.03
☐ 103 Drew Bledsoe	1.00	.45	.12
☐ 104 Bernie Parmalee	.05	.02	.01
☐ 105 Greg Hill	.10	.05	.01
☐ 106 Steve McNair	1.00	.45	.12
☐ 107 Andre Hastings	.10	.05	.01
☐ 108 Eric Metcalf	.10	.05	.01
☐ 109 Kimble Anders	.05	.02	.01
☐ 110 Steve Tasker	.05	.02	.01
☐ 111 Mark Carrier	.05	.02	.01
☐ 112 Jerry Rice	1.00	.45	.12
☐ 113 Joey Galloway	.40	.18	.05
☐ 114 Robert Smith	.10	.05	.01
☐ 115 Hugh Douglas	.05	.02	.01
☐ 116 Willie McGinest	.05	.02	.01
☐ 117 Terrell Davis	1.50	.70	.19
☐ 118 Cortez Kennedy	.10	.05	.01
☐ 119 Marshall Faulk	.20	.09	.03
☐ 120 Michael Haynes	.10	.05	.01
☐ 121 Isaac Bruce	.20	.09	.03
☐ 122 Brian Mitchell	.05	.02	.01
☐ 123 Bryan Cox	.05	.02	.01
☐ 124 Tamarick Vanover	.20	.09	.03
☐ 125 William Floyd	.10	.05	.01
☐ 126 Chris Chandler	.10	.05	.01
☐ 127 Carnell Lake	.05	.02	.01
☐ 128 Aaron Bailey	.05	.02	.01
☐ 129 Darnay Scott	.10	.05	.01
☐ 130 Darren Woodson	.10	.05	.01
☐ 131 Ernie Mills	.05	.02	.01
☐ 132 Charles Haley	.10	.05	.01
☐ 133 Rocket Ismail	.10	.05	.01
☐ 134 Bert Emanuel	.10	.05	.01
☐ 135 Lake Dawson	.10	.05	.01
☐ 136 Jake Reed	.10	.05	.01
☐ 137 Dave Brown	.10	.05	.01
☐ 138 Steve Bono	.10	.05	.01
☐ 139 Terry Allen	.10	.05	.01
☐ 140 Errict Rhett	.10	.05	.01
☐ 141 Rod Woodson	.10	.05	.01
☐ 142 Charles Johnson	.10	.05	.01
☐ 143 Emmitt Smith	2.00	.90	.25
☐ 144 Ki-Jana Carter	.10	.05	.01
☐ 145 Garrison Hearst	.10	.05	.01
☐ 146 Rashaan Salaam	.20	.09	.03
☐ 147 Tony Boselli	.10	.05	.01
☐ 148 Derrick Thomas	.10	.05	.01
☐ 149 Mark Seay	.05	.02	.01
☐ 150 Derrick Alexander DE	.05	.02	.01
☐ 151 Christian Fauria	.05	.02	.01
☐ 152 Aaron Hayden	.05	.02	.01
☐ 153 Chris Warren	.10	.05	.01
☐ 154 Dave Meggett	.05	.02	.01
☐ 155 Jeff George	.10	.05	.01
☐ 156 Jackie Harris	.05	.02	.01
☐ 157 Michael Irvin	.20	.09	.03
☐ 158 Scott Mitchell	.10	.05	.01
☐ 159 Trent Dilfer	.10	.05	.01
☐ 160 Kyle Brady	.10	.05	.01
☐ 161 Dan Marino	2.00	.90	.25
☐ 162 Curtis Martin	1.50	.70	.19
☐ 163 Mario Bates	.10	.05	.01
☐ 164 Erric Pegram	.10	.05	.01
☐ 165 Eric Zeier	.10	.05	.01
☐ 166 Rodney Thomas	.05	.02	.01
☐ 167 Neil O'Donnell	.10	.05	.01
☐ 168 Warren Sapp	.05	.02	.01
☐ 169 Jim Harbaugh	.10	.05	.01
☐ 170 Henry Ellard	.10	.05	.01
☐ 171 Anthony Miller	.10	.05	.01
☐ 172 Derrick Moore	.05	.02	.01
☐ 173 John Elway	.75	.35	.09
☐ 174 Vincent Brisby	.05	.02	.01
☐ 175 Antonio Freeman	.40	.18	.05
☐ 176 Chris Sanders	.10	.05	.01
☐ 177 Steve Young	.75	.35	.09
☐ 178 Shannon Sharpe	.10	.05	.01
☐ 179 Brett Perriman	.10	.05	.01
☐ 180 Orlando Thomas	.05	.02	.01
☐ 181 Eric Bjornson	.05	.02	.01
☐ 182 Natrone Means	.20	.09	.03
☐ 183 Jim Everett	.05	.02	.01
☐ 184 Curtis Conway	.20	.09	.03
☐ 185 Robert Brooks	.20	.09	.03
☐ 186 Tony Martin	.10	.05	.01
☐ 187 Mark Carrier DB	.05	.02	.01
☐ 188 LeShon Johnson	.05	.02	.01
☐ 189 Bernie Kosar	.05	.02	.01
☐ 190 Ray Zellars	.05	.02	.01
☐ 191 Steve Walsh	.05	.02	.01
☐ 192 Craig Erickson	.05	.02	.01
☐ 193 Tommy Maddox	.05	.02	.01
☐ 194 Leslie O'Neal	.05	.02	.01
☐ 195 Harold Green	.05	.02	.01
☐ 196 Steve Beuerlein	.05	.02	.01
☐ 197 Ronald Moore	.05	.02	.01
☐ 198 Leslie Shepherd	.05	.02	.01
☐ 199 Leroy Hoard	.05	.02	.01
☐ 200 Michael Jackson	.10	.05	.01
☐ 201 Will Moore	.05	.02	.01
☐ 202 Ricky Ervins	.05	.02	.01
☐ 203 Keith Jennings	.05	.02	.01
☐ 204 Eric Green	.05	.02	.01
☐ 205 Mark Rypien	.05	.02	.01
☐ 206 Torrance Small	.05	.02	.01
☐ 207 Sean Gilbert	.05	.02	.01
☐ 208 Mike Alstott	.40	.18	.05
☐ 209 Willie Anderson	.05	.02	.01
☐ 210 Alex Molden	.05	.02	.01
☐ 211 Jonathan Ogden	.05	.02	.01
☐ 212 Stepfret Williams	.05	.02	.01
☐ 213 Jeff Lewis	.10	.05	.01
☐ 214 Regan Upshaw	.05	.02	.01
☐ 215 Daryl Gardener	.10	.05	.01
☐ 216 Danny Kanell	.20	.09	.03
☐ 217 John Mobley	.05	.02	.01
☐ 218 Reggie Brown LB	.05	.02	.01
☐ 219 Muhsin Muhammad	1.00	.45	.12
☐ 220 Kevin Hardy	.10	.05	.01
☐ 221 Stanley Pritchett	.10	.05	.01
☐ 222 Cedric Jones	.10	.05	.01
☐ 223 Marco Battaglia	.05	.02	.01
☐ 224 Duane Clemons	.05	.02	.01
☐ 225 Jerald Moore	.05	.02	.01
☐ 226 Simeon Rice	.20	.09	.03
☐ 227 Chris Darkins	.10	.05	.01
☐ 228 Bobby Hoying	.20	.09	.03
☐ 229 Stephen Davis	.20	.09	.03
☐ 230 Walt Harris	.05	.02	.01
☐ 231 Jermane Mayberry	.05	.02	.01
☐ 232 Tony Brackens	.10	.05	.01
☐ 233 Eric Moulds	.75	.35	.09
☐ 234 Alex Van Dyke	.10	.05	.01
☐ 235 Marvin Harrison	1.25	.55	.16
☐ 236 Rickey Dudley	.20	.09	.03
☐ 237 Terrell Owens	1.50	.70	.19
☐ 238 Jerry Rice Checklist Card	.30	.14	.04
☐ 239 Dan Marino Checklist Card	.40	.18	.05
☐ 240 Emmitt Smith Checklist Card	.40	.18	.05

1996 Donruss Press Proofs

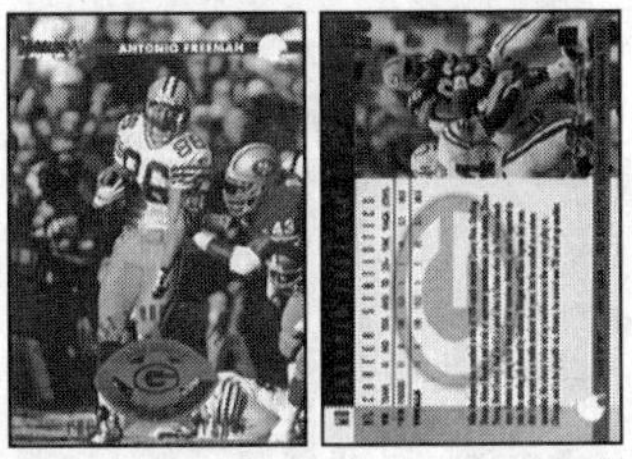

Randomly inserted in packs at a rate of one in five, this set is parallel to the regular set and is similar in design with gold foil highlights. Only 2000 of this set was printed.

	MINT	NRMT	EXC
COMPLETE SET (240)	800.00	350.00	100.00
COMMON CARD (1-240)	1.50	.70	.19
*STARS:15X TO 30X BASIC CARDS			
*YOUNG STARS: 12.5X TO 25X BASIC CARDS			
*RCs: 10X TO 20X BASIC CARDS			

1996 Donruss Elite

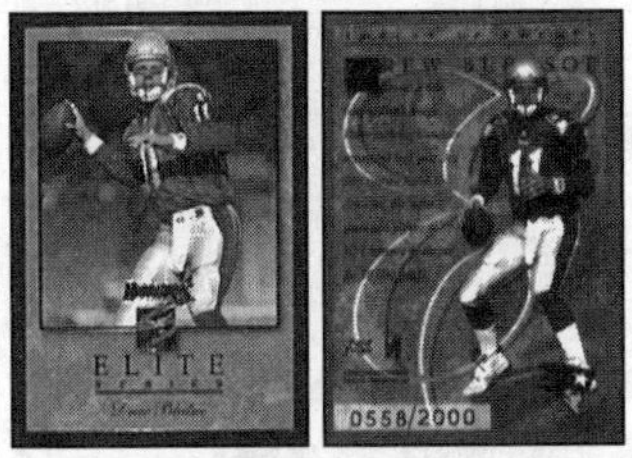

This 20-card set was issued in both a gold and silver version and features color player photos in silver or gold borders. The backs carry another player photo with a paragraph about the player on either a gold or silver background. Only 10,000 of each silver card was produced and only 2,000 of each gold card. Each card is sequentially numbered.

	MINT	NRMT	EXC
COMPLETE SET (20)	250.00	110.00	31.00
COMMON CARD (1-20)	5.00	2.20	.60
COMPLETE GOLD SET (20)	500.00	220.00	60.00
COMMON GOLD CARD	10.00	4.50	1.25
*GOLD STARS: 1X TO 2X BASIC CARDS			
*GOLD YOUNG STARS: .75X TO 1.5X BASIC CARDS			
☐ 1 Emmitt Smith	30.00	13.50	3.70
☐ 2 Barry Sanders	16.00	7.25	2.00
☐ 3 Marshall Faulk	6.00	2.70	.75
☐ 4 Curtis Martin	16.00	7.25	2.00
☐ 5 Junior Seau	5.00	2.20	.60
☐ 6 Troy Aikman	16.00	7.25	2.00
☐ 7 Steve Young	12.00	5.50	1.50
☐ 8 Dan Marino	30.00	13.50	3.70
☐ 9 Brett Favre	30.00	13.50	3.70
☐ 10 John Elway	12.00	5.50	1.50
☐ 11 Kerry Collins	12.00	5.50	1.50
☐ 12 Drew Bledsoe	16.00	7.25	2.00
☐ 13 Jerry Rice	16.00	7.25	2.00
☐ 14 Keyshawn Johnson	8.00	3.60	1.00
☐ 15 Deion Sanders	10.00	4.50	1.25
☐ 16 Isaac Bruce	6.00	2.70	.75
☐ 17 Rashaan Salaam	6.00	2.70	.75
☐ 18 Tim Biakabutuka	6.00	2.70	.75
☐ 19 Lawrence Phillips	5.00	2.20	.60
☐ 20 Robert Brooks	6.00	2.70	.75

1996 Donruss Hit List

Randomly inserted in packs, this 20-card set features color action player photos on a silver foil background. The die cut cards feature team colored borders on two sides. Only 10,000 of each card was produced.

	MINT	NRMT	EXC
COMPLETE SET (20)	150.00	70.00	19.00
COMMON CARD (1-20)	4.00	1.80	.50
☐ 1 Bruce Smith	6.00	2.70	.75
☐ 2 Barry Sanders	12.00	5.50	1.50
☐ 3 Kevin Hardy	4.00	1.80	.50
☐ 4 Greg Lloyd	4.00	1.80	.50
☐ 5 Brett Favre	25.00	11.00	3.10
☐ 6 Emmitt Smith	25.00	11.00	3.10
☐ 7 Kerry Collins	12.00	5.50	1.50
☐ 8 Ken Norton Jr.	4.00	1.80	.50
☐ 9 Steve Atwater	4.00	1.80	.50
☐ 10 Curtis Martin	15.00	6.75	1.85
☐ 11 Chris Warren	4.00	1.80	.50
☐ 12 Steve Young	10.00	4.50	1.25
☐ 13 Marshall Faulk	6.00	2.70	.75

☐ 14 Junior Seau	4.00	1.80	.50
☐ 15 Lawrence Phillips	4.00	1.80	.50
☐ 16 Troy Aikman	12.00	5.50	1.50
☐ 17 Jerry Rice	12.00	5.50	1.50
☐ 18 Dan Marino	25.00	11.00	3.10
☐ 19 Reggie White	6.00	2.70	.75
☐ 20 John Elway	10.00	4.50	1.25

1996 Donruss Rated Rookies

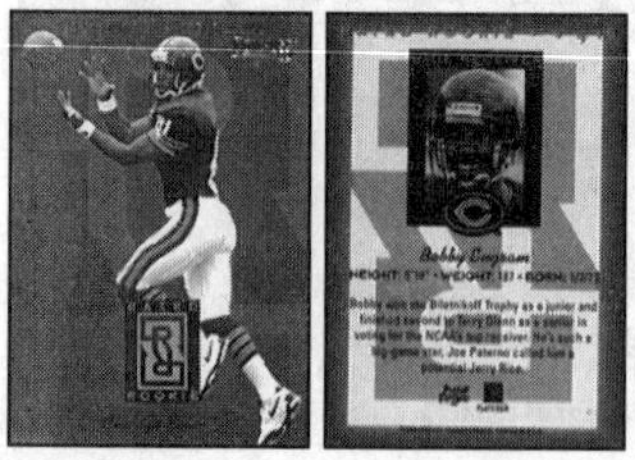

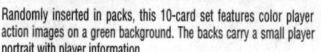

Randomly inserted in packs, this 10-card set features color player action images on a green background. The backs carry a small player portrait with player information.

	MINT	NRMT	EXC
COMPLETE SET (10)	30.00	13.50	3.70
COMMON CARD (1-10)	2.00	.90	.25
☐ 1 Keyshawn Johnson	4.00	1.80	.50
☐ 2 Terry Glenn	6.00	2.70	.75
☐ 3 Tim Biakabutuka	3.00	1.35	.35
☐ 4 Bobby Engram	2.00	.90	.25
☐ 5 Leeland McElroy	2.00	.90	.25
☐ 6 Eddie George	8.00	3.60	1.00
☐ 7 Lawrence Phillips	3.00	1.35	.35
☐ 8 Derrick Mayes	2.00	.90	.25
☐ 9 Karim Abdul-Jabbar	5.00	2.20	.60
☐ 10 Eddie Kennison	4.00	1.80	.50

1996 Donruss Stop Action

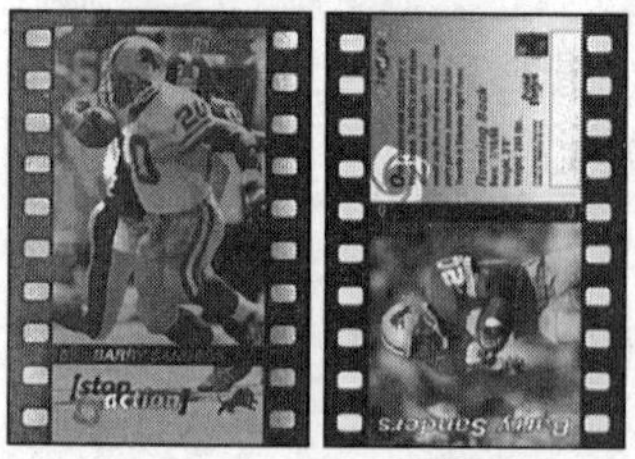

Inserted in jumbo (magazine) packs only, this set features color action player with a film strip border design. The backs carry player information. Only 4000 of this set was printed and are sequentially numbered.

	MINT	NRMT	EXC
COMPLETE SET (10)	300.00	135.00	38.00
COMMON CARD (1-10)	12.00	5.50	1.50
☐ 1 Deion Sanders	18.00	8.00	2.20
☐ 2 Troy Aikman	30.00	13.50	3.70
☐ 3 Brett Favre	60.00	27.00	7.50
☐ 4 Steve Young	20.00	9.00	2.50
☐ 5 Joey Galloway	14.00	6.25	1.75
☐ 6 Dan Marino	60.00	27.00	7.50
☐ 7 Jerry Rice	30.00	13.50	3.70
☐ 8 Emmitt Smith	60.00	27.00	7.50
☐ 9 Isaac Bruce	12.00	5.50	1.50
☐ 10 Barry Sanders	30.00	13.50	3.70

1996 Donruss What If?

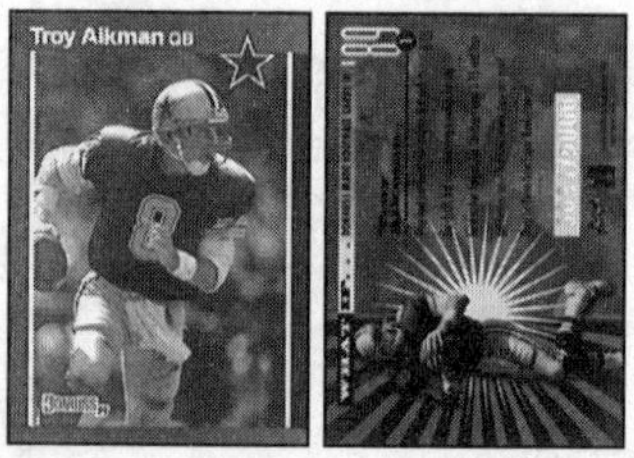

Randomly inserted in hobby packs only, this 10-card set features color player photos on the Donruss card design of the individual year that is stated on each card. The backs carry another player photo on a star burst design along side information about the player. Only 5000 of each card was produced.

	MINT	NRMT	EXC
COMPLETE SET (10)	200.00	90.00	25.00
COMMON CARD (1-10)	10.00	4.50	1.25
☐ 1 Troy Aikman	20.00	9.00	2.50
☐ 2 Jerry Rice	20.00	9.00	2.50
☐ 3 Barry Sanders	20.00	9.00	2.50

☐ 4 Drew Bledsoe	20.00	9.00	2.50
☐ 5 Deion Sanders	10.00	4.50	1.25
☐ 6 Brett Favre	35.00	16.00	4.40
☐ 7 Dan Marino	35.00	16.00	4.40
☐ 8 Steve Young	12.00	5.50	1.50
☐ 9 Emmitt Smith	35.00	16.00	4.40
☐ 10 John Elway	15.00	6.75	1.85

1996 Donruss Will To Win

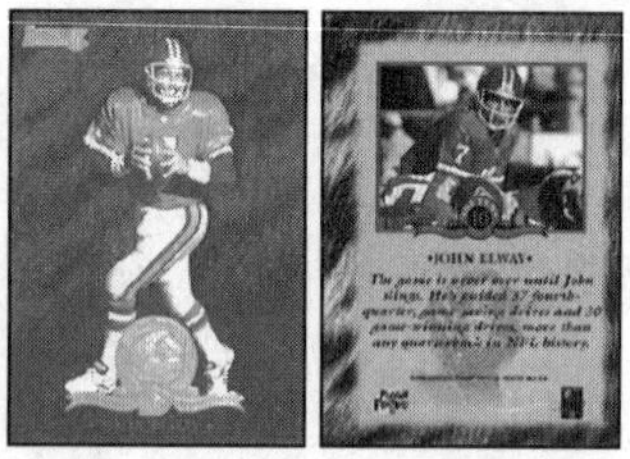

Randomly inserted in retail packs only, this 10-card set features a color player image on a brown-and-black background with copper foil highlights. The backs carry another player photo and a paragraph about the player. Only 5000 of this set was produced.

	MINT	NRMT	EXC
COMPLETE SET (10)	150.00	70.00	19.00
COMMON CARD (1-10)	8.00	3.60	1.00
☐ 1 Emmitt Smith	30.00	13.50	3.70
☐ 2 Brett Favre	30.00	13.50	3.70
☐ 3 Curtis Martin	15.00	6.75	1.85
☐ 4 Jerry Rice	15.00	6.75	1.85
☐ 5 Barry Sanders	15.00	6.75	1.85
☐ 6 Errict Rhett	8.00	3.60	1.00
☐ 7 Troy Aikman	15.00	6.75	1.85
☐ 8 Dan Marino	30.00	13.50	3.70
☐ 9 Steve Young	10.00	4.50	1.25
☐ 10 John Elway	12.00	5.50	1.50

1956 Eagles Team Issue

The Philadelphia Eagles issued and distributed this set of player photos. Each measures approximately 8" by 10" and features a black and white photo on the cardfront with a blank cardback. The player's name, position (abbreviated), height, weight, and college affiliation appear below the photo with the team name above the picture. The checklist is thought to be incomplete. Any additions to this list are greatly appreciated.

	NRMT	VG-E	GOOD
COMPLETE SET (3)	50.00	22.00	6.25
COMMON CARD (1-3)	15.00	6.75	1.85
☐ 1 Eddie Bell	20.00	9.00	2.50
☐ 2 Bob Kelley	15.00	6.75	1.85
☐ 3 Rocky Ryan	15.00	6.75	1.85

1959 Eagles Jay Publishing

This 12-card set features (approximately) 5" by 7" black-and-white player photos. The photos show players in traditional poses with the quarterback preparing to throw, the runner heading downfield, and the defenseman ready for the tackle. These cards were packaged 12 to a packet and originally sold for 25 cents. The backs are blank. The cards are unnumbered and checklisted below in alphabetical order.

	NRMT	VG-E	GOOD
COMPLETE SET (12)	90.00	40.00	11.00
COMMON CARD (1-12)	5.00	2.20	.60
☐ 1 Bill Barnes	5.00	2.20	.60
☐ 2 Chuck Bednarik	15.00	6.75	1.85
☐ 3 Tom Brookshier	7.50	3.40	.95
☐ 4 Marion Campbell	7.50	3.40	.95
☐ 5 Ted Dean	5.00	2.20	.60
☐ 6 Tommy McDonald	10.00	4.50	1.25
☐ 7 Clarence Peaks	5.00	2.20	.60
☐ 8 Pete Retzlaff	7.50	3.40	.95
☐ 9 Jesse Richardson	5.00	2.20	.60
☐ 10 Norm Van Brocklin	15.00	6.75	1.85
☐ 11 Bobby Walston	7.50	3.40	.95
☐ 12 Chuck Weber	5.00	2.20	.60

1960 Eagles Team Issue

This 11-card team-issued set measures approximately 5" by 7" and is printed on thin, slick card stock. The fronts feature black-and-white posed action player photos with white borders. The player's name is printed in black below the picture. The backs are blank. The cards are unnumbered and checklisted below in alphabetical order.

	NRMT	VG-E	GOOD
COMPLETE SET (11)	70.00	32.00	8.75
COMMON CARD (1-11)	5.00	2.20	.60
☐ 1 Maxie Baughan	7.50	3.40	.95
☐ 2 Chuck Bednarik	15.00	6.75	1.85
☐ 3 Don Burroughs	5.00	2.20	.60

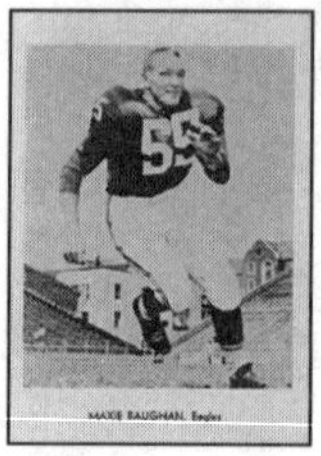

☐ 4 Jimmy Carr	7.50	3.40	.95
☐ 5 Howard Keys	5.00	2.20	.60
☐ 6 Ed Khayat	5.00	2.20	.60
☐ 7 Jim McCusker	5.00	2.20	.60
☐ 8 John Nocera	5.00	2.20	.60
☐ 9 Nick Skorich	7.50	3.40	.95
☐ 10 J.D. Smith	7.50	3.40	.95
☐ 11 John Wittenborn	5.00	2.20	.60

1961 Eagles Jay Publishing

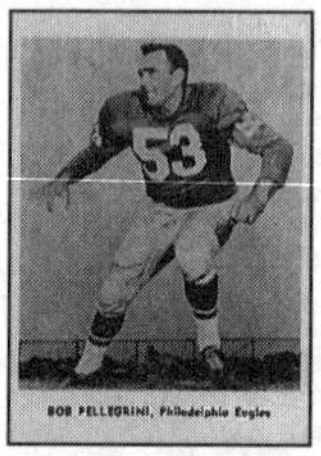

This 12-card set features (approximately) 5" by 7" black-and-white player photos. The photos show players in traditional poses with the quarterback preparing to throw, the runner heading downfield, and the defenseman ready for the tackle. These cards were packaged 12 to a packet and originally sold for 25 cents. The backs are blank. The cards are unnumbered and checklisted below in alphabetical order.

	NRMT	VG-E	GOOD
COMPLETE SET (12)	60.00	27.00	7.50
COMMON CARD (1-12)	5.00	2.20	.60
☐ 1 Maxie Baughan	7.50	3.40	.95
☐ 2 Jim McCusker	5.00	2.20	.60
☐ 3 Tommy McDonald	7.50	3.40	.95
☐ 4 Bob Pellegrini	5.00	2.20	.60
☐ 5 Pete Retzlaff	6.00	2.70	.75
☐ 6 Jesse Richardson	5.00	2.20	.60
☐ 7 Joe Robb	5.00	2.20	.60
☐ 8 Theron Sapp	5.00	2.20	.60
☐ 9 J.D. Smith	6.00	2.70	.75
☐ 10 Bobby Walston	6.00	2.70	.75
☐ 11 Jerry Williams ACO	5.00	2.20	.60
☐ 12 John Wittenborn	5.00	2.20	.60

1961 Eagles Team Issue

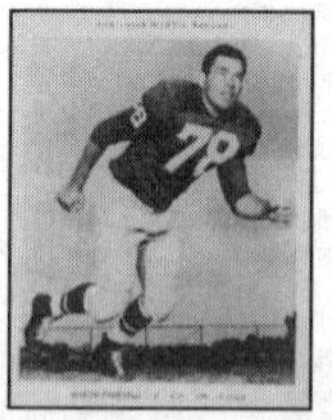

The Eagles issued this set of black and white player photos. Each measures approximately 8" by 10" and features the team name above the player photo with his name, vital statistics and college below. The backs are blank and unnumbered. The checklist below includes the known photos at this time. It's likely there were more produced. Any additions to this list would be appreciated.

	NRMT	VG-E	GOOD
COMPLETE SET (10	50.00	22.00	6.25
COMMON CARD (1-10)	5.00	2.20	.60
☐ 1 Don Burroughs	5.00	2.20	.60
☐ 2 Jimmy Carr	5.00	2.20	.60
☐ 3 King Hill	7.50	3.40	.95
☐ 4 Jim McCusker	5.00	2.20	.60
☐ 5 Clarence Peaks	7.50	3.40	.95
☐ 6 Will Renfro	5.00	2.20	.60
☐ 7 J.D. Smith T	5.00	2.20	.60
☐ 8 Leo Sugar	5.00	2.20	.60
☐ 9 Bobby Walston	7.50	3.40	.95
☐ 10 Chuck Weber	5.00	2.20	.60

1963 Eagles Phillies' Cigars

This attractive color football photo was part of a premium promotion for Phillies Cigars. It measures 6 1/2" by 9" and features a facsimile autograph on the cardfront. The cardback is blank.

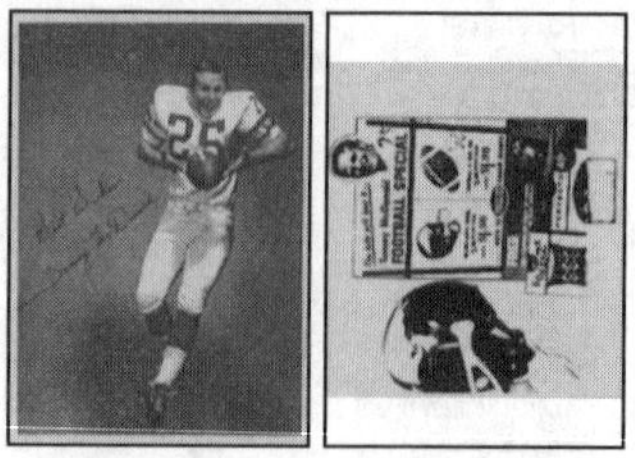

	NRMT	VG-E	GOOD
COMPLETE SET (1)	15.00	6.75	1.85
COMMON CARD	15.00	6.75	1.85
☐ 1 Tommy McDonald	15.00	6.75	1.85

1971 Eagles Postcards

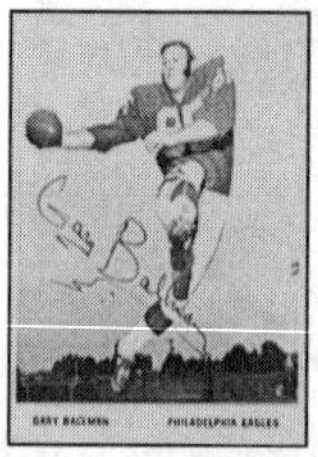

This 17-card set measures approximately 4 1/4" by 5 1/2" and features posed action, black-and-white player photos with white borders. The player's name and team are printed in black in the bottom white margin. Due to variances in printing, the photos were likely issued over a number of years. Several have been found with a Boy Scouts "BSA" logo near the photo while the team name also varies in size from photo to photo. Unless noted below, the backs include a postcard style format. The cards are unnumbered and checklisted below in alphabetical order.

	NRMT-MT	EXC	G-VG
COMPLETE SET (17)	40.00	18.00	5.00
COMMON CARD (1-16)	2.50	1.10	.30
☐ 1 Gary Ballman blankbacked	3.00	1.35	.35
☐ 2 Lee Bouggess	2.50	1.10	.30
☐ 3 Harold Jackson	2.50	1.10	.30
☐ 4 Kent Kramer	3.00	1.35	.35
☐ 5 Tom McNeill	2.50	1.10	.30
☐ 6 Mark Nordquist	2.50	1.10	.30
☐ 7 Ron Porter	2.50	1.10	.30
☐ 8 Steve Preece	3.00	1.35	.35
☐ 9A Tim Rossovich (with facsimile autograph)	3.00	1.35	.35
☐ 9B Tim Rossovich (no facsimile autograph)	3.00	1.35	.35
☐ 10 Jim Skaggs	2.50	1.10	.30
☐ 11 Norm Snead	4.00	1.80	.50
☐ 12 Jim Thrower	2.50	1.10	.30
☐ 13 Mel Tom	3.00	1.35	.35
☐ 14 Jim Ward	2.50	1.10	.30
☐ 15 Adrian Young	2.50	1.10	.30
☐ 16 Don Zimmerman	2.50	1.10	.30

1972-73 Eagles Team Issue

These Philadelphia Eagles team issued photos measure approximately 8" by 10" and feature a black and white player photo on a thin blankbacked card stock. The photos were likely issued over a number of years with many players issued in both a portrait and posed action format. Just the player's name and team name appear below the photo. The checklist is likely incomplete; any additions to this list would be appreciated.

	NRMT-MT	EXC	G-VG
COMPLETE SET (29)	60.00	27.00	7.50
COMMON CARD	2.00	.90	.25
☐ 1 Tom Bailey Portrait	2.00	.90	.25
☐ 2 Herman Ball Director of Personnel	2.00	.90	.25
☐ 3 Bill Bradley Posed Action	4.00	1.80	.50
☐ 4 John Bunting Portrait	3.00	1.35	.35
☐ 5 John Bunting Posed Action	3.00	1.35	.35
☐ 6 Bill Cody Portrait	2.00	.90	.25
☐ 7 Larry Crowe Portrait	2.00	.90	.25
☐ 8 Larry Crowe Posed action	2.00	.90	.25
☐ 9 Albert Davis Portrait	2.00	.90	.25
☐ 10 Albert Davis Posed action	2.00	.90	.25
☐ 11 Stanley Davis Portrait	2.00	.90	.25

	MINT	NRMT	EXC
☐ 12 Stanley Davis	2.00	.90	.25
Posed action			
☐ 13 Mike Dunstan	2.00	.90	.25
Portrait			
☐ 14 Mike Dunstan	2.00	.90	.25
Posed action			
☐ 15 Lawrence Estes	2.00	.90	.25
Portrait			
☐ 16 Pat Gibbs	2.00	.90	.25
Posed Action			
☐ 17 Harold Jackson	5.00	2.20	.60
Posed Action			
☐ 18 Wade Key	2.00	.90	.25
Posed Action			
☐ 19 Kent Kramer	2.00	.90	.25
Portrait			
☐ 20 Randy Logan	2.00	.90	.25
Posed Action			
☐ 21 Tom Luken	2.00	.90	.25
Posed Action			
☐ 22 Tom McNeill	2.00	.90	.25
Jersey 12			
☐ 23 Tom McNeill	2.00	.90	.25
Jersey 36			
☐ 24 Gary Pettigrew	2.00	.90	.25
Posed Action			
☐ 25 Bob Picard	2.00	.90	.25
Posed Action			
☐ 26 Ron Porter	2.00	.90	.25
Posed Action			
☐ 27 Jerry Wampfler CO	2.00	.90	.25
☐ 28 Vern Winfield	2.00	.90	.25
Posed Action			
☐ 29 Steve Zabel	3.00	1.35	.35
Posed Action			

1983 Eagles Frito Lay

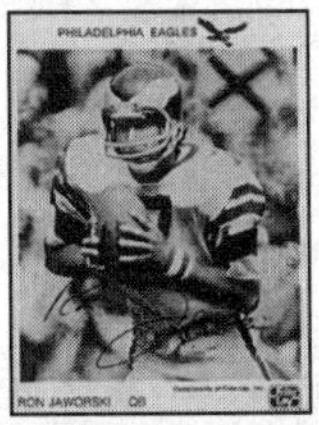

This 34-card set measures approximately 4 1/4" by 5 1/2" and features an action player shot and facsimile autograph enclosed in a white border. The team name and mascot appear in the top border while the player's name, position, and Frito Lay logo appear in the bottom border. The backs of card numbers 5, 27, and 31 are in the postcard format, while the rest of the backs are blank. Frito Lay sponsored several Eagles sets throughout the 1970s and '80s. This release can be differentiated by the full Frito Lay logo in the lower right corner and the 1/8" left and right borders. Because this set is unnumbered, the cards are listed alphabetically.

	MINT	NRMT	EXC
COMPLETE SET (34)	60.00	27.00	7.50
COMMON CARD (1-34)	1.50	.70	.19
☐ 1 Harvey Armstrong	1.50	.70	.19
☐ 2 Ron Baker	1.50	.70	.19
☐ 3 Greg Brown	1.50	.70	.19
☐ 4 Marion Campbell CO	2.00	.90	.25
☐ 5 Harold Carmichael	3.00	1.35	.35
☐ 6 Ken Clarke	1.50	.70	.19
☐ 7 Dennis DeVaughn	1.50	.70	.19
☐ 8 Herman Edwards	2.00	.90	.25
☐ 9 Ray Ellis	1.50	.70	.19
☐ 10 Major Everett	2.00	.90	.25
☐ 11 Anthony Griggs	1.50	.70	.19
☐ 12 Michael Haddix	2.00	.90	.25
☐ 13 Perry Harrington	1.50	.70	.19
☐ 14 Dennis Harrison	1.50	.70	.19
☐ 15 Ron Jaworski	4.00	1.80	.50
☐ 16 Vyto Kab	1.50	.70	.19
☐ 17 Steve Kenney	1.50	.70	.19
☐ 18 Dean Miraldi	1.50	.70	.19
☐ 19 Leonard Mitchell	1.50	.70	.19
☐ 20 Wilbert Montgomery	3.50	1.55	.45
☐ 21 Hubie Oliver	1.50	.70	.19
☐ 22 Joe Pisarcik	2.00	.90	.25
☐ 23 Mike Quick	3.00	1.35	.35
☐ 24 Jerry Robinson	2.00	.90	.25
☐ 25 Max Runager	1.50	.70	.19
☐ 26 Lawrence Sampleton	1.50	.70	.19
☐ 27 Jody Schulz	1.50	.70	.19
☐ 28 Jerry Sisemore	2.00	.90	.25
☐ 29 John Spagnola	2.00	.90	.25
☐ 30 Reggie Wilkes	1.50	.70	.19
☐ 31 Mike Williams	1.50	.70	.19
☐ 32 Tony Woodruff	1.50	.70	.19
☐ 33 Glen Young	1.50	.70	.19
☐ 34 Roynell Young	2.00	.90	.25

1984 Eagles Police

This numbered eight-card set features the Philadelphia Eagles. Backs are printed in black ink with red accent. Cards measure approximately

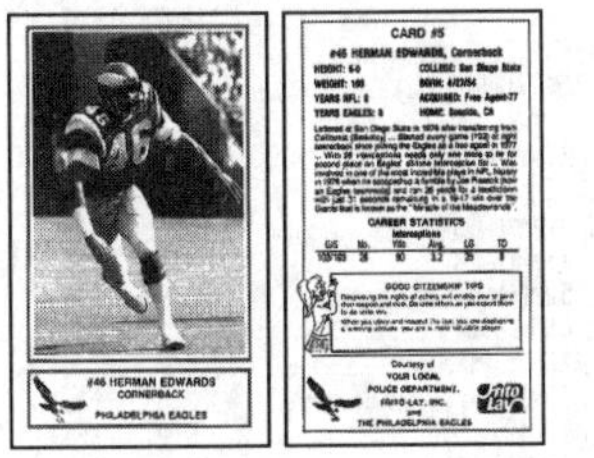

2 5/8" by 4 1/8". The set was sponsored by Frito-Lay, the local police department, and the Philadelphia Eagles.

	MINT	NRMT	EXC
COMPLETE SET (8)	6.00	2.70	.75
COMMON CARD (1-8)	.50	.23	.06
☐ 1 Mike Quick	1.25	.55	.16
☐ 2 Dennis Harrison	.50	.23	.06
☐ 3 Jerry Robinson	.75	.35	.09
☐ 4 Wilbert Montgomery	1.25	.55	.16
☐ 5 Herman Edwards	.50	.23	.06
☐ 6 Kenny Jackson	.75	.35	.09
☐ 7 Anthony Griggs	.50	.23	.06
☐ 8 Ron Jaworski	1.50	.70	.19

1985 Eagles Police

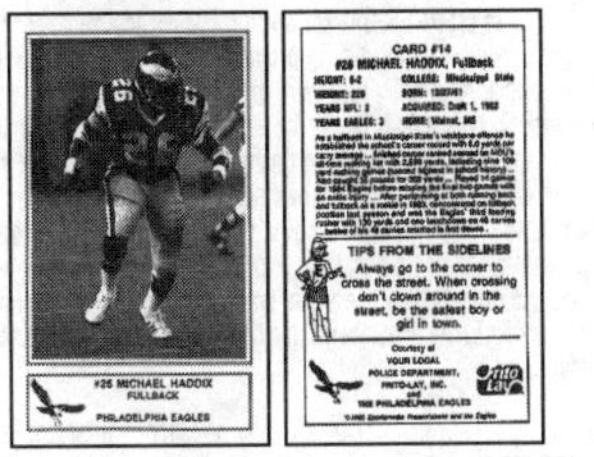

This 16-card set is numbered on the back. The card backs are printed in black and red ink on white card stock. Cards measure 2 5/8" by 4 1/8". The set was sponsored by Frito-Lay, local Police Departments, and the Eagles. Uniform numbers are printed on the card front before the player's name.

	MINT	NRMT	EXC
COMPLETE SET (16)	8.00	3.60	1.00
COMMON CARD (1-16)	.50	.23	.06
☐ 1 Ken Clarke	.50	.23	.06
☐ 2 Roynell Young	.75	.35	.09
☐ 3 Ray Ellis	.50	.23	.06
☐ 4 Ron Baker	.50	.23	.06
☐ 5 John Spagnola	.60	.25	.07
☐ 6 Reggie Wilkes	.50	.23	.06
☐ 7 Ron Jaworski	1.25	.55	.16
☐ 8 Steve Kenney	.50	.23	.06
☐ 9 Paul McFadden	.50	.23	.06
☐ 10 Mike Quick	1.00	.45	.12
☐ 11 Hubie Oliver	.50	.23	.06
☐ 12 Greg Brown	.60	.25	.07
☐ 13 Anthony Griggs	.50	.23	.06
☐ 14 Michael Haddix	.60	.25	.07
☐ 15 Kenny Jackson	.75	.35	.09
☐ 16 Vyto Kab	.50	.23	.06

1985 Eagles Team Issue

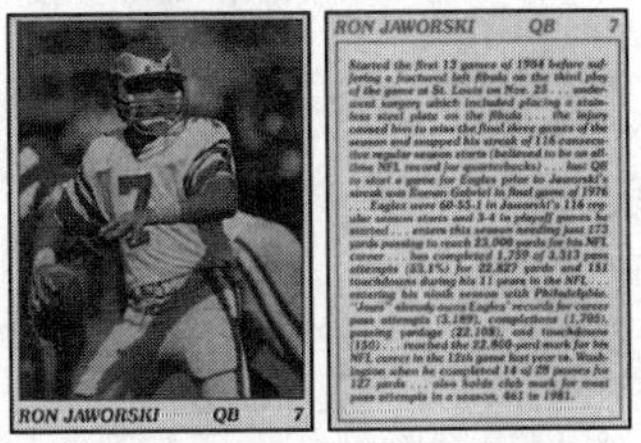

This 53-card team-issued set measures approximately 2 15/16" by 3 7/8". The fronts feature glossy color player photos bordered in white. The wider bottom border contains the player's name, position, and jersey number. Player information again appears on the top of the backs in green print; the career summary is printed in a black box that fills the rest of the backs. The cards are unnumbered and checklisted below alphabetically, with the miscellaneous cards listed at the end.

	MINT	NRMT	EXC
COMPLETE SET (53)	60.00	27.00	7.50
COMMON CARD (1-53)	1.00	.45	.12
☐ 1 Harvey Armstrong	1.00	.45	.12
☐ 2 Ron Baker	1.00	.45	.12
☐ 3 Norman Braman PRES	1.00	.45	.12
☐ 4 Greg Brown	1.00	.45	.12
☐ 5 Marion Campbell CO	1.50	.70	.19
☐ 6 Jeff Christensen	1.00	.45	.12
☐ 7 Ken Clarke	1.00	.45	.12
☐ 8 Evan Cooper	1.00	.45	.12
☐ 9 Byron Darby	1.00	.45	.12
☐ 10 Mark Dennard	1.00	.45	.12
☐ 11 Herman Edwards	1.50	.70	.19
☐ 12 Ray Ellis	1.00	.45	.12
☐ 13 Major Everett	1.50	.70	.19
☐ 14 Gerry Feehery	1.00	.45	.12
☐ 15 Elbert Foules	1.00	.45	.12
☐ 16 Gregg Garrity	1.50	.70	.19
☐ 17 Anthony Griggs	1.00	.45	.12
☐ 18 Michael Haddix	1.00	.45	.12
☐ 19 Andre Hardy	1.00	.45	.12
☐ 20 Dennis Harrison	1.00	.45	.12
☐ 21 Joe Hayes	1.00	.45	.12
☐ 22 Melvin Hoover	1.00	.45	.12
☐ 23 Wes Hopkins	1.50	.70	.19
☐ 24 Mike Horan	1.00	.45	.12
☐ 25 Kenny Jackson	1.50	.70	.19
☐ 26 Ron Jaworski	4.00	1.80	.50
☐ 27 Vyto Kab	1.00	.45	.12
☐ 28 Steve Kenney	1.00	.45	.12
☐ 29 Rich Kraynak	1.00	.45	.12
☐ 30 Dean May	1.00	.45	.12
☐ 31 Paul McFadden	1.00	.45	.12
☐ 32 Dean Miraldi	1.00	.45	.12
☐ 33 Leonard Mitchell	1.00	.45	.12
☐ 34 Wilbert Montgomery	3.00	1.35	.35
☐ 35 Hubie Oliver	1.00	.45	.12
☐ 36 Mike Quick	2.00	.90	.25
☐ 37 Mike Reichenbach	1.00	.45	.12
☐ 38 Jerry Robinson	1.50	.70	.19
☐ 39 Rusty Russell	1.00	.45	.12
☐ 40 Lawrence Sampleton	1.00	.45	.12
☐ 41 Jody Schulz	1.00	.45	.12
☐ 42 John Spagnola	1.50	.70	.19
☐ 43 Tom Strauthers	1.00	.45	.12
☐ 44 Andre Waters	2.00	.90	.25
☐ 45 Reggie Wilkes	1.00	.45	.12
☐ 46 Joel Williams	1.00	.45	.12
☐ 47 Michael Williams	1.00	.45	.12
☐ 48 Brenard Wilson	1.00	.45	.12
☐ 49 Tony Woodruff	1.00	.45	.12
☐ 50 Roynell Young	1.50	.70	.19
☐ 51 Logo Card	1.50	.70	.19
(Eagle holding football on both sides)			
☐ 52 1985 Schedule Card	1.50	.70	.19
(Both sides)			
☐ 53 Title Card 1985-86	1.50	.70	.19
(Eagles' helmet)			

1986 Eagles Frito Lay

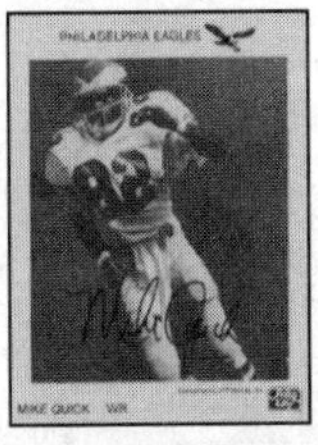

Cards from this set measure approximately 4 1/4" by 5 1/2" and feature an action player shot and facsimile autograph enclosed within a white border. The team name and mascot appear in the top border while the player's name, position, and Frito Lay logo appear in the bottom border. All are blankbacked. Frito Lay sponsored several Eagles sets throughout the 1970s and '80s. This release can be differentiated by the full Frito Lay logo in the lower right corner and the 3/8" left and right borders. Because this set is unnumbered, the cards are listed alphabetically. Any additions to this checklist would be greatly appreciated.

	MINT	NRMT	EXC
COMPLETE SET (7)	15.00	6.75	1.85
COMMON CARD (1-7)	1.00	.45	.12
☐ 1 Wes Hopkins	1.50	.70	.19
☐ 2 Ron Jaworski	4.00	1.80	.50
☐ 3 Ron Johnson WR	1.00	.45	.12
☐ 4 Mike Quick	2.50	1.10	.30
☐ 5 Buddy Ryan CO	4.00	1.80	.50
☐ 6 Tom Strauthers	1.00	.45	.12
☐ 7 Andre Waters	1.50	.70	.19

1986 Eagles Police

This 16-card set is numbered on the card backs, which are printed in black and red ink on white card stock. Cards measure approximately 2 5/8" by 4 1/8". The set was sponsored by Frito-Lay, local Police Departments, and the Eagles. Uniform numbers are printed on the card front before the player's name. Randall Cunningham's card predates his 1987 Topps Rookie Card by one year.

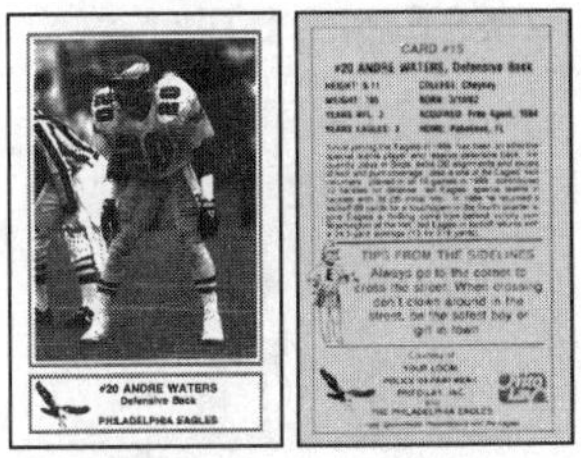

	MINT	NRMT	EXC
COMPLETE SET (16)	10.00	4.50	1.25
COMMON CARD (1-16)	.40	.18	.05
☐ 1 Greg Brown	.50	.23	.06
☐ 2 Reggie White	5.00	2.20	.60
☐ 3 John Spagnola	.50	.23	.06
☐ 4 Mike Quick	.75	.35	.09
☐ 5 Ken Clarke	.40	.18	.05
☐ 6 Ken Reeves	.40	.18	.05
☐ 7 Mike Reichenbach	.40	.18	.05
☐ 8 Wes Hopkins	.60	.25	.07
☐ 9 Roynell Young	.60	.25	.07
☐ 10 Randall Cunningham	3.00	1.35	.35
☐ 11 Paul McFadden	.40	.18	.05
☐ 12 Matt Cavanaugh	.60	.25	.07
☐ 13 Ron Jaworski	1.00	.45	.12
☐ 14 Byron Darby	.40	.18	.05
☐ 15 Andre Waters	.60	.25	.07
☐ 16 Buddy Ryan CO	.75	.35	.09

1987 Eagles Police

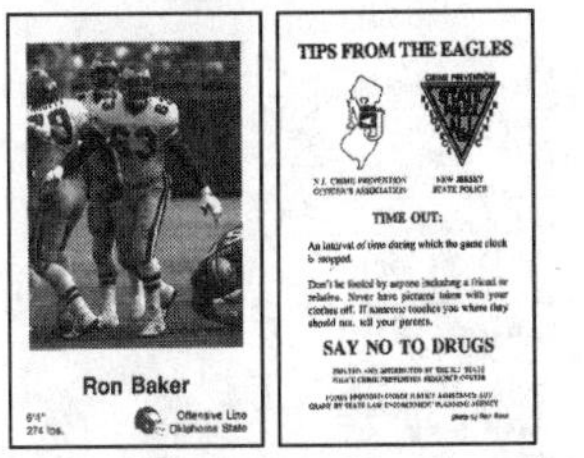

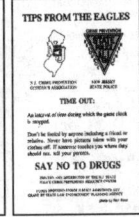

This set of 12 cards featuring Philadelphia Eagles was issued very late in the year and was not widely distributed. Reportedly 10,000 sets were distributed by officers of the New Jersey police force. Cards measure approximately 2 3/4" by 4 1/8" and feature a crime prevention tip on the back. The set was sponsored by the New Jersey State Police Crime Prevention Resource Center. The cards are unnumbered and are listed alphabetically below for reference.

	MINT	NRMT	EXC
COMPLETE SET (12)	75.00	34.00	9.50
COMMON CARD (1-12)	4.00	1.80	.50
☐ 1 Ron Baker	4.00	1.80	.50
☐ 2 Keith Byars	7.50	3.40	.95
☐ 3 Ken Clarke	4.00	1.80	.50
☐ 4 Randall Cunningham	12.00	5.50	1.50
☐ 5 Paul McFadden	4.00	1.80	.50
☐ 6 Mike Quick	5.00	2.20	.60
☐ 7 Mike Reidenbach	4.00	1.80	.50
☐ 8 Buddy Ryan CO	6.00	2.70	.75
☐ 9 John Spagnola	4.00	1.80	.50
☐ 10 Anthony Toney	5.00	2.20	.60
☐ 11 Andre Waters	5.00	2.20	.60
☐ 12 Reggie White	20.00	9.00	2.50

1988 Eagles Police

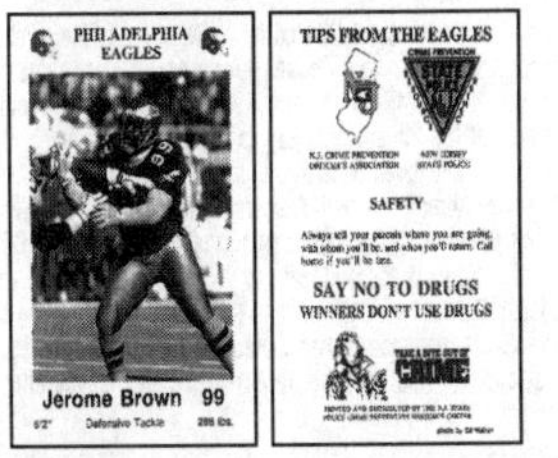

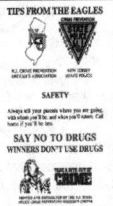

The 1988 Police Philadelphia Eagles set contains 12 unnumbered cards measuring approximately 2 3/4" by 4 1/8". There are 11 player cards and one coach card. The backs have safety tips. The cards are listed below in alphabetical order by subject's name.

	MINT	NRMT	EXC
COMPLETE SET (12)	70.00	32.00	8.75
COMMON CARD (1-12)	4.00	1.80	.50
☐ 1 Jerome Brown	6.00	2.70	.75
☐ 2 Keith Byars	6.00	2.70	.75
☐ 3 Randall Cunningham	7.00	3.10	.85
☐ 4 Matt Darwin	4.00	1.80	.50
☐ 5 Keith Jackson	10.00	4.50	1.25
☐ 6 Seth Joyner	6.00	2.70	.75
☐ 7 Mike Quick	5.00	2.20	.60
☐ 8 Buddy Ryan CO	6.00	2.70	.75
☐ 9 Clyde Simmons	6.00	2.70	.75
☐ 10 John Teltschik	4.00	1.80	.50
☐ 11 Anthony Toney	5.00	2.20	.60
☐ 12 Reggie White	12.00	5.50	1.50

1989 Eagles Daily News

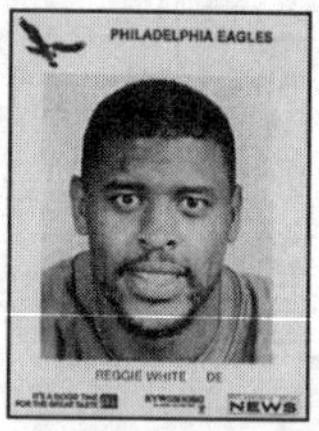

This 24-card set which measures approximately 5 9/16" by 4 1/4" features black and white portrait photos of the players. Above the player's photo is the Eagle logo and the Philadelphia Eagles team name while underneath are advertisments for McDonald's, radio station KYW, and the Philadelphia Daily News. The backs are blank. This was the third season that the Eagles had participated in this project. We have checklisted this set in alphabetical order.

	MINT	NRMT	EXC
COMPLETE SET (24)	40.00	18.00	5.00
COMMON CARD (1-23)	1.00	.45	.12
☐ 1 Eric Allen	1.50	.70	.19
☐ 2 Jerome Brown	2.00	.90	.25
☐ 3 Keith Byars	2.00	.90	.25
☐ 4 Cris Carter UER (Name misspelled Chris on front)	6.00	2.70	.75
☐ 5 Randall Cunningham	3.00	1.35	.35
☐ 6 Matt Darwin	1.00	.45	.12
☐ 7 Gerry Feehery	1.00	.45	.12
☐ 8 Ron Heller	1.00	.45	.12
☐ 9A Terry Hoage (Solid color jersey)	1.50	.70	.19
☐ 9B Terry Hoage (With white collar or undershirt)	1.50	.70	.19
☐ 10 Wes Hopkins	1.50	.70	.19
☐ 11 Keith Jackson	3.00	1.35	.35
☐ 12 Seth Joyner	2.00	.90	.25
☐ 13 Mike Pitts	1.00	.45	.12
☐ 14 Mike Quick	1.50	.70	.19
☐ 15 Mike Reichenbach	1.00	.45	.12
☐ 16 Clyde Simmons	2.00	.90	.25
☐ 17 John Spagnola	1.50	.70	.19
☐ 18 Junior Tautalatasi	1.00	.45	.12
☐ 19 John Teltschik	1.00	.45	.12
☐ 20 Anthony Toney	1.00	.45	.12
☐ 21 Andre Waters	1.50	.70	.19
☐ 22 Reggie White	6.00	2.70	.75
☐ 23 Luis Zendejas	1.00	.45	.12

1989 Eagles Police

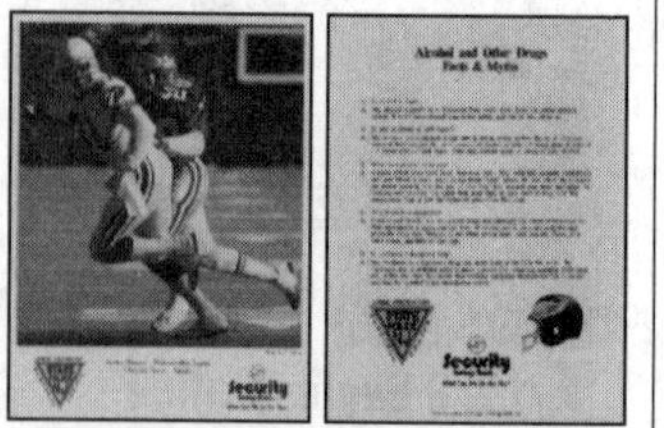

This nine-card set was distributed by the New Jersey State Police in Trenton, New Jersey. These unnumbered cards measure approximately 8 1/2" by 11" and feature action player photos of members of the Philadelphia Eagles inside white borders. Player information is centered beneath the picture between the New Jersey State Police Crime Prevention Resource Center emblem and Security Savings Bank logo. The back carries the title "Alcohol and Other Drugs: Facts and Myths" and features five questions and answers on this topic. Sponsor and team logo at the bottom round out the back. The cards are unnumbered and checklisted below alphabetically. The set is tough to find because, reportedly, it was issued after the season.

	MINT	NRMT	EXC
COMPLETE SET (9)	50.00	22.00	6.25
COMMON CARD (1-9)	4.00	1.80	.50
☐ 1 Cris Carter	15.00	6.75	1.85
☐ 2 Gregg Garrity	4.00	1.80	.50
☐ 3 Mike Golic	5.00	2.20	.60
☐ 4 Keith Jackson	8.00	3.60	1.00
☐ 5 Clyde Simmons	6.00	2.70	.75
☐ 6 John Teltschik	4.00	1.80	.50
☐ 7 Anthony Toney	4.00	1.80	.50
☐ 8 Andre Waters	5.00	2.20	.60
☐ 9 Luis Zendejas	4.00	1.80	.50

1989 Eagles Smokey

This 49-card set features members of the Philadelphia Eagles. The cards measure approximately 3" by 5". The full-color photo on the front covers the complete card, although the player's name, number, and position are overprinted in the lower right corner. Each card back shows a different fire safety cartoon. Backs are printed in green ink in

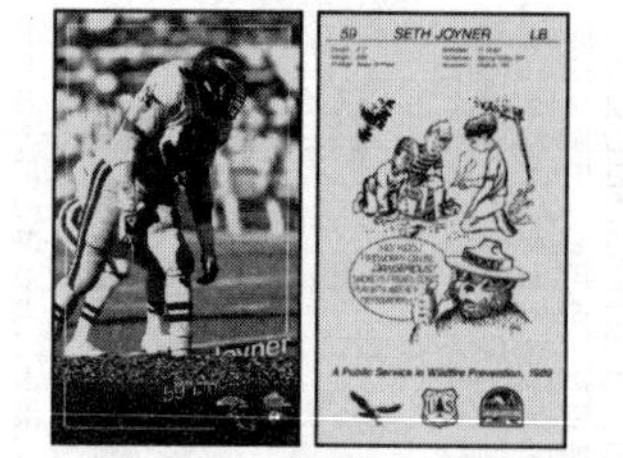

deference to the Eagles colors. Cards are unnumbered, except for uniform number which appears on the card front and back; cards are ordered below by uniform number. In a few cases, there were two cards produced of the same player; typically the two can be distinguished by home and away colors. The complete set price below includes all the variations listed.

	MINT	NRMT	EXC
COMPLETE SET (49)	135.00	60.00	17.00
COMMON CARD	2.00	.90	.25
☐ 6 Matt Cavanaugh	2.50	1.10	.30
☐ 8 Luis Zendejas	2.00	.90	.25
☐ 9 Don McPherson	2.50	1.10	.30
☐ 10 John Teltschik	2.00	.90	.25
☐ 12A Randall Cunningham (White jersey)	10.00	4.50	1.25
☐ 12B Randall Cunningham (Green jersey)	10.00	4.50	1.25
☐ 20 Andre Waters	3.00	1.35	.35
☐ 21 Eric Allen	3.00	1.35	.35
☐ 25 Anthony Toney	2.50	1.10	.30
☐ 33 William Frizzell	2.00	.90	.25
☐ 34 Terry Hoage	2.50	1.10	.30
☐ 35 Mark Konecny	2.00	.90	.25
☐ 41 Keith Byars	4.00	1.80	.50
☐ 42 Eric Everett	2.00	.90	.25
☐ 43 Roynell Young	2.50	1.10	.30
☐ 46 Izel Jenkins	2.00	.90	.25
☐ 48 Wes Hopkins	2.50	1.10	.30
☐ 50 Dave Rimington	2.50	1.10	.30
☐ 52 Todd Bell	2.50	1.10	.30
☐ 53 Dwayne Jiles	2.00	.90	.25
☐ 55 Mike Reichenbach	2.00	.90	.25
☐ 56 Byron Evans	2.50	1.10	.30
☐ 58 Ty Allert	2.00	.90	.25
☐ 59 Seth Joyner	3.00	1.35	.35
☐ 61 Ben Tamburello	2.00	.90	.25
☐ 63 Ron Baker	2.00	.90	.25
☐ 66 Ken Reeves	2.00	.90	.25
☐ 68 Reggie Singletary	2.00	.90	.25
☐ 72 David Alexander	2.00	.90	.25
☐ 73 Ron Heller	2.00	.90	.25
☐ 74 Mike Pitts	2.00	.90	.25
☐ 78 Matt Darwin	2.00	.90	.25
☐ 80 Cris Carter	12.00	5.50	1.50
☐ 81 Kenny Jackson	2.50	1.10	.30
☐ 82A Mike Quick (White jersey)	3.00	1.35	.35
☐ 82B Mike Quick (Green jersey)	3.00	1.35	.35
☐ 83 Jimmie Giles	2.50	1.10	.30
☐ 85 Ron Johnson	2.00	.90	.25
☐ 86 Gregg Garrity	2.00	.90	.25
☐ 88 Keith Jackson	7.50	3.40	.95
☐ 89 David Little	2.50	1.10	.30
☐ 90 Mike Golic	2.50	1.10	.30
☐ 91 Scott Curtis	2.00	.90	.25
☐ 92 Reggie White	15.00	6.75	1.85
☐ 96 Clyde Simmons	3.00	1.35	.35
☐ 97 John Klingel	2.00	.90	.25
☐ 99 Jerome Brown	4.00	1.80	.50
☐ NNO Buddy Ryan CO (Wearing white cap)	6.00	2.70	.75
☐ NNO Buddy Ryan CO (Wearing green cap)	6.00	2.70	.75

1990 Eagles Police

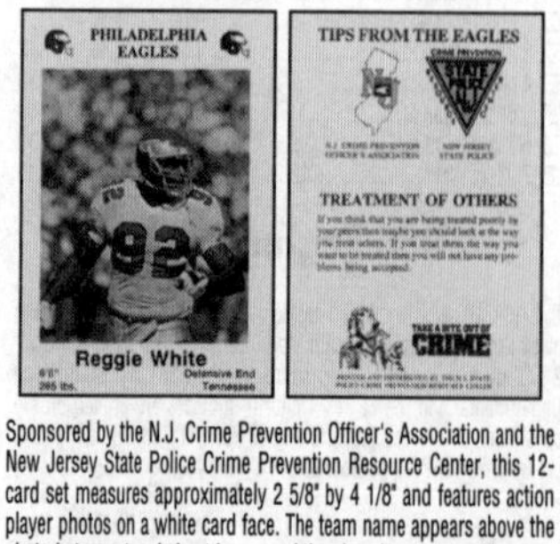

Sponsored by the N.J. Crime Prevention Officer's Association and the New Jersey State Police Crime Prevention Resource Center, this 12-card set measures approximately 2 5/8" by 4 1/8" and features action player photos on a white card face. The team name appears above the photo between two helmet icons, and the player's name, position, and personal information appear below. The backs contains sponsor logos, safety tips, and the slogan "Take a bite out of crime" by McGruff the crime dog. The cards are unnumbered and checklisted below in alphabetical order.

	MINT	NRMT	EXC
COMPLETE SET (12)	45.00	20.00	5.50
COMMON CARD (1-12)	3.00	1.35	.35
☐ 1 David Alexander	3.00	1.35	.35
☐ 2 Eric Allen	4.00	1.80	.50
☐ 3 Randall Cunningham	5.00	2.20	.60
☐ 4 Keith Byars	4.00	1.80	.50
☐ 5 Jeff Feagles	3.00	1.35	.35
☐ 6 Mike Golic	4.00	1.80	.50
☐ 7 Keith Jackson	4.00	1.80	.50
☐ 8 Rich Kotite CO	3.00	1.35	.35
☐ 9 Roger Ruzek	3.00	1.35	.35
☐ 10 Mickey Shuler	4.00	1.80	.50
☐ 11 Clyde Simmons	4.00	1.80	.50
☐ 12 Reggie White	9.00	4.00	1.10

1990 Eagles Sealtest

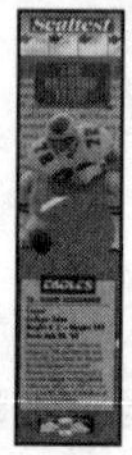

This six-card set (of bookmarks) which measures approximately 2" by 8" was produced by Sealtest to promote reading among children in Philadelphia. Apparently they were given out at The Free Library of Philadelphia on a weekly basis. The basic design of these bookmarks is identical to the 1990 Knudsen Chargers and 49ers bookmark sets. The color action player cut-out overlays a football stadium design. A box at the bottom whose color varies per bookmark gives biographical information and player profile. The backs have sponsor logos and describe two books that are available at the public library. The bookmarks are unnumbered and checklisted below in alphabetical order.

	MINT	NRMT	EXC
COMPLETE SET (6)	15.00	6.75	1.85
COMMON CARD (1-6)	2.50	1.10	.30
☐ 1 David Alexander	2.50	1.10	.30
☐ 2 Eric Allen	3.00	1.35	.35
☐ 3 Keith Byars	3.00	1.35	.35
☐ 4 Randall Cunningham	4.00	1.80	.50
☐ 5 Mike Pitts	2.50	1.10	.30
☐ 6 Mike Quick	3.00	1.35	.35

1992 Eagles Team Issue

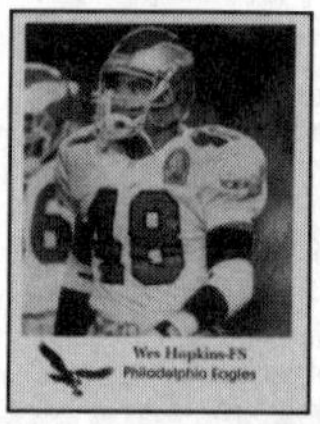

These team issued photos measure approximately 4 1/4" by 5 1/2" and were produced for distribution by the Philadelphia Eagles. Each photo is blankbacked and unnumbered. Several photos were likely issued over a period of years. The set is thought to be complete at 21-photos. Any additions to this list would be appreciated.

	MINT	NRMT	EXC
COMPLETE SET (21)	35.00	16.00	4.40
COMMON CARD (1-21)	1.00	.45	.12
☐ 1 David Alexander	1.00	.45	.12
☐ 2 Eric Allen	2.50	1.10	.30
☐ 3 Fred Barnett	3.00	1.35	.35
☐ 4 Pat Beach	1.00	.45	.12
☐ 5 Keith Byars	2.00	.90	.25
☐ 6 Jeff Feagles	1.00	.45	.12
☐ 7 Mike Golic	1.50	.70	.19
☐ 8 Roy Green	1.50	.70	.19
☐ 9 Britt Hager	1.00	.45	.12
☐ 10 Andy Harmon	1.50	.70	.19
☐ 11 Wes Hopkins	1.00	.45	.12
☐ 12 Izel Jenkins	1.50	.70	.19
☐ 13 Tommy Jeter	1.00	.45	.12
☐ 14 Maurice Johnson	1.00	.45	.12
☐ 15 Jim McMahon	3.00	1.35	.35
☐ 16 Ken Rose	1.00	.45	.12
☐ 17 Clyde Simmons	1.50	.70	.19
☐ 18 Herschel Walker	3.00	1.35	.35
☐ 19 Casey Weldon	2.00	.90	.25
☐ 20 Reggie White	6.00	2.70	.75
☐ 21 Calvin Williams	2.00	.90	.25

1987 English Bears

This 33-card set was made in West Germany (by Ace Fact Pack) for distribution in England. The cards measure approximately 2 1/4" by 3

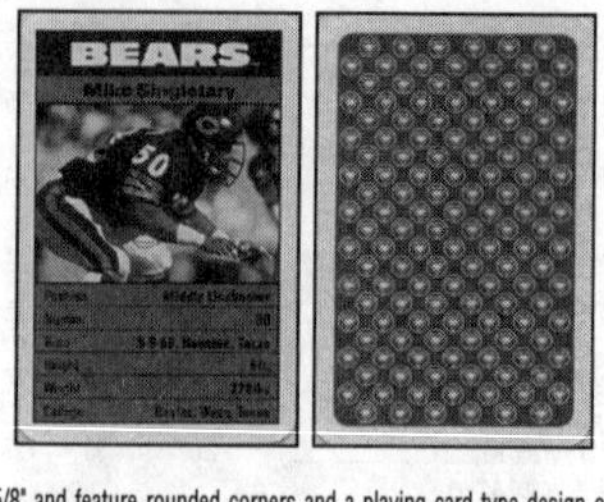

5/8" and feature rounded corners and a playing card type design on the back. The 22 player cards in the set have been checklisted below in alphabetical order.

	MINT	NRMT	EXC
COMPLETE SET (33)	250.00	110.00	31.00
COMMON CARD (1-33)	4.00	1.80	.50
☐ 1 Todd Bell	4.00	1.80	.50
☐ 2 Mark Bortz	4.00	1.80	.50
☐ 3 Kevin Butler	5.00	2.20	.60
☐ 4 Jim Covert	5.00	2.20	.60
☐ 5 Richard Dent	12.00	5.50	1.50
☐ 6 Dave Duerson	4.00	1.80	.50
☐ 7 Gary Fencik	5.00	2.20	.60
☐ 8 Willie Gault	6.00	2.70	.75
☐ 9 Dan Hampton	10.00	4.50	1.25
☐ 10 Jay Hilgenberg	5.00	2.20	.60
☐ 11 Wilber Marshall	5.00	2.20	.60
☐ 12 Jim McMahon	15.00	6.75	1.85
☐ 13 Steve McMichael	7.50	3.40	.95
☐ 14 Emery Moorehead	4.00	1.80	.50
☐ 15 Keith Ortega	4.00	1.80	.50
☐ 16 Walter Payton	100.00	45.00	12.50
☐ 17 William Perry	7.50	3.40	.95
☐ 18 Mike Richardson	4.00	1.80	.50
☐ 19 Mike Singletary	15.00	6.75	1.85
☐ 20 Matt Suhey	5.00	2.20	.60
☐ 21 Keith Van Horne	4.00	1.80	.50
☐ 22 Otis Wilson	4.00	1.80	.50
☐ 23 Bears Helmet	4.00	1.80	.50
☐ 24 Bears Information	4.00	1.80	.50
☐ 25 Bears Uniform	4.00	1.80	.50
☐ 26 Game Record Holders	4.00	1.80	.50
☐ 27 Season Record Holders	4.00	1.80	.50
☐ 28 Career Record Holders	4.00	1.80	.50
☐ 29 Record 1967-86	4.00	1.80	.50
☐ 30 1986 Team Statistics	4.00	1.80	.50
☐ 31 All-Time Greats	4.00	1.80	.50
☐ 32 Roll of Honour	4.00	1.80	.50
☐ 33 Soldier Field	4.00	1.80	.50

1987 English Broncos

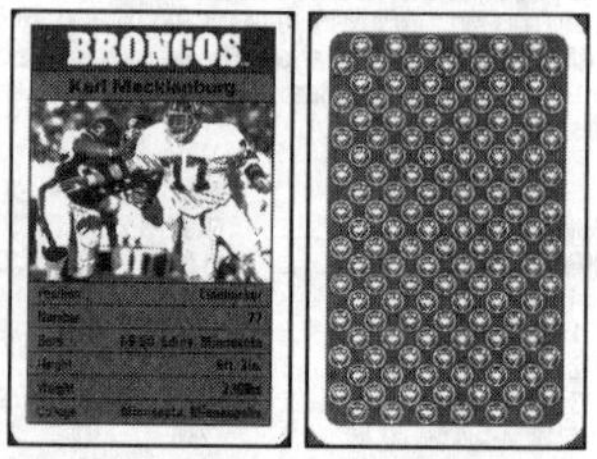

This 33-card set measures approximately 2 1/4" by 3 5/8". This set consists of 22 player cards and 11 organizational cards. These cards, which were issued in Great Britain and made in West Germany (by Ace Fact Pack), have a playing card design on the back. The cards are checklisted below in alphabetical order.

	MINT	NRMT	EXC
COMPLETE SET (33)	200.00	90.00	25.00
COMMON CARD (1-33)	4.00	1.80	.50
☐ 1 Keith Bishop	4.00	1.80	.50
☐ 2 Bill Bryan	4.00	1.80	.50
☐ 3 Mark Cooper	4.00	1.80	.50
☐ 4 John Elway	100.00	45.00	12.50
☐ 5 Steve Foley	4.00	1.80	.50
☐ 6 Mike Harden	4.00	1.80	.50
☐ 7 Ricky Hunley	4.00	1.80	.50
☐ 8 Vance Johnson	5.00	2.20	.60
☐ 9 Rulon Jones	5.00	2.20	.60
☐ 10 Rich Karlis	4.00	1.80	.50
☐ 11 Clarence Kay	4.00	1.80	.50
☐ 12 Ken Lanier	4.00	1.80	.50
☐ 13 Karl Mecklenburg	7.50	3.40	.95
☐ 14 Chris Norman	4.00	1.80	.50
☐ 15 Jim Ryan	4.00	1.80	.50
☐ 16 Dennis Smith	5.00	2.20	.60
☐ 17 Dave Studdard	4.00	1.80	.50
☐ 18 Andre Townsend	4.00	1.80	.50
☐ 19 Steve Watson	5.00	2.20	.60
☐ 20 Gerald Willhite	4.00	1.80	.50
☐ 21 Sammy Winder	5.00	2.20	.60
☐ 22 Louis Wright	5.00	2.20	.60
☐ 23 Broncos Helmet	4.00	1.80	.50
☐ 24 Broncos Information	4.00	1.80	.50
☐ 25 Broncos Uniform	4.00	1.80	.50

	MINT	NRMT	EXC
☐ 26 Game Record Holders	4.00	1.80	.50
☐ 27 Season Record Holders	4.00	1.80	.50
☐ 28 Career Record Holders	4.00	1.80	.50
☐ 29 Record 1967-86	4.00	1.80	.50
☐ 30 1986 Team Statistics	4.00	1.80	.50
☐ 31 All-Time Greats	4.00	1.80	.50
☐ 32 Roll of Honour	4.00	1.80	.50
☐ 33 Denver Mile High Stadium	4.00	1.80	.50

1987 English Cowboys

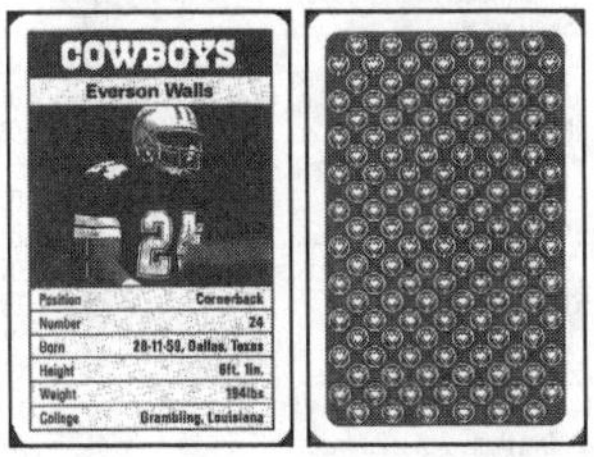

This 33-card set measures approximately 2 1/4" by 3 5/8". This set, which was printed in West Germany (by Ace Fact Pack) for release in Great Britain, has rounded corners and a playing type card back. There were 22 players in this set which we have checklisted alphabetically.

	MINT	NRMT	EXC
COMPLETE SET (33)	225.00	100.00	28.00
COMMON CARD (1-33)	4.00	1.80	.50
☐ 1 Bill Bates	7.50	3.40	.95
☐ 2 Doug Cosbie	5.00	2.20	.60
☐ 3 Tony Dorsett	40.00	18.00	5.00
☐ 4 Michael Downs	4.00	1.80	.50
☐ 5 John Dutton	5.00	2.20	.60
☐ 6 Ron Fellows	4.00	1.80	.50
☐ 7 Mike Hegman	4.00	1.80	.50
☐ 8 Tony Hill	7.50	3.40	.95
☐ 9 Jim Jeffcoat	7.50	3.40	.95
☐ 10 Ed Too Tall Jones	15.00	6.75	1.85
☐ 11 Crawford Ker	4.00	1.80	.50
☐ 12 Eugene Lockhart	4.00	1.80	.50
☐ 13 Phil Pozderac	4.00	1.80	.50
☐ 14 Tom Rafferty	4.00	1.80	.50
☐ 15 Jeff Rohrer	4.00	1.80	.50
☐ 16 Mike Sherrard	7.50	3.40	.95
☐ 17 Glen Titensor	4.00	1.80	.50
☐ 18 Mark Tuinei	6.00	2.70	.75
☐ 19 Herschel Walker	20.00	9.00	2.50
☐ 20 Everson Walls	4.00	1.80	.50
☐ 21 Danny White	12.00	5.50	1.50
☐ 22 Randy White	20.00	9.00	2.50
☐ 23 Cowboys Helmet	4.00	1.80	.50
☐ 24 Cowboys Information	4.00	1.80	.50
☐ 25 Cowboys Uniform	4.00	1.80	.50
☐ 26 Game Record Holders	4.00	1.80	.50
☐ 27 Season Record Holders	4.00	1.80	.50
☐ 28 Career Record Holders	4.00	1.80	.50
☐ 29 Record 1967-86	4.00	1.80	.50
☐ 30 1986 Team Statistics	4.00	1.80	.50
☐ 31 All-Time Greats	4.00	1.80	.50
☐ 32 Roll of Honour	4.00	1.80	.50
☐ 33 Texas Stadium	4.00	1.80	.50

1987 English Dolphins

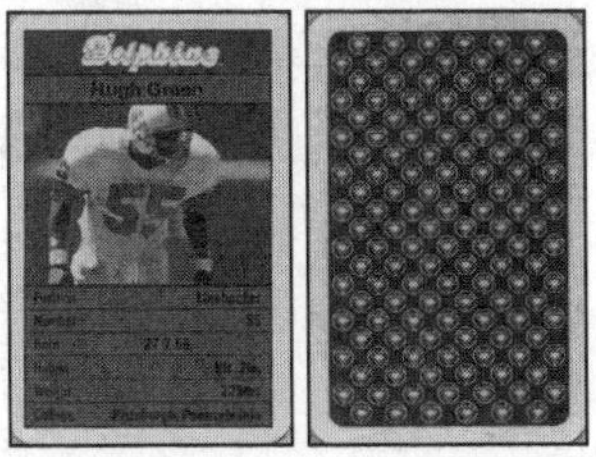

This 33-card set measures approximately 2 1/4" by 3 5/8". The set was printed in West Germany (by Ace Fact Pack) for release in Great Britain. This set features members of the Miami Dolphins and the set has rounded corners on the front and a design for Ace (looks like a playing card) on the back. We have checklisted the set in alphabetical order.

	MINT	NRMT	EXC
COMPLETE SET (33)	400.00	180.00	50.00
COMMON CARD (1-33)	4.00	1.80	.50
☐ 1 Bob Baumhower	5.00	2.20	.60
☐ 2 Woody Bennett	4.00	1.80	.50
☐ 3 Doug Betters	5.00	2.20	.60
☐ 4 Glenn Blackwood	5.00	2.20	.60
☐ 5 Bud Brown	4.00	1.80	.50
☐ 6 Bob Brudzinski	4.00	1.80	.50
☐ 7 Mark Clayton	10.00	4.50	1.25
☐ 8 Mark Duper	10.00	4.50	1.25
☐ 9 Roy Foster	4.00	1.80	.50
☐ 10 Jon Giesler	4.00	1.80	.50
☐ 11 Hugh Green	5.00	2.20	.60
☐ 12 Lorenzo Hampton	4.00	1.80	.50
☐ 13 Bruce Hardy	4.00	1.80	.50
☐ 14 William Judson	4.00	1.80	.50
☐ 15 Greg Koch	4.00	1.80	.50
☐ 16 Paul Lankford	4.00	1.80	.50
☐ 17 George Little	4.00	1.80	.50
☐ 18 Dan Marino	300.00	135.00	38.00
☐ 19 John Offerdahl	5.00	2.20	.60
☐ 20 Dwight Stephenson	5.00	2.20	.60
☐ 21 Don Strock	5.00	2.20	.60
☐ 22 T.J. Turner	4.00	1.80	.50
☐ 23 Dolphins Helmet	4.00	1.80	.50
☐ 24 Dolphins Information	4.00	1.80	.50
☐ 25 Dolphins Uniform	4.00	1.80	.50
☐ 26 Game Record Holders	4.00	1.80	.50
☐ 27 Season Record Holders	4.00	1.80	.50
☐ 28 Career Record Holders	4.00	1.80	.50
☐ 29 Record 1967-86	4.00	1.80	.50
☐ 30 1986 Team Statistics	4.00	1.80	.50
☐ 31 All-Time Greats	4.00	1.80	.50
☐ 32 Roll of Honour	4.00	1.80	.50
☐ 33 Joe Robbie Stadium	4.00	1.80	.50

1987 English 49ers

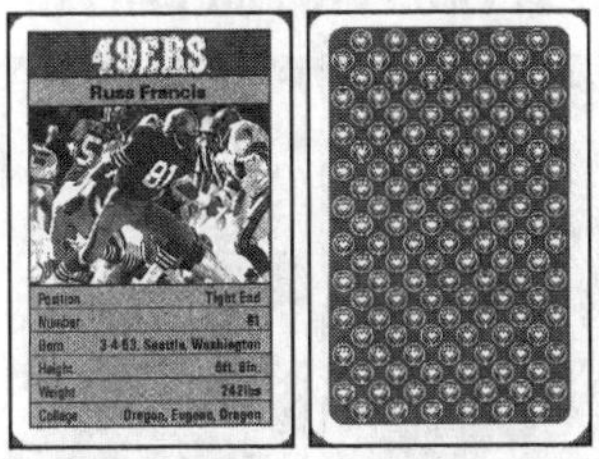

This 33-card set measures approximately 2 1/4" by 3 5/8". This set was manufactured in West Germany (by Ace Fact Pack) for release in Great Britain and features rounded corners and a playing card type of design on the back. There are 22 player cards in this set and we have checklisted those cards in alphabetical order.

	MINT	NRMT	EXC
COMPLETE SET (33)	650.00	300.00	80.00
COMMON CARD (1-33)	4.00	1.80	.50
☐ 1 John Ayers	4.00	1.80	.50
☐ 2 Dwaine Board	4.00	1.80	.50
☐ 3 Michael Carter	5.00	2.20	.60
☐ 4 Dwight Clark	10.00	4.50	1.25
☐ 5 Roger Craig	15.00	6.75	1.85
☐ 6 Joe Cribbs	5.00	2.20	.60
☐ 7 Randy Cross	5.00	2.20	.60
☐ 8 Riki Ellison	4.00	1.80	.50
☐ 9 Jim Fahnhorst	4.00	1.80	.50
☐ 10 Keith Fahnhorst	4.00	1.80	.50
☐ 11 Russ Francis	5.00	2.20	.60
☐ 12 Don Griffin	5.00	2.20	.60
☐ 13 Ronnie Lott	20.00	9.00	2.50
☐ 14 Milt McColl	4.00	1.80	.50
☐ 15 Tim McKyer	5.00	2.20	.60
☐ 16 Joe Montana	250.00	110.00	31.00
☐ 17 Bubba Paris	4.00	1.80	.50
☐ 18 Fred Quillan	4.00	1.80	.50
☐ 19 Jerry Rice	250.00	110.00	31.00
☐ 20 Manu Tuiasosopo	4.00	1.80	.50
☐ 21 Keena Turner	5.00	2.20	.60
☐ 22 Carlton Williamson	4.00	1.80	.50
☐ 23 49ers Helmet	4.00	1.80	.50
☐ 24 49ers Information	4.00	1.80	.50
☐ 25 49ers Uniform	4.00	1.80	.50
☐ 26 Game Record Holders	4.00	1.80	.50
☐ 27 Season Record Holders	4.00	1.80	.50
☐ 28 Career Record Holders	4.00	1.80	.50
☐ 29 Record 1967-86	4.00	1.80	.50
☐ 30 1986 Team Statistics	4.00	1.80	.50
☐ 31 All-Time Greats	4.00	1.80	.50
☐ 32 Roll of Honour	4.00	1.80	.50
☐ 33 Candlestick Park	4.00	1.80	.50

1987 English Giants

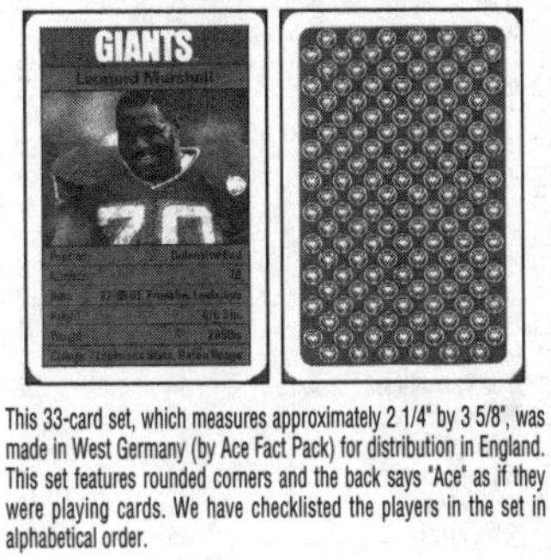

This 33-card set, which measures approximately 2 1/4" by 3 5/8", was made in West Germany (by Ace Fact Pack) for distribution in England. This set features rounded corners and the back says "Ace" as if they were playing cards. We have checklisted the players in the set in alphabetical order.

	MINT	NRMT	EXC
COMPLETE SET (33)	150.00	70.00	19.00
COMMON CARD (1-33)	4.00	1.80	.50
☐ 1 Billy Ard	4.00	1.80	.50
☐ 2 Carl Banks	6.00	2.70	.75
☐ 3 Mark Bavaro	6.00	2.70	.75
☐ 4 Brad Benson	4.00	1.80	.50
☐ 5 Harry Carson	6.00	2.70	.75
☐ 6 Maurice Carthon UER (Misspelled Morris)	5.00	2.20	.60
☐ 7 Mark Collins	5.00	2.20	.60
☐ 8 Chris Godfrey	4.00	1.80	.50
☐ 9 Kenny Hill	4.00	1.80	.50
☐ 10 Erik Howard	5.00	2.20	.60
☐ 11 Bobby Johnson	4.00	1.80	.50
☐ 12 Leonard Marshall	6.00	2.70	.75
☐ 13 George Martin	5.00	2.20	.60
☐ 14 Joe Morris	5.00	2.20	.60
☐ 15 Karl Nelson	4.00	1.80	.50
☐ 16 Bart Oates UER (Misspelled Oakes)	5.00	2.20	.60
☐ 17 Gary Reasons	4.00	1.80	.50
☐ 18 Stacy Robinson	4.00	1.80	.50
☐ 19 Phil Simms	15.00	6.75	1.85
☐ 20 Lawrence Taylor	25.00	11.00	3.10
☐ 21 Herb Welch	4.00	1.80	.50
☐ 22 Perry Williams	4.00	1.80	.50
☐ 23 Giants Helmet	4.00	1.80	.50
☐ 24 Giants Information	4.00	1.80	.50
☐ 25 Giants Uniforms	4.00	1.80	.50
☐ 26 Game Record Holders	4.00	1.80	.50
☐ 27 Season Record Holders	4.00	1.80	.50
☐ 28 Career Record Holders	4.00	1.80	.50
☐ 29 Record 1967-86	4.00	1.80	.50
☐ 30 1986 Team Statistics	4.00	1.80	.50
☐ 31 All-Time Greats	4.00	1.80	.50
☐ 32 Roll of Honour	4.00	1.80	.50
☐ 33 Giants Stadium	4.00	1.80	.50

1987 English Jets

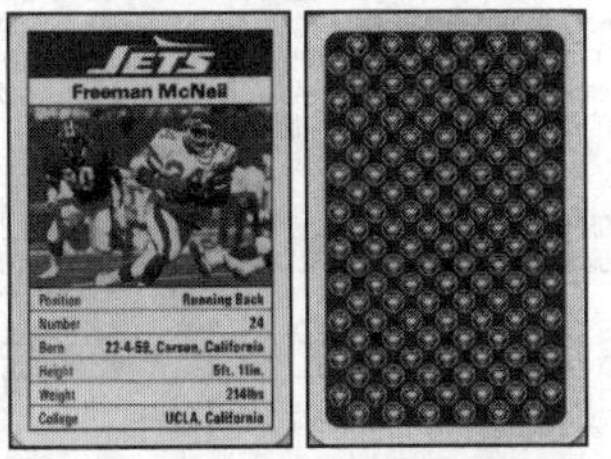

This 33-card set was made in West Germany (by Ace Fact Pack) for sale in England. This set measures approximately 2 1/4" by 3 5/8" and features members of the New York Jets. This set features cards with rounded corners; the card backs have a design for "Ace" like a playing card. We have checklisted the 22 players in the set in alphabetical order.

	MINT	NRMT	EXC
COMPLETE SET (33)	125.00	55.00	15.50
COMMON CARD (1-33)	4.00	1.80	.50
☐ 1 Dan Alexander	4.00	1.80	.50
☐ 2 Tom Baldwin	4.00	1.80	.50
☐ 3 Barry Bennett	4.00	1.80	.50
☐ 4 Russell Carter	5.00	2.20	.60
☐ 5 Kyle Clifton	5.00	2.20	.60
☐ 6 Bob Crable	4.00	1.80	.50
☐ 7 Joe Fields	5.00	2.20	.60
☐ 8 Rusty Guilbeau	4.00	1.80	.50
☐ 9 Harry Hamilton	4.00	1.80	.50
☐ 10 Johnny Hector	5.00	2.20	.60
☐ 11 Jerry Holmes	4.00	1.80	.50
☐ 12 Gordon King	4.00	1.80	.50
☐ 13 Lester Lyles	4.00	1.80	.50
☐ 14 Marty Lyons	5.00	2.20	.60
☐ 15 Kevin McArthur	4.00	1.80	.50
☐ 16 Freeman McNeil	6.00	2.70	.75
☐ 17 Ken O'Brien	6.00	2.70	.75
☐ 18 Tony Paige	5.00	2.20	.60
☐ 19 Mickey Shuler	5.00	2.20	.60
☐ 20 Jim Sweeney	4.00	1.80	.50
☐ 21 Al Toon	7.50	3.40	.95
☐ 22 Wesley Walker	7.50	3.40	.95
☐ 23 Jets Helmet	4.00	1.80	.50
☐ 24 Jets Information	4.00	1.80	.50
☐ 25 Jets Uniform	4.00	1.80	.50
☐ 26 Game Record Holders	4.00	1.80	.50
☐ 27 Season Record Holders	4.00	1.80	.50
☐ 28 Career Record Holders	4.00	1.80	.50
☐ 29 Record 1967-86	4.00	1.80	.50
☐ 30 1986 Team Statistics	4.00	1.80	.50
☐ 31 All-Time Greats	4.00	1.80	.50
☐ 32 Roll of Honour	4.00	1.80	.50
☐ 33 Giants Stadium	4.00	1.80	.50

1987 English Lions

This 33 card set measures approximately 2 1/4" by 3 5/8". This set features members of the Detroit Lions and has rounded corners. The back of the cards features a design for "Ace" like a playing card. These cards were manufactured in West Germany (by Ace Fact Pack) and we have checklisted this set alphabetically.

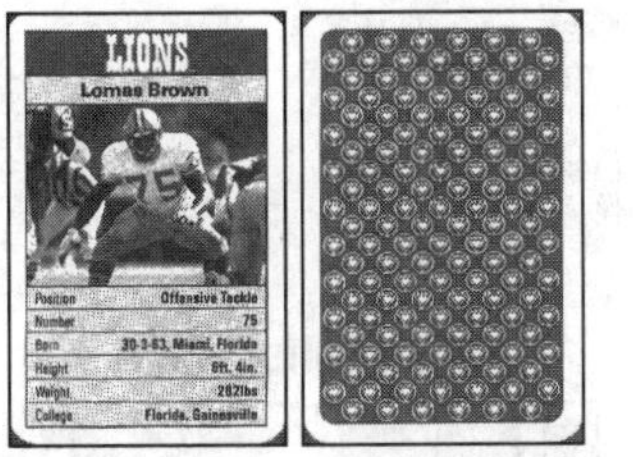

	MINT	NRMT	EXC
COMPLETE SET (33)	100.00	45.00	12.50
COMMON CARD (1-33)	4.00	1.80	.50
☐ 1 Carl Bland	4.00	1.80	.50
☐ 2 Lomas Brown	5.00	2.20	.60
☐ 3 Jeff Chadwick	4.00	1.80	.50
☐ 4 Michael Cofer	4.00	1.80	.50
☐ 5 Keith Dorney	4.00	1.80	.50
☐ 6 Keith Ferguson	4.00	1.80	.50
☐ 7 William Gay	4.00	1.80	.50
☐ 8 James Harrell	4.00	1.80	.50
☐ 9 Eric Hipple	5.00	2.20	.60
☐ 10 Garry James	5.00	2.20	.60
☐ 11 Demetrious Johnson	4.00	1.80	.50
☐ 12 James Jones	5.00	2.20	.60
☐ 13 Chuck Long	5.00	2.20	.60
☐ 14 Vernon Maxwell	4.00	1.80	.50
☐ 15 Bruce McNorton	4.00	1.80	.50
☐ 16 Devon Mitchell	4.00	1.80	.50
☐ 17 Steve Lott	4.00	1.80	.50
☐ 18 Eddie Murray	5.00	2.20	.60
☐ 19 Harvey Salem	4.00	1.80	.50
☐ 20 Rich Stenger	4.00	1.80	.50
☐ 21 Eric Williams	5.00	2.20	.60
☐ 22 Jimmy Williams	4.00	1.80	.50
☐ 23 Lions Helmet	4.00	1.80	.50
☐ 24 Lions Information	4.00	1.80	.50
☐ 25 Lions Uniform	4.00	1.80	.50
☐ 26 Game Record Holders	4.00	1.80	.50
☐ 27 Season Record Holders	4.00	1.80	.50
☐ 28 Career Record Holders	4.00	1.80	.50
☐ 29 Record 1967-86	4.00	1.80	.50
☐ 30 1986 Team Statistics	4.00	1.80	.50
☐ 31 All-Time Greats	4.00	1.80	.50
☐ 32 Championship Seasons	4.00	1.80	.50
☐ 33 Pontiac Silverdome	4.00	1.80	.50

1987 English Packers

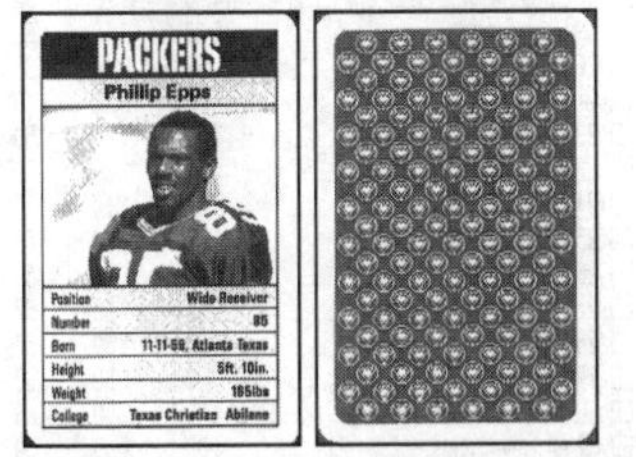

This 33-card set measures approximately 2 1/4" by 3 5/8". These cards feature rounded corners and a playing card type design on the back. There were 22 player cards issued which we have checklisted alphabetically. These cards were made in West Germany (by Ace Fact Pack) for release in Great Britain to capitalize on the popularity of American Football overseas. The set contains members of the Green Bay Packers.

	MINT	NRMT	EXC
COMPLETE SET (33)	125.00	55.00	15.50
COMMON CARD (1-33)	4.00	1.80	.50
☐ 1 John Anderson	4.00	1.80	.50
☐ 2 Robbie Bosco	5.00	2.20	.60
☐ 3 Don Bracken	4.00	1.80	.50
☐ 4 John Cannon	4.00	1.80	.50
☐ 5 Alphonso Carreker	4.00	1.80	.50
☐ 6 Kenneth Davis	6.00	2.70	.75
☐ 7 Al Del Greco	5.00	2.20	.60
☐ 8 Gary Ellerson	4.00	1.80	.50
☐ 9 Gerry Ellis	4.00	1.80	.50
☐ 10 Phillip Epps	5.00	2.20	.60
☐ 11 Ron Hallstrom	4.00	1.80	.50
☐ 12 Mark Lee	4.00	1.80	.50
☐ 13 Bobby Leopold	4.00	1.80	.50
☐ 14 Charles Martin	4.00	1.80	.50
☐ 15 Brian Noble	5.00	2.20	.60
☐ 16 Ken Ruettgers	5.00	2.20	.60
☐ 17 Randy Scott	4.00	1.80	.50
☐ 18 Walter Stanley	4.00	1.80	.50
☐ 19 Ken Stills	4.00	1.80	.50
☐ 20 Keith Uecker	4.00	1.80	.50
☐ 21 Ed West	6.00	2.70	.75
☐ 22 Randy Wright	5.00	2.20	.60
☐ 23 Packers Helmet	4.00	1.80	.50
☐ 24 Packers Information	4.00	1.80	.50
☐ 25 Packers Uniform	4.00	1.80	.50
☐ 26 Game Record Holders	4.00	1.80	.50
☐ 27 Season Record Holders	4.00	1.80	.50

	MINT	NRMT	EXC
□ 28 Career Record Holders	4.00	1.80	.50
□ 29 Record 1967-86	4.00	1.80	.50
□ 30 1986 Team Statistics	4.00	1.80	.50
□ 31 All-Time Greats	4.00	1.80	.50
□ 32 Roll of Honour	4.00	1.80	.50
□ 33 Lambeau Field/ Milwaukee County Stadium	5.00	2.20	.60

1987 English Rams

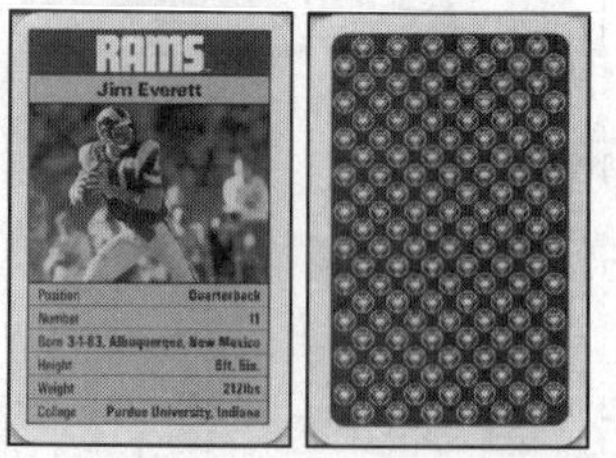

This 33-card set measures approximately 2 1/4" by 3 5/8" and has rounded corners. This set was manufactured in West Germany (by Ace Fact Pack) for release in Great Britain. There are 22 player cards in the set, checklisted below in alphabetical order. The backs of the cards feature a playing card design. The set contains members of the Los Angeles Rams.

	MINT	NRMT	EXC
COMPLETE SET (33)	125.00	55.00	15.50
COMMON CARD (1-33)	4.00	1.80	.50
□ 1 Nolan Cromwell	5.00	2.20	.60
□ 2 Eric Dickerson	15.00	6.75	1.85
□ 3 Reggie Doss	4.00	1.80	.50
□ 4 Carl Ekern	4.00	1.80	.50
□ 5 Henry Ellard	10.00	4.50	1.25
□ 6 Jim Everett	7.50	3.40	.95
□ 7 Jerry Gray	5.00	2.20	.60
□ 8 Dennis Harrah	4.00	1.80	.50
□ 9 David Hill	4.00	1.80	.50
□ 10 Kevin House	5.00	2.20	.60
□ 11 LeRoy Irvin	5.00	2.20	.60
□ 12 Mark Jerue	4.00	1.80	.50
□ 13 Shawn Miller	4.00	1.80	.50
□ 14 Tom Newberry	5.00	2.20	.60
□ 15 Vince Newsome	4.00	1.80	.50
□ 16 Mel Owens	4.00	1.80	.50
□ 17 Irv Pankey	4.00	1.80	.50
□ 18 Doug Reed	4.00	1.80	.50
□ 19 Doug Smith	5.00	2.20	.60
□ 20 Jackie Slater	7.50	3.40	.95
□ 21 Charles White	5.00	2.20	.60
□ 22 Mike Wilcher	4.00	1.80	.50
□ 23 Rams Helmet	4.00	1.80	.50
□ 24 Rams Information	4.00	1.80	.50
□ 25 Rams Uniform	4.00	1.80	.50
□ 26 Game Record Holders	4.00	1.80	.50
□ 27 Season Record Holders	4.00	1.80	.50
□ 28 Career Record Holders	4.00	1.80	.50
□ 29 Record 1967-86	4.00	1.80	.50
□ 30 1986 Team Statistics	4.00	1.80	.50
□ 31 All-Time Greats	4.00	1.80	.50
□ 32 Roll of Honour	4.00	1.80	.50
□ 33 Anaheim Stadium	4.00	1.80	.50

1987 English Redskins

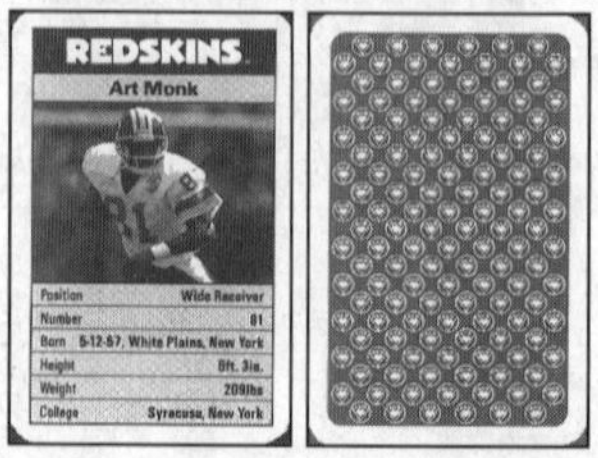

This 33-card set measures approximately 2 1/4" by 3 5/8" and features members of the Washington Redskins. This set was made in West Germany (by Ace Fact Pack) and the card design features rounded corners. We have checklisted the players portrayed in the set in alphabetical order.

	MINT	NRMT	EXC
COMPLETE SET (33)	225.00	100.00	28.00
COMMON CARD (1-33)	4.00	1.80	.50
□ 1 Jeff Bostic	5.00	2.20	.60
□ 2 Dave Butz	6.00	2.70	.75
□ 3 Gary Clark	25.00	11.00	3.10
□ 4 Monte Coleman	5.00	2.20	.60
□ 5 Vernon Dean	4.00	1.80	.50
□ 6 Clint Didier	4.00	1.80	.50
□ 7 Darryl Grant	5.00	2.20	.60
□ 8 Darrell Green	10.00	4.50	1.25
□ 9 Russ Grimm	6.00	2.70	.75
□ 10 Joe Jacoby	7.50	3.40	.95
□ 11 Curtis Jordan	4.00	1.80	.50
□ 12 Dexter Manley	5.00	2.20	.60
□ 13 Charles Mann	7.50	3.40	.95
□ 14 Mark May	5.00	2.20	.60
□ 15 Rich Milot	4.00	1.80	.50
□ 16 Art Monk	50.00	22.00	6.25
□ 17 Neal Olkewicz	4.00	1.80	.50
□ 18 George Rogers	7.50	3.40	.95
□ 19 Jay Schroeder	7.50	3.40	.95
□ 20 R.C. Thielemann	4.00	1.80	.50
□ 21 Alvin Walton	4.00	1.80	.50
□ 22 Don Warren	5.00	2.20	.60
□ 23 Redskins Helmet	4.00	1.80	.50
□ 24 Redskins Information	4.00	1.80	.50
□ 25 Redskins Uniform	4.00	1.80	.50
□ 26 Game Record Holders	4.00	1.80	.50
□ 27 Season Record Holders	4.00	1.80	.50
□ 28 Career Record Holders	4.00	1.80	.50
□ 29 Record 1967-86	4.00	1.80	.50
□ 30 1986 Team Statistics	4.00	1.80	.50
□ 31 All-Time Greats	4.00	1.80	.50
□ 32 Roll of Honour	4.00	1.80	.50
□ 33 Robert F. Kennedy Stadium	5.00	2.20	.60

1987 English Seahawks

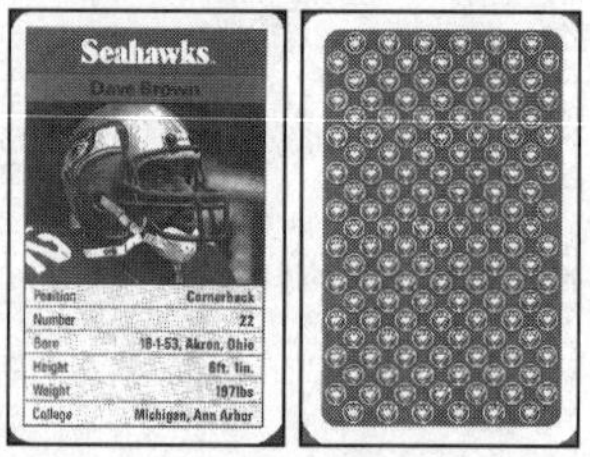

This 33-card set measures approximately 2 1/4" by 3 5/8". This set consists of 33 cards of which 22 are player cards and we have checklisted those cards alphabetically. The cards have rounded corners and a playing card type of design on the back. These cards were manufactured in West Germany (by Ace Fact Pack) and released in Great Britain. The set contains members of the Seattle Seahawks.

	MINT	NRMT	EXC
COMPLETE SET (33)	150.00	70.00	19.00
COMMON CARD (1-33)	4.00	1.80	.50
□ 1 Edwin Bailey	4.00	1.80	.50
□ 2 Dave Brown	4.00	1.80	.50
□ 3 Jeff Bryant	4.00	1.80	.50
□ 4 Blair Bush	4.00	1.80	.50
□ 5 Keith Butler	4.00	1.80	.50
□ 6 Kenny Easley	5.00	2.20	.60
□ 7 Greg Gaines	4.00	1.80	.50
□ 8 Jacob Green	5.00	2.20	.60
□ 9 Norm Johnson	5.00	2.20	.60
□ 10 Dave Krieg	10.00	4.50	1.25
□ 11 Steve Largent	40.00	18.00	5.00
□ 12 Reggie Kinlaw	4.00	1.80	.50
□ 13 Ron Mattes	4.00	1.80	.50
□ 14 Bryan Millard	4.00	1.80	.50
□ 15 Eugene Robinson	5.00	2.20	.60
□ 16 Bruce Scholtz	4.00	1.80	.50
□ 17 Terry Taylor	4.00	1.80	.50
□ 18 Mike Tice	5.00	2.20	.60
□ 19 Daryl Turner	4.00	1.80	.50
□ 20 Curt Warner	6.00	2.70	.75
□ 21 John L. Williams	8.00	3.60	1.00
□ 22 Fredd Young	5.00	2.20	.60
□ 23 Seahawks Helmet	4.00	1.80	.50
□ 24 Seahawks Information	4.00	1.80	.50
□ 25 Seahawks Uniform	4.00	1.80	.50
□ 26 Game Record Holders	4.00	1.80	.50
□ 27 Season Record Holders	4.00	1.80	.50
□ 28 Career Record Holders	4.00	1.80	.50
□ 29 Record 1977-86	4.00	1.80	.50
□ 30 1986 Team Statistics	4.00	1.80	.50
□ 31 All-Time Greats	4.00	1.80	.50
□ 32 Roll of Honour	4.00	1.80	.50
□ 33 Kingdome	4.00	1.80	.50

1991 ENOR Pro Football HOF Promos

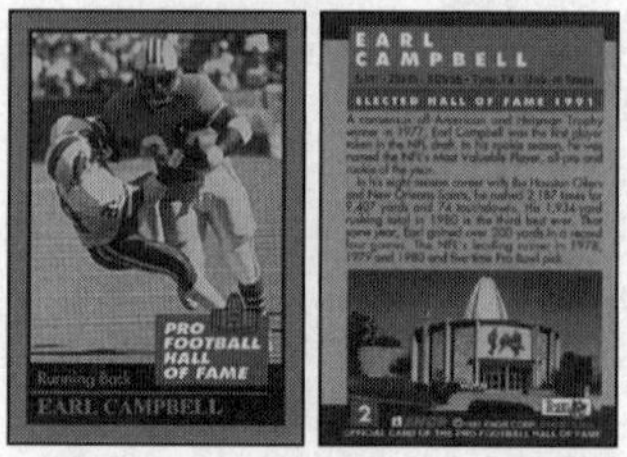

This six-card standard-size promo set was issued to preview the 160-card 1991 ENOR Pro Football Hall of Fame set. Apart from a slightly different shade of colors and card numbering differences, these promo cards differ from their counterparts in that the Team NFL logo on their card backs is black and white, while on the regular series cards, it is red, white, and blue.

	MINT	NRMT	EXC
COMPLETE SET (6)	7.00	3.10	.85
COMMON CARD (1-6)	1.00	.45	.12
□ 1 Pro Football Hall of Fame (Building) (Regular issue card number is also 1)	1.00	.45	.12
□ 2 Earl Campbell (Regular issue card number is 23)	3.00	1.35	.35
□ 3 John Hannah (Regular issue card number is 57)	1.00	.45	.12
□ 4 Stan Jones (Regular issue card number is 74)	1.00	.45	.12
□ 5 Jan Stenerud (Regular issue card number is 131)	1.00	.45	.12
□ 6 Tex Schramm ADM (Regular issue card number is 127)	1.00	.45	.12

1991 ENOR Pro Football HOF

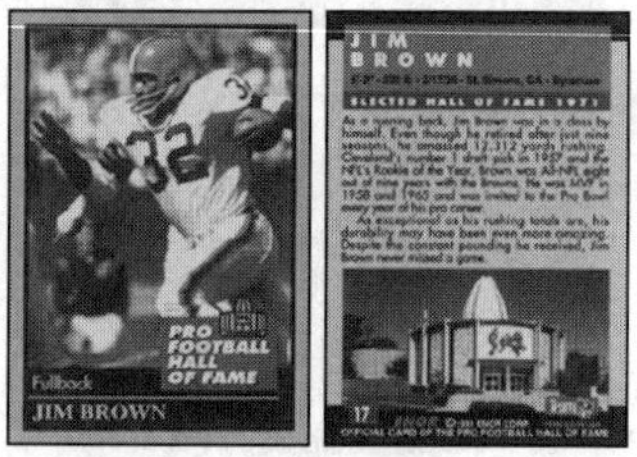

The 1991 Pro Football Hall of Fame set contains 160 standard-size cards. The set, which includes this year's inductees, was issued in factory sets and wax packs. The fronts feature a mix of color or black and white player photos, with black and gold borders (the photos were obtained from the NFL's extensive archives). The player's position and name are given in a black stripe below the picture. A purple box with the words "Pro Football Hall of Fame" in white appears at the lower right corner of the card face. The backs have biography, career summary, and the year the individual was inducted. The backs are predominantly orange in color and have a picture of the Hall of Fame building at the bottom. The numbering is essentially in alphabetical order by subject. Randomly inserted throughout the packs were coupon cards that entitled the collector to receive a free Hall of Fame Album and free admission to the Pro Football Hall of Fame (offer expired December 31, 1993). The front design of the Free Admission card shows four different scenes of the Hall of Fame.

	MINT	NRMT	EXC
COMPLETE SET (160)	12.00	5.50	1.50
COMMON CARD (1-160)	.10	.05	.01
□ 1 Pro Football Hall of Fame (Canton, OH)	.15	.07	.02
□ 1A Free Admission Pro Football Hall of Fame (Canton, OH)	.15	.07	.02
□ 2 Herb Adderley	.15	.07	.02
□ 3 Lance Alworth	.25	.11	.03
□ 4 Doug Atkins	.15	.07	.02
□ 5 Red Badgro	.10	.05	.01
□ 6 Cliff Battles	.15	.07	.02
□ 7 Sammy Baugh	.50	.23	.06
□ 8 Chuck Bednarik	.25	.11	.03
□ 9A Bert Bell FOUND/OWN (Factory set version in coat and tie)	.25	.11	.03
□ 9B Bert Bell FOUND/OWN (Wax pack version in Steelers tee shirt)	.25	.11	.03
□ 10 Bobby Bell	.15	.07	.02
□ 11 Raymond Berry	.25	.11	.03
□ 12 Charles W. Bidwill OWN	.10	.05	.01
□ 13 Fred Biletnikoff	.25	.11	.03
□ 14 George Blanda	.25	.11	.03
□ 15 Mel Blount	.20	.09	.03
□ 16 Terry Bradshaw	.75	.35	.09
□ 17 Jim Brown	.75	.35	.09
□ 18 Paul Brown CO/OWN/ FOUND	.20	.09	.03
□ 19 Roosevelt Brown	.15	.07	.02
□ 20 Willie Brown	.15	.07	.02
□ 21 Buck Buchanan	.15	.07	.02
□ 22 Dick Butkus	.50	.23	.06
□ 23 Earl Campbell	.75	.35	.09
□ 24 Tony Canadeo	.15	.07	.02
□ 25 Joe Carr PRES	.10	.05	.01
□ 26 Guy Chamberlin	.10	.05	.01
□ 27 Jack Christiansen	.15	.07	.02
□ 28 Dutch Clark	.15	.07	.02
□ 29 George Connor	.15	.07	.02
□ 30 Jimmy Conzelman	.10	.05	.01
□ 31 Larry Csonka	.25	.11	.03
□ 32 Willie Davis	.15	.07	.02
□ 33 Len Dawson	.25	.11	.03
□ 34 Mike Ditka	.50	.23	.06
□ 35 Art Donovan	.20	.09	.03
□ 36 Paddy Driscoll	.10	.05	.01
□ 37 Bill Dudley	.15	.07	.02
□ 38 Turk Edwards	.10	.05	.01
□ 39 Weeb Ewbank CO	.10	.05	.01
□ 40 Tom Fears	.15	.07	.02
□ 41 Ray Flaherty CO	.10	.05	.01
□ 42 Len Ford	.15	.07	.02
□ 43 Dan Fortmann	.10	.05	.01
□ 44 Frank Gatski	.10	.05	.01
□ 45 Bill George	.15	.07	.02
□ 46 Frank Gifford	.50	.23	.06
□ 47 Sid Gillman CO	.10	.05	.01
□ 48 Otto Graham	.50	.23	.06
□ 49 Red Grange	.50	.23	.06
□ 50 Joe Greene	.25	.11	.03
□ 51 Forrest Gregg	.15	.07	.02
□ 52 Bob Griese	.30	.14	.04
□ 53 Lou Groza	.20	.09	.03
□ 54 Joe Guyon	.10	.05	.01
□ 55 George Halas CO/OWN FOUND	.25	.11	.03
□ 56 Jack Ham	.25	.11	.03
□ 57 John Hannah	.15	.07	.02
□ 58 Franco Harris	.30	.14	.04
□ 59 Ed Healey	.10	.05	.01
□ 60 Mel Hein	.10	.05	.01
□ 61 Ted Hendricks	.15	.07	.02
□ 62 Pete(Fats) Henry	.15	.07	.02
□ 63 Arnie Herber	.10	.05	.01
□ 64 Bill Hewitt	.10	.05	.01
□ 65 Clarke Hinkle	.10	.05	.01
□ 66 Elroy Hirsch	.20	.09	.03
□ 67 Ken Houston	.15	.07	.02
□ 68 Cal Hubbard	.10	.05	.01
□ 69 Sam Huff	.20	.09	.03
□ 70 Lamar Hunt OWN/FOUND	.15	.07	.02
□ 71 Don Hutson	.20	.09	.03
□ 72 John Henry Johnson	.15	.07	.02
□ 73 Deacon Jones	.20	.09	.03
□ 74 Stan Jones	.15	.07	.02
□ 75 Sonny Jurgensen	.20	.09	.03
□ 76 Walt Kiesling	.10	.05	.01
□ 77 Frank(Bruiser) Kinard	.10	.05	.01
□ 78 Earl(Curly) Lambeau CO/FOUND/OWN	.15	.07	.02
□ 79 Jack Lambert	.30	.14	.04
□ 80 Tom Landry CO	.30	.14	.04
□ 81 Dick Lane	.15	.07	.02
□ 82 Jim Langer	.15	.07	.02
□ 83 Willie Lanier	.15	.07	.02
□ 84 Yale Lary	.15	.07	.02
□ 85 Dante Lavelli	.15	.07	.02
□ 86 Bobby Layne	.40	.18	.05
□ 87 Tuffy Leemans	.10	.05	.01
□ 88 Bob Lilly	.25	.11	.03
□ 89 Sid Luckman	.25	.11	.03
□ 90 Link Lyman	.10	.05	.01
□ 91 Tim Mara FOUND/OWN	.10	.05	.01
□ 92 Gino Marchetti	.15	.07	.02
□ 93 Geo.Preston Marshall FOUND/OWN	.10	.05	.01
□ 94 Don Maynard	.20	.09	.03
□ 95 George McAfee	.15	.07	.02
□ 96 Mike McCormack	.15	.07	.02
□ 97 Johnny(Blood) McNally	.10	.05	.01
□ 98 Mike Michalske	.10	.05	.01
□ 99 Wayne Millner	.10	.05	.01
□ 100 Bobby Mitchell	.20	.09	.03
□ 101 Ron Mix	.15	.07	.02
□ 102 Lenny Moore	.25	.11	.03
□ 103 Marion Motley (See also 130)	.20	.09	.03
□ 104 George Musso	.15	.07	.02
□ 105 Bronko Nagurski	.35	.16	.04
□ 106 Greasy Neale CO	.10	.05	.01
□ 107 Ernie Nevers	.15	.07	.02
□ 108 Ray Nitschke	.25	.11	.03
□ 109 Leo Nomellini	.15	.07	.02
□ 110 Merlin Olsen	.20	.09	.03
□ 111 Jim Otto	.20	.09	.03
□ 112 Steve Owen CO	.10	.05	.01
□ 113 Alan Page	.15	.07	.02
□ 114 Clarence(Ace) Parker	.10	.05	.01
□ 115 Jim Parker	.15	.07	.02
□ 116 1958 NFL Championship	.10	.05	.01
□ 117 Pete Pihos	.15	.07	.02
□ 118 Hugh(Shorty) Ray OFF	.10	.05	.01
□ 119 Dan Reeves OWN	.10	.05	.01
□ 120 Jim Ringo	.15	.07	.02
□ 121 Andy Robustelli	.15	.07	.02
□ 122 Art Rooney FOUND/ADMIN	.15	.07	.02
□ 123 Pete Rozelle COMM	.15	.07	.02
□ 124 Bob St.Clair	.15	.07	.02
□ 125 Gale Sayers	.50	.23	.06
□ 126 Joe Schmidt	.15	.07	.02
□ 127 Tex Schramm ADM	.10	.05	.01
□ 128 Art Shell	.20	.09	.03
□ 129 Roger Staubach	.75	.35	.09
□ 130 Ernie Stautner UER (Numbered as 103)	.20	.09	.03
□ 131 Jan Stenerud	.15	.07	.02

☐ 132 Ken Strong	.15	.07	.02
☐ 133 Joe Stydahar	.10	.05	.01
☐ 134 Fran Tarkenton	.30	.14	.04
☐ 135 Charley Taylor	.15	.07	.02
☐ 136 Jim Taylor	.20	.09	.03
☐ 137 Jim Thorpe	.50	.23	.06
☐ 138 Y.A. Tittle	.35	.16	.04
☐ 139 George Trafton	.10	.05	.01
☐ 140 Charley Trippi	.15	.07	.02
☐ 141 Emlen Tunnell	.15	.07	.02
☐ 142 Bulldog Turner	.20	.09	.03
☐ 143 Johnny Unitas	.60	.25	.07
☐ 144 Gene Upshaw	.15	.07	.02
☐ 145 Norm Van Brocklin	.20	.09	.03
☐ 146 Steve Van Buren	.20	.09	.03
☐ 147 Doak Walker	.20	.09	.03
☐ 148 Paul Warfield	.20	.09	.03
☐ 149 Bob Waterfield	.20	.09	.03
☐ 150 Arnie Weinmeister	.10	.05	.01
☐ 151 Bill Willis	.15	.07	.02
☐ 152 Larry Wilson	.15	.07	.02
☐ 153 Alex Wojciechowicz	.10	.05	.01
☐ 154 Willie Wood	.15	.07	.02
☐ 155 Enshrinement Day Hall of Fame Induction Ceremony	.10	.05	.01
☐ 156 Mementoes Exhibit Enshrinee Mementoes Room	.10	.05	.01
☐ 157 Checklist 1 The Beginning	.10	.05	.01
☐ 158 Checklist 2 The Early Years	.10	.05	.01
☐ 159 Checklist 3 The Modern Era	.10	.05	.01
☐ 160A Checklist 4 Evolution of Uniform includes #133-160	.10	.05	.01

1994 ENOR Pro Football HOF

Packaged with 25 ProGard protective sheets, this six-card standard-size set was issued to commemorate five players and one coach who were inducted into the Football Hall of Fame in 1994. The cards have the same design as those in the 1991 ENOR set, except that they are unnumbered. The cards are listed below in alphabetical order.

	MINT	NRMT	EXC
COMPLETE SET (6)	4.00	1.80	.50
COMMON CARD (1-6)	.50	.23	.06
☐ 1 Tony Dorsett	1.50	.70	.19
☐ 2 Bud Grant CO	.50	.23	.06
☐ 3 Jim Johnson	.50	.23	.06
☐ 4 Leroy Kelly	.50	.23	.06
☐ 5 Jackie Smith	.50	.23	.06
☐ 6 Randy White	.75	.35	.09

1995 ENOR Pro Football HOF

This 5-card standard-size set was issued to commemorate the new inductees into the Pro Football Hall of Fame in 1995. The cards have the same design as those in the 1991 and 1995 ENOR sets, except that they are unnumbered. The cards are listed below in alphabetical order.

	MINT	NRMT	EXC
COMPLETE SET (5)	2.50	1.10	.30
COMMON CARD (1-5)	.50	.23	.06
☐ 1 Jim Finks	.50	.23	.06
☐ 2 Hank Jordan	.50	.23	.06
☐ 3 Steve Largent	.75	.35	.09
☐ 4 Lee Roy Selmon	.50	.23	.06
☐ 5 Kellen Winslow	.60	.25	.07

1995 ENOR Pro Football HOF 180

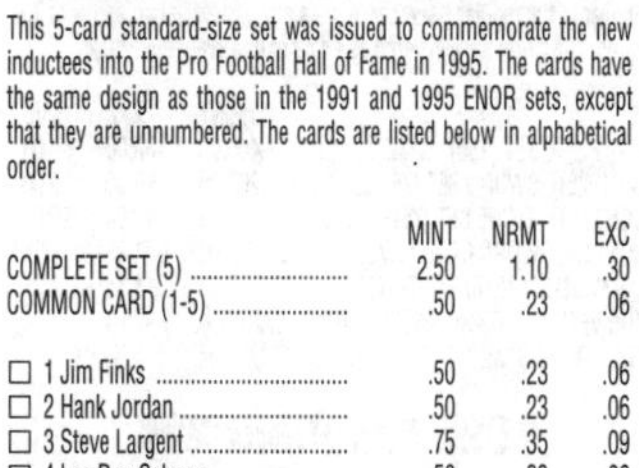

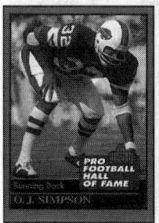

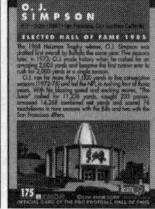

ENOR re-issued its 1991 Pro Football Hall of Fame set in factory set form in 1995. The 1995 release contains the first 159-cards from the 1991 set in original form plus 21 new cards including a re-worked checklist 4. The new cards carry a 1995 copyright date, while the first 159-cards are dated 1991. We've included single card prices for just the 21 new cards. The original 159-cards are priced previously under 1991 ENOR.

	MINT	NRMT	EXC
COMPLETE SET (21)	7.00	3.10	.85
COMMON CARD (160B-180)	.25	.11	.03
☐ 160B Checklist 4 Evolution of Uniform includes 133-180	.35	.16	.04
☐ 161 Lem Barney	.25	.11	.03
☐ 162 Al Davis	.35	.16	.04
☐ 163 John Mackey	.25	.11	.03
☐ 164 John Riggins	.50	.23	.06
☐ 165 Dan Fouts	.50	.23	.06
☐ 166 Larry Little	.25	.11	.03
☐ 167 Chuck Noll	.50	.23	.06
☐ 168 Bill Walsh	.50	.23	.06
☐ 169 Tony Dorsett	.75	.35	.09
☐ 170 Bud Grant	.35	.16	.04
☐ 171 Jim Johnson	.25	.11	.03
☐ 172 Leroy Kelly	.35	.16	.04
☐ 173 Jackie Smith	.25	.11	.03
☐ 174 Randy White	.50	.23	.06
☐ 175 O.J. Simpson	.75	.35	.09
☐ 176 Jim Finks	.25	.11	.03
☐ 177 Hank Jordan	.25	.11	.03
☐ 178 Steve Largent	.75	.35	.09
☐ 179 Lee Roy Selmon	.25	.11	.03
☐ 180 Kellen Winslow	.35	.16	.04

1996 ENOR Pro Football HOF

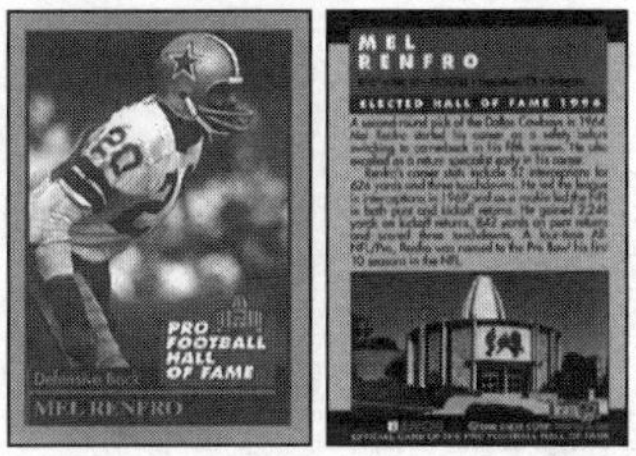

This five-card standard-size set was issued to commemorate the new inductees into the Pro Football Hall of Fame in 1996. The cards have the same design as those in the 1991 and 1995 ENOR sets, except that they are unnumbered. The cards are listed below in alphabetical order.

	MINT	NRMT	EXC
COMPLETE SET (5)	2.50	1.10	.30
COMMON CARD (1-5)	.50	.23	.06
☐ 1 Lou Creekmur	.50	.23	.06
☐ 2 Dan Dierdorf	.60	.25	.07
☐ 3 Joe Gibbs	.50	.23	.06
☐ 4 Charlie Joiner	.60	.25	.07
☐ 5 Mel Renfro	.60	.25	.07

1994 CPC/Enviromint Medallions

To commemorate Joe Montana's career, Chicagoland Processing Corporation/Enviromint issued a silver medallion, a silver collector card, and a gold medallion. Each one-troy ounce medallion is stamped with Montana's likeness, his team name, and his jersey number on the front while the words "Player of the Decade 1980's" are stamped on the reverse. Each 3.5 ounce silver collector card is stamped with a collage of Montana in both 49ers and Chiefs uniforms on the front. Its back carries team logos and the words "All-Time NFL Leader in QB Rating" and "Athlete of the Decade 1980's." The medallions and the card each have their own serial number. The production figures are as follows: silver medallion (7,000); silver collector card (10,000); silver medallion and card set (500); and gold medallion (100). Except for the serial number, the collectibles are unnumbered.

	MINT	EXC	G-VG
COMPLETE SET (4)	375.00	170.00	47.50
COMMON CARD (1-4)	65.00	29.00	8.00
☐ 1 Joe Montana Silver medallion	65.00	29.00	8.00
☐ 2 Joe Montana Silver card	65.00	29.00	8.00
☐ 3 Joe Montana Gold overlay medallion	135.00	60.00	17.00
☐ 4 Joe Montana Gold overlay medallion	135.00	60.00	17.00

1973 Equitable NFL Sketches

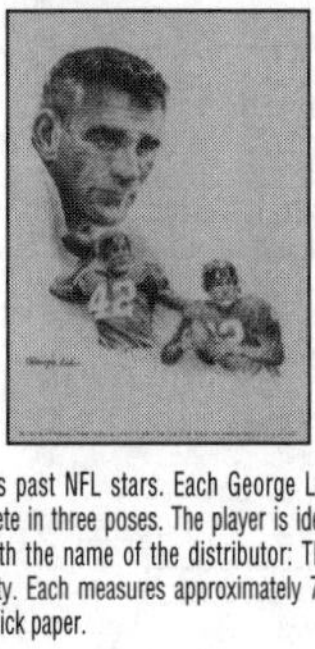

This set features past NFL stars. Each George Loh art rendering includes the athlete in three poses. The player is identified below the picture along with the name of the distributor: The Equitable Life Assurance Society. Each measures approximately 7 3/4" by 11" and was printed on thick paper.

	NRMT-MT	EXC	G-VG
COMPLETE SET (8)	60.00	27.00	7.50
COMMON CARD (1-8)	4.00	1.80	.50
☐ 1 Charley Conerly	5.00	2.20	.60
☐ 2 Roman Gabriel	5.00	2.20	.60
☐ 3 Jerry Kramer	5.00	2.20	.60
☐ 4 Vince Lombardi	15.00	6.75	1.85
☐ 5 Earl Morrall	5.00	2.20	.60
☐ 6 Gale Sayers	15.00	6.75	1.85
☐ 7 Johnny Unitas	15.00	6.75	1.85
☐ 8 Alex Webster	4.00	1.80	.50

1973 Equitable Sketches Sports Legends *

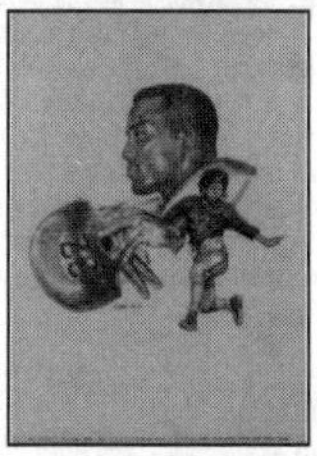

This set features great athletes from a variety of sports. Each Robert Riger art rendering includes the athlete along with a sketch of child. The player is identified below the picture along with the name of the distributor: The Equitable Life Assurance Society. Each measures approximately 7 3/4" by 11" and was printed on thick paper.

	NRMT-MT	EXC	G-VG
COMPLETE SET (16)	125.00	55.00	15.50
COMMON CARD (1-16)	3.00	1.35	.35
☐ 1 Jim Brown	15.00	6.75	1.85
☐ 2 Don Carter Bowler	3.00	1.35	.35
☐ 3 Bob Cousy	10.00	4.50	1.25
☐ 4 Bill Dudley	5.00	2.20	.60
☐ 5 Bob Feller	10.00	4.50	1.25
☐ 6 Althea Gibson Tennis	5.00	2.20	.60
☐ 7 Red Grange	15.00	6.75	1.85
☐ 8 Carol Heiss Skating	3.00	1.35	.35
☐ 9 Elroy Hirsch	6.00	2.70	.75
☐ 10 Carl Hubbell	10.00	4.50	1.25
☐ 11 Bob Mathias Track	3.00	1.35	.35
☐ 12 Bronko Nagurski	15.00	6.75	1.85
☐ 13 Allie Reynolds	3.00	1.35	.35
☐ 14 Babe Ruth	25.00	11.00	3.10
☐ 15 Jim Thorpe	15.00	6.75	1.85
☐ 16 Andy Varipapa Bowling	3.00	1.35	.35

1969 Eskimo Pie

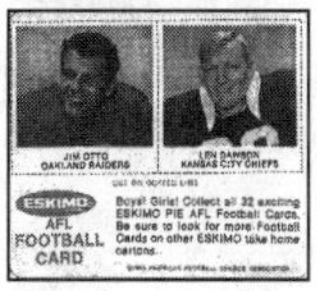

The 1969 Eskimo Pie football card set contains 15 panel pairs of American Football League players. The panels measure approximately 2 1/2" by 3". The cards are actually stickers which could be removed from the cardboard to which they are attached. There are two players per panel. The panels and the players pictured are unnumbered and in color. Numbers have been provided in the checklist below, alphabetically according to the last name of the player on the left since the cards are most commonly found in panels. The names are reversed on the card containing Jim Otto and Len Dawson (card number 14). The catalog designation for this set is F73.

	NRMT-MT	EXC	G-VG
COMPLETE SET (15)	1500.00	700.00	190.00
COMMON CARD (1-15)	75.00	34.00	9.50
☐ 1 Lance Alworth and John Charles	150.00	70.00	19.00
☐ 2 Al Atkinson and George Goeddeke	75.00	34.00	9.50
☐ 3 Marlin Briscoe and Billy Shaw	75.00	34.00	9.50
☐ 4 Gino Cappelletti and Dale Livingston	90.00	40.00	11.00
☐ 5 Eric Crabtree and Jim Dunaway	75.00	34.00	9.50
☐ 6 Ben Davidson and Bob Griese	250.00	110.00	31.00
☐ 7 Hewritt Dixon and Pete Beathard	75.00	34.00	9.50
☐ 8 Mike Garrett and Bob Hunt	90.00	40.00	11.00
☐ 9 Daryle Lamonica and Willie Frazier	90.00	40.00	11.00
☐ 10 Jim Lynch and John Hadl	90.00	40.00	11.00
☐ 11 Kent McCloughan and Tom Regner	75.00	34.00	9.50
☐ 12 Jim Nance and Billy Neighbors	75.00	34.00	9.50
☐ 13 Rick Norton and Paul Costa	75.00	34.00	9.50
☐ 14 Jim Otto and Len Dawson UER (Names reversed)	200.00	90.00	25.00
☐ 15 Matt Snell and Dick Post	90.00	40.00	11.00

1994 Excalibur Elway Promos

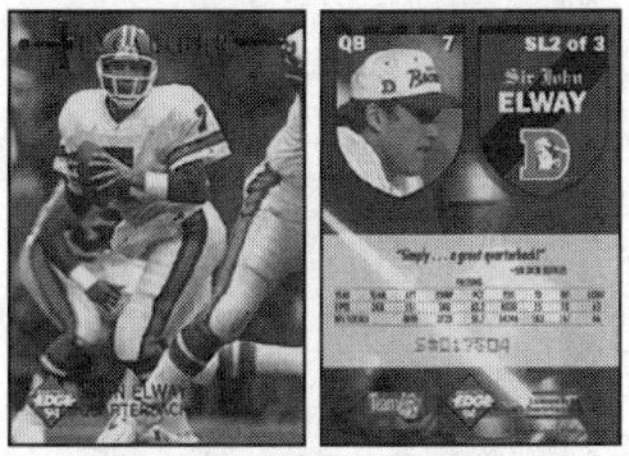

These three standard-size cards were issued to promote the 1994 Excalibur design and feature borderless color action shots of John Elway. The Excalibur logo appears in silver foil at the top; the player's name and position, also in silver foil, appear at the bottom. The back carries a color head shot of Elway in an heraldic shield at the upper left, and his name (preceded by a "Sir") and team logo in another shield at the upper right. A photo of an armored knight holding sword and football forms the background. Elway's career and 1993 stats appear in a ghosted strip below the shields. The "X of 3" numbering on the back is preceded by an "SL" prefix.

	MINT	NRMT	EXC
COMPLETE SET (3)	12.00	5.50	1.50
COMMON CARD (SL1-SL3)	4.00	1.80	.50
☐ SL1 John Elway	4.00	1.80	.50
☐ SL2 John Elway (Looking to pass)	4.00	1.80	.50
☐ SL3 John Elway (Running with football)	4.00	1.80	.50

1994 Excalibur

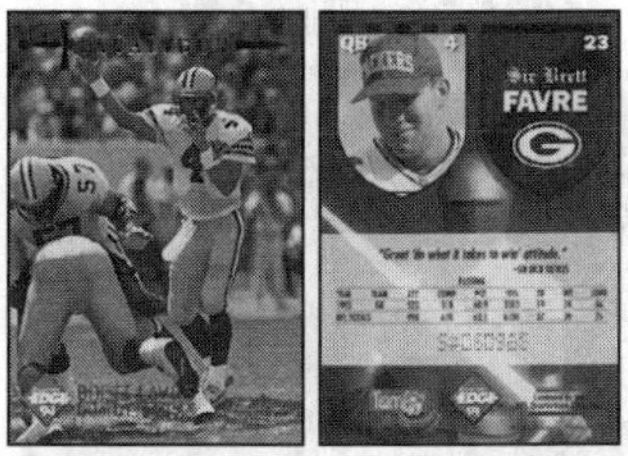

The 1994 Collector's Edge Excalibur set consists of 75 standard-size cards based on the medieval theme of "Excalibur", the silver sword pulled from the stone in the legend of King Arthur. The fronts feature full-bleed color action player photos. The Excalibur logo, player name and position are stamped in bright silver foil. The backs carry player information and a head shot framed in medieval shields at the top with a knight ghosted in the background. Stats for 1993 and NFL career totals appear just below the player commentary by Dick Butkus. Twenty-three NFL teams were represented. The cards are numbered on the back and checklisted alphabetically according to teams. There are no key Rookie Cards in this set.

	MINT	NRMT	EXC
COMPLETE SET (75)	25.00	11.00	3.10
COMMON CARD (1-75)	.15	.07	.02
☐ 1 Bobby Hebert	.15	.07	.02
☐ 2 Deion Sanders	1.50	.70	.19
☐ 3 Andre Rison	.30	.14	.04
☐ 4 Cornelius Bennett	.30	.14	.04
☐ 5 Jim Kelly	.50	.23	.06
☐ 6 Andre Reed	.30	.14	.04
☐ 7 Bruce Smith	.50	.23	.06
☐ 8 Thurman Thomas	.50	.23	.06
☐ 9 Curtis Conway	.50	.23	.06
☐ 10 Richard Dent	.30	.14	.04
☐ 11 Jim Harbaugh	.50	.23	.06
☐ 12 Troy Aikman	2.50	1.10	.30
☐ 13 Michael Irvin	.50	.23	.06
☐ 14 Russell Maryland	.15	.07	.02
☐ 15 Emmitt Smith	5.00	2.20	.60
☐ 16 Steve Atwater	.15	.07	.02
☐ 17 Rod Bernstine	.15	.07	.02
☐ 18 John Elway	2.00	.90	.25
☐ 19 Glyn Milburn	.30	.14	.04
☐ 20 Shannon Sharpe	.30	.14	.04
☐ 21 Barry Sanders	2.50	1.10	.30
☐ 22 Edgar Bennett	.50	.23	.06
☐ 23 Brett Favre	5.00	2.20	.60
☐ 24 Sterling Sharpe	.30	.14	.04
☐ 25 Reggie White	.50	.23	.06
☐ 26 Warren Moon	.50	.23	.06
☐ 27 Wilber Marshall	.15	.07	.02
☐ 28 Haywood Jeffires	.30	.14	.04
☐ 29 Lorenzo White	.15	.07	.02

	MINT	NRMT	EXC
☐ 30 Quentin Coryatt	.15	.07	.02
☐ 31 Roosevelt Potts	.15	.07	.02
☐ 32 Jeff George	.50	.23	.06
☐ 33 Joe Montana	2.50	1.10	.30
☐ 34 Neil Smith	.50	.23	.06
☐ 35 Marcus Allen	.50	.23	.06
☐ 36 Derrick Thomas	.50	.23	.06
☐ 37 Jeff Hostetler	.30	.14	.04
☐ 38 Tim Brown	.50	.23	.06
☐ 39 Rocket Ismail	.30	.14	.04
☐ 40 Randall Cunningham	.30	.14	.04
☐ 41 Jerome Bettis	1.25	.55	.16
☐ 42 Dan Marino	5.00	2.20	.60
☐ 43 Keith Jackson	.15	.07	.02
☐ 44 O.J. McDuffie	.50	.23	.06
☐ 45 Drew Bledsoe	2.50	1.10	.30
☐ 46 Leonard Russell	.15	.07	.02
☐ 47 Wade Wilson	.15	.07	.02
☐ 48 Eric Martin	.15	.07	.02
☐ 49 Phil Simms	.30	.14	.04
☐ 50 Lawrence Taylor	.50	.23	.06
☐ 51 Rodney Hampton	.50	.23	.06
☐ 52 Boomer Esiason	.30	.14	.04
☐ 53 Johnny Johnson	.15	.07	.02
☐ 54 Ronnie Lott	.30	.14	.04
☐ 55 Fred Barnett	.30	.14	.04
☐ 56 Leroy Thompson	.15	.07	.02
☐ 57 Barry Foster	.15	.07	.02
☐ 58 Neil O'Donnell	.50	.23	.06
☐ 59 Stan Humphries	.50	.23	.06
☐ 60 Marion Butts	.15	.07	.02
☐ 61 Anthony Miller	.30	.14	.04
☐ 62 Natrone Means	1.00	.45	.12
☐ 63 Dana Stubblefield	.50	.23	.06
☐ 64 John Taylor	.30	.14	.04
☐ 65 Ricky Watters	.50	.23	.06
☐ 66 Steve Young	2.00	.90	.25
☐ 67 Jerry Rice	2.50	1.10	.30
☐ 68 Tom Rathman	.15	.07	.02
☐ 69 Rick Mirer	.50	.23	.06
☐ 70 Chris Warren	.30	.14	.04
☐ 71 Cortez Kennedy	.30	.14	.04
☐ 72 Mark Rypien	.15	.07	.02
☐ 73 Desmond Howard	.30	.14	.04
☐ 74 Art Monk	.30	.14	.04
☐ 75 Reggie Brooks	.30	.14	.04

1994 Excalibur 22K Gold

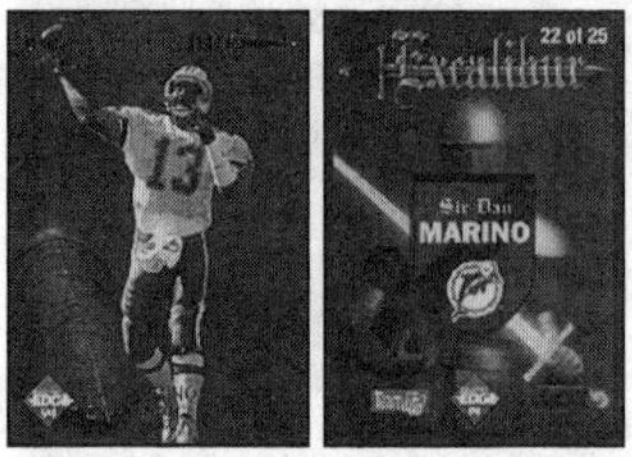

Randomly inserted in packs, this 25-card standard-size insert set showcases some of the NFL's top stars. The card fronts feature a color photo of the player with part of a knight in shining armour as a background. The background serves as a piece of a puzzle. All 25 card backs can be placed together to form a knight. The top of the card features a gold sword and the player's name and position are at the bottom. The card back depicts a knight with a sword and shield with the player's name and team logo superimposed over the knight.

	MINT	NRMT	EXC
COMPLETE SET (25)	40.00	18.00	5.00
COMMON CARD (1-25)	.60	.25	.07
☐ 1 Troy Aikman	4.00	1.80	.50
☐ 2 Michael Irvin	1.50	.70	.19
☐ 3 Emmitt Smith	8.00	3.60	1.00
☐ 4 Edgar Bennett	1.50	.70	.19
☐ 5 Brett Favre	8.00	3.60	1.00
☐ 6 Sterling Sharpe	1.50	.70	.19
☐ 7 Rodney Hampton	1.00	.45	.12
☐ 8 Jerome Bettis	2.50	1.10	.30
☐ 9 Jerry Rice	4.00	1.80	.50
☐ 10 Steve Young	3.00	1.35	.35
☐ 11 Ricky Watters	1.50	.70	.19
☐ 12 Thurman Thomas	1.50	.70	.19
☐ 13 John Elway	3.00	1.35	.35
☐ 14 Shannon Sharpe	1.00	.45	.12
☐ 15 Joe Montana	4.00	1.80	.50
☐ 16 Marcus Allen	1.50	.70	.19
☐ 17 Tim Brown	1.50	.70	.19
☐ 18 Rocket Ismail	1.00	.45	.12
☐ 19 Barry Foster	.60	.25	.07
☐ 20 Natrone Means	2.00	.90	.25
☐ 21 Rick Mirer	1.50	.70	.19
☐ 22 Dan Marino	8.00	3.60	1.00
☐ 23 AFC Card	.60	.25	.07
☐ 24 NFC Card	.60	.25	.07
☐ 25 Excalibur Card	.60	.25	.07

1994 Excalibur EdgeQuest

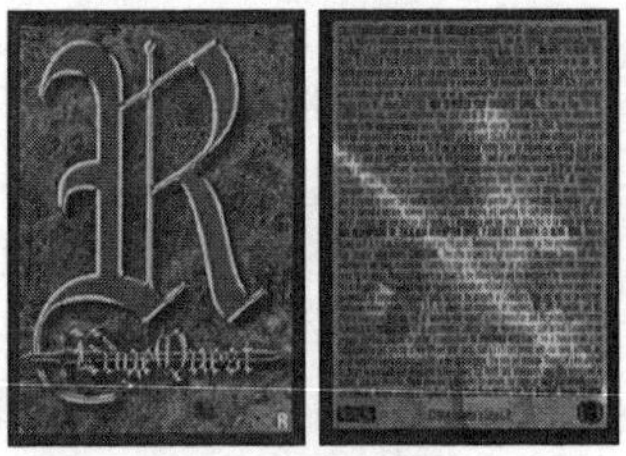

This nine-card standard-size set was issued as a contest as a dealer premium and as an insert in packs. The letter X was issued in shorter quantities in packs and was produced in both silver and gold foil. The letters C, E, L, U were issued both as dealer case promos, and any two of these letters per Collector's Edge Gold foil box. The object of the game was to spell out EXCALIBUR with the cards, which in turn could be redeemed for prizes. Any single card could be redeemed for a Collector's Edge promo card before December 31, 1994. Collectors who completed the set of all nine cards, including a silver X, could win a foil-embossed version of the Excalibur FX set. The gold version of X as part of the set was redeemable for an uncut sheet of the 22K Gold insert cards. The fronts show the letter in large old-style English. Underneath the letter is a sword running through the word "EdgeQuest". The backs have redemption information. The set redemption deadline was March 30, 1995.

	MINT	NRMT	EXC
COMPLETE SET (9)	4.00	1.80	.50
COMMON INSERT (A/B/I/R)	.50	.23	.06
COMMON DEALER (C/E/L/U)	.50	.23	.06
☐ 1 Letter A	.50	.23	.06
☐ 2 Letter B	.50	.23	.06
☐ 3 Letter C	.50	.23	.06
☐ 4 Letter E	.50	.23	.06
☐ 5 Letter I	.50	.23	.06
☐ 6 Letter L	.50	.23	.06
☐ 7 Letter R	.50	.23	.06
☐ 8 Letter U	.50	.23	.06
☐ 9 Letter X SP Expired	2.00	.90	.25

1994 Excalibur FX

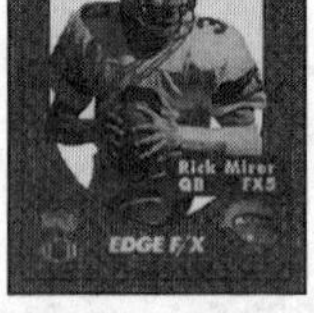

This 7-card standard-size set was randomly inserted in foil packs. On an acetate design, the player emerges from a cutout of a shield. The player's name, position and card number appear in a team colored label at the bottom right of the shield. A team helmet appears at the bottom of the card. Cards with a gold F/X shield impressed on the background were also produced.

	MINT	NRMT	EXC
COMPLETE SET (7)	25.00	11.00	3.10
COMMON CARD (1-7)	2.00	.90	.25
COMPLETE FX GOLD SHIELD (7)	100.00	45.00	12.50
FX GOLD SHIELDS: 2X TO 4X BASIC CARDS			
COMPLETE EQ GOLD SHIELD (7)	25.00	11.00	3.10
*EQ GOLD SHIELDS: SAME VALUE			
COMPLETE EQ SILV.SHIELD (7)	25.00	11.00	3.10
*EQ SILVER SHIELDS: SAME VALUE			
☐ 1 Emmitt Smith	12.00	5.50	1.50
☐ 2 Rodney Hampton	2.00	.90	.25
☐ 3 Jerome Bettis	4.00	1.80	.50
☐ 4 Steve Young	5.00	2.20	.60
☐ 5 Rick Mirer	3.00	1.35	.35
☐ 6 John Elway	5.00	2.20	.60
☐ 7 Troy Aikman UER (RB on front)	6.00	2.70	.75

1995 Excalibur

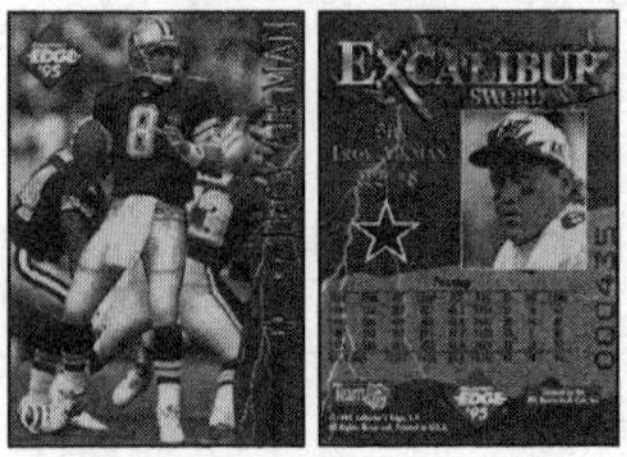

For the second consecutive year, Collector's Edge issued an Excalibur brand. This 150-card medieval-themed card set was released in two series: the Sword (1-75) and the Stone (76-150). Fifteen-hundred, 12-box cases of each series were produced. The suggested retail price for each seven-card pack was $3.49. The fronts feature full-color shots with the player's name and a sword on the right. Both the name and the sword are printed in silver foil. The backs have recent seasonal and career stats and a small inset photo. The cards are grouped alphabetically within teams. Jeff Blake is the only Rookie Card of note in this set.

	MINT	NRMT	EXC
COMPLETE SET (150)	30.00	13.50	3.70
COMPLETE SERIES 1 (75)	15.00	6.75	1.85
COMPLETE SERIES 2 (75)	15.00	6.75	1.85
COMMON CARD (1-150)	.10	.05	.01
☐ 1 Gary Clark	.10	.05	.01
☐ 2 Randal Hill	.10	.05	.01
☐ 3 Anthony Edwards	.10	.05	.01
☐ 4 Terance Mathis	.25	.11	.03
☐ 5 Eric Pegram	.25	.11	.03
☐ 6 Jeff George	.25	.11	.03
☐ 7 Pete Metzelaars	.10	.05	.01
☐ 8 Jim Kelly	.50	.23	.06
☐ 9 Andre Reed	.25	.11	.03
☐ 10 Lewis Tillman	.10	.05	.01
☐ 11 Curtis Conway	.50	.23	.06
☐ 12 Steve Walsh	.10	.05	.01
☐ 13 Derrick Fenner	.10	.05	.01
☐ 14 Harold Green	.10	.05	.01
☐ 15 Michael Jackson	.25	.11	.03
☐ 16 Eric Metcalf	.25	.11	.03
☐ 17 Antonio Langham	.10	.05	.01
☐ 18 Troy Aikman	2.50	1.10	.30
☐ 19 Alvin Harper	.10	.05	.01
☐ 20 Jay Novacek	.25	.11	.03
☐ 21 John Elway	2.00	.90	.25
☐ 22 Glyn Milburn	.10	.05	.01
☐ 23 Steve Atwater	.10	.05	.01
☐ 24 Mel Gray	.10	.05	.01
☐ 25 Herman Moore	.75	.35	.09
☐ 26 Scott Mitchell	.25	.11	.03
☐ 27 Guy McIntyre	.10	.05	.01
☐ 28 Edgar Bennett	.25	.11	.03
☐ 29 Sterling Sharpe	.25	.11	.03
☐ 30 Gary Brown	.10	.05	.01
☐ 31 Haywood Jeffires	.10	.05	.01
☐ 32 Marshall Faulk	1.25	.55	.16
☐ 33 Roosevelt Potts	.10	.05	.01
☐ 34 Marcus Allen	.50	.23	.06
☐ 35 Willie Davis	.25	.11	.03
☐ 36 Lake Dawson	.25	.11	.03
☐ 37 Jeff Hostetler	.25	.11	.03
☐ 38 Rocket Ismail	.25	.11	.03
☐ 39 Troy Drayton	.10	.05	.01
☐ 40 Jerome Bettis	.75	.35	.09
☐ 41 Dan Marino	5.00	2.20	.60
☐ 42 Mark Ingram	.10	.05	.01
☐ 43 O.J. McDuffie	.50	.23	.06
☐ 44 Warren Moon	.25	.11	.03
☐ 45 Qadry Ismail	.25	.11	.03
☐ 46 Jake Reed	.25	.11	.03
☐ 47 Ben Coates	.25	.11	.03
☐ 48 Vincent Brisby	.10	.05	.01
☐ 49 Michael Timpson	.10	.05	.01
☐ 50 Brad Daluiso	.10	.05	.01
☐ 51 Rodney Hampton	.25	.11	.03
☐ 52 Chris Calloway	.10	.05	.01
☐ 53 Rob Moore	.10	.05	.01
☐ 54 Boomer Esiason	.25	.11	.03
☐ 55 Michael Haynes	.25	.11	.03
☐ 56 Vaughn Dunbar	.10	.05	.01
☐ 57 Calvin Williams	.25	.11	.03
☐ 58 Herschel Walker	.25	.11	.03
☐ 59 Charlie Garner	.25	.11	.03
☐ 60 Neil O'Donnell	.25	.11	.03
☐ 61 Deon Figures	.10	.05	.01
☐ 62 Byron Bam Morris	.25	.11	.03
☐ 63 Junior Seau	.50	.23	.06
☐ 64 Leslie O'Neal	.25	.11	.03
☐ 65 Natrone Means	.50	.23	.06
☐ 66 Jerry Rice	2.50	1.10	.30
☐ 67 Deion Sanders	1.50	.70	.19
☐ 68 William Floyd	.50	.23	.06
☐ 69 Chris Warren	.25	.11	.03
☐ 70 Cortez Kennedy	.25	.11	.03
☐ 71 Hardy Nickerson	.10	.05	.01
☐ 72 Craig Erickson	.10	.05	.01
☐ 73 Heath Shuler	.50	.23	.06
☐ 74 Reggie Brooks	.25	.11	.03
☐ 75 Henry Ellard	.25	.11	.03
☐ 76 Garrison Hearst	.50	.23	.06
☐ 77 Steve Beuerlein	.10	.05	.01
☐ 78 Seth Joyner	.10	.05	.01
☐ 79 Andre Rison	.25	.11	.03
☐ 80 Norm Johnson	.10	.05	.01
☐ 81 Craig Heyward	.25	.11	.03
☐ 82 Darryl Talley	.10	.05	.01
☐ 83 Kenneth Davis	.10	.05	.01
☐ 84 Bruce Smith	.50	.23	.06
☐ 85 Tom Waddle	.10	.05	.01
☐ 86 Erik Kramer	.10	.05	.01
☐ 87 Carl Pickens	.50	.23	.06
☐ 88 Dan Wilkinson	.25	.11	.03
☐ 89 Jeff Blake	2.00	.90	.25
☐ 90 Vinny Testaverde	.25	.11	.03
☐ 91 Tommy Vardell	.10	.05	.01
☐ 92 Leroy Hoard	.10	.05	.01
☐ 93 Emmitt Smith	5.00	2.20	.60
☐ 94 Michael Irvin	.50	.23	.06
☐ 95 Daryl Johnston	.25	.11	.03
☐ 96 Shannon Sharpe	.25	.11	.03
☐ 97 Anthony Miller	.25	.11	.03
☐ 98 Leonard Russell	.10	.05	.01
☐ 99 Barry Sanders	2.50	1.10	.30
☐ 100 Brett Perriman	.25	.11	.03
☐ 101 Johnnie Morton	.25	.11	.03
☐ 102 Brett Favre	5.00	2.20	.60
☐ 103 Bryce Paup	.50	.23	.06
☐ 104 Ernest Givins	.10	.05	.01
☐ 105 Webster Slaughter	.10	.05	.01
☐ 106 Jim Harbaugh	.25	.11	.03
☐ 107 Joe Montana	2.50	1.10	.30
☐ 108 J.J. Birden	.10	.05	.01
☐ 109 Steve Bono	.25	.11	.03
☐ 110 James Jett	.25	.11	.03
☐ 111 Tim Brown	.50	.23	.06
☐ 112 Rob Fredrickson	.10	.05	.01
☐ 113 Chris Miller	.10	.05	.01
☐ 114 Bernie Parmalee	.25	.11	.03
☐ 115 Terry Kirby	.25	.11	.03
☐ 116 Bryan Cox	.10	.05	.01
☐ 117 Irving Fryar	.25	.11	.03
☐ 118 Terry Allen	.25	.11	.03
☐ 119 Cris Carter	.50	.23	.06
☐ 120 Fuad Reveiz	.10	.05	.01
☐ 121 Drew Bledsoe	2.50	1.10	.30
☐ 122 Greg McMurtry	18.00	8.00	2.20
☐ 123 Dave Brown	.25	.11	.03
☐ 124 Dave Meggett	.10	.05	.01
☐ 125 Johnny Johnson	.10	.05	.01
☐ 126 Ronnie Lott	.25	.11	.03
☐ 127 Johnny Mitchell	.10	.05	.01
☐ 128 Eric Martin	.10	.05	.01
☐ 129 Jim Everett	.10	.05	.01
☐ 130 Randall Cunningham	.25	.11	.03
☐ 131 Eric Allen	.10	.05	.01
☐ 132 Fred Barnett	.25	.11	.03
☐ 133 Barry Foster	.25	.11	.03
☐ 134 Kevin Greene	.25	.11	.03
☐ 135 Eric Green	.10	.05	.01
☐ 136 Stan Humphries	.25	.11	.03
☐ 137 Mark Seay	.25	.11	.03
☐ 138 Alfred Pupunu	.10	.05	.01
☐ 139 Steve Young	2.00	.90	.25
☐ 140 John Taylor	.10	.05	.01
☐ 141 Ricky Watters	.50	.23	.06
☐ 142 Brian Blades	.25	.11	.03
☐ 143 Rick Mirer	.50	.23	.06
☐ 144 Cortez Kennedy	.25	.11	.03
☐ 145 Jackie Harris	.10	.05	.01
☐ 146 Errict Rhett	.50	.23	.06
☐ 147 Trent Dilfer	.50	.23	.06
☐ 148 Brian Mitchell	.10	.05	.01
☐ 149 Ricky Ervins	.10	.05	.01
☐ 150 Darrell Green	.10	.05	.01

1995 Excalibur Die Cuts

This 150 card die-cut set is a parallel to the basic Excalibur set. Similar to the regular issue, these were also issued in two series of 75 cards. The cards were inserted as a rate of one every nine packs.

	MINT	EXC	G-VG
COMPLETE SET (150)	400.00	180.00	50.00
COMPLETE SWORD SET (75)	200.00	90.00	25.00
COMPLETE STONE SET (75)	200.00	90.00	25.00
COMMON SWORD CARD (1-75)	3.00	1.35	.35
COMMON STONE CARD (76-150)	3.00	1.35	.35
*DC VETERAN STARS: 4X TO 8X BASIC CARDS			
*DC YOUNG STARS: 3X TO 6X BASIC CARDS			

1995 Excalibur 22K

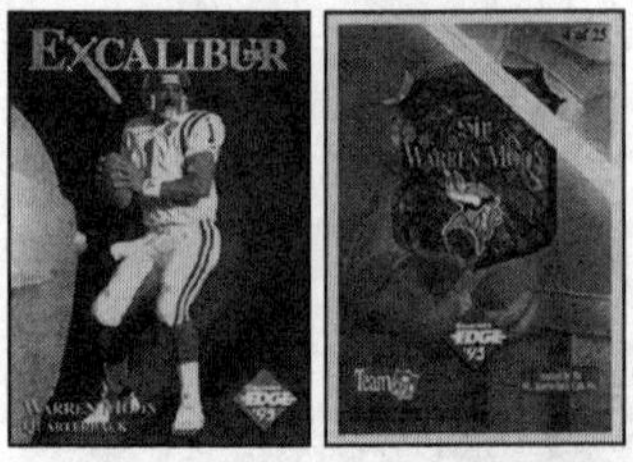

This 50-card standard-size set was randomly inserted into packs. The fronts feature the word "Excalibur" in gold foil across over the player's photo. The player's name is at lower left corner. Medieval themed backs have the player's name with a shield. There was also a prism parallel version of the cards inserted which were limited to 200 of each player. These feature a raindrop look silver prismatic foil on plastic stock and do not contain the Excalibur name at the top of the card. A second and third parallel prism type was produced and released at a later date. Each of these does include the Excalibur name as well as a gold shield surrounding the 22K notation. The second version was printed on a silver prismatic paper stock and the third on a gold prismatic paper stock, each with a prismatic background featuring a circle within a square pattern. The silvers are numbered of 750 sets made and the golds of 250.

	MINT	NRMT	EXC
COMPLETE SET (50)	1000.00	450.00	125.00
COMP.SWORD SER.1 (25)	500.00	220.00	60.00
COMP.STONE SER.2 (25)	500.00	220.00	60.00
COMMON SWORD (1SW-25SW)	10.00	4.50	1.25

	MINT	NRMT	EXC
COMMON STONE (1ST-25ST)	10.00	4.50	1.25
COMPLETE PRISM SET (50)	1500.00	700.00	190.00
COMP.SWORD PRISMS (25)	750.00	350.00	95.00
COMP.STONE PRISMS (25)................	750.00	350.00	95.00
PRISM CARDS: .75X to 1.5X BASIC CARDS			

☐ 1SW Steve Young	35.00	16.00	4.40
☐ 2SW Barry Sanders	50.00	22.00	6.25
☐ 3SW John Elway	40.00	18.00	5.00
☐ 4SW Warren Moon	15.00	6.75	1.85
☐ 5SW Chris Warren	15.00	6.75	1.85
☐ 6SW William Floyd	15.00	6.75	1.85
☐ 7SW Jim Kelly	15.00	6.75	1.85
☐ 8SW Troy Aikman	50.00	22.00	6.25
☐ 9SW Jerome Bettis	15.00	6.75	1.85
☐ 10SW Terance Mathis	15.00	6.75	1.85
☐ 11SW Marcus Allen	15.00	6.75	1.85
☐ 12SW Antonio Langham	10.00	4.50	1.25
☐ 13SW Sterling Sharpe	10.00	4.50	1.25
☐ 14SW Leonard Russell	10.00	4.50	1.25
☐ 15SW Drew Bledsoe	50.00	22.00	6.25
☐ 16SW Rodney Hampton	10.00	4.50	1.25
☐ 17SW Herschel Walker	15.00	6.75	1.85
☐ 18SW Jim Everett	10.00	4.50	1.25
☐ 19SW Terry Allen	15.00	6.75	1.85
☐ 20SW Junior Seau	15.00	6.75	1.85
☐ 21SW Natrone Means	15.00	6.75	1.85
☐ 22SW Deion Sanders	25.00	11.00	3.10
☐ 23SW Charlie Garner	10.00	4.50	1.25
☐ 24SW Marshall Faulk	20.00	9.00	2.50
☐ 25SW Ben Coates	10.00	4.50	1.25
☐ 1ST Emmitt Smith	90.00	40.00	11.00
☐ 2ST Jerry Rice	50.00	22.00	6.25
☐ 3ST Stan Humphries	10.00	4.50	1.25
☐ 4ST Joe Montana	50.00	22.00	6.25
☐ 5ST Steve Atwater	10.00	4.50	1.25
☐ 6ST Eric Metcalf	10.00	4.50	1.25
☐ 7ST Andre Rison	15.00	6.75	1.85
☐ 8ST Brett Favre	90.00	40.00	11.00
☐ 9ST Dan Marino	90.00	40.00	11.00
☐ 10ST Byron Bam Morris	15.00	6.75	1.85
☐ 11ST Heath Shuler	500.00	220.00	60.00
☐ 12ST Trent Dilfer	15.00	6.75	1.85
☐ 13ST Errict Rhett	15.00	6.75	1.85
☐ 14ST Herman Moore	15.00	6.75	1.85
☐ 15ST Eric Allen	10.00	4.50	1.25
☐ 16ST Cris Carter	15.00	6.75	1.85
☐ 17ST Ronnie Lott	10.00	4.50	1.25
☐ 18ST Randall Cunningham ..	10.00	4.50	1.25
☐ 19ST Barry Foster	10.00	4.50	1.25
☐ 20ST John Taylor	10.00	4.50	1.25
☐ 21ST Rick Mirer	15.00	6.75	1.85
☐ 22ST Tim Brown	15.00	6.75	1.85
☐ 23ST Michael Irvin	15.00	6.75	1.85
☐ 24ST Ricky Watters	15.00	6.75	1.85
☐ 25ST Jay Novacek	15.00	6.75	1.85

1995 Excalibur Challengers Draft Day Rookie Redemption

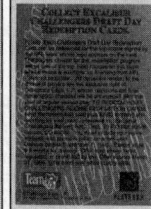

This 30 card standard-size set was randomly inserted into packs. A card is redeemable for the top rookie signed by the NFL team whose logo appears on the card. The front features the team helmet. The back contains redemption information. The cards were redeemable until March 31, 1996. Since the cards are unnumbered, they are sequenced in alphabetical order by team. A gold parallel of the set is also available by redeeming the Edgequest stone set.

	MINT	NRMT	EXC
COMPLETE SILVER SET (31)	40.00	18.00	5.00
COMMON SILVER (DD1-DD31)	1.00	.45	.12
COMPLETE GOLD SET (31)	40.00	18.00	5.00
COMMON GOLD (CR1-CR31)	1.00	.45	.12
*GOLD CARDS: SAME VALUE			

☐ DD1 Derrick Alexander............	1.00	.45	.12
☐ DD2 Tony Boselli	1.50	.70	.19
☐ DD3 Kyle Brady	1.50	.70	.19
☐ DD4 Mark Bruener	1.50	.70	.19
☐ DD5 Jamie Brown	1.00	.45	.12
☐ DD6 Ruben Brown	1.00	.45	.12
☐ DD7 Devin Bush	1.00	.45	.12
☐ DD8 Kevin Carter	1.50	.70	.19
☐ DD9 Ki-Jana Carter	2.00	.90	.25
☐ DD10 Kerry Collins	8.00	3.60	1.00
☐ DD11 Kordell Stewart	8.00	3.60	1.00
☐ DD12 Mark Fields	1.00	.45	.12
☐ DD13 Joey Galloway	5.00	2.20	.60
☐ DD14 Trezelle Jenkins	1.00	.45	.12
☐ DD15 Ellis Johnson	1.00	.45	.12
☐ DD16 Napoleon Kaufman	1.50	.70	.19
☐ DD17 Ty Law	1.50	.70	.19
☐ DD18 Mike Mamula	1.00	.45	.12
☐ DD19 Steve McNair	7.00	3.10	.85
☐ DD20 Billy Milner	1.00	.45	.12
☐ DD21 Craig Newsome	1.50	.70	.19
☐ DD22 Craig Powell	1.00	.45	.12
☐ DD23 Rashaan Salaam	2.50	1.10	.30
☐ DD24 Frank Sanders	1.50	.70	.19
☐ DD25 Warren Sapp	1.50	.70	.19
☐ DD26 Terrance Shaw	1.00	.45	.12
☐ DD27 J.J. Stokes	2.00	.90	.25
☐ DD28 Michael Westbrook ...	1.00	.45	.12
☐ DD29 Tyrone Wheatley	1.50	.70	.19
☐ DD30 Sherman Williams	1.50	.70	.19
☐ DD31 Cover Card	1.00	.45	.12
Checklist back			

1995 Excalibur Dragon Slayers

This fourteen-card standard-size set was randomly inserted into "Stone" or series two packs. Several hobby publications designed two cards each for this set featuring leading NFL players. The cards are unnumbered and, thus, listed alphabetically.

	MINT	NRMT	EXC
COMPLETE SET (14)	60.00	27.00	7.50
COMMON CARD................	2.00	.90	.25

☐ 1 Troy Aikman	6.00	2.70	.75
☐ 2 Jerome Bettis	3.00	1.35	.35
☐ 3 Drew Bledsoe	6.00	2.70	.75
☐ 4 Marshall Faulk	3.50	1.55	.45
☐ 5 Natrone Means	3.00	1.35	.35
☐ 6 Joe Montana	6.00	2.70	.75
☐ 7 Byron Bam Morris	2.00	.90	.25
☐ 8 Errict Rhett	3.00	1.35	.35
☐ 9 Jerry Rice	6.00	2.70	.75
☐ 10 Barry Sanders	6.00	2.70	.75
☐ 11 Deion Sanders	4.00	1.80	.50
☐ 12 Junior Seau............	2.00	.90	.25
☐ 13 Emmitt Smith	10.00	4.50	1.25
☐ 14 Ricky Watters	2.00	.90	.25

1995 Excalibur EdgeQuest

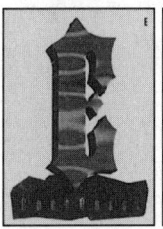
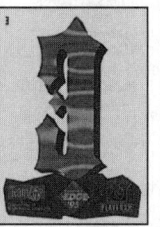

This six-card standard-size insert set was issued both as a dealer promotion and as random inserts in packs. The transparent card features a large letter that is also identified in much smaller print in the upper left corner. The letters D, R and W are in Sword packs, while E, N and T are in Stone packs. Letters S and O were provided free to Edge Excalibur hobby dealers. For completing the word "SWORD", the cards can be redeemed for a Rookie Roundtable set. If a collector completed the word "STONE", they received the Challengers Rookie set. Both words and the short-printed ampersand, can be redeemed for both of the 22K Gold (also known as Knights of the NFL) sheets. The redemption deadline was March 31, 1996. We've assigned numbers to the letters below.

	MINT	NRMT	EXC
COMPLETE SET (9)	4.00	1.80	.50
COMMON BOX INSERT (O/S)	.40	.18	.05
COMMON SWORD INSERT (D/R/W) ..	.40	.18	.05
COMMON STONE INSERT (E/N/T)	.40	.18	.05

☐ 1 Letter D	.40	.18	.05
☐ 2 Letter E	.40	.18	.05
☐ 3 Letter N	.40	.18	.05
☐ 4 Letter O	.40	.18	.05
☐ 5 Letter O	.40	.18	.05
☐ 6 Letter R	.40	.18	.05
☐ 7 Letter S	.40	.18	.05
☐ 8 Letter W	.40	.18	.05
☐ 9 Ampersand	.40	.18	.05

1995 Excalibur EdgeTech

This 12-card standard-size set was randomly inserted in first series "Sword" packs. The fronts have a metallic finish with the player photo superimposed over castle-like background. The word "EdgeTech" is in

red lettering in the lower left corner while the player's name is in the lower right corner. The backs have an inset photo as well as biographical information. The cards are unnumbered and thus are listed alphabetically.

	MINT	NRMT	EXC
COMPLETE SET (12)	250.00	110.00	31.00
COMMON CARD (1-12)	15.00	6.75	1.85

☐ 1 Emmitt Smith	60.00	27.00	7.50
☐ 2 Errict Rhett	20.00	9.00	2.50
☐ 3 Steve Young	20.00	9.00	2.50
☐ 4 Jerry Rice	30.00	13.50	3.70
☐ 5 Ben Coates	15.00	6.75	1.85
☐ 6 Marcus Allen	20.00	9.00	2.50
☐ 7 John Elway	25.00	11.00	3.10
☐ 8 Keith Jackson	15.00	6.75	1.85
☐ 9 Garrison Hearst	20.00	9.00	2.50
☐ 10 Natrone Means	20.00	9.00	2.50
☐ 11 Michael Haynes	15.00	6.75	1.85
☐ 12 Byron Bam Morris	15.00	6.75	1.85

1995 Excalibur Rookie Roundtable

Randomly inserted into packs, this 25-card standard-size set subdivides into Sword Rookie Roundtable (1-13) and Stone Rookie Roundtable (14-25). The sword grouping features defensive players while the stone focuses on offensive players. Hall of Famer Dick Butkus chose the featured rookies and commented on their achievements. The fronts feature posed action shots with the words "Rookie Roundtable" in the upper left corner and the player name at the bottom of the card. The backs include the Butkus quote, biographical and statistical information and an inset player shot.

	MINT	NRMT	EXC
COMPLETE SET (25)	30.00	13.50	3.70
COMPLETE SERIES 1 (13)	12.00	5.50	1.50
COMPLETE SERIES 2 (12)	18.00	8.00	2.20
COMMON CARD (1-25)	.75	.35	.09

☐ 1 Sam Adams	.75	.35	.09
☐ 2 Joe Johnson	.75	.35	.09
☐ 3 Tim Bowens	.75	.35	.09
☐ 4 Bryant Young	1.50	.70	.19
☐ 5 Aubrey Beavers	.75	.35	.09
☐ 6 Willie McGinest	1.50	.70	.19
☐ 7 Rob Fredrickson	.75	.35	.09
☐ 8 Lee Woodall	.75	.35	.09
☐ 9 Antonio Langham	.75	.35	.09
☐ 10 Dewayne Washington	.75	.35	.09
☐ 11 Darryl Morrison	.75	.35	.09
☐ 12 Keith Lyle	.75	.35	.09
☐ 13 Antonio Langham	.75	.35	.09
☐ 14 Darnay Scott	2.00	.90	.25
☐ 15 Derrick Alexander WR.......	1.50	.70	.19
☐ 16 Todd Steussie	.75	.35	.09
☐ 17 Larry Allen	.75	.35	.09
☐ 18 Anthony Redmon	.75	.35	.09
☐ 19 Joe Panos	.75	.35	.09
☐ 20 Kevin Mawae................	.75	.35	.09
☐ 21 Andrew Jordan	.75	.35	.09
☐ 22 Heath Shuler	1.50	.70	.19
☐ 23 Marshall Faulk	3.00	1.35	.35
☐ 24 Errict Rhett	1.50	.70	.19
☐ 25 Marshall Faulk POY	3.00	1.35	.35

1995 Excalibur TekTech

This 12-card standard-size set was randomly inserted in second series "Stone" packs. The fronts have a metallic finish with the player photo superimposed over castle-like background. The word "TekTech" is in red lettering in the lower left corner while the player's name is in the lower right corner. The backs have an inset photo as well as biographical information. The cards are unnumbered and thus are listed in alphabetical order.

	MINT	NRMT	EXC
COMPLETE SET (12)	150.00	70.00	19.00
COMMON CARD (1-12)	6.00	2.70	.75

☐ 1 Troy Aikman	20.00	9.00	2.50
☐ 2 Jerome Bettis	8.00	3.60	1.00
☐ 3 Drew Bledsoe	20.00	9.00	2.50
☐ 4 Tim Brown	8.00	3.60	1.00
☐ 5 Marshall Faulk	10.00	4.50	1.25
☐ 6 Haywood Jeffires	6.00	2.70	.75
☐ 7 Dan Marino	40.00	18.00	5.00
☐ 8 Barry Sanders	20.00	9.00	2.50
☐ 9 Deion Sanders	10.00	4.50	1.25
☐ 10 Junior Seau	8.00	3.60	1.00
☐ 11 Darryl Talley	6.00	2.70	.75
☐ 12 Ricky Watters	8.00	3.60	1.00

1948-52 Exhibit W468

Produced by the Exhibit Supply Company of Chicago, the 1948-52 Football Exhibit cards are unnumbered, blank-backed, thick-stocked cards issued in various colors in vending machines. Advertising panels on the front of these machines displayed from one to three cards and the price for one card; originally one-cent but later raised to two-cents. The cards were first issued in black and white, but later in sepia and several colors (green, red, blue, yellow). The colored cards generally sell for 3-4 times the price of the black and white or sepia cards and we've included notations below for the known color variations. Any additions to this list would be appreciated. Each card measures approximately 3 1/4 by 5 3/8 and features a pro or college player. Cards marked with an * in the checklist below have the same photo as in the Exhibit Sports Champions set of 1948; however, cards in this series do not have the single agate line of type describing the player at the bottom of the card. The cards were issued in three groups of 32 primarily during 1948, 1950, and 1951. We've included what is thought to be the year/years of issue for each card. The 1951 group is the most plentiful as they were reissued intact in sepia tone in 1952 (and perhaps 1953 as well). Some veteran collectors believe the second group may have been issued in 1949 rather than 1950. Cards issued during and after 1951 are marked as DP's as they are quite common compared to the other cards in the set. Several players, such as Creekmur, Houck, and Martin, are rumored to exist, but they have not been verified and are assumed not to exist in the checklist below. The American Card Catalog designation is W468. A football exhibit checklist card has also been found but was apparently produced in very limited quantity in 1950 only. This checklist card is known to exist in green and black-and-white and is identical to the Bednarik card but has the 32 players from the 1950 set listed on its front. Nine-card ad displays also exist; the Bednarik checklist is usually found on these sheets. In the first 32-card printing (1948), the words "Made In USA" measure 5/8". Eleven of these original cards were single prints (Cifers, Comp, Coulter, Horvath, Jacobs, Johnson, LeForce, Mastrangelo, Pritko, Schlinkman, and Wedemeyer) and marked as SP48 below since they were only issued in 1948. These single print cards are much rarer than the six single print cards issued in 1950 (Bednarik, Davis, Hoerner, Justice, Perry, and Ruby) and marked as SP50 below. In the second printing (1950), 11 new cards were produced to replace the original 11 single prints; on these new cards, the words "Made In USA" measure 7/16". The third printing (1951) consisted of only 16 cards; the six single print cards from 1950 and ten cards from 1948 were dropped. In this third printing, the words "Made In USA" measure 1/2".

	NRMT	VG-E	GOOD
COMPLETE SET (59)	3800.00	1700.00	475.00
COMMON CARD DP	7.50	3.40	.95
COMMON CARD................	35.00	16.00	4.40
COMMON CARD SP48	175.00	80.00	22.00
COMMON CARD SP50	60.00	27.00	7.50

☐ 1 Frankie Albert DP	9.00	4.00	1.10
48/50/51/52			
☐ 2 Dick Barwegan DP	7.50	3.40	.95
51/52			
☐ 3 Sammy Baugh * DP	40.00	18.00	5.00
48/50/51/52			
☐ 4 Chuck Bednarik SP50	125.00	55.00	15.50
☐ 5 Tony Canadeo DP	14.00	6.25	1.75
51/52			
☐ 6 Paul Christman	35.00	16.00	4.40
48/50			
☐ 7 Bob Cifers SP48	175.00	80.00	22.00
(green also)			

☐ 8 Irv Comp SP48	175.00	80.00	22.00
☐ 9 Charley Conerly DP 48/50/51/52	18.00	8.00	2.20
☐ 10 George Connor DP 51/52	14.00	6.25	1.75
☐ 11 Tex Coulter SP48	175.00	80.00	22.00
☐ 12 Glenn Davis SP50	90.00	40.00	11.00
☐ 13 Glenn Dobbs * 48/50	35.00	16.00	4.40
☐ 14 John Dottley DP 51/52	7.50	3.40	.95
☐ 15 Bill Dudley 48/50 (red also)	50.00	22.00	6.25
☐ 16 Tom Fears DP 51/52	15.00	6.75	1.85
☐ 17 Joe Geri DP 51/52	7.50	3.40	.95
☐ 18 Otto Graham * DP 48/50/51/52	40.00	18.00	5.00
☐ 19 Pat Harder * 48/50 (blue also)	40.00	18.00	5.00
☐ 20 Elroy Hirsch DP 51/52	18.00	8.00	2.20
☐ 21 Dick Hoerner SP50	60.00	27.00	7.50
☐ 22 Bob Hoernschemeyer DP 51/52	7.50	3.40	.95
☐ 23 Les Horvath SP48	200.00	90.00	25.00
☐ 24 Jack Jacobs * SP48 (green also)	175.00	80.00	22.00
☐ 25 Nate Johnson SP48	175.00	80.00	22.00
☐ 26 Charlie Justice SP50	75.00	34.00	9.50
☐ 27 Bobby Layne DP 48/50/51/52	30.00	13.50	3.70
☐ 28 Clyde LeForce SP48	175.00	80.00	22.00
☐ 29 Sid Luckman * 48/50	75.00	34.00	9.50
☐ 30 Johnny Lujack * 48/50	60.00	27.00	7.50
☐ 31 John Mastrangelo SP48	175.00	80.00	22.00
☐ 32 Ollie Matson DP 51/52	18.00	8.00	2.20
☐ 33 Bill McColl DP 51/52	7.50	3.40	.95
☐ 34 Fred Morrison DP 50/51/52	7.50	3.40	.95
☐ 35 Marion Motley * DP 48/50/51/52	20.00	9.00	2.50
☐ 36 Chuck Ortmann DP 51/52	7.50	3.40	.95
☐ 37 Joe Perry SP50	90.00	40.00	11.00
☐ 38 Pete Pihos 48/50 (yellow also)	50.00	22.00	6.25
☐ 39 Steve Pritko SP48	175.00	80.00	22.00
☐ 40 George Ratterman DP 48/50/51/52	7.50	3.40	.95
☐ 41 Jay Rhodemyre DP 51/52	7.50	3.40	.95
☐ 42 Martin Ruby SP50	60.00	27.00	7.50
☐ 43 Julie Rykovich DP 51/52	7.50	3.40	.95
☐ 44 Walt Schlinkman SP48 (red also)	175.00	80.00	22.00
☐ 45 Emil(Red) Sitko * DP 51/52	7.50	3.40	.95
☐ 46 Vitamin Smith DP 50/51/52	7.50	3.40	.95
☐ 47 Norm Standlee 48/50	35.00	16.00	4.40
☐ 48 George Taliaferro DP 50/51/52	7.50	3.40	.95
☐ 49 Y.A. Tittle HOR 48/50 (green/yellow also)	75.00	34.00	9.50
☐ 50 Charley Trippi DP 48/50/51/52	15.00	6.75	1.85
☐ 51 Frank Tripucka DP 48/50/51/52	9.00	4.00	1.10
☐ 52 Emlen Tunnell DP 51/52	15.00	6.75	1.85
☐ 53 Bulldog Turner DP 48/50/51/52	15.00	6.75	1.85
☐ 54 Steve Van Buren * 48/50	60.00	27.00	7.50
☐ 55 Bob Waterfield * DP 48/50/51/52	25.00	11.00	3.10
☐ 56 Herm Wedemeyer SP48	500.00	220.00	60.00
☐ 57 Bob Williams DP 51/52	7.50	3.40	.95
☐ 58 Claude Buddy Young DP (passing)48/50/51/52	9.00	4.00	1.10
☐ 59 Tank Younger * DP 50/51/52	9.00	4.00	1.10
☐ NNO Checklist Card SP50 Chuck Bednarik pictured	500.00	220.00	60.00

1975 Express Team Issue WFL

The Jacksonville Express of the World Football League distributed this set of player photos. Each photo measures approxmately 4 1/2" by 5" and features a black and white player picture with a blank cardback.

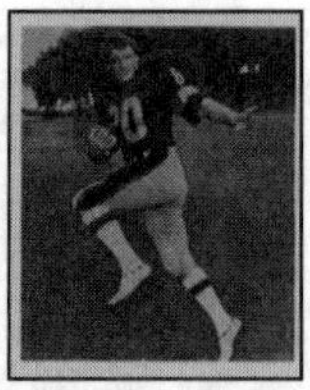

The photos contain no player names nor any other identifying text. We've listed the photos below according to the player's jersey number.

	NRMT-MT	EXC	G-VG
COMPLETE SET (37)	900.00	400.00	110.00
COMMON CARD	25.00	11.00	3.10
☐ 2 Johnny Osborne	25.00	11.00	3.10
☐ 3 Lee McGriff	25.00	11.00	3.10
☐ 6 Dan Callahan	25.00	11.00	3.10
☐ 7 Steve Barrios	25.00	11.00	3.10
☐ 8 Steve Foley	25.00	11.00	3.10
☐ 10 George Mira	30.00	13.50	3.70
☐ 12 David Fowler	25.00	11.00	3.10
☐ 16 Ron Coppenbarger	25.00	11.00	3.10
☐ 18 Abb Ansley	25.00	11.00	3.10
☐ 20 Jimmy Poulos	25.00	11.00	3.10
☐ 21 Tommy Reamon	25.00	11.00	3.10
☐ 23 Alfred Haywood	25.00	11.00	3.10
☐ 30 Jeff Davis	25.00	11.00	3.10
☐ 31 Fletcher Smith	25.00	11.00	3.10
☐ 32 Brian Duncan	25.00	11.00	3.10
☐ 42 Canary Simmons	25.00	11.00	3.10
☐ 44 Skip Johns	25.00	11.00	3.10
☐ 46 Willie Jackson	30.00	13.50	3.70
☐ 50 Rick Thomann	25.00	11.00	3.10
☐ 51 Jay Casey	25.00	11.00	3.10
☐ 52 Glen Gaspard	25.00	11.00	3.10
☐ 54 Howard Kindig	30.00	13.50	3.70
☐ 55 Fred Abbott	25.00	11.00	3.10
☐ 57 Ted Jarnov	25.00	11.00	3.10
☐ 58 Chip Myrtle	30.00	13.50	3.70
☐ 59 Sherman Miller	25.00	11.00	3.10
☐ 63 Tom Walker	25.00	11.00	3.10
☐ 68 Carleton Oats	30.00	13.50	3.70
☐ 70 Buck Baker	25.00	11.00	3.10
☐ 76 Carl Taibi	25.00	11.00	3.10
☐ 77 Joe Jackson	25.00	11.00	3.10
☐ 78 Kenny Moore	25.00	11.00	3.10
☐ 79 Larry Gagner	25.00	11.00	3.10
☐ 80 Dennis Hughes	25.00	11.00	3.10
☐ 81 Charles Hall	25.00	11.00	3.10
☐ 82 Don Brumm	30.00	13.50	3.70
☐ 87 Mike Creaney	25.00	11.00	3.1

1990 FACT Pro Set Cincinnati

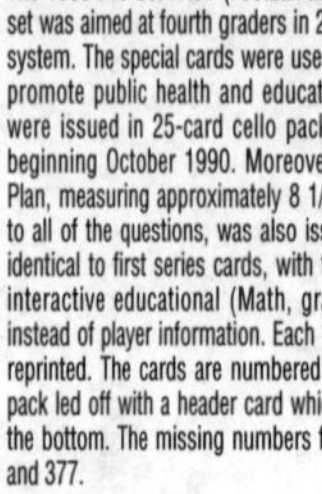

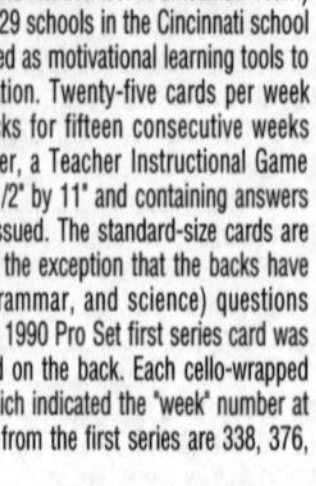

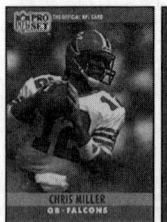

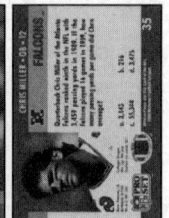

The 1990 Pro Set FACT (Football and Academics: A Cincinnati Team) set was aimed at fourth graders in 29 schools in the Cincinnati school system. The special cards were used as motivational learning tools to promote public health and education. Twenty-five cards per week were issued in 25-card cello packs for fifteen consecutive weeks beginning October 1990. Moreover, a Teacher Instructional Game Plan, measuring approximately 8 1/2" by 11" and containing answers to all of the questions, was also issued. The standard-size cards are identical to first series cards, with the exception that the backs have interactive educational (Math, grammar, and science) questions instead of player information. Each 1990 Pro Set first series card was reprinted. The cards are numbered on the back. Each cello-wrapped pack led off with a header card which indicated the "week" number at the bottom. The missing numbers from the first series are 338, 376, and 377.

	MINT	NRMT	EXC
COMPLETE SET (375)	750.00	350.00	95.00
COMMON CARD (1-375)	1.50	.70	.19
☐ 1 Barry Sanders W1	40.00	18.00	5.00
☐ 2 Joe Montana W1	40.00	18.00	5.00
☐ 3 Lindy Infante W1 UER Coach of the Year (missing Coach next to Packers)	1.50	.70	.19
☐ 4 Warren Moon W1 UER Man of the Year (missing R symbol)	3.00	1.35	.35
☐ 5 Keith Millard W1 Defensive Player of the Year	1.50	.70	.19
☐ 6 Derrick Thomas W1 UER Defensive Rookie of the Year (no 1989 on front banner of card)	3.00	1.35	.35
☐ 7 Ottis Anderson W1 Comeback Player of the Year	2.00	.90	.25
☐ 8 Joe Montana W2 Passing Leader	30.00	13.50	3.70
☐ 9 Christian Okoye W2 Rushing Leader	1.50	.70	.19
☐ 10 Thurman Thomas W2 Total Yardage Leader	3.00	1.35	.35
☐ 11 Mike Cofer W2 Kick Scoring Leader	1.50	.70	.19
☐ 12 Dalton Hilliard W2 UER TD Scoring Leader (O.J. Simpson not listed in stats, but is mentioned in text)	1.50	.70	.19
☐ 13 Sterling Sharpe W2 Receiving Leader	3.00	1.35	.35
☐ 14 Rich Camarillo W3 Punting Leader	1.50	.70	.19
☐ 15 Walter Stanley W3 Punt Return Leader	1.50	.70	.19
☐ 16 Rod Woodson W3 Kickoff Return Leader	3.00	1.35	.35
☐ 17 Felix Wright W3 Interception Leader	1.50	.70	.19
☐ 18 Chris Doleman W3 Sack Leader	1.50	.70	.19
☐ 19 Andre Ware W3 Heisman Trophy	2.00	.90	.25
☐ 20 Mo Elewonibi W4 Outland Trophy	1.50	.70	.19
☐ 21 Percy Snow W4 Lombardi Award	1.50	.70	.19
☐ 22 Anthony Thompson W4 Maxwell Award	2.00	.90	.25
☐ 23 Buck Buchanan W4 (Sacking Bart Starr) 1990 HOF Selection	1.50	.70	.19
☐ 24 Bob Griese W4 1990 HOF Selection	3.00	1.35	.35
☐ 25 Franco Harris W5 1990 HOF Selection	3.00	1.35	.35
☐ 26 Ted Hendricks W4 1990 HOF Selection	2.00	.90	.25
☐ 27 Jack Lambert W5 1990 HOF Selection	2.00	.90	.25
☐ 28 Tom Landry W5 1990 HOF Selection	3.00	1.35	.35
☐ 29 Bob St.Clair W5 1990 HOF Selection	1.50	.70	.19
☐ 30 Aundray Bruce W5 UER (Stats say Falcons)	1.50	.70	.19
☐ 31 Tony Casillas W5 UER (Stats say Falcons)	1.50	.70	.19
☐ 32 Shawn Collins W5	1.50	.70	.19
☐ 33 Marcus Cotton W6	1.50	.70	.19
☐ 34 Bill Fralic W6	1.50	.70	.19
☐ 35 Chris Miller W6	2.00	.90	.25
☐ 36 Deion Sanders W6 UER (Stats say Falcons)	15.00	6.75	1.85
☐ 37 John Settle W6	1.50	.70	.19
☐ 38 Jerry Glanville CO W6	1.50	.70	.19
☐ 39 Cornelius Bennett W7	2.00	.90	.25
☐ 40 Jim Kelly W7	3.00	1.35	.35
☐ 41 Mark Kelso W7 UER (No fumble rec. in '88; mentioned in '89)	1.50	.70	.19
☐ 42 Scott Norwood W7	1.50	.70	.19
☐ 43 Nate Odomes W7	2.00	.90	.25
☐ 44 Scott Radecic W7	1.50	.70	.19
☐ 45 Jim Ritcher W8	1.50	.70	.19
☐ 46 Leonard Smith W8	1.50	.70	.19
☐ 47 Darryl Talley W8	1.50	.70	.19
☐ 48 Marv Levy CO W8	1.50	.70	.19
☐ 49 Neal Anderson W8	2.00	.90	.25
☐ 50 Kevin Butler W8	1.50	.70	.19
☐ 51 Jim Covert W9	1.50	.70	.19
☐ 52 Richard Dent W9	2.00	.90	.25
☐ 53 Jay Hilgenberg W9	1.50	.70	.19
☐ 54 Steve McMichael W9	2.00	.90	.25
☐ 55 Ron Morris W9	1.50	.70	.19
☐ 56 John Roper W9	1.50	.70	.19
☐ 57 Mike Singletary W9	2.00	.90	.25
☐ 58 Keith Van Horne W10	1.50	.70	.19
☐ 59 Mike Ditka CO W10	3.00	1.35	.35
☐ 60 Lewis Billups W10	1.50	.70	.19
☐ 61 Eddie Brown W10	1.50	.70	.19
☐ 62 Jason Buck W10	1.50	.70	.19
☐ 63 Rickey Dixon W10	1.50	.70	.19
☐ 64 Tim McGee W11	1.50	.70	.19
☐ 65 Eric Thomas W11	1.50	.70	.19
☐ 66 Ickey Woods W11	1.50	.70	.19
☐ 67 Carl Zander W11	1.50	.70	.19
☐ 68 Sam Wyche CO W11	1.50	.70	.19
☐ 69 Paul Farren W11	1.50	.70	.19
☐ 70 Thane Gash W12	1.50	.70	.19
☐ 71 David Grayson W12	1.50	.70	.19
☐ 72 Bernie Kosar W12	2.00	.90	.25
☐ 73 Reggie Langhorne W12	1.50	.70	.19
☐ 74 Eric Metcalf W12	3.00	1.35	.35
☐ 75 Ozzie Newsome W12	2.00	.90	.25
☐ 76 Felix Wright W13	1.50	.70	.19
☐ 77 Bud Carson CO W13	1.50	.70	.19
☐ 78 Troy Aikman W13	40.00	18.00	5.00
☐ 79 Michael Irvin W13	4.00	1.80	.50
☐ 80 Jim Jeffcoat W13	1.50	.70	.19
☐ 81 Crawford Ker W13	1.50	.70	.19
☐ 82 Eugene Lockhart W13	1.50	.70	.19
☐ 83 Kelvin Martin W14	2.00	.90	.25
☐ 84 Ken Norton Jr. W14	2.00	.90	.25
☐ 85 Jimmy Johnson CO W14	3.00	1.35	.35
☐ 86 Steve Atwater W14	1.50	.70	.19
☐ 87 Tyrone Braxton W14	1.50	.70	.19
☐ 88 John Elway W14	25.00	11.00	3.10
☐ 89 Simon Fletcher W15	1.50	.70	.19
☐ 90 Ron Holmes W15	1.50	.70	.19
☐ 91 Bobby Humphrey W15	1.50	.70	.19
☐ 92 Vance Johnson W15	1.50	.70	.19
☐ 93 Ricky Nattiel W15	1.50	.70	.19
☐ 94 Dan Reeves CO W15	2.00	.90	.25
☐ 95 Jim Arnold W1	1.50	.70	.19
☐ 96 Jerry Ball W1	1.50	.70	.19
☐ 97 Bennie Blades W1	1.50	.70	.19
☐ 98 Lomas Brown W1	1.50	.70	.19
☐ 99 Michael Cofer W1	1.50	.70	.19
☐ 100 Richard Johnson W4	1.50	.70	.19
☐ 101 Eddie Murray W4	1.50	.70	.19
☐ 102 Barry Sanders W2	40.00	18.00	5.00
☐ 103 Chris Spielman W2	1.50	.70	.19
☐ 104 William White W2	1.50	.70	.19
☐ 105 Eric Williams W2	1.50	.70	.19
☐ 106 Wayne Fontes CO W3 UER (Says born in MO, actually born in MA)	1.50	.70	.19
☐ 107 Brent Fullwood W3	1.50	.70	.19
☐ 108 Ron Hallstrom W3	1.50	.70	.19
☐ 109 Tim Harris W8	1.50	.70	.19
☐ 110 Johnny Holland W8	1.50	.70	.19
☐ 111 Perry Kemp W8	1.50	.70	.19
☐ 112 Don Majkowski W9	1.50	.70	.19
☐ 113 Mark Murphy W9	1.50	.70	.19
☐ 114 Sterling Sharpe W9	4.00	1.80	.50
☐ 115 Ed West W9	2.00	.90	.25
☐ 116 Lindy Infante CO W9	1.50	.70	.19
☐ 117 Steve Brown W9	1.50	.70	.19
☐ 118 Ray Childress W10	1.50	.70	.19
☐ 119 Ernest Givins W10	2.00	.90	.25
☐ 120 John Grimsley W10	1.50	.70	.19
☐ 121 Alonzo Highsmith W10	1.50	.70	.19
☐ 122 Drew Hill W10	2.00	.90	.25
☐ 123 Bubba McDowell W10	2.00	.90	.25
☐ 124 Dean Steinkuhler W10	1.50	.70	.19
☐ 125 Lorenzo White W11	2.00	.90	.25
☐ 126 Tony Zendejas W11	1.50	.70	.19
☐ 127 Jack Pardee CO W11	1.50	.70	.19
☐ 128 Albert Bentley W11	1.50	.70	.19
☐ 129 Dean Biasucci W11	1.50	.70	.19
☐ 130 Duane Bickett W11	1.50	.70	.19
☐ 131 Bill Brooks W12	2.00	.90	.25
☐ 132 Jon Hand W12	1.50	.70	.19
☐ 133 Mike Prior W12	1.50	.70	.19
☐ 134 Andre Rison W12	3.00	1.35	.35
☐ 135 Rohn Stark W12	1.50	.70	.19
☐ 136 Donnell Thompson W12	1.50	.70	.19
☐ 137 Clarence Verdin W13	1.50	.70	.19
☐ 138 Fredd Young W13	1.50	.70	.19
☐ 139 Ron Meyer CO W14	1.50	.70	.19
☐ 140 John Alt W14	1.50	.70	.19
☐ 141 Steve DeBerg W14	2.00	.90	.25
☐ 142 Irv Eatman W1	1.50	.70	.19
☐ 143 Dino Hackett W2	1.50	.70	.19
☐ 144 Nick Lowery W2	1.50	.70	.19
☐ 145 Bill Maas W2	1.50	.70	.19
☐ 146 Stephone Paige W5	1.50	.70	.19
☐ 147 Neil Smith W3	3.00	1.35	.35
☐ 148 Marty Schottenheimer CO W3	1.50	.70	.19
☐ 149 Steve Beuerlein W3	2.00	.90	.25
☐ 150 Tim Brown W4	3.00	1.35	.35
☐ 151 Mike Dyal W4	1.50	.70	.19
☐ 152 Mervyn Fernandez W4	1.50	.70	.19
☐ 153 Willie Gault W4	1.50	.70	.19
☐ 154 Bob Golic W5	1.50	.70	.19
☐ 155 Bo Jackson W5	3.00	1.35	.35
☐ 156 Don Mosebar W5	1.50	.70	.19
☐ 157 Steve Smith W5	1.50	.70	.19
☐ 158 Greg Townsend W5	1.50	.70	.19
☐ 159 Bruce Wilkerson W6	1.50	.70	.19
☐ 160 Steve Wisniewski W6 (Blocking for Bo Jackson)	1.50	.70	.19
☐ 161 Art Shell CO W6	2.00	.90	.25
☐ 162 Flipper Anderson W6	1.50	.70	.19
☐ 163 Greg Bell W6 UER (Stats have 5 catches, should be 9)	1.50	.70	.19
☐ 164 Henry Ellard W6	2.00	.90	.25
☐ 165 Jim Everett W6	2.00	.90	.25
☐ 166 Jerry Gray W7	1.50	.70	.19
☐ 167 Kevin Greene W7	3.00	1.35	.35
☐ 168 Pete Holohan W13	1.50	.70	.19
☐ 169 Larry Kelm W13	1.50	.70	.19
☐ 170 Tom Newberry W13	1.50	.70	.19
☐ 171 Vince Newsome W13	1.50	.70	.19
☐ 172 Irv Pankey W14	1.50	.70	.19
☐ 173 Jackie Slater W14	1.50	.70	.19
☐ 174 Fred Strickland W14	1.50	.70	.19

☐ 175 Mike Wilcher W14 UER (Fumble rec. number different from 1989 Pro Set card)	1.50	.70	.19
☐ 176 John Robinson CO W7 UER (Stats say Rams, should say L.A. Rams)	1.50	.70	.19
☐ 177 Mark Clayton W7	2.00	.90	.25
☐ 178 Roy Foster W7	1.50	.70	.19
☐ 179 Harry Galbreath W7	1.50	.70	.19
☐ 180 Jim C. Jensen W8	1.50	.70	.19
☐ 181 Dan Marino W15	60.00	27.00	7.50
☐ 182 Louis Oliver W15	1.50	.70	.19
☐ 183 Sammie Smith W15	1.50	.70	.19
☐ 184 Brian Sochia W15	1.50	.70	.19
☐ 185 Don Shula CO W15	3.00	1.35	.35
☐ 186 Joey Browner W8	1.50	.70	.19
☐ 187 Anthony Carter W15	2.00	.90	.25
☐ 188 Chris Doleman W8	1.50	.70	.19
☐ 189 Steve Jordan W4	1.50	.70	.19
☐ 190 Carl Lee W4	1.50	.70	.19
☐ 191 Randall McDaniel W5	1.50	.70	.19
☐ 192 Mike Merriweather W5	1.50	.70	.19
☐ 193 Keith Millard W14	1.50	.70	.19
☐ 194 Al Noga W12	1.50	.70	.19
☐ 195 Scott Studwell W5	1.50	.70	.19
☐ 196 Henry Thomas W12	2.00	.90	.25
☐ 197 Herschel Walker W5	2.00	.90	.25
☐ 198 Wade Wilson W5	2.00	.90	.25
☐ 199 Gary Zimmerman W5	1.50	.70	.19
☐ 200 Jerry Burns CO W6	1.50	.70	.19
☐ 201 Vincent Brown W6	1.50	.70	.19
☐ 202 Hart Lee Dykes W14	1.50	.70	.19
☐ 203 Sean Farrell W6	1.50	.70	.19
☐ 204 Fred Marion W6	1.50	.70	.19
☐ 205 Stanley Morgan W15 UER (Text says he reached 10,000 yards fastest; 3 players did it in 10 seasons)	2.00	.90	.25
☐ 206 Eric Sievers W6	1.50	.70	.19
☐ 207 John Stephens W15	1.50	.70	.19
☐ 208 Andre Tippett W15	1.50	.70	.19
☐ 209 Rod Rust CO W15	1.50	.70	.19
☐ 210 Morten Andersen W6	1.50	.70	.19
☐ 211 Brad Edelman W12	1.50	.70	.19
☐ 212 John Fourcade W12	1.50	.70	.19
☐ 213 Dalton Hilliard W13	1.50	.70	.19
☐ 214 Rickey Jackson W13 (Forcing Jim Kelly fumble)	1.50	.70	.19
☐ 215 Vaughan Johnson W13	1.50	.70	.19
☐ 216 Eric Martin W13	2.00	.90	.25
☐ 217 Sam Mills W7	1.50	.70	.19
☐ 218 Pat Swilling W7 UER (Total fumble recoveries listed as 4, should be 5)	2.00	.90	.25
☐ 219 Frank Warren W7	1.50	.70	.19
☐ 220 Jim Wilks W7	1.50	.70	.19
☐ 221 Jim Mora CO W7	1.50	.70	.19
☐ 222 Raul Allegre W2	1.50	.70	.19
☐ 223 Carl Banks W1	1.50	.70	.19
☐ 224 Jumbo Elliott W1	1.50	.70	.19
☐ 225 Erik Howard W7	1.50	.70	.19
☐ 226 Pepper Johnson W2	1.50	.70	.19
☐ 227 Leonard Marshall W7 UER (In Super Bowl XXI, George Martin had the safety)	1.50	.70	.19
☐ 228 Dave Meggett W2	2.00	.90	.25
☐ 229 Bart Oates W3	1.50	.70	.19
☐ 230 Phil Simms W8	2.00	.90	.25
☐ 231 Lawrence Taylor W8	3.00	1.35	.35
☐ 232 Bill Parcells CO W8	2.00	.90	.25
☐ 233 Troy Benson W8	1.50	.70	.19
☐ 234 Kyle Clifton W8 UER (Born: Onley, should be Olney)	1.50	.70	.19
☐ 235 Johnny Hector W8	1.50	.70	.19
☐ 236 Jeff Lageman W9	2.00	.90	.25
☐ 237 Pat Leahy W9	1.50	.70	.19
☐ 238 Freeman McNeil W9	2.00	.90	.25
☐ 239 Ken O'Brien W9	1.50	.70	.19
☐ 240 Al Toon W9	2.00	.90	.25
☐ 241 Jo Jo Townsell W9	1.50	.70	.19
☐ 242 Bruce Coslet CO W10	1.50	.70	.19
☐ 243 Eric Allen W10	1.50	.70	.19
☐ 244 Jerome Brown W10	2.00	.90	.25
☐ 245 Keith Byars W10	2.00	.90	.25
☐ 246 Cris Carter W13	3.00	1.35	.35
☐ 247 Randall Cunningham W13	3.00	1.35	.35
☐ 248 Keith Jackson W14	2.00	.90	.25
☐ 249 Mike Quick W14	2.00	.90	.25
☐ 250 Clyde Simmons W14	2.00	.90	.25
☐ 251 Andre Waters W14	1.50	.70	.19
☐ 252 Reggie White W15	3.00	1.35	.35
☐ 253 Buddy Ryan CO W15	1.50	.70	.19
☐ 254 Rich Camarillo W15	1.50	.70	.19
☐ 255 Earl Ferrell W10 (No mention of retirement on card front)	1.50	.70	.19
☐ 256 Roy Green W10	2.00	.90	.25
☐ 257 Ken Harvey W3	2.00	.90	.25
☐ 258 Ernie Jones W1	1.50	.70	.19
☐ 259 Tim McDonald W11	1.50	.70	.19
☐ 260 Timm Rosenbach W11 UER (Born '67, should be '66)	2.00	.90	.25
☐ 261 Luis Sharpe W3	1.50	.70	.19
☐ 262 Vai Sikahema W3	1.50	.70	.19
☐ 263 J.T. Smith W1	1.50	.70	.19
☐ 264 Ron Wolfley W1 UER (Born Blaisdel, should be Blasdel)	1.50	.70	.19
☐ 265 Joe Bugel CO W11	1.50	.70	.19
☐ 266 Gary Anderson W11	1.50	.70	.19
☐ 267 Bubby Brister W1	2.00	.90	.25
☐ 268 Merril Hoge W11	1.50	.70	.19
☐ 269 Carnell Lake W2	2.00	.90	.25
☐ 270 Louis Lipps W11	1.50	.70	.19
☐ 271 David Little W3	1.50	.70	.19
☐ 272 Greg Lloyd W3	3.00	1.35	.35
☐ 273 Keith Willis W11	1.50	.70	.19
☐ 274 Tim Worley W3	1.50	.70	.19
☐ 275 Chuck Noll CO W4	3.00	1.35	.35
☐ 276 Marion Butts W4	2.00	.90	.25
☐ 277 Gill Byrd W2	1.50	.70	.19
☐ 278 Vencie Glenn W2 UER (Sack total should be 2, not 2.5)	1.50	.70	.19
☐ 279 Burt Grossman W4	1.50	.70	.19
☐ 280 Gary Plummer W4	1.50	.70	.19
☐ 281 Billy Ray Smith W12	1.50	.70	.19
☐ 282 Billy Joe Tolliver W12	1.50	.70	.19
☐ 283 Dan Henning CO W1	1.50	.70	.19
☐ 284 Harris Barton W1	2.00	.90	.25
☐ 285 Michael Carter W1	1.50	.70	.19
☐ 286 Mike Cofer W1	1.50	.70	.19
☐ 287 Roger Craig W1	2.00	.90	.25
☐ 288 Don Griffin W1	1.50	.70	.19
☐ 289 Charles Haley W2	2.00	.90	.25
☐ 290 Pierce Holt W2	2.00	.90	.25
☐ 291 Ronnie Lott W2	2.00	.90	.25
☐ 292 Guy McIntyre W2	2.00	.90	.25
☐ 293 Joe Montana W2	40.00	18.00	5.00
☐ 294 Tom Rathman W2	2.00	.90	.25
☐ 295 Jerry Rice W3	40.00	18.00	5.00
☐ 296 Jesse Sapolu W3	1.50	.70	.19
☐ 297 John Taylor W3	2.00	.90	.25
☐ 298 Michael Walter W3	1.50	.70	.19
☐ 299 George Seifert CO W3	2.00	.90	.25
☐ 300 Jeff Bryant W3	1.50	.70	.19
☐ 301 Jacob Green W4	1.50	.70	.19
☐ 302 Norm Johnson W4 UER (Card shop not in Garden Grove, should say Fullerton)	1.50	.70	.19
☐ 303 Bryan Millard W4	1.50	.70	.19
☐ 304 Joe Nash W4	1.50	.70	.19
☐ 305 Eugene Robinson W4	1.50	.70	.19
☐ 306 John L. Williams W14	1.50	.70	.19
☐ 307 David Wyman W14 (NFL EXP is in caps, inconsistent with rest of the set)	1.50	.70	.19
☐ 308 Chuck Knox CO W14	1.50	.70	.19
☐ 309 Mark Carrier W14	3.00	1.35	.35
☐ 310 Paul Gruber W14	1.50	.70	.19
☐ 311 Harry Hamilton W15	1.50	.70	.19
☐ 312 Bruce Hill W15	1.50	.70	.19
☐ 313 Donald Igwebuike W15	1.50	.70	.19
☐ 314 Kevin Murphy W15	1.50	.70	.19
☐ 315 Ervin Randle W12	1.50	.70	.19
☐ 316 Mark Robinson W12	1.50	.70	.19
☐ 317 Lars Tate W12	1.50	.70	.19
☐ 318 Vinny Testaverde W12	2.00	.90	.25
☐ 319 Ray Perkins CO W12	1.50	.70	.19
☐ 320 Earnest Byner W12	1.50	.70	.19
☐ 321 Gary Clark W12 (Randall Cunningham looking on from sidelines)	3.00	1.35	.35
☐ 322 Darryl Grant W13	1.50	.70	.19
☐ 323 Darrell Green W13	1.50	.70	.19
☐ 324 Jim Lachey W13	1.50	.70	.19
☐ 325 Charles Mann W13	1.50	.70	.19
☐ 326 Wilber Marshall W13	1.50	.70	.19
☐ 327 Ralf Mojsiejenko W13	1.50	.70	.19
☐ 328 Art Monk W15	3.00	1.35	.35
☐ 329 Gerald Riggs W15	2.00	.90	.25
☐ 330 Mark Rypien W14	2.00	.90	.25
☐ 331 Ricky Sanders W4	1.50	.70	.19
☐ 332 Alvin Walton W4	1.50	.70	.19
☐ 333 Joe Gibbs CO W5	2.00	.90	.25
☐ 334 Aloha Stadium W5 Site of Pro Bowl	1.50	.70	.19
☐ 335 Brian Blades PB W5	3.00	1.35	.35
☐ 336 James Brooks PB W5	2.00	.90	.25
☐ 337 Shane Conlan PB W5	1.50	.70	.19
☐ 339 Ray Donaldson PB W5	1.50	.70	.19
☐ 340 Ferrell Edmunds PB W6	1.50	.70	.19
☐ 341 Boomer Esiason PB W6	2.00	.90	.25
☐ 342 David Fulcher PB W6	1.50	.70	.19
☐ 343 Chris Hinton PB W6	1.50	.70	.19
☐ 344 Rodney Holman PB W6	1.50	.70	.19
☐ 345 Kent Hull PB W6	1.50	.70	.19
☐ 346 Tunch Ilkin PB W7	1.50	.70	.19
☐ 347 Mike Johnson PB W7	1.50	.70	.19
☐ 348 Greg Kragen PB W7	1.50	.70	.19
☐ 349 Dave Krieg PB W7	2.00	.90	.25
☐ 350 Albert Lewis PB W1	1.50	.70	.19
☐ 351 Howie Long PB W7	3.00	1.35	.35
☐ 352 Bruce Matthews PB W8	2.00	.90	.25
☐ 353 Clay Matthews PB W8	1.50	.70	.19
☐ 354 Erik McMillan PB W8	1.50	.70	.19
☐ 355 Karl Mecklenburg PB W8	1.50	.70	.19
☐ 356 Anthony Miller PB W8	3.00	1.35	.35
☐ 357 Frank Minnifield PB W8	1.50	.70	.19
☐ 358 Max Montoya PB W8	1.50	.70	.19
☐ 359 Warren Moon PB W10	3.00	1.35	.35
☐ 360 Mike Munchak PB W9	1.50	.70	.19
☐ 361 Anthony Munoz PB W9	3.00	1.35	.35
☐ 362 John Offerdahl PB W9	1.50	.70	.19
☐ 363 Christian Okoye PB W9	1.50	.70	.19
☐ 364 Leslie O'Neal PB W9	2.00	.90	.25
☐ 365 Rufus Porter PB W9 UER (TM logo missing)	1.50	.70	.19
☐ 366 Andre Reed PB W10	2.00	.90	.25
☐ 367 Johnny Rembert PB W10	1.50	.70	.19
☐ 368 Reggie Roby PB W10	1.50	.70	.19
☐ 369 Kevin Ross PB W10	1.50	.70	.19
☐ 370 Webster Slaughter PB W10	1.50	.70	.19
☐ 371 Bruce Smith PB W11	2.00	.90	.25
☐ 372 Dennis Smith PB W11	1.50	.70	.19
☐ 373 Derrick Thomas PB W11	3.00	1.35	.35
☐ 374 Thurman Thomas PB W11	3.00	1.35	.35
☐ 375 David Treadwell PB W11	1.50	.70	.19
☐ 376 Lee Williams PB W11	1.50	.70	.19

1991 FACT Pro Set Mobil

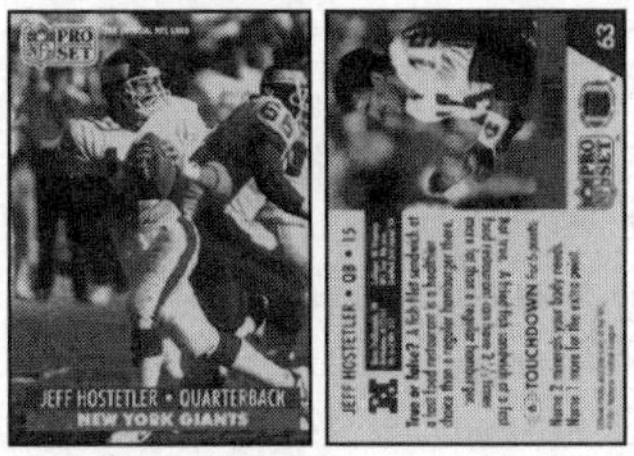

Sponsored by Pro Set and Mobil Oil, the 1991 Pro Set FACT (Football and Academics: A Championship Team) set marks the second year that Pro Set produced cards to serve as motivational learning tools to promote public health and education. This year's program was expanded to include all 26 NFL cities and to target 200,000 fourth grade students in low socio-economic areas. Six monthly lessons were featured in the set, and each lesson had an educational theme. Teachers utilized in-classroom educational materials and distributed a set of 17 Pro Set cards (along with one title/header card) each month, with the reverse sides carrying specific educational lessons corresponding to the educational theme. The standard-size cards are identical to first series cards, with the exception that the backs have interactive educational questions instead of player information. The particular set in which the card was issued is indicated below by S for set number.

	MINT	NRMT	EXC
COMPLETE SET (108)	150.00	70.00	19.00
COMMON CARD	1.00	.45	.12
☐ 3 Joe Montana S1	15.00	6.75	1.85
☐ 5 Mike Singletary S2	1.25	.55	.16
☐ 12 Jay Novacek S3	1.50	.70	.19
☐ 20 Ottis Anderson S2	1.25	.55	.16
☐ 40 Tim Brown S1	1.50	.70	.19
☐ 44 Herschel Walker S1	1.25	.55	.16
☐ 59 Eric Dorsey S3	1.00	.45	.12
☐ 60 Jumbo Elliott S1	1.00	.45	.12
☐ 63 Jeff Hostetler S2	1.50	.70	.19
☐ 69 Eric Moore S4	1.00	.45	.12
☐ 70 Bart Oates S3	1.00	.45	.12
☐ 71 Gary Reasons S4	1.00	.45	.12
☐ 75 Shane Conlan S3	1.00	.45	.12
☐ 78 Jim Kelly S4	3.00	1.35	.35
☐ 84 Darryl Talley S6	1.00	.45	.12
☐ 90 Marv Levy CO S1	1.00	.45	.12
☐ 94 Tim Green S2	1.00	.45	.12
☐ 99 Jerry Glanville CO S3	1.00	.45	.12
☐ 101 Mark Carrier S3	1.00	.45	.12
☐ 104 Jim Harbaugh S6	1.50	.70	.19
☐ 105 Brad Muster S4	1.00	.45	.12
☐ 107 Keith Van Horne S6	1.00	.45	.12
☐ 111 Boomer Esiason S1	1.25	.55	.16
☐ 116 Anthony Munoz S2	1.50	.70	.19
☐ 117 Sam Wyche CO S4	1.00	.45	.12
☐ 118 Paul Farren S6	1.00	.45	.12
☐ 119 Thane Gash S3	1.00	.45	.12
☐ 122 Clay Matthews S2	1.00	.45	.12
☐ 123 Eric Metcalf S6	1.50	.70	.19
☐ 127 Tommie Agee S4	1.00	.45	.12
☐ 128 Troy Aikman S6	15.00	6.75	1.85
☐ 132 Michael Irvin S6	3.00	1.35	.35
☐ 134 Daniel Stubbs S6	1.00	.45	.12
☐ 136 Steve Atwater S1	1.00	.45	.12
☐ 138 John Elway S2	12.00	5.50	1.50
☐ 141 Mark Jackson S6	1.00	.45	.12
☐ 142 Karl Mecklenburg S3	1.00	.45	.12
☐ 143 Doug Widell S2	1.00	.45	.12
☐ 153 Wayne Fontes CO S2	1.00	.45	.12
☐ 156 Don Majkowski S1	1.00	.45	.12
☐ 157 Tony Mandarich S6	1.00	.45	.12
☐ 158 Mark Murphy S6	1.00	.45	.12
☐ 161 Sterling Sharpe S4	3.00	1.35	.35
☐ 162 Lindy Infante CO S3	1.00	.45	.12
☐ 163 Ray Childress S6	1.00	.45	.12
☐ 166 Bruce Matthews S3	1.00	.45	.12
☐ 167 Warren Moon S6	3.00	1.35	.35
☐ 168 Mike Munchak S4	1.00	.45	.12
☐ 169 Al Smith S6	1.00	.45	.12
☐ 174 Bill Brooks S1	1.50	.70	.19
☐ 179 Clarence Verdin S3	1.00	.45	.12
☐ 182 Steve DeBerg S1	1.25	.55	.16
☐ 185 Christian Okoye S3	1.00	.45	.12
☐ 189 M.Schottenheimer CO S1	1.00	.45	.12
☐ 191 Howie Long S2	1.25	.55	.16
☐ 194 Steve Smith S4	1.00	.45	.12
☐ 196 Lionel Washington S6	1.00	.45	.12
☐ 198 Art Shell CO S3	1.25	.55	.16
☐ 203 Buford McGee S2	1.00	.45	.12
☐ 204 Tom Newberry S6	1.00	.45	.12
☐ 205 Frank Stams S1	1.00	.45	.12
☐ 210 Dan Marino S4	25.00	11.00	3.10
☐ 212 John Offerdahl S1	1.00	.45	.12
☐ 216 Don Shula CO S4	1.25	.55	.16
☐ 217 Darrell Fullington S6	1.00	.45	.12
☐ 218 Tim Irwin S2	1.00	.45	.12
☐ 219 Mike Merriweather S3	1.00	.45	.12
☐ 231 Ed Reynolds S3	1.00	.45	.12
☐ 238 Robert Massey S4	1.00	.45	.12
☐ 246 James Hasty S1	1.00	.45	.12
☐ 247 Erik McMillan S2	1.00	.45	.12
☐ 249 Ken O'Brien S4	1.00	.45	.12
☐ 260 Andre Waters S2	1.00	.45	.12
☐ 270 Joe Bugel CO S2	1.00	.45	.12
☐ 271 Gary Anderson S1	1.00	.45	.12
☐ 272 Dermontti Dawson S4	1.25	.55	.16
☐ 275 Tunch Ilkin S2	1.00	.45	.12
☐ 282 Gill Byrd S4	1.00	.45	.12
☐ 290 Michael Carter S2	1.00	.45	.12
☐ 292 Pierce Holt S3	1.00	.45	.12
☐ 297 George Seifert CO S1	1.25	.55	.16
☐ 306 Chuck Knox CO S3	1.00	.45	.12
☐ 310 Harry Hamilton S4	1.00	.45	.12
☐ 321 Martin Mayhew S4	1.00	.45	.12
☐ 322 Mark Rypien S1	1.25	.55	.16
☐ NNO S1 Title Card Stay Fit	1.00	.45	.12
☐ NNO S2 Title Card Eat Smart	1.00	.45	.12
☐ NNO S3 Title Card Stay Off Drugs	1.00	.45	.12
☐ NNO S4 Title Card Stay In Tune	1.00	.45	.12
☐ NNO S5 Title Card Stay True to Yourself	1.00	.45	.12
☐ NNO S6 Title Card Stay In School	1.00	.45	.12

1992 FACT NFL Properties

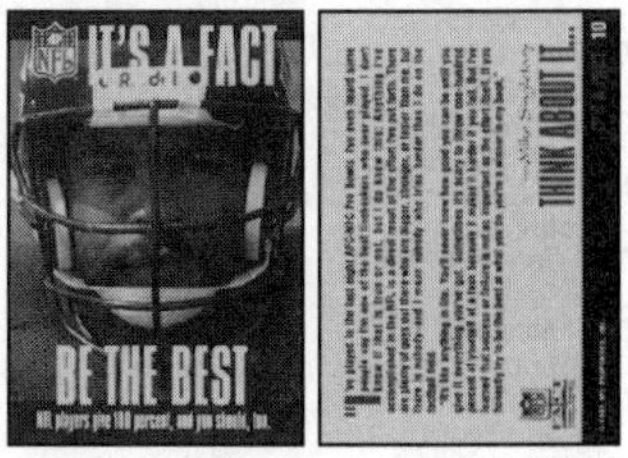

Sponsored by NFL Properties, Inc., this 18-card FACT (Football and Academics: A Championship Team) set measures the standard size and features NFL star players. The color photos on the fronts are full-bleed on the sides but bordered by black above and below. In white block lettering, the top of each card reads "It's A Fact," while the bottom slogan varies from card to card. On a white background with "It's A Fact" printed in pale blue, the horizontal backs have an extended player quote on the theme of the card.

	MINT	NRMT	EXC
COMPLETE SET (18)	35.00	16.00	4.40
COMMON CARD (1-18	1.00	.45	.12
☐ 1 Warren Moon Crack Kills	1.50	.70	.19
☐ 2 Boomer Esiason Think Before You Drink	1.25	.55	.16
☐ 3 Troy Aikman Play It Straight	7.00	3.10	.85
☐ 4 Anthony Munoz Quedate en la Escuela	1.50	.70	.19
☐ 5 Charles Mann Steroids Destroy	1.00	.45	.12
☐ 6 Earnest Byner Never Give Up	1.00	.45	.12
☐ 7 Joe Jacoby Don't Pollute	1.00	.45	.12
☐ 8 Howie Long Aids Kills	1.25	.55	.16
☐ 9 Dan Marino School's The Ticket	12.00	5.50	1.50
☐ 10 Mike Singletary Be The Best	1.25	.55	.16
☐ 11 Cornelius Bennett	1.25	.55	.16

	MINT	NRMT	EXC
Chill			
☐ 12 Chris Doleman	1.25	.55	.16
Turn It Off			
☐ 13 Jim Harbaugh	1.50	.70	.19
Eat To Win			
☐ 14 Chris Hinton	1.00	.45	.12
Say It Don't Spray It			
☐ 15 Nick Lowery	1.00	.45	.12
Heal The Planet			
☐ 16 Rodney Peete	1.25	.55	.16
Respect The Law			
☐ 17 Pat Swilling	1.25	.55	.16
Vote			
☐ 18 Jim Everett	1.25	.55	.16
Study			

1992 FACT Pro Set Mobil

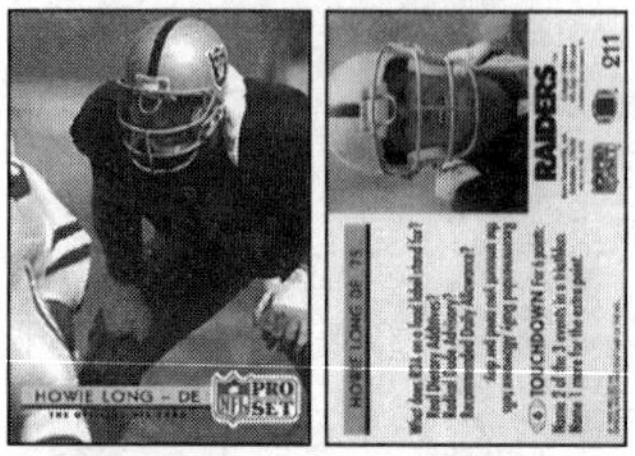

Sponsored by Pro Set and Mobil Oil, the 1992 Pro Set FACT (Football and Academics: A Championship Team) set marks the third year that Pro Set produced cards to serve as motivational learning tools to promote public health and education. Six monthly lessons were featured in the set, and each lesson had an educational theme. Teachers utilized in-classroom educational materials and distributed a set of 18-Pro Set cards (including one title/header card) each month, with the reverse sides carrying specific educational lessons corresponding to the educational theme. The standard-size cards are identical to first series '92 Pro Set cards, with the exception of the backs featuring interactive educational questions instead of player information.

	MINT	NRMT	EXC
COMPLETE SET (108)	75.00	34.00	9.50
COMMON CARD	.75	.35	.09
☐ 10 Michael Irvin	1.00	.45	.12
Season Leader			
☐ 20 Pat Leahy	.75	.35	.09
Milestone			
☐ 76 Andre Collins	.75	.35	.09
☐ 79 Jim Lachey	.75	.35	.09
☐ 82 Martin Mayhew	.75	.35	.09
☐ 83 Matt Millen	.75	.35	.09
☐ 87 Mark Rypien	.75	.35	.09
☐ 90 Joe Gibbs CO	1.00	.45	.12
☐ 98 James Lofton	1.00	.45	.12
☐ 104 Darryl Talley	.75	.35	.09
☐ 108 Marv Levy CO	1.00	.45	.12
☐ 111 Moe Gardner	.75	.35	.09
☐ 117 Jerry Glanville CO	.75	.35	.09
☐ 118 Neal Anderson	.75	.35	.09
☐ 119 Trace Armstrong	.75	.35	.09
☐ 125 Tom Waddle	.75	.35	.09
☐ 132 Anthony Munoz	1.25	.55	.16
☐ 135 David Shula CO	.75	.35	.09
☐ 136 Mike Babb	.75	.35	.09
☐ 137 Brian Brennan	.75	.35	.09
☐ 141 Clay Matthews	.75	.35	.09
☐ 142 Eric Metcalf	1.25	.55	.16
☐ 144 Bill Belichick CO	.75	.35	.09
☐ 145 Steve Beuerlein	.75	.35	.09
☐ 147 Ray Horton	.75	.35	.09
☐ 152 Alexander Wright	.75	.35	.09
☐ 153 Jimmy Johnson CO	1.00	.45	.12
☐ 155 John Elway	2.50	1.10	.30
☐ 158 Karl Mecklenburg	.75	.35	.09
☐ 161 Doug Widell	.75	.35	.09
☐ 170 Chris Spielman	.75	.35	.09
☐ 171 Wayne Fontes	.75	.35	.09
☐ 173 Tony Mandarich	.75	.35	.09
☐ 175 Bryce Paup	1.25	.55	.16
☐ 176 Sterling Sharpe	1.25	.55	.16
☐ 177 Darrell Thompson	.75	.35	.09
☐ 180 Mike Holmgren CO	1.00	.45	.12
☐ 181 Ray Childress	.75	.35	.09
☐ 183 Curtis Duncan	.75	.35	.09
☐ 186 Warren Moon	1.25	.55	.16
☐ 189 Jack Pardee CO	.75	.35	.09
☐ 192 Bill Brooks	.75	.35	.09
☐ 195 Mike Prior	.75	.35	.09
☐ 197 Clarence Verdin	.75	.35	.09
☐ 199 John Alt	.75	.35	.09
☐ 200 Deron Cherry	.75	.35	.09
☐ 202 Nick Lowery	.75	.35	.09
☐ 205 Joe Valerio	.75	.35	.09
☐ 207 Marty Schottenheimer	.75	.35	.09
☐ 210 Tim Brown	1.25	.55	.16
☐ 211 Howie Long	1.25	.55	.16
☐ 212 Ronnie Lott	1.00	.45	.12
☐ 216 Art Shell	1.25	.55	.16
☐ 222 Tom Newberry	.75	.35	.09
☐ 225 Chuck Knox CO	.75	.35	.09
☐ 230 Jim Jensen	.75	.35	.09
☐ 231 Louis Oliver	.75	.35	.09
☐ 234 Don Shula CO	1.25	.55	.16
☐ 238 Steve Jordan	.75	.35	.09
☐ 241 Herschel Walker	1.00	.45	.12
☐ 242 Felix Wright	.75	.35	.09
☐ 243 Dennis Green CO	.75	.35	.09
☐ 248 Hugh Millen	.75	.35	.09
☐ 250 Andre Tippett	.75	.35	.09
☐ 252 Dick MacPherson CO	.75	.35	.09
☐ 254 Bobby Hebert	.75	.35	.09
☐ 259 Floyd Turner	.75	.35	.09
☐ 261 Jim Mora CO	.75	.35	.09
☐ 265 Jeff Hostetler	1.00	.45	.12
☐ 268 Gary Reasons	.75	.35	.09
☐ 269 Everson Walls	.75	.35	.09
☐ 270 Ray Handley CO	.75	.35	.09
☐ 275 Jeff Lageman	.75	.35	.09
☐ 277 Rob Moore	.75	.35	.09
☐ 278 Lonnie Young	.75	.35	.09
☐ 279 Bruce Coslet CO	.75	.35	.09
☐ 283 Keith Jackson	1.00	.45	.12
☐ 286 Andre Waters	.75	.35	.09
☐ 288 Rich Kotite CO	.75	.35	.09
☐ 290 Garth Jax	.75	.35	.09
☐ 291 Ernie Jones	.75	.35	.09
☐ 297 Joe Bugel CO	.75	.35	.09
☐ 298 Gary Anderson K	.75	.35	.09
☐ 300 Eric Green	.75	.35	.09
☐ 301 Bryan Hinkle	.75	.35	.09
☐ 302 Tunch Ilkin	.75	.35	.09
☐ 303 Louis Lipps	.75	.35	.09
☐ 304 Neil O'Donnell	1.25	.55	.16
☐ 306 Bill Cowher CO	1.00	.45	.12
☐ 312 Henry Rolling	.75	.35	.09
☐ 315 Bobby Ross CO	.75	.35	.09
☐ 317 Michael Carter	.75	.35	.09
☐ 320 Brent Jones	1.00	.45	.12
☐ 324 George Seifert CO	1.00	.45	.12
☐ 328 Tommy Kane	.75	.35	.09
☐ 330 Dave Krieg	.75	.35	.09
☐ 333 Tom Flores CO	.75	.35	.09
☐ 336 Reuben Davis	.75	.35	.09
☐ 342 Sam Wyche CO	.75	.35	.09
☐ 375 Steve Atwater	.75	.35	.09
☐ 386 Haywood Jeffires	.75	.35	.09
Pro Bowl			
☐ 398 Richmond Webb	.75	.35	.09
Pro Bowl			
☐ NNO S1 Title Card	.75	.35	.09
Stay in School			
☐ NNO S2 Title Card	.75	.35	.09
Stay Fit			
☐ NNO S3 Title Card	.75	.35	.09
Eat Smart			
☐ NNO S4 Title Card	.75	.35	.09
Stay in Tune			
☐ NNO S5 Title Card	.75	.35	.09
Stay off Drugs			
☐ NNO S6 Title Card	.75	.35	.09
Stay True to Yourself			

1993 FACT Fleer Shell

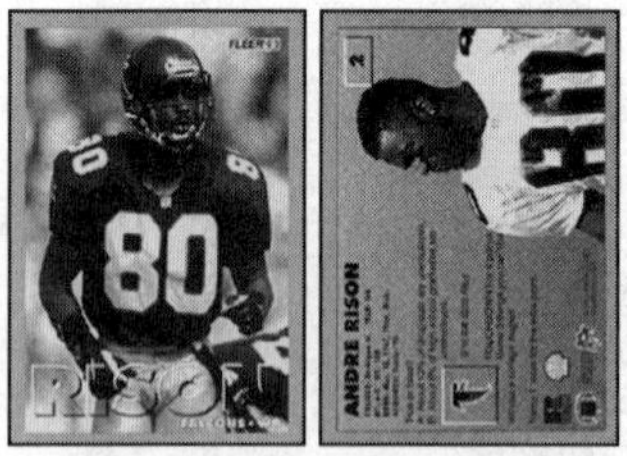

This 108-card set was issued by Fleer and co-sponsored by Shell and Russell Athletic. The FACT (Football and Academics: A Championship Team) sets were originally produced by Pro Set to serve as motivational learning tools to promote public health and education. Teachers utilized in-classroom educational materials and distributed a set of 18 Fleer cards each month, with the reverse sides carrying specific educational lessons corresponding to the educational theme. The standard-size cards are identical to the regular 1993 Fleer set, with the exception that the backs include interactive educational questions along with player information. The cards are numbered on the back with 1-18 being in set 1, 19-36 in set 2, 37-54 in set 3, etc.

	MINT	NRMT	EXC
COMPLETE SET (108)	50.00	22.00	6.25
COMMON CARD (1-108)	.30	.14	.04
☐ 1 Stay in School	.30	.14	.04
Scorecard			
☐ 2 Andre Rison	.75	.35	.09
☐ 3 Jim Kelly	.75	.35	.09
☐ 4 Mark Carrier DB	.30	.14	.04
☐ 5 David Fulcher	.30	.14	.04
☐ 6 Eric Metcalf	.75	.35	.09
☐ 7 Emmitt Smith	6.00	2.70	.75
☐ 8 John Elway	2.50	1.10	.30
☐ 9 Rodney Peete	.40	.18	.05
☐ 10 Brett Favre	6.00	2.70	.75
☐ 11 Warren Moon	.75	.35	.09
Houson Oilers			
☐ 12 Reggie Langhorne	.30	.14	.04
☐ 13 Christian Okoye	.40	.18	.05
☐ 14 Nick Bell	.30	.14	.04
☐ 15 Jim Everett	.40	.18	.05
☐ 16 Dan Marino	6.00	2.70	.75
☐ 17 Chris Doleman	.40	.18	.05
☐ 18 Leonard Russell	.40	.18	.05
☐ 19 Stay Fit	.30	.14	.04
Scorecard			
☐ 20 Sam Mills	.30	.14	.04
☐ 21 Rodney Hampton	.40	.18	.05
☐ 22 Rob Moore	.40	.18	.05
☐ 23 Seth Joyner	.40	.18	.05
☐ 24 Chris Chandler	.40	.18	.05
☐ 25 Barry Foster	.40	.18	.05
☐ 26 Stan Humphries	.75	.35	.09
☐ 27 Steve Young	2.50	1.10	.30
☐ 28 Cortez Kennedy	.40	.18	.05
☐ 29 Reggie Cobb	.30	.14	.04
☐ 30 Mark Rypien	.30	.14	.04
☐ 31 Michael Haynes	.40	.18	.05
☐ 32 Thurman Thomas	.75	.35	.09
☐ 33 Tom Waddle	.30	.14	.04
☐ 34 Harold Green	.30	.14	.04
☐ 35 Tommy Vardell	.30	.14	.04
☐ 36 Michael Irvin	.75	.35	.09
☐ 37 Eat Smart	.30	.14	.04
Scorecard			
☐ 38 Mike Croel	.30	.14	.04
☐ 39 Barry Sanders	3.00	1.35	.35
☐ 40 Sterling Sharpe	.75	.35	.09
☐ 41 Haywood Jeffires	.40	.18	.05
☐ 42 Duane Bickett	.30	.14	.04
☐ 43 Nick Lowery	.30	.14	.04
☐ 44 Greg Townsend	.30	.14	.04
☐ 45 Todd Lyght	.30	.14	.04
☐ 46 Richmond Webb	.30	.14	.04
☐ 47 Cris Carter	.75	.35	.09
☐ 48 Marv Cook	.30	.14	.04
☐ 49 Vaughan Johnson	.30	.14	.04
☐ 50 Pepper Johnson	.30	.14	.04
☐ 51 Kyle Clifton	.30	.14	.04
☐ 52 Fred Barnett	.40	.18	.05
☐ 53 Ken Harvey	.40	.18	.05
☐ 54 Rod Woodson	.75	.35	.09
☐ 55 Stay in Tune	.30	.14	.04
Scorecard			
☐ 56 Marion Butts	.40	.18	.05
☐ 57 Ricky Watters	.75	.35	.09
☐ 58 Brian Blades	.40	.18	.05
☐ 59 Broderick Thomas	.30	.14	.04
☐ 60 Charles Mann	.30	.14	.04
☐ 61 Chris Hinton	.30	.14	.04
☐ 62 Cornelius Bennett	.40	.18	.05
☐ 63 Jim Harbaugh	.75	.35	.09
☐ 64 Tim Krumrie	.30	.14	.04
☐ 65 Bernie Kosar	.40	.18	.05
☐ 66 Troy Aikman	3.00	1.35	.35
☐ 67 Shannon Sharpe	.75	.35	.09
☐ 68 Chris Spielman	.40	.18	.05
☐ 69 Brian Noble	.30	.14	.04
☐ 70 Curtis Duncan	.30	.14	.04
☐ 71 Quentin Coryatt	.40	.18	.05
☐ 72 Derrick Thomas	.75	.35	.09
☐ 73 Stay off Drugs	.30	.14	.04
Scorecard			
☐ 74 Tim Brown	.75	.35	.09
☐ 75 Jackie Slater	.30	.14	.04
☐ 76 Keith Jackson	.40	.18	.05
☐ 77 Terry Allen	.75	.35	.09
☐ 78 Andre Tippett	.30	.14	.04
☐ 79 Morten Andersen	.30	.14	.04
☐ 80 Phil Simms	.40	.18	.05
☐ 81 Jeff Lageman	.30	.14	.04
☐ 82 Randall Cunningham	.40	.18	.05
☐ 83 Randal Hill	.30	.14	.04
☐ 84 Neil O'Donnell	.75	.35	.09
☐ 85 Gill Byrd	.30	.14	.04
☐ 86 John Taylor	.40	.18	.05
☐ 87 Eugene Robinson	.30	.14	.04
☐ 88 Paul Gruber	.30	.14	.04
☐ 89 Andre Collins	.30	.14	.04
☐ 90 Chris Miller	.40	.18	.05
☐ 91 Stay True to Yourself	.30	.14	.04
Scorecard			
☐ 92 Andre Reed	.40	.18	.05
☐ 93 Richard Dent	.40	.18	.05
☐ 94 David Klingler	.30	.14	.04
☐ 95 Jay Novacek	.40	.18	.05
☐ 96 Steve Atwater	.30	.14	.04
☐ 97 Bennie Blades	.30	.14	.04
☐ 98 Terrell Buckley	.30	.14	.04
☐ 99 Ray Childress	.40	.18	.05
☐ 100 Harvey Williams	.40	.18	.05
☐ 101 Howie Long	.75	.35	.09
☐ 102 Lawrence Taylor	.75	.35	.09
☐ 103 Johnny Mitchell	.30	.14	.04
☐ 104 Carnell Lake	.30	.14	.04
☐ 105 Junior Seau	.75	.35	.09
☐ 106 Kevin Fagan	.30	.14	.04
☐ 107 Lawrence Dawsey	.30	.14	.04
☐ 108 Art Monk	.40	.18	.05

1994 FACT Fleer Shell

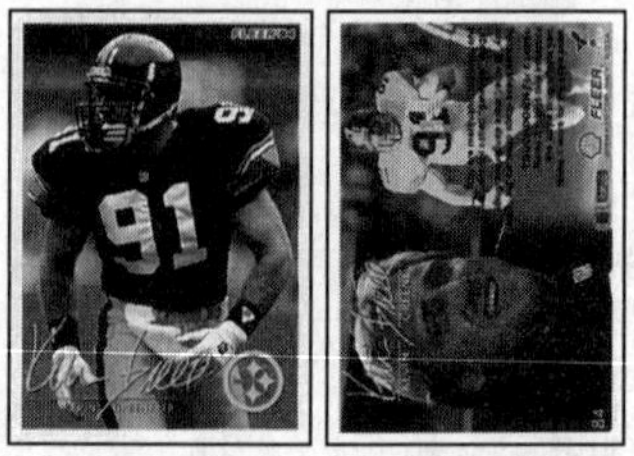

For the second consecutive year, Fleer and Shell Oil teamed up to produce a 108-card FACT (Football and Academics: A Championship Team) set. Consisting of six 18-card subsets, each subset features one title card, 17 player cards, and a different theme. The fronts feature white-bordered color action photos with a gold-foil stamped player signature, name and position, and team logo. The horizontal backs carry a ghosted action shot, and a close-up color photo. The set is arranged according to themes as follows: Stay in School (1-18), Stay Fit (19-36), Eat Smart (37-54), Stay in Tune (55-72), Stay off Drugs (73-90), and Stay True to Yourself (91-108).

	MINT	NRMT	EXC
COMPLETE SET (108)	40.00	18.00	5.00
COMMON CARD (1-108)	.20	.09	.03
☐ 1 Cover Card	.20	.09	.03
Stay in School			
☐ 2 Steve Beuerlein	.30	.14	.04
☐ 3 Erric Pegram	.30	.14	.04
☐ 4 Darryl Talley	.20	.09	.03
☐ 5 Tom Waddle	.20	.09	.03
☐ 6 Darryl Williams	.20	.09	.03
☐ 7 Tony Jones	.20	.09	.03
☐ 8 Jay Novacek	.40	.18	.05
☐ 9 Simon Fletcher	.20	.09	.03
☐ 10 Jason Hanson	.20	.09	.03
☐ 11 Reggie White	.40	.18	.05
☐ 12 Ernest Givins	.20	.09	.03
☐ 13 Kerry Cash	.20	.09	.03
☐ 14 Joe Montana	2.50	1.10	.30
☐ 15 Anthony Smith	.20	.09	.03
☐ 16 Jackie Slater	.20	.09	.03
☐ 17 Terry Kirby	.30	.14	.04
☐ 18 John Randle	.20	.09	.03
☐ 19 Cover Card	.20	.09	.03
Stay Fit			
☐ 20 Drew Bledsoe	2.00	.90	.25
☐ 21 Vaughan Johnson	.20	.09	.03
☐ 22 Greg Jackson	.20	.09	.03
☐ 23 Rob Moore	.30	.14	.04
☐ 24 Byron Evans	.20	.09	.03
☐ 25 Rod Woodson	.40	.18	.05
☐ 26 Junior Seau	.40	.18	.05
☐ 27 Steve Young	1.50	.70	.19
☐ 28 Cortez Kennedy	.30	.14	.04
☐ 29 Paul Gruber	.20	.09	.03
☐ 30 Darrell Green	.20	.09	.03
☐ 31 Tyronne Stowe	.20	.09	.03
☐ 32 Pierce Holt	.20	.09	.03
☐ 33 Steve Tasker	.30	.14	.04
☐ 34 Chris Zorich	.30	.14	.04
☐ 35 Ricardo McDonald	.20	.09	.03
☐ 36 Mark Carrier WR	.30	.14	.04
☐ 37 Cover Card	.20	.09	.03
Eat Smart			
☐ 38 Emmitt Smith	4.00	1.80	.50
☐ 39 Shannon Sharpe	.30	.14	.04
☐ 40 Chris Spielman	.30	.14	.04
☐ 41 Ken Ruettgers	.20	.09	.03
☐ 42 Bubba McDowell	.20	.09	.03
☐ 43 Rohn Stark	.20	.09	.03
☐ 44 Derrick Thomas	.40	.18	.05
☐ 45 Tim Brown	.30	.14	.04
☐ 46 Shane Conlan	.20	.09	.03
☐ 47 Marco Coleman	.20	.09	.03
☐ 48 Steve Jordan	.20	.09	.03
☐ 49 Ben Coates	.30	.14	.04
☐ 50 Willie Roaf	.20	.09	.03
☐ 51 Carlton Bailey	.20	.09	.03
☐ 52 Ronnie Lott	.30	.14	.04
☐ 53 Eric Allen	.20	.09	.03
☐ 54 Dermontti Dawson	.20	.09	.03
☐ 55 Cover Card	.20	.09	.03
Stay in Tune			
☐ 56 Ronnie Harmon	.30	.14	.04
☐ 57 Dana Stubblefield	.40	.18	.05
☐ 58 Rick Mirer	.35	.16	.04
☐ 59 Santana Dotson	.30	.14	.04
☐ 60 Jim Lachey	.20	.09	.03
☐ 61 Ricky Proehl	.20	.09	.03
☐ 62 Jessie Tuggle	.20	.09	.03
☐ 63 Jim Kelly	.40	.18	.05
☐ 64 Mark Carrier DB	.20	.09	.03
☐ 65 David Klingler	.20	.09	.03
☐ 66 Eric Turner	.30	.14	.04
☐ 67 Darrin Smith	.20	.09	.03
☐ 68 Glyn Milburn	.40	.18	.05
☐ 69 Herman Moore	.40	.18	.05
☐ 70 Sterling Sharpe	.40	.18	.05
☐ 71 Ray Childress	.20	.09	.03

☐ 72 Quentin Coryatt	.30	.14	.04
☐ 73 Cover Card Stay off Drugs	.20	.09	.03
☐ 74 Marcus Allen	.40	.18	.05
☐ 75 Jeff Hostetler	.30	.14	.04
☐ 76 Jerome Bettis	.35	.16	.04
☐ 77 Richmond Webb	.20	.09	.03
☐ 78 Randall McDaniel	.20	.09	.03
☐ 79 Maurice Hurst	.20	.09	.03
☐ 80 Morten Andersen	.20	.09	.03
☐ 81 Dave Meggett	.30	.14	.04
☐ 82 Brian Washington	.20	.09	.03
☐ 83 Randall Cunningham	.20	.09	.03
☐ 84 Kevin Greene	.40	.18	.05
☐ 85 Leslie O'Neal	.30	.14	.04
☐ 86 Tim McDonald	.20	.09	.03
☐ 87 Eugene Robinson	.20	.09	.03
☐ 88 Hardy Nickerson	.30	.14	.04
☐ 89 Chip Lohmiller	.20	.09	.03
☐ 90 Jeff George	.40	.18	.05
☐ 91 Cover Card Stay True to Yourself	.20	.09	.03
☐ 92 Cornelius Bennett	.30	.14	.04
☐ 93 Erik Kramer	.20	.09	.03
☐ 94 Tommy Vardell	.20	.09	.03
☐ 95 Troy Aikman	2.00	.90	.25
☐ 96 John Elway	1.50	.70	.19
☐ 97 Barry Sanders	2.00	.90	.25
☐ 98 Dan Saleaumua	.20	.09	.03
☐ 99 Dan Marino	4.00	1.80	.50
☐ 100 Jack Del Rio	.20	.09	.03
☐ 101 Bruce Armstrong	.20	.09	.03
☐ 102 Renaldo Turnbull	.20	.09	.03
☐ 103 Phil Simms	.30	.14	.04
☐ 104 Boomer Esiason	.30	.14	.04
☐ 105 Fred Barnett	.30	.14	.04
☐ 106 Greg Lloyd	.40	.18	.05
☐ 107 John Carney	.20	.09	.03
☐ 108 Jerry Rice	2.00	.90	.25

1994 FACT NFL Properties

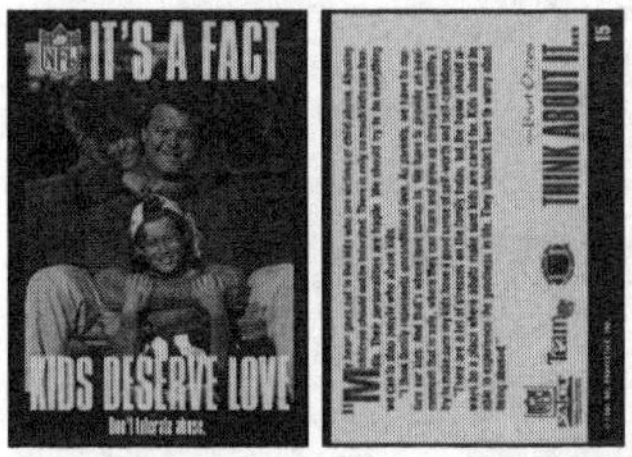

Sponsored by NFL Properties, Inc., this 18-card FACT (Football, Academics: A Championship Team) measures the standard-size and features NFL star players as well as Lesley Visser, a sports journalist. Inside a black picture frame, the fronts feature color posed photos. The words "It's A Fact" appears in white block lettering across the top, while the specific slogan, which varies from card to card, is printed across the bottom. On a white panel edged above and below in black, the backs present an extended player quote on the theme of the card.

	MINT	NRMT	EXC
COMPLETE SET (18)	25.00	11.00	3.10
COMMON CARD (1-18)	.60	.25	.07
☐ 1 Troy Aikman Play It Straight	3.50	1.55	.45
☐ 2 Cornelius Bennett Chill	.75	.35	.09
☐ 3 Lesley Visser ANN Aim High	.75	.35	.09
☐ 4 Junior Seau Eat Smart	1.25	.55	.16
☐ 5 Chris Hinton Clean Up Your Act	.60	.25	.07
☐ 6 Howie Long Plan Ahead	.75	.35	.09
☐ 7 Nick Lowery Heal The Planet	.60	.25	.07
☐ 8 Tony Casillas Guns Are For Fools	.60	.25	.07
☐ 9 Dan Marino School's The Ticket	6.00	2.70	.75
☐ 10 Warren Moon Make A Difference	1.00	.45	.12
☐ 11 Rod Bernstine Jim Kelly We're The Same Inside	.60	.25	.07
☐ 12 Rohn Stark Smoking Is Stupid	.60	.25	.07
☐ 13 Michael Irvin Respect the Law	1.25	.55	.16
☐ 14 Steve Young Education Works	2.50	1.10	.30
☐ 15 Bart Oates Kids Deserve Love	.60	.25	.07
☐ 16 Erik Kramer Be Fit!	.75	.35	.09
☐ 17 Emmitt Smith Don't Quit	6.00	2.70	.75
☐ 18 Steve Beuerlein Think	.75	.35	.09

1994 FACT NFL Properties Artex

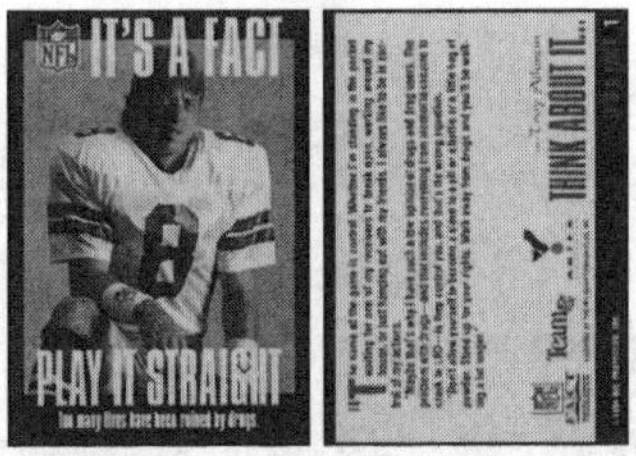

Issued in a cello pack, these three standard-size FACT cards are identical to their counterparts in the 18-card FACT set except for the numbering of cards 2-3 (Marino is #9 and Smith is #17 in the 18-card set) and the Artex Sportswear logo on their back. These sets were also distributed through various K-Mart outlets.

	MINT	NRMT	EXC
COMPLETE SET (3)	10.00	4.50	1.25
COMMON CARD (1-3)	2.00	.90	.25
☐ 1 Troy Aikman Play It Straight	2.00	.90	.25
☐ 2 Dan Marino School's The Ticket	4.00	1.80	.50
☐ 3 Emmitt Smith Don't Quit	4.00	1.80	.50

1995 FACT Fleer Shell

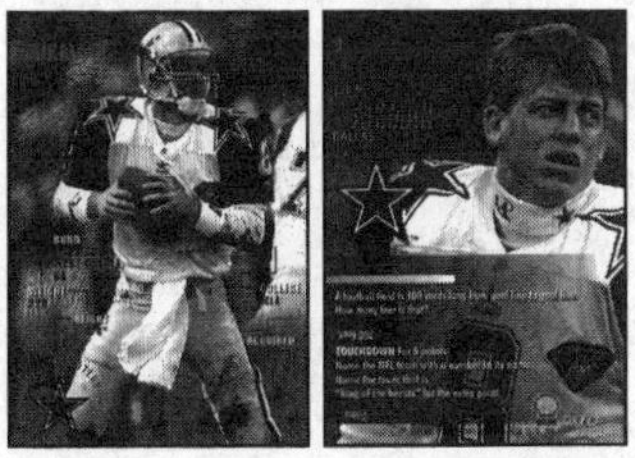

This FACT (Football and Academics: A Championship Team) set was produced by Fleer and Shell Oil and consists of six subsets of 18 cards each. The set features color action player photos with questions relating to the subset theme. The set is arranged according to themes as follows: Stay in School (1-18), Stay Fit (19-36), Eat Smart (37-54), Stay in Tune (55-72), Stay off Drugs (73-90), and Stay True to Yourself (91-108).

	MINT	NRMT	EXC
COMPLETE SET (108)	30.00	13.50	3.70
COMMON CARD (1-108)	.20	.09	.03
SEMISTARS	.30	.14	.04
STARS	.40	.18	.05
☐ 1 Cover Card Stay in School	.20	.09	.03
☐ 2 Seth Joyner	.20	.09	.03
☐ 3 J.J. Birden	.30	.14	.04
☐ 4 Jim Kelly	.40	.18	.05
☐ 5 Pete Metzelaars	.20	.09	.03
☐ 6 Joe Cain	.20	.09	.03
☐ 7 Carl Pickens	.40	.18	.05
☐ 8 Leroy Hoard	.30	.14	.04
☐ 9 Troy Aikman	1.50	.70	.19
☐ 10 Steve Atwater	.20	.09	.03
☐ 11 Bennie Blades	.20	.09	.03
☐ 12 Brett Favre	3.00	1.35	.35
☐ 13 Mel Gray	.20	.09	.03
☐ 14 Tony Bennett	.20	.09	.03
☐ 15 Steve Beuerlein	.30	.14	.04
☐ 16 Marcus Allen	.40	.18	.05
☐ 17 Tim Brown	.40	.18	.05
☐ 18 Tim Bowens	.20	.09	.03
☐ 19 Cover Card Stay Fit	.20	.09	.03
☐ 20 Jack Del Rio	.20	.09	.03
☐ 21 Drew Bledsoe	1.50	.70	.19
☐ 22 Jim Everett	.20	.09	.03
☐ 23 Michael Brooks	.20	.09	.03
☐ 24 Tony Casillas	.20	.09	.03
☐ 25 Fred Barnett	.30	.14	.04
☐ 26 Kevin Greene	.40	.18	.05
☐ 27 Jerome Bettis	.40	.18	.05
☐ 28 John Carney	.20	.09	.03
☐ 29 Ken Norton	.30	.14	.04
☐ 30 Cortez Kennedy	.30	.14	.04
☐ 31 Alvin Harper	.30	.14	.04
☐ 32 Henry Ellard	.30	.14	.04
☐ 33 Aeneas Williams	.20	.09	.03
☐ 34 Jeff George	.40	.18	.05
☐ 35 Bryce Paup	.40	.18	.05
☐ 36 Sam Mills	.30	.14	.04
☐ 37 Cover Card Eat Smart	.20	.09	.03
☐ 38 Mark Carrier	.20	.09	.03
☐ 39 Darnay Scott	.40	.18	.05
☐ 40 Pepper Johnson	.20	.09	.03
☐ 41 Michael Irvin	.40	.18	.05
☐ 42 John Elway	1.00	.45	.12
☐ 43 Herman Moore	.40	.18	.05
☐ 44 John Jurkovic	.20	.09	.03
☐ 45 Al Smith	.20	.09	.03
☐ 46 Steve Emtman	.20	.09	.03
☐ 47 Darren Carrington	.20	.09	.03
☐ 48 Kimble Anders	.20	.09	.03
☐ 49 Jeff Hostetler	.30	.14	.04
☐ 50 Eric Green	.30	.14	.04
☐ 51 Cris Carter	.40	.18	.05
☐ 52 Ben Coates	.30	.14	.04
☐ 53 Michael Haynes	.20	.09	.03
☐ 54 Dave Brown	.30	.14	.04
☐ 55 Cover Card Stay in Tune	.20	.09	.03
☐ 56 Boomer Esiason	.30	.14	.04
☐ 57 Randall Cunningham	.30	.14	.04
☐ 58 Byron Bam Morris	.30	.14	.04
☐ 59 Sean Gilbert	.30	.14	.04
☐ 60 Stan Humphries	.30	.14	.04
☐ 61 Jerry Rice	1.50	.70	.19
☐ 62 Rick Mirer	.40	.18	.05
☐ 63 Hardy Nickerson	.30	.14	.04
☐ 64 Ricky Ervins	.20	.09	.03
☐ 65 Eric Swann	.30	.14	.04
☐ 66 Craig Heyward	.30	.14	.04
☐ 67 Andre Reed	.30	.14	.04
☐ 68 Frank Reich	.30	.14	.04
☐ 69 Steve Walsh	.20	.09	.03
☐ 70 Dan Wilkinson	.20	.09	.03
☐ 71 Vinny Testaverde	.30	.14	.04
☐ 72 Russell Maryland	.20	.09	.03
☐ 73 Cover Card Stay Off Drugs	.20	.09	.03
☐ 74 Shannon Sharpe	.30	.14	.04
☐ 75 Brett Perriman	.30	.14	.04
☐ 76 Reggie White	.40	.18	.05
☐ 77 Mark Stepnoski	.20	.09	.03
☐ 78 Marshall Faulk	.50	.23	.06
☐ 79 Reggie Cobb	.20	.09	.03
☐ 80 Lake Dawson	.20	.09	.03
☐ 81 Rocket Ismail	.30	.14	.04
☐ 82 Dan Marino	3.00	1.35	.35
☐ 83 Warren Moon	.40	.18	.05
☐ 84 Willie McGinest	.30	.14	.04
☐ 85 William Roaf	.20	.09	.03
☐ 86 Rodney Hampton	.40	.18	.05
☐ 87 Marvin Washington	.20	.09	.03
☐ 88 Charlie Garner	.30	.14	.04
☐ 89 Neil O'Donnell	.30	.14	.04
☐ 90 Todd Lyght	.20	.09	.03
☐ 91 Cover Card Stay True to Yourself	.20	.09	.03
☐ 92 Natrone Means	.40	.18	.05
☐ 93 Deion Sanders	.75	.35	.09
☐ 94 Chris Warren	.30	.14	.04
☐ 95 Errict Rhett	.50	.23	.06
☐ 96 Ken Harvey	.20	.09	.03
☐ 97 Bruce Smith	.40	.18	.05
☐ 98 Chris Zorich	.30	.14	.04
☐ 99 Eric Turner	.30	.14	.04
☐ 100 Emmitt Smith	3.00	1.35	.35
☐ 101 Barry Sanders	1.50	.70	.19
☐ 102 Neil Smith	.30	.14	.04
☐ 103 Chester McGlockton	.30	.14	.04
☐ 104 Fuad Reveiz	.20	.09	.03
☐ 105 Thomas Lewis	.20	.09	.03
☐ 106 Rod Woodson	.40	.18	.05
☐ 107 Junior Seau	.40	.18	.05
☐ 108 Steve Young	1.00	.45	.12

1995 FACT NFL Properties

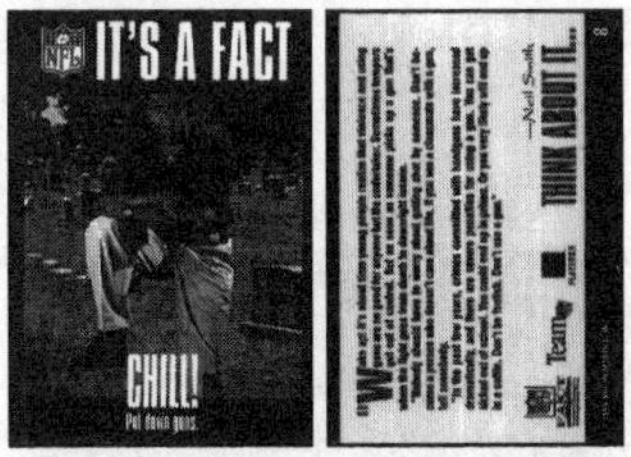

This 18-card set was produced by the NFL to promote it's FACT (Football and Academics: a Championship Team) program. The cards feature black-bordered color player photos with the NFL logo and words, "IT'S A FACT," at the top. The subject and a related message are printed at the bottom. The backs carry a paragraph of the player's thoughts on the card subject.

	MINT	NRMT	EXC
COMPLETE SET (18)	30.00	13.50	3.70
COMMON CARD (1-18)	.60	.25	.07
☐ 1 Troy Aikman	3.00	1.35	.35
☐ 2 Rocket Ismail Qadry Ismail	.75	.35	.09
☐ 3 Robin Roberts	.75	.35	.09
☐ 4 Junior Seau	1.00	.45	.12
☐ 5 Chris Hinton	.60	.25	.07
☐ 6 Sean Jones	.75	.35	.09
☐ 7 Thurman Thomas	1.00	.45	.12
☐ 8 Neil Smith	.75	.35	.09
☐ 9 Dan Marino	6.00	2.70	.75
☐ 10 Reggie Williams	.60	.25	.07
☐ 11 Rob Bernstine Jim Kelly	1.00	.45	.12
☐ 12 Drew Bledsoe	3.00	1.35	.35
☐ 13 Michael Irvin	1.00	.45	.12
☐ 14 Steve Young	2.00	.90	.25
☐ 15 Jerry Rice	3.00	1.35	.35
☐ 16 Herschel Walker	.75	.35	.09
☐ 17 Emmitt Smith	6.00	2.70	.75
☐ 18 Barry Sanders	3.00	1.35	.35

1968-69 Falcons Team Issue

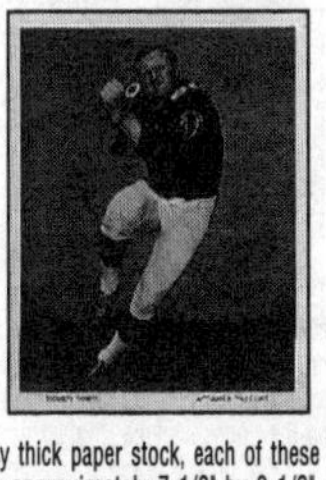

Printed on glossy thick paper stock, each of these black-and-white photos measure approximately 7 1/2" by 9 1/2" and have white borders. With the exception of the Berry photo (a portrait), all the photos are posed action shots. The cardbacks are blank. The photos are unnumbered and checklisted below in alphabetical order. Each includes the player's name and team name below the photo in the card border.

	NRMT-MT	EXC	G-VG
COMPLETE SET (13)	60.00	27.00	7.50
COMMON CARD (1-13)	4.00	1.80	.50
☐ 1 Bob Berry	6.00	2.70	.75
☐ 2 Carlton Dabney	4.00	1.80	.50
☐ 3 Bob Etter	4.00	1.80	.50
☐ 4 Bill Harris	4.00	1.80	.50
☐ 5 Ralph Heck	4.00	1.80	.50
☐ 6 Claude Humphrey	6.00	2.70	.75
☐ 7 Randy Johnson	6.00	2.70	.75
☐ 8 George Kunz (Notre Dame photo)	6.00	2.70	.75
☐ 9 Errol Linden	4.00	1.80	.50
☐ 10 Billy Lothridge	4.00	1.80	.50
☐ 11 Tommy Nobis	15.00	6.75	1.85
☐ 12 Ken Reaves	4.00	1.80	.50
☐ 13 Jerry Shay	4.00	1.80	.50

1975 Falcons Team Sheets

This three-card set was printed on sheets each measuring approximately 8 1/2" by 11" and features black-and-white player portraits. Sheet 1 contains 15 players and the set title. Sheets 2 and 3 contain 16 players each. The backs are blank.

	NRMT-MT	EXC	G-VG
COMPLETE SET (3)	20.00	9.00	2.50
COMMON CARD (1-3)	5.00	2.20	.60
☐ 1 Team Name Rankin Smith Frank Wall Pat Peppler Brad Davis Ray Easterling Wallace Francis Len Gotshalk Fulton Kuykendall Rolland Lawrence Mike Lewis Ron Mabra Oscar Reed Carl Russ Paul Ryczek Royce Smith	5.00	2.20	.60
☐ 2 Marion Campbell Brent Adams Steve Bartkowski Nick Bebout Dave Hampton Don Hansen Dennis Havig Tom Hayes Rosie Manning Jeff Merrow Nick Mike-Mayer Jim Mitchell Haskel Stanback Pat Sullivan Woody Thompson Mike Tilleman	10.00	4.50	1.25
☐ 3 Greg Brezina Ray Brown Ken Burrow Rick Byas Larron Jackson John James Alfred Jenkins	5.00	2.20	.60

Bob Jones
Greg McCrary
Kim McQuilken
Tommy Nobis
Ralph Ortega
Gerald Tinker
Jeff Van Note
Chuck Walker
John Zook

1978 Falcons Kinnett Dairies

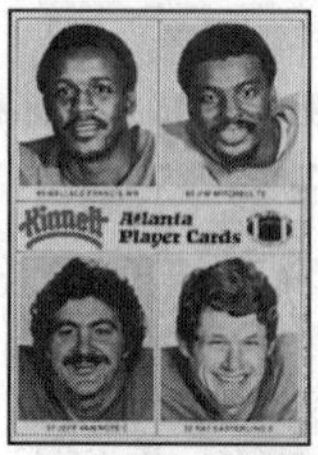

These six blank-backed white panels measure approximately 4 1/4" by 6" and feature four black-and-white player headshots per panel, all framed by a thin red line. A narrow strip running across the center of the panel contains the sponsor name, the words "Atlanta Player Cards," and the NFLPA logo. The cards are unnumbered and checklisted below in the alphabetical order of the players shown in the upper left corners.

	NRMT-MT	EXC	G-VG
COMPLETE SET (6)	40.00	18.00	5.00
COMMON PANEL (1-6)	5.00	2.20	.60
☐ 1 William Andrews Jeff Yeates Wilson Faumuina Phil McKinnely	7.50	3.40	.95
☐ 2 Warren Bryant R.C. Thieleman Steve Bartkowski Frank Reed	10.00	4.50	1.25
☐ 3 Wallace Francis Jim Mitchell Jeff Van Note Ray Easterling	7.50	3.40	.95
☐ 4 Dewey McClain Billy Ryckman Paul Ryczek Bubba Bean	5.00	2.20	.60
☐ 5 Robert Pennywell Dave Scott Jim Bailey John James	5.00	2.20	.60
☐ 6 Haskel Stanback Rick Byas Mike Esposito Tom Moriarty	7.50	3.40	.95

1980 Falcons Police

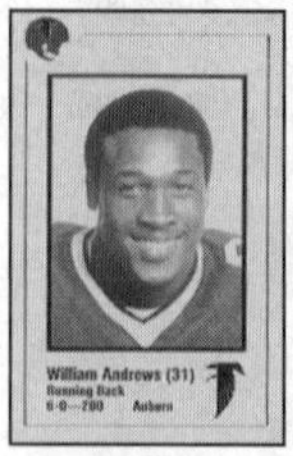

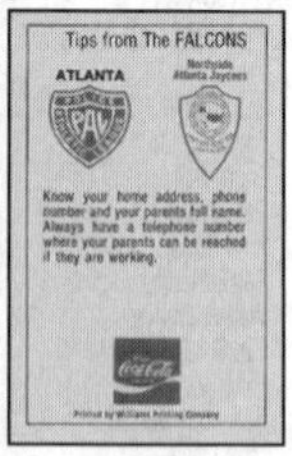

The 1980 Atlanta Falcons set contains 30 unnumbered cards each measuring approximately 2 5/8" by 4 1/8". Although uniform numbers can be found on the front of the cards, the cards have been listed alphabetically on the checklist below for convenience. Logos of the three sponsors, the Atlanta Police Athletic League, the Northside Atlanta Jaycees, and Coca-Cola, can be found on the back of the cards with short "Tips from the Falcons". Card backs have black printing with red accent. The Falcon helmet and stylized logo appear on the front of the cards with the player's name, uniform number, position, height, weight and college.

	MINT	NRMT	EXC
COMPLETE SET (30)	60.00	27.00	7.50
COMMON CARD (1-30)	1.50	.70	.19
☐ 1 William Andrews	5.00	2.20	.60
☐ 2 Steve Bartkowski	10.00	4.50	1.25
☐ 3 Bubba Bean	2.50	1.10	.30
☐ 4 Warren Bryant	1.50	.70	.19
☐ 5 Rick Byas	1.50	.70	.19
☐ 6 Lynn Cain	3.00	1.35	.35
☐ 7 Buddy Curry	1.50	.70	.19
☐ 8 Edgar Fields	1.50	.70	.19
☐ 9 Wallace Francis	3.50	1.55	.45
☐ 10 Alfred Jackson	3.00	1.35	.35
☐ 11 John James	1.50	.70	.19
☐ 12 Alfred Jenkins	4.00	1.80	.50
☐ 13 Kenny Johnson	1.50	.70	.19
☐ 14 Mike Kenn	3.00	1.35	.35
☐ 15 Fulton Kuykendall	2.00	.90	.25
☐ 16 Rolland Lawrence	2.00	.90	.25
☐ 17 Tim Mazzetti	1.50	.70	.19
☐ 18 Dewey McLean	1.50	.70	.19
☐ 19 Jeff Merrow	2.00	.90	.25
☐ 20 Junior Miller	3.00	1.35	.35
☐ 21 Tom Pridemore	1.50	.70	.19
☐ 22 Frank Reed	1.50	.70	.19
☐ 23 Al Richardson	1.50	.70	.19
☐ 24 Dave Scott	1.50	.70	.19
☐ 25 Don Smith	1.50	.70	.19
☐ 26 Reggie Smith	1.50	.70	.19
☐ 27 R.C. Thielemann	2.00	.90	.25
☐ 28 Jeff Van Note	3.00	1.35	.35
☐ 29 Joel Williams	1.50	.70	.19
☐ 30 Jeff Yeates	1.50	.70	.19

1981 Falcons Police

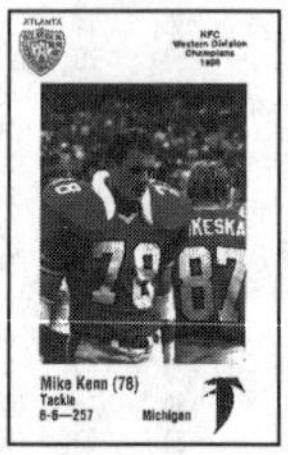

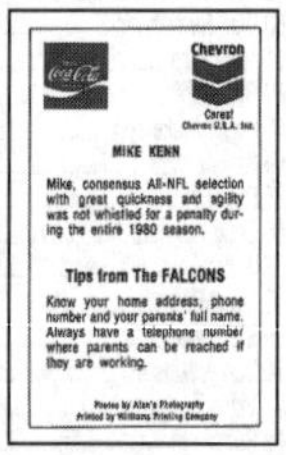

The 1981 Atlanta Falcons 30-card police set is unnumbered but has been listed in the checklist below by player uniform number. The cards measure approximately 2 5/8" by 4 1/8". The set is sponsored by the Atlanta Police Athletic League, whose logo appears on the front, and Coca-Cola and Chevron, whose logos appear on the back. The player's name and brief biographical data, in addition to "Tips from the Falcons," are contained on the backs of the cards. Card backs have black printing with red and blue accent on thin white card stock. The fronts inform the public that the Atlanta Falcons were the NFC Western Division Champions of 1980.

	MINT	NRMT	EXC
COMPLETE SET (30)	15.00	6.75	1.85
COMMON CARD	.40	.18	.05
☐ 6 John James	.40	.18	.05
☐ 10 Steve Bartkowski	3.50	1.55	.45
☐ 16 Reggie Smith	.40	.18	.05
☐ 18 Mick Luckhurst	.40	.18	.05
☐ 21 Lynn Cain	1.00	.45	.12
☐ 23 Bobby Butler	.40	.18	.05
☐ 27 Tom Pridemore	.40	.18	.05
☐ 30 Scott Woerner	.40	.18	.05
☐ 31 William Andrews	1.50	.70	.19
☐ 36 Bob Glazebrook	.40	.18	.05
☐ 37 Kenny Johnson	.40	.18	.05
☐ 50 Buddy Curry	.40	.18	.05
☐ 51 Jim Laughlin	.40	.18	.05
☐ 54 Fulton Kuykendall	.40	.18	.05
☐ 56 Al Richardson	.40	.18	.05
☐ 57 Jeff Van Note	.60	.25	.07
☐ 58 Joel Williams	.40	.18	.05
☐ 65 Don Smith	.40	.18	.05
☐ 66 Warren Bryant	.40	.18	.05
☐ 68 R.C. Thielemann	.40	.18	.05
☐ 70 Dave Scott	.40	.18	.05
☐ 74 Wilson Faumuina	.40	.18	.05
☐ 75 Jeff Merrow	.40	.18	.05
☐ 78 Mike Kenn	.60	.25	.07
☐ 79 Jeff Yeates	.40	.18	.05
☐ 80 Junior Miller	.60	.25	.07
☐ 84 Alfred Jenkins	1.00	.45	.12
☐ 85 Alfred Jackson	.75	.35	.09
☐ 89 Wallace Francis	1.00	.45	.12
☐ NNO Leeman Bennett CO	.40	.18	.05

1993 FCA Super Bowl

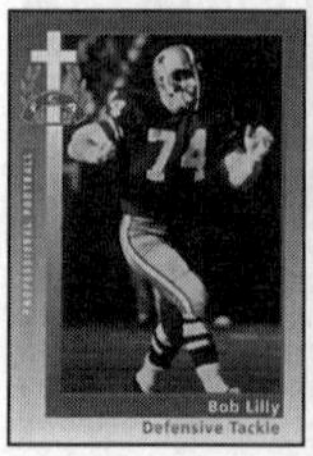

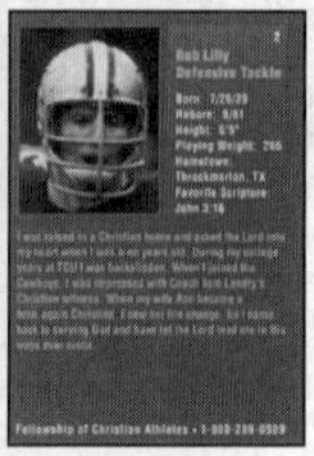

This six-card standard-size set features color player photos on a gradated blue background. The pictures are bordered on three sides by a thin hot pink line. The left side is bordered by a gradated blue border that also runs across the the bottom creating a double hot pink and blue bottom border. At the upper left of the picture is the FCA (Fellowship of Christian Athletes) emblem. The player's name appears in the bottom border, while his position is printed in the bottom margin. A hot pink stripe on the left edge contains the words "Professional Football." The backs are blue and display a color close-up photo, biographical information (including favorite scripture), and the player's testimony in yellow print.

	MINT	NRMT	EXC
COMPLETE SET (6)	6.00	2.70	.75
COMMON CARD (1-5)	.75	.35	.09
☐ 1 Alfred Anderson	.75	.35	.09
☐ 2 Bob Lilly	2.00	.90	.25
☐ 3 Tom Landry CO	2.00	.90	.25
☐ 4 Brent Jones	1.00	.45	.12
☐ 5 Bruce Matthews	.75	.35	.09
☐ 6 Title Card	.75	.35	.09

1992 Finest

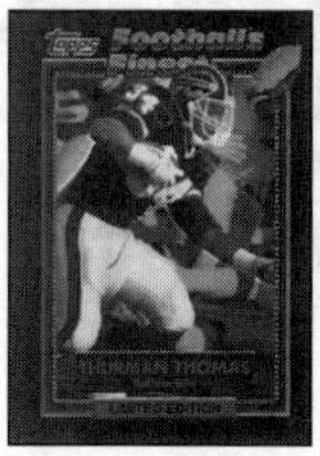

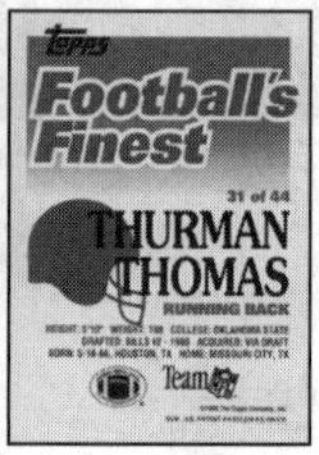

Manufactured with Topps Poly-tech process, this 44-card standard-size set features 33 established NFL stars and 11 top rookies. Three thousand cases were produced, with 20 sets per case. The fronts feature action color player photos with a foil and lacquer finish. The background of each picture has a metallic look. The photos of veteran players are bordered in blue and gold against a black card face. The photos of rookies are bordered in red and gold. The player's name and team appear in a blue bar, and the words "Limited Edition" appear in a gold bar near the bottom. The set name at the top and a football icon round out the front design. The backs are white and show the words "Football's Finest" in white-edged royal blue lettering against a gradated red panel. The player's name appears in large black print and partially overlaps a royal blue helmet icon. Biographical information finishes the back. The cards are numbered on the back and checklisted below alphabetically according to veterans (1-33) and rookies (34-44).

	MINT	NRMT	EXC
COMPLETE FACT.SET (45)	20.00	9.00	2.50
COMMON CARD (1-44)	.30	.14	.04
☐ 1 Neal Anderson	.50	.23	.06
☐ 2 Cornelius Bennett	.50	.23	.06
☐ 3 Marion Butts	.50	.23	.06
☐ 4 Anthony Carter	.50	.23	.06
☐ 5 Mike Croel	.30	.14	.04
☐ 6 John Elway	3.00	1.35	.35
☐ 7 Jim Everett	.50	.23	.06
☐ 8 Ernest Givins	.50	.23	.06
☐ 9 Rodney Hampton	.50	.23	.06
☐ 10 Alvin Harper	.75	.35	.09
☐ 11 Michael Irvin	1.00	.45	.12
☐ 12 Rickey Jackson	.30	.14	.04
☐ 13 Seth Joyner	.50	.23	.06
☐ 14 James Lofton	.50	.23	.06
☐ 15 Ronnie Lott	.50	.23	.06
☐ 16 Eric Metcalf	.75	.35	.09
☐ 17 Chris Miller	.50	.23	.06
☐ 18 Art Monk	.50	.23	.06
☐ 19 Warren Moon	.75	.35	.09
☐ 20 Rob Moore	.50	.23	.06
☐ 21 Anthony Munoz	.50	.23	.06
☐ 22 Christian Okoye	.50	.23	.06
☐ 23 Andre Rison	.75	.35	.09
☐ 24 Leonard Russell	.50	.23	.06
☐ 25 Mark Rypien	.50	.23	.06
☐ 26 Barry Sanders	4.00	1.80	.50
☐ 27 Emmitt Smith	7.50	3.40	.95
☐ 28 Pat Swilling	.50	.23	.06
☐ 29 John Taylor	.50	.23	.06
☐ 30 Derrick Thomas	.75	.35	.09
☐ 31 Thurman Thomas	1.00	.45	.12
☐ 32 Reggie White	.75	.35	.09
☐ 33 Rod Woodson	.75	.35	.09
☐ 34 Edgar Bennett	1.00	.45	.12
☐ 35 Terrell Buckley	.30	.14	.04
☐ 36 Keith Hamilton	.30	.14	.04
☐ 37 Amp Lee	.30	.14	.04
☐ 38 Ricardo McDonald	.30	.14	.04
☐ 39 Chris Mims	.50	.23	.06
☐ 40 Robert Porcher	.50	.23	.06
☐ 41 Leon Searcy	.50	.23	.06
☐ 42 Siran Stacy	.30	.14	.04
☐ 43 Tommy Vardell	.30	.14	.04
☐ 44 Bob Whitfield	.30	.14	.04
☐ NNO Checklist	.30	.14	.04

1994 Finest

The 1994 Finest football set consists of 220 standard-size cards. Specially designed refracting foil cards were produced for each of the 220 cards. One of these foil cards was inserted in approximately every nine packs. Thirty-seven cards displayed a special rookie design, and one of these rookie cards was included in each five-card pack. Moreover, oversized 4" by 6" versions of these 37 rookie cards were produced and inserted at a rate of one in each 24-count box. The fronts feature colorful metallic fronts that carry color player action shots. The player's name appears within a colored bar near the bottom of the frame. The white-bordered horizontal back carries another color player

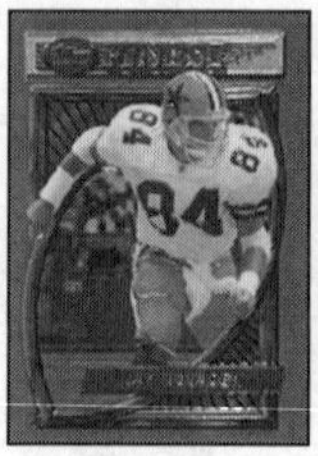

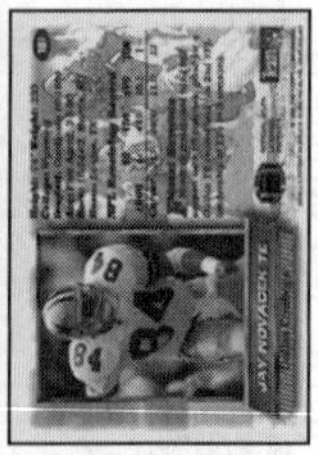

action shot in a simulated picture frame on the left. The back is filled out by biography, statistics, and copy detailing each player's "Finest Moment". There are no key Rookie Cards in this set.

	MINT	NRMT	EXC
COMPLETE SET (220)	110.00	50.00	14.00
COMMON CARD (1-220)	.50	.23	.06
☐ 1 Emmitt Smith	18.00	8.00	2.20
☐ 2 Calvin Williams	1.00	.45	.12
☐ 3 Mark Collins	.50	.23	.06
☐ 4 Steve McMichael	1.00	.45	.12
☐ 5 Jim Kelly	2.00	.90	.25
☐ 6 Michael Dean Perry	1.00	.45	.12
☐ 7 Wayne Simmons	.50	.23	.06
☐ 8 Rocket Ismail	1.00	.45	.12
☐ 9 Mark Rypien	.50	.23	.06
☐ 10 Brian Blades	1.00	.45	.12
☐ 11 Barry Word	.50	.23	.06
☐ 12 Jerry Rice	10.00	4.50	1.25
☐ 13 Derrick Fenner	.50	.23	.06
☐ 14 Karl Mecklenburg	.50	.23	.06
☐ 15 Reggie Cobb	.50	.23	.06
☐ 16 Eric Swann	1.00	.45	.12
☐ 17 Neil Smith	2.00	.90	.25
☐ 18 Barry Foster	.50	.23	.06
☐ 19 Willie Roaf	.50	.23	.06
☐ 20 Troy Drayton	.50	.23	.06
☐ 21 Warren Moon	2.00	.90	.25
☐ 22 Richmond Webb	.50	.23	.06
☐ 23 Anthony Miller	1.00	.45	.12
☐ 24 Chris Slade	.50	.23	.06
☐ 25 Mel Gray	.50	.23	.06
☐ 26 Ronnie Lott	1.00	.45	.12
☐ 27 Andre Rison	1.00	.45	.12
☐ 28 Jeff George	2.00	.90	.25
☐ 29 John Copeland	.50	.23	.06
☐ 30 Derrick Thomas	2.00	.90	.25
☐ 31 Sterling Sharpe	1.00	.45	.12
☐ 32 Chris Doleman	.50	.23	.06
☐ 33 Monte Coleman	.50	.23	.06
☐ 34 Mark Bavaro	.50	.23	.06
☐ 35 Kevin Williams	1.00	.45	.12
☐ 36 Eric Metcalf	1.00	.45	.12
☐ 37 Brent Jones	1.00	.45	.12
☐ 38 Steve Tasker	1.00	.45	.12
☐ 39 Dave Meggett	.50	.23	.06
☐ 40 Howie Long	1.00	.45	.12
☐ 41 Rick Mirer	3.00	1.35	.35
☐ 42 Jerome Bettis	5.00	2.20	.60
☐ 43 Marion Butts	.50	.23	.06
☐ 44 Barry Sanders	10.00	4.50	1.25
☐ 45 Jason Elam	.50	.23	.06
☐ 46 Broderick Thomas	.50	.23	.06
☐ 47 Derek Brown RB	.50	.23	.06
☐ 48 Lorenzo White	.50	.23	.06
☐ 49 Neil O'Donnell	2.00	.90	.25
☐ 50 Chris Burkett	.50	.23	.06
☐ 51 John Offerdahl	.50	.23	.06
☐ 52 Rohn Stark	.50	.23	.06
☐ 53 Neal Anderson	.50	.23	.06
☐ 54 Steve Beuerlein	.50	.23	.06
☐ 55 Bruce Armstrong	.50	.23	.06
☐ 56 Lincoln Kennedy	.50	.23	.06
☐ 57 Darrell Green	.50	.23	.06
☐ 58 Ricardo McDonald	.50	.23	.06
☐ 59 Chris Warren	1.00	.45	.12
☐ 60 Mark Jackson	.50	.23	.06
☐ 61 Pepper Johnson	.50	.23	.06
☐ 62 Chris Spielman	1.00	.45	.12
☐ 63 Marcus Allen	2.00	.90	.25
☐ 64 Jim Everett	1.00	.45	.12
☐ 65 Greg Townsend	.50	.23	.06
☐ 66 Cris Carter	2.00	.90	.25
☐ 67 Don Beebe	.50	.23	.06
☐ 68 Reggie Langhorne	.50	.23	.06
☐ 69 Randall Cunningham	1.00	.45	.12
☐ 70 Johnny Holland	.50	.23	.06
☐ 71 Morten Andersen	.50	.23	.06
☐ 72 Leonard Marshall	.50	.23	.06
☐ 73 Keith Jackson	.50	.23	.06
☐ 74 Leslie O'Neal	.50	.23	.06
☐ 75 Hardy Nickerson	1.00	.45	.12
☐ 76 Dan Williams	.50	.23	.06
☐ 77 Steve Young	7.00	3.10	.85
☐ 78 Deon Figures	.50	.23	.06
☐ 79 Michael Irvin	2.00	.90	.25
☐ 80 Luis Sharpe	.50	.23	.06
☐ 81 Andre Tippett	.50	.23	.06
☐ 82 Ricky Sanders	.50	.23	.06
☐ 83 Erric Pegram	.50	.23	.06
☐ 84 Albert Lewis	.50	.23	.06

☐ 85 Anthony Blaylock	.50	.23	.06
☐ 86 Pat Swilling	.50	.23	.06
☐ 87 Duane Bickett	.50	.23	.06
☐ 88 Myron Guyton	.50	.23	.06
☐ 89 Clay Matthews	.50	.23	.06
☐ 90 Jim McMahon	.50	.23	.06
☐ 91 Bruce Smith	2.00	.90	.25
☐ 92 Reggie White	2.00	.90	.25
☐ 93 Shannon Sharpe	1.00	.45	.12
☐ 94 Rickey Jackson	.50	.23	.06
☐ 95 Ronnie Harmon	.50	.23	.06
☐ 96 Terry McDaniel	.50	.23	.06
☐ 97 Bryan Cox	.50	.23	.06
☐ 98 Webster Slaughter	.50	.23	.06
☐ 99 Boomer Esiason	1.00	.45	.12
☐ 100 Tim Krumrie	.50	.23	.06
☐ 101 Cortez Kennedy	1.00	.45	.12
☐ 102 Henry Ellard	1.00	.45	.12
☐ 103 Clyde Simmons	.50	.23	.06
☐ 104 Craig Erickson	.50	.23	.06
☐ 105 Eric Green	.50	.23	.06
☐ 106 Gary Clark	1.00	.45	.12
☐ 107 Jay Novacek	1.00	.45	.12
☐ 108 Dana Stubblefield	2.00	.90	.25
☐ 109 Mike Johnson	.50	.23	.06
☐ 110 Ray Crockett	.50	.23	.06
☐ 111 Leonard Russell	.50	.23	.06
☐ 112 Robert Smith	3.00	1.35	.35
☐ 113 Art Monk	1.00	.45	.12
☐ 114 Ray Childress	.50	.23	.06
☐ 115 O.J. McDuffie	3.00	1.35	.35
☐ 116 Tim Brown	2.00	.90	.25
☐ 117 Kevin Ross	.50	.23	.06
☐ 118 Richard Dent	1.00	.45	.12
☐ 119 John Elway	7.00	3.10	.85
☐ 120 James Hasty	.50	.23	.06
☐ 121 Gary Plummer	.50	.23	.06
☐ 122 Pierce Holt	.50	.23	.06
☐ 123 Eric Martin	.50	.23	.06
☐ 124 Brett Favre	18.00	8.00	2.20
☐ 125 Cornelius Bennett	1.00	.45	.12
☐ 126 Jessie Hester	.50	.23	.06
☐ 127 Lewis Tillman	.50	.23	.06
☐ 128 Qadry Ismail	2.00	.90	.25
☐ 129 Jay Schroeder	.50	.23	.06
☐ 130 Curtis Conway	3.00	1.35	.35
☐ 131 Santana Dotson	1.00	.45	.12
☐ 132 Nick Lowery	.50	.23	.06
☐ 133 Lomas Brown	.50	.23	.06
☐ 134 Reggie Roby	.50	.23	.06
☐ 135 John L. Williams	.50	.23	.06
☐ 136 Vinny Testaverde	1.00	.45	.12
☐ 137 Seth Joyner	.50	.23	.06
☐ 138 Ethan Horton	.50	.23	.06
☐ 139 Jackie Slater	.50	.23	.06
☐ 140 Rod Bernstine	.50	.23	.06
☐ 141 Rob Moore	1.00	.45	.12
☐ 142 Dan Marino	18.00	8.00	2.20
☐ 143 Ken Harvey	.50	.23	.06
☐ 144 Ernest Givins	1.00	.45	.12
☐ 145 Russell Maryland	.50	.23	.06
☐ 146 Drew Bledsoe	10.00	4.50	1.25
☐ 147 Kevin Greene	2.00	.90	.25
☐ 148 Bobby Hebert	.50	.23	.06
☐ 149 Junior Seau	2.00	.90	.25
☐ 150 Tim McDonald	.50	.23	.06
☐ 151 Thurman Thomas	2.00	.90	.25
☐ 152 Phil Simms	1.00	.45	.12
☐ 153 Terrell Buckley	.50	.23	.06
☐ 154 Sam Mills	.50	.23	.06
☐ 155 Anthony Carter	1.00	.45	.12
☐ 156 Kelvin Martin	.50	.23	.06
☐ 157 Shane Conlan	.50	.23	.06
☐ 158 Irving Fryar	1.00	.45	.12
☐ 159 Demetrius DuBose	.50	.23	.06
☐ 160 David Klingler	.50	.23	.06
☐ 161 Herman Moore	5.00	2.20	.60
☐ 162 Jeff Hostetler	1.00	.45	.12
☐ 163 Tommy Vardell	.50	.23	.06
☐ 164 Craig Heyward	1.00	.45	.12
☐ 165 Wilber Marshall	.50	.23	.06
☐ 166 Quentin Coryatt	.50	.23	.06
☐ 167 Glyn Milburn	1.00	.45	.12
☐ 168 Fred Barnett	1.00	.45	.12
☐ 169 Charles Haley	1.00	.45	.12
☐ 170 Carl Banks	.50	.23	.06
☐ 171 Ricky Proehl	.50	.23	.06
☐ 172 Joe Montana	10.00	4.50	1.25
☐ 173 Johnny Mitchell	.50	.23	.06
☐ 174 Andre Reed	1.00	.45	.12
☐ 175 Marco Coleman	.50	.23	.06
☐ 176 Vaughan Johnson	.50	.23	.06
☐ 177 Carl Pickens	5.00	2.20	.60
☐ 178 Dwight Stone	.50	.23	.06
☐ 179 Ricky Watters	2.00	.90	.25
☐ 180 Michael Haynes	1.00	.45	.12
☐ 181 Roger Craig	1.00	.45	.12
☐ 182 Cleveland Gary	.50	.23	.06
☐ 183 Steve Emtman	.50	.23	.06
☐ 184 Patrick Bates	.50	.23	.06
☐ 185 Mark Carrier WR	1.00	.45	.12
☐ 186 Brad Hopkins	.50	.23	.06
☐ 187 Dennis Smith	.50	.23	.06
☐ 188 Natrone Means	4.00	1.80	.50
☐ 189 Michael Jackson	1.00	.45	.12
☐ 190 Ken Norton Jr.	1.00	.45	.12
☐ 191 Carlton Gray	.50	.23	.06
☐ 192 Edgar Bennett	2.00	.90	.25
☐ 193 Lawrence Taylor	2.00	.90	.25
☐ 194 Marv Cook	.50	.23	.06
☐ 195 Eric Curry	.50	.23	.06
☐ 196 Victor Bailey	.50	.23	.06
☐ 197 Ryan McNeil	.50	.23	.06
☐ 198 Rod Woodson	2.00	.90	.25
☐ 199 Earnest Byner	.50	.23	.06
☐ 200 Marvin Jones	.50	.23	.06
☐ 201 Thomas Smith	.50	.23	.06
☐ 202 Troy Aikman	10.00	4.50	1.25
☐ 203 Audray McMillian	.50	.23	.06
☐ 204 Wade Wilson	.50	.23	.06
☐ 205 George Teague	.50	.23	.06
☐ 206 Deion Sanders	6.00	2.70	.75
☐ 207 Will Shields	.50	.23	.06
☐ 208 John Taylor	1.00	.45	.12
☐ 209 Jim Harbaugh	2.00	.90	.25
☐ 210 Micheal Barrow	.50	.23	.06
☐ 211 Harold Green	.50	.23	.06
☐ 212 Steve Everitt	.50	.23	.06
☐ 213 Flipper Anderson	.50	.23	.06
☐ 214 Rodney Hampton	2.00	.90	.25
☐ 215 Steve Atwater	.50	.23	.06
☐ 216 James Trapp	.50	.23	.06
☐ 217 Terry Kirby	2.00	.90	.25
☐ 218 Garrison Hearst	4.00	1.80	.50
☐ 219 Jeff Bryant	.50	.23	.06
☐ 220 Roosevelt Potts	.50	.23	.06

1994 Finest Refractors

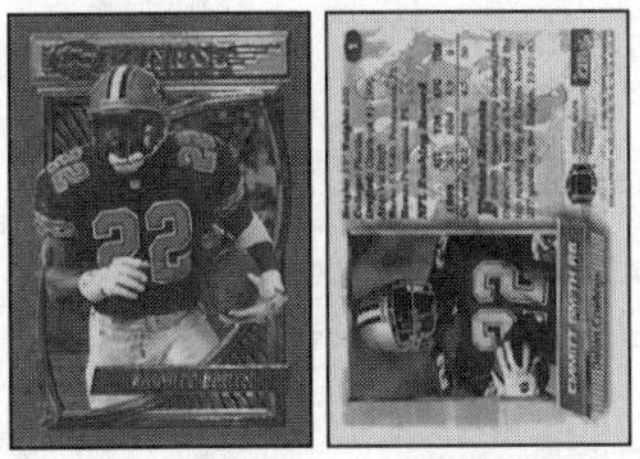

These specially designed refracting foil cards parallel the 220 regular-issue 1994 Finest cards. One of these standard-size foil cards was inserted in every nine packs. The difference can be seen in the rainbow-effect gloss as it stands out from the basic card.

	MINT	NRMT	EXC
COMPLETE SET (220)	2800.00	1250.00	350.00
COMMON CARD (1-220)	4.00	1.80	.50
SEMISTARS	7.00	3.10	.85
UNLISTED STARS	10.00	4.50	1.25
☐ 1 Emmitt Smith	200.00	90.00	25.00
☐ 5 Jim Kelly	20.00	9.00	2.50
☐ 12 Jerry Rice	100.00	45.00	12.50
☐ 21 Warren Moon	20.00	9.00	2.50
☐ 30 Derrick Thomas	15.00	6.75	1.85
☐ 31 Sterling Sharpe	15.00	6.75	1.85
☐ 41 Rick Mirer	40.00	18.00	5.00
☐ 42 Jerome Bettis	75.00	34.00	9.50
☐ 44 Barry Sanders	100.00	45.00	12.50
☐ 59 Chris Warren	15.00	6.75	1.85
☐ 63 Marcus Allen	25.00	11.00	3.10
☐ 66 Cris Carter	20.00	9.00	2.50
☐ 77 Steve Young	80.00	36.00	10.00
☐ 79 Michael Irvin	20.00	9.00	2.50
☐ 91 Bruce Smith	15.00	6.75	1.85
☐ 92 Reggie White	20.00	9.00	2.50
☐ 93 Shannon Sharpe	20.00	9.00	2.50
☐ 112 Robert Smith	25.00	11.00	3.10
☐ 115 O.J. McDuffie	25.00	11.00	3.10
☐ 116 Tim Brown	20.00	9.00	2.50
☐ 119 John Elway	90.00	40.00	11.00
☐ 124 Brett Favre	225.00	100.00	28.00
☐ 130 Curtis Conway	25.00	11.00	3.10
☐ 142 Dan Marino	200.00	90.00	25.00
☐ 146 Drew Bledsoe	160.00	70.00	20.00
☐ 149 Junior Seau	15.00	6.75	1.85
☐ 151 Thurman Thomas	25.00	11.00	3.10
☐ 161 Herman Moore	40.00	18.00	5.00
☐ 172 Joe Montana	125.00	55.00	15.50
☐ 177 Carl Pickens	40.00	18.00	5.00
☐ 179 Ricky Watters	25.00	11.00	3.10
☐ 188 Natrone Means	40.00	18.00	5.00
☐ 192 Edgar Bennett	15.00	6.75	1.85
☐ 198 Rod Woodson	15.00	6.75	1.85
☐ 202 Troy Aikman	100.00	45.00	12.50
☐ 206 Deion Sanders	70.00	32.00	8.75
☐ 209 Jim Harbaugh	20.00	9.00	2.50
☐ 218 Garrison Hearst	40.00	18.00	5.00

1994 Finest Rookie Jumbos

These oversized (4 1/4" by 6") versions of the 37 rookies from the 1994 Finest set were inserted at a rate of one in each 24-count box. Aside from their larger size, the cards are identical to the corresponding basic Finest cards.

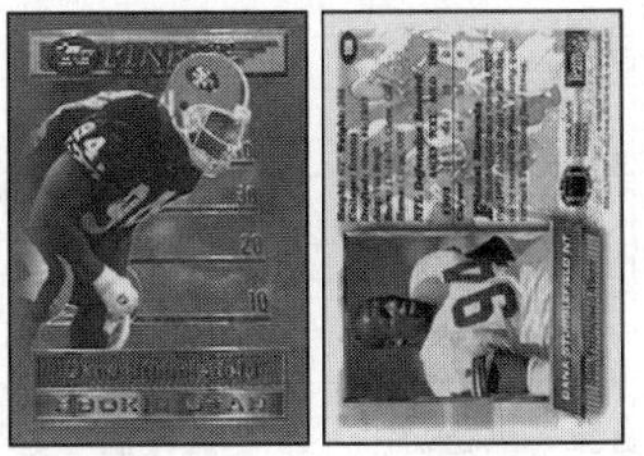

	MINT	NRMT	EXC
COMPLETE SET (37)	200.00	90.00	25.00
COMMON CARD	4.00	1.80	.50
☐ 7 Wayne Simmons	4.00	1.80	.50
☐ 19 Willie Roaf	4.00	1.80	.50
☐ 20 Troy Drayton	6.00	2.70	.75
☐ 24 Chris Slade	6.00	2.70	.75
☐ 29 John Copeland	6.00	2.70	.75
☐ 35 Kevin Williams	8.00	3.60	1.00
☐ 41 Rick Mirer	10.00	4.50	1.25
☐ 42 Jerome Bettis	12.00	5.50	1.50
☐ 45 Jason Elam	4.00	1.80	.50
☐ 47 Derek Brown RB	6.00	2.70	.75
☐ 56 Lincoln Kennedy	4.00	1.80	.50
☐ 78 Deon Figures	6.00	2.70	.75
☐ 108 Dana Stubblefield	6.00	2.70	.75
☐ 112 Robert Smith	8.00	3.60	1.00
☐ 115 O.J. McDuffie	6.00	2.70	.75
☐ 128 Qadry Ismail	6.00	2.70	.75
☐ 130 Curtis Conway	8.00	3.60	1.00
☐ 146 Drew Bledsoe	25.00	11.00	3.10
☐ 159 Demetrius DuBose	4.00	1.80	.50
☐ 167 Glyn Milburn	6.00	2.70	.75
☐ 184 Patrick Bates	4.00	1.80	.50
☐ 186 Brad Hopkins	4.00	1.80	.50
☐ 188 Natrone Means	10.00	4.50	1.25
☐ 191 Carlton Gray	4.00	1.80	.50
☐ 195 Eric Curry	6.00	2.70	.75
☐ 196 Victor Bailey	4.00	1.80	.50
☐ 197 Ryan McNeil	4.00	1.80	.50
☐ 200 Marvin Jones	4.00	1.80	.50
☐ 201 Thomas Smith	4.00	1.80	.50
☐ 205 George Teague	4.00	1.80	.50
☐ 207 Will Shields	4.00	1.80	.50
☐ 210 Micheal Barrow	4.00	1.80	.50
☐ 212 Steve Everitt	4.00	1.80	.50
☐ 216 James Trapp	4.00	1.80	.50
☐ 217 Terry Kirby	8.00	3.60	1.00
☐ 218 Garrison Hearst	10.00	4.50	1.25
☐ 220 Roosevelt Potts	4.00	1.80	.50

1995 Finest

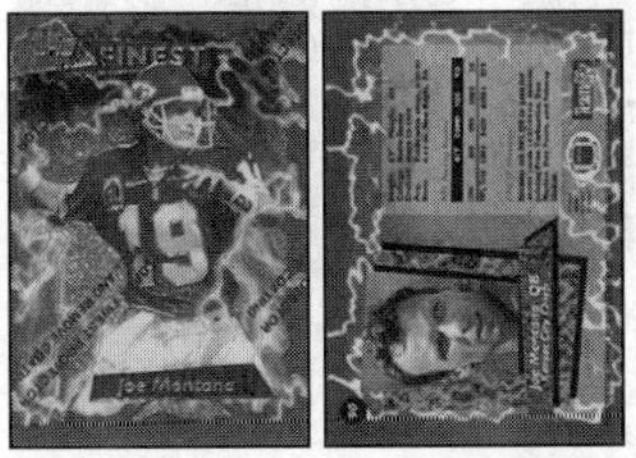

This 275 standard-size set was issued in seven card packs. These packs were in 24 count boxes and had a suggested retail price of $5.00 per pack. These high-tech cards each came with a protective peel-off laminate that prevented the cards from being scratched. The metallic fronts have aqua borders and horizontal backs contain statistics, a small photo and a "Finest Moment". Rookie Cards in this set include Jeff Blake, Ki-Jana Carter, Kerry Collins, Joey Galloway, Curtis Martin, Rashaan Salaam and Michael Westbrook.

	MINT	NRMT	EXC
COMPLETE SET (275)	170.00	75.00	21.00
COMPLETE SERIES 1 (165)	70.00	32.00	8.75
COMPLETE SERIES 2 (110)	100.00	45.00	12.50
COMMON CARD (1-165)	.50	.23	.06
COMMON CARD (166-275)	.50	.23	.06
☐ 1 Natrone Means	1.25	.55	.16
☐ 2 Dave Meggett	.50	.23	.06
☐ 3 Tim Bowens	.50	.23	.06
☐ 4 Jay Novacek	.75	.35	.09
☐ 5 Michael Jackson	.75	.35	.09
☐ 6 Calvin Williams	.75	.35	.09
☐ 7 Neil Smith	.75	.35	.09
☐ 8 Chris Gardocki	.50	.23	.06
☐ 9 Jeff Burris	.50	.23	.06
☐ 10 Warren Moon	.75	.35	.09
☐ 11 Gary Anderson K	.50	.23	.06
☐ 12 Bert Emanuel	1.25	.55	.16
☐ 13 Rick Tuten	.50	.23	.06
☐ 14 Steve Wallace	.50	.23	.06
☐ 15 Marion Butts	.50	.23	.06
☐ 16 Johnnie Morton	.75	.35	.09
☐ 17 Rob Moore	.50	.23	.06
☐ 18 Wayne Gandy	.50	.23	.06
☐ 19 Quentin Coryatt	.75	.35	.09
☐ 20 Richmond Webb	.50	.23	.06
☐ 21 Errict Rhett	1.25	.55	.16
☐ 22 Joe Johnson	.50	.23	.06
☐ 23 Gary Brown	.50	.23	.06
☐ 24 Jeff Hostetler	.75	.35	.09
☐ 25 Larry Centers	.75	.35	.09
☐ 26 Tom Carter	.50	.23	.06
☐ 27 Steve Atwater	.50	.23	.06
☐ 28 Doug Pelfrey	.50	.23	.06
☐ 29 Bryce Paup	1.25	.55	.16
☐ 30 Erik Williams	.50	.23	.06
☐ 31 Henry Jones	.50	.23	.06
☐ 32 Stanley Richard	.50	.23	.06
☐ 33 Marcus Allen	1.25	.55	.16
☐ 34 Antonio Langham	.50	.23	.06
☐ 35 Lewis Tillman	.50	.23	.06
☐ 36 Thomas Randolph	.50	.23	.06
☐ 37 Byron Bam Morris	.75	.35	.09
☐ 38 David Palmer	.75	.35	.09
☐ 39 Ricky Watters	1.25	.55	.16
☐ 40 Brett Perriman	.75	.35	.09
☐ 41 Will Wolford	.50	.23	.06
☐ 42 Burt Grossman	.50	.23	.06
☐ 43 Vincent Brisby	.50	.23	.06
☐ 44 Ronnie Lott	.75	.35	.09
☐ 45 Brian Blades	.75	.35	.09
☐ 46 Brent Jones	.50	.23	.06
☐ 47 Anthony Newman	.50	.23	.06
☐ 48 Willie Roaf	.50	.23	.06
☐ 49 Paul Gruber	.50	.23	.06
☐ 50 Jeff George	.75	.35	.09
☐ 51 Jamir Miller	.50	.23	.06
☐ 52 Anthony Miller	.75	.35	.09
☐ 53 Darrell Green	.50	.23	.06
☐ 54 Steve Wisniewski	.50	.23	.06
☐ 55 Dan Wilkinson	.75	.35	.09
☐ 56 Brett Favre	12.00	5.50	1.50
☐ 57 Leslie O'Neal	.75	.35	.09
☐ 58 Keith Byars	.50	.23	.06
☐ 59 James Washington	.50	.23	.06
☐ 60 Andre Reed	.75	.35	.09
☐ 61 Ken Norton Jr.	.75	.35	.09
☐ 62 John Randle	.50	.23	.06
☐ 63 Lake Dawson	.75	.35	.09
☐ 64 Greg Montgomery	.50	.23	.06
☐ 65 Erric Pegram	.75	.35	.09
☐ 66 Steve Everitt	.50	.23	.06
☐ 67 Chris Brantley	.50	.23	.06
☐ 68 Rod Woodson	.75	.35	.09
☐ 69 Eugene Robinson	.50	.23	.06
☐ 70 Dave Brown	.75	.35	.09
☐ 71 Ricky Reynolds	.50	.23	.06
☐ 72 Rohn Stark	.50	.23	.06
☐ 73 Randal Hill	.50	.23	.06
☐ 74 Brian Washington	.50	.23	.06
☐ 75 Heath Shuler	1.25	.55	.16
☐ 76 Darion Conner	.50	.23	.06
☐ 77 Terry McDaniel	.50	.23	.06
☐ 78 Al Del Greco	.50	.23	.06
☐ 79 Allen Aldridge	.50	.23	.06
☐ 80 Trace Armstrong	.50	.23	.06
☐ 81 Darnay Scott	4.00	1.80	.50
☐ 82 Charlie Garner	.75	.35	.09
☐ 83 Harold Bishop	.50	.23	.06
☐ 84 Reggie White	1.25	.55	.16
☐ 85 Shawn Jefferson	.50	.23	.06
☐ 86 Irving Spikes	.75	.35	.09
☐ 87 Mel Gray	.50	.23	.06
☐ 88 D.J. Johnson	.50	.23	.06
☐ 89 Daryl Johnston	.75	.35	.09
☐ 90 Joe Montana	8.00	3.60	1.00
☐ 91 Michael Strahan	.50	.23	.06
☐ 92 Robert Blackmon	.50	.23	.06
☐ 93 Ryan Yarborough	.75	.35	.09
☐ 94 Terry Allen	.75	.35	.09
☐ 95 Michael Haynes	.75	.35	.09
☐ 96 Jim Harbaugh	.75	.35	.09
☐ 97 Micheal Barrow	.50	.23	.06
☐ 98 John Thierry	.50	.23	.06
☐ 99 Seth Joyner	.50	.23	.06
☐ 100 Deion Sanders	4.00	1.80	.50
☐ 101 Eric Turner	.50	.23	.06
☐ 102 LeShon Johnson	.75	.35	.09
☐ 103 John Copeland	.50	.23	.06
☐ 104 Cornelius Bennett	.75	.35	.09
☐ 105 Sean Gilbert	.75	.35	.09
☐ 106 Herschel Walker	.75	.35	.09
☐ 107 Henry Ellard	.75	.35	.09
☐ 108 Neil O'Donnell	.75	.35	.09
☐ 109 Charles Wilson	.50	.23	.06
☐ 110 Willie McGinest	.75	.35	.09
☐ 111 Tim Brown	1.25	.55	.16
☐ 112 Simon Fletcher	.50	.23	.06
☐ 113 Broderick Thomas	.50	.23	.06
☐ 114 Tom Waddle	.50	.23	.06
☐ 115 Jessie Tuggle	.50	.23	.06
☐ 116 Maurice Hurst	.50	.23	.06
☐ 117 Aubrey Beavers	.50	.23	.06
☐ 118 Donnell Bennett	.50	.23	.06
☐ 119 Shante Carver	.50	.23	.06
☐ 120 Eric Metcalf	.75	.35	.09
☐ 121 John Carney	.50	.23	.06
☐ 122 Thomas Lewis	.75	.35	.09
☐ 123 Johnny Mitchell	.50	.23	.06
☐ 124 Trent Dilfer	1.25	.55	.16

☐ 125 Marshall Faulk	3.00	1.35	.35
☐ 126 Ernest Givins	.50	.23	.06
☐ 127 Aeneas Williams	.50	.23	.06
☐ 128 Bucky Brooks	.50	.23	.06
☐ 129 Todd Steussie	.50	.23	.06
☐ 130 Randall Cunningham	.75	.35	.09
☐ 131 Reggie Brooks	.75	.35	.09
☐ 132 Morten Andersen	.50	.23	.06
☐ 133 James Jett	.75	.35	.09
☐ 134 George Teague	.50	.23	.06
☐ 135 John Taylor	.50	.23	.06
☐ 136 Charles Johnson	.75	.35	.09
☐ 137 Isaac Bruce	3.00	1.35	.35
☐ 138 Jason Elam	.50	.23	.06
☐ 139 Carl Pickens	1.25	.55	.16
☐ 140 Chris Warren	.75	.35	.09
☐ 141 Bruce Armstrong	.50	.23	.06
☐ 142 Mark Carrier DB	.50	.23	.06
☐ 143 Irving Fryar	.75	.35	.09
☐ 144 Van Malone	.50	.23	.06
☐ 145 Charles Haley	.75	.35	.09
☐ 146 Chris Calloway	.50	.23	.06
☐ 147 J.J. Birden	.50	.23	.06
☐ 148 Tony Bennett	.50	.23	.06
☐ 149 Lincoln Kennedy	.50	.23	.06
☐ 150 Stan Humphries	.75	.35	.09
☐ 151 Hardy Nickerson	.50	.23	.06
☐ 152 Randall McDaniel	.50	.23	.06
☐ 153 Marcus Robertson	.50	.23	.06
☐ 154 Ronald Moore	.50	.23	.06
☐ 155 Thurman Thomas	1.25	.55	.16
☐ 156 Tommy Vardell	.50	.23	.06
☐ 157 Ken Ruettgers	.50	.23	.06
☐ 158 Rob Fredrickson	.50	.23	.06
☐ 159 Johnny Bailey	.50	.23	.06
☐ 160 Greg Lloyd	.75	.35	.09
☐ 161 David Alexander	.50	.23	.06
☐ 162 Kevin Mawae	.50	.23	.06
☐ 163 Derek Brown RB	.50	.23	.06
☐ 164 William Floyd	1.25	.55	.16
☐ 165 Aaron Glenn	.50	.23	.06
☐ 166 Joey Galloway	8.00	3.60	1.00
☐ 167 Troy Drayton	.50	.23	.06
☐ 168 Dermontti Dawson	.75	.35	.09
☐ 169 Ronald Moore	.50	.23	.06
☐ 170 Dan Marino	12.00	5.50	1.50
☐ 171 Dennis Gibson	.50	.23	.06
☐ 172 Raymont Harris	.50	.23	.06
☐ 173 Shannon Sharpe	.75	.35	.09
☐ 174 Kevin Williams	.75	.35	.09
☐ 175 Jim Everett	.50	.23	.06
☐ 176 Rocket Ismail	.75	.35	.09
☐ 177 Mark Fields	.50	.23	.06
☐ 178 George Koonce	.50	.23	.06
☐ 179 Chris Hudson	.50	.23	.06
☐ 180 Jerry Rice	7.00	3.10	.85
☐ 181 Dewayne Washington	.75	.35	.09
☐ 182 Dale Carter	.75	.35	.09
☐ 183 Pete Stoyanovich	.50	.23	.06
☐ 184 Blake Brockermeyer	.50	.23	.06
☐ 185 Troy Aikman	7.00	3.10	.85
☐ 186 Jeff Blake	4.00	1.80	.50
☐ 187 Troy Vincent	.50	.23	.06
☐ 188 Lamar Lathon	.50	.23	.06
☐ 189 Tony Boselli	.75	.35	.09
☐ 190 Emmitt Smith	12.00	5.50	1.50
☐ 191 Bobby Houston	.50	.23	.06
☐ 192 Edgar Bennett	.75	.35	.09
☐ 193 Derrick Brooks	.50	.23	.06
☐ 194 Ricky Proehl	.50	.23	.06
☐ 195 Rodney Hampton	.75	.35	.09
☐ 196 Dave Krieg	.50	.23	.06
☐ 197 Vinny Testaverde	.75	.35	.09
☐ 198 Erik Kramer	.50	.23	.06
☐ 199 Ben Coates	.75	.35	.09
☐ 200 Steve Young	6.00	2.70	.75
☐ 201 Glyn Milburn	.50	.23	.06
☐ 202 Bryan Cox	.50	.23	.06
☐ 203 Luther Elliss	.50	.23	.06
☐ 204 Mark McMillian	.50	.23	.06
☐ 205 Jerome Bettis	2.00	.90	.25
☐ 206 Craig Heyward	.75	.35	.09
☐ 207 Ray Buchanan	.50	.23	.06
☐ 208 Kimble Anders	.75	.35	.09
☐ 209 Kevin Greene	.75	.35	.09
☐ 210 Eric Allen	.50	.23	.06
☐ 211 Ricardo McDonald	.50	.23	.06
☐ 212 Ruben Brown	.50	.23	.06
☐ 213 Harvey Williams	.50	.23	.06
☐ 214 Broderick Thomas	.50	.23	.06
☐ 215 Frank Reich	.50	.23	.06
☐ 216 Frank Sanders UER Plays Wide Receiver Defensive Record on Back	3.00	1.35	.35
☐ 217 Craig Newsome	.50	.23	.06
☐ 218 Merton Hanks	.50	.23	.06
☐ 219 Chris Miller	.50	.23	.06
☐ 220 John Elway	6.00	2.70	.75
☐ 221 Ernest Givins	.50	.23	.06
☐ 222 Boomer Esiason	.75	.35	.09
☐ 223 Reggie Roby	.50	.23	.06
☐ 224 Qadry Ismail	.75	.35	.09
☐ 225 Ki-Jana Carter	3.00	1.35	.35
☐ 226 Leon Lett	.50	.23	.06
☐ 227 Eric Hill	.50	.23	.06
☐ 228 Scott Mitchell	.75	.35	.09
☐ 229 Craig Erickson	.50	.23	.06
☐ 230 Drew Bledsoe	7.00	3.10	.85
☐ 231 Sean Landeta	.50	.23	.06
☐ 232 Barrett Brooks	.50	.23	.06
☐ 233 Brian Mitchell	.50	.23	.06
☐ 234 Tyrone Poole	.75	.35	.09
☐ 235 Desmond Howard	.75	.35	.09
☐ 236 Wayne Simmons	.50	.23	.06
☐ 237 Michael Westbrook	4.00	1.80	.50
☐ 238 Quinn Early	.75	.35	.09
☐ 239 Willie Davis	.75	.35	.09
☐ 240 Rashaan Salaam	4.00	1.80	.50
☐ 241 Devin Bush	.50	.23	.06
☐ 242 Dana Stubblefield	1.25	.55	.16
☐ 243 Dexter Carter	.50	.23	.06
☐ 244 Shane Conlan	.50	.23	.06
☐ 245 Keith Elias	.50	.23	.06
☐ 246 Robert Brooks	1.25	.55	.16
☐ 247 Garrison Hearst	1.25	.55	.16
☐ 248 Eric Zeier	1.25	.55	.16
☐ 249 Nate Newton	.75	.35	.09
☐ 250 Barry Sanders	7.00	3.10	.85
☐ 251 Dave Meggett	.50	.23	.06
☐ 252 Courtney Hawkins	.50	.23	.06
☐ 253 Cortez Kennedy	.75	.35	.09
☐ 254 Mario Bates	1.25	.55	.16
☐ 255 Junior Seau	1.25	.55	.16
☐ 256 Brian Washington	.50	.23	.06
☐ 257 Darius Holland	.50	.23	.06
☐ 258 Jeff Graham	.50	.23	.06
☐ 259 Rob Moore	.50	.23	.06
☐ 260 Andre Rison	.75	.35	.09
☐ 261 Kerry Collins	14.00	6.25	1.75
☐ 262 Roosevelt Potts	.50	.23	.06
☐ 263 Cris Carter	1.25	.55	.16
☐ 264 Curtis Martin	14.00	6.25	1.75
☐ 265 Rick Mirer	1.25	.55	.16
☐ 266 Mo Lewis	.50	.23	.06
☐ 267 Mike Sherrard	.50	.23	.06
☐ 268 Herman Moore	4.00	1.80	.50
☐ 269 Eric Metcalf	.75	.35	.09
☐ 270 Ray Childress	.50	.23	.06
☐ 271 Chris Slade	.75	.35	.09
☐ 272 Michael Irvin	1.25	.55	.16
☐ 273 Jim Kelly	1.25	.55	.16
☐ 274 Terance Mathis	.75	.35	.09
☐ 275 LeRoy Butler	.50	.23	.06

1995 Finest Refractors

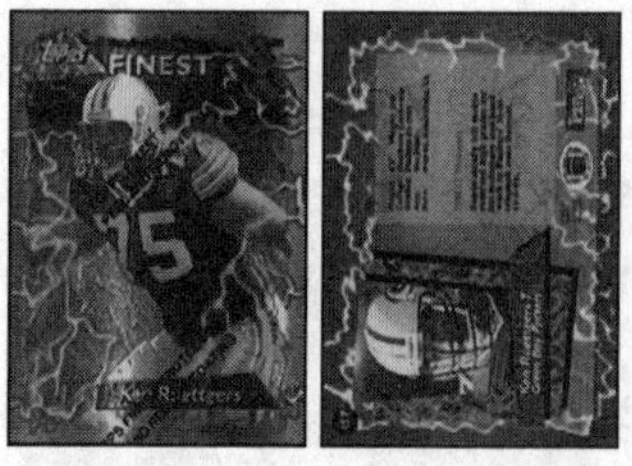

Parallel to the basic Finest set, these cards were randomly inserted at a rate of one in 12 packs. The Refractors are distinguished from the basic card by a "rainbow" foil. The series 2 card backs also contain the letter "R" to distinguish between the two.

	MINT	NRMT	EXC
COMPLETE SET (275)	1800.00	800.00	220.00
COMPLETE SERIES 1 (165)	850.00	375.00	105.00
COMPLETE SERIES 2 (110)	1000.00	450.00	125.00
COMMON CARD (1-275)	3.50	1.55	.45
SEMISTARS	6.00	2.70	.75
UNLISTED STARS	12.00	5.50	1.50
☐ 21 Errict Rhett	20.00	9.00	2.50
☐ 56 Brett Favre	160.00	70.00	20.00
☐ 75 Heath Shuler	15.00	6.75	1.85
☐ 81 Darnay Scott	30.00	13.50	3.70
☐ 90 Joe Montana	90.00	40.00	11.00
☐ 100 Deion Sanders	40.00	18.00	5.00
☐ 125 Marshall Faulk	35.00	16.00	4.40
☐ 137 Isaac Bruce	35.00	16.00	4.40
☐ 166 Joey Galloway	60.00	27.00	7.50
☐ 170 Dan Marino	140.00	65.00	17.50
☐ 180 Jerry Rice	70.00	32.00	8.75
☐ 185 Troy Aikman	70.00	32.00	8.75
☐ 186 Jeff Blake	40.00	18.00	5.00
☐ 190 Emmitt Smith	140.00	65.00	17.50
☐ 200 Steve Young	50.00	22.00	6.25
☐ 205 Jerome Bettis	20.00	9.00	2.50
☐ 216 Frank Sanders	20.00	9.00	2.50
☐ 220 John Elway	60.00	27.00	7.50
☐ 225 Ki-Jana Carter	20.00	9.00	2.50
☐ 230 Drew Bledsoe	70.00	32.00	8.75
☐ 237 Michael Westbrook	40.00	18.00	5.00
☐ 240 Rashaan Salaam	40.00	18.00	5.00
☐ 250 Barry Sanders	70.00	32.00	8.75
☐ 261 Kerry Collins	100.00	45.00	12.50
☐ 264 Curtis Martin	100.00	45.00	12.50
☐ 268 Herman Moore	20.00	9.00	2.50

1995 Finest Fan Favorites

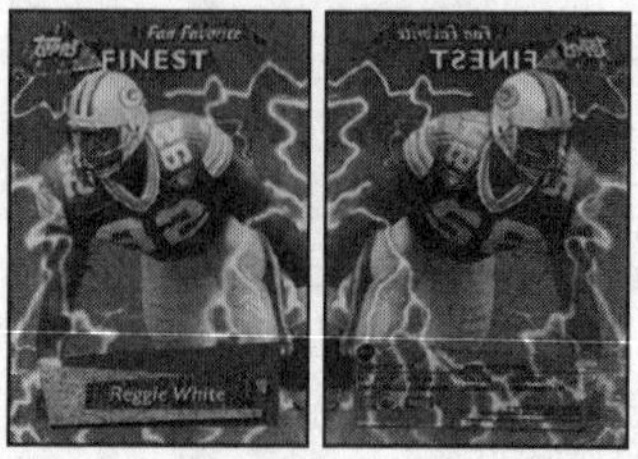

Randomly inserted one in every 12 packs, this 25-card set spotlights some of the NFL's top playmakers. With a front design that is similar to the basic Finest cards, Fan Favorites are transparent with photos surrounded by purple. A Fan Favorite banner is at the top. At the bottom of the back is a brief biography.

	MINT	NRMT	EXC
COMPLETE SET (25)	200.00	90.00	25.00
COMMON CARD (FF1-FF25)	2.50	1.10	.30
☐ FF1 Drew Bledsoe	15.00	6.75	1.85
☐ FF2 Jerome Bettis	6.00	2.70	.75
☐ FF3 Rick Mirer	6.00	2.70	.75
☐ FF4 Andre Rison	4.00	1.80	.50
☐ FF5 Troy Aikman	15.00	6.75	1.85
☐ FF6 Cortez Kennedy	2.50	1.10	.30
☐ FF7 Emmitt Smith	25.00	11.00	3.10
☐ FF8 Sterling Sharpe	4.00	1.80	.50
☐ FF9 Junior Seau	6.00	2.70	.75
☐ FF10 Michael Irvin	6.00	2.70	.75
☐ FF11 Jim Kelly	6.00	2.70	.75
☐ FF12 Steve Young	12.00	5.50	1.50
☐ FF13 John Elway	12.00	5.50	1.50
☐ FF14 Jerry Rice	15.00	6.75	1.85
☐ FF15 Barry Sanders	15.00	6.75	1.85
☐ FF16 Dan Marino	25.00	11.00	3.10
☐ FF17 Dan Wilkinson	2.50	1.10	.30
☐ FF18 Reggie White	6.00	2.70	.75
☐ FF19 Deion Sanders	10.00	4.50	1.25
☐ FF20 Willie McGinest	2.50	1.10	.30
☐ FF21 Stan Humphries	4.00	1.80	.50
☐ FF22 Heath Shuler	6.00	2.70	.75
☐ FF23 Natrone Means	6.00	2.70	.75
☐ FF24 Warren Moon	4.00	1.80	.50
☐ FF25 Marshall Faulk	8.00	3.60	1.00

1995 Finest Landmark

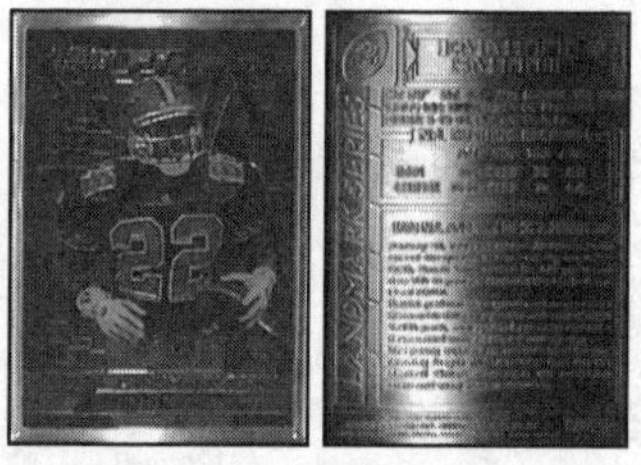

These standard-size "cards" are actually metal cards that were overlaid on a 4-ounce ingot of solid bronze. Using Topps' finest technology, the cards also feature the players personal achievements on the back. The first four cards were originally available only as a set through Topps direct mailers at a cost of $99 plus shipping. Two additional series were released later seperately and re-released together as "series two." These 12-card series two sets were available directly from Topps. We've assigned numbers to the cards alphabetically by series.

	MINT	NRMT	EXC
COMPLETE SET (16)	500.00	220.00	60.00
COMMON CARD (1-16)	25.00	11.00	3.10
☐ 1 Troy Aikman	35.00	16.00	4.40
☐ 2 Jerry Rice	35.00	16.00	4.40
☐ 3 Emmitt Smith	60.00	27.00	7.50
☐ 4 Steve Young	30.00	13.50	3.70
☐ 5 Drew Bledsoe	40.00	18.00	5.00
☐ 6 Randall Cunningham	25.00	11.00	3.10
☐ 7 John Elway	35.00	16.00	4.40
☐ 8 Brett Favre	60.00	27.00	7.50
☐ 9 Michael Irvin	30.00	13.50	3.70
☐ 10 Jim Kelly	30.00	13.50	3.70
☐ 11 Dan Marino	60.00	27.00	7.50
☐ 12 Rick Mirer	30.00	13.50	3.70
☐ 13 Warren Moon	30.00	13.50	3.70
☐ 14 Barry Sanders	40.00	18.00	5.00
☐ 15 Junior Seau	30.00	13.50	3.70
☐ 16 Heath Shuler	25.00	11.00	3.10

1995-96 Finest Pro Bowl Jumbos

This 22-card set measures approximately 4" by 5 5/8". The fronts feature a color player cut-out on a metallic, lightning-effect background with the player's name printed in silver foil on a violet and black marblized band at the bottom. The cards are essentially enlarged versions of regular issue 1995 Finest cards and were distributed at the

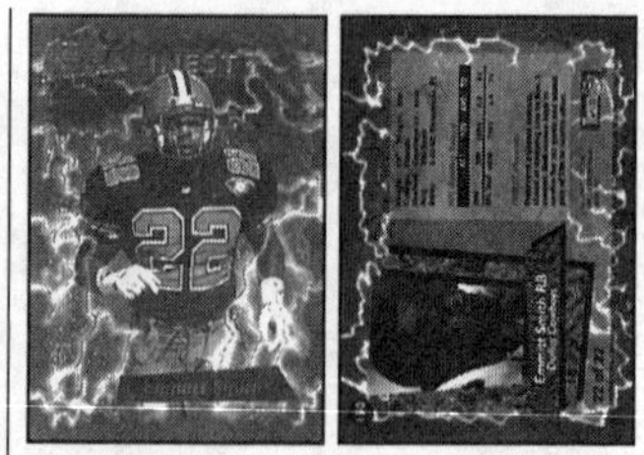

1996 NFL Experience Pro Bowl show in Hawaii. The original card number is included on the backs as well as the new numbering of 22-cards. Refractor parallel versions of each card were produced in much shorter quantities. A poster sized Steve Young Finest promo card was produced as well and distributed at the Pro Bowl Card Show. It is priced separately below.

	MINT	NRMT	EXC
COMPLETE SET (22)	60.00	27.00	7.50
COMMON CARD (1-22)	1.50	.70	.19
☐ 1 Troy Aikman	6.00	2.70	.75
☐ 2 Tim Brown	2.00	.90	.25
☐ 3 Cris Carter	2.00	.90	.25
☐ 4 Marshall Faulk	2.50	1.10	.30
☐ 5 Brett Favre	12.00	5.50	1.50
☐ 6 Merton Hanks	1.50	.70	.19
☐ 7 Michael Irvin	2.00	.90	.25
☐ 8 Greg Lloyd	1.50	.70	.19
☐ 9 Dan Marino	12.00	5.50	1.50
☐ 10 Curtis Martin	7.00	3.10	.85
☐ 11 Herman Moore	2.50	1.10	.30
☐ 12 Terry McDaniel	1.50	.70	.19
☐ 13 Ken Norton	1.50	.70	.19
☐ 14 Bryce Paup	1.50	.70	.19
☐ 15 John Randle	1.50	.70	.19
☐ 16 Jerry Rice	6.00	2.70	.75
☐ 17 Barry Sanders	6.00	2.70	.75
☐ 18 Junior Seau	2.00	.90	.25
☐ 19 Steve Young	5.00	2.20	.60
☐ 20 Reggie White	2.00	.90	.25
☐ 21 Chris Warren	2.00	.90	.25
☐ 22 Emmitt Smith	12.00	5.50	1.50
☐ P1 Steve Young Promo 20" by 14" poster	30.00	13.50	3.70

1995-96 Finest Pro Bowl Jumbos Refractors

This 22-card set is simply the parallel Refractor version of the base Pro Bowl Jumbos set. The cards measure approximately 4" by 5 5/8" and feature a color player photo on a metallic, lightning-effect background with the typical refractor rainbow look. The cards are essentially enlarged versions of regular issue 1995 Finest cards and were distributed at the 1996 NFL Experience Pro Bowl show in Hawaii. The original card number is included on the backs as well as the new numbering of 22-cards.

	MINT	NRMT	EXC
COMPLETE SET (22)	1200.00	550.00	150.00
COMMON CARD (1-22)	25.00	11.00	3.10
*VETERAN STARS: 12X TO 20X BASIC CARDS			
*YOUNG STARS: 9X TO 16X BASIC CARDS			
☐ 1 Troy Aikman	125.00	55.00	15.50
☐ 4 Marshall Faulk	40.00	18.00	5.00
☐ 5 Brett Favre	200.00	90.00	25.00
☐ 9 Dan Marino	200.00	90.00	25.00
☐ 10 Curtis Martin	100.00	45.00	12.50
☐ 16 Jerry Rice	125.00	55.00	15.50
☐ 17 Barry Sanders	125.00	55.00	15.50
☐ 19 Steve Young	100.00	45.00	12.50
☐ 22 Emmitt Smith	200.00	90.00	25.00

1996 Finest

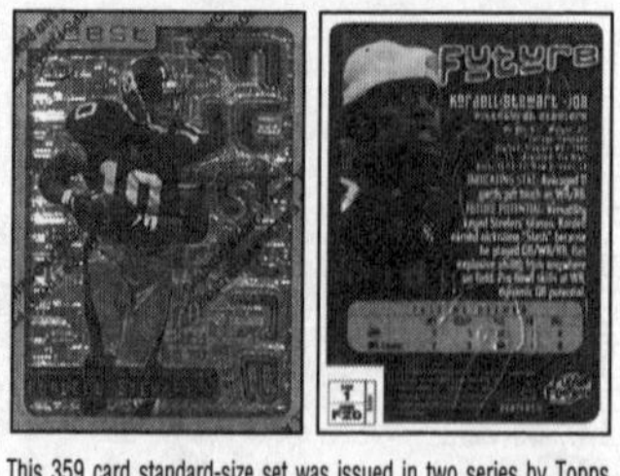

This 359 card standard-size set was issued in two series by Topps. The set was issued in six-card packs and had a suggested retail price of $5 per pack. The set is broken down into a total of 220 bronze cards, 91 silver cards (1:4 packs), and 48 gold cards (1:24 packs). All of the cards feature chromium technology and the "Topps Finest" protector. Cards are numbered on the back both by set order and by card theme.

	MINT	NRMT	EXC
COMPLETE SET (359)	1700.00	750.00	210.00
COMPLETE SER.1 (191)	1000.00	450.00	125.00
COMPLETE SER.2 (168)	700.00	325.00	90.00

COMPLETE BRONZE SET (110)	80.00	36.00	10.00
COMP.BRONZE SER.1 (110)	40.00	18.00	5.00
COMP.BRONZE SER.2 (110)	40.00	18.00	5.00
COMMON BRONZE	.40	.18	.05
COMPLETE GOLD SET (26)	1300.00	575.00	160.00
COMP.GOLD SER.1 (26)	800.00	350.00	100.00
COMP.GOLD SER.2 (22)	500.00	220.00	60.00
COMMON GOLD	15.00	6.75	1.85
COMPLETE SILVER SET (55)	375.00	170.00	47.50
COMP.SILVER SER.1 (55)	225.00	100.00	28.00
COMP.SILVER SER.2 (36)	160.00	70.00	20.00
COMMON SILVER	2.50	1.10	.30

☐ B2 Jay Novacek B	.75	.35	.09
☐ B3 Ray Buchanan B	.40	.18	.05
☐ B5 Phil Hansen B	.40	.18	.05
☐ B6 Mike Mamula B	.40	.18	.05
☐ B9 Bernie Parmalee B	.40	.18	.05
☐ B10 Herman Moore B	1.25	.55	.16
☐ B11 Shawn Jefferson B	.40	.18	.05
☐ B12 Chris Doleman B	.40	.18	.05
☐ B13 Erik Kramer B	.75	.35	.09
☐ B15 Orlando Thomas B	.40	.18	.05
☐ B16 Terrell Davis B	6.00	2.70	.75
☐ B18 Roman Phifer B	.40	.18	.05
☐ B19 Trent Dilfer B	.75	.35	.09
☐ B21 Darnay Scott B	.75	.35	.09
☐ B22 Steve McNair B	4.00	1.80	.50
☐ B23 Lamar Lathon B	.40	.18	.05
☐ B26 Thomas Randolph B	.40	.18	.05
☐ B27 Michael Jackson B	.75	.35	.09
☐ B28 Seth Joyner B	.40	.18	.05
☐ B29 Jeff Lageman B	.40	.18	.05
☐ B30 Darryl Williams B	.40	.18	.05
☐ B32 Erric Pegram B	.75	.35	.09
☐ B34 Sean Dawkins B	.75	.35	.09
☐ B38 Dan Saleaumua B UER	.40	.18	.05
card misnumbered 28			
☐ B39 Henry Thomas B	.40	.18	.05
☐ B43 Pat Swilling B	.40	.18	.05
☐ B44 Marty Carter B	.40	.18	.05
☐ B45 Anthony Miller B	.75	.35	.09
☐ B48 Chris Warren B	.75	.35	.09
☐ B49 Derek Brown B	.40	.18	.05
☐ B51 Blaine Bishop B	.40	.18	.05
☐ B52 Jake Reed B	.75	.35	.09
☐ B55 Vencie Glenn B	.40	.18	.05
☐ B58 Derrick Alexander WR B	.75	.35	.09
☐ B64 Jessie Tuggle B	.40	.18	.05
☐ B65 Terrance Shaw B	.40	.18	.05
☐ B66 David Sloan B	.75	.35	.09
☐ B68 Brent Jones B	.40	.18	.05
☐ B70 William Thomas B	.40	.18	.05
☐ B71 Robert Smith B	.75	.35	.09
☐ B72 Wayne Simmons B	.40	.18	.05
☐ B73 Jim Harbaugh B	.75	.35	.09
☐ B76 Wayne Chrebet B	.75	.35	.09
☐ B77 Chris Hudson B	.40	.18	.05
☐ B79 Stevon Moore B	.40	.18	.05
☐ B80 Chris Calloway B	.40	.18	.05
☐ B81 Tom Carter B	.40	.18	.05
☐ B82 Dave Meggett B	.40	.18	.05
☐ B83 Sam Mills B	.75	.35	.09
☐ B86 Renaldo Turnbull B	.40	.18	.05
☐ B87 Derrick Brooks B	.40	.18	.05
☐ B89 Eugene Robinson B	.40	.18	.05
☐ B91 Rodney Thomas B	.40	.18	.05
☐ B92 Dan Wilkinson B	.40	.18	.05
☐ B93 Mark Fields B	.40	.18	.05
☐ B94 Warren Sapp B	.40	.18	.05
☐ B95 Curtis Martin B	6.00	2.70	.75
☐ B97 Ray Crockett B	.40	.18	.05
☐ B98 Ed McDaniel B	.40	.18	.05
☐ B101 Craig Heyward B	.40	.18	.05
☐ B102 Ellis Johnson B	.40	.18	.05
☐ B104 O.J. McDuffie B	.75	.35	.09
☐ B105 J.J. Stokes B	1.25	.55	.16
☐ B106 Mo Lewis B	.40	.18	.05
☐ B108 Rob Moore B	.40	.18	.05
☐ B110 Tyrone Wheatley B	.75	.35	.09
☐ B111 Ken Harvey B	.40	.18	.05
☐ B113 Willie Green B	.40	.18	.05
☐ B114 Willie Davis B	.75	.35	.09
☐ B115 Andy Harmon B	.40	.18	.05
☐ B117 Bryan Cox B	.40	.18	.05
☐ B119 Bert Emanuel B	.75	.35	.09
☐ B120 Greg Lloyd B	.75	.35	.09
☐ B122 Willie Jackson B	.75	.35	.09
☐ B123 Lorenzo Lynch B	.40	.18	.05
☐ B124 Pepper Johnson B	.40	.18	.05
☐ B128 Tyrone Poole B	.40	.18	.05
☐ B129 Neil Smith B	.75	.35	.09
☐ B130 Eddie Robinson B	.40	.18	.05
☐ B131 Bryce Paup B	.75	.35	.09
☐ B134 Troy Aikman B	5.00	2.20	.60
☐ B136 Chris Sanders B	.75	.35	.09
☐ B138 Jim Everett B	.40	.18	.05
☐ B139 Frank Sanders B	.75	.35	.09
☐ B141 Cortez Kennedy B	.75	.35	.09
☐ B143 Derrick Alexander DE B	.40	.18	.05
☐ B144 Rob Fredrickson B	.40	.18	.05
☐ B145 Chris Zorich B	.40	.18	.05
☐ B146 Devin Bush B	.40	.18	.05
☐ B149 Troy Vincent B	.40	.18	.05
☐ B151 Deion Sanders B	3.00	1.35	.35
☐ B152 James O. Stewart B	.75	.35	.09
☐ B156 Lawrence Dawsey B	.40	.18	.05
☐ B157 Robert Brooks B	1.25	.55	.16
☐ B158 Rashaan Salaam B	1.25	.55	.16
☐ B161 Tim Brown B	.75	.35	.09
☐ B162 Brendan Stai B	.40	.18	.05
☐ B163 Sean Gilbert B	.40	.18	.05
☐ B169 Calvin Williams B	.75	.35	.09
☐ B171 Ruben Brown B	.40	.18	.05
☐ B172 Eric Green B	.40	.18	.05
☐ B175 Jerry Rice B	5.00	2.20	.60
☐ B176 Bruce Smith B	1.25	.55	.16
☐ B177 Mark Bruener B	.40	.18	.05
☐ B179 Lamont Warren B	.40	.18	.05
☐ B180 Tamarick Vanover B	1.25	.55	.16
☐ B182 Scott Mitchell B	.75	.35	.09
☐ B186 Terry Wooden B	.40	.18	.05
☐ B187 Ken Norton B	.75	.35	.09
☐ B188 Jeff Herrod B	.40	.18	.05
☐ B192 Gus Frerotte B	1.25	.55	.16
☐ B194 Brett Maxie B	.40	.18	.05
☐ B198 Eddie Kennison B	4.00	1.80	.50
☐ B201 Marcus Jones B	.40	.18	.05
☐ B202 Terry Allen B	.75	.35	.09
☐ B203 Leroy Hoard B	.40	.18	.05
☐ B205 Reggie White B	1.25	.55	.16
☐ B206 Larry Centers B	.75	.35	.09
☐ B208 Vincent Brisby B	.40	.18	.05
☐ B209 Michael Timpson B	.40	.18	.05
☐ B211 John Mobley B	.40	.18	.05
☐ B212 Clay Matthews B	.75	.35	.09
☐ B213 Shannon Sharpe B	.75	.35	.09
☐ B214 Tony Bennett B	.40	.18	.05
☐ B216 Mickey Washington B	.40	.18	.05
☐ B217 Fred Barnett B	.75	.35	.09
☐ B218 Michael Haynes B	.75	.35	.09
☐ B219 Stan Humphries B	.75	.35	.09
☐ B221 Winston Moss B	.40	.18	.05
☐ B222 Tim Biakabutuka B	3.00	1.35	.35
☐ B223 Leeland McElroy B	2.00	.90	.25
☐ B224 Vinnie Clark B	.40	.18	.05
☐ B225 Keyshawn Johnson B	4.00	1.80	.50
☐ B228 Tony Woods B	.40	.18	.05
☐ B231 Anthony Pleasant B	.40	.18	.05
☐ B232 Jeff George B	.75	.35	.09
☐ B233 Curtis Conway B	1.25	.55	.16
☐ B235 Jeff Lewis B	.75	.35	.09
☐ B236 Edgar Bennett B	.75	.35	.09
☐ B237 Regan Upshaw B	.40	.18	.05
☐ B238 William Fuller B	.40	.18	.05
☐ B241 Willie Anderson B	.40	.18	.05
☐ B242 Derrick Thomas B	.75	.35	.09
☐ B243 Marvin Harrison B	4.00	1.80	.50
☐ B244 Darion Conner B	.40	.18	.05
☐ B245 Antonio Langham B	.40	.18	.05
☐ B246 Rodney Peete B	.40	.18	.05
☐ B247 Tim McDonald B	.40	.18	.05
☐ B248 Robert Jones B	.40	.18	.05
☐ B251 Mark Carrier DB B	.40	.18	.05
☐ B252 Stephen Grant B	.40	.18	.05
☐ B254 Jeff Hostetler B	.75	.35	.09
☐ B255 Darrell Green B	.40	.18	.05
☐ B261 Eric Swann B	.75	.35	.09
☐ B263 Irv Smith B	.40	.18	.05
☐ B264 Tim McKyer B	.40	.18	.05
☐ B266 Sean Jones B	.40	.18	.05
☐ B271 Yancey Thigpen B	.75	.35	.09
☐ B273 Quentin Coryatt B	.40	.18	.05
☐ B274 Hardy Nickerson B	.40	.18	.05
☐ B275 Ricardo McDonald B	.40	.18	.05
☐ B277 Robert Blackmon B	.40	.18	.05
☐ B279 Alonzo Spellman B	.40	.18	.05
☐ B281 Rickey Dudley B	2.00	.90	.25
☐ B282 Joe Cain B	.40	.18	.05
☐ B284 John Randle B	.40	.18	.05
☐ B286 Vinny Testaverde B	.75	.35	.09
☐ B289 Henry Jones B	.40	.18	.05
☐ B290 Simeon Rice B	1.50	.70	.19
☐ B295 Leslie O'Neal B	.40	.18	.05
☐ B297 Greg Hill B	.75	.35	.09
☐ B301 Eric Metcalf B	.75	.35	.09
☐ B303 Jerome Woods B	.40	.18	.05
☐ B306 Anthony Smith B	.40	.18	.05
☐ B307 Darren Perry B	.40	.18	.05
☐ B311 James Hasty B	.40	.18	.05
☐ B312 Cris Carter B	1.25	.55	.16
☐ B314 Lawrence Phillips B	2.50	1.10	.30
☐ B317 Aeneas Williams B	.40	.18	.05
☐ B318 Eric Hill B	.40	.18	.05
☐ B319 Kevin Hardy B	1.50	.70	.19
☐ B321 Chris Chandler B	.75	.35	.09
☐ B322 Rocket Ismail B	.75	.35	.09
☐ B323 Anthony Parker B	.40	.18	.05
☐ B324 John Thierry B	.40	.18	.05
☐ B325 Micheal Barrow B	.40	.18	.05
☐ B326 Henry Ford B	.40	.18	.05
☐ B327 Aaron Hayden B	.40	.18	.05
☐ B328 Terance Mathis B	.40	.18	.05
☐ B329 Kirk Pointer B	.40	.18	.05
☐ B330 Ray Mickens B	.40	.18	.05
☐ B331 Jermane Mayberry B	.40	.18	.05
☐ B332 Mario Bates B	.75	.35	.09
☐ B333 Carlton Gray B	.40	.18	.05
☐ B334 Derek Loville B	.40	.18	.05
☐ B335 Mike Alstott B	2.50	1.10	.30
☐ B336 Eric Guliford B	.40	.18	.05
☐ B337 Marvcus Patton B	.40	.18	.05
☐ B338 Terrell Owens B	6.00	2.70	.75
☐ B339 Lance Johnstone B	.40	.18	.05
☐ B340 Lake Dawson B	.75	.35	.09
☐ B341 Winslow Oliver B	.40	.18	.05
☐ B342 Adrian Murrell B	.75	.35	.09
☐ B343 Jason Belser B	.40	.18	.05
☐ B344 Brian Dawkins B	.40	.18	.05
☐ B345 Reggie Brown B	.40	.18	.05
☐ B346 Shaun Gayle B	.40	.18	.05
☐ B347 Tony Brackens B	1.50	.70	.19
☐ B348 Thomas Lewis B	.40	.18	.05
☐ B349 Kelvin Pritchett B	.40	.18	.05
☐ B350 Bobby Engram B	3.00	1.35	.35
☐ B351 Moe Williams B	.40	.18	.05
☐ B352 Thomas Smith B	.40	.18	.05
☐ B353 Dexter Carter B	.40	.18	.05
☐ B354 Qadry Ismail B	.75	.35	.09
☐ B355 Marco Battaglia B	.40	.18	.05
☐ B356 Levon Kirkland B	.40	.18	.05
☐ B357 Eric Allen B	.40	.18	.05
☐ B358 Bobby Hoying B	1.50	.70	.19
☐ B359 Checklist B	.40	.18	.05
☐ G1 Kordell Stewart G	60.00	27.00	7.50
☐ G7 Kimble Anders G	15.00	6.75	1.85
☐ G8 Merton Hanks G	15.00	6.75	1.85
☐ G17 Rick Mirer G	20.00	9.00	2.50
☐ G33 Craig Newsome G	15.00	6.75	1.85
☐ G36 Bryce Paup G	20.00	9.00	2.50
☐ G40 Dan Marino G	100.00	45.00	12.50
☐ G42 Andre Coleman G	15.00	6.75	1.85
☐ G47 Kevin Carter G	15.00	6.75	1.85
☐ G60 Mark Brunell G	60.00	27.00	7.50
☐ G61 David Palmer G	20.00	9.00	2.50
☐ G75 Carnell Lake G	15.00	6.75	1.85
☐ G96 Joey Galloway G	30.00	13.50	3.70
☐ G112 Melvin Tuten G	15.00	6.75	1.85
☐ G121 Aaron Glenn G	15.00	6.75	1.85
☐ G132 Brett Favre G	100.00	45.00	12.50
☐ G133 Ken Dilger G	20.00	9.00	2.50
☐ G140 Barry Sanders G	60.00	27.00	7.50
☐ G142 Glyn Milburn G	15.00	6.75	1.85
☐ G148 Brett Perriman G	20.00	9.00	2.50
☐ G160 Kerry Collins G	60.00	27.00	7.50
☐ G164 Lee Woodall G	15.00	6.75	1.85
☐ G173 Marshall Faulk G	30.00	13.50	3.70
☐ G178 Troy Aikman G	60.00	27.00	7.50
☐ G190 Drew Bledsoe G	60.00	27.00	7.50
☐ G191 Checklist G	15.00	6.75	1.85
☐ G193 Michael Irvin G	25.00	11.00	3.10
☐ G196 Warren Moon G	20.00	9.00	2.50
☐ G200 Steve Young G	40.00	18.00	5.00
☐ G207 Alex Van Dyke G	20.00	9.00	2.50
☐ G220 Cris Carter G	25.00	11.00	3.10
☐ G230 John Elway G	50.00	22.00	6.25
☐ G234 Charles Haley G	20.00	9.00	2.50
☐ G240 Jim Kelly G	25.00	11.00	3.10
☐ G250 Rodney Hampton G	20.00	9.00	2.50
☐ G256 Errict Rhett G	20.00	9.00	2.50
☐ G257 Alex Molden G	15.00	6.75	1.85
☐ G260 Kevin Hardy G	20.00	9.00	2.50
☐ G267 Bryant Young G	20.00	9.00	2.50
☐ G268 Jeff Blake G	25.00	11.00	3.10
☐ G270 Keyshawn Johnson G	30.00	13.50	3.70
☐ G278 Junior Seau G	25.00	11.00	3.10
☐ G285 Terry Kirby G	20.00	9.00	2.50
☐ G293 Hugh Douglas G	15.00	6.75	1.85
☐ G296 Reggie White G	25.00	11.00	3.10
☐ G298 Elvis Grbac G	25.00	11.00	3.10
☐ G300 Emmitt Smith G	80.00	36.00	10.00
☐ G309 Ricky Watters G	20.00	9.00	2.50
☐ S4 Brett Favre S	35.00	16.00	4.40
☐ S14 Chester McGlockton S	2.50	1.10	.30
☐ S20 Tyrone Hughes S	2.50	1.10	.30
☐ S24 Ty Law S	2.50	1.10	.30
☐ S25 Brian Mitchell S	2.50	1.10	.30
☐ S31 Darren Woodson S	4.00	1.80	.50
☐ S35 Brian Mitchell S	2.50	1.10	.30
☐ S37 Dana Stubblefield S	4.00	1.80	.50
☐ S41 Kerry Collins S	20.00	9.00	2.50
☐ S46 Orlando Thomas S	2.50	1.10	.30
☐ S50 Jerry Rice S	15.00	6.75	1.85
☐ S53 Willie McGinest S	2.50	1.10	.30
☐ S54 Blake Brockermeyer S	2.50	1.10	.30
☐ S56 Michael Westbrook S	6.00	2.70	.75
☐ S57 Garrison Hearst S	6.00	2.70	.75
☐ S59 Kyle Brady S	4.00	1.80	.50
☐ S62 Tim Brown S	4.00	1.80	.50
☐ S63 Jeff Graham S	2.50	1.10	.30
☐ S67 Dan Marino S	30.00	13.50	3.70
☐ S69 Tamarick Vanover S	6.00	2.70	.75
☐ S74 Daryl Johnston S	4.00	1.80	.50
☐ S78 Frank Sanders S	4.00	1.80	.50
☐ S84 Darryll Lewis S	2.50	1.10	.30
☐ S85 Carl Pickens S	6.00	2.70	.75
☐ S88 Jerome Bettis S	6.00	2.70	.75
☐ S90 Terrell Davis S	20.00	9.00	2.50
☐ S99 Napoleon Kaufman S	4.00	1.80	.50
☐ S100 Rashaan Salaam S	6.00	2.70	.75
☐ S103 Barry Sanders S	15.00	6.75	1.85
☐ S107 Tony Boselli S	4.00	1.80	.50
☐ S109 Eric Zeier S	4.00	1.80	.50
☐ S116 Bruce Smith S	6.00	2.70	.75
☐ S118 Zack Crockett S	2.50	1.10	.30
☐ S125 Joey Galloway S	10.00	4.50	1.25
☐ S126 Heath Shuler S	6.00	2.70	.75
☐ S127 Curtis Martin S	20.00	9.00	2.50
☐ S135 Greg Lloyd S	4.00	1.80	.50
☐ S137 Marshall Faulk S	6.00	2.70	.75
☐ S147 Tyrone Poole S	2.50	1.10	.30
☐ S150 J.J. Stokes S	6.00	2.70	.75
☐ S153 Drew Bledsoe S	15.00	6.75	1.85
☐ S154 Terry McDaniel S	2.50	1.10	.30
☐ S155 Terrell Fletcher S	2.50	1.10	.30
☐ S159 Dave Brown S	2.50	1.10	.30
☐ S165 Jim Harbaugh S	4.00	1.80	.50
☐ S166 Larry Brown S	2.50	1.10	.30
☐ S167 Neil Smith S	4.00	1.80	.50
☐ S168 Herman Moore S	6.00	2.70	.75
☐ S170 Deion Sanders S	10.00	4.50	1.25
☐ S174 Mark Chmura S	4.00	1.80	.50
☐ S181 Chris Warren S	4.00	1.80	.50
☐ S183 Robert Brooks S	6.00	2.70	.75
☐ S184 Steve McNair S	15.00	6.75	1.85
☐ S185 Kordell Stewart S	20.00	9.00	2.50
☐ S189 Charlie Garner S	2.50	1.10	.30
☐ S195 Harvey Williams S	2.50	1.10	.30
☐ S197 Jeff George S	4.00	1.80	.50
☐ S199 Ricky Watters S	4.00	1.80	.50
☐ S204 Steve Bono S	4.00	1.80	.50
☐ S210 Jeff Blake S	6.00	2.70	.75
☐ S215 Phillippi Sparks S	2.50	1.10	.30
☐ S226 William Floyd S	4.00	1.80	.50
☐ S227 Troy Drayton S	2.50	1.10	.30
☐ S229 Rodney Hampton S	4.00	1.80	.50
☐ S239 Duane Clemons S	2.50	1.10	.30
☐ S249 Curtis Conway S	6.00	2.70	.75
☐ S253 John Mobley S	2.50	1.10	.30
☐ S258 Chris Slade S	2.50	1.10	.30
☐ S259 Derrick Thomas S	4.00	1.80	.50
☐ S262 Eric Metcalf S	4.00	1.80	.50
☐ S265 Emmitt Smith S	30.00	13.50	3.70
☐ S269 Jeff Hostetler S	4.00	1.80	.50
☐ S272 Thurman Thomas S	6.00	2.70	.75
☐ S276 Steve Atwater S	2.50	1.10	.30
☐ S280 Isaac Bruce S	6.00	2.70	.75
☐ S283 Neil O'Donnell S	4.00	1.80	.50
☐ S287 Jim Kelly S	6.00	2.70	.75
☐ S288 Lawrence Phillips S	6.00	2.70	.75
☐ S291 Terance Mathis S	2.50	1.10	.30
☐ S292 Errict Rhett S	4.00	1.80	.50
☐ S294 Santo Stephens S	2.50	1.10	.30
☐ S299 Walt Harris S	2.50	1.10	.30
☐ S302 Jamir Miller S	2.50	1.10	.30
☐ S304 Ben Coates S	4.00	1.80	.50
☐ S305 Marcus Allen S	6.00	2.70	.75
☐ S308 Jonathan Ogden S	2.50	1.10	.30
☐ S310 John Elway S	15.00	6.75	1.85
☐ S313 Irving Fryar S	4.00	1.80	.50
☐ S315 Junior Seau S	6.00	2.70	.75
☐ S316 Alex Molden S	2.50	1.10	.30
☐ S320 Steve Young S	12.00	5.50	1.50

1996 Finest Refractors

This 359 card standard-size set is a parallel to the regular Finest issue. Similar to the regular set, these cards are broken down into bronze, silver and gold refractors. All of the cards are labeled as refractors, which is different from the early years of the Finest products. The bronze refractors were issued one every 12 packs, the silvers were issued one every 48 packs and the gold were inserted approximately one every 288 packs. Reportedly, less than 150 of each gold refractor was produced.

	MINT	NRMT	EXC
COMPLETE SET (359)	10000.00	4500.00	1250.00
COMPLETE SER.1 (191)	6500.00	2900.00	800.00
COMPLETE SER.2 (168)	3500.00	1600.00	450.00
COMPLETE BRONZE SET (110)	1300.00	575.00	160.00
COMP.BRONZE SER.1 (110)	750.00	350.00	95.00
COMP.BRONZE SER.2 (110)	550.00	250.00	70.00
COMMON BRONZE REF.(1-191)	4.00	1.80	.50
SEMISTARS BRONZE	6.00	2.70	.75
STARS BRONZE	10.00	4.50	1.25
COMPLETE GOLD SET (26)	6000.00	2700.00	750.00
COMP.GOLD SER.2 (22)	2000.00	900.00	250.00
COMMON GOLD REF.(1-191)	30.00	13.50	3.70
SEMISTARS GOLD	50.00	22.00	6.25
STARS GOLD	80.00	36.00	10.00
COMPLETE SILVER SET (55)	3000.00	1350.00	375.00
COMPLETE GOLD SET (26)	2000.00	900.00	250.00
COMP.SILVER SER.2 (36)	1000.00	450.00	125.00
COMMON SILVER REF.(1-191)	15.00	6.75	1.85
SEMISTARS SILVER	25.00	11.00	3.10
STARS SILVER	40.00	18.00	5.00

☐ B16 Terrell Davis B	70.00	32.00	8.75
☐ B22 Steve McNair B	40.00	18.00	5.00
☐ B95 Curtis Martin B	70.00	32.00	8.75
☐ B105 J.J. Stokes B	15.00	6.75	1.85
☐ B134 Troy Aikman B	70.00	32.00	8.75
☐ B151 Deion Sanders B	30.00	13.50	3.70
☐ B175 Jerry Rice B	70.00	32.00	8.75
☐ B198 Eddie Kennison B	30.00	13.50	3.70
☐ B222 Tim Biakabutuka B	18.00	8.00	2.20
☐ B225 Keyshawn Johnson B	30.00	13.50	3.70
☐ B243 Marvin Harrison B	30.00	13.50	3.70
☐ B338 Terrell Owens B	40.00	18.00	5.00
☐ B350 Bobby Engram B	18.00	8.00	2.20
☐ G1 Kordell Stewart G	175.00	80.00	22.00

	MINT	NRMT	EXC
☐ G40 Dan Marino G	500.00	220.00	60.00
☐ G60 Mark Brunell G	300.00	135.00	38.00
☐ G96 Joey Galloway G	125.00	55.00	15.50
☐ G132 Brett Favre G	600.00	275.00	75.00
☐ G140 Barry Sanders G	300.00	135.00	38.00
☐ G160 Kerry Collins G	300.00	135.00	38.00
☐ G173 Marshall Faulk G	100.00	45.00	12.50
☐ G178 Troy Aikman G	300.00	135.00	38.00
☐ G190 Drew Bledsoe G	300.00	135.00	38.00
☐ G200 Steve Young G	200.00	90.00	25.00
☐ G230 John Elway G	250.00	110.00	31.00
☐ G240 Jim Kelly G	100.00	45.00	12.50
☐ G270 Keyshawn Johnson G	150.00	70.00	19.00
☐ G296 Reggie White G	100.00	45.00	12.50
☐ G300 Emmitt Smith G	500.00	220.00	60.00
☐ S4 Brett Favre S	200.00	90.00	25.00
☐ S41 Kerry Collins S	120.00	55.00	15.00
☐ S50 Jerry Rice S	120.00	55.00	15.00
☐ S67 Dan Marino S	200.00	90.00	25.00
☐ S88 Jerome Bettis S	50.00	22.00	6.25
☐ S90 Terrell Davis S	120.00	55.00	15.00
☐ S103 Barry Sanders S	120.00	55.00	15.00
☐ S125 Joey Galloway S	50.00	22.00	6.25
☐ S127 Curtis Martin S	120.00	55.00	15.00
☐ S153 Drew Bledsoe S	120.00	55.00	15.00
☐ S170 Deion Sanders S	60.00	27.00	7.50
☐ S184 Steve McNair S	80.00	36.00	10.00
☐ S185 Kordell Stewart S	120.00	55.00	15.00
☐ S265 Emmitt Smith S	200.00	90.00	25.00
☐ S288 Lawrence Phillips S	50.00	22.00	6.25
☐ S310 John Elway S	80.00	36.00	10.00
☐ S320 Steve Young S	70.00	32.00	8.75

1996-97 Finest Pro Bowl Jumbos

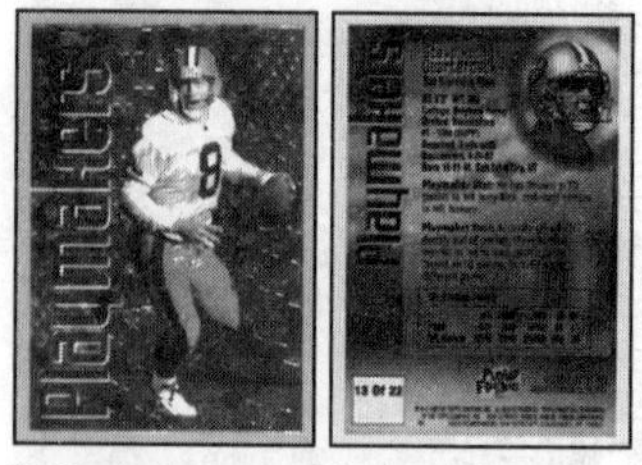

This 22-card set measures approximately 4" by 5 5/8". The fronts feature a color player photo on a metallic background. The cards are essentially enlarged versions of regular issue 1996 Finest gold cards but were distributed at the 1997 NFL Experience Pro Bowl show in Hawaii. Each is numbered "XX of 22" cards. Refractor parallel versions of each card were produced in much shorter quantities.

	MINT	NRMT	EXC
COMPLETE SET (22)	40.00	18.00	5.00
COMMON CARD (1-22)	1.00	.45	.12
*REFRACTORS: 10X TO 18X			
☐ 1 Brett Favre	10.00	4.50	1.25
☐ 2 Herman Moore	2.00	.90	.25
☐ 3 Terrell Davis	5.00	2.20	.60
☐ 4 Jerry Rice	5.00	2.20	.60
☐ 5 Tim Brown	1.50	.70	.19
☐ 6 Dan Marino	10.00	4.50	1.25
☐ 7 Curtis Martin	5.00	2.20	.60
☐ 8 Barry Sanders	5.00	2.20	.60
☐ 9 Bruce Smith	2.00	.90	.25
☐ 10 Troy Aikman	5.00	2.20	.60
☐ 11 Deion Sanders	3.00	1.35	.35
☐ 12 Drew Bledsoe	5.00	2.20	.60
☐ 13 Steve Young	4.00	1.80	.50
☐ 14 Terry Allen	1.50	.70	.19
☐ 15 Reggie White	2.00	.90	.25
☐ 16 Shannon Sharpe	1.50	.70	.19
☐ 17 John Elway	4.00	1.80	.50
☐ 18 Emmitt Smith	10.00	4.50	1.25
☐ 19 Keyshawn Johnson	2.00	.90	.25
☐ 20 Ben Coates	1.50	.70	.19
☐ 21 Ricky Watters	1.50	.70	.19
☐ 22 Junior Seau	2.00	.90	.25

1996-97 Finest Pro Bowl Promos 5X7

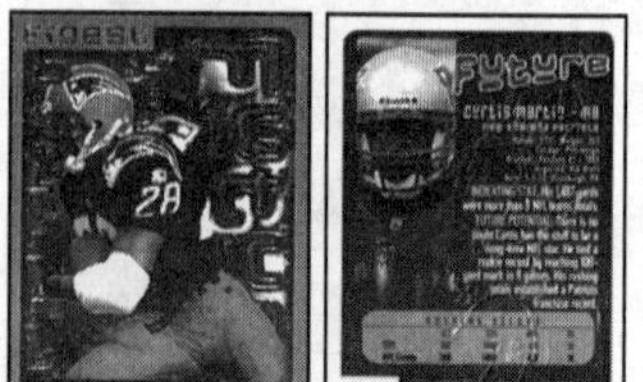

In addition to the 22-card Finest Pro Bowl set, six promo cards were released at the 1997 NFL Experience Pro Bowl Card Show in Hawaii. Each is simply an enlarged (5" by 7") copy of a 1996 Finest card. The backs carry a 1996 copyright date along with a player bio and card number. A Refractor parallel was also produced for each card.

	MINT	NRMT	EXC
COMPLETE SET (6)	35.00	16.00	4.40
COMMON CARD (1-6)	5.00	2.20	.60
*REFRACTORS: 5X TO 10X BASIC CARDS			
☐ 1 Curtis Martin	6.00	2.70	.75
☐ 2 Brett Favre	12.00	5.50	1.50
☐ 3 Barry Sanders	6.00	2.70	.75
☐ 4 Jerry Rice	6.00	2.70	.75
☐ 5 Troy Aikman	6.00	2.70	.75
☐ 6 John Elway	5.00	2.20	.60

1997 Finest

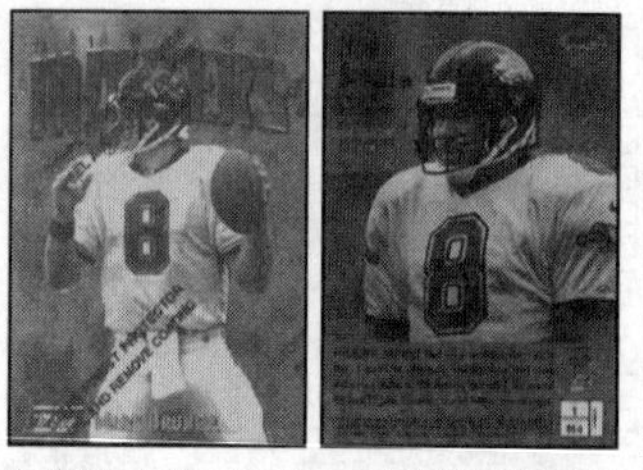

The 1997 Finest set was issued in one series totaling 175 cards and was distributed in six-card packs with a suggested retail price of $5. The set features borderless metallic design with the first 100 cards labeled as Common and highlighted in bronze. Cards #101-150 are labeled as Uncommon and are highlighted in silver with an insertion rate of one in four packs. The last 25 cards (#151-175) are labeled as Rare, are highlighted in gold, and carry an insertion rate of one in 24 packs. The set is also divided into five theme categories: Dynamos, Bulldozers, Masters, Hitmen, and Field Generals. The cards are numbered twice--according to where they fall in the whole set and according to where they fall within each of the five themes.

	MINT	NRMT	EXC
COMPLETE SERIES 1 (175)	800.00	350.00	100.00
COMP.BRONZE SER.1 (100)	35.00	16.00	4.40
COMMON BRONZE (1-100)	.40	.18	.05
COMP.SILVER SER.1 (50)	200.00	90.00	25.00
COMMON SILVER (101-150)	2.00	.90	.25
COMP.GOLD SER.1 (25)	600.00	275.00	75.00
COMMON GOLD (151-175)	12.00	5.50	1.50
☐ 1 Mark Brunell B	4.00	1.80	.50
☐ 2 Chris Slade B	.40	.18	.05
☐ 3 Chris Doleman B	.40	.18	.05
☐ 4 Chris Hudson B	.40	.18	.05
☐ 5 Karim Abdul-Jabbar B	3.00	1.35	.35
☐ 6 Darren Perry B	.40	.18	.05
☐ 7 Daryl Johnston B	.75	.35	.09
☐ 8 Rob Moore B UER listed as uncommon	.40	.18	.05
☐ 9 Robert Smith B	.75	.35	.09
☐ 10 Terry Allen B	.75	.35	.09
☐ 11 Jason Dunn B	.75	.35	.09
☐ 12 Henry Thomas B	.40	.18	.05
☐ 13 Rod Stephens B	.40	.18	.05
☐ 14 Ray Mickens B	.40	.18	.05
☐ 15 Ty Detmer B	.75	.35	.09
☐ 16 Fred Barnett B	.75	.35	.09
☐ 17 Derrick Alexander B	.75	.35	.09
☐ 18 Marcus Robertson B	.40	.18	.05
☐ 19 Robert Blackmon B	.40	.18	.05
☐ 20 Isaac Bruce B	1.25	.55	.16
☐ 21 Chester McGlockton B	.40	.18	.05
☐ 22 Stan Humphries B	.75	.35	.09
☐ 23 Lonnie Marts B	.40	.18	.05
☐ 24 Jason Sehorn B	.40	.18	.05
☐ 25 Bobby Engram B UER listed as uncommon	.75	.35	.09
☐ 26 Brett Perriman B UER listed as uncommon	.75	.35	.09
☐ 27 Stevon Moore B	.40	.18	.05
☐ 28 Jamal Anderson B	.75	.35	.09
☐ 29 Wayne Martin B	.40	.18	.05
☐ 30 Michael Irvin B UER listed as uncommon	1.25	.55	.16
☐ 31 Thomas Smith B	.40	.18	.05
☐ 32 Tony Brackens B	.40	.18	.05
☐ 33 Eric Davis B	.40	.18	.05
☐ 34 James O.Stewart B	.75	.35	.09
☐ 35 Ki-Jana Carter B	.75	.35	.09
☐ 36 Ken Norton B	.40	.18	.05
☐ 37 William Thomas B	.40	.18	.05
☐ 38 Tim Brown B	.75	.35	.09
☐ 39 Lawrence Phillips B	.75	.35	.09
☐ 40 Ricky Watters B	.75	.35	.09
☐ 41 Tony Bennett B	.40	.18	.05
☐ 42 Jessie Armstead B	.40	.18	.05
☐ 43 Trent Dilfer B	.75	.35	.09
☐ 44 Rodney Hampton B	.75	.35	.09
☐ 45 Sam Mills B	.75	.35	.09
☐ 46 Rodney Harrison B	.40	.18	.05
☐ 47 Rob Fredrickson B	.40	.18	.05
☐ 48 Eric Hill B	.40	.18	.05
☐ 49 Bennie Blades B	.40	.18	.05
☐ 50 Eddie George B	6.00	2.70	.75
☐ 51 Dave Brown B	.75	.35	.09
☐ 52 Raymont Harris B	.40	.18	.05
☐ 53 Steve Tovar B	.40	.18	.05
☐ 54 Thurman Thomas B	1.25	.55	.16
☐ 55 Leeland McElroy B	.75	.35	.09
☐ 56 Brian Mitchell B UER listed as uncommon	.40	.18	.05
☐ 57 Eric Allen B	.40	.18	.05
☐ 58 Vinny Testaverde B	.75	.35	.09
☐ 59 Marvin Washington B	.40	.18	.05
☐ 60 Junior Seau B	1.25	.55	.16
☐ 61 Bert Emanuel B	.75	.35	.09
☐ 62 Kevin Carter B	.40	.18	.05
☐ 63 Mark Carrier B	.40	.18	.05
☐ 64 Andre Coleman B	.40	.18	.05
☐ 65 Chris Warren B	.75	.35	.09
☐ 66 Aeneas Williams B	.40	.18	.05
☐ 67 Eugene Robinson B	.40	.18	.05
☐ 68 Darren Woodson B	.75	.35	.09
☐ 69 Anthony Johnson B	.75	.35	.09
☐ 70 Terry Glenn B	4.00	1.80	.50
☐ 71 Troy Vincent B	.40	.18	.05
☐ 72 John Copeland B	.40	.18	.05
☐ 73 Warren Sapp B	.40	.18	.05
☐ 74 Bobby Hebert B	.40	.18	.05
☐ 75 Jeff Hostetler B	.75	.35	.09
☐ 76 Willie Davis B	.75	.35	.09
☐ 77 Mickey Washington B	.40	.18	.05
☐ 78 Cortez Kennedy B	.75	.35	.09
☐ 79 Michael Strahan B	.40	.18	.05
☐ 80 Jerome Bettis B	1.25	.55	.16
☐ 81 Andre Hastings B UER listed as uncommon	.75	.35	.09
☐ 82 Simeon Rice B	.75	.35	.09
☐ 83 Cornelius Bennett B	.75	.35	.09
☐ 84 Napoleon Kaufman B	.75	.35	.09
☐ 85 Jim Harbaugh B	.75	.35	.09
☐ 86 Aaron Hayden B	.40	.18	.05
☐ 87 Gus Frerotte B	1.25	.55	.16
☐ 88 Jeff Blake B	1.25	.55	.16
☐ 89 Anthony Miller B UER listed as uncommon	.75	.35	.09
☐ 90 Deion Sanders B	2.00	.90	.25
☐ 91 Curtis Conway B	1.25	.55	.16
☐ 92 William Floyd B	.75	.35	.09
☐ 93 Eric Moulds B UER listed as uncommon	1.25	.55	.16
☐ 94 Mel Gray B	.40	.18	.05
☐ 95 Andre Rison B UER listed as uncommon	.75	.35	.09
☐ 96 Eugene Daniel B	.40	.18	.05
☐ 97 Jason Belser B	.40	.18	.05
☐ 98 Mike Mamula B	.40	.18	.05
☐ 99 Jim Everett B	.40	.18	.05
☐ 100 Checklist B	.40	.18	.05
☐ 101 Drew Bledsoe S	12.00	5.50	1.50
☐ 102 Shannon Sharpe S	3.00	1.35	.35
☐ 103 Ken Harvey S	2.00	.90	.25
☐ 104 Isaac Bruce S	5.00	2.20	.60
☐ 105 Terry Allen S	3.00	1.35	.35
☐ 106 Lawyer Milloy S	2.00	.90	.25
☐ 107 Ashley Ambrose S	2.00	.90	.25
☐ 108 Alfred Williams S	2.00	.90	.25
☐ 109 Hugh Douglas S	2.00	.90	.25
☐ 110 Junior Seau S	5.00	2.20	.60
☐ 111 Kordell Stewart S	12.00	5.50	1.50
☐ 112 Adrian Murrell S	3.00	1.35	.35
☐ 113 Byron Bam Morris S	3.00	1.35	.35
☐ 114 Terrell Buckley S	2.00	.90	.25
☐ 115 Dan Marino S	25.00	11.00	3.10
☐ 116 Willie Clay S	2.00	.90	.25
☐ 117 Neil Smith S	3.00	1.35	.35
☐ 118 Blaine Bishop S	2.00	.90	.25
☐ 119 John Mobley S	2.00	.90	.25
☐ 120 Herman Moore S	5.00	2.20	.60
☐ 121 Keyshawn Johnson S	6.00	2.70	.75
☐ 122 Boomer Esiason S	3.00	1.35	.35
☐ 123 Marshall Faulk S	5.00	2.20	.60
☐ 124 Keith Jackson S	2.00	.90	.25
☐ 125 Ricky Watters S	3.00	1.35	.35
☐ 126 Carl Pickens S	5.00	2.20	.60
☐ 127 Cris Carter S	5.00	2.20	.60
☐ 128 Mike Alstott S	5.00	2.20	.60
☐ 129 Simeon Rice S	3.00	1.35	.35
☐ 130 Troy Aikman S	12.00	5.50	1.50
☐ 131 Tamarick Vanover S	5.00	2.20	.60
☐ 132 Marquez Pope S	2.00	.90	.25
☐ 133 Winslow Oliver S	2.00	.90	.25
☐ 134 Edgar Bennett S	3.00	1.35	.35
☐ 135 Dave Meggett S	2.00	.90	.25
☐ 136 Marcus Allen S	5.00	2.20	.60
☐ 137 Jerry Rice S	12.00	5.50	1.50
☐ 138 Steve Atwater S	2.00	.90	.25
☐ 139 Tim McDonald S	2.00	.90	.25
☐ 140 Barry Sanders S	12.00	5.50	1.50
☐ 141 Eddie George S	20.00	9.00	2.50
☐ 142 Wesley Walls S	2.00	.90	.25
☐ 143 Jerome Bettis S	5.00	2.20	.60
☐ 144 Kevin Greene S	3.00	1.35	.35
☐ 145 Terrell Davis S	12.00	5.50	1.50
☐ 146 Gus Frerotte S	5.00	2.20	.60
☐ 147 Joey Galloway S	6.00	2.70	.75
☐ 148 Vinny Testaverde S	3.00	1.35	.35
☐ 149 Hardy Nickerson S	2.00	.90	.25
☐ 150 Brett Favre S	25.00	11.00	3.10
☐ 151 Desmond Howard G	15.00	6.75	1.85
☐ 152 Keyshawn Johnson G	30.00	13.50	3.70
☐ 153 Tony Banks G	20.00	9.00	2.50
☐ 154 Chris Spielman G	12.00	5.50	1.50
☐ 155 Reggie White G	20.00	9.00	2.50
☐ 156 Zach Thomas G	20.00	9.00	2.50
☐ 157 Carl Pickens G	20.00	9.00	2.50
☐ 158 Karim Abdul-Jabbar G	30.00	13.50	3.70
☐ 159 Chad Brown G	12.00	5.50	1.50
☐ 160 Kerry Collins G	40.00	18.00	5.00
☐ 161 Marvin Harrison G	20.00	9.00	2.50
☐ 162 Steve Young G	35.00	16.00	4.40
☐ 163 Deion Sanders G	30.00	13.50	3.70
☐ 164 Trent Dilfer G	15.00	6.75	1.85
☐ 165 Barry Sanders G	40.00	18.00	5.00
☐ 166 Cris Carter G	20.00	9.00	2.50
☐ 167 Keenan McCardell G	15.00	6.75	1.85
☐ 168 Terry Glenn G	40.00	18.00	5.00
☐ 169 Emmitt Smith G	80.00	36.00	10.00
☐ 170 John Elway G	35.00	16.00	4.40
☐ 171 Jerry Rice G	40.00	18.00	5.00
☐ 172 Troy Aikman G	40.00	18.00	5.00
☐ 173 Curtis Martin G	40.00	18.00	5.00
☐ 174 Darrell Green G	12.00	5.50	1.50
☐ 175 Mark Brunell G	40.00	18.00	5.00
☐ P5 Karim Abdul-Jabbar Promo	4.00	1.80	.50
☐ P32 Tony Brackens Promo	1.00	.45	.12
☐ P45 Sam Mills Promo	1.00	.45	.12
☐ P70 Terry Glenn Promo	4.00	1.80	.50
☐ P87 Gus Frerotte Promo	2.00	.90	.25

1997 Finest Embossed

Randomly inserted in packs at a rate of one in 16, the first 50 cards from this set are embossed parallel versions of the uncommon or silver cards (1:16 packs, #101-150) in the regular set. The scarcer gold cards (1:96 packs, #151-175) also feature embossed print, but also have die cut edges.

	MINT	NRMT	EXC
COMPLETE SERIES 1 (75)	1600.00	700.00	200.00
COMP.SILVER SER.1 (50)	500.00	220.00	60.00
COMMON SILVER (101-150)	5.00	2.20	.60
SILVER SEMISTARS	8.00	3.60	1.00
SILVER UNLISTED STARS	12.00	5.50	1.50
COMP.GOLD DC SER.1 (25)	1100.00	500.00	140.00
COMMON GOLD DC (151-175)	20.00	9.00	2.50
GOLD SEMISTARS	25.00	11.00	3.10
GOLD DC UNLISTED STARS	30.00	13.50	3.70
☐ 101 Drew Bledsoe S	40.00	18.00	5.00
☐ 111 Kordell Stewart S	30.00	13.50	3.70
☐ 115 Dan Marino S	75.00	34.00	9.50
☐ 130 Troy Aikman S	40.00	18.00	5.00
☐ 137 Jerry Rice S	40.00	18.00	5.00
☐ 140 Barry Sanders S	40.00	18.00	5.00
☐ 141 Eddie George S	50.00	22.00	6.25
☐ 145 Terrell Davis S	40.00	18.00	5.00
☐ 150 Brett Favre S	75.00	34.00	9.50
☐ 158 Karim Abdul-Jabbar G	75.00	34.00	9.50
☐ 160 Kerry Collins G	75.00	34.00	9.50
☐ 162 Steve Young G	70.00	32.00	8.75
☐ 163 Deion Sanders G	60.00	27.00	7.50
☐ 165 Barry Sanders G	90.00	40.00	11.00
☐ 168 Terry Glenn G	90.00	40.00	11.00
☐ 169 Emmitt Smith G	175.00	80.00	22.00
☐ 170 John Elway G	75.00	34.00	9.50
☐ 171 Jerry Rice G	90.00	40.00	11.00
☐ 172 Troy Aikman G	90.00	40.00	11.00
☐ 173 Curtis Martin G	75.00	34.00	9.50
☐ 175 Mark Brunell G	90.00	40.00	11.00

1997 Finest Embossed Refractors

Randomly inserted at the rate of one in 192 packs, the first 50 Silver cards (1:192 packs) from this set parallel the regular Embossed version and are highlighted by a mosaic pattern. The scarcer gold cards (1:1152 packs, #151-175), feature die cut edges coupled with a refractive sheen on front.

	MINT	NRMT	EXC
COMMON SILVER (101-150)	40.00	18.00	5.00
SILVER SEMISTARS	50.00	22.00	6.25
SILVER UNLISTED STARS	60.00	27.00	7.50
COMMON GOLD DC (151-175)	100.00	45.00	12.50
GOLD DC SEMISTARS	125.00	55.00	15.50
GOLD DC UNLISTED STARS	150.00	70.00	19.00
☐ 101 Drew Bledsoe S	250.00	110.00	31.00
☐ 111 Kordell Stewart S	150.00	70.00	19.00
☐ 115 Dan Marino S	450.00	200.00	55.00
☐ 130 Troy Aikman S	250.00	110.00	31.00
☐ 137 Jerry Rice S	250.00	110.00	31.00
☐ 140 Barry Sanders S	250.00	110.00	31.00
☐ 141 Eddie George S	250.00	110.00	31.00
☐ 145 Terrell Davis S	150.00	70.00	19.00
☐ 150 Brett Favre S	450.00	200.00	55.00
☐ 158 Karim Abdul-Jabbar G	300.00	135.00	38.00
☐ 160 Kerry Collins G	400.00	180.00	50.00
☐ 162 Steve Young G	350.00	160.00	45.00
☐ 163 Deion Sanders G	250.00	110.00	31.00
☐ 165 Barry Sanders G	500.00	220.00	60.00
☐ 168 Terry Glenn G	400.00	180.00	50.00
☐ 169 Emmitt Smith G	900.00	400.00	110.00

☐ 170 John Elway G	400.00	180.00	50.00
☐ 171 Jerry Rice G	500.00	220.00	60.00
☐ 172 Troy Aikman G	500.00	220.00	60.00
☐ 173 Curtis Martin G	400.00	180.00	50.00
☐ 175 Mark Brunell G	500.00	220.00	60.00

1997 Finest Refractors

This 175-card set is a parallel version of the entire regular set with a refractive quality. Similar to the regular set, these cards are broken down into common or bronze, uncommon or silver, and rare or gold refractors. The bronze refractors were issued one in every 12 packs; the silver refractors, one in every 48; the gold refractors, one in every 288.

	MINT	NRMT	EXC
COMPLETE SERIES 1 (175)	3500.00	1600.00	450.00
COMP.BRONZE SER.1 (100)	500.00	220.00	60.00
COMMON BRONZE (1-100)	4.00	1.80	.50
BRONZE SEMISTARS	6.00	2.70	.75
BRONZE UNLISTED STARS	10.00	4.50	1.25
COMP.SILVER SER.1 (50)	900.00	400.00	110.00
COMMON SILVER (101-150)	10.00	4.50	1.25
SILVER SEMISTARS	15.00	6.75	1.85
SILVER UNLISTED STARS	20.00	9.00	2.50
COMP.GOLD SER.1 (25)	2200.00	1000.00	275.00
COMMON GOLD (151-175)	40.00	18.00	5.00
GOLD SEMISTARS	60.00	27.00	7.50
GOLD UNLISTED STARS	80.00	36.00	10.00
☐ 1 Mark Brunell B	50.00	22.00	6.25
☐ 5 Karim Abdul-Jabbar B	40.00	18.00	5.00
☐ 50 Eddie George B	60.00	27.00	7.50
☐ 70 Terry Glenn B	50.00	22.00	6.25
☐ 90 Deion Sanders B	25.00	11.00	3.10
☐ 101 Drew Bledsoe S	75.00	34.00	9.50
☐ 111 Kordell Stewart S	60.00	27.00	7.50
☐ 115 Dan Marino S	150.00	70.00	19.00
☐ 130 Troy Aikman S	75.00	34.00	9.50
☐ 137 Jerry Rice S	75.00	34.00	9.50
☐ 140 Barry Sanders S	75.00	34.00	9.50
☐ 141 Eddie George S	100.00	45.00	12.50
☐ 145 Terrell Davis S	60.00	27.00	7.50
☐ 150 Brett Favre S	150.00	70.00	19.00
☐ 158 Karim Abdul-Jabbar G	200.00	90.00	25.00
☐ 160 Kerry Collins G	150.00	70.00	19.00
☐ 162 Steve Young G	140.00	65.00	17.50
☐ 163 Deion Sanders G	125.00	55.00	15.50
☐ 165 Barry Sanders G	200.00	90.00	25.00
☐ 168 Terry Glenn G	175.00	80.00	22.00
☐ 169 Emmitt Smith G	400.00	180.00	50.00
☐ 170 John Elway G	150.00	70.00	19.00
☐ 171 Jerry Rice G	200.00	90.00	25.00
☐ 172 Troy Aikman G	200.00	90.00	25.00
☐ 173 Curtis Martin G	175.00	80.00	22.00
☐ 175 Mark Brunell G	200.00	90.00	25.00

1995 Flair

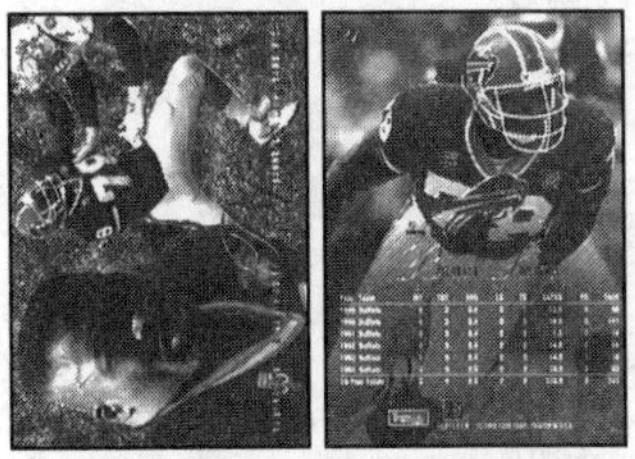

The debut issue for Flair contains 220 cards. The card fronts are horizontal with two player shots over a metallic background. The player's name runs along the bottom of the card with his two initials in script, followed by the team name. Card backs are vertical with the player's statistical information. Rookie Cards include Ki-Jana Carter, Kerry Collins, Curtis Martin, Steve McNair, Rashaan Salaam, J.J. Stokes, Kordell Stewart and Michael Westbrook.

	MINT	NRMT	EXC
COMPLETE SET (220)	60.00	27.00	7.50
COMMON CARD (1-220)	.20	.09	.03
☐ 1 Larry Centers	.35	.16	.04
☐ 2 Garrison Hearst	.60	.25	.07
☐ 3 Seth Joyner	.20	.09	.03
☐ 4 Dave Krieg	.20	.09	.03
☐ 5 Rob Moore	.20	.09	.03
☐ 6 Frank Sanders	2.00	.90	.25
Wearing 18 on front			
Wearing 81 on back			
☐ 7 Eric Swann	.35	.16	.04
☐ 8 Devin Bush	.20	.09	.03
☐ 9 Chris Doleman	.20	.09	.03
☐ 10 Bert Emanuel	.60	.25	.07
☐ 11 Jeff George	.35	.16	.04
☐ 12 Craig Heyward	.35	.16	.04
☐ 13 Terance Mathis	.35	.16	.04
☐ 14 Eric Metcalf	.35	.16	.04
☐ 15 Cornelius Bennett	.35	.16	.04
☐ 16 Jeff Burris	.20	.09	.03
☐ 17 Todd Collins	.60	.25	.07
☐ 18 Russell Copeland	.20	.09	.03
☐ 19 Jim Kelly	.60	.25	.07
☐ 20 Andre Reed	.35	.16	.04
☐ 21 Bruce Smith	.60	.25	.07
☐ 22 Don Beebe	.20	.09	.03
☐ 23 Mark Carrier	.35	.16	.04
☐ 24 Kerry Collins	7.00	3.10	.85
☐ 25 Barry Foster	.35	.16	.04
☐ 26 Pete Metzelaars	.20	.09	.03
☐ 27 Tyrone Poole	.35	.16	.04
☐ 28 Frank Reich	.20	.09	.03
☐ 29 Curtis Conway	.60	.25	.07
☐ 30 Chris Gedney	.20	.09	.03
☐ 31 Jeff Graham	.20	.09	.03
☐ 32 Raymont Harris	.20	.09	.03
☐ 33 Erik Kramer	.20	.09	.03
☐ 34 Rashaan Salaam	2.50	1.10	.30
☐ 35 Lewis Tillman	.20	.09	.03
☐ 36 Michael Timpson	.20	.09	.03
☐ 37 Jeff Blake	2.50	1.10	.30
☐ 38 Ki-Jana Carter	2.00	.90	.25
☐ 39 Tony McGee	.20	.09	.03
☐ 40 Carl Pickens	.60	.25	.07
☐ 41 Corey Sawyer	.20	.09	.03
☐ 42 Darnay Scott	.60	.25	.07
☐ 43 Dan Wilkinson	.35	.16	.04
☐ 44 Derrick Alexander	.60	.25	.07
☐ 45 Leroy Hoard	.20	.09	.03
☐ 46 Michael Jackson	.35	.16	.04
☐ 47 Antonio Langham	.20	.09	.03
☐ 48 Andre Rison	.35	.16	.04
☐ 49 Vinny Testaverde	.35	.16	.04
☐ 50 Eric Turner	.20	.09	.03
☐ 51 Troy Aikman	3.00	1.35	.35
☐ 52 Charles Haley	.35	.16	.04
☐ 53 Michael Irvin	.60	.25	.07
☐ 54 Daryl Johnston	.35	.16	.04
☐ 55 Leon Lett	.20	.09	.03
☐ 56 Jay Novacek	.35	.16	.04
☐ 57 Emmitt Smith	6.00	2.70	.75
☐ 58 Kevin Williams WR	.35	.16	.04
☐ 59 Steve Atwater	.20	.09	.03
☐ 60 Rod Bernstine	.20	.09	.03
☐ 61 John Elway	2.50	1.10	.30
☐ 62 Glyn Milburn	.20	.09	.03
☐ 63 Anthony Miller	.35	.16	.04
☐ 64 Mike Pritchard	.20	.09	.03
☐ 65 Shannon Sharpe	.35	.16	.04
☐ 66 Scott Mitchell	.35	.16	.04
☐ 67 Herman Moore	1.00	.45	.12
☐ 68 Johnnie Morton	.35	.16	.04
☐ 69 Brett Perriman	.35	.16	.04
☐ 70 Barry Sanders	3.00	1.35	.35
☐ 71 Chris Spielman	.35	.16	.04
☐ 72 Edgar Bennett	.35	.16	.04
☐ 73 Robert Brooks	.60	.25	.07
☐ 74 Brett Favre	6.00	2.70	.75
☐ 75 LeShon Johnson	.35	.16	.04
☐ 76 Sean Jones	.20	.09	.03
☐ 77 George Teague	.20	.09	.03
☐ 78 Reggie White	.60	.25	.07
☐ 79 Micheal Barrow	.20	.09	.03
☐ 80 Gary Brown	.20	.09	.03
☐ 81 Mel Gray	.20	.09	.03
☐ 82 Haywood Jeffires	.20	.09	.03
☐ 83 Steve McNair	6.00	2.70	.75
☐ 84 Rodney Thomas	.60	.25	.07
☐ 85 Trev Alberts	.20	.09	.03
☐ 86 Flipper Anderson	.20	.09	.03
☐ 87 Tony Bennett	.20	.09	.03
☐ 88 Quentin Coryatt	.35	.16	.04
☐ 89 Sean Dawkins	.35	.16	.04
☐ 90 Craig Erickson	.20	.09	.03
☐ 91 Marshall Faulk	1.50	.70	.19
☐ 92 Steve Beuerlein	.20	.09	.03
☐ 93 Tony Boselli	.35	.16	.04
☐ 94 Reggie Cobb	.20	.09	.03
☐ 95 Ernest Givins	.20	.09	.03
☐ 96 Desmond Howard	.35	.16	.04
☐ 97 Jeff Lageman	.20	.09	.03
☐ 98 James O.Stewart	.35	.16	.04
☐ 99 Marcus Allen	.60	.25	.07
☐ 100 Steve Bono	.35	.16	.04
☐ 101 Dale Carter	.35	.16	.04
☐ 102 Willie Davis	.35	.16	.04
☐ 103 Lake Dawson	.35	.16	.04
☐ 104 Greg Hill	.35	.16	.04
☐ 105 Neil Smith	.35	.16	.04
☐ 106 Tim Bowens	.20	.09	.03
☐ 107 Bryan Cox	.20	.09	.03
☐ 108 Irving Fryar	.35	.16	.04
☐ 109 Eric Green	.20	.09	.03
☐ 110 Terry Kirby	.35	.16	.04
☐ 111 Dan Marino	6.00	2.70	.75
☐ 112 O.J. McDuffie	.60	.25	.07
☐ 113 Bernie Parmalee	.35	.16	.04
☐ 114 Derrick Alexander	.20	.09	.03
☐ 115 Cris Carter	.60	.25	.07
☐ 116 Qadry Ismail	.35	.16	.04
☐ 117 Warren Moon	.35	.16	.04
☐ 118 Jake Reed	.35	.16	.04
☐ 119 Robert Smith	.60	.25	.07
☐ 120 Dewayne Washington	.35	.16	.04
☐ 121 Drew Bledsoe	3.00	1.35	.35
☐ 122 Vincent Brisby	.20	.09	.03
☐ 123 Ben Coates	.35	.16	.04
☐ 124 Curtis Martin	7.00	3.10	.85
☐ 125 Willie McGinest	.35	.16	.04
☐ 126 Dave Meggett	.20	.09	.03
☐ 127 Chris Slade UER 126	.35	.16	.04
☐ 128 Eric Allen	.20	.09	.03
☐ 129 Mario Bates	.60	.25	.07
☐ 130 Jim Everett	.20	.09	.03
☐ 131 Michael Haynes	.35	.16	.04
☐ 132 Tyrone Hughes	.35	.16	.04
☐ 133 Renaldo Turnbull	.20	.09	.03
☐ 134 Ray Zellars	.35	.16	.04
☐ 135 Michael Brooks	.20	.09	.03
☐ 136 Dave Brown	.35	.16	.04
☐ 137 Rodney Hampton	.35	.16	.04
☐ 138 Thomas Lewis	.35	.16	.04
☐ 139 Mike Sherrard	.20	.09	.03
☐ 140 Herschel Walker	.35	.16	.04
☐ 141 Tyrone Wheatley	1.25	.55	.16
☐ 142 Kyle Brady	.60	.25	.07
☐ 143 Boomer Esiason	.35	.16	.04
☐ 144 Aaron Glenn	.20	.09	.03
☐ 145 Mo Lewis	.20	.09	.03
☐ 146 Johnny Mitchell	.20	.09	.03
☐ 147 Ronald Moore	.20	.09	.03
☐ 148 Joe Aska	.35	.16	.04
☐ 149 Tim Brown	.60	.25	.07
☐ 150 Jeff Hostetler	.35	.16	.04
☐ 151 Rocket Ismail	.35	.16	.04
☐ 152 Napoleon Kaufman	2.00	.90	.25
☐ 153 Chester McGlockton	.35	.16	.04
☐ 154 Harvey Williams	.20	.09	.03
☐ 155 Fred Barnett	.35	.16	.04
☐ 156 Randall Cunningham	.35	.16	.04
☐ 157 Charlie Garner	.35	.16	.04
☐ 158 Mike Mamula	.35	.16	.04
☐ 159 Kevin Turner	.20	.09	.03
☐ 160 Ricky Watters	.60	.25	.07
☐ 161 Calvin Williams	.35	.16	.04
☐ 162 Mark Bruener	.35	.16	.04
☐ 163 Kevin Greene	.35	.16	.04
☐ 164 Charles Johnson	.35	.16	.04
☐ 165 Greg Lloyd	.35	.16	.04
☐ 166 Byron Bam Morris	.35	.16	.04
☐ 167 Neil O'Donnell	.35	.16	.04
☐ 168 Kordell Stewart	6.00	2.70	.75
☐ 169 John L. Williams	.20	.09	.03
☐ 170 Rod Woodson	.35	.16	.04
☐ 171 Jerome Bettis	1.00	.45	.12
☐ 172 Isaac Bruce	1.50	.70	.19
☐ 173 Kevin Carter	.60	.25	.07
☐ 174 Troy Drayton	.20	.09	.03
☐ 175 Sean Gilbert	.35	.16	.04
☐ 176 Carlos Jenkins	.20	.09	.03
☐ 177 Todd Lyght	.20	.09	.03
☐ 178 Chris Miller	.20	.09	.03
☐ 179 Andre Coleman	.20	.09	.03
☐ 180 Stan Humphries	.35	.16	.04
☐ 181 Shawn Jefferson	.20	.09	.03
☐ 182 Natrone Means	.60	.25	.07
☐ 183 Leslie O'Neal	.35	.16	.04
☐ 184 Junior Seau	.60	.25	.07
☐ 185 Mark Seay	.35	.16	.04
☐ 186 William Floyd	.60	.25	.07
☐ 187 Merton Hanks	.20	.09	.03
☐ 188 Brent Jones	.20	.09	.03
☐ 189 Ken Norton	.35	.16	.04
☐ 190 Jerry Rice	3.00	1.35	.35
☐ 191 Deion Sanders	2.00	.90	.25
☐ 192 J.J. Stokes	2.00	.90	.25
☐ 193 Dana Stubblefield	.60	.25	.07
☐ 194 Steve Young	2.50	1.10	.30
☐ 195 Sam Adams	.20	.09	.03
☐ 196 Brian Blades	.35	.16	.04
☐ 197 Joey Galloway	4.00	1.80	.50
☐ 198 Cortez Kennedy	.35	.16	.04
☐ 199 Rick Mirer	.60	.25	.07
☐ 200 Chris Warren	.35	.16	.04
☐ 201 Derrick Brooks	.20	.09	.03
☐ 202 Lawrence Dawsey	.20	.09	.03
☐ 203 Trent Dilfer	.60	.25	.07
☐ 204 Alvin Harper	.20	.09	.03
☐ 205 Jackie Harris	.20	.09	.03
☐ 206 Courtney Hawkins	.20	.09	.03
☐ 207 Hardy Nickerson	.20	.09	.03
☐ 208 Errict Rhett	.60	.25	.07
☐ 209 Warren Sapp	.35	.16	.04
☐ 210 Terry Allen	.35	.16	.04
☐ 211 Tom Carter	.20	.09	.03
☐ 212 Henry Ellard	.35	.16	.04
☐ 213 Darrell Green	.20	.09	.03
☐ 214 Brian Mitchell	.20	.09	.03
☐ 215 Heath Shuler	.60	.25	.07
☐ 216 Michael Westbrook	2.50	1.10	.30
☐ 217 Tydus Winans	.20	.09	.03
☐ 218 Checklist	.20	.09	.03
☐ 219 Checklist	.20	.09	.03
☐ 220 Checklist	.35	.16	.04

1995 Flair Hot Numbers

This 10 card set was randomly inserted into packs at a rate of one in six packs. Card fronts have different color backgrounds similar to the team's colors with different statistical numbers shadowed in the background. At the bottom is the set name followed by the team name and finally, the player's name. Card backs are horizontal with a player shot and a statistical summary of that particular player's prior year.

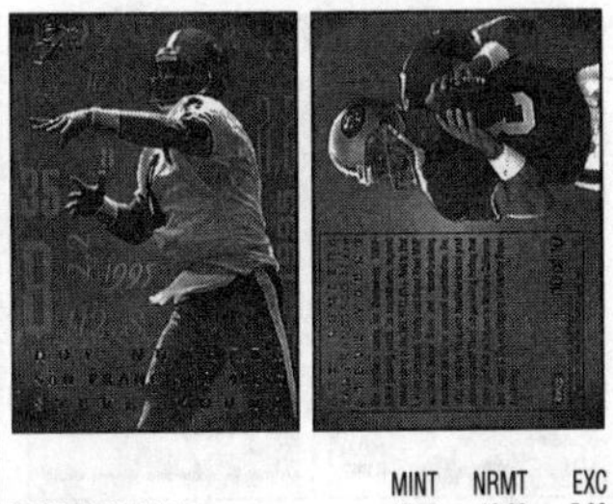

	MINT	NRMT	EXC
COMPLETE SET (10)	40.00	18.00	5.00
COMMON CARD (1-10)	1.25	.55	.16
☐ 1 Jeff Blake	3.00	1.35	.35
☐ 2 Tim Brown	2.00	.90	.25
☐ 3 Drew Bledsoe	6.00	2.70	.75
☐ 4 Ben Coates	1.25	.55	.16
☐ 5 Trent Dilfer	1.25	.55	.16
☐ 6 Brett Favre	12.00	5.50	1.50
☐ 7 Dan Marino	12.00	5.50	1.50
☐ 8 Byron Bam Morris	1.25	.55	.16
☐ 9 Ricky Watters	2.00	.90	.25
☐ 10 Steve Young	5.00	2.20	.60

1995 Flair TD Power

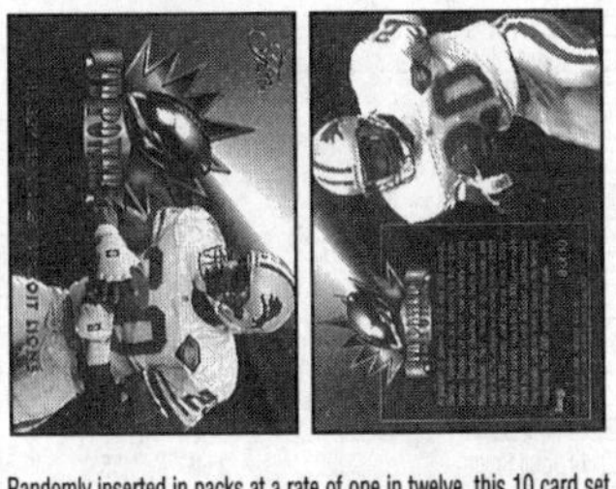

Randomly inserted in packs at a rate of one in twelve, this 10 card set features players who frequent the endzone. Card fronts have silver on one side and purple on the other in the background with a "TD Power" logo beside the player. The player's name and team are located at the bottom of the card. Card backs are similar to the fronts with a statistical summary beside the player.

	MINT	NRMT	EXC
COMPLETE SET (10)	25.00	11.00	3.10
COMMON CARD (1-10)	1.00	.45	.12
☐ 1 Marshall Faulk	2.50	1.10	.30
☐ 2 Natrone Means	1.00	.45	.12
☐ 3 William Floyd	1.00	.45	.12
☐ 4 Byron Bam Morris	1.00	.45	.12
☐ 5 Errict Rhett	1.50	.70	.19
☐ 6 Andre Rison	1.00	.45	.12
☐ 7 Jerry Rice	5.00	2.20	.60
☐ 8 Barry Sanders	5.00	2.20	.60
☐ 9 Emmitt Smith	10.00	4.50	1.25
☐ 10 Chris Warren	1.50	.70	.19

1995 Flair Wave of the Future

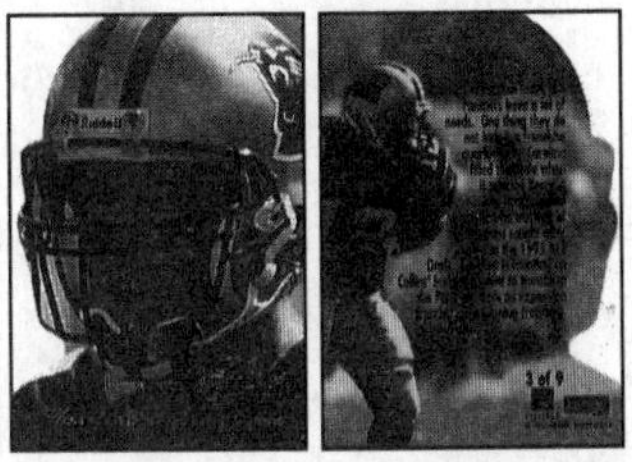

This die cut 10 card set was randomly inserted into packs at a rate of one in 37 and focus on rookie players from 1995. Card fronts contain a die cut head shot of the player with the Wave of the Future logo and the player's name written in script at the bottom. Card backs contain commentary on the player

	MINT	NRMT	EXC
COMPLETE SET (9)	160.00	70.00	20.00
COMMON CARD (1-9)	8.00	3.60	1.00
☐ 1 Kyle Brady	8.00	3.60	1.00
☐ 2 Ki-Jana Carter	12.00	5.50	1.50
☐ 3 Kerry Collins	50.00	22.00	6.25
☐ 4 Joey Galloway	25.00	11.00	3.10
☐ 5 Steve McNair	40.00	18.00	5.00
☐ 6 Rashaan Salaam	15.00	6.75	1.85
☐ 7 James O. Stewart	12.00	5.50	1.50
☐ 8 Michael Westbrook	15.00	6.75	1.85
☐ 9 Tyrone Wheatley	8.00	3.60	1.00

1960 Fleer

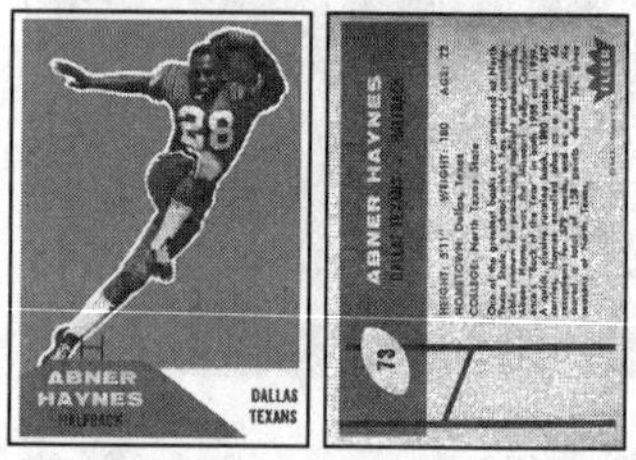

The 1960 Fleer set of 132 standard-size cards was Fleer's first venture into football card production. This set features players of the American Football League's debut season. Several well-known coaches are featured in the set; the set is the last regular issue set to feature coaches (on their own specific card) until the 1989 Pro Set release. The card backs are printed in red and black. The key card in the set is Jack Kemp's Rookie Card. Other Rookie Cards include Sid Gillman, Ron Mix and Hank Stram. The cards are frequently found off-centered as Fleer's first effort into the football card market left much to be desired in the area of quality control. A large quantity of color separations and "proofs" are widely available.

	NRMT	VG-E	GOOD
COMPLETE SET (132)	750.00	350.00	95.00
COMMON CARD (1-132)	3.50	1.55	.45
WRAPPER (5-CENT)	25.00	11.00	3.10

☐ 1 Harvey White	20.00	5.00	1.60
☐ 2 Tom Corky Tharp	3.50	1.55	.45
☐ 3 Dan McGrew	3.50	1.55	.45
☐ 4 Bob White	3.50	1.55	.45
☐ 5 Dick Jamieson	3.50	1.55	.45
☐ 6 Sam Salerno	3.50	1.55	.45
☐ 7 Sid Gillman CO	18.00	8.00	2.20
☐ 8 Ben Preston	3.50	1.55	.45
☐ 9 George Blanch	3.50	1.55	.45
☐ 10 Bob Stransky	3.50	1.55	.45
☐ 11 Fran Curci	3.50	1.55	.45
☐ 12 George Shirkey	3.50	1.55	.45
☐ 13 Paul Larson	3.50	1.55	.45
☐ 14 John Stolte	3.50	1.55	.45
☐ 15 Serafino(Foge) Fazio	5.00	2.20	.60
☐ 16 Tom Dimitroff	3.50	1.55	.45
☐ 17 Elbert Dubenion	12.00	5.50	1.50
☐ 18 Hogan Wharton	3.50	1.55	.45
☐ 19 Tom O'Connell	3.50	1.55	.45
☐ 20 Sammy Baugh CO	45.00	20.00	5.50
☐ 21 Tony Sardisco	3.50	1.55	.45
☐ 22 Alan Cann	3.50	1.55	.45
☐ 23 Mike Hudock	3.50	1.55	.45
☐ 24 Bill Atkins	3.50	1.55	.45
☐ 25 Charlie Jackson	3.50	1.55	.45
☐ 26 Frank Tripucka	5.00	2.20	.60
☐ 27 Tony Teresa	3.50	1.55	.45
☐ 28 Joe Amstutz	3.50	1.55	.45
☐ 29 Bob Fee	3.50	1.55	.45
☐ 30 Jim Baldwin	3.50	1.55	.45
☐ 31 Jim Yates	3.50	1.55	.45
☐ 32 Don Flynn	3.50	1.55	.45
☐ 33 Ken Adamson	3.50	1.55	.45
☐ 34 Ron Drzewiecki	3.50	1.55	.45
☐ 35 J.W. Slack	3.50	1.55	.45
☐ 36 Bob Yates	3.50	1.55	.45
☐ 37 Gary Cobb	3.50	1.55	.45
☐ 38 Jacky Lee	5.00	2.20	.60
☐ 39 Jack Spikes	5.00	2.20	.60
☐ 40 Jim Padgett	3.50	1.55	.45
☐ 41 Jack Larsheid	3.50	1.55	.45
☐ 42 Bob Reifsnyder	3.50	1.55	.45
☐ 43 Fran Rogel	3.50	1.55	.45
☐ 44 Ray Moss	3.50	1.55	.45
☐ 45 Tony Banfield	5.00	2.20	.60
☐ 46 George Herring	3.50	1.55	.45
☐ 47 Willie Smith	3.50	1.55	.45
☐ 48 Buddy Allen	3.50	1.55	.45
☐ 49 Bill Brown	3.50	1.55	.45
☐ 50 Ken Ford	3.50	1.55	.45
☐ 51 Billy Kinard	3.50	1.55	.45
☐ 52 Buddy Mayfield	3.50	1.55	.45
☐ 53 Bill Krisher	3.50	1.55	.45
☐ 54 Frank Bernardi	3.50	1.55	.45
☐ 55 Lou Saban CO	5.00	2.20	.60
☐ 56 Gene Cockrell	3.50	1.55	.45
☐ 57 Sam Sanders	3.50	1.55	.45
☐ 58 George Blanda	45.00	20.00	5.50
☐ 59 Sherrill Headrick	5.00	2.20	.60
☐ 60 Carl Larpenter	3.50	1.55	.45
☐ 61 Gene Prebola	3.50	1.55	.45
☐ 62 Dick Chorovich	3.50	1.55	.45
☐ 63 Bob McNamara	3.50	1.55	.45
☐ 64 Tom Saidock	3.50	1.55	.45
☐ 65 Willie Evans	3.50	1.55	.45
☐ 66 Billy Cannon UER (Hometown: Istruma, should be Istrouma)	18.00	8.00	2.20
☐ 67 Sam McCord	3.50	1.55	.45
☐ 68 Mike Simmons	3.50	1.55	.45
☐ 69 Jim Swink	5.00	2.20	.60
☐ 70 Don Hitt	3.50	1.55	.45
☐ 71 Gerhard Schwedes	3.50	1.55	.45
☐ 72 Thurlow Cooper	3.50	1.55	.45
☐ 73 Abner Haynes	18.00	8.00	2.20
☐ 74 Billy Shoemake	3.50	1.55	.45
☐ 75 Marv Lasater	3.50	1.55	.45
☐ 76 Paul Lowe	16.00	7.25	2.00
☐ 77 Bruce Hartman	3.50	1.55	.45
☐ 78 Blanche Martin	3.50	1.55	.45
☐ 79 Gene Grabosky	3.50	1.55	.45
☐ 80 Lou Rymkus CO	5.00	2.20	.60
☐ 81 Chris Burford	8.00	3.60	1.00
☐ 82 Don Allen	3.50	1.55	.45
☐ 83 Bob Nelson	3.50	1.55	.45
☐ 84 Jim Woodard	3.50	1.55	.45
☐ 85 Tom Rychlec	3.50	1.55	.45
☐ 86 Bob Cox	3.50	1.55	.45
☐ 87 Jerry Cornelison	3.50	1.55	.45
☐ 88 Jack Work	3.50	1.55	.45
☐ 89 Sam DeLuca	3.50	1.55	.45
☐ 90 Rommie Loudd	3.50	1.55	.45
☐ 91 Teddy Edmondson	3.50	1.55	.45
☐ 92 Buster Ramsey CO	3.50	1.55	.45
☐ 93 Doug Asad	3.50	1.55	.45
☐ 94 Jimmy Harris	3.50	1.55	.45
☐ 95 Larry Cundiff	3.50	1.55	.45
☐ 96 Richie Lucas	5.00	2.20	.60
☐ 97 Don Norwood	3.50	1.55	.45
☐ 98 Larry Grantham	5.00	2.20	.60
☐ 99 Bill Mathis	5.00	2.20	.60
☐ 100 Mel Branch	5.00	2.20	.60
☐ 101 Marvin Terrell	3.50	1.55	.45
☐ 102 Charlie Flowers	3.50	1.55	.45
☐ 103 John McMullan	3.50	1.55	.45
☐ 104 Charlie Kaaihue	3.50	1.55	.45
☐ 105 Joe Schaffer	3.50	1.55	.45
☐ 106 Al Day	3.50	1.55	.45
☐ 107 Johnny Carson	3.50	1.55	.45
☐ 108 Alan Goldstein	3.50	1.55	.45
☐ 109 Doug Cline	3.50	1.55	.45
☐ 110 Al Carmichael	3.50	1.55	.45
☐ 111 Bob Dee	3.50	1.55	.45
☐ 112 John Bredice	3.50	1.55	.45
☐ 113 Don Floyd	3.50	1.55	.45
☐ 114 Ronnie Cain	3.50	1.55	.45
☐ 115 Stan Flowers	3.50	1.55	.45
☐ 116 Hank Stram CO	45.00	20.00	5.50
☐ 117 Bob Dougherty	3.50	1.55	.45
☐ 118 Ron Mix	35.00	16.00	4.40
☐ 119 Roger Ellis	3.50	1.55	.45
☐ 120 Elvin Caldwell	3.50	1.55	.45
☐ 121 Bill Kimber	3.50	1.55	.45
☐ 122 Jim Matheny	3.50	1.55	.45
☐ 123 Curley Johnson	3.50	1.55	.45
☐ 124 Jack Kemp	350.00	160.00	45.00
☐ 125 Ed Denk	3.50	1.55	.45
☐ 126 Jerry McFarland	3.50	1.55	.45
☐ 127 Dan Lanphear	3.50	1.55	.45
☐ 128 Paul Maguire	18.00	8.00	2.20
☐ 129 Ray Collins	3.50	1.55	.45
☐ 130 Ron Burton	7.00	3.10	.85
☐ 131 Eddie Erdelatz CO	3.50	1.55	.45
☐ 132 Ron Beagle	15.00	3.70	1.20

1960 Fleer AFL Team Decals

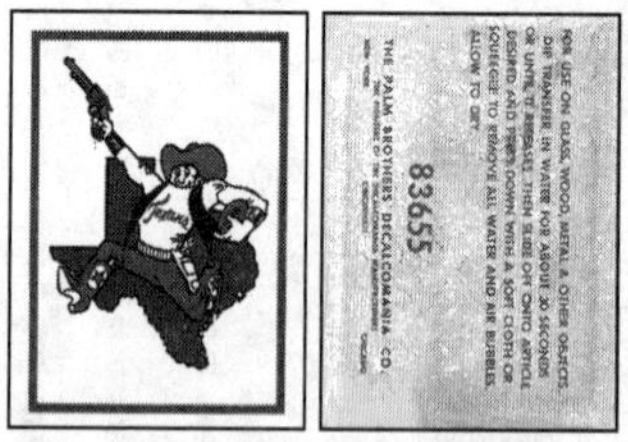

This set of nine logo decals was inserted with the 1960 Fleer regular issue inaugural AFL football set. These inserts measure approximately 2 1/4" by 3" and one decal was to be inserted in each wax pack. The decals are unnumbered and are ordered below alphabetically by team name for convenience. There is one decal for each of the eight AFL teams as well as a decal with the league logo. The backs of the decal backing contained instructions on the proper application of the decal.

	NRMT	VG-E	GOOD
COMPLETE SET (9)	150.00	70.00	19.00
COMMON CARD	12.00	5.50	1.50

☐ 1 AFL Logo	20.00	9.00	2.50
☐ 2 Boston Patriots	12.00	5.50	1.50
☐ 3 Buffalo Bills	15.00	6.75	1.85
☐ 4 Dallas Texans	20.00	9.00	2.50
☐ 5 Denver Broncos	15.00	6.75	1.85
☐ 6 Houston Oilers	12.00	5.50	1.50
☐ 7 Los Angeles Chargers	15.00	6.75	1.85
☐ 8 New York Titans	18.00	8.00	2.20
☐ 9 Oakland Raiders	30.00	13.50	3.70

1960 Fleer College Pennant Decals

This set of 19 pennant decal pairs was distributed as an insert with the 1960 Fleer regular issue inaugural AFL football set along with and at the same time as the AFL Team Decals described immediately

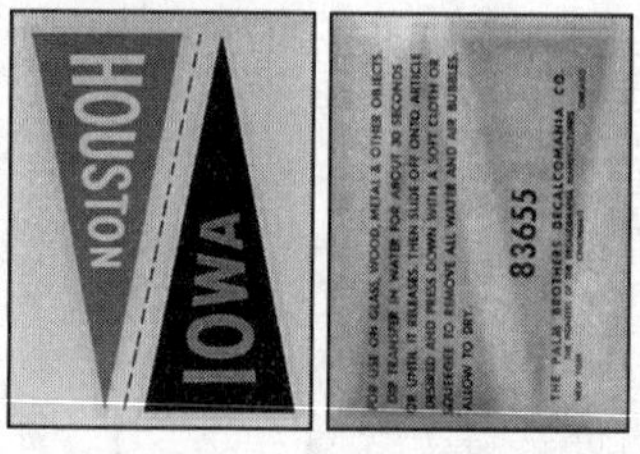

above. Some dealers feel that these college decals are tougher to find than the AFL team decals. These inserts were approximately 2 1/4" by 3" and one decal was to be inserted in each wax pack. The decals are unnumbered and are ordered below alphabetically according to the lower alphabetically of each college pair. The backs of the decal backing contained instructions on the proper application of the decal printed in very light blue.

	NRMT	VG-E	GOOD
COMPLETE SET (19)	175.00	80.00	22.00
COMMON CARD (1-19)	7.50	3.40	.95

☐ 1 Alabama/Yale	12.00	5.50	1.50
☐ 2 Army/Mississippi	7.50	3.40	.95
☐ 3 California/Indiana	7.50	3.40	.95
☐ 4 Duke/Notre Dame	16.00	7.25	2.00
☐ 5 Florida St./Kentucky	12.00	5.50	1.50
☐ 6 Georgia/Oklahoma	12.00	5.50	1.50
☐ 7 Houston/Iowa	7.50	3.40	.95
☐ 8 Idaho St./Penn.	7.50	3.40	.95
☐ 9 Iowa St./Penn State	12.00	5.50	1.50
☐ 10 Kansas/UCLA	10.00	4.50	1.25
☐ 11 Marquette/New Mexico	7.50	3.40	.95
☐ 12 Maryland/Missouri	7.50	3.40	.95
☐ 13 Miss.South./N.Carolina	7.50	3.40	.95
☐ 14 Navy/Stanford	10.00	4.50	1.25
☐ 15 Nebraska/Purdue	12.00	5.50	1.50
☐ 16 Pittsburgh/Utah	7.50	3.40	.95
☐ 17 SMU/West Virginia	7.50	3.40	.95
☐ 18 So.Carolina/USC	10.00	4.50	1.25
☐ 19 Wake Forest/Wisconsin	7.50	3.40	.95

1961 Fleer

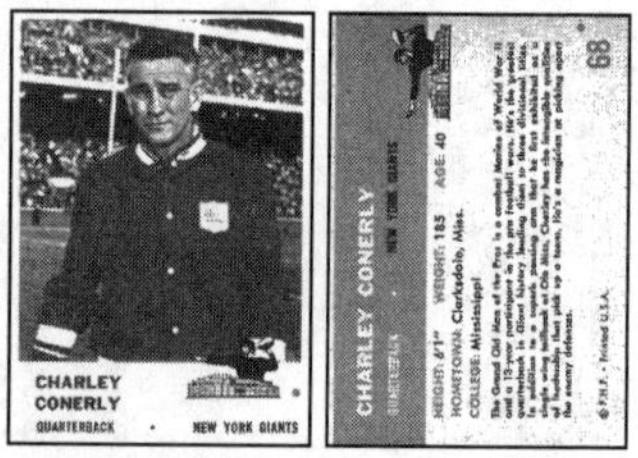

The 1961 Fleer football set contains 220 standard-size cards. The set contains NFL (1-132) and AFL (133-220) players. The cards are grouped alphabetically by team nicknames within league. The backs are printed in black and lime green on a white card stock. The AFL cards are often found in uncut sheet form. The key Rookie Cards in this set are John Brodie, Tom Flores, Don Maynard, Don Meredith, and Jim Otto.

	NRMT	VG-E	GOOD
COMPLETE SET (220)	1600.00	700.00	200.00
COMMON CARD (1-132)	4.00	1.80	.50
COMMON CARD (133-220)	6.00	2.70	.75
WRAPPER (5-CENT, SERIES I)	25.00	11.00	3.10
WRAPPER (5-CENT, SERIES II)	30.00	13.50	3.70

☐ 1 Ed Brown	12.00	3.00	.95
☐ 2 Rick Casares	6.00	2.70	.75
☐ 3 Willie Galimore	6.00	2.70	.75
☐ 4 Jim Dooley	4.00	1.80	.50
☐ 5 Harlon Hill	4.00	1.80	.50
☐ 6 Stan Jones	7.00	3.10	.85
☐ 7 J.C. Caroline	4.00	1.80	.50
☐ 8 Joe Fortunato	4.00	1.80	.50
☐ 9 Doug Atkins	8.00	3.60	1.00
☐ 10 Milt Plum	6.00	2.70	.75
☐ 11 Jim Brown	140.00	65.00	17.50
☐ 12 Bobby Mitchell	10.00	4.50	1.25
☐ 13 Ray Renfro	6.00	2.70	.75
☐ 14 Gern Nagler	4.00	1.80	.50
☐ 15 Jim Shofner	4.00	1.80	.50
☐ 16 Vince Costello	4.00	1.80	.50
☐ 17 Galen Fiss	4.00	1.80	.50
☐ 18 Walt Michaels	6.00	2.70	.75
☐ 19 Bob Gain	4.00	1.80	.50
☐ 20 Mal Hammack	4.00	1.80	.50
☐ 21 Frank Mestnick	4.00	1.80	.50
☐ 22 Bobby Joe Conrad	6.00	2.70	.75
☐ 23 John David Crow	6.00	2.70	.75
☐ 24 Sonny Randle	6.00	2.70	.75
☐ 25 Don Gillis	4.00	1.80	.50
☐ 26 Jerry Norton	4.00	1.80	.50
☐ 27 Bill Stacy	4.00	1.80	.50
☐ 28 Leo Sugar	4.00	1.80	.50
☐ 29 Frank Fuller	4.00	1.80	.50
☐ 30 John Unitas	60.00	27.00	7.50
☐ 31 Alan Ameche	8.00	3.60	1.00
☐ 32 Lenny Moore	15.00	6.75	1.85
☐ 33 Raymond Berry	15.00	6.75	1.85
☐ 34 Jim Mutscheller	4.00	1.80	.50
☐ 35 Jim Parker	8.00	3.60	1.00
☐ 36 Bill Pellington	4.00	1.80	.50
☐ 37 Gino Marchetti	10.00	4.50	1.25
☐ 38 Gene Lipscomb	6.00	2.70	.75
☐ 39 Art Donovan	15.00	6.75	1.85
☐ 40 Eddie LeBaron	6.00	2.70	.75
☐ 41 Don Meredith	160.00	70.00	20.00
☐ 42 Don McIlhenny	4.00	1.80	.50
☐ 43 L.G. Dupre	4.00	1.80	.50
☐ 44 Fred Dugan	4.00	1.80	.50
☐ 45 Billy Howton	6.00	2.70	.75
☐ 46 Duane Putnam	4.00	1.80	.50
☐ 47 Gene Cronin	4.00	1.80	.50
☐ 48 Jerry Tubbs	4.00	1.80	.50
☐ 49 Clarence Peaks	4.00	1.80	.50
☐ 50 Ted Dean	4.00	1.80	.50
☐ 51 Tommy McDonald	6.00	2.70	.75
☐ 52 Bill Barnes	4.00	1.80	.50
☐ 53 Pete Retzlaff	6.00	2.70	.75
☐ 54 Bobby Walston	4.00	1.80	.50
☐ 55 Chuck Bednarik	12.00	5.50	1.50
☐ 56 Maxie Baughan	6.00	2.70	.75
☐ 57 Bob Pellegrini	4.00	1.80	.50
☐ 58 Jesse Richardson	4.00	1.80	.50
☐ 59 John Brodie	50.00	22.00	6.25
☐ 60 J.D. Smith	6.00	2.70	.75
☐ 61 Ray Norton	4.00	1.80	.50
☐ 62 Monty Stickles	4.00	1.80	.50
☐ 63 Bob St. Clair	7.00	3.10	.85
☐ 64 Dave Baker	4.00	1.80	.50
☐ 65 Abe Woodson	4.00	1.80	.50
☐ 66 Matt Hazeltine	4.00	1.80	.50
☐ 67 Leo Nomellini	10.00	4.50	1.25
☐ 68 Charley Conerly	10.00	4.50	1.25
☐ 69 Kyle Rote	6.00	2.70	.75
☐ 70 Jack Stroud	4.00	1.80	.50
☐ 71 Roosevelt Brown	7.00	3.10	.85
☐ 72 Jim Patton	4.00	1.80	.50
☐ 73 Erich Barnes	4.00	1.80	.50
☐ 74 Sam Huff	15.00	6.75	1.85
☐ 75 Andy Robustelli	8.00	3.60	1.00
☐ 76 Dick Modzelewski	4.00	1.80	.50
☐ 77 Roosevelt Grier	7.00	3.10	.85
☐ 78 Earl Morrall	7.00	3.10	.85
☐ 79 Jim Ninowski	4.00	1.80	.50
☐ 80 Nick Pietrosante	6.00	2.70	.75
☐ 81 Howard Cassady	6.00	2.70	.75
☐ 82 Jim Gibbons	4.00	1.80	.50
☐ 83 Gail Cogdill	6.00	2.70	.75
☐ 84 Dick Lane	7.00	3.10	.85
☐ 85 Yale Lary	7.00	3.10	.85
☐ 86 Joe Schmidt	8.00	3.60	1.00
☐ 87 Darris McCord	4.00	1.80	.50
☐ 88 Bart Starr	60.00	27.00	7.50
☐ 89 Jim Taylor	45.00	20.00	5.50
☐ 90 Paul Hornung	55.00	25.00	7.00
☐ 91 Tom Moore	7.00	3.10	.85
☐ 92 Boyd Dowler	12.00	5.50	1.50
☐ 93 Max McGee	7.00	3.10	.85
☐ 94 Forrest Gregg	8.00	3.60	1.00
☐ 95 Jerry Kramer	10.00	4.50	1.25
☐ 96 Jim Ringo	8.00	3.60	1.00
☐ 97 Bill Forester	4.00	1.80	.50
☐ 98 Frank Ryan	6.00	2.70	.75
☐ 99 Ollie Matson	10.00	4.50	1.25
☐ 100 Jon Arnett	6.00	2.70	.75
☐ 101 Dick Bass	6.00	2.70	.75
☐ 102 Jim Phillips	4.00	1.80	.50
☐ 103 Del Shofner	6.00	2.70	.75
☐ 104 Art Hunter	4.00	1.80	.50
☐ 105 Lindon Crow	4.00	1.80	.50
☐ 106 Les Richter	6.00	2.70	.75
☐ 107 Lou Michaels	4.00	1.80	.50
☐ 108 Ralph Guglielmi	4.00	1.80	.50
☐ 109 Don Bosseler	4.00	1.80	.50
☐ 110 John Olszewski	4.00	1.80	.50
☐ 111 Bill Anderson	4.00	1.80	.50
☐ 112 Joe Walton	4.00	1.80	.50
☐ 113 Jim Schrader	4.00	1.80	.50
☐ 114 Gary Glick	4.00	1.80	.50
☐ 115 Ralph Felton	4.00	1.80	.50
☐ 116 Bob Toneff	4.00	1.80	.50
☐ 117 Bobby Layne	35.00	16.00	4.40
☐ 118 John Henry Johnson	8.00	3.60	1.00
☐ 119 Tom Tracy	6.00	2.70	.75
☐ 120 Jimmy Orr	8.00	3.60	1.00
☐ 121 John Nisby	4.00	1.80	.50
☐ 122 Dean Derby	4.00	1.80	.50
☐ 123 John Reger	4.00	1.80	.50
☐ 124 George Tarasovic	4.00	1.80	.50
☐ 125 Ernie Stautner	10.00	4.50	1.25
☐ 126 George Shaw	4.00	1.80	.50
☐ 127 Hugh McElhenny	12.00	5.50	1.50
☐ 128 Dick Haley	4.00	1.80	.50
☐ 129 Dave Middleton	4.00	1.80	.50
☐ 130 Perry Richards	4.00	1.80	.50
☐ 131 Gene Johnson	4.00	1.80	.50
☐ 132 Don Joyce	4.00	1.80	.50
☐ 133 John(Chuck) Green	8.00	3.60	1.00
☐ 134 Wray Carlton	8.00	3.60	1.00
☐ 135 Richie Lucas	8.00	3.60	1.00

☐ 136 Elbert Dubenion	8.00	3.60	1.00
☐ 137 Tom Rychlec	6.00	2.70	.75
☐ 138 Mack Yoho	6.00	2.70	.75
☐ 139 Phil Blazer	6.00	2.70	.75
☐ 140 Dan McGrew	6.00	2.70	.75
☐ 141 Bill Atkins	6.00	2.70	.75
☐ 142 Archie Matsos	6.00	2.70	.75
☐ 143 Gene Grabosky	6.00	2.70	.75
☐ 144 Frank Tripucka	8.00	3.60	1.00
☐ 145 Al Carmichael	6.00	2.70	.75
☐ 146 Bob McNamara	6.00	2.70	.75
☐ 147 Lionel Taylor	14.00	6.25	1.75
☐ 148 Eldon Danenhauer	6.00	2.70	.75
☐ 149 Willie Smith	6.00	2.70	.75
☐ 150 Carl Larpenter	6.00	2.70	.75
☐ 151 Ken Adamson	6.00	2.70	.75
☐ 152 Goose Gonsoulin	10.00	4.50	1.25
☐ 153 Joe Young	6.00	2.70	.75
☐ 154 Gordy Molz	6.00	2.70	.75
☐ 155 Jack Kemp	225.00	100.00	28.00
☐ 156 Charlie Flowers	6.00	2.70	.75
☐ 157 Paul Lowe	12.00	5.50	1.50
☐ 158 Don Norton	6.00	2.70	.75
☐ 159 Howard Clark	6.00	2.70	.75
☐ 160 Paul Maguire	14.00	6.25	1.75
☐ 161 Ernie Wright	10.00	4.50	1.25
☐ 162 Ron Mix	15.00	6.75	1.85
☐ 163 Fred Cole	6.00	2.70	.75
☐ 164 Jim Sears	6.00	2.70	.75
☐ 165 Volney Peters	6.00	2.70	.75
☐ 166 George Blanda	45.00	20.00	5.50
☐ 167 Jacky Lee	8.00	3.60	1.00
☐ 168 Bob White	6.00	2.70	.75
☐ 169 Doug Cline	6.00	2.70	.75
☐ 170 Dave Smith	6.00	2.70	.75
☐ 171 Billy Cannon	14.00	6.25	1.75
☐ 172 Bill Groman	6.00	2.70	.75
☐ 173 Al Jamison	6.00	2.70	.75
☐ 174 Jim Norton	6.00	2.70	.75
☐ 175 Dennit Morris	6.00	2.70	.75
☐ 176 Don Floyd	6.00	2.70	.75
☐ 177 Butch Songin	6.00	2.70	.75
☐ 178 Billy Lott	6.00	2.70	.75
☐ 179 Ron Burton	8.00	3.60	1.00
☐ 180 Jim Colclough	6.00	2.70	.75
☐ 181 Charley Leo	6.00	2.70	.75
☐ 182 Walt Cudzik	6.00	2.70	.75
☐ 183 Fred Bruney	6.00	2.70	.75
☐ 184 Ross O'Hanley	6.00	2.70	.75
☐ 185 Tony Sardisco	6.00	2.70	.75
☐ 186 Harry Jacobs	6.00	2.70	.75
☐ 187 Bob Dee	6.00	2.70	.75
☐ 188 Tom Flores	30.00	13.50	3.70
☐ 189 Jack Larsheid	6.00	2.70	.75
☐ 190 Dick Christy	6.00	2.70	.75
☐ 191 Alan Miller	6.00	2.70	.75
☐ 192 James Smith	6.00	2.70	.75
☐ 193 Gerald Burch	6.00	2.70	.75
☐ 194 Gene Prebola	6.00	2.70	.75
☐ 195 Alan Goldstein	6.00	2.70	.75
☐ 196 Don Manoukian	6.00	2.70	.75
☐ 197 Jim Otto	65.00	29.00	8.00
☐ 198 Wayne Crow	6.00	2.70	.75
☐ 199 Cotton Davidson	8.00	3.60	1.00
☐ 200 Randy Duncan	8.00	3.60	1.00
☐ 201 Jack Spikes	8.00	3.60	1.00
☐ 202 Johnny Robinson	14.00	6.25	1.75
☐ 203 Abner Haynes	14.00	6.25	1.75
☐ 204 Chris Burford	8.00	3.60	1.00
☐ 205 Bill Krisher	6.00	2.70	.75
☐ 206 Marvin Terrell	6.00	2.70	.75
☐ 207 Jimmy Harris	6.00	2.70	.75
☐ 208 Mel Branch	8.00	3.60	1.00
☐ 209 Paul Miller	6.00	2.70	.75
☐ 210 Al Dorow	6.00	2.70	.75
☐ 211 Dick Jamieson	6.00	2.70	.75
☐ 212 Pete Hart	6.00	2.70	.75
☐ 213 Bill Shockley	6.00	2.70	.75
☐ 214 Dewey Bohling	6.00	2.70	.75
☐ 215 Don Maynard	90.00	40.00	11.00
☐ 216 Bob Mischak	6.00	2.70	.75
☐ 217 Mike Hudock	6.00	2.70	.75
☐ 218 Bob Reifsnyder	6.00	2.70	.75
☐ 219 Tom Saidock	6.00	2.70	.75
☐ 220 Sid Youngelman	22.00	5.50	1.75

1961 Fleer Magic Message Blue Inserts

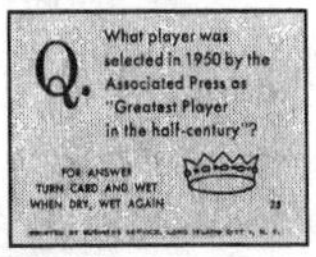

This unattractive set contains 40 cards that were inserted in 1961 Fleer football wax packs. The cards are light blue in color and measure approximately 3" by 2 1/8". The fronts feature a question and a crude line drawing. For the answer, the collector is instructed to "Turn card and wet; when dry, wet again." A tag line at the bottom of the front indicates that the cards were printed by Business Service of Long Island, New York. The backs are blank, and the cards are numbered on the front in the lower right corner.

	NRMT	VG-E	GOOD
COMPLETE SET (40)	150.00	70.00	19.00
COMMON CARD (1-40)	4.00	1.80	.50
☐ 1 When was the first Sugar Bowl game played	4.00	1.80	.50
☐ 2 Which school was famous for its Point-A-Minute team	4.00	1.80	.50
☐ 3 What famous coach was known as Gloomy Gil	4.00	1.80	.50
☐ 4 Which college coach holds the longest record for years coached	4.00	1.80	.50
☐ 5 What is meant by two Platoon System	4.00	1.80	.50
☐ 6 When was the only Sudden Death playoff in NFL history	4.00	1.80	.50
☐ 7 What is a Sudden Death playoff in professional football	4.00	1.80	.50
☐ 8 What is the longest field goal kicked in pro football (place kick)	4.00	1.80	.50
☐ 9 What famous Colorado All-American now holds a key position in President Kennedy's administration (Whizzer White)	4.00	1.80	.50
☐ 10 What Michigan All-American has gained added fame as a radio and television sportscaster (Tom Harmon)	4.00	1.80	.50
☐ 11 The North-South game has become an annual classic. Do you know where it was first played	4.00	1.80	.50
☐ 12 The Army-Navy game has become an annual classic. Do you know when it was first played	4.00	1.80	.50
☐ 13 What slugging major league outfielder was an All-American back during his college days	4.00	1.80	.50
☐ 14 What All-Americans were known as Mr. Inside and Mr. Outside (Glenn Davis and Doc Blanchard)	4.00	1.80	.50
☐ 15 Which team was called the Thundering Herd	4.00	1.80	.50
☐ 16 When was the first championship playoff in the National Football League	4.00	1.80	.50
☐ 17 What is the record for field goals dropkicked in a single game	4.00	1.80	.50
☐ 18 What is the longest winning streak in college football	4.00	1.80	.50
☐ 19 Who was the first collegian gained by draft in the National Football League	4.00	1.80	.50
☐ 20 Which team was the first to use the huddle	4.00	1.80	.50
☐ 21 Who was the first Intercollegiate Champion	4.00	1.80	.50
☐ 22 When was the first broadcast of a football game	4.00	1.80	.50
☐ 23 What is the longest field goal (placement kick) on record	4.00	1.80	.50
☐ 24 What is the origin of the tackling dummy	4.00	1.80	.50
☐ 25 What player was selected in 1950 as Greatest Player in the half-century (Jim Thorpe)	4.00	1.80	.50
☐ 26 What is the record for the most touchdowns in a game	4.00	1.80	.50
☐ 27 What player ran the wrong way in a bowl game	4.00	1.80	.50
☐ 28 When was the first field goal attempted in college football	4.00	1.80	.50
☐ 29 When and by whom was the first All-American team selected	4.00	1.80	.50
☐ 30 When was the forward pass first used	4.00	1.80	.50
☐ 31 What was the first college to put numbers on player's jerseys	4.00	1.80	.50
☐ 32 When was the first professional football game played	4.00	1.80	.50
☐ 33 Where is the Football Hall of Fame to be erected (Canton, Ohio)	4.00	1.80	.50
☐ 34 Who were the Four Horsemen	4.00	1.80	.50
☐ 35 When was the first Rose Bowl game played	4.00	1.80	.50
☐ 36 Who holds the record for the most forward passes attempted in a professional game	4.00	1.80	.50
☐ 37 Who was known as the Galloping Ghost (Red Grange)	4.00	1.80	.50
☐ 38 Has the Rose Bowl always been played in California	4.00	1.80	.50
☐ 39 Which team featured the Seven Blocks of Granite (Fordham)	4.00	1.80	.50
☐ 40 Where and when was the first football game played in the United States	4.00	1.80	.50

1962 Fleer

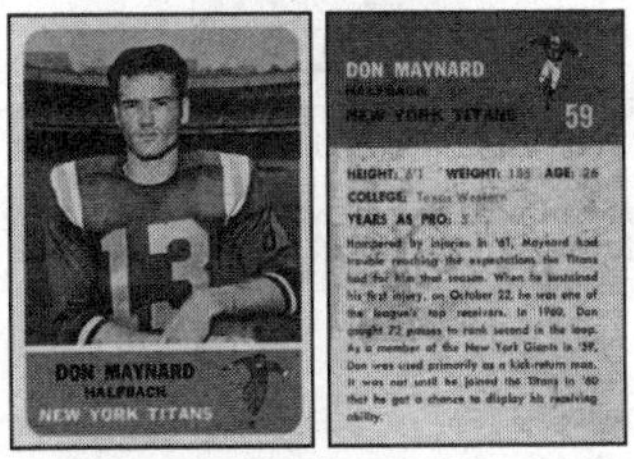

The 1962 Fleer football set contains 88 standard-size cards featuring AFL players only. The set was issued in six-card nickel packs with a slab of bubble gum. Card numbering is alphabetical by team city. The card backs are printed in black and blue on a white card stock. Key Rookie Cards in this set are Gino Cappelletti, Charlie Hennigan, Ernie Ladd and Fred Williamson.

	NRMT	VG-E	GOOD
COMPLETE SET (88)	900.00	400.00	110.00
COMMON CARD (1-88)	7.00	3.10	.85
WRAPPER (5-CENT)	200.00	90.00	25.00
☐ 1 Billy Lott	16.00	4.00	1.30
☐ 2 Ron Burton	8.00	3.60	1.00
☐ 3 Gino Cappelletti	16.00	7.25	2.00
☐ 4 Babe Parilli	8.00	3.60	1.00
☐ 5 Jim Colclough	7.00	3.10	.85
☐ 6 Tony Sardisco	7.00	3.10	.85
☐ 7 Walt Cudzik	7.00	3.10	.85
☐ 8 Bob Dee	7.00	3.10	.85
☐ 9 Tommy Addison	7.00	3.10	.85
☐ 10 Harry Jacobs	7.00	3.10	.85
☐ 11 Ross O'Hanley	7.00	3.10	.85
☐ 12 Art Baker	7.00	3.10	.85
☐ 13 Johnny Green	7.00	3.10	.85
☐ 14 Elbert Dubenion	8.00	3.60	1.00
☐ 15 Tom Rychlec	7.00	3.10	.85
☐ 16 Billy Shaw	8.00	3.60	1.00
☐ 17 Ken Rice	7.00	3.10	.85
☐ 18 Bill Atkins	7.00	3.10	.85
☐ 19 Richie Lucas	7.00	3.10	.85
☐ 20 Archie Matsos	7.00	3.10	.85
☐ 21 Lavern Torczon	7.00	3.10	.85
☐ 22 Warren Rabb	7.00	3.10	.85
☐ 23 Jack Spikes	8.00	3.60	1.00
☐ 24 Cotton Davidson	8.00	3.60	1.00
☐ 25 Abner Haynes	14.00	6.25	1.75
☐ 26 Jimmy Saxton	7.00	3.10	.85
☐ 27 Chris Burford	8.00	3.60	1.00
☐ 28 Bill Miller	7.00	3.10	.85
☐ 29 Sherrill Headrick	8.00	3.60	1.00
☐ 30 E.J. Holub	8.00	3.60	1.00
☐ 31 Jerry Mays	10.00	4.50	1.25
☐ 32 Mel Branch	7.00	3.10	.85
☐ 33 Paul Rochester	7.00	3.10	.85
☐ 34 Frank Tripucka	8.00	3.60	1.00
☐ 35 Gene Mingo	7.00	3.10	.85
☐ 36 Lionel Taylor	10.00	4.50	1.25
☐ 37 Ken Adamson	7.00	3.10	.85
☐ 38 Eldon Danenhauer	7.00	3.10	.85
☐ 39 Goose Gonsoulin	8.00	3.60	1.00
☐ 40 Gordy Holz	7.00	3.10	.85
☐ 41 Bud McFadin	7.00	3.10	.85
☐ 42 Jim Stinnette	7.00	3.10	.85
☐ 43 Bob Hudson	7.00	3.10	.85
☐ 44 George Herring	7.00	3.10	.85
☐ 45 Charley Tolar	7.00	3.10	.85
☐ 46 George Blanda	50.00	22.00	6.25
☐ 47 Billy Cannon	14.00	6.25	1.75
☐ 48 Charlie Hennigan	16.00	7.25	2.00
☐ 49 Bill Groman	7.00	3.10	.85
☐ 50 Al Jamison	7.00	3.10	.85
☐ 51 Tony Banfield	7.00	3.10	.85
☐ 52 Jim Norton	7.00	3.10	.85
☐ 53 Dennit Morris	7.00	3.10	.85
☐ 54 Don Floyd	7.00	3.10	.85
☐ 55 Ed Husmann UER (Misspelled Hussman on both sides)	7.00	3.10	.85
☐ 56 Robert Brooks	7.00	3.10	.85
☐ 57 Al Dorow	7.00	3.10	.85
☐ 58 Dick Christy	7.00	3.10	.85
☐ 59 Don Maynard	50.00	22.00	6.25
☐ 60 Art Powell	10.00	4.50	1.25
☐ 61 Mike Hudock	7.00	3.10	.85
☐ 62 Bill Mathis	7.00	3.10	.85
☐ 63 Butch Songin	7.00	3.10	.85
☐ 64 Larry Grantham	7.00	3.10	.85
☐ 65 Nick Mumley	7.00	3.10	.85
☐ 66 Tom Saidock	7.00	3.10	.85
☐ 67 Alan Miller	7.00	3.10	.85
☐ 68 Tom Flores	14.00	6.25	1.75
☐ 69 Bob Coolbaugh	7.00	3.10	.85
☐ 70 George Fleming	7.00	3.10	.85
☐ 71 Wayne Hawkins	7.00	3.10	.85
☐ 72 Jim Otto	35.00	16.00	4.40
☐ 73 Wayne Crow	7.00	3.10	.85
☐ 74 Fred Williamson	25.00	11.00	3.10
☐ 75 Tom Louderback	7.00	3.10	.85
☐ 76 Volney Peters	7.00	3.10	.85
☐ 77 Charley Powell	7.00	3.10	.85
☐ 78 Don Norton	7.00	3.10	.85
☐ 79 Jack Kemp	250.00	110.00	31.00
☐ 80 Paul Lowe	12.00	5.50	1.50
☐ 81 Dave Kocourek	7.00	3.10	.85
☐ 82 Ron Mix	16.00	7.25	2.00
☐ 83 Ernie Wright	8.00	3.60	1.00
☐ 84 Dick Harris	7.00	3.10	.85
☐ 85 Bill Hudson	7.00	3.10	.85
☐ 86 Ernie Ladd	25.00	11.00	3.10
☐ 87 Earl Faison	8.00	3.60	1.00
☐ 88 Ron Nery	18.00	4.50	1.45

1963 Fleer

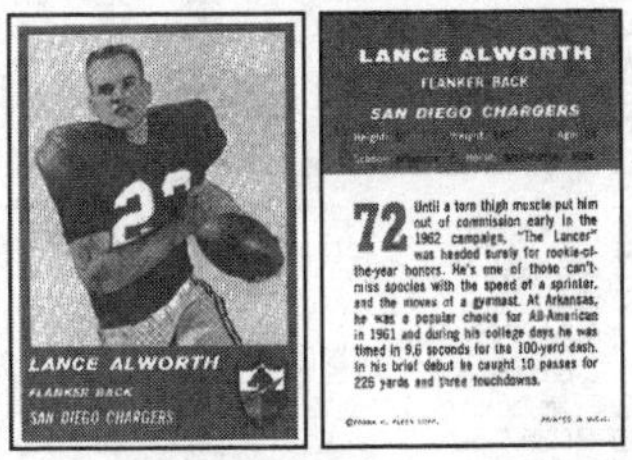

The 1963 Fleer football set of 88 standard-size cards features AFL players only. Card numbering is in team order. Card numbers 6 and 64 are more difficult to obtain than the other cards in the set; their shortage is believed to be attributable to their possible replacement on the printing sheet by the unnumbered checklist. The card backs are printed in red and black on a white card stock. The set price below does not include the checklist card. Cards with numbers divisible by four can be found with or without a red stripe on the bottom of the card back; it is thought that those without the red stripe are in lesser supply. Currently, there is no difference in value. The key Rookie Cards in this set are Lance Alworth, Nick Buoniconti, and Len Dawson.

	NRMT	VG-E	GOOD
COMPLETE SET (88)	1800.00	800.00	220.00
COMMON CARD (1-88)	8.00	3.60	1.00
WRAPPER (5-CENT)	125.00	55.00	15.50
☐ 1 Larry Garron	20.00	5.00	1.60
☐ 2 Babe Parilli	10.00	4.50	1.25
☐ 3 Ron Burton	10.00	4.50	1.25
☐ 4 Jim Colclough	8.00	3.60	1.00
☐ 5 Gino Cappelletti	10.00	4.50	1.25
☐ 6 Charles Long SP	160.00	70.00	20.00
☐ 7 Bill Neighbors	8.00	3.60	1.00
☐ 8 Dick Felt	8.00	3.60	1.00
☐ 9 Tommy Addison	8.00	3.60	1.00
☐ 10 Nick Buoniconti	65.00	29.00	8.00
☐ 11 Larry Eisenhauer	8.00	3.60	1.00
☐ 12 Bill Mathis	8.00	3.60	1.00
☐ 13 Lee Grosscup	10.00	4.50	1.25
☐ 14 Dick Christy	8.00	3.60	1.00
☐ 15 Don Maynard	55.00	25.00	7.00
☐ 16 Alex Kroll	8.00	3.60	1.00
☐ 17 Bob Mischak	8.00	3.60	1.00
☐ 18 Dainard Paulson	8.00	3.60	1.00
☐ 19 Lee Riley	8.00	3.60	1.00
☐ 20 Larry Grantham	10.00	4.50	1.25
☐ 21 Hubert Bobo	8.00	3.60	1.00
☐ 22 Nick Mumley	8.00	3.60	1.00
☐ 23 Cookie Gilchrist	45.00	20.00	5.50

☐ 24 Jack Kemp	250.00	110.00	31.00
☐ 25 Wray Carlton	8.00	3.60	1.00
☐ 26 Elbert Dubenion	10.00	4.50	1.25
☐ 27 Ernie Warlick	8.00	3.60	1.00
☐ 28 Billy Shaw	8.00	3.60	1.00
☐ 29 Ken Rice	8.00	3.60	1.00
☐ 30 Booker Edgerson	8.00	3.60	1.00
☐ 31 Ray Abruzzese	8.00	3.60	1.00
☐ 32 Mike Stratton	10.00	4.50	1.25
☐ 33 Tom Sestak	10.00	4.50	1.25
☐ 34 Charley Tolar	8.00	3.60	1.00
☐ 35 Dave Smith	8.00	3.60	1.00
☐ 36 George Blanda	55.00	25.00	7.00
☐ 37 Billy Cannon	14.00	6.25	1.75
☐ 38 Charlie Hennigan	10.00	4.50	1.25
☐ 39 Bob Talamini	8.00	3.60	1.00
☐ 40 Jim Norton	8.00	3.60	1.00
☐ 41 Tony Banfield	8.00	3.60	1.00
☐ 42 Doug Cline	8.00	3.60	1.00
☐ 43 Don Floyd	8.00	3.60	1.00
☐ 44 Ed Husmann	8.00	3.60	1.00
☐ 45 Curtis McClinton	16.00	7.25	2.00
☐ 46 Jack Spikes	10.00	4.50	1.25
☐ 47 Len Dawson	275.00	125.00	34.00
☐ 48 Abner Haynes	14.00	6.25	1.75
☐ 49 Chris Burford	10.00	4.50	1.25
☐ 50 Fred Arbanas	16.00	7.25	2.00
☐ 51 Johnny Robinson	10.00	4.50	1.25
☐ 52 E.J. Holub	10.00	4.50	1.25
☐ 53 Sherrill Headrick	10.00	4.50	1.25
☐ 54 Mel Branch	10.00	4.50	1.25
☐ 55 Jerry Mays	10.00	4.50	1.25
☐ 56 Cotton Davidson	10.00	4.50	1.25
☐ 57 Clem Daniels	16.00	7.25	2.00
☐ 58 Bo Roberson	8.00	3.60	1.00
☐ 59 Art Powell	12.00	5.50	1.50
☐ 60 Bob Coolbaugh	8.00	3.60	1.00
☐ 61 Wayne Hawkins	8.00	3.60	1.00
☐ 62 Jim Otto	30.00	13.50	3.70
☐ 63 Fred Williamson	12.00	5.50	1.50
☐ 64 Bob Dougherty SP	200.00	90.00	25.00
☐ 65 Dalva Allen	8.00	3.60	1.00
☐ 66 Chuck McMurtry	8.00	3.60	1.00
☐ 67 Gerry McDougall	8.00	3.60	1.00
☐ 68 Tobin Rote	10.00	4.50	1.25
☐ 69 Paul Lowe	12.00	5.50	1.50
☐ 70 Keith Lincoln	40.00	18.00	5.00
☐ 71 Dave Kocourek	8.00	3.60	1.00
☐ 72 Lance Alworth	275.00	125.00	34.00
☐ 73 Ron Mix	25.00	11.00	3.10
☐ 74 Charley McNeil	8.00	3.60	1.00
☐ 75 Emil Karas	8.00	3.60	1.00
☐ 76 Ernie Ladd	20.00	9.00	2.50
☐ 77 Earl Faison	8.00	3.60	1.00
☐ 78 Jim Stinnette	8.00	3.60	1.00
☐ 79 Frank Tripucka	10.00	4.50	1.25
☐ 80 Don Stone	8.00	3.60	1.00
☐ 81 Bob Scarpitto	8.00	3.60	1.00
☐ 82 Lionel Taylor	12.00	5.50	1.50
☐ 83 Jerry Tarr	8.00	3.60	1.00
☐ 84 Eldon Danenhauer	8.00	3.60	1.00
☐ 85 Goose Gonsoulin	10.00	4.50	1.25
☐ 86 Jim Fraser	8.00	3.60	1.00
☐ 87 Chuck Gavin	8.00	3.60	1.00
☐ 88 Bud McFadin	16.00	4.00	1.30
☐ NNO Checklist Card SP	375.00	95.00	30.00

1968 Fleer Big Signs

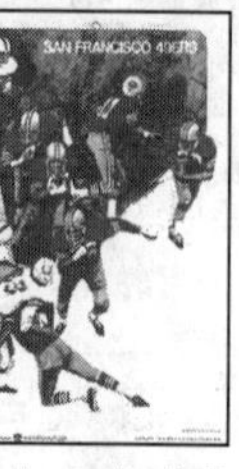

This set of 26 "Big Signs" was produced by Fleer. They are blank backed and measure approximately 7 3/4" by 11 1/2" with rounded corners. They are unnumbered so they are listed below alphabetically by team city name. They are credited at the bottom as 1968 in roman numerals, but in fact were probably issued several years later, perhaps as late as 1974. As another point of reference in dating the set, the New England Patriots changed their name from Boston in 1970. There were two distinct versions of this set, with each version including all 26 teams. The 1970 version was issued in a green box, while the 1974 version was issued in a brown box. Both boxes carry a 1968 copyright date; however, 1974 is generally considered to be the issue date of the second series. Though they are considerably different in design, the size of the collectibles is similar. The generic drawings (of a faceless player from each team) are in color with a white border. The set was licensed by NFL Properties so there are no players shown.

	NRMT-MT	EXC	G-VG
COMPLETE SET (26)	200.00	90.00	25.00
COMMON TEAM (1-26)	7.00	3.10	.85
☐ 1 Atlanta Falcons	7.00	3.10	.85
☐ 2 Baltimore Colts	7.00	3.10	.85
☐ 3 Buffalo Bills	7.00	3.10	.85
☐ 4 Chicago Bears	10.00	4.50	1.25
☐ 5 Cincinnati Bengals	7.00	3.10	.85
☐ 6 Cleveland Browns	7.00	3.10	.85
☐ 7 Dallas Cowboys	12.00	5.50	1.50
☐ 8 Denver Broncos	7.00	3.10	.85
☐ 9 Detroit Lions	7.00	3.10	.85
☐ 10 Green Bay Packers	7.00	3.10	.85
☐ 11 Houston Oilers	7.00	3.10	.85
☐ 12 Kansas City Chiefs	7.00	3.10	.85
☐ 13 Los Angeles Rams	7.00	3.10	.85
☐ 14 Miami Dolphins	10.00	4.50	1.25
☐ 15 Minnesota Vikings	7.00	3.10	.85
☐ 16 New England Patriots	7.00	3.10	.85
☐ 17 New Orleans Saints	7.00	3.10	.85
☐ 18 New York Giants	7.00	3.10	.85
☐ 19 New York Jets	7.00	3.10	.85
☐ 20 Oakland Raiders	12.00	5.50	1.50
☐ 21 Philadelphia Eagles	7.00	3.10	.85
☐ 22 Pittsburgh Steelers	12.00	5.50	1.50
☐ 23 St. Louis Cardinals	7.00	3.10	.85
☐ 24 San Diego Chargers	7.00	3.10	.85
☐ 25 San Francisco 49ers	12.00	5.50	1.50
☐ 26 Washington Redskins	12.00	5.50	1.50

1972 Fleer Quiz

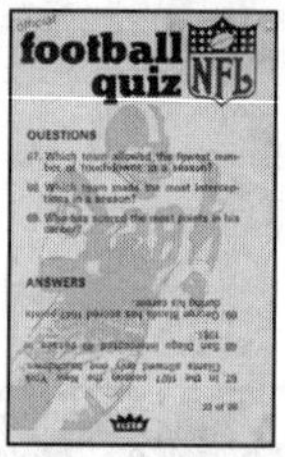

The 28 cards in this set measure approximately 2 1/2" by 4" and feature three questions and (upside down) answers about football players and events. The cards were issued one per pack with Fleer cloth team patches. The words "Official Football Quiz" are printed at the top and are accented by the NFL logo. The backs are blank. The cards are numbered in the lower right hand corner.

	NRMT-MT	EXC	G-VG
COMPLETE SET (28)	50.00	22.00	6.25
COMMON CARD (1-28)	2.00	.90	.25
☐ 1 Questions 1-3	2.00	.90	.25
☐ 2 Questions 4-6	2.00	.90	.25
☐ 3 Questions 7-9	2.00	.90	.25
☐ 4 Questions 10-12	2.00	.90	.25
☐ 5 Questions 13-15	2.00	.90	.25
☐ 6 Questions 16-18	2.00	.90	.25
☐ 7 Questions 19-21	2.00	.90	.25
☐ 8 Questions 22-24	2.00	.90	.25
☐ 9 Questions 25-27	2.00	.90	.25
☐ 10 Questions 28-30	2.00	.90	.25
☐ 11 Questions 31-33	2.00	.90	.25
☐ 12 Questions 34-36	2.00	.90	.25
☐ 13 Questions 37-39	2.00	.90	.25
☐ 14 Questions 40-42	2.00	.90	.25
☐ 15 Questions 43-45	2.00	.90	.25
☐ 16 Questions 46-48	2.00	.90	.25
☐ 17 Questions 49-51	2.00	.90	.25
☐ 18 Questions 52-54	2.00	.90	.25
☐ 19 Questions 55-57	2.00	.90	.25
☐ 20 Questions 58-60	2.00	.90	.25
☐ 21 Questions 61-63	2.00	.90	.25
☐ 22 Questions 64-66	2.00	.90	.25
☐ 23 Questions 67-69	2.00	.90	.25
☐ 24 Questions 70-72	2.00	.90	.25
☐ 25 Questions 73-75	2.00	.90	.25
☐ 26 Questions 76-78	2.00	.90	.25
☐ 27 Questions 79-81	2.00	.90	.25
☐ 28 Questions 82-84	2.00	.90	.25

1973 Fleer Pro Bowl Scouting Report

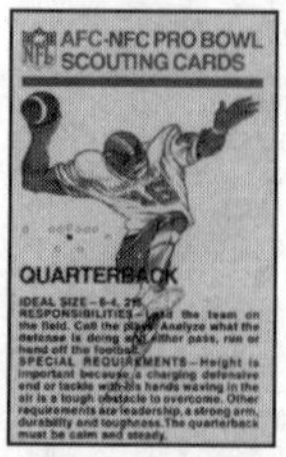

The 14 cards in this set measure approximately 2 1/2" by 4" and feature an explanation of the ideal size, responsibilities, and assignments of each player on the team. Each card shows a different position. Color artwork illustrates examples of how a player might appear. A diagram shows the position on the field. The words "AFC-NFC Pro Bowl Scouting Cards" are printed at the top and are accented by the NFL logo and underscored by a blue stripe. The backs are blank. The cards are unnumbered and checklisted below in alphabetical order. The cards came one per pack with two cloth football logo patches that are dated 1972. It appears that the same cloth patches were sold each year from 1972 to 1975. In the first year, they were sold alone in packs, while in the following years, they were sold again through packs with the Scouting Report and Hall of Fame issues, respectively.

	NRMT-MT	EXC	G-VG
COMPLETE SET (14)	40.00	18.00	5.00
COMMON CARD (1-14)	3.00	1.35	.35
☐ 1 Center	3.00	1.35	.35
☐ 2 Cornerback	3.00	1.35	.35
☐ 3 Defensive End	3.00	1.35	.35
☐ 4 Defensive Tackle	3.00	1.35	.35
☐ 5 Guard	3.00	1.35	.35
☐ 6 Kicker	3.00	1.35	.35
☐ 7 Linebacker	3.00	1.35	.35
☐ 8 Offensive Tackle	3.00	1.35	.35
☐ 9 Punter	3.00	1.35	.35
☐ 10 Quarterback	3.00	1.35	.35
☐ 11 Running Back	3.00	1.35	.35
☐ 12 Safety	3.00	1.35	.35
☐ 13 Tight End	3.00	1.35	.35
☐ 14 Wide Receiver	3.00	1.35	.35

1974 Fleer Big Signs

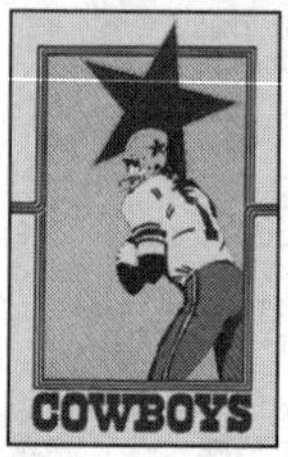

This set of 26 "Big Signs" was produced by Fleer in 1974. They are blank backed and measure approximately 7 3/4" by 11 1/2" with rounded corners. They are unnumbered so they are listed below alphabetically by team city name. They are credited at the bottom as 1968 in roman numerals, but in fact were probably issued several years later, perhaps as late as 1974. As another point of reference in dating the set, the New England Patriots changed their name from Boston in 1970. There were two distinct versions of this set, with each version including all 26 teams. The 1968 version was issued in a green box, while the 1974 version was issued in a brown box. Both boxes carry a 1968 copyright date; however, 1974 is generally considered to be the issue date of this second series. Though they are considerably different in design, the size of the collectibles is similar. The generic drawings (of a faceless player from each team) are in color with a white border. The set was licensed by NFL Properties so there are no players identifiably shown.

	NRMT-MT	EXC	G-VG
COMPLETE SET (26)	50.00	22.00	6.25
COMMON TEAM (1-26)	2.50	1.10	.30
☐ 1 Atlanta Falcons	2.50	1.10	.30
☐ 2 Baltimore Colts	2.50	1.10	.30
☐ 3 Buffalo Bills	2.50	1.10	.30
☐ 4 Chicago Bears	4.00	1.80	.50
☐ 5 Cincinnati Bengals	2.50	1.10	.30
☐ 6 Cleveland Browns	2.50	1.10	.30
☐ 7 Dallas Cowboys	4.00	1.80	.50
☐ 8 Denver Broncos	2.50	1.10	.30
☐ 9 Detroit Lions	2.50	1.10	.30
☐ 10 Green Bay Packers	4.00	1.80	.50
☐ 11 Houston Oilers	2.50	1.10	.30
☐ 12 Kansas City Chiefs	2.50	1.10	.30
☐ 13 Los Angeles Rams	2.50	1.10	.30
☐ 14 Miami Dolphins	4.00	1.80	.50
☐ 15 Minnesota Vikings	2.50	1.10	.30
☐ 16 New England Patriots	2.50	1.10	.30
☐ 17 New Orleans Saints	2.50	1.10	.30
☐ 18 New York Giants	2.50	1.10	.30
☐ 19 New York Jets	2.50	1.10	.30
☐ 20 Oakland Raiders	4.00	1.80	.50
☐ 21 Philadelphia Eagles	2.50	1.10	.30
☐ 22 Pittsburgh Steelers	4.00	1.80	.50
☐ 23 St. Louis Cardinals	2.50	1.10	.30
☐ 24 San Diego Chargers	2.50	1.10	.30
☐ 25 San Francisco 49ers	4.00	1.80	.50
☐ 26 Washington Redskins	4.00	1.80	.50

1974 Fleer Hall of Fame

The 1974 Fleer Hall of Fame football card set contains 50 players inducted into the Pro Football Hall of Fame in Canton, Ohio. The cards measure approximately 2 1/2" by 4". The fronts feature black and white photos, white borders, and a cartoon head of a football player flanked by the words "The Immortal Roll." The backs contain biographical data and a stylized Pro Football Hall of Fame logo. The cards are unnumbered and can be distinguished from cards of the 1975 Fleer Hall of Fame set by this lack of numbering. The cards are arranged and numbered below alphabetically by player's name for convenience. The cards were originally issued in wax packs with one Hall of Fame card and two cloth team logo stickers.

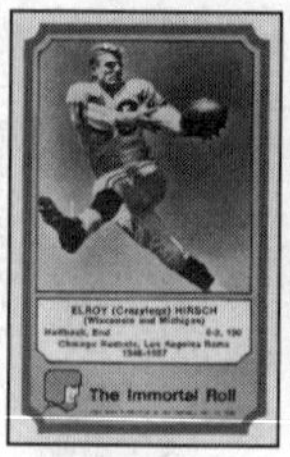

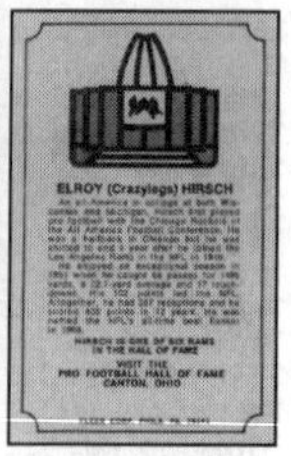

	NRMT-MT	EXC	G-VG
COMPLETE SET (50)	60.00	27.00	7.50
COMMON CARD (1-50)	1.00	.45	.12
☐ 1 Cliff Battles	1.25	.55	.16
☐ 2 Sammy Baugh	3.00	1.35	.35
☐ 3 Chuck Bednarik	1.50	.70	.19
☐ 4 Bert Bell COMM/OWN	1.00	.45	.12
☐ 5 Paul Brown CO/OWN/FOUND	2.00	.90	.25
☐ 6 Joe Carr PRES	1.00	.45	.12
☐ 7 Guy Chamberlin	1.00	.45	.12
☐ 8 Dutch Clark	1.25	.55	.16
☐ 9 Jimmy Conzelman	1.00	.45	.12
☐ 10 Art Donovan	1.50	.70	.19
☐ 11 Paddy Driscoll	1.00	.45	.12
☐ 12 Bill Dudley	1.25	.55	.16
☐ 13 Dan Fortmann	1.00	.45	.12
☐ 14 Otto Graham	3.00	1.35	.35
☐ 15 Red Grange	3.00	1.35	.35
☐ 16 George Halas CO/OWN/ FOUND	2.00	.90	.25
☐ 17 Mel Hein	1.00	.45	.12
☐ 18 Fats Henry	1.00	.45	.12
☐ 19 Bill Hewitt	1.00	.45	.12
☐ 20 Clarke Hinkle	1.00	.45	.12
☐ 21 Elroy(Crazylegs) Hirsch	1.50	.70	.19
☐ 22 Robert(Cal) Hubbard	1.00	.45	.12
☐ 23 Lamar Hunt OWN/FOUND	1.00	.45	.12
☐ 24 Don Hutson	1.25	.55	.16
☐ 25 Earl(Curly) Lambeau CO/ OWN/FOUND	1.00	.45	.12
☐ 26 Bobby Layne	2.50	1.10	.30
☐ 27 Vince Lombardi CO	2.50	1.10	.30
☐ 28 Sid Luckman	2.00	.90	.25
☐ 29 Gino Marchetti	1.25	.55	.16
☐ 30 Ollie Matson	1.50	.70	.19
☐ 31 George McAfee	1.25	.55	.16
☐ 32 Hugh McElhenny	1.50	.70	.19
☐ 33 Johnny(Blood) McNally	1.00	.45	.12
☐ 34 Marion Motley	1.50	.70	.19
☐ 35 Bronko Nagurski	2.50	1.10	.30
☐ 36 Ernie Nevers	1.25	.55	.16
☐ 37 Leo Nomellini	1.25	.55	.16
☐ 38 Steve Owen CO	1.00	.45	.12
☐ 39 Joe Perry	1.50	.70	.19
☐ 40 Pete Pihos	1.25	.55	.16
☐ 41 Andy Robustelli	1.50	.70	.19
☐ 42 Ken Strong	1.25	.55	.16
☐ 43 Jim Thorpe	4.00	1.80	.50
☐ 44 Y.A. Tittle	2.50	1.10	.30
☐ 45 Charley Trippi	1.25	.55	.16
☐ 46 Emlen Tunnell	1.25	.55	.16
☐ 47 Bulldog Turner	1.50	.70	.19
☐ 48 Norm Van Brocklin	2.00	.90	.25
☐ 49 Steve Van Buren	1.50	.70	.19
☐ 50 Bob Waterfield	2.00	.90	.25

1975 Fleer Hall of Fame

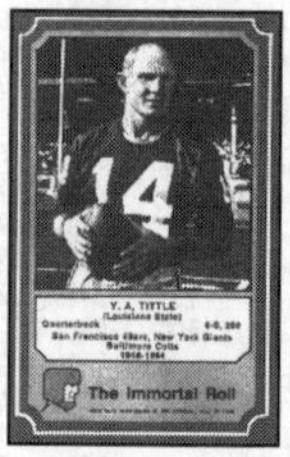

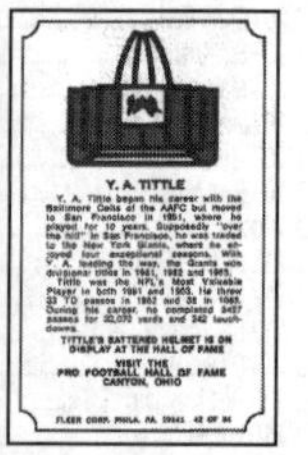

The 1975 Fleer Hall of Fame football card set contains 84 cards. The cards measure 2 1/2" by 4". Except for the change in border color from white to brown and the different set numbering contained on the backs of the cards, fifty of the cards in this set are similar to the cards in the 1974 Fleer set. Thirty-four additional cards have been added to this set in comparison to the 1974 set. These cards are numbered and were issued in wax packs with cloth team logo stickers.

	NRMT-MT	EXC	G-VG
COMPLETE SET (84)	65.00	29.00	8.00
COMMON CARD (1-84)	.75	.35	.09
☐ 1 Jim Thorpe	3.00	1.35	.35
☐ 2 Cliff Battles	1.00	.45	.12
☐ 3 Bronko Nagurski	2.00	.90	.25
☐ 4 Red Grange	2.50	1.10	.30
☐ 5 Guy Chamberlin	.75	.35	.09
☐ 6 Joe Carr PRES	.75	.35	.09
☐ 7 George Halas CO/OWN/ FOUND	1.50	.70	.19
☐ 8 Jimmy Conzelman	.75	.35	.09
☐ 9 George McAfee	1.00	.45	.12
☐ 10 Clarke Hinkle	.75	.35	.09
☐ 11 Paddy Driscoll	.75	.35	.09

□ 12 Mel Hein	.75	.35	.09
□ 13 Johnny(Blood) McNally	.75	.35	.09
□ 14 Dutch Clark	1.00	.45	.12
□ 15 Steve Owen CO	.75	.35	.09
□ 16 Bill Hewitt	.75	.35	.09
□ 17 Robert(Cal) Hubbard	.75	.35	.09
□ 18 Don Hutson	1.25	.55	.16
□ 19 Ernie Nevers	1.00	.45	.12
□ 20 Dan Fortmann	.75	.35	.09
□ 21 Ken Strong	1.00	.45	.12
□ 22 Chuck Bednarik	1.25	.55	.16
□ 23 Bert Bell COMM/OWN	.75	.35	.09
□ 24 Paul Brown CO/OWN/FOUND	1.50	.70	.19
□ 25 Art Donovan	1.25	.55	.16
□ 26 Bill Dudley	1.00	.45	.12
□ 27 Otto Graham	2.00	.90	.25
□ 28 Fats Henry	1.00	.45	.12
□ 29 Elroy Hirsch	1.25	.55	.16
□ 30 Lamar Hunt OWN/FOUND	.75	.35	.09
□ 31 Earl(Curly) Lambeau CO/ OWN/FOUND	.75	.35	.09
□ 32 Vince Lombardi CO	2.00	.90	.25
□ 33 Sid Luckman	1.50	.70	.19
□ 34 Gino Marchetti	1.00	.45	.12
□ 35 Ollie Matson	1.25	.55	.16
□ 36 Hugh McElhenny	1.25	.55	.16
□ 37 Marion Motley	1.00	.45	.12
□ 38 Leo Nomellini	1.00	.45	.12
□ 39 Joe Perry	1.25	.55	.16
□ 40 Andy Robustelli	1.00	.45	.12
□ 41 Pete Pihos	1.00	.45	.12
□ 42 Y.A. Tittle	2.00	.90	.25
□ 43 Charley Trippi	1.00	.45	.12
□ 44 Emlen Tunnell	1.00	.45	.12
□ 45 Bulldog Turner	1.25	.55	.16
□ 46 Norm Van Brocklin	1.50	.70	.19
□ 47 Steve Van Buren	1.25	.55	.16
□ 48 Bob Waterfield	1.50	.70	.19
□ 49 Bobby Layne	2.00	.90	.25
□ 50 Sammy Baugh	2.50	1.10	.30
□ 51 Joe Guyon	.75	.35	.09
□ 52 Roy(Link) Lyman	.75	.35	.09
□ 53 George Trafton	.75	.35	.09
□ 54 Turk Edwards	.75	.35	.09
□ 55 Ed Healey	.75	.35	.09
□ 56 Mike Michalske	.75	.35	.09
□ 57 Alex Wojciechowicz	.75	.35	.09
□ 58 Dante Lavelli	1.25	.55	.16
□ 59 George Connor	1.00	.45	.12
□ 60 Wayne Millner	.75	.35	.09
□ 61 Jack Christiansen	.75	.35	.09
□ 62 Roosevelt Brown	.75	.35	.09
□ 63 Joe Stydahar	.75	.35	.09
□ 64 Ernie Stautner	1.00	.45	.12
□ 65 Jim Parker	1.00	.45	.12
□ 66 Raymond Berry	1.25	.55	.16
□ 67 Geo.Preston Marshall OWN/FOUND	.75	.35	.09
□ 68 Clarence(Ace) Parker	.75	.35	.09
□ 69 Greasy Neale CO	.75	.35	.09
□ 70 Tim Mara OWN/FOUND	.75	.35	.09
□ 71 Hugh(Shorty) Ray OFF	.75	.35	.09
□ 72 Tom Fears	1.00	.45	.12
□ 73 Arnie Herber	.75	.35	.09
□ 74 Walt Kiesling	.75	.35	.09
□ 75 Frank(Bruiser) Kinard	.75	.35	.09
□ 76 Tony Canadeo	.75	.35	.09
□ 77 Bill George	.75	.35	.09
□ 78 Art Rooney FOUND/OWN ADMIN	.75	.35	.09
□ 79 Joe Schmidt	1.00	.45	.12
□ 80 Dan Reeves OWN	.75	.35	.09
□ 81 Lou Groza	1.25	.55	.16
□ 82 Charles W. Bidwill OWN	.75	.35	.09
□ 83 Lenny Moore	1.25	.55	.16
□ 84 Dick(Night Train) Lane	1.00	.45	.12

1976 Fleer Team Action

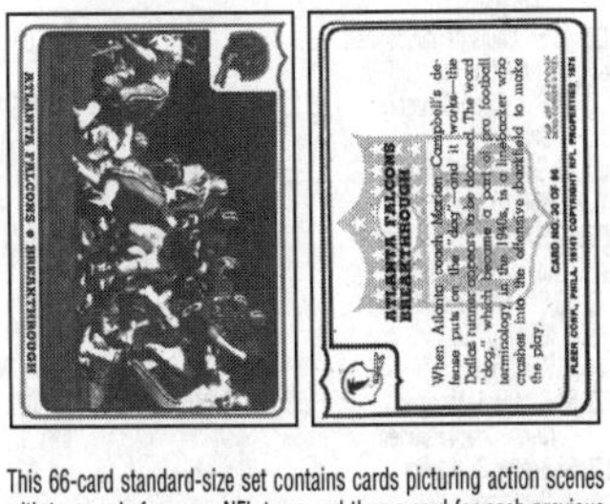

This 66-card standard-size set contains cards picturing action scenes with two cards for every NFL team and then a card for each previous Super Bowl. The first card in each team pair, i.e., the odd-numbered card, is an offensive card; the even-numbered cards are defensive scenes. Cards have a white border with a red outline on the front; the backs are printed with black ink on white cardboard stock with a light blue NFL emblem superimposed in the middle of the write-up on the back of the card. These cards are actually stickers as they may be peeled and stuck. The instructions on the back of the sticker say, "For use as sticker, bend corner and peel." The cards were issued in four-card packs with no inserts, unlike earlier Fleer football issues.

	NRMT-MT	EXC	G-VG
COMPLETE SET (66)	550.00	250.00	70.00
COMMON CARD (1-56)	8.00	3.60	1.00
COMMON SB CARD (57-66)	12.00	5.50	1.50
□ 1 Baltimore Colts High Scorers	9.00	4.00	1.10
□ 2 Baltimore Colts Effective Tackle	8.00	3.60	1.00
□ 3 Buffalo Bills Perfect Blocking	8.00	3.60	1.00
□ 4 Buffalo Bills The Sack	8.00	3.60	1.00
□ 5 Cincinnati Bengals Being Hit Behind The Runner	8.00	3.60	1.00
□ 6 Cincinnati Bengals A Little Help (Tackling Franco Harris)	12.00	5.50	1.50
□ 7 Cleveland Browns Blocking Tight End	8.00	3.60	1.00
□ 8 Cleveland Browns Stopping the Double Threat	8.00	3.60	1.00
□ 9 Denver Broncos The Swing Pass	8.00	3.60	1.00
□ 10 Denver Broncos The Gang Tackle	8.00	3.60	1.00
□ 11 Houston Oilers Short Zone Flood (Dan Pastorini passing)	10.00	4.50	1.25
□ 12 Houston Oilers Run Stoppers (Franco Harris running)	12.00	5.50	1.50
□ 13 Kansas City Chiefs Off On the Ball	8.00	3.60	1.00
□ 14 Kansas City Chiefs Forcing the Scramble	8.00	3.60	1.00
□ 15 Miami Dolphins Pass Protection (Bob Griese)	12.00	5.50	1.50
□ 16 Miami Dolphins Natural Turf	10.00	4.50	1.25
□ 17 New England Patriots Quicker Than the Eye	8.00	3.60	1.00
□ 18 New England Patriots The Rugby Touch	8.00	3.60	1.00
□ 19 New York Jets They Run, Too (John Riggins and Joe Namath)	15.00	6.75	1.85
□ 20 New York Jets The Buck Stops Here (O.J.Simpson tackled)	12.00	5.50	1.50
□ 21 Oakland Raiders A Strong Offense	10.00	4.50	1.25
□ 22 Oakland Raiders High and Low	10.00	4.50	1.25
□ 23 Pittsburgh Steelers The Pitch-Out (Terry Bradshaw, Franco Harris, and Rocky Bleier)	15.00	6.75	1.85
□ 24 Pittsburgh Steelers The Takeaway (Jack Lambert)	12.00	5.50	1.50
□ 25 San Diego Chargers Run to Daylight	8.00	3.60	1.00
□ 26 San Diego Chargers The Swarm	8.00	3.60	1.00
□ 27 Tampa Bay Buccaneers Stadium	8.00	3.60	1.00
□ 28 Tampa Bay Buccaneers Buccaneers Uniform	8.00	3.60	1.00
□ 29 Atlanta Falcons A Key Block	8.00	3.60	1.00
□ 30 Atlanta Falcons Breakthrough (Robert Newhouse)	8.00	3.60	1.00
□ 31 Chicago Bears An Inside Look	8.00	3.60	1.00
□ 32 Chicago Bears Defensive Emphasis	8.00	3.60	1.00
□ 33 Dallas Cowboys Eight-Yard Burst (Robert Newhouse)	10.00	4.50	1.25
□ 34 Dallas Cowboys The Big Return (Cliff Harris)	10.00	4.50	1.25
□ 35 Detroit Lions Power Sweep	8.00	3.60	1.00
□ 36 Detroit Lions A Tough Defense	8.00	3.60	1.00
□ 37 Green Bay Packers Tearaway Gain	8.00	3.60	1.00
□ 38 Green Bay Packers Good Support	8.00	3.60	1.00
□ 39 Los Angeles Rams (Cullen Bryant)	8.00	3.60	1.00
□ 40 Los Angeles Rams Low-Point Defense	8.00	3.60	1.00
□ 41 Minnesota Vikings The Running Guards (Fran Tarkenton and Chuck Foreman)	12.00	5.50	1.50
□ 42 Minnesota Vikings A Stingy Defense	8.00	3.60	1.00
□ 43 New York Giants The Quick Opener	8.00	3.60	1.00
□ 44 New York Giants Defending a Tradition	8.00	3.60	1.00
□ 45 New Orleans Saints Head for the Hole (Archie Manning)	10.00	4.50	1.25
□ 46 New Orleans Saints The Contain Man	8.00	3.60	1.00
□ 47 Philadelphia Eagles Line Signals	8.00	3.60	1.00
□ 48 Philadelphia Eagles Don't Take Sides	8.00	3.60	1.00
□ 49 San Francisco 49ers The Clues	8.00	3.60	1.00
□ 50 San Francisco 49ers Goal-Line Stand	8.00	3.60	1.00
□ 51 St. Louis Cardinals Nonskid Handoff (Jim Hart)	10.00	4.50	1.25
□ 52 St. Louis Cardinals Strong Pursuit	8.00	3.60	1.00
□ 53 Seattle Seahawks Stadium	8.00	3.60	1.00
□ 54 Seattle Seahawks Uniform	8.00	3.60	1.00
□ 55 Washington Redskins A Fancy Passing (Billy Kilmer)	10.00	4.50	1.25
□ 56 Washington Redskins Let's Go Defense (Chris Hanburger)	8.00	3.60	1.00
□ 57 Super Bowl I Green Bay NFL 35 Kansas City AFL 10 (Jim Taylor)	12.00	5.50	1.50
□ 58 Super Bowl II Green Bay NFL 33 Oakland AFL 14 (Ben Davidson)	12.00	5.50	1.50
□ 59 Super Bowl III New York AFL 16 Baltimore NFL 7	12.00	5.50	1.50
□ 60 Super Bowl IV Kansas City AFL 23 Minnesota NFL 7	12.00	5.50	1.50
□ 61 Super Bowl V Baltimore AFC 16 Dallas NFC 13	12.00	5.50	1.50
□ 62 Super Bowl VI Dallas NFC 24 Miami AFC 3 (Walt Garrison and Roger Staubach)	20.00	9.00	2.50
□ 63 Super Bowl VII Miami AFC 14 Washington NFC 7 (Larry Csonka)	14.00	6.25	1.75
□ 64 Super Bowl VIII Miami AFC 24 Minnesota NFC 7 (Larry Csonka diving)	14.00	6.25	1.75
□ 65 Super Bowl IX Pittsburgh AFC 16 Minnesota NFC 6	12.00	5.50	1.50
□ 66 Super Bowl X Pittsburgh AFC 21 Dallas NFC 17 (Terry Bradshaw and Franco Harris)	25.00	11.00	3.10

1977 Fleer Team Action

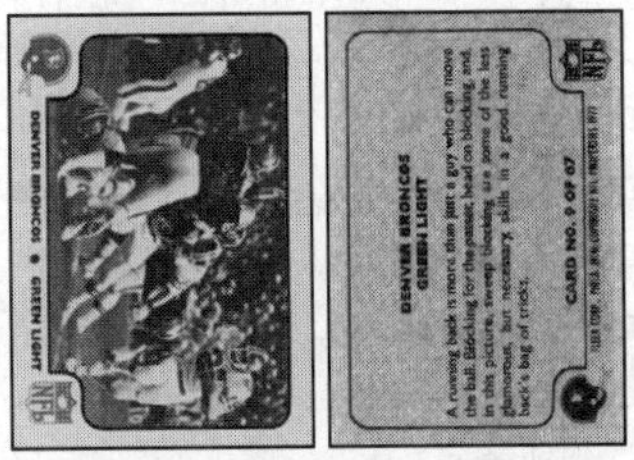

The 1977 Fleer Teams in Action football set contains 67 standard-size cards depicting action scenes. There are two cards for each NFL team and one card for each Super Bowl. The first card in each team pair, i.e., the odd-numbered card, is an offensive card; the even-numbered cards are defensive scenes. The cards have white borders and the backs are printed in dark blue ink on gray stock. The cards are numbered and contain a 1977 copyright date. The cards were issued in four-card wax packs along with four team logo stickers.

	NRMT-MT	EXC	G-VG
COMPLETE SET (67)	80.00	36.00	10.00
COMMON CARD (1-56)	1.25	.55	.16
COMMON SB CARD (57-67)	1.50	.70	.19
□ 1 Baltimore Colts The Easy Chair (Bert Jones)	2.50	1.10	.30
□ 2 Baltimore Colts A Handy Solution	1.25	.55	.16
□ 3 Buffalo Bills Blocking Tight End	1.25	.55	.16
□ 4 Buffalo Bills Search And Destroy	1.25	.55	.16
□ 5 Cincinnati Bengals Cutting on a Rug (Ken Anderson hand off)	2.00	.90	.25
□ 6 Cincinnati Bengals Strength in the Middle	1.25	.55	.16
□ 7 Cleveland Browns Snap, Drop, Set (Brian Sipe)	1.50	.70	.19
□ 8 Cleveland Browns High and Low	1.25	.55	.16
□ 9 Denver Broncos Green Light	1.25	.55	.16
□ 10 Denver Broncos Help From Behind	1.25	.55	.16
□ 11 Houston Oilers Room to Move	1.25	.55	.16
□ 12 Houston Oilers For The Defense	1.25	.55	.16
□ 13 Kansas City Chiefs Chance to Motor	1.25	.55	.16
□ 14 Kansas City Chiefs From the Ground Up	1.25	.55	.16
□ 15 Miami Dolphins Eye of the Storm	1.50	.70	.19
□ 16 Miami Dolphins When Man Takes Flight	1.50	.70	.19
□ 17 New England Patriots Turning the Corner	1.25	.55	.16
□ 18 New England Patriots A Matter of Inches	1.25	.55	.16
□ 19 New York Jets Keeping Him Clean (Joe Namath)	7.00	3.10	.85
□ 20 New York Jets Plugging the Leaks	1.25	.55	.16
□ 21 Oakland Raiders On Solid Ground	1.50	.70	.19
□ 22 Oakland Raiders 3-4, Shut The Door	1.50	.70	.19
□ 23 Pittsburgh Steelers Daylight Saving Time (Rocky Bleier)	2.00	.90	.25
□ 24 Pittsburgh Steelers A Controlled Swarm	1.50	.70	.19
□ 25 San Diego Chargers Youth on the Move (Dan Fouts)	3.50	1.55	.45
□ 26 San Diego Chargers A Rude Housewarming	1.25	.55	.16
□ 27 Seattle Seahawks Play Action Pass (Jim Zorn faking)	2.00	.90	.25
□ 28 Seattle Seahawks Birds of Prey	1.50	.70	.19
□ 29 Atlanta Falcons Ad-Libbing on Offense	1.25	.55	.16
□ 30 Atlanta Falcons A Futile Chase	1.25	.55	.16
□ 31 Chicago Bears Follow Me (Walter Payton blocking)	6.00	2.70	.75
□ 32 Chicago Bears A Nose for the Ball	1.25	.55	.16
□ 33 Dallas Cowboys The Plunge	1.50	.70	.19
□ 34 Dallas Cowboys Unassisted Sack (Ed Too Tall Jones)	2.50	1.10	.30
□ 35 Detroit Lions Motor City Might	1.25	.55	.16
□ 36 Detroit Lions Block Party	1.25	.55	.16
□ 37 Green Bay Packers Another Era	1.25	.55	.16
□ 38 Green Bay Packers Face-to-Face (Walter Payton tackled)	6.00	2.70	.75
□ 39 Los Angeles Rams Personal Escort	1.25	.55	.16
□ 40 Los Angeles Rams A Closed Case	1.25	.55	.16
□ 41 Minnesota Vikings Nothing Fancy	1.25	.55	.16
□ 42 Minnesota Vikings Lending A Hand	1.25	.55	.16
□ 43 New Orleans Saints Ample Protection	1.25	.55	.16
□ 44 New Orleans Saints Well-Timed Contact	1.25	.55	.16
□ 45 New York Giants Quick Pitch	1.25	.55	.16
□ 46 New York Giants In A Pinch	1.25	.55	.16
□ 47 Philadelphia Eagles When to Fly	1.25	.55	.16
□ 48 Philadelphia Eagles Swooping Defense	1.25	.55	.16

☐ 49 St. Louis Cardinals 1.50 .70 .19
Speed Outside
(Jim Hart)

☐ 50 St. Louis Cardinals 1.25 .55 .16
The Circle Tightens

☐ 51 San Francisco 49ers 1.50 .70 .19
Sideline Route
(Gene Washington)

☐ 52 San Francisco 49ers 1.50 .70 .19
The Gold Rush

☐ 53 Tampa Bay Buccaneers 1.25 .55 .16
A Rare Occasion

☐ 54 Tampa Bay Buccaneers 1.25 .55 .16
Expansion Blues

☐ 55 Washington Redskins 2.50 1.10 .30
Splitting the Seam
(Joe Theismann passing)

☐ 56 Washington Redskins 1.50 .70 .19
The Hands of Time

☐ 57 Super Bowl I 1.50 .70 .19
Green Bay NFL 35
Kansas City AFL 10

☐ 58 Super Bowl II 1.50 .70 .19
Green Bay NFL 33
Oakland AFL 14

☐ 59 Super Bowl III 1.50 .70 .19
New York AFL 16
Baltimore NFL 7
(Tom Matte running)

☐ 60 Super Bowl IV 1.50 .70 .19
Kansas City AFL 23
Minnesota NFL 7

☐ 61 Super Bowl V 1.50 .70 .19
Baltimore AFC 16
Dallas NFC 13

☐ 62 Super Bowl VI 4.00 1.80 .50
Dallas NFC 24
Miami AFC 3
(Walt Garrison
running; Roger Staubach
also shown)

☐ 63 Super Bowl VII 2.50 1.10 .30
Miami AFC 14
Washington NFC 7
(Larry Csonka
running)

☐ 64 Super Bowl VIII 2.50 1.10 .30
Miami AFC 24
Minnesota NFC 7
(Larry Csonka
running)

☐ 65 Super Bowl IX 1.50 .70 .19
Pittsburgh AFC 16
Minnesota NFC 6

☐ 66 Super Bowl X 3.50 1.55 .45
Pittsburgh AFC 21
Dallas NFC 17
(Terry Bradshaw
and Franco Harris)

☐ 67 Super Bowl XI 3.50 1.55 .45
Oakland AFC 32
Minnesota NFC 14
(Ken Stabler)

1978 Fleer Team Action

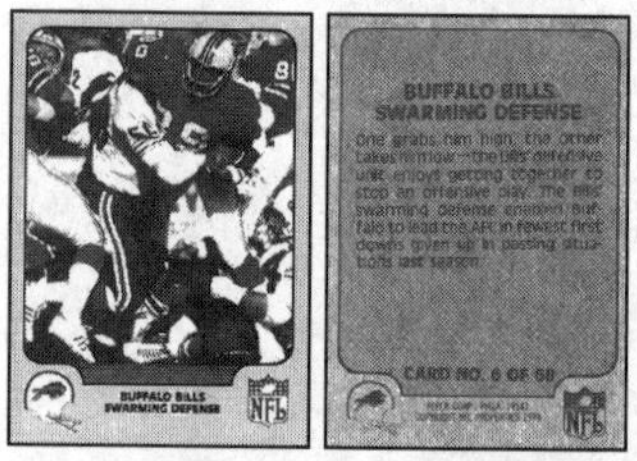

The 1978 Fleer Teams in Action football set contains 68 action scenes. The cards measure the standard size. As in the previous year, each team is depicted on two cards and each Super Bowl is depicted on one card. The additional card in comparison to last year's set comes from the additional Super Bowl which was played during the year. The fronts have yellow borders. The card backs are printed with black ink on gray stock. The cards are numbered and feature a 1978 copyright date. Cards were issued in wax packs of seven team cards plus four team logo stickers.

	NRMT-MT	EXC	G-VG
COMPLETE SET (68)	45.00	20.00	5.50
COMMON CARD (1-56)	.50	.23	.06
COMMON SB CARD (57-68)	.75	.35	.09

☐ 1 Atlanta Falcons 1.25 .55 .16
Sticking to Basics

☐ 2 Atlanta Falcons .50 .23 .06
In Pursuit

☐ 3 Baltimore Colts .50 .23 .06
Forward Plunge

☐ 4 Baltimore Colts .50 .23 .06
Stacking It Up

☐ 5 Buffalo Bills .50 .23 .06
Daylight Breakers

☐ 6 Buffalo Bills .50 .23 .06
Swarming Defense

☐ 7 Chicago Bears 5.00 2.20 .60
Up The Middle
(Walter Payton
running)

☐ 8 Chicago Bears .50 .23 .06
Rejuvenated Defense

☐ 9 Cincinnati Bengals 1.50 .70 .19
Poise and Execution
(Ken Anderson)

☐ 10 Cincinnati Bengals .50 .23 .06
Down-to-Earth

☐ 11 Cleveland Browns .75 .35 .09
Breakaway
(Greg Pruitt)

☐ 12 Cleveland Browns 1.00 .45 .12
Red Dogs
(Ken Anderson tackled)

☐ 13 Dallas Cowboys 6.00 2.70 .75
Up and Over
(Tony Dorsett)

☐ 14 Dallas Cowboys 1.00 .45 .12
Doomsday II

☐ 15 Denver Broncos .50 .23 .06
Mile-High Offense

☐ 16 Denver Broncos 3.50 1.55 .45
Orange Crush
(Walter Payton tackled)

☐ 17 Detroit Lions .50 .23 .06
End-Around

☐ 18 Detroit Lions .50 .23 .06
Special Teams

☐ 19 Green Bay Packers .50 .23 .06
Running Strong

☐ 20 Green Bay Packers .50 .23 .06
Tearin' em Down

☐ 21 Houston Oilers .50 .23 .06
Goal-Line Drive

☐ 22 Houston Oilers .50 .23 .06
Interception

☐ 23 Kansas City Chiefs .50 .23 .06
Running Wide
(Ed Podolak)

☐ 24 Kansas City Chiefs .50 .23 .06
Armed Defense

☐ 25 Los Angeles Rams .50 .23 .06
Rushing Power

☐ 26 Los Angeles Rams .50 .23 .06
Backing the Line

☐ 27 Miami Dolphins 3.00 1.35 .35
Protective Pocket
(Bob Griese passing)

☐ 28 Miami Dolphins .75 .35 .09
Life in the Pit

☐ 29 Minnesota Vikings 1.00 .45 .12
Storm Breakers
(Foreman in snow)

☐ 30 Minnesota Vikings .50 .23 .06
Blocking the Kick

☐ 31 New England Patriots .50 .23 .06
Clearing The Way

☐ 32 New England Patriots .50 .23 .06
One-on-One

☐ 33 New Orleans Saints .50 .23 .06
Extra Yardage

☐ 34 New Orleans Saints .50 .23 .06
Drag-Down Defense

☐ 35 New York Giants .50 .23 .06
Ready, Aim, Fire

☐ 36 New York Giants .50 .23 .06
Meeting of Minds

☐ 37 New York Jets .50 .23 .06
Take-Off

☐ 38 New York Jets .50 .23 .06
Ambush

☐ 39 Oakland Raiders 1.00 .45 .12
Power 31 Left

☐ 40 Oakland Raiders 1.00 .45 .12
Welcoming Committee

☐ 41 Philadelphia Eagles .50 .23 .06
Taking Flight

☐ 42 Philadelphia Eagles .50 .23 .06
Soaring High

☐ 43 Pittsburgh Steelers .75 .35 .09
Ironclad Offense

☐ 44 Pittsburgh Steelers 1.50 .70 .19
Curtain Closes
(Jack Lambert)

☐ 45 St. Louis Cardinals .50 .23 .06
A Good Bet

☐ 46 St. Louis Cardinals .50 .23 .06
Gang Tackle

☐ 47 San Diego Chargers .50 .23 .06
Circus Catch

☐ 48 San Diego Chargers .50 .23 .06
Charge

☐ 49 San Francisco 49ers 1.00 .45 .12
Follow the Block

☐ 50 San Francisco 49ers 1.00 .45 .12
Goal-Line Stand

☐ 51 Seattle Seahawks .50 .23 .06
Finding Daylight

☐ 52 Seattle Seahawks .50 .23 .06
Rushing The Pass

☐ 53 Tampa Bay Buccaneers .50 .23 .06
Play Action

☐ 54 Tampa Bay Buccaneers .50 .23 .06
Youth on the Move

☐ 55 Washington Redskins .75 .35 .09
Renegade Runners

☐ 56 Washington Redskins .75 .35 .09
Dual Action

☐ 57 Super Bowl I 2.00 .90 .25
Green Bay NFL 35
Kansas City AFL 10
(Bart Starr)

☐ 58 Super Bowl II .75 .35 .09
Green Bay NFL 33
Oakland AFL 14

☐ 59 Super Bowl III .75 .35 .09
New York AFL 16
Baltimore NFL 7

☐ 60 Super Bowl IV .75 .35 .09
Kansas City AFL 23
Minnesota NFL 7

☐ 61 Super Bowl V .75 .35 .09
Baltimore AFC 16
Dallas NFC 13

☐ 62 Super Bowl VI .75 .35 .09
Dallas NFC 24
Miami AFC 3

☐ 63 Super Bowl VII .75 .35 .09
Miami AFC 14
Washington NFC 7

☐ 64 Super Bowl VIII 2.00 .90 .25
Miami AFC 24
Minnesota NFC 7
(Larry Csonka
running)

☐ 65 Super Bowl IX 2.50 1.10 .30
Pittsburgh AFC 16
Minnesota NFC 6
(Terry Bradshaw
and Franco Harris)

☐ 66 Super Bowl X .75 .35 .09
Pittsburgh AFC 21
Dallas NFC 17

☐ 67 Super Bowl XI 1.50 .70 .19
Oakland AFC 32
Minnesota NFC 14
(Ken Stabler hand off)

☐ 68 Super Bowl XII 4.00 1.80 .50
Dallas NFC 27
Denver AFC 10
(Roger Staubach and
Tony Dorsett)

1979 Fleer Team Action

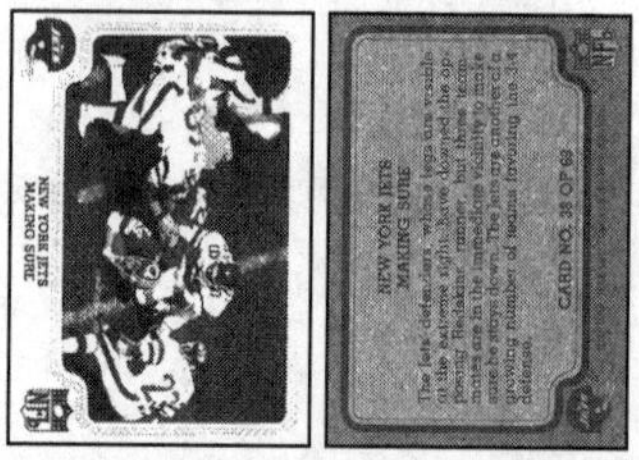

The 1979 Fleer Teams in Action football set mirrors the previous two sets in design (colorful action scenes with specific players not identified) and contains an additional card for the most recent Super Bowl making a total of 69 standard-size cards in the set. The fronts have white borders, and the backs are printed in black ink on gray stock. The backs have a 1979 copyright date. The card numbering follows team name alphabetical order followed by Super Bowl cards in chronological order. Cards were issued in wax packs of seven team cards plus three team logo stickers.

	NRMT-MT	EXC	G-VG
COMPLETE SET (69)	35.00	16.00	4.40
COMMON CARD (1-56)	.40	.18	.05
COMMON SB CARD (57-69)	.60	.25	.07

☐ 1 Atlanta Falcons 1.00 .45 .12
What's Up
Front Counts

☐ 2 Atlanta Falcons .40 .18 .05
Following The
Bouncing Ball

☐ 3 Baltimore Colts .40 .18 .05
Big Enough To Drive
A Truck Through

☐ 4 Baltimore Colts .40 .18 .05
When The Defense
Becomes The Offense

☐ 5 Buffalo Bills .40 .18 .05
Full Steam Ahead

☐ 6 Buffalo Bills .40 .18 .05
Three's A Crowd

☐ 7 Chicago Bears .40 .18 .05
Moving Out As One

☐ 8 Chicago Bears .40 .18 .05
Stack 'Em Up

☐ 9 Cincinnati Bengals .40 .18 .05
Out In The
Open Field

☐ 10 Cincinnati Bengals .40 .18 .05
Sandwiched

☐ 11 Cleveland Browns .40 .18 .05
Protective Pocket

☐ 12 Cleveland Browns .40 .18 .05
Shake Rattle
And Roll

☐ 13 Dallas Cowboys 3.00 1.35 .35
Paving The Way
(Tony Dorsett running)

☐ 14 Dallas Cowboys .60 .25 .07
The Right Place
At The Right Time

☐ 15 Denver Broncos .40 .18 .05
A Stable Of Runners

☐ 16 Denver Broncos .40 .18 .05
Orange Crush

☐ 17 Detroit Lions .40 .18 .05
Through The Line

☐ 18 Detroit Lions .40 .18 .05
Tracked Down

☐ 19 Green Bay Packers .40 .18 .05
Power Play

☐ 20 Green Bay Packers .40 .18 .05
Four-To-One Odds

☐ 21 Houston Oilers 7.00 3.10 .85
Offensive Gusher
(Earl Campbell running)

☐ 22 Houston Oilers .40 .18 .05
Gotcha

☐ 23 Kansas City Chiefs .40 .18 .05
Get Wings

☐ 24 Kansas City Chiefs .40 .18 .05
Ambushed

☐ 25 Los Angeles Rams .40 .18 .05
Men In The Middle

☐ 26 Los Angeles Rams .40 .18 .05
Nowhere To Go
But Down

☐ 27 Miami Dolphins .60 .25 .07
Escort Service

☐ 28 Miami Dolphins .60 .25 .07
All For One

☐ 29 Minnesota Vikings .40 .18 .05
Up And Over

☐ 30 Minnesota Vikings .40 .18 .05
The Purple Gang

☐ 31 New England Patriots .40 .18 .05
Prepare For Takeoff

☐ 32 New England Patriots .40 .18 .05
Dept. Of Defense

☐ 33 New Orleans Saints 1.00 .45 .12
Bombs Away
(Archie Manning)

☐ 34 New Orleans Saints .40 .18 .05
Duel In The Dome

☐ 35 New York Giants .40 .18 .05
Battle Of The Line
Of Scrimmage

☐ 36 New York Giants .40 .18 .05
Piled Up

☐ 37 New York Jets .40 .18 .05
Hitting The Hole

☐ 38 New York Jets .40 .18 .05
Making Sure

☐ 39 Oakland Raiders 2.00 .90 .25
Left-Handed
Strength
(Ken Stabler)

☐ 40 Oakland Raiders .60 .25 .07
Black Sunday

☐ 41 Philadelphia Eagles .40 .18 .05
Ready Aim Fire

☐ 42 Philadelphia Eagles .40 .18 .05
Closing In

☐ 43 Pittsburgh Steelers .60 .25 .07
Anchor Man

☐ 44 Pittsburgh Steelers 1.00 .45 .12
The Steel Curtain

☐ 45 St. Louis Cardinals .60 .25 .07
High Altitude Bomber
(Jim Hart)

☐ 46 St. Louis Cardinals .40 .18 .05
Three On One

☐ 47 San Diego Chargers .40 .18 .05
Charge

☐ 48 San Diego Chargers .40 .18 .05
Special Teams Shot

☐ 49 San Francisco 49ers .60 .25 .07
In For The Score

☐ 50 San Francisco 49ers .60 .25 .07
Nothing But
Red Shirts

☐ 51 Seattle Seahawks .40 .18 .05
North-South Runner

☐ 52 Seattle Seahawks .40 .18 .05
The Sting

☐ 53 Tampa Bay Buccaneers .40 .18 .05
Hitting Paydirt

☐ 54 Tampa Bay Buccaneers .40 .18 .05
Making 'Em Pay
The Price

☐ 55 Washington Redskins .60 .25 .07
On The Warpath

☐ 56 Washington Redskins .60 .25 .07
Drawing A Crowd

☐ 57 Super Bowl I 1.00 .45 .12

Green Bay NFL 35
Kansas City AFL 10
(Jim Taylor running)

		MINT	NRMT	EXC
☐ 58 Super Bowl II		1.25	.55	.16

Green Bay NFL 33
Oakland AFL 14
(Bart Starr passing)

☐ 59 Super Bowl III ..... .60 .25 .07
New York AFL 16
Baltimore NFL 7

☐ 60 Super Bowl IV ..... .60 .25 .07
Kansas City AFL 23
Minnesota NFL 7

☐ 61 Super Bowl V ..... .60 .25 .07
Baltimore AFC 16
Dallas NFC 13

☐ 62 Super Bowl VI ..... 2.00 .90 .25
Dallas NFC 24
Miami AFC 3
(Bob Griese
and Bob Lilly)

☐ 63 Super Bowl VII ..... .60 .25 .07
Miami AFC 14
Washington NFC 7

☐ 64 Super Bowl VIII ..... 2.00 .90 .25
Miami AFC 24
Minnesota NFC 7
(Bob Griese and
Larry Csonka)

☐ 65 Super Bowl IX ..... 3.00 1.35 .35
Pittsburgh AFC 16
Minnesota NFC 6
(Terry Bradshaw and
Franco Harris)

☐ 66 Super Bowl X ..... .60 .25 .07
Pittsburgh AFC 21
Dallas NFC 17

☐ 67 Super Bowl XI ..... .60 .25 .07
Oakland AFC 32
Minnesota NFC 14

☐ 68 Super Bowl XII ..... .60 .25 .07
Dallas NFC 27
Denver AFC 10

☐ 69 Super Bowl XIII ..... 1.25 .55 .16
Pittsburgh AFC 35
Dallas NFC 31

1980 Fleer Team Action

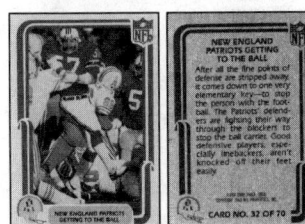

The 1980 Fleer Teams in Action football set continues the tradition of earlier sets but has one additional card for the most recent Super Bowl, i.e., now 70 full color standard-size cards in the set. The fronts have white borders and the backs are printed in black on gray stock. The cards are numbered on back and feature a 1980 copyright date. The card numbering follows team name alphabetical order followed by Super Bowl cards in chronological order. Cards were issued in seven-card wax packs along with three team logo stickers.

	MINT	NRMT	EXC
COMPLETE SET (70)	25.00	11.00	3.10
COMMON CARD (1-56)	.30	.14	.04
COMMON SB CARD (57-70)	.50	.23	.06

☐ 1 Atlanta Falcons ..... .75 .35 .09
Getting The
Extra Yards

☐ 2 Atlanta Falcons ..... .30 .14 .04
Falcons Get
Their Prey

☐ 3 Baltimore Colts ..... .30 .14 .04
Looking For Daylight
(Joe Washington)

☐ 4 Baltimore Colts ..... .30 .14 .04
Ready If Needed

☐ 5 Buffalo Bills ..... .30 .14 .04
You Block For Me and
I'll Block For You

☐ 6 Buffalo Bills ..... .30 .14 .04
Stand Em Up And
Push 'Em Back

☐ 7 Chicago Bears ..... 4.00 1.80 .50
Coming Through
(Walter Payton)

☐ 8 Chicago Bears ..... .30 .14 .04
Four On One

☐ 9 Cincinnati Bengals ..... .30 .14 .04
Power Running

☐ 10 Cincinnati Bengals ..... .30 .14 .04
Out Of Running Room

☐ 11 Cleveland Browns ..... 1.00 .45 .12
End Around
(Ozzie Newsome)

☐ 12 Cleveland Browns ..... .30 .14 .04
Rubber Band Defense

☐ 13 Dallas Cowboys ..... 2.00 .90 .25
Point Of Attack
(Tony Dorsett)

☐ 14 Dallas Cowboys ..... .60 .25 .07
Man In The Middle
(Bob Breunig)

☐ 15 Denver Broncos ..... .30 .14 .04
Strong And Steady

☐ 16 Denver Broncos ..... .30 .14 .04
Orange Power

☐ 17 Detroit Lions ..... .30 .14 .04
On The March

☐ 18 Detroit Lions ..... .30 .14 .04
The Silver Rush

☐ 19 Green Bay Packers ..... .30 .14 .04
Getting Underway

☐ 20 Green Bay Packers ..... .30 .14 .04
The Best Offense
Is A Good Defense

☐ 21 Houston Oilers ..... .30 .14 .04
Airborne

☐ 22 Houston Oilers ..... .30 .14 .04
Search And Destroy

☐ 23 Kansas City Chiefs ..... .30 .14 .04
Blazing The Trail

☐ 24 Kansas City Chiefs ..... .30 .14 .04
Making Sure

☐ 25 Los Angeles Rams ..... .30 .14 .04
One Good Turn
Deserves Another

☐ 26 Los Angeles Rams ..... .30 .14 .04
Shedding The Block

☐ 27 Miami Dolphins ..... .30 .14 .04
Sweeping The Flanks

☐ 28 Miami Dolphins ..... .30 .14 .04
Keep 'Em Busy

☐ 29 Minnesota Vikings ..... .30 .14 .04
One Man To Beat

☐ 30 Minnesota Vikings ..... .30 .14 .04
Purple People
Eaters II

☐ 31 New England Patriots ..... .30 .14 .04
Hitting The Hole

☐ 32 New England Patriots ..... .30 .14 .04
Getting To The Ball

☐ 33 New Orleans Saints ..... .30 .14 .04
Splitting The
Defenders

☐ 34 New Orleans Saints ..... 1.00 .45 .12
Don't Let Him
Get Outside
(Joe Theismann)

☐ 35 New York Giants ..... 2.50 1.10 .30
Audible
(Phil Simms)

☐ 36 New York Giants ..... .30 .14 .04
Wrong Side Up

☐ 37 New York Jets ..... .30 .14 .04
Make Him Miss

☐ 38 New York Jets ..... .30 .14 .04
The Only Way To
Play (Mark Gastineau)

☐ 39 Oakland Raiders ..... .30 .14 .04
Pulling Out All
The Stops

☐ 40 Oakland Raiders ..... .30 .14 .04
Right On

☐ 41 Philadelphia Eagles ..... .30 .14 .04
Not Pretty, But
Still Points

☐ 42 Philadelphia Eagles ..... .30 .14 .04
Applying The Clamps

☐ 43 Pittsburgh Steelers ..... 2.00 .90 .25
All Systems Go
(Franco Harris sweep)

☐ 44 Pittsburgh Steelers ..... .30 .14 .04
Still The Steel
Curtain

☐ 45 St. Louis Cardinals ..... 1.00 .45 .12
On The Move
(Ottis Anderson)

☐ 46 St. Louis Cardinals ..... .30 .14 .04
Long Gone

☐ 47 San Diego Chargers ..... .30 .14 .04
Short-Range Success

☐ 48 San Diego Chargers ..... .30 .14 .04
Pursuit

☐ 49 San Francisco 49ers ..... .30 .14 .04
Getting Field Position

☐ 50 San Francisco 49ers ..... .30 .14 .04
Finding A Nugget

☐ 51 Seattle Seahawks ..... .30 .14 .04
They'll Try
Anything Once

☐ 52 Seattle Seahawks ..... .30 .14 .04
Paying The Price

☐ 53 Tampa Bay Buccaneers ..... .30 .14 .04
Coming Of Age

☐ 54 Tampa Bay Buccaneers ..... 3.00 1.35 .35
3-4 Shut The Door
(Walter Payton
tackled)

☐ 55 Washington Redskins ..... .30 .14 .04

Wide Open

☐ 56 Washington Redskins ..... .30 .14 .04
Rude Reception

☐ 57 Super Bowl I ..... .50 .23 .06
Green Bay NFL 35
Kansas City AFL 10

☐ 58 Super Bowl II ..... 1.00 .45 .12
Green Bay NFL 33
Oakland AFL 14
(Bart Starr)

☐ 59 Super Bowl III ..... 2.50 1.10 .30
New York AFL 16
Baltimore NFL 7
(Joe Namath)

☐ 60 Super Bowl IV ..... .50 .23 .06
Kansas City AFL 23
Minnesota NFL 7

☐ 61 Super Bowl V ..... .50 .23 .06
Baltimore AFC 16
Dallas NFC 13

☐ 62 Super Bowl VI ..... 2.50 1.10 .30
Dallas NFC 24
Miami AFC 3
(Roger Staubach)

☐ 63 Super Bowl VII ..... .50 .23 .06
Miami AFC 14
Washington NFC 7

☐ 64 Super Bowl VIII ..... .50 .23 .06
Miami AFC 24
Minnesota NFC 7

☐ 65 Super Bowl IX ..... 1.50 .70 .19
Pittsburgh AFC 16
Minnesota NFC 6
(Terry Bradshaw
Rocky Bleier)

☐ 66 Super Bowl X ..... 1.00 .45 .12
Pittsburgh AFC 21
Dallas NFC 17
(Jack Lambert)

☐ 67 Super Bowl XI ..... .50 .23 .06
Oakland AFC 44
Minnesota NFC 14
(Chuck Foreman)

☐ 68 Super Bowl XII ..... .50 .23 .06
Dallas NFC 27
Denver AFC 10

☐ 69 Super Bowl XIII ..... 2.00 .90 .25
Pittsburgh AFC 35
Dallas NFC 31
(Terry Bradshaw)

☐ 70 Super Bowl XIV ..... 1.50 .70 .19
Pittsburgh AFC 31
Los Angeles NFC 19
(Franco Harris)

1981 Fleer Team Action

The 1981 Fleer Teams in Action football set deviates from previous years in that, while each team is depicted on two cards and each Super Bowl is depicted on one card, an additional group of cards (72-88) have been added to make the set number 88 standard-size cards, no doubt to accomodate the press sheet size. The card numbering follows team name alphabetical order followed by Super Bowl cards in chronological order and the last group of miscellaneous cards. The card fronts are in full color with white borders, and the card backs are printed in blue and red on white stock. The backs feature a 1981 copyright. Cards were issued in eight-card wax packs along with three team logo stickers.

	MINT	NRMT	EXC
COMPLETE SET (88)	22.00	10.00	2.70
COMMON CARD (1-88)	.25	.11	.03

☐ 1 Atlanta Falcons ..... .50 .23 .06
Out In The Open
(William Andrews)

☐ 2 Atlanta Falcons ..... .25 .11 .03
Grits Blitz

☐ 3 Baltimore Colts ..... .25 .11 .03
Sprung Through
The Line

☐ 4 Baltimore Colts ..... .25 .11 .03
Human Pyramid

☐ 5 Buffalo Bills ..... .25 .11 .03
Buffalo Bills'
Wild West Show

☐ 6 Buffalo Bills ..... .25 .11 .03
Buffaloed

☐ 7 Chicago Bears ..... 2.50 1.10 .30
About To Hit Paydirt
(Walter Payton)

☐ 8 Chicago Bears ..... .25 .11 .03

Bear Trap

☐ 9 Cincinnati Bengals ..... .25 .11 .03
Behind The Wall
(Pete Johnson)

☐ 10 Cincinnati Bengals ..... .25 .11 .03
Black Cloud

☐ 11 Cleveland Browns ..... .35 .16 .04
Point Of Attack
(Mike Pruitt)

☐ 12 Cleveland Browns ..... .50 .23 .06
The Only Way To
Go Is Down
(Rocky Bleier tackled)

☐ 13 Dallas Cowboys ..... .50 .23 .06
Big O In Big D
(Ron Springs fumble)

☐ 14 Dallas Cowboys ..... .50 .23 .06
Headed Off At The Pass

☐ 15 Denver Broncos ..... .25 .11 .03
Man Versus Elements
(Craig Morton in snow)

☐ 16 Denver Broncos ..... .25 .11 .03
The Old High-Low
Treatment

☐ 17 Detroit Lions ..... .50 .23 .06
Play Action
(Billy Sims)

☐ 18 Detroit Lions ..... .25 .11 .03
Into The Lions' Den

☐ 19 Green Bay Packers ..... .25 .11 .03
A Packer Packs
The Pigskin

☐ 20 Green Bay Packers ..... .25 .11 .03
Sandwiched

☐ 21 Houston Oilers ..... .25 .11 .03
Wait A Minute

☐ 22 Houston Oilers ..... .25 .11 .03
3-4 Shut The Door

☐ 23 Kansas City Chiefs ..... .25 .11 .03
On The Ball

☐ 24 Kansas City Chiefs ..... .25 .11 .03
Seeing Red

☐ 25 Los Angeles Rams ..... .25 .11 .03
The Point Of Attack

☐ 26 Los Angeles Rams ..... .25 .11 .03
Get Your Hands Up

☐ 27 Miami Dolphins ..... .35 .16 .04
Plenty Of Time
(David Woodley)

☐ 28 Miami Dolphins ..... .35 .16 .04
Pursuit

☐ 29 Minnesota Vikings ..... .25 .11 .03
Tough Yardage

☐ 30 Minnesota Vikings ..... .25 .11 .03
Purple Avalanche
(Pete Johnson)

☐ 31 New England Patriots ..... .25 .11 .03
In High Gear

☐ 32 New England Patriots ..... 1.00 .45 .12
Keep 'Em Covered
(Ken Stabler)

☐ 33 New Orleans Saints ..... .50 .23 .06
Setting Up
(Archie Manning)

☐ 34 New Orleans Saints ..... .25 .11 .03
Air Ball

☐ 35 New York Giants ..... .25 .11 .03
Off Tackle

☐ 36 New York Giants ..... .25 .11 .03
In The Land Of
The Giants

☐ 37 New York Jets ..... .35 .16 .04
Cleared For Lauching
(Richard Todd)

☐ 38 New York Jets ..... .25 .11 .03
Airborne

☐ 39 Oakland Raiders ..... .35 .16 .04
Off And Running

☐ 40 Oakland Raiders ..... .35 .16 .04
Block That Kick

☐ 41 Philadelphia Eagles ..... .25 .11 .03
About To Take Flight

☐ 42 Philadelphia Eagles ..... .25 .11 .03
Birds Of Prey
(Robert Newhouse)

☐ 43 Pittsburgh Steelers ..... 1.00 .45 .12
Here Come The
Infantry
(Franco Harris)

☐ 44 Pittsburgh Steelers ..... .35 .16 .04
Like A Steel Trap

☐ 45 St. Louis Cardinals ..... .25 .11 .03
Run To Daylight

☐ 46 St. Louis Cardinals ..... .25 .11 .03
Stacked Up And Up

☐ 47 San Diego Chargers ..... .25 .11 .03
Straight-Ahead Power

☐ 48 San Diego Chargers ..... .25 .11 .03
Stonewalled

☐ 49 San Francisco 49ers ..... .35 .16 .04
Follow The Leader

☐ 50 San Francisco 49ers ..... .35 .16 .04
Search And Destroy

☐ 51 Seattle Seahawks ..... .25 .11 .03
Short-Range Success

☐ 52 Seattle Seahawks ..... .25 .11 .03

Take Down
		MINT	NRMT	EXC
☐ 53	Tampa Bay Buccaneers	.25	.11	.03
	Orange Blossom Special			
	(Jerry Eckwood)			
☐ 54	Tampa Bay Buccaneers	.25	.11	.03
	Tropical Storm Buc			
☐ 55	Washington Redskins	.35	.16	.04
	Alone For A Moment			
☐ 56	Washington Redskins	.35	.16	.04
	Ambushed			
☐ 57	Super Bowl I	.50	.23	.06
	Green Bay NFL 35			
	Kansas City AFL 10			
	(Jim Taylor)			
☐ 58	Super Bowl II	.25	.11	.03
	Green Bay NFL 35			
	Oakland AFL 14			
☐ 59	Super Bowl III	.25	.11	.03
	New York AFL 16			
	Baltimore NFL 7			
☐ 60	Super Bowl IV	.25	.11	.03
	Kansas City AFL 23			
	Minnesota NFL 7			
☐ 61	Super Bowl V	.25	.11	.03
	Baltimore AFC 16			
	Dallas NFC 13			
☐ 62	Super Bowl VI	.35	.16	.04
	Dallas NFC 24			
	Miami AFC 3			
☐ 63	Super Bowl VII	.25	.11	.03
	Miami AFC 14			
	Washington NFC 7			
☐ 64	Super Bowl VIII	1.00	.45	.12
	Miami AFC 24			
	Minnesota NFC 7			
	(Larry Csonka running)			
☐ 65	Super Bowl IX	1.00	.45	.12
	Pittsburgh AFC 16			
	Minnesota NFC 6			
	(Franco Harris)			
☐ 66	Super Bowl X	.35	.16	.04
	Pittsburgh AFC 21			
	Dallas NFC 17			
☐ 67	Super Bowl XI	1.00	.45	.12
	Oakland AFC 32			
	Minnesota NFC 14			
	(Ken Stabler)			
☐ 68	Super Bowl XII	2.00	.90	.25
	Dallas NFC 27			
	Denver AFC 10			
	(Roger Staubach and Tony Dorsett)			
☐ 69	Super Bowl XIII	2.50	1.10	.30
	Pittsburgh AFC 35			
	Dallas NFC 31			
	(Roger Staubach and Tony Dorsett)			
☐ 70	Super Bowl XIV	1.00	.45	.12
	Pittsburgh AFC 31			
	Los Angeles NFC 19			
	(Franco Harris)			
☐ 71	Super Bowl XV	.35	.16	.04
	Oakland AFC 27			
	Philadelphia NFC 10			
	(Jim Plunkett)			
☐ 72	Training Camp	.60	.25	.07
	(Steelers)			
	(Chuck Noll)			
☐ 73	Practice Makes Perfect	.25	.11	.03
☐ 74	Airborn Carrier	.25	.11	.03
☐ 75	The National Anthem	.25	.11	.03
	Chargers			
☐ 76	Filling Up	.25	.11	.03
	(Stadium)			
☐ 77	Away In Time	1.50	.70	.19
	(Terry Bradshaw)			
☐ 78	Flat Out	.25	.11	.03
☐ 79	Halftime	.25	.11	.03
	(Band playing)			
☐ 80	Warm Ups Patriots	.25	.11	.03
☐ 81	Getting To The Bottom Of It	.25	.11	.03
☐ 82	Souvenir (Crowd)	.25	.11	.03
☐ 83	A Game Of Inches	.25	.11	.03
	(Officials measuring)			
☐ 84	The Overview	.25	.11	.03
☐ 85	The Dropback	.25	.11	.03
☐ 86	Pregame Huddle	.25	.11	.03
	(Redskins)			
☐ 87	Every Way But Loose UER	.25	.11	.03
	(Giants helmet on back, should be Rams)			
☐ 88	Mudders UER	.35	.16	.04
	(Redskins helmet on back, should be 49ers)			

1982 Fleer Team Action

The 1982 Fleer Teams in Action football set is very similar to the 1981 set (with again 88 standard-size cards) and other Fleer Teams in Action sets of previous years. The backs are printed in yellow and gray on a white stock. These cards feature a 1982 copyright date. The card numbering follows team name alphabetical order followed by

Super Bowl cards in chronological order and NFL Team Highlights cards. Cards were issued in wax packs of seven team cards along with three team logo stickers.

		MINT	NRMT	EXC
	COMPLETE SET (88)	45.00	20.00	5.50
	COMMON CARD (1-88)	.25	.11	.03
☐ 1	Atlanta Falcons	.60	.25	.07
	Running to Daylight			
	(William Andrews)			
☐ 2	Atlanta Falcons	.25	.11	.03
	Airborne Falcons			
☐ 3	Baltimore Colts	.35	.16	.04
	Plenty of Time To Throw (Bert Jones and Mark Gastineau)			
☐ 4	Baltimore Colts	.25	.11	.03
	Lassoing the Opponent			
☐ 5	Buffalo Bills	.35	.16	.04
	Point of Attack (Joe Ferguson)			
☐ 6	Buffalo Bills	.25	.11	.03
	Capturing the Enemy			
☐ 7	Chicago Bears	2.50	1.10	.30
	Three on One (Walter Payton)			
☐ 8	Chicago Bears	.25	.11	.03
	Stretched Out			
☐ 9	Cincinnati Bengals	.25	.11	.03
	About to Hit Paydirt (Pete Johnson)			
☐ 10	Cincinnati Bengals	.25	.11	.03
	Tiger-Striped Attack			
☐ 11	Cleveland Browns	.35	.16	.04
	Reading the Field (Brian Sipe)			
☐ 12	Cleveland Browns	.25	.11	.03
	Covered From All Angles			
☐ 13	Dallas Cowboys	1.25	.55	.16
	Blocking Convoy (Tony Dorsett)			
☐ 14	Dallas Cowboys	.35	.16	.04
	Encircled			
☐ 15	Denver Broncos	.35	.16	.04
	Springing Into Action (Craig Morton)			
☐ 16	Denver Broncos	.25	.11	.03
	High and Low			
☐ 17	Detroit Lions	.25	.11	.03
	Setting Up The Screen Pass			
☐ 18	Detroit Lions	.35	.16	.04
	Poised and Ready To Attack (Doug Williams)			
☐ 19	Green Bay Packers	.25	.11	.03
	Flying Through The Air			
☐ 20	Green Bay Packers	.25	.11	.03
	Hitting The Pack			
☐ 21	Houston Oilers	4.00	1.80	.50
	Waiting For The Hole To Open (Gifford Nielsen and Earl Campbell)			
☐ 22	Houston Oilers	.25	.11	.03
	Biting The Dust			
☐ 23	Kansas City Chiefs	.25	.11	.03
	Going In Untouched			
☐ 24	Kansas City Chiefs	.25	.11	.03
	No Place To Go			
☐ 25	Los Angeles Rams	.25	.11	.03
	Getting To The Outside (Wendell Tyler)			
☐ 26	Los Angeles Rams	.75	.35	.09
	Double Team, Double Trouble (John Riggins tackled)			
☐ 27	Miami Dolphins	.35	.16	.04
	Cutting Back Against The Grain (Tony Nathan)			
☐ 28	Miami Dolphins	.35	.16	.04
	Taking Two Down			
☐ 29	Minnesota Vikings	.25	.11	.03
	Running Inside For Tough Yardage			
☐ 30	Minnesota Vikings	.25	.11	.03
	Bowling Over The Opponent			
☐ 31	New England Patriots	.25	.11	.03
	Leaping For The First Down			
☐ 32	New England Patriots	.25	.11	.03
	Gang Tackling			
☐ 33	New Orleans Saints	.35	.16	.04
	Breaking Into The Clear (George Rogers)			
☐ 34	New Orleans Saints	.25	.11	.03
	Double Jeopardy			
☐ 35	New York Giants	.25	.11	.03

Getting Ready To Hit The Opening
		MINT	NRMT	EXC
☐ 36	New York Giants	1.25	.55	.16
	Negative Yardage (Tony Dorsett)			
☐ 37	New York Jets	.35	.16	.04
	Off To The Races (Freeman McNeil)			
☐ 38	New York Jets	.25	.11	.03
	Sandwiched			
☐ 39	Oakland Raiders	.35	.16	.04
	Throwing The Down and Out (Marc Wilson)			
☐ 40	Oakland Raiders	.35	.16	.04
	The Second Wave Is On The Way			
☐ 41	Philadelphia Eagles	.35	.16	.04
	Blasting Up The Middle (Ron Jaworski)			
☐ 42	Philadelphia Eagles	.75	.35	.09
	Triple-Teaming (Carl Hairston and John Riggins)			
☐ 43	Pittsburgh Steelers	.35	.16	.04
	Stretching For A Score			
☐ 44	Pittsburgh Steelers	.35	.16	.04
	Rising Above The Crowd			
☐ 45	St. Louis Cardinals	.35	.16	.04
	Sweeping To The Right (Jim Hart)			
☐ 46	St. Louis Cardinals	.25	.11	.03
	No Place To Go But Down			
☐ 47	San Diego Chargers	.25	.11	.03
	Looking For Someone To Block			
☐ 48	San Diego Chargers	.25	.11	.03
	Being In The Right Place			
☐ 49	San Francisco 49ers	20.00	9.00	2.50
	Giving Second Effort (Joe Montana)			
☐ 50	San Francisco 49ers	.50	.23	.06
	In Your Face (Steve Bartkowski)			
☐ 51	Seattle Seahawks	.75	.35	.09
	Nothing But Open Space (Jack Lambert)			
☐ 52	Seattle Seahawks	.35	.16	.04
	Attacking From The Blind Side (Brian Sipe)			
☐ 53	Tampa Bay Buccaneers	.35	.16	.04
	Everyone In Motion (Doug Williams)			
☐ 54	Tampa Bay Buccaneers	.25	.11	.03
	Ring Around The Running Back			
☐ 55	Washington Redskins	.75	.35	.09
	Knocking Them Down One-By-One (Joe Theismann)			
☐ 56	Washington Redskins	.35	.16	.04
	Coming From All Directions			
☐ 57	Super Bowl I	.50	.23	.06
	Green Bay NFL 35			
	Kansas City AFL 10			
	(Jim Taylor)			
☐ 58	Super Bowl II	.25	.11	.03
	Green Bay NFL 33			
	Oakland AFL 14			
☐ 59	Super Bowl III	.25	.11	.03
	New York AFL 16			
	Baltimore NFL 7			
☐ 60	Super Bowl IV	.25	.11	.03
	Kansas City AFL 23			
	Minnesota NFL 7			
☐ 61	Super Bowl V	.25	.11	.03
	Baltimore AFC 16			
	Dallas NFC 13			
☐ 62	Super Bowl VI	1.00	.45	.12
	Dallas NFC 24			
	Miami AFC 3			
	(Bob Griese and Bob Lilly)			
☐ 63	Super Bowl VII	.75	.35	.09
	Miami AFC 14			
	Washington NFC 7			
	(Larry Csonka running)			
☐ 64	Super Bowl VIII	1.00	.45	.12
	Miami AFC 24			
	Minnesota NFC 7			
	(Larry Csonka and Paul Warfield)			
☐ 65	Super Bowl IX	.25	.11	.03
	Pittsburgh AFC 16			
	Minnesota NFC 6			
☐ 66	Super Bowl X	2.00	.90	.25
	Pittsburgh AFC 21			

		MINT	NRMT	EXC
	Dallas NFC 17 (Roger Staubach)			
☐ 67	Super Bowl XI	.35	.16	.04
	Oakland AFC 32			
	Minnesota NFC 14			
	(Mark Van Eeghen)			
☐ 68	Super Bowl XII	2.00	.90	.25
	Dallas NFC 27			
	Denver AFC 10			
	(Roger Staubach)			
☐ 69	Super Bowl XIII	1.25	.55	.16
	Pittsburgh AFC 35			
	Dallas NFC 31			
	(Lynn Swann)			
☐ 70	Super Bowl XIV	.25	.11	.03
	Pittsburgh AFC 31			
	Los Angeles NFC 19			
☐ 71	Super Bowl XV	.35	.16	.04
	Oakland AFC 27			
	Philadelphia NFC 10			
	(Jim Plunkett)			
☐ 72	Super Bowl XVI	1.00	.45	.12
	San Francisco NFC 26			
	Cincinnati AFC 21			
	(Dwight Clark)			
☐ 73	NFL Team Highlights	15.00	6.75	1.85
	1982 AFC-NFC Pro Bowl Action (Montana rolling)			
☐ 74	NFL Team Highlights	1.00	.45	.12
	1982 AFC-NFC Pro Bowl Action (Ken Anderson and Anthony Munoz)			
☐ 75	NFL Team Highlights	.25	.11	.03
	Aloha Stadium			
☐ 76	NFL Team Highlights	.25	.11	.03
	On The Field Meeting			
☐ 77	NFL Team Highlights	.60	.25	.07
	First Down (Joe Theismann)			
☐ 78	NFL Team Highlights	.25	.11	.03
	The Man In Charge (Jerry Markbright)			
☐ 79	NFL Team Highlights	.25	.11	.03
	Coming Onto The Field			
☐ 80	NFL Team Highlights	.25	.11	.03
	In The Huddle (Bill Kenney and Carlos Carson)			
☐ 81	NFL Team Highlights	.25	.11	.03
	Lying In Wait (Atlanta defense)			
☐ 82	NFL Team Highlights	.25	.11	.03
	Celebration			
☐ 83	NFL Team Highlights	.25	.11	.03
	Men In Motion			
☐ 84	NFL Team Highlights	.25	.11	.03
	Shotgun Formation			
☐ 85	NFL Team Highlights	.25	.11	.03
	Training Camp			
☐ 86	NFL Team Highlights	1.00	.45	.12
	Halftime Instructions (Bill Walsh in locker room)			
☐ 87	NFL Team Highlights	.25	.11	.03
	Field Goal Attempt (Rolf Benirschke)			
☐ 88	NFL Team Highlights	.35	.16	.04
	Free Kick			

1983 Fleer Team Action

The 1983 Fleer Teams in Action football set contains 88 standard-size cards. There are two cards numbered 67, one of which was obviously intended to be card number 66. The backs are printed in blue on white card stock. These cards feature a 1983 copyright date. The card numbering follows team name alphabetical order followed by Super Bowl cards in chronological order and NFL Team Highlights cards. Cards were issued in seven-card packs along with three team logo stickers.

		MINT	NRMT	EXC
	COMPLETE SET (88)	25.00	11.00	3.10
	COMMON CARD (1-88)	.25	.11	.03
☐ 1	Atlanta Falcons	1.00	.45	.12
	Breaking Away to Daylight (Ronnie Lott)			
☐ 2	Atlanta Falcons	.25	.11	.03
	Piled Up			
☐ 3	Baltimore Colts	.25	.11	.03

Cutting Back
to Daylight
☐ 4 Baltimore Colts .25 .11 .03
Pressuring the QB
(Joe Ferguson)
☐ 5 Buffalo Bills .25 .11 .03
Moving to the Outside
(Roosevelt Leaks running)
☐ 6 Buffalo Bills .25 .11 .03
Buffalo Stampede
☐ 7 Chicago Bears 2.50 1.10 .30
Ready to Let It Fly
(Jim McMahon and
Walter Payton)
☐ 8 Chicago Bears .25 .11 .03
Jump Ball
☐ 9 Cincinnati Bengals .25 .11 .03
Hurdling Into Open
☐ 10 Cincinnati Bengals .25 .11 .03
Hands Up
☐ 11 Cleveland Browns .25 .11 .03
An Open Field Ahead
(Mike Pruitt)
☐ 12 Cleveland Browns .25 .11 .03
Reacting to the
Ball Carrier
☐ 13 Dallas Cowboys 1.25 .55 .16
Mid-Air Ballet
(Tony Dorsett)
☐ 14 Dallas Cowboys .35 .16 .04
3, 2, 1 Takeoff
☐ 15 Denver Broncos .25 .11 .03
Clear Sailing
☐ 16 Denver Broncos .25 .11 .03
Stacking Up Offense
☐ 17 Detroit Lions .25 .11 .03
Hitting the Wall
☐ 18 Detroit Lions .25 .11 .03
Snapping into Action
☐ 19 Green Bay Packers .75 .35 .09
Fingertip Control
(Ed Too Tall Jones)
☐ 20 Green Bay Packers .25 .11 .03
QB Sack
☐ 21 Houston Oilers .25 .11 .03
Sweeping to Outside
☐ 22 Houston Oilers .25 .11 .03
Halting Forward
Progress
(Freeman McNeil)
☐ 23 Kansas City Chiefs .25 .11 .03
Waiting for
the Key Block
☐ 24 Kansas City Chiefs .35 .16 .04
Going Head to Head
(John Hannah)
☐ 25 Los Angeles Raiders .50 .23 .06
Bombs Away
(Jim Plunkett passing)
☐ 26 Los Angeles Raiders .35 .16 .04
Caged Bengal
☐ 27 Los Angeles Rams .25 .11 .03
Clearing Out Middle
☐ 28 Los Angeles Rams .25 .11 .03
One on One Tackle
☐ 29 Miami Dolphins .35 .16 .04
Skating through Hole
☐ 30 Miami Dolphins .35 .16 .04
Follow the Bounc-
ing Ball
☐ 31 Minnesota Vikings .35 .16 .04
Dropping into Pocket
(Tommy Kramer)
☐ 32 Minnesota Vikings .25 .11 .03
Attacking from
All Angles
☐ 33 New England Patriots .25 .11 .03
Touchdown
☐ 34 New England Patriots 2.50 1.10 .30
Pouncing Patriots
(Walter Payton tackled)
☐ 35 New Orleans Saints .25 .11 .03
Only One Man to Beat
☐ 36 New Orleans Saints 1.25 .55 .16
Closing In
(Tony Dorsett)
☐ 37 New York Giants .25 .11 .03
Setting Up to Pass
☐ 38 New York Giants .25 .11 .03
In Pursuit
☐ 39 New York Jets .25 .11 .03
Just Enough Room
☐ 40 New York Jets .25 .11 .03
Wrapping Up Runner
☐ 41 Philadelphia Eagles .35 .16 .04
Play Action Fakers
(Ron Jaworski and
Harry Carson)
☐ 42 Philadelphia Eagles .35 .16 .04
Step Away from Sack
(Archie Manning)
☐ 43 Pittsburgh Steelers 1.00 .45 .12
Exploding Through a
Hole (Franco Harris
and Terry Bradshaw)
☐ 44 Pittsburgh Steelers .75 .35 .09
Outnumbered
(Jack Lambert)
☐ 45 St. Louis Cardinals .25 .11 .03
Keeping His Balance
☐ 46 St. Louis Cardinals .25 .11 .03
Waiting for the
Reinforcements
☐ 47 San Diego Chargers .25 .11 .03
Supercharged Charger
☐ 48 San Diego Chargers .25 .11 .03
Triple Team Tackle
☐ 49 San Francisco 49ers .35 .16 .04
There's No Stopping
Him Now
☐ 50 San Francisco 49ers .35 .16 .04
Heading 'Em Off
at the Pass
☐ 51 Seattle Seahawks .35 .16 .04
Calling the Signals
(Jim Zorn)
☐ 52 Seattle Seahawks .25 .11 .03
The Hands Have It
☐ 53 Tampa Bay Buccaneers .25 .11 .03
Off to the Races
☐ 54 Tampa Bay Buccaneers .25 .11 .03
Buccaneer Sandwich
☐ 55 Washington Redskins .35 .16 .04
Looking for Daylight
☐ 56 Washington Redskins .35 .16 .04
Smothering the
Ball Carrier
☐ 57 Super Bowl I .75 .35 .09
Green Bay NFL 35
Kansas City AFL 10
(Jim Taylor)
☐ 58 Super Bowl II .25 .11 .03
Green Bay NFL 33
Oakland AFL 14
☐ 59 Super Bowl III .25 .11 .03
New York AFL 16
Baltimore NFL 7
☐ 60 Super Bowl IV .25 .11 .03
Kansas City AFL 23
Minnesota NFL 7
☐ 61 Super Bowl V 1.50 .70 .19
Baltimore AFC 16
Dallas NFC 13
(Johnny Unitas)
☐ 62 Super Bowl VI 1.00 .45 .12
Dallas NFC 24
Miami AFC 3
(Bob Griese and
Bob Lilly)
☐ 63 Super Bowl VII .35 .16 .04
Miami AFC 14
Washington NFC 7
(Manny Fernandez)
☐ 64 Super Bowl VIII .75 .35 .09
Miami AFC 24
Minnesota NFC 7
(Larry Csonka diving)
☐ 65 Super Bowl IX 1.00 .45 .12
Pittsburgh AFC 16
Minnesota NFC 6
(Franco Harris)
☐ 66 Super Bowl X UER 1.50 .70 .19
Pittsburgh AFC 21
Dallas NFC 17
(Terry Bradshaw;
number on back 67)
☐ 67 Super Bowl XI .35 .16 .04
Oakland AFC 32
Minnesota NFC 14
(see also card 66)
☐ 68 Super Bowl XII .25 .11 .03
Dallas NFC 27
Denver AFC 10
☐ 69 Super Bowl XIII 1.25 .55 .16
Pittsburgh AFC 35
Dallas NFC 31
(Terry Bradshaw
passing)
☐ 70 Super Bowl XIV .25 .11 .03
Pittsburgh AFC 31
Los Angeles NFC 19
(Vince Ferragamo
passing)
☐ 71 Super Bowl XV .25 .11 .03
Oakland AFC 27
Philadelphia NFC 10
☐ 72 Super Bowl XVI .25 .11 .03
San Francisco NFC 26
Cincinnati AFC 21
☐ 73 Super Bowl XVII .75 .35 .09
Washington NFC 27
Miami AFC 17
(John Riggins running)
☐ 74 NFL Team Highlights 1.00 .45 .12
1983 AFC-NFC
Pro Bowl (Dan Fouts)
☐ 75 NFL Team Highlights .25 .11 .03
Super Bowl XVII
Spectacular
☐ 76 NFL Team Highlights .25 .11 .03
Tampa Stadium: Super
Bowl XVIII
☐ 77 NFL Team Highlights .25 .11 .03
Up, Up, and Away
☐ 78 NFL Team Highlights .35 .16 .04
Sideline Conference
(Steve Bartkowski)
☐ 79 NFL Team Highlights .25 .11 .03
Barefoot Follow-
Through
(Mike Lansford)
☐ 80 NFL Team Highlights .25 .11 .03
Fourth and Long
(Max Runager punting)
☐ 81 NFL Team Highlights .25 .11 .03
Blocked Punt
☐ 82 NFL Team Highlights .25 .11 .03
Fumble
☐ 83 NFL Team Highlights .25 .11 .03
National Anthem
☐ 84 NFL Team Highlights .25 .11 .03
Concentrating on the
Ball (Tony Franklin)
☐ 85 NFL Team Highlights .25 .11 .03
Splashing Around
☐ 86 NFL Team Highlights .25 .11 .03
Loading in Shotgun
☐ 87 NFL Team Highlights .25 .11 .03
Taking the Snap
☐ 88 NFL Team Highlights .35 .16 .04
Line of Scrimmage

1984 Fleer Team Action

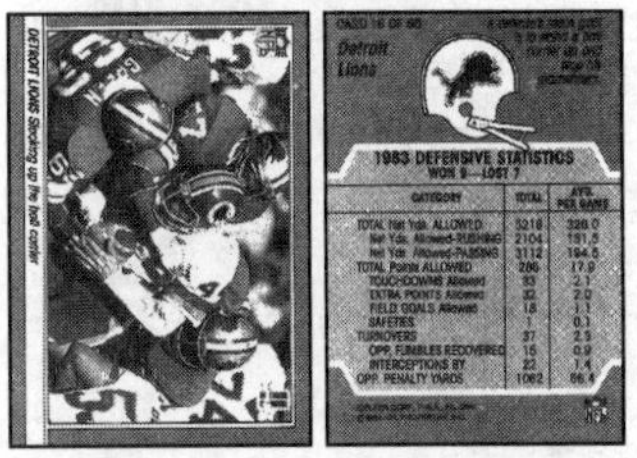

The 1984 Fleer Teams in Action football card set contains 88 standard-size cards. The cards feature a 1984 copyright date. The cards show action scenes with specific players not identified. There is a green border on the fronts of the cards with the title of the card inside a yellow strip; the backs are red and white. The card fronts are in full color. The card numbering follows team name alphabetical order (with the exception of the Indianapolis Colts whose last-minute move from Baltimore aparently put them out of order) followed by Super Bowl cards in chronological order and NFL Team Highlights cards. Cards were issued in seven-card wax packs along with three team logo stickers.

	MINT	NRMT	EXC
COMPLETE SET (88)	22.00	10.00	2.70
COMMON CARD (1-88)	.25	.11	.03

☐ 1 Atlanta Falcons .35 .16 .04
☐ 2 Atlanta Falcons .25 .11 .03
Gang Tackle
☐ 3 Indianapolis Colts .25 .11 .03
About to Break Free
☐ 4 Indianapolis Colts .25 .11 .03
Cutting Off All
the Angles
☐ 5 Buffalo Bills .25 .11 .03
Cracking the First
Line of Defense
☐ 6 Buffalo Bills .25 .11 .03
Getting Help From
A Friend
☐ 7 Chicago Bears 2.50 1.10 .30
Over the Top
(Jim McMahon
and Walter Payton)
☐ 8 Chicago Bears .25 .11 .03
You Grab Him High
I'll Grab Him Low
☐ 9 Cincinnati Bengals .25 .11 .03
Skipping Through
an Opening
☐ 10 Cincinnati Bengals .25 .11 .03
Saying Hello to a QB
(Joe Ferguson)
☐ 11 Cleveland Browns .25 .11 .03
Free Sailing into
the End Zone
(Greg Pruitt)
☐ 12 Cleveland Browns .25 .11 .03
Making Sure of
the Tackle
☐ 13 Dallas Cowboys .50 .23 .06
(Danny White)
☐ 14 Dallas Cowboys .60 .25 .07
Cowboy's Corral
(Ed Too Tall Jones)
☐ 15 Denver Broncos .25 .11 .03
Sprinting into the Open
☐ 16 Denver Broncos .25 .11 .03
Ready to Pounce
(Curt Warner)
☐ 17 Detroit Lions .35 .16 .04
Lion on the Prowl
(Billy Sims)
☐ 18 Detroit Lions .60 .25 .07
Stacking Up
the Ball Carrier
(John Riggins)
☐ 19 Green Bay Packers .25 .11 .03
Waiting For the
Hole to Open
☐ 20 Green Bay Packers .25 .11 .03
Packing Up
Your Opponent
☐ 21 Houston Oilers 4.00 1.80 .50
Nothing But Open
Spaces Ahead
(Earl Campbell)
☐ 22 Houston Oilers .25 .11 .03
Meeting Him Head On
☐ 23 Kansas City Chiefs .25 .11 .03
Going Outside for
Extra Yardage
☐ 24 Kansas City Chiefs .25 .11 .03
A Running Back
in Trouble
☐ 25 Los Angeles Raiders 1.50 .70 .19
No Defenders in Sight
(Marcus Allen)
☐ 26 Los Angeles Raiders 1.00 .45 .12
Rampaging Raiders
(Howie Long and
John Riggins)
☐ 27 Los Angeles Rams .25 .11 .03
Making the Cut
☐ 28 Los Angeles Rams .25 .11 .03
Caught From Behind
☐ 29 Miami Dolphins .35 .16 .04
Sliding Down the Line
☐ 30 Miami Dolphins .35 .16 .04
Making Sure
☐ 31 Minnesota Vikings .25 .11 .03
Stretching For
Touchdown
☐ 32 Minnesota Vikings .25 .11 .03
Hitting the Wall
☐ 33 New England Patriots .35 .16 .04
Straight Up the Middle
(Steve Grogan)
☐ 34 New England Patriots 3.00 1.35 .35
Come here and
Give Me a Hug
(Earl Campbell tackled)
☐ 35 New Orleans Saints .25 .11 .03
One Defender to Beat
☐ 36 New Orleans Saints .25 .11 .03
Saints Sandwich
☐ 37 New York Giants .25 .11 .03
A Six Point Landing
☐ 38 New York Giants .25 .11 .03
Leaping to the Aid
of a Teammate
☐ 39 New York Jets .25 .11 .03
Galloping through
Untouched
☐ 40 New York Jets .25 .11 .03
Capturing the Enemy
☐ 41 Philadelphia Eagles .25 .11 .03
One More Block and
He's Gone
☐ 42 Philadelphia Eagles .25 .11 .03
Meeting an Opponent
With Open Arms
☐ 43 Pittsburgh Steelers .35 .16 .04
The Play Begins
to Develop
☐ 44 Pittsburgh Steelers .35 .16 .04
Rally Around the
Ball Carrier
☐ 45 St. Louis Cardinals .25 .11 .03
Sprinting Around
the Corner
☐ 46 St. Louis Cardinals .25 .11 .03
Overmatched
☐ 47 San Diego Chargers .25 .11 .03
Up, Up, and Away
☐ 48 San Diego Chargers .25 .11 .03
Engulfing the Opponent
☐ 49 San Francisco 49ers .35 .16 .04
Tunneling Up
the Middle
(Wendell Tyler)
☐ 50 San Francisco 49ers .60 .25 .07
Nowhere to Go but
Down (John Riggins)
☐ 51 Seattle Seahawks .25 .11 .03
Letting the Ball Fly
(Jim Zorn)
☐ 52 Seattle Seahawks .25 .11 .03
Handing Out
Some Punishment
☐ 53 Tampa Bay Buccaneers .25 .11 .03
When he Hits the
Ground He's Gone
☐ 54 Tampa Bay Buccaneers .25 .11 .03
One Leg Takedown
☐ 55 Washington Redskins .60 .25 .07
Plenty of Room to Run

(John Riggins)
□ 56 Washington Redskins .... .35 .16 .04
Squashing the Opponent
□ 57 Super Bowl I .... .50 .23 .06
Green Bay NFL 35
Kansas City AFL 10
(Jim Taylor)
□ 58 Super Bowl II .... .75 .35 .09
Green Bay NFL 33
Oakland AFL 14
(Bart Starr)
□ 59 Super Bowl III .... .25 .11 .03
New York AFL 16
Baltimore NFL 7
□ 60 Super Bowl IV .... .25 .11 .03
Kansas City AFL 23
Minnesota NFL 7
□ 61 Super Bowl V .... .50 .23 .06
Baltimore AFC 16
Dallas NFC 13
(Earl Morrall)
□ 62 Super Bowl VI .... 1.25 .55 .16
Dallas NFC 24
Miami AFC 3
(Roger Staubach)
□ 63 Super Bowl VII .... .60 .25 .07
Miami AFC 14
Washington NFC 7
(Jim Kiick and
Bob Griese)
□ 64 Super Bowl VIII .... .75 .35 .09
Miami AFC 24
Minnesota NFC 7
(Larry Csonka diving)
□ 65 Super Bowl IX .... 1.00 .45 .12
Pittsburgh AFC 16
Minnesota NFC 6
(Terry Bradshaw)
□ 66 Super Bowl X .... .75 .35 .09
Pittsburgh AFC 21
Dallas NFC 17
(Franco Harris)
□ 67 Super Bowl XI .... .25 .11 .03
Oakland AFC 32
Minnesota NFC 14
□ 68 Super Bowl XII .... 1.00 .45 .12
Dallas NFC 27
Denver AFC 10
(Tony Dorsett)
□ 69 Super Bowl XIII .... .75 .35 .09
Pittsburgh AFC 35
Dallas NFC 31
(Franco Harris)
□ 70 Super Bowl XIV .... .75 .35 .09
Pittsburgh AFC 31
Los Angeles NFC 19
(Franco Harris)
□ 71 Super Bowl XV .... .25 .11 .03
Oakland AFC 27
Philadelphia NFC 10
(Jim Plunkett)
□ 72 Super Bowl XVI .... .25 .11 .03
San Francisco NFC 26
Cincinnati AFC 21
□ 73 Super Bowl XVII .... .25 .11 .03
Washington NFC 27
Miami AFC 17
□ 74 Super Bowl XVIII .... .75 .35 .09
Los Angeles AFC 38
Washington NFC 9
(Howie Long)
□ 75 NFL Team Highlights .... .25 .11 .03
Official's Conference
□ 76 NFL Team Highlights .... .25 .11 .03
Leaping for the
Ball Carrier
□ 77 NFL Team Highlights .... .25 .11 .03
Setting Up in the
Passing Pocket
(Jim Plunkett)
□ 78 NFL Team Highlights .... .25 .11 .03
Field Goal Block
□ 79 NFL Team Highlights .... .35 .16 .04
Stopped For No Gain
(Steve Grogan)
□ 80 NFL Team Highlights .... .25 .11 .03
Double Team Block
□ 81 NFL Team Highlights .... .25 .11 .03
Kickoff
□ 82 NFL Team Highlights .... .25 .11 .03
Punt Block
□ 83 NFL Team Highlights .... .25 .11 .03
Coaches Signals
□ 84 NFL Team Highlights .... .25 .11 .03
Training Camp
□ 85 NFL Team Highlights .... .25 .11 .03
Fumble
(Dwight Stephenson)
□ 86 NFL Team Highlights .... .25 .11 .03
1984 AFC-NFC Pro Bowl
□ 87 NFL Team Highlights .... .25 .11 .03
Cheerleaders
□ 88 NFL Team Highlights .... .60 .25 .07
In the Huddle
(Joe Theismann)

1985 Fleer Team Action

This 88-card standard-size set, entitled Fleer Teams in Action, is essentially organized alphabetically by the name of the team. There are three cards for each team, the first subtitled "On Offense" with offensive team statistics on the back, the second "On Defense" with defensive team statistics on the back, and the third "In Action" with a team schedule for the upcoming 1985 season. The last four cards feature highlights of the previous three Super Bowls and Pro Bowl. The cards are typically oriented horizontally. The cards feature a 1985 copyright date. The cards show full-color action scenes with specific players not identified. The card backs are printed in orange and black on white card stock. Cards were issued in wax packs of 15 cards and one sticker.

	MINT	NRMT	EXC
COMPLETE SET (88)	30.00	13.50	3.70
COMMON CARD (1-88)	.25	.11	.03

□ 1 Atlanta Falcons .... .35 .16 .04
Nothing But Open
Spaces Ahead
□ 2 Atlanta Falcons .... .25 .11 .03
Leveling Ball Carrier
□ 3 Atlanta Falcons .... .60 .25 .07
Flying Falcon
(John Riggins)
□ 4 Buffalo Bills .... .25 .11 .03
Ducking Under
the Pressure
□ 5 Buffalo Bills .... .25 .11 .03
Swallowing Up
the Opponent
□ 6 Buffalo Bills .... .25 .11 .03
Avoiding Late Hit
□ 7 Chicago Bears .... 2.00 .90 .25
Picking His Spot
(Walter Payton)
□ 8 Chicago Bears .... .25 .11 .03
C'Mon Guys, Give Me
Some Room to Breathe
□ 9 Chicago Bears .... .75 .35 .09
Just Hanging Around
in Case They're Needed
(Richard Dent)
□ 10 Cincinnati Bengals .... .25 .11 .03
Struggling for
Every Extra Yard
□ 11 Cincinnati Bengals .... .25 .11 .03
Making Opponent Pay
□ 12 Cincinnati Bengals .... .25 .11 .03
Just Out of the
Reach of the Defender
□ 13 Cleveland Browns .... .25 .11 .03
Plenty of Time to
Fire the Ball
□ 14 Cleveland Browns .... .25 .11 .03
Hitting the Wall
□ 15 Cleveland Browns .... .25 .11 .03
Look What We Found
□ 16 Dallas Cowboys .... 1.00 .45 .12
Waiting for the Right
Moment to Burst Upfield
(Tony Dorsett and
Wilber Marshall)
□ 17 Dallas Cowboys .... 1.50 .70 .19
Sorry Buddy, This is
the End of the Line
(Ed Too Tall Jones
tackling Walter Payton)
□ 18 Dallas Cowboys .... .60 .25 .07
Following Through
for Three Points
(Ed Too Tall Jones)
□ 19 Denver Broncos .... .25 .11 .03
Blasting Up the Middle
□ 20 Denver Broncos .... .25 .11 .03
Finishing Off
the Tackle
□ 21 Denver Broncos .... .25 .11 .03
About to Hit Paydirt
□ 22 Detroit Lions .... .25 .11 .03
Waiting to Throw
Until the Last Second
(Dexter Manley)
□ 23 Detroit Lions .... .25 .11 .03
Double Trouble on
the Tackle
□ 24 Detroit Lions .... .25 .11 .03
Quick Pitch
□ 25 Green Bay Packers .... .35 .16 .04
Unleashing the

Long Bomb
(Steve McMichael)
□ 26 Green Bay Packers .... 1.00 .45 .12
Encircling the
Ball Carrier
(Marcus Allen)
□ 27 Green Bay Packers .... .25 .11 .03
Piggy-Back Ride
□ 28 Houston Oilers .... 3.50 1.55 .45
Retreating into
the Pocket
(Warren Moon and
Earl Campbell)
□ 29 Houston Oilers .... .25 .11 .03
Punishing the Enemy
□ 30 Houston Oilers .... .25 .11 .03
No Chance to
Block This One
□ 31 Indianapolis Colts .... .25 .11 .03
Getting Ready to
Let It Fly
□ 32 Indianapolis Colts .... .25 .11 .03
Pushing the Ball
Carrier Backward
□ 33 Indianapolis Colts .... .25 .11 .03
Nowhere to Go
□ 34 Kansas City Chiefs .... .25 .11 .03
Cutting Back for
Extra Yardage
□ 35 Kansas City Chiefs .... .25 .11 .03
Reaching for
the Deflection
□ 36 Kansas City Chiefs .... .25 .11 .03
Rising to the Occasion
□ 37 Los Angeles Raiders .... .35 .16 .04
Hurdling Into
the Open Field
□ 38 Los Angeles Raiders .... .35 .16 .04
No Place to Go
□ 39 Los Angeles Raiders .... .35 .16 .04
Standing Tall
In the Pocket
□ 40 Los Angeles Rams .... 1.00 .45 .12
One More Barrier and
He's Off to the Races
(Eric Dickerson)
□ 41 Los Angeles Rams .... .25 .11 .03
Driving A Shoulder
Into the Opponent
□ 42 Los Angeles Rams .... .25 .11 .03
The Kickoff
□ 43 Miami Dolphins .... .35 .16 .04
Sidestepping Trouble
(Tony Nathan)
□ 44 Miami Dolphins .... .35 .16 .04
Hold On, We're Coming
□ 45 Miami Dolphins 12.00 5.50 1.50
The Release Point
(Dan Marino)
□ 46 Minnesota Vikings .... .25 .11 .03
Putting As Much As
He Has Into the Pass
(Tommy Kramer)
□ 47 Minnesota Vikings .... .25 .11 .03
Gang Tackling
□ 48 Minnesota Vikings .... .25 .11 .03
You're Not Getting Away
From Me This Time
□ 49 New England Patriots .... .25 .11 .03
Throwing On the Run
(Tony Eason)
□ 50 New England Patriots .... .25 .11 .03
The Only Place to Go
Is Down
□ 51 New England Patriots .... .25 .11 .03
Standing the Ball
Carrier Up
□ 52 New Orleans Saints .... .25 .11 .03
Going Up the Middle
Under A Full Head
of Steam
□ 53 New Orleans Saints .... .25 .11 .03
Putting Everything
They've Got Into
the Tackle
□ 54 New Orleans Saints .... .25 .11 .03
Getting Off the Ground
to Block the Kick
□ 55 New York Giants .... .25 .11 .03
Over the Top
□ 56 New York Giants .... .25 .11 .03
Rallying Around
the Opposition
□ 57 New York Giants .... .50 .23 .06
The Huddle
(Phil Simms)
□ 58 New York Jets .... .25 .11 .03
Following His Blockers
□ 59 New York Jets .... .25 .11 .03
This Is As Far
As You Go
□ 60 New York Jets .... .25 .11 .03
Looking Over
the Defense
□ 61 Philadelphia Eagles .... .25 .11 .03
Going Through the

Opening Untouched
□ 62 Philadelphia Eagles .... .25 .11 .03
Squashing the Enemy
□ 63 Philadelphia Eagles .... .25 .11 .03
There's No Room
Here, So Let's
Go Outside
□ 64 Pittsburgh Steelers .... .35 .16 .04
Sprinting Around
the End
□ 65 Pittsburgh Steelers .... .35 .16 .04
Mismatch
□ 66 Pittsburgh Steelers .... .35 .16 .04
About to Be Thrown
Back
□ 67 St.Louis Cardinals .... .25 .11 .03
In for Six
□ 68 St.Louis Cardinals .... .25 .11 .03
Piling Up the
Ball Carrier
□ 69 St.Louis Cardinals .... .50 .23 .06
Causing the Fumble
(Joe Theismann tackled)
□ 70 San Diego Chargers .... .25 .11 .03
Plenty of Open
Space Ahead
□ 71 San Diego Chargers .... .25 .11 .03
Ready to Be
Swallowed Up
□ 72 San Diego Chargers .... .25 .11 .03
A Quarterback in
Serious Trouble
□ 73 San Francisco 49ers .... .35 .16 .04
Reading the Hole and
Exploding Through It
□ 74 San Francisco 49ers .... .35 .16 .04
Burying the Opponent
□ 75 San Francisco 49ers .... 7.00 3.10 .85
Waiting to Throw
Until His Receiver
Breaks Free
(Joe Montana and
Russ Francis)
□ 76 Seattle Seahawks .... .35 .16 .04
Getting Just Enough
Time to Pass
(Dave Krieg)
□ 77 Seattle Seahawks .... .35 .16 .04
Capturing the Enemy
(Craig James tackled)
□ 78 Seattle Seahawks .... .25 .11 .03
It's Going to Be
A Footrace Now
□ 79 Tampa Bay Buccaneers .... .25 .11 .03
Heading Outside Away
From Trouble
□ 80 Tampa Bay Buccaneers .... .25 .11 .03
One-On-One Tackle
□ 81 Tampa Bay Buccaneers .... .60 .25 .07
A Buccaneers Sandwich
(Dickerson tackled)
□ 82 Washington Redskins .... .60 .25 .07
Just Enough Room
To Get Through
(John Riggins)
□ 83 Washington Redskins .... .35 .16 .04
Wrapping Up
the Opponent
□ 84 Washington Redskins .... .35 .16 .04
Field-Goal Attempt
(Mark Moseley)
□ 85 Super Bowl XIX .... .60 .25 .07
San Francisco NFC 38
Miami AFC 16
(Roger Craig running)
□ 86 Super Bowl XIX .... 5.00 2.20 .60
San Francisco NFC 38
Miami AFC 16
(Joe Montana passing)
□ 87 Super Bowl XIX .... .35 .16 .04
San Francisco NFC 38
Miami AFC 16
(Tony Nathan tackled)
□ 88 1985 Pro Bowl .... .35 .16 .04
AFC 22, NFC 14
(Runner stopped)

1986 Fleer Team Action

This 88-card standard-size set, entitled "Live Action Football," is essentially organized alphabetically by the name of the team. There are three cards for each team; the first subtitled "On Offense" with offensive team statistics on the back, the second "On Defense" with

defensive team statistics on the back, and the third "In Action" with a team schedule for the upcoming 1986 season. The last four cards feature highlights of the previous three Super Bowls and Pro Bowl. The cards are typically oriented horizontally. The cards feature a 1986 copyright date. The cards show full-color action scenes (with a light blue border around the photo) with specific players not identified. The card backs are printed in blue and black on white card stock. Cards were issued in wax packs of seven team action cards and three team logo stickers.

	MINT	NRMT	EXC
COMPLETE SET (88)	30.00	13.50	3.70
COMMON CARD (1-88)	.25	.11	.03
☐ 1 Atlanta Falcons — Preparing to Make Cut	.35	.16	.04
☐ 2 Atlanta Falcons — Everybody Gets Into the Act	.25	.11	.03
☐ 3 Atlanta Falcons — Where Do You Think You're Going	.25	.11	.03
☐ 4 Buffalo Bills — Turning On the After-Burners	.25	.11	.03
☐ 5 Buffalo Bills — Running Into a Wall of Blue	.25	.11	.03
☐ 6 Buffalo Bills — Up and Over	.25	.11	.03
☐ 7 Chicago Bears — Pocket Forms Around Passer (Jim McMahon and Walter Payton)	1.50	.70	.19
☐ 8 Chicago Bears — Monsters of the Midway II (Richard Dent and Dan Hampton)	.75	.35	.09
☐ 9 Chicago Bears — Blitz in a Blizzard (Mike Singletary)	.75	.35	.09
☐ 10 Cincinnati Bengals — Plowing through Defense (Dave Rimington and Anthony Munoz)	.35	.16	.04
☐ 11 Cincinnati Bengals — Zeroing In for the Hit	.25	.11	.03
☐ 12 Cincinnati Bengals — Oh, No You Don't (Marcus Allen)	.75	.35	.09
☐ 13 Cleveland Browns — Looking for a Hole to Develop (Bernie Kosar and Kevin Mack)	1.00	.45	.12
☐ 14 Cleveland Browns — Buried by the Browns	.25	.11	.03
☐ 15 Cleveland Browns — Another Runner Pounded Into the Turf	.25	.11	.03
☐ 16 Dallas Cowboys — Hole You Could Drive Truck Through (Tony Dorsett)	1.00	.45	.12
☐ 17 Dallas Cowboys — We've Got You Surrounded (Jim Jeffcoat)	.50	.23	.06
☐ 18 Dallas Cowboys — Giving the Referee Some Help (Randy White)	.50	.23	.06
☐ 19 Denver Broncos — The Blockers Spring Into Action (John Elway)	5.00	2.20	.60
☐ 20 Denver Broncos — The Orange Crush Shows Its Stuff	.25	.11	.03
☐ 21 Denver Broncos — A Stampede to Block the Kick	.25	.11	.03
☐ 22 Detroit Lions — A Runner's Eye View of the Situation	.25	.11	.03
☐ 23 Detroit Lions — Levelling the Ball Carrier	.25	.11	.03
☐ 24 Detroit Lions — Going All Out to Get the Quarterback	.25	.11	.03
☐ 25 Green Bay Packers — Sweeping Around the Corner	.25	.11	.03
☐ 26 Green Bay Packers — Not Afraid to Go Head to Head	.25	.11	.03
☐ 27 Green Bay Packers — Taking the Snap	.25	.11	.03
☐ 28 Houston Oilers — Plunging for that Extra Yard	.25	.11	.03
☐ 29 Houston Oilers — Tightening the Vise	.25	.11	.03
☐ 30 Houston Oilers — Launching a Field Goal	.25	.11	.03
☐ 31 Indianapolis Colts — Galloping Out of an Arm-Tackle	.25	.11	.03
☐ 32 Indianapolis Colts — Ball Is Knocked Loose	.25	.11	.03
☐ 33 Indianapolis Colts — Busting Out of the Backfield	.25	.11	.03
☐ 34 Kansas City Chiefs — About to Head Upfield	.25	.11	.03
☐ 35 Kansas City Chiefs — On the Warpath	.25	.11	.03
☐ 36 Kansas City Chiefs — Getting the Point Across	.25	.11	.03
☐ 37 Los Angeles Raiders — Looks Like Clear Sailing Ahead	.25	.11	.03
☐ 38 Los Angeles Raiders — Surrounded by Unfriendly Faces	.25	.11	.03
☐ 39 Los Angeles Raiders — Vaulting for Six Points	.25	.11	.03
☐ 40 Los Angeles Rams — Breaking into an Open Field (Eric Dickerson)	.60	.25	.07
☐ 41 Los Angeles Rams — Swept Away By a Wave of Rams	.25	.11	.03
☐ 42 Los Angeles Rams — Alertly Scooping Up a Fumble	.25	.11	.03
☐ 43 Miami Dolphins — Clearing a Path for the Running Back	.25	.11	.03
☐ 44 Miami Dolphins — Teaching a Painful Lesson	.25	.11	.03
☐ 45 Miami Dolphins — Trying for a Piece of the Ball	.25	.11	.03
☐ 46 Minnesota Vikings — All Day to Throw (Tommy Kramer)	.25	.11	.03
☐ 47 Minnesota Vikings — The Moment before Impact (Walter Payton tackled)	1.50	.70	.19
☐ 48 Minnesota Vikings — Leaving the Competition Behind	.25	.11	.03
☐ 49 New England Patriots — Solid Line of Blockers	.25	.11	.03
☐ 50 New England Patriots — Surprise Attack from the Rear	.25	.11	.03
☐ 51 New England Patriots — Getting a Grip on the Opponent	.25	.11	.03
☐ 52 New Orleans Saints — Look Out, I'm Coming Through	.25	.11	.03
☐ 53 New Orleans Saints — A Furious Assault	.25	.11	.03
☐ 54 New Orleans Saints — Line of Scrimmage	.25	.11	.03
☐ 55 New York Giants — Pass Play Develops (Phil Simms and Joe Morris)	.50	.23	.06
☐ 56 New York Giants — Putting Squeeze on Offense	.25	.11	.03
☐ 57 New York Giants — Using a Great Block to Turn Corner	.25	.11	.03
☐ 58 New York Jets — The Runner Spots Lane	.25	.11	.03
☐ 59 New York Jets — About to Deliver a Headache	.25	.11	.03
☐ 60 New York Jets — Flying Formation	.25	.11	.03
☐ 61 Philadelphia Eagles — Slipping a Tackle (Keith Byars)	.50	.23	.06
☐ 62 Philadelphia Eagles — Airborne Eagles Break Up Pass	.25	.11	.03
☐ 63 Philadelphia Eagles — Connecting on Toss Over Middle (Ron Jaworski passing)	.25	.11	.03
☐ 64 Pittsburgh Steelers — Letting Big Guy Lead The Way	.25	.11	.03
☐ 65 Pittsburgh Steelers — Converging From Every Direction	.35	.16	.04
☐ 66 Pittsburgh Steelers — All Eyes Are on the Football (Gary Anderson K)	.35	.16	.04
☐ 67 St.Louis Cardinals — Calmly Dropping Back to Pass (Neil Lomax and Jim Burt)	.25	.11	.03
☐ 68 St.Louis Cardinals — Applying Some Bruises	.25	.11	.03
☐ 69 St.Louis Cardinals — Looking for Yardage on Interception Return	.25	.11	.03
☐ 70 San Diego Chargers UER — Human Cannonball (reverse negative)	.25	.11	.03
☐ 71 San Diego Chargers — Another One Bites the Dust (Dave Krieg)	.35	.16	.04
☐ 72 San Diego Chargers — A Clean Steal by the Defense	.25	.11	.03
☐ 73 San Francisco 49ers — Looking for Safe Passage (Joe Montana handing off)	6.00	2.70	.75
☐ 74 San Francisco 49ers — An Uplifting Experience	.35	.16	.04
☐ 75 San Francisco 49ers — In Hot Pursuit (Danny White)	.50	.23	.06
☐ 76 Seattle Seahawks — Preparing for Collision	.25	.11	.03
☐ 77 Seattle Seahawks — A Group Effort	.25	.11	.03
☐ 78 Seattle Seahawks — Forcing a Hurried Throw (Dan Fouts)	.60	.25	.07
☐ 79 Tampa Bay Buccaneers — Protecting Quarterback at All Costs	.25	.11	.03
☐ 80 Tampa Bay Buccaneers — Dishing Out Some Punishment	.25	.11	.03
☐ 81 Tampa Bay Buccaneers — No Trespassing	.25	.11	.03
☐ 82 Washington Redskins — Squaring Off in the Trenches	.35	.16	.04
☐ 83 Washington Redskins — Pouncing on the Passer (Danny White)	.50	.23	.06
☐ 84 Washington Redskins — Two Hits Are Better Than One	.35	.16	.04
☐ 85 Super Bowl XX — Chicago NFC 46 New England AFC 10 (Walter Payton running)	1.50	.70	.19
☐ 86 Super Bowl XX — Chicago NFC 46 New England AFC 10 (Jim McMahon passing)	.50	.23	.06
☐ 87 Super Bowl XX — Chicago NFC 46 New England AFC 10 (Bears defense)	.25	.11	.03
☐ 88 Pro Bowl 1986 — NFC 28, AFC 24 (Marcus Allen running)	.75	.35	.09

1987 Fleer Team Action

This 88-card standard-size set, entitled "Live Action Football," is essentially organized alphabetically by the name of the team. There are two cards for each team; basically odd-numbered cards feature the team's offense and even-numbered cards feature the team's defense. The cards are typically oriented horizontally. The cards feature a 1987 copyright date. The cards show full-color action scenes (with a yellow and black border around the photo) with specific players not identified. The card backs are printed in gold and black on white card stock. Cards were issued in wax packs of seven team action cards and three team logo stickers.

	MINT	NRMT	EXC
COMPLETE SET (88)	25.00	11.00	3.10
COMMON CARD (1-88)	.20	.09	.03
☐ 1 Atlanta Falcons — A Clear View Downfield	.30	.14	.04
☐ 2 Atlanta Falcons — Pouncing on a Runner (Roger Craig tackled)	.20	.09	.03
☐ 3 Buffalo Bills — Buffalo Stampede	.20	.09	.03
☐ 4 Buffalo Bills UER — Double Bill (Bengals and Oilers pictured)	.20	.09	.03
☐ 5 Chicago Bears — Stay Out of Our Way (Walter Payton)	1.25	.55	.16
☐ 6 Chicago Bears — Quarterback's Night-mare (Dan Hampton)	.30	.14	.04
☐ 7 Cincinnati Bengals — Irresistible Force (Eddie Brown)	.20	.09	.03
☐ 8 Cincinnati Bengals UER — Bengals on the Prowl (Bills defense tackling Bengal)	.20	.09	.03
☐ 9 Cleveland Browns — Following the Lead Blocker	.20	.09	.03
☐ 10 Cleveland Browns — Block That Kick	.20	.09	.03
☐ 11 Dallas Cowboys — Next Stop...End Zone	.30	.14	.04
☐ 12 Dallas Cowboys — Ride 'em Cowboys	.30	.14	.04
☐ 13 Denver Broncos — Pitchout in Progress (John Elway)	3.00	1.35	.35
☐ 14 Denver Broncos — Broncos' Busters	.20	.09	.03
☐ 15 Detroit Lions — Off to the Races	.20	.09	.03
☐ 16 Detroit Lions — Entering the Lions' Den	.20	.09	.03
☐ 17 Green Bay Packers — Setting the Wheels in Motion	.20	.09	.03
☐ 18 Green Bay Packers — Stack of Packers	.20	.09	.03
☐ 19 Houston Oilers — Making a Cut at the Line of Scrimmage	.20	.09	.03
☐ 20 Houston Oilers — Hit Parade	.20	.09	.03
☐ 21 Indianapolis Colts — The Horses Up Front	.20	.09	.03
☐ 22 Indianapolis Colts — Stopping the Runner in His Tracks	.20	.09	.03
☐ 23 Kansas City Chiefs — It's a Snap	.20	.09	.03
☐ 24 Kansas City Chiefs — Nowhere to Hide (Bo Jackson getting tackled)	.75	.35	.09
☐ 25 Los Angeles Raiders — Looking for Daylight (Bo Jackson running)	1.00	.45	.12
☐ 26 Los Angeles Raiders — Wrapped Up by Raiders	.30	.14	.04
☐ 27 Los Angeles Rams — Movers and Shakers (Jim Everett)	.30	.14	.04
☐ 28 Los Angeles Rams — In the Quarter-back's Face	.20	.09	.03
☐ 29 Miami Dolphins — Full Speed Ahead	.30	.14	.04
☐ 30 Miami Dolphins — Acrobatic Interception	.30	.14	.04
☐ 31 Minnesota Vikings — Solid Line of Protection (Tommy Kramer)	.20	.09	.03
☐ 32 Minnesota Vikings — Bearing a Heavy Load	.20	.09	.03
☐ 33 New England Patriots — The Blockers Fan Out (Craig James)	.30	.14	.04
☐ 34 New England Patriots — Converging Linebackers	.20	.09	.03
☐ 35 New Orleans Saints — Saints Go Diving In (Dalton Hilliard and Jim Burt)	.20	.09	.03
☐ 36 New Orleans Saints — Crash Course	.20	.09	.03
☐ 37 New York Giants — Armed and Dangerous (Phil Simms)	.20	.09	.03
☐ 38 New York Giants — A Giant-sized Hit (Lawrence Taylor)	.75	.35	.09
☐ 39 New York Jets — Jets Prepare for Takeoff (Ken O'Brien)	.20	.09	.03
☐ 40 New York Jets — Showing No Mercy	.20	.09	.03
☐ 41 Philadelphia Eagles — Taking It Straight Up the Middle	.20	.09	.03
☐ 42 Philadelphia Eagles — The Strong Arm of the Defense (Reggie White)	1.25	.55	.16

Card	MINT	NRMT	EXC
43 Pittsburgh Steelers Double-team Trouble	.30	.14	.04
44 Pittsburgh Steelers Caught in a Steel Trap	.30	.14	.04
45 St. Louis Cardinals The kick is up and...it's good	.20	.09	.03
46 St. Louis Cardinals Seeing Red	.20	.09	.03
47 San Diego Chargers Blast Off	.20	.09	.03
48 San Diego Chargers Lightning Strikes (Todd Christensen tackled)	.20	.09	.03
49 San Francisco 49ers UER The Rush Is On (reverse negative photo on front)	.30	.14	.04
50 San Francisco 49ers Shoulder to Shoulder	.30	.14	.04
51 Seattle Seahawks Not a Defender in Sight (Curt Warner)	.20	.09	.03
52 Seattle Seahawks Hard Knocks	.20	.09	.03
53 Tampa Bay Buccaneers Rolling Out Against the Grain (Steve Young)	3.00	1.35	.35
54 Tampa Bay Buccaneers Crunch Time	.20	.09	.03
55 Washington Redskins Getting the Drop on the Defense (Jay Schroeder)	.30	.14	.04
56 Washington Redskins The Blitz Claims Another Victim	.30	.14	.04
57 AFC Championship Game Denver 23, Cleveland 20 (OT)	.20	.09	.03
58 AFC Divisional Playoff Cleveland 23, New York Jets 20 (OT)	.20	.09	.03
59 AFC Divisional Playoff Denver 22, New England 17 (Andre Tippett)	.20	.09	.03
60 AFC Wild Card Game New York Jets 35, Kansas City 15	.20	.09	.03
61 NFC Championship New York Giants 17, Washington 0 (Lawrence Taylor)	.50	.23	.06
62 NFC Divisional Playoff Washington 27, Chicago 13 (William Perry)	.30	.14	.04
63 NFC Divisional Playoff New York Giants 49, San Francisco 3 (Joe Morris)	.30	.14	.04
64 NFC Wild Card Game Washington 19, Los Angeles Rams 7 (Eric Dickerson)	.50	.23	.06
65 Super Bowl I Green Bay NFL 35, Kansas City AFL 10	.20	.09	.03
66 Super Bowl II Green Bay NFL 33, Oakland AFL 14 (Bart Starr)	.50	.23	.06
67 Super Bowl III New York AFL 16, Baltimore NFL 7 (Matt Snell running)	.20	.09	.03
68 Super Bowl IV Kansas City AFL 23, Minnesota NFL 7	.20	.09	.03
69 Super Bowl V Baltimore AFC 16, Dallas NFC 13 (Duane Thomas tackled)	.30	.14	.04
70 Super Bowl VI Dallas NFC 24, Miami AFC 3 (Roger Staubach)	1.25	.55	.16
71 Super Bowl VII Miami AFC 14, Washington NFC 7 (Bob Griese and Jim Kiick)	.50	.23	.06
72 Super Bowl VIII Miami AFC 24, Minnesota NFC 7 (Larry Csonka running)	.50	.23	.06
73 Super Bowl IX Pittsburgh AFC 16, Minnesota NFC 6 (Fran Tarkenton loose ball)	.50	.23	.06
74 Super Bowl X Pittsburgh AFC 21, Dallas NFC 17 (Franco Harris)	.60	.25	.07
75 Super Bowl XI Oakland AFC 32, Minnesota NFC 14 (Chuck Foreman tackled)	.20	.09	.03
76 Super Bowl XII Dallas NFC 27, Denver AFC 10 (Tony Dorsett running)	.75	.35	.09
77 Super Bowl XIII Pittsburgh AFC 35, Dallas NFC 31 (Terry Bradshaw passing)	1.00	.45	.12
78 Super Bowl XIV Pittsburgh AFC 31, Los Angeles NFC 19 (Cullen Bryant tackled)	.30	.14	.04
79 Super Bowl XV Oakland AFC 27, Philadelphia NFC 10 (Jim Plunkett passing)	.30	.14	.04
80 Super Bowl XVI San Francisco NFC 26, Cincinnati AFC 21	.30	.14	.04
81 Super Bowl XVII Washington NFC 27, Miami AFC 17	.20	.09	.03
82 Super Bowl XVIII Los Angeles AFC 38, Washington NFC 9 (Punt blocked)	.20	.09	.03
83 Super Bowl XIX San Francisco NFC 38, Miami AFC 16 (Roger Craig and Joe Montana)	5.00	2.20	.60
84 Super Bowl XX Chicago NFC 46, New England AFC 10 (Wilber Marshall and Richard Dent)	.30	.14	.04
85 Super Bowl XXI New York NFC 39, Denver AFC 20 (Lawrence Taylor)	.60	.25	.07
86 Super Bowl XXI New York NFC 39, Denver AFC 20 (Phil Simms)	.20	.09	.03
87 Super Bowl XXI Giants erupt in 3rd, Score 17 points (Lawrence Taylor and Carl Banks) (Checklist 1-44 on back)	.50	.23	.06
88 Super Bowl XXI Giants Outrun Broncos by only 27 yards (Checklist 45-88 on card back)	.30	.14	.04

1988 Fleer Team Action

This 88-card standard-size set, entitled "Live Action Football," is essentially organized alphabetically by the nickname of the team within each conference. There are two cards for each team. Basically odd-numbered cards feature the team's offense and even-numbered cards feature the team's defense. The Super Bowl cards included in this set are subtitled "Super Bowls of the Decade." The cards are typically oriented horizontally. The cards feature a 1988 copyright date. The cards show full-color action scenes with specific players not identified. The card backs are printed in blue and green on white card stock. Cards were issued in wax packs of seven team action cards and three team logo stickers.

	MINT	NRMT	EXC
COMPLETE SET (88)	20.00	9.00	2.50
COMMON CARD (1-88)	.20	.09	.03

Card	MINT	NRMT	EXC
1 Bengals Offense A Great Wall (Boomer Esiason)	.50	.23	.06
2 Bengals Defense Stacking the Odds	.20	.09	.03
3 Bills Offense Play-Action (Jim Kelly)	1.00	.45	.12
4 Bills Defense Buffalo Soldiers	.20	.09	.03
5 Broncos Offense Sneak Attack (John Elway)	1.25	.55	.16
6 Broncos Defense Crushing the Opposition	.20	.09	.03
7 Browns Offense On the Run (Bernie Kosar and Kevin Mack)	.30	.14	.04
8 Browns Defense Dogs' Day (Eric Dickerson)	.30	.14	.04
9 Chargers Offense A Bolt of Blue (Gary Anderson RB)	.20	.09	.03
10 Chargers Defense That's a Wrap	.20	.09	.03
11 Chiefs Offense Last Line of Offense	.20	.09	.03
12 Chiefs Defense Hard-Hitting in the Heartland	.20	.09	.03
13 Colts Offense An Eye To the End Zone	.20	.09	.03
14 Colts Defense Free Ball	.20	.09	.03
15 Dolphins Offense Miami Scoring Machine (Dan Marino takes snap)	5.00	2.20	.60
16 Dolphins Defense No Mercy	.30	.14	.04
17 Jets Offense On a Roll (Ken O'Brien)	.20	.09	.03
18 Jets Defense Jets Win a Dogfight	.20	.09	.03
19 Oilers Offense Well-Oiled Machine (Warren Moon hands off)	.75	.35	.09
20 Oilers Defense Hard Shoulder	.20	.09	.03
21 Patriots Offense A Clean Sweep (Craig James)	.30	.14	.04
22 Patriots Defense A Fall in New England (Bo Jackson tackled)	.30	.14	.04
23 Raiders Offense Rush Hour in Los Angeles (Bo Jackson)	.50	.23	.06
24 Raiders Defense Cut Me Some Slack (Howie Long)	.30	.14	.04
25 Seahawks Offense Follow the Leader (Curt Warner)	.20	.09	.03
26 Seahawks Defense Pain, But No Gain (Brian Bosworth)	.20	.09	.03
27 Steelers Offense Life in the Fast Lane	.30	.14	.04
28 Steelers Defense No Exit	.30	.14	.04
29 Bears Offense Bearly Audible	.20	.09	.03
30 Bears Defense Here, Kitty, Kitty	.20	.09	.03
31 Buccaneers Offense Letting Loose (Vinny Testaverde)	.30	.14	.04
32 Buccaneers Defense In The Grasp	.20	.09	.03
33 Cardinals Offense You've Gotta Hand It to Him (Neil Lomax)	.20	.09	.03
34 Cardinals Defense Stack of Cards (Roger Craig)	.30	.14	.04
35 Cowboys Offense Take It Away (Herschel Walker)	.30	.14	.04
36 Cowboys Defense Howdy, Pardner (Randy White)	.30	.14	.04
37 Eagles Offense Eagle in Flight (Randall Cunningham)	.50	.23	.06
38 Eagles Defense Buffalo Sandwich (Reggie White)	.75	.35	.09
39 Falcons Offense Rumbling Runner	.20	.09	.03
40 Falcons Defense The Brink of Disaster	.20	.09	.03
41 49ers Offense Move aside (Roger Craig)	.30	.14	.04
42 49ers Defense Bullies by the Bay (Ronnie Lott)	.50	.23	.06
43 Giants Offense Firing a Fastball (Phil Simms passing)	.30	.14	.04
44 Giants Defense A Giant Headache	.20	.09	.03
45 Lions Offense Charge Up the Middle	.20	.09	.03
46 Lions Defense Rocking and Rolling in Motown	.20	.09	.03
47 Packers Offense Gaining Altitude (Carl Lee)	.20	.09	.03
48 Packers Defense This Play is a Hit	.20	.09	.03
49 Rams Offense Rams Lock Horns (Jim Everett)	.20	.09	.03
50 Rams Defense Greetings from L.A.	.20	.09	.03
51 Redskins Offense Capital Gains	.30	.14	.04
52 Redskins Defense No More Mr. Nice Guy	.30	.14	.04
53 Saints Offense Roamin' in the Dome	.20	.09	.03
54 Saints Defense He'll Feel This One Tomorrow	.20	.09	.03
55 Vikings Offense Passing Fancy (Wade Wilson)	.20	.09	.03
56 Vikings Defense A Vikings' Siege	.20	.09	.03
57 Super Bowl XXII Washington 42, Denver 10 (Timmy Smith)	.20	.09	.03
58 Super Bowl Checklist (Timmy Smith running; Checklist 1-50 on back)	.20	.09	.03
59 Super Bowl Checklist (John Elway sacked; Checklist 51-88 on back)	1.00	.45	.12
60 Super Bowl XXI New York Giants 39, Denver 20 (Lawrence Taylor and Carl Banks)	.50	.23	.06
61 Super Bowl XX Chicago 46, New England 10 (Walter Payton)	1.00	.45	.12
62 Super Bowl XIX San Francisco 38, Miami 16 (Roger Craig running)	.30	.14	.04
63 Super Bowl XVIII L.A. Raiders 38, Washington 9 (Marcus Allen running)	.50	.23	.06
64 Super Bowl XVII Washington 27, Miami 17	.20	.09	.03
65 Super Bowl XVI San Francisco 26, Cincinnati 21 (Joe Montana pitching)	2.50	1.10	.30
66 Super Bowl XV Oakland 27, Philadelphia 10 (Jim Plunkett)	.30	.14	.04
67 Super Bowl XIV Pittsburgh 31, Los Angeles Rams 19	.20	.09	.03
68 NFC Championship Washington 17, Minnesota 10	.20	.09	.03
69 AFC Championship Denver 38, Cleveland 33 (John Elway)	1.00	.45	.12
70 NFC Playoff Game Minnesota 36, San Francisco 24 (Joe Montana chased)	2.50	1.10	.30
71 NFC Playoff Game Washington 21, Chicago 17	.20	.09	.03
72 AFC Playoff Game Cleveland 38, Indianapolis 21 (Ozzie Newsome and Kevin Mack)	.30	.14	.04
73 AFC Playoff Game Denver 34, Houston 10	.20	.09	.03
74 NFC Wild Card Game Minnesota 44, New Orleans 10	.20	.09	.03
75 AFC Wild Card Game Houston 23, Seattle 20 (OT)	.20	.09	.03
76 League Leading Team Rushing: 49ers (Roger Craig running)	.30	.14	.04
77 League Leading Team Passing: Dolphins	4.00	1.80	.50

(Dan Marino drops back)
□ 78 League Leading Team .20 .09 .03
Interceptions: Saints
□ 79 League Leading Team .20 .09 .03
Fumble Recovery:
Eagles
□ 80 League Leading Team .30 .14 .04
Sacks: Bears
(Richard Dent)
□ 81 League Leading Team .20 .09 .03
Defense Against
Kickoff Returns: Bills
□ 82 League Leading Team .20 .09 .03
Defense Against
Punt Returns: Jets
□ 83 League Leading Team .20 .09 .03
Punt Returns:
Cardinals
□ 84 League Leading Team .20 .09 .03
Kickoff Returns:
Falcons
□ 85 League Leading Team .20 .09 .03
Fewest Fumbles:
Steelers
□ 86 League Leading Team .30 .14 .04
Fewest Interceptions:
Browns (Bernie Kosar)
□ 87 League Leading Team .20 .09 .03
Fewest Points Allowed:
Colts
□ 88 League Leading Team .50 .23 .06
TD's on Returns: Rams
(Henry Ellard)

1990 Fleer

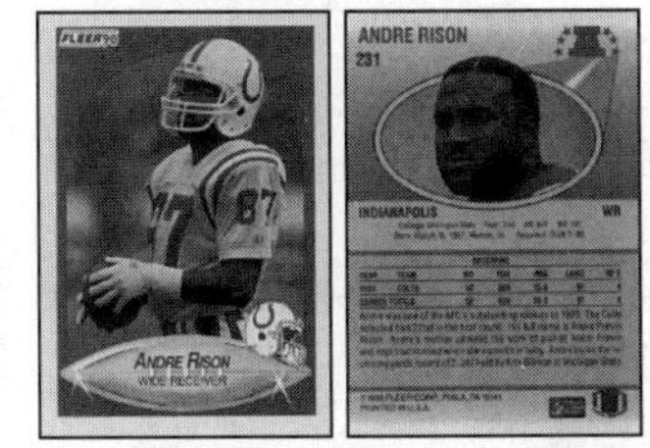

The 1990 Fleer set contains 400 standard-size cards. This set was issued in fifteen-card baggy packs as well as 43 card pre-priced ($1.49) jumbo packs. The fronts have color action photos and team colored inner borders with white outer borders. The vertically oriented backs are multicolored with stats and a color photo. The card numbering is alphabetical within team. The teams are essentially ordered by their respective order of finish during the 1989 season. The following cards have AFC logo location variations: 18, 20-22, 24, 27-30, 32, 49-56, 58, 60, 110-111, 113-117, 119, 122, 124, 198, 200-211, 213-217, and 221-223. Jim Covert (290) and Mark May (162) can be found with or without a thin line just above the text on the back. Rookie Cards include Jeff George and Jeff Hostetler.

	MINT	NRMT	EXC
COMPLETE SET (400)	7.50	3.40	.95
COMMON CARD (1-400)	.04	.02	.01

□ 1 Harris Barton .04 .02 .01
□ 2 Chet Brooks .04 .02 .01
□ 3 Michael Carter .04 .02 .01
□ 4 Mike Cofer UER .04 .02 .01
(FGA and FGM columns
switched)
□ 5 Roger Craig .10 .05 .01
□ 6 Kevin Fagan .04 .02 .01
□ 7 Charles Haley UER .10 .05 .01
(Fumble recoveries
should be 2 in '86
and 5 career, card
says 1 and 4)
□ 8 Pierce Holt .04 .02 .01
□ 9 Ronnie Lott .10 .05 .01
□ 10A Joe Montana ERR 1.00 .45 .12
(31,054 TD's)
□ 10B Joe Montana COR 1.00 .45 .12
(216 TD's)
□ 11 Bubba Paris .04 .02 .01
□ 12 Tom Rathman .04 .02 .01
□ 13 Jerry Rice 1.00 .45 .12
□ 14 John Taylor .25 .11 .03
□ 15 Keena Turner .04 .02 .01
□ 16 Michael Walter .04 .02 .01
□ 17 Steve Young .50 .23 .06
□ 18 Steve Atwater .04 .02 .01
□ 19 Tyrone Braxton .04 .02 .01
□ 20 Michael Brooks .04 .02 .01
□ 21 John Elway .50 .23 .06
□ 22 Simon Fletcher .04 .02 .01
□ 23 Bobby Humphrey .04 .02 .01
□ 24 Mark Jackson .04 .02 .01
□ 25 Vance Johnson .04 .02 .01
□ 26 Greg Kragen .04 .02 .01
□ 27 Ken Lanier .04 .02 .01
□ 28 Karl Mecklenburg .04 .02 .01
□ 29 Orson Mobley .04 .02 .01
□ 30 Steve Sewell .04 .02 .01
□ 31 Dennis Smith .04 .02 .01
□ 32 David Treadwell .04 .02 .01
□ 33 Flipper Anderson .04 .02 .01
□ 34 Greg Bell .04 .02 .01
□ 35 Henry Ellard .10 .05 .01
□ 36 Jim Everett .10 .05 .01
□ 37 Jerry Gray .04 .02 .01
□ 38 Kevin Greene .25 .11 .03
□ 39 Pete Holohan .04 .02 .01
□ 40 LeRoy Irvin .04 .02 .01
□ 41 Mike Lansford .04 .02 .01
□ 42 Buford McGee .04 .02 .01
□ 43 Tom Newberry .04 .02 .01
□ 44 Vince Newsome .04 .02 .01
□ 45 Jackie Slater .04 .02 .01
□ 46 Mike Wilcher .04 .02 .01
□ 47 Matt Bahr .04 .02 .01
□ 48 Brian Brennan .04 .02 .01
□ 49 Thane Gash .04 .02 .01
□ 50 Mike Johnson .04 .02 .01
□ 51 Bernie Kosar .10 .05 .01
□ 52 Reggie Langhorne .04 .02 .01
□ 53 Tim Manoa .04 .02 .01
□ 54 Clay Matthews .10 .05 .01
□ 55 Eric Metcalf .25 .11 .03
□ 56 Frank Minnifield .04 .02 .01
□ 57 Gregg Rakoczy UER .04 .02 .01
(First line of text
calls him Greg)
□ 58 Webster Slaughter .10 .05 .01
□ 59 Bryan Wagner .04 .02 .01
□ 60 Felix Wright .04 .02 .01
□ 61 Raul Allegre .04 .02 .01
□ 62 Ottis Anderson UER .10 .05 .01
(Stats say 9.317 yards,
should be 9,317)
□ 63 Carl Banks .04 .02 .01
□ 64 Mark Bavaro .04 .02 .01
□ 65 Maurice Carthon .04 .02 .01
□ 66 Mark Collins UER .04 .02 .01
(Total fumble recoveries
should be 5, not 3)
□ 67 Jeff Hostetler .40 .18 .05
□ 68 Erik Howard .04 .02 .01
□ 69 Pepper Johnson .04 .02 .01
□ 70 Sean Landeta .04 .02 .01
□ 71 Lionel Manuel .04 .02 .01
□ 72 Leonard Marshall .04 .02 .01
□ 73 Dave Meggett .10 .05 .01
□ 74 Bart Oates .04 .02 .01
□ 75 Doug Riesenberg .04 .02 .01
□ 76 Phil Simms .10 .05 .01
□ 77 Lawrence Taylor .25 .11 .03
□ 78 Eric Allen .04 .02 .01
□ 79 Jerome Brown .04 .02 .01
□ 80 Keith Byars .04 .02 .01
□ 81 Cris Carter .25 .11 .03
□ 82A Byron Evans ERR .15 .07 .02
(should be 83
according to checklist)
□ 82B Randall Cunningham .15 .07 .02
□ 83A Ron Heller ERR .15 .07 .02
(should be 84
according to checklist)
□ 83B Byron Evans COR .15 .07 .02
□ 84 Ron Heller .04 .02 .01
□ 85 Terry Hoage .04 .02 .01
□ 86 Keith Jackson .10 .05 .01
□ 87 Seth Joyner .10 .05 .01
□ 88 Mike Quick .04 .02 .01
□ 89 Mike Schad .04 .02 .01
□ 90 Clyde Simmons .04 .02 .01
□ 91 John Teltschik .04 .02 .01
□ 92 Anthony Toney .04 .02 .01
□ 93 Reggie White .25 .11 .03
□ 94 Ray Berry .04 .02 .01
□ 95 Joey Browner .04 .02 .01
□ 96 Anthony Carter .10 .05 .01
□ 97 Chris Doleman .04 .02 .01
□ 98 Rick Fenney .04 .02 .01
□ 99 Rich Gannon .04 .02 .01
□ 100 Hassan Jones .04 .02 .01
□ 101 Steve Jordan .04 .02 .01
□ 102 Rich Karlis .04 .02 .01
□ 103 Andre Ware .25 .11 .03
□ 104 Kirk Lowdermilk .04 .02 .01
□ 105 Keith Millard .04 .02 .01
□ 106 Scott Studwell .04 .02 .01
□ 107 Herschel Walker .10 .05 .01
□ 108 Wade Wilson .10 .05 .01
□ 109 Gary Zimmerman .04 .02 .01
□ 110 Don Beebe .10 .05 .01
□ 111 Cornelius Bennett .10 .05 .01
□ 112 Shane Conlan .04 .02 .01
□ 113 Jim Kelly .25 .11 .03
□ 114 Scott Norwood UER .04 .02 .01
(FGA and FGM columns
switched)
□ 115 Mark Kelso UER .04 .02 .01
(Some stats added wrong
on back)
□ 116 Larry Kinnebrew .04 .02 .01
□ 117 Pete Metzelaars .04 .02 .01
□ 118 Scott Radecic .04 .02 .01
□ 119 Andre Reed .25 .11 .03
□ 120 Jim Ritcher .04 .02 .01
□ 121 Bruce Smith .25 .11 .03
□ 122 Leonard Smith .04 .02 .01
□ 123 Art Still .04 .02 .01
□ 124 Thurman Thomas .40 .18 .05
□ 125 Steve Brown .04 .02 .01
□ 126 Ray Childress .04 .02 .01
□ 127 Ernest Givins .10 .05 .01
□ 128 John Grimsley .04 .02 .01
□ 129 Alonzo Highsmith .04 .02 .01
□ 130 Drew Hill .04 .02 .01
□ 131 Bruce Matthews .10 .05 .01
□ 132 Johnny Meads .04 .02 .01
□ 133 Warren Moon UER .25 .11 .03
(186 completions in '87
and 1341 career, should
be 184 and 1339)
□ 134 Mike Munchak .04 .02 .01
□ 135 Mike Rozier .04 .02 .01
□ 136 Dean Steinkuhler .04 .02 .01
□ 137 Lorenzo White .04 .02 .01
□ 138 Tony Zendejas .04 .02 .01
□ 139 Gary Anderson K .04 .02 .01
□ 140 Bubby Brister .04 .02 .01
□ 141 Thomas Everett .04 .02 .01
□ 142 Derek Hill .04 .02 .01
□ 143 Merril Hoge .04 .02 .01
□ 144 Tim Johnson .04 .02 .01
□ 145 Louis Lipps .10 .05 .01
□ 146 David Little .04 .02 .01
□ 147 Greg Lloyd .25 .11 .03
□ 148 Mike Mularkey .04 .02 .01
□ 149 John Rienstra .04 .02 .01
□ 150 Gerald Williams UER .04 .02 .01
(Tackles and fumble
recovery headers
are switched)
□ 151 Keith Willis UER .04 .02 .01
(Tackles and fumble
recovery headers
are switched)
□ 152 Rod Woodson .25 .11 .03
□ 153 Tim Worley .04 .02 .01
□ 154 Gary Clark .25 .11 .03
□ 155 Darryl Grant .04 .02 .01
□ 156 Darrell Green .10 .05 .01
□ 157 Joe Jacoby .04 .02 .01
□ 158 Jim Lachey .04 .02 .01
□ 159 Chip Lohmiller .04 .02 .01
□ 160 Charles Mann .04 .02 .01
□ 161 Wilber Marshall .04 .02 .01
□ 162 Mark May .04 .02 .01
□ 163 Ralf Mojsiejenko .04 .02 .01
□ 164 Art Monk UER .10 .05 .01
(No explanation of
How Acquired)
□ 165 Gerald Riggs .10 .05 .01
□ 166 Mark Rypien .10 .05 .01
□ 167 Ricky Sanders .04 .02 .01
□ 168 Don Warren .04 .02 .01
□ 169 Robert Brown .04 .02 .01
□ 170 Blair Bush .04 .02 .01
□ 171 Brent Fullwood .04 .02 .01
□ 172 Tim Harris .04 .02 .01
□ 173 Chris Jacke .04 .02 .01
□ 174 Perry Kemp .04 .02 .01
□ 175 Don Majkowski .04 .02 .01
□ 176 Tony Mandarich .04 .02 .01
□ 177 Mark Murphy .04 .02 .01
□ 178 Brian Noble .04 .02 .01
□ 179 Ken Ruettgers .04 .02 .01
□ 180 Sterling Sharpe .25 .11 .03
□ 181 Ed West .04 .02 .01
□ 182 Keith Woodside .04 .02 .01
□ 183 Morten Andersen .04 .02 .01
□ 184 Stan Brock .04 .02 .01
□ 185 Jim Dombrowski .04 .02 .01
□ 186 John Fourcade .04 .02 .01
□ 187 Bobby Hebert .04 .02 .01
□ 188 Craig Heyward .10 .05 .01
□ 189 Dalton Hilliard .04 .02 .01
□ 190 Rickey Jackson .10 .05 .01
□ 191 Buford Jordan .04 .02 .01
□ 192 Eric Martin .04 .02 .01
□ 193 Robert Massey .04 .02 .01
□ 194 Sam Mills .10 .05 .01
□ 195 Pat Swilling .10 .05 .01
□ 196 Jim Wilks .04 .02 .01
□ 197 John Alt .04 .02 .01
□ 198 Walker Lee Ashley .04 .02 .01
□ 199 Steve DeBerg .04 .02 .01
□ 200 Leonard Griffin .04 .02 .01
□ 201 Albert Lewis .04 .02 .01
□ 202 Nick Lowery .04 .02 .01
□ 203 Bill Maas .04 .02 .01
□ 204 Pete Mandley .04 .02 .01
□ 205 Chris Martin .04 .02 .01
□ 206 Christian Okoye .04 .02 .01
□ 207 Stephone Paige .04 .02 .01
□ 208 Kevin Porter .04 .02 .01
□ 209 Derrick Thomas .25 .11 .03
□ 210 Lewis Billups .04 .02 .01
□ 211 James Brooks .10 .05 .01
□ 212 Jason Buck .04 .02 .01
□ 213 Rickey Dixon .04 .02 .01
□ 214 Boomer Esiason .10 .05 .01
□ 215 David Fulcher .04 .02 .01
□ 216 Rodney Holman .04 .02 .01
□ 217 Lee Johnson .04 .02 .01
□ 218 Tim Krumrie .04 .02 .01
□ 219 Tim McGee .04 .02 .01
□ 220 Anthony Munoz .10 .05 .01
□ 221 Bruce Reimers .04 .02 .01
□ 222 Leon White .04 .02 .01
□ 223 Ickey Woods .04 .02 .01
□ 224 Harvey Armstrong .04 .02 .01
□ 225 Michael Ball .04 .02 .01
□ 226 Chip Banks .04 .02 .01
□ 227 Pat Beach .04 .02 .01
□ 228 Duane Bickett .04 .02 .01
□ 229 Bill Brooks .04 .02 .01
□ 230 Jon Hand .04 .02 .01
□ 231 Andre Rison .25 .11 .03
□ 232 Rohn Stark .04 .02 .01
□ 233 Donnell Thompson .04 .02 .01
□ 234 Jack Trudeau .04 .02 .01
□ 235 Clarence Verdin .04 .02 .01
□ 236 Mark Clayton .10 .05 .01
□ 237 Jeff Cross .04 .02 .01
□ 238 Jeff Dellenbach .04 .02 .01
□ 239 Mark Duper .10 .05 .01
□ 240 Ferrell Edmunds .04 .02 .01
□ 241 Hugh Green UER .04 .02 .01
(Back says Traded '86,
should be '85)
□ 242 E.J. Junior .04 .02 .01
□ 243 Marc Logan .04 .02 .01
□ 244 Dan Marino 1.25 .55 .16
□ 245 John Offerdahl .04 .02 .01
□ 246 Reggie Roby .04 .02 .01
□ 247 Sammie Smith .04 .02 .01
□ 248 Pete Stoyanovich .04 .02 .01
□ 249 Marcus Allen .25 .11 .03
□ 250 Eddie Anderson .04 .02 .01
□ 251 Steve Beuerlein .10 .05 .01
□ 252 Mike Dyal .04 .02 .01
□ 253 Mervyn Fernandez .04 .02 .01
□ 254 Bob Golic .04 .02 .01
□ 255 Mike Harden .04 .02 .01
□ 256 Bo Jackson .25 .11 .03
□ 257 Howie Long UER .10 .05 .01
(Born Sommerville,
should be Somerville)
□ 258 Don Mosebar .04 .02 .01
□ 259 Jay Schroeder .04 .02 .01
□ 260 Steve Smith .04 .02 .01
□ 261 Greg Townsend .04 .02 .01
□ 262 Lionel Washington .04 .02 .01
□ 263 Brian Blades .10 .05 .01
□ 264 Jeff Bryant .04 .02 .01
□ 265 Grant Feasel .04 .02 .01
□ 266 Jacob Green .04 .02 .01
□ 267 James Jefferson .04 .02 .01
□ 268 Norm Johnson .04 .02 .01
□ 269 Dave Krieg UER .10 .05 .01
(Misspelled Kreig
on card front)
□ 270 Travis McNeal .04 .02 .01
□ 271 Joe Nash .04 .02 .01
□ 272 Rufus Porter .04 .02 .01
□ 273 Kelly Stouffer .04 .02 .01
□ 274 John L. Williams .04 .02 .01
□ 275 Jim Arnold .04 .02 .01
□ 276 Jerry Ball .04 .02 .01
□ 277 Bennie Blades .04 .02 .01
□ 278 Lomas Brown .04 .02 .01
□ 279 Michael Cofer .04 .02 .01
□ 280 Bob Gagliano .04 .02 .01
□ 281 Richard Johnson .04 .02 .01
□ 282 Eddie Murray .04 .02 .01
□ 283 Rodney Peete .10 .05 .01
□ 284 Barry Sanders 1.25 .55 .16
□ 285 Eric Sanders .04 .02 .01
□ 286 Chris Spielman .25 .11 .03
□ 287 Eric Williams .04 .02 .01
□ 288 Neal Anderson .10 .05 .01
□ 289A Kevin Butler ERR/ERR .25 .11 .03
(Listed as Punter on
front and back)
□ 289B Kevin Butler COR/ERR .25 .11 .03
(Listed as Placekicker
on front and Punter
on back)
□ 289C Kevin Butler ERR/COR .25 .11 .03
(Listed as Punter on
front and Placekicker
on back)
□ 289D Kevin Butler COR/COR .04 .02 .01
(Listed as Placekicker
on front and back)
□ 290 Jim Covert .04 .02 .01
□ 291 Richard Dent .10 .05 .01
□ 292 Dennis Gentry .04 .02 .01
□ 293 Jim Harbaugh .25 .11 .03
□ 294 Jay Hilgenberg .04 .02 .01
□ 295 Vestee Jackson .04 .02 .01
□ 296 Steve McMichael .10 .05 .01
□ 297 Ron Morris .04 .02 .01
□ 298 Brad Muster .04 .02 .01
□ 299 Mike Singletary .10 .05 .01

☐ 300 James Thornton UER (Missing birthdate)	.04	.02	.01
☐ 301 Mike Tomczak	.10	.05	.01
☐ 302 Keith Van Horne	.04	.02	.01
☐ 303 Chris Bahr UER ('86 FGA and FGM stats are reversed)	.04	.02	.01
☐ 304 Martin Bayless	.04	.02	.01
☐ 305 Marion Butts	.10	.05	.01
☐ 306 Gill Byrd	.04	.02	.01
☐ 307 Arthur Cox	.04	.02	.01
☐ 308 Burt Grossman	.04	.02	.01
☐ 309 Jamie Holland	.04	.02	.01
☐ 310 Jim McMahon	.10	.05	.01
☐ 311 Anthony Miller	.25	.11	.03
☐ 312 Leslie O'Neal	.10	.05	.01
☐ 313 Billy Ray Smith	.04	.02	.01
☐ 314 Tim Spencer	.04	.02	.01
☐ 315 Broderick Thompson	.04	.02	.01
☐ 316 Lee Williams	.04	.02	.01
☐ 317 Bruce Armstrong	.04	.02	.01
☐ 318 Tim Goad	.04	.02	.01
☐ 319 Steve Grogan	.10	.05	.01
☐ 320 Roland James	.04	.02	.01
☐ 321 Cedric Jones	.04	.02	.01
☐ 322 Fred Marion	.04	.02	.01
☐ 323 Stanley Morgan	.04	.02	.01
☐ 324 Robert Perryman (Back says Robert, front says Bob)	.04	.02	.01
☐ 325 Johnny Rembert	.04	.02	.01
☐ 326 Ed Reynolds	.04	.02	.01
☐ 327 Kenneth Sims	.04	.02	.01
☐ 328 John Stephens	.04	.02	.01
☐ 329 Danny Villa	.04	.02	.01
☐ 330 Robert Awalt	.04	.02	.01
☐ 331 Anthony Bell	.04	.02	.01
☐ 332 Rich Camarillo	.04	.02	.01
☐ 333 Earl Ferrell	.04	.02	.01
☐ 334 Roy Green	.10	.05	.01
☐ 335 Gary Hogeboom	.04	.02	.01
☐ 336 Cedric Mack	.04	.02	.01
☐ 337 Freddie Joe Nunn	.04	.02	.01
☐ 338 Luis Sharpe	.04	.02	.01
☐ 339 Vai Sikahema	.04	.02	.01
☐ 340 J.T. Smith	.04	.02	.01
☐ 341 Tom Tupa	.04	.02	.01
☐ 342 Percy Snow	.04	.02	.01
☐ 343 Mark Carrier WR	.25	.11	.03
☐ 344 Randy Grimes	.04	.02	.01
☐ 345 Paul Gruber	.04	.02	.01
☐ 346 Ron Hall	.04	.02	.01
☐ 347 Jeff George	.75	.35	.09
☐ 348 Bruce Hill UER (Photo on back is actually Jerry Bell)	.04	.02	.01
☐ 349 William Howard UER (Yards rec. says 284, should be 285)	.04	.02	.01
☐ 350 Donald Igwebuike	.04	.02	.01
☐ 351 Chris Mohr	.04	.02	.01
☐ 352 Winston Moss	.04	.02	.01
☐ 353 Ricky Reynolds	.04	.02	.01
☐ 354 Mark Robinson	.04	.02	.01
☐ 355 Lars Tate	.04	.02	.01
☐ 356 Vinny Testaverde	.10	.05	.01
☐ 357 Broderick Thomas	.04	.02	.01
☐ 358 Troy Benson	.04	.02	.01
☐ 359 Jeff Criswell	.04	.02	.01
☐ 360 Tony Eason	.04	.02	.01
☐ 361 James Hasty	.04	.02	.01
☐ 362 Johnny Hector	.04	.02	.01
☐ 363 Bobby Humphery UER (Photo on back is actually Bobby Humphrey)	.04	.02	.01
☐ 364 Pat Leahy	.04	.02	.01
☐ 365 Erik McMillan	.04	.02	.01
☐ 366 Freeman McNeil	.04	.02	.01
☐ 367 Ken O'Brien	.04	.02	.01
☐ 368 Ron Stallworth	.04	.02	.01
☐ 369 Al Toon	.10	.05	.01
☐ 370 Blair Thomas	.04	.02	.01
☐ 371 Aundray Bruce	.04	.02	.01
☐ 372 Tony Casillas	.04	.02	.01
☐ 373 Shawn Collins	.04	.02	.01
☐ 374 Evan Cooper	.04	.02	.01
☐ 375 Bill Fralic	.04	.02	.01
☐ 376 Scott Funhage	.04	.02	.01
☐ 377 Mike Gann	.04	.02	.01
☐ 378 Ron Heller	.04	.02	.01
☐ 379 Keith Jones	.04	.02	.01
☐ 380 Mike Kenn	.04	.02	.01
☐ 381 Chris Miller	.25	.11	.03
☐ 382 Deion Sanders UER (Stats say no '89 fumble recoveries, should be 1)	.50	.23	.06
☐ 383 John Settle	.04	.02	.01
☐ 384 Troy Aikman	1.25	.55	.16
☐ 385 Bill Bates	.10	.05	.01
☐ 386 Willie Broughton	.04	.02	.01
☐ 387 Steve Folsom	.04	.02	.01
☐ 388 Ray Horton UER (Extra line after career totals)	.04	.02	.01
☐ 389 Michael Irvin	.25	.11	.03
☐ 390 Jim Jeffcoat	.04	.02	.01
☐ 391 Eugene Lockhart	.04	.02	.01
☐ 392 Kelvin Martin	.04	.02	.01
☐ 393 Nate Newton	.10	.05	.01
☐ 394 Mike Saxon UER (6 career blocked kicks, stats add up to 4)	.04	.02	.01
☐ 395 Derrick Shepard	.04	.02	.01
☐ 396 Steve Walsh UER (Yards Passing 50.2; Percentage and yards data are switched)	.10	.05	.01
☐ 397 Super Bowl MVP's (Jerry Rice and Joe Montana) HOR	.75	.35	.09
☐ 398 Checklist Card UER (Card 103 not listed)	.04	.02	.01
☐ 399 Checklist Card UER (Bengals misspelled)	.04	.02	.01
☐ 400 Checklist Card	.04	.02	.01

1990 Fleer All-Pros

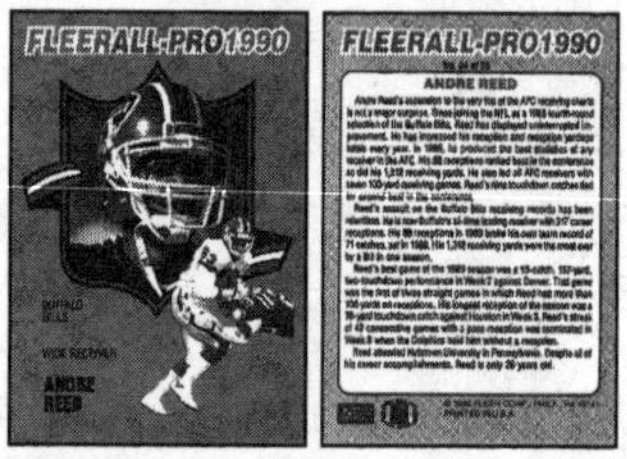

The 1990 Fleer All-Pro set contains 25 standard-size cards. The fronts are silver with a portrait and an action photo. The vertically oriented backs have detailed career information. These cards were randomly distributed in Fleer poly packs, approximately five per box.

	MINT	NRMT	EXC
COMPLETE SET (25)	7.50	3.40	.95
COMMON CARD (1-25)	.25	.11	.03
☐ 1 Joe Montana	2.50	1.10	.30
☐ 2 Jerry Rice UER (photo on front is actually John Taylor)	2.50	1.10	.30
☐ 3 Keith Jackson	.50	.23	.06
☐ 4 Barry Sanders	2.50	1.10	.30
☐ 5 Christian Okoye	.25	.11	.03
☐ 6 Tom Newberry	.25	.11	.03
☐ 7 Jim Covert	.25	.11	.03
☐ 8 Anthony Munoz	.50	.23	.06
☐ 9 Mike Munchak	.25	.11	.03
☐ 10 Jay Hilgenberg	.25	.11	.03
☐ 11 Chris Doleman	.25	.11	.03
☐ 12 Keith Millard	.25	.11	.03
☐ 13 Derrick Thomas	.75	.35	.09
☐ 14 Lawrence Taylor	.50	.23	.06
☐ 15 Karl Mecklenburg	.25	.11	.03
☐ 16 Reggie White	.75	.35	.09
☐ 17 Tim Harris	.25	.11	.03
☐ 18 David Fulcher	.25	.11	.03
☐ 19 Ronnie Lott	.50	.23	.06
☐ 20 Eric Allen	.25	.11	.03
☐ 21 Steve Atwater	.25	.11	.03
☐ 22 Rich Camarillo	.25	.11	.03
☐ 23 Morten Andersen	.25	.11	.03
☐ 24 Andre Reed	.75	.35	.09
☐ 25 Rod Woodson	.75	.35	.09

1990 Fleer Stars'n'Stripes

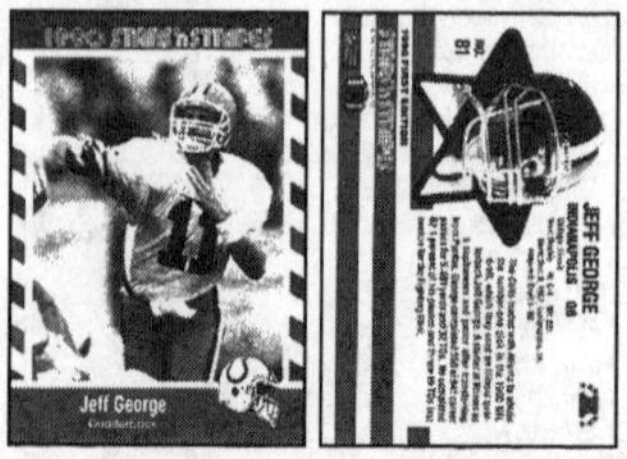

This 90-card standard size set was issued by Fleer in conjunction with their subsidiary, the Asher Candy Company, in a packaging which included two red, white, and blue striped candy sticks as well as eight cards. This set features members of the 1990 Pro Bowl teams as well as ten of the leading rookies in the 1990 season. Cards were arranged as follows, AFC Pro Bowlers (1-39), NFC Pro Bowlers (40-80), and leading draftees (81-90). The fronts of the cards feature an attractive action photo of the player with candy stripes running vertically down each side of the card and the words Stars'n'Stripes on top with the player's name and position underneath the photo and their team identification on the lower right hand corner. While the back of the card is reminiscent of the regular Fleer 1990 issue, the players photo is encased in a star and the identification that this is a Stars'n'Stripes card is also made on the back. Some of the same mistakes made in the regular Fleer set were carried over into the Stars'n'Stripes set including the misspelling of Dave Krieg's name as Kreig. Since this set did not sell that well at the retail level, much of the production was remaindered. However some of these leftover sealed cases are susceptible to damaged cards from the candy "leaking" into or onto the cards.

	MINT	NRMT	EXC
COMPLETE SET (90)	12.00	5.50	1.50
COMMON CARD (1-90)	.15	.07	.02
☐ 1 Warren Moon	.30	.14	.04
☐ 2 Reggie Roby	.15	.07	.02
☐ 3 David Treadwell	.15	.07	.02
☐ 4 Dave Krieg UER (Misspelled Kreig)	.25	.11	.03
☐ 5 James Brooks	.15	.07	.02
☐ 6 Erik McMillan	.15	.07	.02
☐ 7 Rod Woodson	.30	.14	.04
☐ 8 Albert Lewis	.15	.07	.02
☐ 9 Kevin Ross	.15	.07	.02
☐ 10 Frank Minnifield	.15	.07	.02
☐ 11 David Fulcher	.15	.07	.02
☐ 12 Thurman Thomas	.60	.25	.07
☐ 13 Christian Okoye	.15	.07	.02
☐ 14 Dennis Smith	.15	.07	.02
☐ 15 Johnny Rembert	.15	.07	.02
☐ 16 Ray Donaldson	.15	.07	.02
☐ 17 John Offerdahl	.15	.07	.02
☐ 18 Clay Matthews	.15	.07	.02
☐ 19 Shane Conlan	.15	.07	.02
☐ 20 Derrick Thomas	.30	.14	.04
☐ 21 Tunch Ilkin	.15	.07	.02
☐ 22 Mike Munchak	.15	.07	.02
☐ 23 Max Montoya	.15	.07	.02
☐ 24 Kent Hull	.15	.07	.02
☐ 25 Greg Kragen	.15	.07	.02
☐ 26 Bruce Matthews	.15	.07	.02
☐ 27 Howie Long	.25	.11	.03
☐ 28 Chris Hinton	.15	.07	.02
☐ 29 Anthony Munoz	.15	.07	.02
☐ 30 Bruce Smith	.25	.11	.03
☐ 31 Ferrell Edmunds	.15	.07	.02
☐ 32 Rodney Holman	.15	.07	.02
☐ 33 Andre Reed	.25	.11	.03
☐ 34 Webster Slaughter	.15	.07	.02
☐ 35 Anthony Miller	.30	.14	.04
☐ 36 Brian Blades	.15	.07	.02
☐ 37 Leslie O'Neal	.25	.11	.03
☐ 38 Rufus Porter	.15	.07	.02
☐ 39 Lee Williams	.15	.07	.02
☐ 40 Eddie Murray	.15	.07	.02
☐ 41 Mark Rypien	.25	.11	.03
☐ 42 Randall Cunningham	.25	.11	.03
☐ 43 Rich Camarillo	.15	.07	.02
☐ 44 Barry Sanders	2.00	.90	.25
☐ 45 Dalton Hilliard	.15	.07	.02
☐ 46 Eric Allen	.15	.07	.02
☐ 47 Brent Fullwood	.15	.07	.02
☐ 48 Ron Wolfley	.15	.07	.02
☐ 49 Jerry Gray	.15	.07	.02
☐ 50 Dave Meggett	.15	.07	.02
☐ 51 Roger Craig	.25	.11	.03
☐ 52 Carl Lee	.15	.07	.02
☐ 53 Ronnie Lott	.25	.11	.03
☐ 54 Tim McDonald	.15	.07	.02
☐ 55 Joey Browner	.15	.07	.02
☐ 56 Mike Singletary	.25	.11	.03
☐ 57 Vaughan Johnson	.15	.07	.02
☐ 58 Chris Spielman	.15	.07	.02
☐ 59 Doug Smith	.15	.07	.02
☐ 60 Lawrence Taylor	.30	.14	.04
☐ 61 Chris Doleman	.15	.07	.02
☐ 62 Guy McIntyre	.15	.07	.02
☐ 63 Jay Hilgenberg	.15	.07	.02
☐ 64 Randall McDaniel	.15	.07	.02
☐ 65 Gary Zimmerman	.15	.07	.02
☐ 66 Luis Sharpe	.15	.07	.02
☐ 67 Charles Mann	.15	.07	.02
☐ 68 Keith Millard	.15	.07	.02
☐ 69 Jackie Slater	.15	.07	.02
☐ 70 Bill Fralic	.15	.07	.02
☐ 71 Henry Ellard	.25	.11	.03
☐ 72 Jerry Rice	2.00	.90	.25
☐ 73 Steve Jordan	.15	.07	.02
☐ 74 Sterling Sharpe	.30	.14	.04
☐ 75 Keith Jackson	.15	.07	.02
☐ 76 Mark Carrier WR	.25	.11	.03
☐ 77 Kevin Greene	.25	.11	.03
☐ 78 Reggie White	.50	.23	.06
☐ 79 Jerry Ball	.15	.07	.02
☐ 80 Tim Harris	.15	.07	.02
☐ 81 Jeff George	.50	.23	.06
☐ 82 Blair Thomas	.15	.07	.02
☐ 83 Cortez Kennedy	.30	.14	.04
☐ 84 Junior Seau	.50	.23	.06
☐ 85 Mark Carrier DB	.15	.07	.02
☐ 86 Andre Ware	.25	.11	.03
☐ 87 Chris Singleton	.15	.07	.02
☐ 88 Percy Snow	.15	.07	.02
☐ 89 Steve Broussard	.15	.07	.02
☐ 90 Rodney Hampton	.30	.14	.04

1990 Fleer Update

This 120-card standard size set features some of the leading rookies and traded players in their new uniforms. The set is the same design as the regular issue with color photos bordered by a team color. The

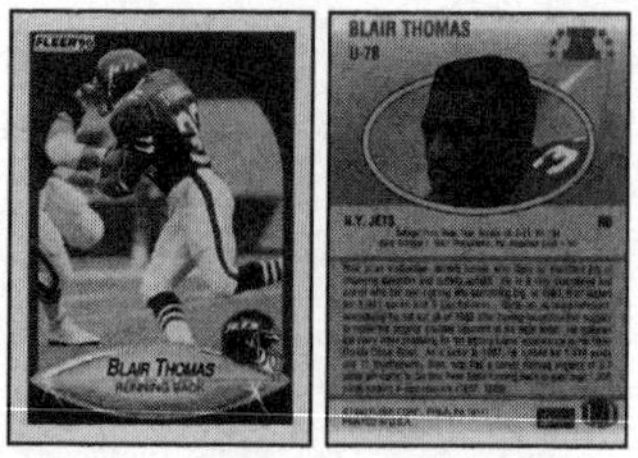

player's name and team helmet are at the bottom. Multicolored backs include text, stats and a color photo. The set is arranged in team order. The cards are numbered on the back with a "U" prefix. Rookie Cards include Brad Baxter, Mark Carrier (DB), Reggie Cobb, Andre Collins, Barry Foster, Eric Green, Harold Green, Rodney Hampton, Leroy Hoard, Stan Humphries, Haywood Jeffires, Johnny Johnson, Brent Jones, Cortez Kennedy, Rob Moore, Ken Norton Jr., Junior Seau, Emmitt Smith and Calvin Williams.

	MINT	NRMT	EXC
COMPLETE FACT.SET (120)	35.00	16.00	4.40
COMMON CARD (U1-U120)	.08	.04	.01
☐ U1 Albert Bentley	.08	.04	.01
☐ U2 Dean Biasucci	.08	.04	.01
☐ U3 Ray Donaldson	.08	.04	.01
☐ U4 Jeff George	2.00	.90	.25
☐ U5 Ray Agnew	.08	.04	.01
☐ U6 Greg McMurtry	.08	.04	.01
☐ U7 Chris Singleton	.08	.04	.01
☐ U8 James Francis	.08	.04	.01
☐ U9 Harold Green	.30	.14	.04
☐ U10 John Elliott	.08	.04	.01
☐ U11 Rodney Hampton	2.50	1.10	.30
☐ U12 Gary Reasons	.08	.04	.01
☐ U13 Lewis Tillman	.08	.04	.01
☐ U14 Everson Walls	.08	.04	.01
☐ U15 David Alexander	.08	.04	.01
☐ U16 Jim McMahon	.15	.07	.02
☐ U17 Ben Smith	.08	.04	.01
☐ U18 Andre Waters	.08	.04	.01
☐ U19 Calvin Williams	.15	.07	.02
☐ U20 Earnest Byner	.08	.04	.01
☐ U21 Andre Collins	.08	.04	.01
☐ U22 Russ Grimm	.08	.04	.01
☐ U23 Stan Humphries	2.50	1.10	.30
☐ U24 Martin Mayhew	.08	.04	.01
☐ U25 Barry Foster	.30	.14	.04
☐ U26 Eric Green	.15	.07	.02
☐ U27 Tunch Ilkin	.08	.04	.01
☐ U28 Hardy Nickerson	.15	.07	.02
☐ U29 Jerrol Williams	.08	.04	.01
☐ U30 Mike Baab	.08	.04	.01
☐ U31 Leroy Hoard	.30	.14	.04
☐ U32 Eddie Johnson	.08	.04	.01
☐ U33 William Fuller	.15	.07	.02
☐ U34 Haywood Jeffires	.30	.14	.04
☐ U35 Don Maggs	.08	.04	.01
☐ U36 Allen Pinkett	.08	.04	.01
☐ U37 Robert Awalt	.08	.04	.01
☐ U38 Dennis McKinnon	.08	.04	.01
☐ U39 Ken Norton	1.50	.70	.19
☐ U40 Emmitt Smith	30.00	13.50	3.70
☐ U41 Alexander Wright	.08	.04	.01
☐ U42 Eric Hill	.08	.04	.01
☐ U43 Johnny Johnson	.15	.07	.02
☐ U44 Timm Rosenbach	.08	.04	.01
☐ U45 Anthony Thompson	.08	.04	.01
☐ U46 Dexter Carter	.08	.04	.01
☐ U47 Eric Davis UER (Listed as WR on front, DB on back)	.15	.07	.02
☐ U48 Keith DeLong	.08	.04	.01
☐ U49 Brent Jones	1.50	.70	.19
☐ U50 Darryl Pollard	.08	.04	.01
☐ U51 Steve Wallace	.30	.14	.04
☐ U52 Bern Brostek	.08	.04	.01
☐ U53 Aaron Cox	.08	.04	.01
☐ U54 Cleveland Gary	.08	.04	.01
☐ U55 Fred Strickland	.08	.04	.01
☐ U56 Pat Terrell	.08	.04	.01
☐ U57 Steve Broussard	.08	.04	.01
☐ U58 Scott Case	.08	.04	.01
☐ U59 Brian Jordan	.15	.07	.02
☐ U60 Andre Rison	.30	.14	.04
☐ U61 Kevin Haverdink	.08	.04	.01
☐ U62 Rueben Mayes	.08	.04	.01
☐ U63 Steve Walsh	.15	.07	.02
☐ U64 Greg Bell	.08	.04	.01
☐ U65 Tim Brown	.30	.14	.04
☐ U66 Willie Gault	.15	.07	.02
☐ U67 Vance Mueller	.08	.04	.01
☐ U68 Bill Pickel	.08	.04	.01
☐ U69 Aaron Wallace	.08	.04	.01
☐ U70 Glenn Parker	.08	.04	.01
☐ U71 Frank Reich	.30	.14	.04
☐ U72 Leon Seals	.08	.04	.01
☐ U73 Darryl Talley	.08	.04	.01
☐ U74 Brad Baxter	.08	.04	.01
☐ U75 Jeff Criswell	.08	.04	.01
☐ U76 Jeff Lageman	.08	.04	.01
☐ U77 Rob Moore	1.25	.55	.16

	MINT	NRMT	EXC
☐ U78 Blair Thomas	.15	.07	.02
☐ U79 Louis Oliver	.08	.04	.01
☐ U80 Tony Paige	.08	.04	.01
☐ U81 Richmond Webb	.08	.04	.01
☐ U82 Robert Blackmon	.08	.04	.01
☐ U83 Derrick Fenner	.08	.04	.01
☐ U84 Andy Heck	.08	.04	.01
☐ U85 Cortez Kennedy	.30	.14	.04
☐ U86 Terry Wooden	.08	.04	.01
☐ U87 Jeff Donaldson	.08	.04	.01
☐ U88 Tim Grunhard	.08	.04	.01
☐ U89 Emile Harry	.08	.04	.01
☐ U90 Dan Saleaumua	.08	.04	.01
☐ U91 Percy Snow	.08	.04	.01
☐ U92 Andre Ware	.30	.14	.04
☐ U93 Darrell Fullington	.08	.04	.01
☐ U94 Mike Merriweather	.08	.04	.01
☐ U95 Henry Thomas	.08	.04	.01
☐ U96 Robert Brown	.08	.04	.01
☐ U97 LeRoy Butler	.30	.14	.04
☐ U98 Anthony Dilweg	.08	.04	.01
☐ U99 Darrell Thompson	.08	.04	.01
☐ U100 Keith Woodside	.08	.04	.01
☐ U101 Gary Plummer	.08	.04	.01
☐ U102 Junior Seau	3.00	1.35	.35
☐ U103 Billy Joe Tolliver	.08	.04	.01
☐ U104 Mark Vlasic	.08	.04	.01
☐ U105 Gary Anderson RB	.08	.04	.01
☐ U106 Ian Beckles	.08	.04	.01
☐ U107 Reggie Cobb	.08	.04	.01
☐ U108 Keith McCants	.08	.04	.01
☐ U109 Mark Bortz	.08	.04	.01
☐ U110 Maury Buford	.08	.04	.01
☐ U111 Mark Carrier DB	.30	.14	.04
☐ U112 Dan Hampton	.15	.07	.02
☐ U113 William Perry	.15	.07	.02
☐ U114 Ron Rivera	.08	.04	.01
☐ U115 Lemuel Stinson	.08	.04	.01
☐ U116 Melvin Bratton	.08	.04	.01
☐ U117 Gary Kubiak	.08	.04	.01
☐ U118 Alton Montgomery	.08	.04	.01
☐ U119 Ricky Nattiel	.08	.04	.01
☐ U120 Checklist 1-132	.08	.04	.01

1991 Fleer

Marcus Allen RAIDERS RB / MARCUS ALLEN

This 432-card standard-size set features color action photos with the player removed from the action. The background is shaded with various colors depending on the player's team. A green border surrounds the card with the player's name, team name and position in a white bar at the bottom. The back has a full-color shot along with complete statistics. Like the front, a green border is prominent. The card numbering is alphabetical by player within team by conference. Subsets include Hot Hitters (396-407), League Leaders (408-419) and Rookie Prospects (420-428). Rookie Cards in this set include Russell Maryland.

	MINT	NRMT	EXC
COMPLETE SET (432)	7.50	3.40	.95
COMMON CARD (1-432)	.04	.02	.01
☐ 1 Shane Conlan	.04	.02	.01
☐ 2 John Davis	.04	.02	.01
☐ 3 Kent Hull	.04	.02	.01
☐ 4 James Lofton	.10	.05	.01
☐ 5 Keith McKeller	.04	.02	.01
☐ 6 Scott Norwood	.04	.02	.01
☐ 7 Nate Odomes	.04	.02	.01
☐ 8 Andre Reed	.10	.05	.01
☐ 9 Jim Ritcher	.04	.02	.01
☐ 10 Leon Seals	.04	.02	.01
☐ 11 Bruce Smith	.25	.11	.03
☐ 12 Leonard Smith	.04	.02	.01
☐ 13 Steve Tasker	.10	.05	.01
☐ 14 Thurman Thomas	.25	.11	.03
☐ 15 Lewis Billups	.04	.02	.01
☐ 16 James Brooks	.10	.05	.01
☐ 17 Eddie Brown	.04	.02	.01
☐ 18 Carl Carter	.04	.02	.01
☐ 19 Boomer Esiason	.10	.05	.01
☐ 20 James Francis	.04	.02	.01
☐ 21 David Fulcher	.04	.02	.01
☐ 22 Harold Green	.10	.05	.01
☐ 23 Rodney Holman	.04	.02	.01
☐ 24 Bruce Kozerski	.04	.02	.01
☐ 25 Tim McGee	.10	.05	.01
☐ 26 Anthony Munoz	.10	.05	.01
☐ 27 Bruce Reimers	.04	.02	.01
☐ 28 Ickey Woods	.04	.02	.01
☐ 29 Carl Zander	.04	.02	.01
☐ 30 Mike Baab	.04	.02	.01
☐ 31 Brian Brennan	.04	.02	.01

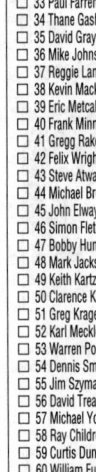
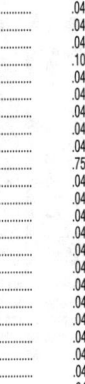

	MINT	NRMT	EXC
☐ 32 Rob Burnett	.04	.02	.01
☐ 33 Paul Farren	.04	.02	.01
☐ 34 Thane Gash	.04	.02	.01
☐ 35 David Grayson	.04	.02	.01
☐ 36 Mike Johnson	.04	.02	.01
☐ 37 Reggie Langhorne	.04	.02	.01
☐ 38 Kevin Mack	.04	.02	.01
☐ 39 Eric Metcalf	.10	.05	.01
☐ 40 Frank Minnifield	.04	.02	.01
☐ 41 Gregg Rakoczy	.04	.02	.01
☐ 42 Felix Wright	.04	.02	.01
☐ 43 Steve Atwater	.04	.02	.01
☐ 44 Michael Brooks	.04	.02	.01
☐ 45 John Elway	.75	.35	.09
☐ 46 Simon Fletcher	.04	.02	.01
☐ 47 Bobby Humphrey	.04	.02	.01
☐ 48 Mark Jackson	.04	.02	.01
☐ 49 Keith Kartz	.04	.02	.01
☐ 50 Clarence Kay	.04	.02	.01
☐ 51 Greg Kragen	.04	.02	.01
☐ 52 Karl Mecklenburg	.04	.02	.01
☐ 53 Warren Powers	.04	.02	.01
☐ 54 Dennis Smith	.04	.02	.01
☐ 55 Jim Szymanski	.04	.02	.01
☐ 56 David Treadwell	.04	.02	.01
☐ 57 Michael Young	.04	.02	.01
☐ 58 Ray Childress	.04	.02	.01
☐ 59 Curtis Duncan	.04	.02	.01
☐ 60 William Fuller	.10	.05	.01
☐ 61 Ernest Givins	.10	.05	.01
☐ 62 Drew Hill	.04	.02	.01
☐ 63 Haywood Jeffires	.10	.05	.01
☐ 64 Richard Johnson	.04	.02	.01
☐ 65 Sean Jones	.10	.05	.01
☐ 66 Don Maggs	.04	.02	.01
☐ 67 Bruce Matthews	.10	.05	.01
☐ 68 Johnny Meads	.04	.02	.01
☐ 69 Greg Montgomery	.04	.02	.01
☐ 70 Warren Moon	.25	.11	.03
☐ 71 Mike Munchak	.04	.02	.01
☐ 72 Allen Pinkett	.04	.02	.01
☐ 73 Lorenzo White	.04	.02	.01
☐ 74 Pat Beach	.04	.02	.01
☐ 75 Albert Bentley	.04	.02	.01
☐ 76 Dean Biasucci	.04	.02	.01
☐ 77 Duane Bickett	.04	.02	.01
☐ 78 Bill Brooks	.04	.02	.01
☐ 79 Sam Clancy	.04	.02	.01
☐ 80 Ray Donaldson	.04	.02	.01
☐ 81 Jeff George	.25	.11	.03
☐ 82 Alan Grant	.04	.02	.01
☐ 83 Jessie Hester	.04	.02	.01
☐ 84 Jeff Herrod	.04	.02	.01
☐ 85 Rohn Stark	.04	.02	.01
☐ 86 Jack Trudeau	.04	.02	.01
☐ 87 Clarence Verdin	.04	.02	.01
☐ 88 John Alt	.04	.02	.01
☐ 89 Steve DeBerg	.04	.02	.01
☐ 90 Tim Grunhard	.04	.02	.01
☐ 91 Dino Hackett	.04	.02	.01
☐ 92 Jonathan Hayes	.04	.02	.01
☐ 93 Albert Lewis	.04	.02	.01
☐ 94 Nick Lowery	.04	.02	.01
☐ 95 Bill Maas UER	.04	.02	.01
(Back photo actually David Szott)			
☐ 96 Christian Okoye	.04	.02	.01
☐ 97 Stephone Paige	.04	.02	.01
☐ 98 Kevin Porter	.04	.02	.01
☐ 99 David Szott	.04	.02	.01
☐ 100 Derrick Thomas	.25	.11	.03
☐ 101 Barry Word	.04	.02	.01
☐ 102 Marcus Allen	.25	.11	.03
☐ 103 Thomas Benson	.04	.02	.01
☐ 104 Tim Brown	.25	.11	.03
☐ 105 Riki Ellison	.04	.02	.01
☐ 106 Mervyn Fernandez	.04	.02	.01
☐ 107 Willie Gault	.10	.05	.01
☐ 108 Bob Golic	.04	.02	.01
☐ 109 Ethan Horton	.04	.02	.01
☐ 110 Bo Jackson	.10	.05	.01
☐ 111 Howie Long	.10	.05	.01
☐ 112 Don Mosebar	.04	.02	.01
☐ 113 Jerry Robinson	.04	.02	.01
☐ 114 Jay Schroeder	.04	.02	.01
☐ 115 Steve Smith	.04	.02	.01
☐ 116 Greg Townsend	.04	.02	.01
☐ 117 Steve Wisniewski	.04	.02	.01
☐ 118 Mark Clayton	.10	.05	.01
☐ 119 Mark Duper	.10	.05	.01
☐ 120 Ferrell Edmunds	.04	.02	.01
☐ 121 Hugh Green	.04	.02	.01
☐ 122 David Griggs	.04	.02	.01
☐ 123 Jim C. Jensen	.04	.02	.01
☐ 124 Dan Marino	1.50	.70	.19
☐ 125 Tim McKyer	.04	.02	.01
☐ 126 John Offerdahl	.04	.02	.01
☐ 127 Louis Oliver	.04	.02	.01
☐ 128 Tony Paige	.04	.02	.01
☐ 129 Reggie Roby	.04	.02	.01
☐ 130 Keith Sims	.04	.02	.01
☐ 131 Sammie Smith	.04	.02	.01
☐ 132 Pete Stoyanovich	.04	.02	.01
☐ 133 Richmond Webb	.04	.02	.01
☐ 134 Bruce Armstrong	.04	.02	.01

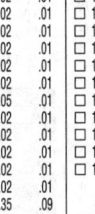

	MINT	NRMT	EXC
☐ 135 Vincent Brown	.04	.02	.01
☐ 136 Hart Lee Dykes	.04	.02	.01
☐ 137 Irving Fryar	.10	.05	.01
☐ 138 Tim Goad	.04	.02	.01
☐ 139 Tommy Hodson	.04	.02	.01
☐ 140 Maurice Hurst	.04	.02	.01
☐ 141 Ronnie Lippett	.04	.02	.01
☐ 142 Greg McMurtry	.04	.02	.01
☐ 143 Ed Reynolds	.04	.02	.01
☐ 144 John Stephens	.04	.02	.01
☐ 145 Andre Tippett	.04	.02	.01
☐ 146 Danny Villa	.04	.02	.01
(Old photo wearing retired number)			
☐ 147 Brad Baxter	.04	.02	.01
☐ 148 Kyle Clifton	.04	.02	.01
☐ 149 Jeff Criswell	.04	.02	.01
☐ 150 James Hasty	.04	.02	.01
☐ 151 Jeff Lageman	.04	.02	.01
☐ 152 Pat Leahy	.04	.02	.01
☐ 153 Rob Moore	.25	.11	.03
☐ 154 Al Toon	.10	.05	.01
☐ 155 Gary Anderson K	.04	.02	.01
☐ 156 Bubby Brister	.04	.02	.01
☐ 157 Chris Calloway	.04	.02	.01
☐ 158 Donald Evans	.04	.02	.01
☐ 159 Eric Green	.04	.02	.01
☐ 160 Bryan Hinkle	.04	.02	.01
☐ 161 Merril Hoge	.04	.02	.01
☐ 162 Tunch Ilkin	.04	.02	.01
☐ 163 Louis Lipps	.04	.02	.01
☐ 164 David Little	.04	.02	.01
☐ 165 Mike Mularkey	.04	.02	.01
☐ 166 Gerald Williams	.04	.02	.01
☐ 167 Warren Williams	.04	.02	.01
☐ 168 Rod Woodson	.25	.11	.03
☐ 169 Tim Worley	.04	.02	.01
☐ 170 Martin Bayless	.04	.02	.01
☐ 171 Marion Butts	.10	.05	.01
☐ 172 Gill Byrd	.04	.02	.01
☐ 173 Frank Cornish	.04	.02	.01
☐ 174 Arthur Cox	.04	.02	.01
☐ 175 Burt Grossman	.04	.02	.01
☐ 176 Anthony Miller	.10	.05	.01
☐ 177 Leslie O'Neal	.10	.05	.01
☐ 178 Gary Plummer	.04	.02	.01
☐ 179 Junior Seau	.40	.18	.05
☐ 180 Billy Joe Tolliver	.04	.02	.01
☐ 181 Derrick Walker	.04	.02	.01
☐ 182 Lee Williams	.04	.02	.01
☐ 183 Robert Blackmon	.04	.02	.01
☐ 184 Brian Blades	.10	.05	.01
☐ 185 Grant Feasel	.04	.02	.01
☐ 186 Derrick Fenner	.04	.02	.01
☐ 187 Andy Heck	.04	.02	.01
☐ 188 Norm Johnson	.04	.02	.01
☐ 189 Tommy Kane	.04	.02	.01
☐ 190 Cortez Kennedy	.25	.11	.03
☐ 191 Dave Krieg	.10	.05	.01
☐ 192 Travis McNeal	.04	.02	.01
☐ 193 Eugene Robinson	.04	.02	.01
☐ 194 Chris Warren	.40	.18	.05
☐ 195 John L. Williams	.04	.02	.01
☐ 196 Steve Broussard	.04	.02	.01
☐ 197 Scott Case	.04	.02	.01
☐ 198 Shawn Collins	.04	.02	.01
☐ 199 Darion Conner UER	.04	.02	.01
(Player on back 8 is not Conner 56)			
☐ 200 Tory Epps	.04	.02	.01
☐ 201 Bill Fralic	.04	.02	.01
☐ 202 Michael Haynes	.25	.11	.03
☐ 203 Chris Hinton	.04	.02	.01
☐ 204 Keith Jones	.04	.02	.01
☐ 205 Brian Jordan	.10	.05	.01
☐ 206 Mike Kenn	.04	.02	.01
☐ 207 Chris Miller	.10	.05	.01
☐ 208 Andre Rison	.10	.05	.01
☐ 209 Mike Rozier	.04	.02	.01
☐ 210 Deion Sanders	.60	.25	.07
☐ 211 Gary Wilkins	.04	.02	.01
☐ 212 Neal Anderson	.10	.05	.01
☐ 213 Trace Armstrong	.04	.02	.01
☐ 214 Mark Bortz	.04	.02	.01
☐ 215 Kevin Butler	.04	.02	.01
☐ 216 Mark Carrier DB	.10	.05	.01
☐ 217 Wendell Davis	.04	.02	.01
☐ 218 Richard Dent	.10	.05	.01
☐ 219 Dennis Gentry	.04	.02	.01
☐ 220 Jim Harbaugh	.25	.11	.03
☐ 221 Jay Hilgenberg	.04	.02	.01
☐ 222 Steve McMichael	.10	.05	.01
☐ 223 Ron Morris	.04	.02	.01
☐ 224 Brad Muster	.04	.02	.01
☐ 225 Mike Singletary	.10	.05	.01
☐ 226 James Thornton	.04	.02	.01
☐ 227 Tommie Agee	.04	.02	.01
☐ 228 Troy Aikman	1.00	.45	.12
☐ 229 Jack Del Rio	.04	.02	.01
☐ 230 Issiac Holt	.04	.02	.01
☐ 231 Ray Horton	.04	.02	.01
☐ 232 Jim Jeffcoat	.04	.02	.01
☐ 233 Eugene Lockhart	.04	.02	.01
☐ 234 Kelvin Martin	.04	.02	.01
☐ 235 Nate Newton	.10	.05	.01

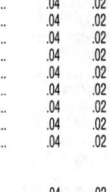
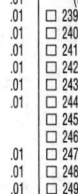
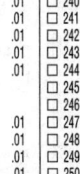
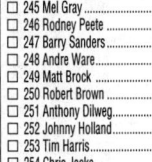
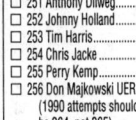
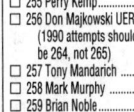
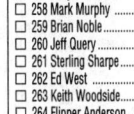
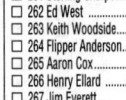
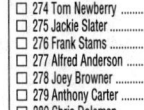
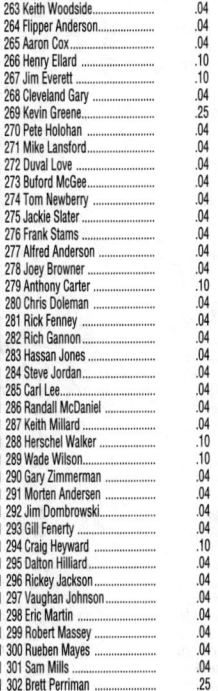

	MINT	NRMT	EXC
☐ 236 Mike Saxon	.04	.02	.01
☐ 237 Emmitt Smith	2.00	.90	.25
☐ 238A Daniel Stubbs	.10	.05	.01
(Danny on back)			
☐ 238B Danny Stubbs	.10	.05	.01
(Daniel on back)			
☐ 239 Jim Arnold	.04	.02	.01
☐ 240 Jerry Ball	.04	.02	.01
☐ 241 Bennie Blades	.04	.02	.01
☐ 242 Lomas Brown	.04	.02	.01
☐ 243 Robert Clark	.04	.02	.01
☐ 244 Mike Cofer	.04	.02	.01
☐ 245 Mel Gray	.10	.05	.01
☐ 246 Rodney Peete	.10	.05	.01
☐ 247 Barry Sanders	1.00	.45	.12
☐ 248 Andre Ware	.10	.05	.01
☐ 249 Matt Brock	.04	.02	.01
☐ 250 Robert Brown	.04	.02	.01
☐ 251 Anthony Dilweg	.04	.02	.01
☐ 252 Johnny Holland	.04	.02	.01
☐ 253 Tim Harris	.04	.02	.01
☐ 254 Chris Jacke	.04	.02	.01
☐ 255 Perry Kemp	.04	.02	.01
☐ 256 Don Majkowski UER	.04	.02	.01
(1990 attempts should be 264, not 265)			
☐ 257 Tony Mandarich	.04	.02	.01
☐ 258 Mark Murphy	.04	.02	.01
☐ 259 Brian Noble	.04	.02	.01
☐ 260 Jeff Query	.04	.02	.01
☐ 261 Sterling Sharpe	.25	.11	.03
☐ 262 Ed West	.04	.02	.01
☐ 263 Keith Woodside	.04	.02	.01
☐ 264 Flipper Anderson	.04	.02	.01
☐ 265 Aaron Cox	.04	.02	.01
☐ 266 Henry Ellard	.10	.05	.01
☐ 267 Jim Everett	.10	.05	.01
☐ 268 Cleveland Gary	.04	.02	.01
☐ 269 Kevin Greene	.25	.11	.03
☐ 270 Pete Holohan	.04	.02	.01
☐ 271 Mike Lansford	.04	.02	.01
☐ 272 Duval Love	.04	.02	.01
☐ 273 Buford McGee	.04	.02	.01
☐ 274 Tom Newberry	.04	.02	.01
☐ 275 Jackie Slater	.04	.02	.01
☐ 276 Frank Stams	.04	.02	.01
☐ 277 Alfred Anderson	.04	.02	.01
☐ 278 Joey Browner	.04	.02	.01
☐ 279 Anthony Carter	.10	.05	.01
☐ 280 Chris Doleman	.04	.02	.01
☐ 281 Rick Fenney	.04	.02	.01
☐ 282 Rich Gannon	.04	.02	.01
☐ 283 Hassan Jones	.04	.02	.01
☐ 284 Steve Jordan	.04	.02	.01
☐ 285 Carl Lee	.04	.02	.01
☐ 286 Randall McDaniel	.04	.02	.01
☐ 287 Keith Millard	.04	.02	.01
☐ 288 Herschel Walker	.10	.05	.01
☐ 289 Wade Wilson	.10	.05	.01
☐ 290 Gary Zimmerman	.04	.02	.01
☐ 291 Morten Andersen	.04	.02	.01
☐ 292 Jim Dombrowski	.04	.02	.01
☐ 293 Gill Fenerty	.04	.02	.01
☐ 294 Craig Heyward	.10	.05	.01
☐ 295 Dalton Hilliard	.04	.02	.01
☐ 296 Rickey Jackson	.04	.02	.01
☐ 297 Vaughan Johnson	.04	.02	.01
☐ 298 Eric Martin	.04	.02	.01
☐ 299 Robert Massey	.04	.02	.01
☐ 300 Rueben Mayes	.04	.02	.01
☐ 301 Sam Mills	.04	.02	.01
☐ 302 Brett Perriman	.25	.11	.03
☐ 303 Pat Swilling	.10	.05	.01
☐ 304 Steve Walsh	.04	.02	.01
☐ 305 Ottis Anderson	.10	.05	.01
☐ 306 Matt Bahr	.04	.02	.01
☐ 307 Mark Bavaro	.04	.02	.01
☐ 308 Maurice Carthon	.04	.02	.01
☐ 309 Mark Collins	.04	.02	.01
☐ 310 John Elliott	.04	.02	.01
☐ 311 Rodney Hampton	.25	.11	.03
☐ 312 Jeff Hostetler	.10	.05	.01
☐ 313 Erik Howard	.04	.02	.01
☐ 314 Pepper Johnson	.04	.02	.01
☐ 315 Sean Landeta	.04	.02	.01
☐ 316 Dave Meggett	.10	.05	.01
☐ 317 Bart Oates	.04	.02	.01
☐ 318 Phil Simms	.10	.05	.01
☐ 319 Lawrence Taylor	.25	.11	.03
☐ 320 Reyna Thompson	.04	.02	.01
☐ 321 Everson Walls	.04	.02	.01
☐ 322 Eric Allen	.04	.02	.01
☐ 323 Fred Barnett	.25	.11	.03
☐ 324 Jerome Brown	.04	.02	.01
☐ 325 Keith Byars	.10	.05	.01
☐ 326 Randall Cunningham	.10	.05	.01
☐ 327 Byron Evans	.04	.02	.01
☐ 328 Ron Heller	.04	.02	.01
☐ 329 Keith Jackson	.10	.05	.01
☐ 330 Seth Joyner	.10	.05	.01
☐ 331 Heath Sherman	.04	.02	.01
☐ 332 Clyde Simmons	.04	.02	.01
☐ 333 Ben Smith	.04	.02	.01
☐ 334 Anthony Toney	.04	.02	.01
☐ 335 Andre Waters	.04	.02	.01

	MINT	NRMT	EXC
☐ 336 Reggie White	.25	.11	.03
☐ 337 Calvin Williams	.10	.05	.01
☐ 338 Anthony Bell	.04	.02	.01
☐ 339 Rich Camarillo	.04	.02	.01
☐ 340 Roy Green	.04	.02	.01
☐ 341 Tim Jorden	.04	.02	.01
☐ 342 Cedric Mack	.04	.02	.01
☐ 343 Dexter Manley	.04	.02	.01
☐ 344 Freddie Joe Nunn	.04	.02	.01
☐ 345 Ricky Proehl	.04	.02	.01
☐ 346 Tootie Robbins	.04	.02	.01
☐ 347 Timm Rosenbach	.04	.02	.01
☐ 348 Luis Sharpe	.04	.02	.01
☐ 349 Vai Sikahema	.04	.02	.01
☐ 350 Anthony Thompson	.04	.02	.01
☐ 351 Lonnie Young	.04	.02	.01
☐ 352 Dexter Carter	.04	.02	.01
☐ 353 Mike Cofer	.04	.02	.01
☐ 354 Kevin Fagan	.04	.02	.01
☐ 355 Don Griffin	.04	.02	.01
☐ 356 Charles Haley UER	.10	.05	.01
(Total fumbles should be 6, not 5)			
☐ 357 Pierce Holt	.04	.02	.01
☐ 358 Brent Jones	.25	.11	.03
☐ 359 Guy McIntyre	.04	.02	.01
☐ 360 Joe Montana	1.00	.45	.12
☐ 361 Darryl Pollard	.04	.02	.01
☐ 362 Tom Rathman	.04	.02	.01
☐ 363 Jerry Rice	1.00	.45	.12
☐ 364 Bill Romanowski	.04	.02	.01
☐ 365 John Taylor	.10	.05	.01
☐ 366 Steve Wallace UER	.10	.05	.01
Listed as a DL on front of card			
☐ 367 Steve Young	.75	.35	.09
☐ 368 Gary Anderson RB	.04	.02	.01
☐ 369 Ian Beckles	.04	.02	.01
☐ 370 Mark Carrier WR	.25	.11	.03
☐ 371 Reggie Cobb	.04	.02	.01
☐ 372 Reuben Davis	.04	.02	.01
☐ 373 Randy Grimes	.04	.02	.01
☐ 374 Wayne Haddix	.04	.02	.01
☐ 375 Ron Hall	.04	.02	.01
☐ 376 Harry Hamilton	.04	.02	.01
☐ 377 Bruce Hill	.04	.02	.01
☐ 378 Keith McCants	.04	.02	.01
☐ 379 Bruce Perkins	.04	.02	.01
☐ 380 Vinny Testaverde UER	.10	.05	.01
(Misspelled Vinnie on card front)			
☐ 381 Broderick Thomas	.04	.02	.01
☐ 382 Jeff Bostic	.04	.02	.01
☐ 383 Earnest Byner	.04	.02	.01
☐ 384 Gary Clark	.25	.11	.03
☐ 385 Darryl Grant	.04	.02	.01
☐ 386 Darrell Green	.04	.02	.01
☐ 387 Stan Humphries	.25	.11	.03
☐ 388 Jim Lachey	.04	.02	.01
☐ 389 Charles Mann	.04	.02	.01
☐ 390 Wilber Marshall	.04	.02	.01
☐ 391 Art Monk	.10	.05	.01
☐ 392 Gerald Riggs	.04	.02	.01
☐ 393 Mark Rypien	.10	.05	.01
☐ 394 Ricky Sanders	.04	.02	.01
☐ 395 Don Warren	.04	.02	.01
☐ 396 Bruce Smith HIT	.10	.05	.01
☐ 397 Reggie White HIT	.10	.05	.01
☐ 398 Lawrence Taylor HIT	.10	.05	.01
☐ 399 David Fulcher HIT	.04	.02	.01
☐ 400 Derrick Thomas HIT	.10	.05	.01
☐ 401 Mark Carrier DB HIT	.04	.02	.01
☐ 402 Mike Singletary HIT	.10	.05	.01
☐ 403 Charles Haley HIT	.04	.02	.01
☐ 404 Jeff Cross HIT	.04	.02	.01
☐ 405 Leslie O'Neal HIT	.10	.05	.01
☐ 406 Tim Harris HIT	.04	.02	.01
☐ 407 Steve Atwater HIT	.04	.02	.01
☐ 408 Joe Montana LL UER	.40	.18	.05
(4th on yardage list, not 3rd)			
☐ 409 Randall Cunningham LL	.10	.05	.01
☐ 410 Warren Moon LL	.10	.05	.01
☐ 411 Andre Rison LL UER	.10	.05	.01
(Card incorrectly numbered as 412 and Michigan State misspelled as Stage)			
☐ 412 Haywood Jeffires LL	.10	.05	.01
(See number 411)			
☐ 413 Stephone Paige LL	.04	.02	.01
☐ 414 Phil Simms LL	.10	.05	.01
☐ 415 Barry Sanders LL	.50	.23	.06
☐ 416 Bo Jackson LL	.10	.05	.01
☐ 417 Thurman Thomas LL	.10	.05	.01
☐ 418 Emmitt Smith LL	1.00	.45	.12
☐ 419 John L. Williams LL	.04	.02	.01
☐ 420 Nick Bell RP	.04	.02	.01
☐ 421 Eric Bieniemy RP	.04	.02	.01
☐ 422 Mike Dumas RP UER	.04	.02	.01
(Returned interception vs. Purdue, not Michigan State)			
☐ 423 Russell Maryland RP	.25	.11	.03
☐ 424 Derek Russell RP	.04	.02	.01
☐ 425 Chris Smith RP UER	.04	.02	.01
(Bengals misspelled as Bengels)			
☐ 426 Mike Stonebreaker RP	.04	.02	.01
☐ 427 Pat Tyrance RP	.04	.02	.01
☐ 428 Kenny Walker RP	.04	.02	.01
(How Acquired has a different style)			
☐ 429 Checklist 1-108 UER	.04	.02	.01
(David Grayson misspelled as Graysor)			
☐ 430 Checklist 109-216	.04	.02	.01
☐ 431 Checklist 217-324	.04	.02	.01
☐ 432 Checklist 325-432	.04	.02	.01

1991 Fleer All-Pros

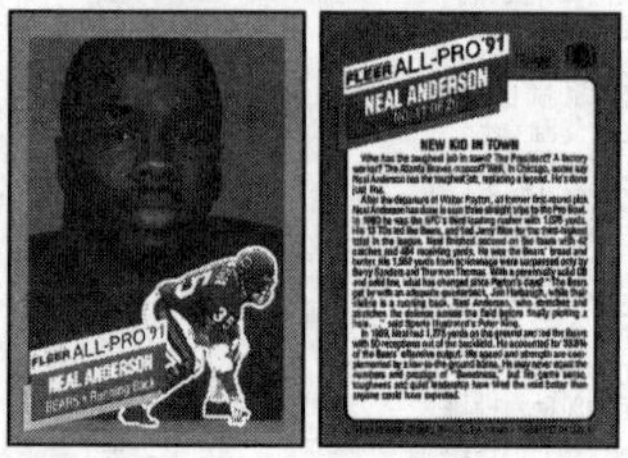

This 26-card standard size set was issued as a random insert in packs. The set features attractive full-color photography. A small player photo is superimposed over a larger up-close player photo on front. A "Fleer All-Pro '91" banner is accompanied by player and team name and position. The card backs contain a large body of text.

	MINT	NRMT	EXC
COMPLETE SET (26)	5.00	2.20	.60
COMMON CARD (1-26)	.15	.07	.02
☐ 1 Andre Reed UER	.30	.14	.04
(Caught 81 passes in '89, should say 88 passes)			
☐ 2 Bobby Humphrey	.15	.07	.02
☐ 3 Kent Hull	.15	.07	.02
☐ 4 Mark Bortz	.15	.07	.02
☐ 5 Bruce Smith	.50	.23	.06
☐ 6 Greg Townsend	.15	.07	.02
☐ 7 Ray Childress	.30	.14	.04
☐ 8 Andre Rison	.50	.23	.06
☐ 9 Barry Sanders	1.50	.70	.19
☐ 10 Bo Jackson	.50	.23	.06
☐ 11 Neal Anderson	.30	.14	.04
☐ 12 Keith Jackson	.30	.14	.04
☐ 13 Derrick Thomas	.50	.23	.06
☐ 14 John Offerdahl	.15	.07	.02
☐ 15 Lawrence Taylor	.50	.23	.06
☐ 16 Darrell Green	.15	.07	.02
☐ 17 Mark Carrier DB UER	.15	.07	.02
(No period in last sentence of bio)			
☐ 18 David Fulcher UER	.15	.07	.02
(Bill Wyche, should be Sam)			
☐ 19 Joe Montana	1.50	.70	.19
☐ 20 Jerry Rice	1.50	.70	.19
☐ 21 Charles Haley	.30	.14	.04
☐ 22 Mike Singletary	.30	.14	.04
☐ 23 Nick Lowery	.15	.07	.02
☐ 24 Jim Lachey UER	.15	.07	.02
(Acquired by trade in '87, not '88)			
☐ 25 Anthony Munoz	.50	.23	.06
☐ 26 Thurman Thomas	.50	.23	.06

1991 Fleer Pro-Visions

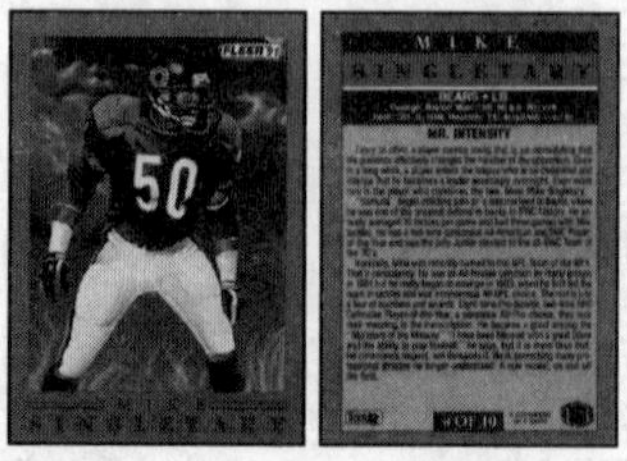

This ten-card standard size set was randomly inserted in packs. The fronts feature artworks with the player's name at the bottom. The backs contain a large write-up describing the player's career highlights.

	MINT	NRMT	EXC
COMPLETE SET (10)	5.00	2.20	.60
COMMON CARD (1-10)	.25	.11	.03
☐ 1 Joe Montana	1.50	.70	.19
☐ 2 Barry Sanders	1.50	.70	.19
☐ 3 Lawrence Taylor	.40	.18	.05
☐ 4 Mike Singletary	.25	.11	.03
☐ 5 Dan Marino	2.00	.90	.25
☐ 6 Bo Jackson	.40	.18	.05
☐ 7 Randall Cunningham	.25	.11	.03
☐ 8 Bruce Smith	.40	.18	.05
☐ 9 Derrick Thomas	.40	.18	.05
☐ 10 Howie Long	.40	.18	.05

1991 Fleer Stars'n'Stripes

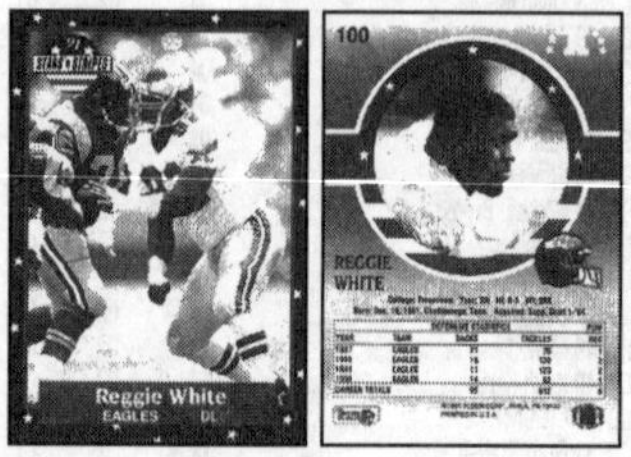

This 140-card standard-size set marked the second year that Fleer, in conjunction with Asher Candy, marketed a set sold with candy sticks. The set features full-color game action shots on the front and a large color portrait, as well as complete statistical information on the back. The cards are arranged by alphabetical team order within each conference.

	MINT	NRMT	EXC
COMPLETE SET (140)	14.00	6.25	1.75
COMMON CARD (1-140)	.10	.05	.01
☐ 1 Shane Conlan	.10	.05	.01
☐ 2 Kent Hull	.10	.05	.01
☐ 3 Andre Reed	.20	.09	.03
☐ 4 Bruce Smith	.20	.09	.03
☐ 5 Thurman Thomas	.40	.18	.05
☐ 6 James Brooks	.10	.05	.01
☐ 7 Boomer Esiason	.20	.09	.03
☐ 8 David Fulcher	.10	.05	.01
☐ 9 Rodney Holman	.10	.05	.01
☐ 10 Anthony Munoz	.20	.09	.03
☐ 11 Reggie Langhorne	.10	.05	.01
☐ 12 Clay Matthews	.10	.05	.01
☐ 13 Eric Metcalf	.25	.11	.03
☐ 14 Gregg Rakoczy	.10	.05	.01
☐ 15 Steve Atwater	.10	.05	.01
☐ 16 John Elway	1.00	.45	.12
☐ 17 Bobby Humphrey	.10	.05	.01
☐ 18 Karl Mecklenburg	.10	.05	.01
☐ 19 Dennis Smith	.10	.05	.01
☐ 20 Ray Childress	.10	.05	.01
☐ 21 Ernest Givins	.10	.05	.01
☐ 22 Haywood Jeffires	.20	.09	.03
☐ 23 Warren Moon	.25	.11	.03
☐ 24 Mike Munchak	.10	.05	.01
☐ 25 Albert Bentley	.10	.05	.01
☐ 26 Jeff George	.25	.11	.03
☐ 27 Rohn Stark	.10	.05	.01
☐ 28 Clarence Verdin	.10	.05	.01
☐ 29 Albert Lewis	.10	.05	.01
☐ 30 Nick Lowery	.10	.05	.01
☐ 31 Christian Okoye	.10	.05	.01
☐ 32 Stephone Paige	.10	.05	.01
☐ 33 Derrick Thomas	.20	.09	.03
☐ 34 Barry Word	.10	.05	.01
☐ 35 Bo Jackson	.25	.11	.03
☐ 36 Howie Long	.20	.09	.03
☐ 37 Greg Townsend	.10	.05	.01
☐ 38 Steve Wisniewski UER	.10	.05	.01
(Acquired by trade in '89, not draft)			
☐ 39 Mark Clayton	.10	.05	.01
☐ 40 Dan Marino	2.50	1.10	.30
☐ 41 John Offerdahl	.10	.05	.01
☐ 42 Richmond Webb	.10	.05	.01
☐ 43 Irving Fryar	.20	.09	.03
☐ 44 Ed Reynolds	.10	.05	.01
☐ 45 John Stephens	.10	.05	.01
☐ 46 Rob Moore	.20	.09	.03
☐ 47 Ken O'Brien	.10	.05	.01
☐ 48 Al Toon	.10	.05	.01
☐ 49 Bubby Brister	.10	.05	.01
☐ 50 Eric Green	.10	.05	.01
☐ 51 Merril Hoge	.10	.05	.01
☐ 52 David Little	.10	.05	.01
☐ 53 Rod Woodson	.20	.09	.03
☐ 54 Marion Butts	.10	.05	.01
☐ 55 Leslie O'Neal	.20	.09	.03
☐ 56 Junior Seau	.40	.18	.05
☐ 57 Billy Joe Tolliver	.10	.05	.01
☐ 58 Cortez Kennedy	.20	.09	.03
☐ 59 Dave Krieg	.10	.05	.01
☐ 60 John L. Williams	.10	.05	.01
☐ 61 Steve Broussard	.10	.05	.01
☐ 62 Bill Fralic	.10	.05	.01
☐ 63 Andre Rison	.20	.09	.03
☐ 64 Neal Anderson	.10	.05	.01
☐ 65 Mark Carrier DB	.10	.05	.01
☐ 66 Richard Dent	.10	.05	.01
☐ 67 Jim Harbaugh	.20	.09	.03
☐ 68 Mike Singletary	.20	.09	.03
☐ 69 Troy Aikman	1.25	.55	.16
☐ 70 Emmitt Smith	2.50	1.10	.30
☐ 71 Mel Gray	.10	.05	.01
☐ 72 Rodney Peete	.10	.05	.01
☐ 73 Barry Sanders	1.25	.55	.16
☐ 74 Tim Harris	.10	.05	.01
☐ 75 Perry Kemp	.10	.05	.01
☐ 76 Sterling Sharpe	.25	.11	.03
☐ 77 Henry Ellard	.20	.09	.03
☐ 78 Jim Everett	.10	.05	.01
☐ 79 Kevin Greene	.20	.09	.03
☐ 80 Jackie Slater	.10	.05	.01
☐ 81 Joey Browner	.10	.05	.01
☐ 82 Chris Doleman	.10	.05	.01
☐ 83 Steve Jordan	.10	.05	.01
☐ 84 Carl Lee	.10	.05	.01
☐ 85 Herschel Walker	.20	.09	.03
☐ 86 Morten Andersen	.10	.05	.01
☐ 87 Dalton Hilliard	.10	.05	.01
☐ 88 Vaughan Johnson	.10	.05	.01
☐ 89 Steve Walsh	.10	.05	.01
☐ 90 Ottis Anderson	.10	.05	.01
☐ 91 John Elliott	.10	.05	.01
☐ 92 Rodney Hampton	.20	.09	.03
☐ 93 Sean Landeta	.10	.05	.01
☐ 94 Dave Meggett	.10	.05	.01
☐ 95 Phil Simms	.20	.09	.03
☐ 96 Lawrence Taylor	.20	.09	.03
☐ 97 Randall Cunningham	.20	.09	.03
☐ 98 Keith Jackson	.10	.05	.01
☐ 99 Seth Joyner	.10	.05	.01
☐ 100 Reggie White	.40	.18	.05
☐ 101 Roy Green	.10	.05	.01
☐ 102 Johnny Johnson	.10	.05	.01
☐ 103 Ricky Proehl	.10	.05	.01
☐ 104 Tootie Robbins	.10	.05	.01
☐ 105 Kevin Fagan UER	.10	.05	.01
(4th round pick in '87, not '86)			
☐ 106 Charles Haley	.20	.09	.03
☐ 107 Guy McIntyre	.10	.05	.01
☐ 108 Joe Montana	1.50	.70	.19
☐ 109 Tom Rathman	.10	.05	.01
☐ 110 Jerry Rice	1.25	.55	.16
☐ 111 John Taylor	.20	.09	.03
☐ 112 Wayne Haddix	.10	.05	.01
☐ 113 Vinny Testaverde	.10	.05	.01
☐ 114 Earnest Byner	.10	.05	.01
☐ 115 Gary Clark	.20	.09	.03
☐ 116 Darrell Green	.10	.05	.01
☐ 117 Jim Lachey	.10	.05	.01
☐ 118 Art Monk	.20	.09	.03
☐ 119 Mark Rypien	.10	.05	.01
☐ 120 Nick Bell	.10	.05	.01
☐ 121 Eric Bieniemy	.10	.05	.01
☐ 122 Jarrod Bunch	.10	.05	.01
☐ 123 Aaron Craver	.10	.05	.01
☐ 124 Lawrence Dawsey	.10	.05	.01
☐ 125 Mike Dumas	.10	.05	.01
☐ 126 Jeff Graham	.25	.11	.03
☐ 127 Paul Justin	.10	.05	.01
☐ 128 Darryll Lewis UER	.10	.05	.01
(Darryll misspelled as Darryl)			
☐ 129 Todd Marinovich	.10	.05	.01
☐ 130 Russell Maryland	.20	.09	.03
☐ 131 Kanavis McGhee	.10	.05	.01
☐ 132 Ernie Mills	.10	.05	.01
☐ 133 Herman Moore	.75	.35	.09
☐ 134 Godfrey Myles	.10	.05	.01
☐ 135 Browning Nagle	.10	.05	.01
☐ 136 Esera Tuaolo	.10	.05	.01
☐ 137 Mark Vander Poel	.10	.05	.01
☐ 138 Harvey Williams	.25	.11	.03
☐ 139 Chris Zorich	.10	.05	.01
☐ 140 Checklist Card UER	.10	.05	.01
(Darryll Lewis misspelled as Darryl)			

1992 Fleer

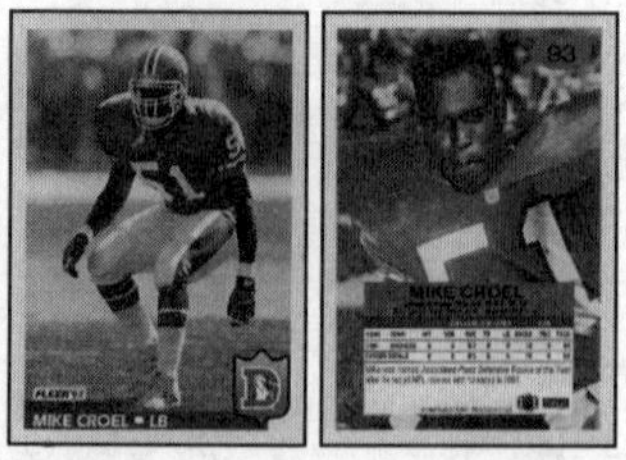

The 1992 Fleer football set contains 480 standard-size cards. The cards were available in 17-card wax packs, 42-card rack packs, and 32-card cello packs. The fronts have color action photos bordered in white. The player's name appears in a color stripe at the bottom of the picture, with the team logo in a shield icon at the lower right corner. The backs carry a close-up color photo, with biography and career statistics in a box on the lower portion of the card. The cards are numbered on the back and checklisted below alphabetically according to teams. Subsets included are Prospects (432-451), League Leaders (452-470), Pro-Visions (471-476), and Checklists (477-480). Rookie Cards include Edgar Bennett, Steve Bono, Amp Lee and Tommy Vardell.

	MINT	NRMT	EXC
COMPLETE SET (480)	10.00	4.50	1.25
COMMON CARD (1-480)	.04	.02	.01

☐ 1 Steve Broussard	.04	.02	.01
☐ 2 Rick Bryan	.04	.02	.01
☐ 3 Scott Case	.04	.02	.01
☐ 4 Tory Epps	.04	.02	.01
☐ 5 Bill Fralic	.04	.02	.01
☐ 6 Moe Gardner	.04	.02	.01
☐ 7 Michael Haynes	.10	.05	.01
☐ 8 Chris Hinton	.04	.02	.01
☐ 9 Brian Jordan	.10	.05	.01
☐ 10 Mike Kenn	.04	.02	.01
☐ 11 Tim McKyer	.04	.02	.01
☐ 12 Chris Miller	.10	.05	.01
☐ 13 Erric Pegram	.10	.05	.01
☐ 14 Mike Pritchard	.10	.05	.01
☐ 15 Andre Rison	.10	.05	.01
☐ 16 Jessie Tuggle	.04	.02	.01
☐ 17 Carlton Bailey	.10	.05	.01
☐ 18 Howard Ballard	.04	.02	.01
☐ 19 Don Beebe	.04	.02	.01
☐ 20 Cornelius Bennett	.10	.05	.01
☐ 21 Shane Conlan	.04	.02	.01
☐ 22 Kent Hull	.04	.02	.01
☐ 23 Mark Kelso	.04	.02	.01
☐ 24 James Lofton	.10	.05	.01
☐ 25 Keith McKeller	.04	.02	.01
☐ 26 Scott Norwood	.04	.02	.01
☐ 27 Nate Odomes	.04	.02	.01
☐ 28 Frank Reich	.10	.05	.01
☐ 29 Jim Ritcher	.04	.02	.01
☐ 30 Leon Seals	.04	.02	.01
☐ 31 Darryl Talley	.04	.02	.01
☐ 32 Steve Tasker	.10	.05	.01
☐ 33 Thurman Thomas	.25	.11	.03
☐ 34 Will Wolford	.04	.02	.01
☐ 35 Neal Anderson	.04	.02	.01
☐ 36 Trace Armstrong	.04	.02	.01
☐ 37 Mark Carrier DB	.04	.02	.01
☐ 38 Richard Dent	.10	.05	.01
☐ 39 Shaun Gayle	.04	.02	.01
☐ 40 Jim Harbaugh	.25	.11	.03
☐ 41 Jay Hilgenberg	.04	.02	.01
☐ 42 Darren Lewis	.04	.02	.01
☐ 43 Steve McMichael	.10	.05	.01
☐ 44 Brad Muster	.04	.02	.01
☐ 45 William Perry	.10	.05	.01
☐ 46 John Roper	.04	.02	.01
☐ 47 Lemuel Stinson	.04	.02	.01
☐ 48 Stan Thomas	.04	.02	.01
☐ 49 Keith Van Horne	.04	.02	.01
☐ 50 Tom Waddle	.04	.02	.01
☐ 51 Donnell Woolford	.04	.02	.01
☐ 52 Chris Zorich	.10	.05	.01
☐ 53 Eddie Brown	.04	.02	.01
☐ 54 James Francis	.04	.02	.01
☐ 55 David Fulcher	.04	.02	.01
☐ 56 David Grant	.04	.02	.01
☐ 57 Harold Green	.04	.02	.01
☐ 58 Rodney Holman	.04	.02	.01
☐ 59 Lee Johnson	.04	.02	.01
☐ 60 Tim Krumrie	.04	.02	.01
☐ 61 Anthony Munoz	.10	.05	.01
☐ 62 Joe Walter	.04	.02	.01
☐ 63 Mike Baab	.04	.02	.01
☐ 64 Stephen Braggs	.04	.02	.01
☐ 65 Richard Brown	.04	.02	.01
☐ 66 Dan Fike	.04	.02	.01
☐ 67 Scott Galbraith	.04	.02	.01
☐ 68 Randy Hilliard	.04	.02	.01
☐ 69 Michael Jackson	.10	.05	.01
☐ 70 Tony Jones	.04	.02	.01
☐ 71 Ed King	.04	.02	.01
☐ 72 Kevin Mack	.04	.02	.01
☐ 73 Clay Matthews	.10	.05	.01
☐ 74 Eric Metcalf	.10	.05	.01
☐ 75 Vince Newsome	.04	.02	.01
☐ 76 John Rienstra	.04	.02	.01
☐ 77 Steve Beuerlein	.04	.02	.01
☐ 78 Larry Brown DB	.04	.02	.01
☐ 79 Tony Casillas	.04	.02	.01
☐ 80 Alvin Harper	.10	.05	.01
☐ 81 Issiac Holt	.04	.02	.01
☐ 82 Ray Horton	.04	.02	.01
☐ 83 Michael Irvin	.25	.11	.03
☐ 84 Daryl Johnston	.25	.11	.03
☐ 85 Kelvin Martin	.04	.02	.01
☐ 86 Nate Newton	.10	.05	.01
☐ 87 Ken Norton	.25	.11	.03
☐ 88 Jay Novacek	.10	.05	.01
☐ 89 Emmitt Smith	2.00	.90	.25
☐ 90 Vinson Smith	.04	.02	.01
☐ 91 Mark Stepnoski	.10	.05	.01
☐ 92 Steve Atwater	.04	.02	.01
☐ 93 Mike Croel	.04	.02	.01
☐ 94 John Elway	.60	.25	.07
☐ 95 Simon Fletcher	.04	.02	.01
☐ 96 Gaston Green	.04	.02	.01
☐ 97 Mark Jackson	.04	.02	.01
☐ 98 Keith Kartz	.04	.02	.01
☐ 99 Greg Kragen	.04	.02	.01
☐ 100 Greg Lewis	.04	.02	.01
☐ 101 Karl Mecklenburg	.04	.02	.01
☐ 102 Derek Russell	.04	.02	.01
☐ 103 Steve Sewell	.04	.02	.01
☐ 104 Dennis Smith	.04	.02	.01
☐ 105 David Treadwell	.04	.02	.01
☐ 106 Kenny Walker	.04	.02	.01
☐ 107 Doug Widell	.04	.02	.01
☐ 108 Michael Young	.04	.02	.01
☐ 109 Jerry Ball	.04	.02	.01
☐ 110 Bennie Blades	.04	.02	.01
☐ 111 Lomas Brown	.04	.02	.01
☐ 112 Scott Conover	.04	.02	.01
☐ 113 Ray Crockett	.04	.02	.01
☐ 114 Mike Farr	.04	.02	.01
☐ 115 Mel Gray	.10	.05	.01
☐ 116 Willie Green	.04	.02	.01
☐ 117 Tracy Hayworth	.04	.02	.01
☐ 118 Erik Kramer	.10	.05	.01
☐ 119 Herman Moore	.75	.35	.09
☐ 120 Dan Owens	.04	.02	.01
☐ 121 Rodney Peete	.10	.05	.01
☐ 122 Brett Perriman	.25	.11	.03
☐ 123 Barry Sanders	1.00	.45	.12
☐ 124 Chris Spielman	.10	.05	.01
☐ 125 Marc Spindler	.04	.02	.01
☐ 126 Tony Bennett	.04	.02	.01
☐ 127 Matt Brock	.04	.02	.01
☐ 128 LeRoy Butler	.04	.02	.01
☐ 129 Johnny Holland	.04	.02	.01
☐ 130 Perry Kemp	.04	.02	.01
☐ 131 Don Majkowski	.04	.02	.01
☐ 132 Mark Murphy	.04	.02	.01
☐ 133 Brian Noble	.04	.02	.01
☐ 134 Bryce Paup	.25	.11	.03
☐ 135 Sterling Sharpe	.25	.11	.03
☐ 136 Scott Stephen	.04	.02	.01
☐ 137 Darrell Thompson	.04	.02	.01
☐ 138 Mike Tomczak	.04	.02	.01
☐ 139 Esera Tuaolo	.04	.02	.01
☐ 140 Keith Woodside	.04	.02	.01
☐ 141 Ray Childress	.04	.02	.01
☐ 142 Cris Dishman	.04	.02	.01
☐ 143 Curtis Duncan	.04	.02	.01
☐ 144 John Flannery	.04	.02	.01
☐ 145 William Fuller	.10	.05	.01
☐ 146 Ernest Givins	.10	.05	.01
☐ 147 Haywood Jeffires	.10	.05	.01
☐ 148 Sean Jones	.10	.05	.01
☐ 149 Lamar Lathon	.04	.02	.01
☐ 150 Bruce Matthews	.04	.02	.01
☐ 151 Bubba McDowell	.04	.02	.01
☐ 152 Johnny Meads	.04	.02	.01
☐ 153 Warren Moon	.25	.11	.03
☐ 154 Mike Munchak	.04	.02	.01
☐ 155 Al Smith	.04	.02	.01
☐ 156 Doug Smith	.04	.02	.01
☐ 157 Lorenzo White	.04	.02	.01
☐ 158 Michael Ball	.04	.02	.01
☐ 159 Chip Banks	.04	.02	.01
☐ 160 Duane Bickett	.04	.02	.01
☐ 161 Bill Brooks	.04	.02	.01
☐ 162 Ken Clark	.04	.02	.01
☐ 163 Jon Hand	.04	.02	.01
☐ 164 Jeff Herrod	.04	.02	.01
☐ 165 Jessie Hester	.04	.02	.01
☐ 166 Scott Radecic	.04	.02	.01
☐ 167 Rohn Stark	.04	.02	.01
☐ 168 Clarence Verdin	.04	.02	.01
☐ 169 John Alt	.04	.02	.01
☐ 170 Tim Barnett	.04	.02	.01
☐ 171 Tim Grunhard	.04	.02	.01
☐ 172 Dino Hackett	.04	.02	.01
☐ 173 Jonathan Hayes	.04	.02	.01
☐ 174 Bill Maas	.04	.02	.01
☐ 175 Chris Martin	.04	.02	.01
☐ 176 Christian Okoye	.04	.02	.01
☐ 177 Stephone Paige	.04	.02	.01
☐ 178 Jayice Pearson	.04	.02	.01
☐ 179 Kevin Porter	.04	.02	.01
☐ 180 Kevin Ross	.04	.02	.01
☐ 181 Dan Saleaumua	.04	.02	.01
☐ 182 Tracy Simien	.04	.02	.01
☐ 183 Neil Smith	.25	.11	.03
☐ 184 Derrick Thomas	.25	.11	.03
☐ 185 Robb Thomas	.04	.02	.01
☐ 186 Mark Vlasic	.04	.02	.01
☐ 187 Barry Word	.04	.02	.01
☐ 188 Marcus Allen	.25	.11	.03
☐ 189 Eddie Anderson	.04	.02	.01
☐ 190 Nick Bell	.04	.02	.01
☐ 191 Tim Brown	.25	.11	.03
☐ 192 Scott Davis	.04	.02	.01
☐ 193 Riki Ellison	.04	.02	.01
☐ 194 Mervyn Fernandez	.04	.02	.01
☐ 195 Willie Gault	.10	.05	.01
☐ 196 Jeff Gossett	.04	.02	.01
☐ 197 Ethan Horton	.04	.02	.01
☐ 198 Jeff Jaeger	.04	.02	.01
☐ 199 Howie Long	.10	.05	.01
☐ 200 Ronnie Lott	.10	.05	.01
☐ 201 Todd Marinovich	.04	.02	.01
☐ 202 Don Mosebar	.04	.02	.01
☐ 203 Jay Schroeder	.04	.02	.01
☐ 204 Greg Townsend	.04	.02	.01
☐ 205 Lionel Washington	.04	.02	.01
☐ 206 Steve Wisniewski	.04	.02	.01
☐ 207 Flipper Anderson	.04	.02	.01
☐ 208 Bern Brostek	.04	.02	.01
☐ 209 Robert Delpino	.04	.02	.01
☐ 210 Henry Ellard	.10	.05	.01
☐ 211 Jim Everett	.10	.05	.01
☐ 212 Cleveland Gary	.04	.02	.01
☐ 213 Kevin Greene	.25	.11	.03
☐ 214 Darryl Henley	.04	.02	.01
☐ 215 Damone Johnson	.04	.02	.01
☐ 216 Larry Kelm	.04	.02	.01
☐ 217 Todd Lyght	.04	.02	.01
☐ 218 Jackie Slater	.04	.02	.01
☐ 219 Michael Stewart	.04	.02	.01
☐ 220 Pat Terrell UER (1991 stats have 74 tackles, text has 64)	.04	.02	.01
☐ 221 Robert Young	.04	.02	.01
☐ 222 Mark Clayton	.10	.05	.01
☐ 223 Bryan Cox	.10	.05	.01
☐ 224 Aaron Craver	.04	.02	.01
☐ 225 Jeff Cross	.04	.02	.01
☐ 226 Mark Duper	.04	.02	.01
☐ 227 Harry Galbreath	.04	.02	.01
☐ 228 David Griggs	.04	.02	.01
☐ 229 Mark Higgs	.04	.02	.01
☐ 230 Vestee Jackson	.04	.02	.01
☐ 231 John Offerdahl	.04	.02	.01
☐ 232 Louis Oliver	.04	.02	.01
☐ 233 Tony Paige	.04	.02	.01
☐ 234 Reggie Roby	.04	.02	.01
☐ 235 Sammie Smith	.04	.02	.01
☐ 236 Pete Stoyanovich	.04	.02	.01
☐ 237 Richmond Webb	.04	.02	.01
☐ 238 Terry Allen	.40	.18	.05
☐ 239 Ray Berry	.04	.02	.01
☐ 240 Joey Browner	.04	.02	.01
☐ 241 Anthony Carter	.10	.05	.01
☐ 242 Cris Carter	.25	.11	.03
☐ 243 Chris Doleman	.04	.02	.01
☐ 244 Rich Gannon	.04	.02	.01
☐ 245 Tim Irwin	.04	.02	.01
☐ 246 Steve Jordan	.04	.02	.01
☐ 247 Carl Lee	.04	.02	.01
☐ 248 Randall McDaniel	.04	.02	.01
☐ 249 Mike Merriweather	.04	.02	.01
☐ 250 Harry Newsome	.04	.02	.01
☐ 251 John Randle	.10	.05	.01
☐ 252 Henry Thomas	.04	.02	.01
☐ 253 Herschel Walker	.10	.05	.01
☐ 254 Ray Agnew	.04	.02	.01
☐ 255 Bruce Armstrong	.04	.02	.01
☐ 256 Vincent Brown	.04	.02	.01
☐ 257 Marv Cook	.04	.02	.01
☐ 258 Irving Fryar	.10	.05	.01
☐ 259 Pat Harlow	.04	.02	.01
☐ 260 Tommy Hodson	.04	.02	.01
☐ 261 Maurice Hurst	.04	.02	.01
☐ 262 Ronnie Lippett	.04	.02	.01
☐ 263 Eugene Lockhart	.04	.02	.01
☐ 264 Greg McMurtry	.04	.02	.01
☐ 265 Hugh Millen	.04	.02	.01
☐ 266 Leonard Russell	.10	.05	.01
☐ 267 Andre Tippett	.04	.02	.01
☐ 268 Brent Williams	.04	.02	.01
☐ 269 Morten Andersen	.04	.02	.01
☐ 270 Gene Atkins	.04	.02	.01
☐ 271 Wesley Carroll	.04	.02	.01
☐ 272 Jim Dombrowski	.04	.02	.01
☐ 273 Quinn Early	.10	.05	.01
☐ 274 Gill Fenerty	.04	.02	.01
☐ 275 Bobby Hebert	.04	.02	.01
☐ 276 Joel Hilgenberg	.04	.02	.01
☐ 277 Rickey Jackson	.04	.02	.01
☐ 278 Vaughan Johnson	.04	.02	.01
☐ 279 Eric Martin	.04	.02	.01
☐ 280 Brett Maxie	.04	.02	.01
☐ 281 Fred McAfee	.04	.02	.01
☐ 282 Sam Mills	.04	.02	.01
☐ 283 Pat Swilling	.10	.05	.01
☐ 284 Floyd Turner	.04	.02	.01
☐ 285 Steve Walsh	.04	.02	.01
☐ 286 Frank Warren	.04	.02	.01
☐ 287 Stephen Baker	.04	.02	.01
☐ 288 Maurice Carthon	.04	.02	.01
☐ 289 Mark Collins	.04	.02	.01
☐ 290 John Elliott	.04	.02	.01
☐ 291 Myron Guyton	.04	.02	.01
☐ 292 Rodney Hampton	.25	.11	.03
☐ 293 Jeff Hostetler	.10	.05	.01
☐ 294 Mark Ingram	.04	.02	.01
☐ 295 Pepper Johnson	.04	.02	.01
☐ 296 Sean Landeta	.04	.02	.01
☐ 297 Leonard Marshall	.04	.02	.01
☐ 298 Dave Meggett	.10	.05	.01
☐ 299 Bart Oates	.04	.02	.01
☐ 300 Phil Simms	.10	.05	.01
☐ 301 Reyna Thompson	.04	.02	.01
☐ 302 Lewis Tillman	.04	.02	.01
☐ 303 Brad Baxter	.04	.02	.01
☐ 304 Kyle Clifton	.04	.02	.01
☐ 305 James Hasty	.04	.02	.01
☐ 306 Joe Kelly	.04	.02	.01
☐ 307 Jeff Lageman	.04	.02	.01
☐ 308 Mo Lewis	.04	.02	.01
☐ 309 Erik McMillan	.04	.02	.01
☐ 310 Rob Moore	.10	.05	.01
☐ 311 Tony Stargell	.04	.02	.01
☐ 312 Jim Sweeney	.04	.02	.01
☐ 313 Marvin Washington	.04	.02	.01
☐ 314 Lonnie Young	.04	.02	.01
☐ 315 Eric Allen	.04	.02	.01
☐ 316 Fred Barnett	.25	.11	.03
☐ 317 Jerome Brown	.04	.02	.01
☐ 318 Keith Byars	.04	.02	.01
☐ 319 Wes Hopkins	.04	.02	.01
☐ 320 Keith Jackson	.10	.05	.01
☐ 321 James Joseph	.04	.02	.01
☐ 322 Seth Joyner	.10	.05	.01
☐ 323 Jeff Kemp	.04	.02	.01
☐ 324 Roger Ruzek	.04	.02	.01
☐ 325 Clyde Simmons	.04	.02	.01
☐ 326 William Thomas	.04	.02	.01
☐ 327 Reggie White	.25	.11	.03
☐ 328 Calvin Williams	.10	.05	.01
☐ 329 Rich Camarillo	.04	.02	.01
☐ 330 Ken Harvey	.04	.02	.01
☐ 331 Eric Hill	.04	.02	.01
☐ 332 Johnny Johnson	.04	.02	.01
☐ 333 Ernie Jones	.04	.02	.01
☐ 334 Tim Jorden	.04	.02	.01
☐ 335 Tim McDonald	.04	.02	.01
☐ 336 Freddie Joe Nunn	.04	.02	.01
☐ 337 Luis Sharpe	.04	.02	.01
☐ 338 Eric Swann	.10	.05	.01
☐ 339 Aeneas Williams	.10	.05	.01
☐ 340 Gary Anderson K	.04	.02	.01
☐ 341 Bubby Brister	.04	.02	.01
☐ 342 Adrian Cooper	.04	.02	.01
☐ 343 Barry Foster	.10	.05	.01
☐ 344 Eric Green	.04	.02	.01
☐ 345 Bryan Hinkle	.04	.02	.01
☐ 346 Tunch Ilkin	.04	.02	.01
☐ 347 Carnell Lake	.04	.02	.01
☐ 348 Louis Lipps	.04	.02	.01
☐ 349 David Little	.04	.02	.01
☐ 350 Greg Lloyd	.25	.11	.03
☐ 351 Neil O'Donnell	.25	.11	.03
☐ 352 Dwight Stone	.04	.02	.01
☐ 353 Rod Woodson	.25	.11	.03
☐ 354 Rod Bernstine	.04	.02	.01
☐ 355 Eric Bieniemy	.04	.02	.01
☐ 356 Marion Butts	.04	.02	.01
☐ 357 Gill Byrd	.04	.02	.01
☐ 358 John Friesz	.10	.05	.01
☐ 359 Burt Grossman	.04	.02	.01
☐ 360 Courtney Hall	.04	.02	.01
☐ 361 Ronnie Harmon	.04	.02	.01
☐ 362 Shawn Jefferson	.04	.02	.01
☐ 363 Nate Lewis	.04	.02	.01
☐ 364 Craig McEwen	.04	.02	.01
☐ 365 Eric Moten	.04	.02	.01
☐ 366 Joe Phillips	.04	.02	.01
☐ 367 Gary Plummer	.04	.02	.01
☐ 368 Henry Rolling	.04	.02	.01
☐ 369 Broderick Thompson	.04	.02	.01
☐ 370 Harris Barton	.04	.02	.01
☐ 371 Steve Bono	.25	.11	.03
☐ 372 Todd Bowles	.04	.02	.01
☐ 373 Dexter Carter	.04	.02	.01
☐ 374 Michael Carter	.04	.02	.01
☐ 375 Mike Cofer	.04	.02	.01
☐ 376 Keith DeLong	.04	.02	.01
☐ 377 Charles Haley	.10	.05	.01
☐ 378 Merton Hanks	.10	.05	.01
☐ 379 Tim Harris	.04	.02	.01
☐ 380 Brent Jones	.10	.05	.01
☐ 381 Guy McIntyre	.04	.02	.01
☐ 382 Tom Rathman	.04	.02	.01
☐ 383 Bill Romanowski	.04	.02	.01
☐ 384 Jesse Sapolu	.04	.02	.01
☐ 385 John Taylor	.10	.05	.01
☐ 386 Steve Young	.60	.25	.07
☐ 387 Robert Blackmon	.04	.02	.01
☐ 388 Brian Blades	.10	.05	.01
☐ 389 Jacob Green	.04	.02	.01
☐ 390 Dwayne Harper	.04	.02	.01
☐ 391 Andy Heck	.04	.02	.01
☐ 392 Tommy Kane	.04	.02	.01
☐ 393 John Kasay	.04	.02	.01
☐ 394 Cortez Kennedy	.10	.05	.01
☐ 395 Bryan Millard	.04	.02	.01
☐ 396 Rufus Porter	.04	.02	.01
☐ 397 Eugene Robinson	.04	.02	.01
☐ 398 John L. Williams	.04	.02	.01
☐ 399 Terry Wooden	.04	.02	.01
☐ 400 Gary Anderson RB	.04	.02	.01
☐ 401 Ian Beckles	.04	.02	.01
☐ 402 Mark Carrier WR	.10	.05	.01
☐ 403 Reggie Cobb	.04	.02	.01
☐ 404 Lawrence Dawsey	.10	.05	.01
☐ 405 Ron Hall	.04	.02	.01
☐ 406 Keith McCants	.04	.02	.01
☐ 407 Charles McRae	.04	.02	.01
☐ 408 Tim Newton	.04	.02	.01
☐ 409 Jesse Solomon	.04	.02	.01
☐ 410 Vinny Testaverde	.10	.05	.01
☐ 411 Broderick Thomas	.04	.02	.01
☐ 412 Robert Wilson	.04	.02	.01
☐ 413 Jeff Bostic	.04	.02	.01
☐ 414 Earnest Byner	.04	.02	.01
☐ 415 Gary Clark	.25	.11	.03
☐ 416 Andre Collins	.04	.02	.01
☐ 417 Brad Edwards	.04	.02	.01
☐ 418 Kurt Gouveia	.04	.02	.01

	MINT	NRMT	EXC
□ 419 Darrell Green	.04	.02	.01
□ 420 Joe Jacoby	.04	.02	.01
□ 421 Jim Lachey	.04	.02	.01
□ 422 Chip Lohmiller	.04	.02	.01
□ 423 Charles Mann	.04	.02	.01
□ 424 Wilber Marshall	.04	.02	.01
□ 425 Ron Middleton	.04	.02	.01
□ 426 Brian Mitchell	.10	.05	.01
□ 427 Art Monk UER (Born in 1967, should say 1957)	.10	.05	.01
□ 428 Mark Rypien	.04	.02	.01
□ 429 Ricky Sanders	.04	.02	.01
□ 430 Mark Schlereth	.04	.02	.01
□ 431 Fred Stokes	.04	.02	.01
□ 432 Edgar Bennett	.75	.35	.09
□ 433 Brian Bollinger	.04	.02	.01
□ 434 Joe Bowden	.04	.02	.01
□ 435 Terrell Buckley	.04	.02	.01
□ 436 Willie Clay	.04	.02	.01
□ 437 Steve Gordon	.04	.02	.01
□ 438 Keith Hamilton	.04	.02	.01
□ 439 Carlos Huerta	.04	.02	.01
□ 440 Matt LaBounty	.04	.02	.01
□ 441 Amp Lee	.04	.02	.01
□ 442 Ricardo McDonald	.04	.02	.01
□ 443 Chris Mims	.10	.05	.01
□ 444 Michael Mooney	.04	.02	.01
□ 445 Patrick Rowe	.04	.02	.01
□ 446 Leon Searcy	.10	.05	.01
□ 447 Siran Stacy	.04	.02	.01
□ 448 Kevin Turner	.04	.02	.01
□ 449 Tommy Vardell	.10	.05	.01
□ 450 Bob Whitfield	.04	.02	.01
□ 451 Darryl Williams	.04	.02	.01
□ 452 Thurman Thomas LL	.10	.05	.01
□ 453 Emmitt Smith LL UER (Thr at start of second paragraph should be the)	1.00	.45	.12
□ 454 Haywood Jeffires LL	.04	.02	.01
□ 455 Michael Irvin LL	.10	.05	.01
□ 456 Mark Clayton LL	.04	.02	.01
□ 457 Barry Sanders LL	.50	.23	.06
□ 458 Pete Stoyanovich LL	.04	.02	.01
□ 459 Chip Lohmiller LL	.04	.02	.01
□ 460 William Fuller LL	.04	.02	.01
□ 461 Pat Swilling LL	.04	.02	.01
□ 462 Ronnie Lott LL	.04	.02	.01
□ 463 Ray Crockett LL	.04	.02	.01
□ 464 Tim McKyer LL	.04	.02	.01
□ 465 Aeneas Williams LL	.04	.02	.01
□ 466 Rod Woodson LL	.10	.05	.01
□ 467 Mel Gray LL	.04	.02	.01
□ 468 Nate Lewis LL	.04	.02	.01
□ 469 Steve Young LL	.30	.14	.04
□ 470 Reggie Roby LL	.04	.02	.01
□ 471 John Elway PV	.30	.14	.04
□ 472 Ronnie Lott PV	.04	.02	.01
□ 473 Art Monk PV UER (Born in 1967, should say 1957)	.04	.02	.01
□ 474 Warren Moon PV	.10	.05	.01
□ 475 Emmitt Smith PV	1.00	.45	.12
□ 476 Thurman Thomas PV	.10	.05	.01
□ 477 Checklist 1-120	.04	.02	.01
□ 478 Checklist 121-240	.04	.02	.01
□ 479 Checklist 241-360	.04	.02	.01
□ 480 Checklist 361-480	.04	.02	.01

1992 Fleer Prototypes

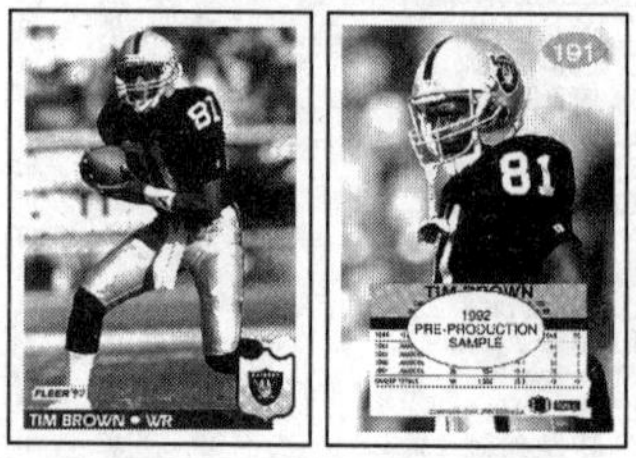

The 1992 Fleer Prototype football set contains six standard-size cards. The cards were distributed as two-card and three-card panels or strips in an attempt to show off the new design features of the 1992 Fleer football cards. The cards prominently pronounce "1992 Pre-Production Sample" in the middle of the reverse.

	MINT	NRMT	EXC
COMPLETE SET (6)	12.00	5.50	1.50
COMMON CARD	1.00	.45	.12
□ 93 Mike Croel	1.00	.45	.12
□ 191 Tim Brown	1.25	.55	.16
□ 428 Mark Rypien	1.00	.45	.12
□ 435 Terrell Buckley	1.00	.45	.12
□ 457 Barry Sanders LL	3.00	1.35	.35
□ 475 Emmitt Smith PV	5.00	2.20	.60

1992 Fleer All-Pros

This 24-card standard-size set was randomly inserted in packs. On a dark blue card face, the fronts feature color player cut outs superimposed on a red, white, and blue NFL logo emblem. The

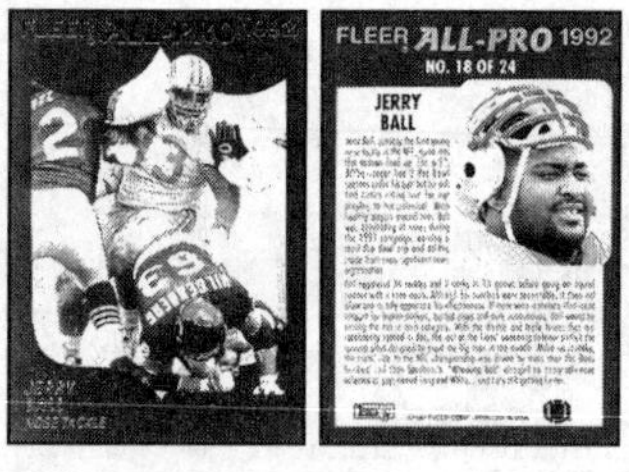

player's name and position appear in gold foil lettering at the lower left corner. The backs carry a color head shot and player profile on a pink background.

	MINT	NRMT	EXC
COMPLETE SET (24)	8.00	3.60	1.00
COMMON CARD (1-24)	.25	.11	.03
□ 1 Marv Cook	.25	.11	.03
□ 2 Mike Kenn	.25	.11	.03
□ 3 Steve Wisniewski	.25	.11	.03
□ 4 Jim Ritcher	.25	.11	.03
□ 5 Jim Lachey	.25	.11	.03
□ 6 Michael Irvin	1.50	.70	.19
□ 7 Andre Rison	.75	.35	.09
□ 8 Thurman Thomas	.75	.35	.09
□ 9 Barry Sanders	4.00	1.80	.50
□ 10 Bruce Matthews	.25	.11	.03
□ 11 Mark Rypien	.25	.11	.03
□ 12 Jeff Jaeger	.25	.11	.03
□ 13 Reggie White	.75	.35	.09
□ 14 Clyde Simmons	.25	.11	.03
□ 15 Pat Swilling	.50	.23	.06
□ 16 Sam Mills	.25	.11	.03
□ 17 Ray Childress	.50	.23	.06
□ 18 Jerry Ball	.25	.11	.03
□ 19 Derrick Thomas	.75	.35	.09
□ 20 Darrell Green	.25	.11	.03
□ 21 Ronnie Lott	.50	.23	.06
□ 22 Steve Atwater	.25	.11	.03
□ 23 Mark Carrier DB	.25	.11	.03
□ 24 Jeff Gossett	.25	.11	.03

1992 Fleer Rookie Sensations

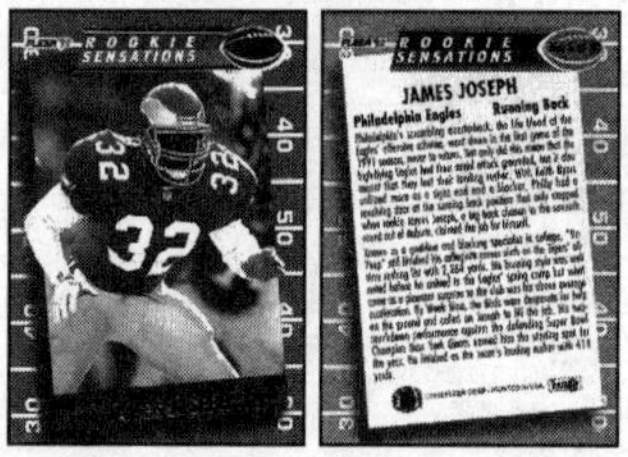

This 20-card standard-size set was inserted in 1992 Fleer cello packs. The color action player photos on the fronts are slightly tilted to the left and have shadow borders on the left and bottom. The card face is designed like a football field, with a green background sectioned off by white yard line markers. At the card top, the words "Rookie Sensations" are accented by gold foil stripes representing the flight of a football, while the player's name appears in gold foil lettering below the picture. The backs have a similar design to the fronts and present a career summary.

	MINT	NRMT	EXC
COMPLETE SET (20)	30.00	13.50	3.70
COMMON CARD (1-20)	1.50	.70	.19
□ 1 Moe Gardner	1.50	.70	.19
□ 2 Mike Pritchard	2.50	1.10	.30
□ 3 Stan Thomas	1.50	.70	.19
□ 4 Larry Brown DB	2.50	1.10	.30
□ 5 Todd Lyght	1.50	.70	.19
□ 6 James Joseph	1.50	.70	.19
□ 7 Aeneas Williams	2.50	1.10	.30
□ 8 Michael Jackson	2.50	1.10	.30
□ 9 Ed King	1.50	.70	.19
□ 10 Mike Croel	1.50	.70	.19
□ 11 Kenny Walker	1.50	.70	.19
□ 12 Tim Barnett	1.50	.70	.19
□ 13 Nick Bell	1.50	.70	.19
□ 14 Todd Marinovich	1.50	.70	.19
□ 15 Leonard Russell	2.50	1.10	.30
□ 16 Pat Harlow	1.50	.70	.19
□ 17 Mo Lewis	2.50	1.10	.30
□ 18 John Kasay	1.50	.70	.19
□ 19 Lawrence Dawsey	2.50	1.10	.30
□ 20 Charles McRae	1.50	.70	.19

1992 Fleer Mark Rypien

This 15-card standard-size set chronicles the career of Mark Rypien, Super Bowl XXVI's Most Valuable Player. The first 12 cards were randomly inserted in packs. Collectors could also obtain three additional cards (13-15) of him by mailing in ten Fleer pack proofs of purchase. Rypien autographed over 2,000 of his cards. The cards

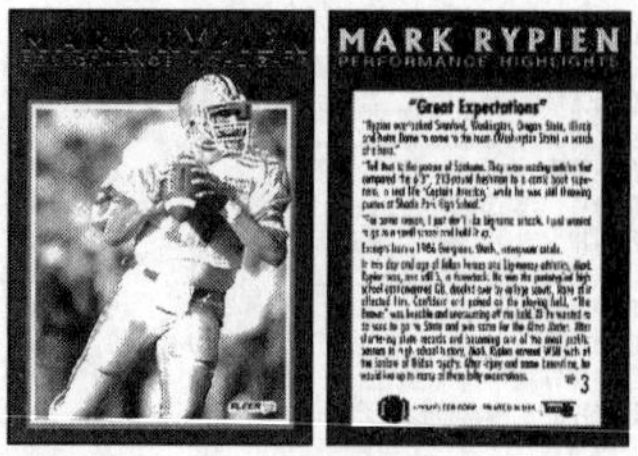

measure the standard size. On a dark blue card face, the fronts feature color action photos outlined in the team's colors. The words "Mark Rypien Performance Highlights" appear in gold-foil lettering above the picture. The backs carry capsule summaries of different phases of Rypien's career.

	MINT	NRMT	EXC
COMPLETE SET (12)	3.00	1.35	.35
COMMON RYPIEN (1-12)	.40	.18	.05
□ 1 A Matter of Faith	.40	.18	.05
□ 2 Mr. Everything	.40	.18	.05
□ 3 Great Expectations	.40	.18	.05
□ 4 Hills and Valleys	.40	.18	.05
□ 5 Breakout Season	.40	.18	.05
□ 6 The End of the Beginning	.40	.18	.05
□ 7 Bowled Over	.40	.18	.05
□ 8 Watching and Waiting	.40	.18	.05
□ 9 QB Controversy	.40	.18	.05
□ 10 Redemption	.40	.18	.05
□ 11 Pain and Pressure	.40	.18	.05
□ 12 Jubilation	.40	.18	.05
□ 13 A Year For The Books	.50	.23	.06
□ 14 No Big Surprise	.50	.23	.06
□ 15 Father Figure	.50	.23	.06
□ AU Mark Rypien AUTO (Certified Autograph)	40.00	18.00	5.00

1992 Fleer Team Leaders

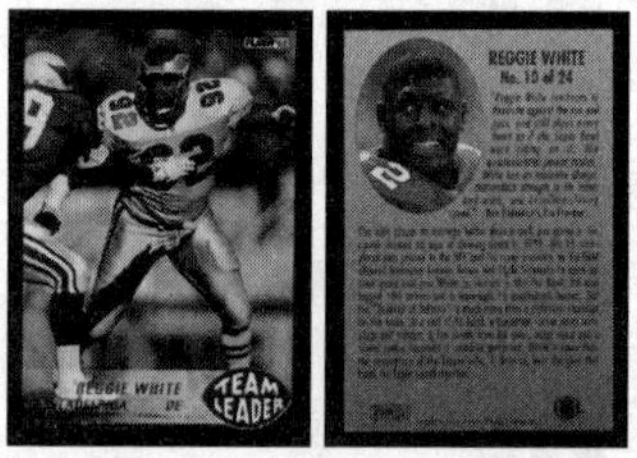

This 24-card standard-size set was inserted in 1992 Fleer rack packs. Each rack contained either a Team Leader card or a Mark Rypien insert. The color action player photos on the fronts are bordered in black and are prone to chipping. The player's name, team, position, and a "Team Leader" logo appear in gold foil lettering toward the bottom of the card face. On a light grayish-blue background, the backs feature a color head shot in an oval frame and present career summary. The cards are arranged alphabetically according to team in the NFC (1-13) and AFC (14-24).

	MINT	NRMT	EXC
COMPLETE SET (24)	90.00	40.00	11.00
COMMON CARD (1-24)	2.00	.90	.25
□ 1 Chris Miller	4.00	1.80	.50
□ 2 Neal Anderson	4.00	1.80	.50
□ 3 Emmitt Smith	40.00	18.00	5.00
□ 4 Chris Spielman	4.00	1.80	.50
□ 5 Brian Noble	2.00	.90	.25
□ 6 Jim Everett	4.00	1.80	.50
□ 7 Joey Browner	2.00	.90	.25
□ 8 Sam Mills	2.00	.90	.25
□ 9 Rodney Hampton	6.00	2.70	.75
□ 10 Reggie White	6.00	2.70	.75
□ 11 Tim McDonald	2.00	.90	.25
□ 12 Charles Haley	4.00	1.80	.50
□ 13 Mark Rypien	4.00	1.80	.50
□ 14 Cornelius Bennett	4.00	1.80	.50
□ 15 Clay Matthews	4.00	1.80	.50
□ 16 John Elway	15.00	6.75	1.85
□ 17 Warren Moon	6.00	2.70	.75
□ 18 Derrick Thomas	6.00	2.70	.75
□ 19 Greg Townsend	2.00	.90	.25
□ 20 Bruce Armstrong	2.00	.90	.25
□ 21 Brad Baxter	2.00	.90	.25
□ 22 Rod Woodson	6.00	2.70	.75
□ 23 Marion Butts	4.00	1.80	.50
□ 24 Rufus Porter	2.00	.90	.25

1993 Fleer

The 1993 Fleer football set consists of 500 standard-size cards. Cards were available in 15 and 29-card packs as well as 27-card rack packs. The color action player photos on the fronts are UV coated and framed by silver metallic borders. At the bottom of the picture, the player's last name is printed in transparent lettering that has an embossed look. The team affiliation and position appear at the lower right corner. On team color-coded panels, the horizontal backs carry a

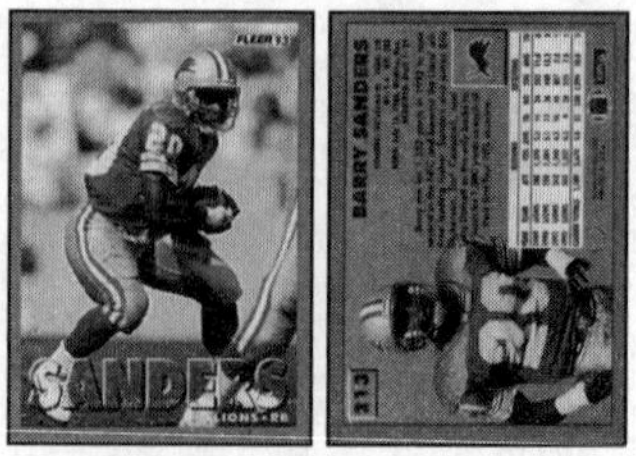

color close-up photo, biography, player profile, team logo, and statistics. Topical subsets featured are Award Winners (236-240, 253-257), League Leaders (241-243, 258-262), and Pro Visions (246-248, 263-264). Rookie Cards include Dave Brown. A Promo Panel with 8-cards was produced and is priced as uncut below.

	MINT	NRMT	EXC
COMPLETE SET (500)	25.00	11.00	3.10
COMMON CARD (1-500)	.05	.02	.01
□ 1 Dan Saleaumua	.05	.02	.01
□ 2 Bryan Cox	.05	.02	.01
□ 3 Dermontti Dawson	.05	.02	.01
□ 4 Michael Jackson	.10	.05	.01
□ 5 Calvin Williams	.10	.05	.01
□ 6 Terry McDaniel	.05	.02	.01
□ 7 Jack Del Rio	.05	.02	.01
□ 8 Steve Atwater	.05	.02	.01
□ 9 Ernie Jones	.05	.02	.01
□ 10 Brad Muster (Signed with New Orleans Saints)	.05	.02	.01
□ 11 Harold Green	.05	.02	.01
□ 12 Eric Bieniemy	.05	.02	.01
□ 13 Eric Dorsey	.05	.02	.01
□ 14 Fred Barnett	.10	.05	.01
□ 15 Cleveland Gary	.05	.02	.01
□ 16 Darion Conner	.05	.02	.01
□ 17 Jerry Ball (Traded to Cleveland Browns)	.05	.02	.01
□ 18 Tony Casillas	.05	.02	.01
□ 19 Brian Blades	.10	.05	.01
□ 20 Tony Bennett	.05	.02	.01
□ 21 Reggie Cobb	.05	.02	.01
□ 22 Kurt Gouveia	.05	.02	.01
□ 23 Greg McMurtry	.05	.02	.01
□ 24 Kyle Clifton	.05	.02	.01
□ 25 Trace Armstrong	.05	.02	.01
□ 26 Terry Allen	.25	.11	.03
□ 27 Steve Bono	.25	.11	.03
□ 28 Barry Word	.05	.02	.01
□ 29 Mark Duper	.05	.02	.01
□ 30 Nate Newton	.10	.05	.01
□ 31 Will Wolford (Signed with Indianapolis Colts)	.05	.02	.01
□ 32 Curtis Duncan	.05	.02	.01
□ 33 Nick Bell	.05	.02	.01
□ 34 Don Beebe	.05	.02	.01
□ 35 Mike Croel	.05	.02	.01
□ 36 Rich Camarillo	.05	.02	.01
□ 37 Wade Wilson (Signed with New Orleans Saints)	.05	.02	.01
□ 38 John Taylor	.10	.05	.01
□ 39 Marion Butts	.05	.02	.01
□ 40 Rodney Hampton	.25	.11	.03
□ 41 Seth Joyner	.05	.02	.01
□ 42 Wilber Marshall	.05	.02	.01
□ 43 Bobby Hebert (Signed with Atlanta Falcons)	.05	.02	.01
□ 44 Bennie Blades	.05	.02	.01
□ 45 Thomas Everett	.05	.02	.01
□ 46 Ricky Sanders	.05	.02	.01
□ 47 Matt Brock	.05	.02	.01
□ 48 Lawrence Dawsey	.05	.02	.01
□ 49 Brad Edwards	.05	.02	.01
□ 50 Vincent Brown	.05	.02	.01
□ 51 Jeff Lageman	.05	.02	.01
□ 52 Mark Carrier DB	.05	.02	.01
□ 53 Cris Carter	.25	.11	.03
□ 54 Brent Jones	.10	.05	.01
□ 55 Barry Foster	.10	.05	.01
□ 56 Derrick Thomas	.25	.11	.03
□ 57 Scott Zolak	.05	.02	.01
□ 58 Mark Stepnoski	.05	.02	.01
□ 59 Eric Metcalf	.10	.05	.01
□ 60 Al Smith	.05	.02	.01
□ 61 Ronnie Harmon	.05	.02	.01
□ 62 Cornelius Bennett	.10	.05	.01
□ 63 Karl Mecklenburg	.05	.02	.01
□ 64 Chris Chandler	.10	.05	.01
□ 65 Toi Cook	.05	.02	.01
□ 66 Tim Krumrie	.05	.02	.01
□ 67 Gill Byrd	.05	.02	.01
□ 68 Mark Jackson (Signed with New York Giants)	.05	.02	.01
□ 69 Tim Harris (Signed with	.05	.02	.01

Philadelphia Eagles)			
☐ 70 Shane Conlan	.05	.02	.01
(Signed with Los Angeles Rams)			
☐ 71 Moe Gardner	.05	.02	.01
☐ 72 Lomas Brown	.05	.02	.01
☐ 73 Charles Haley	.10	.05	.01
☐ 74 Mark Rypien	.05	.02	.01
☐ 75 LeRoy Butler	.05	.02	.01
☐ 76 Steve DeBerg	.05	.02	.01
☐ 77 Darrell Green	.05	.02	.01
☐ 78 Marv Cook	.05	.02	.01
☐ 79 Chris Burkett	.05	.02	.01
☐ 80 Richard Dent	.10	.05	.01
☐ 81 Roger Craig	.10	.05	.01
☐ 82 Amp Lee	.05	.02	.01
☐ 83 Eric Green	.05	.02	.01
☐ 84 Willie Davis	.25	.11	.03
☐ 85 Mark Higgs	.05	.02	.01
☐ 86 Carlton Haselrig	.05	.02	.01
☐ 87 Tommy Vardell	.05	.02	.01
☐ 88 Haywood Jeffires	.10	.05	.01
☐ 89 Tim Brown	.25	.11	.03
☐ 90 Randall McDaniel	.05	.02	.01
☐ 91 John Elway	.75	.35	.09
☐ 92 Ken Harvey	.05	.02	.01
☐ 93 Joel Hilgenberg	.05	.02	.01
☐ 94 Steve Wallace	.05	.02	.01
☐ 95 Stan Humphries	.25	.11	.03
☐ 96 Greg Jackson	.05	.02	.01
☐ 97 Clyde Simmons	.05	.02	.01
☐ 98 Jim Everett	.10	.05	.01
☐ 99 Michael Haynes	.10	.05	.01
☐ 100 Mel Gray	.10	.05	.01
☐ 101 Alvin Harper	.10	.05	.01
☐ 102 Art Monk	.10	.05	.01
☐ 103 Brett Favre	2.00	.90	.25
☐ 104 Keith McCants	.05	.02	.01
☐ 105 Charles Mann	.05	.02	.01
☐ 106 Leonard Russell	.10	.05	.01
☐ 107 Mo Lewis	.05	.02	.01
☐ 108 Shaun Gayle	.05	.02	.01
☐ 109 Chris Doleman	.05	.02	.01
☐ 110 Tim McDonald	.05	.02	.01
(Signed with San Francisco 49ers)			
☐ 111 Louis Oliver	.05	.02	.01
☐ 112 Greg Lloyd	.25	.11	.03
☐ 113 Chip Banks	.05	.02	.01
☐ 114 Sean Jones	.05	.02	.01
☐ 115 Ethan Horton	.05	.02	.01
☐ 116 Kenneth Davis	.05	.02	.01
☐ 117 Simon Fletcher	.05	.02	.01
☐ 118 Johnny Johnson	.05	.02	.01
(Traded to New York Jets)			
☐ 119 Vaughan Johnson	.05	.02	.01
☐ 120 Derrick Fenner	.05	.02	.01
☐ 121 Nate Lewis	.05	.02	.01
☐ 122 Pepper Johnson	.05	.02	.01
☐ 123 Heath Sherman	.05	.02	.01
☐ 124 Darryl Henley	.05	.02	.01
☐ 125 Pierce Holt	.05	.02	.01
(Signed with Atlanta Falcons)			
☐ 126 Herman Moore	.75	.35	.09
☐ 127 Michael Irvin	.25	.11	.03
☐ 128 Tommy Kane	.05	.02	.01
☐ 129 Jackie Harris	.05	.02	.01
☐ 130 Hardy Nickerson	.10	.05	.01
(Signed with Tampa Bay Buccaneers)			
☐ 131 Chip Lohmiller	.05	.02	.01
☐ 132 Andre Tippett	.05	.02	.01
☐ 133 Leonard Marshall	.05	.02	.01
(Signed with New York Jets)			
☐ 134 Craig Heyward	.10	.05	.01
(Signed with Chicago Bears)			
☐ 135 Anthony Carter	.10	.05	.01
☐ 136 Tom Rathman	.05	.02	.01
☐ 137 Lorenzo White	.05	.02	.01
☐ 138 Nick Lowery	.05	.02	.01
☐ 139 John Offerdahl	.05	.02	.01
☐ 140 Neil O'Donnell	.25	.11	.03
☐ 141 Clarence Verdin	.05	.02	.01
☐ 142 Ernest Givins	.10	.05	.01
☐ 143 Todd Marinovich	.05	.02	.01
☐ 144 Jeff Wright	.05	.02	.01
☐ 145 Michael Brooks	.05	.02	.01
☐ 146 Freddie Joe Nunn	.05	.02	.01
☐ 147 William Perry	.10	.05	.01
☐ 148 Daniel Stubbs	.05	.02	.01
☐ 149 Morten Andersen	.05	.02	.01
☐ 150 Dave Meggett	.05	.02	.01
☐ 151 Andre Waters	.05	.02	.01
☐ 152 Todd Lyght	.05	.02	.01
☐ 153 Chris Miller	.10	.05	.01
☐ 154 Rodney Peete	.05	.02	.01
☐ 155 Jim Jeffcoat	.05	.02	.01
☐ 156 Cortez Kennedy	.10	.05	.01
☐ 157 Johnny Holland	.05	.02	.01
☐ 158 Ricky Reynolds	.05	.02	.01
☐ 159 Kevin Greene	.25	.11	.03
(Signed with Pittsburgh Steelers)			
☐ 160 Jeff Herrod	.05	.02	.01
☐ 161 Bruce Matthews	.05	.02	.01
☐ 162 Anthony Smith	.05	.02	.01
☐ 163 Henry Jones	.05	.02	.01
☐ 164 Rob Burnett	.05	.02	.01
☐ 165 Eric Swann	.10	.05	.01
☐ 166 Tom Waddle	.05	.02	.01
☐ 167 Alfred Williams	.05	.02	.01
☐ 168 Darren Carrington	.05	.02	.01
☐ 169 Mike Sherrard	.05	.02	.01
(Signed with New York Giants)			
☐ 170 Frank Reich	.10	.05	.01
☐ 171 Anthony Newman	.05	.02	.01
☐ 172 Mike Pritchard	.10	.05	.01
☐ 173 Andre Ware	.05	.02	.01
☐ 174 Daryl Johnston	.25	.11	.03
☐ 175 Rufus Porter	.05	.02	.01
☐ 176 Reggie White	.25	.11	.03
(Signed with Green Bay Packers)			
☐ 177 Charles Mincy	.05	.02	.01
☐ 178 Pete Stoyanovich	.05	.02	.01
☐ 179 Rod Woodson	.25	.11	.03
☐ 180 Anthony Johnson	.10	.05	.01
☐ 181 Cody Carlson	.05	.02	.01
☐ 182 Gaston Green	.05	.02	.01
(Traded to Los Angeles Raiders)			
☐ 183 Audray McMillian	.05	.02	.01
☐ 184 Mike Johnson	.05	.02	.01
☐ 185 Aeneas Williams	.05	.02	.01
☐ 186 Jarrod Bunch	.05	.02	.01
☐ 187 Dennis Smith	.05	.02	.01
☐ 188 Quinn Early	.10	.05	.01
☐ 189 James Hasty	.05	.02	.01
☐ 190 Darryl Talley	.05	.02	.01
☐ 191 Jon Vaughn	.05	.02	.01
☐ 192 Andre Rison	.10	.05	.01
☐ 193 Kelvin Pritchett	.05	.02	.01
☐ 194 Ken Norton Jr.	.10	.05	.01
☐ 195 Chris Warren	.10	.05	.01
☐ 196 Sterling Sharpe	.25	.11	.03
☐ 197 Christian Okoye	.05	.02	.01
☐ 198 Richmond Webb	.05	.02	.01
☐ 199 James Francis	.05	.02	.01
☐ 200 Reggie Langhorne	.05	.02	.01
☐ 201 J.J. Birden	.05	.02	.01
☐ 202 Aaron Wallace	.05	.02	.01
☐ 203 Henry Thomas	.05	.02	.01
☐ 204 Clay Matthews	.10	.05	.01
☐ 205 Robert Massey	.05	.02	.01
☐ 206 Donnell Woolford	.05	.02	.01
☐ 207 Ricky Watters	.25	.11	.03
☐ 208 Wayne Martin	.05	.02	.01
☐ 209 Rob Moore	.10	.05	.01
☐ 210 Steve Tasker	.10	.05	.01
☐ 211 Jackie Slater	.05	.02	.01
☐ 212 Steve Young	.75	.35	.09
☐ 213 Barry Sanders	1.00	.45	.12
☐ 214 Jay Novacek	.10	.05	.01
☐ 215 Eugene Robinson	.05	.02	.01
☐ 216 Duane Bickett	.05	.02	.01
☐ 217 Broderick Thomas	.05	.02	.01
☐ 218 David Fulcher	.05	.02	.01
☐ 219 Rohn Stark	.05	.02	.01
☐ 220 Warren Moon	.25	.11	.03
☐ 221 Steve Wisniewski	.05	.02	.01
☐ 222 Nate Odomes	.05	.02	.01
☐ 223 Shannon Sharpe	.25	.11	.03
☐ 224 Byron Evans	.05	.02	.01
☐ 225 Mark Collins	.05	.02	.01
☐ 226 Rod Bernstine	.05	.02	.01
(Signed with Denver Broncos)			
☐ 227 Sam Mills	.05	.02	.01
☐ 228 Marvin Washington	.05	.02	.01
☐ 229 Thurman Thomas	.25	.11	.03
☐ 230 Brent Williams	.05	.02	.01
☐ 231 Jessie Tuggle	.05	.02	.01
☐ 232 Chris Spielman	.10	.05	.01
☐ 233 Emmitt Smith	2.00	.90	.25
☐ 234 John L. Williams	.05	.02	.01
☐ 235 Jeff Cross	.05	.02	.01
☐ 236 Chris Doleman AW	.05	.02	.01
☐ 237 John Elway AW	.40	.18	.05
☐ 238 Barry Foster AW	.05	.02	.01
☐ 239 Cortez Kennedy AW	.05	.02	.01
☐ 240 Steve Young AW	.40	.18	.05
☐ 241 Barry Foster LL	.05	.02	.01
☐ 242 Warren Moon LL	.05	.02	.01
☐ 243 Sterling Sharpe LL	.05	.02	.01
☐ 244 Emmitt Smith LL	1.00	.45	.12
☐ 245 Thurman Thomas LL	.10	.05	.01
☐ 246 Michael Irvin PV	.10	.05	.01
☐ 247 Steve Young PV	.40	.18	.05
☐ 248 Barry Foster PV	.05	.02	.01
☐ 249 Checklist	.05	.02	.01
Teams Atlanta through Detroit			
☐ 250 Checklist	.05	.02	.01
Teams Detroit through Miami			
☐ 251 Checklist	.05	.02	.01
Teams Minnesota through Pittsburgh			
☐ 252 Checklist	.05	.02	.01
Teams Pittsburgh through Washington and Specials			
☐ 253 Troy Aikman AW	.50	.23	.06
☐ 254 Jason Hanson AW	.05	.02	.01
☐ 255 Carl Pickens AW	.40	.18	.05
☐ 256 Santana Dotson AW	.05	.02	.01
☐ 257 Dale Carter AW	.05	.02	.01
☐ 258 Clyde Simmons LL	.05	.02	.01
☐ 259 Audray McMillian LL	.05	.02	.01
☐ 260 Henry Jones LL	.05	.02	.01
☐ 261 Deion Sanders LL	.30	.14	.04
☐ 262 Haywood Jeffires LL	.05	.02	.01
☐ 263 Deion Sanders PV	.30	.14	.04
☐ 264 Andre Reed PV	.10	.05	.01
☐ 265 Vince Workman	.05	.02	.01
(Signed with Tampa Bay Buccaneers)			
☐ 266 Robert Brown	.05	.02	.01
☐ 267 Ray Agnew	.05	.02	.01
☐ 268 Ronnie Lott	.10	.05	.01
(Signed with New York Jets)			
☐ 269 Wesley Carroll	.05	.02	.01
☐ 270 John Randle	.05	.02	.01
☐ 271 Rodney Culver	.05	.02	.01
☐ 272 David Alexander	.05	.02	.01
☐ 273 Troy Aikman	1.00	.45	.12
☐ 274 Bernie Kosar	.10	.05	.01
☐ 275 Scott Case	.05	.02	.01
☐ 276 Dan McGwire	.05	.02	.01
☐ 277 John Alt	.05	.02	.01
☐ 278 Dan Marino	2.00	.90	.25
☐ 279 Santana Dotson	.10	.05	.01
☐ 280 Johnny Mitchell	.05	.02	.01
☐ 281 Alonzo Spellman	.05	.02	.01
☐ 282 Adrian Cooper	.05	.02	.01
☐ 283 Gary Clark	.10	.05	.01
(Signed with Phoenix Cardinals)			
☐ 284 Vance Johnson	.05	.02	.01
☐ 285 Eric Martin	.05	.02	.01
☐ 286 Jesse Solomon	.05	.02	.01
☐ 287 Carl Banks	.05	.02	.01
☐ 288 Harris Barton	.05	.02	.01
☐ 289 Jim Harbaugh	.25	.11	.03
☐ 290 Bubba McDowell	.05	.02	.01
☐ 291 Anthony McDowell	.05	.02	.01
☐ 292 Terrell Buckley	.05	.02	.01
☐ 293 Bruce Armstrong	.05	.02	.01
☐ 294 Kurt Barber	.05	.02	.01
☐ 295 Reginald Jones	.05	.02	.01
☐ 296 Steve Jordan	.05	.02	.01
☐ 297 Kerry Cash	.05	.02	.01
☐ 298 Ray Crockett	.05	.02	.01
☐ 299 Keith Byars	.05	.02	.01
☐ 300 Russell Maryland	.05	.02	.01
☐ 301 Johnny Bailey	.05	.02	.01
☐ 302 Vinnie Clark	.05	.02	.01
(Traded to Atlanta Falcons)			
☐ 303 Terry Wooden	.05	.02	.01
☐ 304 Harvey Williams	.10	.05	.01
☐ 305 Marco Coleman	.05	.02	.01
☐ 306 Mark Wheeler	.05	.02	.01
☐ 307 Greg Townsend	.05	.02	.01
☐ 308 Tim McGee	.05	.02	.01
(Signed with Washington Redskins)			
☐ 309 Donald Evans	.05	.02	.01
☐ 310 Randal Hill	.05	.02	.01
☐ 311 Kenny Walker	.05	.02	.01
☐ 312 Dalton Hilliard	.05	.02	.01
☐ 313 Howard Ballard	.05	.02	.01
☐ 314 Phil Simms	.10	.05	.01
☐ 315 Jerry Rice	1.00	.45	.12
☐ 316 Courtney Hall	.05	.02	.01
☐ 317 Darren Lewis	.05	.02	.01
☐ 318 Greg Montgomery	.05	.02	.01
☐ 319 Paul Gruber	.05	.02	.01
☐ 320 George Koonce	.05	.02	.01
☐ 321 Eugene Chung	.05	.02	.01
☐ 322 Mike Brim	.05	.02	.01
☐ 323 Patrick Hunter	.05	.02	.01
☐ 324 Todd Scott	.05	.02	.01
☐ 325 Steve Emtman	.05	.02	.01
☐ 326 Andy Harmon	.10	.05	.01
☐ 327 Larry Brown DB	.05	.02	.01
☐ 328 Chuck Cecil	.05	.02	.01
(Signed with Phoenix Cardinals)			
☐ 329 Tim McKyer	.05	.02	.01
☐ 330 Jeff Bryant	.05	.02	.01
☐ 331 Tim Barnett	.05	.02	.01
☐ 332 Irving Fryar	.10	.05	.01
(Traded to Miami Dolphins)			
☐ 333 Tyji Armstrong	.05	.02	.01
☐ 334 Brad Baxter	.05	.02	.01
☐ 335 Shane Collins	.05	.02	.01
☐ 336 Jeff Graham	.10	.05	.01
☐ 337 Ricky Proehl	.05	.02	.01
☐ 338 Tommy Maddox	.05	.02	.01
☐ 339 Jim Dombrowski	.05	.02	.01
☐ 340 Bill Brooks	.05	.02	.01
(Signed with Buffalo Bills)			
☐ 341 Dave Brown	.25	.11	.03
☐ 342 Eric Davis	.05	.02	.01
☐ 343 Leslie O'Neal	.10	.05	.01
☐ 344 Jim Morrissey	.05	.02	.01
☐ 345 Mike Munchak	.05	.02	.01
☐ 346 Ron Hall	.05	.02	.01
☐ 347 Brian Noble	.05	.02	.01
☐ 348 Chris Singleton	.05	.02	.01
☐ 349 Boomer Esiason UER	.10	.05	.01
(Signed with New York Jets) (Card front notes he was signed instead of traded)			
☐ 350 Ray Roberts	.05	.02	.01
☐ 351 Gary Zimmerman	.05	.02	.01
☐ 352 Quentin Coryatt	.10	.05	.01
☐ 353 Willie Green	.05	.02	.01
☐ 354 Randall Cunningham	.10	.05	.01
☐ 355 Kevin Smith	.10	.05	.01
☐ 356 Michael Dean Perry	.10	.05	.01
☐ 357 Tim Green	.05	.02	.01
☐ 358 Dwayne Harper	.05	.02	.01
☐ 359 Dale Carter	.05	.02	.01
☐ 360 Keith Jackson	.10	.05	.01
☐ 361 Martin Mayhew	.05	.02	.01
(Signed with Tampa Bay Buccaneers)			
☐ 362 Brian Washington	.05	.02	.01
☐ 363 Earnest Byner	.05	.02	.01
☐ 364 D.J. Johnson	.05	.02	.01
☐ 365 Timm Rosenbach	.05	.02	.01
☐ 366 Doug Widell	.05	.02	.01
☐ 367 Vaughn Dunbar	.05	.02	.01
☐ 368 Phil Hansen	.05	.02	.01
☐ 369 Mike Fox	.05	.02	.01
☐ 370 Dana Hall	.05	.02	.01
☐ 371 Junior Seau	.25	.11	.03
☐ 372 Steve McMichael	.10	.05	.01
☐ 373 Eddie Robinson	.05	.02	.01
☐ 374 Milton Mack	.05	.02	.01
☐ 375 Mike Prior	.05	.02	.01
(Signed with Green Bay Packers)			
☐ 376 Jerome Henderson	.05	.02	.01
☐ 377 Scott Mersereau	.05	.02	.01
☐ 378 Neal Anderson	.05	.02	.01
☐ 379 Harry Newsome	.05	.02	.01
☐ 380 John Baylor	.05	.02	.01
☐ 381 Bill Fralic	.05	.02	.01
(Signed with Detroit Lions)			
☐ 382 Mark Bavaro	.05	.02	.01
(Signed with Philadelphia Eagles)			
☐ 383 Robert Jones	.05	.02	.01
☐ 384 Tyronne Stowe	.05	.02	.01
☐ 385 Deion Sanders	.60	.25	.07
☐ 386 Robert Blackmon	.05	.02	.01
☐ 387 Neil Smith	.25	.11	.03
☐ 388 Mark Ingram	.05	.02	.01
(Signed with Miami Dolphins)			
☐ 389 Mark Carrier WR	.10	.05	.01
(Signed with Cleveland Browns)			
☐ 390 Browning Nagle	.05	.02	.01
☐ 391 Ricky Ervins	.05	.02	.01
☐ 392 Carnell Lake	.05	.02	.01
☐ 393 Luis Sharpe	.05	.02	.01
☐ 394 Greg Kragen	.05	.02	.01
☐ 395 Tommy Barnhardt	.05	.02	.01
☐ 396 Mark Kelso	.05	.02	.01
☐ 397 Kent Graham	.25	.11	.03
☐ 398 Bill Romanowski	.05	.02	.01
☐ 399 Anthony Miller	.10	.05	.01
☐ 400 John Roper	.05	.02	.01
☐ 401 Lamar Rogers	.05	.02	.01
☐ 402 Troy Auzenne	.05	.02	.01
☐ 403 Webster Slaughter	.05	.02	.01
☐ 404 David Brandon	.05	.02	.01
☐ 405 Chris Hinton	.05	.02	.01
☐ 406 Andy Heck	.05	.02	.01
☐ 407 Tracy Simien	.05	.02	.01
☐ 408 Troy Vincent	.05	.02	.01
☐ 409 Jason Hanson	.05	.02	.01
☐ 410 Rod Jones	.05	.02	.01
☐ 411 Al Noga	.05	.02	.01
(Signed with Washington Redskins)			
☐ 412 Ernie Mills	.05	.02	.01
☐ 413 Willie Gault	.05	.02	.01
☐ 414 Henry Ellard	.10	.05	.01
☐ 415 Rickey Jackson	.05	.02	.01
☐ 416 Bruce Smith	.25	.11	.03
☐ 417 Derek Brown TE	.05	.02	.01
☐ 418 Kevin Fagan	.05	.02	.01
☐ 419 Gary Plummer	.05	.02	.01
☐ 420 Wendell Davis	.05	.02	.01
☐ 421 Craig Thompson	.05	.02	.01
☐ 422 Wes Hopkins	.05	.02	.01
☐ 423 Ray Childress	.05	.02	.01
☐ 424 Pat Harlow	.05	.02	.01

☐ 425 Howie Long	.10	.05	.01
☐ 426 Shane Dronett	.05	.02	.01
☐ 427 Sean Salisbury	.05	.02	.01
☐ 428 Dwight Hollier	.05	.02	.01
☐ 429 Brett Perriman	.25	.11	.03
☐ 430 Donald Hollas	.05	.02	.01
☐ 431 Jim Lachey	.05	.02	.01
☐ 432 Darren Perry	.05	.02	.01
☐ 433 Lionel Washington	.05	.02	.01
☐ 434 Sean Gilbert	.10	.05	.01
☐ 435 Gene Atkins	.05	.02	.01
☐ 436 Jim Kelly	.25	.11	.03
☐ 437 Ed McCaffrey	.05	.02	.01
☐ 438 Don Griffin	.05	.02	.01
☐ 439 Jerrol Williams	.05	.02	.01
(Signed with			
San Diego Chargers)			
☐ 440 Bryce Paup	.25	.11	.03
☐ 441 Darryl Williams	.05	.02	.01
☐ 442 Vai Sikahema	.05	.02	.01
☐ 443 Cris Dishman	.05	.02	.01
☐ 444 Kevin Mack	.05	.02	.01
☐ 445 Winston Moss	.05	.02	.01
☐ 446 Tyrone Braxton	.05	.02	.01
☐ 447 Mike Merriweather	.05	.02	.01
☐ 448 Tony Paige	.05	.02	.01
☐ 449 Robert Porcher	.05	.02	.01
☐ 450 Ricardo McDonald	.05	.02	.01
☐ 451 Danny Copeland	.05	.02	.01
☐ 452 Tony Tolbert	.05	.02	.01
☐ 453 Eric Dickerson	.10	.05	.01
☐ 454 Flipper Anderson	.05	.02	.01
☐ 455 Dave Krieg	.10	.05	.01
☐ 456 Brad Lamb	.05	.02	.01
☐ 457 Bart Oates	.05	.02	.01
☐ 458 Guy McIntyre	.05	.02	.01
☐ 459 Stanley Richard	.05	.02	.01
☐ 460 Edgar Bennett	.25	.11	.03
☐ 461 Pat Carter	.05	.02	.01
☐ 462 Eric Allen	.05	.02	.01
☐ 463 William Fuller	.05	.02	.01
☐ 464 James Jones	.05	.02	.01
☐ 465 Chester McGlockton	.10	.05	.01
☐ 466 Charles Dimry	.05	.02	.01
☐ 467 Tim Grunhard	.05	.02	.01
☐ 468 Jarvis Williams	.05	.02	.01
☐ 469 Tracy Scroggins	.05	.02	.01
☐ 470 David Klingler	.05	.02	.01
☐ 471 Andre Collins	.05	.02	.01
☐ 472 Erik Williams	.05	.02	.01
☐ 473 Eddie Anderson	.05	.02	.01
☐ 474 Marc Boutte	.05	.02	.01
☐ 475 Joe Montana	1.00	.45	.12
☐ 476 Andre Reed	.10	.05	.01
☐ 477 Lawrence Taylor	.25	.11	.03
☐ 478 Jeff George	.25	.11	.03
☐ 479 Chris Mims	.05	.02	.01
☐ 480 Ken Ruettgers	.05	.02	.01
☐ 481 Roman Phifer	.05	.02	.01
☐ 482 William Thomas	.05	.02	.01
☐ 483 Lamar Lathon	.05	.02	.01
☐ 484 Vinny Testaverde	.10	.05	.01
(Signed with			
Cleveland Browns)			
☐ 485 Mike Kenn	.05	.02	.01
☐ 486 Greg Lewis	.05	.02	.01
☐ 487 Chris Martin	.05	.02	.01
(Traded to			
Los Angeles Rams)			
☐ 488 Maurice Hurst	.05	.02	.01
☐ 489 Pat Swilling	.05	.02	.01
(Traded to			
Detroit Lions)			
☐ 490 Carl Pickens	.75	.35	.09
☐ 491 Tony Smith	.05	.02	.01
☐ 492 James Washington	.05	.02	.01
☐ 493 Jeff Hostetler	.10	.05	.01
(Signed with			
Los Angeles Raiders)			
☐ 494 Jeff Chadwick	.05	.02	.01
☐ 495 Kevin Ross	.05	.02	.01
☐ 496 Jim Ritcher	.05	.02	.01
☐ 497 Jessie Hester	.05	.02	.01
☐ 498 Burt Grossman	.05	.02	.01
☐ 499 Keith Van Horne	.05	.02	.01
☐ 500 Gerald Robinson	.05	.02	.01
☐ P1 Promo Panel	5.00	2.20	.60
Steve Young			
Kenny Walker			
Chip Lohmiller			
Kevin Greene			
Craig Heyward			
Ernie Jones			
Emmitt Smith			
Keith Byars			

1993 Fleer All-Pros

Randomly inserted into foil packs, this 25-card standard-size set features the best of the NFL at each offensive and defensive position. Inside white borders, the horizontal fronts feature a color player cut out superimposed on a black-and-white action shot of the player. The "Fleer All-Pro" logo and the player's name are gold foil stamped on the picture. On team color-coded panels, the horizontal backs present career summary. The set is checklisted in alphabetical order.

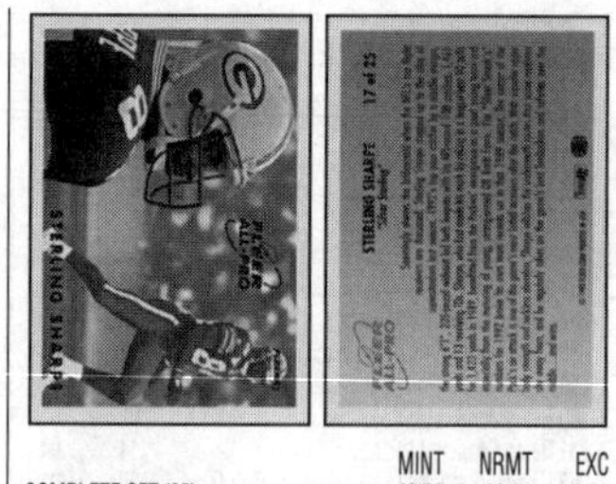

	MINT	NRMT	EXC
COMPLETE SET (25)	40.00	18.00	5.00
COMMON CARD (1-25)	.50	.23	.06
☐ 1 Steve Atwater	.50	.23	.06
☐ 2 Rich Camarillo	.50	.23	.06
☐ 3 Ray Childress	.75	.35	.09
☐ 4 Chris Doleman	.75	.35	.09
☐ 5 Barry Foster	.75	.35	.09
☐ 6 Henry Jones	.50	.23	.06
☐ 7 Cortez Kennedy	.75	.35	.09
☐ 8 Nick Lowery	.50	.23	.06
☐ 9 Wilber Marshall	.50	.23	.06
☐ 10 Bruce Matthews	.50	.23	.06
☐ 11 Randall McDaniel	.50	.23	.06
☐ 12 Audray McMillian	.50	.23	.06
☐ 13 Sam Mills	.50	.23	.06
☐ 14 Jay Novacek	.75	.35	.09
☐ 15 Jerry Rice	8.00	3.60	1.00
☐ 16 Junior Seau	1.50	.70	.19
☐ 17 Sterling Sharpe	.75	.35	.09
☐ 18 Clyde Simmons	.50	.23	.06
☐ 19 Emmitt Smith	16.00	7.25	2.00
☐ 20 Derrick Thomas	1.50	.70	.19
☐ 21 Steve Wallace	.50	.23	.06
☐ 22 Richmond Webb	.50	.23	.06
☐ 23 Steve Wisniewski	.50	.23	.06
☐ 24 Rod Woodson	1.50	.70	.19
☐ 25 Steve Young	6.00	2.70	.75

1993 Fleer Prospects

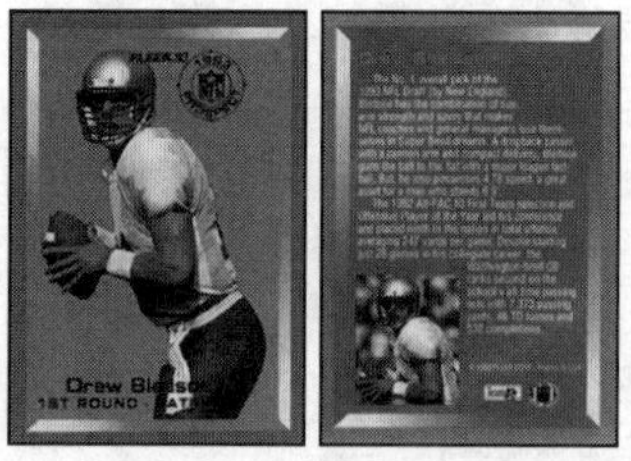

Randomly inserted into foil packs, this 30-card standard-size set features the top 1993 NFL draft picks. The fronts feature color player cut outs on a gold panel with sky blue borders. Gold foil stamped on the picture are Fleer's "1993 NFL Prospect" emblem, the player's name, the round he was drafted, and the team name. The backs reverse the colors on the front and carry player profile and a color close-up shot. The set started Fleer's tradition of issuing cards of current year rookies as an insert.

	MINT	NRMT	EXC
COMPLETE SET (30)	60.00	27.00	7.50
COMMON CARD (1-30)	1.00	.45	.12
☐ 1 Drew Bledsoe	20.00	9.00	2.50
☐ 2 Garrison Hearst	10.00	4.50	1.25
☐ 3 John Copeland	2.00	.90	.25
☐ 4 Eric Curry	2.00	.90	.25
☐ 5 Curtis Conway	6.00	2.70	.75
☐ 6 Lincoln Kennedy	1.00	.45	.12
☐ 7 Jerome Bettis	12.00	5.50	1.50
☐ 8 Patrick Bates	1.00	.45	.12
☐ 9 Brad Hopkins	1.00	.45	.12
☐ 10 Tom Carter	2.00	.90	.25
☐ 11 Irv Smith	2.00	.90	.25
☐ 12 Robert Smith	6.00	2.70	.75
☐ 13 Deon Figures	2.00	.90	.25
☐ 14 Leonard Renfro	1.00	.45	.12
☐ 15 O.J. McDuffie	6.00	2.70	.75
☐ 16 Dana Stubblefield	4.00	1.80	.50
☐ 17 Todd Kelly	1.00	.45	.12
☐ 18 George Teague	2.00	.90	.25
☐ 19 Demetrius DuBose	1.00	.45	.12
☐ 20 Coleman Rudolph	1.00	.45	.12
☐ 21 Carlton Gray	1.00	.45	.12
☐ 22 Troy Drayton	2.00	.90	.25
☐ 23 Natrone Means UER	10.00	4.50	1.25
(San Diego Chargers			
Receiver spelled Reveiver)			
☐ 24 Qadry Ismail	4.00	1.80	.50
☐ 25 Gino Torretta	2.00	.90	.25
☐ 26 Carl Simpson	1.00	.45	.12
☐ 27 Glyn Milburn	2.00	.90	.25
☐ 28 Chad Brown	2.00	.90	.25
☐ 29 Reggie Brooks	2.00	.90	.25
☐ 30 Billy Joe Hobert	2.00	.90	.25

1993 Fleer Rookie Sensations

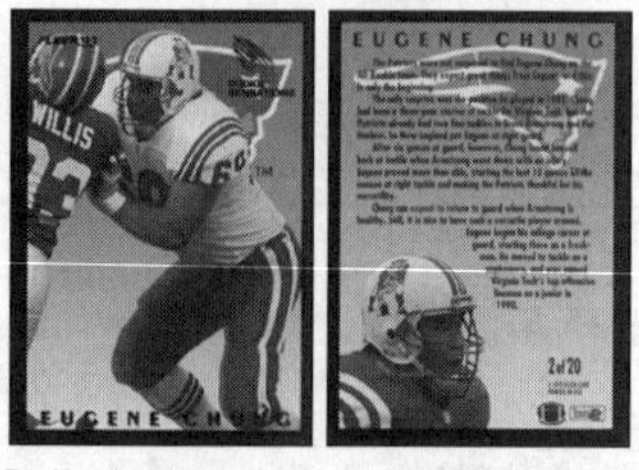

This 20-card standard-size set was randomly inserted in jumbo packs. Black-bordered fronts have color action photos with backgound colors that are consistent with the player's team. The card backs contain a write-up, a player photo and backgrounds consistent with the fronts. The set is checklisted in alphabetical order.

	MINT	NRMT	EXC
COMPLETE SET (20)	125.00	55.00	15.50
COMMON CARD (1-20)	6.00	2.70	.75
☐ 1 Dale Carter	8.00	3.60	1.00
☐ 2 Eugene Chung	6.00	2.70	.75
☐ 3 Marco Coleman	8.00	3.60	1.00
☐ 4 Quentin Coryatt	8.00	3.60	1.00
☐ 5 Santana Dotson	6.00	2.70	.75
☐ 6 Vaughn Dunbar	8.00	3.60	1.00
☐ 7 Steve Emtman	8.00	3.60	1.00
☐ 8 Sean Gilbert	8.00	3.60	1.00
☐ 9 Dana Hall	8.00	3.60	1.00
☐ 10 Jason Hanson	6.00	2.70	.75
☐ 11 Robert Jones	6.00	2.70	.75
☐ 12 David Klingler	8.00	3.60	1.00
☐ 13 Amp Lee	6.00	2.70	.75
☐ 14 Troy Auzenne	6.00	2.70	.75
☐ 15 Ricardo McDonald	6.00	2.70	.75
☐ 16 Chris Mims	8.00	3.60	1.00
☐ 17 Johnny Mitchell	8.00	3.60	1.00
☐ 18 Carl Pickens	25.00	11.00	3.10
☐ 19 Darren Perry	6.00	2.70	.75
☐ 20 Troy Vincent	8.00	3.60	1.00

1993 Fleer Team Leaders

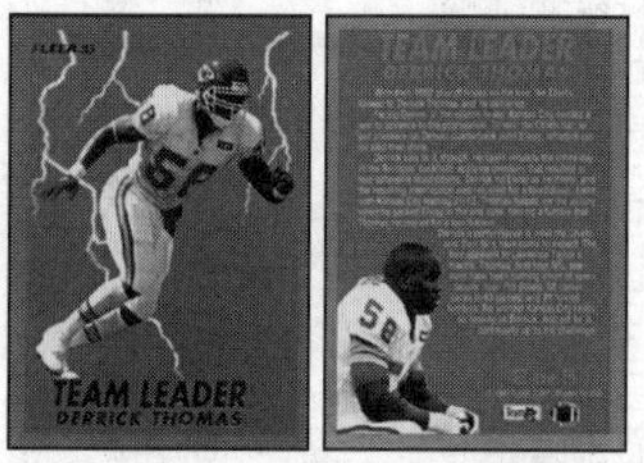

Randomly inserted into foil packs, this five-card standard-size set showcases 1992's brightest stars. On a sky blue background laced with lightning streaks, the fronts feature full-bleed color action player cut outs. The words "Team Leader" and the player's name are gold foil stamped at the bottom. Inside a gold border on a sky blue panel, the backs present a player profile and a second color player cut out.

	MINT	NRMT	EXC
COMPLETE SET (5)	40.00	18.00	5.00
COMMON CARD (1-5)	3.00	1.35	.35
☐ 1 Brett Favre	20.00	9.00	2.50
☐ 2 Derrick Thomas	3.00	1.35	.35
☐ 3 Steve Young	10.00	4.50	1.25
☐ 4 John Elway	10.00	4.50	1.25
☐ 5 Cortez Kennedy	3.00	1.35	.35

1993 Fleer Steve Young

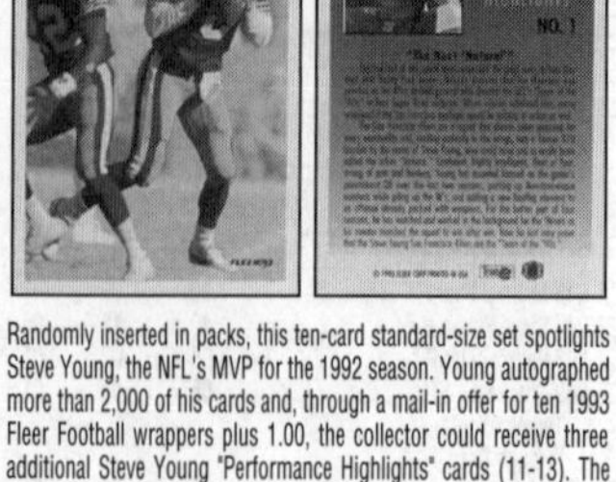

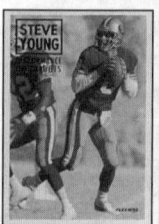

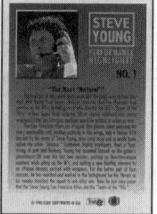

Randomly inserted in packs, this ten-card standard-size set spotlights Steve Young, the NFL's MVP for the 1992 season. Young autographed more than 2,000 of his cards and, through a mail-in offer for ten 1993 Fleer Football wrappers plus 1.00, the collector could receive three additional Steve Young "Performance Highlights" cards (11-13). The fronts feature color action player photos bordered in white. The player's name and "Performance Highlights" are gold-foil stamped at the upper left corner. Inside white borders, a red panel carries a color close-up shot and player profile.

	MINT	NRMT	EXC
COMPLETE SET (10)	10.00	4.50	1.25
COMMON YOUNG (1-10)	1.00	.45	.12
☐ 1 Steve Young	1.00	.45	.12
The Next Natural			
☐ 2 Steve Young	1.00	.45	.12
Judging the Book			
☐ 3 Steve Young	1.00	.45	.12
Understudy to Stardom			
☐ 4 Steve Young	1.00	.45	.12
Express to Success			
☐ 5 Steve Young	1.00	.45	.12
NFL			
☐ 6 Steve Young	1.00	.45	.12
Full-Time Football			
☐ 7 Steve Young	1.00	.45	.12
Learning To Fly			
☐ 8 Steve Young	1.00	.45	.12
Ringbearer			
☐ 9 Steve Young	1.00	.45	.12
Showtime			
☐ 10 Steve Young	1.00	.45	.12
Top Gun			
☐ 11 Steve Young	2.00	.90	.25
Man for All Seasons			
☐ 12 Steve Young	2.00	.90	.25
Quips and Quotes			
☐ 13 Steve Young	2.00	.90	.25
1992 MVP			
☐ NNO Steve Young AU	125.00	55.00	15.50
(Certified autograph)			

1993 Fleer Fruit of the Loom

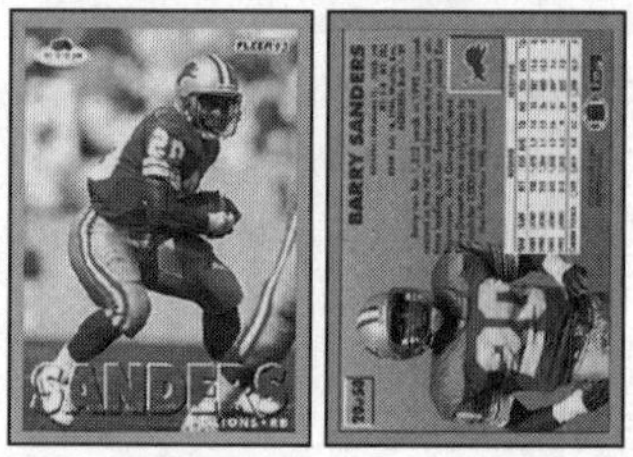

This 50-card standard-size set issued by Fleer was sponsored by Fruit of the Loom. Each specially marked underwear package contained six cards. The color action player photos on the fronts are framed with silver metallic borders. At the bottom of the photo, the player's last name is printed in transparent lettering that has an embossed look. The team affiliation and position appear at the lower right corner. Fruit of the Loom's logo is in the upper left corner. On a team color-coded panel, the horizontal backs carry a close-up color shot, biography, player profile, team logo, and statistics.

	MINT	NRMT	EXC
COMPLETE SET (50)	90.00	40.00	11.00
COMMON CARD (1-50)	1.00	.45	.12
☐ 1 Andre Rison	2.00	.90	.25
☐ 2 Deion Sanders	6.00	2.70	.75
☐ 3 Neal Anderson	1.50	.70	.19
☐ 4 Jim Harbaugh	2.00	.90	.25
☐ 5 Bernie Kosar	1.50	.70	.19
☐ 6 Eric Metcalf	2.00	.90	.25
☐ 7 John Elway	7.00	3.10	.85
☐ 8 Karl Mecklenburg	1.00	.45	.12
☐ 9 Sterling Sharpe	2.00	.90	.25
☐ 10 Reggie White	2.00	.90	.25
(Traded to Green Bay			
Packers)			
☐ 11 Steve Emtman	1.00	.45	.12
☐ 12 Jeff George	2.50	1.10	.30
☐ 13 Willie Gault	1.00	.45	.12
☐ 14 Jim Kelly	2.00	.90	.25
☐ 15 Thurman Thomas	2.50	1.10	.30
☐ 16 Harold Green	1.50	.70	.19
☐ 17 Carl Pickens	2.50	1.10	.30
☐ 18 Troy Aikman	8.00	3.60	1.00
☐ 19 Emmitt Smith	16.00	7.25	2.00
☐ 20 Barry Sanders	8.00	3.60	1.00
☐ 21 Pat Swilling	1.00	.45	.12
(Traded to Detroit Lions)			
☐ 22 Haywood Jeffires	1.50	.70	.19
☐ 23 Warren Moon	2.00	.90	.25
☐ 24 Derrick Thomas	2.00	.90	.25
☐ 25 Christian Okoye	1.00	.45	.12
☐ 26 Flipper Anderson	1.00	.45	.12
☐ 27 Jim Everett	1.50	.70	.19
☐ 28 Keith Jackson	1.00	.45	.12
☐ 29 Dan Marino	16.00	7.25	2.00
☐ 30 Andre Tippett	1.00	.45	.12
☐ 31 Lawrence Taylor	2.00	.90	.25
☐ 32 Randall Cunningham	1.50	.70	.19
☐ 33 Barry Foster	1.50	.70	.19
☐ 34 Rod Woodson	2.00	.90	.25
☐ 35 Jerry Rice	8.00	3.60	1.00
☐ 36 Steve Young	7.00	3.10	.85
☐ 37 Reggie Cobb	1.00	.45	.12
☐ 38 Roger Craig	1.50	.70	.19
☐ 39 Chris Doleman	1.00	.45	.12
☐ 40 Morten Andersen	1.00	.45	.12

☐ 41 Dalton Hilliard	1.00	.45	.12
☐ 42 Ronnie Lott (Traded to New York Jets)	1.50	.70	.19
☐ 43 Chris Chandler	1.50	.70	.19
☐ 44 Stan Humphries	2.00	.90	.25
☐ 45 Junior Seau	2.50	1.10	.30
☐ 46 Brian Blades	1.00	.45	.12
☐ 47 Cortez Kennedy	1.50	.70	.19
☐ 48 Wilber Marshall	1.00	.45	.12
☐ 49 Art Monk	1.50	.70	.19
☐ 50 Checklist Card	1.00	.45	.12

1994 Fleer

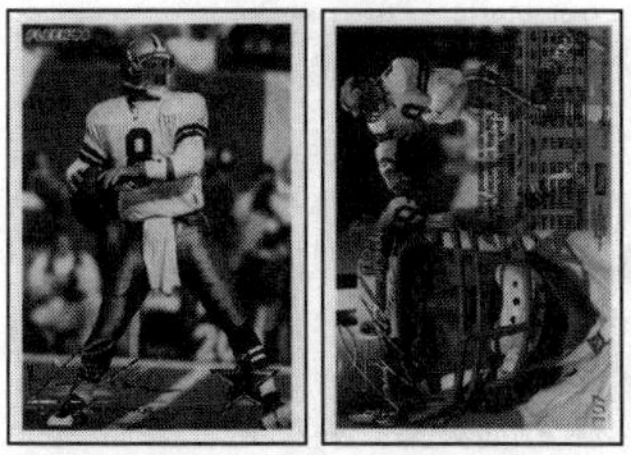

The 1994 Fleer set consists of 480 standard-size cards. The fronts feature white-bordered color action player photos with a gold-foil stamped player signature, name and position, and team logo. The horizontal backs carry a ghosted action shot, and a close-up color player portrait. Complete stats are printed over the ghosted action photo. The cards are numbered on the back, grouped alphabetically within teams, and checklisted below alphabetically according to teams. A "Fleer Hot Pack" was inserted in about every other box. It looks like a regular pack but it is filled with 15 insert cards. Otherwise, one insert card was included per pack. Cards were available in 15 and 21-card packs.There are no key Rookie Cards in this set. A Jerome Bettis prototype/promo card was produced and priced below.

	MINT	NRMT	EXC
COMPLETE SET (480)	25.00	11.00	3.10
COMMON CARD (1-480)	.05	.02	.01
☐ 1 Michael Bankston	.05	.02	.01
☐ 2 Steve Beuerlein	.05	.02	.01
☐ 3 John Booty	.05	.02	.01
☐ 4 Rich Camarillo	.05	.02	.01
☐ 5 Chuck Cecil	.05	.02	.01
☐ 6 Larry Centers	.20	.09	.03
☐ 7 Gary Clark	.10	.05	.01
☐ 8 Garrison Hearst	.40	.18	.05
☐ 9 Eric Hill	.05	.02	.01
☐ 10 Randal Hill	.05	.02	.01
☐ 11 Ronald Moore	.05	.02	.01
☐ 12 Ricky Proehl	.05	.02	.01
☐ 13 Luis Sharpe	.05	.02	.01
☐ 14 Clyde Simmons	.05	.02	.01
☐ 15 Tyronne Stowe	.05	.02	.01
☐ 16 Eric Swann	.10	.05	.01
☐ 17 Aeneas Williams	.05	.02	.01
☐ 18 Darion Conner	.05	.02	.01
☐ 19 Moe Gardner	.05	.02	.01
☐ 20 Jumpy Geathers	.05	.02	.01
☐ 21 Jeff George	.20	.09	.03
☐ 22 Roger Harper	.05	.02	.01
☐ 23 Bobby Hebert	.05	.02	.01
☐ 24 Pierce Holt	.05	.02	.01
☐ 25 D.J. Johnson	.05	.02	.01
☐ 26 Mike Kenn	.05	.02	.01
☐ 27 Lincoln Kennedy	.05	.02	.01
☐ 28 Erric Pegram	.05	.02	.01
☐ 29 Mike Pritchard	.05	.02	.01
☐ 30 Andre Rison	.10	.05	.01
☐ 31 Deion Sanders	.60	.25	.07
☐ 32 Tony Smith	.05	.02	.01
☐ 33 Jesse Solomon	.05	.02	.01
☐ 34 Jessie Tuggle	.05	.02	.01
☐ 35 Don Beebe	.05	.02	.01
☐ 36 Cornelius Bennett	.10	.05	.01
☐ 37 Bill Brooks	.05	.02	.01
☐ 38 Kenneth Davis	.05	.02	.01
☐ 39 John Fina	.05	.02	.01
☐ 40 Phil Hansen	.05	.02	.01
☐ 41 Kent Hull	.05	.02	.01
☐ 42 Henry Jones	.05	.02	.01
☐ 43 Jim Kelly	.20	.09	.03
☐ 44 Pete Metzelaars	.05	.02	.01
☐ 45 Marvcus Patton	.05	.02	.01
☐ 46 Andre Reed	.10	.05	.01
☐ 47 Frank Reich	.10	.05	.01
☐ 48 Bruce Smith	.20	.09	.03
☐ 49 Thomas Smith	.05	.02	.01
☐ 50 Darryl Talley	.05	.02	.01
☐ 51 Steve Tasker	.10	.05	.01
☐ 52 Thurman Thomas	.20	.09	.03
☐ 53 Jeff Wright	.05	.02	.01
☐ 54 Neal Anderson	.05	.02	.01
☐ 55 Trace Armstrong	.05	.02	.01
☐ 56 Troy Auzenne	.05	.02	.01
☐ 57 Joe Cain	.05	.02	.01
☐ 58 Mark Carrier DB	.05	.02	.01
☐ 59 Curtis Conway	.20	.09	.03
☐ 60 Richard Dent	.10	.05	.01
☐ 61 Shaun Gayle	.05	.02	.01
☐ 62 Andy Heck	.05	.02	.01
☐ 63 Dante Jones	.05	.02	.01
☐ 64 Erik Kramer	.10	.05	.01
☐ 65 Steve McMichael	.10	.05	.01
☐ 66 Terry Obee	.05	.02	.01
☐ 67 Vinson Smith	.05	.02	.01
☐ 68 Alonzo Spellman	.05	.02	.01
☐ 69 Tom Waddle	.05	.02	.01
☐ 70 Donnell Woolford	.05	.02	.01
☐ 71 Tim Worley	.05	.02	.01
☐ 72 Chris Zorich	.05	.02	.01
☐ 73 Mike Brim	.05	.02	.01
☐ 74 John Copeland	.05	.02	.01
☐ 75 Derrick Fenner	.05	.02	.01
☐ 76 James Francis	.05	.02	.01
☐ 77 Harold Green	.05	.02	.01
☐ 78 Rod Jones	.05	.02	.01
☐ 79 David Klingler	.05	.02	.01
☐ 80 Bruce Kozerski	.05	.02	.01
☐ 81 Tim Krumrie	.05	.02	.01
☐ 82 Ricardo McDonald	.05	.02	.01
☐ 83 Tim McGee	.05	.02	.01
☐ 84 Tony McGee	.05	.02	.01
☐ 85 Louis Oliver	.05	.02	.01
☐ 86 Carl Pickens	.50	.23	.06
☐ 87 Jeff Query	.05	.02	.01
☐ 88 Daniel Stubbs	.05	.02	.01
☐ 89 Steve Tovar	.05	.02	.01
☐ 90 Alfred Williams	.05	.02	.01
☐ 91 Darryl Williams	.05	.02	.01
☐ 92 Rob Burnett	.05	.02	.01
☐ 93 Mark Carrier WR	.10	.05	.01
☐ 94 Leroy Hoard	.05	.02	.01
☐ 95 Michael Jackson	.10	.05	.01
☐ 96 Mike Johnson	.05	.02	.01
☐ 97 Pepper Johnson	.05	.02	.01
☐ 98 Tony Jones	.05	.02	.01
☐ 99 Clay Matthews	.05	.02	.01
☐ 100 Eric Metcalf	.10	.05	.01
☐ 101 Stevon Moore	.05	.02	.01
☐ 102 Michael Dean Perry	.10	.05	.01
☐ 103 Anthony Pleasant	.05	.02	.01
☐ 104 Vinny Testaverde	.10	.05	.01
☐ 105 Eric Turner	.05	.02	.01
☐ 106 Tommy Vardell	.05	.02	.01
☐ 107 Troy Aikman	1.00	.45	.12
☐ 108 Larry Brown DB	.05	.02	.01
☐ 109 Dixon Edwards	.05	.02	.01
☐ 110 Charles Haley	.10	.05	.01
☐ 111 Alvin Harper	.10	.05	.01
☐ 112 Michael Irvin	.20	.09	.03
☐ 113 Jim Jeffcoat	.05	.02	.01
☐ 114 Daryl Johnston	.10	.05	.01
☐ 115 Leon Lett	.05	.02	.01
☐ 116 Russell Maryland	.05	.02	.01
☐ 117 Nate Newton	.05	.02	.01
☐ 118 Ken Norton Jr.	.10	.05	.01
☐ 119 Jay Novacek	.10	.05	.01
☐ 120 Darrin Smith	.05	.02	.01
☐ 121 Emmitt Smith	2.00	.90	.25
☐ 122 Kevin Smith	.05	.02	.01
☐ 123 Mark Stepnoski	.05	.02	.01
☐ 124 Tony Tolbert	.05	.02	.01
☐ 125 Erik Williams	.05	.02	.01
☐ 126 Kevin Williams	.10	.05	.01
☐ 127 Darren Woodson	.10	.05	.01
☐ 128 Steve Atwater	.05	.02	.01
☐ 129 Rod Bernstine	.05	.02	.01
☐ 130 Ray Crockett	.05	.02	.01
☐ 131 Mike Croel	.05	.02	.01
☐ 132 Robert Delpino	.05	.02	.01
☐ 133 Shane Dronett	.05	.02	.01
☐ 134 Jason Elam	.05	.02	.01
☐ 135 John Elway	.75	.35	.09
☐ 136 Simon Fletcher	.05	.02	.01
☐ 137 Greg Kragen	.05	.02	.01
☐ 138 Karl Mecklenburg	.05	.02	.01
☐ 139 Glyn Milburn	.10	.05	.01
☐ 140 Anthony Miller	.10	.05	.01
☐ 141 Derek Russell	.05	.02	.01
☐ 142 Shannon Sharpe	.10	.05	.01
☐ 143 Dennis Smith	.05	.02	.01
☐ 144 Dan Williams	.05	.02	.01
☐ 145 Gary Zimmerman	.05	.02	.01
☐ 146 Bennie Blades	.05	.02	.01
☐ 147 Lomas Brown	.05	.02	.01
☐ 148 Bill Fralic	.05	.02	.01
☐ 149 Mel Gray	.05	.02	.01
☐ 150 Willie Green	.05	.02	.01
☐ 151 Jason Hanson	.05	.02	.01
☐ 152 Robert Massey	.05	.02	.01
☐ 153 Ryan McNeil	.10	.05	.01
☐ 154 Scott Mitchell	.20	.09	.03
☐ 155 Derrick Moore	.05	.02	.01
☐ 156 Herman Moore	.40	.18	.05
☐ 157 Brett Perriman	.10	.05	.01
☐ 158 Robert Porcher	.05	.02	.01
☐ 159 Kelvin Pritchett	.05	.02	.01
☐ 160 Barry Sanders	1.00	.45	.12
☐ 161 Tracy Scroggins	.05	.02	.01
☐ 162 Chris Spielman	.10	.05	.01
☐ 163 Pat Swilling	.05	.02	.01
☐ 164 Edgar Bennett	.20	.09	.03
☐ 165 Robert Brooks	.40	.18	.05
☐ 166 Terrell Buckley	.05	.02	.01
☐ 167 LeRoy Butler	.05	.02	.01
☐ 168 Brett Favre	2.00	.90	.25
☐ 169 Harry Galbreath	.05	.02	.01
☐ 170 Jackie Harris	.05	.02	.01
☐ 171 Johnny Holland	.05	.02	.01
☐ 172 Chris Jacke	.05	.02	.01
☐ 173 George Koonce	.05	.02	.01
☐ 174 Bryce Paup	.20	.09	.03
☐ 175 Ken Ruettgers	.05	.02	.01
☐ 176 Sterling Sharpe	.10	.05	.01
☐ 177 Wayne Simmons	.05	.02	.01
☐ 178 George Teague	.05	.02	.01
☐ 179 Darrell Thompson	.05	.02	.01
☐ 180 Reggie White	.20	.09	.03
☐ 181 Gary Brown	.05	.02	.01
☐ 182 Cody Carlson	.05	.02	.01
☐ 183 Ray Childress	.05	.02	.01
☐ 184 Cris Dishman	.05	.02	.01
☐ 185 Ernest Givins	.10	.05	.01
☐ 186 Haywood Jeffires	.10	.05	.01
☐ 187 Sean Jones	.05	.02	.01
☐ 188 Lamar Lathon	.05	.02	.01
☐ 189 Bruce Matthews	.05	.02	.01
☐ 190 Bubba McDowell	.05	.02	.01
☐ 191 Glenn Montgomery	.05	.02	.01
☐ 192 Greg Montgomery	.05	.02	.01
☐ 193 Warren Moon	.20	.09	.03
☐ 194 Bo Orlando	.05	.02	.01
☐ 195 Marcus Robertson	.05	.02	.01
☐ 196 Eddie Robinson	.05	.02	.01
☐ 197 Webster Slaughter	.05	.02	.01
☐ 198 Lorenzo White	.05	.02	.01
☐ 199 John Baylor	.05	.02	.01
☐ 200 Jason Belser	.05	.02	.01
☐ 201 Tony Bennett	.05	.02	.01
☐ 202 Dean Biasucci	.05	.02	.01
☐ 203 Ray Buchanan	.05	.02	.01
☐ 204 Kerry Cash	.05	.02	.01
☐ 205 Quentin Coryatt	.05	.02	.01
☐ 206 Eugene Daniel	.05	.02	.01
☐ 207 Steve Emtman	.05	.02	.01
☐ 208 Jon Hand	.05	.02	.01
☐ 209 Jim Harbaugh	.20	.09	.03
☐ 210 Jeff Herrod	.05	.02	.01
☐ 211 Anthony Johnson	.10	.05	.01
☐ 212 Roosevelt Potts	.05	.02	.01
☐ 213 Rohn Stark	.05	.02	.01
☐ 214 Will Wolford	.05	.02	.01
☐ 215 Marcus Allen	.20	.09	.03
☐ 216 John Alt	.05	.02	.01
☐ 217 Kimble Anders	.10	.05	.01
☐ 218 J.J. Birden	.05	.02	.01
☐ 219 Dale Carter	.05	.02	.01
☐ 220 Keith Cash	.05	.02	.01
☐ 221 Tony Casillas	.05	.02	.01
☐ 222 Willie Davis	.10	.05	.01
☐ 223 Tim Grunhard	.05	.02	.01
☐ 224 Nick Lowery	.05	.02	.01
☐ 225 Charles Mincy	.05	.02	.01
☐ 226 Joe Montana	1.00	.45	.12
☐ 227 Dan Saleaumua	.05	.02	.01
☐ 228 Tracy Simien	.05	.02	.01
☐ 229 Neil Smith	.20	.09	.03
☐ 230 Derrick Thomas	.20	.09	.03
☐ 231 Eddie Anderson	.05	.02	.01
☐ 232 Tim Brown	.20	.09	.03
☐ 233 Nolan Harrison	.05	.02	.01
☐ 234 Jeff Hostetler	.10	.05	.01
☐ 235 Rocket Ismail	.10	.05	.01
☐ 236 Jeff Jaeger	.05	.02	.01
☐ 237 James Jett	.05	.02	.01
☐ 238 Joe Kelly	.05	.02	.01
☐ 239 Albert Lewis	.05	.02	.01
☐ 240 Terry McDaniel	.05	.02	.01
☐ 241 Chester McGlockton	.05	.02	.01
☐ 242 Winston Moss	.05	.02	.01
☐ 243 Gerald Perry	.05	.02	.01
☐ 244 Greg Robinson	.05	.02	.01
☐ 245 Anthony Smith	.05	.02	.01
☐ 246 Steve Smith	.05	.02	.01
☐ 247 Greg Townsend	.05	.02	.01
☐ 248 Lionel Washington	.05	.02	.01
☐ 249 Steve Wisniewski	.05	.02	.01
☐ 250 Alexander Wright	.05	.02	.01
☐ 251 Flipper Anderson	.05	.02	.01
☐ 252 Jerome Bettis	.50	.23	.06
☐ 253 Marc Boutte	.05	.02	.01
☐ 254 Shane Conlan	.05	.02	.01
☐ 255 Troy Drayton	.05	.02	.01
☐ 256 Henry Ellard	.10	.05	.01
☐ 257 Sean Gilbert	.05	.02	.01
☐ 258 Nate Lewis	.05	.02	.01
☐ 259 Todd Lyght	.05	.02	.01
☐ 260 Chris Miller	.05	.02	.01
☐ 261 Anthony Newman	.05	.02	.01
☐ 262 Roman Phifer	.05	.02	.01
☐ 263 Henry Rolling	.05	.02	.01
☐ 264 T.J. Rubley	.05	.02	.01
☐ 265 Jackie Slater	.05	.02	.01
☐ 266 Fred Stokes	.05	.02	.01
☐ 267 Robert Young	.05	.02	.01
☐ 268 Gene Atkins	.05	.02	.01
☐ 269 J.B. Brown	.05	.02	.01
☐ 270 Keith Byars	.05	.02	.01
☐ 271 Marco Coleman	.05	.02	.01
☐ 272 Bryan Cox	.05	.02	.01
☐ 273 Jeff Cross	.05	.02	.01
☐ 274 Irving Fryar	.10	.05	.01
☐ 275 Mark Higgs	.05	.02	.01
☐ 276 Dwight Hollier	.05	.02	.01
☐ 277 Mark Ingram	.05	.02	.01
☐ 278 Keith Jackson	.05	.02	.01
☐ 279 Terry Kirby	.20	.09	.03
☐ 280 Bernie Kosar	.10	.05	.01
☐ 281 Dan Marino	2.00	.90	.25
☐ 282 O.J. McDuffie	.20	.09	.03
☐ 283 Keith Sims	.05	.02	.01
☐ 284 Pete Stoyanovich	.05	.02	.01
☐ 285 Troy Vincent	.05	.02	.01
☐ 286 Richmond Webb	.05	.02	.01
☐ 287 Terry Allen	.10	.05	.01
☐ 288 Anthony Carter	.10	.05	.01
☐ 289 Cris Carter	.20	.09	.03
☐ 290 Jack Del Rio	.05	.02	.01
☐ 291 Chris Doleman	.05	.02	.01
☐ 292 Vencie Glenn	.05	.02	.01
☐ 293 Scottie Graham	.10	.05	.01
☐ 294 Chris Hinton	.05	.02	.01
☐ 295 Qadry Ismail	.20	.09	.03
☐ 296 Carlos Jenkins	.05	.02	.01
☐ 297 Steve Jordan	.05	.02	.01
☐ 298 Carl Lee	.05	.02	.01
☐ 299 Randall McDaniel	.05	.02	.01
☐ 300 John Randle	.05	.02	.01
☐ 301 Todd Scott	.05	.02	.01
☐ 302 Robert Smith	.20	.09	.03
☐ 303 Fred Strickland	.05	.02	.01
☐ 304 Henry Thomas	.05	.02	.01
☐ 305 Bruce Armstrong	.05	.02	.01
☐ 306 Harlon Barnett	.05	.02	.01
☐ 307 Drew Bledsoe	1.25	.55	.16
☐ 308 Vincent Brown	.05	.02	.01
☐ 309 Ben Coates	.20	.09	.03
☐ 310 Todd Collins	.05	.02	.01
☐ 311 Myron Guyton	.05	.02	.01
☐ 312 Pat Harlow	.05	.02	.01
☐ 313 Maurice Hurst	.05	.02	.01
☐ 314 Leonard Russell	.05	.02	.01
☐ 315 Chris Slade	.05	.02	.01
☐ 316 Michael Timpson	.05	.02	.01
☐ 317 Andre Tippett	.05	.02	.01
☐ 318 Morten Andersen	.05	.02	.01
☐ 319 Derek Brown RB	.05	.02	.01
☐ 320 Vince Buck	.05	.02	.01
☐ 321 Toi Cook	.05	.02	.01
☐ 322 Quinn Early	.10	.05	.01
☐ 323 Jim Everett	.10	.05	.01
☐ 324 Michael Haynes	.10	.05	.01
☐ 325 Tyrone Hughes	.10	.05	.01
☐ 326 Rickey Jackson	.05	.02	.01
☐ 327 Vaughan Johnson	.05	.02	.01
☐ 328 Eric Martin	.05	.02	.01
☐ 329 Wayne Martin	.05	.02	.01
☐ 330 Sam Mills	.05	.02	.01
☐ 331 Willie Roaf	.05	.02	.01
☐ 332 Irv Smith	.05	.02	.01
☐ 333 Keith Taylor	.05	.02	.01
☐ 334 Renaldo Turnbull	.05	.02	.01
☐ 335 Carlton Bailey	.05	.02	.01
☐ 336 Michael Brooks	.05	.02	.01
☐ 337 Jarrod Bunch	.05	.02	.01
☐ 338 Chris Calloway	.05	.02	.01
☐ 339 Mark Collins	.05	.02	.01
☐ 340 Howard Cross	.05	.02	.01
☐ 341 Stacey Dillard	.05	.02	.01
☐ 342 John Elliott	.05	.02	.01
☐ 343 Rodney Hampton	.20	.09	.03
☐ 344 Greg Jackson	.05	.02	.01
☐ 345 Mark Jackson	.05	.02	.01
☐ 346 Dave Meggett	.05	.02	.01
☐ 347 Corey Miller	.05	.02	.01
☐ 348 Mike Sherrard	.05	.02	.01
☐ 349 Phil Simms	.10	.05	.01
☐ 350 Lewis Tillman	.05	.02	.01
☐ 351 Brad Baxter	.05	.02	.01
☐ 352 Kyle Clifton	.05	.02	.01
☐ 353 Boomer Esiason	.10	.05	.01
☐ 354 James Hasty	.05	.02	.01
☐ 355 Bobby Houston	.05	.02	.01
☐ 356 Johnny Johnson	.05	.02	.01
☐ 357 Jeff Lageman	.05	.02	.01
☐ 358 Mo Lewis	.05	.02	.01
☐ 359 Ronnie Lott	.10	.05	.01
☐ 360 Leonard Marshall	.05	.02	.01
☐ 361 Johnny Mitchell	.05	.02	.01
☐ 362 Rob Moore	.10	.05	.01
☐ 363 Eric Thomas	.05	.02	.01
☐ 364 Brian Washington	.05	.02	.01
☐ 365 Marvin Washington	.05	.02	.01
☐ 366 Eric Allen	.05	.02	.01
☐ 367 Fred Barnett	.10	.05	.01
☐ 368 Bubby Brister	.05	.02	.01
☐ 369 Randall Cunningham	.10	.05	.01
☐ 370 Byron Evans	.05	.02	.01
☐ 371 William Fuller	.05	.02	.01
☐ 372 Andy Harmon	.05	.02	.01
☐ 373 Seth Joyner	.05	.02	.01
☐ 374 William Perry	.10	.05	.01
☐ 375 Leonard Renfro	.05	.02	.01
☐ 376 Heath Sherman	.05	.02	.01
☐ 377 Ben Smith	.05	.02	.01

☐ 378 William Thomas	.05	.02	.01
☐ 379 Herschel Walker	.10	.05	.01
☐ 380 Calvin Williams	.10	.05	.01
☐ 381 Chad Brown	.05	.02	.01
☐ 382 Dermontti Dawson	.05	.02	.01
☐ 383 Deon Figures	.05	.02	.01
☐ 384 Barry Foster	.05	.02	.01
☐ 385 Jeff Graham	.05	.02	.01
☐ 386 Eric Green	.05	.02	.01
☐ 387 Kevin Greene	.20	.09	.03
☐ 388 Carlton Haselrig	.05	.02	.01
☐ 389 Levon Kirkland	.05	.02	.01
☐ 390 Carnell Lake	.05	.02	.01
☐ 391 Greg Lloyd	.20	.09	.03
☐ 392 Neil O'Donnell	.20	.09	.03
☐ 393 Darren Perry	.05	.02	.01
☐ 394 Dwight Stone	.05	.02	.01
☐ 395 Leroy Thompson	.05	.02	.01
☐ 396 Rod Woodson	.20	.09	.03
☐ 397 Marion Butts	.05	.02	.01
☐ 398 John Carney	.05	.02	.01
☐ 399 Darren Carrington	.05	.02	.01
☐ 400 Burt Grossman	.05	.02	.01
☐ 401 Courtney Hall	.05	.02	.01
☐ 402 Ronnie Harmon	.05	.02	.01
☐ 403 Stan Humphries	.20	.09	.03
☐ 404 Shawn Jefferson	.05	.02	.01
☐ 405 Vance Johnson	.05	.02	.01
☐ 406 Chris Mims	.05	.02	.01
☐ 407 Leslie O'Neal	.05	.02	.01
☐ 408 Stanley Richard	.05	.02	.01
☐ 409 Junior Seau	.20	.09	.03
☐ 410 Harris Barton	.05	.02	.01
☐ 411 Dennis Brown	.05	.02	.01
☐ 412 Eric Davis	.05	.02	.01
☐ 413 Merton Hanks	.10	.05	.01
☐ 414 John Johnson	.05	.02	.01
☐ 415 Brent Jones	.10	.05	.01
☐ 416 Marc Logan	.05	.02	.01
☐ 417 Tim McDonald	.05	.02	.01
☐ 418 Gary Plummer	.05	.02	.01
☐ 419 Tom Rathman	.05	.02	.01
☐ 420 Jerry Rice	1.00	.45	.12
☐ 421 Bill Romanowski	.05	.02	.01
☐ 422 Jesse Sapolu	.05	.02	.01
☐ 423 Dana Stubblefield	.20	.09	.03
☐ 424 John Taylor	.10	.05	.01
☐ 425 Steve Wallace	.05	.02	.01
☐ 426 Ted Washington	.05	.02	.01
☐ 427 Ricky Watters	.20	.09	.03
☐ 428 Troy Wilson	.05	.02	.01
☐ 429 Steve Young	.75	.35	.09
☐ 430 Howard Ballard	.05	.02	.01
☐ 431 Michael Bates	.05	.02	.01
☐ 432 Robert Blackmon	.05	.02	.01
☐ 433 Brian Blades	.10	.05	.01
☐ 434 Ferrell Edmunds	.05	.02	.01
☐ 435 Carlton Gray	.05	.02	.01
☐ 436 Patrick Hunter	.05	.02	.01
☐ 437 Cortez Kennedy	.10	.05	.01
☐ 438 Kelvin Martin	.05	.02	.01
☐ 439 Rick Mirer	.20	.09	.03
☐ 440 Nate Odomes	.05	.02	.01
☐ 441 Ray Roberts	.05	.02	.01
☐ 442 Eugene Robinson	.05	.02	.01
☐ 443 Rod Stephens	.05	.02	.01
☐ 444 Chris Warren	.10	.05	.01
☐ 445 John L. Williams	.05	.02	.01
☐ 446 Terry Wooden	.05	.02	.01
☐ 447 Marty Carter	.05	.02	.01
☐ 448 Reggie Cobb	.05	.02	.01
☐ 449 Lawrence Dawsey	.05	.02	.01
☐ 450 Santana Dotson	.10	.05	.01
☐ 451 Craig Erickson	.05	.02	.01
☐ 452 Thomas Everett	.05	.02	.01
☐ 453 Paul Gruber	.05	.02	.01
☐ 454 Courtney Hawkins	.05	.02	.01
☐ 455 Martin Mayhew	.05	.02	.01
☐ 456 Hardy Nickerson	.10	.05	.01
☐ 457 Ricky Reynolds	.05	.02	.01
☐ 458 Vince Workman	.05	.02	.01
☐ 459 Reggie Brooks	.10	.05	.01
☐ 460 Earnest Byner	.05	.02	.01
☐ 461 Andre Collins	.05	.02	.01
☐ 462 Brad Edwards	.05	.02	.01
☐ 463 Kurt Gouveia	.05	.02	.01
☐ 464 Darrell Green	.05	.02	.01
☐ 465 Ken Harvey	.05	.02	.01
☐ 466 Ethan Horton	.05	.02	.01
☐ 467 A.J. Johnson	.05	.02	.01
☐ 468 Tim Johnson	.05	.02	.01
☐ 469 Jim Lachey	.05	.02	.01
☐ 470 Chip Lohmiller	.05	.02	.01
☐ 471 Art Monk	.10	.05	.01
☐ 472 Sterling Palmer	.05	.02	.01
☐ 473 Mark Rypien	.05	.02	.01
☐ 474 Ricky Sanders	.05	.02	.01
☐ 475 Checklist 1-106	.05	.02	.01
☐ 476 Checklist 107-214	.05	.02	.01
☐ 477 Checklist 215-317	.05	.02	.01
☐ 478 Checklist 318-409	.05	.02	.01
☐ 479 Checklist 410-480/Inserts	.05	.02	.01
☐ 480 Inserts Checklist	.05	.02	.01
☐ P244 Jerome Bettis Promo Numbered 244	1.00	.45	.12

1994 Fleer All-Pros

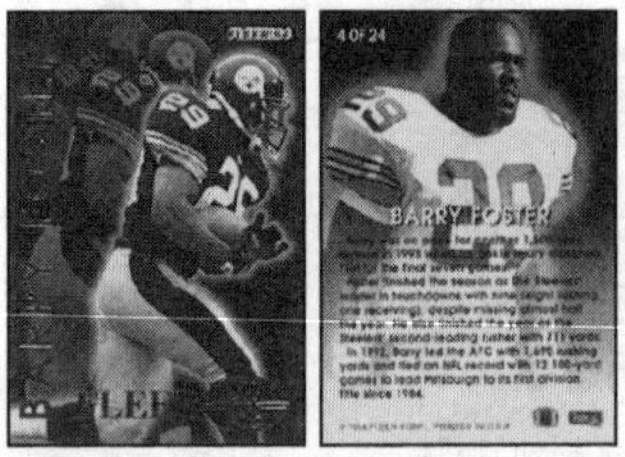

Randomly inserted in packs, these 24 standard-size cards present Fleer's choices for leading offensive and defensive players from both conferences. The borderless fronts feature color action player cutouts with multiple ghosted "echoes" of the player's image. The player's name appears vertically in gold foil near the left edge. The borderless back carries a color player closeup surrounded by a colorful "aura." Career highlights appear near the bottom. The cards are numbered on the back as "X of 24."

	MINT	NRMT	EXC
COMPLETE SET (24)	25.00	11.00	3.10
COMMON CARD (1-24)	.30	.14	.04
☐ 1 Troy Aikman	3.00	1.35	.35
☐ 2 Eric Allen	.30	.14	.04
☐ 3 Jerome Bettis	1.50	.70	.19
☐ 4 Barry Foster	.30	.14	.04
☐ 5 Michael Irvin	.75	.35	.09
☐ 6 Cortez Kennedy	.30	.14	.04
☐ 7 Joe Montana	3.00	1.35	.35
☐ 8 Hardy Nickerson	.30	.14	.04
☐ 9 Jerry Rice	3.00	1.35	.35
☐ 10 Andre Rison	.50	.23	.06
☐ 11 Barry Sanders	3.00	1.35	.35
☐ 12 Deion Sanders	1.50	.70	.19
☐ 13 Junior Seau	.75	.35	.09
☐ 14 Shannon Sharpe	.50	.23	.06
☐ 15 Sterling Sharpe	.50	.23	.06
☐ 16 Bruce Smith	.50	.23	.06
☐ 17 Emmitt Smith	6.00	2.70	.75
☐ 18 Neil Smith	.50	.23	.06
☐ 19 Derrick Thomas	.75	.35	.09
☐ 20 Thurman Thomas	.75	.35	.09
☐ 21A Renaldo Turnbull ERR (Photo of Reggie White)	.75	.35	.09
☐ 21B Renaldo Turnbull COR	.50	.23	.06
☐ 22 Reggie White	.75	.35	.09
☐ 23 Rod Woodson	.50	.23	.06
☐ 24 Steve Young	2.00	.90	.25

1994 Fleer Award Winners

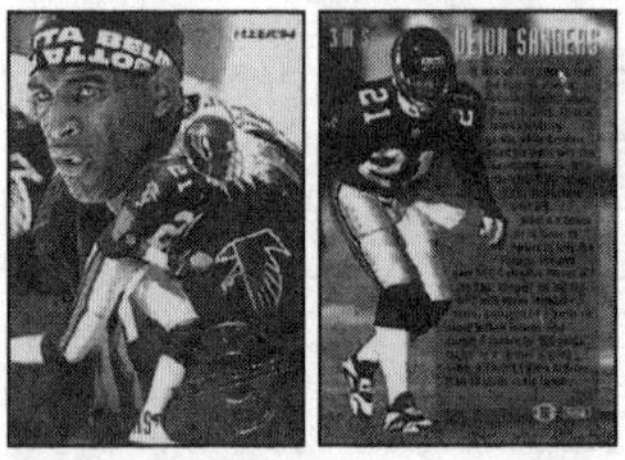

Randomly inserted in packs, this five-card standard-size set focuses on the Super Bowl MVP, the AFC and NFC Offensive Rookies of the Year, the NFL Defensive Player of the Year and the NFL Rookie of the Year. Each borderless front features a color action player cutout. This is set on a background of a black-and-white player close-up, which is color-screened near the bottom. The player's name appears in gold foil at the lower left. The borderless back carries a color player action shot, the background of which is faded to black-and-white. Career highlights appear within a color-screened rectangle set off to one side. The cards are numbered on the back as "X of 5." The set is checklisted in alphabetical order.

	MINT	NRMT	EXC
COMPLETE SET (5)	4.00	1.80	.50
COMMON CARD (1-5)	.30	.14	.04
☐ 1 Jerome Bettis	.50	.23	.06
☐ 2 Rick Mirer	.75	.35	.09
☐ 3 Deion Sanders	1.00	.45	.12
☐ 4 Emmitt Smith	2.50	1.10	.30
☐ 5 Dana Stubblefield	.30	.14	.04

1994 Fleer Jerome Bettis

Randomly inserted in packs, this 12-card standard-size set details Jerome Bettis' achievements at Notre Dame and as a 1993 rookie star with the Los Angeles Rams. Each standard-size card features a color action player cutout set on a colorized abstract design. The player's name and likeness appear in gold foil at the bottom. A horizontal back features a color action shot of Bettis as well as career highlights. Three mail-in cards (13-15) could be obtained for 10 1994 Fleer Football wrappers plus 1.50.

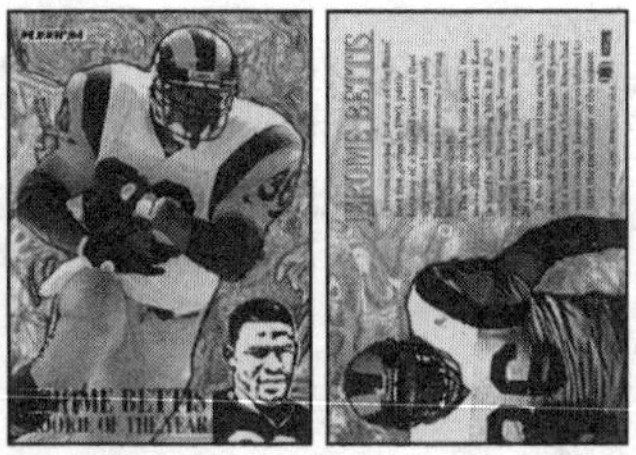

	MINT	NRMT	EXC
COMPLETE SET (12)	6.00	2.70	.75
COMMON BETTIS (1-12)	.60	.25	.07
☐ 1 Jerome Bettis Wearing Notre Dame uniform	.60	.25	.07
☐ 2 Jerome Bettis Draft day	.60	.25	.07
☐ 3 Jerome Bettis Rushing; right side profile	.60	.25	.07
☐ 4 Jerome Bettis Hurdling tackler	.60	.25	.07
☐ 5 Jerome Bettis Rushing; holding ball with both hands	.60	.25	.07
☐ 6 Jerome Bettis Rushing; left arm across body	.60	.25	.07
☐ 7 Jerome Bettis Rushing; side view	.60	.25	.07
☐ 8 Jerome Bettis Rushing straight ahead	.60	.25	.07
☐ 9 Jerome Bettis Rushing; hand in front of face	.60	.25	.07
☐ 10 Jerome Bettis Rushing; shot from left side	.60	.25	.07
☐ 11 Jerome Bettis Rushing; closeup shot	.60	.25	.07
☐ 12 Jerome Bettis In Pro Bowl uniform	.60	.25	.07
☐ 13 Jerome Bettis Rushing; left arm extended	1.00	.45	.12
☐ 14 Jerome Bettis Seated; wearing LA Rams t-shirt	1.00	.45	.12
☐ 15 Jerome Bettis Celebrating; arms extended upward	1.00	.45	.12

1994 Fleer League Leaders

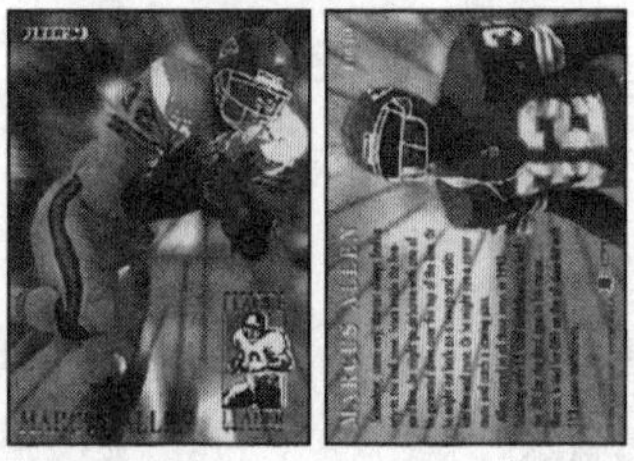

The 1994 Fleer League Leaders 10-card, standard-size set highlights top-ranked players in passing, rushing and receiving from the 1993 campaign. The card fronts feature color photos of players that emerge from a blurred background. Player name and the League Leader logo adorn the front. Card backs contain a small color photo and 1993 achievements. The cards were randomly inserted in packs. The set is checklisted in alphabetical order.

	MINT	NRMT	EXC
COMPLETE SET (10)	10.00	4.50	1.25
COMMON CARD (1-10)	.40	.18	.05
☐ 1 Marcus Allen	.75	.35	.09
☐ 2 Tim Brown	.60	.25	.07
☐ 3 John Elway	1.50	.70	.19
☐ 4 Tyrone Hughes	.40	.18	.05
☐ 5 Jerry Rice	2.00	.90	.25
☐ 6 Sterling Sharpe	.60	.25	.07
☐ 7 Emmitt Smith	4.00	1.80	.50
☐ 8 Neil Smith	.40	.18	.05
☐ 9 Thurman Thomas	.75	.35	.09
☐ 10 Steve Young	1.50	.70	.19

1994 Fleer Living Legends

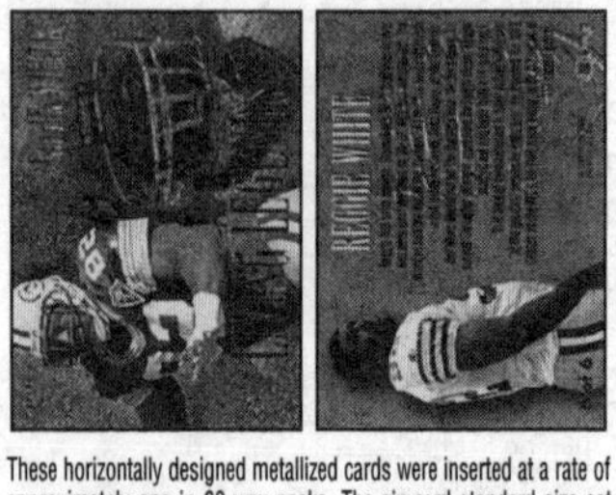

These horizontally designed metallized cards were inserted at a rate of approximately one in 60 wax packs. The six-card standard size set features NFL stars with long records of achievement in the league. The fronts have a silver background with a color player photo to the left or right. A holographic likeness of the player is on the opposite side. The backs have a color photo with career highlights. The set is checklisted in alphabetical order.

	MINT	NRMT	EXC
COMPLETE SET (6)	50.00	22.00	6.25
COMMON CARD (1-6)	4.00	1.80	.50
☐ 1 Marcus Allen	4.00	1.80	.50
☐ 2 John Elway	10.00	4.50	1.25
☐ 3 Joe Montana	12.00	5.50	1.50
☐ 4 Jerry Rice	12.00	5.50	1.50
☐ 5 Emmitt Smith	20.00	9.00	2.50
☐ 6 Reggie White	4.00	1.80	.50

1994 Fleer Pro-Visions

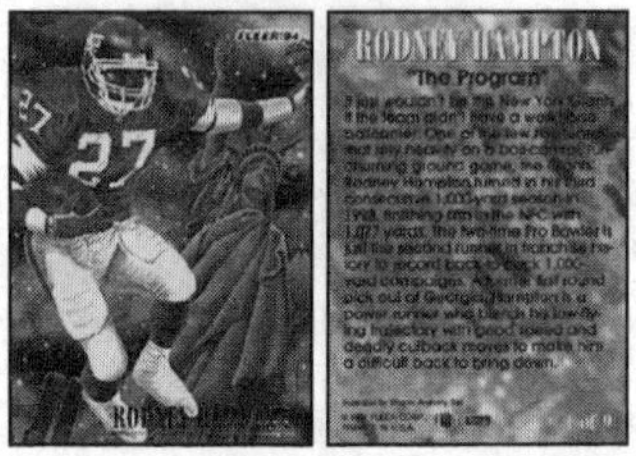

This nine-card standard-size set was randomly inserted in packs. In keeping with the Pro-Visions theme established in prior years, selected stars of the NFL are presented artistically. When placed together, they form a colorful puzzle. The back contains career highlights. The nine-card jumbo parallel set was distributed one set per hobby case.

	MINT	NRMT	EXC
COMPLETE SET (9)	6.00	2.70	.75
COMMON CARD (1-9)	.30	.14	.04
COMPLETE JUMBO SET (9)	20.00	9.00	2.50
*JUMBO CARDS: 2X to 3.5X BASIC CARDS			
☐ 1 Rodney Hampton	.50	.23	.06
☐ 2 Ricky Watters	.75	.35	.09
☐ 3 Rick Mirer	.75	.35	.09
☐ 4 Brett Favre	2.50	1.10	.30
☐ 5 Troy Aikman	1.50	.70	.19
☐ 6 Jerome Bettis	.75	.35	.09
☐ 7 Joe Montana	1.50	.70	.19
☐ 8 Cornelius Bennett	.30	.14	.04
☐ 9 Rod Woodson	.50	.23	.06

1994 Fleer Prospects

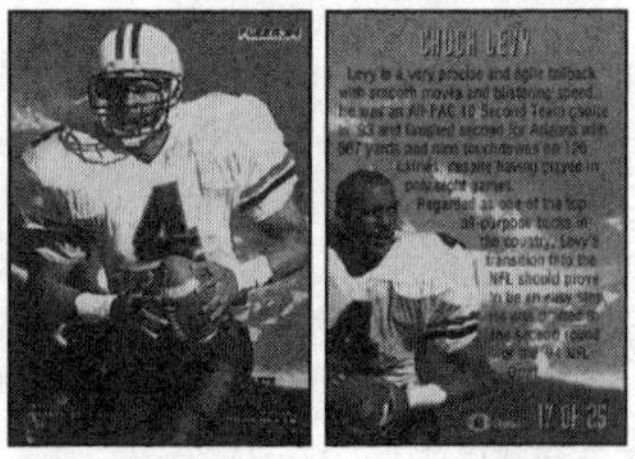

Randomly inserted in packs, this 25-card standard size set features leading 1994 rookie prospects. Pictured in his collegiate uniform, the player is superimposed over a the fiery background of a steel mill. The backs have a smaller player photo with a like background. Collegiate highlights are provided in the text on back. The set is checklisted in alphabetical order.

	MINT	NRMT	EXC
COMPLETE SET (25)	25.00	11.00	3.10
COMMON CARD (1-25)	.50	.23	.06
☐ 1 Sam Adams	.75	.35	.09
☐ 2 Trev Alberts	.75	.35	.09
☐ 3 Derrick Alexander WR	1.25	.55	.16
☐ 4 Mario Bates	1.25	.55	.16
☐ 5 Jeff Burris	.75	.35	.09
☐ 6 Shante Carver	.50	.23	.06
☐ 7 Marshall Faulk	5.00	2.20	.60
☐ 8 William Floyd	1.50	.70	.19
☐ 9 Rob Fredrickson	.75	.35	.09
☐ 10 Wayne Gandy	.50	.23	.06
☐ 11 Charlie Garner	1.25	.55	.16
☐ 12 Aaron Glenn	.75	.35	.09
☐ 13 Charles Johnson	1.25	.55	.16
☐ 14 Joe Johnson	.50	.23	.06
☐ 15 Tre Johnson	.50	.23	.06
☐ 16 Antonio Langham	.75	.35	.09
☐ 17 Chuck Levy	.50	.23	.06
☐ 18 Willie McGinest	1.25	.55	.16
☐ 19 David Palmer	1.25	.55	.16
☐ 20 Errict Rhett UER (Florida played in '94 Sugar Bowl, not Copper Bowl)	2.00	.90	.25
☐ 21 Jason Sehorn	.75	.35	.09
☐ 22 Heath Shuler	1.50	.70	.19
☐ 23 Charlie Ward Not Drafted	1.25	.55	.16
☐ 24 Dewayne Washington	.75	.35	.09
☐ 25 Bryant Young	1.25	.55	.16

1994 Fleer Rookie Exchange

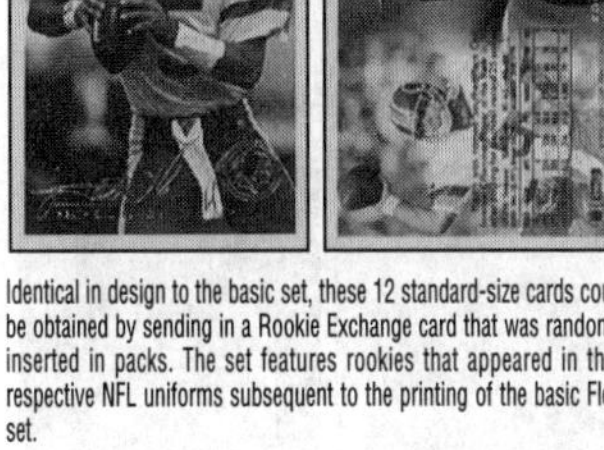

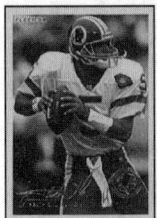

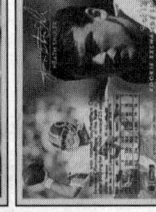

Identical in design to the basic set, these 12 standard-size cards could be obtained by sending in a Rookie Exchange card that was randomly inserted in packs. The set features rookies that appeared in their respective NFL uniforms subsequent to the printing of the basic Fleer set.

	MINT	NRMT	EXC
COMPLETE SET (12)	20.00	9.00	2.50
COMMON CARD (1-12)	.60	.25	.07
☐ 1 Derrick Alexander WR	1.00	.45	.12
☐ 2 Trent Dilfer	1.50	.70	.19
☐ 3 Marshall Faulk	6.00	2.70	.75
☐ 4 Charlie Garner	.60	.25	.07
☐ 5 Greg Hill	1.50	.70	.19
☐ 6 Charles Johnson	1.50	.70	.19
☐ 7 Antonio Langham	.60	.25	.07
☐ 8 Willie McGinest	.60	.25	.07
☐ 9 Heath Shuler	2.00	.90	.25
☐ 10 Dewayne Washington	1.00	.45	.12
☐ 11 Dan Wilkinson	1.00	.45	.12
☐ 12 Bryant Young	1.50	.70	.19
☐ NNO Rookie Exchange Expired	.50	.23	.06

1994 Fleer Rookie Sensations

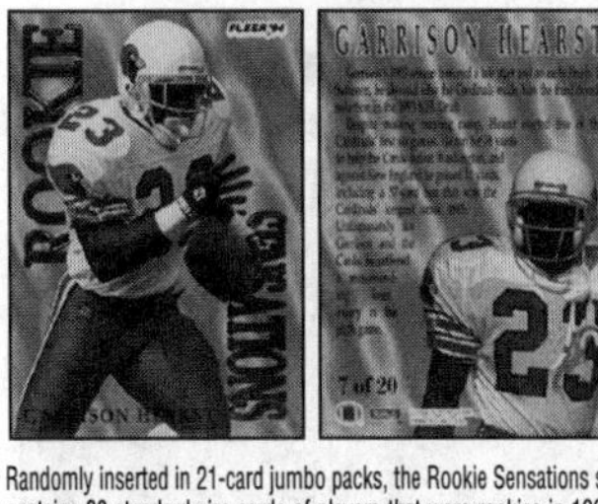

Randomly inserted in 21-card jumbo packs, the Rookie Sensations set contains 20 standard size cards of players that were rookies in 1993. A color player photo on the front has a wavy background in the dominant color of his team. The backs also have a team colored background with a small player photo and bio. The set is checklisted in alphabetical order.

	MINT	NRMT	EXC
COMPLETE SET (20)	180.00	80.00	22.00
COMMON CARD (1-20)	6.00	2.70	.75
☐ 1 Jerome Bettis	25.00	11.00	3.10
☐ 2 Drew Bledsoe	50.00	22.00	6.25
☐ 3 Reggie Brooks	10.00	4.50	1.25
☐ 4 Tom Carter	6.00	2.70	.75
☐ 5 John Copeland	6.00	2.70	.75
☐ 6 Jason Elam	6.00	2.70	.75
☐ 7 Garrison Hearst	20.00	9.00	2.50
☐ 8 Tyrone Hughes	6.00	2.70	.75
☐ 9 James Jett	6.00	2.70	.75
☐ 10 Lincoln Kennedy	6.00	2.70	.75
☐ 11 Terry Kirby	10.00	4.50	1.25
☐ 12 Glyn Milburn	10.00	4.50	1.25
☐ 13 Rick Mirer	20.00	9.00	2.50
☐ 14 Ronald Moore	6.00	2.70	.75
☐ 15 Willie Roaf	6.00	2.70	.75
☐ 16 Wayne Simmons	6.00	2.70	.75
☐ 17 Chris Slade	6.00	2.70	.75
☐ 18 Darrin Smith	6.00	2.70	.75
☐ 19 Dana Stubblefield	10.00	4.50	1.25
☐ 20 George Teague	6.00	2.70	.75

1994 Fleer Scoring Machines

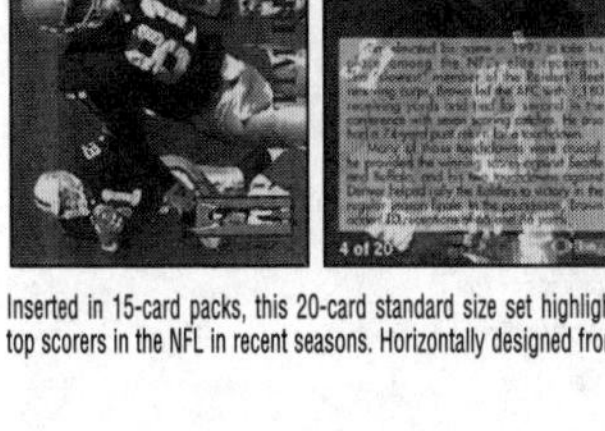

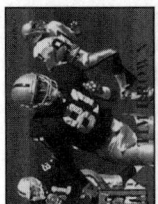

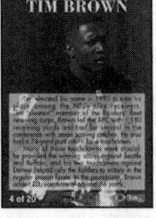

Inserted in 15-card packs, this 20-card standard size set highlights top scorers in the NFL in recent seasons. Horizontally designed fronts feature three player photos with a background consistent with his team colors. The backs are vertical with a player photo and career highlights. The set is checklisted in alphabetical order.

	MINT	NRMT	EXC
COMPLETE SET (20)	140.00	65.00	17.50
COMMON CARD (1-20)	2.00	.90	.25
☐ 1 Marcus Allen	5.00	2.20	.60
☐ 2 Natrone Means	6.00	2.70	.75
☐ 3 Jerome Bettis	8.00	3.60	1.00
☐ 4 Tim Brown	4.00	1.80	.50
☐ 5 Barry Foster	2.00	.90	.25
☐ 6 Rodney Hampton	4.00	1.80	.50
☐ 7 Michael Irvin	5.00	2.20	.60
☐ 8 Nick Lowery	2.00	.90	.25
☐ 9 Dan Marino	25.00	11.00	3.10
☐ 10 Joe Montana	15.00	6.75	1.85
☐ 11 Warren Moon	4.00	1.80	.50
☐ 12 Andre Reed	4.00	1.80	.50
☐ 13 Jerry Rice	15.00	6.75	1.85
☐ 14 Andre Rison	4.00	1.80	.50
☐ 15 Barry Sanders	15.00	6.75	1.85
☐ 16 Shannon Sharpe	2.00	.90	.25
☐ 17 Sterling Sharpe	4.00	1.80	.50
☐ 18 Emmitt Smith	25.00	11.00	3.10
☐ 19 Thurman Thomas	5.00	2.20	.60
☐ 20 Ricky Watters	4.00	1.80	.50

1995 Fleer

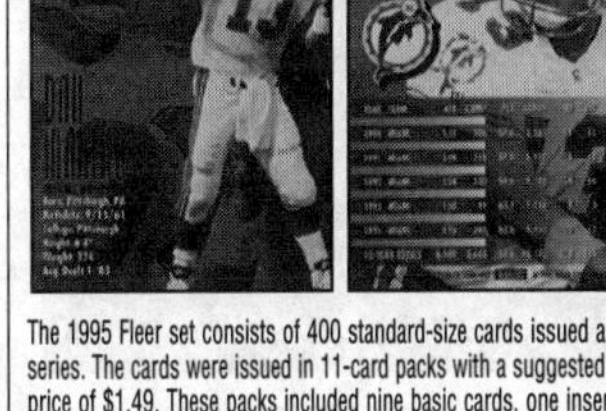

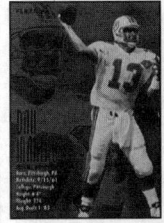

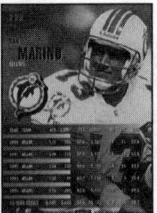

The 1995 Fleer set consists of 400 standard-size cards issued as one series. The cards were issued in 11-card packs with a suggested retail price of $1.49. These packs included nine basic cards, one insert and one Flair preview card. Hot packs containing only insert cards were included one out of 72 packs. Seventeen-card jumbo ($2.29) included 15 basic cards, one insert as well as one Flair preview. Full-bleed fronts have two photos, including a silhouette of the color photo. Atypical of football card fronts, biographical information such as height, weight and how acquired is included. The backs are in the team colors and contain yearly statistics, a brief write-up and another photo. The cards are grouped alphabetically within teams, and checklisted below alphabetically according to teams. Jeff Blake is the key Rookie Card in this set. A Promo Panel of 3-cards was produced and is priced below as an uncut panel.

	MINT	NRMT	EXC
COMPLETE SET (400)	25.00	11.00	3.10
COMMON CARD (1-400)	.05	.02	.01
☐ 1 Michael Bankston	.05	.02	.01
☐ 2 Larry Centers	.10	.05	.01
☐ 3 Gary Clark	.05	.02	.01
☐ 4 Eric Hill	.05	.02	.01
☐ 5 Seth Joyner	.05	.02	.01
☐ 6 Dave Krieg	.05	.02	.01
☐ 7 Lorenzo Lynch	.05	.02	.01
☐ 8 Jamir Miller	.05	.02	.01
☐ 9 Ronald Moore	.05	.02	.01
☐ 10 Ricky Proehl	.05	.02	.01
☐ 11 Clyde Simmons	.05	.02	.01
☐ 12 Eric Swann	.10	.05	.01
☐ 13 Aeneas Williams	.05	.02	.01
☐ 14 J.J. Birden	.05	.02	.01
☐ 15 Chris Doleman	.05	.02	.01
☐ 16 Bert Emanuel	.20	.09	.03
☐ 17 Jumpy Geathers	.05	.02	.01
☐ 18 Jeff George	.10	.05	.01
☐ 19 Roger Harper	.05	.02	.01
☐ 20 Craig Heyward	.10	.05	.01
☐ 21 Pierce Holt	.05	.02	.01
☐ 22 D.J. Johnson	.05	.02	.01
☐ 23 Terance Mathis	.10	.05	.01
☐ 24 Clay Matthews	.10	.05	.01
☐ 25 Andre Rison	.10	.05	.01
☐ 26 Chuck Smith	.05	.02	.01
☐ 27 Jessie Tuggle	.05	.02	.01
☐ 28 Cornelius Bennett	.10	.05	.01
☐ 29 Bucky Brooks	.05	.02	.01
☐ 30 Jeff Burris	.05	.02	.01
☐ 31 Russell Copeland	.05	.02	.01
☐ 32 Matt Darby	.05	.02	.01
☐ 33 Phil Hansen	.05	.02	.01
☐ 34 Henry Jones	.05	.02	.01
☐ 35 Jim Kelly	.20	.09	.03
☐ 36 Mark Maddox	.05	.02	.01
☐ 37 Bryce Paup	.20	.09	.03
☐ 38 Andre Reed	.10	.05	.01
☐ 39 Bruce Smith	.20	.09	.03
☐ 40 Darryl Talley	.05	.02	.01
☐ 41 Dewell Brewer	.05	.02	.01
☐ 42 Mike Fox	.05	.02	.01
☐ 43 Eric Guliford	.05	.02	.01
☐ 44 Lamar Lathon	.05	.02	.01
☐ 45 Pete Metzelaars	.05	.02	.01
☐ 46 Sam Mills	.10	.05	.01
☐ 47 Frank Reich	.05	.02	.01
☐ 48 Rod Smith DB	.10	.05	.01
☐ 49 Jack Trudeau	.05	.02	.01
☐ 50 Trace Armstrong	.05	.02	.01
☐ 51 Joe Cain	.05	.02	.01
☐ 52 Mark Carrier DB	.05	.02	.01
☐ 53 Curtis Conway	.20	.09	.03
☐ 54 Shaun Gayle	.05	.02	.01
☐ 55 Jeff Graham	.05	.02	.01
☐ 56 Raymont Harris	.05	.02	.01
☐ 57 Erik Kramer	.05	.02	.01
☐ 58 Lewis Tillman	.05	.02	.01
☐ 59 Tom Waddle	.05	.02	.01
☐ 60 Steve Walsh	.05	.02	.01
☐ 61 Donnell Woolford	.05	.02	.01
☐ 62 Chris Zorich	.05	.02	.01
☐ 63 Jeff Blake	1.25	.55	.16
☐ 64 Mike Brim	.05	.02	.01
☐ 65 Steve Broussard	.05	.02	.01
☐ 66 James Francis	.05	.02	.01
☐ 67 Ricardo McDonald	.05	.02	.01
☐ 68 Tony McGee	.05	.02	.01
☐ 70 Darnay Scott	.20	.09	.03
☐ 71 Steve Tovar	.05	.02	.01
☐ 72 Dan Wilkinson	.10	.05	.01
☐ 73 Alfred Williams	.05	.02	.01
☐ 74 Darryl Williams	.05	.02	.01
☐ 75 Derrick Alexander WR	.20	.09	.03
☐ 76 Randy Baldwin	.05	.02	.01
☐ 77 Carl Banks	.05	.02	.01
☐ 78 Rob Burnett	.05	.02	.01
☐ 79 Steve Everitt	.05	.02	.01
☐ 80 Leroy Hoard	.05	.02	.01
☐ 81 Michael Jackson	.10	.05	.01
☐ 82 Pepper Johnson	.05	.02	.01
☐ 83 Tony Jones	.05	.02	.01
☐ 84 Antonio Langham	.05	.02	.01
☐ 85 Eric Metcalf	.10	.05	.01
☐ 86 Stevon Moore	.05	.02	.01
☐ 87 Anthony Pleasant	.05	.02	.01
☐ 88 Vinny Testaverde	.10	.05	.01
☐ 89 Eric Turner	.05	.02	.01
☐ 90 Troy Aikman	1.00	.45	.12
☐ 91 Charles Haley	.10	.05	.01
☐ 92 Michael Irvin	.20	.09	.03
☐ 93 Daryl Johnston	.10	.05	.01
☐ 94 Robert Jones	.05	.02	.01
☐ 95 Leon Lett	.05	.02	.01
☐ 96 Russell Maryland	.05	.02	.01
☐ 97 Nate Newton	.10	.05	.01
☐ 98 Jay Novacek	.10	.05	.01
☐ 99 Darrin Smith	.05	.02	.01
☐ 100 Emmitt Smith	2.00	.90	.25
☐ 101 Kevin Smith	.05	.02	.01
☐ 102 Erik Williams	.05	.02	.01
☐ 103 Kevin Williams WR	.10	.05	.01
☐ 104 Darren Woodson	.10	.05	.01
☐ 105 Elijah Alexander	.05	.02	.01
☐ 106 Steve Atwater	.05	.02	.01
☐ 107 Ray Crockett	.05	.02	.01
☐ 108 Shane Dronett	.05	.02	.01
☐ 109 Jason Elam	.05	.02	.01
☐ 110 John Elway	.75	.35	.09
☐ 111 Simon Fletcher	.05	.02	.01
☐ 112 Glyn Milburn	.05	.02	.01
☐ 113 Anthony Miller	.10	.05	.01
☐ 114 Michael Dean Perry	.05	.02	.01
☐ 115 Mike Pritchard	.05	.02	.01
☐ 116 Derek Russell	.05	.02	.01
☐ 117 Leonard Russell	.05	.02	.01
☐ 118 Shannon Sharpe	.10	.05	.01
☐ 119 Gary Zimmerman	.05	.02	.01
☐ 120 Bennie Blades	.05	.02	.01
☐ 121 Lomas Brown	.05	.02	.01
☐ 122 Willie Clay	.05	.02	.01
☐ 123 Mike Johnson	.05	.02	.01
☐ 124 Robert Massey	.05	.02	.01
☐ 125 Scott Mitchell	.10	.05	.01
☐ 126 Herman Moore	.40	.18	.05
☐ 127 Brett Perriman	.10	.05	.01
☐ 128 Robert Porcher	.05	.02	.01
☐ 129 Barry Sanders	1.00	.45	.12
☐ 130 Chris Spielman	.10	.05	.01
☐ 131 Henry Thomas	.05	.02	.01
☐ 132 Edgar Bennett	.10	.05	.01
☐ 134 LeRoy Butler	.05	.02	.01
☐ 135 Brett Favre	2.00	.90	.25
☐ 136 Sean Jones	.05	.02	.01
☐ 137 John Jurkovic	.05	.02	.01
☐ 138 George Koonce	.05	.02	.01
☐ 139 Wayne Simmons	.05	.02	.01
☐ 140 George Teague	.05	.02	.01
☐ 141 Reggie White	.20	.09	.03
☐ 142 Micheal Barrow	.05	.02	.01
☐ 143 Gary Brown	.05	.02	.01
☐ 144 Cody Carlson	.05	.02	.01
☐ 145 Ray Childress	.05	.02	.01
☐ 146 Cris Dishman	.05	.02	.01
☐ 147 Ernest Givins	.05	.02	.01
☐ 148 Mel Gray	.05	.02	.01
☐ 149 Darryll Lewis	.05	.02	.01
☐ 150 Bruce Matthews	.05	.02	.01
☐ 151 Marcus Robertson	.05	.02	.01
☐ 152 Webster Slaughter	.05	.02	.01
☐ 153 Al Smith	.05	.02	.01
☐ 154 Mark Stepnoski	.05	.02	.01
☐ 155 Trev Alberts	.05	.02	.01
☐ 156 Flipper Anderson	.05	.02	.01
☐ 157 Jason Belser	.05	.02	.01
☐ 158 Tony Bennett	.05	.02	.01
☐ 159 Ray Buchanan	.05	.02	.01
☐ 160 Quentin Coryatt	.10	.05	.01
☐ 161 Sean Dawkins	.10	.05	.01
☐ 162 Steve Emtman	.05	.02	.01
☐ 163 Marshall Faulk	.50	.23	.06
☐ 164 Stephen Grant	.05	.02	.01
☐ 165 Jim Harbaugh	.10	.05	.01
☐ 166 Jeff Herrod	.05	.02	.01
☐ 167 Tony Siragusa	.05	.02	.01
☐ 168 Steve Beuerlein	.05	.02	.01
☐ 169 Darren Carrington	.05	.02	.01
☐ 170 Reggie Cobb	.05	.02	.01
☐ 171 Kelvin Martin	.05	.02	.01
☐ 172 Kelvin Pritchett	.05	.02	.01
☐ 173 Joel Smeenge	.05	.02	.01
☐ 174 James Williams	.05	.02	.01
☐ 175 Marcus Allen	.20	.09	.03
☐ 176 Kimble Anders	.10	.05	.01
☐ 177 Dale Carter	.10	.05	.01
☐ 178 Mark Collins	.05	.02	.01
☐ 179 Willie Davis	.10	.05	.01
☐ 180 Lake Dawson	.10	.05	.01
☐ 181 Greg Hill	.10	.05	.01
☐ 182 Darren Mickell	.05	.02	.01
☐ 183 Joe Montana	1.00	.45	.12
☐ 184 Tracy Simien	.05	.02	.01
☐ 185 Neil Smith	.10	.05	.01
☐ 186 William White	.05	.02	.01
☐ 187 Greg Biekert	.05	.02	.01
☐ 188 Tim Brown	.20	.09	.03
☐ 189 Rob Fredrickson	.05	.02	.01
☐ 190 Andrew Glover	.05	.02	.01
☐ 191 Nolan Harrison	.05	.02	.01
☐ 192 Jeff Hostetler	.10	.05	.01
☐ 193 Rocket Ismail	.10	.05	.01
☐ 194 Terry McDaniel	.05	.02	.01
☐ 195 Chester McGlockton	.10	.05	.01
☐ 196 Winston Moss	.05	.02	.01
☐ 197 Anthony Smith	.05	.02	.01
☐ 198 Harvey Williams	.05	.02	.01
☐ 199 Steve Wisniewski	.05	.02	.01
☐ 200 Johnny Bailey	.05	.02	.01
☐ 201 Jerome Bettis	.30	.14	.04
☐ 202 Isaac Bruce	.50	.23	.06
☐ 203 Shane Conlan	.05	.02	.01
☐ 204 Troy Drayton	.05	.02	.01
☐ 205 Sean Gilbert	.10	.05	.01
☐ 206 Jessie Hester	.05	.02	.01
☐ 207 Jimmie Jones	.05	.02	.01
☐ 208 Todd Lyght	.05	.02	.01
☐ 209 Chris Miller	.05	.02	.01
☐ 210 Roman Phifer	.05	.02	.01
☐ 211 Marquez Pope	.05	.02	.01
☐ 212 Robert Young	.05	.02	.01
☐ 213 Gene Atkins	.05	.02	.01
☐ 214 Aubrey Beavers	.05	.02	.01
☐ 215 Tim Bowens	.05	.02	.01
☐ 216 Bryan Cox	.05	.02	.01
☐ 217 Jeff Cross	.05	.02	.01
☐ 218 Irving Fryar	.10	.05	.01
☐ 219 Eric Green	.05	.02	.01
☐ 220 Mark Ingram	.05	.02	.01
☐ 221 Terry Kirby	.10	.05	.01
☐ 222 Dan Marino	2.00	.90	.25
☐ 223 O.J. McDuffie	.20	.09	.03
☐ 224 Bernie Parmalee	.10	.05	.01
☐ 225 Keith Sims	.05	.02	.01
☐ 226 Irving Spikes	.10	.05	.01
☐ 227 Michael Stewart	.05	.02	.01
☐ 228 Troy Vincent	.05	.02	.01
☐ 229 Richmond Webb	.05	.02	.01
☐ 230 Terry Allen	.10	.05	.01
☐ 231 Cris Carter	.20	.09	.03
☐ 232 Jack Del Rio	.05	.02	.01
☐ 233 Vencie Glenn	.05	.02	.01
☐ 234 Qadry Ismail	.10	.05	.01
☐ 235 Carlos Jenkins	.05	.02	.01
☐ 236 Ed McDaniel	.05	.02	.01
☐ 237 Randall McDaniel	.05	.02	.01
☐ 238 Warren Moon	.10	.05	.01
☐ 239 Anthony Parker	.05	.02	.01
☐ 240 John Randle	.05	.02	.01
☐ 241 Jake Reed	.10	.05	.01
☐ 242 Fuad Reveiz	.05	.02	.01
☐ 243 Broderick Thomas	.05	.02	.01
☐ 244 Dewayne Washington	.10	.05	.01
☐ 245 Bruce Armstrong	.05	.02	.01
☐ 246 Drew Bledsoe	1.00	.45	.12
☐ 247 Vincent Brisby	.05	.02	.01
☐ 248 Vincent Brown	.05	.02	.01
☐ 249 Marion Butts	.05	.02	.01
☐ 250 Ben Coates	.10	.05	.01
☐ 251 Tim Goad	.05	.02	.01
☐ 252 Myron Guyton	.05	.02	.01
☐ 253 Maurice Hurst	.05	.02	.01
☐ 254 Mike Jones	.05	.02	.01

☐ 255 Willie McGinest	.10	.05	.01
☐ 256 Dave Meggett	.05	.02	.01
☐ 257 Ricky Reynolds	.05	.02	.01
☐ 258 Chris Slade	.10	.05	.01
☐ 259 Michael Timpson	.05	.02	.01
☐ 260 Mario Bates	.20	.09	.03
☐ 261 Derek Brown RB	.05	.02	.01
☐ 262 Darion Conner	.05	.02	.01
☐ 263 Quinn Early	.10	.05	.01
☐ 264 Jim Everett	.05	.02	.01
☐ 265 Michael Haynes	.10	.05	.01
☐ 266 Tyrone Hughes	.10	.05	.01
☐ 267 Joe Johnson	.05	.02	.01
☐ 268 Wayne Martin	.05	.02	.01
☐ 269 Willie Roaf	.05	.02	.01
☐ 270 Irv Smith	.05	.02	.01
☐ 271 Jimmy Spencer	.05	.02	.01
☐ 272 Winfred Tubbs	.05	.02	.01
☐ 273 Renaldo Turnbull	.05	.02	.01
☐ 274 Michael Brooks	.05	.02	.01
☐ 275 Dave Brown	.10	.05	.01
☐ 276 Chris Calloway	.05	.02	.01
☐ 277 Jesse Campbell	.05	.02	.01
☐ 278 Howard Cross	.05	.02	.01
☐ 279 John Elliott	.05	.02	.01
☐ 280 Keith Hamilton	.05	.02	.01
☐ 281 Rodney Hampton	.10	.05	.01
☐ 282 Thomas Lewis	.10	.05	.01
☐ 283 Thomas Randolph	.05	.02	.01
☐ 284 Mike Sherrard	.05	.02	.01
☐ 285 Michael Strahan	.05	.02	.01
☐ 286 Brad Baxter	.05	.02	.01
☐ 287 Tony Casillas	.05	.02	.01
☐ 288 Kyle Clifton	.05	.02	.01
☐ 289 Boomer Esiason	.10	.05	.01
☐ 290 Aaron Glenn	.05	.02	.01
☐ 291 Bobby Houston	.05	.02	.01
☐ 292 Johnny Johnson	.05	.02	.01
☐ 293 Jeff Lageman	.05	.02	.01
☐ 294 Mo Lewis	.05	.02	.01
☐ 295 Johnny Mitchell	.05	.02	.01
☐ 296 Rob Moore	.05	.02	.01
☐ 297 Marcus Turner	.05	.02	.01
☐ 298 Marvin Washington	.05	.02	.01
☐ 299 Eric Allen	.05	.02	.01
☐ 300 Fred Barnett	.10	.05	.01
☐ 301 Randall Cunningham	.10	.05	.01
☐ 302 Byron Evans	.05	.02	.01
☐ 303 William Fuller	.05	.02	.01
☐ 304 Charlie Garner	.10	.05	.01
☐ 305 Andy Harmon	.05	.02	.01
☐ 306 Greg Jackson	.05	.02	.01
☐ 307 Bill Romanowski	.05	.02	.01
☐ 308 William Thomas	.05	.02	.01
☐ 309 Herschel Walker	.10	.05	.01
☐ 310 Calvin Williams	.10	.05	.01
☐ 311 Michael Zordich	.05	.02	.01
☐ 312 Chad Brown	.10	.05	.01
☐ 313 Dermontti Dawson	.10	.05	.01
☐ 314 Barry Foster	.10	.05	.01
☐ 315 Kevin Greene	.10	.05	.01
☐ 316 Charles Johnson	.10	.05	.01
☐ 317 Levon Kirkland	.05	.02	.01
☐ 318 Carnell Lake	.05	.02	.01
☐ 319 Greg Lloyd	.10	.05	.01
☐ 320 Byron Bam Morris	.10	.05	.01
☐ 321 Neil O'Donnell	.10	.05	.01
☐ 322 Darren Perry	.05	.02	.01
☐ 323 Ray Seals	.05	.02	.01
☐ 324 John L. Williams	.05	.02	.01
☐ 325 Rod Woodson	.10	.05	.01
☐ 326 John Carney	.05	.02	.01
☐ 327 Andre Coleman	.05	.02	.01
☐ 328 Courtney Hall	.05	.02	.01
☐ 329 Ronnie Harmon	.05	.02	.01
☐ 330 Dwayne Harper	.05	.02	.01
☐ 331 Stan Humphries	.10	.05	.01
☐ 332 Shawn Jefferson	.05	.02	.01
☐ 333 Tony Martin	.10	.05	.01
☐ 334 Natrone Means	.20	.09	.03
☐ 335 Chris Mims	.05	.02	.01
☐ 336 Leslie O'Neal	.10	.05	.01
☐ 337 Alfred Pupunu	.05	.02	.01
☐ 338 Junior Seau	.20	.09	.03
☐ 339 Mark Seay	.10	.05	.01
☐ 340 Eric Davis	.05	.02	.01
☐ 341 William Floyd	.20	.09	.03
☐ 342 Merton Hanks	.05	.02	.01
☐ 343 Rickey Jackson	.05	.02	.01
☐ 344 Brent Jones	.05	.02	.01
☐ 345 Tim McDonald	.05	.02	.01
☐ 346 Ken Norton Jr.	.10	.05	.01
☐ 347 Gary Plummer	.05	.02	.01
☐ 348 Jerry Rice	1.00	.45	.12
☐ 349 Deion Sanders	.60	.25	.07
☐ 350 Jesse Sapolu	.05	.02	.01
☐ 351 Dana Stubblefield	.20	.09	.03
☐ 352 John Taylor	.05	.02	.01
☐ 353 Steve Wallace	.05	.02	.01
☐ 354 Ricky Watters	.20	.09	.03
☐ 355 Lee Woodall	.05	.02	.01
☐ 356 Bryant Young	.10	.05	.01
☐ 357 Steve Young	.75	.35	.09
☐ 358 Sam Adams	.05	.02	.01
☐ 359 Howard Ballard	.05	.02	.01
☐ 360 Robert Blackmon	.05	.02	.01
☐ 361 Brian Blades	.10	.05	.01
☐ 362 Carlton Gray	.05	.02	.01
☐ 363 Cortez Kennedy	.10	.05	.01
☐ 364 Rick Mirer	.20	.09	.03
☐ 365 Eugene Robinson	.05	.02	.01
☐ 366 Chris Warren	.10	.05	.01
☐ 367 Terry Wooden	.05	.02	.01
☐ 368 Brad Culpepper	.05	.02	.01
☐ 369 Lawrence Dawsey	.05	.02	.01
☐ 370 Trent Dilfer	.20	.09	.03
☐ 371 Santana Dotson	.05	.02	.01
☐ 372 Craig Erickson	.05	.02	.01
☐ 373 Thomas Everett	.05	.02	.01
☐ 374 Paul Gruber	.05	.02	.01
☐ 375 Alvin Harper	.05	.02	.01
☐ 376 Jackie Harris	.05	.02	.01
☐ 377 Courtney Hawkins	.05	.02	.01
☐ 378 Martin Mayhew	.05	.02	.01
☐ 379 Hardy Nickerson	.05	.02	.01
☐ 380 Errict Rhett	.20	.09	.03
☐ 381 Charles Wilson	.05	.02	.01
☐ 382 Reggie Brooks	.10	.05	.01
☐ 383 Tom Carter	.05	.02	.01
☐ 384 Andre Collins	.05	.02	.01
☐ 385 Henry Ellard	.10	.05	.01
☐ 386 Ricky Ervins	.05	.02	.01
☐ 387 Darrell Green	.05	.02	.01
☐ 388 Ken Harvey	.05	.02	.01
☐ 389 Brian Mitchell	.05	.02	.01
☐ 390 Stanley Richard	.05	.02	.01
☐ 391 Heath Shuler	.20	.09	.03
☐ 392 Rod Stephens	.05	.02	.01
☐ 393 Tyronne Stowe	.05	.02	.01
☐ 394 Tydus Winans	.05	.02	.01
☐ 395 Tony Woods	.05	.02	.01
☐ 396 Checklist (1-104)	.05	.02	.01
☐ 397 Checklist (105-212)	.05	.02	.01
☐ 398 Checklist (213-298)	.05	.02	.01
☐ 399 Checklist (299-400)	.05	.02	.01
☐ 400 Checklist (Inserts)	.05	.02	.01
☐ P1 Promo Panel Reggie Brooks Jerome Bettis Rick Mirer	2.00	.90	.25

1995 Fleer Aerial Attack

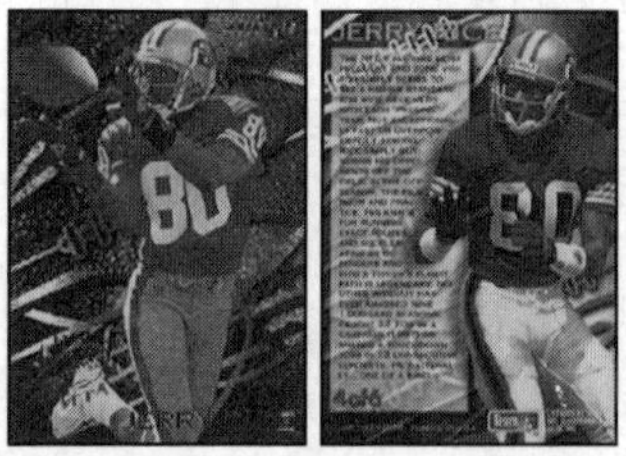

This six-card standard-size set was randomly inserted into packs at a rate of one in 37. Featured in this set are leading passers and receivers. These cards contain a player photo against a metallic, etched foil design. The words "Aerial Attack" are in the lower left corner in gold foil. The player's name is identified in gold foil across the bottom. The back is divided between player information as well as another photo.

	MINT	NRMT	EXC
COMPLETE SET (6)	35.00	16.00	4.40
COMMON CARD (1-6)	2.00	.90	.25
☐ 1 Tim Brown	3.00	1.35	.35
☐ 2 Dan Marino	16.00	7.25	2.00
☐ 3 Joe Montana	8.00	3.60	1.00
☐ 4 Jerry Rice	8.00	3.60	1.00
☐ 5 Andre Rison	2.00	.90	.25
☐ 6 Sterling Sharpe	2.00	.90	.25

1995 Fleer Flair Preview

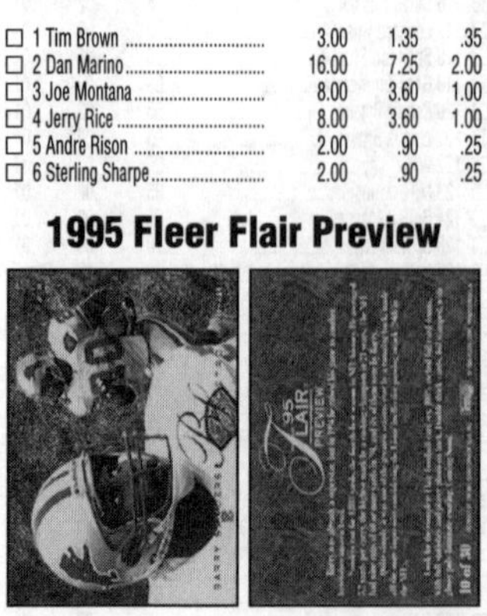

As a preview to the 1995 Flair issue, these 30 standard-size cards were inserted one per Fleer regular and jumbo pack. The fronts feature two photos on an etched foil surface with glossy polylaminate coating. The player's name and team name are on the bottom of the card. The backs mention that the card is a 1995 Flair Preview and gives some player highlights.

	MINT	NRMT	EXC
COMPLETE SET (30)	20.00	9.00	2.50
COMMON CARD (1-30)	.25	.11	.03
☐ 1 Aeneas Williams	.25	.11	.03
☐ 2 Jeff George	.75	.35	.09
☐ 3 Andre Reed	.40	.18	.05
☐ 4 Kerry Collins	2.50	1.10	.30
☐ 5 Mark Carrier DB	.25	.11	.03
☐ 6 Jeff Blake	1.00	.45	.12
☐ 7 Leroy Hoard	.25	.11	.03
☐ 8 Emmitt Smith	4.00	1.80	.50
☐ 9 Shannon Sharpe	.75	.35	.09
☐ 10 Barry Sanders	2.00	.90	.25
☐ 11 Reggie White	.75	.35	.09
☐ 12 Bruce Matthews	.25	.11	.03
☐ 13 Marshall Faulk	1.00	.45	.12
☐ 14 Tony Boselli	.40	.18	.05
☐ 15 Joe Montana	2.00	.90	.25
☐ 16 Tim Brown	.40	.18	.05
☐ 17 Jerome Bettis	.75	.35	.09
☐ 18 Dan Marino	4.00	1.80	.50
☐ 19 Cris Carter	.75	.35	.09
☐ 20 Drew Bledsoe	2.00	.90	.25
☐ 21 Willie Roaf	.25	.11	.03
☐ 22 Rodney Hampton	.40	.18	.05
☐ 23 Rob Moore	.25	.11	.03
☐ 24 Fred Barnett	.40	.18	.05
☐ 25 Rod Woodson	.40	.18	.05
☐ 26 Natrone Means	.75	.35	.09
☐ 27 Jerry Rice	2.00	.90	.25
☐ 28 Chris Warren	.40	.18	.05
☐ 29 Errict Rhett	.40	.18	.05
☐ 30 Henry Ellard	.25	.11	.03

1995 Fleer Gridiron Leaders

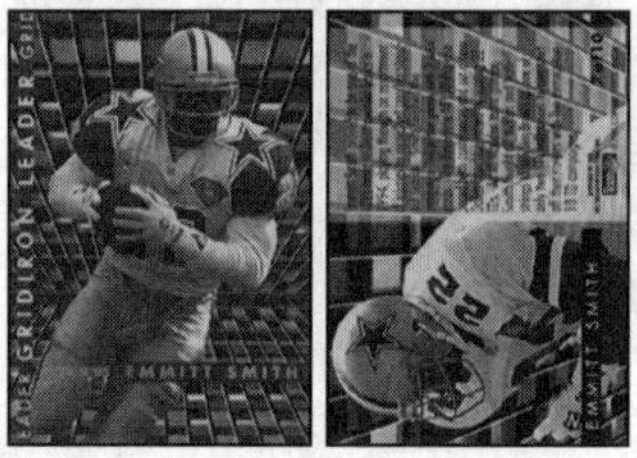

This 10-card standard-size set was inserted at a ratio of one in every four packs. The fronts feature the player's photo set against a geometric background. The words "Gridiron Leader" run vertically across the left border, while the player is identified in the bottom right corner. The back has a player close-up along with career highlights.

	MINT	NRMT	EXC
COMPLETE SET (10)	8.00	3.60	1.00
COMMON CARD (1-10)	.25	.11	.03
☐ 1 Cris Carter	.40	.18	.05
☐ 2 Ben Coates	.25	.11	.03
☐ 3 Marshall Faulk	.60	.25	.07
☐ 4 Jerry Rice	1.25	.55	.16
☐ 5 Barry Sanders	1.25	.55	.16
☐ 6 Deion Sanders	.75	.35	.09
☐ 7 Emmitt Smith	2.50	1.10	.30
☐ 8 Eric Turner	.25	.11	.03
☐ 9 Chris Warren	.40	.18	.05
☐ 10 Steve Young	1.00	.45	.12

1995 Fleer Prospects

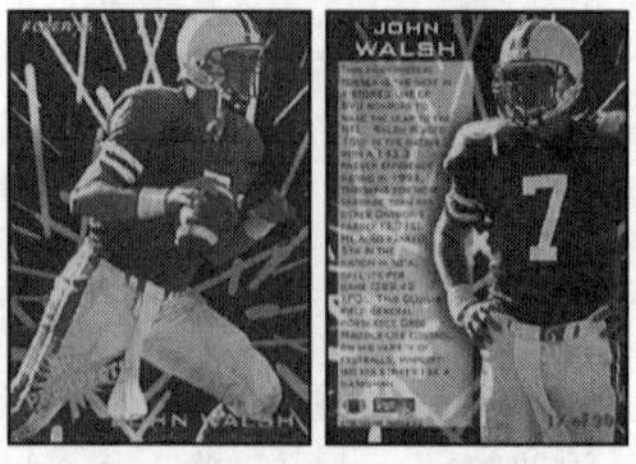

This 20-card standard-size set was inserted one in every six packs. Players featured were expected by Fleer to go high in the 1995 draft. The fronts have a player photo against a multi-colored background. "NFL Prospects" is in the lower left corner with the player name at the bottom. The back contains another shot as well as some pertinent information.

	MINT	NRMT	EXC
COMPLETE SET (20)	25.00	11.00	3.10
COMMON CARD (1-20)	.50	.23	.06
☐ 1 Tony Boselli	.75	.35	.09
☐ 2 Kyle Brady	.75	.35	.09
☐ 3 Ruben Brown	.50	.23	.06
☐ 4 Kevin Carter	1.50	.70	.19
☐ 5 Ki-Jana Carter	1.50	.70	.19
☐ 6 Kerry Collins	5.00	2.20	.60
☐ 7 Luther Elliss	.50	.23	.06
☐ 8 Jimmy Hitchcock	.50	.23	.06
☐ 9 Jack Jackson	.50	.23	.06
☐ 10 Ellis Johnson	.50	.23	.06
☐ 11 Rob Johnson	.50	.23	.06
☐ 12 Steve McNair	4.00	1.80	.50
☐ 13 Rashaan Salaam	2.00	.90	.25
☐ 14 Warren Sapp	.50	.23	.06
☐ 15 J.J. Stokes	1.50	.70	.19
☐ 16 Bobby Taylor	.75	.35	.09
☐ 17 John Walsh	.50	.23	.06
☐ 18 Michael Westbrook	2.00	.90	.25
☐ 19 Tyrone Wheatley	.75	.35	.09
☐ 20 Sherman Williams	.75	.35	.09

1995 Fleer Pro-Visions

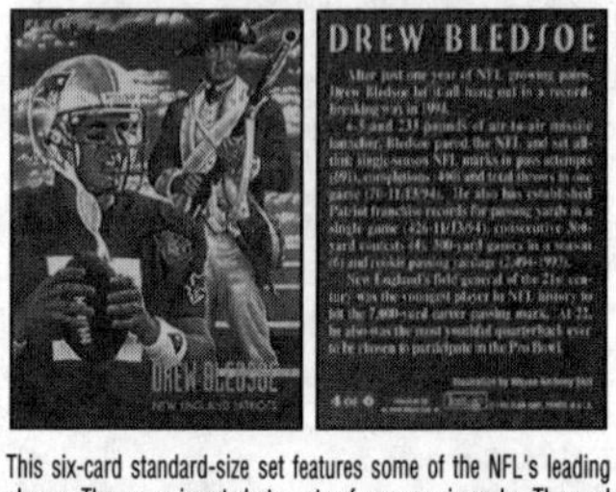

This six-card standard-size set features some of the NFL's leading players. They were inserted at a rate of one per six packs. The card illustrations on front were done by sports artist Wayne Anthony Still. The artwork is consistent with the team nickname. The player's name and team is identified in gold-foil in the lower right corner. The back contains player profile information.

	MINT	NRMT	EXC
COMPLETE SET (6)	3.00	1.35	.35
COMMON CARD (1-6)	.25	.11	.03
☐ 1 Natrone Means	.40	.18	.05
☐ 2 Sterling Sharpe	.25	.11	.03
☐ 3 Ken Norton	.25	.11	.03
☐ 4 Drew Bledsoe	1.25	.55	.16
☐ 5 Marshall Faulk	1.25	.55	.16
☐ 6 Tim Brown	.40	.18	.05

1995 Fleer Rookie Sensations

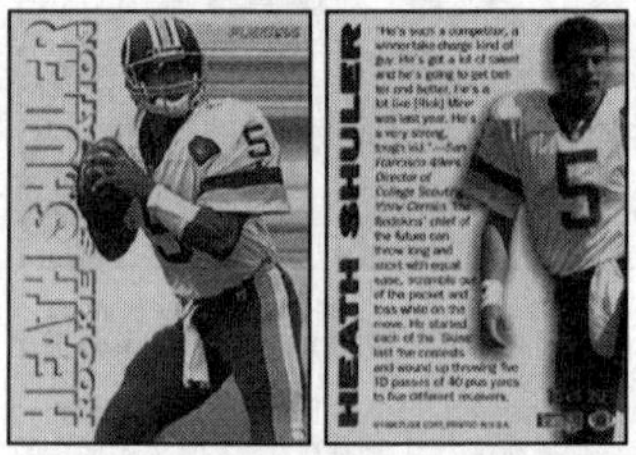

This 20-card standard-size set was issued in jumbo packs only. They were released at a rate of one every three packs. Players featured in this set were among the best 1994 rookies. Fronts feature an embossed player photo with player name and the words "Rookie Sensation" on the left side. The back contains a player profile and player photo.

	MINT	NRMT	EXC
COMPLETE SET (20)	60.00	27.00	7.50
COMMON CARD (1-20)	2.50	1.10	.30
☐ 1 Derrick Alexander WR	4.00	1.80	.50
☐ 2 Mario Bates	2.50	1.10	.30
☐ 3 Tim Bowens	2.50	1.10	.30
☐ 4 Lake Dawson	2.50	1.10	.30
☐ 5 Bert Emanuel	4.00	1.80	.50
☐ 6 Marshall Faulk	8.00	3.60	1.00
☐ 7 William Floyd	2.50	1.10	.30
☐ 8 Rob Fredrickson	2.50	1.10	.30
☐ 9 Greg Hill	4.00	1.80	.50
☐ 10 Charles Johnson	4.00	1.80	.50
☐ 11 Antonio Langham	2.50	1.10	.30
☐ 12 Willie McGinest	4.00	1.80	.50
☐ 13 Byron Bam Morris	2.50	1.10	.30
☐ 14 Errict Rhett	4.00	1.80	.50
☐ 15 Darnay Scott	6.00	2.70	.75
☐ 16 Heath Shuler	4.00	1.80	.50
☐ 17 Dewayne Washington	2.50	1.10	.30
☐ 18 Dan Wilkinson	2.50	1.10	.30
☐ 19 Lee Woodall	2.50	1.10	.30
☐ 20 Bryant Young	2.50	1.10	.30

1995 Fleer TD Sensations

This 10-card standard-size set was issued in 11-card packs at a rate of one in every three packs. Players featured in this set excelled in getting the ball into the end zone. The borderless fronts feature action shots of the player. The backs are split between another action shot as well as some highlights.

	MINT	NRMT	EXC
COMPLETE SET (10)	10.00	4.50	1.25
COMMON CARD (1-10)	.25	.11	.03

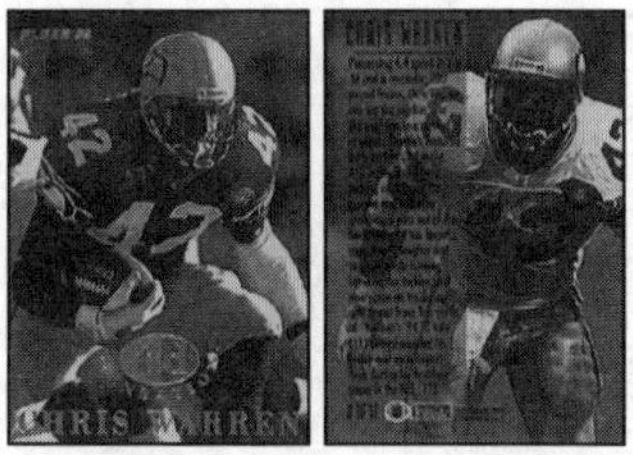

☐ 1 Marshall Faulk	.60	.25	.07
☐ 2 Dan Marino	2.50	1.10	.30
☐ 3 Natrone Means	.25	.11	.03
☐ 4 Herman Moore	.60	.25	.07
☐ 5 Jerry Rice	1.25	.55	.16
☐ 6 Sterling Sharpe	.25	.11	.03
☐ 7 Emmitt Smith	2.50	1.10	.30
☐ 8 Chris Warren	.40	.18	.05
☐ 9 Ricky Watters	.40	.18	.05
☐ 10 Steve Young	1.00	.45	.12

1995 Fleer Bettis/Mirer Sheet

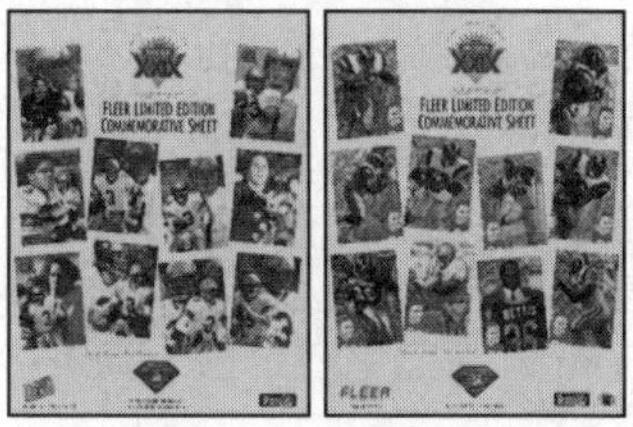

At the Super Bowl card show in Miami, commemorative sheets of Bettis and Mirer insert cards could be purchased for five wrappers and 1.00. Just 2,500 were produced; 400 of these were signed by one of the two players and sold for 25.00. The sheets measure 8 1/2" by 11". One side features ten insert cards of Jerome Bettis, while the other side shows ten Rick Mirer insert cards.

	MINT	NRMT	EXC
COMPLETE SET	2.00	.90	.25
COMMON CARD	2.00	.90	.25
☐ 1 Jerome Bettis	2.00	.90	.25
Rick Mirer			

1995 Fleer Shell

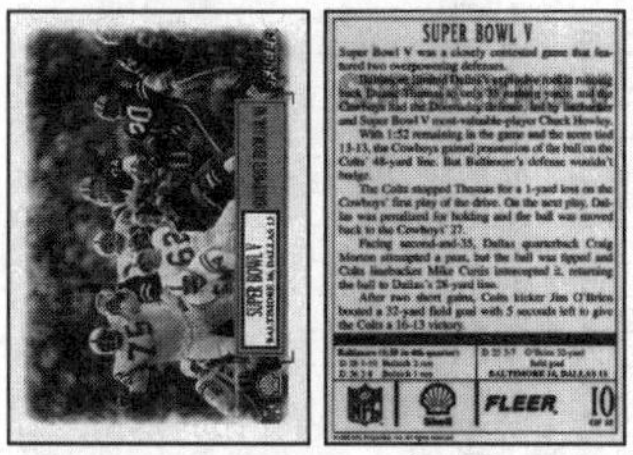

Produced by Fleer, this 10-card set was issued by Shell in the "Drive to the Super Bowl XXX" sweepstakes. The standard-size cards are perforated at one end and were originally attached to a tab card of equal size. The tab features three rub-offs on its front and abbreviated rules on its back. The three rub-offs were titled "your score," "their score," and "prize." If the first rub-off had a higher score than the second one, then the holder could scratch the prize box to determine the prize. The contest expired 9/17/95. The cards themselves feature horizontal fronts with either color or black-and-white action photos that fade along the edges into white borders. The card title and final game score are presented in a yellow rectangle at the bottom. The circumstances surrounding the particular game are summarized on the back. Reportedly, 65 million game pieces (cards) were created.

	MINT	NRMT	EXC
COMPLETE SET (10)	8.00	3.60	1.00
COMMON CARD (1-10)	.75	.35	.09
☐ 1 Super Bowl XXIII	2.00	.90	.25
Joe Montana's drive			
☐ 2 1967 NFL Championship	1.00	.45	.12
Bart Starr's TD			
☐ 3 1986 AFC Championship	.75	.35	.09
The Drive			
Mark Jackson			
☐ 4 Super Bowl XIII	1.25	.55	.16
Steeler's drive			
Terry Bradshaw			
Franco Harris			
☐ 5 1975 NFC Divisional Playoffs	.75	.35	.09
Cowboy's drive			
Doug Dennison featured			
☐ 6 1968 AFL Championship	.75	.35	.09
Jet's drive			
☐ 7 1981 NFC Championship	1.00	.45	.12
49ers team shot			
☐ 8 1983 NFC Championship	1.00	.45	.12
Redskins' drive			
John Riggins' TD			
☐ 9 1969 AFL Divisional Playoffs	1.00	.45	.12
Len Dawson in huddle			
☐ 10 Super Bowl V	1.00	.45	.12
Colts' field goal			
Bob Lilly and			
Mel Renfro pictured			

1996 Fleer

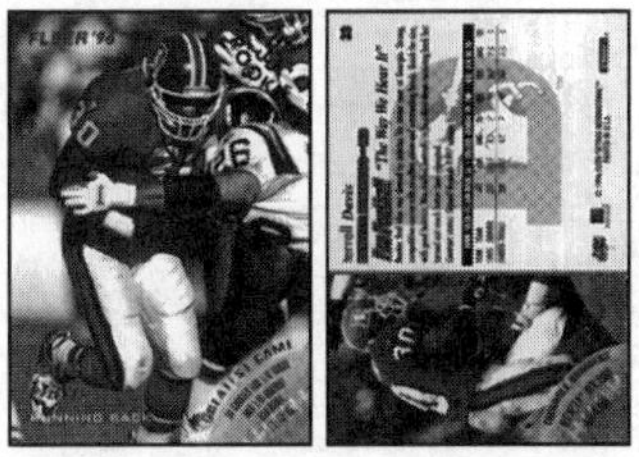

The 1996 Fleer set was issued in one series totalling 200 cards. The 11-card packs retail for $1.49 each. The cards are grouped alphabetically within teams and checklisted below alphabetically according to teams. The set contains the topical subsets: Rookies (141-180) and PFW Weekly Previews (181-197). A three-card promo sheet (cards numbered S1-S3) was produced and is priced below in complete sheet form.

	MINT	NRMT	EXC
COMPLETE SET (200)	20.00	9.00	2.50
COMMON CARD (1-200)	.05	.02	.01
☐ 1 Garrison Hearst	.10	.05	.01
☐ 2 Rob Moore	.05	.02	.01
☐ 3 Frank Sanders	.10	.05	.01
☐ 4 Eric Swann	.10	.05	.01
☐ 5 Aeneas Williams	.05	.02	.01
☐ 6 Jeff George	.10	.05	.01
☐ 7 Craig Heyward	.05	.02	.01
☐ 8 Terance Mathis	.05	.02	.01
☐ 9 Eric Metcalf	.10	.05	.01
☐ 10 Michael Jackson	.10	.05	.01
☐ 11 Andre Rison	.10	.05	.01
☐ 12 Vinny Testaverde	.10	.05	.01
☐ 13 Eric Turner	.05	.02	.01
☐ 14 Darick Holmes	.10	.05	.01
☐ 15 Jim Kelly	.20	.09	.03
☐ 16 Bryce Paup	.10	.05	.01
☐ 17 Bruce Smith	.20	.09	.03
☐ 18 Thurman Thomas	.20	.09	.03
☐ 19 Kerry Collins	.75	.35	.09
☐ 20 Lamar Lathon	.05	.02	.01
☐ 21 Derrick Moore	.05	.02	.01
☐ 22 Tyrone Poole	.05	.02	.01
☐ 23 Curtis Conway	.20	.09	.03
☐ 24 Bryan Cox	.05	.02	.01
☐ 25 Erik Kramer	.05	.02	.01
☐ 26 Rashaan Salaam	.20	.09	.03
☐ 27 Jeff Blake	.20	.09	.03
☐ 28 Ki-Jana Carter	.10	.05	.01
☐ 29 Carl Pickens	.20	.09	.03
☐ 30 Darnay Scott	.10	.05	.01
☐ 31 Troy Aikman	.75	.35	.09
☐ 32 Charles Haley	.10	.05	.01
☐ 33 Michael Irvin	.20	.09	.03
☐ 34 Daryl Johnston	.10	.05	.01
☐ 35 Jay Novacek	.10	.05	.01
☐ 36 Deion Sanders	.40	.18	.05
☐ 37 Emmitt Smith	1.50	.70	.19
☐ 38 Steve Atwater	.05	.02	.01
☐ 39 Terrell Davis	1.00	.45	.12
☐ 40 John Elway	.60	.25	.07
☐ 41 Anthony Miller	.10	.05	.01
☐ 42 Shannon Sharpe	.10	.05	.01
☐ 43 Scott Mitchell	.10	.05	.01
☐ 44 Herman Moore	.20	.09	.03
☐ 45 Johnnie Morton	.10	.05	.01
☐ 46 Brett Perriman	.10	.05	.01
☐ 47 Barry Sanders	.75	.35	.09
☐ 48 Edgar Bennett	.10	.05	.01
☐ 49 Robert Brooks	.20	.09	.03
☐ 50 Mark Chmura	.10	.05	.01
☐ 51 Brett Favre	1.50	.70	.19
☐ 52 Reggie White	.20	.09	.03
☐ 53 Mel Gray	.05	.02	.01
☐ 54 Steve McNair	.50	.23	.06
☐ 55 Chris Sanders	.10	.05	.01
☐ 56 Rodney Thomas	.05	.02	.01
☐ 57 Quentin Coryatt	.05	.02	.01
☐ 58 Sean Dawkins	.05	.02	.01
☐ 59 Ken Dilger	.10	.05	.01
☐ 60 Marshall Faulk	.20	.09	.03
☐ 61 Jim Harbaugh	.10	.05	.01
☐ 62 Tony Boselli	.10	.05	.01
☐ 63 Mark Brunell	.75	.35	.09
☐ 64 Natrone Means	.20	.09	.03
☐ 65 James O.Stewart	.10	.05	.01
☐ 66 Marcus Allen	.20	.09	.03
☐ 67 Steve Bono	.10	.05	.01
☐ 68 Neil Smith	.10	.05	.01
☐ 69 Derrick Thomas	.10	.05	.01
☐ 70 Tamarick Vanover	.20	.09	.03
☐ 71 Fred Barnett	.10	.05	.01
☐ 72 Eric Green	.05	.02	.01
☐ 73 Dan Marino	1.50	.70	.19
☐ 74 O.J. McDuffie	.10	.05	.01
☐ 75 Bernie Parmalee	.05	.02	.01
☐ 76 Cris Carter	.20	.09	.03
☐ 77 Qadry Ismail	.10	.05	.01
☐ 78 Warren Moon	.10	.05	.01
☐ 79 Jake Reed	.10	.05	.01
☐ 80 Robert Smith	.10	.05	.01
☐ 81 Drew Bledsoe	.75	.35	.09
☐ 82 Vincent Brisby	.05	.02	.01
☐ 83 Ben Coates	.10	.05	.01
☐ 84 Curtis Martin	1.00	.45	.12
☐ 85 Dave Meggett	.05	.02	.01
☐ 86 Mario Bates	.10	.05	.01
☐ 87 Jim Everett	.05	.02	.01
☐ 88 Michael Haynes	.10	.05	.01
☐ 89 Renaldo Turnbull	.05	.02	.01
☐ 90 Dave Brown	.10	.05	.01
☐ 91 Rodney Hampton	.10	.05	.01
☐ 92 Thomas Lewis	.05	.02	.01
☐ 93 Tyrone Wheatley	.10	.05	.01
☐ 94 Kyle Brady	.10	.05	.01
☐ 95 Hugh Douglas	.05	.02	.01
☐ 96 Aaron Glenn	.05	.02	.01
☐ 97 Jeff Graham	.05	.02	.01
☐ 98 Adrian Murrell	.10	.05	.01
☐ 99 Neil O'Donnell	.10	.05	.01
☐ 100 Tim Brown	.10	.05	.01
☐ 101 Jeff Hostetler	.10	.05	.01
☐ 102 Napoleon Kaufman	.10	.05	.01
☐ 103 Chester McGlockton	.05	.02	.01
☐ 104 Harvey Williams	.05	.02	.01
☐ 105 William Fuller	.05	.02	.01
☐ 106 Charlie Garner	.05	.02	.01
☐ 107 Ricky Watters	.10	.05	.01
☐ 108 Calvin Williams	.05	.02	.01
☐ 109 Jerome Bettis	.20	.09	.03
☐ 110 Greg Lloyd	.10	.05	.01
☐ 111 Byron Bam Morris	.10	.05	.01
☐ 112 Kordell Stewart	.75	.35	.09
☐ 113 Yancey Thigpen	.10	.05	.01
☐ 114 Rod Woodson	.10	.05	.01
☐ 115 Isaac Bruce	.20	.09	.03
☐ 116 Troy Drayton	.05	.02	.01
☐ 117 Leslie O'Neal	.05	.02	.01
☐ 118 Steve Walsh	.05	.02	.01
☐ 119 Marco Coleman	.05	.02	.01
☐ 120 Aaron Hayden	.05	.02	.01
☐ 121 Stan Humphries	.10	.05	.01
☐ 122 Junior Seau	.20	.09	.03
☐ 123 William Floyd	.10	.05	.01
☐ 124 Brent Jones	.05	.02	.01
☐ 125 Ken Norton	.10	.05	.01
☐ 126 Jerry Rice	.75	.35	.09
☐ 127 J.J. Stokes	.20	.09	.03
☐ 128 Steve Young	.60	.25	.07
☐ 129 Brian Blades	.10	.05	.01
☐ 130 Joey Galloway	.30	.14	.04
☐ 131 Rick Mirer	.10	.05	.01
☐ 132 Chris Warren	.10	.05	.01
☐ 133 Trent Dilfer	.10	.05	.01
☐ 134 Alvin Harper	.05	.02	.01
☐ 135 Hardy Nickerson	.05	.02	.01
☐ 136 Errict Rhett	.10	.05	.01
☐ 137 Terry Allen	.10	.05	.01
☐ 138 Henry Ellard	.10	.05	.01
☐ 139 Heath Shuler	.20	.09	.03
☐ 140 Michael Westbrook	.20	.09	.03
☐ 141 Karim Abdul-Jabbar	1.50	.70	.19
☐ 142 Mike Alstott	.40	.18	.05
☐ 143 Marco Battaglia	.05	.02	.01
☐ 144 Tim Biakabutuka	.50	.23	.06
☐ 145 Tony Brackens	.10	.05	.01
☐ 146 Duane Clemons	.05	.02	.01
☐ 147 Ernie Conwell	.05	.02	.01
☐ 148 Chris Darkins	.10	.05	.01
☐ 149 Stephen Davis	.20	.09	.03
☐ 150 Brian Dawkins	.05	.02	.01
☐ 151 Rickey Dudley	.20	.09	.03
☐ 152 Jason Dunn	.10	.05	.01
☐ 153 Bobby Engram	.50	.23	.06
☐ 154 Daryl Gardener	.10	.05	.01
☐ 155 Eddie George	2.50	1.10	.30
☐ 156 Terry Glenn	2.00	.90	.25
☐ 157 Kevin Hardy	.10	.05	.01
☐ 158 Walt Harris	.05	.02	.01
☐ 159 Marvin Harrison	1.00	.45	.12
☐ 160 Bobby Hoying	.20	.09	.03
☐ 161 Keyshawn Johnson	1.00	.45	.12
☐ 162 Cedric Jones	.10	.05	.01
☐ 163 Marcus Jones	.05	.02	.01
☐ 164 Eddie Kennison	1.00	.45	.12
☐ 165 Ray Lewis	.05	.02	.01
☐ 166 Derrick Mayes	.50	.23	.06
☐ 167 Leeland McElroy	.20	.09	.03
☐ 168 Johnny McWilliams	.05	.02	.01
☐ 169 John Mobley	.05	.02	.01
☐ 170 Alex Molden	.05	.02	.01
☐ 171 Eric Moulds	.50	.23	.06
☐ 172 Muhsin Muhammad	.75	.35	.09
☐ 173 Jonathan Ogden	.05	.02	.01
☐ 174 Lawrence Phillips	.40	.18	.05
☐ 175 Stanley Pritchett	.10	.05	.01
☐ 176 Simeon Rice	.20	.09	.03
☐ 177 Bryan Still	.05	.02	.01
☐ 178 Amani Toomer	.20	.09	.03
☐ 179 Regan Upshaw	.05	.02	.01
☐ 180 Alex Van Dyke	.10	.05	.01
☐ 181 Barry Sanders PFW	.40	.18	.05
☐ 182 Marcus Allen PFW	.20	.09	.03
☐ 183 Bryce Paup PFW	.10	.05	.01
☐ 184 Jerry Rice PFW	.40	.18	.05
☐ 185 Desmond Howard PFW	.10	.05	.01
Bob Christian			
☐ 186 Leon Lett PFW	.05	.02	.01
☐ 187 Brett Favre PFW	.75	.35	.09
☐ 188 Greg Lloyd PFW	.05	.02	.01
Derrick Thomas			
☐ 189 Jeff Blake PFW	.10	.05	.01
☐ 190 Emmitt Smith PFW	.75	.35	.09
☐ 191 John Elway PFW	.25	.11	.03
Jeff Hostetler			
☐ 192 Chiefs PFW	.05	.02	.01
☐ 193 Marshall Faulk PFW	.10	.05	.01
☐ 194 Troy Aikman PFW	.40	.18	.05
Steve Young			
☐ 195 Dan Marino PFW	.75	.35	.09
☐ 196 Donta Jones PFW	.05	.02	.01
☐ 197 Jim Kelly PFW	.20	.09	.03
☐ 198 Checklist	.05	.02	.01
☐ 199 Checklist	.05	.02	.01
☐ 200 Checklist	.05	.02	.01
☐ P1 Promo Sheet	3.00	1.35	.35
William Floyd			
Trent Dilfer			
Brett Favre			

1996 Fleer Breakthroughs

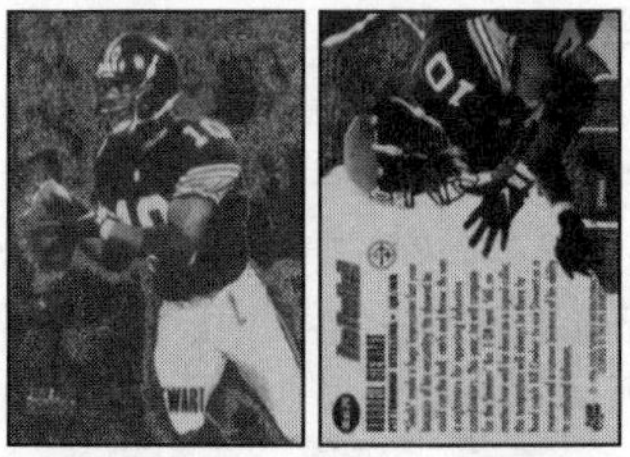

Randomly inserted in packs at the rate of one in three, this 24-card set features photos of players chosen by Pro Football Weekly to have had career seasons, including some '96 rookies highlighted in 100% etched foil design.

	MINT	NRMT	EXC
COMPLETE SET (24)	25.00	11.00	3.10
COMMON CARD (1-24)	.75	.35	.09
☐ 1 Tim Bowens	.75	.35	.09
☐ 2 Kyle Brady	1.25	.55	.16
☐ 3 Devin Bush	.75	.35	.09
☐ 4 Kevin Carter	.75	.35	.09
☐ 5 Ki-Jana Carter	1.25	.55	.16
☐ 6 Kerry Collins	4.00	1.80	.50
☐ 7 Trent Dilfer	1.25	.55	.16
☐ 8 Ken Dilger	.75	.35	.09
☐ 9 Joey Galloway	2.00	.90	.25
☐ 10 Aaron Hayden	.75	.35	.09
☐ 11 Napoleon Kaufman	1.25	.55	.16
☐ 12 Craig Newsome	.75	.35	.09
☐ 13 Tyrone Poole	.75	.35	.09
☐ 14 Jake Reed	.75	.35	.09
☐ 15 Rashaan Salaam	1.50	.70	.19
☐ 16 Chris Sanders	1.25	.55	.16
☐ 17 Frank Sanders	1.25	.55	.16
☐ 18 Kordell Stewart	4.00	1.80	.50
☐ 19 J.J. Stokes	1.25	.55	.16
☐ 20 Bobby Taylor	.75	.35	.09
☐ 21 Orlando Thomas	.75	.35	.09
☐ 22 Michael Timpson	.75	.35	.09
☐ 23 Tamarick Vanover	1.50	.70	.19
☐ 24 Michael Westbrook	1.50	.70	.19

1996 Fleer RAC Pack

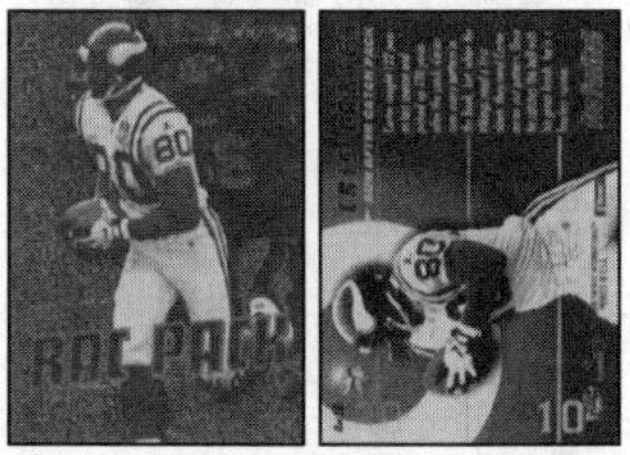

Randomly inserted in packs at the rate of one in 18, this 10-card set features photos of receivers who excel at racking up Run After Catch yardage in 100% etched foil and color foil stamped design.

	MINT	NRMT	EXC
COMPLETE SET (10)	20.00	9.00	2.50
COMMON CARD (1-10)	1.00	.45	.12
☐ 1 Robert Brooks	2.00	.90	.25
☐ 2 Tim Brown	2.00	.90	.25
☐ 3 Isaac Bruce	3.00	1.35	.35
☐ 4 Cris Carter	2.00	.90	.25
☐ 5 Curtis Conway	1.00	.45	.12
☐ 6 Michael Irvin	2.00	.90	.25
☐ 7 Eric Metcalf	1.00	.45	.12
☐ 8 Herman Moore	2.50	1.10	.30
☐ 9 Carl Pickens	2.00	.90	.25
☐ 10 Jerry Rice	10.00	4.50	1.25

1996 Fleer Rookie Sensations

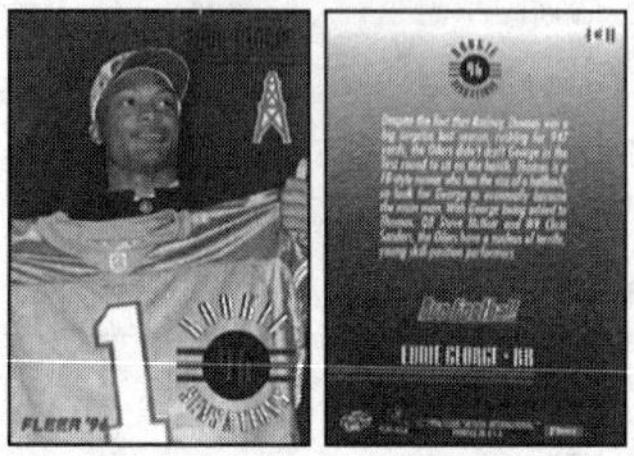

Randomly inserted at the rate of one in 72 packs, this 11-card set features color photos of some of the NFL's best 1996 rookies printed on colorful plastic cards. Seeded 1:960 packs was a special Rookie Sensations Hot Packs containing specially marked versions of all 11 Rookie Sensations insert cards with a special Hot Packs logo.

	MINT	NRMT	EXC
COMPLETE SET (11)	150.00	70.00	19.00
COMMON CARD (1-11)	6.00	2.70	.75
COMP.HOT PACK SET (11)	100.00	45.00	12.50
*HOT PACK CARDS: .35X TO .75X BASIC CARDS			
☐ 1 Karim Abdul-Jabbar	25.00	11.00	3.10
☐ 2 Tim Biakabutuka	10.00	4.50	1.25
☐ 3 Rickey Dudley	6.00	2.70	.75
☐ 4 Eddie George	40.00	18.00	5.00
☐ 5 Terry Glenn	30.00	13.50	3.70
☐ 6 Kevin Hardy	6.00	2.70	.75
☐ 7 Marvin Harrison	15.00	6.75	1.85
☐ 8 Keyshawn Johnson	15.00	6.75	1.85
☐ 9 Jonathan Ogden	6.00	2.70	.75
☐ 10 Lawrence Phillips	10.00	4.50	1.25
☐ 11 Simeon Rice	6.00	2.70	.75

1996 Fleer Rookie Signatures

Randomly inserted in hobby packs only at a rate of one in 288, this three-card autographed set features players that Fleer felt would make an impact in their Rookie season.

	MINT	NRMT	EXC
COMPLETE SET (3)	200.00	90.00	25.00
COMMON CARD (A1-A3)	50.00	22.00	6.25
BLUE SIGNATURES: 1.5X BASIC CARDS			
☐ A1 Tim Biakabutuka	50.00	22.00	6.25
☐ A2 Eddie George	100.00	45.00	12.50
☐ A3 Leeland McElroy	50.00	22.00	6.25

1996 Fleer Rookie Write-Ups

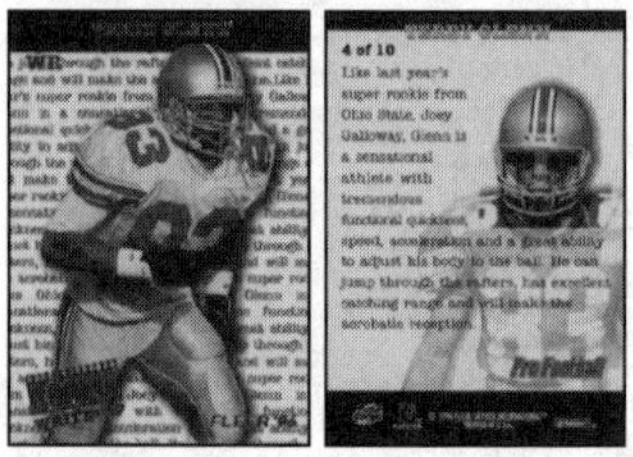

Randomly inserted in hobby packs only at the rate of one in 12, this 10-card set features color player images of rookies entering the NFL in '96 whose scouting reports are similar to those of previous rookies. The backs carry a player head photo with a paragraph stating the name of the previous rookie and why he and the pictured rookie are similar.

	MINT	NRMT	EXC
COMPLETE SET (10)	30.00	13.50	3.70
COMMON CARD (1-10)	1.50	.70	.19
☐ 1 Tim Biakabutuka	2.50	1.10	.30
☐ 2 Rickey Dudley	1.50	.70	.19
☐ 3 Eddie George	8.00	3.60	1.00
☐ 4 Terry Glenn	7.00	3.10	.85
☐ 5 Kevin Hardy	1.50	.70	.19
☐ 6 Marvin Harrison	4.00	1.80	.50
☐ 7 Keyshawn Johnson	4.00	1.80	.50
☐ 8 Leeland McElroy	1.50	.70	.19
☐ 9 Lawrence Phillips	2.50	1.10	.30
☐ 10 Simeon Rice	1.50	.70	.19

1996 Fleer Statistically Speaking

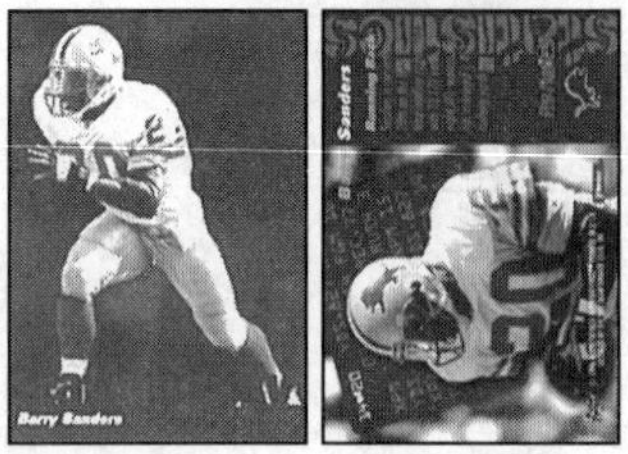

Randomly inserted in packs at the rate of one in 37, this 20-card set features player images of the NFL's statistical standouts printed on plastic cards in hot colors with statistics as the background.

	MINT	NRMT	EXC
COMPLETE SET (20)	135.00	60.00	17.00
COMMON CARD (1-20)	2.00	.90	.25
☐ 1 Troy Aikman	10.00	4.50	1.25
☐ 2 Larry Centers	2.00	.90	.25
☐ 3 Ben Coates	2.00	.90	.25
☐ 4 Brett Favre	20.00	9.00	2.50
☐ 5 Joey Galloway	4.00	1.80	.50
☐ 6 Rodney Hampton	2.00	.90	.25
☐ 7 Dan Marino	20.00	9.00	2.50
☐ 8 Curtis Martin	15.00	6.75	1.85
☐ 9 Anthony Miller	2.00	.90	.25
☐ 10 Brian Mitchell	2.00	.90	.25
☐ 11 Herman Moore	3.00	1.35	.35
☐ 12 Errict Rhett	2.00	.90	.25
☐ 13 Rashaan Salaam	3.00	1.35	.35
☐ 14 Barry Sanders	10.00	4.50	1.25
☐ 15 Deion Sanders	6.00	2.70	.75
☐ 16 Emmitt Smith	20.00	9.00	2.50
☐ 17 Kordell Stewart	12.00	5.50	1.50
☐ 18 Chris Warren	2.00	.90	.25
☐ 19 Ricky Watters	3.00	1.35	.35
☐ 20 Steve Young	8.00	3.60	1.00

1997 Fleer

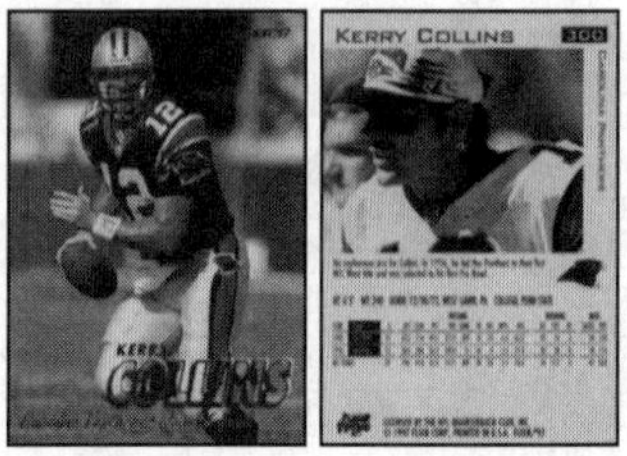

The 1997 Fleer set was issued in one series totaling 450 cards and features full-bleed action player photos with the Textured Legend matte finish making the cards especially suitable for autographs. The player's name is printed in gold foil block type with his team and position in gold foil script below. The set was distributed in 10-card foil packs with a suggested retail price of $1.49.

	MINT	NRMT	EXC
COMPLETE SET (450)	40.00	18.00	5.00
COMMON CARD (1-450)	.10	.05	.01
☐ 1 Mark Brunell	1.50	.70	.19
☐ 2 Andre Reed	.20	.09	.03
☐ 3 Darrell Green	.10	.05	.01
☐ 4 Mario Bates	.20	.09	.03
☐ 5 Eddie George	2.50	1.10	.30
☐ 6 Cris Carter	.30	.14	.04
☐ 7 Terrell Owens	1.00	.45	.12
☐ 8 Bill Romanowski	.10	.05	.01
☐ 9 Isaac Bruce	.30	.14	.04
☐ 10 Eric Curry	.10	.05	.01
☐ 11 Danny Kanell	.20	.09	.03
☐ 12 Ki-Jana Carter	.20	.09	.03
☐ 13 Antonio Freeman	.50	.23	.06
☐ 14 Ricky Watters	.20	.09	.03
☐ 15 Ty Law	.10	.05	.01
☐ 16 Alonzo Spellman	.10	.05	.01
☐ 17 Kordell Stewart	1.25	.55	.16
☐ 18 Jerry Rice	1.50	.70	.19
☐ 19 Derrick Alexander WR	.20	.09	.03
☐ 20 Barry Sanders	1.50	.70	.19
☐ 21 Keyshawn Johnson	.75	.35	.09
☐ 22 Emmitt Smith	3.00	1.35	.35
☐ 23 Ricky Proehl	.10	.05	.01
☐ 24 Daryl Gardener	.20	.09	.03
☐ 25 Dan Saleaumua	.10	.05	.01
☐ 26 Kevin Greene	.20	.09	.03
☐ 27 Junior Seau	.30	.14	.04
☐ 28 Randall McDaniel	.10	.05	.01
☐ 29 Marshall Faulk	.30	.14	.04
☐ 30 Lorenzo Lynch	.10	.05	.01
☐ 31 Terance Mathis	.10	.05	.01
☐ 32 Warren Sapp	.10	.05	.01
☐ 33 Chris Sanders	.20	.09	.03
☐ 34 Tom Carter	.10	.05	.01
☐ 35 Aeneas Williams	.10	.05	.01
☐ 36 Lawrence Phillips	.20	.09	.03
☐ 37 John Elway	1.25	.55	.16
☐ 38 Stanley Richard	.10	.05	.01
☐ 39 Darryl Williams	.10	.05	.01
☐ 40 Phillippi Sparks	.10	.05	.01
☐ 41 Tedy Bruschi	.10	.05	.01
☐ 42 Merton Hanks	.10	.05	.01
☐ 43 Ray Lewis	.10	.05	.01
☐ 44 Erik Williams	.10	.05	.01
☐ 45 Jason Gildon	.10	.05	.01
☐ 46 George Koonce	.10	.05	.01
☐ 47 Louis Oliver	.10	.05	.01
☐ 48 Muhsin Muhammad	.50	.23	.06
☐ 49 Daryl Hobbs	.10	.05	.01
☐ 50 Terry Glenn	1.50	.70	.19
☐ 51 Marvin Harrison	.75	.35	.09
☐ 52 Brian Dawkins	.10	.05	.01
☐ 53 Dale Carter	.10	.05	.01
☐ 54 Alex Molden	.10	.05	.01
☐ 55 Raymont Harris	.10	.05	.01
☐ 56 Jeff Burris	.10	.05	.01
☐ 57 Don Beebe	.10	.05	.01
☐ 58 Jamir Miller	.10	.05	.01
☐ 59 Carl Pickens	.30	.14	.04
☐ 60 Antonio London	.10	.05	.01
☐ 61 Courtney Hall	.10	.05	.01
☐ 62 Derrick Brooks	.10	.05	.01
☐ 63 Chris Boniol	.10	.05	.01
☐ 64 Jeff Lageman	.10	.05	.01
☐ 65 Roy Barker	.10	.05	.01
☐ 66 Devin Bush	.10	.05	.01
☐ 67 Aaron Glenn	.10	.05	.01
☐ 68 Wayne Simmons	.10	.05	.01
☐ 69 Steve Atwater	.10	.05	.01
☐ 70 Jimmie Jones	.10	.05	.01
☐ 71 Mark Carrier WR	.20	.09	.03
☐ 72 Chris Chandler	.20	.09	.03
☐ 73 Andy Harmon	.10	.05	.01
☐ 74 John Friesz	.10	.05	.01
☐ 75 Karim Abdul-Jabbar	1.25	.55	.16
☐ 76 Levon Kirkland	.10	.05	.01
☐ 77 Torrance Small	.10	.05	.01
☐ 78 Harvey Williams	.10	.05	.01
☐ 79 Chris Calloway	.10	.05	.01
☐ 80 Vinny Testaverde	.20	.09	.03
☐ 81 Bryant Young	.20	.09	.03
☐ 82 Ray Buchanan	.10	.05	.01
☐ 83 Robert Smith	.20	.09	.03
☐ 84 Robert Brooks	.30	.14	.04
☐ 85 Ray Crockett	.10	.05	.01
☐ 86 Bennie Blades	.10	.05	.01
☐ 87 Mark Carrier DB	.10	.05	.01
☐ 88 Mike Tomczak	.10	.05	.01
☐ 89 Darick Holmes	.20	.09	.03
☐ 90 Drew Bledsoe	1.50	.70	.19
☐ 91 Darren Woodson	.20	.09	.03
☐ 92 Dan Wilkinson	.10	.05	.01
☐ 93 Charles Way	.10	.05	.01
☐ 94 Ray Farmer	.10	.05	.01
☐ 95 Marcus Allen	.30	.14	.04
☐ 96 Marco Coleman	.10	.05	.01
☐ 97 Zach Thomas	.50	.23	.06
☐ 98 Wesley Walls	.10	.05	.01
☐ 99 Frank Wycheck	.10	.05	.01
☐ 100 Troy Aikman	1.50	.70	.19
☐ 101 Clyde Simmons	.10	.05	.01
☐ 102 Courtney Hawkins	.10	.05	.01
☐ 103 Chuck Smith	.10	.05	.01
☐ 104 Neil O'Donnell	.20	.09	.03
☐ 105 Kevin Carter	.10	.05	.01
☐ 106 Chris Slade	.10	.05	.01
☐ 107 Jessie Armstead	.10	.05	.01
☐ 108 Sean Dawkins	.10	.05	.01
☐ 109 Robert Blackmon	.10	.05	.01
☐ 110 Kevin Smith	.10	.05	.01
☐ 111 Lonnie Johnson	.10	.05	.01
☐ 112 Craig Newsome	.10	.05	.01
☐ 113 Jonathan Ogden	.10	.05	.01
☐ 114 Chris Zorich	.10	.05	.01
☐ 115 Tim Brown	.20	.09	.03
☐ 116 Fred Barnett	.20	.09	.03
☐ 117 Michael Haynes	.20	.09	.03
☐ 118 Eric Hill	.10	.05	.01
☐ 119 Ronnie Harmon	.10	.05	.01
☐ 120 Sean Gilbert	.10	.05	.01
☐ 121 Derrick Alexander DE	.10	.05	.01
☐ 122 Derrick Thomas	.20	.09	.03
☐ 123 Tyrone Wheatley	.20	.09	.03
☐ 124 Cortez Kennedy	.20	.09	.03
☐ 125 Jeff George	.20	.09	.03
☐ 126 Chad Cota	.10	.05	.01
☐ 127 Gary Zimmerman	.10	.05	.01
☐ 128 Johnnie Morton	.20	.09	.03
☐ 129 Chad Brown	.20	.09	.03
☐ 130 Marvcus Patton	.10	.05	.01
☐ 131 James O.Stewart	.20	.09	.03
☐ 132 Terry Kirby	.20	.09	.03
☐ 133 Chris Mims	.10	.05	.01
☐ 134 William Thomas	.10	.05	.01
☐ 135 Steve Tasker	.10	.05	.01
☐ 136 Jason Belser	.10	.05	.01
☐ 137 Bryan Cox	.10	.05	.01
☐ 138 Jessie Tuggle	.10	.05	.01
☐ 139 Ashley Ambrose	.10	.05	.01
☐ 140 Mark Chmura	.20	.09	.03
☐ 141 Jeff Hostetler	.20	.09	.03
☐ 142 Rich Owens	.10	.05	.01
☐ 143 Willie Davis	.20	.09	.03
☐ 144 Hardy Nickerson	.10	.05	.01
☐ 145 Curtis Martin	1.50	.70	.19
☐ 146 Ken Norton	.10	.05	.01
☐ 147 Victor Green	.10	.05	.01
☐ 148 Anthony Miller	.20	.09	.03
☐ 149 John Kasay	.10	.05	.01
☐ 150 O.J. McDuffie	.20	.09	.03
☐ 151 Darren Perry	.10	.05	.01
☐ 152 Luther Elliss	.10	.05	.01
☐ 153 Greg Hill	.20	.09	.03
☐ 154 John Randle	.10	.05	.01
☐ 155 Stephen Grant	.10	.05	.01
☐ 156 Leon Lett	.10	.05	.01
☐ 157 Darrien Gordon	.10	.05	.01
☐ 158 Ray Zellars	.10	.05	.01
☐ 159 Michael Jackson	.20	.09	.03
☐ 160 Leslie O'Neal	.10	.05	.01
☐ 161 Bruce Smith	.30	.14	.04
☐ 162 Santana Dotson	.10	.05	.01
☐ 163 Bobby Hebert	.10	.05	.01
☐ 164 Keith Hamilton	.10	.05	.01
☐ 165 Tony Boselli	.20	.09	.03
☐ 166 Alfred Williams	.10	.05	.01
☐ 167 Ty Detmer	.20	.09	.03
☐ 168 Chester McGlockton	.10	.05	.01
☐ 169 William Floyd	.20	.09	.03
☐ 170 Bruce Matthews	.10	.05	.01
☐ 171 Simeon Rice	.20	.09	.03
☐ 172 Scott Mitchell	.20	.09	.03
☐ 173 Ricardo McDonald	.10	.05	.01
☐ 174 Tyrone Poole	.10	.05	.01
☐ 175 Greg Lloyd	.20	.09	.03
☐ 176 Bruce Armstrong	.10	.05	.01
☐ 177 Erik Kramer	.10	.05	.01
☐ 178 Kimble Anders	.10	.05	.01
☐ 179 Lamar Smith	.10	.05	.01
☐ 180 Tony Tolbert	.10	.05	.01
☐ 181 Joe Aska	.10	.05	.01
☐ 182 Eric Allen	.10	.05	.01
☐ 183 Eric Turner	.10	.05	.01
☐ 184 Brad Johnson	.20	.09	.03
☐ 185 Tony Martin	.20	.09	.03
☐ 186 Mike Mamula	.10	.05	.01
☐ 187 Irving Spikes	.10	.05	.01
☐ 188 Keith Jackson	.10	.05	.01
☐ 189 Carlton Bailey	.10	.05	.01
☐ 190 Tyrone Braxton	.10	.05	.01
☐ 191 Chad Bratzke	.10	.05	.01
☐ 192 Adrian Murrell	.20	.09	.03
☐ 193 Roman Phifer	.10	.05	.01
☐ 194 Todd Collins	.20	.09	.03
☐ 195 Chris Warren	.20	.09	.03
☐ 196 Kevin Hardy	.20	.09	.03
☐ 197 Rick Mirer	.20	.09	.03
☐ 198 Cornelius Bennett	.20	.09	.03
☐ 199 Jimmy Hitchcock	.10	.05	.01
☐ 200 Michael Irvin	.30	.14	.04
☐ 201 Quentin Coryatt	.10	.05	.01
☐ 202 Reggie White	.30	.14	.04
☐ 203 Larry Centers	.20	.09	.03
☐ 204 Rodney Thomas	.10	.05	.01
☐ 205 Dana Stubblefield	.20	.09	.03
☐ 206 Rod Woodson	.20	.09	.03
☐ 207 Rhett Hall	.10	.05	.01
☐ 208 Steve Tovar	.10	.05	.01
☐ 209 Michael Westbrook	.30	.14	.04
☐ 210 Steve Wisniewski	.10	.05	.01
☐ 211 Carlester Crumpler	.10	.05	.01
☐ 212 Elvis Grbac	.20	.09	.03
☐ 213 Tim Bowens	.10	.05	.01
☐ 214 Robert Porcher	.10	.05	.01
☐ 215 John Carney	.10	.05	.01
☐ 216 Anthony Newman	.10	.05	.01
☐ 217 Earnest Byner	.10	.05	.01
☐ 218 Dewayne Washington	.10	.05	.01
☐ 219 Willie Green	.10	.05	.01
☐ 220 Terry Allen	.20	.09	.03
☐ 221 William Fuller	.10	.05	.01
☐ 222 Al Del Greco	.10	.05	.01
☐ 223 Trent Dilfer	.20	.09	.03
☐ 224 Michael Dean Perry	.10	.05	.01
☐ 225 Larry Allen	.10	.05	.01
☐ 226 Mark Bruener	.10	.05	.01
☐ 227 Clay Matthews	.20	.09	.03
☐ 228 Ruben Brown	.10	.05	.01
☐ 229 Edgar Bennett	.20	.09	.03
☐ 230 Neil Smith	.20	.09	.03
☐ 231 Ken Harvey	.10	.05	.01
☐ 232 Kyle Brady	.10	.05	.01
☐ 233 Corey Miller	.10	.05	.01
☐ 234 Tony Siragusa	.10	.05	.01
☐ 235 Todd Sauerbrun	.10	.05	.01
☐ 236 Daniel Stubbs	.10	.05	.01
☐ 237 Robb Thomas	.10	.05	.01
☐ 238 Jimmy Smith	.20	.09	.03
☐ 239 Marquez Pope	.10	.05	.01
☐ 240 Tim Biakabutuka	.30	.14	.04

☐ 241 Jamie Asher	.20	.09	.03
☐ 242 Steve McNair	1.00	.45	.12
☐ 243 Harold Green	.10	.05	.01
☐ 244 Frank Sanders	.20	.09	.03
☐ 245 Joe Johnson	.10	.05	.01
☐ 246 Eric Bieniemy	.10	.05	.01
☐ 247 Kevin Turner	.10	.05	.01
☐ 248 Rickey Dudley	.20	.09	.03
☐ 249 Orlando Thomas	.10	.05	.01
☐ 250 Dan Marino	3.00	1.35	.35
☐ 251 Deion Sanders	.75	.35	.09
☐ 252 Dan Williams	.10	.05	.01
☐ 253 Sam Gash	.10	.05	.01
☐ 254 Lonnie Marts	.10	.05	.01
☐ 255 Mo Lewis	.10	.05	.01
☐ 256 Charles Johnson	.20	.09	.03
☐ 257 Chris Jacke	.10	.05	.01
☐ 258 Keenan McCardell	.20	.09	.03
☐ 259 Donnell Woolford	.10	.05	.01
☐ 260 Terrance Shaw	.10	.05	.01
☐ 261 Jason Dunn	.20	.09	.03
☐ 262 Willie McGinest	.10	.05	.01
☐ 263 Ken Dilger	.20	.09	.03
☐ 264 Keith Lyle	.10	.05	.01
☐ 265 Antonio Langham	.10	.05	.01
☐ 266 Carlton Gray	.10	.05	.01
☐ 267 LeShon Johnson	.10	.05	.01
☐ 268 Thurman Thomas	.30	.14	.04
☐ 269 Jesse Campbell	.10	.05	.01
☐ 270 Carnell Lake	.10	.05	.01
☐ 271 Cris Dishman	.10	.05	.01
☐ 272 Kevin Williams	.10	.05	.01
☐ 273 Troy Brown	.10	.05	.01
☐ 274 William Roaf	.10	.05	.01
☐ 275 Terrell Davis	1.50	.70	.19
☐ 276 Herman Moore	.30	.14	.04
☐ 277 Walt Harris	.10	.05	.01
☐ 278 Mark Collins	.10	.05	.01
☐ 279 Bert Emanuel	.20	.09	.03
☐ 280 Qadry Ismail	.20	.09	.03
☐ 281 Phil Hansen	.10	.05	.01
☐ 282 Steve Young	1.00	.45	.12
☐ 283 Michael Sinclair	.10	.05	.01
☐ 284 Jeff Graham	.10	.05	.01
☐ 285 Sam Mills	.20	.09	.03
☐ 286 Terry McDaniel	.10	.05	.01
☐ 287 Eugene Robinson	.10	.05	.01
☐ 288 Tony Bennett	.10	.05	.01
☐ 289 Daryl Johnston	.20	.09	.03
☐ 290 Eric Swann	.20	.09	.03
☐ 291 Byron Bam Morris	.20	.09	.03
☐ 292 Thomas Lewis	.10	.05	.01
☐ 293 Terrell Fletcher	.10	.05	.01
☐ 294 Gus Frerotte	.30	.14	.04
☐ 295 Stanley Pritchett	.10	.05	.01
☐ 296 Mike Alstott	.30	.14	.04
☐ 297 Will Shields	.10	.05	.01
☐ 298 Errict Rhett	.20	.09	.03
☐ 299 Garrison Hearst	.20	.09	.03
☐ 300 Kerry Collins	1.25	.55	.16
☐ 301 Darryll Lewis	.10	.05	.01
☐ 302 Chris T. Jones	.30	.14	.04
☐ 303 Yancey Thigpen	.20	.09	.03
☐ 304 Jackie Harris	.10	.05	.01
☐ 305 Steve Christie	.10	.05	.01
☐ 306 Gilbert Brown	.20	.09	.03
☐ 307 Terry Wooden	.10	.05	.01
☐ 308 Pete Mitchell	.10	.05	.01
☐ 309 Tim McDonald	.10	.05	.01
☐ 310 Jake Reed	.20	.09	.03
☐ 311 Ed McCaffrey	.10	.05	.01
☐ 312 Chris Doleman	.10	.05	.01
☐ 313 Eric Metcalf	.20	.09	.03
☐ 314 Ricky Reynolds	.10	.05	.01
☐ 315 David Sloan	.20	.09	.03
☐ 316 Marvin Washington	.10	.05	.01
☐ 317 Herschel Walker	.20	.09	.03
☐ 318 Michael Timpson	.10	.05	.01
☐ 319 Blaine Bishop	.10	.05	.01
☐ 320 Irv Smith	.10	.05	.01
☐ 321 Seth Joyner	.10	.05	.01
☐ 322 Terrell Buckley	.10	.05	.01
☐ 323 Michael Strahan	.10	.05	.01
☐ 324 Sam Adams	.10	.05	.01
☐ 325 Leslie Shepherd	.10	.05	.01
☐ 326 James Jett	.10	.05	.01
☐ 327 Anthony Pleasant	.10	.05	.01
☐ 328 Lee Woodall	.10	.05	.01
☐ 329 Shannon Sharpe	.20	.09	.03
☐ 330 Jamal Anderson	.20	.09	.03
☐ 331 Andre Hastings	.20	.09	.03
☐ 332 Troy Vincent	.10	.05	.01
☐ 333 Sean LaChapelle	.10	.05	.01
☐ 334 Winslow Oliver	.10	.05	.01
☐ 335 Sean Jones	.10	.05	.01
☐ 336 Darnay Scott	.20	.09	.03
☐ 337 Todd Lyght	.10	.05	.01
☐ 338 Leonard Russell	.10	.05	.01
☐ 339 Nate Newton	.10	.05	.01
☐ 340 Zack Crockett	.10	.05	.01
☐ 341 Amp Lee	.10	.05	.01
☐ 342 Bobby Engram	.20	.09	.03
☐ 343 Mike Hollis	.10	.05	.01
☐ 344 Rodney Hampton	.20	.09	.03
☐ 345 Mel Gray	.10	.05	.01
☐ 346 Van Malone	.10	.05	.01
☐ 347 Aaron Craver	.10	.05	.01
☐ 348 Jim Everett	.10	.05	.01
☐ 349 Trace Armstrong	.10	.05	.01
☐ 350 Pat Swilling	.10	.05	.01
☐ 351 Brent Jones	.10	.05	.01
☐ 352 Chris Spielman	.20	.09	.03
☐ 353 Brett Perriman	.20	.09	.03
☐ 354 Brian Kinchen	.10	.05	.01
☐ 355 Joey Galloway	.50	.23	.06
☐ 356 Henry Ellard	.20	.09	.03
☐ 357 Ben Coates	.20	.09	.03
☐ 358 Dorsey Levens	.20	.09	.03
☐ 359 Charlie Garner	.10	.05	.01
☐ 360 Erric Pegram	.10	.05	.01
☐ 361 Anthony Johnson	.20	.09	.03
☐ 362 Rashaan Salaam	.30	.14	.04
☐ 363 Jeff Blake	.30	.14	.04
☐ 364 Kent Graham	.20	.09	.03
☐ 365 Broderick Thomas	.10	.05	.01
☐ 366 Richmond Webb	.10	.05	.01
☐ 367 Alfred Pupunu	.10	.05	.01
☐ 368 Mark Stepnoski	.10	.05	.01
☐ 369 David Dunn	.10	.05	.01
☐ 370 Bobby Houston	.10	.05	.01
☐ 371 Anthony Parker	.10	.05	.01
☐ 372 Quinn Early	.10	.05	.01
☐ 373 LeRoy Butler	.10	.05	.01
☐ 374 Kurt Gouveia	.10	.05	.01
☐ 375 Greg Biekert	.10	.05	.01
☐ 376 Jim Harbaugh	.20	.09	.03
☐ 377 Eric Bjornson	.10	.05	.01
☐ 378 Craig Heyward	.10	.05	.01
☐ 379 Steve Bono	.10	.05	.01
☐ 380 Tony Banks	.50	.23	.06
☐ 381 John Mobley	.10	.05	.01
☐ 382 Irving Fryar	.20	.09	.03
☐ 383 Dermontti Dawson	.10	.05	.01
☐ 384 Eric Davis	.10	.05	.01
☐ 385 Natrone Means	.30	.14	.04
☐ 386 Jason Sehorn	.10	.05	.01
☐ 387 Michael McCrary	.10	.05	.01
☐ 388 Corwin Brown	.10	.05	.01
☐ 389 Kevin Glover	.10	.05	.01
☐ 390 Jerris McPhail	.10	.05	.01
☐ 391 Bobby Taylor	.20	.09	.03
☐ 392 Tony McGee	.10	.05	.01
☐ 393 Curtis Conway	.30	.14	.04
☐ 394 Napoleon Kaufman	.20	.09	.03
☐ 395 Brian Blades	.20	.09	.03
☐ 396 Richard Dent	.10	.05	.01
☐ 397 Dave Brown	.20	.09	.03
☐ 398 Stan Humphries	.20	.09	.03
☐ 399 Stevon Moore	.10	.05	.01
☐ 400 Brett Favre	3.00	1.35	.35
☐ 401 Jerome Bettis	.30	.14	.04
☐ 402 Darrin Smith	.10	.05	.01
☐ 403 Chris Penn	.10	.05	.01
☐ 404 Rob Moore	.10	.05	.01
☐ 405 Micheal Barrow	.10	.05	.01
☐ 406 Tony Brackens	.10	.05	.01
☐ 407 Wayne Martin	.10	.05	.01
☐ 408 Warren Moon	.20	.09	.03
☐ 409 Jason Elam	.10	.05	.01
☐ 410 J.J. Birden	.10	.05	.01
☐ 411 Hugh Douglas	.10	.05	.01
☐ 412 Lamar Lathon	.10	.05	.01
☐ 413 John Kidd	.10	.05	.01
☐ 414 Bryce Paup	.10	.05	.01
☐ 415 Shawn Jefferson	.10	.05	.01
☐ 416 Leeland McElroy SS	.20	.09	.03
☐ 417 Elbert Shelley SS	.10	.05	.01
☐ 418 Jermaine Lewis SS	.10	.05	.01
☐ 419 Eric Moulds SS	.30	.14	.04
☐ 420 Michael Bates SS	.10	.05	.01
☐ 421 John Mangum SS	.10	.05	.01
☐ 422 Corey Sawyer SS	.10	.05	.01
☐ 423 Jim Schwantz SS	.10	.05	.01
☐ 424 Rod Smith WR SS	.10	.05	.01
☐ 425 Glyn Milburn SS	.10	.05	.01
☐ 426 Desmond Howard SS	.20	.09	.03
☐ 427 John Henry Mills SS	.10	.05	.01
☐ 428 Cary Blanchard SS	.10	.05	.01
☐ 429 Chris Hudson SS	.10	.05	.01
☐ 430 Tamarick Vanover SS	.20	.09	.03
☐ 431 Kirby Dar Dar SS	.10	.05	.01
☐ 432 David Palmer SS	.20	.09	.03
☐ 433 Dave Meggett SS	.10	.05	.01
☐ 434 Tyrone Hughes SS	.10	.05	.01
☐ 435 Amani Toomer SS	.20	.09	.03
☐ 436 Wayne Chrebet SS	.10	.05	.01
☐ 437 Carl Kidd SS	.10	.05	.01
☐ 438 Derrick Witherspoon SS	.10	.05	.01
☐ 439 Jahine Arnold SS	.10	.05	.01
☐ 440 Andre Coleman SS	.10	.05	.01
☐ 441 Jeff Wilkins SS	.10	.05	.01
☐ 442 Jay Bellamy SS	.10	.05	.01
☐ 443 Eddie Kennison SS	.75	.35	.09
☐ 444 Nilo Silvan SS	.10	.05	.01
☐ 445 Brian Mitchell SS	.10	.05	.01
☐ 446 Garrison Hearst	.20	.09	.03
Checklist back			
☐ 447 Napoleon Kaufman	.20	.09	.03
Checklist back			
☐ 448 Brian Mitchell	.10	.05	.01
Checklist back			
☐ 449 Rodney Hampton	.20	.09	.03
Checklist back			
☐ 450 Edgar Bennett	.10	.05	.01
Checklist back			
☐ S1 Mark Chmura Sample	1.00	.45	.12

1997 Fleer Crystal Silver

Randomly inserted in hobby packs only at a rate of one in two, this 445-card set is a parallel version of the basic set player cards with glossy UV coating and silver foil detailing.

	MINT	NRMT	EXC
COMPLETE SET (445)	150.00	70.00	19.00
COMMON CARD (1-445)	.40	.18	.05

*CRYSTAL SILVER STARS: 1.5X TO 3X BASIC CARDS
*CRYSTAL SILVER STARS: 1.25X TO 2.5X BASIC CARDS

1997 Fleer Tiffany Blue

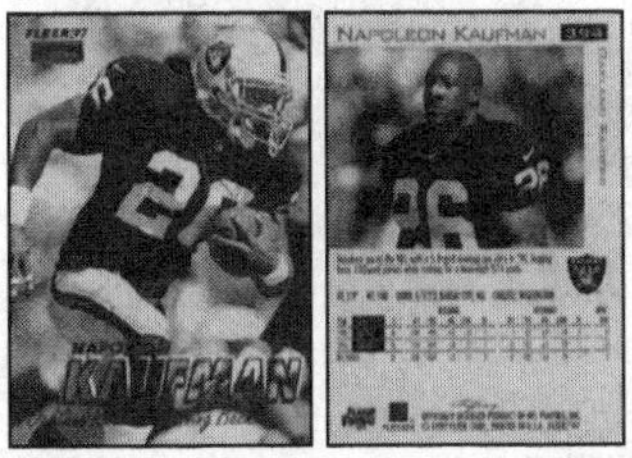

Randomly inserted in hobby packs only at a rate of one in 20, this 445-card set is a limited-edition parallel version of all basic set player cards with glossy UV coating and holographic foil detailing.

	MINT	NRMT	EXC
COMPLETE SET (445)	800.00	350.00	100.00
COMMON CARD (1-445)	2.00	.90	.25

*TIFFANY BLUE STARS: 12X TO 25X BASIC CARDS
*TIFFANY BLUE YOUNG STARS: 10X TO 20X BASIC CARDS

1997 Fleer All-Pro

Randomly inserted in retail packs only at a rate of one in 36, this 24-card set features color player photos of first-time and regular All-Pro players.

	MINT	NRMT	EXC
COMPLETE SET (24)	175.00	80.00	22.00
COMMON CARD (1-24)	2.00	.90	.25
☐ 1 Troy Aikman	20.00	9.00	2.50
☐ 2 Larry Allen	2.00	.90	.25
☐ 3 Drew Bledsoe	20.00	9.00	2.50
☐ 4 Terrell Davis	20.00	9.00	2.50
☐ 5 Dermontti Dawson	2.00	.90	.25
☐ 6 John Elway	15.00	6.75	1.85
☐ 7 Brett Favre	35.00	16.00	4.40
☐ 8 Herman Moore	5.00	2.20	.60
☐ 9 Jerry Rice	20.00	9.00	2.50
☐ 10 Barry Sanders	20.00	9.00	2.50
☐ 11 Shannon Sharpe	3.00	1.35	.35
☐ 12 Erik Williams	2.00	.90	.25
☐ 13 Ashley Ambrose	2.00	.90	.25
☐ 14 Chad Brown	2.00	.90	.25
☐ 15 LeRoy Butler	2.00	.90	.25
☐ 16 Kevin Greene	3.00	1.35	.35
☐ 17 Sam Mills	2.00	.90	.25
☐ 18 John Randle	2.00	.90	.25
☐ 19 Deion Sanders	10.00	4.50	1.25
☐ 20 Junior Seau	5.00	2.20	.60
☐ 21 Bruce Smith	5.00	2.20	.60
☐ 22 Alfred Williams	2.00	.90	.25
☐ 23 Darren Woodson	3.00	1.35	.35
☐ 24 Bryant Young	3.00	1.35	.35

1997 Fleer Decade of Excellence

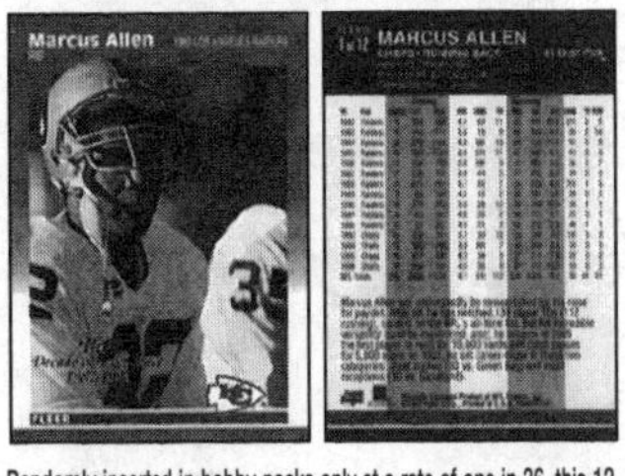

Randomly inserted in hobby packs only at a rate of one in 36, this 12-card set pays tribute to players whose careers began in 1987 or earlier and features 1987 photography and design details.

	MINT	NRMT	EXC
COMPLETE SET (12)	80.00	36.00	10.00
COMMON CARD (1-12)	3.00	1.35	.35
☐ 1 Marcus Allen	5.00	2.20	.60
☐ 2 Cris Carter	4.00	1.80	.50
☐ 3 John Elway	12.00	5.50	1.50
☐ 4 Irving Fryar	3.00	1.35	.35
☐ 5 Darrell Green	3.00	1.35	.35
☐ 6 Dan Marino	25.00	11.00	3.10
☐ 7 Jerry Rice	15.00	6.75	1.85
☐ 8 Bruce Smith	5.00	2.20	.60
☐ 9 Herschel Walker	3.00	1.35	.35
☐ 10 Reggie White	5.00	2.20	.60
☐ 11 Rod Woodson	4.00	1.80	.50
☐ 12 Steve Young	10.00	4.50	1.25

1997 Fleer Game Breakers

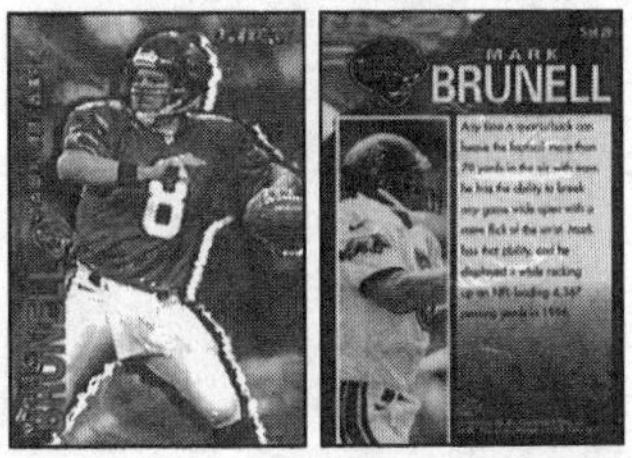

Randomly inserted in retail packs only at a rate of one in two, this 20-card set features color photos of players who can break a game wide open. The tougher Supreme parallels combines a matte-finish background with a fully sculptured embossed player image covered in glossy UV coating. They were inserted at the rate of 1:18 hobby and retail packs.

	MINT	NRMT	EXC
COMPLETE SET (20)	20.00	9.00	2.50
COMMON CARD (1-20)	.40	.18	.05

*SUPREME CARDS: 2X TO 5X BASIC CARDS

☐ 1 Troy Aikman	2.00	.90	.25
☐ 2 Jerome Bettis	.75	.35	.09
☐ 3 Drew Bledsoe	2.00	.90	.25
☐ 4 Isaac Bruce	.75	.35	.09
☐ 5 Mark Brunell	2.00	.90	.25
☐ 6 Kerry Collins	1.50	.70	.19
☐ 7 Terrell Davis	2.00	.90	.25
☐ 8 Marshall Faulk	.75	.35	.09
☐ 9 Antonio Freeman	.75	.35	.09
☐ 10 Joey Galloway	.75	.35	.09
☐ 11 Terry Glenn	2.00	.90	.25
☐ 12 Desmond Howard	.40	.18	.05
☐ 13 Keyshawn Johnson	.75	.35	.09
☐ 14 Eddie Kennison	1.00	.45	.12
☐ 15 Curtis Martin	2.00	.90	.25
☐ 16 Herman Moore	.75	.35	.09
☐ 17 Lawrence Phillips	.60	.25	.07
☐ 18 Barry Sanders	2.00	.90	.25
☐ 19 Shannon Sharpe	.40	.18	.05
☐ 20 Emmitt Smith	4.00	1.80	.50

1997 Fleer Million Dollar Moments

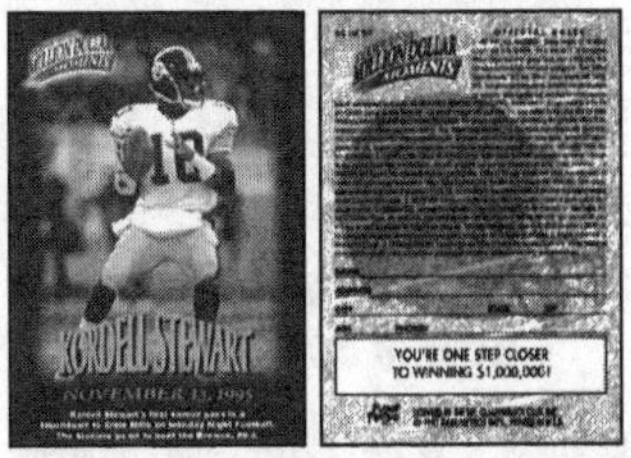

Each 1997 Fleer and Ultra pack included one Million Dollar Moments game piece as part of a Sweepstakes promotion with a $1 million top prize. Ten free game pieces could be received via mail as well. The contest ends April 30, 1998. The cards include a notable NFL event on the fronts (along with the player's photo) with the game rules on the card backs. Cards #46-49 pulled from packs were the contest winner cards and could be exchanged (along with the other 45-cards) for a chance to win various prizes including $1000 hobby shopping sprees. Card #50 could be redeemed (with the other 49-cards) for the $1 million dollar prize. Finally, the first 45-cards could be redeemed along with $5.95 for a special print version of the final 5-cards to help collectors fill out their sets.

	MINT	NRMT	EXC
COMPLETE SET (45)	5.00	2.20	.60
COMMON CARD (1-45)	.05	.02	.01
☐ 1 Checklist Card	.05	.02	.01
☐ 2 Troy Aikman	.50	.23	.06
☐ 3 Sid Luckman	.10	.05	.01
☐ 4 Barry Sanders	.50	.23	.06
☐ 5 Tom Fears	.10	.05	.01
☐ 6 Reggie White	.20	.09	.03
☐ 7 Lou Groza	.10	.05	.01
not shown in photo			
☐ 8 John Elway	.40	.18	.05
☐ 9 Raymond Berry	.10	.05	.01
☐ 10 Marcus Allen	.20	.09	.03
☐ 11 Paul Hornung	.20	.09	.03
☐ 12 Herschel Walker	.05	.02	.01
☐ 13 Norm Van Brocklin	.10	.05	.01

☐ 14 Bruce Smith	.20	.09	.03
☐ 15 Bill Wade	.05	.02	.01
☐ 16 Andre Reed	.10	.05	.01
☐ 17 Gale Sayers	.20	.09	.03
☐ 18 Terrell Davis	.50	.23	.06
☐ 19 Jim Bakken	.05	.02	.01
☐ 20 Marshall Faulk	.20	.09	.03
☐ 21 Tom Dempsey	.05	.02	.01
☐ 22 Dan Marino	1.00	.45	.12
☐ 23 Garo Yepremian	.05	.02	.01
☐ 24 Jerry Rice	.50	.23	.06
☐ 25 Herman Edwards	.05	.02	.01
☐ 26 Derrick Thomas	.10	.05	.01
☐ 27 Kellen Winslow	.10	.05	.01
☐ 28 Steve Young	.30	.14	.04
☐ 29 Tony Dorsett	.20	.09	.03
☐ 30 Desmond Howard	.05	.02	.01
☐ 31 Roger Craig	.05	.02	.01
☐ 32 Drew Bledsoe	.50	.23	.06
☐ 33 Doug Williams	.05	.02	.01
☐ 34 Jerome Bettis	.20	.09	.03
☐ 35 Bobby Layne	.10	.05	.01
☐ 36 Junior Seau	.20	.09	.03
☐ 37 Roman Gabriel	.05	.02	.01
☐ 38 Cris Carter	.05	.02	.01
☐ 39 Drew Pearson	.10	.05	.01
☐ 40 Warren Moon	.10	.05	.01
☐ 41 Wesley Walker	.05	.02	.01
☐ 42 Ricky Watters	.10	.05	.01
☐ 43 Carl Eller	.05	.02	.01
☐ 44 Kordell Stewart	.40	.18	.05
☐ 45 John Mackey	.05	.02	.01

1997 Fleer Prospects

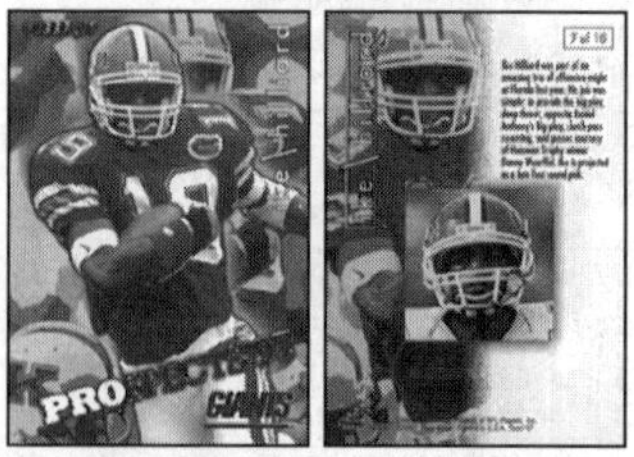

Randomly inserted in packs at a rate of one in six, this 10-card set features color photos of the top prospects from the 1997 NFL draft with college statistics and commentary on their anticipated impact as pros.

	MINT	NRMT	EXC
COMPLETE SET (10)	15.00	6.75	1.85
COMMON CARD (1-10)	1.00	.45	.12
☐ 1 Peter Boulware	1.00	.45	.12
☐ 2 Rae Carruth	2.00	.90	.25
☐ 3 Jim Druckenmiller	4.00	1.80	.50
☐ 4 Warrick Dunn	5.00	2.20	.60
☐ 5 Tony Gonzalez	1.50	.70	.19
☐ 6 Yatil Green	3.00	1.35	.35
☐ 7 Ike Hilliard	3.00	1.35	.35
☐ 8 Orlando Pace	1.50	.70	.19
☐ 9 Darrell Russell	1.00	.45	.12
☐ 10 Shawn Springs	1.50	.70	.19

1997 Fleer Rookie Sensations

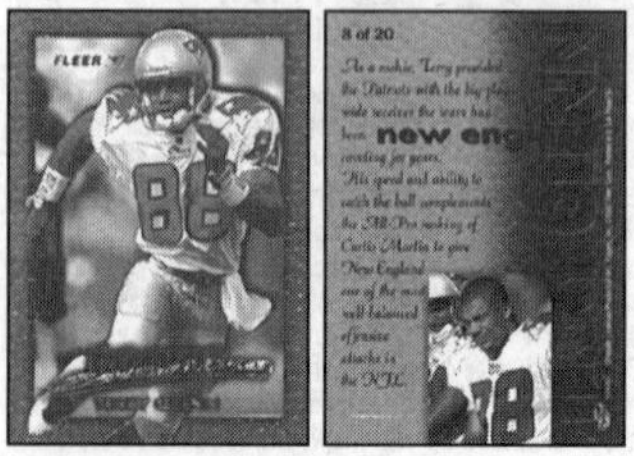

Randomly inserted in packs at a rate of one in four, this 20-card set features color photos of high-impact rookies from the 1996 season. The card design includes textured border and single-level embossed player image.

	MINT	NRMT	EXC
COMPLETE SET (20)	30.00	13.50	3.70
COMMON CARD (1-20)	.75	.35	.09
☐ 1 Karim Abdul-Jabbar	4.00	1.80	.50
☐ 2 Mike Alstott	1.50	.70	.19
☐ 3 Tony Banks	2.00	.90	.25
☐ 4 Tony Brackens	.75	.35	.09
☐ 5 Rickey Dudley	1.50	.70	.19
☐ 6 Bobby Engram	1.00	.45	.12
☐ 7 Eddie George	8.00	3.60	1.00
☐ 8 Terry Glenn	5.00	2.20	.60
☐ 9 Kevin Hardy	1.00	.45	.12
☐ 10 Marvin Harrison	2.50	1.10	.30
☐ 11 Keyshawn Johnson	2.50	1.10	.30
☐ 12 Eddie Kennison	2.50	1.10	.30
☐ 13 Jermaine Lewis	.75	.35	.09
☐ 14 Ray Lewis	.75	.35	.09
☐ 15 John Mobley	.75	.35	.09
☐ 16 Eric Moulds	.75	.35	.09
☐ 17 Jonathan Ogden	.75	.35	.09
☐ 18 Lawrence Phillips	1.00	.45	.12
☐ 19 Simeon Rice	.75	.35	.09
☐ 20 Zach Thomas	2.00	.90	.25

1997 Fleer Thrill Seekers

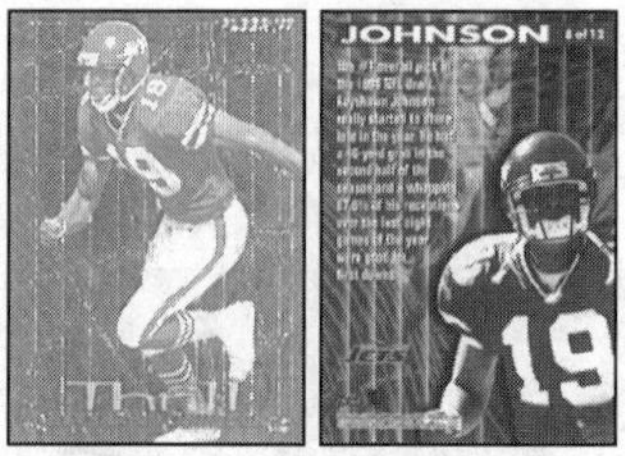

Randomly inserted in packs at a rate of one in 288, this 12-card set features color photos of players who are known for making the big play. Both player image and background have a shimmery metallic look.

	MINT	NRMT	EXC
COMPLETE SET (12)	600.00	275.00	75.00
COMMON CARD (1-12)	15.00	6.75	1.85
☐ 1 Karim Abdul-Jabbar	35.00	16.00	4.40
☐ 2 Jerome Bettis	15.00	6.75	1.85
☐ 3 Terrell Davis	50.00	22.00	6.25
☐ 4 John Elway	40.00	18.00	5.00
☐ 5 Brett Favre	100.00	45.00	12.50
☐ 6 Eddie George	70.00	32.00	8.75
☐ 7 Terry Glenn	50.00	22.00	6.25
☐ 8 Keyshawn Johnson	15.00	6.75	1.85
☐ 9 Dan Marino	100.00	45.00	12.50
☐ 10 Curtis Martin	50.00	22.00	6.25
☐ 11 Deion Sanders	25.00	11.00	3.10
☐ 12 Emmitt Smith	100.00	45.00	12.50

1997 Fleer Goudey

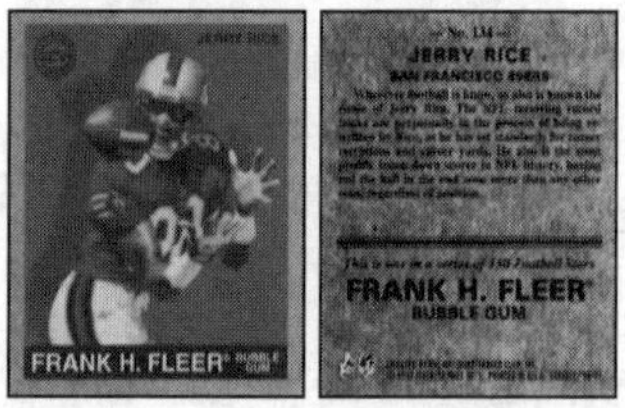

The 1997 Fleer Goudey set was issued in one series totaling 150 cards. The cards measured the small almost square shape (2 3/8" x 2 7/8") the same as the 1930's Goudey sets. Inspired by the classic look of the 1930's cards these cards have the same "Art Deco-style" graphics and same matte finish. The cards were issued in 10 card packs in 36 count hobby boxes. An unnumbered base card of Brett Favre was released to promote the set.

	MINT	NRMT	EXC
COMPLETE SET (150)	18.00	8.00	2.20
COMMON CARD (1-150)	.05	.02	.01
☐ 1 Michael Jackson	.10	.05	.01
☐ 2 Ray Lewis	.05	.02	.01
☐ 3 Vinny Testaverde	.10	.05	.01
☐ 4 Eric Turner	.05	.02	.01
☐ 5 Jim Kelly	.20	.09	.03
☐ 6 Bryce Paup	.05	.02	.01
☐ 7 Andre Reed	.10	.05	.01
☐ 8 Bruce Smith	.20	.09	.03
☐ 9 Thurman Thomas	.20	.09	.03
☐ 10 Jeff Blake	.20	.09	.03
☐ 11 Ki-Jana Carter	.10	.05	.01
☐ 12 Carl Pickens	.20	.09	.03
☐ 13 Darnay Scott	.10	.05	.01
☐ 14 Terrell Davis	1.00	.45	.12
☐ 15 John Elway	.75	.35	.09
☐ 16 Anthony Miller	.10	.05	.01
☐ 17 John Mobley	.05	.02	.01
☐ 18 Shannon Sharpe	.10	.05	.01
☐ 19 Chris Chandler	.10	.05	.01
☐ 20 Eddie George	1.50	.70	.19
☐ 21 Steve McNair	.60	.25	.07
☐ 22 Chris Sanders	.10	.05	.01
☐ 23 Quentin Coryatt	.05	.02	.01
☐ 24 Sean Dawkins	.05	.02	.01
☐ 25 Ken Dilger	.10	.05	.01
☐ 26 Marshall Faulk	.20	.09	.03
☐ 27 Jim Harbaugh	.10	.05	.01
☐ 28 Marvin Harrison	.50	.23	.06
☐ 29 Tony Brackens	.05	.02	.01
☐ 30 Mark Brunell	1.00	.45	.12
☐ 31 Kevin Hardy	.10	.05	.01
☐ 32 Keenan McCardell	.10	.05	.01
☐ 33 James O.Stewart	.10	.05	.01
☐ 34 Marcus Allen	.20	.09	.03
☐ 35 Steve Bono	.05	.02	.01
☐ 36 Dale Carter	.05	.02	.01
☐ 37 Neil Smith	.10	.05	.01
☐ 38 Derrick Thomas	.10	.05	.01
☐ 39 Tamarick Vanover	.10	.05	.01
☐ 40 Karim Abdul-Jabbar	.75	.35	.09
☐ 41 Dan Marino	2.00	.90	.25
☐ 42 O.J. McDuffie	.10	.05	.01
☐ 43 Stanley Pritchett	.05	.02	.01
☐ 44 Zach Thomas	.30	.14	.04
☐ 45 Drew Bledsoe	1.00	.45	.12
☐ 46 Ben Coates	.10	.05	.01
☐ 47 Terry Glenn	1.00	.45	.12
☐ 48 Shawn Jefferson	.05	.02	.01
☐ 49 Curtis Martin	1.00	.45	.12
☐ 50 Dave Meggett	.05	.02	.01
☐ 51 Hugh Douglas	.05	.02	.01
☐ 52 Keyshawn Johnson	.50	.23	.06
☐ 53 Adrian Murrell	.10	.05	.01
☐ 54 Tim Brown	.10	.05	.01
☐ 55 Rickey Dudley	.10	.05	.01
☐ 56 Jeff Hostetler	.10	.05	.01
☐ 57 Napoleon Kaufman	.10	.05	.01
☐ 58 Chester McGlockton	.05	.02	.01
☐ 59 Jerome Bettis	.20	.09	.03
☐ 60 Andre Hastings	.10	.05	.01
☐ 61 Greg Lloyd	.10	.05	.01
☐ 62 Kordell Stewart	.75	.35	.09
☐ 63 Yancey Thigpen	.10	.05	.01
☐ 64 Rod Woodson	.10	.05	.01
☐ 65 Andre Coleman	.05	.02	.01
☐ 66 Stan Humphries	.10	.05	.01
☐ 67 Tony Martin	.10	.05	.01
☐ 68 Leonard Russell	.05	.02	.01
☐ 69 Junior Seau	.20	.09	.03
☐ 70 Brian Blades	.10	.05	.01
☐ 71 Joey Galloway	.30	.14	.04
☐ 72 Chris Warren	.10	.05	.01
☐ 73 Larry Centers	.10	.05	.01
☐ 74 Leeland McElroy	.10	.05	.01
☐ 75 Simeon Rice	.10	.05	.01
☐ 76 Frank Sanders	.10	.05	.01
☐ 77 Eric Swann	.10	.05	.01
☐ 78 Jamal Anderson	.10	.05	.01
☐ 79 Bert Emanuel	.10	.05	.01
☐ 80 Terance Mathis	.05	.02	.01
☐ 81 Eric Metcalf	.10	.05	.01
☐ 82 Tim Biakabutuka	.20	.09	.03
☐ 83 Kerry Collins	.75	.35	.09
☐ 84 Kevin Greene	.10	.05	.01
☐ 85 Muhsin Muhammad	.30	.14	.04
☐ 86 Wesley Walls	.05	.02	.01
☐ 87 Curtis Conway	.20	.09	.03
☐ 88 Bryan Cox	.05	.02	.01
☐ 89 Walt Harris	.05	.02	.01
☐ 90 Erik Kramer	.05	.02	.01
☐ 91 Rashaan Salaam	.20	.09	.03
☐ 92 Troy Aikman	1.00	.45	.12
☐ 93 Michael Irvin	.20	.09	.03
☐ 94 Daryl Johnston	.10	.05	.01
☐ 95 Leon Lett	.05	.02	.01
☐ 96 Deion Sanders	.50	.23	.06
☐ 97 Emmitt Smith	2.00	.90	.25
☐ 98 Scott Mitchell	.10	.05	.01
☐ 99 Herman Moore	.20	.09	.03
☐ 100 Johnnie Morton	.10	.05	.01
☐ 101 Brett Perriman	.10	.05	.01
☐ 102 Barry Sanders	1.00	.45	.12
☐ 103 Edgar Bennett	.10	.05	.01
☐ 104 Robert Brooks	.20	.09	.03
☐ 105 Brett Favre	2.00	.90	.25
☐ 106 Antonio Freeman	.30	.14	.04
☐ 107 Keith Jackson	.05	.02	.01
☐ 108 Reggie White	.20	.09	.03
☐ 109 Cris Carter	.20	.09	.03
☐ 110 Warren Moon	.10	.05	.01
☐ 111 John Randle	.05	.02	.01
☐ 112 Jake Reed	.10	.05	.01
☐ 113 Robert Smith	.10	.05	.01
☐ 114 Jim Everett	.05	.02	.01
☐ 115 Michael Haynes	.10	.05	.01
☐ 116 Alex Molden	.05	.02	.01
☐ 117 Ray Zellars	.05	.02	.01
☐ 118 Chris Calloway	.05	.02	.01
☐ 119 Rodney Hampton	.10	.05	.01
☐ 120 Phillippi Sparks	.05	.02	.01
☐ 121 Amani Toomer	.10	.05	.01
☐ 122 Ty Detmer	.10	.05	.01
☐ 123 Jason Dunn	.10	.05	.01
☐ 124 Irving Fryar	.10	.05	.01
☐ 125 Chris T. Jones	.20	.09	.03
☐ 126 Ricky Watters	.10	.05	.01
☐ 127 Tony Banks	.30	.14	.04
☐ 128 Isaac Bruce	.20	.09	.03
☐ 129 Eddie Kennison	.50	.23	.06
☐ 130 Lawrence Phillips	.10	.05	.01
☐ 131 Merton Hanks	.05	.02	.01
☐ 132 Terry Kirby	.10	.05	.01
☐ 133 Ken Norton	.05	.02	.01
☐ 134 Jerry Rice	1.00	.45	.12
☐ 135 J.J. Stokes	.10	.05	.01
☐ 136 Steve Young	.60	.25	.07
☐ 137 Alvin Harper	.05	.02	.01
☐ 138 Jackie Harris	.05	.02	.01
☐ 139 Hardy Nickerson	.05	.02	.01
☐ 140 Errict Rhett	.10	.05	.01
☐ 141 Terry Allen	.10	.05	.01
☐ 142 Henry Ellard	.10	.05	.01
☐ 143 Gus Frerotte	.20	.09	.03
☐ 144 Brian Mitchell	.05	.02	.01
☐ 145 Michael Westbrook	.20	.09	.03
☐ 146 Chuck Bednarik	.10	.05	.01
☐ 147 Y.A. Tittle	.10	.05	.01
☐ 148 Checklist	.05	.02	.01
☐ 149 Checklist	.05	.02	.01
☐ 150 Checklist	.05	.02	.01
☐ P1 Brett Favre Promo unnumbered base card	2.00	.90	.25

1997 Fleer Goudey Bednarik Says

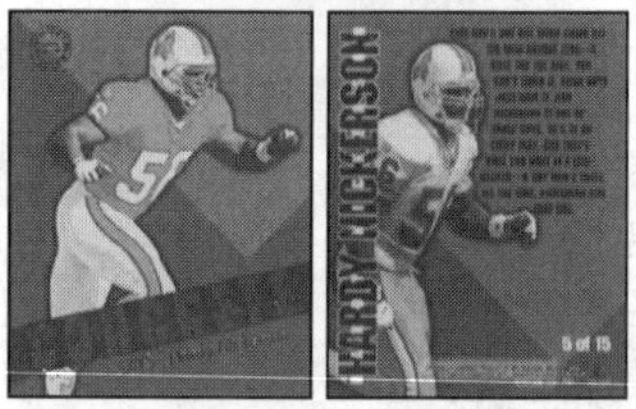

Inserted at the rate of one in 60 hobby and one in 72 retail packs, this 15 card insert highlights Bednarik's personally chosen Top 15 current day defenders. The cards measure 2 3/8" x 2 7/8".

	MINT	NRMT	EXC
COMPLETE SET (15)	110.00	50.00	14.00
COMMON CARD (1-15)	2.50	1.10	.30
☐ 1 Kevin Greene	4.00	1.80	.50
☐ 2 Ray Lewis	2.50	1.10	.30
☐ 3 Greg Lloyd	4.00	1.80	.50
☐ 4 Chester McGlockton	2.50	1.10	.30
☐ 5 Hardy Nickerson	2.50	1.10	.30
☐ 6 Bryce Paup	4.00	1.80	.50
☐ 7 Simeon Rice	4.00	1.80	.50
☐ 8 Deion Sanders	12.00	5.50	1.50
☐ 9 Junior Seau	6.00	2.70	.75
☐ 10 Bruce Smith	6.00	2.70	.75
☐ 11 Derrick Thomas	4.00	1.80	.50
☐ 12 Zach Thomas	10.00	4.50	1.25
☐ 13 Eric Turner	2.50	1.10	.30
☐ 14 Reggie White	8.00	3.60	1.00
☐ 15 Rod Woodson	4.00	1.80	.50

1997 Fleer Goudey Gridiron Greats

Randomly inserted at a rate of one in three packs, this was a '90's' parallel to the basic set. The cards are enhanced with UV coating, foil stamping and full bleed photos. The checklists were not used in this set. Also, the Chuck Bednarik and Y.A. Tittle cards were only produced as autographed inserts. The cards measure 2 3/8" x 2 7/8".

	MINT	NRMT	EXC
COMPLETE SET (145)	80.00	36.00	10.00
COMMON CARD (1-145)	.20	.09	.03

*GRID.GREATS STARS: 2.5X TO 5X BASIC CARDS
*GRID.GREATS YOU. STARS: 1.75X TO 3.5X BASIC CARDS

1997 Fleer Goudey Heads Up

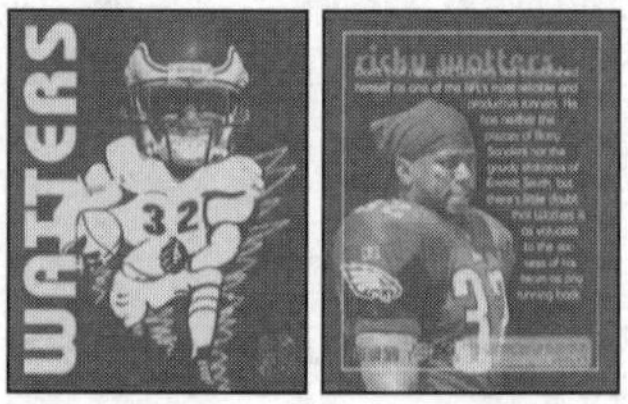

This 20 card insert can be found in one in 30 hobby and one in 36 retail packs. Inspired by Goudey's 1938 "Heads Up" cards, the set's design has oversized head photos on black and white cartoon body drawings on a foil enhanced card stock. The cards measure 2 3/8" x 2 7/8".

	MINT	NRMT	EXC
COMPLETE SET (20)	135.00	60.00	17.00
COMMON CARD (1-20)	4.00	1.80	.50
☐ 1 Troy Aikman	12.00	5.50	1.50
☐ 2 Marcus Allen	6.00	2.70	.75
☐ 3 Tim Biakabutuka	6.00	2.70	.75
☐ 4 Robert Brooks	6.00	2.70	.75
☐ 5 Isaac Bruce	6.00	2.70	.75
☐ 6 Kerry Collins	10.00	4.50	1.25
☐ 7 Terrell Davis	12.00	5.50	1.50
☐ 8 Brett Favre	25.00	11.00	3.10
☐ 9 Terry Glenn	15.00	6.75	1.85
☐ 10 Rodney Hampton	4.00	1.80	.50
☐ 11 Michael Irvin	6.00	2.70	.75

	MINT	NRMT	EXC
12 Chris T. Jones	6.00	2.70	.75
13 Carl Pickens	4.00	1.80	.50
14 Barry Sanders	12.00	5.50	1.50
15 Kordell Stewart	10.00	4.50	1.25
16 Thurman Thomas	6.00	2.70	.75
17 Tamarick Vanover	6.00	2.70	.75
18 Chris Warren	4.00	1.80	.50
19 Ricky Watters	4.00	1.80	.50
20 Steve Young	10.00	4.50	1.25

1997 Fleer Goudey Pigskin 2000

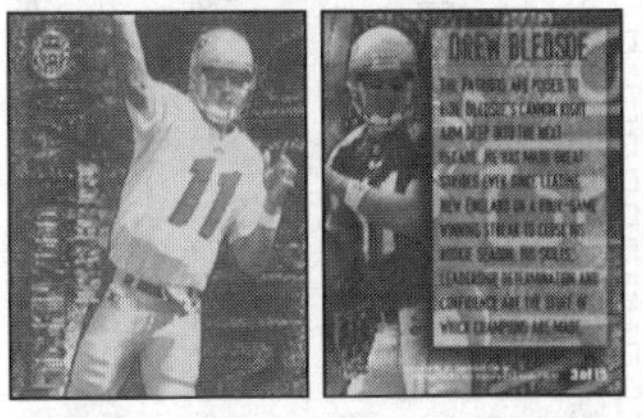

Inserted at a rate of one 360 hobby packs, this 15 card set highlights up-and-coming players that could be the future of the NFL in the year 2000. The cards utilize a multi-colored foil style that Fleer says embodies the "card of the future" design. The cards measure 2 3/8" x 2 7/8".

	MINT	NRMT	EXC
COMPLETE SET (15)	250.00	110.00	31.00
COMMON CARD (1-15)	10.00	4.50	1.25
1 Karim Abdul-Jabbar	25.00	11.00	3.10
2 Jeff Blake	10.00	4.50	1.25
3 Drew Bledsoe	40.00	18.00	5.00
4 Robert Brooks	10.00	4.50	1.25
5 Terrell Davis	30.00	13.50	3.70
6 Marshall Faulk	15.00	6.75	1.85
7 Joey Galloway	15.00	6.75	1.85
8 Eddie George	40.00	18.00	5.00
9 Terry Glenn	30.00	13.50	3.70
10 Keyshawn Johnson	15.00	6.75	1.85
11 Chris T. Jones	10.00	4.50	1.25
12 Curtis Martin	30.00	13.50	3.70
13 Steve McNair	15.00	6.75	1.85
14 Lawrence Phillips	10.00	4.50	1.25
15 Kordell Stewart	25.00	11.00	3.10

1997 Fleer Goudey Tittle Says

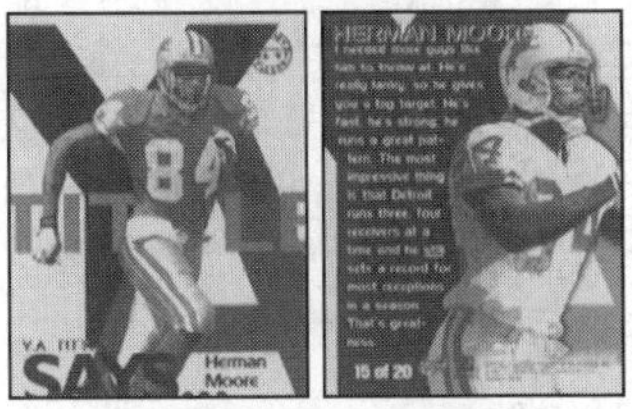

Coming out of packs at the rate of one in 72 hobby and one in 85 retail packs, this 20 card set highlights Tittle's personal Top 20 current day offensive players. The cards measuring 2 3/8" x 2 7/8", show a picture of the player on a white background that also includes a large "Y" and "A" on the card fronts. The player's name is written in gold foil stamping.

	MINT	NRMT	EXC
COMPLETE SET (20)	200.00	90.00	25.00
COMMON CARD (1-20)	4.00	1.80	.50
1 Karim Abdul-Jabbar	12.00	5.50	1.50
2 Jerome Bettis	8.00	3.60	1.00
3 Tim Brown	6.00	2.70	.75
4 Isaac Bruce	8.00	3.60	1.00
5 Cris Carter	4.00	1.80	.50
6 Curtis Conway	4.00	1.80	.50
7 John Elway	10.00	4.50	1.25
8 Marshall Faulk	8.00	3.60	1.00
9 Brett Favre	25.00	11.00	3.10
10 Joey Galloway	8.00	3.60	1.00
11 Eddie George	20.00	9.00	2.50
12 Keyshawn Johnson	10.00	4.50	1.25
13 Dan Marino	25.00	11.00	3.10
14 Curtis Martin	15.00	6.75	1.85
15 Herman Moore	8.00	3.60	1.00
16 Jerry Rice	12.00	5.50	1.50
17 Barry Sanders	12.00	5.50	1.50
18 Emmitt Smith	25.00	11.00	3.10
19 Thurman Thomas	8.00	3.60	1.00
20 Ricky Watters	6.00	2.70	.75

1995 FlickBall NFL Helmets

FlickBall produced its first full set of "paper footballs" in 1995 as NFL Team Helmets. Each flickball features an NFL helmet and were packaged 6 per pack. There were two special inaugural season expansion team flickballs (#61-62) randomly inserted at the rate of 1:48 packs. They are not considered part of the complete set price.

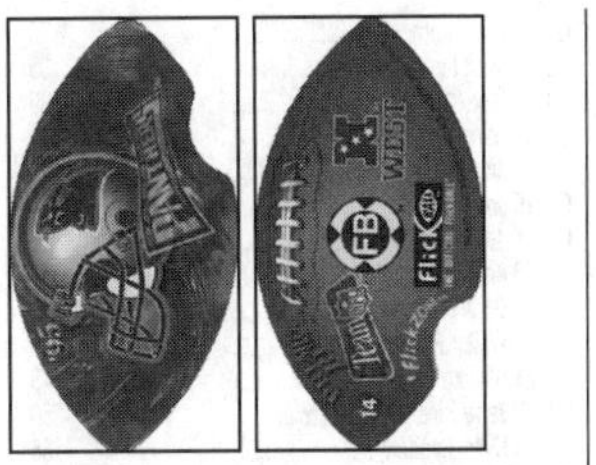

	MINT	NRMT	EXC
COMPLETE SET (60)	20.00	9.00	2.50
COMMON CARD (1-62)	.30	.14	.04
1 Dallas Cowboys	.50	.23	.06
2 New York Giants	.30	.14	.04
3 Arizona Cardinals	.30	.14	.04
4 Philadelphia Eagles	.30	.14	.04
5 Washington Redskins	.50	.23	.06
6 Minnesota Vikings	.30	.14	.04
7 Chicago Bears	.30	.14	.04
8 Green Bay Packers	.50	.23	.06
9 Detroit Lions	.30	.14	.04
10 Tampa Bay Buccaneers	.30	.14	.04
11 San Francisco 49ers	.50	.23	.06
12 New Orleans Saints	.30	.14	.04
13 Atlanta Falcons	.30	.14	.04
14 Carolina Panthers	.50	.23	.06
15 St.Louis Rams	.30	.14	.04
16 New England Patriots	.30	.14	.04
17 Miami Dolphins	.50	.23	.06
18 Buffalo Bills	.30	.14	.04
19 Indianapolis Colts	.30	.14	.04
20 New York Jets	.30	.14	.04
21 Pittsburgh Steelers	.50	.23	.06
22 Cleveland Browns	.30	.14	.04
23 Cincinnati Bengals	.30	.14	.04
24 Jacksonville Jaguars	.50	.23	.06
25 Houston Oilers	.30	.14	.04
26 San Diego Chargers	.30	.14	.04
27 Oakland Raiders	.50	.23	.06
28 Kansas City Chiefs	.30	.14	.04
29 Denver Broncos	.30	.14	.04
30 Seattle Seahawks	.30	.14	.04
31 Super Bowl I	.30	.14	.04
32 Super Bowl II	.30	.14	.04
33 Super Bowl III	.30	.14	.04
34 Super Bowl IV	.30	.14	.04
35 Super Bowl V	.30	.14	.04
36 Super Bowl VI	.30	.14	.04
37 Super Bowl VII	.30	.14	.04
38 Super Bowl VIII	.30	.14	.04
39 Super Bowl IX	.30	.14	.04
40 Super Bowl X	.30	.14	.04
41 Super Bowl XI	.30	.14	.04
42 Super Bowl XII	.30	.14	.04
43 Super Bowl XIII	.30	.14	.04
44 Super Bowl XIV	.30	.14	.04
45 Super Bowl XV	.30	.14	.04
46 Super Bowl XVI	.30	.14	.04
47 Super Bowl XVII	.30	.14	.04
48 Super Bowl XVIII	.30	.14	.04
49 Super Bowl XIX	.30	.14	.04
50 Super Bowl XX	.30	.14	.04
51 Super Bowl XXI	.30	.14	.04
52 Super Bowl XXII	.30	.14	.04
53 Super Bowl XXIII	.30	.14	.04
54 Super Bowl XXIV	.30	.14	.04
55 Super Bowl XXV	.30	.14	.04
56 Super Bowl XXVI	.30	.14	.04
57 Super Bowl XXVII	.30	.14	.04
58 Super Bowl XXVIII	.30	.14	.04
59 Super Bowl XXIX	.30	.14	.04
60 Super Bowl XXX Logo	.30	.14	.04
61 Carolina Panthers Inaugural Season	1.00	.45	.12
62 Jacksonville Jaguars Inaugural Season	1.00	.45	.12

1995 FlickBall Prototypes

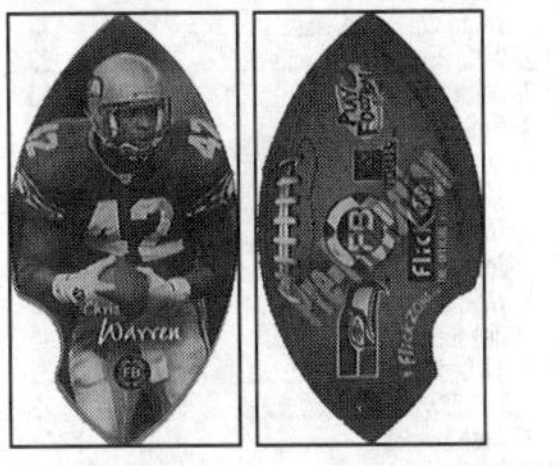

FlickBall produced this set as Prototypes for its 1996 premier FlickBall release. The 10-card, football-shaped set measures approximately 2 1/4" by 1 1/4" and features a finger-size cut-out space called the "flick zone" used to "flick" the card (ball) as part of a football game. The fronts feature color player photos while the backs include logos and the "Pre-Production" title. Card number seven is called a "Double Flick" and has a different player on each side. The cards are unnumbered and checklisted below in alphabetical order.

	MINT	NRMT	EXC
COMPLETE SET (10)	5.00	2.20	.60
COMMON CARD	.20	.09	.03
1 Bill Bates	.20	.09	.03
2 Jeff Blake	.50	.23	.06
3 Drew Bledsoe	.75	.35	.09
4 Brett Favre	2.00	.90	.25
5 Kevin Greene	.20	.09	.03
6 Daryl Johnston	.20	.09	.03
7 Steve McNair Kerry Collins	1.00	.45	.12
8 Jerry Rice	1.00	.45	.12
9 Tamarick Vanover	.50	.23	.06
10 Chris Warren	.30	.14	.04

1996 FlickBall

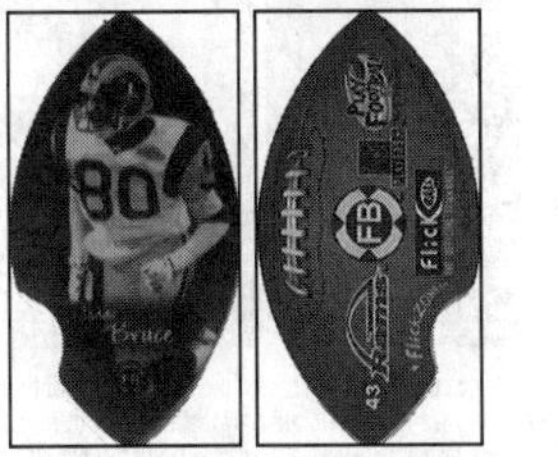

FlickBall produced a complete 100-card set in 1996. The flickballs were packaged seven to a blister pack and included several random insert sets.

	MINT	NRMT	EXC
COMPLETE SET (100)	30.00	13.50	3.70
COMMON CARD (1-100)	.15	.07	.02
1 Troy Aikman	1.50	.70	.19
2 Emmitt Smith	3.00	1.35	.35
3 Michael Irvin	.40	.18	.05
4 Deion Sanders	1.00	.45	.12
5 Bill Bates	.15	.07	.02
6 Rodney Peete	.25	.11	.03
7 Ricky Watters	.40	.18	.05
8 Fred Barnett	.25	.11	.03
9 Dave Krieg	.15	.07	.02
10 Larry Centers	.15	.07	.02
11 Garrison Hearst	.40	.18	.05
12 Dave Brown	.25	.11	.03
13 Rodney Hampton	.40	.18	.05
14 Mike Sherrard	.15	.07	.02
15 Gus Frerotte	.25	.11	.03
16 Henry Ellard	.25	.11	.03
17 Darrell Green	.15	.07	.02
18 Scott Mitchell	.40	.18	.05
19 Barry Sanders	1.50	.70	.19
20 Herman Moore	.50	.23	.06
21 Erik Kramer	.25	.11	.03
22 Curtis Conway	.40	.18	.05
23 Jeff Graham	.25	.11	.03
24 Brett Favre	3.00	1.35	.35
25 Edgar Bennett	.25	.11	.03
26 Robert Brooks	.40	.18	.05
27 Reggie White	.40	.18	.05
28 Warren Moon	.40	.18	.05
29 Robert Smith	.25	.11	.03
30 Cris Carter	.40	.18	.05
31 Trent Dilfer	.40	.18	.05
32 Errict Rhett	.50	.23	.06
33 Santana Dotson	.15	.07	.02
34 Steve Young	1.25	.55	.16
35 Jerry Rice	1.50	.70	.19
36 Merton Hanks	.15	.07	.02
37 Ken Norton	.25	.11	.03
38 Jesse Sapolu	.15	.07	.02
39 Jim Everett	.25	.11	.03
40 Willie Roaf	.15	.07	.02
41 Tyrone Hughes	.25	.11	.03
42 Chris Miller	.25	.11	.03
43 Isaac Bruce	.50	.23	.06
44 Shane Conlan	.15	.07	.02
45 Jeff George	.40	.18	.05
46 Eric Metcalf	.40	.18	.05
47 Craig Heyward	.25	.11	.03
48 Sam Mills	.15	.07	.02
49 Mark Carrier WR	.25	.11	.03
50 Brett Maxie	.15	.07	.02
51 Jim Kelly	.40	.18	.05
52 Andre Reed	.25	.11	.03
53 Bruce Smith	.25	.11	.03
54 Bryce Paup	.25	.11	.03
55 Jim Harbaugh	.40	.18	.05
56 Marshall Faulk	.60	.25	.07
57 Sean Dawkins	.25	.11	.03
58 Dan Marino	3.00	1.35	.35
59 Terry Kirby	.25	.11	.03
60 O.J. McDuffie	.40	.18	.05
61 Bernie Parmalee	.25	.11	.03
62 Wayne Chrebet	.40	.18	.05
63 Adrian Murrell	.25	.11	.03
64 Ronald Moore	.25	.11	.03
65 Drew Bledsoe	1.50	.70	.19
66 Vincent Brisby	.25	.11	.03
67 Vincent Brown	.15	.07	.02
68 Neil O'Donnell UER name spelled Niel	.40	.18	.05
69 Erric Pegram	.25	.11	.03
70 Rohn Stark	.15	.07	.02
71 Kevin Greene	.25	.11	.03
72 Greg Lloyd	.40	.18	.05
73 Todd McNair	.15	.07	.02
74 Mark Stepnoski	.15	.07	.02
75 Bruce Matthews	.15	.07	.02
76 Jeff Blake	.75	.35	.09
77 Carl Pickens	.40	.18	.05
78 John Copeland	.15	.07	.02
79 Vinny Testaverde	.15	.07	.02
80 Andre Rison	.25	.11	.03
81 Leroy Hoard	.15	.07	.02
82 Mark Brunell	.40	.18	.05
83 Cedric Tillman	.15	.07	.02
84 Desmond Howard	.25	.11	.03
85 Stan Humphries	.40	.18	.05
86 Natrone Means	.25	.11	.03
87 Junior Seau	.40	.18	.05
88 Steve Bono	.40	.18	.05
89 Marcus Allen	.25	.11	.03
90 Derrick Thomas	.25	.11	.03
91 Neil Smith	.25	.11	.03
92 Rick Mirer	.40	.18	.05
93 Chris Warren	.40	.18	.05
94 Cortez Kennedy	.25	.11	.03
95 Jeff Hostetler	.25	.11	.03
96 Tim Brown	.40	.18	.05
97 Terry McDaniel	.15	.07	.02
98 John Elway	1.25	.55	.16
99 Shannon Sharpe	.25	.11	.03
100 Steve Atwater	.15	.07	.02

1996 FlickBall Commemoratives

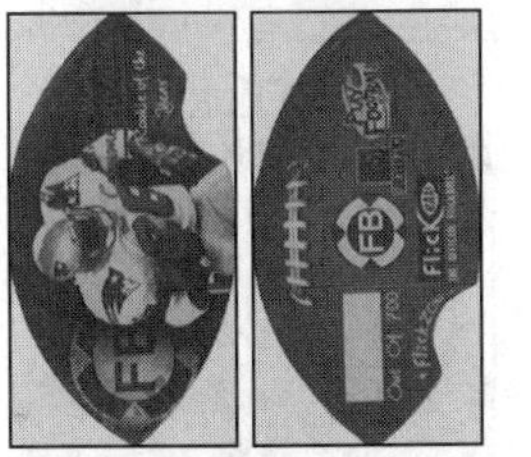

These four inserts into 1996 FlickBall blister packs were hand numbered of 700. They feature four standout NFL players and were inserted at the rate of 1:357 packs.

	MINT	NRMT	EXC
COMPLETE SET (4)	70.00	32.00	8.75
COMMON CARD (C1-C4)	15.00	6.75	1.85
C1 Emmitt Smith 25 Touchdowns	20.00	9.00	2.50
C2 Dan Marino Most passing yards	20.00	9.00	2.50
C3 Brett Favre MVP	20.00	9.00	2.50
C4 Curtis Martin Rookie of the Year	15.00	6.75	1.85

1996 FlickBall DoubleFlicks

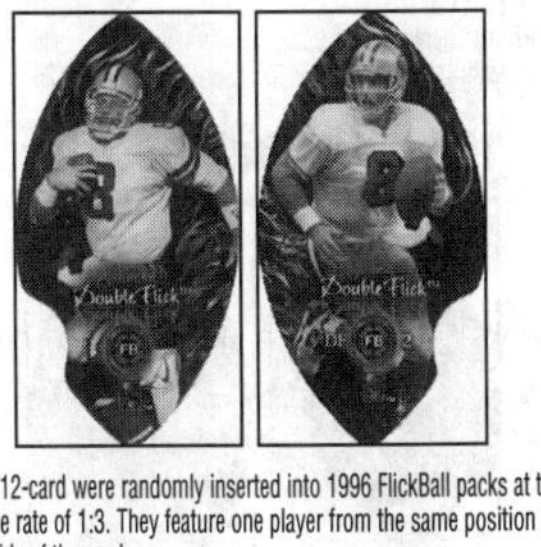

These 12-card were randomly inserted into 1996 FlickBall packs at the average rate of 1:3. They feature one player from the same position on each side of the card.

	MINT	NRMT	EXC
COMPLETE SET (12)	20.00	9.00	2.50
COMMON CARD (DF1-DF12)	1.00	.45	.12
DF1 Dan Marino Drew Bledsoe	4.00	1.80	.50
DF2 Troy Aikman Steve Young	2.50	1.10	.30
DF3 Kerry Collins Steve McNair	2.00	.90	.25
DF4 Eric Zeier Kordell Stewart	2.00	.90	.25
DF5 Emmitt Smith Marshall Faulk	4.00	1.80	.50
DF6 Barry Sanders Errict Rhett	2.00	.90	.25

		MINT	NRMT	EXC
☐	DF7 Curtis Martin / Terrell Davis	3.00	1.35	.35
☐	DF8 Rashaan Salaam / Napoleon Kaufman	1.50	.70	.19
☐	DF9 Michael Irvin / Jerry Rice	2.00	.90	.25
☐	DF10 Tim Brown / Cris Carter	1.00	.45	.12
☐	DF11 Joey Galloway / J.J. Stokes	1.50	.70	.19
☐	DF12 Frank Sanders / Michael Westbrook	1.50	.70	.19

1996 FlickBall Hawaiian Flicks

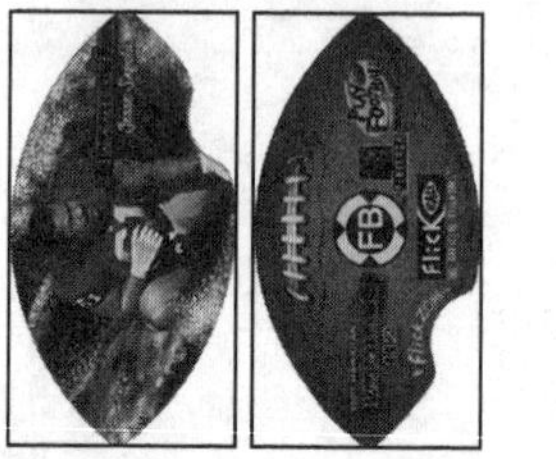

These 4-cards were randomly inserted into 1996 FlickBall blister packs at the rate of 1:8. They feature NFL players native to Hawaii.

	MINT	NRMT	EXC
COMPLETE SET (4)	5.00	2.20	.60
COMMON CARD (H1-H4)	1.00	.45	.12
☐ H1 Mark Tuinei	1.00	.45	.12
☐ H2 Jesse Sapolu	1.00	.45	.12
☐ H3 Jason Elam	1.00	.45	.12
☐ H4 Junior Seau	2.00	.90	.25

1996 FlickBall PreviewFlick Cowboys

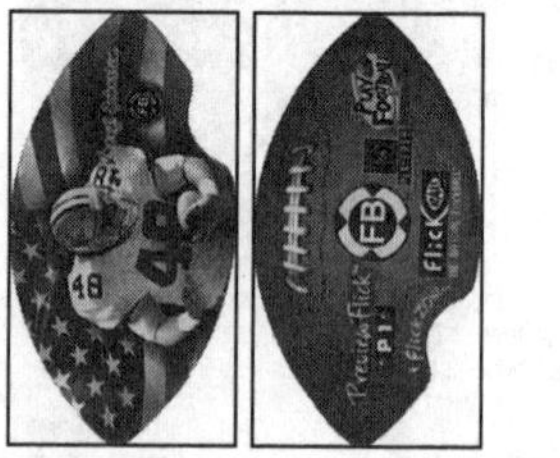

Random 1996 FlickBall packs contained these 8-cards. They feature Dallas Cowboys players and carry a "P" card number prefix. The insertion ratio was 1:4 packs.

	MINT	NRMT	EXC
COMPLETE SET (8)	6.00	2.70	.75
COMMON CARD (P1-P8)	.75	.35	.09
☐ P1 Daryl Johnston	1.00	.45	.12
☐ P2 Jay Novacek	1.00	.45	.12
☐ P3 Kevin Williams WR	.75	.35	.09
☐ P4 Charles Haley	1.00	.45	.12
☐ P5 Darren Woodson	.75	.35	.09
☐ P6 Leon Lett	.75	.35	.09
☐ P7 Chad Hennings	.75	.35	.09
☐ P8 Mark Tuinei	.75	.35	.09

1996 FlickBall Rookies

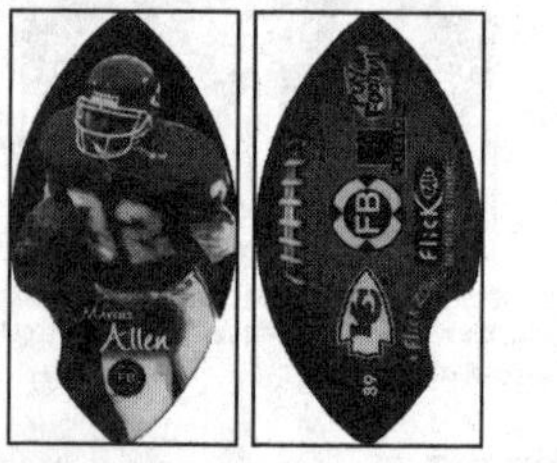

Randomly inserted into 1996 FlickBall packs at the rate of 1:2, these 20-cards feature top 1995 NFL rookies.

	MINT	NRMT	EXC
COMPLETE SET (20)	15.00	6.75	1.85
COMMON CARD (R1-R20)	.30	.14	.04
☐ R1 Sherman Williams	.30	.14	.04
☐ R2 Mike Mamula	.30	.14	.04
☐ R3 Frank Sanders	.40	.18	.05
☐ R4 Steve Stenstrom	.30	.14	.04
☐ R5 Michael Westbrook	.50	.23	.06
☐ R6 Warren Sapp	.30	.14	.04
☐ R7 Rashaan Salaam	.50	.23	.06
☐ R8 J.J. Stokes	.50	.23	.06
☐ R9 Kevin Carter	.30	.14	.04
☐ R10 Kerry Collins	2.50	1.10	.30
☐ R11 Curtis Martin	2.50	1.10	.30
☐ R12 Kordell Stewart	2.50	1.10	.30
☐ R13 Steve McNair	2.00	.90	.25
☐ R14 Rodney Thomas	.40	.18	.05
☐ R15 Eric Zeier	.40	.18	.05
☐ R16 Tony Boselli	.40	.18	.05
☐ R17 Tamarick Vanover	.50	.23	.06
☐ R18 Joey Galloway	.75	.35	.09
☐ R19 Napoleon Kaufman	.40	.18	.05
☐ R20 Terrell Davis	2.50	1.10	.30

1996 FlickBall Team Sets

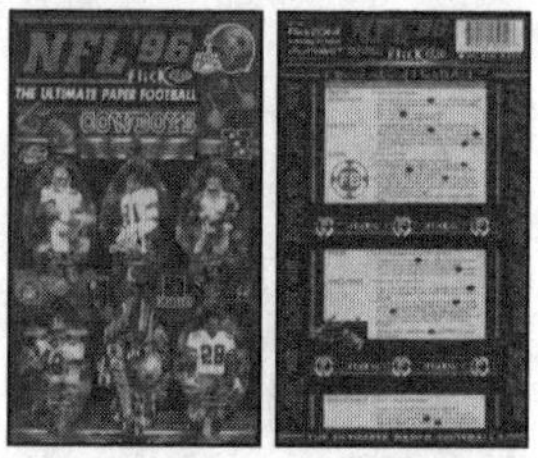

MGwhiz, Inc., the makers or FlickBall products, developed this set as a test. The three teams were primarily distributed in their respective areas. Each team was individually packaged with five players and one team helmet mounted on a display backer board. We've added the team name initials to the card numbers below to assist with cataloging. There are no prefixes on the actual card numbers.

	MINT	NRMT	EXC
COMPLETE SET (18)	16.00	7.25	2.00
COMP.COWBOYS SET (6)	7.00	3.10	.85
COMP.VIKINGS SET (6)	3.50	1.55	.45
COMP.PACKERS SET (6)	6.00	2.70	.75
COMMON CARD	.50	.23	.06
☐ DC1 Troy Aikman	2.00	.90	.25
☐ DC2 Deion Sanders	1.25	.55	.16
☐ DC3 Emmitt Smith	4.00	1.80	.50
☐ DC4 Daryl Johnston	.75	.35	.09
☐ DC5 Cowboys Helmet	.50	.23	.06
☐ DC6 Darren Woodson	.50	.23	.06
☐ MV1 Warren Moon	.75	.35	.09
☐ MV2 Cris Carter	.75	.35	.09
☐ MV3 Robert Smith	.75	.35	.09
☐ MV4 Qadry Ismail	.50	.23	.06
☐ MV5 Vikings Helmet	.50	.23	.06
☐ MV6 David Palmer	.50	.23	.06
☐ GBP1 Brett Favre	4.00	1.80	.50
☐ GBP2 Edgar Bennett	.75	.35	.09
☐ GBP3 Reggie White	1.00	.45	.12
☐ GBP4 Robert Brooks	1.50	.70	.19
☐ GBP5 Packers Helmet	.50	.23	.06
☐ GBP6 George Teague	.50	.23	.06

1988 Football Heroes Sticker Book

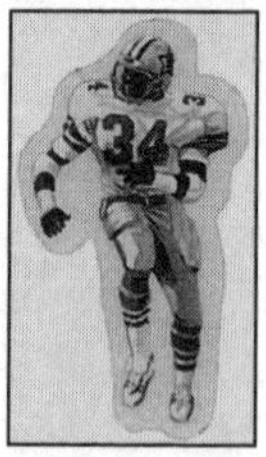

This sticker book contains 20 pages and measures approximately 9 1/4" by 12 1/2". It serves as an introduction to American football, with a discussion of how the game is played and a glossary of terms. The bulk of the book discusses various positions (e.g., quarterbacks, running backs, tight ends, wide receivers, kickers, offensive linemen, and defensive linemen), and outstanding NFL players who fill these positions. The stickers are approximately 3" in height and issued on two sheets, with 15 stickers per sheet. They are to be pasted on a glossy "Football Heroes" poster, which has an imitation-wood picture frame and slots for only 15 player stickers. The cards are unnumbered and checklisted below in alphabetical order.

	MINT	NRMT	EXC
COMPLETE SET (30)	50.00	22.00	6.25
COMMON CARD (1-30)	.75	.35	.09
SEMISTARS	1.00	.45	.12
☐ 1 Marcus Allen	2.00	.90	.25
☐ 2 Gary Anderson K	.75	.35	.09
☐ 3 Brian Bosworth	.75	.35	.09
☐ 4 Anthony Carter	1.00	.45	.12
☐ 5 Deron Cherry	.75	.35	.09
☐ 6 Eric Dickerson	1.00	.45	.12
☐ 7 John Elway	7.50	3.40	.95
☐ 8 Bo Jackson	3.00	1.35	.35
☐ 9 Rich Karlis	.75	.35	.09
☐ 10 Bernie Kosar	1.00	.45	.12
☐ 11 Steve Largent	5.00	2.20	.60
☐ 12 Mick Luckhurst	.75	.35	.09
☐ 13 Dexter Manley	.75	.35	.09
☐ 14 Dan Marino	15.00	6.75	1.85
☐ 15 Jim McMahon	1.00	.45	.12
☐ 16 Joe Montana	10.00	4.50	1.25
☐ 17 Joe Morris	.75	.35	.09
☐ 18 Anthony Munoz	1.00	.45	.12
☐ 19 Ozzie Newsome	1.00	.45	.12
☐ 20 Walter Payton	7.50	3.40	.95
☐ 21 William Perry	1.00	.45	.12
☐ 22 Jerry Rice	10.00	4.50	1.25
☐ 23 Ricky Sanders	.75	.35	.09
☐ 24 Phil Simms	1.00	.45	.12
☐ 25 Mike Singletary	1.00	.45	.12
☐ 26 Dwight Stephenson	.75	.35	.09
☐ 27 Lawrence Taylor	2.00	.90	.25
☐ 28 Herschel Walker	2.00	.90	.25
☐ 29 Doug Williams	1.00	.45	.12
☐ 30 Kellen Winslow	1.00	.45	.12

1985-87 Football Immortals

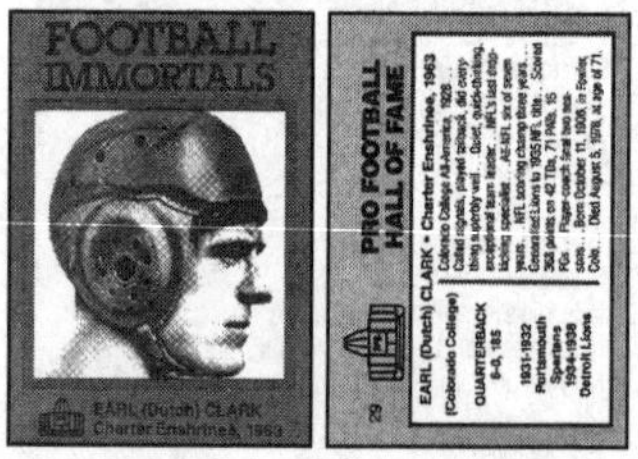

This set was produced in 1985 and 1987; since the majority of the cards in the sets are exactly the same both years, the sets are lumped together below. The 1985 set had 135 cards and the 1987 had 142 cards. In the checklist below the variation cards are listed using the following convention, that the A (or first) variety is from 1985 and the B variety is the version that was released with the 1987 set. Cards 6-128 are essentially in alphabetical order by subject's name. The cards are standard size. The horizontal card backs are light green and black on white card stock. The card photos are in black and white inside two color borders. The outer, thicker border is gold metallic. The inner border is color coded according to the number of the card, red border (1-45), blue border (46-90), green border (91-135), and yellow border (136-142). The set is titled "Football Immortals" at the top of every obverse. Since all members of the set are Football Hall of Famers, their year of induction is given on the front and back of each card. The complete set price below includes all listed variations.

	MINT	NRMT	EXC
COMPLETE SET (147)	75.00	34.00	9.50
COMMON CARD (1-135)	.35	.16	.04
COMMON CARD (136-142)	1.50	.70	.19
☐ 1 Pete Rozelle	.60	.25	.07
☐ 2 Joe Namath	1.50	.70	.19
☐ 3 Frank Gatski	.35	.16	.04
☐ 4 O.J. Simpson	1.00	.45	.12
☐ 5 Roger Staubach	1.25	.55	.16
☐ 6 Herb Adderley	.50	.23	.06
☐ 7 Lance Alworth	.60	.25	.07
☐ 8 Doug Atkins	.50	.23	.06
☐ 9 Red Badgro	.35	.16	.04
☐ 10 Cliff Battles	.35	.16	.04
☐ 11 Sammy Baugh	1.00	.45	.12
☐ 12 Raymond Berry	.60	.25	.07
☐ 13 Charles W. Bidwill	.35	.16	.04
☐ 14 Chuck Bednarik	.60	.25	.07
☐ 15 Bert Bell	.35	.16	.04
☐ 16 Bobby Bell	.50	.23	.06
☐ 17 George Blanda	.60	.25	.07
☐ 18 Jim Brown	1.25	.55	.16
☐ 19 Paul Brown	.75	.35	.09
☐ 20 Roosevelt Brown	.50	.23	.06
☐ 21 Ray Flaherty	.35	.16	.04
☐ 22 Len Ford	.35	.16	.04
☐ 23 Dan Fortmann	.35	.16	.04
☐ 24 Bill George	.50	.23	.06
☐ 25 Art Donovan	.60	.25	.07
☐ 26 Paddy Driscoll	.35	.16	.04
☐ 27 Jimmy Conzelman	.35	.16	.04
☐ 28 Willie Davis	.50	.23	.06
☐ 29 Dutch Clark	.50	.23	.06
☐ 30 George Connor	.50	.23	.06
☐ 31 Guy Chamberlin	.35	.16	.04
☐ 32 Jack Christiansen	.50	.23	.06
☐ 33 Tony Canadeo	.50	.23	.06
☐ 34 Joe Carr	.35	.16	.04
☐ 35 Willie Brown	.50	.23	.06
☐ 36 Dick Butkus	1.00	.45	.12
☐ 37 Bill Dudley	.50	.23	.06
☐ 38 Turk Edwards	.50	.23	.06
☐ 39 Weeb Ewbank	.35	.16	.04
☐ 40 Tom Fears	.50	.23	.06
☐ 41 Otto Graham	1.00	.45	.12
☐ 42 Red Grange	1.00	.45	.12
☐ 43 Frank Gifford	1.00	.45	.12
☐ 44 Sid Gillman	.35	.16	.04
☐ 45 Forrest Gregg	.50	.23	.06
☐ 46 Lou Groza	.75	.35	.09
☐ 47 Joe Guyon	.35	.16	.04
☐ 48 George Halas	.75	.35	.09
☐ 49 Ed Healey	.35	.16	.04
☐ 50 Mel Hein	.35	.16	.04
☐ 51 Fats Henry	.50	.23	.06
☐ 52 Arnie Herber	.35	.16	.04
☐ 53 Bill Hewitt	.35	.16	.04
☐ 54 Clarke Hinkle	.35	.16	.04
☐ 55 Elroy Hirsch	.60	.25	.07
☐ 56 Robert(Cal) Hubbard	.35	.16	.04
☐ 57 Sam Huff	.50	.23	.06
☐ 58 Lamar Hunt	.35	.16	.04
☐ 59 Don Hutson	.50	.23	.06
☐ 60 Dave(Deacon) Jones	.50	.23	.06
☐ 61 Sonny Jurgensen	.50	.23	.06
☐ 62 Walt Kiesling	.35	.16	.04
☐ 63 Frank(Bruiser) Kinard	.35	.16	.04
☐ 64 Earl(Curly) Lambeau	.35	.16	.04
☐ 65 Dick(Night Train)Lane	.50	.23	.06
☐ 66 Yale Lary	.50	.23	.06
☐ 67 Dante Lavelli	.50	.23	.06
☐ 68 Bobby Layne	1.00	.45	.12
☐ 69 Tuffy Leemans	.35	.16	.04
☐ 70 Bob Lilly	.50	.23	.06
☐ 71 Vince Lombardi	.75	.35	.09
☐ 72 Sid Luckman	1.00	.45	.12
☐ 73 Link Lyman	.35	.16	.04
☐ 74 Tim Mara	.35	.16	.04
☐ 75 Gino Marchetti	.50	.23	.06
☐ 76 Geo.Preston Marshall	.35	.16	.04
☐ 77 Ollie Matson	.60	.25	.07
☐ 78 George McAfee	.50	.23	.06
☐ 79 Mike McCormack	.50	.23	.06
☐ 80 Hugh McElhenny	.60	.25	.07
☐ 81 Johnny(Blood) McNally	.35	.16	.04
☐ 82 Mike Michalske	.35	.16	.04
☐ 83 Wayne Millner	.35	.16	.04
☐ 84 Bobby Mitchell	.50	.23	.06
☐ 85 Ron Mix	.50	.23	.06
☐ 86 Lenny Moore	.60	.25	.07
☐ 87 Marion Motley	.60	.25	.07
☐ 88 George Musso	.35	.16	.04
☐ 89 Bronko Nagurski	.75	.35	.09
☐ 90 Greasy Neale	.35	.16	.04
☐ 91 Ernie Nevers	.50	.23	.06
☐ 92 Ray Nitschke	.50	.23	.06
☐ 93 Leo Nomellini	.50	.23	.06
☐ 94 Merlin Olsen	.50	.23	.06
☐ 95 Jim Otto	.50	.23	.06
☐ 96 Steve Owen	.35	.16	.04
☐ 97 Clarence(Ace) Parker	.35	.16	.04
☐ 98 Jim Parker	.50	.23	.06
☐ 99 Joe Perry	.60	.25	.07
☐ 100 Pete Pihos	.50	.23	.06
☐ 101 Hugh(Shorty) Ray	.35	.16	.04
☐ 102 Dan Reeves OWN	.35	.16	.04
☐ 103 Jim Ringo	.50	.23	.06
☐ 104 Andy Robustelli	.50	.23	.06
☐ 105 Art Rooney	.35	.16	.04
☐ 106 Gale Sayers	1.00	.45	.12
☐ 107 Joe Schmidt	.50	.23	.06
☐ 108 Bart Starr	1.00	.45	.12
☐ 109 Ernie Stautner	.50	.23	.06
☐ 110 Ken Strong	.50	.23	.06
☐ 111 Joe Stydahar	.35	.16	.04
☐ 112 Charley Taylor	.50	.23	.06
☐ 113 Jim Taylor	.60	.25	.07
☐ 114 Jim Thorpe	1.00	.45	.12
☐ 115 Y.A. Tittle	1.00	.45	.12
☐ 116 George Trafton	.35	.16	.04
☐ 117 Charley Trippi	.50	.23	.06
☐ 118 Emlen Tunnell	.50	.23	.06
☐ 119 Bulldog Turner	.50	.23	.06
☐ 120 Johnny Unitas	1.25	.55	.16
☐ 121 Norm Van Brocklin	.75	.35	.09
☐ 122 Steve Van Buren	.60	.25	.07
☐ 123 Paul Warfield	.50	.23	.06
☐ 124 Bob Waterfield	.75	.35	.09
☐ 125 Arnie Weinmeister	.35	.16	.04
☐ 126 Bill Willis	.35	.16	.04
☐ 127 Larry Wilson	.50	.23	.06
☐ 128 Alex Wojciechowicz	.35	.16	.04
☐ 129 Pro Football Hall of Fame (Entrance pictured)	.35	.16	.04
☐ 130A Jim Thorpe Statue	1.25	.55	.16
☐ 130B Doak Walker	3.00	1.35	.35
☐ 131A Enshrinement Galleries	1.00	.45	.12
☐ 131B Willie Lanier	2.00	.90	.25
☐ 132 Pro Football Hall of Fame on Enshrinement Day (Aerial shot of crowd)	.35	.16	.04
☐ 133A Eric Dickerson Display	1.25	.55	.16
☐ 133B Paul Hornung	4.00	1.80	.50
☐ 134A Walter Payton Display	1.25	.55	.16
☐ 134B Ken Houston	2.00	.90	.25
☐ 135A Super Bowl Display	1.00	.45	.12
☐ 135B Fran Tarkenton	5.00	2.20	.60
☐ 136 Don Maynard	2.50	1.10	.30
☐ 137 Larry Csonka	4.00	1.80	.50
☐ 138 Joe Greene	4.00	1.80	.50
☐ 139 Len Dawson	3.50	1.55	.45

☐ 140 Gene Upshaw	2.00	.90	.25
☐ 141 Jim Langer	1.50	.70	.19
☐ 142 John Henry Johnson	2.00	.90	.25

1966 Fortune Shoes

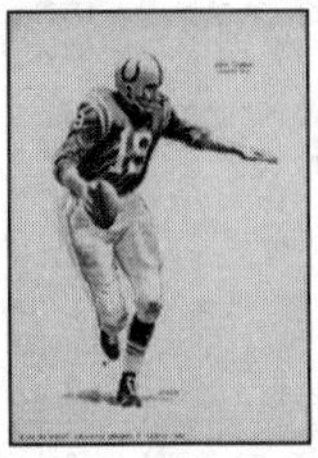

Fortune Shoe Company sponsored this set of 9" by 12" black-and-white pencil sketches. The unnumbered cards are blankbacked and were printed on thick paper stock. The set is likely larger than the below cataloged cards. Any additions to this list would be appreciated.

	NRMT	VG-E	GOOD
COMPLETE SET (7)	125.00	55.00	15.50
COMMON CARD (1-7)	10.00	4.50	1.25
☐ 1 Roman Gabriel	10.00	4.50	1.25
☐ 2 Charlie Johnson	10.00	4.50	1.25
☐ 3 John Henry Johnson	15.00	6.75	1.85
☐ 4 Don Meredith	25.00	11.00	3.10
☐ 5 Frank Ryan	10.00	4.50	1.25
☐ 6 Gale Sayers	40.00	18.00	5.00
☐ 7 John Unitas	25.00	11.00	3.10

1955 49ers Team Issue

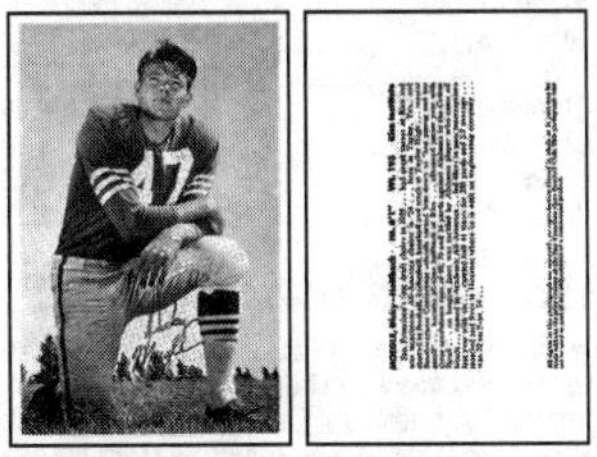

This 38-card set measures approximately 4 1/4" by 6 1/4". The front features a black and white posed action photo enclosed by a white border, with the player's signature across the bottom portion of the picture. The back of the card lists the player's name, position, height, weight, and college, along with basic biographical information. Many of the cards in this and the other similar team issue sets are only distinguishable as to year by comparing text on the card back; the first few words of text are provided for many of the cards parenthetically below. The set was available direct from the team as part of a package for their fans. The cards are unnumbered and hence are listed alphabetically for convenience.

	NRMT	VG-E	GOOD
COMPLETE SET (38)	250.00	110.00	31.00
COMMON CARD (1-38)	4.00	1.80	.50
☐ 1 Frankie Albert CO	5.00	2.20	.60
(One of Red ...)			
☐ 2 Joe Arenas	4.00	1.80	.50
(The All-Time ...)			
☐ 3 Harry Babcock	4.00	1.80	.50
☐ 4 Ed Beatty	4.00	1.80	.50
(After searching ...)			
☐ 5 Phil Bengtson CO	5.00	2.20	.60
(An All-America ...)			
☐ 6 Rex Berry	4.00	1.80	.50
(One of the ...)			
☐ 7 Hardy Brown	12.00	5.50	1.50
☐ 8 Marion Campbell	6.00	2.70	.75
☐ 9 Al Carapella	4.00	1.80	.50
☐ 10 Paul Carr	4.00	1.80	.50
(Drafted by ...)			
☐ 11 Maury Duncan	4.00	1.80	.50
☐ 12 Bob Hantla	4.00	1.80	.50
☐ 13 Carroll Hardy	5.00	2.20	.60
☐ 14 Matt Hazeltine	5.00	2.20	.60
(Won All-America ...)			
☐ 15 Howard(Red) Hickey CO	5.00	2.20	.60
(After 14 years ...)			
☐ 16 Doug Hogland	4.00	1.80	.50
☐ 17 Bill Johnson	4.00	1.80	.50
(Here's one ... with ten lines of text)			
☐ 18 John Henry Johnson	25.00	11.00	3.10
☐ 19 Eldred Kraemer	4.00	1.80	.50
☐ 20 Bud Laughlin	4.00	1.80	.50
☐ 21 Bobby Luna	4.00	1.80	.50
☐ 22 George Maderos	4.00	1.80	.50
(The greatest ...)			
☐ 23 Clay Matthews Sr.	6.00	2.70	.75
☐ 24 Hugh McElhenny	25.00	11.00	3.10
(NFL Commissioner ...)			
☐ 25 Dick Moegle	5.00	2.20	.60
(25 text lines)			
☐ 26 Leo Nomellini	20.00	9.00	2.50
(Leo was ...)			
☐ 27 Lou Palatella	4.00	1.80	.50
(Like Eldred ...)			
☐ 28 Joe Perry	25.00	11.00	3.10
(First man ...)			
☐ 29 Charley Powell	5.00	2.20	.60
(Charley, ...)			
☐ 30 Gordy Soltau	4.00	1.80	.50
(One of the ...)			
☐ 31 Bob St. Clair	20.00	9.00	2.50
(In two years ...)			
☐ 32 Tom Stolhandske	4.00	1.80	.50
☐ 33 Roy Storey ANN, Bob Fouts ANN, and Red Strader CO	4.00	1.80	.50
☐ 34 Red Strader CO	4.00	1.80	.50
☐ 35 Y.A. Tittle	35.00	16.00	4.40
(Jinxed by ...)			
☐ 36 Bob Toneff	4.00	1.80	.50
(Rated the ...)			
☐ 37 Billy Wilson	6.00	2.70	.75
(Named the ...)			
☐ 38 Sid Youngelman	4.00	1.80	.50

1956 49ers Team Issue

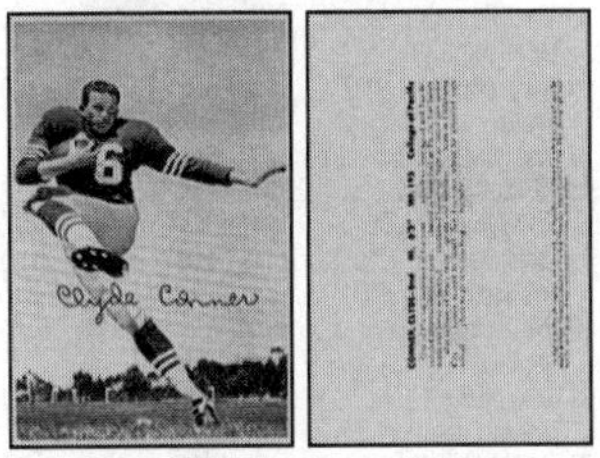

This 29-card set measures approximately 4 1/8" by 6 1/4". The front features a black and white posed action photo enclosed by a white border, with the player's signature across the bottom portion of the picture. The back of the card lists the player's name, position, height, weight, and college, along with basic biographical information. Many of the cards in this and the other similar team issue sets are only distinguishable as to year by comparing text on the card back; the first few words of text are provided for many of the cards parenthetically below. The set was available direct from the team as part of a package for their fans. The cards are unnumbered and hence are listed alphabetically for convenience.

	NRMT	VG-E	GOOD
COMPLETE SET (29)	160.00	70.00	20.00
COMMON CARD (1-29)	4.00	1.80	.50
☐ 1 Frankie Albert CO	5.00	2.20	.60
(Frank Culling Albert, who ...)			
☐ 2 Ed Beatty	4.00	1.80	.50
(Traded by ...)			
☐ 3 Phil Bengtson CO	5.00	2.20	.60
(Phil is known ...)			
☐ 4 Rex Berry	4.00	1.80	.50
(Unanimously ...)			
☐ 5 Bruce Bosley	5.00	2.20	.60
(Bosley was ...)			
☐ 6 Fred Bruney	4.00	1.80	.50
☐ 7 Paul Carr	4.00	1.80	.50
(A "redshirt" ...)			
☐ 8 Clyde Conner	4.00	1.80	.50
(One of the ...)			
☐ 9 Paul Goad	4.00	1.80	.50
☐ 10 Matt Hazeltine	5.00	2.20	.60
(Matt reported ...)			
☐ 11 Ed Henke	4.00	1.80	.50
(After attending ...)			
☐ 12 Bill Herchman	4.00	1.80	.50
(Bill was ...)			
☐ 13 Howard(Red) Hickey CO	5.00	2.20	.60
(Red Hickey ...)			
☐ 14 Bill Jessup	4.00	1.80	.50
(Bill is one ...)			
☐ 15 Bill Johnson	4.00	1.80	.50
(Here's one ... with nine lines of text)			
☐ 16 George Maderos	4.00	1.80	.50
(A 21st ...)			
☐ 17 Dick Moegle	5.00	2.20	.60
(San ... with 11 lines of text)			
☐ 18 George Morris	4.00	1.80	.50
☐ 19 Leo Nomellini	20.00	9.00	2.50
(A 49er standby ...)			
☐ 20 Lou Palatella	4.00	1.80	.50
(Most ... same as 1957)			
☐ 21 Joe Perry	25.00	11.00	3.10
(Joe is ...)			
☐ 22 Charley Powell	5.00	2.20	.60
(Equipped ...)			
☐ 23 Leo Rucka	4.00	1.80	.50
☐ 24 Ed Sharkey	4.00	1.80	.50
☐ 25 Charles Smith	4.00	1.80	.50
☐ 26 Gordy Soltau	4.00	1.80	.50
(No all-time ...)			
☐ 27 Bob St. Clair	15.00	6.75	1.85
(Tallest man ...)			
☐ 28 Bob Toneff	4.00	1.80	.50
(Another ...)			
☐ 29 Billy Wilson	5.00	2.20	.60
(Billy is ...)			

1957 49ers Team Issue

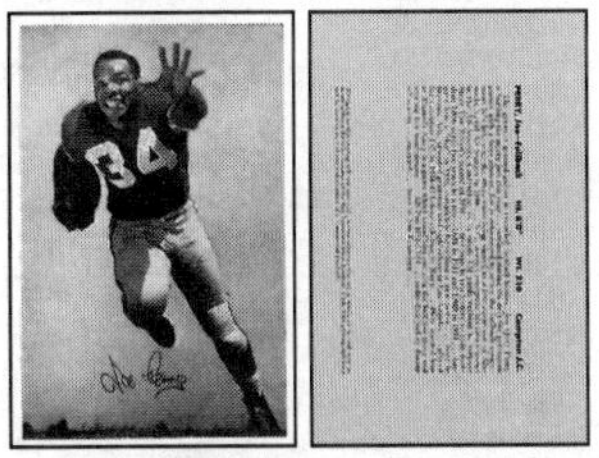

This 43-card set measures approximately 4 1/8" by 6 1/4". The front features a black and white posed action photo enclosed by a white border, with the player's signature across the bottom portion of the picture. For those players who were included in the 1956 set, the same photos were used in the 1957 set, with the exception of Bill Johnson, who appears as a coach in the 1957 set. The back lists the player's name, position, height, weight, and college, along with basic biographical information. Many of the cards in this and the other similar team issue sets are only distinguishable as to year by comparing text on the card back; the first few words of text are provided for many of the cards parenthetically below. The set was available direct from the team as part of a package for their fans. The John Brodie card in this set predates his Topps and Fleer Rookie Cards by four years. The cards are unnumbered and hence are listed alphabetically for convenience.

	NRMT	VG-E	GOOD
COMPLETE SET (43)	250.00	110.00	31.00
COMMON CARD (1-43)	4.00	1.80	.50
☐ 1 Frankie Albert CO	5.00	2.20	.60
(Frank Culling Albert played ... same as 1958)			
☐ 2 Joe Arenas	4.00	1.80	.50
(Again in 1956 ...)			
☐ 3 Gene Babb	4.00	1.80	.50
(Drafted 19th ...)			
☐ 4 Larry Barnes	4.00	1.80	.50
☐ 5 Phil Bengtson CO	5.00	2.20	.60
(Beginning his eighth ...)			
☐ 6 Bruce Bosley	5.00	2.20	.60
(After a ... same as 1958)			
☐ 7 John Brodie	35.00	16.00	4.40
(According to ...)			
☐ 8 Paul Carr	4.00	1.80	.50
(Versatile on ...)			
☐ 9 Clyde Conner	4.00	1.80	.50
(Football ...)			
☐ 10 Ted Connolly	4.00	1.80	.50
(The 49er ...)			
☐ 11 Bobby Cross	4.00	1.80	.50
☐ 12 Mark Duncan CO	4.00	1.80	.50
(Mark ... same as 1958)			
☐ 13 Bob Fouts ANN, Lon Simmons ANN, and Frankie Albert CO	4.00	1.80	.50
(Same as 1958)			
☐ 14 John Gonzaga	4.00	1.80	.50
(One of the ...)			
☐ 15 Tom Harmon ANN	7.50	3.40	.95
(Kids' ages are 11, 8, and 5)			
☐ 16 Matt Hazeltine	5.00	2.20	.60
(An All-American ...)			
☐ 17 Ed Henke	4.00	1.80	.50
(Studious-looking ...)			
☐ 18 Bill Herchman	4.00	1.80	.50
(The 49ers' ...)			
☐ 19 Howard(Red) Hickey CO	5.00	2.20	.60
(After 14 campaigns ... same as 1958)			
☐ 20 Bob Holladay	4.00	1.80	.50
☐ 21 Bill Jessup	4.00	1.80	.50
(One of the ...)			
☐ 22 Bill Johnson CO	4.00	1.80	.50
(No all-time ... same as 1958)			
☐ 23 Marv Matuszak	5.00	2.20	.60
(Traded to ...)			
☐ 24 Hugh McElhenny	20.00	9.00	2.50
(Sidelined ...)			
☐ 25 Dick Moegle	5.00	2.20	.60
(An ... with 11 lines of text)			
☐ 26 Frank Morze	4.00	1.80	.50
(The 49ers, used ...)			
☐ 27 Leo Nomellini	15.00	6.75	1.85
(He was ...)			
☐ 28 R.C. Owens	7.50	3.40	.95
(If the ...)			
☐ 29 Lou Palatella	4.00	1.80	.50
(Most ... same as 1956)			
☐ 30 Joe Perry	20.00	9.00	2.50
(The greatest ...)			
☐ 31 Charley Powell	5.00	2.20	.60
(Name almost ...)			
☐ 32 Jim Ridlon	4.00	1.80	.50
(Teaming with ...)			
☐ 33 Karl Rubke	4.00	1.80	.50
(The 16th ...)			
☐ 34 J.D. Smith	5.00	2.20	.60
(J.D.'s football ...)			
☐ 35 Gordy Soltau	4.00	1.80	.50
(Already listed ...)			
☐ 36 Bob St. Clair	12.50	5.50	1.55
(A born leader ...)			
☐ 37 Bill Stits	4.00	1.80	.50
(An All-American ...)			
☐ 38 Y.A. Tittle	30.00	13.50	3.70
(For sheer ...)			
☐ 39 Bob Toneff	4.00	1.80	.50
(After a ...)			
☐ 40 Lynn Waldorf	4.00	1.80	.50
Director of Personnel (Vertical text, same as 1958)			
☐ 41 Val Joe Walker	4.00	1.80	.50
☐ 42 Billy Wilson	5.00	2.20	.60
(Born on ...)			
☐ 43 49ers Coaches	5.00	2.20	.60
Bill Johnson, Phil Bengtson, Frankie Albert, Mark Duncan, Howard(Red) Hickey (Blank back, same as 1958)			

1958 49ers Team Issue

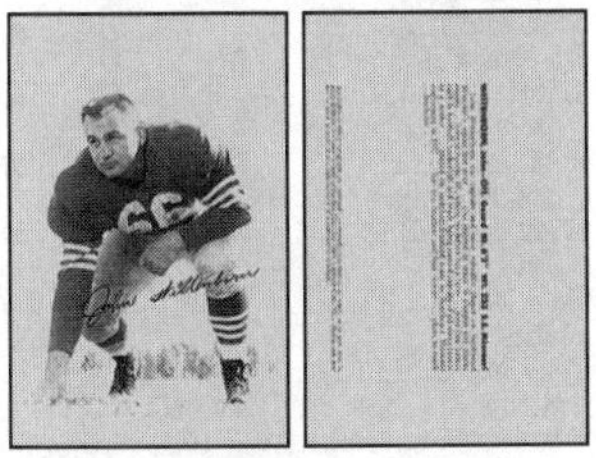

This 44-card set measures approximately 4 1/8" by 6 1/4". The front features a black and white posed action photo enclosed by a white border, with the player's signature across the bottom portion of the picture. The back lists the player's name, position, height, weight, and college, along with basic biographical information. Many of the cards in this and the other similar team issue sets are only distinguishable as to year by comparing text on the card back; the first few words of text are provided for many of the cards parenthetically below. The set was available direct from the team as part of a package for their fans. The John Brodie card in this set holds particular interest to some collectors in that it precedes Brodie's Topps and Fleer Rookie Cards by three years. The cards are unnumbered and hence are listed alphabetically for convenience.

	NRMT	VG-E	GOOD
COMPLETE SET (44)	250.00	110.00	31.00
COMMON CARD (1-44)	4.00	1.80	.50
☐ 1 Frankie Albert CO	5.00	2.20	.60
(Frank Culling Albert played ... same as 1957)			
☐ 2 Bill Atkins	4.00	1.80	.50
(Alabama ...)			
☐ 3 Gene Babb	4.00	1.80	.50
(A great ...)			
☐ 4 Phil Bengtson CO	5.00	2.20	.60
(Beginning his 9th ...)			
☐ 5 Bruce Bosley	5.00	2.20	.60
(After a ... same as 1957)			
☐ 6 John Brodie	25.00	11.00	3.10
(With John ...)			
☐ 7 Clyde Conner	4.00	1.80	.50
(In signing ... running pose)			
☐ 8 Ted Connolly	4.00	1.80	.50
(When Santa Clara ...)			
☐ 9 Fred Dugan	4.00	1.80	.50
("Butch" Dugan ...)			
☐ 10 Mark Duncan CO	4.00	1.80	.50
(Mark ... same as 1957)			
☐ 11 Bob Fouts ANN, Lon Simmons ANN, and Frankie Albert CO	4.00	1.80	.50
(Same as 1957)			
☐ 12 John Gonzaga	4.00	1.80	.50
(Recommended ...)			
☐ 13 Tom Harmon ANN	6.00	2.70	.75
(Kids' ages are			

Column 1

12, 9, and 6)

- 14 Matt Hazeltine .... 5.00 2.20 .60
  (Improved ...)
- 15 Ed Henke .... 4.00 1.80 .50
  (The "Frank Buck" ...)
- 16 Bill Herchman .... 4.00 1.80 .50
  (A lineman's ...)
- 17 Howard(Red) Hickey CO .... 5.00 2.20 .60
  (After 14 campaigns ... same as 1957)
- 18 Bill Jessup .... 4.00 1.80 .50
  (Hard luck ...)
- 19 Bill Johnson CO .... 4.00 1.80 .50
  (No all-time ... same as 1957)
- 20 Marv Matuszak .... 5.00 2.20 .60
  (The best ...)
- 21 Hugh McElhenny 20.00 9.00 2.50
  (More people ...)
- 22 Jerry Mertens .... 4.00 1.80 .50
  (A 20th draft selection, Jerry ...)
- 23 Dick Moegle .... 5.00 2.20 .60
  (13 text lines)
- 24 Dennit Morris .... 4.00 1.80 .50
- 25 Frank Morze .... 4.00 1.80 .50
  (The 49ers drafted ...)
- 26 Leo Nomellini 15.00 6.75 1.85
  (Defensive ...)
- 27 R.C. Owens .... 6.00 2.70 .75
  (There's always ...)
- 28 Jim Pace .... 4.00 1.80 .50
- 29 Lou Palatella .... 4.00 1.80 .50
  (When ...)
- 30 Joe Perry 20.00 9.00 2.50
  (The all-time ...)
- 31 Jim Ridlon .... 4.00 1.80 .50
  (After a ...)
- 32 Karl Rubke .... 4.00 1.80 .50
  (Desperately ...)
- 33 J.D. Smith .... 5.00 2.20 .60
  (Used mainly ...)
- 34 Gordy Soltau .... 4.00 1.80 .50
  (In his eight ...)
- 35 Bob St. Clair 12.00 5.50 1.50
  (The only ...)
- 36 Bill Stits .... 4.00 1.80 .50
  (When the ...)
- 37 John Thomas .... 4.00 1.80 .50
  (This is ...)
- 38 Y.A. Tittle 25.00 11.00 3.10
  (His real ...)
- 39 Bob Toneff .... 4.00 1.80 .50
  (A chronic ...)
- 40 Lynn Waldorf .... 4.00 1.80 .50
  Director of Personnel
  (Vertical text, same as 1957)
- 41 Billy Wilson .... 5.00 2.20 .60
  (Em Tunnell, great ...)
- 42 John Wittenborn .... 4.00 1.80 .50
  (John ...)
- 43 Abe Woodson .... 6.00 2.70 .75
  (The 49ers ...)
- 44 49ers Coaches .... 5.00 2.20 .60
  Bill Johnson
  Phil Bengtson
  Frankie Albert
  Mark Duncan
  Howard(Red) Hickey
  (Blank back, same as 1957)

Column 2

(Played defensive ...)

- 2 Dave Baker .... 5.00 2.20 .60
- 3 Bruce Bosley .... 5.00 2.20 .60
  (Starred as ...)
- 4 John Brodie 25.00 11.00 3.10
  (Led NFL ...)
- 5 Jack Christiansen CO 12.00 5.50 1.50
- 6 Monte Clark .... 6.00 2.70 .75
- 7 Clyde Conner .... 4.00 1.80 .50
  (Standing pose, uniform number 88)
- 8 Ted Connolly .... 4.00 1.80 .50
  (Realized his ...)
- 9 Tommy Davis .... 5.00 2.20 .60
- 10 Eddie Dove .... 4.00 1.80 .50
- 11 Fred Dugan .... 4.00 1.80 .50
  (Made ...)
- 12 Mark Duncan CO .... 4.00 1.80 .50
  (A versatile ...)
- 13 Bob Fouts ANN .... 4.00 1.80 .50
- 14 John Gonzaga .... 4.00 1.80 .50
  (One of few ...)
- 15 Bob Harrison .... 4.00 1.80 .50
- 16 Matt Hazeltine .... 5.00 2.20 .60
  (One of the ...)
- 17 Ed Henke .... 4.00 1.80 .50
  (Suffered a ...)
- 18 Bill Herchman .... 4.00 1.80 .50
  (Starting ...)
- 19 Howard(Red) Hickey CO .... 5.00 2.20 .60
  (Baseball ...)
- 20 Russ Hodges ANN .... 5.00 2.20 .60
- 21 Bill Johnson CO .... 4.00 1.80 .50
  (Bill Johnson ...)
- 22 Charlie Krueger .... 5.00 2.20 .60
- 23 Lenny Lyles .... 4.00 1.80 .50
- 24 Hugh McElhenny 20.00 9.00 2.50
  (One of the ...)
- 25 Jerry Mertens .... 4.00 1.80 .50
  (A 20th draft selection last ...)
- 26 Dick Moegle .... 5.00 2.20 .60
  (7 text lines)
- 27 Frank Morze .... 4.00 1.80 .50
  (Transferred ...)
- 28 Leo Nomellini 15.00 6.75 1.85
  (Has never ...)
- 29 Clancy Osborne .... 5.00 2.20 .60
- 30 R.C. Owens .... 6.00 2.70 .75
  (Have football ...)
- 31 Joe Perry 20.00 9.00 2.50
  (Football's ...)
- 32 Jim Ridlon .... 4.00 1.80 .50
  (Showed ...)
- 33 Karl Rubke .... 4.00 1.80 .50
  (Started his ...)
- 34 Bob St.Clair 12.00 5.50 1.50
  (Tallest player ...)
- 35 Henry Schmidt .... 4.00 1.80 .50
- 36 Bob Shaw CO .... 4.00 1.80 .50
- 37 Lon Simmons ANN .... 4.00 1.80 .50
- 38 J.D. Smith .... 5.00 2.20 .60
  (One of the ...)
- 39 John Thomas .... 4.00 1.80 .50
  (Didn't make ...)
- 40 Y.A. Tittle 25.00 11.00 3.10
  (In 11 years ...)
- 41 Jerry Tubbs .... 6.00 2.70 .75
- 42 Lynn Waldorf .... 4.00 1.80 .50
  Director of Personnel
  (Horizontal text)
- 43 Billy Wilson .... 5.00 2.20 .60
  (Emlen Tunnell, 12-year ...)
- 44 John Wittenborn .... 4.00 1.80 .50
  (Handy ...)
- 45 Abe Woodson .... 5.00 2.20 .60
  (Received ...)

Column 3

- 1 Dave Baker .... 5.00 2.20 .60
  (David Lee Baker ...)
- 2 Bruce Bosley .... 5.00 2.20 .60
  (Born in Fresno ...)
- 3 John Brodie 20.00 9.00 2.50
  (This could be ...)
- 4 Jack Christiansen ACO 12.00 5.50 1.50
  (A special chapter ...)
- 5 Monte Clark .... 5.00 2.20 .60
- 6 Dan Colchico .... 4.00 1.80 .50
  (Big Dan ...)
- 7 Clyde Conner .... 4.00 1.80 .50
  (Clyde Raymond ...)
- 8 Ted Connolly .... 4.00 1.80 .50
  (When Theodore ...)
- 9 Tommy Davis .... 5.00 2.20 .60
  (San Francisco ...)
- 10 Eddie Dove .... 4.00 1.80 .50
  (Edward Everett ...)
- 11 Mark Duncan ACO .... 4.00 1.80 .50
  (A versatile ...)
- 12 Bob Fouts ANN .... 4.00 1.80 .50
- 13 Bob Harrison .... 4.00 1.80 .50
  (There is no more ...)
- 14 Matt Hazeltine .... 5.00 2.20 .60
  (Matthew Hazeltine ...)
- 15 Ed Henke .... 4.00 1.80 .50
  (Desire and ...)
- 16 Howard(Red) Hickey CO .... 5.00 2.20 .60
  (Baseball ...)
- 17 Russ Hodges ANN .... 5.00 2.20 .60
- 18 Bill Johnson CO .... 4.00 1.80 .50
  (Bill Johnson ...)
- 19 Gordon Kelley .... 4.00 1.80 .50
  (This Southern ...)
- 20 Charlie Krueger .... 5.00 2.20 .60
  (The 49ers' ...)
- 21 Lenny Lyles .... 4.00 1.80 .50
  (Leonard Lyles ...)
- 22 Hugh McElhenny 20.00 9.00 2.50
  (San Francisco's ...)
- 23 Mike Magac .... 4.00 1.80 .50
  (Mike was ...)
- 24 Jerry Mertens .... 4.00 1.80 .50
  (Jerome William ...)
- 25 Frank Morze .... 4.00 1.80 .50
  (Anyone with ...)
- 26 Leo Nomellini 15.00 6.75 1.85
  (Leo played ...)
- 27 Clancy Osborne .... 5.00 2.20 .60
  ("Desire" ...)
- 28 R.C. Owens .... 6.00 2.70 .75
  (Few players ...)
- 29 Jim Ridlon .... 4.00 1.80 .50
  (James Ridlon ...)
- 30 C.R. Roberts .... 4.00 1.80 .50
  (After trials ...)
- 31 Len Rohde .... 4.00 1.80 .50
  (Len, a three- ...)
- 32 Karl Rubke .... 4.00 1.80 .50
  (Only 20 years ...)
- 33 Bob St.Clair 12.00 5.50 1.50
  (Robert Bruce ...)
- 34 Henry Schmidt .... 4.00 1.80 .50
  (After two years ...)
- 35 Lon Simmons ANN .... 4.00 1.80 .50
- 36 J.D. Smith .... 5.00 2.20 .60
  (In J.D. Smith ...)
- 37 Gordy Soltau ANN .... 4.00 1.80 .50
- 38 Monty Stickles .... 5.00 2.20 .60
  (The football ...)
- 39 John Thomas .... 4.00 1.80 .50
  (Noted more ...)
- 40 Y.A. Tittle 25.00 11.00 3.10
  (When Yelberton ...)
- 41 Lynn(Pappy) Waldorf .... 4.00 1.80 .50
  (Director of Personnel)
- 42 Bobby Waters .... 5.00 2.20 .60
  (A smart, ...)
- 43 Billy Wilson .... 5.00 2.20 .60
  (Only Don Hutson ...)
- 44 Abe Woodson .... 5.00 2.20 .60
  (A Big 10 ...)

Column 4

is printed in black and silver. It also appears in the white border below the player information. Because this set is unnumbered, the players and coaches are listed alphabetically. Steve Spurrier's card predates his Rookie Card by four years.

	NRMT-MT	EXC	G-VG
COMPLETE SET (35)	175.00	80.00	22.00
COMMON CARD (1-35)	2.50	1.10	.30

- 1 Kermit Alexander .... 4.00 1.80 .50
- 2 Cas Banaszek .... 2.50 1.10 .30
- 3 Ed Beard .... 2.50 1.10 .30
- 4 Forrest Blue .... 4.00 1.80 .50
- 5 Bruce Bosley .... 4.00 1.80 .50
- 6 John Brodie 15.00 6.75 1.85
  posed action photo
- 7 Elmer Collett .... 2.50 1.10 .30
- 8 Doug Cunningham .... 4.00 1.80 .50
- 9 Tommy Davis .... 4.00 1.80 .50
- 10 Kevin Hardy .... 2.50 1.10 .30
- 11 Matt Hazeltine .... 4.00 1.80 .50
- 12 Stan Hindman .... 2.50 1.10 .30
- 13 Tom Holzer .... 2.50 1.10 .30
- 14 Jim Johnson 10.00 4.50 1.25
- 15 Charlie Krueger .... 4.00 1.80 .50
- 16 Roland Lakes .... 2.50 1.10 .30
- 17 Gary Lewis .... 2.50 1.10 .30
- 18 Kay McFarland .... 2.50 1.10 .30
- 19 Clifton McNeil .... 4.00 1.80 .50
- 20 George Mira .... 6.00 2.70 .75
- 21 Howard Mudd .... 2.50 1.10 .30
- 22 Dick Nolan CO .... 4.00 1.80 .50
- 23 Frank Nunley .... 2.50 1.10 .30
- 24 Don Parker .... 2.50 1.10 .30
- 25 Mel Phillips .... 4.00 1.80 .50
- 26 Al Randolph .... 2.50 1.10 .30
- 27 Len Rohde .... 2.50 1.10 .30
- 28 Steve Spurrier 40.00 18.00 5.00
- 29 John Thomas .... 2.50 1.10 .30
- 30 Bill Tucker .... 2.50 1.10 .30
- 31 Dave Wilcox .... 6.00 2.70 .75
- 32 Ken Willard .... 6.00 2.70 .75
- 33 Bob Windsor .... 4.00 1.80 .50
- 34 Dick Witcher .... 4.00 1.80 .50
- 35 Team Photo 15.00 6.75 1.85

1969 49ers Team Issue 4X5

These small (roughly 4" by 5") black and white photos look very similar to the 1971 release. Each includes a player photo along with his team name, player name, and position. The cardbacks are blank. We've noted text or photo differences below on players that were included in both sets.

	NRMT-MT	EXC	G-VG
COMPLETE SET (20)	50.00	22.00	6.25
COMMON CARD (1-20)	2.50	1.10	.30

- 1 Elmer Collett .... 2.50 1.10 .30
  no comma after team
- 2 Tommy Davis .... 4.00 1.80 .50
- 3 Earl Edwards .... 2.50 1.10 .30
  listed as DE
- 4 Johnny Fuller .... 2.50 1.10 .30
  comma after team
- 5 Harold Hays .... 2.50 1.10 .30
- 6 Stan Hindman .... 2.50 1.10 .30
  jersey number hidden
- 7 Roland Lakes .... 2.50 1.10 .30
- 8 Gary Lewis .... 2.50 1.10 .30
- 9 Frank Nunley .... 2.50 1.10 .30
  listed as LB
- 10 Clifton McNeil .... 4.00 1.80 .50
- 11 Mel Phillips .... 4.00 1.80 .50
  listed as DB
- 12 Al Randolph .... 2.50 1.10 .30
- 13 Len Rohde .... 2.50 1.10 .30
  smiling in photo
- 14 Jim Sniadecki .... 2.50 1.10 .30
  no comma after name
- 15 Sam Silas .... 2.50 1.10 .30
- 16 Jimmy Thomas .... 2.50 1.10 .30
  team name missing
  listed as RB
- 17 Bill Tucker .... 2.50 1.10 .30
- 18 Bob Windsor .... 4.00 1.80 .50
  (team name 'SF 49ers')
- 19 Dick Witcher .... 4.00 1.80 .50
  listed as FL
- 20 John Woitt .... 2.50 1.10 .30

1971 49ers Team Issue 4X5

These small (roughly 4" by 5") black and white photos look very similar to the 1969 release. Each includes a player photo along with his team name, player name, and position. The cardbacks are blank. We've noted text or photo differences below on players that were included in both sets.

	NRMT-MT	EXC	G-VG
COMPLETE SET (20)	50.00	22.00	6.25
COMMON CARD (1-20)	2.50	1.10	.30

- 1 Elmer Collett .... 2.50 1.10 .30
  comma after team name
- 2 Earl Edwards .... 2.50 1.10 .30

1959 49ers Team Issue

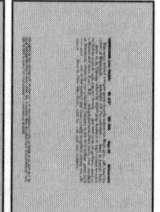

This 45-card set measures approximately 4 1/8" by 6 1/4". The front features a black and white posed action photo enclosed by a white border, with the player's signature across the bottom portion of the picture. The back lists the player's name, position, height, weight, and college, along with basic biographical information. Many of the cards in this and the other similar team issue sets are only distinguishable as to year by comparing text on the card back; the first few words of text are provided for many of the cards parenthetically below. The set was available direct from the team as part of a package for their fans. The cards are unnumbered and hence are listed alphabetically for convenience.

	NRMT	VG-E	GOOD
COMPLETE SET (45)	250.00	110.00	31.00
COMMON CARD (1-45)	4.00	1.80	.50

- 1 Bill Atkins .... 4.00 1.80 .50

1960 49ers Team Issue

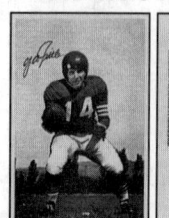
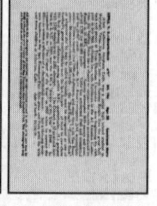

This 44-card set measures approximately 4 1/8" by 6 1/4". The front features a black-and-white posed action photo with white borders. The player's facsimile autograph is inscribed across the picture. The back lists the player's name, position, height, weight, age, college, along with career summary and biographical notes. The set was available direct from the team as part of a package for their fans. The photos are unnumbered and checklisted below in alphabetical order.

	NRMT	VG-E	GOOD
COMPLETE SET (44)	250.00	110.00	31.00
COMMON CARD (1-44)	4.00	1.80	.50

1968 49ers Team Issue

This 35-card team issue set measures approximately 8 1/2" by 11" and features black and white posed action photos of the San Francisco 49ers on thin card stock. The backs are blank. The player's name, position, height, and weight are printed in the white lower border in all caps. The set is very similar to the 1971-72 release, but the team logo

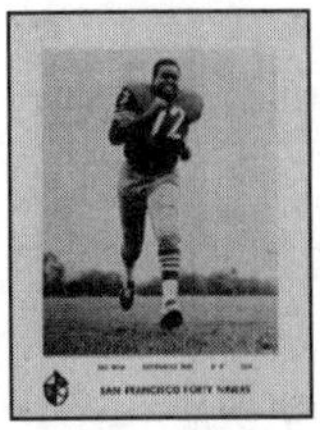

listed as DT			
☐ 3 Johnny Fuller	2.50	1.10	.30
no comma after team			
☐ 4 Tony Harris	2.50	1.10	.30
☐ 5 Tommy Hart	5.00	2.20	.60
☐ 6 Stan Hindman	2.50	1.10	.30
jersey number showing			
☐ 7 Bob Hoskins	2.50	1.10	.30
☐ 8 John Isenbarger	2.50	1.10	.30
☐ 9 Jim McCann	2.50	1.10	.30
☐ 10 Frank Nunley	2.50	1.10	.30
listed as MLB			
☐ 11 Mel Phillips	4.00	1.80	.50
listed as S			
☐ 12 Preston Riley	2.50	1.10	.30
☐ 13 Len Rohde	2.50	1.10	.30
not smiling in photo			
☐ 14 Larry Schrieber	2.50	1.10	.30
☐ 15 Mike Simpson	2.50	1.10	.30
☐ 16 Jim Sniadecki	2.50	1.10	.30
comma after name			
☐ 17 Jimmy Thomas	2.50	1.10	.30
listed as WR			
☐ 18 Vic Washington	4.00	1.80	.50
☐ 19 Bob Windsor	4.00	1.80	.50
(team name "SF 49er")			
☐ 20 Dick Witcher	4.00	1.80	.50
listed as WR			

1971 49ers Postcards

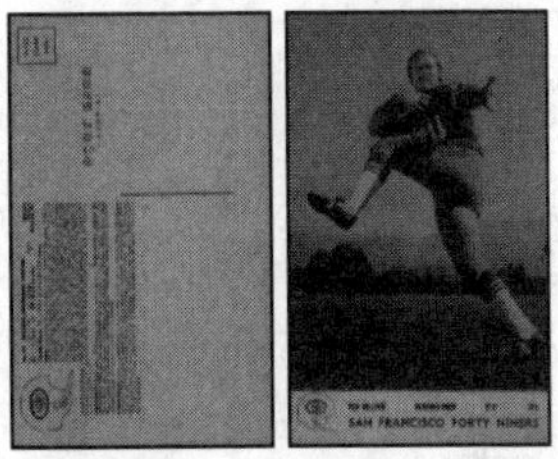

The San Francisco 49ers distributed this set of oversized postcards in 1971. Each measures approximately 5 3/4" by 9" and features a black and white player photo on front with a postcard style back. The cardbacks also contain extensive player career information and stats. The checklist below is thought to be incomplete. Any additions to this list are welcomed.

	NRMT-MT	EXC	G-VG
COMPLETE SET (4)	60.00	27.00	7.50
COMMON CARD (1-4)	15.00	6.75	1.85
☐ 1 Bruce Gossett	15.00	6.75	1.85
☐ 2 Frank Nunley	15.00	6.75	1.85
☐ 3 Len Rohde	15.00	6.75	1.85
☐ 4 Ken Willard	20.00	9.00	2.50

1971-72 49ers Team Issue

This team issue set measures approximately 8 1/2" by 11" and features black and white posed action photos of the San Francisco 49ers on thin card stock. The backs are blank. The player's name, position, height, and weight are printed in the white lower border in all caps. The set is very similar to the 1968 release, but the team logo is printed in all black and appears in the white border below the player information. Because this set is unnumbered, the players are listed alphabetically.

	NRMT-MT	EXC	G-VG
COMPLETE SET (4)	30.00	13.50	3.70
COMMON CARD (1-4)	5.00	2.20	.60
☐ 1 Ed Beard	5.00	2.20	.60
☐ 2 Bill Belk	5.00	2.20	.60
☐ 3 John Brodie	15.00	6.75	1.85
head and shoulder shot			
☐ 4 Bruce Gossett	5.00	2.20	.60

1972 49ers Redwood City Tribune

This set of six (approximately) 3" by 5 1/2" facsimile autograph cards features black-and-white head shots with white borders. The player's name is printed beneath the picture and in a large space immediately beneath, the card carries the player's signature. The bottom of the front reads "49er autograph card courtesy of Redwood City Tribune." The cards are unnumbered and checklisted below in alphabetical order. The set's date is bracketed by the fact that Frank Edwards last year with the San Francisco 49ers was 1972 and Larry Schreiber's first year with the 49ers was 1971.

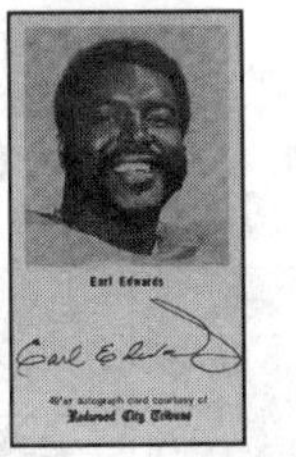

	NRMT-MT	EXC	G-VG
COMPLETE SET (6)	75.00	34.00	9.50
COMMON CARD (1-6)	7.50	3.40	.95
☐ 1 Frank Edwards	7.50	3.40	.95
☐ 2 Frank Nunley	7.50	3.40	.95
☐ 3 Len Rohde	7.50	3.40	.95
☐ 4 Larry Schrieber	7.50	3.40	.95
☐ 5 Steve Spurrier	40.00	18.00	5.00
☐ 6 Gene Washington	12.50	5.50	1.55

1972-75 49ers Team Issue

The 49ers released similar player photos over a period of years in the 1970s. For ease in cataloging, we've included them together below. There are likely many missing from the checklist, any additions to the list would be appreciated. Each photo measures approximately 7" by 11" and was printed on very thin stock. The fronts feature black-and-white action player photos on a white background. The player's picture measures roughly 6 1/4" by 7 1/2" and the cardbacks are blanks. The player's name, biographical information, career highlights, and a personal profile are printed in the white margin at the bottom. Most also include a 49ers helmet logo. This helps with identifying the year of issue. The cards are unnumbered and checklisted below in alphabetical order.

	NRMT-MT	EXC	G-VG
COMPLETE SET (7)	60.00	27.00	7.50
COMMON CARD (1-7)	5.00	2.20	.60
☐ 1 Windlan Hall 74	5.00	2.20	.60
☐ 2 Wilbur Jackson 74	7.50	3.40	.95
no helmet on front			
☐ 3 Jim Johnson 74	10.00	4.50	1.25
☐ 4 Manfred Moore 74	5.00	2.20	.60
no helmet on front			
☐ 5 Mel Phillips 72	5.00	2.20	.60
☐ 6 Steve Spurrier 74	25.00	11.00	3.10
☐ 7 Gene Washington 75	7.50	3.40	.95

1982 49ers Team Issue

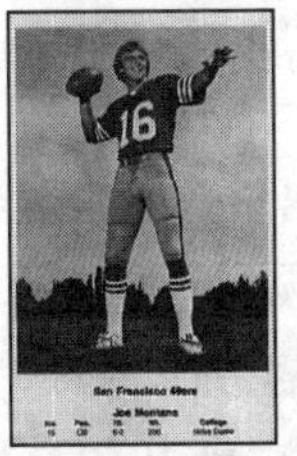

This 44-card team issue set of the San Francisco 49ers measures approximately 5" by 8" and features a black-and-white player photo in a white border. The players name, jersey number, height, weight, and college are printed in the wide bottom margin. The backs are blank. The cards are unnumbered and checklisted below in alphabetical order. The set features an early Joe Montana card.

	MINT	NRMT	EXC
COMPLETE SET (46)	75.00	34.00	9.50
COMMON CARD (1-46)	1.00	.45	.12
☐ 1 Dan Audick	1.00	.45	.12
☐ 2 John Ayers	1.00	.45	.12
☐ 3 Guy Benjamin	1.00	.45	.12
☐ 4 Dwaine Board	1.50	.70	.19
☐ 5 Ken Bungarda	1.00	.45	.12
☐ 6 Dan Bunz	1.00	.45	.12
☐ 7 Dwight Clark	6.00	2.70	.75
☐ 8 Ricky Churchman	1.00	.45	.12
☐ 9 Earl Cooper	1.50	.70	.19
☐ 10 Randy Cross	2.00	.90	.25
☐ 11 Johnny Davis	1.00	.45	.12
☐ 12 Fred Dean	1.50	.70	.19
☐ 13 Walt Downing	1.00	.45	.12
☐ 14 Walt Easley	1.00	.45	.12
☐ 15 Lenvil Elliott	1.00	.45	.12
☐ 16 Keith Fahnhorst	1.50	.70	.19
☐ 17 Rick Gervais	1.00	.45	.12
☐ 18 Willie Harper	1.00	.45	.12
☐ 19 John Harty	1.00	.45	.12
☐ 20 Dwight Hicks	2.00	.90	.25
☐ 21 Pete Kugler	1.50	.70	.19
☐ 22 Amos Lawrence	1.00	.45	.12
☐ 23 Bobby Leopold	1.00	.45	.12
☐ 24 Ronnie Lott	10.00	4.50	1.25
☐ 25 Saladin Martin	1.00	.45	.12
☐ 26 Milt McColl	1.00	.45	.12
☐ 27 Jim Miller	1.00	.45	.12
☐ 28 Joe Montana	30.00	13.50	3.70
☐ 29 Ricky Patton	1.00	.45	.12
☐ 30 Lawrence Pillers	1.00	.45	.12
☐ 31 Craig Puki	1.00	.45	.12
☐ 32 Fred Quillan	1.50	.70	.19
☐ 33 Eason Ramson	1.00	.45	.12
☐ 34 Archie Reese	1.00	.45	.12
☐ 35 Jack Reynolds	2.00	.90	.25
☐ 36 Mike Shumann	1.00	.45	.12
☐ 37 Freddie Solomon	2.50	1.10	.30
☐ 38 Scott Stauch	1.00	.45	.12
☐ 39 Jim Stuckey	1.00	.45	.12
☐ 40 Lynn Thomas	1.00	.45	.12
☐ 41 Keena Turner	2.00	.90	.25
☐ 42 Ray Wersching	1.00	.45	.12
☐ 43 Carlton Williamson	1.50	.70	.19
☐ 44 Mike Wilson	1.00	.45	.12
☐ 45 Eric Wright	2.00	.90	.25
☐ 46 Charlie Young	1.50	.70	.19

1984 49ers Police

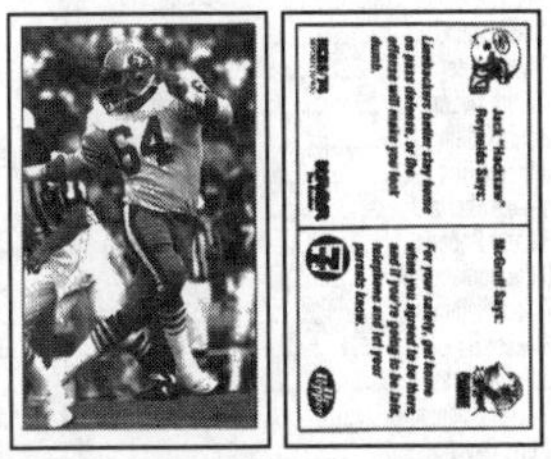

This set of 12 cards was issued in three panels of four cards each. Individual cards measure approximately 2 1/2" by 4 1/16" and feature the San Francisco 49ers. Since the cards are unnumbered, they are ordered and numbered below alphabetically by the subject's name. The set is sponsored by 7-Eleven, Dr. Pepper, and KCBS.

	MINT	NRMT	EXC
COMPLETE SET (12)	25.00	11.00	3.10
COMMON CARD (1-12)	.75	.35	.09
☐ 1 Dwaine Board	.75	.35	.09
☐ 2 Roger Craig	5.00	2.20	.60
☐ 3 Riki Ellison	.75	.35	.09
☐ 4 Keith Fahnhorst	.75	.35	.09
☐ 5 Joe Montana and Dwight Clark	15.00	6.75	1.85
☐ 6 Jack Reynolds	1.00	.45	.12
☐ 7 Freddie Solomon	1.00	.45	.12
☐ 8 Keena Turner	1.00	.45	.12
☐ 9 Wendell Tyler	1.00	.45	.12
☐ 10 Bill Walsh CO	4.00	1.80	.50
☐ 11 Ray Wersching	.75	.35	.09
☐ 12 Eric Wright	.75	.35	.09

1985 49ers Police

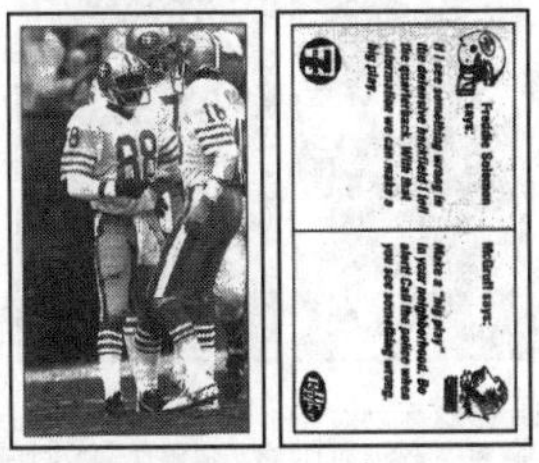

This set of 16 cards was issued in four panels of four cards each. Individual cards measure approximately 2 1/2" by 4" and feature the San Francisco 49ers. Since the cards are unnumbered, they are ordered and numbered below alphabetically by the subject's name. The set is differentiated from the similar 1984 Police 49ers set since this 1985 set is only sponsored by 7-Eleven and Dr. Pepper.

	MINT	NRMT	EXC
COMPLETE SET (16)	20.00	9.00	2.50
COMMON CARD (1-16)	.40	.18	.05
☐ 1 John Ayers	.40	.18	.05
☐ 2 Roger Craig	2.00	.90	.25
☐ 3 Fred Dean	.75	.35	.09
☐ 4 Riki Ellison	.50	.23	.06
☐ 5 Keith Fahnhorst	.40	.18	.05
☐ 6 Russ Francis	.75	.35	.09
☐ 7 Dwight Hicks	.50	.23	.06
☐ 8 Ronnie Lott	2.00	.90	.25
☐ 9 Dana McLemore	.40	.18	.05
☐ 10 Joe Montana	12.00	5.50	1.50
☐ 11 Todd Shell	.50	.23	.06
☐ 12 Freddie Solomon	.75	.35	.09
☐ 13 Keena Turner	.50	.23	.06
☐ 14 Bill Walsh CO	1.25	.55	.16
☐ 15 Ray Wersching	.40	.18	.05
☐ 16 Eric Wright	.50	.23	.06

1985 49ers Smokey

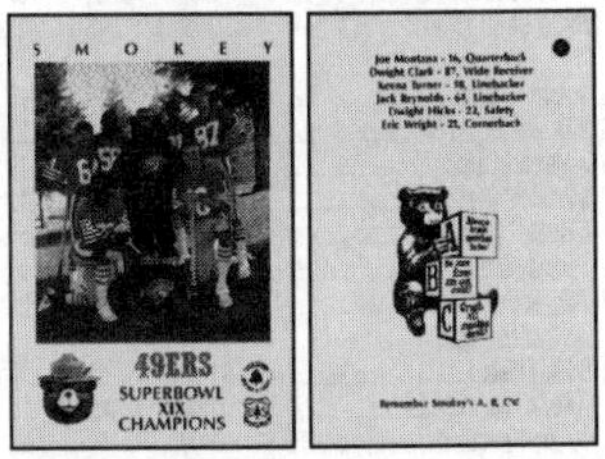

This set of seven large (approximately 2 15/16" by 4 3/8") cards was issued in the Summer of 1985 and features the San Francisco 49ers and Smokey Bear. The card backs are printed in black on a thin white card stock. Card backs have a cartoon fire safety message and a facsimile autograph of the player. Smokey Bear is pictured on each card along with the player (or players).

	MINT	NRMT	EXC
COMPLETE SET (7)	50.00	22.00	6.25
COMMON CARD (1-7)	2.00	.90	.25
☐ 1 Group Picture with Smokey (Player list on back of card)	10.00	4.50	1.25
☐ 2 Joe Montana	30.00	13.50	3.70
☐ 3 Jack Reynolds	3.00	1.35	.35
☐ 4 Eric Wright	2.00	.90	.25
☐ 5 Dwight Hicks	2.00	.90	.25
☐ 6 Dwight Clark	5.00	2.20	.60
☐ 7 Keena Turner	2.00	.90	.25

1988 49ers Police

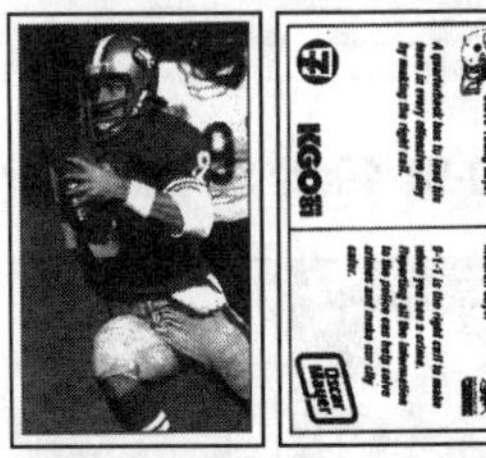

The 1988 Police San Francisco 49ers set contains 20 unnumbered cards measuring approximately 2 1/2" by 4". There are 19 player cards and one coach card. The fronts are basically "pure" with white borders. The backs have a football tip and a McGruff crime tip. The cards are listed below in alphabetical order by subject's name. The set is sponsored by 7-Eleven and Oscar Mayer, which differentiates this set from the similar-looking 1985 Police 49ers set.

	MINT	NRMT	EXC
COMPLETE SET (20)	30.00	13.50	3.70
COMMON CARD (1-20)	.50	.23	.06
☐ 1 Harris Barton	.75	.35	.09
☐ 2 Dwaine Board	.50	.23	.06
☐ 3 Michael Carter	.75	.35	.09
☐ 4 Roger Craig	1.50	.70	.19
☐ 5 Randy Cross	.75	.35	.09
☐ 6 Riki Ellison	.50	.23	.06
☐ 7 John Frank	.75	.35	.09
☐ 8 Jeff Fuller	.50	.23	.06
☐ 9 Pete Kugler	.50	.23	.06
☐ 10 Ronnie Lott	2.50	1.10	.30
☐ 11 Joe Montana	10.00	4.50	1.25
☐ 12 Tom Rathman	2.50	1.10	.30
☐ 13 Jerry Rice	10.00	4.50	1.25
☐ 14 Jeff Stover	.50	.23	.06
☐ 15 Keena Turner	.75	.35	.09
☐ 16 Bill Walsh CO	1.25	.55	.16
☐ 17 Michael Walter	.50	.23	.06
☐ 18 Mike Wilson	.50	.23	.06
☐ 19 Eric Wright	.75	.35	.09
☐ 20 Steve Young	7.50	3.40	.95

1988 49ers Smokey

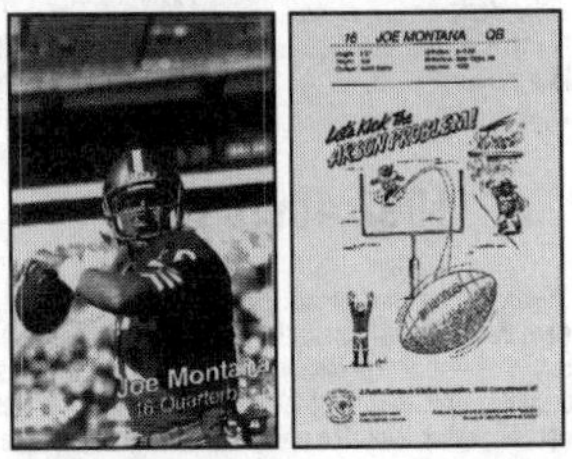

This 35-card set features members of the San Francisco 49ers. The cards measure approximately 5" by 8". The printing on the card back is in black ink on white card stock. The cards are unnumbered except for uniform number; they are ordered below alphabetically for convenience. Each card back contains a fire safety cartoon (usually) featuring Smokey. Reportedly the Dwaine Board card is more difficult to find than the other cards in the set.

	MINT	NRMT	EXC
COMPLETE SET (35)	125.00	55.00	15.50
COMMON CARD (1-35)	1.00	.45	.12
☐ 1 Harris Barton	1.50	.70	.19
☐ 2 Dwaine Board SP	10.00	4.50	1.25
☐ 3 Michael Carter	1.50	.70	.19
☐ 4 Bruce Collie	1.00	.45	.12
☐ 5 Roger Craig	4.00	1.80	.50
☐ 6 Randy Cross	2.00	.90	.25
☐ 7 Eddie DeBartolo Jr. (Owner/President)	2.00	.90	.25
☐ 8 Riki Ellison	1.00	.45	.12
☐ 9 Kevin Fagan	1.00	.45	.12
☐ 10 Jim Fahnhorst	1.00	.45	.12
☐ 11 John Frank	1.50	.70	.19
☐ 12 Jeff Fuller	1.00	.45	.12
☐ 13 Don Griffin	1.50	.70	.19
☐ 14 Charles Haley	4.00	1.80	.50
☐ 15 Ron Heller	1.00	.45	.12
☐ 16 Tom Holmoe	1.00	.45	.12
☐ 17 Pete Kugler	1.00	.45	.12
☐ 18 Ronnie Lott	5.00	2.20	.60
☐ 19 Tim McKyer	1.50	.70	.19
☐ 20 Joe Montana	30.00	13.50	3.70
☐ 21 Tory Nixon	1.00	.45	.12
☐ 22 Bubba Paris	1.50	.70	.19
☐ 23 John Paye	1.00	.45	.12
☐ 24 Tom Rathman	3.00	1.35	.35
☐ 25 Jerry Rice	30.00	13.50	3.70
☐ 26 Jeff Stover	1.00	.45	.12
☐ 27 Harry Sydney	1.00	.45	.12
☐ 28 John Taylor	4.00	1.80	.50
☐ 29 Keena Turner	1.50	.70	.19
☐ 30 Steve Wallace	1.50	.70	.19
☐ 31 Bill Walsh CO	3.00	1.35	.35
☐ 32 Michael Walter	1.00	.45	.12
☐ 33 Mike Wilson	1.00	.45	.12
☐ 34 Eric Wright	1.50	.70	.19
☐ 35 Steve Young	25.00	11.00	3.10

1990-91 49ers SF Examiner

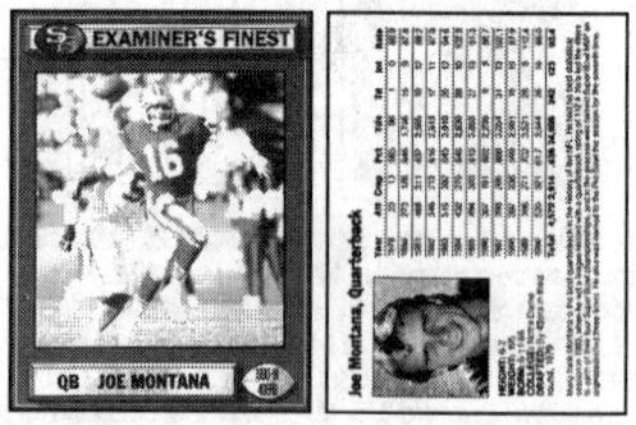

This 16-card San Francisco Examiner 49ers set was issued on two unperforated sheets measuring approximately 14" by 11". Each sheet featured eight cards, with a newspaper headline at the top of the sheet reading "San Francisco Examiner Salutes the 49ers' Finest". If the cards were cut, they would measure approximately 3 1/4" by 4 1/8". The front design has color game shots, with a thin orange border on a red card face. A gold plaque at the card top reads "SF Examiner's Finest," while the gold plaque at the bottom has the player's position and name. The horizontally oriented backs have a black and white head shot, biographical information, statistics, and player profile. The cards are unnumbered and checklisted below in alphabetical order.

	MINT	NRMT	EXC
COMPLETE SET (16)	20.00	9.00	2.50
COMMON CARD (1-16)	.60	.25	.07
☐ 1 Harris Barton	.75	.35	.09
☐ 2 Michael Carter	.60	.25	.07
☐ 3 Mike Cofer	.60	.25	.07
☐ 4 Roger Craig	1.00	.45	.12
☐ 5 Kevin Fagan	.60	.25	.07
☐ 6 Don Griffin	.60	.25	.07
☐ 7 Charles Haley	1.25	.55	.16
☐ 8 Pierce Holt	.75	.35	.09
☐ 9 Brent Jones	1.25	.55	.16
☐ 10 Ronnie Lott	1.50	.70	.19
☐ 11 Guy McIntyre	.60	.25	.07
☐ 12 Matt Millen	.75	.35	.09
☐ 13 Joe Montana	6.00	2.70	.75
☐ 14 Tom Rathman	1.00	.45	.12
☐ 15 Jerry Rice	6.00	2.70	.75
☐ 16 John Taylor	1.25	.55	.16

1992 49ers FBI

This 40-card standard-size set was sponsored by the San Francisco 49ers and the FBI (Federal Bureau of Investigation). According to the title card, a different pack of cards was available free with the 49ers' edition of GameDay Magazine at regular season home games each week at Candlestick Park. The fronts display color action player photos with white borders. In red and white lettering, the player's first and last names are overprinted on the photo at the upper left and lower right corners respectively. The team helmet at the lower left corner rounds out the front. Inside white borders on brick-red background, the backs feature a color close-up photo (inside a football helmet design), biographical information, and a public service message in the form of a player quote.

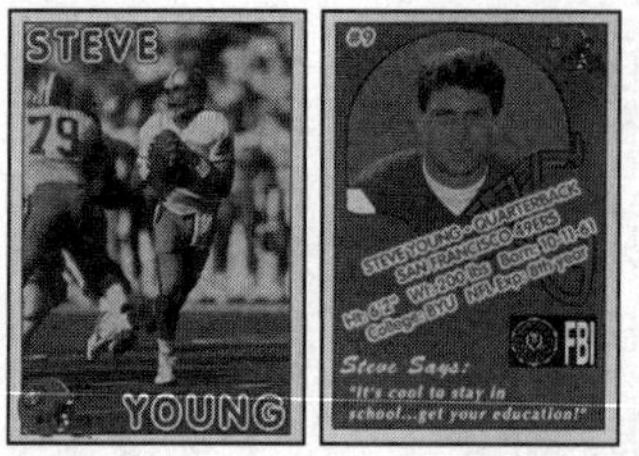

	MINT	NRMT	EXC
COMPLETE SET (40)	45.00	20.00	5.50
COMMON CARD (1-39)	.50	.23	.06
☐ 1 Michael Carter	.50	.23	.06
☐ 2 Kevin Fagan	.50	.23	.06
☐ 3 Charles Haley	1.00	.45	.12
☐ 4 Guy McIntyre	.50	.23	.06
☐ 5 George Seifert CO	1.00	.45	.12
☐ 6 Harry Sydney	.50	.23	.06
☐ 7 John Taylor	1.25	.55	.16
☐ 8 Michael Walter	.50	.23	.06
☐ 9 Steve Young	10.00	4.50	1.25
☐ 10 Mike Cofer	.50	.23	.06
☐ 11 Keith DeLong	.50	.23	.06
☐ 12 Don Griffin	.50	.23	.06
☐ 13 Pierce Holt	.75	.35	.09
☐ 14 Mike Sherrard	1.00	.45	.12
☐ 15 Larry Roberts	.50	.23	.06
☐ 16 Bill Romanowski	.50	.23	.06
☐ 17 Tom Rathman	1.00	.45	.12
☐ 18 Jesse Sapolu	.75	.35	.09
☐ 19 Brent Jones	1.25	.55	.16
☐ 20 Brian Bollinger	.50	.23	.06
☐ 21 Eric Davis	.50	.23	.06
☐ 22 Antonio Goss	.50	.23	.06
☐ 23 Alan Grant	.50	.23	.06
☐ 24 Harris Barton	.75	.35	.09
☐ 25 Ricky Watters	4.00	1.80	.50
☐ 26 Darin Jordan	.50	.23	.06
☐ 27 Odessa Turner	.50	.23	.06
☐ 28 David Wilkins	.50	.23	.06
☐ 29 Merton Hanks	1.00	.45	.12
☐ 30 David Whitmore	.50	.23	.06
☐ 31 Joe Montana	12.00	5.50	1.50
☐ 32 Klaus Wilmsmeyer	.50	.23	.06
☐ 33 Tim Harris	.75	.35	.09
☐ 34 Roy Foster	.50	.23	.06
☐ 35 Bill Musgrave	1.00	.45	.12
☐ 36 Dana Hall	1.00	.45	.12
☐ 37 Steve Wallace	.75	.35	.09
☐ 38 Steve Bono	2.00	.90	.25
☐ 39 Jerry Rice	12.00	5.50	1.50
☐ NNO Title Card	.75	.35	.09

1994 49ers Pro Mags/Pro Tags

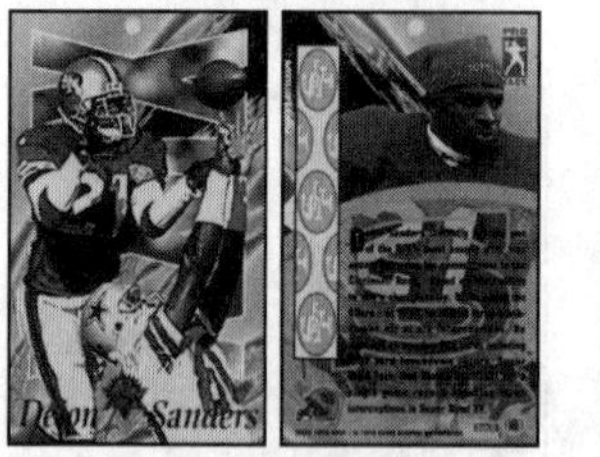

Issued in a black cardboard box and featuring the San Francisco 49ers, this set consists of six Pro Mags and six Pro Tags, both with rounded corners and measuring 2 1/8" by 3 3/8". Each box was individually numbered out of 750. On a team color-coded background, the magnet fronts display borderless color action player photos. The player's name in big gold-foil letters appears along the left side, with the team name below. A gold-foil Super Bowl XXIX logo is printed in the lower right corner. On a computerized team color-coded background, the tag fronts feature a color action player cutout superimposed on the Roman numerals XXIX printed vertically in block lettering. The player's name is gold foil-stamped across the bottom, with a gold-foil Super Bowl XXIX logo between the first and last name. The backs carry a color closeup photo, an autograph strip, and player profile. The magnets and tags are unnumbered and checklisted below in alphabetical order, first the magnets (1-6) and then the tags (7-12).

	MINT	NRMT	EXC
COMPLETE SET (12)	20.00	9.00	2.50
COMMON CARD (1-12)	1.25	.55	.16
☐ 1 Ken Norton Jr.	1.25	.55	.16
☐ 2 Jerry Rice	3.00	1.35	.35
☐ 3 Deion Sanders	2.00	.90	.25
☐ 4 John Taylor	1.25	.55	.16
☐ 5 Ricky Watters	1.50	.70	.19
☐ 6 Steve Young	2.50	1.10	.30
☐ 7 Ken Norton Jr.	1.25	.55	.16
☐ 8 Jerry Rice	3.00	1.35	.35
☐ 9 Deion Sanders	2.00	.90	.25
☐ 10 John Taylor	1.25	.55	.16
☐ 11 Ricky Watters	1.50	.70	.19
☐ 12 Steve Young	2.50	1.10	.30

1996 49ers Save Mart Cards/Coins

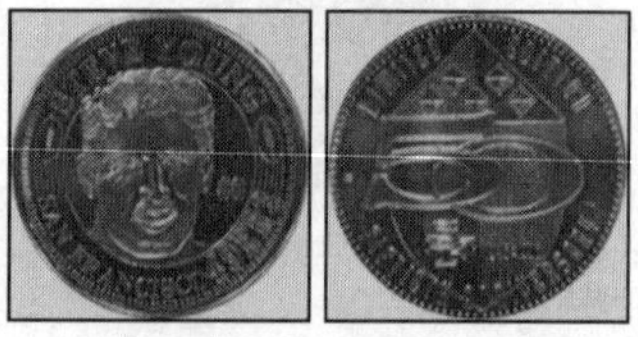

The San Francisco 49ers, in conjunction with Save Mart Supermarkets, produced this 9-card and 9-coin set commemorating the team's Super Bowl teams past and present. The card fronts feature color action player photos with the player's name printed diagonally on one side of the cardfront. The backs display the complete 9-card checklist and individual card numbers. We've listed the cards below using a "CA" prefix. The coin fronts feature a player likeness with the player's name and jersey number. The backs display the 49ers team logo. The coins are unnumbered but have been listed below alphabetically using a "CO" prefix. A cardboard holder featuring Jerry Rice and Steve Young was produced to house the set.

	MINT	NRMT	EXC
COMP.CARD/COIN SET (18)	40.00	18.00	5.00
COMPLETE CARD SET (9)	20.00	9.00	2.50
COMPLETE COIN SET (9)	20.00	9.00	2.50
COMMON CARD (CA1-CA9)	1.50	.70	.19
COMMON COIN (CO1-CO9)	1.50	.70	.19
☐ CA1 Steve Young	4.00	1.80	.50
☐ CA2 Roger Craig	2.00	.90	.25
☐ CA3 Jerry Rice	5.00	2.20	.60
☐ CA4 Ronnie Lott	2.50	1.10	.30
☐ CA5 Ken Norton	1.50	.70	.19
☐ CA6 Dwight Clark	2.00	.90	.25
☐ CA7 Brent Jones	1.50	.70	.19
☐ CA8 Joe Montana	5.00	2.20	.60
☐ CA9 Steve Young Jerry Rice Super Bowl XXIX	4.00	1.80	.50
☐ CO1 Dwight Clark	2.00	.90	.25
☐ CO2 Roger Craig	2.00	.90	.25
☐ CO3 Brent Jones	1.50	.70	.19
☐ CO4 Ronnie Lott	2.50	1.10	.30
☐ CO5 Joe Montana	5.00	2.20	.60
☐ CO6 Ken Norton	1.50	.70	.19
☐ CO7 Jerry Rice	5.00	2.20	.60
☐ CO8 Steve Young	4.00	1.80	.50
☐ CO9 Super Bowl XXIX Trophy Gold colored coin	3.00	1.35	.35
☐ NNO Set Display Holder Jerry Rice Steve Young	4.00	1.80	.50

1989 Franchise Game

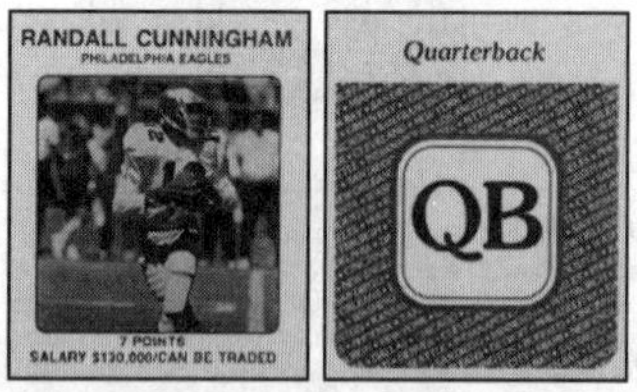

The 1989 NFL Franchise Game was produced by Rohrwood Enterprises of Loveland, Colorado. The game is modeled after Monopoly, in that players begin with a sum of money (54.5 million dollars) and travel around the board, acquiring "property" (i.e., players) in exchange for money. The object of the game is to build a team of 23 players who fill all the different positions required by the team and who are under contract. The game cards measure approximately 3" by 3 1/2" and feature action player photos with rounded corners and white borders. Some collectors have observed a variation in photographic quality. The player's name and team appear above the picture, while the draft round, number of points player is worth to the franchise, and his salary are printed below the picture. The card backs display a teal panel printed with the home cities of NFL teams. A large numeral or acronym appears in the center of the panel. The player's position is printed across the top. The cards are unnumbered and checklisted below alphabetically acccording to and within teams. In addition to these player cards, the set includes 28 unnumbered team cards displaying the team helmet and 13 generic coaches' cards.

	MINT	NRMT	EXC
COMPLETE SET (332)	200.00	90.00	25.00
COMMON CARD (1-304)	.60	.25	.07
COMMON TEAM (T1-T28)	.50	.23	.06
☐ 1 Neal Anderson	1.00	.45	.12
☐ 2 Kevin Butler	.60	.25	.07
☐ 3 Jim Covert	.60	.25	.07
☐ 4 Dave Duerson	.60	.25	.07
☐ 5 Dan Hampton	1.00	.45	.12
☐ 6 Jay Hilgenberg	.60	.25	.07
☐ 7 Mike Richardson	.60	.25	.07
☐ 8 Ron Rivera	.60	.25	.07
☐ 9 Mike Singletary	1.00	.45	.12
☐ 10 Mike Tomczak	1.00	.45	.12
☐ 11 Keith Van Horne	.60	.25	.07
☐ 12 Lewis Billups	.60	.25	.07
☐ 13 Jim Breech	.60	.25	.07
☐ 14 James Brooks	1.00	.45	.12
☐ 15 Eddie Brown	.75	.35	.09
☐ 16 Ross Browner	.60	.25	.07
☐ 17 Jason Buck	.60	.25	.07
☐ 18 Cris Collinsworth	.75	.35	.09
☐ 19 Eddie Edwards	.60	.25	.07
☐ 20 Boomer Esiason	1.00	.45	.12
☐ 21 David Fulcher	.75	.35	.09
☐ 22 Ray Horton	.60	.25	.07
☐ 23 Tim Krumrie	.75	.35	.09
☐ 24 Max Montoya	.60	.25	.07
☐ 25 Anthony Munoz	1.50	.70	.19
☐ 26 Jim Skow	.60	.25	.07
☐ 27 Reggie Williams	.75	.35	.09
☐ 28 Ickey Woods	.75	.35	.09
☐ 29 Cornelius Bennett	1.00	.45	.12
☐ 30 Shane Conlan	1.00	.45	.12
☐ 31 Joe Devlin	.60	.25	.07
☐ 32 Nate Odomes	.60	.25	.07
☐ 33 Scott Norwood	.60	.25	.07
☐ 34 Andre Reed	1.50	.70	.19
☐ 35 Jim Ritcher	.60	.25	.07
☐ 36 Fred Smerlas	.60	.25	.07
☐ 37 Bruce Smith	1.50	.70	.19
☐ 38 Art Still	.60	.25	.07
☐ 39 Keith Bishop	.60	.25	.07
☐ 40 Bill Bryan	.60	.25	.07
☐ 41 Tony Dorsett	3.00	1.35	.35
☐ 42 Simon Fletcher	.75	.35	.09
☐ 43 Mike Harden	.60	.25	.07
☐ 44 Mark Haynes	.60	.25	.07
☐ 45 Mike Horan	.60	.25	.07
☐ 46 Vance Johnson	1.00	.45	.12
☐ 47 Rulon Jones	.60	.25	.07
☐ 48 Rich Karlis	.60	.25	.07
☐ 49 Karl Mecklenburg	1.00	.45	.12
☐ 50 Dennis Smith	.75	.35	.09
☐ 51 Dave Studdard	.60	.25	.07
☐ 52 Andre Townsend	.60	.25	.07
☐ 53 Steve Watson	.60	.25	.07
☐ 54 Sammy Winder	.60	.25	.07
☐ 55 Matt Bahr	.60	.25	.07
☐ 56 Rickey Bolden	.60	.25	.07
☐ 57 Earnest Byner	1.00	.45	.12
☐ 58 Sam Clancy	.60	.25	.07
☐ 59 Hanford Dixon	.60	.25	.07
☐ 60 Bob Golic	.75	.35	.09
☐ 61 Carl Hairston	.75	.35	.09
☐ 62 Eddie Johnson	.60	.25	.07
☐ 63 Kevin Mack	.75	.35	.09
☐ 64 Clay Matthews	1.00	.45	.12
☐ 65 Frank Minnifield	.75	.35	.09
☐ 66 Ozzie Newsome	1.00	.45	.12
☐ 67 Cody Risien	.60	.25	.07
☐ 68 John Cannon	.60	.25	.07
☐ 69 Ron Holmes	.60	.25	.07
☐ 70 Winston Moss	.60	.25	.07
☐ 71 Rob Taylor	.60	.25	.07
☐ 72 Joe Bostic	.60	.25	.07
☐ 73 Roy Green	1.00	.45	.12
☐ 74 Ricky Hunley	.60	.25	.07
☐ 75 E.J. Junior	.60	.25	.07
☐ 76 Neil Lomax	.60	.25	.07
☐ 77 Tim McDonald	.60	.25	.07
☐ 78 Cedric Mack	.60	.25	.07
☐ 79 Freddie Joe Nunn	.60	.25	.07
☐ 80 Gary Anderson	.75	.35	.09
☐ 81 Keith Baldwin	.60	.25	.07
☐ 82 Gill Byrd	.75	.35	.09
☐ 83 Elvis Patterson	.60	.25	.07
☐ 84 Gary Plummer	.60	.25	.07
☐ 85 Billy Ray Smith	.60	.25	.07
☐ 86 Lee Williams	.75	.35	.09
☐ 87 Mike Bell	.60	.25	.07
☐ 88 Lloyd Burruss	.60	.25	.07
☐ 89 Carlos Carson	.60	.25	.07
☐ 90 Deron Cherry	.75	.35	.09
☐ 91 Jack Del Rio	.75	.35	.09
☐ 92 Irv Eatman	.60	.25	.07
☐ 93 Dino Hackett	.60	.25	.07
☐ 94 Bill Kenney	.60	.25	.07
☐ 95 Albert Lewis	.60	.25	.07
☐ 96 David Lutz	.60	.25	.07
☐ 97 Bill Maas	.60	.25	.07
☐ 98 Stephone Paige	1.00	.45	.12
☐ 99 Neil Smith	1.50	.70	.19
☐ 100 Dean Biasucci	.60	.25	.07
☐ 101 Duane Bickett	.75	.35	.09
☐ 102 Chris Chandler	1.50	.70	.19
☐ 103 Eugene Daniel	.60	.25	.07
☐ 104 Ray Donaldson	.60	.25	.07
☐ 105 Jon Hand	.60	.25	.07
☐ 106 Chris Hinton	.60	.25	.07
☐ 107 Joe Klecko	.60	.25	.07
☐ 108 Cliff Odom	.60	.25	.07
☐ 109 Rohn Stark	.60	.25	.07
☐ 110 Donnell Thompson	.60	.25	.07
☐ 111 Willie Tullis	.60	.25	.07

☐ 112 Freddie Young	.60	.25	.07
☐ 113 Michael Downs	.60	.25	.07
☐ 114 Michael Irvin	3.00	1.35	.35
☐ 115 Jim Jeffcoat	.60	.25	.07
☐ 116 Ed(Too Tall) Jones	1.00	.45	.12
☐ 117 Tom Rafferty	.60	.25	.07
☐ 118 Herschel Walker	1.50	.70	.19
☐ 119 Everson Walls	.60	.25	.07
☐ 120 Danny White	.75	.35	.09
☐ 121 Randy White	1.50	.70	.19
☐ 122 Bob Brudzinski	.60	.25	.07
☐ 123 Mark Clayton	1.00	.45	.12
☐ 124 Mark Duper	1.00	.45	.12
☐ 125 Ron Jaworski	1.00	.45	.12
☐ 126 Paul Lankford	.60	.25	.07
☐ 127 Dan Marino	15.00	6.75	1.85
☐ 128 John Offerdahl	.60	.25	.07
☐ 129 Reggie Roby	.60	.25	.07
☐ 130 Dwight Stephenson	.75	.35	.09
☐ 131 Randall Cunningham	1.00	.45	.12
☐ 132 Ron Heller	.60	.25	.07
☐ 133 Mike Quick	.75	.35	.09
☐ 134 Ken Reeves	.60	.25	.07
☐ 135 Dave Rimington	.60	.25	.07
☐ 136 Reggie Singletary	.60	.25	.07
☐ 137 Andre Waters	.60	.25	.07
☐ 138 Reggie White	4.00	1.80	.50
☐ 139 Roynell Young	.60	.25	.07
☐ 140 Aundray Bruce	.60	.25	.07
☐ 141 Bobby Butler	.60	.25	.07
☐ 142 Bill Fralic	.60	.25	.07
☐ 143 Mike Kenn	.60	.25	.07
☐ 144 Chris Miller	1.50	.70	.19
☐ 145 John Settle	.60	.25	.07
☐ 146 George Yarno	.60	.25	.07
☐ 147 Michael Carter	.60	.25	.07
☐ 148 Wes Chandler	1.00	.45	.12
☐ 149 Roger Craig	1.50	.70	.19
☐ 150 Randy Cross	.60	.25	.07
☐ 151 Riki Ellison	.60	.25	.07
☐ 152 Jim Fahnhorst	.60	.25	.07
☐ 153 Charles Haley	1.50	.70	.19
☐ 154 Barry Helton	.60	.25	.07
☐ 155 Guy McIntyre	.75	.35	.09
☐ 156 Tim McKyer	.60	.25	.07
☐ 157 Joe Montana	10.00	4.50	1.25
☐ 158 Jerry Rice	10.00	4.50	1.25
☐ 159 Keena Turner	.60	.25	.07
☐ 160 Eric Wright	.60	.25	.07
☐ 161 Steve Young	8.00	3.60	1.00
☐ 162 Raul Allegre	.60	.25	.07
☐ 163 Ottis Anderson	1.00	.45	.12
☐ 164 Billy Ard	.60	.25	.07
☐ 165 Carl Banks	.75	.35	.09
☐ 166 Mark Bavaro	1.00	.45	.12
☐ 167 Jim Burt	.60	.25	.07
☐ 168 Harry Carson	.75	.35	.09
☐ 169 John Elliott	.60	.25	.07
☐ 170 Terry Kinard	.60	.25	.07
☐ 171 Sean Landeta	.60	.25	.07
☐ 172 Lionel Manuel	.60	.25	.07
☐ 173 Joe Morris	.75	.35	.09
☐ 174 Bart Oates	.60	.25	.07
☐ 175 Phil Simms	1.00	.45	.12
☐ 176 Pat Leahy	.60	.25	.07
☐ 177 Marty Lyons	.60	.25	.07
☐ 178 Erik McMillan	.60	.25	.07
☐ 179 Freeman McNeil	1.00	.45	.12
☐ 180 Scott Mersereau	.60	.25	.07
☐ 181 Ken O'Brien	.75	.35	.09
☐ 182 Jim Sweeney	.60	.25	.07
☐ 183 Al Toon	1.00	.45	.12
☐ 184 Wesley Walker	1.00	.45	.12
☐ 185 Jim Arnold	.60	.25	.07
☐ 186 Bennie Blades	1.00	.45	.12
☐ 187 Mike Cofer	.60	.25	.07
☐ 188 Keith Ferguson	.60	.25	.07
☐ 189 Steve Mott	.60	.25	.07
☐ 190 Eddie Murray	.60	.25	.07
☐ 191 Harvey Salem	.60	.25	.07
☐ 192 Bobby Watkins	.60	.25	.07
☐ 193 Keith Bostic	.60	.25	.07
☐ 194 Richard Byrd	.60	.25	.07
☐ 195 Ray Childress	.75	.35	.09
☐ 196 Ernest Givins	1.00	.45	.12
☐ 197 Kenny Johnson	.60	.25	.07
☐ 198 Sean Jones	.75	.35	.09
☐ 199 Robert Lyles	.60	.25	.07
☐ 200 Bruce Matthews	.75	.35	.09
☐ 201 Johnny Meads	.60	.25	.07
☐ 202 Warren Moon	2.00	.90	.25
☐ 203 Mike Munchak	1.00	.45	.12
☐ 204 Mike Rozier	.75	.35	.09
☐ 205 Dean Steinkuhler	.60	.25	.07
☐ 206 Tony Zendejas	.60	.25	.07
☐ 207 Mark Cannon	.60	.25	.07
☐ 208 Alphonso Carreker	.60	.25	.07
☐ 209 Phillip Epps	.60	.25	.07
☐ 210 Tim Harris	.75	.35	.09
☐ 211 Brian Noble	.60	.25	.07
☐ 212 Raymond Clayborn	.60	.25	.07
☐ 213 Steve Grogan	1.00	.45	.12
☐ 214 Roland James	.60	.25	.07
☐ 215 Fred Marion	.60	.25	.07
☐ 216 Stanley Morgan	1.00	.45	.12
☐ 217 Kenneth Sims	.60	.25	.07
☐ 218 Andre Tippett	1.00	.45	.12
☐ 219 Marcus Allen	4.00	1.80	.50
☐ 220 Chris Bahr	.60	.25	.07
☐ 221 Steve Beuerlein	1.00	.45	.12
☐ 222 Tim Brown	4.00	1.80	.50
☐ 223 Todd Christensen	.75	.35	.09
☐ 224 Ron Fellows	.60	.25	.07
☐ 225 Willie Gault	.75	.35	.09
☐ 226 Mike Haynes	.75	.35	.09
☐ 227 Bo Jackson	2.00	.90	.25
☐ 228 James Lofton	2.00	.90	.25
☐ 229 Howie Long	1.50	.70	.19
☐ 230 Vann McElroy	.60	.25	.07
☐ 231 Rod Martin	.60	.25	.07
☐ 232 Matt Millen	.75	.35	.09
☐ 233 Bill Pickel	.60	.25	.07
☐ 234 Jay Schroeder	1.00	.45	.12
☐ 235 Stacey Toran	.60	.25	.07
☐ 236 Greg Townsend	.75	.35	.09
☐ 237 Greg Bell	.60	.25	.07
☐ 238 Henry Ellard	1.50	.70	.19
☐ 239 Jerry Gray	.60	.25	.07
☐ 240 LeRoy Irvin	.60	.25	.07
☐ 241 Gary Jeter	.60	.25	.07
☐ 242 Johnnie Johnson	.60	.25	.07
☐ 243 Larry Kelm	.60	.25	.07
☐ 244 Mike Lansford	.60	.25	.07
☐ 245 Shawn Miller	.60	.25	.07
☐ 246 Mel Owens	.60	.25	.07
☐ 247 Jackie Slater	.60	.25	.07
☐ 248 Charles White	.75	.35	.09
☐ 249 Jeff Bostic	.60	.25	.07
☐ 250 Kelvin Bryant	.60	.25	.07
☐ 251 Dave Butz	.60	.25	.07
☐ 252 Gary Clark	1.50	.70	.19
☐ 253 Steve Cox	.60	.25	.07
☐ 254 Darryl Grant	.60	.25	.07
☐ 255 Darrell Green	1.00	.45	.12
☐ 256 Joe Jacoby	.60	.25	.07
☐ 257 Mel Kaufman	.60	.25	.07
☐ 258 Jim Lachey	.60	.25	.07
☐ 259 Dexter Manley	.60	.25	.07
☐ 260 Charles Mann	.75	.35	.09
☐ 261 Mark May	.60	.25	.07
☐ 262 Art Monk	1.50	.70	.19
☐ 263 Ricky Sanders	1.00	.45	.12
☐ 264 Alvin Walton	.60	.25	.07
☐ 265 Doug Williams	1.00	.45	.12
☐ 266 Morten Andersen	.75	.35	.09
☐ 267 Bruce Clark	.60	.25	.07
☐ 268 Jim Dombrowski	.60	.25	.07
☐ 269 Mel Gray	1.00	.45	.12
☐ 270 Bobby Hebert	1.00	.45	.12
☐ 271 Rickey Jackson	.75	.35	.09
☐ 272 Van Jakes	.60	.25	.07
☐ 273 Steve Korte	.60	.25	.07
☐ 274 Rueben Mayes	.60	.25	.07
☐ 275 Sam Mills	1.00	.45	.12
☐ 276 Dave Waymer	.60	.25	.07
☐ 277 Jeff Bryant	.60	.25	.07
☐ 278 Blair Bush	.60	.25	.07
☐ 279 Jacob Green	.60	.25	.07
☐ 280 Melvin Jenkins	.60	.25	.07
☐ 281 Norm Johnson	.60	.25	.07
☐ 282 Dave Krieg	1.00	.45	.12
☐ 283 Bryan Millard	.60	.25	.07
☐ 284 Ruben Rodriguez	.60	.25	.07
☐ 285 Terry Taylor	.60	.25	.07
☐ 286 Curt Warner	1.00	.45	.12
☐ 287 Tony Woods	.60	.25	.07
☐ 288 Gary Anderson	.60	.25	.07
☐ 289 Tunch Ilkin	.60	.25	.07
☐ 290 Earnest Jackson	.60	.25	.07
☐ 291 Louis Lipps	1.00	.45	.12
☐ 292 Mike Webster	1.50	.70	.19
☐ 293 Rod Woodson	4.00	1.80	.50
☐ 294 Joey Browner	.60	.25	.07
☐ 295 Anthony Carter	1.50	.70	.19
☐ 296 Chris Doleman	1.00	.45	.12
☐ 297 Tim Irwin	.60	.25	.07
☐ 298 Tommy Kramer	.75	.35	.09
☐ 299 Carl Lee	.60	.25	.07
☐ 300 Kirk Lowdermilk	.60	.25	.07
☐ 301 Keith Millard	.60	.25	.07
☐ 302 Scott Studwell	.60	.25	.07
☐ 303 Wade Wilson	.75	.35	.09
☐ 304 Gary Zimmerman	.60	.25	.07
☐ T1 Atlanta Falcons Team Helmet	.50	.23	.06
☐ T2 Buffalo Bills Team Helmet	.50	.23	.06
☐ T3 Chicago Bears Team Helmet	.50	.23	.06
☐ T4 Cincinnati Bengals Team Helmet	.50	.23	.06
☐ T5 Cleveland Browns Team Helmet	.50	.23	.06
☐ T6 Dallas Cowboys Team Helmet	.75	.35	.09
☐ T7 Denver Broncos Team Helmet	.50	.23	.06
☐ T8 Detroit Lions Team Helmet	.50	.23	.06
☐ T9 Green Bay Packers Team Helmet	.50	.23	.06
☐ T10 Houston Oilers Team Helmet	.50	.23	.06
☐ T11 Indianapolis Colts Team Helmet	.50	.23	.06
☐ T12 Kansas City Chiefs Team Helmet	.50	.23	.06
☐ T13 Los Angeles Raiders Team Helmet	.75	.35	.09
☐ T14 Los Angeles Rams Team Helmet	.50	.23	.06
☐ T15 Miami Dolphins Team Helmet	.75	.35	.09
☐ T16 Minnesota Vikings Team Helmet	.50	.23	.06
☐ T17 New England Patriots Team Helmet	.50	.23	.06
☐ T18 New Orleans Saints Team Helmet	.50	.23	.06
☐ T19 New York Giants Team Helmet	.50	.23	.06
☐ T20 New York Jets Team Helmet	.50	.23	.06
☐ T21 Philadelphia Eagles Team Helmet	.50	.23	.06
☐ T22 Phoenix Cardinals Team Helmet	.50	.23	.06
☐ T23 Pittsburgh Steelers Team Helmet	.50	.23	.06
☐ T24 San Diego Chargers Team Helmet	.50	.23	.06
☐ T25 San Francisco 49ers Team Helmet	.50	.23	.06
☐ T26 Seattle Seahawks Team Helmet	.50	.23	.06
☐ T27 Tampa Bay Buccaneers Team Helmet	.50	.23	.06
☐ T28 Washington Redskins Team Helme	.50	.23	.06

1992 GameDay Draft Day Promos

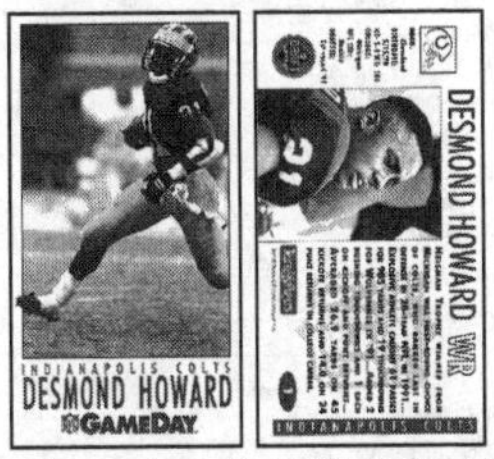

This 13-card promo set was produced by NFL Properties. In the May 1, 1992 edition of USA Today, an ad ran offering to the public 2,500 sets for 50.00 each with the proceeds going to NFL Charities. Other unnumbered sets (originally reported as 10,000 sets but later discovered to be only a small percentage of the original reported amount with many of these other sets missing one player) were also available through various media and dealer channels. The cards were patterned after 1965 Topps football and thus measure approximately 2 1/2" by 4 11/16". Several cards of the same player were issued to reflect different draft day scenarios; 13 different combos existed. Card fronts feature a full-color action picture in a small colored border enclosed by a white border. The team name beneath the photo is in gray lettering, while the player's name appears in block lettering. The title "NFL GameDay" is below the name. Horizontal backs feature the player's team helmet in a box, biography, and the NFL Draft logo in the white border on the far left. A full-color photo is also on the back along with a summary of the player's collegiate career. Although all the cards are numbered "1" on the back, they are checklisted below in alphabetical order according to the player's last name.

	MINT	NRMT	EXC
COMPLETE SET (13)	20.00	9.00	2.50
COMMON CARD (1A-1M)	1.25	.55	.16
☐ 1A Quentin Coryatt (Rams)	3.00	1.35	.35
☐ 1B Vaughn Dunbar (Falcons)	1.25	.55	.16
☐ 1C Vaughn Dunbar (49ers)	1.25	.55	.16
☐ 1D Vaughn Dunbar (Seahawks)	1.25	.55	.16
☐ 1E Steve Emtman (Colts)	1.25	.55	.16
☐ 1F Steve Emtman (Rams)	1.25	.55	.16
☐ 1G Desmond Howard (Colts)	2.50	1.10	.30
☐ 1H Desmond Howard (Redskins)	2.50	1.10	.30
☐ 1I David Klingler (Chiefs)	1.50	.70	.19
☐ 1J David Klingler (Giants)	1.50	.70	.19
☐ 1K Troy Vincent (Bengals)	1.25	.55	.16
☐ 1L Troy Vincent (Colts)	1.25	.55	.16
☐ 1M Troy Vincent (Packers)	1.25	.55	.16

1992 GameDay

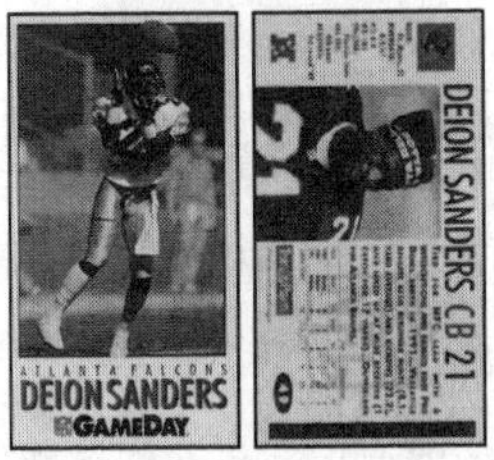

This 500-card set measures 2 1/2" by 4 11/16" and was issued in 12-card packs. In terms of card size, it is the largest basic issue set since 1965 Topps. The fronts feature color action player photos that stand out from a black-and-white background. The photo is bordered by a color that corresponds to the player's team. The border of the card is white with the player's name and team at the bottom. Horizontal backs carry close-up color player photos surrounded by biography, statistics and career highlights. The player's name, position, uniform number, team name and helmet icon complete the back. The backs are done in team colors. The set includes 14 multi-player special cards which feature 56 rookies chosen after the third round of the 1992 draft. Rookie Cards include Edgar Bennett, Steve Bono, Robert Brooks, Terrell Buckley, Mark Chmura, Marco Coleman, Quentin Coryatt, Steve Emtman, Chester McGlockton, Johnny Mitchell, Carl Pickens, and Tommy Vardell.

	MINT	NRMT	EXC
COMPLETE SET (500)	20.00	9.00	2.50
COMMON CARD (1-500)	.08	.04	.01
☐ 1 Jim Kelly	.30	.14	.04
☐ 2 Mark Ingram	.08	.04	.01
☐ 3 Travis McNeal	.08	.04	.01
☐ 4 Ricky Ervins	.08	.04	.01
☐ 5 Joe Montana	2.50	1.10	.30
☐ 6 Broderick Thompson	.08	.04	.01
☐ 7 Darion Conner	.08	.04	.01
☐ 8 Jim Harbaugh	.30	.14	.04
☐ 9 Harvey Williams	.30	.14	.04
☐ 10 Chip Banks	.08	.04	.01
☐ 11 Henry Thomas	.08	.04	.01
☐ 12 Derek Brown TE	.08	.04	.01
☐ 13 James Joseph	.08	.04	.01
☐ 14 Kevin Fagan	.08	.04	.01
☐ 15 Chuck Klingbeil	.08	.04	.01
☐ 16 Harlon Barnett	.08	.04	.01
☐ 17 Jim Price	.08	.04	.01
☐ 18 Terrell Buckley	.08	.04	.01
☐ 19 Paul McJulien	.08	.04	.01
☐ 20 James Hasty	.08	.04	.01
☐ 21 James Francis	.08	.04	.01
☐ 22 Andre Tippett	.08	.04	.01
☐ 23 John Elway	1.50	.70	.19
☐ 24 Eric Dickerson	.15	.07	.02
☐ 25 James Jefferson	.08	.04	.01
☐ 26 Danny Noonan	.08	.04	.01
☐ 27 Warren Moon	.30	.14	.04
☐ 28 Gene Atkins	.08	.04	.01
☐ 29 Jessie Hester	.08	.04	.01
☐ 30 Mike Mooney Kevin Smith RB Ron Humphrey Tracy Boyd	.08	.04	.01
☐ 31 Toby Caston	.08	.04	.01
☐ 32 Howard Dinkins	.08	.04	.01
☐ 33 James Patton	.08	.04	.01
☐ 34 Walter Reeves	.08	.04	.01
☐ 35 Johnny Mitchell	.08	.04	.01
☐ 36 Mike Brim	.08	.04	.01
☐ 37 Irving Fryar	.15	.07	.02
☐ 38 Lewis Billups	.08	.04	.01
☐ 39 Alonzo Spellman	.15	.07	.02
☐ 40 John Friesz	.15	.07	.02
☐ 41 Patrick Hunter	.08	.04	.01
☐ 42 Reuben Davis	.08	.04	.01
☐ 43 Tom Myslinski Shawn Harper Mark Thomas Mike Frier	.08	.04	.01
☐ 44 Siran Stacy	.08	.04	.01
☐ 45 Stephone Paige	.08	.04	.01
☐ 46 Eddie Robinson	.08	.04	.01
☐ 47 Tracy Scroggins	.08	.04	.01
☐ 48 David Klingler	.15	.07	.02
☐ 49A Deion Sanders ERR (Last line of card says outfielder)	1.25	.55	.16
☐ 49B Deion Sanders COR (Last line of card says plays outfield)	1.25	.55	.16
☐ 50 Tom Waddle	.08	.04	.01
☐ 51 Gary Anderson RB	.08	.04	.01
☐ 52 Kevin Butler	.08	.04	.01
☐ 53 Bruce Smith	.30	.14	.04
☐ 54 Steve Sewell	.08	.04	.01
☐ 55 Wesley Walls	.08	.04	.01
☐ 56 Lawrence Taylor	.30	.14	.04
☐ 57 Mike Merriweather	.08	.04	.01
☐ 58 Roman Phifer	.08	.04	.01
☐ 59 Shaun Gayle	.08	.04	.01

☐ 60 Marc Boutte	.08	.04	.01
☐ 61 Tony Mayberry	.08	.04	.01
☐ 62 Antone Davis UER	.08	.04	.01
(Card has 9th pick in '91 draft, was 8th)			
☐ 63 Rod Bernstine	.08	.04	.01
☐ 64 Shane Collins	.08	.04	.01
☐ 65 Martin Bayless	.08	.04	.01
☐ 66 Corey Harris	.08	.04	.01
☐ 67 Jason Hanson	.15	.07	.02
☐ 68 John Fina	.08	.04	.01
☐ 69 Cornelius Bennett	.15	.07	.02
☐ 70 Mark Bortz	.08	.04	.01
☐ 71 Gary Anderson K	.08	.04	.01
☐ 72 Paul Siever	.08	.04	.01
☐ 73 Flipper Anderson	.08	.04	.01
☐ 74 Shane Dronett	.08	.04	.01
☐ 75 Brian Noble	.08	.04	.01
☐ 76 Tim Green	.08	.04	.01
☐ 77 Percy Snow	.08	.04	.01
☐ 78 Greg McMurtry	.08	.04	.01
☐ 79 Dana Hall	.15	.07	.02
☐ 80 Tyji Armstrong	.08	.04	.01
☐ 81 Gary Clark	.30	.14	.04
☐ 82 Steve Emtman	.08	.04	.01
☐ 83 Eric Moore	.08	.04	.01
☐ 84 Brent Jones	.15	.07	.02
☐ 85 Ray Seals	.08	.04	.01
☐ 86 James Jones	.08	.04	.01
☐ 87 Jeff Hostetler	.15	.07	.02
☐ 88 Keith Jackson	.15	.07	.02
☐ 89 Gary Plummer	.08	.04	.01
☐ 90 Robert Blackmon	.08	.04	.01
☐ 91 Larry Tharpe	.08	.04	.01
Michael Brandon			
Anthony Hamlet			
Mike Pawlawski			
☐ 92 Greg Skrepenak	.08	.04	.01
☐ 93 Kevin Call	.08	.04	.01
☐ 94 Clarence Kay	.08	.04	.01
☐ 95 William Fuller	.15	.07	.02
☐ 96 Troy Auzenne	.08	.04	.01
☐ 97 Carl Pickens	3.00	1.35	.35
☐ 98 Lorenzo White	.08	.04	.01
☐ 99 Doug Smith	.08	.04	.01
☐ 100 Dale Carter	.30	.14	.04
☐ 101 Fred McAfee	.08	.04	.01
☐ 102 Jack Del Rio	.08	.04	.01
☐ 103 Vaughn Dunbar	.08	.04	.01
☐ 104 J.J. Birden	.08	.04	.01
☐ 105 Harris Barton	.08	.04	.01
☐ 106 Ray Ethridge	.08	.04	.01
☐ 107 John Gesek	.08	.04	.01
☐ 108 Mike Singletary	.15	.07	.02
☐ 109 Mark Rypien	.08	.04	.01
☐ 110 Robb Thomas	.08	.04	.01
☐ 111 Joe Kelly	.08	.04	.01
☐ 112 Ben Smith	.08	.04	.01
☐ 113 Neil O'Donnell	.30	.14	.04
☐ 114 John L. Williams	.08	.04	.01
☐ 115 Mike Sherrard	.08	.04	.01
☐ 116 Chad Hennings	.15	.07	.02
☐ 117 Henry Ellard	.15	.07	.02
☐ 118 Jay Hilgenberg	.08	.04	.01
☐ 119 Charles Dimry	.08	.04	.01
☐ 120 Chuck Smith	.08	.04	.01
☐ 121 Brian Mitchell	.15	.07	.02
☐ 122 Eric Allen	.08	.04	.01
☐ 123 Nate Lewis	.08	.04	.01
☐ 124 Kevin Ross	.08	.04	.01
☐ 125 Jimmy Smith	.30	.14	.04
☐ 126 Kevin Smith	.30	.14	.04
☐ 127 Larry Webster	.08	.04	.01
☐ 128 Marv Cook	.08	.04	.01
☐ 129 Calvin Williams	.15	.07	.02
☐ 130 Harry Swayne	.08	.04	.01
☐ 131 Jimmie Jones	.08	.04	.01
☐ 132 Ethan Horton	.08	.04	.01
☐ 133 Chris Mims	.15	.07	.02
☐ 134 Derrick Thomas	.30	.14	.04
☐ 135 Gerald Dixon	.08	.04	.01
☐ 136 Gary Zimmerman	.08	.04	.01
☐ 137 Robert Jones	.08	.04	.01
☐ 138 Steve Broussard	.08	.04	.01
☐ 139 David Wyman	.08	.04	.01
☐ 140 Ian Beckles	.08	.04	.01
☐ 141 Steve Bono	.50	.23	.06
☐ 142 Cris Carter	.30	.14	.04
☐ 143 Anthony Carter	.15	.07	.02
☐ 144 Greg Townsend	.08	.04	.01
☐ 145 Al Smith	.08	.04	.01
☐ 146 Troy Vincent	.15	.07	.02
☐ 147 Jessie Tuggle	.08	.04	.01
☐ 148 David Fulcher	.08	.04	.01
☐ 149 Johnny Rembert	.08	.04	.01
☐ 150 Ernie Jones	.08	.04	.01
☐ 151 Mark Royals	.08	.04	.01
☐ 152 Jeff Bryant	.08	.04	.01
☐ 153 Vai Sikahema	.08	.04	.01
☐ 154 Tony Woods	.08	.04	.01
☐ 155 Joe Bowden	.08	.04	.01
Doug Rigby			
Marcus Dowdell			
Ostell Miles			
☐ 156 Mark Carrier WR	.15	.07	.02
☐ 157 Joe Nash	.08	.04	.01
☐ 158 Keith Van Horne	.08	.04	.01
☐ 159 Kelvin Martin	.08	.04	.01
☐ 160 Peter Tom Willis	.08	.04	.01
☐ 161 Richard Johnson	.08	.04	.01
☐ 162 Louis Oliver	.08	.04	.01
☐ 163 Nick Lowery	.08	.04	.01
☐ 164 Ricky Proehl	.08	.04	.01
☐ 165 Terance Mathis	.15	.07	.02
☐ 166 Keith Sims	.08	.04	.01
☐ 167 E.J. Junior	.08	.04	.01
☐ 168 Scott Mersereau	.08	.04	.01
☐ 169 Tom Rathman	.08	.04	.01
☐ 170 Robert Harris	.08	.04	.01
☐ 171 Ashley Ambrose	.15	.07	.02
☐ 172 David Treadwell	.08	.04	.01
☐ 173 Mark Green	.08	.04	.01
☐ 174 Clayton Holmes	.08	.04	.01
☐ 175 Tony Sacca	.08	.04	.01
☐ 176 Wes Hopkins	.08	.04	.01
☐ 177 Mark Wheeler	.08	.04	.01
☐ 178 Robert Clark	.08	.04	.01
☐ 179 Eugene Daniel	.08	.04	.01
☐ 180 Rob Burnett	.08	.04	.01
☐ 181 Al Edwards	.08	.04	.01
☐ 182 Clarence Verdin	.08	.04	.01
☐ 183 Tom Newberry	.08	.04	.01
☐ 184 Mike Jones	.08	.04	.01
☐ 185 Roy Foster	.08	.04	.01
☐ 186 Leslie O'Neal	.15	.07	.02
☐ 187 Izel Jenkins	.08	.04	.01
☐ 188 Willie Clay	.40	.18	.05
Ty Detmer			
Mike Evans			
Ed McDaniel			
☐ 189 Mike Tomczak	.08	.04	.01
☐ 190 Leonard Wheeler	.08	.04	.01
☐ 191 Gaston Green	.08	.04	.01
☐ 192 Maury Buford	.08	.04	.01
☐ 193 Jeremy Lincoln	.08	.04	.01
☐ 194 Todd Collins	.08	.04	.01
☐ 195 Billy Ray Smith	.08	.04	.01
☐ 196 Renaldo Turnbull	.08	.04	.01
☐ 197 Michael Carter	.08	.04	.01
☐ 198 Rod Milstead	.08	.04	.01
Dion Lambert			
Hesham Ismail			
Reggie E. White			
☐ 199 Shawn Collins	.08	.04	.01
☐ 200 Issiac Holt	.08	.04	.01
☐ 201 Irv Eatman	.08	.04	.01
☐ 202 Anthony Thompson	.08	.04	.01
☐ 203 Chester McGlockton	.30	.14	.04
☐ 204 Greg Biggs	.08	.04	.01
Chris Crooms			
Ephesians Bartley			
Curtis Whitley			
☐ 205 James Brown	.08	.04	.01
☐ 206 Marvin Washington	.08	.04	.01
☐ 207 Richard Cooper	.08	.04	.01
☐ 208 Jim C. Jensen	.08	.04	.01
☐ 209 Sam Seale	.08	.04	.01
☐ 210 Andre Reed	.15	.07	.02
☐ 211 Thane Gash	.08	.04	.01
☐ 212 Randal Hill	.08	.04	.01
☐ 213 Brad Baxter	.08	.04	.01
☐ 214 Michael Cofer	.08	.04	.01
☐ 215 Ray Crockett	.08	.04	.01
☐ 216 Tony Mandarich	.08	.04	.01
☐ 217 Warren Williams	.08	.04	.01
☐ 218 Erik Kramer	.15	.07	.02
☐ 219 Bubby Brister	.08	.04	.01
☐ 220 Steve Young	1.50	.70	.19
☐ 221 Jeff George	.30	.14	.04
☐ 222 James Washington	.08	.04	.01
☐ 223 Bruce Alexander	.08	.04	.01
☐ 224 Broderick Thomas	.08	.04	.01
☐ 225 Bern Brostek	.08	.04	.01
☐ 226 Brian Blades	.15	.07	.02
☐ 227 Troy Aikman	2.50	1.10	.30
☐ 228 Aaron Wallace	.08	.04	.01
☐ 229 Tommy Jeter	.08	.04	.01
☐ 230 Russell Maryland	.15	.07	.02
☐ 231 Charles Haley	.15	.07	.02
☐ 232 James Lofton	.15	.07	.02
☐ 233 William White	.08	.04	.01
☐ 234 Tim McGee	.08	.04	.01
☐ 235 Haywood Jeffires	.15	.07	.02
☐ 236 Charles Mann	.08	.04	.01
☐ 237 Robert Lyles	.08	.04	.01
☐ 238 Rohn Stark	.08	.04	.01
☐ 239 Jim Morrissey	.08	.04	.01
☐ 240 Mel Gray	.15	.07	.02
☐ 241 Barry Word	.08	.04	.01
☐ 242 Dave Widell	.08	.04	.01
☐ 243 Sean Gilbert	.30	.14	.04
☐ 244 Tommy Maddox	.08	.04	.01
☐ 245 Bernie Kosar	.15	.07	.02
☐ 246 John Roper	.08	.04	.01
☐ 247 Mark Higgs	.08	.04	.01
☐ 248 Rob Moore	.15	.07	.02
☐ 249 Dan Fike	.08	.04	.01
☐ 250 Dan Saleaumua	.08	.04	.01
☐ 251 Tim Krumrie	.08	.04	.01
☐ 252 Tony Casillas	.08	.04	.01
☐ 253 Jayice Pearson	.08	.04	.01
☐ 254 Dan Marino	4.00	1.80	.50
☐ 255 Tony Martin	.30	.14	.04
☐ 256 Mike Fox	.08	.04	.01
☐ 257 Courtney Hawkins	.15	.07	.02
☐ 258 Leonard Marshall	.08	.04	.01
☐ 259 Willie Gault	.15	.07	.02
☐ 260 Al Toon	.15	.07	.02
☐ 261 Browning Nagle	.08	.04	.01
☐ 262 Ronnie Lott	.15	.07	.02
☐ 263 Sean Jones	.15	.07	.02
☐ 264 Ernest Givins	.15	.07	.02
☐ 265 Ray Donaldson	.08	.04	.01
☐ 266 Vaughan Johnson	.08	.04	.01
☐ 267 Tommy Hodson	.08	.04	.01
☐ 268 Chris Doleman	.08	.04	.01
☐ 269 Pat Swilling	.15	.07	.02
☐ 270 Merril Hoge	.08	.04	.01
☐ 271 Bill Maas	.08	.04	.01
☐ 272 Sterling Sharpe	.30	.14	.04
☐ 273 Mitchell Price	.08	.04	.01
☐ 274 Richard Brown	.08	.04	.01
☐ 275 Randall Cunningham	.15	.07	.02
☐ 276 Chris Martin	.08	.04	.01
☐ 277 Courtney Hall	.08	.04	.01
☐ 278 Michael Walter	.08	.04	.01
☐ 279 Ricardo McDonald	.08	.04	.01
David Wilson			
Sean Lumpkin			
Tony Brooks			
☐ 280 Bill Brooks	.08	.04	.01
☐ 281 Jay Schroeder	.08	.04	.01
☐ 282 John Stephens	.08	.04	.01
☐ 283 William Perry	.15	.07	.02
☐ 284 Floyd Turner	.08	.04	.01
☐ 285 Carnell Lake	.08	.04	.01
☐ 286 Joel Steed	.08	.04	.01
☐ 287 Vinnie Clark	.08	.04	.01
☐ 288 Ken Norton	.30	.14	.04
☐ 289 Eric Thomas	.08	.04	.01
☐ 290 Derrick Fenner	.08	.04	.01
☐ 291 Tony Smith	.08	.04	.01
☐ 292 Eric Metcalf	.15	.07	.02
☐ 293 Roger Craig	.15	.07	.02
☐ 294 Leon Searcy	.15	.07	.02
☐ 295 Tyrone Legette	.08	.04	.01
☐ 296 Rob Taylor	.08	.04	.01
☐ 297 Eric Williams	.08	.04	.01
☐ 298 David Little	.08	.04	.01
☐ 299 Wayne Martin	.08	.04	.01
☐ 300 Eric Martin	.08	.04	.01
☐ 301 Jim Everett	.15	.07	.02
☐ 302 Michael Dean Perry	.15	.07	.02
☐ 303 Dwayne White	.08	.04	.01
☐ 304 Greg Lloyd	.30	.14	.04
☐ 305 Ricky Reynolds	.08	.04	.01
☐ 306 Anthony Smith	.08	.04	.01
☐ 307 Robert Delpino	.08	.04	.01
☐ 308 Ken Clark	.08	.04	.01
☐ 309 Chris Jacke	.08	.04	.01
☐ 310 Reggie Dwight	.08	.04	.01
Anthony McCoy			
Craig Thompson			
Klaus Wilmsmeyer			
☐ 311 Doug Widell	.08	.04	.01
☐ 312 Sammie Smith	.08	.04	.01
☐ 313 Ken O'Brien	.08	.04	.01
☐ 314 Timm Rosenbach	.08	.04	.01
☐ 315 Jesse Sapolu	.08	.04	.01
☐ 316 Ronnie Harmon	.08	.04	.01
☐ 317 Bill Pickel	.08	.04	.01
☐ 318 Lonnie Young	.08	.04	.01
☐ 319 Chris Burkett	.08	.04	.01
☐ 320 Ervin Randle	.08	.04	.01
☐ 321 Ed West	.08	.04	.01
☐ 322 Tom Thayer	.08	.04	.01
☐ 323 Keith McKeller	.08	.04	.01
☐ 324 Webster Slaughter	.08	.04	.01
☐ 325 Duane Bickett	.08	.04	.01
☐ 326 Howie Long	.15	.07	.02
☐ 327 Sam Mills	.08	.04	.01
☐ 328 Mike Golic	.08	.04	.01
☐ 329 Bruce Armstrong	.08	.04	.01
☐ 330 Pat Terrell	.08	.04	.01
☐ 331 Mike Pritchard	.15	.07	.02
☐ 332 Audray McMillian	.08	.04	.01
☐ 333 Marquez Pope	.08	.04	.01
☐ 334 Pierce Holt	.08	.04	.01
☐ 335 Erik Howard	.08	.04	.01
☐ 336 Jerry Rice	2.50	1.10	.30
☐ 337 Vinny Testaverde	.15	.07	.02
☐ 338 Bart Oates	.08	.04	.01
☐ 339 Nolan Harrison	.08	.04	.01
☐ 340 Chris Goode	.08	.04	.01
☐ 341 Ken Ruettgers	.08	.04	.01
☐ 342 Brad Muster	.08	.04	.01
☐ 343 Paul Farren	.08	.04	.01
☐ 344 Corey Miller	.08	.04	.01
☐ 345 Brian Washington	.08	.04	.01
☐ 346 Jim Sweeney	.08	.04	.01
☐ 347 Keith McCants	.08	.04	.01
☐ 348 Louis Lipps	.08	.04	.01
☐ 349 Keith Byars	.08	.04	.01
☐ 350 Steve Walsh	.08	.04	.01
☐ 351 Jeff Jaeger	.08	.04	.01
☐ 352 Christian Okoye	.08	.04	.01
☐ 353 Cris Dishman	.08	.04	.01
☐ 354 Keith Kartz	.08	.04	.01
☐ 355 Harold Green	.08	.04	.01
☐ 356 Richard Shelton	.08	.04	.01
☐ 357 Jacob Green	.08	.04	.01
☐ 358 Al Noga	.08	.04	.01
☐ 359 Dean Biasucci	.08	.04	.01
☐ 360 Jeff Herrod	.08	.04	.01
☐ 361 Bennie Blades	.08	.04	.01
☐ 362 Mark Vlasic	.08	.04	.01
☐ 363 Chris Miller	.15	.07	.02
☐ 364 Bubba McDowell	.08	.04	.01
☐ 365 Tyronne Stowe	.08	.04	.01
☐ 366 Jon Vaughn	.08	.04	.01
☐ 367 Winston Moss	.08	.04	.01
☐ 368 Levon Kirkland	.08	.04	.01
☐ 369 Ted Washington	.08	.04	.01
☐ 370 Cortez Kennedy	.15	.07	.02
☐ 371 Jeff Feagles	.08	.04	.01
☐ 372 Aundray Bruce	.08	.04	.01
☐ 373 Michael Irvin	.30	.14	.04
☐ 374 Lemuel Stinson	.08	.04	.01
☐ 375 Billy Joe Tolliver	.08	.04	.01
☐ 376 Anthony Munoz	.15	.07	.02
☐ 377 Nate Newton	.15	.07	.02
☐ 378 Steve Smith	.08	.04	.01
☐ 379 Eugene Chung	.08	.04	.01
☐ 380 Bryan Hinkle	.08	.04	.01
☐ 381 Dan McGwire	.08	.04	.01
☐ 382 Jeff Cross	.08	.04	.01
☐ 383 Ferrell Edmunds	.08	.04	.01
☐ 384 Craig Heyward	.15	.07	.02
☐ 385 Shannon Sharpe	.30	.14	.04
☐ 386 Anthony Miller	.15	.07	.02
☐ 387 Eugene Lockhart	.08	.04	.01
☐ 388 Darryl Henley	.08	.04	.01
☐ 389 LeRoy Butler	.08	.04	.01
☐ 390 Scott Fulhage	.08	.04	.01
☐ 391 Andre Ware	.08	.04	.01
☐ 392 Lionel Washington	.08	.04	.01
☐ 393 Rick Fenney	.08	.04	.01
☐ 394 John Taylor	.15	.07	.02
☐ 395 Chris Singleton	.08	.04	.01
☐ 396 Monte Coleman	.08	.04	.01
☐ 397 Brett Perriman	.30	.14	.04
☐ 398 Hugh Millen	.08	.04	.01
☐ 399 Dennis Gentry	.08	.04	.01
☐ 400 Eddie Anderson	.08	.04	.01
☐ 401 Lance Olberding	.15	.07	.02
Eddie Miller			
Dwayne Sabb			
Corey Widmer			
☐ 402 Brent Williams	.08	.04	.01
☐ 403 Tony Zendejas	.08	.04	.01
☐ 404 Donnell Woolford	.08	.04	.01
☐ 405 Boomer Esiason	.15	.07	.02
☐ 406 Gill Fenerty	.08	.04	.01
☐ 407 Kurt Barber	.08	.04	.01
☐ 408 William Thomas	.08	.04	.01
☐ 409 Keith Henderson	.08	.04	.01
☐ 410 Paul Gruber	.08	.04	.01
☐ 411 Alfred Oglesby	.08	.04	.01
☐ 412 Wendell Davis	.08	.04	.01
☐ 413 Robert Brooks	2.50	1.10	.30
☐ 414 Ken Willis	.08	.04	.01
☐ 415 Aaron Cox	.08	.04	.01
☐ 416 Thurman Thomas	.30	.14	.04
☐ 417 Alton Montgomery	.08	.04	.01
☐ 418 Mike Prior	.08	.04	.01
☐ 419 Albert Bentley	.08	.04	.01
☐ 420 John Randle	.15	.07	.02
☐ 421 Dermontti Dawson	.08	.04	.01
☐ 422 Phillippi Sparks	.08	.04	.01
☐ 423 Michael Jackson	.15	.07	.02
☐ 424 Carl Banks	.08	.04	.01
☐ 425 Chris Zorich	.15	.07	.02
☐ 426 Dwight Stone	.08	.04	.01
☐ 427 Bryan Millard	.08	.04	.01
☐ 428 Neal Anderson	.08	.04	.01
☐ 429 Michael Haynes	.15	.07	.02
☐ 430 Michael Young	.08	.04	.01
☐ 431 Dennis Byrd	.08	.04	.01
☐ 432 Fred Barnett	.30	.14	.04
☐ 433 Junior Seau	.30	.14	.04
☐ 434 Mark Clayton	.15	.07	.02
☐ 435 Marco Coleman	.15	.07	.02
☐ 436 Lee Williams	.08	.04	.01
☐ 437 Stan Thomas	.08	.04	.01
☐ 438 Lawrence Dawsey	.15	.07	.02
☐ 439 Tommy Vardell	.15	.07	.02
☐ 440 Steve Israel	.08	.04	.01
☐ 441 Ray Childress	.08	.04	.01
☐ 442 Darren Woodson	.30	.14	.04
☐ 443 Lamar Lathon	.08	.04	.01
☐ 444 Reggie Roby	.08	.04	.01
☐ 445 Eric Green	.08	.04	.01
☐ 446 Mark Carrier DB	.08	.04	.01
☐ 447 Kevin Walker	.08	.04	.01
☐ 448 Vince Workman	.15	.07	.02
☐ 449 Leonard Griffin	.08	.04	.01
☐ 450 Robert Porcher	.15	.07	.02
☐ 451 Hart Lee Dykes	.08	.04	.01
☐ 452 Thomas McLemore	.08	.04	.01
☐ 453 Jamie Dukes	.08	.04	.01

	MINT	NRMT	EXC
☐ 454 Bill Romanowski	.08	.04	.01
☐ 455 Deron Cherry	.08	.04	.01
☐ 456 Burt Grossman	.08	.04	.01
☐ 457 Lance Smith	.08	.04	.01
☐ 458 Jay Novacek	.15	.07	.02
☐ 459 Eric Pegram	.15	.07	.02
☐ 460 Reggie Rutland	.08	.04	.01
☐ 461 Rickey Jackson	.08	.04	.01
☐ 462 Dennis Brown	.08	.04	.01
☐ 463 Neil Smith	.30	.14	.04
☐ 464 Rich Gannon	.08	.04	.01
☐ 465 Herman Moore	1.50	.70	.19
☐ 466 Rodney Peete	.15	.07	.02
☐ 467 Alvin Harper	.15	.07	.02
☐ 468 Andre Rison	.15	.07	.02
☐ 469 Rufus Porter	.08	.04	.01
☐ 470 Robert Wilson	.08	.04	.01
☐ 471 Phil Simms	.15	.07	.02
☐ 472 Art Monk	.15	.07	.02
☐ 473 Mike Tice	.08	.04	.01
☐ 474 Quentin Coryatt	.30	.14	.04
☐ 475 Chris Hinton	.08	.04	.01
☐ 476 Vance Johnson	.08	.04	.01
☐ 477 Kyle Clifton	.08	.04	.01
☐ 478 Garth Jax	.08	.04	.01
☐ 479 Ray Agnew	.08	.04	.01
☐ 480 Patrick Rowe	.08	.04	.01
☐ 481 Joe Jacoby	.08	.04	.01
☐ 482 Bruce Pickens	.08	.04	.01
☐ 483 Keith DeLong	.08	.04	.01
☐ 484 Eric Swann	.15	.07	.02
☐ 485 Steve McMichael	.15	.07	.02
☐ 486 Leroy Hoard	.15	.07	.02
☐ 487 Rickey Dixon	.08	.04	.01
☐ 488 Robert Perryman	.08	.04	.01
☐ 489 Darryl Williams	.08	.04	.01
☐ 490 Emmitt Smith	5.00	2.20	.60
☐ 491 Dino Hackett	.08	.04	.01
☐ 492 Earnest Byner	.08	.04	.01
☐ 493 Bucky Richardson	.08	.04	.01
Bernard Dafney			
Anthony Davis			
Tony Brown			
☐ 494 Bill Johnson	.08	.04	.01
☐ 495 Darryl Ashmore	.08	.04	.01
Joe Campbell			
Kelvin Harris			
Tim Lester			
☐ 496 Nick Bell	.08	.04	.01
☐ 497 Jerry Ball	.08	.04	.01
☐ 498 Edgar Bennett	4.00	1.80	.50
Mark Chmura			
Chris Holder			
Mazio Royster			
☐ 499 Steve Christie	.08	.04	.01
☐ 500 Kenneth Davis	.08	.04	.01

1992 GameDay Box Tops

The GameDay foil pack display boxes featured four different box tops. Each box lid measures approximately 5 1/2" by 11 5/8" and displays four GameDay player cards. While most of the cards featured differ from one box top to another, the Randall Cunningham card is found on all four box tops. The backs of the box tops are blank. The box tops are unnumbered and the individual cards are checklisted below beginning in the upper left corner and ending in the lower right corner.

	MINT	NRMT	EXC
COMPLETE SET (4)	2.00	.90	.25
COMMON PANEL (1-4)	.50	.23	.06
☐ 1 Randall Cunningham	.50	.23	.06
Anthony Munoz			
Earnest Byner			
Jim Everett			
☐ 2 Haywood Jeffires	.50	.23	.06
Randall Cunningham			
Mark Carrier DB			
Vinny Testaverde			
☐ 3 Howie Long	.50	.23	.06
Thurman Thomas			
Randall Cunningham			
Jerry Rice			
☐ 4 Christian Okoye	.50	.23	.06
Pat Swilling			
Steve Emtman			
Randall Cunningham			

1992 GameDay National

The cards in this 46-card preview set were given away during the 13th National Sports Card Convention in Atlanta, Georgia. An attractive black vinyl notebook with a cardboard slip cover was available to hold the cards. Like the 1965 Topps football set, these cards measure approximately 2 1/2" by 4 11/16". The players featured on each card front are in color against a black and white background. The horizontally oriented backs have career statistics, biography, and a color head shot. The cards are numbered on the back. Reportedly the cards of Deron Cherry, Mark Rypien, and Deion Sanders were individually distributed in limited quantities at the National in Atlanta.

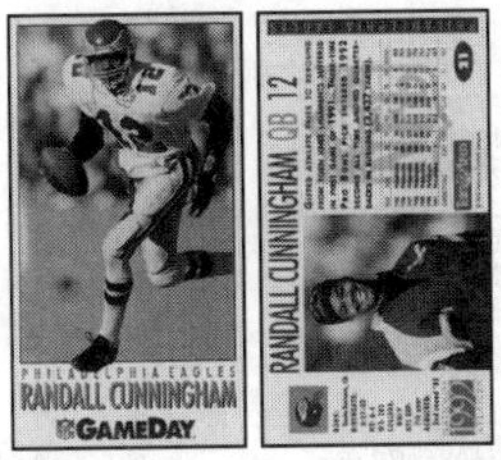

	MINT	NRMT	EXC
COMPLETE SET (46)	40.00	18.00	5.00
COMMON CARD (1-46)	.25	.11	.03
☐ 1 Deion Sanders SP	4.00	1.80	.50
☐ 2 Jim Kelly	.50	.23	.06
☐ 3 Jim Harbaugh	.50	.23	.06
☐ 4 Boomer Esiason	.30	.14	.04
☐ 5 Bernie Kosar	.30	.14	.04
☐ 6 Troy Aikman	5.00	2.20	.60
☐ 7 John Elway	4.00	1.80	.50
☐ 8 Rodney Peete	.30	.14	.04
☐ 9 Sterling Sharpe	1.00	.45	.12
☐ 10 Warren Moon	.50	.23	.06
☐ 11 Jeff George	.50	.23	.06
☐ 12 Derrick Thomas	.30	.14	.04
☐ 13 Howie Long	.30	.14	.04
☐ 14 Jim Everett	.30	.14	.04
☐ 15 Dan Marino	10.00	4.50	1.25
☐ 16 Chris Doleman	.25	.11	.03
☐ 17 Irving Fryar	.30	.14	.04
☐ 18 Pat Swilling	.25	.11	.03
☐ 19 Lawrence Taylor	.50	.23	.06
☐ 20 Ken O'Brien	.25	.11	.03
☐ 21 Randall Cunningham	.30	.14	.04
☐ 22 Timm Rosenbach	.25	.11	.03
☐ 23 Bubby Brister	.25	.11	.03
☐ 24 John Friesz	.25	.11	.03
☐ 25 Joe Montana	6.00	2.70	.75
☐ 26 Dan McGwire	.25	.11	.03
☐ 27 Vinny Testaverde	.25	.11	.03
☐ 28 Mark Rypien SP	1.00	.45	.12
☐ 29 Ronnie Lott	.30	.14	.04
☐ 30 Marco Coleman	.30	.14	.04
☐ 31 Rob Moore	.30	.14	.04
☐ 32 Bill Pickel	.25	.11	.03
☐ 33 Brad Baxter	.25	.11	.03
☐ 34 Steve Broussard	.25	.11	.03
☐ 35 Darion Conner	.25	.11	.03
☐ 36 Chris Hinton	.25	.11	.03
☐ 37 Eric Pegram	.30	.14	.04
☐ 38 Jessie Tuggle	.25	.11	.03
☐ 39 Billy Joe Tolliver	.25	.11	.03
☐ 40 David Klingler	.30	.14	.04
☐ 41 Michael Irvin	1.00	.45	.12
☐ 42 Emmitt Smith	10.00	4.50	1.25
☐ 43 Quentin Coryatt	.50	.23	.06
☐ 44 Steve Emtman	.30	.14	.04
☐ 45 Deron Cherry SP	1.00	.45	.12
☐ 46 Ricky Ervins	.25	.11	.03

1992-93 GameDay Gamebreakers

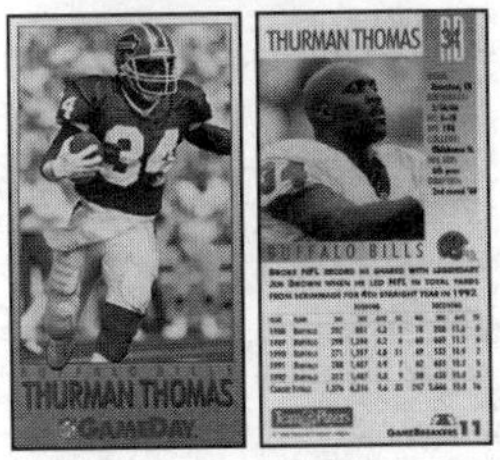

This 14-card set was first made available at the Super Bowl card show to preview the 1993 design. The cards, patterned after 1965 Topps football, measure approximately 2 1/2" by 4 11/16". The checklist card is printed with the individual number of the set and the total number produced (5,000). The fronts feature action player photos with the featured player in color against a black-and-white background. The pictures are bordered by a thin team color-coded line, and they rest on backgrounds that are pale versions of the team color at the bottom and fade to white toward the top. The team name and player's name are printed below the picture in the other team color. The backs carry a close-up player picture bordered on the right and bottom by a pale, team color-coded border that fades to white where they intersect at the team helmet icon. The borders contain the team name and biographical information. Below the picture, on a white background, are career highlights and statistics. The player's name, position, and jersey number appear at the top.

	MINT	NRMT	EXC
COMPLETE SET (14)	8.00	3.60	1.00
COMMON CARD (1-14)	.20	.09	.03
☐ 1 Marco Coleman	.20	.09	.03
☐ 2 Bill Cowher CO	.20	.09	.03
☐ 3 John Elway	1.50	.70	.19
☐ 4 Barry Foster	.30	.14	.04
☐ 5 Cortez Kennedy	.40	.18	.05
☐ 6 James Lofton	.30	.14	.04
☐ 7 Art Monk	.30	.14	.04
☐ 8 Jerry Rice	2.00	.90	.25
☐ 9 Sterling Sharpe	.50	.23	.06
☐ 10 Emmitt Smith	4.00	1.80	.50
☐ 11 Thurman Thomas	.60	.25	.07
☐ 12 Gino Torretta	.20	.09	.03
☐ 13 Steve Young	1.50	.70	.19
☐ 14 Checklist Card	.20	.09	.03

1992-93 GameDay SB Program

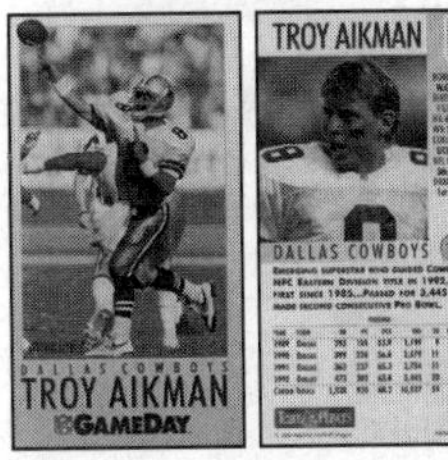

This six-card promo set was inserted one card per 1993 Super Bowl program. Each card measures approximately 2 1/2" by 4 3/4". The fronts feature action player photos with the featured player in color against a black-and-white background. The borders shade from white to the team's dominant color, and the team, name, player's name, and producer's name are printed in the team's second color in the bottom border. The backs carry a color close-up photo, biography, career summary, and season-by-season statistics. The cards are numbered on the back, arranged, in alphabetical order, and identified as promo cards.

	MINT	NRMT	EXC
COMPLETE SET (6)	12.00	5.50	1.50
COMMON CARD (1-6)	1.25	.55	.16
☐ 1 Troy Aikman	5.00	2.20	.60
☐ 2 Terry Allen	2.00	.90	.25
☐ 3 Ray Childress	1.25	.55	.16
☐ 4 Marco Coleman	1.25	.55	.16
☐ 5 Barry Foster	1.25	.55	.16
☐ 6 Sterling Sharpe	2.00	.90	.25

1993 GameDay

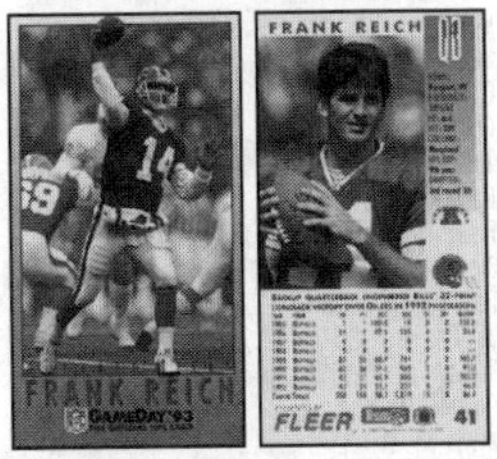

Issued by Fleer in 12-card packs, this set consists of 480 cards measuring approximately 2 1/2" by 4 3/4". The fronts feature team-colored borders that surround color action player photos. The photos stand out against black-and-white game-action backgrounds. The team name appears at the bottom of the picture and the player's name appears in team colors within the lower border. The backs carry close-up color player shots, biography, statistics and career highlights. Rookie Cards include Jerome Bettis, Drew Bledsoe, Reggie Brooks, Curtis Conway, Andre Hastings, Garrison Hearst, Qadry Ismail, Terry Kirby, O.J. McDuffie, Natrone Means, Glyn Milburn, Rick Mirer, Roosevelt Potts, Robert Smith, Dana Stubblefield and Kevin Williams. A six-card promo sheet was produced and priced below.

	MINT	NRMT	EXC
COMPLETE SET (480)	55.00	25.00	7.00
COMMON CARD (1-480)	.10	.05	.01
☐ 1 Troy Aikman	2.50	1.10	.30
☐ 2 Terry Allen	.40	.18	.05
☐ 3 Ray Childress	.10	.05	.01
☐ 4 Marco Coleman	.10	.05	.01
☐ 5 Barry Foster	.20	.09	.03
☐ 6 Sterling Sharpe	.40	.18	.05
☐ 7 Steve McMichael	.20	.09	.03
☐ 8 Steve Young	1.50	.70	.19
☐ 9 Derrick Thomas	.40	.18	.05
☐ 10 John Elway	1.50	.70	.19
☐ 11 Drew Bledsoe	7.00	3.10	.85
☐ 12 Jim Kelly	.40	.18	.05
☐ 13 Dan Marino	4.00	1.80	.50
☐ 14 Mo Lewis	.10	.05	.01
☐ 15 David Klingler	.10	.05	.01
☐ 16 Darrell Green	.10	.05	.01
☐ 17 James Francis	.10	.05	.01
☐ 18 John Copeland	.20	.09	.03
☐ 19 Terry McDaniel	.10	.05	.01
☐ 20 Barry Sanders	2.50	1.10	.30
☐ 21 Deion Sanders	1.50	.70	.19
☐ 22 Emmitt Smith	4.00	1.80	.50
☐ 23 Marion Butts	.10	.05	.01
☐ 24 Darryl Talley	.10	.05	.01
☐ 25 Randall Cunningham	.20	.09	.03
☐ 26 Rod Woodson	.40	.18	.05
☐ 27 Terrell Buckley	.10	.05	.01
☐ 28 Michael Haynes	.20	.09	.03
☐ 29 Tony Jones	.10	.05	.01
☐ 30 Santana Dotson	.20	.09	.03
☐ 31 Lomas Brown	.10	.05	.01
☐ 32 Eric Metcalf	.20	.09	.03
☐ 33 Morten Andersen	.10	.05	.01
☐ 34 Reggie Cobb	.10	.05	.01
☐ 35 Ferrell Edmunds	.10	.05	.01
☐ 36 Joe Montana	2.50	1.10	.30
☐ 37 Ken Harvey	.10	.05	.01
☐ 38 Rodney Hampton	.40	.18	.05
☐ 39 Kurt Gouveia	.10	.05	.01
☐ 40 Ken Norton Jr.	.20	.09	.03
☐ 41 Frank Reich	.20	.09	.03
☐ 42 Kevin Greene	.40	.18	.05
☐ 43 Cleveland Gary	.10	.05	.01
☐ 44 Maurice Hurst	.10	.05	.01
☐ 45 Troy Vincent	.10	.05	.01
☐ 46 Eric Curry	.10	.05	.01
☐ 47 Curtis Conway	2.00	.90	.25
☐ 48 Christian Okoye	.10	.05	.01
☐ 49 Tunch Ilkin	.10	.05	.01
☐ 50 Michael Irvin	.40	.18	.05
☐ 51 Bart Oates	.10	.05	.01
☐ 52 Pepper Johnson	.10	.05	.01
☐ 53 Vaughan Johnson	.10	.05	.01
☐ 54 Lawrence Taylor	.40	.18	.05
☐ 55 Junior Seau	.40	.18	.05
☐ 56 Michael Brooks	.10	.05	.01
☐ 57 Neal Anderson	.10	.05	.01
☐ 58 D.J. Johnson	.10	.05	.01
☐ 59 Seth Joyner	.10	.05	.01
☐ 60 Marvin Washington	.10	.05	.01
☐ 61 Ernest Givins	.20	.09	.03
☐ 62 Jaime Fields	.10	.05	.01
☐ 63 Vincent Brown	.10	.05	.01
☐ 64 Randall McDaniel	.10	.05	.01
☐ 65 Tommy Maddox	.10	.05	.01
☐ 66 Steve Everitt	.10	.05	.01
☐ 67 Brian Noble	.10	.05	.01
☐ 68 Bryce Paup	.40	.18	.05
☐ 69 Brad Baxter	.10	.05	.01
☐ 70 Demetrius DuBose	.10	.05	.01
☐ 71 Duane Bickett	.10	.05	.01
☐ 72 Mark Rypien	.10	.05	.01
☐ 73 Harris Barton	.10	.05	.01
☐ 74 Bruce Matthews	.10	.05	.01
☐ 75 Irving Fryar	.20	.09	.03
☐ 76 Steve Wisniewski	.10	.05	.01
☐ 77 Will Shields	.10	.05	.01
☐ 78 Tom Carter	.20	.09	.03
☐ 79 Steve Emtman	.10	.05	.01
☐ 80 Jerry Rice	2.50	1.10	.30
☐ 81 Art Monk	.20	.09	.03
☐ 82 Tony Tolbert	.10	.05	.01
☐ 83 Johnny Mitchell	.10	.05	.01
☐ 84 Deon Figures	.20	.09	.03
☐ 85 Marv Cook	.10	.05	.01
☐ 86 Darion Conner	.10	.05	.01
☐ 87 Ricky Proehl	.10	.05	.01
☐ 88 Tony Bennett	.10	.05	.01
☐ 89 Jay Schroeder	.10	.05	.01
☐ 90 Neil Smith	.40	.18	.05
☐ 91 Jarvis Williams	.10	.05	.01
☐ 92 James Hasty	.10	.05	.01
☐ 93 Anthony Miller	.20	.09	.03
☐ 94 Thomas Smith	.20	.09	.03
☐ 95 Richard Dent	.20	.09	.03
☐ 96 Henry Jones	.10	.05	.01
☐ 97 Renaldo Turnbull	.10	.05	.01
☐ 98 Jason Hanson	.10	.05	.01
☐ 99 Cortez Kennedy	.20	.09	.03
☐ 100 Brett Favre	4.00	1.80	.50
☐ 101 Anthony Carter	.20	.09	.03
☐ 102 Cris Carter	.40	.18	.05
☐ 103 Dana Stubblefield	.40	.18	.05
☐ 104 Nick Bell	.10	.05	.01
☐ 105 Marcus Allen	.40	.18	.05
☐ 106 Neil O'Donnell	.40	.18	.05
☐ 107 Steve DeBerg	.10	.05	.01
☐ 108 Leonard Russell	.20	.09	.03
☐ 109 Ethan Horton	.10	.05	.01
☐ 110 William Perry	.20	.09	.03
☐ 111 Don Griffin UER	.10	.05	.01
(No.104 on back,			
No.111 does not exist)			
☐ 112 Clarence Verdin	.10	.05	.01
☐ 113 Amp Lee	.10	.05	.01
☐ 114 Earnest Byner	.10	.05	.01
☐ 115 Ricky Reynolds	.10	.05	.01
☐ 116 Tom Waddle	.10	.05	.01
☐ 117 Robert Jones	.10	.05	.01
☐ 118 Willie Davis	.40	.18	.05
☐ 119 Chris Miller	.20	.09	.03
☐ 120 Drew Hill	.10	.05	.01
☐ 121 Warren Moon	.40	.18	.05
☐ 122 Flipper Anderson	.10	.05	.01
☐ 123 George Teague	.20	.09	.03
☐ 124 John L. Williams	.10	.05	.01
☐ 125 Ed McCaffrey	.10	.05	.01
☐ 126 Eric Green	.10	.05	.01
☐ 127 Scott Mersereau	.10	.05	.01
☐ 128 Charles Mann	.10	.05	.01
☐ 129 Todd Lyght	.10	.05	.01
☐ 130 Rodney Culver	.10	.05	.01

☐ 131 Richmond Webb	.10	.05	.01
☐ 132 John Parrella	.10	.05	.01
☐ 133 Reggie Brooks	.20	.09	.03
☐ 134 Lincoln Kennedy	.10	.05	.01
☐ 135 Tim Johnson	.10	.05	.01
☐ 136 Robert Massey	.10	.05	.01
☐ 137 Keith Jackson	.20	.09	.03
☐ 138 Alfred Williams	.10	.05	.01
☐ 139 Leroy Hoard	.20	.09	.03
☐ 140 Jessie Tuggle	.10	.05	.01
☐ 141 Chris Mims	.10	.05	.01
☐ 142 Herschel Walker	.20	.09	.03
☐ 143 Clyde Simmons	.10	.05	.01
☐ 144 Dana Hall	.10	.05	.01
☐ 145 Nate Newton	.20	.09	.03
☐ 146 Dennis Smith	.10	.05	.01
☐ 147 Rich Camarillo	.10	.05	.01
☐ 148 Chris Spielman	.20	.09	.03
☐ 149 Jim Dombrowski	.10	.05	.01
☐ 150 Steve Beuerlein	.10	.05	.01
☐ 151 Mark Clayton	.10	.05	.01
☐ 152 Lee Williams	.10	.05	.01
☐ 153 Robert Smith	2.00	.90	.25
☐ 154 Greg Jackson	.10	.05	.01
☐ 155 Jay Hilgenberg	.10	.05	.01
☐ 156 Howard Ballard	.10	.05	.01
☐ 157 Mike Compton	.10	.05	.01
☐ 158 Brent Williams	.10	.05	.01
☐ 159 Tommy Kane	.10	.05	.01
☐ 160 Barry Word	.10	.05	.01
☐ 161 Darren Lewis	.10	.05	.01
☐ 162 Steve Atwater	.10	.05	.01
☐ 163 Gary Clark	.20	.09	.03
☐ 164 Donnell Woolford	.10	.05	.01
☐ 165 Henry Thomas	.10	.05	.01
☐ 166 Tim Brown	.40	.18	.05
☐ 167 Andre Ware	.10	.05	.01
☐ 168 Jackie Harris	.10	.05	.01
☐ 169 Browning Nagle	.10	.05	.01
☐ 170 Chris Singleton	.10	.05	.01
☐ 171 Ronnie Lott	.20	.09	.03
☐ 172 Leonard Marshall	.10	.05	.01
☐ 173 Dale Carter	.10	.05	.01
☐ 174 Bruce Armstrong	.10	.05	.01
☐ 175 Tommy Vardell	.10	.05	.01
☐ 176 Bubba McDowell	.10	.05	.01
☐ 177 Patrick Bates	.10	.05	.01
☐ 178 Tyji Armstrong	.10	.05	.01
☐ 179 Keith Byars	.10	.05	.01
☐ 180 Boomer Esiason	.20	.09	.03
☐ 181 Ricky Watters	.40	.18	.05
☐ 182 Keith Sims	.10	.05	.01
☐ 183 Burt Grossman	.10	.05	.01
☐ 184 Richard Cooper	.10	.05	.01
☐ 185 Marc Boutte	.10	.05	.01
☐ 186 Shane Conlan	.10	.05	.01
☐ 187 Luis Sharpe	.10	.05	.01
☐ 188 O.J. McDuffie	2.00	.90	.25
☐ 189 Harvey Williams	.20	.09	.03
☐ 190 Blair Thomas	.10	.05	.01
☐ 191 Charles Haley	.20	.09	.03
☐ 192 Chip Lohmiller	.10	.05	.01
☐ 193 Vinny Testaverde	.20	.09	.03
☐ 194 Desmond Howard	.20	.09	.03
☐ 195 Johnny Johnson	.10	.05	.01
☐ 196 Bennie Blades	.10	.05	.01
☐ 197 Jeff Wright	.10	.05	.01
☐ 198 Cody Carlson	.10	.05	.01
☐ 199 Micheal Barrow	.10	.05	.01
☐ 200 Pat Swilling	.10	.05	.01
☐ 201 Willie Roaf	.20	.09	.03
☐ 202 Michael Walter	.10	.05	.01
☐ 203 Kevin Fagan	.10	.05	.01
☐ 204 Nate Odomes	.10	.05	.01
☐ 205 Michael Dean Perry	.20	.09	.03
☐ 206 Bruce Pickens	.10	.05	.01
☐ 207 Mel Gray	.20	.09	.03
☐ 208 Jack Trudeau	.10	.05	.01
☐ 209 Ricky Sanders	.10	.05	.01
☐ 210 Bobby Hebert	.10	.05	.01
☐ 211 Craig Heyward	.20	.09	.03
☐ 212 Eric Bieniemy	.10	.05	.01
☐ 213 Andre Rison	.20	.09	.03
☐ 214 Bernie Kosar	.20	.09	.03
☐ 215 Lester Holmes	.10	.05	.01
☐ 216 Marcus Buckley	.10	.05	.01
☐ 217 Tony Casillas	.10	.05	.01
☐ 218 Cornelius Bennett	.20	.09	.03
☐ 219 Kyle Clifton	.10	.05	.01
☐ 220 Kirk Lowdermilk	.10	.05	.01
☐ 221 Leon Searcy	.10	.05	.01
☐ 222 Gary Anderson K	.10	.05	.01
☐ 223 Tim Barnett	.10	.05	.01
☐ 224 Gene Atkins	.10	.05	.01
☐ 225 Jeff Cross	.10	.05	.01
☐ 226 Darrin Smith	.20	.09	.03
☐ 227 Rohn Stark	.10	.05	.01
☐ 228 Chris Warren	.20	.09	.03
☐ 229 Eric Allen	.10	.05	.01
☐ 230 Wayne Simmons	.10	.05	.01
☐ 231 Al Smith	.10	.05	.01
☐ 232 Reggie Rivers	.10	.05	.01
☐ 233 Kevin Smith	.20	.09	.03
☐ 234 Vince Workman	.10	.05	.01
☐ 235 Thurman Thomas	.40	.18	.05
☐ 236 Kevin Williams	.60	.25	.07
☐ 237 Dan McGwire	.10	.05	.01
☐ 238 Greg Lloyd	.40	.18	.05
☐ 239 Ray Buchanan	.10	.05	.01
☐ 240 Shannon Sharpe	.40	.18	.05
☐ 241 Ricardo McDonald	.10	.05	.01
☐ 242 Aaron Wallace	.10	.05	.01
☐ 243 Chris Hinton	.10	.05	.01
☐ 244 Bill Romanowski	.10	.05	.01
☐ 245 Randal Hill	.10	.05	.01
☐ 246 Ray Agnew	.10	.05	.01
☐ 247 Todd Kelly	.10	.05	.01
☐ 248 John Stephens	.10	.05	.01
☐ 249 Sean Salisbury	.10	.05	.01
☐ 250 Roger Craig	.20	.09	.03
☐ 251 Dave Krieg	.20	.09	.03
☐ 252 Brian Blades	.20	.09	.03
☐ 253 Jarrod Bunch	.10	.05	.01
☐ 254 Phil Simms	.20	.09	.03
☐ 255 Keith Van Horne	.10	.05	.01
☐ 256 Jim Price	.10	.05	.01
☐ 257 Garrison Hearst	3.00	1.35	.35
☐ 258 Derrick Walker	.10	.05	.01
☐ 259 Mike Pritchard	.20	.09	.03
☐ 260 Leonard Renfro	.10	.05	.01
☐ 261 Rodney Peete	.10	.05	.01
☐ 262 Jeff Bryant	.10	.05	.01
☐ 263 Dermontti Dawson	.10	.05	.01
☐ 264 Greg McMurtry	.10	.05	.01
☐ 265 Wendell Davis	.10	.05	.01
☐ 266 Kerry Cash	.10	.05	.01
☐ 267 Jackie Slater	.10	.05	.01
☐ 268 Sam Mills	.10	.05	.01
☐ 269 Carlton Bailey	.10	.05	.01
☐ 270 Mark Wheeler	.10	.05	.01
☐ 271 Darren Perry	.10	.05	.01
☐ 272 Todd Scott	.10	.05	.01
☐ 273 Johnny Holland	.10	.05	.01
☐ 274 Mike Croel	.10	.05	.01
☐ 275 Shane Dronett	.10	.05	.01
☐ 276 Andre Collins	.10	.05	.01
☐ 277 Eric Swann	.20	.09	.03
☐ 278 Jessie Hester	.10	.05	.01
☐ 279 Bryan Cox	.10	.05	.01
☐ 280 Mark Jackson	.10	.05	.01
☐ 281 Thomas Everett	.10	.05	.01
☐ 282 James Lofton	.20	.09	.03
☐ 283 Carl Pickens	1.50	.70	.19
☐ 284 Mark Carrier WR	.20	.09	.03
☐ 285 Heath Sherman	.10	.05	.01
☐ 286 Chris Burkett	.10	.05	.01
☐ 287 Coleman Rudolph	.10	.05	.01
☐ 288 Todd Marinovich	.10	.05	.01
☐ 289 Nate Lewis	.10	.05	.01
☐ 290 Fred Barnett	.20	.09	.03
☐ 291 Jim Lachey	.10	.05	.01
☐ 292 Jerry Ball	.10	.05	.01
☐ 293 Jeff George	.40	.18	.05
☐ 294 William Fuller	.10	.05	.01
☐ 295 Courtney Hawkins	.10	.05	.01
☐ 296 Kelvin Martin	.10	.05	.01
☐ 297 Trace Armstrong	.10	.05	.01
☐ 298 Carl Banks	.10	.05	.01
☐ 299 Terry Kirby	.60	.25	.07
☐ 300 John Offerdahl	.10	.05	.01
☐ 301 Harry Swayne	.10	.05	.01
☐ 302 Wilber Marshall	.10	.05	.01
☐ 303 Guy McIntyre	.10	.05	.01
☐ 304 Steve Wallace	.10	.05	.01
☐ 305 Chris Slade	.20	.09	.03
☐ 306 Anthony Newman	.10	.05	.01
☐ 307 Chip Banks	.10	.05	.01
☐ 308 Carlton Gray	.10	.05	.01
☐ 309 Wayne Martin	.10	.05	.01
☐ 310 Tom Rathman	.10	.05	.01
☐ 311 Shaun Gayle	.10	.05	.01
☐ 312 Billy Joe Hobert	1.00	.45	.12
☐ 313 Matt Brock	.10	.05	.01
☐ 314 Arthur Marshall	.10	.05	.01
☐ 315 Wade Wilson	.10	.05	.01
☐ 316 Michael Jackson	.20	.09	.03
☐ 317 Bruce Kozerski	.10	.05	.01
☐ 318 Reggie Langhorne	.10	.05	.01
☐ 319 Jerrol Williams	.10	.05	.01
☐ 320 Aeneas Williams	.10	.05	.01
☐ 321 Tony McGee	.20	.09	.03
☐ 322 Carl Simpson	.10	.05	.01
☐ 323 Russell Maryland	.10	.05	.01
☐ 324 Nick Lowery	.10	.05	.01
☐ 325 Steve Tasker	.20	.09	.03
☐ 326 Alvin Harper	.20	.09	.03
☐ 327 Haywood Jeffires	.20	.09	.03
☐ 328 Hardy Nickerson	.20	.09	.03
☐ 329 Alonzo Spellman	.10	.05	.01
☐ 330 Eric Dickerson	.20	.09	.03
☐ 331 Scott Zolak	.10	.05	.01
☐ 332 Darryl Henley	.10	.05	.01
☐ 333 Daniel Stubbs	.10	.05	.01
☐ 334 Andy Heck	.10	.05	.01
☐ 335 Mark May	.10	.05	.01
☐ 336 Roosevelt Potts	.10	.05	.01
☐ 337 Erik Howard	.10	.05	.01
☐ 338 Sean Gilbert	.20	.09	.03
☐ 339 Jerome Bettis	3.50	1.55	.45
☐ 340 Darren Carrington	.10	.05	.01
☐ 341 Gill Byrd	.10	.05	.01
☐ 342 John Friesz	.20	.09	.03
☐ 343 Roger Harper	.10	.05	.01
☐ 344 Fred Stokes	.10	.05	.01
☐ 345 Stanley Richard	.10	.05	.01
☐ 346 Johnny Bailey	.10	.05	.01
☐ 347 David Wyman	.10	.05	.01
☐ 348 Merril Hoge	.10	.05	.01
☐ 349 Brett Perriman	.40	.18	.05
☐ 350 Kelvin Pritchett	.10	.05	.01
☐ 351 Rod Bernstine	.10	.05	.01
☐ 352 Jim Ritcher	.10	.05	.01
☐ 353 Mark Stepnoski	.10	.05	.01
☐ 354 Jeff Lageman	.10	.05	.01
☐ 355 Darrien Gordon	.10	.05	.01
☐ 356 Don Mosebar	.10	.05	.01
☐ 357 Simon Fletcher	.10	.05	.01
☐ 358 Charles Mincy	.10	.05	.01
☐ 359 Ron Hall	.10	.05	.01
☐ 360 Brent Jones	.20	.09	.03
☐ 361 Byron Evans	.10	.05	.01
☐ 362 Dan Footman	.10	.05	.01
☐ 363 Mark Higgs	.10	.05	.01
☐ 364 Brian Washington	.10	.05	.01
☐ 365 Brad Hopkins	.10	.05	.01
☐ 366 Tracy Simien	.10	.05	.01
☐ 367 Derrick Fenner	.10	.05	.01
☐ 368 Lorenzo White	.10	.05	.01
☐ 369 Marvin Jones	.10	.05	.01
☐ 370 Chris Doleman	.10	.05	.01
☐ 371 Jeff Herrod	.10	.05	.01
☐ 372 Jim Harbaugh	.40	.18	.05
☐ 373 Jim Jeffcoat	.10	.05	.01
☐ 374 Michael Strahan	.10	.05	.01
☐ 375 Ricky Ervins	.10	.05	.01
☐ 376 Joel Hilgenberg	.10	.05	.01
☐ 377 Curtis Duncan	.10	.05	.01
☐ 378 Glyn Milburn	.40	.18	.05
☐ 379 Jack Del Rio	.10	.05	.01
☐ 380 Eric Martin	.10	.05	.01
☐ 381 Dave Meggett	.10	.05	.01
☐ 382 Jeff Hostetler	.20	.09	.03
☐ 383 Greg Townsend	.10	.05	.01
☐ 384 Brad Muster	.10	.05	.01
☐ 385 Irv Smith	.10	.05	.01
☐ 386 Chris Jacke	.10	.05	.01
☐ 387 Ernest Dye	.10	.05	.01
☐ 388 Henry Ellard	.20	.09	.03
☐ 389 John Taylor	.20	.09	.03
☐ 390 Chris Chandler	.20	.09	.03
☐ 391 Larry Centers	.60	.25	.07
☐ 392 Henry Rolling	.10	.05	.01
☐ 393 Dan Saleaumua	.10	.05	.01
☐ 394 Moe Gardner	.10	.05	.01
☐ 395 Darryl Williams	.10	.05	.01
☐ 396 Paul Gruber	.10	.05	.01
☐ 397 Dwayne Harper	.10	.05	.01
☐ 398 Pat Harlow	.10	.05	.01
☐ 399 Rickey Jackson	.10	.05	.01
☐ 400 Quentin Coryatt	.20	.09	.03
☐ 401 Steve Jordan	.10	.05	.01
☐ 402 Rick Mirer	3.00	1.35	.35
☐ 403 Howard Cross	.10	.05	.01
☐ 404 Mike Johnson	.10	.05	.01
☐ 405 Broderick Thomas	.10	.05	.01
☐ 406 Stan Humphries	.40	.18	.05
☐ 407 Ronnie Harmon	.10	.05	.01
☐ 408 Andy Harmon	.20	.09	.03
☐ 409 Troy Drayton	.20	.09	.03
☐ 410 Dan Williams	.10	.05	.01
☐ 411 Mark Bavaro	.10	.05	.01
☐ 412 Bruce Smith	.40	.18	.05
☐ 413 Elbert Shelley	.10	.05	.01
☐ 414 Tim McGee	.10	.05	.01
☐ 415 Tim Harris	.10	.05	.01
☐ 416 Rob Moore	.20	.09	.03
☐ 417 Rob Burnett	.10	.05	.01
☐ 418 Howie Long	.20	.09	.03
☐ 419 Chuck Cecil	.10	.05	.01
☐ 420 Carl Lee	.10	.05	.01
☐ 421 Anthony Smith	.10	.05	.01
☐ 422 Jeff Graham	.20	.09	.03
☐ 423 Clay Matthews	.20	.09	.03
☐ 424 Jay Novacek	.20	.09	.03
☐ 425 Phil Hansen	.10	.05	.01
☐ 426 Andre Hastings	.40	.18	.05
☐ 427 Toi Cook	.10	.05	.01
☐ 428 Rufus Porter	.10	.05	.01
☐ 429 Mike Pitts	.10	.05	.01
☐ 430 Eddie Robinson	.10	.05	.01
☐ 431 Herman Moore	1.50	.70	.19
☐ 432 Erik Kramer	.20	.09	.03
☐ 433 Mark Carrier DB	.10	.05	.01
☐ 434 Natrone Means	3.00	1.35	.35
☐ 435 Carnell Lake	.10	.05	.01
☐ 436 Carlton Haselrig	.10	.05	.01
☐ 437 John Randle	.10	.05	.01
☐ 438 Louis Oliver	.10	.05	.01
☐ 439 Ray Roberts	.10	.05	.01
☐ 440 Leslie O'Neal	.20	.09	.03
☐ 441 Reggie White	.40	.18	.05
☐ 442 Dalton Hilliard	.10	.05	.01
☐ 443 Tim Krumrie	.10	.05	.01
☐ 444 LeRoy Butler	.10	.05	.01
☐ 445 Greg Kragen	.10	.05	.01
☐ 446 Anthony Johnson	.20	.09	.03
☐ 447 Audray McMillian	.10	.05	.01
☐ 448 Lawrence Dawsey	.10	.05	.01
☐ 449 Pierce Holt	.10	.05	.01
☐ 450 Brad Edwards	.10	.05	.01
☐ 451 J.J. Birden	.10	.05	.01
☐ 452 Mike Munchak	.10	.05	.01
☐ 453 Tracy Scroggins	.10	.05	.01
☐ 454 Mike Tomczak	.10	.05	.01
☐ 455 Harold Green	.10	.05	.01
☐ 456 Vaughn Dunbar	.10	.05	.01
☐ 457 Calvin Williams	.20	.09	.03
☐ 458 Pete Stoyanovich	.10	.05	.01
☐ 459 Willie Gault	.10	.05	.01
☐ 460 Ken Ruettgers	.10	.05	.01
☐ 461 Eugene Robinson	.10	.05	.01
☐ 462 Larry Brown DB	.10	.05	.01
☐ 463 Antonio London	.10	.05	.01
☐ 464 Andre Reed	.20	.09	.03
☐ 465 Daryl Johnston	.40	.18	.05
☐ 466 Karl Mecklenburg	.10	.05	.01
☐ 467 David Lang	.10	.05	.01
☐ 468 Bill Brooks	.10	.05	.01
☐ 469 Jim Everett	.20	.09	.03
☐ 470 Qadry Ismail	.40	.18	.05
☐ 471 Vai Sikahema	.10	.05	.01
☐ 472 Andre Tippett	.10	.05	.01
☐ 473 Eugene Chung	.10	.05	.01
☐ 474 Cris Dishman	.10	.05	.01
☐ 475 Tim McDonald	.10	.05	.01
☐ 476 Freddie Joe Nunn	.10	.05	.01
☐ 477 Checklist 1-134	.10	.05	.01
☐ 478 Checklist 135-268	.10	.05	.01
☐ 479 Checklist 269-402	.10	.05	.01
☐ 480 CL 403-480/Inserts	.10	.05	.01
☐ P1 Promo Sheet	4.00	1.80	.50

Steve Young
Thurman Thomas
Junior Seau
Jay Novacek
Terrell Buckley
Rick Mirer

1993 GameDay Gamebreakers

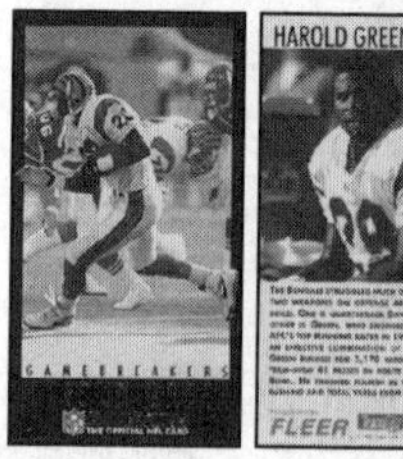

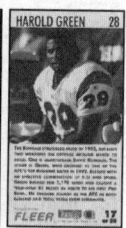

The GameDay Gamebreakers set consists of 20 cards measuring approximately 2 1/2" by 4 3/4". Randomly inserted in packs at a rate of one in four, this set spotlights top stars who can break open a game. The black bordered fronts feature color action player photos against black-and-white game-action backgrounds. Stamped in gold foil at the bottom of the picture are the set name and the player's name. The white borderless backs carry a close-up color player picture, the player's name and highlights of the 1992 season. The cards are numbered as "X" of 20.

	MINT	NRMT	EXC
COMPLETE SET (20)	30.00	13.50	3.70
COMMON CARD (1-20)	.50	.23	.06
☐ 1 Troy Aikman	4.00	1.80	.50
☐ 2 Brett Favre	6.00	2.70	.75
☐ 3 Steve Young	3.00	1.35	.35
☐ 4 Dan Marino	6.00	2.70	.75
☐ 5 Joe Montana	4.00	1.80	.50
☐ 6 Jim Kelly	1.50	.70	.19
☐ 7 Emmitt Smith	6.00	2.70	.75
☐ 8 Ricky Watters	1.50	.70	.19
☐ 9 Barry Foster	1.00	.45	.12
☐ 10 Barry Sanders	4.00	1.80	.50
☐ 11 Michael Irvin	1.50	.70	.19
☐ 12 Thurman Thomas	1.50	.70	.19
☐ 13 Sterling Sharpe	1.50	.70	.19
☐ 14 Jerry Rice	4.00	1.80	.50
☐ 15 Andre Rison	1.50	.70	.19
☐ 16 Deion Sanders	2.50	1.10	.30
☐ 17 Harold Green	.50	.23	.06
☐ 18 Lorenzo White	1.00	.45	.12
☐ 19 Terry Allen	1.50	.70	.19
☐ 20 Haywood Jeffires	1.00	.45	.12

1993 GameDay Rookie Standouts

The GameDay Rookie Standouts set consists of 16 cards measuring approximately 2 1/2" by 4 3/4". Randomly inserted in packs at a rate of one in four, the set spotlights top picks of the 1993 NFL Draft. The dark blue-bordered fronts feature color action player photos against black-and-white game-action backgrounds. Stamped in gold foil at the bottom of the picture are the set name and the player's name. The

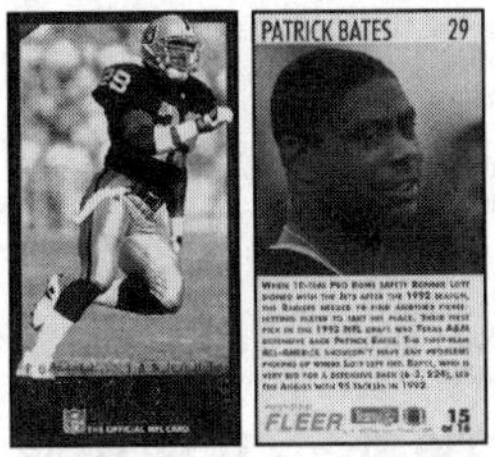

white borderless backs carry a close-up color player picture, the player's name, jersey number, and highlights of the 1992 season. The cards are numbered as "X" of 16.

	MINT	NRMT	EXC
COMPLETE SET (16)	30.00	13.50	3.70
COMMON CARD (1-16)	.50	.23	.06
☐ 1 Drew Bledsoe	10.00	4.50	1.25
☐ 2 Rick Mirer	3.00	1.35	.35
☐ 3 Garrison Hearst	3.00	1.35	.35
☐ 4 Jerome Bettis	5.00	2.20	.60
☐ 5 Marvin Jones	1.00	.45	.12
☐ 6 Reggie Brooks	1.50	.70	.19
☐ 7 O.J. McDuffie	2.50	1.10	.30
☐ 8 Qadry Ismail	1.50	.70	.19
☐ 9 Glyn Milburn	1.50	.70	.19
☐ 10 Andre Hastings	1.50	.70	.19
☐ 11 Curtis Conway	2.50	1.10	.30
☐ 12 Eric Curry	1.00	.45	.12
☐ 13 John Copeland	1.00	.45	.12
☐ 14 Kevin Williams	1.50	.70	.19
☐ 15 Patrick Bates	.50	.23	.06
☐ 16 Lincoln Kennedy	.50	.23	.06

1993 GameDay Second Year Stars

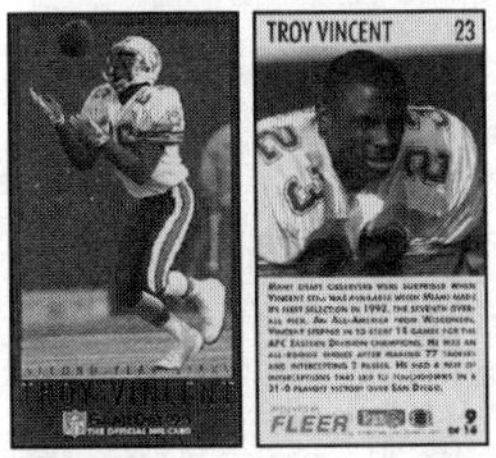

The GameDay Second Year Stars set consists of 16 cards measuring approximately 2 1/2" by 4 3/4". Randomly inserted in packs at a rate of one in four, the set spotlights 1992 rookies. The green-bordered fronts feature color action player photos against black-and-white game-action backgrounds. Stamped in gold foil at the bottom of the picture are the set name and the player's name. The white borderless backs carry a close-up color player picture, the player's name, jersey number, and highlights of the 1992 season.

	MINT	NRMT	EXC
COMPLETE SET (16)	8.00	3.60	1.00
COMMON CARD (1-16)	.50	.23	.06
☐ 1 Carl Pickens	2.00	.90	.25
☐ 2 David Klingler	.75	.35	.09
☐ 3 Santana Dotson	.75	.35	.09
☐ 4 Chris Mims	.75	.35	.09
☐ 5 Steve Emtman	.50	.23	.06
☐ 6 Marco Coleman	.75	.35	.09
☐ 7 Robert Jones	.50	.23	.06
☐ 8 Dale Carter	.75	.35	.09
☐ 9 Troy Vincent	.75	.35	.09
☐ 10 Tracy Scroggins	.50	.23	.06
☐ 11 Vaughn Dunbar	.50	.23	.06
☐ 12 Quentin Coryatt	1.00	.45	.12
☐ 13 Dana Hall	.50	.23	.06
☐ 14 Terrell Buckley	.50	.23	.06
☐ 15 Tommy Vardell	.50	.23	.06
☐ 16 Johnny Mitchell	.75	.35	.09

1994 GameDay

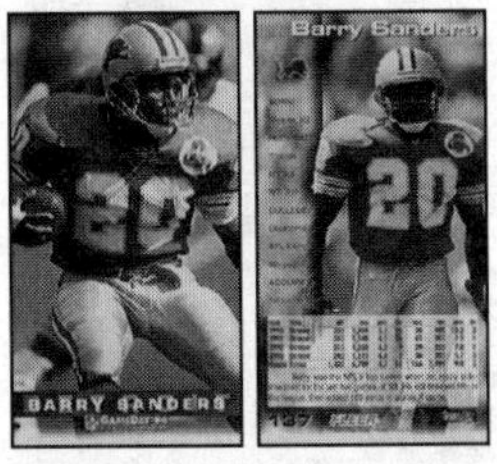

Measuring 2 1/2" by 4 3/4", this 420-card set features full-bleed action photos on front with the player's name and team name at the bottom. The backs have a player photo with statistics and a write-up at the bottom. Biographical information runs along the right border. The players are grouped alphabetically within teams, and checklisted below alphabetically according to teams. Rookie Cards in this set include Mario Bates, Isaac Bruce, Bert Emanuel, Marshall Faulk, Errict Rhett, Darnay Scott and Heath Shuler. A Reggie Brooks promo card was produced and is priced below.

	MINT	NRMT	EXC
COMPLETE SET (420)	40.00	18.00	5.00
COMMON CARD (1-420)	.10	.05	.01
☐ 1 Michael Bankston	.10	.05	.01
☐ 2 Steve Beuerlein	.10	.05	.01
☐ 3 Gary Clark	.20	.09	.03
☐ 4 Garrison Hearst	.75	.35	.09
☐ 5 Eric Hill	.10	.05	.01
☐ 6 Randal Hill	.10	.05	.01
☐ 7 Seth Joyner	.10	.05	.01
☐ 8 Jim McMahon	.10	.05	.01
☐ 9 Jamir Miller	.10	.05	.01
☐ 10 Ronald Moore	.10	.05	.01
☐ 11 Ricky Proehl	.10	.05	.01
☐ 12 Luis Sharpe	.10	.05	.01
☐ 13 Clyde Simmons	.10	.05	.01
☐ 14 Eric Swann	.20	.09	.03
☐ 15 Aeneas Williams	.10	.05	.01
☐ 16 Chris Doleman	.10	.05	.01
☐ 17 Bert Emanuel	1.50	.70	.19
☐ 18 Moe Gardner	.10	.05	.01
☐ 19 Jeff George	.30	.14	.04
☐ 20 Roger Harper	.10	.05	.01
☐ 21 Pierce Holt	.10	.05	.01
☐ 22 Lincoln Kennedy	.10	.05	.01
☐ 23 Erric Pegram	.10	.05	.01
☐ 24 Andre Rison	.20	.09	.03
☐ 25 Deion Sanders	1.25	.55	.16
☐ 26 Tony Smith	.10	.05	.01
☐ 27 Jessie Tuggle	.10	.05	.01
☐ 28 Don Beebe	.10	.05	.01
☐ 29 Cornelius Bennett	.20	.09	.03
☐ 30 Bill Brooks	.10	.05	.01
☐ 31 Bucky Brooks	.10	.05	.01
☐ 32 Jeff Burris	.20	.09	.03
☐ 33 Kenneth Davis	.10	.05	.01
☐ 34 Phil Hansen	.10	.05	.01
☐ 35 Kent Hull	.10	.05	.01
☐ 36 Henry Jones	.10	.05	.01
☐ 37 Jim Kelly	.30	.14	.04
☐ 38 Pete Metzelaars	.10	.05	.01
☐ 39 Marvcus Patton	.10	.05	.01
☐ 40 Andre Reed	.20	.09	.03
☐ 41 Bruce Smith	.30	.14	.04
☐ 42 Thomas Smith	.10	.05	.01
☐ 43 Darryl Talley	.10	.05	.01
☐ 44 Steve Tasker	.20	.09	.03
☐ 45 Thurman Thomas	.30	.14	.04
☐ 46 Jeff Wright	.10	.05	.01
☐ 47 Trace Armstrong	.10	.05	.01
☐ 48 Joe Cain	.10	.05	.01
☐ 49 Mark Carrier DB	.10	.05	.01
☐ 50 Curtis Conway	.30	.14	.04
☐ 51 Shaun Gayle	.10	.05	.01
☐ 52 Dante Jones	.10	.05	.01
☐ 53 Erik Kramer	.20	.09	.03
☐ 54 Terry Obee	.10	.05	.01
☐ 55 Vinson Smith	.10	.05	.01
☐ 56 Alonzo Spellman	.10	.05	.01
☐ 57 John Thierry	.10	.05	.01
☐ 58 Tom Waddle	.10	.05	.01
☐ 59 Donnell Woolford	.10	.05	.01
☐ 60 Tim Worley	.10	.05	.01
☐ 61 Chris Zorich	.10	.05	.01
☐ 62 Mike Brim	.10	.05	.01
☐ 63 John Copeland	.10	.05	.01
☐ 64 Derrick Fenner	.10	.05	.01
☐ 65 James Francis	.10	.05	.01
☐ 66 Harold Green	.10	.05	.01
☐ 67 David Klingler	.10	.05	.01
☐ 68 Ricardo McDonald	.10	.05	.01
☐ 69 Tony McGee	.10	.05	.01
☐ 70 Carl Pickens	.75	.35	.09
☐ 71 Jeff Query	.10	.05	.01
☐ 72 Darnay Scott	2.50	1.10	.30
☐ 73 Steve Tovar	.10	.05	.01
☐ 74 Dan Wilkinson	.20	.09	.03
☐ 75 Alfred Williams	.10	.05	.01
☐ 76 Darryl Williams	.10	.05	.01
☐ 77 Derrick Alexander WR	.30	.14	.04
☐ 78 Rob Burnett	.10	.05	.01
☐ 79 Steve Everitt	.10	.05	.01
☐ 80 Michael Jackson	.20	.09	.03
☐ 81 Pepper Johnson	.10	.05	.01
☐ 82 Tony Jones	.10	.05	.01
☐ 83 Antonio Langham	.20	.09	.03
☐ 84 Eric Metcalf	.20	.09	.03
☐ 85 Stevon Moore	.10	.05	.01
☐ 86 Michael Dean Perry	.20	.09	.03
☐ 87 Anthony Pleasant	.10	.05	.01
☐ 88 Vinny Testaverde	.20	.09	.03
☐ 89 Eric Turner	.10	.05	.01
☐ 90 Tommy Vardell	.10	.05	.01
☐ 91 Troy Aikman	2.00	.90	.25
☐ 92 Larry Brown DB	.10	.05	.01
☐ 93 Shante Carver	.10	.05	.01
☐ 94 Charles Haley	.20	.09	.03
☐ 95 Alvin Harper	.20	.09	.03
☐ 96 Michael Irvin	.30	.14	.04
☐ 97 Daryl Johnston	.20	.09	.03
☐ 98 Leon Lett	.10	.05	.01
☐ 99 Russell Maryland	.10	.05	.01
☐ 100 Nate Newton	.10	.05	.01
☐ 101 Jay Novacek	.20	.09	.03
☐ 102 Darrin Smith	.10	.05	.01
☐ 103 Emmitt Smith	4.00	1.80	.50
☐ 104 Kevin Smith	.10	.05	.01
☐ 105 Mark Stepnoski	.10	.05	.01
☐ 106 Tony Tolbert	.10	.05	.01
☐ 107 Erik Williams	.10	.05	.01
☐ 108 Kevin Williams	.20	.09	.03
☐ 109 Darren Woodson	.20	.09	.03
☐ 110 Allen Aldridge	.10	.05	.01
☐ 111 Steve Atwater	.10	.05	.01
☐ 112 Rod Bernstine	.10	.05	.01
☐ 113 Ray Crockett	.10	.05	.01
☐ 114 Mike Croel	.10	.05	.01
☐ 115 Robert Delpino	.10	.05	.01
☐ 116 Shane Dronett	.10	.05	.01
☐ 117 Jason Elam	.10	.05	.01
☐ 118 John Elway	1.50	.70	.19
☐ 119 Simon Fletcher	.10	.05	.01
☐ 120 Glyn Milburn	.20	.09	.03
☐ 121 Anthony Miller	.20	.09	.03
☐ 122 Mike Pritchard	.10	.05	.01
☐ 123 Shannon Sharpe	.20	.09	.03
☐ 124 Dan Williams	.10	.05	.01
☐ 125 Bennie Blades	.10	.05	.01
☐ 126 Lomas Brown	.10	.05	.01
☐ 127 Anthony Carter	.20	.09	.03
☐ 128 Mel Gray	.10	.05	.01
☐ 129 Jason Hanson	.10	.05	.01
☐ 130 Robert Massey	.10	.05	.01
☐ 131 Ryan McNeil	.10	.05	.01
☐ 132 Scott Mitchell	.30	.14	.04
☐ 133 Herman Moore	.75	.35	.09
☐ 134 Johnnie Morton	.75	.35	.09
☐ 135 Brett Perriman	.20	.09	.03
☐ 136 Robert Porcher	.10	.05	.01
☐ 137 Barry Sanders	2.00	.90	.25
☐ 138 Tracy Scroggins	.10	.05	.01
☐ 139 Chris Spielman	.20	.09	.03
☐ 140 Pat Swilling	.10	.05	.01
☐ 141 Edgar Bennett	.30	.14	.04
☐ 142 Robert Brooks	.60	.25	.07
☐ 143 Terrell Buckley	.10	.05	.01
☐ 144 LeRoy Butler	.10	.05	.01
☐ 145 Reggie Cobb	.10	.05	.01
☐ 146 Curtis Duncan	.10	.05	.01
☐ 147 Brett Favre	4.00	1.80	.50
☐ 148 Sean Jones	.10	.05	.01
☐ 149 George Koonce	.10	.05	.01
☐ 150 Ken Ruettgers	.10	.05	.01
☐ 151 Sterling Sharpe	.20	.09	.03
☐ 152 Wayne Simmons	.10	.05	.01
☐ 153 Aaron Taylor	.10	.05	.01
☐ 154 George Teague	.10	.05	.01
☐ 155 Reggie White	.30	.14	.04
☐ 156 Micheal Barrow	.10	.05	.01
☐ 157 Gary Brown	.10	.05	.01
☐ 158 Rich Camarillo	.10	.05	.01
☐ 159 Cody Carlson	.10	.05	.01
☐ 160 Ray Childress	.10	.05	.01
☐ 161 Cris Dishman	.10	.05	.01
☐ 162 Henry Ford	.10	.05	.01
☐ 163 Ernest Givins	.20	.09	.03
☐ 164 Steve Jackson	.10	.05	.01
☐ 165 Haywood Jeffires	.20	.09	.03
☐ 166 Bruce Matthews	.10	.05	.01
☐ 167 Bubba McDowell	.10	.05	.01
☐ 168 Marcus Robertson	.10	.05	.01
☐ 169 Gerald Robinson	.10	.05	.01
☐ 170 Webster Slaughter	.10	.05	.01
☐ 171 Trev Alberts	.20	.09	.03
☐ 172 Tony Bennett	.10	.05	.01
☐ 173 Ray Buchanan	.10	.05	.01
☐ 174 Kerry Cash	.10	.05	.01
☐ 175 Quentin Coryatt	.10	.05	.01
☐ 176 Eugene Daniel	.10	.05	.01
☐ 177 Sean Dawkins	.75	.35	.09
☐ 178 Steve Emtman	.10	.05	.01
☐ 179 Marshall Faulk	4.00	1.80	.50
☐ 180 Jon Hand	.10	.05	.01
☐ 181 Jim Harbaugh	.30	.14	.04
☐ 182 Jeff Herrod	.10	.05	.01
☐ 183 Roosevelt Potts	.10	.05	.01
☐ 184 Rohn Stark	.10	.05	.01
☐ 185 Marcus Allen	.30	.14	.04
☐ 186 Donnell Bennett	.10	.05	.01
☐ 187 J.J. Birden	.10	.05	.01
☐ 188 Dale Carter	.10	.05	.01
☐ 189 Mark Collins	.10	.05	.01
☐ 190 Willie Davis	.20	.09	.03
☐ 191 Lake Dawson	1.00	.45	.12
☐ 192 Tim Grunhard	.10	.05	.01
☐ 193 Greg Hill	1.00	.45	.12
☐ 194 Joe Montana	2.00	.90	.25
☐ 195 Tracy Simien	.10	.05	.01
☐ 196 Neil Smith	.30	.14	.04
☐ 197 Derrick Thomas	.30	.14	.04
☐ 198 Tim Brown	.30	.14	.04
☐ 199 James Folston	.10	.05	.01
☐ 200 Rob Fredrickson	.20	.09	.03
☐ 201 Nolan Harrison	.10	.05	.01
☐ 202 Jeff Hostetler	.20	.09	.03
☐ 203 Rocket Ismail	.20	.09	.03
☐ 204 Jeff Jaeger	.10	.05	.01
☐ 205 James Jett	.10	.05	.01
☐ 206 Terry McDaniel	.10	.05	.01
☐ 207 Chester McGlockton	.10	.05	.01
☐ 208 Winston Moss	.10	.05	.01
☐ 209 Tom Rathman	.10	.05	.01
☐ 210 Anthony Smith	.10	.05	.01
☐ 211 Harvey Williams	.20	.09	.03
☐ 212 Steve Wisniewski	.10	.05	.01
☐ 213 Alexander Wright	.10	.05	.01
☐ 214 Flipper Anderson	.10	.05	.01
☐ 215 Jerome Bettis	1.00	.45	.12
☐ 216 Isaac Bruce	4.00	1.80	.50
☐ 217 Troy Drayton	.10	.05	.01
☐ 218 Wayne Gandy	.10	.05	.01
☐ 219 Sean Gilbert	.10	.05	.01
☐ 220 Nate Lewis	.10	.05	.01
☐ 221 Todd Lyght	.10	.05	.01
☐ 222 Chris Miller	.10	.05	.01
☐ 223 Anthony Newman	.10	.05	.01
☐ 224 Roman Phifer	.10	.05	.01
☐ 225 Henry Rolling	.10	.05	.01
☐ 226 Jackie Slater	.10	.05	.01
☐ 227 Fred Stokes	.10	.05	.01
☐ 228 Gene Atkins	.10	.05	.01
☐ 229 Aubrey Beavers	.10	.05	.01
☐ 230 Tim Bowens	.20	.09	.03
☐ 231 J.B. Brown	.10	.05	.01
☐ 232 Keith Byars	.10	.05	.01
☐ 233 Marco Coleman	.10	.05	.01
☐ 234 Bryan Cox	.10	.05	.01
☐ 235 Jeff Cross	.10	.05	.01
☐ 236 Irving Fryar	.20	.09	.03
☐ 237 Mark Ingram	.10	.05	.01
☐ 238 Keith Jackson	.10	.05	.01
☐ 239 Terry Kirby	.30	.14	.04
☐ 240 Dan Marino	4.00	1.80	.50
☐ 241 Michael Stewart	.10	.05	.01
☐ 242 Troy Vincent	.10	.05	.01
☐ 243 Richmond Webb	.10	.05	.01
☐ 244 Terry Allen	.20	.09	.03
☐ 245 Cris Carter	.30	.14	.04
☐ 246 Jack Del Rio	.10	.05	.01
☐ 247 Vencie Glenn	.10	.05	.01
☐ 248 Chris Hinton	.10	.05	.01
☐ 249 Qadry Ismail	.30	.14	.04
☐ 250 Carlos Jenkins	.10	.05	.01
☐ 251 Randall McDaniel	.10	.05	.01
☐ 252 Warren Moon	.30	.14	.04
☐ 253 David Palmer	.20	.09	.03
☐ 254 John Randle	.10	.05	.01
☐ 255 Jake Reed	.20	.09	.03
☐ 256 Todd Scott	.10	.05	.01
☐ 257 Todd Steussie	.20	.09	.03
☐ 258 Henry Thomas	.10	.05	.01
☐ 259 Dewayne Washington	.20	.09	.03
☐ 260 Bruce Armstrong	.10	.05	.01
☐ 261 Drew Bledsoe	2.00	.90	.25
☐ 262 Vincent Brisby	.30	.14	.04
☐ 263 Vincent Brown	.10	.05	.01
☐ 264 Marion Butts	.10	.05	.01
☐ 265 Ben Coates	.30	.14	.04
☐ 266 Pat Harlow	.10	.05	.01
☐ 267 Maurice Hurst	.10	.05	.01
☐ 268 Willie McGinest	.30	.14	.04
☐ 269 Chris Slade	.10	.05	.01
☐ 270 Michael Timpson	.10	.05	.01
☐ 271 Morten Andersen	.10	.05	.01
☐ 272 Mario Bates	.75	.35	.09
☐ 273 Derek Brown RB	.10	.05	.01
☐ 274 Quinn Early	.20	.09	.03
☐ 275 Jim Everett	.20	.09	.03
☐ 276 Michael Haynes	.20	.09	.03
☐ 277 Tyrone Hughes	.20	.09	.03
☐ 278 Joe Johnson	.10	.05	.01
☐ 279 Eric Martin	.10	.05	.01
☐ 280 Wayne Martin	.10	.05	.01
☐ 281 Sam Mills	.10	.05	.01
☐ 282 Willie Roaf	.10	.05	.01
☐ 283 Irv Smith	.10	.05	.01
☐ 284 Renaldo Turnbull	.10	.05	.01
☐ 285 Carlton Bailey	.10	.05	.01
☐ 286 Michael Brooks	.10	.05	.01
☐ 287 Dave Brown	.20	.09	.03
☐ 288 Jarrod Bunch	.10	.05	.01
☐ 289 Howard Cross	.10	.05	.01
☐ 290 John Elliott	.10	.05	.01
☐ 291 Keith Hamilton	.10	.05	.01
☐ 292 Rodney Hampton	.30	.14	.04
☐ 293 Mark Jackson	.10	.05	.01
☐ 294 Thomas Lewis	.20	.09	.03
☐ 295 Dave Meggett	.10	.05	.01
☐ 296 Corey Miller	.10	.05	.01
☐ 297 Mike Sherrard	.10	.05	.01
☐ 298 Brad Baxter	.10	.05	.01
☐ 299 Kyle Clifton	.10	.05	.01
☐ 300 Boomer Esiason	.20	.09	.03
☐ 301 Aaron Glenn	.20	.09	.03
☐ 302 James Hasty	.10	.05	.01
☐ 303 Johnny Johnson	.10	.05	.01
☐ 304 Jeff Lageman	.10	.05	.01
☐ 305 Mo Lewis	.10	.05	.01
☐ 306 Ronnie Lott	.20	.09	.03
☐ 307 Johnny Mitchell	.10	.05	.01

☐ 308 Art Monk	.20	.09	.03
☐ 309 Rob Moore	.20	.09	.03
☐ 310 Brian Washington	.10	.05	.01
☐ 311 Marvin Washington	.10	.05	.01
☐ 312 Ryan Yarborough	.10	.05	.01
☐ 313 Eric Allen	.10	.05	.01
☐ 314 Victor Bailey	.10	.05	.01
☐ 315 Fred Barnett	.20	.09	.03
☐ 316 Mark Bavaro	.10	.05	.01
☐ 317 Randall Cunningham	.20	.09	.03
☐ 318 Byron Evans	.10	.05	.01
☐ 319 William Fuller	.10	.05	.01
☐ 320 Charlie Garner	.20	.09	.03
☐ 321 Andy Harmon	.10	.05	.01
☐ 322 Vaughn Hebron	.10	.05	.01
☐ 323 Mark McMillian	.10	.05	.01
☐ 324 Bill Romanowski	.10	.05	.01
☐ 325 William Thomas	.10	.05	.01
☐ 326 Greg Townsend	.10	.05	.01
☐ 327 Herschel Walker	.20	.09	.03
☐ 328 Bernard Williams	.10	.05	.01
☐ 329 Calvin Williams	.20	.09	.03
☐ 330 Dermontti Dawson	.10	.05	.01
☐ 331 Deon Figures	.10	.05	.01
☐ 332 Barry Foster	.10	.05	.01
☐ 333 Eric Green	.10	.05	.01
☐ 334 Kevin Greene	.30	.14	.04
☐ 335 Carlton Haselrig	.10	.05	.01
☐ 336 Charles Johnson	.75	.35	.09
☐ 337 Levon Kirkland	.10	.05	.01
☐ 338 Carnell Lake	.10	.05	.01
☐ 339 Greg Lloyd	.30	.14	.04
☐ 340 Neil O'Donnell	.30	.14	.04
☐ 341 Darren Perry	.10	.05	.01
☐ 342 Dwight Stone	.10	.05	.01
☐ 343 John L. Williams	.10	.05	.01
☐ 344 Rod Woodson	.30	.14	.04
☐ 345 John Carney	.10	.05	.01
☐ 346 Darren Carrington	.10	.05	.01
☐ 347 Isaac Davis	.10	.05	.01
☐ 348 Courtney Hall	.10	.05	.01
☐ 349 Ronnie Harmon	.10	.05	.01
☐ 350 Dwayne Harper	.10	.05	.01
☐ 351 Stan Humphries	.30	.14	.04
☐ 352 Shawn Jefferson	.10	.05	.01
☐ 353 Vance Johnson	.10	.05	.01
☐ 354 Natrone Means	.75	.35	.09
☐ 355 Chris Mims	.10	.05	.01
☐ 356 Leslie O'Neal	.10	.05	.01
☐ 357 Stanley Richard	.10	.05	.01
☐ 358 Junior Seau	.30	.14	.04
☐ 359 Harris Barton	.10	.05	.01
☐ 360 Eric Davis	.10	.05	.01
☐ 361 Richard Dent	.20	.09	.03
☐ 362 William Floyd	1.50	.70	.19
☐ 363 Merton Hanks	.20	.09	.03
☐ 364 Brent Jones	.20	.09	.03
☐ 365 Marc Logan	.10	.05	.01
☐ 366 Tim McDonald	.10	.05	.01
☐ 367 Ken Norton	.20	.09	.03
☐ 368 Jerry Rice	2.00	.90	.25
☐ 369 Jesse Sapolu	.10	.05	.01
☐ 370 Dana Stubblefield	.30	.14	.04
☐ 371 John Taylor	.20	.09	.03
☐ 372 Ricky Watters	.30	.14	.04
☐ 373 Bryant Young	.75	.35	.09
☐ 374 Steve Young	1.50	.70	.19
☐ 375 Sam Adams	.20	.09	.03
☐ 376 Michael Bates	.10	.05	.01
☐ 377 Robert Blackmon	.10	.05	.01
☐ 378 Brian Blades	.20	.09	.03
☐ 379 Ferrell Edmunds	.10	.05	.01
☐ 380 John Kasay	.10	.05	.01
☐ 381 Cortez Kennedy	.20	.09	.03
☐ 382 Kelvin Martin	.10	.05	.01
☐ 383 Rick Mirer	.30	.14	.04
☐ 384 Rufus Porter	.10	.05	.01
☐ 385 Eugene Robinson	.10	.05	.01
☐ 386 Rod Stephens	.10	.05	.01
☐ 387 Chris Warren	.20	.09	.03
☐ 388 Marty Carter	.10	.05	.01
☐ 389 Horace Copeland	.10	.05	.01
☐ 390 Eric Curry	.10	.05	.01
☐ 391 Lawrence Dawsey	.10	.05	.01
☐ 392 Trent Dilfer	1.25	.55	.16
☐ 393 Santana Dotson	.20	.09	.03
☐ 394 Craig Erickson	.10	.05	.01
☐ 395 Thomas Everett	.10	.05	.01
☐ 396 Paul Gruber	.10	.05	.01
☐ 397 Jackie Harris	.10	.05	.01
☐ 398 Courtney Hawkins	.10	.05	.01
☐ 399 Martin Mayhew	.10	.05	.01
☐ 400 Hardy Nickerson	.20	.09	.03
☐ 401 Errict Rhett	2.00	.90	.25
☐ 402 Vince Workman	.10	.05	.01
☐ 403 Reggie Brooks	.20	.09	.03
☐ 404 Tom Carter	.10	.05	.01
☐ 405 Andre Collins	.10	.05	.01
☐ 406 Henry Ellard	.20	.09	.03
☐ 407 Kurt Gouveia	.10	.05	.01
☐ 408 Darrell Green	.10	.05	.01
☐ 409 Ken Harvey	.10	.05	.01
☐ 410 Ethan Horton	.10	.05	.01
☐ 411 Desmond Howard	.20	.09	.03
☐ 412 Jim Lachey	.10	.05	.01
☐ 413 Sterling Palmer	.10	.05	.01
☐ 414 Heath Shuler	1.50	.70	.19
☐ 415 Tyronne Stowe	.10	.05	.01
☐ 416 Tony Woods	.10	.05	.01
☐ 417 Checklist 1-124	.10	.05	.01
☐ 418 Checklist 125-243	.10	.05	.01
☐ 419 Checklist 244-358	.10	.05	.01
☐ 420 CL 359-420/Inserts	.10	.05	.01
☐ P1 Reggie Brooks Promo Numbered 000	1.00	.45	.12

1994 GameDay Flashing Stars

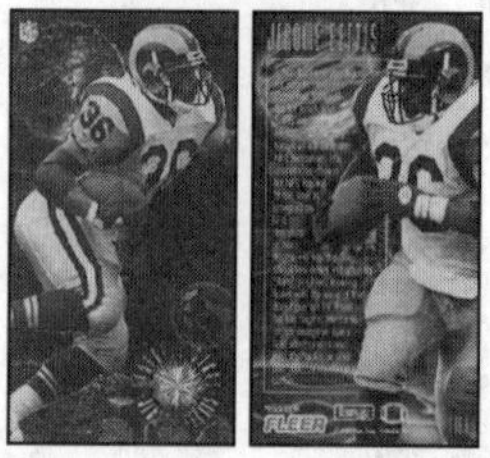

Randomly inserted in packs, this four-card set spotlights outstanding young players. The cards measure 2 1/2" by 4 3/4". Prismatic foil fronts contain a player photo and the Flashing Stars logo. The backs have a photo and a write-up. The set is numbered as "X" of 4 and is sequenced in alphabetical order.

	MINT	NRMT	EXC
COMPLETE SET (4)	60.00	27.00	7.50
COMMON CARD (1-4)	6.00	2.70	.75
☐ 1 Jerome Bettis	10.00	4.50	1.25
☐ 2 Rick Mirer	6.00	2.70	.75
☐ 3 Jerry Rice	18.00	8.00	2.20
☐ 4 Emmitt Smith	30.00	13.50	3.70

1994 GameDay Gamebreakers

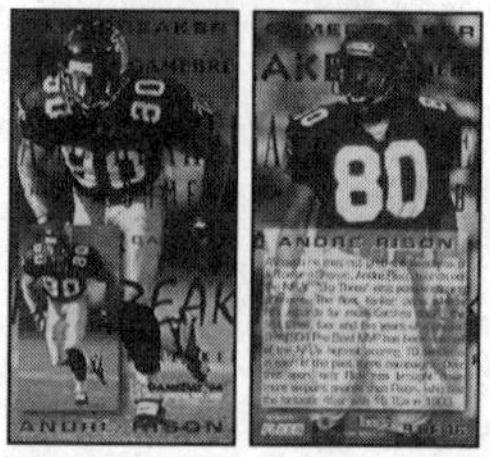

Randomly inserted in packs, this 16-card set spotlights clutch running backs, quarterbacks and receivers. The cards measure 2 1/2" by 4 3/4". Card fronts contain a large black and white photo with the same photo in color toward the bottom left. The word "Gamebreaker" runs across the card. The backs have a color player photo with a write-up. The set is numbered as "X" of 16 and is sequenced in alphabetical order.

	MINT	NRMT	EXC
COMPLETE SET (16)	20.00	9.00	2.50
COMMON CARD (1-16)	.40	.18	.05
☐ 1 Troy Aikman	2.50	1.10	.30
☐ 2 Marcus Allen	.75	.35	.09
☐ 3 Tim Brown	.60	.25	.07
☐ 4 John Elway	2.00	.90	.25
☐ 5 Michael Irvin	.75	.35	.09
☐ 6 Dan Marino	5.00	2.20	.60
☐ 7 Joe Montana	2.50	1.10	.30
☐ 8 Jerry Rice	2.50	1.10	.30
☐ 9 Andre Rison	.60	.25	.07
☐ 10 Barry Sanders	2.50	1.10	.30
☐ 11 Deion Sanders	2.00	.90	.25
☐ 12 Sterling Sharpe	.40	.18	.05
☐ 13 Emmitt Smith	5.00	2.20	.60
☐ 14 Thurman Thomas	.75	.35	.09
☐ 15 Rod Woodson	.40	.18	.05
☐ 16 Steve Young	2.00	.90	.25

1994 GameDay Rookie Standouts

Randomly inserted in packs, this 16-card set contains top 1994 rookies. The cards measure 2 1/2" by 4 3/4". These cards are distinguished by a "3-D embossed" design on front. The player photo occupies the entire front with the player's name in gold letters at the bottom. The backs have a close-up photo with highlights. The set is numbered as "X" of 16 and is sequenced in alphabetical order.

	MINT	NRMT	EXC
COMPLETE SET (16)	16.00	7.25	2.00
COMMON CARD (1-16)	.50	.23	.06
☐ 1 Sam Adams	.50	.23	.06
☐ 2 Trev Alberts	1.00	.45	.12
☐ 3 Lake Dawson	1.00	.45	.12

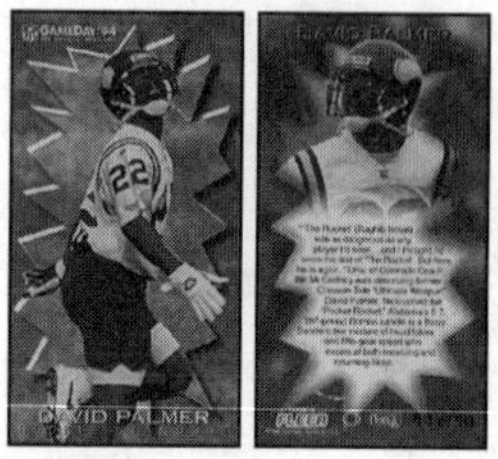

☐ 4 Trent Dilfer	1.50	.70	.19
☐ 5 Marshall Faulk	5.00	2.20	.60
☐ 6 Aaron Glenn	.50	.23	.06
☐ 7 Charles Johnson	1.00	.45	.12
☐ 8 Willie McGinest	1.00	.45	.12
☐ 9 Jamir Miller	.50	.23	.06
☐ 10 Johnnie Morton	1.00	.45	.12
☐ 11 David Palmer	1.00	.45	.12
☐ 12 Errict Rhett	2.00	.90	.25
☐ 13 Heath Shuler	1.50	.70	.19
☐ 14 John Thierry	.50	.23	.06
☐ 15 Dan Wilkinson	1.00	.45	.12
☐ 16 Bryant Young	1.00	.45	.12

1994 GameDay Second Year Stars

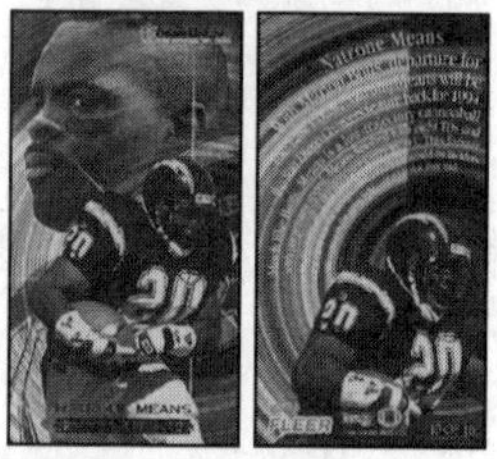

Looking back on top rookies from 1993, this 16-card set was randomly inserted in packs. Action oriented fronts contain two photos and the player's name in gold foil. Background color is consistent with team colors. The backs are designed much like the front, except for one photo and highlights. The cards are numbered as "X" of 16 and are sequenced in alphabetical order.

	MINT	NRMT	EXC
COMPLETE SET (16)	12.00	5.50	1.50
COMMON CARD (1-16)	.50	.23	.06
☐ 1 Jerome Bettis	1.50	.70	.19
☐ 2 Drew Bledsoe	3.00	1.35	.35
☐ 3 Reggie Brooks	.75	.35	.09
☐ 4 Tom Carter	.50	.23	.06
☐ 5 Eric Curry	.50	.23	.06
☐ 6 Steve Everitt	.50	.23	.06
☐ 7 Tyrone Hughes	.50	.23	.06
☐ 8 James Jett	.50	.23	.06
☐ 9 Terry Kirby	.75	.35	.09
☐ 10 Natrone Means	1.00	.45	.12
☐ 11 Rick Mirer	1.50	.70	.19
☐ 12 Ronald Moore	.50	.23	.06
☐ 13 Willie Roaf	.50	.23	.06
☐ 14 Chris Slade	.50	.23	.06
☐ 15 Darrin Smith	.50	.23	.06
☐ 16 Dana Stubblefield	.75	.35	.09

1971 Gatorade Team Lids

These lids were actually the tops on bottles of Gatorade during the 1971 season. The white lids had a dark outline of a helmet with the team name underneath.

	NRMT-MT	EXC	G-VG
COMPLETE SET (26)	125.00	55.00	15.50
COMMON CAP (1-26)	5.00	2.20	.60
☐ 1 Atlanta Falcons	5.00	2.20	.60
☐ 2 Baltimore Colts	5.00	2.20	.60
☐ 3 Buffalo Bills	5.00	2.20	.60
☐ 4 Chicago Bears	6.00	2.70	.75
☐ 5 Cincinnati Bengals	5.00	2.20	.60
☐ 6 Cleveland Browns	5.00	2.20	.60
☐ 7 Dallas Cowboys	9.00	4.00	1.10
☐ 8 Denver Broncos	6.00	2.70	.75
☐ 9 Detroit Lions	5.00	2.20	.60
☐ 10 Green Bay Packers	5.00	2.20	.60
☐ 11A Houston Oilers Blue Helmet	5.00	2.20	.60
☐ 11B Houston Oilers Gray Helmet	5.00	2.20	.60
☐ 12 Kansas City Chiefs	5.00	2.20	.60
☐ 13A Los Angeles Rams white Rams horns	5.00	2.20	.60
☐ 13B Los Angeles Rams yellow Rams horns	5.00	2.20	.60
☐ 14 Miami Dolphins	6.00	2.70	.75
☐ 15 Minnesota Vikings	5.00	2.20	.60
☐ 16 New England Patriots	5.00	2.20	.60
☐ 17 New Orleans Saints	5.00	2.20	.60
☐ 18 New York Giants	5.00	2.20	.60
☐ 19 New York Jets	5.00	2.20	.60
☐ 20 Oakland Raiders	9.00	4.00	1.10
☐ 21 Philadelphia Eagles	6.00	2.70	.75
☐ 22 Pittsburgh Steelers	6.00	2.70	.75
☐ 23 San Diego Chargers	5.00	2.20	.60
☐ 24 San Francisco 49ers	6.00	2.70	.75
☐ 25 St. Louis Cardinals	5.00	2.20	.60
☐ 26A Washington Redskins ("R" logo old style)	6.00	2.70	.75
☐ 26B Washington Redskins (Indian head logo new style)	6.00	2.70	.75

1956 Giants Team Issue

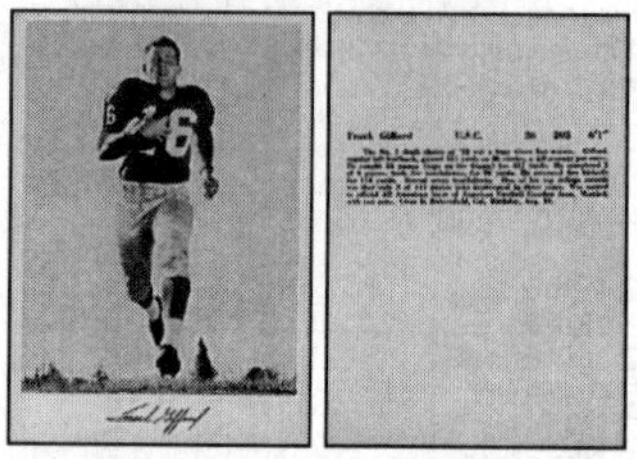

The 1956 Giants Team Issue set contains 36 cards measuring approximately 4 7/8" by 6 7/8". The fronts have black and white posed player photos with white borders. A facsimile autograph appears below the picture. The backs have brief biographical information and career highlights. The cards are unnumbered and checklisted below in alphabetical order.

	NRMT	VG-E	GOOD
COMPLETE SET (36)	250.00	110.00	31.00
COMMON CARD (1-36)	5.00	2.20	.60
☐ 1 Bill Austin	5.00	2.20	.60
☐ 2 Ray Beck	5.00	2.20	.60
☐ 3 Roosevelt Brown	15.00	6.75	1.85
☐ 4 Hank Burnine	5.00	2.20	.60
☐ 5 Don Chandler	6.00	2.70	.75
☐ 6 Bobby Clatterbuck	5.00	2.20	.60
☐ 7 Charley Conerly	25.00	11.00	3.10
☐ 8 Frank Gifford	40.00	18.00	5.00
☐ 9 Roosevelt Grier	15.00	6.75	1.85
☐ 10 Don Heinrich	6.00	2.70	.75
☐ 11 John Hermann	5.00	2.20	.60
☐ 12 Jim Lee Howell CO	6.00	2.70	.75
☐ 13 Sam Huff	20.00	9.00	2.50
☐ 14 Ed Hughes	5.00	2.20	.60
☐ 15 Gerald Huth	5.00	2.20	.60
☐ 16 Jim Katcavage	6.00	2.70	.75
☐ 17 Gene Kirby ANN	5.00	2.20	.60
☐ 18 Ken MacAfee	6.00	2.70	.75
☐ 19 Dick Modzelewski (Misspelled Modelewski on the reverse)	6.00	2.70	.75
☐ 20 Henry Moore	5.00	2.20	.60
☐ 21 Dick Nolan	6.00	2.70	.75
☐ 22 Jimmy Patton	6.00	2.70	.75
☐ 23 Andy Robustelli	15.00	6.75	1.85
☐ 24 Kyle Rote	12.00	5.50	1.50
☐ 25 Chris Schenkel ANN	6.00	2.70	.75
☐ 26 Bob Schnelker	5.00	2.20	.60
☐ 27 Jack Stroud	5.00	2.20	.60
☐ 28 Harland Svare	6.00	2.70	.75
☐ 29 Bill Svoboda	5.00	2.20	.60
☐ 30 Bob Topp	5.00	2.20	.60
☐ 31 Mel Triplett	6.00	2.70	.75
☐ 32 Emlen Tunnell	15.00	6.75	1.85
☐ 33 Alex Webster	7.50	3.40	.95
☐ 34 Ray Wietecha	5.00	2.20	.60
☐ 35 Dick Yelvington	5.00	2.20	.60
☐ 36 Walt Yowarsky	5.00	2.20	.60

1957 Giants Team Issue

This 40-card set measures approximately 4 7/8" by 6 7/8". The front has a black and white photo on glossy stock with a white border. The back gives biographical and statistical information. This set features one of the earliest Vince Lombardi cards. The cards are unnumbered and checklisted below in alphabetical order.

	NRMT	VG-E	GOOD
COMPLETE SET (40)	325.00	145.00	40.00
COMMON CARD (1-40)	4.00	1.80	.50
☐ 1 Ben Agajanian	5.00	2.20	.60
☐ 2 Bill Austin	4.00	1.80	.50
☐ 3 Ray Beck	4.00	1.80	.50
☐ 4 John Bookman	4.00	1.80	.50
☐ 5 Roosevelt Brown	12.00	5.50	1.50
☐ 6 Don Chandler	5.00	2.20	.60
☐ 7 Bobby Clatterbuck	4.00	1.80	.50
☐ 8 Charley Conerly	20.00	9.00	2.50
☐ 9 John Dell Isola CO	4.00	1.80	.50
☐ 10 Gene Filipski	5.00	2.20	.60
☐ 11 Frank Gifford	30.00	13.50	3.70
☐ 12 Don Heinrich	5.00	2.20	.60
☐ 13 Jim Lee Howell CO	5.00	2.20	.60
☐ 14 Sam Huff	15.00	6.75	1.85
☐ 15 Ed Hughes	4.00	1.80	.50
☐ 16 Gerald Huth	4.00	1.80	.50

☐ 17 Jim Katcavage	5.00	2.20	.60
☐ 18 Ken Kavanaugh CO	5.00	2.20	.60
☐ 19 Les Keiter ANN	4.00	1.80	.50
☐ 20 Tom Landry CO	50.00	22.00	6.25
☐ 21 Cliff Livingston	4.00	1.80	.50
☐ 22 Vince Lombardi CO	60.00	27.00	7.50
☐ 23 Ken MacAfee	5.00	2.20	.60
☐ 24 Dennis Mendyk	4.00	1.80	.50
☐ 25 Dick Modzelewski	5.00	2.20	.60
☐ 26 Dick Nolan	5.00	2.20	.60
☐ 27 Jim Patton	5.00	2.20	.60
☐ 28 Andy Robustelli	15.00	6.75	1.85
☐ 29 Kyle Rote	10.00	4.50	1.25
☐ 30 Chris Schenkel ANN	5.00	2.20	.60
☐ 31 Jack Spinks	4.00	1.80	.50
☐ 32 Jack Stroud	4.00	1.80	.50
☐ 33 Harland Svare	4.00	1.80	.50
☐ 34 Bill Svoboda	4.00	1.80	.50
☐ 35 Mel Triplett	5.00	2.20	.60
☐ 36 Emlen Tunnell	12.00	5.50	1.50
☐ 37 Alex Webster	6.00	2.70	.75
☐ 38 Ray Wietecha	5.00	2.20	.60
☐ 39 Dick Yelvington	4.00	1.80	.50
☐ 40 Walt Yowarsky	4.00	1.80	.50

1960 Giants Jay Publishing

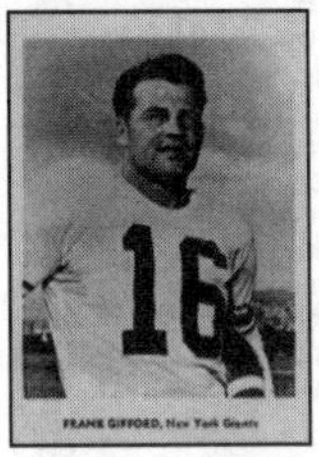

This 12-card set features (approximately) 5" by 7" black-and-white player photos. The photos show players in traditional poses with the quarterback preparing to throw, the runner heading downfield, and the defenseman ready for the tackle. These cards were packaged 12 to a packet and originally sold for 25 cents. The backs are blank. The cards are unnumbered and checklisted in alphabetical order.

	NRMT	VG-E	GOOD
COMPLETE SET (12)	100.00	45.00	12.50
COMMON CARD (1-12)	4.00	1.80	.50
☐ 1 Roosevelt Brown	10.00	4.50	1.25
☐ 2 Don Chandler	4.00	1.80	.50
☐ 3 Charley Conerly	15.00	6.75	1.85
☐ 4 Frank Gifford	25.00	11.00	3.10
☐ 5 Roosevelt Grier	8.00	3.60	1.00
☐ 6 Sam Huff	15.00	6.75	1.85
☐ 7 Phil King	4.00	1.80	.50
☐ 8 Andy Robustelli	10.00	4.50	1.25
☐ 9 Kyle Rote	8.00	3.60	1.00
☐ 10 Bob Schnelker	4.00	1.80	.50
☐ 11 Pat Summerall	10.00	4.50	1.25
☐ 12 Alex Webster	5.00	2.20	.60

1960 Giants Shell/Riger Posters

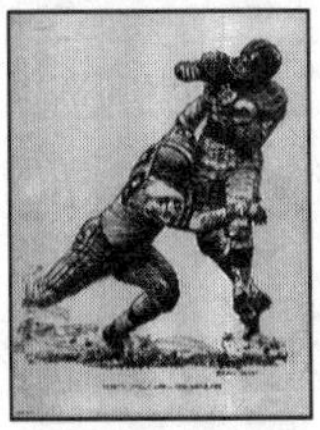

This set of ten posters was distributed by Shell Oil in 1960. The pictures are black and white drawings by Robert Riger, and measure approximately 11 3/4" by 13 3/4". The unnumbered posters are arranged alphabetically by the player's last name and feature members of the New York Giants.

	NRMT	VG-E	GOOD
COMPLETE SET (10)	175.00	80.00	22.00
COMMON CARD (1-10)	10.00	4.50	1.25
☐ 1 Charley Conerly	25.00	11.00	3.10
☐ 2 Frank Gifford	40.00	18.00	5.00
☐ 3 Sam Huff	20.00	9.00	2.50
☐ 4 Dick Modzelewski	10.00	4.50	1.25
☐ 5 Jim Patton	10.00	4.50	1.25
☐ 6 Andy Robustelli	18.00	8.00	2.20
☐ 7 Kyle Rote	15.00	6.75	1.85
☐ 8 Bob Schnelker	10.00	4.50	1.25
☐ 9 Pat Summerall	20.00	9.00	2.50
☐ 10 Alex Webster and Roosevelt Brown	15.00	6.75	1.85

1961 Giants Jay Publishing

This 12-card set features (approximately) 5" by 7" black-and-white player photos. The photos show players in traditional poses with the quarterback preparing to throw, the runner heading downfield, and the defenseman ready for the tackle. These cards were packaged 12 to a packet and originally sold for 25 cents. The backs are blank. The cards are unnumbered and checklisted below in alphabetical order.

	NRMT	VG-E	GOOD
COMPLETE SET (12)	75.00	34.00	9.50
COMMON CARD (1-12)	4.00	1.80	.50
☐ 1 Roosevelt Brown	8.00	3.60	1.00
☐ 2 Don Chandler	4.00	1.80	.50
☐ 3 Charley Conerly	12.00	5.50	1.50
☐ 4 Roosevelt Grier	7.00	3.10	.85
☐ 5 Sam Huff	12.00	5.50	1.50
☐ 6 Dick Modzelewski	4.00	1.80	.50
☐ 7 Jimmy Patton	5.00	2.20	.60
☐ 8 Jim Podoley	4.00	1.80	.50
☐ 9 Andy Robustelli	8.00	3.60	1.00
☐ 10 Allie Sherman CO	4.00	1.80	.50
☐ 11 Del Shofner	5.00	2.20	.60
☐ 12 Y.A. Tittle	20.00	9.00	2.50

1962 Giants Team Issue

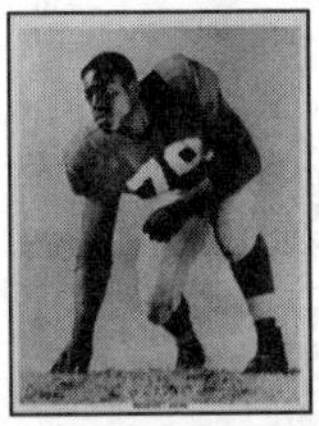

The New York Giants issued this set of player photos in 1962. Each measures approximately 8" by 10" and features a black and white photo with the player's name directly below. The cards are blankbacked and unnumbered.

	NRMT	VG-E	GOOD
COMPLETE SET (10)	125.00	55.00	15.50
COMMON CARD (1-10)	10.00	4.50	1.25
☐ 1 Roosevelt Brown	15.00	6.75	1.85
☐ 2 Don Chandler	10.00	4.50	1.25
☐ 3 Frank Gifford	35.00	16.00	4.40
☐ 4 Sam Huff	20.00	9.00	2.50
☐ 5 Dick Lynch	10.00	4.50	1.25
☐ 6 Jim Patton	12.00	5.50	1.50
☐ 7 Andy Robustelli	20.00	9.00	2.50
☐ 8 Del Shofner	12.00	5.50	1.50
☐ 9 Y.A. Tittle	25.00	11.00	3.10
☐ 10 Alex Webster	12.00	5.50	1.50

1973 Giants Color Litho

Each of these color lithos measures approximately 8 1/2" by 11" and is blank backed. There is no card border and a facsimile autograph appears within a white triangle below the player photo.

	NRMT-MT	EXC	G-VG
COMPLETE SET (8)	50.00	22.00	6.25
COMMON CARD (1-8)	6.00	2.70	.75
☐ 1 Jim Files	6.00	2.70	.75
☐ 2 Jack Gregory	6.00	2.70	.75
☐ 3 Ron Johnson	7.50	3.40	.95
☐ 4 Greg Larson	6.00	2.70	.75
☐ 5 Spider Lockhart	7.50	3.40	.95
☐ 6 Norm Snead	10.00	4.50	1.25
☐ 7 Bob Tucker	7.50	3.40	.95
☐ 8 Brad Van Pelt	7.50	3.40	.95

1987 Giants Police

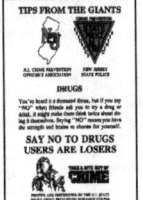

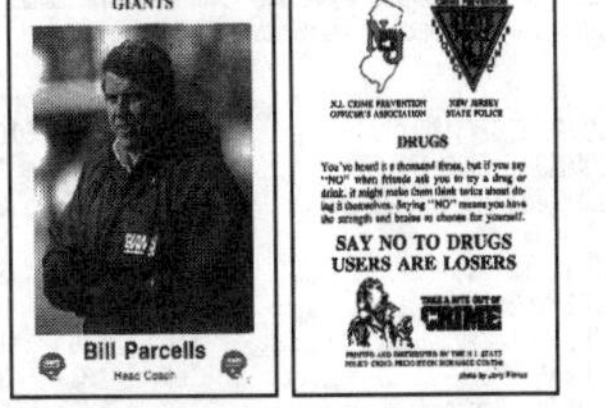
NEW YORK GIANTS
Bill Parcells
TIPS FROM THE GIANTS
DRUGS
SAY NO TO DRUGS USERS ARE LOSERS

This set of 12 cards featuring New York Giants was issued very late in the year and was not widely distributed. Reportedly 10,000 sets were distributed by officers of the New Jersey police force. Cards measure approximately 2 3/4" by 4 1/8" and feature a crime prevention tip on the back. The set was sponsored by the New Jersey State Police Crime Prevention Resource Center. The Giants helmet appears below the player photo which differentiates this set from the very similar 1988 Police Giants set. These unnumbered cards are listed alphabetically in the checklist below.

	MINT	NRMT	EXC
COMPLETE SET (12)	75.00	34.00	9.50
COMMON CARD (1-12)	4.00	1.80	.50
☐ 1 Carl Banks	6.00	2.70	.75
☐ 2 Mark Bavaro	5.00	2.20	.60
☐ 3 Brad Benson	4.00	1.80	.50
☐ 4 Jim Burt	5.00	2.20	.60
☐ 5 Harry Carson	5.00	2.20	.60
☐ 6 Maurice Carthon	4.00	1.80	.50
☐ 7 Sean Landeta	4.00	1.80	.50
☐ 8 Leonard Marshall	5.00	2.20	.60
☐ 9 George Martin	4.00	1.80	.50
☐ 10 Joe Morris	6.00	2.70	.75
☐ 11 Bill Parcells CO	10.00	4.50	1.25
☐ 12 Phil Simms	20.00	9.00	2.50

1988 Giants Police

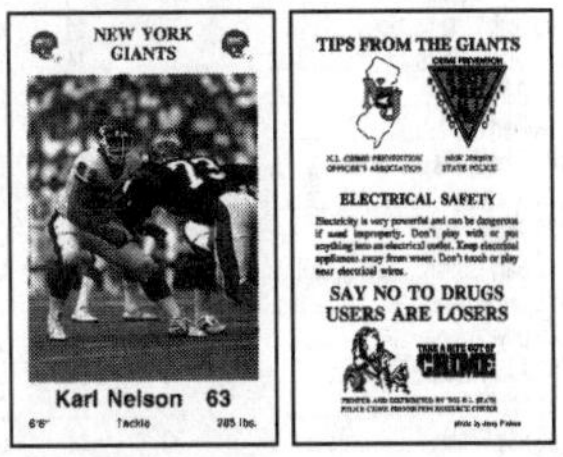
NEW YORK GIANTS
Karl Nelson 63
TIPS FROM THE GIANTS
ELECTRICAL SAFETY
SAY NO TO DRUGS USERS ARE LOSERS

The 1988 Police New York Giants set contains 12 unnumbered cards measuring approximately 2 3/4" by 4 1/8". There are 11 player cards and one coach card. The backs have safety tips. The cards are listed below in alphabetical order by subject's name. The Giants team name and helmets appear above the player photo which differentiates this set from the very similar 1987 Police Giants set.

	MINT	NRMT	EXC
COMPLETE SET (12)	65.00	29.00	8.00
COMMON CARD (1-12)	4.00	1.80	.50
☐ 1 Billy Ard	4.00	1.80	.50
☐ 2 Jim Burt	4.00	1.80	.50
☐ 3 Harry Carson	6.00	2.70	.75
☐ 4 Maurice Carthon	4.00	1.80	.50
☐ 5 Leonard Marshall	5.00	2.20	.60
☐ 6 George Martin	4.00	1.80	.50
☐ 7 Phil McConkey	4.00	1.80	.50
☐ 8 Joe Morris	6.00	2.70	.75
☐ 9 Karl Nelson	4.00	1.80	.50
☐ 10 Bart Oates	5.00	2.20	.60
☐ 11 Bill Parcells CO	7.50	3.40	.95
☐ 12 Phil Simms	15.00	6.75	1.85

1990 Giants Police

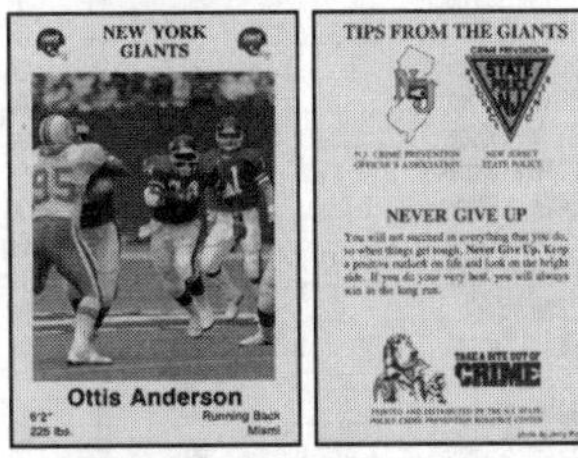
NEW YORK GIANTS
Ottis Anderson
TIPS FROM THE GIANTS
NEVER GIVE UP

This 12-card set was printed and distributed by the New Jersey State Police Crime Prevention Resource Center. The cards measure approxiamtely 2 3/4" by 4 1/8". The fronts display color action player photos bordered in white. The team name appears at the top between two representations of the team helmet, while player information is printed beneath the picture. In dark blue print on white, the backs carry logos, "Tips from the Giants" in the form of public service announcements, and the McGruff the Crime Dog "Take a Bite out of Crime" slogan. The cards are unnumbered and checklisted below in alphabetical order.

	MINT	NRMT	EXC
COMPLETE SET (12)	50.00	22.00	6.25
COMMON CARD (1-12)	3.00	1.35	.35
☐ 1 Ottis Anderson	6.00	2.70	.75
☐ 2 Matt Bahr	3.00	1.35	.35
☐ 3 Eric Dorsey	3.00	1.35	.35
☐ 4 John Elliott	3.00	1.35	.35
☐ 5 Ray Handley CO	3.00	1.35	.35
☐ 6 Jeff Hostetler	7.50	3.40	.95
☐ 7 Erik Howard	3.00	1.35	.35
☐ 8 Pepper Johnson	4.00	1.80	.50
☐ 9 Leonard Marshall	4.00	1.80	.50
☐ 10 Bart Oates	4.00	1.80	.50
☐ 11 Gary Reasons	3.00	1.35	.35
☐ 12 Phil Simms	10.00	4.50	1.25

1992 Giants Police

This 12-card police set was printed and distributed by the New Jersey State Police Crime Prevention Resource Center. The cards measure approximately 2 3/4" by 4 1/8". The fronts feature color action player photos bordered in white. The team name appears above the picture, while the player's name and brief biographical information are printed below it. The backs carry sponsor logos, "Tips from the Giants" in the form of public service announcements, and the McGruff crime dog slogan "Take a Bite Out of Crime." The cards are unnumbered and checklisted below in alphabetical order.

	MINT	NRMT	EXC
COMPLETE SET (12)	25.00	11.00	3.10
COMMON CARD (1-12)	1.50	.70	.19
☐ 1 Ottis Anderson	2.50	1.10	.30
☐ 2 Matt Bahr	1.50	.70	.19
☐ 3 Eric Dorsey	1.50	.70	.19
☐ 4 John Elliott	1.50	.70	.19
☐ 5 Ray Handley CO	1.50	.70	.19
☐ 6 Jeff Hostetler	4.00	1.80	.50
☐ 7 Erik Howard	1.50	.70	.19
☐ 8 Pepper Johnson	2.00	.90	.25
☐ 9 Leonard Marshall	2.00	.90	.25
☐ 10 Bart Oates	2.00	.90	.25
☐ 11 Gary Reasons	1.50	.70	.19
☐ 12 Phil Simms	5.00	2.20	.60

1969 Glendale Stamps

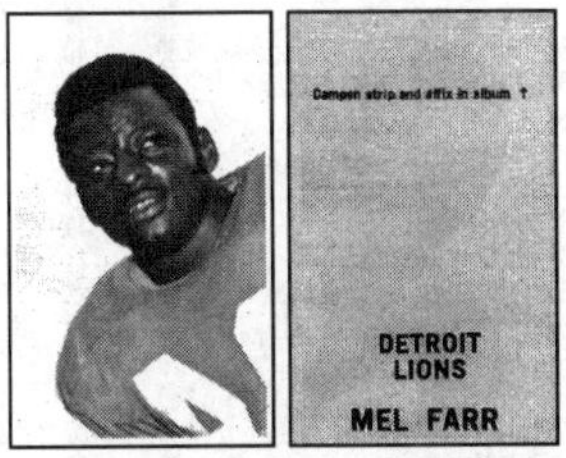
DETROIT LIONS
MEL FARR

This set contains 312 stamps featuring NFL players each measuring approximately 1 13/16" by 2 15/16". The stamps were meant to be pasted in an accompanying album, which itself measures approximately 9" by 12". The stamps and the album positions are unnumbered so the stamps are ordered and numbered below according to the team order that they appear in the book. The team order is alphabetical as well, according to the city name. The stamp of O.J. Simpson predates his 1970 Topps Rookie Card by one year and the stamp of Gene Upshaw predates his Rookie Card by three years.

	NRMT-MT	EXC	G-VG
COMPLETE SET (312)	300.00	135.00	38.00
COMMON CARD (1-312)	.30	.14	.04
☐ 1 Bob Berry	.30	.14	.04
☐ 2 Clark Miller	.30	.14	.04
☐ 3 Jim Butler	.30	.14	.04
☐ 4 Junior Coffey	.30	.14	.04
☐ 5 Paul Flatley	.30	.14	.04
☐ 6 Randy Johnson	.30	.14	.04
☐ 7 Charlie Bryant	.30	.14	.04
☐ 8 Billy Lothridge	.30	.14	.04
☐ 9 Tommy Nobis	1.50	.70	.19
☐ 10 Claude Humphrey	.30	.14	.04
☐ 11 Ken Reaves	.30	.14	.04
☐ 12 Jerry Simmons	.30	.14	.04
☐ 13 Mike Curtis	.50	.23	.06
☐ 14 Dennis Gaubatz	.30	.14	.04
☐ 15 Jerry Logan	.30	.14	.04
☐ 16 Lenny Lyles	.30	.14	.04
☐ 17 John Mackey	2.00	.90	.25
☐ 18 Tom Matte	.30	.14	.04
☐ 19 Lou Michaels	.30	.14	.04
☐ 20 Jimmy Orr	.30	.14	.04
☐ 21 Willie Richardson	.30	.14	.04
☐ 22 Don Shinnick	.30	.14	.04
☐ 23 Dan Sullivan	.30	.14	.04
☐ 24 Johnny Unitas	15.00	6.75	1.85
☐ 25 Houston Antwine	.30	.14	.04
☐ 26 John Bramlett	.30	.14	.04
☐ 27 Aaron Marsh	.30	.14	.04
☐ 28 R.C. Gamble	.30	.14	.04
☐ 29 Gino Cappelletti	.50	.23	.06
☐ 30 John Charles	.30	.14	.04
☐ 31 Larry Eisenhauer	.30	.14	.04
☐ 32 Jon Morris	.30	.14	.04
☐ 33 Jim Nance	.50	.23	.06
☐ 34 Len St. Jean	.30	.14	.04
☐ 35 Mike Taliaferro	.30	.14	.04
☐ 36 Jim Whalen	.30	.14	.04
☐ 37 Stew Barber	.30	.14	.04
☐ 38 Al Bemiller	.30	.14	.04
☐ 39 George(Butch) Byrd	.30	.14	.04
☐ 40 Booker Edgerson	.30	.14	.04
☐ 41 Harry Jacobs	.30	.14	.04
☐ 42 Jack Kemp	20.00	9.00	2.50
☐ 43 Ron McDole	.30	.14	.04
☐ 44 Joe O'Donnell	.30	.14	.04
☐ 45 John Pitts	.30	.14	.04
☐ 46 George Saimes	.30	.14	.04
☐ 47 Mike Stratton	.30	.14	.04
☐ 48 O.J. Simpson	20.00	9.00	2.50
☐ 49 Ron Bull	.30	.14	.04
☐ 50 Dick Butkus	12.50	5.50	1.55
☐ 51 Jim Cadile	.30	.14	.04
☐ 52 Jack Concannon	.30	.14	.04
☐ 53 Dick Evey	.30	.14	.04
☐ 54 Bennie McRae	.30	.14	.04
☐ 55 Ed O'Bradovich	.30	.14	.04
☐ 56 Brian Piccolo	25.00	11.00	3.10
☐ 57 Mike Pyle	.30	.14	.04
☐ 58 Gale Sayers	12.50	5.50	1.55
☐ 59 Dick Gordon	.30	.14	.04

☐ 60 Roosevelt Taylor	.30	.14	.04
☐ 61 Al Beauchamp	.30	.14	.04
☐ 62 Dave Middendorf	.30	.14	.04
☐ 63 Harry Gunner	.30	.14	.04
☐ 64 Bobby Hunt	.30	.14	.04
☐ 65 Bob Johnson	.30	.14	.04
☐ 66 Charley King	.30	.14	.04
☐ 67 Andy Rice	.30	.14	.04
☐ 68 Paul Robinson	.30	.14	.04
☐ 69 Bill Staley	.30	.14	.04
☐ 70 Pat Matson	.30	.14	.04
☐ 71 Bob Trumpy	1.00	.45	.12
☐ 72 Sam Wyche	5.00	2.20	.60
☐ 73 Erich Barnes	.30	.14	.04
☐ 74 Gary Collins	.30	.14	.04
☐ 75 Ben Davis	.30	.14	.04
☐ 76 John Demarie	.30	.14	.04
☐ 77 Gene Hickerson	.30	.14	.04
☐ 78 Jim Houston	.30	.14	.04
☐ 79 Ernie Kellerman	.30	.14	.04
☐ 80 Leroy Kelly	2.50	1.10	.30
☐ 81 Dale Lindsey	.30	.14	.04
☐ 82 Bill Nelsen	.30	.14	.04
☐ 83 Jim Kanicki	.30	.14	.04
☐ 84 Dick Schafrath	.30	.14	.04
☐ 85 George Andrie	.30	.14	.04
☐ 86 Mike Clark	.30	.14	.04
☐ 87 Cornell Green	.50	.23	.06
☐ 88 Bob Hayes	2.00	.90	.25
☐ 89 Chuck Howley	.75	.35	.09
☐ 90 Lee Roy Jordan	1.50	.70	.19
☐ 91 Bob Lilly	4.00	1.80	.50
☐ 92 Craig Morton	.75	.35	.09
☐ 93 John Niland	.30	.14	.04
☐ 94 Dan Reeves	5.00	2.20	.60
☐ 95 Mel Renfro	2.00	.90	.25
☐ 96 Lance Rentzel	.30	.14	.04
☐ 97 Tom Beer	.30	.14	.04
☐ 98 Billy Van Heusen	.30	.14	.04
☐ 99 Mike Current	.30	.14	.04
☐ 100 Al Denson	.30	.14	.04
☐ 101 Pete Duranko	.30	.14	.04
☐ 102 George Goeddeke	.30	.14	.04
☐ 103 John Huard	.30	.14	.04
☐ 104 Rich Jackson	.30	.14	.04
☐ 105 Pete Jacques	.30	.14	.04
☐ 106 Fran Lynch	.30	.14	.04
☐ 107 Floyd Little	1.50	.70	.19
☐ 108 Steve Tensi	.30	.14	.04
☐ 109 Lem Barney	2.50	1.10	.30
☐ 110 Nick Eddy	.30	.14	.04
☐ 111 Mel Farr	.30	.14	.04
☐ 112 Ed Flanagan	.30	.14	.04
☐ 113 Larry Hand	.30	.14	.04
☐ 114 Alex Karras	2.50	1.10	.30
☐ 115 Dick LeBeau	.30	.14	.04
☐ 116 Mike Lucci	.30	.14	.04
☐ 117 Earl McCullouch	.30	.14	.04
☐ 118 Bill Munson	.30	.14	.04
☐ 119 Jerry Rush	.30	.14	.04
☐ 120 Wayne Walker	.30	.14	.04
☐ 121 Herb Adderley	2.00	.90	.25
☐ 122 Donny Anderson	.50	.23	.06
☐ 123 Lee Roy Caffey	.30	.14	.04
☐ 124 Carroll Dale	.30	.14	.04
☐ 125 Willie Davis	2.00	.90	.25
☐ 126 Boyd Dowler	.30	.14	.04
☐ 127 Marv Fleming	.30	.14	.04
☐ 128 Bob Jeter	.30	.14	.04
☐ 129 Hank Jordan	2.00	.90	.25
☐ 130 Dave Robinson	.30	.14	.04
☐ 131 Bart Starr	12.50	5.50	1.55
☐ 132 Willie Wood	2.00	.90	.25
☐ 133 Pete Beathard	.50	.23	.06
☐ 134 Jim Beirne	.30	.14	.04
☐ 135 Garland Boyette	.30	.14	.04
☐ 136 Woody Campbell	.30	.14	.04
☐ 137 Miller Farr	.30	.14	.04
☐ 138 Hoyle Granger	.30	.14	.04
☐ 139 Mac Haik	.30	.14	.04
☐ 140 Ken Houston	2.50	1.10	.30
☐ 141 Bobby Maples	.30	.14	.04
☐ 142 Alvin Reed	.30	.14	.04
☐ 143 Don Trull	.30	.14	.04
☐ 144 George Webster	.50	.23	.06
☐ 145 Bobby Bell	2.00	.90	.25
☐ 146 Aaron Brown	.30	.14	.04
☐ 147 Buck Buchanan	2.00	.90	.25
☐ 148 Len Dawson	5.00	2.20	.60
☐ 149 Mike Garrett	.50	.23	.06
☐ 150 Robert Holmes	.30	.14	.04
☐ 151 Willie Lanier	2.50	1.10	.30
☐ 152 Frank Pitts	.30	.14	.04
☐ 153 Johnny Robinson	.50	.23	.06
☐ 154 Jan Stenerud	2.50	1.10	.30
☐ 155 Otis Taylor	.75	.35	.09
☐ 156 Jim Tyrer	.30	.14	.04
☐ 157 Dick Bass	.30	.14	.04
☐ 158 Maxie Baughan	.30	.14	.04
☐ 159 Richie Petitbon	.30	.14	.04
☐ 160 Roger Brown	.30	.14	.04
☐ 161 Roman Gabriel	1.00	.45	.12
☐ 162 Bruce Gossett	.30	.14	.04
☐ 163 Deacon Jones	2.00	.90	.25
☐ 164 Tom Mack	1.00	.45	.12
☐ 165 Tommy Mason	.30	.14	.04
☐ 166 Ed Meador	.30	.14	.04
☐ 167 Merlin Olsen	2.50	1.10	.30
☐ 168 Pat Studstill	.30	.14	.04
☐ 169 Jack Clancy	.30	.14	.04
☐ 170 Maxie Williams	.30	.14	.04
☐ 171 Larry Csonka	12.50	5.50	1.55
☐ 172 Jim Warren	.30	.14	.04
☐ 173 Norm Evans	.30	.14	.04
☐ 174 Rick Norton	.30	.14	.04
☐ 175 Bob Griese	10.00	4.50	1.25
☐ 176 Howard Twilley	.30	.14	.04
☐ 177 Billy Neighbors	.30	.14	.04
☐ 178 Nick Buoniconti	1.50	.70	.19
☐ 179 Tom Goode	.30	.14	.04
☐ 180 Dick Westmoreland	.30	.14	.04
☐ 181 Grady Alderman	.30	.14	.04
☐ 182 Bill Brown	.50	.23	.06
☐ 183 Fred Cox	.30	.14	.04
☐ 184 Clint Jones	.30	.14	.04
☐ 185 Joe Kapp	.75	.35	.09
☐ 186 Paul Krause	.75	.35	.09
☐ 187 Gary Larsen	.30	.14	.04
☐ 188 Jim Marshall	2.00	.90	.25
☐ 189 Dave Osborn	.30	.14	.04
☐ 190 Alan Page	5.00	2.20	.60
☐ 191 Mick Tingelhoff	.50	.23	.06
☐ 192 Roy Winston	.30	.14	.04
☐ 193 Dan Abramowicz	.30	.14	.04
☐ 194 Doug Atkins	2.00	.90	.25
☐ 195 Bo Burris	.30	.14	.04
☐ 196 John Douglas	.30	.14	.04
☐ 197 Don Shy	.30	.14	.04
☐ 198 Billy Kilmer	.75	.35	.09
☐ 199 Tony Lorick	.30	.14	.04
☐ 200 Dave Parks	.30	.14	.04
☐ 201 Dave Rowe	.30	.14	.04
☐ 202 Monty Stickles	.30	.14	.04
☐ 203 Steve Stonebreaker	.30	.14	.04
☐ 204 Del Williams	.30	.14	.04
☐ 205 Pete Case	.30	.14	.04
☐ 206 Tommy Crutcher	.30	.14	.04
☐ 207 Scott Eaton	.30	.14	.04
☐ 208 Tucker Frederickson	.30	.14	.04
☐ 209 Pete Gogolak	.30	.14	.04
☐ 210 Homer Jones	.30	.14	.04
☐ 211 Ernie Koy	.30	.14	.04
☐ 212 Spider Lockhart	.30	.14	.04
☐ 213 Bruce Maher	.30	.14	.04
☐ 214 Aaron Thomas	.30	.14	.04
☐ 215 Fran Tarkenton	10.00	4.50	1.25
☐ 216 Jim Katcavage	.30	.14	.04
☐ 217 Al Atkinson	.30	.14	.04
☐ 218 Emerson Boozer	.30	.14	.04
☐ 219 John Elliott	.30	.14	.04
☐ 220 Dave Herman	.30	.14	.04
☐ 221 Winston Hill	.30	.14	.04
☐ 222 Jim Hudson	.30	.14	.04
☐ 223 Pete Lammons	.30	.14	.04
☐ 224 Gerry Philbin	.30	.14	.04
☐ 225 George Sauer Jr.	.30	.14	.04
☐ 226 Joe Namath	25.00	11.00	3.10
☐ 227 Matt Snell	.50	.23	.06
☐ 228 Jim Turner	.30	.14	.04
☐ 229 Fred Biletnikoff	4.00	1.80	.50
☐ 230 Willie Brown	2.00	.90	.25
☐ 231 Billy Cannon	.50	.23	.06
☐ 232 Dan Conners	.30	.14	.04
☐ 233 Ben Davidson	.50	.23	.06
☐ 234 Hewritt Dixon	.30	.14	.04
☐ 235 Daryle Lamonica	1.00	.45	.12
☐ 236 Ike Lassiter	.30	.14	.04
☐ 237 Kent McCloughan	.30	.14	.04
☐ 238 Jim Otto	2.00	.90	.25
☐ 239 Harry Schuh	.30	.14	.04
☐ 240 Gene Upshaw	2.50	1.10	.30
☐ 241 Gary Ballman	.30	.14	.04
☐ 242 Joe Carollo	.30	.14	.04
☐ 243 Dave Lloyd	.30	.14	.04
☐ 244 Fred Hill	.30	.14	.04
☐ 245 Al Nelson	.30	.14	.04
☐ 246 Joe Scarpati	.30	.14	.04
☐ 247 Sam Baker	.30	.14	.04
☐ 248 Fred Brown	.30	.14	.04
☐ 249 Floyd Peters	.30	.14	.04
☐ 250 Nate Ramsey	.30	.14	.04
☐ 251 Norm Snead	.50	.23	.06
☐ 252 Tom Woodeshick	.30	.14	.04
☐ 253 John Hilton	.30	.14	.04
☐ 254 Kent Nix	.30	.14	.04
☐ 255 Paul Martha	.30	.14	.04
☐ 256 Ben McGee	.30	.14	.04
☐ 257 Andy Russell	.50	.23	.06
☐ 258 Dick Shiner	.30	.14	.04
☐ 259 J.R. Wilburn	.30	.14	.04
☐ 260 Marv Woodson	.30	.14	.04
☐ 261 Earl Gros	.30	.14	.04
☐ 262 Dick Hoak	.30	.14	.04
☐ 263 Roy Jefferson	.30	.14	.04
☐ 264 Larry Gagner	.30	.14	.04
☐ 265 Johnny Roland	.50	.23	.06
☐ 266 Jackie Smith	2.00	.90	.25
☐ 267 Jim Bakken	.30	.14	.04
☐ 268 Don Brumm	.30	.14	.04
☐ 269 Bob DeMarco	.30	.14	.04
☐ 270 Irv Goode	.30	.14	.04
☐ 271 Ken Gray	.30	.14	.04
☐ 272 Charlie Johnson	.50	.23	.06
☐ 273 Ernie McMillan	.30	.14	.04
☐ 274 Larry Stallings	.30	.14	.04
☐ 275 Jerry Stovall	.30	.14	.04
☐ 276 Larry Wilson	1.50	.70	.19
☐ 277 Chuck Allen	.30	.14	.04
☐ 278 Lance Alworth	5.00	2.20	.60
☐ 279 Kenny Graham	.30	.14	.04
☐ 280 Steve DeLong	.30	.14	.04
☐ 281 Willie Frazier	.30	.14	.04
☐ 282 Gary Garrison	.30	.14	.04
☐ 283 Sam Gruneisen	.30	.14	.04
☐ 284 John Hadl	.75	.35	.09
☐ 285 Brad Hubbert	.30	.14	.04
☐ 286 Ron Mix	1.50	.70	.19
☐ 287 Dick Post	.30	.14	.04
☐ 288 Walt Sweeney	.30	.14	.04
☐ 289 Kermit Alexander	.30	.14	.04
☐ 290 Ed Beard	.30	.14	.04
☐ 291 Bruce Bosley	.30	.14	.04
☐ 292 John Brodie	2.50	1.10	.30
☐ 293 Stan Hindman	.30	.14	.04
☐ 294 Jim Johnson	2.00	.90	.25
☐ 295 Charlie Krueger	.30	.14	.04
☐ 296 Clifton McNeil	.30	.14	.04
☐ 297 Gary Lewis	.30	.14	.04
☐ 298 Howard Mudd	.30	.14	.04
☐ 299 Dave Wilcox	.30	.14	.04
☐ 300 Ken Willard	.30	.14	.04
☐ 301 Charlie Gogolak	.30	.14	.04
☐ 302 Len Hauss	.30	.14	.04
☐ 303 Sonny Jurgensen	4.00	1.80	.50
☐ 304 Carl Kammerer	.30	.14	.04
☐ 305 Walter Rock	.30	.14	.04
☐ 306 Ray Schoenke	.30	.14	.04
☐ 307 Chris Hanburger	.50	.23	.06
☐ 308 Tom Brown	.30	.14	.04
☐ 309 Sam Huff	2.50	1.10	.30
☐ 310 Bob Long	.30	.14	.04
☐ 311 Vince Promuto	.30	.14	.04
☐ 312 Pat Richter	.30	.14	.04
☐ NNO Stamp Album	20.00	9.00	2.50

1989-97 Goal Line HOF

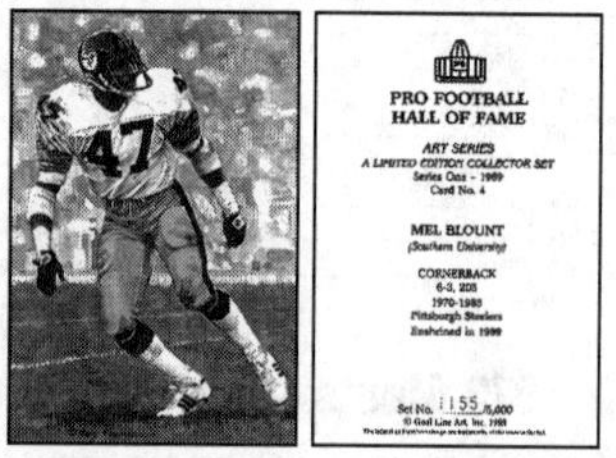

These attractive cards were issued by subscription per series of 30. They were sent out one series at a time in a custom box. The cards are postcard-size drawings (a full-color action painting) measuring approximately 4" by 6". The card backs contain brief biographical information and are printed in black on white card stock. Each card contains the specific set number out of 5,000 at the bottom of the reverse of every card in the set as well as the player's name, college, position, years, pro team, and the date he was enshrined in the Hall of Fame. The players featured are all members of the Pro Football Hall of Fame in Canton, Ohio. It was reported that 5,000 of the each series were produced and distributed. The second series was produced in 1990, the third series in 1991, and so forth. Collectors who ordered series five before August 31, 1993, received a free commemorative ticket signed by Pete Elliott (Commissioner of the Pro Football Hall of Fame) and were entered into a drawing for one of three uncut sheets of series five. In total, 50 fifth series uncut sheets were produced, and they were signed and numbered by the artist. Within each series the cards have been numbered alphabetically. They are considered ideal for autographing and are often found signed. The artist for the set was Gary Thomas. Collectors who have been purchasing this set over the years have the continuation right to receive the same serial numbered card whenever the next series is issued.

	MINT	NRMT	EXC
COMPLETE SET (189)	500.00	220.00	60.00
COMMON CARD (1-173, 175)	1.50	.70	.19
COMMON CARD (174, 176-189)	3.00	1.35	.35
☐ 1 Lance Alworth	3.00	1.35	.35
☐ 2 Red Badgro	2.50	1.10	.30
☐ 3 Cliff Battles	1.50	.70	.19
☐ 4 Mel Blount	3.00	1.35	.35
☐ 5 Terry Bradshaw	7.50	3.40	.95
☐ 6 Jim Brown	10.00	4.50	1.25
☐ 7 George Connor	2.50	1.10	.30
☐ 8 Turk Edwards	1.50	.70	.19
☐ 9 Tom Fears	2.50	1.10	.30
☐ 10 Frank Gifford	7.00	3.10	.85
☐ 11 Otto Graham	6.00	2.70	.75
☐ 12 Red Grange	5.00	2.20	.60
☐ 13 George Halas	3.00	1.35	.35
☐ 14 Clarke Hinkle	1.50	.70	.19
☐ 15 Robert(Cal) Hubbard	1.50	.70	.19
☐ 16 Sam Huff	3.00	1.35	.35
☐ 17 Frank(Bruiser) Kinard	1.50	.70	.19
☐ 18 Dick(Night Train) Lane	2.50	1.10	.30
☐ 19 Sid Luckman	5.00	2.20	.60
☐ 20 Bobby Mitchell	2.50	1.10	.30
☐ 21 Merlin Olsen	4.00	1.80	.50
☐ 22 Jim Parker	2.50	1.10	.30
☐ 23 Joe Perry	3.00	1.35	.35
☐ 24 Pete Rozelle	2.50	1.10	.30
☐ 25 Art Shell	2.50	1.10	.30
☐ 26 Fran Tarkenton	6.00	2.70	.75
☐ 27 Jim Thorpe	5.00	2.20	.60
☐ 28 Paul Warfield	3.00	1.35	.35
☐ 29 Larry Wilson	2.50	1.10	.30
☐ 30 Willie Wood	2.50	1.10	.30
☐ 31 Doug Atkins	2.50	1.10	.30
☐ 32 Bobby Bell	2.50	1.10	.30
☐ 33 Raymond Berry	3.00	1.35	.35
☐ 34 Paul Brown	1.50	.70	.19
☐ 35 Guy Chamberlin	1.50	.70	.19
☐ 36 Dutch Clark	1.50	.70	.19
☐ 37 Jimmy Conzelman	1.50	.70	.19
☐ 38 Len Dawson	3.00	1.35	.35
☐ 39 Mike Ditka	6.00	2.70	.75
☐ 40 Dan Fortmann	1.50	.70	.19
☐ 41 Frank Gatski	2.50	1.10	.30
☐ 42 Bill George	1.50	.70	.19
☐ 43 Elroy Hirsch	3.00	1.35	.35
☐ 44 Paul Hornung	4.00	1.80	.50
☐ 45 John Henry Johnson	2.50	1.10	.30
☐ 46 Walt Kiesling	1.50	.70	.19
☐ 47 Yale Lary	2.50	1.10	.30
☐ 48 Bobby Layne	3.00	1.35	.35
☐ 49 Tuffy Leemans	1.50	.70	.19
☐ 50 Geo.Preston Marshall	1.50	.70	.19
☐ 51 George McAfee	2.50	1.10	.30
☐ 52 Wayne Millner	1.50	.70	.19
☐ 53 Bronko Nagurski	4.00	1.80	.50
☐ 54 Joe Namath	12.00	5.50	1.50
☐ 55 Ray Nitschke	3.00	1.35	.35
☐ 56 Jim Ringo	2.50	1.10	.30
☐ 57 Art Rooney	1.50	.70	.19
☐ 58 Joe Stydahar	1.50	.70	.19
☐ 59 Charley Taylor	3.00	1.35	.35
☐ 60 Charley Trippi	2.50	1.10	.30
☐ 61 Fred Biletnikoff	3.00	1.35	.35
☐ 62 Buck Buchanan	1.50	.70	.19
☐ 63 Dick Butkus	6.00	2.70	.75
☐ 64 Earl Campbell	7.00	3.10	.85
☐ 65 Tony Canadeo	2.50	1.10	.30
☐ 66 Art Donovan	3.00	1.35	.35
☐ 67 Ray Flaherty	1.50	.70	.19
☐ 68 Forrest Gregg	2.50	1.10	.30
☐ 69 Lou Groza	3.00	1.35	.35
☐ 70 John Hannah	2.50	1.10	.30
☐ 71 Don Hutson	2.50	1.10	.30
☐ 72 Deacon Jones	3.00	1.35	.35
☐ 73 Stan Jones	2.50	1.10	.30
☐ 74 Sonny Jurgensen	3.00	1.35	.35
☐ 75 Vince Lombardi	3.00	1.35	.35
☐ 76 Tim Mara	1.50	.70	.19
☐ 77 Ollie Matson	2.50	1.10	.30
☐ 78 Mike McCormack	2.50	1.10	.30
☐ 79 Johnny(Blood) McNally	1.50	.70	.19
☐ 80 Marion Motley	3.00	1.35	.35
☐ 81 George Musso	2.50	1.10	.30
☐ 82 Greasy Neale	1.50	.70	.19
☐ 83 Clarence(Ace) Parker	2.50	1.10	.30
☐ 84 Pete Pihos	2.50	1.10	.30
☐ 85 Tex Schramm	2.50	1.10	.30
☐ 86 Roger Staubach	10.00	4.50	1.25
☐ 87 Jan Stenerud	2.50	1.10	.30
☐ 88 Y.A. Tittle	4.00	1.80	.50
☐ 89 Bulldog Turner	2.50	1.10	.30
☐ 90 Steve Van Buren	2.50	1.10	.30
☐ 91 Herb Adderley	2.50	1.10	.30
☐ 92 Lem Barney	2.50	1.10	.30
☐ 93 Sammy Baugh	5.00	2.20	.60
☐ 94 Chuck Bednarik	3.00	1.35	.35
☐ 95 Charles W. Bidwill	1.50	.70	.19
☐ 96 Willie Brown	3.00	1.35	.35
☐ 97 Al Davis	4.00	1.80	.50
☐ 98 Bill Dudley	2.50	1.10	.30
☐ 99 Weeb Ewbank	2.50	1.10	.30
☐ 100 Len Ford	1.50	.70	.19
☐ 101 Sid Gillman	2.50	1.10	.30
☐ 102 Jack Ham	3.00	1.35	.35
☐ 103 Mel Hein	1.50	.70	.19
☐ 104 Bill Hewitt	1.50	.70	.19
☐ 105 Dante Lavelli	2.50	1.10	.30
☐ 106 Bob Lilly	3.00	1.35	.35
☐ 107 John Mackey	2.50	1.10	.30
☐ 108 Hugh McElhenny	3.00	1.35	.35
☐ 109 Mike Michalske	1.50	.70	.19
☐ 110 Ron Mix	2.50	1.10	.30
☐ 111 Leo Nomellini	2.50	1.10	.30
☐ 112 Steve Owen	1.50	.70	.19
☐ 113 Alan Page	3.00	1.35	.35
☐ 114 Dan Reeves OWN	1.50	.70	.19
☐ 115 John Riggins	3.00	1.35	.35
☐ 116 Gale Sayers	5.00	2.20	.60
☐ 117 Ken Strong	1.50	.70	.19
☐ 118 Gene Upshaw	2.50	1.10	.30
☐ 119 Norm Van Brocklin	4.00	1.80	.50
☐ 120 Alex Wojciechowicz	1.50	.70	.19
☐ 121 Bert Bell COMM	1.50	.70	.19
☐ 122 George Blanda	4.00	1.80	.50

☐ 123 Joe Carr	1.50	.70	.19
☐ 124 Larry Csonka	4.00	1.80	.50
☐ 125 Paddy Driscoll	1.50	.70	.19
☐ 126 Dan Fouts	3.00	1.35	.35
☐ 127 Bob Griese	4.00	1.80	.50
☐ 128 Ed Healey	1.50	.70	.19
☐ 129 Wilbur(Fats) Henry	1.50	.70	.19
☐ 130 Ken Houston	2.50	1.10	.30
☐ 131 Lamar Hunt OWN	2.50	1.10	.30
☐ 132 Jack Lambert	3.00	1.35	.35
☐ 133 Tom Landry	4.00	1.80	.50
☐ 134 Willie Lanier	2.50	1.10	.30
☐ 135 Larry Little	2.50	1.10	.30
☐ 136 Don Maynard	2.50	1.10	.30
☐ 137 Lenny Moore	3.00	1.35	.35
☐ 138 Chuck Noll CO	3.00	1.35	.35
☐ 139 Jim Otto	3.00	1.35	.35
☐ 140 Walter Payton	7.50	3.40	.95
☐ 141 Hugh(Shorty) Ray OFF	1.50	.70	.19
☐ 142 Andy Robustelli	2.50	1.10	.30
☐ 143 Bob St. Clair	2.50	1.10	.30
☐ 144 Joe Schmidt	3.00	1.35	.35
☐ 145 Jim Taylor	3.00	1.35	.35
☐ 146 Doak Walker	3.00	1.35	.35
☐ 147 Bill Walsh CO	3.00	1.35	.35
☐ 148 Bob Waterfield	3.00	1.35	.35
☐ 149 Arnie Weinmeister	2.50	1.10	.30
☐ 150 Bill Willis	2.50	1.10	.30
☐ 151 Roosevelt Brown	2.50	1.10	.30
☐ 152 Jack Christiansen	1.50	.70	.19
☐ 153 Willie Davis	2.50	1.10	.30
☐ 154 Tony Dorsett	5.00	2.20	.60
☐ 155 Bud Grant	2.50	1.10	.30
☐ 156 Joe Greene	4.00	1.80	.50
☐ 157 Joe Guyon	1.50	.70	.19
☐ 158 Franco Harris	4.00	1.80	.50
☐ 159 Ted Hendricks	3.00	1.35	.35
☐ 160 Arnie Herber	1.50	.70	.19
☐ 161 Jim Johnson	2.50	1.10	.30
☐ 162 Leroy Kelly	3.00	1.35	.35
☐ 163 Curly Lambeau	1.50	.70	.19
☐ 164 Jim Langer	2.50	1.10	.30
☐ 165 Link Lyman	1.50	.70	.19
☐ 166 Gino Marchetti	2.50	1.10	.30
☐ 167 Ernie Nevers	3.00	1.35	.35
☐ 168 O.J. Simpson	6.00	2.70	.75
☐ 169 Jackie Smith	2.50	1.10	.30
☐ 170 Bart Starr	5.00	2.20	.60
☐ 171 Ernie Stautner	3.00	1.35	.35
☐ 172 George Trafton	1.50	.70	.19
☐ 173 Emlen Tunnell	1.50	.70	.19
☐ 174 Johnny Unitas	10.00	4.50	1.25
☐ 175 Randy White	3.00	1.35	.35
☐ 176 Jim Finks	3.00	1.35	.35
☐ 177 Hank Jordan	3.00	1.35	.35
☐ 178 Steve Largent	6.00	2.70	.75
☐ 179 Lee Roy Selmon	4.00	1.80	.50
☐ 180 Kellen Winslow	5.00	2.20	.60
☐ 181 Lou Creekmur	4.00	1.80	.50
☐ 182 Dan Dierdorf	5.00	2.20	.60
☐ 183 Joe Gibbs	4.00	1.80	.50
☐ 184 Charlie Joiner	5.00	2.20	.60
☐ 185 Mel Renfro	5.00	2.20	.60
☐ 186 Mike Haynes	4.00	1.80	.50
☐ 187 Wellington Mara	3.00	1.35	.35
☐ 188 Don Shula	6.00	2.70	.75
☐ 189 Mike Webster	4.00	1.80	.50

1991 Greenleaf Puzzles

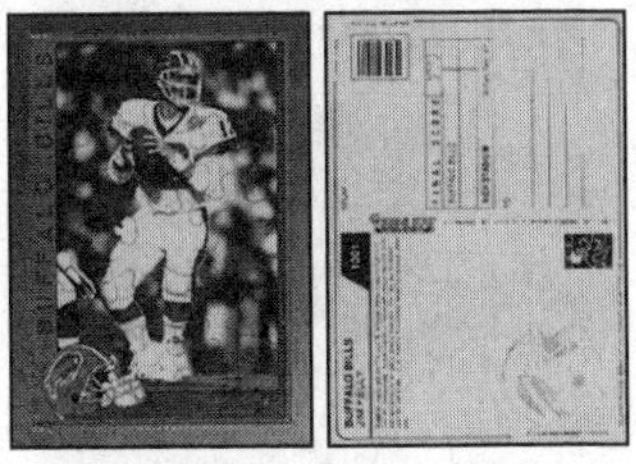

Greenleaf Steel Rule Die Corp. produced these NFL player puzzles. Each measures roughly 4-1/2" by 6-3/8" and is sealed within a cardboard frame and thick plastic cover. The puzzle backs contain a postcard style format along with a short write-up on the featured player. The checklist below is presumed to be incomplete.

	MINT	NRMT	EXC
COMPLETE SET (6)	15.00	6.75	1.85
COMMON PUZZLE	2.00	.90	.25
☐ 1001 Jim Kelly	3.00	1.35	.35
☐ 1005 Dan Marino	6.00	2.70	.75
☐ 1010 Lawrence Taylor	3.00	1.35	.35
☐ 1013 Randall Cunningham	2.00	.90	.25
☐ 1015 Troy Aikman	4.00	1.80	.50
☐ 1016 Thurman Thomas	3.00	1.35	.35

1939 Gridiron Greats Blotters

This set of 12 ink blotters was sponsored by Louis F. Dow Company in honor of great college football players. The legal size blotters measure approximately 9" by 3 7/8" and were issued in a brown paper

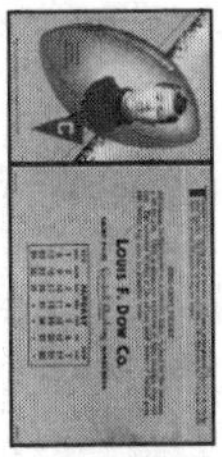

sleeve. The left portion of the blotter front has a head and shoulders sepia-toned drawing, with the player wearing either a red or a blue jersey. This drawing is superimposed on a football, and the player's college letter appears in a banner below the picture. The right portion of the blotter has a brief player profile, a blotter advertisement, and a monthly calendar (a different month on each of the 12 blotters). The backs are blank and done in medium blue. The blotters are numbered on the front.

	EX-MT	VG-E	GOOD
COMPLETE SET (12)	4500.00	2000.00	550.00
COMMON CARD	150.00	70.00	19.00
☐ B3941 Jim Thorpe	600.00	275.00	75.00
☐ B3942 Walter Eckersall	150.00	70.00	19.00
☐ B3943 Edward Mahan	150.00	70.00	19.00
☐ B3944 Sammy Baugh	600.00	275.00	75.00
☐ B3945 Thomas Shevlin	150.00	70.00	19.00
☐ B3946 Red Grange	600.00	275.00	75.00
☐ B3947 Ernie Nevers	400.00	180.00	50.00
☐ B3948 George Gipp	600.00	275.00	75.00
☐ B3949 Pudge Heffelfinger	200.00	90.00	25.00
☐ B3950 Bronko Nagurski	700.00	325.00	90.00
☐ B3951 Willie Heston	150.00	70.00	19.00
☐ B3952 Jay Berwanger	200.00	90.00	25.00

1991 GTE Super Bowl Theme Art

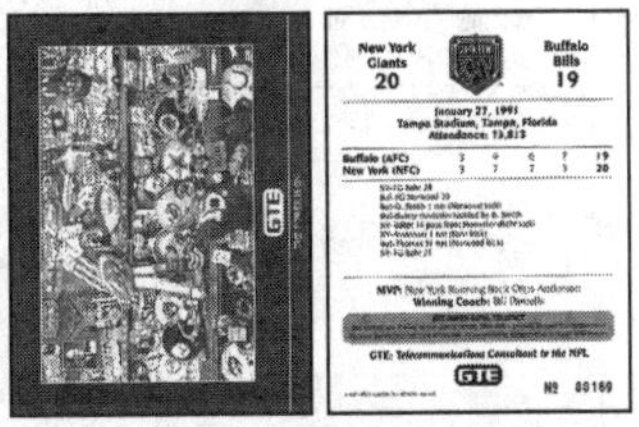

This limited edition set of approximately 4 5/8" by 6" cards was issued on the occasion of Super Bowl XXV and sponsored by GTE, whose company logo appears at the bottom on the front of each card above a full color reproduction of the Super Bowl program cover enframed by black borders. The back includes information on the Super Bowl for that particular year, including location, teams, score, winning coach, MVP, and a GTE Super Bowl Telefact.

	MINT	NRMT	EXC
COMPLETE SET (25)	6.00	2.70	.75
COMMON CARD (1-25)	.30	.14	.04
☐ 1 Super Bowl I	.50	.23	.06
☐ 2 Super Bowl II	.30	.14	.04
☐ 3 Super Bowl III	.30	.14	.04
☐ 4 Super Bowl IV	.30	.14	.04
☐ 5 Super Bowl V	.30	.14	.04
☐ 6 Super Bowl VI	.30	.14	.04
☐ 7 Super Bowl VII	.30	.14	.04
☐ 8 Super Bowl VIII	.30	.14	.04
☐ 9 Super Bowl IX	.30	.14	.04
☐ 10 Super Bowl X	.30	.14	.04
☐ 11 Super Bowl XI	.30	.14	.04
☐ 12 Super Bowl XII	.30	.14	.04
☐ 13 Super Bowl XIII	.30	.14	.04
☐ 14 Super Bowl XIV	.30	.14	.04
☐ 15 Super Bowl XV	.30	.14	.04
☐ 16 Super Bowl XVI	.30	.14	.04
☐ 17 Super Bowl XVII	.30	.14	.04
☐ 18 Super Bowl XVIII	.30	.14	.04
☐ 19 Super Bowl XIX	.30	.14	.04
☐ 20 Super Bowl XX	.30	.14	.04
☐ 21 Super Bowl XXI	.30	.14	.04
☐ 22 Super Bowl XXII	.30	.14	.04
☐ 23 Super Bowl XXIII	.30	.14	.04
☐ 24 Super Bowl XXIV	.30	.14	.04
☐ 25 Super Bowl XXV	.50	.23	.06

1995 GTE Super Bowl XXIX Phone Cards

GTE produced and distributed these two cards for the 1995 NFL Experience Super Bowl Card Show in Miami. Each measures 3 3/8" by 2 1/8" and has rounded corners. Card #1 originally could be purchased for $8.85 and provided 15-units of long distance. Card #2 sold initially for $17.11 and provided 29-units. Each one was issued in a clear cellophane pack. The backs have instructions on how to use the calling card feature. Each is numbered of 3000 produced and expired on 12/31/95.

	MINT	NRMT	EXC
COMPLETE SET (2)	4.00	1.80	.50
COMMON CARD (1-2)	2.00	.90	.25
☐ 1 Super Bowl XXIX Teams Chargers Helmet 49ers Helmet	2.00	.90	.25
☐ 2 Super Bowl XXIX Logo	2.00	.90	.25

1995 GTE/Shell Super Bowl Phone Cards

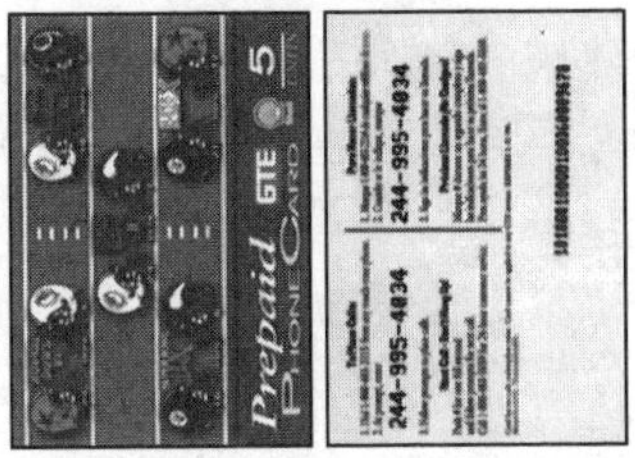

GTE produced this phone card set sponsored and distributed by Shell Oil Co. Each card was valued at 5-units of GTE phone time that expired on January 31, 1996. Five previous Super Bowl game scores are included on each of the first five cards and four games on the last card.

	MINT	NRMT	EXC
COMPLETE SET (6)	15.00	6.75	1.85
COMMON CARD (1-6)	2.50	1.10	.30
☐ 1 Super Bowl I-V	2.50	1.10	.30
☐ 2 Super Bowl VI-X	2.50	1.10	.30
☐ 3 Super Bowl XI-XV	2.50	1.10	.30
☐ 4 Super Bowl XVI-XX	2.50	1.10	.30
☐ 5 Super Bowl XXI-XXV	2.50	1.10	.30
☐ 6 Super Bowl XXVI-XIX	2.50	1.10	.30

1982-96 Hall of Fame Metallics

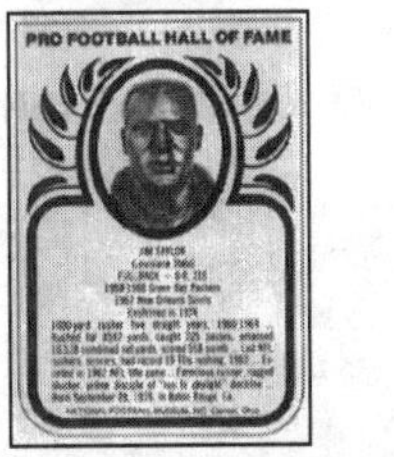

This set features Pro Football Hall of Fame enshrinees and was distributed in separate series with each series containing the inductees for specific years. Only 2,000 of each series were produced and a purchase of a complete run of series' included a Letter of Authenticity. Each 10 mil 2 1/2" by 3 1/2" silver-toned metallic card carries an imprinted reproduction of the enshrinee's bust from the Hall of Fame along with appropriate statistical data of the enshrinee's football career. The first fifteen series' were produced together in 1982-83 and sold separately as 8-card series'. Subsequent series' were sold as that year's enshrinees were announced, therefore they vary in number of cards. We've assigned numbers to the unnumbered cards below according to alphabetical order within series.

	MINT	NRMT	EXC
COMPLETE SET (181)	750.00	350.00	95.00
COMMON CARD	3.00	1.35	.35
☐ 1 Sammy Baugh	10.00	4.50	1.25
☐ 2 Joe Carr	3.00	1.35	.35
☐ 3 George Halas	8.00	3.60	1.00
☐ 4 Mel Hein	3.00	1.35	.35
☐ 5 Dick Lane	4.00	1.80	.50
☐ 6 Bob Lilly	10.00	4.50	1.25
☐ 7 Marion Motley	5.00	2.20	.60
☐ 8 Jim Thorpe	10.00	4.50	1.25
☐ 9 Herb Adderley	4.00	1.80	.50
☐ 10 Dutch Clark	4.00	1.80	.50
☐ 11 Red Grange	10.00	4.50	1.25
☐ 12 Vince Lombardi	10.00	4.50	1.25
☐ 13 Joe Perry	5.00	2.20	.60
☐ 14 Art Rooney	4.00	1.80	.50
☐ 15 Joe Schmidt	4.00	1.80	.50
☐ 16 Bill Willis	4.00	1.80	.50
☐ 17 Paul Brown	5.00	2.20	.60
☐ 18 Fats Henry	3.00	1.35	.35
☐ 19 Elroy Hirsch	5.00	2.20	.60
☐ 20 Bronko Nagurski	10.00	4.50	1.25
☐ 21 Leo Nomellini	4.00	1.80	.50
☐ 22 Jim Ringo	4.00	1.80	.50
☐ 23 Joe Stydahar	3.00	1.35	.35
☐ 24 Y.A. Tittle	8.00	3.60	1.00
☐ 25 Guy Chamberlin	3.00	1.35	.35
☐ 26 George Connor	4.00	1.80	.50
☐ 27 Willie Davis	4.00	1.80	.50
☐ 28 Frank Gifford	3.00	1.35	.35
☐ 29 Clarke Hinkle	3.00	1.35	.35
☐ 30 Lamar Hunt	4.00	1.80	.50
☐ 31 Bruiser Kinard	4.00	1.80	.50
☐ 32 Curly Lambeau	4.00	1.80	.50
☐ 33 Weeb Ewbank	3.00	1.35	.35
☐ 34 Dan Fortmann	3.00	1.35	.35
☐ 35 Yale Lary	4.00	1.80	.50
☐ 36 Sid Luckman	8.00	3.60	1.00
☐ 37 Lenny Moore	8.00	3.60	1.00
☐ 38 Ernie Nevers	4.00	1.80	.50
☐ 39 Jim Parker	4.00	1.80	.50
☐ 40 Ernie Stautner	5.00	2.20	.60
☐ 41 Lance Alworth	8.00	3.60	1.00
☐ 42 Red Badgro	3.00	1.35	.35
☐ 43 Chuck Bednarik	6.00	2.70	.75
☐ 44 Roosevelt Brown	4.00	1.80	.50
☐ 45 Bill Dudley	4.00	1.80	.50
☐ 46 Bobby Layne	8.00	3.60	1.00
☐ 47 Link Lyman	3.00	1.35	.35
☐ 48 Steve Owen	3.00	1.35	.35
☐ 49 Paddy Driscoll	3.00	1.35	.35
☐ 50 Len Ford	4.00	1.80	.50
☐ 51 Sam Huff	5.00	2.20	.60
☐ 52 Deacon Jones	5.00	2.20	.60
☐ 53 Dante Lavelli	4.00	1.80	.50
☐ 54 Tuffy Leemans	3.00	1.35	.35
☐ 55 Dan Reeves	3.00	1.35	.35
☐ 56 Bulldog Turner	5.00	2.20	.60
☐ 57 Doug Atkins	4.00	1.80	.50
☐ 58 George Blanda	10.00	4.50	1.25
☐ 59 Dick Butkus	10.00	4.50	1.25
☐ 60 Joe Guyon	3.00	1.35	.35
☐ 61 Arnie Herber	3.00	1.35	.35
☐ 62 Don Hutson	5.00	2.20	.60
☐ 63 Walt Kiesling	3.00	1.35	.35
☐ 64 Ron Mix	4.00	1.80	.50
☐ 65 Cliff Battles	4.00	1.80	.50
☐ 66 Jim Brown	15.00	6.75	1.85
☐ 67 Lou Groza	5.00	2.20	.60
☐ 68 Ed Healey	3.00	1.35	.35
☐ 69 Jim Otto	5.00	2.20	.60
☐ 70 Pete Pihos	4.00	1.80	.50
☐ 71 Hugh Shorty Ray	3.00	1.35	.35
☐ 72 Bob Waterfield	5.00	2.20	.60
☐ 73 Raymond Berry	6.00	2.70	.75
☐ 74 Turk Edwards	3.00	1.35	.35
☐ 75 Johnny Blood McNally	3.00	1.35	.35
☐ 76 Greasy Neale	3.00	1.35	.35
☐ 77 Ace Parker	3.00	1.35	.35
☐ 78 Andy Robustelli	4.00	1.80	.50
☐ 79 Charley Trippi	4.00	1.80	.50
☐ 80 Larry Wilson	3.00	1.35	.35
☐ 81 Art Donovan	5.00	2.20	.60
☐ 82 Forrest Gregg	4.00	1.80	.50
☐ 83 Tim Mara	3.00	1.35	.35
☐ 84 Mike Michalske	3.00	1.35	.35
☐ 85 Wayne Millner	3.00	1.35	.35
☐ 86 Gale Sayers	10.00	4.50	1.25
☐ 87 Ken Strong	4.00	1.80	.50
☐ 88 Norm Van Brocklin	5.00	2.20	.60
☐ 89 Charles Bidwill	3.00	1.35	.35
☐ 90 Bill George	4.00	1.80	.50
☐ 91 Bill Hewitt	3.00	1.35	.35
☐ 92 Hugh McElhenny	5.00	2.20	.60
☐ 93 Bart Starr	10.00	4.50	1.25
☐ 94 George Trafton	3.00	1.35	.35
☐ 95 Steve Van Buren	5.00	2.20	.60
☐ 96 Alex Wojciechowicz	3.00	1.35	.35
☐ 97 Tony Canadeo	4.00	1.80	.50
☐ 98 Jack Christiansen	4.00	1.80	.50
☐ 99 Gino Marchetti	4.00	1.80	.50
☐ 100 George Preston Marshall	3.00	1.35	.35
☐ 101 Ollie Matson	4.00	1.80	.50
☐ 102 George Musso	4.00	1.80	.50
☐ 103 Ray Nitschke	8.00	3.60	1.00
☐ 104 Johnny Unitas	10.00	4.50	1.25
☐ 105 Bert Bell	3.00	1.35	.35
☐ 106 Tom Fears	4.00	1.80	.50
☐ 107 Ray Flaherty	3.00	1.35	.35
☐ 108 Otto Graham	10.00	4.50	1.25
☐ 109 Cal Hubbard	3.00	1.35	.35
☐ 110 George McAfee	4.00	1.80	.50
☐ 111 Merlin Olsen	5.00	2.20	.60
☐ 112 Jim Taylor	5.00	2.20	.60
☐ 113 Bobby Bell	4.00	1.80	.50
☐ 114 Jimmy Conzelman	3.00	1.35	.35
☐ 115 Sid Gillman	3.00	1.35	.35
☐ 116 Sonny Jurgensen	6.00	2.70	.75
☐ 117 Bobby Mitchell	5.00	2.20	.60
☐ 118 Emlen Tunnell	4.00	1.80	.50
☐ 119 Paul Warfield	5.00	2.20	.60
☐ 120 Hall of Fame logo	3.00	1.35	.35
☐ 121 Willie Brown	4.00	1.80	.50
☐ 122 Mike McCormack	4.00	1.80	.50
☐ 123 Charley Taylor	4.00	1.80	.50
☐ 124 Arnie Weinmeister	3.00	1.35	.35
☐ 125 Frank Gatski	3.00	1.35	.35
☐ 126 Joe Namath	15.00	6.75	1.85
☐ 127 Pete Rozelle	4.00	1.80	.50
☐ 128 O.J. Simpson	10.00	4.50	1.25
☐ 129 Roger Staubach	15.00	6.75	1.85
☐ 130 Paul Hornung	10.00	4.50	1.25
☐ 131 Ken Houston	4.00	1.80	.50
☐ 132 Willie Lanier	4.00	1.80	.50
☐ 133 Fran Tarkenton	8.00	3.60	1.00
☐ 134 Doak Walker	5.00	2.20	.60

	MINT	NRMT	EXC
☐ 135 Larry Csonka	8.00	3.60	1.00
☐ 136 Len Dawson	6.00	2.70	.75
☐ 137 Joe Greene	8.00	3.60	1.00
☐ 138 John Henry Johnson	4.00	1.80	.50
☐ 139 Jim Langer	4.00	1.80	.50
☐ 140 Don Maynard	5.00	2.20	.60
☐ 141 Gene Upshaw	4.00	1.80	.50
☐ 142 Fred Biletnikoff	6.00	2.70	.75
☐ 143 Mike Ditka	10.00	4.50	1.25
☐ 144 Jack Ham	6.00	2.70	.75
☐ 145 Alan Page	4.00	1.80	.50
☐ 146 Mel Blount	5.00	2.20	.60
☐ 147 Terry Bradshaw	15.00	6.75	1.85
☐ 148 Art Shell	5.00	2.20	.60
☐ 149 Willie Wood	4.00	1.80	.50
☐ 150 Buck Buchanan	4.00	1.80	.50
☐ 151 Bob Griese	8.00	3.60	1.00
☐ 152 Franco Harris	8.00	3.60	1.00
☐ 153 Ted Hendricks	4.00	1.80	.50
☐ 154 Jack Lambert	8.00	3.60	1.00
☐ 155 Tom Landry	10.00	4.50	1.25
☐ 156 Bob St. Clair	4.00	1.80	.50
☐ 157 Earl Campbell	15.00	6.75	1.85
☐ 158 John Hannah	4.00	1.80	.50
☐ 159 Stan Jones	3.00	1.35	.35
☐ 160 Tex Schramm	3.00	1.35	.35
☐ 161 Jan Stenerud	4.00	1.80	.50
☐ 162 Lem Barney	3.00	1.35	.35
☐ 163 Al Davis	5.00	2.20	.60
☐ 164 John Mackey	3.00	1.35	.35
☐ 165 John Riggins	3.00	1.35	.35
☐ 166 Dan Fouts	6.00	2.70	.75
☐ 167 Larry Little	3.00	1.35	.35
☐ 168 Chuck Noll	5.00	2.20	.60
☐ 169 Walter Payton	15.00	6.75	1.85
☐ 170 Bill Walsh	6.00	2.70	.75
☐ 171 Tony Dorsett	10.00	4.50	1.25
☐ 172 Bud Grant	6.00	2.70	.75
☐ 173 Jim Johnson	3.00	1.35	.35
☐ 174 Leroy Kelly	6.00	2.70	.75
☐ 175 Jackie Smith	3.00	1.35	.35
☐ 176 Randy White	8.00	3.60	1.00
☐ 177 Jim Finks	3.00	1.35	.35
☐ 178 Hank Jordan	4.00	1.80	.50
☐ 179 Steve Largent	6.00	2.70	.75
☐ 180 Lee Roy Selmon	3.00	1.35	.35
☐ 181 Kellen Winslow	3.00	1.35	.35

1990 Hall of Fame Stickers

Jim Thorpe, HB

This 80-sticker set is actually part of a book; the individual stickers in the book measure approximately 1 7/8" by 2 1/8". The book was entitled "The Official Pro Football Hall of Fame Fun and Fact Sticker Book." The original artwork from which the stickers were derived was performed by noted hobbyist Mark Rucker and featured 80 members of the Pro Football Hall of Fame.

	MINT	NRMT	EXC
COMPLETE SET (80)	10.00	4.50	1.25
COMMON CARD (1-80)	.15	.07	.02
☐ 1 Wilbur(Fats) Henry	.20	.09	.03
☐ 2 George Trafton	.15	.07	.02
☐ 3 Mike Michalske	.15	.07	.02
☐ 4 Turk Edwards	.15	.07	.02
☐ 5 Bill Hewitt	.15	.07	.02
☐ 6 Mel Hein	.15	.07	.02
☐ 7 Joe Stydahar	.15	.07	.02
☐ 8 Dan Fortmann	.15	.07	.02
☐ 9 Alex Wojciechowicz	.15	.07	.02
☐ 10 George Connor	.20	.09	.03
☐ 11 Jim Thorpe	.30	.14	.04
☐ 12 Ernie Nevers	.20	.09	.03
☐ 13 Johnny(Blood) McNally	.15	.07	.02
☐ 14 Ken Strong	.20	.09	.03
☐ 15 Bronko Nagurski	.50	.23	.06
☐ 16 Clarke Hinkle	.15	.07	.02
☐ 17 Clarence(Ace) Parker	.15	.07	.02
☐ 18 Bill Dudley	.20	.09	.03
☐ 19 Don Hutson	.25	.11	.03
☐ 20 Dante Lavelli	.20	.09	.03
☐ 21 Elroy Hirsch	.25	.11	.03
☐ 22 Raymond Berry	.30	.14	.04
☐ 23 Bobby Mitchell	.25	.11	.03
☐ 24 Don Maynard	.25	.11	.03
☐ 25 Mike Ditka	.60	.25	.07
☐ 26 Lance Alworth	.30	.14	.04
☐ 27 Charley Taylor	.25	.09	.03
☐ 28 Paul Warfield	.25	.11	.03
☐ 29 Lou Groza	.25	.11	.03
☐ 30 Art Donovan	.25	.11	.03
☐ 31 Leo Nomellini	.20	.09	.03
☐ 32 Andy Robustelli	.20	.09	.03
☐ 33 Gino Marchetti	.25	.09	.03

	MINT	NRMT	EXC
☐ 34 Forrest Gregg	.20	.09	.03
☐ 35 Jim Otto	.25	.11	.03
☐ 36 Ron Mix	.20	.09	.03
☐ 37 Deacon Jones	.25	.11	.03
☐ 38 Bob Lilly	.30	.14	.04
☐ 39 Merlin Olsen	.25	.11	.03
☐ 40 Alan Page	.20	.09	.03
☐ 41 Joe Greene	.30	.14	.04
☐ 42 Art Shell	.25	.11	.03
☐ 43 Sammy Baugh	.60	.25	.07
☐ 44 Sid Luckman	.30	.14	.04
☐ 45 Bob Waterfield	.25	.11	.03
☐ 46 Bobby Layne	.50	.23	.06
☐ 47 Norm Van Brocklin	.25	.11	.03
☐ 48 Y.A. Tittle	.40	.18	.05
☐ 49 Johnny Unitas	.75	.35	.09
☐ 50 Bart Starr	.35	.16	.04
☐ 51 Sonny Jurgensen	.25	.11	.03
☐ 52 Joe Namath	1.25	.55	.16
☐ 53 Roger Staubach	1.00	.45	.12
☐ 54 Terry Bradshaw	1.00	.45	.12
☐ 55 Steve Van Buren	.30	.14	.04
☐ 56 Marion Motley	.25	.11	.03
☐ 57 Joe Perry	.25	.11	.03
☐ 58 Hugh McElhenny	.25	.11	.03
☐ 59 Frank Gifford	.60	.25	.07
☐ 60 Jim Brown	1.00	.45	.12
☐ 61 Jim Taylor	.25	.11	.03
☐ 62 Gale Sayers	.60	.25	.07
☐ 63 Larry Csonka	.30	.14	.04
☐ 64 Emlen Tunnell	.20	.09	.03
☐ 65 Jack Christiansen	.20	.09	.03
☐ 66 Dick(Night Train) Lane	.20	.09	.03
☐ 67 Sam Huff	.25	.11	.03
☐ 68 Ray Nitschke	.30	.14	.04
☐ 69 Larry Wilson	.20	.09	.03
☐ 70 Willie Wood	.20	.09	.03
☐ 71 Bobby Bell	.20	.09	.03
☐ 72 Willie Brown	.20	.09	.03
☐ 73 Dick Butkus	.50	.23	.06
☐ 74 Jack Ham	.30	.14	.04
☐ 75 George Halas	.35	.16	.04
☐ 76 Steve Owen	.15	.07	.02
☐ 77 Art Rooney	.20	.09	.03
☐ 78 Bert Bell	.15	.07	.02
☐ 79 Paul Brown	.25	.11	.03
☐ 80 Pete Rozelle	.20	.09	.03

1993 Heads and Tails SB XXVII

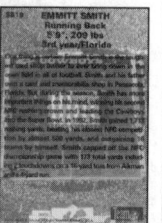

Designed and produced by Heads and Tails Inc., this 25-card standard-size set features the best past and current players that the Super Bowl has to offer as well as some 1993 NFL Pro Bowl picks. The production run was reportedly 200,000 sets, and these sets were sold through Wal-Mart and other retailers. Randomly inserted throughout the product were 10,000 sets featuring gold foil stamping on the words 'Rose Bowl' and on the stem of the Rose Bowl insignia. The remaining 190,000 sets have silver foil stamping instead of gold. Gold sets are valued at two to three times the values listed below. Each set was packed in a special box that contained foil packs with over 200 cards from other NFL licensed trading card producers (Topps, Fleer Ultra, GameDay, Proline, and Wild Card). The cards feature full-bleed color action player photos. The Pro Bowl picks have the player's name embossed in foil at the bottom. The Super Bowl player cards display the player's name in white printed vertically down one edge, a Rose Bowl foil embossed emblem, and an icon showing the Super Bowl they played in. On a background consisting of a ghosted picture of the Rose Bowl, the backs summarize the player's performance. After a checklist/header card, the set is arranged as follows: NFL Salutes (2-3), '93 Pro Bowl Picks (4-7), Super Bowl MVP's of the Past (8-11), AFC Champions Buffalo Bills (12-18), and NFC Champions Dallas Cowboys (19-25). The cards are numbered with an 'SB' prefix.

	MINT	NRMT	EXC
COMPLETE SET (25)	12.00	5.50	1.50
COMMON CARD (1-25)	.25	.11	.03
☐ 1 Title Card CL	.25	.11	.03
☐ 2 Lawrence Taylor	.40	.18	.05
Mike Singletary			
☐ 3 Dennis Byrd	.25	.11	.03
☐ 4 Junior Seau	.50	.23	.06
☐ 5 Steve Young	1.00	.45	.12
☐ 6 Sterling Sharpe	.40	.18	.05
☐ 7 Cortez Kennedy	.40	.18	.05
☐ 8 Terry Bradshaw	.75	.35	.09
☐ 9 Fred Biletnikoff	.40	.18	.05
☐ 10 John Riggins	.40	.18	.05
☐ 11 Phil Simms	.40	.18	.05
☐ 12 Cornelius Bennett	.40	.18	.05

	MINT	NRMT	EXC
☐ 13 Jim Kelly	.60	.25	.07
☐ 14 Bruce Smith	.40	.18	.05
☐ 15 Andre Reed	.40	.18	.05
☐ 16 Keith McKeller	.25	.11	.03
☐ 17 James Lofton	.40	.18	.05
☐ 18 Thurman Thomas	.60	.25	.07
☐ 19 Emmitt Smith	2.50	1.10	.30
☐ 20 Kelvin Martin	.25	.11	.03
☐ 21 Troy Aikman	1.50	.70	.19
☐ 22 Charles Haley	.25	.11	.03
☐ 23 Alvin Harper	.40	.18	.05
☐ 24 Michael Irvin	.60	.25	.07
☐ 25 Jay Novacek	.40	.18	.05

1991 Heisman Collection I

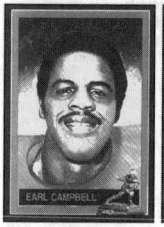

The first series of the Heisman Collection contains 20 standard-size cards honoring former Heisman Trophy winners. One hundred thousand sets were produced, and each set contains a title card with a unique serial number. Each of the 1,000 cases (100 sets per case) contained two personally autographed cards from a former Heisman Trophy winner. The front design features a color posed shot of the player, bordered in gold and black. The player's name appears in a black stripe at the bottom of the picture, with a picture of the Heisman Trophy in the lower right corner of the card face. The horizontally oriented back has a larger picture of the Heisman Trophy and a summary of the player's career. The year the player won the trophy is indicated in a gold stripe on the right side of the card back. The cards are skip-numbered and arranged chronologically from older to more recent Heisman trophy winners. There also exists a promo card for Bo Jackson marked "Sample" on the back. It was issued as part of a 10" by 3 1/2" strip with set and ordering information on it. The sample card is not considered part of the complete set.

	MINT	NRMT	EXC
COMPLETE SET (21)	5.00	2.20	.60
COMMON CARD	.15	.07	.02
☐ 1 Jay Berwanger	.15	.07	.02
☐ 6 Tom Harmon	.25	.11	.03
☐ 9 Angelo Bertelli	.15	.07	.02
☐ 11 Doc Blanchard	.25	.11	.03
☐ 13 Johnny Lujack	.35	.16	.04
☐ 15 Leon Hart	.25	.11	.03
☐ 16 Vic Janowicz	.35	.16	.04
☐ 19 John Lattner	.25	.11	.03
☐ 23 John David Crow	.15	.07	.02
☐ 26 Joe Bellino	.15	.07	.02
☐ 30 John Huarte	.15	.07	.02
☐ 32 Steve Spurrier	2.00	.90	.25
☐ 36 Jim Plunkett	.35	.16	.04
☐ 40 Archie Griffin	.25	.11	.03
☐ 42 Tony Dorsett	1.00	.45	.12
☐ 43 Earl Campbell	1.00	.45	.12
☐ 45 Charles White	.15	.07	.02
☐ 48 Herschel Walker	.50	.23	.06
☐ 51 Bo Jackson	.75	.35	.09
☐ 53 Tim Brown	.50	.23	.06
☐ NNO Title Card	.15	.07	.02
☐ SAM Bo Jackson	2.00	.90	.25
Sample Promo			

1991 Heisman Collection I Autographs

The 1991 series of Heisman Collection cards contained randomly signed cards of 10 of the Heisman Trophy winners pictured in the set. These cards were inserted at a ratio of 1:50 sets, and at first glance appear identical to the cards within the set, other than the player autograph on the front. However, these cards are printed on a linen finish, with the number of the particular card out of 200 between the legs of the Heisman Trophy statute on the reverse of the card. Other differences between the regular cards and the autograph cards include bolder, larger (and sometimes different) text on the back of the autographed cards, no number on the autographed cards, and the copyright listed as College Classics, as opposed to the regular cards, which were copyrighted by The Downtown Athletic Club of New York City, Inc. Since these cards are unnumbered, they are checklisted below in alphabetical order.

	MINT	NRMT	EXC
COMPLETE SET (10)	350.00	160.00	45.00
COMMON CARD	20.00	9.00	2.50
☐ 1 Joe Bellino	20.00	9.00	2.50
☐ 2 Angelo Bertelli	30.00	13.50	3.70
☐ 3 Jay Berwanger	35.00	16.00	4.40
☐ 4 Tim Brown	30.00	13.50	3.70
☐ 5 Archie Griffin	30.00	13.50	3.70
☐ 6 Leon Hart	30.00	13.50	3.70

1992 Heisman Collection II

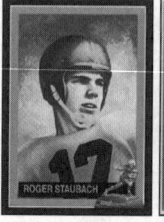

For the second year, College Classics in association with The Downtown Athletic Club of New York issued a series consisting of 20 cards honoring Heisman Trophy winners. One hundred thousand sets were produced, and each one included a consecutively numbered card from 1-100,000. The set was issued in a sturdy cardboard box with an unnumbered checklist on its back. Two-card strips measuring approximately 3 1/2" by 7 1/2" and featuring either Barry Sanders or Roger Staubach were issued to promote the set. The Sanders and Staubach promos are different in that the card number on the back of the regular issue has been replaced by the word "Sample." The sample cards are not considered part of the set. The front design features a color player portrait bordered in black and gold. The player's name appears in a black stripe that cuts across the bottom of the picture, intersecting a picture of the Heisman Trophy at the lower right corner. The horizontal back has a larger picture of the Heisman Trophy and a summary of the player's career. The year the player won the trophy is printed vertically in a gold stripe running down the right side. The cards are skip-numbered and arranged chronologically from older to more recent Heisman trophy winners.

	MINT	NRMT	EXC
COMPLETE SET (21)	12.00	5.50	1.50
COMMON CARD	.50	.23	.06
☐ 2 Larry Kelley	.50	.23	.06
☐ 3 Clint Frank	.50	.23	.06
☐ 5 Nile Kinnick	.75	.35	.09
☐ 7 Bruce Smith	.50	.23	.06
☐ 10 Les Horvath	.50	.23	.06
☐ 14 Doak Walker	.75	.35	.09
☐ 17 Dick Kazmaier	.50	.23	.06
☐ 20 Alan Ameche	.50	.23	.06
☐ 21 Howard Cassady	.50	.23	.06
☐ 25 Billy Cannon	.75	.35	.09
☐ 27 Ernie Davis	2.00	.90	.25
☐ 29 Roger Staubach	2.50	1.10	.30
☐ 31 Mike Garrett	.50	.23	.06
☐ 35 Steve Owens	.50	.23	.06
☐ 38 Johnny Rodgers	.75	.35	.09
☐ 39 John Cappelletti	.50	.23	.06
☐ 44 Billy Sims	.75	.35	.09
☐ 50 Doug Flutie	1.00	.45	.12
☐ 52 Vinny Testaverde	.50	.23	.06
☐ 54 Barry Sanders	2.00	.90	.25
☐ NNO Title Card	.50	.23	.06
☐ SAM Barry Sanders	7.50	3.40	.95
Sample Promo			
☐ SAM Roger Staubach	10.00	4.50	1.25
Sample Promo			

1970 Hi-C Mini-Posters

This set of ten posters were the insides of the Hi-C drink can labels. They are numbered very subtly below the player's picture but they are listed below in alphabetical order. The players selected for the set were leaders at their positions during the 1969 season. The mini-posters measure approximately 6 5/8" by 13 3/4".

	NRMT-MT	EXC	G-VG
COMPLETE SET (10)	650.00	300.00	80.00
COMMON POSTER (1-10)	50.00	22.00	6.25
☐ 1 Greg Cook	75.00	34.00	9.50
☐ 2 Fred Cox	60.00	27.00	7.50
☐ 3 Sonny Jurgensen	110.00	50.00	14.00
☐ 4 David Lee	50.00	22.00	6.25
☐ 5 Dennis Partee	50.00	22.00	6.25
☐ 6 Dick Post	50.00	22.00	6.25
☐ 7 Mel Renfro	100.00	45.00	12.50
☐ 8 Gale Sayers	150.00	70.00	19.00
☐ 9 Emmitt Thomas	50.00	22.00	6.25
☐ 10 Jim Turner	50.00	22.00	6.25

1991 Homers

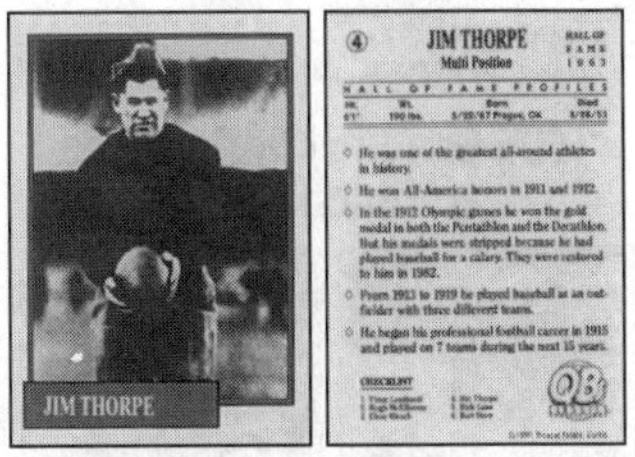

This six-card standard-size set was sponsored by Legend Food Products in honor of the listed Hall of Famers. One free card was randomly inserted in either 3 1/2 or 10 oz. boxes of QB's Cookies. The vanilla-flavored cookies came in six player shapes (wide receiver, kicker, linebacker, tackle, running back, and quarterback), with a trivia quiz and secret message featured on each box. The card fronts display sepia-toned photos enclosed by bronze borders on a white card face. The player's name appears in a bronze bar at the lower left corner. The backs present year of induction into the Pro Football Hall of Fame, biography, career highlights, and a checklist for the set.

	MINT	NRMT	EXC
COMPLETE SET (6)	15.00	6.75	1.85
COMMON CARD (1-6)	1.50	.70	.19
☐ 1 Vince Lombardi CO	3.00	1.35	.35
☐ 2 Hugh McElhenny	2.00	.90	.25
☐ 3 Elroy Hirsch	2.00	.90	.25
☐ 4 Jim Thorpe	4.00	1.80	.50
☐ 5 Dick Lane	1.50	.70	.19
☐ 6 Bart Starr	4.00	1.80	.50

1994 Images

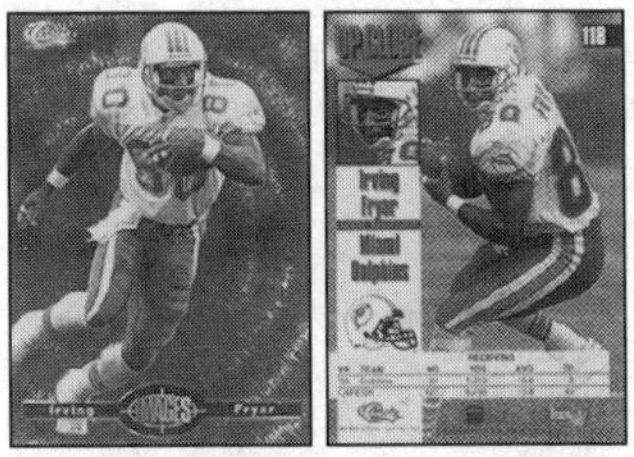

This premier edition of Classic Images features 125 standard-size cards. Production was limited to 1,994 cases. The full-bleed color action photos on the fronts have a metallic sheen to them. The player's name is printed toward the bottom, with the "Images" logo between the first and last name. A second black-and-white photo appears on the back, along with the player's name, position, team name and statistics, as well as a small color headshot on the left side. The cards were sold six cards to a pack, with no jumbo or periodical versions produced. Rookie Cards in this set include Derrick Alexander, Isaac Bruce, Trent Dilfer, Marshall Faulk, William Floyd, Greg Hill, Charles Johnson, Byron Bam Morris, Errict Rhett, Darnay Scott and Heath Shuler. The Emmitt Smith (one per box chiptopper) and Drew Bledsoe Throwbacks (random insert in packs) NFL Experience preview cards were included in the Images product. An Emmitt Smith Images promo card was produced as well and is priced below.

	MINT	NRMT	EXC
COMPLETE SET (125)	50.00	22.00	6.25
COMMON CARD (1-125)	.20	.09	.03
☐ 1 Emmitt Smith	5.00	2.20	.60
☐ 2 Reggie White	.50	.23	.06
☐ 3 Michael Haynes	.30	.14	.04
☐ 4 Chris Warren	.30	.14	.04
☐ 5 Jeff George	.50	.23	.06
☐ 6 Sean Gilbert	.20	.09	.03
☐ 7 Ricky Watters	.50	.23	.06
☐ 8 Eric Metcalf	.30	.14	.04
☐ 9 Randall Cunningham	.30	.14	.04
☐ 10 Tim Brown	.50	.23	.06
☐ 11 Trent Dilfer	1.25	.55	.16
☐ 12 Marshall Faulk	6.00	2.70	.75
☐ 13 David Klingler	.20	.09	.03
☐ 14 Barry Foster	.20	.09	.03
☐ 15 John Elway	2.00	.90	.25
☐ 16 Joe Montana	3.00	1.35	.35
☐ 17 Rodney Hampton	.50	.23	.06
☐ 18 Todd Steussie	.30	.14	.04
☐ 19 Bruce Smith	.50	.23	.06
☐ 20 Wayne Gandy	.20	.09	.03
☐ 21 Anthony Miller	.30	.14	.04
☐ 22 Reggie Brooks	.30	.14	.04
☐ 23 Johnny Johnson	.20	.09	.03
☐ 24 Byron Bam Morris	.50	.23	.06
☐ 25 Drew Bledsoe	3.00	1.35	.35
☐ 26 Jeff Hostetler	.30	.14	.04
☐ 27 Alvin Harper	.30	.14	.04
☐ 28 Cris Carter	.50	.23	.06
☐ 29 Bert Emanuel	2.00	.90	.25
☐ 30 Errict Rhett	2.50	1.10	.30
☐ 31 Scott Mitchell	.50	.23	.06
☐ 32 Deion Sanders	2.00	.90	.25
☐ 33 Lewis Tillman	.20	.09	.03
☐ 34 Tim Bowens	.30	.14	.04
☐ 35 Charles Haley	.30	.14	.04
☐ 36 Stan Humphries	.50	.23	.06
☐ 37 Haywood Jeffires	.30	.14	.04
☐ 38 Andre Reed	.30	.14	.04
☐ 39 Charles Johnson	1.00	.45	.12
☐ 40 Ronald Moore	.20	.09	.03
☐ 41 Jim Everett	.30	.14	.04
☐ 42 Greg Hill	1.25	.55	.16
☐ 43 Thurman Thomas	.50	.23	.06
☐ 44 Willie McGinest	.50	.23	.06
☐ 45 Aaron Glenn	.30	.14	.04
☐ 46 Erric Pegram	.20	.09	.03
☐ 47 Terry Kirby	.50	.23	.06
☐ 48 Warren Moon	.50	.23	.06
☐ 49 Clyde Simmons	.20	.09	.03
☐ 50 Eric Turner	.20	.09	.03
☐ 51 Heath Shuler	2.00	.90	.25
☐ 52 Rickey Jackson	.20	.09	.03
☐ 53 Johnnie Morton	1.00	.45	.12
☐ 54 Charlie Garner	.30	.14	.04
☐ 55 Mark Collins	.20	.09	.03
☐ 56 Mike Pritchard	.20	.09	.03
☐ 57 Bryant Young	1.00	.45	.12
☐ 58 Joe Johnson	.20	.09	.03
☐ 59 Erik Kramer	.30	.14	.04
☐ 60 Barry Sanders	3.00	1.35	.35
☐ 61 Rod Woodson	.50	.23	.06
☐ 62 Dave Brown	.30	.14	.04
☐ 63 Gary Brown	.20	.09	.03
☐ 64 Brett Favre	5.00	2.20	.60
☐ 65 Isaac Bruce	6.00	2.70	.75
☐ 66 Boomer Esiason	.30	.14	.04
☐ 67 Jim Harbaugh	.50	.23	.06
☐ 68 Jackie Harris	.20	.09	.03
☐ 69 Art Monk	.30	.14	.04
☐ 70 Jamir Miller	.20	.09	.03
☐ 71 Neil O'Donnell	.50	.23	.06
☐ 72 Neil Smith	.50	.23	.06
☐ 73 Junior Seau	.50	.23	.06
☐ 74 Jerome Bettis	1.50	.70	.19
☐ 75 Bernard Williams	.20	.09	.03
☐ 76 Jeff Burris	.30	.14	.04
☐ 77 Henry Ellard	.30	.14	.04
☐ 78 Reggie Cobb	.20	.09	.03
☐ 79 Shante Carver	.20	.09	.03
☐ 80 Terry Allen	.30	.14	.04
☐ 81 Cortez Kennedy	.30	.14	.04
☐ 82 Trev Alberts	.30	.14	.04
☐ 83 Michael Irvin	.50	.23	.06
☐ 84 Herschel Walker	.30	.14	.04
☐ 85 Dan Marino	5.00	2.20	.60
☐ 86 Dave Meggett	.20	.09	.03
☐ 87 Herman Moore	1.25	.55	.16
☐ 88 Darnay Scott	3.50	1.55	.45
☐ 89 Dewayne Washington	.30	.14	.04
☐ 90 Rob Fredrickson	.30	.14	.04
☐ 91 Rick Mirer	.50	.23	.06
☐ 92 Thomas Lewis	.30	.14	.04
☐ 93 Chris Miller	.20	.09	.03
☐ 94 Marion Butts	.20	.09	.03
☐ 95 Sam Adams	.30	.14	.04
☐ 96 Jerry Rice	3.00	1.35	.35
☐ 97 Ben Coates	.50	.23	.06
☐ 98 David Palmer	.30	.14	.04
☐ 99 Antonio Langham	.30	.14	.04
☐ 100 Curtis Conway	.50	.23	.06
☐ 101 Derrick Thomas	.50	.23	.06
☐ 102 Ken Norton Jr.	.30	.14	.04
☐ 103 Ronnie Lott	.30	.14	.04
☐ 104 Sterling Sharpe	.30	.14	.04
☐ 105 Troy Aikman	3.00	1.35	.35
☐ 106 Shannon Sharpe	.30	.14	.04
☐ 107 Natrone Means	1.25	.55	.16
☐ 108 Derek Brown RB	.20	.09	.03
☐ 109 Dan Wilkinson	.30	.14	.04
☐ 110 Andre Rison	.30	.14	.04
☐ 111 Quentin Coryatt	.20	.09	.03
☐ 112 Cody Carlson	.20	.09	.03
☐ 113 William Floyd	2.00	.90	.25
☐ 114 Marcus Allen	.50	.23	.06
☐ 115 Steve Young	2.00	.90	.25
☐ 116 Jim Kelly	.50	.23	.06
☐ 117 LeShon Johnson	.30	.14	.04
☐ 118 Irving Fryar	.30	.14	.04
☐ 119 Carl Pickens	1.50	.70	.19
☐ 120 Keith Jackson	.20	.09	.03
☐ 121 John Thierry	.20	.09	.03
☐ 122 Vinny Testaverde	.30	.14	.04
☐ 123 Derrick Alexander WR	.50	.23	.06
☐ 124 Seth Joyner	.20	.09	.03
☐ 125 Checklist	.20	.09	.03
☐ IF1 Emmitt Smith Promo Numbered IF1	3.00	1.35	.35
☐ TP1 Drew Bledsoe NFL Experience Throwbacks preview card	50.00	22.00	6.25
☐ NNO Emmitt Smith NFL Experience Sneak Preview card	12.00	5.50	1.50

1994 Images All-Pro

Featuring Perennial All-Pros and All-Pro Prospects, this 25-card set measures the standard size. Two All-Pro insert packs containing six cards were inserted in every case, while two additional All-Pro cards

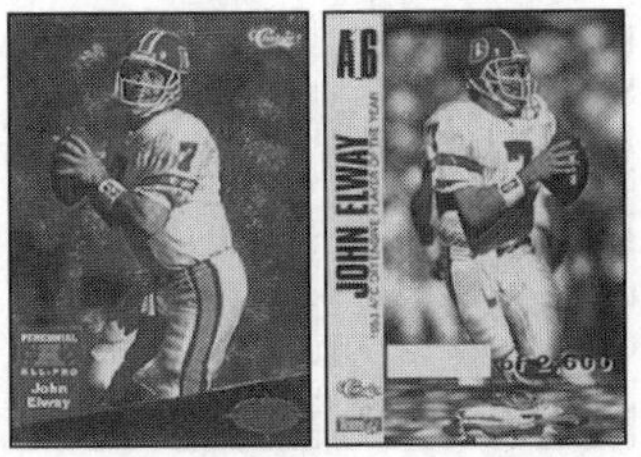

were inserted in every box. Just 2,600 of each insert card were produced. The first 12 cards of this set highlight AFC players, while the last 13 showcase NFC players. The fronts are foil stamped in either red or blue to designate the AFC or NFC. The full-bleed color action photos on the front have a metallic sheen to them. The player's name is printed toward the bottom. A second photo appears on the back, along with the player's name and his accomplishment which establishes his place as a Perennial All-Pro or All-Pro Prospect, as well as a smaller, black-and-white version of this photo underneath.

	MINT	NRMT	EXC
COMPLETE SET (25)	350.00	160.00	45.00
COMMON CARD (A1-A25)	5.00	2.20	.60
☐ A1 Heath Shuler	8.00	3.60	1.00
☐ A2 Steve Young	20.00	9.00	2.50
☐ A3 Trent Dilfer	8.00	3.60	1.00
☐ A4 Troy Aikman	25.00	11.00	3.10
☐ A5 Emmitt Smith	50.00	22.00	6.25
☐ A6 Barry Sanders	25.00	11.00	3.10
☐ A7 Jerome Bettis	12.00	5.50	1.50
☐ A8 Errict Rhett	8.00	3.60	1.00
☐ A9 Jerry Rice	25.00	11.00	3.10
☐ A10 Michael Irvin	8.00	3.60	1.00
☐ A11 Andre Rison	6.00	2.70	.75
☐ A12 Sterling Sharpe	6.00	2.70	.75
☐ A13 Reggie White	8.00	3.60	1.00
☐ A14 Rick Mirer	8.00	3.60	1.00
☐ A15 Drew Bledsoe	25.00	11.00	3.10
☐ A16 John Elway	20.00	9.00	2.50
☐ A17 Joe Montana	25.00	11.00	3.10
☐ A18 Dan Marino	50.00	22.00	6.25
☐ A19 Thurman Thomas	8.00	3.60	1.00
☐ A20 Marshall Faulk	20.00	9.00	2.50
☐ A21 Marcus Allen	8.00	3.60	1.00
☐ A22 Charles Johnson	5.00	2.20	.60
☐ A23 Tim Brown	6.00	2.70	.75
☐ A24 Anthony Miller	5.00	2.20	.60
☐ A25 Derrick Thomas	6.00	2.70	.75

1994-95 Images Update

These ten standard-size cards were randomly inserted in retail packs of 1995 Classic Images 4-Sport. These cards feature some leading NFL players and were numbered in continuation of the 1994 Classic Images set.

	MINT	NRMT	EXC
COMPLETE SET (10)	100.00	45.00	12.50
COMMON CARD (126-135)	4.00	1.80	.50
☐ 126 Emmitt Smith	25.00	11.00	3.10
☐ 127 Troy Aikman	12.00	5.50	1.50
☐ 128 Steve Young	10.00	4.50	1.25
☐ 129 Deion Sanders	8.00	3.60	1.00
☐ 130 Ben Coates	4.00	1.80	.50
☐ 131 Natrone Means	5.00	2.20	.60
☐ 132 Drew Bledsoe	12.00	5.50	1.50
☐ 133 Cris Carter	5.00	2.20	.60
☐ 134 Marshall Faulk	10.00	4.50	1.25
☐ 135 Errict Rhett	5.00	2.20	.60

1995 Images Limited/Live

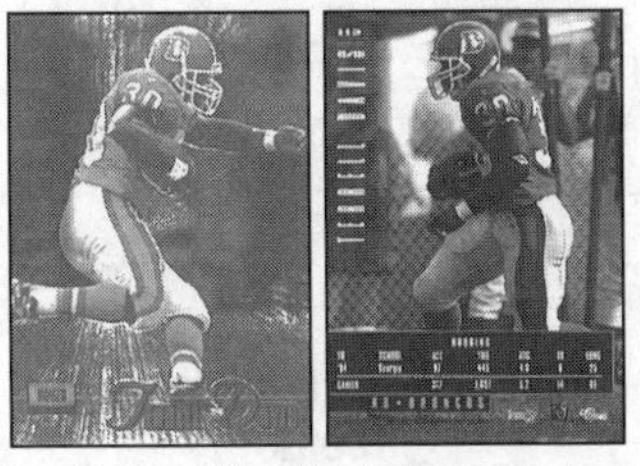

Classic issued Images NFL as a 125-card set in two seperate releases: Live and Limited. Each set had different action photos of the same player on 24-point micro-lined foil-board cards. A few cards were issued in only one version, as noted below with an "LM" or "LV" suffix on the card number. Card fronts have a silver background with the player's name along the bottom of the card. The Live version also contains the word "Live!" along the left side of the card. Limited card backs feature a full bleed shot with the player's name on the left of the card and statistical information at the bottom. Live card backs contain a player shot in a diagonal photo with the player's name and statistics at the bottom. Rookie Cards in this set include Jeff Blake, Ki-Jana Carter, Kerry Collins, Joey Galloway, Curtis Martin, Steve McNair, Rashaan Salaam, Kordell Stewart, J.J. Stokes and Michael Westbrook. Another bonus feature was Hot Boxes, where each pack contained approximately 50% inserts. Hot Boxes were specially marked and could be found in every five cases. Drew Bledsoe Live and Limited Promo cards were produced and priced below.

	MINT	NRMT	EXC
COMPLETE SET (125)	25.00	11.00	3.10
COMMON CARD (1-125)	.10	.05	.01
☐ 1 Emmitt Smith	2.50	1.10	.30
☐ 2 Steve Young	1.00	.45	.12
☐ 3 Drew Bledsoe	1.25	.55	.16
☐ 4 Dan Marino	2.50	1.10	.30
☐ 5 John Elway	1.00	.45	.12
☐ 6 Barry Sanders	1.25	.55	.16
☐ 7 Brett Favre	2.50	1.10	.30
☐ 8 Troy Aikman	1.25	.55	.16
☐ 9 Jim Kelly	.30	.14	.04
☐ 10 Marshall Faulk	.60	.25	.07
☐ 11 Jerry Rice	1.25	.55	.16
☐ 12 Warren Moon	.15	.07	.02
☐ 13 Jim Everett	.10	.05	.01
☐ 14 Rodney Hampton	.15	.07	.02
☐ 15 Jeff Hostetler	.15	.07	.02
☐ 16 Errict Rhett	.30	.14	.04
☐ 17 Jerome Bettis	.50	.23	.06
☐ 18 Byron Bam Morris	.15	.07	.02
☐ 19 Randall Cunningham	.15	.07	.02
☐ 20 Rick Mirer	.30	.14	.04
☐ 21 Natrone Means	.30	.14	.04
☐ 22 Jeff George	.15	.07	.02
☐ 23 Garrison Hearst	.30	.14	.04
☐ 24 Michael Irvin	.30	.14	.04
☐ 25 Cris Carter	.30	.14	.04
☐ 26 Irving Fryar	.15	.07	.02
☐ 27 Jeff Blake	1.25	.55	.16
☐ 28 Bruce Smith	.30	.14	.04
☐ 29 Shannon Sharpe	.15	.07	.02
☐ 30 Steve Beuerlein	.10	.05	.01
☐ 31 Stan Humphries	.15	.07	.02
☐ 32 Chris Warren	.15	.07	.02
☐ 33 Ben Coates	.15	.07	.02
☐ 34 Boomer Esiason	.15	.07	.02
☐ 35 Trent Dilfer	.30	.14	.04
☐ 36 Chris Miller	.10	.05	.01
☐ 37 Dave Brown	.15	.07	.02
☐ 38 Herman Moore	.60	.25	.07
☐ 39 Anthony Miller	.15	.07	.02
☐ 40 Andre Reed	.15	.07	.02
☐ 41 Reggie White	.30	.14	.04
☐ 42 Darnay Scott	.30	.14	.04
☐ 43 Erik Kramer	.10	.05	.01
☐ 44 Leroy Hoard	.10	.05	.01
☐ 45 Fred Barnett	.15	.07	.02
☐ 46 Junior Seau	.30	.14	.04
☐ 47 Vinny Testaverde	.15	.07	.02
☐ 48 Gus Frerotte	.60	.25	.07
☐ 49 William Floyd	.30	.14	.04
☐ 50 Mo Lewis	.10	.05	.01
☐ 51 Tim Brown	.30	.14	.04
☐ 52 Greg Lloyd	.15	.07	.02
☐ 53 Chester McGlockton	.15	.07	.02
☐ 54 Heath Shuler	.30	.14	.04
☐ 55 Rod Woodson	.15	.07	.02
☐ 56 Don Beebe	.10	.05	.01
☐ 57 Carl Pickens	.30	.14	.04
☐ 58 Charles Haley	.15	.07	.02
☐ 59 Steve Bono	.15	.07	.02
☐ 60 Harvey Williams	.10	.05	.01
☐ 61 Greg Hill	.15	.07	.02
☐ 62 Eric Metcalf	.15	.07	.02
☐ 63 Mario Bates	.30	.14	.04
☐ 64 Terry Allen	.15	.07	.02
☐ 65 Michael Timpson	.10	.05	.01
☐ 66 Mark Stepnoski	.10	.05	.01
☐ 67 Jeff Lageman	.10	.05	.01
☐ 68 Robert Smith	.30	.14	.04
☐ 69 Eric Allen	.10	.05	.01
☐ 70 Ricky Watters	.30	.14	.04
☐ 71 Derek Loville	.10	.05	.01
☐ 72 Bernie Parmalee	.15	.07	.02
☐ 73 Bryce Paup	.30	.14	.04
☐ 74 Frank Reich	.10	.05	.01
☐ 75 Henry Thomas	.10	.05	.01
☐ 76 Craig Erickson	.10	.05	.01
☐ 77 Eric Green	.10	.05	.01
☐ 78 Dave Meggett	.10	.05	.01
☐ 79 Deion Sanders	.75	.35	.09
☐ 80 Herschel Walker	.15	.07	.02
☐ 81 Andre Rison	.15	.07	.02
☐ 82 Ki-Jana Carter	1.00	.45	.12
☐ 83 Tony Boselli	.15	.07	.02
☐ 84 Steve McNair	3.00	1.35	.35
☐ 85 Michael Westbrook	1.25	.55	.16
☐ 86 Kerry Collins	4.00	1.80	.50
☐ 87 Kevin Carter	.30	.14	.04
☐ 88 Warren Sapp	.15	.07	.02
☐ 89 Joey Galloway	2.00	.90	.25
☐ 90 J.J. Stokes	1.00	.45	.12
☐ 91 Derrick Brooks	.10	.05	.01
☐ 92 Kyle Brady	.30	.14	.04
☐ 93 Napoleon Kaufman	1.00	.45	.12
☐ 94 Tyrone Wheatley	.50	.23	.06
☐ 95 Mike Mamula	.15	.07	.02
☐ 96 Desmond Howard	.15	.07	.02
☐ 97 James O.Stewart	.15	.07	.02
☐ 98 Craig Newsome	.10	.05	.01
☐ 99 Ty Law	.15	.07	.02

☐ 100 Ellis Johnson	.10	.05	.01
☐ 101 Hugh Douglas	.15	.07	.02
☐ 102 Mark Bruener	.15	.07	.02
☐ 103 Tyrone Poole	.15	.07	.02
☐ 104 Luther Elliss	.10	.05	.01
☐ 105 Mark Fields	.10	.05	.01
☐ 106 Frank Sanders	.30	.14	.04
☐ 107 Rashaan Salaam	1.25	.55	.16
☐ 108 Craig Powell	.10	.05	.01
☐ 109 Sherman Williams	.10	.05	.01
☐ 110 Chad May	.10	.05	.01
☐ 111 Rob Johnson	.10	.05	.01
☐ 112 Todd Collins	.30	.14	.04
☐ 113 Terrell Davis	4.00	1.80	.50
☐ 114 Eric Zeier	.30	.14	.04
☐ 115 Curtis Martin	4.00	1.80	.50
☐ 116 Kordell Stewart	3.00	1.35	.35
☐ 117 Troy Vincent	.10	.05	.01
☐ 118 Ray Zellars	.15	.07	.02
☐ 119LM Dave Krieg	.10	.05	.01
☐ 119LV Mark Brunell	1.25	.55	.16
☐ 120LM Mike Sherrard	.10	.05	.01
☐ 120LV Keenan McCardell	.30	.14	.04
☐ 121LM Willie Davis	.15	.07	.02
☐ 121LV Terry Kirby	.15	.07	.02
☐ 122LM Robert Brooks	.30	.14	.04
☐ 122LV Marcus Allen	.30	.14	.04
☐ 123LM Chris Sanders	1.25	.55	.16
☐ 123LV Charlie Garner	.15	.07	.02
☐ 124 Checklist #1 Drew Bledsoe	.60	.25	.07
☐ 125 Checklist #2 Emmitt Smith	1.00	.45	.12
☐ LT1 Drew Bledsoe Promo numbered LT1, ad back	1.50	.70	.19
☐ LV1 Drew Bledsoe Promo numbered LV1, ad back	1.50	.70	.19

1995 Images Limited/Live Die Cuts

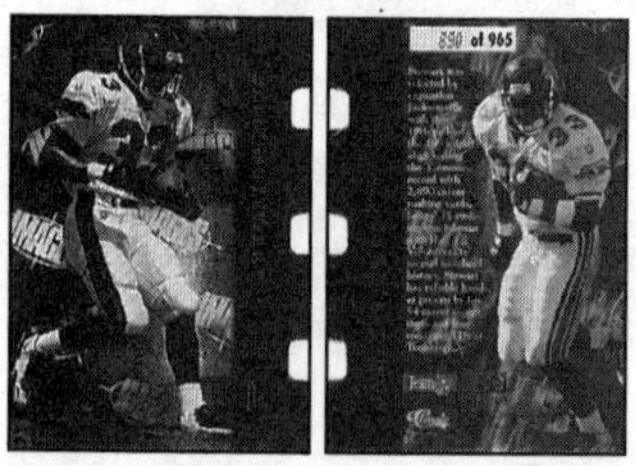

This 30 card set was randomly inserted into both Limited and Live packs at a rate of one in 99 packs. Cards DC1-DC15 were randomly inserted in Limited packs, while cards DC16-DC30 were found in Live packs. There are no other differences between the cards. Card fronts are die cut on the right side on a black background and have a silver-foil background on the rest. Card backs are numbered out of 965 at the top with a black and green background. A brief statistical summary is also included.

	MINT	NRMT	EXC
COMPLETE SET (30)	500.00	220.00	60.00
COMPLETE SERIES 1 (15)	250.00	110.00	31.00
COMPLETE SERIES 2 (15)	250.00	110.00	31.00
COMMON CARD (DC1-DC30)	8.00	3.60	1.00
☐ DC1 Jim Kelly	12.00	5.50	1.50
☐ DC2 Kerry Collins	35.00	16.00	4.40
☐ DC3 Michael Irvin	12.00	5.50	1.50
☐ DC4 Troy Aikman	30.00	13.50	3.70
☐ DC5 John Elway	25.00	11.00	3.10
☐ DC6 Barry Sanders	30.00	13.50	3.70
☐ DC7 Marshall Faulk	15.00	6.75	1.85
☐ DC8 James O.Stewart	12.00	5.50	1.50
☐ DC9 Drew Bledsoe	30.00	13.50	3.70
☐ DC10 Herman Moore	15.00	6.75	1.85
☐ DC11 Byron Bam Morris	8.00	3.60	1.00
☐ DC12 Jerry Rice	30.00	13.50	3.70
☐ DC13 Joey Galloway	25.00	11.00	3.10
☐ DC14 Rick Mirer	12.00	5.50	1.50
☐ DC15 Errict Rhett	12.00	5.50	1.50
☐ DC16 Rob Moore	8.00	3.60	1.00
☐ DC17 Jeff George	12.00	5.50	1.50
☐ DC18 Rashaan Salaam	15.00	6.75	1.85
☐ DC19 Andre Rison	8.00	3.60	1.00
☐ DC20 Emmitt Smith	60.00	27.00	7.50
☐ DC21 Brett Favre	60.00	27.00	7.50
☐ DC22 Dan Marino	60.00	27.00	7.50
☐ DC23 Warren Moon	12.00	5.50	1.50
☐ DC24 Dave Brown	8.00	3.60	1.00
☐ DC25 Napoleon Kaufman	8.00	3.60	1.00
☐ DC26 Natrone Means	12.00	5.50	1.50
☐ DC27 Steve Young	20.00	9.00	2.50
☐ DC28 Reggie White	12.00	5.50	1.50
☐ DC29 Jerome Bettis	12.00	5.50	1.50
☐ DC30 Michael Westbrook	15.00	6.75	1.85

1995 Images Limited/Live Focused

This 30 card set was inserted as a special one-card pack in both sets at a rate of one in every box. The cards feature two star players from

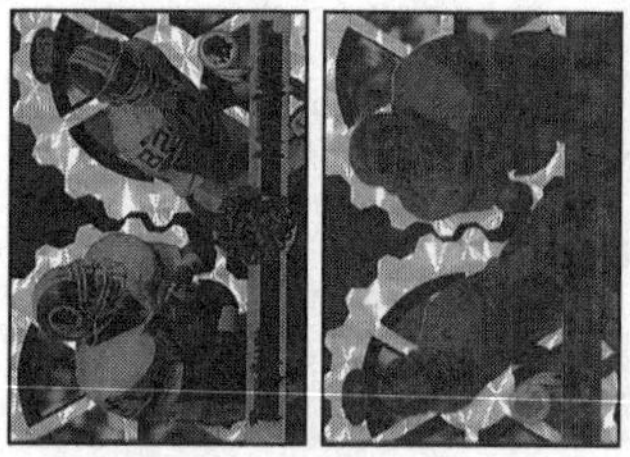

the same team and are printed on 24-point acetate material. Card fronts from the Limited set have two gold gears in the background with a shot of each player over each gear. The player's names are listed at the bottom of the card on a white and blue background with the "Focused" logo in between them. Live card fronts vary slightly with the gear background using a clear holographic pattern instead of the gold. Card backs on both are clear with the same background image of the player and the card numbered with a "F" prefix.

	MINT	NRMT	EXC
COMPLETE SET (30)	160.00	70.00	20.00
COMMON CARD (F1-F30)	3.00	1.35	.35
☐ F1 Rashaan Salaam Erik Kramer	6.00	2.70	.75
☐ F2 Kerry Collins Frank Reich	10.00	4.50	1.25
☐ F3 Jim Kelly Andre Reed	5.00	2.20	.60
☐ F4 Jeff George Craig Heyward	3.00	1.35	.35
☐ F5 Garrison Hearst Dave Krieg	5.00	2.20	.60
☐ F6 Barry Sanders Herman Moore	12.00	5.50	1.50
☐ F7 John Elway Shannon Sharpe	12.00	5.50	1.50
☐ F8 Emmitt Smith Troy Aikman	20.00	9.00	2.50
☐ F9 Andre Rison Leroy Hoard	3.00	1.35	.35
☐ F10 Carl Pickens Jeff Blake	6.00	2.70	.75
☐ F11 Willie Davis Steve Bono	3.00	1.35	.35
☐ F12 James O.Stewart Steve Beuerlein	3.00	1.35	.35
☐ F13 Marshall Faulk Craig Erickson	6.00	2.70	.75
☐ F14 Steve McNair Chris Chandler	8.00	3.60	1.00
☐ F15 Brett Favre Reggie White	20.00	9.00	2.50
☐ F16 Rodney Hampton Dave Brown	3.00	1.35	.35
☐ F17 Mario Bates Jim Everett	3.00	1.35	.35
☐ F18 Drew Bledsoe Ben Coates	12.00	5.50	1.50
☐ F19 Warren Moon Cris Carter	5.00	2.20	.60
☐ F20 Dan Marino Irving Fryar	20.00	9.00	2.50
☐ F21 Natrone Means Stan Humphries	5.00	2.20	.60
☐ F22 Byron Bam Morris Kevin Greene	3.00	1.35	.35
☐ F23 Ricky Watters Randall Cunningham	5.00	2.20	.60
☐ F24 Tim Brown Jeff Hostetler	3.00	1.35	.35
☐ F25 Boomer Esiason Kyle Brady	3.00	1.35	.35
☐ F26 Michael Westbrook Terry Allen	5.00	2.20	.60
☐ F27 Errict Rhett Trent Dilfer	5.00	2.20	.60
☐ F28 Jerome Bettis Kevin Carter	5.00	2.20	.60
☐ F29 Steve Young Jerry Rice	15.00	6.75	1.85
☐ F30 Joey Galloway Rick Mirer	7.00	3.10	.85

1995 Images Limited/Live Icons

This 20 card set was randomly inserted in Limited packs only at a rate of one in 20 packs. The card fronts have a fabric backgound with the player's name and "Icons" logo in foil. Card backs are numbered with an "I" prefix and have a brief commentary surrounded by an orange border.

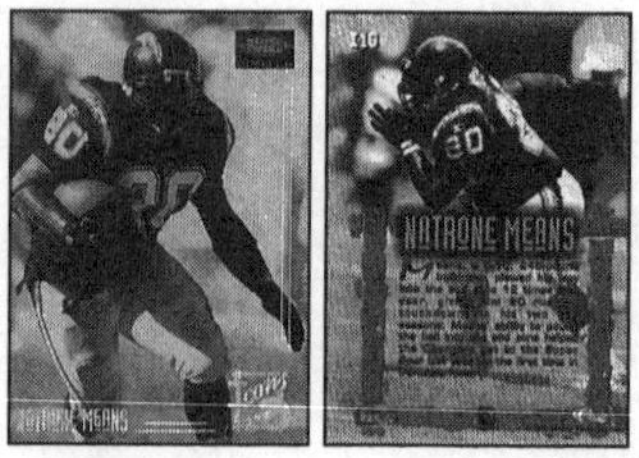

	MINT	NRMT	EXC
COMPLETE SET (20)	160.00	70.00	20.00
COMMON CARD (I1-I20)	3.00	1.35	.35
☐ I1 Jim Kelly	5.00	2.20	.60
☐ I2 Rashaan Salaam	7.00	3.10	.85
☐ I3 Andre Rison	3.00	1.35	.35
☐ I4 Troy Aikman	12.00	5.50	1.50
☐ I5 Emmitt Smith	25.00	11.00	3.10
☐ I6 John Elway	10.00	4.50	1.25
☐ I7 Barry Sanders	12.00	5.50	1.50
☐ I8 Brett Favre	25.00	11.00	3.10
☐ I9 Marshall Faulk	6.00	2.70	.75
☐ I10 Irving Fryar	3.00	1.35	.35
☐ I11 Dan Marino	25.00	11.00	3.10
☐ I12 Drew Bledsoe	12.00	5.50	1.50
☐ I13 Rodney Hampton	5.00	2.20	.60
☐ I14 Ricky Watters	5.00	2.20	.60
☐ I15 Byron Bam Morris	3.00	1.35	.35
☐ I16 Natrone Means	5.00	2.20	.60
☐ I17 Steve Young	10.00	4.50	1.25
☐ I18 Jerry Rice	12.00	5.50	1.50
☐ I19 Errict Rhett	5.00	2.20	.60
☐ I20 Michael Westbrook	7.00	3.10	.85

1995 Images Limited/Live Sculpted Previews

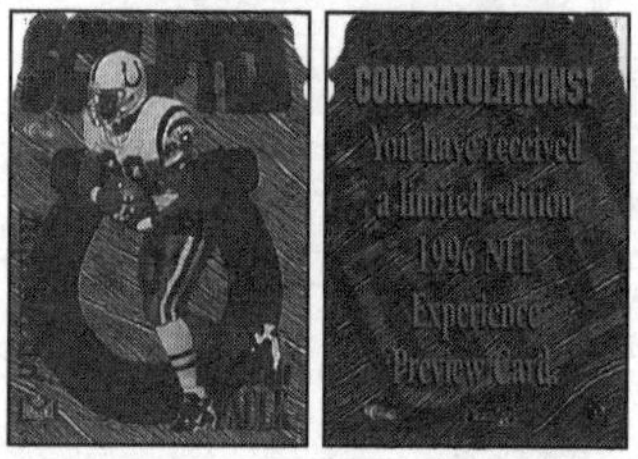

This five card set was randomly inserted in Limited packs only at a rate of 24 packs. The cards are preview cards of the "Sculpted" insert set that was released in the 1996 Classic NFL Experience product. Card fronts are die cut at the top with the word "Sculpted" across the top and a wood grain background. The photo of the player is in the center of the card with the team's logo in the background. The word "preview" runs along the left side of the card and the player's name is located on the bottom right side. Card backs have an NFL logo in the background with the phrase "Congratulations! You have received a limited edition 1996 NFL Experience Preview Card. Card backs also have a "NX" prefix.

	MINT	NRMT	EXC
COMPLETE SET (5)	30.00	13.50	3.70
COMMON CARD (NX1-NX5)	4.00	1.80	.50
☐ NX1 Emmitt Smith	15.00	6.75	1.85
☐ NX2 Drew Bledsoe	7.00	3.10	.85
☐ NX3 Steve Young	6.00	2.70	.75
☐ NX4 Rashaan Salaam	4.00	1.80	.50
☐ NX5 Marshall Faulk	4.00	1.80	.50

1995 Images Limited/Live Silks

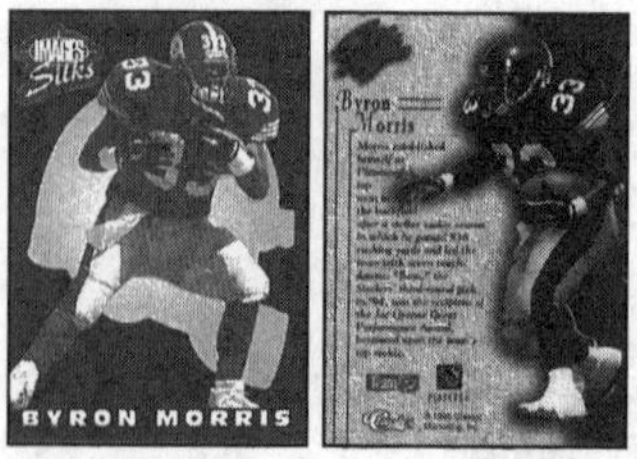

This 10 card set was randomly inserted in both Limited and Live packs at a rate of one in 375 packs. Card numbers S1-S5 were inserted in Live packs and numbers S6-S10 were inserted in Limited packs. Card fronts have an orange die cut background surrounded by a black background. The image of the player is made with a silk material. The player's name is in white at the bottom of the card. Card backs contain a statistical summary and the cards are numbered with a "S" prefix.

	MINT	NRMT	EXC
COMPLETE SET (10)	500.00	220.00	60.00
COMPLETE SERIES 1 (5)	200.00	90.00	25.00
COMPLETE SERIES 2 (5)	300.00	135.00	38.00
COMMON CARD (S1-S10)	15.00	6.75	1.85
☐ S1 Troy Aikman	75.00	34.00	9.50
☐ S2 Marshall Faulk	40.00	18.00	5.00
☐ S3 Drew Bledsoe	75.00	34.00	9.50
☐ S4 Byron Bam Morris	15.00	6.75	1.85
☐ S5 James O.Stewart	15.00	6.75	1.85
☐ S6 Emmitt Smith	150.00	70.00	19.00
☐ S7 Steve Young	50.00	22.00	6.25
☐ S8 Rashaan Salaam	25.00	11.00	3.10
☐ S9 Natrone Means	20.00	9.00	2.50
☐ S10 Michael Westbrook	25.00	11.00	3.10

1995 Images Limited/Live Untouchables

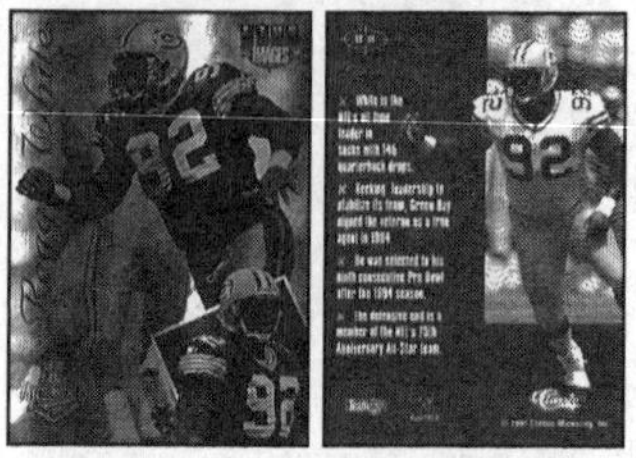

This 25 card set was randomly inserted into Live packs only and is printed on three-dimensional holographic foil board. Card fronts contain the player's name on the left side with the "NFL Untouchables" logo underneath it. A full shot of the player is shown with an additional head shot in the bottom right corner. Card backs have mostly a black background with bullet-point information about the player on the left side. Cards are numbered with a "U" prefix.

	MINT	NRMT	EXC
COMPLETE SET (25)	200.00	90.00	25.00
COMMON CARD (U1-U25)	4.00	1.80	.50
☐ U1 Jim Kelly	6.00	2.70	.75
☐ U2 Kerry Collins	15.00	6.75	1.85
☐ U3 Rashaan Salaam	7.00	3.10	.85
☐ U4 Troy Aikman	15.00	6.75	1.85
☐ U5 Emmitt Smith	30.00	13.50	3.70
☐ U6 John Elway	12.00	5.50	1.50
☐ U7 Barry Sanders	15.00	6.75	1.85
☐ U8 Reggie White	6.00	2.70	.75
☐ U9 Steve McNair	12.00	5.50	1.50
☐ U10 Marshall Faulk	8.00	3.60	1.00
☐ U11 Dan Marino	30.00	13.50	3.70
☐ U12 Drew Bledsoe	15.00	6.75	1.85
☐ U13 Ben Coates	4.00	1.80	.50
☐ U14 Tyrone Wheatley	4.00	1.80	.50
☐ U15 Chester McGlockton	4.00	1.80	.50
☐ U16 Ricky Watters	6.00	2.70	.75
☐ U17 Junior Seau	6.00	2.70	.75
☐ U18 Natrone Means	6.00	2.70	.75
☐ U19 Steve Young	12.00	5.50	1.50
☐ U20 Jerry Rice	15.00	6.75	1.85
☐ U21 Rick Mirer	6.00	2.70	.75
☐ U22 Jerome Bettis	6.00	2.70	.75
☐ U23 Warren Sapp	4.00	1.80	.50
☐ U24 Michael Westbrook	6.00	2.70	.75
☐ U25 Heath Shuler	6.00	2.70	.75

1992-93 Intimidator Bio Sheets

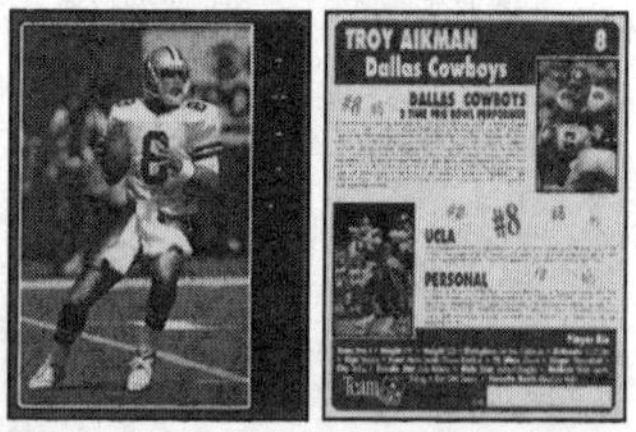

Produced by Intimidator, each of these 36 bio sheets measures approximately 8 1/2" by 11" and is printed on card stock. The fronts display a large glossy color player photo framed by black and white inner borders. The right side of the photo is edged by a gold foil stripe that presents the player's name, team name, Intimidator logo, and uniform number. The surrounding card face, which constitutes the outer border, is team color-coded. The backs carry two black-and-white player photos, pro career summary, college career summary, and personal as well as biographical information. An autograph slot at the lower right corner rounds out the back. The bio sheets are unnumbered and checklisted below in alphabetical order.

	MINT	NRMT	EXC
COMPLETE SET (36)	100.00	45.00	12.50
COMMON CARD (1-36)	1.50	.70	.19
☐ 1 Troy Aikman	8.00	3.60	1.00
☐ 2 Jerry Ball	1.50	.70	.19
☐ 3 Cornelius Bennett	2.00	.90	.25
☐ 4 Earnest Byner	1.50	.70	.19
☐ 5 Randall Cunningham	2.00	.90	.25
☐ 6 Chris Doleman	2.00	.90	.25
☐ 7 John Elway	6.00	2.70	.75
☐ 8 Jim Everett	2.00	.90	.25
☐ 9 Michael Irvin	3.00	1.35	.35
☐ 10 Jim Kelly	3.00	1.35	.35
☐ 11 James Lofton	2.00	.90	.25
☐ 12 Howie Long	2.00	.90	.25
☐ 13 Ronnie Lott	2.00	.90	.25
☐ 14 Nick Lowery	1.50	.70	.19

☐ 15 Charles Mann	1.50	.70	.19
☐ 16 Dan Marino	15.00	6.75	1.85
☐ 17 Art Monk	2.00	.90	.25
☐ 18 Joe Montana	8.00	3.60	1.00
☐ 19 Warren Moon	3.00	1.35	.35
☐ 20 Christian Okoye	2.00	.90	.25
☐ 21 Leslie O'Neal	2.00	.90	.25
☐ 22 Andre Reed	3.00	1.35	.35
☐ 23 Jerry Rice	8.00	3.60	1.00
☐ 24 Andre Rison	3.00	1.35	.35
☐ 25 Deion Sanders	5.00	2.20	.60
☐ 26 Junior Seau	3.00	1.35	.35
☐ 27 Mike Singletary	2.00	.90	.25
☐ 28 Bruce Smith	3.00	1.35	.35
☐ 29 Emmitt Smith	15.00	6.75	1.85
☐ 30 Neil Smith	3.00	1.35	.35
☐ 31 Pat Swilling	2.00	.90	.25
☐ 32 Lawrence Taylor	3.00	1.35	.35
☐ 33 Broderick Thomas	1.50	.70	.19
☐ 34 Derrick Thomas	3.00	1.35	.35
☐ 35 Thurman Thomas	3.00	1.35	.35
☐ 36 Lorenzo White	2.00	.90	.25

1984 Invaders Smokey

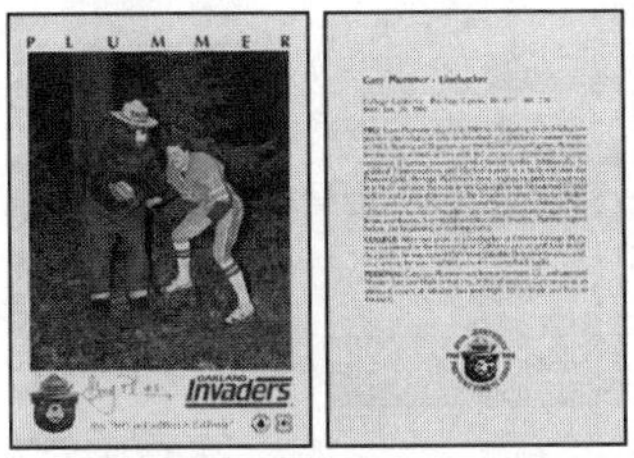

This five-card set features the Oakland Invaders of the USFL. The theme of the set is Forestry, i.e., Smokey the Bear is pictured on each card. The set commemorates the 40th birthday of Smokey Bear and is sponsored by the California Forestry Department in conjunction with the U.S. Forest Service. The cards measure approximately 5" by 7". The front features a color posed photo of the football player with Smokey Bear. The player's signature, jersey number, and a public service announcement concerning wildfire prevention occur below the picture. Biographical information is provided on the back.

	MINT	NRMT	EXC
COMPLETE SET (5)	75.00	34.00	9.50
COMMON CARD (1-5)	15.00	6.75	1.85
☐ 1 Dupre Marshall	15.00	6.75	1.85
☐ 2 Gary Plummer	20.00	9.00	2.50
☐ 3 David Shaw	15.00	6.75	1.85
☐ 4 Kevin Shea	15.00	6.75	1.85
☐ 5 Smokey Bear (With players above)	15.00	6.75	1.85

1986 Jeno's Pizza

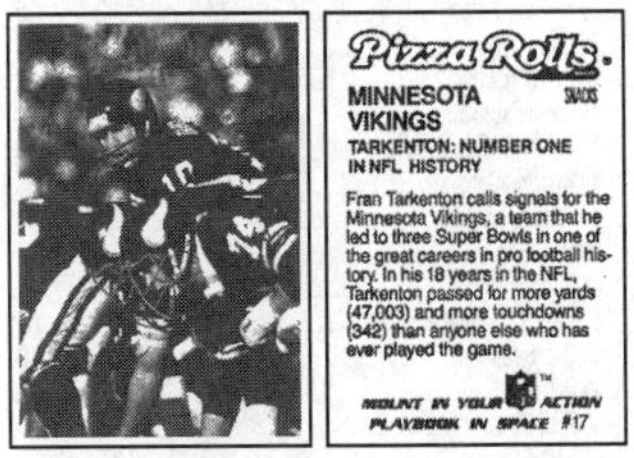

The 1986 Jeno's Pizza football set contains 56 cards (two for each of the 28 teams). The two cards for each team typically represent a retired star and a current player. The cards are standard sized (2 1/2" by 3 1/2") and were printed horizontally (most of them) on thin card stock. The cards were distributed as a promotion with one card, sealed in plastic, contained in each special Jeno's box. Reportedly 10,000 sets were produced. There was also issued a Terry Bradshaw Action Play Book; one had to send in a coupon to receive the book. The set price below includes the book.

	MINT	NRMT	EXC
COMPLETE SET (56)	20.00	9.00	2.50
COMMON CARD (1-56)	.20	.09	.03
☐ 1 Duane Thomas	.30	.14	.04
☐ 2 Butch Johnson	.30	.14	.04
☐ 3 Andy Headen	.20	.09	.03
☐ 4 Joe Morris	.30	.14	.04
☐ 5 Wilbert Montgomery	.30	.14	.04
☐ 6 Harold Carmichael	.40	.18	.05
☐ 7 Ottis Anderson	.40	.18	.05
☐ 8 Roy Green	.20	.09	.03
☐ 9 Mark Murphy	.20	.09	.03
☐ 10 Joe Theismann	.60	.25	.07
☐ 11 Jim McMahon	.60	.25	.07
☐ 12 Walter Payton	2.50	1.10	.30
☐ 13 Billy Sims	.40	.18	.05
☐ 14 James Jones	.20	.09	.03
☐ 15 Willie Davis	.40	.18	.05
☐ 16 Eddie Lee Ivery	.20	.09	.03
☐ 17 Fran Tarkenton	1.00	.45	.12
☐ 18 Alan Page	.40	.18	.05
☐ 19 Ricky Bell	.30	.14	.04
☐ 20 Cecil Johnson	.20	.09	.03
☐ 21 Bubba Bean	.20	.09	.03
☐ 22 Gerald Riggs	.20	.09	.03
☐ 23 Eric Dickerson and Barry Redden	.60	.25	.07
☐ 24 Jack Reynolds	.30	.14	.04
☐ 25 Archie Manning	.40	.18	.05
☐ 26 Wayne Wilson	.30	.14	.04
☐ 27 Dan Bunz and Pete Johnson	.20	.09	.03
☐ 28 Roger Craig	.60	.25	.07
☐ 29 O.J. Simpson	2.50	1.10	.30
☐ 30 Joe Cribbs	.30	.14	.04
☐ 31 Rick Volk and Leroy Kelly	.40	.18	.05
☐ 32 Earl Morrall	.30	.14	.04
☐ 33 Jim Kiick	.30	.14	.04
☐ 34 Dan Marino	5.00	2.20	.60
☐ 35 Craig James	.40	.18	.05
☐ 36 Julius Adams	.20	.09	.03
☐ 37 Joe Namath	3.00	1.35	.35
☐ 38 Freeman McNeil	.30	.14	.04
☐ 39 Pete Johnson	.20	.09	.03
☐ 40 Larry Kinnebrew	.20	.09	.03
☐ 41 Brian Sipe	.30	.14	.04
☐ 42 Kevin Mack and Earnest Byner	.30	.14	.04
☐ 43 Dan Pastorini	.30	.14	.04
☐ 44 Elvin Bethea and Carter Hartwig	.20	.09	.03
☐ 45 Fran Tarkenton and Jack Lambert	1.00	.45	.12
☐ 46 Terry Bradshaw	2.50	1.10	.30
☐ 47 Randy Gradishar and Steve Foley	.30	.14	.04
☐ 48 Sammy Winder	.20	.09	.03
☐ 49 Robert Holmes	.20	.09	.03
☐ 50 Buck Buchanan and Curley Culp	.40	.18	.05
☐ 51 Willie Jones and Cedrick Hardman	.20	.09	.03
☐ 52 Marcus Allen	.75	.35	.09
☐ 53 Dan Fouts and Don Macek	.60	.25	.07
☐ 54 Dan Fouts	1.25	.55	.16
☐ 55 Blair Bush	.20	.09	.03
☐ 56 Steve Largent	1.25	.55	.16
☐ NNO Play Book (Terry Bradshaw)	3.00	1.35	.35

1966 Jets Team Issue

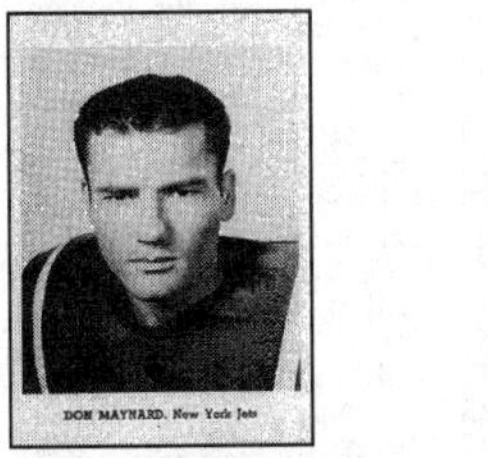

This nine-card set of the New York Jets measures approximately 5" by 7" and follow the usual team issue photo format. The fronts feature black-and-white player photos in traditional poses with the quarterback preparing to throw, the runner heading downfield, and the defenseman ready for the tackle. The backs are blank. The cards are unnumbered and checklisted below in alphabetical order.

	NRMT	VG-E	GOOD
COMPLETE SET (9)	100.00	45.00	12.50
COMMON CARD	5.00	2.20	.60
☐ 1 Ralph Baker	5.00	2.20	.60
☐ 2 Larry Grantham	7.50	3.40	.95
☐ 3 Bill Mathis	5.00	2.20	.60
☐ 4 Don Maynard	12.50	5.50	1.55
☐ 5 Joe Namath	50.00	22.00	6.25
☐ 6 Gerry Philbin	7.50	3.40	.95
☐ 7 Mark Smolinski	5.00	2.20	.60
☐ 8 Matt Snell	10.00	4.50	1.25
☐ 9 Bake Turner	5.00	2.20	.60

1969 Jets Tasco Prints

Tasco Associates produced this set of New York Jets prints. The fronts feature a large color artist's rendering of the player along with the player's name and position. The backs are blank. The prints measure approximately 11" by 16."

	NRMT-MT	EXC	G-VG
COMPLETE SET (6)	100.00	45.00	12.50
COMMON PRINT (1-6)	10.00	4.50	1.25
☐ 1 Winston Hill	10.00	4.50	1.25
☐ 2 Joe Namath	50.00	22.00	6.25
☐ 3 Gerry Philbin	12.00	5.50	1.50

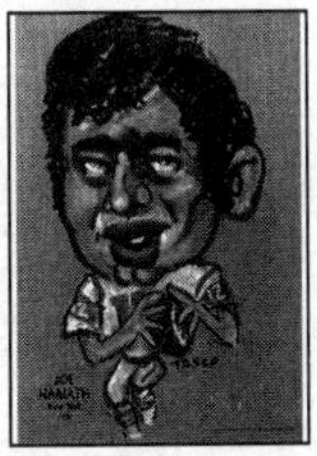

☐ 4 Johnny Sample	10.00	4.50	1.25
☐ 5 Matt Snell	10.00	4.50	1.25
☐ 6 Jim Turner	10.00	4.50	1.25

1981 Jets Police

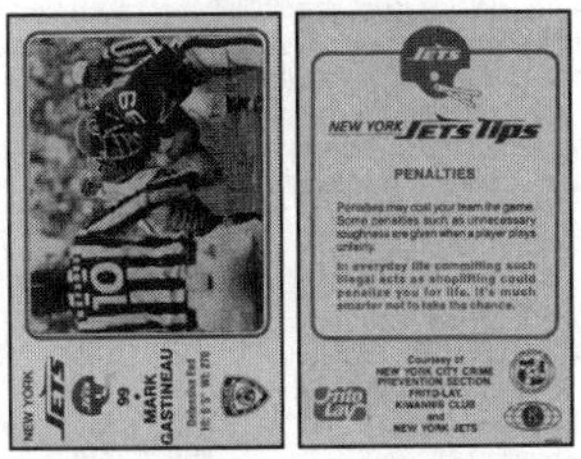

This unnumbered Police issue is complete at ten cards. Cards measure approximately 2 5/8" by 4 1/8" and have a green border around the photo on the front of the cards. The set was sponsored by New York City Crime Prevention Section, Frito-Lay, Kiwanis Club, and the New York Jets. The backs each contain a safety tip printed in red ink. The 1981 date is printed on the card backs. Apparently these Jets Police cards were printed on a sheet such that six of the cards were double printed and four of the cards were single printed. The single-printed cards, which are more difficult to find, are indicated below by SP.

	MINT	NRMT	EXC
COMPLETE SET (10)	25.00	11.00	3.10
COMMON CARD	1.25	.55	.16
☐ 14 Richard Todd SP	4.00	1.80	.50
☐ 42 Bruce Harper	1.25	.55	.16
☐ 51 Greg Buttle	1.25	.55	.16
☐ 73 Joe Klecko	2.50	1.10	.30
☐ 79 Marvin Powell	2.00	.90	.25
☐ 80 Johnny Lam Jones SP	3.50	1.55	.45
☐ 85 Wesley Walker SP	6.00	2.70	.75
☐ 93 Marty Lyons	2.50	1.10	.30
☐ 99 Mark Gastineau	2.50	1.10	.30
☐ NNO Team Effort SP	2.50	1.10	.30

1959 Kahn's

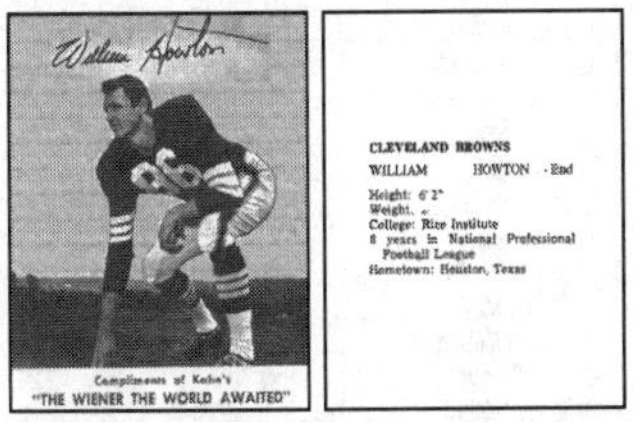

The 1959 Kahn's football set of 31 black and white cards features players from the Cleveland Browns and the Pittsburgh Steelers. The cards measure approximately 3 1/4" by 3 15/16". The backs contain height, weight and short football career data. The statistics on the back are single spaced. The cards are unnumbered and hence are listed below alphabetically for convenience.

	NRMT	VG-E	GOOD
COMPLETE SET (31)	1600.00	700.00	200.00
COMMON CARD (1-31)	35.00	16.00	4.40
☐ 1 Dick Alban	35.00	16.00	4.40
☐ 2 Jim Brown	400.00	180.00	50.00
☐ 3 Jack Butler	35.00	16.00	4.40
☐ 4 Lew Carpenter	35.00	16.00	4.40
☐ 5 Preston Carpenter	35.00	16.00	4.40
☐ 6 Vince Costello	35.00	16.00	4.40
☐ 7 Dale Dodrill	35.00	16.00	4.40
☐ 8 Bob Gain	40.00	18.00	5.00
☐ 9 Gary Glick	35.00	16.00	4.40
☐ 10 Lou Groza	75.00	34.00	9.50
☐ 11 Gene Hickerson	40.00	18.00	5.00
☐ 12 Bill Howton	40.00	18.00	5.00
☐ 13 Art Hunter	35.00	16.00	4.40
☐ 14 Joe Krupa	35.00	16.00	4.40
☐ 15 Bobby Layne	100.00	45.00	12.50
☐ 16 Joe Lewis	35.00	16.00	4.40
☐ 17 Jack McClairen	35.00	16.00	4.40
☐ 18 Mike McCormack	50.00	22.00	6.25
☐ 19 Walt Michaels	40.00	18.00	5.00
☐ 20 Bobby Mitchell	75.00	34.00	9.50
☐ 21 Jim Ninowski	35.00	16.00	4.40
☐ 22 Chuck Noll	150.00	70.00	19.00
☐ 23 Jimmy Orr	40.00	18.00	5.00
☐ 24 Milt Plum	40.00	18.00	5.00
☐ 25 Ray Renfro	40.00	18.00	5.00
☐ 26 Mike Sandusky	35.00	16.00	4.40
☐ 27 Billy Ray Smith	35.00	16.00	4.40
☐ 28 Jim Ray Smith	35.00	16.00	4.40
☐ 29 Ernie Stautner	60.00	27.00	7.50
☐ 30 Tom Tracy	40.00	18.00	5.00
☐ 31 Frank Varrichione	35.00	16.00	4.40

1960 Kahn's

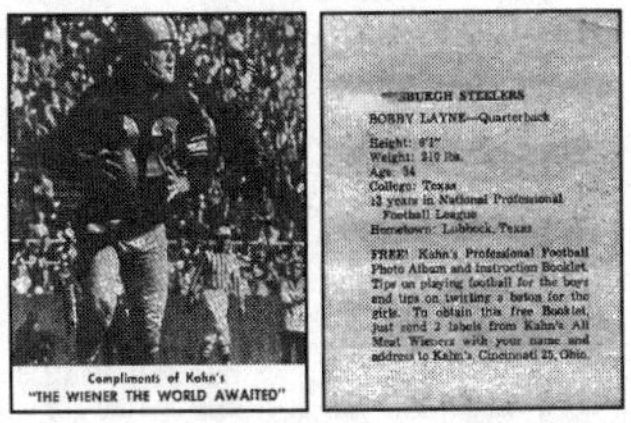

The 1960 Kahn's football set of 38 cards features Cleveland Browns and Pittsburgh Steelers. The cards measure approximately 3 1/4" by 3 15/16". In addition to data similar to the backs of the 1959 Kahn's cards, the backs of the 1960 Kahn's cards contain an ad for a free professional album and instruction booklet, which could be obtained by sending two labels to Kahn's. The cards are unnumbered and hence are listed below alphabetically for convenience. Willie Davis' card predates his 1964 Philadelphia Rookie Card by four years.

	NRMT	VG-E	GOOD
COMPLETE SET (38)	1400.00	650.00	180.00
COMMON CARD (1-38)	25.00	11.00	3.10
☐ 1 Sam Baker	25.00	11.00	3.10
☐ 2 Jim Brown	300.00	135.00	38.00
☐ 3 Ray Campbell	25.00	11.00	3.10
☐ 4 Preston Carpenter	25.00	11.00	3.10
☐ 5 Vince Costello	25.00	11.00	3.10
☐ 6 Willie Davis	75.00	34.00	9.50
☐ 7 Galen Fiss	25.00	11.00	3.10
☐ 8 Bob Gain	30.00	13.50	3.70
☐ 9 Lou Groza	60.00	27.00	7.50
☐ 10 Gene Hickerson	30.00	13.50	3.70
☐ 11 John Henry Johnson	50.00	22.00	6.25
☐ 12 Rich Kreitling	25.00	11.00	3.10
☐ 13 Joe Krupa	25.00	11.00	3.10
☐ 14 Bobby Layne	75.00	34.00	9.50
☐ 15 Jack McClairen	25.00	11.00	3.10
☐ 16 Mike McCormack	40.00	18.00	5.00
☐ 17 Walt Michaels	30.00	13.50	3.70
☐ 18 Bobby Mitchell	50.00	22.00	6.25
☐ 19 Dick Moegle	30.00	13.50	3.70
☐ 20 John Morrow	25.00	11.00	3.10
☐ 21 Gern Nagler	25.00	11.00	3.10
☐ 22 John Nisby	25.00	11.00	3.10
☐ 23 Jimmy Orr	30.00	13.50	3.70
☐ 24 Bernie Parrish	25.00	11.00	3.10
☐ 25 Milt Plum	35.00	16.00	4.40
☐ 26 John Reger	25.00	11.00	3.10
☐ 27 Ray Renfro	30.00	13.50	3.70
☐ 28 Will Renfro	25.00	11.00	3.10
☐ 29 Mike Sandusky	25.00	11.00	3.10
☐ 30 Dick Schafrath	25.00	11.00	3.10
☐ 31 Jim Ray Smith	25.00	11.00	3.10
☐ 32 Billy Ray Smith	30.00	13.50	3.70
☐ 33 Ernie Stautner	50.00	22.00	6.25
☐ 34 George Tarasovic	25.00	11.00	3.10
☐ 35 Tom Tracy	30.00	13.50	3.70
☐ 36 Frank Varrichione	25.00	11.00	3.10
☐ 37 John Wooten	25.00	11.00	3.10
☐ 38 Lowe W. Wren	25.00	11.00	3.10

1961 Kahn's

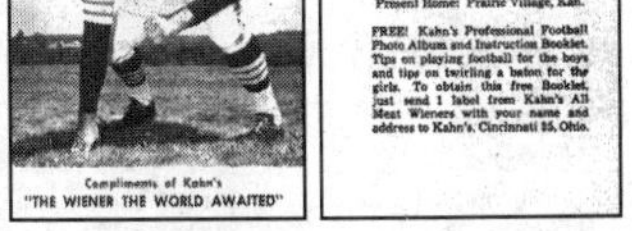

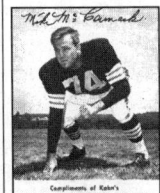

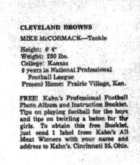

The 1961 Kahn's football set of 36 cards features Cleveland and Pittsburgh players. The cards measure approximately 3 1/4" by 4 1/16". The backs are the same as the 1960 Kahn's cards; however, the free booklet ad requires but one label to be sent in rather than the two labels required for the 1960 offer. Pictures of Larry Krutko and Tom Tracy are reversed. The cards are unnumbered and hence are listed below alphabetically for convenience.

	NRMT	VG-E	GOOD
COMPLETE SET (36)	1000.00	450.00	125.00
COMMON CARD (1-36)	20.00	9.00	2.50
☐ 1 Sam Baker	20.00	9.00	2.50
☐ 2 Jim Brown	250.00	110.00	31.00

☐ 3 Preston Carpenter	20.00	9.00	2.50
☐ 4 Vince Costello	20.00	9.00	2.50
☐ 5 Dean Derby	20.00	9.00	2.50
☐ 6 Buddy Dial	25.00	11.00	3.10
☐ 7 Don Fleming	20.00	9.00	2.50
☐ 8 Bob Gain	20.00	9.00	2.50
☐ 9 Bobby Joe Green	20.00	9.00	2.50
☐ 10 Gene Hickerson	25.00	11.00	3.10
☐ 11 Jim Houston	20.00	9.00	2.50
☐ 12 Dan James	20.00	9.00	2.50
☐ 13 John Henry Johnson	35.00	16.00	4.40
☐ 14 Rich Kreitling	20.00	9.00	2.50
☐ 15 Joe Krupa	20.00	9.00	2.50
☐ 16 Larry Krutko UER (Photo actually Tom Tracy)	20.00	9.00	2.50
☐ 17 Bobby Layne	60.00	27.00	7.50
☐ 18 Joe Lewis	20.00	9.00	2.50
☐ 19 Gene Lipscomb	40.00	18.00	5.00
☐ 20 Mike McCormack	30.00	13.50	3.70
☐ 21 Bobby Mitchell	40.00	18.00	5.00
☐ 22 John Morrow	20.00	9.00	2.50
☐ 23 John Nisby	20.00	9.00	2.50
☐ 24 Jimmy Orr	25.00	11.00	3.10
☐ 25 Milt Plum	25.00	11.00	3.10
☐ 26 John Reger	20.00	9.00	2.50
☐ 27 Ray Renfro	25.00	11.00	3.10
☐ 28 Will Renfro	20.00	9.00	2.50
☐ 29 Mike Sandusky	20.00	9.00	2.50
☐ 30 Dick Schafrath	20.00	9.00	2.50
☐ 31 Jim Ray Smith	20.00	9.00	2.50
☐ 32 Ernie Stautner	40.00	18.00	5.00
☐ 33 George Tarasovic	20.00	9.00	2.50
☐ 34 Tom Tracy UER (Photo actually Larry Krutko)	25.00	11.00	3.10
☐ 35 Frank Varrichione	20.00	9.00	2.50
☐ 36 John Wooten	20.00	9.00	2.50

1962 Kahn's

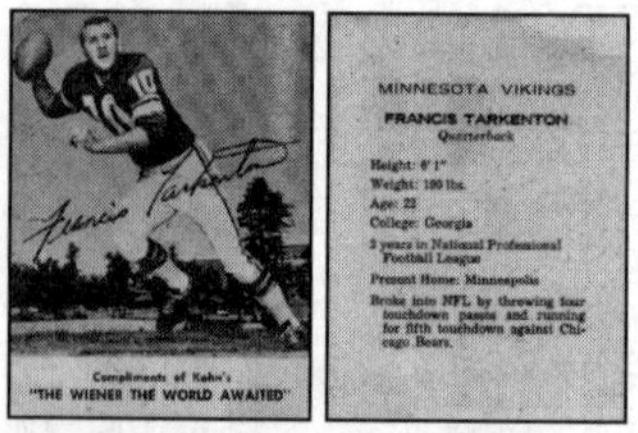

The 1962 Kahn's football card set contains 38 players from eight different teams. New teams added in this year's set are the Chicago Bears, Detroit Lions, and Minnesota Vikings. The cards measure approximately 3 1/4" by 4 3/16". The backs contain information comparable to the backs of previous years; however, the statistics are double spaced, and the player's name on the back is in bold-faced type. The cards are unnumbered and hence are listed below alphabetically for convenienece. One of the most interesting cards in this set is that of Fran Tarkenton; Kahn's issued one of the few Tarkenton cards available in 1962; his rookie year for cards.

	NRMT	VG-E	GOOD
COMPLETE SET (38)	1200.00	550.00	150.00
COMMON CARD (1-38)	20.00	9.00	2.50
☐ 1 Maxie Baughan	25.00	11.00	3.10
☐ 2 Charley Britt	20.00	9.00	2.50
☐ 3 Jim Brown	200.00	90.00	25.00
☐ 4 Preston Carpenter	20.00	9.00	2.50
☐ 5 Pete Case	20.00	9.00	2.50
☐ 6 Howard Cassady	30.00	13.50	3.70
☐ 7 Vince Costello	20.00	9.00	2.50
☐ 8 Buddy Dial	25.00	11.00	3.10
☐ 9 Gene Hickerson	25.00	11.00	3.10
☐ 10 Jim Houston	25.00	11.00	3.10
☐ 11 Dan James	20.00	9.00	2.50
☐ 12 Rich Kreitling	20.00	9.00	2.50
☐ 13 Joe Krupa	20.00	9.00	2.50
☐ 14 Bobby Layne	50.00	22.00	6.25
☐ 15 Ray Lemek	20.00	9.00	2.50
☐ 16 Gene Lipscomb	35.00	16.00	4.40
☐ 17 Dave Lloyd	20.00	9.00	2.50
☐ 18 Lou Michaels	25.00	11.00	3.10
☐ 19 Larry Morris	20.00	9.00	2.50
☐ 20 John Morrow	20.00	9.00	2.50
☐ 21 Jim Ninowski	20.00	9.00	2.50
☐ 22 Buzz Nutter	20.00	9.00	2.50
☐ 23 Jimmy Orr	25.00	11.00	3.10
☐ 24 Bernie Parrish	20.00	9.00	2.50
☐ 25 Milt Plum	25.00	11.00	3.10
☐ 26 Myron Pottios	20.00	9.00	2.50
☐ 27 John Reger	20.00	9.00	2.50
☐ 28 Ray Renfro	25.00	11.00	3.10
☐ 29 Frank Ryan	30.00	13.50	3.70
☐ 30 Johnny Sample	25.00	11.00	3.10
☐ 31 Mike Sandusky	20.00	9.00	2.50
☐ 32 Dick Schafrath	25.00	11.00	3.10
☐ 33 Jim Shofner	25.00	11.00	3.10
☐ 34 Jim Ray Smith	25.00	11.00	3.10
☐ 35 Ernie Stautner	35.00	16.00	4.40
☐ 36 Fran Tarkenton	250.00	110.00	31.00
☐ 37 Paul Wiggin	25.00	11.00	3.10
☐ 38 John Wooten	25.00	11.00	3.10

1963 Kahn's

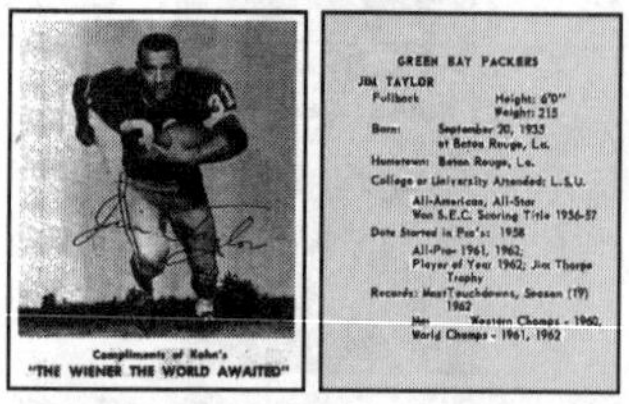

The 1963 Kahn's football card set includes players from six new teams not appearing in previous Kahn sets. All 14 NFL teams are represented in this set. The new teams are Dallas Cowboys, Green Bay Packers, New York Giants, St. Louis Cardinals, San Francisco 49ers and Washington Redskins. The cards measure approximately 3 1/4" by 4 3/16". The backs contain player statistics comparable to previous years; however, this set may be distinguished from Kahn's sets of other years because it is the only Kahn's football card set that has a distinct white border surrounding the picture on the obverse. With a total of 92 different cards, this is the largest Kahn's football issue. The cards are unnumbered and hence are listed below alphabetically for convenience.

	NRMT	VG-E	GOOD
COMPLETE SET (92)	2200.00	1000.00	275.00
COMMON CARD (1-92)	15.00	6.75	1.85
☐ 1 Bill Barnes	15.00	6.75	1.85
☐ 2 Erich Barnes	20.00	9.00	2.50
☐ 3 Dick Bass	20.00	9.00	2.50
☐ 4 Don Bosseler	15.00	6.75	1.85
☐ 5 Jim Brown	175.00	80.00	22.00
☐ 6 Roger Brown	15.00	6.75	1.85
☐ 7 Roosevelt Brown	25.00	11.00	3.10
☐ 8 Ron Bull	20.00	9.00	2.50
☐ 9 Preston Carpenter	15.00	6.75	1.85
☐ 10 Frank Clarke	20.00	9.00	2.50
☐ 11 Gail Cogdill	15.00	6.75	1.85
☐ 12 Bobby Joe Conrad	20.00	9.00	2.50
☐ 13 John David Crow	25.00	11.00	3.10
☐ 14 Dan Currie	15.00	6.75	1.85
☐ 15 Buddy Dial	18.00	8.00	2.20
☐ 16 Mike Ditka	100.00	45.00	12.50
☐ 17 Fred Dugan	15.00	6.75	1.85
☐ 18 Galen Fiss	15.00	6.75	1.85
☐ 19 Bill Forester	18.00	8.00	2.20
☐ 20 Bob Gain	15.00	6.75	1.85
☐ 21 Willie Galimore	20.00	9.00	2.50
☐ 22 Bill George	25.00	11.00	3.10
☐ 23 Frank Gifford	80.00	36.00	10.00
☐ 24 Bill Glass	18.00	8.00	2.20
☐ 25 Forrest Gregg	25.00	11.00	3.10
☐ 26 Fred Hageman	15.00	6.75	1.85
☐ 27 Jimmy Hill	15.00	6.75	1.85
☐ 28 Sam Huff	35.00	16.00	4.40
☐ 29 Dan James	15.00	6.75	1.85
☐ 30 John Henry Johnson	25.00	11.00	3.10
☐ 31 Sonny Jurgensen	40.00	18.00	5.00
☐ 32 Jim Katcavage	18.00	8.00	2.20
☐ 33 Ron Kostelnik	15.00	6.75	1.85
☐ 34 Jerry Kramer	25.00	11.00	3.10
☐ 35 Ron Kramer	18.00	8.00	2.20
☐ 36 Dick Lane	25.00	11.00	3.10
☐ 37 Yale Lary	25.00	11.00	3.10
☐ 38 Eddie LeBaron	25.00	11.00	3.10
☐ 39 Dick Lynch	15.00	6.75	1.85
☐ 40 Tommy Mason	20.00	9.00	2.50
☐ 41 Tommy McDonald	20.00	9.00	2.50
☐ 42 Lou Michaels	18.00	8.00	2.20
☐ 43 Bobby Mitchell	30.00	13.50	3.70
☐ 44 Dick Modzelewski	18.00	8.00	2.20
☐ 45 Lenny Moore	35.00	16.00	4.40
☐ 46 John Morrow	15.00	6.75	1.85
☐ 47 John Nisby	15.00	6.75	1.85
☐ 48 Ray Nitschke	40.00	18.00	5.00
☐ 49 Leo Nomellini	25.00	11.00	3.10
☐ 50 Jimmy Orr	20.00	9.00	2.50
☐ 51 John Paluck	15.00	6.75	1.85
☐ 52 Jim Parker	25.00	11.00	3.10
☐ 53 Bernie Parrish	15.00	6.75	1.85
☐ 54 Jim Patton	15.00	6.75	1.85
☐ 55 Don Perkins	25.00	11.00	3.10
☐ 56 Richie Petitbon	20.00	9.00	2.50
☐ 57 Jim Phillips	15.00	6.75	1.85
☐ 58 Nick Pietrosante	15.00	6.75	1.85
☐ 59 Milt Plum	20.00	9.00	2.50
☐ 60 Myron Pottios	15.00	6.75	1.85
☐ 61 Sonny Randle	20.00	9.00	2.50
☐ 62 John Reger	15.00	6.75	1.85
☐ 63 Ray Renfro	20.00	9.00	2.50
☐ 64 Pete Retzlaff	20.00	9.00	2.50
☐ 65 Pat Richter	18.00	8.00	2.20
☐ 66 Jim Ringo	25.00	11.00	3.10
☐ 67 Andy Robustelli	30.00	13.50	3.70
☐ 68 Joe Rutgens	15.00	6.75	1.85
☐ 69 Bob St. Clair	25.00	11.00	3.10
☐ 70 Johnny Sample	20.00	9.00	2.50
☐ 71 Lonnie Sanders	15.00	6.75	1.85
☐ 72 Dick Schafrath	15.00	6.75	1.85
☐ 73 Joe Schmidt	30.00	13.50	3.70
☐ 74 Del Shofner	20.00	9.00	2.50
☐ 75 J.D. Smith	15.00	6.75	1.85
☐ 76 Norm Snead	20.00	9.00	2.50
☐ 77 Bill Stacy	15.00	6.75	1.85
☐ 78 Bart Starr	60.00	27.00	7.50
☐ 79 Ernie Stautner	30.00	13.50	3.70
☐ 80 Jim Steffen	15.00	6.75	1.85
☐ 81 Andy Stynchula	15.00	6.75	1.85
☐ 82 Fran Tarkenton	90.00	40.00	11.00
☐ 83 Jim Taylor	40.00	18.00	5.00
☐ 84 Clendon Thomas	15.00	6.75	1.85
☐ 85 Fuzzy Thurston	25.00	11.00	3.10
☐ 86 Y.A. Tittle	60.00	27.00	7.50
☐ 87 Bob Toneff	15.00	6.75	1.85
☐ 88 Jerry Tubbs	20.00	9.00	2.50
☐ 89 Johnny Unitas	90.00	40.00	11.00
☐ 90 Bill Wade	20.00	9.00	2.50
☐ 91 Willie Wood	25.00	11.00	3.10
☐ 92 Abe Woodson	20.00	9.00	2.50

1964 Kahn's

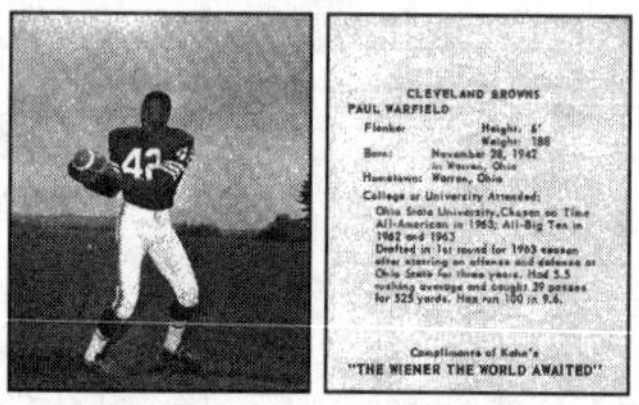

The 1964 Kahn's football card set of 53 is the only Kahn's football card set in full color. It is also the only set which does not contain the statement "Compliments of Kahn's, the Wiener the World Awaited" on the cardfront. This slogan is contained on the back of the card which also contains player data similar to cards of other years. The cards measure approximately 3" by 3 5/8". The cards are unnumbered and hence are listed below alphabetically for convenience. Paul Warfield's card holds special interest in that it was issued very early in his career.

	NRMT	VG-E	GOOD
COMPLETE SET (53)	1400.00	650.00	180.00
COMMON CARD (1-53)	15.00	6.75	1.85
☐ 1 Doug Atkins	25.00	11.00	3.10
☐ 2 Terry Barr	15.00	6.75	1.85
☐ 3 Dick Bass	20.00	9.00	2.50
☐ 4 Ordell Braase	15.00	6.75	1.85
☐ 5 Ed Brown	20.00	9.00	2.50
☐ 6 Jimmy Brown	150.00	70.00	19.00
☐ 7 Gary Collins	20.00	9.00	2.50
☐ 8 Bobby Joe Conrad	20.00	9.00	2.50
☐ 9 Mike Ditka	75.00	34.00	9.50
☐ 10 Galen Fiss	15.00	6.75	1.85
☐ 11 Paul Flatley	20.00	9.00	2.50
☐ 12 Joe Fortunato	20.00	9.00	2.50
☐ 13 Bill George	22.00	10.00	2.70
☐ 14 Bill Glass	20.00	9.00	2.50
☐ 15 Ernie Green	20.00	9.00	2.50
☐ 16 Dick Hoak	15.00	6.75	1.85
☐ 17 Paul Hornung	50.00	22.00	6.25
☐ 18 Sam Huff	30.00	13.50	3.70
☐ 19 Charlie Johnson	20.00	9.00	2.50
☐ 20 John Henry Johnson	25.00	11.00	3.10
☐ 21 Alex Karras	30.00	13.50	3.70
☐ 22 Jim Katcavage	20.00	9.00	2.50
☐ 23 Joe Krupa	15.00	6.75	1.85
☐ 24 Dick Lane	22.00	10.00	2.70
☐ 25 Tommy Mason	20.00	9.00	2.50
☐ 26 Don Meredith	70.00	32.00	8.75
☐ 27 Bobby Mitchell	25.00	11.00	3.10
☐ 28 Larry Morris	15.00	6.75	1.85
☐ 29 Jimmy Orr	20.00	9.00	2.50
☐ 30 Jim Parker	25.00	11.00	3.10
☐ 31 Bernie Parrish	15.00	6.75	1.85
☐ 32 Don Perkins	20.00	9.00	2.50
☐ 33 Jim Phillips	15.00	6.75	1.85
☐ 34 Sonny Randle	15.00	6.75	1.85
☐ 35 Pete Retzlaff	20.00	9.00	2.50
☐ 36 Jim Ringo	22.00	10.00	2.70
☐ 37 Frank Ryan	20.00	9.00	2.50
☐ 38 Dick Schafrath	15.00	6.75	1.85
☐ 39 Joe Schmidt	25.00	11.00	3.10
☐ 40 Del Shofner	20.00	9.00	2.50
☐ 41 J.D. Smith	15.00	6.75	1.85
☐ 42 Norm Snead	20.00	9.00	2.50
☐ 43 Bart Starr	50.00	22.00	6.25
☐ 44 Fran Tarkenton	70.00	32.00	8.75
☐ 45 Jim Taylor	30.00	13.50	3.70
☐ 46 Clendon Thomas	15.00	6.75	1.85
☐ 47 Y.A. Tittle	50.00	22.00	6.25
☐ 48 Jerry Tubbs	20.00	9.00	2.50
☐ 49 Johnny Unitas	75.00	34.00	9.50
☐ 50 Bill Wade	20.00	9.00	2.50
☐ 51 Paul Warfield	60.00	27.00	7.50
☐ 52 Alex Webster	20.00	9.00	2.50
☐ 53 Abe Woodson	15.00	6.75	1.85

1970 Kellogg's

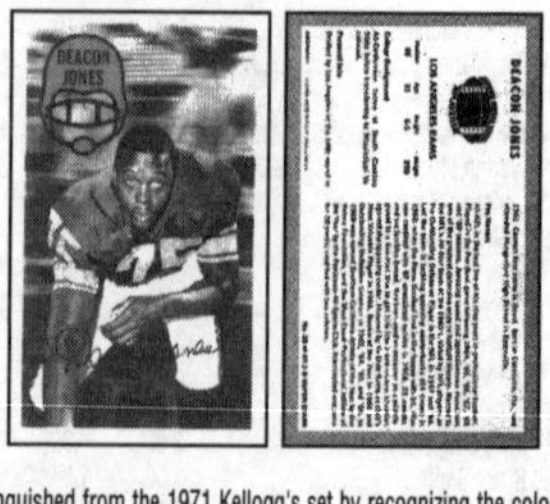

The 1970 Kellogg's football set of 60 cards was Kellogg's first football issue. The cards have a 3D effect and are approximately 2 1/4" by 3 1/2". The cards could be obtained from boxes of cereal or as a set from a box top offer. The 1970 Kellogg's set can easily be distinguished from the 1971 Kellogg's set by recognizing the color of the helmet logo on the front of each card. In the 1970 set this helmet logo is blue, whereas with the 1971 set the helmet logo is red. The 1971 set also is distinguished by its thick blue (with white spots) border on each card front as well as by the small inset photo in the upper left corner of each reverse. The key card in the set is O.J. Simpson as 1970 was O.J.'s rookie year for cards.

	NRMT-MT	EXC	G-VG
COMPLETE SET (60)	75.00	34.00	9.50
COMMON CARD (1-60)	.50	.23	.06
☐ 1 Carl Eller	1.25	.55	.16
☐ 2 Jim Otto	1.00	.45	.12
☐ 3 Tom Matte	.75	.35	.09
☐ 4 Bill Nelsen	.50	.23	.06
☐ 5 Travis Williams	.50	.23	.06
☐ 6 Len Dawson	3.00	1.35	.35
☐ 7 Gene Washington	.50	.23	.06
☐ 8 Jim Nance	.50	.23	.06
☐ 9 Norm Snead	.75	.35	.09
☐ 10 Dick Butkus	6.00	2.70	.75
☐ 11 George Sauer Jr.	.75	.35	.09
☐ 12 Billy Kilmer	.75	.35	.09
☐ 13 Alex Karras	2.50	1.10	.30
☐ 14 Larry Wilson	1.00	.45	.12
☐ 15 Dave Robinson	.50	.23	.06
☐ 16 Bill Brown	.50	.23	.06
☐ 17 Bob Griese	5.00	2.20	.60
☐ 18 Al Denson	.50	.23	.06
☐ 19 Dick Post	.50	.23	.06
☐ 20 Jan Stenerud	1.00	.45	.12
☐ 21 Paul Warfield	3.00	1.35	.35
☐ 22 Mel Farr	.50	.23	.06
☐ 23 Mel Renfro	1.00	.45	.12
☐ 24 Roy Jefferson	.50	.23	.06
☐ 25 Mike Garrett	.50	.23	.06
☐ 26 Harry Jacobs	.50	.23	.06
☐ 27 Carl Garrett	.50	.23	.06
☐ 28 Dave Wilcox	.50	.23	.06
☐ 29 Matt Snell	.75	.35	.09
☐ 30 Tom Woodeshick	.50	.23	.06
☐ 31 Leroy Kelly	1.25	.55	.16
☐ 32 Floyd Little	.75	.35	.09
☐ 33 Ken Willard	.50	.23	.06
☐ 34 John Mackey	1.25	.55	.16
☐ 35 Merlin Olsen	2.50	1.10	.30
☐ 36 Dave Grayson	.50	.23	.06
☐ 37 Lem Barney	2.00	.90	.25
☐ 38 Deacon Jones	2.00	.90	.25
☐ 39 Bob Hayes	1.25	.55	.16
☐ 40 Lance Alworth	3.00	1.35	.35
☐ 41 Larry Csonka	4.00	1.80	.50
☐ 42 Bobby Bell	1.50	.70	.19
☐ 43 George Webster	.50	.23	.06
☐ 44 Johnny Roland	.50	.23	.06
☐ 45 Dick Shiner	.50	.23	.06
☐ 46 Bubba Smith	2.00	.90	.25
☐ 47 Daryle Lamonica	.75	.35	.09
☐ 48 O.J. Simpson	25.00	11.00	3.10
☐ 49 Calvin Hill	1.00	.45	.12
☐ 50 Fred Biletnikoff	2.50	1.10	.30
☐ 51 Gale Sayers	6.00	2.70	.75
☐ 52 Homer Jones	.50	.23	.06
☐ 53 Sonny Jurgensen	3.00	1.35	.35
☐ 54 Bob Lilly	3.00	1.35	.35
☐ 55 Johnny Unitas	8.00	3.60	1.00
☐ 56 Tommy Nobis	1.00	.45	.12
☐ 57 Ed Meador	.50	.23	.06
☐ 58 Spider Lockhart	.50	.23	.06
☐ 59 Don Maynard	2.00	.90	.25
☐ 60 Greg Cook	.50	.23	.06

1971 Kellogg's

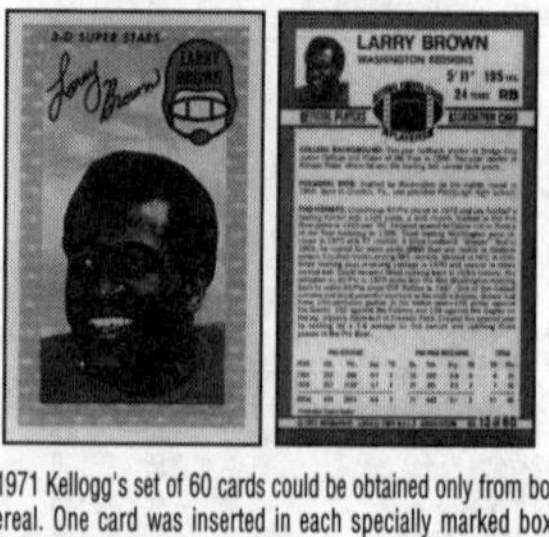

The 1971 Kellogg's set of 60 cards could be obtained only from boxes of cereal. One card was inserted in each specially marked box of Kellogg's Corn Flakes and Kellogg's Raisin Bran cereals. The cards measure approximately 2 1/4" by 3 1/2". This set is much more

difficult to obtain than the previous Kellogg's set since no box top offer was available. The 1971 Kellogg's set can easily be distinguished from the 1970 Kellogg's set by recognizing the color of the helmet logo on the front of each card. In the 1970 set this helmet logo is blue, whereas with the 1971 set the helmet logo is red. The 1971 set also is distinguished by its thick blue (with white spots) border on each card front as well as by the small inset photo in the uppper left corner of each reverse. Among the key cards in the set is Joe Greene as 1971 was "Mean" Joe's rookie year for cards.

	NRMT-MT	EXC	G-VG
COMPLETE SET (60)	350.00	160.00	45.00
COMMON CARD (1-60)	5.00	2.20	.60
□ 1 Tom Barrington	5.00	2.20	.60
□ 2 Chris Hanburger	6.00	2.70	.75
□ 3 Frank Nunley	5.00	2.20	.60
□ 4 Houston Antwine	5.00	2.20	.60
□ 5 Ron Johnson	6.00	2.70	.75
□ 6 Craig Morton	8.00	3.60	1.00
□ 7 Jack Snow	6.00	2.70	.75
□ 8 Mel Renfro	8.00	3.60	1.00
□ 9 Les Josephson	5.00	2.20	.60
□ 10 Gary Garrison	5.00	2.20	.60
□ 11 Dave Herman	5.00	2.20	.60
□ 12 Fred Dryer	8.00	3.60	1.00
□ 13 Larry Brown	7.00	3.10	.85
□ 14 Gene Washington	6.00	2.70	.75
□ 15 Joe Greene	20.00	9.00	2.50
□ 16 Marlin Briscoe	5.00	2.20	.60
□ 17 Bob Grant	5.00	2.20	.60
□ 18 Dan Conners	5.00	2.20	.60
□ 19 Mike Curtis	6.00	2.70	.75
□ 20 Harry Schuh	5.00	2.20	.60
□ 21 Rich Jackson	5.00	2.20	.60
□ 22 Clint Jones	5.00	2.20	.60
□ 23 Hewritt Dixon	5.00	2.20	.60
□ 24 Jess Phillips	5.00	2.20	.60
□ 25 Gary Cuozzo	5.00	2.20	.60
□ 26 Bo Scott	5.00	2.20	.60
□ 27 Glen Ray Hines	5.00	2.20	.60
□ 28 Johnny Unitas	25.00	11.00	3.10
□ 29 John Gilliam	5.00	2.20	.60
□ 30 Harmon Wages	5.00	2.20	.60
□ 31 Walt Sweeney	5.00	2.20	.60
□ 32 Bruce Taylor	5.00	2.20	.60
□ 33 George Blanda	20.00	9.00	2.50
□ 34 Ken Bowman	5.00	2.20	.60
□ 35 Johnny Robinson	6.00	2.70	.75
□ 36 Ed Podolak	5.00	2.20	.60
□ 37 Curley Culp	5.00	2.20	.60
□ 38 Jim Hart	7.00	3.10	.85
□ 39 Dick Butkus	22.00	10.00	2.70
□ 40 Floyd Little	7.00	3.10	.85
□ 41 Nick Buoniconti	8.00	3.60	1.00
□ 42 Larry Smith	5.00	2.20	.60
□ 43 Wayne Walker	6.00	2.70	.75
□ 44 MacArthur Lane	5.00	2.20	.60
□ 45 John Brodie	12.00	5.50	1.50
□ 46 Dick LeBeau	5.00	2.20	.60
□ 47 Claude Humphrey	5.00	2.20	.60
□ 48 Jerry LeVias	5.00	2.20	.60
□ 49 Erich Barnes	5.00	2.20	.60
□ 50 Andy Russell	6.00	2.70	.75
□ 51 Donny Anderson	6.00	2.70	.75
□ 52 Mike Reid	8.00	3.60	1.00
□ 53 Al Atkinson	5.00	2.20	.60
□ 54 Tom Dempsey	5.00	2.20	.60
□ 55 Bob Griese	20.00	9.00	2.50
□ 56 Dick Gordon	5.00	2.20	.60
□ 57 Charlie Sanders	6.00	2.70	.75
□ 58 Doug Cunningham	5.00	2.20	.60
□ 59 Cyril Pinder	5.00	2.20	.60
□ 60 Dave Osborn	5.00	2.20	.60

1978 Kellogg's Stickers

These stickers measure approximately 2 1/2" by 2 5/8". The fronts feature color team helmets with the team's name below. The backs carry a short team history and a quiz about referee's signals. The stickers are numbered on the back "X of 28."

	NRMT-MT	EXC	G-VG
COMPLETE SET (28)	30.00	13.50	3.70
COMMON CARD (1-28)	1.00	.45	.12
□ 1 Atlanta Falcons	1.00	.45	.12
□ 2 Baltimore Colts	1.00	.45	.12
□ 3 Buffalo Bills	1.00	.45	.12
□ 4 Chicago Bears	1.00	.45	.12
□ 5 Cincinnati Bengals	1.00	.45	.12
□ 6 Cleveland Browns	1.00	.45	.12
□ 7 Dallas Cowboys	1.50	.70	.19
□ 8 Denver Broncos	1.00	.45	.12
□ 9 Detroit Lions	1.00	.45	.12
□ 10 Green Bay Packers	1.00	.45	.12
□ 11 Houston Oilers	1.00	.45	.12
□ 12 Kansas City Chiefs	1.00	.45	.12
□ 13 Los Angeles Rams	1.00	.45	.12
□ 14 Miami Dolphins	1.50	.70	.19
□ 15 Minnesota Vikings	1.00	.45	.12
□ 16 New England Patriots	1.00	.45	.12
□ 17 New Orleans Saints	1.00	.45	.12
□ 18 New York Giants	1.00	.45	.12
□ 19 New York Jets	1.00	.45	.12
□ 20 Oakland Raiders	1.50	.70	.19
□ 21 Philadelphia Eagles	1.00	.45	.12
□ 22 Pittsburgh Steelers	1.50	.70	.19
□ 23 St. Louis Cardinals	1.00	.45	.12
□ 24 San Diego Chargers	1.00	.45	.12
□ 25 San Francisco 49ers	1.50	.70	.19
□ 26 Seattle Seahawks	1.00	.45	.12
□ 27 Tampa Bay Buccaneers	1.00	.45	.12
□ 28 Washington Redskins	1.50	.70	.19

1982 Kellogg's Panels

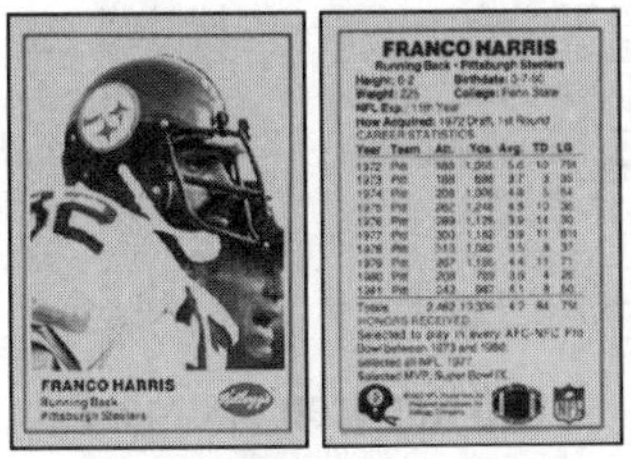

The 1982 Kellogg's National Football League set of 24 cards was issued in eight panels of three cards each. The cards measure 2 1/2" by 3 1/2" and the panels are approximately 4 1/8" by 7 1/2". The cards came with Kellogg's Raisin Bran cereal and contain statistics on the back. Cards are in color and contain the Kellogg's logo in the lower right corner of the front of the card. While not numbered, the cards have been listed in the checklist below alphabetically according to the left hand side player, when the panel is viewed from the front. Prices below are for full panels of three. It is possible (but not recommended) to separate the cards at the perforation marks. No value for individual cards is given. Sharp-eyed Cowboy fans will notice that the photos for Harvey Martin and Billy Joe DuPree were erroneously switched.

	MINT	NRMT	EXC
COMPLETE SET (8)	8.00	3.60	1.00
COMMON PANEL (1-8)	1.00	.45	.12
□ 1 Ken Anderson Frank Lewis Gifford Nielsen	1.00	.45	.12
□ 2 Ottis Anderson Cris Collinsworth Franco Harris	2.00	.90	.25
□ 3 William Andrews Brian Sipe Fred Smerlas	1.00	.45	.12
□ 4 Steve Bartkowski Robert Brazile Jack Rudnay	1.00	.45	.12
□ 5 Tony Dorsett Eric Hipple Pat McInally	2.00	.90	.25
□ 6 Billy Joe DuPree UER (Photo actually Harvey Martin) David Hill John Stallworth	1.25	.55	.16
□ 7 Harvey Martin UER (Photo actually Billy Joe DuPree) Mike Pruitt Joe Senser	1.00	.45	.12
□ 8 Art Still Mel Gray Tommy Kramer	1.00	.45	.12

1982 Kellogg's Teams

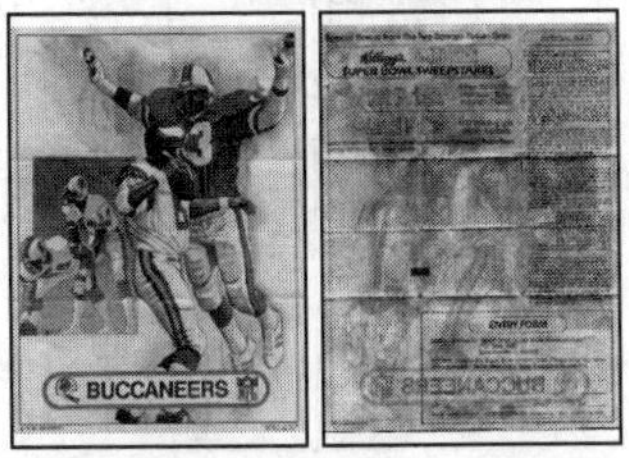

These 28 NFL team posters were inserted in specially marked boxes of Kellogg's Raisin Bran cereal. Each poster measures approximately 8" by 10 1/2" and is printed on thin paper stock. Inside a thin black border, the fronts feature a color painting of an action scene, with a smaller painting of another scene placed over to the side. The team name appears inside a bar at the bottom of the picture. The back carries the official contest rules and an entry form for the Kellogg's "Raisin Bran Super Bowl Sweepstakes". If the team pictured on the poster was the winning team in the 1983 Super Bowl, the collector was to print his name and address on the entry form and mail in the entire poster so that it would be received between January 30 and March 19, 1983. From the entries, the winners would be selected in a random drawing to receive one of four trips for two to the 1984 Super Bowl (1st prize) or one of 500 Spalding leather footballs (2nd prize). The posters are unnumbered and checklisted below alphabetically according to the team's city name. The NFL properties logo is prominently displayed on the card front. The posters are typically found with fold marks as they were folded into three parts both horizontally and vertically. The posters are copyrighted 1982 on the front. No players are explicitly identified on the cards. The poster backs are printed in light blue ink.

	MINT	NRMT	EXC
COMPLETE SET (28)	125.00	55.00	15.50
COMMON TEAM (1-28)	6.00	2.70	.75
□ 1 Atlanta Falcons	6.00	2.70	.75
□ 2 Buffalo Bills	6.00	2.70	.75
□ 3 Chicago Bears	6.00	2.70	.75
□ 4 Cincinnati Bengals	6.00	2.70	.75
□ 5 Cleveland Browns	6.00	2.70	.75
□ 6 Dallas Cowboys	7.50	3.40	.95
□ 7 Denver Broncos	6.00	2.70	.75
□ 8 Detroit Lions	6.00	2.70	.75
□ 9 Green Bay Packers	6.00	2.70	.75
□ 10 Houston Oilers	6.00	2.70	.75
□ 11 Indianapolis Colts	6.00	2.70	.75
□ 12 Kansas City Chiefs	6.00	2.70	.75
□ 13 Los Angeles Raiders	7.50	3.40	.95
□ 14 Los Angeles Rams	6.00	2.70	.75
□ 15 Miami Dolphins	7.50	3.40	.95
□ 16 Minnesota Vikings	6.00	2.70	.75
□ 17 New England Patriots	6.00	2.70	.75
□ 18 New Orleans Saints	6.00	2.70	.75
□ 19 New York Giants	6.00	2.70	.75
□ 20 New York Jets	6.00	2.70	.75
□ 21 Philadelphia Eagles	6.00	2.70	.75
□ 22 Pittsburgh Steelers	7.50	3.40	.95
□ 23 St. Louis Cardinals	6.00	2.70	.75
□ 24 San Diego Chargers	6.00	2.70	.75
□ 25 San Francisco 49ers	7.50	3.40	.95
□ 26 Seattle Seahawks	6.00	2.70	.75
□ 27 Tampa Bay Buccaneers	6.00	2.70	.75
□ 28 Washington Redskins WIN	12.00	5.50	1.50

1989 King B Discs

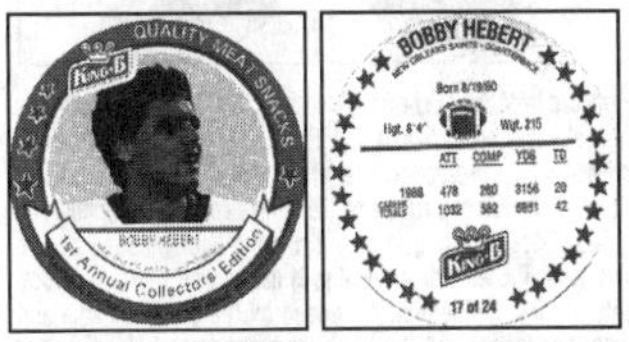

The 1989 King B Football Discs set has 24 red-bordered 2 3/8" diameter round discs. The fronts have helmetless color mug shots; the backs are white and have sparse bio and stats. One disc was included in each specially marked can of King B beef jerky. The discs are numbered on the back. The set is arranged alphabetically by teams, one player per team, with only 24 of the 28 NFL teams represented. The set, which was produced by Michael Schechter Associates, was apparently endorsed only by the NFLPA. There are many quarterbacks included in the set. The discs are referred to as "1st Annual Collectors Edition." It has been estimated that 500,000 total discs were produced for this issue.

	MINT	NRMT	EXC
COMPLETE SET (24)	50.00	22.00	6.25
COMMON CARD (1-24)	1.00	.45	.12
□ 1 Chris Miller	2.00	.90	.25
□ 2 Shane Conlan	1.50	.70	.19
□ 3 Richard Dent	1.50	.70	.19
□ 4 Boomer Esiason	1.50	.70	.19
□ 5 Frank Minnifield	1.50	.70	.19
□ 6 Herschel Walker	2.00	.90	.25
□ 7 Karl Mecklenburg	1.50	.70	.19
□ 8 Mike Cofer	1.00	.45	.12
□ 9 Warren Moon	2.00	.90	.25
□ 10 Chris Chandler	2.00	.90	.25
□ 11 Deron Cherry	1.50	.70	.19
□ 12 Bo Jackson	2.00	.90	.25
□ 13 Jim Everett	2.00	.90	.25
□ 14 Dan Marino	20.00	9.00	2.50
□ 15 Anthony Carter	2.00	.90	.25
□ 16 Andre Tippett	1.50	.70	.19
□ 17 Bobby Hebert	1.50	.70	.19
□ 18 Phil Simms	1.50	.70	.19
□ 19 Al Toon	1.50	.70	.19
□ 20 Gary Anderson RB	1.00	.45	.12
□ 21 Joe Montana	12.00	5.50	1.50
□ 22 Dave Krieg	1.50	.70	.19
□ 23 Randall Cunningham	1.50	.70	.19
□ 24 Bubby Brister	1.50	.70	.19

1990 King B Discs

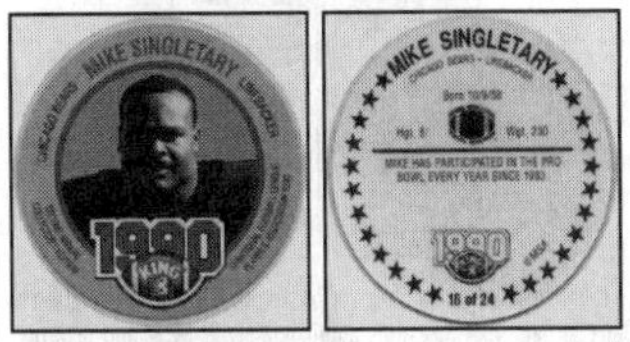

The 1990 King B Discs set contains 24 discs each measuring approximately 2 3/8" in diameter. The fronts have color head shots of the players (without helmets), encircled by a red border on a yellow background. The year "1990" in green block lettering and a King B football icon overlay the bottom of the picture. On the backs, the biographical and statistical information is encircled by a ring of stars. The style of the set is very similar to the previous year.

	MINT	NRMT	EXC
COMPLETE SET (24)	50.00	22.00	6.25
COMMON CARD (1-24)	1.00	.45	.12
□ 1 Jim Everett	1.50	.70	.19
□ 2 Marcus Allen	2.00	.90	.25
□ 3 Brian Blades	1.50	.70	.19
□ 4 Bubby Brister	1.50	.70	.19
□ 5 Mark Carrier WR	1.50	.70	.19
□ 6 Steve Jordan	1.50	.70	.19
□ 7 Barry Sanders	10.00	4.50	1.25
□ 8 Ronnie Lott	1.50	.70	.19
□ 9 Howie Long	2.00	.90	.25
□ 10 Steve Atwater	1.50	.70	.19
□ 11 Dan Marino	16.00	7.25	2.00
□ 12 Boomer Esiason	1.50	.70	.19
□ 13 Dalton Hilliard	1.00	.45	.12
□ 14 Phil Simms	1.50	.70	.19
□ 15 Jim Kelly	2.00	.90	.25
□ 16 Mike Singletary	1.50	.70	.19
□ 17 John Stephens	1.00	.45	.12
□ 18 Christian Okoye	1.50	.70	.19
□ 19 Art Monk	2.00	.90	.25
□ 20 Chris Miller	2.00	.90	.25
□ 21 Roger Craig	1.50	.70	.19
□ 22 Duane Bickett	1.00	.45	.12
□ 23 Don Majkowski	1.50	.70	.19
□ 24 Eric Metcalf	2.00	.90	.25

1991 King B Discs

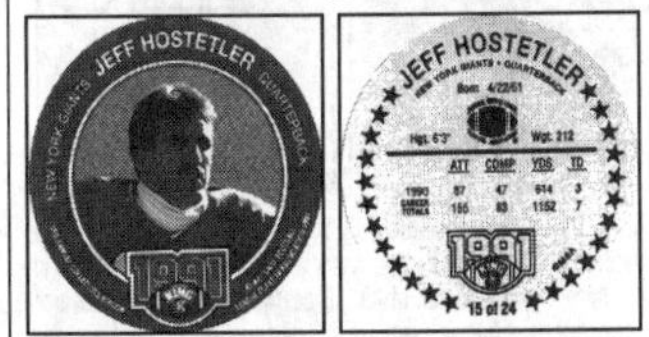

This set of 24 discs was produced by Michael Schechter Associates, and each one measures approximately 2 5/8" in diameter. One disc was included in each specially marked can of King B beef jerky. The front features a head shot of the player, his name, position, and team name printed in gold in the magenta border. The year and the King B logo are printed at the base of each picture. The circular backs are printed in scarlet and carry biographical and statistical information encircled by stars.

	MINT	NRMT	EXC
COMPLETE SET (24)	35.00	16.00	4.40
COMMON CARD (1-24)	1.00	.45	.12
□ 1 Mark Rypien	1.25	.55	.16
□ 2 Art Monk	1.25	.55	.16
□ 3 Sean Jones	1.25	.55	.16
□ 4 Bubby Brister	1.25	.55	.16
□ 5 Warren Moon	1.50	.70	.19
□ 6 Andre Rison	1.50	.70	.19
□ 7 Emmitt Smith	10.00	4.50	1.25
□ 8 Mervyn Fernandez	1.00	.45	.12
□ 9 Rickey Jackson	1.25	.55	.16
□ 10 Bruce Armstrong	1.00	.45	.12
□ 11 Neal Anderson	1.25	.55	.16
□ 12 Christian Okoye	1.25	.55	.16
□ 13 Thurman Thomas	1.50	.70	.19
□ 14 Bruce Smith	1.50	.70	.19
□ 15 Jeff Hostetler	1.25	.55	.16
□ 16 Barry Sanders	6.00	2.70	.75
□ 17 Andre Reed	1.50	.70	.19
□ 18 Derrick Thomas	1.50	.70	.19
□ 19 Jim Everett	1.25	.55	.16
□ 20 Boomer Esiason	1.25	.55	.16
□ 21 Merril Hoge	1.00	.45	.12
□ 22 Steve Atwater	1.00	.45	.12
□ 23 Dan Marino	10.00	4.50	1.25
□ 24 Mark Collins	1.00	.45	.12

1992 King B Discs

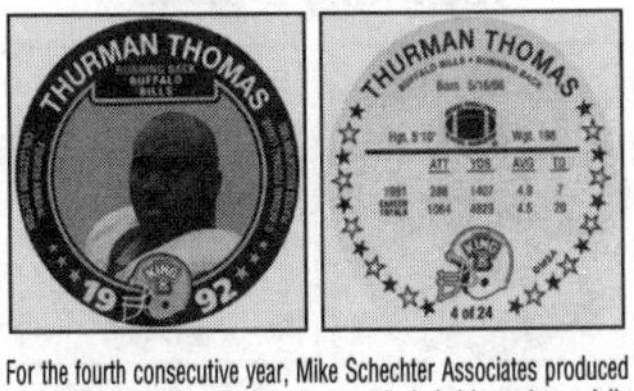

For the fourth consecutive year, Mike Schechter Associates produced a 24-disc set for King B. One disc was included in each specially marked can of King B beef jerky. The discs measure approximately 2 3/8" in diameter. The fronts feature posed color player photos edged by a bright yellow border on a black face. The player's name appears in white at the top with his position and team name immediately below. The year in white block lettering and a bright yellow King B helmet icon are at the base of the picture. The backs are white with black print, and they carry biography, statistics, the player's name, and the King B helmet icon. The left and right edges are detailed with solid black and black outline stars.

	MINT	NRMT	EXC
COMPLETE SET (24)	20.00	9.00	2.50
COMMON CARD (1-24)	.75	.35	.09
☐ 1 Derrick Thomas	1.25	.55	.16
☐ 2 Wilber Marshall	.75	.35	.09
☐ 3 Andre Rison	1.25	.55	.16
☐ 4 Thurman Thomas	1.25	.55	.16
☐ 5 Emmitt Smith	6.00	2.70	.75
☐ 6 Charles Mann	.75	.35	.09
☐ 7 Michael Irvin	1.25	.55	.16
☐ 8 Jim Everett	1.00	.45	.12
☐ 9 Gary Anderson RB	.75	.35	.09
☐ 10 Trace Armstrong	.75	.35	.09
☐ 11 John Elway	3.00	1.35	.35
☐ 12 Chip Lohmiller	.75	.35	.09
☐ 13 Bobby Hebert	1.00	.45	.12
☐ 14 Cornelius Bennett	1.00	.45	.12
☐ 15 Chris Miller	1.00	.45	.12
☐ 16 Warren Moon	1.25	.55	.16
☐ 17 Charles Haley	1.00	.45	.12
☐ 18 Mark Rypien	1.00	.45	.12
☐ 19 Darrell Green	.75	.35	.09
☐ 20 Barry Sanders	4.00	1.80	.50
☐ 21 Rodney Hampton	1.25	.55	.16
☐ 22 Shane Conlan	.75	.35	.09
☐ 23 Jerry Ball	.75	.35	.09
☐ 24 Morten Andersen	.75	.35	.09

1993 King B Discs

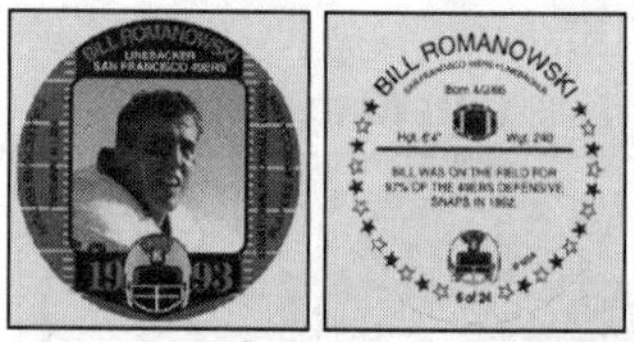

This Fifth Annual Collectors Edition of the King B Discs set was produced by Michael Schechter Associates. One disc was included in each specially marked can of King B beef jerky. Each disc measures approximately 2 3/8" in diameter and features on its front a posed color player head shot bordered on the sides by a green gridiron design. The player's name, position, and team appear in orange and white lettering within the black margin above the photo. The year of the set, 1993, and a blue football helmet icon bearing the King B logo rest in the black margin at the bottom. The backs are white with black print, and they carry the player's name, team, position, biography, statistics (or highlights), and the King B helmet icon. The left and right edges are detailed with solid black and black outline stars. This set was also issued in an uncut sheet measuring 17 1/4" by 12 3/4".

	MINT	NRMT	EXC
COMPLETE SET (24)	20.00	9.00	2.50
COMMON CARD (1-24)	.75	.35	.09
☐ 1 Luis Sharpe	.75	.35	.09
☐ 2 Erik McMillan	.75	.35	.09
☐ 3 Chris Doleman	1.00	.45	.12
☐ 4 Cortez Kennedy	1.00	.45	.12
☐ 5 Howie Long	1.00	.45	.12
☐ 6 Bill Romanowski	.75	.35	.09
☐ 7 Andre Tippett	.75	.35	.09
☐ 8 Simon Fletcher	.75	.35	.09
☐ 9 Derrick Thomas	1.25	.55	.16
☐ 10 Rodney Peete	1.00	.45	.12
☐ 11 Ronnie Lott	1.00	.45	.12
☐ 12 Duane Bickett	.75	.35	.09
☐ 13 Steve Walsh	1.00	.45	.12
☐ 14 Stan Humphries	1.25	.55	.16
☐ 15 Jeff George	1.50	.70	.19
☐ 16 Jay Novacek	1.25	.55	.16
☐ 17 Andre Reed	1.25	.55	.16
☐ 18 Andre Rison	1.25	.55	.16
☐ 19 Emmitt Smith	5.00	2.20	.60
☐ 20 Neal Anderson	1.00	.45	.12
☐ 21 Ricky Sanders	.75	.35	.09
☐ 22 Thurman Thomas	1.25	.55	.16
☐ 23 Lorenzo White	1.00	.45	.12
☐ 24 Barry Foster	1.00	.45	.12

1994 King B Discs

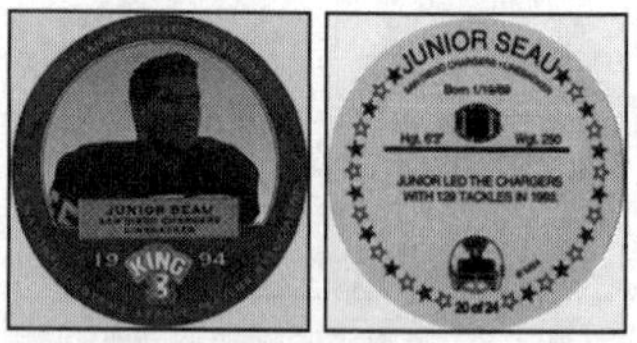

Produced by Michael Schechter Associates, this was the Sixth Annual Collectors Edition of 1994 King B discs. One disc was included in each specially-marked can of King B beef jerky. The discs measure approximately 2 3/8" in diameter. On a green background, the fronts feature posed color closeups. The player's name, position and the team name appear inside a yellow ochre bar across the bottom part of the photo. The year 1994 and the King B logo are below. The backs are white with green print and carry player biography and statistics. The discs are basically arranged alphabetically and numbered on the back as "X of 24."

	MINT	NRMT	EXC
COMPLETE SET (24)	20.00	9.00	2.50
COMMON CARD (1-24)	.75	.35	.09
☐ 1 Marcus Allen	1.25	.55	.16
☐ 2 Jerome Bettis	1.50	.70	.19
☐ 3 Terrell Buckley	.75	.35	.09
☐ 4 Craig Erickson	.75	.35	.09
☐ 5 Brett Favre	6.00	2.70	.75
☐ 6 Barry Foster	.75	.35	.09
☐ 7 Irving Fryar	1.00	.45	.12
☐ 8 Gary Brown	.75	.35	.09
☐ 9 Rodney Hampton	1.00	.45	.12
☐ 10 Qadry Ismail	1.25	.55	.16
☐ 11 Jim Jeffcoat	.75	.35	.09
☐ 12 Jim Lachey	.75	.35	.09
☐ 13 Natrone Means	1.50	.70	.19
☐ 14 Tony Meola	1.00	.45	.12
☐ 15 Pete Metzelaars	.75	.35	.09
☐ 16 Scott Mitchell	1.25	.55	.16
☐ 17 Ronald Moore	.75	.35	.09
☐ 18 Andre Rison	1.25	.55	.16
☐ 19 Jay Schroeder	.75	.35	.09
☐ 20 Junior Seau	1.25	.55	.16
☐ 21 Shannon Sharpe	1.00	.45	.12
☐ 22 Sterling Sharpe	1.00	.45	.12
☐ 23 Tim Brown	1.00	.45	.12
☐ 24 Chris Warren	1.25	.55	.16

1995 King-B Discs

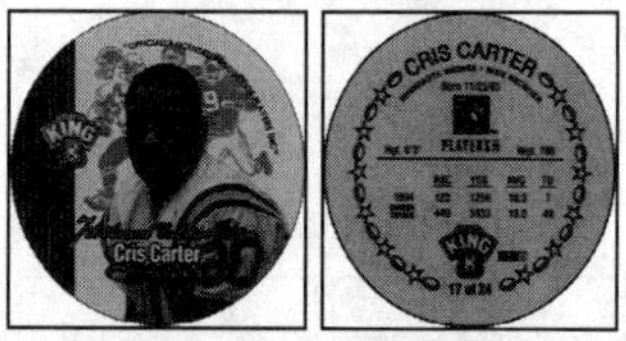

Produced by Michael Schechter Associates, the "7th Annual Collectors Edition" was issued both as a 17 1/4" by 12 1/2" collector sheet and as individual discs in shredded beef jerky containers. The discs measure 2 5/8" in diameter and feature on their fronts color closeup photos on a white back picturing in gray a running back pursued by two defenders. The left side of the disc is dark brown with thin vertical gold stripes. Inside a circle formed by the player's name and alternating football and star icons, the backs present biography and statistics. The discs are numbered on the back "X of 24."

	MINT	NRMT	EXC
COMPLETE SET (24)	15.00	6.75	1.85
COMMON DISC (1-24)	.60	.25	.07
☐ 1 Errict Rhett	1.50	.70	.19
☐ 2 Andre Reed	.75	.35	.09
☐ 3 Rodney Hampton	1.00	.45	.12
☐ 4 Kevin Greene	1.00	.45	.12
☐ 5 Merton Hanks	.60	.25	.07
☐ 6 Jerome Bettis	1.00	.45	.12
☐ 7 Johnny Johnson	.75	.35	.09
☐ 8 Ricky Watters	1.00	.45	.12
☐ 9 Harvey Williams	.75	.35	.09
☐ 10 Mel Gray	.75	.35	.09
☐ 11 Craig Erickson	.75	.35	.09
☐ 12 Stan Humphries	.75	.35	.09
☐ 13 Natrone Means	1.00	.45	.12
☐ 14 Terance Mathis	.75	.35	.09
☐ 15 Ken Harvey	.60	.25	.07
☐ 16 Brian Mitchell	.75	.35	.09
☐ 17 Cris Carter	1.00	.45	.12
☐ 18 Tim Brown	1.00	.45	.12
☐ 19 Marshall Faulk	1.50	.70	.19
☐ 20 Eric Turner	.75	.35	.09
☐ 21 Terry Allen	.75	.35	.09
☐ 22 Chris Warren	1.00	.45	.12
☐ 23 Randy Baldwin	.60	.25	.07
☐ 24 Ben Coates	1.00	.45	.12

1989 Knudsen Raiders

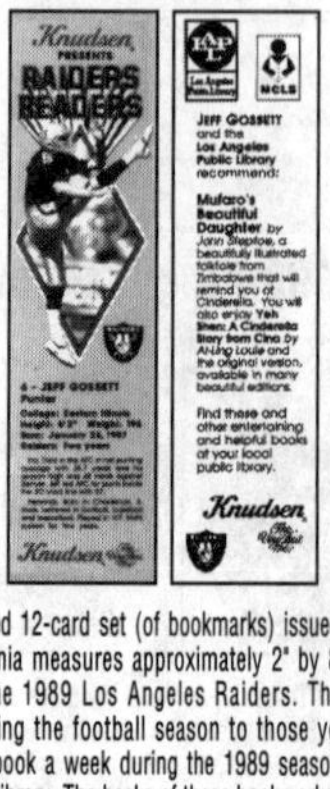

This unnumbered 12-card set (of bookmarks) issued by Knudsen's Dairy in California measures approximately 2" by 8" and features members of the 1989 Los Angeles Raiders. These sets were distributed during the football season to those youngsters who checked out a book a week during the 1989 season from the Los Angeles Public Library. The backs of these bookmarks feature various reading tips for the youth to follow. The set is checklisted below by player's uniform number. The Shanahan card was apparently undistributed or withdrawn after he left the team.

	MINT	NRMT	EXC
COMPLETE SET (14)	35.00	16.00	4.40
COMMON CARD	2.00	.90	.25
☐ 6 Jeff Gossett	2.00	.90	.25
☐ 13 Jay Schroeder	2.50	1.10	.30
☐ 26 Vann McElroy	2.00	.90	.25
☐ 35 Steve Smith	2.50	1.10	.30
☐ 36 Terry McDaniel	2.50	1.10	.30
☐ 70 Scott Davis	2.00	.90	.25
☐ 72 Don Mosebar	2.00	.90	.25
☐ 75 Howie Long	3.00	1.35	.35
☐ 76 Steve Wisniewski	2.50	1.10	.30
☐ 81 Tim Brown	5.00	2.20	.60
☐ 83 Willie Gault	2.50	1.10	.30
☐ NNO Mike Shanahan SP CO	15.00	6.75	1.85
☐ NNO Raiders/Super Bowl	2.00	.90	.25
☐ NNO Raiderettes SP	3.00	1.35	.35

1990 Knudsen Chargers

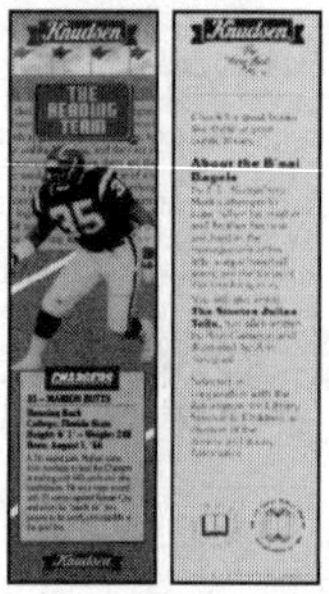

This six-card set (of bookmarks) which measures approximately 2" by 8" was produced by Knudsen's to help promote readership by people under 15 years old in the San Diego area. They were given out in San Diego libraries on a weekly basis. The set was sponsored by Knudsen, American Library Association, and the San Diego Public Library. Between the Knudsen company name, the front features a color action photo of the player superimposed on a football stadium. The field is green, the bleachers are yellow with gray print, and the scoreboard above the player reads "The Reading Team". The box below the player gives brief biographical information and player highlights. The back has logos of the sponsors and describes two books that are available at the public library. We have checklisted this set in alphabetical order because they are otherwise unnumbered except for the player's uniform number displayed on the card front.

	MINT	NRMT	EXC
COMPLETE SET (6)	12.00	5.50	1.50
COMMON CARD (1-6)	2.00	.90	.25
☐ 1 Marion Butts	2.50	1.10	.30
☐ 2 Anthony Miller	3.00	1.35	.35
☐ 3 Leslie O'Neal	2.50	1.10	.30
☐ 4 Gary Plummer	2.50	1.10	.30
☐ 5 Billy Ray Smith	2.00	.90	.25
☐ 6 Billy Joe Tolliver	2.00	.90	.25

1990 Knudsen 49ers

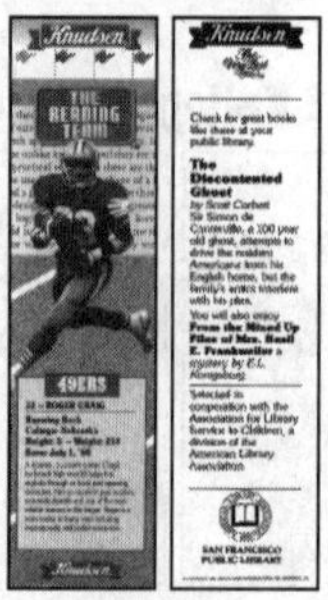

This six-card set (of bookmarks) which measures approximately 2" by 8" was produced by Knudsen's to help promote readership by people under 15 years old in the San Francisco area. They were given out in San Francisco libraries on a weekly basis. Between the Knudsen company name, the front features a color action photo of the player superimposed on a football stadium. The field is green, the bleachers are yellow with gray print, and the scoreboard above the player reads "The Reading Team". The box below the player gives brief biographical information and player highlights. The back has logos of the sponsors and describes two books that are available at the public library. We have checklisted this set in alphabetical order because they are otherwise unnumbered except for the player's uniform number displayed on the card front.

	MINT	NRMT	EXC
COMPLETE SET (6)	35.00	16.00	4.40
COMMON CARD (1-6)	2.00	.90	.25
SEMISTARS	3.00	1.35	.35
☐ 1 Roger Craig	3.00	1.35	.35
☐ 2 Ronnie Lott	4.00	1.80	.50
☐ 3 Joe Montana	15.00	6.75	1.85
☐ 4 Jerry Rice	15.00	6.75	1.85
☐ 5 George Siefert CO	3.00	1.35	.35
☐ 6 Michael Walter	2.00	.90	.25

1990 Knudsen/Sealtest Patriots

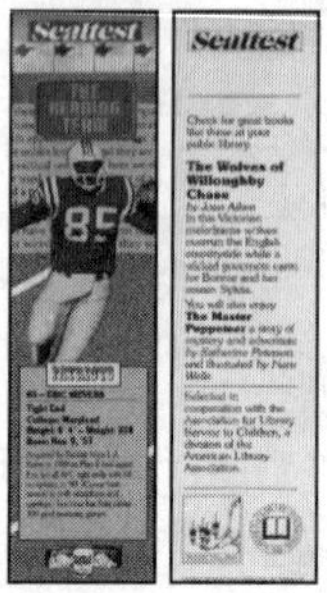

This six-card set (of bookmarks) which measures approximately 2" by 8" was produced by Knudsen's and Sealtest to help promote readership by people under 15 years old in the New England area. Between the Knudsen or Sealtest company name, the front features a color action photo of the player superimposed on a football stadium. The field is green, the bleachers are yellow with gray print, and the scoreboard above the player reads "The Reading Team". The box below the player gives brief biographical information and player highlights. The back has logos of the sponsors and describes two books that are available at the public library. We have checklisted this set in alphabetical order because they are otherwise unnumbered except for the player's uniform number displayed on the card front.

	MINT	NRMT	EXC
COMPLETE SET (6)	25.00	11.00	3.10
COMMON CARD (1-6)	4.00	1.80	.50
☐ 1 Steve Grogan	6.00	2.70	.75
☐ 2 Ronnie Lippett	5.00	2.20	.60
☐ 3 Eric Sievers	4.00	1.80	.50
☐ 4 Mosi Tatupu	4.00	1.80	.50
☐ 5 Andre Tippett	6.00	2.70	.75
☐ 6 Garin Veris	4.00	1.80	.50

1990 Knudsen Rams

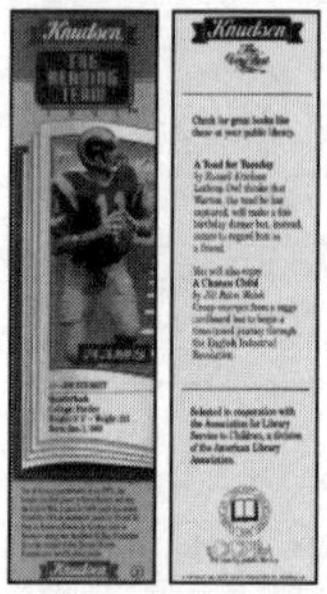

This six-card set (of bookmarks) which measures approximately 2" by 8" was produced by Knudsen's to help promote readership by people under 15 years old in the Los Angeles area. Between the Knudsen company name, the front features a color action photo of the player superimposed on a football stadium. The field is green, the bleachers are yellow with gray print, and the scoreboard above the player reads "The Reading Team". The box below the player gives brief biographical information and player highlights. The back has logos of the sponsors and describes two books that are available at the public library. We have checklisted this set in alphabetical order because they are otherwise unnumbered except for the player's uniform number displayed on the card front.

	MINT	NRMT	EXC
COMPLETE SET (6)	25.00	11.00	3.10
COMMON CARD (1-6)	4.00	1.80	.50
☐ 1 Henry Ellard	6.00	2.70	.75
☐ 2 Jim Everett	6.00	2.70	.75
☐ 3 Jerry Gray	4.00	1.80	.50
☐ 4 Pete Holohan	4.00	1.80	.50
☐ 5 Mike Lansford	4.00	1.80	.50
☐ 6 Irv Pankey	4.00	1.80	.50

1991 Knudsen

This 18-card set (of bookmarks) produced by Knudsen's Dairy in California measures approximately 2" by 8". They were presented to youngsters who checked out library books during the 1991 football season in order to promote reading. The fronts feature a player photo superimposed on the page of a book, with biography and career summary below. Card numbers appear in circles in the lower right corner of each card. The backs have logos of the sponsors and

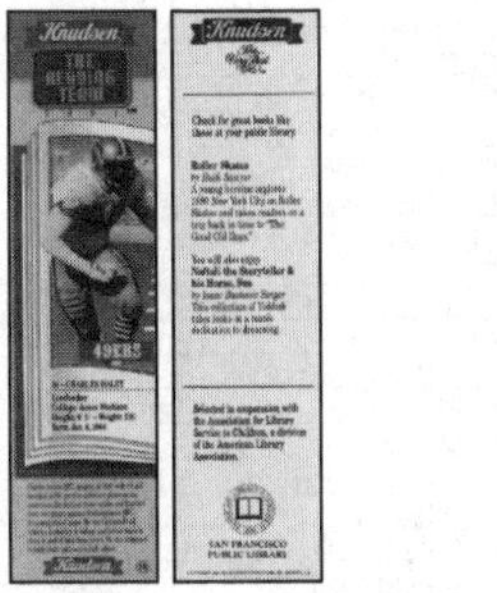

describe two books that are available at the public library. The bookmarks were distributed in the team's respective areas, San Diego Chargers (1-6), Los Angeles Rams (7-12), and San Francisco 49ers (13-18).

	MINT	NRMT	EXC
COMPLETE SET (18)	40.00	18.00	5.00
COMMON CARD (1-18)	1.50	.70	.19
☐ 1 Gill Byrd	1.50	.70	.19
☐ 2 Courtney Hall	1.50	.70	.19
☐ 3 Ronnie Harmon	2.00	.90	.25
☐ 4 Anthony Miller	2.50	1.10	.30
☐ 5 Joe Phillips	1.50	.70	.19
☐ 6 Junior Seau	4.00	1.80	.50
☐ 7 Jim Everett	2.50	1.10	.30
☐ 8 Kevin Greene	2.50	1.10	.30
☐ 9 Damone Johnson	1.50	.70	.19
☐ 10 Tom Newberry	1.50	.70	.19
☐ 11 John Robinson CO	2.00	.90	.25
☐ 12 Michael Stewart	1.50	.70	.19
☐ 13 Michael Carter	1.50	.70	.19
☐ 14 Charles Haley	2.50	1.10	.30
☐ 15 Joe Montana	10.00	4.50	1.25
☐ 16 Tom Rathman	2.00	.90	.25
☐ 17 Jerry Rice	10.00	4.50	1.25
☐ 18 George Seifert CO	2.00	.90	.25

1976 Landsman Portraits

These 8 1/2" by 11" black-and-white portraits were issued in approximately 1976 by the artist Landsman. This checklist, is thought to be complete any additional information would be appreciated.

	MINT	NRMT	EXC
COMPLETE SET (3)	50.00	22.00	6.25
COMMON CARD (1-3)	10.00	4.50	1.25
☐ 1 Chuck Foreman	10.00	4.50	1.25
☐ 2 Ken Stabler	25.00	11.00	3.10
☐ 3 Fran Tarkenton	15.00	6.75	1.85

1996 Laser View

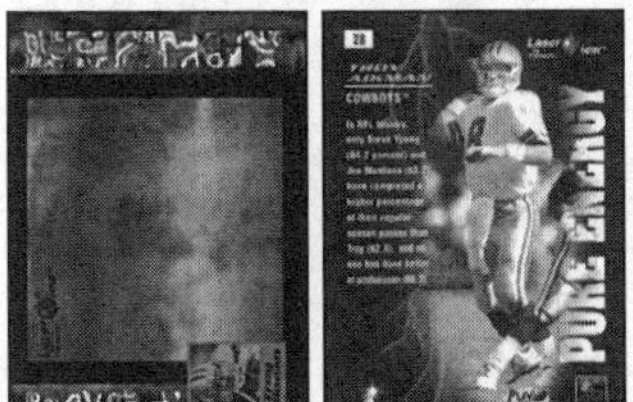

The 1996 Laser View set was issued in one series totalling 40 cards and features 3.5 seconds of actual game footage printed on super premium 20pt. card stock with full-motion hologram technology. The one-card packs retail for $4.99 each.

	MINT	NRMT	EXC
COMPLETE SET (40)	60.00	27.00	7.50
COMMON CARD (1-40)	.75	.35	.09
☐ 1 Jim Kelly	1.50	.70	.19
☐ 2 Troy Aikman	5.00	2.20	.60
☐ 3 Michael Irvin	1.50	.70	.19
☐ 4 Emmitt Smith	10.00	4.50	1.25
☐ 5 John Elway	4.00	1.80	.50
☐ 6 Barry Sanders	5.00	2.20	.60
☐ 7 Brett Favre	10.00	4.50	1.25
☐ 8 Jim Harbaugh	1.00	.45	.12
☐ 9 Dan Marino	10.00	4.50	1.25
☐ 10 Warren Moon	1.00	.45	.12
☐ 11 Drew Bledsoe	5.00	2.20	.60
☐ 12 Jim Everett	.75	.35	.09
☐ 13 Jeff Hostetler	1.00	.45	.12
☐ 14 Neil O'Donnell	1.00	.45	.12
☐ 15 Junior Seau	1.50	.70	.19
☐ 16 Jerry Rice	5.00	2.20	.60
☐ 17 Steve Young	4.00	1.80	.50
☐ 18 Rick Mirer	1.00	.45	.12
☐ 19 Boomer Esiason	1.00	.45	.12
☐ 20 Bernie Kosar	.75	.35	.09
☐ 21 Heath Shuler	1.50	.70	.19
☐ 22 Dave Brown	1.00	.45	.12
☐ 23 Jeff Blake	1.50	.70	.19
☐ 24 Kerry Collins	5.00	2.20	.60
☐ 25 Kordell Stewart	5.00	2.20	.60
☐ 26 Scott Mitchell	1.00	.45	.12
☐ 27 Kerry Collins PE	3.00	1.35	.35
☐ 28 Troy Aikman PE	3.00	1.35	.35
☐ 29 Kordell Stewart PE	3.00	1.35	.35
☐ 30 Michael Irvin PE	1.00	.45	.12
☐ 31 Emmitt Smith PE	6.00	2.70	.75
☐ 32 John Elway PE	2.50	1.10	.30
☐ 33 Barry Sanders PE	3.00	1.35	.35
☐ 34 Brett Favre PE	6.00	2.70	.75
☐ 35 Dan Marino PE	6.00	2.70	.75
☐ 36 Drew Bledsoe PE	3.00	1.35	.35
☐ 37 Neil O'Donnell PE	1.00	.45	.12
☐ 38 Jerry Rice PE	3.00	1.35	.35
☐ 39 Steve Young PE	2.50	1.10	.30
☐ 40 Jeff Blake PE	1.00	.45	.12
☐ P5 John Elway Promo	2.50	1.10	.30

1996 Laser View Gold

Randomly inserted at the rate of one in 12 packs, this 40-card set is a parallel gold-foil, full motion hologram version of the regular 1996 Laser View set.

	MINT	NRMT	EXC
COMPLETE SET (40)	3.00	1.35	.35
COMMON CARD (1-40)	300.00	135.00	38.00

*STARS: 1.25X TO 2.5X BASIC CARDS
*YOUNG STARS: 1X TO 2X BASIC CARDS

1996 Laser View Eye on the Prize

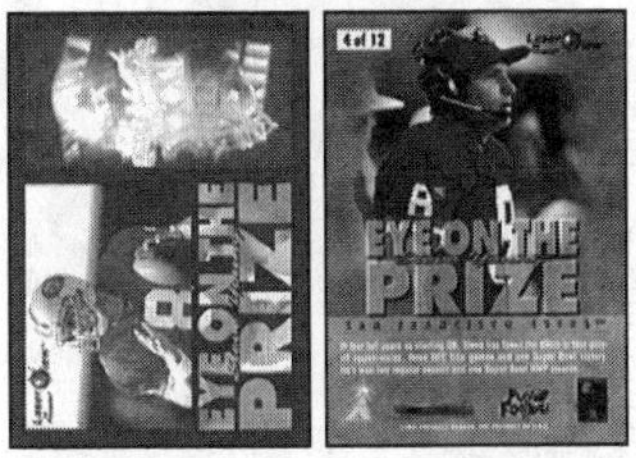

Randomly inserted in packs at a rate of one in 24, this 12-card set spotlights on the league's superstar elite as they compete for the coveted Lombardi Trophy.

	MINT	NRMT	EXC
COMPLETE SET (12)	100.00	45.00	12.50
COMMON CARD (1-12)	2.50	1.10	.30
☐ 1 Troy Aikman	12.00	5.50	1.50
☐ 2 Emmitt Smith	25.00	11.00	3.10
☐ 3 Michael Irvin	4.00	1.80	.50
☐ 4 Steve Young	10.00	4.50	1.25
☐ 5 Jerry Rice	12.00	5.50	1.50
☐ 6 Dan Marino	25.00	11.00	3.10
☐ 7 John Elway	10.00	4.50	1.25
☐ 8 Junior Seau	2.50	1.10	.30
☐ 9 Neil O'Donnell	2.50	1.10	.30
☐ 10 Jeff Hostetler	2.50	1.10	.30
☐ 11 Jim Kelly	4.00	1.80	.50
☐ 12 Kordell Stewart	12.00	5.50	1.50

1996 Laser View Inscriptions

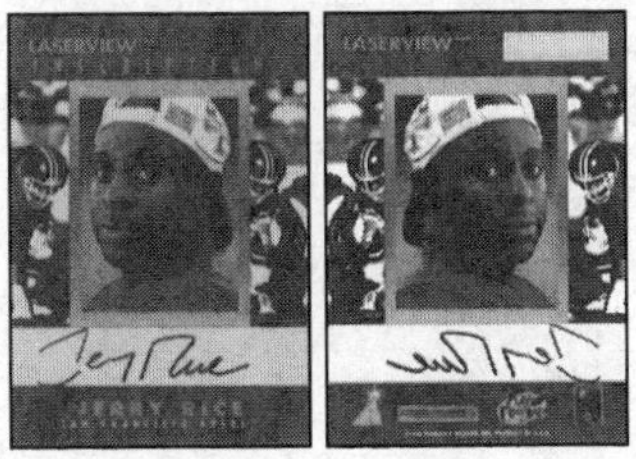

Randomly inserted in packs at a rate of one in 24, this set is a 25-card, sequentially numbered set featuring autographs of some of the top players in the NFL. The cards are unnumbered and listed below alphabetically. The number of autographs that each player signed is listed after his name.

	MINT	NRMT	EXC
COMPLETE SET (25)	1400.00	650.00	180.00
COMMON CARD (1-25)	20.00	9.00	2.50
☐ 1 Jeff Blake/3125	35.00	16.00	4.40
☐ 2 Drew Bledsoe/2775	100.00	45.00	12.50
☐ 3 Dave Brown/3100	20.00	9.00	2.50
☐ 4 Mark Brunell/3200	100.00	45.00	12.50
☐ 5 Kerry Collins/3000	80.00	36.00	10.00
☐ 6 John Elway/3100	75.00	34.00	9.50
☐ 7 Boomer Esiason/1500	130.00	57.50	16.00
☐ 8 Jim Everett/3100	20.00	9.00	2.50
☐ 9 Brett Favre/4850	125.00	55.00	15.50
☐ 10 Jeff George/2900	25.00	11.00	3.10
☐ 11 Jim Harbaugh/3500	30.00	13.50	3.70
☐ 12 Jeff Hostetler/3750	20.00	9.00	2.50
☐ 13 Michael Irvin/3050	30.00	13.50	3.70
☐ 14 Jim Kelly/3100	40.00	18.00	5.00
☐ 15 Bernie Kosar/3200	20.00	9.00	2.50
☐ 16 Erik Kramer/3150	20.00	9.00	2.50
☐ 17 Rick Mirer/3150	30.00	13.50	3.70
☐ 18 Scott Mitchell/4900	20.00	9.00	2.50
☐ 19 Warren Moon/2800	30.00	13.50	3.70
☐ 20 Neil O'Donnell/1600	40.00	18.00	5.00
☐ 21 Jerry Rice/900	350.00	160.00	45.00
☐ 22 Barry Sanders/2900	100.00	45.00	12.50
☐ 23 Junior Seau/3000	25.00	11.00	3.10
☐ 24 Heath Shuler/3100	25.00	11.00	3.10
☐ 25 Steve Young/1950	110.00	50.00	14.00

1983 Latrobe Police

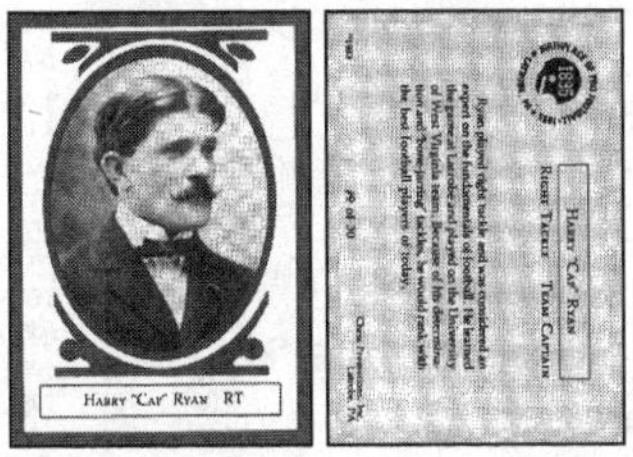

This 30-card standard-size set is subtitled "The Birth of Professional Football" in Latrobe, Pennsylvania. Cards were not printed in full color, rather either sepia or black and white. The set is not attractive and, hence, has never been very aggressively pursued by collectors. The set is available with two kinds of backs. There is no difference in value between the two sets of backs although the set with safety tips on the back seems to be more in demand due to the many collectors of police issues.

	MINT	NRMT	EXC
COMPLETE SET (30)	8.00	3.60	1.00
COMMON CARD (1-30)	.30	.14	.04
☐ 1 John Kinport Brallier	1.00	.45	.12
☐ 2 John K. Brallier	.50	.23	.06
☐ 3 Latrobe YMCA Team 1895	.50	.23	.06
☐ 4 Brallier and Team at W and J 1895	.50	.23	.06
☐ 5 Latrobe A.A. Team 1896	.50	.23	.06
☐ 6 Latrobe A.A. 1897	.50	.23	.06
☐ 7 1st All Pro Team 1897	.50	.23	.06
☐ 8 David J. Berry Mgr.	.30	.14	.04
☐ 9 Harry Cap Ryan RT	.30	.14	.04
☐ 10 Walter Okeson LE	.30	.14	.04
☐ 11 Edward Wood RE	.30	.14	.04
☐ 12 E.Big Bill Hammer C	.30	.14	.04
☐ 13 Marcus Saxman LH	.30	.14	.04
☐ 14 Charles Shumaker SUB	.30	.14	.04
☐ 15 Charles McDyre LE	.30	.14	.04
☐ 16 Edward Abbatticchio FB	.30	.14	.04
☐ 17 George Flickinger C/LT	.30	.14	.04
☐ 18 Walter Howard RH	.30	.14	.04
☐ 19 Thomas Trenchard	.50	.23	.06
☐ 20 John Kinport Brallier QB	.75	.35	.09
☐ 21 Jack Gass LH	.30	.14	.04
☐ 22 Dave Campbell LT	.30	.14	.04
☐ 23 Edward Blair RH	.30	.14	.04
☐ 24 John Johnston RG	.30	.14	.04
☐ 25 Sam Johnston LG	.30	.14	.04
☐ 26 Alex Laird SUB	.30	.14	.04
☐ 27 Latrobe A.A. 1897 Team	.50	.23	.06
☐ 28 Pro Football Memorial Plaque	.30	.14	.04
☐ 29 Commemorative Medallion	.30	.14	.04
☐ 30 Birth of Pro Football Checklist Card	.50	.23	.06

1975 Laughlin Flaky Football

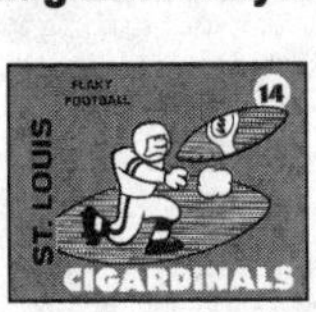

This 26-card set measures approximately 2 1/2" by 3 3/8". The title card indicates that the set was copyrighted in 1975 by noted artist, R.G. Laughlin. The typical orientation of the cards is that the city name is printed on the top of the card, with the mock team name running from top to bottom down the left side. The cartoon pictures are oriented horizontally inside the right angle formed by these two lines of text. The cards are numbered in the lower right hand corner (usually) and the backs of the cards are blank.

	NRMT-MT	EXC	G-VG
COMPLETE SET (27)	150.00	70.00	19.00
COMMON CARD (1-26)	7.00	3.10	.85
☐ 1 Pittsburgh Stealers	10.00	4.50	1.25
☐ 2 Minnesota Spikings	7.00	3.10	.85
☐ 3 Cincinnati Bungles	7.00	3.10	.85
☐ 4 Chicago Bares	7.00	3.10	.85
☐ 5 Miami Dullfins	10.00	4.50	1.25
☐ 6 Philadelphia Eggles	7.00	3.10	.85
☐ 7 Cleveland Brawns	7.00	3.10	.85
☐ 8 New York Gianuts	7.00	3.10	.85
☐ 9 Buffalo Bulls	7.00	3.10	.85
☐ 10 Dallas Plowboys	10.00	4.50	1.25
☐ 11 New England Pastry Nuts	7.00	3.10	.85
☐ 12 Green Bay Porkers	7.00	3.10	.85
☐ 13 Denver Bongos	7.00	3.10	.85
☐ 14 St. Louis Cigardinals	7.00	3.10	.85
☐ 15 New York Jests	7.00	3.10	.85
☐ 16 Washington Redshins	10.00	4.50	1.25
☐ 17 Oakland Waders	10.00	4.50	1.25
☐ 18 Los Angeles Yams	7.00	3.10	.85
☐ 19 Baltimore Kilts	7.00	3.10	.85
☐ 20 New Orleans Scents	7.00	3.10	.85
☐ 21 San Diego Charges	7.00	3.10	.85
☐ 22 Detroit Loins	7.00	3.10	.85
☐ 23 Kansas City Chefs	7.00	3.10	.85
☐ 24 Atlanta Fakin's	7.00	3.10	.85
☐ 25 Houston Owlers	7.00	3.10	.85
☐ 26 San Francisco 40 Miners	10.00	4.50	1.25
☐ NNO Title Card Flaky Football	10.00	4.50	1.25

1948 Leaf

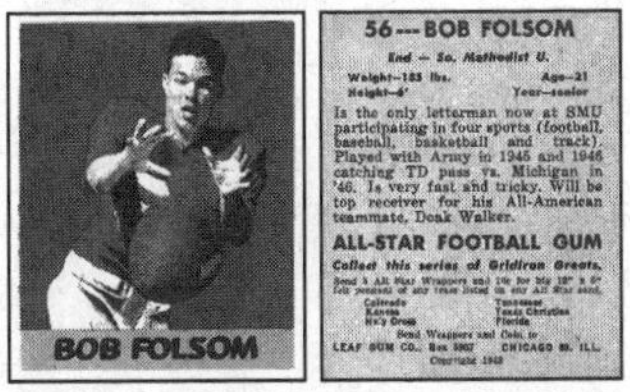

The 1948 Leaf set of 98 cards features black and white player portraits against a solid color background. The player's uniforms were painted.The cards measure approximately 2 3/8" by 2 7/8". The cards can be found on either gray or cream colored card stock. The backs contain a small write-up and bio. The second series (50-98) cards are much more difficult to obtain than the first series (1-49). This set features the Rookie Cards of many football stars since it was, along with the 1948 Bowman set, the first major post-war set. The set included NFL players as well as college stars. Such Rookie Cards include Sammy Baugh, Chuck Bednarik, Charley Conerly, Leon Hart, Jackie Jensen, Bobby Layne, Sid Luckman, Johnny Lujack, Leo Nomellini, Steve Van Buren, Doak Walker and Bob Waterfield.

	NRMT	VG-E	GOOD
COMPLETE SET (98)	6000.00	2700.00	750.00
COMMON CARD (1-49)	25.00	11.00	3.10
COMMON CARD (50-98)	120.00	55.00	15.00
WRAPPER (5-CENT)	250.00	110.00	31.00
☐ 1 Sid Luckman	350.00	90.00	35.00
☐ 2 Steve Suhey	25.00	11.00	3.10
☐ 3A Bulldog Turner (Reddish background)	110.00	50.00	14.00
☐ 3B Bulldog Turner (White background)	110.00	50.00	14.00
☐ 4 Doak Walker	160.00	70.00	20.00
☐ 5 Levi Jackson	30.00	13.50	3.70
☐ 6 Bobby Layne UER (Name spelled Bobbie on front)	325.00	145.00	40.00
☐ 7 Bill Fischer	25.00	11.00	3.10
☐ 8A Vince Banonis (White name on front)	25.00	11.00	3.10
☐ 8B Vince Banonis (Black name on front)	25.00	11.00	3.10
☐ 9 Tommy Thompson	30.00	13.50	3.70
☐ 10 Perry Moss	25.00	11.00	3.10
☐ 11 Terry Brennan	30.00	13.50	3.70
☐ 12A William Swiacki (White name on front)	25.00	11.00	3.10
☐ 12B William Swiacki (Black name on front)	25.00	11.00	3.10
☐ 13 Johnny Lujack	160.00	70.00	20.00
☐ 14A Mal Kutner (White name on front)	25.00	11.00	3.10
☐ 14B Mal Kutner (Black name on front)	30.00	13.50	3.70
☐ 15 Charlie Justice	90.00	40.00	11.00
☐ 16 Pete Pihos	100.00	45.00	12.50
☐ 17A Kenny Washington (White name on front)	50.00	22.00	6.25
☐ 17B Kenny Washington (Black name on front)	50.00	22.00	6.25
☐ 18 Harry Gilmer	35.00	16.00	4.40
☐ 19A George McAfee ERR (Listed as Gorgeous George on front)	120.00	55.00	15.00
☐ 19B George McAfee COR	100.00	45.00	12.50
☐ 20 George Taliaferro	30.00	13.50	3.70
☐ 21 Paul Christman	40.00	18.00	5.00
☐ 22 Steve Van Buren	160.00	70.00	20.00
☐ 23 Ken Kavanaugh	30.00	13.50	3.70
☐ 24 Jim Martin	30.00	13.50	3.70
☐ 25 Elmer Bud Angsman	30.00	13.50	3.70
☐ 26 Bob Waterfield	225.00	100.00	28.00
☐ 27A Fred Davis (Yellow background)	25.00	11.00	3.10

☐ 27B Fred Davis (White background)	25.00	11.00	3.10
☐ 28 Whitey Wistert	30.00	13.50	3.70
☐ 29 Charley Trippi	110.00	50.00	14.00
☐ 30 Paul Governali	30.00	13.50	3.70
☐ 31 Tom McWilliams	25.00	11.00	3.10
☐ 32 Larry Zimmerman	25.00	11.00	3.10
☐ 33 Pat Harder UER (Misspelled Harber)	50.00	22.00	6.25
☐ 34 Sammy Baugh	450.00	200.00	55.00
☐ 35 Ted Fritsch Sr.	30.00	13.50	3.70
☐ 36 Bill Dudley	110.00	50.00	14.00
☐ 37 George Connor	75.00	34.00	9.50
☐ 38 Frank Dancewicz	25.00	11.00	3.10
☐ 39 Billy Dewell	25.00	11.00	3.10
☐ 40 John Nolan	25.00	11.00	3.10
☐ 41A Harry Szulborski Yellow jersey	25.00	11.00	3.10
☐ 41B Harry Szulborski Orange jersey	25.00	11.00	3.10
☐ 42 Tex Coulter	30.00	13.50	3.70
☐ 43A Robert Nussbaumer (Maroon Jersey)	25.00	11.00	3.10
☐ 43B Robert Nussbaumer (Red Jersey)	25.00	11.00	3.10
☐ 44 Bob Mann	25.00	11.00	3.10
☐ 45 Jim White	25.00	11.00	3.10
☐ 46 Jack Jacobs	25.00	11.00	3.10
☐ 47 John Clement	25.00	11.00	3.10
☐ 48 Frank Reagan	25.00	11.00	3.10
☐ 49 Frank Tripucka	40.00	18.00	5.00
☐ 50 John Rauch	120.00	55.00	15.00
☐ 51 Mike Dimitro	120.00	55.00	15.00
☐ 52 Leo Nomellini	350.00	160.00	45.00
☐ 53 Charley Conerly	350.00	160.00	45.00
☐ 54 Chuck Bednarik	400.00	180.00	50.00
☐ 55 Chick Jagade	120.00	55.00	15.00
☐ 56 Bob Folsom	125.00	55.00	15.50
☐ 57 Eugene Rossides	125.00	55.00	15.50
☐ 58 Art Weiner	120.00	55.00	15.00
☐ 59 Alex Sarkistian	120.00	55.00	15.00
☐ 60 Dick Harris	120.00	55.00	15.00
☐ 61 Len Younce	120.00	55.00	15.00
☐ 62 Gene Derricotte	120.00	55.00	15.00
☐ 63 Roy Rebel Steiner	120.00	55.00	15.00
☐ 64 Frank Seno	120.00	55.00	15.00
☐ 65 Bob Hendren	120.00	55.00	15.00
☐ 66 Jack Cloud	120.00	55.00	15.00
☐ 67 Harrell Collins	120.00	55.00	15.00
☐ 68 Clyde LeForce	120.00	55.00	15.00
☐ 69 Larry Joe	120.00	55.00	15.00
☐ 70 Phil O'Reilly	120.00	55.00	15.00
☐ 71 Paul Campbell	120.00	55.00	15.00
☐ 72 Ray Evans	120.00	55.00	15.00
☐ 73 Jackie Jensen UER Spelled Jackey on card front	350.00	160.00	45.00
☐ 74 Russ Steger	120.00	55.00	15.00
☐ 75 Tony Minisi	120.00	55.00	15.00
☐ 76 Clayton Tonnemaker	120.00	55.00	15.00
☐ 77 George Savitsky	120.00	55.00	15.00
☐ 78 Clarence Self	120.00	55.00	15.00
☐ 79 Rod Franz	120.00	55.00	15.00
☐ 80 Jim Youle	120.00	55.00	15.00
☐ 81 Billy Bye	120.00	55.00	15.00
☐ 82 Fred Enke	120.00	55.00	15.00
☐ 83 Fred Folger	120.00	55.00	15.00
☐ 84 Jug Girard	100.00	45.00	12.50
☐ 85 Joe Scott	120.00	55.00	15.00
☐ 86 Bob Demoss	120.00	55.00	15.00
☐ 87 Dave Templeton	120.00	55.00	15.00
☐ 88 Herb Siegert	120.00	55.00	15.00
☐ 89 Bucky O'Conner	120.00	55.00	15.00
☐ 90 Joe Whisler	120.00	55.00	15.00
☐ 91 Leon Hart	200.00	90.00	25.00
☐ 92 Earl Banks	120.00	55.00	15.00
☐ 93 Frank Aschenbrenner	120.00	55.00	15.00
☐ 94 John Goldsberry	120.00	55.00	15.00
☐ 95 Porter Payne	120.00	55.00	15.00
☐ 96 Pete Perini	120.00	55.00	15.00
☐ 97 Jay Rhodemyre	120.00	55.00	15.00
☐ 98 Al DiMarco	200.00	50.00	20.00

1949 Leaf

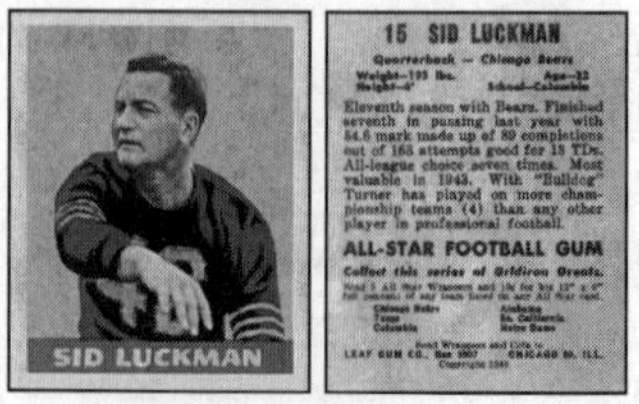

Measuring approximately 2 3/8" by 2 7/8", the 1949 Leaf set contains 49 cards that are skip-numbered from 1 to 150. Designed much like the 1948 issue (use of many of the same portraits), the fronts feature player portraits againts a solid background. The player's name is at the bottom. The backs carry career highlights and a bio. The cards can be found on either gray or cream colored card stock. The card backs detail an offer to send in five wrappers and a dime for a 12" by 6" felt pennant of one of the teams listed on the different card backs including college and pro teams. Unlike the 1948 set, all the players portrayed were in the NFL. There are no key Rookie Cards in this set as virtually all of the players in the 1949 set were also in the 1948 Leaf set.

	NRMT	VG-E	GOOD
COMPLETE SET (49)	2200.00	1000.00	275.00
COMMON CARD (1-150)	25.00	11.00	3.10
WRAPPER (5-CENT)	300.00	135.00	38.00
☐ 1 Bob Hendren	80.00	20.00	8.00
☐ 2 Joe Scott	25.00	11.00	3.10
☐ 3 Frank Reagan	25.00	11.00	3.10
☐ 4 John Rauch	25.00	11.00	3.10
☐ 7 Bill Fischer	25.00	11.00	3.10
☐ 9 Elmer Bud Angsman	35.00	16.00	4.40
☐ 10 Billy Dewell	25.00	11.00	3.10
☐ 13 Tommy Thompson	35.00	16.00	4.40
☐ 15 Sid Luckman	125.00	55.00	15.50
☐ 16 Charley Trippi	55.00	25.00	7.00
☐ 17 Bob Mann	25.00	11.00	3.10
☐ 19 Paul Christman	35.00	16.00	4.40
☐ 22 Bill Dudley	55.00	25.00	7.00
☐ 23 Clyde LeForce	25.00	11.00	3.10
☐ 26 Sammy Baugh	275.00	125.00	34.00
☐ 28 Pete Pihos	55.00	25.00	7.00
☐ 31 Tex Coulter	35.00	16.00	4.40
☐ 32 Mal Kutner	35.00	16.00	4.40
☐ 35 Whitey Wistert	35.00	16.00	4.40
☐ 37 Ted Fritsch Sr.	35.00	16.00	4.40
☐ 38 Vince Banonis	25.00	11.00	3.10
☐ 39 Jim White	25.00	11.00	3.10
☐ 40 George Connor	50.00	22.00	6.25
☐ 41 George McAfee	50.00	22.00	6.25
☐ 43 Frank Tripucka	35.00	16.00	4.40
☐ 47 Fred Enke	25.00	11.00	3.10
☐ 49 Charley Conerly	100.00	45.00	12.50
☐ 51 Ken Kavanaugh	35.00	16.00	4.40
☐ 52 Bob Demoss	25.00	11.00	3.10
☐ 56 John Lujack	90.00	40.00	11.00
☐ 57 Jim Youle	25.00	11.00	3.10
☐ 62 Harry Gilmer	35.00	16.00	4.40
☐ 65 Robert Nussbaumer	25.00	11.00	3.10
☐ 67 Bobby Layne	160.00	70.00	20.00
☐ 70 Herb Siegert	25.00	11.00	3.10
☐ 74 Tony Minisi	25.00	11.00	3.10
☐ 79 Steve Van Buren	90.00	40.00	11.00
☐ 81 Perry Moss	25.00	11.00	3.10
☐ 89 Bob Waterfield	100.00	45.00	12.50
☐ 90 Jack Jacobs	25.00	11.00	3.10
☐ 95 Kenny Washington	40.00	18.00	5.00
☐ 101 Pat Harder UER (Misspelled Harber on card front)	35.00	16.00	4.40
☐ 110 Bill Swiacki	35.00	16.00	4.40
☐ 118 Fred Davis	25.00	11.00	3.10
☐ 126 Jay Rhodemyre	25.00	11.00	3.10
☐ 127 Frank Seno	25.00	11.00	3.10
☐ 134 Chuck Bednarik	125.00	55.00	15.50
☐ 144 George Savitsky	25.00	11.00	3.10
☐ 150 Bulldog Turner	125.00	31.00	12.50

1983 Leaf Football Facts Booklets

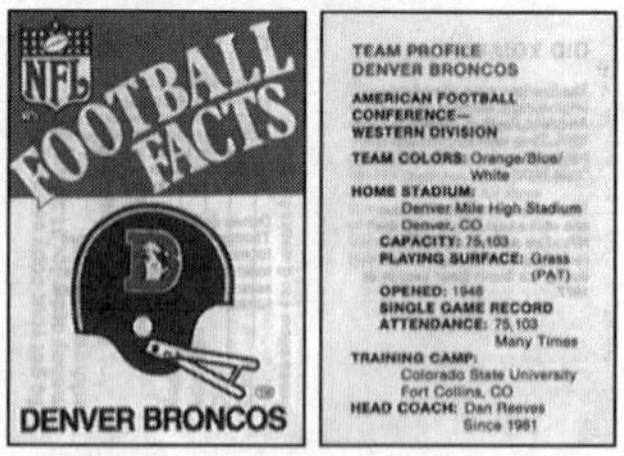

(from Athleticards (he sold at $3-8), need to verify Raiders and Colts!!) One Football Facts Booklet for each NFL team was produced by Leaf in 1983. They were distributed one per small box of Leaf bubble gum and unfold to reveal team history and statistics. The booklets are unnumbered.

	MINT	NRMT	EXC
COMPLETE SET (28)	75.00	34.00	9.50
COMMON CARD (1-28)	3.00	1.35	.35
☐ 1 Atlanta Falcons	3.00	1.35	.35
☐ 2 Baltimore Colts	3.00	1.35	.35
☐ 3 Buffalo Bills	3.00	1.35	.35
☐ 4 Chicago Bears	5.00	2.20	.60
☐ 5 Cincinnati Bengals	3.00	1.35	.35
☐ 6 Cleveland Browns	3.00	1.35	.35
☐ 7 Dallas Cowboys	6.00	2.70	.75
☐ 8 Denver Broncos	3.00	1.35	.35
☐ 9 Detroit Lions	3.00	1.35	.35
☐ 10 Green Bay Packers	6.00	2.70	.75
☐ 11 Houston Oilers	3.00	1.35	.35
☐ 12 Kansas City Chiefs	3.00	1.35	.35
☐ 13 Los Angeles Rams	3.00	1.35	.35
☐ 14 Miami Dolphins	6.00	2.70	.75
☐ 15 Minnesota Vikings	3.00	1.35	.35
☐ 16 New England Patriots	3.00	1.35	.35
☐ 17 New Orleans Saints	3.00	1.35	.35
☐ 18 New York Giants	3.00	1.35	.35
☐ 19 New York Jets	3.00	1.35	.35
☐ 20 Oakland Raiders	6.00	2.70	.75
☐ 21 Philadelphia Eagles	3.00	1.35	.35
☐ 22 Pittsburgh Steelers	6.00	2.70	.75
☐ 23 St. Louis Cardinals	3.00	1.35	.35
☐ 24 San Diego Chargers	3.00	1.35	.35
☐ 25 San Francisco 49ers	6.00	2.70	.75
☐ 26 Seattle Seahawks	3.00	1.35	.35
☐ 27 Tampa Bay Buccaneers	3.00	1.35	.35
☐ 28 Washington Redskins	6.00	2.70	.75

1996 Leaf

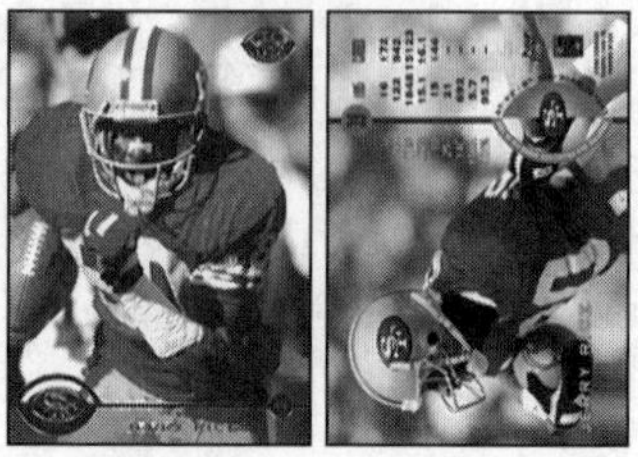

This 190-card set was distributed in 10-card packs with a suggested retail price of $2.99. The fronts feature borderless action color player photos. The backs carry another player photo with career statistics.

	MINT	NRMT	EXC
COMPLETE SET (190)	25.00	11.00	3.10
COMMON CARD (1-190)	.08	.04	.01
☐ 1 Troy Aikman	1.25	.55	.16
☐ 2 Ricky Watters	.15	.07	.02
☐ 3 Robert Brooks	.30	.14	.04
☐ 4 Ki-Jana Carter	.15	.07	.02
☐ 5 Drew Bledsoe	1.25	.55	.16
☐ 6 Eric Swann	.15	.07	.02
☐ 7 Hardy Nickerson	.08	.04	.01
☐ 8 Tony Martin	.15	.07	.02
☐ 9 Garrison Hearst	.15	.07	.02
☐ 10 Bernie Parmalee	.08	.04	.01
☐ 11 Neil Smith	.15	.07	.02
☐ 12 Aaron Craver	.08	.04	.01
☐ 13 Rashaan Salaam	.30	.14	.04
☐ 14 Greg Hill	.15	.07	.02
☐ 15 Charlie Garner	.08	.04	.01
☐ 16 Kimble Anders	.08	.04	.01
☐ 17 Steve McNair	1.25	.55	.16
☐ 18 Neil O'Donnell	.15	.07	.02
☐ 19 Greg Lloyd	.15	.07	.02
☐ 20 Warren Moon	.15	.07	.02
☐ 21 Bernie Kosar	.08	.04	.01
☐ 22 Derrick Thomas	.15	.07	.02
☐ 23 Andre Hastings	.15	.07	.02
☐ 24 Wayne Chrebet	.15	.07	.02
☐ 25 Mark Seay	.08	.04	.01
☐ 26 Eric Metcalf	.15	.07	.02
☐ 27 Shawn Jefferson	.08	.04	.01
☐ 28 Napoleon Kaufman	.15	.07	.02
☐ 29 Steve Walsh	.08	.04	.01
☐ 30 Derrick Alexander DE	.08	.04	.01
☐ 31 Rodney Peete	.08	.04	.01
☐ 32 Terance Mathis	.08	.04	.01
☐ 33 Michael Westbrook	.30	.14	.04
☐ 34 Kevin Carter	.15	.07	.02
☐ 35 Aaron Hayden	.08	.04	.01
☐ 36 J.J. Stokes	.30	.14	.04
☐ 37 Andre Reed	.15	.07	.02
☐ 38 Chris Warren	.15	.07	.02
☐ 39 Jerry Rice	1.25	.55	.16
☐ 40 Ben Coates	.15	.07	.02
☐ 41 Reggie White	.30	.14	.04
☐ 42 Joey Galloway	.50	.23	.06
☐ 43 Sean Dawkins	.08	.04	.01
☐ 44 Brett Favre	2.50	1.10	.30
☐ 45 Jeff George	.15	.07	.02
☐ 46 Robert Smith	.15	.07	.02
☐ 47 Ken Dilger	.15	.07	.02
☐ 48 Larry Centers	.15	.07	.02
☐ 49 Jackie Harris	.08	.04	.01
☐ 50 Hugh Douglas	.08	.04	.01
☐ 51 Herschel Walker	.15	.07	.02
☐ 52 Kerry Collins	1.50	.70	.19
☐ 53 Michael Irvin	.30	.14	.04
☐ 54 Willie McGinest	.08	.04	.01
☐ 55 Herman Moore	.30	.14	.04
☐ 56 Leroy Hoard	.08	.04	.01
☐ 57 Scott Mitchell	.15	.07	.02
☐ 58 Terrell Davis	2.00	.90	.25
☐ 59 Kevin Greene	.15	.07	.02
☐ 60 Yancey Thigpen	.15	.07	.02
☐ 61 Kevin Smith	.08	.04	.01
☐ 62 Trent Dilfer	.15	.07	.02
☐ 63 Cortez Kennedy	.15	.07	.02
☐ 64 Carnell Lake	.08	.04	.01
☐ 65 Quinn Early	.08	.04	.01
☐ 66 Kyle Brady	.15	.07	.02
☐ 67 Marshall Faulk	.30	.14	.04
☐ 68 Fred Barnett	.15	.07	.02
☐ 69 Quentin Coryatt	.08	.04	.01
☐ 70 Dan Marino	2.50	1.10	.30
☐ 71 Junior Seau	.30	.14	.04
☐ 72 Andre Coleman	.08	.04	.01
☐ 73 Terry Kirby	.15	.07	.02
☐ 74 Curtis Martin	2.00	.90	.25
☐ 75 Isaac Bruce	.30	.14	.04
☐ 76 Mark Chmura	.15	.07	.02
☐ 77 Edgar Bennett	.15	.07	.02
☐ 78 Mario Bates	.15	.07	.02
☐ 79 Eric Zeier	.15	.07	.02
☐ 80 Adrian Murrell	.15	.07	.02
☐ 81 Mark Brunell	1.25	.55	.16
☐ 82 Mark Rypien	.08	.04	.01
☐ 83 Erric Pegram	.15	.07	.02
☐ 84 Bryan Cox	.08	.04	.01
☐ 85 Heath Shuler	.30	.14	.04
☐ 86 Lake Dawson	.15	.07	.02
☐ 87 O.J. McDuffie	.15	.07	.02
☐ 88 Emmitt Smith	2.50	1.10	.30
☐ 89 Jim Harbaugh	.15	.07	.02
☐ 90 Aaron Bailey	.08	.04	.01
☐ 91 Jim Kelly	.30	.14	.04
☐ 92 Rodney Hampton	.15	.07	.02
☐ 93 Cris Carter	.30	.14	.04
☐ 94 Henry Ellard	.15	.07	.02
☐ 95 Darnay Scott	.15	.07	.02
☐ 96 Daryl Johnston	.15	.07	.02
☐ 97 Tamarick Vanover	.30	.14	.04
☐ 98 Jeff Blake	.30	.14	.04
☐ 99 Anthony Miller	.15	.07	.02
☐ 100 Darren Woodson	.15	.07	.02
☐ 101 Irving Fryar	.15	.07	.02
☐ 102 Craig Hayward	.08	.04	.01
☐ 103 Derek Loville	.08	.04	.01
☐ 104 Ernie Mills	.08	.04	.01
☐ 105 Brian Blades	.15	.07	.02
☐ 106 Gus Frerotte	.30	.14	.04
☐ 107 Alvin Harper	.08	.04	.01
☐ 108 Tyrone Wheatley	.15	.07	.02
☐ 109 John Elway	1.00	.45	.12
☐ 110 Charles Haley	.15	.07	.02
☐ 111 Terrell Fletcher	.08	.04	.01
☐ 112 Vincent Brisby	.08	.04	.01
☐ 113 Jerome Bettis	.30	.14	.04
☐ 114 Barry Sanders	1.25	.55	.16
☐ 115 Ken Norton Jr.	.15	.07	.02
☐ 116 Sherman Williams	.08	.04	.01
☐ 117 Antonio Freeman	.50	.23	.06
☐ 118 Bert Emanuel	.15	.07	.02
☐ 119 Marcus Allen	.30	.14	.04
☐ 120 Stan Humphries	.15	.07	.02
☐ 121 Chris Sanders	.15	.07	.02
☐ 122 Jeff Graham	.08	.04	.01
☐ 123 Jay Novacek	.15	.07	.02
☐ 124 Aeneas Williams	.08	.04	.01
☐ 125 Kordell Stewart	1.50	.70	.19
☐ 126 Steve Young	1.00	.45	.12
☐ 127 Jake Reed	.15	.07	.02
☐ 128 Rick Mirer	.15	.07	.02
☐ 129 Jeff Hostetler	.15	.07	.02
☐ 130 Tim Brown	.15	.07	.02
☐ 131 Shannon Sharpe	.15	.07	.02
☐ 132 Dave Brown	.15	.07	.02
☐ 133 Harvey Williams	.08	.04	.01
☐ 134 Rodney Thomas	.08	.04	.01
☐ 135 Frank Sanders	.15	.07	.02
☐ 136 Brett Perriman	.15	.07	.02
☐ 137 Steve Bono	.15	.07	.02
☐ 138 Steve Atwater	.08	.04	.01
☐ 139 Andre Rison	.15	.07	.02
☐ 140 Orlando Thomas	.08	.04	.01
☐ 141 Terry Allen	.15	.07	.02
☐ 142 Carl Pickens	.30	.14	.04
☐ 143 William Floyd	.15	.07	.02
☐ 144 Bryce Paup	.15	.07	.02
☐ 145 James Stewart	.15	.07	.02
☐ 146 Eric Bjornson	.08	.04	.01
☐ 147 Errict Rhett	.15	.07	.02
☐ 148 Darick Holmes	.15	.07	.02
☐ 149 Brian Mitchell	.08	.04	.01
☐ 150 Brent Jones	.08	.04	.01
☐ 151 Natrone Means	.30	.14	.04
☐ 152 Rod Woodson	.15	.07	.02
☐ 153 Bruce Smith	.30	.14	.04
☐ 154 Deion Sanders	.75	.35	.09
☐ 155 Kevin Williams	.08	.04	.01
☐ 156 Erik Kramer	.08	.04	.01
☐ 157 Jim Everett	.08	.04	.01
☐ 158 Vinny Testaverde	.15	.07	.02
☐ 159 Boomer Esiason	.15	.07	.02
☐ 160 Leslie O'Neal	.08	.04	.01
☐ 161 Curtis Conway	.30	.14	.04
☐ 162 Thurman Thomas	.30	.14	.04
☐ 163 Tony Brackens	.15	.07	.02
☐ 164 Stepfret Williams	.08	.04	.01
☐ 165 Alex Van Dyke	.15	.07	.02
☐ 166 Cedric Jones	.15	.07	.02
☐ 167 Stanley Pritchett	.15	.07	.02
☐ 168 Willie Anderson	.08	.04	.01
☐ 169 Regan Upshaw	.08	.04	.01
☐ 170 Daryl Gardener	.15	.07	.02
☐ 171 Alex Molden	.08	.04	.01
☐ 172 John Mobley	.08	.04	.01
☐ 173 Danny Kanell	.30	.14	.04
☐ 174 Marco Battaglia	.08	.04	.01
☐ 175 Simeon Rice	.30	.14	.04
☐ 176 Tony Banks RC	1.25	.55	.16

☐ 177 Stephen Davis	.30	.14	.04
☐ 178 Walt Harris	.08	.04	.01
☐ 179 Amani Toomer	.30	.14	.04
☐ 180 Derrick Mayes	1.00	.45	.12
☐ 181 Jeff Lewis	.15	.07	.02
☐ 182 Chris Darkins	.15	.07	.02
☐ 183 Rickey Dudley	.30	.14	.04
☐ 184 Jonathan Ogden	.08	.04	.01
☐ 185 Mike Alstott	.50	.23	.06
☐ 186 Eric Moulds	1.00	.45	.12
☐ 187 Karim Abdul-Jabbar	3.00	1.35	.35
☐ 188 Jerry Rice Checklist Card	.35	.16	.04
☐ 189 Dan Marino Checklist Card	.50	.23	.06
☐ 190 Emmitt Smith Checklist Card	.50	.23	.06

1996 Leaf Collector's Edition

This 190-card set is a parallel version of the regular Leaf set with gold foil highlights and the words "Collectors Edition" printed across the top of the horizontal back.

	MINT	NRMT	EXC
COMPLETE SET (190)	40.00	18.00	5.00
COMMON CARD (1-190)	.10	.05	.01

*COLLECT.EDITION CARDS: .6X TO 1.25X

1996 Leaf Press Proofs

This 190-card set is a die-cut, gold foil parallel version of the regular Leaf set. Each card is serial numbered as one of 2,000 cards produced.

	MINT	NRMT	EXC
COMPLETE SET (190)	800.00	350.00	100.00
COMMON CARD (1-190)	2.00	.90	.25

*STARS: 15X TO 30X BASIC CARDS ..
*YOUNG STARS: 12.5X TO 25X BASIC CARDS
*RCs: 10X TO 20X BASIC CARDS ......

1996 Leaf American All-Stars

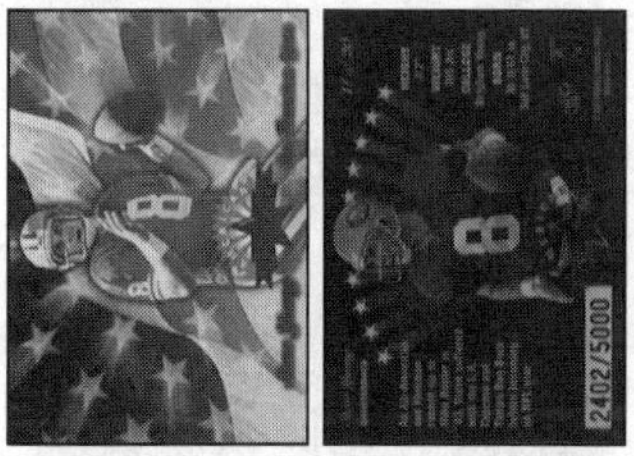

This 20-card set features color player photos of top former All-American NFL players printed on simulated sail cloth card stock with the look and feel of a real American flag. Only 5000 of this set were produced, and each card is sequentially numbered.

	MINT	NRMT	EXC
COMPLETE SET (20)	350.00	160.00	45.00
COMMON CARD (1-20)	6.00	2.70	.75

*GOLD CARDS: 1X TO 2X BASIC CARDS

☐ 1 Emmitt Smith	50.00	22.00	6.25
☐ 2 Drew Bledsoe	20.00	9.00	2.50
☐ 3 Jerry Rice	20.00	9.00	2.50
☐ 4 Kerry Collins	20.00	9.00	2.50
☐ 5 Eddie George	25.00	11.00	3.10
☐ 6 Keyshawn Johnson	10.00	4.50	1.25
☐ 7 Lawrence Phillips	6.00	2.70	.75
☐ 8 Rashaan Salaam	8.00	3.60	1.00
☐ 9 Deion Sanders	12.00	5.50	1.50
☐ 10 Marshall Faulk	8.00	3.60	1.00
☐ 11 Steve Young	15.00	6.75	1.85
☐ 12 Ki-Jana Carter	6.00	2.70	.75
☐ 13 Curtis Martin	20.00	9.00	2.50
☐ 14 Joey Galloway	8.00	3.60	1.00
☐ 15 Troy Aikman	20.00	9.00	2.50
☐ 16 Barry Sanders	20.00	9.00	2.50
☐ 17 Dan Marino	50.00	22.00	6.25
☐ 18 John Elway	15.00	6.75	1.85
☐ 19 Steve McNair	10.00	4.50	1.25
☐ 20 Tim Biakabutuka	8.00	3.60	1.00

1996 Leaf Collector's Edition Autographs

Randomly inserted at the rate of at least one per set, this 14-card set features authentic player autographs. Reportedly, no more than 2,000 autographs were produced of any of the players. The cards are checklisted below alphabetically.

	MINT	NRMT	EXC
COMPLETE SET (14)	300.00	135.00	38.00
COMMON CARD (1-14)	12.00	5.50	1.50

☐ 1 Karim Abdul-Jabbar	35.00	16.00	4.40
☐ 2 Tony Banks	15.00	6.75	1.85
☐ 3 Tim Biakabutuka	15.00	6.75	1.85
☐ 4 Isaac Bruce	15.00	6.75	1.85
☐ 5 Terrell Davis	50.00	22.00	6.25
☐ 6 Bobby Engram	12.00	5.50	1.50
☐ 7 Joey Galloway	25.00	11.00	3.10
☐ 8 Eddie George	60.00	27.00	7.50
☐ 9 Marvin Harrison	15.00	6.75	1.85
☐ 10 Eddie Kennison	20.00	9.00	2.50
☐ 11 Leeland McElroy	12.00	5.50	1.50
☐ 12 Lawrence Phillips	15.00	6.75	1.85
☐ 13 Rashaan Salaam	15.00	6.75	1.85
☐ 14 Tamarick Vanover	15.00	6.75	1.85

1996 Leaf Gold Leaf Rookies

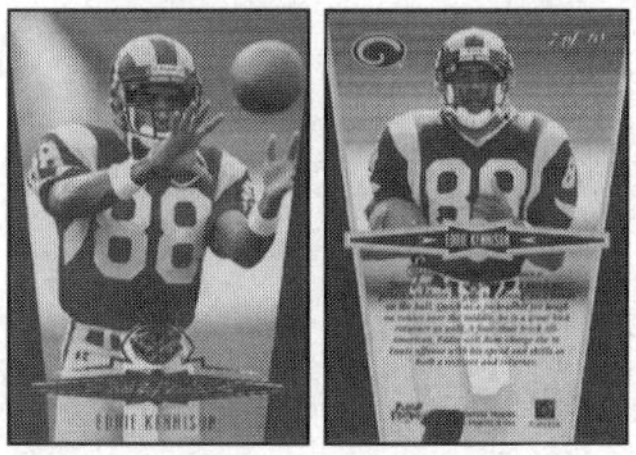

This 10-card set features color photos of ten standout newcomers with gold foil triangular side borders. The backs carry another player photo with team color triangular side borders and a paragraph about the player.

	MINT	NRMT	EXC
COMPLETE SET (10)	30.00	13.50	3.70
COMMON CARD (1-10)	2.00	.90	.25

☐ 1 Leeland McElroy	2.00	.90	.25
☐ 2 Marvin Harrison	4.00	1.80	.50
☐ 3 Lawrence Phillips	3.00	1.35	.35
☐ 4 Bobby Engram	2.00	.90	.25
☐ 5 Kevin Hardy	2.00	.90	.25
☐ 6 Keyshawn Johnson	4.00	1.80	.50
☐ 7 Eddie Kennison	4.00	1.80	.50
☐ 8 Tim Biakabutuka	3.00	1.35	.35
☐ 9 Eddie George	12.00	5.50	1.50
☐ 10 Terry Glenn	8.00	3.60	1.00

1996 Leaf Gold Leaf Stars

Randomly inserted in retail packs only, this 15-card set features color player photos on a gold foil background with a 22 karat gold seal. The backs carry a small player photo and a paragraph about the player. Only 2500 of this set were produced.

	MINT	NRMT	EXC
COMPLETE SET (15)	500.00	220.00	60.00
COMMON CARD (1-15)	12.00	5.50	1.50

☐ 1 Drew Bledsoe	40.00	18.00	5.00
☐ 2 Jerry Rice	40.00	18.00	5.00
☐ 3 Emmitt Smith	70.00	32.00	8.75
☐ 4 Dan Marino	70.00	32.00	8.75
☐ 5 Isaac Bruce	15.00	6.75	1.85
☐ 6 Kerry Collins	35.00	16.00	4.40
☐ 7 Barry Sanders	40.00	18.00	5.00
☐ 8 Keyshawn Johnson	15.00	6.75	1.85
☐ 9 Errict Rhett	12.00	5.50	1.50
☐ 10 Joey Galloway	18.00	8.00	2.20
☐ 11 Brett Favre	70.00	32.00	8.75
☐ 12 Curtis Martin	35.00	16.00	4.40
☐ 13 Steve Young	30.00	13.50	3.70
☐ 14 Troy Aikman	40.00	18.00	5.00
☐ 15 John Elway	35.00	16.00	4.40

1996 Leaf Grass Roots

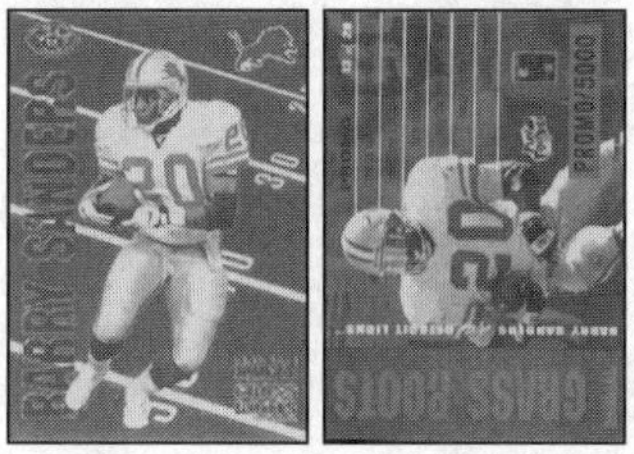

This 20-card set features color images of some of the NFL's top running backs on a simulated artificial turf look and feel background. The backs carry another player photo and a paragraph about the player's running ability. Only 5000 of this set were produced.

	MINT	NRMT	EXC
COMPLETE SET (20)	150.00	70.00	19.00
COMMON CARD (1-20)	5.00	2.20	.60

☐ 1 Thurman Thomas	8.00	3.60	1.00
☐ 2 Eddie George	25.00	11.00	3.10
☐ 3 Rodney Hampton	5.00	2.20	.60
☐ 4 Rashaan Salaam	8.00	3.60	1.00
☐ 5 Natrone Means	6.00	2.70	.75
☐ 6 Errict Rhett	6.00	2.70	.75
☐ 7 Leeland McElroy	5.00	2.20	.60
☐ 8 Emmitt Smith	30.00	13.50	3.70
☐ 9 Marshall Faulk	8.00	3.60	1.00
☐ 10 Ricky Watters	6.00	2.70	.75
☐ 11 Chris Warren	5.00	2.20	.60
☐ 12 Tim Biakabutuka	8.00	3.60	1.00
☐ 13 Barry Sanders	15.00	6.75	1.85
☐ 14 Karim Abdul-Jabbar	15.00	6.75	1.85
☐ 15 Darick Holmes	5.00	2.20	.60
☐ 16 Terrell Davis	15.00	6.75	1.85
☐ 17 Lawrence Phillips	8.00	3.60	1.00
☐ 18 Ki-Jana Carter	5.00	2.20	.60
☐ 19 Curtis Martin	15.00	6.75	1.85
☐ 20 Kordell Stewart	15.00	6.75	1.85

1996 Leaf Shirt Off My Back

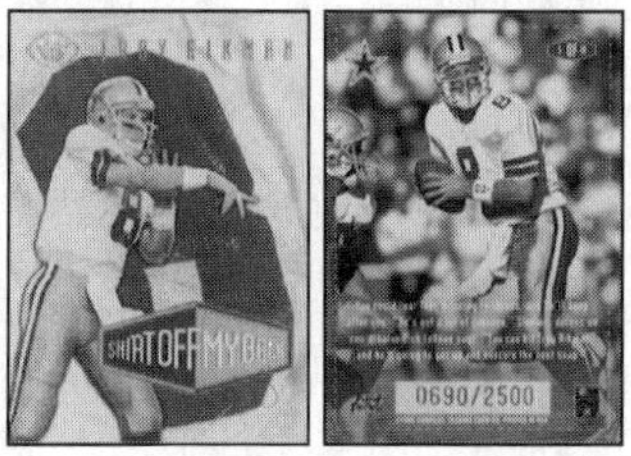

Randomly inserted in magazine packs only, this 10-card set features color images of the league's top quarterbacks with each team jersey and number as a background and is printed on card stock that simulates jersey material. Only 2500 of each card were produced and are sequentially numbered.

	MINT	NRMT	EXC
COMPLETE SET (10)	250.00	110.00	31.00
COMMON CARD (1-10)	10.00	4.50	1.25

☐ 1 Steve Young	20.00	9.00	2.50
☐ 2 Jeff Blake	10.00	4.50	1.25
☐ 3 Drew Bledsoe	30.00	13.50	3.70
☐ 4 Kordell Stewart	25.00	11.00	3.10
☐ 5 Troy Aikman	30.00	13.50	3.70
☐ 6 Steve McNair	20.00	9.00	2.50
☐ 7 John Elway	25.00	11.00	3.10
☐ 8 Dan Marino	60.00	27.00	7.50
☐ 9 Kerry Collins	25.00	11.00	3.10
☐ 10 Brett Favre	60.00	27.00	7.50

1996 Leaf Statistical Standouts

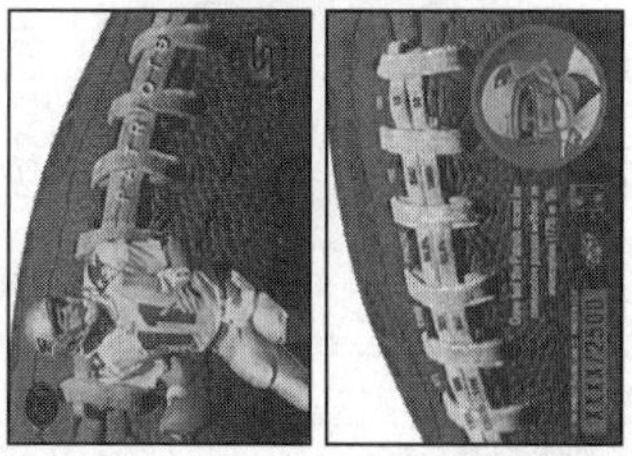

Randomly inserted in hobby packs only, this 15-card set features color player images printed on a simulated leather football die-cut card. The backs carry a small player circular head photo with season and career statistics. Only 2500 of each card were produced and are sequentially numbered.

	MINT	NRMT	EXC
COMPLETE SET (15)	450.00	200.00	55.00
COMMON CARD (1-15)	12.00	5.50	1.50

☐ 1 John Elway	30.00	13.50	3.70
☐ 2 Jerry Rice	40.00	18.00	5.00
☐ 3 Reggie White	15.00	6.75	1.85
☐ 4 Drew Bledsoe	40.00	18.00	5.00
☐ 5 Chris Warren	12.00	5.50	1.50
☐ 6 Bruce Smith	15.00	6.75	1.85
☐ 7 Barry Sanders	40.00	18.00	5.00
☐ 8 Greg Lloyd	12.00	5.50	1.50
☐ 9 Emmitt Smith	75.00	34.00	9.50
☐ 10 Dan Marino	75.00	34.00	9.50
☐ 11 Steve Young	25.00	11.00	3.10
☐ 12 Steve Atwater	12.00	5.50	1.50
☐ 13 Isaac Bruce	15.00	6.75	1.85
☐ 14 Deion Sanders	25.00	11.00	3.10
☐ 15 Brett Favre	75.00	34.00	9.50

1993-94 Legendary Foils

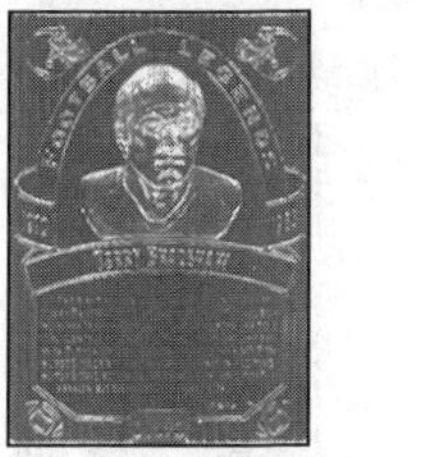

The Legendary Foils Sport Series was intended to be a monthly series featuring Pro Football Hall of Famers. The cards measure approximately 3 1/2" by 5" and were issued in a green and black custom designed folder. The embossed fronts carry the players portrait and a short career summary. The gold edition cards are completely gold foil layered on a matte gold background, while the colored edition cards have a green background. Production was limited to no more than 95,000 for the colored edition and 5,000 for the gold edition. The serial number also appears on the front. The backs are silver and carry Legendary Foil logos. There were no card numbers. We've included single card prices below for the colored version.

	MINT	NRMT	EXC
COMPLETE SET (2)	6.00	2.70	.75
COMMON CARD (1-2)	2.00	.90	.25

☐ 1 Morris Red Badgro	2.00	.90	.25
☐ 2 Terry Bradshaw	4.00	1.80	.50
☐ P1 Terry Bradshaw Promo	4.00	1.80	.50

1950 Lions Matchbooks

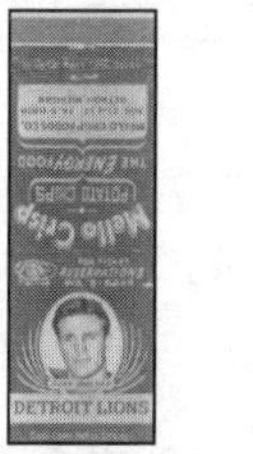

Universal Match Corp. produced these Detroit Lions matchcovers. Each measures approximately 1 1/2" by 4 1/2" (when completely folded out) and features a blue bordered front with the player's photo in black and white along with an advertisement for either Mello Crisp Potato Chips or Ray Whyte Chevy. Backs contain the 1950 Lions' sesaon schedule. The prices given are for full covers (with strikers) missing the actual matches. This is the form in which the matchbooks are most commonly found. Complete books with matches typically carry a 50% premium. Books missing the striker are considered VG at best.

	NRMT	VG-E	GOOD
COMPLETE SET (2)	25.00	11.00	3.10
COMMON MATCHBOOK	10.00	4.50	1.25

☐ 1 Leon Hart	10.00	4.50	1.25
☐ 2 Doak Walker	15.00	6.75	1.85

1961 Lions Jay Publishing

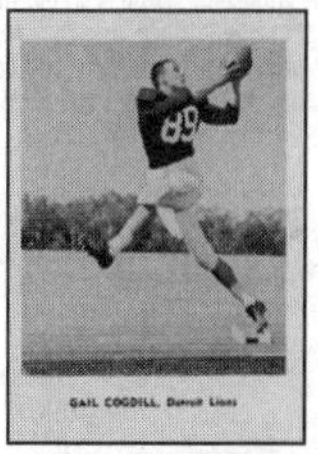

This 12-card set features (approximately) 5" by 7" black-and-white player photos. The photos show players in traditional poses with the quarterback preparing to throw, the runner heading downfield, and the defenseman ready for the tackle. These cards were packaged 12 to a packet and originally sold for 25 cents. The backs are blank. The cards are unnumbered and checklisted below in alphabetical order.

	NRMT	VG-E	GOOD
COMPLETE SET (12)	75.00	34.00	[illegible]
COMMON CARD (1-12)	5.00	2.20	[illegible]

☐ 1 Carl Brettschneider	5.00	2.20	[illegible]
☐ 2 Howard Cassady	6.00	2.70	[illegible]
☐ 3 Gail Cogdill	5.00	2.20	[illegible]
☐ 4 Jim Gibbons	6.00	2.70	[illegible]
☐ 5 Alex Karras	10.00	4.50	[illegible]
☐ 6 Yale Lary	7.50	3.40	[illegible]
☐ 7 Jim Martin	5.00	2.20	[illegible]
☐ 8 Earl Morrall	7.50	3.40	[illegible]
☐ 9 Jim Ninowski	6.00	2.70	[illegible]
☐ 10 Nick Pietrosante	6.00	2.70	[illegible]

☐ 11 Joe Schmidt	10.00	4.50	1.25
☐ 12 George Wilson CO	5.00	2.20	.60

1964 Lions Team Issue

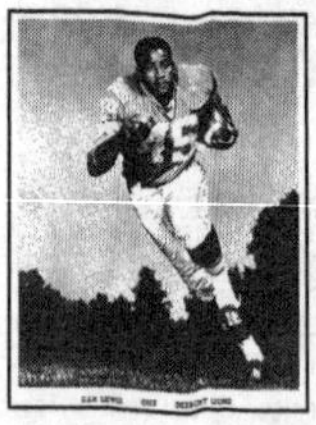

This 24 card team issue set consists of glossy black and white 7 3/8" by 9 3/8" posed action photos enclosed in a white border. Player's name and position are printed on one line with the team name in black ink along the bottom portion of the white border. The set is unnumbered and thus the cards are listed below alphabetically. Some of the players may have been reissued in later years as some of the cards can be found with a dated stamp on the back.

	NRMT	VG-E	GOOD
COMPLETE SET (24)	100.00	45.00	12.50
COMMON CARD (1-24)	4.00	1.80	.50
☐ 1 Dick Compton	4.00	1.80	.50
☐ 2 Larry Ferguson	4.00	1.80	.50
☐ 3 Dennis Gaubatz	4.00	1.80	.50
☐ 4 Jim Gibbons	5.00	2.20	.60
☐ 5 John Gonzaga	4.00	1.80	.50
☐ 6 John Gordy	5.00	2.20	.60
☐ 7 Tom Hall	4.00	1.80	.50
☐ 8 Roger LaLonde	4.00	1.80	.50
☐ 9 Dan LaRose	4.00	1.80	.50
☐ 10 Yale Lary	10.00	4.50	1.25
☐ 11 Dan Lewis	5.00	2.20	.60
☐ 12 Gary Lowe	4.00	1.80	.50
☐ 13 Bruce Maher	5.00	2.20	.60
☐ 14 Hugh McInnis	4.00	1.80	.50
☐ 15 Max Messner	4.00	1.80	.50
☐ 16 Floyd Peters	6.00	2.70	.75
☐ 17 Daryl Sanders	4.00	1.80	.50
☐ 18 Joe Schmidt	12.00	5.50	1.50
☐ 19 Bob Scholtz	4.00	1.80	.50
☐ 20 James Simon	4.00	1.80	.50
☐ 21 J.D. Smith	5.00	2.20	.60
☐ 22 Bill Quinlan	4.00	1.80	.50
☐ 23 Bob Whitlow	4.00	1.80	.50
☐ 24 Sam Williams	4.00	1.80	.50

1966 Lions Marathon Oil

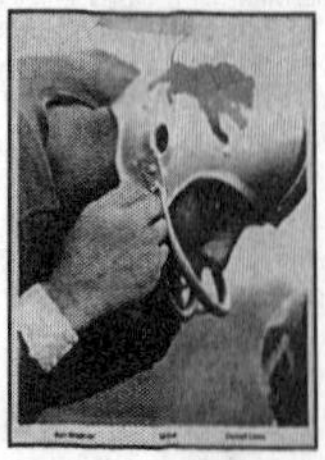

This set consists of seven photos measuring approximately 5" by 7" thought to have been released by Marathon Oil. The fronts feature black-and-white photos with white borders. The player's name, position, and team name are printed in the bottom border. The backs are blank. The cards are unnumbered and checklisted below in alphabetical order.

	NRMT	VG-E	GOOD
COMPLETE SET (7)	45.00	20.00	5.50
COMMON CARD (1-7)	5.00	2.20	.60
☐ 1 Gail Cogdill	6.00	2.70	.75
☐ 2 John Gordy	5.00	2.20	.60
☐ 3 Alex Karras	15.00	6.75	1.85
☐ 4 Ron Kramer	6.00	2.70	.75
☐ 5 Milt Plum	8.00	3.60	1.00
☐ 6 Wayne Rasmussen	5.00	2.20	.60
☐ 7 Daryl Sanders	5.00	2.20	.60

1966 Lions Team Issue

The Detroit Lions issued this set of large photos to Lions' fans who requested player pictures in 1966. Each measures approximately 7 1/2" by 9 1/2" and features a black and white photo. The player's name, position, and team name appear below the photo.

	NRMT	VG-E	GOOD
COMPLETE SET (41)	200.00	90.00	25.00
COMMON CARD (1-41)	4.00	1.80	.50
☐ 1 Mike Alford	4.00	1.80	.50
☐ 2 Roger Brown	5.00	2.20	.60
☐ 3 Ernie Clark	4.00	1.80	.50
☐ 4 Bill Cody	4.00	1.80	.50
☐ 5 Gail Cogdill	5.00	2.20	.60
☐ 6 Ed Flanagan	4.00	1.80	.50
☐ 7 Jim Gibbons	4.00	1.80	.50
☐ 8 John Gordy	4.00	1.80	.50
☐ 9 Larry Hand	5.00	2.20	.60
☐ 10 John Henderson	4.00	1.80	.50
☐ 11 Wally Hilgenberg	5.00	2.20	.60
☐ 12 Alex Karras	15.00	6.75	1.85
☐ 13 Bob Kowalkowski	4.00	1.80	.50
☐ 14 Ron Kramer	6.00	2.70	.75
☐ 15 Dick LeBeau	6.00	2.70	.75
☐ 16 Joe Don Looney	10.00	4.50	1.25
☐ 17 Mike Lucci	6.00	2.70	.75
☐ 18 Bruce Maher	4.00	1.80	.50
☐ 19 Bill Malinchak	4.00	1.80	.50
☐ 20 Amos Marsh	5.00	2.20	.60
☐ 21 Jerry Mazzanti	4.00	1.80	.50
☐ 22 Darris McCord	5.00	2.20	.60
☐ 23 Bruce McLenna	4.00	1.80	.50
☐ 24 Tom Nowatzke	5.00	2.20	.60
☐ 25 Milt Plum	8.00	3.60	1.00
☐ 26 Wayne Rasmussen	4.00	1.80	.50
☐ 27 Johnnie Robinson DB	5.00	2.20	.60
☐ 28 Jerry Rush	5.00	2.20	.60
☐ 29 Daryl Sanders	4.00	1.80	.50
☐ 30 Bobby Smith	4.00	1.80	.50
☐ 31 J.D. Smith	6.00	2.70	.75
☐ 32 Pat Studstill	5.00	2.20	.60
☐ 33 Karl Sweetan	5.00	2.20	.60
☐ 34 Bobby Thompson	4.00	1.80	.50
☐ 35 Jim Todd	4.00	1.80	.50
☐ 36 Doug Van Horn	5.00	2.20	.60
☐ 37 Tom Vaughn	4.00	1.80	.50
☐ 38 Wayne Walker	5.00	2.20	.60
☐ 39 Willie Walker	4.00	1.80	.50
☐ 40 Tom Watkins	4.00	1.80	.50
☐ 41 Coaching Staff John North Lou Rymkus Harry Gilmer Carl Taseff Carl Brettschneider Sammy Baugh Joe Schmidt	15.00	6.75	1.85

1986 Lions Police

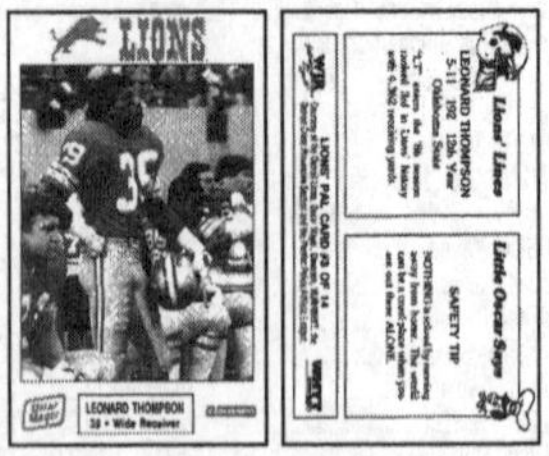

This 14-card set of Detroit Lions is numbered on the card backs, which are printed in black ink on white card stock. Cards measure approximately 2 5/8" by 4 1/8". The set was sponsored by the Detroit Lions, Oscar Mayer, Claussen, WJR/WHYT, the Detroit Crime Prevention Section, and the Pontiac Police Athletic League. Uniform numbers are printed on the card front along with the player's name and position.

	MINT	NRMT	EXC
COMPLETE SET (14)	6.00	2.70	.75
COMMON CARD (1-14)	.50	.23	.06
☐ 1 William Gay	.50	.23	.06
☐ 2 Pontiac Silverdome	.60	.25	.07
☐ 3 Leonard Thompson	.60	.25	.07
☐ 4 Eddie Murray	.75	.35	.09
☐ 5 Eric Hipple	.75	.35	.09
☐ 6 James Jones	.75	.35	.09
☐ 7 Darryl Rogers CO	.50	.23	.06
☐ 8 Chuck Long	.75	.35	.09
☐ 9 Garry James	.60	.25	.07
☐ 10 Michael Cofer	.60	.25	.07
☐ 11 Jeff Chadwick	.60	.25	.07
☐ 12 Jimmy Williams	.50	.23	.06
☐ 13 Keith Dorney	.50	.23	.06
☐ 14 Bobby Watkins	.50	.23	.06

1987 Lions Police

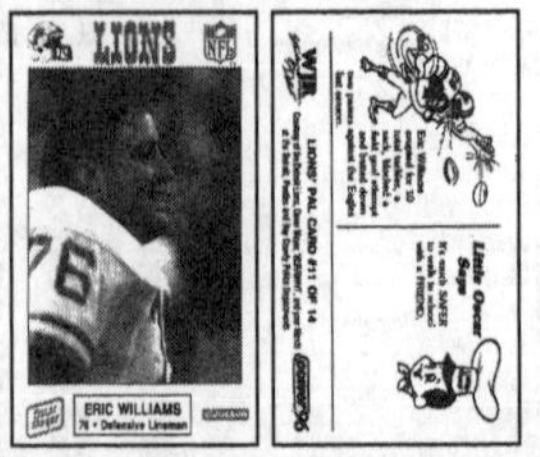

This 14-card set of Detroit Lions is numbered on the back. The card backs are printed in blue ink on white card stock and contain a safety tip entitled "Little Oscar Says". Cards measure approximately 2 5/8" by 4 1/8". The set was sponsored by the Detroit Lions, Oscar Mayer, Claussen Pickles, WJR/WHYT, the Detroit Crime Prevention Section, and the Pontiac Police Athletic League. Uniform numbers are printed on the card front along with the player's name and position. Reportedly, nearly three million cards were distributed through the participating police agencies. The Lions team name appears above the player photo which differentiates this set from the 1988 Police Lions set.

	MINT	NRMT	EXC
COMPLETE SET (14)	6.00	2.70	.75
COMMON CARD (1-14)	.40	.18	.05
☐ 1 Michael Cofer Vernon Maxwell William Gay	.50	.23	.06
☐ 2 Rich Strenger	.40	.18	.05
☐ 3 Keith Ferguson	.40	.18	.05
☐ 4 James Jones	.60	.25	.07
☐ 5 Jeff Chadwick	.50	.23	.06
☐ 6 Devon Mitchell	.40	.18	.05
☐ 7 Eddie Murray	.60	.25	.07
☐ 8 Reggie Rogers	.50	.23	.06
☐ 9 Chuck Long	.60	.25	.07
☐ 10 Jimmie Giles	.60	.25	.07
☐ 11 Eric Williams	.40	.18	.05
☐ 12 Lomas Brown	.50	.23	.06
☐ 13 Jimmy Williams	.40	.18	.05
☐ 14 Garry James	.50	.23	.06

1988 Lions Police

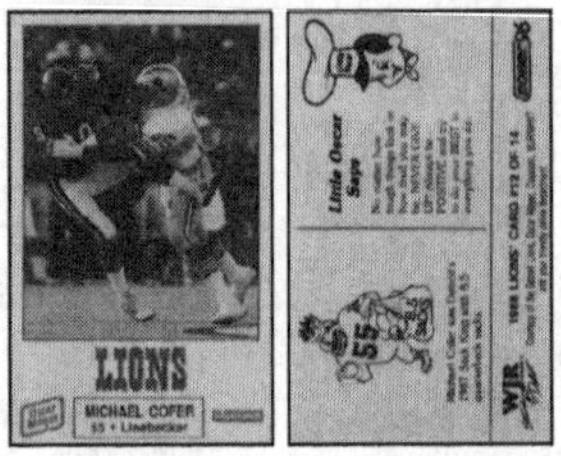

The 1988 Police Detroit Lions set contains 14 numbered cards measuring approximately 2 5/8" by 4 1/8". There are 13 single player cards plus one for Detroit's top three 1988 draft picks. The backs have career highlights and safety tips. The Lions team name appears below the player photo which differentiates this set from the similar-looking 1987 Police Lions set.

	MINT	NRMT	EXC
COMPLETE SET (14)	6.00	2.70	.75
COMMON CARD (1-14)	.50	.23	.06
☐ 1 Rob Rubick	.50	.23	.06
☐ 2 Paul Butcher	.50	.23	.06
☐ 3 Pete Mandley	.60	.25	.07
☐ 4 Jimmy Williams	.50	.23	.06
☐ 5 Harvey Salem	.50	.23	.06
☐ 6 Chuck Long	.60	.25	.07
☐ 7 Pat Carter Bennie Blades Chris Spielman	1.25	.55	.16
☐ 8 Jerry Ball	.75	.35	.09
☐ 9 Lomas Brown	.60	.25	.07
☐ 10 Dennis Gibson	.50	.23	.06
☐ 11 Jim Arnold	.50	.23	.06
☐ 12 Michael Cofer	.50	.23	.06
☐ 13 James Jones	.60	.25	.07
☐ 14 Steve Mott	.50	.23	.06

1989 Lions Police

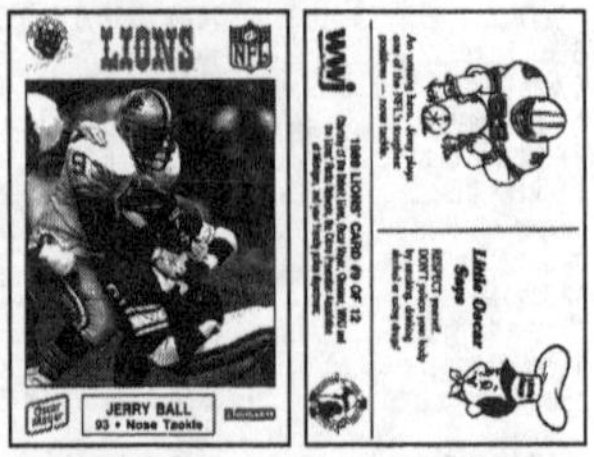

The 1989 Police Detroit Lions set contains 12 numbered cards measuring approximately 2 5/8" by 4 1/8". The set was also sponsored by Oscar Mayer. The fronts have white borders and color action photos; some are horizontally oriented, others are vertically oriented. The horizontally oriented backs have safety tips and brief career highlights. These cards were printed on very thin stock. The set is notable for a card of Barry Sanders, showing a photo of him at his postdraft press conference. It has been reported that three million cards were given away during this program by police officers in Michigan and Ontario.

	MINT	NRMT	EXC
COMPLETE SET (12)	12.00	5.50	1.50
COMMON CARD (1-12)	.35	.16	.04
☐ 1 George Jamison	.35	.16	.04
☐ 2 Wayne Fontes CO	.50	.23	.06
☐ 3 Kevin Glover	.35	.16	.04
☐ 4 Chris Spielman	1.00	.45	.12
☐ 5 Eddie Murray	.50	.23	.06
☐ 6 Bennie Blades	.75	.35	.09
☐ 7 Joe Milinichik	.35	.16	.04
☐ 8 Michael Cofer	.35	.16	.04
☐ 9 Jerry Ball	.50	.23	.06
☐ 10 Dennis Gibson	.35	.16	.04
☐ 11 Barry Sanders	10.00	4.50	1.25
☐ 12 Jim Arnold	.35	.16	.04

1990 Lions Police

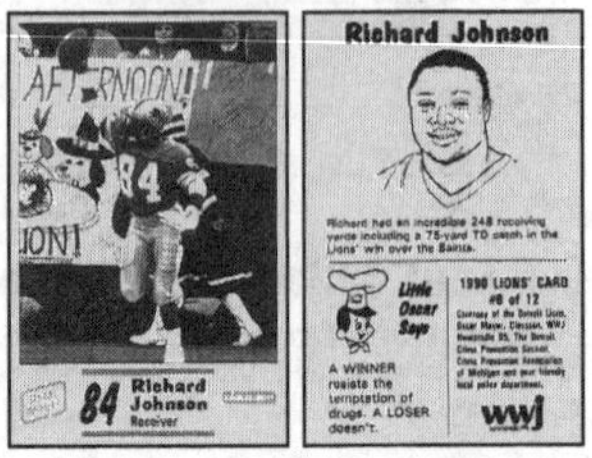

This 12-card set was issued by Oscar Mayer in conjunction with the Detroit Lions, Claussen, WWJ radio station, the Detroit Crime Prevention Society, and the Crime Prevention Association of Michigan. The fronts of the cards feature an action photo of the player on the front and a drawing of the player along with a brief note about the player on the back. In addition there is a safety tip from Little Oscar (the symbol for Oscar Mayer) on the back. The cards measure approximately 2 5/8" by 4 1/8".

	MINT	NRMT	EXC
COMPLETE SET (12)	7.00	3.10	.85
COMMON CARD (1-12)	.35	.16	.04
☐ 1 William White	.35	.16	.04
☐ 2 Chris Spielman	.75	.35	.09
☐ 3 Rodney Peete	1.00	.45	.12
☐ 4 Jimmy Williams	.35	.16	.04
☐ 5 Bennie Blades	.50	.23	.06
☐ 6 Barry Sanders	4.00	1.80	.50
☐ 7 Jerry Ball	.50	.23	.06
☐ 8 Richard Johnson	.50	.23	.06
☐ 9 Michael Cofer	.35	.16	.04
☐ 10 Lomas Brown	.50	.23	.06
☐ 11 Joe Schmidt GM Andre Ware Wayne Fontes CO	.75	.35	.09
☐ 12 Eddie Murray	.50	.23	.06

1991 Lions Police

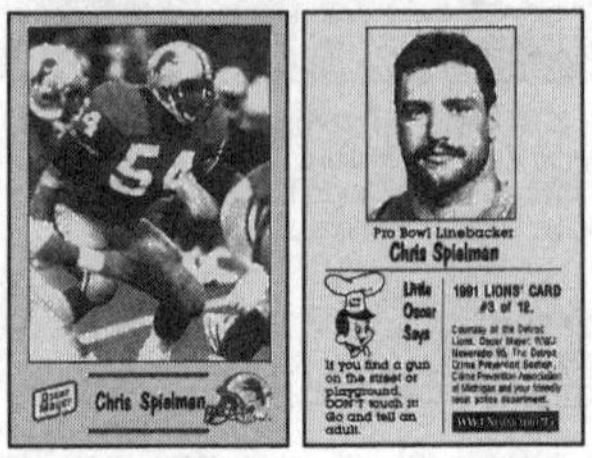

This 12-card Police Lions set was distributed during the season by participating Michigan police departments. The cards measure approximately 2 5/8" by 4 1/8" and feature color action shots of each player enclosed in a yellow border on thin card stock. Oscar Mayer's logo, player's name, and team helmet appearing at the bottom of each card are highlighted by blue lines above and below. Card backs, printed vertically, carry a black and white head shot of the player, player information, while a safety tip from the main sponsor appears at the bottom left half of card. The bottom right half lists card numbers and other sponsor names.

	MINT	NRMT	EXC
COMPLETE SET (12)	6.00	2.70	.75
COMMON CARD (1-12)	.35	.16	.04
☐ 1 Mel Gray	.60	.25	.07
☐ 2 Ken Dallafior	.35	.16	.04
☐ 3 Chris Spielman	.60	.25	.07
☐ 4 Bennie Blades	.50	.23	.06
☐ 5 Robert Clark	.50	.23	.06
☐ 6 Eric Andolsek	.50	.23	.06
☐ 7 Rodney Peete	.75	.35	.09
☐ 8 William White	.35	.16	.04
☐ 9 Lomas Brown	.50	.23	.06
☐ 10 Jerry Ball	.50	.23	.06
☐ 11 Michael Cofer	.35	.16	.04
☐ 12 Barry Sanders	3.00	1.35	.35

1993 Lions 60th Season Commemorative

These 16 standard-size 60th-season commemorative cards feature borderless player photos on their fronts. Some photos are color, others are black-and-white; some are action shots, others are posed. The player's name (or the card's title), the rectangle it appears in, and the 60th season logo, all appear in team colors. The white backs carry black-and-white head shots of the players. Also appearing are the players' names, the years they played for the Lions, position, and

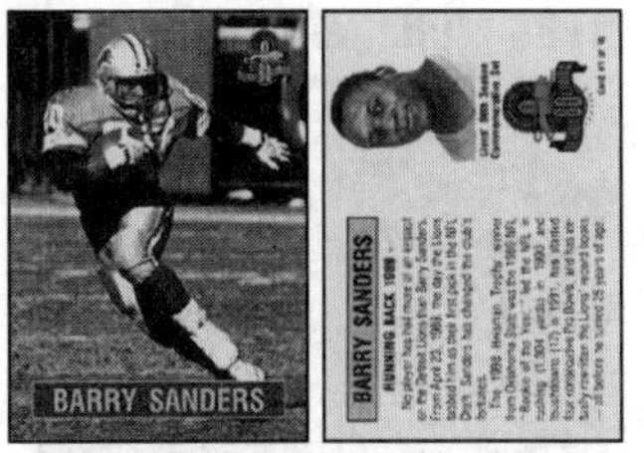

career highlights. The team color-coded 60th season logo reappears in a lower corner. The cards came with their own approximately 6" by 8" four-page black vinyl card holder emblazoned with the Lions' 60th season logo.

	MINT	NRMT	EXC
COMPLETE SET (16)	15.00	6.75	1.85
COMMON CARD (1-16)	.50	.23	.06
☐ 1 Barry Sanders	4.00	1.80	.50
☐ 2 Joe Schmidt	1.25	.55	.16
☐ 3 The Fearsome Foursome	.75	.35	.09
Sam Williams			
Roger Brown			
Alex Karras			
Darris McCord			
☐ 4 Chris Spielman	.75	.35	.09
☐ 5 Billy Sims	.75	.35	.09
☐ 6 '40s Phenoms	.75	.35	.09
Alex Wojciechowicz			
Byron(Whizzer) White			
☐ 7 Thunder and Lightning	.50	.23	.06
Bennie Blades			
Mel Gray			
☐ 8 Bobby Layne	1.50	.70	.19
☐ 9 Dutch Clark	.75	.35	.09
☐ 10 Great Games	.50	.23	.06
Thanksgiving 1962			
☐ 11 Charlie Sanders	.75	.35	.09
☐ 12 Lomas Brown	.50	.23	.06
☐ 13 Doug English	.75	.35	.09
☐ 14 Doak Walker	1.50	.70	.19
☐ 15 Roaring '20s	2.00	.90	.25
Lem Barney			
Billy Sims			
Barry Sanders			
☐ 16 Anniversary Card	.50	.23	.06

1990 Little Big Leaguers

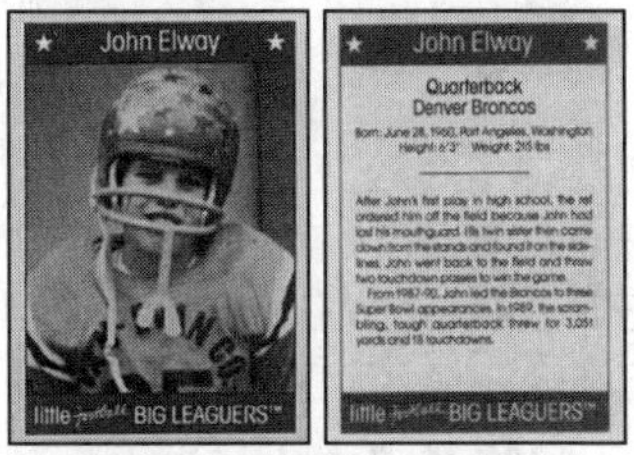

This 95-page book/album was published by Simon and Schuster and includes boyhood stories of today's pro football players. Moreover, five 8 1/2" by 11" sheets of cards (nine cards per sheet) are inserted at the end of the album; after perforation, the cards measure the standard size. The fronts feature black and white photos of these players as kids. The cards have blue and white borders, and in the thicker blue borders above and below the picture, one finds the player's name and the words "Little Football Big Leaguers" respectively. The backs have the same design, only with biography and career summary in place of the picture. The cards are unnumbered and checklisted below in alphabetical order.

	MINT	NRMT	EXC
COMPLETE SET (45)	40.00	18.00	5.00
COMMON CARD (1-45)	.50	.23	.06
☐ 1 Troy Aikman	9.00	4.00	1.10
☐ 2 Morten Andersen	.50	.23	.06
☐ 3 Jerry Ball	.50	.23	.06
☐ 4 Carl Banks	.75	.35	.09
☐ 5 Bennie Blades	.50	.23	.06
☐ 6 Brian Blades	.75	.35	.09
☐ 7 Joey Browner	.50	.23	.06
☐ 8 Keith Byars	.75	.35	.09
☐ 9 Anthony Carter	.75	.35	.09
☐ 10 Deron Cherry	.50	.23	.06
☐ 11 Roger Craig	.75	.35	.09
☐ 12 John Elway	7.50	3.40	.95
☐ 13 Doug Flutie	1.00	.45	.12
☐ 14 Tim Goad	.50	.23	.06
☐ 15 Bob Golic	.50	.23	.06
☐ 16 Dino Hackett	.50	.23	.06
☐ 17 Dan Hampton	.75	.35	.09
☐ 18 Bobby Hebert	.75	.35	.09
☐ 19 Darryl Henley	.50	.23	.06
☐ 20 Wes Hopkins	.50	.23	.06
☐ 21 Hank Ilesic	.50	.23	.06
☐ 22 Tunch Ilkin	.50	.23	.06
☐ 23 Perry Kemp	.50	.23	.06
☐ 24 Bernie Kosar	.75	.35	.09
☐ 25 Mike Lansford	.50	.23	.06
☐ 26 Shawn Lee	.50	.23	.06
☐ 27 Charles Mann	.75	.35	.09
☐ 28 Dan Marino	15.00	6.75	1.85
☐ 29 Bruce Matthews	.75	.35	.09
☐ 30 Clay Matthews	.75	.35	.09
☐ 31 Freeman McNeil	.75	.35	.09
☐ 32 Warren Moon	1.50	.70	.19
☐ 33 Anthony Munoz	1.00	.45	.12
☐ 34 Andre Reed	1.00	.45	.12
☐ 35 Andre Rison	1.00	.45	.12
☐ 36 Phil Simms	.75	.35	.09
☐ 37 Mike Singletary	.75	.35	.09
☐ 38 Rohn Stark	.50	.23	.06
☐ 39 Kelly Stouffer	.50	.23	.06
☐ 40 Vinny Testaverde	.75	.35	.09
☐ 41 Doug Williams	.50	.23	.06
☐ 42 Marc Wilson	.50	.23	.06
☐ 43 Craig Wolfley	.50	.23	.06
☐ 44 Ron Wolfley	.50	.23	.06
☐ 45 Steve Young	7.50	3.40	.95

1977 Marketcom Test

The 1977 Marketcom Test set includes 2 known mini-posters measuring approximately 5 1/2" by 8 1/2". They were printed on paper-thin stock and are virtually always found with fold creases. Marketcom is credited at the bottom of each blank-backed poster along with the year 1977. These posters are unnumbered and listed below in alphabetical order.

	NRMT-MT	EXC	G-VG
COMPLETE SET (2)	100.00	45.00	12.50
COMMON CARD (1-2)	50.00	22.00	6.25
☐ 1 Greg Pruitt	50.00	22.00	6.25
☐ 2 Jack Youngblood	50.00	22.00	6.25

1978-79 Marketcom Test

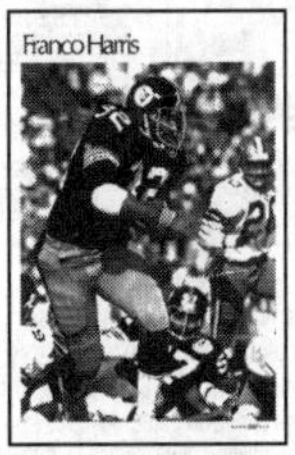

The 1978 Marketcom set includes mini-posters measuring approximately 5 1/2" by 8 1/2". They were printed on paper-thin stock and are virtually always found with fold creases. Marketcom is credited at the bottom of each blank-backed poster. These posters are unnumbered and listed below in alphabetical order.

	NRMT-MT	EXC	G-VG
COMPLETE SET (32)	450.00	200.00	55.00
COMMON CARD (1-32)	6.00	2.70	.75
☐ 1 Otis Armstrong SP	10.00	4.50	1.25
☐ 2 Steve Bartkowski SP	12.00	5.50	1.50
☐ 3 Terry Bradshaw SP	40.00	18.00	5.00
☐ 4 Earl Campbell	30.00	13.50	3.70
☐ 5 Dave Casper	8.00	3.60	1.00
☐ 6 Dan Dierdorf SP	12.00	5.50	1.50
☐ 7 Dan Fouts SP	25.00	11.00	3.10
☐ 8 Tony Galbreath	6.00	2.70	.75
☐ 9 Randy Gradishar SP	10.00	4.50	1.25
☐ 10 Bob Griese SP	25.00	11.00	3.10
☐ 11 Steve Grogan	8.00	3.60	1.00
☐ 12 Ray Guy	8.00	3.60	1.00
☐ 13 Pat Haden SP	12.00	5.50	1.50
☐ 14 Jack Ham	12.00	5.50	1.50
☐ 15 Cliff Harris SP	10.00	4.50	1.25
☐ 16 Franco Harris	15.00	6.75	1.85
☐ 17 Jim Hart	8.00	3.60	1.00
☐ 18 Ron Jaworski	8.00	3.60	1.00
☐ 19 Bert Jones SP	12.00	5.50	1.50
☐ 20 Jack Lambert SP	20.00	9.00	2.50
☐ 21 Reggie McKenzie	6.00	2.70	.75
☐ 22 Karl Mecklenburg SP	10.00	4.50	1.25
☐ 23 Craig Morton	8.00	3.60	1.00
☐ 24 Dan Pastorini	6.00	2.70	.75
☐ 25 Walter Payton SP	40.00	18.00	5.00
☐ 26 Lee Roy Selmon	10.00	4.50	1.25
☐ 27 Roger Staubach SP	40.00	18.00	5.00
☐ 28 Joe Theismann UER	12.00	5.50	1.50
(Misspelled Theisman			
on card)			
☐ 29 Wesley Walker SP	10.00	4.50	1.25
☐ 30 Randy White	12.00	5.50	1.50
☐ 31 Jack Youngblood SP	10.00	4.50	1.25
☐ 32 Jim Zorn	8.00	3.60	1.00

1980 Marketcom

In 1980, Marketcom issued a set of 50 Football Mini-Posters. These 5 1/2" by 8 1/2" cards are very attractive, featuring a large full color (action scene) picture of each player with a white border. The cards have the player's name on front at top and have a facsimile autograph on the picture as well; cards are numbered on the back at the bottom as "x of 50". A very tough to find Rocky Bleier card (numbered 51) was produced as well, but is not listed below due to lack of market information.

	MINT	NRMT	EXC
COMPLETE SET (50)	50.00	22.00	6.25
COMMON CARD (1-50)	.50	.23	.06
☐ 1 Ottis Anderson	1.50	.70	.19
☐ 2 Brian Sipe	.60	.25	.07
☐ 3 Lawrence McCutcheon	.60	.25	.07
☐ 4 Ken Anderson	1.50	.70	.19
☐ 5 Roland Harper	.50	.23	.06
☐ 6 Chuck Foreman	.60	.25	.07
☐ 7 Gary Danielson	.50	.23	.06
☐ 8 Wallace Francis	.50	.23	.06
☐ 9 John Jefferson	.75	.35	.09
☐ 10 Charlie Waters	.75	.35	.09
☐ 11 Jack Ham	1.50	.70	.19
☐ 12 Jack Lambert	1.50	.70	.19
☐ 13 Walter Payton	6.00	2.70	.75
☐ 14 Bert Jones	.75	.35	.09
☐ 15 Harvey Martin	.60	.25	.07
☐ 16 Jim Hart	.60	.25	.07
☐ 17 Craig Morton	.75	.35	.09
☐ 18 Reggie McKenzie	.50	.23	.06
☐ 19 Keith Wortman	.50	.23	.06
☐ 20 Otis Armstrong	.60	.25	.07
☐ 21 Steve Grogan	.75	.35	.09
☐ 22 Jim Zorn	.60	.25	.07
☐ 23 Bob Griese	2.00	.90	.25
☐ 24 Tony Dorsett	3.00	1.35	.35
☐ 25 Wesley Walker	.60	.25	.07
☐ 26 Dan Fouts	2.00	.90	.25
☐ 27 Dan Dierdorf	1.50	.70	.19
☐ 28 Steve Bartkowski	.75	.35	.09
☐ 29 Archie Manning	.75	.35	.09
☐ 30 Randy Gradishar	.60	.25	.07
☐ 31 Randy White	1.50	.70	.19
☐ 32 Joe Theismann	1.50	.70	.19
☐ 33 Tony Galbreath	.50	.23	.06
☐ 34 Cliff Harris	.75	.35	.09
☐ 35 Ray Guy	.75	.35	.09
☐ 36 Dave Casper	.60	.25	.07
☐ 37 Ron Jaworski	.75	.35	.09
☐ 38 Greg Pruitt	.60	.25	.07
☐ 39 Ken Burrough	.60	.25	.07
☐ 40 Robert Brazile	.50	.23	.06
☐ 41 Pat Haden	.75	.35	.09
☐ 42 Dan Pastorini	.60	.25	.07
☐ 43 Lee Roy Selmon	1.50	.70	.19
☐ 44 Franco Harris	2.00	.90	.25
☐ 45 Jack Youngblood	1.00	.45	.12
☐ 46 Terry Bradshaw	6.00	2.70	.75
☐ 47 Roger Staubach	6.00	2.70	.75
☐ 48 Earl Campbell	6.00	2.70	.75
☐ 49 Phil Simms	3.00	1.35	.35
☐ 50 Delvin Williams	.50	.23	.06

1981 Marketcom

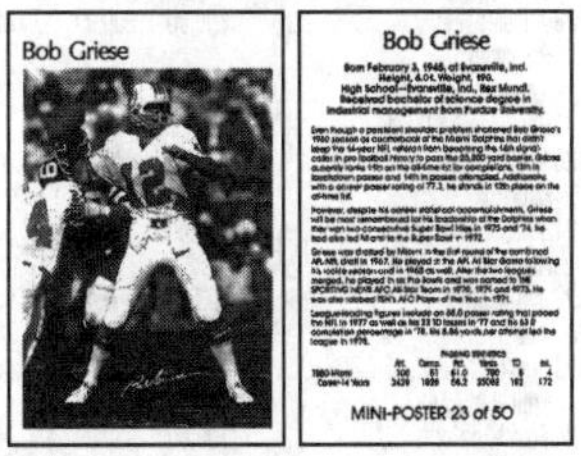

In 1981, Marketcom issued a set of 50 Football Mini-Posters. These 5 1/2" by 8 1/2" cards are very attractive, featuring a large full color (action scene) picture of each player with a white border. The cards have player's name on front at top and have a facsimile autograph on the picture as well; cards are numbered on the back at the bottom. This set can be distinguished from the set of the previous year by the presence of statistics and text on the backs of this issue.

	MINT	NRMT	EXC
COMPLETE SET (50)	40.00	18.00	5.00
COMMON CARD (1-50)	.50	.23	.06
☐ 1 Ottis Anderson	1.00	.45	.12
☐ 2 Brian Sipe	.60	.25	.07
☐ 3 Rocky Bleier	1.00	.45	.12
☐ 4 Ken Anderson	1.50	.70	.19
☐ 5 Roland Harper	.50	.23	.06
☐ 6 Steve Furness	.50	.23	.06
☐ 7 Gary Danielson	.50	.23	.06
☐ 8 Wallace Francis	.60	.25	.07
☐ 9 John Jefferson	.60	.25	.07
☐ 10 Charlie Waters	.75	.35	.09
☐ 11 Jack Ham	1.00	.45	.12
☐ 12 Jack Lambert	1.50	.70	.19
☐ 13 Walter Payton	5.00	2.20	.60
☐ 14 Bert Jones	.75	.35	.09
☐ 15 Harvey Martin	.75	.35	.09
☐ 16 Jim Hart	.75	.35	.09
☐ 17 Craig Morton	.75	.35	.09
☐ 18 Reggie McKenzie	.50	.23	.06
☐ 19 Keith Wortman	.50	.23	.06
☐ 20 Joe Greene	1.50	.70	.19
☐ 21 Steve Grogan	.75	.35	.09
☐ 22 Jim Zorn	.60	.25	.07
☐ 23 Bob Griese	2.00	.90	.25
☐ 24 Tony Dorsett	3.00	1.35	.35
☐ 25 Wesley Walker	.60	.25	.07
☐ 26 Dan Fouts	2.00	.90	.25
☐ 27 Dan Dierdorf	1.00	.45	.12
☐ 28 Steve Bartkowski	.75	.35	.09
☐ 29 Archie Manning	.75	.35	.09
☐ 30 Randy Gradishar	.60	.25	.07
☐ 31 Randy White	1.50	.70	.19
☐ 32 Joe Theismann	1.50	.70	.19
☐ 33 Tony Galbreath	.50	.23	.06
☐ 34 Cliff Harris	.75	.35	.09
☐ 35 Ray Guy	.75	.35	.09
☐ 36 Joe Ferguson	.60	.25	.07
☐ 37 Ron Jaworski	.75	.35	.09
☐ 38 Greg Pruitt	.60	.25	.07
☐ 39 Ken Burrough	.60	.25	.07
☐ 40 Robert Brazile	.50	.23	.06
☐ 41 Pat Haden	.75	.35	.09
☐ 42 Ken Stabler	2.50	1.10	.30
☐ 43 Lee Roy Selmon	1.50	.70	.19
☐ 44 Franco Harris	2.00	.90	.25
☐ 45 Jack Youngblood	1.00	.45	.12
☐ 46 Terry Bradshaw	5.00	2.20	.60
☐ 47 Roger Staubach	5.00	2.20	.60
☐ 48 Earl Campbell	5.00	2.20	.60
☐ 49 Phil Simms	1.50	.70	.19
☐ 50 Delvin Williams	.50	.23	.06

1982 Marketcom

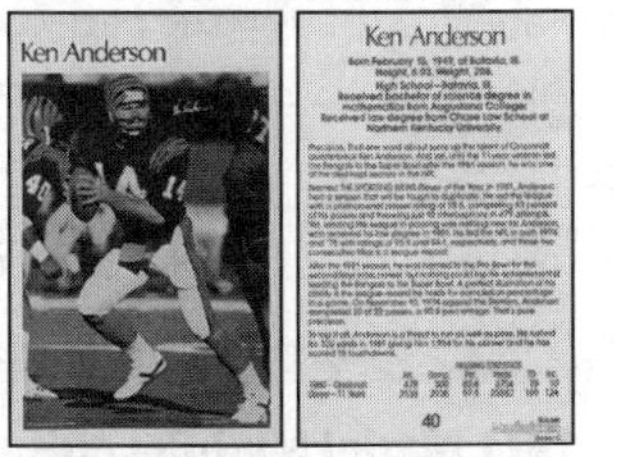

In 1982, Marketcom issued a set of 48 Football Mini-Posters. These 5 1/2" by 8 1/2" cards are very attractive, featuring a large full color (action scene) picture of each player with a white border. The cards have player's name on front at top and have a facsimile autograph on the picture as well; cards are numbered on the back at the bottom. The back carries biographical information, player profile, and statistics. The lower right corner of the card back indicates "St. Louis - Marketcom - Series C". There are no licensing logos or credits on the front which may be a clue as to why this particular year of Marketcom is much tougher to find than the others.

	MINT	NRMT	EXC
COMPLETE SET (48)	400.00	180.00	50.00
COMMON CARD (1-48)	4.00	1.80	.50
☐ 1 Joe Ferguson	5.00	2.20	.60
☐ 2 Kellen Winslow	8.00	3.60	1.00
☐ 3 Jim Hart	5.00	2.20	.60
☐ 4 Archie Manning	5.00	2.20	.60
☐ 5 Earl Campbell	30.00	13.50	3.70
☐ 6 Wallace Francis	5.00	2.20	.60
☐ 7 Randy Gradishar	5.00	2.20	.60
☐ 8 Ken Stabler	20.00	9.00	2.50
☐ 9 Danny White	6.00	2.70	.75
☐ 10 Jack Ham	6.00	2.70	.75
☐ 11 Lawrence Taylor	35.00	16.00	4.40
☐ 12 Eric Hipple	4.00	1.80	.50
☐ 13 Ron Jaworski	5.00	2.20	.60
☐ 14 George Rogers	5.00	2.20	.60
☐ 15 Jack Lambert	10.00	4.50	1.25
☐ 16 Randy White	10.00	4.50	1.25
☐ 17 Terry Bradshaw	35.00	16.00	4.40
☐ 18 Ray Guy	5.00	2.20	.60
☐ 19 Rob Carpenter	4.00	1.80	.50
☐ 20 Reggie McKenzie	4.00	1.80	.50
☐ 21 Tony Dorsett	20.00	9.00	2.50
☐ 22 Wesley Walker	5.00	2.20	.60
☐ 23 Tommy Kramer	5.00	2.20	.60
☐ 24 Dwight Clark	5.00	2.20	.60
☐ 25 Franco Harris	10.00	4.50	1.25
☐ 26 Craig Morton	5.00	2.20	.60
☐ 27 Harvey Martin	5.00	2.20	.60
☐ 28 Jim Zorn	5.00	2.20	.60
☐ 29 Steve Bartkowski	5.00	2.20	.60
☐ 30 Joe Theismann	8.00	3.60	1.00
☐ 31 Dan Dierdorf	6.00	2.70	.75
☐ 32 Walter Payton	35.00	16.00	4.40
☐ 33 John Jefferson	5.00	2.20	.60
☐ 34 Phil Simms	6.00	2.70	.75
☐ 35 Lee Roy Selmon	8.00	3.60	1.00
☐ 36 Joe Montana	60.00	27.00	7.50
☐ 37 Robert Brazile	4.00	1.80	.50
☐ 38 Steve Grogan	5.00	2.20	.60
☐ 39 Dave Logan	4.00	1.80	.50
☐ 40 Ken Anderson	6.00	2.70	.75
☐ 41 Richard Todd	5.00	2.20	.60
☐ 42 Jack Youngblood	6.00	2.70	.75

☐ 43 Ottis Anderson	5.00	2.20	.60
☐ 44 Brian Sipe	5.00	2.20	.60
☐ 45 Mark Gastineau	5.00	2.20	.60
☐ 46 Mike Pruitt	4.00	1.80	.50
☐ 47 Cris Collinsworth	5.00	2.20	.60
☐ 48 Dan Fouts	12.00	5.50	1.50

1982 Marketcom Cowboys

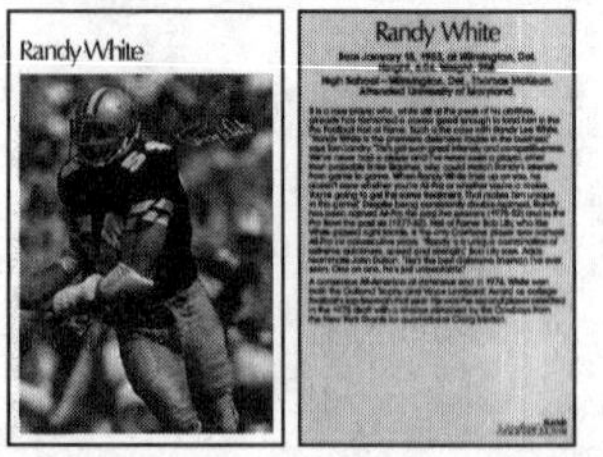

In 1982 Marketcom issued a set of 48 NFL football Mini-Posters, as well as a separate team set for the Cowboys. These 5 1/2" by 8 1/2" cards feature a large full color picture of each player with a white border. Similar to the regular 48-card issue, the Cowboys cards have the player's name on front at top and a facsimile autograph on the picture. The cards are unnumbered and the cardbacks carry biographical information, player profile, and statistics. The lower right corner of the card back indicates "St. Louis - Marketcom", but omits "Series C" found on the other 1982 cards. The set is thought to contain 10-cards.

	MINT	NRMT	EXC
COMPLETE SET (9)	50.00	22.00	6.25
COMMON CARD (1-9)	5.00	2.20	.60
☐ 1 Bob Breunig	5.00	2.20	.60
☐ 2 Pat Donovan	5.00	2.20	.60
☐ 3 Michael Downs	5.00	2.20	.60
☐ 4 Butch Johnson	6.00	2.70	.75
☐ 5 Harvey Martin	6.00	2.70	.75
☐ 6 Timmy Newsome	5.00	2.20	.60
☐ 7 Drew Pearson	7.50	3.40	.95
☐ 8 Danny White	7.50	3.40	.95
☐ 9 Randy White	10.00	4.50	1.25

1971 Mattel Mini-Records

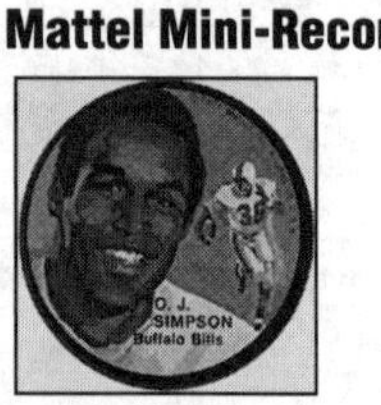

This 17-disc set was designed to be played on a special Mattel mini-record player, which is not included in the complete set price. One four-pack contained Butkus, Lamonica, Mackey, and Simpson, while another four-pack contained Brodie, Hayes, Olsen, and Sayers. These eight discs are easier to find than the others and are marked by DP in the checklist below. Packaging also included eight discs with a booklet featuring either Bart Starr or Joe Namath. Each black plastic disc, approximately 2 1/2" in diameter, features a recording on one side and a color drawing of the player on the other. The picture appears on a paper disk that is glued onto the smooth unrecorded side of the mini-record. On the recorded side, the player's name and the set's subtitle, "Instant Replay," appear in arcs stamped in the central portion of the mini-record. The hand-engraved player's name appears again along with a production number, copyright symbol, and the Mattel name and year of production in the ring between the central portion of the record and the grooves. Bart Starr also exists as a two-sided white plastic disc. The discs are unnumbered and checklisted below in alphabetical order.

	NRMT-MT	EXC	G-VG
COMPLETE SET (17)	200.00	90.00	25.00
COMMON CARD (1-17)	4.00	1.80	.50
☐ 1 Donny Anderson	4.00	1.80	.50
☐ 2 Lem Barney	6.00	2.70	.75
☐ 3 John Brodie DP	6.00	2.70	.75
☐ 4 Dick Butkus DP	15.00	6.75	1.85
☐ 5 Bob Hayes DP	6.00	2.70	.75
☐ 6 Sonny Jurgensen	10.00	4.50	1.25
☐ 7 Alex Karras	10.00	4.50	1.25
☐ 8 Leroy Kelly	9.00	4.00	1.10
☐ 9 Daryle Lamonica DP	4.00	1.80	.50
☐ 10 John Mackey DP	6.00	2.70	.75
☐ 11 Earl Morrall	4.00	1.80	.50
☐ 12 Joe Namath	50.00	22.00	6.25
☐ 13 Merlin Olsen DP	6.00	2.70	.75
☐ 14 Alan Page	9.00	4.00	1.10
☐ 15 Gale Sayers DP	20.00	9.00	2.50
☐ 16 O.J. Simpson DP	25.00	11.00	3.10
☐ 17 Bart Starr	30.00	13.50	3.70
☐ NNO Record Player	100.00	45.00	12.50

1894 Mayo

The 1894 Mayo College Football series contains 35 cards of college players from the Ivy League. The catalog designation is #302. The cards are sepia photos of the player surrounded with a black border,

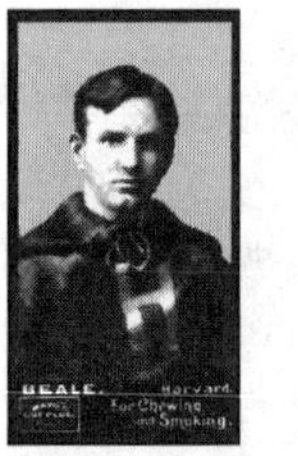

in which the player's name, his college, and a Mayo Cut Plug ad appears. The cards have black backs and measure approximately 1 5/8" by 2 7/8". The cards are unnumbered, but have been alphabetically numbered in the checklist below for your convenience. One of the cards has no identification of the player and is listed below as being anonymous. Those players who were All-American selections are listed below with the last two digits of their year(s) of selection. The Poe in the set is a direct descendant of the famous writer Edgar Allan Poe.

	EX	VG	GOOD
COMPLETE SET (35)	25000.00	12500.00	5000.00
COMMON CARD (1-35)	600.00	300.00	120.00
☐ 1 R. Acton Harvard	600.00	300.00	120.00
☐ 2 George Adee Yale AA94	600.00	300.00	120.00
☐ 3 R. Armstrong Yale	600.00	300.00	120.00
☐ 4 H.W.Barnett Princeton	600.00	300.00	120.00
☐ 5 A.M.Beale Harvard	600.00	300.00	120.00
☐ 6 Anson Beard Yale	700.00	350.00	140.00
☐ 7 Charles Brewer Harvard AA92/93/95	700.00	350.00	140.00
☐ 8 Brown Princeton	600.00	300.00	120.00
☐ 9 Burt Princeton	600.00	300.00	120.00
☐ 10 Frank Butterworth Yale AA93/94	700.00	350.00	140.00
☐ 11 Eddie Crowdis Princeton	600.00	300.00	120.00
☐ 12 Robert Emmons Harvard	600.00	300.00	120.00
☐ 13 M.G.Gonterman UER Harvard (Misspelled Gouterman)	600.00	300.00	120.00
☐ 14 G.A.Grey Harvard	600.00	300.00	120.00
☐ 15 John Greenway Yale	600.00	300.00	120.00
☐ 16 William Hickok Yale AA93/94	700.00	350.00	140.00
☐ 17 Frank Hinkey Yale AA91/92/93/94	900.00	450.00	180.00
☐ 18 Augustus Holly Princeton	600.00	300.00	120.00
☐ 19 Langdon Lea Princeton AA93/94/95	700.00	350.00	140.00
☐ 20 W.C. Mackie Harvard	600.00	300.00	120.00
☐ 21 T.J. Manahan Harvard	600.00	300.00	120.00
☐ 22 Jim McCrea Yale	600.00	300.00	120.00
☐ 23 Frank Morse Princeton AA93	600.00	300.00	120.00
☐ 24 Fred Murphy Yale AA95/96	700.00	350.00	140.00
☐ 25 Poe Princeton thought to be Neilson or Arthur	1000.00	500.00	200.00
☐ 26 Dudley Riggs Princeton AA95	700.00	350.00	140.00
☐ 27 Phillip Stillman Yale AA94	600.00	300.00	120.00
☐ 28 Knox Taylor Princeton	600.00	300.00	120.00
☐ 29 Brinck Thorne Yale AA95	600.00	300.00	120.00
☐ 30 Thomas Trenchard Princeton AA93	700.00	350.00	140.00
☐ 31 William Ward Princeton	600.00	300.00	120.00
☐ 32 Bert Waters Harvard AA92/94	700.00	350.00	140.00
☐ 33 Arthur Wheeler Princeton AA92/93/94	700.00	350.00	140.00
☐ 34 Edgar Wrightington Harvard AA96	600.00	300.00	120.00
☐ 35 Anonymous John Dunlop Harvard	5000.00	2800.00	1450.00

1975 McDonald's Quarterbacks

The 1975 McDonald's Quarterbacks set contains four cards, each of which was used as a promotion for McDonald's hamburger

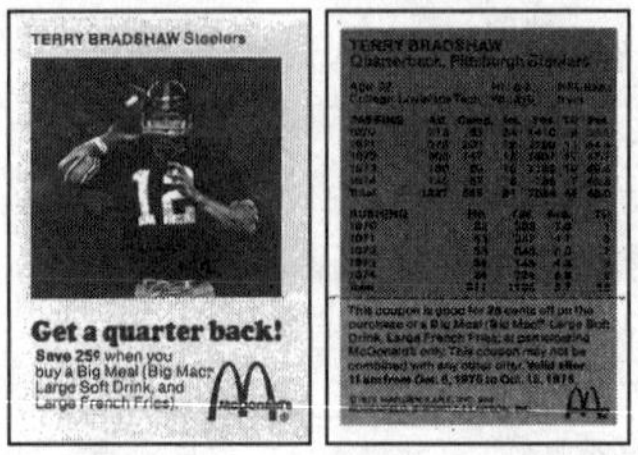

restaurants. The cards measure 2 1/2" by 3 7/16". One might get a quarter back if the coupon at the bottom of the card were presented at one of McDonald's retail establishments. Each coupon was valid for only one week, that particular week clearly marked on the coupon. The cards themselves are in color with yellow borders on the front and statistics on the back. The back of each card is a different color. Statistics are given for each of the quarterback's previous seasons record passing and rushing. The prices below are for the cards with coupons intact as that is the way they are usually found.

	NRMT-MT	EXC	G-VG
COMPLETE SET (4)	15.00	6.75	1.85
COMMON CARD (1-4)	.60	.25	.07
☐ 1 Terry Bradshaw	7.50	3.40	.95
☐ 2 Joe Ferguson	1.50	.70	.19
☐ 3 Ken Stabler	6.00	2.70	.75
☐ 4 Al Woodall	.60	.25	.07

1985 McDonald's Bears

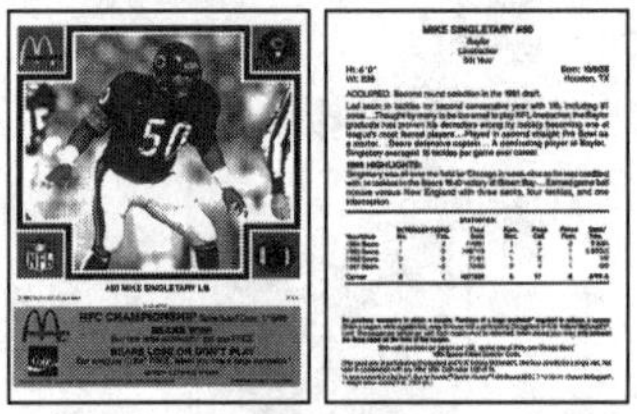

This set of 32 cards featuring the Chicago Bears was available with three different tab colors. Yellow tabs referenced the Super Bowl. Orange tabs referenced the NFC Championship Game. Blue tabs referenced the Divisional Playoff game. All three sets contain the same 32 players. The cards measure approximately 4 1/2" by 5 7/8" with the tab intact and 4 1/2" by 4 3/8" without the tab, noticeably larger than the McDonald's cards of 1986. Apparently this set was a test market which evidently was successful enough for McDonald's to distribute all 28 teams (plus All-Stars) in 1986. Apparently, this promotion was intended to last until the Bears were eliminated from the playoffs, but they never were; they won the Super Bowl in convincing fashion. Individual player card prices below refer to that player's value in the least expensive color tab. For individual prices on the more expensive color tabs, merely apply the ratio of that color's set price to the base (cheapest) color set price and use the resulting multiple on the individual prices for that color. Prices listed are for cards with tabs intact.

	MINT	NRMT	EXC
COMPLETE SET (BLUE)	40.00	18.00	5.00
COMPLETE SET (ORANGE)	25.00	11.00	3.10
COMPLETE SET (YELLOW)	20.00	9.00	2.50
COMMON CARD	.50	.23	.06
☐ 4 Steve Fuller	.75	.35	.09
☐ 6 Kevin Butler	.75	.35	.09
☐ 8 Maury Buford	.50	.23	.06
☐ 9 Jim McMahon	2.00	.90	.25
☐ 21 Leslie Frazier	.50	.23	.06
☐ 22 Dave Duerson	.50	.23	.06
☐ 26 Matt Suhey	.75	.35	.09
☐ 27 Mike Richardson	.50	.23	.06
☐ 29 Dennis Gentry	.50	.23	.06
☐ 33 Calvin Thomas	.50	.23	.06
☐ 34 Walter Payton	6.00	2.70	.75
☐ 45 Gary Fencik	.75	.35	.09
☐ 50 Mike Singletary	2.00	.90	.25
☐ 55 Otis Wilson	.50	.23	.06
☐ 58 Wilber Marshall	1.00	.45	.12
☐ 62 Mark Bortz	.50	.23	.06
☐ 63 Jay Hilgenberg	.75	.35	.09
☐ 72 William Perry	1.00	.45	.12
☐ 73 Mike Hartenstine	.50	.23	.06
☐ 74 Jim Covert	.75	.35	.09
☐ 75 Stefan Humphries	.50	.23	.06
☐ 76 Steve McMichael	1.00	.45	.12
☐ 78 Keith Van Horne	.50	.23	.06
☐ 80 Tim Wrightman	.50	.23	.06
☐ 82 Ken Margerum	.50	.23	.06
☐ 83 Willie Gault	1.00	.45	.12
☐ 85 Dennis McKinnon	.75	.35	.09
☐ 87 Emery Moorehead	.50	.23	.06
☐ 95 Richard Dent	2.00	.90	.25
☐ 99 Dan Hampton	2.00	.90	.25
☐ xx0 Mike Ditka CO	2.00	.90	.25
☐ xx0 Buddy Ryan ACO	1.00	.45	.12

1986 McDonald's All-Stars

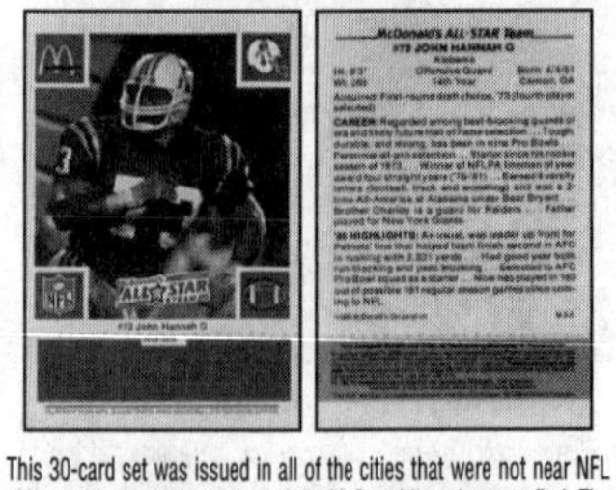

This 30-card set was issued in all of the cities that were not near NFL cities and hence is the easiest of the McDonald's subsets to find. The set was issued over a four-week period with blue tabs the first week, black (or gray) tabs the second week, gold (or orange) tabs the third week, and green tabs the fourth week. The cards measure approximately 3 1/16" by 4 11/16" with the tab intact and 3 1/16" by 3 5/8" without the tab. The value of cards without tabs or tabs scratched off is F-G at best. All-Stars were printed on a 30-card sheet; hence, there are no DP cards, unlike the situation with the team subsets, where six cards were double printed. Since the cards are unnumbered, they are listed below by uniform number; in several instances, players on different teams have the same number.

	MINT	NRMT	EXC
COMPLETE SET (BLUE)	6.00	2.70	.75
COMPLETE SET (BLACK)	6.00	2.70	.75
COMPLETE SET (GOLD)	6.00	2.70	.75
COMPLETE SET (GREEN)	6.00	2.70	.75
COMMON CARD	.15	.07	.02
☐ 9 Jim McMahon	.35	.16	.04
☐ 11 Phil Simms	.35	.16	.04
☐ 13 Dan Marino	3.00	1.35	.35
☐ 14 Dan Fouts	.35	.16	.04
☐ 16 Joe Montana	2.00	.90	.25
☐ 20A Deron Cherry	.15	.07	.02
☐ 20B Joe Morris	.15	.07	.02
☐ 32 Marcus Allen	.35	.16	.04
☐ 33 Roger Craig	.25	.11	.03
☐ 34A Kevin Mack	.15	.07	.02
☐ 34B Walter Payton	1.50	.70	.19
☐ 42 Gerald Riggs	.15	.07	.02
☐ 45 Kenny Easley	.15	.07	.02
☐ 47A Joey Browner	.15	.07	.02
☐ 47B LeRoy Irvin	.15	.07	.02
☐ 52 Mike Webster	.25	.11	.03
☐ 54A E.J. Junior	.15	.07	.02
☐ 54B Randy White	.25	.11	.03
☐ 56 Lawrence Taylor	.35	.16	.04
☐ 63 Mike Munchak	.15	.07	.02
☐ 66 Joe Jacoby	.15	.07	.02
☐ 73 John Hannah	.25	.11	.03
☐ 75A Chris Hinton	.15	.07	.02
☐ 75B Rulon Jones	.15	.07	.02
☐ 75C Howie Long	.25	.11	.03
☐ 78 Anthony Munoz	.25	.11	.03
☐ 81 Art Monk	.35	.16	.04
☐ 82A Ozzie Newsome	.35	.16	.04
☐ 82B Mike Quick	.15	.07	.02
☐ 99 Mark Gastineau	.15	.07	.02

1986 McDonald's Bears

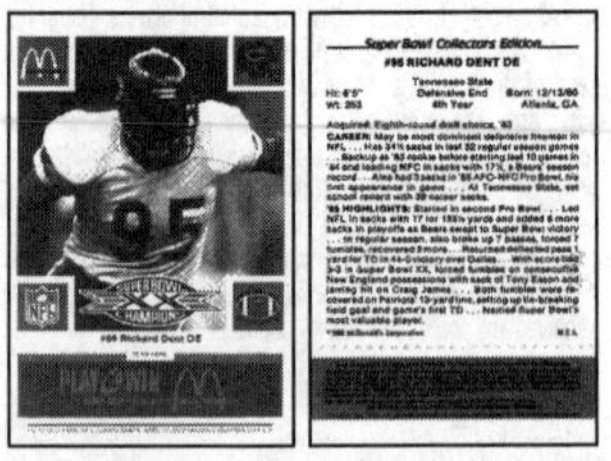

This 24-card set was issued in McDonald's Hamburger restaurants around Chicago. The set was issued over a four-week period with blue tabs the first week, black (or gray) tabs the second week, gold (or orange) tabs the third week, and green tabs the fourth week. The cards measure approximately 3 1/16" by 4 11/16" with the tab intact and 3 1/16" by 3 5/8" without the tab. The cards are numbered below by uniform number. The value of cards without tabs or tabs scratched off is F-G at best. The cards were printed on a 30-card sheet; hence, there are six double-printed cards listed DP in the checklist below. For individual prices on the more expensive color tabs, merely apply the ratio of that color's set price to the base (cheapest) color set price and use the resulting multiple on the individual prices for that color.

	MINT	NRMT	EXC
COMPLETE SET (BLUE)	15.00	6.75	1.85
COMPLETE SET (BLACK)	7.50	3.40	.95
COMPLETE SET (GOLD)	7.50	3.40	.95
COMPLETE SET (GREEN)	7.50	3.40	.95
COMMON CARD	.30	.14	.04
☐ 6 Kevin Butler DP	.40	.18	.05
☐ 8 Maury Buford	.30	.14	.04
☐ 9 Jim McMahon DP	1.00	.45	.12
☐ 22 Dave Duerson	.30	.14	.04

Card	MINT	NRMT	EXC
☐ 26 Matt Suhey	.40	.18	.05
☐ 27 Mike Richardson	.30	.14	.04
☐ 34 Walter Payton DP	1.50	.70	.19
☐ 45 Gary Fencik	.40	.18	.05
☐ 50 Mike Singletary DP	1.00	.45	.12
☐ 55 Otis Wilson	.30	.14	.04
☐ 57 Tom Thayer	.30	.14	.04
☐ 58 Wilber Marshall	.50	.23	.06
☐ 62 Mark Bortz DP	.30	.14	.04
☐ 63 Jay Hilgenberg	.40	.18	.05
☐ 72 William Perry DP	.50	.23	.06
☐ 74 Jim Covert	.40	.18	.05
☐ 76 Steve McMichael	.50	.23	.06
☐ 78 Keith Van Horne	.30	.14	.04
☐ 80 Tim Wrightman	.30	.14	.04
☐ 82 Ken Margerum	.30	.14	.04
☐ 83 Willie Gault	.50	.23	.06
☐ 87 Emery Moorehead	.30	.14	.04
☐ 95 Richard Dent	1.00	.45	.12
☐ 99 Dan Hampton	1.00	.45	.12

1986 McDonald's Bengals

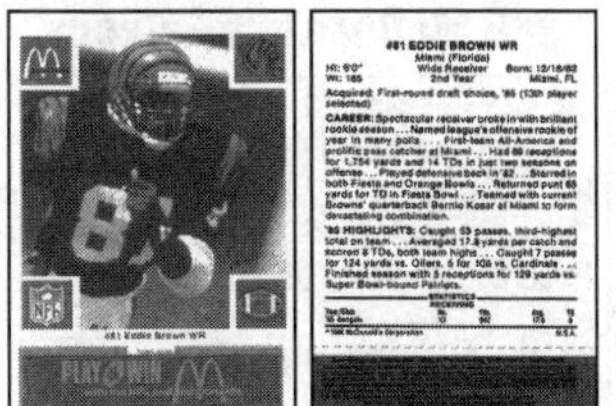

This 24-card set was issued in McDonald's Hamburger restaurants around Cincinnati. The set was issued over a four-week period with blue tabs the first week, black (or gray) tabs the second week, gold (or orange) tabs the third week, and green tabs the fourth week. The cards measure approximately 3 1/16" by 4 11/16" with the tab intact and 3 1/16" by 3 5/8" without the tab. The cards are numbered below by uniform number. The value of cards without tabs or tabs scratched off is F-G at best. The cards were printed on a 30-card sheet; hence, there are six double-printed cards listed DP in the checklist below. For individual prices on the more expensive color tabs, merely apply the ratio of that color's set price to the base (cheapest) color set price and use the resulting multiple on the individual prices for that color. Boomer Esiason appears in his Rookie Card year.

	MINT	NRMT	EXC
COMPLETE SET (BLUE)	25.00	11.00	3.10
COMPLETE SET (BLACK)	12.50	5.50	1.55
COMPLETE SET (GOLD)	12.50	5.50	1.55
COMPLETE SET (GREEN)	12.50	5.50	1.55
COMMON CARD	.50	.23	.06

Card	MINT	NRMT	EXC
☐ 7 Boomer Esiason	3.00	1.35	.35
☐ 14 Ken Anderson DP	1.25	.55	.16
☐ 20 Ray Horton	.60	.25	.07
☐ 21 James Brooks DP	1.00	.45	.12
☐ 22 James Griffin	.50	.23	.06
☐ 28 Larry Kinnebrew	.60	.25	.07
☐ 34 Louis Breeden DP	.50	.23	.06
☐ 37 Robert Jackson	.50	.23	.06
☐ 40 Charles Alexander DP	.50	.23	.06
☐ 52 Dave Rimington	.60	.25	.07
☐ 57 Reggie Williams	1.00	.45	.12
☐ 65 Max Montoya	.60	.25	.07
☐ 69 Tim Krumrie	.75	.35	.09
☐ 73 Eddie Edwards	.60	.25	.07
☐ 74 Brian Blados DP	.50	.23	.06
☐ 77 Mike Wilson	.50	.23	.06
☐ 78 Anthony Munoz	1.50	.70	.19
☐ 79 Ross Browner	.60	.25	.07
☐ 80 Cris Collinsworth	1.00	.45	.12
☐ 81 Eddie Brown DP	.75	.35	.09
☐ 82 Rodney Holman	.60	.25	.07
☐ 83 M.L. Harris	.50	.23	.06
☐ 90 Emanuel King	.50	.23	.06
☐ 91 Carl Zander	.50	.23	.06

1986 McDonald's Bills

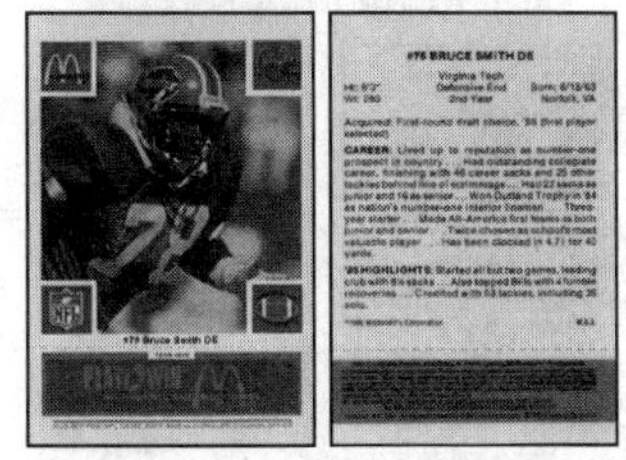

This 24-card set was issued in McDonald's Hamburger restaurants around Buffalo. The set was issued over a four-week period with blue tabs the first week, black (or gray) tabs the second week, gold (or orange) tabs the third week, and green tabs the fourth week. The cards measure approximately 3 1/16" by 4 11/16" with the tab intact and 3 1/16" by 3 5/8" without the tab. The cards are numbered below by uniform number. The value of cards without tabs or tabs scratched off is F-G at best. The cards were printed on a 30-card sheet; hence, there are six double-printed cards listed DP in the checklist below. For individual prices on the more expensive color tabs, merely apply the ratio of that color's set price to the base (cheapest) color set price and use the resulting multiple on the individual prices for that color. Andre Reed and Bruce Smith appear in their Rookie Card year.

	MINT	NRMT	EXC
COMPLETE SET (BLUE)	150.00	70.00	19.00
COMPLETE SET (BLACK)	30.00	13.50	3.70
COMPLETE SET (GOLD)	15.00	6.75	1.85
COMPLETE SET (GREEN)	15.00	6.75	1.85
COMMON CARD	.75	.35	.09

Card	MINT	NRMT	EXC
☐ 4 John Kidd	.75	.35	.09
☐ 7 Bruce Mathison	.75	.35	.09
☐ 11 Scott Norwood	1.00	.45	.12
☐ 22 Steve Freeman	.75	.35	.09
☐ 26 Charles Romes	.75	.35	.09
☐ 28 Greg Bell DP	1.00	.45	.12
☐ 29 Derrick Burroughs DP	.75	.35	.09
☐ 43 Martin Bayless DP	.75	.35	.09
☐ 51 Jim Ritcher	1.00	.45	.12
☐ 54 Eugene Marve	.75	.35	.09
☐ 55 Jim Haslett	.75	.35	.09
☐ 57 Lucius Sanford	.75	.35	.09
☐ 63 Justin Cross DP	.75	.35	.09
☐ 65 Tim Vogler	.75	.35	.09
☐ 70 Joe Devlin	.75	.35	.09
☐ 72 Ken Jones	.75	.35	.09
☐ 76 Fred Smerlas	1.00	.45	.12
☐ 77 Ben Williams	1.00	.45	.12
☐ 78 Bruce Smith	4.00	1.80	.50
☐ 80 Jerry Butler DP	1.00	.45	.12
☐ 83 Andre Reed	4.00	1.80	.50
☐ 85 Chris Burkett DP	1.00	.45	.12
☐ 87 Eason Ramson	.75	.35	.09
☐ 95 Sean McNanie	.75	.35	.09

1986 McDonald's Broncos

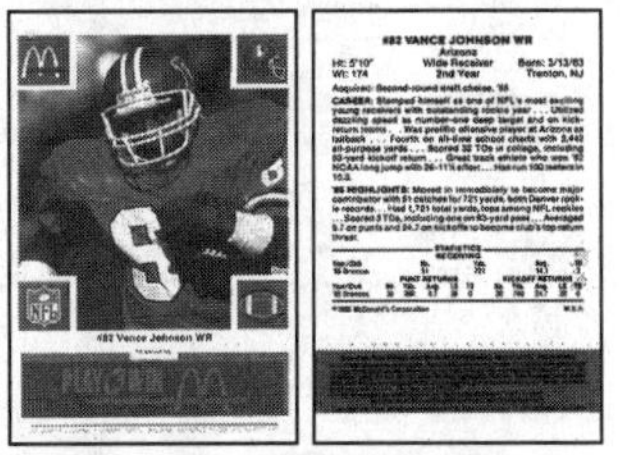

This 24-card set was issued in McDonald's Hamburger restaurants around Denver. The set was issued over a four-week period with blue tabs the first week, black (or gray) tabs the second week, gold (or orange) tabs the third week, and green tabs the fourth week. The cards measure approximately 3 1/16" by 4 11/16" with the tab intact and 3 1/16" by 3 5/8" without the tab. The cards are numbered below by uniform number. The value of cards without tabs or tabs scratched off is F-G at best. The cards were printed on a 30-card sheet; hence, there are six double-printed cards listed DP in the checklist below. For individual prices on the more expensive color tabs, merely apply the ratio of that color's set price to the base (cheapest) color set price and use the resulting multiple on the individual prices for that color.

	MINT	NRMT	EXC
COMPLETE SET (BLUE)	30.00	13.50	3.70
COMPLETE SET (BLACK)	10.00	4.50	1.25
COMPLETE SET (GOLD)	10.00	4.50	1.25
COMPLETE SET (GREEN)	10.00	4.50	1.25
COMMON CARD	.30	.14	.04

Card	MINT	NRMT	EXC
☐ 3 Rich Karlis	.30	.14	.04
☐ 7 John Elway DP	3.00	1.35	.35
☐ 20 Louis Wright	.40	.18	.05
☐ 22 Tony Lilly	.30	.14	.04
☐ 23 Sammy Winder	.40	.18	.05
☐ 30 Steve Sewell	.40	.18	.05
☐ 31 Mike Harden	.40	.18	.05
☐ 43 Steve Foley	.40	.18	.05
☐ 47 Gerald Willhite	.40	.18	.05
☐ 49 Dennis Smith	.50	.23	.06
☐ 50 Jim Ryan	.30	.14	.04
☐ 54 Keith Bishop DP	.30	.14	.04
☐ 55 Rick Dennison DP	.30	.14	.04
☐ 57 Tom Jackson	1.00	.45	.12
☐ 60 Paul Howard	.30	.14	.04
☐ 64 Bill Bryan DP	.30	.14	.04
☐ 68 Rubin Carter DP	.30	.14	.04
☐ 70 Dave Studdard	.30	.14	.04
☐ 75 Rulon Jones	.40	.18	.05
☐ 77 Karl Mecklenburg	.60	.25	.07
☐ 79 Barney Chavous DP	.30	.14	.04
☐ 81 Steve Watson	.40	.18	.05
☐ 82 Vance Johnson	.60	.25	.07
☐ 84 Clint Sampson	.30	.14	.04

1986 McDonald's Browns

This 24-card set was issued in McDonald's Hamburger restaurants around Cleveland. The set was issued over a four-week period with blue tabs the first week, black (or gray) tabs the second week, gold (or orange) tabs the third week, and green tabs the fourth week. The cards measure approximately 3 1/16" by 4 11/16" with the tab intact and 3 1/16" by 3 5/8" without the tab. The cards are numbered below by uniform number. The value of cards without tabs or tabs scratched off is F-G at best. The cards were printed on a 30-card sheet; hence, there are six double-printed cards listed DP in the checklist below. For individual prices on the more expensive color tabs, merely apply the ratio of that color's set price to the base (cheapest) color set price and use the resulting multiple on the individual prices for that color. Bernie Kosar appears in his Rookie Card year.

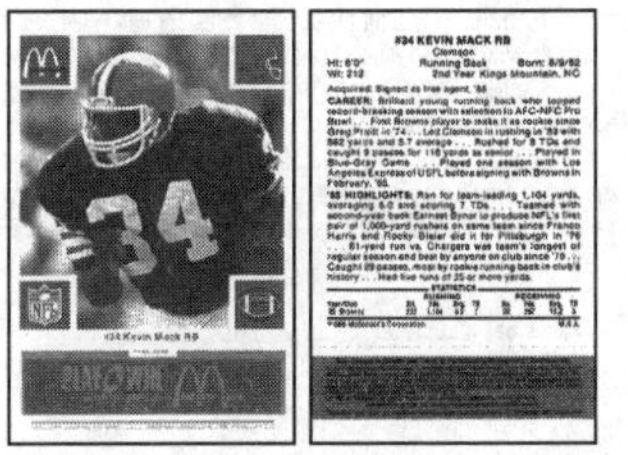

	MINT	NRMT	EXC
COMPLETE SET (BLUE)	12.00	5.50	1.50
COMPLETE SET (BLACK)	6.00	2.70	.75
COMPLETE SET (GOLD)	6.00	2.70	.75
COMPLETE SET (GREEN)	6.00	2.70	.75
COMMON CARD	.25	.11	.03

Card	MINT	NRMT	EXC
☐ 9 Matt Bahr DP	.25	.11	.03
☐ 18 Gary Danielson	.25	.11	.03
☐ 19 Bernie Kosar DP	2.00	.90	.25
☐ 27 Al Gross	.25	.11	.03
☐ 29 Hanford Dixon	.35	.16	.04
☐ 31 Frank Minnifield	.35	.16	.04
☐ 34 Kevin Mack	.50	.23	.06
☐ 37 Chris Rockins	.25	.11	.03
☐ 44 Earnest Byner	.75	.35	.09
☐ 51 Eddie Johnson	.25	.11	.03
☐ 55 Curtis Weathers	.25	.11	.03
☐ 56 Chip Banks DP	.25	.11	.03
☐ 57 Clay Matthews	.50	.23	.06
☐ 60 Tom Cousineau	.25	.11	.03
☐ 61 Mike Baab DP	.25	.11	.03
☐ 63 Cody Risien	.35	.16	.04
☐ 77 Rickey Bolden DP	.25	.11	.03
☐ 78 Carl Hairston	.25	.11	.03
☐ 79 Bob Golic	.35	.16	.04
☐ 82 Ozzie Newsome	1.00	.45	.12
☐ 84 Glen Young	.25	.11	.03
☐ 85 Clarence Weathers	.25	.11	.03
☐ 86 Brian Brennan DP	.35	.16	.04
☐ 96 Reggie Camp	.25	.11	.03

1986 McDonald's Buccaneers

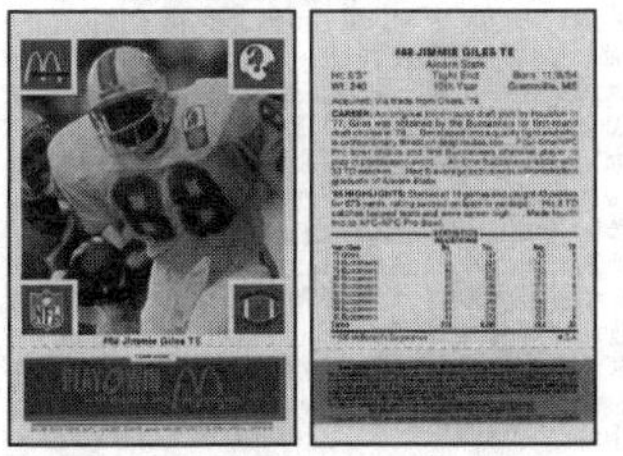

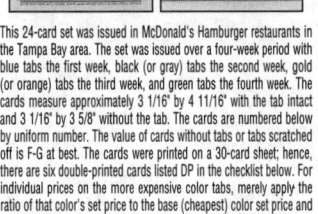

This 24-card set was issued in McDonald's Hamburger restaurants in the Tampa Bay area. The set was issued over a four-week period with blue tabs the first week, black (or gray) tabs the second week, gold (or orange) tabs the third week, and green tabs the fourth week. The cards measure approximately 3 1/16" by 4 11/16" with the tab intact and 3 1/16" by 3 5/8" without the tab. The cards are numbered below by uniform number. The value of cards without tabs or tabs scratched off is F-G at best. The cards were printed on a 30-card sheet; hence, there are six double-printed cards listed DP in the checklist below. For individual prices on the more expensive color tabs, merely apply the ratio of that color's set price to the base (cheapest) color set price and use the resulting multiple on the individual prices for that color. Steve Young appears in his NFL Rookie Card year.

	MINT	NRMT	EXC
COMPLETE SET (BLUE)	18.00	8.00	2.20
COMPLETE SET (BLACK)	18.00	8.00	2.20
COMPLETE SET (GOLD)	18.00	8.00	2.20
COMPLETE SET (GREEN)	18.00	8.00	2.20
COMMON CARD	.30	.14	.04

Card	MINT	NRMT	EXC
☐ 1 Donald Igwebuike	.30	.14	.04
☐ 8 Steve Young	10.00	4.50	1.25
☐ 17 Steve DeBerg	.75	.35	.09
☐ 21 John Holt	.30	.14	.04
☐ 23 Jeremiah Castille DP	.30	.14	.04
☐ 30 David Greenwood	.30	.14	.04
☐ 32 James Wilder	.50	.23	.06
☐ 44 Ivory Sully	.30	.14	.04
☐ 51 Chris Washington	.30	.14	.04
☐ 52 Scot Brantley DP	.30	.14	.04
☐ 54 Ervin Randle	.30	.14	.04
☐ 58 Jeff Davis DP	.30	.14	.04
☐ 60 Randy Grimes	.30	.14	.04
☐ 62 Sean Farrell	.40	.18	.05

Card	MINT	NRMT	EXC
☐ 66 George Yarno	.30	.14	.04
☐ 73 Ron Heller	.30	.14	.04
☐ 76 David Logan	.30	.14	.04
☐ 78 John Cannon DP	.30	.14	.04
☐ 82 Jerry Bell DP	.30	.14	.04
☐ 86 Calvin Magee	.30	.14	.04
☐ 87 Gerald Carter DP	.30	.14	.04
☐ 88 Jimmie Giles	.50	.23	.06
☐ 89 Kevin House	.50	.23	.06
☐ 90 Ron Holmes	.40	.18	.05

1986 McDonald's Cardinals

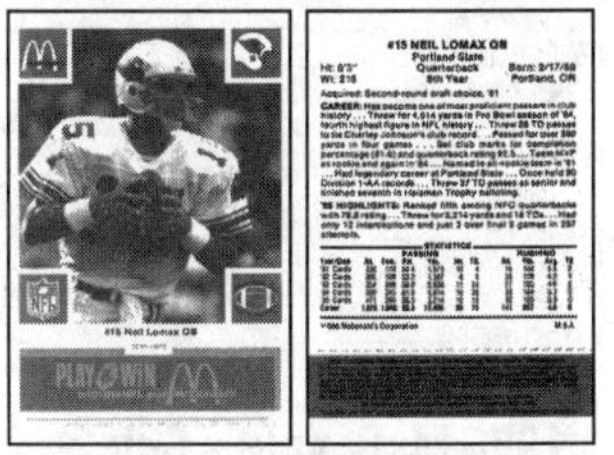

This 24-card set was issued in McDonald's Hamburger restaurants around St. Louis. The set was issued over a four-week period with blue tabs the first week, black (or gray) tabs the second week, gold (or orange) tabs the third week, and green tabs the fourth week. The cards measure approximately 3 1/16" by 4 11/16" with the tab intact and 3 1/16" by 3 5/8" without the tab. The cards are numbered below by uniform number. The value of cards without tabs or tabs scratched off is F-G at best. The cards were printed on a 30-card sheet; hence, there are six double-printed cards listed DP in the checklist below. For individual prices on the more expensive color tabs, merely apply the ratio of that color's set price to the base (cheapest) color set price and use the resulting multiple on the individual prices for that color.

	MINT	NRMT	EXC
COMPLETE SET (BLUE)	10.00	4.50	1.25
COMPLETE SET (BLACK)	6.00	2.70	.75
COMPLETE SET (GOLD)	6.00	2.70	.75
COMPLETE SET (GREEN)	6.00	2.70	.75
COMMON CARD	.25	.11	.03

Card	MINT	NRMT	EXC
☐ 15 Neil Lomax	.50	.23	.06
☐ 18 Carl Birdsong DP	.25	.11	.03
☐ 30 Stump Mitchell	.35	.16	.04
☐ 32 Ottis Anderson DP	.75	.35	.09
☐ 43 Lonnie Young	.25	.11	.03
☐ 45 Leonard Smith	.25	.11	.03
☐ 47 Cedric Mack	.25	.11	.03
☐ 48 Lionel Washington	.25	.11	.03
☐ 53 Freddie Joe Nunn	.35	.16	.04
☐ 54 E.J. Junior	.35	.16	.04
☐ 57 Niko Noga	.25	.11	.03
☐ 60 Al Bubba Baker DP	.35	.16	.04
☐ 63 Tootie Robbins	.25	.11	.03
☐ 65 David Galloway	.25	.11	.03
☐ 66 Doug Dawson DP	.25	.11	.03
☐ 67 Luis Sharpe	.25	.11	.03
☐ 71 Joe Bostic DP	.25	.11	.03
☐ 73 Mark Duda DP	.25	.11	.03
☐ 75 Curtis Greer	.25	.11	.03
☐ 80 Doug Marsh	.25	.11	.03
☐ 81 Roy Green	.50	.23	.06
☐ 83 Pat Tilley	.25	.11	.03
☐ 84 J.T. Smith	.35	.16	.04
☐ 89 Greg LaFleur	.25	.11	.03

1986 McDonald's Chargers

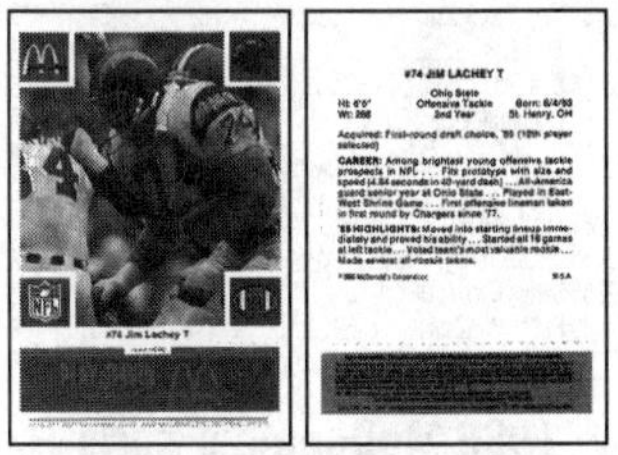

This 24-card set was issued in McDonald's Hamburger restaurants around San Diego. The set was issued over a four-week period with blue tabs the first week, black (or gray) tabs the second week, gold (or orange) tabs the third week, and green tabs the fourth week. The cards measure approximately 3 1/16" by 4 11/16" with the tab intact and 3 1/16" by 3 5/8" without the tab. The cards are numbered below by uniform number. The value of cards without tabs or tabs scratched off is F-G at best. The cards were printed on a 30-card sheet; hence, there are six double-printed cards listed DP in the checklist below. For individual prices on the more expensive color tabs, merely apply the ratio of that color's set price to the base (cheapest) color set price and use the resulting multiple on the individual prices for that color.

	MINT	NRMT	EXC
COMPLETE SET (BLUE)	25.00	11.00	3.10
COMPLETE SET (BLACK)	20.00	9.00	2.50
COMPLETE SET (GOLD)	12.00	5.50	1.50
COMPLETE SET (GREEN)	12.00	5.50	1.50
COMMON CARD	.40	.18	.05

	MINT	NRMT	EXC
☐ 9 Mark Herrmann	.40	.18	.05
☐ 14 Dan Fouts DP	1.50	.70	.19
☐ 18 Charlie Joiner	1.00	.45	.12
☐ 21 Buford McGee	.40	.18	.05
☐ 22 Gill Byrd DP	.50	.23	.06
☐ 26 Lionel James	.50	.23	.06
☐ 29 John Hendy	.40	.18	.05
☐ 37 Jeffery Dale DP	.40	.18	.05
☐ 40 Gary Anderson RB DP	.75	.35	.09
☐ 43 Tim Spencer	.40	.18	.05
☐ 51 Woodrow Lowe	.40	.18	.05
☐ 54 Billy Ray Smith	.50	.23	.06
☐ 60 Dennis McKnight	.40	.18	.05
☐ 62 Don Macek	.40	.18	.05
☐ 67 Ed White	.40	.18	.05
☐ 74 Jim Lachey	1.00	.45	.12
☐ 78 Chuck Ehin DP	.40	.18	.05
☐ 80 Kellen Winslow	1.50	.70	.19
☐ 83 Trumaine Johnson	.40	.18	.05
☐ 85 Eric Sievers	.40	.18	.05
☐ 88 Pete Holohan	.50	.23	.06
☐ 89 Wes Chandler DP	.50	.23	.06
☐ 93 Earl Wilson	.40	.18	.05
☐ 99 Lee Williams	.50	.23	.06

1986 McDonald's Chiefs

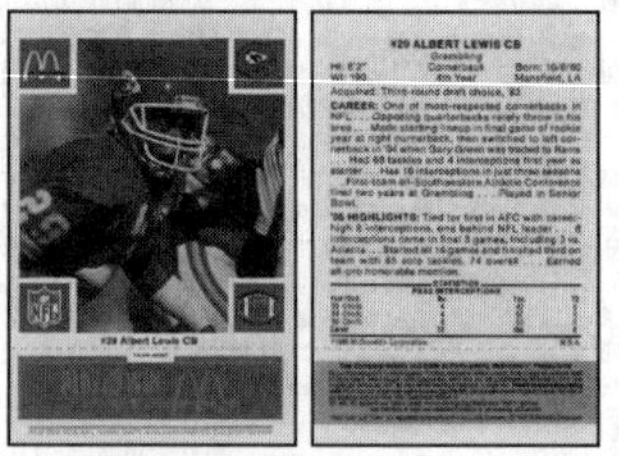

This 24-card set was issued in McDonald's Hamburger restaurants around Kansas City. The set was issued over a four-week period with blue tabs the first week, black (or gray) tabs the second week, gold (or orange) tabs the third week, and green tabs the fourth week. The cards measure approximately 3 1/16" by 4 11/16" with the tab intact and 3 1/16" by 3 5/8" without the tab. The cards are numbered below by uniform number. The value of cards without tabs or tabs scratched off is F-G at best. The cards were printed on a 30-card sheet; hence, there are six double-printed cards listed DP in the checklist below. For individual prices on the more expensive color tabs, merely apply the ratio of that color's set price to the base (cheapest) color set price and use the resulting multiple on the individual prices for that color.

	MINT	NRMT	EXC
COMPLETE SET (BLUE)	20.00	9.00	2.50
COMPLETE SET (BLACK)	40.00	18.00	5.00
COMPLETE SET (GOLD)	18.00	8.00	2.20
COMPLETE SET (GREEN)	18.00	8.00	2.20
COMMON CARD	.75	.35	.09
☐ 6 Jim Arnold DP	.75	.35	.09
☐ 8 Nick Lowery	1.00	.45	.12
☐ 9 Bill Kenney	.75	.35	.09
☐ 14 Todd Blackledge DP	1.00	.45	.12
☐ 20 Deron Cherry DP	1.25	.55	.16
☐ 29 Albert Lewis	1.50	.70	.19
☐ 31 Kevin Ross	1.25	.55	.16
☐ 34 Lloyd Burruss DP	.75	.35	.09
☐ 41 Garcia Lane	.75	.35	.09
☐ 42 Jeff Smith	.75	.35	.09
☐ 43 Mike Pruitt	1.00	.45	.12
☐ 44 Herman Heard	.75	.35	.09
☐ 50 Calvin Daniels	.75	.35	.09
☐ 59 Gary Spani	.75	.35	.09
☐ 63 Bill Maas	.75	.35	.09
☐ 64 Bob Olderman	.75	.35	.09
☐ 66 Brad Budde DP	.75	.35	.09
☐ 67 Art Still	.75	.35	.09
☐ 72 David Lutz	.75	.35	.09
☐ 83 Stephone Paige	1.25	.55	.16
☐ 85 Jonathan Hayes	1.00	.45	.12
☐ 88 Carlos Carson DP	1.00	.45	.12
☐ 89 Henry Marshall	.75	.35	.09
☐ 97 Scott Radecic	.75	.35	.09

1986 McDonald's Colts

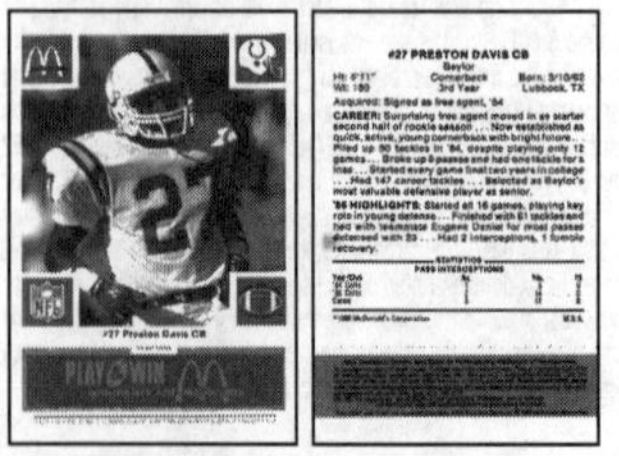

This 24-card set was issued in McDonald's Hamburger restaurants around Indianapolis. The set was issued over a four-week period with blue tabs the first week, black (or gray) tabs the second week, gold (or orange) tabs the third week, and green tabs the fourth week. The cards measure approximately 3 1/16" by 4 11/16" with the tab intact and 3 1/16" by 3 5/8" without the tab. The cards are numbered below by uniform number. The value of cards without tabs or tabs scratched off is F-G at best. The cards were printed on a 30-card sheet; hence, there are six double-printed cards listed DP in the checklist below. For individual prices on the more expensive color tabs, merely apply the ratio of that color's set price to the base (cheapest) color set price and use the resulting multiple on the individual prices for that color.

	MINT	NRMT	EXC
COMPLETE SET (BLUE)	100.00	45.00	12.50
COMPLETE SET (BLACK)	18.00	8.00	2.20
COMPLETE SET (GOLD)	15.00	6.75	1.85
COMPLETE SET (GREEN)	18.00	8.00	2.20
COMMON CARD	.60	.25	.07
☐ 2 Raul Allegre DP	.60	.25	.07
☐ 3 Rohn Stark	.75	.35	.09
☐ 25 Nesby Glasgow	.60	.25	.07
☐ 27 Preston Davis	.60	.25	.07
☐ 32 Randy McMillan	.75	.35	.09
☐ 34 George Wonsley	.60	.25	.07
☐ 38 Eugene Daniel	.75	.35	.09
☐ 44 Owen Gill	.60	.25	.07
☐ 47 Leonard Coleman	.60	.25	.07
☐ 50 Duane Bickett DP	1.00	.45	.12
☐ 53 Ray Donaldson	.75	.35	.09
☐ 55 Barry Krauss	.60	.25	.07
☐ 64 Ben Utt	.60	.25	.07
☐ 66 Ron Solt	.60	.25	.07
☐ 72 Karl Baldischwiler DP	.60	.25	.07
☐ 75 Chris Hinton	.75	.35	.09
☐ 81 Pat Beach DP	.60	.25	.07
☐ 85 Matt Bouza DP	.60	.25	.07
☐ 87 Wayne Capers DP	.60	.25	.07
☐ 88 Robbie Martin	.60	.25	.07
☐ 92 Brad White	.60	.25	.07
☐ 93 Cliff Odom	.60	.25	.07
☐ 96 Blaise Winter	.60	.25	.07
☐ 98 Johnie Cooks	.60	.25	.07

1986 McDonald's Cowboys

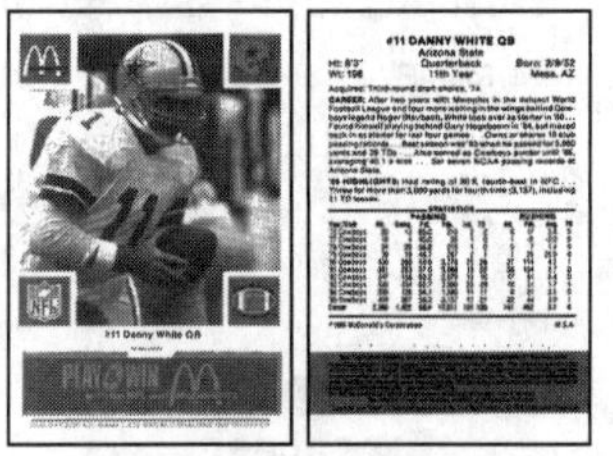

This 25-card set was issued in McDonald's Hamburger restaurants around Dallas. The set was issued over a four-week period with blue tabs the first week, black (or gray) tabs the second week, gold (or orange) tabs the third week, and green tabs the fourth week. The cards measure approximately 3 1/16" by 4 11/16" with the tab intact and 3 1/16" by 3 5/8" without the tab. The cards are numbered below by uniform number. The Herschel Walker card was produced later due to his popularity. Walker's card was produced only with a green tab without any coating on the tab to be scratched off; hence his cards are typically found in nice condition. The value of cards without tabs or tabs scratched off is F-G at best. The cards (other than Herschel Walker) were printed on a 30-card sheet; hence, there are six double-printed cards listed DP in the checklist below. For individual prices on the more expensive color tabs, merely apply the ratio of that color's set price to the base (cheapest) color set price and use the resulting multiple on the individual prices for that color.

	MINT	NRMT	EXC
COMPLETE SET (BLUE)	10.00	4.50	1.25
COMPLETE SET (BLACK)	10.00	4.50	1.25
COMPLETE SET (GOLD)	10.00	4.50	1.25
COMPLETE SET (GREEN)	10.00	4.50	1.25
COMMON CARD	.25	.11	.03
☐ 1 Rafael Septien	.25	.11	.03
☐ 11 Danny White	.50	.23	.06
☐ 24 Everson Walls	.35	.16	.04
☐ 26 Michael Downs DP	.25	.11	.03
☐ 27 Ron Fellows	.25	.11	.03
☐ 30 Timmy Newsome	.25	.11	.03
☐ 33 Tony Dorsett DP	1.00	.45	.12
☐ 34 Herschel Walker	2.00	.90	.25
☐ 40 Bill Bates DP	.50	.23	.06
☐ 47 Dextor Clinkscale DP	.25	.11	.03
☐ 50 Jeff Rohrer	.25	.11	.03
☐ 54 Randy White	.75	.35	.09
☐ 56 Eugene Lockhart	.35	.16	.04
☐ 58 Mike Hegman	.25	.11	.03
☐ 61 Jim Cooper DP	.25	.11	.03
☐ 63 Glen Titensor	.25	.11	.03
☐ 64 Tom Rafferty	.25	.11	.03
☐ 65 Kurt Petersen	.25	.11	.03
☐ 72 Ed Too Tall Jones	.75	.35	.09
☐ 75 Phil Pozderac	.25	.11	.03
☐ 77 Jim Jeffcoat	.50	.23	.06
☐ 78 John Dutton	.35	.16	.04
☐ 80 Tony Hill	.35	.16	.04
☐ 82 Mike Renfro	.25	.11	.03
☐ 84 Doug Cosbie DP	.25	.11	.03

1986 McDonald's Dolphins

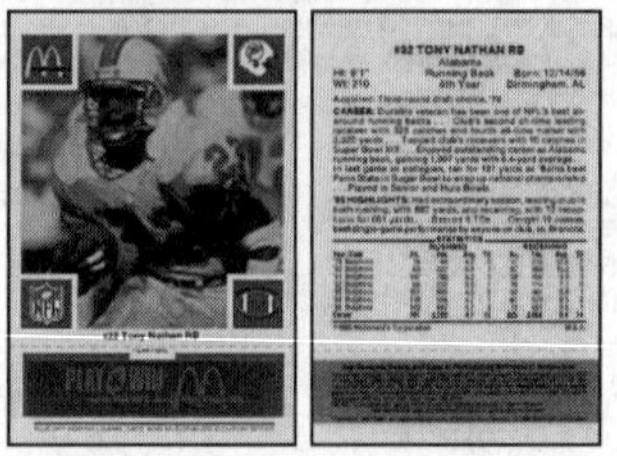

This 25-card set was issued in McDonald's Hamburger restaurants around Miami. The set was issued over a four-week period with blue tabs the first week, black (or gray) tabs the second week, gold (or orange) tabs the third week, and green tabs the fourth week. The cards measure approximately 3 1/16" by 4 11/16" with the tab intact and 3 1/16" by 3 5/8" without the tab. The cards are numbered below by uniform number. Joe Carter and Tony Nathan have photos reversed so that there are 25 different cards, but since this error happened on a double-printed player, no additional value is assigned. The value of cards without tabs or tabs scratched off is F-G at best. The cards were printed on a 30-card sheet; hence, there are five double-printed cards listed DP in the checklist below. For individual prices on the more expensive color tabs, merely apply the ratio of that color's set price to the base (cheapest) color set price and use the resulting multiple on the individual prices for that color.

	MINT	NRMT	EXC
COMPLETE SET (BLUE)	45.00	20.00	5.50
COMPLETE SET (BLACK)	25.00	11.00	3.10
COMPLETE SET (GOLD)	25.00	11.00	3.10
COMPLETE SET (GREEN)	25.00	11.00	3.10
COMMON CARD	.60	.25	.07
☐ 4 Reggie Roby	.75	.35	.09
☐ 7 Fuad Reveiz	1.00	.45	.12
☐ 10 Don Strock	.75	.35	.09
☐ 13 Dan Marino	15.00	6.75	1.85
☐ 22 Tony Nathan	.75	.35	.09
☐ 23A Joe Carter ERR (Photo actually Tony Nathan 22)	.75	.35	.09
☐ 23B Joe Carter COR	.60	.25	.07
☐ 27 Lorenzo Hampton	.60	.25	.07
☐ 30 Ron Davenport	.60	.25	.07
☐ 43 Bud Brown DP	.60	.25	.07
☐ 47 Glenn Blackwood DP	.60	.25	.07
☐ 49 William Judson	.60	.25	.07
☐ 55 Hugh Green	.75	.35	.09
☐ 57 Dwight Stephenson	.75	.35	.09
☐ 58 Kim Bokamper DP	.60	.25	.07
☐ 59 Bob Brudzinski DP	.60	.25	.07
☐ 61 Roy Foster	.60	.25	.07
☐ 71 Mike Charles	.60	.25	.07
☐ 75 Doug Betters DP	.60	.25	.07
☐ 79 Jon Giesler	.60	.25	.07
☐ 83 Mark Clayton	1.50	.70	.19
☐ 84 Bruce Hardy	.60	.25	.07
☐ 85 Mark Duper	1.00	.45	.12
☐ 89 Nat Moore	.75	.35	.09
☐ 91 Mack Moore	.60	.25	.07

1986 McDonald's Eagles

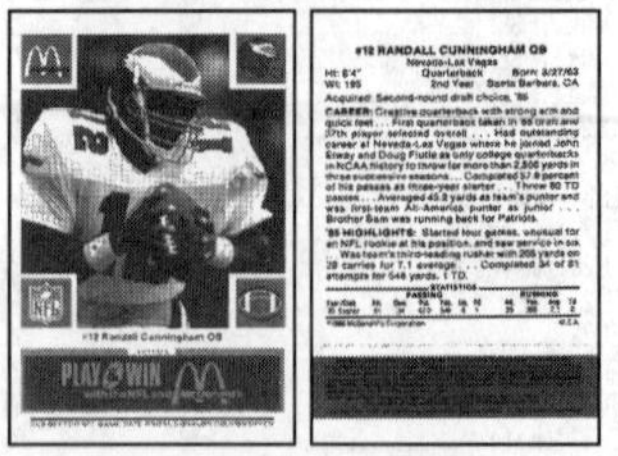

This 24-card set was issued in McDonald's Hamburger restaurants around Philadelphia. The set was issued over a four-week period with blue tabs the first week, black (or gray) tabs the second week, gold (or orange) tabs the third week, and green tabs the fourth week. The cards measure approximately 3 1/16" by 4 11/16" with the tab intact and 3 1/16" by 3 5/8" without the tab. The cards are numbered below by uniform number. The value of cards without tabs or tabs scratched off is F-G at best. The cards were printed on a 30-card sheet; hence, there are six double-printed cards listed DP in the checklist below. For individual prices on the more expensive color tabs, merely apply the ratio of that color's set price to the base (cheapest) color set price and use the resulting multiple on the individual prices for that color. Randall Cunningham appears in this set, a year before his Topps Rookie Card.

	MINT	NRMT	EXC
COMPLETE SET (BLUE)	60.00	27.00	7.50
COMPLETE SET (BLACK)	20.00	9.00	2.50
COMPLETE SET (GOLD)	10.00	4.50	1.25
COMPLETE SET (GREEN)	10.00	4.50	1.25
COMMON CARD	.25	.11	.03
☐ 7 Ron Jaworski	.50	.23	.06
☐ 8 Paul McFadden	.25	.11	.03
☐ 12 Randall Cunningham DP	2.00	.90	.25
☐ 22 Brenard Wilson	.25	.11	.03
☐ 24 Ray Ellis	.25	.11	.03
☐ 29 Elbert Foules	.25	.11	.03
☐ 36 Herman Hunter	.25	.11	.03
☐ 41 Earnest Jackson	.35	.16	.04
☐ 43 Roynell Young	.35	.16	.04
☐ 48 Wes Hopkins	.35	.16	.04
☐ 50 Garry Cobb DP	.25	.11	.03
☐ 63 Ron Baker DP	.25	.11	.03
☐ 66 Ken Reeves	.25	.11	.03
☐ 71 Ken Clarke DP	.25	.11	.03
☐ 73 Steve Kenney	.25	.11	.03
☐ 74 Leonard Mitchell	.25	.11	.03
☐ 81 Kenny Jackson	.35	.16	.04
☐ 82 Mike Quick	.35	.16	.04
☐ 85 Ron Johnson	.25	.11	.03
☐ 88 John Spagnola	.25	.11	.03
☐ 91 Reggie White	3.00	1.35	.35
☐ 93 Tom Strauthers	.25	.11	.03
☐ 94 Byron Darby DP	.25	.11	.03
☐ 98 Greg Brown DP	.25	.11	.03

1986 McDonald's Falcons

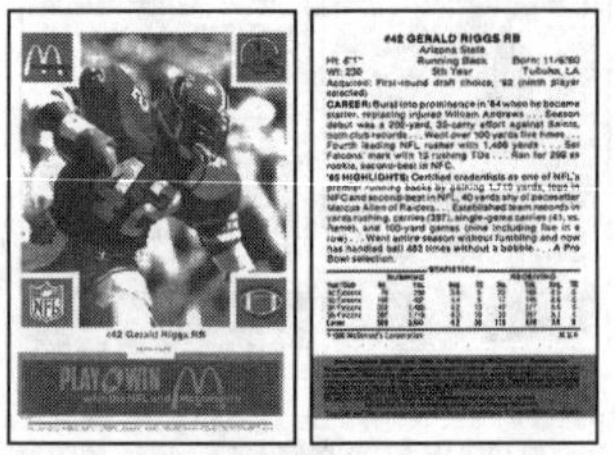

This 24-card set was issued in McDonald's Hamburger restaurants around Atlanta. The set was issued over a four-week period with blue tabs the first week, black (or gray) tabs the second week, gold (or orange) tabs the third week, and green tabs the fourth week. The cards measure approximately 3 1/16" by 4 11/16" with the tab intact and 3 1/16" by 3 5/8" without the tab. The cards are numbered below by uniform number. The value of cards without tabs or tabs scratched off is F-G at best. The cards were printed on a 30-card sheet; hence, there are six double-printed cards listed DP in the checklist below. For individual prices on the more expensive color tabs, merely apply the ratio of that color's set price to the base (cheapest) color set price and use the resulting multiple on the individual prices for that color.

	MINT	NRMT	EXC
COMPLETE SET (BLUE)	60.00	27.00	7.50
COMPLETE SET (BLACK)	225.00	100.00	28.00
COMPLETE SET (GOLD)	40.00	18.00	5.00
COMPLETE SET (GREEN)	15.00	6.75	1.85
COMMON CARD	.60	.25	.07
☐ 3 Rick Donnelly	.60	.25	.07
☐ 16 David Archer DP	1.00	.45	.12
☐ 18 Mick Luckhurst	.60	.25	.07
☐ 23 Bobby Butler	.60	.25	.07
☐ 26 James Britt DP	.60	.25	.07
☐ 37 Kenny Johnson	.60	.25	.07
☐ 39 Cliff Austin DP	.60	.25	.07
☐ 42 Gerald Riggs	.75	.35	.09
☐ 50 Buddy Curry	.60	.25	.07
☐ 56 Al Richardson	.60	.25	.07
☐ 57 Jeff Van Note	.75	.35	.09
☐ 58 David Frye	.60	.25	.07
☐ 61 John Scully	.60	.25	.07
☐ 62 Brett Miller	.60	.25	.07
☐ 74 Mike Pitts	.60	.25	.07
☐ 76 Mike Gann	.60	.25	.07
☐ 77 Rick Bryan	.60	.25	.07
☐ 78 Mike Kenn	.75	.35	.09
☐ 79 Bill Fralic	1.00	.45	.12
☐ 81 Billy Johnson	.75	.35	.09
☐ 82 Stacey Bailey DP	.60	.25	.07
☐ 87 Cliff Benson DP	.60	.25	.07
☐ 88 Arthur Cox	.60	.25	.07
☐ 89 Charlie Brown DP	.75	.35	.09

1986 McDonald's 49ers

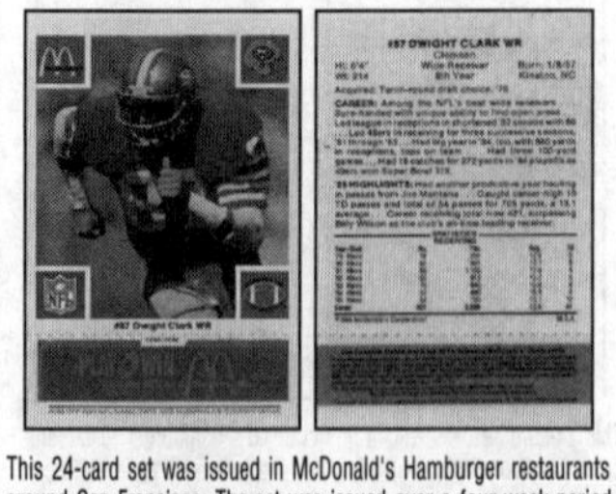

This 24-card set was issued in McDonald's Hamburger restaurants around San Francisco. The set was issued over a four-week period with blue tabs the first week, black (or gray) tabs the second week, gold (or orange) tabs the third week, and green tabs the fourth week. The cards measure approximately 3 1/16" by 4 11/16" with the tab intact and 3 1/16" by 3 5/8" without the tab. The cards are numbered below by uniform number. The value of cards without tabs or tabs

scratched off is F-G at best. The cards were printed on a 30-card sheet; hence, there are six double-printed cards listed DP in the checklist below. For individual prices on the more expensive color tabs, merely apply the ratio of that color's set price to the base (cheapest) color set price and use the resulting multiple on the individual prices for that color. Jerry Rice appears in his Rookie Card year.

	MINT	NRMT	EXC
COMPLETE SET (BLUE)	50.00	22.00	6.25
COMPLETE SET (BLACK)	25.00	11.00	3.10
COMPLETE SET (GOLD)	25.00	11.00	3.10
COMPLETE SET (GREEN)	25.00	11.00	3.10
COMMON CARD	.75	.35	.09
☐ 16 Joe Montana	12.00	5.50	1.50
☐ 21 Eric Wright	1.00	.45	.12
☐ 26 Wendell Tyler	1.00	.45	.12
☐ 27 Carlton Williamson	.75	.35	.09
☐ 33 Roger Craig DP	1.25	.55	.16
☐ 42 Ronnie Lott	2.00	.90	.25
☐ 49 Jeff Fuller	.75	.35	.09
☐ 50 Riki Ellison	.75	.35	.09
☐ 51 Randy Cross DP	1.00	.45	.12
☐ 56 Fred Quillan	.75	.35	.09
☐ 58 Keena Turner	.75	.35	.09
☐ 62 Guy McIntyre	.75	.35	.09
☐ 68 John Ayers DP	.75	.35	.09
☐ 71 Keith Fahnhorst	.75	.35	.09
☐ 72 Jeff Stover	.75	.35	.09
☐ 76 Dwaine Board DP	.75	.35	.09
☐ 77 Bubba Paris	.75	.35	.09
☐ 78 Manu Tuiasosopo	.75	.35	.09
☐ 80 Jerry Rice	15.00	6.75	1.85
☐ 81 Russ Francis	1.00	.45	.12
☐ 86 John Frank	.75	.35	.09
☐ 87 Dwight Clark DP	1.00	.45	.12
☐ 90 Todd Shell	.75	.35	.09
☐ 95 Michael Carter DP	1.00	.45	.12

1986 McDonald's Giants

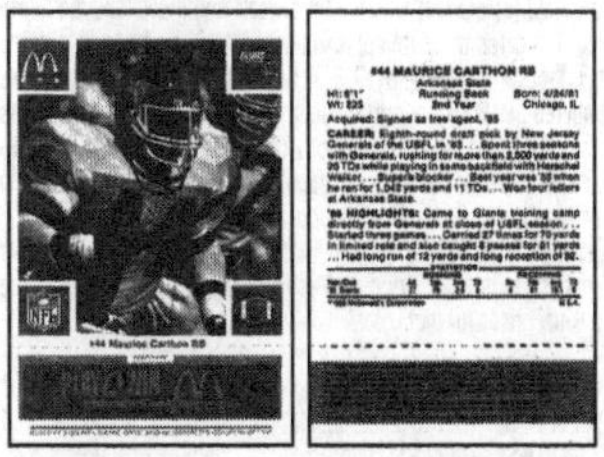

This 24-card set was issued in McDonald's Hamburger restaurants around New York. The set was issued over a four-week period with blue tabs the first week, black (or gray) tabs the second week, gold (or orange) tabs the third week, and green tabs the fourth week. The cards measure approximately 3 1/16" by 4 11/16" with the tab intact and 3 1/16" by 3 5/8" without the tab. The cards are numbered below by uniform number. The value of cards without tabs or tabs scratched off is F-G at best. The cards were printed on a 30-card sheet; hence, there are six double-printed cards listed DP in the checklist below. For individual prices on the more expensive color tabs, merely apply the ratio of that color's set price to the base (cheapest) color set price and use the resulting multiple on the individual prices for that color.

	MINT	NRMT	EXC
COMPLETE SET (BLUE)	12.00	5.50	1.50
COMPLETE SET (BLACK)	9.00	4.00	1.10
COMPLETE SET (GOLD)	6.00	2.70	.75
COMPLETE SET (GREEN)	6.00	2.70	.75
COMMON CARD	.25	.11	.03
☐ 5 Sean Landeta	.35	.16	.04
☐ 11 Phil Simms	1.25	.55	.16
☐ 20 Joe Morris	.50	.23	.06
☐ 23 Perry Williams	.25	.11	.03
☐ 26 Rob Carpenter DP	.25	.11	.03
☐ 33 George Adams DP	.25	.11	.03
☐ 34 Elvis Patterson	.35	.16	.04
☐ 43 Terry Kinard	.25	.11	.03
☐ 44 Maurice Carthon	.25	.11	.03
☐ 48 Kenny Hill	.25	.11	.03
☐ 53 Harry Carson	.35	.16	.04
☐ 54 Andy Headen	.25	.11	.03
☐ 56 Lawrence Taylor	1.50	.70	.19
☐ 60 Brad Benson DP	.25	.11	.03
☐ 63 Karl Nelson	.25	.11	.03
☐ 64 Jim Burt DP	.35	.16	.04
☐ 67 Billy Ard DP	.25	.11	.03
☐ 70 Leonard Marshall	.35	.16	.04
☐ 75 George Martin	.35	.16	.04
☐ 80 Phil McConkey	.35	.16	.04
☐ 84 Zeke Mowatt	.25	.11	.03
☐ 85 Don Hasselbeck	.25	.11	.03
☐ 86 Lionel Manuel	.35	.16	.04
☐ 89 Mark Bavaro DP	.35	.16	.04

1986 McDonald's Jets

This 24-card set was issued in McDonald's Hamburger restaurants around New York. The set was issued over a four-week period with blue tabs the first week, black (or gray) tabs the second week, gold (or orange) tabs the third week, and green tabs the fourth week. The

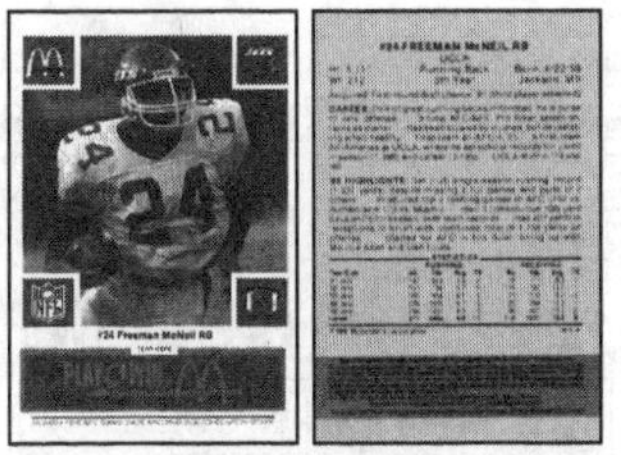

cards measure approximately 3 1/16" by 4 11/16" with the tab intact and 3 1/16" by 3 5/8" without the tab. The cards are numbered below by uniform number. The value of cards without tabs or tabs scratched off is F-G at best. The cards were printed on a 30-card sheet; hence, there are six double-printed cards listed DP in the checklist below. For individual prices on the more expensive color tabs, merely apply the ratio of that color's set price to the base (cheapest) color set price and use the resulting multiple on the individual prices for that color.

	MINT	NRMT	EXC
COMPLETE SET (BLUE)	150.00	70.00	19.00
COMPLETE SET (BLACK)	150.00	70.00	19.00
COMPLETE SET (GOLD)	30.00	13.50	3.70
COMPLETE SET (GREEN)	30.00	13.50	3.70
COMMON CARD	1.25	.55	.16
☐ 5 Pat Leahy	1.25	.55	.16
☐ 7 Ken O'Brien	1.50	.70	.19
☐ 21 Kirk Springs	1.25	.55	.16
☐ 24 Freeman McNeil	2.00	.90	.25
☐ 27 Russell Carter DP	1.25	.55	.16
☐ 29 Johnny Lynn	1.25	.55	.16
☐ 34 Johnny Hector	1.50	.70	.19
☐ 39 Harry Hamilton	1.25	.55	.16
☐ 49 Tony Paige	1.50	.70	.19
☐ 53 Jim Sweeney	1.25	.55	.16
☐ 56 Lance Mehl	1.25	.55	.16
☐ 59 Kyle Clifton DP	1.50	.70	.19
☐ 60 Dan Alexander DP	1.25	.55	.16
☐ 65 Joe Fields DP	1.25	.55	.16
☐ 73 Joe Klecko	1.50	.70	.19
☐ 78 Barry Bennett DP	1.25	.55	.16
☐ 80 Johnny Lam Jones	1.25	.55	.16
☐ 82 Mickey Shuler	1.25	.55	.16
☐ 85 Wesley Walker	1.50	.70	.19
☐ 87 Kurt Sohn	1.25	.55	.16
☐ 88 Al Toon	2.00	.90	.25
☐ 89 Rocky Klever	1.25	.55	.16
☐ 93 Marty Lyons	1.50	.70	.19
☐ 99 Mark Gastineau DP	1.50	.70	.19

1986 McDonald's Lions

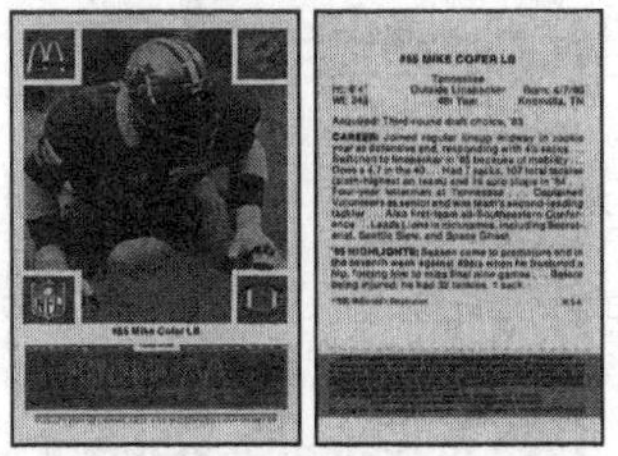

This 24-card set was issued in McDonald's Hamburger restaurants around Detroit. The set was issued over a four-week period with blue tabs the first week, black (or gray) tabs the second week, gold (or orange) tabs the third week, and green tabs the fourth week. The cards measure approximately 3 1/16" by 4 11/16" with the tab intact and 3 1/16" by 3 5/8" without the tab. The cards are numbered below by uniform number. The value of cards without tabs or tabs scratched off is F-G at best. The cards were printed on a 30-card sheet; hence, there are six double-printed cards listed DP in the checklist below. For individual prices on the more expensive color tabs, merely apply the ratio of that color's set price to the base (cheapest) color set price and use the resulting multiple on the individual prices for that color.

	MINT	NRMT	EXC
COMPLETE SET (BLUE)	6.00	2.70	.75
COMPLETE SET (BLACK)	6.00	2.70	.75
COMPLETE SET (GOLD)	6.00	2.70	.75
COMPLETE SET (GREEN)	6.00	2.70	.75
COMMON CARD	.25	.11	.03
☐ 3 Eddie Murray	.35	.16	.04
☐ 11 Michael Black DP	.25	.11	.03
☐ 17 Eric Hipple	.35	.16	.04
☐ 20 Billy Sims	.50	.23	.06
☐ 21 Demetrious Johnson	.25	.11	.03
☐ 27 Bobby Watkins	.25	.11	.03
☐ 29 Bruce McNorton	.25	.11	.03
☐ 30 James Jones	.35	.16	.04
☐ 33 William Graham	.25	.11	.03
☐ 35 Alvin Hall	.25	.11	.03
☐ 39 Leonard Thompson	.35	.16	.04
☐ 50 August Curley DP	.25	.11	.03
☐ 52 Steve Mott	.25	.11	.03
☐ 55 Mike Cofer DP	.35	.16	.04
☐ 59 Jimmy Williams	.25	.11	.03
☐ 70 Keith Dorney DP	.25	.11	.03
☐ 71 Rich Strenger	.25	.11	.03
☐ 75 Lomas Brown DP	.35	.16	.04
☐ 76 Eric Williams	.25	.11	.03
☐ 79 William Gay	.25	.11	.03
☐ 82 Pete Mandley	.25	.11	.03
☐ 86 Mark Nichols	.25	.11	.03
☐ 87 David Lewis	.25	.11	.03
☐ 89 Jeff Chadwick DP	.25	.11	.03

1986 McDonald's Oilers

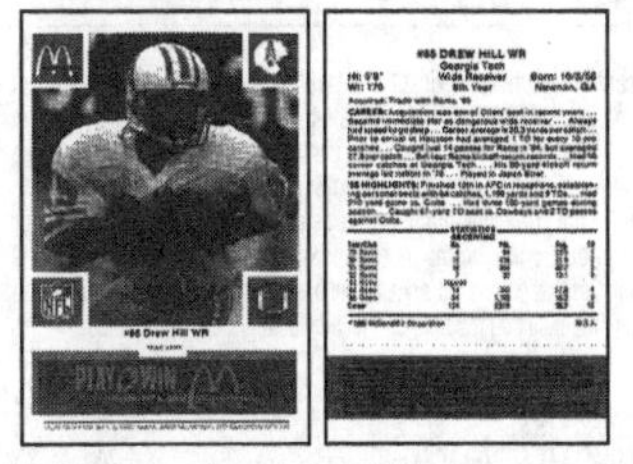

This 24-card set was issued in McDonald's Hamburger restaurants around Houston. The set was issued over a four-week period with blue tabs the first week, black (or gray) tabs the second week, gold (or orange) tabs the third week, and green tabs the fourth week. The cards measure approximately 3 1/16" by 4 11/16" with the tab intact and 3 1/16" by 3 5/8" without the tab. The cards are numbered below by uniform number. The value of cards without tabs or tabs scratched off is F-G at best. The cards were printed on a 30-card sheet; hence, there are six double-printed cards listed DP in the checklist below. For individual prices on the more expensive color tabs, merely apply the ratio of that color's set price to the base (cheapest) color set price and use the resulting multiple on the individual prices for that color.

	MINT	NRMT	EXC
COMPLETE SET (BLUE)	12.00	5.50	1.50
COMPLETE SET (BLACK)	8.00	3.60	1.00
COMPLETE SET (GOLD)	8.00	3.60	1.00
COMPLETE SET (GREEN)	8.00	3.60	1.00
COMMON CARD	.30	.14	.04
☐ 1 Warren Moon	4.00	1.80	.50
☐ 7 Tony Zendejas	.30	.14	.04
☐ 10 Oliver Luck	.40	.18	.05
☐ 21 Bo Eason	.30	.14	.04
☐ 23 Richard Johnson	.30	.14	.04
☐ 24 Steve Brown DP	.30	.14	.04
☐ 25 Keith Bostic DP	.30	.14	.04
☐ 29 Patrick Allen DP	.30	.14	.04
☐ 33 Mike Rozier	.50	.23	.06
☐ 40 Butch Woolfolk	.30	.14	.04
☐ 53 Avon Riley	.30	.14	.04
☐ 56 Robert Abraham DP	.30	.14	.04
☐ 63 Mike Munchak	.40	.18	.05
☐ 67 Mike Stensrud	.30	.14	.04
☐ 70 Dean Steinkuhler	.40	.18	.05
☐ 71 Richard Byrd DP	.30	.14	.04
☐ 73 Harvey Salem	.30	.14	.04
☐ 74 Bruce Matthews	.75	.35	.09
☐ 79 Ray Childress	.75	.35	.09
☐ 83 Tim Smith	.30	.14	.04
☐ 85 Drew Hill	.75	.35	.09
☐ 87 Jamie Williams	.30	.14	.04
☐ 91 Johnny Meads	.30	.14	.04
☐ 94 Frank Bush DP	.30	.14	.04

1986 McDonald's Packers

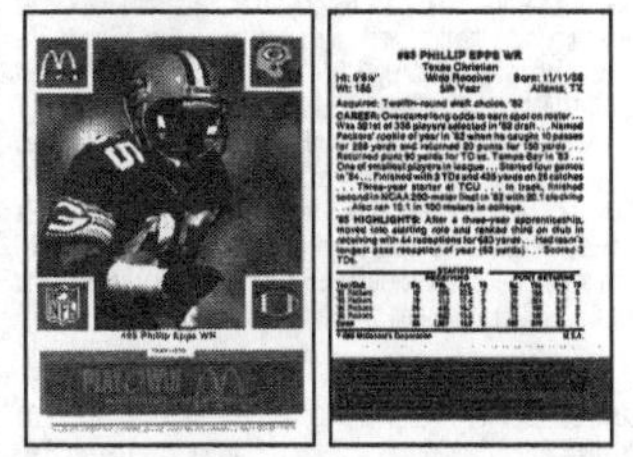

This 24-card set was issued in McDonald's Hamburger restaurants around Green Bay and Milwaukee. The set was issued over a four-week period with blue tabs the first week, black (or gray) tabs the second week, gold (or orange) tabs the third week, and green tabs the fourth week. The cards measure approximately 3 1/16" by 4 11/16" with the tab intact and 3 1/16" by 3 5/8" without the tab. The cards are numbered below by uniform number. The value of cards without tabs or tabs scratched off is F-G at best. The cards were printed on a 30-card sheet; hence, there are six double-printed cards listed DP in the checklist below. For individual prices on the more expensive color tabs, merely apply the ratio of that color's set price to the base (cheapest) color set price and use the resulting multiple on the individual prices for that color.

	MINT	NRMT	EXC
COMPLETE SET (BLUE)	6.00	2.70	.75
COMPLETE SET (BLACK)	6.00	2.70	.75
COMPLETE SET (GOLD)	6.00	2.70	.75
COMPLETE SET (GREEN)	6.00	2.70	.75
COMMON CARD	.25	.11	.03
☐ 10 Al Del Greco DP	.25	.11	.03
☐ 12 Lynn Dickey	.35	.16	.04
☐ 16 Randy Wright	.35	.16	.04
☐ 18 Jim Zorn	.35	.16	.04
☐ 22 Mark Lee	.25	.11	.03
☐ 26 Tim Lewis	.25	.11	.03
☐ 31 Gerry Ellis	.25	.11	.03
☐ 33 Jessie Clark DP	.25	.11	.03
☐ 37 Mark Murphy	.35	.16	.04
☐ 41 Tom Flynn	.25	.11	.03
☐ 42 Gary Ellerson	.25	.11	.03
☐ 53 Mike Douglass	.25	.11	.03
☐ 55 Randy Scott	.25	.11	.03
☐ 59 John Anderson DP	.25	.11	.03
☐ 67 Karl Swanke	.25	.11	.03
☐ 75 Ken Ruettgers	.25	.11	.03
☐ 76 Alphonso Carreker DP	.25	.11	.03
☐ 77 Mike Butler DP	.25	.11	.03
☐ 79 Donnie Humphrey	.25	.11	.03
☐ 82 Paul Coffman DP	.25	.11	.03
☐ 85 Phillip Epps	.35	.16	.04
☐ 90 Ezra Johnson	.25	.11	.03
☐ 91 Brian Noble	.35	.16	.04
☐ 94 Charles Martin	.25	.11	.03

1986 McDonald's Patriots

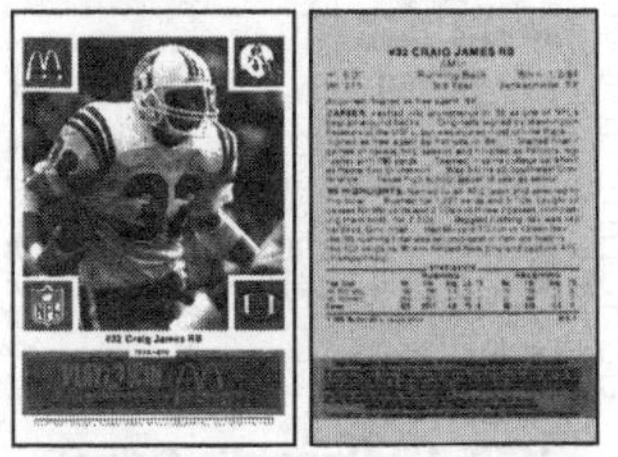

This 24-card set was issued in McDonald's Hamburger restaurants around New England. The set was issued over a four-week period with blue tabs the first week, black (or gray) tabs the second week, gold (or orange) tabs the third week, and green tabs the fourth week. The cards measure approximately 3 1/16" by 4 11/16" with the tab intact and 3 1/16" by 3 5/8" without the tab. The cards are numbered below by uniform number. The value of cards without tabs or tabs scratched off is F-G at best. The cards were printed on a 30-card sheet; hence, there are six double-printed cards listed DP in the checklist below. For individual prices on the more expensive color tabs, merely apply the ratio of that color's set price to the base (cheapest) color set price and use the resulting multiple on the individual prices for that color.

	MINT	NRMT	EXC
COMPLETE SET (BLUE)	6.00	2.70	.75
COMPLETE SET (BLACK)	6.00	2.70	.75
COMPLETE SET (GOLD)	6.00	2.70	.75
COMPLETE SET (GREEN)	6.00	2.70	.75
COMMON CARD	.25	.11	.03
☐ 3 Rich Camarillo DP	.25	.11	.03
☐ 11 Tony Eason DP	.35	.16	.04
☐ 14 Steve Grogan	.50	.23	.06
☐ 24 Robert Weathers	.25	.11	.03
☐ 26 Raymond Clayborn DP	.25	.11	.03
☐ 30 Mosi Tatupu	.25	.11	.03
☐ 31 Fred Marion	.25	.11	.03
☐ 32 Craig James	.50	.23	.06
☐ 33 Tony Collins DP	.35	.16	.04
☐ 38 Roland James	.25	.11	.03
☐ 42 Ronnie Lippett	.25	.11	.03
☐ 50 Larry McGrew	.25	.11	.03
☐ 55 Don Blackmon DP	.25	.11	.03
☐ 56 Andre Tippett	.50	.23	.06
☐ 57 Steve Nelson	.25	.11	.03
☐ 58 Pete Brock DP	.25	.11	.03
☐ 60 Garin Veris	.25	.11	.03
☐ 61 Ron Wooten	.25	.11	.03
☐ 73 John Hannah	.50	.23	.06
☐ 77 Kenneth Sims	.25	.11	.03
☐ 80 Irving Fryar	1.00	.45	.12
☐ 81 Stephen Starring	.25	.11	.03
☐ 83 Cedric Jones	.25	.11	.03
☐ 86 Stanley Morgan	.50	.23	.06

1986 McDonald's Raiders

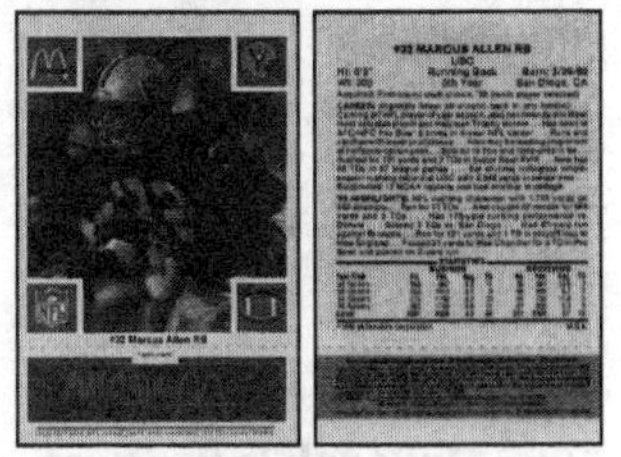

This 24-card set was issued in McDonald's Hamburger restaurants around Los Angeles. The set was issued over a four-week period with blue tabs the first week, black (or gray) tabs the second week, gold (or orange) tabs the third week, and green tabs the fourth week. The cards measure approximately 3 1/16" by 4 11/16" with the tab intact

and 3 1/16" by 3 5/8" without the tab. The cards are numbered below by uniform number. The value of cards without tabs or tabs scratched off is F-G at best. The cards were printed on a 30-card sheet; hence, there are six double-printed cards listed DP in the checklist below. For individual prices on the more expensive color tabs, merely apply the ratio of that color's set price to the base (cheapest) color set price and use the resulting multiple on the individual prices for that color.

	MINT	NRMT	EXC
COMPLETE SET (BLUE)	20.00	9.00	2.50
COMPLETE SET (BLACK)	15.00	6.75	1.85
COMPLETE SET (GOLD)	8.00	3.60	1.00
COMPLETE SET (GREEN)	8.00	3.60	1.00
COMMON CARD	.25	.11	.03
☐ 1 Marc Wilson	.35	.16	.04
☐ 8 Ray Guy DP	.50	.23	.06
☐ 10 Chris Bahr DP	.25	.11	.03
☐ 16 Jim Plunkett	.50	.23	.06
☐ 22 Mike Haynes	.35	.16	.04
☐ 26 Vann McElroy	.25	.11	.03
☐ 27 Frank Hawkins	.25	.11	.03
☐ 32 Marcus Allen DP	1.25	.55	.16
☐ 36 Mike Davis DP	.25	.11	.03
☐ 37 Lester Hayes	.35	.16	.04
☐ 46 Todd Christensen DP	.50	.23	.06
☐ 53 Rod Martin	.35	.16	.04
☐ 54 Reggie McKenzie	.25	.11	.03
☐ 55 Matt Millen	.35	.16	.04
☐ 70 Henry Lawrence	.25	.11	.03
☐ 71 Bill Pickel	.25	.11	.03
☐ 72 Don Mosebar	.35	.16	.04
☐ 73 Charley Hannah	.25	.11	.03
☐ 75 Howie Long	1.00	.45	.12
☐ 79 Bruce Davis DP	.25	.11	.03
☐ 84 Jessie Hester	.50	.23	.06
☐ 85 Dokie Williams	.25	.11	.03
☐ 91 Brad Van Pelt	.25	.11	.03
☐ 99 Sean Jones	.50	.23	.06

1986 McDonald's Rams

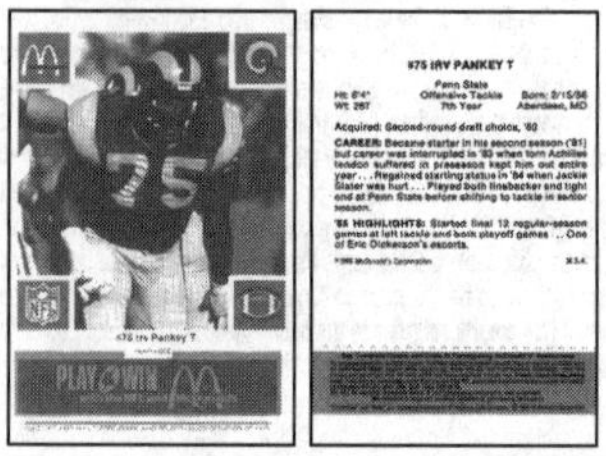

This 24-card set was issued in McDonald's Hamburger restaurants around Los Angeles. The set was issued over a four-week period with blue tabs the first week, black (or gray) tabs the second week, gold (or orange) tabs the third week, and green tabs the fourth week. The cards measure approximately 3 1/16" by 4 11/16" with the tab intact and 3 1/16" by 3 5/8" without the tab. The cards are numbered below by uniform number. The value of cards without tabs or tabs scratched off is F-G at best. The cards were printed on a 30-card sheet; hence, there are six double-printed cards listed DP in the checklist below. For individual prices on the more expensive color tabs, merely apply the ratio of that color's set price to the base (cheapest) color set price and use the resulting multiple on the individual prices for that color.

	MINT	NRMT	EXC
COMPLETE SET (BLUE)	9.00	4.00	1.10
COMPLETE SET (BLACK)	6.00	2.70	.75
COMPLETE SET (GOLD)	6.00	2.70	.75
COMPLETE SET (GREEN)	6.00	2.70	.75
COMMON CARD	.25	.11	.03
☐ 1 Mike Lansford	.25	.11	.03
☐ 3 Dale Hatcher	.25	.11	.03
☐ 5 Dieter Brock DP	.25	.11	.03
☐ 20 Johnnie Johnson	.25	.11	.03
☐ 21 Nolan Cromwell DP	.35	.16	.04
☐ 22 Vince Newsome	.25	.11	.03
☐ 27 Gary Green	.25	.11	.03
☐ 29 Eric Dickerson DP	1.00	.45	.12
☐ 44 Mike Guman	.25	.11	.03
☐ 47 LeRoy Irvin	.35	.16	.04
☐ 50 Jim Collins DP	.25	.11	.03
☐ 54 Mike Wilcher	.25	.11	.03
☐ 55 Carl Ekern	.25	.11	.03
☐ 56 Doug Smith	.25	.11	.03
☐ 58 Mel Owens	.25	.11	.03
☐ 60 Dennis Harrah	.25	.11	.03
☐ 71 Reggie Doss DP	.25	.11	.03
☐ 72 Kent Hill	.25	.11	.03
☐ 75 Irv Pankey	.25	.11	.03
☐ 78 Jackie Slater	.50	.23	.06
☐ 80 Henry Ellard	1.00	.45	.12
☐ 81 David Hill	.25	.11	.03
☐ 87 Tony Hunter	.25	.11	.03
☐ 89 Ron Brown DP	.35	.16	.04

1986 McDonald's Redskins

This 24-card set was issued in McDonald's Hamburger restaurants around Washington. The set was issued over a four-week period with blue tabs the first week, black (or gray) tabs the second week, gold (or orange) tabs the third week, and green tabs the fourth week. The

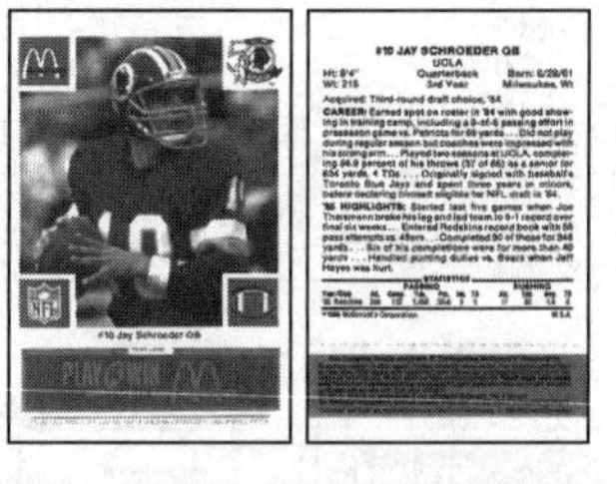

cards measure approximately 3 1/16" by 4 11/16" with the tab intact and 3 1/16" by 3 5/8" without the tab. The cards are numbered below by uniform number. The value of cards without tabs or tabs scratched off is F-G at best. The cards were printed on a 30-card sheet; hence, there are six double-printed cards listed DP in the checklist below. For individual prices on the more expensive color tabs, merely apply the ratio of that color's set price to the base (cheapest) color set price and use the resulting multiple on the individual prices for that color.

	MINT	NRMT	EXC
COMPLETE SET (BLUE)	6.00	2.70	.75
COMPLETE SET (BLACK)	6.00	2.70	.75
COMPLETE SET (GOLD)	6.00	2.70	.75
COMPLETE SET (GREEN)	6.00	2.70	.75
COMMON CARD	.25	.11	.03
☐ 3 Mark Moseley	.25	.11	.03
☐ 10 Jay Schroeder	.50	.23	.06
☐ 22 Curtis Jordan	.25	.11	.03
☐ 28 Darrell Green	.50	.23	.06
☐ 32 Vernon Dean DP	.25	.11	.03
☐ 35 Keith Griffin	.25	.11	.03
☐ 37 Raphel Cherry DP	.25	.11	.03
☐ 38 George Rogers	.35	.16	.04
☐ 51 Monte Coleman DP	.35	.16	.04
☐ 52 Neal Olkewicz	.25	.11	.03
☐ 53 Jeff Bostic DP	.25	.11	.03
☐ 55 Mel Kaufman	.25	.11	.03
☐ 57 Rich Milot	.25	.11	.03
☐ 65 Dave Butz DP	.35	.16	.04
☐ 66 Joe Jacoby	.35	.16	.04
☐ 68 Russ Grimm	.35	.16	.04
☐ 71 Charles Mann	.50	.23	.06
☐ 72 Dexter Manley	.35	.16	.04
☐ 73 Mark May	.35	.16	.04
☐ 77 Darryl Grant	.25	.11	.03
☐ 81 Art Monk	1.00	.45	.12
☐ 84 Gary Clark DP	1.00	.45	.12
☐ 85 Don Warren	.35	.16	.04
☐ 86 Clint Didier	.25	.11	.03

1986 McDonald's Saints

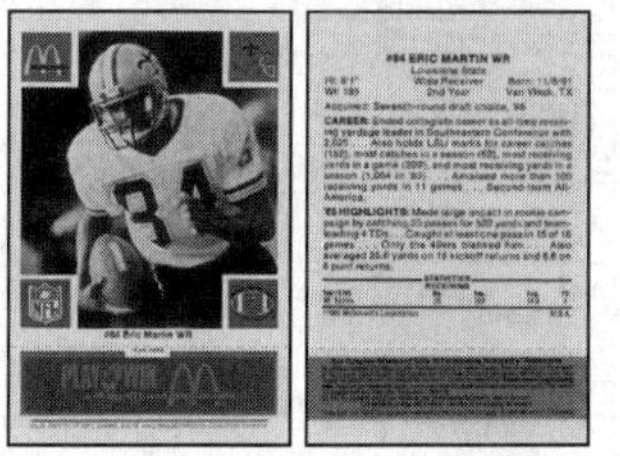

This 24-card set was issued in McDonald's Hamburger restaurants around New Orleans. The set was issued over a four-week period with blue tabs the first week, black (or gray) tabs the second week, gold (or orange) tabs the third week, and green tabs the fourth week. The cards measure approximately 3 1/16" by 4 11/16" with the tab intact and 3 1/16" by 3 5/8" without the tab. The cards are numbered below by uniform number. The value of cards without tabs or tabs scratched off is F-G at best. The cards were printed on a 30-card sheet; hence, there are six double-printed cards listed DP in the checklist below. For individual prices on the more expensive color tabs, merely apply the ratio of that color's set price to the base (cheapest) color set price and use the resulting multiple on the individual prices for that color.

	MINT	NRMT	EXC
COMPLETE SET (BLUE)	150.00	70.00	19.00
COMPLETE SET (BLACK)	30.00	13.50	3.70
COMPLETE SET (GOLD)	20.00	9.00	2.50
COMPLETE SET (GREEN)	25.00	11.00	3.10
COMMON CARD	.75	.35	.09
☐ 3 Bobby Hebert	2.00	.90	.25
☐ 7 Morten Andersen DP	1.25	.55	.16
☐ 10 Brian Hansen	.75	.35	.09
☐ 18 Dave Wilson	.75	.35	.09
☐ 20 Russell Gary	.75	.35	.09
☐ 25 Johnnie Poe	.75	.35	.09
☐ 30 Wayne Wilson	.75	.35	.09
☐ 44 Dave Waymer	1.00	.45	.12
☐ 46 Hokie Gajan	.75	.35	.09
☐ 49 Frank Wattelett	.75	.35	.09
☐ 50 Jack Del Rio DP	1.25	.55	.16
☐ 57 Rickey Jackson	1.25	.55	.16
☐ 60 Steve Korte	.75	.35	.09
☐ 61 Joel Hilgenberg	.75	.35	.09
☐ 63 Brad Edelman DP	.75	.35	.09
☐ 64 Dave Lafary	.75	.35	.09
☐ 67 Stan Brock DP	1.00	.45	.12
☐ 73 Frank Warren	.75	.35	.09
☐ 75 Bruce Clark DP	.75	.35	.09
☐ 84 Eric Martin	2.00	.90	.25
☐ 85 Hoby Brenner DP	.75	.35	.09
☐ 88 Eugene Goodlow	.75	.35	.09
☐ 89 Tyrone Young	.75	.35	.09
☐ 99 Tony Elliott	.75	.35	.09

1986 McDonald's Seahawks

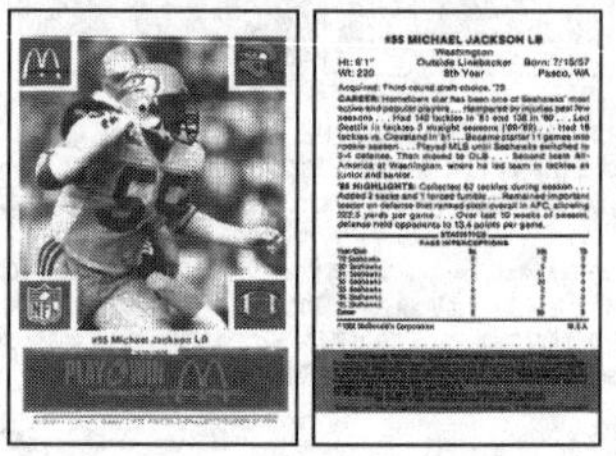

This 24-card set was issued in McDonald's Hamburger restaurants around Seattle. The set was issued over a four-week period with blue tabs the first week, black (or gray) tabs the second week, gold (or orange) tabs the third week, and green tabs the fourth week. The cards measure approximately 3 1/16" by 4 11/16" with the tab intact and 3 1/16" by 3 5/8" without the tab. The cards are numbered below by uniform number. The value of cards without tabs or tabs scratched off is F-G at best. The cards were printed on a 30-card sheet; hence, there are six double-printed cards listed DP in the checklist below. For individual prices on the more expensive color tabs, merely apply the ratio of that color's set price to the base (cheapest) color set price and use the resulting multiple on the individual prices for that color.

	MINT	NRMT	EXC
COMPLETE SET (BLUE)	10.00	4.50	1.25
COMPLETE SET (BLACK)	7.00	3.10	.85
COMPLETE SET (GOLD)	7.00	3.10	.85
COMPLETE SET (GREEN)	7.00	3.10	.85
COMMON CARD	.25	.11	.03
☐ 9 Norm Johnson	.35	.16	.04
☐ 17 Dave Krieg	.50	.23	.06
☐ 20 Terry Taylor	.25	.11	.03
☐ 22 Dave Brown DP	.25	.11	.03
☐ 28 Curt Warner	.50	.23	.06
☐ 33 Dan Doornink	.25	.11	.03
☐ 44 John Harris	.25	.11	.03
☐ 45 Kenny Easley	.35	.16	.04
☐ 46 David Hughes	.25	.11	.03
☐ 50 Fredd Young	.25	.11	.03
☐ 53 Keith Butler DP	.25	.11	.03
☐ 55 Michael Jackson	.25	.11	.03
☐ 58 Bruce Scholtz	.25	.11	.03
☐ 59 Blair Bush DP	.25	.11	.03
☐ 61 Robert Pratt	.25	.11	.03
☐ 64 Ron Essink	.25	.11	.03
☐ 65 Edwin Bailey DP	.25	.11	.03
☐ 72 Joe Nash	.25	.11	.03
☐ 77 Jeff Bryant DP	.25	.11	.03
☐ 78 Bob Cryder DP	.25	.11	.03
☐ 79 Jacob Green	.35	.16	.04
☐ 80 Steve Largent	2.00	.90	.25
☐ 81 Daryl Turner	.25	.11	.03
☐ 82 Paul Skansi	.25	.11	.03

1986 McDonald's Steelers

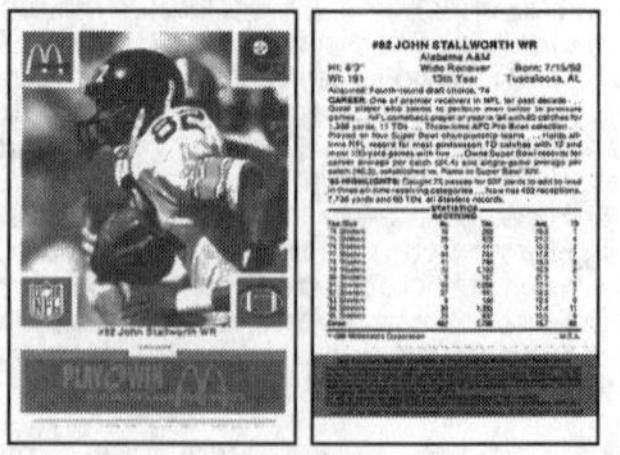

This 24-card set was issued in McDonald's Hamburger restaurants around Pittsburgh. The set was issued over a four-week period with blue tabs the first week, black (or gray) tabs the second week, gold (or orange) tabs the third week, and green tabs the fourth week. The cards measure approximately 3 1/16" by 4 11/16" with the tab intact and 3 1/16" by 3 5/8" without the tab. The cards are numbered below by uniform number. The value of cards without tabs or tabs scratched off is F-G at best. The cards were printed on a 30-card sheet; hence, there are six double-printed cards listed DP in the checklist below. For individual prices on the more expensive color tabs, merely apply the ratio of that color's set price to the base (cheapest) color set price and use the resulting multiple on the individual prices for that color.

	MINT	NRMT	EXC
COMPLETE SET (BLUE)	50.00	22.00	6.25
COMPLETE SET (BLACK)	25.00	11.00	3.10
COMPLETE SET (GOLD)	10.00	4.50	1.25
COMPLETE SET (GREEN)	10.00	4.50	1.25
COMMON CARD	.40	.18	.05
☐ 1 Gary Anderson K DP	.50	.23	.06
☐ 16 Mark Malone	.50	.23	.06
☐ 21 Eric Williams	.40	.18	.05
☐ 24 Rich Erenberg DP	.40	.18	.05
☐ 30 Frank Pollard	.40	.18	.05
☐ 31 Donnie Shell	.50	.23	.06
☐ 34 Walter Abercrombie DP	.40	.18	.05
☐ 49 Dwayne Woodruff	.40	.18	.05
☐ 50 David Little	.40	.18	.05
☐ 52 Mike Webster	.50	.23	.06
☐ 53 Bryan Hinkle	.50	.23	.06
☐ 56 Robin Cole DP	.40	.18	.05
☐ 57 Mike Merriweather	.50	.23	.06
☐ 62 Tunch Ilkin	.40	.18	.05
☐ 65 Ray Pinney	.40	.18	.05
☐ 67 Gary Dunn DP	.40	.18	.05
☐ 73 Craig Wolfley	.40	.18	.05
☐ 74 Terry Long	.40	.18	.05
☐ 82 John Stallworth	.75	.35	.09
☐ 83 Louis Lipps	.75	.35	.09
☐ 87 Weegie Thompson	.40	.18	.05
☐ 92 Keith Gary DP	.40	.18	.05
☐ 93 Keith Willis	.40	.18	.05
☐ 99 Darryl Sims	.40	.18	.05

1986 McDonald's Vikings

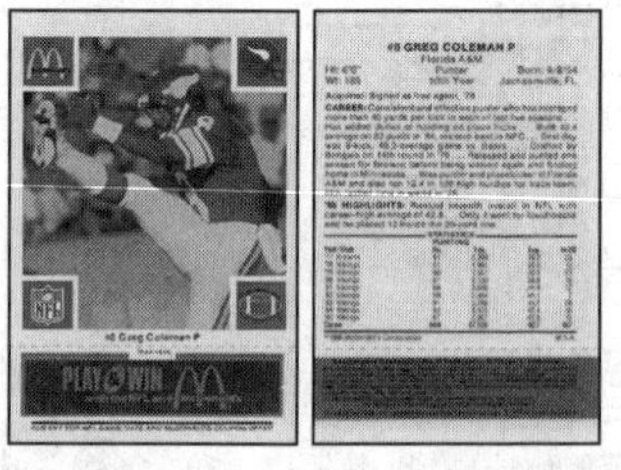

This 24-card set was issued in McDonald's Hamburger restaurants around Minneapolis and St. Paul. The set was issued over a four-week period with blue tabs the first week, black (or gray) tabs the second week, gold (or orange) tabs the third week, and green tabs the fourth week. The cards measure approximately 3 1/16" by 4 11/16" with the tab intact and 3 1/16" by 3 5/8" without the tab. The cards are numbered below by uniform number. The value of cards without tabs or tabs scratched off is F-G at best. The cards were printed on a 30-card sheet; hence, there are six double-printed cards listed DP in the checklist below. For individual prices on the more expensive color tabs, merely apply the ratio of that color's set price to the base (cheapest) color set price and use the resulting multiple on the individual prices for that color.

	MINT	NRMT	EXC
COMPLETE SET (BLUE)	45.00	20.00	5.50
COMPLETE SET (BLACK)	35.00	16.00	4.40
COMPLETE SET (GOLD)	15.00	6.75	1.85
COMPLETE SET (GREEN)	15.00	6.75	1.85
COMMON CARD	.60	.25	.07
☐ 8 Greg Coleman DP	.60	.25	.07
☐ 9 Tommy Kramer	.75	.35	.09
☐ 11 Wade Wilson	1.00	.45	.12
☐ 20 Darrin Nelson	.75	.35	.09
☐ 23 Ted Brown DP	.60	.25	.07
☐ 37 Willie Teal	.60	.25	.07
☐ 39 Carl Lee	.75	.35	.09
☐ 46 Alfred Anderson DP	.60	.25	.07
☐ 47 Joey Browner DP	1.00	.45	.12
☐ 55 Scott Studwell	.60	.25	.07
☐ 56 Chris Doleman	1.00	.45	.12
☐ 59 Matt Blair DP	.75	.35	.09
☐ 67 Dennis Swilley	.60	.25	.07
☐ 68 Curtis Rouse	.60	.25	.07
☐ 75 Keith Millard	1.00	.45	.12
☐ 76 Tim Irwin	.60	.25	.07
☐ 77 Mark Mullaney	.60	.25	.07
☐ 79 Doug Martin	.60	.25	.07
☐ 81 Anthony Carter DP	1.25	.55	.16
☐ 83 Steve Jordan	1.00	.45	.12
☐ 87 Leo Lewis	.75	.35	.09
☐ 89 Mike Jones	.60	.25	.07
☐ 96 Tim Newton	.60	.25	.07
☐ 99 David Howard	.60	.25	.07

1993 McDonald's GameDay

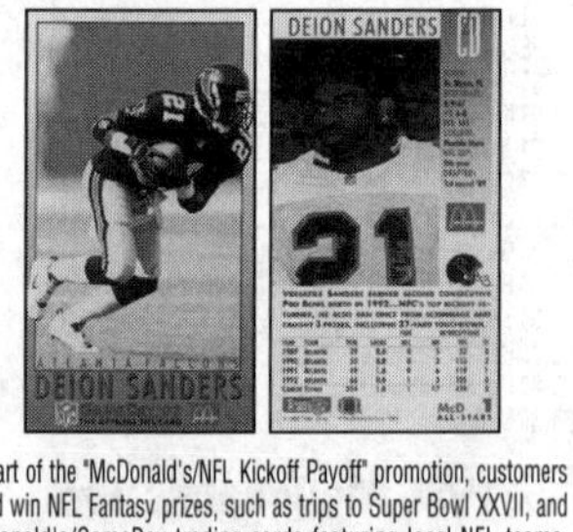

As part of the "McDonald's/NFL Kickoff Payoff" promotion, customers could win NFL Fantasy prizes, such as trips to Super Bowl XXVII, and McDonald's/GameDay trading cards featuring local NFL teams. Customers received a pull-tab gamepiece on packages of large and extra-large french fries, hash browns, 21- and 32-oz. soft drinks, and 16-oz. coffee. Every gamepiece won free food, an instant-win NFL

Fantasy prize, or NFL Point Values of six (touchdown), three (field goal), or one (extra point). The Point Values could be collected and redeemed for trading cards or special discounts on merchandise. For ten points, customers received a six-card sheet at participating McDonald's restaurants while supplies lasted. Measuring approximately 2 1/2" by 4 3/4", the GameDay cards are similar to the regular issues, except that they have McDonald's logos on both sides, and on the backs are renumbered with a "McD" prefix. Three sheets make a complete team set. Most McDonald's restaurants in a region offered cards of the local NFL team(s). In addition, many restaurants offered an All-Star set of 18 NFL superstars. Each NFL team has 18 cards in total on three different sheets (A, B, and C), and the cards are listed below in alphabetical team order, preceded by the All-Star set. One sheet was distributed per week for three weeks during the promotion.

	MINT	NRMT	EXC
COMPLETE SET (87)	50.00	22.00	6.25
COMMON PANEL (1-87)	.75	.35	.09

☐ 1 All-Stars A .... 1.25 .55 .16
Deion Sanders
Thurman Thomas
Troy Aikman
John Elway
Barry Sanders
Sterling Sharpe
☐ 2 All-Stars B .... 1.25 .55 .16
Derrick Thomas
Howie Long
Dan Marino
Chris Doleman
Vaughan Johnson
Phil Simms
☐ 3 All-Stars C .... 1.00 .45 .12
Randall Cunningham
Barry Foster
Jerry Rice
Junior Seau
Cortez Kennedy
Mark Rypien
☐ 4 Atlanta Falcons A .... 1.50 .70 .19
Deion Sanders
Moe Gardner
Tim Green
Michael Haynes
Chris Hinton
Tim McKyer
☐ 5 Atlanta Falcons B .... 1.00 .45 .12
Chris Miller
Bruce Pickens
Mike Pritchard
Andre Rison
Darion Conner
Jessie Tuggle
☐ 6 Atlanta Falcons C .... .75 .35 .09
Drew Hill
Pierce Holt
Elbert Shelley
Jesse Solomon
Bobby Hebert
Lincoln Kennedy
☐ 7 Buffalo Bills A .... 1.00 .45 .12
Howard Ballard
Don Beebe
Cornelius Bennett
Phil Hansen
Henry Jones
Jim Kelly
☐ 8 Buffalo Bills B .... 1.00 .45 .12
Nate Odomes
Andre Reed
Frank Reich
Bruce Smith
Darryl Talley
Steve Tasker
☐ 9 Buffalo Bills C .... 1.25 .55 .16
Bill Brooks
Jim Ritcher
Thurman Thomas
Kenneth Davis
Jeff Wright
Thomas Smith
☐ 10 Chicago Bears A .... .75 .35 .09
Neal Anderson
Trace Armstrong
Mark Carrier DB
Wendell Davis
Richard Dent
Shaun Gayle
☐ 11 Chicago Bears B .... .75 .35 .09
Jim Harbaugh
Darren Lewis
Jim Morrissey
William Perry
Alonzo Spellman
Tom Waddle
☐ 12 Chicago Bears C .... 1.00 .45 .12
Steve McMichael
Craig Heyward
Lemuel Stinson
Keith Van Horne
Donnell Woolford
Curtis Conway
☐ 13 Cincinnati Bengals A .... .75 .35 .09
Derrick Fenner
James Francis
David Fulcher
Harold Green
Rod Jones CB
David Klingler
☐ 14 Cincinnati Bengals B .... 1.25 .55 .16
Bruce Kozerski
Tim Krumrie
Ricardo McDonald
Carl Pickens
Reggie Rembert
Daniel Stubbs
☐ 15 Cincinnati Bengals C .... .75 .35 .09
Eddie Brown
Gary Reasons
Lamar Rogers
Alfred Williams
Darryl Williams
John Copeland
☐ 16 Cleveland Browns A .... 1.00 .45 .12
Rob Burnett
Jay Hilgenberg
Leroy Hoard
Michael Jackson
Mike Johnson
Bernie Kosar
☐ 17 Cleveland Browns B .... 1.00 .45 .12
Eric Metcalf
Michael Dean Perry
Clay Matthews
Lawyer Tillman
Eric Turner
Tommy Vardell
☐ 18 Cleveland Browns C .... .75 .35 .09
David Brandon
Tony Jones T
Scott Galbraith
James Jones DT
Vinny Testaverde
Steve Everitt
☐ 19 Dallas Cowboys A .... 1.50 .70 .19
Troy Aikman
Tony Casillas
Thomas Everett
Charles Haley
Alvin Harper
Michael Irvin
☐ 20 Dallas Cowboys B .... 1.00 .45 .12
Jim Jeffcoat
Daryl Johnston
Robert Jones
Nate Newton
Ken Norton Jr.
Jay Novacek
☐ 21 Dallas Cowboys C .... 2.00 .90 .25
Russell Maryland
Emmitt Smith
Kevin Smith
Mark Stepnoski
Tony Tolbert
Larry Brown DB
☐ 22 Denver Broncos A .... 1.50 .70 .19
Steve Atwater
Mike Croel
Shane Dronett
John Elway
Simon Fletcher
Reggie Rivers
☐ 23 Denver Broncos B .... .75 .35 .09
Vance Johnson
Greg Lewis
Tommy Maddox
Arthur Marshall
Shannon Sharpe
Dennis Smith
☐ 24 Denver Broncos C .... .75 .35 .09
Rod Bernstine
Michael Brooks
Wymon Henderson
Greg Kragen
Karl Mecklenburg
Dan Williams
☐ 25 Detroit Lions A .... .75 .35 .09
Bennie Blades
Michael Cofer
Ray Crockett
Mel Gray
Willie Green
Jason Hanson
☐ 26 Detroit Lions B .... 1.50 .70 .19
Herman Moore
Rodney Peete
Brett Perriman
Kelvin Pritchett
Barry Sanders
Tracy Scroggins
☐ 27 Detroit Lions C .... 1.00 .45 .12
Pat Swilling
Lomas Brown
Erik Kramer
Chris Spielman
Andre Ware
William White
☐ 28 Green Bay Packers A .... 1.25 .55 .16
Tony Bennett
Matt Brock
Terrell Buckley
LeRoy Butler
Chris Jacke
Brett Favre
☐ 29 Green Bay Packers B .... 1.00 .45 .12
Jackie Harris
Brian Noble
Bryce Paup
Sterling Sharpe
Ed West
Johnny Holland
☐ 30 Green Bay Packers C .... 1.25 .55 .16
Tunch Ilkin
George Teague
Reggie White
Ken O'Brien
John Stephens
Wayne Simmons
☐ 31 Houston Oilers A .... .75 .35 .09
Cody Carlson
Ray Childress
Curtis Duncan
William Fuller
Haywood Jeffires
Lamar Lathon
☐ 32 Houston Oilers B .... 1.00 .45 .12
Bruce Matthews
Bubba McDowell
Warren Moon
Mike Munchak
Eddie Robinson
Webster Slaughter
☐ 33 Houston Oilers C .... .75 .35 .09
Ernest Givins
Cris Dishman
Al Smith
Lorenzo White
Lee Williams
Brad Hopkins
☐ 34 Indianapolis Colts A .... .75 .35 .09
Chip Banks
Kerry Cash
Quentin Coryatt
Rodney Culver
Steve Emtman
Reggie Langhorne
☐ 35 Indianapolis Colts B .... 1.00 .45 .12
Jeff Herrod
Anthony Johnson
Jeff George
Rohn Stark
Jack Trudeau
Clarence Verdin
☐ 36 Indianapolis Colts C .... .75 .35 .09
Duane Bickett
Eugene Daniel
Jessie Hester
Chris Goode
Kirk Lowdermilk
Sean Dawkins
☐ 37 Kansas City Chiefs A .... .75 .35 .09
Dale Carter
Willie Davis
Dave Krieg
Albert Lewis
Nick Lowery
J.J. Birden
☐ 38 Kansas City Chiefs B .... .75 .35 .09
Charles Mincy
Christian Okoye
Kevin Ross
Dan Saleaumua
Tracy Simien
Harvey Williams
☐ 39 Kansas City Chiefs C .... 1.50 .70 .19
Todd McNair
Neil Smith
Derrick Thomas
Leonard Griffin
Barry Word
Joe Montana
☐ 40 Los Angeles Raiders A .... .75 .35 .09
Eddie Anderson
Jeff Gossett
Ethan Horton
Jeff Jaeger
Howie Long
Todd Marinovich
☐ 41 Los Angeles Raiders B .... .75 .35 .09
Terry McDaniel
Don Mosebar
Anthony Smith
Greg Townsend
Aaron Wallace
Steve Wisniewski
☐ 42 Los Angeles Raiders C .... 1.00 .45 .12
Nick Bell
Tim Brown
Eric Dickerson
James Lofton
Jeff Hostetler
Patrick Bates
☐ 43 Los Angeles Rams A .... .75 .35 .09
Flipper Anderson
Marc Boutte
Henry Ellard
Bill Hawkins
Cleveland Gary
David Lang
☐ 44 Los Angeles Rams B .... 1.00 .45 .12
Jim Everett
Darryl Henley
Todd Lyght
Anthony Newman
Roman Phifer
Jim Price
☐ 45 Los Angeles Rams C .... 1.25 .55 .16
Shane Conlan
Henry Rolling
Larry Kelm
Jackie Slater
Fred Stokes
Jerome Bettis
☐ 46 Miami Dolphins A .... .75 .35 .09
Marco Coleman
Bryan Cox
Jeff Cross
Mark Duper
Keith Sims
Mark Higgs
☐ 47 Miami Dolphins B .... 2.00 .90 .25
Keith Jackson
Dan Marino
John Offerdahl
Louis Oliver
Tony Paige
Pete Stoyanovich
☐ 48 Miami Dolphins C .... 1.00 .45 .12
Tony Martin
Irving Fryar
Troy Vincent
Richmond Webb
Jarvis Williams
O.J. McDuffie
☐ 49 Minnesota Vikings A .... 1.00 .45 .12
Terry Allen
Anthony Carter
Cris Carter
Jack Del Rio
Chris Doleman
Rich Gannon
☐ 50 Minnesota Vikings B .... .75 .35 .09
Steve Jordan
Carl Lee
Randall McDaniel
John Randle
Sean Salisbury
Todd Scott
☐ 51 Minnesota Vikings C .... .75 .35 .09
Jim McMahon
Audray McMillian
Mike Merriweather
Henry Thomas
Gary Zimmerman
Robert Smith
☐ 52 New England Patriots A .... .75 .35 .09
Ray Agnew
Bruce Armstrong
Vincent Brown
Eugene Chung
Marv Cook
Maurice Hurst
☐ 53 New England Patriots B .... 1.00 .45 .12
Pat Harlow
Eugene Lockhart
Greg McMurtry
Scott Zolak
Leonard Russell
Andre Tippett
☐ 54 New England Patriots C .... 2.00 .90 .25
David Howard
Johnny Rembert
Jon Vaughn
Brent Williams
Scott Secules
Drew Bledsoe
☐ 55 New Orleans Saints A .... .75 .35 .09
Morten Andersen
Gene Atkins
Toi Cook
Richard Cooper
Jim Dombrowski
Vaughn Dunbar
☐ 56 New Orleans Saints B .... .75 .35 .09
Joel Hilgenberg
Rickey Jackson
Vaughan Johnson
Wayne Martin
Renaldo Turnbull
Frank Warren
☐ 57 New Orleans Saints C .... .75 .35 .09
Irv Smith
Brad Muster
Dalton Hilliard
Eric Martin
Sam Mills
Willie Roaf
☐ 58 New York Giants A .... 1.00 .45 .12
Jarrod Bunch
Mark Collins
Howard Cross
Rodney Hampton

Erik Howard			
Greg Jackson			
☐ 59 New York Giants B	1.00	.45	.12
Pepper Johnson			
Sean Landeta			
Ed McCaffrey			
Dave Meggett			
Bart Oates			
Phil Simms			
☐ 60 New York Giants C	1.00	.45	.12
Carlton Bailey			
Carl Banks			
John Elliott			
Eric Dorsey			
Lawrence Taylor			
Mike Sherrard			
☐ 61 New York Jets A	.75	.35	.09
Brad Baxter			
Scott Mersereau			
Chris Burkett			
Kyle Clifton			
Jeff Lageman			
Mo Lewis			
☐ 62 New York Jets B	.75	.35	.09
Johnny Mitchell			
Rob Moore			
Browning Nagle			
Blair Thomas			
Brian Washington			
Marvin Washington			
☐ 63 New York Jets C	1.00	.45	.12
Boomer Esiason			
James Hasty			
Ronnie Lott			
Leonard Marshall			
Terance Mathis			
Marvin Jones			
☐ 64 Philadelphia Eagles A	1.00	.45	.12
Eric Allen			
Fred Barnett			
Randall Cunningham			
Byron Evans			
Andy Harmon			
Seth Joyner			
☐ 65 Philadelphia Eagles B	1.00	.45	.12
Heath Sherman			
Vai Sikahema			
Clyde Simmons			
Herschel Walker			
Andre Waters			
Calvin Williams			
☐ 66 Philadelphia Eagles C	.75	.35	.09
Keith Byars			
Mike Golic			
Leonard Renfro			
William Thomas			
Antone Davis			
Lester Holmes			
☐ 67 Phoenix Cardinals A	.75	.35	.09
Johnny Bailey			
Rich Camarillo			
Larry Centers			
Chris Chandler			
Ken Harvey			
Randal Hill			
☐ 68 Phoenix Cardinals B	1.00	.45	.12
Mark May			
Robert Massey			
Freddie Joe Nunn			
Ricky Proehl			
Eric Hill			
Eric Swann			
☐ 69 Phoenix Cardinals C	1.25	.55	.16
Gary Clark			
John Booty			
Chuck Cecil			
Steve Beuerlein			
Ernest Dye			
Garrison Hearst			
☐ 70 Pittsburgh Steelers A	1.00	.45	.12
Dermontti Dawson			
Barry Foster			
Jeff Graham			
Eric Green			
Carlton Haselrig			
Bryan Hinkle			
☐ 71 Pittsburgh Steelers B	1.00	.45	.12
Merril Hoge			
D.J. Johnson			
Carnell Lake			
David Little			
Neil O'Donnell			
Darren Perry			
☐ 72 Pittsburgh Steelers C	1.00	.45	.12
Bubby Brister			
Kevin Greene			
Greg Lloyd			
Leon Searcy			
Rod Woodson			
Deon Figures			
☐ 73 San Diego Chargers A	1.25	.55	.16
Eric Bieniemy			
Marion Butts			
Burt Grossman			
Ronnie Harmon			
Stan Humphries			
Nate Lewis			
☐ 74 San Diego Chargers B	1.25	.55	.16
Chris Mims			
Leslie O'Neal			
Stanley Richard			
Junior Seau			
Harry Swayne			
Derrick Walker			
☐ 75 San Diego Chargers C	1.00	.45	.12
Jerrol Williams			
Gill Byrd			
John Friesz			
Anthony Miller			
Gary Plummer			
Darrien Gordon			
☐ 76 San Francisco 49ers A	1.00	.45	.12
Ricky Watters			
Michael Carter			
Don Griffin			
Dana Hall			
Brent Jones			
Harris Barton			
☐ 77 San Francisco 49ers B	1.50	.70	.19
Tom Rathman			
Jerry Rice			
Bill Romanowski			
John Taylor			
Steve Wallace			
Michael Walter			
☐ 78 San Francisco 49ers C	1.50	.70	.19
Kevin Fagan			
Todd Kelly			
Guy McIntyre			
Tim McDonald			
Steve Young			
Dana Stubblefield			
☐ 79 Seattle Seahawks A	.75	.35	.09
Robert Blackmon			
Brian Blades			
Jeff Bryant			
Dwayne Harper			
Andy Heck			
Tommy Kane			
☐ 80 Seattle Seahawks B	1.00	.45	.12
Cortez Kennedy			
Dan McGwire			
Rufus Porter			
Ray Roberts			
Eugene Robinson			
Chris Warren			
☐ 81 Seattle Seahawks C	1.25	.55	.16
Ferrell Edmunds			
Kelvin Martin			
John L. Williams			
Tony Woods			
David Wyman			
Rick Mirer			
☐ 82 Tampa Bay Buccaneers A	.75	.35	.09
Gary Anderson RB			
Tyji Armstrong			
Reggie Cobb			
Lawrence Dawsey			
Steve DeBerg			
Santana Dotson			
☐ 83 Tampa Bay Buccaneers B	.75	.35	.09
Ron Hall			
Courtney Hawkins			
Keith McCants			
Charles McRae			
Ricky Reynolds			
Broderick Thomas			
☐ 84 Tampa Bay Buccaneers C	.75	.35	.09
Vince Workman			
Paul Gruber			
Hardy Nickerson			
Marty Carter			
Mark Wheeler			
Eric Curry			
☐ 85 Washington Redskins A	1.00	.45	.12
Earnest Byner			
Andre Collins			
Brad Edwards			
Ricky Ervins			
Darrell Green			
Desmond Howard			
☐ 86 Washington Redskins B	1.00	.45	.12
Tim Johnson			
Jim Lachey			
Chip Lohmiller			
Mark Rypien			
Ricky Sanders			
Mark Schlereth			
☐ 87 Washington Redskins C	1.00	.45	.12
Al Noga			
Kurt Gouveia			
Charles Mann			
Wilber Marshall			
Art Monk			
Tom Carter			

1996 McDonald's Looney Tunes Cups

These cups were available at participating McDonald's restaurants during the 1996 Season. Each player cup has a corresponding Looney Tunes character on the cup with them.

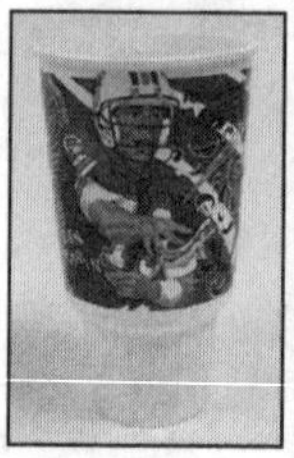
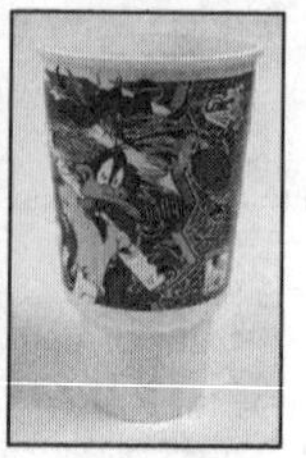

	MINT	NRMT	EXC
COMPLETE SET (4)	6.00	2.70	.75
COMMON CUP (1-4)	1.25	.55	.16
☐ 1 Drew Bledsoe	1.25	.55	.16
Wile E. Coyote			
☐ 2 Dan Marino	2.00	.90	.25
Daffy Duck			
☐ 3 Barry Sanders	1.25	.55	.16
Tazmanian Devil			
☐ 4 Emmitt Smith	2.00	.90	.25
Bugs Bunny			

1995 Metal

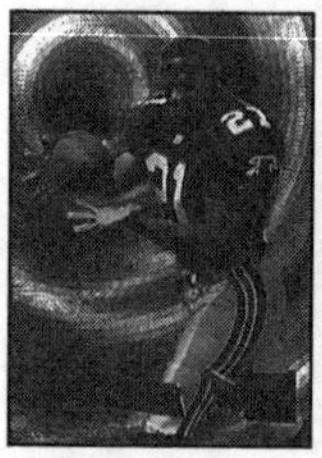
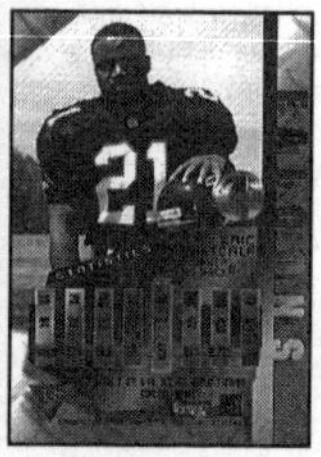

This set marked the debut season for the 200 card all foil-etched standard-size set. Cards were available in 8 card packs for the suggested retail price of $2.49. Card fronts feature different silver-etched backgrounds with the player's name and "Fleer Metal" logo at the bottom. Card backs are "machine-like" with player statistics and biographical information. The set is ordered by teams. Rookie Cards include Jeff Blake, Ki-Jana Carter, Kerry Collins, Joey Galloway, Steve McNair, Rashaan Salaam, J.J. Stokes and Michael Westbrook. Also included in random packs was an instant winner card for a trip to Super Bowl XXX. A Trent Dilfer Sample card was produced and priced below.

	MINT	NRMT	EXC
COMPLETE SET (200)	30.00	13.50	3.70
COMMON CARD (1-200)	.15	.07	.02
☐ 1 Garrison Hearst	.40	.18	.05
☐ 2 Seth Joyner	.15	.07	.02
☐ 3 Dave Krieg	.15	.07	.02
☐ 4 Lorenzo Lynch	.15	.07	.02
☐ 5 Rob Moore	.15	.07	.02
☐ 6 Eric Swann	.25	.11	.03
☐ 7 Aeneas Williams	.15	.07	.02
☐ 8 Chris Doleman	.15	.07	.02
☐ 9 Bert Emanuel	.40	.18	.05
☐ 10 Jeff George	.25	.11	.03
☐ 11 Craig Heyward	.25	.11	.03
☐ 12 Terance Mathis	.25	.11	.03
☐ 13 Eric Metcalf	.25	.11	.03
☐ 14 Cornelius Bennett	.25	.11	.03
☐ 15 Bucky Brooks	.15	.07	.02
☐ 16 Jeff Burris	.15	.07	.02
☐ 17 Jim Kelly	.40	.18	.05
☐ 18 Andre Reed	.25	.11	.03
☐ 19 Bruce Smith	.40	.18	.05
☐ 20 Don Beebe	.15	.07	.02
☐ 21 Kerry Collins	5.00	2.20	.60
☐ 22 Barry Foster	.25	.11	.03
☐ 23 Lamar Lathon	.15	.07	.02
☐ 24 Sam Mills	.25	.11	.03
☐ 25 Tyrone Poole	.25	.11	.03
☐ 26 Frank Reich	.15	.07	.02
☐ 27 Joe Cain	.15	.07	.02
☐ 28 Curtis Conway	.40	.18	.05
☐ 29 Jeff Graham	.15	.07	.02
☐ 30 Erik Kramer	.15	.07	.02
☐ 31 Rashaan Salaam	2.00	.90	.25
☐ 32 Lewis Tillman	.15	.07	.02
☐ 33 Chris Zorich	.15	.07	.02
☐ 34 Jeff Blake	2.00	.90	.25
☐ 35 Ki-Jana Carter	1.50	.70	.19
☐ 36 Carl Pickens	.40	.18	.05
☐ 37 Corey Sawyer	.15	.07	.02
☐ 38 Darnay Scott	.40	.18	.05
☐ 39 Dan Wilkinson	.25	.11	.03
☐ 40 Darryl Williams	.15	.07	.02
☐ 41 Derrick Alexander WR	.40	.18	.05
☐ 42 Leroy Hoard	.15	.07	.02
☐ 43 Michael Jackson	.25	.11	.03
☐ 44 Antonio Langham	.15	.07	.02
☐ 45 Andre Rison	.25	.11	.03
☐ 46 Vinny Testaverde	.25	.11	.03
☐ 47 Eric Turner	.15	.07	.02
☐ 48 Troy Aikman	2.00	.90	.25
☐ 49 Charles Haley	.25	.11	.03
☐ 50 Michael Irvin	.40	.18	.05
☐ 51 Daryl Johnston	.25	.11	.03
☐ 52 Jay Novacek	.25	.11	.03
☐ 53 Emmitt Smith	4.00	1.80	.50
☐ 54 Kevin Williams WR	.25	.11	.03
☐ 55 Steve Atwater	.15	.07	.02
☐ 56 Rod Bernstine	.15	.07	.02
☐ 57 John Elway	1.50	.70	.19
☐ 58 Glyn Milburn	.15	.07	.02
☐ 59 Anthony Miller	.25	.11	.03
☐ 60 Mike Pritchard	.15	.07	.02
☐ 61 Shannon Sharpe	.25	.11	.03
☐ 62 Mike Johnson	.15	.07	.02
☐ 63 Scott Mitchell	.25	.11	.03
☐ 64 Herman Moore	1.00	.45	.12
☐ 65 Brett Perriman	.25	.11	.03
☐ 66 Barry Sanders	2.00	.90	.25
☐ 67 Chris Spielman	.25	.11	.03
☐ 68 Edgar Bennett	.25	.11	.03
☐ 69 Robert Brooks	.40	.18	.05
☐ 70 Brett Favre	4.00	1.80	.50
☐ 71 LeShon Johnson	.25	.11	.03
☐ 72 George Koonce	.15	.07	.02
☐ 73 Reggie White	.40	.18	.05
☐ 74 Gary Brown	.15	.07	.02
☐ 75 Cris Dishman	.15	.07	.02
☐ 76 Mel Gray	.15	.07	.02
☐ 77 Steve McNair	4.00	1.80	.50
☐ 78 Webster Slaughter	.15	.07	.02
☐ 79 Rodney Thomas	.40	.18	.05
☐ 80 Trev Alberts	.15	.07	.02
☐ 81 Quentin Coryatt	.25	.11	.03
☐ 82 Sean Dawkins	.25	.11	.03
☐ 83 Craig Erickson	.15	.07	.02
☐ 84 Marshall Faulk	1.00	.45	.12
☐ 85 Stephen Grant	.15	.07	.02
☐ 86 Steve Beuerlein	.15	.07	.02
☐ 87 Tony Boselli	.25	.11	.03
☐ 88 Desmond Howard	.25	.11	.03
☐ 89 James O.Stewart	.25	.11	.03
☐ 90 Marcus Allen	.40	.18	.05
☐ 91 Kimble Anders	.25	.11	.03
☐ 92 Steve Bono	.25	.11	.03
☐ 93 Lake Dawson	.25	.11	.03
☐ 94 Greg Hill	.25	.11	.03
☐ 95 Neil Smith	.25	.11	.03
☐ 96 William White	.15	.07	.02
☐ 97 Tim Bowens	.15	.07	.02
☐ 98 Bryan Cox	.15	.07	.02
☐ 99 Irving Fryar	.25	.11	.03
☐ 100 Eric Green	.15	.07	.02
☐ 101 Dan Marino	4.00	1.80	.50
☐ 102 O.J. McDuffie	.40	.18	.05
☐ 103 Bernie Parmalee	.25	.11	.03
☐ 104 Cris Carter	.40	.18	.05
☐ 105 Jack Del Rio	.15	.07	.02
☐ 106 Rocket Ismail	.25	.11	.03
☐ 107 Warren Moon	.25	.11	.03
☐ 108 Jake Reed	.25	.11	.03
☐ 109 Dewayne Washington	.25	.11	.03
☐ 110 Bruce Armstrong	.15	.07	.02
☐ 111 Drew Bledsoe	2.00	.90	.25
☐ 112 Vincent Brisby	.15	.07	.02
☐ 113 Ben Coates	.25	.11	.03
☐ 114 Willie McGinest	.25	.11	.03
☐ 115 Dave Meggett	.15	.07	.02
☐ 116 Chris Slade	.25	.11	.03
☐ 117 Mario Bates	.40	.18	.05
☐ 118 Quinn Early	.25	.11	.03
☐ 119 Jim Everett	.15	.07	.02
☐ 120 Michael Haynes	.25	.11	.03
☐ 121 Tyrone Hughes	.25	.11	.03
☐ 122 Renaldo Turnbull	.15	.07	.02
☐ 123 Ray Zellers	.25	.11	.03
☐ 124 Dave Brown	.25	.11	.03
☐ 125 Chris Calloway	.15	.07	.02
☐ 126 Rodney Hampton	.25	.11	.03
☐ 127 Thomas Lewis	.25	.11	.03
☐ 128 Phillippi Sparks	.15	.07	.02
☐ 129 Tyrone Wheatley	.75	.35	.09
☐ 130 Kyle Brady	.40	.18	.05
☐ 131 Boomer Esiason	.25	.11	.03
☐ 132 Aaron Glenn	.15	.07	.02
☐ 133 Bobby Houston	.15	.07	.02
☐ 134 Mo Lewis	.15	.07	.02
☐ 135 Johnny Mitchell	.15	.07	.02
☐ 136 Ronald Moore	.15	.07	.02
☐ 137 Greg Biekert	.15	.07	.02
☐ 138 Tim Brown	.40	.18	.05
☐ 139 Jeff Hostetler	.25	.11	.03
☐ 140 Rocket Ismail	.25	.11	.03
☐ 141 Napoleon Kaufman	1.50	.70	.19
☐ 142 Chester McGlockton	.25	.11	.03
☐ 143 Harvey Williams	.15	.07	.02
☐ 144 Fred Barnett	.25	.11	.03
☐ 145 Randall Cunningham	.25	.11	.03
☐ 146 William Fuller	.15	.07	.02
☐ 147 Charlie Garner	.25	.11	.03
☐ 148 Andy Harmon	.15	.07	.02
☐ 149 Ricky Watters	.40	.18	.05
☐ 150 Calvin Williams	.25	.11	.03
☐ 151 Kevin Greene	.25	.11	.03
☐ 152 Charles Johnson	.25	.11	.03
☐ 153 Greg Lloyd	.25	.11	.03

☐ 154 Byron Bam Morris	.25	.11	.03
☐ 155 Neil O'Donnell	.25	.11	.03
☐ 156 Darren Perry	.15	.07	.02
☐ 157 Rod Woodson	.25	.11	.03
☐ 158 Jerome Bettis	.60	.25	.07
☐ 159 Isaac Bruce	1.00	.45	.12
☐ 160 Troy Drayton	.15	.07	.02
☐ 161 Sean Gilbert	.25	.11	.03
☐ 162 Todd Lyght	.15	.07	.02
☐ 163 Chris Miller	.15	.07	.02
☐ 164 Andre Coleman	.15	.07	.02
☐ 165 Stan Humphries	.25	.11	.03
☐ 166 Shawn Jefferson	.15	.07	.02
☐ 167 Natrone Means	.40	.18	.05
☐ 168 Leslie O'Neal	.25	.11	.03
☐ 169 Junior Seau	.40	.18	.05
☐ 170 Mark Seay	.25	.11	.03
☐ 171 William Floyd	.40	.18	.05
☐ 172 Merton Hanks	.15	.07	.02
☐ 173 Brent Jones	.15	.07	.02
☐ 174 Jerry Rice	2.00	.90	.25
☐ 175 Deion Sanders UER	1.25	.55	.16
Card lists him as a linebacker			
☐ 176 J.J. Stokes	1.50	.70	.19
☐ 177 Lee Woodall	.15	.07	.02
☐ 178 Bryant Young	.25	.11	.03
☐ 179 Steve Young	1.50	.70	.19
☐ 180 Brian Blades	.25	.11	.03
☐ 181 Joey Galloway	3.00	1.35	.35
☐ 182 Cortez Kennedy	.25	.11	.03
☐ 183 Kevin Mawae	.15	.07	.02
☐ 184 Rick Mirer	.40	.18	.05
☐ 185 Chris Warren	.25	.11	.03
☐ 186 Lawrence Dawsey	.15	.07	.02
☐ 187 Trent Dilfer	.40	.18	.05
☐ 188 Paul Gruber	.15	.07	.02
☐ 189 Hardy Nickerson	.15	.07	.02
☐ 190 Errict Rhett	.40	.18	.05
☐ 191 Warren Sapp	.25	.11	.03
☐ 192 Tom Carter	.15	.07	.02
☐ 193 Henry Ellard	.25	.11	.03
☐ 194 Darrell Green	.15	.07	.02
☐ 195 Brian Mitchell	.15	.07	.02
☐ 196 Heath Shuler	.40	.18	.05
☐ 197 Michael Westbrook	2.00	.90	.25
☐ 198 Checklist 1-96	.15	.07	.02
☐ 199 Checklist 97-200	.15	.07	.02
☐ 200 Checklist Inserts	.15	.07	.02
☐ S1 Trent Dilfer Sample	1.00	.45	.12

1995 Metal Gold Blasters

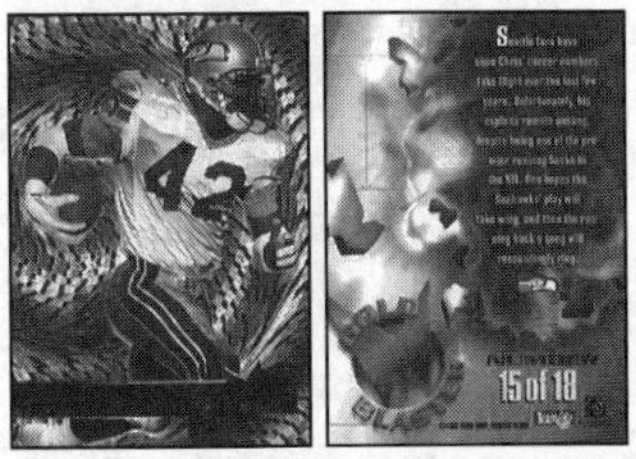

This 18 card set was randomly inserted into packs at a rate of one in approximately six packs and highlights players who have had a major impact on the NFL. Card fronts have a gold-swirl background with some highlighting of the team's colors. Backs contain a melted yellow-orange background. In the melted area is a brief commentary on the featured player.

	MINT	NRMT	EXC
COMPLETE SET (18)	60.00	27.00	7.50
COMMON CARD (1-18)	1.00	.45	.12
☐ 1 Troy Aikman	6.00	2.70	.75
☐ 2 Jerome Bettis	2.00	.90	.25
☐ 3 Tim Brown	2.00	.90	.25
☐ 4 Ben Coates	1.00	.45	.12
☐ 5 John Elway	5.00	2.20	.60
☐ 6 Brett Favre	12.00	5.50	1.50
☐ 7 William Floyd	1.00	.45	.12
☐ 8 Joey Galloway	4.00	1.80	.50
☐ 9 Rodney Hampton	2.00	.90	.25
☐ 10 Dan Marino	12.00	5.50	1.50
☐ 11 Steve McNair	5.00	2.20	.60
☐ 12 Herman Moore	3.00	1.35	.35
☐ 13 Errict Rhett	2.00	.90	.25
☐ 14 Rashaan Salaam	2.50	1.10	.30
☐ 15 Chris Warren	2.00	.90	.25
☐ 16 Michael Westbrook	2.50	1.10	.30
☐ 17 Rod Woodson	1.00	.45	.12
☐ 18 Steve Young	5.00	2.20	.60

1995 Metal Platinum Portraits

This 12 card set was randomly inserted at a rate of one in nine packs and is billed as a "serious heavy metal set" of 12 of the NFL's elite players. Card fronts contain a silver foil-etched background with a shot of the player and a circular-etched image of the player in action. Card backs have an orange and silver backgound with a player summary at the top of the card.

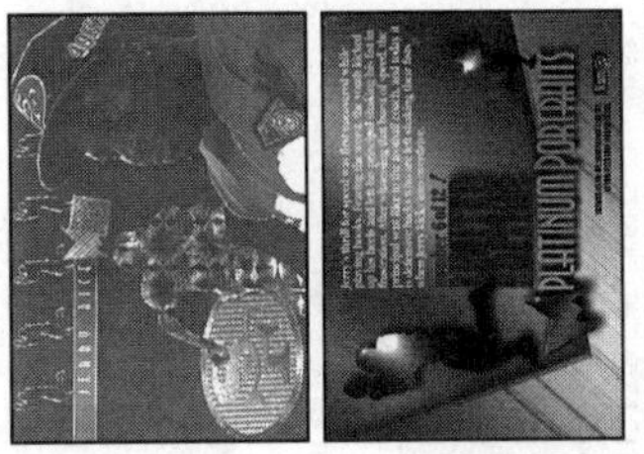

	MINT	NRMT	EXC
COMPLETE SET (12)	50.00	22.00	6.25
COMMON CARD (1-12)	2.00	.90	.25
☐ 1 Drew Bledsoe	6.00	2.70	.75
☐ 2 Ki-Jana Carter	2.00	.90	.25
☐ 3 Marshall Faulk	4.00	1.80	.50
☐ 4 Natrone Means	3.00	1.35	.35
☐ 5 Byron Bam Morris	3.00	1.35	.35
☐ 6 Jerry Rice	6.00	2.70	.75
☐ 7 Andre Rison	2.00	.90	.25
☐ 8 Barry Sanders	6.00	2.70	.75
☐ 9 Deion Sanders	4.00	1.80	.50
☐ 10 Emmitt Smith	12.00	5.50	1.50
☐ 11 J.J. Stokes	2.00	.90	.25
☐ 12 Ricky Watters	3.00	1.35	.35

1995 Metal Silver Flashers

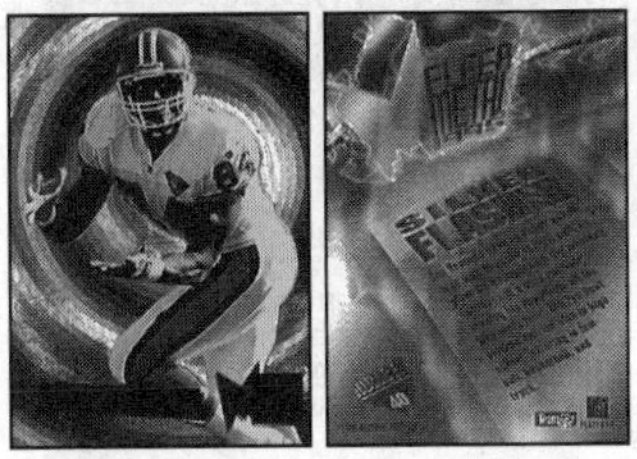

This 50 card set was randomly inserted at a rate of one in every two packs and features the NFL's flashiest performers. Card fronts have a silver foil-etched background with several different designs ranging from circular to squares to waves. The player's name is located at the bottom left corner of the card. Card backs feature the "Fleer Metal 1995" logo electrified with a melting orange and silver background. A brief player commentary is also on the back.

	MINT	NRMT	EXC
COMPLETE SET (50)	70.00	32.00	8.75
COMMON CARD (1-50)	.75	.35	.09
☐ 1 Troy Aikman	4.00	1.80	.50
☐ 2 Marcus Allen	1.50	.70	.19
☐ 3 Jerome Bettis	1.50	.70	.19
☐ 4 Drew Bledsoe	4.00	1.80	.50
☐ 5 Tim Brown	1.50	.70	.19
☐ 6 Cris Carter	1.50	.70	.19
☐ 7 Ki-Jana Carter	1.25	.55	.16
☐ 8 Ben Coates	1.25	.55	.16
☐ 9 Kerry Collins	6.00	2.70	.75
☐ 10 Randall Cunningham	.75	.35	.09
☐ 11 Lake Dawson	.75	.35	.09
☐ 12 Trent Dilfer	.75	.35	.09
☐ 13 John Elway	3.00	1.35	.35
☐ 14 Jim Everett	.75	.35	.09
☐ 15 Marshall Faulk	1.50	.70	.19
☐ 16 Brett Favre	8.00	3.60	1.00
☐ 17 William Floyd	1.25	.55	.16
☐ 18 Jeff George	1.50	.70	.19
☐ 19 Rodney Hampton	1.25	.55	.16
☐ 20 Jeff Hostetler	.75	.35	.09
☐ 21 Stan Humphries	.75	.35	.09
☐ 22 Michael Irvin	1.50	.70	.19
☐ 23 Cortez Kennedy	.75	.35	.09
☐ 24 Dan Marino	8.00	3.60	1.00
☐ 25 Terance Mathis	.75	.35	.09
☐ 26 Willie McGinest	.75	.35	.09
☐ 27 Natrone Means	1.50	.70	.19
☐ 28 Rick Mirer	1.50	.70	.19
☐ 29 Warren Moon	1.25	.55	.16
☐ 30 Herman Moore	1.50	.70	.19
☐ 31 Byron Bam Morris	1.25	.55	.16
☐ 32 Carl Pickens	1.50	.70	.19
☐ 33 Errict Rhett	1.50	.70	.19
☐ 34 Jerry Rice	4.00	1.80	.50
☐ 35 Andre Rison	.75	.35	.09
☐ 36 Rashaan Salaam	2.00	.90	.25
☐ 37 Barry Sanders	4.00	1.80	.50
☐ 38 Deion Sanders	2.50	1.10	.30
☐ 39 Junior Seau	1.50	.70	.19
☐ 40 Shannon Sharpe	1.50	.70	.19
☐ 41 Heath Shuler	1.50	.70	.19
☐ 42 Emmitt Smith	8.00	3.60	1.00
☐ 43 J.J. Stokes	2.00	.90	.25
☐ 44 Chris Warren	1.25	.55	.16
☐ 45 Ricky Watters	1.50	.70	.19
☐ 46 Michael Westbrook	1.50	.70	.19
☐ 47 Tyrone Wheatley	1.25	.55	.16
☐ 48 Reggie White	1.50	.70	.19
☐ 49 Rod Woodson	1.25	.55	.16
☐ 50 Steve Young	3.00	1.35	.35

1996 Metal

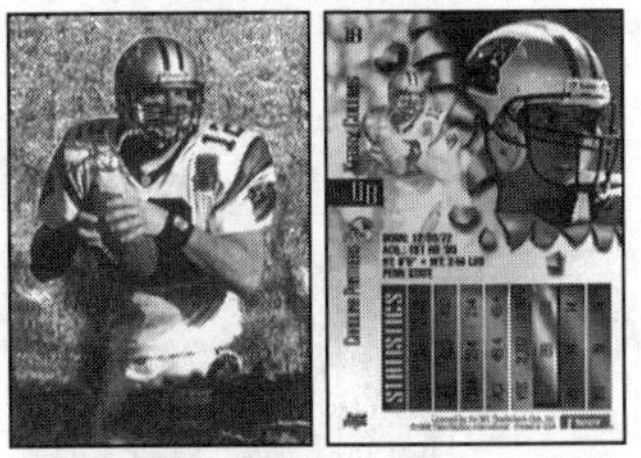

The 1996 Fleer Metal set was issued in one series totalling 150 cards and features metallized foil engraved by hand on each card front making no two player cards alike. The eight-card packs retail for $2.49 each. The set contains the subset Rookies (124-148).

	MINT	NRMT	EXC
COMPLETE SET (150)	30.00	13.50	3.70
COMMON CARD (1-150)	.08	.04	.01
☐ 1 Garrison Hearst	.15	.07	.02
☐ 2 Rob Moore	.08	.04	.01
☐ 3 Frank Sanders	.15	.07	.02
☐ 4 Eric Swann	.15	.07	.02
☐ 5 Jeff George	.15	.07	.02
☐ 6 Craig Heyward	.08	.04	.01
☐ 7 Terance Mathis	.08	.04	.01
☐ 8 Eric Metcalf	.15	.07	.02
☐ 9 Derrick Alexander WR	.15	.07	.02
☐ 10 Andre Rison	.15	.07	.02
☐ 11 Vinny Testaverde	.15	.07	.02
☐ 12 Eric Turner	.08	.04	.01
☐ 13 Jim Kelly	.30	.14	.04
☐ 14 Bryce Paup	.15	.07	.02
☐ 15 Bruce Smith	.30	.14	.04
☐ 16 Thurman Thomas	.30	.14	.04
☐ 17 Bob Christian	.08	.04	.01
☐ 18 Kerry Collins	1.50	.70	.19
☐ 19 Lamar Lathon	.08	.04	.01
☐ 20 Tyrone Poole	.08	.04	.01
☐ 21 Curtis Conway	.30	.14	.04
☐ 22 Bryan Cox	.08	.04	.01
☐ 23 Erik Kramer	.08	.04	.01
☐ 24 Rashaan Salaam	.30	.14	.04
☐ 25 Jeff Blake	.30	.14	.04
☐ 26 Ki-Jana Carter	.15	.07	.02
☐ 27 Carl Pickens	.30	.14	.04
☐ 28 Darnay Scott	.15	.07	.02
☐ 29 Troy Aikman	1.25	.55	.16
☐ 30 Michael Irvin	.30	.14	.04
☐ 31 Daryl Johnston	.15	.07	.02
☐ 32 Deion Sanders	.75	.35	.09
☐ 33 Emmitt Smith	2.50	1.10	.30
☐ 34 Terrell Davis	2.00	.90	.25
☐ 35 John Elway	1.00	.45	.12
☐ 36 Anthony Miller	.15	.07	.02
☐ 37 Shannon Sharpe	.15	.07	.02
☐ 38 Scott Mitchell	.15	.07	.02
☐ 39 Herman Moore	.30	.14	.04
☐ 40 Brett Perriman	.15	.07	.02
☐ 41 Barry Sanders	1.25	.55	.16
☐ 42 Edgar Bennett	.15	.07	.02
☐ 43 Robert Brooks	.30	.14	.04
☐ 44 Mark Chmura	.15	.07	.02
☐ 45 Brett Favre	2.50	1.10	.30
☐ 46 Reggie White	.30	.14	.04
☐ 47 Mel Gray	.08	.04	.01
☐ 48 Steve McNair	1.25	.55	.16
☐ 49 Chris Sanders	.15	.07	.02
☐ 50 Rodney Thomas	.08	.04	.01
☐ 51 Quentin Coryatt	.08	.04	.01
☐ 52 Sean Dawkins	.08	.04	.01
☐ 53 Ken Dilger	.15	.07	.02
☐ 54 Marshall Faulk	.30	.14	.04
☐ 55 Jim Harbaugh	.15	.07	.02
☐ 56 Tony Boselli	.15	.07	.02
☐ 57 Mark Brunell	1.25	.55	.16
☐ 58 Natrone Means	.30	.14	.04
☐ 59 James O.Stewart	.15	.07	.02
☐ 60 Marcus Allen	.30	.14	.04
☐ 61 Steve Bono	.15	.07	.02
☐ 62 Neil Smith	.15	.07	.02
☐ 63 Tamarick Vanover	.30	.14	.04
☐ 64 Eric Green	.08	.04	.01
☐ 65 Terry Kirby	.15	.07	.02
☐ 66 Dan Marino	2.50	1.10	.30
☐ 67 O.J. McDuffie	.15	.07	.02
☐ 68 Cris Carter	.30	.14	.04
☐ 69 Qadry Ismail	.15	.07	.02
☐ 70 Warren Moon	.15	.07	.02
☐ 71 Jake Reed	.15	.07	.02
☐ 72 Drew Bledsoe	1.25	.55	.16
☐ 73 Ben Coates	.15	.07	.02
☐ 74 Curtis Martin	2.00	.90	.25
☐ 75 Dave Meggett	.08	.04	.01
☐ 76 Mario Bates	.15	.07	.02
☐ 77 Jim Everett	.08	.04	.01
☐ 78 Michael Haynes	.15	.07	.02
☐ 79 Tyrone Hughes	.08	.04	.01
☐ 80 Dave Brown	.15	.07	.02
☐ 81 Rodney Hampton	.15	.07	.02
☐ 82 Thomas Lewis	.08	.04	.01
☐ 83 Tyrone Wheatley	.15	.07	.02
☐ 84 Kyle Brady	.15	.07	.02
☐ 85 Hugh Douglas	.08	.04	.01
☐ 86 Adrian Murrell	.15	.07	.02
☐ 87 Neil O'Donnell	.15	.07	.02
☐ 88 Tim Brown	.15	.07	.02
☐ 89 Jeff Hostetler	.15	.07	.02
☐ 90 Napoleon Kaufman	.15	.07	.02
☐ 91 Harvey Williams	.08	.04	.01
☐ 92 Charlie Garner	.08	.04	.01
☐ 93 Rodney Peete	.08	.04	.01
☐ 94 Ricky Watters	.15	.07	.02
☐ 95 Calvin Williams	.08	.04	.01
☐ 96 Jerome Bettis	.30	.14	.04
☐ 97 Greg Lloyd	.15	.07	.02
☐ 98 Kordell Stewart	1.50	.70	.19
☐ 99 Yancey Thigpen	.15	.07	.02
☐ 100 Rod Woodson	.15	.07	.02
☐ 101 Isaac Bruce	.30	.14	.04
☐ 102 Kevin Carter	.15	.07	.02
☐ 103 Steve Walsh	.08	.04	.01
☐ 104 Aaron Hayden	.08	.04	.01
☐ 105 Stan Humphries	.15	.07	.02
☐ 106 Junior Seau	.30	.14	.04
☐ 107 William Floyd	.15	.07	.02
☐ 108 Brent Jones	.08	.04	.01
☐ 109 Jerry Rice	1.25	.55	.16
☐ 110 J.J. Stokes	.30	.14	.04
☐ 111 Steve Young	1.00	.45	.12
☐ 112 Brian Blades	.15	.07	.02
☐ 113 Joey Galloway	.60	.25	.07
☐ 114 Rick Mirer	.15	.07	.02
☐ 115 Chris Warren	.15	.07	.02
☐ 116 Trent Dilfer	.15	.07	.02
☐ 117 Alvin Harper	.08	.04	.01
☐ 118 Hardy Nickerson	.08	.04	.01
☐ 119 Errict Rhett	.15	.07	.02
☐ 120 Terry Allen	.15	.07	.02
☐ 121 Brian Mitchell	.08	.04	.01
☐ 122 Heath Shuler	.30	.14	.04
☐ 123 Michael Westbrook	.30	.14	.04
☐ 124 Karim Abdul-Jabbar	2.50	1.10	.30
☐ 125 Tim Biakabutuka	1.00	.45	.12
☐ 126 Duane Clemons	.08	.04	.01
☐ 127 Stephen Davis	.30	.14	.04
☐ 128 Rickey Dudley	.30	.14	.04
☐ 129 Bobby Engram	1.00	.45	.12
☐ 130 Daryl Gardener	.15	.07	.02
☐ 131 Eddie George	4.00	1.80	.50
☐ 132 Terry Glenn	3.00	1.35	.35
☐ 133 Kevin Hardy	.15	.07	.02
☐ 134 Walt Harris	.08	.04	.01
☐ 135 Marvin Harrison	1.50	.70	.19
☐ 136 Keyshawn Johnson	1.50	.70	.19
☐ 137 Cedric Jones	.15	.07	.02
☐ 138 Eddie Kennison	1.50	.70	.19
☐ 139 Sam Manuel	.08	.04	.01
Sean Manuel			
☐ 140 Leeland McElroy	.30	.14	.04
☐ 141 Ray Mickens	.08	.04	.01
☐ 142 Jonathan Ogden	.08	.04	.01
☐ 143 Lawrence Phillips	.50	.23	.06
☐ 144 Kavika Pittman	.08	.04	.01
☐ 145 Simeon Rice	.30	.14	.04
☐ 146 Regan Upshaw	.08	.04	.01
☐ 147 Alex Van Dyke	.15	.07	.02
☐ 148 Stepfret Williams	.08	.04	.01
☐ 149 Checklist	.08	.04	.01
☐ 150 Checklist	.08	.04	.01

1996 Metal Precious Metal

Inserted one per box, this 148-card set is a rare parallel version of the regular Metal set excluding the two checklist cards. Each card features an all-silver solid foil etched front, with the letters "PM" preceding the card number on the back.

	MINT	NRMT	EXC
COMPLETE SET (148)	750.00	350.00	95.00
COMMON CARD (1PM-148PM)	3.00	1.35	.35
*STARS: 12.5X TO 25X BASIC CARDS			
*YOUNG STARS: 10X TO 20X BASIC CARDS			
*RCs: 7.5X TO 15X BASIC CARDS			

1996 Metal Freshly Forged

Randomly inserted in hobby packs only at a rate of one in 80, this 10-card set featues color player photos of second-year standouts and flashy rookies on acrylic cards. The backs carry a paragraph about the player.

	MINT	NRMT	EXC
COMPLETE SET (10)	100.00	45.00	12.50
COMMON CARD (1-10)	5.00	2.20	.60
☐ 1 Tim Biakabutuka	10.00	4.50	1.25
☐ 2 Jeff Blake	8.00	3.60	1.00
☐ 3 Ki-Jana Carter	5.00	2.20	.60
☐ 4 Eddie George	25.00	11.00	3.10
☐ 5 Terry Glenn	20.00	9.00	2.50
☐ 6 Keyshawn Johnson	10.00	4.50	1.25
☐ 7 Curtis Martin	20.00	9.00	2.50

	MINT	NRMT	EXC
☐ 8 Leeland McElroy	5.00	2.20	.60
☐ 9 Lawrence Phillips	8.00	3.60	1.00
☐ 10 Kordell Stewart	15.00	6.75	1.85

1996 Metal Goldfingers

Randomly inserted in packs at a rate of one in eight, this 12-card set is a 24-karat etched gold foil stamped collection of top-flight receivers. A color player image is set over a gold foil hand background. The backs carry another player photo and a paragraph about the player.

	MINT	NRMT	EXC
COMPLETE SET (12)	35.00	16.00	4.40
COMMON CARD (1-12)	2.50	1.10	.30
☐ 1 Isaac Bruce	4.00	1.80	.50
☐ 2 Joey Galloway	5.00	2.20	.60
☐ 3 Michael Irvin	4.00	1.80	.50
☐ 4 Herman Moore	4.00	1.80	.50
☐ 5 Carl Pickens	2.50	1.10	.30
☐ 6 Jerry Rice	8.00	3.60	1.00
☐ 7 Chris Sanders	2.50	1.10	.30
☐ 8 Frank Sanders	2.50	1.10	.30
☐ 9 J.J. Stokes	4.00	1.80	.50
☐ 10 Yancey Thigpen	2.50	1.10	.30
☐ 11 Tamarick Vanover	4.00	1.80	.50
☐ 12 Michael Westbrook	4.00	1.80	.50

1996 Metal Goldflingers

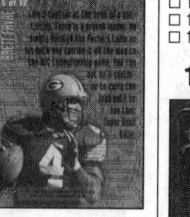

Randomly inserted in retail packs only at the rate of one in 12, this 12-card set features color player images on a gold foil background of some of the NFL's best quarterbacks. The backs carry another player photo and a paragraph about the player.

	MINT	NRMT	EXC
COMPLETE SET (12)	50.00	22.00	6.25
COMMON CARD (1-12)	2.50	1.10	.30
☐ 1 Troy Aikman	8.00	3.60	1.00
☐ 2 Steve Bono	2.50	1.10	.30
☐ 3 Kerry Collins	8.00	3.60	1.00
☐ 4 Trent Dilfer	2.50	1.10	.30
☐ 5 Brett Favre	15.00	6.75	1.85
☐ 6 Gus Frerotte	4.00	1.80	.50
☐ 7 Stan Humphries	2.50	1.10	.30
☐ 8 Dan Marino	15.00	6.75	1.85
☐ 9 Steve McNair	6.00	2.70	.75
☐ 10 Scott Mitchell	2.50	1.10	.30
☐ 11 Steve Young	6.00	2.70	.75
☐ 12 Eric Zeier	2.50	1.10	.30

1996 Metal Molten Metal

Randomly inserted in packs at a rate of one in 120, this 10-card set features foil embossed cards of very hot players. The backs carry a paragraph about the player.

	MINT	NRMT	EXC
COMPLETE SET (10)	225.00	100.00	28.00
COMMON CARD (1-10)	12.00	5.50	1.50
☐ 1 Troy Aikman	30.00	13.50	3.70
☐ 2 Ki-Jana Carter	12.00	5.50	1.50
☐ 3 Kerry Collins	30.00	13.50	3.70

	MINT	NRMT	EXC
☐ 4 Terrell Davis	30.00	13.50	3.70
☐ 5 Marshall Faulk			
☐ 6 Brett Favre	50.00	22.00	6.25
☐ 7 Keyshawn Johnson	18.00	8.00	2.20
☐ 8 Curtis Martin	30.00	13.50	3.70
☐ 9 Deion Sanders	18.00	8.00	2.20
☐ 10 Emmitt Smith	50.00	22.00	6.25

1996 Metal Platinum Portraits

Fleer inserted the first 10-cards of the set into packs of 1996 Metal. The insertion ratio was one in 50. Additonally, the final two cards were later released via a mail redemption. They featured the two NFL Rookie of the Year Award winners. Both cards could be had for ten Metal wrappers plus $25. The offer expired June 30, 1997.

	MINT	NRMT	EXC
COMPLETE SET (10)	90.00	40.00	11.00
COMMON CARD (1-10)	4.00	1.80	.50
☐ 1 Isaac Bruce	6.00	2.70	.75
☐ 2 Terrell Davis	20.00	9.00	2.50
☐ 3 John Elway	16.00	7.25	2.00
☐ 4 Joey Galloway	8.00	3.60	1.00
☐ 5 Steve McNair	12.00	5.50	1.50
☐ 6 Errict Rhett	4.00	1.80	.50
☐ 7 Rashaan Salaam	6.00	2.70	.75
☐ 8 Barry Sanders	20.00	9.00	2.50
☐ 9 Chris Warren	4.00	1.80	.50
☐ 10 Steve Young	16.00	7.25	2.00
☐ 11 Eddie George	30.00	13.50	3.70
☐ 12 Simeon Rice	6.00	2.70	.75

1992 Metallic Images Tins

Designed by Metallic Images Inc. and sold through participating 7-Eleven stores, these four collector tins each contained two decks of playing cards. The tins are unnumbered and listed below alphabetically.

	MINT	NRMT	EXC
COMPLETE SET (4)	25.00	11.00	3.10
COMMON TIN (1-4)	3.00	1.35	.35
☐ 1 Dan Marino	12.00	5.50	1.50
☐ 2 Warren Moon	5.00	2.20	.60
☐ 3 Y.A. Tittle	4.00	1.80	.50
☐ 4 Johnny Unitas	6.00	2.70	.75

1993 Metallic Images QB Legends

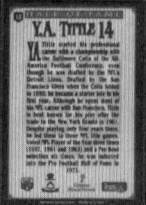

An offshoot of CUI, a Wilmington-based maker of collectible ceramic and glassware products, Metallic Images Inc. produced these 20 metal cards to honor outstanding NFL quarterbacks. Only 49,000 numbered sets were produced, each accompanied by a certificate of authenticity and packaged in a collectors tin featuring graphics on the sides and lid. These metallic cards measure approximately 2 9/16" by 3 9/16" and have rolled metal edges. The fronts display a color action shot cutout and superimposed on a team color-coded background with gold pinstripes. A black-and-white headshot appears in an oval at the upper left corner, while the team logo and uniform number are below. On a pinstripe panel inside a team color-coded border, the backs present career summary.

	MINT	NRMT	EXC
COMPLETE SET (20)	45.00	20.00	5.50
COMMON CARD (1-20)	1.50	.70	.19
☐ 1 Steve Bartkowski	2.00	.90	.25
☐ 2 John Brodie	2.00	.90	.25
☐ 3 Charley Conerly	2.00	.90	.25
☐ 4 Lynn Dickey	1.50	.70	.19
☐ 5 Tom Flores	2.00	.90	.25
☐ 6 Roman Gabriel	2.00	.90	.25
☐ 7 Bob Griese	5.00	2.20	.60
☐ 8 Steve Grogan	2.00	.90	.25
☐ 9 James Harris	1.50	.70	.19
☐ 10 Jim Hart	1.50	.70	.19
☐ 11 Sonny Jurgensen	3.00	1.35	.35
☐ 12 Billy Kilmer	2.00	.90	.25
☐ 13 Daryle Lamonica	2.50	1.10	.30
☐ 14 Archie Manning	2.50	1.10	.30
☐ 15 Craig Morton	2.00	.90	.25
☐ 16 Dan Pastorini	1.50	.70	.19
☐ 17 Jim Plunkett	2.00	.90	.25
☐ 18 Y.A. Tittle	5.00	2.20	.60
☐ 19 Johnny Unitas	7.50	3.40	.95
☐ 20 Danny White	2.00	.90	.25

1985 Miller Lite Beer

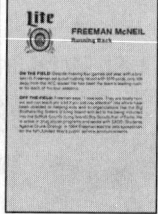

These oversized cards measure approximately 4 3/4" by 7" and feature on their fronts white-bordered posed player photos. The player's name and position, along with logos for his team and Miller Lite appear within the wide bottom margin. The logos reappear on the white backs, along with the player's career highlights. The cards are unnumbered and checklisted below in alphabetical order.

	MINT	NRMT	EXC
COMPLETE SET (6)	150.00	70.00	19.00
COMMON CARD (1-6)	15.00	6.75	1.85
☐ 1 Larry Csonka	25.00	11.00	3.10
☐ 2 John Hadl CO	15.00	6.75	1.85
☐ 3 Freeman McNeil NFL Man of the Year	15.00	6.75	1.85
☐ 4 Jack Reynolds Lite Beer All-Stars	15.00	6.75	1.85
☐ 5 Steve Young USFL Man of the Year	75.00	34.00	9.50
☐ 6 1985 LA Express Cheerleaders	15.00	6.75	1.85

1988 Monty Gum

This 100-card set was made in Europe by Monty Gum. The cards measure approximately 1 15/16" by 2 3/4" and contain thick yellow borders around a color photo. There was also an album issued with the set. The cards do not feature specific players, only generic team action scenes; hence they are not very popular with collectors. The cards have blank backs. The cards are numbered and subtitled at the bottom inside a black box. There is a blank-backed sticker version, a thin paper version and a white cardboard version of each card in the set. The sticker backs actually have a white paper cover that is removable. Otherwise, they are the same as the card versions; the stickers are valued at double the prices listed below.

	MINT	NRMT	EXC
COMPLETE SET (100)	100.00	45.00	12.50
COMMON TEAM (1-79)	1.25	.55	.16
COMMON CARD (80-100)	1.00	.45	.12
☐ 1 Atlanta Falcons Atlanta Stadium	1.50	.70	.19
☐ 2 Atlanta Falcons Defense	1.25	.55	.16
☐ 3 Atlanta Falcons Offense	1.25	.55	.16
☐ 4 Buffalo Bills Blocked Punt	1.25	.55	.16
☐ 5 Chicago Bears At the Scrimmage Line	1.25	.55	.16
☐ 6 Chicago Bears	1.25	.55	.16

	MINT	NRMT	EXC
☐ 7 Cincinnati Bengals Riverfront Stadium	1.25	.55	.16
☐ 8 Cincinnati Bengals Inside the Stadium	1.25	.55	.16
☐ 9 Cincinnati Bengals Goal Line Stand (Walter Payton diving)	6.00	2.70	.75
☐ 10 Cincinnati Bengals (Action shot)	1.25	.55	.16
☐ 11 Cincinnati Bengals Cheerleader	1.50	.70	.19
☐ 12 Cleveland Browns Cleveland Stadium	1.25	.55	.16
☐ 13 Cleveland Browns QB Rollout (Bernie Kosar)	1.50	.70	.19
☐ 14 Cleveland Browns Head Coach	1.25	.55	.16
☐ 15 Cleveland Browns Fans	1.25	.55	.16
☐ 16 Dallas Cowboys Texas Stadium	1.50	.70	.19
☐ 17 Dallas Cowboys Touchdown Reception	1.50	.70	.19
☐ 18 Dallas Cowboys Cheerleader	1.50	.70	.19
☐ 19 Denver Broncos Mile High Stadium	1.25	.55	.16
☐ 20 Denver Broncos Swarming Defense	1.25	.55	.16
☐ 21 Denver Broncos (Randy Gradishar)	1.25	.55	.16
☐ 22 Detroit Lions QB Sack Celebration	1.25	.55	.16
☐ 23 Green Bay Packers On the Run	1.25	.55	.16
☐ 24 Green Bay Packers (Action shot)	1.25	.55	.16
☐ 25 Houston Oilers Houston Astrodome	1.25	.55	.16
☐ 26 Houston Oilers Tackled from behind	1.25	.55	.16
☐ 27 Indianapolis Colts Field Goal Attempt	1.25	.55	.16
☐ 28 Kansas City Chiefs Up the Middle	1.25	.55	.16
☐ 29 Kansas City Chiefs (Action shot)	1.25	.55	.16
☐ 30 Kansas City Chiefs Cheerleader	1.50	.70	.19
☐ 31 Los Angeles Raiders L.A. Memorial Coliseum	1.50	.70	.19
☐ 32 Los Angeles Raiders Inside the Stadium	1.50	.70	.19
☐ 33 Los Angeles Raiders In the Pocket	1.50	.70	.19
☐ 34 Los Angeles Raiders (Marcus Allen; Super Bowl shot)	2.50	1.10	.30
☐ 35 Los Angeles Rams Anaheim Stadium	1.25	.55	.16
☐ 36 Los Angeles Rams Power Blocking (Eric Dickerson running)	1.50	.70	.19
☐ 37 Los Angeles Rams (Action shot)	1.25	.55	.16
☐ 38 Miami Dolphins Attacking the Zone#[(Dan Marino)	20.00	9.00	2.50
☐ 39 Miami Dolphins (Action shot)	1.50	.70	.19
☐ 40 Minnesota Vikings (Metrodome)	1.25	.55	.16
☐ 41 Minnesota Vikings Halfback Handoff	1.25	.55	.16
☐ 42 New England Patriots Sullivan Stadium	1.25	.55	.16
☐ 43 New England Patriots Throwing Deep (Steve Grogan)	1.50	.70	.19
☐ 44 New England Patriots (Earl Campbell running)	5.00	2.20	.60
☐ 45 New Orleans Saints Swarming Linebackers (Roger Craig running)	2.00	.90	.25
☐ 46 New Orleans Saints UER (Photo actually shows Washington and Michigan in '81 Rose Bowl game)	1.50	.70	.19
☐ 47 New York Giants Turning the Corner	1.50	.70	.19
☐ 48 New York Giants (Action shot)	1.25	.55	.16
☐ 49 New York Jets Breaking Loose	1.25	.55	.16
☐ 50 New York Jets (Line photo)	1.25	.55	.16
☐ 51 Philadelphia Eagles Veterans Stadium	1.25	.55	.16
☐ 52 Philadelphia Eagles Power Right	1.25	.55	.16
☐ 53 Philadelphia Eagles (Action shot)	1.25	.55	.16
☐ 54 Philadelphia Eagles Fans	1.25	.55	.16
☐ 55 Pittsburgh Steelers	1.50	.70	.19

Three Rivers Stadium			
☐ 56 Pittsburgh Steelers .... Swarming to the Ball	1.50	.70	.19
☐ 57 Pittsburgh Steelers .... (Action shot) Jack Lambert and Donnie Shell	2.00	.90	.25
☐ 58 St.Louis Cardinals........ Busch Stadium	1.25	.55	.16
☐ 59 St.Louis Cardinals........ Setting Up	1.25	.55	.16
☐ 60 St.Louis Cardinals........ (Action shot)	1.25	.55	.16
☐ 61 St.Louis Cardinals UER........ (Photo actually shows Saints vs. Browns game)	1.25	.55	.16
☐ 62 San Diego Chargers .... Jack Murphy Stadium (Outside of stadium)	1.25	.55	.16
☐ 63 San Diego Chargers .... Jack Murphy Stadium (Inside of stadium)	1.25	.55	.16
☐ 64 San Diego Chargers .... Going for the Bomb; Dan Fouts	2.50	1.10	.30
☐ 65 San Diego Chargers .... Fans	1.25	.55	.16
☐ 66 San Francisco 49ers .... Candlestick Park	1.50	.70	.19
☐ 67 San Francisco 49ers .... Nose Guard on Attack	1.50	.70	.19
☐ 68 San Francisco 49ers .... (Joe Montana)	15.00	6.75	1.85
☐ 69 San Francisco 49ers .... (Joe Montana)	15.00	6.75	1.85
☐ 70 Seattle Seahawks .... Shutting down the run	1.25	.55	.16
☐ 71 Seattle Seahawks .... (Action shot)	1.25	.55	.16
☐ 72 Tampa Bay Buccaneers........ Tampa Stadium	1.25	.55	.16
☐ 73 Tampa Bay Buccaneers........ Tampa Stadium	1.25	.55	.16
☐ 74 Tampa Bay Buccaneers........ Breaking Free	1.25	.55	.16
☐ 75 Tampa Bay Buccaneers........ Defense	1.25	.55	.16
☐ 76 Washington Redskins........ R.F.Kennedy Stadium	1.50	.70	.19
☐ 77 Washington Redskins........ Redskins at the 50	1.50	.70	.19
☐ 78 Washington Redskins........ (Action shot)	1.50	.70	.19
☐ 79 Washington Redskins........ Fans	1.50	.70	.19
☐ 80 Official NFL Football	1.00	.45	.12
☐ 81 Helmets:Falcons/Bills	1.00	.45	.12
☐ 82 Helmets:Bears/Bengals........	1.00	.45	.12
☐ 83 Helmets:Browns/ .... Cowboys	1.00	.45	.12
☐ 84 Helmets:Broncos/Lions........	1.00	.45	.12
☐ 85 Helmets:Packers/ .... Oilers	1.00	.45	.12
☐ 86 Helmets:Colts/Chiefs........	1.00	.45	.12
☐ 87 Helmets:Raiders/Rams	1.00	.45	.12
☐ 88 Helmets:Dolphins/ .... Vikings	1.00	.45	.12
☐ 89 Helmets:Patriots/ .... Saints	1.00	.45	.12
☐ 90 Helmets:Giants/Jets	1.00	.45	.12
☐ 91 Philadelphia Eagles........ Helmet	1.00	.45	.12
☐ 92 Pittsburgh Steelers .... Helmet	1.00	.45	.12
☐ 93 St. Louis Cardinals .... Helmet	1.00	.45	.12
☐ 94 San Diego Chargers .... Helmet	1.00	.45	.12
☐ 95 San Francisco 49ers .... Helmet	1.00	.45	.12
☐ 96 Seattle Seahawks .... Helmet	1.00	.45	.12
☐ 97 Tampa Bay Buccaneers........ Helmet	1.00	.45	.12
☐ 98 Washington Redskins........ Helmet	1.00	.45	.12
☐ 99 National Football........ League Logo	1.00	.45	.12
☐ 100 American Football Fans........	1.25	.55	.16

1996 MotionVision

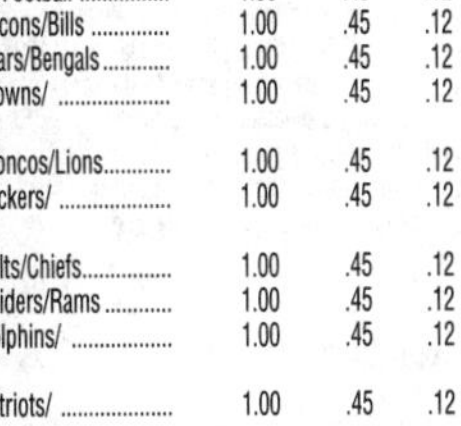

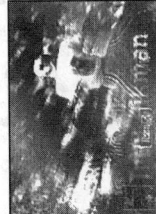

The 1996 MotionVision set was issued in two series of 12 cards each for a total of 24 cards and was distributed in one-card packs with a suggested retail price of $5.99 each. Only 25,000 of each player card was produced. Created on thick plastic, the cards feature Digital Film imaging technology which takes live actual game day footage from the NFL films, transfers them to a film emulsion, and plays back the action sequence on the card with the flick of a wrist. Each Digital Replay was individually packaged in its own see-through custom designed CD jewel case for maximum protection. A Super Bowl XXXI Promo card was distributed at the Super Bowl in New Orleans. It features NFC and AFC helmets crashing in action.

	MINT	NRMT	EXC
COMPLETE SET (24)	250.00	110.00	31.00
COMPLETE SERIES 1 (12)	125.00	55.00	15.50
COMPLETE SERIES 2 (12)	125.00	55.00	15.50
COMMON CARD (1-24)	6.00	2.70	.75
☐ 1 Troy Aikman	12.00	5.50	1.50
☐ 2 Dan Marino	20.00	9.00	2.50
☐ 3 Steve Young	10.00	4.50	1.25
☐ 4 Emmitt Smith	20.00	9.00	2.50
☐ 5 Drew Bledsoe	12.00	5.50	1.50
☐ 6 Kordell Stewart	12.00	5.50	1.50
☐ 7 Jerry Rice	12.00	5.50	1.50
☐ 8 Warren Moon	6.00	2.70	.75
☐ 9 Junior Seau........	6.00	2.70	.75
☐ 10 Barry Sanders........	12.00	5.50	1.50
☐ 11 Jim Harbaugh	6.00	2.70	.75
☐ 12 John Elway	10.00	4.50	1.25
☐ 13 Brett Favre	20.00	9.00	2.50
☐ 14 Brett Favre	20.00	9.00	2.50
☐ 15 Troy Aikman	12.00	5.50	1.50
☐ 16 Emmitt Smith	20.00	9.00	2.50
☐ 17 Dan Marino........	20.00	9.00	2.50
☐ 18 Kordell Stewart........	12.00	5.50	1.50
☐ 19 John Elway	10.00	4.50	1.25
☐ 20 Kerry Collins........	12.00	5.50	1.50
☐ 21 Jim Kelly........	8.00	3.60	1.00
☐ 22 Drew Bledsoe	12.00	5.50	1.50
☐ 23 Mark Brunell........	12.00	5.50	1.50
☐ 24 Jerry Rice	12.00	5.50	1.50
☐ NNO Super Bowl XXXI Promo .... (issued at the game)	10.00	4.50	1.25

1996 MotionVision Limited Digital Replays

The MotionVision Limited Digital Replays were randomly inserted into packs. Series one cards were produced in quantities of 2500 each, with series two at 3500 of each. They are easily distinguishable from the regular cards by the addition of a standard card-like back

	MINT	NRMT	EXC
COMPLETE SET (10)	400.00	180.00	50.00
COMPLETE SERIES 1 (6)........	225.00	100.00	28.00
COMPLETE SERIES 2 (4)........	200.00	90.00	25.00
COMMON CARD (LDR1-LDR10)	25.00	11.00	3.10
☐ LDR1 Troy Aikman........	30.00	13.50	3.70
☐ LDR1A Troy Aikman AUTO	325.00	145.00	40.00
☐ LDR2 Dan Marino	60.00	27.00	7.50
☐ LDR3 Steve Young........	25.00	11.00	3.10
☐ LDR3A Steve Young AUTO	275.00	125.00	34.00
☐ LDR4 Emmitt Smith........	60.00	27.00	7.50
☐ LDR5 Drew Bledsoe........	30.00	13.50	3.70
☐ LDR5A Drew Bledsoe AUTO	250.00	110.00	31.00
☐ LDR6 Kordell Stewart	30.00	13.50	3.70
☐ LDR6A Kordell Stewart AUTO	250.00	110.00	31.00
☐ LDR7 Brett Favre	60.00	27.00	7.50
☐ LDR8 Brett Favre	60.00	27.00	7.50
☐ LDR9 Emmitt Smith........	55.00	25.00	7.00
☐ LDR10 Kerry Collins	30.00	13.50	3.70

1997 MotionVision Super Bowl XXXI

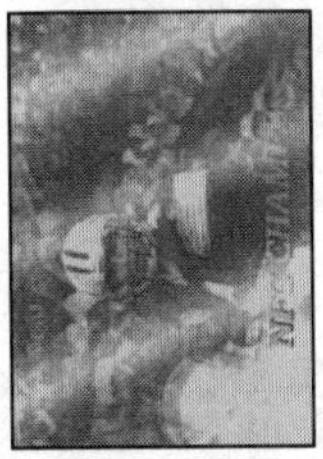

These four cards were made available via a redemption offer in 1996 MotionVision series 2 packs. There was one card made commemorating each Conference Championship game and one for Super Bowl XXXI. The fourth card features Favre during the Super Bowl using a jumbo format (roughly 5 5/8" by 3 3/4"). Each is numbered of 5000 cards produced.

	MINT	NRMT	EXC
COMPLETE SET (4)	75.00	34.00	9.50
COMMON CARD (1-4)	15.00	6.75	1.85
☐ 1 Drew Bledsoe .... AFC Championship Game	15.00	6.75	1.85
☐ 2 Brett Favre .... NFC Championship Game	20.00	9.00	2.50
☐ 3 Brett Favre .... Super Bowl XXXI	20.00	9.00	2.50
☐ 4 Brett Favre Jumbo .... Super Bowl XXXI	20.00	9.00	2.50

1981 MSA Holsum Discs

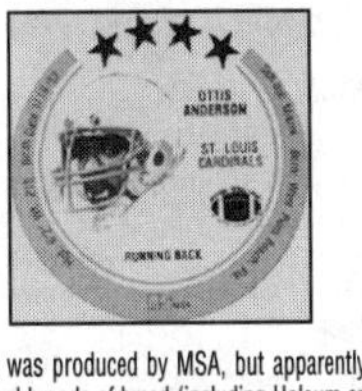

This 32-disc set was produced by MSA, but apparently not widely distributed. Several brands of bread (including Holsum and Gardner's in Wisconsin) carried one football disc per specially marked loaf during the promotion. The discs are blank backed and are approximately 2 3/4" in diameter. Since they are unnumbered, they are listed below in alphabetical order. The discs are licensed only by the NFL Players Association and carry no sponsor logos or identification. There were also two different posters (Holsum and Gardner's) produced for holding and displaying the set. The key card in the set depicts Joe Montana in his rookie year for cards.

	MINT	NRMT	EXC
COMPLETE SET (32)	225.00	100.00	28.00
COMMON CARD (1-32)	2.50	1.10	.30
☐ 1 Ken Anderson........	5.00	2.20	.60
☐ 2 Ottis Anderson	3.00	1.35	.35
☐ 3 Steve Bartkowski	3.00	1.35	.35
☐ 4 Ricky Bell	2.50	1.10	.30
☐ 5 Terry Bradshaw........	20.00	9.00	2.50
☐ 6 Harold Carmichael	3.00	1.35	.35
☐ 7 Joe Cribbs........	2.50	1.10	.30
☐ 8 Gary Danielson	2.50	1.10	.30
☐ 9 Lynn Dickey	2.50	1.10	.30
☐ 10 Dan Doornink	2.50	1.10	.30
☐ 11 Vince Evans	2.50	1.10	.30
☐ 12 Joe Ferguson	3.00	1.35	.35
☐ 13 Vagas Ferguson	2.50	1.10	.30
☐ 14 Dan Fouts	10.00	4.50	1.25
☐ 15 Steve Fuller........	2.50	1.10	.30
☐ 16 Archie Griffin........	3.00	1.35	.35
☐ 17 Steve Grogan	3.00	1.35	.35
☐ 18 Bruce Harper........	2.50	1.10	.30
☐ 19 Jim Hart	3.00	1.35	.35
☐ 20 Jim Jensen	2.50	1.10	.30
☐ 21 Bert Jones........	3.00	1.35	.35
☐ 22 Archie Manning........	4.00	1.80	.50
☐ 23 Ted McKnight	2.50	1.10	.30
☐ 24 Joe Montana........	150.00	70.00	19.00
☐ 25 Craig Morton........	4.00	1.80	.50
☐ 26 Robert Newhouse	3.00	1.35	.35
☐ 27 Phil Simms	10.00	4.50	1.25
☐ 28 Billy Taylor	2.50	1.10	.30
☐ 29 Joe Theismann	5.00	2.20	.60
☐ 30 Mark Van Eeghen	2.50	1.10	.30
☐ 31 Delvin Williams........	2.50	1.10	.30
☐ 32 Tim Wilson	2.50	1.10	.30

1990 MSA Superstars

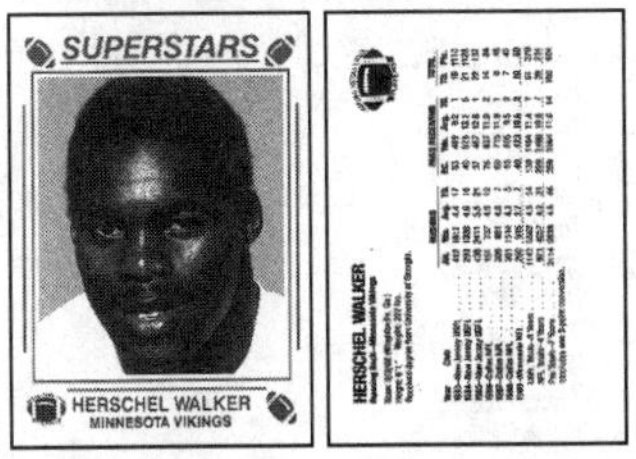

This 12-card, 2 1/2" by 3 3/8", set was issued in boxes of (Ralston Purina) Staff and Food Club Frosted Flakes cereal. The cards were released as two cards in every box and a coupon was also inserted that enabled collectors to mail away and receive the set for 2 UPC symbol codes and postage and handling. These cards are unnumbered so we have checklisted them alphabetically. The fronts of the cards have the word "Superstars" on top of the players photo and his name and team underneath. The back of the card features personal information about the player and statistical information in a textual style. There are no team logos on the card as the cards apparently were issued with only the permission of the National Football League Players Association. There is no mention of MSA on the cards, but they are very similar to the Mike Schechter baseball issue for Ralston Purina so they have been cataloged as such.

	MINT	NRMT	EXC
COMPLETE SET (12)	15.00	6.75	1.85
COMMON CARD (1-12)	.75	.35	.09
☐ 1 Carl Banks........	.75	.35	.09
☐ 2 Cornelius Bennett	1.00	.45	.12
☐ 3 Roger Craig........	1.00	.45	.12
☐ 4 Jim Everett	1.00	.45	.12
☐ 5 Bo Jackson........	1.50	.70	.19
☐ 6 Ronnie Lott........	1.00	.45	.12
☐ 7 Don Majkowski	.75	.35	.09
☐ 8 Dan Marino........	10.00	4.50	1.25
☐ 9 Karl Mecklenburg	.75	.35	.09
☐ 10 Christian Okoye........	.75	.35	.09
☐ 11 Mike Singletary........	1.00	.45	.12
☐ 12 Herschel Walker	1.50	.70	.19

1935 National Chicle

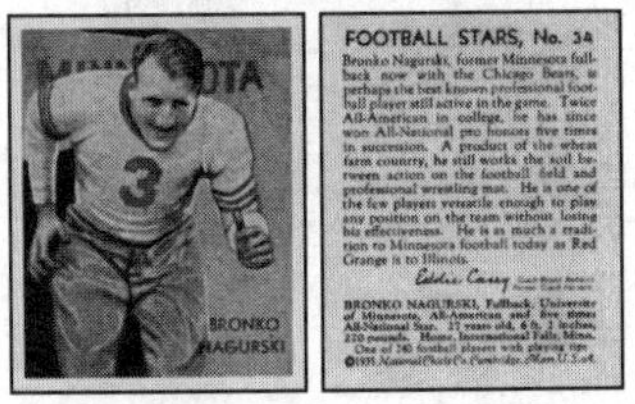

The 1935 National Chicle set was the first nationally distributed bubble gum set dedicated exclusively to football players. The cards measure 2 3/8" by 2 7/8". Card numbers 25 to 36 are more difficult to obtain than other cards in this set. The Knute Rockne and Bronco Nagurski cards are two of the most valuable football cards in existence. The set features NFL players except for the Rockne card. There are variations on the back of nearly every card with respect to the size of Eddie Casey's facsimile signature. It was printed in either small or large letters.

	EX-MT	VG-E	GOOD
COMPLETE SET (36)	15000.00	6800.00	1900.00
COMMON CARD (1-24)	125.00	55.00	15.50
COMMON CARD (25-36)	400.00	180.00	50.00
☐ 1 Dutch Clark........	500.00	220.00	60.00
☐ 2 Bo Molenda........	125.00	55.00	15.50
☐ 3 George Kenneally	125.00	55.00	15.50
☐ 4 Ed Matesic	125.00	55.00	15.50
☐ 5 Glenn Presnell........	125.00	55.00	15.50
☐ 6 Pug Rentner	125.00	55.00	15.50
☐ 7 Ken Strong	400.00	180.00	50.00
☐ 8 Jim Zyntell	125.00	55.00	15.50
☐ 9 Knute Rockne CO	1500.00	700.00	190.00
☐ 10 Cliff Battles........	350.00	160.00	45.00
☐ 11 Turk Edwards	350.00	160.00	45.00
☐ 12 Tom Hupke	125.00	55.00	15.50
☐ 13 Homer Griffiths........	125.00	55.00	15.50
☐ 14 Phil Sarboe UER .... (Misspelled Sorboe on both sides of card)	125.00	55.00	15.50
☐ 15 Ben Ciccone	125.00	55.00	15.50
☐ 16 Ben Smith........	125.00	55.00	15.50
☐ 17 Potsy Jones	125.00	55.00	15.50
☐ 18 Mike Mikulak........	125.00	55.00	15.50
☐ 19 Ralph G. Kercheval	125.00	55.00	15.50
☐ 20 Warren Heller	125.00	55.00	15.50
☐ 21 Cliff Montgomery	125.00	55.00	15.50
☐ 22 Shipwreck Kelly UER .... Name spelled Kelley on card	150.00	70.00	19.00
☐ 23 Beattie Feathers	250.00	110.00	31.00
☐ 24 Clarke Hinkle........	400.00	180.00	50.00
☐ 25 Dale Burnett	400.00	180.00	50.00
☐ 26 John Dell Isola .... (Dell omitted from name on card front)	400.00	180.00	50.00
☐ 27 Bull Tosi	400.00	180.00	50.00
☐ 28 Stan Kostka........	400.00	180.00	50.00
☐ 29 Jim MacMurdo	400.00	180.00	50.00
☐ 30 Ernie Caddel	400.00	180.00	50.00
☐ 31 Nic Niccola	400.00	180.00	50.00
☐ 32 Swede Johnston........	400.00	180.00	50.00
☐ 33 Ernie Smith........	400.00	180.00	50.00
☐ 34 Bronko Nagurski........	5000.00	2200.00	600.00
☐ 35 Luke Johnsos	400.00	180.00	50.00
☐ 36 Bernie Masterson	1000.00	450.00	125.00

1992 NewSport

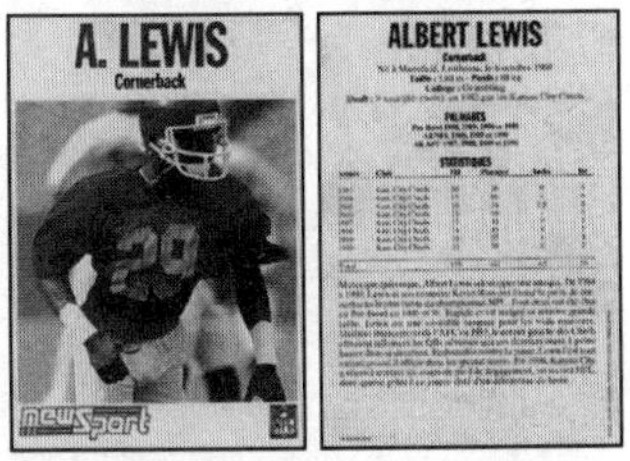

This set of 32 glossy player photos was sponsored by NewSport and issued in France. The month when each card was issued is printed as a tagline on the card back; four cards were issued per month from November 1991 to June 1992. The set was also available in four-card uncut strips. The cards measure approximately 4" by 6" and display glossy color player photos with white borders. The player's name and position appear in the top border, while the NewSport and NFL logos adorn the bottom of the card face. In French, the backs present biography, complete statistics, and career summary. The cards are unnumbered and checklisted below in alphabetical order.

	MINT	NRMT	EXC
COMPLETE SET (32)	200.00	90.00	25.00
COMMON CARD (1-32)	5.00	2.20	.60
☐ 1 Bubby Brister	7.50	3.40	.95
☐ 2 James Brooks........	7.50	3.40	.95
☐ 3 Joey Browner	5.00	2.20	.60
☐ 4 Gill Byrd	5.00	2.20	.60
☐ 5 Eric Dickerson........	10.00	4.50	1.25

☐ 6 Henry Ellard	7.50	3.40	.95
☐ 7 John Elway	25.00	11.00	3.10
☐ 8 Mervyn Fernandez	5.00	2.20	.60
☐ 9 David Fulcher	5.00	2.20	.60
☐ 10 Ernest Givins	7.50	3.40	.95
☐ 11 Jay Hilgenberg	5.00	2.20	.60
☐ 12 Michael Irvin	10.00	4.50	1.25
☐ 13 Dave Krieg	7.50	3.40	.95
☐ 14 Albert Lewis	5.00	2.20	.60
☐ 15 James Lofton	7.50	3.40	.95
☐ 16 Dan Marino	40.00	18.00	5.00
☐ 17 Wilber Marshall	5.00	2.20	.60
☐ 18 Freeman McNeil	7.50	3.40	.95
☐ 19 Karl Mecklenburg	5.00	2.20	.60
☐ 20 Joe Montana	30.00	13.50	3.70
☐ 21 Christian Okoye	7.50	3.40	.95
☐ 22 Michael Dean Perry	7.50	3.40	.95
☐ 23 Tom Rathman	5.00	2.20	.60
☐ 24 Mark Rypien	7.50	3.40	.95
☐ 25 Barry Sanders	30.00	13.50	3.70
☐ 26 Deion Sanders	20.00	9.00	2.50
☐ 27 Sterling Sharpe	10.00	4.50	1.25
☐ 28 Pat Swilling	7.50	3.40	.95
☐ 29 Lawrence Taylor	10.00	4.50	1.25
☐ 30 Vinny Testaverde	7.50	3.40	.95
☐ 31 Andre Tippett	5.00	2.20	.60
☐ 32 Reggie White	10.00	4.50	1.25

1991-92 NFL Experience

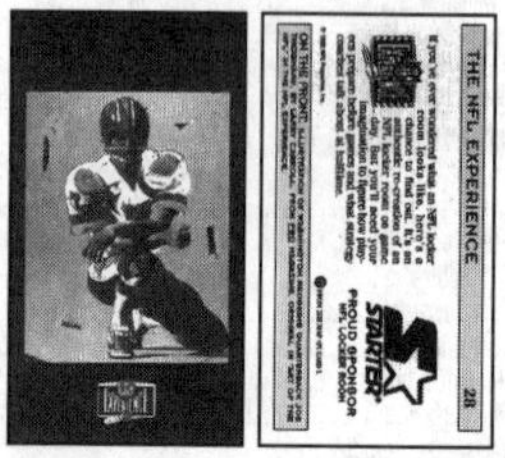

This 28-card set measures approximately 2 1/2" by 4 3/4" and has black borders around each picture. Produced by the NFL, this stylized card set highlights Super Bowl players and scenes. Card fronts run either horizontally or vertically and carry the NFL Experience logo at the bottom center. The backs are printed horizontally with the words "The NFL Experience" and card number appearing in black in a light pink bar at the top. The bottom pink bar carries a description of front artwork, while the center portion describes some aspect of NFL life. Sponsors' logos appear on the right portion of each back.

	MINT	NRMT	EXC
COMPLETE SET (28)	4.00	1.80	.50
COMMON CARD	.20	.09	.03
☐ 1 NFL Experience	.30	.14	.04
Theme Art			
☐ 2 Super Bowl I	.20	.09	.03
Max McGee			
☐ 3 Super Bowl II	.50	.23	.06
Vince Lombardi			
Bart Starr			
☐ 4 Super Bowl III	.75	.35	.09
Don Shula			
Joe Namath			
☐ 5 Super Bowl IV	.20	.09	.03
☐ 6 Super Bowl V	.20	.09	.03
Colts/Cowboys			
☐ 7 Super Bowl VI	.60	.25	.07
Duane Thomas			
Bob Lilly			
Roger Staubach			
Tom Landry			
Tex Schramm			
☐ 8 Super Bowl VII	.20	.09	.03
☐ 9 Super Bowl VIII	.30	.14	.04
Larry Csonka			
☐ 10 Super Bowl IX	.20	.09	.03
☐ 11 Super Bowl X	.30	.14	.04
Lynn Swann			
Jack Lambert			
☐ 12 Super Bowl XI	.30	.14	.04
John Madden			
Raiders/Vikings			
☐ 13 Super Bowl XIII	.30	.14	.04
Randy White			
Harvey Martin			
Craig Morton			
☐ 14 Super Bowl XIII	.20	.09	.03
Steelers/Cowboys			
☐ 15 Super Bowl XIV	.60	.25	.07
Terry Bradshaw			
☐ 16 Super Bowl XV	.20	.09	.03
Raiders/Eagles			
☐ 17 Super Bowl XVI	.20	.09	.03
49ers/Bengals			
☐ 18 Super Bowl XVII	.30	.14	.04
John Riggins			
☐ 19 Super Bowl XVIII	.30	.14	.04
Marcus Allen			
☐ 20 Super Bowl XIX	.20	.09	.03
49ers/Dolphins			
☐ 21 Super Bowl XX	.30	.14	.04
Richard Dent			
☐ 22 Super Bowl XXI	.20	.09	.03
☐ 23 Super Bowl XXII	.30	.14	.04
John Elway			
Doug Williams			
☐ 24 Super Bowl XXIII	.20	.09	.03
49ers/Bengals			
☐ 25 Super Bowl XXIV	1.00	.45	.12
Joe Montana			
☐ 26 Super Bowl XXV	.20	.09	.03
Collage of 25			
Super Bowls			
☐ 27 Super Bowl XXVI	.20	.09	.03
Lombardi Trophy			
☐ 28 Joe Theismann	.30	.14	.04

1993 NFL Properties Santa Claus

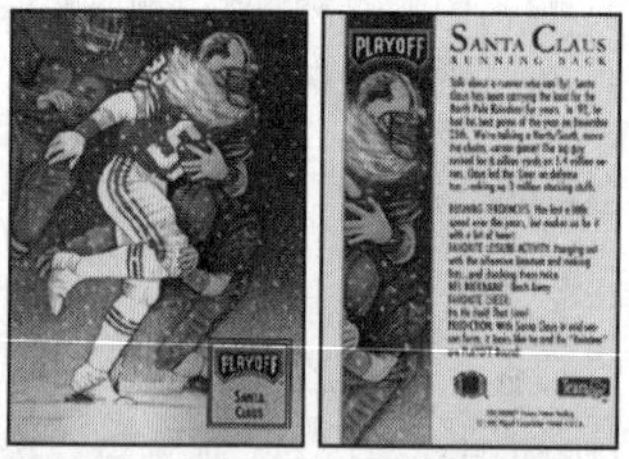

The first Santa Claus card produced by an NFL trading card licensee was in 1989. In 1993, each of the 12 trading card licensees produced an NFL Santa Claus Card, and the entire set, which included a checklist card issued by NFL Properties, was offered through a special mail-away offer for any 30 1993 NFL trading card wrappers and 1.50 for postage and handling. The cards were sent out to dealers along with a season's greeting card. All the cards measure the standard size and feature different artistic renderings of Santa Claus on their fronts and season's greetings on their backs. Although some cards are numbered while others are not, the cards are checklisted below alphabetically according to the licensee's name.

	MINT	NRMT	EXC
COMPLETE SET (13)	16.00	7.25	2.00
COMMON CARD (1-13)	1.50	.70	.19
☐ 1 Santa Claus	1.50	.70	.19
Action Packed			
☐ 2 Santa Claus	1.50	.70	.19
Classic			
☐ 3 Santa Claus	1.50	.70	.19
Collector's Edge			
☐ 4 Santa Claus	1.50	.70	.19
Fleer			
☐ 5 Santa Claus	1.50	.70	.19
Pacific			
☐ 6 Santa Claus	1.50	.70	.19
Pinnacle			
☐ 7 Santa Claus	1.50	.70	.19
Playoff			
☐ 8 Santa Claus	1.50	.70	.19
Pro Set			
☐ 9 Santa Claus	1.50	.70	.19
SkyBox			
☐ 10 Santa Claus	1.50	.70	.19
Topps			
☐ 11 Santa Claus	1.50	.70	.19
Upper Deck			
☐ 12 Santa Claus	1.50	.70	.19
Wild Card			
☐ 13 Checklist Card	1.50	.70	.19
NFL Properties			

1993-95 NFL Properties Show Redemption Cards

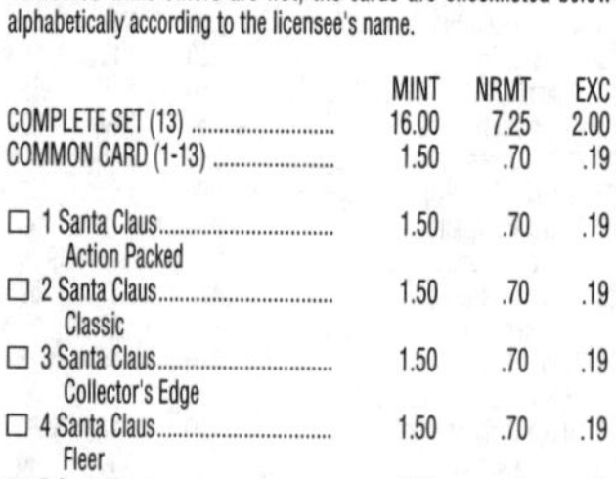

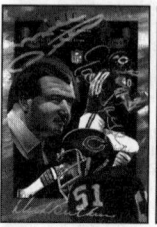

Produced by NFL Properties and handed out to attendees at card shows, these oversized cards measure approximately 3 1/2" by 5" and feature on their fronts collages of player portraits and/or photos. A banner at the top of each card carries the city and dates that the show was held. On the card given out at the National in Chicago, each of the honored players has signed the card in silver ink. The card given out in St. Louis, listed below as 4B, replaced 4A, which was done to commemorate the St. Louis Stallions NFL franchise that never materialized and so was not released. One thousand of 4B were distributed each of the three days of the show, making a total of 3,000. The white back of each card carries text about the players depicted on the front (except card number 2, the back of which carries the 49ers 1993 schedule) and the individual serial number out of the total produced. Card 4B also carries the date that the card was distributed next to the "X of 1000" production figure. Except for the first card, the cards are numbered on the back in Roman numerals. The 49ers card was available at the Team NFL booth at the 1993 San Francisco Labor Day Sports Collector's Convention in exchange for ten wrappers from any licensed 1993 NFL card product. Card number 6A was given to attendees of the Cocktail Reception sponsored by NFL Properties at the 15th National Sports Collectors Convention. The three featured players autographed the card in blue ink. Card number 6B was issued as part of a Back-to-School promotion; collectors redeemed two proofs-of-purchase for this oversized Elway card and an NFL FACT card.

	MINT	NRMT	EXC
COMPLETE SET (9)	900.00	400.00	110.00
COMMON CARD	10.00	4.50	1.25
☐ 1 Chicago Bears	150.00	70.00	19.00
Saluting Hall of Famers			
7/24/93 (200)			
Dick Butkus			
Mike Ditka			
Gale Sayers			
(Signed in silver ink)			
☐ 2 San Francisco 49ers	20.00	9.00	2.50
Labor Day Weekend			
9/93 (1,000)			
NFL Kickoff '93			
Ricky Watters			
Steve Young			
Keith DeLong			
Jerry Rice			
John Taylor			
Tim McDonald			
(1993 49er schedule			
on card back)			
☐ 3 San Francisco 49ers	15.00	6.75	1.85
Labor Day Weekend			
9/93 (1,000)			
Saluting Bay			
Area Legends			
Y.A. Tittle			
Ken Stabler			
(Career summaries			
on back)			
☐ 3AU San Francisco 49ers AUTO	200.00	90.00	25.00
Labor Day Weekend			
9/93 (100)			
Saluting Bay			
Area Legends			
Y.A. Tittle			
Ken Stabler			
Signed by both players			
☐ 4B St. Louis Cardinals	10.00	4.50	1.25
Saluting Three Decades of			
Gateway City QBs			
10/29-31/93 (3000)			
Jim Hart			
Charlie Johnson			
Neil Lomax			
☐ 5 Dallas Cowboys	15.00	6.75	1.85
Saluting the Super Bowl Champions			
11/19-21/93 (3000)			
Michael Irvin			
Troy Aikman			
Emmitt Smith			
Jay Novacek			
Russell Maryland			
Ken Norton Jr.			
☐ 6A Houston Oilers	200.00	90.00	25.00
Saluting a Trio of			
Oilers Legends (Autographed)			
8/4-7/94 (200)			
Earl Campbell			
Dan Pastorini			
Ken Stabler			
☐ 6B John Elway	150.00	70.00	19.00
1995 Spokesman NFL			
Trading Cards			
Autographed (300)			
☐ 7 Joe Namath	200.00	90.00	25.00
John Elway			
Autographed (300)			

1994 NFL Properties Back-to-School

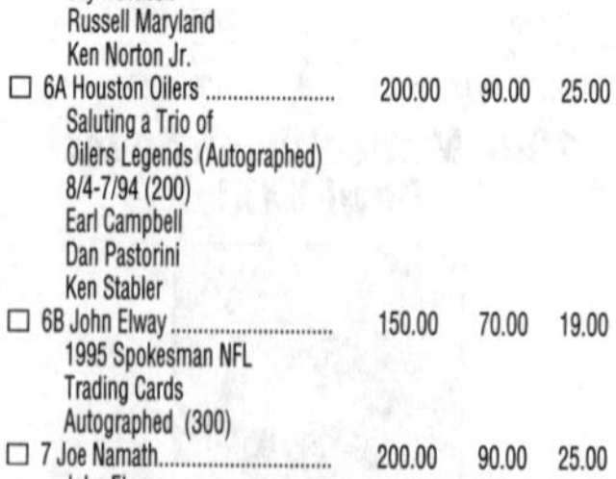

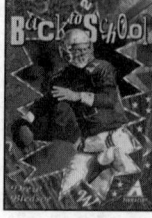

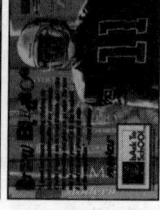

The NFL developed this 11-card standard-size set for football fans and card collectors. The set was available to collectors who sent 20 wrappers from any NFL-licensed trading cards to the NFL '94 Back-to-School Offer address in Minnesota by Nov. 30, 1994. The set features one standard-size card from each of the major licensed football card manufacturers. As originally conceived, the set included a Brett Favre card by Pro Set, but NFL Properties was unable to include this card in the set since Pro Set went out of business. All cards feature on their backs the NFL Back-to-School logo and a message on the importance of staying in school. Only the Action Packed (BS1) and Upper Deck (#19) cards are numbered on the backs. The cards are checklisted below alphabetically according to card manufacturers.

	MINT	NRMT	EXC
COMPLETE SET (11)	16.00	7.25	2.00
COMMON CARD	.50	.23	.06
☐ 1 NFL Quarterback Club	1.50	.70	.19
Action Packed			
☐ 2 Emmitt Smith	4.00	1.80	.50
Classic			
☐ 3 John Elway	1.25	.55	.16
Collector's Edge			
☐ 4 Jerome Bettis	1.00	.45	.12
Fleer			
☐ 5 Sterling Sharpe	.75	.35	.09
Pacific			
☐ 6 Drew Bledsoe	2.50	1.10	.30
Pinnacle			
☐ 7 Dana Stubblefield	.75	.35	.09
Playoff			
☐ 8 Jim Kelly	.75	.35	.09
SkyBox			
☐ 9 Jerry Rice	2.00	.90	.25
Topps			
☐ 10 Joe Montana	2.50	1.10	.30
Upper Deck			
☐ 11 Checklist	.50	.23	.06
NFL Properties			

1994 NFL Properties Santa Claus

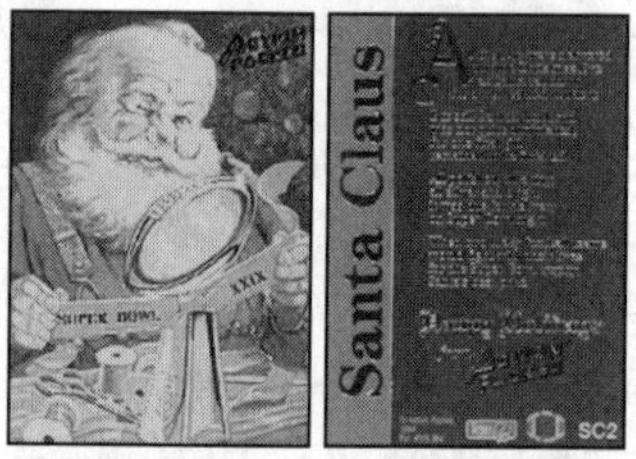

In 1994, each of the ten trading card licensees produced an NFL Santa Claus card. Collectors could obtain the set by sending in 20 wrappers of any participating football card manufacturer and 1.50 for postage and handling. The offer expired on March 31, 1995, or earlier should NFL Properties run out of cards. All the cards measure the standard-size and feature different artistic renderings of Santa Claus on their fronts and season's greetings on their backs. Though some cards are numbered while others are not, all the cards are listed below alphabetically according to licensee's name.

	MINT	NRMT	EXC
COMPLETE SET (11)			
COMMON CARD (1-11)	1.25	.55	.16
☐ 1 Santa Claus	1.25	.55	.16
Action Packed			
☐ 2 Santa Claus	1.25	.55	.16
Classic			
☐ 3 Santa Claus	1.25	.55	.16
Collector's Edge			
☐ 4 Santa Claus	1.25	.55	.16
Fleer			
☐ 5 Santa Claus	1.25	.55	.16
Pacific			
☐ 6 Santa Claus	1.25	.55	.16
Pinnacle			
☐ 7 Santa Claus	1.25	.55	.16
Playoff			
☐ 8 Santa Claus	1.25	.55	.16
SkyBox			
☐ 9 Santa Claus	1.25	.55	.16
Topps			
☐ 10 Santa Claus	1.25	.55	.16
Upper Deck			
☐ 11 Checklist Card	1.25	.55	.16
NFL Properties			

1995 NFL Properties Santa Claus

This nine-card set consists of Santa Claus cards produced by the eight NFL trading card licensees and features different artistic renderings of Santa Claus and season's greetings. The cards are listed below alphabetically according to the licensee's name. Collectors could obtain the set by sending in 20 wrappers of any participating football card manufacturer and $1.50 for postage and handling. The offer expired on March 31, 1996.

	MINT	NRMT	EXC
COMPLETE SET (9)	12.00	5.50	1.50
COMMON CARD	1.00	.45	.12
☐ 1 Title Card	1.00	.45	.12
Santa and friend			

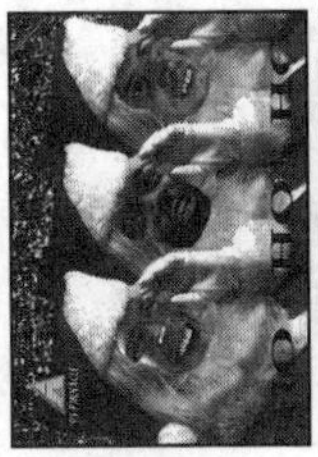

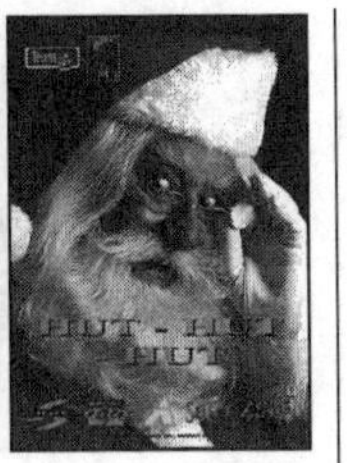

□ 2 Santa Claus Classic Proline with Emmitt Smith and Drew Bledsoe	2.50	1.10	.30
□ 3 Santa Claus Collector's Edge	1.00	.45	.12
□ 4 Santa Claus Pacific	1.00	.45	.12
□ 5 Santa Claus Pinnacle with Dan Marino Emmitt Smith Steve Young	3.00	1.35	.35
□ 6 Santa Claus Playoff	1.00	.45	.12
□ 7 Santa Claus Skybox	1.00	.45	.12
□ 8 Santa Claus Topps	1.00	.45	.12
□ 9 Santa Claus Upper Deck	1.00	.45	.12

1996 NFL Properties Back-to-School

The NFL developed this 9-card standard-size set to promote football card collecting. The set was available to collectors who sent 20 wrappers from any NFL-licensed trading card set and $1.50 postage to the NFL '96 Back-to-School Collector's Set address in Minnesota by Nov. 30, 1996. The set features one standard-size card from each of the major licensed football card manufacturers. The cards are checklisted below alphabetically.

	MINT	NRMT	EXC
COMPLETE SET (9)	10.00	4.50	1.25
COMMON CARD (1-9)	.75	.35	.09
□ 1 Steve Bono Collector's Edge	.75	.35	.09
□ 2 John Elway NFL Properties	1.50	.70	.19
□ 3 Brett Favre Fleer	2.50	1.10	.30
□ 4 Dan Marino Upper Deck	2.50	1.10	.30
□ 5 Dan Marino Steve Young Pinnacle	2.00	.90	.25
□ 6 Deion Sanders Playoff	1.00	.45	.12
□ 7 Emmitt Smith Classic	2.50	1.10	.30
□ 8 Chris Warren Pacific	.75	.35	.09
□ 9 Steve Young Topps	1.25	.55	.16

1996 NFL Properties Santa Claus

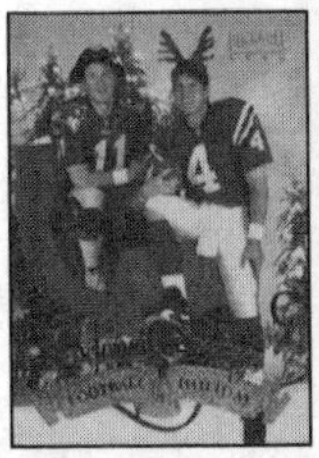

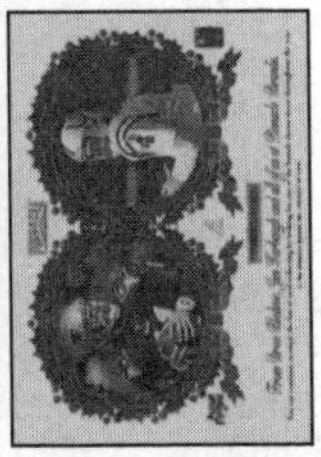

This nine-card set consists of Santa Claus cards produced by the eight NFL trading card licensees and features different artistic renderings of Santa Claus and season's greetings. The cards are listed below alphabetically according to the licensee's name. Collectors could obtain the set by sending in 20 wrappers of any participating football card manufacturer and $1.50 for postage and handling. The offer expired on March 31, 1997.

	MINT	NRMT	EXC
COMPLETE SET (9)	8.00	3.60	1.00
COMMON CARD	1.00	.45	.12
□ 1 Title Card Santa Claus	1.00	.45	.12
□ 2 Santa Claus Collector's Edge with Jeff Blake and Steve Bono	1.00	.45	.12
□ 3 Santa Claus Fleer/Skybox with Brett Favre on back	1.00	.45	.12
□ 4 Santa Claus Pacific	1.00	.45	.12
□ 5 Santa Claus Pinnacle with Drew Bledsoe and Jim Harbaugh	1.00	.45	.12
□ 6 Santa Claus Playoff	1.00	.45	.12
□ 7 Santa Claus Score Board with Troy Aikman	1.00	.45	.12
□ 8 Santa Claus Topps	1.00	.45	.12
□ 9 Santa Claus Upper Deck	1.00	.45	.12

1996 NFL Properties 7-Eleven

NFL Properties and 7-Eleven stores teamed to distribute this 9-card set promoting football card collecting. Each card was available through 7-Eleven stores three per month (October-December) during the 1996 NFL season. A collector was required to send in two football card wrappers and a sales receipt from the 7-Eleven store along with $1 postage to receive one of the nine cards. A different NFL licensed trading card manufacturer produced each card.

	MINT	NRMT	EXC
COMPLETE SET (9)	25.00	11.00	3.10
COMMON CARD (1-9)	1.00	.45	.12
□ 1 John Elway	2.00	.90	.25
□ 2 Jerry Rice	3.00	1.35	.35
□ 3 Dan Marino	5.00	2.20	.60
□ 4 Barry Sanders	3.00	1.35	.35
□ 5 Kordell Stewart	2.50	1.10	.30
□ 6 Steve Young	2.00	.90	.25
□ 7 Joe Namath	3.00	1.35	.35
□ 8 Brett Favre	5.00	2.20	.60
□ 9 Trent Dilfer	1.00	.45	.12

1972 NFLPA Wonderful World Stamps

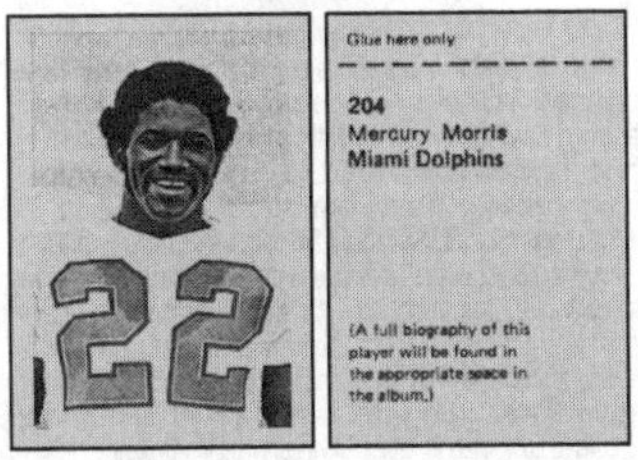

This set of 390 stamps was issued in both 1971 and 1972 under the auspices of the NFL Players Association in conjunction with an album entitled "The Wonderful World of Pro Football USA". The stamps are numbered and are approximately 1 15/16" by 2 7/8". The team order of the album is arranged alphabetically according to the city name and then alphabetically by player name within each team The picture stamp album contains 30 pages measuring approximately 9 1/2" by 13 1/4". The text narrates the story of pro football in the United States. The album includes spaces for 390 color player stamps. The checklist and stamp numbering below is according to the album. There are some numbering and very slight text variations between the 1971 and 1972 issues on some stamps, as noted below.

	NRMT-MT	EXC	G-VG
COMPLETE SET (390)	350.00	160.00	45.00
COMMON CARD (1-390)	.40	.18	.05
□ 1 Bob Berry	.50	.23	.06
□ 2 Greg Brezina	.40	.18	.05
□ 3 Ken Burrow	.40	.18	.05
□ 4 Jim Butler	.40	.18	.05
□ 5 Wes Chesson	.40	.18	.05
□ 6 Claude Humphrey	.50	.23	.06
□ 7 George Kunz	.50	.23	.06
□ 8 Tom McCauley	.40	.18	.05
□ 9 Jim Mitchell	.50	.23	.06
□ 10 Tommy Nobis	1.50	.70	.19
□ 11 Ken Reaves	.40	.18	.05
□ 12 Bill Sandeman	.40	.18	.05
□ 13 John Small	.40	.18	.05
□ 14 Harmon Wages	.40	.18	.05
□ 15 John Zook	.50	.23	.06
□ 16 Norm Bulaich	.50	.23	.06
□ 17 Bill Curry	.50	.23	.06
□ 18 Mike Curtis	.50	.23	.06
□ 19 Ted Hendricks	2.00	.90	.25
□ 20 Roy Hilton	.40	.18	.05
□ 21 Eddie Hinton	.40	.18	.05
□ 22 David Lee	.40	.18	.05
□ 23 Jerry Logan	.40	.18	.05
□ 24 John Mackey	2.00	.90	.25
□ 25 Tom Matte	.75	.35	.09
□ 26 Jim O'Brien	.50	.23	.06
□ 27 Glenn Ressler	.40	.18	.05
□ 28 Johnny Unitas	12.00	5.50	1.50
□ 29 Bob Vogel	.50	.23	.06
□ 30 Rick Volk	.50	.23	.06
□ 31 Paul Costa	.40	.18	.05
□ 32 Jim Dunaway	.40	.18	.05
□ 33 Paul Guidry	.40	.18	.05
□ 34 Jim Harris	.40	.18	.05
□ 35 Robert James	.40	.18	.05
□ 36 Mike McBath	.40	.18	.05
□ 37 Haven Moses	.75	.35	.09
□ 38 Wayne Patrick	.40	.18	.05
□ 39 John Pitts	.40	.18	.05
□ 40 Jim Reilly	.40	.18	.05
□ 41 Pete Richardson	.40	.18	.05
□ 42 Dennis Shaw	.50	.23	.06
□ 43 O.J. Simpson	15.00	6.75	1.85
□ 44 Mike Stratton	.40	.18	.05
□ 45 Bob Tatarek	.40	.18	.05
□ 46 Dick Butkus	10.00	4.50	1.25
□ 47 Jim Cadile	.40	.18	.05
□ 48 Jack Concannon	.50	.23	.06
□ 49 Bobby Douglass	.50	.23	.06
□ 50 George Farmer	.40	.18	.05
□ 51 Dick Gordon	.50	.23	.06
□ 52 Bobby Joe Green	.40	.18	.05
□ 53 Ed O'Bradovich	.40	.18	.05
□ 54 Mac Percival	.40	.18	.05
□ 55 Gale Sayers	10.00	4.50	1.25
□ 56 George Seals	.40	.18	.05
□ 57 Jim Seymour	.40	.18	.05
□ 58 Ron Smith	.50	.23	.06
□ 59 Bill Staley	.40	.18	.05
□ 60 Cecil Turner	.40	.18	.05
□ 61 Al Beauchamp	.40	.18	.05
□ 62 Virgil Carter	.50	.23	.06
□ 63 Vern Holland	.40	.18	.05
□ 64 Bob Johnson	.50	.23	.06
□ 65 Ron Lamb	.40	.18	.05
□ 66 Dave Lewis	.40	.18	.05
□ 67 Rufus Mayes	.40	.18	.05
□ 68 Horst Muhlmann	.40	.18	.05
□ 69 Lemar Parrish	.75	.35	.09
□ 70 Jess Phillips	.40	.18	.05
□ 71 Mike Reid	2.00	.90	.25
□ 72 Ken Riley	.75	.35	.09
□ 73 Paul Robinson	.40	.18	.05
□ 74 Bob Trumpy	1.25	.55	.16
□ 75 Fred Willis	.40	.18	.05
□ 76 Don Cockroft	.50	.23	.06
□ 77 Gary Collins	.50	.23	.06
□ 78 Gene Hickerson	.40	.18	.05
□ 79 Fair Hooker	.50	.23	.06
□ 80 Jim Houston	.50	.23	.06
□ 81 Walter Johnson	.50	.23	.06
□ 82 Joe Jones	.40	.18	.05
□ 83 Leroy Kelly	2.00	.90	.25
□ 84 Milt Morin	.40	.18	.05
□ 85 Reece Morrison	.40	.18	.05
□ 86 Bill Nelsen	.50	.23	.06
□ 87 Mike Phipps	.75	.35	.09
□ 88 Bo Scott	.50	.23	.06
□ 89 Jerry Sherk	.50	.23	.06
□ 90 Ron Snidow	.40	.18	.05
□ 91 Herb Adderley	2.00	.90	.25
□ 92 George Andrie	.50	.23	.06
□ 93 Mike Clark	.40	.18	.05
□ 94 Dave Edwards	.50	.23	.06
□ 95 Walt Garrison	.75	.35	.09
□ 96 Cornell Green	.50	.23	.06
□ 97 Bob Hayes	2.00	.90	.25
□ 98 Calvin Hill	1.50	.70	.19
□ 99 Chuck Howley	.75	.35	.09
□ 100 Lee Roy Jordan	2.00	.90	.25
□ 101 Dave Manders	.40	.18	.05
□ 102 Craig Morton	1.25	.55	.16
□ 103 Ralph Neely	.50	.23	.06
□ 104 Mel Renfro	2.00	.90	.25
□ 105 Roger Staubach	20.00	9.00	2.50
□ 106 Bob Anderson	.50	.23	.06
□ 107 Sam Brunelli	.40	.18	.05
□ 108 Dave Costa	.40	.18	.05
□ 109 Mike Current	.40	.18	.05
□ 110 Pete Duranko	.40	.18	.05
□ 111 George Goeddeke	.40	.18	.05
□ 112 Cornell Gordon	.40	.18	.05
□ 113 Don Horn	.40	.18	.05
□ 114 Rich Jackson	.40	.18	.05
□ 115 Larry Kaminski	.40	.18	.05
□ 116 Floyd Little	1.25	.55	.16
□ 117 Marv Montgomery	.40	.18	.05
□ 118 Steve Ramsey	.40	.18	.05
□ 119 Paul Smith	.50	.23	.06
□ 120 Bill Thompson	.50	.23	.06
□ 121 Lem Barney	2.00	.90	.25
□ 122 Nick Eddy	.40	.18	.05
□ 123 Mel Farr	.50	.23	.06
□ 124 Ed Flanagan	.40	.18	.05
□ 125 Larry Hand	.40	.18	.05
□ 126 Greg Landry	.75	.35	.09
□ 127 Dick LeBeau	.50	.23	.06
□ 128 Mike Lucci	.50	.23	.06
□ 129 Earl McCullouch	.50	.23	.06
□ 130 Bill Munson	.50	.23	.06
□ 131 Wayne Rasmussen	.40	.18	.05
□ 132 Joe Robb	.40	.18	.05
□ 133 Jerry Rush	.40	.18	.05
□ 134 Altie Taylor	.50	.23	.06
□ 135 Wayne Walker	.50	.23	.06
□ 136 Ken Bowman	.40	.18	.05
□ 137 John Brockington	.75	.35	.09
□ 138 Fred Carr	.50	.23	.06
□ 139 Carroll Dale	.50	.23	.06
□ 140 Ken Ellis	.40	.18	.05
□ 141 Gale Gillingham	.50	.23	.06
□ 142 Dave Hampton	.40	.18	.05
□ 143 Doug Hart	.40	.18	.05
□ 144 MacArthur Lane	.75	.35	.09
□ 145 Mike McCoy	.50	.23	.06
□ 146 Ray Nitschke	2.00	.90	.25
□ 147 Frank Patrick	.40	.18	.05
□ 148 Francis Peay	.40	.18	.05
□ 149 Dave Robinson	.50	.23	.06
□ 150 Bart Starr name misspelled Part	10.00	4.50	1.25
□ 151 Bob Atkins	.40	.18	.05
□ 152 Elvin Bethea	.50	.23	.06
□ 153 Garland Boyette	.40	.18	.05
□ 154 Ken Burrough	.75	.35	.09
□ 155 Woody Campbell	.40	.18	.05
□ 156 John Charles	.40	.18	.05
□ 157 Lynn Dickey	.75	.35	.09
□ 158 Elbert Drungo	.40	.18	.05
□ 159 Gene Ferguson	.40	.18	.05
□ 160 Charlie Johnson	.75	.35	.09
□ 161 Charlie Joiner	2.50	1.10	.30
□ 162 Dan Pastorini	1.00	.45	.12
□ 163 Ron Pritchard	.40	.18	.05
□ 164 Walt Suggs	.40	.18	.05
□ 165 Mike Tilleman	.40	.18	.05
□ 166 Bobby Bell	2.00	.90	.25
□ 167 Aaron Brown	.40	.18	.05
□ 168 Buck Buchanan	2.00	.90	.25
□ 169 Ed Budde	.50	.23	.06
□ 170 Curley Culp	.50	.23	.06
□ 171 Len Dawson	5.00	2.20	.60
□ 172 Willie Lanier	2.00	.90	.25
□ 173 Jim Lynch	.50	.23	.06
□ 174 Jim Marsalis	.50	.23	.06
□ 175 Mo Moorman	.40	.18	.05
□ 176 Ed Podolak	.50	.23	.06
□ 177 Johnny Robinson	.75	.35	.09
□ 178 Jan Stenerud	1.50	.70	.19
□ 179 Otis Taylor	1.00	.45	.12
□ 180 Jim Tyrer	.50	.23	.06
□ 181 Kermit Alexander	.50	.23	.06
□ 182 Coy Bacon	.50	.23	.06
□ 183 Dick Buzin	.40	.18	.05
□ 184 Roman Gabriel	1.25	.55	.16
□ 185 Gene Howard	.40	.18	.05
□ 186 Ken Iman	.40	.18	.05
□ 187 Les Josephson	.50	.23	.06
□ 188 Marlin McKeever	.40	.18	.05
□ 189 Merlin Olsen	4.00	1.80	.50
□ 190 Phil Olsen	.40	.18	.05
□ 191 David Ray	.40	.18	.05
□ 192 Lance Rentzel	.50	.23	.06
□ 193 Isiah Robertson	.50	.23	.06
□ 194 Larry Smith	.40	.18	.05
□ 195 Jack Snow	1.00	.45	.12
□ 196 Nick Buoniconti	2.00	.90	.25
□ 197 Doug Crusan	.40	.18	.05
□ 198 Larry Csonka	10.00	4.50	1.25
□ 199 Bob DeMarco	.50	.23	.06
□ 200 Marv Fleming	.50	.23	.06
□ 201 Bob Griese	8.00	3.60	1.00
□ 202 Jim Kiick	1.00	.45	.12
□ 203 Bob Kuechenberg	1.00	.45	.12
□ 204 Mercury Morris	1.50	.70	.19
□ 205 John Richardson	.40	.18	.05
□ 206 Jim Riley	.40	.18	.05
□ 207 Jake Scott	.75	.35	.09
□ 208 Howard Twilley	.50	.23	.06
□ 209 Paul Warfield	4.00	1.80	.50
□ 210 Garo Yepremian	.50	.23	.06
□ 211 Grady Alderman	.50	.23	.06
□ 212 John Beasley	.40	.18	.05
□ 213 John Henderson	.40	.18	.05
□ 214 Wally Hilgenberg	.40	.18	.05
□ 215 Clint Jones	.40	.18	.05
□ 216 Karl Kassulke	.40	.18	.05
□ 217 Paul Krause	1.25	.55	.16
□ 218 Dave Osborn	.50	.23	.06
□ 219 Alan Page	2.00	.90	.25
□ 220 Ed Sharockman	.40	.18	.05
□ 221 Fran Tarkenton	8.00	3.60	1.00
□ 222 Mick Tingelhoff	.75	.35	.09
□ 223 Charlie West	.40	.18	.05
□ 224 Lonnie Warwick	.40	.18	.05
□ 225 Gene Washington	.50	.23	.06
□ 226 Hank Barton	.40	.18	.05
□ 227 Ron Berger	.40	.18	.05
□ 228 Larry Carwell	.40	.18	.05
□ 229 Jim Cheyunski	.50	.23	.06
□ 230 Carl Garrett	.50	.23	.06
□ 231 Rickie Harris	.40	.18	.05
□ 232 Daryle Johnson	.40	.18	.05
□ 233 Steve Kiner	.40	.18	.05
□ 234 Jon Morris	.40	.18	.05
□ 235 Jim Nance	.75	.35	.09
□ 236 Tom Neville	.40	.18	.05
□ 237 Jim Plunkett	2.50	1.10	.30
□ 238 Ron Sellers	.40	.18	.05

☐ 239 Len St. Jean	.40	.18	.05
☐ 240 Don Webb	.40	.18	.05
☐ 241 Dan Abramowicz	.50	.23	.06
☐ 242 Dick Absher	.40	.18	.05
☐ 243 Leo Carroll	.40	.18	.05
☐ 244 Jim Duncan	.40	.18	.05
☐ 245 Al Dodd	.40	.18	.05
☐ 246 Jim Flanigan	.40	.18	.05
☐ 247 Hoyle Granger	.40	.18	.05
☐ 248 Edd Hargett	.50	.23	.06
☐ 249 Glen Ray Hines	.40	.18	.05
☐ 250 Hugo Hollas	.40	.18	.05
☐ 251 Jake Kupp	.40	.18	.05
☐ 252 Dave Long	.40	.18	.05
☐ 253 Mike Morgan	.40	.18	.05
☐ 254 Tom Roussel	.40	.18	.05
☐ 255 Del Williams	.40	.18	.05
☐ 256 Otto Brown	.40	.18	.05
☐ 257 Bobby Duhon	.40	.18	.05
☐ 258 Scott Eaton	.40	.18	.05
☐ 259 Jim Files	.40	.18	.05
☐ 260 Tucker Frederickson	.50	.23	.06
☐ 261A Don Herrmann	.40	.18	.05
☐ 261B Pete Gogolak	.50	.23	.06
☐ 262 Bob Grim	.50	.23	.06
☐ 263 Don Herrmann	.40	.18	.05
☐ 264A Ernie Koy	.50	.23	.06
☐ 264B Ron Johnson	.50	.23	.06
☐ 265A Spider Lockhart	.50	.23	.06
☐ 265B Jim Kanicki	.40	.18	.05
☐ 266 Spider Lockhart	.50	.23	.06
☐ 267 Joe Morrison	.50	.23	.06
☐ 268 Bob Tucker	.75	.35	.09
☐ 269 Willie Williams	.40	.18	.05
☐ 270 Willie Young	.40	.18	.05
☐ 271 Al Atkinson	.40	.18	.05
☐ 272 Ralph Baker	.40	.18	.05
☐ 273 Emerson Boozer	.75	.35	.09
☐ 274 John Elliott	.40	.18	.05
☐ 275 Dave Herman	.40	.18	.05
☐ 276A Dave Herman	.40	.18	.05
☐ 276B Winston Hill	.50	.23	.06
☐ 277 Gus Hollomon	.40	.18	.05
☐ 278 Bobby Howfield	.40	.18	.05
☐ 279 Pete Lammons	.40	.18	.05
☐ 280 Joe Namath	20.00	9.00	2.50
☐ 281A Gerry Philbin	.50	.23	.06
☐ 281B Joe Namath	20.00	9.00	2.50
☐ 282 Matt Snell	.75	.35	.09
☐ 282B Gerry Philbin UER Spelled Jerry	.50	.23	.06
☐ 283 Steve Tannen	.40	.18	.05
☐ 284 Earlie Thomas	.40	.18	.05
☐ 285 Al Woodall	.40	.18	.05
☐ 286 Fred Biletnikoff	4.00	1.80	.50
☐ 287 George Blanda	6.00	2.70	.75
☐ 288 Willie Brown	2.00	.90	.25
☐ 289 Raymond Chester	.50	.23	.06
☐ 290 Tony Cline	.40	.18	.05
☐ 291 Dan Conners	.40	.18	.05
☐ 292 Ben Davidson	1.00	.45	.12
☐ 293 Hewritt Dixon	.50	.23	.06
☐ 294 Tom Keating	.40	.18	.05
☐ 295 Daryle Lamonica	1.50	.70	.19
☐ 296 Gus Otto	.40	.18	.05
☐ 297 Jim Otto	2.00	.90	.25
☐ 298 Rod Sherman	.40	.18	.05
☐ 299 Charlie Smith	.40	.18	.05
☐ 300A Warren Wells	.40	.18	.05
☐ 300B Gene Upshaw	2.00	.90	.25
☐ 301 Rick Arrington	.40	.18	.05
☐ 302 Gary Ballman	.40	.18	.05
☐ 303 Lee Bouggess	.40	.18	.05
☐ 304 Bill Bradley	.50	.23	.06
☐ 305A Richard Harris	.40	.18	.05
☐ 305B Happy Feller	.40	.18	.05
☐ 306A Ben Hawkins	.40	.18	.05
☐ 306B Richard Harris	.40	.18	.05
☐ 307 Ben Hawkins	.40	.18	.05
☐ 308 Harold Jackson	1.25	.55	.16
☐ 309 Pete Liske	.50	.23	.06
☐ 310 Al Nelson	.40	.18	.05
☐ 311 Gary Pettigrew	.40	.18	.05
☐ 312 Tim Rossovich	.50	.23	.06
☐ 313 Tom Woodeshick	.50	.23	.06
☐ 314 Adrian Young	.40	.18	.05
☐ 315 Steve Zabel	.40	.18	.05
☐ 316 Chuck Allen	.50	.23	.06
☐ 317 Warren Bankston	.40	.18	.05
☐ 318 Chuck Beatty	.40	.18	.05
☐ 319 Terry Bradshaw	20.00	9.00	2.50
☐ 320 John Fuqua	.50	.23	.06
☐ 321 Terry Hanratty	.75	.35	.09
☐ 322 Ray Mansfield	.40	.18	.05
☐ 323 Ben McGee	.40	.18	.05
☐ 324 John Rowser	.40	.18	.05
☐ 325 Andy Russell	.50	.23	.06
☐ 326 Ron Shanklin	.40	.18	.05
☐ 327 Dave Smith	.40	.18	.05
☐ 328 Bruce Van Dyke	.40	.18	.05
☐ 329 Lloyd Voss	.40	.18	.05
☐ 330 Bobby Walden	.40	.18	.05
☐ 331 Donny Anderson	.50	.23	.06
☐ 332 Jim Bakken	.50	.23	.06
☐ 333 Pete Beathard	.50	.23	.06
☐ 334A Mel Gray	1.00	.45	.12
☐ 334B Miller Farr	.40	.18	.05
☐ 335A Jim Hart	1.00	.45	.12
☐ 335B Mel Gray	1.00	.45	.12
☐ 336 Jim Hart	1.00	.45	.12
☐ 337A Chuck Latourette	.40	.18	.05
☐ 337B Rolf Krueger	.40	.18	.05
☐ 338 Chuck Latourette	.40	.18	.05
☐ 339A Bob Reynolds	.40	.18	.05
☐ 339B Ernie McMillan	.50	.23	.06
☐ 340 Bob Reynolds	.40	.18	.05
☐ 341 Jackie Smith	2.00	.90	.25
☐ 342 Larry Stallings	.40	.18	.05
☐ 343 Chuck Walker	.40	.18	.05
☐ 344 Roger Wehrli	.75	.35	.09
☐ 345 Larry Wilson	2.00	.90	.25
☐ 346 Bob Babich	.40	.18	.05
☐ 347 Pete Barnes	.40	.18	.05
☐ 348A Marty Domres	.40	.18	.05
☐ 348B Steve DeLong	.50	.23	.06
☐ 349 Marty Domres	.40	.18	.05
☐ 350 Gary Garrison	.50	.23	.06
☐ 351A Walker Gillette	.40	.18	.05
☐ 351B John Hadl	1.25	.55	.16
☐ 352 Kevin Hardy	.40	.18	.05
☐ 353 Bob Howard	.40	.18	.05
☐ 354A Jim Hill	.40	.18	.05
☐ 354B Deacon Jones	2.50	1.10	.30
☐ 355 Terry Owens	.50	.23	.06
☐ 356 Dennis Partee	.40	.18	.05
☐ 357A Dennis Partee	.40	.18	.05
☐ 357B Jeff Queen	.40	.18	.05
☐ 358 Jim Tolbert	.40	.18	.05
☐ 359 Russ Washington	.40	.18	.05
☐ 360 Doug Wilkerson	.40	.18	.05
☐ 361 John Brodie	2.50	1.10	.30
☐ 362 Doug Cunningham	.40	.18	.05
☐ 363 Bruce Gossett	.40	.18	.05
☐ 364 Stan Hindman	.40	.18	.05
☐ 365 John Isenbarger	.40	.18	.05
☐ 366 Charlie Krueger	.50	.23	.06
☐ 367 Frank Nunley	.40	.18	.05
☐ 368 Woody Peoples	.40	.18	.05
☐ 369 Len Rohde	.40	.18	.05
☐ 370 Steve Spurrier	12.00	5.50	1.50
☐ 371 Gene Washington	1.00	.45	.12
☐ 372 Dave Wilcox	.75	.35	.09
☐ 373 Ken Willard	.50	.23	.06
☐ 374 Bob Windsor	.40	.18	.05
☐ 375 Dick Witcher	.40	.18	.05
☐ 376 Verlon Biggs	.50	.23	.06
☐ 377 Larry Brown	1.50	.70	.19
☐ 378 Speedy Duncan	.40	.18	.05
☐ 379 Chris Hanburger	.75	.35	.09
☐ 380 Charlie Harraway	.40	.18	.05
☐ 381 Sonny Jurgensen	4.00	1.80	.50
☐ 382 Billy Kilmer	1.50	.70	.19
☐ 383 Tommy Mason	.50	.23	.06
☐ 384 Ron McDole	.50	.23	.06
☐ 385 Brig Owens	.40	.18	.05
☐ 386 Jack Pardee	1.00	.45	.12
☐ 387 Myron Pottios	.40	.18	.05
☐ 388 Jerry Smith	.50	.23	.06
☐ 389 Diron Talbert	.50	.23	.06
☐ 390 Charley Taylor	3.00	1.35	.35
☐ NNO Wonderful World Album	20.00	9.00	2.50

1972 NFLPA Fabric Cards

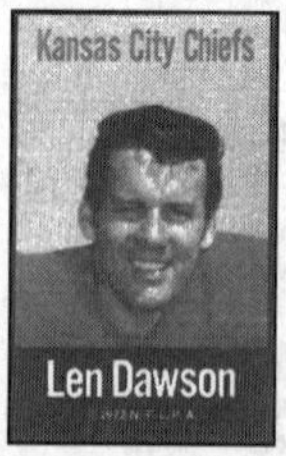
Kansas City Chiefs
Len Dawson

The 1972 NFLPA Fabric Cards set includes 35 cards printed on cloth. These thin fabric cards measure approximately 2 1/4" by 3 1/2" and are blank backed. The cards are sometimes referred to as "Iron Ons" as they were intended to be semi-permanently ironed on to clothes. The full color portrait of the player is surrounded by a black border. Below the player's name at the bottom of the card is indicated copyright by the NFL Players Association in 1972. The cards may have been illegally reprinted. There is some additional interest in the Staubach card due to the fact that his 1972 Topps card (that same year) is considered his Rookie Card. Since they are unnumbered, they are listed below in alphabetical order according to the player's name. These fabric cards were originally available in vending machines at retail stores and other outlets.

	NRMT-MT	EXC	G-VG
COMPLETE SET (35)	150.00	70.00	19.00
COMMON CARD (1-35)	1.50	.70	.19
☐ 1 Donny Anderson	1.50	.70	.19
☐ 2 George Blanda	6.00	2.70	.75
☐ 3 Terry Bradshaw	18.00	8.00	2.20
☐ 4 John Brockington	1.50	.70	.19
☐ 5 John Brodie	4.00	1.80	.50
☐ 6 Dick Butkus	10.00	4.50	1.25
☐ 7 Larry Csonka	6.00	2.70	.75
☐ 8 Mike Curtis	1.50	.70	.19
☐ 9 Len Dawson	5.00	2.20	.60
☐ 10 Carl Eller	2.50	1.10	.30
☐ 11 Mike Garrett	1.50	.70	.19
☐ 12 Joe Greene	6.00	2.70	.75
☐ 13 Bob Griese	6.00	2.70	.75
☐ 14 Dick Gordon	1.50	.70	.19
☐ 15 John Hadl	2.00	.90	.25
☐ 16 Bob Hayes	2.50	1.10	.30
☐ 17 Ron Johnson	1.50	.70	.19
☐ 18 Deacon Jones	3.00	1.35	.35
☐ 19 Sonny Jurgensen	5.00	2.20	.60
☐ 20 Leroy Kelly	3.00	1.35	.35
☐ 21 Jim Kiick	2.00	.90	.25
☐ 22 Greg Landry	1.50	.70	.19
☐ 23 Floyd Little	2.00	.90	.25
☐ 24 Mike Lucci	1.50	.70	.19
☐ 25 Archie Manning	4.00	1.80	.50
☐ 26 Joe Namath	25.00	11.00	3.10
☐ 27 Tommy Nobis	2.50	1.10	.30
☐ 28 Alan Page	3.00	1.35	.35
☐ 29 Jim Plunkett	4.00	1.80	.50
☐ 30 Gale Sayers	10.00	4.50	1.25
☐ 31 O.J. Simpson	18.00	8.00	2.20
☐ 32 Roger Staubach	25.00	11.00	3.10
☐ 33 Duane Thomas	2.00	.90	.25
☐ 34 Johnny Unitas	15.00	6.75	1.85
☐ 35 Paul Warfield	5.00	2.20	.60

1972 NFLPA Vinyl Stickers

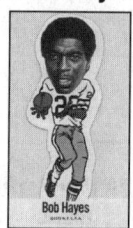

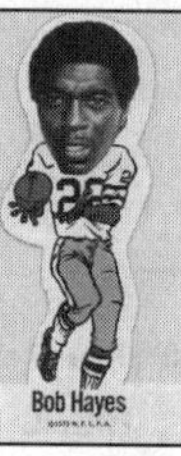
Bob Hayes

The 1972 NFLPA Vinyl Stickers set contains 20 stand-up type stickers depicting the players in a caricature-like style with big heads. These irregularly shaped stickers are approximately 2 3/4" by 4 3/4". Below the player's name at the bottom of the card is indicated copyright by the NFL Players Association in 1972. The set is sometimes offered as a short set excluding the shorter-printed cards, i.e., those listed by SP in the checklist below. Since they are unnumbered, they are listed below in alphabetical order according to the player's name. The Roger Staubach card holds special interest in that 1972 represents Roger's rookie year for cards. These stickers were originally available in vending machines at retail stores and other outlets. The Dick Butkus and Joe Namath stickers exist as reverse negatives. The set is considered complete with either Butkus or Namath variation.

	NRMT-MT	EXC	G-VG
COMPLETE SET (20)	100.00	45.00	12.50
COMMON CARD (1-20)	2.50	1.10	.30
☐ 1 Donny Anderson	2.50	1.10	.30
☐ 2 George Blanda	6.00	2.70	.75
☐ 3 Terry Bradshaw	20.00	9.00	2.50
☐ 4 John Brockington	2.50	1.10	.30
☐ 5 John Brodie	5.00	2.20	.60
☐ 6A Dick Butkus Reversed Negative	10.00	4.50	1.25
☐ 6B Dick Butkus	10.00	4.50	1.25
☐ 7 Dick Gordon	2.50	1.10	.30
☐ 8 Joe Greene	6.00	2.70	.75
☐ 9 John Hadl	3.50	1.55	.45
☐ 10 Bob Hayes	4.00	1.80	.50
☐ 11 Ron Johnson SP	8.00	3.60	1.00
☐ 12 Floyd Little	3.50	1.55	.45
☐ 13A Joe Namath Reversed Negative	25.00	11.00	3.10
☐ 13B Joe Namath	25.00	11.00	3.10
☐ 14 Tommy Nobis	4.00	1.80	.50
☐ 15 Alan Page SP	12.00	5.50	1.50
☐ 16 Jim Plunkett	5.00	2.20	.60
☐ 17 Gale Sayers	12.00	5.50	1.50
☐ 18 Roger Staubach	25.00	11.00	3.10
☐ 19 Johnny Unitas	16.00	7.25	2.00
☐ 20 Paul Warfield	5.00	2.20	.60

1979 NFLPA Pennant Stickers

The 1979 NFL Football Pennant Stickers set contains 51 stickers measuring approximately 2 1/2" by 5". The pennant-shaped stickers show a circular (black and white) photo of the player next to the NFL Players Association football logo. The set was apparently not approved by the NFL as the team logos are not shown on the cards. The player's name, position, and team are given at the bottom of the card. The backs are blank as it is a peel-off backing only. Some of the stickers can be found with more than one color background and have been listed accordingly below.

	NRMT-MT	EXC	G-VG
COMPLETE SET (51)	500.00	220.00	60.00
COMMON CARD (1-51)	5.00	2.20	.60

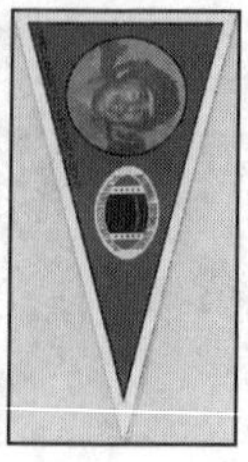

☐ 1 Lyle Alzado (Red)	6.00	2.70	.75
☐ 2 Ken Anderson (Blue)	7.50	3.40	.95
☐ 3 Steve Bartkowski SP (Yellow)	18.00	8.00	2.20
☐ 4 Ricky Bell (Red)	6.00	2.70	.75
☐ 5 Elvin Bethea (Blue)	5.00	2.20	.60
☐ 6 Tom Blanchard (Blue, red, or yellow)	5.00	2.20	.60
☐ 7 Terry Bradshaw (Red or yellow)	35.00	16.00	4.40
☐ 8 Bob Breunig (Red or yellow)	5.00	2.20	.60
☐ 9 Greg Brezina (Purple, red or yellow)	5.00	2.20	.60
☐ 10 Doug Buffone SP (Green)	15.00	6.75	1.85
☐ 11 Earl Campbell (Yellow)	35.00	16.00	4.40
☐ 12 John Cappelletti (Green)	5.00	2.20	.60
☐ 13 Harold Carmichael (Blue)	6.00	2.70	.75
☐ 14 Chuck Crist SP (Green)	15.00	6.75	1.85
☐ 15 Sam Cunningham (Green)	5.00	2.20	.60
☐ 16 Joe DeLamielleure (Blue)	5.00	2.20	.60
☐ 17 Tom Dempsey (Blue, red, or yellow)	5.00	2.20	.60
☐ 18 Tony Dorsett (Yellow)	15.00	6.75	1.85
☐ 19 Dan Fouts SP (Green)	25.00	11.00	3.10
☐ 20 Roy Gerela (Red or yellow)	5.00	2.20	.60
☐ 21 Bob Griese UER (Purple; Greise)	12.00	5.50	1.50
☐ 22 Franco Harris (Red or yellow)	12.00	5.50	1.50
☐ 23 Jim Hart SP	18.00	8.00	2.20
☐ 24 Charlie Joiner (Green)	6.00	2.70	.75
☐ 25 Paul Krause (Green)	6.00	2.70	.75
☐ 26 Bob Kuechenberg (Purple)	5.00	2.20	.60
☐ 27 Greg Landry (Purple)	6.00	2.70	.75
☐ 28 Archie Manning (Blue)	6.00	2.70	.75
☐ 29 Chester Marcol (Purple)	5.00	2.20	.60
☐ 30 Harvey Martin (Red)	6.00	2.70	.75
☐ 31 Lawrence McCutcheon SP (Yellow)	18.00	8.00	2.20
☐ 32 Craig Morton (Green)	6.00	2.70	.75
☐ 33 Haven Moses (Green)	5.00	2.20	.60
☐ 34 Steve Odom (Purple)	5.00	2.20	.60
☐ 35 Morris Owens (Green)	5.00	2.20	.60
☐ 36 Dan Pastorini SP	18.00	8.00	2.20
☐ 37 Walter Payton (Green)	35.00	16.00	4.40
☐ 38 Greg Pruitt SP (Green)	18.00	8.00	2.20
☐ 39 John Riggins (Purple)	10.00	4.50	1.25
☐ 40 Jake Scott (Red)	5.00	2.20	.60
☐ 41 Jerry Sherk SP	15.00	6.75	1.85
☐ 42 Ken Stabler SP (Blue)	35.00	16.00	4.40
☐ 43 Roger Staubach (Yellow)	35.00	16.00	4.40
☐ 44 Jan Stenerud (Purple)	6.00	2.70	.75
☐ 45 Art Still SP	15.00	6.75	1.85
☐ 46 Mick Tingelhoff (Blue)	5.00	2.20	.60
☐ 47 Richard Todd (Yellow)	5.00	2.20	.60
☐ 48 Phil Villapiano SP (Purple)	15.00	6.75	1.85

☐ 49 Wesley Walker (Red or yellow)	6.00	2.70	.75
☐ 50 Roger Wehrli SP (Purple)	15.00	6.75	1.85
☐ 51 Jim Zorn SP (Red)	18.00	8.00	2.20

1995 NFLPA Super Bowl Player's Party

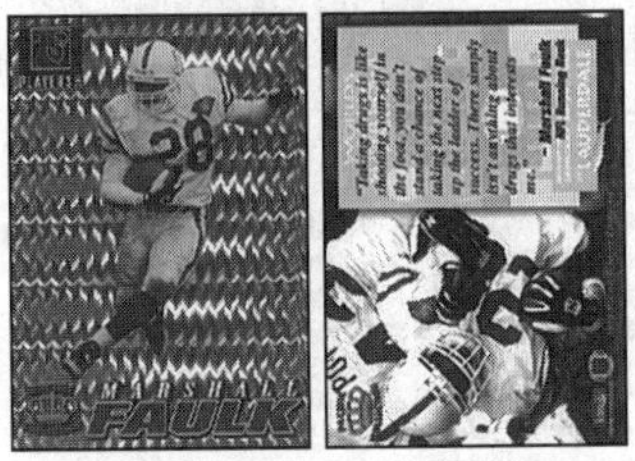

These ten standard-size cards were given away at a NFLPA Super Bowl XXIX player's party. Each card company produced one card; reportedly, the set was limited to 500 of each card. The cards are unnumbered and checklisted below in alphabetical order.

	MINT	NRMT	EXC
COMPLETE SET (10)	200.00	90.00	25.00
COMMON CARD (1-10)	10.00	4.50	1.25
☐ 1 Marcus Allen Pinnacle	12.00	5.50	1.50
☐ 2 Jerome Bettis Fleer	10.00	4.50	1.25
☐ 3 Tim Brown Collector's Edge	10.00	4.50	1.25
☐ 4 Trent Dilfer SkyBox	15.00	6.75	1.85
☐ 5 Marshall Faulk Pacific	40.00	18.00	5.00
☐ 6 Ronnie Lott Classic	10.00	4.50	1.25
☐ 7 Dan Marino Upper Deck	75.00	34.00	9.50
☐ 8 Junior Seau Stadium Club	12.00	5.50	1.50
☐ 9 Sterling Sharpe Action Packed	10.00	4.50	1.25
☐ 10 Heath Shuler Playoff	25.00	11.00	3.10

1996 NFLPA Super Bowl Player's Party

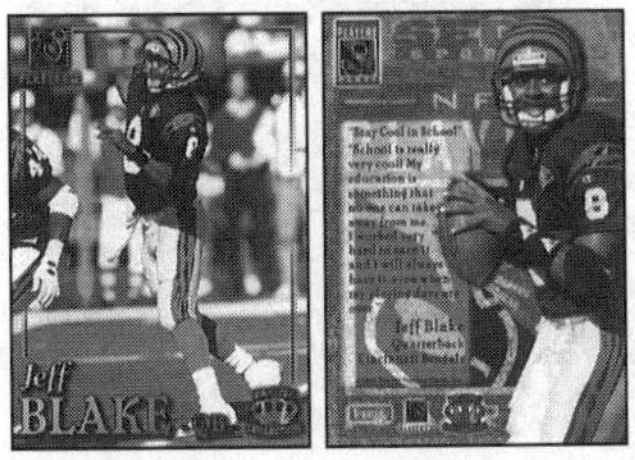

This 12-card set was given away at a NFLPA Super Bowl XXX player's party. Each card company produced a card for one or more of their brands and each card carries the Players, Inc. logo. The cards are unnumbered and checklisted below in alphabetical order.

	MINT	NRMT	EXC
COMPLETE SET (12)	15.00	6.75	1.85
COMMON CARD (1-12)	.75	.35	.09
☐ 1 Marcus Allen Ronnie Lott Collector's Edge	1.00	.45	.12
☐ 2 Steve Beuerlein Topps	.75	.35	.09
☐ 3 Jeff Blake Pacific	1.50	.70	.19
☐ 4 Tim Brown Action Packed	1.00	.45	.12
☐ 5 Kerry Collins Classic	2.50	1.10	.30
☐ 6 Kevin Greene Playoff	.75	.35	.09
☐ 7 Garrison Hearst Fleer Metal	1.00	.45	.12
☐ 8 Daryl Johnston SkyBox Impact	.75	.35	.09
☐ 9 Joe Montana Upper Deck	3.00	1.35	.35
☐ 10 Deion Sanders Donruss Red Zone	1.50	.70	.19
☐ 11 Herschel Walker Pinnacle	1.00	.45	.12
☐ 12 Logo Card Checklist back	.75	.35	.09

1997 NFLPA Super Bowl Player's Party

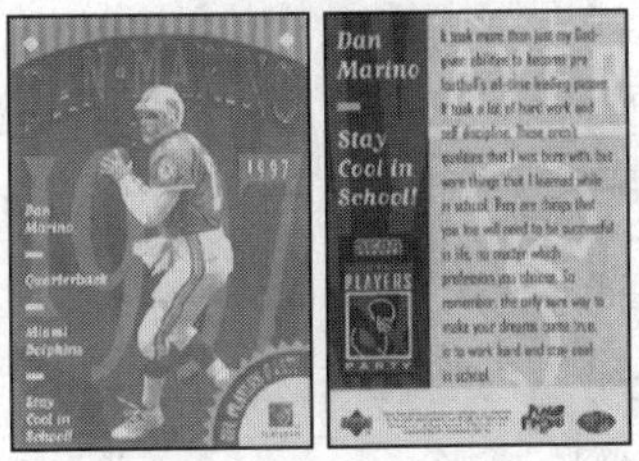

This 11-card set was distributed at the NFL Player's Association Super Bowl player's party in New Orleans. Each card company produced one or two cards for the set with each carrying the Player's Party logo. The cards are unnumbered and checklisted below in alphabetical order.

	MINT	NRMT	EXC
COMPLETE SET (11)	12.00	5.50	1.50
COMMON CARD (1-11)	.75	.35	.09
☐ 1 Morten Andersen SkyBox	.75	.35	.09
☐ 2 Steve Bono Collector's Edge	.75	.35	.09
☐ 3 Robert Brooks Pacific	1.25	.55	.16
☐ 4 Tony Dorsett Topps	1.50	.70	.19
☐ 5 Gus Frerotte Donruss	1.00	.45	.12
☐ 6 Kevin Hardy Pinnacle	.75	.35	.09
☐ 7 Tyrone Hughes Score Board	.75	.35	.09
☐ 8 Dan Marino Upper Deck	3.00	1.35	.35
☐ 9 Curtis Martin SkyBox	2.00	.90	.25
☐ 10 Deion Sanders Playoff	1.50	.70	.19
☐ 11 Checklist Card Upper Deck	.75	.35	.09

1961 Oilers Jay Publishing

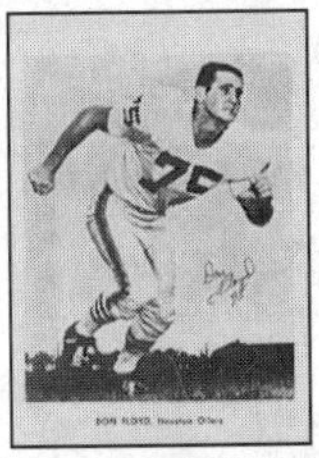

This 24-card set features (approximately) 5" by 7" black-and-white player photos. The photos show players in traditional poses with the quarterback preparing to throw, the runner heading downfield, and the defenseman ready for the tackle. These cards were packaged 12 to a packet and originally sold for 25 cents. The backs are blank. The cards are unnumbered and checklisted below in alphabetical order.

	NRMT	VG-E	GOOD
COMPLETE SET (24)	140.00	65.00	17.50
COMMON CARD (1-24)	5.00	2.20	.60
☐ 1 Dalva Allen	5.00	2.20	.60
☐ 2 Tony Banfield	5.00	2.20	.60
☐ 3 George Blanda	20.00	9.00	2.50
☐ 4 Billy Cannon	10.00	4.50	1.25
☐ 5 Doug Cline	5.00	2.20	.60
☐ 6 Willard Dewveall	5.00	2.20	.60
☐ 7 Mike Dukes	5.00	2.20	.60
☐ 8 Don Floyd	6.00	2.70	.75
☐ 9 Freddy Glick	6.00	2.70	.75
☐ 10 Bill Groman	6.00	2.70	.75
☐ 11 Charlie Hennigan	8.00	3.60	1.00
☐ 12 Ed Husmann	5.00	2.20	.60
☐ 13 Al Jamison	5.00	2.20	.60
☐ 14 Mark Johnston	5.00	2.20	.60
☐ 15 Jacky Lee	6.00	2.70	.75
☐ 16 Bob McLeod	5.00	2.20	.60
☐ 17 Rich Michael	5.00	2.20	.60
☐ 18 Dennit Morris	5.00	2.20	.60
☐ 19 Jim Norton	6.00	2.70	.75
☐ 20 Bob Schmidt	5.00	2.20	.60
☐ 21 Dave Smith	5.00	2.20	.60
☐ 22 Bob Talamini	6.00	2.70	.75
☐ 23 Charley Tolar	6.00	2.70	.75
☐ 24 Hogan Wharton	5.00	2.20	.60

1964-65 Oilers Color Team Issue

This team-issued set of 16 player photos measures approximately 7 3/4" by 9 3/4" and features color posed shots of players in uniform.

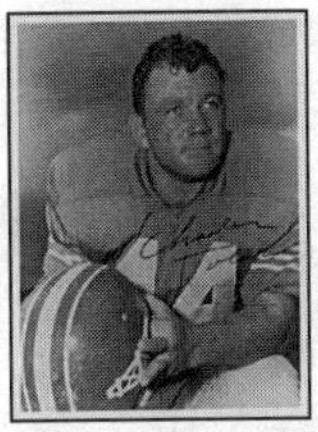

Eight photos were grouped together as a set and packaged in plastic bags; set 1 and 2 each originally sold for 50 cents. The year 1964 was Scott Appleton, Ode Burrell, and Don Trull's first year with the Oilers. The photos are printed on thin paper stock, and white borders frame each picture. A facsimile autograph is inscribed across the pictures in black ink. The backs are blank. The photos are unnumbered and checklisted below in alphabetical order.

	NRMT	VG-E	GOOD
COMPLETE SET (16)	100.00	45.00	12.50
COMMON CARD (1-16)	5.00	2.20	.60
☐ 1 Scott Appleton	6.00	2.70	.75
☐ 2 Tony Banfield	6.00	2.70	.75
☐ 3 Sonny Bishop	6.00	2.70	.75
☐ 4 George Blanda	20.00	9.00	2.50
☐ 5 Sid Blanks	6.00	2.70	.75
☐ 6 Danny Brabham	5.00	2.20	.60
☐ 7 Ode Burrell	6.00	2.70	.75
☐ 8 Doug Cline	5.00	2.20	.60
☐ 9 Don Floyd	6.00	2.70	.75
☐ 10 Freddy Glick	6.00	2.70	.75
☐ 11 Charlie Hennigan	10.00	4.50	1.25
☐ 12 Ed Husmann	5.00	2.20	.60
☐ 13 Walt Suggs	6.00	2.70	.75
☐ 14 Bob Talamini	5.00	2.20	.60
☐ 15 Charley Tolar	6.00	2.70	.75
☐ 16 Don Trull	6.00	2.70	.75

1967 Oilers Team Issue

This 14-card set of the Houston Oilers measures approximately 5 1/8" by 7" and features black-and-white player photos. The backs are blank. The cards are unnumbered and checklisted below in alphabetical order.

	NRMT	VG-E	GOOD
COMPLETE SET (14)	60.00	27.00	7.50
COMMON CARD (1-14)	5.00	2.20	.60
☐ 1 Pete Barnes	5.00	2.20	.60
☐ 2 Sonny Bishop	6.00	2.70	.75
☐ 3 Ode Burrell	6.00	2.70	.75
☐ 4 Ronnie Caveness	5.00	2.20	.60
☐ 5 Joe Childress CO	5.00	2.20	.60
☐ 6 Glen Ray Hines	6.00	2.70	.75
☐ 7 Pat Holmes	5.00	2.20	.60
☐ 8 Bobby Jancik	6.00	2.70	.75
☐ 9 Pete Johns	5.00	2.20	.60
☐ 10 Jim Norton	6.00	2.70	.75
☐ 11 Willie Parker	5.00	2.20	.60
☐ 12 Bob Poole	5.00	2.20	.60
☐ 13 Alvin Reed	5.00	2.20	.60
☐ 14 Olen Underwood	5.00	2.20	.60

1968 Oilers Team Issue

These approximately 8" by 10" black-and-white photos have white borders. Most of the photos feature posed action shots. The player's name, position (initials), and team name are printed in the bottom white border in upper and lower case letters. The backs are blank and the photos are unnumbered and checklisted below in alphabetical order.

	NRMT-MT	EXC	G-VG
COMPLETE SET (3)	10.00	4.50	1.25
COMMON CARD (1-3)	3.00	1.35	.35
☐ 1 Jim Beirne position "SE"	4.00	1.80	.50
☐ 2 Jim LeMoine	3.00	1.35	.35
☐ 3 Wayne Walker	4.00	1.80	.50

1969 Oilers Team Issue

These approximately 8" by 10" black-and-white photos have white borders. Most of the photos feature posed action shots. The player's name, position (initials), and team name are printed in the bottom white border in all caps. The backs are blank and the photos are unnumbered and checklisted below in alphabetical order.

	NRMT-MT	EXC	G-VG
COMPLETE SET (33)	125.00	55.00	15.50
COMMON CARD (1-33)	4.00	1.80	.50
☐ 1 Jim Beirne position "WR"	5.00	2.20	.60
☐ 3 Elvin Bethea	6.00	2.70	.75
☐ 4 Sonny Bishop	5.00	2.20	.60
☐ 5 Garland Boyette	5.00	2.20	.60
☐ 6 Ode Burrell	5.00	2.20	.60
☐ 7 Ed Carrington	4.00	1.80	.50
☐ 8 Joe Childress CO	4.00	1.80	.50
☐ 9 Bob Davis	4.00	1.80	.50
☐ 10 Hugh Devore CO	4.00	1.80	.50
☐ 11 Tom Domres	4.00	1.80	.50
☐ 12 F.A. Dry CO	4.00	1.80	.50
☐ 13 Miller Farr	5.00	2.20	.60
☐ 14 Mac Haik (Action shot)	4.00	1.80	.50
☐ 15 Mac Haik (Portrait)	4.00	1.80	.50
☐ 16 W.K. Hicks	4.00	1.80	.50
☐ 17 Glen Ray Hines	5.00	2.20	.60
☐ 18 Pat Holmes	4.00	1.80	.50
☐ 19 Roy Hopkins	4.00	1.80	.50
☐ 22 Bobby Maples	5.00	2.20	.60
☐ 23 Richard Marshall	4.00	1.80	.50
☐ 24 Zeke Moore	5.00	2.20	.60
☐ 25 Willie Parker	4.00	1.80	.50
☐ 26 Johnny Peacock	4.00	1.80	.50
☐ 29 Ron Pritchard (Preparing to fend off blocker)	4.00	1.80	.50
☐ 30 Tom Regner	4.00	1.80	.50
☐ 31 George Rice	4.00	1.80	.50
☐ 32 George Rice	4.00	1.80	.50
☐ 33 Bob Robertson	4.00	1.80	.50
☐ 34 Walt Suggs	4.00	1.80	.50
☐ 35 Don Trull	5.00	2.20	.60
☐ 36 Olen Underwood	4.00	1.80	.50
☐ 37 Loyd Wainscott	4.00	1.80	.50
☐ 39 Glenn Woods	4.00	1.80	.50

1971 Oilers Team Issue

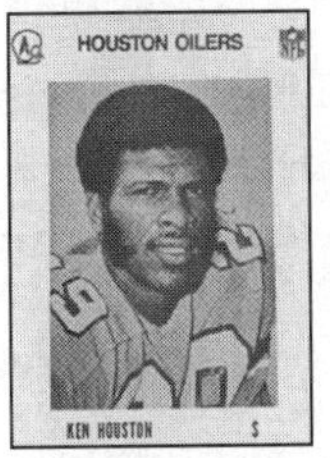

This 23-card set measures approximately 4" by 5 1/2" and features black-and-white, close-up, player photos, bordered in white and printed on a textured paper stock. The team name appears at the top between an Oilers helmet and the NFL logo, while the player's name and position are printed in the bottom border. The cards are unnumbered and checklisted below in alphabetical order. The set's date is defined by the fact that Willie Alexander, Ron Billingsley, Ken Burrough, Lynn Dickey, Robert Holmes, Dan Pastorini, Floyd Rice, Mike Tilleman's first year with the Houston Oilers was 1971, and Charlie Johnson's last year with the Oilers was 1971.

	NRMT-MT	EXC	G-VG
COMPLETE SET (23)	75.00	34.00	9.50
COMMON CARD (1-23)	2.00	.90	.25
☐ 1 Willie Alexander	2.50	1.10	.30
☐ 2 Jim Beirne	2.50	1.10	.30
☐ 3 Elvin Bethea	3.00	1.35	.35
☐ 4 Ron Billingsley	2.00	.90	.25
☐ 5 Garland Boyette	2.50	1.10	.30
☐ 6 Leo Brooks	2.00	.90	.25
☐ 7 Ken Burrough	4.00	1.80	.50
☐ 8 Woody Campbell	2.00	.90	.25
☐ 9 Lynn Dickey	4.00	1.80	.50
☐ 10 Elbert Drungo	2.00	.90	.25
☐ 11 Pat Holmes	2.00	.90	.25
☐ 12 Robert Holmes	2.50	1.10	.30
☐ 13 Ken Houston	12.00	5.50	1.50
☐ 14 Charlie Johnson	4.00	1.80	.50
☐ 15 Charlie Joiner	15.00	6.75	1.85
☐ 16 Zeke Moore	2.50	1.10	.30
☐ 17 Mark Moseley	4.00	1.80	.50
☐ 18 Dan Pastorini	5.00	2.20	.60
☐ 19 Alvin Reed	2.00	.90	.25
☐ 20 Tom Regner	2.00	.90	.25
☐ 21 Floyd Rice	2.00	.90	.25
☐ 22 Mike Tilleman	2.00	.90	.25
☐ 23 George Webster	3.00	1.35	.35

1972 Oilers Team Issue

This 11-card set of the Houston Oilers measures approximately 5" by 7" and features borderless black-and-white player photos. The backs are blank. The cards are unnumbered and checklisted below in alphabetical order.

	NRMT-MT	EXC	G-VG
COMPLETE SET (11)	20.00	9.00	2.50
COMMON CARD	2.00	.90	.25
☐ 1 Ron Billingsley	2.00	.90	.25
☐ 2 Garland Boyette	2.50	1.10	.30
☐ 3 Levert Carr	2.00	.90	.25
☐ 4 Walter Highsmith	2.00	.90	.25
☐ 5 Albert Johnson	2.00	.90	.25
☐ 6 Benny Johnson	2.00	.90	.25
☐ 7 Guy Murdock	2.00	.90	.25
☐ 8 Ron Saul	2.50	1.10	.30
☐ 9 Mike Tilleman	2.00	.90	.25

☐ 10 Ward Walsh	2.00	.90	.25
☐ 11 George Webster	3.00	1.35	.35

1973 Oilers McDonald's

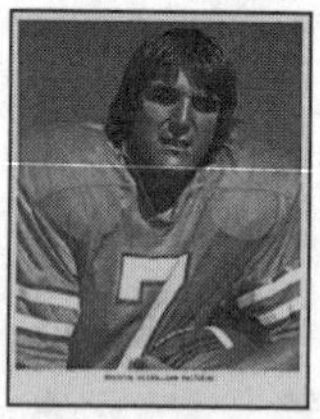

This set of three photos was sponsored by McDonald's. Each photo measures approximately 8" by 10" and features a posed color close-up photo bordered in white. The player's name and team name are printed in black in the bottom white border. The top portion of the back has biographical information, career summary, and career statistics. The bottom portion carries the Oilers 1973 game schedule. The photos are unnumbered and are checklisted below alphabetically.

	NRMT-MT	EXC	G-VG
COMPLETE SET (3)	25.00	11.00	3.10
COMMON CARD (1-3)	7.50	3.40	.95
☐ 1 John Matuszak	15.00	6.75	1.85
☐ 2 Zeke Moore	7.50	3.40	.95
☐ 3 Dan Pastorini	15.00	6.75	1.85

1973 Oilers Team Issue

This 17-card set of the Houston Oilers measures approximately 5" by 8" and features black-and-white player photos with a white border. The backs are blank. The cards are unnumbered and checklisted below in alphabetical order.

	NRMT-MT	EXC	G-VG
COMPLETE SET (17)	35.00	16.00	4.40
COMMON CARD (1-17)	2.00	.90	.25
☐ 1 Mack Alston	2.00	.90	.25
☐ 2 Bob Atkins	2.00	.90	.25
☐ 3 Skip Butler	2.00	.90	.25
☐ 4 Al Cowlings	2.50	1.10	.30
☐ 5 Lynn Dickey	3.50	1.55	.45
☐ 6 Mike Fanucci	2.00	.90	.25
☐ 7 Edd Hargett	2.50	1.10	.30
☐ 8 Lewis Jolley	2.00	.90	.25
☐ 9 Clifton McNeil	2.50	1.10	.30
☐ 10 Ralph Miller	2.00	.90	.25
☐ 11 Zeke Moore	2.50	1.10	.30
☐ 12 Dave Parks	2.50	1.10	.30
☐ 13 Willie Rodgers	2.00	.90	.25
☐ 14 Greg Sampson	2.00	.90	.25
☐ 15 Finn Seemann	2.00	.90	.25
☐ 16 Jeff Severson	2.00	.90	.25
☐ 17 Fred Willis	2.50	1.10	.30

1980 Oilers Police

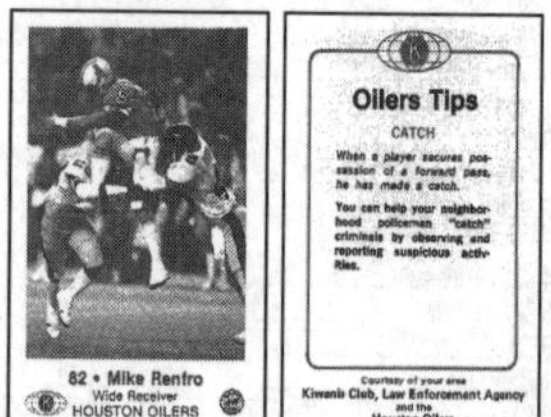

The 14-card set of the 1980 Houston Oilers is unnumbered and checklist below in alphabetical order. The cards measure approximately 2 5/8" by 4 1/8". The Kiwanis Club, the local law enforcement agency, and the Houston Oilers sponsored this set. The backs feature "Oilers Tips" and a Kiwanis logo. The fronts feature logos of the Kiwanis and the City of Houston.

	MINT	NRMT	EXC
COMPLETE SET (14)	15.00	6.75	1.85
COMMON CARD	.75	.35	.09
☐ 1 Gregg Bingham	1.00	.45	.12
☐ 2 Robert Brazile	.75	.35	.09
☐ 3 Ken Burrough	1.50	.70	.19
☐ 4 Rob Carpenter	1.00	.45	.12
☐ 5 Ronnie Coleman	1.00	.45	.12
☐ 6 Curley Culp	1.00	.45	.12
☐ 7 Carter Hartwig	.75	.35	.09
☐ 8 Billy Johnson	1.50	.70	.19
☐ 9 Carl Mauck	.75	.35	.09
☐ 10 Gifford Nielsen	1.00	.45	.12
☐ 11 Cliff Parsley	.75	.35	.09
☐ 12 Bum Phillips CO	1.00	.45	.12
☐ 13 Mike Renfro	1.00	.45	.12
☐ 14 Ken Stabler	5.00	2.20	.60

1984 Pacific Legends

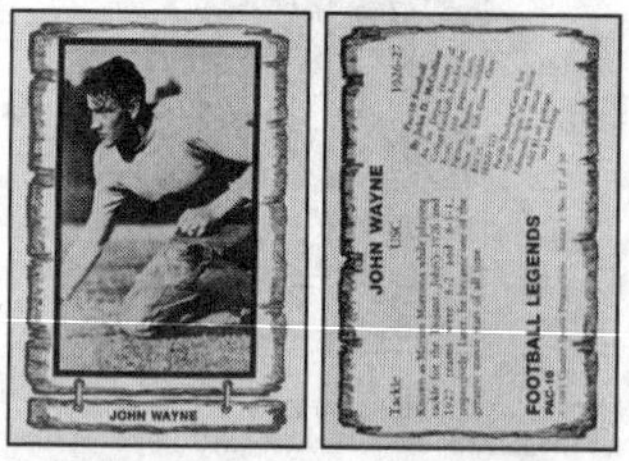

This 30-card set (produced by Pacific Trading Cards in 1984) has a yellowish tone to the front of the cards, similar to Cramer's Baseball Legends, but is entitled "Football Legends." The cards measure approximately 2 1/2" by 3 1/2". The set features prominent individuals who played football at universities in the Pac 10 conference (and its predecessors).

	MINT	NRMT	EXC
COMPLETE SET (30)	20.00	9.00	2.50
COMMON CARD (1-30)	.30	.14	.04
☐ 1 O.J. Simpson	4.00	1.80	.50
☐ 2 Mike Garrett	.50	.23	.06
☐ 3 Pop Warner	.50	.23	.06
☐ 4 Bob Schloredt	.30	.14	.04
☐ 5 Pat Haden	.60	.25	.07
☐ 6 Ernie Nevers	.50	.23	.06
☐ 7 Jackie Robinson	4.00	1.80	.50
☐ 8 Arnie Weinmeister	.50	.23	.06
☐ 9 Gary Beban	.50	.23	.06
☐ 10 Jim Plunkett	.60	.25	.07
☐ 11 Bobby Grayson	.30	.14	.04
☐ 12 Craig Morton	.50	.23	.06
☐ 13 Ben Davidson	.60	.25	.07
☐ 14 Jim Hardy	.30	.14	.04
☐ 15 Vern Burke	.30	.14	.04
☐ 16 Hugh McElhenny	.75	.35	.09
☐ 17 John Wayne	6.00	2.70	.75
☐ 18 Ricky Bell UER Name spelled Rickey on both sides	.50	.23	.06
☐ 19 George Wildcat Wilson	.30	.14	.04
☐ 20 Bob Waterfield	.75	.35	.09
☐ 21 Charlie Mitchell	.30	.14	.04
☐ 22 Donn Moomaw	.30	.14	.04
☐ 23 Don Heinrich	.30	.14	.04
☐ 24 Terry Baker	.50	.23	.06
☐ 25 Jack Thompson	.50	.23	.06
☐ 26 Charles White	.50	.23	.06
☐ 27 Frank Gifford	2.00	.90	.25
☐ 28 Lynn Swann	3.00	1.35	.35
☐ 29 Brick Muller	.30	.14	.04
☐ 30 Ron Yary	.50	.23	.06

1989 Pacific Steve Largent

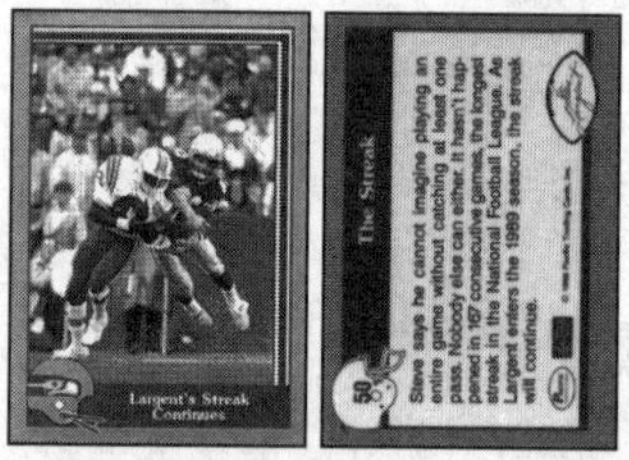

The 1989 Pacific Trading Cards Steve Largent set contains 110 standard-size cards, 85 of which are numbered. The numbered cards have silver borders on the fronts with photos of various career highlights; some are horizontally oriented, others are vertically oriented. The backs all are horizontally oriented and have light blue borders with information about the highlight shown on the front. The other 25 unnumbered cards are actually puzzle pieces which form a 12 1/2" by 17 1/2" poster of Largent in action. The cards were distributed as factory sets and in ten-card wax packs.

	MINT	NRMT	EXC
COMPLETE SET (110)	25.00	11.00	3.10
COMMON CARD (1-85)	.25	.11	.03
COMMON PUZZLE PIECE	.15	.07	.02
☐ 1 Title Card (checklist 1-42 on back)	.75	.35	.09
☐ 2 Santa, Can You Please	.25	.11	.03
☐ 3 Age 9	.25	.11	.03
☐ 4 Junior High 1968	.25	.11	.03
☐ 5 High School 1971	.25	.11	.03
☐ 6 Baseball or Football	.25	.11	.03
☐ 7 Tulsa, Senior Bowl	.25	.11	.03
☐ 8 Led Nation in TD's	.25	.11	.03
☐ 9 Coach Patera and Coach Jerry Rhome	.40	.18	.05
☐ 10 Rookie 1976	.75	.35	.09
☐ 11 First NFL TD	.25	.11	.03
☐ 12 Seahawks' First Win	.25	.11	.03
☐ 13 First Team All-Rookie	.40	.18	.05
☐ 14 Beats Buffalo 56-7	.25	.11	.03
☐ 15 The Huddle	.25	.11	.03
☐ 16 Captains Largent and Norm Evans	.40	.18	.05
☐ 17 First Win Against Raiders	.25	.11	.03
☐ 18 3000 Yards Receiving	.25	.11	.03
☐ 19 Jerry Rhome and Largent	.75	.35	.09
☐ 20 Great Hands	.25	.11	.03
☐ 21 Climbs Mt. Rainier	.25	.11	.03
☐ 22 Zorn Connection	.40	.18	.05
☐ 23 Steve Largent and Jim Zorn (in jeans)	.40	.18	.05
☐ 24 First Team All-AFC	.25	.11	.03
☐ 25 Seahawks MVP 1981	.40	.18	.05
☐ 26 Strike Season 1982	.25	.11	.03
☐ 27 Training Camp 1983	.25	.11	.03
☐ 28 Chuck Knox Head Coach	.40	.18	.05
☐ 29 50 Career TD's	.25	.11	.03
☐ 30 7000 Yards Receiving	.25	.11	.03
☐ 31 Tilley and Largent UER Two Greats From Tulsa (card back refers to Howard Twilley)	.75	.35	.09
☐ 32 Cold Day in Cincy	.25	.11	.03
☐ 33 Catches 3 TD Passes	.25	.11	.03
☐ 34 Seahawks 12-4 in 1984	.25	.11	.03
☐ 35 Defeated in AFC Championships	.25	.11	.03
☐ 36 Preparing for 1985 Season	.25	.11	.03
☐ 37 Career High 79 Catches	.25	.11	.03
☐ 38 Career High 1287 Yards	.25	.11	.03
☐ 39 10000 Yards Receiving	.25	.11	.03
☐ 40 Throws a Pass	.25	.11	.03
☐ 41 Game Day 1985	.25	.11	.03
☐ 42 Seattle Sports Star of the Year	.40	.18	.05
☐ 43 A Very Sore Elbow	.25	.11	.03
☐ 44 The Concentration	.25	.11	.03
☐ 45 Steve and Eugene Robinson	.40	.18	.05
☐ 46 Breaks Carmichael's Record	.25	.11	.03
☐ 47 Seahawks 37, Raiders 0	.25	.11	.03
☐ 48 11000 Yards Receiving	.25	.11	.03
☐ 49 Rough Game	.25	.11	.03
☐ 50 Streak Continues	.25	.11	.03
☐ 51 Captains Lane, Brown, and Largent	.40	.18	.05
☐ 52 Steve and Kyle Catch a Big One	.25	.11	.03
☐ 53 Krieg Connection	.40	.18	.05
☐ 54 Steve and Kyle at Seahawk Camp	.25	.11	.03
☐ 55 NFL All-Time Leading Receiver	.40	.18	.05
☐ 56 Hall of Fame Ball	.25	.11	.03
☐ 57 Steve and Coach Knox	.40	.18	.05
☐ 58 1987 Seahawks MVP	.40	.18	.05
☐ 59 Largent at Quarterback	.75	.35	.09
☐ 60 NFL All-Time Great	.40	.18	.05
☐ 61 Travelers' NFL Man of the Year 1988	.40	.18	.05
☐ 62 Steve and Terry Largent (exercising)	.25	.11	.03
☐ 63 Holding for Norm Johnson	.40	.18	.05
☐ 64 Great Moves	.25	.11	.03
☐ 65 Great Hands	.25	.11	.03
☐ 66 Seven-Time Pro Bowl Selection	.25	.11	.03
☐ 67 Agee, Largent, and Paul Skansi	.40	.18	.05
☐ 68 Signing for Fans	.25	.11	.03
☐ 69 Miller, Joe Nash, Largent, and Bryan Millard	.25	.11	.03
☐ 70 Pro Bowl Greats, Largent and John Elway	2.00	.90	.25
☐ 71 Hanging onto the Ball	.25	.11	.03
☐ 72 1618 Career Yards vs. Denver	.25	.11	.03
☐ 73 17 Pro Bowl Receptions	.25	.11	.03
☐ 74 Jim Zorn and Largent in Hawaii	.40	.18	.05
☐ 75 Mr. Seahawk	.40	.18	.05
☐ 76 Sets NFL Career Yardage Record	.40	.18	.05
☐ 77 Two of the Greatest (with Charlie Joiner)	.75	.35	.09
☐ 78 Steve Largent, Jerry Rhome, and Charlie Joiner	.75	.35	.09
☐ 79 NFL All-Time Leader in Receptions	.40	.18	.05
☐ 80 NFL All-Time Leader in Consecutive Game Receptions	.40	.18	.05
☐ 81 NFL All-Time Leader 12686 Receiving Yards	.25	.11	.03
☐ 82 NFL All-Time Leader 1000 Yard Seasons	.40	.18	.05
☐ 83 First Recipient of the Bart Starr Trophy	.75	.35	.09
☐ 84 Steve Largent, Wide Receiver	.40	.18	.05
☐ 85 Future Hall of Famer	1.00	.45	.12

1991 Pacific Prototypes

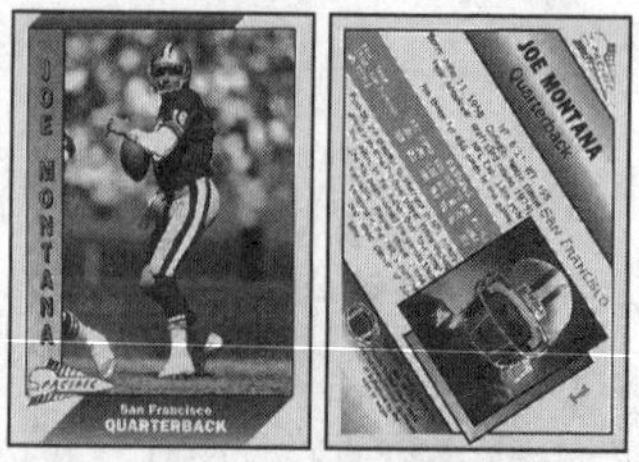

This five-card standard-size set was sent out by Pacific Trading Cards to prospective dealers prior to the general release of their debut set of NFL football cards. The cards are styled almost exactly like the regular issue Pacific cards that followed shortly thereafter. These prototype cards are distinguished from the regular issue cards by their different card numbers and the presence of zeroes for the stat totals on the prototype card backs. The cards are numbered on the back. The production run reportedly was approximately 5,000 sets, and these sets were distributed to dealers in the Pacific network with the rest being used as sales samples.

	MINT	NRMT	EXC
COMPLETE SET (5)	150.00	70.00	19.00
COMMON CARD (1-5)	15.00	6.75	1.85
☐ 1 Joe Montana (Different border from regular card)	60.00	27.00	7.50
☐ 32 Bo Jackson	15.00	6.75	1.85
☐ 66 Eric Metcalf	15.00	6.75	1.85
☐ 100 Barry Sanders (Different photo from regular card)	40.00	18.00	5.00
☐ 232 Troy Aikman	40.00	18.00	5.00

1991 Pacific

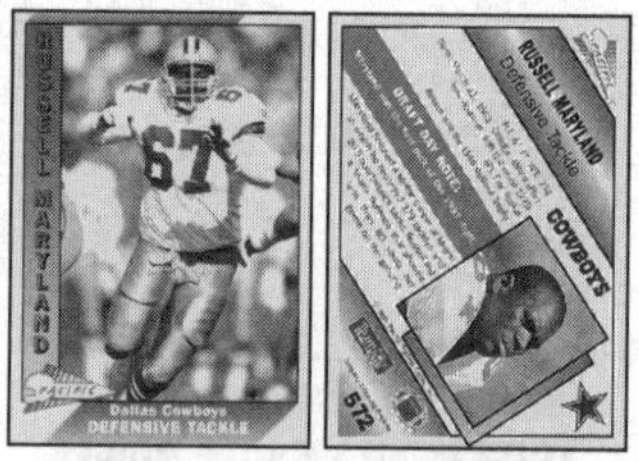

This 660-card standard size set was the first full football set issued by Pacific Trading Cards. The cards were issued in two series of 550 and 110 cards with packs containing 10 cards. Factory sets were also produced for each series. The cards feature a full-color glossy front with the name on the left hand side of the card. The left border of the card is in the same colors as the team's helmet. In the lower left hand corner of the card there is a Pacific pennant. The team identity and player's position is under the player's picture. The back of the card has an approximate 45 degree tilt to it and includes a full-color portrait of the player, complete biographical information, and interesting facts about the players. Rookie Cards include Mike Croel, Lawrence Dawsey, Craig Erickson (his only Rookie Card), Ricky Ervins, Brett Favre, Jeff Graham, Mark Higgs, Randal Hill, Michael Jackson, Herman Moore, Erric Pegram, Mike Pritchard, Leonard Russell and Harvey Williams.

	MINT	NRMT	EXC
COMPLETE SET (660)	15.00	6.75	1.85
COMPLETE SERIES 1 (550)	8.00	3.60	1.00
COMP.FACT.SERIES 1 (550)	8.00	3.60	1.00
COMPLETE SERIES 2 (110)	8.00	3.60	1.00
COMP.FACT.SERIES 2 (110)	8.00	3.60	1.00
COMMON CARD (1-660)	.05	.02	.01
COMP.CHECKLIST SET (5)	15.00	6.75	1.85
☐ 1 Deion Sanders	.60	.25	.07
☐ 2 Steve Broussard	.05	.02	.01
☐ 3 Aundray Bruce	.05	.02	.01
☐ 4 Rick Bryan	.05	.02	.01
☐ 5 John Rade	.05	.02	.01
☐ 6 Scott Case	.05	.02	.01
☐ 7 Tony Casillas	.05	.02	.01
☐ 8 Shawn Collins	.05	.02	.01
☐ 9 Darion Conner	.05	.02	.01
☐ 10 Tory Epps	.05	.02	.01
☐ 11 Bill Fralic	.05	.02	.01
☐ 12 Mike Gann	.05	.02	.01
☐ 13 Tim Green UER (Listed as DT should say DE)	.05	.02	.01
☐ 14 Chris Hinton	.05	.02	.01
☐ 15 Houston Hoover UER (Deion misspelled as Deon on card back)	.05	.02	.01
☐ 16 Chris Miller	.10	.05	.01
☐ 17 Andre Rison	.10	.05	.01
☐ 18 Mike Rozier	.05	.02	.01
☐ 19 Jessie Tuggle	.05	.02	.01
☐ 20 Don Beebe	.05	.02	.01
☐ 21 Ray Bentley	.05	.02	.01

☐ 22 Shane Conlan .05 .02 .01
☐ 23 Kent Hull .05 .02 .01
☐ 24 Mark Kelso .05 .02 .01
☐ 25 James Lofton UER .10 .05 .01
(Photo on front
actually Flip Johnson)
☐ 26 Scott Norwood .05 .02 .01
☐ 27 Andre Reed .10 .05 .01
☐ 28 Leonard Smith .05 .02 .01
☐ 29 Bruce Smith .25 .11 .03
☐ 30 Leon Seals .05 .02 .01
☐ 31 Darryl Talley .05 .02 .01
☐ 32 Steve Tasker .10 .05 .01
☐ 33 Thurman Thomas .25 .11 .03
☐ 34 James Williams .05 .02 .01
☐ 35 Will Wolford .05 .02 .01
☐ 36 Frank Reich .10 .05 .01
☐ 37 Jeff Wright .05 .02 .01
☐ 38 Neal Anderson .10 .05 .01
☐ 39 Trace Armstrong .05 .02 .01
☐ 40 Johnny Bailey UER .05 .02 .01
(Gained 5320 yards in
college, should be 6320)
☐ 41 Mark Bortz UER .05 .02 .01
(Johnny Bailey misspelled
as Johnny on cardback)
☐ 42 Cap Boso .05 .02 .01
☐ 43 Kevin Butler .05 .02 .01
☐ 44 Mark Carrier DB .10 .05 .01
☐ 45 Jim Covert .05 .02 .01
☐ 46 Wendell Davis .05 .02 .01
☐ 47 Richard Dent .10 .05 .01
☐ 48 Shaun Gayle .05 .02 .01
☐ 49 Jim Harbaugh .25 .11 .03
☐ 50 Jay Hilgenberg .05 .02 .01
☐ 51 Brad Muster .05 .02 .01
☐ 52 William Perry .10 .05 .01
☐ 53 Mike Singletary UER .10 .05 .01
(No College listed
should say Baylor)
☐ 54 Peter Tom Willis .05 .02 .01
☐ 55 Donnell Woolford .05 .02 .01
☐ 56 Steve McMichael .10 .05 .01
☐ 57 Eric Ball .05 .02 .01
☐ 58 Lewis Billups .05 .02 .01
☐ 59 Jim Breech .05 .02 .01
☐ 60 James Brooks .10 .05 .01
☐ 61 Eddie Brown .05 .02 .01
☐ 62 Rickey Dixon .05 .02 .01
☐ 63 Boomer Esiason .10 .05 .01
☐ 64 James Francis .05 .02 .01
☐ 65 David Fulcher .05 .02 .01
☐ 66 David Grant .05 .02 .01
☐ 67 Harold Green UER .05 .02 .01
(Misplaced apostrophe
in Gamecocks)
☐ 68 Rodney Holman .05 .02 .01
☐ 69 Stanford Jennings .05 .02 .01
☐ 70A Tim Krumrie ERR .10 .05 .01
(Misspelled Krumprie
on card front)
☐ 70B Tim Krumrie COR .10 .05 .01
☐ 71 Tim McGee .05 .02 .01
☐ 72 Anthony Munoz .10 .05 .01
☐ 73 Mitchell Price .05 .02 .01
☐ 74 Eric Thomas .05 .02 .01
☐ 75 Ickey Woods .05 .02 .01
☐ 76 Mike Baab .05 .02 .01
☐ 77 Thane Gash .05 .02 .01
☐ 78 David Grayson .05 .02 .01
☐ 79 Mike Johnson .05 .02 .01
☐ 80 Reggie Langhorne .05 .02 .01
☐ 81 Kevin Mack .05 .02 .01
☐ 82 Clay Matthews .10 .05 .01
☐ 83A Eric Metcalf ERR .10 .05 .01
("Terry is the son of Terry")
☐ 83B Eric Metcalf COR .10 .05 .01
("Eric is the son of Terry")
☐ 84 Frank Minnifield .05 .02 .01
☐ 85 Mike Oliphant .05 .02 .01
☐ 86 Mike Pagel .05 .02 .01
☐ 87 John Talley .05 .02 .01
☐ 88 Lawyer Tillman .05 .02 .01
☐ 89 Gregg Rakoczy UER .05 .02 .01
(Misspelled Greg on
both sides of card)
☐ 90 Bryan Wagner .05 .02 .01
☐ 91 Rob Burnett .05 .02 .01
☐ 92 Tommie Agee .05 .02 .01
☐ 93 Troy Aikman UER 1.00 .45 .12
(4328 yards is career
total not season; text
has him breaking passing
record which is not true)
☐ 94A Bill Bates ERR .10 .05 .01
(Black line on cardfront)
☐ 94B Bill Bates COR .10 .05 .01
(No black line
on cardfront)
☐ 95 Jack Del Rio .05 .02 .01
☐ 96 Issiac Holt UER .05 .02 .01
(Photo on back
actually Timmy Newsome)
☐ 97 Michael Irvin .25 .11 .03
☐ 98 Jim Jeffcoat UER .05 .02 .01
(On back, red line
has Jeff not Jim)
☐ 99 Jimmie Jones .05 .02 .01
☐ 100 Kelvin Martin .05 .02 .01
☐ 101 Nate Newton .10 .05 .01
☐ 102 Danny Noonan .05 .02 .01
☐ 103 Ken Norton Jr. .25 .11 .03
☐ 104 Jay Novacek .25 .11 .03
☐ 105 Mike Saxon .05 .02 .01
☐ 106 Derrick Shepard .05 .02 .01
☐ 107 Emmitt Smith 2.00 .90 .25
☐ 108 Daniel Stubbs .05 .02 .01
☐ 109 Tony Tolbert .05 .02 .01
☐ 110 Alexander Wright .05 .02 .01
☐ 111 Steve Atwater .05 .02 .01
☐ 112 Melvin Bratton .05 .02 .01
☐ 113 Tyrone Braxton UER .05 .02 .01
(Went to North Dakota
State, not South Dakota)
☐ 114 Alphonso Carreker .05 .02 .01
☐ 115 John Elway .75 .35 .09
☐ 116 Simon Fletcher .05 .02 .01
☐ 117 Bobby Humphrey .05 .02 .01
☐ 118 Mark Jackson .05 .02 .01
☐ 119 Vance Johnson .05 .02 .01
☐ 120 Greg Kragen UER .05 .02 .01
(Recovered 20 fumbles
in '89, yet 11 in career)
☐ 121 Karl Mecklenburg UER .05 .02 .01
(Misspelled Mecklenberg
on card front)
☐ 122A Orson Mobley ERR .50 .23 .06
(Misspelled Orsen)
☐ 122B Orson Mobley COR .10 .05 .01
☐ 123 Alton Montgomery .05 .02 .01
☐ 124 Ricky Nattiel .05 .02 .01
☐ 125 Steve Sewell .05 .02 .01
☐ 126 Shannon Sharpe .50 .23 .06
☐ 127 Dennis Smith .05 .02 .01
☐ 128A Andre Townsend ERR .50 .23 .06
(Misspelled Andie
on card front)
☐ 128B Andre Townsend COR .10 .05 .01
☐ 129 Mike Horan .05 .02 .01
☐ 130 Jerry Ball .05 .02 .01
☐ 131 Bennie Blades .05 .02 .01
☐ 132 Lomas Brown .05 .02 .01
☐ 133 Jeff Campbell UER .05 .02 .01
(No NFL totals line)
☐ 134 Robert Clark .05 .02 .01
☐ 135 Michael Cofer .05 .02 .01
☐ 136 Dennis Gibson .05 .02 .01
☐ 137 Mel Gray .10 .05 .01
☐ 138 LeRoy Irvin UER .05 .02 .01
(Misspelled LEROY;
spent 10 years with
Rams, not 11)
☐ 139 George Jamison .05 .02 .01
☐ 140 Richard Johnson .05 .02 .01
☐ 141 Eddie Murray .05 .02 .01
☐ 142 Dan Owens .05 .02 .01
☐ 143 Rodney Peete .10 .05 .01
☐ 144 Barry Sanders 1.00 .45 .12
☐ 145 Chris Spielman .10 .05 .01
☐ 146 Marc Spindler .05 .02 .01
☐ 147 Andre Ware .10 .05 .01
☐ 148 William White .05 .02 .01
☐ 149 Tony Bennett .10 .05 .01
☐ 150 Robert Brown .05 .02 .01
☐ 151 LeRoy Butler .10 .05 .01
☐ 152 Anthony Dilweg .05 .02 .01
☐ 153 Michael Haddix .05 .02 .01
☐ 154 Ron Hallstrom .05 .02 .01
☐ 155 Tim Harris .05 .02 .01
☐ 156 Johnny Holland .05 .02 .01
☐ 157 Chris Jacke .05 .02 .01
☐ 158 Perry Kemp .05 .02 .01
☐ 159 Mark Lee .05 .02 .01
☐ 160 Don Majkowski .05 .02 .01
☐ 161 Tony Mandarich UER .05 .02 .01
(United Stated on back)
☐ 162 Mark Murphy .05 .02 .01
☐ 163 Brian Noble .05 .02 .01
☐ 164 Shawn Patterson .05 .02 .01
☐ 165 Jeff Query .05 .02 .01
☐ 166 Sterling Sharpe .25 .11 .03
☐ 167 Darrell Thompson .05 .02 .01
☐ 168 Ed West .05 .02 .01
☐ 169 Ray Childress UER .05 .02 .01
(Front DE, back DT)
☐ 170A Cris Dishman ERR .10 .05 .01
(Misspelled Chris
on both sides)
☐ 170B Cris Dishman COR/ERR .10 .05 .01
(Misspelled Chris
on back only)
☐ 170C Cris Dishman COR .10 .05 .01
☐ 171 Curtis Duncan .05 .02 .01
☐ 172 William Fuller .10 .05 .01
☐ 173 Ernest Givins UER .10 .05 .01
(Missing a highlight
line on back)
☐ 174 Drew Hill .05 .02 .01
☐ 175A Haywood Jeffires ERR .25 .11 .03
(Misspelled Jeffries
on both sides of card)
☐ 175B Haywood Jeffires COR .25 .11 .03
☐ 176 Sean Jones .10 .05 .01
☐ 177 Lamar Lathon .05 .02 .01
☐ 178 Bruce Matthews .10 .05 .01
☐ 179 Bubba McDowell .05 .02 .01
☐ 180 Johnny Meads .05 .02 .01
☐ 181 Warren Moon UER .25 .11 .03
(Birth listed as '65,
should be '56)
☐ 182 Mike Munchak .05 .02 .01
☐ 183 Allen Pinkett .05 .02 .01
☐ 184 Dean Steinkuhler UER .05 .02 .01
(Oakland, should
be Outland)
☐ 185 Lorenzo White UER .05 .02 .01
(Rout misspelled as
route on card back)
☐ 186A John Grimsley ERR .10 .05 .01
(Misspelled Grimsby)
☐ 186B John Grimsley COR .10 .05 .01
☐ 187 Pat Beach .05 .02 .01
☐ 188 Albert Bentley .05 .02 .01
☐ 189 Dean Biasucci .05 .02 .01
☐ 190 Duane Bickett .05 .02 .01
☐ 191 Bill Brooks .05 .02 .01
☐ 192 Eugene Daniel .05 .02 .01
☐ 193 Jeff George .25 .11 .03
☐ 194 Jon Hand .05 .02 .01
☐ 195 Jeff Herrod .05 .02 .01
☐ 196A Jessie Hester ERR .30 .14 .04
(Misspelled Jesse)
☐ 196B Jessie Hester ERR .10 .05 .01
(Name corrected;
6-year player, not 7;
no NFL total line)
☐ 197 Mike Prior .05 .02 .01
☐ 198 Stacey Simmons .05 .02 .01
☐ 199 Rohn Stark .05 .02 .01
☐ 200 Pat Tomberlin .05 .02 .01
☐ 201 Clarence Verdin .05 .02 .01
☐ 202 Keith Taylor .05 .02 .01
☐ 203 Jack Trudeau .05 .02 .01
☐ 204 Chip Banks .05 .02 .01
☐ 205 John Alt .05 .02 .01
☐ 206 Deron Cherry .05 .02 .01
☐ 207 Steve DeBerg .05 .02 .01
☐ 208 Tim Grunhard .05 .02 .01
☐ 209 Albert Lewis .05 .02 .01
☐ 210 Nick Lowery UER .05 .02 .01
(12 years NFL exp.,
should be 13)
☐ 211 Bill Maas .05 .02 .01
☐ 212 Chris Martin .05 .02 .01
☐ 213 Todd McNair .05 .02 .01
☐ 214 Christian Okoye .05 .02 .01
☐ 215 Stephone Paige .05 .02 .01
☐ 216 Steve Pelluer .05 .02 .01
☐ 217 Kevin Porter .05 .02 .01
☐ 218 Kevin Ross .05 .02 .01
☐ 219 Dan Saleaumua .05 .02 .01
☐ 220 Neil Smith .25 .11 .03
☐ 221 David Szott UER .05 .02 .01
(Listed as Off. Guard)
☐ 222 Derrick Thomas .25 .11 .03
☐ 223 Barry Word .05 .02 .01
☐ 224 Percy Snow .05 .02 .01
☐ 225 Marcus Allen .25 .11 .03
☐ 226 Eddie Anderson UER .05 .02 .01
(Began career with
Seahawks, not Raiders)
☐ 227 Steve Beuerlein UER .10 .05 .01
(Not injured during '90
season, but was inactive)
☐ 228A Tim Brown ERR .25 .11 .03
(No position on card)
☐ 228B Tim Brown COR .25 .11 .03
☐ 229 Scott Davis .05 .02 .01
☐ 230 Mike Dyal .05 .02 .01
☐ 231 Mervyn Fernandez UER .05 .02 .01
(Card says free agent
in '87, but was
drafted in '83)
☐ 232 Willie Gault UER .05 .02 .01
(Text says 60 catches
in '90, stats say 50)
☐ 233 Ethan Horton UER .05 .02 .01
(No height and
weight listings)
☐ 234 Bo Jackson UER .25 .11 .03
(Drafted in '87, not '86)
☐ 235 Howie Long .10 .05 .01
☐ 236 Terry McDaniel .05 .02 .01
☐ 237 Max Montoya .05 .02 .01
☐ 238 Don Mosebar .05 .02 .01
☐ 239 Jay Schroeder .05 .02 .01
☐ 240 Steve Smith .05 .02 .01
☐ 241 Greg Townsend .05 .02 .01
☐ 242 Aaron Wallace .05 .02 .01
☐ 243 Lionel Washington .05 .02 .01
☐ 244A Steve Wisniewski ERR .10 .05 .01
(Misspelled Winsnlewski
on both sides;
Drafted, should say
traded to)
☐ 244B Steve Wisniewski ERR 1.00 .45 .12
(Misspelled Winsniewski
on card back)
☐ 244C Steve Wisniewski COR .10 .05 .01
☐ 245 Flipper Anderson .05 .02 .01
☐ 246 Latin Berry .05 .02 .01
☐ 247 Robert Delpino .05 .02 .01
☐ 248 Marcus Dupree .05 .02 .01
☐ 249 Henry Ellard .10 .05 .01
☐ 250 Jim Everett .10 .05 .01
☐ 251 Cleveland Gary .05 .02 .01
☐ 252 Jerry Gray .05 .02 .01
☐ 253 Kevin Greene .25 .11 .03
☐ 254 Pete Holohan UER .05 .02 .01
(Photo on back
actually Kevin Greene)
☐ 255 Buford McGee .05 .02 .01
☐ 256 Tom Newberry .05 .02 .01
☐ 257A Irv Pankey ERR .10 .05 .01
(Misspelled as Panky
on both sides of card)
☐ 257B Irv Pankey COR .10 .05 .01
☐ 258 Jackie Slater .05 .02 .01
☐ 259 Doug Smith .05 .02 .01
☐ 260 Frank Stams .05 .02 .01
☐ 261 Michael Stewart .05 .02 .01
☐ 262 Fred Strickland .05 .02 .01
☐ 263 J.B. Brown UER .05 .02 .01
(No periods after
initials on card front)
☐ 264 Mark Clayton .10 .05 .01
☐ 265 Jeff Cross .05 .02 .01
☐ 266 Mark Dennis .05 .02 .01
☐ 267 Mark Duper .10 .05 .01
☐ 268 Ferrell Edmunds .05 .02 .01
☐ 269 Dan Marino 1.50 .70 .19
☐ 270 John Offerdahl .05 .02 .01
☐ 271 Louis Oliver .05 .02 .01
☐ 272 Tony Paige .05 .02 .01
☐ 273 Reggie Roby .05 .02 .01
☐ 274 Sammie Smith .05 .02 .01
(Picture is sideways
on the card)
☐ 275 Keith Sims .05 .02 .01
☐ 276 Brian Sochia .05 .02 .01
☐ 277 Pete Stoyanovich .05 .02 .01
☐ 278 Richmond Webb .05 .02 .01
☐ 279 Jarvis Williams .05 .02 .01
☐ 280 Tim McKyer .05 .02 .01
☐ 281A Jim C. Jensen ERR .10 .05 .01
(Misspelled Jenson
on card back)
☐ 281B Jim C. Jensen COR .10 .05 .01
(Plays a skill position,
not skilled)
☐ 282 Scott Secules .05 .02 .01
☐ 283 Ray Berry .05 .02 .01
☐ 284 Joey Browner UER .05 .02 .01
(Safetys, sic)
☐ 285 Anthony Carter .10 .05 .01
☐ 286A Cris Carter ERR .25 .11 .03
(Misspelled Chris
on both sides)
☐ 286B Cris Carter ERR/COR 1.50 .70 .19
(Misspelled Chris
on card back)
☐ 286C Cris Carter COR .25 .11 .03
☐ 287 Chris Doleman .05 .02 .01
☐ 288 Mark Dusbabek UER .05 .02 .01
(Front DT, back LB)
☐ 289 Hassan Jones .05 .02 .01
☐ 290 Steve Jordan .05 .02 .01
☐ 291 Carl Lee .05 .02 .01
☐ 292 Kirk Lowdermilk .05 .02 .01
☐ 293 Randall McDaniel .05 .02 .01
☐ 294 Mike Merriweather .05 .02 .01
☐ 295A Keith Millard UER .10 .05 .01
(No position on card)
☐ 295B Keith Millard COR .10 .05 .01
☐ 296 Al Noga UER .05 .02 .01
(Card says DT,
should say DE)
☐ 297 Scott Studwell UER .05 .02 .01
(83 career tackles,
but bio says 156
tackles in '81 season)
☐ 298 Henry Thomas .05 .02 .01
☐ 299 Herschel Walker .10 .05 .01
☐ 300 Gary Zimmerman .05 .02 .01
☐ 301 Rick Gannon .05 .02 .01
☐ 302 Wade Wilson UER .10 .05 .01
(Led AFC, should
say led NFC)
☐ 303 Vincent Brown .05 .02 .01
☐ 304 Marv Cook .05 .02 .01
☐ 305 Hart Lee Dykes .05 .02 .01
☐ 306 Irving Fryar .10 .05 .01
☐ 307 Tommy Hodson UER .05 .02 .01
(No NFL totals line)
☐ 308 Maurice Hurst .05 .02 .01
☐ 309 Ronnie Lippett UER .05 .02 .01
(On back,reserves
should be reserve)
☐ 310 Fred Marion .05 .02 .01
☐ 311 Greg McMurtry .05 .02 .01
☐ 312 Johnny Rembert .05 .02 .01
☐ 313 Chris Singleton .05 .02 .01

☐ 314 Ed Reynolds	.05	.02	.01
☐ 315 Andre Tippett	.05	.02	.01
☐ 316 Garin Veris	.05	.02	.01
☐ 317 Brent Williams	.05	.02	.01
☐ 318A John Stephens ERR (Misspelled Stevens on both sides of card)	.10	.05	.01
☐ 318B John Stephens COR/ERR (Misspelled Stevens on card back)	1.00	.45	.12
☐ 318C John Stephens COR	.10	.05	.01
☐ 319 Sammy Martin	.05	.02	.01
☐ 320 Bruce Armstrong	.05	.02	.01
☐ 321A Morten Andersen ERR (Misspelled Anderson on both sides of card)	.30	.14	.04
☐ 321B Morten Andersen ERR/COR (Misspelled Anderson on card back)	1.00	.45	.12
☐ 321C Morten Andersen COR	.10	.05	.01
☐ 322 Gene Atkins UER (No NFL Exp. line)	.05	.02	.01
☐ 323 Vince Buck	.05	.02	.01
☐ 324 John Fourcade	.05	.02	.01
☐ 325 Kevin Haverdink	.05	.02	.01
☐ 326 Bobby Hebert	.05	.02	.01
☐ 327 Craig Heyward	.10	.05	.01
☐ 328 Dalton Hilliard	.05	.02	.01
☐ 329 Rickey Jackson	.05	.02	.01
☐ 330A Vaughan Johnson ERR (Misspelled Vaughn)	.10	.05	.01
☐ 330B Vaughan Johnson COR	.10	.05	.01
☐ 331 Eric Martin	.05	.02	.01
☐ 332 Wayne Martin	.05	.02	.01
☐ 333 Rueben Mayes UER (Misspelled Reuben on card back)	.05	.02	.01
☐ 334 Sam Mills	.05	.02	.01
☐ 335 Brett Perriman	.25	.11	.03
☐ 336 Pat Swilling	.10	.05	.01
☐ 337 Renaldo Turnbull	.05	.02	.01
☐ 338 Lonzell Hill	.05	.02	.01
☐ 339 Steve Walsh UER (19 of 20 for 70.3, should be 95 percent)	.05	.02	.01
☐ 340 Carl Banks UER (Led defensive in tackles should say defense)	.05	.02	.01
☐ 341 Mark Bavaro UER (Weight on back 145, should say 245)	.05	.02	.01
☐ 342 Maurice Carthon	.05	.02	.01
☐ 343 Pat Harlow	.05	.02	.01
☐ 344 Eric Dorsey	.05	.02	.01
☐ 345 John Elliott	.05	.02	.01
☐ 346 Rodney Hampton	.25	.11	.03
☐ 347 Jeff Hostetler	.10	.05	.01
☐ 348 Erik Howard UER (Listed as DT, should be NT)	.05	.02	.01
☐ 349 Pepper Johnson	.05	.02	.01
☐ 350A Sean Landeta ERR (Misspelled Landetta on both sides of card)	.10	.05	.01
☐ 350B Sean Landeta COR	.50	.23	.06
☐ 351 Leonard Marshall	.05	.02	.01
☐ 352 Dave Meggett	.10	.05	.01
☐ 353A Bart Oates ERR (Misspelled Oats on both sides; misspelled Megget in Did You Know)	.10	.05	.01
☐ 353B Bart Oates COR/ERR (Misspelled Oats on card back; misspelled Megget in Did You Know)	1.00	.45	.12
☐ 353C Bart Oates COR (Dave Meggett still misspelled as Megget)	.10	.05	.01
☐ 354 Gary Reasons	.05	.02	.01
☐ 355 Phil Simms	.10	.05	.01
☐ 356 Lawrence Taylor	.25	.11	.03
☐ 357 Reyna Thompson	.05	.02	.01
☐ 358 Brian Williams UER (Front C-G, back G)	.05	.02	.01
☐ 359 Matt Bahr	.05	.02	.01
☐ 360 Mark Ingram	.10	.05	.01
☐ 361 Brad Baxter	.05	.02	.01
☐ 362 Mark Boyer	.05	.02	.01
☐ 363 Dennis Byrd	.05	.02	.01
☐ 364 Dave Cadigan UER (Terance misspelled as Terrance on back)	.05	.02	.01
☐ 365 Kyle Clifton	.05	.02	.01
☐ 366 James Hasty	.05	.02	.01
☐ 367 Joe Kelly UER (Front 50, back 58)	.05	.02	.01
☐ 368 Jeff Lageman	.05	.02	.01
☐ 369 Pat Leahy UER (Career-best FG in '65, should say '85)	.05	.02	.01
☐ 370 Terance Mathis	.10	.05	.01
☐ 371 Erik McMillan	.05	.02	.01
☐ 372 Rob Moore	.25	.11	.03
☐ 373 Ken O'Brien	.05	.02	.01
☐ 374 Tony Stargell	.05	.02	.01
☐ 375 Jim Sweeney UER (Landetta, sic)	.05	.02	.01
☐ 376 Al Toon	.10	.05	.01
☐ 377 Johnny Hector	.05	.02	.01
☐ 378 Jeff Criswell	.05	.02	.01
☐ 379 Mike Haight	.05	.02	.01
☐ 380 Troy Benson	.05	.02	.01
☐ 381 Eric Allen	.05	.02	.01
☐ 382 Fred Barnett	.25	.11	.03
☐ 383 Jerome Brown	.05	.02	.01
☐ 384 Keith Byars	.05	.02	.01
☐ 385 Randall Cunningham	.10	.05	.01
☐ 386 Byron Evans	.05	.02	.01
☐ 387 Wes Hopkins	.05	.02	.01
☐ 388 Keith Jackson	.10	.05	.01
☐ 389 Seth Joyner UER (Fumble recovery line not aligned)	.10	.05	.01
☐ 390 Bobby Wilson	.05	.02	.01
☐ 391 Heath Sherman	.05	.02	.01
☐ 392 Clyde Simmons UER (Listed as DT, should say DE)	.05	.02	.01
☐ 393 Ben Smith	.05	.02	.01
☐ 394 Andre Waters	.05	.02	.01
☐ 395 Reggie White UER (Derrick Thomas holds NFL record with 7 sacks)	.25	.11	.03
☐ 396 Calvin Williams	.10	.05	.01
☐ 397 Al Harris	.05	.02	.01
☐ 398 Anthony Toney	.05	.02	.01
☐ 399 Mike Quick	.05	.02	.01
☐ 400 Anthony Bell	.05	.02	.01
☐ 401 Rich Camarillo	.05	.02	.01
☐ 402 Roy Green	.05	.02	.01
☐ 403 Ken Harvey	.10	.05	.01
☐ 404 Eric Hill	.05	.02	.01
☐ 405 Garth Jax UER (Should have comma before "the" and after "Cowboys" on cardback)	.05	.02	.01
☐ 406 Ernie Jones	.05	.02	.01
☐ 407A Cedric Mack ERR (Misspelled Cedrick on card front)	.10	.05	.01
☐ 407B Cedric Mack COR (NFL Exp. line is red instead of black)	.10	.05	.01
☐ 408 Dexter Manley	.05	.02	.01
☐ 409 Tim McDonald	.05	.02	.01
☐ 410 Freddie Joe Nunn	.05	.02	.01
☐ 411 Ricky Proehl	.05	.02	.01
☐ 412 Moe Gardner	.05	.02	.01
☐ 413 Timm Rosenbach	.05	.02	.01
☐ 414 Luis Sharpe UER (Lomiller, sic)	.05	.02	.01
☐ 415 Vai Sikahema UER (Front RB, back PR)	.05	.02	.01
☐ 416 Anthony Thompson	.05	.02	.01
☐ 417 Ron Wolfley UER (Missing NFL fact line under vital stats)	.05	.02	.01
☐ 418 Lonnie Young	.05	.02	.01
☐ 419 Gary Anderson K	.05	.02	.01
☐ 420 Bubby Brister	.05	.02	.01
☐ 421 Thomas Everett	.05	.02	.01
☐ 422 Eric Green	.05	.02	.01
☐ 423 Delton Hall	.05	.02	.01
☐ 424 Bryan Hinkle	.05	.02	.01
☐ 425 Merril Hoge	.05	.02	.01
☐ 426 Carnell Lake	.05	.02	.01
☐ 427 Louis Lipps	.05	.02	.01
☐ 428 David Little	.05	.02	.01
☐ 429 Greg Lloyd	.25	.11	.03
☐ 430 Mike Mularkey	.05	.02	.01
☐ 431 Keith Willis UER (No period after C in L.C. Greenwood on back)	.05	.02	.01
☐ 432 Dwayne Woodruff	.05	.02	.01
☐ 433 Rod Woodson UER (No NFL experience listed on card)	.25	.11	.03
☐ 434 Tim Worley	.05	.02	.01
☐ 435 Warren Williams	.05	.02	.01
☐ 436 Terry Long UER (Not 5th NFL team, tied for 7th)	.05	.02	.01
☐ 437 Martin Bayless	.05	.02	.01
☐ 438 Jarrod Bunch	.05	.02	.01
☐ 439 Marion Butts	.10	.05	.01
☐ 440 Gill Byrd UER (Pickoffs misspelled as two words)	.05	.02	.01
☐ 441 Arthur Cox	.05	.02	.01
☐ 442 John Friesz	.25	.11	.03
☐ 443 Leo Goeas	.05	.02	.01
☐ 444 Burt Grossman	.05	.02	.01
☐ 445 Courtney Hall UER (In DYK section, is should be in)	.05	.02	.01
☐ 446 Ronnie Harmon	.05	.02	.01
☐ 447 Nate Lewis	.05	.02	.01
☐ 448 Anthony Miller	.10	.05	.01
☐ 449 Leslie O'Neal	.10	.05	.01
☐ 450 Gary Plummer	.05	.02	.01
☐ 451 Junior Seau	.40	.18	.05
☐ 452 Billy Ray Smith	.05	.02	.01
☐ 453 Billy Joe Tolliver	.05	.02	.01
☐ 454 Broderick Thompson	.05	.02	.01
☐ 455 Lee Williams	.05	.02	.01
☐ 456 Michael Carter	.05	.02	.01
☐ 457 Mike Cofer	.05	.02	.01
☐ 458 Kevin Fagan	.05	.02	.01
☐ 459 Charles Haley	.10	.05	.01
☐ 460 Pierce Holt	.05	.02	.01
☐ 461 Johnnie Jackson UER (Johnny on front)	.05	.02	.01
☐ 462 Brent Jones	.25	.11	.03
☐ 463 Guy McIntyre	.05	.02	.01
☐ 464 Joe Montana	1.00	.45	.12
☐ 465A Bubba Paris ERR (Misspelled Parris; reversed negative)	.10	.05	.01
☐ 465B Bubba Paris ERR/COR (Misspelled Parris; photo corrected)	.50	.23	.06
☐ 465C Bubba Paris COR	.10	.05	.01
☐ 466 Tom Rathman UER (Born 10/7/62, not 11/7/62)	.05	.02	.01
☐ 467 Jerry Rice UER (4th to catch 100, should say 2nd)	1.00	.45	.12
☐ 468 Mike Sherrard	.05	.02	.01
☐ 469 John Taylor UER (AL1-Time, sic)	.10	.05	.01
☐ 470 Steve Young	.75	.35	.09
☐ 471 Dennis Brown	.05	.02	.01
☐ 472 Dexter Carter	.05	.02	.01
☐ 473 Bill Romanowski	.05	.02	.01
☐ 474 Dave Waymer	.05	.02	.01
☐ 475 Robert Blackmon	.05	.02	.01
☐ 476 Derrick Fenner	.05	.02	.01
☐ 477 Nesby Glasgow UER (Missing total line for fumbles)	.05	.02	.01
☐ 478 Jacob Green	.05	.02	.01
☐ 479 Andy Heck	.05	.02	.01
☐ 480 Norm Johnson UER (They own and operate card store, not run)	.05	.02	.01
☐ 481 Tommy Kane	.05	.02	.01
☐ 482 Cortez Kennedy	.25	.11	.03
☐ 483A Dave Krieg ERR (Misspelled Kreig on both sides)	.10	.05	.01
☐ 483B Dave Krieg COR	.10	.05	.01
☐ 484 Bryan Millard	.05	.02	.01
☐ 485 Joe Nash	.05	.02	.01
☐ 486 Rufus Porter	.05	.02	.01
☐ 487 Eugene Robinson	.05	.02	.01
☐ 488 Mike Tice	.05	.02	.01
☐ 489 Chris Warren	.40	.18	.05
☐ 490 John L. Williams UER (No period after L on card front)	.05	.02	.01
☐ 491 Terry Wooden	.05	.02	.01
☐ 492 Tony Woods	.05	.02	.01
☐ 493 Brian Blades	.10	.05	.01
☐ 494 Paul Skansi	.05	.02	.01
☐ 495 Gary Anderson RB	.05	.02	.01
☐ 496 Mark Carrier WR	.25	.11	.03
☐ 497 Chris Chandler	.10	.05	.01
☐ 498 Steve Christie	.05	.02	.01
☐ 499 Reggie Cobb	.05	.02	.01
☐ 500 Reuben Davis	.05	.02	.01
☐ 501 Willie Drewrey UER (Misspelled Drewery on both sides of card)	.05	.02	.01
☐ 502 Randy Grimes	.05	.02	.01
☐ 503 Paul Gruber	.05	.02	.01
☐ 504 Wayne Haddix	.05	.02	.01
☐ 505 Ron Hall	.05	.02	.01
☐ 506 Harry Hamilton	.05	.02	.01
☐ 507 Bruce Hill	.05	.02	.01
☐ 508 Eugene Marve	.05	.02	.01
☐ 509 Keith McCants	.05	.02	.01
☐ 510 Winston Moss	.05	.02	.01
☐ 511 Kevin Murphy	.05	.02	.01
☐ 512 Mark Robinson	.05	.02	.01
☐ 513 Vinny Testaverde	.10	.05	.01
☐ 514 Broderick Thomas	.05	.02	.01
☐ 515A Jeff Bostic UER (Lomiller, sic; on back, word "goal" touches lower border)	.08	.04	.01
☐ 515B Jeff Bostic UER (Lomiller, sic; on back, word "goal" is away from border)	.08	.04	.01
☐ 516 Todd Bowles	.05	.02	.01
☐ 517 Earnest Byner	.05	.02	.01
☐ 518 Gary Clark	.25	.11	.03
☐ 519 Craig Erickson	.25	.11	.03
☐ 520 Darryl Grant	.05	.02	.01
☐ 521 Darrell Green	.05	.02	.01
☐ 522 Russ Grimm	.05	.02	.01
☐ 523 Stan Humphries	.25	.11	.03
☐ 524 Joe Jacoby UER (Lomiller, sic)	.05	.02	.01
☐ 525 Jim Lachey	.05	.02	.01
☐ 526 Chip Lohmiller	.05	.02	.01
☐ 527 Charles Mann	.05	.02	.01
☐ 528 Wilber Marshall	.05	.02	.01
☐ 529A Art Monk (On back, "y" in history touches copyright symbol)	.08	.04	.01
☐ 529B Art Monk (On back, "y" in history is away from symbol)	.08	.04	.01
☐ 530 Tracy Rocker	.05	.02	.01
☐ 531 Mark Rypien	.10	.05	.01
☐ 532 Ricky Sanders UER (Stats say caught 56, text says 57)	.05	.02	.01
☐ 533 Alvin Walton UER (Listed as WR, should be S)	.05	.02	.01
☐ 534 Todd Marinovich UER (17 percent, should be 71 percent)	.05	.02	.01
☐ 535 Mike Dumas	.05	.02	.01
☐ 536A Russell Maryland ERR (No highlight line)	.25	.11	.03
☐ 536B Russell Maryland COR (Highlight line added)	.25	.11	.03
☐ 537 Eric Turner UER (Don Rogers misspelled as Rodgers)	.10	.05	.01
☐ 538 Ernie Mills	.10	.05	.01
☐ 539 Ed King	.05	.02	.01
☐ 540 Mike Stonebreaker	.05	.02	.01
☐ 541 Chris Zorich	.25	.11	.03
☐ 542A Mike Croel UER (Missing highlight line under bio notes; front photo reversed negative; on back, "y" in weekly inside copyright)	.05	.02	.01
☐ 542B Mike Croel UER (Missing highlight line under bio notes; front photo reversed negative; on back, "y" in weekly barely touches copyright)	.05	.02	.01
☐ 543 Eric Moten	.05	.02	.01
☐ 544 Dan McGwire	.05	.02	.01
☐ 545 Keith Cash	.05	.02	.01
☐ 546 Kenny Walker UER (Drafted 8th round, not 7th)	.05	.02	.01
☐ 547 Leroy Hoard UER (LeROY on card; not a draft pick)	.10	.05	.01
☐ 548 Luis Cristobal UER (front LB, back G)	.05	.02	.01
☐ 549 Stacy Danley	.05	.02	.01
☐ 550 Todd Lyght	.05	.02	.01
☐ 551 Brett Favre	4.00	1.80	.50
☐ 552 Mike Pritchard	.25	.11	.03
☐ 553 Moe Gardner	.05	.02	.01
☐ 554 Tim McKyer	.05	.02	.01
☐ 555 Erric Pegram	.25	.11	.03
☐ 556 Norm Johnson	.05	.02	.01
☐ 557 Bruce Pickens	.05	.02	.01
☐ 558 Henry Jones	.10	.05	.01
☐ 559 Phil Hansen	.05	.02	.01
☐ 560 Cornelius Bennett	.10	.05	.01
☐ 561 Stan Thomas	.05	.02	.01
☐ 562 Chris Zorich	.10	.05	.01
☐ 563 Anthony Morgan	.05	.02	.01
☐ 564 Darren Lewis	.05	.02	.01
☐ 565 Mike Stonebreaker	.05	.02	.01
☐ 566 Alfred Williams	.05	.02	.01
☐ 567 Lamar Rogers	.05	.02	.01
☐ 568 Erik Wilhelm UER (No NFL Experience line on card back)	.05	.02	.01
☐ 569 Ed King	.05	.02	.01
☐ 570 Michael Jackson	.25	.11	.03
☐ 571 James Jones	.05	.02	.01
☐ 572 Russell Maryland	.25	.11	.03
☐ 573 Dixon Edwards	.05	.02	.01
☐ 574 Darrick Brownlow	.05	.02	.01
☐ 575 Larry Brown DB	.10	.05	.01
☐ 576 Mike Croel	.05	.02	.01
☐ 577 Keith Traylor	.05	.02	.01
☐ 578 Kenny Walker	.05	.02	.01
☐ 579 Reggie Johnson	.05	.02	.01
☐ 580 Herman Moore	2.00	.90	.25
☐ 581 Kelvin Pritchett	.10	.05	.01
☐ 582 Kevin Scott	.05	.02	.01
☐ 583 Vinnie Clark	.05	.02	.01
☐ 584 Esera Tuaolo	.05	.02	.01
☐ 585 Don Davey	.05	.02	.01
☐ 586 Blair Kiel	.05	.02	.01
☐ 587 Mike Dumas	.05	.02	.01
☐ 588 Darryll Lewis	.10	.05	.01
☐ 589 John Flannery	.05	.02	.01
☐ 590 Kevin Donnalley	.05	.02	.01
☐ 591 Shane Curry	.05	.02	.01
☐ 592 Mark Vander Poel	.05	.02	.01
☐ 593 Dave McCloughan	.05	.02	.01

☐ 594 Mel Agee	.05	.02	.01
☐ 595 Kerry Cash	.05	.02	.01
☐ 596 Harvey Williams	.25	.11	.03
☐ 597 Joe Valerio	.05	.02	.01
☐ 598 Tim Barnett UER (Harvey Williams pictured on front)	.05	.02	.01
☐ 599 Todd Marinovich	.10	.05	.01
☐ 600 Nick Bell	.05	.02	.01
☐ 601 Roger Craig	.10	.05	.01
☐ 602 Ronnie Lott	.10	.05	.01
☐ 603 Mike Jones	.05	.02	.01
☐ 604 Todd Lyght	.05	.02	.01
☐ 605 Roman Phifer	.05	.02	.01
☐ 606 David Lang	.05	.02	.01
☐ 607 Aaron Craver	.05	.02	.01
☐ 608 Mark Higgs	.05	.02	.01
☐ 609 Chris Green	.05	.02	.01
☐ 610 Randy Baldwin	.05	.02	.01
☐ 611 Pat Harlow	.05	.02	.01
☐ 612 Leonard Russell	.25	.11	.03
☐ 613 Jerome Henderson	.05	.02	.01
☐ 614 Scott Zolak UER (Bio says drafted in 1984, should be 1991)	.05	.02	.01
☐ 615 Jon Vaughn	.05	.02	.01
☐ 616 Harry Colon	.05	.02	.01
☐ 617 Wesley Carroll	.05	.02	.01
☐ 618 Quinn Early	.10	.05	.01
☐ 619 Reginald Jones	.05	.02	.01
☐ 620 Jarrod Bunch	.05	.02	.01
☐ 621 Kanavis McGhee	.05	.02	.01
☐ 622 Ed McCaffrey	.10	.05	.01
☐ 623 Browning Nagle	.05	.02	.01
☐ 624 Mo Lewis	.10	.05	.01
☐ 625 Blair Thomas	.05	.02	.01
☐ 626 Antone Davis	.05	.02	.01
☐ 627 Jim McMahon	.10	.05	.01
☐ 628 Scott Kowalkowski	.05	.02	.01
☐ 629 Brad Goebel	.05	.02	.01
☐ 630 William Thomas	.05	.02	.01
☐ 631 Eric Swann	.25	.11	.03
☐ 632 Mike Jones	.05	.02	.01
☐ 633 Aeneas Williams	.25	.11	.03
☐ 634 Dexter Davis	.05	.02	.01
☐ 635 Tom Tupa UER (Did play in 1990, but not as QB)	.05	.02	.01
☐ 636 Johnny Johnson	.05	.02	.01
☐ 637 Randal Hill	.10	.05	.01
☐ 638 Jeff Graham	.25	.11	.03
☐ 639 Ernie Mills	.05	.02	.01
☐ 640 Adrian Cooper	.05	.02	.01
☐ 641 Stanley Richard	.05	.02	.01
☐ 642 Eric Bieniemy	.05	.02	.01
☐ 643 Eric Moten	.05	.02	.01
☐ 644 Shawn Jefferson	.10	.05	.01
☐ 645 Ted Washington	.05	.02	.01
☐ 646 John Johnson	.05	.02	.01
☐ 647 Dan McGwire	.05	.02	.01
☐ 648 Doug Thomas	.05	.02	.01
☐ 649 David Daniels	.05	.02	.01
☐ 650 John Kasay	.10	.05	.01
☐ 651 Jeff Kemp	.05	.02	.01
☐ 652 Charles McRae	.05	.02	.01
☐ 653 Lawrence Dawsey	.10	.05	.01
☐ 654 Robert Wilson	.05	.02	.01
☐ 655 Dexter Manley	.05	.02	.01
☐ 656 Chuck Weatherspoon	.05	.02	.01
☐ 657 Tim Ryan	.05	.02	.01
☐ 658 Bobby Wilson	.05	.02	.01
☐ 659 Ricky Ervins	.10	.05	.01
☐ 660 Matt Millen	.10	.05	.01

1991 Pacific Picks The Pros

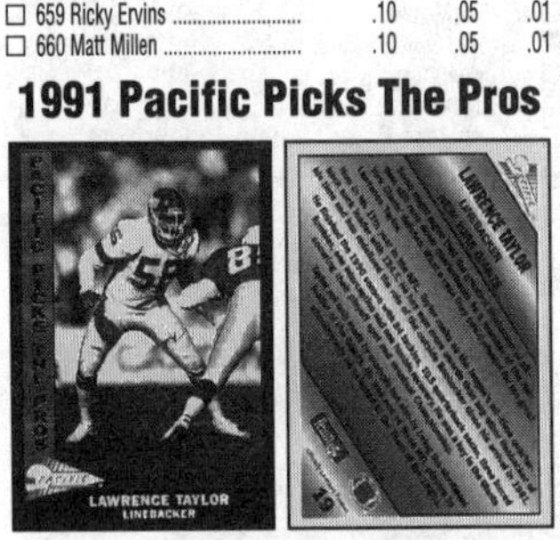

Randomly inserted in packs, this 25-card standard-size set features the best player for each offensive and defensive position. A card of first pick Russell Maryland is also included. The cards have color action player photos on the fronts, with either gold or silver foil borders. There were 10,000 cards produced with a gold foil border and an equal number with a silver foil border. The silver foil cards were randomly inserted into jumbo packs, while the gold foil cards were randomly inserted into the wax and foil packs. There is no difference in price. The words "Pacific Picks the Pros" are printed vertically in a blue and red colored stripe on the left side of the picture. The horizontally oriented backs present career summaries in a diagonal direction on a red and blue background.

	MINT	NRMT	EXC
COMPLETE SET (25)	60.00	27.00	7.50
COMMON CARD (1-25)	2.00	.90	.25
*GOLD/SILVER: SAME PRICE			

☐ 1 Russell Maryland	3.00	1.35	.35
☐ 2 Andre Reed	4.00	1.80	.50
☐ 3 Jerry Rice	12.00	5.50	1.50
☐ 4 Keith Jackson	3.00	1.35	.35
☐ 5 Jim Lachey	2.00	.90	.25
☐ 6 Anthony Munoz	4.00	1.80	.50
☐ 7 Randall McDaniel	2.00	.90	.25
☐ 8 Bruce Matthews	3.00	1.35	.35
☐ 9 Kent Hull	2.00	.90	.25
☐ 10 Joe Montana	10.00	4.50	1.25
☐ 11 Barry Sanders	12.00	5.50	1.50
☐ 12 Thurman Thomas	4.00	1.80	.50
☐ 13 Morten Andersen	2.00	.90	.25
☐ 14 Jerry Ball	2.00	.90	.25
☐ 15 Jerome Brown	3.00	1.35	.35
☐ 16 Reggie White	4.00	1.80	.50
☐ 17 Bruce Smith	4.00	1.80	.50
☐ 18 Derrick Thomas	4.00	1.80	.50
☐ 19 Lawrence Taylor	4.00	1.80	.50
☐ 20 Charles Haley	3.00	1.35	.35
☐ 21 Albert Lewis	2.00	.90	.25
☐ 22 Rod Woodson	4.00	1.80	.50
☐ 23 David Fulcher	2.00	.90	.25
☐ 24 Joey Browner	2.00	.90	.25
☐ 25 Sean Landeta	2.00	.90	.25

1991 Pacific Flash Cards

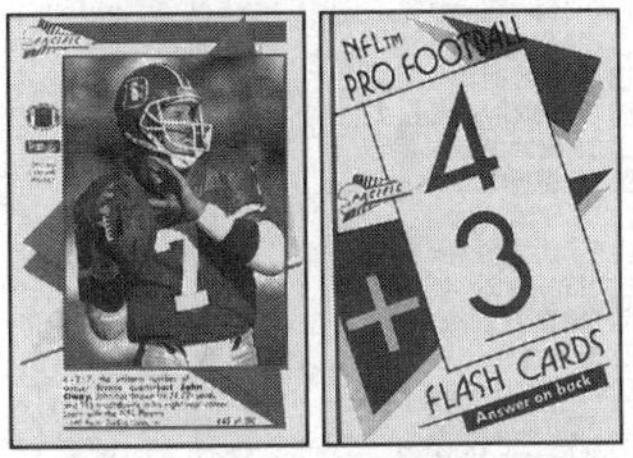

The 1991 Pacific Flash Cards football set contains 110 standard-size cards. The front design has brightly colored triangles on a white card face and a math problem involving addition, subtraction, multiplication, or division. By performing one of these operations on the two numbers, one arrives at the uniform number of the player featured on the backs. The back design is similar to the front but has a glossy color game shot of the player, with either career summary or last year's highlights below the picture.

	MINT	NRMT	EXC
COMPLETE SET (110)	6.00	2.70	.75
COMMON CARD (1-110)	.05	.02	.01

☐ 1 Steve Young	.60	.25	.07
☐ 2 Hart Lee Dykes	.05	.02	.01
☐ 3 Timm Rosenbach	.10	.05	.01
☐ 4 Andre Collins	.05	.02	.01
☐ 5 Johnny Johnson	.10	.05	.01
☐ 6 Nick Lowery	.05	.02	.01
☐ 7 John Stephens	.05	.02	.01
☐ 8 Jim Arnold	.05	.02	.01
☐ 9 Steve DeBerg	.10	.05	.01
☐ 10 Christian Okoye	.10	.05	.01
☐ 11 Eric Swann	.15	.07	.02
☐ 12 Jerry Robinson	.05	.02	.01
☐ 13 Steve Wisniewski	.05	.02	.01
☐ 14 Jim Harbaugh	.20	.09	.03
☐ 15 Steve Broussard	.05	.02	.01
☐ 16 Mike Singletary UER (Joined Bears in '80, should say '81)	.10	.05	.01
☐ 17 Tim Green	.05	.02	.01
☐ 18 Roger Craig	.10	.05	.01
☐ 19 Maury Buford	.05	.02	.01
☐ 20 Marcus Allen	.15	.07	.02
☐ 21 Deion Sanders	.50	.23	.06
☐ 22 Chris Miller	.10	.05	.01
☐ 23 Joey Browner	.05	.02	.01
☐ 24 Bubby Brister	.10	.05	.01
☐ 25 Buford McGee	.05	.02	.01
☐ 26 Ed West	.10	.05	.01
☐ 27 Mark Murphy	.05	.02	.01
☐ 28 Tim Worley	.05	.02	.01
☐ 29 Keith Willis	.05	.02	.01
☐ 30 Rich Gannon	.10	.05	.01
☐ 31 Jim Everett	.10	.05	.01
☐ 32 Duval Love	.05	.02	.01
☐ 33 Bob Nelson	.05	.02	.01
☐ 34 Anthony Munoz	.10	.05	.01
☐ 35 Boomer Esiason	.10	.05	.01
☐ 36 Kenny Walker	.05	.02	.01
☐ 37 Mike Horan	.05	.02	.01
☐ 38 Gary Kubiak	.05	.02	.01
☐ 39 David Treadwell	.05	.02	.01
☐ 40 Robert Wilson	.05	.02	.01
☐ 41 Lewis Billups	.05	.02	.01
☐ 42 Kevin Mack	.05	.02	.01
☐ 43 John Elway	.60	.25	.07
☐ 44 Lee Johnson	.05	.02	.01
☐ 45 Ken Willis	.05	.02	.01
☐ 46 Herman Moore	.75	.35	.09
☐ 47 Eddie Murray	.05	.02	.01
☐ 48 Mike Saxon	.05	.02	.01
☐ 49 John L. Williams	.10	.05	.01
☐ 50 Barry Sanders	.75	.35	.09
☐ 51 Andre Ware	.10	.05	.01
☐ 52 Dave Krieg	.10	.05	.01
☐ 53 Cortez Kennedy	.15	.07	.02
☐ 54 Bo Jackson	.20	.09	.03
☐ 55 Derrick Fenner	.05	.02	.01
☐ 56 Steve Walsh	.10	.05	.01
☐ 57 Brett Maxie	.05	.02	.01
☐ 58 Stan Brock	.05	.02	.01
☐ 59 DeMond Winston	.05	.02	.01
☐ 60 Sam Mills	.05	.02	.01
☐ 61 Eric Martin	.05	.02	.01
☐ 62 Michael Carter	.05	.02	.01
☐ 63 Steve Wallace	.10	.05	.01
☐ 64 Jesse Sapolu	.05	.02	.01
☐ 65 Bill Romanowski	.05	.02	.01
☐ 66 Joe Montana	.75	.35	.09
☐ 67 Sean Landeta	.05	.02	.01
☐ 68 Doug Riesenberg	.05	.02	.01
☐ 69 Myron Guyton	.05	.02	.01
☐ 70 Andre Reed	.15	.07	.02
☐ 71 John Elliott	.05	.02	.01
☐ 72 Jeff Hostetler	.10	.05	.01
☐ 73 Rohn Stark	.05	.02	.01
☐ 74 Jeff George	.20	.09	.03
☐ 75 Duane Bickett	.05	.02	.01
☐ 76 Emmitt Smith	1.25	.55	.16
☐ 77 Michael Irvin	.20	.09	.03
☐ 78 Tony Stargell	.05	.02	.01
☐ 79 Kyle Clifton	.05	.02	.01
☐ 80 John Booty	.05	.02	.01
☐ 81 Fred Barnett	.15	.07	.02
☐ 82 Blair Thomas	.10	.05	.01
☐ 83 Erik McMillan	.05	.02	.01
☐ 84 Broderick Thomas	.05	.02	.01
☐ 85 Jim Skow	.05	.02	.01
☐ 86 Gary Anderson RB	.05	.02	.01
☐ 87 Mark Robinson	.05	.02	.01
☐ 88 Steve Christie	.05	.02	.01
☐ 89 Cody Carlson	.10	.05	.01
☐ 90 Warren Moon	.15	.07	.02
☐ 91 Lorenzo White	.10	.05	.01
☐ 92 Reggie Roby	.05	.02	.01
☐ 93 Jim C. Jensen	.05	.02	.01
☐ 94 Mark Clayton	.10	.05	.01
☐ 95 Willie Gault	.10	.05	.01
☐ 96 Don Mosebar	.05	.02	.01
☐ 97 Gary Plummer	.05	.02	.01
☐ 98 Leslie O'Neal	.15	.07	.02
☐ 99 Neal Anderson	.10	.05	.01
☐ 100 Derrick Thomas	.15	.07	.02
☐ 101 Luis Sharpe	.05	.02	.01
☐ 102 D.J. Dozier	.05	.02	.01
☐ 103 Jarrod Bunch	.05	.02	.01
☐ 104 Mark Ingram	.10	.05	.01
☐ 105 James Lofton	.15	.07	.02
☐ 106 Jay Schroeder	.05	.02	.01
☐ 107 Ronnie Lott	.10	.05	.01
☐ 108 Todd Marinovich	.05	.02	.01
☐ 109 Chris Zorich	.10	.05	.01
☐ 110 Charles McRae	.05	.02	.01

1992 Pacific Prototypes

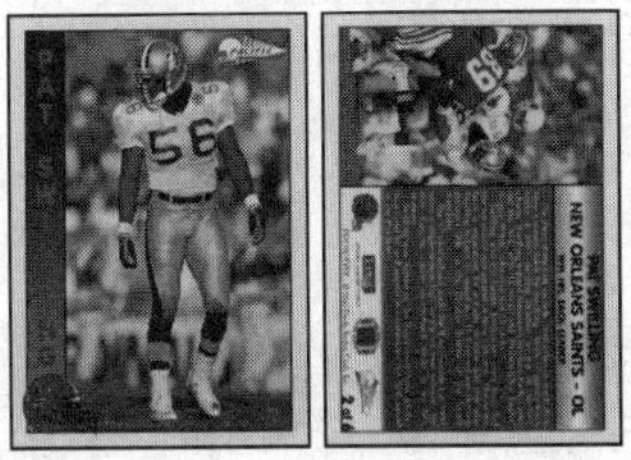

The 1992 Pacific prototypes were given away at the Super Bowl card show in Minneapolis and used as sales samples. The cards measure the standard size. The cards were intended to be a preview for the upcoming 1992 Pacific set since they used the new card design. The production run was approximately 5,000 sets. The fronts feature glossy color action player photos enclosed by white borders. The player's name is printed vertically in a color stripe running down the left side of the picture, with the team helmet in the lower left corner. In a horizontal format, the backs have a second color photo and player profile.

	MINT	NRMT	EXC
COMPLETE SET (6)	25.00	11.00	3.10
COMMON CARD (1-6)	4.00	1.80	.50

☐ 1 Warren Moon	5.00	2.20	.60
☐ 2 Pat Swilling	4.00	1.80	.50
☐ 3 Michael Irvin	5.00	2.20	.60
☐ 4 Haywood Jeffires	4.00	1.80	.50
☐ 5 Thurman Thomas	5.00	2.20	.60
☐ 6 Leonard Russell	4.00	1.80	.50

1992 Pacific

The 1992 Pacific set consists of 660 standard-size cards. The set was issued in two series of 330 cards. A factory set consisted of every card. Cards were issued in 14-card packs and 24-card jumbo packs for each series. Factory sets included a 30-card Statistical Leaders set. The fronts feature glossy color action player photos enclosed by

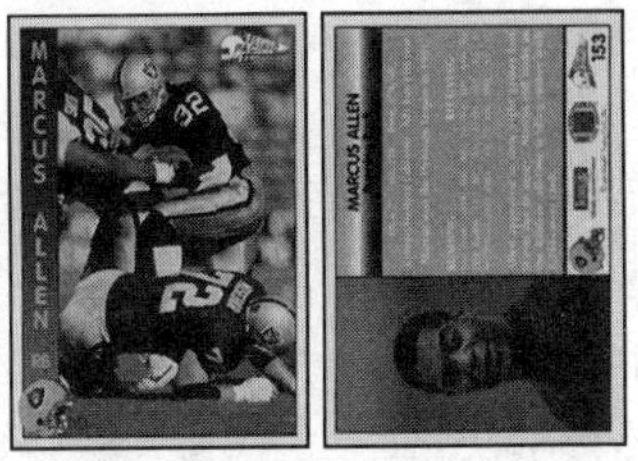

white borders. The player's name is printed vertically in a color stripe running down the left side of the picture, with the team helmet in the lower left corner. In a horizontal format, the backs have a second color photo and player profile. The cards are numbered on the back and checklisted below alphabetically according to teams. Cards 320-330 and 649-660 are Draft Picks. Rookie Cards include Steve Bono, Ben Coates (exclusive to Pacific), Terrell Buckley, Chris Mims, Leroy Thompson and Michael Timpson. Separately numbered checklist cards were also randomly inserted in packs.

	MINT	NRMT	EXC
COMPLETE SET (660)	16.00	7.25	2.00
COMPLETE FACT.SET (690)	25.00	11.00	3.10
COMPLETE SERIES 1 (330)	8.00	3.60	1.00
COMPLETE SERIES 2 (330)	8.00	3.60	1.00
COMMON CARD (1-660)	.04	.02	.01
COMPLETE CHECKLIST SET (5)	3.00	1.35	.35

☐ 1 Steve Broussard	.04	.02	.01
☐ 2 Darion Conner	.04	.02	.01
☐ 3 Tory Epps	.04	.02	.01
☐ 4 Michael Haynes	.10	.05	.01
☐ 5 Chris Hinton	.04	.02	.01
☐ 6 Mike Kenn	.04	.02	.01
☐ 7 Tim McKyer	.04	.02	.01
☐ 8 Chris Miller	.10	.05	.01
☐ 9 Eric Pegram	.10	.05	.01
☐ 10 Mike Pritchard	.10	.05	.01
☐ 11 Moe Gardner	.04	.02	.01
☐ 12 Tim Green	.04	.02	.01
☐ 13 Norm Johnson	.04	.02	.01
☐ 14 Don Beebe	.04	.02	.01
☐ 15 Cornelius Bennett	.10	.05	.01
☐ 16 Al Edwards	.04	.02	.01
☐ 17 Mark Kelso	.04	.02	.01
☐ 18 James Lofton	.10	.05	.01
☐ 19 Frank Reich	.10	.05	.01
☐ 20 Leon Seals	.04	.02	.01
☐ 21 Darryl Talley	.04	.02	.01
☐ 22 Thurman Thomas	.25	.11	.03
☐ 23 Kent Hull	.04	.02	.01
☐ 24 Jeff Wright	.04	.02	.01
☐ 25 Nate Odomes	.04	.02	.01
☐ 26 Carwell Gardner	.04	.02	.01
☐ 27 Neal Anderson	.04	.02	.01
☐ 28 Mark Carrier DB	.04	.02	.01
☐ 29 Johnny Bailey	.04	.02	.01
☐ 30 Jim Harbaugh	.25	.11	.03
☐ 31 Jay Hilgenberg	.04	.02	.01
☐ 32 William Perry	.10	.05	.01
☐ 33 Wendell Davis	.04	.02	.01
☐ 34 Donnell Woolford	.04	.02	.01
☐ 35 Keith Van Horne	.04	.02	.01
☐ 36 Shaun Gayle	.04	.02	.01
☐ 37 Tom Waddle	.04	.02	.01
☐ 38 Chris Zorich	.10	.05	.01
☐ 39 Tom Thayer	.04	.02	.01
☐ 40 Rickey Dixon	.04	.02	.01
☐ 41 James Francis	.04	.02	.01
☐ 42 David Fulcher	.04	.02	.01
☐ 43 Reggie Rembert	.04	.02	.01
☐ 44 Anthony Munoz	.10	.05	.01
☐ 45 Harold Green	.04	.02	.01
☐ 46 Mitchell Price	.04	.02	.01
☐ 47 Rodney Holman	.04	.02	.01
☐ 48 Bruce Kozerski	.04	.02	.01
☐ 49 Bruce Reimers	.04	.02	.01
☐ 50 Erik Wilhelm	.04	.02	.01
☐ 51 Harlon Barnett	.04	.02	.01
☐ 52 Mike Johnson	.04	.02	.01
☐ 53 Brian Brennan	.04	.02	.01
☐ 54 Ed King	.04	.02	.01
☐ 55 Reggie Langhorne	.04	.02	.01
☐ 56 James Jones	.04	.02	.01
☐ 57 Mike Baab	.04	.02	.01
☐ 58 Dan Fike	.04	.02	.01
☐ 59 Frank Minnifield	.04	.02	.01
☐ 60 Clay Matthews	.10	.05	.01
☐ 61 Kevin Mack	.04	.02	.01
☐ 62 Tony Casillas	.04	.02	.01
☐ 63 Jay Novacek	.10	.05	.01
☐ 64 Larry Brown DB	.04	.02	.01
☐ 65 Michael Irvin	.25	.11	.03
☐ 66 Jack Del Rio	.04	.02	.01
☐ 67 Ken Willis	.04	.02	.01
☐ 68 Emmitt Smith	2.00	.90	.25
☐ 69 Alan Veingrad	.04	.02	.01
☐ 70 John Gesek	.04	.02	.01
☐ 71 Steve Beuerlein	.04	.02	.01
☐ 72 Vinson Smith	.04	.02	.01
☐ 73 Steve Atwater	.04	.02	.01
☐ 74 Mike Croel	.04	.02	.01

☐ 75 John Elway .60 .25 .07
☐ 76 Gaston Green .04 .02 .01
☐ 77 Mike Horan .04 .02 .01
☐ 78 Vance Johnson .04 .02 .01
☐ 79 Karl Mecklenburg .04 .02 .01
☐ 80 Shannon Sharpe .25 .11 .03
☐ 81 David Treadwell .04 .02 .01
☐ 82 Kenny Walker .04 .02 .01
☐ 83 Greg Lewis .04 .02 .01
☐ 84 Shawn Moore .04 .02 .01
☐ 85 Alton Montgomery .04 .02 .01
☐ 86 Michael Young .04 .02 .01
☐ 87 Jerry Ball .04 .02 .01
☐ 88 Bennie Blades .04 .02 .01
☐ 89 Mel Gray .10 .05 .01
☐ 90 Herman Moore .75 .35 .09
☐ 91 Erik Kramer .10 .05 .01
☐ 92 Willie Green .04 .02 .01
☐ 93 George Jamison .04 .02 .01
☐ 94 Chris Spielman .10 .05 .01
☐ 95 Kelvin Pritchett .04 .02 .01
☐ 96 William White .04 .02 .01
☐ 97 Mike Utley .10 .05 .01
☐ 98 Tony Bennett .04 .02 .01
☐ 99 LeRoy Butler .04 .02 .01
☐ 100 Vinnie Clark .04 .02 .01
☐ 101 Ron Hallstrom .04 .02 .01
☐ 102 Chris Jacke .04 .02 .01
☐ 103 Tony Mandarich .04 .02 .01
☐ 104 Sterling Sharpe .25 .11 .03
☐ 105 Don Majkowski .04 .02 .01
☐ 106 Johnny Holland .04 .02 .01
☐ 107 Esera Tuaolo .04 .02 .01
☐ 108 Darrell Thompson .04 .02 .01
☐ 109 Bubba McDowell .04 .02 .01
☐ 110 Curtis Duncan .04 .02 .01
☐ 111 Lamar Lathon .04 .02 .01
☐ 112 Drew Hill .04 .02 .01
☐ 113 Bruce Matthews .04 .02 .01
☐ 114 Bo Orlando .04 .02 .01
☐ 115 Don Maggs .04 .02 .01
☐ 116 Lorenzo White .04 .02 .01
☐ 117 Ernest Givins .10 .05 .01
☐ 118 Tony Jones .04 .02 .01
☐ 119 Dean Steinkuhler .04 .02 .01
☐ 120 Dean Biasucci .04 .02 .01
☐ 121 Duane Bickett .04 .02 .01
☐ 122 Bill Brooks .04 .02 .01
☐ 123 Ken Clark .04 .02 .01
☐ 124 Jessie Hester .04 .02 .01
☐ 125 Anthony Johnson .10 .05 .01
☐ 126 Chip Banks .04 .02 .01
☐ 127 Mike Prior .04 .02 .01
☐ 128 Rohn Stark .04 .02 .01
☐ 129 Jeff Herrod .04 .02 .01
☐ 130 Clarence Verdin .04 .02 .01
☐ 131 Tim Manoa .04 .02 .01
☐ 132 Brian Baldinger .04 .02 .01
☐ 133 Tim Barnett .04 .02 .01
☐ 134 J.J. Birden .04 .02 .01
☐ 135 Deron Cherry .04 .02 .01
☐ 136 Steve DeBerg .04 .02 .01
☐ 137 Nick Lowery .04 .02 .01
☐ 138 Todd McNair .04 .02 .01
☐ 139 Christian Okoye .04 .02 .01
☐ 140 Mark Vlasic .04 .02 .01
☐ 141 Dan Saleaumua .04 .02 .01
☐ 142 Neil Smith .25 .11 .03
☐ 143 Robb Thomas .04 .02 .01
☐ 144 Eddie Anderson .04 .02 .01
☐ 145 Nick Bell .04 .02 .01
☐ 146 Tim Brown .25 .11 .03
☐ 147 Roger Craig .10 .05 .01
☐ 148 Jeff Gossett .04 .02 .01
☐ 149 Ethan Horton .04 .02 .01
☐ 150 Jamie Holland .04 .02 .01
☐ 151 Jeff Jaeger .04 .02 .01
☐ 152 Todd Marinovich .04 .02 .01
☐ 153 Marcus Allen .25 .11 .03
☐ 154 Steve Smith .04 .02 .01
☐ 155 Flipper Anderson .04 .02 .01
☐ 156 Robert Delpino .04 .02 .01
☐ 157 Cleveland Gary .04 .02 .01
☐ 158 Kevin Greene .25 .11 .03
☐ 159 Dale Hatcher .04 .02 .01
☐ 160 Duval Love .04 .02 .01
☐ 161 Ron Brown .04 .02 .01
☐ 162 Jackie Slater .04 .02 .01
☐ 163 Doug Smith .04 .02 .01
☐ 164 Aaron Cox .04 .02 .01
☐ 165 Larry Kelm .04 .02 .01
☐ 166 Mark Clayton .10 .05 .01
☐ 167 Louis Oliver .04 .02 .01
☐ 168 Mark Higgs .04 .02 .01
☐ 169 Aaron Craver .04 .02 .01
☐ 170 Sammie Smith .04 .02 .01
☐ 171 Tony Paige .04 .02 .01
☐ 172 Jeff Cross .04 .02 .01
☐ 173 David Griggs .04 .02 .01
☐ 174 Richmond Webb .04 .02 .01
☐ 175 Vestee Jackson .04 .02 .01
☐ 176 Jim C. Jensen .04 .02 .01
☐ 177 Anthony Carter .10 .05 .01
☐ 178 Cris Carter .25 .11 .03
☐ 179 Chris Doleman .04 .02 .01
☐ 180 Rich Gannon .04 .02 .01
☐ 181 Al Noga .04 .02 .01
☐ 182 Randall McDaniel .04 .02 .01
☐ 183 Todd Scott .04 .02 .01
☐ 184 Henry Thomas .04 .02 .01
☐ 185 Felix Wright .04 .02 .01
☐ 186 Gary Zimmerman .04 .02 .01
☐ 187 Herschel Walker .10 .05 .01
☐ 188 Vincent Brown .04 .02 .01
☐ 189 Harry Colon .04 .02 .01
☐ 190 Irving Fryar .10 .05 .01
☐ 191 Marv Cook .04 .02 .01
☐ 192 Leonard Russell .10 .05 .01
☐ 193 Hugh Millen .04 .02 .01
☐ 194 Pat Harlow .04 .02 .01
☐ 195 Jon Vaughn .04 .02 .01
☐ 196 Ben Coates 2.00 .90 .25
☐ 197 Johnny Rembert .04 .02 .01
☐ 198 Greg McMurtry .04 .02 .01
☐ 199 Morten Andersen .04 .02 .01
☐ 200 Tommy Barnhardt .04 .02 .01
☐ 201 Bobby Hebert .04 .02 .01
☐ 202 Dalton Hilliard .04 .02 .01
☐ 203 Sam Mills .04 .02 .01
☐ 204 Pat Swilling .10 .05 .01
☐ 205 Rickey Jackson .04 .02 .01
☐ 206 Stan Brock .04 .02 .01
☐ 207 Reginald Jones .04 .02 .01
☐ 208 Gill Fenerty .04 .02 .01
☐ 209 Eric Martin .04 .02 .01
☐ 210 Matt Bahr .04 .02 .01
☐ 211 Rodney Hampton .25 .11 .03
☐ 212 Jeff Hostetler .10 .05 .01
☐ 213 Pepper Johnson .04 .02 .01
☐ 214 Leonard Marshall .04 .02 .01
☐ 215 Doug Riesenberg .04 .02 .01
☐ 216 Stephen Baker .04 .02 .01
☐ 217 Mike Fox .04 .02 .01
☐ 218 Bart Oates .04 .02 .01
☐ 219 Everson Walls .04 .02 .01
☐ 220 Gary Reasons .04 .02 .01
☐ 221 Jeff Lageman .04 .02 .01
☐ 222 Joe Kelly .04 .02 .01
☐ 223 Mo Lewis .04 .02 .01
☐ 224 Tony Stargell .04 .02 .01
☐ 225 Jim Sweeney .04 .02 .01
☐ 226 Freeman McNeil .04 .02 .01
☐ 227 Brian Washington .04 .02 .01
☐ 228 Johnny Hector .04 .02 .01
☐ 229 Terance Mathis .10 .05 .01
☐ 230 Rob Moore .10 .05 .01
☐ 231 Brad Baxter .04 .02 .01
☐ 232 Eric Allen .04 .02 .01
☐ 233 Fred Barnett .25 .11 .03
☐ 234 Jerome Brown .04 .02 .01
☐ 235 Keith Byars .04 .02 .01
☐ 236 William Thomas .04 .02 .01
☐ 237 Jessie Small .04 .02 .01
☐ 238 Robert Drummond .04 .02 .01
☐ 239 Reggie White .25 .11 .03
☐ 240 James Joseph .04 .02 .01
☐ 241 Brad Goebel .04 .02 .01
☐ 242 Clyde Simmons .04 .02 .01
☐ 243 Rich Camarillo .04 .02 .01
☐ 244 Ken Harvey .04 .02 .01
☐ 245 Garth Jax .04 .02 .01
☐ 246 Johnny Johnson UER .04 .02 .01
(Photo on back not him)
☐ 247 Mike Jones .04 .02 .01
☐ 248 Ernie Jones .04 .02 .01
☐ 249 Tom Tupa .04 .02 .01
☐ 250 Ron Wolfley .04 .02 .01
☐ 251 Luis Sharpe .04 .02 .01
☐ 252 Eric Swann .10 .05 .01
☐ 253 Anthony Thompson .04 .02 .01
☐ 254 Gary Anderson K .04 .02 .01
☐ 255 Dermontti Dawson .04 .02 .01
☐ 256 Jeff Graham .25 .11 .03
☐ 257 Eric Green .04 .02 .01
☐ 258 Louis Lipps .04 .02 .01
☐ 259 Neil O'Donnell .25 .11 .03
☐ 260 Rod Woodson .25 .11 .03
☐ 261 Dwight Stone .04 .02 .01
☐ 262 Aaron Jones .04 .02 .01
☐ 263 Keith Willis .04 .02 .01
☐ 264 Ernie Mills .04 .02 .01
☐ 265 Martin Bayless .04 .02 .01
☐ 266 Rod Bernstine .04 .02 .01
☐ 267 John Carney .04 .02 .01
☐ 268 John Friesz .10 .05 .01
☐ 269 Nate Lewis .04 .02 .01
☐ 270 Shawn Jefferson .04 .02 .01
☐ 271 Burt Grossman .04 .02 .01
☐ 272 Eric Moten .04 .02 .01
☐ 273 Gary Plummer .04 .02 .01
☐ 274 Henry Rolling .04 .02 .01
☐ 275 Steve Hendrickson .04 .02 .01
☐ 276 Michael Carter .04 .02 .01
☐ 277 Steve Bono .25 .11 .03
☐ 278 Dexter Carter .04 .02 .01
☐ 279 Mike Cofer .04 .02 .01
☐ 280 Charles Haley .10 .05 .01
☐ 281 Tom Rathman .04 .02 .01
☐ 282 Guy McIntyre .04 .02 .01
☐ 283 John Taylor .10 .05 .01
☐ 284 Dave Waymer .04 .02 .01
☐ 285 Steve Wallace .04 .02 .01
☐ 286 Jamie Williams .04 .02 .01
☐ 287 Brian Blades .10 .05 .01
☐ 288 Jeff Bryant .04 .02 .01
☐ 289 Grant Feasel .04 .02 .01
☐ 290 Jacob Green .04 .02 .01
☐ 291 Andy Heck .04 .02 .01
☐ 292 Kelly Stouffer .04 .02 .01
☐ 293 John Kasay .04 .02 .01
☐ 294 Cortez Kennedy .10 .05 .01
☐ 295 Bryan Millard .04 .02 .01
☐ 296 Eugene Robinson .04 .02 .01
☐ 297 Tony Woods .04 .02 .01
☐ 298 Jesse Anderson UER .04 .02 .01
(Should have Tight
End, not TIGHT END)
☐ 299 Gary Anderson RB .04 .02 .01
☐ 300 Mark Carrier WR .10 .05 .01
☐ 301 Reggie Cobb .04 .02 .01
☐ 302 Robert Wilson .04 .02 .01
☐ 303 Jesse Solomon .04 .02 .01
☐ 304 Broderick Thomas .04 .02 .01
☐ 305 Lawrence Dawsey .10 .05 .01
☐ 306 Charles McRae .04 .02 .01
☐ 307 Paul Gruber .04 .02 .01
☐ 308 Vinny Testaverde .10 .05 .01
☐ 309 Brian Mitchell .10 .05 .01
☐ 310 Darrell Green .04 .02 .01
☐ 311 Art Monk .10 .05 .01
☐ 312 Russ Grimm .04 .02 .01
☐ 313 Mark Rypien .04 .02 .01
☐ 314 Bobby Wilson .04 .02 .01
☐ 315 Wilber Marshall .04 .02 .01
☐ 316 Gerald Riggs .04 .02 .01
☐ 317 Chip Lohmiller .04 .02 .01
☐ 318 Joe Jacoby .04 .02 .01
☐ 319 Martin Mayhew .04 .02 .01
☐ 320 Amp Lee .04 .02 .01
☐ 321 Terrell Buckley .04 .02 .01
☐ 322 Tommy Vardell .10 .05 .01
☐ 323 Ricardo McDonald .04 .02 .01
☐ 324 Joe Bowden .04 .02 .01
☐ 325 Darryl Williams .04 .02 .01
☐ 326 Carlos Huerta .04 .02 .01
☐ 327 Patrick Rowe .04 .02 .01
☐ 328 Siran Stacy .04 .02 .01
☐ 329 Dexter McNabb .04 .02 .01
☐ 330 Willie Clay .04 .02 .01
☐ 331 Oliver Barnett .04 .02 .01
☐ 332 Aundray Bruce .04 .02 .01
☐ 333 Ken Tippins .04 .02 .01
☐ 334 Jessie Tuggle .04 .02 .01
☐ 335 Brian Jordan .10 .05 .01
☐ 336 Andre Rison .10 .05 .01
☐ 337 Houston Hoover .04 .02 .01
☐ 338 Bill Fralic .04 .02 .01
☐ 339 Pat Chaffey .04 .02 .01
☐ 340 Keith Jones .04 .02 .01
☐ 341 Jamie Dukes .04 .02 .01
☐ 342 Chris Mohr .04 .02 .01
☐ 343 John Davis .04 .02 .01
☐ 344 Ray Bentley .04 .02 .01
☐ 345 Scott Norwood .04 .02 .01
☐ 346 Shane Conlan .04 .02 .01
☐ 347 Steve Tasker .10 .05 .01
☐ 348 Will Wolford .04 .02 .01
☐ 349 Gary Baldinger .04 .02 .01
☐ 350 Kirby Jackson .04 .02 .01
☐ 351 Jamie Mueller .04 .02 .01
☐ 352 Pete Metzelaars .04 .02 .01
☐ 353 Richard Dent .10 .05 .01
☐ 354 Ron Rivera .04 .02 .01
☐ 355 Jim Morrissey .04 .02 .01
☐ 356 John Roper .04 .02 .01
☐ 357 Steve McMichael .10 .05 .01
☐ 358 Ron Morris .04 .02 .01
☐ 359 Darren Lewis .04 .02 .01
☐ 360 Anthony Morgan .04 .02 .01
☐ 361 Stan Thomas .04 .02 .01
☐ 362 James Thornton .04 .02 .01
☐ 363 Brad Muster .04 .02 .01
☐ 364 Tim Krumrie .04 .02 .01
☐ 365 Lee Johnson .04 .02 .01
☐ 366 Eric Ball .04 .02 .01
☐ 367 Alonzo Mitz .04 .02 .01
☐ 368 David Grant .04 .02 .01
☐ 369 Lynn James .04 .02 .01
☐ 370 Lewis Billups .04 .02 .01
☐ 371 Jim Breech .04 .02 .01
☐ 372 Alfred Williams .04 .02 .01
☐ 373 Wayne Haddix .04 .02 .01
☐ 374 Tim McGee .04 .02 .01
☐ 375 Michael Jackson .10 .05 .01
☐ 376 Leroy Hoard .10 .05 .01
☐ 377 Tony Jones .04 .02 .01
☐ 378 Vince Newsome .04 .02 .01
☐ 379 Todd Philcox .04 .02 .01
☐ 380 Eric Metcalf .10 .05 .01
☐ 381 John Rienstra .04 .02 .01
☐ 382 Matt Stover .04 .02 .01
☐ 383 Brian Hansen .04 .02 .01
☐ 384 Joe Morris .04 .02 .01
☐ 385 Anthony Pleasant .04 .02 .01
☐ 386 Mark Stepnoski .10 .05 .01
☐ 387 Erik Williams .04 .02 .01
☐ 388 Jimmie Jones .04 .02 .01
☐ 389 Kevin Gogan .04 .02 .01
☐ 390 Manny Hendrix .04 .02 .01
☐ 391 Issiac Holt .04 .02 .01
☐ 392 Ken Norton .25 .11 .03
☐ 393 Tommie Agee .04 .02 .01
☐ 394 Alvin Harper .10 .05 .01
☐ 395 Alexander Wright .04 .02 .01
☐ 396 Mike Saxon .04 .02 .01
☐ 397 Michael Brooks .04 .02 .01
☐ 398 Bobby Humphrey .04 .02 .01
☐ 399 Ken Lanier .04 .02 .01
☐ 400 Steve Sewell .04 .02 .01
☐ 401 Robert Perryman .04 .02 .01
☐ 402 Wymon Henderson .04 .02 .01
☐ 403 Keith Kartz .04 .02 .01
☐ 404 Clarence Kay .04 .02 .01
☐ 405 Keith Traylor .04 .02 .01
☐ 406 Doug Widell .04 .02 .01
☐ 407 Dennis Smith .04 .02 .01
☐ 408 Marc Spindler .04 .02 .01
☐ 409 Lomas Brown .04 .02 .01
☐ 410 Robert Clark .04 .02 .01
☐ 411 Eric Andolsek .04 .02 .01
☐ 412 Mike Farr .04 .02 .01
☐ 413 Ray Crockett .04 .02 .01
☐ 414 Jeff Campbell .04 .02 .01
☐ 415 Dan Owens .04 .02 .01
☐ 416 Jim Arnold .04 .02 .01
☐ 417 Barry Sanders 1.00 .45 .12
☐ 418 Eddie Murray .04 .02 .01
☐ 419 Vince Workman .10 .05 .01
☐ 420 Ed West .04 .02 .01
☐ 421 Charles Wilson .04 .02 .01
☐ 422 Perry Kemp .04 .02 .01
☐ 423 Chuck Cecil .04 .02 .01
☐ 424 James Campen .04 .02 .01
☐ 425 Robert Brown .04 .02 .01
☐ 426 Brian Noble .04 .02 .01
☐ 427 Rich Moran .04 .02 .01
☐ 428 Vai Sikahema .04 .02 .01
☐ 429 Allen Rice .04 .02 .01
☐ 430 Haywood Jeffires .10 .05 .01
☐ 431 Warren Moon .25 .11 .03
☐ 432 Greg Montgomery .04 .02 .01
☐ 433 Sean Jones .10 .05 .01
☐ 434 Richard Johnson .04 .02 .01
☐ 435 Al Smith .04 .02 .01
☐ 436 Johnny Meads .04 .02 .01
☐ 437 William Fuller .10 .05 .01
☐ 438 Mike Munchak .04 .02 .01
☐ 439 Ray Childress .04 .02 .01
☐ 440 Cody Carlson .04 .02 .01
☐ 441 Scott Radecic .04 .02 .01
☐ 442 Quintus McDonald .04 .02 .01
☐ 443 Eugene Daniel .04 .02 .01
☐ 444 Mark Herrmann .04 .02 .01
☐ 445 John Baylor .04 .02 .01
☐ 446 Dave McCloughan .04 .02 .01
☐ 447 Mark Vander Poel .04 .02 .01
☐ 448 Randy Dixon .04 .02 .01
☐ 449 Keith Taylor .04 .02 .01
☐ 450 Alan Grant .04 .02 .01
☐ 451 Tony Siragusa .04 .02 .01
☐ 452 Rich Baldinger .04 .02 .01
☐ 453 Derrick Thomas .25 .11 .03
☐ 454 Bill Jones .04 .02 .01
☐ 455 Troy Stradford .04 .02 .01
☐ 456 Barry Word .04 .02 .01
☐ 457 Tim Grunhard .04 .02 .01
☐ 458 Chris Martin .04 .02 .01
☐ 459 Jayice Pearson .04 .02 .01
☐ 460 Dino Hackett .04 .02 .01
☐ 461 David Lutz .04 .02 .01
☐ 462 Albert Lewis .04 .02 .01
☐ 463 Fred Jones .04 .02 .01
☐ 464 Winston Moss .04 .02 .01
☐ 465 Sam Graddy .04 .02 .01
☐ 466 Steve Wisniewski .04 .02 .01
☐ 467 Jay Schroeder .04 .02 .01
☐ 468 Ronnie Lott .10 .05 .01
☐ 469 Willie Gault .10 .05 .01
☐ 470 Greg Townsend .04 .02 .01
☐ 471 Max Montoya .04 .02 .01
☐ 472 Howie Long .10 .05 .01
☐ 473 Lionel Washington .04 .02 .01
☐ 474 Riki Ellison .04 .02 .01
☐ 475 Tom Newberry .04 .02 .01
☐ 476 Damone Johnson .04 .02 .01
☐ 477 Pat Terrell .04 .02 .01
☐ 478 Marcus Dupree .04 .02 .01
☐ 479 Todd Lyght .04 .02 .01
☐ 480 Buford McGee .04 .02 .01
☐ 481 Bern Brostek .04 .02 .01
☐ 482 Jim Price .04 .02 .01
☐ 483 Robert Young .04 .02 .01
☐ 484 Tony Zendejas .04 .02 .01
☐ 485 Robert Bailey .04 .02 .01
☐ 486 Alvin Wright .04 .02 .01
☐ 487 Pat Carter .04 .02 .01
☐ 488 Pete Stoyanovich .04 .02 .01
☐ 489 Reggie Roby .04 .02 .01
☐ 490 Harry Galbreath .04 .02 .01
☐ 491 Mike McGruder .04 .02 .01

☐ 492 J.B. Brown	.04	.02	.01
☐ 493 E.J. Junior	.04	.02	.01
☐ 494 Ferrell Edmunds	.04	.02	.01
☐ 495 Scott Secules	.04	.02	.01
☐ 496 Greg Baty	.04	.02	.01
☐ 497 Mike Iaquaniello	.04	.02	.01
☐ 498 Keith Sims	.04	.02	.01
☐ 499 John Randle	.10	.05	.01
☐ 500 Joey Browner	.04	.02	.01
☐ 501 Steve Jordan	.04	.02	.01
☐ 502 Darrin Nelson	.04	.02	.01
☐ 503 Audray McMillian	.04	.02	.01
☐ 504 Harry Newsome	.04	.02	.01
☐ 505 Hassan Jones	.04	.02	.01
☐ 506 Ray Berry	.04	.02	.01
☐ 507 Mike Merriweather	.04	.02	.01
☐ 508 Leo Lewis	.04	.02	.01
☐ 509 Tim Irwin	.04	.02	.01
☐ 510 Kirk Lowdermilk	.04	.02	.01
☐ 511 Alfred Anderson	.04	.02	.01
☐ 512 Michael Timpson	.10	.05	.01
☐ 513 Jerome Henderson	.04	.02	.01
☐ 514 Andre Tippett	.04	.02	.01
☐ 515 Chris Singleton	.04	.02	.01
☐ 516 John Stephens	.04	.02	.01
☐ 517 Ronnie Lippett	.04	.02	.01
☐ 518 Bruce Armstrong	.04	.02	.01
☐ 519 Marion Hobby	.04	.02	.01
☐ 520 Tim Goad	.04	.02	.01
☐ 521 Mickey Washington	.04	.02	.01
☐ 522 Fred Smerlas	.04	.02	.01
☐ 523 Wayne Martin	.04	.02	.01
☐ 524 Frank Warren	.04	.02	.01
☐ 525 Floyd Turner	.04	.02	.01
☐ 526 Wesley Carroll	.04	.02	.01
☐ 527 Gene Atkins	.04	.02	.01
☐ 528 Vaughan Johnson	.04	.02	.01
☐ 529 Hoby Brenner	.04	.02	.01
☐ 530 Renaldo Turnbull	.04	.02	.01
☐ 531 Joel Hilgenberg	.04	.02	.01
☐ 532 Craig Heyward	.10	.05	.01
☐ 533 Vince Buck	.04	.02	.01
☐ 534 Jim Dombrowski	.04	.02	.01
☐ 535 Fred McAfee	.04	.02	.01
☐ 536 Phil Simms	.10	.05	.01
☐ 537 Lewis Tillman	.04	.02	.01
☐ 538 John Elliott	.04	.02	.01
☐ 539 Dave Meggett	.10	.05	.01
☐ 540 Mark Collins	.04	.02	.01
☐ 541 Ottis Anderson	.10	.05	.01
☐ 542 Bobby Abrams	.04	.02	.01
☐ 543 Sean Landeta	.04	.02	.01
☐ 544 Brian Williams	.04	.02	.01
☐ 545 Erik Howard	.04	.02	.01
☐ 546 Mark Ingram	.04	.02	.01
☐ 547 Kanavis McGhee	.04	.02	.01
☐ 548 Kyle Clifton	.04	.02	.01
☐ 549 Marvin Washington	.04	.02	.01
☐ 550 Jeff Criswell	.04	.02	.01
☐ 551 Dave Cadigan	.04	.02	.01
☐ 552 Chris Burkett	.04	.02	.01
☐ 553 Erik McMillan	.04	.02	.01
☐ 554 James Hasty	.04	.02	.01
☐ 555 Louie Aguiar	.04	.02	.01
☐ 556 Troy Johnson	.04	.02	.01
☐ 557 Troy Taylor	.04	.02	.01
☐ 558 Pat Kelly	.04	.02	.01
☐ 559 Heath Sherman	.04	.02	.01
☐ 560 Roger Ruzek	.04	.02	.01
☐ 561 Andre Waters	.04	.02	.01
☐ 562 Izel Jenkins	.04	.02	.01
☐ 563 Keith Jackson	.10	.05	.01
☐ 564 Byron Evans	.04	.02	.01
☐ 565 Wes Hopkins	.04	.02	.01
☐ 566 Rich Miano	.04	.02	.01
☐ 567 Seth Joyner	.10	.05	.01
☐ 568 Thomas Sanders	.04	.02	.01
☐ 569 David Alexander	.04	.02	.01
☐ 570 Jeff Kemp	.04	.02	.01
☐ 571 Jock Jones	.04	.02	.01
☐ 572 Craig Patterson	.04	.02	.01
☐ 573 Robert Massey	.04	.02	.01
☐ 574 Bill Lewis	.04	.02	.01
☐ 575 Freddie Joe Nunn	.04	.02	.01
☐ 576 Aeneas Williams	.10	.05	.01
☐ 577 John Jackson	.04	.02	.01
☐ 578 Tim McDonald	.04	.02	.01
☐ 579 Michael Zordich	.04	.02	.01
☐ 580 Eric Hill	.04	.02	.01
☐ 581 Lorenzo Lynch	.04	.02	.01
☐ 582 Vernice Smith	.04	.02	.01
☐ 583 Greg Lloyd	.25	.11	.03
☐ 584 Carnell Lake	.04	.02	.01
☐ 585 Hardy Nickerson	.10	.05	.01
☐ 586 Delton Hall	.04	.02	.01
☐ 587 Gerald Williams	.04	.02	.01
☐ 588 Bryan Hinkle	.04	.02	.01
☐ 589 Barry Foster	.10	.05	.01
☐ 590 Bubby Brister	.04	.02	.01
☐ 591 Rick Strom	.04	.02	.01
☐ 592 David Little	.04	.02	.01
☐ 593 Leroy Thompson	.04	.02	.01
☐ 594 Eric Bieniemy	.04	.02	.01
☐ 595 Courtney Hall	.04	.02	.01
☐ 596 George Thornton	.04	.02	.01
☐ 597 Donnie Elder	.04	.02	.01
☐ 598 Billy Ray Smith	.04	.02	.01
☐ 599 Gill Byrd	.04	.02	.01
☐ 600 Marion Butts	.04	.02	.01
☐ 601 Ronnie Harmon	.04	.02	.01
☐ 602 Anthony Shelton	.04	.02	.01
☐ 603 Mark May	.04	.02	.01
☐ 604 Craig McEwen	.04	.02	.01
☐ 605 Steve Young	.60	.25	.07
☐ 606 Keith Henderson	.04	.02	.01
☐ 607 Pierce Holt	.04	.02	.01
☐ 608 Roy Foster	.04	.02	.01
☐ 609 Don Griffin	.04	.02	.01
☐ 610 Harry Sydney	.04	.02	.01
☐ 611 Todd Bowles	.04	.02	.01
☐ 612 Ted Washington	.04	.02	.01
☐ 613 Johnnie Jackson	.04	.02	.01
☐ 614 Jesse Sapolu	.04	.02	.01
☐ 615 Brent Jones	.10	.05	.01
☐ 616 Travis McNeal	.04	.02	.01
☐ 617 Darrick Brilz	.04	.02	.01
☐ 618 Terry Wooden	.04	.02	.01
☐ 619 Tommy Kane	.04	.02	.01
☐ 620 Nesby Glasgow	.04	.02	.01
☐ 621 Dwayne Harper	.04	.02	.01
☐ 622 Rick Tuten	.04	.02	.01
☐ 623 Chris Warren	.25	.11	.03
☐ 624 John L. Williams	.04	.02	.01
☐ 625 Rufus Porter	.04	.02	.01
☐ 626 David Daniels	.04	.02	.01
☐ 627 Keith McCants	.04	.02	.01
☐ 628 Reuben Davis	.04	.02	.01
☐ 629 Mark Royals	.04	.02	.01
☐ 630 Marty Carter	.04	.02	.01
☐ 631 Ian Beckles	.04	.02	.01
☐ 632 Ron Hall	.04	.02	.01
☐ 633 Eugene Marve	.04	.02	.01
☐ 634 Willie Drewrey	.04	.02	.01
☐ 635 Tom McHale	.04	.02	.01
☐ 636 Kevin Murphy	.04	.02	.01
☐ 637 Robert Hardy	.04	.02	.01
☐ 638 Ricky Sanders	.04	.02	.01
☐ 639 Gary Clark	.25	.11	.03
☐ 640 Andre Collins	.04	.02	.01
☐ 641 Brad Edwards	.04	.02	.01
☐ 642 Monte Coleman	.04	.02	.01
☐ 643 Clarence Vaughn	.04	.02	.01
☐ 644 Fred Stokes	.04	.02	.01
☐ 645 Charles Mann	.04	.02	.01
☐ 646 Earnest Byner	.04	.02	.01
☐ 647 Jim Lachey	.04	.02	.01
☐ 648 Jeff Bostic	.04	.02	.01
☐ 649 Chris Mims	.10	.05	.01
☐ 650 George Williams	.04	.02	.01
☐ 651 Ed Cunningham	.04	.02	.01
☐ 652 Tony Smith	.04	.02	.01
☐ 653 Will Furrer	.04	.02	.01
☐ 654 Matt Elliott	.04	.02	.01
☐ 655 Mike Mooney	.04	.02	.01
☐ 656 Eddie Blake	.04	.02	.01
☐ 657 Leon Searcy	.10	.05	.01
☐ 658 Kevin Turner	.04	.02	.01
☐ 659 Keith Hamilton	.04	.02	.01
☐ 660 Alan Haller	.04	.02	.01

1992 Pacific Bob Griese

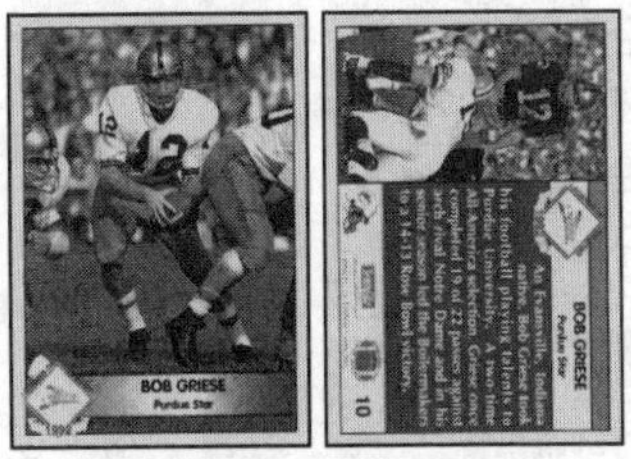

This nine-card standard-size set captures highlights from the career of Hall of Famer Bob Griese. These cards were randomly inserted in second series foil and jumbo packs. They were also randomly inserted in triple folder and five-card change-maker packs. Griese personally autographed 1,000 cards. These cards are individually numbered on the back. The color action player photos on the fronts have white borders, with the player's name and a caption in a multicolored stripe cutting across the bottom of the picture. In a horizontal format, the backs carry another color photo and career summary. The cards are numbered on the back (10-18) continuing with the numbering of the Legends of the Game (Steve) Largent series.

	MINT	NRMT	EXC
COMPLETE SET (9)	5.00	2.20	.60
COMMON GRIESE (10-18)	.60	.25	.07
☐ 10 Purdue Star	.60	.25	.07
☐ 11 AFL Star	.60	.25	.07
☐ 12 Super Bowl Star	.60	.25	.07
☐ 13 Thinking Man's QB	.60	.25	.07
☐ 14 349 Yards	.60	.25	.07
☐ 15 All-Star	.60	.25	.07
☐ 16 The 25,000 Yard Club	.60	.25	.07
☐ 17 Number 12 Retired	.60	.25	.07
☐ 18 Hall of Fame	.60	.25	.07
☐ AU0 Bob Griese AU (Certified autograph)	90.00	40.00	11.00

1992 Pacific Steve Largent

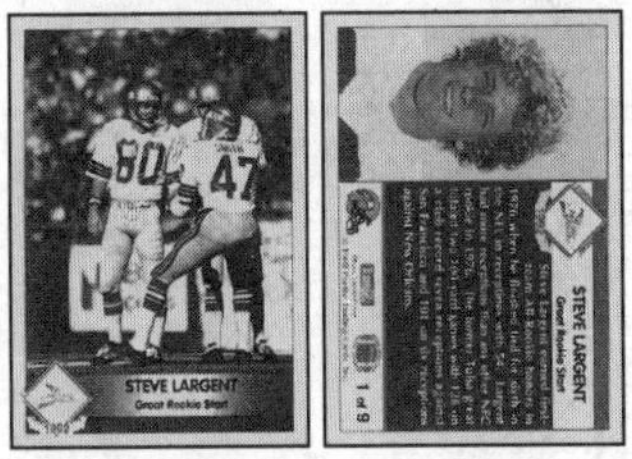

This nine-card standard-size set captures highlights from the career of Hall of Famer Steve Largent. The cards were randomly inserted in first series packs as well as Triple Holder and change-maker packs. Largent personally autographed 1,000 cards and these cards are individually numbered on the back. The color action photos on the fronts have white borders, with the player's name and a caption in a multicolored stripe cutting across the bottom of the picture. In a horizontal format, the backs carry another color photo and career summary.

	MINT	NRMT	EXC
COMPLETE SET (9)	5.00	2.20	.60
COMMON LARGENT (1-9)	.60	.25	.07
☐ 1 Great Rookie Start	.60	.25	.07
☐ 2 Largent Leads NFL	.60	.25	.07
☐ 3 Hi-Steppin'	.60	.25	.07
☐ 4 NFL Leader	.60	.25	.07
☐ 5 Team Captain	.60	.25	.07
☐ 6 Pro Bowl	.60	.25	.07
☐ 7 Man of the Year	.60	.25	.07
☐ 8 The Final Season	.60	.25	.07
☐ 9 Retirement Celebration	.60	.25	.07
☐ AU0 Steve Largent AU (Certified autograph)	90.00	40.00	11.00

1992 Pacific Picks The Pros

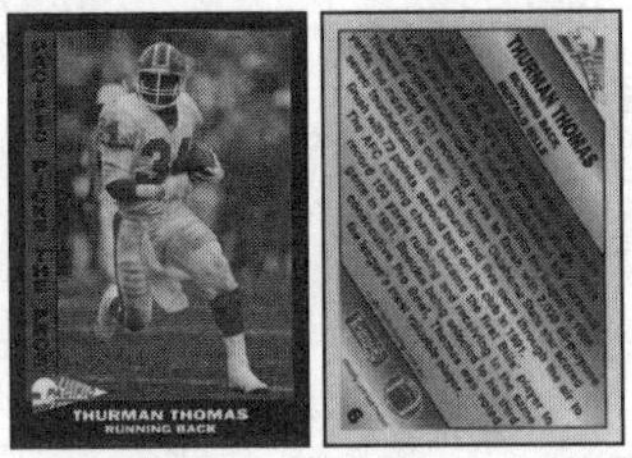

This 25-card standard-size set features Pacific's picks for the top player at each position. The color action player photos on the fronts have either gold or silver foil borders, with the words "Pacific Picks the Pros" in corresponding foil lettering in a multicolored stripe running down the left side of the picture. The gold foil cards were randomly inserted in first series foil packs, while the silver foil cards were found in first series jumbo packs. There is no difference in value between the two versions. On a background of different shades of red and yellow, the diagonally oriented backs present career summaries.

	MINT	NRMT	EXC
COMPLETE SET (25)	35.00	16.00	4.40
COMMON CARD (1-25)	1.00	.45	.12
*GOLD/SILVER: SAME PRICE			
☐ 1 Mark Rypien	2.00	.90	.25
☐ 2 Marv Cook	1.00	.45	.12
☐ 3 Jim Lachey	1.00	.45	.12
☐ 4 Darrell Green	1.00	.45	.12
☐ 5 Derrick Thomas	2.50	1.10	.30
☐ 6 Thurman Thomas	2.50	1.10	.30
☐ 7 Kent Hull	1.00	.45	.12
☐ 8 Tim McDonald	1.00	.45	.12
☐ 9 Mike Croel	1.00	.45	.12
☐ 10 Anthony Munoz	2.50	1.10	.30
☐ 11 Jerome Brown	2.00	.90	.25
☐ 12 Reggie White	2.50	1.10	.30
☐ 13 Gill Byrd	1.00	.45	.12
☐ 14 Jessie Tuggle	1.00	.45	.12
☐ 15 Randall McDaniel	1.00	.45	.12
☐ 16 Sam Mills	1.00	.45	.12
☐ 17 Pat Swilling	2.00	.90	.25
☐ 18 Eugene Robinson	1.00	.45	.12
☐ 19 Michael Irvin	1.00	.45	.12
☐ 20 Emmitt Smith	15.00	6.75	1.85
☐ 21 Jeff Gossett	1.00	.45	.12
☐ 22 Jeff Jaeger	1.00	.45	.12
☐ 23 William Fuller	2.00	.90	.25
☐ 24 Mike Munchak	1.00	.45	.12
☐ 25 Andre Rison	2.50	1.10	.30

1992 Pacific Prism Inserts

This ten-card standard-size set features top NFL running backs. According to Pacific, 10,000 of each card were produced. They were

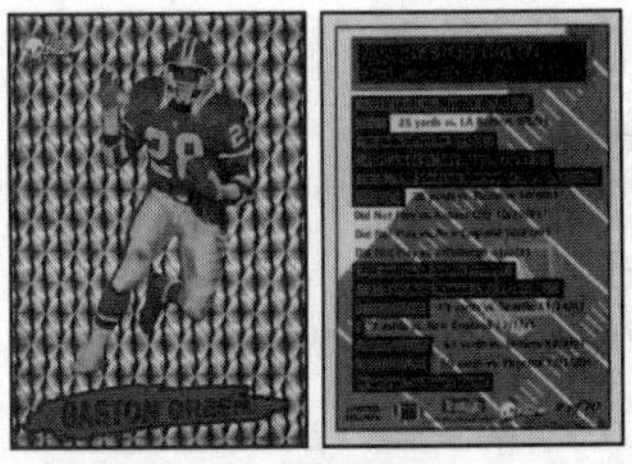

randomly inserted into second series foil packs and Triple Folder card packs. The fronts display color action player photos cut out and superimposed on a prism-patterned background. The player's name appears in a colored streak toward the bottom of the front. On a background consisting of a pastel green football field, the backs use team-color coded bar graphs to present the player's yardage for each game of the 1991 season.

	MINT	NRMT	EXC
COMPLETE SET (10)	18.00	8.00	2.20
COMMON CARD (1-10)	1.00	.45	.12
☐ 1 Thurman Thomas	2.00	.90	.25
☐ 2 Gaston Green	1.00	.45	.12
☐ 3 Christian Okoye	1.50	.70	.19
☐ 4 Leonard Russell	1.50	.70	.19
☐ 5 Mark Higgs	1.00	.45	.12
☐ 6 Emmitt Smith	5.00	2.20	.60
☐ 7 Barry Sanders	3.00	1.35	.35
☐ 8 Rodney Hampton	2.00	.90	.25
☐ 9 Earnest Byner	1.00	.45	.12
☐ 10 Herschel Walker	1.50	.70	.19

1992 Pacific Statistical Leaders

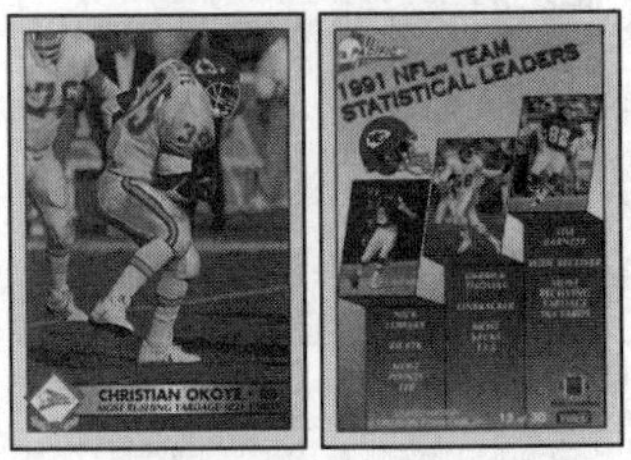

This 30-card standard-size set features the team statistical leaders from the 28 NFL teams, plus two cards devoted to the AFC and NFC rushing leaders. The cards were randomly inserted into both series foil packs, Triple Folder card packs, and change-maker (25 cents) packs. The whole set of these Stat Leaders was included as an insert with 1992 Pacific factory sets. The fronts display glossy color action photos bordered in white. At the bottom of the picture, the player's name and accomplishment appear in a multi-colored stripe. The backs reflect the team's colors and have mini-photos of three other team leaders. The cards are numbered on the back and the team leader cards are checklisted alphabetically according to team name.

	MINT	NRMT	EXC
COMPLETE SET (30)	10.00	4.50	1.25
COMMON CARD (1-30)	.30	.14	.04
☐ 1 Chris Miller	.50	.23	.06
☐ 2 Thurman Thomas	.75	.35	.09
☐ 3 Jim Harbaugh	.75	.35	.09
☐ 4 Jim Breech	.30	.14	.04
☐ 5 Kevin Mack	.30	.14	.04
☐ 6 Emmitt Smith	4.00	1.80	.50
☐ 7 Gaston Green	.30	.14	.04
☐ 8 Barry Sanders	2.00	.90	.25
☐ 9 Tony Bennett	.30	.14	.04
☐ 10 Warren Moon	.75	.35	.09
☐ 11 Bill Brooks	.50	.23	.06
☐ 12 Christian Okoye	.50	.23	.06
☐ 13 Jay Schroeder	.30	.14	.04
☐ 14 Robert Delpino	.30	.14	.04
☐ 15 Mark Higgs	.30	.14	.04
☐ 16 John Randle	.50	.23	.06
☐ 17 Leonard Russell	.50	.23	.06
☐ 18 Pat Swilling	.50	.23	.06
☐ 19 Rodney Hampton	.75	.35	.09
☐ 20 Terance Mathis	.50	.23	.06
☐ 21 Fred Barnett	.75	.35	.09
☐ 22 Aeneas Williams	.50	.23	.06
☐ 23 Neil O'Donnell	.50	.23	.06
☐ 24 Marion Butts	.50	.23	.06
☐ 25 Steve Young	1.00	.45	.12
☐ 26 John L. Williams	.30	.14	.04
☐ 27 Reggie Cobb	.30	.14	.04
☐ 28 Mark Rypien	.50	.23	.06
☐ 29 Thurman Thomas AFC Rushing Leaders	.75	.35	.09
☐ 30 Emmitt Smith NFC Rushing Leaders	2.00	.90	.25

1993 Pacific Prototypes

These five standard-size cards were issued to preview the design of the 1993 Pacific Plus football series. Each card was packed in a cello

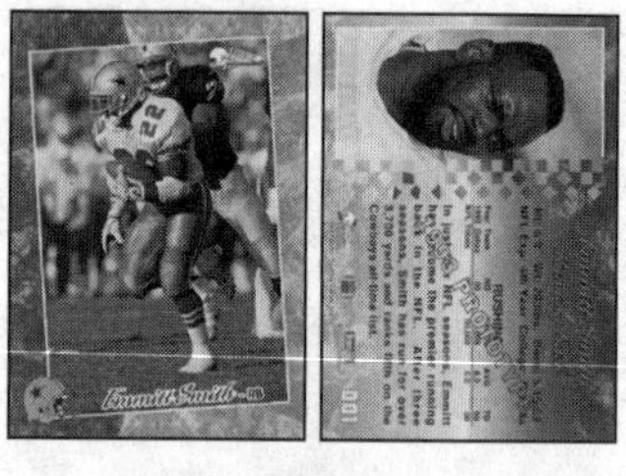

pack with an ad card. The color action photos on the fronts are tilted slightly to the left and set on a two-color marbleized card face reflecting the team's colors. The player's name appears in script at the bottom of the picture, with the team helmet in the lower left corner. On two-toned marbelized background, the horizontal backs carry a color close-up shot, biography, statistics, and career highlights. Running across the text portion are the words "1993 Prototypes." The cards were given away at the July 1993 National Sports Collectors Convention in Chicago and used as sales samples. The production run was reportedly 5,000 sets.

	MINT	NRMT	EXC
COMPLETE SET (5)	20.00	9.00	2.50
COMMON CARD (1-5)	1.50	.70	.19
□ 1 Emmitt Smith	8.00	3.60	1.00
□ 2 Barry Sanders	5.00	2.20	.60
□ 3 Derrick Thomas	2.00	.90	.25
□ 4 Jim Everett	1.50	.70	.19
□ 5 Steve Young	4.00	1.80	.50

1993 Pacific

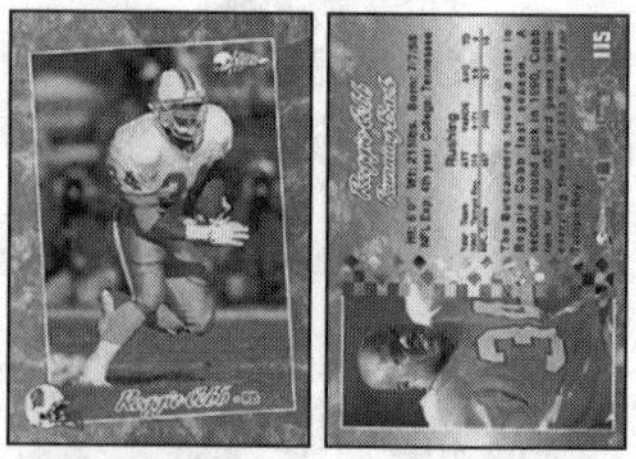

The 1993 Pacific football set consists of 440 standard-size cards. Just 5,000 cases or 99,000 of each card were reportedly produced. Randomly inserted throughout the 12-card foil packs were a 25-card Pacific Picks the Pros gold foil set and a 20-card Prism set. The production run on the insert sets was 8,000 each. The color action photos on the fronts are tilted slightly to the left and set on a two-color marbleized card face reflecting the team's colors. The player's name appears in script at the bottom of the picture, with the team helmet in the lower left corner. On two-toned marbelized background, the horizontal backs carry a color close-up shot, biography, statistics, and career highlights. The cards are numbered on the back and checklisted below according to NFC and AFC divisional alignments. The set closes with the following topical subsets: NFL Stars (393-417) and Rookies (418-440). Rookie Cards include Jerome Bettis, Drew Bledsoe, Reggie Brooks, Curtis Conway, Garrison Hearst, O.J. McDuffie, Natrone Means, Glyn Milburn, Rick Mirer, Robert Smith and Kevin Williams. Separately numbered checklist cards were also randomly inserted into packs.

	MINT	NRMT	EXC
COMPLETE SET (440)	20.00	9.00	2.50
COMMON CARD (1-440)	.05	.02	.01
COMPLETE CHECKLIST SET (4)	4.00	1.80	.50
□ 1 Emmitt Smith	2.00	.90	.25
□ 2 Troy Aikman	1.00	.45	.12
□ 3 Larry Brown DB	.05	.02	.01
□ 4 Tony Casillas	.05	.02	.01
□ 5 Thomas Everett	.05	.02	.01
□ 6 Alvin Harper	.10	.05	.01
□ 7 Michael Irvin	.25	.11	.03
□ 8 Charles Haley	.10	.05	.01
□ 9 Leon Lett	.10	.05	.01
□ 10 Kevin Smith	.10	.05	.01
□ 11 Robert Jones	.05	.02	.01
□ 12 Jimmy Smith	.10	.05	.01
□ 13 Derrick Gainer	.05	.02	.01
□ 14 Lin Elliott	.05	.02	.01
□ 15 William Thomas	.05	.02	.01
□ 16 Clyde Simmons	.05	.02	.01
□ 17 Seth Joyner	.05	.02	.01
□ 18 Randall Cunningham	.10	.05	.01
□ 19 Byron Evans	.05	.02	.01
□ 20 Fred Barnett	.10	.05	.01
□ 21 Calvin Williams	.10	.05	.01
□ 22 James Joseph	.05	.02	.01
□ 23 Heath Sherman	.05	.02	.01
□ 24 Siran Stacy	.05	.02	.01
□ 25 Andy Harmon	.10	.05	.01
□ 26 Eric Allen	.05	.02	.01
□ 27 Herschel Walker	.10	.05	.01
□ 28 Vai Sikahema	.05	.02	.01
□ 29 Earnest Byner	.05	.02	.01
□ 30 Jeff Bostic	.05	.02	.01
□ 31 Monte Coleman	.05	.02	.01
□ 32 Ricky Ervins	.05	.02	.01
□ 33 Darrell Green	.05	.02	.01
□ 34 Mark Schlereth	.05	.02	.01
□ 35 Mark Rypien	.05	.02	.01
□ 36 Art Monk	.10	.05	.01
□ 37 Brian Mitchell	.10	.05	.01
□ 38 Chip Lohmiller	.05	.02	.01
□ 39 Charles Mann	.05	.02	.01
□ 40 Shane Collins	.05	.02	.01
□ 41 Jim Lachey	.05	.02	.01
□ 42 Desmond Howard	.10	.05	.01
□ 43 Rodney Hampton	.25	.11	.03
□ 44 Dave Brown	.25	.11	.03
□ 45 Mark Collins	.05	.02	.01
□ 46 Jarrod Bunch	.05	.02	.01
□ 47 William Roberts	.05	.02	.01
□ 48 Sean Landeta	.05	.02	.01
□ 49 Lawrence Taylor	.25	.11	.03
□ 50 Ed McCaffrey	.05	.02	.01
□ 51 Bart Oates	.05	.02	.01
□ 52 Pepper Johnson	.05	.02	.01
□ 53 Eric Dorsey	.05	.02	.01
□ 54 Erik Howard	.05	.02	.01
□ 55 Phil Simms	.10	.05	.01
□ 56 Derek Brown TE	.05	.02	.01
□ 57 Johnny Bailey	.05	.02	.01
□ 58 Rich Camarillo	.05	.02	.01
□ 59 Larry Centers	.40	.18	.05
□ 60 Chris Chandler	.10	.05	.01
□ 61 Randal Hill	.05	.02	.01
□ 62 Ricky Proehl	.05	.02	.01
□ 63 Freddie Joe Nunn	.05	.02	.01
□ 64 Robert Massey	.05	.02	.01
□ 65 Aeneas Williams	.05	.02	.01
□ 66 Luis Sharpe	.05	.02	.01
□ 67 Eric Swann	.10	.05	.01
□ 68 Timm Rosenbach	.05	.02	.01
□ 69 Anthony Edwards	.05	.02	.01
□ 70 Greg Davis	.05	.02	.01
□ 71 Terry Allen	.25	.11	.03
□ 72 Anthony Carter	.10	.05	.01
□ 73 Cris Carter	.25	.11	.03
□ 74 Roger Craig	.10	.05	.01
□ 75 Jack Del Rio	.05	.02	.01
□ 76 Chris Doleman	.05	.02	.01
□ 77 Rich Gannon	.05	.02	.01
□ 78 Hassan Jones	.05	.02	.01
□ 79 Steve Jordan	.05	.02	.01
□ 80 Randall McDaniel	.05	.02	.01
□ 81 Sean Salisbury	.05	.02	.01
□ 82 Harry Newsome	.05	.02	.01
□ 83 Carlos Jenkins	.05	.02	.01
□ 84 Jake Reed	.25	.11	.03
□ 85 Edgar Bennett	.25	.11	.03
□ 86 Tony Bennett	.05	.02	.01
□ 87 Terrell Buckley	.05	.02	.01
□ 88 Ty Detmer	.25	.11	.03
□ 89 Brett Favre	2.00	.90	.25
□ 90 Chris Jacke	.05	.02	.01
□ 91 Sterling Sharpe	.25	.11	.03
□ 92 James Campen	.05	.02	.01
□ 93 Brian Noble	.05	.02	.01
□ 94 Lester Archambeau	.05	.02	.01
□ 95 Harry Sydney	.05	.02	.01
□ 96 Corey Harris	.05	.02	.01
□ 97 Don Majkowski	.05	.02	.01
□ 98 Ken Ruettgers	.05	.02	.01
□ 99 Lomas Brown	.05	.02	.01
□ 100 Jason Hanson	.05	.02	.01
□ 101 Robert Porcher	.05	.02	.01
□ 102 Chris Spielman	.10	.05	.01
□ 103 Erik Kramer	.10	.05	.01
□ 104 Tracy Scroggins	.05	.02	.01
□ 105 Rodney Peete	.05	.02	.01
□ 106 Barry Sanders	1.00	.45	.12
□ 107 Herman Moore	.75	.35	.09
□ 108 Brett Perriman	.25	.11	.03
□ 109 Mel Gray	.10	.05	.01
□ 110 Dennis Gibson	.05	.02	.01
□ 111 Bennie Blades	.05	.02	.01
□ 112 Andre Ware	.05	.02	.01
□ 113 Gary Anderson RB	.05	.02	.01
□ 114 Tyji Armstrong	.05	.02	.01
□ 115 Reggie Cobb	.05	.02	.01
□ 116 Marty Carter	.05	.02	.01
□ 117 Lawrence Dawsey	.05	.02	.01
□ 118 Steve DeBerg	.05	.02	.01
□ 119 Ron Hall	.05	.02	.01
□ 120 Courtney Hawkins	.05	.02	.01
□ 121 Broderick Thomas	.05	.02	.01
□ 122 Keith McCants	.05	.02	.01
□ 123 Bruce Reimers	.05	.02	.01
□ 124 Darrick Brownlow	.05	.02	.01
□ 125 Mark Wheeler	.05	.02	.01
□ 126 Ricky Reynolds	.05	.02	.01
□ 127 Neal Anderson	.05	.02	.01
□ 128 Trace Armstrong	.05	.02	.01
□ 129 Mark Carrier DB	.05	.02	.01
□ 130 Richard Dent	.10	.05	.01
□ 131 Wendell Davis	.05	.02	.01
□ 132 Darren Lewis	.05	.02	.01
□ 133 Tom Waddle	.05	.02	.01
□ 134 Jim Harbaugh	.25	.11	.03
□ 135 Steve McMichael	.10	.05	.01
□ 136 William Perry	.10	.05	.01
□ 137 Alonzo Spellman	.05	.02	.01
□ 138 John Roper	.05	.02	.01
□ 139 Peter Tom Willis	.05	.02	.01
□ 140 Dante Jones	.05	.02	.01
□ 141 Harris Barton	.05	.02	.01
□ 142 Michael Carter	.05	.02	.01
□ 143 Eric Davis	.05	.02	.01
□ 144 Dana Hall	.05	.02	.01
□ 145 Amp Lee	.05	.02	.01
□ 146 Don Griffin	.05	.02	.01
□ 147 Jerry Rice	1.00	.45	.12
□ 148 Ricky Watters	.25	.11	.03
□ 149 Steve Young	.75	.35	.09
□ 150 Bill Romanowski	.05	.02	.01
□ 151 Klaus Wilmsmeyer	.05	.02	.01
□ 152 Steve Bono	.25	.11	.03
□ 153 Tom Rathman	.05	.02	.01
□ 154 Odessa Turner	.05	.02	.01
□ 155 Morten Andersen	.05	.02	.01
□ 156 Richard Cooper	.05	.02	.01
□ 157 Toi Cook	.05	.02	.01
□ 158 Quinn Early	.10	.05	.01
□ 159 Vaughn Dunbar	.05	.02	.01
□ 160 Rickey Jackson	.05	.02	.01
□ 161 Wayne Martin	.05	.02	.01
□ 162 Hoby Brenner	.05	.02	.01
□ 163 Joel Hilgenberg	.05	.02	.01
□ 164 Mike Buck	.05	.02	.01
□ 165 Torrance Small	.05	.02	.01
□ 166 Eric Martin	.05	.02	.01
□ 167 Vaughan Johnson	.05	.02	.01
□ 168 Sam Mills	.05	.02	.01
□ 169 Steve Broussard	.05	.02	.01
□ 170 Darion Conner	.05	.02	.01
□ 171 Drew Hill	.05	.02	.01
□ 172 Chris Hinton	.05	.02	.01
□ 173 Chris Miller	.10	.05	.01
□ 174 Tim McKyer	.05	.02	.01
□ 175 Norm Johnson	.05	.02	.01
□ 176 Mike Pritchard	.10	.05	.01
□ 177 Andre Rison	.10	.05	.01
□ 178 Deion Sanders	.60	.25	.07
□ 179 Tony Smith	.05	.02	.01
□ 180 Bruce Pickens	.05	.02	.01
□ 181 Michael Haynes	.10	.05	.01
□ 182 Jessie Tuggle	.05	.02	.01
□ 183 Marc Boutte	.05	.02	.01
□ 184 Don Bracken	.05	.02	.01
□ 185 Bern Brostek	.05	.02	.01
□ 186 Henry Ellard	.10	.05	.01
□ 187 Jim Everett	.10	.05	.01
□ 188 Sean Gilbert	.10	.05	.01
□ 189 Cleveland Gary	.05	.02	.01
□ 190 Todd Kinchen	.05	.02	.01
□ 191 Pat Terrell	.05	.02	.01
□ 192 Jackie Slater	.05	.02	.01
□ 193 David Lang	.05	.02	.01
□ 194 Flipper Anderson	.05	.02	.01
□ 195 Tony Zendejas	.05	.02	.01
□ 196 Roman Phifer	.05	.02	.01
□ 197 Steve Christie	.05	.02	.01
□ 198 Cornelius Bennett	.10	.05	.01
□ 199 Phil Hansen	.05	.02	.01
□ 200 Don Beebe	.05	.02	.01
□ 201 Mark Kelso	.05	.02	.01
□ 202 Bruce Smith	.25	.11	.03
□ 203 Darryl Talley	.05	.02	.01
□ 204 Andre Reed	.10	.05	.01
□ 205 Mike Lodish	.05	.02	.01
□ 206 Jim Kelly	.25	.11	.03
□ 207 Thurman Thomas	.25	.11	.03
□ 208 Kenneth Davis	.05	.02	.01
□ 209 Frank Reich	.05	.02	.01
□ 210 Kent Hull	.05	.02	.01
□ 211 Marco Coleman	.05	.02	.01
□ 212 Bryan Cox	.05	.02	.01
□ 213 Jeff Cross	.05	.02	.01
□ 214 Mark Higgs	.05	.02	.01
□ 215 Keith Jackson	.10	.05	.01
□ 216 Scott Miller	.05	.02	.01
□ 217 John Offerdahl	.05	.02	.01
□ 218 Dan Marino	2.00	.90	.25
□ 219 Keith Sims	.05	.02	.01
□ 220 Chuck Klingbeil	.05	.02	.01
□ 221 Troy Vincent	.05	.02	.01
□ 222 Mike Williams	.05	.02	.01
□ 223 Pete Stoyanovich	.05	.02	.01
□ 224 J.B. Brown	.05	.02	.01
□ 225 Ashley Ambrose	.05	.02	.01
□ 226 Jason Belser	.05	.02	.01
□ 227 Jeff George	.25	.11	.03
□ 228 Quentin Coryatt	.10	.05	.01
□ 229 Duane Bickett	.05	.02	.01
□ 230 Steve Emtman	.05	.02	.01
□ 231 Anthony Johnson	.10	.05	.01
□ 232 Rohn Stark	.05	.02	.01
□ 233 Jessie Hester	.05	.02	.01
□ 234 Reggie Langhorne	.05	.02	.01
□ 235 Clarence Verdin	.05	.02	.01
□ 236 Dean Biasucci	.05	.02	.01
□ 237 Jack Trudeau	.05	.02	.01
□ 238 Tony Siragusa	.05	.02	.01
□ 239 Chris Burkett	.05	.02	.01
□ 240 Brad Baxter	.05	.02	.01
□ 241 Rob Moore	.10	.05	.01
□ 242 Browning Nagle	.05	.02	.01
□ 243 Jim Sweeney	.05	.02	.01
□ 244 Kurt Barber	.05	.02	.01
□ 245 Siupeli Malamala	.05	.02	.01
□ 246 Mike Brim	.05	.02	.01
□ 247 Mo Lewis	.05	.02	.01
□ 248 Johnny Mitchell	.05	.02	.01
□ 249 Ken Whisenhunt	.05	.02	.01
□ 250 James Hasty	.05	.02	.01
□ 251 Kyle Clifton	.05	.02	.01
□ 252 Terance Mathis	.10	.05	.01
□ 253 Ray Agnew	.05	.02	.01
□ 254 Eugene Chung	.05	.02	.01
□ 255 Marv Cook	.05	.02	.01
□ 256 Johnny Rembert	.05	.02	.01
□ 257 Maurice Hurst	.05	.02	.01
□ 258 Jon Vaughn	.05	.02	.01
□ 259 Leonard Russell	.10	.05	.01
□ 260 Pat Harlow	.05	.02	.01
□ 261 Andre Tippett	.05	.02	.01
□ 262 Michael Timpson	.05	.02	.01
□ 263 Greg McMurtry	.05	.02	.01
□ 264 Chris Singleton	.05	.02	.01
□ 265 Reggie Redding	.05	.02	.01
□ 266 Walter Stanley	.05	.02	.01
□ 267 Gary Anderson K	.05	.02	.01
□ 268 Merril Hoge	.05	.02	.01
□ 269 Barry Foster	.10	.05	.01
□ 270 Charles Davenport	.05	.02	.01
□ 271 Jeff Graham	.10	.05	.01
□ 272 Adrian Cooper	.05	.02	.01
□ 273 David Little	.05	.02	.01
□ 274 Neil O'Donnell	.25	.11	.03
□ 275 Rod Woodson	.25	.11	.03
□ 276 Ernie Mills	.05	.02	.01
□ 277 Dwight Stone	.05	.02	.01
□ 278 Darren Perry	.05	.02	.01
□ 279 Dermontti Dawson	.05	.02	.01
□ 280 Carlton Haselrig	.05	.02	.01
□ 281 Pat Coleman	.05	.02	.01
□ 282 Ernest Givins	.10	.05	.01
□ 283 Warren Moon	.25	.11	.03
□ 284 Haywood Jeffires	.10	.05	.01
□ 285 Cody Carlson	.05	.02	.01
□ 286 Ray Childress	.05	.02	.01
□ 287 Bruce Matthews	.05	.02	.01
□ 288 Webster Slaughter	.05	.02	.01
□ 289 Bo Orlando	.05	.02	.01
□ 290 Lorenzo White	.05	.02	.01
□ 291 Eddie Robinson	.05	.02	.01
□ 292 Bubba McDowell	.05	.02	.01
□ 293 Bucky Richardson	.05	.02	.01
□ 294 Sean Jones	.05	.02	.01
□ 295 David Brandon	.05	.02	.01
□ 296 Shawn Collins	.05	.02	.01
□ 297 Lawyer Tillman	.05	.02	.01
□ 298 Bob Dahl	.05	.02	.01
□ 299 Kevin Mack	.05	.02	.01
□ 300 Bernie Kosar	.10	.05	.01
□ 301 Tommy Vardell	.05	.02	.01
□ 302 Jay Hilgenberg	.05	.02	.01
□ 303 Michael Dean Perry	.10	.05	.01
□ 304 Michael Jackson	.10	.05	.01
□ 305 Eric Metcalf	.10	.05	.01
□ 306 Rico Smith	.05	.02	.01
□ 307 Stevon Moore	.05	.02	.01
□ 308 Leroy Hoard	.10	.05	.01
□ 309 Eric Ball	.05	.02	.01
□ 310 Derrick Fenner	.05	.02	.01
□ 311 James Francis	.05	.02	.01
□ 312 Ricardo McDonald	.05	.02	.01
□ 313 Tim Krumrie	.05	.02	.01
□ 314 Carl Pickens	.75	.35	.09
□ 315 David Klingler	.05	.02	.01
□ 316 Donald Hollas	.05	.02	.01
□ 317 Harold Green	.05	.02	.01
□ 318 Daniel Stubbs	.05	.02	.01
□ 319 Alfred Williams	.05	.02	.01
□ 320 Darryl Williams	.05	.02	.01
□ 321 Mike Arthur	.05	.02	.01
□ 322 Leonard Wheeler	.05	.02	.01
□ 323 Gill Byrd	.05	.02	.01
□ 324 Eric Bieniemy	.05	.02	.01
□ 325 Marion Butts	.05	.02	.01
□ 326 John Carney	.05	.02	.01
□ 327 Stan Humphries	.25	.11	.03
□ 328 Ronnie Harmon	.05	.02	.01
□ 329 Junior Seau	.25	.11	.03
□ 330 Nate Lewis	.05	.02	.01
□ 331 Harry Swayne	.05	.02	.01
□ 332 Leslie O'Neal	.10	.05	.01
□ 333 Eric Moten	.05	.02	.01
□ 334 Blaise Winter	.05	.02	.01
□ 335 Anthony Miller	.10	.05	.01
□ 336 Gary Plummer	.05	.02	.01
□ 337 Willie Davis	.25	.11	.03
□ 338 J.J. Birden	.05	.02	.01
□ 339 Tim Barnett	.05	.02	.01
□ 340 Dave Krieg	.10	.05	.01
□ 341 Barry Word	.05	.02	.01
□ 342 Tracy Simien	.05	.02	.01
□ 343 Christian Okoye	.05	.02	.01
□ 344 Todd McNair	.05	.02	.01
□ 345 Dan Saleaumua	.05	.02	.01
□ 346 Derrick Thomas	.25	.11	.03
□ 347 Harvey Williams	.10	.05	.01

☐ 348 Kimble Anders	.25	.11	.03
☐ 349 Tim Grunhard	.05	.02	.01
☐ 350 Tony Hargain UER (Hargrain on front)	.05	.02	.01
☐ 351 Simon Fletcher	.05	.02	.01
☐ 352 John Elway	.75	.35	.09
☐ 353 Mike Croel	.05	.02	.01
☐ 354 Steve Atwater	.05	.02	.01
☐ 355 Tommy Maddox	.05	.02	.01
☐ 356 Karl Mecklenburg	.05	.02	.01
☐ 357 Shane Dronett	.05	.02	.01
☐ 358 Kenny Walker	.05	.02	.01
☐ 359 Reggie Rivers	.05	.02	.01
☐ 360 Cedric Tillman	.05	.02	.01
☐ 361 Arthur Marshall	.05	.02	.01
☐ 362 Greg Lewis	.05	.02	.01
☐ 363 Shannon Sharpe	.25	.11	.03
☐ 364 Doug Widell	.05	.02	.01
☐ 365 Todd Marinovich	.05	.02	.01
☐ 366 Nick Bell	.05	.02	.01
☐ 367 Eric Dickerson	.10	.05	.01
☐ 368 Max Montoya	.05	.02	.01
☐ 369 Winston Moss	.05	.02	.01
☐ 370 Howie Long	.10	.05	.01
☐ 371 Willie Gault	.05	.02	.01
☐ 372 Tim Brown	.25	.11	.03
☐ 373 Steve Smith	.05	.02	.01
☐ 374 Steve Wisniewski	.05	.02	.01
☐ 375 Alexander Wright	.05	.02	.01
☐ 376 Ethan Horton	.05	.02	.01
☐ 377 Napoleon McCallum	.05	.02	.01
☐ 378 Terry McDaniel	.05	.02	.01
☐ 379 Patrick Hunter	.05	.02	.01
☐ 380 Robert Blackmon	.05	.02	.01
☐ 381 John Kasay	.05	.02	.01
☐ 382 Cortez Kennedy	.10	.05	.01
☐ 383 Andy Heck	.05	.02	.01
☐ 384 Bill Hitchcock	.05	.02	.01
☐ 385 Rick Mirer	1.25	.55	.16
☐ 386 Jeff Bryant	.05	.02	.01
☐ 387 Eugene Robinson	.05	.02	.01
☐ 388 John L. Williams	.05	.02	.01
☐ 389 Chris Warren	.10	.05	.01
☐ 390 Rufus Porter	.05	.02	.01
☐ 391 Joe Tofflemire	.05	.02	.01
☐ 392 Dan McGwire	.05	.02	.01
☐ 393 Boomer Esiason	.10	.05	.01
☐ 394 Brad Muster	.05	.02	.01
☐ 395 James Lofton	.10	.05	.01
☐ 396 Tim McGee	.05	.02	.01
☐ 397 Steve Beuerlein	.05	.02	.01
☐ 398 Gaston Green	.05	.02	.01
☐ 399 Bill Brooks	.05	.02	.01
☐ 400 Ronnie Lott	.10	.05	.01
☐ 401 Jay Schroeder	.05	.02	.01
☐ 402 Marcus Allen	.25	.11	.03
☐ 403 Kevin Greene	.25	.11	.03
☐ 404 Kirk Lowdermilk	.05	.02	.01
☐ 405 Hugh Millen	.05	.02	.01
☐ 406 Pat Swilling	.05	.02	.01
☐ 407 Bobby Hebert	.05	.02	.01
☐ 408 Carl Banks	.05	.02	.01
☐ 409 Jeff Hostetler	.10	.05	.01
☐ 410 Leonard Marshall	.05	.02	.01
☐ 411 Ken O'Brien	.05	.02	.01
☐ 412 Joe Montana	1.00	.45	.12
☐ 413 Reggie White	.25	.11	.03
☐ 414 Gary Clark	.10	.05	.01
☐ 415 Johnny Johnson	.05	.02	.01
☐ 416 Tim McDonald	.05	.02	.01
☐ 417 Pierce Holt	.05	.02	.01
☐ 418 Gino Torretta	.10	.05	.01
☐ 419 Glyn Milburn	.25	.11	.03
☐ 420 O.J. McDuffie	.75	.35	.09
☐ 421 Coleman Rudolph	.05	.02	.01
☐ 422 Reggie Brooks	.10	.05	.01
☐ 423 Garrison Hearst	1.25	.55	.16
☐ 424 Leonard Renfro	.05	.02	.01
☐ 425 Kevin Williams	.25	.11	.03
☐ 426 Demetrius DuBose	.05	.02	.01
☐ 427 Elvis Grbac	1.25	.55	.16
☐ 428 Lincoln Kennedy	.05	.02	.01
☐ 429 Carlton Gray	.05	.02	.01
☐ 430 Micheal Barrow	.05	.02	.01
☐ 431 George Teague	.10	.05	.01
☐ 432 Curtis Conway	.75	.35	.09
☐ 433 Natrone Means	1.25	.55	.16
☐ 434 Jerome Bettis	1.50	.70	.19
☐ 435 Drew Bledsoe	3.00	1.35	.35
☐ 436 Robert Smith	.75	.35	.09
☐ 437 Deon Figures	.10	.05	.01
☐ 438 Qadry Ismail	.25	.11	.03
☐ 439 Chris Slade	.10	.05	.01
☐ 440 Dana Stubblefield	.25	.11	.03

1993 Pacific Picks the Pros Gold

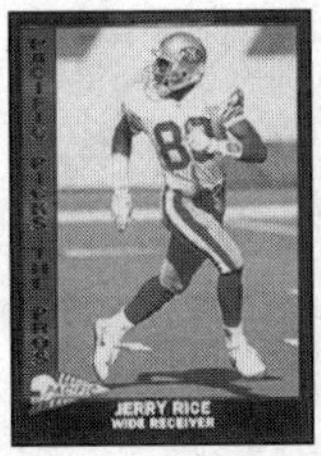

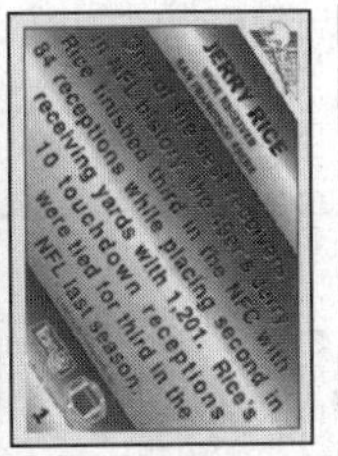

These 25 standard-size cards showcasing Pacific's picks at each position were random inserts in 1993 Pacific packs. Cards from the parallel silver version of this set were randomly inserted in packs of 1993 Pacific Triple Folders. The fronts feature gold foil-bordered color action photos. The player's name and position appear in white lettering in the gold foil margin beneath the photo. The horizontal white bordered back carries the player's name, position, team name and season highlights in diagonal black lettering set on a gray and blue background.

	MINT	NRMT	EXC
COMPLETE SET (25)	70.00	32.00	8.75
COMMON CARD (1-25)	2.00	.90	.25
*SILVER CARDS: SAME PRICE			
☐ 1 Jerry Rice	12.00	5.50	1.50
☐ 2 Sterling Sharpe	4.00	1.80	.50
☐ 3 Richmond Webb	2.00	.90	.25
☐ 4 Harris Barton	2.00	.90	.25
☐ 5 Randall McDaniel	2.00	.90	.25
☐ 6 Steve Wisniewski	2.00	.90	.25
☐ 7 Mark Stepnoski	2.00	.90	.25
☐ 8 Steve Young	8.00	3.60	1.00
☐ 9 Emmitt Smith	25.00	11.00	3.10
☐ 10 Barry Foster	3.00	1.35	.35
☐ 11 Nick Lowery	2.00	.90	.25
☐ 12 Reggie White	4.00	1.80	.50
☐ 13 Leslie O'Neal	3.00	1.35	.35
☐ 14 Cortez Kennedy	3.00	1.35	.35
☐ 15 Ray Childress	3.00	1.35	.35
☐ 16 Vaughan Johnson	2.00	.90	.25
☐ 17 Wilber Marshall	2.00	.90	.25
☐ 18 Junior Seau	4.00	1.80	.50
☐ 19 Sam Mills	2.00	.90	.25
☐ 20 Rod Woodson	4.00	1.80	.50
☐ 21 Ricky Reynolds	2.00	.90	.25
☐ 22 Steve Atwater	2.00	.90	.25
☐ 23 Chuck Cecil	2.00	.90	.25
☐ 24 Rich Camarillo	2.00	.90	.25
☐ 25 Dale Carter	3.00	1.35	.35

1993 Pacific Silver Prism Inserts

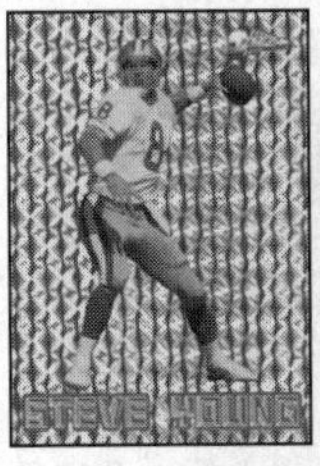

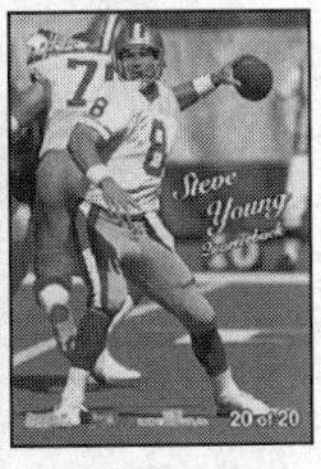

There are three slightly different versions of this 20-card standard-size set. The difference involves the prismatic backgrounds. The standard 1993 Pacific Prism Inserts were produced with triangular prismatic backgrounds in quantities of 8,000 cards each. They were randomly inserted in regular (12-card maroon-colored) Pacific packs as well as Triple Folder packs. The circular versions of the prismatic background cards were inserted one per special (gold-colored) retail packs. They carry the same value as the basic prism cards. The third version uses a gold triangular prismatic background. The production of these cards was reportedly limited to 1,000 each, and they were randomly inserted in 1993 Pacific Triple Folder packs. The fronts feature color player action cut-outs over borderless prismatic foil backgrounds. The player's name appears in team-colored block lettering at the bottom. The borderless back carries the same player photo, but this time with its original on-field background. The player's name appears in white cursive lettering near a lower corner. The set features 20 of the NFL's top players on a "Prism" background that makes the player contrast sharply with the background. The backs display a full-bleed color action player photo with the player's name and position in script. The cards are numbered on the back at the lower right "X of 20."

	MINT	NRMT	EXC
COMPLETE SET (20)	90.00	40.00	11.00
COMMON CARD (1-20)	2.00	.90	.25
COMP.CIRCULAR SET (20)	90.00	40.00	11.00
*CIRCULAR BACKGROUND: SAME PRICE			
COMP.GOLD SET (20)	300.00	135.00	38.00
*GOLD: 2X to 3.5X SILVER CARDS			
☐ 1 Troy Aikman	8.00	3.60	1.00
☐ 2 Jerome Bettis	5.00	2.20	.60
☐ 3 Drew Bledsoe	10.00	4.50	1.25
☐ 4 Reggie Brooks	2.00	.90	.25
☐ 5 Brett Favre	14.00	6.25	1.75
☐ 6 Barry Foster	2.00	.90	.25
☐ 7 Garrison Hearst	4.00	1.80	.50
☐ 8 Michael Irvin	4.00	1.80	.50
☐ 9 Cortez Kennedy	3.00	1.35	.35
☐ 10 David Klingler	2.00	.90	.25
☐ 11 Dan Marino	14.00	6.25	1.75
☐ 12 Rick Mirer	4.00	1.80	.50
☐ 13 Joe Montana	8.00	3.60	1.00
☐ 14 Jay Novacek	3.00	1.35	.35
☐ 15 Jerry Rice	8.00	3.60	1.00
☐ 16 Barry Sanders	8.00	3.60	1.00
☐ 17 Sterling Sharpe	4.00	1.80	.50
☐ 18 Emmitt Smith	14.00	6.25	1.75
☐ 19 Thurman Thomas	4.00	1.80	.50
☐ 20 Steve Young	6.00	2.70	.75

1994 Pacific

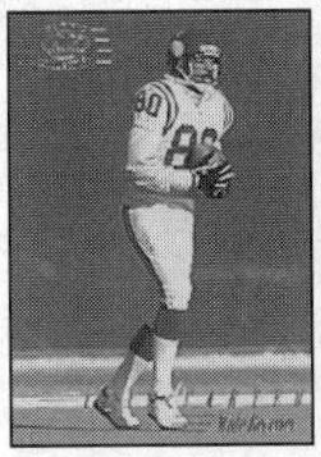

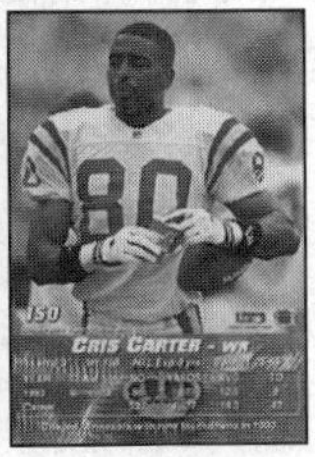

This set consists of 450 standard size cards featuring full-bleed color photos. The player's name and position are in gold foil at the bottom. The backs are dominated by a color with statistics at the bottom. The players are grouped alphabetically within their team subsets. The set closes with a Rookies (417-450) subset. Rookie Cards in this set include Mario Bates, Lake Dawson, Trent Dilfer, Marshall Faulk, William Floyd, Greg Hill. Charles Johnson, Errict Rhett, Darnay Scott, and Heath Shuler. A Sterling Sharpe Promo card was produced and priced below.

	MINT	NRMT	EXC
COMPLETE SET (450)	30.00	13.50	3.70
COMMON CARD (1-450)	.05	.02	.01
☐ 1 Troy Aikman	1.00	.45	.12
☐ 2 Charles Haley	.10	.05	.01
☐ 3 Alvin Harper	.10	.05	.01
☐ 4 Michael Irvin	.20	.09	.03
☐ 5 Jim Jeffcoat	.05	.02	.01
☐ 6 Daryl Johnston	.10	.05	.01
☐ 7 Robert Jones	.05	.02	.01
☐ 8 Brock Marion	.05	.02	.01
☐ 9 Russell Maryland	.05	.02	.01
☐ 10 Ken Norton	.10	.05	.01
☐ 11 Jay Novacek	.10	.05	.01
☐ 12 Emmitt Smith	2.00	.90	.25
☐ 13 Kevin Smith	.05	.02	.01
☐ 14 Tony Tolbert	.05	.02	.01
☐ 15 Kevin Williams WR	.10	.05	.01
☐ 16 Don Beebe	.05	.02	.01
☐ 17 Cornelius Bennett	.10	.05	.01
☐ 18 Bill Brooks	.05	.02	.01
☐ 19 Steve Christie	.05	.02	.01
☐ 20 Russell Copeland	.05	.02	.01
☐ 21 Kenneth Davis	.05	.02	.01
☐ 22 Kent Hull	.05	.02	.01
☐ 23 Jim Kelly	.20	.09	.03
☐ 24 Pete Metzelaars	.05	.02	.01
☐ 25 Andre Reed	.10	.05	.01
☐ 26 Frank Reich	.10	.05	.01
☐ 27 Bruce Smith	.20	.09	.03
☐ 28 Darryl Talley	.05	.02	.01
☐ 29 Steve Tasker	.10	.05	.01
☐ 30 Thurman Thomas	.20	.09	.03
☐ 31 Steve Bono	.10	.05	.01
☐ 32 Dexter Carter	.05	.02	.01
☐ 33 Kevin Fagan	.05	.02	.01
☐ 34 Dana Hall	.05	.02	.01
☐ 35 Brent Jones	.10	.05	.01
☐ 36 Amp Lee	.05	.02	.01
☐ 37 Marc Logan	.05	.02	.01
☐ 38 Tim McDonald	.05	.02	.01
☐ 39 Guy McIntyre	.05	.02	.01
☐ 40 Tom Rathman	.05	.02	.01
☐ 41 Jerry Rice	1.00	.45	.12
☐ 42 Dana Stubblefield	.20	.09	.03
☐ 43 Steve Wallace	.05	.02	.01
☐ 44 Ricky Watters	.20	.09	.03
☐ 45 Steve Young	.75	.35	.09
☐ 46 Marcus Allen	.20	.09	.03
☐ 47 Kimble Anders	.10	.05	.01
☐ 48 Tim Barnett	.05	.02	.01
☐ 49 J.J. Birden	.05	.02	.01
☐ 50 Dale Carter	.05	.02	.01
☐ 51 Jonathan Hayes	.05	.02	.01
☐ 52 Dave Krieg	.10	.05	.01
☐ 53 Albert Lewis	.05	.02	.01
☐ 54 Nick Lowery	.05	.02	.01
☐ 55 Joe Montana	1.00	.45	.12
☐ 56 Neil Smith	.20	.09	.03
☐ 57 John Stephens	.05	.02	.01
☐ 58 Derrick Thomas	.20	.09	.03
☐ 59 Harvey Williams	.10	.05	.01
☐ 60 Micheal Barrow	.05	.02	.01
☐ 61 Gary Brown	.05	.02	.01
☐ 62 Cody Carlson	.05	.02	.01
☐ 63 Ray Childress	.05	.02	.01
☐ 64 Curtis Duncan	.05	.02	.01
☐ 65 Ernest Givins	.10	.05	.01
☐ 66 Haywood Jeffires	.10	.05	.01
☐ 67 Wilber Marshall	.05	.02	.01
☐ 68 Bubba McDowell	.05	.02	.01
☐ 69 Warren Moon	.20	.09	.03
☐ 70 Mike Munchak	.05	.02	.01
☐ 71 Marcus Robertson	.05	.02	.01
☐ 72 Webster Slaughter	.05	.02	.01
☐ 73 Gary Wellman	.05	.02	.01
☐ 74 Lorenzo White	.05	.02	.01
☐ 75 Ray Crockett	.05	.02	.01
☐ 76 Jason Hanson	.05	.02	.01
☐ 77 Rodney Holman	.05	.02	.01
☐ 78 George Jamison	.05	.02	.01
☐ 79 Erik Kramer	.10	.05	.01
☐ 80 Ryan McNeil	.05	.02	.01
☐ 81 Derrick Moore	.05	.02	.01
☐ 82 Herman Moore	.50	.23	.06
☐ 83 Rodney Peete	.05	.02	.01
☐ 84 Brett Perriman	.10	.05	.01
☐ 85 Barry Sanders	1.00	.45	.12
☐ 86 Chris Spielman	.10	.05	.01
☐ 87 Pat Swilling	.05	.02	.01
☐ 88 Vernon Turner	.05	.02	.01
☐ 89 Andre Ware	.05	.02	.01
☐ 90 Michael Brooks	.05	.02	.01
☐ 91 Dave Brown	.10	.05	.01
☐ 92 Derek Brown TE	.05	.02	.01
☐ 93 Jarrod Bunch	.05	.02	.01
☐ 94 Chris Calloway	.05	.02	.01
☐ 95 Kent Graham	.10	.05	.01
☐ 96 Rodney Hampton	.20	.09	.03
☐ 97 Mark Jackson	.05	.02	.01
☐ 98 Ed McCaffrey	.05	.02	.01
☐ 99 Dave Meggett	.05	.02	.01
☐ 100 Aaron Pierce	.05	.02	.01
☐ 101 Mike Sherrard	.05	.02	.01
☐ 102 Phil Simms	.10	.05	.01
☐ 103 Lewis Tillman	.05	.02	.01
☐ 104 Eddie Anderson	.05	.02	.01
☐ 105 Patrick Bates	.05	.02	.01
☐ 106 Nick Bell	.05	.02	.01
☐ 107 Tim Brown	.20	.09	.03
☐ 108 Willie Gault	.05	.02	.01
☐ 109 Jeff Gossett	.05	.02	.01
☐ 110 Ethan Horton	.05	.02	.01
☐ 111 Jeff Hostetler	.10	.05	.01
☐ 112 Rocket Ismail	.10	.05	.01
☐ 113 Chester McGlockton	.05	.02	.01
☐ 114 Anthony Smith	.05	.02	.01
☐ 115 Steve Smith	.05	.02	.01
☐ 116 Greg Townsend	.05	.02	.01
☐ 117 Steve Wisniewski	.05	.02	.01
☐ 118 Alexander Wright	.05	.02	.01
☐ 119 Steve Atwater	.05	.02	.01
☐ 120 Rod Bernstine	.05	.02	.01
☐ 121 Mike Croel	.05	.02	.01
☐ 122 Shane Dronett	.05	.02	.01
☐ 123 Jason Elam	.05	.02	.01
☐ 124 John Elway	.75	.35	.09
☐ 125 Brian Habib	.05	.02	.01
☐ 126 Rondell Jones	.05	.02	.01
☐ 127 Tommy Maddox	.05	.02	.01
☐ 128 Karl Mecklenburg	.05	.02	.01
☐ 129 Glyn Milburn	.10	.05	.01
☐ 130 Derek Russell	.05	.02	.01
☐ 131 Shannon Sharpe	.10	.05	.01
☐ 132 Dennis Smith	.05	.02	.01
☐ 133 Edgar Bennett	.20	.09	.03
☐ 134 Tony Bennett	.05	.02	.01
☐ 135 Robert Brooks	.40	.18	.05
☐ 136 Terrell Buckley	.05	.02	.01
☐ 137 LeRoy Butler	.05	.02	.01
☐ 138 Mark Clayton	.05	.02	.01
☐ 139 Ty Detmer	.10	.05	.01
☐ 140 Brett Favre	2.00	.90	.25
☐ 141 John Jurkovic	.10	.05	.01
☐ 142 Bryce Paup	.20	.09	.03
☐ 143 Sterling Sharpe	.10	.05	.01
☐ 144 George Teague	.05	.02	.01
☐ 145 Darrell Thompson	.05	.02	.01
☐ 146 Ed West	.05	.02	.01
☐ 147 Reggie White	.20	.09	.03
☐ 148 Terry Allen	.10	.05	.01
☐ 149 Anthony Carter	.10	.05	.01
☐ 150 Cris Carter	.20	.09	.03
☐ 151 Roger Craig	.10	.05	.01
☐ 152 Jack Del Rio	.05	.02	.01
☐ 153 Chris Doleman	.05	.02	.01
☐ 154 Scottie Graham	.10	.05	.01
☐ 155 Eric Guliford	.05	.02	.01
☐ 156 Qadry Ismail	.20	.09	.03
☐ 157 Steve Jordan	.05	.02	.01
☐ 158 Randall McDaniel	.05	.02	.01
☐ 159 Jim McMahon	.05	.02	.01
☐ 160 Audray McMillian	.05	.02	.01
☐ 161 Sean Salisbury	.05	.02	.01
☐ 162 Robert Smith	.20	.09	.03
☐ 163 Henry Thomas	.05	.02	.01
☐ 164 Gary Anderson K	.05	.02	.01
☐ 165 Deon Figures	.05	.02	.01
☐ 166 Barry Foster	.05	.02	.01
☐ 167 Jeff Graham	.05	.02	.01
☐ 168 Kevin Greene	.20	.09	.03
☐ 169 Dave Hoffman	.05	.02	.01
☐ 170 Merril Hoge	.05	.02	.01
☐ 171 Gary Jones	.05	.02	.01

☐ 172 Greg Lloyd	.20	.09	.03
☐ 173 Ernie Mills	.05	.02	.01
☐ 174 Neil O'Donnell	.20	.09	.03
☐ 175 Darren Perry	.05	.02	.01
☐ 176 Leon Searcy	.05	.02	.01
☐ 177 Leroy Thompson	.05	.02	.01
☐ 178 Willie Williams	.05	.02	.01
☐ 179 Rod Woodson	.20	.09	.03
☐ 180 Keith Byars	.05	.02	.01
☐ 181 Marco Coleman	.05	.02	.01
☐ 182 Bryan Cox	.05	.02	.01
☐ 183 Irving Fryar	.10	.05	.01
☐ 184 John Grimsley	.05	.02	.01
☐ 185 Mark Higgs	.05	.02	.01
☐ 186 Mark Ingram	.05	.02	.01
☐ 187 Keith Jackson	.05	.02	.01
☐ 188 Terry Kirby	.20	.09	.03
☐ 189 Dan Marino	2.00	.90	.25
☐ 190 O.J. McDuffie	.20	.09	.03
☐ 191 Scott Mitchell	.20	.09	.03
☐ 192 Pete Stoyanovich	.05	.02	.01
☐ 193 Troy Vincent	.05	.02	.01
☐ 194 Richmond Webb	.05	.02	.01
☐ 195 Brad Baxter	.05	.02	.01
☐ 196 Chris Burkett	.05	.02	.01
☐ 197 Rob Carpenter	.05	.02	.01
☐ 198 Boomer Esiason	.10	.05	.01
☐ 199 Johnny Johnson	.05	.02	.01
☐ 200 Jeff Lageman	.05	.02	.01
☐ 201 Mo Lewis	.05	.02	.01
☐ 202 Ronnie Lott	.10	.05	.01
☐ 203 Leonard Marshall	.05	.02	.01
☐ 204 Terance Mathis	.10	.05	.01
☐ 205 Johnny Mitchell	.05	.02	.01
☐ 206 Rob Moore	.10	.05	.01
☐ 207 Anthony Prior	.05	.02	.01
☐ 208 Blair Thomas	.05	.02	.01
☐ 209 Brian Washington	.05	.02	.01
☐ 210 Eric Bieniemy	.05	.02	.01
☐ 211 Marion Butts	.05	.02	.01
☐ 212 Gill Byrd	.05	.02	.01
☐ 213 John Carney	.05	.02	.01
☐ 214 Darren Carrington	.05	.02	.01
☐ 215 John Friesz	.10	.05	.01
☐ 216 Ronnie Harmon	.05	.02	.01
☐ 217 Stan Humphries	.20	.09	.03
☐ 218 Nate Lewis	.05	.02	.01
☐ 219 Natrone Means	.50	.23	.06
☐ 220 Anthony Miller	.10	.05	.01
☐ 221 Chris Mims	.05	.02	.01
☐ 222 Eric Moten	.05	.02	.01
☐ 223 Leslie O'Neal	.05	.02	.01
☐ 224 Junior Seau	.20	.09	.03
☐ 225 Morten Andersen	.05	.02	.01
☐ 226 Gene Atkins	.05	.02	.01
☐ 227 Derek Brown RB	.05	.02	.01
☐ 228 Toi Cook	.05	.02	.01
☐ 229 Vaughn Dunbar	.05	.02	.01
☐ 230 Quinn Early	.10	.05	.01
☐ 231 Reggie Freeman	.05	.02	.01
☐ 232 Tyrone Hughes	.10	.05	.01
☐ 233 Rickey Jackson	.05	.02	.01
☐ 234 Eric Martin	.05	.02	.01
☐ 235 Sam Mills	.05	.02	.01
☐ 236 Brad Muster	.05	.02	.01
☐ 237 Torrance Small	.05	.02	.01
☐ 238 Irv Smith	.05	.02	.01
☐ 239 Wade Wilson	.05	.02	.01
☐ 240 Eric Allen	.05	.02	.01
☐ 241 Victor Bailey	.05	.02	.01
☐ 242 Fred Barnett	.10	.05	.01
☐ 243 Mark Bavaro	.05	.02	.01
☐ 244 Bubby Brister	.05	.02	.01
☐ 245 Randall Cunningham	.10	.05	.01
☐ 246 Antone Davis	.05	.02	.01
☐ 247 Britt Hager	.05	.02	.01
☐ 248 Vaughn Hebron	.05	.02	.01
☐ 249 James Joseph	.05	.02	.01
☐ 250 Seth Joyner	.05	.02	.01
☐ 251 Rich Miano	.05	.02	.01
☐ 252 Heath Sherman	.05	.02	.01
☐ 253 Clyde Simmons	.05	.02	.01
☐ 254 Herschel Walker	.10	.05	.01
☐ 255 Calvin Williams	.10	.05	.01
☐ 256 Jerry Ball	.05	.02	.01
☐ 257 Mark Carrier WR	.10	.05	.01
☐ 258 Michael Jackson	.10	.05	.01
☐ 259 Mike Johnson	.05	.02	.01
☐ 260 James Jones	.05	.02	.01
☐ 261 Brian Kinchen	.10	.05	.01
☐ 262 Clay Matthews	.05	.02	.01
☐ 263 Eric Metcalf	.10	.05	.01
☐ 264 Stevon Moore	.05	.02	.01
☐ 265 Michael Dean Perry	.10	.05	.01
☐ 266 Todd Philcox	.05	.02	.01
☐ 267 Anthony Pleasant	.05	.02	.01
☐ 268 Vinny Testaverde	.10	.05	.01
☐ 269 Eric Turner	.05	.02	.01
☐ 270 Tommy Vardell	.05	.02	.01
☐ 271 Neal Anderson	.05	.02	.01
☐ 272 Trace Armstrong	.05	.02	.01
☐ 273 Mark Carrier DB	.05	.02	.01
☐ 274 Bob Christian	.05	.02	.01
☐ 275 Curtis Conway	.20	.09	.03
☐ 276 Richard Dent	.10	.05	.01

☐ 277 Robert Green	.05	.02	.01
☐ 278 Jim Harbaugh	.20	.09	.03
☐ 279 Craig Heyward	.10	.05	.01
☐ 280 Terry Obee	.05	.02	.01
☐ 281 Alonzo Spellman	.05	.02	.01
☐ 282 Tom Waddle	.05	.02	.01
☐ 283 Peter Tom Willis	.05	.02	.01
☐ 284 Donnell Woolford	.05	.02	.01
☐ 285 Tim Worley	.05	.02	.01
☐ 286 Chris Zorich	.05	.02	.01
☐ 287 Steve Broussard	.05	.02	.01
☐ 288 Darion Conner	.05	.02	.01
☐ 289 Jumpy Geathers	.05	.02	.01
☐ 290 Michael Haynes	.10	.05	.01
☐ 291 Bobby Hebert	.05	.02	.01
☐ 292 Lincoln Kennedy	.05	.02	.01
☐ 293 Chris Miller	.05	.02	.01
☐ 294 David Mims	.05	.02	.01
☐ 295 Erric Pegram	.05	.02	.01
☐ 296 Mike Pritchard	.05	.02	.01
☐ 297 Andre Rison	.10	.05	.01
☐ 298 Deion Sanders	.60	.25	.07
☐ 299 Chuck Smith	.05	.02	.01
☐ 300 Tony Smith	.05	.02	.01
☐ 301 Johnny Bailey	.05	.02	.01
☐ 302 Steve Beuerlein	.05	.02	.01
☐ 303 Chuck Cecil	.05	.02	.01
☐ 304 Chris Chandler	.10	.05	.01
☐ 305 Gary Clark	.10	.05	.01
☐ 306 Rick Cunningham	.05	.02	.01
☐ 307 Ken Harvey	.05	.02	.01
☐ 308 Garrison Hearst	.50	.23	.06
☐ 309 Randal Hill	.05	.02	.01
☐ 310 Robert Massey	.05	.02	.01
☐ 311 Ronald Moore	.05	.02	.01
☐ 312 Ricky Proehl	.05	.02	.01
☐ 313 Eric Swann	.10	.05	.01
☐ 314 Aeneas Williams	.05	.02	.01
☐ 315 Michael Bates	.05	.02	.01
☐ 316 Brian Blades	.10	.05	.01
☐ 317 Carlton Gray	.05	.02	.01
☐ 318 Paul Green	.05	.02	.01
☐ 319 Patrick Hunter	.05	.02	.01
☐ 320 John Kasay	.05	.02	.01
☐ 321 Cortez Kennedy	.10	.05	.01
☐ 322 Kelvin Martin	.05	.02	.01
☐ 323 Dan McGwire	.05	.02	.01
☐ 324 Rick Mirer	.20	.09	.03
☐ 325 Eugene Robinson	.05	.02	.01
☐ 326 Rick Tuten	.05	.02	.01
☐ 327 Chris Warren	.10	.05	.01
☐ 328 John L. Williams	.05	.02	.01
☐ 329 Reggie Cobb	.05	.02	.01
☐ 330 Horace Copeland	.05	.02	.01
☐ 331 Lawrence Dawsey	.05	.02	.01
☐ 332 Santana Dotson	.10	.05	.01
☐ 333 Craig Erickson	.05	.02	.01
☐ 334 Ron Hall	.05	.02	.01
☐ 335 Courtney Hawkins	.05	.02	.01
☐ 336 Keith McCants	.05	.02	.01
☐ 337 Hardy Nickerson	.10	.05	.01
☐ 338 Mazio Royster	.05	.02	.01
☐ 339 Broderick Thomas	.05	.02	.01
☐ 340 Casey Weldon	.20	.09	.03
☐ 341 Mark Wheeler	.05	.02	.01
☐ 342 Vince Workman	.05	.02	.01
☐ 343 Flipper Anderson	.05	.02	.01
☐ 344 Jerome Bettis	.60	.25	.07
☐ 345 Richard Buchanan	.05	.02	.01
☐ 346 Shane Conlan	.05	.02	.01
☐ 347 Troy Drayton	.05	.02	.01
☐ 348 Henry Ellard	.10	.05	.01
☐ 349 Jim Everett	.10	.05	.01
☐ 350 Cleveland Gary	.05	.02	.01
☐ 351 Sean Gilbert	.05	.02	.01
☐ 352 David Lang	.05	.02	.01
☐ 353 Todd Lyght	.05	.02	.01
☐ 354 T.J. Rubley	.05	.02	.01
☐ 355 Jackie Slater	.05	.02	.01
☐ 356 Russell White	.10	.05	.01
☐ 357 Bruce Armstrong	.05	.02	.01
☐ 358 Drew Bledsoe	1.25	.55	.16
☐ 359 Vincent Brisby	.20	.09	.03
☐ 360 Vincent Brown	.05	.02	.01
☐ 361 Ben Coates	.20	.09	.03
☐ 362 Marv Cook	.05	.02	.01
☐ 363 Ray Crittenden	.05	.02	.01
☐ 364 Corey Croom	.05	.02	.01
☐ 365 Pat Harlow	.05	.02	.01
☐ 366 Dion Lambert	.05	.02	.01
☐ 367 Greg McMurtry	.05	.02	.01
☐ 368 Leonard Russell	.10	.05	.01
☐ 369 Scott Secules	.05	.02	.01
☐ 370 Chris Slade	.05	.02	.01
☐ 371 Michael Timpson	.05	.02	.01
☐ 372 Kevin Turner	.05	.02	.01
☐ 373 Ashley Ambrose	.05	.02	.01
☐ 374 Dean Biasucci	.05	.02	.01
☐ 375 Duane Bickett	.05	.02	.01
☐ 376 Quentin Coryatt	.05	.02	.01
☐ 377 Rodney Culver	.05	.02	.01
☐ 378 Sean Dawkins	.20	.09	.03
☐ 379 Jeff George	.20	.09	.03
☐ 380 Jeff Herrod	.05	.02	.01
☐ 381 Jessie Hester	.05	.02	.01

☐ 382 Anthony Johnson	.10	.05	.01
☐ 383 Reggie Langhorne	.05	.02	.01
☐ 384 Roosevelt Potts	.05	.02	.01
☐ 385 William Schultz	.05	.02	.01
☐ 386 Rohn Stark	.05	.02	.01
☐ 387 Clarence Verdin	.05	.02	.01
☐ 388 Carl Banks	.05	.02	.01
☐ 389 Reggie Brooks	.10	.05	.01
☐ 390 Earnest Byner	.05	.02	.01
☐ 391 Tom Carter	.05	.02	.01
☐ 392 Cary Conklin	.05	.02	.01
☐ 393 Pat Eilers	.05	.02	.01
☐ 394 Ricky Ervins	.05	.02	.01
☐ 395 Rich Gannon	.05	.02	.01
☐ 396 Darrell Green	.05	.02	.01
☐ 397 Desmond Howard	.10	.05	.01
☐ 398 Chip Lohmiller	.05	.02	.01
☐ 399 Sterling Palmer	.05	.02	.01
☐ 400 Mark Rypien	.05	.02	.01
☐ 401 Ricky Sanders	.05	.02	.01
☐ 402 Johnny Thomas	.05	.02	.01
☐ 403 John Copeland	.05	.02	.01
☐ 404 Derrick Fenner	.05	.02	.01
☐ 405 Alex Gordon	.05	.02	.01
☐ 406 Harold Green	.05	.02	.01
☐ 407 Lance Gunn	.05	.02	.01
☐ 408 David Klingler	.05	.02	.01
☐ 409 Ricardo McDonald	.05	.02	.01
☐ 410 Tim McGee	.05	.02	.01
☐ 411 Reggie Rembert	.05	.02	.01
☐ 412 Patrick Robinson	.05	.02	.01
☐ 413 Jay Schroeder	.05	.02	.01
☐ 414 Erik Wilhelm	.05	.02	.01
☐ 415 Alfred Williams	.05	.02	.01
☐ 416 Darryl Williams	.05	.02	.01
☐ 417 Sam Adams	.10	.05	.01
☐ 418 Mario Bates	.50	.23	.06
☐ 419 James Bostic	.05	.02	.01
☐ 420 Bucky Brooks	.05	.02	.01
☐ 421 Jeff Burris	.10	.05	.01
☐ 422 Shante Carver	.05	.02	.01
☐ 423 Jeff Cothran	.05	.02	.01
☐ 424 Lake Dawson	.60	.25	.07
☐ 425 Trent Dilfer	.60	.25	.07
☐ 426 Marshall Faulk	3.00	1.35	.35
☐ 427 Cory Fleming	.05	.02	.01
☐ 428 William Floyd	1.00	.45	.12
☐ 429 Glenn Foley	.05	.02	.01
☐ 430 Rob Fredrickson	.10	.05	.01
☐ 431 Charlie Garner	.10	.05	.01
☐ 432 Greg Hill	.20	.09	.03
☐ 433 Charles Johnson	.20	.09	.03
☐ 434 Calvin Jones	.05	.02	.01
☐ 435 Jimmy Klingler	.10	.05	.01
☐ 436 Antonio Langham	.10	.05	.01
☐ 437 Kevin Lee	.05	.02	.01
☐ 438 Chuck Levy	.05	.02	.01
☐ 439 Willie McGinest	.20	.09	.03
☐ 440 Jamir Miller	.05	.02	.01
☐ 441 Johnnie Morton	.20	.09	.03
☐ 442 David Palmer	.10	.05	.01
☐ 443 Errict Rhett	1.25	.55	.16
☐ 444 Cory Sawyer	.05	.02	.01
☐ 445 Darnay Scott	2.00	.90	.25
☐ 446 Heath Shuler	1.00	.45	.12
☐ 447 Lamar Smith	.05	.02	.01
☐ 448 Dan Wilkinson	.10	.05	.01
☐ 449 Bernard Williams	.05	.02	.01
☐ 450 Bryant Young	.20	.09	.03
☐ P1 Sterling Sharpe Promo Numbered 000	1.00	.45	.12

1994 Pacific Crystalline

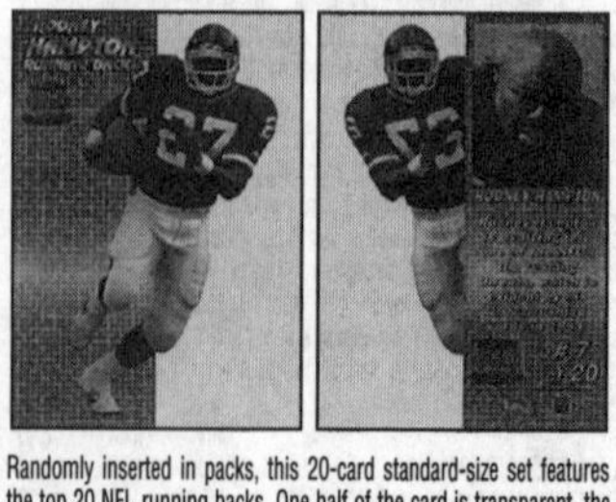

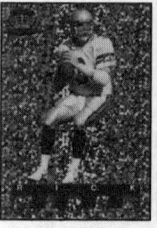

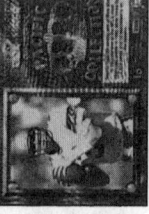

Randomly inserted in packs, this 20-card standard-size set features the top 20 NFL running backs. One half of the card is transparent, the other half has a color action-packed image placed in the center. That portion of the back has a small photo and 1993 highlights. Only 7,000 sets were produced.

	MINT	NRMT	EXC
COMPLETE SET (20)	80.00	36.00	10.00
COMMON CARD (1-20)	1.50	.70	.19
☐ 1 Emmitt Smith	30.00	13.50	3.70
☐ 2 Jerome Bettis	8.00	3.60	1.00
☐ 3 Thurman Thomas	5.00	2.20	.60
☐ 4 Erric Pegram	3.00	1.35	.35
☐ 5 Barry Sanders	20.00	9.00	2.50
☐ 6 Leonard Russell	1.50	.70	.19
☐ 7 Rodney Hampton	3.00	1.35	.35
☐ 8 Chris Warren	3.00	1.35	.35
☐ 9 Reggie Brooks	1.50	.70	.19
☐ 10 Ronald Moore	1.50	.70	.19
☐ 11 Gary Brown	1.50	.70	.19
☐ 12 Ricky Watters	5.00	2.20	.60
☐ 13 Johnny Johnson	1.50	.70	.19
☐ 14 Rod Bernstine	1.50	.70	.19
☐ 15 Marcus Allen	5.00	2.20	.60
☐ 16 Leroy Thompson	1.50	.70	.19
☐ 17 Marion Butts	3.00	1.35	.35
☐ 18 Herschel Walker	3.00	1.35	.35
☐ 19 Barry Foster	1.50	.70	.19
☐ 20 Roosevelt Potts	1.50	.70	.19

1994 Pacific Gems of the Crown

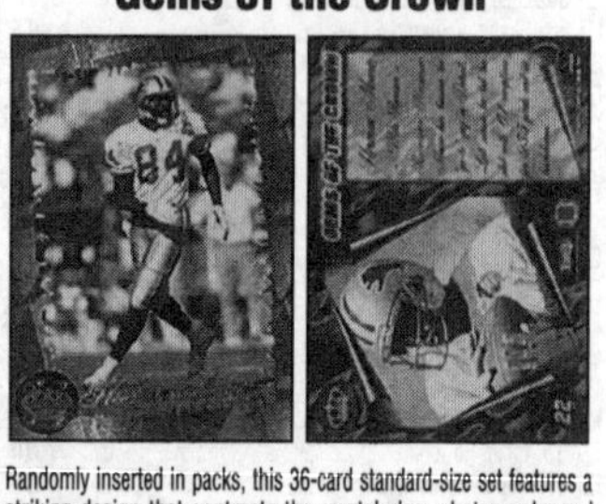

Randomly inserted in packs, this 36-card standard-size set features a striking design that contrasts the crystal-clear photography and etched gold foil frame. Horizontal backs contain a photo and 1993 highlights. Only 7,000 sets were produced. The set is sequenced in alphabetical order.

	MINT	NRMT	EXC
COMPLETE SET (36)	140.00	65.00	17.50
COMMON CARD (1-36)	1.50	.70	.19
☐ 1 Troy Aikman	10.00	4.50	1.25
☐ 2 Marcus Allen	5.00	2.20	.60
☐ 3 Jerome Bettis	7.00	3.10	.85
☐ 4 Drew Bledsoe	10.00	4.50	1.25
☐ 5 Reggie Brooks	1.50	.70	.19
☐ 6 Gary Brown	1.50	.70	.19
☐ 7 Tim Brown	3.00	1.35	.35
☐ 8 Cody Carlson	1.50	.70	.19
☐ 9 John Elway	8.00	3.60	1.00
☐ 10 Boomer Esiason	3.00	1.35	.35
☐ 11 Brett Favre	20.00	9.00	2.50
☐ 12 Rodney Hampton	3.00	1.35	.35
☐ 13 Alvin Harper	1.50	.70	.19
☐ 14 Jeff Hostetler	3.00	1.35	.35
☐ 15 Jim Kelly	5.00	2.20	.60
☐ 16 Dan Marino	20.00	9.00	2.50
☐ 17 Eric Martin	1.50	.70	.19
☐ 18 O.J. McDuffie	5.00	2.20	.60
☐ 19 Natrone Means	7.00	3.10	.85
☐ 20 Rick Mirer	5.00	2.20	.60
☐ 21 Joe Montana	10.00	4.50	1.25
☐ 22 Herman Moore	7.00	3.10	.85
☐ 23 Ronald Moore	1.50	.70	.19
☐ 24 Neil O'Donnell	3.00	1.35	.35
☐ 25 Erric Pegram	3.00	1.35	.35
☐ 26 Roosevelt Potts	1.50	.70	.19
☐ 27 Jerry Rice	10.00	4.50	1.25
☐ 28 Barry Sanders	10.00	4.50	1.25
☐ 29 Shannon Sharpe	3.00	1.35	.35
☐ 30 Sterling Sharpe	3.00	1.35	.35
☐ 31 Emmitt Smith	20.00	9.00	2.50
☐ 32 Thurman Thomas	5.00	2.20	.60
☐ 33 Herschel Walker	3.00	1.35	.35
☐ 34 Chris Warren	3.00	1.35	.35
☐ 35 Ricky Watters	5.00	2.20	.60
☐ 36 Steve Young	8.00	3.60	1.00

1994 Pacific Knights of the Gridiron

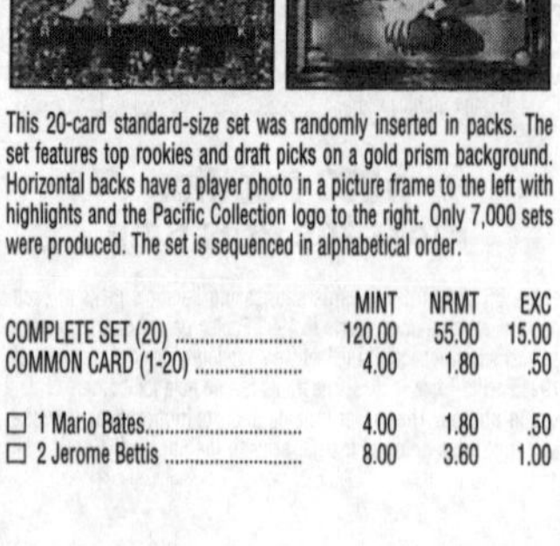

This 20-card standard-size set was randomly inserted in packs. The set features top rookies and draft picks on a gold prism background. Horizontal backs have a player photo in a picture frame to the left with highlights and the Pacific Collection logo to the right. Only 7,000 sets were produced. The set is sequenced in alphabetical order.

	MINT	NRMT	EXC
COMPLETE SET (20)	120.00	55.00	15.00
COMMON CARD (1-20)	4.00	1.80	.50
☐ 1 Mario Bates	4.00	1.80	.50
☐ 2 Jerome Bettis	8.00	3.60	1.00

	MINT	NRMT	EXC
☐ 3 Drew Bledsoe	16.00	7.25	2.00
☐ 4 Vincent Brisby	4.00	1.80	.50
☐ 5 Reggie Brooks	4.00	1.80	.50
☐ 6 Derek Brown RB	4.00	1.80	.50
☐ 7 Jeff Burris	4.00	1.80	.50
☐ 8 Trent Dilfer	6.00	2.70	.75
☐ 9 Troy Drayton	4.00	1.80	.50
☐ 10 Marshall Faulk	12.00	5.50	1.50
☐ 11 William Floyd	6.00	2.70	.75
☐ 12 Rocket Ismail	4.00	1.80	.50
☐ 13 Terry Kirby	6.00	2.70	.75
☐ 14 Thomas Lewis	4.00	1.80	.50
☐ 15 Natrone Means	8.00	3.60	1.00
☐ 16 Rick Mirer	6.00	2.70	.75
☐ 17 David Palmer	4.00	1.80	.50
☐ 18 Errict Rhett	6.00	2.70	.75
☐ 19 Darnay Scott	8.00	3.60	1.00
☐ 20 Heath Shuler	6.00	2.70	.75

1994 Pacific Marquee Prisms

This 36 card standard-size set was produced in both silver and gold. These cards were inserted one per marquee prism pack. Although either a silver or gold card was issued in each pack, gold cards are much more difficult to obtain. They were inserted approximately two per box. In either case, the player is superimposed over the silver or gold background. A marquee design with the player's name and position is at the bottom. Backs have a player photo to the left and a marquee with the player's name to the right. The set is sequenced in alphabetical order.

	MINT	NRMT	EXC
COMPLETE SET (36)	30.00	13.50	3.70
COMMON CARD (1-36)	.40	.18	.05
COMP.GOLD SET (36)	250.00	110.00	31.00

*GOLD STARS: 3X to 6X BASIC CARDS
*GOLD YOUNG STARS: 2X to 4X BASIC CARDS

	MINT	NRMT	EXC
☐ 1 Troy Aikman	2.50	1.10	.30
☐ 2 Marcus Allen	.75	.35	.09
☐ 3 Jerome Bettis	1.25	.55	.16
☐ 4 Drew Bledsoe	2.50	1.10	.30
☐ 5 Reggie Brooks	.40	.18	.05
☐ 6 Dave Brown	.50	.23	.06
☐ 7 Ben Coates	.75	.35	.09
☐ 8 Reggie Cobb	.40	.18	.05
☐ 9 Curtis Conway	.75	.35	.09
☐ 10 John Elway	1.50	.70	.19
☐ 11 Marshall Faulk	2.50	1.10	.30
☐ 12 Brett Favre	4.00	1.80	.50
☐ 13 Barry Foster	.40	.18	.05
☐ 14 Rodney Hampton	.50	.23	.06
☐ 15 Michael Irvin	.75	.35	.09
☐ 16 Terry Kirby	.75	.35	.09
☐ 17 Dan Marino	4.00	1.80	.50
☐ 18 Natrone Means	1.00	.45	.12
☐ 19 Rick Mirer	.75	.35	.09
☐ 20 Joe Montana	2.50	1.10	.30
☐ 21 Warren Moon	.75	.35	.09
☐ 22 Ronald Moore	.40	.18	.05
☐ 23 David Palmer	.40	.18	.05
☐ 24 Errict Rhett	1.25	.55	.16
☐ 25 Jerry Rice	2.50	1.10	.30
☐ 26 Bucky Richardson	.40	.18	.05
☐ 27 Barry Sanders	2.50	1.10	.30
☐ 28 Shannon Sharpe	.50	.23	.06
☐ 29 Sterling Sharpe	.50	.23	.06
☐ 30 Heath Shuler	.75	.35	.09
☐ 31 Emmitt Smith	4.00	1.80	.50
☐ 32 Irving Spikes	.50	.23	.06
☐ 33 Thurman Thomas	.75	.35	.09
☐ 34 Chris Warren	.75	.35	.09
☐ 35 Ricky Watters	.75	.35	.09
☐ 36 Steve Young	1.50	.70	.19

1995 Pacific

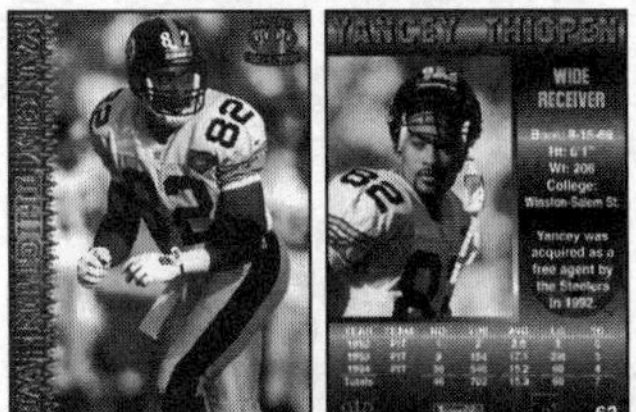

This 450 card set was issued in one series and featured 12 cards per pack. Card fronts contain a full bleed shot of the player with the player's name and position on gold foil along the left side of the card. Card back backgrounds are in the team's colors with statistical and biographical information. Two parallels of the set were also issued: Blue and Royal Platinum. The blue versions were randomly inserted at a rate of nine in 37 retail packs, while the platinum versions were randomly inserted at a rate of nine in 37 hobby packs. Rookie Cards in this set include Jeff Blake, Kerry Collins, Joey Galloway, Steve McNair, Rashaan Salaam, Kordell Stewart, J.J Stokes, Yancey Thigpen and Michael Westbrook. Natrone Means standard sized and jumbo (7" by 9 3/4") promo cards were produced and are included below.

	MINT	NRMT	EXC
COMPLETE SET (450)	30.00	13.50	3.70
COMMON CARD (1-450)	.05	.02	.01

	MINT	NRMT	EXC
☐ 1 Randy Baldwin	.05	.02	.01
☐ 2 Tommy Barnhardt	.05	.02	.01
☐ 3 Tim McKyer	.05	.02	.01
☐ 4 Sam Mills	.10	.05	.01
☐ 5 Brian O'Neal	.05	.02	.01
☐ 6 Frank Reich	.05	.02	.01
☐ 7 Jack Trudeau	.05	.02	.01
☐ 8 Vernon Turner	.05	.02	.01
☐ 9 Kerry Collins	3.00	1.35	.35
☐ 10 Shawn King	.05	.02	.01
☐ 11 Steve Beuerlein	.05	.02	.01
☐ 12 Derek Brown	.05	.02	.01
☐ 13 Reggie Clark	.05	.02	.01
☐ 14 Reggie Cobb	.05	.02	.01
☐ 15 Desmond Howard	.10	.05	.01
☐ 16 Jeff Lageman	.05	.02	.01
☐ 17 Kelvin Pritchett	.05	.02	.01
☐ 18 Cedric Tillman	.05	.02	.01
☐ 19 Tony Boselli	.10	.05	.01
☐ 20 James Stewart	.20	.09	.03
☐ 21 Eric Davis	.05	.02	.01
☐ 22 William Floyd	.20	.09	.03
☐ 23 Elvis Grbac	.20	.09	.03
☐ 24 Brent Jones	.05	.02	.01
☐ 25 Ken Norton, Jr.	.10	.05	.01
☐ 26 Bart Oates	.05	.02	.01
☐ 27 Jerry Rice	1.00	.45	.12
☐ 28 Deion Sanders	.60	.25	.07
☐ 29 John Taylor	.05	.02	.01
☐ 30 Adam Walker	.05	.02	.01
☐ 31 Steve Wallace	.05	.02	.01
☐ 32 Ricky Watters	.20	.09	.03
☐ 33 Lee Woodall	.05	.02	.01
☐ 34 Bryant Young	.10	.05	.01
☐ 35 Steve Young	.75	.35	.09
☐ 36 J.J. Stokes	1.00	.45	.12
☐ 37 Troy Aikman	1.00	.45	.12
☐ 38 Larry Allen	.10	.05	.01
☐ 39 Chris Boniol	.05	.02	.01
☐ 40 Lincoln Coleman	.05	.02	.01
☐ 41 Charles Haley	.10	.05	.01
☐ 42 Alvin Harper	.05	.02	.01
☐ 43 Chad Hennings	.10	.05	.01
☐ 44 Michael Irvin	.20	.09	.03
☐ 45 Daryl Johnston	.10	.05	.01
☐ 46 Leon Lett	.05	.02	.01
☐ 47 Nate Newton	.10	.05	.01
☐ 48 Jay Novacek	.10	.05	.01
☐ 49 Emmitt Smith	2.00	.90	.25
☐ 50 James Washington	.05	.02	.01
☐ 51 Kevin Williams	.10	.05	.01
☐ 52 Sherman Williams	.05	.02	.01
☐ 53 Barry Foster	.10	.05	.01
☐ 54 Eric Green	.05	.02	.01
☐ 55 Kevin Greene	.10	.05	.01
☐ 56 Andre Hastings	.10	.05	.01
☐ 57 Charles Johnson	.10	.05	.01
☐ 58 Greg Lloyd	.10	.05	.01
☐ 59 Ernie Mills	.05	.02	.01
☐ 60 Byron Bam Morris	.10	.05	.01
☐ 61 Neil O'Donnell	.10	.05	.01
☐ 62 Darren Perry	.05	.02	.01
☐ 63 Yancey Thigpen	1.00	.45	.12
☐ 64 Mike Tomczak	.05	.02	.01
☐ 65 John L. Williams	.05	.02	.01
☐ 66 Rod Woodson	.10	.05	.01
☐ 67 Mark Bruener	.10	.05	.01
☐ 68 Kordell Stewart	3.00	1.35	.35
☐ 69 Jeff Brohm	.05	.02	.01
☐ 70 Andre Coleman	.05	.02	.01
☐ 71 Reuben Davis	.05	.02	.01
☐ 72 Dennis Gibson	.05	.02	.01
☐ 73 Darrien Gordon	.05	.02	.01
☐ 74 Stan Humphries	.10	.05	.01
☐ 75 Shawn Jefferson	.05	.02	.01
☐ 76 Tony Martin	.10	.05	.01
☐ 77 Natrone Means	.20	.09	.03
☐ 78 Shannon Mitchell	.05	.02	.01
☐ 79 Leslie O'Neal	.10	.05	.01
☐ 80 Alfred Pupunu	.05	.02	.01
☐ 81 Stanley Richard	.05	.02	.01
☐ 82 Junior Seau	.20	.09	.03
☐ 83 Mark Seay	.10	.05	.01
☐ 84 Derrick Alexander WR	.20	.09	.03
☐ 85 Carl Banks	.05	.02	.01
☐ 86 Isaac Booth	.05	.02	.01
☐ 87 Rob Burnett	.05	.02	.01
☐ 88 Earnest Byner	.05	.02	.01
☐ 89 Steve Everitt	.05	.02	.01
☐ 90 Leroy Hoard	.05	.02	.01
☐ 91 Pepper Johnson	.05	.02	.01
☐ 92 Antonio Langham	.05	.02	.01
☐ 93 Eric Metcalf	.10	.05	.01
☐ 94 Anthony Pleasant	.05	.02	.01
☐ 95 Frank Stams	.05	.02	.01
☐ 96 Vinny Testaverde	.10	.05	.01
☐ 97 Eric Turner	.05	.02	.01
☐ 98 Mike Miller	.05	.02	.01
☐ 99 Craig Powell	.05	.02	.01
☐ 100 Gene Atkins	.05	.02	.01
☐ 101 Aubrey Beavers	.05	.02	.01
☐ 102 Tim Bowens	.05	.02	.01
☐ 103 Keith Byars	.05	.02	.01
☐ 104 Bryan Cox	.05	.02	.01
☐ 105 Aaron Craver	.05	.02	.01
☐ 106 Jeff Cross	.05	.02	.01
☐ 107 Irving Fryar	.10	.05	.01
☐ 108 Dan Marino	2.00	.90	.25
☐ 109 O.J. McDuffie	.20	.09	.03
☐ 110 Bernie Parmalee	.10	.05	.01
☐ 111 James Saxon	.05	.02	.01
☐ 112 Keith Sims	.05	.02	.01
☐ 113 Irving Spikes	.10	.05	.01
☐ 114 Pete Mitchell	.10	.05	.01
☐ 115 Terry Allen	.10	.05	.01
☐ 116 Cris Carter	.20	.09	.03
☐ 117 Adrian Cooper	.05	.02	.01
☐ 118 Bernard Dafney	.05	.02	.01
☐ 119 Jack Del Rio	.05	.02	.01
☐ 120 Vencie Glenn	.05	.02	.01
☐ 121 Qadry Ismail	.10	.05	.01
☐ 122 Carlos Jenkins	.05	.02	.01
☐ 123 Andrew Jordan	.05	.02	.01
☐ 124 Ed McDaniel	.05	.02	.01
☐ 125 Warren Moon	.10	.05	.01
☐ 126 David Palmer	.10	.05	.01
☐ 127 John Randle	.05	.02	.01
☐ 128 Jake Reed	.10	.05	.01
☐ 129 Derrick Alexander DE	.05	.02	.01
☐ 130 Chad May	.05	.02	.01
☐ 131 Korey Stringer	.05	.02	.01
☐ 132 Bruce Armstrong	.05	.02	.01
☐ 133 Drew Bledsoe	1.00	.45	.12
☐ 134 Vincent Brisby	.05	.02	.01
☐ 135 Troy Brown	.05	.02	.01
☐ 136 Vincent Brown	.05	.02	.01
☐ 137 Marion Butts	.05	.02	.01
☐ 138 Ben Coates	.10	.05	.01
☐ 139 Ray Crittenden	.05	.02	.01
☐ 140 Maurice Hurst	.05	.02	.01
☐ 141 Aaron Jones	.05	.02	.01
☐ 142 Willie McGinest	.10	.05	.01
☐ 143 Marty Moore	.05	.02	.01
☐ 144 Mike Pitts	.05	.02	.01
☐ 145 Leroy Thompson	.05	.02	.01
☐ 146 Michael Timpson	.05	.02	.01
☐ 147 Bennie Blades	.05	.02	.01
☐ 148 Jocelyn Borgella	.05	.02	.01
☐ 149 Anthony Carter	.10	.05	.01
☐ 150 Willie Clay	.05	.02	.01
☐ 151 Mel Gray	.05	.02	.01
☐ 152 Mike Johnson	.05	.02	.01
☐ 153 Dave Krieg	.05	.02	.01
☐ 154 Robert Massey	.05	.02	.01
☐ 155 Scott Mitchell	.10	.05	.01
☐ 156 Herman Moore	.50	.23	.06
☐ 157 Johnnie Morton	.10	.05	.01
☐ 158 Barry Sanders	1.00	.45	.12
☐ 159 Chris Spielman	.10	.05	.01
☐ 160 Broderick Thomas	.05	.02	.01
☐ 161 Cory Schlesinger	.05	.02	.01
☐ 162 Marcus Allen	.20	.09	.03
☐ 163 Donnell Bennett	.05	.02	.01
☐ 164 J.J. Birden	.05	.02	.01
☐ 165 Matt Blundin	.05	.02	.01
☐ 166 Steve Bono	.10	.05	.01
☐ 167 Dale Carter	.10	.05	.01
☐ 168 Lake Dawson	.10	.05	.01
☐ 169 Ron Dickerson	.05	.02	.01
☐ 170 Lin Elliott	.05	.02	.01
☐ 171 Jaime Fields	.05	.02	.01
☐ 172 Greg Hill	.10	.05	.01
☐ 173 Danan Hughes	.05	.02	.01
☐ 174 Neil Smith	.10	.05	.01
☐ 175 Steve Stenstrom	.05	.02	.01
☐ 176 Edgar Bennett	.10	.05	.01
☐ 177 Robert Brooks	.20	.09	.03
☐ 178 Mark Brunell	1.00	.45	.12
☐ 179 Doug Evans	.05	.02	.01
☐ 180 Brett Favre	2.00	.90	.25
☐ 181 Corey Harris	.05	.02	.01
☐ 182 LeShon Johnson	.10	.05	.01
☐ 183 Sean Jones	.05	.02	.01
☐ 184 Lenny McGill	.05	.02	.01
☐ 185 Terry Mickens	.05	.02	.01
☐ 186 Sterling Sharpe	.10	.05	.01
☐ 187 Joe Sims	.05	.02	.01
☐ 188 Darrell Thompson	.05	.02	.01
☐ 189 Reggie White	.20	.09	.03
☐ 190 Craig Newsome	.05	.02	.01
☐ 191 Tim Brown	.20	.09	.03
☐ 192 Vince Evans	.05	.02	.01
☐ 193 Rob Fredrickson	.05	.02	.01
☐ 194 Andrew Glover	.05	.02	.01
☐ 195 Jeff Hostetler	.10	.05	.01
☐ 196 Rocket Ismail	.10	.05	.01
☐ 197 Jeff Jaeger	.05	.02	.01
☐ 198 James Jett	.10	.05	.01
☐ 199 Chester McGlockton	.10	.05	.01
☐ 200 Don Mosebar	.05	.02	.01
☐ 201 Tom Rathman	.05	.02	.01
☐ 202 Harvey Williams	.05	.02	.01
☐ 203 Steve Wisniewski	.05	.02	.01
☐ 204 Alexander Wright	.05	.02	.01
☐ 205 Napoleon Kaufman	1.00	.45	.12
☐ 206 Trace Armstrong	.05	.02	.01
☐ 207 Curtis Conway	.20	.09	.03
☐ 208 Raymont Harris	.05	.02	.01
☐ 209 Erik Kramer	.05	.02	.01
☐ 210 Nate Lewis	.05	.02	.01
☐ 211 Shane Matthews	.05	.02	.01
☐ 212 John Thierry	.05	.02	.01
☐ 213 Lewis Tillman	.05	.02	.01
☐ 214 Tom Waddle	.05	.02	.01
☐ 215 Steve Walsh	.05	.02	.01
☐ 216 James Williams	.05	.02	.01
☐ 217 Donnell Woolford	.05	.02	.01
☐ 218 Chris Zorich	.05	.02	.01
☐ 219 Rashaan Salaam	1.25	.55	.16
☐ 220 John Booty	.05	.02	.01
☐ 221 Michael Brooks	.05	.02	.01
☐ 222 Dave Brown	.10	.05	.01
☐ 223 Chris Calloway	.05	.02	.01
☐ 224 Gary Downs	.05	.02	.01
☐ 225 Kent Graham	.10	.05	.01
☐ 226 Keith Hamilton	.05	.02	.01
☐ 227 Rodney Hampton	.10	.05	.01
☐ 228 Brian Kozlowski	.05	.02	.01
☐ 229 Thomas Lewis	.10	.05	.01
☐ 230 Dave Meggett	.05	.02	.01
☐ 231 Aaron Pierce	.05	.02	.01
☐ 232 Mike Sherrard	.05	.02	.01
☐ 233 Phillippi Sparks	.05	.02	.01
☐ 234 Tyrone Wheatley	.50	.23	.06
☐ 235 Trev Alberts	.05	.02	.01
☐ 236 Aaron Bailey	.05	.02	.01
☐ 237 Jason Belser	.05	.02	.01
☐ 238 Tony Bennett	.05	.02	.01
☐ 239 Kerry Cash	.05	.02	.01
☐ 240 Marshall Faulk	.50	.23	.06
☐ 241 Stephen Grant	.05	.02	.01
☐ 242 Jeff Herrod	.05	.02	.01
☐ 243 Ronald Humphrey	.05	.02	.01
☐ 244 Kirk Lowdermilk	.05	.02	.01
☐ 245 Don Majkowski	.05	.02	.01
☐ 246 Tony McCoy	.05	.02	.01
☐ 247 Floyd Turner	.05	.02	.01
☐ 248 Lamont Warren	.05	.02	.01
☐ 249 Zack Crockett	.05	.02	.01
☐ 250 Michael Bankston	.05	.02	.01
☐ 251 Larry Centers	.10	.05	.01
☐ 252 Gary Clark	.05	.02	.01
☐ 253 Ed Cunningham	.05	.02	.01
☐ 254 Garrison Hearst	.20	.09	.03
☐ 255 Eric Hill	.05	.02	.01
☐ 256 Terry Irving	.05	.02	.01
☐ 257 Lorenzo Lynch	.05	.02	.01
☐ 258 Jamir Miller	.05	.02	.01
☐ 259 Ronald Moore	.05	.02	.01
☐ 260 Terry Samuels	.05	.02	.01
☐ 261 Jay Schroeder	.05	.02	.01
☐ 262 Eric Swann	.10	.05	.01
☐ 263 Aeneas Williams	.05	.02	.01
☐ 264 Frank Sanders	.20	.09	.03
☐ 265 Morten Andersen	.05	.02	.01
☐ 266 Mario Bates	.20	.09	.03
☐ 267 Derek Brown	.05	.02	.01
☐ 268 Darion Conner	.05	.02	.01
☐ 269 Quinn Early	.10	.05	.01
☐ 270 Jim Everett	.05	.02	.01
☐ 271 Michael Haynes	.10	.05	.01
☐ 272 Wayne Martin	.05	.02	.01
☐ 273 Derrell Mitchell	.05	.02	.01
☐ 274 Lorenzo Neal	.05	.02	.01
☐ 275 Jimmy Spencer	.05	.02	.01
☐ 276 Winfred Tubbs	.05	.02	.01
☐ 277 Renaldo Turnbull	.05	.02	.01
☐ 278 Jeff Uhlenhake	.05	.02	.01
☐ 279 Steve Atwater	.05	.02	.01
☐ 280 Keith Burns	.05	.02	.01
☐ 281 Butler By'Not'e	.05	.02	.01
☐ 282 Jeff Campbell	.05	.02	.01
☐ 283 Derrick Clark	.05	.02	.01
☐ 284 Shane Dronett	.05	.02	.01
☐ 285 Jason Elam	.05	.02	.01
☐ 286 John Elway	.75	.35	.09
☐ 287 Jerry Evans	.05	.02	.01
☐ 288 Karl Mecklenburg	.05	.02	.01
☐ 289 Glyn Milburn	.05	.02	.01
☐ 290 Anthony Miller	.10	.05	.01
☐ 291 Tom Rouen	.05	.02	.01
☐ 292 Leonard Russell	.05	.02	.01
☐ 293 Shannon Sharpe	.10	.05	.01
☐ 294 Steve Russ	.05	.02	.01
☐ 295 Mel Agee	.05	.02	.01
☐ 296 Lester Archambeau	.05	.02	.01
☐ 297 Bert Emanuel	.20	.09	.03
☐ 298 Jeff George	.10	.05	.01
☐ 299 Craig Heyward	.10	.05	.01
☐ 300 Bobby Hebert	.05	.02	.01
☐ 301 D.J. Johnson	.05	.02	.01

☐ 302 Mike Kenn	.05	.02	.01
☐ 303 Terance Mathis	.10	.05	.01
☐ 304 Clay Matthews	.10	.05	.01
☐ 305 Erric Pegram	.10	.05	.01
☐ 306 Andre Rison	.10	.05	.01
☐ 307 Chuck Smith	.05	.02	.01
☐ 308 Jessie Tuggle	.05	.02	.01
☐ 309 Lorenzo Styles	.05	.02	.01
☐ 310 Cornelius Bennett	.10	.05	.01
☐ 311 Bill Brooks	.05	.02	.01
☐ 312 Jeff Burris	.05	.02	.01
☐ 313 Carwell Gardner	.05	.02	.01
☐ 314 Kent Hull	.05	.02	.01
☐ 315 Yonel Jourdain	.05	.02	.01
☐ 316 Jim Kelly	.20	.09	.03
☐ 317 Vince Marrow	.05	.02	.01
☐ 318 Pete Metzelaars	.05	.02	.01
☐ 319 Andre Reed	.10	.05	.01
☐ 320 Kurt Schulz	.05	.02	.01
☐ 321 Bruce Smith	.20	.09	.03
☐ 322 Darryl Talley	.05	.02	.01
☐ 323 Matt Darby	.05	.02	.01
☐ 324 Justin Armour	.05	.02	.01
☐ 325 Todd Collins	.20	.09	.03
☐ 326 David Alexander DE	.05	.02	.01
☐ 327 Eric Allen	.05	.02	.01
☐ 328 Fred Barnett	.10	.05	.01
☐ 329 Randall Cunningham	.10	.05	.01
☐ 330 William Fuller	.05	.02	.01
☐ 331 Charlie Garner	.10	.05	.01
☐ 332 Vaughn Hebron	.05	.02	.01
☐ 333 James Joseph	.05	.02	.01
☐ 334 Bill Romanowski	.05	.02	.01
☐ 335 Ken Rose	.05	.02	.01
☐ 336 Jeff Snyder	.05	.02	.01
☐ 337 William Thomas	.05	.02	.01
☐ 338 Herschel Walker	.10	.05	.01
☐ 339 Calvin Williams	.10	.05	.01
☐ 340 Dave Barr	.05	.02	.01
☐ 341 Chidi Ahanotu	.05	.02	.01
☐ 342 Barney Bussey	.05	.02	.01
☐ 343 Horace Copeland	.05	.02	.01
☐ 344 Trent Dilfer	.20	.09	.03
☐ 345 Craig Erickson	.05	.02	.01
☐ 346 Paul Gruber	.05	.02	.01
☐ 347 Courtney Hawkins	.05	.02	.01
☐ 348 Lonnie Marts	.05	.02	.01
☐ 349 Martin Mayhew	.05	.02	.01
☐ 350 Hardy Nickerson	.05	.02	.01
☐ 351 Errict Rhett	.20	.09	.03
☐ 352 Lamar Thomas	.05	.02	.01
☐ 353 Charles Wilson	.05	.02	.01
☐ 354 Vince Workman	.05	.02	.01
☐ 355 Derrick Brooks	.05	.02	.01
☐ 356 Warren Sapp	.10	.05	.01
☐ 357 Sam Adams	.05	.02	.01
☐ 358 Michael Bates	.05	.02	.01
☐ 359 Brian Blades	.10	.05	.01
☐ 360 Carlton Gray	.05	.02	.01
☐ 361 Bill Hitchcock	.05	.02	.01
☐ 362 Cortez Kennedy	.10	.05	.01
☐ 363 Rick Mirer	.20	.09	.03
☐ 364 Eugene Robinson	.05	.02	.01
☐ 365 Michael Sinclair	.05	.02	.01
☐ 366 Steve Smith	.05	.02	.01
☐ 367 Bob Spitulski	.05	.02	.01
☐ 368 Rick Tuten	.05	.02	.01
☐ 369 Chris Warren	.10	.05	.01
☐ 370 Terrence Warren	.05	.02	.01
☐ 371 Christian Fauria	.05	.02	.01
☐ 372 Joey Galloway	2.00	.90	.25
☐ 373 Boomer Esiason	.10	.05	.01
☐ 374 Aaron Glenn	.05	.02	.01
☐ 375 Victor Green	.05	.02	.01
☐ 376 Johnny Johnson	.05	.02	.01
☐ 377 Mo Lewis	.05	.02	.01
☐ 378 Ronnie Lott	.10	.05	.01
☐ 379 Nick Lowery	.05	.02	.01
☐ 380 Johnny Mitchell	.05	.02	.01
☐ 381 Rob Moore	.05	.02	.01
☐ 382 Adrian Murrell	.10	.05	.01
☐ 383 Anthony Prior	.05	.02	.01
☐ 384 Brian Washington	.05	.02	.01
☐ 385 Matt Willig	.05	.02	.01
☐ 386 Kyle Brady	.20	.09	.03
☐ 387 Flipper Anderson	.05	.02	.01
☐ 388 Johnny Bailey	.05	.02	.01
☐ 389 Jerome Bettis	.30	.14	.04
☐ 390 Isaac Bruce	.50	.23	.06
☐ 391 Shane Conlan	.05	.02	.01
☐ 392 Troy Drayton	.05	.02	.01
☐ 393 D'Marco Farr	.05	.02	.01
☐ 394 Jessie Hester	.05	.02	.01
☐ 395 Todd Kinchen	.05	.02	.01
☐ 396 Ron Middleton	.05	.02	.01
☐ 397 Chris Miller	.05	.02	.01
☐ 398 Marquez Pope	.05	.02	.01
☐ 399 Robert Young	.05	.02	.01
☐ 400 Tony Zendejas	.05	.02	.01
☐ 401 Kevin Carter	.20	.09	.03
☐ 402 Reggie Brooks	.10	.05	.01
☐ 403 Tom Carter	.05	.02	.01
☐ 404 Andre Collins	.05	.02	.01
☐ 405 Pat Eilers	.05	.02	.01
☐ 406 Henry Ellard	.10	.05	.01
☐ 407 Ricky Ervins	.05	.02	.01
☐ 408 Gus Frerotte	.50	.23	.06
☐ 409 Ken Harvey	.05	.02	.01
☐ 410 Jim Lachey	.05	.02	.01
☐ 411 Brian Mitchell	.05	.02	.01
☐ 412 Reggie Roby	.05	.02	.01
☐ 413 Heath Shuler	.20	.09	.03
☐ 414 Tyronne Stowe	.05	.02	.01
☐ 415 Tydus Winans	.05	.02	.01
☐ 416 Cory Raymer	.05	.02	.01
☐ 417 Michael Westbrook	1.25	.55	.16
☐ 418 Jeff Blake	1.25	.55	.16
☐ 419 Steve Broussard	.05	.02	.01
☐ 420 Dave Cadigan	.05	.02	.01
☐ 421 Jeff Cothran	.05	.02	.01
☐ 422 Derrick Fenner	.05	.02	.01
☐ 423 James Francis	.05	.02	.01
☐ 424 Lee Johnson	.05	.02	.01
☐ 425 Louis Oliver	.05	.02	.01
☐ 426 Carl Pickens	.20	.09	.03
☐ 427 Jeff Query	.05	.02	.01
☐ 428 Corey Sawyer	.05	.02	.01
☐ 429 Darnay Scott	.20	.09	.03
☐ 430 Dan Wilkinson	.10	.05	.01
☐ 431 Alfred Williams	.05	.02	.01
☐ 432 Ki-Jana Carter	1.00	.45	.12
☐ 433 David Dunn	.05	.02	.01
☐ 434 John Walsh	.05	.02	.01
☐ 435 Gary Brown	.05	.02	.01
☐ 436 Pat Carter	.05	.02	.01
☐ 437 Ray Childress	.05	.02	.01
☐ 438 Ernest Givins	.05	.02	.01
☐ 439 Haywood Jeffires	.05	.02	.01
☐ 440 Lamar Lathon	.05	.02	.01
☐ 441 Bruce Matthews	.05	.02	.01
☐ 442 Marcus Robertson	.05	.02	.01
☐ 443 Eddie Robinson	.05	.02	.01
☐ 444 Malcolm Seabron	.05	.02	.01
☐ 445 Webster Slaughter	.05	.02	.01
☐ 446 Al Smith	.05	.02	.01
☐ 447 Billy Joe Tolliver	.05	.02	.01
☐ 448 Lorenzo White	.05	.02	.01
☐ 449 Steve McNair	2.50	1.10	.30
☐ 450 Rodney Thomas	.20	.09	.03
☐ P1 Natrone Means Promo	1.50	.70	.19
☐ P1J Natrone Means Promo Jumbo card 7" by 9 3/4"	2.00	.90	.25

1995 Pacific Blue/Platinum

These two 450-card parallel sets were randomly inserted into packs at a rate of nine in 37. Blue foil cards could be found in retail packs with Platinum versions found in hobby packs. The retail Blue version brings a slight premium over the Platinum version.

	MINT	NRMT	EXC
COMPLETE BLUE SET (450)	250.00	110.00	31.00
COMMON CARD	.35	.16	.04
*VETERAN STARS: 3.5X TO 7X BASIC CARDS			
*YOUNG STARS: 2.5X TO 5X BASIC CARDS			
*RCs: 2X TO 4X BASIC CARDS			
COMPLETE PLATINUM SET	225.00	100.00	28.00
COMMON PLATINUM (1-450)	.30	.14	.04
*VETERAN STARS: 3X TO 6X BASIC CARDS			
*YOUNG STARS: 2X TO 4X BASIC CARDS			
*RCs: 1.5X TO 3X BASIC CARDS			

1995 Pacific Cramer's Choice

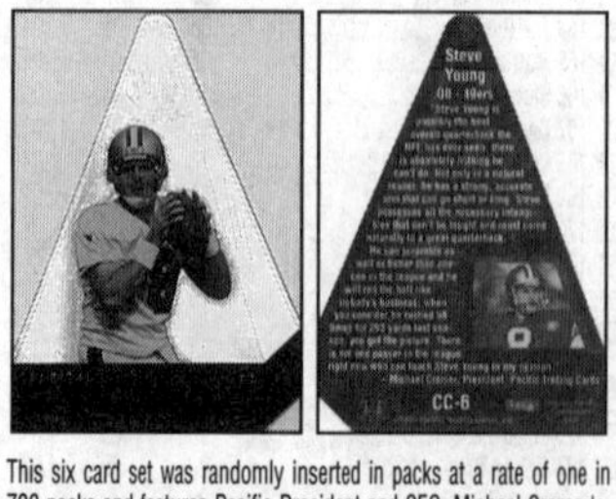

This six card set was randomly inserted in packs at a rate of one in 720 packs and features Pacific President and CEO, Michael Cramer's, selection of the top NFL players in six different categories including top running back, top defensive player, top rookie, etc. Card fronts are die cut in the shape of a trophy with a holographic background. The bottom of the card front has a black marble background with the card title, player's name and their category. Card backs feature a small head shot of the player with commentary. Cards are numbered with a "CC" prefix.

	MINT	NRMT	EXC
COMPLETE SET (6)	600.00	275.00	75.00
COMMON CARD (CC1-CC6)	50.00	22.00	6.25
☐ CC1 Ki-Jana Carter	50.00	22.00	6.25
☐ CC2 Emmitt Smith	200.00	90.00	25.00
☐ CC3 Marshall Faulk	70.00	32.00	8.75
☐ CC4 Jerry Rice	135.00	60.00	17.00
☐ CC5 Deion Sanders	70.00	32.00	8.75
☐ CC6 Steve Young	100.00	45.00	12.50

1995 Pacific Gems of the Crown

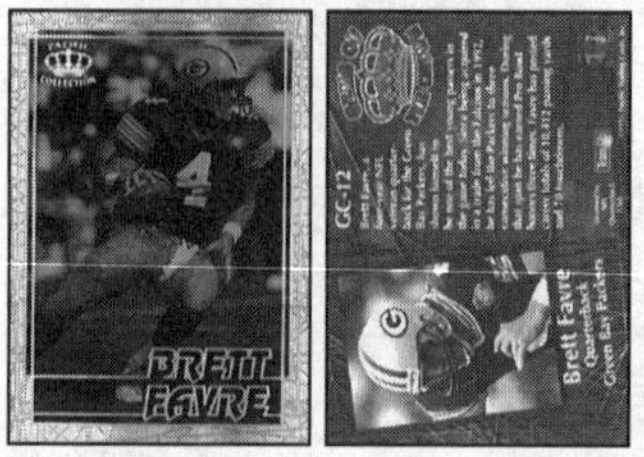

This 36 card set was randomly inserted in packs at a rate of two in 37 packs and features superstars within a holographic foil-etched design. Card fronts also contain a shot of the player against a regular background with the player's name blocked in foil at the bottom. Card backs are horizontal with a navy background and feature a shot of the player and a brief summary. Cards are numbered with a "GC" prefix.

	MINT	NRMT	EXC
COMPLETE SET (36)	175.00	80.00	22.00
COMMON CARD (GC1-GC36)	2.50	1.10	.30
☐ GC1 Jim Kelly	4.00	1.80	.50
☐ GC2 Kerry Collins	15.00	6.75	1.85
☐ GC3 Darnay Scott	4.00	1.80	.50
☐ GC4 Jeff Blake	6.00	2.70	.75
☐ GC5 Terry Allen	4.00	1.80	.50
☐ GC6 Emmitt Smith	20.00	9.00	2.50
☐ GC7 Michael Irvin	4.00	1.80	.50
☐ GC8 Troy Aikman	12.00	5.50	1.50
☐ GC9 John Elway	10.00	4.50	1.25
☐ GC10 Dave Krieg	2.50	1.10	.30
☐ GC11 Barry Sanders	12.00	5.50	1.50
☐ GC12 Brett Favre	20.00	9.00	2.50
☐ GC13 Marshall Faulk	6.00	2.70	.75
☐ GC14 Marcus Allen	4.00	1.80	.50
☐ GC15 Tim Brown	4.00	1.80	.50
☐ GC16 Bernie Parmalee	2.50	1.10	.30
☐ GC17 Dan Marino	20.00	9.00	2.50
☐ GC18 Cris Carter	4.00	1.80	.50
☐ GC19 Drew Bledsoe	12.00	5.50	1.50
☐ GC20 Mario Bates	2.50	1.10	.30
☐ GC21 Rodney Hampton	4.00	1.80	.50
☐ GC22 Ben Coates	2.50	1.10	.30
☐ GC23 Charles Johnson	2.50	1.10	.30
☐ GC24 Byron Bam Morris	2.50	1.10	.30
☐ GC25 Stan Humphries	4.00	1.80	.50
☐ GC26 Deion Sanders	8.00	3.60	1.00
☐ GC27 Jerry Rice	12.00	5.50	1.50
☐ GC28 Ricky Watters	4.00	1.80	.50
☐ GC29 Steve Young	10.00	4.50	1.25
☐ GC30 Natrone Means	4.00	1.80	.50
☐ GC31 William Floyd	2.50	1.10	.30
☐ GC32 Chris Warren	4.00	1.80	.50
☐ GC33 Rick Mirer	4.00	1.80	.50
☐ GC34 Jerome Bettis	4.00	1.80	.50
☐ GC35 Errict Rhett	4.00	1.80	.50
☐ GC36 Heath Shuler	4.00	1.80	.50

1995 Pacific G-Force

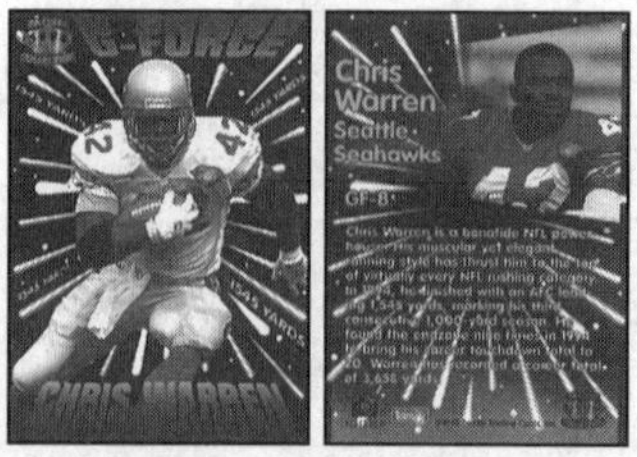

This 10 card set was randomly inserted in packs at a ratio of one in 37 and feature the top running backs of the NFL. Card fronts have a black background with different colors shooting out from the center. The word "G-Force" is located at the top of the card and the player's name is located at the bottom. Their total rushing numbers from 1994 are also listed in four different areas on the front of the card. Card backs contain the same background with a headshot of the player and a brief commentary. Cards are numbered with a "GF" prefix.

	MINT	NRMT	EXC
COMPLETE SET (10)	40.00	18.00	5.00
COMMON CARD (GF1-GF10)	2.00	.90	.25
☐ GF1 Marcus Allen	3.00	1.35	.35
☐ GF2 Terry Allen	3.00	1.35	.35
☐ GF3 Emmitt Smith	15.00	6.75	1.85
☐ GF4 Barry Sanders	8.00	3.60	1.00
☐ GF5 Marshall Faulk	4.00	1.80	.50
☐ GF6 Rodney Hampton	2.00	.90	.25
☐ GF7 Natrone Means	3.00	1.35	.35
☐ GF8 Chris Warren	2.00	.90	.25
☐ GF9 Jerome Bettis	3.00	1.35	.35
☐ GF10 Errict Rhett	3.00	1.35	.35

1995 Pacific Gold Crown Die Cuts

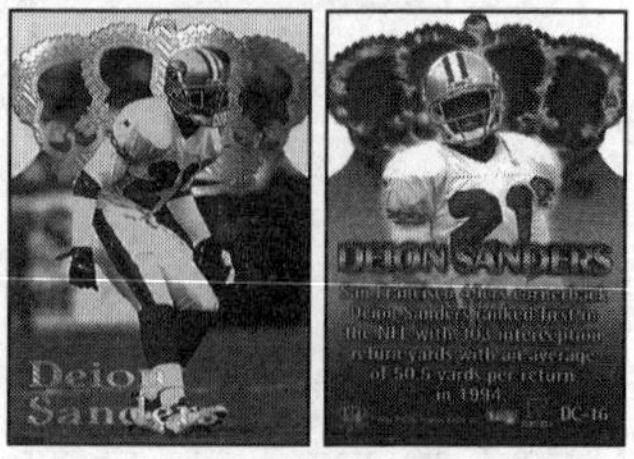

This 20 card set was randomly inserted into packs at a rate of one in 37 packs and features the top players in the NFL. Card fronts are die cut in the shape of a crown at the top and feature either holographic gold foil or flat gold foil. Card fronts also contain the player's name at the bottom of the card in the same holographic gold foil or flat gold foil. Card backs feature a shot of the player, his name and a brief commentary.

	MINT	NRMT	EXC
COMP.HOLOFOIL SET (20)	350.00	160.00	45.00
COMMON HOLOFOIL (DC1-DC20)	8.00	3.60	1.00
COMP.FLAT GOLD SET (20)	750.00	350.00	95.00
*FLAT GOLD CARDS: 1X TO 2X BASIC CARDS			
☐ DC1 Ki-Jana Carter	8.00	3.60	1.00
☐ DC2 Michael Irvin	12.00	5.50	1.50
☐ DC3 Emmitt Smith	40.00	18.00	5.00
☐ DC4 Troy Aikman	25.00	11.00	3.10
☐ DC5 John Elway	20.00	9.00	2.50
☐ DC6 Barry Sanders	25.00	11.00	3.10
☐ DC7 Marshall Faulk	14.00	6.25	1.75
☐ DC8 Dan Marino	40.00	18.00	5.00
☐ DC9 Ben Coates	8.00	3.60	1.00
☐ DC10 Drew Bledsoe	25.00	11.00	3.10
☐ DC11 Byron Bam Morris	8.00	3.60	1.00
☐ DC12 Jerry Rice	25.00	11.00	3.10
☐ DC13 William Floyd	8.00	3.60	1.00
☐ DC14 Steve Young	20.00	9.00	2.50
☐ DC15 Natrone Means	12.00	5.50	1.50
☐ DC16 Deion Sanders	16.00	7.25	2.00
☐ DC17 Rick Mirer	12.00	5.50	1.50
☐ DC18 Chris Warren	8.00	3.60	1.00
☐ DC19 Jerome Bettis	12.00	5.50	1.50
☐ DC20 Errict Rhett	12.00	5.50	1.50

1995 Pacific Hometown Heroes

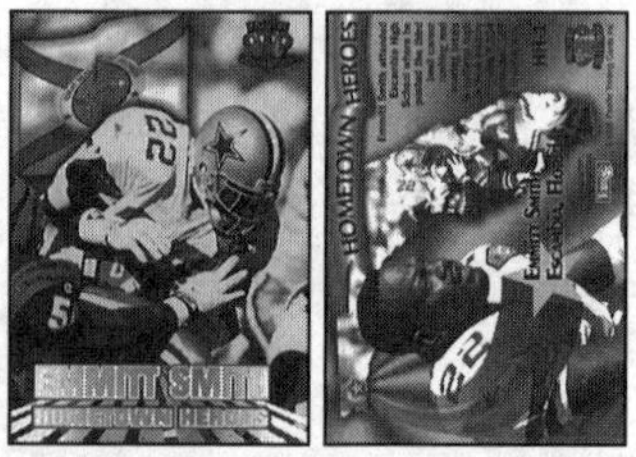

This 10 card set was randomly inserted in packs at a ratio of one in 37 packs and features information on where top players went to high school and where they started their football careers. Card fronts feature a full bleed photo with the player's name and the "Hometown Heroes" slogan in blue holographic foil at the bottom. There is also a flag on the left side of the card that represents the state where the player played. Card backs are horizontal with an orange background and contains two shots of the player - one literally in the state he played and another on the side of it. The also contain a brief commentary. Cards are numbered with a "HH" prefix.

	MINT	NRMT	EXC
COMPLETE SET (10)	40.00	18.00	5.00
COMMON CARD (HH1-HH10)	1.50	.70	.19
☐ HH1 Emmitt Smith	10.00	4.50	1.25
☐ HH2 Troy Aikman	5.00	2.20	.60
☐ HH3 Barry Sanders	5.00	2.20	.60
☐ HH4 Marshall Faulk	2.00	.90	.25
☐ HH5 Dan Marino	10.00	4.50	1.25
☐ HH6 Drew Bledsoe	5.00	2.20	.60
☐ HH7 Natrone Means	1.50	.70	.19
☐ HH8 Steve Young	4.00	1.80	.50
☐ HH9 Jerry Rice	5.00	2.20	.60
☐ HH10 Errict Rhett	1.50	.70	.19

1995 Pacific Rookies

This 20 card set was randomly inserted into packs at a rate of two in 37 packs and features Pacific's choices of the top rookies of 1995. Card fronts feature the rookies in their college uniforms with their pro team's helmet in the lower right hand corner. The rookie's name is listed horizontally along the side in a prism-foil. Card backs contain a head shot of the player in his college uniform in the top left hand corner. A brief commentary on the player is listed under the shot.

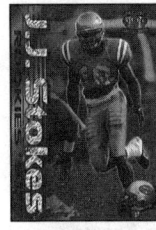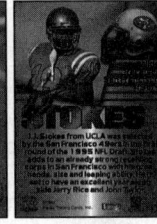

J.J. Stokes from UCLA was selected by the San Francisco 49ers in the first round of the 1995 NFL Draft. Stokes adds to an already strong receiving corps in San Francisco with his blazing speed, size and hands, giving him a shot to have an excellent year even while Jerry Rice and John Taylor...

	MINT	NRMT	EXC
COMPLETE SET (20)	40.00	18.00	5.00
COMMON CARD (1-20)	1.00	.45	.12
☐ 1 Dave Barr	1.00	.45	.12
☐ 2 Kyle Brady	1.00	.45	.12
☐ 3 Mark Bruener	1.00	.45	.12
☐ 4 Ki-Jana Carter	2.00	.90	.25
☐ 5 Kerry Collins	8.00	3.60	1.00
☐ 6 Todd Collins	2.00	.90	.25
☐ 7 Christian Fauria	1.00	.45	.12
☐ 8 Joey Galloway	5.00	2.20	.60
☐ 9 Chris T. Jones	3.00	1.35	.35
☐ 10 Napoleon Kaufman	2.00	.90	.25
☐ 11 Chad May	1.00	.45	.12
☐ 12 Steve McNair	6.00	2.70	.75
☐ 13 Rashaan Salaam	4.00	1.80	.50
☐ 14 Warren Sapp	1.00	.45	.12
☐ 15 James O.Stewart	2.00	.90	.25
☐ 16 Kordell Stewart	8.00	3.60	1.00
☐ 17 J.J. Stokes	3.00	1.35	.35
☐ 18 Michael Westbrook	3.00	1.35	.35
☐ 19 Tyrone Wheatley	2.00	.90	.25
☐ 20 Sherman Williams	1.00	.45	.12

1995 Pacific Young Warriors

This 20 card set was randomly inserted in packs at a rate of two in 37 packs and features Pacific's selection of the best second year players in the NFL. Card fronts contain a full foil gold background with the player's name in their team colors along the bottom. The set name "Young Warriors" is etched in the gold foil along the right side of the card. Card backs have an orange-brown background with an outline of the player nestled between two columns and brief statistical fact underneath it.

	MINT	NRMT	EXC
COMPLETE SET (20)	20.00	9.00	2.50
COMMON CARD (1-20)	1.00	.45	.12
☐ 1 Bert Emanuel	1.00	.45	.12
☐ 2 Darnay Scott	2.50	1.10	.30
☐ 3 Dan Wilkinson	1.00	.45	.12
☐ 4 Derrick Alexander WR	2.00	.90	.25
☐ 5 Willie McGinest	1.00	.45	.12
☐ 6 Marshall Faulk	4.00	1.80	.50
☐ 7 Lake Dawson	2.00	.90	.25
☐ 8 Greg Hill	2.00	.90	.25
☐ 9 Tim Bowens	1.00	.45	.12
☐ 10 David Palmer	1.00	.45	.12
☐ 11 Aaron Glenn	1.00	.45	.12
☐ 12 Mario Bates	1.00	.45	.12
☐ 13 Charles Johnson	1.00	.45	.12
☐ 14 Byron Bam Morris	2.00	.90	.25
☐ 15 William Floyd	2.00	.90	.25
☐ 16 Adam Walker	1.00	.45	.12
☐ 17 Bryant Young	1.00	.45	.12
☐ 18 Trent Dilfer	2.00	.90	.25
☐ 19 Errict Rhett	2.00	.90	.25
☐ 20 Heath Shuler	2.00	.90	.25

1996 Pacific

This 450-card set was issued in one series and distributed in 12-card packs. The set features borderless color action player photos with gold foil highlights. Two parallel sets were also issued: Red Foil and Blue Foil. The scorching red foil version was inserted in retail only packs at the rate of nine in 37. The electric blue foil version was inserted in the same rate in hobby only packs. The cards are grouped alphabetically within teams and checklisted below alphabetically according to teams.

	MINT	NRMT	EXC
COMPLETE SET (450)	40.00	18.00	5.00
COMMON CARD (1-450)	.05	.02	.01
☐ 1 Jeff Feagles	.05	.02	.01
☐ 2 Rob Moore	.05	.02	.01
☐ 3 Clyde Simmons	.05	.02	.01
☐ 4 Mike Buck	.05	.02	.01
☐ 5 Aeneas Williams	.05	.02	.01
☐ 6 Simeon Rice	.20	.09	.03
☐ 7 Garrison Hearst	.10	.05	.01
☐ 8 Eric Swann	.10	.05	.01
☐ 9 Dave Krieg	.05	.02	.01
☐ 10 Leeland McElroy	.20	.09	.03
☐ 11 Oscar McBride	.05	.02	.01
☐ 12 Frank Sanders	.10	.05	.01
☐ 13 Larry Centers	.10	.05	.01
☐ 14 Seth Joyner	.05	.02	.01
☐ 15 Stevie Anderson	.05	.02	.01
☐ 16 Craig Heyward	.05	.02	.01
☐ 17 Devin Bush	.05	.02	.01
☐ 18 Eric Metcalf	.10	.05	.01
☐ 19 Jeff George	.10	.05	.01
☐ 20 Richard Huntley	.05	.02	.01
☐ 21 Jamal Anderson	.75	.35	.09
☐ 22 Bert Emanuel	.10	.05	.01
☐ 23 Terance Mathis	.05	.02	.01
☐ 24 Roman Fortin	.05	.02	.01
☐ 25 Jessie Tuggle	.05	.02	.01
☐ 26 Morten Andersen	.05	.02	.01
☐ 27 Chris Doleman	.05	.02	.01
☐ 28 D.J. Johnson	.05	.02	.01
☐ 29 Kevin Ross	.05	.02	.01
☐ 30 Michael Jackson	.10	.05	.01
☐ 31 Eric Zeier	.10	.05	.01
☐ 32 Jonathan Ogden	.05	.02	.01
☐ 33 Eric Turner	.05	.02	.01
☐ 34 Andre Rison	.10	.05	.01
☐ 35 Lorenzo White	.05	.02	.01
☐ 36 Earnest Byner	.05	.02	.01
☐ 37 Derrick Alexander WR	.10	.05	.01
☐ 38 Brian Kinchen	.05	.02	.01
☐ 39 Anthony Pleasant	.05	.02	.01
☐ 40 Vinny Testaverde	.10	.05	.01
☐ 41 Pepper Johnson	.05	.02	.01
☐ 42 Frank Hartley	.05	.02	.01
☐ 43 Craig Powell	.05	.02	.01
☐ 44 Leroy Hoard	.05	.02	.01
☐ 45 Kent Hull	.05	.02	.01
☐ 46 Bryce Paup	.10	.05	.01
☐ 47 Andre Reed	.10	.05	.01
☐ 48 Darick Holmes	.10	.05	.01
☐ 49 Russell Copeland	.05	.02	.01
☐ 50 Jerry Ostroski	.05	.02	.01
☐ 51 Chris Green	.05	.02	.01
☐ 52 Eric Moulds	.75	.35	.09
☐ 53 Justin Armour	.05	.02	.01
☐ 54 Jim Kelly	.20	.09	.03
☐ 55 Cornelius Bennett	.10	.05	.01
☐ 56 Steve Tasker	.05	.02	.01
☐ 57 Thurman Thomas	.20	.09	.03
☐ 58 Bruce Smith	.20	.09	.03
☐ 59 Todd Collins	.10	.05	.01
☐ 60 Shawn King	.05	.02	.01
☐ 61 Don Beebe	.05	.02	.01
☐ 62 John Kasay	.05	.02	.01
☐ 63 Tim McKyer	.05	.02	.01
☐ 64 Darion Conner	.05	.02	.01
☐ 65 Pete Metzelaars	.05	.02	.01
☐ 66 Derrick Moore	.05	.02	.01
☐ 67 Blake Brockermeyer	.05	.02	.01
☐ 68 Tim Biakabutuka	.75	.35	.09
☐ 69 Sam Mills	.10	.05	.01
☐ 70 Vince Workman	.05	.02	.01
☐ 71 Kerry Collins	1.25	.55	.16
☐ 72 Carlton Bailey	.05	.02	.01
☐ 73 Mark Carrier WR	.10	.05	.01
☐ 74 Donnell Woolford	.05	.02	.01
☐ 75 Walt Harris	.05	.02	.01
☐ 76 John Thierry	.05	.02	.01
☐ 77 Al Fontenot	.05	.02	.01
☐ 78 Lewis Tillman	.05	.02	.01
☐ 79 Curtis Conway	.20	.09	.03
☐ 80 Chris Zorich	.05	.02	.01
☐ 81 Mark Carrier DB	.05	.02	.01
☐ 82 Bobby Engram	.75	.35	.09
☐ 83 Alonzo Spellman	.05	.02	.01
☐ 84 Rashaan Salaam	.20	.09	.03
☐ 85 Michael Timpson	.05	.02	.01
☐ 86 Nate Lewis	.05	.02	.01
☐ 87 James Williams	.05	.02	.01
☐ 88 Jeff Graham	.05	.02	.01
☐ 89 Erik Kramer	.05	.02	.01
☐ 90 Willie Anderson	.05	.02	.01
☐ 91 Tony McGee	.05	.02	.01
☐ 92 Marco Battaglia	.05	.02	.01
☐ 93 Dan Wilkinson	.05	.02	.01
☐ 94 John Walsh	.05	.02	.01
☐ 95 Eric Bieniemy	.05	.02	.01
☐ 96 Ricardo McDonald	.05	.02	.01
☐ 97 Carl Pickens	.20	.09	.03
☐ 98 Kevin Sargent	.05	.02	.01
☐ 99 David Dunn	.05	.02	.01
☐ 100 Jeff Blake	.20	.09	.03
☐ 101 Harold Green	.05	.02	.01
☐ 102 James Francis	.05	.02	.01
☐ 103 John Copeland	.05	.02	.01
☐ 104 Darnay Scott	.10	.05	.01
☐ 105 Darren Woodson	.05	.02	.01
☐ 106 Jay Novacek	.10	.05	.01
☐ 107 Charles Haley	.10	.05	.01
☐ 108 Mark Tuinei	.05	.02	.01
☐ 109 Michael Irvin	.20	.09	.03
☐ 110 Troy Aikman	1.00	.45	.12
☐ 111 Chris Boniol	.05	.02	.01
☐ 112 Sherman Williams	.05	.02	.01
☐ 113 Deion Sanders	.60	.25	.07
☐ 114 Emmitt Smith	2.00	.90	.25
☐ 115 Eric Bjornson	.05	.02	.01
☐ 116 Nate Newton	.05	.02	.01
☐ 117 Larry Allen	.05	.02	.01
☐ 118 Kevin Williams	.05	.02	.01
☐ 119 Leon Lett	.05	.02	.01
☐ 120 John Mobley	.05	.02	.01
☐ 121 Anthony Miller	.10	.05	.01
☐ 122 Brian Habib	.05	.02	.01
☐ 123 Aaron Craver	.05	.02	.01
☐ 124 Glyn Milburn	.05	.02	.01
☐ 125 Shannon Sharpe	.10	.05	.01
☐ 126 Steve Atwater	.05	.02	.01
☐ 127 Jason Elam	.05	.02	.01
☐ 128 John Elway	.75	.35	.09
☐ 129 Reggie Rivers	.05	.02	.01
☐ 130 Mike Pritchard	.05	.02	.01
☐ 131 Vance Johnson	.05	.02	.01
☐ 132 Terrell Davis	1.50	.70	.19
☐ 133 Tyrone Braxton	.05	.02	.01
☐ 134 Ed McCaffrey	.05	.02	.01
☐ 135 Brett Perriman	.10	.05	.01
☐ 136 Chris Spielman	.05	.02	.01
☐ 137 Luther Elliss	.05	.02	.01
☐ 138 Johnnie Morton	.10	.05	.01
☐ 139 Zefross Moss	.05	.02	.01
☐ 140 Barry Sanders	1.00	.45	.12
☐ 141 Lomas Brown	.05	.02	.01
☐ 142 Cory Schlesinger	.05	.02	.01
☐ 143 Jason Hanson	.05	.02	.01
☐ 144 Kevin Glover	.05	.02	.01
☐ 145 Ron Rivers	.05	.02	.01
☐ 146 Aubrey Matthews	.05	.02	.01
☐ 147 Reggie Brown LB	.05	.02	.01
☐ 148 Herman Moore	.20	.09	.03
☐ 149 Scott Mitchell	.10	.05	.01
☐ 150 Brett Favre	2.00	.90	.25
☐ 151 Sean Jones	.05	.02	.01
☐ 152 LeRoy Butler	.05	.02	.01
☐ 153 Mark Chmura	.10	.05	.01
☐ 154 Derrick Mayes	.75	.35	.09
☐ 155 Mark Ingram	.05	.02	.01
☐ 156 Antonio Freeman	.40	.18	.05
☐ 157 Chris Darkins	.10	.05	.01
☐ 158 Robert Brooks	.20	.09	.03
☐ 159 William Henderson	.05	.02	.01
☐ 160 George Koonce	.05	.02	.01
☐ 161 Craig Newsome	.05	.02	.01
☐ 162 Darius Holland	.05	.02	.01
☐ 163 George Teague	.05	.02	.01
☐ 164 Edgar Bennett	.10	.05	.01
☐ 165 Reggie White	.20	.09	.03
☐ 166 Micheal Barrow	.05	.02	.01
☐ 167 Mel Gray	.05	.02	.01
☐ 168 Anthony Dorsett	.05	.02	.01
☐ 169 Roderick Lewis	.05	.02	.01
☐ 170 Henry Ford	.05	.02	.01
☐ 171 Mark Stepnoski	.05	.02	.01
☐ 172 Chris Sanders	.10	.05	.01
☐ 173 Anthony Cook	.05	.02	.01
☐ 174 Eddie Robinson	.05	.02	.01
☐ 175 Steve McNair	1.00	.45	.12
☐ 176 Haywood Jeffires	.05	.02	.01
☐ 177 Eddie George	4.00	1.80	.50
☐ 178 Marion Butts	.05	.02	.01
☐ 179 Malcolm Seabron	.05	.02	.01
☐ 180 Rodney Thomas	.05	.02	.01
☐ 181 Ken Dilger	.10	.05	.01
☐ 182 Zack Crockett	.05	.02	.01
☐ 183 Tony Bennett	.05	.02	.01
☐ 184 Quentin Coryatt	.05	.02	.01
☐ 185 Marshall Faulk	.20	.09	.03
☐ 186 Sean Dawkins	.05	.02	.01
☐ 187 Jim Harbaugh	.10	.05	.01
☐ 188 Eugene Daniel	.05	.02	.01
☐ 189 Roosevelt Potts	.05	.02	.01
☐ 190 Lamont Warren	.05	.02	.01
☐ 191 Will Wolford	.05	.02	.01
☐ 192 Tony Siragusa	.05	.02	.01
☐ 193 Aaron Bailey	.05	.02	.01
☐ 194 Trev Alberts	.05	.02	.01
☐ 195 Kevin Hardy	.10	.05	.01
☐ 196 Greg Spann	.05	.02	.01
☐ 197 Steve Beuerlein	.05	.02	.01
☐ 198 Steve Taneyhill	.05	.02	.01
☐ 199 Vaughn Dunbar	.05	.02	.01
☐ 200 Mark Brunell	1.00	.45	.12
☐ 201 Bernard Carter	.05	.02	.01
☐ 202 James O. Stewart	.20	.09	.03
☐ 203 Tony Boselli	.10	.05	.01
☐ 204 Chris Doering	.05	.02	.01
☐ 205 Willie Jackson	.10	.05	.01
☐ 206 Tony Brackens	.10	.05	.01
☐ 207 Ernest Givins	.05	.02	.01
☐ 208 Le'Shai Maston	.05	.02	.01
☐ 209 Pete Mitchell	.05	.02	.01
☐ 210 Desmond Howard	.10	.05	.01
☐ 211 Vinnie Clark	.05	.02	.01
☐ 212 Jeff Lageman	.05	.02	.01
☐ 213 Derrick Walker	.05	.02	.01
☐ 214 Dan Saleaumua	.05	.02	.01
☐ 215 Derrick Thomas	.10	.05	.01
☐ 216 Neil Smith	.10	.05	.01
☐ 217 Willie Davis	.10	.05	.01
☐ 218 Mark Collins	.05	.02	.01
☐ 219 Lake Dawson	.10	.05	.01
☐ 220 Greg Hill	.10	.05	.01
☐ 221 Anthony Davis	.05	.02	.01
☐ 222 Kimble Anders	.05	.02	.01
☐ 223 Webster Slaughter	.05	.02	.01
☐ 224 Tamarick Vanover	.20	.09	.03
☐ 225 Marcus Allen	.20	.09	.03
☐ 226 Steve Bono	.10	.05	.01
☐ 227 Will Shields	.05	.02	.01
☐ 228 Karim Abdul-Jabbar	2.50	1.10	.30
☐ 229 Tim Bowens	.05	.02	.01
☐ 230 Keith Sims	.05	.02	.01
☐ 231 Terry Kirby	.10	.05	.01
☐ 232 Gene Atkins	.05	.02	.01
☐ 233 Dan Marino	2.00	.90	.25
☐ 234 Richmond Webb	.05	.02	.01
☐ 235 Gary Clark	.05	.02	.01
☐ 236 O.J. McDuffie	.10	.05	.01
☐ 237 Marco Coleman	.05	.02	.01
☐ 238 Bernie Parmalee	.05	.02	.01
☐ 239 Randal Hill	.05	.02	.01
☐ 240 Bryan Cox	.05	.02	.01
☐ 241 Irving Fryar	.10	.05	.01
☐ 242 Derrick Alexander DE	.05	.02	.01
☐ 243 Qadry Ismail	.10	.05	.01
☐ 244 Warren Moon	.10	.05	.01
☐ 245 Cris Carter	.20	.09	.03
☐ 246 Chad May	.05	.02	.01
☐ 247 Robert Smith	.05	.02	.01
☐ 248 Fuad Reveiz	.05	.02	.01
☐ 249 Orlando Thomas	.05	.02	.01
☐ 250 Chris Hinton	.05	.02	.01
☐ 251 Jack Del Rio	.05	.02	.01
☐ 252 Moe Williams	.05	.02	.01
☐ 253 Roy Barker	.05	.02	.01
☐ 254 Jake Reed	.10	.05	.01
☐ 255 Adrian Cooper	.05	.02	.01
☐ 256 Curtis Martin	1.50	.70	.19
☐ 257 Ben Coates	.10	.05	.01
☐ 258 Drew Bledsoe	1.00	.45	.12
☐ 259 Maurice Hurst	.05	.02	.01
☐ 260 Troy Brown	.05	.02	.01
☐ 261 Bruce Armstrong	.05	.02	.01
☐ 262 Myron Guyton	.05	.02	.01
☐ 263 Dave Meggett	.05	.02	.01
☐ 264 Terry Glenn	3.00	1.35	.35
☐ 265 Chris Slade	.05	.02	.01
☐ 266 Vincent Brisby	.05	.02	.01
☐ 267 Willie McGinest	.05	.02	.01
☐ 268 Vincent Brown	.05	.02	.01
☐ 269 Will Moore	.05	.02	.01
☐ 270 Jay Barker	.05	.02	.01
☐ 271 Ray Zellars	.05	.02	.01
☐ 272 Derek Brown RB	.05	.02	.01
☐ 273 William Roaf	.05	.02	.01
☐ 274 Quinn Early	.05	.02	.01
☐ 275 Michael Haynes	.10	.05	.01
☐ 276 Rufus Porter	.05	.02	.01
☐ 277 Renaldo Turnbull	.05	.02	.01
☐ 278 Wayne Martin	.05	.02	.01
☐ 279 Tyrone Hughes	.05	.02	.01
☐ 280 Irv Smith	.05	.02	.01
☐ 281 Eric Allen	.05	.02	.01
☐ 282 Mark Fields	.05	.02	.01
☐ 283 Mario Bates	.10	.05	.01
☐ 284 Jim Everett	.05	.02	.01
☐ 285 Vince Buck	.05	.02	.01
☐ 286 Alex Molden	.05	.02	.01
☐ 287 Tyrone Wheatley	.10	.05	.01
☐ 288 Chris Calloway	.05	.02	.01
☐ 289 Jessie Armstead	.05	.02	.01
☐ 290 Arthur Marshall	.05	.02	.01
☐ 291 Aaron Pierce	.05	.02	.01
☐ 292 Dave Brown	.10	.05	.01
☐ 293 Rodney Hampton	.10	.05	.01
☐ 294 Jumbo Elliott	.05	.02	.01
☐ 295 Mike Sherrard	.05	.02	.01
☐ 296 Howard Cross	.05	.02	.01
☐ 297 Michael Brooks	.05	.02	.01
☐ 298 Herschel Walker	.10	.05	.01
☐ 299 Danny Kanell	.20	.09	.03
☐ 300 Keith Elias	.05	.02	.01
☐ 301 Bobby Houston	.05	.02	.01
☐ 302 Dexter Carter	.05	.02	.01
☐ 303 Tony Casillas	.05	.02	.01
☐ 304 Kyle Brady	.10	.05	.01
☐ 305 Glenn Foley	.05	.02	.01
☐ 306 Ronald Moore	.05	.02	.01
☐ 307 Ryan Yarborough	.05	.02	.01

☐ 308 Aaron Glenn	.05	.02	.01
☐ 309 Adrian Murrell	.10	.05	.01
☐ 310 Boomer Esiason	.10	.05	.01
☐ 311 Kyle Clifton	.05	.02	.01
☐ 312 Wayne Chrebet	.10	.05	.01
☐ 313 Erik Howard	.05	.02	.01
☐ 314 Keyshawn Johnson	1.50	.70	.19
☐ 315 Marvin Washington	.05	.02	.01
☐ 316 Johnny Mitchell	.05	.02	.01
☐ 317 Alex Van Dyke	.10	.05	.01
☐ 318 Billy Joe Hobert	.10	.05	.01
☐ 319 Andrew Glover	.05	.02	.01
☐ 320 Vince Evans	.05	.02	.01
☐ 321 Chester McGlockton	.05	.02	.01
☐ 322 Pat Swilling	.05	.02	.01
☐ 323 Rocket Ismail	.10	.05	.01
☐ 324 Eddie Anderson	.05	.02	.01
☐ 325 Rickey Dudley	.20	.09	.03
☐ 326 Steve Wisniewski	.05	.02	.01
☐ 327 Harvey Williams	.05	.02	.01
☐ 328 Napoleon Kaufman	.10	.05	.01
☐ 329 Tim Brown	.10	.05	.01
☐ 330 Jeff Hostetler	.10	.05	.01
☐ 331 Anthony Smith	.05	.02	.01
☐ 332 Terry McDaniel	.05	.02	.01
☐ 333 Charlie Garner	.05	.02	.01
☐ 334 Ricky Watters	.10	.05	.01
☐ 335 Brian Dawkins	.05	.02	.01
☐ 336 Randall Cunningham	.10	.05	.01
☐ 337 Gary Anderson	.05	.02	.01
☐ 338 Calvin Williams	.05	.02	.01
☐ 339 Chris T. Jones	.20	.09	.03
☐ 340 Bobby Hoying	.20	.09	.03
☐ 341 William Fuller	.05	.02	.01
☐ 342 William Thomas	.05	.02	.01
☐ 343 Mike Mamula	.05	.02	.01
☐ 344 Fred Barnett	.10	.05	.01
☐ 345 Rodney Peete	.05	.02	.01
☐ 346 Mark McMillian	.05	.02	.01
☐ 347 Bobby Taylor	.10	.05	.01
☐ 348 Yancey Thigpen	.10	.05	.01
☐ 349 Neil O'Donnell	.10	.05	.01
☐ 350 Rod Woodson	.10	.05	.01
☐ 351 Kordell Stewart	1.25	.55	.16
☐ 352 Dermontti Dawson	.05	.02	.01
☐ 353 Norm Johnson	.05	.02	.01
☐ 354 Ernie Mills	.05	.02	.01
☐ 355 Byron Bam Morris	.10	.05	.01
☐ 356 Mark Bruener	.05	.02	.01
☐ 357 Kevin Greene	.10	.05	.01
☐ 358 Greg Lloyd	.10	.05	.01
☐ 359 Andre Hastings	.10	.05	.01
☐ 360 Erric Pegram	.10	.05	.01
☐ 361 Carnell Lake	.05	.02	.01
☐ 362 Dwayne Harper	.05	.02	.01
☐ 363 Ronnie Harmon	.05	.02	.01
☐ 364 Leslie O'Neal	.05	.02	.01
☐ 365 John Carney	.05	.02	.01
☐ 366 Stan Humphries	.10	.05	.01
☐ 367 Brian Roche	.05	.02	.01
☐ 368 Terrell Fletcher	.05	.02	.01
☐ 369 Shaun Gayle	.05	.02	.01
☐ 370 Alfred Pupunu	.05	.02	.01
☐ 371 Shawn Jefferson	.05	.02	.01
☐ 372 Junior Seau	.20	.09	.03
☐ 373 Mark Seay	.05	.02	.01
☐ 374 Aaron Hayden	.05	.02	.01
☐ 375 Tony Martin	.10	.05	.01
☐ 376 Steve Young	.75	.35	.09
☐ 377 J.J. Stokes	.20	.09	.03
☐ 378 Jerry Rice	1.00	.45	.12
☐ 379 Derek Loville	.05	.02	.01
☐ 380 Lee Woodall	.05	.02	.01
☐ 381 Terrell Owens	2.00	.90	.25
☐ 382 Elvis Grbac	.20	.09	.03
☐ 383 Ricky Ervins	.05	.02	.01
☐ 384 Eric Davis	.05	.02	.01
☐ 385 Dana Stubblefield	.10	.05	.01
☐ 386 Gary Plummer	.05	.02	.01
☐ 387 Tim McDonald	.05	.02	.01
☐ 388 William Floyd	.10	.05	.01
☐ 389 Ken Norton Jr.	.10	.05	.01
☐ 390 Merton Hanks	.05	.02	.01
☐ 391 Bart Oates	.05	.02	.01
☐ 392 Brent Jones	.05	.02	.01
☐ 393 Steve Broussard	.05	.02	.01
☐ 394 Robert Blackmon	.05	.02	.01
☐ 395 Rick Tuten	.05	.02	.01
☐ 396 Pete Kendall	.05	.02	.01
☐ 397 John Friesz	.05	.02	.01
☐ 398 Terry Wooden	.05	.02	.01
☐ 399 Rick Mirer	.10	.05	.01
☐ 400 Chris Warren	.10	.05	.01
☐ 401 Joey Galloway	.40	.18	.05
☐ 402 Howard Ballard	.05	.02	.01
☐ 403 Jason Kyle	.05	.02	.01
☐ 404 Kevin Mawae	.05	.02	.01
☐ 405 Mack Strong	.05	.02	.01
☐ 406 Reggie Brown RB	.05	.02	.01
☐ 407 Cortez Kennedy	.10	.05	.01
☐ 408 Sean Gilbert	.05	.02	.01
☐ 409 J.T. Thomas	.05	.02	.01
☐ 410 Shane Conlan	.05	.02	.01
☐ 411 Johnny Bailey	.05	.02	.01
☐ 412 Mark Rypien	.05	.02	.01
☐ 413 Leonard Russell	.05	.02	.01
☐ 414 Troy Drayton	.05	.02	.01
☐ 415 Jerome Bettis	.20	.09	.03
☐ 416 Jessie Hester	.05	.02	.01
☐ 417 Isaac Bruce	.20	.09	.03
☐ 418 Roman Phifer	.05	.02	.01
☐ 419 Todd Kinchen	.05	.02	.01
☐ 420 Alexander Wright	.05	.02	.01
☐ 421 Marcus Jones	.05	.02	.01
☐ 422 Horace Copeland	.05	.02	.01
☐ 423 Eric Curry	.05	.02	.01
☐ 424 Courtney Hawkins	.05	.02	.01
☐ 425 Alvin Harper	.05	.02	.01
☐ 426 Derrick Brooks	.05	.02	.01
☐ 427 Errict Rhett	.10	.05	.01
☐ 428 Trent Dilfer	.10	.05	.01
☐ 429 Hardy Nickerson	.05	.02	.01
☐ 430 Brad Culpepper	.05	.02	.01
☐ 431 Warren Sapp	.05	.02	.01
☐ 432 Reggie Roby	.05	.02	.01
☐ 433 Santana Dotson	.05	.02	.01
☐ 434 Jerry Ellison	.05	.02	.01
☐ 435 Lawrence Dawsey	.05	.02	.01
☐ 436 Heath Shuler	.20	.09	.03
☐ 437 Stanley Richard	.05	.02	.01
☐ 438 Rod Stephens	.05	.02	.01
☐ 439 Stephen Davis	.20	.09	.03
☐ 440 Terry Allen	.10	.05	.01
☐ 441 Michael Westbrook	.20	.09	.03
☐ 442 Ken Harvey	.05	.02	.01
☐ 443 Coleman Bell	.05	.02	.01
☐ 444 Marvcus Patton	.05	.02	.01
☐ 445 Gus Frerotte	.20	.09	.03
☐ 446 Leslie Shepherd	.05	.02	.01
☐ 447 Tom Carter	.05	.02	.01
☐ 448 Brian Mitchell	.05	.02	.01
☐ 449 Darrell Green	.05	.02	.01
☐ 450 Tony Woods	.05	.02	.01

1996 Pacific Blue

Randomly inserted in hobby only packs at the rate of nine in 37, this 450-card set is a blue foil parallel version of the regular Pacific set.

	MINT	NRMT	EXC
COMPLETE SET (450)	300.00	135.00	38.00
COMMON CARD (1-450)	.40	.18	.05
*STARS: 4X TO 8X BASIC CARDS			
*YOUNG STARS: 2.5X TO 5X			
*RCs: 2X TO 4X			

1996 Pacific Red

Randomly inserted in retail only packs at the rate of nine in 37, this 450 card set is a red foil parallel version of the regular Pacific set.

	MINT	NRMT	EXC
COMPLETE SET (450)	400.00	180.00	50.00
COMMON CARD (1-450)	.60	.25	.07
*STARS: 5X TO 10X BASIC CARDS			
*YOUNG STARS: 3.5X TO 7X			
*RCs: 2.5X TO 5X			

1996 Pacific Silver

This 450-card set is a silver foil parallel version of the regular Pacific set. The silver parallel was inserted in special retail packs.

	MINT	NRMT	EXC
COMPLETE SET (450)	300.00	135.00	38.00
COMMON CARD (1-450)	.40	.18	.05
*STARS: 4X TO 8X BASIC CARDS			
*YOUNG STARS: 2.5X TO 5X			
*RCs: 2X TO 4X			

1996 Pacific Bomb Squad

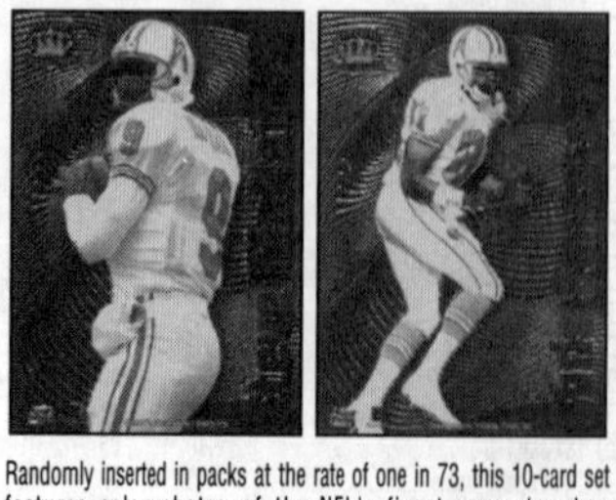

Randomly inserted in packs at the rate of one in 73, this 10-card set features color photos of the NFL's finest passer/receiver combinations. One player is displayed on each side for a double sided card.

	MINT	NRMT	EXC
COMPLETE SET (10)	200.00	90.00	25.00
COMMON CARD (1-10)	12.00	5.50	1.50

☐ 1 Jeff Blake	12.00	5.50	1.50
Carl Pickens			
☐ 2 John Elway	20.00	9.00	2.50
Anthony Miller			
☐ 3 Scott Mitchell	15.00	6.75	1.85
Herman Moore			
☐ 4 Troy Aikman	25.00	11.00	3.10
Jay Novacek			
☐ 5 Brett Favre	50.00	22.00	6.25
Robert Brooks			
☐ 6 Steve McNair	20.00	9.00	2.50
Chris Sanders			
☐ 7 Dan Marino	50.00	22.00	6.25
Irving Fryar			
☐ 8 Drew Bledsoe	30.00	13.50	3.70
Terry Glenn			
☐ 9 Kordell Stewart	25.00	11.00	3.10
Kordell Stewart			
☐ 10 Steve Young	30.00	13.50	3.70
Jerry Rice			

1996 Pacific Card-Supials

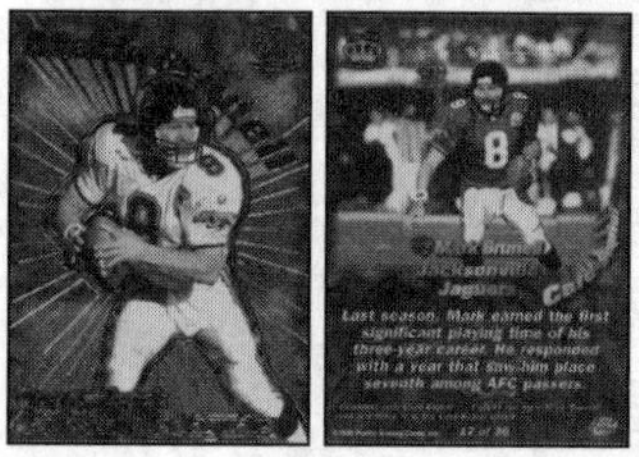

Randomly inserted in packs at a rate of one in 37, this 36-paired-card insert set features color action player photos with gold foil highlights of some of the greatest NFL players. A smaller card was made to pair with the regular size card of the same player. The backs carry a slot for insertion of the small card which completes the color picture.

	MINT	NRMT	EXC
COMPLETE SET (72)	550.00	250.00	70.00
COMPLETE LARGE SET (36)	350.00	165.00	45.00
COMPLETE SMALL SET (36)	200.00	90.00	25.00
COMMON LARGE CARD (1-36)	3.00	1.35	.35
SMALL CARDS: 3.5X TO 7X LARGE CARDS			

☐ 1 Garrison Hearst	5.00	2.20	.60
☐ 2 Jeff George	5.00	2.20	.60
☐ 3 Eric Zeier	3.00	1.35	.35
☐ 4 Jim Kelly	7.00	3.10	.85
☐ 5 Kerry Collins	15.00	6.75	1.85
☐ 6 Rashaan Salaam	7.00	3.10	.85
☐ 7 Jeff Blake	7.00	3.10	.85
☐ 8 Troy Aikman	15.00	6.75	1.85
☐ 9 Emmitt Smith	30.00	13.50	3.70
☐ 10 Terrell Davis	20.00	9.00	2.50
☐ 11 John Elway	12.00	5.50	1.50
☐ 12 Deion Sanders	10.00	4.50	1.25
☐ 13 Barry Sanders	15.00	6.75	1.85
☐ 14 Brett Favre	30.00	13.50	3.70
☐ 15 Steve McNair	12.00	5.50	1.50
☐ 16 Marshall Faulk	7.00	3.10	.85
☐ 17 Mark Brunell	15.00	6.75	1.85
☐ 18 Tamarick Vanover	5.00	2.20	.60
☐ 19 Dan Marino	30.00	13.50	3.70
☐ 20 Cris Carter	5.00	2.20	.60
☐ 21 Keyshawn Johnson	7.00	3.10	.85
☐ 22 Rodney Hampton	5.00	2.20	.60
☐ 23 Curtis Martin	20.00	9.00	2.50
☐ 24 Drew Bledsoe	15.00	6.75	1.85
☐ 25 Mario Bates	3.00	1.35	.35
☐ 26 Napoleon Kaufman	3.00	1.35	.35
☐ 27 Ricky Watters	5.00	2.20	.60
☐ 28 Kordell Stewart	15.00	6.75	1.85
☐ 29 Junior Seau	5.00	2.20	.60
☐ 30 Steve Young	12.00	5.50	1.50
☐ 31 Jerry Rice	15.00	6.75	1.85
☐ 32 Isaac Bruce	7.00	3.10	.85
☐ 33 Joey Galloway	8.00	3.60	1.00
☐ 34 Chris Warren	5.00	2.20	.60
☐ 35 Errict Rhett	5.00	2.20	.60
☐ 36 Michael Westbrook	7.00	3.10	.85

1996 Pacific Cramer's Choice Awards

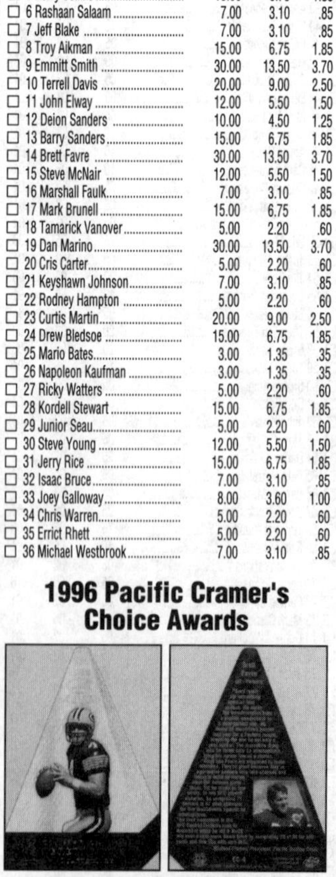

Randomly inserted in packs at the rate of one in 721, this 10-card set features Michael Cramer's, Pacific Trading Cards President, selection of the top NFL players. Cards are die cut in the shape of a trophy with a color player image on a silver foil background. The bottom of the card has a brown marble border with gold foil printing. The backs carry a small player head shot with commentary.

	MINT	NRMT	EXC
COMPLETE SET (10)	1400.00	650.00	180.00
COMMON CARD (1-10)	50.00	22.00	6.25

☐ 1 Emmitt Smith	250.00	110.00	31.00
☐ 2 John Elway	100.00	45.00	12.50
☐ 3 Barry Sanders	150.00	70.00	19.00
☐ 4 Brett Favre	250.00	110.00	31.00
☐ 5 Reggie White	60.00	27.00	7.50
☐ 6 Dan Marino	250.00	110.00	31.00
☐ 7 Curtis Martin	130.00	57.50	16.00
☐ 8 Keyshawn Johnson	50.00	22.00	6.25
☐ 9 Kordell Stewart	135.00	60.00	17.00
☐ 10 Jerry Rice	150.00	70.00	19.00

1996 Pacific Gems of the Crown

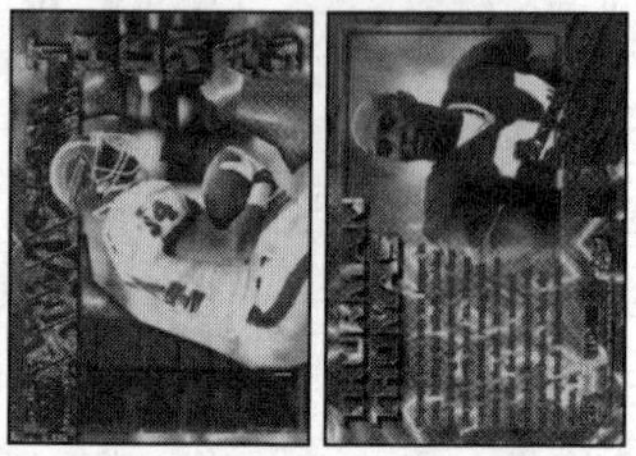

This 36-card standard-size set features leading NFL players. The horizontal fronts have the player's photo framed by the team name on the left and his last name on the right. The horizontal backs have some textual information as well as another player photo. The cards are numbered with a "GC" prefix. Cards #1-18 were inserted approximately two every 37 Pacific Dynagon packs and cards #19-36 were random inserts in the regular 1996 Pacific issue.

	MINT	NRMT	EXC
COMPLETE SET (36)	250.00	110.00	31.00
COMPLETE SERIES 1 SET (18)	100.00	45.00	12.50
COMPLETE SERIES 2 SET (18)	150.00	70.00	19.00
COMMON CARD (GC1-GC36)	2.00	.90	.25

☐ GC1 Kerry Collins	10.00	4.50	1.25
☐ GC2 Rashaan Salaam	4.00	1.80	.50
☐ GC3 Steve Young	8.00	3.60	1.00
☐ GC4 Rodney Thomas	2.00	.90	.25
☐ GC5 Michael Westbrook	4.00	1.80	.50
☐ GC6 Cris Carter	3.00	1.35	.35
☐ GC7 Jerry Rice	10.00	4.50	1.25
☐ GC8 Drew Bledsoe	10.00	4.50	1.25
☐ GC9 Steve McNair	8.00	3.60	1.00
☐ GC10 Terrell Davis	12.00	5.50	1.50
☐ GC11 Barry Sanders	10.00	4.50	1.25
☐ GC12 Robert Brooks	4.00	1.80	.50
☐ GC13 Chris Warren	3.00	1.35	.35
☐ GC14 Marshall Faulk	4.00	1.80	.50
☐ GC15 John Elway	8.00	3.60	1.00
☐ GC16 Isaac Bruce	4.00	1.80	.50
☐ GC17 Emmitt Smith	20.00	9.00	2.50
☐ GC18 Thurman Thomas	3.00	1.35	.35
☐ GC19 Garrison Hearst	4.00	1.80	.50
☐ GC20 Jeff Blake	3.00	1.35	.35
☐ GC21 Troy Aikman	10.00	4.50	1.25
☐ GC22 Deion Sanders	6.00	2.70	.75
☐ GC23 Brett Favre	20.00	9.00	2.50
☐ GC24 Robert Smith	2.00	.90	.25
☐ GC25 Mario Bates	2.00	.90	.25
☐ GC26 Napoleon Kaufman	2.00	.90	.25
☐ GC27 Kordell Stewart	10.00	4.50	1.25
☐ GC28 Jim Kelly	4.00	1.80	.50
☐ GC29 Jim Harbaugh	3.00	1.35	.35
☐ GC30 Tamarick Vanover	4.00	1.80	.50
☐ GC31 Dan Marino	20.00	9.00	2.50
☐ GC32 Warren Moon	2.00	.90	.25
☐ GC33 Curtis Martin	12.00	5.50	1.50
☐ GC34 Rodney Hampton	2.00	.90	.25
☐ GC35 Ricky Watters	3.00	1.35	.35
☐ GC36 Joey Galloway	5.00	2.20	.60

1996 Pacific Gold Crown Die-Cuts

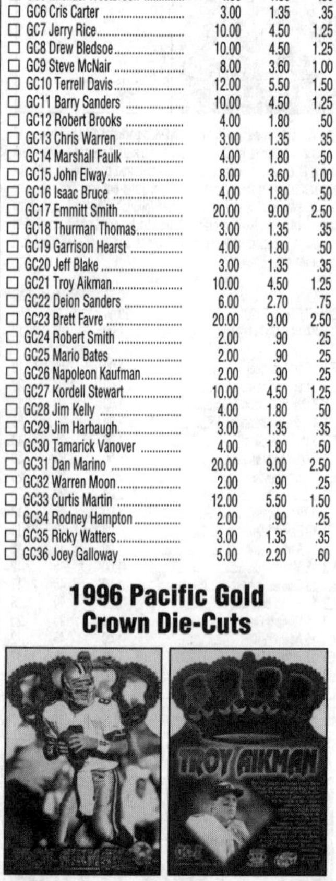

Randomly inserted in packs at the rate of one in 37, this 20-card set features color player photos with a die cut crown at the top of the card and gold foil highlights. The backs carry a small player head photo with a paragraph about the player. A Platinum version was produced as well and distributed through boxes sold on the Shop at Home television network. The platinum cards included new photos and were numbered with a PC prefix.

	MINT	NRMT	EXC
COMPLETE SET (20)	400.00	180.00	50.00

COMMON CARD (1-20)	8.00	3.60	1.00
*PLATINUM CARDS: 1X TO 2X			
☐ 1 Emmitt Smith	40.00	18.00	5.00
☐ 2 Troy Aikman	20.00	9.00	2.50
☐ 3 Barry Sanders	20.00	9.00	2.50
☐ 4 Kerry Collins	20.00	9.00	2.50
☐ 5 Jeff Blake	10.00	4.50	1.25
☐ 6 John Elway	15.00	6.75	1.85
☐ 7 Terrell Davis	25.00	11.00	3.10
☐ 8 Deion Sanders	12.00	5.50	1.50
☐ 9 Brett Favre	40.00	18.00	5.00
☐ 10 Dan Marino	40.00	18.00	5.00
☐ 11 Eddie George	25.00	11.00	3.10
☐ 12 Curtis Martin	25.00	11.00	3.10
☐ 13 Drew Bledsoe	20.00	9.00	2.50
☐ 14 Keyshawn Johnson	12.00	5.50	1.50
☐ 15 Napoleon Kaufman	8.00	3.60	1.00
☐ 16 Kordell Stewart	20.00	9.00	2.50
☐ 17 Steve Young	15.00	6.75	1.85
☐ 18 Jerry Rice	20.00	9.00	2.50
☐ 19 Joey Galloway	12.00	5.50	1.50
☐ 20 Chris Warren	8.00	3.60	1.00

1996 Pacific Power Corps

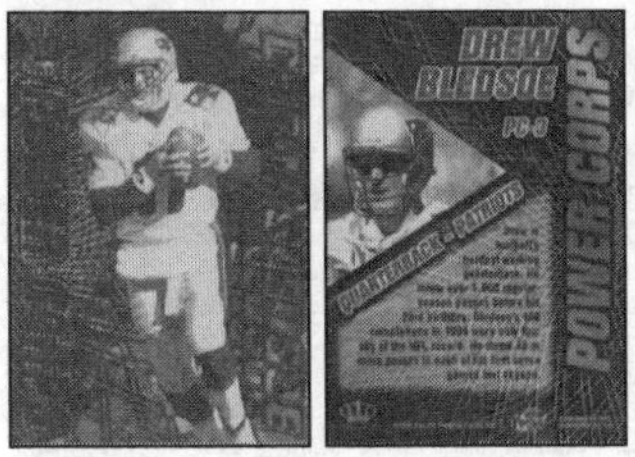

Randomly inserted in special retail packs only available at Wal-Mart stores, this 20-card set features color player photos of some of the best players of the 1995 season on a gold highlighted background. The backs carry a small triangular head photo with information as to why this player was selected for this set. Six players' cards are available in a foiling variation.

	MINT	NRMT	EXC
COMPLETE SET (20)	75.00	34.00	9.50
COMMON CARD (PC1-PC20)	2.00	.90	.25
FOIL PARAL(1/11/14/17-19):1.25X to 2.5X			
☐ PC1 Troy Aikman	5.00	2.20	.60
☐ PC2 Jeff Blake	3.00	1.35	.35
☐ PC3 Drew Bledsoe	5.00	2.20	.60
☐ PC4 Kerry Collins	5.00	2.20	.60
☐ PC5 Terrell Davis	6.00	2.70	.75
☐ PC6 John Elway	4.00	1.80	.50
☐ PC7 Marshall Faulk	3.00	1.35	.35
☐ PC8 Brett Favre	10.00	4.50	1.25
☐ PC9 Joey Galloway	3.00	1.35	.35
☐ PC10 Garrison Hearst	2.00	.90	.25
☐ PC11 Dan Marino	10.00	4.50	1.25
☐ PC12 Curtis Martin	6.00	2.70	.75
☐ PC13 Steve McNair	4.00	1.80	.50
☐ PC14 Jerry Rice	5.00	2.20	.60
☐ PC15 Rashaan Salaam	3.00	1.35	.35
☐ PC16 Barry Sanders	5.00	2.20	.60
☐ PC17 Emmitt Smith	10.00	4.50	1.25
☐ PC18 Kordell Stewart	5.00	2.20	.60
☐ PC19 Chris Warren	2.00	.90	.25
☐ PC20 Steve Young	4.00	1.80	.50

1996 Pacific The Zone

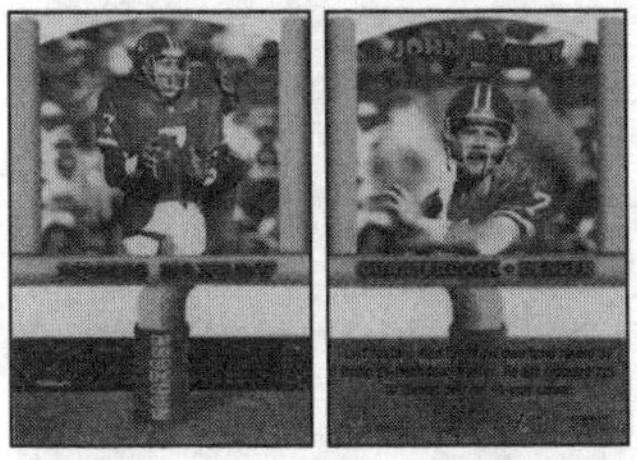

Randomly inserted in packs at the rate of one in 145, this 20-card set features color photos of some of last season's most productive NFL players. The cards are die cut in the shape of a football goal post with the player's name and team name printed in gold foil on the post. The backs carry a player head photo with his playing position and city of the team.

	MINT	NRMT	EXC
COMPLETE SET (20)	750.00	350.00	95.00
COMMON CARD (1-20)	15.00	6.75	1.85
☐ 1 Jim Kelly	20.00	9.00	2.50
☐ 2 Rashaan Salaam	20.00	9.00	2.50
☐ 3 Carl Pickens	15.00	6.75	1.85
☐ 4 Jeff Blake	20.00	9.00	2.50
☐ 5 Kerry Collins	50.00	22.00	6.25
☐ 6 Emmitt Smith	100.00	45.00	12.50
☐ 7 Troy Aikman	60.00	27.00	7.50
☐ 8 John Elway	50.00	22.00	6.25
☐ 9 Barry Sanders	60.00	27.00	7.50
☐ 10 Herman Moore	20.00	9.00	2.50
☐ 11 Scott Mitchell	15.00	6.75	1.85
☐ 12 Brett Favre	100.00	45.00	12.50
☐ 13 Robert Brooks	20.00	9.00	2.50
☐ 14 Marshall Faulk	20.00	9.00	2.50
☐ 15 Dan Marino	100.00	45.00	12.50
☐ 16 Drew Bledsoe	60.00	27.00	7.50
☐ 17 Curtis Martin	50.00	22.00	6.25
☐ 18 Steve Young	40.00	18.00	5.00
☐ 19 Jerry Rice	60.00	27.00	7.50
☐ 20 Chris Warren	15.00	6.75	1.85

1996 Pacific Super Bowl

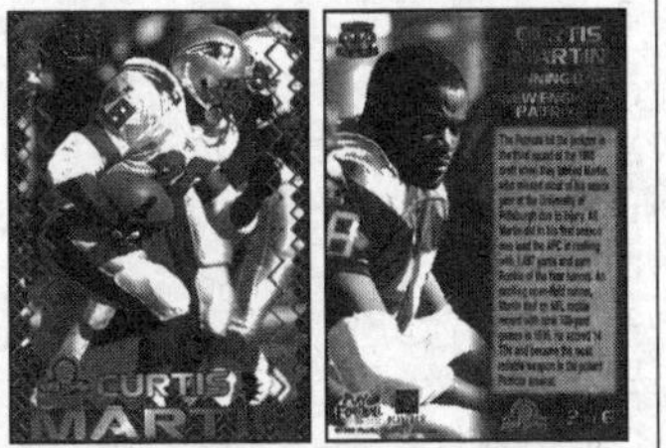

This six-card set was produced with both a gold and bronze foil border. The bronze set was made available through a special wrapper redemption program at the 1996 Super Bowl Card Show in Phoenix. Collectors with five wrappers would receive one card and 30-pack wrappers were good for a complete set. The fronts feature color action player photos with a bronze foil overlay going up the sides of the card along with the Super Bowl Card Show logo. The gold foil set was available via a wrapper redemption program with 1995 Triple Folders. Collectors could receive a complete set by sending 18 Triple Folders wrappers to Pacific along with $5.95. The gold cards are basically a parallel to the bronze issue, but contain a Super Bowl XXX logo on the cardfronts.

	MINT	NRMT	EXC
COMP.GOLD SET (6)	15.00	6.75	1.85
COMP.BRONZE SET (6)	15.00	6.75	1.85
COMMON BRONZE CARD (1-6)	1.00	.45	.12
*BRONZE CARDS: SAME PRICE			
☐ 1 Chris Warren	1.50	.70	.19
☐ 2 Kordell Stewart	1.50	.70	.19
☐ 3 Curtis Martin	6.00	2.70	.75
☐ 4 Errict Rhett	1.50	.70	.19
☐ 5 Neil O'Donnell	1.50	.70	.19
☐ 6 Barry Sanders	1.50	.70	.19

1995 Pacific Crown Royale

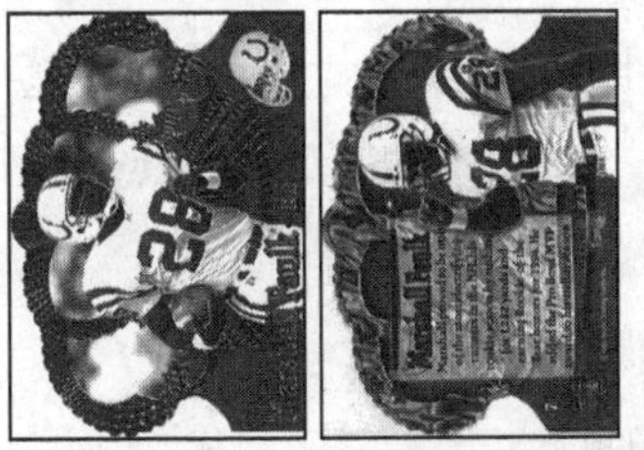

This set is actually a spin-off of the popular Gold Crown Die Cuts insert from the regular Pacific product. It contains 144 cards and was issued in four card packs. Every card in the set is die cut in the shape of a crown horizontally and the crown portion is finished in gold-etched foil. Card backs have the same outline of the crown die cut with a teal background and contain a brief statistical summary of the player. Two parallels of the regular set exist: a Copper version and a Blue Holofoil version. The copper parallel was randomly inserted in hobby packs, while the blue holofoil was inserted into retail packs. Some boxes of Crown Royale also contained one instant win card redeemable for a trip to Super Bowl XXX.

	MINT	NRMT	EXC
COMPLETE SET (144)	150.00	70.00	19.00
COMMON CARD (1-144)	.60	.25	.07
☐ 1 Lake Dawson	1.00	.45	.12
☐ 2 Steve Beuerlein	.60	.25	.07
☐ 3 Jake Reed	1.00	.45	.12
☐ 4 Jim Everett	.60	.25	.07
☐ 5 Sean Dawkins	1.00	.45	.12
☐ 6 Jeff Hostetler	1.00	.45	.12
☐ 7 Marshall Faulk	3.00	1.35	.35
☐ 8 Jeff Blake	6.00	2.70	.75
☐ 9 Dave Brown	1.00	.45	.12
☐ 10 Frank Reich	.60	.25	.07
☐ 11 Rocket Ismail	1.00	.45	.12
☐ 12 Jerry Jones OWN UER Built is spelled bulit	5.00	2.20	.60
☐ 13 Dan Marino	12.00	5.50	1.50
☐ 14 Ricky Watters	2.00	.90	.25
☐ 15 Herman Moore	3.00	1.35	.35
☐ 16 Daryl Johnston	1.00	.45	.12
☐ 17 Craig Erickson	.60	.25	.07
☐ 18 Alexander Wright	.60	.25	.07
☐ 19 Reggie White	2.00	.90	.25
☐ 20 Andre Rison	1.00	.45	.12
☐ 21 Fred Barnett	1.00	.45	.12
☐ 22 Tyrone Wheatley	2.50	1.10	.30
☐ 23 Charles Johnson	1.00	.45	.12
☐ 24 Rashaan Salaam	5.00	2.20	.60
☐ 25 Mark Brunell	6.00	2.70	.75
☐ 26 Derek Loville	.60	.25	.07
☐ 27 Garrison Hearst	2.00	.90	.25
☐ 28 Ken Norton Jr.	1.00	.45	.12
☐ 29 Kerry Collins	12.00	5.50	1.50
☐ 30 Isaac Bruce	3.00	1.35	.35
☐ 31 Andre Reed	1.00	.45	.12
☐ 32 Leon Lett	.60	.25	.07
☐ 33 Deion Sanders	4.00	1.80	.50
☐ 34 Terance Mathis	1.00	.45	.12
☐ 35 Tim Bowens	.60	.25	.07
☐ 36 Shannon Sharpe	1.00	.45	.12
☐ 37 Quinn Early	1.00	.45	.12
☐ 38 Jerry Rice	6.00	2.70	.75
☐ 39 Bruce Smith	2.00	.90	.25
☐ 40 Drew Bledsoe	6.00	2.70	.75
☐ 41 Alvin Harper	.60	.25	.07
☐ 42 Jim Kelly	2.00	.90	.25
☐ 43 Napoleon Kaufman	4.00	1.80	.50
☐ 44 Errict Rhett	2.00	.90	.25
☐ 45 Henry Ellard	1.00	.45	.12
☐ 46 Barry Sanders	6.00	2.70	.75
☐ 47 Vincent Brisby	.60	.25	.07
☐ 48 Chris Zorich	.60	.25	.07
☐ 49 Zack Crockett	.60	.25	.07
☐ 50 Haywood Jeffires	.60	.25	.07
☐ 51 Byron Bam Morris	1.00	.45	.12
☐ 52 John Kasay	.60	.25	.07
☐ 53 Scott Mitchell	1.00	.45	.12
☐ 54 Boomer Esiason	1.00	.45	.12
☐ 55 Eric Metcalf	1.00	.45	.12
☐ 56 Kevin Greene	1.00	.45	.12
☐ 57 Courtney Hawkins	.60	.25	.07
☐ 58 Johnny Johnson	.60	.25	.07
☐ 59 Larry Centers	1.00	.45	.12
☐ 60 Leroy Hoard	.60	.25	.07
☐ 61 Lorenzo White	.60	.25	.07
☐ 62 Chris Spielman	1.00	.45	.12
☐ 63 Carl Pickens	2.00	.90	.25
☐ 64 Steve Young	5.00	2.20	.60
☐ 65 Trent Dilfer	2.00	.90	.25
☐ 66 Erik Kramer	.60	.25	.07
☐ 67 Cortez Kennedy	1.00	.45	.12
☐ 68 Ray Childress	.60	.25	.07
☐ 69 Rick Mirer	2.00	.90	.25
☐ 70 Kevin Williams WR	1.00	.45	.12
☐ 71 Joey Galloway	8.00	3.60	1.00
☐ 72 Dan Wilkinson	1.00	.45	.12
☐ 73 Antonio Freeman	8.00	3.60	1.00
☐ 74 Curtis Conway	2.00	.90	.25
☐ 75 Troy Aikman	6.00	2.70	.75
☐ 76 Natrone Means	2.00	.90	.25
☐ 77 Jeff George	1.00	.45	.12
☐ 78 Curtis Martin	12.00	5.50	1.50
☐ 79 William Floyd	2.00	.90	.25
☐ 80 Anthony Miller	1.00	.45	.12
☐ 81 Greg Hill	1.00	.45	.12
☐ 82 Craig Heyward	1.00	.45	.12
☐ 83 Brian Mitchell	.60	.25	.07
☐ 84 Anthony Carter	1.00	.45	.12
☐ 85 Jerome Bettis	2.50	1.10	.30
☐ 86 Jim Harbaugh	1.00	.45	.12
☐ 87 Harvey Williams	.60	.25	.07
☐ 88 Tony Martin	1.00	.45	.12
☐ 89 Rob Moore	.60	.25	.07
☐ 90 Neil O'Donnell	1.00	.45	.12
☐ 91 Cris Carter	2.00	.90	.25
☐ 92 Warren Sapp	1.00	.45	.12
☐ 93 Terry Allen	1.00	.45	.12
☐ 94 Michael Irvin	2.00	.90	.25
☐ 95 Heath Shuler	2.00	.90	.25
☐ 96 Cornelius Bennett	1.00	.45	.12
☐ 97 Randy Baldwin	.60	.25	.07
☐ 98 Vince Workman	.60	.25	.07
☐ 99 Irving Fryar	1.00	.45	.12
☐ 100 Randall Cunningham	1.00	.45	.12
☐ 101 James O.Stewart	2.00	.90	.25
☐ 102 Stan Humphries	1.00	.45	.12
☐ 103 Mario Bates	2.00	.90	.25
☐ 104 Ben Coates	1.00	.45	.12
☐ 105 Charlie Garner	1.00	.45	.12
☐ 106 Todd Collins	2.00	.90	.25
☐ 107 Tim Brown	2.00	.90	.25
☐ 108 Edgar Bennett	1.00	.45	.12
☐ 109 J.J. Stokes	4.00	1.80	.50
☐ 110 Michael Timpson	.60	.25	.07
☐ 111 Junior Seau	2.00	.90	.25
☐ 112 Bernie Parmalee	1.00	.45	.12
☐ 113 Willie McGinest	1.00	.45	.12
☐ 114 David Dunn	.60	.25	.07
☐ 115 Kyle Brady	2.00	.90	.25
☐ 116 Vinny Testaverde	1.00	.45	.12
☐ 117 Ernest Givins	.60	.25	.07
☐ 118 Eric Zeier	2.00	.90	.25
☐ 119 Michael Jackson	1.00	.45	.12
☐ 120 Chad May	.60	.25	.07
☐ 121 Dave Krieg	.60	.25	.07
☐ 122 Rodney Hampton	1.00	.45	.12
☐ 123 Darnay Scott	3.00	1.35	.35
☐ 124 Chris Miller	.60	.25	.07
☐ 125 Emmitt Smith	12.00	5.50	1.50
☐ 126 Steve McNair	10.00	4.50	1.25
☐ 127 Warren Moon	1.00	.45	.12
☐ 128 Robert Brooks	2.00	.90	.25
☐ 129 Bert Emanuel	2.00	.90	.25
☐ 130 John Elway	5.00	2.20	.60
☐ 131 Chris Warren	1.00	.45	.12
☐ 132 Herschel Walker	1.00	.45	.12
☐ 133 Terry Kirby	1.00	.45	.12
☐ 134 Michael Westbrook	5.00	2.20	.60
☐ 135 Kordell Stewart	10.00	4.50	1.25
☐ 136 Terrell Davis	12.00	5.50	1.50
☐ 137 Desmond Howard	1.00	.45	.12
☐ 138 Rodney Thomas	2.00	.90	.25
☐ 139 Brett Favre	12.00	5.50	1.50
☐ 140 Ray Zellars	1.00	.45	.12
☐ 141 Marcus Allen	2.00	.90	.25
☐ 142 Gus Frerotte	3.00	1.35	.35
☐ 143 Steve Bono	1.00	.45	.12
☐ 144 Aaron Craver	.60	.25	.07
☐ P144 Natrone Means Promo Jumbo card 7" by 9 3/4"	2.00	.90	.25

1995 Pacific Crown Royale Blue Holofoil

This 144 card parallel set was randomly inserted into retail packs and contains a blue holographic background rather than the standard gold foil on the die cut crown at the top of the card.

	MINT	NRMT	EXC
COMPLETE SET (144)	1200.00	550.00	150.00
COMMON CARD (1-144)	4.00	1.80	.50
*VETERAN STARS: 4X TO 8X BASIC CARDS			
*YOUNG STARS: 3X TO 6X BASIC CARDS			
*RCs: 2.5X TO 5X BASIC CARDS			

1995 Pacific Crown Royale Copper

This 144 card parallel set was randomly inserted into hobby packs and contains a copper foil rather than the standard gold on the die cut crown design at the top of the card.

	MINT	NRMT	EXC
COMPLETE SET (144)	700.00	325.00	90.00
COMMON CARD (1-144)	2.50	1.10	.30
*VETERAN STARS: 2.5X TO 5X BASIC CARDS			
*YOUNG STARS: 2X TO 4X BASIC CARDS			
*RCs: 1.5X TO 3X BASIC CARDS			

1995 Pacific Crown Royale Cramer's Choice Jumbos

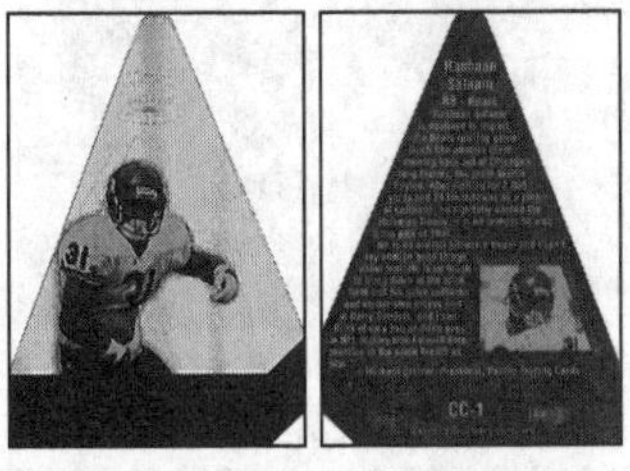

This oversized version was made due to the tremendous response to the regular sized insert set that was randomly inserted in the 1995 Pacific product. This six card set was randomly inserted as a chiptopper in boxes of Crown Royale at a rate of one in every 16 boxes. The card fronts are die cut in the shape of a trophy with most of the background being holographic. The bottom portion of the card contains the player's name with other information. Backs of the card contain a summary on the player and a head shot. Cards are numbered with a "CC" prefix.

	MINT	NRMT	EXC
COMPLETE SET (6)	400.00	180.00	50.00
COMMON CARD (CC1-CC6)	40.00	18.00	5.00
☐ CC1 Rashaan Salaam	40.00	18.00	5.00
☐ CC2 Emmitt Smith	150.00	70.00	19.00
☐ CC3 Marshall Faulk	80.00	36.00	10.00
☐ CC4 Jerry Rice	90.00	40.00	11.00
☐ CC5 Deion Sanders	50.00	22.00	6.25
☐ CC6 Steve Young	70.00	32.00	8.75

1995 Pacific Crown Royale Pride of the NFL

This 36 card set was randomly inserted in packs at a rate of three in 25 packs and features some of the NFL's greatest players. Card fronts have a gold foil-etched design that runs around the back of the player and onto the bottom of the card. The player's name is blocked into the gold foil, but contains no foil. Card backs are horizontal with a shot of the player and a summary. Cards are numbered with a "PN" prefix.

	MINT	NRMT	EXC
COMPLETE SET (36)	300.00	135.00	38.00
COMMON CARD (PN1-PN36)	5.00	2.20	.60

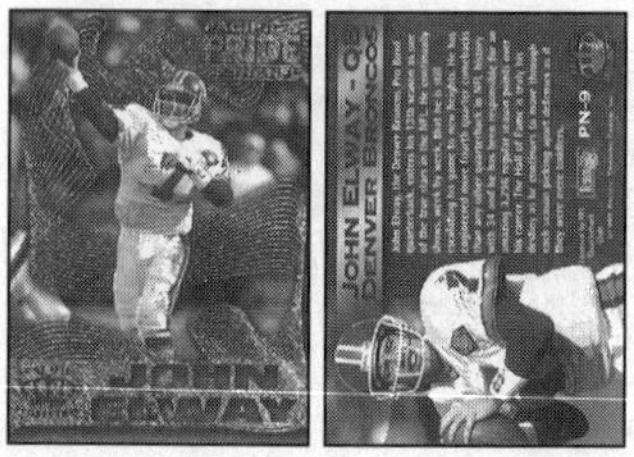

	MINT	NRMT	EXC
PN1 Jim Kelly	7.00	3.10	.85
PN2 Kerry Collins	20.00	9.00	2.50
PN3 Darnay Scott	5.00	2.20	.60
PN4 Jeff Blake	8.00	3.60	1.00
PN5 Terry Allen	7.00	3.10	.85
PN6 Emmitt Smith	30.00	13.50	3.70
PN7 Michael Irvin	7.00	3.10	.85
PN8 Troy Aikman	16.00	7.25	2.00
PN9 John Elway	14.00	6.25	1.75
PN10 Napoleon Kaufman	7.00	3.10	.85
PN11 Barry Sanders	16.00	7.25	2.00
PN12 Brett Favre	30.00	13.50	3.70
PN13 Michael Westbrook	8.00	3.60	1.00
PN14 Marcus Allen	7.00	3.10	.85
PN15 Tim Brown	7.00	3.10	.85
PN16 Bernie Parmalee	5.00	2.20	.60
PN17 Dan Marino	30.00	13.50	3.70
PN18 Cris Carter	7.00	3.10	.85
PN19 Drew Bledsoe	16.00	7.25	2.00
PN20 Mario Bates	5.00	2.20	.60
PN21 Rodney Hampton	5.00	2.20	.60
PN22 Ben Coates	5.00	2.20	.60
PN23 Charles Johnson	5.00	2.20	.60
PN24 Byron Bam Morris	7.00	3.10	.85
PN25 Stan Humphries	5.00	2.20	.60
PN26 Rashaan Salaam	8.00	3.60	1.00
PN27 Jerry Rice	16.00	7.25	2.00
PN28 Ricky Watters	7.00	3.10	.85
PN29 Steve Young	14.00	6.25	1.75
PN30 Natrone Means	7.00	3.10	.85
PN31 William Floyd	5.00	2.20	.60
PN32 Chris Warren	7.00	3.10	.85
PN33 Rick Mirer	7.00	3.10	.85
PN34 Jerome Bettis	7.00	3.10	.85
PN35 Errict Rhett	7.00	3.10	.85
PN36 Heath Shuler	7.00	3.10	.85

1995 Pacific Crown Royale Pro Bowl Die Cuts

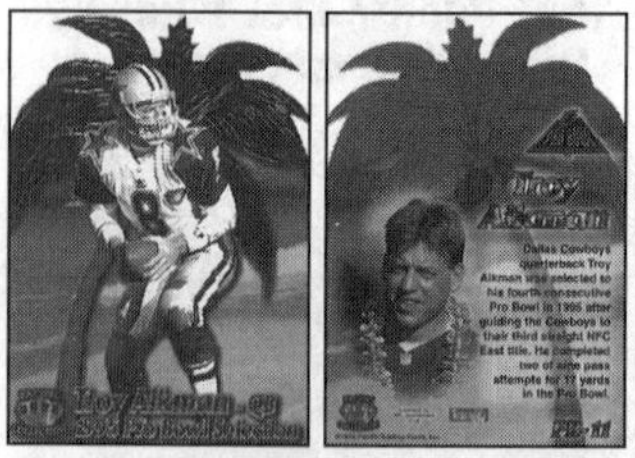

This 20 card set was randomly inserted into packs at a rate of one in 25 packs and features the top players selected to the 1995 Pro Bowl. Card fronts are die cut in the shape of a palm tree on the top of the card and contain green etched foil. The background is a beach scene with the player's name in green and yellow at the bottom of the card. Card backs feature a head shot of the player in a oval with a brief commentary on the player beside it. Cards are numbered with a "PB" prefix. Cards are also condition sensitive due to the complex die cut design.

	MINT	NRMT	EXC
COMPLETE SET (20)	750.00	350.00	95.00
COMMON CARD (PB1-PB20)	15.00	6.75	1.85
PB1 Drew Bledsoe	60.00	27.00	7.50
PB2 Ben Coates	15.00	6.75	1.85
PB3 John Elway	50.00	22.00	6.25
PB4 Marshall Faulk	30.00	13.50	3.70
PB5 Dan Marino	135.00	60.00	17.00
PB6 Natrone Means	20.00	9.00	2.50
PB7 Junior Seau	20.00	9.00	2.50
PB8 Chris Warren	15.00	6.75	1.85
PB9 Rod Woodson	15.00	6.75	1.85
PB10 Tim Brown	20.00	9.00	2.50
PB11 Troy Aikman	60.00	27.00	7.50
PB12 Jerome Bettis	20.00	9.00	2.50
PB13 Michael Irvin	20.00	9.00	2.50
PB14 Jerry Rice	60.00	27.00	7.50
PB15 Barry Sanders	60.00	27.00	7.50
PB16 Deion Sanders	30.00	13.50	3.70
PB17 Emmitt Smith	135.00	60.00	17.00
PB18 Steve Young	40.00	18.00	5.00
PB19 Reggie White	20.00	9.00	2.50
PB20 Cris Carter	20.00	9.00	2.50

1996 Pacific Crown Royale

The 1996 Pacific Crown Royale set was issued in one series totalling 144 cards and was distributed in five-card packs. The set features

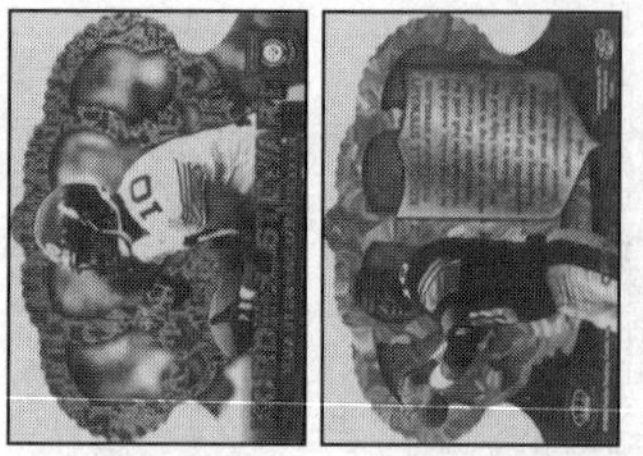

color player images on an etched die cut gold crown background with the player's name and position printed at the bottom beside the team logo.

	MINT	NRMT	EXC
COMPLETE SET (144)	150.00	70.00	19.00
COMMON CARD (1-144)	.75	.35	.09
1 Dan Marino	12.00	5.50	1.50
2 Frank Sanders	1.25	.55	.16
3 Bobby Engram	4.00	1.80	.50
4 Cornelius Bennett	1.25	.55	.16
5 Steve Bono	1.25	.55	.16
6 Aaron Hayden	.75	.35	.09
7 Leroy Hoard	.75	.35	.09
8 Brett Perriman	1.25	.55	.16
9 Irv Smith	.75	.35	.09
10 Jim Kelly	2.00	.90	.25
11 Rodney Thomas	.75	.35	.09
12 Eric Bieniemy	.75	.35	.09
13 Darnay Scott	1.25	.55	.16
14 Ki-Jana Carter	1.25	.55	.16
15 Kerry Collins	8.00	3.60	1.00
16 Shannon Sharpe	1.25	.55	.16
17 Michael Westbrook	2.00	.90	.25
18 Steve McNair	6.00	2.70	.75
19 Tony Banks	4.00	1.80	.50
20 Rashaan Salaam	2.00	.90	.25
21 Terrell Fletcher	.75	.35	.09
22 Michael Timpson	.75	.35	.09
23 Bobby Hoying	2.50	1.10	.30
24 Quinn Early	.75	.35	.09
25 Warren Moon	1.25	.55	.16
26 Tommy Vardell	.75	.35	.09
27 Marvin Harrison	6.00	2.70	.75
28 Lake Dawson	1.25	.55	.16
29 Karim Abdul-Jabbar	10.00	4.50	1.25
30 Chris Warren	1.25	.55	.16
31 Heath Shuler	2.00	.90	.25
32 Bert Emanuel	1.25	.55	.16
33 Howard Griffith	.75	.35	.09
34 Alex Van Dyke	1.25	.55	.16
35 Isaac Bruce	2.00	.90	.25
36 Mark Brunell	6.00	2.70	.75
37 Winslow Oliver	.75	.35	.09
38 O.J. McDuffie	1.25	.55	.16
39 Terrell Owens	7.00	3.10	.85
40 Jerry Rice	6.00	2.70	.75
41 Henry Ellard	1.25	.55	.16
42 Chris Sanders	1.25	.55	.16
43 Craig Heyward	.75	.35	.09
44 Eddie Kennison	6.00	2.70	.75
45 Terrell Davis	10.00	4.50	1.25
46 Rodney Hampton	1.25	.55	.16
47 Bryan Still	.75	.35	.09
48 Tim Brown	1.25	.55	.16
49 Keyshawn Johnson	6.00	2.70	.75
50 Barry Sanders	6.00	2.70	.75
51 Terry Allen	1.25	.55	.16
52 Sean Dawkins	.75	.35	.09
53 Bryce Paup	1.25	.55	.16
54 Brett Favre	12.00	5.50	1.50
55 Deion Sanders	4.00	1.80	.50
56 Kevin Hardy	2.50	1.10	.30
57 Kevin Williams	.75	.35	.09
58 Jeff George	1.25	.55	.16
59 Tim Biakabutuka	4.00	1.80	.50
60 Drew Bledsoe	6.00	2.70	.75
61 Michael Jackson	1.25	.55	.16
62 James Stewart	2.00	.90	.25
63 Mario Bates	1.25	.55	.16
64 Daryl Johnston	1.25	.55	.16
65 Herman Moore	2.00	.90	.25
66 Ben Coates	1.25	.55	.16
67 Terry Glenn	12.00	5.50	1.50
68 Robert Smith	1.25	.55	.16
69 Irving Fryar	1.25	.55	.16
70 Napoleon Kaufman	1.25	.55	.16
71 Rickey Dudley	2.50	1.10	.30
72 Bernie Parmalee	.75	.35	.09
73 Kyle Brady	1.25	.55	.16
74 Neil O'Donnell	1.25	.55	.16
75 Lawrence Phillips	3.00	1.35	.35
76 Hardy Nickerson	.75	.35	.09
77 John Elway	5.00	2.20	.60
78 Pete Mitchell	.75	.35	.09
79 Jason Dunn	1.25	.55	.16
80 Reggie White	2.00	.90	.25
81 J.J. Stokes	2.00	.90	.25
82 Jake Reed	1.25	.55	.16
83 Yancey Thigpen	1.25	.55	.16
84 Jonathan Ogden	.75	.35	.09
85 Larry Centers	1.25	.55	.16
86 Scott Mitchell	1.25	.55	.16
87 Eric Zeier	1.25	.55	.16
88 Anthony Miller	1.25	.55	.16
89 Brian Blades	1.25	.55	.16
90 Cris Carter	2.00	.90	.25
91 Kordell Stewart	8.00	3.60	1.00
92 Charles Way	.75	.35	.09
93 Jeff Hostetler	1.25	.55	.16
94 Brad Johnson	1.25	.55	.16
95 Marcus Allen	2.00	.90	.25
96 Errict Rhett	1.25	.55	.16
97 Stan Humphries	1.25	.55	.16
98 Michael Haynes	1.25	.55	.16
99 Curtis Martin	10.00	4.50	1.25
100 Troy Aikman	6.00	2.70	.75
101 Earnest Byner	.75	.35	.09
102 Vincent Brisby	.75	.35	.09
103 Zack Crockett	.75	.35	.09
104 Haywood Jeffires	.75	.35	.09
105 Joey Galloway	4.00	1.80	.50
106 Carl Pickens	2.00	.90	.25
107 Leeland McElroy	2.50	1.10	.30
108 Adrian Murrell	1.25	.55	.16
109 Joe Horn	.75	.35	.09
110 Steve Young	5.00	2.20	.60
111 Andre Rison	1.25	.55	.16
112 Jim Everett	.75	.35	.09
113 Jamie Asher	2.50	1.10	.30
114 Steve Walsh	.75	.35	.09
115 Robert Brooks	2.00	.90	.25
116 Eric Moulds	4.00	1.80	.50
117 Edgar Bennett	1.25	.55	.16
118 Greg Lloyd	1.25	.55	.16
119 Jerris McPhail	.75	.35	.09
120 Marshall Faulk	2.00	.90	.25
121 Dave Brown	1.25	.55	.16
122 Harvey Williams	.75	.35	.09
123 Trent Dilfer	1.25	.55	.16
124 Eddie George	14.00	6.25	1.75
125 Jeff Blake	2.00	.90	.25
126 Mark Chmura	1.25	.55	.16
127 Boomer Esiason	1.25	.55	.16
128 Jim Harbaugh	1.25	.55	.16
129 Bryan Cox	.75	.35	.09
130 Ricky Watters	1.25	.55	.16
131 Amani Toomer	2.50	1.10	.30
132 Jim Miller	.75	.35	.09
133 Cortez Kennedy	1.25	.55	.16
134 Courtney Hawkins	.75	.35	.09
135 Junior Seau	2.00	.90	.25
136 Tamarick Vanover	2.00	.90	.25
137 Jerome Bettis	2.00	.90	.25
138 Chris Calloway	.75	.35	.09
139 Rick Mirer	1.25	.55	.16
140 Thurman Thomas	2.00	.90	.25
141 Sheddrick Wilson	.75	.35	.09
142 Charlie Garner	.75	.35	.09
143 Erik Kramer	.75	.35	.09
144 Emmitt Smith	12.00	5.50	1.50

1996 Pacific Crown Royale Blue

Randomly inserted in hobby packs only at a rate of four in 25, this 144-card die cut set is a parallel blue foil version of the regular 1996 Pacific Crown Royale set.

	MINT	NRMT	EXC
COMPLETE SET (144)	2.50	1.10	.30
COMMON CARD (1-144)	700.00	325.00	90.00

*STARS: 2.5X TO 5X BASIC CARDS
*YOUNG STARS:2X TO 4X BASIC CARDS
*RCs: 1.5X TO 3X BASIC CARDS

1996 Pacific Crown Royale Silver

Randomly inserted in retail packs only at a rate of four in 25, this 144-card die cut set is a parallel silver foil version of the regular 1996 Pacific Crown Royale set.

	MINT	NRMT	EXC
COMPLETE SET (144)	1200.00	550.00	150.00
COMMON CARD (1-144)	4.00	1.80	.50

*STARS: 4X TO 8X BASIC CARDS
*YOUNG STARS: 3X TO 6X BASIC CARDS
*RCs: 2.5X TO 5X BASIC CARDS

1996 Pacific Crown Royale Cramer's Choice Jumbos

This 10-card serial-numbered set measuring approximately 4" by 5.5" is die cut in the shape of a trophy with a color player image on a silver foil background. The bottom of the card has a brown marble border with gold foil printing. Redemption cards seeded in random packs of Pacific Trading Cards' Crown Royale at the rate of one in 385 could be redeemed for these premium-sized cards.

	MINT	NRMT	EXC
COMPLETE SET (10)	750.00	350.00	95.00
COMMON CARD (1-10)	40.00	18.00	5.00
1 John Elway	70.00	32.00	8.75
2 Brett Favre	125.00	55.00	15.50
3 Keyshawn Johnson *	40.00	18.00	5.00
4 Dan Marino	125.00	55.00	15.50
5 Curtis Martin *	80.00	36.00	10.00
6 Jerry Rice	80.00	36.00	10.00
7 Barry Sanders *	80.00	36.00	10.00
8 Emmitt Smith	125.00	55.00	15.50
9 Kordell Stewart *	70.00	32.00	8.75
10 Reggie White *	40.00	18.00	5.00

1996 Pacific Crown Royale Field Force

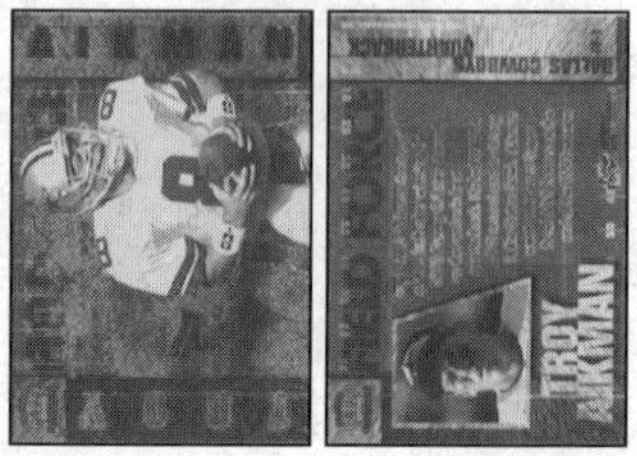

Randomly inserted in packs at a rate of one in 49, this 20-card set features color player images on a football field background and printed in a new Etch-Tech design with explosive graphics.

	MINT	NRMT	EXC
COMPLETE SET (20)	900.00	400.00	110.00
COMMON CARD (1-20)	20.00	9.00	2.50
1 Troy Aikman	60.00	27.00	7.50
2 Karim Abdul-Jabbar	50.00	22.00	6.25
3 Jeff Blake	25.00	11.00	3.10
4 Drew Bledsoe	60.00	27.00	7.50
5 Lawrence Phillips	25.00	11.00	3.10
6 Kerry Collins	60.00	27.00	7.50
7 Terrell Davis	60.00	27.00	7.50
8 John Elway	50.00	22.00	6.25
9 Brett Favre	100.00	45.00	12.50
10 Eddie George	60.00	27.00	7.50
11 Dan Marino	100.00	45.00	12.50
12 Curtis Martin	60.00	27.00	7.50
13 Jerry Rice	60.00	27.00	7.50
14 Rashaan Salaam	25.00	11.00	3.10
15 Barry Sanders	60.00	27.00	7.50
16 Deion Sanders	40.00	18.00	5.00
17 Emmitt Smith	100.00	45.00	12.50
18 Kordell Stewart	60.00	27.00	7.50
19 Chris Warren	20.00	9.00	2.50
20 Steve Young	40.00	18.00	5.00

1996 Pacific Crown Royale NFL Regime

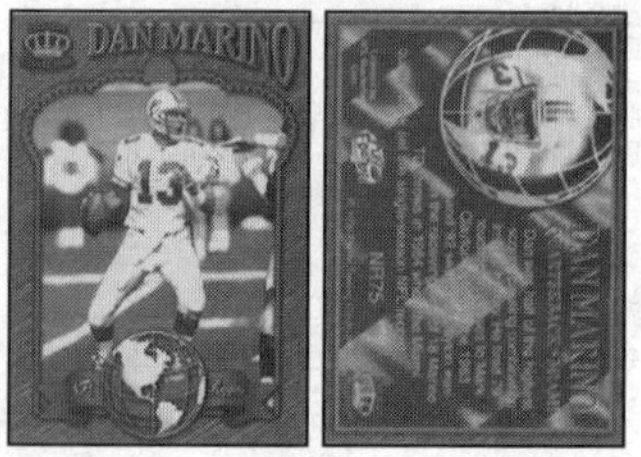

Inserted one in every pack, this 110-card set features color action player photos inside a crown-shaped border of some of the league's old and new unsung heroes of the game.

	MINT	NRMT	EXC
COMPLETE SET (110)	25.00	11.00	3.10
COMMON CARD (1-110)	.15	.07	.02
1 Steve Young	1.00	.45	.12
2 Jamir Miller	.15	.07	.02
3 Tyrone Brown	.15	.07	.02
4 Chris Shelling	.15	.07	.02
5 Warren Moon	.20	.09	.03
6 Shane Bonham	.15	.07	.02
7 Gary Brown T	.15	.07	.02
8 Chris Chandler	.20	.09	.03
9 Bradford Banta	.15	.07	.02
10 John Elway	1.00	.45	.12
11 Tom McManus	.15	.07	.02
12 Alfred Jackson	.15	.07	.02
13 Jay Barker	.15	.07	.02
14 Kirk Botkin	.15	.07	.02
15 Jim Kelly	.40	.18	.05
16 Lou Benfatti	.15	.07	.02
17 Billy Joe Hobert	.20	.09	.03
18 John Jackson	.15	.07	.02
19 Torin Dorn	.15	.07	.02
20 Drew Bledsoe	1.25	.55	.16
21 Gale Gilbert	.15	.07	.02
22 James Atkins	.15	.07	.02
23 John Lynch	.15	.07	.02
24 James Jenkins	.15	.07	.02
25 Kerry Collins	1.25	.55	.16
26 Eric Swann	.20	.09	.03

☐ 27 Dan Stryzinski	.15	.07	.02
☐ 28 Mike Groh	.15	.07	.02
☐ 29 Tim Tindale	.15	.07	.02
☐ 30 Kordell Stewart	1.25	.55	.16
☐ 31 Frank Garcia	.15	.07	.02
☐ 32 Mill Coleman	.15	.07	.02
☐ 33 Bracey Walker	.15	.07	.02
☐ 34 Ryan McNeil	.15	.07	.02
☐ 35 Rodney Hampton	.20	.09	.03
☐ 36 John Mobley	.15	.07	.02
☐ 37 Derek Russell	.15	.07	.02
☐ 38 Jeff George	.20	.09	.03
☐ 39 Steve Morrison	.15	.07	.02
☐ 40 Rashaan Salaam	.40	.18	.05
☐ 41 Ryan Christopherson	.15	.07	.02
☐ 42 Darren Anderson	.15	.07	.02
☐ 43 Ronnie Williams	.15	.07	.02
☐ 44 Scottie Graham	.15	.07	.02
☐ 45 Thurman Thomas	.40	.18	.05
☐ 46 Corwin Brown	.15	.07	.02
☐ 47 Lee DeRamus	.15	.07	.02
☐ 48 Ray Agnew	.15	.07	.02
☐ 49 Erik Howard	.15	.07	.02
☐ 50 Emmitt Smith	2.50	1.10	.30
☐ 51 Dan Land	.15	.07	.02
☐ 52 Vinny Testaverde	.20	.09	.03
☐ 53 Myron Bell	.15	.07	.02
☐ 54 Keith Lyle	.15	.07	.02
☐ 55 Aaron Hayden	.15	.07	.02
☐ 56 Jeff Brohm	.15	.07	.02
☐ 57 Ronnie Harris	.15	.07	.02
☐ 58 Trent Dilfer	.20	.09	.03
☐ 59 Browning Nagle	.15	.07	.02
☐ 60 Jeff Blake	.40	.18	.05
☐ 61 Rich Owens	.15	.07	.02
☐ 62 Anthony Edwards	.15	.07	.02
☐ 63 Orlando Brown	.15	.07	.02
☐ 64 Matthew Campbell	.15	.07	.02
☐ 65 Ricky Watters	.20	.09	.03
☐ 66 Travis Hannah	.15	.07	.02
☐ 67 Melvin Tuten	.15	.07	.02
☐ 68 Aaron Taylor	.15	.07	.02
☐ 69 Dale Hellestrae	.15	.07	.02
☐ 70 Marshall Faulk	.40	.18	.05
☐ 71 Gary Anderson	.15	.07	.02
☐ 72 David Williams	.15	.07	.02
☐ 73 Jim Harbaugh	.20	.09	.03
☐ 74 Ray Hall	.15	.07	.02
☐ 75 Dan Marino	2.50	1.10	.30
☐ 76 Chris Mims	.15	.07	.02
☐ 77 Matt Blundin	.15	.07	.02
☐ 78 Roy Barker	.15	.07	.02
☐ 79 John Burke	.15	.07	.02
☐ 80 Troy Aikman	1.25	.55	.16
☐ 81 Ed King	.15	.07	.02
☐ 82 Stan White	.15	.07	.02
☐ 83 Vance Joseph	.15	.07	.02
☐ 84 David Klingler	.15	.07	.02
☐ 85 Terrell Davis	1.50	.70	.19
☐ 86 Bobby Hoying	.40	.18	.05
☐ 87 Lethon Flowers	.15	.07	.02
☐ 88 Dwayne White	.15	.07	.02
☐ 89 Vaughn Parker	.15	.07	.02
☐ 90 Jerry Rice	1.25	.55	.16
☐ 91 Casey Weldon	.20	.09	.03
☐ 92 Rick Mirer	.20	.09	.03
☐ 93 Jim Pyne	.15	.07	.02
☐ 94 Matt Turk	.15	.07	.02
☐ 95 Marcus Allen	.40	.18	.05
☐ 96 Rob Moore	.15	.07	.02
☐ 97 Ruben Brown	.15	.07	.02
☐ 98 Zach Thomas	1.00	.45	.12
☐ 99 Carwell Gardner	.15	.07	.02
☐ 100 Barry Sanders	1.25	.55	.16
☐ 101 Ben Coleman	.15	.07	.02
☐ 102 Steve Rhem	.15	.07	.02
☐ 103 Everett McIver	.15	.07	.02
☐ 104 Cole Ford	.15	.07	.02
☐ 105 Dave Krieg	.15	.07	.02
☐ 106 Anthony Parker	.15	.07	.02
☐ 107 Michael Brandon	.15	.07	.02
☐ 108 Michael McCrary	.15	.07	.02
☐ 109 Chad Fann	.15	.07	.02
☐ 110 Brett Favre	2.50	1.10	.30

1996 Pacific Crown Royale Pro Bowl Die Cuts

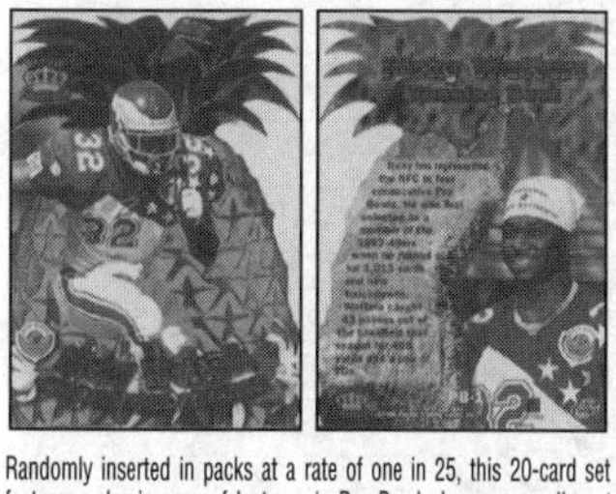

Randomly inserted in packs at a rate of one in 25, this 20-card set features color images of last year's Pro Bowl players on a die cut pineapple shaped background.

	MINT	NRMT	EXC
COMPLETE SET (20)	500.00	220.00	60.00
COMMON CARD (1-20)	10.00	4.50	1.25
☐ 1 Jeff Blake	15.00	6.75	1.85
☐ 2 Mark Chmura	10.00	4.50	1.25
☐ 3 Marshall Faulk	15.00	6.75	1.85
☐ 4 Brett Favre	100.00	45.00	12.50
☐ 5 Charles Haley	10.00	4.50	1.25
☐ 6 Merton Hanks	10.00	4.50	1.25
☐ 7 Greg Lloyd	10.00	4.50	1.25
☐ 8 Dan Marino	100.00	45.00	12.50
☐ 9 Curtis Martin	60.00	27.00	7.50
☐ 10 Anthony Miller	10.00	4.50	1.25
☐ 11 Herman Moore	15.00	6.75	1.85
☐ 12 Bryce Paup	10.00	4.50	1.25
☐ 13 Jerry Rice	50.00	22.00	6.25
☐ 14 Barry Sanders	50.00	22.00	6.25
☐ 15 Junior Seau	15.00	6.75	1.85
☐ 16 Emmitt Smith	100.00	45.00	12.50
☐ 17 Yancey Thigpen	10.00	4.50	1.25
☐ 18 Chris Warren	10.00	4.50	1.25
☐ 19 Ricky Watters	10.00	4.50	1.25
☐ 20 Steve Young	30.00	13.50	3.70

1996 Pacific Crown Royale Triple Crown Die Cuts

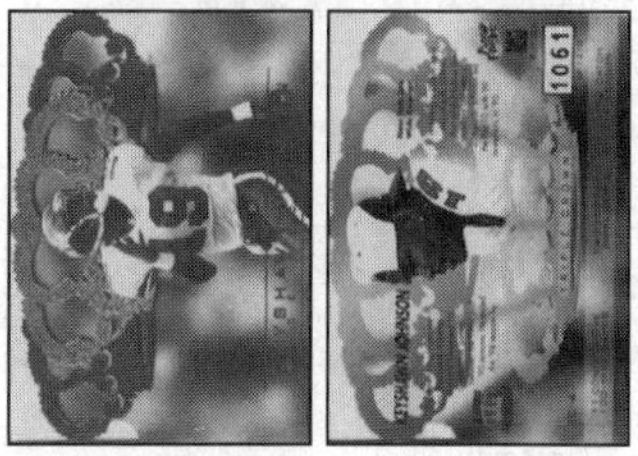

Randomly inserted in packs at a rate of one in 73, this 10-card set honors players who have led the league in a least three different categories. The serial-numbered set features color player images on a gold die cut triple crown background.

	MINT	NRMT	EXC
COMPLETE SET (10)	600.00	275.00	75.00
COMMON CARD (1-10)	30.00	13.50	3.70
☐ 1 Troy Aikman	50.00	22.00	6.25
☐ 2 John Elway	40.00	18.00	5.00
☐ 3 Brett Favre	100.00	45.00	12.50
☐ 4 Keyshawn Johnson	30.00	13.50	3.70
☐ 5 Dan Marino	100.00	45.00	12.50
☐ 6 Curtis Martin	70.00	32.00	8.75
☐ 7 Jerry Rice	50.00	22.00	6.25
☐ 8 Barry Sanders	50.00	22.00	6.25
☐ 9 Emmitt Smith	100.00	45.00	12.50
☐ 10 Steve Young	30.00	13.50	3.70

1996 Pacific Dynagon

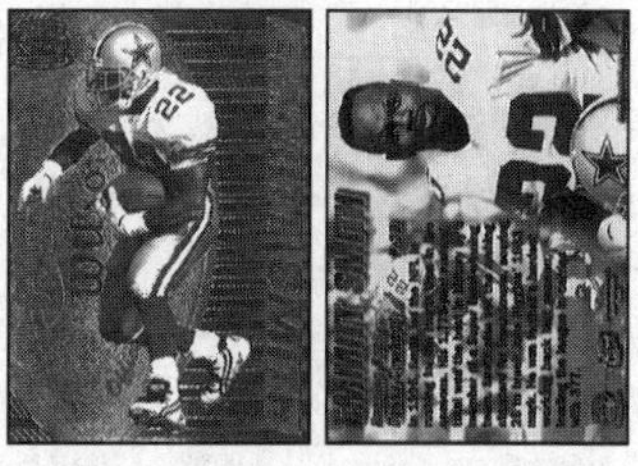

The 1996 Dynagon Prism set was issued in one series totalling 144 cards. The set was issued in two card packs with 36 packs in a box and 20 boxes in a case. Against a gold background which includes a NFL football, the player's photo is shown. The player's name is printed on the right. The horizontal backs include another photo as well as some text. The set is sequenced in alphabetical order within alphabetical team order. Rookie Cards include Tim Biakabutuka, Eddie George, Terry Glenn, Keyshawn Johnson and Lawrence Phillips.

	MINT	NRMT	EXC
COMPLETE SET (144)	125.00	55.00	15.50
COMMON CARD (1-144)	.75	.35	.09
☐ 1 Larry Centers	1.00	.45	.12
☐ 2 Garrison Hearst	1.00	.45	.12
☐ 3 Dave Krieg	.75	.35	.09
☐ 4 Frank Sanders	1.00	.45	.12
☐ 5 Jeff George	1.00	.45	.12
☐ 6 Craig Heyward	.75	.35	.09
☐ 7 Terance Mathis	.75	.35	.09
☐ 8 Eric Metcalf	1.00	.45	.12
☐ 9 Todd Collins	1.00	.45	.12
☐ 10 Darick Holmes	1.00	.45	.12
☐ 11 Jim Kelly	1.25	.55	.16
☐ 12 Eric Moulds	2.00	.90	.25
☐ 13 Bryce Paup	1.00	.45	.12
☐ 14 Thurman Thomas	1.25	.55	.16
☐ 15 Tim Biakabutuka	2.00	.90	.25
☐ 16 Blake Brockermeyer	.75	.35	.09
☐ 17 Mark Carrier WR	1.00	.45	.12
☐ 18 Kerry Collins	6.00	2.70	.75
☐ 19 Derrick Moore	.75	.35	.09
☐ 20 Bobby Engram	2.00	.90	.25
☐ 21 Jeff Graham	.75	.35	.09
☐ 22 Erik Kramer	.75	.35	.09
☐ 23 Rashaan Salaam	1.25	.55	.16
☐ 24 Steve Stenstrom	.75	.35	.09
☐ 25 Chris Zorich	.75	.35	.09
☐ 26 Jeff Blake	1.25	.55	.16
☐ 27 David Dunn	.75	.35	.09
☐ 28 Carl Pickens	1.25	.55	.16
☐ 29 Darnay Scott	1.00	.45	.12
☐ 30 Earnest Byner	.75	.35	.09
☐ 31 Leroy Hoard	.75	.35	.09
☐ 32 Keenan McCardell	1.25	.55	.16
☐ 33 Eric Zeier	1.00	.45	.12
☐ 34 Troy Aikman	5.00	2.20	.60
☐ 35 Chris Boniol	.75	.35	.09
☐ 36 Michael Irvin	1.25	.55	.16
☐ 37 Daryl Johnston	1.00	.45	.12
☐ 38 Deion Sanders	3.00	1.35	.35
☐ 39 Emmitt Smith	10.00	4.50	1.25
☐ 40 Stepfret Williams	.75	.35	.09
☐ 41 John Elway	4.00	1.80	.50
☐ 42 Terrell Davis	8.00	3.60	1.00
☐ 43 Anthony Miller	1.00	.45	.12
☐ 44 Shannon Sharpe	1.00	.45	.12
☐ 45 Scott Mitchell	1.00	.45	.12
☐ 46 Herman Moore	1.25	.55	.16
☐ 47 Brett Perriman	1.00	.45	.12
☐ 48 Barry Sanders	5.00	2.20	.60
☐ 49 Cory Schlesinger	.75	.35	.09
☐ 50 Edgar Bennett	1.00	.45	.12
☐ 51 Robert Brooks	1.25	.55	.16
☐ 52 Mark Chmura	1.00	.45	.12
☐ 53 Brett Favre	10.00	4.50	1.25
☐ 54 Reggie White	1.25	.55	.16
☐ 55 Eddie George	10.00	4.50	1.25
☐ 56 Steve McNair	5.00	2.20	.60
☐ 57 Chris Sanders	1.00	.45	.12
☐ 58 Rodney Thomas	.75	.35	.09
☐ 59 Ben Bronson	.75	.35	.09
☐ 60 Zack Crockett	.75	.35	.09
☐ 61 Marshall Faulk	1.25	.55	.16
☐ 62 Jim Harbaugh	1.00	.45	.12
☐ 63 Mark Brunell	5.00	2.20	.60
☐ 64 Kevin Hardy	1.25	.55	.16
☐ 65 Willie Jackson	1.00	.45	.12
☐ 66 Pete Mitchell	.75	.35	.09
☐ 67 James O.Stewart	1.25	.55	.16
☐ 68 Marcus Allen	1.25	.55	.16
☐ 69 Steve Bono	1.00	.45	.12
☐ 70 Lake Dawson	1.00	.45	.12
☐ 71 Neil Smith	1.00	.45	.12
☐ 72 Tamarick Vanover	1.25	.55	.16
☐ 73 Irving Fryar	1.00	.45	.12
☐ 74 Terry Kirby	1.00	.45	.12
☐ 75 Dan Marino	10.00	4.50	1.25
☐ 76 O.J. McDuffie	1.00	.45	.12
☐ 77 Bernie Parmalee	.75	.35	.09
☐ 78 Stanley Pritchett	1.00	.45	.12
☐ 79 Cris Carter	1.25	.55	.16
☐ 80 Qadry Ismail	1.00	.45	.12
☐ 81 Chad May	.75	.35	.09
☐ 82 Warren Moon	1.00	.45	.12
☐ 83 Robert Smith	1.00	.45	.12
☐ 84 Drew Bledsoe	5.00	2.20	.60
☐ 85 Ben Coates	1.00	.45	.12
☐ 86 Terry Glenn	8.00	3.60	1.00
☐ 87 Curtis Martin	8.00	3.60	1.00
☐ 88 Willie McGinest	.75	.35	.09
☐ 89 Mario Bates	1.00	.45	.12
☐ 90 Jim Everett	.75	.35	.09
☐ 91 Wayne Martin	.75	.35	.09
☐ 92 Shane Pahukoa	1.00	.45	.12
☐ 93 Ray Zellars	.75	.35	.09
☐ 94 Dave Brown	1.00	.45	.12
☐ 95 Chris Calloway	.75	.35	.09
☐ 96 Rodney Hampton	1.00	.45	.12
☐ 97 Tyrone Wheatley	1.00	.45	.12
☐ 98 Wayne Chrebet	1.00	.45	.12
☐ 99 Glenn Foley	.75	.35	.09
☐ 100 Keyshawn Johnson	3.00	1.35	.35
☐ 101 Adrian Murrell	1.00	.45	.12
☐ 102 Alex Van Dyke	1.00	.45	.12
☐ 103 Tim Brown	1.00	.45	.12
☐ 104 Billy Joe Hobert	1.00	.45	.12
☐ 105 Rocket Ismail	1.00	.45	.12
☐ 106 Napoleon Kaufman	1.00	.45	.12
☐ 107 Harvey Williams	.75	.35	.09
☐ 108 Charlie Garner	.75	.35	.09
☐ 109 Rodney Peete	.75	.35	.09
☐ 110 Ricky Watters	1.00	.45	.12
☐ 111 Calvin Williams	.75	.35	.09
☐ 112 Mark Bruener	.75	.35	.09
☐ 113 Kevin Greene	1.00	.45	.12
☐ 114 Ernie Mills	.75	.35	.09
☐ 115 Kordell Stewart	6.00	2.70	.75
☐ 116 Yancey Thigpen	1.00	.45	.12
☐ 117 Dave Barr	.75	.35	.09
☐ 118 Jerome Bettis	1.25	.55	.16
☐ 119 Isaac Bruce	1.25	.55	.16
☐ 120 Lawrence Phillips	2.00	.90	.25
☐ 121 J.T. Thomas	.75	.35	.09
☐ 122 Ronnie Harmon	.75	.35	.09
☐ 123 Aaron Hayden	1.00	.45	.12
☐ 124 Stan Humphries	1.00	.45	.12
☐ 125 Junior Seau	1.25	.55	.16
☐ 126 William Floyd	1.25	.55	.16
☐ 127 Elvis Grbac	1.25	.55	.16
☐ 128 Jerry Rice	5.00	2.20	.60
☐ 129 J.J. Stokes	1.25	.55	.16
☐ 130 Steve Young	4.00	1.80	.50
☐ 131 Joey Galloway	3.00	1.35	.35
☐ 132 Cortez Kennedy	1.00	.45	.12
☐ 133 Kevin Mawae	.75	.35	.09
☐ 134 Rick Mirer	1.00	.45	.12
☐ 135 Chris Warren	1.00	.45	.12
☐ 136 Trent Dilfer	1.00	.45	.12
☐ 137 Jerry Ellison	.75	.35	.09
☐ 138 Alvin Harper	.75	.35	.09
☐ 139 Errict Rhett	1.00	.45	.12
☐ 140 Terry Allen	1.00	.45	.12
☐ 141 Brian Mitchell	.75	.35	.09
☐ 142 Gus Frerotte	1.25	.55	.16
☐ 143 Michael Westbrook	1.25	.55	.16
☐ 144 Heath Shuler	1.25	.55	.16

1996 Pacific Dynagon Best Kept Secrets

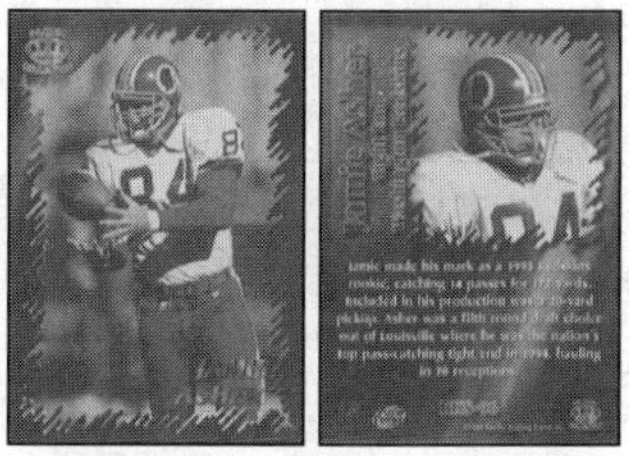

Issued one per pack, these 100 standard-size cards feature many lesser known players who rarely get proper recognition for their skills. The players photo is in the middle with his name in the lower right. The back features another photo as well as some text information. The cards were numbered with a "BKS" prefix.

	MINT	NRMT	EXC
COMPLETE SET (100)	16.00	7.25	2.00
COMMON CARD (1-100)	.20	.09	.03
☐ 1 Wendall Gaines	.20	.09	.03
☐ 2 Randy Kirk	.20	.09	.03
☐ 3 Anthony Redmon	.20	.09	.03
☐ 4 Bernard Wilson	.20	.09	.03
☐ 5 Ron Davis	.20	.09	.03
☐ 6 Roell Preston	.40	.18	.05
☐ 7 Robbie Tobeck	.20	.09	.03
☐ 8 Harold Bishop	.20	.09	.03
☐ 9 Dan Footman	.20	.09	.03
☐ 10 Ernest Hunter	.20	.09	.03
☐ 11 Tony Cline	.20	.09	.03
☐ 12 Kurt Schulz	.20	.09	.03
☐ 13 Alex Van Pelt	.60	.25	.07
☐ 14 Howard Griffith	.20	.09	.03
☐ 15 Mark Thomas	.20	.09	.03
☐ 16 Keshon Johnson	.20	.09	.03
☐ 17 Kevin Miniefield	.20	.09	.03
☐ 18 Steve Stenstrom	.40	.18	.05
☐ 19 Jeff Cothran	.40	.18	.05
☐ 20 Jeff Hill	.20	.09	.03
☐ 21 Alundis Brice	.20	.09	.03
☐ 22 Cory Fleming	.40	.18	.05
☐ 23 Kendell Watkins	.20	.09	.03
☐ 24 Charlie Williams	.20	.09	.03
☐ 25 Byron Chamberlain	.20	.09	.03
☐ 26 Jerry Evans	.20	.09	.03
☐ 27 Rod Smith WR	.40	.18	.05
☐ 28 Kevin Hickman	.20	.09	.03
☐ 29 Ron Rivers	.20	.09	.03
☐ 30 Henry Thomas	.40	.18	.05
☐ 31 Keith Crawford	.20	.09	.03
☐ 32 Doug Evans	.20	.09	.03
☐ 33 William Henderson	.20	.09	.03
☐ 34 John Jurkovic	.20	.09	.03
☐ 35 Blaine Bishop	.40	.18	.05
☐ 36 Kenny Davidson	.20	.09	.03
☐ 37 Erik Norgard	.20	.09	.03
☐ 38 Derwin Gray	.20	.09	.03
☐ 39 Ellis Johnson	.20	.09	.03
☐ 40 Tony McCoy	.20	.09	.03
☐ 41 Glen Sanders	.20	.09	.03
☐ 42 Bernard Whittington	.20	.09	.03
☐ 43 Travis Davis	.20	.09	.03
☐ 44 Rogerick Green	.20	.09	.03
☐ 45 Rob Johnson	.20	.09	.03
☐ 46 Curtis Marsh	.20	.09	.03
☐ 47 Matt Blundin	.40	.18	.05
☐ 48 Lin Elliott	.20	.09	.03
☐ 49 Pellom McDaniels	.20	.09	.03
☐ 50 Kirby Dar Dar	.20	.09	.03
☐ 51 Jeff Kopp	.20	.09	.03
☐ 52 Billy Milner	.40	.18	.05
☐ 53 Tuineau Alipate	.20	.09	.03
☐ 54 Jeff Brady	.20	.09	.03
☐ 55 David Dixon	.20	.09	.03

☐ 56 Mike Morris	.20	.09	.03
☐ 57 Max Lane	.20	.09	.03
☐ 58 Tim Roberts	.20	.09	.03
☐ 59 Reggie E.White	.20	.09	.03
☐ 60 Tommy Hodson	.20	.09	.03
☐ 61 Joe Johnson	.20	.09	.03
☐ 62 Gary Downs	.20	.09	.03
☐ 63 Gary Harrell	.20	.09	.03
☐ 64 Robert Harris	.40	.18	.05
☐ 65 Kenyon Rasheed	.40	.18	.05
☐ 66 Richie Anderson	.20	.09	.03
☐ 67 Matt Brock	.20	.09	.03
☐ 68 Hugh Douglas	.60	.25	.07
☐ 69 Jeff Gossett	.20	.09	.03
☐ 70 Mike Jones	.20	.09	.03
☐ 71 Mike Morton	.20	.09	.03
☐ 72 Anthony Smith	.40	.18	.05
☐ 73 Jay Fiedler	.20	.09	.03
☐ 74 Frank Wainright	.20	.09	.03
☐ 75 Marc Woodard	.20	.09	.03
☐ 76 Eric Zomalt	.20	.09	.03
☐ 77 Chad Brown	.40	.18	.05
☐ 78 James Parrish	.20	.09	.03
☐ 79 Justin Strzelczyk	.20	.09	.03
☐ 80 Darryl Ashmore	.40	.18	.05
☐ 81 Gerald McBurrows	.20	.09	.03
☐ 82 Lovell Pinkney	.20	.09	.03
☐ 83 Lewis Bush	.20	.09	.03
☐ 84 Eric Castle	.20	.09	.03
☐ 85 Terrance Shaw	.40	.18	.05
☐ 86 Frank Pollack	.20	.09	.03
☐ 87 Kirk Scrafford	.20	.09	.03
☐ 88 Alfred Williams	.20	.09	.03
☐ 89 Carlton Gray	.20	.09	.03
☐ 90 James McKnight	.20	.09	.03
☐ 91 Todd Peterson	.20	.09	.03
☐ 92 Dean Wells	.20	.09	.03
☐ 93 Curtis Buckley	.20	.09	.03
☐ 94 Thomas Everett	.40	.18	.05
☐ 95 Pete Pierson	.20	.09	.03
☐ 96 Jamie Asher	.20	.09	.03
☐ 97 William Bell	.20	.09	.03
☐ 98 Trent Green	.60	.25	.07
☐ 99 Richard Huntley	.20	.09	.03
☐ 100 Terrell Owens	1.00	.45	.12

1996 Pacific Dynagon Dynamic Duos

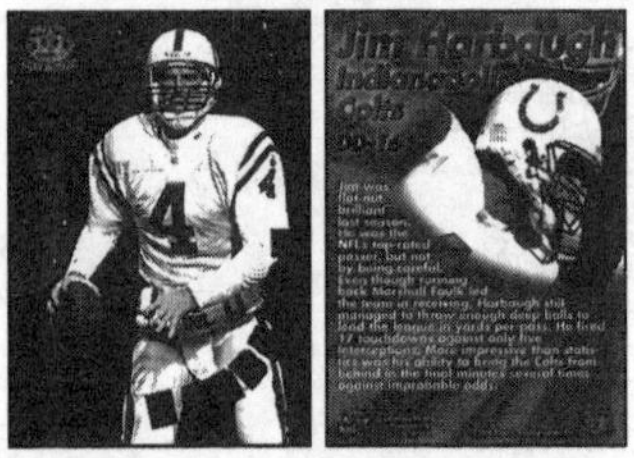

This 24 card standard-size insert set features pairs of teammates. In a novel twist, the first half of the pair is located in hobby packs while the second half is located in retail packs. The hobby inserts are "DD1-DD12" while the retail inserts are "DD13-DD24". These cards were inserted into each type of pack at a rate of one in 37.

	MINT	NRMT	EXC
COMPLETE SET (24)	250.00	110.00	31.00
COMMON CARD (DD1-DD24)	5.00	2.20	.60
☐ DD1 Troy Aikman	20.00	9.00	2.50
☐ DD2 Jerry Rice	20.00	9.00	2.50
☐ DD3 Brett Favre	35.00	16.00	4.40
☐ DD4 Marshall Faulk	10.00	4.50	1.25
☐ DD5 Carl Pickens	8.00	3.60	1.00
☐ DD6 Terrell Davis	20.00	9.00	2.50
☐ DD7 Curtis Martin	20.00	9.00	2.50
☐ DD8 Dan Marino	35.00	16.00	4.40
☐ DD9 Herman Moore	10.00	4.50	1.25
☐ DD10 Kordell Stewart	15.00	6.75	1.85
☐ DD11 Emmitt Smith	35.00	16.00	4.40
☐ DD12 Trent Dilfer	8.00	3.60	1.00
☐ DD13 Deion Sanders	12.00	5.50	1.50
☐ DD14 Steve Young	15.00	6.75	1.85
☐ DD15 Robert Brooks	10.00	4.50	1.25
☐ DD16 Jim Harbaugh	8.00	3.60	1.00
☐ DD17 Jeff Blake	10.00	4.50	1.25
☐ DD18 John Elway	15.00	6.75	1.85
☐ DD19 Drew Bledsoe	20.00	9.00	2.50
☐ DD20 Bernie Parmalee	5.00	2.20	.60
☐ DD21 Barry Sanders	20.00	9.00	2.50
☐ DD22 Kevin Greene	5.00	2.20	.60
☐ DD23 Sherman Williams	5.00	2.20	.60
☐ DD24 Errict Rhett	8.00	3.60	1.00

1996 Pacific Dynagon Kings of the NFL

This 10-card standard-size set was inserted approximately one every 361 packs. The player's name is on top with a crown and the crowning achievement printed in gold foil on the bottom. In the

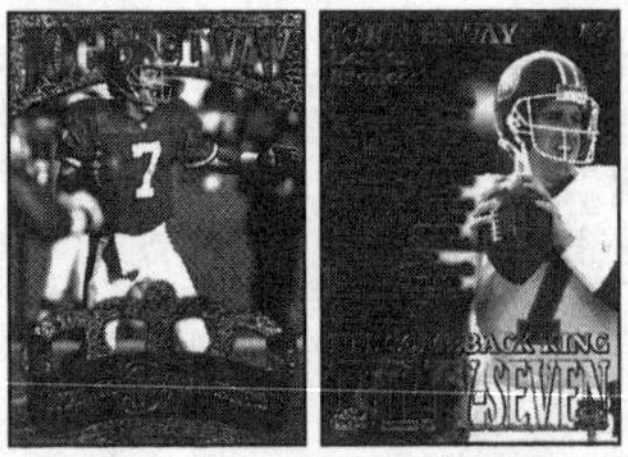

middle is the player photo. The back has more details about that record as well as another photo. The cards are numbered with a "K" prefix.

	MINT	NRMT	EXC
COMPLETE SET (10)	600.00	275.00	75.00
COMMON CARD (K1-K10)	40.00	18.00	5.00
☐ K1 Emmitt Smith	100.00	45.00	12.50
☐ K2 Dan Marino	100.00	45.00	12.50
☐ K3 Barry Sanders	60.00	27.00	7.50
☐ K4 Curtis Martin	70.00	32.00	8.75
☐ K5 Brett Favre	100.00	45.00	12.50
☐ K6 Kordell Stewart	60.00	27.00	7.50
☐ K7 Emmitt Smith	100.00	45.00	12.50
☐ K8 Jerry Rice	60.00	27.00	7.50
☐ K9 John Elway	40.00	18.00	5.00
☐ K10 Dan Marino	100.00	45.00	12.50

1996 Pacific Dynagon Tandems

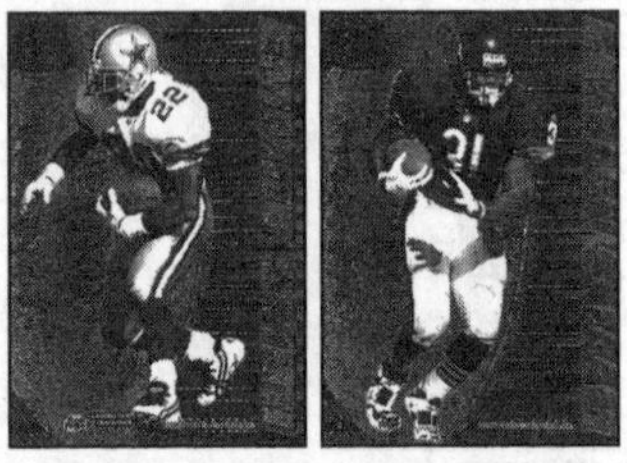

This 72 card standard-size set is a mini-parallel to the regular Pacific Dynagon set. Unlike the regular issue, these cards are not sequenced in the same order. They are numbered in white ink in the lower left corner and feature two base brand Dynagon cards back-to-back. The cards were inserted at the rate of 1:37 packs.

	MINT	NRMT	EXC
COMPLETE SET (72)	1600.00	700.00	200.00
COMMON CARD (1-72)	12.00	5.50	1.50
☐ 1 Dan Marino Troy Aikman	160.00	70.00	20.00
☐ 2 Emmitt Smith Rashaan Salaam	120.00	55.00	15.00
☐ 3 Jim Kelly John Elway	60.00	27.00	7.50
☐ 4 Steve Young Brett Favre	140.00	65.00	17.50
☐ 5 Curtis Martin Terrell Davis	60.00	27.00	7.50
☐ 6 Kordell Stewart Napoleon Kaufman	50.00	22.00	6.25
☐ 7 Barry Sanders Jerry Rice	90.00	40.00	11.00
☐ 8 Joey Galloway J.J.Stokes	25.00	11.00	3.10
☐ 9 Kerry Collins Jeff Blake	50.00	22.00	6.25
☐ 10 Deion Sanders Reggie White	40.00	18.00	5.00
☐ 11 Herman Moore Mark Chmura	20.00	9.00	2.50
☐ 12 Eric Zeier Tyrone Wheatley	20.00	9.00	2.50
☐ 13 Errict Rhett Robert Brooks	20.00	9.00	2.50
☐ 14 Trent Dilfer Steve McNair	40.00	18.00	5.00
☐ 15 Marshall Faulk Drew Bledsoe	60.00	27.00	7.50
☐ 16 Tamarick Vanover Michael Westbrook	20.00	9.00	2.50
☐ 17 Heath Shuler Jerome Bettis	20.00	9.00	2.50
☐ 18 Isaac Bruce Tim Brown	20.00	9.00	2.50
☐ 19 Terry Allen Chris Warren	15.00	6.75	1.85
☐ 20 Brian Mitchell Alex Van Dyke	15.00	6.75	1.85
☐ 21 Jerry Ellison Kevin Mawae	12.00	5.50	1.50
☐ 22 Alvin Harper Stanley Pritchett	15.00	6.75	1.85
☐ 23 Rick Mirer Elvis Grbac	20.00	9.00	2.50
☐ 24 Cortez Kennedy Junior Seau	20.00	9.00	2.50
☐ 25 William Floyd Aaron Hayden	15.00	6.75	1.85
☐ 26 Stan Humphries Dave Barr	15.00	6.75	1.85
☐ 27 J.T.Thomas Sherman Williams	12.00	5.50	1.50
☐ 28 Ronnie Harmon Yancey Thigpen	15.00	6.75	1.85
☐ 29 Ernie Mills Calvin Williams	12.00	5.50	1.50
☐ 30 Mark Bruener Eddie George	50.00	22.00	6.25
☐ 31 Kevin Greene Eric Moulds	20.00	9.00	2.50
☐ 32 Ricky Watters Harvey Williams	15.00	6.75	1.85
☐ 33 Rodney Peete Keyshawn Johnson	30.00	13.50	3.70
☐ 34 Charlie Garner Adrian Murrell	15.00	6.75	1.85
☐ 35 Rocket Ismail Wayne Chrebet	15.00	6.75	1.85
☐ 36 Billy Joe Hobert Glenn Foley	12.00	5.50	1.50
☐ 37 Rodney Hampton Ben Coates	15.00	6.75	1.85
☐ 38 Chris Calloway Qadry Ismail	15.00	6.75	1.85
☐ 39 Dave Brown Warren Moon	20.00	9.00	2.50
☐ 40 Ray Zellars Robert Smith	15.00	6.75	1.85
☐ 41 Shane Pahukoa Bernie Parmalee	12.00	5.50	1.50
☐ 42 Wayne Martin Neil Smith	12.00	5.50	1.50
☐ 43 Jim Everett Steve Bono	15.00	6.75	1.85
☐ 44 Mario Bates Terry Kirby	15.00	6.75	1.85
☐ 45 Willie McGinest Lawrence Phillips	20.00	9.00	2.50
☐ 46 Chad May Mark Brunell	50.00	22.00	6.25
☐ 47 Cris Carter O.J. McDuffie	20.00	9.00	2.50
☐ 48 Irving Fryar Lake Dawson	15.00	6.75	1.85
☐ 49 Marcus Allen James O.Stewart	20.00	9.00	2.50
☐ 50 Willie Jackson Terry Glenn	40.00	18.00	5.00
☐ 51 Pete Mitchell Kevin Hardy	15.00	6.75	1.85
☐ 52 Jim Harbaugh Scott Mitchell	20.00	9.00	2.50
☐ 53 Zack Crockett Rodney Thomas	15.00	6.75	1.85
☐ 54 Ben Bronson Chris Sanders	15.00	6.75	1.85
☐ 55 Edgar Bennett Tim Biakabutuka	20.00	9.00	2.50
☐ 56 Brett Perriman Anthony Miller	15.00	6.75	1.85
☐ 57 Cory Schlesinger Daryl Johnston	15.00	6.75	1.85
☐ 58 Shannon Sharpe Michael Irvin	20.00	9.00	2.50
☐ 59 Chris Boniol Thurman Thomas	20.00	9.00	2.50
☐ 60 Keenan McCardell Darnay Scott	15.00	6.75	1.85
☐ 61 Leroy Hoard Chris Zorich	12.00	5.50	1.50
☐ 62 Earnest Byner Jeff Graham	15.00	6.75	1.85
☐ 63 Carl Pickens Darick Holmes	20.00	9.00	2.50
☐ 64 David Dunn Mark Carrier WR	15.00	6.75	1.85
☐ 65 Steve Stenstrom Todd Collins	15.00	6.75	1.85
☐ 66 Erik Kramer Derrick Moore	15.00	6.75	1.85
☐ 67 Larry Centers Bobby Engram	15.00	6.75	1.85
☐ 68 Garrison Hearst Jeff George	20.00	9.00	2.50
☐ 69 Dave Krieg Craig Heyward	15.00	6.75	1.85
☐ 70 Frank Sanders Terance Mathis	20.00	9.00	2.50
☐ 71 Gus Frerotte Eric Metcalf	20.00	9.00	2.50
☐ 72 Bryce Paup Blake Brockermeyer	12.00	5.50	1.50

1997 Pacific Dynagon

This 144-card set was issued in three card packs and recognizes some of the hottest players in the NFL. The fronts feature action color player images on a background of a football helmet and rays foiled in gold. The backs carry player information.

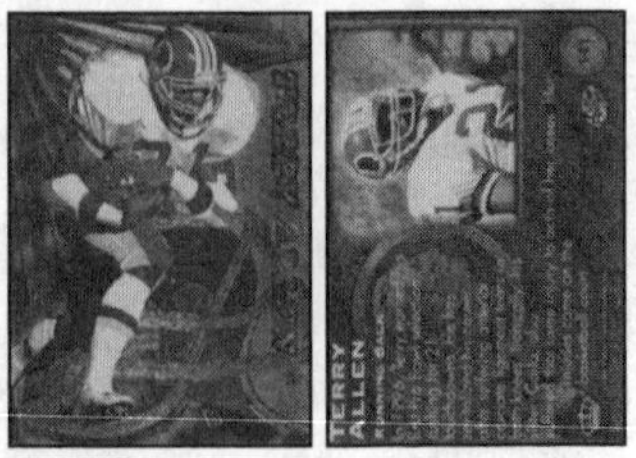

	MINT	NRMT	EXC
COMPLETE SET (144)	140.00	65.00	17.50
COMMON CARD (1-144)	.60	.25	.07
☐ 1 Larry Centers	.75	.35	.09
☐ 2 Kent Graham	.75	.35	.09
☐ 3 Leeland McElroy	.75	.35	.09
☐ 4 Frank Sanders	.75	.35	.09
☐ 5 Jamal Anderson	.75	.35	.09
☐ 6 Bert Emanuel	.75	.35	.09
☐ 7 Bobby Hebert	.60	.25	.07
☐ 8 Terance Mathis	.60	.25	.07
☐ 9 Eric Metcalf	.75	.35	.09
☐ 10 Derrick Alexander WR	.75	.35	.09
☐ 11 Earnest Byner	.60	.25	.07
☐ 12 Michael Jackson	.75	.35	.09
☐ 13 Vinny Testaverde	.75	.35	.09
☐ 14 Quinn Early	.60	.25	.07
☐ 15 Jim Kelly	1.25	.55	.16
☐ 16 Eric Moulds	1.25	.55	.16
☐ 17 Andre Reed	.75	.35	.09
☐ 18 Bruce Smith	1.25	.55	.16
☐ 19 Thurman Thomas	1.25	.55	.16
☐ 20 Tim Biakabutuka	1.25	.55	.16
☐ 21 Mark Carrier	.60	.25	.07
☐ 22 Kerry Collins	4.00	1.80	.50
☐ 23 Kevin Greene	.75	.35	.09
☐ 24 Anthony Johnson	.75	.35	.09
☐ 25 Wesley Walls	.60	.25	.07
☐ 26 Curtis Conway	1.25	.55	.16
☐ 27 Bobby Engram	.75	.35	.09
☐ 28 Raymont Harris	.60	.25	.07
☐ 29 Dave Krieg	.60	.25	.07
☐ 30 Rashaan Salaam	1.25	.55	.16
☐ 31 Jeff Blake	1.25	.55	.16
☐ 32 Ki-Jana Carter	.75	.35	.09
☐ 33 Garrison Hearst	.75	.35	.09
☐ 34 Carl Pickens	1.25	.55	.16
☐ 35 Darnay Scott	.75	.35	.09
☐ 36 Troy Aikman	5.00	2.20	.60
☐ 37 Chris Boniol	.60	.25	.07
☐ 38 Michael Irvin	1.25	.55	.16
☐ 39 Deion Sanders	3.00	1.35	.35
☐ 40 Emmitt Smith	10.00	4.50	1.25
☐ 41 Herschel Walker	.75	.35	.09
☐ 42 Terrell Davis	5.00	2.20	.60
☐ 43 John Elway	4.00	1.80	.50
☐ 44 Ed McCaffrey	.60	.25	.07
☐ 45 Shannon Sharpe	.75	.35	.09
☐ 46 Alfred Williams	.60	.25	.07
☐ 47 Scott Mitchell	.75	.35	.09
☐ 48 Herman Moore	1.25	.55	.16
☐ 49 Brett Perriman	.75	.35	.09
☐ 50 Barry Sanders	5.00	2.20	.60
☐ 51 Edgar Bennett	.75	.35	.09
☐ 52 Robert Brooks	1.25	.55	.16
☐ 53 Mark Chmura	.75	.35	.09
☐ 54 Brett Favre	10.00	4.50	1.25
☐ 55 Antonio Freeman	2.00	.90	.25
☐ 56 Desmond Howard	.75	.35	.09
☐ 57 Reggie White	1.25	.55	.16
☐ 58 Chris Chandler	.75	.35	.09
☐ 59 Eddie George	8.00	3.60	1.00
☐ 60 James McKeehan	.60	.25	.07
☐ 61 Steve McNair	3.00	1.35	.35
☐ 62 Chris Sanders	.75	.35	.09
☐ 63 Sean Dawkins	.60	.25	.07
☐ 64 Ken Dilger	.75	.35	.09
☐ 65 Marshall Faulk	1.25	.55	.16
☐ 66 Jim Harbaugh	.75	.35	.09
☐ 67 Marvin Harrison	4.00	1.80	.50
☐ 68 Tony Boselli	.75	.35	.09
☐ 69 Mark Brunell	5.00	2.20	.60
☐ 70 Keenan McCardell	.75	.35	.09
☐ 71 Natrone Means	1.25	.55	.16
☐ 72 Jimmy Smith	.75	.35	.09
☐ 73 Marcus Allen	1.25	.55	.16
☐ 74 Kimble Anders	.60	.25	.07
☐ 75 Dale Carter	.60	.25	.07
☐ 76 Greg Hill	.75	.35	.09
☐ 77 Derrick Thomas	.75	.35	.09
☐ 78 Tamarick Vanover	.75	.35	.09
☐ 79 Karim Abdul-Jabbar	5.00	2.20	.60
☐ 80 Dan Marino	10.00	4.50	1.25
☐ 81 O.J. McDuffie	.75	.35	.09
☐ 82 Jerris McPhail	.60	.25	.07
☐ 83 Zach Thomas	2.50	1.10	.30
☐ 84 Cris Carter	1.25	.55	.16
☐ 85 Brad Johnson	.75	.35	.09
☐ 86 Jake Reed	.75	.35	.09
☐ 87 Robert Smith	.75	.35	.09
☐ 88 Drew Bledsoe	5.00	2.20	.60

☐ 89 Ben Coates	.75	.35	.09
☐ 90 Terry Glenn	6.00	2.70	.75
☐ 91 Curtis Martin	5.00	2.20	.60
☐ 92 Willie McGinest	.60	.25	.07
☐ 93 Jim Everett	.60	.25	.07
☐ 94 Michael Haynes	.75	.35	.09
☐ 95 Haywood Jeffires	.60	.25	.07
☐ 96 Ray Zellars	.60	.25	.07
☐ 97 Dave Brown	.75	.35	.09
☐ 98 Rodney Hampton	.75	.35	.09
☐ 99 Danny Kanell	.75	.35	.09
☐ 100 Thomas Lewis	.60	.25	.07
☐ 101 Wayne Chrebet	.60	.25	.07
☐ 102 Keyshawn Johnson	4.00	1.80	.50
☐ 103 Adrian Murrell	.75	.35	.09
☐ 104 Neil O'Donnell	.75	.35	.09
☐ 105 Tim Brown	.75	.35	.09
☐ 106 Rickey Dudley	.75	.35	.09
☐ 107 Jeff Hostetler	.75	.35	.09
☐ 108 Napoleon Kaufman	.75	.35	.09
☐ 109 Ty Detmer	.75	.35	.09
☐ 110 Jason Dunn	.75	.35	.09
☐ 111 Irving Fryar	.75	.35	.09
☐ 112 Chris T. Jones	1.25	.55	.16
☐ 113 Ricky Watters	.75	.35	.09
☐ 114 Jerome Bettis	1.25	.55	.16
☐ 115 Chad Brown	.75	.35	.09
☐ 116 Kordell Stewart	4.00	1.80	.50
☐ 117 Mike Tomczak	.60	.25	.07
☐ 118 Rod Woodson	.75	.35	.09
☐ 119 Tony Banks	2.50	1.10	.30
☐ 120 Isaac Bruce	1.25	.55	.16
☐ 121 Eddie Kennison	4.00	1.80	.50
☐ 122 Lawrence Phillips	.75	.35	.09
☐ 123 Terrell Fletcher	.60	.25	.07
☐ 124 Stan Humphries	.75	.35	.09
☐ 125 Tony Martin	.75	.35	.09
☐ 126 Junior Seau	1.25	.55	.16
☐ 127 Elvis Grbac	.75	.35	.09
☐ 128 Terrell Owens	5.00	2.20	.60
☐ 129 Ted Popson	.60	.25	.07
☐ 130 Jerry Rice	5.00	2.20	.60
☐ 131 Steve Young	4.00	1.80	.50
☐ 132 John Friesz	.60	.25	.07
☐ 133 Joey Galloway	2.00	.90	.25
☐ 134 Michael McCrary	.60	.25	.07
☐ 135 Lamar Smith	.60	.25	.07
☐ 136 Chris Warren	.75	.35	.09
☐ 137 Mike Alstott	1.25	.55	.16
☐ 138 Trent Dilfer	.75	.35	.09
☐ 139 Courtney Hawkins	.60	.25	.07
☐ 140 Errict Rhett	.75	.35	.09
☐ 141 Terry Allen	.75	.35	.09
☐ 142 Henry Ellard	.75	.35	.09
☐ 143 Gus Frerotte	1.25	.55	.16
☐ 144 Leslie Shepherd	.60	.25	.07

1997 Pacific Dynagon Copper

Randomly inserted at the rate of two in 37 hobby only packs, this 144-card set is a parallel version of the regular set and is similar in design. The distinction is found in the copper foil highlights.

	MINT	NRMT	EXC
COMPLETE SET (144)	700.00	325.00	90.00
COMMON CARD (1-144)	3.00	1.35	.35

*COPPER STARS: 3X TO 6X BASIC CARDS
*COPPER YOUNG STARS: 2.5X TO 5X BASIC CARDS

1997 Pacific Dynagon Silver

Randomly inserted at the rate of two in 37 retail only packs, this 144-card set is a parallel version of the regular set and is similar in design. The distinction is found in the silver foil highlights.

	MINT	NRMT	EXC
COMPLETE SET (144)	800.00	350.00	100.00
COMMON CARD (1-144)	4.00	1.80	.50

*SILVER STARS: 3.5X TO 7X BASIC CARDS
*SILVER YOUNG STARS: 3X TO 6X BASIC CARDS

1997 Pacific Dynagon Best Kept Secrets

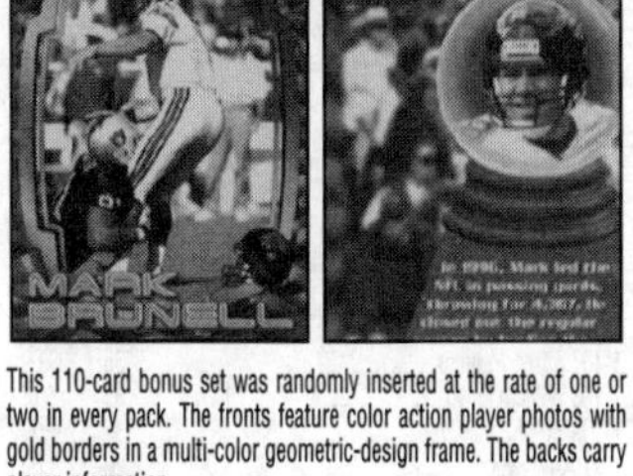

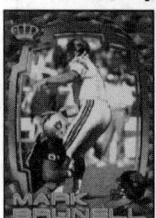

This 110-card bonus set was randomly inserted at the rate of one or two in every pack. The fronts feature color action player photos with gold borders in a multi-color geometric-design frame. The backs carry player information.

	MINT	NRMT	EXC
COMPLETE SET (110)	25.00	11.00	3.10
COMMON CARD (1-110)	.10	.05	.01
☐ 1 Mark Brunell	1.25	.55	.16
☐ 2 Bob Dahl	.10	.05	.01
☐ 3 Tommy Bennett	.10	.05	.01
☐ 4 Jamal Anderson	.20	.09	.03
☐ 5 Jermaine Lewis	.10	.05	.01
☐ 6 Chris Brantley	.10	.05	.01
☐ 7 Mathew Campbell	.10	.05	.01
☐ 8 Jeff Jaeger	.10	.05	.01
☐ 9 Marco Battaglia	.10	.05	.01
☐ 10 Troy Aikman	1.25	.55	.16
☐ 11 Terrell Davis	1.25	.55	.16
☐ 12 Jeff Hartings	.10	.05	.01
☐ 13 Brett Favre	2.50	1.10	.30
☐ 14 Eddie George	2.00	.90	.25
☐ 15 Elijah Alexander	.10	.05	.01
☐ 16 Bryan Barker	.10	.05	.01
☐ 17 Louie Aguiar	.10	.05	.01
☐ 18 Karim Abdul-Jabbar	1.25	.55	.16
☐ 19 Greg DeLong	.10	.05	.01
☐ 20 Drew Bledsoe	1.25	.55	.16
☐ 21 Jim Everett	.10	.05	.01
☐ 22 Keith Elias	.10	.05	.01
☐ 23 Richie Anderson	.10	.05	.01
☐ 24 Joe Aska	.10	.05	.01
☐ 25 Barrett Brooks	.10	.05	.01
☐ 26 Jerome Bettis	.40	.18	.05
☐ 27 Darryl Ashmore	.10	.05	.01
☐ 28 Tony Berti	.10	.05	.01
☐ 29 Frank Pollack	.10	.05	.01
☐ 30 Joey Galloway	.40	.18	.05
☐ 31 Jason Maniecki	.10	.05	.01
☐ 32 Trent Green	.20	.09	.03
☐ 33 Pat Carter	.10	.05	.01
☐ 34 Ruben Brown	.10	.05	.01
☐ 35 Kerry Collins	1.00	.45	.12
☐ 36 Keith Jennings	.10	.05	.01
☐ 37 Randall Godfrey	.10	.05	.01
☐ 38 David Diaz-Infante	.10	.05	.01
☐ 39 Derek Price	.10	.05	.01
☐ 40 William Henderson	.10	.05	.01
☐ 41 James Ritchey	.10	.05	.01
☐ 42 Richard Dent	.10	.05	.01
☐ 43 Ben Coleman	.10	.05	.01
☐ 44 Shane Burton	.10	.05	.01
☐ 45 Dixon Edwards	.10	.05	.01
☐ 46 Ted Johnson	.10	.05	.01
☐ 47 Harry Boatswain	.10	.05	.01
☐ 48 Derrick Fenner	.10	.05	.01
☐ 49 Ty Detmer	.20	.09	.03
☐ 50 Corey Holliday	.10	.05	.01
☐ 51 Jerry Rice	1.25	.55	.16
☐ 52 Boomer Esiason	.20	.09	.03
☐ 53 Jeff Pahukoa	.10	.05	.01
☐ 54 Scott Otis	.10	.05	.01
☐ 55 Darick Holmes	.20	.09	.03
☐ 56 Frank Garcia	.10	.05	.01
☐ 57 Michael Lowery	.10	.05	.01
☐ 58 Jeff Blake	.40	.18	.05
☐ 59 Dale Hellestrae	.10	.05	.01
☐ 60 John Elway	1.00	.45	.12
☐ 61 Barry Sanders	1.25	.55	.16
☐ 62 Dorsey Levens	.20	.09	.03
☐ 63 James Roberson	.10	.05	.01
☐ 64 Jim Harbaugh	.20	.09	.03
☐ 65 Travis Davis	.10	.05	.01
☐ 66 Marcus Allen	.40	.18	.05
☐ 67 Steve Emtman	.10	.05	.01
☐ 68 Martin Harrison	.10	.05	.01
☐ 69 Curtis Martin	1.25	.55	.16
☐ 70 Anthony Newman	.10	.05	.01
☐ 71 Ron Stone	.10	.05	.01
☐ 72 Reggie Cobb	.10	.05	.01
☐ 73 Robert Jenkins	.10	.05	.01
☐ 74 Morris Unutoa	.10	.05	.01
☐ 75 Kordell Stewart	1.00	.45	.12
☐ 76 Raylee Johnson	.10	.05	.01
☐ 77 Tommy Thompson	.10	.05	.01
☐ 78 Dou Innocent	.10	.05	.01
☐ 79 Jim Pyne	.10	.05	.01
☐ 80 Jim Kelly	.40	.18	.05
☐ 81 Leeland McElroy	.20	.09	.03
☐ 82 Dan Stryzinski	.10	.05	.01
☐ 83 James Roe	.10	.05	.01
☐ 84 Anthony Johnson	.20	.09	.03
☐ 85 Chris Villarrial	.10	.05	.01
☐ 86 Kerry Joseph	.10	.05	.01
☐ 87 Emmitt Smith	2.50	1.10	.30
☐ 88 Jeff Lewis	.20	.09	.03
☐ 89 Kerwin Waldroup	.10	.05	.01
☐ 90 Aaron Taylor	.10	.05	.01
☐ 91 Sheddrick Wilson	.10	.05	.01
☐ 92 Chris Hetherington	.10	.05	.01
☐ 93 Bryan Schwartz	.10	.05	.01
☐ 94 Reggie Tongue	.10	.05	.01
☐ 95 Dan Marino	2.50	1.10	.30
☐ 96 Warren Moon	.20	.09	.03
☐ 97 Pio Sagapolutele	.10	.05	.01
☐ 98 Austin Robbins	.10	.05	.01
☐ 99 Stan White	.10	.05	.01
☐ 100 Keyshawn Johnson	.40	.18	.05
☐ 101 Napoleon Kaufman	.20	.09	.03
☐ 102 Ricky Watters	.20	.09	.03
☐ 103 Jon Witman	.20	.09	.03
☐ 104 Jermaine Ross	.10	.05	.01
☐ 105 Leonard Russell	.10	.05	.01
☐ 106 Iheanyi Uwaezuoke	.20	.09	.03
☐ 107 Gino Torretta	.20	.09	.03
☐ 108 Robb Thomas	.10	.05	.01
☐ 109 Shar Pourdanesh	.10	.05	.01
☐ 110 Gabe Northern	.10	.05	.01

1997 Pacific Dynagon Careers

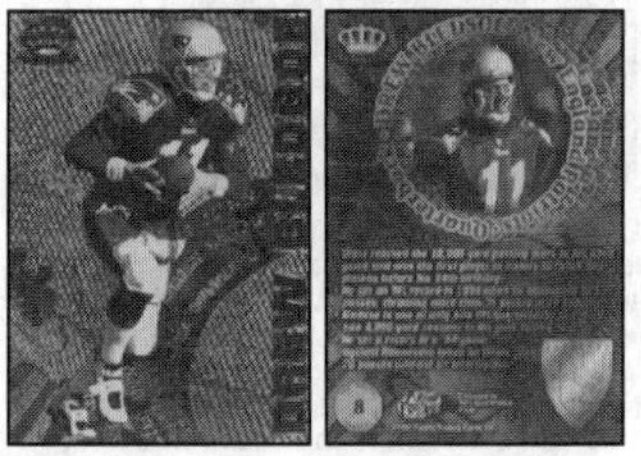

Randomly inserted in packs at a rate of two in 271, this set honors ten of the NFL's all-time greats and their individual achievements. Foiled in gold, the fronts feature color action player images on a football background. The backs carry information about the player's achievements.

	MINT	NRMT	EXC
COMPLETE SET (10)	700.00	325.00	90.00
COMMON CARD (1-10)	40.00	18.00	5.00

*COLOR CARDS: 2X TO 4X BASIC CARDS

☐ 1 Jim Kelly	50.00	22.00	6.25
☐ 2 Emmitt Smith	150.00	70.00	19.00
☐ 3 John Elway	75.00	34.00	9.50
☐ 4 Barry Sanders	80.00	36.00	10.00
☐ 5 Brett Favre	150.00	70.00	19.00
☐ 6 Reggie White	40.00	18.00	5.00
☐ 7 Dan Marino	150.00	70.00	19.00
☐ 8 Drew Bledsoe	80.00	36.00	10.00
☐ 9 Jerry Rice	80.00	36.00	10.00
☐ 10 Steve Young	70.00	32.00	8.75

1997 Pacific Dynagon Player of the Week

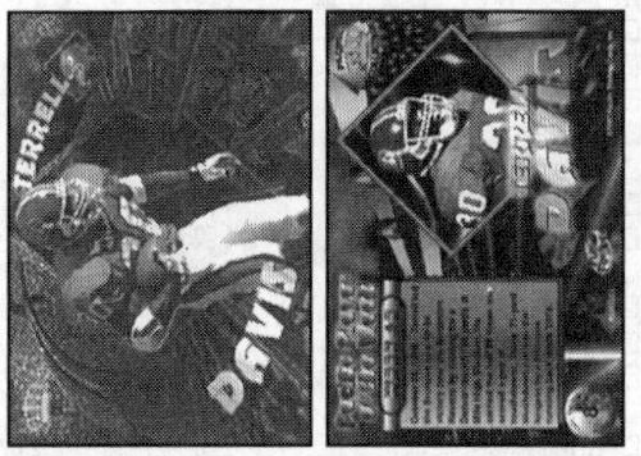

Randomly inserted in packs at a rate of one in 37, this 20-card set features color action player images of the weekly winners from the 1996 season, as voted on by visitors to the Pacific Trading Cards website, and a 1996 MVP, Super Bowl MVP, and Pro Bowl MVP.

	MINT	NRMT	EXC
COMPLETE SET (20)	400.00	180.00	50.00
COMMON CARD (1-20)	8.00	3.60	1.00
☐ 1 Karim Abdul-Jabbar	20.00	9.00	2.50
☐ 2 Eddie George	30.00	13.50	3.70
☐ 3 Curtis Martin	20.00	9.00	2.50
☐ 4 Mark Brunell	20.00	9.00	2.50
☐ 5 John Elway	15.00	6.75	1.85
☐ 6 Drew Bledsoe	20.00	9.00	2.50
☐ 7 Emmitt Smith	40.00	18.00	5.00
☐ 8 Terrell Davis	20.00	9.00	2.50
☐ 9 Troy Aikman	20.00	9.00	2.50
☐ 10 Jerry Rice	20.00	9.00	2.50
☐ 11 Dan Marino	40.00	18.00	5.00
☐ 12 Barry Sanders	20.00	9.00	2.50
☐ 13 Brett Favre	40.00	18.00	5.00
☐ 14 Steve Young	15.00	6.75	1.85
☐ 15 Kerry Collins	20.00	9.00	2.50
☐ 16 Eddie Kennison	10.00	4.50	1.25
☐ 17 Terry Allen	8.00	3.60	1.00
☐ 18 Brett Favre	40.00	18.00	5.00
☐ 19 Desmond Howard	8.00	3.60	1.00
☐ 20 Mark Brunell	20.00	9.00	2.50

1997 Pacific Dynagon Royal Connections

Randomly inserted in packs at a rate of one in 73, this 30-card set features color player photos of 15 of the best quarterback-receiver combinations in the league. Each card is die-cut and can stand alone or be matched up with its companion card to form a complete pair.

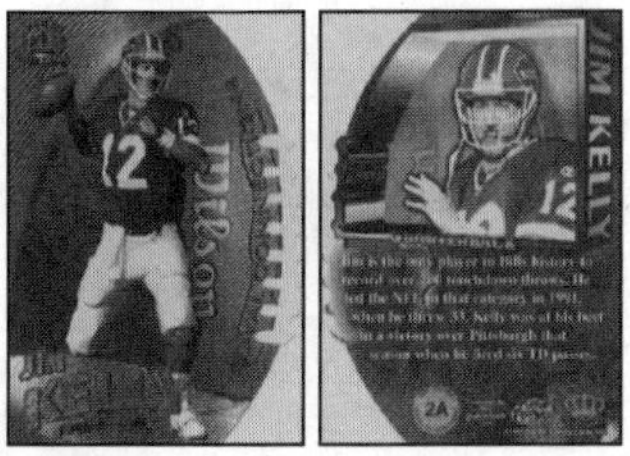

	MINT	NRMT	EXC
COMPLETE SET (30)	500.00	220.00	60.00
COMMON CARD (1A-15B)	10.00	4.50	1.25
☐ 1A Kent Graham	10.00	4.50	1.25
☐ 1B Larry Centers	10.00	4.50	1.25
☐ 2A Jim Kelly	20.00	9.00	2.50
☐ 2B Andre Reed	15.00	6.75	1.85
☐ 3A Kerry Collins	40.00	18.00	5.00
☐ 3B Wesley Walls	10.00	4.50	1.25
☐ 4A Jeff Blake	15.00	6.75	1.85
☐ 4B Carl Pickens	15.00	6.75	1.85
☐ 5A Troy Aikman	40.00	18.00	5.00
☐ 5B Michael Irvin	20.00	9.00	2.50
☐ 6A John Elway	30.00	13.50	3.70
☐ 6B Shannon Sharpe	10.00	4.50	1.25
☐ 7A Brett Favre	75.00	34.00	9.50
☐ 7B Antonio Freeman	20.00	9.00	2.50
☐ 8A Mark Brunell	40.00	18.00	5.00
☐ 8B Keenan McCardell	10.00	4.50	1.25
☐ 9A Dan Marino	75.00	34.00	9.50
☐ 9B O.J. McDuffie	15.00	6.75	1.85
☐ 10A Brad Johnson	10.00	4.50	1.25
☐ 10B Jake Reed	10.00	4.50	1.25
☐ 11A Drew Bledsoe	40.00	18.00	5.00
☐ 11B Terry Glenn	30.00	13.50	3.70
☐ 12A Ty Detmer	15.00	6.75	1.85
☐ 12B Irving Fryar	10.00	4.50	1.25
☐ 13A Kordell Stewart	30.00	13.50	3.70
☐ 13B Charles Johnson	10.00	4.50	1.25
☐ 14A Tony Banks	20.00	9.00	2.50
☐ 14B Isaac Bruce	20.00	9.00	2.50
☐ 15A Steve Young	25.00	11.00	3.10
☐ 15B Jerry Rice	40.00	18.00	5.00

1997 Pacific Dynagon Tandems

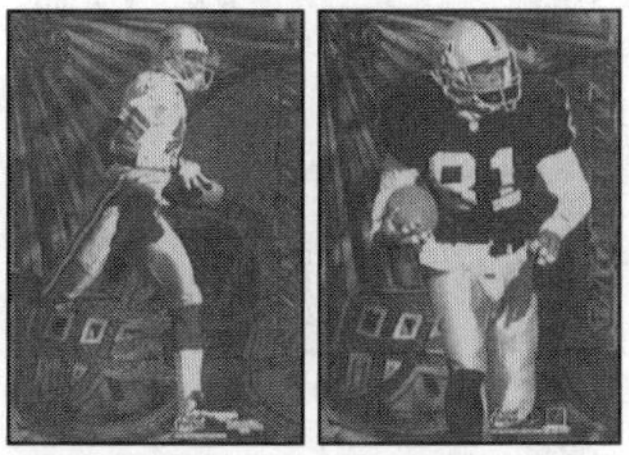

Randomly inserted at the rate of one in 37 packs, this 72-card set features the same 144 players from the main set but are matched up to form 72 "double-fronted" cards that are foiled in emerald.

	MINT	NRMT	EXC
COMPLETE SET (72)	1400.00	650.00	180.00
COMMON CARD (1-72)	12.00	5.50	1.50
☐ 1 Jerome Bettis Eddie George	100.00	45.00	12.50
☐ 2 Jamal Anderson Eric Moulds	20.00	9.00	2.50
☐ 3 Kerry Collins Kordell Stewart	70.00	32.00	8.75
☐ 4 Jeff Blake Ty Detmer	20.00	9.00	2.50
☐ 5 Michael Irvin Tim Brown	20.00	9.00	2.50
☐ 6 Deion Sanders Ray Zellars	30.00	13.50	3.70
☐ 7 Emmitt Smith Steve Young	140.00	65.00	17.50
☐ 8 Terrell Davis Barry Sanders	80.00	36.00	10.00
☐ 9 John Elway Dan Marino	150.00	70.00	19.00
☐ 10 Robert Brooks Eddie Kennison	30.00	13.50	3.70
☐ 11 Mark Chmura Shannon Sharpe	15.00	6.75	1.85
☐ 12 Brett Favre Mark Brunell	150.00	70.00	19.00
☐ 13 Antonio Freeman Isaac Bruce	20.00	9.00	2.50
☐ 14 Desmond Howard Natrone Means	20.00	9.00	2.50
☐ 15 Reggie White Keyshawn Johnson	20.00	9.00	2.50
☐ 16 Edgar Bennett Chris Sanders	12.00	5.50	1.50
☐ 17 Terry Glenn Jerry Rice	80.00	36.00	10.00
☐ 18 Steve McNair Karim Abdul-Jabbar	50.00	22.00	6.25
☐ 19 Marshall Faulk Tamarick Vanover	20.00	9.00	2.50
☐ 20 Gus Frerotte	20.00	9.00	2.50

Brad Johnson			
□ 21 Jim Kelly	30.00	13.50	3.70
Tim Biakabutuka			
□ 22 Lawrence Phillips	15.00	6.75	1.85
Ben Coates			
□ 23 Napoleon Kaufman	30.00	13.50	3.70
Terrell Owens			
□ 24 Elvis Grbac	15.00	6.75	1.85
Junior Seau			
□ 25 Drew Bledsoe	80.00	36.00	10.00
Tony Banks			
□ 26 Curtis Martin	80.00	36.00	10.00
Troy Aikman			
□ 27 Curtis Conway	15.00	6.75	1.85
Brett Perriman			
□ 28 Bobby Engram	12.00	5.50	1.50
Larry Centers			
□ 29 Raymont Harris	12.00	5.50	1.50
Eric Metcalf			
□ 30 Dave Krieg	12.00	5.50	1.50
Derrick Alexander			
□ 31 Rashaan Salaam	20.00	9.00	2.50
Leeland McElroy			
□ 32 Ki-Jana Carter	20.00	9.00	2.50
Herman Moore			
□ 33 Garrison Hearst	15.00	6.75	1.85
Earnest Byner			
□ 34 Carl Pickens	15.00	6.75	1.85
Frank Sanders			
□ 35 Darnay Scott	15.00	6.75	1.85
Michael Jackson			
□ 36 Chris Boniol	12.00	5.50	1.50
Kent Graham			
□ 37 Herschel Walker	20.00	9.00	2.50
Thurman Thomas			
□ 38 Ed McCaffrey	12.00	5.50	1.50
Quinn Early			
□ 39 Aeneas Williams	15.00	6.75	1.85
Mike Alstott			
□ 40 Scott Mitchell	12.00	5.50	1.50
Mark Carrier			
□ 41 Bert Emanuel	12.00	5.50	1.50
Henry Ellard			
□ 42 Bobby Hebert	15.00	6.75	1.85
Trent Dilfer			
□ 43 Terence Mathis	15.00	6.75	1.85
Andre Reed			
□ 44 Vinny Testaverde	15.00	6.75	1.85
Chris Warren			
□ 45 Bruce Smith	20.00	9.00	2.50
Kevin Greene			
□ 46 Anthony Johnson	15.00	6.75	1.85
Terry Allen			
□ 47 Wesley Walls	15.00	6.75	1.85
Errict Rhett			
□ 48 John Friesz	12.00	5.50	1.50
Jeff Hostetler			
□ 49 Joey Galloway	20.00	9.00	2.50
Leslie Shepherd			
□ 50 Michael McCrary	12.00	5.50	1.50
Cedric Jones			
□ 51 Lamar Smith	12.00	5.50	1.50
Courtney Hawkins			
□ 52 Rickey Dudley	15.00	6.75	1.85
Jason Dunn			
□ 53 Irving Fryar	12.00	5.50	1.50
Tony Martin			
□ 54 Ted Popson	15.00	6.75	1.85
Ricky Watters			
□ 55 Chad Brown	15.00	6.75	1.85
Zach Thomas			
□ 56 Mike Tomczak	15.00	6.75	1.85
Stan Humphries			
□ 57 Rod Woodson	15.00	6.75	1.85
Willie McGinest			
□ 58 Terrell Fletcher	12.00	5.50	1.50
Jerris McPhail			
□ 59 O.J. McDuffie	15.00	6.75	1.85
Cris Carter			
□ 60 Jake Reed	20.00	9.00	2.50
Marcus Allen			
□ 61 Robert Smith	15.00	6.75	1.85
Greg Hill			
□ 62 Jim Everett	12.00	5.50	1.50
Dave Brown			
□ 63 Michael Haynes	12.00	5.50	1.50
James McKeehan			
□ 64 Haywood Jeffires	12.00	5.50	1.50
Sean Dawkins			
□ 65 Rodney Hampton	15.00	6.75	1.85
Adrian Murrell			
□ 66 Danny Kanell	30.00	13.50	3.70
Marvin Harrison			
□ 67 Thomas Lewis	12.00	5.50	1.50
Dale Carter			
□ 68 Wayne Chrebet	12.00	5.50	1.50
Ken Dilger			
□ 69 Neil O'Donnell	15.00	6.75	1.85
Chris Chandler			
□ 70 Jim Harbaugh	20.00	9.00	2.50
Jimmy Smith			
□ 71 Derrick Thomas	20.00	9.00	2.50
Tony Boselli			
□ 72 Keenan McCardell	15.00	6.75	1.85
Kimble Anders			

1995 Pacific Gridiron

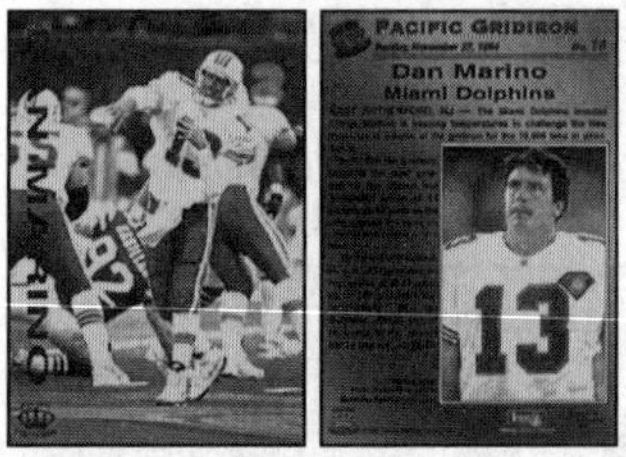

Pacific produced 750 hobby cases (blue foil) and 750 retail cases (red foil). Each set also had a parallel set representing 10 percent of the sets produced. The hobby parallel set was stamped in platinum foil, while the retail parallel set was stamped in copper foil. Just 30 "presidential gold" sets were produced, with two gold cards seeded per hobby or retail case.This 100-card set measures 3 1/2" by 5". The fronts feature full-color action shots which bleed to the borders. The backs have a write-up of the player's performance in the game pictured in the front photo. The back also has an inset photo. Pacific founders Mike and Cheryl Cramer took many of the photos used in this set. Rookie Cards in this set include Jeff Blake, Ki-Jana Carter, and Steve McNair. Natrone Means appears on four different promo cards as listed below.

	MINT	NRMT	EXC
COMP. BLUE/RED SET (100)	125.00	55.00	15.50
COMMON BLUE/RED (1-100)	1.00	.45	.12
□ 1 Natrone Means	2.00	.90	.25
□ 2 Dave Meggett	1.00	.45	.12
□ 3 Curtis Conway	2.00	.90	.25
□ 4 Sam Adams	1.00	.45	.12
□ 5 Qadry Ismail	1.50	.70	.19
□ 6 Steve Young	4.00	1.80	.50
□ 7 Errict Rhett	2.00	.90	.25
□ 8 Nate Lewis	1.00	.45	.12
□ 9 Barry Sanders	5.00	2.20	.60
□ 10 Sterling Sharpe	1.50	.70	.19
□ 11 Steve Beuerlein	1.00	.45	.12
□ 12 Irving Spikes	1.50	.70	.19
□ 13 Byron Bam Morris	1.50	.70	.19
□ 14 Eric Metcalf	1.50	.70	.19
□ 15 Michael Irvin	2.00	.90	.25
□ 16 Dan Marino	10.00	4.50	1.25
□ 17 Stan Humphries	1.50	.70	.19
□ 18 Leroy Hoard	1.00	.45	.12
□ 19 Marcus Allen	2.00	.90	.25
□ 20 Barry Foster	1.50	.70	.19
□ 21 Ronald Moore	1.00	.45	.12
□ 22 Rodney Hampton	1.50	.70	.19
□ 23 Ben Coates	1.50	.70	.19
□ 24 Vernon Turner	1.00	.45	.12
□ 25 Shannon Sharpe	1.50	.70	.19
□ 26 Larry Centers	1.50	.70	.19
□ 27 Mack Strong	1.00	.45	.12
□ 28 Reggie White	2.00	.90	.25
□ 29 Harvey Williams	1.00	.45	.12
□ 30 Darnay Scott	2.00	.90	.25
□ 31 Drew Bledsoe	5.00	2.20	.60
□ 32 Marshall Faulk	3.00	1.35	.35
□ 33 Troy Aikman	5.00	2.20	.60
□ 34 Boomer Esiason	1.50	.70	.19
□ 35 Bobby Hebert	1.00	.45	.12
□ 36 Brian Mitchell	1.00	.45	.12
□ 37 Andre Rison	1.50	.70	.19
□ 38 Brett Favre	10.00	4.50	1.25
□ 39 Don Majkowski	1.00	.45	.12
□ 40 Johnny Johnson	1.00	.45	.12
□ 41 Mark Carrier WR	1.50	.70	.19
□ 42 James Joseph	1.00	.45	.12
□ 43 Mario Bates	2.00	.90	.25
□ 44 Craig Heyward	1.50	.70	.19
□ 45 Henry Ellard	1.50	.70	.19
□ 46 Thurman Thomas	2.00	.90	.25
□ 47 Jerome Bettis	2.50	1.10	.30
□ 48 Dave Brown	1.50	.70	.19
□ 49 Lorenzo White	1.00	.45	.12
□ 50 Joe Montana	5.00	2.20	.60
□ 51 Vinny Testaverde	1.50	.70	.19
□ 52 Lake Dawson	1.50	.70	.19
□ 53 Michael Timpson	1.00	.45	.12
□ 54 Ricky Ervins	1.00	.45	.12
□ 55 Cris Carter	2.00	.90	.25
□ 56 Raymont Harris	1.00	.45	.12
□ 57 Andre Coleman	1.00	.45	.12
□ 58 Craig Erickson	1.00	.45	.12
□ 59 Jeff Hostetler	1.50	.70	.19
□ 60 Deion Sanders	3.00	1.35	.35
□ 61 Eric Turner	1.00	.45	.12
□ 62 Daryl Johnston	1.50	.70	.19
□ 63 Bernie Parmalee	1.50	.70	.19
□ 64 Ricky Watters	2.00	.90	.25
□ 65 David Palmer	1.50	.70	.19
□ 66 Aaron Glenn	1.00	.45	.12
□ 67 Todd Kinchen	1.00	.45	.12
□ 68 Edgar Bennett	1.50	.70	.19
□ 69 Mel Gray	1.00	.45	.12
□ 70 Randall Cunningham	1.50	.70	.19
□ 71 Michael Haynes	1.50	.70	.19
□ 72 Chris Miller	1.00	.45	.12
□ 73 Glyn Milburn	1.00	.45	.12
□ 74 Steve McNair	7.00	3.10	.85
□ 75 Lewis Tillman	1.00	.45	.12
□ 76 Chuck Levy	1.00	.45	.12
□ 77 Carl Pickens	2.00	.90	.25
□ 78 Michael Bates	1.00	.45	.12
□ 79 Jeff Blake	3.00	1.35	.35
□ 80 O.J. McDuffie	2.00	.90	.25
□ 81 Tim Brown	2.00	.90	.25
□ 82 Haywood Jeffires	1.00	.45	.12
□ 83 Jeff Burris	1.00	.45	.12
□ 84 John Elway	4.00	1.80	.50
□ 85 Charles Johnson	1.50	.70	.19
□ 86 Emmitt Smith	10.00	4.50	1.25
□ 87 William Floyd	2.00	.90	.25
□ 88 Herschel Walker	1.50	.70	.19
□ 89 Rick Mirer	2.00	.90	.25
□ 90 Roosevelt Potts	1.00	.45	.12
□ 91 Rod Woodson	1.50	.70	.19
□ 92 Greg Hill	1.50	.70	.19
□ 93 Junior Seau	2.00	.90	.25
□ 94 Dave Krieg	1.00	.45	.12
□ 95 Jim Kelly	2.00	.90	.25
□ 96 Warren Moon	1.50	.70	.19
□ 97 Leroy Thompson	1.00	.45	.12
□ 98 Ki-Jana Carter	3.00	1.35	.35
□ 99 Herman Moore	3.00	1.35	.35
□ 100 Jerry Rice	5.00	2.20	.60
□ P1 Natrone Means	2.00	.90	.25
Bronze Foil			
Numbered 100			
□ P2 Natrone Means	2.00	.90	.25
Gold Foil			
Numbered 100			
□ P3 Natrone Means	2.00	.90	.25
Red Foil			
Numbered 100			
□ P4 Natrone Means	2.00	.90	.25
Blue Foil			
Numbered 100			

1995 Pacific Gridiron Copper/Platinum

This 100 card parallel is differentiated from the basic card by having platinum/copper foil on the front of the card rather than the standard blue foil. The copper were inserted into hobby packs only and represent only 10% of the sets produced. The platinum parallel were inserted into retail packs at the same rate.

	MINT	NRMT	EXC
COMPLETE SET (100)	800.00	350.00	100.00
COMMON CARD (1-100)	4.00	1.80	.50

*VETERAN STARS: 4X TO 8X BASIC CARDS
*YOUNG STARS: 3X TO 6X BASIC CARDS
*RCs: 2X TO 4X BASIC CARDS

1995 Pacific Gridiron Gold

This 100 card parallel is differentiated from the basic card by having gold foil on the front of the card rather than the standard red foil. These were inserted into retail packs and represent only 10% of the sets produced.

	MINT	NRMT	EXC
COMMON CARD (1-100)	50.00	22.00	6.25
SEMISTARS	100.00	45.00	12.50

*VETERAN STARS: 75X TO 150X BASIC CARDS
*YOUNG STARS/RCs: 40X TO 80X BASIC CARDS

1996 Pacific Gridiron

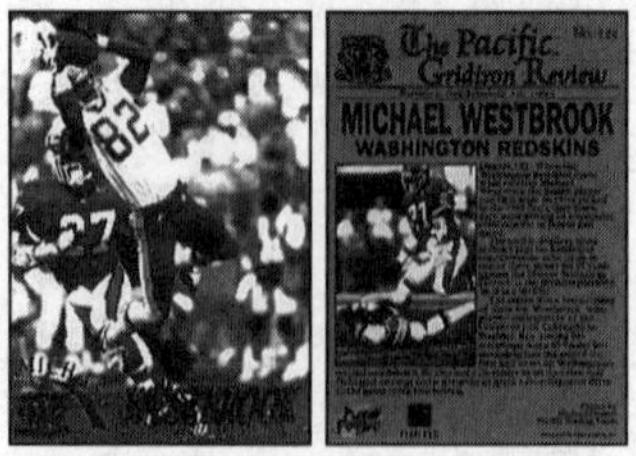

The 1996 Pacific Gridiron set was issued in one series totalling 125 cards. The set was issued in 2-card packs, with 36 packs per box and 20 boxes per case. The oversized set measures 3 1/2" by 5". The set is sequenced in alphabetical order within alphabetical team order. Aaron Hayden is the only Rookie Card of note in this set. A Chris Warren Sample card was produced and priced below.

	MINT	NRMT	EXC
COMPLETE SET (125)	100.00	45.00	12.50
COMMON CARD (1-125)	.75	.35	.09
□ 1 Larry Centers	1.25	.55	.16
□ 2 Garrison Hearst	1.25	.55	.16
□ 3 Dave Krieg	.75	.35	.09
□ 4 Frank Sanders	1.25	.55	.16
□ 5 Jamal Anderson	4.00	1.80	.50
□ 6 J.J. Birden	.75	.35	.09
□ 7 Eric Metcalf	1.25	.55	.16
□ 8 Jeff George	1.25	.55	.16
□ 9 Cornelius Bennett	1.25	.55	.16
□ 10 Todd Collins	1.25	.55	.16
□ 11 Darick Holmes	1.25	.55	.16
□ 12 Jim Kelly	2.00	.90	.25
□ 13 Bryce Paup	1.25	.55	.16
□ 14 Bob Christian	.75	.35	.09
□ 15 Kerry Collins	7.00	3.10	.85
□ 16 Pete Metzelaars	.75	.35	.09
□ 17 Derrick Moore	.75	.35	.09
□ 18 Curtis Conway	2.00	.90	.25
□ 19 Jim Flanigan	.75	.35	.09
□ 20 Erik Kramer	.75	.35	.09
□ 21 Rashaan Salaam	2.00	.90	.25
□ 22 Eric Bieniemy	.75	.35	.09
□ 23 Jeff Blake	2.00	.90	.25
□ 24 Tony McGee	.75	.35	.09
□ 25 Darnay Scott	1.25	.55	.16
□ 26 Vashone Adams	.75	.35	.09
□ 27 Leroy Hoard	.75	.35	.09
□ 28 Andre Rison	1.25	.55	.16
□ 29 Tommy Vardell	.75	.35	.09
□ 30 Troy Aikman	5.00	2.20	.60
□ 31 Michael Irvin	2.00	.90	.25
□ 32 Daryl Johnston	1.25	.55	.16
□ 33 Deion Sanders	3.00	1.35	.35
□ 34 Emmitt Smith	10.00	4.50	1.25
□ 35 Terrell Davis	8.00	3.60	1.00
□ 36 John Elway	4.00	1.80	.50
□ 37 Ed McCaffrey	.75	.35	.09
□ 38 Anthony Miller	1.25	.55	.16
□ 39 Scott Mitchell	1.25	.55	.16
□ 40 Brett Perriman	1.25	.55	.16
□ 41 Barry Sanders	5.00	2.20	.60
□ 42 Chris Spielman	1.25	.55	.16
□ 43 Edgar Bennett	1.25	.55	.16
□ 44 Robert Brooks	2.00	.90	.25
□ 45 Brett Favre	10.00	4.50	1.25
□ 46 Antonio Freeman	3.00	1.35	.35
□ 47 Reggie White	2.00	.90	.25
□ 48 Haywood Jeffires	.75	.35	.09
□ 49 Steve McNair	5.00	2.20	.60
□ 50 Rodney Thomas	.75	.35	.09
□ 51 Frank Wycheck	.75	.35	.09
□ 52 Ashley Ambrose	.75	.35	.09
□ 53 Mark Brunell	5.00	2.20	.60
□ 54 Ken Dilger	1.25	.55	.16
□ 55 Marshall Faulk	2.00	.90	.25
□ 56 Jim Harbaugh	1.25	.55	.16
□ 57 Tony Boselli	1.25	.55	.16
□ 58 Pete Mitchell	.75	.35	.09
□ 59 James O.Stewart	2.00	.90	.25
□ 60 Marcus Allen	2.00	.90	.25
□ 61 Steve Bono	1.25	.55	.16
□ 62 Lake Dawson	1.25	.55	.16
□ 63 Tamarick Vanover	2.00	.90	.25
□ 64 Bryan Cox	.75	.35	.09
□ 65 Dan Marino	10.00	4.50	1.25
□ 66 O.J. McDuffie	1.25	.55	.16
□ 67 Bernie Parmalee	.75	.35	.09
□ 68 Cris Carter	2.00	.90	.25
□ 69 Rocket Ismail	1.25	.55	.16
□ 70 Warren Moon	1.25	.55	.16
□ 71 Robert Smith	1.25	.55	.16
□ 72 Drew Bledsoe	5.00	2.20	.60
□ 73 Vincent Brisby	.75	.35	.09
□ 74 Ben Coates	1.25	.55	.16
□ 75 Curtis Martin	8.00	3.60	1.00
□ 76 Mario Bates	1.25	.55	.16
□ 77 Derek Brown RB	.75	.35	.09
□ 78 Jim Everett	.75	.35	.09
□ 79 Dave Brown	1.25	.55	.16
□ 80 Chris Calloway	.75	.35	.09
□ 81 Rodney Hampton	1.25	.55	.16
□ 82 Tyrone Wheatley	1.25	.55	.16
□ 83 Kyle Brady	1.25	.55	.16
□ 84 Wayne Chrebet	1.25	.55	.16
□ 85 Adrian Murrell	1.25	.55	.16
□ 86 Tim Brown	1.25	.55	.16
□ 87 Rob Carpenter	.75	.35	.09
□ 88 Charlie Garner	.75	.35	.09
□ 89 Daryl Hobbs	.75	.35	.09
□ 90 Napoleon Kaufman	1.25	.55	.16
□ 91 Rodney Peete	.75	.35	.09
□ 92 Ricky Watters	1.25	.55	.16
□ 93 Calvin Williams	2.00	.90	.25
□ 94 Kevin Greene	1.25	.55	.16
□ 95 Greg Lloyd	1.25	.55	.16
□ 96 Neil O'Donnell	1.25	.55	.16
□ 97 Erric Pegram	1.25	.55	.16
□ 98 Kordell Stewart	6.00	2.70	.75
□ 99 Yancey Thigpen	1.25	.55	.16
□ 100 Rod Woodson	1.25	.55	.16
□ 101 Isaac Bruce	2.00	.90	.25
□ 102 Jerome Bettis	2.00	.90	.25
□ 103 J.T. Thomas	.75	.35	.09
□ 104 Ronnie Harmon	.75	.35	.09
□ 105 Aaron Hayden	1.25	.55	.16
□ 106 Stan Humphries	1.25	.55	.16
□ 107 Alfred Pupunu	.75	.35	.09
□ 108 William Floyd	1.25	.55	.16
□ 109 Brent Jones	.75	.35	.09
□ 110 Jerry Rice	5.00	2.20	.60
□ 111 J.J. Stokes	2.00	.90	.25
□ 112 John Taylor	.75	.35	.09
□ 113 Steve Young	4.00	1.80	.50
□ 114 Harvey Williams	.75	.35	.09

	MINT	NRMT	EXC
☐ 115 John Friesz	.75	.35	.09
☐ 116 Joey Galloway	3.00	1.35	.35
☐ 117 Cortez Kennedy	1.25	.55	.16
☐ 118 Rick Mirer	1.25	.55	.16
☐ 119 Chris Warren	1.25	.55	.16
☐ 120 Trent Dilfer	1.25	.55	.16
☐ 121 Alvin Harper	.75	.35	.09
☐ 122 Errict Rhett	1.25	.55	.16
☐ 123 Terry Allen	1.25	.55	.16
☐ 124 Gus Frerotte	2.00	.90	.25
☐ 125 Michael Westbrook	2.00	.90	.25
☐ S1 Chris Warren Sample	1.50	.70	.19

1996 Pacific Gridiron Gold

This 125-card set is also a parallel to the regular Pacific Gridiron issue. These cards were inserted at a ratio of approximately two in 721 packs. According to the manufacturer, only 30 gold sets were produced.

	MINT	NRMT	EXC
COMMON CARD (1-125)	50.00	22.00	6.25
SEMISTARS	100.00	45.00	12.50

*STARS: 75X TO 150X BASIC CARDS
*YOUNG STARS: 40X TO 80X BASIC CARDS

1996 Pacific Gridiron Driving Force

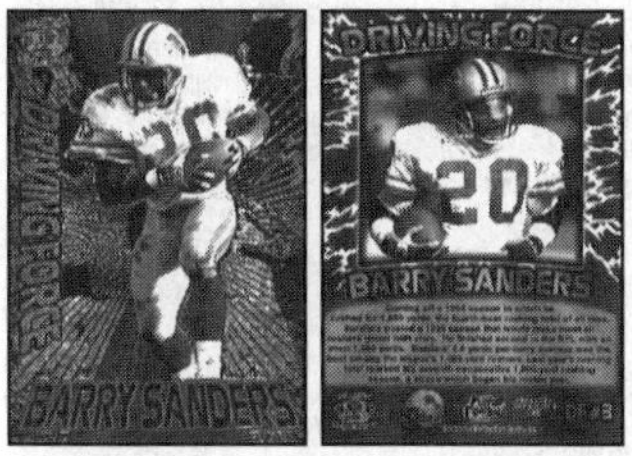

Randomly inserted in packs at a rate of one in 73, this 10-card set turns the spotlight towards some of the NFL's top running backs. The busy fronts include the words "Driving Force" on the left and the player's name on the bottom. The back contains another photo as well as some career textual information. The cards are numbered with a "DF" prefix

	MINT	NRMT	EXC
COMPLETE SET (10)	200.00	90.00	25.00
COMMON CARD (DF1-DF10)	12.00	5.50	1.50
☐ DF1 Chris Warren	12.00	5.50	1.50
☐ DF2 Emmitt Smith	50.00	22.00	6.25
☐ DF3 Barry Sanders	25.00	11.00	3.10
☐ DF4 Rashaan Salaam	16.00	7.25	2.00
☐ DF5 Errict Rhett	14.00	6.25	1.75
☐ DF6 Curtis Martin	30.00	13.50	3.70
☐ DF7 Garrison Hearst	14.00	6.25	1.75
☐ DF8 Marshall Faulk	16.00	7.25	2.00
☐ DF9 Terrell Davis	30.00	13.50	3.70
☐ DF10 Edgar Bennett	12.00	5.50	1.50

1996 Pacific Gridiron Gems

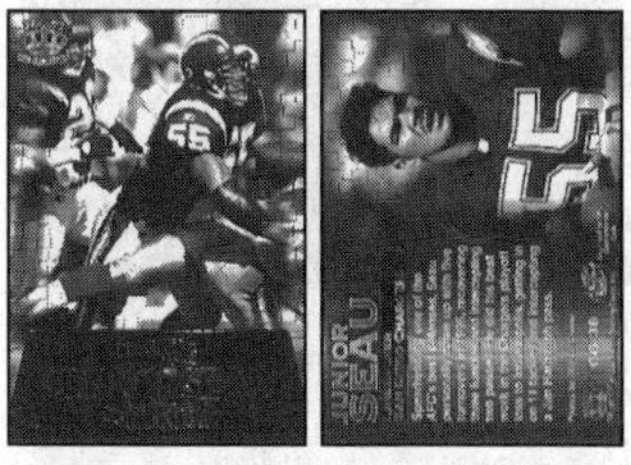

Randomly inserted in packs at a rate of three in four, this 50-card set contains photographs of leading NFL players. The cards are numbered with a "GG" prefix.

	MINT	NRMT	EXC
COMPLETE SET (50)	40.00	18.00	5.00
COMMON CARD (GG1-GG50)	.75	.35	.09
☐ GG1 J.J. Birden	.75	.35	.09
☐ GG2 Garrison Hearst	1.25	.55	.16
☐ GG3 Bryce Paup	.75	.35	.09
☐ GG4 Kerry Collins	3.00	1.35	.35
☐ GG5 Alonzo Spellman	.75	.35	.09
☐ GG6 Chris Zorich	.75	.35	.09
☐ GG7 Harold Green	.75	.35	.09
☐ GG8 Lee Johnson	.75	.35	.09
☐ GG9 Eric Zeier	.75	.35	.09
☐ GG10 Troy Aikman	3.00	1.35	.35
☐ GG11 Deion Sanders	2.00	.90	.25
☐ GG12 Emmitt Smith	6.00	2.70	.75
☐ GG13 John Elway	2.50	1.10	.30
☐ GG14 Mike Pritchard	.75	.35	.09
☐ GG15 Shane Bonham	.75	.35	.09
☐ GG16 Barry Sanders	3.00	1.35	.35
☐ GG17 Edgar Bennett	1.25	.55	.16
☐ GG18 Brett Favre	6.00	2.70	.75
☐ GG19 Reggie White	1.50	.70	.19
☐ GG20 Eddie Robinson	.75	.35	.09
☐ GG21 Marshall Faulk	1.50	.70	.19
☐ GG22 Brian Stablein	.75	.35	.09
☐ GG23 Don Davey	.75	.35	.09
☐ GG24 Neil Smith	.75	.35	.09
☐ GG25 Derrick Thomas	1.25	.55	.16
☐ GG26 Eric Green	.75	.35	.09
☐ GG27 Jake Reed	.75	.35	.09
☐ GG28 Troy Brown	.75	.35	.09
☐ GG29 Will Moore	.75	.35	.09
☐ GG30 Wesley Walls	.75	.35	.09
☐ GG31 Herschel Walker	.75	.35	.09
☐ GG32 Keyshawn Johnson	2.00	.90	.25
☐ GG33 Billy Joe Hobert	.75	.35	.09
☐ GG34 Ricky Watters	1.25	.55	.16
☐ GG35 Ernie Mills	.75	.35	.09
☐ GG36 Kordell Stewart	3.00	1.35	.35
☐ GG37 Terrell Fletcher	.75	.35	.09
☐ GG38 Junior Seau	1.50	.70	.19
☐ GG39 Elvis Grbac	.75	.35	.09
☐ GG40 Gary Plummer	.75	.35	.09
☐ GG41 Jerry Rice	3.00	1.35	.35
☐ GG42 Steve Young	2.50	1.10	.30
☐ GG43 Carlester Crumpler	.75	.35	.09
☐ GG44 Joey Galloway	1.50	.70	.19
☐ GG45 Cortez Kennedy	.75	.35	.09
☐ GG46 Chris Warren	1.25	.55	.16
☐ GG47 Greg Robinson	.75	.35	.09
☐ GG48 Errict Rhett	1.25	.55	.16
☐ GG49 Terry Allen	1.25	.55	.16
☐ GG50 Stanley Richard	.75	.35	.09

1996 Pacific Gridiron Gold Crown Die Cut Redemption

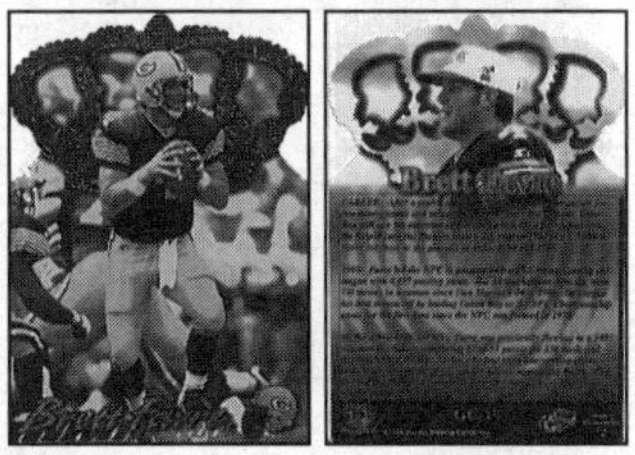

Randomly inserted in packs at a rate of one in 37, this 20-card set is available via redemption card only. Each redemption card bears one player's name and card number -- collectors can redeem their card for that player's Gold Crown Die-Cut. The cards, when received, are numbered with a "GC" prefix.

	MINT	NRMT	EXC
COMPLETE SET (20)	350.00	160.00	45.00
COMMON CARD (GC1-GC20)	10.00	4.50	1.25
☐ GC1 Barry Sanders	30.00	13.50	3.70
☐ GC2 Ricky Watters	10.00	4.50	1.25
☐ GC3 Troy Aikman	30.00	13.50	3.70
☐ GC4 Deion Sanders	20.00	9.00	2.50
☐ GC5 Kerry Collins	30.00	13.50	3.70
☐ GC6 Dan Marino	50.00	22.00	6.25
☐ GC7 Steve Young	20.00	9.00	2.50
☐ GC8 Drew Bledsoe	30.00	13.50	3.70
☐ GC9 Jerry Rice	30.00	13.50	3.70
☐ GC10 Steve McNair	25.00	11.00	3.10
☐ GC11 Joey Galloway	20.00	9.00	2.50
☐ GC12 John Elway	25.00	11.00	3.10
☐ GC13 Terrell Davis	35.00	16.00	4.40
☐ GC14 Rashaan Salaam	15.00	6.75	1.85
☐ GC15 Kordell Stewart	30.00	13.50	3.70
☐ GC16 Emmitt Smith	50.00	22.00	6.25
☐ GC17 Curtis Martin	35.00	16.00	4.40
☐ GC18 Marshall Faulk	20.00	9.00	2.50
☐ GC19 Brett Favre	50.00	22.00	6.25
☐ GC20 Chris Warren	10.00	4.50	1.25

1996 Pacific Gridiron Rock Solid Rookies

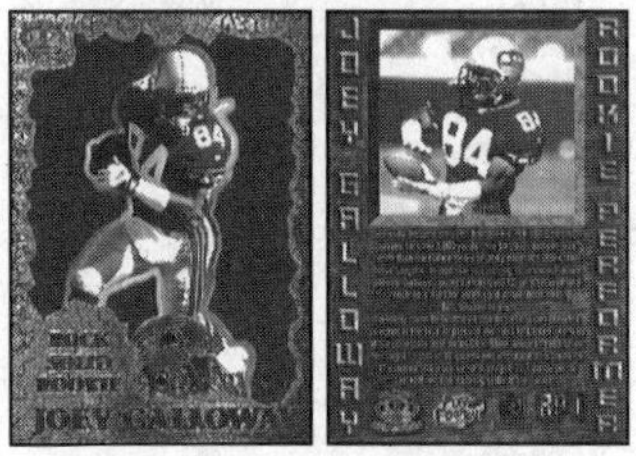

Randomly inserted in packs at a rate of one in 121, this six-card set features leading 1995 rookies. Similar to other Pacific Gridiron cards, they measure 3 1/2" by 5". The cards are numbered with an "RP" prefix.

	MINT	NRMT	EXC
COMPLETE SET (6)	150.00	70.00	19.00
COMMON CARD (RP1-RP6)	20.00	9.00	2.50
☐ RP1 Joey Galloway	30.00	13.50	3.70
☐ RP2 Napoleon Kaufman	20.00	9.00	2.50
☐ RP3 Michael Westbrook	25.00	11.00	3.10
☐ RP4 Kerry Collins	40.00	18.00	5.00
☐ RP5 Aaron Hayden	20.00	9.00	2.50
☐ RP6 Kordell Stewart	40.00	18.00	5.00

1996 Pacific Invincible

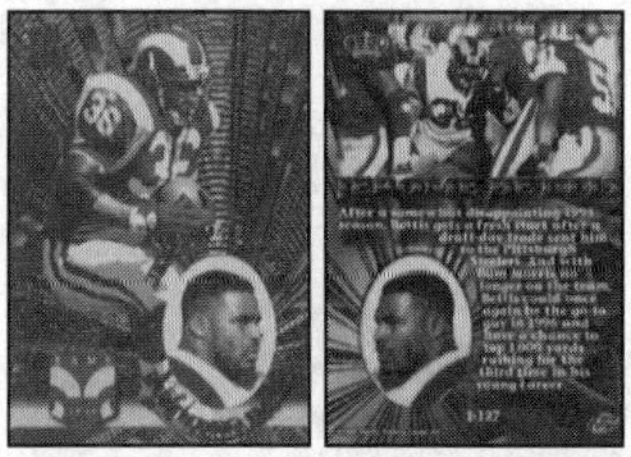

The 1996 Pacific Invincible set was issued in one series totalling 150 cards and distributed in three-card packs. The set offers a "cel" inlay in each of the 150 cards. Each card carried an "I" prefix on the card number. Several parallel card versions were also produced: bronze foil for hobby and silver foil for retail. There was a Platinum Blue series made which parallels both hobby and retail that was more difficult to pull.

	MINT	NRMT	EXC
COMPLETE SET (150)	175.00	80.00	22.00
COMMON CARD (1-150)	.75	.35	.09
☐ 1 Larry Centers	1.25	.55	.16
☐ 2 Garrison Hearst	1.25	.55	.16
☐ 3 Seth Joyner	.75	.35	.09
☐ 4 Simeon Rice	2.50	1.10	.30
☐ 5 Eric Swann	1.25	.55	.16
☐ 6 Bert Emanuel	1.25	.55	.16
☐ 7 Jeff George	1.25	.55	.16
☐ 8 Craig Heyward	.75	.35	.09
☐ 9 Terance Mathis	.75	.35	.09
☐ 10 Eric Metcalf	1.25	.55	.16
☐ 11 Derrick Alexander WR	1.25	.55	.16
☐ 12 Leroy Hoard	.75	.35	.09
☐ 13 Andre Rison	1.25	.55	.16
☐ 14 Tommy Vardell	.75	.35	.09
☐ 15 Eric Zeier	1.25	.55	.16
☐ 16 Jim Kelly	2.00	.90	.25
☐ 17 Eric Moulds	4.00	1.80	.50
☐ 18 Bryce Paup	1.25	.55	.16
☐ 19 Bruce Smith	2.00	.90	.25
☐ 20 Thurman Thomas	2.00	.90	.25
☐ 21 Tim Biakabutuka	4.00	1.80	.50
☐ 22 Blake Brockermeyer	.75	.35	.09
☐ 23 Kerry Collins	8.00	3.60	1.00
☐ 24 Howard Griffith	.75	.35	.09
☐ 25 Lamar Lathon	.75	.35	.09
☐ 26 Mark Carrier DB	.75	.35	.09
☐ 27 Curtis Conway	2.00	.90	.25
☐ 28 Erik Kramer	.75	.35	.09
☐ 29 Rashaan Salaam	2.00	.90	.25
☐ 30 Alonzo Spellman	.75	.35	.09
☐ 32 Harold Green	.75	.35	.09
☐ 33 Carl Pickens	2.00	.90	.25
☐ 34 Darnay Scott	1.25	.55	.16
☐ 35 Dan Wilkinson	.75	.35	.09
☐ 36 Troy Aikman	6.00	2.70	.75
☐ 37 Jay Novacek	1.25	.55	.16
☐ 38 Deion Sanders	4.00	1.80	.50
☐ 39 Emmitt Smith	12.00	5.50	1.50
☐ 40 Kevin Williams	.75	.35	.09
☐ 41 Terrell Davis	10.00	4.50	1.25
☐ 42 John Elway	5.00	2.20	.60
☐ 43 Anthony Miller	1.25	.55	.16
☐ 44 Michael Dean Perry	.75	.35	.09
☐ 45 Shannon Sharpe	1.25	.55	.16
☐ 46 Scott Mitchell	1.25	.55	.16
☐ 47 Herman Moore	2.00	.90	.25
☐ 48 Brett Perriman	1.25	.55	.16
☐ 49 Barry Sanders	6.00	2.70	.75
☐ 50 Chris Spielman	1.25	.55	.16
☐ 51 Edgar Bennett	1.25	.55	.16
☐ 52 Robert Brooks	2.00	.90	.25
☐ 53 Brett Favre	12.00	5.50	1.50
☐ 54 Derrick Mayes	4.00	1.80	.50
☐ 55 Reggie White	2.00	.90	.25
☐ 56 Eddie George	12.00	5.50	1.50
☐ 57 Haywood Jeffires	.75	.35	.09
☐ 58 Steve McNair	6.00	2.70	.75
☐ 59 Chris Sanders	1.25	.55	.16
☐ 60 Rodney Thomas	.75	.35	.09
☐ 61 Tony Bennett	.75	.35	.09
☐ 62 Quentin Coryatt	.75	.35	.09
☐ 63 Ken Dilger	1.25	.55	.16
☐ 64 Marshall Faulk	2.00	.90	.25
☐ 65 Jim Harbaugh	1.25	.55	.16
☐ 66 Tony Boselli	1.25	.55	.16
☐ 67 Mark Brunell	6.00	2.70	.75
☐ 68 Kevin Hardy	1.25	.55	.16
☐ 69 Desmond Howard	1.25	.55	.16
☐ 70 James O.Stewart	2.00	.90	.25
☐ 71 Marcus Allen	2.00	.90	.25
☐ 72 Steve Bono	1.25	.55	.16
☐ 73 Neil Smith	1.25	.55	.16
☐ 74 Derrick Thomas	1.25	.55	.16
☐ 75 Tamarick Vanover	2.00	.90	.25
☐ 76 Karim Abdul-Jabbar	8.00	3.60	1.00
☐ 77 Irving Fryar	1.25	.55	.16
☐ 78 Eric Green	.75	.35	.09
☐ 79 Dan Marino	12.00	5.50	1.50
☐ 80 Bernie Parmalee	.75	.35	.09
☐ 81 Cris Carter	2.00	.90	.25
☐ 82 Warren Moon	1.25	.55	.16
☐ 83 Jake Reed	1.25	.55	.16
☐ 84 Robert Smith	1.25	.55	.16
☐ 85 Moe Williams	.75	.35	.09
☐ 86 Drew Bledsoe	6.00	2.70	.75
☐ 87 Ben Coates	1.25	.55	.16
☐ 88 Terry Glenn	10.00	4.50	1.25
☐ 89 Curtis Martin	10.00	4.50	1.25
☐ 90 Dave Meggett	.75	.35	.09
☐ 91 Mario Bates	1.25	.55	.16
☐ 92 Jim Everett	.75	.35	.09
☐ 93 Michael Haynes	1.25	.55	.16
☐ 94 Torrance Small	.75	.35	.09
☐ 95 Ray Zellars	.75	.35	.09
☐ 96 Kyle Brady	1.25	.55	.16
☐ 97 Wayne Chrebet	1.25	.55	.16
☐ 98 Keyshawn Johnson	5.00	2.20	.60
☐ 99 Adrian Murrell	1.25	.55	.16
☐ 100 Alex Van Dyke	1.25	.55	.16
☐ 101 Michael Brooks	.75	.35	.09
☐ 102 Dave Brown	1.25	.55	.16
☐ 103 Chris Calloway	.75	.35	.09
☐ 104 Rodney Hampton	1.25	.55	.16
☐ 105 Amani Toomer	2.50	1.10	.30
☐ 106 Tyrone Wheatley	1.25	.55	.16
☐ 107 Tim Brown	1.25	.55	.16
☐ 108 Rickey Dudley	2.50	1.10	.30
☐ 109 Billy Joe Hobert	1.25	.55	.16
☐ 110 Rocket Ismail	1.25	.55	.16
☐ 111 Napoleon Kaufman	1.25	.55	.16
☐ 112 Harvey Williams	.75	.35	.09
☐ 113 Charlie Garner	.75	.35	.09
☐ 114 Bobby Hoying	2.50	1.10	.30
☐ 115 Rodney Peete	.75	.35	.09
☐ 116 Ricky Watters	1.25	.55	.16
☐ 117 Greg Lloyd	1.25	.55	.16
☐ 118 Erric Pegram	1.25	.55	.16
☐ 119 Kordell Stewart	8.00	3.60	1.00
☐ 120 Yancey Thigpen	1.25	.55	.16
☐ 121 Jon Witman	1.25	.55	.16
☐ 122 Aaron Hayden	.75	.35	.09
☐ 123 Stan Humphries	1.25	.55	.16
☐ 124 Tony Martin	1.25	.55	.16
☐ 125 Leslie O'Neal	.75	.35	.09
☐ 126 Junior Seau	2.00	.90	.25
☐ 127 Jerome Bettis	2.00	.90	.25
☐ 128 Isaac Bruce	2.00	.90	.25
☐ 129 Ernie Conwell	.75	.35	.09
☐ 130 Lawrence Phillips	3.00	1.35	.35
☐ 131 William Floyd	1.25	.55	.16
☐ 132 Terrell Owens	6.00	2.70	.75
☐ 133 Jerry Rice	6.00	2.70	.75
☐ 134 J.J. Stokes	2.00	.90	.25
☐ 135 Steve Young	5.00	2.20	.60
☐ 136 Brian Blades	1.25	.55	.16
☐ 137 Christian Fauria	.75	.35	.09
☐ 138 Joey Galloway	4.00	1.80	.50
☐ 139 Rick Mirer	1.25	.55	.16
☐ 140 Chris Warren	1.25	.55	.16
☐ 141 Horace Copeland	.75	.35	.09
☐ 142 Trent Dilfer	1.25	.55	.16
☐ 143 Alvin Harper	.75	.35	.09
☐ 144 Dave Moore	.75	.35	.09
☐ 145 Errict Rhett	1.25	.55	.16
☐ 146 Terry Allen	1.25	.55	.16
☐ 147 Gus Frerotte	2.00	.90	.25
☐ 148 Brian Mitchell	.75	.35	.09
☐ 149 Heath Shuler	2.00	.90	.25
☐ 150 Michael Westbrook	2.00	.90	.25

1996 Pacific Invincible Bronze

Randomly inserted in hobby packs only at the rate of four in 25, this 149-card set is a bronze parallel version of the regular 1996 Pacific Invincible set. This parallel set does not contain card #31 Jeff Blake.

	MINT	NRMT	EXC
COMPLETE SET (149)	900.00	400.00	110.00
COMMON CARD (1-150)	5.00	2.20	.60

*STARS: 2.5X TO 5X BASIC CARDS
*YOUNG STARS: 2X TO 4X BASIC CARDS
*RCs:1.5X TO 3X BASIC CARDS

1996 Pacific Invincible Platinum Blue

Randomly inserted in packs at the rate of one in 25, this 149-card set is a platinum parallel version of the regular 1996 Pacific Invincible set. This set does not contain card #31, Jeff Blake.

	MINT	NRMT	EXC
COMPLETE SET (149)	2500.00	1100.00	300.00
COMMON CARD (1-150)	12.00	5.50	1.50

*STARS: 7X TO 14X BASIC CARDS

*YOUNG STARS: 5X TO 10X BASIC CARDS
*RCs:4X TO 8X BASIC CARDS...........

1996 Pacific Invincible Silver

Randomly inserted in retail packs only at the rate of four in 25, this 149-card set is a silver parallel version of the regular 1996 Pacific Invincible set. This parallel set does not contain card #31, Jeff Blake.

	MINT	NRMT	EXC
COMPLETE SET (149)	1000.00	450.00	125.00
COMMON CARD (1-150)	6.00	2.70	.75

*STARS: 3X TO 6X BASIC CARDS......
*YOUNG STARS: 2.5X TO 5X BASIC CARDS
*RCs: 2X TO 4X BASIC CARDS ....

1996 Pacific Invincible Kick Starter Die Cuts

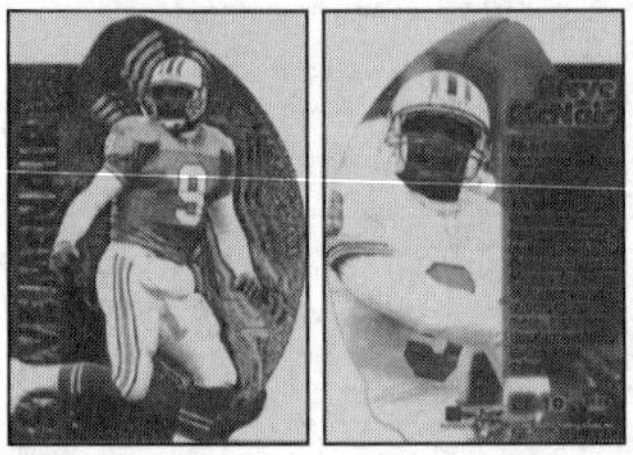

Randomly inserted in packs at a rate of one in 49, this 20-card set features color action player images on a die cut gold foil football background. The backs carry another player photo with a paragraph about the player.

	MINT	NRMT	EXC
COMPLETE SET (20)	500.00	220.00	60.00
COMMON CARD (KS1-KS20)	10.00	4.50	1.25
☐ KS1 Jeff Blake	15.00	6.75	1.85
☐ KS2 Tim Brown	10.00	4.50	1.25
☐ KS3 Kerry Collins	35.00	16.00	4.40
☐ KS4 John Elway	30.00	13.50	3.70
☐ KS5 Marshall Faulk	15.00	6.75	1.85
☐ KS6 Brett Favre	70.00	32.00	8.75
☐ KS7 Keyshawn Johnson	20.00	9.00	2.50
☐ KS8 Dan Marino	70.00	32.00	8.75
☐ KS9 Curtis Martin	35.00	16.00	4.40
☐ KS10 Steve McNair	30.00	13.50	3.70
☐ KS11 Errict Rhett	10.00	4.50	1.25
☐ KS12 Jerry Rice	40.00	18.00	5.00
☐ KS13 Rashaan Salaam	15.00	6.75	1.85
☐ KS14 Barry Sanders	40.00	18.00	5.00
☐ KS15 Deion Sanders	25.00	11.00	3.10
☐ KS16 Emmitt Smith	70.00	32.00	8.75
☐ KS17 Kordell Stewart	30.00	13.50	3.70
☐ KS18 Tamarick Vanover	15.00	6.75	1.85
☐ KS19 Chris Warren	10.00	4.50	1.25
☐ KS20 Ricky Watters	10.00	4.50	1.25

1996 Pacific Invincible Pro Bowl

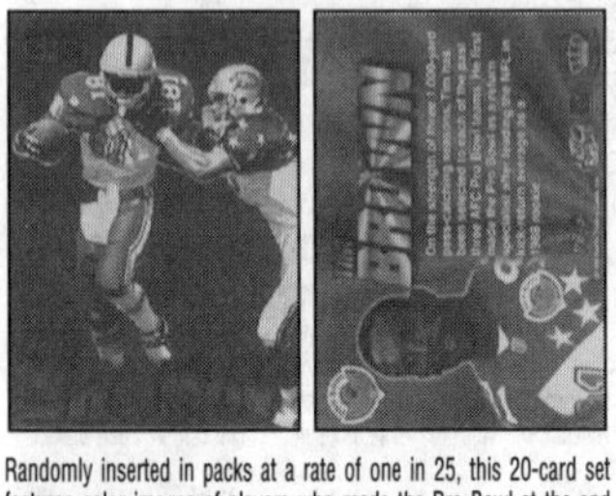

Randomly inserted in packs at a rate of one in 25, this 20-card set features color images of players who made the Pro Bowl at the end last season and are printed on a metallic football field background. The backs another player photo with a paragraph about the player.

	MINT	NRMT	EXC
COMPLETE SET (20)	200.00	90.00	25.00
COMMON CARD (1-20)	5.00	2.20	.60
☐ 1 Jeff Blake	8.00	3.60	1.00
☐ 2 Steve Bono	5.00	2.20	.60
☐ 3 Tim Brown	5.00	2.20	.60
☐ 4 Cris Carter	5.00	2.20	.60
☐ 5 Ben Coates	5.00	2.20	.60
☐ 6 Brett Favre	35.00	16.00	4.40
☐ 7 Jim Harbaugh	5.00	2.20	.60
☐ 8 Curtis Martin	25.00	11.00	3.10
☐ 9 Warren Moon	5.00	2.20	.60
☐ 10 Herman Moore	8.00	3.60	1.00
☐ 11 Carl Pickens	5.00	2.20	.60
☐ 12 Jerry Rice	20.00	9.00	2.50
☐ 13 Barry Sanders	20.00	9.00	2.50
☐ 14 Shannon Sharpe	5.00	2.20	.60
☐ 15 Emmitt Smith	35.00	16.00	4.40
☐ 16 Yancey Thigpen	5.00	2.20	.60
☐ 17 Chris Warren	5.00	2.20	.60
☐ 18 Ricky Watters	5.00	2.20	.60
☐ 19 Reggie White	8.00	3.60	1.00
☐ 20 Steve Young	15.00	6.75	1.85

1996 Pacific Invincible Smash Mouth

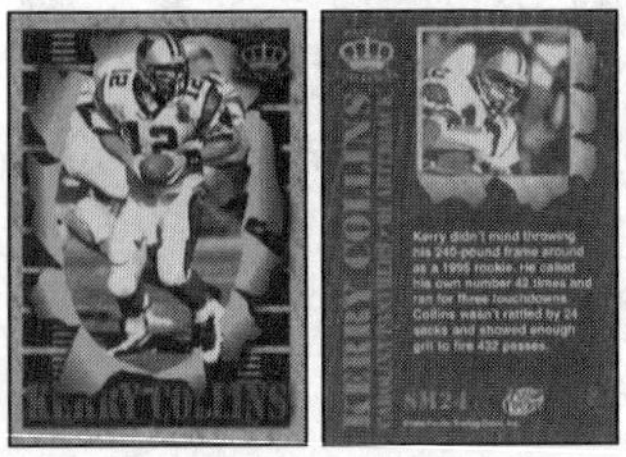

Inserted at the rate of approximately two per pack of the 1996 Pacific Invincible regular set, this 180-card set features color player images printed to look as if they are crashing out of the card. The backs carry a small player head photo and a paragraph about the player.

	MINT	NRMT	EXC
COMPLETE SET (180)	20.00	9.00	2.50
COMMON CARD (SM1-SM180)	.15	.07	.02
☐ 1 Marcus Dowdell	.15	.07	.02
☐ 2 Karl Dunbar	.15	.07	.02
☐ 3 Eric England	.15	.07	.02
☐ 4 Garrison Hearst	.20	.09	.03
☐ 5 Bryan Reeves	.15	.07	.02
☐ 6 Simeon Rice	.40	.18	.05
☐ 7 Jeff George	.20	.09	.03
☐ 8 Bobby Hebert	.15	.07	.02
☐ 9 Craig Heyward	.15	.07	.02
☐ 10 David Richards	.15	.07	.02
☐ 11 Elbert Shelley	.15	.07	.02
☐ 12 Lonnie Johnson	.15	.07	.02
☐ 13 Jim Kelly	.40	.18	.05
☐ 14 Corbin Lacina	.15	.07	.02
☐ 15 Bryce Paup	.20	.09	.03
☐ 16 Sam Rogers	.15	.07	.02
☐ 17 Bruce Smith	.40	.18	.05
☐ 18 Thurman Thomas	.40	.18	.05
☐ 19 Carl Banks	.15	.07	.02
☐ 20 Dan Footman	.15	.07	.02
☐ 21 Louis Riddick	.15	.07	.02
☐ 22 Matt Stover	.15	.07	.02
☐ 23 Tommy Barnhardt	.15	.07	.02
☐ 24 Kerry Collins	1.25	.55	.16
☐ 25 Mark Dennis	.15	.07	.02
☐ 26 Matt Elliott	.15	.07	.02
☐ 27 Eric Guliford	.15	.07	.02
☐ 28 Lamar Lathon	.15	.07	.02
☐ 29 Joe Cain	.15	.07	.02
☐ 30 Marty Carter	.15	.07	.02
☐ 31 Robert Green	.15	.07	.02
☐ 32 Erik Kramer	.15	.07	.02
☐ 33 Todd Perry	.15	.07	.02
☐ 34 Rashaan Salaam	.40	.18	.05
☐ 35 Alonzo Spellman	.15	.07	.02
☐ 36 Jeff Blake	.40	.18	.05
☐ 37 Andre Collins	.15	.07	.02
☐ 38 Todd Kelly	.15	.07	.02
☐ 39 Carl Pickens	.40	.18	.05
☐ 40 Kevin Sargent	.15	.07	.02
☐ 41 Troy Aikman	1.00	.45	.12
☐ 42 Charles Haley	.20	.09	.03
☐ 43 Daryl Johnston	.20	.09	.03
☐ 44 Nate Newton	.15	.07	.02
☐ 45 Deion Sanders	.60	.25	.07
☐ 46 Emmitt Smith	2.00	.90	.25
☐ 47 Steve Atwater	.15	.07	.02
☐ 48 Terrell Davis	1.50	.70	.19
☐ 49 John Elway	.75	.35	.09
☐ 50 Michael Dean Perry	.15	.07	.02
☐ 51 Shannon Sharpe	.20	.09	.03
☐ 52 David Wyman	.15	.07	.02
☐ 53 Bennie Blades	.15	.07	.02
☐ 54 Kevin Glover	.15	.07	.02
☐ 55 Herman Moore	.40	.18	.05
☐ 56 Robert Porcher	.15	.07	.02
☐ 57 Barry Sanders	1.00	.45	.12
☐ 58 Henry Thomas	.15	.07	.02
☐ 59 Edgar Bennett	.20	.09	.03
☐ 60 Robert Brooks	.40	.18	.05
☐ 61 Brett Favre	2.00	.90	.25
☐ 62 Harry Galbreath	.15	.07	.02
☐ 63 Sean Jones	.15	.07	.02
☐ 64 Reggie White	.40	.18	.05
☐ 65 Blaine Bishop	.15	.07	.02
☐ 66 Chuck Cecil	.15	.07	.02
☐ 67 Cris Dishman	.15	.07	.02
☐ 68 Steve McNair	1.00	.45	.12
☐ 69 Rodney Thomas	.15	.07	.02
☐ 70 Jason Belser	.15	.07	.02
☐ 71 Ray Buchanan	.15	.07	.02
☐ 72 Quentin Coryatt	.15	.07	.02
☐ 73 Marshall Faulk	.40	.18	.05
☐ 74 Jim Harbaugh	.20	.09	.03
☐ 75 Devon McDonald	.15	.07	.02
☐ 76 Tony Boselli	.20	.09	.03
☐ 77 Tony Brackens	.20	.09	.03
☐ 78 Mark Brunell	1.00	.45	.12
☐ 79 Don Davey	.15	.07	.02
☐ 80 Rich Griffith	.15	.07	.02
☐ 81 Kevin Hardy	.20	.09	.03
☐ 82 Mickey Washington	.15	.07	.02
☐ 83 Louie Aguiar	.15	.07	.02
☐ 84 Dan Saleaumua	.15	.07	.02
☐ 85 Will Shields	.15	.07	.02
☐ 86 Neil Smith	.20	.09	.03
☐ 87 Derrick Thomas	.20	.09	.03
☐ 88 Tamarick Vanover	.40	.18	.05
☐ 89 Gene Atkins	.15	.07	.02
☐ 90 Bryan Cox	.15	.07	.02
☐ 91 Steve Emtman	.15	.07	.02
☐ 92 Chris Gray	.15	.07	.02
☐ 93 Dan Marino	2.00	.90	.25
☐ 94 Derrick Alexander DE	.15	.07	.02
☐ 95 Cris Carter	.40	.18	.05
☐ 96 Jeff Christy	.15	.07	.02
☐ 97 Robert Smith	.20	.09	.03
☐ 98 Korey Stringer	.15	.07	.02
☐ 99 Orlando Thomas	.15	.07	.02
☐ 100 Esera Tuaolo	.15	.07	.02
☐ 101 Drew Bledsoe	1.00	.45	.12
☐ 102 Eddie Cade	.15	.07	.02
☐ 103 Mike Jones	.15	.07	.02
☐ 104 Curtis Martin	1.50	.70	.19
☐ 105 Willie McGinest	.15	.07	.02
☐ 106 Chris Slade	.15	.07	.02
☐ 107 Eric Allen	.15	.07	.02
☐ 108 Mario Bates	.20	.09	.03
☐ 109 Jim Dombrowski	.15	.07	.02
☐ 110 Wayne Martin	.15	.07	.02
☐ 111 William Roaf	.15	.07	.02
☐ 112 Irv Smith	.15	.07	.02
☐ 113 Michael Brooks	.15	.07	.02
☐ 114 Stacey Dillard	.15	.07	.02
☐ 115 Rodney Hampton	.20	.09	.03
☐ 116 Doug Riesenberg	.15	.07	.02
☐ 117 Coleman Rudolph	.15	.07	.02
☐ 118 Tyrone Wheatley	.20	.09	.03
☐ 119 Kyle Brady	.20	.09	.03
☐ 120 Roger Duffy	.15	.07	.02
☐ 121 Keyshawn Johnson	.75	.35	.09
☐ 122 Gary Jones	.15	.07	.02
☐ 123 Eddie Anderson	.15	.07	.02
☐ 124 Rickey Dudley	.40	.18	.05
☐ 125 Napoleon Kaufman	.20	.09	.03
☐ 126 Greg Skrepenak	.15	.07	.02
☐ 127 Pat Swilling	.15	.07	.02
☐ 128 Steve Wisniewski	.15	.07	.02
☐ 129 William Fuller	.15	.07	.02
☐ 130 Kurt Gouveia	.15	.07	.02
☐ 131 Andy Harmon	.15	.07	.02
☐ 132 Mike Mamula	.15	.07	.02
☐ 133 Guy McIntyre	.15	.07	.02
☐ 134 Ricky Watters	.20	.09	.03
☐ 135 Kevin Greene	.20	.09	.03
☐ 136 Bill Johnson	.15	.07	.02
☐ 137 Carnell Lake	.15	.07	.02
☐ 138 Greg Lloyd	.20	.09	.03
☐ 139 Erric Pegram	.20	.09	.03
☐ 140 Leon Searcy	.15	.07	.02
☐ 141 Shane Conlan	.15	.07	.02
☐ 142 Troy Drayton	.15	.07	.02
☐ 143 Wayne Gandy	.15	.07	.02
☐ 144 Sean Gilbert	.15	.07	.02
☐ 145 Carlos Jenkins	.15	.07	.02
☐ 146 Lawrence Phillips	.40	.18	.05
☐ 147 Aaron Hayden	.15	.07	.02
☐ 148 Stan Humphries	.20	.09	.03
☐ 149 Leslie O'Neal	.15	.07	.02
☐ 150 Bo Orlando	.15	.07	.02
☐ 151 Junior Seau	.40	.18	.05
☐ 152 Harry Swayne	.15	.07	.02
☐ 153 Harris Barton	.15	.07	.02
☐ 154 Merton Hanks	.15	.07	.02
☐ 155 Rod Milstead	.15	.07	.02
☐ 156 Ken Norton Jr.	.20	.09	.03
☐ 157 Gary Plummer	.15	.07	.02
☐ 158 Jerry Rice	1.00	.45	.12
☐ 159 Steve Wallace	.15	.07	.02
☐ 160 Steve Young	.75	.35	.09
☐ 161 James Atkins	.15	.07	.02
☐ 162 Brian Blades	.20	.09	.03
☐ 163 Matt Joyce	.15	.07	.02
☐ 164 Cortez Kennedy	.20	.09	.03
☐ 165 Kevin Mawae	.15	.07	.02
☐ 166 Winston Moss	.15	.07	.02
☐ 167 Chris Warren	.20	.09	.03
☐ 168 Derrick Brooks	.15	.07	.02
☐ 169 Trent Dilfer	.20	.09	.03
☐ 170 Santana Dotson	.15	.07	.02
☐ 171 Alvin Harper	.15	.07	.02
☐ 172 Hardy Nickerson	.15	.07	.02
☐ 173 Errict Rhett	.20	.09	.03
☐ 174 Warren Sapp	.15	.07	.02
☐ 175 Terry Allen	.20	.09	.03
☐ 176 John Gesek	.15	.07	.02
☐ 177 Ken Harvey	.15	.07	.02
☐ 178 Tre Johnson	.15	.07	.02
☐ 179 Rod Stephens	.15	.07	.02
☐ 180 Michael Westbrook	.40	.18	.05

1996 Pacific Invincible Chris Warren

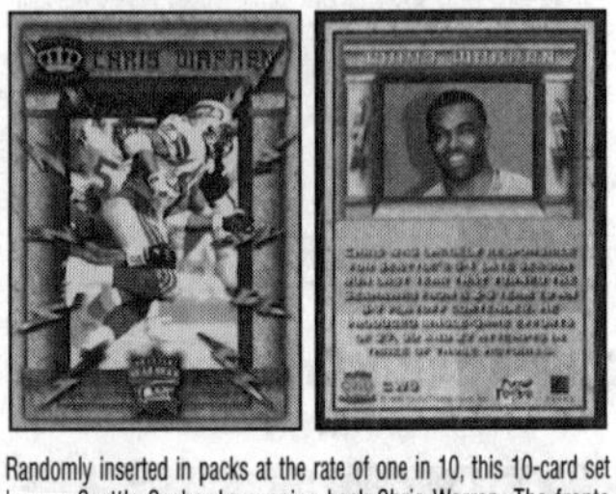

Randomly inserted in packs at the rate of one in 10, this 10-card set honors Seattle Seahawks running back Chris Warren. The fronts feature color action player photos with a simulated stone column inside border and gold marble outside border. The backs each carry different small head photos and paragraphs about his outstanding efforts and career.

	MINT	NRMT	EXC
COMPLETE SET (10)	10.00	4.50	1.25
COMMON CARD (CW1-CW10)	1.25	.55	.16
☐ CW1 Chris Warren Blocking	1.25	.55	.16
☐ CW2 Chris Warren Horizontal Card	1.25	.55	.16
☐ CW3 Chris Warren Running, No Ball	1.25	.55	.16
☐ CW4 Chris Warren Running against Jaguars	1.25	.55	.16
☐ CW5 Chris Warren Running, ball in right hand	1.25	.55	.16
☐ CW6 Chris Warren	1.25	.55	.16
☐ CW7 Chris Warren Being Tackled by Chief	1.25	.55	.16
☐ CW8 Chris Warren Running low to ground	1.25	.55	.16
☐ CW9 Chris Warren Tracy Simien in background	1.25	.55	.16
☐ CW10 Chris Warren Pro Bowl uniform	1.25	.55	.16

1996 Pacific Litho-Cel

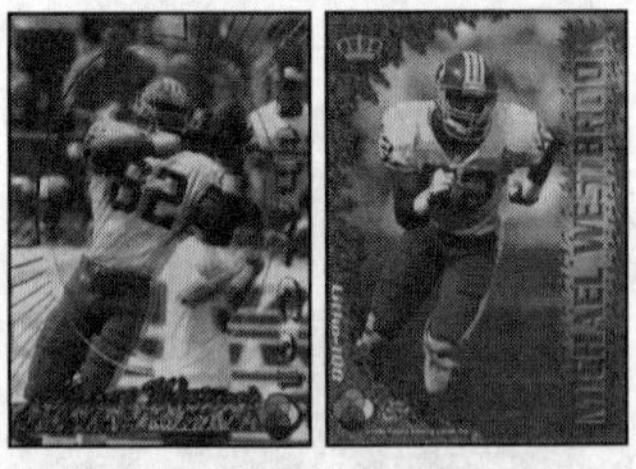

This 100-card set was distributed in three-card packs and features action player photos on the front of the Litho card with a different action photo of the same player on the back only in full color. A Cel card is made to be combined with a Litho card to make the front photo of the player magically appear in full color.

	MINT	NRMT	EXC
COMPLETE SET (100)	200.00	90.00	25.00
COMMON CARD (1-100)	1.00	.45	.12
ALL CARDS PRICED AS PAIRS			
SINGLE CARDS: HALF VALUE			
☐ 1 Kent Graham	1.50	.70	.19
☐ 2 LeShon Johnson	1.00	.45	.12
☐ 3 Leeland McElroy	3.00	1.35	.35
☐ 4 Frank Sanders	1.50	.70	.19
☐ 5 Jamal Anderson	4.00	1.80	.50
☐ 6 Cornelius Bennett	1.50	.70	.19
☐ 7 Bobby Hebert	1.00	.45	.12
☐ 8 Earnest Byner	1.00	.45	.12
☐ 9 Michael Jackson	1.50	.70	.19
☐ 10 Vinny Testaverde	1.50	.70	.19
☐ 11 Jim Kelly	2.00	.90	.25
☐ 12 Andre Reed	1.50	.70	.19
☐ 13 Bruce Smith	2.00	.90	.25
☐ 14 Thurman Thomas	2.00	.90	.25
☐ 15 Kerry Collins	8.00	3.60	1.00
☐ 16 Lamar Lathon	1.00	.45	.12
☐ 17 Kevin Greene	1.50	.70	.19
☐ 18 Bobby Engram	4.00	1.80	.50

☐ 19 Erik Kramer	1.00	.45	.12
☐ 20 Rashaan Salaam	2.00	.90	.25
☐ 21 Jeff Blake	2.00	.90	.25
☐ 22 Garrison Hearst	1.50	.70	.19
☐ 23 Carl Pickens	2.00	.90	.25
☐ 24 Darnay Scott	1.50	.70	.19
☐ 25 Troy Aikman	8.00	3.60	1.00
☐ 26 Eric Bjornson	1.00	.45	.12
☐ 27 Deion Sanders	4.00	1.80	.50
☐ 28 Emmitt Smith	14.00	6.25	1.75
☐ 29 Terrell Davis	10.00	4.50	1.25
☐ 30 John Elway	6.00	2.70	.75
☐ 31 Anthony Miller	1.50	.70	.19
☐ 32 John Mobley	1.00	.45	.12
☐ 33 Scott Mitchell	1.50	.70	.19
☐ 34 Herman Moore	2.00	.90	.25
☐ 35 Brett Perriman	1.50	.70	.19
☐ 36 Barry Sanders	8.00	3.60	1.00
☐ 37 Edgar Bennett	1.50	.70	.19
☐ 38 Robert Brooks	2.00	.90	.25
☐ 39 Brett Favre	14.00	6.25	1.75
☐ 40 Reggie White	2.00	.90	.25
☐ 41 Chris Chandler	1.50	.70	.19
☐ 42 Eddie George	16.00	7.25	2.00
☐ 43 Steve McNair	6.00	2.70	.75
☐ 44 Chris Sanders	1.50	.70	.19
☐ 45 Ken Dilger	1.50	.70	.19
☐ 46 Marshall Faulk	2.00	.90	.25
☐ 47 Jim Harbaugh	1.50	.70	.19
☐ 48 Mark Brunell	8.00	3.60	1.00
☐ 49 Keenan McCardell	2.00	.90	.25
☐ 50 James O.Stewart	1.50	.70	.19
☐ 51 Marcus Allen	2.00	.90	.25
☐ 52 Steve Bono	1.50	.70	.19
☐ 53 Greg Hill	1.50	.70	.19
☐ 54 Tamarick Vanover	2.00	.90	.25
☐ 55 Karim Abdul-Jabbar	10.00	4.50	1.25
☐ 56 Dan Marino	14.00	6.25	1.75
☐ 57 Zach Thomas	4.00	1.80	.50
☐ 58 Cris Carter	2.00	.90	.25
☐ 59 Warren Moon	1.50	.70	.19
☐ 60 Robert Smith	1.50	.70	.19
☐ 61 Drew Bledsoe	8.00	3.60	1.00
☐ 62 Terry Glenn	14.00	6.25	1.75
☐ 63 Curtis Martin	10.00	4.50	1.25
☐ 64 Mario Bates	1.50	.70	.19
☐ 65 Jim Everett	1.00	.45	.12
☐ 66 Haywood Jeffires	1.00	.45	.12
☐ 67 Dave Brown	1.50	.70	.19
☐ 68 Rodney Hampton	1.50	.70	.19
☐ 69 Amani Toomer	2.50	1.10	.30
☐ 70 Adrian Murrell	1.50	.70	.19
☐ 71 Neil O'Donnell	1.50	.70	.19
☐ 72 Alex Van Dyke	1.50	.70	.19
☐ 73 Tim Brown	1.50	.70	.19
☐ 74 Jeff Hostetler	1.50	.70	.19
☐ 75 Napoleon Kaufman	1.50	.70	.19
☐ 76 Irving Fryar	1.50	.70	.19
☐ 77 Chris T. Jones	2.00	.90	.25
☐ 78 Ricky Watters	1.50	.70	.19
☐ 79 Jerome Bettis	2.00	.90	.25
☐ 80 Kordell Stewart	8.00	3.60	1.00
☐ 81 Tony Banks	4.00	1.80	.50
☐ 82 Eddie Kennison	6.00	2.70	.75
☐ 83 Lawrence Phillips	3.00	1.35	.35
☐ 84 Stan Humphries	1.50	.70	.19
☐ 85 Tony Martin	1.50	.70	.19
☐ 86 Leonard Russell	1.00	.45	.12
☐ 87 Junior Seau	2.00	.90	.25
☐ 88 Jerry Rice	8.00	3.60	1.00
☐ 89 J.J. Stokes	2.00	.90	.25
☐ 90 Tommy Vardell	1.00	.45	.12
☐ 91 Steve Young	6.00	2.70	.75
☐ 92 Joey Galloway	4.00	1.80	.50
☐ 93 Rick Mirer	1.50	.70	.19
☐ 94 Chris Warren	1.50	.70	.19
☐ 95 Mike Alstott	2.00	.90	.25
☐ 96 Trent Dilfer	1.50	.70	.19
☐ 97 Nilo Silvan	1.00	.45	.12
☐ 98 Terry Allen	1.50	.70	.19
☐ 99 Gus Frerotte	2.00	.90	.25
☐ 100 Michael Westbrook	2.00	.90	.25
☐ P1 Chris Warren Promo Blue Litho Card	.75	.35	.09
☐ P2 Chris Warren Promo Red Litho Card	.75	.35	.09
☐ P3 Chris Warren Promo Blue Cel Card	.75	.35	.09
☐ P4 Chris Warren Promo Red Cel Card	.75	.35	.09

1996 Pacific Litho-Cel Bronze

Randomly inserted in retail packs only at the rate of three in 25, this 100-card set is a bronze Cel parallel version of the regular Cel set.

	MINT	NRMT	EXC
COMPLETE SET (100)	1000.00	450.00	125.00
COMMON CARD (1-100)	4.00	1.80	.50
*STARS: 2X TO 4X BASIC CARDS			
*YOUNG STARS: 1.5X TO 3X BASIC CARDS			
*RCs: 1X TO 2X BASIC CARDS			

1996 Pacific Litho-Cel Silver

Randomly inserted in hobby packs only at the rate of three in 25, this 100-card set is a silver Cel parallel version of the regular Cel set.

	MINT	NRMT	EXC
COMPLETE SET (100)	800.00	350.00	100.00
COMMON CARD (1-100)	3.00	1.35	.35
*STARS: 1.5X TO 3X BASIC CARDS			
*YOUNG STARS: 1.25X TO 2.5X BASIC CARDS			
*RCs:1X TO 2X BASIC CARDS			

1996 Pacific Litho-Cel Feature Performers

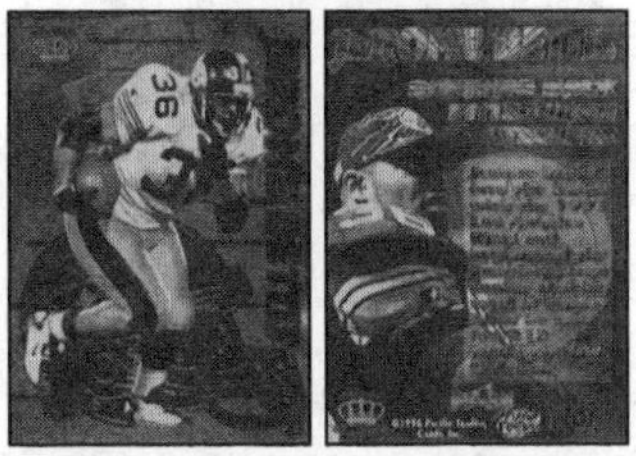

Randomly inserted in packs at a rate of one in 25, this 20-card set features top NFL player images on a gold foil background with the outline of the team's helmet imprinted on the lower half. The backs carry a paragraph about the player beside a color player photo.

	MINT	NRMT	EXC
COMPLETE SET (20)	350.00	160.00	45.00
COMMON CARD (FP1-FP20)	10.00	4.50	1.25
☐ FP1 Jim Kelly	12.00	5.50	1.50
☐ FP2 Troy Aikman	25.00	11.00	3.10
☐ FP3 Deion Sanders	15.00	6.75	1.85
☐ FP4 Emmitt Smith	40.00	18.00	5.00
☐ FP5 Terrell Davis	30.00	13.50	3.70
☐ FP6 John Elway	20.00	9.00	2.50
☐ FP7 Herman Moore	12.00	5.50	1.50
☐ FP8 Barry Sanders	25.00	11.00	3.10
☐ FP9 Robert Brooks	12.00	5.50	1.50
☐ FP10 Brett Favre	40.00	18.00	5.00
☐ FP11 Eddie George	25.00	11.00	3.10
☐ FP12 Jim Harbaugh	10.00	4.50	1.25
☐ FP13 Marcus Allen	12.00	5.50	1.50
☐ FP14 Karim Abdul-Jabbar	15.00	6.75	1.85
☐ FP15 Dan Marino	40.00	18.00	5.00
☐ FP16 Joey Galloway	12.00	5.50	1.50
☐ FP17 Curtis Martin	30.00	13.50	3.70
☐ FP18 Jerome Bettis	12.00	5.50	1.50
☐ FP19 Jerry Rice	25.00	11.00	3.10
☐ FP20 Steve Young	20.00	9.00	2.50

1996 Pacific Litho-Cel Game Time

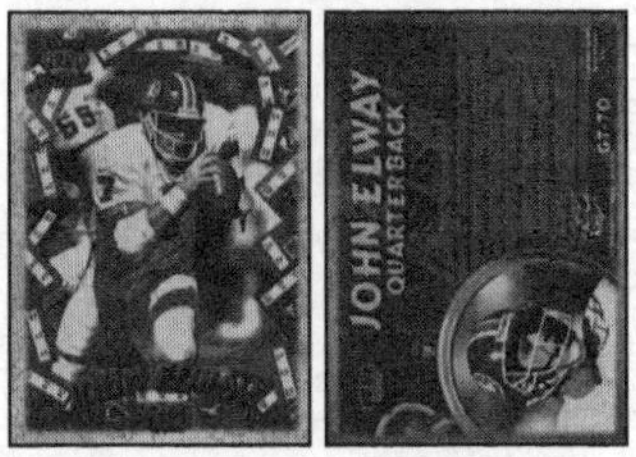

Randomly inserted one in every pack, this 96-card set features color player photos on the fronts with a border of different team ticket stubs. Cards #GT97-GT100 are printed with a gold foil border. The backs carry a player head photo in a stopwatch frame with a paragraph about the player.

	MINT	NRMT	EXC
COMPLETE SET (100)	25.00	11.00	3.10
COMMON CARD (GT1-GT96)	.15	.07	.02
FOIL CARDS (GT97-GT100)	.30	.14	.04
☐ GT1 Eddie George	2.00	.90	.25
☐ GT2 Larry Bowie	.15	.07	.02
☐ GT3 Jarius Hayes	.15	.07	.02
☐ GT4 Jamal Anderson	.50	.23	.06
☐ GT5 Ernest Hunter	.15	.07	.02
☐ GT6 Darick Holmes	.25	.11	.03
☐ GT7 Kerry Collins	1.25	.55	.16
☐ GT8 Raymont Harris	.15	.07	.02
☐ GT9 Jeff Blake	.50	.23	.06
☐ GT10 Troy Aikman	1.25	.55	.16
☐ GT11 Terrell Davis	1.50	.70	.19
☐ GT12 Kevin Glover	.15	.07	.02
☐ GT13 Brett Favre	2.50	1.10	.30
☐ GT14 Al Del Greco	.15	.07	.02
☐ GT15 Marshall Faulk	.50	.23	.06
☐ GT16 Bryan Barker	.15	.07	.02
☐ GT17 Rich Gannon	.15	.07	.02
☐ GT18 Dwight Hollier	.15	.07	.02
☐ GT19 Dixon Edwards	.15	.07	.02
☐ GT20 Drew Bledsoe	1.25	.55	.16
☐ GT21 Paul Green	.15	.07	.02
☐ GT22 Lawrence Dawsey	.15	.07	.02
☐ GT23 Ron Carpenter	.15	.07	.02
☐ GT24 Joe Aska	.15	.07	.02
☐ GT25 Joe Panos	.15	.07	.02
☐ GT26 Norm Johnson	.15	.07	.02
☐ GT27 Tony Banks	.50	.23	.06
☐ GT28 Darren Bennett	.15	.07	.02
☐ GT29 Steve Israel	.15	.07	.02
☐ GT30 Michael Barber	.15	.07	.02
☐ GT31 Dexter Nottage	.15	.07	.02
☐ GT32 Kwamie Lassiter	.15	.07	.02
☐ GT33 Travis Hall	.15	.07	.02
☐ GT34 Greg Montgomery	.15	.07	.02
☐ GT35 Jim Kelly	.50	.23	.06
☐ GT36 Matt Elliott	.15	.07	.02
☐ GT37 Jack Jackson	.15	.07	.02
☐ GT38 Ki-Jana Carter	.25	.11	.03
☐ GT39 Deion Sanders	.75	.35	.09
☐ GT40 Jason Elam	.15	.07	.02
☐ GT41 Johnnie Morton	.25	.11	.03
☐ GT42 Darius Holland	.15	.07	.02
☐ GT43 Sheddrick Wilson	.15	.07	.02
☐ GT44 Derrick Frazier	.15	.07	.02
☐ GT45 Travis Davis	.15	.07	.02
☐ GT46 Pellom McDaniels	.15	.07	.02
☐ GT47 Dan Marino	2.50	1.10	.30
☐ GT48 Ben Hanks	.15	.07	.02
☐ GT49 Tedy Bruschi	.15	.07	.02
☐ GT50 Tommy Hodson	.15	.07	.02
☐ GT51 Amani Toomer	.50	.23	.06
☐ GT52 Brian Hansen	.15	.07	.02
☐ GT53 Paul Butcher	.15	.07	.02
☐ GT54 Kevin Turner	.15	.07	.02
☐ GT55 Darren Perry	.15	.07	.02
☐ GT56 Mike Gruttadauria	.15	.07	.02
☐ GT57 Charlie Jones	.15	.07	.02
☐ GT58 Iheanyi Uwaezuoke	.15	.07	.02
☐ GT59 Glenn Montgomery	.15	.07	.02
☐ GT60 Mike Alstott	.50	.23	.06
☐ GT61 Joe Patton	.15	.07	.02
☐ GT62 Leeland McElroy	.50	.23	.06
☐ GT63 Robbie Tobeck	.15	.07	.02
☐ GT64 Vinny Testaverde	.25	.11	.03
☐ GT65 Chris Spielman	.25	.11	.03
☐ GT66 Anthony Johnson	.25	.11	.03
☐ GT67 Todd Sauerbrun	.15	.07	.02
☐ GT68 Jeff Hill	.15	.07	.02
☐ GT69 Emmitt Smith	2.50	1.10	.30
☐ GT70 John Elway	1.00	.45	.12
☐ GT71 Barry Sanders	1.25	.55	.16
☐ GT72 Brian Williams	.15	.07	.02
☐ GT73 Chris Gardocki	.15	.07	.02
☐ GT74 Jimmy Smith	.25	.11	.03
☐ GT75 Ricky Siglar	.15	.07	.02
☐ GT76 Tim Ruddy	.15	.07	.02
☐ GT77 Moe Williams	.15	.07	.02
☐ GT78 Willie Clay	.15	.07	.02
☐ GT79 Henry Lusk	.15	.07	.02
☐ GT80 Brian Williams	.15	.07	.02
☐ GT81 Ronald Moore	.15	.07	.02
☐ GT82 Trey Junkin	.15	.07	.02
☐ GT83 James Willis	.15	.07	.02
☐ GT84 Joel Steed	.15	.07	.02
☐ GT85 Jamie Martin	.25	.11	.03
☐ GT86 Shawn Lee	.15	.07	.02
☐ GT87 Steve Young	1.00	.45	.12
☐ GT88 Barrett Robbins	.15	.07	.02
☐ GT89 Charles Dimry	.15	.07	.02
☐ GT90 Darryl Pounds	.15	.07	.02
☐ GT91 Herschel Walker	.25	.11	.03
☐ GT92 Bill Romanowski	.15	.07	.02
☐ GT93 David Tate	.15	.07	.02
☐ GT94 Marrio Grier	.15	.07	.02
☐ GT95 Rodney Young	.15	.07	.02
☐ GT96 Lamar Smith	.15	.07	.02
☐ GT97 Don Beebe	.15	.07	.02
☐ GT98 Ty Detmer	.25	.11	.03
☐ GT99 Ted Popson	.15	.07	.02
☐ GT100 Natrone Means	.50	.23	.06

1996 Pacific Litho-Cel Litho-Proof

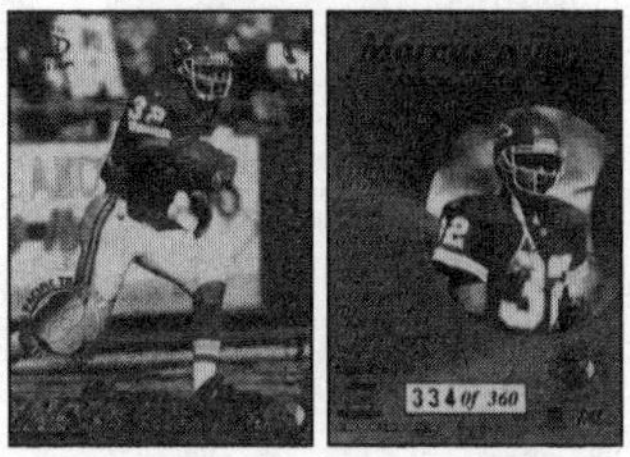

Randomly inserted in packs at a rate of one in 97, this 36-card set features borderless color action player photos with the words "Litho-Proof" printed down the right side. Only 360 of each card was produced and is sequentially numbered.

	MINT	NRMT	EXC
COMPLETE SET (36)	1800.00	800.00	220.00
COMMON CARD (1-36)	20.00	9.00	2.50
*CERTIFIED CARDS: 1.5X TO 4X BASIC CARDS			
☐ 1 Jim Kelly	30.00	13.50	3.70
☐ 2 Kerry Collins	90.00	40.00	11.00
☐ 3 Rashaan Salaam	30.00	13.50	3.70
☐ 4 Jeff Blake	30.00	13.50	3.70
☐ 5 Carl Pickens	20.00	9.00	2.50
☐ 6 Troy Aikman	90.00	40.00	11.00
☐ 7 Deion Sanders	60.00	27.00	7.50
☐ 8 Emmitt Smith	175.00	80.00	22.00
☐ 9 Terrell Davis	90.00	40.00	11.00
☐ 10 John Elway	80.00	36.00	10.00
☐ 11 Herman Moore	30.00	13.50	3.70
☐ 12 Barry Sanders	90.00	40.00	11.00
☐ 13 Robert Brooks	30.00	13.50	3.70
☐ 14 Brett Favre	175.00	80.00	22.00
☐ 15 Reggie White	30.00	13.50	3.70
☐ 16 Eddie George	100.00	45.00	12.50
☐ 17 Marshall Faulk	30.00	13.50	3.70
☐ 18 Jim Harbaugh	20.00	9.00	2.50
☐ 19 Mark Brunell	90.00	40.00	11.00
☐ 20 Marcus Allen	30.00	13.50	3.70
☐ 21 Steve Bono	20.00	9.00	2.50
☐ 22 Karim Abdul-Jabbar	70.00	32.00	8.75
☐ 23 Dan Marino	175.00	80.00	22.00
☐ 24 Warren Moon	20.00	9.00	2.50
☐ 25 Drew Bledsoe	90.00	40.00	11.00
☐ 26 Curtis Martin	90.00	40.00	11.00
☐ 27 Amani Toomer	30.00	13.50	3.70
☐ 28 Tim Brown	20.00	9.00	2.50
☐ 29 Napoleon Kaufman	20.00	9.00	2.50
☐ 30 Ricky Watters	20.00	9.00	2.50
☐ 31 Jerome Bettis	30.00	13.50	3.70
☐ 32 Kordell Stewart	90.00	40.00	11.00
☐ 33 Jerry Rice	90.00	40.00	11.00
☐ 34 Steve Young	70.00	32.00	8.75
☐ 35 Joey Galloway	40.00	18.00	5.00
☐ 36 Terry Allen	20.00	9.00	2.50

1996 Pacific Litho-Cel Moments in Time

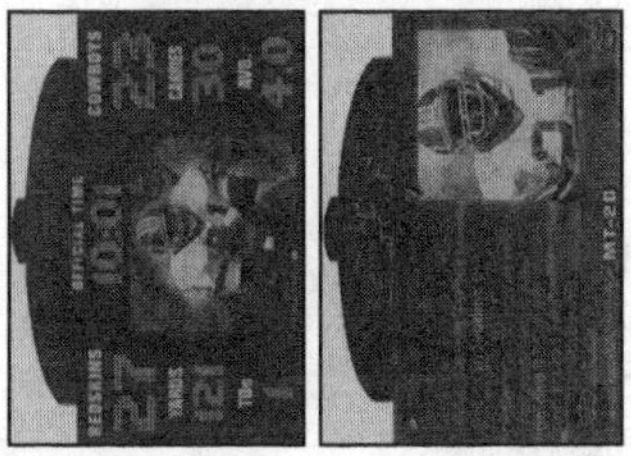

Randomly inserted in packs at a rate of one in 49, this 20-card set features action color player photos on a diecut card with a billboard designed border. The backs carry another player photo with the particular game date and a paragraph about the pictured player's great moments of that game.

	MINT	NRMT	EXC
COMPLETE SET (20)	600.00	275.00	75.00
COMMON CARD (MT1-MT20)	12.00	5.50	1.50
☐ MT1 Jim Kelly	18.00	8.00	2.20
☐ MT2 Kerry Collins	50.00	22.00	6.25
☐ MT3 Rashaan Salaam	18.00	8.00	2.20
☐ MT4 Troy Aikman	50.00	22.00	6.25
☐ MT5 Deion Sanders	30.00	13.50	3.70
☐ MT6 Emmitt Smith	90.00	40.00	11.00
☐ MT7 Terrell Davis	50.00	22.00	6.25
☐ MT8 John Elway	40.00	18.00	5.00
☐ MT9 Barry Sanders	50.00	22.00	6.25
☐ MT10 Robert Brooks	18.00	8.00	2.20
☐ MT11 Brett Favre	90.00	40.00	11.00
☐ MT12 Marshall Faulk	18.00	8.00	2.20
☐ MT13 Jim Harbaugh	12.00	5.50	1.50
☐ MT14 Steve Bono	12.00	5.50	1.50
☐ MT15 Dan Marino	90.00	40.00	11.00
☐ MT16 Drew Bledsoe	50.00	22.00	6.25
☐ MT17 Curtis Martin	50.00	22.00	6.25
☐ MT18 Jerry Rice	50.00	22.00	6.25
☐ MT19 Steve Young	30.00	13.50	3.70
☐ MT20 Terry Allen	12.00	5.50	1.50

1997 Pacific Philadelphia

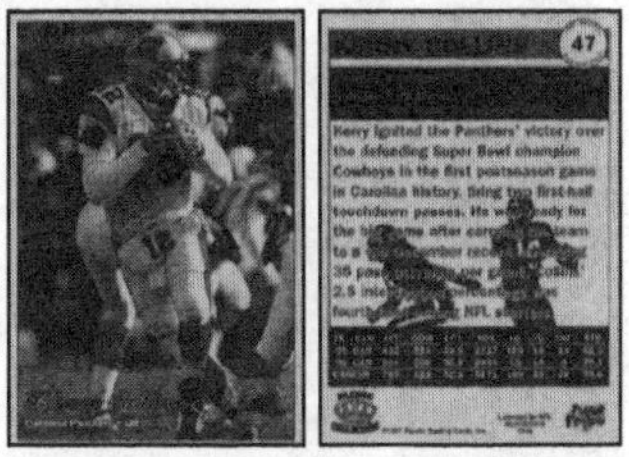

The 1997 Pacific Philadelphia set was issued in one series totaling 330 cards and was distributed in eight-card packs with a suggested retail of $1.49. Each pack contained five regular series cards with

either three bonus cards or two bonus and one insert card. The fronts feature color action player photos in a white border. The backs carry player information and career statistics.

	MINT	NRMT	EXC
COMPLETE SET (330)	30.00	13.50	3.70
COMMON CARD (1-330)	.10	.05	.01
☐ 1 Kevin Butler	.10	.05	.01
☐ 2 Larry Centers	.15	.07	.02
☐ 3 Kent Graham	.15	.07	.02
☐ 4 Leeland McElroy	.15	.07	.02
☐ 5 Ronald McKinnon	.10	.05	.01
☐ 6 Johnny McWilliams	.10	.05	.01
☐ 7 Brad Otis	.10	.05	.01
☐ 8 Frank Sanders	.15	.07	.02
☐ 9 Rob Selby	.10	.05	.01
☐ 10 Cedric Smith	.10	.05	.01
☐ 11 Joe Staysniak	.10	.05	.01
☐ 12 Cornelius Bennett	.15	.07	.02
☐ 13 David Brandon	.10	.05	.01
☐ 14 Tyrone Brown	.10	.05	.01
☐ 15 John Burrough	.10	.05	.01
☐ 16 Browning Nagle	.10	.05	.01
☐ 17 Dan Owens	.10	.05	.01
☐ 18 Anthony Phillips	.10	.05	.01
☐ 19 Roell Preston	.10	.05	.01
☐ 20 Darnell Walker	.10	.05	.01
☐ 21 Bob Whitfield	.10	.05	.01
☐ 22 Mike Zandofsky	.10	.05	.01
☐ 23 Vashone Adams	.10	.05	.01
☐ 24 Derrick Alexander WR	.15	.07	.02
☐ 25 Harold Bishop	.10	.05	.01
☐ 26 Jeff Blackshear	.10	.05	.01
☐ 27 Donny Brady	.10	.05	.01
☐ 28 Mike Frederick	.10	.05	.01
☐ 29 Tim Goad	.10	.05	.01
☐ 30 DeRon Jenkins	.10	.05	.01
☐ 31 Ray Lewis	.10	.05	.01
☐ 32 Rick Lyle	.10	.05	.01
☐ 33 Byron Bam Morris	.15	.07	.02
☐ 34 Chris Brantley	.10	.05	.01
☐ 35 Jeff Burris	.10	.05	.01
☐ 36 Todd Collins	.15	.07	.02
☐ 37 Rob Coons	.10	.05	.01
☐ 38 Corbin Lacina	.10	.05	.01
☐ 39 Emanuel Martin	.10	.05	.01
☐ 40 Marlo Perry	.10	.05	.01
☐ 41 Shawn Price	.10	.05	.01
☐ 42 Thomas Smith	.10	.05	.01
☐ 43 Matt Stevens	.10	.05	.01
☐ 44 Thurman Thomas	.30	.14	.04
☐ 45 Jay Barker	.10	.05	.01
☐ 46 Tim Biakabutuka	.30	.14	.04
☐ 47 Kerry Collins	.75	.35	.09
☐ 48 Matt Elliott	.10	.05	.01
☐ 49 Howard Griffith	.10	.05	.01
☐ 50 Anthony Johnson	.15	.07	.02
☐ 51 John Kasay	.10	.05	.01
☐ 52 Muhsin Muhammad	.40	.18	.05
☐ 53 Winslow Oliver	.10	.05	.01
☐ 54 Walter Rasby	.10	.05	.01
☐ 55 Gerald Williams	.10	.05	.01
☐ 56 Mark Butterfield	.10	.05	.01
☐ 57 Bryan Cox	.10	.05	.01
☐ 58 Mike Faulkerson	.10	.05	.01
☐ 59 Paul Grasmanis	.10	.05	.01
☐ 60 Robert Green	.10	.05	.01
☐ 61 Jack Jackson	.10	.05	.01
☐ 62 Bobby Neely	.10	.05	.01
☐ 63 Todd Perry	.10	.05	.01
☐ 64 Evan Pilgrim	.10	.05	.01
☐ 65 Octus Polk	.10	.05	.01
☐ 66 Rashaan Salaam	.30	.14	.04
☐ 67 Willie Anderson	.10	.05	.01
☐ 68 Jeff Blake	.30	.14	.04
☐ 69 Scott Brumfield	.10	.05	.01
☐ 70 Jeff Cothran	.10	.05	.01
☐ 71 Gerald Dixon	.10	.05	.01
☐ 72 Garrison Hearst	.15	.07	.02
☐ 73 James Hundon	.10	.05	.01
☐ 74 Brian Milne	.10	.05	.01
☐ 75 Troy Sadowski	.10	.05	.01
☐ 76 Tom Tumulty	.10	.05	.01
☐ 77 Kimo von Oelhoffen	.10	.05	.01
☐ 78 Troy Aikman	1.00	.45	.12
☐ 79 Dale Hellestrae	.10	.05	.01
☐ 80 Roger Harper	.10	.05	.01
☐ 81 Michael Irvin	.30	.14	.04
☐ 82 John Jett	.10	.05	.01
☐ 83 Kelvin Martin	.10	.05	.01
☐ 84 Deion Sanders	.50	.23	.06
☐ 85 Darrin Smith	.10	.05	.01
☐ 86 Emmitt Smith	2.00	.90	.25
☐ 87 Herschel Walker	.15	.07	.02
☐ 88 Charlie Williams	.10	.05	.01
☐ 89 Glenn Cadrez	.10	.05	.01
☐ 90 Dwayne Carswell	.10	.05	.01
☐ 91 Terrell Davis	1.00	.45	.12
☐ 92 David Diaz-infante	.10	.05	.01
☐ 93 John Elway	.75	.35	.09
☐ 94 Harald Hasselback	.10	.05	.01
☐ 95 Tory James	.10	.05	.01
☐ 96 Bill Musgrave	.10	.05	.01
☐ 97 Ralph Tamm	.10	.05	.01
☐ 98 Maa Tanuvasa	.10	.05	.01
☐ 99 Gary Zimmerman	.10	.05	.01
☐ 100 Shane Bonham	.10	.05	.01
☐ 101 Stephen Boyd	.10	.05	.01
☐ 102 Jeff Hartings	.10	.05	.01
☐ 103 Hessley Hempstead	.10	.05	.01
☐ 104 Scott Kowalkowski	.10	.05	.01
☐ 105 Herman Moore	.30	.14	.04
☐ 106 Barry Sanders	1.00	.45	.12
☐ 107 Tony Semple	.10	.05	.01
☐ 108 Ryan Stewart	.10	.05	.01
☐ 109 Mike Wells	.10	.05	.01
☐ 110 Richard Woodley	.10	.05	.01
☐ 111 Brett Favre	2.00	.90	.25
☐ 112 Bernardo Harris	.10	.05	.01
☐ 113 Keith McKenzie	.10	.05	.01
☐ 114 Terry Mickens	.10	.05	.01
☐ 115 Doug Pederson	.10	.05	.01
☐ 116 Jeff Thomason	.10	.05	.01
☐ 117 Adam Timmerman	.10	.05	.01
☐ 118 Reggie White	.30	.14	.04
☐ 119 Bruce Wilkerson	.10	.05	.01
☐ 120 Gabe Wilkins	.10	.05	.01
☐ 121 Tyrone Williams	.10	.05	.01
☐ 122 Al Del Greco	.10	.05	.01
☐ 123 Anthony Dorsett	.10	.05	.01
☐ 124 Josh Evans	.10	.05	.01
☐ 125 Eddie George	1.50	.70	.19
☐ 126 Lemanski Hall	.10	.05	.01
☐ 127 Ronnie Harmon	.10	.05	.01
☐ 128 Steve McNair	.60	.25	.07
☐ 129 Michael Roan	.10	.05	.01
☐ 130 Marcus Robertson	.10	.05	.01
☐ 131 Jon Runyan	.10	.05	.01
☐ 132 Chris Sanders	.15	.07	.02
☐ 133 Kerwin Bell	.10	.05	.01
☐ 134 Marshall Faulk	.30	.14	.04
☐ 135 Clif Groce	.10	.05	.01
☐ 136 Jim Harbaugh	.15	.07	.02
☐ 137 Marvin Harrison	.50	.23	.06
☐ 138 Eric Mahlum	.10	.05	.01
☐ 139 Tony Mandarich	.10	.05	.01
☐ 140 Dedric Mathis	.10	.05	.01
☐ 141 Marcus Pollard	.10	.05	.01
☐ 142 Scott Slutzker	.10	.05	.01
☐ 143 Mark Stock	.10	.05	.01
☐ 144 Bucky Brooks	.10	.05	.01
☐ 145 Mark Brunell	1.00	.45	.12
☐ 146 Kendricke Bullard	.10	.05	.01
☐ 147 Randy Jordan	.10	.05	.01
☐ 148 Jeff Kopp	.10	.05	.01
☐ 149 Le'Shai Maston	.10	.05	.01
☐ 150 Keenan McCardell	.15	.07	.02
☐ 151 Clyde Simmons	.10	.05	.01
☐ 152 Jimmy Smith	.15	.07	.02
☐ 153 Rich Tylski	.10	.05	.01
☐ 154 Dave Widell	.10	.05	.01
☐ 155 Marcus Allen	.30	.14	.04
☐ 156 Keith Cash	.10	.05	.01
☐ 157 Donnie Edwards	.10	.05	.01
☐ 158 Trezelle Jenkins	.10	.05	.01
☐ 159 Sean LaChapelle	.10	.05	.01
☐ 160 Greg Manusky	.10	.05	.01
☐ 161 Steve Matthews	.10	.05	.01
☐ 162 Pellom McDaniels	.10	.05	.01
☐ 163 Chris Penn	.10	.05	.01
☐ 164 Danny Villa	.10	.05	.01
☐ 165 Jerome Woods	.10	.05	.01
☐ 166 Karim Abdul-Jabbar	.75	.35	.09
☐ 167 John Bock	.10	.05	.01
☐ 168 O.J. Brigance	.10	.05	.01
☐ 169 Norman Hand	.10	.05	.01
☐ 170 Anthony Harris	.10	.05	.01
☐ 171 Larry Izzo	.10	.05	.01
☐ 172 Charles Jordan	.10	.05	.01
☐ 173 Dan Marino	2.00	.90	.25
☐ 174 Everett McIver	.10	.05	.01
☐ 175 Joe Nedney	.10	.05	.01
☐ 176 Robert Wilson	.10	.05	.01
☐ 177 David Dixon	.10	.05	.01
☐ 178 Charles Evans	.10	.05	.01
☐ 179 Hunter Goodwin	.10	.05	.01
☐ 180 Ben Hanks	.10	.05	.01
☐ 181 Warren Moon	.15	.07	.02
☐ 182 Harold Morrow	.10	.05	.01
☐ 183 Fernando Smith	.10	.05	.01
☐ 184 Robert Smith	.15	.07	.02
☐ 185 Sean Vanhorse	.10	.05	.01
☐ 186 Jay Walker	.10	.05	.01
☐ 187 Dewayne Washington	.10	.05	.01
☐ 188 Moe Williams	.10	.05	.01
☐ 189 Mike Bartrum	.10	.05	.01
☐ 190 Drew Bledsoe	1.00	.45	.12
☐ 191 Troy Brown	.10	.05	.01
☐ 192 Chad Eaton	.10	.05	.01
☐ 193 Sam Gash	.10	.05	.01
☐ 194 Mike Gisler	.10	.05	.01
☐ 195 Curtis Martin	1.00	.45	.12
☐ 196 David Richards	.10	.05	.01
☐ 197 Todd Rucci	.10	.05	.01
☐ 198 Chris Sullivan	.10	.05	.01
☐ 199 Adam Vinatieri	.10	.05	.01
☐ 200 Doug Brien	.10	.05	.01
☐ 201 Derek Brown	.10	.05	.01
☐ 202 Lee DeRamus	.10	.05	.01
☐ 203 Jim Everett	.10	.05	.01
☐ 204 Mercury Hayes	.10	.05	.01
☐ 205 Joe Johnson	.10	.05	.01
☐ 206 Henry Lusk	.10	.05	.01
☐ 207 Andy McCollum	.10	.05	.01
☐ 208 Alex Molden	.10	.05	.01
☐ 209 Ray Zellars	.10	.05	.01
☐ 210 Marcus Buckley	.10	.05	.01
☐ 211 Doug Coleman	.10	.05	.01
☐ 212 Percy Ellsworth	.10	.05	.01
☐ 213 Rodney Hampton	.15	.07	.02
☐ 214 Brian Saxton	.10	.05	.01
☐ 215 Jason Sehorn	.10	.05	.01
☐ 216 Stan White	.10	.05	.01
☐ 217 Corey Widmer	.10	.05	.01
☐ 218 Rodney Young	.10	.05	.01
☐ 219 Rob Zatechka	.10	.05	.01
☐ 220 Henry Bailey	.10	.05	.01
☐ 221 Chad Cascadden	.10	.05	.01
☐ 222 Wayne Chrebet	.10	.05	.01
☐ 223 Tyrone Davis	.10	.05	.01
☐ 224 Kwame Ellis	.10	.05	.01
☐ 225 Glenn Foley	.10	.05	.01
☐ 226 Erik Howard	.10	.05	.01
☐ 227 Gary Jones	.10	.05	.01
☐ 228 Adrian Murrell	.15	.07	.02
☐ 229 Marc Spindler	.10	.05	.01
☐ 230 Lonnie Young	.10	.05	.01
☐ 231 Eric Zomalt	.10	.05	.01
☐ 232 Tim Brown	.15	.07	.02
☐ 233 Aundray Bruce	.10	.05	.01
☐ 234 Darren Carrington	.10	.05	.01
☐ 235 Rick Cunningham	.10	.05	.01
☐ 236 Rob Homberg	.10	.05	.01
☐ 237 Jeff Hostetler	.15	.07	.02
☐ 238 Lorenzo Lynch	.10	.05	.01
☐ 239 Barrett Robbins	.10	.05	.01
☐ 240 Dan Turk	.10	.05	.01
☐ 241 Harvey Williams	.10	.05	.01
☐ 242 Brian Dawkins	.10	.05	.01
☐ 243 Ty Detmer	.15	.07	.02
☐ 244 Troy Drake	.10	.05	.01
☐ 245 Rhett Hall	.10	.05	.01
☐ 246 Joe Panos	.10	.05	.01
☐ 247 Johnny Thomas	.10	.05	.01
☐ 248 Kevin Turner	.10	.05	.01
☐ 249 Ricky Watters	.15	.07	.02
☐ 250 Derrick Witherspoon	.10	.05	.01
☐ 251 Sylvester Wright	.10	.05	.01
☐ 252 Jerome Bettis	.30	.14	.04
☐ 253 Carlos Emmons	.10	.05	.01
☐ 254 Jason Gildon	.10	.05	.01
☐ 255 Jonathan Hayes	.10	.05	.01
☐ 256 Kevin Henry	.10	.05	.01
☐ 257 Jerry Olsavsky	.10	.05	.01
☐ 258 Erric Pegram	.10	.05	.01
☐ 259 Brendan Stai	.10	.05	.01
☐ 260 Justin Strzelczyk	.10	.05	.01
☐ 261 Mike Tomczak	.10	.05	.01
☐ 262 Tony Banks	.40	.18	.05
☐ 263 Hayward Clay	.10	.05	.01
☐ 264 Percell Gaskins	.10	.05	.01
☐ 265 Eddie Kennison	.60	.25	.07
☐ 266 Aaron Laing	.10	.05	.01
☐ 267 Keith Lyle	.10	.05	.01
☐ 268 Jamie Martin	.15	.07	.02
☐ 269 Lawrence Phillips	.15	.07	.02
☐ 270 Zach Wiegert	.10	.05	.01
☐ 271 Toby Wright	.10	.05	.01
☐ 272 Darren Bennett	.10	.05	.01
☐ 273 Tony Berti	.10	.05	.01
☐ 274 Freddie Bradley	.10	.05	.01
☐ 275 Joe Cocozzo	.10	.05	.01
☐ 276 Andre Coleman	.10	.05	.01
☐ 277 Marco Coleman	.10	.05	.01
☐ 278 Rodney Harrison	.10	.05	.01
☐ 279 David Hendrix	.10	.05	.01
☐ 280 Leonard Russell	.10	.05	.01
☐ 281 Sean Salisbury	.10	.05	.01
☐ 282 Dennis Brown	.10	.05	.01
☐ 283 Chris Dalman	.10	.05	.01
☐ 284 Brent Jones	.10	.05	.01
☐ 285 Sean Manuel	.10	.05	.01
☐ 286 Marquez Pope	.10	.05	.01
☐ 287 Jerry Rice	1.00	.45	.12
☐ 288 Kirk Scrafford	.10	.05	.01
☐ 289 Iheanyi Uwaezuoke	.10	.05	.01
☐ 290 Tommy Vardell	.10	.05	.01
☐ 291 Steve Young	.75	.35	.09
☐ 292 James Atkins	.10	.05	.01
☐ 293 T.J. Cunningham	.10	.05	.01
☐ 294 Stan Gelbaugh	.10	.05	.01
☐ 295 James Logan	.10	.05	.01
☐ 296 James McKnight	.10	.05	.01
☐ 297 Rick Mirer	.15	.07	.02
☐ 298 Todd Peterson	.10	.05	.01
☐ 299 Fred Thomas	.10	.05	.01
☐ 300 Rick Tuten	.10	.05	.01
☐ 301 Chris Warren	.15	.07	.02
☐ 302 Donnie Abraham	.10	.05	.01
☐ 303 Trent Dilfer	.15	.07	.02
☐ 304 Kenneth Gant	.10	.05	.01
☐ 305 Jeff Gooch	.10	.05	.01
☐ 306 Courtney Hawkins	.10	.05	.01
☐ 307 Tyoka Jackson	.10	.05	.01
☐ 308 Melvin Johnson	.10	.05	.01
☐ 309 Lonnie Marts	.10	.05	.01
☐ 310 Hardy Nickerson	.10	.05	.01
☐ 311 Errict Rhett	.15	.07	.02
☐ 312 Terry Allen	.15	.07	.02
☐ 313 Flipper Anderson	.10	.05	.01
☐ 314 William Bell	.10	.05	.01
☐ 315 Scott Blanton	.10	.05	.01
☐ 316 Leomont Evans	.10	.05	.01
☐ 317 Gus Frerotte	.30	.14	.04
☐ 318 Darryl Morrison	.10	.05	.01
☐ 319 Matt Turk	.10	.05	.01
☐ 320 Jeff Uhlenhake	.10	.05	.01
☐ 321 Bryan Walker	.10	.05	.01
☐ 322 Mark Brunell LL	.50	.23	.06
☐ 323 Barry Sanders LL	.50	.23	.06
☐ 324 Isaac Bruce LL	.30	.14	.04
☐ 325 Terry Allen LL	.15	.07	.02
☐ 326 Steve Young LL	.40	.18	.05
☐ 327 Jerry Rice LL	.50	.23	.06
☐ 328 Ricky Watters LL	.15	.07	.02
☐ 329 Kevin Greene LL	.15	.07	.02
☐ 330 Brett Favre LL	1.00	.45	.12
☐ S1 Mark Brunell Promo marked "Sample" on back	1.00	.45	.12

1997 Pacific Philadelphia Gold

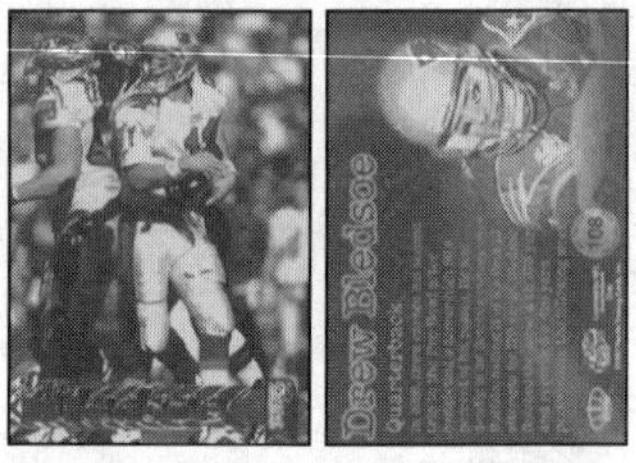

Inserted in packs at the rate of three per pack, this 200-card bonus set features borderless color player action photos with gold foil highlights. The backs carry player information.

	MINT	NRMT	EXC
COMPLETE SET (200)	30.00	13.50	3.70
COMMON CARD (1-200)	.15	.07	.02
*COPPERS: 2X TO 4X BASIC CARDS..			
*SILVERS: 3.5X TO 7X BASIC CARDS			
☐ 1 Ryan Christopherson	.15	.07	.02
☐ 2 James Dexter	.15	.07	.02
☐ 3 Boomer Esiason	.25	.11	.03
☐ 4 Jarius Hayes	.15	.07	.02
☐ 5 Eric Hill	.15	.07	.02
☐ 6 Trey Junkin	.15	.07	.02
☐ 7 Kwamie Lassiter	.15	.07	.02
☐ 8 Patrick Bates	.15	.07	.02
☐ 9 Brad Edwards	.15	.07	.02
☐ 10 Roman Fortin	.15	.07	.02
☐ 11 Harper Le Bel	.15	.07	.02
☐ 12 Lorenzo Styles	.15	.07	.02
☐ 13 Robbie Tobeck	.15	.07	.02
☐ 14 Mike Caldwell	.15	.07	.02
☐ 15 Eric Green	.15	.07	.02
☐ 16 Brian Kinchen	.15	.07	.02
☐ 17 Eric Turner	.15	.07	.02
☐ 18 Jerrol Williams	.15	.07	.02
☐ 19 Eric Zeier	.25	.11	.03
☐ 20 Darick Holmes	.25	.11	.03
☐ 21 Ken Irvin	.15	.07	.02
☐ 22 Jerry Ostroski	.15	.07	.02
☐ 23 Andre Reed	.25	.11	.03
☐ 24 Steve Tasker	.15	.07	.02
☐ 25 Thurman Thomas	.40	.18	.05
☐ 26 Steve Beuerlein	.15	.07	.02
☐ 27 Kerry Collins	.75	.35	.09
☐ 28 Eric Davis	.15	.07	.02
☐ 29 Norberto Garrido	.15	.07	.02
☐ 30 Lamar Lathon	.15	.07	.02
☐ 31 Andre Royal	.15	.07	.02
☐ 32 Tony Carter	.15	.07	.02
☐ 33 Jerry Fontenot	.15	.07	.02
☐ 34 Raymont Harris	.15	.07	.02
☐ 35 Anthony Marshall	.15	.07	.02
☐ 36 Barry Minter	.15	.07	.02
☐ 37 Steve Stenstrom	.15	.07	.02
☐ 38 Donnell Woolford	.15	.07	.02
☐ 39 Ken Blackman	.15	.07	.02
☐ 40 Jeff Blake	.40	.18	.05
☐ 41 Carl Pickens	.40	.18	.05
☐ 42 Artie Smith	.15	.07	.02
☐ 43 Ramondo Stallings	.15	.07	.02
☐ 44 Melvin Tuten	.15	.07	.02
☐ 45 Joe Walter	.15	.07	.02
☐ 46 Troy Aikman	1.00	.45	.12
☐ 47 Billy Davis	.15	.07	.02
☐ 48 Chad Hennings	.25	.11	.03
☐ 49 Emmitt Smith	2.00	.90	.25
☐ 50 George Teague	.15	.07	.02
☐ 51 Kevin Williams	.15	.07	.02
☐ 52 Terrell Davis	1.00	.45	.12
☐ 53 John Elway	.75	.35	.09
☐ 54 Tom Naten	.15	.07	.02

☐ 55 Bill Romanowski	.15	.07	.02
☐ 56 Rod Smith WR	.15	.07	.02
☐ 57 Dan Williams	.15	.07	.02
☐ 58 Mike Compton	.15	.07	.02
☐ 59 Eric Lynch	.15	.07	.02
☐ 60 Aubrey Matthews	.15	.07	.02
☐ 61 Pete Metzelaars	.15	.07	.02
☐ 62 Herman Moore	.40	.18	.05
☐ 63 Barry Sanders	1.00	.45	.12
☐ 64 Keith Washington	.15	.07	.02
☐ 65 Edgar Bennett	.25	.11	.03
☐ 66 Brett Favre	2.00	.90	.25
☐ 67 Lamont Hollinquest	.15	.07	.02
☐ 68 Keith Jackson	.15	.07	.02
☐ 69 Derrick Mayes	.25	.11	.03
☐ 70 Andre Rison	.25	.11	.03
☐ 71 Eddie George	1.50	.70	.19
☐ 72 Mel Gray	.15	.07	.02
☐ 73 Darryll Lewis	.15	.07	.02
☐ 74 John Henry Mills	.15	.07	.02
☐ 75 Rodney Thomas	.15	.07	.02
☐ 76 Gary Walker	.15	.07	.02
☐ 77 Troy Auzenne	.15	.07	.02
☐ 78 Sammie Burroughs	.15	.07	.02
☐ 79 Jim Harbaugh	.25	.11	.03
☐ 80 Tony McCoy	.15	.07	.02
☐ 81 Brian Stablein	.15	.07	.02
☐ 82 Kipp Vickers	.15	.07	.02
☐ 83 Aaron Beasley	.15	.07	.02
☐ 84 Mark Brunell	1.00	.45	.12
☐ 85 Don Davey	.15	.07	.02
☐ 86 Chris Hudson	.15	.07	.02
☐ 87 Greg Huntington	.15	.07	.02
☐ 88 Ernie Logan	.15	.07	.02
☐ 89 Donnell Bennett	.15	.07	.02
☐ 90 Anthony Davis	.15	.07	.02
☐ 91 Tim Grunhard	.15	.07	.02
☐ 92 Danan Hughes	.15	.07	.02
☐ 93 Tony Richardson	.15	.07	.02
☐ 94 Tracy Simien	.15	.07	.02
☐ 95 Karim Abdul-Jabbar	1.00	.45	.12
☐ 96 Dwight Hollier	.15	.07	.02
☐ 97 John Kidd	.15	.07	.02
☐ 98 Dan Marino	2.00	.90	.25
☐ 99 Jerris McPhail	.15	.07	.02
☐ 100 Irving Spikes	.15	.07	.02
☐ 101 Richmond Webb	.15	.07	.02
☐ 102 Jeff Brady	.15	.07	.02
☐ 103 Richard Brown	.15	.07	.02
☐ 104 Corey Fuller	.15	.07	.02
☐ 105 John Gerak	.15	.07	.02
☐ 106 Scottie Graham	.15	.07	.02
☐ 107 Amp Lee	.15	.07	.02
☐ 108 Drew Bledsoe	1.00	.45	.12
☐ 109 Tedy Bruschi	.15	.07	.02
☐ 110 Todd Collins	.25	.11	.03
☐ 111 Bob Kratch	.15	.07	.02
☐ 112 Curtis Martin	1.00	.45	.12
☐ 113 Dave Meggett	.15	.07	.02
☐ 114 Tom Tupa	.15	.07	.02
☐ 115 Eric Allen	.15	.07	.02
☐ 116 Mario Bates	.25	.11	.03
☐ 117 Clarence Jones	.15	.07	.02
☐ 118 Sean Lumpkin	.15	.07	.02
☐ 119 Doug Nussmeier	.15	.07	.02
☐ 120 Irv Smith	.15	.07	.02
☐ 121 Winfred Tubbs	.15	.07	.02
☐ 122 Willie Beamon	.15	.07	.02
☐ 123 Greg Bishop	.15	.07	.02
☐ 124 Dave Brown	.25	.11	.03
☐ 125 Gary Downs	.15	.07	.02
☐ 126 Thomas Lewis	.15	.07	.02
☐ 127 Michael Strahan	.15	.07	.02
☐ 128 Tyrone Wheatley	.25	.11	.03
☐ 129 Matt Brock	.15	.07	.02
☐ 130 Mike Chalenski	.15	.07	.02
☐ 131 Roger Duffy	.15	.07	.02
☐ 132 John Hudson	.15	.07	.02
☐ 133 Frank Reich	.15	.07	.02
☐ 134 David Williams	.15	.07	.02
☐ 135 Greg Biekert	.15	.07	.02
☐ 136 Mike Jones	.15	.07	.02
☐ 137 Napoleon Kaufman	.25	.11	.03
☐ 138 Carl Kidd	.15	.07	.02
☐ 139 Terry McDaniel	.15	.07	.02
☐ 140 Mike Morton	.15	.07	.02
☐ 141 Olanda Truitt	.15	.07	.02
☐ 142 Gary Anderson	.15	.07	.02
☐ 143 Richard Cooper	.15	.07	.02
☐ 144 Jimmie Johnson	.15	.07	.02
☐ 145 Joe Kelly	.15	.07	.02
☐ 146 William Thomas	.15	.07	.02
☐ 147 Ricky Watters	.25	.11	.03
☐ 148 Ed West	.15	.07	.02
☐ 149 Michael Zordich	.15	.07	.02
☐ 150 Jerome Bettis	.40	.18	.05
☐ 151 Dermontti Dawson	.15	.07	.02
☐ 152 Lethon Flowers	.15	.07	.02
☐ 153 Charles Johnson	.25	.11	.03
☐ 154 Darren Perry	.15	.07	.02
☐ 155 Kordell Stewart	.75	.35	.09
☐ 156 Will Wolford	.15	.07	.02
☐ 157 Isaac Bruce	.40	.18	.05
☐ 158 Kevin Carter	.15	.07	.02
☐ 159 Torin Dorn	.15	.07	.02
☐ 160 Leo Goeas	.15	.07	.02
☐ 161 Gerald McBurrows	.15	.07	.02
☐ 162 Chuck Osborne	.15	.07	.02
☐ 163 J.T. Thomas	.15	.07	.02
☐ 164 Dwayne Gordon	.15	.07	.02
☐ 165 Stan Humphries	.25	.11	.03
☐ 166 Shawn Lee	.15	.07	.02
☐ 167 Chris Mims	.15	.07	.02
☐ 168 John Parrella	.15	.07	.02
☐ 169 Junior Seau	.40	.18	.05
☐ 170 Bryan Still	.15	.07	.02
☐ 171 Curtis Buckley	.15	.07	.02
☐ 172 William Floyd	.25	.11	.03
☐ 173 Merton Hanks	.15	.07	.02
☐ 174 Terry Kirby	.25	.11	.03
☐ 175 Jerry Rice	1.00	.45	.12
☐ 176 J.J. Stokes	.25	.11	.03
☐ 177 Jeff Wilkins	.15	.07	.02
☐ 178 Bryant Young	.25	.11	.03
☐ 179 Sam Adams	.15	.07	.02
☐ 180 John Friesz	.15	.07	.02
☐ 181 Joey Galloway	.40	.18	.05
☐ 182 Pete Kendall	.15	.07	.02
☐ 183 Jason Kyle	.15	.07	.02
☐ 184 Darryl Williams	.15	.07	.02
☐ 185 Ronnie Williams	.15	.07	.02
☐ 186 Mike Alstott	.40	.18	.05
☐ 187 Trent Dilfer	.25	.11	.03
☐ 188 Tyrone Legette	.15	.07	.02
☐ 189 Martin Mayhew	.15	.07	.02
☐ 190 Jason Odom	.15	.07	.02
☐ 191 Warren Sapp	.15	.07	.02
☐ 192 Karl Williams	.15	.07	.02
☐ 193 Terry Allen	.25	.11	.03
☐ 194 Romeo Bandison	.15	.07	.02
☐ 195 Alcides Catanho	.15	.07	.02
☐ 196 Gus Frerotte	.40	.18	.05
☐ 197 William Gaines	.15	.07	.02
☐ 198 Ken Harvey	.15	.07	.02
☐ 199 Trevor Matich	.15	.07	.02
☐ 200 Scott Turner	.15	.07	.02
☐ S1 Mark Brunell Promo marked "Sample" on back	2.00	.90	.25

1997 Pacific Philadelphia Heart of the Game

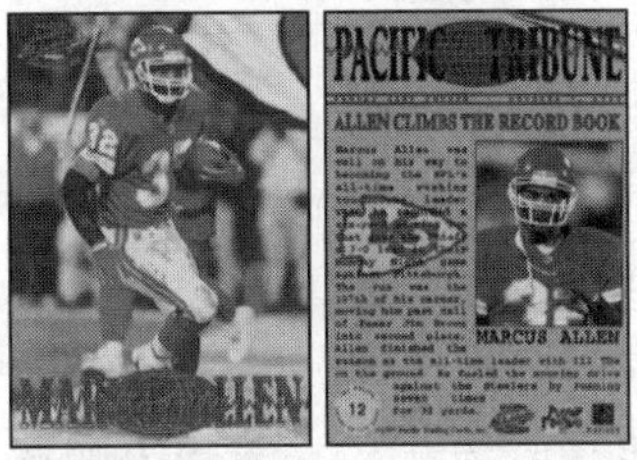

Randomly inserted in packs at a rate of one in 73, this 20-card set features borderless color action player photos on the fronts with player information on the backs.

	MINT	NRMT	EXC
COMPLETE SET (20)	300.00	135.00	38.00
COMMON CARD (1-20)	8.00	3.60	1.00
☐ 1 Thurman Thomas	12.00	5.50	1.50
☐ 2 Kerry Collins	20.00	9.00	2.50
☐ 3 Troy Aikman	20.00	9.00	2.50
☐ 4 Emmitt Smith	40.00	18.00	5.00
☐ 5 Terrell Davis	20.00	9.00	2.50
☐ 6 John Elway	15.00	6.75	1.85
☐ 7 Barry Sanders	20.00	9.00	2.50
☐ 8 Brett Favre	40.00	18.00	5.00
☐ 9 Antonio Freeman	12.00	5.50	1.50
☐ 10 Marshall Faulk	12.00	5.50	1.50
☐ 11 Mark Brunell	20.00	9.00	2.50
☐ 12 Marcus Allen	12.00	5.50	1.50
☐ 13 Dan Marino	40.00	18.00	5.00
☐ 14 Drew Bledsoe	20.00	9.00	2.50
☐ 15 Curtis Martin	20.00	9.00	2.50
☐ 16 Napoleon Kaufman	8.00	3.60	1.00
☐ 17 Jerome Bettis	12.00	5.50	1.50
☐ 18 Isaac Bruce	12.00	5.50	1.50
☐ 19 Jerry Rice	20.00	9.00	2.50
☐ 20 Steve Young	15.00	6.75	1.85

1997 Pacific Philadelphia Milestones

Randomly inserted in packs at a rate of one in 37, this 20-card set features color action player images on a team-color helmet with a gold ribbon running from the top of the card to the bottom stating the player's accomplishment and name. The backs carry additional player information.

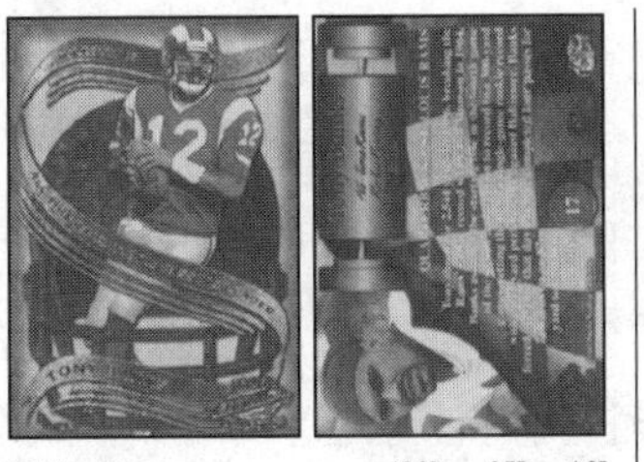

	MINT	NRMT	EXC
COMPLETE SET (20)	250.00	110.00	31.00
COMMON CARD (1-20)	4.00	1.80	.50
☐ 1 Simeon Rice	4.00	1.80	.50
☐ 2 Thurman Thomas	8.00	3.60	1.00
☐ 3 Troy Aikman	15.00	6.75	1.85
☐ 4 Emmitt Smith	30.00	13.50	3.70
☐ 5 Terrell Davis	15.00	6.75	1.85
☐ 6 John Elway	12.00	5.50	1.50
☐ 7 Brett Favre	30.00	13.50	3.70
☐ 8 Desmond Howard	4.00	1.80	.50
☐ 9 Reggie White	8.00	3.60	1.00
☐ 10 Mark Brunell	15.00	6.75	1.85
☐ 11 Marcus Allen	8.00	3.60	1.00
☐ 12 Karim Abdul-Jabbar	12.00	5.50	1.50
☐ 13 Dan Marino	30.00	13.50	3.70
☐ 14 Drew Bledsoe	15.00	6.75	1.85
☐ 15 Terry Glenn	15.00	6.75	1.85
☐ 16 Curtis Martin	15.00	6.75	1.85
☐ 17 Tony Banks	8.00	3.60	1.00
☐ 18 Jerry Rice	15.00	6.75	1.85
☐ 19 Steve Young	12.00	5.50	1.50
☐ 20 Terry Allen	6.00	2.70	.75

1997 Pacific Philadelphia Photoengravings

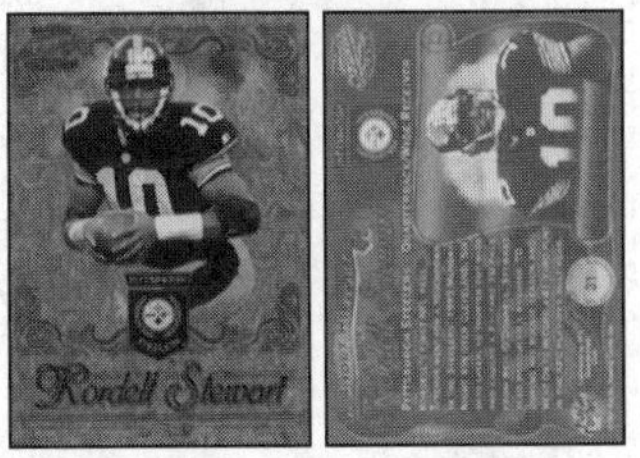

Randomly inserted in packs at a rate of two in 37, this 36-card set with rounded corners features color action photos of players from the waist up set in a thin frame on a background with engraved-looking abstract design. The backs carry information about the player.

	MINT	NRMT	EXC
COMPLETE SET (36)	250.00	110.00	31.00
COMMON CARD (1-36)	2.50	1.10	.30
☐ 1 Thurman Thomas	6.00	2.70	.75
☐ 2 Kerry Collins	10.00	4.50	1.25
☐ 3 Jeff Blake	4.00	1.80	.50
☐ 4 Troy Aikman	12.00	5.50	1.50
☐ 5 Deion Sanders	7.00	3.10	.85
☐ 6 Emmitt Smith	25.00	11.00	3.10
☐ 7 Terrell Davis	10.00	4.50	1.25
☐ 8 John Elway	10.00	4.50	1.25
☐ 9 Herman Moore	6.00	2.70	.75
☐ 10 Barry Sanders	12.00	5.50	1.50
☐ 11 Brett Favre	25.00	11.00	3.10
☐ 12 Desmond Howard	2.50	1.10	.30
☐ 13 Dorsey Levens	2.50	1.10	.30
☐ 14 Eddie George	18.00	8.00	2.20
☐ 15 Marshall Faulk	6.00	2.70	.75
☐ 16 Jim Harbaugh	4.00	1.80	.50
☐ 17 Marvin Harrison	6.00	2.70	.75
☐ 18 Mark Brunell	12.00	5.50	1.50
☐ 19 Keenan McCardell	2.50	1.10	.30
☐ 20 Karim Abdul-Jabbar	10.00	4.50	1.25
☐ 21 Dan Marino	25.00	11.00	3.10
☐ 22 Brad Johnson	2.50	1.10	.30
☐ 23 Drew Bledsoe	12.00	5.50	1.50
☐ 24 Terry Glenn	12.00	5.50	1.50
☐ 25 Curtis Martin	10.00	4.50	1.25
☐ 26 Keyshawn Johnson	6.00	2.70	.75
☐ 27 Tim Brown	4.00	1.80	.50
☐ 28 Napoleon Kaufman	2.50	1.10	.30
☐ 29 Ricky Watters	4.00	1.80	.50
☐ 30 Jerome Bettis	6.00	2.70	.75
☐ 31 Kordell Stewart	10.00	4.50	1.25
☐ 32 Eddie Kennison	6.00	2.70	.75
☐ 33 Jerry Rice	12.00	5.50	1.50
☐ 34 Steve Young	10.00	4.50	1.25
☐ 35 Chris Warren	4.00	1.80	.50
☐ 36 Terry Allen	4.00	1.80	.50

1993 Pacific Prisms

After debuting as an insert set in the 1992 Pacific NFL series, Pacific decided to release a 108-card (plus one checklist) set of Prism cards. The standard-size cards comprising this set were issued in one-card packs and feature on their fronts color player action cut-outs over borderless triangular prismatic foil backgrounds. The player's name, the characters of which resemble hand-printed upper case lettering, appears in team colors at the bottom. The horizontal back carries two color player photos, a helmet bearing his team's logo, and player profile, all superposed upon a grayish background. Seventeen thousand of each card were produced. The cards are numbered on the back and checklisted below alphabetically according to teams. Rookie Cards include Jerome Bettis, Drew Bledsoe, Reggie Brooks, Garrison Hearst, Rick Mirer and Robert Smith. Two promo cards (Emmitt Smith and Drew Bledsoe) were produced and are listed below. They were released primarily at the Chicago National Card Collectors Convention and each looks very similar to its regular issue card. The promos however differ slightly on the backs in relation to the small player and helmet photos. The player photo is touching the helmet and the helmet photo is smaller on the promo cards. Reportedly 5,500 of each promo was produced.

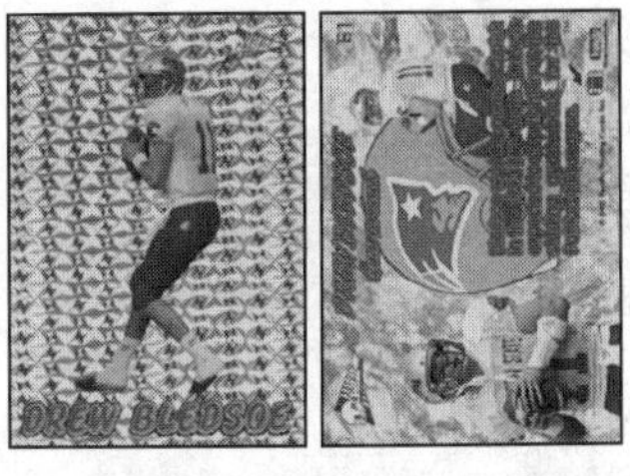

	MINT	NRMT	EXC
COMPLETE SET (109)	120.00	55.00	15.00
COMMON CARD (1-108)	.75	.35	.09
☐ 1 Chris Miller	1.25	.55	.16
☐ 2 Mike Pritchard	1.25	.55	.16
☐ 3 Andre Rison	1.25	.55	.16
☐ 4 Deion Sanders	5.00	2.20	.60
☐ 5 Tony Smith	.75	.35	.09
☐ 6 Jim Kelly	2.00	.90	.25
☐ 7 Andre Reed	1.25	.55	.16
☐ 8 Thurman Thomas	2.00	.90	.25
☐ 9 Neal Anderson	.75	.35	.09
☐ 10 Jim Harbaugh	2.00	.90	.25
☐ 11 Donnell Woolford	.75	.35	.09
☐ 12 David Klingler	.75	.35	.09
☐ 13 Carl Pickens	4.00	1.80	.50
☐ 14 Alfred Williams	.75	.35	.09
☐ 15 Michael Jackson	1.25	.55	.16
☐ 16 Bernie Kosar	1.25	.55	.16
☐ 17 Tommy Vardell	.75	.35	.09
☐ 18 Troy Aikman	8.00	3.60	1.00
☐ 19 Alvin Harper	1.25	.55	.16
☐ 20 Michael Irvin	2.00	.90	.25
☐ 21 Russell Maryland	.75	.35	.09
☐ 22 Emmitt Smith	12.00	5.50	1.50
☐ 23 John Elway	6.00	2.70	.75
☐ 24 Tommy Maddox	.75	.35	.09
☐ 25 Shannon Sharpe	2.00	.90	.25
☐ 26 Herman Moore	5.00	2.20	.60
☐ 27 Rodney Peete	.75	.35	.09
☐ 28 Barry Sanders	8.00	3.60	1.00
☐ 29 Pat Swilling	.75	.35	.09
☐ 30 Terrell Buckley	.75	.35	.09
☐ 31 Brett Favre	12.00	5.50	1.50
☐ 32 Sterling Sharpe	2.00	.90	.25
☐ 33 Reggie White	2.00	.90	.25
☐ 34 Ernest Givins	1.25	.55	.16
☐ 35 Haywood Jeffires	1.25	.55	.16
☐ 36 Warren Moon	2.00	.90	.25
☐ 37 Lorenzo White	.75	.35	.09
☐ 38 Steve Emtman	.75	.35	.09
☐ 39 Jeff George	2.00	.90	.25
☐ 40 Reggie Langhorne	.75	.35	.09
☐ 41 Dale Carter	.75	.35	.09
☐ 42 Joe Montana	8.00	3.60	1.00
☐ 43 Derrick Thomas	2.00	.90	.25
☐ 44 Barry Word	.75	.35	.09
☐ 45 Nick Bell	.75	.35	.09
☐ 46 Eric Dickerson	1.25	.55	.16
☐ 47 Jeff Jaeger	.75	.35	.09
☐ 48 Jerome Bettis	7.00	3.10	.85
☐ 49 Henry Ellard	1.25	.55	.16
☐ 50 Jim Everett	1.25	.55	.16
☐ 51 Cleveland Gary	.75	.35	.09
☐ 52 Marco Coleman	.75	.35	.09
☐ 53 Mark Higgs	.75	.35	.09
☐ 54 Keith Jackson	1.25	.55	.16
☐ 55 Dan Marino	12.00	5.50	1.50
☐ 56 Troy Vincent	.75	.35	.09
☐ 57 Terry Allen	2.00	.90	.25
☐ 58 Jack Del Rio	.75	.35	.09
☐ 59 Sean Salisbury	.75	.35	.09
☐ 60 Robert Smith	4.00	1.80	.50
☐ 61 Drew Bledsoe	14.00	6.25	1.75
☐ 62 Marv Cook	.75	.35	.09
☐ 63 Irving Fryar	1.25	.55	.16
☐ 64 Leonard Russell	1.25	.55	.16
☐ 65 Andre Tippett	.75	.35	.09
☐ 66 Morten Andersen	.75	.35	.09
☐ 67 Vaughn Dunbar	.75	.35	.09
☐ 68 Eric Martin	.75	.35	.09
☐ 69 David Brown	2.00	.90	.25
☐ 70 Rodney Hampton	2.00	.90	.25
☐ 71 Phil Simms	1.25	.55	.16
☐ 72 Lawrence Taylor	2.00	.90	.25
☐ 73 Ronnie Lott	1.25	.55	.16
☐ 74 Johnny Mitchell	.75	.35	.09
☐ 75 Rob Moore	1.25	.55	.16
☐ 76 Browning Nagle	.75	.35	.09

☐ 77 Fred Barnett	1.25	.55	.16
☐ 78 Randall Cunningham	1.25	.55	.16
☐ 79 Herschel Walker	1.25	.55	.16
☐ 80 Gary Clark	1.25	.55	.16
☐ 81 Ken Harvey	.75	.35	.09
☐ 82 Garrison Hearst	6.00	2.70	.75
☐ 83 Ricky Proehl	.75	.35	.09
☐ 84 Barry Foster	1.25	.55	.16
☐ 85 Ernie Mills	.75	.35	.09
☐ 86 Neil O'Donnell	2.00	.90	.25
☐ 87 Stan Humphries	2.00	.90	.25
☐ 88 Leslie O'Neal	1.25	.55	.16
☐ 89 Junior Seau	2.00	.90	.25
☐ 90 Amp Lee	.75	.35	.09
☐ 91 Jerry Rice	8.00	3.60	1.00
☐ 92 Ricky Watters	2.00	.90	.25
☐ 93 Steve Young	6.00	2.70	.75
☐ 94 Cortez Kennedy	1.25	.55	.16
☐ 95 Rick Mirer	6.00	2.70	.75
☐ 96 Eugene Robinson	.75	.35	.09
☐ 97 Chris Warren	1.25	.55	.16
☐ 98 John L. Williams	.75	.35	.09
☐ 99 Reggie Cobb	.75	.35	.09
☐ 100 Lawrence Dawsey	.75	.35	.09
☐ 101 Santana Dotson	1.25	.55	.16
☐ 102 Courtney Hawkins	.75	.35	.09
☐ 103 Reggie Brooks	1.25	.55	.16
☐ 104 Ricky Ervins	.75	.35	.09
☐ 105 Desmond Howard	1.25	.55	.16
☐ 106 Art Monk	1.25	.55	.16
☐ 107 Mark Rypien	.75	.35	.09
☐ 108 Ricky Sanders	.75	.35	.09
☐ P22 Emmitt Smith Promo	15.00	6.75	1.85
☐ P61 Drew Bledsoe Promo	20.00	9.00	2.50
☐ NNO Checklist Card	.50	.23	.06

1994 Pacific Prisms

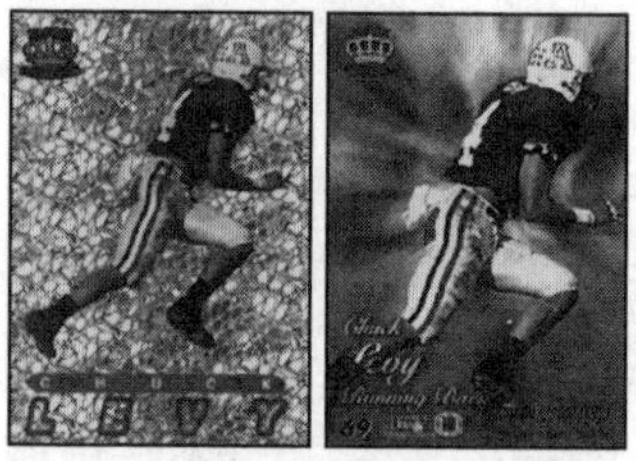

These 128 standard-size cards feature borderless fronts with color action player photos cut out and superimposed on a prism-patterned background. The player's name appears at the bottom beneath the action cutout. The back contains the same color action player photo with a blurred background. There were reportedly 16,000 of each card produced in silver foil and 1,138 of each card produced in gold foil. Each pack contained either a silver or gold Prism card. Rookie Cards include Mario Bates, Marshall Faulk, William Floyd, Greg Hill, Charles Johnson, Errict Rhett and Heath Shuler.

	MINT	NRMT	EXC
COMPLETE SET (128)	140.00	65.00	17.50
COMMON CARD (1-126)	.50	.23	.06
☐ 1 Troy Aikman UER (Text on back indicates he led Cowboys to victory in Super Bowl XXV. The Giants won SB XXV)	6.00	2.70	.75
☐ 2 Marcus Allen	1.50	.70	.19
☐ 3 Morten Andersen	.50	.23	.06
☐ 4 Fred Barnett	1.00	.45	.12
☐ 5 Mario Bates	2.50	1.10	.30
☐ 6 Edgar Bennett	1.50	.70	.19
☐ 7 Rod Bernstine	.50	.23	.06
☐ 8 Jerome Bettis	3.00	1.35	.35
☐ 9 Steve Beuerlein	.50	.23	.06
☐ 10 Brian Blades	1.00	.45	.12
☐ 11 Drew Bledsoe	6.00	2.70	.75
☐ 12 Vincent Brisby	1.00	.45	.12
☐ 13 Reggie Brooks	1.00	.45	.12
☐ 14 Derek Brown RB	.50	.23	.06
☐ 15 Gary Brown	.50	.23	.06
☐ 16 Tim Brown	1.00	.45	.12
☐ 17 Marion Butts	.50	.23	.06
☐ 18 Keith Byars	.50	.23	.06
☐ 19 Cody Carlson	.50	.23	.06
☐ 20 Anthony Carter	1.00	.45	.12
☐ 21 Tom Carter	.50	.23	.06
☐ 22 Gary Clark	1.00	.45	.12
☐ 23 Ben Coates	1.50	.70	.19
☐ 24 Reggie Cobb	.50	.23	.06
☐ 25 Curtis Conway	1.00	.45	.12
☐ 26 John Copeland	.50	.23	.06
☐ 27 Randall Cunningham	1.00	.45	.12
☐ 28 Willie Davis	1.00	.45	.12
☐ 29 Sean Dawkins	2.50	1.10	.30
☐ 30 Lawrence Dawsey	.50	.23	.06
☐ 31 Richard Dent	1.00	.45	.12
☐ 32 Trent Dilfer	3.00	1.35	.35
☐ 33 Troy Drayton	.50	.23	.06
☐ 34 Vaughn Dunbar	.50	.23	.06
☐ 35 Henry Ellard	1.00	.45	.12
☐ 36 John Elway	5.00	2.20	.60
☐ 37 Craig Erickson	.50	.23	.06
☐ 38 Boomer Esiason	1.00	.45	.12
☐ 39 Marshall Faulk	6.00	2.70	.75
☐ 40 Brett Favre	12.00	5.50	1.50
☐ 41 William Floyd	3.00	1.35	.35
☐ 42 Glenn Foley	.50	.23	.06
☐ 43 Barry Foster	.50	.23	.06
☐ 44 Irving Fryar	1.00	.45	.12
☐ 45 Jeff George	1.50	.70	.19
☐ 46 Scottie Graham	1.00	.45	.12
☐ 47 Rodney Hampton	1.00	.45	.12
☐ 48 Jim Harbaugh	1.50	.70	.19
☐ 49 Alvin Harper	1.00	.45	.12
☐ 50 Courtney Hawkins	.50	.23	.06
☐ 51 Garrison Hearst	2.50	1.10	.30
☐ 52 Vaughn Hebron	.50	.23	.06
☐ 53 Greg Hill	3.00	1.35	.35
☐ 54 Jeff Hostetler	1.00	.45	.12
☐ 55 Michael Irvin	1.50	.70	.19
☐ 56 Qadry Ismail	1.00	.45	.12
☐ 57 Rocket Ismail	1.00	.45	.12
☐ 58 Anthony Johnson	1.00	.45	.12
☐ 59 Charles Johnson	2.50	1.10	.30
☐ 60 Johnny Johnson	.50	.23	.06
☐ 61 Brent Jones	1.00	.45	.12
☐ 62 Kyle Clifton	.50	.23	.06
☐ 63 Jim Kelly	1.00	.45	.12
☐ 64 Cortez Kennedy	1.00	.45	.12
☐ 65 Terry Kirby	1.50	.70	.19
☐ 66 David Klingler	.50	.23	.06
☐ 67 Erik Kramer	1.00	.45	.12
☐ 68 Reggie Langhorne	.50	.23	.06
☐ 69 Chuck Levy	.50	.23	.06
☐ 70 Dan Marino	12.00	5.50	1.50
☐ 71 O.J. McDuffie	1.50	.70	.19
☐ 72 Natrone Means	2.50	1.10	.30
☐ 73 Eric Metcalf	1.00	.45	.12
☐ 74 Glyn Milburn	1.00	.45	.12
☐ 75 Anthony Miller	1.00	.45	.12
☐ 76 Rick Mirer	1.50	.70	.19
☐ 77 Johnny Mitchell	.50	.23	.06
☐ 78 Scott Mitchell	1.50	.70	.19
☐ 79 Joe Montana	6.00	2.70	.75
☐ 80 Warren Moon	1.00	.45	.12
☐ 81 Derrick Moore	.50	.23	.06
☐ 82 Herman Moore	3.00	1.35	.35
☐ 83 Rob Moore	1.00	.45	.12
☐ 84 Ronald Moore	.50	.23	.06
☐ 85 Johnnie Morton	2.50	1.10	.30
☐ 86 Neil O'Donnell	1.00	.45	.12
☐ 87 David Palmer	1.00	.45	.12
☐ 88 Erric Pegram	.50	.23	.06
☐ 89 Carl Pickens	3.00	1.35	.35
☐ 90 Anthony Pleasant	.50	.23	.06
☐ 91 Roosevelt Potts	.50	.23	.06
☐ 92 Mike Pritchard	.50	.23	.06
☐ 93 Andre Reed	1.00	.45	.12
☐ 94 Errict Rhett	4.00	1.80	.50
☐ 95 Jerry Rice	6.00	2.70	.75
☐ 96 Andre Rison	1.00	.45	.12
☐ 97 Greg Robinson	.50	.23	.06
☐ 98 T.J. Rubley	.50	.23	.06
☐ 99 Leonard Russell	.50	.23	.06
☐ 100 Barry Sanders	6.00	2.70	.75
☐ 101 Deion Sanders	4.00	1.80	.50
☐ 102 Ricky Sanders	.50	.23	.06
☐ 103 Junior Seau	1.00	.45	.12
☐ 104 Shannon Sharpe	1.00	.45	.12
☐ 105 Sterling Sharpe	1.00	.45	.12
☐ 106 Heath Shuler	3.00	1.35	.35
☐ 107 Phil Simms	1.00	.45	.12
☐ 108 Webster Slaughter	.50	.23	.06
☐ 109 Bruce Smith	1.50	.70	.19
☐ 110 Emmitt Smith	12.00	5.50	1.50
☐ 111 Irv Smith	.50	.23	.06
☐ 112 Robert Smith	1.00	.45	.12
☐ 113 Vinny Testaverde	1.00	.45	.12
☐ 114 Derrick Thomas	1.00	.45	.12
☐ 115 Thurman Thomas	1.00	.45	.12
☐ 116 Leroy Thompson	.50	.23	.06
☐ 117 Lewis Tillman	.50	.23	.06
☐ 118 Michael Timpson	.50	.23	.06
☐ 119 Herschel Walker	1.00	.45	.12
☐ 120 Chris Warren	1.00	.45	.12
☐ 121 Ricky Watters	1.50	.70	.19
☐ 122 Lorenzo White	.50	.23	.06
☐ 123 Reggie White	1.50	.70	.19
☐ 124 Dan Wilkinson	1.00	.45	.12
☐ 125 Kevin Williams	1.00	.45	.12
☐ 126 Steve Young	5.00	2.20	.60
☐ CL1 Checklist 1	.30	.14	.04
☐ CL2 Checklist 2	.30	.14	.04
☐ S1 Sterling Sharpe Promo numbered S-1	1.50	.70	.19

1994 Pacific Prisms Gold

These 126 standard-size cards form a parallel to the regular Pacific Prism issue. These cards were reportedly produced in gold foil at a rate of less than ten percent of the total print run (1138 of each gold card).

	MINT	NRMT	EXC
COMPLETE SET (126)	900.00	400.00	110.00
COMMON CARD (1-126)	2.50	1.10	.30

*VETERAN STARS: 2.5X TO 5X BASIC CARDS
*YOUNG STARS/RCs: 1.5X TO 3X BASIC CARDS

1994 Pacific Prisms Team Helmets

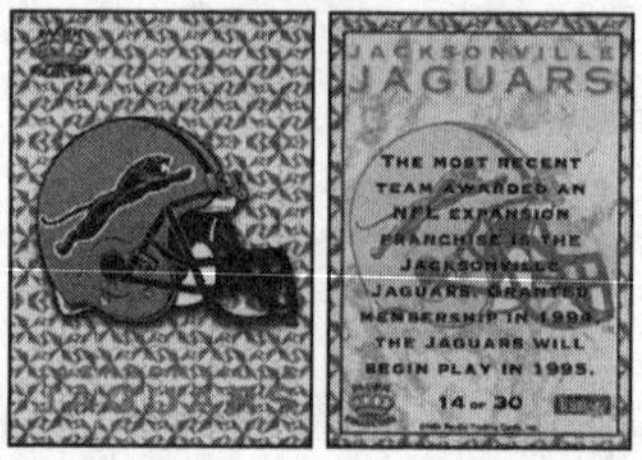

Randomly inserted in foil packs, this 30-card standard size set features a borderless front with a colored picture of a team helmet set against a silver tiled background. The team's name appears at the bottom. The back features a brief history of the team on a background consisting of a ghosted version of the team helmet. The cards are numbered on the back by "X of 30".

	MINT	NRMT	EXC
COMPLETE SET (30)	5.00	2.20	.60
COMMON CARD (1-30)	.20	.09	.03
☐ 1 Arizona Cardinals	.20	.09	.03
☐ 2 Atlanta Falcons	.20	.09	.03
☐ 3 Buffalo Bills	.20	.09	.03
☐ 4 Carolina Panthers	.25	.11	.03
☐ 5 Chicago Bears	.20	.09	.03
☐ 6 Cincinnati Bengals	.20	.09	.03
☐ 7 Cleveland Browns	.20	.09	.03
☐ 8 Dallas Cowboys	.30	.14	.04
☐ 9 Denver Broncos	.20	.09	.03
☐ 10 Detroit Lions	.20	.09	.03
☐ 11 Green Bay Packers	.30	.14	.04
☐ 12 Houston Oilers	.20	.09	.03
☐ 13 Indianapolis Colts	.20	.09	.03
☐ 14 Jacksonville Jaguars	.20	.09	.03
☐ 15 Kansas City Chiefs	.20	.09	.03
☐ 16 Los Angeles Raiders	.25	.11	.03
☐ 17 Los Angeles Rams	.20	.09	.03
☐ 18 Miami Dolphins	.30	.14	.04
☐ 19 Minnesota Vikings	.20	.09	.03
☐ 20 New England Patriots	.20	.09	.03
☐ 21 New Orleans Saints	.20	.09	.03
☐ 22 New York Giants	.20	.09	.03
☐ 23 New York Jets	.20	.09	.03
☐ 24 Philadelphia Eagles	.20	.09	.03
☐ 25 Pittsburgh Steelers	.30	.14	.04
☐ 26 San Diego Chargers	.20	.09	.03
☐ 27 San Francisco 49ers	.30	.14	.04
☐ 28 Seattle Seahawks	.20	.09	.03
☐ 29 Tampa Bay Buccaneers	.20	.09	.03
☐ 30 Washington Redskins	.30	.14	.04

1995 Pacific Prisms

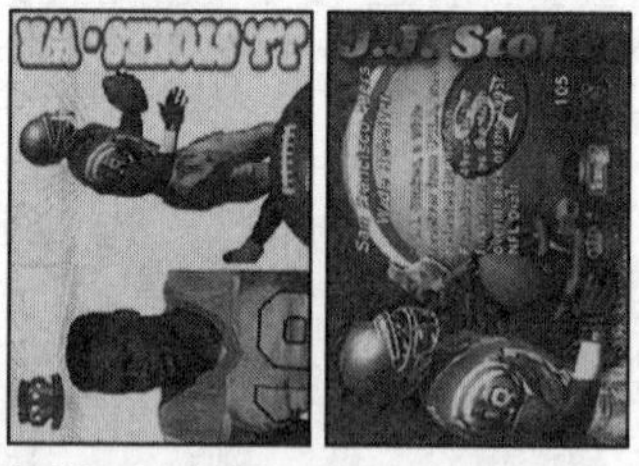

This 216 card standard-size set was issued in two-card packs including one player card and either a Super Bowl information card, a team card or a uniform card. The set was issued in two series, both containing 108 cards each. The horizontal fronts feature two player photos with the player's name up the right side. The horizontal backs feature another player photo as well as a few career highlights set against the team's helmet. There was also a parallel set issued: a gold foil set. These singles were randomly inserted at a rate of two in 37 packs. Rookie Cards in this set include Jeff Blake, Ki-Jana Carter, Kerry Collins, Joey Galloway, Curtis Martin, Steve McNair, Rashaan Salaam, Kordell Stewart, J.J. Stokes and Michael Westbrook. A John Elway autograph card, featuring an embossed Pacific logo, was also randomly inserted in the series 2 product. The card was hand signed and numbered (of 50) and was from the 1994 Pacific Gems of the Crown insert set. It could be found approximately one in every 43,200 packs. Finally, a two card unnumbered expansion set was issued in regular packs that contain a red foil-etched background. The two players represented were Steve Beuerlein and Barry Foster. A Natrone Means Promo card (#1) was produced in both silver and gold foil and priced below.

	MINT	NRMT	EXC
COMPLETE SET (216)	200.00	90.00	25.00
COMPLETE SERIES 1 (108)	100.00	45.00	12.50
COMPLETE SERIES 2 (108)	100.00	45.00	12.50
COMMON CARD (1-216)	.75	.35	.09
COMPLETE HELMET SET (30)	4.00	1.80	.50
COMPLETE SB LOGOS (30)	4.00	1.80	.50
COMPLETE UNIFORM SET (30)	4.00	1.80	.50
☐ 1 Chuck Levy	.75	.35	.09
☐ 2 Ronald Moore	.75	.35	.09
☐ 3 Jay Schroeder	.75	.35	.09
☐ 4 Bert Emanuel	2.00	.90	.25
☐ 5 Terance Mathis	1.00	.45	.12
☐ 6 Andre Rison	1.00	.45	.12
☐ 7 Bucky Brooks	.75	.35	.09
☐ 8 Jeff Burris	.75	.35	.09
☐ 9 Jim Kelly	2.00	.90	.25
☐ 10 Lewis Tillman	.75	.35	.09
☐ 11 Steve Walsh	.75	.35	.09
☐ 12 Chris Zorich	.75	.35	.09
☐ 13 Jeff Blake	5.00	2.20	.60
☐ 14 Steve Broussard	.75	.35	.09
☐ 15 Jeff Cothran	.75	.35	.09
☐ 16 Earnset Byner	.75	.35	.09
☐ 17 Leroy Hoard	.75	.35	.09
☐ 18 Vinny Testaverde	1.00	.45	.12
☐ 19 Troy Aikman	8.00	3.60	1.00
☐ 20 Alvin Harper	.75	.35	.09
☐ 21 Leon Lett	.75	.35	.09
☐ 22 Jay Novacek	1.00	.45	.12
☐ 23 John Elway	6.00	2.70	.75
☐ 24 Karl Mecklenburg	.75	.35	.09
☐ 25 Leonard Russell	.75	.35	.09
☐ 26 Mel Gray	.75	.35	.09
☐ 27 Dave Krieg	.75	.35	.09
☐ 28 Barry Sanders	8.00	3.60	1.00
☐ 29 Chris Spielman	1.00	.45	.12
☐ 30 Robert Brooks	2.00	.90	.25
☐ 31 LeShon Johnson	1.00	.45	.12
☐ 32 Sterling Sharpe	1.00	.45	.12
☐ 33 Ernest Givins	.75	.35	.09
☐ 34 Billy Joe Tolliver	.75	.35	.09
☐ 35 Lorenzo White	.75	.35	.09
☐ 36 Charles Arbuckle	.75	.35	.09
☐ 37 Sean Dawkins	1.00	.45	.12
☐ 38 Marshall Faulk	4.00	1.80	.50
☐ 39 Marcus Allen	2.00	.90	.25
☐ 40 Donnell Bennett	.75	.35	.09
☐ 41 Matt Blundin	.75	.35	.09
☐ 42 Greg Hill	1.00	.45	.12
☐ 43 Tim Brown	2.00	.90	.25
☐ 44 Billy Joe Hobert	1.00	.45	.12
☐ 45 Rocket Ismail	1.00	.45	.12
☐ 46 James Jett	1.00	.45	.12
☐ 47 Tim Bowens	.75	.35	.09
☐ 48 Irving Fryar	1.00	.45	.12
☐ 49 O.J. McDuffie	2.00	.90	.25
☐ 50 Irving Spikes	1.00	.45	.12
☐ 51 Terry Allen	1.00	.45	.12
☐ 52 Cris Carter	2.00	.90	.25
☐ 53 Amp Lee	.75	.35	.09
☐ 54 Drew Bledsoe	8.00	3.60	1.00
☐ 55 Willie McGinest	1.00	.45	.12
☐ 56 Leroy Thompson	.75	.35	.09
☐ 57 Michael Timpson	.75	.35	.09
☐ 58 Michael Haynes	1.00	.45	.12
☐ 59 Derrell Mitchell	.75	.35	.09
☐ 60 Dave Brown	1.00	.45	.12
☐ 61 Thomas Lewis	1.00	.45	.12
☐ 62 Dave Meggett	.75	.35	.09
☐ 63 Boomer Esiason	1.00	.45	.12
☐ 64 Aaron Glenn	.75	.35	.09
☐ 65 Ronnie Lott	1.00	.45	.12
☐ 66 Randall Cunningham	1.00	.45	.12
☐ 67 Charlie Garner	1.00	.45	.12
☐ 68 Herschel Walker	1.00	.45	.12
☐ 69 Barry Foster	1.00	.45	.12
☐ 70 Charles Johnson	1.00	.45	.12
☐ 71 Jim Miller	1.00	.45	.12
☐ 72 Rod Woodson	1.00	.45	.12
☐ 73 Andre Coleman	.75	.35	.09
☐ 74 Natrone Means	2.00	.90	.25
☐ 75 Shannon Mitchell	.75	.35	.09
☐ 76 Junior Seau	2.00	.90	.25
☐ 77 Elvis Grbac	2.00	.90	.25
☐ 78 Deion Sanders	4.00	1.80	.50
☐ 79 Adam Walker	.75	.35	.09
☐ 80 Ricky Watters	2.00	.90	.25
☐ 81 Michael Bates	.75	.35	.09
☐ 82 Brian Blades	1.00	.45	.12
☐ 83 Eugene Robinson	.75	.35	.09
☐ 84 Chris Warren	1.00	.45	.12
☐ 85 Jerome Bettis	2.50	1.10	.30
☐ 86 Troy Drayton	.75	.35	.09
☐ 87 Chris Miller	.75	.35	.09
☐ 88 Trent Dilfer	2.00	.90	.25
☐ 89 Hardy Nickerson	.75	.35	.09
☐ 90 Errict Rhett	2.00	.90	.25
☐ 91 Henry Ellard	1.00	.45	.12
☐ 92 Gus Frerotte	3.00	1.35	.35
☐ 93 Ricky Ervins	.75	.35	.09
☐ 94 Dave Barr	.75	.35	.09
☐ 95 Kyle Brady	2.00	.90	.25
☐ 96 Mark Bruener	1.00	.45	.12
☐ 97 Ki-Jana Carter	3.00	1.35	.35
☐ 98 Kerry Collins	12.00	5.50	1.50
☐ 99 Joey Galloway	8.00	3.60	1.00
☐ 100 Napoleon Kaufman	3.00	1.35	.35
☐ 101 Steve McNair	10.00	4.50	1.25
☐ 102 Craig Newsome	.75	.35	.09
☐ 103 Rashaan Salaam	5.00	2.20	.60
☐ 104 Kordell Stewart	10.00	4.50	1.25
☐ 105 J.J. Stokes	3.00	1.35	.35
☐ 106 Rodney Thomas	2.00	.90	.25
☐ 107 Michael Westbrook	5.00	2.20	.60

☐ 108 Tyrone Wheatley	2.00	.90	.25
☐ 109 Larry Centers	1.00	.45	.12
☐ 110 Garrison Hearst	2.00	.90	.25
☐ 111 Jamir Miller	.75	.35	.09
☐ 112 Jeff George	1.00	.45	.12
☐ 113 Craig Heyward	1.00	.45	.12
☐ 114 Cornelius Bennett	1.00	.45	.12
☐ 115 Andre Reed	1.00	.45	.12
☐ 116 Randy Baldwin	.75	.35	.09
☐ 117 Tommy Barnhardt	.75	.35	.09
☐ 118 Sam Mills	1.00	.45	.12
☐ 119 Brian O'Neal	.75	.35	.09
☐ 120 Frank Reich	.75	.35	.09
☐ 121 Tony Smith	.75	.35	.09
☐ 122 Lawyer Tillman	.75	.35	.09
☐ 123 Jack Trudeau	.75	.35	.09
☐ 124 Vernon Turner	.75	.35	.09
☐ 125 Curtis Conway	2.00	.90	.25
☐ 126 Erik Kramer	.75	.35	.09
☐ 127 Nate Lewis	.75	.35	.09
☐ 128 Carl Pickens	2.00	.90	.25
☐ 129 Darnay Scott	2.50	1.10	.30
☐ 130 Dan Wilkinson	1.00	.45	.12
☐ 131 Derrick Alexander WR	2.00	.90	.25
☐ 132 Carl Banks	.75	.35	.09
☐ 133 Michael Irvin	2.00	.90	.25
☐ 134 Emmitt Smith	15.00	6.75	1.85
☐ 135 Kevin Williams WR	1.00	.45	.12
☐ 136 Glyn Milburn	.75	.35	.09
☐ 137 Anthony Miller	1.00	.45	.12
☐ 138 Shannon Sharpe	1.00	.45	.12
☐ 139 Scott Mitchell	1.00	.45	.12
☐ 140 Herman Moore	3.00	1.35	.35
☐ 141 Edgar Bennett	1.00	.45	.12
☐ 142 Brett Favre	15.00	6.75	1.85
☐ 143 Reggie White	2.00	.90	.25
☐ 144 Gary Brown	.75	.35	.09
☐ 145 Haywood Jeffires	.75	.35	.09
☐ 146 Webster Slaughter	.75	.35	.09
☐ 147 Craig Erickson	.75	.35	.09
☐ 148 Paul Justin	.75	.35	.09
☐ 149 Lamont Warren	.75	.35	.09
☐ 150 Steve Beuerlein	.75	.35	.09
☐ 151 Derek Brown TE	.75	.35	.09
☐ 152 Mark Brunell	8.00	3.60	1.00
☐ 153 Reggie Cobb	.75	.35	.09
☐ 154 Desmond Howard	1.00	.45	.12
☐ 155 Kelvin Pritchett	.75	.35	.09
☐ 156 James O.Stewart	2.00	.90	.25
☐ 157 Cedric Tillman	.75	.35	.09
☐ 158 Kimble Anders	1.00	.45	.12
☐ 159 Lake Dawson	1.00	.45	.12
☐ 160 Keith Byars	.75	.35	.09
☐ 161 Dan Marino	15.00	6.75	1.85
☐ 162 Bernie Parmalee	1.00	.45	.12
☐ 163 Qadry Ismail	1.00	.45	.12
☐ 164 Warren Moon	1.00	.45	.12
☐ 165 Jake Reed	1.00	.45	.12
☐ 166 Marion Butts	.75	.35	.09
☐ 167 Ben Coates	1.00	.45	.12
☐ 168 Mario Bates	2.00	.90	.25
☐ 169 Quinn Early	1.00	.45	.12
☐ 170 Jim Everett	.75	.35	.09
☐ 171 Rodney Hampton	1.00	.45	.12
☐ 172 Mike Horan	.75	.35	.09
☐ 173 Mike Sherrard	.75	.35	.09
☐ 174 Johnny Johnson	.75	.35	.09
☐ 175 Adrian Murrell	1.00	.45	.12
☐ 176 Andrew Glover	.75	.35	.09
☐ 177 Jeff Hostetler	1.00	.45	.12
☐ 178 Harvey Williams	.75	.35	.09
☐ 179 Fred Barnett	1.00	.45	.12
☐ 180 Vaughn Hebron	.75	.35	.09
☐ 181 Jeff Sydner	.75	.35	.09
☐ 182 Kevin Greene	1.00	.45	.12
☐ 183 Byron Bam Morris	1.00	.45	.12
☐ 184 Neil O'Donnell	1.00	.45	.12
☐ 185 Stan Humphries	1.00	.45	.12
☐ 186 Tony Martin	1.00	.45	.12
☐ 187 Mark Seay	1.00	.45	.12
☐ 188 William Floyd	2.00	.90	.25
☐ 189 Rickey Jackson	.75	.35	.09
☐ 190 Jerry Rice	8.00	3.60	1.00
☐ 191 Steve Young	6.00	2.70	.75
☐ 192 Cortez Kennedy	1.00	.45	.12
☐ 193 Rick Mirer	2.00	.90	.25
☐ 194 Jessie Hester	.75	.35	.09
☐ 195 Curtis Martin	12.00	5.50	1.50
☐ 196 Horace Copeland	.75	.35	.09
☐ 197 Charles Wilson	.75	.35	.09
☐ 198 Reggie Brooks	1.00	.45	.12
☐ 199 Brian Mitchell	.75	.35	.09
☐ 200 Heath Shuler	2.00	.90	.25
☐ 201 Justin Armour	.75	.35	.09
☐ 202 Jay Barker	.75	.35	.09
☐ 203 Zack Crockett	.75	.35	.09
☐ 204 Christian Fauria	.75	.35	.09
☐ 205 Antonio Freeman	8.00	3.60	1.00
☐ 206 Chad May	.75	.35	.09
☐ 207 Frank Sanders	3.00	1.35	.35
☐ 208 Steve Stenstrom	.75	.35	.09
☐ 209 Lorenzo Styles	.75	.35	.09
☐ 210 Sherman Williams	.75	.35	.09
☐ 211 Ray Zellars	1.00	.45	.12
☐ 212 Eric Zeier	2.00	.90	.25
☐ 213 Joey Galloway	4.00	1.80	.50
☐ 214 Napoleon Kaufman	2.00	.90	.25
☐ 215 Rashaan Salaam	2.50	1.10	.30
☐ 216 J.J. Stokes	2.00	.90	.25
☐ NNO Steve Beuerlein EE	3.00	1.35	.35
☐ NNO Barry Foster EE	4.00	1.80	.50
☐ AU9 John Elway AUTO 1994 Gems of the Crown signed card	200.00	90.00	25.00
☐ P1 Natrone Means Promo Silver foil	2.00	.90	.25
☐ P2 Natrone Means Promo Gold foil	3.00	1.35	.35

1995 Pacific Prisms Gold

This 216 card parallel set was randomly inserted into packs at a rate of two per 37 packs. The cards are differentiated by having a gold design in the background rather than the standard silver.

	MINT	NRMT	EXC
COMPLETE SET (216)	1600.00	700.00	200.00
COMMON CARD (1-216)	3.00	1.35	.35

*VETERAN STARS: 2.5X TO 5X BASIC CARDS
*YOUNG STARS: 2X TO 4X BASIC CARDS
*RCs: 1.75X TO 3.5X BASIC CARDS ..

1995 Pacific Prisms Connections

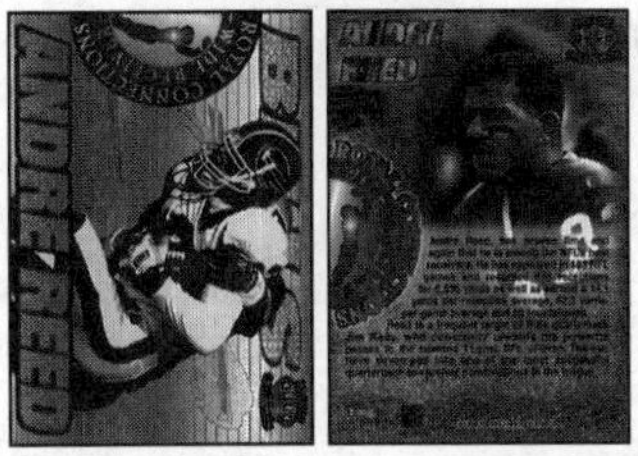

This 20 card set was randomly inserted in series 2 hobby and retail packs at a rate of one in 73 packs. Cards 1A-10A were randomly inserted in retail packs while cards 1B-10B were inserted into hobby. Each individual card had a quarterback/receiver combination with the quarterbacks using the "A" prefix and the receivers the "B" prefix. Card fronts have either a green etched foil background or a blue holofoil background. The Blue Holofoil background is a parallel that was randomly inserted. According to Pacific, less than 200 of the sets exist. Card fronts also have the player's team across the top and the player's name across the bottom. When the "A" and the "B" cards are linked they form the "Royal Connections" logo in the middle of the card. Card backs are vertical with a photo of the player in an oval with a statistical summary underneath. Cards are numbered with a "RC" prefix.

	MINT	NRMT	EXC
COMPLETE SET (20)	350.00	160.00	45.00
COMMON CARD (1-10)	12.00	5.50	1.50
COMMON CARD BLUE HOLO.	25.00	11.00	3.10

*BLUE HOLOFOILS: 2.5X TO 4X GREEN CARDS
*WR BLUE HOLO.(B): 1.5X TO 3X BASIC CARDS

☐ 1A Steve Young	30.00	13.50	3.70
☐ 1B Jerry Rice	40.00	18.00	5.00
☐ 2A Dan Marino	80.00	36.00	10.00
☐ 2B Irving Fryar	12.00	5.50	1.50
☐ 3A Drew Bledsoe	40.00	18.00	5.00
☐ 3B Ben Coates	12.00	5.50	1.50
☐ 4A John Elway	35.00	16.00	4.40
☐ 4B Shannon Sharpe	16.00	7.25	2.00
☐ 5A Jeff Hostetler	12.00	5.50	1.50
☐ 5B Tim Brown	16.00	7.25	2.00
☐ 6A Warren Moon	16.00	7.25	2.00
☐ 6B Cris Carter	16.00	7.25	2.00
☐ 7A Neil O'Donnell	12.00	5.50	1.50
☐ 7B Charles Johnson	12.00	5.50	1.50
☐ 8A Troy Aikman	40.00	18.00	5.00
☐ 8B Michael Irvin	16.00	7.25	2.00
☐ 9A Stan Humphries	12.00	5.50	1.50
☐ 9B Shawn Jefferson	12.00	5.50	1.50
☐ 10A Jim Kelly	16.00	7.25	2.00
☐ 10B Andre Reed	12.00	5.50	1.50

1995 Pacific Prisms Kings of the NFL

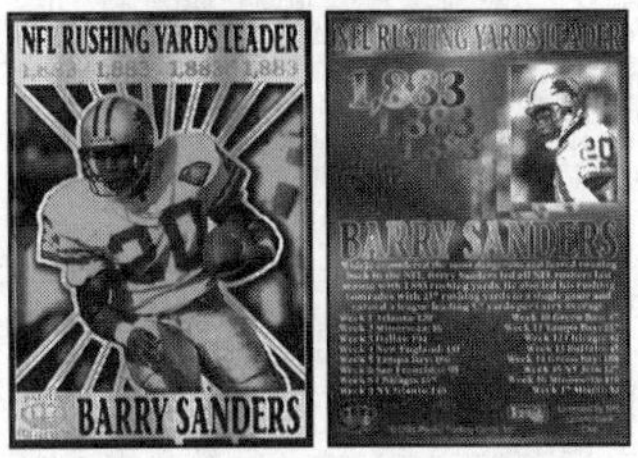

This 10 card set was randomly inserted into series 2 packs at a rate of one in 361 packs and features the leaders in ten different NFL categories. Card fronts contain a full bleed photo with a gold holographic foil design at the top, bottom and running behind the player. The top of the card signifies what the player led the NFL in and the player's name is at the bottom. Card backs contain a head shot of the player with the player's name underneath it, followed by a summary of the previous season.

	MINT	NRMT	EXC
COMPLETE SET (10)	800.00	350.00	100.00
COMMON CARD (1-10)	40.00	18.00	5.00

☐ 1 Emmitt Smith	135.00	60.00	17.00
☐ 2 Steve Young	60.00	27.00	7.50
☐ 3 Jerry Rice	75.00	34.00	9.50
☐ 4 Deion Sanders	50.00	22.00	6.25
☐ 5 Emmitt Smith	135.00	60.00	17.00
☐ 6 Dan Marino	135.00	60.00	17.00
☐ 7 Drew Bledsoe	75.00	34.00	9.50
☐ 8 Barry Sanders	75.00	34.00	9.50
☐ 9 Marshall Faulk	50.00	22.00	6.25
☐ 10 Marshall Faulk Natrone Means	40.00	18.00	5.00

1995 Pacific Prisms Red Hot Rookies

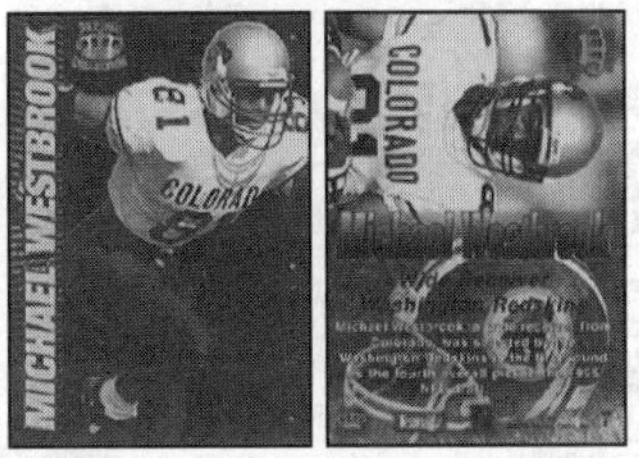

This nine-card standard-size set, featuring leading prospects, was inserted one in every 73 hobby packs. The player's image is featured against a metallic red background and features the rookies in their college uniforms. The player's name is located up the left side. The backs contain a player photo and highlights.

	MINT	NRMT	EXC
COMPLETE SET (9)	225.00	100.00	28.00
COMMON CARD (1-9)	16.00	7.25	2.00

☐ 1 Ki-Jana Carter	16.00	7.25	2.00
☐ 2 Joey Galloway	30.00	13.50	3.70
☐ 3 Steve McNair	40.00	18.00	5.00
☐ 4 Tyrone Wheatley	16.00	7.25	2.00
☐ 5 Kerry Collins	50.00	22.00	6.25
☐ 6 Rashaan Salaam	25.00	11.00	3.10
☐ 7 Michael Westbrook	20.00	9.00	2.50
☐ 8 J.J. Stokes	20.00	9.00	2.50
☐ 9 Napoleon Kaufman	16.00	7.25	2.00

1995 Pacific Prisms Red Hot Stars

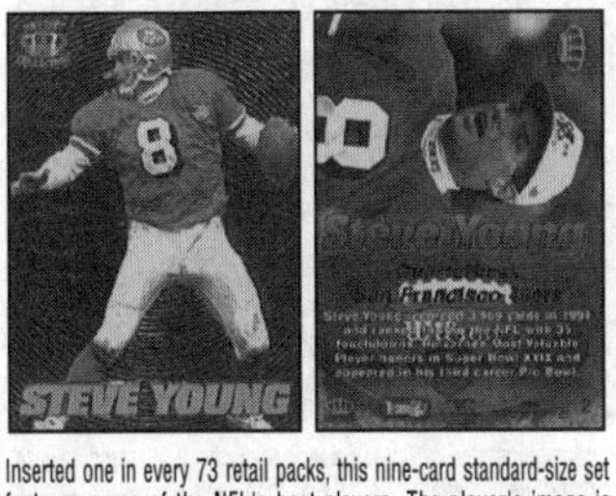

Inserted one in every 73 retail packs, this nine-card standard-size set features some of the NFL's best players. The player's image is featured against a red foil-etched background. The player's name is at the bottom of the card. The backs feature a player photo and highlights.

	MINT	NRMT	EXC
COMPLETE SET (9)	400.00	180.00	50.00
COMMON CARD (1-9)	25.00	11.00	3.10

☐ 1 Barry Sanders	50.00	22.00	6.25
☐ 2 Steve Young	40.00	18.00	5.00
☐ 3 Emmitt Smith	80.00	36.00	10.00
☐ 4 Drew Bledsoe	50.00	22.00	6.25
☐ 5 Natrone Means	25.00	11.00	3.10
☐ 6 Dan Marino	80.00	36.00	10.00
☐ 7 Marshall Faulk	30.00	13.50	3.70
☐ 8 Jerry Rice	50.00	22.00	6.25
☐ 9 Errict Rhett	25.00	11.00	3.10

1995 Pacific Prisms Super Bowl Logos

This set was one of the "insert" backers in Pacific Prism backs. This set has on the front a Super Bowl logo for each game played. The back has details about the game. The cards are unnumbered so we have sequenced them in chronological order.

	MINT	NRMT	EXC
COMPLETE SET (30)	4.00	1.80	.50
COMMON CARD (1-30)	.15	.07	.02

☐ 1 Super Bowl I	.15	.07	.02
☐ 2 Super Bowl II	.15	.07	.02
☐ 3 Super Bowl III	.15	.07	.02
☐ 4 Super Bowl IV	.15	.07	.02
☐ 5 Super Bowl V	.15	.07	.02
☐ 6 Super Bowl VI	.15	.07	.02
☐ 7 Super Bowl VII	.15	.07	.02
☐ 8 Super Bowl VIII	.15	.07	.02
☐ 9 Super Bowl IX	.15	.07	.02
☐ 10 Super Bowl X	.15	.07	.02
☐ 11 Super Bowl XI	.15	.07	.02
☐ 12 Super Bowl XII	.15	.07	.02
☐ 13 Super Bowl XIII	.15	.07	.02
☐ 14 Super Bowl XIV	.15	.07	.02
☐ 15 Super Bowl XV	.15	.07	.02
☐ 16 Super Bowl XVI	.15	.07	.02
☐ 17 Super Bowl XVII	.15	.07	.02
☐ 18 Super Bowl XVIII	.15	.07	.02
☐ 19 Super Bowl XIX	.15	.07	.02
☐ 20 Super Bowl XX	.15	.07	.02
☐ 21 Super Bowl XXI	.15	.07	.02
☐ 22 Super Bowl XXII	.15	.07	.02
☐ 23 Super Bowl XXIII	.15	.07	.02
☐ 24 Super Bowl XXIV	.15	.07	.02
☐ 25 Super Bowl XXV	.15	.07	.02
☐ 26 Super Bowl XXVI	.15	.07	.02
☐ 27 Super Bowl XXVII	.15	.07	.02
☐ 28 Super Bowl XXVIII	.15	.07	.02
☐ 29 Super Bowl XXIX	.15	.07	.02
☐ 30 Super Bowl XXX	.15	.07	.02

1995 Pacific Prisms Team Helmets

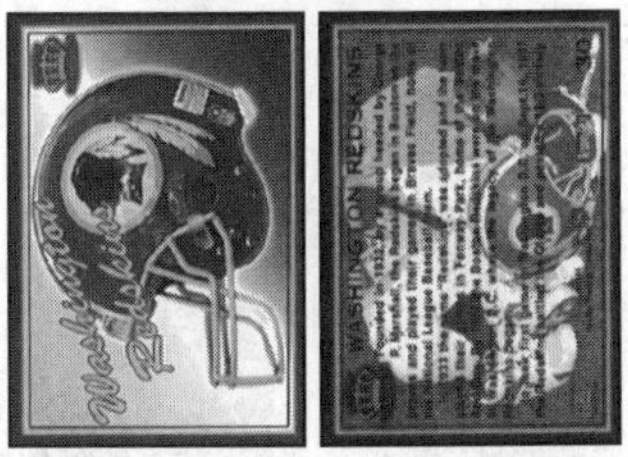

These horizontal cards feature each NFL's team helmet. The team name is also printed on the front of the card. The back gives some history about each franchise. This set was issued as another "Backer Insert" set in Pacific Prism.

	MINT	NRMT	EXC
COMPLETE SET (30)	4.00	1.80	.50
COMMON CARD (1-30)	.15	.07	.02

☐ 1 Arizona Cardinals	.15	.07	.02
☐ 2 Atlanta Falcons	.15	.07	.02
☐ 3 Buffalo Bills	.15	.07	.02
☐ 4 Carolina Panthers	.20	.09	.03
☐ 5 Chicago Bears	.15	.07	.02
☐ 6 Cincinnati Bengals	.15	.07	.02
☐ 7 Cleveland Browns	.15	.07	.02
☐ 8 Dallas Cowboys	.25	.11	.03
☐ 9 Denver Broncos	.15	.07	.02
☐ 10 Detroit Lions	.15	.07	.02
☐ 11 Green Bay Packers	.25	.11	.03
☐ 12 Detroit Lions	.15	.07	.02
☐ 13 Indianapolis Colts	.15	.07	.02
☐ 14 Jacksonville Jaguars	.15	.07	.02
☐ 15 Kansas City Chiefs	.15	.07	.02
☐ 16 Los Angeles Raiders	.20	.09	.03
☐ 17 Miami Dolphins	.25	.11	.03
☐ 18 Minnesota Vikings	.15	.07	.02
☐ 19 New England Patriots	.15	.07	.02
☐ 20 New Orleans Saints	.15	.07	.02
☐ 21 New York Giants	.15	.07	.02
☐ 22 New York Jets	.15	.07	.02
☐ 23 Philadelphia Eagles	.15	.07	.02
☐ 24 Pittsburgh Steelers	.25	.11	.03
☐ 25 San Diego Chargers	.15	.07	.02
☐ 26 San Francisco 49ers	.25	.11	.03
☐ 27 Seattle Seahawks	.15	.07	.02
☐ 28 St.Louis Rams	.15	.07	.02
☐ 29 Tampa Bay Buccaneers	.15	.07	.02
☐ 30 Washington Redskins	.25	.11	.03

1995 Pacific Prisms Team Uniforms

These horizontal cards were issued as backer cards in Pacific Prism packs. The fronts feature various parts of each teams uniforms while the backs give various histories about the team.

	MINT	NRMT	EXC
COMPLETE SET (30)	4.00	1.80	.50
COMMON CARD (1-30)	.15	.07	.02

☐ 1 Arizona Cardinals	.15	.07	.02
☐ 2 Atlanta Falcons	.15	.07	.02

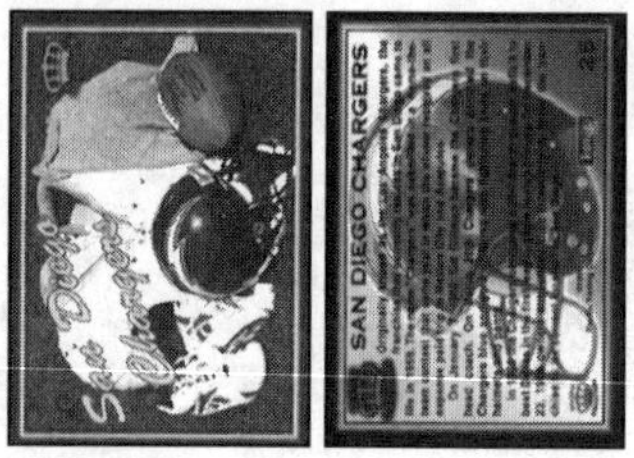

☐ 3 Buffalo Bills	.15	.07	.02
☐ 4 Carolina Panthers	.20	.09	.03
☐ 5 Chicago Bears	.15	.07	.02
☐ 6 Cincinnati Bengals	.15	.07	.02
☐ 7 Cleveland Browns	.15	.07	.02
☐ 8 Dallas Cowboys	.25	.11	.03
☐ 9 Denver Broncos	.15	.07	.02
☐ 10 Detroit Lions	.15	.07	.02
☐ 11 Green Bay Packers	.25	.11	.03
☐ 12 Houston Oilers	.15	.07	.02
☐ 13 Indianapolis Colts	.15	.07	.02
☐ 14 Jacksonville Jaguars	.15	.07	.02
☐ 15 Kansas City Chiefs	.15	.07	.02
☐ 16 Los Angeles Raiders	.20	.09	.03
☐ 17 Miami Dolphins	.25	.11	.03
☐ 18 Minnesota Vikings	.15	.07	.02
☐ 19 New England Patriots	.15	.07	.02
☐ 20 New Orleans Saints	.15	.07	.02
☐ 21 New York Giants	.15	.07	.02
☐ 22 New York Jets	.15	.07	.02
☐ 23 Philadelphia Eagles	.15	.07	.02
☐ 24 Pittsburgh Steelers	.25	.11	.03
☐ 25 San Diego Chargers	.15	.07	.02
☐ 26 San Francisco 49ers	.25	.11	.03
☐ 27 Seattle Seahawks	.15	.07	.02
☐ 28 St.Louis Rams	.15	.07	.02
☐ 29 Tampa Bay Buccaneers	.15	.07	.02
☐ 30 Washington Redskins	.25	.11	.03

1992 Pacific Triple Folders

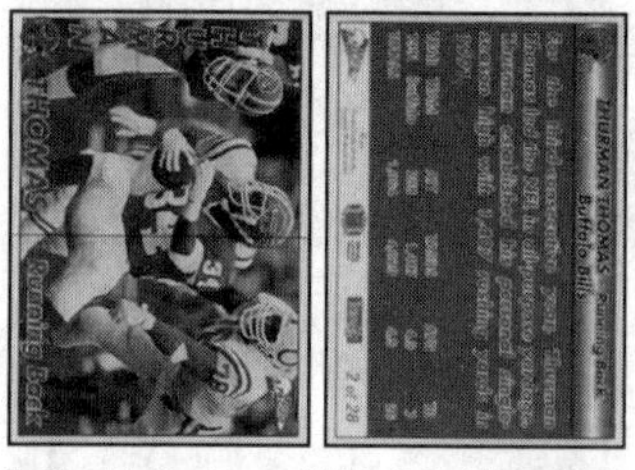

The 28 cards in this set measure 3 1/2" by 5" when folded and display a glossy action color player photo on the front. The player's name and position are printed in block letters. The two panels that make up the front photo are split down the center and can be opened to reveal three separate photos on the inside. The center panel carries an action color player photo and the player's name in block letters. The left inside panel has an action player photo while the right inside panel has a posed close-up shot. The backs carry career highlights and statistics. The background and lettering are team color-coded. The players chosen represent each of the 28 NFL teams, and the cards are arranged alphabetically according to team name. Each triple folder card pack contained a bonus card from one of the following insert sets: Steve Largent subset, Bob Griese subset, team Statistical Leader subset, gold and silver foil subset, Rushing Leader Prism subset, or Checklist Card subset.

	MINT	NRMT	EXC
COMPLETE SET (28)	25.00	11.00	3.10
COMMON CARD (1-28)	.50	.23	.06
☐ 1 Chris Miller	.75	.35	.09
☐ 2 Thurman Thomas	1.25	.55	.16
☐ 3 Neal Anderson	.50	.23	.06
☐ 4 Tim McGee	.50	.23	.06
☐ 5 Kevin Mack	.50	.23	.06
☐ 6 Emmitt Smith	5.00	2.20	.60
☐ 7 John Elway	2.00	.90	.25
☐ 8 Barry Sanders	2.50	1.10	.30
☐ 9 Sterling Sharpe	1.00	.45	.12
☐ 10 Warren Moon	.75	.35	.09
☐ 11 Bill Brooks	.75	.35	.09
☐ 12 Christian Okoye	.50	.23	.06
☐ 13 Nick Bell	.50	.23	.06
☐ 14 Robert Delpino	.50	.23	.06
☐ 15 Mark Higgs	.50	.23	.06
☐ 16 Rich Gannon	.50	.23	.06
☐ 17 Leonard Russell	.75	.35	.09
☐ 18 Pat Swilling	.75	.35	.09
☐ 19 Rodney Hampton	1.00	.45	.12
☐ 20 Rob Moore	.75	.35	.09
☐ 21 Reggie White	1.25	.55	.16
☐ 22 Johnny Johnson	.50	.23	.06
☐ 23 Neil O'Donnell	1.00	.45	.12
☐ 24 Marion Butts	.50	.23	.06
☐ 25 Steve Young	2.00	.90	.25
☐ 26 John L. Williams	.50	.23	.06
☐ 27 Reggie Cobb	.50	.23	.06
☐ 28 Mark Rypien	.50	.23	.06

1993 Pacific Triple Folders

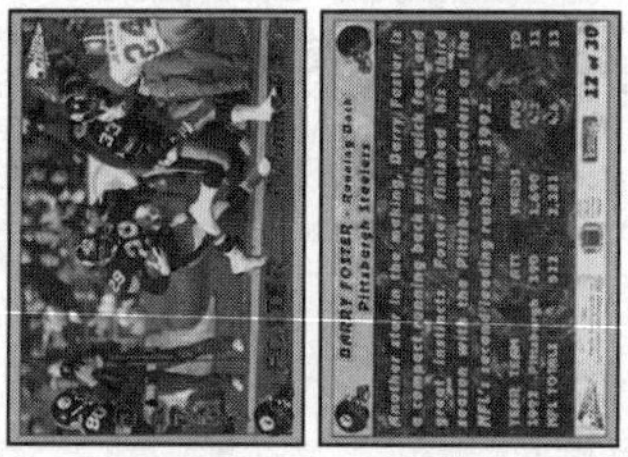

These 30 cards measure approximately 3 1/2" by 10 1/8" when folded out and feature gray-bordered color player action shots on all of their panels, except the backs. When the front panels are closed they merge into a single color player action photo, with the player's name and position printed in team color-coded marbleized lettering down the left side and along the bottom. On a team color-coded marbleized background, the back carries the player's name, position, team, career highlights, and 1992 stats. There were reportedly only 2,500 cases of Triple Folders produced by Pacific.

	MINT	NRMT	EXC
COMPLETE SET (30)	25.00	11.00	3.10
COMMON CARD (1-30)	.50	.23	.06
☐ 1 Thurman Thomas	.75	.35	.09
☐ 2 Carl Pickens	.75	.35	.09
☐ 3 Glyn Milburn	.75	.35	.09
☐ 4 Lorenzo White	.50	.23	.06
☐ 5 Anthony Johnson	.50	.23	.06
☐ 6 Joe Montana	2.00	.90	.25
☐ 7 Nick Bell	.50	.23	.06
☐ 8 Dan Marino	3.50	1.55	.45
☐ 9 Anthony Carter	.50	.23	.06
☐ 10 Drew Bledsoe	2.00	.90	.25
☐ 11 Rob Moore	.50	.23	.06
☐ 12 Barry Foster	.50	.23	.06
☐ 13 Stan Humphries	.75	.35	.09
☐ 14 Cortez Kennedy	.75	.35	.09
☐ 15 Rick Mirer	.75	.35	.09
☐ 16 Deion Sanders	1.25	.55	.16
☐ 17 Curtis Conway	1.00	.45	.12
☐ 18 Tommy Vardell	.50	.23	.06
☐ 19 Emmitt Smith	3.50	1.55	.45
☐ 20 Barry Sanders	2.00	.90	.25
☐ 21 Brett Favre	3.50	1.55	.45
☐ 22 Cleveland Gary	.50	.23	.06
☐ 23 Morten Andersen	.50	.23	.06
☐ 24 Marcus Buckley	.50	.23	.06
☐ 25 Rodney Hampton	.75	.35	.09
☐ 26 Herschel Walker	.75	.35	.09
☐ 27 Garrison Hearst	1.00	.45	.12
☐ 28 Jerry Rice	2.00	.90	.25
☐ 29 Lawrence Dawsey	.50	.23	.06
☐ 30 Desmond Howard	.75	.35	.09

1993 Pacific Triple Folder Rookies/Stars

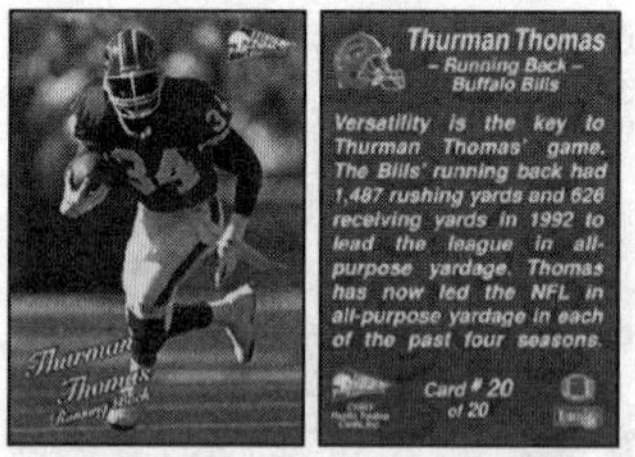

Randomly inserted in Triple Folder packs, these 20 standard-size cards feature borderless color player action shots on their fronts. The player's name and position appears in white cursive lettering in a lower corner. On a team-colored background consisting of football icons, the back carries the player's name, position, team name and helmet, and 1992 season highlights. Card numbers 2-8, 11, 13, and 19 are rookies; the remainder are superstars.

	MINT	NRMT	EXC
COMPLETE SET (20)	20.00	9.00	2.50
COMMON CARD (1-20)	.50	.23	.06
☐ 1 Troy Aikman	2.50	1.10	.30
☐ 2 Victor Bailey	.50	.23	.06
☐ 3 Jerome Bettis	.75	.35	.09
☐ 4 Drew Bledsoe	2.50	1.10	.30
☐ 5 Reggie Brooks	.75	.35	.09
☐ 6 Derek Brown RB	.75	.35	.09
☐ 7 Marcus Buckley	.50	.23	.06
☐ 8 Curtis Conway	1.00	.45	.12
☐ 9 Brett Favre	4.00	1.80	.50
☐ 10 Barry Foster	.75	.35	.09
☐ 11 Garrison Hearst	1.25	.55	.16
☐ 12 Cortez Kennedy	.75	.35	.09
☐ 13 Rick Mirer	.75	.35	.09
☐ 14 Joe Montana	2.50	1.10	.30
☐ 15 Jerry Rice	2.50	1.10	.30
☐ 16 Barry Sanders	2.50	1.10	.30
☐ 17 Sterling Sharpe	.75	.35	.09
☐ 18 Emmitt Smith	4.00	1.80	.50
☐ 19 Robert Smith	1.00	.45	.12
☐ 20 Thurman Thomas	.75	.35	.09

1994 Pacific Triple Folders

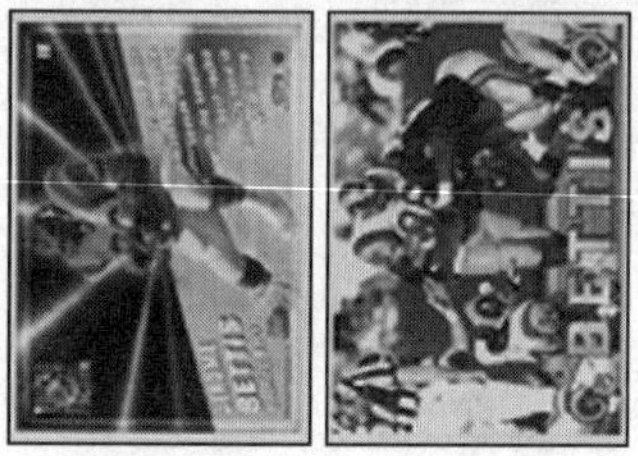

These 33 cards measure approximately 3 1/2" by 5" when folded and feature white-bordered color action player shots on all of their panels. When the front panels are closed, they merge into a single color action player photo with the player's first name printed on the bottom. When opened, the inside reveals another color action player photo. The player's last name is printed on the bottom with a team helmet on the left and right. On a team color-coded background, the backs carry the player's name and position and a career highlight. The set is arranged in alphabetical order by teams. In addition to a Triple Folder card, each pack included one bonus card from either the Gems of the Crown, Crown Collection Crystalline, or Knights of the Gridiron subsets. Also, randomly inserted in Triple Folder packs only were the Rookies and Stars 40-card insert. Less than 2,999 individually-numbered cases were produced.

	MINT	NRMT	EXC
COMPLETE SET (33)	25.00	11.00	3.10
COMMON CARD (1-33)	.50	.23	.06
☐ 1 Ronald Moore	.75	.35	.09
☐ 2 Erric Pegram	.50	.23	.06
☐ 3 Jim Kelly	1.00	.45	.12
☐ 4 Thurman Thomas	1.00	.45	.12
☐ 5 Curtis Conway	1.00	.45	.12
☐ 6 Vinny Testaverde	.50	.23	.06
☐ 7 Troy Aikman	2.00	.90	.25
☐ 8 Emmitt Smith	3.50	1.55	.45
☐ 9 John Elway	1.50	.70	.19
☐ 10 Shannon Sharpe	.75	.35	.09
☐ 11 Barry Sanders	2.00	.90	.25
☐ 12 Brett Favre	3.50	1.55	.45
☐ 13 Sterling Sharpe	.75	.35	.09
☐ 14 Gary Brown	.50	.23	.06
☐ 15 Marshall Faulk	1.25	.55	.16
☐ 16 Joe Montana	2.00	.90	.25
☐ 17 Rocket Ismail	.75	.35	.09
☐ 18 Jerome Bettis	1.00	.45	.12
☐ 19 Dan Marino	3.50	1.55	.45
☐ 20 David Palmer	.50	.23	.06
☐ 21 Drew Bledsoe	2.00	.90	.25
☐ 22 Ben Coates	.75	.35	.09
☐ 23 Derrick Ned	.50	.23	.06
☐ 24 Rodney Hampton	.75	.35	.09
☐ 25 Boomer Esiason	.75	.35	.09
☐ 26 Barry Foster	.50	.23	.06
☐ 27 Charles Johnson	.75	.35	.09
☐ 28 Natrone Means	1.00	.45	.12
☐ 29 Steve Young	1.50	.70	.19
☐ 30 Rick Mirer	1.00	.45	.12
☐ 31 Chris Warren	.75	.35	.09
☐ 32 Trent Dilfer	1.00	.45	.12
☐ 33 Heath Shuler	1.00	.45	.12

1994 Pacific Triple Folders Rookies/Stars

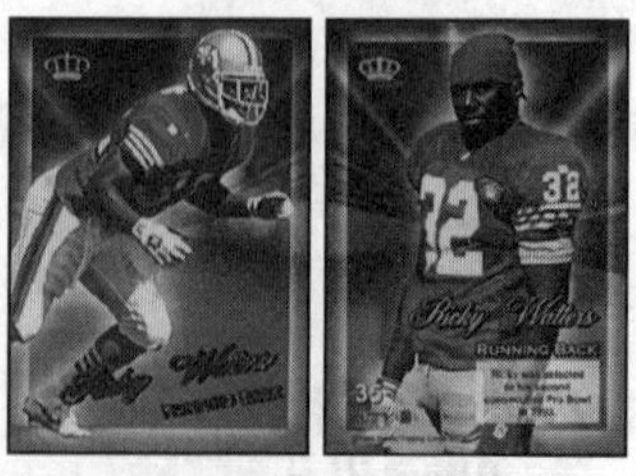

This 40-card standard-size set was randomly inserted only in Triple Folder packs. The fronts feature color action player shots with a computer generated backgound. The player's name and position in gold-foil appears on the bottom. On the same background, the backs carry a posed color action photo with the player's name, position and a career highlight. The set is arranged in team alphabetical order.

	MINT	NRMT	EXC
COMPLETE SET (40)	25.00	11.00	3.10
COMMON CARD (1-40)	.30	.14	.04
☐ 1 Ronald Moore	.50	.23	.06
☐ 2 Jeff George	.50	.23	.06
☐ 3 Jim Kelly	.50	.23	.06
☐ 4 Thurman Thomas	.50	.23	.06
☐ 5 Curtis Conway	.75	.35	.09
☐ 6 Darnay Scott	.60	.25	.07
☐ 7 Vinny Testaverde	.30	.14	.04
☐ 8 Troy Aikman	2.00	.90	.25
☐ 9 Emmitt Smith	3.50	1.55	.45
☐ 10 John Elway	1.25	.55	.16
☐ 11 Shannon Sharpe	.30	.14	.04
☐ 12 Barry Sanders	2.00	.90	.25
☐ 13 LeShon Johnson	.30	.14	.04
☐ 14 Sterling Sharpe	.50	.23	.06
☐ 15 Gary Brown	.30	.14	.04
☐ 16 Marshall Faulk	1.00	.45	.12
☐ 17 Lake Dawson	.60	.25	.07
☐ 18 Greg Hill	.60	.25	.07
☐ 19 Joe Montana	2.00	.90	.25
☐ 20 Tim Brown	.50	.23	.06
☐ 21 Jerome Bettis	.60	.25	.07
☐ 22 Dan Marino	3.50	1.55	.45
☐ 23 Terry Allen	.50	.23	.06
☐ 24 David Palmer	.50	.23	.06
☐ 25 Drew Bledsoe	2.00	.90	.25
☐ 26 Ben Coates	.50	.23	.06
☐ 27 Michael Haynes	.30	.14	.04
☐ 28 Rodney Hampton	.50	.23	.06
☐ 29 Thomas Lewis	.50	.23	.06
☐ 30 Aaron Glenn	.50	.23	.06
☐ 31 Charlie Garner	.50	.23	.06
☐ 32 Charles Johnson	.50	.23	.06
☐ 33 Byron Bam Morris	.50	.23	.06
☐ 34 Natrone Means	.60	.25	.07
☐ 35 Ricky Watters	.50	.23	.06
☐ 36 Steve Young	1.25	.55	.16
☐ 37 Rick Mirer	.60	.25	.07
☐ 38 Trent Dilfer	1.00	.45	.12
☐ 39 Errict Rhett	.75	.35	.09
☐ 40 Heath Shuler	.75	.35	.09

1995 Pacific Triple Folders

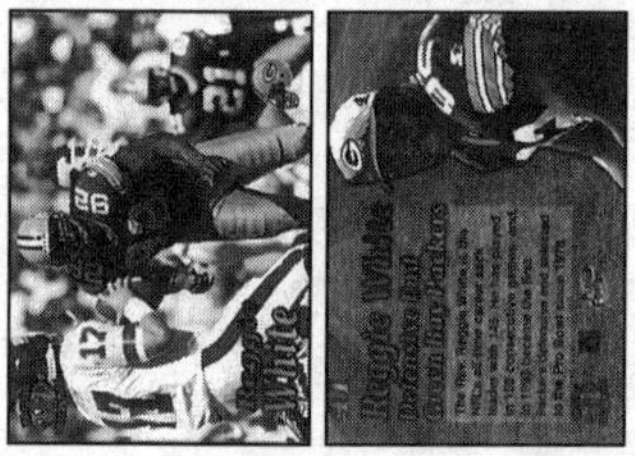

This 48 card set was issued late in 1995 by Pacific and is the first Triple Folder set that features cards that are standard sized when folded. When opened, the length of the cards double in size while the width remains the same as a standard card. The card fronts are full bleed horizontal game shots of the player with the player's name in the lower left hand corner. When opened, the card forms three panels. The left and right panel both feature individual player shots, while the middle shows another full bleed shot showing the completion of the play the folded shot showed. Card backs feature a field in the background with a shot of the player and a brief commentary. Packs include one insert each. In addition, a Super Bowl XXX Wrapper Redemption was offered. Collectors could get a special six-card set by sending in 18 1995 Triple Folder wrappers plus $5.95 for shipping and handling. A Natrone Means promo card was produced and priced below.

	MINT	NRMT	EXC
COMPLETE SET (48)	22.00	10.00	2.70
COMMON CARD (1-48)	.25	.11	.03
☐ 1 Garrison Hearst	.50	.23	.06
☐ 2 Kerry Collins	2.00	.90	.25
☐ 3 Jeff George	.50	.23	.06
☐ 4 Herschel Walker	.25	.11	.03
☐ 5 Lake Dawson	.40	.18	.05
☐ 6 Cris Carter	.50	.23	.06
☐ 7 Byron Bam Morris	.40	.18	.05
☐ 8 Jim Kelly	.50	.23	.06
☐ 9 Rashaan Salaam	1.25	.55	.16
☐ 10 Eric Zeier	.50	.23	.06
☐ 11 Curtis Martin	3.00	1.35	.35
☐ 12 Jerry Rice	2.00	.90	.25
☐ 13 Chris Warren	.50	.23	.06
☐ 14 Trent Dilfer	.50	.23	.06
☐ 15 Terry Allen	.40	.18	.05
☐ 16 Jeff Blake	.50	.23	.06
☐ 17 Drew Bledsoe	2.00	.90	.25
☐ 18 Tim Brown	.50	.23	.06
☐ 19 Wayne Chrebet	.50	.23	.06
☐ 20 Bernie Parmalee	.40	.18	.05
☐ 21 Stan Humphries	.50	.23	.06
☐ 22 Jerome Bettis	.50	.23	.06
☐ 23 Michael Westbrook	1.25	.55	.16
☐ 24 Charlie Garner	.25	.11	.03
☐ 25 Mario Bates	.50	.23	.06
☐ 26 Marcus Allen	.50	.23	.06
☐ 27 James O.Stewart	.50	.23	.06
☐ 28 Ben Coates	.50	.23	.06
☐ 29 Tyrone Wheatley	.50	.23	.06
☐ 30 Steve Young	1.50	.70	.19
☐ 31 Natrone Means	.50	.23	.06
☐ 32 Terrell Davis	2.50	1.10	.30
☐ 33 Napoleon Kaufman	.50	.23	.06
☐ 34 Charles Johnson	.40	.18	.05

☐ 35 Barry Sanders	2.00	.90	.25
☐ 36 John Elway	1.50	.70	.19
☐ 37 Joey Galloway	1.00	.45	.12
☐ 38 Bret Favre	4.00	1.80	.50
☐ 39 Errict Rhett	.50	.23	.06
☐ 40 Gary Brown	.25	.11	.03
☐ 41 Reggie White	.50	.23	.06
☐ 42 Steve Bono	.50	.23	.06
☐ 43 Marshall Faulk	2.00	.90	.25
☐ 44 Dan Marino	4.00	1.80	.50
☐ 45 Emmitt Smith	4.00	1.80	.50
☐ 46 Troy Aikman	2.00	.90	.25
☐ 47 Ricky Watters	.50	.23	.06
☐ 48 Michael Irvin	.50	.23	.06
☐ P1 Natrone Means Promo	1.00	.45	.12

1995 Pacific Triple Folders Big Guns

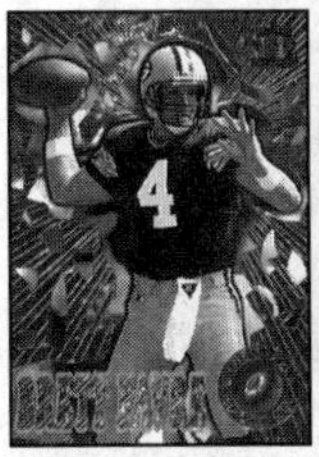
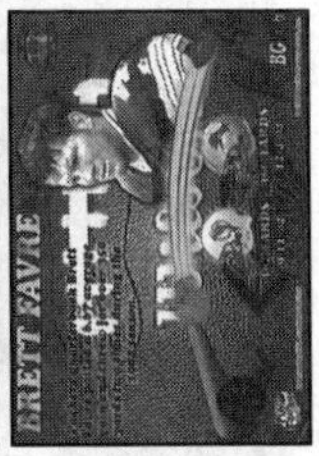

Inserted two in every 37 packs, this 12 card set features NFL quarterbacks who passed for 350 yards or more in at least one game the previous season. Card fronts contain almost a full holographic foil background with a shot of the player in the center and the player's name on the bottom in the same foil. The "Big Guns of the NFL" logo is located in the bottom right of the card. Card backs are horizontal with a football in the background and a brief commentary on the game the player threw for at least 350 yards in.

	MINT	NRMT	EXC
COMPLETE SET (12)	100.00	45.00	12.50
COMMON CARD (BG1-BG12)	3.00	1.35	.35
☐ BG1 Drew Bledsoe	12.00	5.50	1.50
☐ BG2 Dan Marino	25.00	11.00	3.10
☐ BG3 Warren Moon	4.00	1.80	.50
☐ BG4 John Elway	10.00	4.50	1.25
☐ BG5 Jeff Blake	8.00	3.60	1.00
☐ BG6 Brett Favre	25.00	11.00	3.10
☐ BG7 Steve Young	10.00	4.50	1.25
☐ BG8 Boomer Esiason	3.00	1.35	.35
☐ BG9 Jim Everett	3.00	1.35	.35
☐ BG10 Jim Kelly	4.00	1.80	.50
☐ BG11 Jeff George	4.00	1.80	.50
☐ BG12 Dave Krieg	3.00	1.35	.35

1995 Pacific Triple Folders Careers

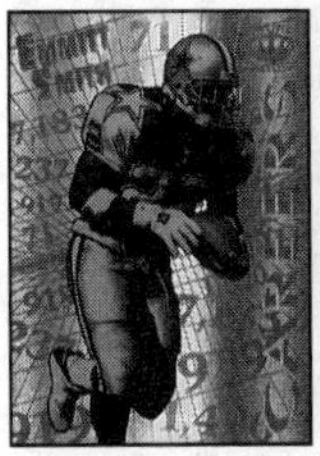
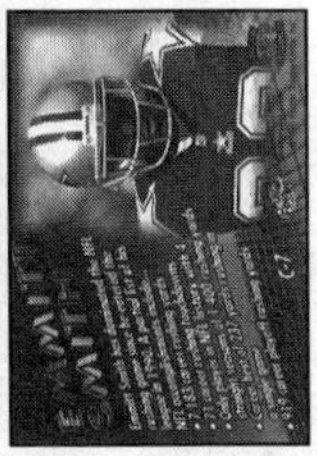

This eight card set was randomly inserted into packs at a rate of one in 181 or four per case. Card fronts have a holographic gold foil background with the player's name etched into it. Cardbacks are horizontal with a head shot of the player and some bullet point information about the player's accomplishments. Cards are numbered with a "C" prefix.

	MINT	NRMT	EXC
COMPLETE SET (8)	400.00	180.00	50.00
COMMON CARD (C1-C8)	15.00	6.75	1.85
☐ C1 Troy Aikman	50.00	22.00	6.25
☐ C2 Marcus Allen	15.00	6.75	1.85
☐ C3 John Elway	40.00	18.00	5.00
☐ C4 Dan Marino	100.00	45.00	12.50
☐ C5 Jerry Rice	50.00	22.00	6.25
☐ C6 Barry Sanders	50.00	22.00	6.25
☐ C7 Emmitt Smith	100.00	45.00	12.50
☐ C8 Steve Young	40.00	18.00	5.00

1995 Pacific Triple Folders Crystalline

This 20 card set was randomly inserted into packs at a rate of four in 37 and have an acetate design. Cards fronts are clear at the top and are colored in the team's colors at the botton. The player's name is in gold foil and the player's team name appears in clear block letters at the botton. Card backs contain biographical information and a brief commentary. Cards are numbered with a "Cr" prefix.

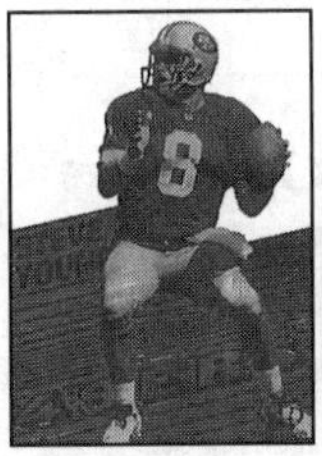
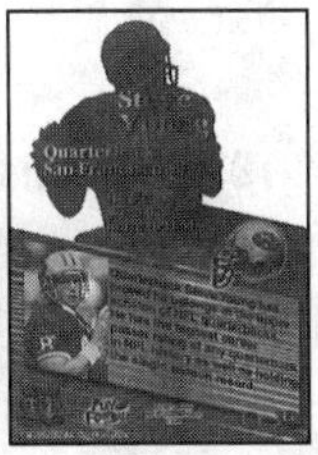

	MINT	NRMT	EXC
COMPLETE SET (20)	135.00	60.00	17.00
COMMON CARD (CR1-CR20)	2.50	1.10	.30
☐ CR1 Troy Aikman	10.00	4.50	1.25
☐ CR2 Jeff Blake	6.00	2.70	.75
☐ CR3 Drew Bledsoe	10.00	4.50	1.25
☐ CR4 Kerry Collins	12.00	5.50	1.50
☐ CR5 John Elway	8.00	3.60	1.00
☐ CR6 Marshall Faulk	3.50	1.55	.45
☐ CR7 Gus Frerotte	3.50	1.55	.45
☐ CR8 Joey Galloway	6.00	2.70	.75
☐ CR9 Garrison Hearst	3.50	1.55	.45
☐ CR10 Jeff Hostetler	2.50	1.10	.30
☐ CR11 Dan Marino	20.00	9.00	2.50
☐ CR12 Natrone Means	3.50	1.55	.45
☐ CR13 Errict Rhett	3.50	1.55	.45
☐ CR14 Rashaan Salaam	3.50	1.55	.45
☐ CR15 Barry Sanders	10.00	4.50	1.25
☐ CR16 Deion Sanders	7.00	3.10	.85
☐ CR17 Emmitt Smith UER All Vital Statistics are Wrong	20.00	9.00	2.50
☐ CR18 J.J. Stokes	3.50	1.55	.45
☐ CR19 Steve Young	8.00	3.60	1.00
☐ CR20 Eric Zeier	2.50	1.10	.30

1995 Pacific Triple Folders Rookies and Stars

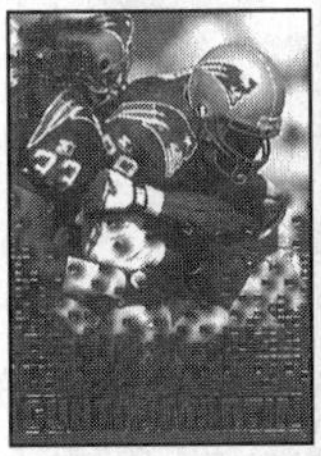
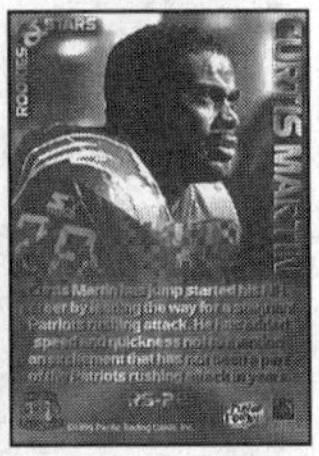

This 36 card set was randomly inserted in packs at a rate of three in four packs and features top rookies and stars from the NFL. Card fronts are a full bleed photo with gold foil checkered from the middle down to the bottom of the card. The player's name is located at the bottom of the card. Card backs feature a photo of the player and information about him. Three different parallels of this set exist: a Blue, a Raspberry and a Silver. Across the production run, the Raspberry and Silver parallels were inserted at a rate of three in 37 packs. The Blue parallel was inserted in retail packs (3:4 packs), the Raspberry in hobby packs and the Silver in retail packs.

	MINT	NRMT	EXC
COMPLETE GOLD SET (36)	35.00	16.00	4.40
COMMON GOLD CARD (1-36)	.50	.23	.06
COMPLETE BLUE SET (36)	35.00	16.00	4.40
*BLUE CARDS: SAME PRICE			
*RASPBERRY CARDS: 2.5X TO 5X BASIC CARDS			
*SILVER CARDS: 2.5X TO 5X BASIC CARDS			
☐ 1 Garrison Hearst	.75	.35	.09
☐ 2 Darick Holmes	.75	.35	.09
☐ 3 Kerry Collins	3.00	1.35	.35
☐ 4 Rashaan Salaam	.75	.35	.09
☐ 5 Jeff Blake	1.00	.45	.12
☐ 6 Eric Zeier	.50	.23	.06
☐ 7 Troy Aikman	1.50	.70	.19
☐ 8 Eric Bjornson	.50	.23	.06
☐ 9 Deion Sanders	1.00	.45	.12
☐ 10 Emmitt Smith	3.00	1.35	.35
☐ 11 Sherman Williams	.50	.23	.06
☐ 12 Terrell Davis	3.00	1.35	.35
☐ 13 John Elway	1.25	.55	.16
☐ 14 Barry Sanders	1.50	.70	.19
☐ 15 Steve McNair	2.50	1.10	.30
☐ 16 Marshall Faulk	.75	.35	.09
☐ 17 James O.Stewart	.50	.23	.06
☐ 18 Steve Bono	.50	.23	.06
☐ 19 Tamarick Vanover	.75	.35	.09
☐ 20 Dan Marino	3.00	1.35	.35
☐ 21 Drew Bledsoe	1.50	.70	.19
☐ 22 Curtis Martin	3.00	1.35	.35
☐ 23 Tyrone Wheatley	.50	.23	.06
☐ 24 Tim Brown	.75	.35	.09
☐ 25 Napoleon Kaufman	.50	.23	.06
☐ 26 Ricky Watters	.75	.35	.09
☐ 27 Natrone Means	.75	.35	.09
☐ 28 Jerry Rice	1.50	.70	.19
☐ 29 J.J. Stokes	.75	.35	.09
☐ 30 Steve Young	1.25	.55	.16
☐ 31 Joey Galloway	1.25	.55	.16
☐ 32 Chris Warren	.75	.35	.09
☐ 33 Jerome Bettis	.75	.35	.09
☐ 34 Errict Rhett	.75	.35	.09
☐ 35 Terry Allen	.75	.35	.09
☐ 36 Michael Westbrook	.75	.35	.09

1995 Pacific Triple Folders Teams

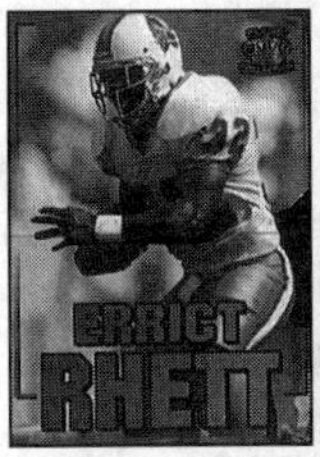
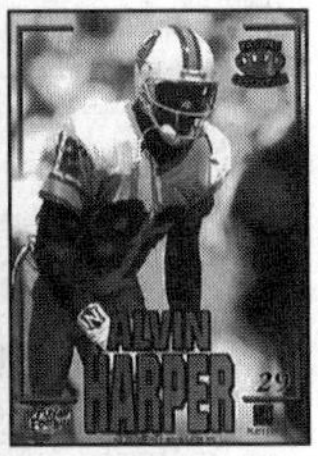

Inserted at a rate of nine in 37 packs, this 30 card set features a different card for each NFL team, highlighting each team's three highest profile players on one card. Card fronts contain a full bleed shot of the first player with his name at the bottom. Card backs contain the same design with a different player. When opened the card forms a larger shot of the third player with the same design, except the player's name is located at the top in gold-etched foil and the team name and logo is located in a circular gold-etched design at the bottom.

	MINT	NRMT	EXC
COMPLETE SET (30)	40.00	18.00	5.00
COMMON CARD (1-30)	.75	.35	.09
☐ 1 Garrison Hearst Dave Krieg Rob Moore	1.00	.45	.12
☐ 2 Jeff George Terance Mathis Eric Metcalf	1.00	.45	.12
☐ 3 Darick Holmes Jim Kelly Andre Reed	1.00	.45	.12
☐ 4 Edgar Bennett Brett Favre Reggie White	5.00	2.20	.60
☐ 5 Haywood Jeffires Chris Chandler Steve McNair	2.00	.90	.25
☐ 6 Marshall Faulk Jim Harbaugh Sean Dawkins	2.50	1.10	.30
☐ 7 Bob Christian Tim McKyer Kerry Collins	2.50	1.10	.30
☐ 8 Rashaan Salaam Erik Kramer Michael Timpson	1.00	.45	.12
☐ 9 Carl Pickens Jeff Blake Darnay Scott	1.50	.70	.19
☐ 10 Leroy Hoard Andre Rison Vinny Testaverde	.75	.35	.09
☐ 11 Troy Aikman Michael Irvin Emmitt Smith	5.00	2.20	.60
☐ 12 John Elway Terrell Davis Shannon Sharpe	2.00	.90	.25
☐ 13 Scott Mitchell Herman Moore Barry Sanders	2.50	1.10	.30
☐ 14 James O.Stewart Mark Brunell Desmond Howard	1.00	.45	.12
☐ 15 Marcus Allen Steve Bono Greg Hill	1.00	.45	.12
☐ 16 Bernie Parmalee Dan Marino Irving Fryar	5.00	2.20	.60
☐ 17 Robert Smith Warren Moon Cris Carter	.75	.35	.09
☐ 18 Curtis Martin Drew Bledsoe Ben Coates	4.00	1.80	.50
☐ 19 Mario Bates Jim Everett Michael Haynes	.75	.35	.09
☐ 20 Rodney Hampton Dave Brown Herschel Walker	.75	.35	.09
☐ 21 Wayne Chrebet Kyle Brady Adrian Murrell	.75	.35	.09
☐ 22 Napoleon Kaufman Jeff Hostetler Tim Brown	.75	.35	.09
☐ 23 Ricky Watters Charlie Garner Mike Mamula	.75	.35	.09
☐ 24 Byron Bam Morris Mike Tomczak Charles Johnson	.75	.35	.09
☐ 25 Natrone Means Stan Humphries Tony Martin	.75	.35	.09
☐ 26 Jerry Rice Steve Young J.J. Stokes	4.00	1.80	.50
☐ 27 Chris Warren Rick Mirer Joey Galloway	1.00	.45	.12
☐ 28 Jerome Bettis Kevin Carter Isaac Bruce	1.50	.70	.19
☐ 29 Errict Rhett Trent Dilfer Alvin Harper	1.00	.45	.12
☐ 30 Terry Allen Gus Frerotte Michael Westbrook	1.50	.70	.19

1961 Packers Lake to Lake

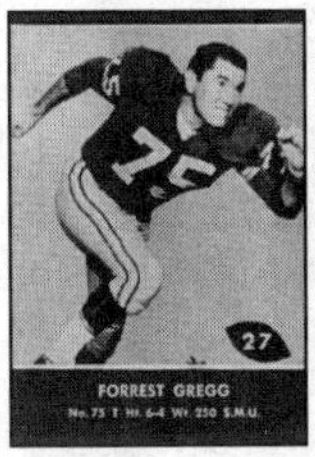

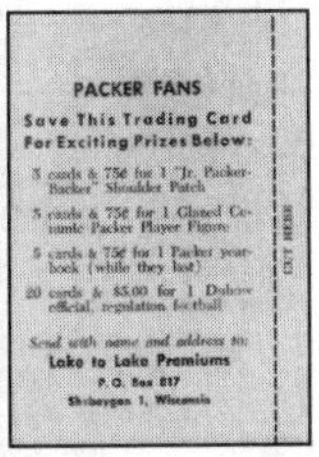

The 1961 Lake to Lake Green Bay Packers set consists of 36 unnumbered, green and white cards each measuring approximately 2 1/2" by 3 1/4". The fronts contain the card number, the player's uniform number, his position, and his height, weight, and college. The backs contain advertisements for the Packer fans to obtain Lake to Lake premiums. Card numbers 1-8 and 17-24 are more difficult to obtain than other cards in the set. Lineman Ken Iman's card was issued ten years before his Rookie Card; Defensive back Herb Adderley's card was issued three years before his Rookie Card.

	NRMT	VG-E	GOOD
COMPLETE SET (36)	700.00	325.00	90.00
COMMON CARD (1-8/17-24)	25.00	11.00	3.10
COMMON CARD (9-16/25-32)	2.50	1.10	.30
COMMON CARD (33-36)	5.00	2.20	.60
COMMON SP	25.00	11.00	3.10
☐ 1 Jerry Kramer SP	40.00	18.00	5.00
☐ 2 Norm Masters SP	25.00	11.00	3.10
☐ 3 Willie Davis SP	50.00	22.00	6.25
☐ 4 Bill Quinlan SP	25.00	11.00	3.10
☐ 5 Jim Temp SP	25.00	11.00	3.10
☐ 6 Emlen Tunnell SP	40.00	18.00	5.00
☐ 7 Gary Knafelc SP	25.00	11.00	3.10
☐ 8 Hank Jordan SP	40.00	18.00	5.00
☐ 9 Bill Forester	10.00	4.50	1.25
☐ 10 Paul Hornung	20.00	9.00	2.50
☐ 11 Jesse Whittenton	2.50	1.10	.30
☐ 12 Andy Cvercko	2.50	1.10	.30
☐ 13 Jim Taylor	15.00	6.75	1.85
☐ 14 Hank Gremminger	2.50	1.10	.30
☐ 15 Tom Moore	3.00	1.35	.35
☐ 16 John Symank	2.50	1.10	.30
☐ 17 Max McGee SP	35.00	16.00	4.40
☐ 18 Bart Starr SP	100.00	45.00	12.50
☐ 19 Ray Nitschke SP	75.00	34.00	9.50
☐ 20 Dave Hanner SP	30.00	13.50	3.70
☐ 21 Tom Bettis SP	25.00	11.00	3.10
☐ 22 Fuzzy Thurston SP	30.00	13.50	3.70
☐ 23 Lew Carpenter SP	25.00	11.00	3.10
☐ 24 Boyd Dowler SP	30.00	13.50	3.70
☐ 25 Ken Iman	2.50	1.10	.30
☐ 26 Bob Skoronski	2.50	1.10	.30
☐ 27 Forrest Gregg	10.00	4.50	1.25
☐ 28 Jim Ringo	10.00	4.50	1.25
☐ 29 Ron Kramer	3.00	1.35	.35
☐ 30 Herb Adderley	15.00	6.75	1.85
☐ 31 Dan Currie	2.50	1.10	.30
☐ 32 John Roach	2.50	1.10	.30
☐ 33 Dale Hackbart	5.00	2.20	.60
☐ 34 Larry Hickman	5.00	2.20	.60
☐ 35 Nelson Toburen	5.00	2.20	.60
☐ 36 Willie Wood	15.00	6.75	1.85

1966 Packers Mobil Posters

This eight-poster set of the Green Bay Packers measures approximately 11" by 14" and features art prints suitable for framing of various game action pictures. The fronts carry a color action art piece and the backs are blank. The posters were distributed in envelopes that included the title of the artwork and the poster number. Although players are not specifically identified, we've made attempts to identify some key players. The prints are listed below according to the number and title on the envelope.

	NRMT	VG-E	GOOD
COMPLETE SET (8)	75.00	34.00	9.50
COMMON CARD (1-8)	10.00	4.50	1.25

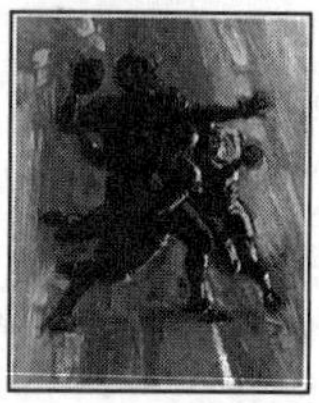

☐ 1 The Pass Bart Starr back to pass	25.00	11.00	3.10
☐ 2 The Block Jerry Kramer blocking for Elijah Pitts	12.00	5.50	1.50
☐ 3 The Punt Don Chandler punting	10.00	4.50	1.25
☐ 4 The Sweep Jim Taylor following blocking	15.00	6.75	1.85
☐ 5 The Catch Boyd Dowler	12.00	5.50	1.50
☐ 6 The Tackle	10.00	4.50	1.25
☐ 7 The Touchdown Tom Moore scoring	10.00	4.50	1.25
☐ 8 The Extra Point Don Chandler with Bart Starr holding	10.00	4.50	1.25

1968-69 Packers Team Issue

This team-issued set consists of black-and-white player photos with each measuring approximately 8" by 10". They were printed on thin glossy paper. The player's name, position, and team name are printed in black in the bottom white border. Although they are very similar to the 1971-72 release, the printing used for the text is generally larger. The team name is approximately 1 3/4" to 2" long. The cardbacks are blank. The photos are unnumbered and checklisted below in alphabetical order.

	NRMT-MT	EXC	G-VG
COMPLETE SET (12)	60.00	27.00	7.50
COMMON CARD (1-12)	2.50	1.10	.30
☐ 1 Herb Adderley	6.00	2.70	.75
☐ 2 Ken Bowman	2.50	1.10	.30
☐ 3 Lee Roy Caffey	3.00	1.35	.35
☐ 4 Fred Carr	3.00	1.35	.35
☐ 5 Carroll Dale	4.00	1.80	.50
☐ 6 Wille Davis	6.00	2.70	.75
☐ 7 Boyd Dowler	4.00	1.80	.50
☐ 9 Bob Hyland	2.50	1.10	.30
☐ 10 Jerry Kramer	5.00	2.20	.60
☐ 12 Max McGee	5.00	2.20	.60
☐ 15 Bart Starr	15.00	6.75	1.85
☐ 17 Travis Williams	5.00	2.20	.60

1969 Packers Drenks Potato Chip Pins

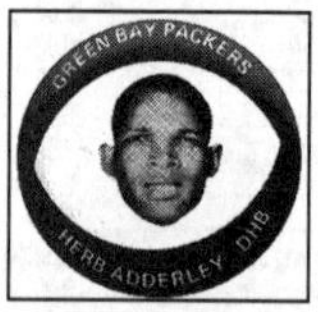

The 1969 Packers Drenks Potato Chip set contains 20 pins, each measuring approximately 1 1/8" in diameter. The fronts have a green and white background, with a black and white headshot in the center of the white football-shaped area. The team name at the top and player information at the bottom follow the curve of the pin. The pins are unnumbered and checklisted below in alphabetical order.

	NRMT-MT	EXC	G-VG
COMPLETE SET (20)	90.00	40.00	11.00
COMMON PIN (1-20)	2.00	.90	.25
☐ 1 Herb Adderley	7.50	3.40	.95
☐ 2 Lionel Aldridge	3.00	1.35	.35
☐ 3 Donny Anderson	4.00	1.80	.50
☐ 4 Ken Bowman	2.00	.90	.25
☐ 5 Carroll Dale	3.00	1.35	.35
☐ 6 Willie Davis	7.50	3.40	.95
☐ 7 Boyd Dowler	4.00	1.80	.50
☐ 8 Marv Fleming	4.00	1.80	.50
☐ 9 Gale Gillingham	3.00	1.35	.35
☐ 10 Jim Grabowski	4.00	1.80	.50
☐ 11 Forrest Gregg	7.50	3.40	.95
☐ 12 Don Horn	2.00	.90	.25
☐ 13 Bob Jeter	3.00	1.35	.35
☐ 14 Hank Jordan	7.50	3.40	.95
☐ 15 Ray Nitschke	10.00	4.50	1.25
☐ 16 Elijah Pitts	4.00	1.80	.50
☐ 17 Dave Robinson	4.00	1.80	.50
☐ 18 Bart Starr	15.00	6.75	1.85
☐ 19 Travis Williams	4.00	1.80	.50
☐ 20 Willie Wood	7.50	3.40	.95

1969 Packers Tasco Prints

Tasco Associates produced this set of Green Bay Packers prints. The fronts feature a large color artist's rendering of the player along with the player's name and position. The backs are blank and unnumbered. The prints measure approximately 11" by 16."

	NRMT-MT	EXC	G-VG
COMPLETE SET (7)	100.00	45.00	12.50
COMMON PRINT	10.00	4.50	1.25
☐ 1 Donny Anderson	12.00	5.50	1.50
☐ 2 Boyd Dowler	12.00	5.50	1.50
☐ 3 Jim Grabowski	10.00	4.50	1.25
☐ 4 Hank Jordan	15.00	6.75	1.85
☐ 5 Ray Nitschke	18.00	8.00	2.20
☐ 6 Bart Starr	25.00	11.00	3.10
☐ 7 Willie Wood	15.00	6.75	1.85

1971-72 Packers Team Issue

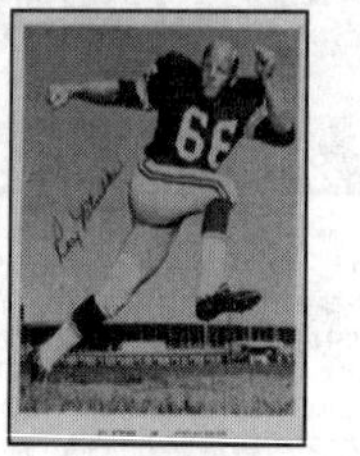

This team-issued set consists of black-and-white player photos with each measuring approximately 8" by 10". They were printed on thin glossy paper. The player's name, position, and team name are printed in black in the bottom white border. Although they are very similar to the 1968-69 release, the printing used for the text is generally smaller. The team name is approximately 1 1/2" long. The cardbacks are blank. Several players have two photos in the set: Dale, Hudson, Thomas, Snider, and Widby. Furthermore, Napper never played in the NFL, and Pittman never played for the Packers, suggesting that these photos may have been taken during training camp or preseason. The photos are unnumbered and checklisted below in alphabetical order.

	NRMT-MT	EXC	G-VG
COMPLETE SET (42)	110.00	50.00	14.00
COMMON CARD (1-42)	2.50	1.10	.30
☐ 1 John Brockington	5.00	2.20	.60
☐ 2 Bob Brown DT	3.00	1.35	.35
☐ 3 Willie Buchanon	4.00	1.80	.50
☐ 4 Jim Carter	3.00	1.35	.35
☐ 5 Carroll Dale (Action pose)	4.00	1.80	.50
☐ 6 Dan Devine CO/GM	4.00	1.80	.50
☐ 7 Ken Ellis	2.50	1.10	.30
☐ 8 Len Garrett	2.50	1.10	.30
☐ 9 Gale Gillingham	3.00	1.35	.35
☐ 10 Leland Glass	2.50	1.10	.30
☐ 11 Charlie Hall	2.50	1.10	.30
☐ 12 Jim Hill	3.00	1.35	.35
☐ 13 Dick Himes	2.50	1.10	.30
☐ 14 Bob Hudson (Head shot)	2.50	1.10	.30
☐ 15 Bob Hudson (Kneeling pose)	2.50	1.10	.30
☐ 16 Kevin Hunt	2.50	1.10	.30
☐ 17 Scott Hunter	4.00	1.80	.50
☐ 18 Dave Kopay	2.50	1.10	.30
☐ 19 Bob Kroll	2.50	1.10	.30
☐ 20 Pete Lammons	2.50	1.10	.30
☐ 21 MacArthur Lane	4.00	1.80	.50
☐ 22 Bill Lueck	2.50	1.10	.30
☐ 23 Al Matthews	2.50	1.10	.30
☐ 24 Mike McCoy	3.00	1.35	.35
☐ 25 Rich McGeorge	3.00	1.35	.35
☐ 26 Charlie Napper	2.50	1.10	.30
☐ 27 Ray Nitschke	10.00	4.50	1.25
☐ 28 Charlie Pittman	4.00	1.80	.50
☐ 29 Alden Roche	2.50	1.10	.30
☐ 30 Malcolm Snider (Action pose; Falcons' uniform)	2.50	1.10	.30
☐ 31 Malcolm Snider (Kneeling pose)	2.50	1.10	.30
☐ 32 Jon Staggers	4.00	1.80	.50
☐ 33 Jerry Tagge	4.00	1.80	.50
☐ 34 Isaac Thomas (Action pose) (Cowboys uniform)	2.50	1.10	.30
☐ 35 Isaac Thomas (Kneeling pose)	2.50	1.10	.30
☐ 36 Vern Vanoy	2.50	1.10	.30
☐ 37 Ron Widby (Action pose) (Cowboys' uniform)	2.50	1.10	.30
☐ 38 Ron Widby (Kneeling pose)	2.50	1.10	.30
☐ 39 Clarence Williams	2.50	1.10	.30
☐ 40 Perry Williams	2.50	1.10	.30
☐ 41 Keith Wortman	3.00	1.35	.35
☐ 42 Coaching Staff Bart Starr Hank Kuhlmann Dave Hanner Burt Gustafson John Polonchek Don Doll Red Cochran Dan Devine Rollie Dotsch	10.00	4.50	1.25

1975 Packers Team Issue

The Green Bay Packers issued this set of 14-photos along with a saver album. A space for Al Mathews is included in the album, but the photo is not yet known to exist. Each measures approximately 6" by 9". The fronts feature posed color photos of the players kneeling with their right hand resting on their helmets. Facsimile autographs are inscribed across the pictures. The backs are blank. The cards are unnumbered and checklisted below in alphabetical order.

	NRMT-MT	EXC	G-VG
COMPLETE SET (14)	60.00	27.00	7.50
COMMON CARD (1-14)	3.00	1.35	.35
☐ 1 John Brockington	5.00	2.20	.60
☐ 2 Willie Buchanon	4.00	1.80	.50
☐ 3 Fred Carr	4.00	1.80	.50
☐ 4 Jim Carter	4.00	1.80	.50
☐ 5 Jack Concannon	4.00	1.80	.50
☐ 6 Bill Curry	5.00	2.20	.60
☐ 7 John Hadl	5.00	2.20	.60
☐ 8 Bill Lueck	3.00	1.35	.35
☐ 9 Chester Marcol	4.00	1.80	.50
☐ 10 Rich McGeorge	4.00	1.80	.50
☐ 11 Alden Roche	3.00	1.35	.35
☐ 12 Barry Smith	3.00	1.35	.35
☐ 13 Barty Smith	3.00	1.35	.35
☐ 14 Clarence Williams	3.00	1.35	.35
☐ NNO Saver Album	20.00	9.00	2.50

1983 Packers Police

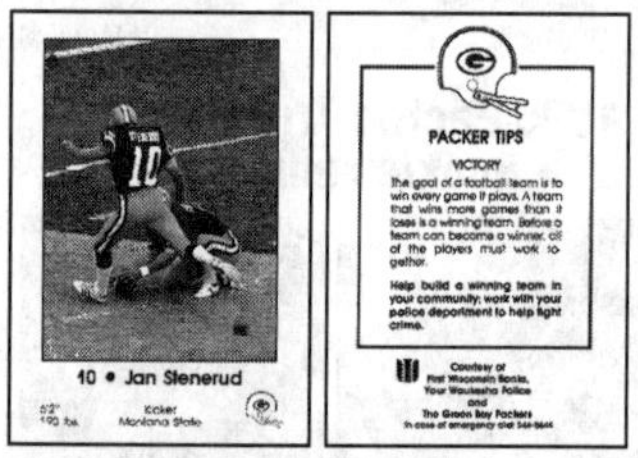

This 19-card set is somewhat more difficult to find than the other Packers Police sets. There are three different types of backs: First Wisconsin Banks, without First Wisconsin Banks, and Waukesha P.D. The hardest to get of these three is the set without First Wisconsin Banks. All cards are approximately 2 5/8" by 4 1/8". Card backs are printed in green ink on white card stock. A safety tip ("Packer Tips") is given on the back. Cards are unnumbered except for uniform number.

	MINT	NRMT	EXC
COMPLETE SET (19)	25.00	11.00	3.10
COMMON CARD	1.00	.45	.12
☐ 10 Jan Stenerud	2.50	1.10	.30
☐ 12 Lynn Dickey	1.50	.70	.19
☐ 24 Johnnie Gray	1.00	.45	.12
☐ 29 Mike McCoy	1.25	.55	.16
☐ 31 Gerry Ellis	1.00	.45	.12
☐ 40 Eddie Lee Ivery	1.50	.70	.19
☐ 52 George Cumby	1.00	.45	.12
☐ 53 Mike Douglass	1.25	.55	.16
☐ 54 Larry McCarren	1.00	.45	.12
☐ 59 John Anderson	1.25	.55	.16
☐ 63 Terry Jones	1.00	.45	.12
☐ 64 Syd Kitson	1.00	.45	.12
☐ 68 Greg Koch	1.00	.45	.12
☐ 80 James Lofton	4.00	1.80	.50
☐ 82 Paul Coffman	1.50	.70	.19
☐ 83 John Jefferson	2.00	.90	.25
☐ 85 Phillip Epps	1.50	.70	.19
☐ 90 Ezra Johnson	1.00	.45	.12
☐ NNO Bart Starr CO	4.00	1.80	.50

1984 Packers Police

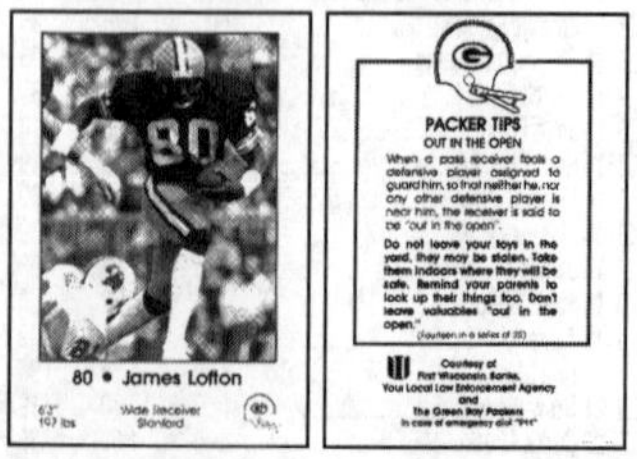

This 25-card set is numbered on the back. The card backs were printed in green ink. Cards were sponsored by First Wisconsin banks, the local law enforcement agency, and the Green Bay Packers. The cards measure approximately 2 5/8" by 4".

	MINT	NRMT	EXC
COMPLETE SET (25)	12.00	5.50	1.50
COMMON CARD (1-25)	.40	.18	.05
☐ 1 John Jefferson	.60	.25	.07
☐ 2 Forrest Gregg CO	2.00	.90	.25
☐ 3 John Anderson	.50	.23	.06
☐ 4 Eddie Garcia	.40	.18	.05
☐ 5 Tim Lewis	.40	.18	.05
☐ 6 Jessie Clark	.40	.18	.05
☐ 7 Karl Swanke	.40	.18	.05
☐ 8 Lynn Dickey	.75	.35	.09
☐ 9 Eddie Lee Ivery	.60	.25	.07
☐ 10 Dick Modzelewski CO (Defensive Coord.)	.40	.18	.05
☐ 11 Mark Murphy	.40	.18	.05
☐ 12 David Drechsler	.40	.18	.05
☐ 13 Mike Douglass	.40	.18	.05
☐ 14 James Lofton	3.00	1.35	.35
☐ 15 Bucky Scribner	.40	.18	.05
☐ 16 Randy Scott	.40	.18	.05
☐ 17 Mark Lee	.50	.23	.06
☐ 18 Gerry Ellis	.40	.18	.05
☐ 19 Terry Jones	.40	.18	.05
☐ 20 Greg Koch	.40	.18	.05
☐ 21 Bob Schnelker CO (Offensive Coord.)	.40	.18	.05
☐ 22 George Cumby	.40	.18	.05
☐ 23 Larry McCarren	.40	.18	.05
☐ 24 Syd Kitson	.40	.18	.05
☐ 25 Paul Coffman	.50	.23	.06

1985 Packers Police

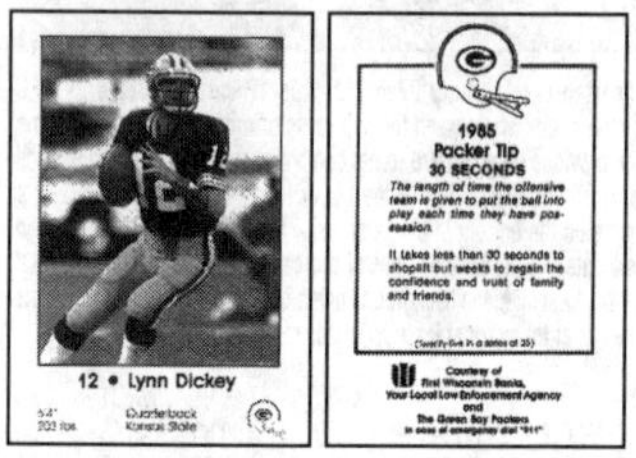

This 25-card set of Green Bay Packers is numbered on the back. Cards measure approximately 2 3/4" by 4". The backs contain a "1985 Packer Tip". Each player's uniform number is given on the card front.

	MINT	NRMT	EXC
COMPLETE SET (25)	8.00	3.60	1.00
COMMON CARD (1-25)	.40	.18	.05
☐ 1 Forrest Gregg CO	1.50	.70	.19
☐ 2 Paul Coffman	.60	.25	.07
☐ 3 Terry Jones	.40	.18	.05
☐ 4 Ron Hallstrom	.40	.18	.05
☐ 5 Eddie Lee Ivery	.60	.25	.07
☐ 6 John Anderson	.50	.23	.06
☐ 7 Tim Lewis	.40	.18	.05
☐ 8 Bob Schnelker CO (Offensive Coord.)	.40	.18	.05
☐ 9 Al Del Greco	.40	.18	.05
☐ 10 Mark Murphy	.50	.23	.06
☐ 11 Tim Huffman	.40	.18	.05
☐ 12 Del Rodgers	.40	.18	.05
☐ 13 Mark Lee	.50	.23	.06
☐ 14 Tom Flynn	.40	.18	.05
☐ 15 Dick Modzelewski CO (Defensive Coord.)	.40	.18	.05
☐ 16 Randy Scott	.40	.18	.05
☐ 17 Bucky Scribner	.40	.18	.05
☐ 18 George Cumby	.40	.18	.05
☐ 19 James Lofton	2.00	.90	.25
☐ 20 Mike Douglass	.50	.23	.06
☐ 21 Alphonso Carreker	.40	.18	.05
☐ 22 Greg Koch	.40	.18	.05
☐ 23 Gerry Ellis	.40	.18	.05
☐ 24 Ezra Johnson	.40	.18	.05
☐ 25 Lynn Dickey	.75	.35	.09

1986 Packers Police

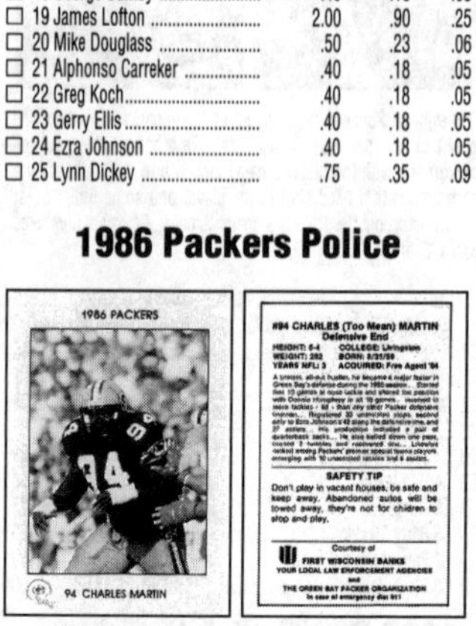

This 25-card set of Green Bay Packers is unnumbered except for uniform number. Cards measure approximately 2 3/4" by 4" and the backs contain a "Safety Tip". The fronts features the prominent heading "1986 Packers". Card backs are written in green ink on white card stock.

	MINT	NRMT	EXC
COMPLETE SET (25)	8.00	3.60	1.00
COMMON CARD	.35	.16	.04

	MINT	NRMT	EXC
□ 10 Al Del Greco	.35	.16	.04
□ 12 Lynn Dickey	.60	.25	.07
□ 16 Randy Wright	.60	.25	.07
□ 26 Tim Lewis	.35	.16	.04
□ 31 Gerry Ellis	.35	.16	.04
□ 33 Jessie Clark	.35	.16	.04
□ 37 Mark Murphy	.50	.23	.06
□ 40 Eddie Lee Ivery	.50	.23	.06
□ 41 Tom Flynn	.35	.16	.04
□ 42 Gary Ellerson	.35	.16	.04
□ 55 Randy Scott	.35	.16	.04
□ 58 Mark Cannon	.35	.16	.04
□ 59 John Anderson	.50	.23	.06
□ 65 Ron Hallstrom	.35	.16	.04
□ 67 Karl Swanke	.35	.16	.04
□ 76 Alphonso Carreker	.35	.16	.04
□ 80 James Lofton	1.50	.70	.19
□ 82 Paul Coffman	.50	.23	.06
□ 85 Phillip Epps	.50	.23	.06
□ 90 Ezra Johnson	.35	.16	.04
□ 91 Brian Noble	.50	.23	.06
□ 93 Robert Brown	.35	.16	.04
□ 94 Charles Martin	.35	.16	.04
□ 99 John Dorsey	.35	.16	.04
□ NNO Forrest Gregg CO	1.25	.55	.16

1987 Packers Police

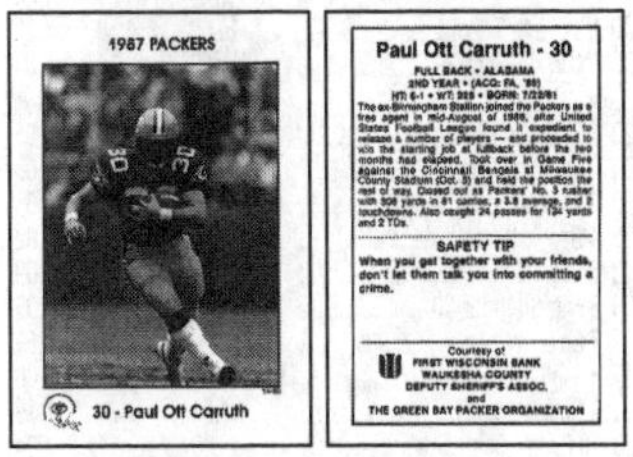

This 22-card set of Green Bay Packers is numbered on the front in the lower right corner below the photo. Sponsors were the Employers Health Insurance Company, Arson Task Force, local law enforcement agencies, and the Green Bay Packers. Cards measure 2 3/4" by 4". The backs contain a "Safety Tip". The fronts features the prominent heading "1987 Packers". Card backs are written in green ink on white card stock. Cards 5, 6, and 20 were never issued as apparently they were scheduled to be players who were later cut and released from the team. Reportedly 35,000 sets were distributed.

	MINT	NRMT	EXC
COMPLETE SET (22)	8.00	3.60	1.00
COMMON CARD (1-25)	.35	.16	.04
□ 1 Forrest Gregg CO	1.00	.45	.12
□ 2 George Greene	.35	.16	.04
□ 3 Ron Hallstrom	.35	.16	.04
□ 4 Ezra Johnson	.35	.16	.04
□ 7 Robert Brown	.35	.16	.04
□ 8 Tom Neville	.35	.16	.04
□ 9 Rich Moran	.35	.16	.04
□ 10 Ken Ruettgers	.50	.23	.06
□ 11 Alan Veingrad	.35	.16	.04
□ 12 Mark Lee	.50	.23	.06
□ 13 John Dorsey	.35	.16	.04
□ 14 Paul Ott Carruth	.35	.16	.04
□ 15 Randy Wright	.50	.23	.06
□ 16 Phillip Epps	.50	.23	.06
□ 17 Al Del Greco	.35	.16	.04
□ 18 Tim Harris	1.00	.45	.12
□ 19 Kenneth Davis	1.00	.45	.12
□ 21 John Anderson	.50	.23	.06
□ 22 Mark Murphy	.50	.23	.06
□ 23 Ken Stills	.35	.16	.04
□ 24 Brian Noble	.50	.23	.06
□ 25 Mark Cannon	.35	.16	.04

1988 Packers Police

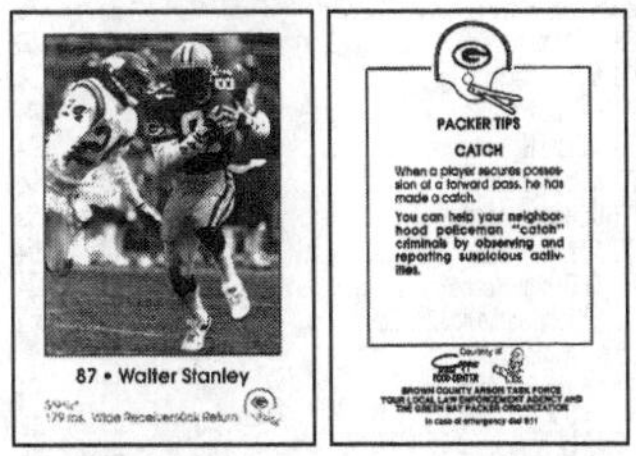

The 1988 Police Green Bay Packers set contains 25 cards measuring approximately 2 3/4" by 4". There are 24 player cards and one coach card. The backs have football tips and safety tips. The cards are unnumbered so they are listed below in alphabetical order.

	MINT	NRMT	EXC
COMPLETE SET (25)	10.00	4.50	1.25
COMMON CARD (1-25)	.40	.18	.05
□ 1 John Anderson	.50	.23	.06
□ 2 Jerry Boyarsky	.40	.18	.05
□ 3 Don Bracken	.40	.18	.05
□ 4 Dave Brown	.40	.18	.05
□ 5 Mark Cannon	.40	.18	.05
□ 6 Alphonso Carreker	.40	.18	.05
□ 7 Paul Ott Carruth	.40	.18	.05
□ 8 Kenneth Davis	.75	.35	.09
□ 9 John Dorsey	.40	.18	.05
□ 10 Brent Fullwood	.50	.23	.06
□ 11 Tiger Greene	.40	.18	.05
□ 12 Ron Hallstrom	.40	.18	.05
□ 13 Tim Harris	.75	.35	.09
□ 14 Johnny Holland	.50	.23	.06
□ 15 Lindy Infante CO	.60	.25	.07
□ 16 Mark Lee	.50	.23	.06
□ 17 Don Majkowski	1.00	.45	.12
□ 18 Rich Moran	.40	.18	.05
□ 19 Mark Murphy	.40	.18	.05
□ 20 Ken Ruettgers	.50	.23	.06
□ 21 Walter Stanley	.60	.25	.07
□ 22 Keith Uecker	.40	.18	.05
□ 23 Ed West	.50	.23	.06
□ 24 Randy Wright	.40	.18	.05
□ 25 Max Zendejas	.40	.18	.05

1989 Packers Police

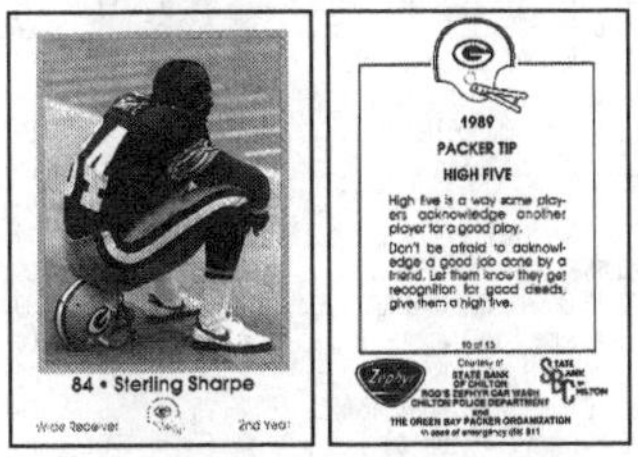

The 1989 Police Green Bay Packers set contains 15 numbered cards measuring approximately 2 3/4" by 4". The fronts have white borders and color action photos bordered in Packers yellow; the vertically oriented backs have safety tips. These cards were printed on very thin stock. Sterling Sharpe appears in his Rookie Card year.

	MINT	NRMT	EXC
COMPLETE SET (15)	6.00	2.70	.75
COMMON CARD (1-15)	.35	.16	.04
□ 1 Lindy Infante CO	.50	.23	.06
□ 2 Don Majkowski	.60	.25	.07
□ 3 Brent Fullwood	.35	.16	.04
□ 4 Mark Lee	.50	.23	.06
□ 5 Dave Brown	.35	.16	.04
□ 6 Mark Murphy	.50	.23	.06
□ 7 Johnny Holland	.50	.23	.06
□ 8 John Anderson	.50	.23	.06
□ 9 Ken Ruettgers	.50	.23	.06
□ 10 Sterling Sharpe	2.00	.90	.25
□ 11 Ed West	.35	.16	.04
□ 12 Walter Stanley	.50	.23	.06
□ 13 Brian Noble	.50	.23	.06
□ 14 Shawn Patterson	.35	.16	.04
□ 15 Tim Harris	.50	.23	.06

1990 Packers Police

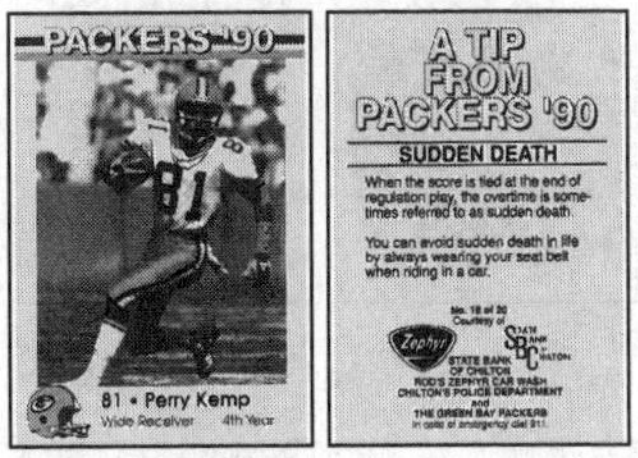

This 20-card set, which measures approximately 2 3/4" by 4", was issued by police departments in Wisconsin and featured members of the 1990 Green Bay Packers. The fronts have white borders with a "Packers '90" title on the front and the name of the subject along with their position and NFL experience. The backs of the card feature a safety tip and small ads for the sponsors of the set.

	MINT	NRMT	EXC
COMPLETE SET (20)	6.00	2.70	.75
COMMON CARD (1-20)	.25	.11	.03
□ 1 Lindy Infante CO	.35	.16	.04
□ 2 Keith Woodside	.25	.11	.03
□ 3 Chris Jacke	.35	.16	.04
□ 4 Chuck Cecil	.35	.16	.04
□ 5 Tony Mandarich	.25	.11	.03
□ 6 Brent Fullwood	.25	.11	.03
□ 7 Robert Brown	.25	.11	.03
□ 8 Scott Stephen	.25	.11	.03
□ 9 Anthony Dilweg	.25	.11	.03
□ 10 Mark Murphy	.25	.11	.03
□ 11 Johnny Holland	.35	.16	.04
□ 12 Sterling Sharpe	1.00	.45	.12
□ 13 Tim Harris	.35	.16	.04
□ 14 Ed West	.25	.11	.03
□ 15 Jeff Query	.25	.11	.03
□ 16 Mark Lee	.25	.11	.03
□ 17 Rich Moran	.25	.11	.03
□ 18 Perry Kemp	.35	.16	.04
□ 19 Brian Noble	.35	.16	.04
□ 20 Don Majkowski	.50	.23	.06

1990 Packers 25th Anniversary

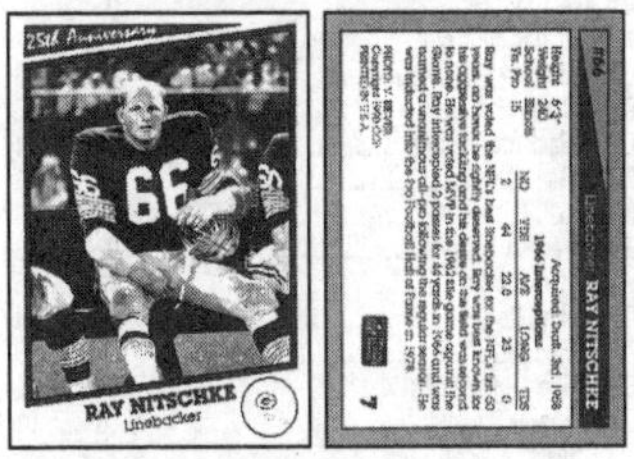

This 45-card standard size set was issued by Champion Cards of Owosso, Michigan and produced by Pacific Trading Cards, Inc. This set celebrated the 25th anniversary of the 1966 Green Bay Packers, the first team to win the Super Bowl. This set has a mix of color and sepia-toned photos and a mix of action and portrait shots on the front with a biography of the player on the back of the card. The only member of the 1966 Packers not featured in this set is Paul Hornung.

	MINT	NRMT	EXC
COMPLETE SET (45)	15.00	6.75	1.85
COMMON CARD (1-45)	.25	.11	.03
□ 1 Introduction Card	.50	.23	.06
□ 2 Bart Starr	2.00	.90	.25
□ 3 Herb Adderley	.75	.35	.09
□ 4 Bob Skoronski	.25	.11	.03
□ 5 Tom Brown	.35	.16	.04
□ 6 Lee Roy Caffey	.35	.16	.04
□ 7 Ray Nitschke	1.00	.45	.12
□ 8 Carroll Dale	.35	.16	.04
□ 9 Jim Taylor	1.25	.55	.16
□ 10 Ken Bowman	.25	.11	.03
□ 11 Gale Gillingham	.35	.16	.04
□ 12 Jim Grabowski	.50	.23	.06
□ 13 Dave Robinson	.50	.23	.06
□ 14 Donny Anderson	.50	.23	.06
□ 15 Willie Wood	.75	.35	.09
□ 16 Zeke Bratkowski	.50	.23	.06
□ 17 Doug Hart	.25	.11	.03
□ 18 Jerry Kramer	.75	.35	.09
□ 19 Marv Fleming	.35	.16	.04
□ 20 Lionel Aldridge	.35	.16	.04
□ 21 Bill Red Mack UER (Text reads returned to football before the following season, should be retired)	.25	.11	.03
□ 22 Ron Kostelnik	.25	.11	.03
□ 23 Boyd Dowler	.50	.23	.06
□ 24 Vince Lombardi CO	1.50	.70	.19
□ 25 Forrest Gregg	.75	.35	.09
□ 26 Max McGee Superstar	.35	.16	.04
□ 27 Fuzzy Thurston	.50	.23	.06
□ 28 Bob Brown DT	.35	.16	.04
□ 29 Willie Davis	.75	.35	.09
□ 30 Elijah Pitts	.50	.23	.06
□ 31 Hank Jordan	.75	.35	.09
□ 32 Bart Starr	2.00	.90	.25
□ 33 Super Bowl I (Jim Taylor)	.75	.35	.09
□ 34 1966 Packers	.50	.23	.06
□ 35 Max McGee	.50	.23	.06
□ 36 Jim Weatherwax	.25	.11	.03
□ 37 Bob Long	.25	.11	.03
□ 38 Don Chandler	.35	.16	.04
□ 39 Bill Anderson	.25	.11	.03
□ 40 Tommy Crutcher	.35	.16	.04
□ 41 Dave Hathcock	.25	.11	.03
□ 42 Steve Wright	.25	.11	.03
□ 43 Phil Vandersea	.25	.11	.03
□ 44 Bill Curry	.50	.23	.06
□ 45 Bob Jeter	.35	.16	.04

1991 Packers Police

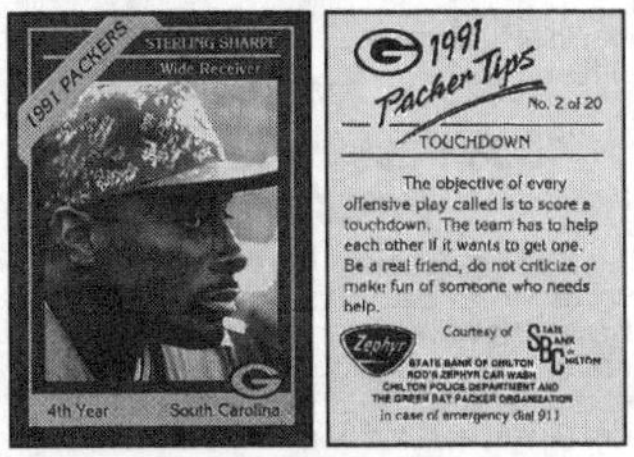

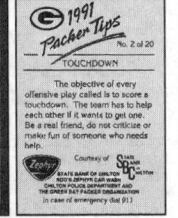

This 20-card standard-size set was printed on white card stock. These cards feature player action shots on the fronts enclosed by yellow and green borders. A yellow banner design in the top left corner has "1991 Packers" printed in black. Player's name and position appear in gold in the top right green border. College team and years played with Packers are noted in a gold band at bottom. The backs are printed in green ink and have Packer (safety) tips based on the player's position. Sponsor names appear at the bottom of card. Only card number 1 is printed horizontally front and back.

	MINT	NRMT	EXC
COMPLETE SET (20)	7.00	3.10	.85
COMMON CARD (1-20)	.30	.14	.04
□ 1 Lambeau Field	.30	.14	.04
□ 2 Sterling Sharpe	.75	.35	.09
□ 3 James Campen	.30	.14	.04
□ 4 Chuck Cecil	.40	.18	.05
□ 5 Lindy Infante CO	.40	.18	.05
□ 6 Keith Woodside	.30	.14	.04
□ 7 Perry Kemp	.30	.14	.04
□ 8 Johnny Holland	.40	.18	.05
□ 9 Don Majkowski	.40	.18	.05
□ 10 Tony Bennett	.50	.23	.06
□ 11 LeRoy Butler	.40	.18	.05
□ 12 Tony Mandarich	.30	.14	.04
□ 13 Darrell Thompson	.40	.18	.05
□ 14 Matt Brock	.30	.14	.04
□ 15 Charles Wilson	.50	.23	.06
□ 16 Brian Noble	.40	.18	.05
□ 17 Ed West	.30	.14	.04
□ 18 Chris Jacke	.30	.14	.04
□ 19 Blair Kiel	.40	.18	.05
□ 20 Mark Murphy	.30	.14	.04

1991 Packers Super Bowl II

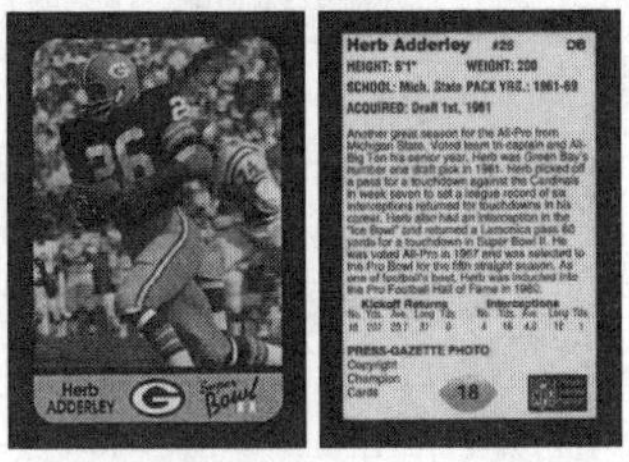

This 50-card Green Bay Packers set was released by Sportscards of Michigan and commemorates the 25th anniversary of the team's win in Super Bowl II. The cards are printed on thin card stock and measure the standard size (2 1/2" by 3 1/2"). The fronts feature either black and white or color player photos with dark green borders. The player's name, team logo, and "Super Bowl II" appear in a yellow stripe below the picture. The backs have biography and career highlights. The cards are numbered on the back.

	MINT	NRMT	EXC
COMPLETE SET (50)	12.00	5.50	1.50
COMMON CARD (1-49)	.25	.11	.03
□ 1 Intro Card Super Bowl Trophy	.50	.23	.06
□ 2 Steve Wright	.25	.11	.03
□ 3 Jim Flanigan	.25	.11	.03
□ 4 Tom Brown	.35	.16	.04
□ 5 Tommy Joe Crutcher	.35	.16	.04
□ 6 Doug Hart	.35	.16	.04
□ 7 Bob Hyland	.25	.11	.03
□ 8 John Rowser	.25	.11	.03
□ 9 Bob Skoronski	.25	.11	.03
□ 10 Jim Weatherwax	.25	.11	.03
□ 11 Ben Wilson	.25	.11	.03
□ 12 Don Horn	.35	.16	.04
□ 13 Allen Brown	.25	.11	.03
□ 14 Dick Capp	.25	.11	.03
□ 15 Super Bowl II Action Donny Anderson	.50	.23	.06
□ 16 Ice Bowl: The Play Bart Starr	1.50	.70	.19
□ 17 Chuck Mercein	.35	.16	.04
□ 18 Herb Adderley	.75	.35	.09
□ 19 Ken Bowman	.25	.11	.03
□ 20 Lee Roy Caffey	.35	.16	.04
□ 21 Carroll Dale	.35	.16	.04
□ 22 Marv Fleming	.35	.16	.04
□ 23 Jim Grabowski	.50	.23	.06
□ 24 Bob Jeter	.35	.16	.04
□ 25 Jerry Kramer	.75	.35	.09
□ 26 Max McGee	.50	.23	.06
□ 27 Elijah Pitts	.50	.23	.06
□ 28 Bart Starr	1.50	.70	.19
□ 29 Fuzzy Thurston	.50	.23	.06
□ 30 Willie Wood	.75	.35	.09
□ 31 Lionel Aldridge	.35	.16	.04
□ 32 Donny Anderson	.50	.23	.06
□ 33 Zeke Bratkowski	.50	.23	.06
□ 34 Bob Brown DT	.35	.16	.04
□ 35 Don Chandler	.35	.16	.04
□ 36 Willie Davis	.75	.35	.09
□ 37 Boyd Dowler	.50	.23	.06
□ 38 Gale Gillingham	.35	.16	.04
□ 39 Hank Jordan	.75	.35	.09
□ 40 Ron Kostelnik	.25	.11	.03
□ 41 Vince Lombardi CO	1.25	.55	.16
□ 42 Bob Long	.25	.11	.03
□ 43 Ray Nitschke	1.00	.45	.12
□ 44 Dave Robinson	.50	.23	.06

	MINT	NRMT	EXC
☐ 45 Bart Starr MVP	1.25	.55	.16
☐ 46 Travis Williams	.35	.16	.04
☐ 47 1967 Packers Team	.50	.23	.06
☐ 48 Ice Bowl Game Summary	.25	.11	.03
☐ 49 Ice Bowl	.25	.11	.03
☐ NNO Packer Pro Shop	.25	.11	.03

1992 Packers Hall of Fame

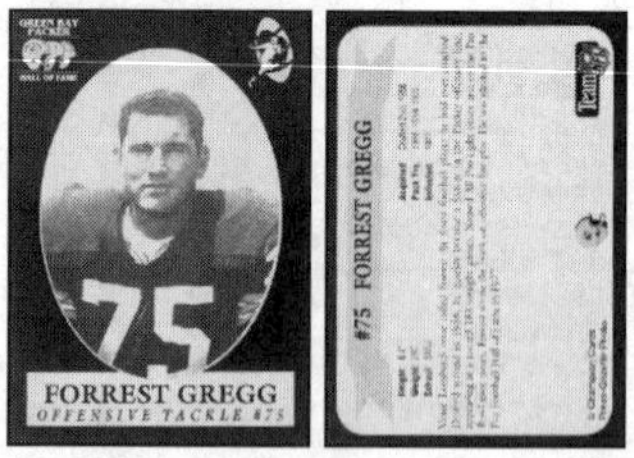

This 110-card standard-size set features all 106 Packer Hall of Fame inductees. It was available to collectors exclusively at the Packer Hall of Fame gift shop, and yearly updates will be issued as new members are selected for induction to the Hall of Fame. The cards are printed on thin cardboard stock. The fronts display black and white or color player photos enclosed by an oval gold border on a dark green card face. The player's name, position, and jersey number are in a gold band beneath the picture. The horizontally oriented backs carry biography and career highlights. The player's name appears in green in a gold banner at the top, while the card number is printed on a small helmet at the bottom center. There is no number 1 card, but there are two number 45's.

	MINT	NRMT	EXC
COMPLETE SET (110)	20.00	9.00	2.50
COMMON CARD (1-108)	.10	.05	.01
☐ 2 Red Dunn	.20	.09	.03
☐ 3 Mike Michalske	.50	.23	.06
☐ 4 Cal Hubbard	.50	.23	.06
☐ 5 Johnny(Blood) McNally	.50	.23	.06
☐ 6 Verne Lewellen	.10	.05	.01
☐ 7 Cub Buck	.10	.05	.01
☐ 8 Whitey Woodin	.10	.05	.01
☐ 9 Jug Earp	.10	.05	.01
☐ 10 Charlie Mathys	.10	.05	.01
☐ 11 Andrew Turnbull PRES	.10	.05	.01
☐ 12 Curly Lambeau Founder/Coach	.50	.23	.06
☐ 13 George Calhoun PUB	.10	.05	.01
☐ 14 Boob Darling	.10	.05	.01
☐ 15 Eddie Jankowski	.10	.05	.01
☐ 16 Swede Johnston	.10	.05	.01
☐ 17 George Svendsen	.10	.05	.01
☐ 18 Bob Monnett	.10	.05	.01
☐ 19 Joe Laws	.10	.05	.01
☐ 20 Tiny Engebretsen	.10	.05	.01
☐ 21 Milt Gantenbein	.10	.05	.01
☐ 22 Hank Bruder	.10	.05	.01
☐ 23 Clarke Hinkle	.50	.23	.06
☐ 24 Lon Evans	.10	.05	.01
☐ 25 Buckets Goldenberg	.10	.05	.01
☐ 26 Nate Barrager	.10	.05	.01
☐ 27 Arnie Herber	.30	.14	.04
☐ 28 Lee Joannes PRES	.10	.05	.01
☐ 29 Jerry Clifford VP	.10	.05	.01
☐ 30 Pete Tinsley	.10	.05	.01
☐ 31 Buford Ray	.10	.05	.01
☐ 32 Andy Uram	.10	.05	.01
☐ 33 Larry Craig	.10	.05	.01
☐ 34 Charles Brock	.10	.05	.01
☐ 35 Ted Fritsch Sr.	.20	.09	.03
☐ 36 Lou Brock	.10	.05	.01
☐ 37 Carl Mulleneaux	.10	.05	.01
☐ 38 Harry Jacunski	.10	.05	.01
☐ 39 Cecil Isbell	.30	.14	.04
☐ 40 Bud Svendsen	.10	.05	.01
☐ 41 Russ Letlow	.10	.05	.01
☐ 42 Don Hutson	1.00	.45	.12
☐ 43 Irv Comp	.10	.05	.01
☐ 44 John Martinkovic	.10	.05	.01
☐ 45A Bobby Dillon	.20	.09	.03
☐ 45B Lavern Dilweg UER (Back is that of card 45 card, Bobby Dillon)	.50	.23	.06
☐ 46 Wilner Burke Band Director	.10	.05	.01
☐ 47 Dick Wildung	.10	.05	.01
☐ 48 Bill Howton	.30	.14	.04
☐ 49 Tobin Rote	.30	.14	.04
☐ 50 Jim Ringo	.50	.23	.06
☐ 51 Deral Teteak	.10	.05	.01
☐ 52 Bob Forte	.10	.05	.01
☐ 53 Tony Canadeo	.50	.23	.06
☐ 54 Al Carmichael	.10	.05	.01
☐ 55 Bob Mann	.10	.05	.01
☐ 56 Jack Vainisi Scout	.10	.05	.01
☐ 57 Ken Bowman	.10	.05	.01
☐ 58 Bob Skoronski	.10	.05	.01
☐ 59 Dave Hanner	.20	.09	.03
☐ 60 Bill Forester	.20	.09	.03
☐ 61 Fred Cone	.10	.05	.01
☐ 62 Lionel Aldridge	.20	.09	.03
☐ 63 Carroll Dale	.20	.09	.03
☐ 64 Howard Ferguson	.10	.05	.01
☐ 65 Gary Knafelc	.10	.05	.01
☐ 66 Ron Kramer	.20	.09	.03
☐ 67 Forrest Gregg	.50	.23	.06
☐ 68 Phil Bengtson CO	.10	.05	.01
☐ 69 Dan Currie	.10	.05	.01
☐ 70 Al Schneider Contributor	.10	.05	.01
☐ 71 Bob Jeter	.20	.09	.03
☐ 72 Jesse Whittenton	.20	.09	.03
☐ 73 Hank Gremminger	.10	.05	.01
☐ 74 Ron Kostelnik	.10	.05	.01
☐ 75 Gale Gillingham	.20	.09	.03
☐ 76 Lee Roy Caffey	.20	.09	.03
☐ 77 Hank Jordan	.50	.23	.06
☐ 78 Boyd Dowler	.30	.14	.04
☐ 79 Fred Carr	.20	.09	.03
☐ 80 Bud Jorgensen TR	.10	.05	.01
☐ 81 Eugene Brusky Team Physician	.10	.05	.01
☐ 82 Fred Trowbridge Executive Committee	.10	.05	.01
☐ 83 Jan Stenerud	.50	.23	.06
☐ 84 Jerry Atkinson Contributor	.10	.05	.01
☐ 85 Larry McCarren	.10	.05	.01
☐ 86 Fred Leicht Executive Committee	.10	.05	.01
☐ 87 Max McGee	.30	.14	.04
☐ 88 Zeke Bratkowski	.30	.14	.04
☐ 89 Dave Robinson	.30	.14	.04
☐ 90 Herb Adderley	.50	.23	.06
☐ 91 Dominic Olejniczak President	.20	.09	.03
☐ 92 Jerry Kramer	.50	.23	.06
☐ 93 Super Bowl I	.20	.09	.03
☐ 94 Don Chandler	.10	.05	.01
☐ 95 John Brockington	.30	.14	.04
☐ 96 Lynn Dickey	.20	.09	.03
☐ 97 Bart Starr	1.25	.55	.16
☐ 98 Willie Wood	.75	.35	.09
☐ 99 Packer Hall of Fame	.20	.09	.03
☐ 100 Donny Anderson	.20	.09	.03
☐ 101 Chester Marcol	.20	.09	.03
☐ 102 Fuzzy Thurston	.20	.09	.03
☐ 103 Paul Hornung	1.00	.45	.12
☐ 104 Jim Taylor	1.00	.45	.12
☐ 105 Vince Lombardi CO	1.00	.45	.12
☐ 106 Willie Davis	.50	.23	.06
☐ 107 Ray Nitschke	.75	.35	.09
☐ 108 Elijah Pitts	.20	.09	.03
☐ NNO Honor Roll Checklist Card	.20	.09	.03
☐ NNO Packer Hall of Fame Catalog Order Form	.20	.09	.03

1992 Packers Police

This 20-card set features players of the Packers. The cards were printed with a green border and color player photograph on front. Cardbacks are white with green printing. We've assigned numbers to the unnumbered issue according to alphabetical order.

	MINT	NRMT	EXC
COMPLETE SET (20)	12.00	5.50	1.50
COMMON CARD	.25	.11	.03
☐ 1 Tony Bennett	.50	.23	.06
☐ 2 Matt Brock	.25	.11	.03
☐ 3 Leroy Butler	.25	.11	.03
☐ 4 Vinnie Clark	.35	.16	.04
☐ 5 Brett Favre	8.00	3.60	1.00
☐ 6 Jackie Harris	.50	.23	.06
☐ 7 Johnny Holland	.25	.11	.03
☐ 8 Mike Holmgren CO	1.00	.45	.12
☐ 9 Chris Jacke	.25	.11	.03
☐ 10 Sherman Lewis CO	.25	.11	.03
☐ 11 Don Majkowski	.35	.16	.04
☐ 12 Tony Mandarich	.25	.11	.03
☐ 13 Paul McJulien	.25	.11	.03
☐ 14 Bryce Paup	1.50	.70	.19
☐ 14 Brian Noble	.35	.16	.04
☐ 16 Ray Rhodes CO	1.00	.45	.12
☐ 17 Tootie Robbins	.25	.11	.03
☐ 18 Sterling Sharpe	.75	.35	.09
☐ 19 Darrell Thompson	.25	.11	.03
☐ 20 Ron Wolf GM	.35	.16	.04

1993 Packers Archives Postcards

These 40 postcards were made by Champion Cards of Green Bay to commemorate the Packers' 75th anniversary and, except for the unnumbered title card, measure approximately 3 1/2" by 5 1/2". The white-bordered postcards are framed by team color-coded lines and feature mostly black-and-white archival photos of Packer players and teams of yesteryear. Most of the cards display the Packers' 75th anniversary logo in the lower left. The horizontal white backs carry on their left sides information about the subject depicted on the front. On the right side is a ghosted Champion Cards logo. The postcards are numbered on the back within a football icon that appears at the bottom.

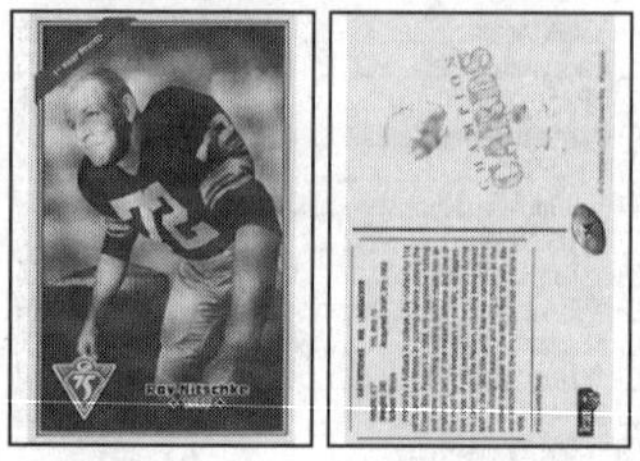

	MINT	NRMT	EXC
COMPLETE SET (40)	15.00	6.75	1.85
COMMON CARD (1-39)	.50	.23	.06
☐ 1 The First Team 1919	.75	.35	.09
☐ 2 The 1920s	.50	.23	.06
☐ 3 The 1930s	.50	.23	.06
☐ 4 The 1940s	.50	.23	.06
☐ 5 The 1950s	.50	.23	.06
☐ 6 The 1960s	.50	.23	.06
☐ 7 The 1970s	.50	.23	.06
☐ 8 The 1980s	.50	.23	.06
☐ 9 The 1990s	.50	.23	.06
☐ 10 Curly Lambeau 1919	.75	.35	.09
☐ 11 Jim Ringo 1953	.75	.35	.09
☐ 12 Ice Bowl 1967	.75	.35	.09
☐ 13 Jerry Kramer 1958	.75	.35	.09
☐ 14 Ray Nitschke 1958	1.00	.45	.12
☐ 15 Fuzzy Thurston 1959	.75	.35	.09
☐ 16 James Lofton 1978-86	.75	.35	.09
☐ 17 Super Bowl I Action	.75	.35	.09
☐ 18 Don Hutson 1935-45	1.00	.45	.12
☐ 19 Tony Canadeo '41-43/46-52	.75	.35	.09
☐ 20 Bobby Dillon 1952-59	.50	.23	.06
☐ 21 The Quarterback	.75	.35	.09
☐ 22 Willie Wood 1960-71	.75	.35	.09
☐ 23 Dave Beverly 1975-80	.50	.23	.06
☐ 24 James Lofton 1978	.75	.35	.09
☐ 25 Tim Harris 1986-90	.75	.35	.09
☐ 26 1929 Championship Team	.50	.23	.06
☐ 27 1930 Championship Team	.50	.23	.06
☐ 28 1931 Championship Team	.50	.23	.06
☐ 29 1936 Championship Team	.50	.23	.06
☐ 30 1939 Championship Team	.50	.23	.06
☐ 31 1944 Championship Team	.50	.23	.06
☐ 32 1961 Championship Team	.75	.35	.09
☐ 33 1962 Championship Team	.75	.35	.09
☐ 34 1965 Championship Team	.75	.35	.09
☐ 35 1966 Championship Team	.75	.35	.09
☐ 36 1967 Championship Team	.75	.35	.09
☐ 37 Old City Stadium	.50	.23	.06
☐ 38 New City Stadium	.50	.23	.06
☐ 39 Lambeau Field - 1992	.50	.23	.06
☐ NNO Title card (3 3/4" by 5 3/4")	.75	.35	.09

1993 Packers Police

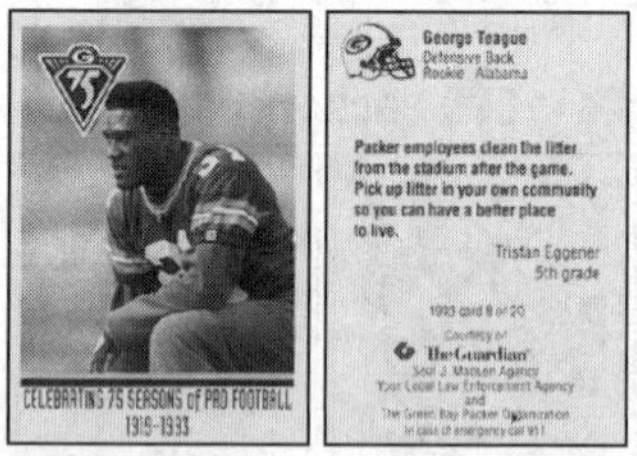

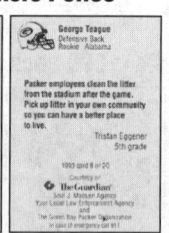

These 20 standard-size cards were issued to commemorate the Packers' 75th anniversary and feature on their fronts white-bordered color player photos. Two team color-coded stripes edge the pictures at the bottom. The 75th anniversary logo appears at the upper left, and the words "Celebrating 75 Years of Pro Football 1919-1993" appear below the photo. The white back carries the player's name, position, years in the NFL, alma mater, and Packers helmet at the upper left. Below are safety messages written by area grade schoolers.

	MINT	NRMT	EXC
COMPLETE SET (20)	10.00	4.50	1.25
COMMON CARD (1-20)	.25	.11	.03
☐ 1 Ron Wolf GM	.25	.11	.03
☐ 2 Wayne Simmons	.35	.16	.04
☐ 3 James Campen	.25	.11	.03
☐ 4 Matt Brock	.25	.11	.03
☐ 5 Mike Holmgren CO	.75	.35	.09
☐ 6 Brian Noble	.35	.16	.04
☐ 7 Ken O'Brien	.35	.16	.04
☐ 8 George Teague	.35	.16	.04
☐ 9 Brett Favre	5.00	2.20	.60
☐ 10 LeRoy Butler	.35	.16	.04
☐ 11 Harry Galbreath	.25	.11	.03
☐ 12 Chris Jacke	.35	.16	.04
☐ 13 Sterling Sharpe	.75	.35	.09
☐ 14 Terrell Buckley	.35	.16	.04
☐ 15 Ken Ruettgers	.35	.16	.04
☐ 16 Johnny Holland	.35	.16	.04
☐ 17 Edgar Bennett	1.00	.45	.12
☐ 18 Jackie Harris	.50	.23	.06
☐ 19 Tony Bennett	.50	.23	.06
☐ 20 Reggie White	1.00	.45	.12

1994 Packers Police

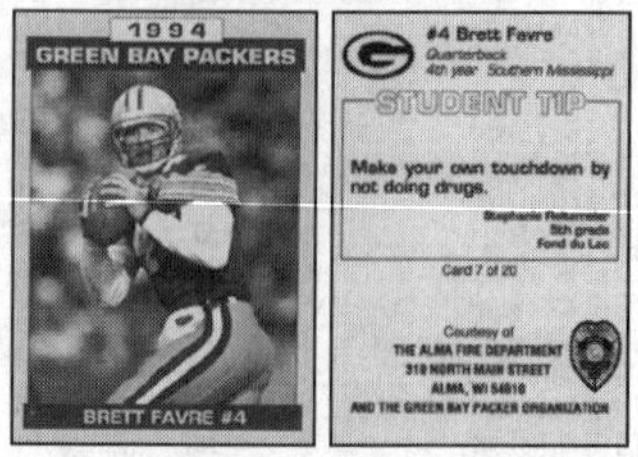

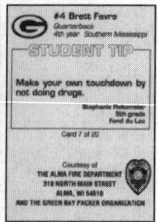

This 20-card standard-size set was issued courtesy of the Alma Fire Department and the Green Bay Packer Organization. The fronts display color player photos accented by team color-coded borders. The player's name and uniform number are printed in the green bar beneath the picture. On a white background in dark green print, the backs carry a student tip by Fond du Lac elementary school children and list the set's sponsors.

	MINT	NRMT	EXC
COMPLETE SET (20)	10.00	4.50	1.25
COMMON CARD (1-20)	.30	.14	.04
☐ 1 Sherman Lewis	.40	.18	.05
☐ 2 Sterling Sharpe	.60	.25	.07
☐ 3 Ken Ruettgers	.40	.18	.05
☐ 4 Reggie White	.75	.35	.09
☐ 5 Edgar Bennett	.75	.35	.09
☐ 6 Fritz Shurmur CO	.40	.18	.05
☐ 7 Brett Favre	4.00	1.80	.50
☐ 8 John Jurkovic	.50	.23	.06
☐ 9 Robert Brooks	1.50	.70	.19
☐ 10 Reggie Cobb	.30	.14	.04
☐ 11 Bryce Paup	.75	.35	.09
☐ 12 Harry Galbreath	.30	.14	.04
☐ 13 Mike Holmgren CO	.50	.23	.06
☐ 14 Ed West	.30	.14	.04
☐ 15 Sean Jones	.50	.23	.06
☐ 16 Ron Wolf GM	.30	.14	.04
☐ 17 Chris Jacke	.40	.18	.05
☐ 18 Wayne Simmons	.40	.18	.05
☐ 19 LeRoy Butler	.30	.14	.04
☐ 20 George Teague	.40	.18	.05

1995 Packers Safety Fritsch

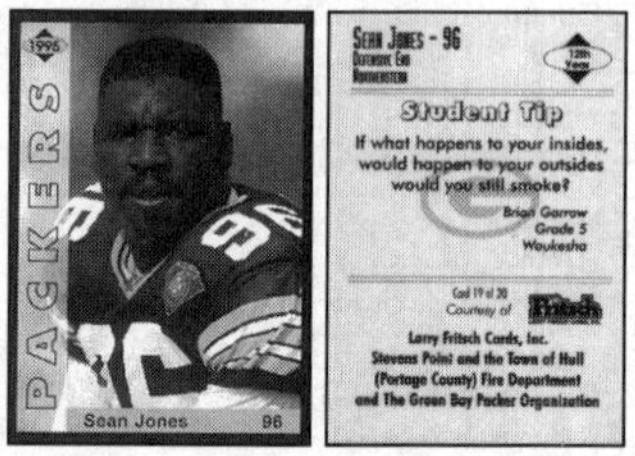

This 20-card set of the Green Pay Packers features color action player photos in a thin green border. The set was produced by Larry Fritsch Cards and sponsored by the local Fire Department. The backs carry a student safety tip.

	MINT	NRMT	EXC
COMPLETE SET (20)	8.00	3.60	1.00
COMMON CARD (1-20)	.30	.14	.04
☐ 1 Mike Holmgren CO	.50	.23	.06
☐ 2 Ron Wolf VP/GM	.30	.14	.04
☐ 3 Brett Favre	3.00	1.35	.35
☐ 4 Ty Detmer	.50	.23	.06
☐ 5 Chris Jacke	.50	.23	.06
☐ 6 Craig Hentrich	.30	.14	.04
☐ 7 Craig Newsome	.30	.14	.04
☐ 8 George Teague	.50	.23	.06
☐ 9 Edgar Bennett	.75	.35	.09
☐ 10 LeRoy Butler	.30	.14	.04
☐ 11 George Koonce	.30	.14	.04
☐ 12 John Jurkovic	.50	.23	.06
☐ 13 Aaron Taylor	.30	.14	.04
☐ 14 Ken Ruettgers	.30	.14	.04
☐ 15 Robert Brooks	1.00	.45	.12
☐ 16 Mark Chmura	1.25	.55	.16
☐ 17 Reggie White	1.00	.45	.12
☐ 18 Doug Evans	.30	.14	.04
☐ 19 Sean Jones	.50	.23	.06
☐ 20 Wayne Simmons	.50	.23	.06

1996 Packers Police

The Green Bay Packers issued this set in 1996 sponsored by Citgo. The cards feature a green border with the team and year "Packers 1996" at the top of the cardfront. The cardbacks feature green text on white card stock.

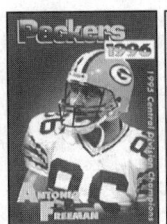

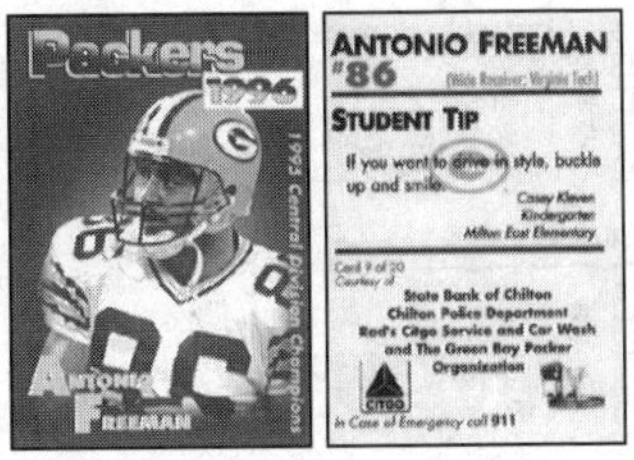

	MINT	NRMT	EXC
COMPLETE SET (20)	10.00	4.50	1.25
COMMON CARD (1-20)	.30	.14	.04

☐ 1 Edgar Bennett	.75	.35	.09
☐ 2 Robert Brooks	1.00	.45	.12
☐ 3 Gilbert Brown	.75	.35	.09
☐ 4 Leroy Butler	.50	.23	.06
☐ 5 Mark Chmura	.75	.35	.09
☐ 6 Earl Dotson	.30	.14	.04
☐ 7 Doug Evans	.30	.14	.04
☐ 8 Brett Favre	3.00	1.35	.35
☐ 9 Antonio Freeman	1.50	.70	.19
☐ 10 Craig Hentrich	.30	.14	.04
☐ 11 Chris Jacke	.50	.23	.06
☐ 12 Wayne Simmons	.50	.23	.06
☐ 13 George Koonce	.30	.14	.04
☐ 14 Craig Newsome	.30	.14	.04
☐ 15 Ken Ruettgers	.30	.14	.04
☐ 16 Keith Jackson	.50	.23	.06
☐ 17 Aaron Taylor	.30	.14	.04
☐ 18 Reggie White	1.00	.45	.12
☐ 19 Mike Holmgren	.50	.23	.06
☐ 20 Ron Wolf	.30	.14	.04

1997 Packers Playoff

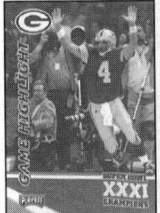 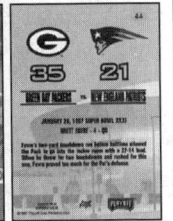

This 50-card set honors the 1997 Super Bowl XXXI World Champions, the Green Bay Packers. The fronts feature borderless color action player photos with the Super Bowl logo printed at the bottom and player's name on one side. The backs carry the score of the championship game with the New England Patriots and player information on a faint background of the dome in New Orleans.

	MINT	NRMT	EXC
COMPLETE SET (50)	30.00	13.50	3.70
COMMON CARD (1-50)	.40	.18	.05

☐ 1 Super Bowl XXXI Champions Scoreboard Photo	.50	.23	.06
☐ 2 Brett Favre MVP	3.00	1.35	.35
☐ 3 Reggie White Minister of Defense	1.50	.70	.19
☐ 4 Desmond Howard MVP	.50	.23	.06
☐ 5 NFC Championship Trophy Presentation	.40	.18	.05
☐ 6 Mike Holmgren CO	.50	.23	.06
☐ 7 Brett Favre	5.00	2.20	.60
☐ 8 Chris Jacke	.50	.23	.06
☐ 9 Craig Hentrich	.40	.18	.05
☐ 10 Craig Newsome	.50	.23	.06
☐ 11 Dorsey Levens	2.00	.90	.25
☐ 12 Doug Evans	.40	.18	.05
☐ 13 Edgar Bennett	.75	.35	.09
☐ 14 Leroy Butler	.50	.23	.06
☐ 15 Eugene Robinson	.40	.18	.05
☐ 16 Brian Williams	.40	.18	.05
☐ 17 Frank Winters	.40	.18	.05
☐ 18 Ron Cox	.40	.18	.05
☐ 19 Wayne Simmons	.50	.23	.06
☐ 20 Adam Timmerman	.40	.18	.05
☐ 21 Bruce Wilkerson	.40	.18	.05
☐ 22 Santana Dotson	.50	.23	.06
☐ 23 Earl Dotson	.40	.18	.05
☐ 24 Aaron Taylor	.40	.18	.05
☐ 25 Desmond Howard	.50	.23	.06
☐ 26 Don Beebe	.50	.23	.06
☐ 27 Andre Rison	.50	.23	.06
☐ 28 Antonio Freeman	2.00	.90	.25
☐ 29 Terry Mickens	.40	.18	.05
☐ 30 Keith Jackson	.50	.23	.06
☐ 31 Mark Chmura	1.00	.45	.12
☐ 32 Reggie White	1.50	.70	.19
☐ 33 Gilbert Brown	.50	.23	.06
☐ 34 Sean Jones	.50	.23	.06
☐ 35 Robert Brooks George Koonce	1.00	.45	.12
☐ 36 Derrick Mayes Gary Brown	.50	.23	.06

☐ 37 Jim McMahon	.50	.23	.06
☐ 38 William Henderson	.40	.18	.05
☐ 39 Travis Jervey Roderick Mullen	.50	.23	.06
☐ 40 Tyrone Williams	.40	.18	.05
☐ 41 John Michels	.50	.23	.06
☐ 42 Mike Prior	.40	.18	.05
☐ 43 Calvin Jones Jeff Thomason	.40	.18	.05
☐ 44 Brett Favre	3.00	1.35	.35
☐ 45 Jeff Dellenbach	.40	.18	.05
☐ 46 Bernardo Harris	.40	.18	.05
☐ 47 Darius Holland	.40	.18	.05
☐ 48 Lamont Hollinquest	.40	.18	.05
☐ 49 Lindsay Knapp	.40	.18	.05
☐ 50 Gabe Wilkins	.40	.18	.05

1997 Packers Shopko

This 90 card standard-sized set was distributed and produced for Shopko, a retailer who has stores in the Wisconsin area.

	MINT	NRMT	EXC
COMPLETE SET (90)	50.00	22.00	6.25
COMMON CARD (GB1-GB90)	.30	.14	.04

☐ GB1 Robert Brooks	1.00	.45	.12
☐ GB2 Antonio Freeman	1.00	.45	.12
☐ GB3 Keith Jackson	.75	.35	.09
☐ GB4 Mark Chmura	.60	.25	.07
☐ GB5 Brett Favre	2.00	.90	.25
☐ GB6 Reggie White	1.00	.45	.12
☐ GB7 Leroy Butler	.40	.18	.05
☐ GB8 Craig Newsome	.40	.18	.05
☐ GB9 Sean Jones	.40	.18	.05
☐ GB10 Edgar Bennett	.75	.35	.09
☐ GB11 William Henderson	.40	.18	.05
☐ GB12 Dorsey Levens	1.00	.45	.12
☐ GB13 Travis Jervey	.40	.18	.05
☐ GB14 Jim McMahon	.40	.18	.05
☐ GB15 Aaron Taylor	.30	.14	.04
☐ GB16 Brian Winters	.30	.14	.04
☐ GB17 Earl Dotson	.30	.14	.04
☐ GB18 Andy Timmerman	.30	.14	.04
☐ GB19 Bruce Wilkerson	.30	.14	.04
☐ GB20 John Michels	.40	.18	.05
☐ GB21 Don Beebe	.40	.18	.05
☐ GB22 Andre Rison	.40	.18	.05
☐ GB23 Desmond Howard	.40	.18	.05
☐ GB24 Terry Mickens	.30	.14	.04
☐ GB25 Derrick Mayes	.75	.35	.09
☐ GB26 Chris Jacke	.40	.18	.05
☐ GB27 Gilbert Brown	.75	.35	.09
☐ GB28 Santana Dotson	.40	.18	.05
☐ GB29 George Koonce	.30	.14	.04
☐ GB30 Wayne Simmons	.40	.18	.05
☐ GB31 Brian Williams	.40	.18	.05
☐ GB32 Ron Cox	.30	.14	.04
☐ GB33 Doug Evans	.30	.14	.04
☐ GB34 Eugene Robinson	.30	.14	.04
☐ GB35 Mike Prior	.30	.14	.04
☐ GB36 Tyrone Williams	.30	.14	.04
☐ GB37 Sherman Lewis	.40	.18	.05
☐ GB38 Fritz Shurmer	.75	.35	.09
☐ GB39 Gordon(Red) Batty	.30	.14	.04
☐ GB40 Lambeau Field	.75	.35	.09
☐ GB41 Brett Favre	2.00	.90	.25
☐ GB42 Brett Favre	2.00	.90	.25
☐ GB43 Edgar Bennett	.75	.35	.09
☐ GB44 Edgar Bennett	.75	.35	.09
☐ GB45 Antonio Freeman	1.00	.45	.12
☐ GB46 Antonio Freeman	1.00	.45	.12
☐ GB47 Dorsey Levens	1.00	.45	.12
☐ GB48 Andre Rison	.40	.18	.05
☐ GB49 Keith Jackson	.75	.35	.09
☐ GB50 Don Beebe	.40	.18	.05
☐ GB51 Reggie White	1.00	.45	.12
☐ GB52 Packer Defense	.30	.14	.04
☐ GB53 Craig Newsome	.40	.18	.05
☐ GB54 Eugene Robinson	.30	.14	.04
☐ GB55 Desmond Howard	.40	.18	.05
☐ GB56 Robert Brooks	1.00	.45	.12
☐ GB57 Chris Jacke	.40	.18	.05
☐ GB58 Mike Holmgren	.40	.18	.05
☐ GB59 Ron Wolf	.30	.14	.04
☐ GB60 Brett Favre	2.00	.90	.25
☐ GB61 Brett Favre	2.00	.90	.25
☐ GB62 Edgar Bennett	.75	.35	.09
☐ GB63 Edgar Bennett	.75	.35	.09
☐ GB64 Dorsey Levens	1.00	.45	.12
☐ GB65 Dorsey Levens	1.00	.45	.12
☐ GB66 Antonio Freeman	1.00	.45	.12
☐ GB67 Antonio Freeman	1.00	.45	.12
☐ GB68 Andre Rison	.40	.18	.05
☐ GB69 Don Beebe	.40	.18	.05
☐ GB70 Mark Chmura	.60	.25	.07
☐ GB71 Reggie White	1.00	.45	.12
☐ GB72 Eugene Robinson	.30	.14	.04
☐ GB73 Desmond Howard	.40	.18	.05
☐ GB74 Desmond Howard	.40	.18	.05
☐ GB75 Craig Newsome	.40	.18	.05
☐ GB76 Tyrone Williams	.30	.14	.04
☐ GB77 Chris Jacke	.40	.18	.05
☐ GB78 Wayne Simmons	.40	.18	.05
☐ GB79 Offensive Line	.30	.14	.04
☐ GB80 Brett Favre	2.00	.90	.25

☐ GB81 Antonio Freeman	1.00	.45	.12
☐ GB82 Reggie White	1.00	.45	.12
☐ GB83 Wayne Simmons	.40	.18	.05
☐ GB84 Edgar Bennett	.75	.35	.09
☐ GB85 Andre Rison	.40	.18	.05
☐ GB86 Dorsey Levens	1.00	.45	.12
☐ GB87 Chris Jacke	.40	.18	.05
☐ GB88 The Secondary	.30	.14	.04
☐ GB89 Desmond Howard	.40	.18	.05
☐ GB90 Checklist	.30	.14	.04

1988 Panini Stickers

 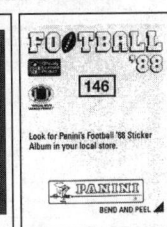

This set of 433 different stickers (457 including half stickers) was issued in 1988 by Panini. Panini had been producing stickers under Topps license but, beginning with this set, Panini established its own trade name in this country separate from Topps. The stickers measure approximately 2 1/8" by 2 3/4", are numbered on both the front and the back, and are in alphabetical order by team. The album for the set is easily obtainable. It is organized in team order like the sticker numbering. On the inside back cover of the sticker album the company offered (via direct mail-order) up to 30 different stickers of your choice for either ten cents each (only in Canada) or in trade one-for-one for your unwanted extra stickers (only in the United States) plus 1.00 for postage and handling; this is one reason why the values of the most popular players in these sticker sets are somewhat depressed compared to traditional card set prices. Each sticker pack included one foil sticker. Team name foils were produced in pairs; the other member of the pair is listed parenthetically. The team name foils contain a referee signal on the sticker back, the helmet foils have the team's stadium on the back, and the uniform foils include a team "Huddles" cartoon card on the back. The album for the set features John Elway on the cover. Bo Jackson appears in his Rookie Football Card year and Simon Fletcher appears one year prior to his Rookie Cards.

	MINT	NRMT	EXC
COMPLETE SET (447)	30.00	13.50	3.70
COMMON CARD (1-447)	.05	.02	.01

☐ 1 Super Bowl XXII Program Cover	.05	.02	.01
☐ 2 Buffalo Bills Helmet FOIL	.05	.02	.01
☐ 3 Buffalo Bills Action	.05	.02	.01
☐ 4 Cornelius Bennett	.20	.09	.03
☐ 5 Chris Burkett	.05	.02	.01
☐ 6 Derrick Burroughs	.05	.02	.01
☐ 7 Shane Conlan	.20	.09	.03
☐ 8 Ronnie Harmon	.10	.05	.01
☐ 9 Jim Kelly	.25	.11	.03
☐ 10 Buffalo Bills FOIL (240)	.05	.02	.01
☐ 11 Mark Kelso	.05	.02	.01
☐ 12 Nate Odomes	.10	.05	.01
☐ 13 Andre Reed	.20	.09	.03
☐ 14 Fred Smerlas	.05	.02	.01
☐ 15 Bruce Smith	.20	.09	.03
☐ 16 Buffalo Bills Uniform FOIL	.05	.02	.01
☐ 17 Cincinnati Bengals Helmet FOIL	.05	.02	.01
☐ 18 Cincinnati Bengals Action	.05	.02	.01
☐ 19 Jim Breech	.05	.02	.01
☐ 20 James Brooks	.10	.05	.01
☐ 21 Eddie Brown	.10	.05	.01
☐ 22 Cris Collinsworth	.10	.05	.01
☐ 23 Boomer Esiason	.20	.09	.03
☐ 24 Rodney Holman	.10	.05	.01
☐ 25 Cincinnati Bengals FOIL (255)	.05	.02	.01
☐ 26 Larry Kinnebrew	.05	.02	.01
☐ 27 Tim Krumrie	.05	.02	.01
☐ 28 Anthony Munoz	.20	.09	.03
☐ 29 Reggie Williams	.10	.05	.01
☐ 30 Carl Zander	.05	.02	.01
☐ 31 Cincinnati Bengals Uniform FOIL	.05	.02	.01
☐ 32 Cleveland Browns Helmet FOIL	.05	.02	.01
☐ 33 Browns Action (Bernie Kosar)	.05	.02	.01
☐ 34 Earnest Byner	.20	.09	.03
☐ 35 Hanford Dixon	.05	.02	.01
☐ 36 Bob Golic	.05	.02	.01
☐ 37 Mike Johnson	.05	.02	.01
☐ 38 Bernie Kosar	.20	.09	.03
☐ 39 Kevin Mack	.10	.05	.01
☐ 40 Cleveland Browns FOIL (270)	.05	.02	.01
☐ 41 Clay Matthews	.10	.05	.01
☐ 42 Gerald McNeil	.05	.02	.01
☐ 43 Frank Minnifield	.05	.02	.01
☐ 44 Ozzie Newsome	.20	.09	.03
☐ 45 Cody Risien	.05	.02	.01
☐ 46 Cleveland Browns Uniform FOIL			

☐ 47 Denver Broncos Helmet FOIL	.05	.02	.01
☐ 48 Denver Broncos Action	.05	.02	.01
☐ 49 Keith Bishop	.05	.02	.01
☐ 50 Tony Dorsett	.20	.09	.03
☐ 51 John Elway	1.25	.55	.16
☐ 52 Simon Fletcher	.10	.05	.01
☐ 53 Mark Jackson	.10	.05	.01
☐ 54 Vance Johnson	.10	.05	.01
☐ 55 Denver Broncos FOIL (285)	.05	.02	.01
☐ 56 Rulon Jones	.05	.02	.01
☐ 57 Rich Karlis	.05	.02	.01
☐ 58 Karl Mecklenburg	.10	.05	.01
☐ 59 Ricky Nattiel	.10	.05	.01
☐ 60 Sammy Winder	.05	.02	.01
☐ 61 Denver Broncos Uniform FOIL	.05	.02	.01
☐ 62 Houston Oilers Helmet FOIL	.05	.02	.01
☐ 63 Oilers Action (Warren Moon)	.20	.09	.03
☐ 64 Keith Bostic	.05	.02	.01
☐ 65 Steve Brown	.05	.02	.01
☐ 66 Ray Childress	.10	.05	.01
☐ 67 Jeff Donaldson	.05	.02	.01
☐ 68 John Grimsley	.05	.02	.01
☐ 69 Robert Lyles	.05	.02	.01
☐ 70 Houston Oilers FOIL (300)	.05	.02	.01
☐ 71 Drew Hill	.10	.05	.01
☐ 72 Warren Moon	.50	.23	.06
☐ 73 Mike Munchak	.05	.02	.01
☐ 74 Mike Rozier	.05	.02	.01
☐ 75 Johnny Meads	.05	.02	.01
☐ 76 Houston Oilers Uniform FOIL	.05	.02	.01
☐ 77 Indianapolis Colts Helmet FOIL	.05	.02	.01
☐ 78 Colts Action (Eric Dickerson)	.05	.02	.01
☐ 79 Albert Bentley	.05	.02	.01
☐ 80 Dean Biasucci	.10	.05	.01
☐ 81 Duane Bickett	.05	.02	.01
☐ 82 Bill Brooks	.10	.05	.01
☐ 83 Johnie Cooks	.05	.02	.01
☐ 84 Eric Dickerson	.20	.09	.03
☐ 85 Indianapolis Colts FOIL (315)	.05	.02	.01
☐ 86 Ray Donaldson	.05	.02	.01
☐ 87 Chris Hinton	.05	.02	.01
☐ 88 Cliff Odom	.05	.02	.01
☐ 89 Barry Krauss	.05	.02	.01
☐ 90 Jack Trudeau	.05	.02	.01
☐ 91 Indianapolis Colts Uniform FOIL	.05	.02	.01
☐ 92 Kansas City Chiefs Helmet FOIL	.05	.02	.01
☐ 93 Kansas City Chiefs Action	.05	.02	.01
☐ 94 Carlos Carson	.05	.02	.01
☐ 95 Deron Cherry	.05	.02	.01
☐ 96 Dino Hackett	.05	.02	.01
☐ 97 Bill Kenney	.05	.02	.01
☐ 98 Albert Lewis	.20	.09	.03
☐ 99 Nick Lowery	.10	.05	.01
☐ 100 Kansas City Chiefs FOIL (330)		.05	.02
.01			
☐ 101 Bill Maas	.05	.02	.01
☐ 102 Christian Okoye	.20	.09	.03
☐ 103 Stephone Paige	.05	.02	.01
☐ 104 Paul Palmer	.05	.02	.01
☐ 105 Kevin Ross	.10	.05	.01
☐ 106 Kansas City Chiefs Uniform FOIL	.05	.02	.01
☐ 107 Los Angeles Raiders Helmet FOIL	.05	.02	.01
☐ 108 Raiders Action (Bo Jackson)	.20	.09	.03
☐ 109 Marcus Allen	.30	.14	.04
☐ 110 Todd Christensen	.10	.05	.01
☐ 111 Mike Haynes	.10	.05	.01
☐ 112 Bo Jackson	.20	.09	.03
☐ 113 James Lofton	.20	.09	.03
☐ 114 Howie Long	.20	.09	.03
☐ 115 Los Angeles Raiders FOIL (345)	.05	.02	.01
☐ 116 Rod Martin	.10	.05	.01
☐ 117 Vann McElroy	.05	.02	.01
☐ 118 Bill Pickel	.05	.02	.01
☐ 119 Don Mosebar	.10	.05	.01
☐ 120 Stacey Toran	.05	.02	.01
☐ 121 Los Angeles Raiders Uniform FOIL	.05	.02	.01
☐ 122 Miami Dolphins Helmet FOIL	.05	.02	.01
☐ 123 Miami Dolphins Action	.05	.02	.01
☐ 124 John Bosa	.05	.02	.01
☐ 125 Mark Clayton	.10	.05	.01
☐ 126 Mark Duper	.10	.05	.01
☐ 127 Lorenzo Hampton	.05	.02	.01
☐ 128 William Judson	.05	.02	.01
☐ 129 Dan Marino	3.00	1.35	.35
☐ 130 Miami Dolphins FOIL (360)	.05	.02	.01
☐ 131 John Offerdahl	.10	.05	.01
☐ 132 Reggie Roby	.05	.02	.01
☐ 133 Jackie Shipp	.05	.02	.01
☐ 134 Dwight Stephenson	.05	.02	.01
☐ 135 Troy Stradford	.05	.02	.01
☐ 136 Miami Dolphins Uniform FOIL	.05	.02	.01
☐ 137 New England Patriots Helmet FOIL	.05	.02	.01
☐ 138 New England Patriots Action	.05	.02	.01

☐ 139 Bruce Armstrong	.05	.02	.01
☐ 140 Raymond Clayborn	.05	.02	.01
☐ 141 Reggie Dupard	.05	.02	.01
☐ 142 Steve Grogan	.10	.05	.01
☐ 143 Craig James	.10	.05	.01
☐ 144 Ronnie Lippett	.05	.02	.01
☐ 145 New England Patriots FOIL (375)	.05	.02	.01
☐ 146 Fred Marion	.05	.02	.01
☐ 147 Stanley Morgan	.10	.05	.01
☐ 148 Mosi Tatupu	.05	.02	.01
☐ 149 Andre Tippett	.10	.05	.01
☐ 150 Garin Veris	.05	.02	.01
☐ 151 New England Patriots Uniform FOIL	.05	.02	.01
☐ 152 New York Jets Helmet FOIL	.05	.02	.01
☐ 153 Jets Action (Ken O'Brien)	.05	.02	.01
☐ 154 Bob Crable	.05	.02	.01
☐ 155 Mark Gastineau	.10	.05	.01
☐ 156 Pat Leahy	.05	.02	.01
☐ 157 Johnny Hector	.05	.02	.01
☐ 158 Marty Lyons	.05	.02	.01
☐ 159 Freeman McNeil	.10	.05	.01
☐ 160 New York Jets FOIL (390)	.05	.02	.01
☐ 161 Ken O'Brien	.10	.05	.01
☐ 162 Mickey Shuler	.05	.02	.01
☐ 163 Al Toon	.10	.05	.01
☐ 164 Roger Vick	.05	.02	.01
☐ 165 Wesley Walker	.10	.05	.01
☐ 166 New York Jets Uniform FOIL	.05	.02	.01
☐ 167 Pittsburgh Steelers Helmet FOIL	.05	.02	.01
☐ 168 Pittsburgh Steelers Action	.05	.02	.01
☐ 169 Walter Abercrombie	.05	.02	.01
☐ 170 Gary Anderson K	.05	.02	.01
☐ 171 Todd Blackledge	.05	.02	.01
☐ 172 Thomas Everett	.10	.05	.01
☐ 173 Delton Hall	.05	.02	.01
☐ 174 Bryan Hinkle	.05	.02	.01
☐ 175 Pittsburgh Steelers FOIL (405)	.05	.02	.01
☐ 176 Earnest Jackson	.05	.02	.01
☐ 177 Louis Lipps	.10	.05	.01
☐ 178 David Little	.05	.02	.01
☐ 179 Mike Merriweather	.05	.02	.01
☐ 180 Mike Webster	.10	.05	.01
☐ 181 Pittsburgh Steelers Uniform FOIL	.05	.02	.01
☐ 182 San Diego Chargers Helmet FOIL	.05	.02	.01
☐ 183 San Diego Chargers Action	.05	.02	.01
☐ 184 Gary Anderson RB	.10	.05	.01
☐ 185 Chip Banks	.05	.02	.01
☐ 186 Martin Bayless	.05	.02	.01
☐ 187 Chuck Ehin	.05	.02	.01
☐ 188 Vencie Glenn	.10	.05	.01
☐ 189 Lionel James	.05	.02	.01
☐ 190 San Diego Chargers FOIL (420)	.05	.02	.01
☐ 191 Mark Malone	.05	.02	.01
☐ 192 Ralf Mojsiejenko	.05	.02	.01
☐ 193 Billy Ray Smith	.05	.02	.01
☐ 194 Lee Williams	.05	.02	.01
☐ 195 Kellen Winslow	.20	.09	.03
☐ 196 San Diego Chargers Uniform FOIL	.05	.02	.01
☐ 197 Seattle Seahawks Helmet FOIL	.05	.02	.01
☐ 198 Seahawks Action (Dave Krieg)	.10	.05	.01
☐ 199 Eugene Robinson	.05	.02	.01
☐ 200 Jeff Bryant	.05	.02	.01
☐ 201 Raymond Butler	.05	.02	.01
☐ 202 Jacob Green	.05	.02	.01
☐ 203 Norm Johnson	.05	.02	.01
☐ 204 Dave Krieg	.10	.05	.01
☐ 205 Seahawks FOIL (435)	.05	.02	.01
☐ 206 Steve Largent	.50	.23	.06
☐ 207 Joe Nash	.05	.02	.01
☐ 208 Curt Warner	.10	.05	.01
☐ 209 Bobby Joe Edmonds	.05	.02	.01
☐ 210 Daryl Turner	.05	.02	.01
☐ 211 Seattle Seahawks Uniform FOIL	.05	.02	.01
☐ 212 AFC Logo	.05	.02	.01
☐ 213 Bernie Kosar	.20	.09	.03
☐ 214 Curt Warner	.10	.05	.01
☐ 215 Jerry Rice and Steve Largent	1.50	.70	.19
☐ 216 Mark Bavaro and Anthony Munoz	.10	.05	.01
☐ 217 Gary Zimmerman and Bill Fralic	.05	.02	.01
☐ 218 Dwight Stephenson and Mike Munchak	.05	.02	.01
☐ 219 Joe Montana	2.00	.90	.25
☐ 220 Charles White and Eric Dickerson	.25	.11	.03
☐ 221 Morten Andersen and Vai Sikahema	.10	.05	.01
☐ 222 Bruce Smith and Reggie White	.30	.14	.04
☐ 223 Michael Carter and Steve McMichael	.05	.02	.01
☐ 224 Jim Arnold	.05	.02	.01
☐ 225 Carl Banks and Andre Tippett	.05	.02	.01
☐ 226 Barry Wilburn and Mike Singletary	.05	.02	.01
☐ 227 Hanford Dixon and Frank Minnifield	.05	.02	.01
☐ 228 Ronnie Lott and Joey Browner	.20	.09	.03
☐ 229 NFC Logo	.05	.02	.01
☐ 230 Gary Clark	.20	.09	.03
☐ 231 Richard Dent	.20	.09	.03
☐ 232 Atlanta Falcons Helmet FOIL	.05	.02	.01
☐ 233 Atlanta Falcons Action	.05	.02	.01
☐ 234 Rick Bryan	.05	.02	.01
☐ 235 Bobby Butler	.05	.02	.01
☐ 236 Tony Casillas	.10	.05	.01
☐ 237 Floyd Dixon	.05	.02	.01
☐ 238 Rick Donnelly	.05	.02	.01
☐ 239 Bill Fralic	.10	.05	.01
☐ 240 Atlanta Falcons FOIL (10)	.05	.02	.01
☐ 241 Mike Gann	.05	.02	.01
☐ 242 Chris Miller	.20	.09	.03
☐ 243 Robert Moore	.05	.02	.01
☐ 244 John Rade	.05	.02	.01
☐ 245 Gerald Riggs	.10	.05	.01
☐ 246 Atlanta Falcons Uniform FOIL	.05	.02	.01
☐ 247 Chicago Bears Helmet FOIL	.05	.02	.01
☐ 248 Bears Action (Jim McMahon)	.05	.02	.01
☐ 249 Neal Anderson	.20	.09	.03
☐ 250 Jim Covert	.05	.02	.01
☐ 251 Richard Dent	.20	.09	.03
☐ 252 Dave Duerson	.05	.02	.01
☐ 253 Dennis Gentry	.05	.02	.01
☐ 254 Jay Hilgenberg	.05	.02	.01
☐ 255 Chicago Bears FOIL (25)	.05	.02	.01
☐ 256 Jim McMahon	.20	.09	.03
☐ 257 Steve McMichael	.10	.05	.01
☐ 258 Matt Suhey	.05	.02	.01
☐ 259 Mike Singletary	.20	.09	.03
☐ 260 Otis Wilson	.05	.02	.01
☐ 261 Chicago Bears Uniform FOIL	.05	.02	.01
☐ 262 Dallas Cowboys Helmet FOIL	.05	.02	.01
☐ 263 Cowboys Action (Herschel Walker)	.05	.02	.01
☐ 264 Bill Bates	.10	.05	.01
☐ 265 Doug Cosbie	.05	.02	.01
☐ 266 Ron Francis	.05	.02	.01
☐ 267 Jim Jeffcoat	.05	.02	.01
☐ 268 Ed Too Tall Jones	.20	.09	.03
☐ 269 Eugene Lockhart	.05	.02	.01
☐ 270 Dallas Cowboys FOIL (40)	.05	.02	.01
☐ 271 Danny Noonan	.05	.02	.01
☐ 272 Steve Pelluer	.05	.02	.01
☐ 273 Herschel Walker	.20	.09	.03
☐ 274 Everson Walls	.05	.02	.01
☐ 275 Randy White	.20	.09	.03
☐ 276 Dallas Cowboys Uniform FOIL	.05	.02	.01
☐ 277 Detroit Lions Helmet FOIL	.05	.02	.01
☐ 278 Detroit Lions Action	.05	.02	.01
☐ 279 Jim Arnold	.05	.02	.01
☐ 280 Jerry Ball	.05	.02	.01
☐ 281 Michael Cofer	.05	.02	.01
☐ 282 Keith Ferguson	.05	.02	.01
☐ 283 Dennis Gibson	.05	.02	.01
☐ 284 James Griffin	.05	.02	.01
☐ 285 Detroit Lions FOIL (55)	.05	.02	.01
☐ 286 James Jones	.05	.02	.01
☐ 287 Chuck Long	.10	.05	.01
☐ 288 Pete Mandley	.05	.02	.01
☐ 289 Eddie Murray	.05	.02	.01
☐ 290 Garry James	.05	.02	.01
☐ 291 Detroit Lions Uniform FOIL	.05	.02	.01
☐ 292 Green Bay Packers Helmet FOIL	.05	.02	.01
☐ 293 Green Bay Packers Action	.05	.02	.01
☐ 294 John Anderson	.05	.02	.01
☐ 295 Dave Brown	.05	.02	.01
☐ 296 Alphonso Carreker	.05	.02	.01
☐ 297 Kenneth Davis	.10	.05	.01
☐ 298 Phillip Epps	.05	.02	.01
☐ 299 Brent Fullwood	.05	.02	.01
☐ 300 Green Bay Packers FOIL (70)	.05	.02	.01
☐ 301 Tim Harris	.10	.05	.01
☐ 302 Johnny Holland	.10	.05	.01
☐ 303 Mark Murphy	.05	.02	.01
☐ 304 Brian Noble	.05	.02	.01
☐ 305 Walter Stanley	.05	.02	.01
☐ 306 Green Bay Packers Uniform FOIL	.05	.02	.01
☐ 307 Los Angeles Rams Helmet FOIL	.05	.02	.01
☐ 308 Los Angeles Rams Action	.05	.02	.01
☐ 309 Jim Collins	.05	.02	.01
☐ 310 Henry Ellard	.25	.11	.03
☐ 311 Jim Everett	.20	.09	.03
☐ 312 Jerry Gray	.05	.02	.01
☐ 313 LeRoy Irvin	.05	.02	.01
☐ 314 Mike Lansford	.05	.02	.01
☐ 315 Los Angeles Rams FOIL (85)	.05	.02	.01
☐ 316 Mel Owens	.05	.02	.01
☐ 317 Jackie Slater	.10	.05	.01
☐ 318 Doug Smith	.05	.02	.01
☐ 319 Charles White	.10	.05	.01
☐ 320 Mike Wilcher	.05	.02	.01
☐ 321 Los Angeles Rams Uniform FOIL	.05	.02	.01
☐ 322 Minnesota Vikings Helmet FOIL	.05	.02	.01
☐ 323 Minnesota Vikings Action	.05	.02	.01
☐ 324 Joey Browner	.05	.02	.01
☐ 325 Anthony Carter	.10	.05	.01
☐ 326 Chris Doleman	.20	.09	.03
☐ 327 D.J. Dozier	.10	.05	.01
☐ 328 Steve Jordan	.10	.05	.01
☐ 329 Tommy Kramer	.10	.05	.01
☐ 330 Minnesota Vikings FOIL (100)	.05	.02	.01
☐ 331 Darrin Nelson	.05	.02	.01
☐ 332 Jesse Solomon	.05	.02	.01
☐ 333 Scott Studwell	.05	.02	.01
☐ 334 Wade Wilson	.10	.05	.01
☐ 335 Gary Zimmerman	.05	.02	.01
☐ 336 Minnesota Vikings Uniform FOIL	.05	.02	.01
☐ 337 New Orleans Saints Helmet FOIL	.05	.02	.01
☐ 338 Saints Action (Bobby Hebert)	.05	.02	.01
☐ 339 Morten Andersen	.10	.05	.01
☐ 340 Bruce Clark	.05	.02	.01
☐ 341 Brad Edelman	.05	.02	.01
☐ 342 Bobby Hebert	.10	.05	.01
☐ 343 Dalton Hilliard	.05	.02	.01
☐ 344 Rickey Jackson	.10	.05	.01
☐ 345 New Orleans Saints FOIL (115)	.05	.02	.01
☐ 346 Vaughan Johnson	.10	.05	.01
☐ 347 Rueben Mayes	.05	.02	.01
☐ 348 Sam Mills	.20	.09	.03
☐ 349 Pat Swilling	.20	.09	.03
☐ 350 Dave Waymer	.05	.02	.01
☐ 351 New Orleans Saints Uniform FOIL	.05	.02	.01
☐ 352 New York Giants Helmet FOIL	.05	.02	.01
☐ 353 New York Giants Action	.05	.02	.01
☐ 354 Carl Banks	.10	.05	.01
☐ 355 Mark Bavaro	.10	.05	.01
☐ 356 Jim Burt	.05	.02	.01
☐ 357 Harry Carson	.05	.02	.01
☐ 358 Terry Kinard	.05	.02	.01
☐ 359 Lionel Manuel	.05	.02	.01
☐ 360 New York Giants FOIL (130)	.05	.02	.01
☐ 361 Leonard Marshall	.10	.05	.01
☐ 362 George Martin	.05	.02	.01
☐ 363 Joe Morris	.10	.05	.01
☐ 364 Phil Simms	.25	.11	.03
☐ 365 George Adams	.05	.02	.01
☐ 366 New York Giants Uniform FOIL	.05	.02	.01
☐ 367 Philadelphia Eagles Helmet FOIL	.05	.02	.01
☐ 368 Eagles Action (Randall Cunningham)	.20	.09	.03
☐ 369 Jerome Brown	.20	.09	.03
☐ 370 Keith Byars	.20	.09	.03
☐ 371 Randall Cunningham	.20	.09	.03
☐ 372 Terry Hoage	.05	.02	.01
☐ 373 Seth Joyner	.20	.09	.03
☐ 374 Mike Quick	.10	.05	.01
☐ 375 Philadelphia Eagles FOIL (145)	.05	.02	.01
☐ 376 Clyde Simmons	.10	.05	.01
☐ 377 Anthony Toney	.05	.02	.01
☐ 378 Andre Waters	.10	.05	.01
☐ 379 Reggie White	.25	.11	.03
☐ 380 Roynell Young	.05	.02	.01
☐ 381 Philadelphia Eagles Uniform FOIL	.05	.02	.01
☐ 382 Phoenix Cardinals Helmet FOIL	.05	.02	.01
☐ 383 Phoenix Cardinals Action	.05	.02	.01
☐ 384 Robert Awalt	.05	.02	.01
☐ 385 Roy Green	.10	.05	.01
☐ 386 Neil Lomax	.10	.05	.01
☐ 387 Stump Mitchell	.05	.02	.01
☐ 388 Niko Noga	.05	.02	.01
☐ 389 Freddie Joe Nunn	.05	.02	.01
☐ 390 Phoenix Cardinals FOIL (160)	.05	.02	.01
☐ 391 Luis Sharpe	.05	.02	.01
☐ 392 Vai Sikahema	.05	.02	.01
☐ 393 J.T. Smith	.05	.02	.01
☐ 394 Leonard Smith	.05	.02	.01
☐ 395 Lonnie Young	.05	.02	.01
☐ 396 Phoenix Cardinals Uniform FOIL	.05	.02	.01
☐ 397 San Francisco 49ers Helmet FOIL	.05	.02	.01
☐ 398 49ers Action (Joe Montana)	.75	.35	.09
☐ 399 Dwaine Board	.05	.02	.01
☐ 400 Michael Carter	.05	.02	.01
☐ 401 Roger Craig	.10	.05	.01
☐ 402 Jeff Fuller	.05	.02	.01
☐ 403 Don Griffin	.05	.02	.01
☐ 404 Ronnie Lott	.20	.09	.03
☐ 405 San Francisco 49ers FOIL (175)	.05	.02	.01
☐ 406 Joe Montana	2.00	.90	.25
☐ 407 Tom Rathman	.20	.09	.03
☐ 408 Jerry Rice	1.50	.70	.19
☐ 409 Keena Turner	.05	.02	.01
☐ 410 Michael Walter	.05	.02	.01
☐ 411 San Francisco 49ers Uniform FOIL	.05	.02	.01
☐ 412 Tampa Bay Bucs Helmet FOIL	.05	.02	.01
☐ 413 Tampa Bay Bucs Action	.05	.02	.01
☐ 414 Mark Carrier WR	.20	.09	.03
☐ 415 Gerald Carter	.05	.02	.01
☐ 416 Ron Holmes	.05	.02	.01
☐ 417 Rod Jones	.05	.02	.01
☐ 418 Calvin Magee	.05	.02	.01
☐ 419 Ervin Randle	.05	.02	.01
☐ 420 Tampa Bay Buccaneers FOIL (190)	.05	.02	.01
☐ 421 Donald Igwebuike	.05	.02	.01
☐ 422 Vinny Testaverde	.20	.09	.03
☐ 423 Jackie Walker	.05	.02	.01
☐ 424 Chris Washington	.05	.02	.01
☐ 425 James Wilder	.05	.02	.01
☐ 426 Tampa Bay Bucs Uniform FOIL	.05	.02	.01
☐ 427 Washington Redskins Helmet FOIL	.05	.02	.01
☐ 428 Redskins Action (Doug Williams)	.10	.05	.01
☐ 429 Gary Clark	.20	.09	.03
☐ 430 Monte Coleman	.05	.02	.01
☐ 431 Darrell Green	.20	.09	.03
☐ 432 Charles Mann	.10	.05	.01
☐ 433 Kelvin Bryant	.10	.05	.01
☐ 434 Art Monk	.20	.09	.03
☐ 435 Washington Redskins FOIL (205)	.05	.02	.01
☐ 436 Ricky Sanders	.20	.09	.03
☐ 437 Jay Schroeder	.05	.02	.01
☐ 438 Alvin Walton	.05	.02	.01
☐ 439 Barry Wilburn	.05	.02	.01
☐ 440 Doug Williams	.20	.09	.03
☐ 441 Washington Redskins Uniform FOIL	.05	.02	.01
☐ 442 Super Bowl action (Left half)	.05	.02	.01
☐ 443 Super Bowl action (Right half)	.05	.02	.01
☐ 444 Doug Williams (Super Bowl MVP)	.10	.05	.01
☐ 445 Super Bowl action	.05	.02	.01
☐ 446 Super Bowl action (Left half)	.05	.02	.01
☐ 447 Super Bowl action (Right half)	.05	.02	.01
☐ NNO Panini Album (John Elway on cover)	2.50	1.10	.30

1989 Panini Stickers

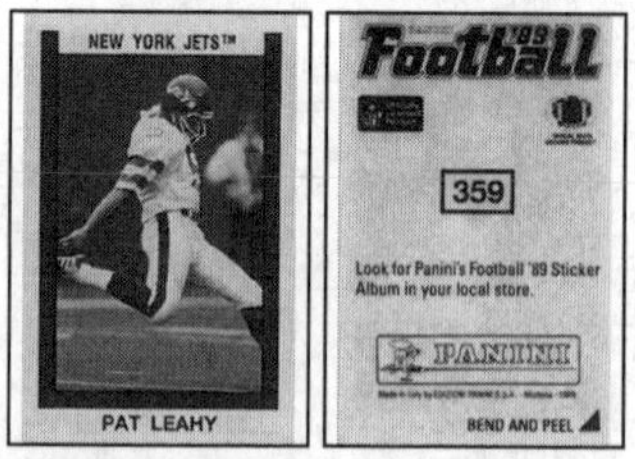

This set of 416 stickers was issued in 1989 by Panini. The stickers measure approximately 1 15/16" by 3" and are numbered on the front and on the back. The album for the set is easily obtainable. It is organized in team order like the sticker numbering. On the inside back cover of the sticker album the company offered (via direct mail-order) up to 30 different stickers of your choice for either ten cents each (only in Canada) or in trade one-for-one for your unwanted extra stickers (only in the United States) plus 1.00 for postage and handling; this is one reason why the values of the most popular players in these sticker sets are somewhat depressed compared to traditional card set prices. The album for the set features Joe Montana on the cover. Tim Brown, Cris Carter, Michael Irvin, Keith Jackson, Jay Novacek, Sterling Sharpe, Thurman Thomas, Rod Woodson appear in their Rookie Card year. The stickers were also issued in a UK version which is distinguished by the presence of stats printed on the sticker backs. The UK version album also features Joe Montana as well as the TV-4 logo.

	MINT	NRMT	EXC
COMPLETE SET (416)	15.00	6.75	1.85
COMMON CARD (1-416)	.05	.02	.01
☐ 1 SB XXIII Program	.05	.02	.01
☐ 2 SB XXIII Program	.05	.02	.01
☐ 3 Floyd Dixon	.05	.02	.01
☐ 4 Tony Casillas	.05	.02	.01

☐ 5 Bill Fralic	.05	.02	.01
☐ 6 Aundray Bruce	.05	.02	.01
☐ 7 Scott Case	.05	.02	.01
☐ 8 Rick Donnelly	.05	.02	.01
☐ 9 Atlanta Falcons Logo FOIL	.05	.02	.01
☐ 10 Atlanta Falcons Helmet FOIL	.05	.02	.01
☐ 11 Marcus Cotton	.05	.02	.01
☐ 12 Chris Miller	.10	.05	.01
☐ 13 Robert Moore	.05	.02	.01
☐ 14 Bobby Butler	.05	.02	.01
☐ 15 Rick Bryan	.05	.02	.01
☐ 16 John Settle	.05	.02	.01
☐ 17 Jim McMahon	.10	.05	.01
☐ 18 Neal Anderson	.10	.05	.01
☐ 19 Dave Duerson	.05	.02	.01
☐ 20 Steve McMichael	.05	.02	.01
☐ 21 Jay Hilgenberg	.05	.02	.01
☐ 22 Dennis McKinnon	.05	.02	.01
☐ 23 Chicago Bears Logo FOIL	.05	.02	.01
☐ 24 Chicago Bears Helmet FOIL	.05	.02	.01
☐ 25 Richard Dent	.10	.05	.01
☐ 26 Dennis Gentry	.05	.02	.01
☐ 27 Mike Singletary	.10	.05	.01
☐ 28 Vestee Jackson	.05	.02	.01
☐ 29 Mike Tomczak	.10	.05	.01
☐ 30 Dan Hampton	.10	.05	.01
☐ 31 Michael Irvin	.50	.23	.06
☐ 32 Eugene Lockhart	.05	.02	.01
☐ 33 Herschel Walker	.10	.05	.01
☐ 34 Kelvin Martin	.05	.02	.01
☐ 35 Jim Jeffcoat	.05	.02	.01
☐ 36 Everson Walls	.05	.02	.01
☐ 37 Dallas Cowboys Logo FOIL	.05	.02	.01
☐ 38 Dallas Cowboys Helmet FOIL	.05	.02	.01
☐ 39 Danny Noonan	.05	.02	.01
☐ 40 Ray Alexander	.05	.02	.01
☐ 41 Garry Cobb	.05	.02	.01
☐ 42 Ed Too Tall Jones	.10	.05	.01
☐ 43 Kevin Brooks	.05	.02	.01
☐ 44 Bill Bates	.10	.05	.01
☐ 45 Detroit Lions Logo FOIL	.05	.02	.01
☐ 46 Chuck Long	.05	.02	.01
☐ 47 Jim Arnold	.05	.02	.01
☐ 48 Michael Cofer	.05	.02	.01
☐ 49 Eddie Murray	.05	.02	.01
☐ 50 Keith Ferguson	.05	.02	.01
☐ 51 Pete Mandley	.05	.02	.01
☐ 52 Detroit Lions Helmet FOIL	.05	.02	.01
☐ 53 Jerry Ball	.05	.02	.01
☐ 54 Bennie Blades	.10	.05	.01
☐ 55 Dennis Gibson	.05	.02	.01
☐ 56 Chris Spielman	.20	.09	.03
☐ 57 Eric Williams	.05	.02	.01
☐ 58 Lomas Brown	.05	.02	.01
☐ 59 Johnny Holland	.05	.02	.01
☐ 60 Tim Harris	.05	.02	.01
☐ 61 Mark Murphy	.05	.02	.01
☐ 62 Walter Stanley	.05	.02	.01
☐ 63 Brent Fullwood	.05	.02	.01
☐ 64 Ken Ruettgers	.05	.02	.01
☐ 65 Green Bay Packers Logo FOIL	.05	.02	.01
☐ 66 Green Bay Packers Helmet FOIL	.05	.02	.01
☐ 67 John Anderson	.05	.02	.01
☐ 68 Brian Noble	.05	.02	.01
☐ 69 Sterling Sharpe	.40	.18	.05
☐ 70 Keith Woodside	.05	.02	.01
☐ 71 Mark Lee	.05	.02	.01
☐ 72 Don Majkowski	.10	.05	.01
☐ 73 Aaron Cox	.05	.02	.01
☐ 74 LeRoy Irvin	.05	.02	.01
☐ 75 Jim Everett	.10	.05	.01
☐ 76 Mike Lansford	.05	.02	.01
☐ 77 Mike Wilcher	.05	.02	.01
☐ 78 Henry Ellard	.20	.09	.03
☐ 79 Los Angeles Rams Helmet FOIL	.05	.02	.01
☐ 80 Jerry Gray	.05	.02	.01
☐ 81 Doug Smith	.05	.02	.01
☐ 82 Tom Newberry	.05	.02	.01
☐ 83 Jackie Slater	.05	.02	.01
☐ 84 Greg Bell	.05	.02	.01
☐ 85 Kevin Greene	.25	.11	.03
☐ 86 Chris Doleman	.10	.05	.01
☐ 87 Steve Jordan	.05	.02	.01
☐ 88 Jesse Solomon	.05	.02	.01
☐ 89 Randall McDaniel	.05	.02	.01
☐ 90 Hassan Jones	.05	.02	.01
☐ 91 Joey Browner	.05	.02	.01
☐ 92 Minnesota Vikings Logo FOIL	.05	.02	.01
☐ 93 Minnesota Vikings Helmet FOIL	.05	.02	.01
☐ 94 Anthony Carter	.20	.09	.03
☐ 95 Gary Zimmerman	.05	.02	.01
☐ 96 Wade Wilson	.10	.05	.01
☐ 97 Scott Studwell	.05	.02	.01
☐ 98 Keith Millard	.05	.02	.01
☐ 99 Carl Lee	.05	.02	.01
☐ 100 Morten Andersen	.05	.02	.01
☐ 101 Bobby Hebert	.10	.05	.01
☐ 102 Rueben Mayes	.05	.02	.01
☐ 103 Sam Mills	.10	.05	.01
☐ 104 Vaughan Johnson	.10	.05	.01
☐ 105 Pat Swilling	.10	.05	.01
☐ 106 New Orleans Saints Logo FOIL	.05	.02	.01
☐ 107 New Orleans Saints Helmet FOIL	.05	.02	.01
☐ 108 Brad Edelman	.05	.02	.01
☐ 109 Craig Heyward	.10	.05	.01
☐ 110 Eric Martin	.10	.05	.01
☐ 111 Dalton Hilliard	.05	.02	.01
☐ 112 Lonzell Hill	.05	.02	.01
☐ 113 Rickey Jackson	.10	.05	.01
☐ 114 Erik Howard	.05	.02	.01
☐ 115 Phil Simms	.10	.05	.01
☐ 116 Leonard Marshall	.10	.05	.01
☐ 117 Joe Morris	.10	.05	.01
☐ 118 Bart Oates	.05	.02	.01
☐ 119 Mark Bavaro	.10	.05	.01
☐ 120 New York Giants Logo FOIL	.05	.02	.01
☐ 121 New York Giants Helmet FOIL	.05	.02	.01
☐ 122 Terry Kinard	.05	.02	.01
☐ 123 Carl Banks	.10	.05	.01
☐ 124 Lionel Manuel	.05	.02	.01
☐ 125 Stephen Baker	.05	.02	.01
☐ 126 Pepper Johnson	.05	.02	.01
☐ 127 Jim Burt	.05	.02	.01
☐ 128 Cris Carter	.50	.23	.06
☐ 129 Mike Quick	.10	.05	.01
☐ 130 Terry Hoage	.05	.02	.01
☐ 131 Keith Jackson	.20	.09	.03
☐ 132 Clyde Simmons	.10	.05	.01
☐ 133 Eric Allen	.10	.05	.01
☐ 134 Philadelphia Eagles Logo FOIL	.05	.02	.01
☐ 135 Philadelphia Eagles Helmet FOIL	.05	.02	.01
☐ 136 Randall Cunningham	.10	.05	.01
☐ 137 Mike Pitts	.05	.02	.01
☐ 138 Keith Byars	.10	.05	.01
☐ 139 Seth Joyner	.10	.05	.01
☐ 140 Jerome Brown	.20	.09	.03
☐ 141 Reggie White	.20	.09	.03
☐ 142 Jay Novacek	.30	.14	.04
☐ 143 Neil Lomax	.05	.02	.01
☐ 144 Ken Harvey	.10	.05	.01
☐ 145 Freddie Joe Nunn	.05	.02	.01
☐ 146 Robert Awalt	.05	.02	.01
☐ 147 Niko Noga	.05	.02	.01
☐ 148 Phoenix Cardinals Logo FOIL	.05	.02	.01
☐ 149 Phoenix Cardinals Helmet FOIL	.05	.02	.01
☐ 150 Tim McDonald	.05	.02	.01
☐ 151 Roy Green	.10	.05	.01
☐ 152 Stump Mitchell	.05	.02	.01
☐ 153 J.T. Smith	.10	.05	.01
☐ 154 Luis Sharpe	.05	.02	.01
☐ 155 Vai Sikahema	.05	.02	.01
☐ 156 Jeff Fuller	.05	.02	.01
☐ 157 Joe Montana	1.25	.55	.16
☐ 158 Harris Barton	.10	.05	.01
☐ 159 Michael Carter	.05	.02	.01
☐ 160 Jeff Fuller	.05	.02	.01
☐ 161 Jerry Rice	1.00	.45	.12
☐ 162 San Francisco 49ers Logo FOIL	.05	.02	.01
☐ 163 San Francisco 49ers Helmet FOIL	.05	.02	.01
☐ 164 Tom Rathman	.10	.05	.01
☐ 165 Roger Craig	.20	.09	.03
☐ 166 Ronnie Lott	.20	.09	.03
☐ 167 Charles Haley	.20	.09	.03
☐ 168 John Taylor	.20	.09	.03
☐ 169 Michael Walter	.05	.02	.01
☐ 170 Ron Hall	.05	.02	.01
☐ 171 Ervin Randle	.05	.02	.01
☐ 172 James Wilder	.05	.02	.01
☐ 173 Ron Holmes	.05	.02	.01
☐ 174 Mark Carrier WR	.20	.09	.03
☐ 175 William Howard	.05	.02	.01
☐ 176 Tampa Bay Bucs Logo FOIL	.05	.02	.01
☐ 177 Tampa Bay Bucs Helmet FOIL	.05	.02	.01
☐ 178 Lars Tate	.05	.02	.01
☐ 179 Vinny Testaverde	.20	.09	.03
☐ 180 Paul Gruber	.10	.05	.01
☐ 181 Bruce Hill	.05	.02	.01
☐ 182 Reuben Davis	.05	.02	.01
☐ 183 Ricky Reynolds	.05	.02	.01
☐ 184 Ricky Sanders	.10	.05	.01
☐ 185 Gary Clark	.20	.09	.03
☐ 186 Mark May	.05	.02	.01
☐ 187 Darrell Green	.10	.05	.01
☐ 188 Jim Lachey	.05	.02	.01
☐ 189 Doug Williams	.10	.05	.01
☐ 190 Washington Redskins Helmet FOIL	.05	.02	.01
☐ 191 Washington Redskins Logo FOIL	.05	.02	.01
☐ 192 Kelvin Bryant	.05	.02	.01
☐ 193 Charles Mann	.10	.05	.01
☐ 194 Alvin Walton	.05	.02	.01
☐ 195 Art Monk	.20	.09	.03
☐ 196 Barry Wilburn	.05	.02	.01
☐ 197 Mark Rypien	.10	.05	.01
☐ 198 NFC Logo	.05	.02	.01
☐ 199 Scott Case	.05	.02	.01
☐ 200 Herschel Walker	.10	.05	.01
☐ 201 Herschel Walker and Roger Craig	.20	.09	.03
☐ 202 Henry Ellard and Jerry Rice	.50	.23	.06
☐ 203 Bruce Matthews and Tom Newberry	.10	.05	.01
☐ 204 Gary Zimmerman and Anthony Munoz	.05	.02	.01
☐ 205 Boomer Esiason	.10	.05	.01
☐ 206 Jay Hilgenberg	.05	.02	.01
☐ 207 Keith Jackson	.20	.09	.03
☐ 208 Reggie White and Bruce Smith	.20	.09	.03
☐ 209 Keith Millard and Tim Krumrie	.05	.02	.01
☐ 210 Carl Lee and Frank Minnifield	.05	.02	.01
☐ 211 Joey Browner and Deron Cherry	.05	.02	.01
☐ 212 Shane Conlan	.10	.05	.01
☐ 213 Mike Singletary	.10	.05	.01
☐ 214 Cornelius Bennett	.10	.05	.01
☐ 215 AFC Logo	.05	.02	.01
☐ 216 Boomer Esiason	.10	.05	.01
☐ 217 Erik McMillan	.05	.02	.01
☐ 218 Jim Kelly	.25	.11	.03
☐ 219 Cornelius Bennett	.10	.05	.01
☐ 220 Fred Smerlas	.05	.02	.01
☐ 221 Shane Conlan	.10	.05	.01
☐ 222 Scott Norwood	.05	.02	.01
☐ 223 Mark Kelso	.05	.02	.01
☐ 224 Buffalo Bills Logo FOIL	.05	.02	.01
☐ 225 Buffalo Bills Helmet FOIL	.05	.02	.01
☐ 226 Thurman Thomas	.60	.25	.07
☐ 227 Pete Metzelaars	.10	.05	.01
☐ 228 Bruce Smith	.20	.09	.03
☐ 229 Art Still	.05	.02	.01
☐ 230 Kent Hull	.05	.02	.01
☐ 231 Andre Reed	.20	.09	.03
☐ 232 Tim Krumrie	.10	.05	.01
☐ 233 Boomer Esiason	.10	.05	.01
☐ 234 Ickey Woods	.10	.05	.01
☐ 235 Eric Thomas	.05	.02	.01
☐ 236 Rodney Holman	.05	.02	.01
☐ 237 Jim Skow	.05	.02	.01
☐ 238 Cincinnati Bengals Helmet FOIL	.05	.02	.01
☐ 239 James Brooks	.10	.05	.01
☐ 240 David Fulcher	.10	.05	.01
☐ 241 Carl Zander	.05	.02	.01
☐ 242 Eddie Brown	.10	.05	.01
☐ 243 Max Montoya	.05	.02	.01
☐ 244 Anthony Munoz	.20	.09	.03
☐ 245 Felix Wright	.05	.02	.01
☐ 246 Clay Matthews	.10	.05	.01
☐ 247 Hanford Dixon	.05	.02	.01
☐ 248 Ozzie Newsome	.10	.05	.01
☐ 249 Bernie Kosar	.10	.05	.01
☐ 250 Kevin Mack	.05	.02	.01
☐ 251 Cincinnati Bengals Helmet FOIL	.05	.02	.01
☐ 252 Brian Brennan	.05	.02	.01
☐ 253 Reggie Langhorne	.05	.02	.01
☐ 254 Cody Risien	.05	.02	.01
☐ 255 Webster Slaughter	.10	.05	.01
☐ 256 Mike Johnson	.05	.02	.01
☐ 257 Frank Minnifield	.10	.05	.01
☐ 258 Mike Horan	.05	.02	.01
☐ 259 Dennis Smith	.10	.05	.01
☐ 260 Ricky Nattiel	.05	.02	.01
☐ 261 Karl Mecklenburg	.10	.05	.01
☐ 262 Keith Bishop	.05	.02	.01
☐ 263 John Elway	.75	.35	.09
☐ 264 Denver Broncos Helmet FOIL	.05	.02	.01
☐ 265 Denver Broncos Logo FOIL	.05	.02	.01
☐ 266 Simon Fletcher	.10	.05	.01
☐ 267 Vance Johnson	.10	.05	.01
☐ 268 Tony Dorsett	.05	.02	.01
☐ 269 Greg Kragen	.05	.02	.01
☐ 270 Mike Harden	.05	.02	.01
☐ 271 Mark Jackson	.10	.05	.01
☐ 272 Warren Moon	.20	.09	.03
☐ 273 Mike Rozier	.10	.05	.01
☐ 274 Houston Oilers Logo FOIL	.05	.02	.01
☐ 275 Allen Pinkett	.10	.05	.01
☐ 276 Tony Zendejas	.05	.02	.01
☐ 277 Alonzo Highsmith	.05	.02	.01
☐ 278 Johnny Meads	.05	.02	.01
☐ 279 Houston Oilers Helmet FOIL	.05	.02	.01
☐ 280 Mike Munchak	.10	.05	.01
☐ 281 John Grimsley	.05	.02	.01
☐ 282 Ernest Givins	.10	.05	.01
☐ 283 Drew Hill	.10	.05	.01
☐ 284 Bruce Matthews	.10	.05	.01
☐ 285 Ray Childress	.10	.05	.01
☐ 286 Indianapolis Colts Logo FOIL	.05	.02	.01
☐ 287 Chris Hinton	.10	.05	.01
☐ 288 Clarence Verdin	.10	.05	.01
☐ 289 Jon Hand	.05	.02	.01
☐ 290 Chris Chandler	.20	.09	.03
☐ 291 Eugene Daniel	.10	.05	.01
☐ 292 Dean Biasucci	.05	.02	.01
☐ 293 Indianapolis Colts Helmet FOIL	.05	.02	.01
☐ 294 Duane Bickett	.10	.05	.01
☐ 295 Rohn Stark	.05	.02	.01
☐ 296 Albert Bentley	.05	.02	.01
☐ 297 Bill Brooks	.10	.05	.01
☐ 298 O'Brien Alston	.05	.02	.01
☐ 299 Ray Donaldson	.05	.02	.01
☐ 300 Carlos Carson	.05	.02	.01
☐ 301 Lloyd Burruss	.05	.02	.01
☐ 302 Steve DeBerg	.10	.05	.01
☐ 303 Irv Eatman	.05	.02	.01
☐ 304 Dino Hackett	.05	.02	.01
☐ 305 Albert Lewis	.05	.02	.01
☐ 306 Kansas City Chiefs Helmet FOIL	.05	.02	.01
☐ 307 Kansas City Chiefs Logo FOIL	.05	.02	.01
☐ 308 Deron Cherry	.10	.05	.01
☐ 309 Paul Palmer	.05	.02	.01
☐ 310 Neil Smith	.25	.11	.03
☐ 311 Christian Okoye	.20	.09	.03
☐ 312 Stephone Paige	.10	.05	.01
☐ 313 Bill Maas	.05	.02	.01
☐ 314 Marcus Allen	.20	.09	.03
☐ 315 Vann McElroy	.05	.02	.01
☐ 316 Mervyn Fernandez	.05	.02	.01
☐ 317 Bill Pickel	.05	.02	.01
☐ 318 Greg Townsend	.10	.05	.01
☐ 319 Tim Brown	.50	.23	.06
☐ 320 Los Angeles Raiders Logo FOIL	.05	.02	.01
☐ 321 Los Angeles Raiders Helmet FOIL	.05	.02	.01
☐ 322 James Lofton	.20	.09	.03
☐ 323 Willie Gault	.10	.05	.01
☐ 324 Jay Schroeder	.10	.05	.01
☐ 325 Matt Millen	.10	.05	.01
☐ 326 Howie Long	.10	.05	.01
☐ 327 Bo Jackson	.25	.11	.03
☐ 328 Lorenzo Hampton	.05	.02	.01
☐ 329 Jarvis Williams	.05	.02	.01
☐ 330 Jim C. Jensen	.05	.02	.01
☐ 331 Dan Marino	2.00	.90	.25
☐ 332 John Offerdahl	.05	.02	.01
☐ 333 Brian Sochia	.05	.02	.01
☐ 334 Miami Dolphins Logo FOIL	.05	.02	.01
☐ 335 Miami Dolphins Helmet FOIL	.05	.02	.01
☐ 336 Ferrell Edmunds	.05	.02	.01
☐ 337 Mark Brown	.05	.02	.01
☐ 338 Mark Duper	.10	.05	.01
☐ 339 Troy Stradford	.05	.02	.01
☐ 340 T.J. Turner	.05	.02	.01
☐ 341 Mark Clayton	.10	.05	.01
☐ 342 New England Patriots Logo FOIL	.05	.02	.01
☐ 343 Johnny Rembert	.05	.02	.01
☐ 344 Garin Veris	.05	.02	.01
☐ 345 Stanley Morgan	.10	.05	.01
☐ 346 John Stephens	.05	.02	.01
☐ 347 Fred Marion	.05	.02	.01
☐ 348 Irving Fryar	.20	.09	.03
☐ 349 New England Patriots Helmet FOIL	.05	.02	.01
☐ 350 Andre Tippett	.10	.05	.01
☐ 351 Roland James	.05	.02	.01
☐ 352 Brent Williams	.05	.02	.01
☐ 353 Raymond Clayborn	.05	.02	.01
☐ 354 Tony Eason	.05	.02	.01
☐ 355 Bruce Armstrong	.10	.05	.01
☐ 356 New York Jets Logo FOIL	.05	.02	.01
☐ 357 Marty Lyons	.05	.02	.01
☐ 358 Bobby Humphery	.05	.02	.01
☐ 359 Pat Leahy	.05	.02	.01
☐ 360 Mickey Shuler	.05	.02	.01
☐ 361 James Hasty	.05	.02	.01
☐ 362 Ken O'Brien	.10	.05	.01
☐ 363 New York Jets Helmet FOIL	.05	.02	.01
☐ 364 Alex Gordon	.05	.02	.01
☐ 365 Al Toon	.10	.05	.01
☐ 366 Erik McMillan	.05	.02	.01
☐ 367 Johnny Hector	.05	.02	.01
☐ 368 Wesley Walker	.10	.05	.01
☐ 369 Freeman McNeil	.10	.05	.01
☐ 370 Pittsburgh Steelers Logo FOIL	.05	.02	.01
☐ 371 Gary Anderson K	.05	.02	.01
☐ 372 Rodney Carter	.05	.02	.01
☐ 373 Merril Hoge	.05	.02	.01
☐ 374 David Little	.05	.02	.01
☐ 375 Bubby Brister	.10	.05	.01
☐ 376 Thomas Everett	.10	.05	.01
☐ 377 Pittsburgh Steelers Helmet FOIL	.05	.02	.01
☐ 378 Rod Woodson	.40	.18	.05
☐ 379 Bryan Hinkle	.05	.02	.01
☐ 380 Tunch Ilkin	.05	.02	.01
☐ 381 Aaron Jones	.05	.02	.01

☐ 382 Louis Lipps	.10	.05	.01
☐ 383 Warren Williams	.05	.02	.01
☐ 384 Anthony Miller	.30	.14	.04
☐ 385 Gary Anderson RB	.05	.02	.01
☐ 386 Lee Williams	.10	.05	.01
☐ 387 Lionel James	.05	.02	.01
☐ 388 Gary Plummer	.05	.02	.01
☐ 389 Gill Byrd	.10	.05	.01
☐ 390 San Diego Chargers Helmet FOIL	.05	.02	.01
☐ 391 Ralf Mojsiejenko	.05	.02	.01
☐ 392 Rod Bernstine	.10	.05	.01
☐ 393 Keith Browner	.05	.02	.01
☐ 394 Billy Ray Smith	.05	.02	.01
☐ 395 Leslie O'Neal	.10	.05	.01
☐ 396 Jamie Holland	.05	.02	.01
☐ 397 Tony Woods	.05	.02	.01
☐ 398 Bruce Scholtz	.05	.02	.01
☐ 399 Joe Nash	.05	.02	.01
☐ 400 Curt Warner	.10	.05	.01
☐ 401 John L. Williams	.10	.05	.01
☐ 402 Bryan Millard	.05	.02	.01
☐ 403 Seattle Seahawks Logo FOIL	.05	.02	.01
☐ 404 Seattle Seahawks Helmet FOIL	.05	.02	.01
☐ 405 Steve Largent	.30	.14	.04
☐ 406 Norm Johnson	.05	.02	.01
☐ 407 Jacob Green	.05	.02	.01
☐ 408 Dave Krieg	.10	.05	.01
☐ 409 Paul Moyer	.05	.02	.01
☐ 410 Brian Blades	.30	.14	.04
☐ 411 SB XXIII	.05	.02	.01
☐ 412 Jerry Rice	1.00	.45	.12
☐ 413 SB XXIII	.05	.02	.01
☐ 414 SB XXIII	.05	.02	.01
☐ 415 SB XXIII	.05	.02	.01
☐ 416 SB XXIII	.05	.02	.01
☐ NNO Panini Album (Joe Montana on cover)	3.00	1.35	.35

1990 Panini Stickers

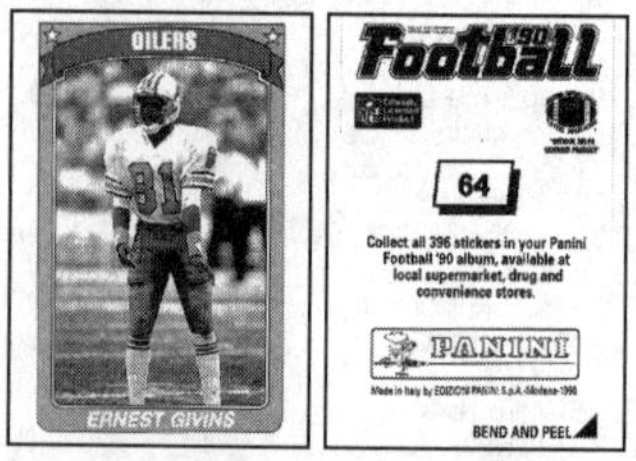

This set contains 396 colorful stickers. The stickers are numbered in team order. Each sticker measures approximately 1 7/8" by 2 15/16". The cover of the album contains pictures of Mike Singletary, Ronnie Lott, and Lawrence Taylor as the theme is "The Hitters." The stickers were also issued in a UK version which is distinguished by the presence of stats printed on the sticker backs.

	MINT	NRMT	EXC
COMPLETE SET (396)	15.00	6.75	1.85
COMMON CARD (1-396)	.05	.02	.01
☐ 1 Super Bowl XXIV FOIL Program Cover (top)	.05	.02	.01
☐ 2 Super Bowl XXIV FOIL Program Cover (bottom)	.05	.02	.01
☐ 3 Buffalo Bills Crest FOIL	.05	.02	.01
☐ 4 Thurman Thomas	.30	.14	.04
☐ 5 Nate Odomes	.05	.02	.01
☐ 6 Jim Kelly	.25	.11	.03
☐ 7 Cornelius Bennett	.10	.05	.01
☐ 8 Scott Norwood	.05	.02	.01
☐ 9 Mark Kelso	.05	.02	.01
☐ 10 Kent Hull	.05	.02	.01
☐ 11 Jim Ritcher	.05	.02	.01
☐ 12 Darryl Talley	.10	.05	.01
☐ 13 Bruce Smith	.20	.09	.03
☐ 14 Shane Conlan	.10	.05	.01
☐ 15 Andre Reed	.20	.09	.03
☐ 16 Jason Buck	.05	.02	.01
☐ 17 David Fulcher	.05	.02	.01
☐ 18 Jim Skow	.05	.02	.01
☐ 19 Anthony Munoz	.20	.09	.03
☐ 20 Eric Thomas	.05	.02	.01
☐ 21 Eric Ball	.05	.02	.01
☐ 22 Tim Krumrie	.10	.05	.01
☐ 23 James Brooks	.10	.05	.01
☐ 24 Cincinnati Bengals Crest FOIL	.05	.02	.01
☐ 25 Rodney Holman	.05	.02	.01
☐ 26 Boomer Esiason	.10	.05	.01
☐ 27 Eddie Brown	.10	.05	.01
☐ 28 Tim McGee	.05	.02	.01
☐ 29 Cleveland Browns Crest FOIL	.05	.02	.01
☐ 30 Mike Johnson	.05	.02	.01
☐ 31 David Grayson	.05	.02	.01
☐ 32 Thane Gash	.05	.02	.01
☐ 33 Robert Banks	.05	.02	.01
☐ 34 Eric Metcalf	.20	.09	.03
☐ 35 Kevin Mack	.05	.02	.01
☐ 36 Reggie Langhorne	.05	.02	.01
☐ 37 Webster Slaughter	.10	.05	.01
☐ 38 Felix Wright	.05	.02	.01
☐ 39 Bernie Kosar	.10	.05	.01
☐ 40 Frank Minnifield	.05	.02	.01
☐ 41 Clay Matthews	.10	.05	.01
☐ 42 Vance Johnson	.05	.02	.01
☐ 43 Ron Holmes	.05	.02	.01
☐ 44 Melvin Bratton	.05	.02	.01
☐ 45 Greg Kragen	.05	.02	.01
☐ 46 Karl Mecklenburg	.10	.05	.01
☐ 47 Dennis Smith	.05	.02	.01
☐ 48 Bobby Humphrey	.05	.02	.01
☐ 49 Simon Fletcher	.05	.02	.01
☐ 50 Denver Broncos Crest FOIL	.05	.02	.01
☐ 51 Michael Brooks	.05	.02	.01
☐ 52 Steve Atwater	.10	.05	.01
☐ 53 John Elway	1.00	.45	.12
☐ 54 David Treadwell	.05	.02	.01
☐ 55 Houston Oilers Crest FOIL	.05	.02	.01
☐ 56 Bubba McDowell	.10	.05	.01
☐ 57 Ray Childress	.10	.05	.01
☐ 58 Bruce Matthews	.10	.05	.01
☐ 59 Allen Pinkett	.05	.02	.01
☐ 60 Warren Moon	.20	.09	.03
☐ 61 John Grimsley	.05	.02	.01
☐ 62 Alonzo Highsmith	.05	.02	.01
☐ 63 Mike Munchak	.05	.02	.01
☐ 64 Ernest Givins	.10	.05	.01
☐ 65 Johnny Meads	.05	.02	.01
☐ 66 Drew Hill	.10	.05	.01
☐ 67 William Fuller	.10	.05	.01
☐ 68 Duane Bickett	.05	.02	.01
☐ 69 Jack Trudeau	.05	.02	.01
☐ 70 Jon Hand	.05	.02	.01
☐ 71 Chris Hinton	.10	.05	.01
☐ 72 Bill Brooks	.10	.05	.01
☐ 73 Donnell Thompson	.05	.02	.01
☐ 74 Jeff Herrod	.05	.02	.01
☐ 75 Andre Rison	.20	.09	.03
☐ 76 Indianapolis Colts Crest FOIL	.05	.02	.01
☐ 77 Chris Chandler	.20	.09	.03
☐ 78 Ray Donaldson	.05	.02	.01
☐ 79 Albert Bentley	.05	.02	.01
☐ 80 Keith Taylor	.05	.02	.01
☐ 81 Kansas City Chiefs Crest FOIL	.05	.02	.01
☐ 82 Leonard Griffin	.05	.02	.01
☐ 83 Dino Hackett	.05	.02	.01
☐ 84 Christian Okoye	.10	.05	.01
☐ 85 Chris Martin	.05	.02	.01
☐ 86 John Alt	.05	.02	.01
☐ 87 Kevin Ross	.05	.02	.01
☐ 88 Steve DeBerg	.10	.05	.01
☐ 89 Albert Lewis	.05	.02	.01
☐ 90 Stephone Paige	.05	.02	.01
☐ 91 Derrick Thomas	.20	.09	.03
☐ 92 Neil Smith	.20	.09	.03
☐ 93 Pete Mandley	.05	.02	.01
☐ 94 Howie Long	.10	.05	.01
☐ 95 Greg Townsend	.10	.05	.01
☐ 96 Mervyn Fernandez	.05	.02	.01
☐ 97 Scott Davis	.05	.02	.01
☐ 98 Steve Beuerlein	.10	.05	.01
☐ 99 Mike Dyal	.05	.02	.01
☐ 100 Willie Gault	.05	.02	.01
☐ 101 Eddie Anderson	.05	.02	.01
☐ 102 Los Angeles Raiders Crest FOIL	.05	.02	.01
☐ 103 Terry McDaniel	.10	.05	.01
☐ 104 Bo Jackson	.25	.11	.03
☐ 105 Steve Wisniewski	.10	.05	.01
☐ 106 Steve Smith	.05	.02	.01
☐ 107 Miami Dolphins Crest FOIL	.05	.02	.01
☐ 108 Mark Clayton	.10	.05	.01
☐ 109 Louis Oliver	.05	.02	.01
☐ 110 Jarvis Williams	.05	.02	.01
☐ 111 Ferrell Edmunds	.05	.02	.01
☐ 112 Jeff Cross	.05	.02	.01
☐ 113 John Offerdahl	.05	.02	.01
☐ 114 Brian Sochia	.05	.02	.01
☐ 115 Dan Marino	2.50	1.10	.30
☐ 116 Jim C. Jensen	.05	.02	.01
☐ 117 Sammie Smith	.05	.02	.01
☐ 118 Reggie Roby	.05	.02	.01
☐ 119 Roy Foster	.05	.02	.01
☐ 120 Bruce Armstrong	.05	.02	.01
☐ 121 Steve Grogan	.10	.05	.01
☐ 122 Hart Lee Dykes	.05	.02	.01
☐ 123 Andre Tippett	.05	.02	.01
☐ 124 Johnny Rembert	.05	.02	.01
☐ 125 Ed Reynolds	.05	.02	.01
☐ 126 Cedric Jones	.05	.02	.01
☐ 127 Vincent Brown	.20	.09	.03
☐ 128 New England Patriots Crest FOIL	.05	.02	.01
☐ 129 Brent Williams	.05	.02	.01
☐ 130 John Stephens	.05	.02	.01
☐ 131 Eric Sievers	.05	.02	.01
☐ 132 Maurice Hurst	.05	.02	.01
☐ 133 Jets Crest FOIL	.05	.02	.01
☐ 134 Johnny Hector	.05	.02	.01
☐ 135 Erik McMillan	.05	.02	.01
☐ 136 Jeff Lageman	.10	.05	.01
☐ 137 Al Toon	.10	.05	.01
☐ 138 James Hasty	.05	.02	.01
☐ 139 Kyle Clifton	.05	.02	.01
☐ 140 Ken O'Brien	.10	.05	.01
☐ 141 Jim Sweeney	.05	.02	.01
☐ 142 Jo Jo Townsell	.05	.02	.01
☐ 143 Dennis Byrd	.10	.05	.01
☐ 144 Mickey Shuler	.05	.02	.01
☐ 145 Alex Gordon	.05	.02	.01
☐ 146 Keith Willis	.05	.02	.01
☐ 147 Louis Lipps	.10	.05	.01
☐ 148 David Little	.05	.02	.01
☐ 149 Greg Lloyd	.20	.09	.03
☐ 150 Carnell Lake	.10	.05	.01
☐ 151 Tim Worley	.05	.02	.01
☐ 152 Dwayne Woodruff	.05	.02	.01
☐ 153 Gerald Williams	.05	.02	.01
☐ 154 Pittsburgh Steelers Crest FOIL	.05	.02	.01
☐ 155 Merril Hoge	.05	.02	.01
☐ 156 Bubby Brister	.10	.05	.01
☐ 157 Tunch Ilkin	.05	.02	.01
☐ 158 Rod Woodson	.20	.09	.03
☐ 159 San Diego Chargers Crest FOIL	.05	.02	.01
☐ 160 Leslie O'Neal	.10	.05	.01
☐ 161 Billy Ray Smith	.05	.02	.01
☐ 162 Marion Butts	.10	.05	.01
☐ 163 Lee Williams	.05	.02	.01
☐ 164 Gill Byrd	.05	.02	.01
☐ 165 Jim McMahon	.10	.05	.01
☐ 166 Courtney Hall	.05	.02	.01
☐ 167 Burt Grossman	.05	.02	.01
☐ 168 Gary Plummer	.05	.02	.01
☐ 169 Anthony Miller	.20	.09	.03
☐ 170 Billy Joe Tolliver	.05	.02	.01
☐ 171 Vencie Glenn	.05	.02	.01
☐ 172 Andy Heck	.05	.02	.01
☐ 173 Brian Blades	.10	.05	.01
☐ 174 Bryan Millard	.05	.02	.01
☐ 175 Tony Woods	.05	.02	.01
☐ 176 Rufus Porter	.05	.02	.01
☐ 177 David Wyman	.05	.02	.01
☐ 178 John L. Williams	.05	.02	.01
☐ 179 Jacob Green	.05	.02	.01
☐ 180 Seattle Seahawks Crest FOIL	.05	.02	.01
☐ 181 Eugene Robinson	.05	.02	.01
☐ 182 Jeff Bryant	.05	.02	.01
☐ 183 Dave Krieg	.10	.05	.01
☐ 184 Joe Nash	.05	.02	.01
☐ 185 Christian Okoye LL	.05	.02	.01
☐ 186 Felix Wright LL	.05	.02	.01
☐ 187 Rod Woodson LL	.20	.09	.03
☐ 188 Barry Sanders AP and Christian Okoye AP	.50	.23	.06
☐ 189 Jerry Rice AP and Sterling Sharpe AP	.60	.25	.07
☐ 190 Bruce Matthews AP	.05	.02	.01
☐ 191 Jay Hilgenberg AP	.05	.02	.01
☐ 192 Tom Newberry AP	.05	.02	.01
☐ 193 Anthony Munoz AP	.20	.09	.03
☐ 194 Jim Lachey AP	.05	.02	.01
☐ 195 Keith Jackson AP	.05	.02	.01
☐ 196 Joe Montana AP	1.25	.55	.16
☐ 197 David Fulcher AP and Ronnie Lott AP	.05	.02	.01
☐ 198 Albert Lewis AP and Eric Allen AP	.05	.02	.01
☐ 199 Reggie White AP	.20	.09	.03
☐ 200 Keith Millard AP	.05	.02	.01
☐ 201 Chris Doleman AP	.05	.02	.01
☐ 202 Mike Singletary AP	.10	.05	.01
☐ 203 Tim Harris AP	.05	.02	.01
☐ 204 Lawrence Taylor AP	.20	.09	.03
☐ 205 Rich Camarillo AP	.05	.02	.01
☐ 206 Sterling Sharpe LL	.20	.09	.03
☐ 207 Chris Doleman LL	.05	.02	.01
☐ 208 Barry Sanders LL	.50	.23	.06
☐ 209 Atlanta Falcons Crest FOIL	.05	.02	.01
☐ 210 Michael Haynes	.20	.09	.03
☐ 211 Scott Case	.05	.02	.01
☐ 212 Marcus Cotton	.05	.02	.01
☐ 213 Chris Miller	.20	.09	.03
☐ 214 Keith Jones	.05	.02	.01
☐ 215 Tim Green	.05	.02	.01
☐ 216 Deion Sanders	.75	.35	.09
☐ 217 Shawn Collins	.05	.02	.01
☐ 218 John Settle	.05	.02	.01
☐ 219 Bill Fralic	.05	.02	.01
☐ 220 Aundray Bruce	.05	.02	.01
☐ 221 Jessie Tuggle	.05	.02	.01
☐ 222 James Thornton	.05	.02	.01
☐ 223 Dennis Gentry	.05	.02	.01
☐ 224 Richard Dent	.10	.05	.01
☐ 225 Jay Hilgenberg	.05	.02	.01
☐ 226 Steve McMichael	.05	.02	.01
☐ 227 Brad Muster	.05	.02	.01
☐ 228 Donnell Woolford	.10	.05	.01
☐ 229 Mike Singletary	.10	.05	.01
☐ 230 Chicago Bears Crest FOIL	.05	.02	.01
☐ 231 Mark Bortz	.05	.02	.01
☐ 232 Kevin Butler	.05	.02	.01
☐ 233 Neal Anderson	.10	.05	.01
☐ 234 Trace Armstrong	.05	.02	.01
☐ 235 Dallas Cowboys Crest FOIL	.05	.02	.01
☐ 236 Mark Tuinei	.05	.02	.01
☐ 237 Tony Tolbert	.10	.05	.01
☐ 238 Eugene Lockhart	.05	.02	.01
☐ 239 Daryl Johnston	.20	.09	.03
☐ 240 Troy Aikman	1.25	.55	.16
☐ 241 Jim Jeffcoat	.05	.02	.01
☐ 242 James Dixon	.05	.02	.01
☐ 243 Jesse Solomon	.05	.02	.01
☐ 244 Ken Norton Jr.	.20	.09	.03
☐ 245 Kelvin Martin	.05	.02	.01
☐ 246 Danny Noonan	.05	.02	.01
☐ 247 Michael Irvin	.30	.14	.04
☐ 248 Eric Williams	.05	.02	.01
☐ 249 Richard Johnson	.05	.02	.01
☐ 250 Michael Cofer	.05	.02	.01
☐ 251 Chris Spielman	.20	.09	.03
☐ 252 Rodney Peete	.10	.05	.01
☐ 253 Bennie Blades	.05	.02	.01
☐ 254 Jerry Ball	.05	.02	.01
☐ 255 Eddie Murray	.05	.02	.01
☐ 256 Detroit Lions Crest FOIL	.05	.02	.01
☐ 257 Barry Sanders	1.25	.55	.16
☐ 258 Jerry Holmes	.05	.02	.01
☐ 259 Dennis Gibson	.05	.02	.01
☐ 260 Lomas Brown	.05	.02	.01
☐ 261 Packers Crest FOIL	.05	.02	.01
☐ 262 Dave Brown	.05	.02	.01
☐ 263 Mark Murphy	.05	.02	.01
☐ 264 Perry Kemp	.05	.02	.01
☐ 265 Don Majkowski	.10	.05	.01
☐ 266 Chris Jacke	.05	.02	.01
☐ 267 Keith Woodside	.05	.02	.01
☐ 268 Tony Mandarich	.05	.02	.01
☐ 269 Robert Brown	.05	.02	.01
☐ 270 Sterling Sharpe	.20	.09	.03
☐ 271 Tim Harris	.05	.02	.01
☐ 272 Brent Fullwood	.05	.02	.01
☐ 273 Brian Noble	.05	.02	.01
☐ 274 Alvin Wright	.05	.02	.01
☐ 275 Flipper Anderson	.10	.05	.01
☐ 276 Jackie Slater	.05	.02	.01
☐ 277 Kevin Greene	.20	.09	.03
☐ 278 Pete Holohan	.05	.02	.01
☐ 279 Tom Newberry	.05	.02	.01
☐ 280 Jerry Gray	.05	.02	.01
☐ 281 Henry Ellard	.10	.05	.01
☐ 282 Rams Crest FOIL	.05	.02	.01
☐ 283 LeRoy Irvin	.05	.02	.01
☐ 284 Jim Everett	.10	.05	.01
☐ 285 Greg Bell	.05	.02	.01
☐ 286 Doug Smith	.05	.02	.01
☐ 287 Minnesota Vikings Crest FOIL	.05	.02	.01
☐ 288 Joey Browner	.05	.02	.01
☐ 289 Wade Wilson	.10	.05	.01
☐ 290 Chris Doleman	.10	.05	.01
☐ 291 Al Noga	.05	.02	.01
☐ 292 Herschel Walker	.10	.05	.01
☐ 293 Henry Thomas	.10	.05	.01
☐ 294 Steve Jordan	.10	.05	.01
☐ 295 Anthony Carter	.10	.05	.01
☐ 296 Keith Millard	.05	.02	.01
☐ 297 Carl Lee	.05	.02	.01
☐ 298 Randall McDaniel	.05	.02	.01
☐ 299 Gary Zimmerman	.05	.02	.01
☐ 300 Morten Andersen	.05	.02	.01
☐ 301 Rickey Jackson	.10	.05	.01
☐ 302 Sam Mills	.10	.05	.01
☐ 303 Hoby Brenner	.05	.02	.01
☐ 304 Dalton Hilliard	.05	.02	.01
☐ 305 Robert Massey	.05	.02	.01
☐ 306 John Fourcade	.05	.02	.01
☐ 307 Lonzell Hill	.05	.02	.01
☐ 308 Saints Crest FOIL	.05	.02	.01
☐ 309 Jim Dombrowski	.05	.02	.01
☐ 310 Pat Swilling	.10	.05	.01
☐ 311 Vaughan Johnson	.10	.05	.01
☐ 312 Eric Martin	.05	.02	.01
☐ 313 Giants Crest FOIL	.05	.02	.01
☐ 314 Ottis Anderson	.10	.05	.01
☐ 315 Myron Guyton	.05	.02	.01
☐ 316 Terry Kinard	.05	.02	.01
☐ 317 Mark Bavaro	.05	.02	.01
☐ 318 Phil Simms	.10	.05	.01
☐ 319 Lawrence Taylor	.20	.09	.03
☐ 320 Odessa Turner	.05	.02	.01
☐ 321 Erik Howard	.05	.02	.01
☐ 322 Mark Collins	.05	.02	.01
☐ 323 Dave Meggett	.10	.05	.01
☐ 324 Leonard Marshall	.10	.05	.01
☐ 325 Carl Banks	.10	.05	.01
☐ 326 Anthony Toney	.05	.02	.01
☐ 327 Seth Joyner	.10	.05	.01
☐ 328 Cris Carter	.20	.09	.03
☐ 329 Eric Allen	.10	.05	.01
☐ 330 Keith Jackson	.10	.05	.01
☐ 331 Clyde Simmons	.10	.05	.01
☐ 332 Byron Evans	.05	.02	.01
☐ 333 Keith Byars	.10	.05	.01
☐ 334 Philadelphia Eagles Crest FOIL	.05	.02	.01
☐ 335 Reggie White	.20	.09	.03
☐ 336 Izel Jenkins	.05	.02	.01
☐ 337 Jerome Brown	.10	.05	.01
☐ 338 David Alexander	.05	.02	.01

☐ 339 Phoenix Cardinals Crest FOIL	.05	.02	.01
☐ 340 Rich Camarillo	.05	.02	.01
☐ 341 Ken Harvey	.10	.05	.01
☐ 342 Luis Sharpe	.05	.02	.01
☐ 343 Timm Rosenbach	.05	.02	.01
☐ 344 Tim McDonald	.05	.02	.01
☐ 345 Vai Sikahema	.05	.02	.01
☐ 346 Freddie Joe Nunn	.05	.02	.01
☐ 347 Ernie Jones	.05	.02	.01
☐ 348 J.T. Smith	.05	.02	.01
☐ 349 Eric Hill	.05	.02	.01
☐ 350 Roy Green	.10	.05	.01
☐ 351 Anthony Bell	.05	.02	.01
☐ 352 Kevin Fagan	.05	.02	.01
☐ 353 Roger Craig	.10	.05	.01
☐ 354 Ronnie Lott	.10	.05	.01
☐ 355 Mike Cofer	.05	.02	.01
☐ 356 John Taylor	.20	.09	.03
☐ 357 Joe Montana	2.00	.90	.25
☐ 358 Charles Haley	.20	.09	.03
☐ 359 Guy McIntyre	.05	.02	.01
☐ 360 49ers Crest FOIL	.05	.02	.01
☐ 361 Pierce Holt	.05	.02	.01
☐ 362 Tom Rathman	.10	.05	.01
☐ 363 Jerry Rice	1.25	.55	.16
☐ 364 Michael Carter	.05	.02	.01
☐ 365 Buccaneers Crest FOIL	.05	.02	.01
☐ 366 Lars Tate	.05	.02	.01
☐ 367 Paul Gruber	.05	.02	.01
☐ 368 Winston Moss	.05	.02	.01
☐ 369 Reuben Davis	.05	.02	.01
☐ 370 Mark Robinson	.05	.02	.01
☐ 371 Bruce Hill	.05	.02	.01
☐ 372 Kevin Murphy	.05	.02	.01
☐ 373 Ricky Reynolds	.05	.02	.01
☐ 374 Harry Hamilton	.05	.02	.01
☐ 375 Vinny Testaverde	.10	.05	.01
☐ 376 Mark Carrier WR	.10	.05	.01
☐ 377 Ervin Randle	.05	.02	.01
☐ 378 Ricky Sanders	.10	.05	.01
☐ 379 Charles Mann	.10	.05	.01
☐ 380 Jim Lachey	.05	.02	.01
☐ 381 Wilber Marshall	.05	.02	.01
☐ 382 A.J. Johnson	.05	.02	.01
☐ 383 Darrell Green	.10	.05	.01
☐ 384 Mark Rypien	.05	.02	.01
☐ 385 Gerald Riggs	.10	.05	.01
☐ 386 Washington Redskins Crest FOIL	.05	.02	.01
☐ 387 Alvin Walton	.05	.02	.01
☐ 388 Art Monk	.20	.09	.03
☐ 389 Gary Clark	.20	.09	.03
☐ 390 Earnest Byner	.10	.05	.01
☐ 391 SB XXIV Action FOIL (Jerry Rice)	.75	.35	.09
☐ 392 SB XXIV Action FOIL (49er Offensive Line)	.05	.02	.01
☐ 393 SB XXIV Action FOIL (Tom Rathman)	.05	.02	.01
☐ 394 SB XXIV Action FOIL (Chet Brooks)	.05	.02	.01
☐ 395 SB XXIV Action FOIL (John Elway)	.75	.35	.09
☐ 396 Joe Montana FOIL SB XXIV MVP	2.50	1.10	.30
☐ NNO Panini Album	2.00	.90	.25

1995 Panthers SkyBox

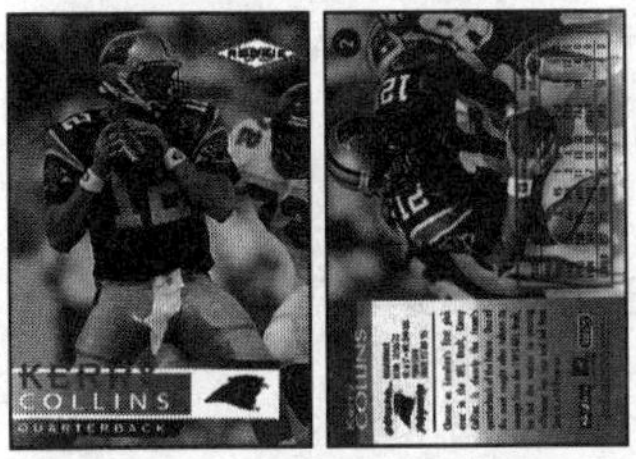

This 21-card set of the Carolina Panthers features borderless color action player photos with the player's name and position in team color stripes at the bottom. The backs carry another color player picture along with player biographical information. The set includes 20 numbered player cards and one unnumbered cover/checklist card.

	MINT	NRMT	EXC
COMPLETE SET (21)	20.00	9.00	2.50
COMMON CARD (1-20)	.75	.35	.09
☐ 1 John Kasay	1.00	.45	.12
☐ 2 Kerry Collins	5.00	2.20	.60
☐ 3 Frank Reich	1.00	.45	.12
☐ 4 Rod Smith	1.50	.70	.19
☐ 5 Tim McKyer	.75	.35	.09
☐ 6 Randy Baldwin	.75	.35	.09
☐ 7 Bubba McDowell	.75	.35	.09
☐ 8 Tyrone Poole	1.50	.70	.19
☐ 9 Sam Mills	1.25	.55	.16
☐ 10 Carlton Bailey	.75	.35	.09
☐ 11 Darion Conner	.75	.35	.09
☐ 12 Lamar Lathon	1.00	.45	.12
☐ 13 Blake Brockermeyer	1.00	.45	.12
☐ 14 Mike Fox	.75	.35	.09
☐ 15 Don Beebe	1.00	.45	.12
☐ 16 Mark Carrier	1.50	.70	.19
☐ 17 Pete Metzelaars	.75	.35	.09
☐ 18 Shawn King	.75	.35	.09
☐ 19 Howard Griffith	.75	.35	.09
☐ 20 Bob Christian	1.00	.45	.12
☐ NNO Cover Card Checklist back	.75	.35	.09

1996 Panthers Fleer/SkyBox Impact Promo Sheet

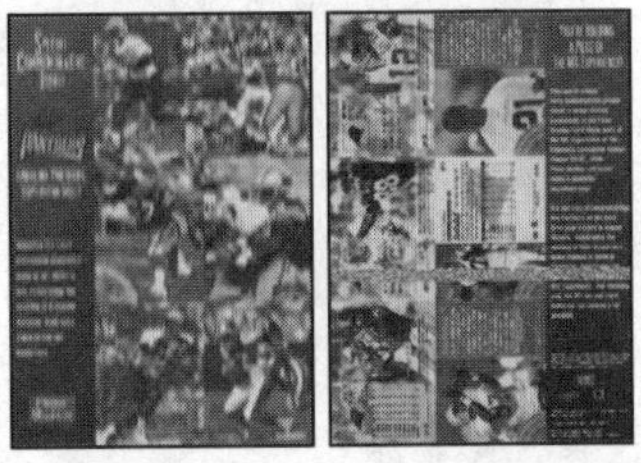

Fleer/SkyBox distributed this promo sheet primarily at the NFL Experience Card Show at the Charlotte Convention Center August 29-31, 1996. The sheet features six Panthers' players with individual card numbers CP1-CP6. We've included only a complete sheet price which is the form most commonly sold.

	MINT	NRMT	EXC
COMPLETE SET (1)	5.00	2.20	.60
COMMON SHEET	5.00	2.20	.60
☐ 1 Promo Sheet Tim Biakabutuka Lamar Lathon Muhsin Muhammad Kerry Collins Tyrone Poole Mark Carrier WR	5.00	2.20	.60

1974 Parker Brothers Pro Draft

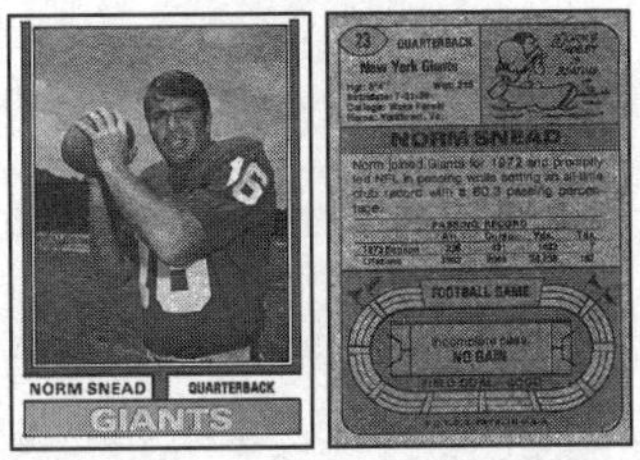

This 50-card standard-size set was printed by Topps for distribution by Parker Brothers in early 1974 as part of a football board game. The only players in this set (game) are offensive players (with an emphasis on the skill positions) and all come from the first 132 cards in the 1974 Topps football card set. The cards are very similar and often confused with the 1974 Topps regular issue football cards. There are several notable differences between these cards and the 1974 Topps regular issue; those cards with 1972 statistics on the back (unlike the 1974 Topps regular issue) are indicated in the checklist below with an asterisk. Those cards with pose variations (different from the 1974 Topps) are noted as well parenthetically; these six pose variations are numbers 23, 49, 116, 124, 126, and 127. Parker Brothers game cards can also be distinguished by the presence of two asterisks rather than one on the copyright line. However, there are cards in the regular 1974 Topps set that do have two asterisks but are not Parker Brothers Pro Draft cards. Cards in the 1974 Topps regular set with two asterisks include 26, 129, 130, 156, 162, 219, 265-364, 367-422, and 424-528; the rest have only one asterisk. The Parker Brothers cards are skip-numbered with the number on the back corresponding to that player's number in the Topps regular issue.

	NRMT-MT	EXC	G-VG
COMPLETE SET (50)	100.00	45.00	12.50
COMMON CARD	1.00	.45	.12
COMMON CARD (WITH *)	2.00	.90	.25
☐ 4 Ken Bowman	1.00	.45	.12
☐ 6 Jerry Smith *	2.00	.90	.25
☐ 7 Ed Podolak *	2.00	.90	.25
☐ 9 Pat Matson	1.00	.45	.12
☐ 11 Frank Pitts *	2.00	.90	.25
☐ 15 Winston Hill	1.00	.45	.12
☐ 18 Rich Coady *	2.00	.90	.25
☐ 19 Ken Willard *	2.50	1.10	.30
☐ 21 Ben Hawkins *	2.00	.90	.25
☐ 23 Norm Snead * (Vertical pose; Topps has horizontal pose)	8.00	3.60	1.00
☐ 24 Jim Yarbrough *	2.00	.90	.25
☐ 28 Bob Hayes *	5.00	2.20	.60
☐ 32 Dan Dierdorf *	6.00	2.70	.75
☐ 35 Essex Johnson *	2.00	.90	.25
☐ 39 Mike Siani	1.00	.45	.12
☐ 42 Del Williams	1.00	.45	.12
☐ 43 Don McCauley *	2.00	.90	.25
☐ 44 Randy Jackson *	2.00	.90	.25
☐ 46 Gene Washington *	3.00	1.35	.35
☐ 49 Bob Windsor * (Vertical pose; Topps has horizontal pose)	5.00	2.20	.60
☐ 50 John Hadl *	4.00	1.80	.50
☐ 52 Steve Owens *	3.50	1.55	.45
☐ 54 Rayfield Wright *	2.00	.90	.25
☐ 57 Milt Sunde *	2.00	.90	.25
☐ 58 Billy Kilmer *	5.00	2.20	.60
☐ 61 Rufus Mayes *	2.00	.90	.25
☐ 63 Gene Washington *	2.50	1.10	.30
☐ 65 Gene Upshaw	5.00	2.20	.60
☐ 75 Fred Willis *	2.00	.90	.25
☐ 77 Tom Neville	1.00	.45	.12
☐ 78 Ted Kwalick *	2.50	1.10	.30
☐ 80 John Niland *	2.00	.90	.25
☐ 81 Ted Fritsch Jr.	1.00	.45	.12
☐ 83 Jack Snow *	3.00	1.35	.35
☐ 87 Mike Phipps *	3.00	1.35	.35
☐ 90 MacArthur Lane *	3.00	1.35	.35
☐ 95 Calvin Hill *	4.00	1.80	.50
☐ 98 Len Rohde	1.00	.45	.12
☐ 101 Gary Garrison *	2.00	.90	.25
☐ 103 Len St. Jean	1.00	.45	.12
☐ 107 Jim Mitchell *	2.00	.90	.25
☐ 109 Harry Schuh	1.00	.45	.12
☐ 110 Greg Pruitt *	5.00	2.20	.60
☐ 111 Ed Flanagan	1.00	.45	.12
☐ 113 Chuck Foreman *	5.00	2.20	.60
☐ 116 Charlie Johnson * (Vertical pose; Topps has horizontal pose)	6.00	2.70	.75
☐ 119 Roy Jefferson *	2.50	1.10	.30
☐ 124 Forrest Blue * (Not All-Pro on card; Topps card is All-Pro)	6.00	2.70	.75
☐ 126 Tom Mack * (Not All-Pro on card; Topps card is All-Pro)	7.50	3.40	.95
☐ 127 Bob Tucker * (Not All-Pro on card; Topps card is All-Pro)	6.00	2.70	.75

1989 Parker Brothers Talking Football

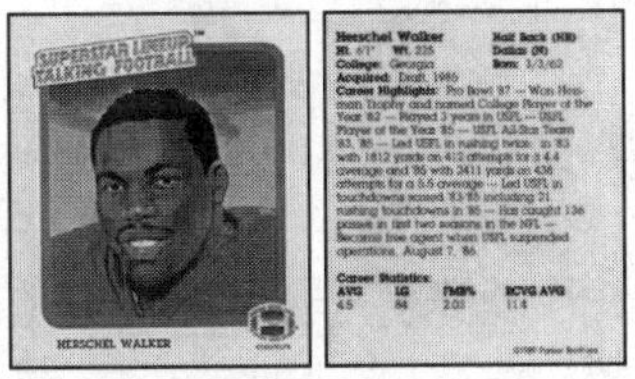

Measuring approximately 2 5/8" by 3", this 34-card set was licensed only by the NFL Players Association. When players are shown together on a card, it relates to their respective position(s). The cards are unnumbered so they are listed below in alphabetical order according to the AFC (1-17) and the NFC (18-34). For cards with more than one subject, those players are in turn alphabetically listed so that they can be alphabetized consistently along with the single player cards.

	MINT	NRMT	EXC
COMPLETE SET (34)	150.00	70.00	19.00
COMMON CARD (1-34)	2.00	.90	.25
☐ 1 AFC Team Roster	2.00	.90	.25
☐ 2 Marcus Allen	10.00	4.50	1.25
☐ 3 Cornelius Bennett John Offerdahl	4.00	1.80	.50
☐ 4 Keith Bishop Mike Munchak	2.00	.90	.25
☐ 5 Keith Bostic Deron Cherry Hanford Dixon	2.00	.90	.25
☐ 6 Carlos Carson Stanley Morgan	2.00	.90	.25
☐ 7 Todd Christensen Mickey Shuler	3.00	1.35	.35
☐ 8 Eric Dickerson	7.50	3.40	.95
☐ 9 Ray Donaldson Irving Fryar	2.00	.90	.25
☐ 10 Jacob Green Bruce Smith	4.00	1.80	.50
☐ 11 Mark Haynes Frank Minnifield Dennis Smith	2.00	.90	.25
☐ 12 Chris Hinton Anthony Munoz	3.00	1.35	.35
☐ 13 Steve Largent Al Toon	8.00	3.60	1.00
☐ 14 Howie Long Bill Maas	5.00	2.20	.60
☐ 15 Nick Lowery Reggie Roby	2.00	.90	.25
☐ 16 Dan Marino	40.00	18.00	5.00
☐ 17 Karl Mecklenburg Andre Tippett	3.00	1.35	.35
☐ 18 NFC Team Roster	2.00	.90	.25
☐ 19 Morten Andersen Jim Arnold	2.00	.90	.25
☐ 20 Carl Banks Mike Singletary	4.00	1.80	.50
☐ 21 Mark Bavaro Doug Cosbie	3.00	1.35	.35
☐ 22 Joey Browner Darrell Green Leonard Smith	3.00	1.35	.35
☐ 23 Anthony Carter Jerry Rice	25.00	11.00	3.10
☐ 24 Gary Clark Mike Quick	6.00	2.70	.75
☐ 25 Richard Dent Chris Doleman	4.00	1.80	.50
☐ 26 Brad Edelman Bill Fralic	2.00	.90	.25
☐ 27 Carl Ekern Rickey Jackson	2.00	.90	.25
☐ 28 Jerry Gray LeRoy Irvin Ronnie Lott	3.00	1.35	.35
☐ 29 Mel Gray Jay Hilgenberg	4.00	1.80	.50
☐ 30 Dexter Manley Reggie White	3.00	1.35	.35
☐ 31 Rueben Mayes	2.00	.90	.25
☐ 32 Joe Montana	35.00	16.00	4.40
☐ 33 Jackie Slater Gary Zimmerman	2.00	.90	.25
☐ 34 Herschel Walker	4.00	1.80	.50

1983 Patriots Frito Lay

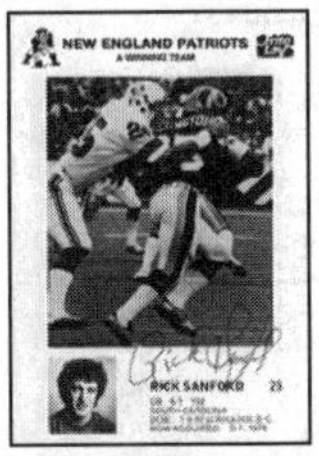

The New England Patriots issued this set sponsored by Frito Lay. The cards are blankbacked, measure approximately 4" by 6", and contain black and white player photos. The cards can be distinguished from other Patriots Frito Lay issues by the title line "A Winning Team" contained at the top of the cardfront. This issue also contains two player photos per card instead of one. Any additional information on this checklist would be greatly appreciated.

	MINT	NRMT	EXC
COMPLETE SET (3	10.00	4.50	1.25
COMMON CARD (1-3)	3.00	1.35	.35
☐ 1 Roland James	3.00	1.35	.35
☐ 2 Rick Sanford	3.00	1.35	.35
☐ 3 John Smith	4.00	1.80	.50

1985 Patriots Frito Lay

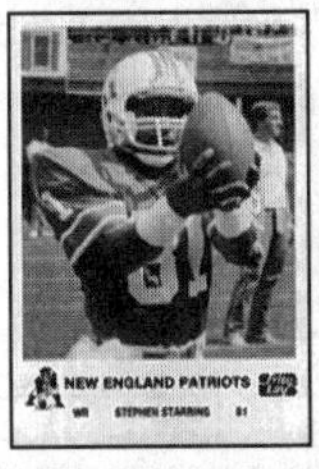

The New England Patriots issued this set sponsored by Frito Lay. The cards are blankbacked, measure approximately 4" by 6", and contain black and white player photos. The cards can be distinguished from other Patriots Frito Lay issues by the lack of any set title something commonly found on the other releases. The complete set is likely more than 10-cards. Any additions to this list would be appreciated.

	MINT	NRMT	EXC
COMPLETE SET (10)	25.00	11.00	3.10
COMMON CARD (1-10)	2.50	1.10	.30
☐ 1 Darryl Haley	2.50	1.10	.30
☐ 2 Brian Ingram	2.50	1.10	.30
☐ 3 Cedric Jones WR	2.50	1.10	.30
☐ 4 Ronnie Lippett	3.00	1.35	.35
☐ 5 Larry McGrew	2.50	1.10	.30
☐ 6 Steve Moore	2.50	1.10	.30
☐ 7 Stanley Morgan	4.00	1.80	.50
☐ 8 Kenneth Sims	3.00	1.35	.35
☐ 9 Stephen Starring	2.50	1.10	.30
☐ 10 Clayton Weishuhn	2.50	1.10	.30

1986 Patriots Frito Lay

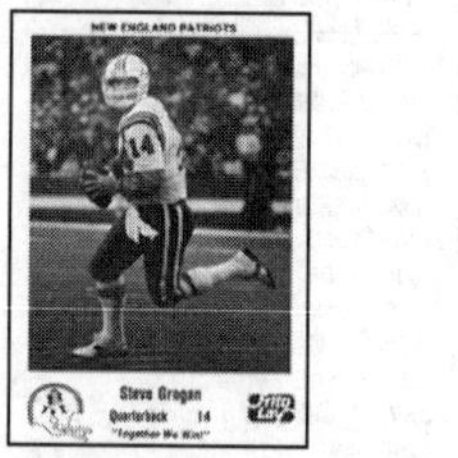

The New England Patriots issued this set sponsored by Frito Lay. The cards are blankbacked, measure approximately 4" by 6", and contain black and white player photos. The cards can be distinguished from other Patriots Frito Lay issues by the title "Together We Win" printed at the bottom of the cardfront. The set is thought to be complete at 41-cards. Any additions to the list would be appreciated.

	MINT	NRMT	EXC
COMPLETE SET (41)	75.00	34.00	9.50
COMMON CARD (1-41)	2.00	.90	.25
☐ 1 Greg Baty	2.00	.90	.25
☐ 2 Raymond Berry CO	3.00	1.35	.35
☐ 3 Don Blackmon	2.00	.90	.25
☐ 4 Jim Bowman	2.00	.90	.25
☐ 5 Pete Brock	2.00	.90	.25
☐ 6 Raymond Clayborn	3.00	1.35	.35
☐ 7 Tony Collins	2.50	1.10	.30
☐ 8 Rich Camarillo	2.50	1.10	.30
☐ 9 Steve Doig	2.00	.90	.25
☐ 10 Reggie Dupard	2.50	1.10	.30
☐ 11 Tony Eason	3.00	1.35	.35
☐ 12 Sean Farrell	2.50	1.10	.30
☐ 13 Tony Franklin	2.00	.90	.25
☐ 14 Ernest Gibson	2.00	.90	.25
☐ 15 Steve Grogan	4.00	1.80	.50
☐ 16 Greg Hawthorne	2.00	.90	.25
☐ 17 Brian Holloway	2.00	.90	.25
☐ 18 Craig James	3.00	1.35	.35
☐ 19 Eric Jordan	2.00	.90	.25
☐ 20 Roland James	2.00	.90	.25
☐ 21 Fred Marion	2.50	1.10	.30
☐ 22 Trevor Matich	2.00	.90	.25
☐ 23 Rod McSwain	2.00	.90	.25
☐ 24 Guy Morriss	2.00	.90	.25
☐ 25 Steve Nelson	2.00	.90	.25
☐ 26 Dennis Owens	2.00	.90	.25
☐ 27 Eugene Profit	2.00	.90	.25
☐ 28 Tom Ramsey	2.00	.90	.25
☐ 29 Johnny Rembert	2.00	.90	.25
☐ 30 Ed Reynolds	2.50	1.10	.30
☐ 31 Mike Ruth	2.00	.90	.25
☐ 32 Stephen Starring	2.00	.90	.25
☐ 33 Willie Scott	2.00	.90	.25
☐ 34 Mosi Tatupu	2.50	1.10	.30
☐ 35 Andre Tippett	3.00	1.35	.35
☐ 36 Garin Veris	2.50	1.10	.30
☐ 37 Robert Weathers	2.00	.90	.25
☐ 38 Brent Williams	2.50	1.10	.30
☐ 39 Derwin Williams	2.00	.90	.25
☐ 40 Toby Williams	2.00	.90	.25
☐ 41 Ron Wooten	2.00	.90	.25

1988 Patriots Holsum

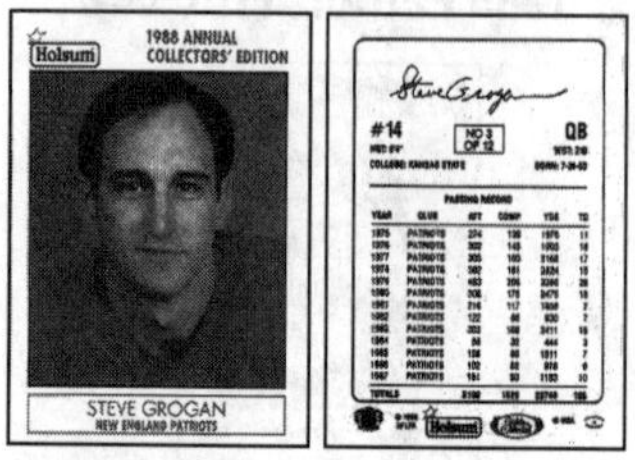

This 12-card standard-size full-color set features players of the New England Patriots; cards were available only in Holsum Bread packages. The set was co-produced by Mike Schechter Associates on behalf of the NFL Players Association. Card fronts have a color photo within a green border and the backs are printed in black ink on white card stock.

	MINT	NRMT	EXC
COMPLETE SET (12)	45.00	20.00	5.50
COMMON CARD (1-12)	4.00	1.80	.50
☐ 1 Andre Tippett	5.00	2.20	.60
☐ 2 Stanley Morgan	6.00	2.70	.75
☐ 3 Steve Grogan	6.00	2.70	.75
☐ 4 Ronnie Lippett	4.00	1.80	.50
☐ 5 Kenneth Sims	4.00	1.80	.50
☐ 6 Pete Brock	4.00	1.80	.50
☐ 7 Sean Farrell	4.00	1.80	.50
☐ 8 Garin Veris	4.00	1.80	.50
☐ 9 Mosi Tatupu	4.00	1.80	.50
☐ 10 Raymond Clayborn	5.00	2.20	.60
☐ 11 Tony Franklin	4.00	1.80	.50
☐ 12 Reggie Dupard	4.00	1.80	.50

1988 Walter Payton Commemorative

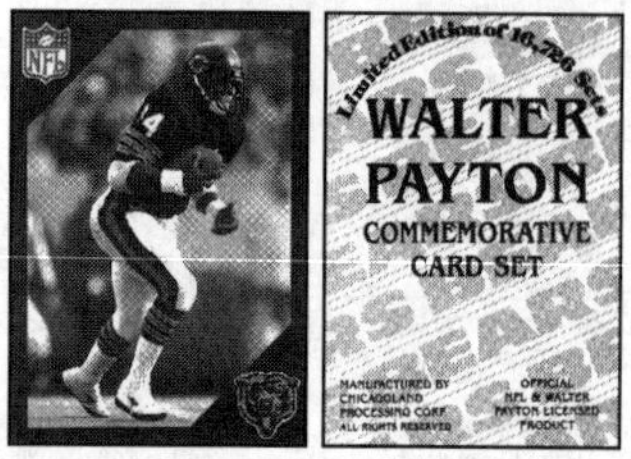

Each of the 132 standard-size cards in this set pictures and features Walter Payton in some aspect of his great career. Cards listed below are generally listed by the title on the card back. Each set was packaged inside its own numbered dark blue plastic box. Card fronts carry the NFL logo in the upper left corner and the Bears logo in the lower right corner. The set was issued in conjunction with a soft-cover book, "Sweetness".

	MINT	NRMT	EXC
COMPLETE SET (132)	45.00	20.00	5.50
COMMON CARD (1-132)	.50	.23	.06
☐ 1 Leading Scorer in NCAA History	1.00	.45	.12
☐ 2 1975 Game-by-Game	.50	.23	.06
☐ 3 Vs. New York Jets	.50	.23	.06
☐ 4 Vs. Miami Dolphins	.50	.23	.06
☐ 5 Vs. Baltimore/	.50	.23	.06
☐ 6 Vs. Buffalo Bills	.50	.23	.06
☐ 7 Vs. New England Patriots	.50	.23	.06
☐ 8 Vs. Houston Oilers	.50	.23	.06
☐ 9 Vs. Pittsburgh Steelers	.50	.23	.06
☐ 10 Vs. Cincinnati Bengals	.50	.23	.06
☐ 11 Vs. Cleveland Browns	.50	.23	.06
☐ 12 Vs. Kansas City Chiefs	.50	.23	.06
☐ 13 Vs. Oakland/	.50	.23	.06
☐ 14 Vs. San Diego Chargers	.50	.23	.06
☐ 15 Vs. Denver Broncos	.50	.23	.06
☐ 16 Vs. Seattle Seahawks	.50	.23	.06
☐ 17 Vs. Washington Redskins	.50	.23	.06
☐ 18 Vs. New York Giants	.50	.23	.06
☐ 19 Vs. Dallas Cowboys	.50	.23	.06
☐ 20 Vs. St. Louis Cardinals	.50	.23	.06
☐ 21 Vs. Philadelphia Eagles	.50	.23	.06
☐ 22 Vs. New Orleans Saints	.50	.23	.06
☐ 23 Vs. Atlanta Falcons	.50	.23	.06
☐ 24 Vs. Los Angeles Rams	.50	.23	.06
☐ 25 Vs. San Francisco 49ers	.50	.23	.06
☐ 26 Vs. Detroit Lions	.50	.23	.06
☐ 27 Vs. Minnesota Vikings	.50	.23	.06
☐ 28 Vs. Tampa Bay Buccaneers	.50	.23	.06
☐ 29 Vs. Green Bay Packers	.50	.23	.06
☐ 30 1976 Game-By-Game	.50	.23	.06
☐ 31 Appears in Nine Pro Bowls	.50	.23	.06
☐ 32 Post-Season Stats	.50	.23	.06
☐ 33 Owns 23 Bear Records	.50	.23	.06
☐ 34 Season-by-Season Statistics	.50	.23	.06
☐ 35 1977 Game-By-Game	.50	.23	.06
☐ 36 NFL Record for Most Yards Gained, Rushing	.50	.23	.06
☐ 37 NFL Record for Most Combined Yards, Career	.50	.23	.06
☐ 38 NFL Record for Most Rushing Touchdowns	.50	.23	.06
☐ 39 NFL Record for Most Games, 100 Yards Rushing, Career	.50	.23	.06
☐ 40 NFL Record for Most Consecutive Combined 2000-Yard Seasons (3)	.50	.23	.06
☐ 41 NFL Record for Most Yards Gained, Rushing, Game (275)	.50	.23	.06
☐ 42 NFL Record for Most Rushing Attempts, Career (3838)	.50	.23	.06
☐ 43 NFL Record for Most Combined Attempts, Career (4347)	.50	.23	.06
☐ 44 NFL Record for Most Seasons, 1000 Yards Rushing (10)	.50	.23	.06
☐ 45 1978 Game-By-Game	.50	.23	.06
☐ 46 The Top 10 Average Per Carry Days 1 vs. Saints 12/14/80	.50	.23	.06
☐ 47 The Top 10 Average Per Carry Days 2 vs. Broncos 9/9/84	.50	.23	.06
☐ 48 The Top 10 Average Per Carry Days 3 at Green Bay 10/30/77	.50	.23	.06
☐ 49 The Top 10 Average Per Carry Days 4 vs. Vikings 9/9/79	.50	.23	.06
☐ 50 The Top 10 Average Per Carry Days 5 vs. Minnesota 10/10/76	.50	.23	.06
☐ 51 The Top 10 Average Per Carry Days 6 vs. Saints 10/2/76	.50	.23	.06
☐ 52 The Top 10 Average Per Carry Days 7 at Denver 10/16/78	.50	.23	.06
☐ 53 The Top 10 Average Per Carry Days 8 at San Francisco 10/28/79	.50	.23	.06
☐ 54 The Top 10 Average Per Carry Days 9 vs. Lions 9/18/77	.50	.23	.06
☐ 55 The Top 10 Average Per Carry Days 10 at Tampa Bay 11/9/86	.50	.23	.06
☐ 56 1979 Game-By-Game	.50	.23	.06
☐ 57 In Training Didn't Play Until 11th Grade	.50	.23	.06
☐ 58 In Training Running the Hill	.50	.23	.06
☐ 59 In Training Jumping Rope	.50	.23	.06
☐ 60 In Training	.50	.23	.06
☐ 61 Personal Life Interests include ...	.50	.23	.06
☐ 62 Personal Life Corporate Spokesman	.50	.23	.06
☐ 63 Personal Life Family Man	.50	.23	.06
☐ 64 Personal Life Relatives in NFL	.50	.23	.06
☐ 65 Personal Life "Sweetness" autobiography written, 1978	.50	.23	.06
☐ 66 Personal Life National Committee for Prevention of Child Abuse	.50	.23	.06
☐ 67 Personal Life Chicago 1986 Sports Father of the Year	.50	.23	.06
☐ 68 Personal Life Active in Many Charities	.50	.23	.06
☐ 69 Personal Life Parade Grand Marshall	.50	.23	.06
☐ 70 1980 Game-By-Game	.50	.23	.06
☐ 71 Nobody Did It Better 1976 TSN NFC Player of the Year	.50	.23	.06
☐ 72 Nobody Did It Better 1976 Chicago Red Cloud Athlete of the Year	.50	.23	.06
☐ 73 Nobody Did It Better 1977 UPI Athlete of the Year	.50	.23	.06
☐ 74 Nobody Did It Better 1977 PFWA NFL MVP	.50	.23	.06
☐ 75 Nobody Did It Better 1977 UPI and TSN NFC Player of the Year	.50	.23	.06
☐ 76 Nobody Did It Better 1977 All Pro Pick AP, UPI, and NEA	.50	.23	.06
☐ 77 Nobody Did It Better 1977 PFWA, NEA, Mutual Radio, AP, FB Digest, Sport Magazine NFL Player of the Year	.50	.23	.06
☐ 78 Nobody Did It Better TSN NFC All-Star 1976-79	.50	.23	.06
☐ 79 Nobody Did It Better TSN NFL All-Star 1980, 1984, and 1985	.50	.23	.06
☐ 80 1981 Game-By-Game	.50	.23	.06
☐ 81 As Quarterback	.50	.23	.06
☐ 82 Kickoff Return	.50	.23	.06
☐ 83 Complete Player	.50	.23	.06
☐ 84 Touchdown	.50	.23	.06
☐ 85 1982 Game-By-Game	.50	.23	.06
☐ 86 Most Consecutive Games, Career (176)	.50	.23	.06
☐ 87 Five Longest Runs	.50	.23	.06
☐ 88 Pass Receiving	.50	.23	.06
☐ 89 Ditka On Payton	1.00	.45	.12
☐ 90 1983 Game-By-Game	.50	.23	.06
☐ 91 Breaks Career Rushing Record 10/7/84	.50	.23	.06
☐ 92 Breaks Career Rushing	.50	.23	.06
☐ 93 Breaks Career Rushing	.50	.23	.06
☐ 94 Breaks Career Rushing	.50	.23	.06
☐ 95 1984 Game-By-Game	.50	.23	.06
☐ 96 Bears Win 1985 NFC Championship over Rams	.50	.23	.06
☐ 97 Super Bowl XX	.50	.23	.06
☐ 98 Super Bowl XX	.50	.23	.06
☐ 99 Super Bowl XX	.50	.23	.06
☐ 100 Super Bowl XX	.50	.23	.06
☐ 101 1985 Game-By-Game	.50	.23	.06
☐ 102 Sweetness	.50	.23	.06
☐ 103 Sweetness Unanimous Choice to Pro Bowl Squad 1977	.50	.23	.06
☐ 104 Sweetness	.50	.23	.06
☐ 105 Sweetness 1979 Pro Bowl Starter, AP All-NFC	.50	.23	.06
☐ 106 Sweetness	.50	.23	.06
☐ 107 Sweetness	.50	.23	.06
☐ 108 Sweetness	.50	.23	.06
☐ 109 Sweetness	.50	.23	.06
☐ 110 1986 Game-By-Game	.50	.23	.06
☐ 111 Final Season Goodbye to Green Bay	.50	.23	.06
☐ 112 Final Season	.50	.23	.06
☐ 113 Last Regular Season Home Game	.50	.23	.06
☐ 114 Last Regular Season Home Game Number Retired	.50	.23	.06
☐ 115 Last Regular Season Home Game Presented with Portrait	.50	.23	.06
☐ 116 Last Regular Season Home Game	.50	.23	.06
☐ 117 Last Regular Season Home Game Soldier Field Has Been Known as Payton's Place	.50	.23	.06
☐ 118 Last Regular Season Home Game	.50	.23	.06
☐ 119 Last Regular Season Game vs. Raiders	.50	.23	.06
☐ 120 Last Regular Season Game	.50	.23	.06
☐ 121 Last Regular Season Game, Catches Two Passes	.50	.23	.06
☐ 122 Last Regular Season Game	.50	.23	.06
☐ 123 Last Regular Season Game	.50	.23	.06
☐ 124 Last Regular Season Game, Plays 190th Game, Bears' All-Time Record	.50	.23	.06
☐ 125 Last Regular Season Game	.50	.23	.06
☐ 126 Last Regular Season Game, Ends Career with 21,803 Combined Yards	.50	.23	.06
☐ 127 Last Regular Season Game, Finishes With 4542 Career Receiving Yards	.50	.23	.06
☐ 128 Last Regular Season Game, 16,726 Career Rushing Yards	.50	.23	.06
☐ 129 1987 Game-By-Game	.50	.23	.06
☐ 130 The End Of An Era	.50	.23	.06
☐ 131 Thanks For The Memories	.50	.23	.06
☐ 132 Last Few Moments	1.00	.45	.12

1976 Pepsi Discs

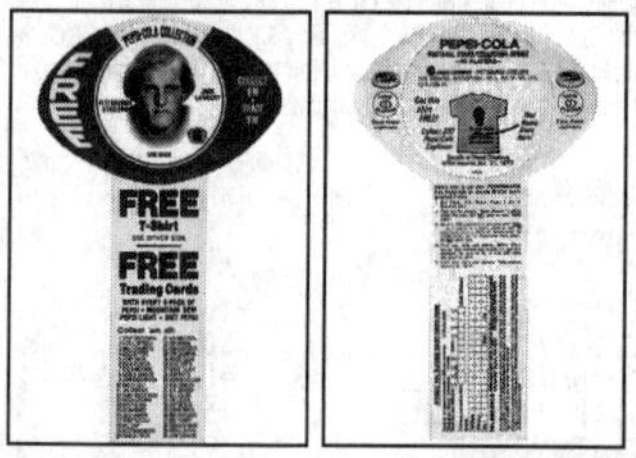

The 1976 Pepsi Discs set contains 40 numbered discs, each measuring approximately 3 1/2" in diameter. Each disc has a player photo, biographical information, and 1975 statistics. Disc numbers 1-20 are from many different teams and are known as "All-Stars." Numbers 21-40 feature Cincinnati Bengals, since this set was a regional issue produced in the Cincinnati area. Numbers 1, 5, 7, 8, and 14 are much scarcer than the other 35 and are marked SP in the

checklist below. Ed Marinaro also exists as a New York Jet, which is very difficult to find. It has been reported that Ed Marinaro may be a sixth SP. The checklist for the set is printed on the tab; the checklist below values the discs with the tabs intact as that is the way they are most commonly found.

	NRMT-MT	EXC	G-VG
COMPLETE SET (40)	140.00	65.00	17.50
COMMON CARD (1-40)	1.00	.45	.12
☐ 1 Steve Bartkowski SP	20.00	9.00	2.50
☐ 2 Lydell Mitchell	1.50	.70	.19
☐ 3 Wally Chambers	1.00	.45	.12
☐ 4 Doug Buffone	1.00	.45	.12
☐ 5 Jerry Sherk SP	25.00	11.00	3.10
☐ 6 Drew Pearson	2.50	1.10	.30
☐ 7 Otis Armstrong SP	15.00	6.75	1.85
☐ 8 Charlie Sanders SP	15.00	6.75	1.85
☐ 9 John Brockington	1.50	.70	.19
☐ 10 Curley Culp	1.50	.70	.19
☐ 11 Jan Stenerud	2.00	.90	.25
☐ 12 Lawrence McCutcheon	1.50	.70	.19
☐ 13 Chuck Foreman	2.00	.90	.25
☐ 14 Bob Pollard SP	15.00	6.75	1.85
☐ 15 Ed Marinaro	12.00	5.50	1.50
☐ 16 Jack Lambert	7.50	3.40	.95
☐ 17 Terry Metcalf	1.50	.70	.19
☐ 18 Mel Gray	1.50	.70	.19
☐ 19 Russ Washington	1.00	.45	.12
☐ 20 Charley Taylor	2.50	1.10	.30
☐ 21 Ken Anderson	2.50	1.10	.30
☐ 22 Bob Brown DT	1.00	.45	.12
☐ 23 Ron Carpenter	1.00	.45	.12
☐ 24 Tommy Casanova	1.50	.70	.19
☐ 25 Boobie Clark	1.50	.70	.19
☐ 26 Isaac Curtis	1.50	.70	.19
☐ 27 Lenvil Elliott	1.00	.45	.12
☐ 28 Stan Fritts	1.00	.45	.12
☐ 29 Vern Holland	1.00	.45	.12
☐ 30 Bob Johnson	1.50	.70	.19
☐ 31 Ken Johnson	1.00	.45	.12
☐ 32 Bill Kollar	1.00	.45	.12
☐ 33 Jim LeClair	1.00	.45	.12
☐ 34 Chip Myers	1.00	.45	.12
☐ 35 Lemar Parrish	1.50	.70	.19
☐ 36 Ron Pritchard	1.00	.45	.12
☐ 37 Bob Trumpy	2.00	.90	.25
☐ 38 Sherman White	1.00	.45	.12
☐ 39 Archie Griffin	2.00	.90	.25
☐ 40 John Shinners	1.00	.45	.12

1964 Philadelphia

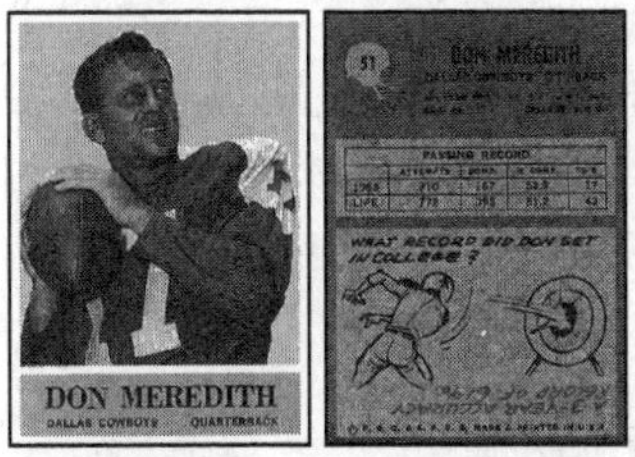

The 1964 Philadelphia Gum set of 198 standard-size cards, featuring National Football League players, is the first of four annual issues released by the company. The cards were issued in one-card penny packs, six-card nickel packs, as well as cello packs. Each card has a question about that player in a cartoon at the bottom of the reverse; the answer is given upside down in blue ink. Each team has a team picture card as well as a card diagramming one of the team's plays; this "play card" shows a small black and white picture of the team's coach on the front of the card. The card backs are printed in blue and black on a gray card stock. Within each team group the players are arranged alphabetically by last name. The two checklist cards erroneously say "Official 1963 Checklist" at the top. The key Rookie Cards in this set are Herb Adderley, Willie Davis, Jim Johnson, John Mackey and Merlin Olsen. Tatoo Transfers sheets were included as inserts in packs.

	NRMT	VG-E	GOOD
COMPLETE SET (198)	900.00	400.00	110.00
COMMON CARD (1-198)	2.50	1.10	.30
WRAPPER (1-CENT)	35.00	16.00	4.40
WRAPPER (5-CENT)	15.00	6.75	1.85
☐ 1 Raymond Berry	20.00	9.00	2.50
☐ 2 Tom Gilburg	2.50	1.10	.30
☐ 3 John Mackey	30.00	13.50	3.70
☐ 4 Gino Marchetti	5.00	2.20	.60
☐ 5 Jim Martin	2.50	1.10	.30
☐ 6 Tom Matte	6.00	2.70	.75
☐ 7 Jimmy Orr	2.50	1.10	.30
☐ 8 Jim Parker	5.00	2.20	.60
☐ 9 Bill Pellington	2.50	1.10	.30
☐ 10 Alex Sandusky	2.50	1.10	.30
☐ 11 Dick Szymanski	2.50	1.10	.30
☐ 12 John Unitas	45.00	20.00	5.50
☐ 13 Baltimore Colts Team Card	3.00	1.35	.35
☐ 14 Baltimore Colts Play Card (Don Shula)	35.00	16.00	4.40
☐ 15 Doug Atkins	5.00	2.20	.60
☐ 16 Ron Bull	2.50	1.10	.30
☐ 17 Mike Ditka	40.00	18.00	5.00
☐ 18 Joe Fortunato	2.50	1.10	.30
☐ 19 Willie Galimore	3.00	1.35	.35
☐ 20 Joe Marconi	2.50	1.10	.30
☐ 21 Bennie McRae	2.50	1.10	.30
☐ 22 Johnny Morris	2.50	1.10	.30
☐ 23 Richie Petitbon	3.00	1.35	.35
☐ 24 Mike Pyle	2.50	1.10	.30
☐ 25 Roosevelt Taylor	5.00	2.20	.60
☐ 26 Bill Wade	3.00	1.35	.35
☐ 27 Chicago Bears Team Card	3.00	1.35	.35
☐ 28 Chicago Bears Play Card (George Halas)	12.00	5.50	1.50
☐ 29 Johnny Brewer	2.50	1.10	.30
☐ 30 Jim Brown	80.00	36.00	10.00
☐ 31 Gary Collins	8.00	3.60	1.00
☐ 32 Vince Costello	2.50	1.10	.30
☐ 33 Galen Fiss	2.50	1.10	.30
☐ 34 Bill Glass	2.50	1.10	.30
☐ 35 Ernie Green	3.00	1.35	.35
☐ 36 Rich Kreitling	2.50	1.10	.30
☐ 37 John Morrow	2.50	1.10	.30
☐ 38 Frank Ryan	3.00	1.35	.35
☐ 39 Charlie Scales	2.50	1.10	.30
☐ 40 Dick Schafrath	2.50	1.10	.30
☐ 41 Cleveland Browns Team Card	3.00	1.35	.35
☐ 42 Cleveland Browns Play Card (Blanton Collier)	2.50	1.10	.30
☐ 43 Don Bishop	2.50	1.10	.30
☐ 44 Frank Clarke	3.00	1.35	.35
☐ 45 Mike Connelly	2.50	1.10	.30
☐ 46 Lee Folkins	2.50	1.10	.30
☐ 47 Cornell Green	6.00	2.70	.75
☐ 48 Bob Lilly	40.00	18.00	5.00
☐ 49 Amos Marsh	2.50	1.10	.30
☐ 50 Tommy McDonald	3.00	1.35	.35
☐ 51 Don Meredith	30.00	13.50	3.70
☐ 52 Pettis Norman	3.00	1.35	.35
☐ 53 Don Perkins	3.00	1.35	.35
☐ 54 Guy Reese	2.50	1.10	.30
☐ 55 Dallas Cowboys Team Card	3.00	1.35	.35
☐ 56 Dallas Cowboys Play Card (Tom Landry)	16.00	7.25	2.00
☐ 57 Terry Barr	2.50	1.10	.30
☐ 58 Roger Brown	3.00	1.35	.35
☐ 59 Gail Cogdill	2.50	1.10	.30
☐ 60 John Gordy	2.50	1.10	.30
☐ 61 Dick Lane	5.00	2.20	.60
☐ 62 Yale Lary	4.00	1.80	.50
☐ 63 Dan Lewis	2.50	1.10	.30
☐ 64 Darris McCord	2.50	1.10	.30
☐ 65 Earl Morrall	3.00	1.35	.35
☐ 66 Joe Schmidt	5.00	2.20	.60
☐ 67 Pat Studstill	3.00	1.35	.35
☐ 68 Wayne Walker	3.00	1.35	.35
☐ 69 Detroit Lions Team Card	3.00	1.35	.35
☐ 70 Detroit Lions Play Card (George Wilson CO)	2.50	1.10	.30
☐ 71 Herb Adderley	30.00	13.50	3.70
☐ 72 Willie Davis	30.00	13.50	3.70
☐ 73 Forrest Gregg	5.00	2.20	.60
☐ 74 Paul Hornung	35.00	16.00	4.40
☐ 75 Hank Jordan	5.00	2.20	.60
☐ 76 Jerry Kramer	6.00	2.70	.75
☐ 77 Tom Moore	3.00	1.35	.35
☐ 78 Jim Ringo UER (Green Bay on front, Philadelphia on back)	5.00	2.20	.60
☐ 79 Bart Starr	45.00	20.00	5.50
☐ 80 Jim Taylor	20.00	9.00	2.50
☐ 81 Jesse Whittenton	3.00	1.35	.35
☐ 82 Willie Wood	8.00	3.60	1.00
☐ 83 Green Bay Packers Team Card	5.00	2.20	.60
☐ 84 Green Bay Packers Play Card (Vince Lombardi)	30.00	13.50	3.70
☐ 85 Jon Arnett	3.00	1.35	.35
☐ 86 Pervis Atkins	2.50	1.10	.30
☐ 87 Dick Bass	3.00	1.35	.35
☐ 88 Carroll Dale	3.00	1.35	.35
☐ 89 Roman Gabriel	6.00	2.70	.75
☐ 90 Ed Meador	2.50	1.10	.30
☐ 91 Merlin Olsen	45.00	20.00	5.50
☐ 92 Jack Pardee	5.00	2.20	.60
☐ 93 Jim Phillips	2.50	1.10	.30
☐ 94 Carver Shannon	2.50	1.10	.30
☐ 95 Frank Varrichione	2.50	1.10	.30
☐ 96 Danny Villanueva	2.50	1.10	.30
☐ 97 Los Angeles Rams Team Card	3.00	1.35	.35
☐ 98 Los Angeles Rams Play Card (Harland Svare)	2.50	1.10	.30
☐ 99 Grady Alderman	3.00	1.35	.35
☐ 100 Larry Bowie	2.50	1.10	.30
☐ 101 Bill Brown	6.00	2.70	.75
☐ 102 Paul Flatley	2.50	1.10	.30
☐ 103 Rip Hawkins	2.50	1.10	.30
☐ 104 Jim Marshall	8.00	3.60	1.00
☐ 105 Tommy Mason	3.00	1.35	.35
☐ 106 Jim Prestel	2.50	1.10	.30
☐ 107 Jerry Reichow	2.50	1.10	.30
☐ 108 Ed Sharockman	2.50	1.10	.30
☐ 109 Fran Tarkenton	25.00	11.00	3.10
☐ 110 Mick Tingelhoff	5.00	2.20	.60
☐ 111 Minnesota Vikings Team Card	3.00	1.35	.35
☐ 112 Minnesota Vikings Play Card (Norm Van Brocklin)	4.00	1.80	.50
☐ 113 Erich Barnes	2.50	1.10	.30
☐ 114 Roosevelt Brown	4.00	1.80	.50
☐ 115 Don Chandler	2.50	1.10	.30
☐ 116 Darrell Dess	2.50	1.10	.30
☐ 117 Frank Gifford	30.00	13.50	3.70
☐ 118 Dick James	2.50	1.10	.30
☐ 119 Jim Katcavage	2.50	1.10	.30
☐ 120 John Lovetere	2.50	1.10	.30
☐ 121 Dick Lynch	3.00	1.35	.35
☐ 122 Jim Patton	2.50	1.10	.30
☐ 123 Del Shofner	3.00	1.35	.35
☐ 124 Y.A. Tittle	20.00	9.00	2.50
☐ 125 New York Giants Team Card	3.00	1.35	.35
☐ 126 New York Giants Play Card (Allie Sherman)	2.50	1.10	.30
☐ 127 Sam Baker	2.50	1.10	.30
☐ 128 Maxie Baughan	2.50	1.10	.30
☐ 129 Timmy Brown	3.00	1.35	.35
☐ 130 Mike Clark	2.50	1.10	.30
☐ 131 Irv Cross	3.00	1.35	.35
☐ 132 Ted Dean	2.50	1.10	.30
☐ 133 Ron Goodwin	2.50	1.10	.30
☐ 134 King Hill	2.50	1.10	.30
☐ 135 Clarence Peaks	2.50	1.10	.30
☐ 136 Pete Retzlaff	3.00	1.35	.35
☐ 137 Jim Schrader	2.50	1.10	.30
☐ 138 Norm Snead	3.00	1.35	.35
☐ 139 Philadelphia Eagles Team Card	3.00	1.35	.35
☐ 140 Philadelphia Eagles Play Card (Nick Skorich)	2.50	1.10	.30
☐ 141 Gary Ballman	2.50	1.10	.30
☐ 142 Charley Bradshaw	2.50	1.10	.30
☐ 143 Ed Brown	3.00	1.35	.35
☐ 144 John Henry Johnson	5.00	2.20	.60
☐ 145 Joe Krupa	2.50	1.10	.30
☐ 146 Bill Mack	2.50	1.10	.30
☐ 147 Lou Michaels	2.50	1.10	.30
☐ 148 Buzz Nutter	2.50	1.10	.30
☐ 149 Myron Pottios	2.50	1.10	.30
☐ 150 John Reger	2.50	1.10	.30
☐ 151 Mike Sandusky	2.50	1.10	.30
☐ 152 Clendon Thomas	2.50	1.10	.30
☐ 153 Pittsburgh Steelers Team Card	3.00	1.35	.35
☐ 154 Pittsburgh Steelers Play Card (Buddy Parker)	2.50	1.10	.30
☐ 155 Kermit Alexander	3.00	1.35	.35
☐ 156 Bernie Casey	3.00	1.35	.35
☐ 157 Dan Colchico	2.50	1.10	.30
☐ 158 Clyde Conner	2.50	1.10	.30
☐ 159 Tommy Davis	2.50	1.10	.30
☐ 160 Matt Hazeltine	2.50	1.10	.30
☐ 161 Jim Johnson	16.00	7.25	2.00
☐ 162 Don Lisbon	2.50	1.10	.30
☐ 163 Lamar McHan	2.50	1.10	.30
☐ 164 Bob St. Clair	4.00	1.80	.50
☐ 165 J.D. Smith	2.50	1.10	.30
☐ 166 Abe Woodson	2.50	1.10	.30
☐ 167 San Francisco 49ers Team Card	3.00	1.35	.35
☐ 168 San Francisco 49ers Play Card (Red Hickey)	2.50	1.10	.30
☐ 169 Garland Boyette UER (Photo on front is not Boyette)	2.50	1.10	.30
☐ 170 Bobby Joe Conrad	3.00	1.35	.35
☐ 171 Bob DeMarco	2.50	1.10	.30
☐ 172 Ken Gray	2.50	1.10	.30
☐ 173 Jimmy Hill	2.50	1.10	.30
☐ 174 Charlie Johnson UER (Misspelled Charley on both sides)	3.00	1.35	.35
☐ 175 Ernie McMillan	2.50	1.10	.30
☐ 176 Dale Meinert	2.50	1.10	.30
☐ 177 Luke Owens	2.50	1.10	.30
☐ 178 Sonny Randle	2.50	1.10	.30
☐ 179 Joe Robb	2.50	1.10	.30
☐ 180 Bill Stacy	2.50	1.10	.30
☐ 181 St. Louis Cardinals Team Card	3.00	1.35	.35
☐ 182 St. Louis Cardinals Play Card (Wally Lemm)	2.50	1.10	.30
☐ 183 Bill Barnes	2.50	1.10	.30
☐ 184 Don Bosseler	2.50	1.10	.30
☐ 185 Sam Huff	6.00	2.70	.75
☐ 186 Sonny Jurgensen	18.00	8.00	2.20
☐ 187 Bob Khayat	2.50	1.10	.30
☐ 188 Riley Mattson	2.50	1.10	.30
☐ 189 Bobby Mitchell	6.00	2.70	.75
☐ 190 John Nisby	2.50	1.10	.30
☐ 191 Vince Promuto	2.50	1.10	.30
☐ 192 Joe Rutgens	2.50	1.10	.30
☐ 193 Lonnie Sanders	2.50	1.10	.30
☐ 194 Jim Steffen	2.50	1.10	.30
☐ 195 Washington Redskins Team Card	3.00	1.35	.35
☐ 196 Washington Redskins Play Card (Bill McPeak)	2.50	1.10	.30
☐ 197 Checklist 1 UER (Dated 1963)	30.00	13.50	3.70
☐ 198 Checklist 2 UER (Dated 1963, 174 Charley Johnson should be Charlie)	55.00	25.00	7.00

1965 Philadelphia

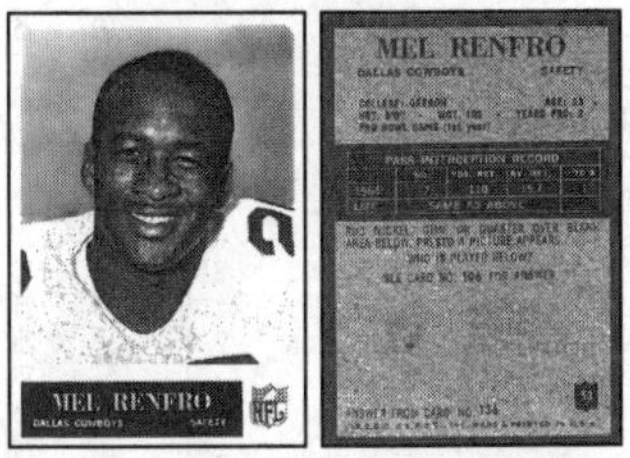

The 1965 Philadelphia Gum set of NFL players consists of 198 standard-size cards. The cards were issued in six-card nickel packs and cello packs. The card fronts have the player's name, team name and position in a black box beneath the photo. The NFL logo is at bottom right. The card backs feature statistics and a question and answer section that requires a coin to rub and reveal the answer. The card backs are printed in maroon on a gray card stock. Each team has a team picture card as well as a card featuring a diagram of one of the team's plays; this play card shows a small coach's picture in black and white on the front of the card. The card backs are printed in maroon on a gray card stock. The cards are numbered within team with the players arranged alphabetically by last name. The key Rookie Cards in this set are Carl Eller, Paul Krause, Mel Renfro, Charley Taylor, and Paul Warfield. Comic Transfers sheets were included as inserts into packs.

	NRMT	VG-E	GOOD
COMPLETE SET (198)	800.00	350.00	100.00
COMMON CARD (1-198)	2.00	.90	.25
WRAPPER (5-CENT)	15.00	6.75	1.85
☐ 1 Baltimore Colts Team Card	14.00	6.25	1.75
☐ 2 Raymond Berry	8.00	3.60	1.00
☐ 3 Bob Boyd	2.00	.90	.25
☐ 4 Wendell Harris	2.00	.90	.25
☐ 5 Jerry Logan	2.00	.90	.25
☐ 6 Tony Lorick	2.00	.90	.25
☐ 7 Lou Michaels	2.00	.90	.25
☐ 8 Lenny Moore	8.00	3.60	1.00
☐ 9 Jimmy Orr	3.00	1.35	.35
☐ 10 Jim Parker	4.00	1.80	.50
☐ 11 Dick Szymanski	2.00	.90	.25
☐ 12 John Unitas	35.00	16.00	4.40
☐ 13 Bob Vogel	2.00	.90	.25
☐ 14 Baltimore Colts Play Card (Don Shula)	20.00	9.00	2.50
☐ 15 Chicago Bears Team Card	3.00	1.35	.35
☐ 16 Jon Arnett	2.00	.90	.25
☐ 17 Doug Atkins	5.00	2.20	.60
☐ 18 Rudy Bukich	3.00	1.35	.35
☐ 19 Mike Ditka	30.00	13.50	3.70
☐ 20 Dick Evey	2.00	.90	.25
☐ 21 Joe Fortunato	2.00	.90	.25
☐ 22 Bobby Joe Green	2.00	.90	.25
☐ 23 Johnny Morris	2.00	.90	.25
☐ 24 Mike Pyle	2.00	.90	.25
☐ 25 Roosevelt Taylor	3.00	1.35	.35
☐ 26 Bill Wade	3.00	1.35	.35
☐ 27 Bob Wetoska	2.00	.90	.25
☐ 28 Chicago Bears Play Card (George Halas)	8.00	3.60	1.00
☐ 29 Cleveland Browns Team Card	3.00	1.35	.35
☐ 30 Walter Beach	2.00	.90	.25
☐ 31 Jim Brown	70.00	32.00	8.75
☐ 32 Gary Collins	3.00	1.35	.35
☐ 33 Bill Glass	2.00	.90	.25
☐ 34 Ernie Green	2.00	.90	.25
☐ 35 Jim Houston	2.00	.90	.25
☐ 36 Dick Modzelewski	2.00	.90	.25
☐ 37 Bernie Parrish	2.00	.90	.25
☐ 38 Walter Roberts	2.00	.90	.25

☐ 39 Frank Ryan	3.00	1.35	.35
☐ 40 Dick Schafrath	2.00	.90	.25
☐ 41 Paul Warfield	75.00	34.00	9.50
☐ 42 Cleveland Browns Play Card (Blanton Collier)	2.00	.90	.25
☐ 43 Dallas Cowboys Team Card UER (Cowboys Dallas on back)	3.00	1.35	.35
☐ 44 Frank Clarke	3.00	1.35	.35
☐ 45 Mike Connelly	2.00	.90	.25
☐ 46 Buddy Dial	2.00	.90	.25
☐ 47 Bob Lilly	25.00	11.00	3.10
☐ 48 Tony Liscio	2.00	.90	.25
☐ 49 Tommy McDonald	3.00	1.35	.35
☐ 50 Don Meredith	25.00	11.00	3.10
☐ 51 Pettis Norman	2.00	.90	.25
☐ 52 Don Perkins	3.00	1.35	.35
☐ 53 Mel Renfro	35.00	16.00	4.40
☐ 54 Jim Ridlon	2.00	.90	.25
☐ 55 Jerry Tubbs	2.00	.90	.25
☐ 56 Dallas Cowboys Play Card (Tom Landry)	12.00	5.50	1.50
☐ 57 Detroit Lions Team Card	3.00	1.35	.35
☐ 58 Terry Barr	2.00	.90	.25
☐ 59 Roger Brown	2.00	.90	.25
☐ 60 Gail Cogdill	2.00	.90	.25
☐ 61 Jim Gibbons	2.00	.90	.25
☐ 62 John Gordy	2.00	.90	.25
☐ 63 Yale Lary	4.00	1.80	.50
☐ 64 Dick LeBeau	3.00	1.35	.35
☐ 65 Earl Morrall	3.00	1.35	.35
☐ 66 Nick Pietrosante	2.00	.90	.25
☐ 67 Pat Studstill	2.00	.90	.25
☐ 68 Wayne Walker	3.00	1.35	.35
☐ 69 Tom Watkins	2.00	.90	.25
☐ 70 Detroit Lions Play Card (George Wilson CO)	2.00	.90	.25
☐ 71 Green Bay Packers Team Card	5.00	2.20	.60
☐ 72 Herb Adderley	8.00	3.60	1.00
☐ 73 Willie Davis	8.00	3.60	1.00
☐ 74 Boyd Dowler	3.00	1.35	.35
☐ 75 Forrest Gregg	5.00	2.20	.60
☐ 76 Paul Hornung	30.00	13.50	3.70
☐ 77 Hank Jordan	5.00	2.20	.60
☐ 78 Tom Moore	3.00	1.35	.35
☐ 79 Ray Nitschke	16.00	7.25	2.00
☐ 80 Elijah Pitts	8.00	3.60	1.00
☐ 81 Bart Starr	35.00	16.00	4.40
☐ 82 Jim Taylor	20.00	9.00	2.50
☐ 83 Willie Wood	6.00	2.70	.75
☐ 84 Green Bay Packers Play Card (Vince Lombardi)	18.00	8.00	2.20
☐ 85 Los Angeles Rams Team Card	3.00	1.35	.35
☐ 86 Dick Bass	3.00	1.35	.35
☐ 87 Roman Gabriel	5.00	2.20	.60
☐ 88 Roosevelt Grier	4.00	1.80	.50
☐ 89 Deacon Jones	10.00	4.50	1.25
☐ 90 Lamar Lundy	4.00	1.80	.50
☐ 91 Marlin McKeever	2.00	.90	.25
☐ 92 Ed Meador	2.00	.90	.25
☐ 93 Bill Munson	4.00	1.80	.50
☐ 94 Merlin Olsen	16.00	7.25	2.00
☐ 95 Bobby Smith	2.00	.90	.25
☐ 96 Frank Varrichione	2.00	.90	.25
☐ 97 Ben Wilson	2.00	.90	.25
☐ 98 Los Angeles Rams Play Card (Harland Svare)	2.00	.90	.25
☐ 99 Minnesota Vikings Team Card	3.00	1.35	.35
☐ 100 Grady Alderman	2.00	.90	.25
☐ 101 Hal Bedsole	2.00	.90	.25
☐ 102 Bill Brown	3.00	1.35	.35
☐ 103 Bill Butler	2.00	.90	.25
☐ 104 Fred Cox	3.00	1.35	.35
☐ 105 Carl Eller	25.00	11.00	3.10
☐ 106 Paul Flatley	2.00	.90	.25
☐ 107 Jim Marshall	6.00	2.70	.75
☐ 108 Tommy Mason	2.00	.90	.25
☐ 109 George Rose	2.00	.90	.25
☐ 110 Fran Tarkenton	20.00	9.00	2.50
☐ 111 Mick Tingelhoff	3.00	1.35	.35
☐ 112 Minnesota Vikings Play Card (Norm Van Brocklin)	4.00	1.80	.50
☐ 113 New York Giants Team Card	3.00	1.35	.35
☐ 114 Erich Barnes	2.00	.90	.25
☐ 115 Roosevelt Brown	4.00	1.80	.50
☐ 116 Clarence Childs	2.00	.90	.25
☐ 117 Jerry Hillebrand	2.00	.90	.25
☐ 118 Greg Larson	2.00	.90	.25
☐ 119 Dick Lynch	2.00	.90	.25
☐ 120 Joe Morrison	4.00	1.80	.50
☐ 121 Lou Slaby	2.00	.90	.25
☐ 122 Aaron Thomas	2.00	.90	.25
☐ 123 Steve Thurlow	2.00	.90	.25
☐ 124 Ernie Wheelwright	2.00	.90	.25
☐ 125 Gary Wood	2.00	.90	.25
☐ 126 New York Giants Play Card (Allie Sherman)	2.00	.90	.25
☐ 127 Philadelphia Eagles Team Card	3.00	1.35	.35
☐ 128 Sam Baker	2.00	.90	.25
☐ 129 Maxie Baughan	2.00	.90	.25
☐ 130 Timmy Brown	3.00	1.35	.35
☐ 131 Jack Concannon	2.00	.90	.25
☐ 132 Irv Cross	3.00	1.35	.35
☐ 133 Earl Gros	2.00	.90	.25
☐ 134 Dave Lloyd	2.00	.90	.25
☐ 135 Floyd Peters	2.00	.90	.25
☐ 136 Nate Ramsey	2.00	.90	.25
☐ 137 Pete Retzlaff	3.00	1.35	.35
☐ 138 Jim Ringo	4.00	1.80	.50
☐ 139 Norm Snead	3.00	1.35	.35
☐ 140 Philadelphia Eagles Play Card (Joe Kuharich)	2.00	.90	.25
☐ 141 Pittsburgh Steelers Team Card	3.00	1.35	.35
☐ 142 John Baker	2.00	.90	.25
☐ 143 Gary Ballman	2.00	.90	.25
☐ 144 Charley Bradshaw	2.00	.90	.25
☐ 145 Ed Brown	2.00	.90	.25
☐ 146 Dick Haley	2.00	.90	.25
☐ 147 John Henry Johnson	5.00	2.20	.60
☐ 148 Brady Keys	2.00	.90	.25
☐ 149 Ray Lemek	2.00	.90	.25
☐ 150 Ben McGee	2.00	.90	.25
☐ 151 Clarence Peaks	2.00	.90	.25
☐ 152 Myron Pottios	2.00	.90	.25
☐ 153 Clendon Thomas	2.00	.90	.25
☐ 154 Pittsburgh Steelers Play Card (Buddy Parker)	2.00	.90	.25
☐ 155 St. Louis Cardinals Team Card	3.00	1.35	.35
☐ 156 Jim Bakken	3.00	1.35	.35
☐ 157 Joe Childress	2.00	.90	.25
☐ 158 Bobby Joe Conrad	3.00	1.35	.35
☐ 159 Bob DeMarco	2.00	.90	.25
☐ 160 Pat Fischer	4.00	1.80	.50
☐ 161 Irv Goode	2.00	.90	.25
☐ 162 Ken Gray	2.00	.90	.25
☐ 163 Charlie Johnson UER (Misspelled Charley on both sides)	3.00	1.35	.35
☐ 164 Bill Koman	2.00	.90	.25
☐ 165 Dale Meinert	2.00	.90	.25
☐ 166 Jerry Stovall	3.00	1.35	.35
☐ 167 Abe Woodson	2.00	.90	.25
☐ 168 St. Louis Cardinals Play Card (Wally Lemm)	2.00	.90	.25
☐ 169 San Francisco 49ers Team Card	3.00	1.35	.35
☐ 170 Kermit Alexander	2.00	.90	.25
☐ 171 John Brodie	10.00	4.50	1.25
☐ 172 Bernie Casey	3.00	1.35	.35
☐ 173 John David Crow	3.00	1.35	.35
☐ 174 Tommy Davis	2.00	.90	.25
☐ 175 Matt Hazeltine	2.00	.90	.25
☐ 176 Jim Johnson	4.00	1.80	.50
☐ 177 Charlie Krueger	2.00	.90	.25
☐ 178 Roland Lakes	2.00	.90	.25
☐ 179 George Mira	3.00	1.35	.35
☐ 180 Dave Parks	3.00	1.35	.35
☐ 181 John Thomas	2.00	.90	.25
☐ 182 San Francisco 49ers Play Card (Jack Christiansen)	2.00	.90	.25
☐ 183 Washington Redskins Team Card	3.00	1.35	.35
☐ 184 Pervis Atkins	2.00	.90	.25
☐ 185 Preston Carpenter	2.00	.90	.25
☐ 186 Angelo Coia	2.00	.90	.25
☐ 187 Sam Huff	6.00	2.70	.75
☐ 188 Sonny Jurgensen	14.00	6.25	1.75
☐ 189 Paul Krause	16.00	7.25	2.00
☐ 190 Jim Martin	2.00	.90	.25
☐ 191 Bobby Mitchell	5.00	2.20	.60
☐ 192 John Nisby	2.00	.90	.25
☐ 193 John Paluck	2.00	.90	.25
☐ 194 Vince Promuto	2.00	.90	.25
☐ 195 Charley Taylor	50.00	22.00	6.25
☐ 196 Washington Redskins Play Card (Bill McPeak)	2.00	.90	.25
☐ 197 Checklist 1	30.00	13.50	3.70
☐ 198 Checklist 2 UER (163 Charley Johnson should be Charlie)	50.00	22.00	6.25

1966 Philadelphia

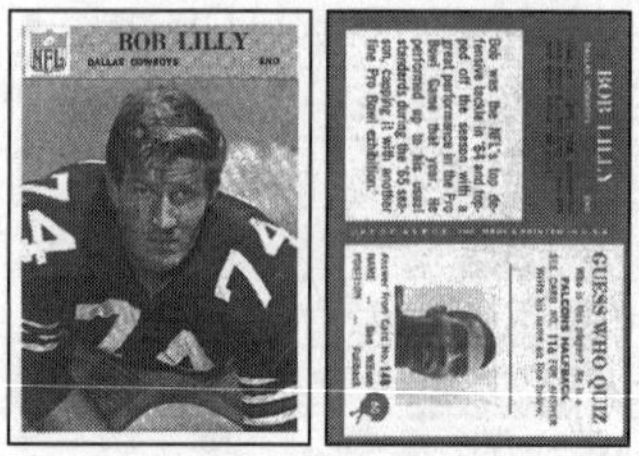

The 1966 Philadelphia Gum football card set contains 198 standard-size cards featuring NFL players. The cards were issued in six-card nickel packs and cello packs. The card fronts feature the player's name, team name and position in a color bar above the photo. The NFL logo is at upper left. The card backs are printed in green and black on a white card stock. The backs contain the player's name, a card number, a short biography, and a "Guess Who" quiz. The quiz answer is found on another card. The last two cards in the set are checklist cards. Each team's "play card" shows a color photo of actual game action, described on the back. The cards are numbered within team with the players arranged alphabetically by last name. The set features the debut of Hall of Fame Chicago Bears' greats Dick Butkus and Gale Sayers. Other Rookie Cards include Cowboys Bob Hayes and Chuck Howley. Comic Transfers sheets were included as inserts into packs.

	NRMT	VG-E	GOOD
COMPLETE SET (198)	900.00	400.00	110.00
COMMON CARD (1-198)	2.00	.90	.25
WRAPPER (5-CENT)	15.00	6.75	1.85
☐ 1 Atlanta Falcons Insignia	12.00	5.50	1.50
☐ 2 Larry Benz	2.00	.90	.25
☐ 3 Dennis Claridge	2.00	.90	.25
☐ 4 Perry Lee Dunn	2.00	.90	.25
☐ 5 Dan Grimm	2.00	.90	.25
☐ 6 Alex Hawkins	2.00	.90	.25
☐ 7 Ralph Heck	2.00	.90	.25
☐ 8 Frank Lasky	2.00	.90	.25
☐ 9 Guy Reese	2.00	.90	.25
☐ 10 Bob Richards	2.00	.90	.25
☐ 11 Ron Smith	2.00	.90	.25
☐ 12 Ernie Wheelwright	2.00	.90	.25
☐ 13 Atlanta Falcons Roster	3.00	1.35	.35
☐ 14 Baltimore Colts Team Card	3.00	1.35	.35
☐ 15 Raymond Berry	8.00	3.60	1.00
☐ 16 Bob Boyd	2.00	.90	.25
☐ 17 Jerry Logan	2.00	.90	.25
☐ 18 John Mackey	7.00	3.10	.85
☐ 19 Tom Matte	3.00	1.35	.35
☐ 20 Lou Michaels	2.00	.90	.25
☐ 21 Lenny Moore	8.00	3.60	1.00
☐ 22 Jimmy Orr	2.00	.90	.25
☐ 23 Jim Parker	3.50	1.55	.45
☐ 24 John Unitas	35.00	16.00	4.40
☐ 25 Bob Vogel	2.00	.90	.25
☐ 26 Baltimore Colts Play Card (Lenny Moore Jim Parker)	3.50	1.55	.45
☐ 27 Chicago Bears Team Card	3.00	1.35	.35
☐ 28 Doug Atkins	4.00	1.80	.50
☐ 29 Rudy Bukich	2.00	.90	.25
☐ 30 Ron Bull	2.00	.90	.25
☐ 31 Dick Butkus	225.00	100.00	28.00
☐ 32 Mike Ditka	30.00	13.50	3.70
☐ 33 Joe Fortunato	2.00	.90	.25
☐ 34 Bobby Joe Green	2.00	.90	.25
☐ 35 Roger LeClerc	2.00	.90	.25
☐ 36 Johnny Morris	2.00	.90	.25
☐ 37 Mike Pyle	2.00	.90	.25
☐ 38 Gale Sayers	200.00	90.00	25.00
☐ 39 Chicago Bears Play Card (Gale Sayers)	30.00	13.50	3.70
☐ 40 Cleveland Browns Team Card	3.00	1.35	.35
☐ 41 Jim Brown	70.00	32.00	8.75
☐ 42 Gary Collins	3.00	1.35	.35
☐ 43 Ross Fichtner	2.00	.90	.25
☐ 44 Ernie Green	2.00	.90	.25
☐ 45 Gene Hickerson	3.00	1.35	.35
☐ 46 Jim Houston	2.00	.90	.25
☐ 47 John Morrow	2.00	.90	.25
☐ 48 Walter Roberts	2.00	.90	.25
☐ 49 Frank Ryan	3.00	1.35	.35
☐ 50 Dick Schafrath	2.00	.90	.25
☐ 51 Paul Wiggin	2.00	.90	.25
☐ 52 Cleveland Browns Play Card (Ernie Green sweep)	2.00	.90	.25
☐ 53 Dallas Cowboys Team Card	3.00	1.35	.35
☐ 54 George Andrie UER (Text says startling, should be starting)	2.00	.90	.25
☐ 55 Frank Clarke	3.00	1.35	.35
☐ 56 Mike Connelly	2.00	.90	.25
☐ 57 Cornell Green	3.00	1.35	.35
☐ 58 Bob Hayes	45.00	20.00	5.50
☐ 59 Chuck Howley	14.00	6.25	1.75
☐ 60 Bob Lilly	18.00	8.00	2.20
☐ 61 Don Meredith	25.00	11.00	3.10
☐ 62 Don Perkins	3.00	1.35	.35
☐ 63 Mel Renfro	10.00	4.50	1.25
☐ 64 Danny Villanueva	2.00	.90	.25
☐ 65 Dallas Cowboys Play Card (Danny Villanueva)	2.00	.90	.25
☐ 66 Detroit Lions Team Card	3.00	1.35	.35
☐ 67 Roger Brown	2.00	.90	.25
☐ 68 John Gordy	2.00	.90	.25
☐ 69 Alex Karras	10.00	4.50	1.25
☐ 70 Dick LeBeau	2.00	.90	.25
☐ 71 Amos Marsh	2.00	.90	.25
☐ 72 Milt Plum	3.00	1.35	.35
☐ 73 Bobby Smith	2.00	.90	.25
☐ 74 Wayne Rasmussen	2.00	.90	.25
☐ 75 Pat Studstill	2.00	.90	.25
☐ 76 Wayne Walker	2.00	.90	.25
☐ 77 Tom Watkins	2.00	.90	.25
☐ 78 Detroit Lions Play Card (George Izo pass)	2.00	.90	.25
☐ 79 Green Bay Packers Team Card	4.00	1.80	.50
☐ 80 Herb Adderley UER (Adderly on back)	6.00	2.70	.75
☐ 81 Lee Roy Caffey	3.50	1.55	.45
☐ 82 Don Chandler	3.00	1.35	.35
☐ 83 Willie Davis	6.00	2.70	.75
☐ 84 Boyd Dowler	3.00	1.35	.35
☐ 85 Forrest Gregg	4.00	1.80	.50
☐ 86 Tom Moore	3.00	1.35	.35
☐ 87 Ray Nitschke	12.00	5.50	1.50
☐ 88 Bart Starr	35.00	16.00	4.40
☐ 89 Jim Taylor	20.00	9.00	2.50
☐ 90 Willie Wood	5.00	2.20	.60
☐ 91 Green Bay Packers Play Card (Don Chandler FG)	2.00	.90	.25
☐ 92 Los Angeles Rams Team Card	3.00	1.35	.35
☐ 93 Willie Brown WR	2.00	.90	.25
☐ 94 Dick Bass and Roman Gabriel	4.00	1.80	.50
☐ 95 Bruce Gossett (Tom Landry small photo on back)	3.00	1.35	.35
☐ 96 Deacon Jones	6.00	2.70	.75
☐ 97 Tommy McDonald	3.00	1.35	.35
☐ 98 Marlin McKeever	2.00	.90	.25
☐ 99 Aaron Martin	2.00	.90	.25
☐ 100 Ed Meador	2.00	.90	.25
☐ 101 Bill Munson	3.00	1.35	.35
☐ 102 Merlin Olsen	8.00	3.60	1.00
☐ 103 Jim Stiger	2.00	.90	.25
☐ 104 Los Angeles Rams Play Card (Willie Brown run)	3.00	1.35	.35
☐ 105 Minnesota Vikings Team Card	3.00	1.35	.35
☐ 106 Grady Alderman	2.00	.90	.25
☐ 107 Bill Brown	3.00	1.35	.35
☐ 108 Fred Cox	2.00	.90	.25
☐ 109 Paul Flatley	2.00	.90	.25
☐ 110 Rip Hawkins	2.00	.90	.25
☐ 111 Tommy Mason	2.00	.90	.25
☐ 112 Ed Sharockman	2.00	.90	.25
☐ 113 Gordon Smith	2.00	.90	.25
☐ 114 Fran Tarkenton	20.00	9.00	2.50
☐ 115 Mick Tingelhoff	3.00	1.35	.35
☐ 116 Bobby Walden	2.00	.90	.25
☐ 117 Minnesota Vikings Play Card (Bill Brown run)	2.00	.90	.25
☐ 118 New York Giants Team Card	3.00	1.35	.35
☐ 119 Roosevelt Brown	3.50	1.55	.45
☐ 120 Henry Carr	3.00	1.35	.35
☐ 121 Clarence Childs	2.00	.90	.25
☐ 122 Tucker Frederickson	3.00	1.35	.35
☐ 123 Jerry Hillebrand	2.00	.90	.25
☐ 124 Greg Larson	2.00	.90	.25
☐ 125 Spider Lockhart	3.00	1.35	.35
☐ 126 Dick Lynch	2.00	.90	.25
☐ 127 Earl Morrall and Bob Scholtz	3.00	1.35	.35
☐ 128 Joe Morrison	2.00	.90	.25
☐ 129 Steve Thurlow	2.00	.90	.25
☐ 130 New York Giants Play Card (Chuck Mercein over)	2.00	.90	.25
☐ 131 Philadelphia Eagles Team Card	3.00	1.35	.35
☐ 132 Sam Baker	2.00	.90	.25
☐ 133 Maxie Baughan	2.00	.90	.25
☐ 134 Bob Brown OT	6.00	2.70	.75
☐ 135 Timmy Brown (Lou Groza small photo on back)	3.00	1.35	.35
☐ 136 Irv Cross	3.00	1.35	.35
☐ 137 Earl Gros	2.00	.90	.25
☐ 138 Ray Poage	2.00	.90	.25
☐ 139 Nate Ramsey	2.00	.90	.25
☐ 140 Pete Retzlaff	3.00	1.35	.35
☐ 141 Jim Ringo (Joe Schmidt small photo on back)	3.50	1.55	.45
☐ 142 Norm Snead	3.00	1.35	.35

(Norm Van Brocklin
small photo on back)

☐ 143 Philadelphia Eagles	2.00	.90	.25
Play Card			
(Earl Gros tackled)			
☐ 144 Pittsburgh Steelers	3.00	1.35	.35
Team Card			
(Lee Roy Jordan small photo on back)			
☐ 145 Gary Ballman	2.00	.90	.25
☐ 146 Charley Bradshaw	2.00	.90	.25
☐ 147 Jim Butler	2.00	.90	.25
☐ 148 Mike Clark	2.00	.90	.25
☐ 149 Dick Hoak	2.00	.90	.25
☐ 150 Roy Jefferson	3.00	1.35	.35
☐ 151 Frank Lambert	2.00	.90	.25
☐ 152 Mike Lind	2.00	.90	.25
☐ 153 Bill Nelsen	4.00	1.80	.50
☐ 154 Clarence Peaks	2.00	.90	.25
☐ 155 Clendon Thomas	2.00	.90	.25
☐ 156 Pittsburgh Steelers	2.00	.90	.25
Play Card			
(Gary Ballman scores)			
☐ 157 St. Louis Cardinals	3.00	1.35	.35
Team Card			
☐ 158 Jim Bakken	2.00	.90	.25
☐ 159 Bobby Joe Conrad	3.00	1.35	.35
☐ 160 Willis Crenshaw	2.00	.90	.25
☐ 161 Bob DeMarco	2.00	.90	.25
☐ 162 Pat Fischer	3.00	1.35	.35
☐ 163 Charlie Johnson UER	3.00	1.35	.35
(Misspelled Charley on both sides)			
☐ 164 Dale Meinert	2.00	.90	.25
☐ 165 Sonny Randle	2.00	.90	.25
☐ 166 Sam Silas	2.00	.90	.25
☐ 167 Bill Triplett	2.00	.90	.25
☐ 168 Larry Wilson	3.50	1.55	.45
☐ 169 St. Louis Cardinals	2.00	.90	.25
Play Card			
(Bill Triplett tackled by Roosevelt Davis and Roger LaLonde)			
☐ 170 San Francisco 49ers	3.00	1.35	.35
Team Card			
(Vince Lombardi small photo on back)			
☐ 171 Kermit Alexander	2.00	.90	.25
☐ 172 Bruce Bosley	2.00	.90	.25
☐ 173 John Brodie	6.00	2.70	.75
☐ 174 Bernie Casey	3.00	1.35	.35
☐ 175 John David Crow	3.00	1.35	.35
(Don Shula small photo on back)			
☐ 176 Tommy Davis	2.00	.90	.25
☐ 177 Jim Johnson	4.00	1.80	.50
☐ 178 Gary Lewis	2.00	.90	.25
☐ 179 Dave Parks	2.00	.90	.25
☐ 180 Walter Rock	3.00	1.35	.35
(Paul Hornung small photo on back)			
☐ 181 Ken Willard	4.00	1.80	.50
(George Halas small photo on back)			
☐ 182 San Francisco 49ers	2.00	.90	.25
Play Card			
(Tommy Davis FG)			
☐ 183 Washington Redskins	3.00	1.35	.35
Team Card			
☐ 184 Rickie Harris	2.00	.90	.25
☐ 185 Sonny Jurgensen	8.00	3.60	1.00
☐ 186 Paul Krause	6.00	2.70	.75
☐ 187 Bobby Mitchell	5.00	2.20	.60
☐ 188 Vince Promuto	2.00	.90	.25
☐ 189 Pat Richter	2.00	.90	.25
(Craig Morton small photo on back)			
☐ 190 Joe Rutgens	2.00	.90	.25
☐ 191 Johnny Sample	2.00	.90	.25
☐ 192 Lonnie Sanders	2.00	.90	.25
☐ 193 Jim Steffen	2.00	.90	.25
☐ 194 Charley Taylor UER	18.00	8.00	2.20
(Called Charley and Charlie on card back)			
☐ 195 Washington Redskins	2.00	.90	.25
Play Card			
(Dan Lewis tackled by Roger LaLonde)			
☐ 196 Referee Signals	3.00	1.35	.35
☐ 197 Checklist 1	25.00	11.00	3.10
☐ 198 Checklist 2 UER	50.00	22.00	6.25
(163 Charley Johnson should be Charlie)			

1967 Philadelphia

The 1967 Philadelphia Gum set of NFL players consists of 198 standard-size cards. It was the company's last issue. Cards were issued in six-card nickel packs and cello packs. This set is easily distinguished from the other Philadelphia football sets by its yellow border on the fronts of the cards. The player's name, team name and position are at the bottom in a color bar. The NFL logo is at the top right or left. Horizontally designed backs are printed in brown on a white card stock. The left side of the back contains a trivia question that requires a coin to scratch to reveal the answer. The right side has a brief write-up. The cards are numbered within team with players

arranged alphabetically by last name. The key Rookie Cards in this set are Lee Roy Jordan, Leroy Kelly, Tommy Nobis, Dan Reeves and Jackie Smith.

	NRMT	VG-E	GOOD
COMPLETE SET (198)	650.00	300.00	80.00
COMMON CARD (1-198)	2.00	.90	.25
WRAPPER (5-CENT)	15.00	6.75	1.85

☐ 1 Atlanta Falcons	10.00	4.50	1.25
Team Card			
☐ 2 Junior Coffey	3.00	1.35	.35
☐ 3 Alex Hawkins	2.00	.90	.25
☐ 4 Randy Johnson	3.00	1.35	.35
☐ 5 Lou Kirouac	2.00	.90	.25
☐ 6 Billy Martin	2.00	.90	.25
☐ 7 Tommy Nobis	20.00	9.00	2.50
☐ 8 Jerry Richardson	5.00	2.20	.60
☐ 9 Marion Rushing	2.00	.90	.25
☐ 10 Ron Smith	2.00	.90	.25
☐ 11 Ernie Wheelwright UER	2.00	.90	.25
(Misspelled Wheelright on both sides)			
☐ 12 Atlanta Falcons	2.00	.90	.25
Insignia			
☐ 13 Baltimore Colts	3.00	1.35	.35
Team Card			
☐ 14 Raymond Berry UER	7.00	3.10	.85
(Photo actually Bob Boyd)			
☐ 15 Bob Boyd	2.00	.90	.25
☐ 16 Ordell Braase	2.00	.90	.25
☐ 17 Alvin Haymond	2.00	.90	.25
☐ 18 Tony Lorick	2.00	.90	.25
☐ 19 Lenny Lyles	2.00	.90	.25
☐ 20 John Mackey	5.00	2.20	.60
☐ 21 Tom Matte	3.00	1.35	.35
☐ 22 Lou Michaels	2.00	.90	.25
☐ 23 John Unitas	30.00	13.50	3.70
☐ 24 Baltimore Colts	2.00	.90	.25
Insignia			
☐ 25 Chicago Bears	3.00	1.35	.35
Team Card			
☐ 26 Rudy Bukich UER	2.00	.90	.25
(Misspelled Buckich on card back)			
☐ 27 Ron Bull	2.00	.90	.25
☐ 28 Dick Butkus	75.00	34.00	9.50
☐ 29 Mike Ditka	25.00	11.00	3.10
☐ 30 Dick Gordon	3.00	1.35	.35
☐ 31 Roger LeClerc	2.00	.90	.25
☐ 32 Bennie McRae	2.00	.90	.25
☐ 33 Richie Petitbon	3.00	1.35	.35
☐ 34 Mike Pyle	2.00	.90	.25
☐ 35 Gale Sayers	70.00	32.00	8.75
☐ 36 Chicago Bears	2.00	.90	.25
Insignia			
☐ 37 Cleveland Browns	3.00	1.35	.35
Team Card			
☐ 38 Johnny Brewer	2.00	.90	.25
☐ 39 Gary Collins	3.00	1.35	.35
☐ 40 Ross Fichtner	2.00	.90	.25
☐ 41 Ernie Green	2.00	.90	.25
☐ 42 Gene Hickerson	2.00	.90	.25
☐ 43 Leroy Kelly	35.00	16.00	4.40
☐ 44 Frank Ryan	3.00	1.35	.35
☐ 45 Dick Schafrath	2.00	.90	.25
☐ 46 Paul Warfield	20.00	9.00	2.50
☐ 47 John Wooten	2.00	.90	.25
☐ 48 Cleveland Browns	2.00	.90	.25
Insignia			
☐ 49 Dallas Cowboys	3.00	1.35	.35
Team Card			
☐ 50 George Andrie	2.00	.90	.25
☐ 51 Cornell Green	3.00	1.35	.35
☐ 52 Bob Hayes	15.00	6.75	1.85
☐ 53 Chuck Howley	5.00	2.20	.60
☐ 54 Lee Roy Jordan	20.00	9.00	2.50
☐ 55 Bob Lilly	14.00	6.25	1.75
☐ 56 Dave Manders	3.00	1.35	.35
☐ 57 Don Meredith	25.00	11.00	3.10
☐ 58 Dan Reeves	30.00	13.50	3.70
☐ 59 Mel Renfro	6.00	2.70	.75
☐ 60 Dallas Cowboys	2.00	.90	.25
Insignia			
☐ 61 Detroit Lions	3.00	1.35	.35
Team Card			
☐ 62 Roger Brown	3.00	1.35	.35
☐ 63 Gail Cogdill	2.00	.90	.25
☐ 64 John Gordy	2.00	.90	.25
☐ 65 Ron Kramer	2.00	.90	.25
☐ 66 Dick LeBeau	2.00	.90	.25
☐ 67 Mike Lucci	4.00	1.80	.50

☐ 68 Amos Marsh	2.00	.90	.25
☐ 69 Tom Nowatzke	2.00	.90	.25
☐ 70 Pat Studstill	2.00	.90	.25
☐ 71 Karl Sweetan	2.00	.90	.25
☐ 72 Detroit Lions	2.00	.90	.25
Insignia			
☐ 73 Green Bay Packers	4.00	1.80	.50
Team Card			
☐ 74 Herb Adderley UER	5.00	2.20	.60
(Adderly on back)			
☐ 75 Lee Roy Caffey	3.00	1.35	.35
☐ 76 Willie Davis	5.00	2.20	.60
☐ 77 Forrest Gregg	4.00	1.80	.50
☐ 78 Hank Jordan	4.00	1.80	.50
☐ 79 Ray Nitschke	10.00	4.50	1.25
☐ 80 Dave Robinson	6.00	2.70	.75
☐ 81 Bob Skoronski	3.00	1.35	.35
☐ 82 Bart Starr	30.00	13.50	3.70
☐ 83 Willie Wood	4.00	1.80	.50
☐ 84 Green Bay Packers	2.00	.90	.25
Insignia			
☐ 85 Los Angeles Rams	3.00	1.35	.35
Team Card			
☐ 86 Dick Bass	3.00	1.35	.35
☐ 87 Maxie Baughan	2.00	.90	.25
☐ 88 Roman Gabriel	3.50	1.55	.45
☐ 89 Bruce Gossett	2.00	.90	.25
☐ 90 Deacon Jones	5.00	2.20	.60
☐ 91 Tommy McDonald	3.00	1.35	.35
☐ 92 Marlin McKeever	2.00	.90	.25
☐ 93 Tom Moore	2.00	.90	.25
☐ 94 Merlin Olsen	6.00	2.70	.75
☐ 95 Clancy Williams	2.00	.90	.25
☐ 96 Los Angeles Rams	2.00	.90	.25
Insignia			
☐ 97 Minnesota Vikings	3.00	1.35	.35
Team Card			
☐ 98 Grady Alderman	2.00	.90	.25
☐ 99 Bill Brown	3.00	1.35	.35
☐ 100 Fred Cox	2.00	.90	.25
☐ 101 Paul Flatley	2.00	.90	.25
☐ 102 Dale Hackbart	2.00	.90	.25
☐ 103 Jim Marshall	4.00	1.80	.50
☐ 104 Tommy Mason	2.00	.90	.25
☐ 105 Milt Sunde	2.00	.90	.25
☐ 106 Fran Tarkenton	18.00	8.00	2.20
☐ 107 Mick Tingelhoff	3.00	1.35	.35
☐ 108 Minnesota Vikings	2.00	.90	.25
Insignia			
☐ 109 New York Giants	3.00	1.35	.35
Team Card			
☐ 110 Henry Carr	2.00	.90	.25
☐ 111 Clarence Childs	2.00	.90	.25
☐ 112 Allen Jacobs	2.00	.90	.25
☐ 113 Homer Jones	3.00	1.35	.35
☐ 114 Tom Kennedy	2.00	.90	.25
☐ 115 Spider Lockhart	2.00	.90	.25
☐ 116 Joe Morrison	2.00	.90	.25
☐ 117 Francis Peay	2.00	.90	.25
☐ 118 Jeff Smith	2.00	.90	.25
☐ 119 Aaron Thomas	2.00	.90	.25
☐ 120 New York Giants	2.00	.90	.25
Insignia			
☐ 121 New Orleans Saints	2.00	.90	.25
Insignia			
(See also card 132)			
☐ 122 Charley Bradshaw	2.00	.90	.25
☐ 123 Paul Hornung	22.00	10.00	2.70
☐ 124 Elbert Kimbrough	2.00	.90	.25
☐ 125 Earl Leggett	2.00	.90	.25
☐ 126 Obert Logan	2.00	.90	.25
☐ 127 Riley Mattson	2.00	.90	.25
☐ 128 John Morrow	2.00	.90	.25
☐ 129 Bob Scholtz	2.00	.90	.25
☐ 130 Dave Whitsell	2.00	.90	.25
☐ 131 Gary Wood	2.00	.90	.25
☐ 132 New Orleans Saints	3.00	1.35	.35
Roster UER			
(121 on back)			
☐ 133 Philadelphia Eagles	3.00	1.35	.35
Team Card			
☐ 134 Sam Baker	2.00	.90	.25
☐ 135 Bob Brown OT	3.00	1.35	.35
☐ 136 Timmy Brown	3.00	1.35	.35
☐ 137 Earl Gros	2.00	.90	.25
☐ 138 Dave Lloyd	2.00	.90	.25
☐ 139 Floyd Peters	2.00	.90	.25
☐ 140 Pete Retzlaff	3.00	1.35	.35
☐ 141 Joe Scarpati	2.00	.90	.25
☐ 142 Norm Snead	3.00	1.35	.35
☐ 143 Jim Skaggs	2.00	.90	.25
☐ 144 Philadelphia Eagles	2.00	.90	.25
Insignia			
☐ 145 Pittsburgh Steelers	3.00	1.35	.35
Team Card			
☐ 146 Bill Asbury	2.00	.90	.25
☐ 147 John Baker	2.00	.90	.25
☐ 148 Gary Ballman	2.00	.90	.25
☐ 149 Mike Clark	2.00	.90	.25
☐ 150 Riley Gunnels	2.00	.90	.25
☐ 151 John Hilton	2.00	.90	.25
☐ 152 Roy Jefferson	3.00	1.35	.35
☐ 153 Brady Keys	2.00	.90	.25
☐ 154 Ben McGee	2.00	.90	.25
☐ 155 Bill Nelsen	3.00	1.35	.35

☐ 156 Pittsburgh Steelers	2.00	.90	.25
Insignia			
☐ 157 St. Louis Cardinals	3.00	1.35	.35
Team Card			
☐ 158 Jim Bakken	2.00	.90	.25
☐ 159 Bobby Joe Conrad	3.00	1.35	.35
☐ 160 Ken Gray	2.00	.90	.25
☐ 161 Charlie Johnson UER	3.00	1.35	.35
(Misspelled Charley on both sides)			
☐ 162 Joe Robb	2.00	.90	.25
☐ 163 Johnny Roland	3.00	1.35	.35
☐ 164 Roy Shivers	2.00	.90	.25
☐ 165 Jackie Smith	16.00	7.25	2.00
☐ 166 Jerry Stovall	2.00	.90	.25
☐ 167 Larry Wilson	3.50	1.55	.45
☐ 168 St. Louis Cardinals	2.00	.90	.25
Insignia			
☐ 169 San Francisco 49ers	3.00	1.35	.35
Team Card			
☐ 170 Kermit Alexander	2.00	.90	.25
☐ 171 Bruce Bosley	2.00	.90	.25
☐ 172 John Brodie	6.00	2.70	.75
☐ 173 Bernie Casey	3.00	1.35	.35
☐ 174 Tommy Davis	2.00	.90	.25
☐ 175 Howard Mudd	2.00	.90	.25
☐ 176 Dave Parks	2.00	.90	.25
☐ 177 John Thomas	2.00	.90	.25
☐ 178 Dave Wilcox	4.00	1.80	.50
☐ 179 Ken Willard	3.00	1.35	.35
☐ 180 San Francisco 49ers	2.00	.90	.25
Insignia			
☐ 181 Washington Redskins	3.00	1.35	.35
Team Card			
☐ 182 Charlie Gogolak	3.00	1.35	.35
☐ 183 Chris Hanburger	8.00	3.60	1.00
☐ 184 Len Hauss	3.00	1.35	.35
☐ 185 Sonny Jurgensen	7.00	3.10	.85
☐ 186 Bobby Mitchell	5.00	2.20	.60
☐ 187 Brig Owens	2.00	.90	.25
☐ 188 Jim Shorter	2.00	.90	.25
☐ 189 Jerry Smith	3.00	1.35	.35
☐ 190 Charley Taylor	8.00	3.60	1.00
☐ 191 A.D. Whitfield	2.00	.90	.25
☐ 192 Washington Redskins	2.00	.90	.25
Insignia			
☐ 193 Cleveland Browns	6.00	2.70	.75
Play Card			
(Leroy Kelly)			
☐ 194 New York Giants	2.00	.90	.25
Play Card			
(Joe Morrison)			
☐ 195 Atlanta Falcons	2.00	.90	.25
Play Card			
(Ernie Wheelright)			
☐ 196 Referee Signals	3.00	1.35	.35
☐ 197 Checklist 1	20.00	9.00	2.50
☐ 198 Checklist 2 UER	40.00	18.00	5.00
(161 Charley Johnson should be Charlie)			

1991 Pinnacle Promo Panels

These (approximately) 5" by 7" promo panels each feature four cards to show the design of the 1991 Pinnacle series cards. They were introduced and initially distributed at the Super Bowl XXVI Card Show. The cards, which would measure the standard size if cut, display two color photos on a black panel with white borders. The backs carry a color cut-out action shot, biography, player profile, and statistics. The cards are numbered on the back as in the regular series; the panels themselves, however, are unnumbered. The panels are listed below alphabetically according to the player's name on the card featured at upper left corner of each panel.

	MINT	NRMT	EXC
COMPLETE SET (18)	100.00	45.00	12.50
COMMON PANEL (1-18)	3.00	1.35	.35

☐ 1 John Alt	3.00	1.35	.35
Eric Green			
Don Mosebar			
Greg Townsend			
☐ 2 Bruce Armstrong	12.00	5.50	1.50
Joe Montana			
Jim Lachey			
Bruce Matthews			
☐ 3 Don Beebe	4.00	1.80	.50
Irving Fryar			
Ricky Proehl			
Vinny Testaverde			
☐ 4 Duane Bickett	3.00	1.35	.35
Tony Bennett			

John Friesz			
Rob Burnett			
☐ 5 Mark Bortz	4.00	1.80	.50
Warren Moon			
Jim Breech			
Eric Metcalf			
☐ 6 Roger Craig	3.00	1.35	.35
Issiac Holt			
Kevin Mack			
Shane Conlan			
☐ 7 Wendell Davis	3.00	1.35	.35
Gaston Green			
Tony Mandarich			
Merril Hoge			
☐ 8 Dermontti Dawson	3.00	1.35	.35
Jerry Gray			
Nick Lowery			
Scott Case			
☐ 9 Chris Doleman	10.00	4.50	1.25
Troy Aikman			
Sterling Sharpe			
Sean Landeta			
☐ 10 Darryl Henley	4.00	1.80	.50
Karl Mecklenburg			
Sam Mills			
Rod Woodson			
☐ 11 Mark Higgs	4.00	1.80	.50
Jay Schroeder			
Mark Carrier DB			
Jim Everett			
☐ 12 Jay Hilgenburg	20.00	9.00	2.50
Dan Marino			
Anthony Carter			
Howie Long			
☐ 13 Louis Lipps	4.00	1.80	.50
John Offerdahl			
Herschel Walker			
Jeff George			
☐ 14 Greg McMurtry	4.00	1.80	.50
Henry Ellard			
Brian Mitchell			
Mark Clayton			
☐ 15 Nate Odomes	3.00	1.35	.35
Allen Pinkett			
Don Majkowski			
Dave Meggett			
☐ 16 Andre Rison	4.00	1.80	.50
Jeff Hostetler			
Hugh Millen			
Jack Del Rio			
☐ 17 Emmit Smith	20.00	9.00	2.50
Dennis Smith			
Bill Brooks			
Bobby Hebert			
☐ 18 Reyna Thompson	4.00	1.80	.50
Louis Oliver			
Steve Broussard			
Andre Reed			

1991 Pinnacle

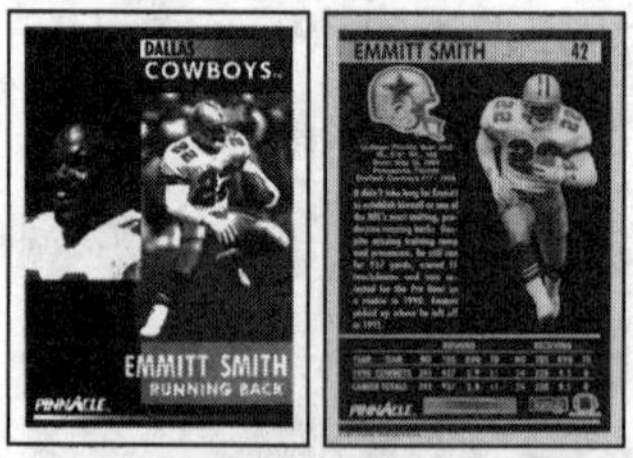

The premier edition of the 1991 Pinnacle set contains 415 standard-size cards. Cards were issued in 12-card packs. The front design of the veteran player cards features two color photos, an action photo and a head shot, on a black background with white borders. The card backs have a color action shot superimposed on a black background. The rookie cards have the same design, except with a green background on the front, and head shots rather than action shots on the back. The backs also include a biography, player profile, and statistics (where appropriate). The set includes 58 rookies (253, 281-336, 393) and four special cards. Special subsets featured are Head to Head (351-355), Technicians (356-362), Gamewinners (363-371), Idols (372-386), and Sideline (394-415). A patented anti-counterfeit device appears on the bottom border of each card back. Rookie Cards in this set include Bryan Cox, Lawrence Dawsey, Ricky Ervins, Jeff Graham, Randal Hill, Russell Maryland, Bryce Paup, Eric Pegram, Mike Pritchard, Leonard Russell, and Harvey Williams. An Emmitt Smith promo card was produced as well and listed below. It can be differentiated from the regular issue Smith card by the mention of his "holdout" on the cardback.

	MINT	NRMT	EXC
COMPLETE SET (415)	25.00	11.00	3.10
COMMON CARD (1-415)	.10	.05	.01

☐ 1 Warren Moon	.40	.18	.05
☐ 2 Morten Andersen	.10	.05	.01
☐ 3 Rohn Stark	.10	.05	.01
☐ 4 Mark Bortz	.10	.05	.01
☐ 5 Mark Higgs	.10	.05	.01
☐ 6 Troy Aikman	3.00	1.35	.35
☐ 7 John Elway	2.50	1.10	.30
☐ 8 Neal Anderson	.20	.09	.03
☐ 9 Chris Doleman	.10	.05	.01
☐ 10 Jay Schroeder	.10	.05	.01
☐ 11 Sterling Sharpe	.40	.18	.05
☐ 12 Steve DeBerg	.10	.05	.01
☐ 13 Ronnie Lott	.20	.09	.03
☐ 14 Sean Landeta	.10	.05	.01
☐ 15 Jim Everett	.20	.09	.03
☐ 16 Jim Breech	.10	.05	.01
☐ 17 Barry Foster	.20	.09	.03
☐ 18 Mike Merriweather	.10	.05	.01
☐ 19 Eric Metcalf	.20	.09	.03
☐ 20 Mark Carrier DB	.20	.09	.03
☐ 21 James Brooks	.20	.09	.03
☐ 22 Nate Odomes	.10	.05	.01
☐ 23 Rodney Hampton	.40	.18	.05
☐ 24 Chris Miller	.20	.09	.03
☐ 25 Roger Craig	.20	.09	.03
☐ 26 Louis Oliver	.10	.05	.01
☐ 27 Allen Pinkett	.10	.05	.01
☐ 28 Bubby Brister	.10	.05	.01
☐ 29 Reyna Thompson	.10	.05	.01
☐ 30 Issiac Holt	.10	.05	.01
☐ 31 Steve Broussard	.10	.05	.01
☐ 32 Christian Okoye	.10	.05	.01
☐ 33 Dave Meggett	.20	.09	.03
☐ 34 Andre Reed	.20	.09	.03
☐ 35 Shane Conlan	.10	.05	.01
☐ 36 Eric Ball	.10	.05	.01
☐ 37 Johnny Bailey	.10	.05	.01
☐ 38 Don Majkowski	.10	.05	.01
☐ 39 Gerald Williams	.10	.05	.01
☐ 40 Kevin Mack	.10	.05	.01
☐ 41 Jeff Herrod	.10	.05	.01
☐ 42 Emmitt Smith	6.00	2.70	.75
☐ 43 Wendell Davis	.10	.05	.01
☐ 44 Lorenzo White	.10	.05	.01
☐ 45 Andre Rison	.20	.09	.03
☐ 46 Jerry Gray	.10	.05	.01
☐ 47 Dennis Smith	.10	.05	.01
☐ 48 Gaston Green	.10	.05	.01
☐ 49 Dermontti Dawson	.10	.05	.01
☐ 50 Jeff Hostetler	.20	.09	.03
☐ 51 Nick Lowery	.10	.05	.01
☐ 52 Merril Hoge	.10	.05	.01
☐ 53 Bobby Hebert	.10	.05	.01
☐ 54 Scott Case	.10	.05	.01
☐ 55 Jack Del Rio	.10	.05	.01
☐ 56 Cornelius Bennett	.20	.09	.03
☐ 57 Tony Mandarich	.10	.05	.01
☐ 58 Bill Brooks	.10	.05	.01
☐ 59 Jessie Tuggle	.10	.05	.01
☐ 60 Hugh Millen	.10	.05	.01
☐ 61 Tony Bennett	.20	.09	.03
☐ 62 Cris Dishman	.10	.05	.01
☐ 63 Darryl Henley	.10	.05	.01
☐ 64 Duane Bickett	.10	.05	.01
☐ 65 Jay Hilgenberg	.10	.05	.01
☐ 66 Joe Montana	3.00	1.35	.35
☐ 67 Bill Fralic	.10	.05	.01
☐ 68 Sam Mills	.10	.05	.01
☐ 69 Bruce Armstrong	.10	.05	.01
☐ 70 Dan Marino	5.00	2.20	.60
☐ 71 Jim Lachey	.10	.05	.01
☐ 72 Rod Woodson	.40	.18	.05
☐ 73 Simon Fletcher	.10	.05	.01
☐ 74 Bruce Matthews	.20	.09	.03
☐ 75 Howie Long	.20	.09	.03
☐ 76 John Friesz	.40	.18	.05
☐ 77 Karl Mecklenburg	.10	.05	.01
☐ 78 John L. Williams UER	.10	.05	.01
(Two photos show			
42 Chris Warren)			
☐ 79 Rob Burnett	.10	.05	.01
☐ 80 Anthony Carter	.20	.09	.03
☐ 81 Henry Ellard	.20	.09	.03
☐ 82 Don Beebe	.10	.05	.01
☐ 83 Louis Lipps	.10	.05	.01
☐ 84 Greg McMurtry	.10	.05	.01
☐ 85 Will Wolford	.10	.05	.01
☐ 86 Eric Green	.10	.05	.01
☐ 87 Irving Fryar	.20	.09	.03
☐ 88 John Offerdahl	.10	.05	.01
☐ 89 John Alt	.10	.05	.01
☐ 90 Tom Tupa	.10	.05	.01
☐ 91 Don Mosebar	.10	.05	.01
☐ 92 Jeff George	.40	.18	.05
☐ 93 Vinny Testaverde	.20	.09	.03
☐ 94 Greg Townsend	.10	.05	.01
☐ 95 Derrick Fenner	.10	.05	.01
☐ 96 Brian Mitchell	.20	.09	.03
☐ 97 Herschel Walker	.20	.09	.03
☐ 98 Ricky Proehl	.10	.05	.01
☐ 99 Mark Clayton	.20	.09	.03
☐ 100 Derrick Thomas	.40	.18	.05
☐ 101 Jim Harbaugh	.40	.18	.05
☐ 102 Barry Word	.10	.05	.01
☐ 103 Jerry Rice	3.00	1.35	.35
☐ 104 Keith Byars	.10	.05	.01
☐ 105 Marion Butts	.20	.09	.03
☐ 106 Rich Moran	.10	.05	.01
☐ 107 Thurman Thomas	.40	.18	.05
☐ 108 Stephone Paige	.10	.05	.01
☐ 109 D.J. Johnson	.10	.05	.01
☐ 110 William Perry	.20	.09	.03
☐ 111 Haywood Jeffires	.20	.09	.03
☐ 112 Rodney Peete	.20	.09	.03
☐ 113 Andy Heck	.10	.05	.01
☐ 114 Kevin Ross	.10	.05	.01
☐ 115 Michael Carter	.10	.05	.01
☐ 116 Tim McKyer	.10	.05	.01
☐ 117 Kenneth Davis	.10	.05	.01
☐ 118 Richmond Webb	.10	.05	.01
☐ 119 Rich Camarillo	.10	.05	.01
☐ 120 James Francis	.10	.05	.01
☐ 121 Craig Heyward	.20	.09	.03
☐ 122 Hardy Nickerson	.20	.09	.03
☐ 123 Michael Brooks	.10	.05	.01
☐ 124 Fred Barnett	.40	.18	.05
☐ 125 Cris Carter	.40	.18	.05
☐ 126 Brian Jordan	.20	.09	.03
☐ 127 Pat Leahy	.10	.05	.01
☐ 128 Kevin Greene	.40	.18	.05
☐ 129 Trace Armstrong	.10	.05	.01
☐ 130 Eugene Lockhart	.10	.05	.01
☐ 131 Albert Lewis	.10	.05	.01
☐ 132 Ernie Jones	.10	.05	.01
☐ 133 Eric Martin	.10	.05	.01
☐ 134 Anthony Thompson	.10	.05	.01
☐ 135 Tim Krumrie	.10	.05	.01
☐ 136 James Lofton	.20	.09	.03
☐ 137 John Taylor	.20	.09	.03
☐ 138 Jeff Cross	.10	.05	.01
☐ 139 Tommy Kane	.10	.05	.01
☐ 140 Robb Thomas	.10	.05	.01
☐ 141 Gary Anderson K	.10	.05	.01
☐ 142 Mark Murphy	.10	.05	.01
☐ 143 Rickey Jackson	.10	.05	.01
☐ 144 Ken O'Brien	.10	.05	.01
☐ 145 Ernest Givins	.20	.09	.03
☐ 146 Jessie Hester	.10	.05	.01
☐ 147 Deion Sanders	2.00	.90	.25
☐ 148 Keith Henderson	.10	.05	.01
☐ 149 Chris Singleton	.10	.05	.01
☐ 150 Rod Bernstine	.10	.05	.01
☐ 151 Quinn Early	.20	.09	.03
☐ 152 Boomer Esiason	.20	.09	.03
☐ 153 Mike Gann	.10	.05	.01
☐ 154 Dino Hackett	.10	.05	.01
☐ 155 Perry Kemp	.10	.05	.01
☐ 156 Mark Ingram	.20	.09	.03
☐ 157 Daryl Johnston	1.00	.45	.12
☐ 158 Eugene Daniel	.10	.05	.01
☐ 159 Dalton Hilliard	.10	.05	.01
☐ 160 Rufus Porter	.10	.05	.01
☐ 161 Tunch Ilkin	.10	.05	.01
☐ 162 James Hasty	.10	.05	.01
☐ 163 Keith McKeller	.10	.05	.01
☐ 164 Heath Sherman	.10	.05	.01
☐ 165 Vai Sikahema	.10	.05	.01
☐ 166 Pat Terrell	.10	.05	.01
☐ 167 Anthony Munoz	.20	.09	.03
☐ 168 Brad Edwards	.10	.05	.01
☐ 169 Tom Rathman	.10	.05	.01
☐ 170 Steve McMichael	.20	.09	.03
☐ 171 Vaughan Johnson	.10	.05	.01
☐ 172 Nate Lewis	.10	.05	.01
☐ 173 Mark Rypien	.20	.09	.03
☐ 174 Rob Moore	.40	.18	.05
☐ 175 Tim Green	.10	.05	.01
☐ 176 Tony Casillas	.10	.05	.01
☐ 177 Jon Hand	.10	.05	.01
☐ 178 Todd McNair	.10	.05	.01
☐ 179 Toi Cook	.10	.05	.01
☐ 180 Eddie Brown	.10	.05	.01
☐ 181 Mark Jackson	.10	.05	.01
☐ 182 Pete Stoyanovich	.10	.05	.01
☐ 183 Bryce Paup	1.25	.55	.16
☐ 184 Anthony Miller	.20	.09	.03
☐ 185 Dan Saleaumua	.10	.05	.01
☐ 186 Guy McIntyre	.10	.05	.01
☐ 187 Broderick Thomas	.10	.05	.01
☐ 188 Frank Warren	.10	.05	.01
☐ 189 Drew Hill	.10	.05	.01
☐ 190 Reggie White	.40	.18	.05
☐ 191 Chris Hinton	.10	.05	.01
☐ 192 David Little	.10	.05	.01
☐ 193 David Fulcher	.10	.05	.01
☐ 194 Clarence Verdin	.10	.05	.01
☐ 195 Junior Seau	.75	.35	.09
☐ 196 Blair Thomas	.10	.05	.01
☐ 197 Stan Brock	.10	.05	.01
☐ 198 Gary Clark	.40	.18	.05
☐ 199 Michael Irvin	.40	.18	.05
☐ 200 Ronnie Harmon	.10	.05	.01
☐ 201 Steve Young	2.50	1.10	.30
☐ 202 Brian Noble	.10	.05	.01
☐ 203 Dan Stryzinski	.10	.05	.01
☐ 204 Darryl Talley	.10	.05	.01
☐ 205 David Alexander	.10	.05	.01
☐ 206 Pat Swilling	.20	.09	.03
☐ 207 Gary Plummer	.10	.05	.01
☐ 208 Robert Delpino	.10	.05	.01
☐ 209 Norm Johnson	.10	.05	.01
☐ 210 Mike Singletary	.20	.09	.03
☐ 211 Anthony Johnson	.40	.18	.05
☐ 212 Eric Allen	.10	.05	.01
☐ 213 Gill Fenerty	.10	.05	.01
☐ 214 Neil Smith	.40	.18	.05
☐ 215 Joe Phillips	.10	.05	.01
☐ 216 Ottis Anderson	.20	.09	.03
☐ 217 LeRoy Butler	.20	.09	.03
☐ 218 Ray Childress	.10	.05	.01
☐ 219 Rodney Holman	.10	.05	.01
☐ 220 Kevin Fagan	.10	.05	.01
☐ 221 Bruce Smith	.40	.18	.05
☐ 222 Brad Muster	.10	.05	.01
☐ 223 Mike Horan	.10	.05	.01
☐ 224 Steve Atwater	.10	.05	.01
☐ 225 Rich Gannon	.10	.05	.01
☐ 226 Anthony Pleasant	.10	.05	.01
☐ 227 Steve Jordan	.10	.05	.01
☐ 228 Lomas Brown	.10	.05	.01
☐ 229 Jackie Slater	.10	.05	.01
☐ 230 Brad Baxter	.10	.05	.01
☐ 231 Joe Morris	.10	.05	.01
☐ 232 Marcus Allen	.40	.18	.05
☐ 233 Chris Warren	.75	.35	.09
☐ 234 Johnny Johnson	.10	.05	.01
☐ 235 Phil Simms	.20	.09	.03
☐ 236 Dave Krieg	.20	.09	.03
☐ 237 Jim McMahon	.20	.09	.03
☐ 238 Richard Dent	.20	.09	.03
☐ 239 John Washington	.10	.05	.01
☐ 240 Sammie Smith	.10	.05	.01
☐ 241 Brian Brennan	.10	.05	.01
☐ 242 Cortez Kennedy	.40	.18	.05
☐ 243 Tim McDonald	.10	.05	.01
☐ 244 Charles Haley	.20	.09	.03
☐ 245 Joey Browner	.10	.05	.01
☐ 246 Eddie Murray	.10	.05	.01
☐ 247 Bob Golic	.10	.05	.01
☐ 248 Myron Guyton	.10	.05	.01
☐ 249 Dennis Byrd	.10	.05	.01
☐ 250 Barry Sanders	3.00	1.35	.35
☐ 251 Clay Matthews	.20	.09	.03
☐ 252 Pepper Johnson	.10	.05	.01
☐ 253 Eric Swann	.40	.18	.05
☐ 254 Lamar Lathon	.10	.05	.01
☐ 255 Andre Tippett	.10	.05	.01
☐ 256 Tom Newberry	.10	.05	.01
☐ 257 Kyle Clifton	.10	.05	.01
☐ 258 Leslie O'Neal	.20	.09	.03
☐ 259 Bubba McDowell	.10	.05	.01
☐ 260 Scott Davis	.10	.05	.01
☐ 261 Wilber Marshall	.10	.05	.01
☐ 262 Marv Cook	.10	.05	.01
☐ 263 Jeff Lageman	.10	.05	.01
☐ 264 Michael Young	.10	.05	.01
☐ 265 Gary Zimmerman	.10	.05	.01
☐ 266 Mike Munchak	.10	.05	.01
☐ 267 David Treadwell	.10	.05	.01
☐ 268 Steve Wisniewski	.10	.05	.01
☐ 269 Mark Duper	.20	.09	.03
☐ 270 Chris Spielman	.20	.09	.03
☐ 271 Brett Perriman	.40	.18	.05
☐ 272 Lionel Washington	.10	.05	.01
☐ 273 Lawrence Taylor	.40	.18	.05
☐ 274 Mark Collins	.10	.05	.01
☐ 275 Mark Carrier WR	.40	.18	.05
☐ 276 Paul Gruber	.10	.05	.01
☐ 277 Earnest Byner	.10	.05	.01
☐ 278 Andre Collins	.10	.05	.01
☐ 279 Reggie Cobb	.10	.05	.01
☐ 280 Art Monk	.20	.09	.03
☐ 281 Henry Jones	.20	.09	.03
☐ 282 Mike Pritchard	.40	.18	.05
☐ 283 Moe Gardner	.10	.05	.01
☐ 284 Chris Zorich	.40	.18	.05
☐ 285 Keith Traylor	.10	.05	.01
☐ 286 Mike Dumas	.10	.05	.01
☐ 287 Ed King	.10	.05	.01
☐ 288 Russell Maryland	.40	.18	.05
☐ 289 Alfred Williams	.10	.05	.01
☐ 290 Derek Russell	.10	.05	.01
☐ 291 Vinnie Clark	.10	.05	.01
☐ 292 Mike Croel	.10	.05	.01
☐ 293 Todd Marinovich	.10	.05	.01
☐ 294 Phil Hansen	.10	.05	.01
☐ 295 Aaron Craver	.10	.05	.01
☐ 296 Nick Bell	.10	.05	.01
☐ 297 Kenny Walker	.10	.05	.01
☐ 298 Roman Phifer	.10	.05	.01
☐ 299 Kanavis McGhee	.10	.05	.01
☐ 300 Ricky Ervins	.20	.09	.03
☐ 301 Jim Price	.10	.05	.01
☐ 302 John Johnson	.10	.05	.01
☐ 303 George Thornton	.10	.05	.01
☐ 304 Huey Richardson	.10	.05	.01
☐ 305 Harry Colon	.10	.05	.01
☐ 306 Antone Davis	.10	.05	.01
☐ 307 Todd Lyght	.10	.05	.01
☐ 308 Bryan Cox	.40	.18	.05
☐ 309 Brad Goebel	.10	.05	.01
☐ 310 Eric Moten	.10	.05	.01
☐ 311 John Kasay	.20	.09	.03
☐ 312 Esera Tuaolo	.10	.05	.01
☐ 313 Bobby Wilson	.10	.05	.01
☐ 314 Mo Lewis	.20	.09	.03
☐ 315 Harvey Williams	.40	.18	.05
☐ 316 Mike Stonebreaker	.10	.05	.01
☐ 317 Charles McRae	.10	.05	.01
☐ 318 John Flannery	.10	.05	.01
☐ 319 Ted Washington	.10	.05	.01
☐ 320 Stanley Richard	.10	.05	.01

☐ 321 Browning Nagle	.10	.05	.01
☐ 322 Ed McCaffery	.20	.09	.03
☐ 323 Jeff Graham	1.00	.45	.12
☐ 324 Stan Thomas	.10	.05	.01
☐ 325 Lawrence Dawsey	.20	.09	.03
☐ 326 Eric Bieniemy	.10	.05	.01
☐ 327 Tim Barnett	.10	.05	.01
☐ 328 Erric Pegram	.40	.18	.05
☐ 329 Lamar Rogers	.10	.05	.01
☐ 330 Ernie Mills	.20	.09	.03
☐ 331 Pat Harlow	.10	.05	.01
☐ 332 Greg Lewis	.10	.05	.01
☐ 333 Jarrod Bunch	.10	.05	.01
☐ 334 Dan McGwire	.10	.05	.01
☐ 335 Randal Hill	.20	.09	.03
☐ 336 Leonard Russell	.40	.18	.05
☐ 337 Carnell Lake	.10	.05	.01
☐ 338 Brian Blades	.20	.09	.03
☐ 339 Darrell Green	.10	.05	.01
☐ 340 Bobby Humphrey	.10	.05	.01
☐ 341 Mervyn Fernandez	.10	.05	.01
☐ 342 Ricky Sanders	.10	.05	.01
☐ 343 Keith Jackson	.20	.09	.03
☐ 344 Carl Banks	.10	.05	.01
☐ 345 Gill Byrd	.10	.05	.01
☐ 346 Al Toon	.20	.09	.03
☐ 347 Stephen Baker	.10	.05	.01
☐ 348 Randall Cunningham	.20	.09	.03
☐ 349 Flipper Anderson	.10	.05	.01
☐ 350 Jay Novacek	.40	.18	.05
☐ 351 Steve Young HH vs. Bruce Smith	.40	.18	.05
☐ 352 Barry Sanders HH vs. Joey Browner	.75	.35	.09
☐ 353 Joe Montana HH vs. Mark Carrier	.50	.23	.06
☐ 354 Thurman Thomas HH vs. Lawrence Taylor	.20	.09	.03
☐ 355 Jerry Rice HH vs. Darrell Green	.60	.25	.07
☐ 356 Warren Moon TECH	.20	.09	.03
☐ 357 Anthony Munoz TECH	.10	.05	.01
☐ 358 Barry Sanders TECH	1.50	.70	.19
☐ 359 Jerry Rice TECH	1.50	.70	.19
☐ 360 Joey Browner TECH	.10	.05	.01
☐ 361 Morten Andersen TECH	.10	.05	.01
☐ 362 Sean Landeta TECH	.10	.05	.01
☐ 363 Thurman Thomas GW	.40	.18	.05
☐ 364 Emmitt Smith GW	3.00	1.35	.35
☐ 365 Gaston Green GW	.10	.05	.01
☐ 366 Barry Sanders GW	2.00	.90	.25
☐ 367 Christian Okoye GW	.10	.05	.01
☐ 368 Earnest Byner GW	.10	.05	.01
☐ 369 Neal Anderson GW	.10	.05	.01
☐ 370 Herschel Walker GW	.20	.09	.03
☐ 371 Rodney Hampton GW	.40	.18	.05
☐ 372 Darryl Talley IDOL Ted Hendricks	.10	.05	.01
☐ 373 Mark Carrier IDOL Ronnie Lott	.10	.05	.01
☐ 374 Jim Breech IDOL Jan Stenerud	.10	.05	.01
☐ 375 Rodney Hampton IDOL Ottis Anderson	.10	.05	.01
☐ 376 Kevin Mack IDOL Earnest Byner	.10	.05	.01
☐ 377 Steve Jordan IDOL Oscar Robertson	.10	.05	.01
☐ 378 Boomer Esiason IDOL Bert Jones	.10	.05	.01
☐ 379 Steve DeBerg IDOL Roman Gabriel	.20	.09	.03
☐ 380 Al Toon IDOL Wesley Walker	.10	.05	.01
☐ 381 Ronnie Lott IDOL Charley Taylor	.20	.09	.03
☐ 382 Henry Ellard IDOL Bob Hayes	.10	.05	.01
☐ 383 Troy Aikman IDOL Roger Staubach	1.50	.70	.19
☐ 384 Thurman Thomas IDOL Earl Campbell	.40	.18	.05
☐ 385 Dan Marino IDOL Terry Bradshaw	2.00	.90	.25
☐ 386 Howie Long IDOL Joe Greene	.20	.09	.03
☐ 387 Franco Harris Immaculate Reception	.20	.09	.03
☐ 388 Esera Tuaolo	.10	.05	.01
☐ 389 Super Bowl XXVI (Super Bowl Records)	.10	.05	.01
☐ 390 Charles Mann	.10	.05	.01
☐ 391 Kenny Walker	.10	.05	.01
☐ 392 Reggie Roby	.10	.05	.01
☐ 393 Bruce Pickens	.10	.05	.01
☐ 394 Ray Childress SIDE	.10	.05	.01
☐ 395 Karl Mecklenburg SIDE	.10	.05	.01
☐ 396 Dean Biasucci SIDE	.10	.05	.01
☐ 397 John Alt SIDE	.10	.05	.01
☐ 398 Marcus Allen SIDE	.20	.09	.03
☐ 399 John Offerdahl SIDE	.10	.05	.01
☐ 400 Richard Tardits SIDE	.10	.05	.01
☐ 401 Al Toon SIDE	.10	.05	.01
☐ 402 Joey Browner SIDE	.10	.05	.01
☐ 403 Spencer Tillman SIDE	.10	.05	.01
☐ 404 Jay Novacek SIDE	.20	.09	.03
☐ 405 Stephen Braggs SIDE	.10	.05	.01
☐ 406 Mike Tice SIDE	.10	.05	.01
☐ 407 Kevin Greene SIDE	.20	.09	.03
☐ 408 Reggie White SIDE	.20	.09	.03
☐ 409 Brian Noble SIDE	.10	.05	.01
☐ 410 Bart Oates SIDE	.10	.05	.01
☐ 411 Art Monk SIDE	.20	.09	.03
☐ 412 Ron Wolfley SIDE	.10	.05	.01
☐ 413 Louis Lipps SIDE	.10	.05	.01
☐ 414 Dante Jones SIDE	.20	.09	.03
☐ 415 Kenneth Davis SIDE	.10	.05	.01
☐ P1 Emmitt Smith Promo numbered 42 Mentions holdout on back	25.00	11.00	3.10

1992 Pinnacle Samples

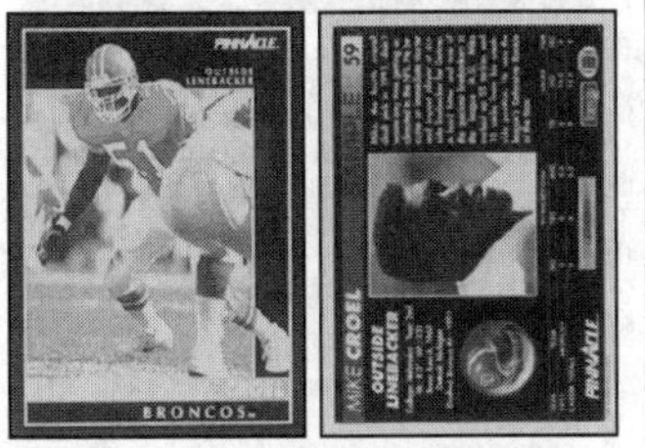

This six-card sample standard-size set features action color player photos on a black card face. The image of the player is partially cut out and extends beyond the photo background. A thin white line forms a frame near the card edge. The player's name appears at the bottom in a gradated bar that reflects the team's color. The horizontally oriented backs have white borders and black backgrounds. A gradated purple bar at the top contains the player's name, the word "sample," and the card number. A close-up player photo appears in the center. The back is rounded out with biography, statistics (1991 and career), player profile, and a picture of the team helmet in a circular format.

	MINT	NRMT	EXC
COMPLETE SET (6)	6.00	2.70	.75
COMMON CARD	1.00	.45	.12
☐ 1 Reggie White	2.00	.90	.25
☐ 5 Pepper Johnson	1.00	.45	.12
☐ 19 Chris Spielman	1.00	.45	.12
☐ 59 Mike Croel	1.00	.45	.12
☐ 100 Bobby Hebert	1.00	.45	.12
☐ 102 Rodney Hampton	1.50	.70	.19

1992 Pinnacle

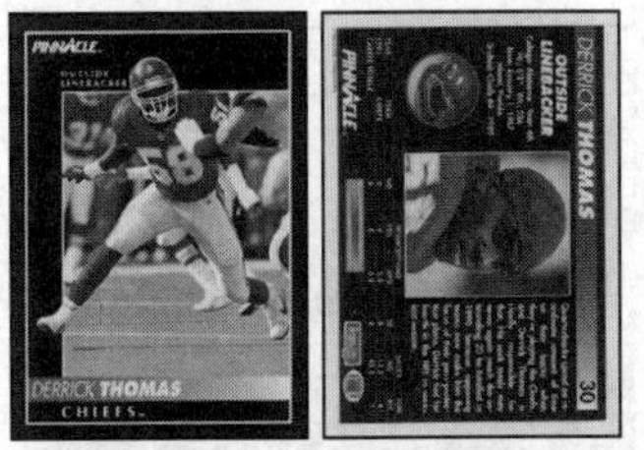

The 1992 Pinnacle set consists of 360 standard-size cards. Cards were issued in 16-card and 27-card super packs. The fronts feature action color player photos on a black card face. The image of the player is partially cut out and extends beyond the photo background. A thin white line forms a frame near the card edge. The player's name appears at the bottom in a gradated bar that matches the player's uniform. The horizontally oriented backs have white borders and black backgrounds. A gradated purple bar at the top contains the player's name. A close-up player photo appears in the center. The back is rounded out with biographical and statistical information, and a player profile. The set closes with the following subsets: Rookies (314-330), Sidelines (331-334), Gamewinners (335-344), Hall of Famers (345-347), and Idols (348-357). Rookie Cards include Steve Bono, Edgar Bennett, Amp Lee and Tommy Vardell. An 8-card Promo Panel was produced and distributed at the Super Bowl XXVII Card Show in Pasadena.

	MINT	NRMT	EXC
COMPLETE SET (360)	25.00	11.00	3.10
COMMON CARD (1-360)	.08	.04	.01
☐ 1 Reggie White	.30	.14	.04
☐ 2 Eric Green	.08	.04	.01
☐ 3 Craig Heyward	.15	.07	.02
☐ 4 Phil Simms	.15	.07	.02
☐ 5 Pepper Johnson	.08	.04	.01
☐ 6 Sean Landeta	.08	.04	.01
☐ 7 Dino Hackett	.08	.04	.01
☐ 8 Andre Ware	.08	.04	.01
☐ 9 Ricky Nattiel	.08	.04	.01
☐ 10 Jim Price	.08	.04	.01
☐ 11 Jim Ritcher	.08	.04	.01
☐ 12 Kelly Stouffer	.08	.04	.01
☐ 13 Ray Crockett	.08	.04	.01
☐ 14 Steve Tasker	.15	.07	.02
☐ 15 Barry Sanders	3.00	1.35	.35
☐ 16 Pat Swilling	.15	.07	.02
☐ 17 Moe Gardner	.08	.04	.01
☐ 18 Steve Young	2.00	.90	.25
☐ 19 Chris Spielman	.15	.07	.02
☐ 20 Richard Dent	.15	.07	.02
☐ 21 Anthony Munoz	.15	.07	.02
☐ 22 Thurman Thomas	.30	.14	.04
☐ 23 Ricky Sanders	.08	.04	.01
☐ 24 Steve Atwater	.08	.04	.01
☐ 25 Tony Tolbert	.08	.04	.01
☐ 26 Haywood Jeffires	.15	.07	.02
☐ 27 Duane Bickett	.08	.04	.01
☐ 28 Tim McDonald	.08	.04	.01
☐ 29 Cris Carter	.30	.14	.04
☐ 30 Derrick Thomas	.30	.14	.04
☐ 31 Hugh Millen	.08	.04	.01
☐ 32 Bart Oates	.08	.04	.01
☐ 33 Darryl Talley	.08	.04	.01
☐ 34 Marion Butts	.08	.04	.01
☐ 35 Pete Stoyanovich	.08	.04	.01
☐ 36 Ronnie Lott	.15	.07	.02
☐ 37 Simon Fletcher	.08	.04	.01
☐ 38 Morten Andersen	.08	.04	.01
☐ 39 Clyde Simmons	.08	.04	.01
☐ 40 Mark Rypien	.08	.04	.01
☐ 41 Henry Ellard	.15	.07	.02
☐ 42 Michael Irvin	.30	.14	.04
☐ 43 Louis Lipps	.08	.04	.01
☐ 44 John L. Williams	.08	.04	.01
☐ 45 Broderick Thomas	.08	.04	.01
☐ 46 Don Majkowski	.08	.04	.01
☐ 47 William Perry	.15	.07	.02
☐ 48 David Fulcher	.08	.04	.01
☐ 49 Tony Bennett	.08	.04	.01
☐ 50 Clay Matthews	.15	.07	.02
☐ 51 Warren Moon	.30	.14	.04
☐ 52 Bruce Armstrong	.08	.04	.01
☐ 53 Bill Brooks	.08	.04	.01
☐ 54 Greg Townsend	.08	.04	.01
☐ 55 Steve Broussard	.08	.04	.01
☐ 56 Mel Gray	.15	.07	.02
☐ 57 Kevin Mack	.08	.04	.01
☐ 58 Emmitt Smith	5.00	2.20	.60
☐ 59 Mike Croel	.08	.04	.01
☐ 60 Brian Mitchell	.15	.07	.02
☐ 61 Bennie Blades	.08	.04	.01
☐ 62 Carnell Lake	.08	.04	.01
☐ 63 Cornelius Bennett	.15	.07	.02
☐ 64 Darrell Thompson	.08	.04	.01
☐ 65 Jessie Hester	.08	.04	.01
☐ 66 Marv Cook	.08	.04	.01
☐ 67 Tim Brown	.30	.14	.04
☐ 68 Mark Duper	.08	.04	.01
☐ 69 Robert Delpino	.08	.04	.01
☐ 70 Eric Martin	.08	.04	.01
☐ 71 Wendell Davis	.08	.04	.01
☐ 72 Vaughan Johnson	.08	.04	.01
☐ 73 Brian Blades	.15	.07	.02
☐ 74 Ed King	.08	.04	.01
☐ 75 Gaston Green	.08	.04	.01
☐ 76 Christian Okoye	.08	.04	.01
☐ 77 Rohn Stark	.08	.04	.01
☐ 78 Kevin Greene	.30	.14	.04
☐ 79 Jay Novacek	.15	.07	.02
☐ 80 Chip Lohmiller	.08	.04	.01
☐ 81 Cris Dishman	.08	.04	.01
☐ 82 Ethan Horton	.08	.04	.01
☐ 83 Pat Harlow	.08	.04	.01
☐ 84 Mark Ingram	.08	.04	.01
☐ 85 Mark Carrier DB	.08	.04	.01
☐ 86 Sam Mills	.08	.04	.01
☐ 87 Mark Higgs	.08	.04	.01
☐ 88 Keith Jackson	.15	.07	.02
☐ 89 Gary Anderson K	.08	.04	.01
☐ 90 Ken Harvey	.08	.04	.01
☐ 91 Anthony Carter	.15	.07	.02
☐ 92 Randall McDaniel	.08	.04	.01
☐ 93 Johnny Johnson	.08	.04	.01
☐ 94 Shane Conlan	.08	.04	.01
☐ 95 Sterling Sharpe	.30	.14	.04
☐ 96 Guy McIntyre	.08	.04	.01
☐ 97 Albert Lewis	.08	.04	.01
☐ 98 Chris Doleman	.08	.04	.01
☐ 99 Andre Rison	.15	.07	.02
☐ 100 Bobby Hebert	.08	.04	.01
☐ 101 Dan Owens	.08	.04	.01
☐ 102 Rodney Hampton	.30	.14	.04
☐ 103 Ernie Jones	.08	.04	.01
☐ 104 Reggie Cobb	.08	.04	.01
☐ 105 Wilber Marshall	.08	.04	.01
☐ 106 Mike Munchak	.08	.04	.01
☐ 107 Cortez Kennedy	.15	.07	.02
☐ 108 Todd Lyght	.08	.04	.01
☐ 109 Burt Grossman	.08	.04	.01
☐ 110 Ferrell Edmunds	.08	.04	.01
☐ 111 Jim Everett	.15	.07	.02
☐ 112 Hardy Nickerson	.15	.07	.02
☐ 113 Andre Tippett	.08	.04	.01
☐ 114 Ronnie Harmon	.08	.04	.01
☐ 115 Andre Waters	.08	.04	.01
☐ 116 Ernest Givins	.15	.07	.02
☐ 117 Eric Hill	.08	.04	.01
☐ 118 Erric Pegram	.15	.07	.02
☐ 119 Jarrod Bunch	.08	.04	.01
☐ 120 Marcus Allen	.30	.14	.04
☐ 121 Barry Foster	.15	.07	.02
☐ 122 Kent Hull	.08	.04	.01
☐ 123 Neal Anderson	.08	.04	.01
☐ 124 Stephen Braggs	.08	.04	.01
☐ 125 Nick Lowery	.08	.04	.01
☐ 126 Jeff Hostetler	.15	.07	.02
☐ 127 Michael Carter	.08	.04	.01
☐ 128 Don Warren	.08	.04	.01
☐ 129 Brad Baxter	.08	.04	.01
☐ 130 John Taylor	.15	.07	.02
☐ 131 Harold Green	.08	.04	.01
☐ 132 Mike Merriweather	.08	.04	.01
☐ 133 Gary Clark	.30	.14	.04
☐ 134 Vince Buck	.08	.04	.01
☐ 135 Dan Saleaumua	.08	.04	.01
☐ 136 Gary Zimmerman	.08	.04	.01
☐ 137 Richmond Webb	.08	.04	.01
☐ 138 Art Monk	.15	.07	.02
☐ 139 Mervyn Fernandez	.08	.04	.01
☐ 140 Mark Jackson	.08	.04	.01
☐ 141 Freddie Joe Nunn	.08	.04	.01
☐ 142 Jeff Lageman	.08	.04	.01
☐ 143 Kenny Walker	.08	.04	.01
☐ 144 Mark Carrier WR	.15	.07	.02
☐ 145 Jon Vaughn	.08	.04	.01
☐ 146 Greg Davis	.08	.04	.01
☐ 147 Bubby Brister	.08	.04	.01
☐ 148 Mo Lewis	.08	.04	.01
☐ 149 Howie Long	.15	.07	.02
☐ 150 Rod Bernstine	.08	.04	.01
☐ 151 Nick Bell	.08	.04	.01
☐ 152 Terry Allen	.75	.35	.09
☐ 153 William Fuller	.15	.07	.02
☐ 154 Dexter Carter	.08	.04	.01
☐ 155 Gene Atkins	.08	.04	.01
☐ 156 Don Beebe	.08	.04	.01
☐ 157 Mark Collins	.08	.04	.01
☐ 158 Jerry Ball	.08	.04	.01
☐ 159 Fred Barnett	.30	.14	.04
☐ 160 Rodney Holman	.08	.04	.01
☐ 161 Stephen Baker	.08	.04	.01
☐ 162 Jeff Graham	.30	.14	.04
☐ 163 Leonard Russell	.15	.07	.02
☐ 164 Jeff Gossett	.08	.04	.01
☐ 165 Vinny Testaverde	.15	.07	.02
☐ 166 Maurice Hurst	.08	.04	.01
☐ 167 Louis Oliver	.08	.04	.01
☐ 168 Jim Morrissey	.08	.04	.01
☐ 169 Greg Kragen	.08	.04	.01
☐ 170 Andre Collins	.08	.04	.01
☐ 171 Dave Meggett	.15	.07	.02
☐ 172 Keith Henderson	.08	.04	.01
☐ 173 Vince Newsome	.08	.04	.01
☐ 174 Chris Hinton	.08	.04	.01
☐ 175 James Hasty	.08	.04	.01
☐ 176 John Offerdahl	.08	.04	.01
☐ 177 Lomas Brown	.08	.04	.01
☐ 178 Neil O'Donnell	.30	.14	.04
☐ 179 Leonard Marshall	.08	.04	.01
☐ 180 Bubba McDowell	.08	.04	.01
☐ 181 Herman Moore	2.00	.90	.25
☐ 182 Rob Moore	.15	.07	.02
☐ 183 Earnest Byner	.08	.04	.01
☐ 184 Keith McCants	.08	.04	.01
☐ 185 Floyd Turner	.08	.04	.01
☐ 186 Steve Jordan	.08	.04	.01
☐ 187 Nate Odomes	.08	.04	.01
☐ 188 Jeff Herrod	.08	.04	.01
☐ 189 Jim Harbaugh	.30	.14	.04
☐ 190 Jessie Tuggle	.08	.04	.01
☐ 191 Al Smith	.08	.04	.01
☐ 192 Lawrence Dawsey	.15	.07	.02
☐ 193 Steve Bono	.50	.23	.06
☐ 194 Greg Lloyd	.30	.14	.04
☐ 195 Steve Wisniewski	.08	.04	.01
☐ 196 Larry Kelm	.08	.04	.01
☐ 197 Tommy Kane	.08	.04	.01
☐ 198 Mark Schlereth	.08	.04	.01
☐ 199 Ray Childress	.08	.04	.01
☐ 200 Vincent Brown	.08	.04	.01
☐ 201 Rodney Peete	.15	.07	.02
☐ 202 Dennis Smith	.08	.04	.01
☐ 203 Bruce Matthews	.08	.04	.01
☐ 204 Rickey Jackson	.08	.04	.01
☐ 205 Eric Allen	.08	.04	.01
☐ 206 Rich Camarillo	.08	.04	.01
☐ 207 Jim Lachey	.08	.04	.01
☐ 208 Kevin Ross	.08	.04	.01
☐ 209 Irving Fryar	.15	.07	.02
☐ 210 Mark Clayton	.15	.07	.02
☐ 211 Keith Byars	.08	.04	.01
☐ 212 John Elway	2.00	.90	.25
☐ 213 Harris Barton	.08	.04	.01
☐ 214 Aeneas Williams	.15	.07	.02
☐ 215 Rich Gannon	.08	.04	.01
☐ 216 Toi Cook	.08	.04	.01
☐ 217 Rod Woodson	.30	.14	.04
☐ 218 Gary Anderson RB	.08	.04	.01
☐ 219 Reggie Roby	.08	.04	.01
☐ 220 Karl Mecklenburg	.08	.04	.01
☐ 221 Rufus Porter	.08	.04	.01
☐ 222 Jon Hand	.08	.04	.01
☐ 223 Tim Barnett	.08	.04	.01
☐ 224 Eric Swann	.15	.07	.02
☐ 225 Eugene Robinson	.08	.04	.01

☐ 226 Michael Young	.08	.04	.01
☐ 227 Frank Warren	.08	.04	.01
☐ 228 Mike Kenn	.08	.04	.01
☐ 229 Tim Green	.08	.04	.01
☐ 230 Barry Word	.08	.04	.01
☐ 231 Mike Pritchard	.15	.07	.02
☐ 232 John Kasay	.08	.04	.01
☐ 233 Derek Russell	.08	.04	.01
☐ 234 Jim Breech	.08	.04	.01
☐ 235 Pierce Holt	.08	.04	.01
☐ 236 Tim Krumrie	.08	.04	.01
☐ 237 William Roberts	.08	.04	.01
☐ 238 Erik Kramer	.15	.07	.02
☐ 239 Brett Perriman	.30	.14	.04
☐ 240 Reyna Thompson	.08	.04	.01
☐ 241 Chris Miller	.15	.07	.02
☐ 242 Drew Hill	.08	.04	.01
☐ 243 Curtis Duncan	.08	.04	.01
☐ 244 Seth Joyner	.15	.07	.02
☐ 245 Ken Norton Jr.	.30	.14	.04
☐ 246 Calvin Williams	.15	.07	.02
☐ 247 James Joseph	.08	.04	.01
☐ 248 Bennie Thompson	.08	.04	.01
☐ 249 Tunch Ilkin	.08	.04	.01
☐ 250 Brad Edwards	.08	.04	.01
☐ 251 Jeff Jaeger	.08	.04	.01
☐ 252 Gill Byrd	.08	.04	.01
☐ 253 Jeff Feagles	.08	.04	.01
☐ 254 Jamie Dukes	.08	.04	.01
☐ 255 Greg McMurtry	.08	.04	.01
☐ 256 Anthony Johnson	.15	.07	.02
☐ 257 Lamar Lathon	.08	.04	.01
☐ 258 John Roper	.08	.04	.01
☐ 259 Lorenzo White	.08	.04	.01
☐ 260 Brian Noble	.08	.04	.01
☐ 261 Chris Singleton	.08	.04	.01
☐ 262 Todd Marinovich	.08	.04	.01
☐ 263 Jay Hilgenberg	.08	.04	.01
☐ 264 Kyle Clifton	.08	.04	.01
☐ 265 Tony Casillas	.08	.04	.01
☐ 266 James Francis	.08	.04	.01
☐ 267 Eddie Anderson	.08	.04	.01
☐ 268 Tim Harris	.08	.04	.01
☐ 269 James Lofton	.15	.07	.02
☐ 270 Jay Schroeder	.08	.04	.01
☐ 271 Ed West	.08	.04	.01
☐ 272 Don Mosebar	.08	.04	.01
☐ 273 Jackie Slater	.08	.04	.01
☐ 274 Fred McAfee	.08	.04	.01
☐ 275 Steve Sewell	.08	.04	.01
☐ 276 Charles Mann	.08	.04	.01
☐ 277 Ron Hall	.08	.04	.01
☐ 278 Darrell Green	.08	.04	.01
☐ 279 Jeff Cross	.08	.04	.01
☐ 280 Jeff Wright	.08	.04	.01
☐ 281 Issiac Holt	.08	.04	.01
☐ 282 Dermontti Dawson	.08	.04	.01
☐ 283 Michael Haynes	.15	.07	.02
☐ 284 Tony Mandarich	.08	.04	.01
☐ 285 Leroy Hoard	.15	.07	.02
☐ 286 Darryl Henley	.08	.04	.01
☐ 287 Tim McGee	.08	.04	.01
☐ 288 Willie Gault	.15	.07	.02
☐ 289 Dalton Hilliard	.08	.04	.01
☐ 290 Tim McKyer	.08	.04	.01
☐ 291 Tom Waddle	.08	.04	.01
☐ 292 Eric Thomas	.08	.04	.01
☐ 293 Herschel Walker	.15	.07	.02
☐ 294 Donnell Woolford	.08	.04	.01
☐ 295 James Brooks	.15	.07	.02
☐ 296 Brad Muster	.08	.04	.01
☐ 297 Brent Jones	.15	.07	.02
☐ 298 Erik Howard	.08	.04	.01
☐ 299 Alvin Harper UER (Born in Frostproof, not Frostfree)	.15	.07	.02
☐ 300 Joey Browner	.08	.04	.01
☐ 301 Jack Del Rio	.08	.04	.01
☐ 302 Cleveland Gary	.08	.04	.01
☐ 303 Brett Favre	6.00	2.70	.75
☐ 304 Freeman McNeil	.08	.04	.01
☐ 305 Willie Green	.08	.04	.01
☐ 306 Percy Snow	.08	.04	.01
☐ 307 Neil Smith	.30	.14	.04
☐ 308 Eric Bieniemy	.08	.04	.01
☐ 309 Keith Traylor	.08	.04	.01
☐ 310 Ernie Mills	.08	.04	.01
☐ 311 Will Wolford	.08	.04	.01
☐ 312 Robert Young	.08	.04	.01
☐ 313 Anthony Smith	.08	.04	.01
☐ 314 Robert Porcher	.15	.07	.02
☐ 315 Leon Searcy	.15	.07	.02
☐ 316 Amp Lee	.08	.04	.01
☐ 317 Siran Stacy	.08	.04	.01
☐ 318 Patrick Rowe	.08	.04	.01
☐ 319 Chris Mims	.15	.07	.02
☐ 320 Matt Elliott	.08	.04	.01
☐ 321 Ricardo McDonald	.08	.04	.01
☐ 322 Keith Hamilton	.08	.04	.01
☐ 323 Edgar Bennett	1.50	.70	.19
☐ 324 Chris Hakel	.08	.04	.01
☐ 325 Dexter McNabb	.08	.04	.01
☐ 326 Rod Milstead	.08	.04	.01
☐ 327 Joe Bowden	.08	.04	.01
☐ 328 Brian Bollinger	.08	.04	.01
☐ 329 Darryl Williams	.08	.04	.01
☐ 330 Tommy Vardell	.15	.07	.02
☐ 331 Glenn Parker SIDE Mitch Frerotte	.08	.04	.01
☐ 332 Herschel Walker SIDE	.08	.04	.01
☐ 333 Mike Cofer SIDE	.08	.04	.01
☐ 334 Mark Rypien SIDE	.08	.04	.01
☐ 335 Andre Rison GW	.15	.07	.02
☐ 336 Henry Ellard GW	.08	.04	.01
☐ 337 Rob Moore GW	.08	.04	.01
☐ 338 Fred Barnett GW	.08	.04	.01
☐ 339 Mark Clayton GW	.08	.04	.01
☐ 340 Eric Martin GW	.08	.04	.01
☐ 341 Irving Fryar GW	.08	.04	.01
☐ 342 Tim Brown GW	.15	.07	.02
☐ 343 Sterling Sharpe GW	.15	.07	.02
☐ 344 Gary Clark GW	.08	.04	.01
☐ 345 John Mackey HOF	.08	.04	.01
☐ 346 Lem Barney HOF	.08	.04	.01
☐ 347 John Riggins HOF	.15	.07	.02
☐ 348 Marion Butts IDOL William Andrews	.08	.04	.01
☐ 349 Jeff Lageman IDOL Jack Lambert	.08	.04	.01
☐ 350 Eric Green IDOL Sam Rutigliano	.08	.04	.01
☐ 351 Reggie White IDOL Bobby Jones	.15	.07	.02
☐ 352 Marv Cook IDOL Dan Gable	.08	.04	.01
☐ 353 John Elway IDOL Roger Staubach	1.00	.45	.12
☐ 354 Steve Tasker IDOL Ed Podolak	.08	.04	.01
☐ 355 Nick Lowery IDOL Jan Stenerud	.08	.04	.01
☐ 356 Mark Clayton IDOL Paul Warfield	.08	.04	.01
☐ 357 Warren Moon IDOL Roman Gabriel	.15	.07	.02
☐ 358 Eric Metcalf	.15	.07	.02
☐ 359 Charles Haley	.15	.07	.02
☐ 360 Terrell Buckley	.08	.04	.01
☐ P1 Promo Panel Super Bowl XXVII promo John Elway Sterling Sharpe Warren Moon Tommy Vardell Derrick Thomas Pat Swilling Neil Smith Cortez Kennedy	5.00	2.20	.60

1992 Pinnacle Team Pinnacle

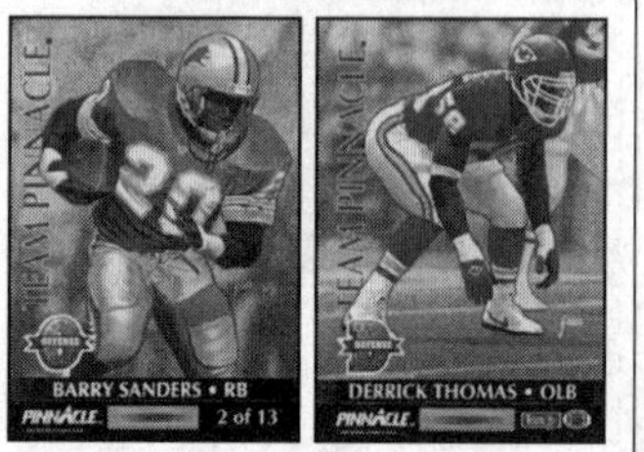

These 13 standard-size cards feature paintings by sports artist Christopher Greco. The cards were randomly inserted into Pinnacle packs at an approximate rate of one in 36. One side showcases the best offensive player by position while the other side has his defensive counterpart. On both sides, a gold foil stripe carrying the player's name and position and a black stripe appear beneath the portrait. The card number is printed on the back in the black stripe.

	MINT	NRMT	EXC
COMPLETE SET (13)	90.00	40.00	11.00
COMMON PAIR (1-13)	4.00	1.80	.50
☐ 1 Mark Rypien Ronnie Lott	6.00	2.70	.75
☐ 2 Barry Sanders Derrick Thomas	20.00	9.00	2.50
☐ 3 Thurman Thomas Pat Swilling	8.00	3.60	1.00
☐ 4 Eric Green Steve Atwater	6.00	2.70	.75
☐ 5 Haywood Jeffires Darrell Green	6.00	2.70	.75
☐ 6 Michael Irvin Eric Allen	8.00	3.60	1.00
☐ 7 Bruce Matthews Jerry Ball	4.00	1.80	.50
☐ 8 Steve Wisniewski Pepper Johnson	4.00	1.80	.50
☐ 9 William Roberts Karl Mecklenburg	4.00	1.80	.50
☐ 10 Jim Lachey William Fuller	4.00	1.80	.50
☐ 11 Anthony Munoz Reggie White	8.00	3.60	1.00
☐ 12 Mel Gray Steve Tasker	6.00	2.70	.75
☐ 13 Jeff Jaeger Jeff Gossett	4.00	1.80	.50

1992 Pinnacle Team 2000

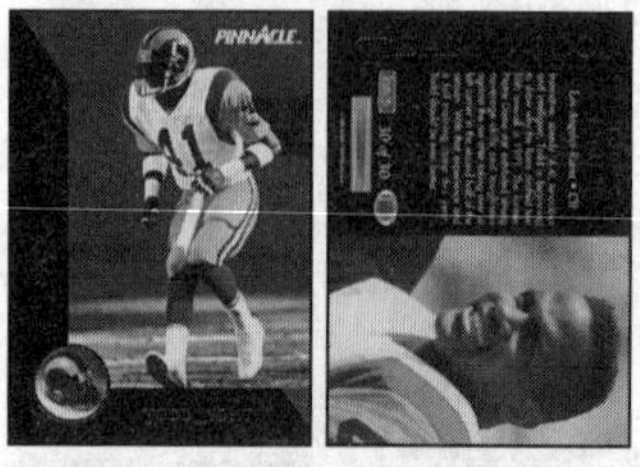

This 30-card standard-size set focuses on young players who were expected to be the NFL's major stars in the year 2000. The cards were inserted two per 27-card jumbo pack. The cards are bordered by a 1/2" black stripe that runs along the left edge and bottom forming a right angle. The two ends of the black stripe are sloped. The words "Team 2000" and the player's name appear in gold foil in the stripe. The team helmet is displayed in the lower left corner. The horizontally oriented backs show a close-up color player photo and a career summary on a black background.

	MINT	NRMT	EXC
COMPLETE SET (30)	15.00	6.75	1.85
COMMON CARD (1-30)	.25	.11	.03
☐ 1 Todd Marinovich	.25	.11	.03
☐ 2 Rodney Hampton	.75	.35	.09
☐ 3 Mike Croel	.25	.11	.03
☐ 4 Leonard Russell	.40	.18	.05
☐ 5 Herman Moore	1.25	.55	.16
☐ 6 Rob Moore	.40	.18	.05
☐ 7 Jon Vaughn	.25	.11	.03
☐ 8 Lamar Lathon	.25	.11	.03
☐ 9 Ed King	.25	.11	.03
☐ 10 Moe Gardner	.25	.11	.03
☐ 11 Barry Foster	.40	.18	.05
☐ 12 Eric Green	.40	.18	.05
☐ 13 Kenny Walker	.25	.11	.03
☐ 14 Tim Barnett	.25	.11	.03
☐ 15 Derrick Thomas	.75	.35	.09
☐ 16 Steve Atwater	.25	.11	.03
☐ 17 Nick Bell	.25	.11	.03
☐ 18 John Friesz	.40	.18	.05
☐ 19 Emmitt Smith	4.00	1.80	.50
☐ 20 Eric Swann	.75	.35	.09
☐ 21 Barry Sanders	2.00	.90	.25
☐ 22 Mark Carrier DB	.25	.11	.03
☐ 23 Brett Favre	5.00	2.20	.60
☐ 24 James Francis	.25	.11	.03
☐ 25 Lawrence Dawsey	.40	.18	.05
☐ 26 Keith McCants	.25	.11	.03
☐ 27 Broderick Thomas	.25	.11	.03
☐ 28 Mike Pritchard	.40	.18	.05
☐ 29 Bruce Pickens	.25	.11	.03
☐ 30 Todd Lyght	.25	.11	.03

1993 Pinnacle Samples

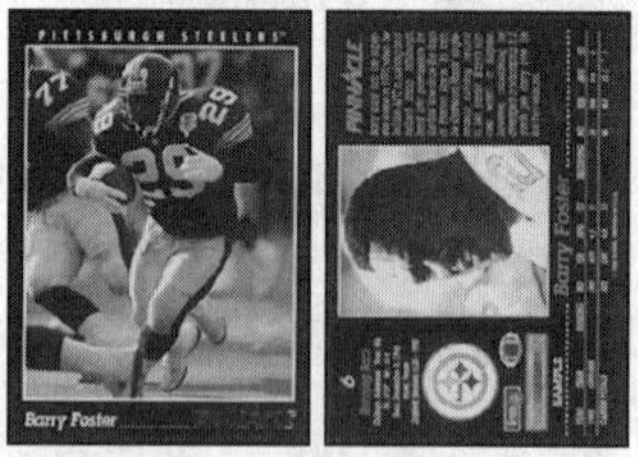

This sample panel measures approximately 7 1/2" by 7" and features two rows of three cards each. If cut, the cards would measure the standard size. The fronts display color action player photos on a black card face accented by thin white picture frames. The team name and the player's name are printed above and below the picture respectively; the gold-foil stamped Pinnacle logo at the lower right corner rounds out the card face. On a black background, the horizontal backs carry a color close-up photo, biography, career summary, and 1992 season statistics. The cards are numbered at the upper left corner, and the word "Sample" is printed just below Score's anti-counterfeiting device.

	MINT	NRMT	EXC
COMPLETE SET (6)	8.00	3.60	1.00
COMMON CARD (1-6)	1.00	.45	.12
☐ 1 Brett Favre	5.00	2.20	.60
☐ 2 Tommy Vardell	1.00	.45	.12
☐ 3 Jarrod Bunch	1.00	.45	.12
☐ 4 Mike Croel	1.00	.45	.12
☐ 5 Morten Andersen	1.00	.45	.12
☐ 6 Barry Foster	1.00	.45	.12

1993 Pinnacle

The 1993 Pinnacle set consists of 360 standard-size cards that were issued in 15 and 27-card packs. The black-bordered fronts display color action player photos framed by a thin white line. The team name and the player's name are printed above and below the picture, respectively. On a black background, the horizontal backs carry a color close-up player portrait, biography, career summary, team logo, and 1992 season and career statistics. The set closes with the Hall of Fame (353-356) and Hometown Hero (357-360) subsets. Rookie Cards include Dave Brown. For each order of 20 boxes, Pinnacle would send one of 3,000 autographed cards of its spokesman, Franco Harris.

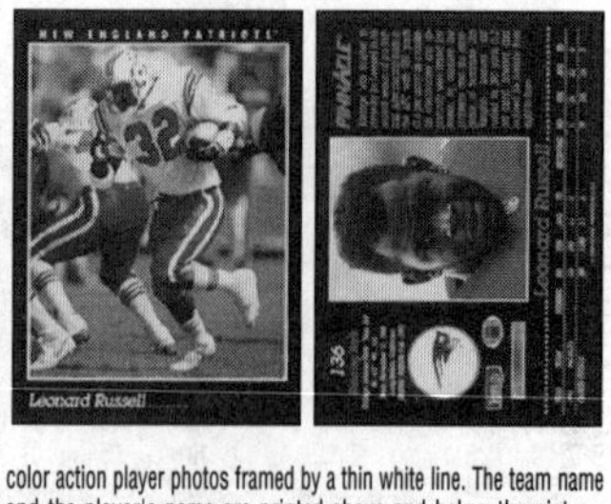

	MINT	NRMT	EXC
COMPLETE SET (360)	30.00	13.50	3.70
COMMON CARD (1-360)	.10	.05	.01
☐ 1 Brett Favre	4.00	1.80	.50
☐ 2 Tommy Vardell	.10	.05	.01
☐ 3 Jarrod Bunch	.10	.05	.01
☐ 4 Mike Croel	.10	.05	.01
☐ 5 Morten Andersen	.10	.05	.01
☐ 6 Barry Foster	.20	.09	.03
☐ 7 Chris Spielman	.20	.09	.03
☐ 8 Jim Jeffcoat	.10	.05	.01
☐ 9 Ken Ruettgers	.10	.05	.01
☐ 10 Cris Dishman	.10	.05	.01
☐ 11 Ricky Watters	.40	.18	.05
☐ 12 Alfred Williams	.10	.05	.01
☐ 13 Mark Kelso	.10	.05	.01
☐ 14 Moe Gardner	.10	.05	.01
☐ 15 Terry Allen	.40	.18	.05
☐ 16 Willie Gault	.10	.05	.01
☐ 17 Bubba McDowell	.10	.05	.01
☐ 18 Brian Mitchell	.20	.09	.03
☐ 19 Karl Mecklenburg	.10	.05	.01
☐ 20 Jim Everett	.20	.09	.03
☐ 21 Bobby Humphrey	.10	.05	.01
☐ 22 Tim Krumrie	.10	.05	.01
☐ 23 Ken Norton Jr.	.20	.09	.03
☐ 24 Wendell Davis	.10	.05	.01
☐ 25 Brad Baxter	.10	.05	.01
☐ 26 Mel Gray	.20	.09	.03
☐ 27 Jon Vaughn	.10	.05	.01
☐ 28 James Hasty	.10	.05	.01
☐ 29 Chris Warren	.20	.09	.03
☐ 30 Tim Harris	.10	.05	.01
☐ 31 Eric Metcalf	.20	.09	.03
☐ 32 Rob Moore	.20	.09	.03
☐ 33 Charles Haley	.20	.09	.03
☐ 34 Leonard Marshall	.10	.05	.01
☐ 35 Jeff Graham	.20	.09	.03
☐ 36 Eugene Robinson	.10	.05	.01
☐ 37 Darryl Talley	.10	.05	.01
☐ 38 Brent Jones	.20	.09	.03
☐ 39 Reggie Roby	.10	.05	.01
☐ 40 Bruce Armstrong	.10	.05	.01
☐ 41 Audray McMillian	.10	.05	.01
☐ 42 Bern Brostek	.10	.05	.01
☐ 43 Tony Bennett	.10	.05	.01
☐ 44 Albert Lewis	.10	.05	.01
☐ 45 Derrick Thomas	.40	.18	.05
☐ 46 Cris Carter	.40	.18	.05
☐ 47 Richmond Webb	.10	.05	.01
☐ 48 Sean Landeta	.10	.05	.01
☐ 49 Cleveland Gary	.10	.05	.01
☐ 50 Mark Carrier DB	.10	.05	.01
☐ 51 Lawrence Dawsey	.10	.05	.01
☐ 52 Lamar Lathon	.10	.05	.01
☐ 53 Nick Bell	.10	.05	.01
☐ 54 Curtis Duncan	.10	.05	.01
☐ 55 Irving Fryar	.20	.09	.03
☐ 56 Seth Joyner	.10	.05	.01
☐ 57 Jay Novacek	.20	.09	.03
☐ 58 John L. Williams	.10	.05	.01
☐ 59 Amp Lee	.10	.05	.01
☐ 60 Marion Butts	.10	.05	.01
☐ 61 Clyde Simmons	.10	.05	.01
☐ 62 Rich Gannon	.10	.05	.01
☐ 63 Anthony Johnson	.20	.09	.03
☐ 64 Dave Meggett	.10	.05	.01
☐ 65 James Francis	.10	.05	.01
☐ 66 Trace Armstrong	.10	.05	.01
☐ 67 Mo Lewis	.10	.05	.01
☐ 68 Cornelius Bennett	.20	.09	.03
☐ 69 Mark Duper	.10	.05	.01
☐ 70 Frank Reich	.20	.09	.03
☐ 71 Eric Green	.10	.05	.01
☐ 72 Bruce Matthews	.10	.05	.01
☐ 73 Steve Broussard	.10	.05	.01
☐ 74 Anthony Carter	.20	.09	.03
☐ 75 Sterling Sharpe	.40	.18	.05
☐ 76 Mike Kenn	.10	.05	.01
☐ 77 Andre Rison	.20	.09	.03
☐ 78 Todd Marinovich	.10	.05	.01

☐ 79 Vincent Brown	.10	.05	.01
☐ 80 Harold Green	.10	.05	.01
☐ 81 Art Monk	.20	.09	.03
☐ 82 Reggie Cobb	.10	.05	.01
☐ 83 Johnny Johnson	.10	.05	.01
☐ 84 Tommy Kane	.10	.05	.01
☐ 85 Rohn Stark	.10	.05	.01
☐ 86 Steve Tasker	.20	.09	.03
☐ 87 Ronnie Harmon	.10	.05	.01
☐ 88 Pepper Johnson	.10	.05	.01
☐ 89 Hardy Nickerson	.20	.09	.03
☐ 90 Alvin Harper	.20	.09	.03
☐ 91 Louis Oliver	.10	.05	.01
☐ 92 Rod Woodson	.40	.18	.05
☐ 93 Sam Mills	.10	.05	.01
☐ 94 Randall McDaniel	.10	.05	.01
☐ 95 Johnny Holland	.10	.05	.01
☐ 96 Jackie Slater	.10	.05	.01
☐ 97 Don Mosebar	.10	.05	.01
☐ 98 Andre Ware	.10	.05	.01
☐ 99 Kelvin Martin	.10	.05	.01
☐ 100 Emmitt Smith	4.00	1.80	.50
☐ 101 Michael Brooks	.10	.05	.01
☐ 102 Dan Saleaumua	.10	.05	.01
☐ 103 John Elway	1.50	.70	.19
☐ 104 Henry Jones	.10	.05	.01
☐ 105 William Perry	.20	.09	.03
☐ 106 James Lofton	.20	.09	.03
☐ 107 Carnell Lake	.10	.05	.01
☐ 108 Chip Lohmiller	.10	.05	.01
☐ 109 Andre Tippett	.10	.05	.01
☐ 110 Barry Word	.10	.05	.01
☐ 111 Haywood Jeffires	.20	.09	.03
☐ 112 Kenny Walker	.10	.05	.01
☐ 113 John Randle	.10	.05	.01
☐ 114 Donnell Woolford	.10	.05	.01
☐ 115 Johnny Bailey	.10	.05	.01
☐ 116 Marcus Allen	.40	.18	.05
☐ 117 Mark Jackson	.10	.05	.01
☐ 118 Ray Agnew	.10	.05	.01
☐ 119 Gill Byrd	.10	.05	.01
☐ 120 Kyle Clifton	.10	.05	.01
☐ 121 Marv Cook	.10	.05	.01
☐ 122 Jerry Ball	.10	.05	.01
☐ 123 Steve Jordan	.10	.05	.01
☐ 124 Shannon Sharpe	.40	.18	.05
☐ 125 Brian Blades	.20	.09	.03
☐ 126 Rodney Hampton	.40	.18	.05
☐ 127 Bobby Hebert	.10	.05	.01
☐ 128 Jessie Tuggle	.10	.05	.01
☐ 129 Tom Newberry	.10	.05	.01
☐ 130 Keith McCants	.10	.05	.01
☐ 131 Richard Dent	.20	.09	.03
☐ 132 Herman Moore	1.50	.70	.19
☐ 133 Michael Irvin	.40	.18	.05
☐ 134 Ernest Givins	.20	.09	.03
☐ 135 Mark Rypien	.10	.05	.01
☐ 136 Leonard Russell	.20	.09	.03
☐ 137 Reggie White	.40	.18	.05
☐ 138 Thurman Thomas	.40	.18	.05
☐ 139 Nick Lowery	.10	.05	.01
☐ 140 Al Smith	.10	.05	.01
☐ 141 Jackie Harris	.10	.05	.01
☐ 142 Duane Bickett	.10	.05	.01
☐ 143 Lawyer Tillman	.10	.05	.01
☐ 144 Steve Wisniewski	.10	.05	.01
☐ 145 Derrick Fenner	.10	.05	.01
☐ 146 Harris Barton	.10	.05	.01
☐ 147 Rich Camarillo	.10	.05	.01
☐ 148 John Offerdahl	.10	.05	.01
☐ 149 Mike Johnson	.10	.05	.01
☐ 150 Ricky Reynolds	.10	.05	.01
☐ 151 Fred Barnett	.20	.09	.03
☐ 152 Nate Newton	.20	.09	.03
☐ 153 Chris Doleman	.10	.05	.01
☐ 154 Todd Scott	.10	.05	.01
☐ 155 Tim McKyer	.10	.05	.01
☐ 156 Ken Harvey	.10	.05	.01
☐ 157 Jeff Feagles	.10	.05	.01
☐ 158 Vince Workman	.10	.05	.01
☐ 159 Bart Oates	.10	.05	.01
☐ 160 Chris Miller	.20	.09	.03
☐ 161 Pete Stoyanovich	.10	.05	.01
☐ 162 Steve Wallace	.10	.05	.01
☐ 163 Dermontti Dawson	.10	.05	.01
☐ 164 Kenneth Davis	.10	.05	.01
☐ 165 Mike Munchak	.10	.05	.01
☐ 166 George Jamison	.10	.05	.01
☐ 167 Christian Okoye	.10	.05	.01
☐ 168 Chris Hinton	.10	.05	.01
☐ 169 Vaughan Johnson	.10	.05	.01
☐ 170 Gaston Green	.10	.05	.01
☐ 171 Kevin Greene	.40	.18	.05
☐ 172 Rob Burnett	.10	.05	.01
☐ 173 Norm Johnson	.10	.05	.01
☐ 174 Eric Hill	.10	.05	.01
☐ 175 Lomas Brown	.10	.05	.01
☐ 176 Chip Banks	.10	.05	.01
☐ 177 Greg Townsend	.10	.05	.01
☐ 178 David Fulcher	.10	.05	.01
☐ 179 Gary Anderson RB	.10	.05	.01
☐ 180 Brian Washington	.10	.05	.01
☐ 181 Brett Perriman	.40	.18	.05
☐ 182 Chris Chandler	.20	.09	.03
☐ 183 Phil Hansen	.10	.05	.01
☐ 184 Mark Clayton	.10	.05	.01
☐ 185 Frank Warren	.10	.05	.01
☐ 186 Tim Brown	.40	.18	.05
☐ 187 Mark Stepnoski	.10	.05	.01
☐ 188 Bryan Cox	.10	.05	.01
☐ 189 Gary Zimmerman	.10	.05	.01
☐ 190 Neil O'Donnell	.40	.18	.05
☐ 191 Anthony Smith	.10	.05	.01
☐ 192 Craig Heyward	.20	.09	.03
☐ 193 Keith Byars	.10	.05	.01
☐ 194 Sean Salisbury	.10	.05	.01
☐ 195 Todd Lyght	.10	.05	.01
☐ 196 Jessie Hester	.10	.05	.01
☐ 197 Rufus Porter	.10	.05	.01
☐ 198 Steve Christie	.10	.05	.01
☐ 199 Nate Lewis	.10	.05	.01
☐ 200 Barry Sanders	2.50	1.10	.30
☐ 201 Michael Haynes	.20	.09	.03
☐ 202 John Taylor	.20	.09	.03
☐ 203 John Friesz	.20	.09	.03
☐ 204 William Fuller	.10	.05	.01
☐ 205 Dennis Smith	.10	.05	.01
☐ 206 Adrian Cooper	.10	.05	.01
☐ 207 Henry Thomas	.10	.05	.01
☐ 208 Gerald Williams	.10	.05	.01
☐ 209 Chris Burkett	.10	.05	.01
☐ 210 Broderick Thomas	.10	.05	.01
☐ 211 Marvin Washington	.10	.05	.01
☐ 212 Bennie Blades	.10	.05	.01
☐ 213 Tony Casillas	.10	.05	.01
☐ 214 Bubby Brister	.10	.05	.01
☐ 215 Don Griffin	.10	.05	.01
☐ 216 Jeff Cross	.10	.05	.01
☐ 217 Derrick Walker	.10	.05	.01
☐ 218 Lorenzo White	.10	.05	.01
☐ 219 Ricky Sanders	.10	.05	.01
☐ 220 Rickey Jackson	.10	.05	.01
☐ 221 Simon Fletcher	.10	.05	.01
☐ 222 Troy Vincent	.10	.05	.01
☐ 223 Gary Clark	.20	.09	.03
☐ 224 Stanley Richard	.10	.05	.01
☐ 225 Dave Krieg	.20	.09	.03
☐ 226 Warren Moon	.40	.18	.05
☐ 227 Reggie Langhorne	.10	.05	.01
☐ 228 Kent Hull	.10	.05	.01
☐ 229 Ferrell Edmunds	.10	.05	.01
☐ 230 Cortez Kennedy	.20	.09	.03
☐ 231 Hugh Millen	.10	.05	.01
☐ 232 Eugene Chung	.10	.05	.01
☐ 233 Rodney Peete	.10	.05	.01
☐ 234 Tom Waddle	.10	.05	.01
☐ 235 David Klingler	.10	.05	.01
☐ 236 Mark Carrier WR	.20	.09	.03
☐ 237 Jay Schroeder	.10	.05	.01
☐ 238 James Jones	.10	.05	.01
☐ 239 Phil Simms	.20	.09	.03
☐ 240 Steve Atwater	.10	.05	.01
☐ 241 Jeff Herrod	.10	.05	.01
☐ 242 Dale Carter	.10	.05	.01
☐ 243 Glenn Cadrez	.10	.05	.01
☐ 244 Wayne Martin	.10	.05	.01
☐ 245 Willie Davis	.40	.18	.05
☐ 246 Lawrence Taylor	.40	.18	.05
☐ 247 Stan Humphries	.40	.18	.05
☐ 248 Byron Evans	.10	.05	.01
☐ 249 Wilber Marshall	.10	.05	.01
☐ 250 Michael Bankston	.10	.05	.01
☐ 251 Steve McMichael	.20	.09	.03
☐ 252 Brad Edwards	.10	.05	.01
☐ 253 Will Wolford	.10	.05	.01
☐ 254 Paul Gruber	.10	.05	.01
☐ 255 Steve Young	1.50	.70	.19
☐ 256 Chuck Cecil	.10	.05	.01
☐ 257 Pierce Holt	.10	.05	.01
☐ 258 Anthony Miller	.20	.09	.03
☐ 259 Carl Banks	.10	.05	.01
☐ 260 Brad Muster	.10	.05	.01
☐ 261 Clay Matthews	.20	.09	.03
☐ 262 Rod Bernstine	.10	.05	.01
☐ 263 Tim Barnett	.10	.05	.01
☐ 264 Greg Lloyd	.40	.18	.05
☐ 265 Sean Jones	.10	.05	.01
☐ 266 J.J. Birden	.10	.05	.01
☐ 267 Tim McDonald	.10	.05	.01
☐ 268 Charles Mann	.10	.05	.01
☐ 269 Bruce Smith	.40	.18	.05
☐ 270 Sean Gilbert	.20	.09	.03
☐ 271 Ricardo McDonald	.10	.05	.01
☐ 272 Jeff Hostetler	.20	.09	.03
☐ 273 Russell Maryland	.10	.05	.01
☐ 274 Dave Brown	.40	.18	.05
☐ 275 Ronnie Lott	.20	.09	.03
☐ 276 Jim Kelly	.40	.18	.05
☐ 277 Joe Montana	2.50	1.10	.30
☐ 278 Eric Allen	.10	.05	.01
☐ 279 Browning Nagle	.10	.05	.01
☐ 280 Neal Anderson	.10	.05	.01
☐ 281 Troy Aikman	2.50	1.10	.30
☐ 282 Ed McCaffrey	.10	.05	.01
☐ 283 Robert Jones	.10	.05	.01
☐ 284 Dalton Hilliard	.10	.05	.01
☐ 285 Johnny Mitchell	.10	.05	.01
☐ 286 Jay Hilgenberg	.10	.05	.01
☐ 287 Eric Martin	.10	.05	.01
☐ 288 Steve Emtman	.10	.05	.01
☐ 289 Vaughn Dunbar	.10	.05	.01
☐ 290 Mark Wheeler	.10	.05	.01
☐ 291 Leslie O'Neal	.20	.09	.03
☐ 292 Jerry Rice	2.50	1.10	.30
☐ 293 Neil Smith	.40	.18	.05
☐ 294 Kerry Cash	.10	.05	.01
☐ 295 Dan McGwire	.10	.05	.01
☐ 296 Carl Pickens	1.50	.70	.19
☐ 297 Terrell Buckley	.10	.05	.01
☐ 298 Randall Cunningham	.20	.09	.03
☐ 299 Santana Dotson	.20	.09	.03
☐ 300 Keith Jackson	.20	.09	.03
☐ 301 Jim Lachey	.10	.05	.01
☐ 302 Dan Marino	4.00	1.80	.50
☐ 303 Lee Williams	.10	.05	.01
☐ 304 Burt Grossman	.10	.05	.01
☐ 305 Kevin Mack	.10	.05	.01
☐ 306 Pat Swilling	.10	.05	.01
☐ 307 Arthur Marshall	.10	.05	.01
☐ 308 Jim Harbaugh	.40	.18	.05
☐ 309 Kurt Barber	.10	.05	.01
☐ 310 Harvey Williams	.20	.09	.03
☐ 311 Ricky Ervins	.10	.05	.01
☐ 312 Flipper Anderson	.10	.05	.01
☐ 313 Bernie Kosar	.20	.09	.03
☐ 314 Boomer Esiason	.20	.09	.03
☐ 315 Deion Sanders	1.50	.70	.19
☐ 316 Ray Childress	.10	.05	.01
☐ 317 Howie Long	.20	.09	.03
☐ 318 Henry Ellard	.20	.09	.03
☐ 319 Marco Coleman	.10	.05	.01
☐ 320 Chris Mims	.10	.05	.01
☐ 321 Quentin Coryatt	.20	.09	.03
☐ 322 Jason Hanson	.10	.05	.01
☐ 323 Ricky Proehl	.10	.05	.01
☐ 324 Randal Hill	.10	.05	.01
☐ 325 Vinny Testaverde	.20	.09	.03
☐ 326 Jeff George	.40	.18	.05
☐ 327 Junior Seau	.40	.18	.05
☐ 328 Earnest Byner	.10	.05	.01
☐ 329 Andre Reed	.20	.09	.03
☐ 330 Phillippi Sparks	.10	.05	.01
☐ 331 Kevin Ross	.10	.05	.01
☐ 332 Clarence Verdin	.10	.05	.01
☐ 333 Darryl Henley	.10	.05	.01
☐ 334 Dana Hall	.10	.05	.01
☐ 335 Greg McMurtry	.10	.05	.01
☐ 336 Ron Hall	.10	.05	.01
☐ 337 Darrell Green	.10	.05	.01
☐ 338 Carlton Bailey	.10	.05	.01
☐ 339 Irv Eatman	.10	.05	.01
☐ 340 Greg Kragen	.10	.05	.01
☐ 341 Wade Wilson	.10	.05	.01
☐ 342 Klaus Wilmsmeyer	.10	.05	.01
☐ 343 Derek Brown TE	.10	.05	.01
☐ 344 Erik Williams	.10	.05	.01
☐ 345 Jim McMahon	.10	.05	.01
☐ 346 Mike Sherrard	.10	.05	.01
☐ 347 Mark Bavaro	.10	.05	.01
☐ 348 Anthony Munoz	.20	.09	.03
☐ 349 Eric Dickerson	.20	.09	.03
☐ 350 Steve Beuerlein	.10	.05	.01
☐ 351 Tim McGee	.10	.05	.01
☐ 352 Terry McDaniel	.10	.05	.01
☐ 353 Dan Fouts HOF	.10	.05	.01
☐ 354 Chuck Noll HOF	.20	.09	.03
☐ 355 Bill Walsh HOF	.20	.09	.03
☐ 356 Larry Little HOF	.10	.05	.01
☐ 357 Todd Marinovich HH	.10	.05	.01
☐ 358 Jeff George HH	.40	.18	.05
☐ 359 Bernie Kosar HH	.20	.09	.03
☐ 360 Rob Moore HH	.20	.09	.03
☐ NNO Franco Harris AU/3000	30.00	13.50	3.70

1993 Pinnacle Men of Autumn

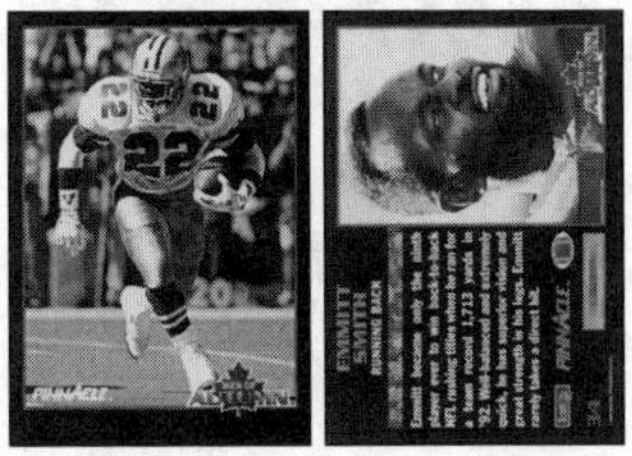

The 1993 Pinnacle Men of Autumn set consists of 55 standard-size cards. Not available in regular Pinnacle packs, one of these cards was inserted into each 16-card 1993 Score football foil pack. The fronts feature color on-field action shots on a glossy black laminate. The photos are edged with a red line and the borders are of the glossy black backing. The player's name and position appears in gold foil in the bottom margin, and the Men of Autumn logo rests at the bottom of the photo. The horizontal backs display a red-edged, black-bordered player close-up on the right half, while a brief review of the player's performance appears on the left half. The cards are arranged in alphabetical order within an alphabetical team order.

	MINT	NRMT	EXC
COMPLETE SET (55)	12.00	5.50	1.50
COMMON CARD (1-55)	.25	.11	.03

☐ 1 Andre Rison	.40	.18	.05
☐ 2 Thurman Thomas	.60	.25	.07
☐ 3 Wendell Davis	.25	.11	.03
☐ 4 Harold Green	.25	.11	.03
☐ 5 Eric Metcalf	.60	.25	.07
☐ 6 Michael Irvin	.60	.25	.07
☐ 7 John Elway	1.50	.70	.19
☐ 8 Barry Sanders	2.00	.90	.25
☐ 9 Sterling Sharpe	.60	.25	.07
☐ 10 Warren Moon	.60	.25	.07
☐ 11 Rohn Stark	.25	.11	.03
☐ 12 Derrick Thomas	.60	.25	.07
☐ 13 Terry McDaniel	.25	.11	.03
☐ 14 Cleveland Gary	.25	.11	.03
☐ 15 Dan Marino	3.00	1.35	.35
☐ 16 Terry Allen	.60	.25	.07
☐ 17 Marv Cook	.25	.11	.03
☐ 18 Bobby Hebert	.25	.11	.03
☐ 19 Rodney Hampton	.40	.18	.05
☐ 20 Brad Baxter	.25	.11	.03
☐ 21 Reggie White	.60	.25	.07
☐ 22 Ricky Proehl	.25	.11	.03
☐ 23 Barry Foster	.40	.18	.05
☐ 24 Junior Seau	.60	.25	.07
☐ 25 Steve Young	1.50	.70	.19
☐ 26 Cortez Kennedy	.40	.18	.05
☐ 27 Reggie Cobb	.25	.11	.03
☐ 28 Mark Rypien	.40	.18	.05
☐ 29 Deion Sanders	1.50	.70	.19
☐ 30 Bruce Smith	.60	.25	.07
☐ 31 Richard Dent	.40	.18	.05
☐ 32 Alfred Williams	.25	.11	.03
☐ 33 Clay Matthews	.25	.11	.03
☐ 34 Emmitt Smith	3.00	1.35	.35
☐ 35 Simon Fletcher	.25	.11	.03
☐ 36 Chris Spielman	.40	.18	.05
☐ 37 Brett Favre	3.00	1.35	.35
☐ 38 Bruce Matthews	.25	.11	.03
☐ 39 Jeff Herrod	.25	.11	.03
☐ 40 Nick Lowery	.25	.11	.03
☐ 41 Steve Wisniewski	.25	.11	.03
☐ 42 Jim Everett	.40	.18	.05
☐ 43 Keith Jackson	.40	.18	.05
☐ 44 Chris Doleman	.25	.11	.03
☐ 45 Irving Fryar	.40	.18	.05
☐ 46 Rickey Jackson	.25	.11	.03
☐ 47 Pepper Johnson	.25	.11	.03
☐ 48 Randall Cunningham	.40	.18	.05
☐ 49 Rich Camarillo	.25	.11	.03
☐ 50 Rod Woodson	.60	.25	.07
☐ 51 Ronnie Harmon	.25	.11	.03
☐ 52 Ricky Watters	.60	.25	.07
☐ 53 Chris Warren	.60	.25	.07
☐ 54 Lawrence Dawsey	.25	.11	.03
☐ 55 Wilber Marshall	.25	.11	.03

1993 Pinnacle Rookies

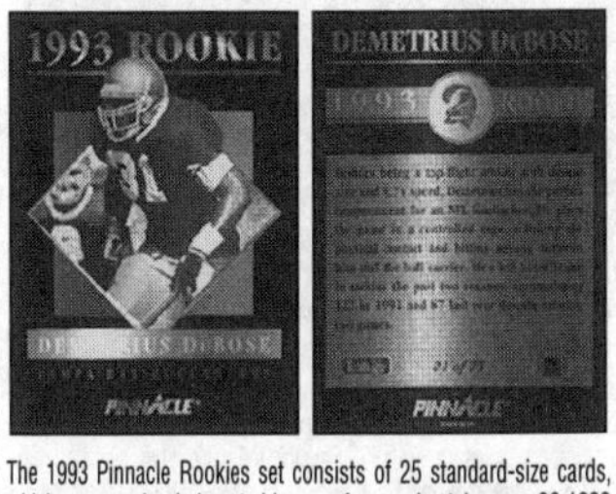

The 1993 Pinnacle Rookies set consists of 25 standard-size cards, which were randomly inserted in one of approximately every 36 1993 Pinnacle foil packs. The black fronts feature a color action player cut-out emerging from a diamond-shaped "FX" metallic design in the center of the card. The set title and the Pinnacle logo are stamped in copper-foil above and below the picture, respectively. The player's name appears on a team color-coded metallic bar below the picture, with the team name below. The black backs carry a copper-colored panel containing career highlights with the copper-colored player's name at the top of the card. The cards are numbered on the back "X of 25."

	MINT	NRMT	EXC
COMPLETE SET (25)	400.00	180.00	50.00
COMMON CARD (1-25)	6.00	2.70	.75

☐ 1 Drew Bledsoe UER Card has drafted in 92 He was 1st pick of 93 draft	175.00	80.00	22.00
☐ 2 Garrison Hearst	35.00	16.00	4.40
☐ 3 John Copeland	6.00	2.70	.75
☐ 4 Eric Curry	8.00	3.60	1.00
☐ 5 Curtis Conway	20.00	9.00	2.50
☐ 6 Lincoln Kennedy	6.00	2.70	.75
☐ 7 Jerome Bettis	60.00	27.00	7.50
☐ 8 Dan Williams	6.00	2.70	.75
☐ 9 Patrick Bates	6.00	2.70	.75
☐ 10 Brad Hopkins	6.00	2.70	.75
☐ 11 Wayne Simmons	6.00	2.70	.75
☐ 12 Rick Mirer	30.00	13.50	3.70
☐ 13 Tom Carter	6.00	2.70	.75
☐ 14 Irv Smith	8.00	3.60	1.00
☐ 15 Marvin Jones	6.00	2.70	.75

☐ 16 Deon Figures	6.00	2.70	.75
☐ 17 Leonard Renfro	6.00	2.70	.75
☐ 18 O.J.McDuffie	20.00	9.00	2.50
☐ 19 Dana Stubblefield	10.00	4.50	1.25
☐ 20 Carlton Gray	6.00	2.70	.75
☐ 21 Demetrius DuBose	6.00	2.70	.75
☐ 22 Troy Drayton	6.00	2.70	.75
☐ 23 Natrone Means	35.00	16.00	4.40
☐ 24 Reggie Brooks	8.00	3.60	1.00
☐ 25 Glyn Milburn	10.00	4.50	1.25

1993 Pinnacle Super Bowl XXVII

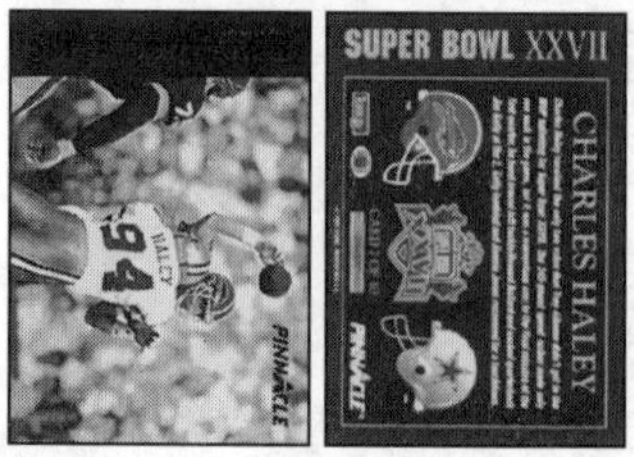

The 1993 Pinnacle Super Bowl XXVII set consists of ten standard-size cards commemorating the 1993 Super Bowl Champion Dallas Cowboys. The cards were issued one per hobby box. The horizontal front features a color action player shot that is borderless, except on the left, where a dark blue stripe carries the set title in blue-foil. Within a black panel, the horizontal back carries the player's name, game highlights, SB XXVII logo, and helmets of the Bills and the Cowboys. The cards are numbered on the back "X of 10."

	MINT	NRMT	EXC
COMPLETE SET (10)	125.00	55.00	15.50
COMMON CARD (1-10)	8.00	3.60	1.00
☐ 1 Rose Bowl	8.00	3.60	1.00
☐ 2 Thomas Everett	8.00	3.60	1.00
☐ 3 Emmitt Smith	40.00	18.00	5.00
☐ 4 Ken Norton Jr.	10.00	4.50	1.25
☐ 5 Michael Irvin	15.00	6.75	1.85
☐ 6 Jay Novacek	10.00	4.50	1.25
☐ 7 Charles Haley	10.00	4.50	1.25
☐ 8 Leon Lett	10.00	4.50	1.25
☐ 9 Alvin Harper	10.00	4.50	1.25
☐ 10 Tony Casillas	8.00	3.60	1.00

1993 Pinnacle Team Pinnacle

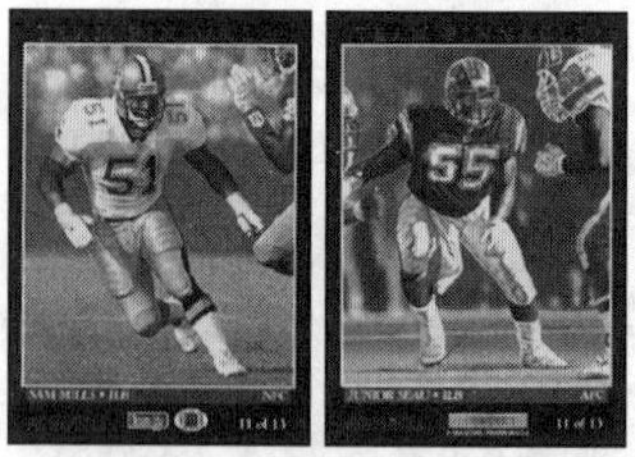

The 1993 Pinnacle Team Pinnacle set consists of 13 two-player standard-size cards. One side showcases the best player by position for the AFC, while the flip side carries his NFC counterpart. The cards were randomly inserted in 1993 Pinnacle foil packs at an insertion rate of at least one in 90 packs. Both sides display black-bordered color action player paintings framed by a thin white line. The player's name, position, and conference designation appear on a gray stripe along the bottom of the portrait. Both sides of the card are numbered "X of 13."

	MINT	NRMT	EXC
COMPLETE SET (13)	250.00	110.00	31.00
COMMON PAIR (1-13)	10.00	4.50	1.25
☐ 1 Troy Aikman Joe Montana	125.00	55.00	15.50
☐ 2 Thurman Thomas Emmitt Smith	60.00	27.00	7.50
☐ 3 Rodney Hampton Barry Foster	14.00	6.25	1.75
☐ 4 Sterling Sharpe Anthony Miller	14.00	6.25	1.75
☐ 5 Haywood Jeffires Michael Irvin	10.00	4.50	1.25
☐ 6 Jay Novacek Keith Jackson	14.00	6.25	1.75
☐ 7 Richmond Webb Steve Wallace	10.00	4.50	1.25
☐ 8 Reggie White Leslie O'Neal	14.00	6.25	1.75
☐ 9 Cortez Kennedy Sean Gilbert	10.00	4.50	1.25
☐ 10 Derrick Thomas Wilber Marshall	14.00	6.25	1.75
☐ 11 Sam Mills Junior Seau	10.00	4.50	1.25
☐ 12 Rod Woodson Deion Sanders	25.00	11.00	3.10
☐ 13 Steve Atwater Tim McDonald	10.00	4.50	1.25

1993 Pinnacle Team 2001

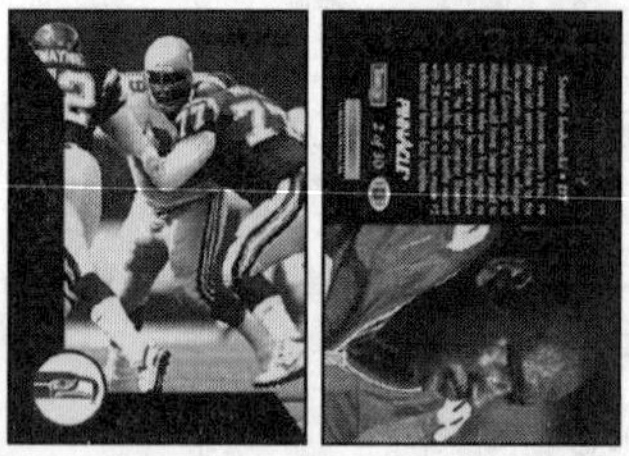

The 1993 Pinnacle Team 2001 set consists of 30 standard-size cards showcasing the league's young players who were expected to be the NFL's major stars in the year 2001. The cards were inserted one per 27-card super pack of 1993 Pinnacle. The front features a color action player photo bordered by a wide black stripe that runs along the left and bottom edges. The gold-foil set title appears along the left border; the player's name is gold-foil stamped within the lower border. The team logo appears at the lower left. The horizontal back displays a close-up player shot on one side, and a black panel on the other containing the gold-foil player's name, team name, position, and 1992 season highlights. The cards are numbered on the back "X of 30."

	MINT	NRMT	EXC
COMPLETE SET (30)	15.00	6.75	1.85
COMMON CARD (1-30)	.30	.14	.04
☐ 1 Junior Seau	1.00	.45	.12
☐ 2 Cortez Kennedy	.50	.23	.06
☐ 3 Carl Pickens	3.00	1.35	.35
☐ 4 David Klingler	.50	.23	.06
☐ 5 Santana Dotson	.50	.23	.06
☐ 6 Sean Gilbert	.50	.23	.06
☐ 7 Brett Favre	7.00	3.10	.85
☐ 8 Steve Emtman	.30	.14	.04
☐ 9 Rodney Hampton	.50	.23	.06
☐ 10 Browning Nagle	.30	.14	.04
☐ 11 Amp Lee	.30	.14	.04
☐ 12 Vaughn Dunbar	.30	.14	.04
☐ 13 Quentin Coryatt	.50	.23	.06
☐ 14 Marco Coleman	.30	.14	.04
☐ 15 Johnny Mitchell	.30	.14	.04
☐ 16 Arthur Marshall	.30	.14	.04
☐ 17 Dale Carter	.50	.23	.06
☐ 18 Henry Jones	.30	.14	.04
☐ 19 Terrell Buckley	.30	.14	.04
☐ 20 Tommy Vardell	.30	.14	.04
☐ 21 Tommy Maddox	.30	.14	.04
☐ 22 Barry Foster	.50	.23	.06
☐ 23 Herman Moore	3.50	1.55	.45
☐ 24 Ricky Watters	1.00	.45	.12
☐ 25 Mike Croel	.30	.14	.04
☐ 26 Russell Maryland	.50	.23	.06
☐ 27 Terry Allen	1.00	.45	.12
☐ 28 Jon Vaughn	.30	.14	.04
☐ 29 Todd Marinovich	.30	.14	.04
☐ 30 Jeff Graham	.50	.23	.06

1994 Pinnacle Samples

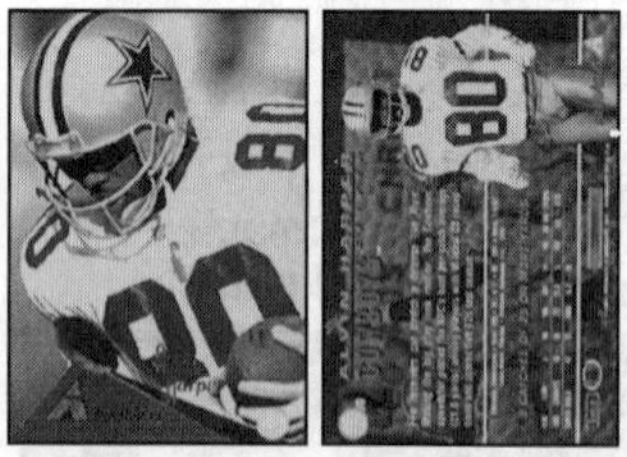

This ten-card standard-size set was issued to promote the 1994 Pinnacle football series. The cards are virtually identical to their counterparts in the regular series, with only a very slight difference when examined closely. We've noted the minor differences below. The sample cards also are punched in one corner to indicate that they are promotional samples not for sale.

	MINT	NRMT	EXC
COMPLETE SET (10)	8.00	3.60	1.00
COMMON CARD	.50	.23	.06
☐ 1 Deion Sanders last line of text reads "es for a 17.7-yard..."	1.50	.70	.19
☐ 3 Barry Sanders Trophy Collection name in brown ink on back	3.00	1.35	.35
☐ 24 Sean Gilbert last line of text reads "mage to earn..."	.50	.23	.06
☐ 30 Alvin Harper last line of text reads "tions and scored..."	.50	.23	.06
☐ 32 Derrick Thomas last line of text reads "bles last season."	.75	.35	.09
☐ 85 James Jett hometown/drafted line 1-3/16" long instead of 1-5/16"	.50	.23	.06
☐ 214 Chuck Levy card number in white letters	.50	.23	.06
☐ DP8 William Floyd last line of text reads "over would-be tacklers."	.75	.35	.09
☐ NNO Pick Pinnacle Redemp.Card no player name on front	.50	.23	.06
☐ NNO Ad Card	.50	.23	.06

1994 Pinnacle

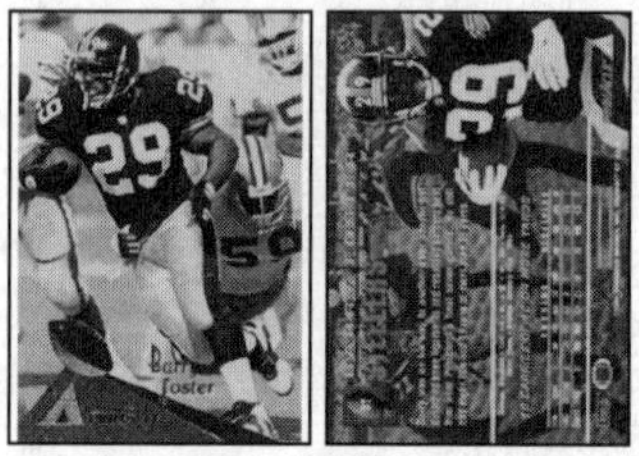

The 1994 Pinnacle football set consists of 270 standard-size cards. The fronts feature full-bleed photos with the player's name and Pinnacle logo in gold foil at the bottom. Horizontal backs have a player photo, a brief write-up and statistics. Cards 190-221 comprise of a Rookies subset. Card 271, Jerry Rice, was issued only in jumbo packs. The set is considered complete without it. Odds of finding the Drew Bledsoe Pinnacle Passer were one in approximately 360 hobby packs. Rookie Cards in this set include Mario Bates, Trent Dilfer, Marshall Faulk, William Floyd, Byron Bam Morris, Errict Rhett, Darnay Scott and Heath Shuler.

	MINT	NRMT	EXC
COMPLETE SET (270)	20.00	9.00	2.50
COMMON CARD (1-270)	.08	.04	.01
☐ 1 Deion Sanders	1.25	.55	.16
☐ 2 Eric Metcalf	.15	.07	.02
☐ 3 Barry Sanders	2.00	.90	.25
☐ 4 Ernest Givins	.15	.07	.02
☐ 5 Phil Simms	.15	.07	.02
☐ 6 Rod Woodson	.30	.14	.04
☐ 7 Michael Irvin	.30	.14	.04
☐ 8 Cortez Kennedy	.15	.07	.02
☐ 9 Eric Martin	.08	.04	.01
☐ 10 Jeff Hostetler	.15	.07	.02
☐ 11 Sterling Sharpe	.15	.07	.02
☐ 12 John Elway	1.50	.70	.19
☐ 13 Neal Anderson	.08	.04	.01
☐ 14 Terry Kirby	.30	.14	.04
☐ 15 Jim Everett	.15	.07	.02
☐ 16 Lawrence Dawsey	.08	.04	.01
☐ 17 Kelvin Martin	.08	.04	.01
☐ 18 Tim McGee	.08	.04	.01
☐ 19 Cris Carter	.30	.14	.04
☐ 20 Ronnie Harmon	.08	.04	.01
☐ 21 Jim Kelly	.30	.14	.04
☐ 22 Steve Young	1.50	.70	.19
☐ 23 Johnny Johnson	.08	.04	.01
☐ 24 Sean Gilbert	.08	.04	.01
☐ 25 Brian Mitchell	.08	.04	.01
☐ 26 Carl Pickens	.75	.35	.09
☐ 27 Tim Brown	.30	.14	.04
☐ 28 Reggie Langhorne	.08	.04	.01
☐ 29 Webster Slaughter	.08	.04	.01
☐ 30 Alvin Harper	.15	.07	.02
☐ 31 Andre Rison	.15	.07	.02
☐ 32 Derrick Thomas	.30	.14	.04
☐ 33 Irving Fryar	.15	.07	.02
☐ 34 Vinny Testaverde	.15	.07	.02
☐ 35 Steve Beuerlein	.08	.04	.01
☐ 36 Brett Favre	4.00	1.80	.50
☐ 37 Barry Foster	.08	.04	.01
☐ 38 Vaughan Johnson	.08	.04	.01
☐ 39 Carlton Bailey	.08	.04	.01
☐ 40 Steve Emtman	.08	.04	.01
☐ 41 Anthony Miller	.15	.07	.02
☐ 42 Jeff Cross	.08	.04	.01
☐ 43 Trace Armstrong	.08	.04	.01
☐ 44 Derek Russell	.08	.04	.01
☐ 45 Vincent Brisby	.30	.14	.04
☐ 46 Mark Jackson	.08	.04	.01
☐ 47 Eugene Robinson	.08	.04	.01
☐ 48 John Friesz	.15	.07	.02
☐ 49 Scott Mitchell	.30	.14	.04
☐ 50 Steve Atwater	.08	.04	.01
☐ 51 Ken Norton	.15	.07	.02
☐ 52 Vincent Brown	.08	.04	.01
☐ 53 Morten Andersen	.08	.04	.01
☐ 54 Gary Anderson K	.08	.04	.01
☐ 55 Eric Curry	.08	.04	.01
☐ 56 Henry Jones	.08	.04	.01
☐ 57 Flipper Anderson	.08	.04	.01
☐ 58 Pat Swilling	.08	.04	.01
☐ 59 Erric Pegram	.08	.04	.01
☐ 60 Bruce Matthews	.08	.04	.01
☐ 61 Willie Davis	.15	.07	.02
☐ 62 O.J. McDuffie	.30	.14	.04
☐ 63 Qadry Ismail	.30	.14	.04
☐ 64 Anthony Smith	.08	.04	.01
☐ 65 Eric Allen	.08	.04	.01
☐ 66 Marion Butts	.08	.04	.01
☐ 67 Chris Miller	.08	.04	.01
☐ 68 Terrell Buckley	.08	.04	.01
☐ 69 Thurman Thomas	.30	.14	.04
☐ 70 Roosevelt Potts	.08	.04	.01
☐ 71 Tony McGee	.08	.04	.01
☐ 72 Jason Hanson	.08	.04	.01
☐ 73 Victor Bailey	.08	.04	.01
☐ 74 Albert Lewis	.08	.04	.01
☐ 75 Nate Odomes	.08	.04	.01
☐ 76 Ben Coates	.30	.14	.04
☐ 77 Warren Moon	.30	.14	.04
☐ 78 Derek Brown RB	.08	.04	.01
☐ 79 David Klingler	.08	.04	.01
☐ 80 Cleveland Gary	.08	.04	.01
☐ 81 Emmitt Smith	4.00	1.80	.50
☐ 82 Jay Novacek	.15	.07	.02
☐ 83 Dana Stubblefield	.30	.14	.04
☐ 84 Michael Brooks	.08	.04	.01
☐ 85 James Jett	.08	.04	.01
☐ 86 J.J. Birden	.08	.04	.01
☐ 87 William Fuller	.08	.04	.01
☐ 88 Glyn Milburn	.15	.07	.02
☐ 89 Tim Worley	.08	.04	.01
☐ 90 Brett Perriman	.15	.07	.02
☐ 91 Randall Cunningham	.15	.07	.02
☐ 92 Drew Bledsoe	2.00	.90	.25
☐ 93 Jerome Bettis	1.00	.45	.12
☐ 94 Boomer Esiason	.15	.07	.02
☐ 95 Garrison Hearst	.75	.35	.09
☐ 96 Bruce Smith	.30	.14	.04
☐ 97 Jackie Harris	.08	.04	.01
☐ 98 Jeff George	.30	.14	.04
☐ 99 Tom Waddle	.08	.04	.01
☐ 100 John Copeland	.08	.04	.01
☐ 101 Bobby Hebert	.08	.04	.01
☐ 102 Joe Montana	2.00	.90	.25
☐ 103 Herman Moore	.75	.35	.09
☐ 104 Rick Mirer	.30	.14	.04
☐ 105 Ricky Watters	.30	.14	.04
☐ 106 Neil O'Donnell	.30	.14	.04
☐ 107 Herschel Walker	.15	.07	.02
☐ 108 Rob Moore	.15	.07	.02
☐ 109 Reggie Brooks	.15	.07	.02
☐ 110 Tommy Vardell	.08	.04	.01
☐ 111 Eric Green	.08	.04	.01
☐ 112 Stan Humphries	.30	.14	.04
☐ 113 Greg Robinson	.08	.04	.01
☐ 114 Eric Swann	.15	.07	.02
☐ 115 Courtney Hawkins	.08	.04	.01
☐ 116 Andre Reed	.15	.07	.02
☐ 117 Steve McMichael	.15	.07	.02
☐ 118 Gary Brown	.08	.04	.01
☐ 119 Terry Allen	.15	.07	.02
☐ 120 Dan Marino	4.00	1.80	.50
☐ 121 Gary Clark	.15	.07	.02
☐ 122 Chris Warren	.15	.07	.02
☐ 123 Pierce Holt	.08	.04	.01
☐ 124 Anthony Carter	.15	.07	.02
☐ 125 Quentin Coryatt	.08	.04	.01
☐ 126 Harold Green	.08	.04	.01
☐ 127 Leonard Russell	.08	.04	.01
☐ 128 Tim McDonald	.08	.04	.01
☐ 129 Chris Spielman	.15	.07	.02
☐ 130 Cody Carlson	.08	.04	.01
☐ 131 Ronald Moore	.08	.04	.01
☐ 132 Renaldo Turnbull	.08	.04	.01
☐ 133 Ronnie Lott	.15	.07	.02
☐ 134 Natrone Means	.75	.35	.09
☐ 135 Keith Byars	.08	.04	.01
☐ 136 Henry Ellard	.15	.07	.02
☐ 137 Steve Jordan	.08	.04	.01
☐ 138 Calvin Williams	.15	.07	.02
☐ 139 Brian Blades	.15	.07	.02
☐ 140 Michael Jackson	.15	.07	.02
☐ 141 Charles Haley	.15	.07	.02
☐ 142 Curtis Conway	.30	.14	.04
☐ 143 Nick Lowery	.08	.04	.01
☐ 144 Bill Brooks	.08	.04	.01
☐ 145 Michael Haynes	.15	.07	.02
☐ 146 Willie Green	.08	.04	.01
☐ 147 Duane Bickett	.08	.04	.01
☐ 148 Shannon Sharpe	.15	.07	.02
☐ 149 Ricky Proehl	.08	.04	.01
☐ 150 Troy Aikman	2.00	.90	.25
☐ 151 Mike Sherrard	.08	.04	.01
☐ 152 Reggie Cobb	.08	.04	.01
☐ 153 Norm Johnson	.08	.04	.01
☐ 154 Neil Smith	.30	.14	.04
☐ 155 James Francis	.08	.04	.01
☐ 156 Greg McMurtry	.08	.04	.01
☐ 157 Greg Townsend	.08	.04	.01
☐ 158 Mel Gray	.08	.04	.01
☐ 159 Rocket Ismail	.15	.07	.02
☐ 160 Leslie O'Neal	.08	.04	.01
☐ 161 Johnny Mitchell	.08	.04	.01
☐ 162 Brent Jones	.15	.07	.02
☐ 163 Chris Doleman	.08	.04	.01
☐ 164 Seth Joyner	.08	.04	.01
☐ 165 Marco Coleman	.08	.04	.01
☐ 166 Mark Higgs	.08	.04	.01

	MINT	NRMT	EXC
☐ 167 John L. Williams	.08	.04	.01
☐ 168 Darrell Green	.08	.04	.01
☐ 169 Mark Carrier WR	.15	.07	.02
☐ 170 Reggie White	.30	.14	.04
☐ 171 Darryl Talley	.08	.04	.01
☐ 172 Russell Maryland	.08	.04	.01
☐ 173 Mark Collins	.08	.04	.01
☐ 174 Chris Jacke	.08	.04	.01
☐ 175 Richard Dent	.15	.07	.02
☐ 176 John Taylor	.15	.07	.02
☐ 177 Rodney Hampton	.30	.14	.04
☐ 178 Dwight Stone	.08	.04	.01
☐ 179 Cornelius Bennett	.15	.07	.02
☐ 180 Cris Dishman	.08	.04	.01
☐ 181 Jerry Rice	2.00	.90	.25
☐ 182 Rod Bernstine	.08	.04	.01
☐ 183 Keith Hamilton	.08	.04	.01
☐ 184 Keith Jackson	.08	.04	.01
☐ 185 Craig Erickson	.08	.04	.01
☐ 186 Marcus Allen	.30	.14	.04
☐ 187 Marcus Robertson	.08	.04	.01
☐ 188 Junior Seau	.30	.14	.04
☐ 189 LeShon Johnson	.15	.07	.02
☐ 190 Perry Klein	.08	.04	.01
☐ 191 Bryant Young	.75	.35	.09
☐ 192 Byron Bam Morris	.30	.14	.04
☐ 193 Jeff Cothran	.08	.04	.01
☐ 194 Lamar Smith	.08	.04	.01
☐ 195 Calvin Jones	.08	.04	.01
☐ 196 James Bostic	.08	.04	.01
☐ 197 Dan Wilkinson	.15	.07	.02
☐ 198 Marshall Faulk	4.00	1.80	.50
☐ 199 Heath Shuler	1.50	.70	.19
☐ 200 Willie McGinest	.30	.14	.04
☐ 201 Trev Alberts	.15	.07	.02
☐ 202 Trent Dilfer	1.25	.55	.16
☐ 203 Sam Adams	.15	.07	.02
☐ 204 Charles Johnson	.75	.35	.09
☐ 205 Johnnie Morton	.75	.35	.09
☐ 206 Thomas Lewis	.15	.07	.02
☐ 207 Greg Hill	1.00	.45	.12
☐ 208 William Floyd	1.50	.70	.19
☐ 209 Derrick Alexander WR	.30	.14	.04
☐ 210 Darnay Scott	2.50	1.10	.30
☐ 211 Lake Dawson	1.00	.45	.12
☐ 212 Errict Rhett	2.00	.90	.25
☐ 213 Kevin Lee	.08	.04	.01
☐ 214 Chuck Levy	.08	.04	.01
☐ 215 David Palmer	.15	.07	.02
☐ 216 Ryan Yarborough	.08	.04	.01
☐ 217 Charlie Garner	.15	.07	.02
☐ 218 Mario Bates	.75	.35	.09
☐ 219 Jamir Miller	.08	.04	.01
☐ 220 Bucky Brooks	.08	.04	.01
☐ 221 Donnell Bennett	.08	.04	.01
☐ 222 Kevin Greene	.30	.14	.04
☐ 223 LeRoy Butler	.08	.04	.01
☐ 224 Anthony Pleasant	.08	.04	.01
☐ 225 Steve Christie	.08	.04	.01
☐ 226 Bill Romanowski	.08	.04	.01
☐ 227 Darren Carrington	.08	.04	.01
☐ 228 Chester McGlockton	.08	.04	.01
☐ 229 Jack Del Rio	.08	.04	.01
☐ 230 Kevin Smith	.08	.04	.01
☐ 231 Chris Zorich	.08	.04	.01
☐ 232 Donnell Woolford	.08	.04	.01
☐ 233 Tony Casillas	.08	.04	.01
☐ 234 Terry McDaniel	.08	.04	.01
☐ 235 Ray Childress	.08	.04	.01
☐ 236 John Randle	.08	.04	.01
☐ 237 Clyde Simmons	.08	.04	.01
☐ 238 Dante Jones	.08	.04	.01
☐ 239 Karl Mecklenburg	.08	.04	.01
☐ 240 Daryl Johnston	.15	.07	.02
☐ 241 Hardy Nickerson	.15	.07	.02
☐ 242 Jeff Lageman	.08	.04	.01
☐ 243 Lewis Tillman	.08	.04	.01
☐ 244 Jim McMahon	.08	.04	.01
☐ 245 Mike Pritchard	.08	.04	.01
☐ 246 Harvey Williams	.15	.07	.02
☐ 247 Sean Jones	.08	.04	.01
☐ 248 Stevon Moore	.08	.04	.01
☐ 249 Pete Metzelaars	.08	.04	.01
☐ 250 Mike Johnson	.08	.04	.01
☐ 251 Chris Slade	.08	.04	.01
☐ 252 Jessie Hester	.08	.04	.01
☐ 253 Louis Oliver	.08	.04	.01
☐ 254 Ken Harvey	.08	.04	.01
☐ 255 Bryan Cox	.08	.04	.01
☐ 256 Erik Kramer	.15	.07	.02
☐ 257 Andy Harmon	.08	.04	.01
☐ 258 Rickey Jackson	.08	.04	.01
☐ 259 Mark Carrier DB	.08	.04	.01
☐ 260 Greg Lloyd	.30	.14	.04
☐ 261 Robert Brooks	.60	.25	.07
☐ 262 Dave Brown	.15	.07	.02
☐ 263 Dennis Smith	.08	.04	.01
☐ 264 Michael Dean Perry	.15	.07	.02
☐ 265 Dan Saleaumua	.08	.04	.01
☐ 266 Mo Lewis	.08	.04	.01
☐ 267 AFC Checklist	.08	.04	.01
☐ 268 AFC Checklist	.08	.04	.01
☐ 269 NFC Checklist	.08	.04	.01
☐ 270 NFC Checklist	.08	.04	.01
☐ 271SP Jerry Rice TD King	8.00	3.60	1.00
☐ NNO Drew Bledsoe Pinnacle Passer	60.00	27.00	7.50

1994 Pinnacle Trophy Collection

This 270-card standard-size set is a Dufex version of the regular series cards. Odds of finding a Trophy Collection card were approximately one in four count goods packs. The backs differ from the basic cards with a Trophy Collection logo on the back.

	MINT	NRMT	EXC
COMPLETE SET (270)	400.00	180.00	50.00
COMMON CARD (1-270)	1.50	.70	.19
*STARS: 8X TO 16X BASIC CARDS			
*RCs: 5X TO 10X BASIC CARDS			

1994 Pinnacle Draft Pinnacle

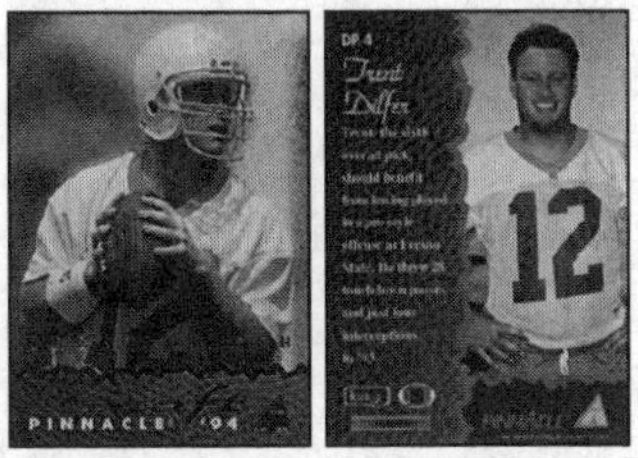

Randomly inserted in hobby packs only, this 10-card standard-size set features ten top draft choices in their NFL uniforms. Odds of finding a Draft Pinnacle card are approximately one in every 24 hobby packs. The fronts display full-bleed color action photos except at the bottom, where a gold foil jagged line separates a pebblegrain area carrying the set title. A jagged foil line divides the half in back, with player profile on a pebblegrain background on the left, and a narrowly-cropped color player photo on the right. The cards also have a dufex parallel that could be obtained through the "Pick Pinnacle" redemption program.

	MINT	NRMT	EXC
COMPLETE SET (10)	70.00	32.00	8.75
COMMON CARD (DP1-DP10)	3.00	1.35	.35
COMP.DUFEX SET (10)	70.00	32.00	8.75
EXPIRED PICK PINN.CARDS	.75	.35	.09
*DUFEX CARDS: SAME PRICE			
☐ DP1 Dan Wilkinson	3.00	1.35	.35
☐ DP2 Marshall Faulk	20.00	9.00	2.50
☐ DP3 Heath Shuler	6.00	2.70	.75
☐ DP4 Trent Dilfer	6.00	2.70	.75
☐ DP5 Charles Johnson	5.00	2.20	.60
☐ DP6 Johnnie Morton	5.00	2.20	.60
☐ DP7 Darnay Scott	12.00	5.50	1.50
☐ DP8 William Floyd	5.00	2.20	.60
☐ DP9 Errict Rhett	8.00	3.60	1.00
☐ DP10 Chuck Levy	3.00	1.35	.35

1994 Pinnacle Performers

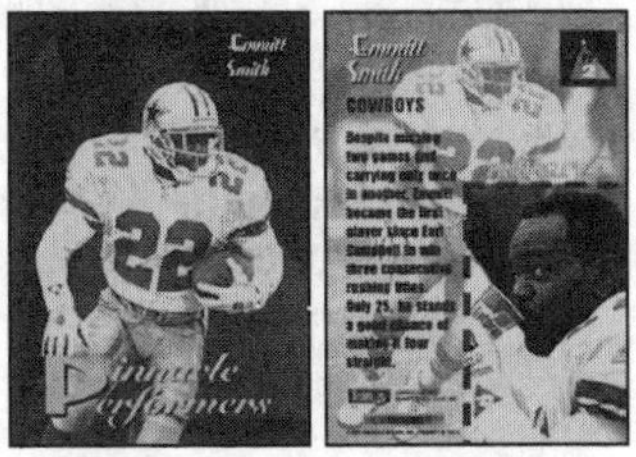

Randomly inserted in jumbo packs at a rate of one in four, this 18-card standard-size set spotlights some of the NFL's superstars. Card fronts feature a player photo superimposed over an enlarged Pinnacle gold pyramid logo. The back has a small color photo and highlights over a ghosted black and white photo. The cards are numbered on the back with a "PP" prefix.

	MINT	NRMT	EXC
COMPLETE SET (18)	60.00	27.00	7.50
COMMON CARD (PP1-PP18)	1.25	.55	.16
☐ PP1 Troy Aikman	6.00	2.70	.75
☐ PP2 Emmitt Smith	10.00	4.50	1.25
☐ PP3 Sterling Sharpe	1.25	.55	.16
☐ PP4 Barry Sanders	6.00	2.70	.75
☐ PP5 Jerry Rice	6.00	2.70	.75
☐ PP6 Steve Young	4.00	1.80	.50
☐ PP7 John Elway	4.00	1.80	.50
☐ PP8 Michael Irvin	3.00	1.35	.35
☐ PP9 Jerome Bettis	3.00	1.35	.35
☐ PP10 Tim Brown	2.00	.90	.25
☐ PP11 Joe Montana	6.00	2.70	.75
☐ PP12 Reggie Brooks	1.25	.55	.16
☐ PP13 Brett Favre	10.00	4.50	1.25
☐ PP14 Drew Bledsoe	6.00	2.70	.75
☐ PP15 Ricky Watters	2.00	.90	.25
☐ PP16 Garrison Hearst	3.00	1.35	.35
☐ PP17 Rodney Hampton	1.25	.55	.16
☐ PP18 Dan Marino	10.00	4.50	1.25

1994 Pinnacle Team Pinnacle

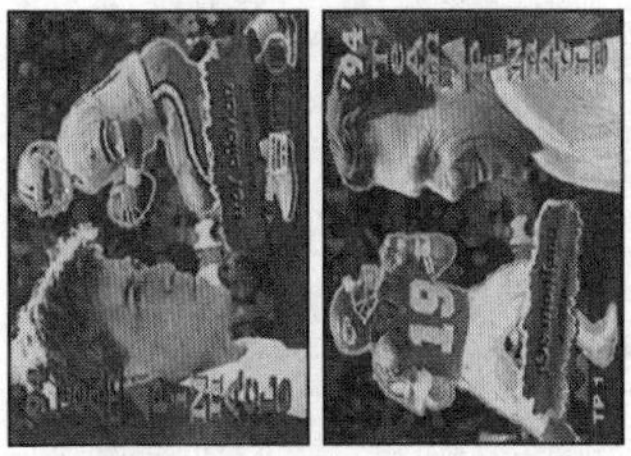

Randomly inserted in retail and hobby packs at a rate of one in 90, this 10-card standard-size set showcases a top AFC player on one side with his NFC counterpart on the flipside. With a Dufex design, the horizontally designed cards have two player photos on either side. The cards are numbered with a "TP" prefix.

	MINT	NRMT	EXC
COMPLETE SET (10)	250.00	110.00	31.00
COMMON CARD (TP1-TP10)	10.00	4.50	1.25
☐ TP1 Troy Aikman Joe Montana	70.00	32.00	8.75
☐ TP2 Brett Favre Rick Mirer	50.00	22.00	6.25
☐ TP3 Emmitt Smith Thurman Thomas	50.00	22.00	6.25
☐ TP4 Barry Sanders Barry Foster	35.00	16.00	4.40
☐ TP5 Jerome Bettis Natrone Means	20.00	9.00	2.50
☐ TP6 Sterling Sharpe Tim Brown	12.00	5.50	1.50
☐ TP7 Jerry Rice Anthony Miller	35.00	16.00	4.40
☐ TP8 Michael Irvin James Jett	15.00	6.75	1.85
☐ TP9 Reggie White Bruce Smith	15.00	6.75	1.85
☐ TP10 Sean Gilbert Cortez Kennedy	10.00	4.50	1.25

1994 Pinnacle Canton Bound

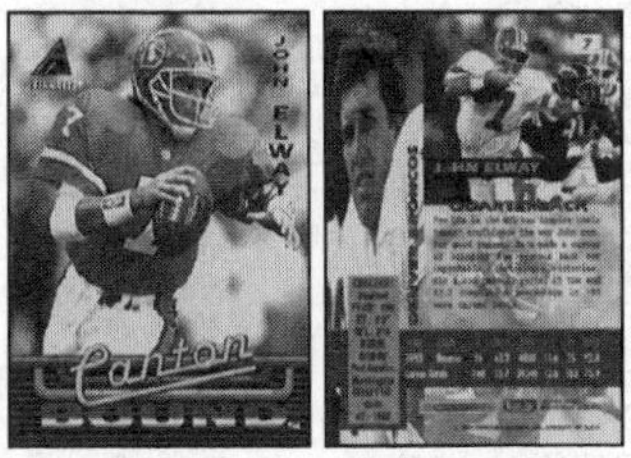

These 25 standard-size cards feature Pinnacle's picks for future Hall of Fame inductees. Production was limited to 100,000 sets, and each set contained a numbered certificate of authenticity. The fronts feature color player action shots that are borderless, and carry the player's name in vertical gold-foil lettering near the right edge. On a borderless back composed of multiple player photos, the back carries the player's biography, career highlights, and statistics. A Ronnie Lott Sample card was produced as well and is listed below, but is not considered part of the set.

	MINT	NRMT	EXC
COMPLETE SET (25)	10.00	4.50	1.25
COMMON CARD (1-25)	.20	.09	.03
☐ 1 Troy Aikman	1.50	.70	.19
☐ 2 Emmitt Smith	3.00	1.35	.35
☐ 3 Barry Sanders	1.50	.70	.19
☐ 4 Jerry Rice	1.50	.70	.19
☐ 5 Sterling Sharpe	.35	.16	.04
☐ 6 Ronnie Lott	.35	.16	.04
☐ 7 John Elway	1.00	.45	.12
☐ 8 Joe Montana	1.50	.70	.19
☐ 9 Reggie White	.35	.16	.04
☐ 10 Thurman Thomas	.50	.23	.06
☐ 11 Bruce Smith	.35	.16	.04
☐ 12 Cortez Kennedy	.20	.09	.03
☐ 13 Dan Marino	3.00	1.35	.35
☐ 14 James Lofton	.35	.16	.04
☐ 15 Art Monk	.35	.16	.04
☐ 16 Warren Moon	.35	.16	.04
☐ 17 Barry Foster	.20	.09	.03
☐ 18 Steve Young	1.00	.45	.12
☐ 19 Phil Simms	.35	.16	.04
☐ 20 Richard Dent	.20	.09	.03
☐ 21 Marcus Allen	.35	.16	.04
☐ 22 Junior Seau	.35	.16	.04
☐ 23 Michael Irvin	.50	.23	.06
☐ 24 Deion Sanders	.75	.35	.09
☐ 25 Jerome Bettis	.50	.23	.06
☐ S1 Ronnie Lott Sample	1.50	.70	.19

1994 Pinnacle/Sportflics Super Bowl

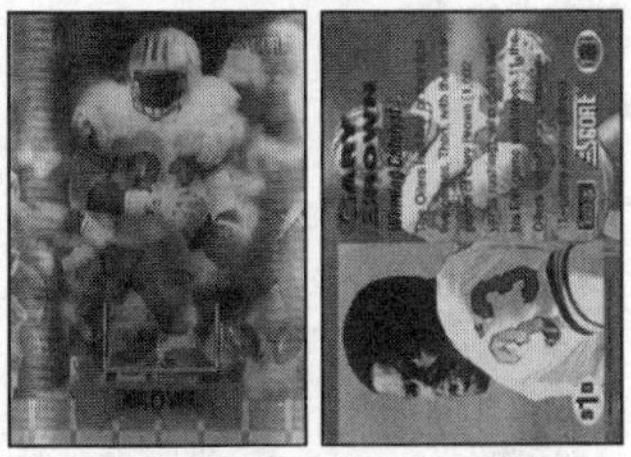

This seven-card 1994 Magic Motion standard-size set was issued by Pinnacle Brands, Inc. (Score) at the 1994 Super Bowl Card Show in Atlanta. Cards were distributed individually by exchanging three Pinnacle Brands wrappers from foil packs. The cards were produced and distributed in the following quantities: 3,000 for Gary Brown and Emmitt Smith; 2,000 for Sterling Sharpe, Jerome Bettis/Reggie Brooks, and Drew Bledsoe/Rick Mirer; and 1,000 for Jerry Rice and Deion Sanders. The "Magic Motion" process is an improved version of the old Sportflics. The full-bleed fronts when tilted can show two different action pictures of the same player, with footballs moving over the goal posts under the photo. The player's last name appears in a blue rectangle which also changes from bold size lettering to reduced size lettering. The horizontal backs have a player portrait on the left side with a ghosted action shot on the right. Season highlights for the player are superimposed over the ghosted photo. An "S" prefix and a "B" suffix appear on either side of the card number printed on a yellow oval on the card back.

	MINT	NRMT	EXC
COMPLETE SET (7)	275.00	125.00	34.00
COMMON CARD (1-7)	15.00	6.75	1.85
☐ 1 Gary Brown/3000	15.00	6.75	1.85
☐ 2 Emmitt Smith/3000	60.00	27.00	7.50
☐ 3 Sterling Sharpe/2000	20.00	9.00	2.50
☐ 4 Jerome Bettis/2000 Reggie Brooks	30.00	13.50	3.70
☐ 5 Drew Bledsoe/2000 Rick Mirer	40.00	18.00	5.00
☐ 6 Jerry Rice/1000	75.00	34.00	9.50
☐ 7 Deion Sanders/1000	50.00	22.00	6.25

1995 Pinnacle Promos

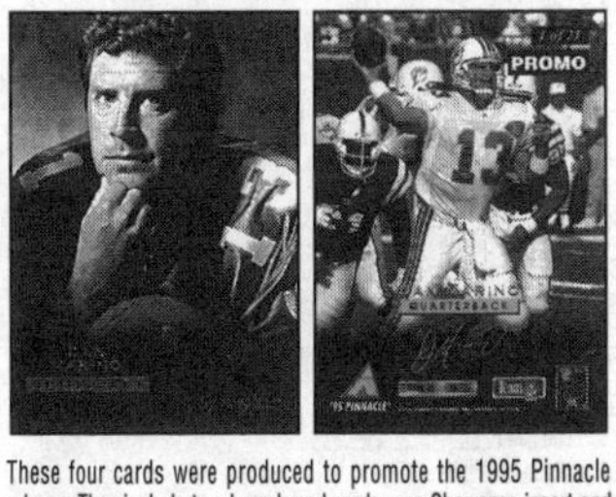

These four cards were produced to promote the 1995 Pinnacle release. They include two base brand cards, one Showcase insert and an ad card.

	MINT	NRMT	EXC
COMPLETE SET (4)	7.00	3.10	.85
COMMON CARD	.50	.23	.06
☐ 1 Dan Marino Showcase Card	4.00	1.80	.50
☐ 39 Barry Sanders	2.00	.90	.25
☐ 62 Steve Young	1.25	.55	.16
☐ NNO Ad Card	.50	.23	.06

1995 Pinnacle

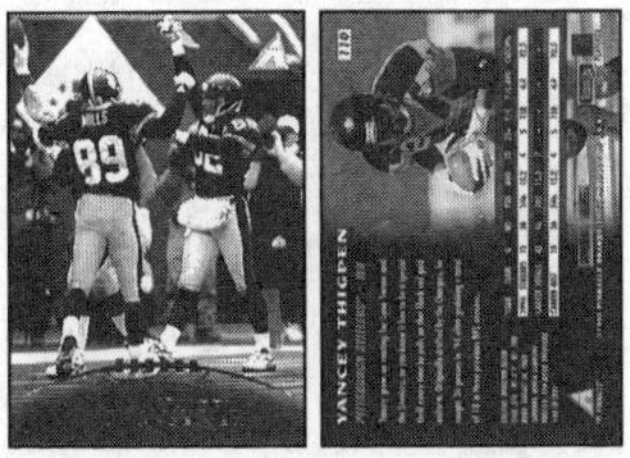

This 250 card set was issued by Pinnacle Brands and was available in 12 card packs for hobby and retail. Jumbo packs were also available. Card fronts feature a full bleed shot with a shadow of a football at the bottom with the top lacing in gold foil. The player's name and position are also in foil against the shadow background. Card backs contain statistical and biographical data on each player. A special Deion Sanders card was issued only in jumbo packs and numbered 251SP. It features Sanders with his new team - the Dallas Cowboys. The set also contains a parallel called Trophy Collection, which features the same player shots with an all-foil dufex background. Trophy Collection cards were randomly inserted into packs at a rate of one in four. The Joe Montana Trophy Collection card (#193) is unique from

the other cards because it does not have an Artist Proof parallel. Rookie Cards include Jeff Blake, Ki-Jana Carter, Kerry Collins, Joey Galloway, Steve McNair, Rashaan Salaam, Kordell Stewart, J.J. Stokes and Michael Westbrook

	MINT	NRMT	EXC
COMPLETE SET (250)	20.00	9.00	2.50
COMMON CARD (1-250)	.10	.05	.01
□ 1 Reggie White	.30	.14	.04
□ 2 Troy Aikman	1.50	.70	.19
□ 3 Willie Davis	.15	.07	.02
□ 4 Jerry Rice	1.50	.70	.19
□ 5 Bruce Smith	.30	.14	.04
□ 6 Keith Byars	.10	.05	.01
□ 7 Chris Warren	.15	.07	.02
□ 8 Erik Kramer	.10	.05	.01
□ 9 Leon Lett	.10	.05	.01
□ 10 Greg Lloyd	.15	.07	.02
□ 11 Jackie Harris	.10	.05	.01
□ 12 Irving Fryar	.15	.07	.02
□ 13 Rodney Hampton	.15	.07	.02
□ 14 Michael Irvin	.30	.14	.04
□ 15 Michael Haynes	.15	.07	.02
□ 16 Irving Spikes	.15	.07	.02
□ 17 Calvin Williams	.15	.07	.02
□ 18 Ken Norton Jr.	.15	.07	.02
□ 19 Herman Moore	.75	.35	.09
□ 20 Lewis Tillman	.10	.05	.01
□ 21 Cortez Kennedy	.15	.07	.02
□ 22 Dan Marino	3.00	1.35	.35
□ 23 Erric Pegram	.15	.07	.02
□ 24 Tim Brown	.30	.14	.04
□ 25 Jeff Blake	1.50	.70	.19
□ 26 Brett Favre	3.00	1.35	.35
□ 27 Garrison Hearst	.30	.14	.04
□ 28 Ronnie Harmon	.10	.05	.01
□ 29 Qadry Ismail	.15	.07	.02
□ 30 Ben Coates	.15	.07	.02
□ 31 Deion Sanders	1.00	.45	.12
□ 32 John Elway	1.25	.55	.16
□ 33 Natrone Means	.30	.14	.04
□ 34 Derrick Alexander WR	.30	.14	.04
□ 35 Craig Heyward	.15	.07	.02
□ 36 Jake Reed	.15	.07	.02
□ 37 Steve Walsh	.10	.05	.01
□ 38 John Randle	.10	.05	.01
□ 39 Barry Sanders	1.50	.70	.19
□ 40 Tydus Winans	.10	.05	.01
□ 41 Thomas Lewis	.15	.07	.02
□ 42 Jim Kelly	.30	.14	.04
□ 43 Gus Frerotte	.75	.35	.09
□ 44 Cris Carter	.30	.14	.04
□ 45 Kevin Williams WR	.15	.07	.02
□ 46 Dave Meggett	.10	.05	.01
□ 47 Pat Swilling	.10	.05	.01
□ 48 Neil O'Donnell	.15	.07	.02
□ 49 Terance Mathis	.15	.07	.02
□ 50 Desmond Howard	.15	.07	.02
□ 51 Bryant Young	.15	.07	.02
□ 52 Stan Humphries	.15	.07	.02
□ 53 Alvin Harper	.10	.05	.01
□ 54 Henry Ellard	.15	.07	.02
□ 55 Jessie Hester	.10	.05	.01
□ 56 Lorenzo White	.10	.05	.01
□ 57 John Friesz	.15	.07	.02
□ 58 Anthony Smith	.10	.05	.01
□ 59 Bert Emanuel	.30	.14	.04
□ 60 Gary Clark	.10	.05	.01
□ 61 Bill Brooks	.10	.05	.01
□ 62 Steve Young	1.25	.55	.16
□ 63 Jerome Bettis	.50	.23	.06
□ 64 John Taylor	.10	.05	.01
□ 65 Ricky Proehl	.10	.05	.01
□ 66 Junior Seau	.30	.14	.04
□ 67 Bubby Brister	.10	.05	.01
□ 68 Neil Smith	.15	.07	.02
□ 69 Dan McGwire	.10	.05	.01
□ 70 Brett Perriman	.15	.07	.02
□ 71 Chris Spielman	.15	.07	.02
□ 72 Jeff George	.15	.07	.02
□ 73 Emmitt Smith	3.00	1.35	.35
□ 74 Chris Penn	.10	.05	.01
□ 75 Derrick Fenner	.10	.05	.01
□ 76 Reggie Brooks	.15	.07	.02
□ 77 Chris Chandler	.15	.07	.02
□ 78 Rod Woodson	.15	.07	.02
□ 79 Isaac Bruce	.75	.35	.09
□ 80 Reggie Cobb	.10	.05	.01
□ 81 Bryce Paup	.30	.14	.04
□ 82 Warren Moon	.15	.07	.02
□ 83 Bryan Reeves	.10	.05	.01
□ 84 Lake Dawson	.15	.07	.02
□ 85 Larry Centers	.15	.07	.02
□ 86 Marshall Faulk	.75	.35	.09
□ 87 Jim Harbaugh	.15	.07	.02
□ 88 Ray Childress	.10	.05	.01
□ 89 Eric Metcalf	.15	.07	.02
□ 90 Ernie Mills	.10	.05	.01
□ 91 Lamar Lathon	.10	.05	.01
□ 92 Errict Rhett	.30	.14	.04
□ 93 David Klingler	.15	.07	.02
□ 94 Vincent Brown	.15	.07	.02
□ 95 Andre Rison	.15	.07	.02
□ 96 Brian Mitchell	.10	.05	.01
□ 97 Mark Rypien	.10	.05	.01
□ 98 Eugene Robinson	.10	.05	.01
□ 99 Eric Green	.10	.05	.01
□ 100 Rocket Ismail	.15	.07	.02
□ 101 Flipper Anderson	.10	.05	.01
□ 102 Randall Cunningham	.15	.07	.02
□ 103 Ricky Watters	.30	.14	.04
□ 104 Amp Lee	.10	.05	.01
□ 105 Ernest Givins	.10	.05	.01
□ 106 Daryl Johnston	.15	.07	.02
□ 107 Dave Krieg	.10	.05	.01
□ 108 Dana Stubblefield	.30	.14	.04
□ 109 Torrance Small	.10	.05	.01
□ 110 Yancey Thigpen	1.25	.55	.16
□ 111 Chester McGlockton	.15	.07	.02
□ 112 Craig Erickson	.10	.05	.01
□ 113 Herschel Walker	.15	.07	.02
□ 114 Mike Sherrard	.10	.05	.01
□ 115 Tony McGee	.10	.05	.01
□ 116 Adrian Murrell	.15	.07	.02
□ 117 Frank Reich	.10	.05	.01
□ 118 Hardy Nickerson	.10	.05	.01
□ 119 Andre Reed	.15	.07	.02
□ 120 Leonard Russell	.10	.05	.01
□ 121 Eric Allen	.10	.05	.01
□ 122 Jeff Hostetler	.15	.07	.02
□ 123 Barry Foster	.15	.07	.02
□ 124 Anthony Miller	.15	.07	.02
□ 125 Shawn Jefferson	.10	.05	.01
□ 126 Richie Anderson	.10	.05	.01
□ 127 Steve Bono	.15	.07	.02
□ 128 Seth Joyner	.10	.05	.01
□ 129 Darnay Scott	.30	.14	.04
□ 130 Johnny Mitchell	.10	.05	.01
□ 131 Eric Swann	.15	.07	.02
□ 132 Drew Bledsoe	1.50	.70	.19
□ 133 Marcus Allen	.30	.14	.04
□ 134 Carl Pickens	.30	.14	.04
□ 135 Michael Brooks	.10	.05	.01
□ 136 John L. Williams	.10	.05	.01
□ 137 Steve Beuerlein	.10	.05	.01
□ 138 Robert Smith	.30	.14	.04
□ 139 O.J. McDuffie	.30	.14	.04
□ 140 Haywood Jeffires	.10	.05	.01
□ 141 Aeneas Williams	.10	.05	.01
□ 142 Rick Mirer	.30	.14	.04
□ 143 William Floyd	.30	.14	.04
□ 144 Fred Barnett	.15	.07	.02
□ 145 Leroy Hoard	.10	.05	.01
□ 146 Terry Kirby	.15	.07	.02
□ 147 Boomer Esiason	.15	.07	.02
□ 148 Ken Harvey	.10	.05	.01
□ 149 Cleveland Gary	.10	.05	.01
□ 150 Brian Blades	.15	.07	.02
□ 151 Eric Turner	.10	.05	.01
□ 152 Vinny Testaverde	.15	.07	.02
□ 153 Ronald Moore UER card pictures Rob Moore	.10	.05	.01
□ 154 Curtis Conway	.30	.14	.04
□ 155 Johnnie Morton	.15	.07	.02
□ 156 Kenneth Davis	.10	.05	.01
□ 157 Scott Mitchell	.15	.07	.02
□ 158 Sean Gilbert	.15	.07	.02
□ 159 Shannon Sharpe	.15	.07	.02
□ 160 Mark Seay	.15	.07	.02
□ 161 Cornelius Bennett	.15	.07	.02
□ 162 Heath Shuler	.30	.14	.04
□ 163 Byron Bam Morris	.15	.07	.02
□ 164 Robert Brooks	.30	.14	.04
□ 165 Glyn Milburn	.10	.05	.01
□ 166 Gary Brown	.10	.05	.01
□ 167 Jim Everett	.10	.05	.01
□ 168 Steve Atwater	.10	.05	.01
□ 169 Darren Woodson	.15	.07	.02
□ 170 Mark Ingram	.10	.05	.01
□ 171 Donnell Woolford	.10	.05	.01
□ 172 Trent Dilfer	.30	.14	.04
□ 173 Charlie Garner	.15	.07	.02
□ 174 Charles Johnson	.15	.07	.02
□ 175 Mike Pritchard	.10	.05	.01
□ 176 Derek Brown RB	.10	.05	.01
□ 177 Chris Miller	.10	.05	.01
□ 178 Charles Haley	.15	.07	.02
□ 179 J.J. Birden	.10	.05	.01
□ 180 Jeff Graham	.10	.05	.01
□ 181 Bernie Parmalee	.15	.07	.02
□ 182 Mark Brunell	1.50	.70	.19
□ 183 Greg Hill	.15	.07	.02
□ 184 Michael Timpson	.10	.05	.01
□ 185 Terry Allen	.15	.07	.02
□ 186 Ricky Ervins	.10	.05	.01
□ 187 Dave Brown	.15	.07	.02
□ 188 Dan Wilkinson	.15	.07	.02
□ 189 Jay Novacek	.15	.07	.02
□ 190 Harvey Williams	.10	.05	.01
□ 191 Mario Bates	.30	.14	.04
□ 192 Steve Young	.60	.25	.07
□ 193 Joe Montana	1.50	.70	.19
□ 194 Steve Young PP	.60	.25	.07
□ 195 Troy Aikman PP	.75	.35	.09
□ 196 Drew Bledsoe PP	.75	.35	.09
□ 197 Dan Marino PP	1.25	.55	.16
□ 198 John Elway PP	.60	.25	.07
□ 199 Brett Favre PP	1.25	.55	.16
□ 200 Heath Shuler PP	.30	.14	.04
□ 201 Warren Moon PP	.10	.05	.01
□ 202 Jim Kelly PP	.30	.14	.04
□ 203 Jeff Hostetler PP	.15	.07	.02
□ 204 Rick Mirer PP	.15	.07	.02
□ 205 Dave Brown PP	.15	.07	.02
□ 206 Randall Cunningham PP	.15	.07	.02
□ 207 Neil O'Donnell PP	.15	.07	.02
□ 208 Jim Everett PP	.10	.05	.01
□ 209 Ki-Jana Carter	1.25	.55	.16
□ 210 Steve McNair	3.00	1.35	.35
□ 211 Michael Westbrook	1.50	.70	.19
□ 212 Kerry Collins	4.00	1.80	.50
□ 213 Joey Galloway	2.50	1.10	.30
□ 214 Kyle Brady	.30	.14	.04
□ 215 J.J. Stokes	1.25	.55	.16
□ 216 Tyrone Wheatley	.60	.25	.07
□ 217 Rashaan Salaam	1.50	.70	.19
□ 218 Napoleon Kaufman	1.25	.55	.16
□ 219 Frank Sanders	.30	.14	.04
□ 220 Stoney Case	.10	.05	.01
□ 221 Todd Collins	.30	.14	.04
□ 222 Warren Sapp	.15	.07	.02
□ 223 Sherman Williams	.10	.05	.01
□ 224 Rob Johnson	.10	.05	.01
□ 225 Mark Bruener	.15	.07	.02
□ 226 Derrick Brooks	.10	.05	.01
□ 227 Chad May	.10	.05	.01
□ 228 James A.Stewart	.10	.05	.01
□ 229 Ray Zellars	.15	.07	.02
□ 230 Dave Barr	.10	.05	.01
□ 231 Kordell Stewart	4.00	1.80	.50
□ 232 Jimmy Oliver	.10	.05	.01
□ 233 Tony Boselli	.15	.07	.02
□ 234 James O.Stewart	.30	.14	.04
□ 235 Derrick Alexander DE	.10	.05	.01
□ 236 Lovell Pinkney	.10	.05	.01
□ 237 John Walsh	.10	.05	.01
□ 238 Tyrone Davis	.10	.05	.01
□ 239 Joe Aska	.15	.07	.02
□ 240 Korey Stringer	.10	.05	.01
□ 241 Hugh Douglas	.15	.07	.02
□ 242 Christian Fauria	.10	.05	.01
□ 243 Terrell Fletcher	.10	.05	.01
□ 244 Dan Marino	.75	.35	.09
□ 245 Drew Bledsoe	.40	.18	.05
□ 246 John Elway	.30	.14	.04
□ 247 Emmitt Smith	.75	.35	.09
□ 248 Steve Young	.30	.14	.04
□ 249 Barry Sanders	.40	.18	.05
□ 250 Jerry Rice CL Junior Seau CL	.40	.18	.05
□ 251SP Deion Sanders SP	4.00	1.80	.50

1995 Pinnacle Artist's Proofs

Inserted one in 48 packs, this 249 card set is a parallel of the parallel Trophy Collection set. The cards feature the same all-foil dufex printing technology, but are identified by an round seal, which says "Artist's Proof" in the middle. There are only 249 parallel cards rather than 250, due to the fact that Joe Montana did not have an Artist Proof card.

	MINT	NRMT	EXC
COMPLETE SET (249)	2800.00	1250.00	350.00
COMMON CARD (1-250)	5.00	2.20	.60

193 MONTANA AP NOT ISSUED
*AP VETERAN STARS: 30X TO 60X BASIC CARDS
*AP YOUNG STARS: 20X TO 40X BASIC CARDS
*AP RCs: 15X TO 30X BASIC CARDS

1995 Pinnacle Trophy Collection

This 250 card parallel set was randomly inserted into packs at a rate of one in four and feature the same basic card fronts with "Dufex" technology in the background. Card backs also have the card name "Trophy Collection".

	MINT	NRMT	EXC
COMPLETE SET (250)	400.00	180.00	50.00
COMMON CARD (1-250)	1.00	.45	.12

*VETERAN STARS: 3X TO 6X BASIC CARDS
*YOUNG STARS: 2.5X TO 5X BASIC CARDS
*RCs: 2X TO 4X BASIC CARDS

	MINT	NRMT	EXC
JOE MONTANA TC	175.00	80.00	22.00

1995 Pinnacle Black 'N Blue

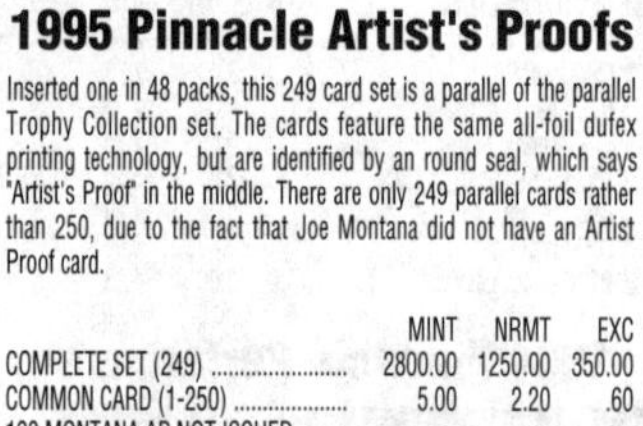

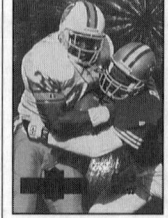

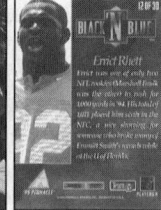

Inserted at a rate of one in 18 jumbo packs only, this 30 card set features an all-foil silver dufex background with the "Black 'N' Blue" logo at the bottom left of the card. The player's name is listed directly to the right of the logo. Card backs are numbered out of 30 and feature a player shot on the left side of the card with a brief commentary to the right.

	MINT	NRMT	EXC
COMPLETE SET (30)	150.00	70.00	19.00
COMMON CARD (1-30)	3.00	1.35	.35
□ 1 Junior Seau	5.00	2.20	.60
□ 2 Byron Bam Morris	5.00	2.20	.60
□ 3 Craig Heyward	3.00	1.35	.35
□ 4 Drew Bledsoe	15.00	6.75	1.85
□ 5 Barry Sanders	15.00	6.75	1.85
□ 6 Jerome Bettis	6.00	2.70	.75
□ 7 William Floyd	5.00	2.20	.60
□ 8 Greg Lloyd	3.00	1.35	.35
□ 9 John Elway	12.00	5.50	1.50
□ 10 Jerry Rice	15.00	6.75	1.85
□ 11 Kevin Greene	3.00	1.35	.35
□ 12 Errict Rhett	6.00	2.70	.75
□ 13 Steve Young	12.00	5.50	1.50
□ 14 Bruce Smith	5.00	2.20	.60
□ 15 Steve Atwater	3.00	1.35	.35
□ 16 Natrone Means	6.00	2.70	.75
□ 17 Ben Coates	5.00	2.20	.60
□ 18 Reggie White	6.00	2.70	.75
□ 19 Ken Harvey	3.00	1.35	.35
□ 20 Dan Marino	30.00	13.50	3.70
□ 21 Marshall Faulk	8.00	3.60	1.00
□ 22 Seth Joyner	3.00	1.35	.35
□ 23 Rod Woodson	5.00	2.20	.60
□ 24 Hardy Nickerson	3.00	1.35	.35
□ 25 Brett Favre	30.00	13.50	3.70
□ 26 Bryan Cox	3.00	1.35	.35
□ 27 Rodney Hampton	5.00	2.20	.60
□ 28 Jeff Hostetler	3.00	1.35	.35
□ 29 Brent Jones	3.00	1.35	.35
□ 30 Emmitt Smith	30.00	13.50	3.70

1995 Pinnacle Clear Shots

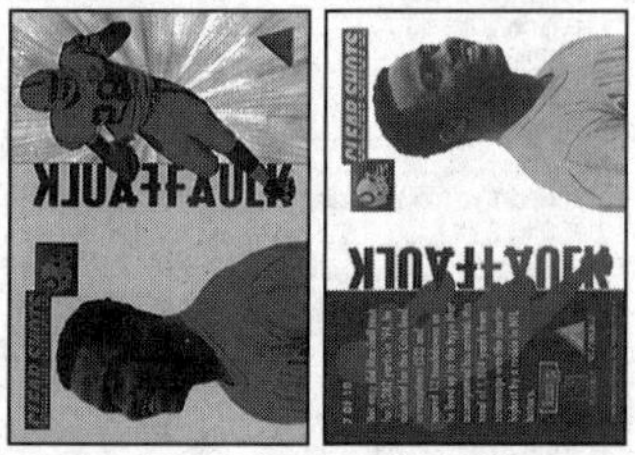

Inserted at a rate of one in 60 hobby and one in 33 retail packs, this 10 card set features eight of the league's hottest veteran players and two promising rookies using a clear plastic card stock overprinted with rainbow holographic foil. Card fronts contain a head shot of the player on the left under the "Clear Shots" logo. The right side of the card features an action shot of the player against the rainbow foil. Card backs feature the same head shot of the player reversed on the right side and commentary on the player to the left against a black background. Cards are numbered out of 10.

	MINT	NRMT	EXC
COMPLETE SET (10)	100.00	45.00	12.50
COMMON CARD (1-10)	4.00	1.80	.50
□ 1 Jerry Rice	12.00	5.50	1.50
□ 2 Dan Marino	25.00	11.00	3.10
□ 3 Steve Young	10.00	4.50	1.25
□ 4 Drew Bledsoe	12.00	5.50	1.50
□ 5 Emmitt Smith	25.00	11.00	3.10
□ 6 Barry Sanders	12.00	5.50	1.50
□ 7 Marshall Faulk	6.00	2.70	.75
□ 8 Troy Aikman	12.00	5.50	1.50
□ 9 Ki-Jana Carter	4.00	1.80	.50
□ 10 Steve McNair	12.00	5.50	1.50

1995 Pinnacle Gamebreakers

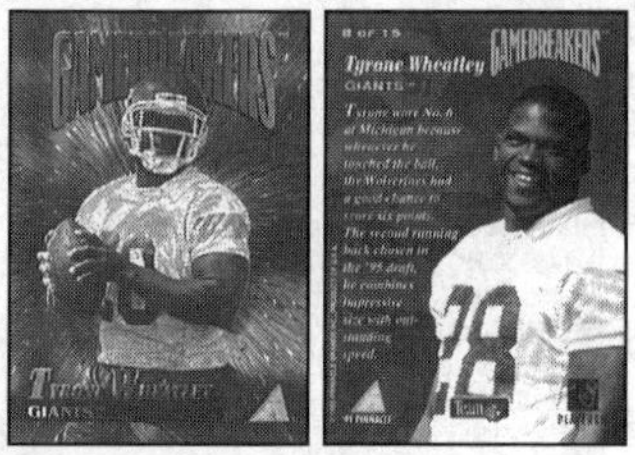

This 15 card set was randomly inserted into packs at a rate of one in 24 hobby packs. Card fronts feature the shot of the player against different color dufexed backgrounds. The title "Gamebreakers" is located above the shot and the player's name and team are located in the bottom left corner. Card backs include a shot of the player in a tan background with another color shot and a brief commentary. Cards are numbered out of 15.

	MINT	NRMT	EXC
COMPLETE SET (15)	150.00	70.00	19.00
COMMON CARD (1-15)	2.00	.90	.25
□ 1 Marshall Faulk	6.00	2.70	.75
□ 2 Emmitt Smith	25.00	11.00	3.10
□ 3 Steve Young	10.00	4.50	1.25

☐ 4 Ki-Jana Carter	3.00	1.35	.35
☐ 5 Drew Bledsoe	12.00	5.50	1.50
☐ 6 Troy Aikman	12.00	5.50	1.50
☐ 7 Rashaan Salaam	4.00	1.80	.50
☐ 8 Tyrone Wheatley	2.00	.90	.25
☐ 9 Dan Marino	25.00	11.00	3.10
☐ 10 Natrone Means	4.00	1.80	.50
☐ 11 Barry Sanders	12.00	5.50	1.50
☐ 12 Jerry Rice	12.00	5.50	1.50
☐ 13 Byron Bam Morris	2.00	.90	.25
☐ 14 Steve McNair	10.00	4.50	1.25
☐ 15 Kerry Collins	12.00	5.50	1.50

1995 Pinnacle Showcase

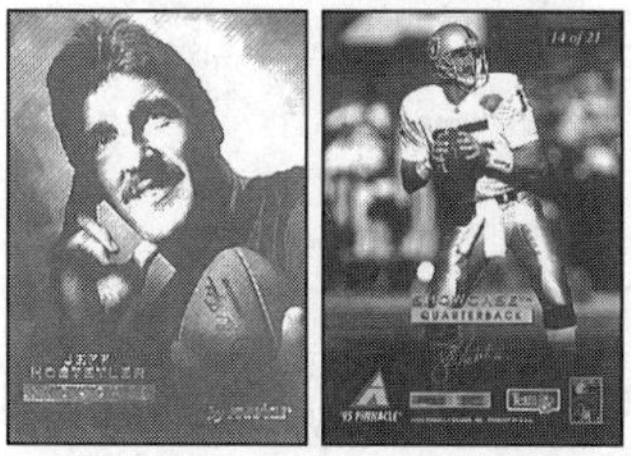

This 21 card black and white set was randomly inserted into one in every 18 hobby, one in every 10 retail packs and one in every 14 jumbo packs. Card fronts feature a posed shot of the player with his name in silver foil on the left side. Card backs feature an action shot of the player with a facsimile autograph in gold at the bottom.

	MINT	NRMT	EXC
COMPLETE SET (21)	50.00	22.00	6.25
COMMON CARD (1-21)	1.00	.45	.12
☐ 1 Drew Bledsoe	5.00	2.20	.60
☐ 2 Joey Galloway	2.50	1.10	.30
☐ 3 Steve Young	4.00	1.80	.50
☐ 4 Joe Aska	1.00	.45	.12
☐ 5 Barry Sanders	5.00	2.20	.60
☐ 6 Troy Aikman	5.00	2.20	.60
☐ 7 Dan Marino	10.00	4.50	1.25
☐ 8 Randall Cunningham	1.00	.45	.12
☐ 9 John Elway	4.00	1.80	.50
☐ 10 Brett Favre	10.00	4.50	1.25
☐ 11 Jim Kelly	2.00	.90	.25
☐ 12 Warren Moon	2.00	.90	.25
☐ 13 Dave Brown	1.00	.45	.12
☐ 14 Jeff Hostetler	1.00	.45	.12
☐ 15 Rick Mirer	2.00	.90	.25
☐ 16 Ki-Jana Carter	2.00	.90	.25
☐ 17 Kerry Collins	5.00	2.20	.60
☐ 18 J.J. Stokes	2.00	.90	.25
☐ 19 Kordell Stewart	5.00	2.20	.60
☐ 20 Michael Westbrook	2.00	.90	.25
☐ 21 Todd Collins	1.00	.45	.12

1995 Pinnacle Team Pinnacle

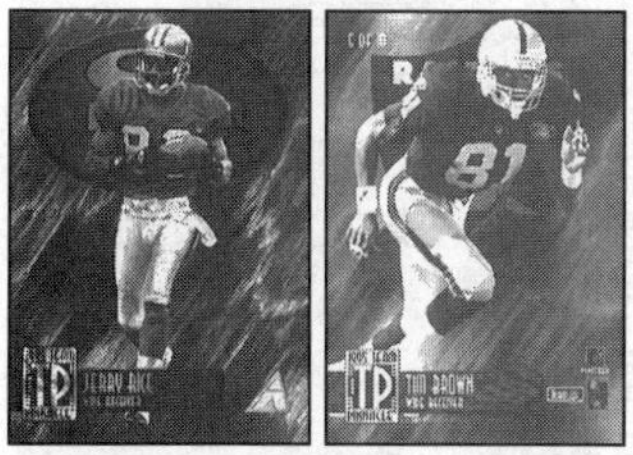

Inserted one in every 90 hobby and one in every 49 retail packs, this 10 card set features the hottest NFC and AFC players back-to-back by position. Each card features one side printed with all-foil dufex. The cards have an orange/brown/yellow color with the player's team logo in the background. The "Team Pinnacle" logo, player's name and position is located on the bottom left of the card against a green and black marble background. Cards are numbered out of 10.

	MINT	NRMT	EXC
COMPLETE SET (10)	250.00	110.00	31.00
COMMON CARD (1-10)	15.00	6.75	1.85
☐ 1 Steve Young Drew Bledsoe	30.00	13.50	3.70
☐ 2 Emmitt Smith Marshall Faulk	50.00	22.00	6.25
☐ 3 Barry Sanders Natrone Means	30.00	13.50	3.70
☐ 4 Dan Marino Troy Aikman	60.00	27.00	7.50
☐ 5 Jerry Rice Tim Brown	30.00	13.50	3.70
☐ 6 Errict Rhett Byron Bam Morris	20.00	9.00	2.50
☐ 7 Brett Favre John Elway	50.00	22.00	6.25
☐ 8 Rashaan Salaam Ki-Jana Carter	15.00	6.75	1.85
☐ 9 Kery Collins Steve McNair	30.00	13.50	3.70
☐ 10 Joey Galloway Michael Westbrook	20.00	9.00	2.50

1995 Pinnacle Club Collection Promos

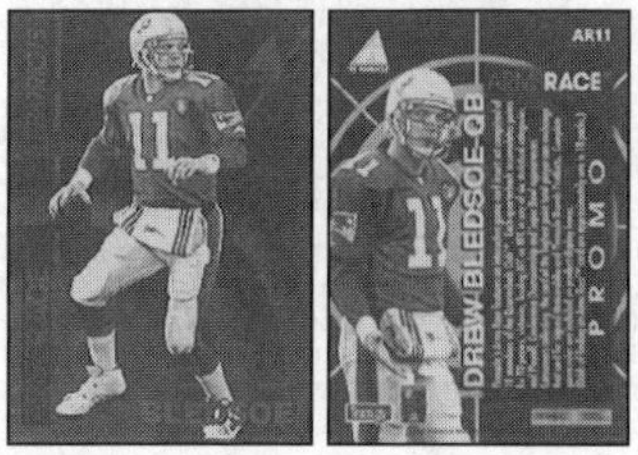

Issued in a cello pack, this 4-card standard-size set promoted the 1995 Pinnacle Club Collection series. The set features two regular issue cards, one "Arms Race" card, and an ad card. The backs of the player cards are clearly marked by the word "Promo" in white block lettering.

	MINT	NRMT	EXC
COMPLETE SET (4)	10.00	4.50	1.25
COMMON CARD	.50	.23	.06
☐ 1 Steve Young	2.00	.90	.25
☐ 11 Dan Marino	5.00	2.20	.60
☐ AR11 Drew Bledsoe Arm's Race	3.00	1.35	.35
☐ NNO Pinnacle Ad Card	.50	.23	.06

1995 Pinnacle Club Collection

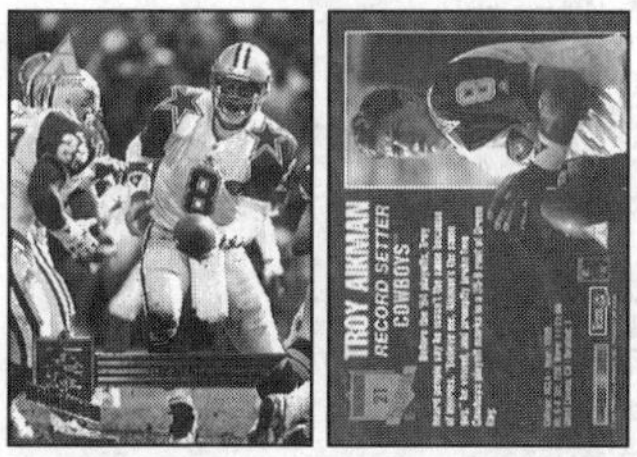

The debut set contains 261 cards with each member of the NFL Quarterback Club having nine cards each. Basic card fronts feature an all bleed photograph with the "Quarterback Club" logo and the player's name listed at the bottom against a gold foil background. Card backs are horizontal with the player's statistical information in yellow at the top and a statistical summary in yellow at the bottom. The cards are numbered against a blue marble background in the upper left corner of the card. The packs also included 20 Pin Redemption cards that were randomly inserted at a rate of one in 24. Collectors could receive a collectible pin of the Quarterback Club member pictured on the card by exchanging it with $1.95 before February 28, 1996. A John Elway signed card (75 autographed) was released as part of the prize list for Arms Race contest winners. The card is virtually identical to card #68 of the base set except for the gold foil being printed with a holographic foil pattern.

	MINT	NRMT	EXC
COMPLETE SET (261)	20.00	9.00	2.50
COMMON CARD (1-261)	.04	.02	.01
☐ 1 Steve Young	.30	.14	.04
☐ 2 Steve Young	.30	.14	.04
☐ 3 Steve Young	.30	.14	.04
☐ 4 Steve Young	.30	.14	.04
☐ 5 Steve Young	.30	.14	.04
☐ 6 Steve Young	.30	.14	.04
☐ 7 Steve Young	.30	.14	.04
☐ 8 Steve Young	.30	.14	.04
☐ 9 Steve Young	.30	.14	.04
☐ 10 Dan Marino	.75	.35	.09
☐ 11 Dan Marino	.75	.35	.09
☐ 12 Dan Marino	.75	.35	.09
☐ 13 Dan Marino	.75	.35	.09
☐ 14 Dan Marino	.75	.35	.09
☐ 15 Dan Marino	.75	.35	.09
☐ 16 Dan Marino	.75	.35	.09
☐ 17 Dan Marino	.75	.35	.09
☐ 18 Dan Marino	.75	.35	.09
☐ 19 Troy Aikman	.40	.18	.05
☐ 20 Troy Aikman	.40	.18	.05
☐ 21 Troy Aikman	.40	.18	.05
☐ 22 Troy Aikman	.40	.18	.05
☐ 23 Troy Aikman	.40	.18	.05
☐ 24 Troy Aikman	.40	.18	.05
☐ 25 Troy Aikman	.40	.18	.05
☐ 26 Troy Aikman	.40	.18	.05
☐ 27 Troy Aikman	.40	.18	.05
☐ 28 Drew Bledsoe	.40	.18	.05
☐ 29 Drew Bledsoe	.40	.18	.05
☐ 30 Drew Bledsoe	.40	.18	.05
☐ 31 Drew Bledsoe	.40	.18	.05
☐ 32 Drew Bledsoe	.40	.18	.05
☐ 33 Drew Bledsoe	.40	.18	.05
☐ 34 Drew Bledsoe	.40	.18	.05
☐ 35 Drew Bledsoe	.40	.18	.05
☐ 36 Drew Bledsoe	.40	.18	.05
☐ 37 Bubby Brister	.04	.02	.01
☐ 38 Bubby Brister	.04	.02	.01
☐ 39 Bubby Brister	.04	.02	.01
☐ 40 Bubby Brister	.04	.02	.01
☐ 41 Bubby Brister	.04	.02	.01
☐ 42 Bubby Brister	.04	.02	.01
☐ 43 Bubby Brister	.04	.02	.01
☐ 44 Bubby Brister	.04	.02	.01
☐ 45 Bubby Brister	.04	.02	.01
☐ 46 Dave Brown	.04	.02	.01
☐ 47 Dave Brown	.04	.02	.01
☐ 48 Dave Brown	.04	.02	.01
☐ 49 Dave Brown	.04	.02	.01
☐ 50 Dave Brown	.04	.02	.01
☐ 51 Dave Brown	.04	.02	.01
☐ 52 Dave Brown	.04	.02	.01
☐ 53 Dave Brown	.04	.02	.01
☐ 54 Dave Brown	.04	.02	.01
☐ 55 Randall Cunningham	.04	.02	.01
☐ 56 Randall Cunningham	.04	.02	.01
☐ 57 Randall Cunningham	.04	.02	.01
☐ 58 Randall Cunningham	.04	.02	.01
☐ 59 Randall Cunningham	.04	.02	.01
☐ 60 Randall Cunningham	.04	.02	.01
☐ 61 Randall Cunningham	.04	.02	.01
☐ 62 Randall Cunningham	.04	.02	.01
☐ 63 Randall Cunningham	.04	.02	.01
☐ 64 John Elway	.30	.14	.04
☐ 65 John Elway	.30	.14	.04
☐ 66 John Elway	.30	.14	.04
☐ 67 John Elway	.30	.14	.04
☐ 68 John Elway	.30	.14	.04
☐ 69 John Elway	.30	.14	.04
☐ 70 John Elway	.30	.14	.04
☐ 71 John Elway	.30	.14	.04
☐ 72 John Elway	.30	.14	.04
☐ 73 Boomer Esiason	.08	.04	.01
☐ 74 Boomer Esiason	.08	.04	.01
☐ 75 Boomer Esiason	.08	.04	.01
☐ 76 Boomer Esiason	.08	.04	.01
☐ 77 Boomer Esiason	.08	.04	.01
☐ 78 Boomer Esiason	.08	.04	.01
☐ 79 Boomer Esiason	.08	.04	.01
☐ 80 Boomer Esiason	.08	.04	.01
☐ 81 Boomer Esiason	.08	.04	.01
☐ 82 Jim Everett	.04	.02	.01
☐ 83 Jim Everett	.04	.02	.01
☐ 84 Jim Everett	.04	.02	.01
☐ 85 Jim Everett	.04	.02	.01
☐ 86 Jim Everett	.04	.02	.01
☐ 87 Jim Everett	.04	.02	.01
☐ 88 Jim Everett	.04	.02	.01
☐ 89 Jim Everett	.04	.02	.01
☐ 90 Jim Everett	.04	.02	.01
☐ 91 Brett Favre	.75	.35	.09
☐ 92 Brett Favre	.75	.35	.09
☐ 93 Brett Favre	.75	.35	.09
☐ 94 Brett Favre	.75	.35	.09
☐ 95 Brett Favre	.75	.35	.09
☐ 96 Brett Favre	.75	.35	.09
☐ 97 Brett Favre	.75	.35	.09
☐ 98 Brett Favre	.75	.35	.09
☐ 99 Brett Favre	.75	.35	.09
☐ 100 Jim Harbaugh	.08	.04	.01
☐ 101 Jim Harbaugh	.08	.04	.01
☐ 102 Jim Harbaugh	.08	.04	.01
☐ 103 Jim Harbaugh	.08	.04	.01
☐ 104 Jim Harbaugh	.08	.04	.01
☐ 105 Jim Harbaugh	.08	.04	.01
☐ 106 Jim Harbaugh	.08	.04	.01
☐ 107 Jim Harbaugh	.08	.04	.01
☐ 108 Jim Harbaugh	.08	.04	.01
☐ 109 Jeff Hostetler	.04	.02	.01
☐ 110 Jeff Hostetler	.04	.02	.01
☐ 111 Jeff Hostetler	.04	.02	.01
☐ 112 Jeff Hostetler	.04	.02	.01
☐ 113 Jeff Hostetler	.04	.02	.01
☐ 114 Jeff Hostetler	.04	.02	.01
☐ 115 Jeff Hostetler	.04	.02	.01
☐ 116 Jeff Hostetler	.04	.02	.01
☐ 117 Jeff Hostetler	.04	.02	.01
☐ 118 Michael Irvin	.15	.07	.02
☐ 119 Michael Irvin	.15	.07	.02
☐ 120 Michael Irvin	.15	.07	.02
☐ 121 Michael Irvin	.15	.07	.02
☐ 122 Michael Irvin	.15	.07	.02
☐ 123 Michael Irvin	.15	.07	.02
☐ 124 Michael Irvin	.15	.07	.02
☐ 125 Michael Irvin	.15	.07	.02
☐ 126 Michael Irvin	.15	.07	.02
☐ 127 Jim Kelly	.15	.07	.02
☐ 128 Jim Kelly	.15	.07	.02
☐ 129 Jim Kelly	.15	.07	.02
☐ 130 Jim Kelly	.15	.07	.02
☐ 131 Jim Kelly	.15	.07	.02
☐ 132 Jim Kelly	.15	.07	.02
☐ 133 Jim Kelly	.15	.07	.02
☐ 134 Jim Kelly	.15	.07	.02
☐ 135 Jim Kelly	.15	.07	.02
☐ 136 David Klingler	.04	.02	.01
☐ 137 David Klingler	.04	.02	.01
☐ 138 David Klingler	.04	.02	.01
☐ 139 David Klingler	.04	.02	.01
☐ 140 David Klingler	.04	.02	.01
☐ 141 David Klingler	.04	.02	.01
☐ 142 David Klingler	.04	.02	.01
☐ 143 David Klingler	.04	.02	.01
☐ 144 David Klingler	.04	.02	.01
☐ 145 Bernie Kosar	.04	.02	.01
☐ 146 Bernie Kosar	.04	.02	.01
☐ 147 Bernie Kosar	.04	.02	.01
☐ 148 Bernie Kosar	.04	.02	.01
☐ 149 Bernie Kosar	.04	.02	.01
☐ 150 Bernie Kosar	.04	.02	.01
☐ 151 Bernie Kosar	.04	.02	.01
☐ 152 Bernie Kosar	.04	.02	.01
☐ 153 Bernie Kosar	.04	.02	.01
☐ 154 Chris Miller	.04	.02	.01
☐ 155 Chris Miller	.04	.02	.01
☐ 156 Chris Miller	.04	.02	.01
☐ 157 Chris Miller	.04	.02	.01
☐ 158 Chris Miller	.04	.02	.01
☐ 159 Chris Miller	.04	.02	.01
☐ 160 Chris Miller	.04	.02	.01
☐ 161 Chris Miller	.04	.02	.01
☐ 162 Chris Miller	.04	.02	.01
☐ 163 Rick Mirer	.15	.07	.02
☐ 164 Rick Mirer	.15	.07	.02
☐ 165 Rick Mirer	.15	.07	.02
☐ 166 Rick Mirer	.15	.07	.02
☐ 167 Rick Mirer	.08	.04	.01
☐ 168 Rick Mirer	.15	.07	.02
☐ 169 Rick Mirer	.15	.07	.02
☐ 170 Rick Mirer	.15	.07	.02
☐ 171 Rick Mirer	.15	.07	.02
☐ 172 Warren Moon	.08	.04	.01
☐ 173 Warren Moon	.08	.04	.01
☐ 174 Warren Moon	.08	.04	.01
☐ 175 Warren Moon	.08	.04	.01
☐ 176 Warren Moon	.08	.04	.01
☐ 177 Warren Moon	.08	.04	.01
☐ 178 Warren Moon	.08	.04	.01
☐ 179 Warren Moon	.08	.04	.01
☐ 180 Warren Moon	.08	.04	.01
☐ 181 Neil O'Donnell	.08	.04	.01
☐ 182 Neil O'Donnell	.08	.04	.01
☐ 183 Neil O'Donnell	.08	.04	.01
☐ 184 Neil O'Donnell	.08	.04	.01
☐ 185 Neil O'Donnell	.08	.04	.01
☐ 186 Neil O'Donnell	.08	.04	.01
☐ 187 Neil O'Donnell	.08	.04	.01
☐ 188 Neil O'Donnell	.08	.04	.01
☐ 189 Neil O'Donnell	.08	.04	.01
☐ 190 Jerry Rice	.40	.18	.05
☐ 191 Jerry Rice	.40	.18	.05
☐ 192 Jerry Rice	.40	.18	.05
☐ 193 Jerry Rice	.40	.18	.05
☐ 194 Jerry Rice	.40	.18	.05
☐ 195 Jerry Rice	.40	.18	.05
☐ 196 Jerry Rice	.40	.18	.05
☐ 197 Jerry Rice	.40	.18	.05
☐ 198 Jerry Rice	.40	.18	.05
☐ 199 Mark Rypien	.04	.02	.01
☐ 200 Mark Rypien	.04	.02	.01
☐ 201 Mark Rypien	.04	.02	.01
☐ 202 Mark Rypien	.04	.02	.01
☐ 203 Mark Rypien	.04	.02	.01
☐ 204 Mark Rypien	.04	.02	.01
☐ 205 Mark Rypien	.04	.02	.01
☐ 206 Mark Rypien	.04	.02	.01
☐ 207 Mark Rypien	.04	.02	.01
☐ 208 Barry Sanders	.40	.18	.05
☐ 209 Barry Sanders	.40	.18	.05
☐ 210 Barry Sanders	.40	.18	.05
☐ 211 Barry Sanders	.40	.18	.05
☐ 212 Barry Sanders	.40	.18	.05
☐ 213 Barry Sanders	.40	.18	.05
☐ 214 Barry Sanders	.40	.18	.05
☐ 215 Barry Sanders	.40	.18	.05
☐ 216 Barry Sanders	.40	.18	.05
☐ 217 Junior Seau	.08	.04	.01
☐ 218 Junior Seau	.08	.04	.01
☐ 219 Junior Seau	.08	.04	.01
☐ 220 Junior Seau	.08	.04	.01
☐ 221 Junior Seau	.08	.04	.01
☐ 222 Junior Seau	.08	.04	.01
☐ 223 Junior Seau	.08	.04	.01
☐ 224 Junior Seau	.08	.04	.01
☐ 225 Junior Seau	.08	.04	.01
☐ 226 Emmitt Smith	.75	.35	.09
☐ 227 Emmitt Smith	.75	.35	.09
☐ 228 Emmitt Smith	.75	.35	.09
☐ 229 Emmitt Smith	.75	.35	.09
☐ 230 Emmitt Smith	.75	.35	.09
☐ 231 Emmitt Smith	.75	.35	.09
☐ 232 Emmitt Smith	.75	.35	.09
☐ 233 Emmitt Smith	.75	.35	.09
☐ 234 Emmitt Smith	.75	.35	.09
☐ 235 Phil Simms	.08	.04	.01
☐ 236 Phil Simms	.08	.04	.01
☐ 237 Phil Simms	.08	.04	.01
☐ 238 Phil Simms	.08	.04	.01
☐ 239 Phil Simms	.08	.04	.01
☐ 240 Phil Simms	.08	.04	.01
☐ 241 Phil Simms	.08	.04	.01

	MINT	NRMT	EXC
☐ 242 Phil Simms	.08	.04	.01
☐ 243 Phil Simms	.08	.04	.01
☐ 244 Heath Shuler	.25	.11	.03
☐ 245 Heath Shuler	.25	.11	.03
☐ 246 Heath Shuler	.25	.11	.03
☐ 247 Heath Shuler	.25	.11	.03
☐ 248 Heath Shuler	.25	.11	.03
☐ 249 Heath Shuler	.25	.11	.03
☐ 250 Heath Shuler	.25	.11	.03
☐ 251 Heath Shuler	.25	.11	.03
☐ 252 Heath Shuler	.25	.11	.03
☐ 253 Frank Reich	.04	.02	.01
☐ 254 Frank Reich	.04	.02	.01
☐ 255 Frank Reich	.04	.02	.01
☐ 256 Frank Reich	.04	.02	.01
☐ 257 Frank Reich	.04	.02	.01
☐ 258 Frank Reich	.04	.02	.01
☐ 259 Frank Reich	.04	.02	.01
☐ 260 Frank Reich	.04	.02	.01
☐ 261 Frank Reich	.04	.02	.01
☐ AU68 John Elway AUTO	200.00	90.00	25.00
Holographical foil pattern used			

1995 Pinnacle Club Collection Aerial Assault

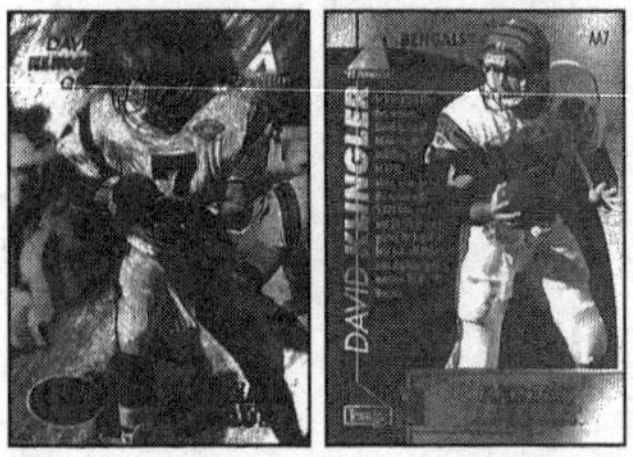

Inserted one in every 36 packs, this 18 card set features members of the Quarterback Club against a silver all-foil dufex "X-ed" background. The player's name is located at the top left of the card while the team logo is located at the bottom left. The set name "Aerial Assault" is in red foil on the bottom right. Card backs feature a gold and black background with the player's name running vertical along the left side of the card and a brief commentary. Cards are numbered with an "AA" prefix.

	MINT	NRMT	EXC
COMPLETE SET (18)	120.00	55.00	15.00
COMMON CARD (AA1-AA18)	3.00	1.35	.35
☐ AA1 Troy Aikman	12.00	5.50	1.50
☐ AA2 Dave Brown	3.00	1.35	.35
☐ AA3 Drew Bledsoe	12.00	5.50	1.50
☐ AA4 Randall Cunningham	3.00	1.35	.35
☐ AA5 Jim Everett	3.00	1.35	.35
☐ AA6 Jeff Hostetler	3.00	1.35	.35
☐ AA7 David Klingler	3.00	1.35	.35
☐ AA8 Dan Marino	25.00	11.00	3.10
☐ AA9 Rick Mirer	4.00	1.80	.50
☐ AA10 Neil O'Donnell	4.00	1.80	.50
☐ AA11 Brett Favre	25.00	11.00	3.10
☐ AA12 Boomer Esiason	3.00	1.35	.35
☐ AA13 Jim Harbaugh	4.00	1.80	.50
☐ AA14 John Elway	10.00	4.50	1.25
☐ AA15 Steve Young	10.00	4.50	1.25
☐ AA16 Warren Moon	4.00	1.80	.50
☐ AA17 Jim Kelly	4.00	1.80	.50
☐ AA18 Heath Shuler	6.00	2.70	.75

1995 Pinnacle Club Collection Arms Race

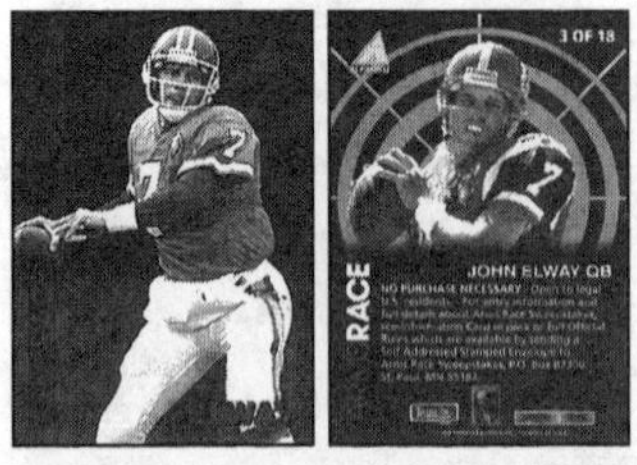

This 18 card interactive set was randomly inserted into packs at a rate of one in 18. Card fronts feature a shot of the player against a gold and brown background with the player's name in the lower right corner and the set name "Arms Race" running vertically along the left. Card backs feature a head shot against a bullseye background with basic information about the interactive element at the bottom. Basic information about the game: each quarterback would accumulate points for touchdown passes, victories, leading the AFC or NFC in any of six statistical categories, and Playoff, Conference Championship and Super Bowl appearances. Consumers that collected the card of the highest point total player could exchange that card for a chance to win a trip to the Foot Action NFL Quarterback Challenge and signed memorabilia. There was only one grand prize of the trip, 50 first prizes of official NFL footballs bearing the signatures of all the members of the Quarterback Club and 75 second prizes of John Elway signed cards.

	MINT	NRMT	EXC
COMPLETE SET (18)	50.00	22.00	6.25
COMMON CARD (1-18)	1.25	.55	.16
☐ 1 Steve Young	4.00	1.80	.50
☐ 2 Troy Aikman	6.00	2.70	.75
☐ 3 John Elway	4.00	1.80	.50
☐ 4 Dan Marino	12.00	5.50	1.50
☐ 5 Brett Favre	12.00	5.50	1.50
☐ 6 Heath Shuler	3.00	1.35	.35
☐ 7 Jim Kelly	2.00	.90	.25
☐ 8 Randall Cunningham	1.25	.55	.16
☐ 9 Dave Brown	1.25	.55	.16
☐ 10 Jim Everett	1.25	.55	.16
☐ 11 Drew Bledsoe	6.00	2.70	.75
☐ 12 Rick Mirer	2.00	.90	.25
☐ 13 Jeff Hostetler	1.25	.55	.16
☐ 14 Neil O'Donnell	2.00	.90	.25
☐ 15 Warren Moon	2.00	.90	.25
☐ 16 Boomer Esiason	1.25	.55	.16
☐ 17 Chris Miller	1.25	.55	.16
☐ 18 David Klingler	1.25	.55	.16

1995 Pinnacle Club Collection Spotlight

This five card set was randomly inserted at a rate of one in 90 packs and is a set focused on the five Quarterback Club superstars who are not quarterbacks. Card fronts feature an all-foil dufex silver background.

	MINT	NRMT	EXC
COMPLETE SET (5)	50.00	22.00	6.25
COMMON CARD (1-5)	4.00	1.80	.50
☐ 1 Emmitt Smith	25.00	11.00	3.10
☐ 2 Barry Sanders	12.00	5.50	1.50
☐ 3 Jerry Rice	12.00	5.50	1.50
☐ 4 Michael Irvin	6.00	2.70	.75
☐ 5 Junior Seau	4.00	1.80	.50

1995 Pinnacle Dial Corporation

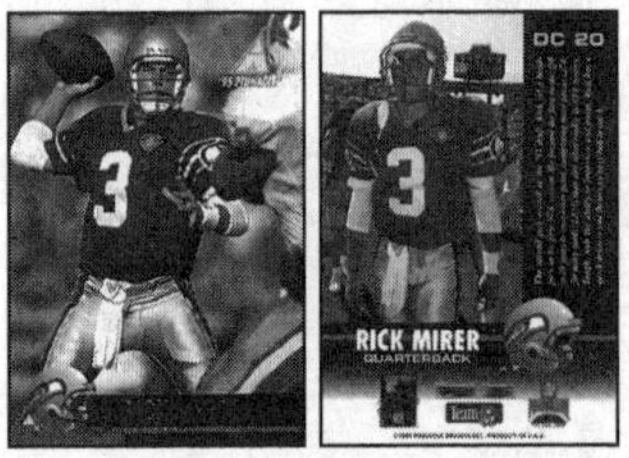

This 30-card standard-size set was sponsored by Dial and Purex and carries a Pinnacle '95 logo. It could be obtained by sending in UPC symbols from three Dial soap and Purex laundry products plus 2.50 to cover shipping and handling. The offer expired 1/31/96, or earlier if supplies became exhausted. The fronts feature full-bleed color action photos, with biography and statistical information on the backs. As part of a Dial Soap Super Bowl Contest, uncut sheets of the cards were issued as prizes. These sheets include 90-cards (3 complete sets) with one of the Bruce Smith cards autographed.

	MINT	NRMT	EXC
COMPLETE SET (30)	25.00	11.00	3.10
COMMON CARD (DC1-DC30)	.30	.14	.04
☐ DC1 Troy Aikman	2.00	.90	.25
☐ DC2 Frank Reich	.30	.14	.04
☐ DC3 Drew Bledsoe	2.00	.90	.25
☐ DC4 Bubby Brister	.30	.14	.04
☐ DC5 Dave Brown	.30	.14	.04
☐ DC6 Randall Cunningham	.30	.14	.04
☐ DC7 John Elway	1.25	.55	.16
☐ DC8 Boomer Esiason	.30	.14	.04
☐ DC9 Jim Everett	.30	.14	.04
☐ DC10 Bruce Smith	.50	.23	.06
☐ DC11 Brett Favre	4.00	1.80	.50
☐ DC12 Jim Harbaugh	.75	.35	.09
☐ DC13 Jeff Hostetler	.30	.14	.04
☐ DC14 Michael Irvin	.75	.35	.09
☐ DC15 Jim Kelly	.75	.35	.09
☐ DC16 David Klingler	.30	.14	.04
☐ DC17 Bernie Kosar	.30	.14	.04
☐ DC18 Dan Marino	4.00	1.80	.50
☐ DC19 Chris Miller	.30	.14	.04
☐ DC20 Rick Mirer	.75	.35	.09
☐ DC21 Warren Moon	.50	.23	.06
☐ DC22 Neil O'Donnell	.50	.23	.06
☐ DC23 Jerry Rice	2.00	.90	.25
☐ DC24 Mark Rypien	.30	.14	.04
☐ DC25 Barry Sanders	2.00	.90	.25
☐ DC26 Junior Seau	.75	.35	.09
☐ DC27 Heath Shuler	.75	.35	.09
☐ DC28 Phil Simms	.30	.14	.04
☐ DC29 Emmitt Smith	4.00	1.80	.50
☐ DC30 Steve Young	1.25	.55	.16
☐ P1 Uncut Sheet Prize	50.00	22.00	6.25

1996 Pinnacle

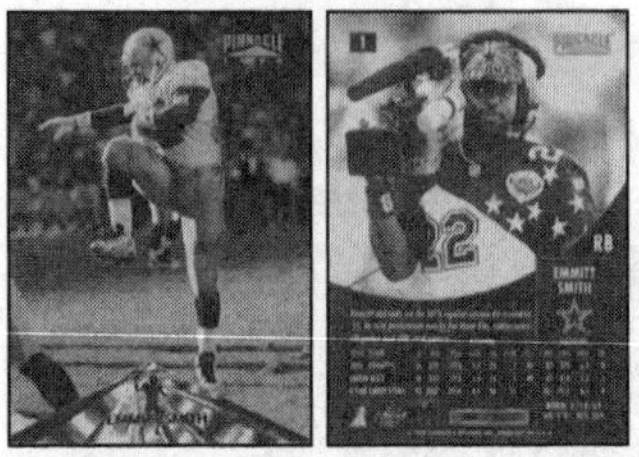

The 1996 Pinnacle set was issued in one series totalling 200 cards. The 10-card packs retail for $2.49 each. The following subsets are included in the set: Rookies (153-182), Bid for 6 (183-194) and Checklists (195-199). The fronts feature borderless action player photos with the player's name printed in a triangular design at the bottom. The backs carry another player photo and career statistics.

	MINT	NRMT	EXC
COMPLETE SET (200)	25.00	11.00	3.10
COMMON CARD (1-200)	.08	.04	.01
☐ 1 Emmitt Smith	2.00	.90	.25
☐ 2 Robert Brooks	.25	.11	.03
☐ 3 Joey Galloway	.40	.18	.05
☐ 4 Dan Marino	2.00	.90	.25
☐ 5 Frank Sanders	.15	.07	.02
☐ 6 Cris Carter	.25	.11	.03
☐ 7 Jeff Blake	.25	.11	.03
☐ 8 Steve McNair	1.00	.45	.12
☐ 9 Tamarick Vanover	.25	.11	.03
☐ 10 Andre Reed	.15	.07	.02
☐ 11 Junior Seau	.25	.11	.03
☐ 12 Alvin Harper	.08	.04	.01
☐ 13 Trent Dilfer	.15	.07	.02
☐ 14 Kordell Stewart	1.25	.55	.16
☐ 15 Kyle Brady	.15	.07	.02
☐ 16 Charles Haley	.15	.07	.02
☐ 17 Greg Lloyd	.15	.07	.02
☐ 18 Mario Bates	.15	.07	.02
☐ 19 Shannon Sharpe	.15	.07	.02
☐ 20 Scott Mitchell	.15	.07	.02
☐ 21 Craig Heyward	.08	.04	.01
☐ 22 Marcus Allen	.25	.11	.03
☐ 23 Curtis Martin	1.50	.70	.19
☐ 24 Drew Bledsoe	1.00	.45	.12
☐ 25 Jerry Rice	1.00	.45	.12
☐ 26 Charlie Garner	.08	.04	.01
☐ 27 Michael Irvin	.25	.11	.03
☐ 28 Curtis Conway	.25	.11	.03
☐ 29 Terrell Davis	1.50	.70	.19
☐ 30 Jeff Hostetler	.15	.07	.02
☐ 31 Neil O'Donnell	.15	.07	.02
☐ 32 Errict Rhett	.15	.07	.02
☐ 33 Stan Humphries	.15	.07	.02
☐ 34 Jeff Graham	.08	.04	.01
☐ 35 Floyd Turner	.08	.04	.01
☐ 36 Vincent Brisby	.08	.04	.01
☐ 37 Steve Young	.75	.35	.09
☐ 38 Carl Pickens	.25	.11	.03
☐ 39 Terance Mathis	.08	.04	.01
☐ 40 Brett Favre	2.00	.90	.25
☐ 41 Ki-Jana Carter	.15	.07	.02
☐ 42 Jim Everett	.08	.04	.01
☐ 43 Marshall Faulk	.25	.11	.03
☐ 44 William Floyd	.15	.07	.02
☐ 45 Deion Sanders	.60	.25	.07
☐ 46 Garrison Hearst	.15	.07	.02
☐ 47 Chris Sanders	.15	.07	.02
☐ 48 Isaac Bruce	.25	.11	.03
☐ 49 Natrone Means	.25	.11	.03
☐ 50 Troy Aikman	1.00	.45	.12
☐ 51 Ben Coates	.15	.07	.02
☐ 52 Tony Martin	.15	.07	.02
☐ 53 Rod Woodson	.15	.07	.02
☐ 54 Edgar Bennett	.15	.07	.02
☐ 55 Eric Zeier	.15	.07	.02
☐ 56 Steve Bono	.15	.07	.02
☐ 57 Tim Brown	.15	.07	.02
☐ 58 Kevin Williams	.08	.04	.01
☐ 59 Erik Kramer	.08	.04	.01
☐ 60 Jim Kelly	.25	.11	.03
☐ 61 Larry Centers	.15	.07	.02
☐ 62 Terrell Fletcher	.08	.04	.01
☐ 63 Michael Westbrook	.25	.11	.03
☐ 64 Kerry Collins	1.25	.55	.16
☐ 65 Jay Novacek	.15	.07	.02
☐ 66 J.J. Stokes	.25	.11	.03
☐ 67 John Elway	.75	.35	.09
☐ 68 Jim Harbaugh	.15	.07	.02
☐ 69 Aeneas Williams	.08	.04	.01
☐ 70 Tyrone Wheatley	.15	.07	.02
☐ 71 Chris Warren	.15	.07	.02
☐ 72 Rodney Thomas	.08	.04	.01
☐ 73 Jeff George	.15	.07	.02
☐ 74 Rick Mirer	.15	.07	.02
☐ 75 Yancey Thigpen	.15	.07	.02
☐ 76 Herman Moore	.25	.11	.03
☐ 77 Gus Frerotte	.25	.11	.03
☐ 78 Anthony Miller	.15	.07	.02
☐ 79 Ricky Watters	.15	.07	.02
☐ 80 Sherman Williams	.08	.04	.01
☐ 81 Hardy Nickerson	.08	.04	.01
☐ 82 Henry Ellard	.15	.07	.02
☐ 83 Aaron Craver	.08	.04	.01
☐ 84 Rodney Peete	.08	.04	.01
☐ 85 Eric Metcalf	.15	.07	.02
☐ 86 Brian Blades	.15	.07	.02
☐ 87 Rob Moore	.08	.04	.01
☐ 88 Kimble Anders	.08	.04	.01
☐ 89 Harvey Williams	.08	.04	.01
☐ 90 Thurman Thomas	.25	.11	.03
☐ 91 Dave Brown	.15	.07	.02
☐ 92 Terry Allen	.15	.07	.02
☐ 93 Ken Norton Jr.	.15	.07	.02
☐ 94 Reggie White	.25	.11	.03
☐ 95 Mark Chmura	.15	.07	.02
☐ 96 Bert Emanuel	.15	.07	.02
☐ 97 Brett Perriman	.15	.07	.02
☐ 98 Antonio Freeman	.40	.18	.05
☐ 99 Brian Mitchell	.08	.04	.01
☐ 100 Orlando Thomas	.08	.04	.01
☐ 101 Aaron Hayden	.08	.04	.01
☐ 102 Quinn Early	.08	.04	.01
☐ 103 Lovell Pinkney	.08	.04	.01
☐ 104 Napoleon Kaufman	.15	.07	.02
☐ 105 Daryl Johnston	.15	.07	.02
☐ 106 Steve Tasker	.08	.04	.01
☐ 107 Brent Jones	.08	.04	.01
☐ 108 Mark Brunell	1.00	.45	.12
☐ 109 Leslie O'Neal	.08	.04	.01
☐ 110 Irving Fryar	.15	.07	.02
☐ 111 Jim Miller	.08	.04	.01
☐ 112 Sean Dawkins	.08	.04	.01
☐ 113 Boomer Esiason	.15	.07	.02
☐ 114 Heath Shuler	.25	.11	.03
☐ 115 Bruce Smith	.25	.11	.03
☐ 116 Russell Maryland	.08	.04	.01
☐ 117 Jake Reed	.15	.07	.02
☐ 118 O.J. McDuffie	.15	.07	.02
☐ 119 Erik Williams	.08	.04	.01
☐ 120 Willie McGinest	.08	.04	.01
☐ 121 Terry Kirby	.15	.07	.02
☐ 122 Fred Barnett	.15	.07	.02
☐ 123 Andre Hastings	.15	.07	.02
☐ 124 Dale Hellestrae	.08	.04	.01
☐ 125 Darren Woodson	.15	.07	.02
☐ 126 Steve Atwater	.08	.04	.01
☐ 127 Quentin Coryatt	.08	.04	.01
☐ 128 Derrick Thomas	.15	.07	.02
☐ 129 Nate Newton	.08	.04	.01
☐ 130 Kevin Greene	.15	.07	.02
☐ 131 Barry Sanders	1.00	.45	.12
☐ 132 Warren Moon	.15	.07	.02
☐ 133 Rashaan Salaam	.25	.11	.03
☐ 134 Rodney Hampton	.15	.07	.02
☐ 135 James O.Stewart	.25	.11	.03
☐ 136 Erric Pegram	.15	.07	.02
☐ 137 Bryan Cox	.08	.04	.01
☐ 138 Adrian Murrell	.15	.07	.02
☐ 139 Robert Smith	.15	.07	.02
☐ 140 Bernie Parmalee	.08	.04	.01
☐ 141 Bryce Paup	.15	.07	.02
☐ 142 Darick Holmes	.15	.07	.02
☐ 143 Hugh Douglas	.08	.04	.01
☐ 144 Ken Dilger	.15	.07	.02
☐ 145 Derek Loville	.08	.04	.01
☐ 146 Horace Copeland	.08	.04	.01
☐ 147 Wayne Chrebet	.15	.07	.02
☐ 148 Andre Coleman	.08	.04	.01
☐ 149 Greg Hill	.15	.07	.02
☐ 150 Eric Swann	.15	.07	.02
☐ 151 Tyrone Hughes	.08	.04	.01
☐ 152 Ernie Mills	.08	.04	.01
☐ 153 Terry Glenn	3.00	1.35	.35
☐ 154 Cedric Jones	.15	.07	.02
☐ 155 Leeland McElroy	.25	.11	.03
☐ 156 Bobby Engram	.75	.35	.09
☐ 157 Willie Anderson	.08	.04	.01
☐ 158 Mike Alstott	.50	.23	.06
☐ 159 Alex Van Dyke	.15	.07	.02
☐ 160 Jeff Lewis	.15	.07	.02
☐ 161 Keyshawn Johnson	1.50	.70	.19
☐ 162 Regan Upshaw	.08	.04	.01
☐ 163 Eric Moulds	.75	.35	.09
☐ 164 Tim Biakabutuka	.75	.35	.09
☐ 165 Kevin Hardy	.15	.07	.02
☐ 166 Marvin Harrison	1.50	.70	.19
☐ 167 Karim Abdul-Jabbar	2.50	1.10	.30
☐ 168 Tony Brackens	.15	.07	.02
☐ 169 Stepfret Williams	.08	.04	.01
☐ 170 Eddie George	4.00	1.80	.50
☐ 171 Lawrence Phillips	.50	.23	.06
☐ 172 Danny Kanell	.25	.11	.03
☐ 173 Derrick Mayes	.75	.35	.09
☐ 174 Daryl Gardener	.15	.07	.02
☐ 175 Jonathan Ogden	.08	.04	.01
☐ 176 Alex Molden	.08	.04	.01
☐ 177 Chris Darkins	.15	.07	.02
☐ 178 Stephen Davis	.25	.11	.03
☐ 179 Rickey Dudley	.25	.11	.03
☐ 180 Eddie Kennison	1.50	.70	.19
☐ 181 Simeon Rice	.25	.11	.03
☐ 182 Bobby Hoying	.25	.11	.03
☐ 183 Troy Aikman BF6	.50	.23	.06
☐ 184 Emmitt Smith BF6	1.00	.45	.12

☐ 185 Michael Irvin BF6	.15	.07	.02
☐ 186 Deion Sanders BF6	.30	.14	.04
☐ 187 Daryl Johnston BF6	.15	.07	.02
☐ 188 Jay Novacek BF6	.15	.07	.02
☐ 189 Steve Young BF6	.35	.16	.04
☐ 190 Jerry Rice BF6	.50	.23	.06
☐ 191 J.J. Stokes BF6	.25	.11	.03
☐ 192 Ken Norton BF6	.15	.07	.02
☐ 193 William Floyd BF6	.08	.04	.01
☐ 194 Brent Jones BF6	.08	.04	.01
☐ 195 Dan Marino CL	.40	.18	.05
☐ 196 Brett Favre CL	.40	.18	.05
☐ 197 Emmitt Smith CL	.40	.18	.05
☐ 198 Barry Sanders CL	.30	.14	.04
☐ 199 Dan Marino CL	.30	.14	.04
Emmitt Smith CL			
Brett Favre CL			
Barry Sanders CL			
☐ 200 Brett Favre	2.00	.90	.25
Packer Backer			

1996 Pinnacle Artist's Proofs

Randomly inserted at the rate of one in 48 packs, this 200-card set is a gold foil parallel version of the regular 1996 Pinnacle set stamped with the holographic gold foil Artist's Proof logo.

	MINT	NRMT	EXC
COMP.AP SET (200)	2000.00	900.00	250.00
COMMON CARD (1-200)	4.00	1.80	.50
*AP STARS: 40X TO 75X BASIC CARDS			
*AP YOUNG STARS: 30X TO 50X			
*AP RCs: 17.5X TO 25X			

1996 Pinnacle Premium Stock

This 200-card set is a hobby-only parallel version of the regular Pinnacle set and was available at hobby dealers in 25-card packs with a suggested retail price of $6.99. The set was printed on 24-point card stock with silver foil stamping.

	MINT	NRMT	EXC
COMPLETE SET (200)	50.00	22.00	6.25
COMMON CARD (1-200)	.20	.09	.03
*PREMIUM STOCK: 1.25X TO 2X BASIC CARDS			

1996 Pinnacle Trophy Collection

Randomly inserted in packs at the rate of one in five, this 200-card set is an all-foil Dufex print version of the regular 1996 Pinnacle set.

	MINT	NRMT	EXC
COMPLETE SET (200)	1.25	.55	.16
COMMON CARD (1-200)	500.00	220.00	60.00
*TC STARS: 8X TO 16X			
*TC YOUNG STARS: 6X TO 12X			
*TC RCs: 4X TO 8X			

1996 Pinnacle Black 'N Blue

Randomly inserted in magazine all-foil packs only at a rate of one in 33, this 25-card set features borderless color player photos on the top two-thirds of the all-foil fronts with a black-and-white player image at the bottom. The backs carry a black-and-white player photo with a paragraph indicating why the player was selected for this set.

	MINT	NRMT	EXC
COMPLETE SET (25)	300.00	135.00	38.00
COMMON CARD (1-25)	4.00	1.80	.50
☐ 1 Steve Young	15.00	6.75	1.85
☐ 2 Troy Aikman	20.00	9.00	2.50
☐ 3 Dan Marino	35.00	16.00	4.40
☐ 4 Michael Irvin	6.00	2.70	.75
☐ 5 Jerry Rice	20.00	9.00	2.50
☐ 6 Emmitt Smith	35.00	16.00	4.40
☐ 7 Brett Favre	35.00	16.00	4.40
☐ 8 Drew Bledsoe	20.00	9.00	2.50
☐ 9 John Elway	15.00	6.75	1.85
☐ 10 Barry Sanders	20.00	9.00	2.50
☐ 11 Cris Carter	4.00	1.80	.50
☐ 12 Jeff Blake	6.00	2.70	.75
☐ 13 Chris Warren	4.00	1.80	.50
☐ 14 Kerry Collins	16.00	7.25	2.00
☐ 15 Natrone Means	6.00	2.70	.75
☐ 16 Herman Moore	6.00	2.70	.75
☐ 17 Steve McNair	12.00	5.50	1.50
☐ 18 Ricky Watters	6.00	2.70	.75
☐ 19 Tamarick Vanover	6.00	2.70	.75
☐ 20 Deion Sanders	12.00	5.50	1.50

☐ 21 Terrell Davis	20.00	9.00	2.50
☐ 22 Rodney Thomas	4.00	1.80	.50
☐ 23 Rashaan Salaam	6.00	2.70	.75
☐ 24 Darick Holmes	4.00	1.80	.50
☐ 25 Eric Zeier	4.00	1.80	.50

1996 Pinnacle Die Cut Jerseys

Randomly inserted in hobby packs only at a rate of one in 24, this 20-card set features action color player images printed on a die cut card of the player's game jersey as background. A parallel exclusive rainbow holographic foil version of this set was randomly inserted in Pinnacle Premium Stock packs at the rate of one in six.

	MINT	NRMT	EXC
COMPLETE SET (20)	150.00	70.00	19.00
COMMON CARD (1-20)	3.00	1.35	.35
COMP.HOLOFOIL SET (20)	275.00	125.00	34.00
COMMON HOLOFOIL (1-20)	5.00	2.20	.60
*HOLOFOILS: .75X TO 1.5X BASIC CARDS			
☐ 1 Errict Rhett	3.00	1.35	.35
☐ 2 Marshall Faulk	4.00	1.80	.50
☐ 3 Isaac Bruce	4.00	1.80	.50
☐ 4 William Floyd	3.00	1.35	.35
☐ 5 Heath Shuler	3.00	1.35	.35
☐ 6 Kerry Collins	16.00	7.25	2.00
☐ 7 Kordell Stewart	16.00	7.25	2.00
☐ 8 Rashaan Salaam	4.00	1.80	.50
☐ 9 Terrell Davis	20.00	9.00	2.50
☐ 10 Rodney Thomas	3.00	1.35	.35
☐ 11 Curtis Martin	20.00	9.00	2.50
☐ 12 Steve McNair	12.00	5.50	1.50
☐ 13 J.J. Stokes	4.00	1.80	.50
☐ 14 Joey Galloway	6.00	2.70	.75
☐ 15 Michael Westbrook	4.00	1.80	.50
☐ 16 Keyshawn Johnson	10.00	4.50	1.25
☐ 17 Lawrence Phillips	6.00	2.70	.75
☐ 18 Terry Glenn	16.00	7.25	2.00
☐ 19 Tim Biakabutuka	6.00	2.70	.75
☐ 20 Eddie George	20.00	9.00	2.50

1996 Pinnacle Double Disguise

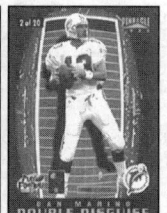

Randomly inserted in packs at a rate of one in 18, this double-sided 20-card set features color photos of five players in different combinations with each other and an opaque peel-off wrapper covering both sides of the cards. Prices below are for peeled cards.

	MINT	NRMT	EXC
COMPLETE SET (20)	150.00	70.00	19.00
COMMON CARD (1-20)	4.00	1.80	.50
☐ 1 Emmitt Smith	12.00	5.50	1.50
Emmitt Smith			
☐ 2 Emmitt Smith	12.00	5.50	1.50
Dan Marino			
☐ 3 Emmitt Smith	12.00	5.50	1.50
Brett Favre			
☐ 4 Emmitt Smith	10.00	4.50	1.25
Steve Young			
☐ 5 Dan Marino	12.00	5.50	1.50
Dan Marino			
☐ 6 Dan Marino	12.00	5.50	1.50
Emmitt Smith			
☐ 7 Dan Marino	10.00	4.50	1.25
Kerry Collins			
☐ 8 Dan Marino	10.00	4.50	1.25
Steve Young			
☐ 9 Kerry Collins	6.00	2.70	.75
Kerry Collins			
☐ 10 Kerry Collins	10.00	4.50	1.25
Dan Marino			
☐ 11 Kerry Collins	10.00	4.50	1.25
Brett Favre			
☐ 12 Kerry Collins	6.00	2.70	.75

Steve Young			
☐ 13 Brett Favre	12.00	5.50	1.50
Brett Favre			
☐ 14 Brett Favre	10.00	4.50	1.25
Kerry Collins			
☐ 15 Brett Favre	12.00	5.50	1.50
Dan Marino			
☐ 16 Brett Favre	12.00	5.50	1.50
Emmitt Smith			
☐ 17 Steve Young	4.00	1.80	.50
Steve Young			
☐ 18 Steve Young	10.00	4.50	1.25
Brett Favre			
☐ 19 Steve Young	10.00	4.50	1.25
Emmitt Smith			
☐ 20 Steve Young	6.00	2.70	.75
Kerry Collins			

1996 Pinnacle On The Line

Randomly inserted in retail packs only at a rate of one in 23, this Dufex printed 15-card set features color player photos of top NFL receivers.

	MINT	NRMT	EXC
COMPLETE SET (15)	120.00	55.00	15.00
COMMON CARD (1-15)	4.00	1.80	.50
☐ 1 Michael Irvin	6.00	2.70	.75
☐ 2 Robert Brooks	6.00	2.70	.75
☐ 3 Herman Moore	6.00	2.70	.75
☐ 4 Cris Carter	4.00	1.80	.50
☐ 5 Chris Sanders	4.00	1.80	.50
☐ 6 Jerry Rice	25.00	11.00	3.10
☐ 7 Michael Westbrook	6.00	2.70	.75
☐ 8 Carl Pickens	4.00	1.80	.50
☐ 9 Bobby Engram	8.00	3.60	1.00
☐ 10 Alex Van Dyke	4.00	1.80	.50
☐ 11 Keyshawn Johnson	10.00	4.50	1.25
☐ 12 Terry Glenn	25.00	11.00	3.10
☐ 13 Eric Moulds	8.00	3.60	1.00
☐ 14 Marvin Harrison	10.00	4.50	1.25
☐ 15 Eddie Kennison	10.00	4.50	1.25

1996 Pinnacle Team Pinnacle

Randomly inserted in packs at a rate of one in 90, this 10-card set features color player images of the best AFC player at each position with the top NFC position player on the flip side with each image set on a facsimile football background.

	MINT	NRMT	EXC
COMPLETE SET (10)	250.00	110.00	31.00
COMMON CARD (1-10)	15.00	6.75	1.85
☐ 1 Troy Aikman	30.00	13.50	3.70
Drew Bledsoe			
☐ 2 Steve Young	20.00	9.00	2.50
Jeff Blake			
☐ 3 Brett Favre	50.00	22.00	6.25
John Elway			
☐ 4 Kerry Collins	50.00	22.00	6.25
Dan Marino			
☐ 5 Emmitt Smith	50.00	22.00	6.25
Curtis Martin			
☐ 6 Barry Sanders	25.00	11.00	3.10
Chris Warren			
☐ 7 Errict Rhett	15.00	6.75	1.85
Marshall Faulk			
☐ 8 Jerry Rice	25.00	11.00	3.10
Carl Pickens			
☐ 9 Michael Irvin	18.00	8.00	2.20
Joey Galloway			
☐ 10 Isaac Bruce	25.00	11.00	3.10
Kordell Stewart			

1996 Pinnacle Bimbo Bread

These small (approximately 1 1/2" by 2 1/2") magic motion cards were distributed in Mexico through Bimbo Bakery snack products. The cardfronts feature a magic motion action photo of the player with the Bimbo logo. The backs are green with a player photo and player bio written in spanish.

	MINT	NRMT	EXC
COMPLETE SET (30)	300.00	135.00	38.00
COMMON CARD (1-30)	4.00	1.80	.50
☐ 1 Troy Aikman	30.00	13.50	3.70
☐ 2 Michael Irvin	8.00	3.60	1.00
☐ 3 Emmitt Smith	60.00	27.00	7.50
☐ 4 Jim Kelly	8.00	3.60	1.00
☐ 5 John Elway	25.00	11.00	3.10
☐ 6 Barry Sanders	30.00	13.50	3.70
☐ 7 Brett Favre	60.00	27.00	7.50
☐ 8 Jim Harbaugh	6.00	2.70	.75
☐ 9 Dan Marino	60.00	27.00	7.50
☐ 10 Warren Moon	6.00	2.70	.75
☐ 11 Drew Bledsoe	30.00	13.50	3.70
☐ 12 Jim Everett	4.00	1.80	.50
☐ 13 Jeff Hostetler	4.00	1.80	.50
☐ 14 Neil O'Donnell	4.00	1.80	.50
☐ 15 Junior Seau	6.00	2.70	.75
☐ 16 Jerry Rice	30.00	13.50	3.70
☐ 17 Steve Young	20.00	9.00	2.50
☐ 18 Rick Mirer	6.00	2.70	.75
☐ 19 Jeff Blake	8.00	3.60	1.00
☐ 20 David Klingler	4.00	1.80	.50
☐ 21 Boomer Esiason	6.00	2.70	.75
☐ 22 Heath Shuler	6.00	2.70	.75
☐ 23 Dave Brown	4.00	1.80	.50
☐ 24 Bernie Kosar	4.00	1.80	.50
☐ 25 Kordell Stewart	30.00	13.50	3.70
☐ 26 Mark Brunell	30.00	13.50	3.70
☐ 27 Kerry Collins	30.00	13.50	3.70
☐ 28 Scott Mitchell	4.00	1.80	.50
☐ 29 Erik Kramer	4.00	1.80	.50
☐ 30 Jeff George	6.00	2.70	.75

1996 Pinnacle Super Bowl Card Show

This 15-card standard-size set features color action player photos on a metallic dufex background. The player's last name is printed in a metallic gold band with the Super Bowl XXX Card Show logo at the bottom. The horizontal backs carry the player's name, team, a career highlight, nickname, and sponsor logos on a dark blue marblized background. Pinnacle offered three-card packs to each Card Show attendee in exchange for two football card wrappers from 1995 Pinnacle football products. Although the cards carry a 1995 copyright date, the cards were released in January 1996 at the Tempe, Arizona Super Bowl Card Show.

	MINT	NRMT	EXC
COMPLETE SET (15)	25.00	11.00	3.10
COMMON CARD (1-15)	.50	.23	.06
☐ 1 Steve Young	1.50	.70	.19
☐ 2 Dan Marino	5.00	2.20	.60
☐ 3 Troy Aikman	2.50	1.10	.30
☐ 4 Drew Bledsoe	2.50	1.10	.30
☐ 5 John Elway	2.00	.90	.25
☐ 6 Brett Favre	5.00	2.20	.60
☐ 7 Jim Harbaugh	.50	.23	.06
☐ 8 Jeff Hostetler	.50	.23	.06
☐ 9 Michael Irvin	1.00	.45	.12
☐ 10 Jim Kelly	1.00	.45	.12
☐ 11 Warren Moon	.50	.23	.06
☐ 12 Jerry Rice	2.50	1.10	.30
☐ 13 Barry Sanders	2.50	1.10	.30
☐ 14 Junior Seau	1.00	.45	.12
☐ 15 Emmitt Smith	5.00	2.20	.60

1997 Pinnacle Rembrandt

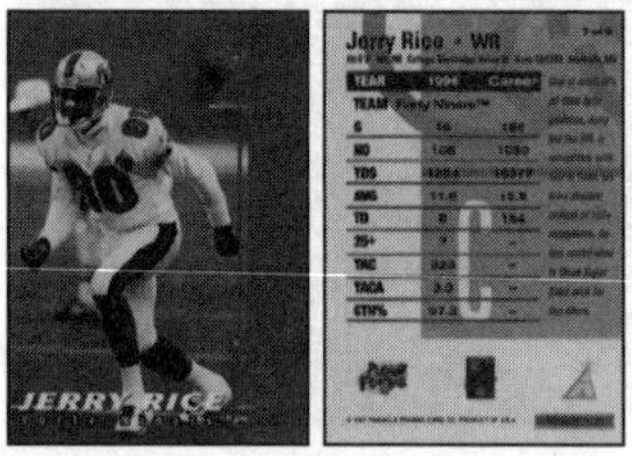

Pinnacle produced this set of 9-cards distributed by Rembrandt, Inc. with their line of Ultra-PRO plastic sheets. Each included a player photo with a bronze colored foil section to the right of the photo containing the Pinnacle and QB Club logos. One card was inserted into each box of sheets. There were also Silver and Gold parallel sets produced. As part of the promotion, collectors who assembled a complete Gold set could send the set to Rembrandt for $250 cash. A set of Silver cards could be redeemed for a gift box of Ultra-PRO products. A set of Bronze cards could be redeemed for a gold/silver/bronze set of one of the nine players. All sets sent in were returned with a cancelled stamp.

	MINT	NRMT	EXC
COMPLETE SET (9)	20.00	9.00	2.50
COMMON CARD (1-9)	1.50	.70	.19
*GOLD CARDS: 6X TO 12X BASIC CARD			
*SILVER CARDS: 3X TO 6X BASIC CARD			

☐ 1 Brett Favre	4.00	1.80	.50
☐ 2 Troy Aikman	2.00	.90	.25
☐ 3 John Elway	1.50	.70	.19
☐ 4 Dan Marino	4.00	1.80	.50
☐ 5 Drew Bledsoe	2.00	.90	.25
☐ 6 Emmitt Smith	4.00	1.80	.50
☐ 7 Jerry Rice	2.00	.90	.25
☐ 8 Barry Sanders	2.00	.90	.25
☐ 9 Mark Brunell	2.00	.90	.25

1996 Pinnacle Mint

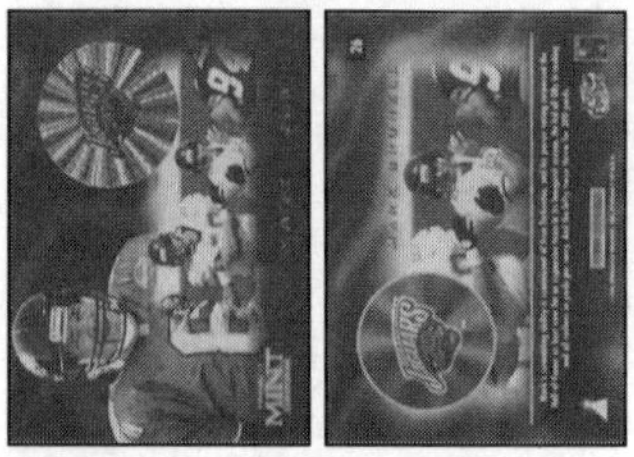

The 1996 Pinnacle Mint Collection set was issued in one series of 30-cards and 30-coins. The two-coin/three-card packs carried a suggested retail price of $3.99 each. The challenge was to fit the coins with the die-cut cards that pictured the same player. Two die-cut cards and two coins were inserted in each pack. Either one bronze, silver or gold card was also included in each pack. The fronts feature color action player photos with a cut-out area for the matching coin. Die cut cards are listed below.

	MINT	NRMT	EXC
COMP.DIE CUT SET (30)	20.00	9.00	2.50
COMMON CARD DC (1-30)	.25	.11	.03

☐ 1 Troy Aikman	1.25	.55	.16
☐ 2 John Elway	1.00	.45	.12
☐ 3 Jim Kelly	.60	.25	.07
☐ 4 Dan Marino	2.50	1.10	.30
☐ 5 Warren Moon	.40	.18	.05
☐ 6 Steve Young	1.00	.45	.12
☐ 7 Boomer Esiason	.40	.18	.05
☐ 8 Jim Everett	.25	.11	.03
☐ 9 Brett Favre	2.50	1.10	.30
☐ 10 Jim Harbaugh	.40	.18	.05
☐ 11 Jeff Hostetler	.40	.18	.05
☐ 12 Neil O'Donnell	.40	.18	.05
☐ 13 Drew Bledsoe	1.25	.55	.16
☐ 14 Rick Mirer	.40	.18	.05
☐ 15 Emmitt Smith	2.50	1.10	.30
☐ 16 Jerry Rice	1.25	.55	.16
☐ 17 Barry Sanders	1.25	.55	.16
☐ 18 Junior Seau	.60	.25	.07
☐ 19 Dave Brown	.40	.18	.05
☐ 20 Heath Shuler	.60	.25	.07
☐ 21 Jeff Blake	.60	.25	.07
☐ 22 Kerry Collins	1.25	.55	.16
☐ 23 Scott Mitchell	.40	.18	.05
☐ 24 Kordell Stewart	1.25	.55	.16
☐ 25 Jeff George	.40	.18	.05
☐ 26 Mark Brunell	1.25	.55	.16
☐ 27 Erik Kramer	.25	.11	.03
☐ 28 Bernie Kosar	.25	.11	.03
☐ 29 Frank Reich	.25	.11	.03
☐ 30 Randall Cunningham	.40	.18	.05

1996 Pinnacle Mint Bronze

Each pack of 1996 Pinnacle Mint contained either one bronze, silver or gold card. The bronze versions are the most common. Each bronze card features a color player action photo with a large player portrait in the background. The player's team logo is embossed in a bronze coin replica placed where the coin is to be inserted in the die cut version.

	MINT	NRMT	EXC
COMP.BRONZE SET (30)	40.00	18.00	5.00
COMMON BRONZE CARD	.50	.23	.06
*BRONZE CARDS: 1X TO 2X DIE CUTS			

1996 Pinnacle Mint Gold

Randomly inserted in packs at a rate of one in 48, this 30-card set is a parallel Gold-foil dufex version of the regular set.

	MINT	NRMT	EXC
COMP.GOLD SET (30)	400.00	180.00	50.00
COMMON GOLD CARD (1-30)	5.00	2.20	.60
*GOLD CARDS: 10X TO 20X DIE CUTS			

1996 Pinnacle Mint Silver

Randomly inserted in packs at a rate of one in 20, this 30-card set is a silver-foil parallel version of the regular set.

	MINT	NRMT	EXC
COMP.SILVER SET (30)	150.00	70.00	19.00
COMMON SILVER CARD (1-30)	2.00	.90	.25
*SILVER CARDS: 4X TO 8X DIE CUTS			

1996 Pinnacle Mint Coins

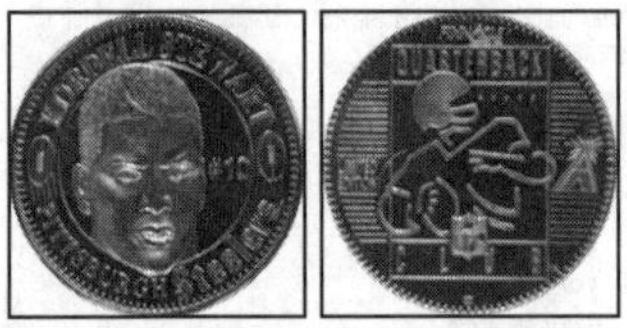

Each pack of Pinnacle Mint contained two coins (a mixture of Brass, Nickel and Gold Plated). The Brass coins were the most common. This set features coins minted in brass with embossed player heads and were made to be matched with the die cut card version of the same player.

	MINT	NRMT	EXC
COMP.BRASS SET (30)	60.00	27.00	7.50
COMMON BRASS COIN	1.00	.45	.12
COMP.NICKEL SET (30)	250.00	110.00	31.00
COMMON NICKEL COIN	4.00	1.80	.50
*NICKEL COINS: 2X TO 4X BRASS			
COMP.GOLD PLATED (30)	600.00	275.00	75.00
COMMON GOLD PLATED	10.00	4.50	1.25
*GOLD PLATED: 5X TO 10X BRASS			

☐ 1 Troy Aikman	5.00	2.20	.60
☐ 2 John Elway	4.00	1.80	.50
☐ 3 Jim Kelly	2.00	.90	.25
☐ 4 Dan Marino	10.00	4.50	1.25
☐ 5 Warren Moon	1.00	.45	.12
☐ 6 Steve Young	4.00	1.80	.50
☐ 7 Boomer Esiason	1.50	.70	.19
☐ 8 Jim Everett	1.00	.45	.12
☐ 9 Brett Favre	10.00	4.50	1.25
☐ 10 Jim Harbaugh	1.50	.70	.19
☐ 11 Jeff Hostetler	1.00	.45	.12
☐ 12 Neil O'Donnell	1.00	.45	.12
☐ 13 Drew Bledsoe	5.00	2.20	.60
☐ 14 Rick Mirer	1.50	.70	.19
☐ 15 Emmitt Smith	10.00	4.50	1.25
☐ 16 Jerry Rice	5.00	2.20	.60
☐ 17 Barry Sanders	5.00	2.20	.60
☐ 18 Junior Seau	1.50	.70	.19
☐ 19 Dave Brown	1.00	.45	.12
☐ 20 Heath Shuler	1.50	.70	.19
☐ 21 Jeff Blake	2.00	.90	.25
☐ 22 Kerry Collins	5.00	2.20	.60
☐ 23 Scott Mitchell	1.00	.45	.12
☐ 24 Kordell Stewart	5.00	2.20	.60
☐ 25 Jeff George	1.50	.70	.19
☐ 26 Mark Brunell	5.00	2.20	.60
☐ 27 Erik Kramer	1.00	.45	.12
☐ 28 Bernie Kosar	1.00	.45	.12
☐ 29 Frank Reich	1.00	.45	.12
☐ 30 David Klingler	1.00	.45	.12
☐ SP1 Randall Cunningham	3.00	1.35	.35

1992 Playoff Promos

These seven standard-size cards were issued to give collectors a preview of the forthcoming 1992 Playoff series. These cards are distinguished from other cards by the Tekchrome printing process, which enhances the action photography and gives the cards a three-dimensional appearance, and by their thicker (22 point) card stock. The fronts feature glossy full-bleed color player photos that exhibit a metallic-like sheen. The player's name appears in silver lettering in a black bar toward the bottom of the photo. The backs have a full-bleed color close-up photo with the player's name in a team color-coded vertical bar that descends from the top edge. The cards are numbered on the back "X of 6 Promo".

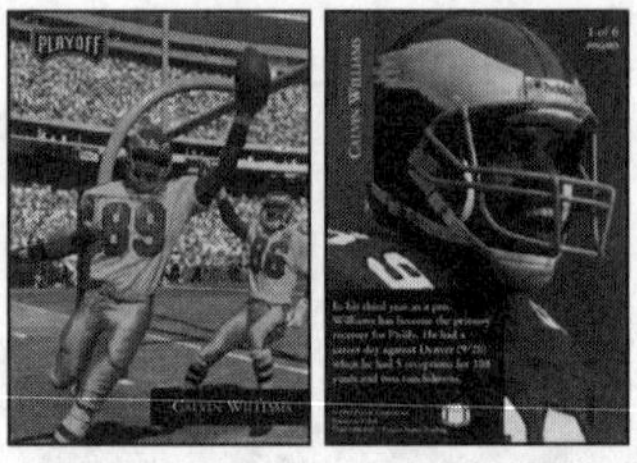

	MINT	NRMT	EXC
COMPLETE SET (7)	12.00	5.50	1.50
COMMON CARD (1-6)	.75	.35	.09

☐ 1 Calvin Williams	1.00	.45	.12
☐ 2 John Elway	3.00	1.35	.35
☐ 3 Dalton Hilliard	.75	.35	.09
☐ 4 Steve Young	3.00	1.35	.35
☐ 5 Emmitt Smith	6.00	2.70	.75
☐ 6 Mike Golic	.75	.35	.09
☐ NNO Header/Intro Card	.75	.35	.09

1992 Playoff

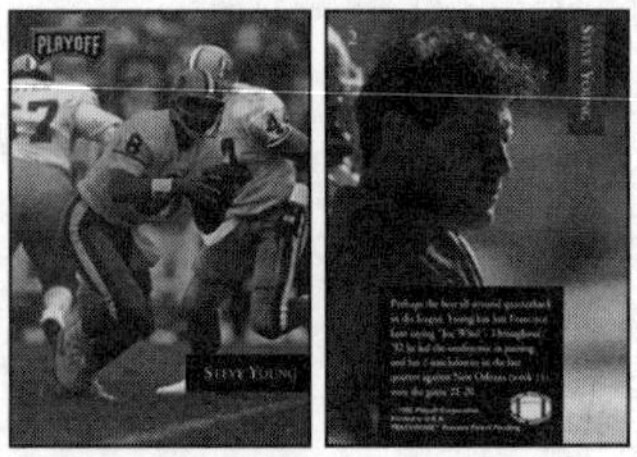

The 150 standard-size cards were issued in eight-card packs. The fronts display full-bleed, metallic player photos accented by the player's name in a black bar near the bottom. The backs have a full-bleed color close-up photo with the player's name in a team color-coded vertical bar that descends from the top edge. A black box centered at the bottom presents a detailed look at the player's performance during a key game in the 1992 season. Twelve different versions of the display box were produced, each featuring a different football player. Rookie Cards in this set include Steve Bono, Terrell Buckley, Willie Davis and Amp Lee.

	MINT	NRMT	EXC
COMPLETE SET (150)	40.00	18.00	5.00
COMMON CARD (1-150)	.25	.11	.03

☐ 1 Emmitt Smith	10.00	4.50	1.25
☐ 2 Steve Young	3.00	1.35	.35
☐ 3 Jack Del Rio	.25	.11	.03
☐ 4 Bobby Hebert	.25	.11	.03
☐ 5 Shannon Sharpe	.60	.25	.07
☐ 6 Gary Clark	.60	.25	.07
☐ 7 Christian Okoye	.25	.11	.03
☐ 8 Ernest Givins	.40	.18	.05
☐ 9 Mike Horan	.25	.11	.03
☐ 10 Dennis Gentry	.25	.11	.03
☐ 11 Michael Irvin	.60	.25	.07
☐ 12 Eric Floyd	.25	.11	.03
☐ 13 Brent Jones	.40	.18	.05
☐ 14 Anthony Carter	.40	.18	.05
☐ 15 Tony Martin	.60	.25	.07
☐ 16 Greg Lewis UER ("Returning" should be "returned" on back)	.25	.11	.03
☐ 17 Todd McNair	.25	.11	.03
☐ 18 Earnest Byner	.25	.11	.03
☐ 19 Steve Beuerlein	.25	.11	.03
☐ 20 Roger Craig	.40	.18	.05
☐ 21 Mark Higgs	.25	.11	.03
☐ 22 Guy McIntyre	.25	.11	.03
☐ 23 Don Warren	.25	.11	.03
☐ 24 Alvin Harper	.40	.18	.05
☐ 25 Mark Jackson	.25	.11	.03
☐ 26 Chris Doleman	.25	.11	.03
☐ 27 Jesse Sapolu	.25	.11	.03
☐ 28 Tony Tolbert	.25	.11	.03
☐ 29 Wendell Davis	.25	.11	.03
☐ 30 Dan Saleaumua	.25	.11	.03
☐ 31 Jeff Bostic	.25	.11	.03
☐ 32 Jay Novacek	.40	.18	.05
☐ 33 Cris Carter	.60	.25	.07
☐ 34 Tony Paige	.25	.11	.03
☐ 35 Greg Kragen	.25	.11	.03
☐ 36 Jeff Dellenbach	.25	.11	.03
☐ 37 Keith DeLong	.25	.11	.03
☐ 38 Todd Scott	.25	.11	.03
☐ 39 Jeff Feagles	.25	.11	.03
☐ 40 Mike Saxon	.25	.11	.03
☐ 41 Martin Mayhew	.25	.11	.03
☐ 42 Steve Bono	.75	.35	.09
☐ 43 Willie Davis	.75	.35	.09
☐ 44 Mark Stepnoski	.40	.18	.05
☐ 45 Harry Newsome	.25	.11	.03
☐ 46 Thane Gash	.25	.11	.03
☐ 47 Gaston Green	.25	.11	.03
☐ 48 James Washington	.25	.11	.03
☐ 49 Kenny Walker	.25	.11	.03
☐ 50 Jeff Davidson	.25	.11	.03
☐ 51 Shane Conlan	.25	.11	.03
☐ 52 Richard Dent	.40	.18	.05
☐ 53 Haywood Jeffires	.40	.18	.05
☐ 54 Harry Galbreath	.25	.11	.03
☐ 55 Terry Allen	1.50	.70	.19
☐ 56 Tommy Barnhardt	.25	.11	.03
☐ 57 Mike Golic	.25	.11	.03
☐ 58 Dalton Hilliard	.25	.11	.03
☐ 59 Danny Copeland	.25	.11	.03
☐ 60 Jerry Fontenot	.25	.11	.03
☐ 61 Kelvin Martin	.25	.11	.03
☐ 62 Mark Kelso	.25	.11	.03
☐ 63 Wymon Henderson	.25	.11	.03
☐ 64 Mark Rypien	.25	.11	.03
☐ 65 Bobby Humphrey	.25	.11	.03
☐ 66 Rich Gannon UER (Tarkington misspelled; Minneapolis instead of Minnesota on back)	.25	.11	.03
☐ 67 Darren Lewis	.25	.11	.03
☐ 68 Barry Foster	.40	.18	.05
☐ 69 Ken Norton Jr.	.60	.25	.07
☐ 70 James Lofton	.40	.18	.05
☐ 71 Trace Armstrong	.25	.11	.03
☐ 72 Vestee Jackson	.25	.11	.03
☐ 73 Clyde Simmons	.25	.11	.03
☐ 74 Brad Muster	.25	.11	.03
☐ 75 Cornelius Bennett	.40	.18	.05
☐ 76 Mike Merriweather	.25	.11	.03
☐ 77 John Elway	3.00	1.35	.35
☐ 78 Herschel Walker	.40	.18	.05
☐ 79 Hassan Jones UER (Minneapolis instead of Minnesota on back)	.25	.11	.03
☐ 80 Jim Harbaugh	.60	.25	.07
☐ 81 Issiac Holt	.25	.11	.03
☐ 82 David Alexander	.25	.11	.03
☐ 83 Brian Mitchell	.40	.18	.05
☐ 84 Mark Tuinei	.25	.11	.03
☐ 85 Tom Rathman	.25	.11	.03
☐ 86 Reggie White	.60	.25	.07
☐ 87 William Perry	.40	.18	.05
☐ 88 Jeff Wright	.25	.11	.03
☐ 89 Keith Kartz	.25	.11	.03
☐ 90 Andre Waters	.25	.11	.03
☐ 91 Darryl Talley	.25	.11	.03
☐ 92 Morten Andersen	.25	.11	.03
☐ 93 Tom Waddle	.25	.11	.03
☐ 94 Felix Wright UER (Minneapolis instead of Minnesota on back)	.25	.11	.03
☐ 95 Keith Jackson	.40	.18	.05
☐ 96 Art Monk	.40	.18	.05
☐ 97 Seth Joyner	.40	.18	.05
☐ 98 Steve McMichael	.40	.18	.05
☐ 99 Thurman Thomas	.60	.25	.07
☐ 100 Warren Moon	.60	.25	.07
☐ 101 Tony Casillas	.25	.11	.03
☐ 102 Vance Johnson	.25	.11	.03
☐ 103 Doug Dawson	.25	.11	.03
☐ 104 Bill Maas	.25	.11	.03
☐ 105 Mark Clayton	.40	.18	.05
☐ 106 Hoby Brenner	.25	.11	.03
☐ 107 Gary Anderson K	.25	.11	.03
☐ 108 Marc Logan	.25	.11	.03
☐ 109 Ricky Sanders	.25	.11	.03
☐ 110 Vai Sikahema	.25	.11	.03
☐ 111 Neil Smith	.60	.25	.07
☐ 112 Cody Carlson	.25	.11	.03
☐ 113 Jimmie Jones	.25	.11	.03
☐ 114 Pat Swilling	.40	.18	.05
☐ 115 Neil O'Donnell	.60	.25	.07
☐ 116 Chip Lohmiller	.25	.11	.03
☐ 117 Mike Croel	.25	.11	.03
☐ 118 Pete Metzelaars	.25	.11	.03
☐ 119 Ray Childress	.25	.11	.03
☐ 120 Fred Banks	.25	.11	.03
☐ 121 Derek Kennard	.25	.11	.03
☐ 122 Daryl Johnston	.60	.25	.07
☐ 123 Lorenzo White UER (Minneapolis instead of Minnesota on back)	.25	.11	.03
☐ 124 Hardy Nickerson	.40	.18	.05
☐ 125 Derrick Thomas	.60	.25	.07
☐ 126 Steve Walsh	.25	.11	.03
☐ 127 Doug Widell	.25	.11	.03
☐ 128 Calvin Williams	.40	.18	.05
☐ 129 Tim Harris	.25	.11	.03
☐ 130 Rod Woodson	.60	.25	.07
☐ 131 Craig Heyward	.40	.18	.05
☐ 132 Barry Word	.25	.11	.03
☐ 133 Mark Duper	.25	.11	.03
☐ 134 Tim Johnson	.25	.11	.03
☐ 135 John Gesek	.25	.11	.03
☐ 136 Steve Jackson	.25	.11	.03
☐ 137 Dave Krieg	.40	.18	.05
☐ 138 Barry Sanders UER (Won Heisman in 1988, not 1986)	5.00	2.20	.60
☐ 139 Michael Haynes	.40	.18	.05
☐ 140 Eric Metcalf	.40	.18	.05
☐ 141 Stan Humphries	.60	.25	.07
☐ 142 Sterling Sharpe	.60	.25	.07

	MINT	NRMT	EXC
☐ 143 Todd Marinovich	.25	.11	.03
☐ 144 Rodney Hampton	.60	.25	.07
☐ 145 Rodney Peete	.40	.18	.05
☐ 146 Darryl Williams	.25	.11	.03
☐ 147 Darren Perry	.25	.11	.03
☐ 148 Terrell Buckley	.25	.11	.03
☐ 149 Amp Lee	.25	.11	.03
☐ 150 Ricky Watters	1.50	.70	.19

1993 Playoff Promos

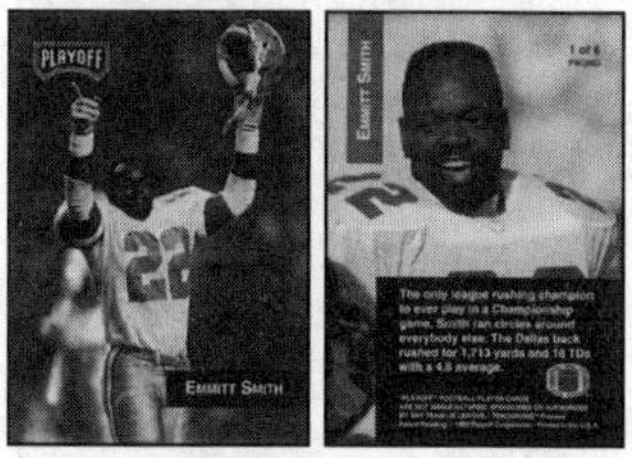

Measuring the standard-size, these six cards were issued to preview the design of the 1993 Playoff Collectors Edition football set. Printed on a thicker (22 point) card using the Tekchrome printing process, the action player photos on the fronts are full-bleed and have a metallic sheen to them. The player's name appears in silver lettering on a short black bar that overlays the bottom of the picture. On a full-bleed color close-up photo, the backs have the player's name on a brick-red vertical bar and a brief player profile on a black panel. The cards are numbered "X of 6 Promo."

	MINT	NRMT	EXC
COMPLETE SET (6)	12.00	5.50	1.50
COMMON CARD (1-6)	.75	.35	.09
☐ 1 Emmitt Smith	6.00	2.70	.75
☐ 2 Barry Foster	.75	.35	.09
☐ 3 Quinn Early	.75	.35	.09
☐ 4 Tim Brown	1.25	.55	.16
☐ 5 Steve Young	3.00	1.35	.35
☐ 6 Sterling Sharpe	1.25	.55	.16

1993 Playoff

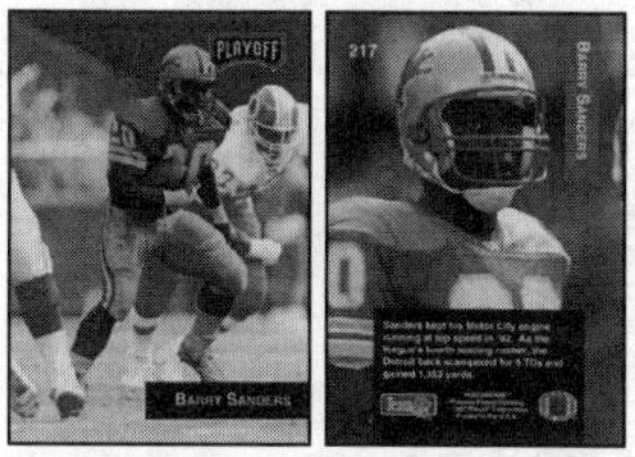

The 1993 Playoff set consists of 315 standard-size cards that were issued in eight-card packs. Card fronts contain full-bleed metallic color photos with the player's name in a black bar at the bottom. The backs also have a full-bleed photo that occupies most of the card. A black box at the bottom contains highlights. Subsets featured include The Backs (277-282), Connections (283-292), and Rookies (293-315). Rookie Cards include Jerome Bettis, Drew Bledsoe, Reggie Brooks, Curtis Conway, Garrison Hearst, O.J. McDuffie, Rick Mirer, Ronald Moore and Kevin Williams.

	MINT	NRMT	EXC
COMPLETE SET (315)	50.00	22.00	6.25
COMMON CARD (1-315)	.15	.07	.02
☐ 1 Troy Aikman	4.00	1.80	.50
☐ 2 Jerry Rice	4.00	1.80	.50
☐ 3 Keith Jackson	.30	.14	.04
☐ 4 Sean Gilbert	.30	.14	.04
☐ 5 Jim Kelly	.50	.23	.06
☐ 6 Junior Seau	.50	.23	.06
☐ 7 Deion Sanders	2.50	1.10	.30
☐ 8 Joe Montana	4.00	1.80	.50
☐ 9 Terrell Buckley	.15	.07	.02
☐ 10 Emmitt Smith	6.00	2.70	.75
☐ 11 Pete Stoyanovich	.15	.07	.02
☐ 12 Randall Cunningham	.30	.14	.04
☐ 13 Boomer Esiason	.30	.14	.04
☐ 14 Mike Saxon	.15	.07	.02
☐ 15 Chuck Cecil	.15	.07	.02
☐ 16 Vinny Testaverde	.30	.14	.04
☐ 17 Jeff Hostetler	.30	.14	.04
☐ 18 Mark Clayton	.15	.07	.02
☐ 19 Nick Bell	.15	.07	.02
☐ 20 Frank Reich	.30	.14	.04
☐ 21 Henry Ellard	.30	.14	.04
☐ 22 Andre Reed	.30	.14	.04
☐ 23 Mark Ingram	.15	.07	.02
☐ 24 Mike Brim	.15	.07	.02
☐ 25A Bernie Kosar UER (Name spelled Kozar on both sides)	.30	.14	.04
☐ 25B Bernie Kosar COR	.30	.14	.04
☐ 26 Jeff George	.50	.23	.06
☐ 27 Tommy Maddox	.15	.07	.02
☐ 28 Kent Graham	.50	.23	.06
☐ 29 David Klingler	.15	.07	.02
☐ 30 Robert Delpino	.15	.07	.02
☐ 31 Kevin Fagan	.15	.07	.02
☐ 32 Mark Bavaro	.15	.07	.02
☐ 33 Harold Green	.15	.07	.02
☐ 34 Shawn McCarthy	.15	.07	.02
☐ 35 Ricky Proehl	.15	.07	.02
☐ 36 Eugene Robinson	.15	.07	.02
☐ 37 Phil Simms	.30	.14	.04
☐ 38 David Lang	.15	.07	.02
☐ 39 Santana Dotson	.30	.14	.04
☐ 40 Brett Perriman	.50	.23	.06
☐ 41 Jim Harbaugh	.50	.23	.06
☐ 42 Keith Byars	.15	.07	.02
☐ 43 Quentin Coryatt	.30	.14	.04
☐ 44 Louis Oliver	.15	.07	.02
☐ 45 Howie Long	.30	.14	.04
☐ 46 Mike Sherrard	.15	.07	.02
☐ 47 Earnest Byner	.15	.07	.02
☐ 48 Neil Smith	.50	.23	.06
☐ 49 Audray McMillian	.15	.07	.02
☐ 50 Vaughn Dunbar	.15	.07	.02
☐ 51 Ronnie Lott	.30	.14	.04
☐ 52 Clyde Simmons	.15	.07	.02
☐ 53 Kevin Scott	.15	.07	.02
☐ 54 Bubby Brister	.15	.07	.02
☐ 55 Randal Hill	.15	.07	.02
☐ 56 Pat Swilling	.15	.07	.02
☐ 57 Steve Beuerlein	.15	.07	.02
☐ 58 Gary Clark	.30	.14	.04
☐ 59 Brian Noble	.15	.07	.02
☐ 60 Leslie O'Neal	.30	.14	.04
☐ 61 Vincent Brown	.15	.07	.02
☐ 62 Edgar Bennett	.50	.23	.06
☐ 63 Anthony Carter	.30	.14	.04
☐ 64 Glenn Cadrez UER (Name misspelled Cadez on front)	.15	.07	.02
☐ 65 Dalton Hilliard	.15	.07	.02
☐ 66 James Lofton	.30	.14	.04
☐ 67 Walter Stanley	.15	.07	.02
☐ 68 Tim Harris	.15	.07	.02
☐ 69 Carl Banks	.15	.07	.02
☐ 70 Andre Ware	.15	.07	.02
☐ 71 Karl Mecklenburg	.15	.07	.02
☐ 72 Russell Maryland	.15	.07	.02
☐ 73 Leroy Thompson	.15	.07	.02
☐ 74 Tommy Kane	.15	.07	.02
☐ 75 Dan Marino	6.00	2.70	.75
☐ 76 Darrell Fullington	.15	.07	.02
☐ 77 Jessie Tuggle	.15	.07	.02
☐ 78 Bruce Smith	.50	.23	.06
☐ 79 Neal Anderson	.15	.07	.02
☐ 80 Kevin Mack	.15	.07	.02
☐ 81 Shane Dronett	.15	.07	.02
☐ 82 Nick Lowery	.15	.07	.02
☐ 83 Sheldon White	.15	.07	.02
☐ 84 Flipper Anderson	.15	.07	.02
☐ 85 Jeff Herrod	.15	.07	.02
☐ 86 Dwight Stone	.15	.07	.02
☐ 87 Dave Krieg	.30	.14	.04
☐ 88 Bryan Cox	.15	.07	.02
☐ 89 Greg McMurtry	.15	.07	.02
☐ 90 Rickey Jackson	.15	.07	.02
☐ 91 Ernie Mills	.15	.07	.02
☐ 92 Browning Nagle	.15	.07	.02
☐ 93 John Taylor	.30	.14	.04
☐ 94 Eric Dickerson	.30	.14	.04
☐ 95 Johnny Holland	.15	.07	.02
☐ 96 Anthony Miller	.30	.14	.04
☐ 97 Fred Barnett	.30	.14	.04
☐ 98 Ricky Ervins UER (Name misspelled Rickey on back)	.15	.07	.02
☐ 99 Leonard Russell	.30	.14	.04
☐ 100 Lawrence Taylor	.50	.23	.06
☐ 101 Tony Casillas	.15	.07	.02
☐ 102 John Elway	2.50	1.10	.30
☐ 103 Bennie Blades	.15	.07	.02
☐ 104 Harry Sydney	.15	.07	.02
☐ 105 Bubba McDowell	.15	.07	.02
☐ 106 Todd McNair	.15	.07	.02
☐ 107 Steve Smith	.15	.07	.02
☐ 108 Jim Everett	.30	.14	.04
☐ 109 Bobby Humphrey	.15	.07	.02
☐ 110 Rich Gannon	.15	.07	.02
☐ 111 Marv Cook	.15	.07	.02
☐ 112 Wayne Martin	.15	.07	.02
☐ 113 Sean Landeta	.15	.07	.02
☐ 114 Brad Baxter UER (Reversed negative on front)	.15	.07	.02
☐ 115 Reggie White	.50	.23	.06
☐ 116 Johnny Johnson	.15	.07	.02
☐ 117 Jeff Graham	.30	.14	.04
☐ 118 Darren Carrington	.15	.07	.02
☐ 119 Ricky Watters	.50	.23	.06
☐ 120 Art Monk UER (Reversed negative on back)	.30	.14	.04
☐ 121 Cornelius Bennett	.30	.14	.04
☐ 122 Wade Wilson	.15	.07	.02
☐ 123 Daniel Stubbs	.15	.07	.02
☐ 124 Brad Muster	.15	.07	.02
☐ 125 Mike Tomczak	.15	.07	.02
☐ 126 Jay Novacek	.30	.14	.04
☐ 127 Shannon Sharpe	.50	.23	.06
☐ 128 Rodney Peete	.15	.07	.02
☐ 129 Daryl Johnston	.50	.23	.06
☐ 130 Warren Moon	.50	.23	.06
☐ 131 Willie Gault	.15	.07	.02
☐ 132 Tony Martin	.50	.23	.06
☐ 133 Terry Allen	.50	.23	.06
☐ 134 Hugh Millen	.15	.07	.02
☐ 135 Rob Moore	.30	.14	.04
☐ 136 Andy Harmon	.30	.14	.04
☐ 137 Kelvin Martin	.15	.07	.02
☐ 138 Rod Woodson	.50	.23	.06
☐ 139 Nate Lewis	.15	.07	.02
☐ 140 Darryl Talley	.15	.07	.02
☐ 141 Guy McIntyre	.15	.07	.02
☐ 142 John L. Williams	.15	.07	.02
☐ 143 Brad Edwards	.15	.07	.02
☐ 144 Trace Armstrong	.15	.07	.02
☐ 145 Kenneth Davis	.15	.07	.02
☐ 146 Clay Matthews	.30	.14	.04
☐ 147 Gaston Green	.15	.07	.02
☐ 148 Chris Spielman	.30	.14	.04
☐ 149 Cody Carlson	.15	.07	.02
☐ 150 Derrick Thomas	.50	.23	.06
☐ 151 Terry McDaniel	.15	.07	.02
☐ 152 Kevin Greene	.50	.23	.06
☐ 153 Roger Craig	.30	.14	.04
☐ 154 Craig Heyward	.30	.14	.04
☐ 155 Rodney Hampton	.50	.23	.06
☐ 156 Heath Sherman	.15	.07	.02
☐ 157 Mark Stepnoski	.15	.07	.02
☐ 158 Chris Chandler	.30	.14	.04
☐ 159 Rod Bernstine	.15	.07	.02
☐ 160 Pierce Holt	.15	.07	.02
☐ 161 Wilber Marshall	.15	.07	.02
☐ 162 Reggie Cobb	.15	.07	.02
☐ 163 Tom Rathman	.15	.07	.02
☐ 164 Michael Haynes	.30	.14	.04
☐ 165 Nate Odomes	.15	.07	.02
☐ 166 Tom Waddle	.15	.07	.02
☐ 167 Eric Ball	.15	.07	.02
☐ 168 Brett Favre UER (Photo of Don Majkowski on back)	6.00	2.70	.75
☐ 169 Michael Jackson	.30	.14	.04
☐ 170 Lorenzo White	.15	.07	.02
☐ 171 Cleveland Gary	.15	.07	.02
☐ 172 Jay Schroeder	.15	.07	.02
☐ 173 Tony Paige	.15	.07	.02
☐ 174 Jack Del Rio	.15	.07	.02
☐ 175 Jon Vaughn	.15	.07	.02
☐ 176 Morten Andersen UER (Misspelled Morton)	.15	.07	.02
☐ 177 Chris Burkett	.15	.07	.02
☐ 178 Vai Sikahema	.15	.07	.02
☐ 179 Ronnie Harmon	.15	.07	.02
☐ 180 Amp Lee	.15	.07	.02
☐ 181 Chip Lohmiller	.15	.07	.02
☐ 182 Steve Broussard	.15	.07	.02
☐ 183 Don Beebe	.15	.07	.02
☐ 184 Tommy Vardell	.15	.07	.02
☐ 185 Keith Jennings	.15	.07	.02
☐ 186 Simon Fletcher	.15	.07	.02
☐ 187 Mel Gray	.30	.14	.04
☐ 188 Vince Workman	.15	.07	.02
☐ 189 Haywood Jeffires	.30	.14	.04
☐ 190 Barry Word	.15	.07	.02
☐ 191 Ethan Horton	.15	.07	.02
☐ 192 Mark Higgs	.15	.07	.02
☐ 193 Irving Fryar	.30	.14	.04
☐ 194 Charles Haley	.30	.14	.04
☐ 195 Steve Bono	.50	.23	.06
☐ 196 Mike Golic	.15	.07	.02
☐ 197 Gary Anderson K	.15	.07	.02
☐ 198 Sterling Sharpe	.50	.23	.06
☐ 199 Andre Tippett	.15	.07	.02
☐ 200 Thurman Thomas	.50	.23	.06
☐ 201 Chris Miller	.30	.14	.04
☐ 202 Henry Jones	.15	.07	.02
☐ 203 Mo Lewis	.15	.07	.02
☐ 204 Marion Butts	.15	.07	.02
☐ 205 Mike Johnson	.15	.07	.02
☐ 206 Alvin Harper	.30	.14	.04
☐ 207 Ray Childress	.15	.07	.02
☐ 208 Anthony Johnson	.30	.14	.04
☐ 209 Tony Bennett	.15	.07	.02
☐ 210 Anthony Newman	.15	.07	.02
☐ 211 Christian Okoye	.15	.07	.02
☐ 212 Marcus Allen	.50	.23	.06
☐ 213 Jackie Harris	.15	.07	.02
☐ 214 Mark Duper	.15	.07	.02
☐ 215 Cris Carter	.50	.23	.06
☐ 216 John Stephens	.15	.07	.02
☐ 217 Barry Sanders	4.00	1.80	.50
☐ 218A Herman Moore ERR (First name misspelled Sherman)	3.00	1.35	.35
☐ 218B Herman Moore COR name spelled correctly	3.50	1.55	.45
☐ 219 Marvin Washington	.15	.07	.02
☐ 220 Calvin Williams	.30	.14	.04
☐ 221 John Randle	.15	.07	.02
☐ 222 Marco Coleman	.15	.07	.02
☐ 223 Eric Martin	.15	.07	.02
☐ 224 Dave Meggett	.15	.07	.02
☐ 225 Brian Washington	.15	.07	.02
☐ 226 Barry Foster	.30	.14	.04
☐ 227 Michael Zordich	.15	.07	.02
☐ 228 Stan Humphries	.50	.23	.06
☐ 229 Mike Cofer	.15	.07	.02
☐ 230 Chris Warren	.30	.14	.04
☐ 231 Keith McCants	.15	.07	.02
☐ 232 Mark Rypien	.15	.07	.02
☐ 233 James Francis	.15	.07	.02
☐ 234 Andre Rison	.30	.14	.04
☐ 235 William Perry	.30	.14	.04
☐ 236 Chip Banks	.15	.07	.02
☐ 237 Willie Davis	.50	.23	.06
☐ 238 Chris Doleman	.15	.07	.02
☐ 239 Tim Brown	.50	.23	.06
☐ 240 Darren Perry	.15	.07	.02
☐ 241 Johnny Bailey	.15	.07	.02
☐ 242 Ernest Givins UER (Spelled Givens on back)	.30	.14	.04
☐ 243 John Carney	.15	.07	.02
☐ 244 Cortez Kennedy	.30	.14	.04
☐ 245 Lawrence Dawsey	.15	.07	.02
☐ 246 Martin Mayhew	.15	.07	.02
☐ 247 Shane Conlan	.15	.07	.02
☐ 248 J.J. Birden	.15	.07	.02
☐ 249 Quinn Early	.30	.14	.04
☐ 250 Michael Irvin	.50	.23	.06
☐ 251 Neil O'Donnell	.50	.23	.06
☐ 252 Stan Gelbaugh	.15	.07	.02
☐ 253 Drew Hill	.15	.07	.02
☐ 254 Wendell Davis	.15	.07	.02
☐ 255 Tim Johnson	.15	.07	.02
☐ 256 Seth Joyner	.15	.07	.02
☐ 257 Derrick Fenner	.15	.07	.02
☐ 258 Steve Young	2.50	1.10	.30
☐ 259 Jackie Slater	.15	.07	.02
☐ 260 Eric Metcalf	.30	.14	.04
☐ 261 Rufus Porter	.15	.07	.02
☐ 262 Ken Norton Jr.	.30	.14	.04
☐ 263 Tim McDonald	.15	.07	.02
☐ 264 Mark Jackson	.15	.07	.02
☐ 265 Hardy Nickerson	.30	.14	.04
☐ 266 Anthony Munoz	.30	.14	.04
☐ 267 Mark Carrier WR	.30	.14	.04
☐ 268 Mike Pritchard	.30	.14	.04
☐ 269 Steve Emtman	.15	.07	.02
☐ 270 Ricky Sanders	.15	.07	.02
☐ 271 Robert Massey	.15	.07	.02
☐ 272 Pete Metzelaars	.15	.07	.02
☐ 273 Reggie Langhorne	.15	.07	.02
☐ 274 Tim McGee	.15	.07	.02
☐ 275 Reggie Rivers	.15	.07	.02
☐ 276 Jimmie Jones	.15	.07	.02
☐ 277 Lorenzo White TB	.15	.07	.02
☐ 278 Emmitt Smith TB	3.00	1.35	.35
☐ 279 Thurman Thomas TB	.50	.23	.06
☐ 280 Barry Sanders TB UER (Ten TD's in '92; should be nine)	2.00	.90	.25
☐ 281 Rodney Hampton TB	.30	.14	.04
☐ 282 Barry Foster TB	.30	.14	.04
☐ 283 Troy Aikman PC	2.00	.90	.25
☐ 284 Michael Irvin PC	.30	.14	.04
☐ 285 Brett Favre PC	3.00	1.35	.35
☐ 286 Sterling Sharpe PC	.30	.14	.04
☐ 287 Steve Young PC	1.50	.70	.19
☐ 288 Jerry Rice PC	2.00	.90	.25
☐ 289 Stan Humphries PC	.30	.14	.04
☐ 290 Anthony Miller PC	.30	.14	.04
☐ 291 Dan Marino PC	3.00	1.35	.35
☐ 292 Keith Jackson PC	.15	.07	.02
☐ 293 Patrick Bates	.15	.07	.02
☐ 294 Jerome Bettis	4.00	1.80	.50
☐ 295 Drew Bledsoe	8.00	3.60	1.00
☐ 296 Tom Carter	.30	.14	.04
☐ 297 Curtis Conway	2.50	1.10	.30
☐ 298 John Copeland	.30	.14	.04
☐ 299 Eric Curry	.15	.07	.02
☐ 300 Reggie Brooks	.30	.14	.04
☐ 301 Steve Everitt	.15	.07	.02
☐ 302 Deon Figures	.30	.14	.04
☐ 303 Garrison Hearst	3.50	1.55	.45
☐ 304 Qadry Ismail UER (Misspelled Quadry on both sides)	.50	.23	.06
☐ 305 Marvin Jones	.15	.07	.02
☐ 306 Lincoln Kennedy	.15	.07	.02
☐ 307 O.J. McDuffie	2.50	1.10	.30
☐ 308 Rick Mirer	3.50	1.55	.45
☐ 309 Wayne Simmons	.15	.07	.02
☐ 310 Irv Smith	.15	.07	.02
☐ 311 Robert Smith	2.50	1.10	.30
☐ 312 Dana Stubblefield	.50	.23	.06
☐ 313 George Teague	.30	.14	.04
☐ 314 Dan Williams	.15	.07	.02
☐ 315 Kevin Williams	.75	.35	.09
☐ NNO Santa Claus	2.00	.90	.25

1993 Playoff Checklists

These eight standard-size cards were randomly inserted in packs. The fronts feature full-bleed color action player photos. Overlaying the picture at the bottom is a silver box edged on its left by a black stripe carrying the words "Check It Out." The silver box carries statistical highlights on the featured player(s). The checklist on the backs is printed on a white panel bordered on the top by a red stripe and on the bottom by a black stripe.

	MINT	NRMT	EXC
COMPLETE SET (8)	6.00	2.70	.75
COMMON CARD (1-8)	.30	.14	.04

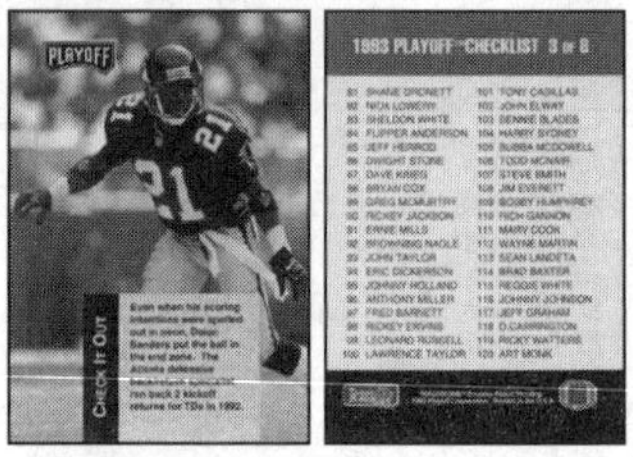

	MINT	NRMT	EXC
☐ 1A Warren Moon UER	.50	.23	.06
(Kosar misspelled Kozar)			
☐ 1B Warren Moon COR	.50	.23	.06
☐ 2 Barry Sanders	2.50	1.10	.30
☐ 3 Deion Sanders	1.25	.55	.16
☐ 4 Rod Woodson	.50	.23	.06
☐ 5 Junior Seau	.75	.35	.09
☐ 6 Mark Rypien	.30	.14	.04
☐ 7 Derrick Thomas	.50	.23	.06
☐ 8 Dallas Players UER	.75	.35	.09
Daryl Johnston			
Alvin Harper			
Michael Irvin			
(Stan Humphries listed as 299; should be 289)			

1993 Playoff Club

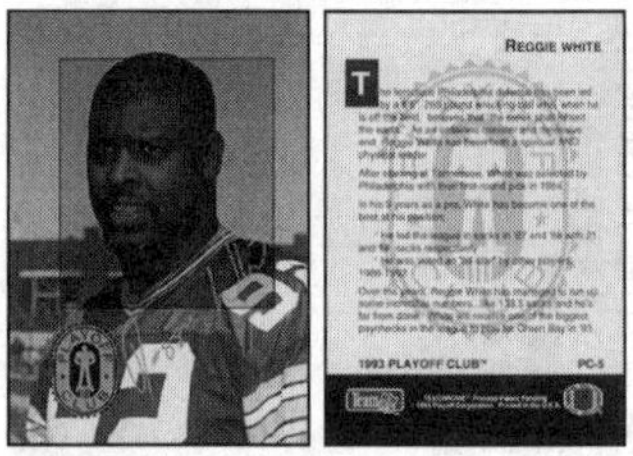

Featuring all-time great, still active football players, this seven-card, standard-size set was available in both hobby and retail packs. On the fronts, the color head shots inside a picture frame contrast with the black-and-white surrounding photo. The gold Playoff Club emblem appears at the lower left corner, and the player's signature is inscribed in gold ink across the picture. On the backs, a career summary is overprinted on a white panel with a gray Playoff Club emblem. The cards are numbered on the back with a "PC" prefix.

	MINT	NRMT	EXC
COMPLETE SET (7)	25.00	11.00	3.10
COMMON CARD (PC1-PC7)	2.00	.90	.25
☐ PC1 Joe Montana	15.00	6.75	1.85
☐ PC2 Art Monk	3.00	1.35	.35
☐ PC3 Lawrence Taylor	3.00	1.35	.35
☐ PC4 Ronnie Lott	3.00	1.35	.35
☐ PC5 Reggie White	4.00	1.80	.50
☐ PC6 Anthony Munoz	2.00	.90	.25
☐ PC7 Jackie Slater	2.00	.90	.25

1993 Playoff Brett Favre

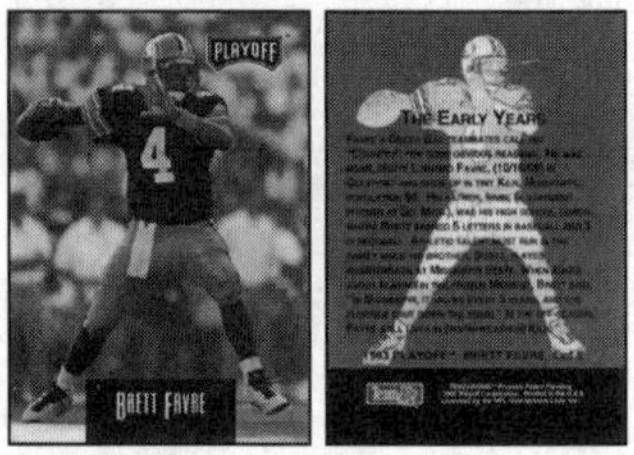

Randomly inserted in hobby packs, these five standard-size cards trace the career of Brett Favre, quarterback of the Green Bay Packers. The fronts display full-bleed color action player photos with a metallic sheen to them. The player's name appears in a black box at the bottom. On a green panel displaying a ghosted silhouette of Favre preparing to pass, the backs present season highlights. The cards are numbered on the back as "X of 5."

	MINT	NRMT	EXC
COMPLETE SET (5)	100.00	45.00	12.50
COMMON FAVRE (1-5)	20.00	9.00	2.50
☐ 1 Brett Favre	20.00	9.00	2.50
The Early Years			
☐ 2 Brett Favre	20.00	9.00	2.50
The College Years			
☐ 3 Brett Favre	20.00	9.00	2.50
Turning Pro			
☐ 4 Brett Favre	20.00	9.00	2.50
Green Bay Star			
☐ 5 Brett Favre	20.00	9.00	2.50
1992: The Storybook Season			

1993 Playoff Headliners Redemption

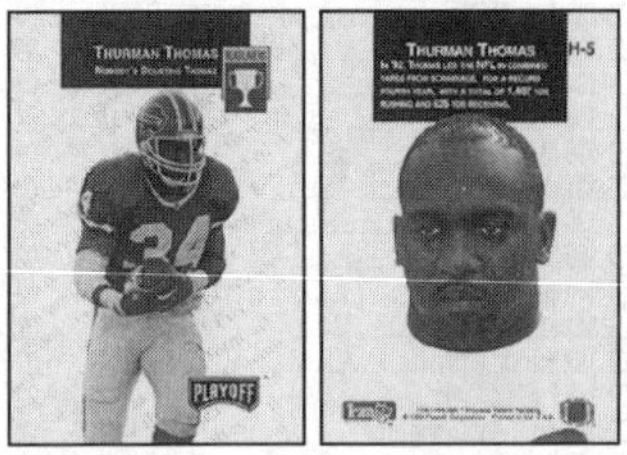

A special trade card randomly inserted in retail foil packs, entitled collector to receive these six standard-size cards. The redemption offer expired July 31, 1994. A similar card randomly inserted in hobby foil packs entitled the collector to receive a ten-card Rookie Roundup set. According to the card back, 48,475 trade cards were produced for random insertion. The borderless fronts feature metallic color player action shots that are cut out and superimposed upon a gray background with oblique silver newspaper type. The player's name appears in silver-colored lettering within a black rectangle at the top. The set's logo is shown at the upper right. The borderless back carries a color player headshot superposed upon a white background with oblique beige-colored logos of the player's team. The player's name and 1992 season highlights appear in white lettering within the black rectangle at the top. The cards are numbered on the back with an "H" prefix.

	MINT	NRMT	EXC
COMPLETE SET (6)	20.00	9.00	2.50
COMMON CARD (H1-H6)	1.25	.55	.16
☐ H1 Brett Favre	10.00	4.50	1.25
☐ H2 Sterling Sharpe	2.00	.90	.25
☐ H3 Emmitt Smith	10.00	4.50	1.25
☐ H4 Jerry Rice	6.00	2.70	.75
☐ H5 Thurman Thomas	3.00	1.35	.35
☐ H6 David Klingler	1.25	.55	.16
☐ NNO Headliner Redemption	.50	.23	.06

1993 Playoff Promo Inserts

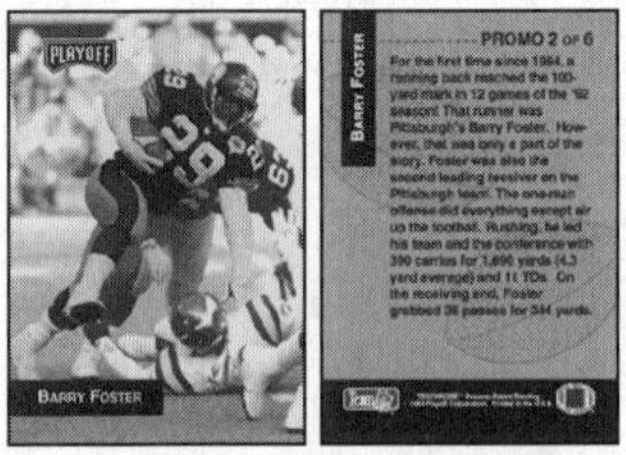

One Playoff Promo Insert (or Playoff Ricky Watters card) was inserted in every special retail pack of 1993 Playoff. The six standard-size promos feature borderless player action shots on their fronts. The featured player is in color, but the background is black-and-white. The player's name appears in silver-colored lettering within a black bar at the lower left. The back carries the player's career highlights on a colored panel. His name appears vertically in white lettering within a black bar at the upper left. The cards are numbered on the back as "Promo X of 6."

	MINT	NRMT	EXC
COMPLETE SET (6)	10.00	4.50	1.25
COMMON CARD (1-6)	1.50	.70	.19
☐ 1 Michael Irvin	2.50	1.10	.30
☐ 2 Barry Foster	1.50	.70	.19
☐ 3 Quinn Early	1.50	.70	.19
☐ 4 Tim Brown	2.50	1.10	.30
☐ 5 Reggie White	2.50	1.10	.30
☐ 6 Sterling Sharpe	1.50	.70	.19

1993 Playoff Rookie Roundup Redemption

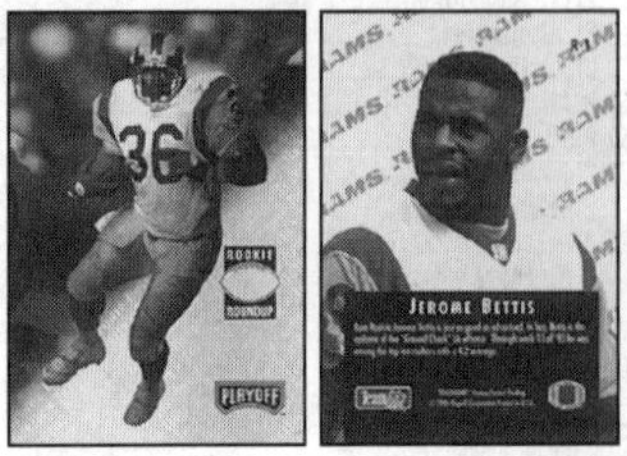

A special insert card (1993 Playoff Rookie Roundup Redemption) found in hobby foil packs could be redeemed through a mail-in offer for this ten-card, standard-size set. The expiration date was July 3, 1994. These cards showcase the ten hottest rookies of the 1993 NFL season. According to the card back, 15,683 trade cards were produced. The borderless fronts feature metallic color player action shots that are cut out and superimposed on a gray background with oblique silver newspaper type. The player's name appears in the silver-colored lower right corner in silver metallic lettering. The Rookie Roundup logo is printed on the right edge. The borderless back carries a color player headshot superimposed on a white background with oblique gray-colored logos of the player's team. The player's name and 1993 season highlights appear in white lettering within the black rectangle at the bottom. The cards are numbered on the back with an "R" prefix.

	MINT	NRMT	EXC
COMPLETE SET (10)	40.00	18.00	5.00
COMMON CARD (R1-R10)	2.00	.90	.25
☐ R1 Jerome Bettis	8.00	3.60	1.00
☐ R2 Drew Bledsoe	15.00	6.75	1.85
☐ R3 Reggie Brooks	3.00	1.35	.35
☐ R4 Derek Brown RB	2.00	.90	.25
☐ R5 Garrison Hearst	6.00	2.70	.75
☐ R6 Terry Kirby	4.00	1.80	.50
☐ R7 Glyn Milburn	3.00	1.35	.35
☐ R8 Rick Mirer	6.00	2.70	.75
☐ R9 Roosevelt Potts	2.00	.90	.25
☐ R10 Dana Stubblefield	3.00	1.35	.35
☐ NNO Rookie Roundup	.50	.23	.06
Redemption Card			

1993 Playoff Ricky Watters

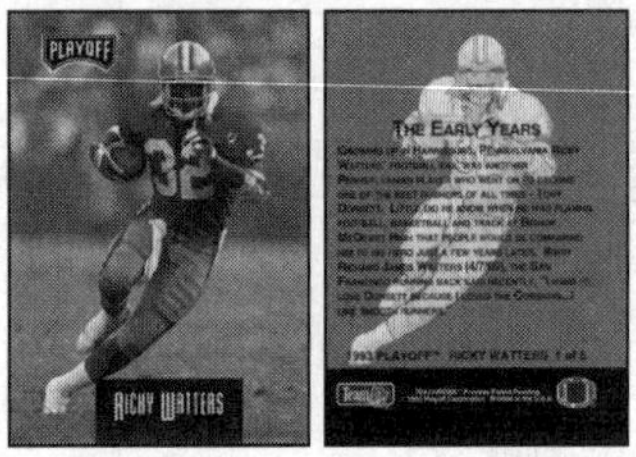

Randomly inserted in retail packs, these five standard-size cards trace the career of San Francisco running back Ricky Watters. The fronts display full-bleed color action player photos with a metallic sheen to them. The player's name appears in a black box at the bottom. On a tan panel displaying a ghosted silhouette of Watters running, the backs present season highlights. The cards are numbered on the back as "X of 5."

	MINT	NRMT	EXC
COMPLETE SET (5)	20.00	9.00	2.50
COMMON WATTERS (1-5)	4.00	1.80	.50
☐ 1 Ricky Watters	4.00	1.80	.50
The Early Years			
☐ 2 Ricky Watters	4.00	1.80	.50
Irish Eyes Were Smiling			
☐ 3 Ricky Watters	4.00	1.80	.50
The Bay Watters			
☐ 4 Ricky Watters	4.00	1.80	.50
A Second-Year Rookie			
☐ 5 Ricky Watters	4.00	1.80	.50
Rookie of the Year			

1994 Playoff Prototypes

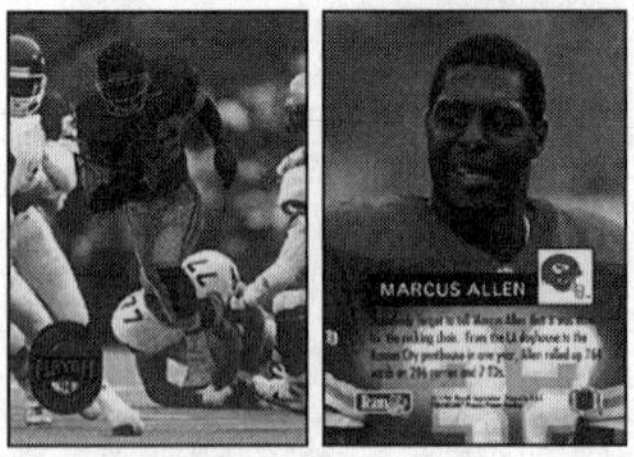

These six standard-size prototypes feature on their fronts borderless metallic color player action shots. The player's name appears within an oval emblem in one corner. The borderless back carries a color closeup with the player's name, team helmet, and career highlights. The cards are unnumbered and checklisted below in alphabetical order.

	MINT	NRMT	EXC
COMPLETE SET (6)	8.00	3.60	1.00
COMMON CARD (1-6)	.75	.35	.09
☐ 1 Marcus Allen	.75	.35	.09
☐ 2 Rick Mirer	.75	.35	.09
☐ 3 Barry Sanders	2.00	.90	.25
☐ 4 Junior Seau	.75	.35	.09
☐ 5 Sterling Sharpe	.75	.35	.09
☐ 6 Emmitt Smith	4.00	1.80	.50

1994 Playoff

These 336 standard-size feature borderless card fronts with metallic color player action shots. The cards were issued in eight-card hobby, retail and four-star packs. The player's name appears within an oval emblem in one corner. The borderless backs carry a color closeup with the player's name, team helmet, and career highlights. Topical subsets featured are Sack Pack (226-232), Ground Attack (233-262),

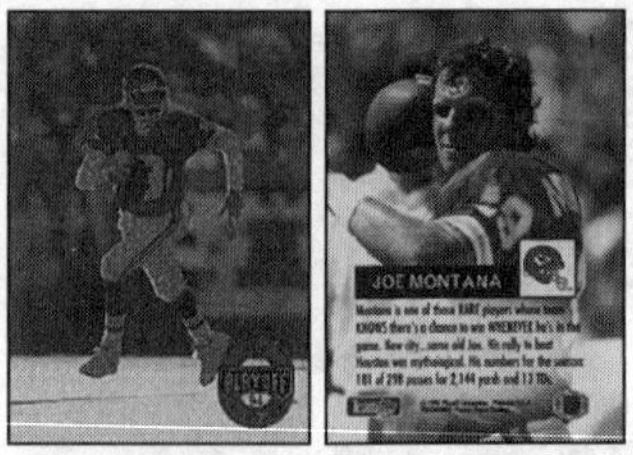

Summerall's Best (263-290), and Rookies (291-336). Rookie Cards include Derrick Alexander, Isaac Bruce, Trent Dilfer, Marshall Faulk, William Floyd, Greg Hill, Charles Johnson, Errict Rhett, Darnay Scott and Heath Shuler.

	MINT	NRMT	EXC
COMPLETE SET (336)	50.00	22.00	6.25
COMMON CARD (1-336)	.10	.05	.01
☐ 1 Joe Montana	2.50	1.10	.30
☐ 2 Derrick Thomas	.30	.14	.04
☐ 3 Dan Marino	5.00	2.20	.60
☐ 4 Cris Carter	.30	.14	.04
☐ 5 Boomer Esiason	.20	.09	.03
☐ 6 Bruce Smith	.30	.14	.04
☐ 7 Andre Rison	.20	.09	.03
☐ 8 Curtis Conway	.30	.14	.04
☐ 9 Michael Irvin	.30	.14	.04
☐ 10 Shannon Sharpe	.20	.09	.03
☐ 11 Pat Swilling	.10	.05	.01
☐ 12 John Parrella	.10	.05	.01
☐ 13 Mel Gray	.10	.05	.01
☐ 14 Ray Childress	.10	.05	.01
☐ 15 Willie Davis	.20	.09	.03
☐ 16 Rocket Ismail	.20	.09	.03
☐ 17 Jim Everett	.20	.09	.03
☐ 18 Mark Higgs	.10	.05	.01
☐ 19 Trace Armstrong	.10	.05	.01
☐ 20 Jim Kelly	.30	.14	.04
☐ 21 Rob Burnett	.10	.05	.01
☐ 22 Jay Novacek	.20	.09	.03
☐ 23 Robert Delpino	.10	.05	.01
☐ 24 Brett Perriman	.20	.09	.03
☐ 25 Troy Aikman	2.50	1.10	.30
☐ 26 Reggie White	.30	.14	.04
☐ 27 Lorenzo White	.10	.05	.01
☐ 28 Bubba McDowell	.10	.05	.01
☐ 29 Steve Emtman	.10	.05	.01
☐ 30 Brett Favre	5.00	2.20	.60
☐ 31 Derek Russell	.10	.05	.01
☐ 32 Jeff Hostetler	.20	.09	.03
☐ 33 Henry Ellard	.20	.09	.03
☐ 34 Jack Del Rio	.10	.05	.01
☐ 35 Mike Saxon	.10	.05	.01
☐ 36 Rickey Jackson	.10	.05	.01
☐ 37 Phil Simms	.20	.09	.03
☐ 38 Quinn Early	.20	.09	.03
☐ 39 Russell Copeland	.10	.05	.01
☐ 40 Carl Pickens	1.00	.45	.12
☐ 41 Lance Gunn	.10	.05	.01
☐ 42 Bernie Kosar	.20	.09	.03
☐ 43 John Elway	2.00	.90	.25
☐ 44 George Teague	.10	.05	.01
☐ 45 Nick Lowery	.10	.05	.01
☐ 46 Haywood Jeffires	.20	.09	.03
☐ 47 Will Shields	.10	.05	.01
☐ 48 Daryl Johnston	.20	.09	.03
☐ 49 Pete Metzelaars	.10	.05	.01
☐ 50 Warren Moon	.30	.14	.04
☐ 51 Cornelius Bennett	.20	.09	.03
☐ 52 Vinny Testaverde	.20	.09	.03
☐ 53 John Mangum	.10	.05	.01
☐ 54 Tommy Vardell	.10	.05	.01
☐ 55 Lincoln Coleman	.10	.05	.01
☐ 56 Karl Mecklenburg	.10	.05	.01
☐ 57 Jackie Harris	.10	.05	.01
☐ 58 Curtis Duncan	.10	.05	.01
☐ 59 Quentin Coryatt	.10	.05	.01
☐ 60 Tim Brown	.30	.14	.04
☐ 61 Irving Fryar	.20	.09	.03
☐ 62 Sean Gilbert	.10	.05	.01
☐ 63 Qadry Ismail	.30	.14	.04
☐ 64 Irv Smith	.10	.05	.01
☐ 65 Mark Jackson	.10	.05	.01
☐ 66 Ronnie Lott	.20	.09	.03
☐ 67 Henry Jones	.10	.05	.01
☐ 68 Horace Copeland	.10	.05	.01
☐ 69 John Copeland	.10	.05	.01
☐ 70 Mark Carrier WR	.20	.09	.03
☐ 71 Michael Jackson	.20	.09	.03
☐ 72 Jason Elam	.10	.05	.01
☐ 73 Rod Bernstine	.10	.05	.01
☐ 74 Wayne Simmons	.10	.05	.01
☐ 75 Cody Carlson	.10	.05	.01
☐ 76 Alexander Wright	.10	.05	.01
☐ 77 Shane Conlan	.10	.05	.01
☐ 78 Keith Jackson	.10	.05	.01
☐ 79 Sean Salisbury	.10	.05	.01
☐ 80 Vaughan Johnson	.10	.05	.01
☐ 81 Rob Moore	.20	.09	.03
☐ 82 Andre Reed	.20	.09	.03
☐ 83 David Klinger	.10	.05	.01

☐ 84 Jim Harbaugh	.30	.14	.04
☐ 85 John Jett	.10	.05	.01
☐ 86 Sterling Sharpe	.20	.09	.03
☐ 87 Webster Slaughter	.10	.05	.01
☐ 88 J.J. Birden	.10	.05	.01
☐ 89 O.J. McDuffie	.30	.14	.04
☐ 90 Andre Tippett	.10	.05	.01
☐ 91 Don Beebe	.10	.05	.01
☐ 92 Mark Stepnoski	.10	.05	.01
☐ 93 Neil Smith	.30	.14	.04
☐ 94 Terry Kirby	.30	.14	.04
☐ 95 Wade Wilson	.10	.05	.01
☐ 96 Darryl Talley	.10	.05	.01
☐ 97 Anthony Smith	.10	.05	.01
☐ 98 Willie Roaf	.10	.05	.01
☐ 99 Mo Lewis	.10	.05	.01
☐ 100 James Washington	.10	.05	.01
☐ 101 Nate Odomes	.10	.05	.01
☐ 102 Chris Gedney	.10	.05	.01
☐ 103 Joe Walter	.10	.05	.01
☐ 104 Alvin Harper	.20	.09	.03
☐ 105 Simon Fletcher	.10	.05	.01
☐ 106 Rodney Peete	.10	.05	.01
☐ 107 Terrell Buckley	.10	.05	.01
☐ 108 Jeff George	.30	.14	.04
☐ 109 James Jett	.10	.05	.01
☐ 110 Tony Casillas	.10	.05	.01
☐ 111 Marco Coleman	.10	.05	.01
☐ 112 Anthony Carter	.20	.09	.03
☐ 113 Lincoln Kennedy	.10	.05	.01
☐ 114 Chris Calloway	.10	.05	.01
☐ 115 Randall Cunningham	.20	.09	.03
☐ 116 Steve Beuerlein	.10	.05	.01
☐ 117 Neil O'Donnell	.30	.14	.04
☐ 118 Stan Humphries	.30	.14	.04
☐ 119 John Taylor	.20	.09	.03
☐ 120 Cortez Kennedy	.20	.09	.03
☐ 121 Santana Dotson	.20	.09	.03
☐ 122 Thomas Smith	.10	.05	.01
☐ 123 Kevin Williams	.20	.09	.03
☐ 124 Andre Ware	.10	.05	.01
☐ 125 Ethan Horton	.10	.05	.01
☐ 126 Mike Sherrard	.10	.05	.01
☐ 127 Fred Barnett	.20	.09	.03
☐ 128 Ricky Proehl	.10	.05	.01
☐ 129 Kevin Greene	.30	.14	.04
☐ 130 John Carney	.10	.05	.01
☐ 131 Tim McDonald	.10	.05	.01
☐ 132 Rick Mirer	.30	.14	.04
☐ 133 Blair Thomas	.10	.05	.01
☐ 134 Hardy Nickerson	.20	.09	.03
☐ 135 Heath Sherman	.10	.05	.01
☐ 136 Andre Hastings	.20	.09	.03
☐ 137 Randal Hill	.10	.05	.01
☐ 138 Mike Cofer	.10	.05	.01
☐ 139 Brian Blades	.20	.09	.03
☐ 140 Earnest Byner	.10	.05	.01
☐ 141 Bill Bates	.20	.09	.03
☐ 142 Junior Seau	.30	.14	.04
☐ 143 Johnny Bailey	.10	.05	.01
☐ 144 Dwight Stone	.10	.05	.01
☐ 145 Todd Kelly	.10	.05	.01
☐ 146 Tyrone Montgomery	.10	.05	.01
☐ 147 Herschel Walker	.20	.09	.03
☐ 148 Gary Clark	.20	.09	.03
☐ 149 Eric Green	.10	.05	.01
☐ 150 Steve Young	2.00	.90	.25
☐ 151 Anthony Miller	.20	.09	.03
☐ 152 Dana Stubblefield	.30	.14	.04
☐ 153 Dean Wells	.10	.05	.01
☐ 154 Vincent Brisby	.30	.14	.04
☐ 155 Chris Chandler	.20	.09	.03
☐ 156 Clyde Simmons	.10	.05	.01
☐ 157 Rod Woodson	.30	.14	.04
☐ 158 Nate Lewis	.10	.05	.01
☐ 159 Martin Harrison	.10	.05	.01
☐ 160 Kelvin Martin	.10	.05	.01
☐ 161 Craig Erickson	.10	.05	.01
☐ 162 Johnny Mitchell	.10	.05	.01
☐ 163 Calvin Williams	.20	.09	.03
☐ 164 Deon Figures	.10	.05	.01
☐ 165 Tom Rathman	.10	.05	.01
☐ 166 Rick Hamilton	.10	.05	.01
☐ 167 John L. Williams	.10	.05	.01
☐ 168 Demetrius DuBose	.10	.05	.01
☐ 169 Michael Brooks	.10	.05	.01
☐ 170 Marion Butts	.10	.05	.01
☐ 171 Brent Jones	.20	.09	.03
☐ 172 Bobby Hebert	.10	.05	.01
☐ 173 Brad Edwards	.10	.05	.01
☐ 174 David Wyman	.10	.05	.01
☐ 175 Herman Moore	1.25	.55	.16
☐ 176 LeRoy Butler	.10	.05	.01
☐ 177 Reggie Langhorne	.10	.05	.01
☐ 178 Dave Krieg	.20	.09	.03
☐ 179 Patrick Bates	.10	.05	.01
☐ 180 Erik Kramer	.20	.09	.03
☐ 181 Troy Drayton	.10	.05	.01
☐ 182 Dave Meggett	.10	.05	.01
☐ 183 Eric Allen	.10	.05	.01
☐ 184 Mark Bavaro	.10	.05	.01
☐ 185 Leslie O'Neal	.10	.05	.01
☐ 186 Jerry Rice	2.50	1.10	.30
☐ 187 Desmond Howard	.20	.09	.03
☐ 188 Deion Sanders	2.00	.90	.25
☐ 189 Bill Maas	.10	.05	.01
☐ 190 Frank Wycheck	.10	.05	.01
☐ 191 Ernest Givins	.20	.09	.03
☐ 192 Terry McDaniel	.10	.05	.01
☐ 193 Bryan Cox	.10	.05	.01
☐ 194 Guy McIntyre	.10	.05	.01
☐ 195 Pierce Holt	.10	.05	.01
☐ 196 Fred Stokes	.10	.05	.01
☐ 197 Mike Pritchard	.10	.05	.01
☐ 198 Terry Obee	.10	.05	.01
☐ 199 Mark Collins	.10	.05	.01
☐ 200 Drew Bledsoe	2.50	1.10	.30
☐ 201 Barry Word	.10	.05	.01
☐ 202 Derrick Lassic	.10	.05	.01
☐ 203 Chris Spielman	.20	.09	.03
☐ 204 John Jurkovic	.20	.09	.03
☐ 205 Ken Norton Jr.	.20	.09	.03
☐ 206 Dale Carter	.10	.05	.01
☐ 207 Chris Doleman	.10	.05	.01
☐ 208 Keith Hamilton	.10	.05	.01
☐ 209 Andy Harmon	.10	.05	.01
☐ 210 John Friesz	.20	.09	.03
☐ 211 Steve Bono	.20	.09	.03
☐ 212 Mark Rypien	.10	.05	.01
☐ 213 Ricky Sanders	.10	.05	.01
☐ 214 Michael Haynes	.20	.09	.03
☐ 215 Todd McNair	.10	.05	.01
☐ 216 Leon Lett	.10	.05	.01
☐ 217 Scott Mitchell	.30	.14	.04
☐ 218 Mike Morris	.10	.05	.01
☐ 219 Darrin Smith	.10	.05	.01
☐ 220 Jim McMahon	.10	.05	.01
☐ 221 Garrison Hearst	1.00	.45	.12
☐ 222 Leroy Thompson	.10	.05	.01
☐ 223 Darren Carrington	.10	.05	.01
☐ 224 Pete Stoyanovich	.10	.05	.01
☐ 225 Chris Miller	.10	.05	.01
☐ 226 Bruce Smith SP	.20	.09	.03
☐ 227 Simon Fletcher SP	.10	.05	.01
☐ 228 Reggie White SP	.30	.14	.04
☐ 229 Neil Smith SP	.30	.14	.04
☐ 230 Chris Doleman SP	.10	.05	.01
☐ 231 Keith Hamilton SP	.10	.05	.01
☐ 232 Dana Stubblefield SP	.10	.05	.01
☐ 233 Erric Pegram GA	.10	.05	.01
☐ 234 Thurman Thomas GA	.30	.14	.04
☐ 235 Lewis Tillman GA	.10	.05	.01
☐ 236 Harold Green GA	.10	.05	.01
☐ 237 Eric Metcalf GA	.20	.09	.03
☐ 238 Emmitt Smith GA	5.00	2.20	.60
☐ 239 Glyn Milburn GA	.20	.09	.03
☐ 240 Barry Sanders GA	2.50	1.10	.30
☐ 241 Edgar Bennett GA	.20	.09	.03
☐ 242 Gary Brown GA	.10	.05	.01
☐ 243 Roosevelt Potts GA	.10	.05	.01
☐ 244 Marcus Allen GA	.30	.14	.04
☐ 245 Greg Robinson GA	.10	.05	.01
☐ 246 Jerome Bettis GA	1.25	.55	.16
☐ 247 Keith Byars GA	.10	.05	.01
☐ 248 Robert Smith GA	.20	.09	.03
☐ 249 Leonard Russell GA	.10	.05	.01
☐ 250 Derek Brown RB GA	.10	.05	.01
☐ 251 Rodney Hampton GA	.20	.09	.03
☐ 252 Johnny Johnson GA	.10	.05	.01
☐ 253 Vaughn Hebron GA	.10	.05	.01
☐ 254 Ronald Moore GA	.10	.05	.01
☐ 255 Barry Foster GA	.10	.05	.01
☐ 256 Natrone Means GA	1.00	.45	.12
☐ 257 Ricky Watters GA	.30	.14	.04
☐ 258 Chris Warren GA	.30	.14	.04
☐ 259 Vince Workman GA	.10	.05	.01
☐ 260 Reggie Brooks GA	.10	.05	.01
☐ 261 Carolina Panthers Logo	.30	.14	.04
☐ 262 Jacksonville Jaguars Logo	.10	.05	.01
☐ 263 Troy Aikman SB	1.25	.55	.16
☐ 264 Barry Sanders SB	1.25	.55	.16
☐ 265 Emmitt Smith SB	2.50	1.10	.30
☐ 266 Michael Irvin SB	.30	.14	.04
☐ 267 Jerry Rice SB	1.25	.55	.16
☐ 268 Shannon Sharpe SB	.20	.09	.03
☐ 269 Bob Kratch SB	.10	.05	.01
☐ 270 Howard Ballard SB	.10	.05	.01
☐ 271 Erik Williams SB	.10	.05	.01
☐ 272 Guy McIntyre SB	.10	.05	.01
☐ 273 Kelvin Williams SB	.20	.09	.03
☐ 274 Mel Gray SB	.10	.05	.01
☐ 275 Eddie Murray SB	.10	.05	.01
☐ 276 Mark Stepnoski SB	.10	.05	.01
☐ 277 Tommy Barnhardt SB	.10	.05	.01
☐ 278 Derrick Thomas SB	.20	.09	.03
☐ 279 Ken Norton Jr. SB	.20	.09	.03
☐ 280 Chris Spielman SB	.10	.05	.01
☐ 281 Deion Sanders SB	1.00	.45	.12
☐ 282 Mark Collins SB	.10	.05	.01
☐ 283 Bruce Smith SB	.20	.09	.03
☐ 284 Reggie White SB	.30	.14	.04
☐ 285 Sean Gilbert SB	.10	.05	.01
☐ 286 Cortez Kennedy SB	.20	.09	.03
☐ 287 Steve Atwater SB	.10	.05	.01
☐ 288 Tim McDonald SB	.10	.05	.01
☐ 289 Jerome Bettis SB	.60	.25	.07
☐ 290 Dana Stubblefield SB	.20	.09	.03
☐ 291 Bert Emanuel	1.50	.70	.19
☐ 292 Jeff Burris	.20	.09	.03
☐ 293 Bucky Brooks	.10	.05	.01
☐ 294 Dan Wilkinson	.20	.09	.03
☐ 295 Darnay Scott	2.50	1.10	.30
☐ 296 Derrick Alexander WR	.30	.14	.04
☐ 297 Antonio Langham	.20	.09	.03
☐ 298 Shante Carver	.10	.05	.01
☐ 299 Shelby Hill	.10	.05	.01
☐ 300 Larry Allen	.20	.09	.03
☐ 301 Johnnie Morton	.75	.35	.09
☐ 302 Van Malone	.10	.05	.01
☐ 303 Aaron Taylor	.10	.05	.01
☐ 304 Marshall Faulk	4.00	1.80	.50
☐ 305 Eric Mahlum	.10	.05	.01
☐ 306 Trev Alberts	.20	.09	.03
☐ 307 Greg Hill	1.00	.45	.12
☐ 308 Donnell Bennett	.10	.05	.01
☐ 309 Rob Fredrickson	.20	.09	.03
☐ 310 James Folston	.10	.05	.01
☐ 311 Isaac Bruce	4.00	1.80	.50
☐ 312 Tim Ruddy	.10	.05	.01
☐ 313 Aubrey Beavers	.10	.05	.01
☐ 314 David Palmer	.20	.09	.03
☐ 315 Dewayne Washington	.20	.09	.03
☐ 316 Willie McGinest	.30	.14	.04
☐ 317 Mario Bates	.75	.35	.09
☐ 318 Kevin Lee	.10	.05	.01
☐ 319 Jason Sehorn	.10	.05	.01
☐ 320 Thomas Randolph	.10	.05	.01
☐ 321 Ryan Yarborough	.10	.05	.01
☐ 322 Bernard Williams	.10	.05	.01
☐ 323 Chuck Levy	.10	.05	.01
☐ 324 Jamir Miller	.10	.05	.01
☐ 325 Charles Johnson	.75	.35	.09
☐ 326 Bryant Young	.75	.35	.09
☐ 327 William Floyd	1.50	.70	.19
☐ 328 Kevin Mitchell	.10	.05	.01
☐ 329 Sam Adams	.20	.09	.03
☐ 330 Kevin Mawae	.10	.05	.01
☐ 331 Errict Rhett	2.00	.90	.25
☐ 332 Trent Dilfer	1.25	.55	.16
☐ 333 Heath Shuler	1.50	.70	.19
☐ 334 Aaron Glenn	.20	.09	.03
☐ 335 Todd Steussie	.20	.09	.03
☐ 336 Toby Wright	.10	.05	.01
☐ NNO Gale Sayers Player's Club	8.00	3.60	1.00
☐ NNO Gale Sayers AUTO signed Player's Club	150.00	70.00	19.00

1994 Playoff Jerome Bettis

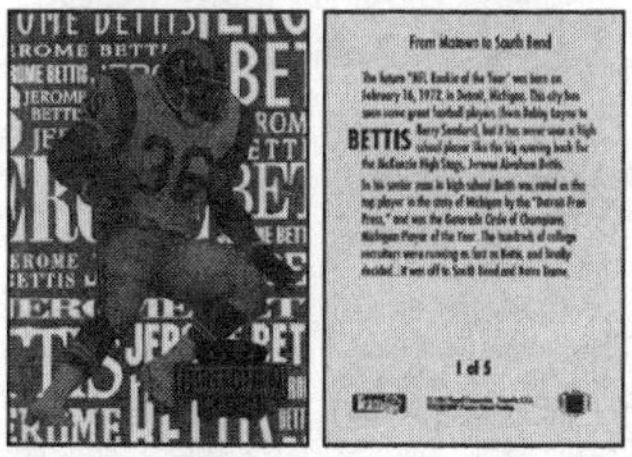

Randomly inserted in regular issue packs, this standard-size five-card set highlights Jerome Bettis. The cards were printed on thick card stock. On a silver foil background carrying his name in different white fonts, the fronts feature color action player photos with the "1994 Playoff Collection" logo in a lower corner. On a bright yellow background, the backs carry biographical information. The cards are numbered on the back with "x of 5".

	MINT	NRMT	EXC
COMPLETE SET (5)	60.00	27.00	7.50
COMMON BETTIS (1-5)	12.00	5.50	1.50
☐ 1 Jerome Bettis From Motown to South Bend	12.00	5.50	1.50
☐ 2 Jerome Bettis The Luck of the Irish	12.00	5.50	1.50
☐ 3 Jerome Bettis I Love LA	12.00	5.50	1.50
☐ 4 Jerome Bettis Welcome to the NFL	12.00	5.50	1.50
☐ 5 Jerome Bettis The Rookie of the Year	12.00	5.50	1.50

1994 Playoff Checklists

Randomly inserted in regular issue packs, these ten standard-size cards feature on their fronts borderless metallic color action shots with player information in a silver foil box at the bottom. The backs carry the set's checklists. The cards are numbered on the back as "X of 10".

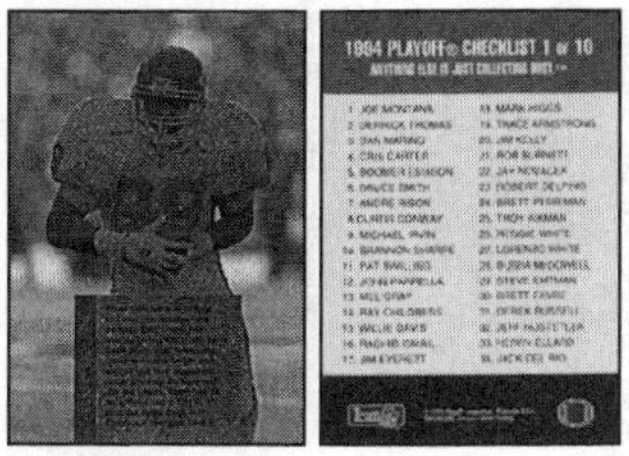

	MINT	NRMT	EXC
COMPLETE SET (10)	5.00	2.20	.60
COMMON CARD (1-10)	.50	.23	.06
☐ 1 Keith Cash	.50	.23	.06
☐ 2 Kerry Cash	.50	.23	.06
☐ 3 Qadry Ismail	.75	.35	.09
☐ 4 Rocket Ismail	.75	.35	.09
☐ 5 Bruce Matthews	.50	.23	.06
☐ 6 Clay Matthews	.50	.23	.06
☐ 7 Shannon Sharpe	.50	.23	.06
☐ 8 Sterling Sharpe	1.00	.45	.12
☐ 9 John Taylor	.50	.23	.06
☐ 10 Keith Taylor	.50	.23	.06

1994 Playoff Club

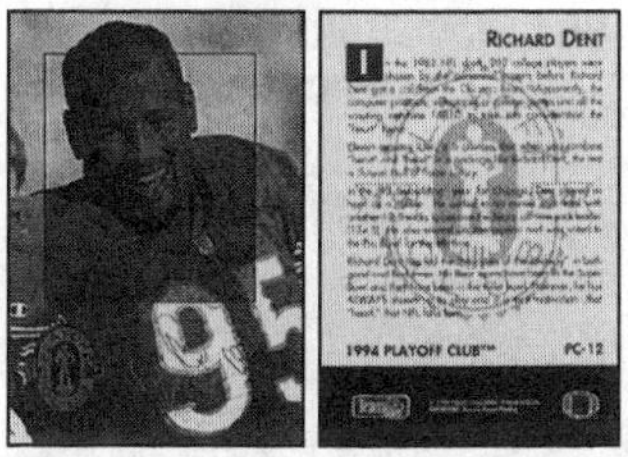

Randomly inserted in packs at a rate of one in 20, these six standard-size cards feature metallic color action shots. The words "Playoff Club" appear within an oval emblem in one corner, while the player's facsimile signature appears in the other corner. On a white background, the backs carry the player's name and career highlights. The cards are numbered on the back with a "PC" prefix.

	MINT	NRMT	EXC
COMPLETE SET (6)	25.00	11.00	3.10
COMMON CARD (PC8-PC13)	2.50	1.10	.30
☐ PC8 Jerry Rice	15.00	6.75	1.85
☐ PC9 Marcus Allen	4.00	1.80	.50
☐ PC10 Howie Long	2.50	1.10	.30
☐ PC11 Clay Matthews	2.50	1.10	.30
☐ PC12 Richard Dent	2.50	1.10	.30
☐ PC13 Morten Andersen	2.50	1.10	.30

1994 Playoff Headliners Redemption

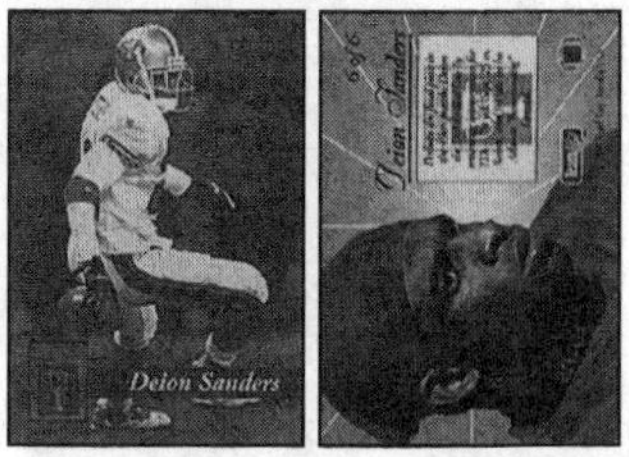

Issued one set per redemption card, this set consists of six standard-size cards of player that reached milestones in 1994. Full-bleed prism fronts have the Headliners logo and player name at the bottom. Horizontal backs have a close-up photo with a brief write-up on the milestone.

	MINT	NRMT	EXC
COMPLETE SET (6)	20.00	9.00	2.50
COMMON CARD (1-6)	2.00	.90	.25
☐ 1 Tim Brown	3.00	1.35	.35
☐ 2 Bernie Parmalee	2.00	.90	.25
☐ 3 Sterling Sharpe	3.00	1.35	.35
☐ 4 Natrone Means	4.00	1.80	.50
☐ 5 Alvin Harper	2.00	.90	.25
☐ 6 Deion Sanders	6.00	2.70	.75
☐ NNO Headliners Redemption	.50	.23	.06

1994 Playoff Jerry Rice

Randomly inserted in retail packs, this five-card standard-size set chronicles the career of the 49ers Jerry Rice. Card fronts feature an action photo superimposed over a silver background. The backs detail highlights of his career.

	MINT	NRMT	EXC
COMPLETE SET (5)	100.00	45.00	12.50
COMMON RICE (1-5)	20.00	9.00	2.50
☐ 1 Jerry Rice Born to Run	20.00	9.00	2.50
☐ 2 Jerry Rice All American	20.00	9.00	2.50

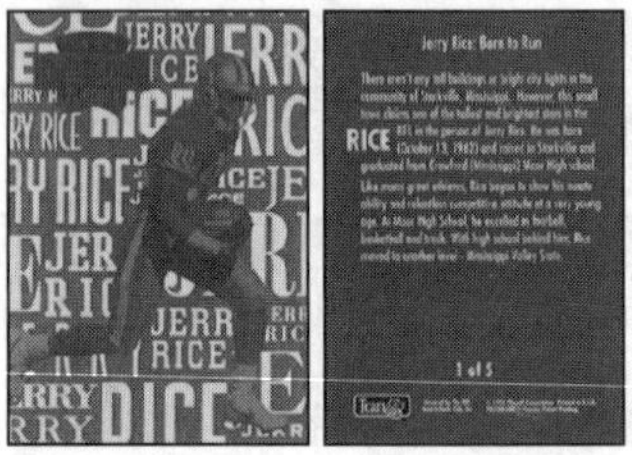

☐ 3 Jerry Rice The 49ers Start the Dynasty	20.00	9.00	2.50
☐ 4 Jerry Rice The Offensive Player of the Year (Again)	20.00	9.00	2.50
☐ 5 Jerry Rice Breaking Jim Brown's Record	20.00	9.00	2.50

1994 Playoff Rookie Roundup Redemption

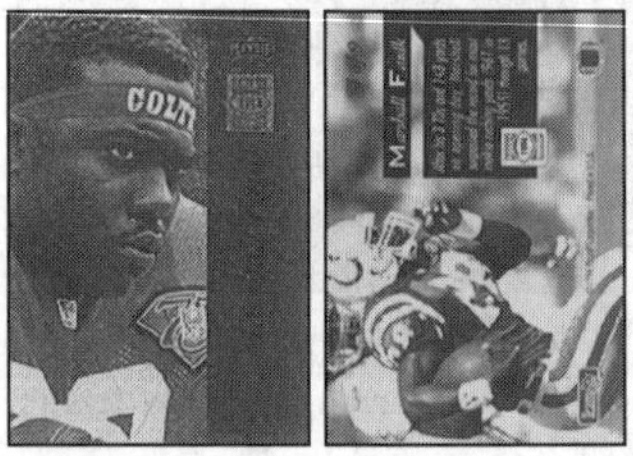

A special trade card randomly inserted in packs, could be redeemed through a mail-in offer by the collector for this nine-card, standard-size set. This set was redeemable until December 31, 1995. The fronts feature the player's photo with a solid left or right border that is consistent with team colors. The horizontal backs have a full-color player photo with his name and biographical information as an inset. Popular rookies in this set include Marshall Faulk, Errict Rhett and Heath Shuler.

	MINT	NRMT	EXC
COMPLETE SET (9)	40.00	18.00	5.00
COMMON CARD (1-9)	3.00	1.35	.35
☐ 1 Heath Shuler	4.00	1.80	.50
☐ 2 David Palmer	4.00	1.80	.50
☐ 3 Dan Wilkinson	3.00	1.35	.35
☐ 4 Marshall Faulk	10.00	4.50	1.25
☐ 5 Charlie Garner	3.00	1.35	.35
☐ 6 Errict Rhett	6.00	2.70	.75
☐ 7 Trent Dilfer	4.00	1.80	.50
☐ 8 Antonio Langham	3.00	1.35	.35
☐ 9 Gus Frerotte	6.00	2.70	.75
☐ NNO Redemption Card	.50	.23	.06

1994 Playoff Barry Sanders

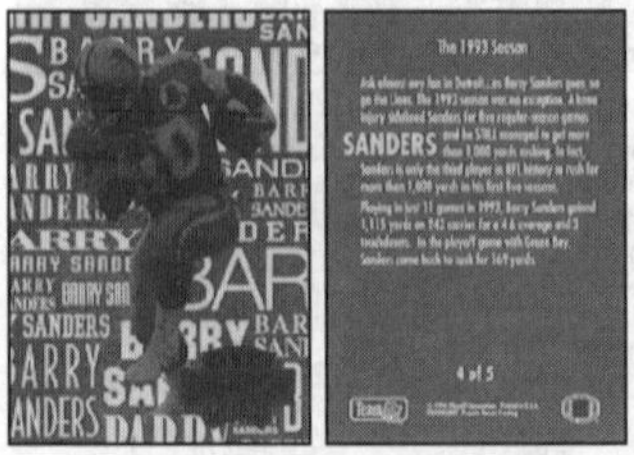

Randomly inserted in four star packs, this five-card standard-size set chronicles the career of Lions running back Barry Sanders. Card fronts have an action photo superimposed over a silver background The backs detail different parts of his career.

	MINT	NRMT	EXC
COMPLETE SET (5)	100.00	45.00	12.50
COMMON B.SANDERS (1-5)	20.00	9.00	2.50
☐ 1 Barry Sanders The Wichita Line-Mangler	20.00	9.00	2.50
☐ 2 Barry Sanders The Fastest Cowboy in Oklahoma	20.00	9.00	2.50
☐ 3 Barry Sanders Detroit Gets the Franchise	20.00	9.00	2.50
☐ 4 Barry Sanders The 1993 Season	20.00	9.00	2.50
☐ 5 Barry Sanders What a Career!	20.00	9.00	2.50

1994 Playoff Super Bowl Redemption

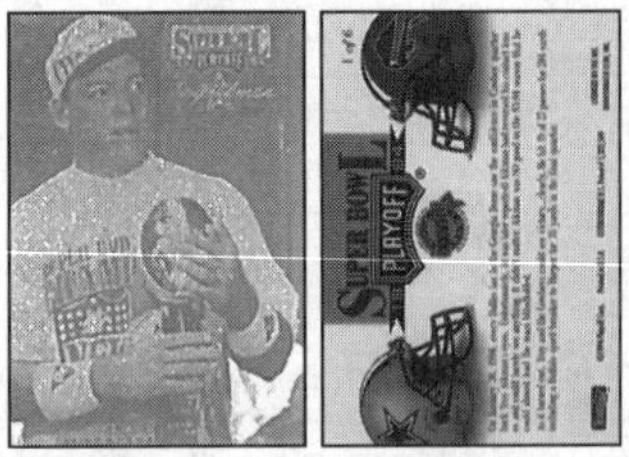

A special trade card randomly inserted in packs could be redeemed through a mail-in offer by the collector for a special six-card standard-size set. This set was redeemable until December 31, 1995. The Dallas Cowboys won Super Bowl XXVIII, therefore Cowboy players are featured in this set. The borderless fronts have metallic color player action photos while the backs describe personal highlights from the contest.

	MINT	NRMT	EXC
COMPLETE SET (6)	30.00	13.50	3.70
COMMON CARD (1-6)	2.00	.90	.25
☐ 1 Troy Aikman	12.00	5.50	1.50
☐ 2 Emmitt Smith	20.00	9.00	2.50
☐ 3 Leon Lett	2.00	.90	.25
☐ 4 Michael Irvin	3.00	1.35	.35
☐ 5 James Washington	2.00	.90	.25
☐ 6 Darrin Smith	2.00	.90	.25
☐ NNO Super Bowl Redemp.	.50	.23	.06

1994 Playoff Julie Bell Art Redemption

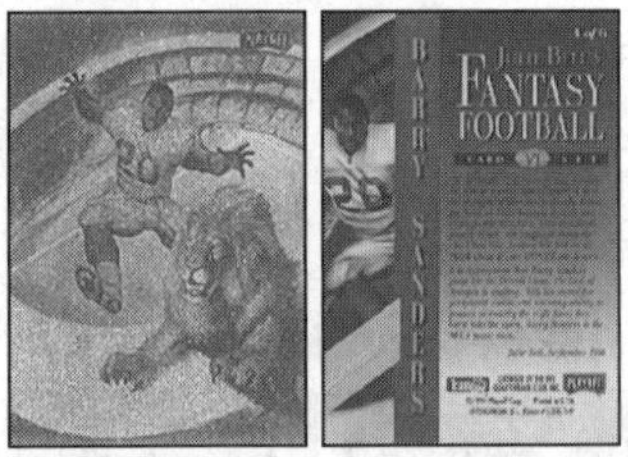

This six-card standard-size set was available through mail redemption. Full-bleed, metallic card fronts contain Julie Bell's artwork of top players. The backs contain a quote from Bell that ties in with the theme on front.

	MINT	NRMT	EXC
COMPLETE SET (6)	20.00	9.00	2.50
COMMON CARD (1-6)	2.00	.90	.25
☐ 1 Emmitt Smith	8.00	3.60	1.00
☐ 2 Marcus Allen	3.00	1.35	.35
☐ 3 Junior Seau	2.00	.90	.25
☐ 4 Barry Sanders	4.00	1.80	.50
☐ 5 Rick Mirer	2.00	.90	.25
☐ 6 Sterling Sharpe	2.00	.90	.25

1994 Playoff Super Bowl Promos

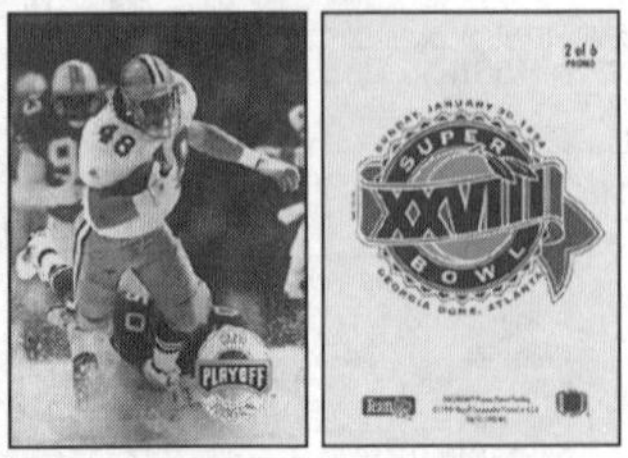

This six-card standard-size set was issued by Playoff to commemorate the 1994 Super Bowl. The fronts display borderless color action shots that have a metallic sheen. The player's name appears above and below the Playoff logo, both within a silver-colored oval in a lower corner. The white backs carry the 1994 Super Bowl logo in the center. The cards are numbered in the upper right corner with the word "Promo" printed below the number.

	MINT	NRMT	EXC
COMPLETE SET (6)	12.00	5.50	1.50
COMMON CARD (1-6)	1.25	.55	.16
☐ 1 Jerry Rice	5.00	2.20	.60
☐ 2 Daryl Johnston	1.25	.55	.16
☐ 3 Herschel Walker	1.25	.55	.16
☐ 4 Reggie White	2.00	.90	.25
☐ 5 Scott Mitchell	1.25	.55	.16
☐ 6 Thurman Thomas	2.00	.90	.25

1995 Playoff Absolute/Prime

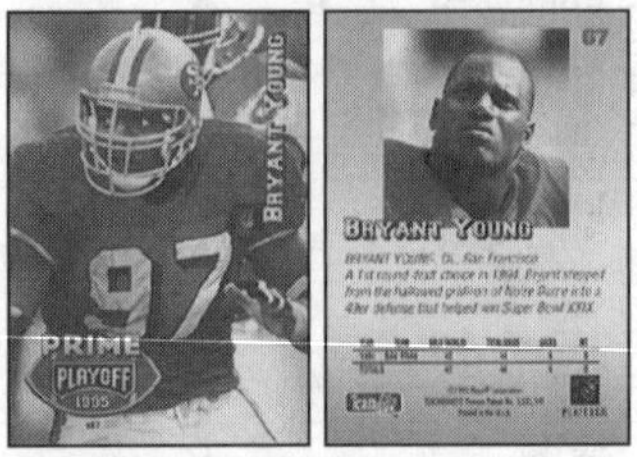

This 200-card standard-size set was released both through hobby and retail packaging. The hobby product was called Absolute while the retail product was titled Prime. The hobby boxes contained 24 packs per box with eight cards per pack. The fronts of the "Absolute" cards feature a player's photo against a solid silver background. The player's name is printed in yellow lettering across the bottom. The backs contain a player photo, some personal information as well as 1994 and career statistics. Cards 179-200 are dedicated to a draft pick subset. These "Absolute" draft pick cards are easy to differentiate from the regular cards as the words "Draft Picks" are emblazoned in large letters at the bottom of the card. In between the words "Draft Picks", the player is identified in white lettering against a black background. The "Prime" cards features full-bleed photos. The player is identified in the upper right corner and the words "Prime Playoff" are in the lower left corner. Against a yellowish background, the backs feature a player photo, some information as well as seasonal and career stats. Two special cards of both Tony Boselli and Kerry Collins were also inserted into both types of packs. Boselli cards were DP1G for the gold version and DP1S for the silver and Collins cards were DP2G for the gold and DP2S for the silver. Rookie Cards include Jeff Blake, Ki-Jana Carter, Kerry Collins, Joey Galloway, Napoleon Kaufman, Steve McNair, Rashaan Salaam, J.J. Stokes, Michael Westbrook and Tyrone Wheatley.

	MINT	NRMT	EXC
COMP.ABSOLUTE SET (200)	30.00	13.50	3.70
COMMON ABSOLUTE (1-200)	.20	.09	.03
COMPLETE PRIME SET (200)	15.00	6.75	1.85
*PRIME CARDS: .2X TO .5X ABSOLUTES			
☐ 1 John Elway	1.50	.70	.19
☐ 2 Reggie White	.40	.18	.05
☐ 3 Errict Rhett	.40	.18	.05
☐ 4 Deion Sanders	1.25	.55	.16
☐ 5 Rocket Ismail	.30	.14	.04
☐ 6 Jerome Bettis	.60	.25	.07
☐ 7 Randall Cunningham	.30	.14	.04
☐ 8 Mario Bates	.40	.18	.05
☐ 9 Dave Brown	.30	.14	.04
☐ 10 Stan Humphries	.30	.14	.04
☐ 11 Drew Bledsoe	2.00	.90	.25
☐ 12 Neil O'Donnell	.30	.14	.04
☐ 13 Dan Marino	4.00	1.80	.50
☐ 14 Larry Centers	.30	.14	.04
☐ 15 Craig Heyward	.30	.14	.04
☐ 16 Bruce Smith	.40	.18	.05
☐ 17 Erik Kramer	.20	.09	.03
☐ 18 Jeff Blake	2.00	.90	.25
☐ 19 Vinny Testaverde	.30	.14	.04
☐ 20 Barry Sanders	2.00	.90	.25
☐ 21 Boomer Esiason	.30	.14	.04
☐ 22 Emmitt Smith	4.00	1.80	.50
☐ 23 Warren Moon	.30	.14	.04
☐ 24 Junior Seau	.40	.18	.05
☐ 25 Heath Shuler	.40	.18	.05
☐ 26 Jackie Harris	.20	.09	.03
☐ 27 Terance Mathis	.30	.14	.04
☐ 28 Raymont Harris	.20	.09	.03
☐ 29 Jim Kelly	.40	.18	.05
☐ 30 Dan Wilkinson	.30	.14	.04
☐ 31 Herman Moore	1.00	.45	.12
☐ 32 Shannon Sharpe	.30	.14	.04
☐ 33 Antonio Langham	.20	.09	.03
☐ 34 Charles Haley	.30	.14	.04
☐ 35 Brett Favre	4.00	1.80	.50
☐ 36 Marshall Faulk	1.00	.45	.12
☐ 37 Neil Smith	.30	.14	.04
☐ 38 Harvey Williams	.20	.09	.03
☐ 39 Johnny Bailey	.20	.09	.03
☐ 40 O.J. McDuffie	.40	.18	.05
☐ 41 David Palmer	.30	.14	.04
☐ 42 Willie McGinest	.30	.14	.04
☐ 43 Quinn Early	.30	.14	.04
☐ 44 Johnny Johnson	.20	.09	.03
☐ 45 Derek Brown TE	.20	.09	.03
☐ 46 Charlie Garner	.30	.14	.04
☐ 47 Byron Bam Morris	.30	.14	.04
☐ 48 Natrone Means	.40	.18	.05
☐ 49 Ken Norton Jr.	.30	.14	.04
☐ 50 Troy Aikman	2.00	.90	.25
☐ 51 Reggie Brooks	.30	.14	.04
☐ 52 Trent Dilfer	.40	.18	.05
☐ 53 Cortez Kennedy	.30	.14	.04
☐ 54 Chuck Levy	.20	.09	.03
☐ 55 Jeff George	.30	.14	.04
☐ 56 Steve Young	1.50	.70	.19
☐ 57 Lewis Tillman	.20	.09	.03
☐ 58 Carl Pickens	.40	.18	.05
☐ 59 Brett Perriman	.30	.14	.04
☐ 60 Jay Novacek	.30	.14	.04
☐ 61 Greg Hill	.30	.14	.04
☐ 62 James Jett	.30	.14	.04
☐ 63 Terry Kirby	.30	.14	.04
☐ 64 Qadry Ismail	.30	.14	.04
☐ 65 Ben Coates	.30	.14	.04
☐ 66 Kevin Greene	.30	.14	.04
☐ 67 Bryant Young	.30	.14	.04
☐ 68 Brian Mitchell	.20	.09	.03
☐ 69 Steve Walsh	.20	.09	.03
☐ 70 Darnay Scott	.40	.18	.05
☐ 71 Daryl Johnston	.30	.14	.04
☐ 72 Glyn Milburn	.20	.09	.03
☐ 73 Tim Brown	.40	.18	.05
☐ 74 Isaac Bruce	1.00	.45	.12
☐ 75 Bernie Parmalee	.30	.14	.04
☐ 76 Terry Allen	.30	.14	.04
☐ 77 Jim Everett	.20	.09	.03
☐ 78 Thomas Lewis	.30	.14	.04
☐ 79 Vaughn Hebron	.20	.09	.03
☐ 80 Rod Woodson	.30	.14	.04
☐ 81 Rick Mirer	.40	.18	.05
☐ 82 Dana Stubblefield	.40	.18	.05
☐ 83 Bert Emanuel	.40	.18	.05
☐ 84 Andre Reed	.30	.14	.04
☐ 85 Jeff Graham	.20	.09	.03
☐ 86 Johnnie Morton	.30	.14	.04
☐ 87 LeShon Johnson	.30	.14	.04
☐ 88 Michael Irvin	.40	.18	.05
☐ 89 Derrick Alexander WR	.40	.18	.05
☐ 90 Lake Dawson	.30	.14	.04
☐ 91 Cody Carlson	.20	.09	.03
☐ 92 Chris Warren	.30	.14	.04
☐ 93 William Floyd	.40	.18	.05
☐ 94 Charles Johnson	.30	.14	.04
☐ 95 Roosevelt Potts	.20	.09	.03
☐ 96 Cris Carter	.40	.18	.05
☐ 97 Aaron Glenn	.20	.09	.03
☐ 98 Curtis Conway	.40	.18	.05
☐ 99 Kevin Williams WR	.30	.14	.04
☐ 100 Jerry Rice	2.00	.90	.25
☐ 101 Frank Reich	.20	.09	.03
☐ 102 Harold Green	.20	.09	.03
☐ 103 Russell Copeland	.20	.09	.03
☐ 104 Rob Moore	.20	.09	.03
☐ 105 Edgar Bennett	.30	.14	.04
☐ 106 Darren Carrington	.20	.09	.03
☐ 107 Tommy Maddox	.20	.09	.03
☐ 108 Dave Meggett	.20	.09	.03
☐ 109 Fred Barnett	.30	.14	.04
☐ 110 Mark Seay	.30	.14	.04
☐ 111 Gus Frerotte	1.00	.45	.12
☐ 112 Brent Jones	.20	.09	.03
☐ 113 Chris Miller	.20	.09	.03
☐ 114 Cedric Tillman	.20	.09	.03
☐ 115 Mark Ingram	.20	.09	.03
☐ 116 Eric Turner	.20	.09	.03
☐ 117 Mark Carrier WR	.30	.14	.04
☐ 118 Garrison Hearst	.40	.18	.05
☐ 119 Craig Erickson	.20	.09	.03
☐ 120 Derek Russell	.20	.09	.03
☐ 121 Mike Sherrard	.20	.09	.03
☐ 122 Horace Copeland	.20	.09	.03
☐ 123 Jack Trudeau	.20	.09	.03
☐ 124 Leroy Hoard	.20	.09	.03
☐ 125 Gary Brown	.20	.09	.03
☐ 126 Mel Gray	.20	.09	.03
☐ 127 Steve Beuerlein	.20	.09	.03
☐ 128 Marcus Allen	.40	.18	.05
☐ 129 Irving Fryar	.30	.14	.04
☐ 130 Marion Butts	.20	.09	.03
☐ 131 Ricky Watters	.40	.18	.05
☐ 132 Tony Martin	.30	.14	.04
☐ 133 Lawrence Dawsey	.20	.09	.03
☐ 134 Ronnie Harmon	.20	.09	.03
☐ 135 Herschel Walker	.30	.14	.04
☐ 136 Michael Haynes	.30	.14	.04
☐ 137 Eric Green	.20	.09	.03
☐ 138 Steve Bono	.30	.14	.04
☐ 139 Jamir Miller	.20	.09	.03
☐ 140 Rod Smith DB	.30	.14	.04
☐ 141 Andre Rison	.30	.14	.04
☐ 142 Eric Metcalf	.30	.14	.04
☐ 143 Michael Timpson	.20	.09	.03
☐ 144 Cornelius Bennett	.30	.14	.04
☐ 145 Sean Dawkins	.30	.14	.04
☐ 146 Scott Mitchell	.30	.14	.04
☐ 147 Ray Childress	.20	.09	.03
☐ 148 Jim Harbaugh	.30	.14	.04
☐ 149 Reggie Cobb	.20	.09	.03
☐ 150 Willie Roaf	.20	.09	.03
☐ 151 Stevie Anderson	.20	.09	.03
☐ 152 Barry Foster	.30	.14	.04
☐ 153 Joe Montana	2.00	.90	.25
☐ 154 David Klingler	.30	.14	.04
☐ 155 Chris Chandler	.30	.14	.04
☐ 156 Carnell Lake	.20	.09	.03
☐ 157 Calvin Williams	.30	.14	.04
☐ 158 Kenneth Davis	.20	.09	.03
☐ 159 Tydus Winans	.20	.09	.03
☐ 160 Sam Adams	.20	.09	.03
☐ 161 Ronald Moore	.20	.09	.03
☐ 162 Vincent Brisby	.20	.09	.03
☐ 163 Alvin Harper	.20	.09	.03
☐ 164 Jake Reed	.30	.14	.04
☐ 165 Jeff Hostetler	.30	.14	.04

☐ 166 Mark Brunell	2.00	.90	.25
☐ 167 Leonard Russell	.20	.09	.03
☐ 168 Greg Truitt	.20	.09	.03
☐ 169 Pete Metzelaars	.20	.09	.03
☐ 170 Dave Krieg	.20	.09	.03
☐ 171 Lorenzo White	.20	.09	.03
☐ 172 Robert Brooks	.40	.18	.05
☐ 173 Willie Davis	.30	.14	.04
☐ 174 Irving Spikes	.30	.14	.04
☐ 175 Rodney Hampton	.30	.14	.04
☐ 176 Erric Pegram	.30	.14	.04
☐ 177 Brian Blades	.30	.14	.04
☐ 178 Shawn Jefferson	.20	.09	.03
☐ 179 Tyrone Poole	.30	.14	.04
☐ 180 Rob Johnson	.20	.09	.03
☐ 181 Ki-Jana Carter	1.50	.70	.19
☐ 182 Steve McNair	5.00	2.20	.60
☐ 183 Michael Westbrook	2.00	.90	.25
☐ 184 Kerry Collins	6.00	2.70	.75
☐ 185 Kevin Carter	.40	.18	.05
☐ 186 Tony Boselli	.30	.14	.04
☐ 187 Joey Galloway	3.00	1.35	.35
☐ 188 Kyle Brady	.40	.18	.05
☐ 189 J.J. Stokes	1.50	.70	.19
☐ 190 Warren Sapp	.30	.14	.04
☐ 191 Tyrone Wheatley	.75	.35	.09
☐ 192 Napolean Kaufman	1.50	.70	.19
☐ 193 James O.Stewart	.40	.18	.05
☐ 194 Rashaan Salaam	2.00	.90	.25
☐ 195 Ray Zellars	.30	.14	.04
☐ 196 Todd Collins	.40	.18	.05
☐ 197 Sherman Williams	.20	.09	.03
☐ 198 Frank Sanders	1.50	.70	.19
☐ 199 Terrell Fletcher	.20	.09	.03
☐ 200 Chad May	.20	.09	.03
☐ DP1G Tony Boselli Draft Gold	3.00	1.35	.35
☐ DP1S Tony Boselli Draft Silver	2.00	.90	.25
☐ DP2G Kerry Collins Draft Gold	20.00	9.00	2.50
☐ DP2S Kerry Collins Draft Silver	15.00	6.75	1.85

1995 Playoff Absolute/Prime Die Cut Helmets

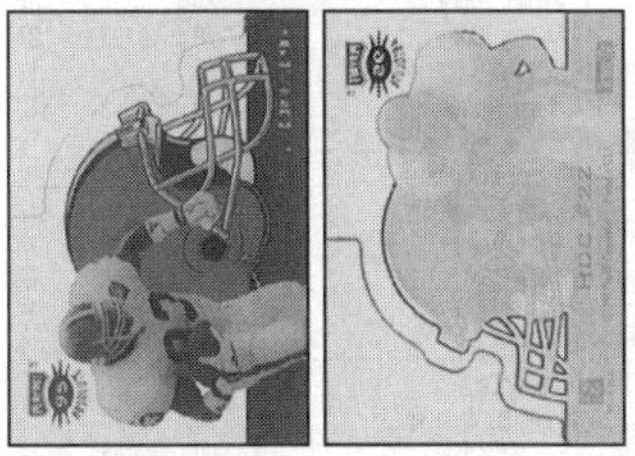

This 30 card set was inserted only in "Absolute" packs at a rate of one in 25. Leading NFL players are featured in this set. These are acetate cards with a die-cut outline of a NFL helmet. The player is featured on the left of the card. The "Playoff Absolute" logo is imprinted in gold in the upper left corner. The cards are numbered on the back with a "HDC" prefix.

	MINT	NRMT	EXC
COMPLETE SET (30)	450.00	200.00	55.00
COMMON CARD (1-30)	6.00	2.70	.75
☐ 1 Garrison Hearst	12.00	5.50	1.50
☐ 2 Jim Kelly	12.00	5.50	1.50
☐ 3 Jeff Blake	12.00	5.50	1.50
☐ 4 Emmitt Smith	60.00	27.00	7.50
☐ 5 John Elway	30.00	13.50	3.70
☐ 6 Brett Favre	60.00	27.00	7.50
☐ 7 Marshall Faulk	20.00	9.00	2.50
☐ 8 Marcus Allen	12.00	5.50	1.50
☐ 9 Jerome Bettis	12.00	5.50	1.50
☐ 10 Dan Marino	60.00	27.00	7.50
☐ 11 Cris Carter	8.00	3.60	1.00
☐ 12 Drew Bledsoe	40.00	18.00	5.00
☐ 13 Jim Everett	6.00	2.70	.75
☐ 14 Rodney Hampton	8.00	3.60	1.00
☐ 15 Natrone Means	12.00	5.50	1.50
☐ 16 Steve Young	25.00	11.00	3.10
☐ 17 Rick Mirer	12.00	5.50	1.50
☐ 18 Errict Rhett	12.00	5.50	1.50
☐ 19 Heath Shuler	12.00	5.50	1.50
☐ 20 Lewis Tillman	6.00	2.70	.75
☐ 21 Barry Sanders	35.00	16.00	4.40
☐ 22 Leroy Hoard	6.00	2.70	.75
☐ 23 Rod Woodson	8.00	3.60	1.00
☐ 24 Gary Brown	6.00	2.70	.75
☐ 25 Terance Mathis	6.00	2.70	.75
☐ 26 Frank Reich	6.00	2.70	.75
☐ 27 Steve Beuerlein	6.00	2.70	.75
☐ 28 Rocket Ismail	6.00	2.70	.75
☐ 29 Johnny Johnson	6.00	2.70	.75
☐ 30 Charlie Garner	6.00	2.70	.75

1995 Playoff Absolute/Prime Fantasy Team

This 20-card standard-size set was randomly inserted into "Prime" packs. The players featured are often taken early in "rotisserie" drafts and were printed on clear plastic with the letters from the set name

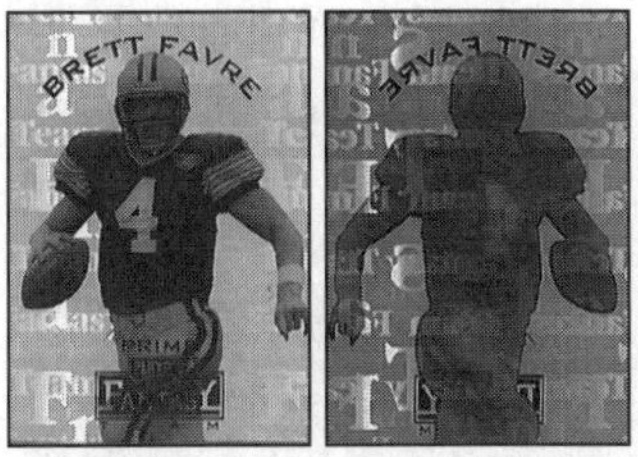

"Fantasy Team" in foil jumbled in the background. The player's name is in gold foil above the shot of the player. Card backs are numbered with an "FT" prefix.

	MINT	NRMT	EXC
COMPLETE SET (20)	200.00	90.00	25.00
COMMON CARD (FT1-FT20)	2.50	1.10	.30
☐ FT1 Jerome Bettis	6.00	2.70	.75
☐ FT2 Shannon Sharpe	2.50	1.10	.30
☐ FT3 Fuad Reveiz	2.50	1.10	.30
☐ FT4 John Carney	2.50	1.10	.30
☐ FT5 Steve Young	15.00	6.75	1.85
☐ FT6 Brett Favre	35.00	16.00	4.40
☐ FT7 Tim Brown	4.00	1.80	.50
☐ FT8 Ben Coates	4.00	1.80	.50
☐ FT9 Marshall Faulk	10.00	4.50	1.25
☐ FT10 Stan Humphries	4.00	1.80	.50
☐ FT11 Dan Marino	35.00	16.00	4.40
☐ FT12 Jerry Rice	20.00	9.00	2.50
☐ FT13 Errict Rhett	6.00	2.70	.75
☐ FT14 Chris Warren	4.00	1.80	.50
☐ FT15 Barry Sanders	20.00	9.00	2.50
☐ FT16 Cris Carter	4.00	1.80	.50
☐ FT17 Michael Irvin	6.00	2.70	.75
☐ FT18 Emmitt Smith	35.00	16.00	4.40
☐ FT19 Terance Mathis	2.50	1.10	.30
☐ FT20 Herman Moore	6.00	2.70	.75

1995 Playoff Absolute/Prime Minis

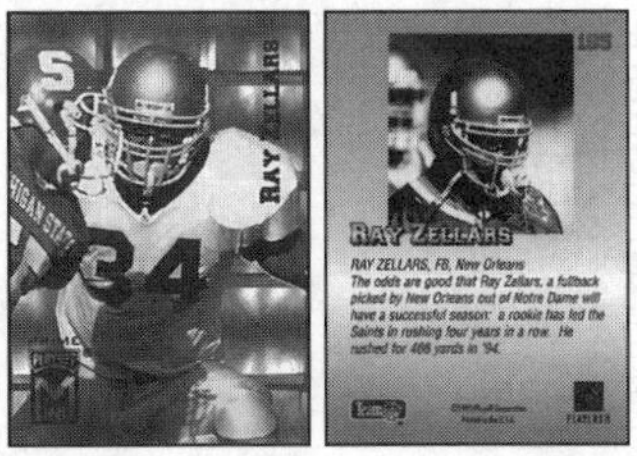

This 200 card set is a parallel of the basic "Prime" set and is smaller than a standard-sized card. Card fronts feature a silver holographic foil square background with the player's name running vertically along the top right and the "Mini" logo on the lower left. Card backs are identical to the basic "Prime" card.

	MINT	NRMT	EXC
COMPLETE SET (200)	700.00	325.00	90.00
COMMON CARD (1-200)	1.50	.70	.19
SEMISTARS	3.00	1.35	.35
UNLISTED STARS	6.00	2.70	.75
☐ 1 John Elway	20.00	9.00	2.50
☐ 4 Deion Sanders	15.00	6.75	1.85
☐ 6 Jerome Bettis	8.00	3.60	1.00
☐ 11 Drew Bledsoe	30.00	13.50	3.70
☐ 13 Dan Marino	50.00	22.00	6.25
☐ 18 Jeff Blake	10.00	4.50	1.25
☐ 20 Barry Sanders	30.00	13.50	3.70
☐ 22 Emmitt Smith	50.00	22.00	6.25
☐ 31 Herman Moore	12.00	5.50	1.50
☐ 35 Brett Favre	50.00	22.00	6.25
☐ 36 Marshall Faulk	12.00	5.50	1.50
☐ 50 Troy Aikman	30.00	13.50	3.70
☐ 56 Steve Young	20.00	9.00	2.50
☐ 70 Darnay Scott	8.00	3.60	1.00
☐ 74 Isaac Bruce	12.00	5.50	1.50
☐ 100 Jerry Rice	30.00	13.50	3.70
☐ 111 Gus Frerotte	12.00	5.50	1.50
☐ 153 Joe Montana	30.00	13.50	3.70
☐ 166 Mark Brunell	30.00	13.50	3.70
☐ 181 Ki-Jana Carter	8.00	3.60	1.00
☐ 182 Steve McNair	20.00	9.00	2.50
☐ 183 Michael Westbrook	10.00	4.50	1.25
☐ 184 Kerry Collins	25.00	11.00	3.10
☐ 187 Joey Galloway	15.00	6.75	1.85
☐ 189 J.J. Stokes	8.00	3.60	1.00
☐ 192 Napolean Kaufman	8.00	3.60	1.00
☐ 194 Rashaan Salaam	10.00	4.50	1.25
☐ 198 Frank Sanders	8.00	3.60	1.00

1995 Playoff Absolute/Prime Pigskin Previews

This 12-card standard-size set includes a section made with real leather. This set was issued in both 'Absolute' packs (cards 1-6) and

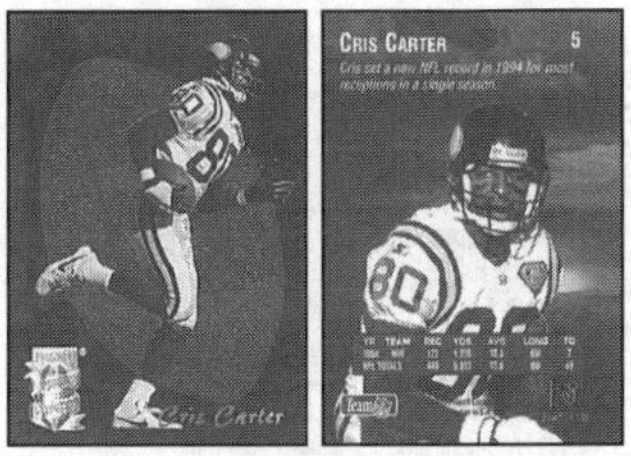

"Prime" packs (cards 7-12). Card fronts have a green and black background with the player shot over the leather portion. The "Pigskin Preview" logo is at the bottom left and the player's name is written on the lower right. Both have holographic foil. Card backs include a commentary and statistical information.

	MINT	NRMT	EXC
COMPLETE SET (12)	500.00	220.00	60.00
COMPLETE SERIES 1 (6)	300.00	135.00	38.00
COMPLETE SERIES 2 (6)	200.00	90.00	25.00
COMMON CARD (1-6)	20.00	9.00	2.50
COMMON CARD (7-12)	16.00	7.25	2.00
☐ 1 Emmitt Smith	120.00	55.00	15.00
☐ 2 Steve Young	50.00	22.00	6.25
☐ 3 Barry Sanders	80.00	36.00	10.00
☐ 4 Deion Sanders	30.00	13.50	3.70
☐ 5 Cris Carter	20.00	9.00	2.50
☐ 6 Errict Rhett	20.00	9.00	2.50
☐ 7 Dan Marino	90.00	40.00	11.00
☐ 8 Marshall Faulk	25.00	11.00	3.10
☐ 9 Natrone Means	16.00	7.25	2.00
☐ 10 Tim Brown	16.00	7.25	2.00
☐ 11 Drew Bledsoe	60.00	27.00	7.50
☐ 12 Marcus Allen	20.00	9.00	2.50

1995 Playoff Absolute/Prime Quad Series

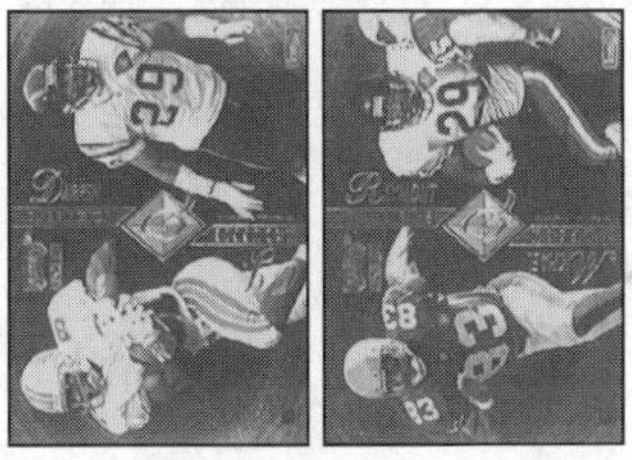

This 50-card standard-size set features only players in the base Playoff "Absolute" set. All cards have 4 players pictured on them. Most cards have a common theme. The theme is they play the same position or play for the same team. This set was randomly inserted into hobby packs. Each card has two photos on each side. The cards are numbered with a "Q" prefix.

	MINT	NRMT	EXC
COMPLETE SET (50)	1400.00	650.00	180.00
COMMON QUAD (Q1-Q50)	8.00	3.60	1.00
☐ Q1 Joe Montana	200.00	90.00	25.00
Dan Marino			
Steve Young			
John Elway			
☐ Q2 Troy Aikman	200.00	90.00	25.00
Brett Favre			
Drew Bledsoe			
Rick Mirer			
☐ Q3 Trent Dilfer	60.00	27.00	7.50
Heath Shuler			
Mark Brunell			
Jeff Blake			
☐ Q4 Randall Cunningham	8.00	3.60	1.00
Warren Moon			
Jim Kelly			
Boomer Esiason			
☐ Q5 Jeff George	12.00	5.50	1.50
Dave Brown			
Stan Humphries			
Jim Everett			
☐ Q6 Barry Sanders	175.00	80.00	22.00
Emmitt Smith			
Marshall Faulk			
Errict Rhett			
☐ Q7 Marcus Allen	20.00	9.00	2.50
Ricky Watters			
William Floyd			
Natrone Means			
☐ Q8 Garrison Hearst	12.00	5.50	1.50
Jerome Bettis			
Lewis Tillman			
Gary Brown			
☐ Q9 Michael Irvin	80.00	36.00	10.00
Jerry Rice			
Tim Brown			
Cris Carter			
☐ Q10 Pete Metzelaars	12.00	5.50	1.50
Byron Bam Morris			
Ben Coates			
Andre Rison			
☐ Q11 Reggie White	40.00	18.00	5.00
Bruce Smith			
Deion Sanders			
Junior Seau			
☐ Q12 Rob Moore	12.00	5.50	1.50
Larry Centers			
Jamir Miller			
Chuck Levy			
☐ Q13 Craig Heyward UER	12.00	5.50	1.50
Terance Mathis			
Bert Emanuel			
Eric Metcalf			
☐ Q14 Kenneth Davis	12.00	5.50	1.50
Andre Reed			
Russell Copeland			
Cornelius Bennett			
☐ Q15 Frank Reich	12.00	5.50	1.50
Jack Trudeau			
Mark Carrier WR			
Tyrone Poole			
☐ Q16 Jeff Graham	12.00	5.50	1.50
Curtis Conway			
Erik Kramer			
Steve Walsh			
☐ Q17 Carl Pickens	12.00	5.50	1.50
Darnay Scott			
Harold Green			
David Klingler			
☐ Q18 Vinny Testaverde	8.00	3.60	1.00
Derrick Alexander WR			
Leroy Hoard			
Lorenzo White			
☐ Q19 Charles Haley	12.00	5.50	1.50
Kevin Williams WR			
Daryl Johnston			
Jay Novacek			
☐ Q20 Glyn Milburn	8.00	3.60	1.00
Leonard Russell			
Derek Russell			
Shannon Sharpe			
☐ Q21 Scott Mitchell	20.00	9.00	2.50
Brett Perriman			
Herman Moore			
Johnnie Morton			
☐ Q22 Edgar Bennett	12.00	5.50	1.50
LeShon Johnson			
Robert Brooks			
Mark Ingram			
☐ Q23 Cody Carlson	8.00	3.60	1.00
Mel Gray			
Chris Chandler			
Ray Childress			
☐ Q24 Craig Erickson	12.00	5.50	1.50
Jim Harbaugh			
Roosevelt Potts			
Sean Dawkins			
☐ Q25 Steve Beuerlein	12.00	5.50	1.50
Rob Johnson			
Cedric Tillman			
Reggie Cobb			
☐ Q26 Greg Hill	12.00	5.50	1.50
Willie Davis			
Lake Dawson			
Steve Bono			
☐ Q27 Harvey Williams	8.00	3.60	1.00
Jeff Hostetler			
James Jett			
Rocket Ismail			
☐ Q28 Bernie Parmalee	8.00	3.60	1.00
Irving Spikes			
Terry Kirby			
Irving Fryar			
☐ Q29 Terry Allen	8.00	3.60	1.00
David Palmer			
Qadry Ismail			
Jake Reed			
☐ Q30 Marion Butts	8.00	3.60	1.00
Vincent Brisby			
Dave Meggett			
Willie McGinest			
☐ Q31 Willie Roaf	8.00	3.60	1.00
Mario Bates			
Quinn Early			
Michael Haynes			
☐ Q32 Herschel Walker	8.00	3.60	1.00
Mike Sherrard			
Derek Brown TE			
Thomas Lewis			
☐ Q33 Stevie Anderson	8.00	3.60	1.00
Aaron Glenn			
Johnny Johnson			
Ron Moore			
☐ Q34 Calvin Williams	12.00	5.50	1.50
Fred Barnett			
Vaughn Hebron			
Charlie Garner			
☐ Q35 Charles Johnson	12.00	5.50	1.50
Neil O'Donnell			
Rod Woodson			
Erric Pegram			
☐ Q36 Ronnie Harmon	8.00	3.60	1.00
Shawn Jefferson			
Tony Martin			
Mark Seay			

		MINT	NRMT	EXC
Q37	Brent Jones	12.00	5.50	1.50
	Dana Stubblefield			
	Bryant Young			
	Ken Norton			
Q38	Chris Warren	12.00	5.50	1.50
	Cortez Kennedy			
	Sam Adams			
	Brian Blades			
Q39	Tommy Maddox	35.00	16.00	4.40
	Chris Miller			
	Johnny Bailey			
	Isaac Bruce			
Q40	Lawrence Dawsey	8.00	3.60	1.00
	Alvin Harper			
	Jackie Harris			
	Horace Copeland			
Q41	Gus Frerotte	25.00	11.00	3.10
	Brian Mitchell			
	Reggie Brooks			
	Tydus Winans			
Q42	Steve McNair	100.00	45.00	12.50
	Kerry Collins			
	Todd Collins			
	Chad May			
Q43	Ki-Jana Carter	30.00	13.50	3.70
	Tyrone Wheatley			
	Napoleon Kaufman			
	Rashaan Salaam			
Q44	Terrell Fletcher	20.00	9.00	2.50
	Sherman Williams			
	Ray Zellars			
	James O.Stewart			
Q45	Michael Westbrook	50.00	22.00	6.25
	Joey Galloway			
	J.J. Stokes			
	Frank Sanders			
Q46	Kevin Carter	12.00	5.50	1.50
	Tony Boselli			
	Warren Sapp			
	Kyle Brady			
Q47	Greg Truitt	8.00	3.60	1.00
	Dan Wilkinson			
	Eric Turner			
	Antonio Langham			
Q48	Carnell Lake	12.00	5.50	1.50
	Neil Smith			
	Rod Smith DB			
	Kevin Greene			
Q49	O.J. McDuffie	12.00	5.50	1.50
	Darren Carrington			
	Michael Timpson			
	Raymont Harris			
Q50	Rodney Hampton	8.00	3.60	1.00
	Dave Krieg			
	Barry Foster			
	Eric Green			

1995 Playoff Absolute/Prime Unsung Heroes

 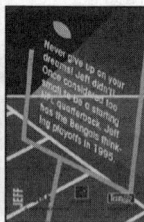

This 28-card standard-size set was randomly inserted in both "Absolute" and "Prime" packs. This set features players who do not garner heavy publicity. The set is checklisted in alphabetical order by team. Card fronts feature a colorful green background with the player's name in the lower left corner. Card backs feature a brief commentary on the player in between a yellow goal post. Cards were available in both gold and silver foils, with gold inserted into "Absolute" packs and silver inserted into "Prime" packs.

		MINT	NRMT	EXC
	COMPLETE SET (28)	25.00	11.00	3.10
	COMMON CARD (1-28)	.50	.23	.06
	*GOLD/SILVER: SAME VALUE			
1	Garth Jax	.50	.23	.06
2	Craig Heyward	.75	.35	.09
3	Steve Tasker	.75	.35	.09
4	Raymont Harris	.50	.23	.06
5	Jeff Blake	5.00	2.20	.60
6	Bob Dahl	.50	.23	.06
7	Jason Garrett	.50	.23	.06
8	Gary Zimmerman	.50	.23	.06
9	Tom Beer	.50	.23	.06
10	John Jurkovic	.50	.23	.06
11	Spencer Tillman	.50	.23	.06
12	Devon McDonald	.50	.23	.06
13	John Alt	.50	.23	.06
14	Steve Wisniewski	.50	.23	.06
15	Tim Bowens	.50	.23	.06

		MINT	NRMT	EXC
16	Amp Lee	.50	.23	.06
17	Todd Rucci	.50	.23	.06
18	Tyrone Hughes	.75	.35	.09
19	Michael Strahan	.50	.23	.06
20	Brad Baxter	.50	.23	.06
21	Mark Bavaro	.50	.23	.06
22	Yancey Thigpen	4.00	1.80	.50
23	Courtney Hall	.50	.23	.06
24	Eric Davis	.50	.23	.06
25	Rufus Porter	.50	.23	.06
26	Jackie Slater	.75	.35	.09
27	Courtney Hawkins	.75	.35	.09
28	Gus Frerotte	3.00	1.35	.35

1995 Playoff Night of the Stars

This 6-card standard-size was given away during the Tuesday night Trade Show preceding the National Sports Collectors Convention in St. Louis. Collectors could also obtain the set by exchanging ten wrappers for one of the six cards at the Playoff Booth. The fronts feature full-bleed color action player photos, with the set title, player's name, manufacturer's name, and football icon gold foil stamped across the bottom. The pro players are pictured in their pro uniforms, and the rookies in their collegiate uniforms. Though each back sports the same geometric design in a different color, all display on a black panel an advertisement for the National Sports Collectors Convention.

		MINT	NRMT	EXC
	COMPLETE SET (6)	20.00	9.00	2.50
	COMMON CARD (1-6)	2.00	.90	.25
1	Jerome Bettis	4.00	1.80	.50
2	Ben Coates	2.00	.90	.25
3	Deion Sanders	4.00	1.80	.50
4	Ki-Jana Carter	3.00	1.35	.35
5	Steve McNair	6.00	2.70	.75
6	Errict Rhett	2.50	1.10	.30

1995 Playoff Super Bowl Card Show

 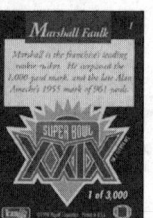

This eight-card standard-size set were given away during the Super Bowl XXIX Card Show. The fronts feature borderless metallic color action player cutouts superposed over a metallic red, silver and gold background. The player's name in silver-foil letters appears in the top left corner. On a black background, the backs carry the player's name, season highlights and the Super Bowl XXIX logo. Only 3,000 of each card was produced.

		MINT	NRMT	EXC
	COMPLETE SET (8)	20.00	9.00	2.50
	COMMON CARD (1-8)	2.00	.90	.25
1	Marshall Faulk	6.00	2.70	.75
2	Heath Shuler	3.00	1.35	.35
3	David Palmer	2.00	.90	.25
4	Errict Rhett	4.00	1.80	.50
5	Charlie Garner	2.00	.90	.25
6	Irving Spikes	2.00	.90	.25
7	Shante Carver	2.00	.90	.25
8	Greg Hill	3.00	1.35	.35

1996 Playoff Absolute Promos

These promo cards were issued to preview the 1996 Playoff Absolute release. Each is very similar to its base brand card in design, except for the word "sample" where the card number otherwise would be.

		MINT	NRMT	EXC
	COMPLETE SET (3)	8.00	3.60	1.00
	COMMON CARD (1-3)	1.50	.70	.19
1	Terrell Davis	5.00	2.20	.60
2	Rashaan Salaam	2.00	.90	.25
3	Tamarick Vanover	1.50	.70	.19

1996 Playoff Absolute

 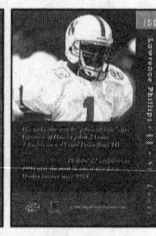

The 1996 Playoff Absolute set was issued in one series totalling 200 cards. The 6-card packs retailed for $3.75 each. Within every pack is five cards and an additional inner pack, featuring one collectible card. This concept from Playoff created three levels of color coded insertion ratios for the base cards: red, white and blue. The red level (1-100) are the most frequently inserted cards. The white level cards (101-150) appear in white inner packs which are found inside the Absolute pack. With one card per pack, the white packs appear approximately 18 per box. The blue level cards (151-200) are the hardest to find and also contain one card per pack. Approximately six packs per box will contain a blue pack, in place of the white pack. Rookie Cards in this set include Tim Biakabutuka, Terry Glenn, Eddie George, Keshawn Johnson, Leeland McElroy, Eric Moulds and Lawrence Phillips.

	MINT	NRMT	EXC
COMPLETE SET (200)	200.00	90.00	25.00
COMPLETE RED SET (100)	15.00	6.75	1.85
COMMON RED CARD (1-100)	.15	.07	.02
COMPLETE WHITE SET (50)	40.00	18.00	5.00
COMMON WHITE CARD (101-150)	.60	.25	.07
COMPLETE BLUE SET (50)	150.00	70.00	19.00
COMMON BLUE CARD (151-200)	1.25	.55	.16

		MINT	NRMT	EXC
1	Jim Kelly	.30	.14	.04
2	Michael Irvin	.30	.14	.04
3	Jim Harbaugh	.20	.09	.03
4	Warren Moon	.20	.09	.03
5	Rick Mirer	.20	.09	.03
6	Drew Bledsoe	1.50	.70	.19
7	Steve Young	1.25	.55	.16
8	Junior Seau	.30	.14	.04
9	Sherman Williams	.15	.07	.02
10	Jay Novacek	.20	.09	.03
11	Bill Brooks	.15	.07	.02
12	Steve Bono	.20	.09	.03
13	Leroy Hoard	.15	.07	.02
14	Willie Jackson	.20	.09	.03
15	Irving Fryar	.20	.09	.03
16	Tony McGee	.15	.07	.02
17	Neil O'Donnell	.20	.09	.03
18	Fred Barnett	.20	.09	.03
19	Erric Pegram	.20	.09	.03
20	Derrick Moore	.15	.07	.02
21	Johnnie Morton	.20	.09	.03
22	James Jett	.15	.07	.02
23	Tim Brown	.20	.09	.03
24	Kevin Miniefield	.15	.07	.02
25	Jim McMahon	.15	.07	.02
26	Brian Blades	.20	.09	.03
27	Henry Ellard	.20	.09	.03
28	Calvin Williams	.30	.14	.04
29	Chris Chandler	.20	.09	.03
30	Rod Woodson	.20	.09	.03
31	Ronnie Harmon	.15	.07	.02
32	Brent Jones	.15	.07	.02
33	Qadry Ismail	.20	.09	.03
34	Steve Tasker	.15	.07	.02
35	Eric Green	.15	.07	.02
36	Brian Mitchell	.15	.07	.02
37	Herschel Walker	.20	.09	.03
38	Sean Dawkins	.15	.07	.02
39	Bryce Paup	.20	.09	.03
40	Dorsey Levens	.20	.09	.03
41	Andre Rison	.20	.09	.03
42	Lamont Warren	.15	.07	.02
43	Earnest Byner	.15	.07	.02
44	Bobby Engram	1.00	.45	.12
45	Simeon Rice	.40	.18	.05
46	Michael Jackson	.20	.09	.03
47	Marvin Harrison	1.50	.70	.19
48	Thurman Thomas	.30	.14	.04
49	Charles Haley	.20	.09	.03
50	Rob Moore	.15	.07	.02
51	Bryan Cox	.15	.07	.02
52	Horace Copeland	.15	.07	.02
53	Rodney Peete	.15	.07	.02
54	Jeff Graham	.15	.07	.02
55	Charles Johnson	.20	.09	.03
56	Natrone Means	.30	.14	.04
57	Terrell Fletcher	.15	.07	.02
58	Eric Bieniemy	.15	.07	.02
59	Karim Abdul-Jabbar	2.50	1.10	.30
60	Quinn Early	.15	.07	.02
61	Mark Bruener	.15	.07	.02
62	Shawn Jefferson	.15	.07	.02
63	Vinny Testaverde	.20	.09	.03
64	Derrick Mayes	1.00	.45	.12
65	Mario Bates	.20	.09	.03
66	J.J. Birden	.15	.07	.02
67	Eddie Kennison	1.50	.70	.19

		MINT	NRMT	EXC
68	Steve Walsh	.15	.07	.02
69	Mark Chmura	.20	.09	.03
70	Mike Sherrard	.15	.07	.02
71	Boomer Esiason	.20	.09	.03
72	Alex Van Dyke	.20	.09	.03
73	Jake Reed	.20	.09	.03
74	Jackie Harris	.15	.07	.02
75	Mark Rypien	.15	.07	.02
76	Chris Calloway	.15	.07	.02
77	Amani Toomer	.40	.18	.05
78	Terrell Davis	3.00	1.35	.35
79	Rocket Ismail	.20	.09	.03
80	Derek Loville	.15	.07	.02
81	Ben Coates	.20	.09	.03
82	Kyle Brady	.15	.07	.02
83	Willie Green	.15	.07	.02
84	Randall Cunningham	.20	.09	.03
85	Amp Lee	.15	.07	.02
86	Bert Emanuel	.20	.09	.03
87	Jason Dunn	.20	.09	.03
88	Michael Haynes	.20	.09	.03
89	Robert Green	.15	.07	.02
90	Willie Davis	.20	.09	.03
91	O.J. McDuffie	.20	.09	.03
92	Harold Green	.15	.07	.02
93	Ken Dilger	.20	.09	.03
94	Brett Perriman	.20	.09	.03
95	Eric Zeier	.20	.09	.03
96	Jerome Bettis	.30	.14	.04
97	Rickey Dudley	.60	.25	.07
98	Darnay Scott	.20	.09	.03
99	Mark Brunell	1.50	.70	.19
100	Christian Fauria	.15	.07	.02
101	Jeff Blake	1.50	.70	.19
102	Troy Aikman	5.00	2.20	.60
103	John Elway	3.00	1.35	.35
104	Barry Sanders	5.00	2.20	.60
105	Curtis Conway	1.50	.70	.19
106	Wayne Chrebet	1.00	.45	.12
107	Lake Dawson	1.00	.45	.12
108	Jerry Rice	5.00	2.20	.60
109	Kevin Williams	.60	.25	.07
110	Zack Crockett	.60	.25	.07
111	Vincent Brisby	.60	.25	.07
112	Rodney Thomas	.60	.25	.07
113	Rodney Hampton	1.00	.45	.12
114	Adrian Murrell	1.00	.45	.12
115	Bruce Smith	1.50	.70	.19
116	Napoleon Kaufman	1.00	.45	.12
117	Byron Bam Morris	1.00	.45	.12
118	Anthony Miller	1.00	.45	.12
119	Aaron Hayden	1.00	.45	.12
120	Joey Galloway	3.00	1.35	.35
121	Trent Dilfer	1.00	.45	.12
122	Stoney Case	.60	.25	.07
123	Tamarick Vanover	1.50	.70	.19
124	Eric Metcalf	1.00	.45	.12
125	Marcus Allen	1.50	.70	.19
126	James O. Stewart	1.50	.70	.19
127	Charlie Garner	.60	.25	.07
128	Yancey Thigpen	1.00	.45	.12
129	William Floyd	1.00	.45	.12
130	Terry Allen	1.00	.45	.12
131	Robert Smith	1.00	.45	.12
132	Todd Kinchen	.60	.25	.07
133	Gus Frerotte	1.50	.70	.19
134	Frank Sanders	1.00	.45	.12
135	Scott Mitchell	1.00	.45	.12
136	Greg Hill	1.00	.45	.12
137	Edgar Bennett	1.00	.45	.12
138	Alvin Harper	.60	.25	.07
139	Reggie White	1.50	.70	.19
140	Craig Heyward	.60	.25	.07
141	Todd Collins	1.00	.45	.12
142	Ernie Mills	.60	.25	.07
143	Keyshawn Johnson	4.00	1.80	.50
144	Mark Carrier	.60	.25	.07
145	Robert Brooks	.60	.25	.07
146	Bernie Parmalee	.60	.25	.07
147	Carl Pickens	1.50	.70	.19
148	Kevin Hardy	2.00	.90	.25
149	Jonathan Ogden	.60	.25	.07
150	Lawrence Phillips	3.00	1.35	.35
151	Emmitt Smith	20.00	9.00	2.50
152	Brett Favre	20.00	9.00	2.50
153	Dan Marino	20.00	9.00	2.50
154	Jim Everett	1.25	.55	.16
155	Dave Brown	2.00	.90	.25
156	Jeff Hostetler	2.00	.90	.25
157	Heath Shuler	3.00	1.35	.35
158	Daryl Johnston	2.00	.90	.25
159	Terance Mathis	1.25	.55	.16
160	Curtis Martin	16.00	7.25	2.00
161	Ray Zellars	1.25	.55	.16
162	Ricky Watters	2.00	.90	.25
163	Chris Warren	2.00	.90	.25
164	Larry Centers	2.00	.90	.25
165	Steve McNair	10.00	4.50	1.25
166	Terry Kirby	2.00	.90	.25
167	Rob Johnson	1.25	.55	.16
168	Dave Meggett	2.00	.90	.25
169	Antonio Freeman	5.00	2.20	.60
170	Marshall Faulk	3.00	1.35	.35
171	Andre Hastings	2.00	.90	.25
172	Stan Humphries	2.00	.90	.25

☐ 173 Errict Rhett	2.00	.90	.25
☐ 174 Michael Westbrook	3.00	1.35	.35
☐ 175 Deion Sanders	6.00	2.70	.75
☐ 176 Jeff George	2.00	.90	.25
☐ 177 Cris Carter	3.00	1.35	.35
☐ 178 Chris Sanders	2.00	.90	.25
☐ 179 Ki-Jana Carter	2.00	.90	.25
☐ 180 Kordell Stewart	14.00	6.25	1.75
☐ 181 Isaac Bruce	3.00	1.35	.35
☐ 182 Terry Glenn	12.00	5.50	1.50
☐ 183 Garrison Hearst	2.00	.90	.25
☐ 184 Erik Kramer	1.25	.55	.16
☐ 185 Leeland McElroy	3.50	1.55	.45
☐ 186 Rashaan Salaam	3.00	1.35	.35
☐ 187 Kimble Anders	1.25	.55	.16
☐ 188 Chad May	1.25	.55	.16
☐ 189 Tony Martin	2.00	.90	.25
☐ 190 J.J. Stokes	3.00	1.35	.35
☐ 191 Darick Holmes	2.00	.90	.25
☐ 192 Eric Moulds	4.00	1.80	.50
☐ 193 Shannon Sharpe	2.00	.90	.25
☐ 194 Tim Biakabutuka	4.00	1.80	.50
☐ 195 Eddie George	15.00	6.75	1.85
☐ 196 Mike Alstott	3.00	1.35	.35
☐ 197 Kerry Collins	14.00	6.25	1.75
☐ 198 Harvey Williams	1.25	.55	.16
☐ 199 Herman Moore	5.00	2.20	.60
☐ 200 Tyrone Wheatley	2.00	.90	.25

1996 Playoff Absolute Metal XL

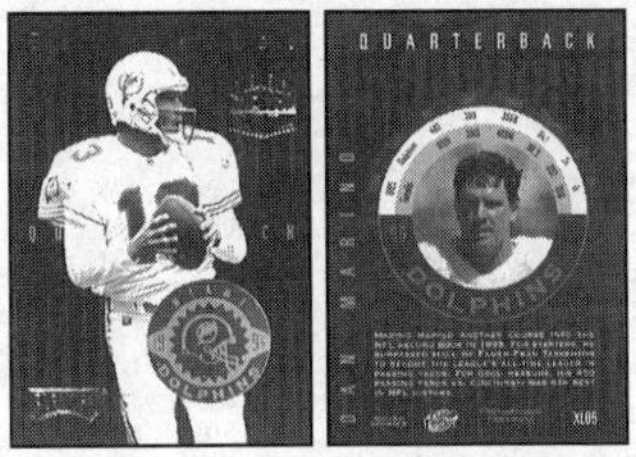

Series one cards were randomly inserted into Absolute packs at a rate of one in 96-blue packs, while series two card were random inserts in Prime packs. A metal coin commemorating each player's team was inset in the standard-size cards. Each is numbered with an "XL" prefix.

	MINT	NRMT	EXC
COMPLETE SET (36)	800.00	350.00	100.00
COMP.SERIES 1 SET (18)	500.00	220.00	60.00
COMP.SERIES 2 SET (18)	300.00	135.00	38.00
COMMON CARD (1-36)	8.00	3.60	1.00
☐ 1 Troy Aikman	40.00	18.00	5.00
☐ 2 Emmitt Smith	80.00	36.00	10.00
☐ 3 Barry Sanders	40.00	18.00	5.00
☐ 4 Brett Favre	80.00	36.00	10.00
☐ 5 Dan Marino	80.00	36.00	10.00
☐ 6 Jerry Rice	40.00	18.00	5.00
☐ 7 Marshall Faulk	16.00	7.25	2.00
☐ 8 Curtis Martin	40.00	18.00	5.00
☐ 9 Rashaan Salaam	16.00	7.25	2.00
☐ 10 Harvey Williams	8.00	3.60	1.00
☐ 11 Ricky Watters	12.00	5.50	1.50
☐ 12 Yancey Thigpen	8.00	3.60	1.00
☐ 13 Chris Warren	12.00	5.50	1.50
☐ 14 Errict Rhett	12.00	5.50	1.50
☐ 15 Terry Allen	12.00	5.50	1.50
☐ 16 Robert Brooks	16.00	7.25	2.00
☐ 17 Anthony Miller	8.00	3.60	1.00
☐ 18 Erik Kramer	8.00	3.60	1.00
☐ 19 Michael Irvin	16.00	7.25	2.00
☐ 20 John Elway	30.00	13.50	3.70
☐ 21 Jim Harbaugh	12.00	5.50	1.50
☐ 22 Steve Young	25.00	11.00	3.10
☐ 23 Deion Sanders	25.00	11.00	3.10
☐ 24 Terrell Davis	40.00	18.00	5.00
☐ 25 Reggie White	16.00	7.25	2.00
☐ 26 Herman Moore	16.00	7.25	2.00
☐ 27 Rodney Hampton	12.00	5.50	1.50
☐ 28 Cris Carter	12.00	5.50	1.50
☐ 29 Isaac Bruce	16.00	7.25	2.00
☐ 30 Kordell Stewart	40.00	18.00	5.00
☐ 31 Brett Perriman	8.00	3.60	1.00
☐ 32 Joey Galloway	20.00	9.00	2.50
☐ 33 Drew Bledsoe	40.00	18.00	5.00
☐ 34 J.J. Stokes	16.00	7.25	2.00
☐ 35 Napoleon Kaufman	8.00	3.60	1.00
☐ 36 Tim Brown	12.00	5.50	1.50

1996 Playoff Absolute Quad Series

Randomly inserted in packs at a rate of one in 24 red packs, this 35-card set features popular players from each team. There are also some rookie-only quad cards. Cards 1-30 are sequenced in alphabetical team order while cards 31-35 are the rookie only quads.

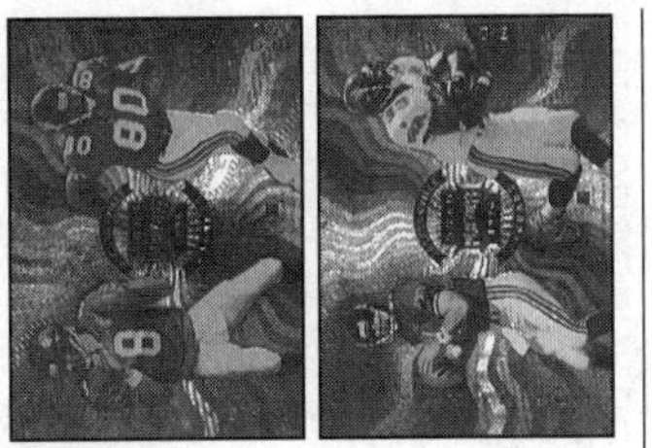

	MINT	NRMT	EXC
COMPLETE SET (35)	700.00	325.00	90.00
COMMON CARD (1-35)	10.00	4.50	1.25
☐ 1 Stoney Case	14.00	6.25	1.75
Garrison Hearst			
Rob Moore			
Frank Sanders			
☐ 2 J.J.Birden	10.00	4.50	1.25
Bert Emanuel			
Jeff George			
Craig Heyward			
☐ 3 Todd Collins	20.00	9.00	2.50
Bill Brooks			
Jim Kelly			
Bryce Paup			
☐ 4 Mark Carrier WR	40.00	18.00	5.00
Kerry Collins			
Willie Green			
Derrick Moore			
☐ 5 Curtis Conway	14.00	6.25	1.75
Robert Green			
Erik Kramer			
Kevin Miniefield			
☐ 6 Eric Bieniemy	20.00	9.00	2.50
Jeff Blake			
Harold Green			
Tony McGee			
☐ 7 Earnest Byner	10.00	4.50	1.25
Michael Jackson			
Andre Rison			
Eric Zeier			
☐ 8 Michael Irvin	25.00	11.00	3.10
Jay Novacek			
Deion Sanders			
Kevin Williams			
☐ 9 Terrell Davis	50.00	22.00	6.25
John Elway			
Anthony Miller			
Shannon Sharpe			
☐ 10 Scott Mitchell	20.00	9.00	2.50
Herman Moore			
Johnnie Morton			
Brett Perriman			
☐ 11 Edgar Bennett	25.00	11.00	3.10
Mark Chmura			
Antonio Freeman			
Reggie White			
☐ 12 Chris Chandler	30.00	13.50	3.70
Steve McNair			
Chris Sanders			
Rodney Thomas			
☐ 13 Zack Crockett	14.00	6.25	1.75
Sean Dawkins			
Ken Dilger			
Jim Harbaugh			
☐ 14 Mark Brunell	30.00	13.50	3.70
Willie Jackson			
Rob Johnson			
James O.Stewart			
☐ 15 Marcus Allen	20.00	9.00	2.50
Kimble Anders			
Lake Dawson			
Tamarick Vanover			
☐ 16 Eric Green	14.00	6.25	1.75
Terry Kirby			
O.J. McDuffie			
Bernie Parmalee			
☐ 17 Cris Carter	14.00	6.25	1.75
Warren Moon			
Robert Smith			
Chad May			
☐ 18 Drew Bledsoe	40.00	18.00	5.00
Vincent Brisby			
Ben Coates			
Dave Meggett			
☐ 19 Mario Bates	10.00	4.50	1.25
Jim Everett			
Michael Haynes			
Ray Zellars			
☐ 20 Dave Brown	14.00	6.25	1.75
Chris Calloway			
Rodney Hampton			
Tyrone Wheatley			
☐ 21 Kyle Brady	14.00	6.25	1.75
Wayne Chrebet			
Adrian Murrell			
Neil O'Donnell			
☐ 22 Tim Brown	14.00	6.25	1.75
Jeff Hostetler			
Rocket Ismail			
Napoleon Kaufman			
☐ 23 Charlie Garner	14.00	6.25	1.75
Rodney Peete			
Ricky Watters			
Calvin Williams			
☐ 24 Andre Hastings	40.00	18.00	5.00
Ernie Mills			
Kordell Stewart			
Rod Woodson			
☐ 25 Terrell Fletcher	20.00	9.00	2.50
Ronnie Harmon			
Aaron Hayden			
Junior Seau			
☐ 26 William Floyd	40.00	18.00	5.00
Derek Loville			
J.J.Stokes			
Steve Young			
☐ 27 Brian Blades	25.00	11.00	3.10
Christian Fauria			
Joey Galloway			
Rick Mirer			
☐ 28 Mark Rypien	20.00	9.00	2.50
Isaac Bruce			
Todd Kinchen			
Steve Walsh			
☐ 29 Horace Copeland	14.00	6.25	1.75
Trent Dilfer			
Alvin Harper			
James Harris			
☐ 30 Henry Ellard	20.00	9.00	2.50
Gus Frerotte			
Heath Shuler			
Michael Westbrook			
☐ 31 Keyshawn Johnson	40.00	18.00	5.00
Kevin Hardy			
Simeon Rice			
Jonathan Ogden			
☐ 32 Lawrence Phillips	50.00	22.00	6.25
Tim Biakabutuka			
Terry Glenn			
Rickey Dudley			
☐ 33 Eddie George	65.00	29.00	8.00
Marvin Harrison			
Eric Moulds			
Eddie Kennison			
☐ 34 Derrick Mayes	40.00	18.00	5.00
Karim Abdul-Jabbar			
Alex Van Dyke			
Bobby Engram			
☐ 35 Leeland McElroy	20.00	9.00	2.50
Jason Dunn			
Mike Alstott			
Amani Toomer			

1996 Playoff Absolute Unsung Heroes

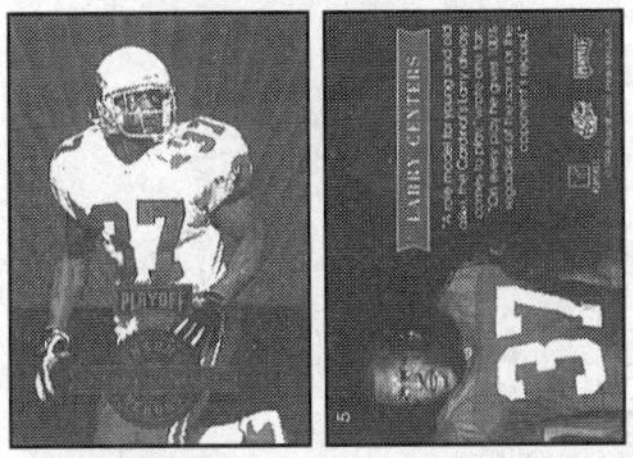

Randomly inserted in Absolute or Prime packs at a rate of one in 24 red packs, this 30-card standard-size set is a special insert honoring players chosen by the fans and teammates. One player from each NFC team is featured in Absolute packs while the AFC players were honored in the Prime packs. These cards are sequenced in alpahabetical order.

	MINT	NRMT	EXC
COMPLETE SET (30)	30.00	13.50	3.70
COMP.SERIES 1 SET (15)	12.00	5.50	1.50
COMP.SERIES 2 SET (15)	18.00	8.00	2.20
COMMON CARD (1-30)	.75	.35	.09
☐ 1 Bill Bates	1.25	.55	.16
☐ 2 Jeff Brady	.75	.35	.09
☐ 3 Ray Brown	.75	.35	.09
☐ 4 Isaac Bruce	2.00	.90	.25
☐ 5 Larry Centers	1.25	.55	.16
☐ 6 Mark Chmura	1.50	.70	.19
☐ 7 Keith Elias	.75	.35	.09
☐ 8 Robert Green	.75	.35	.09
☐ 9 Andy Harmon	.75	.35	.09
☐ 10 Rodney Holman	.75	.35	.09
☐ 11 Derek Loville	1.25	.55	.16
☐ 12 J.J. McCleskey	.75	.35	.09
☐ 13 Sam Mills	1.25	.55	.16
☐ 14 Hardy Nickerson	1.25	.55	.16
☐ 15 Jessie Tuggle	.75	.35	.09
☐ 16 Eric Bieniemy	.75	.35	.09
☐ 17 Blaine Bishop	.75	.35	.09
☐ 18 Mark Brunell	6.00	2.70	.75
☐ 19 Wayne Chrebet	1.25	.55	.16
☐ 20 Vince Evans	.75	.35	.09
☐ 21 Sam Gash	.75	.35	.09
☐ 22 Tim Grunhard	.75	.35	.09
☐ 23 Jim Harbaugh	1.25	.55	.16
☐ 24 Dwayne Harper	.75	.35	.09
☐ 25 Bernie Parmalee	1.25	.55	.16
☐ 26 Reggie Rivers	.75	.35	.09
☐ 27 Eugene Robinson	.75	.35	.09
☐ 28 Kordell Stewart	8.00	3.60	1.00
☐ 29 Steve Tasker	.75	.35	.09
☐ 30 Bennie Thompson	.75	.35	.09

1996 Playoff Absolute Xtreme Team

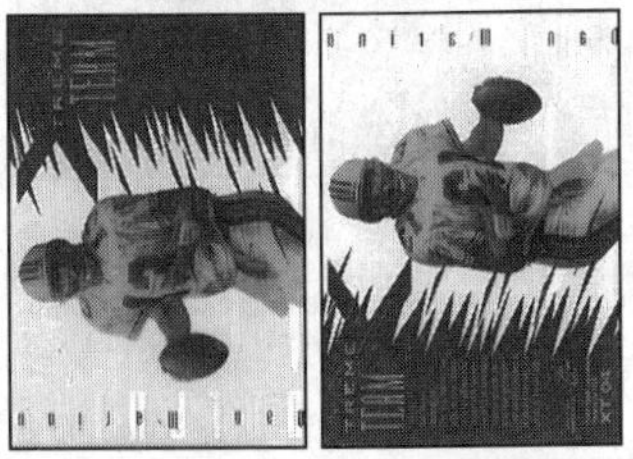

Randomly inserted in packs at a rate of one in 24 white packs, this 30-card standard-size set features some of Football's best players. The cards are issued on clear-plastic which have been foil-enhanced. The cards are numbered with an "TX" prefix.

	MINT	NRMT	EXC
COMPLETE SET (30)	300.00	135.00	38.00
COMMON CARD (1-30)	5.00	2.20	.60
☐ 1 Troy Aikman	20.00	9.00	2.50
☐ 2 Emmitt Smith	35.00	16.00	4.40
☐ 3 Jerry Rice	20.00	9.00	2.50
☐ 4 Dan Marino	35.00	16.00	4.40
☐ 5 Brett Favre	35.00	16.00	4.40
☐ 6 Barry Sanders	20.00	9.00	2.50
☐ 7 Michael Irvin	10.00	4.50	1.25
☐ 8 John Elway	15.00	6.75	1.85
☐ 9 Joey Galloway	12.00	5.50	1.50
☐ 10 Steve Young	15.00	6.75	1.85
☐ 11 Deion Sanders	12.00	5.50	1.50
☐ 12 Terrell Davis	20.00	9.00	2.50
☐ 13 Herman Moore	10.00	4.50	1.25
☐ 14 Reggie White	10.00	4.50	1.25
☐ 15 Cris Carter	8.00	3.60	1.00
☐ 16 Rodney Hampton	5.00	2.20	.60
☐ 17 Isaac Bruce	10.00	4.50	1.25
☐ 18 Brett Perriman	5.00	2.20	.60
☐ 19 Curtis Conway	8.00	3.60	1.00
☐ 20 Scott Mitchell	5.00	2.20	.60
☐ 21 Rashaan Salaam	10.00	4.50	1.25
☐ 22 Robert Brooks	10.00	4.50	1.25
☐ 23 Marshall Faulk	10.00	4.50	1.25
☐ 24 Curtis Martin	20.00	9.00	2.50
☐ 25 Harvey Williams	5.00	2.20	.60
☐ 26 Yancey Thigpen	8.00	3.60	1.00
☐ 27 Chris Warren	8.00	3.60	1.00
☐ 28 Errict Rhett	8.00	3.60	1.00
☐ 29 Terry Allen	8.00	3.60	1.00
☐ 30 Carl Pickens	8.00	3.60	1.00

1996 Playoff National Promos

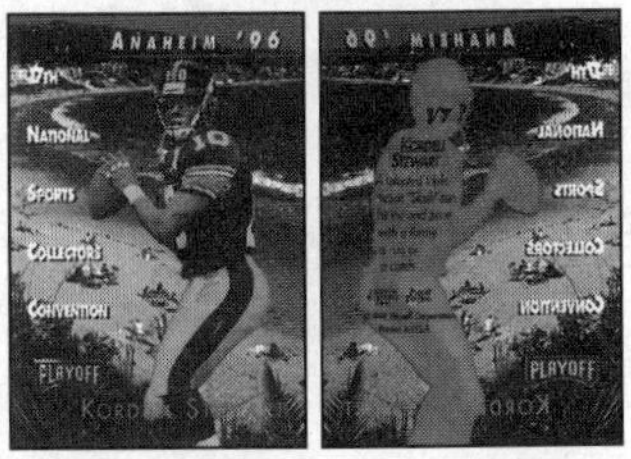

This seven-card set was distributed at the 1996 National Sports Collectors Convention in Anaheim as part of a wrapper redemption program. Collectors could redeem three wrappers from any Playoff product for one card, or a foil box worth of wrappers for a complete set. The Kordell Stewart card was only available as part of the complete set offer.

	MINT	NRMT	EXC
COMPLETE SET (7)	40.00	18.00	5.00
COMMON CARD (1-7)	3.00	1.35	.35
☐ 1 Kordell Stewart	10.00	4.50	1.25
☐ 2 Curtis Martin	12.00	5.50	1.50
☐ 3 Tyrone Wheatley	3.00	1.35	.35
☐ 4 Joey Galloway	5.00	2.20	.60
☐ 5 Steve McNair	8.00	3.60	1.00
☐ 6 Kerry Collins	10.00	4.50	1.25
☐ 7 Napoleon Kaufman	3.00	1.35	.35

1996 Playoff Super Bowl Card Show

This six-card set features borderless color action player photos superimposed over an Arizona desert background. The player's name and Super Bowl Card Show logo rounds out the front design. The backs carry the card name, player's name, and a highlight from the 1995 season. Playoff offered one card to each Card Show attendee

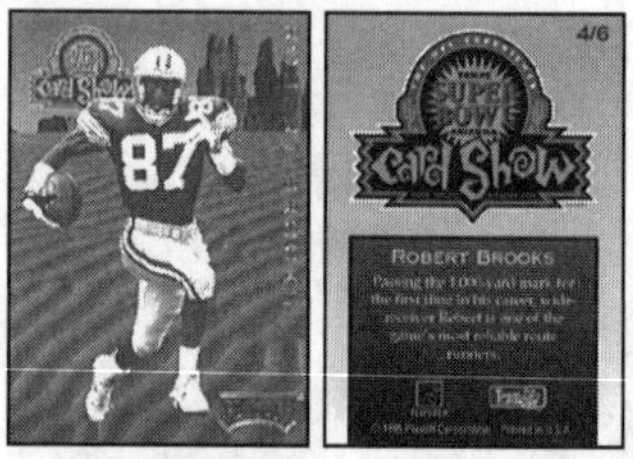

each day in exchange for one Playoff football card wrapper. Ten wrappers were good for a complete set any day of the show. Although the cards carry a 1995 copyright date, the cards were released in January 1996 at the Tempe, Arizona Super Bowl Card Show. Reportedly, 5500 sets were produced.

	MINT	NRMT	EXC
COMPLETE SET (6)	20.00	9.00	2.50
COMMON CARD (1-6)	2.00	.90	.25
☐ 1 Deion Sanders	3.00	1.35	.35
☐ 2 Rashaan Salaam	3.00	1.35	.35
☐ 3 Garrison Hearst	2.50	1.10	.30
☐ 4 Robert Brooks	2.00	.90	.25
☐ 5 Barry Sanders	8.00	3.60	1.00
☐ 6 Errict Rhett	3.00	1.35	.35

1996 Playoff Unsung Heroes Banquet

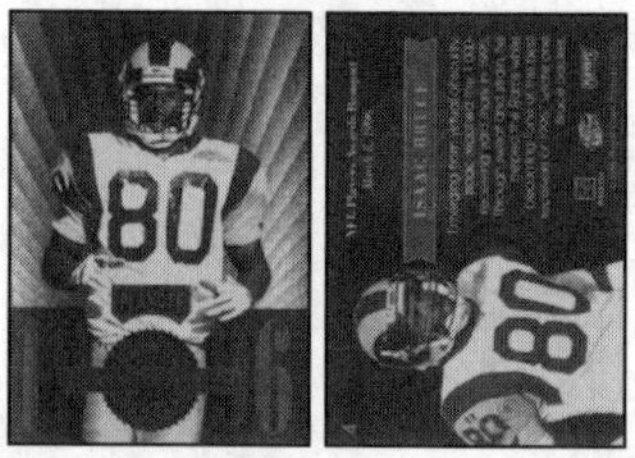

Playoff issued this set to attendees of the March 8, 1996 NFL Players Award Banquet in Washington D.C. The 30-cards feature color action player cut-outs over a purple striped metallic background. The backs carry a color player portrait with a quote about the player.

	MINT	NRMT	EXC
COMPLETE SET (30)	30.00	13.50	3.70
COMMON CARD (1-30)	.50	.23	.06
☐ 1 Bill Bates	.75	.35	.09
☐ 2 Jeff Brady	.50	.23	.06
☐ 3 Ray Brown	.50	.23	.06
☐ 4 Isaac Bruce	3.00	1.35	.35
☐ 5 Larry Centers	.75	.35	.09
☐ 6 Mark Chmura	1.50	.70	.19
☐ 7 Keith Elias	.50	.23	.06
☐ 8 Robert Green	.50	.23	.06
☐ 9 Andy Harmon	.50	.23	.06
☐ 10 Rodney Holman	.50	.23	.06
☐ 11 Derek Loville	.75	.35	.09
☐ 12 J.J. McCleskey	.50	.23	.06
☐ 13 Sam Mills	.75	.35	.09
☐ 14 Hardy Nickerson	.75	.35	.09
☐ 15 Jessie Tuggle	.50	.23	.06
☐ 16 Eric Bieniemy	.50	.23	.06
☐ 17 Blaine Bishop	.50	.23	.06
☐ 18 Mark Brunell	8.00	3.60	1.00
☐ 19 Wayne Chrebet	1.00	.45	.12
☐ 20 Vince Evans	.50	.23	.06
☐ 21 Sam Gash	.50	.23	.06
☐ 22 Tim Grunhard	.50	.23	.06
☐ 23 Jim Harbaugh	.75	.35	.09
☐ 24 Dwayne Harper	.50	.23	.06
☐ 25 Bernie Parmalee	.50	.23	.06
☐ 26 Reggie Rivers	.50	.23	.06
☐ 27 Eugene Robinson	.50	.23	.06
☐ 28 Kordell Stewart	6.00	2.70	.75
☐ 29 Steve Tasker	.50	.23	.06
☐ 30 Bennie Thompson	.50	.23	.06

1997 Playoff Absolute

The 1997 Playoff Absolute set was issued together as three series totaling 200 cards. The first 100-cards (green bordered) were the easiest to pull with the second 50 (blue bordered) slightly tougher and the final 50 (red bordered) the most difficult to pull. Several insert sets were included with the product which was packaged 5-cards and one Chip Shot per pack with 24-packs per box.

	MINT	NRMT	EXC
COMPLETE SET (200)	180.00	80.00	22.00
COMP.GREEN SET (100)	25.00	11.00	3.10
COMP.BLUE SET (50)	35.00	16.00	4.40

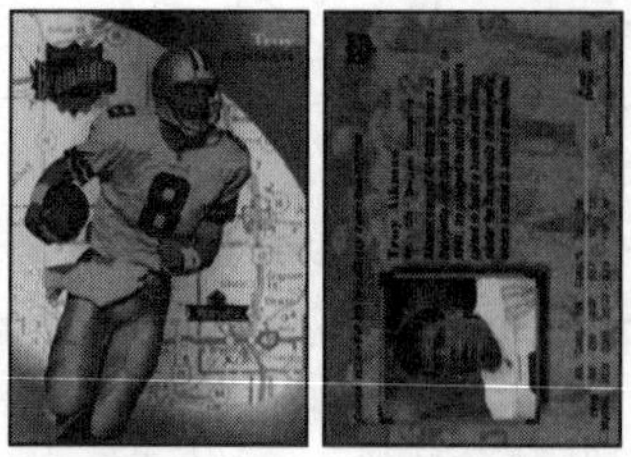

	MINT	NRMT	EXC
COMP.RED SET (50)	125.00	55.00	15.50
COMMON GREEN (1-100)	.15	.07	.02
COMMON BLUE (101-150)	.50	.23	.06
COMMON RED (151-200)	.75	.35	.09
☐ 1 Marcus Allen	.40	.18	.05
☐ 2 Eric Bieniemy	.15	.07	.02
☐ 3 Jason Dunn	.25	.11	.03
☐ 4 Jim Harbaugh	.25	.11	.03
☐ 5 Michael Westbrook	.40	.18	.05
☐ 6 Tiki Barber	1.25	.55	.16
☐ 7 Frank Reich	.15	.07	.02
☐ 8 Irving Fryar	.25	.11	.03
☐ 9 Courtney Hawkins	.15	.07	.02
☐ 10 Eric Zeier	.25	.11	.03
☐ 11 Kent Graham	.25	.11	.03
☐ 12 Trent Dilfer	.25	.11	.03
☐ 13 Neil O'Donnell	.25	.11	.03
☐ 14 Reidel Anthony	2.50	1.10	.30
☐ 15 Jeff Hostetler	.25	.11	.03
☐ 16 Lawrence Phillips	.25	.11	.03
☐ 17 Dave Brown	.25	.11	.03
☐ 18 Mike Tomczak	.15	.07	.02
☐ 19 Jake Reed	.25	.11	.03
☐ 20 Anthony Miller	.25	.11	.03
☐ 21 Eric Metcalf	.25	.11	.03
☐ 22 Sedrick Shaw	1.25	.55	.16
☐ 23 Anthony Johnson	.25	.11	.03
☐ 24 Mario Bates	.25	.11	.03
☐ 25 Dorsey Levens	.25	.11	.03
☐ 26 Stan Humphries	.25	.11	.03
☐ 27 Ben Coates	.25	.11	.03
☐ 28 Tyrone Wheatley	.25	.11	.03
☐ 29 Adrian Murrell	.25	.11	.03
☐ 30 William Henderson	.15	.07	.02
☐ 31 Warrick Dunn	4.00	1.80	.50
☐ 32 LeShon Johnson	.15	.07	.02
☐ 33 James O.Stewart	.25	.11	.03
☐ 34 Edgar Bennett	.25	.11	.03
☐ 35 Raymont Harris	.15	.07	.02
☐ 36 LeRoy Butler	.15	.07	.02
☐ 37 Darren Woodson	.25	.11	.03
☐ 38 Darnell Autry	1.25	.55	.16
☐ 39 Johnnie Morton	.25	.11	.03
☐ 40 William Floyd	.25	.11	.03
☐ 41 Terrell Fletcher	.15	.07	.02
☐ 42 Leonard Russell	.15	.07	.02
☐ 43 Henry Ellard	.25	.11	.03
☐ 44 Terrell Owens	1.00	.45	.12
☐ 45 John Friesz	.15	.07	.02
☐ 46 Antowain Smith	1.25	.55	.16
☐ 47 Charles Johnson	.25	.11	.03
☐ 48 Rickey Dudley	.25	.11	.03
☐ 49 Lake Dawson	.25	.11	.03
☐ 50 Bert Emanuel	.25	.11	.03
☐ 51 Zach Thomas	.60	.25	.07
☐ 52 Earnest Byner	.15	.07	.02
☐ 53 Yatil Green	2.50	1.10	.30
☐ 54 Chris Spielman	.25	.11	.03
☐ 55 Muhsin Muhammad	.60	.25	.07
☐ 56 Bobby Engram	.25	.11	.03
☐ 57 Eric Bjornson	.15	.07	.02
☐ 58 Willie Green	.15	.07	.02
☐ 59 Derrick Mayes	.25	.11	.03
☐ 60 Chris Sanders	.25	.11	.03
☐ 61 Jimmy Smith	.25	.11	.03
☐ 62 Tony Gonzalez	1.25	.55	.16
☐ 63 Rich Gannon	.15	.07	.02
☐ 64 Stanley Pritchett	.15	.07	.02
☐ 65 Brad Johnson	.25	.11	.03
☐ 66 Rodney Peete	.15	.07	.02
☐ 67 Sam Gash	.15	.07	.02
☐ 68 Chris Calloway	.15	.07	.02
☐ 69 Chris T. Jones	.40	.18	.05
☐ 70 Will Blackwell	.75	.35	.09
☐ 71 Mark Bruener	.15	.07	.02
☐ 72 Terry Kirby	.25	.11	.03
☐ 73 Brian Blades	.25	.11	.03
☐ 74 Craig Heyward	.15	.07	.02
☐ 75 Jamie Asher	.25	.11	.03
☐ 76 Terance Mathis	.15	.07	.02
☐ 77 Troy Davis	2.00	.90	.25
☐ 78 Bruce Smith	.40	.18	.05
☐ 79 Simeon Rice	.25	.11	.03
☐ 80 Fred Barnett	.25	.11	.03
☐ 81 Tim Brown	.25	.11	.03
☐ 82 James Jett	.15	.07	.02
☐ 83 Mark Carrier	.25	.11	.03
☐ 84 Shawn Jefferson	.15	.07	.02
☐ 85 Ken Dilger	.25	.11	.03
☐ 86 Rae Carruth	1.50	.70	.19
☐ 87 Keenan McCardell	.25	.11	.03
☐ 88 Michael Irvin	.40	.18	.05
☐ 89 Mark Chmura	.25	.11	.03
☐ 90 Derrick Alexander WR	.25	.11	.03
☐ 91 Andre Reed	.25	.11	.03
☐ 92 Ed McCaffrey	.15	.07	.02
☐ 93 Erik Kramer	.15	.07	.02
☐ 94 Albert Connell	.15	.07	.02
☐ 95 Frank Wycheck	.15	.07	.02
☐ 96 Zack Crockett	.15	.07	.02
☐ 97 Jim Everett	.15	.07	.02
☐ 98 Michael Haynes	.25	.11	.03
☐ 99 Jeff Graham	.15	.07	.02
☐ 100 Brent Jones	.25	.11	.03
☐ 101 Troy Aikman	4.00	1.80	.50
☐ 102 Byron Hanspard	3.00	1.35	.35
☐ 103 Robert Brooks	1.25	.55	.16
☐ 104 Karim Abdul-Jabbar	3.00	1.35	.35
☐ 105 Drew Bledsoe	4.00	1.80	.50
☐ 106 Napoleon Kaufman	.75	.35	.09
☐ 107 Steve Young	3.00	1.35	.35
☐ 108 Leeland McElroy	.75	.35	.09
☐ 109 Jamal Anderson	.75	.35	.09
☐ 110 David LaFleur	2.00	.90	.25
☐ 111 Vinny Testaverde	.75	.35	.09
☐ 112 Eric Moulds	1.25	.55	.16
☐ 113 Tim Biakabutuka	1.25	.55	.16
☐ 114 Rick Mirer	.75	.35	.09
☐ 115 Jeff Blake	1.25	.55	.16
☐ 116 Jim Schwantz	.50	.23	.06
☐ 117 Herman Moore	1.25	.55	.16
☐ 118 Ike Hilliard	5.00	2.20	.60
☐ 119 Reggie White	1.25	.55	.16
☐ 120 Steve McNair	3.00	1.35	.35
☐ 121 Marshall Faulk	1.25	.55	.16
☐ 122 Natrone Means	1.25	.55	.16
☐ 123 Greg Hill	.75	.35	.09
☐ 124 O.J. McDuffie	.75	.35	.09
☐ 125 Robert Smith	.75	.35	.09
☐ 126 Bryant Westbrook	1.25	.55	.16
☐ 127 Ray Zellars	.50	.23	.06
☐ 128 Rodney Hampton	.75	.35	.09
☐ 129 Wayne Chrebet	.50	.23	.06
☐ 130 Desmond Howard	.75	.35	.09
☐ 131 Ty Detmer	.75	.35	.09
☐ 132 Erric Pegram	.50	.23	.06
☐ 133 Yancey Thigpen	.75	.35	.09
☐ 134 Danny Wuerffel	7.00	3.10	.85
☐ 135 Charlie Jones	.50	.23	.06
☐ 136 Chris Warren	.75	.35	.09
☐ 137 Isaac Bruce	1.25	.55	.16
☐ 138 Errict Rhett	.75	.35	.09
☐ 139 Gus Frerotte	1.25	.55	.16
☐ 140 Frank Sanders	.75	.35	.09
☐ 141 Todd Collins	.75	.35	.09
☐ 142 Jake Plummer	2.00	.90	.25
☐ 143 Darnay Scott	.75	.35	.09
☐ 144 Rashaan Salaam	1.25	.55	.16
☐ 145 Terrell Davis	4.00	1.80	.50
☐ 146 Scott Mitchell	.75	.35	.09
☐ 147 Junior Seau	1.25	.55	.16
☐ 148 Warren Moon	.75	.35	.09
☐ 149 Wesley Walls	.50	.23	.06
☐ 150 Daryl Johnston	.75	.35	.09
☐ 151 Brett Favre	15.00	6.75	1.85
☐ 152 Emmitt Smith	15.00	6.75	1.85
☐ 153 Dan Marino	15.00	6.75	1.85
☐ 154 Larry Centers	1.25	.55	.16
☐ 155 Michael Jackson	1.25	.55	.16
☐ 156 Kerry Collins	7.00	3.10	.85
☐ 157 Curtis Conway	2.00	.90	.25
☐ 158 Peter Boulware	1.25	.55	.16
☐ 159 Carl Pickens	2.00	.90	.25
☐ 160 Shannon Sharpe	1.25	.55	.16
☐ 161 Brett Perriman	1.25	.55	.16
☐ 162 Eddie George	10.00	4.50	1.25
☐ 163 Mark Brunell	8.00	3.60	1.00
☐ 164 Tamarick Vanover	1.25	.55	.16
☐ 165 Cris Carter	2.00	.90	.25
☐ 166 Corey Dillon	6.00	2.70	.75
☐ 167 Curtis Martin	8.00	3.60	1.00
☐ 168 Amani Toomer	1.25	.55	.16
☐ 169 Jeff George	1.25	.55	.16
☐ 170 Kordell Stewart	7.00	3.10	.85
☐ 171 Garrison Hearst	1.25	.55	.16
☐ 172 Tony Banks	3.00	1.35	.35
☐ 173 Mike Alstott	2.00	.90	.25
☐ 174 Jim Druckenmiller	12.00	5.50	1.50
☐ 175 Chris Chandler	1.25	.55	.16
☐ 176 Byron Bam Morris	1.25	.55	.16
☐ 177 Billy Joe Hobert	1.25	.55	.16
☐ 178 Ernie Mills	.75	.35	.09
☐ 179 Ki-Jana Carter	1.25	.55	.16
☐ 180 Deion Sanders	4.00	1.80	.50
☐ 181 Ricky Watters	1.25	.55	.16
☐ 182 Shawn Springs	3.00	1.35	.35
☐ 183 Barry Sanders	8.00	3.60	1.00
☐ 184 Antonio Freeman	3.00	1.35	.35
☐ 185 Marvin Harrison	4.00	1.80	.50
☐ 186 Elvis Grbac	1.25	.55	.16
☐ 187 Terry Glenn	7.00	3.10	.85
☐ 188 Willie Roaf	.75	.35	.09
☐ 189 Keyshawn Johnson	4.00	1.80	.50
☐ 190 Orlando Pace	3.00	1.35	.35
☐ 191 Jerome Bettis	2.00	.90	.25
☐ 192 Tony Martin	1.25	.55	.16
☐ 193 Jerry Rice	8.00	3.60	1.00
☐ 194 Joey Galloway	3.00	1.35	.35
☐ 195 Terry Allen	1.25	.55	.16
☐ 196 Eddie Kennison	4.00	1.80	.50
☐ 197 Thurman Thomas	2.00	.90	.25
☐ 198 Darrell Russell	1.25	.55	.16
☐ 199 Rob Moore	.75	.35	.09
☐ 200 John Elway	7.00	3.10	.85

1997 Playoff Absolute Chip Shots

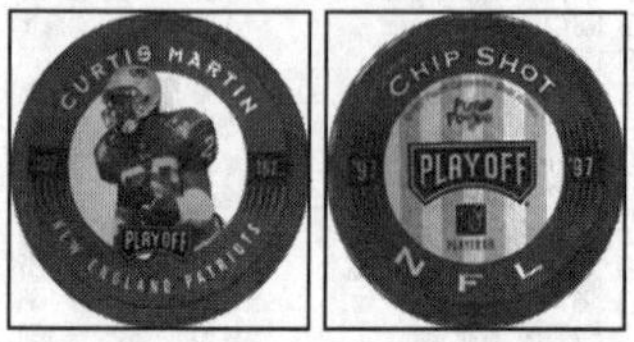

This 200 coin set was inserted one per 1997 Playoff Absolute pack and is a parallel to the same players in the base set. The players are randomly assigned a colored poker chip style of blue, dark green, or red. All players appear to have a chip for each color, and no premium is set for one color over another.

	MINT	NRMT	EXC
COMPLETE SET (200)	250.00	110.00	31.00
COMMON COIN (1-200)	.50	.23	.06
SEMISTARS	1.00	.45	.12
UNLISTED STARS	2.00	.90	.25
☐ 14 Reidel Anthony	5.00	2.20	.60
☐ 31 Warrick Dunn	10.00	4.50	1.25
☐ 44 Terrell Owens	5.00	2.20	.60
☐ 53 Yatil Green	5.00	2.20	.60
☐ 77 Troy Davis	4.00	1.80	.50
☐ 86 Rae Carruth	3.00	1.35	.35
☐ 101 Troy Aikman	8.00	3.60	1.00
☐ 102 Byron Hanspard	3.00	1.35	.35
☐ 104 Karim Abdul-Jabbar	6.00	2.70	.75
☐ 105 Drew Bledsoe	8.00	3.60	1.00
☐ 107 Steve Young	5.00	2.20	.60
☐ 118 Ike Hilliard	5.00	2.20	.60
☐ 120 Steve McNair	5.00	2.20	.60
☐ 134 Danny Wuerffel	8.00	3.60	1.00
☐ 145 Terrell Davis	8.00	3.60	1.00
☐ 151 Brett Favre	15.00	6.75	1.85
☐ 152 Emmitt Smith	15.00	6.75	1.85
☐ 153 Dan Marino	15.00	6.75	1.85
☐ 156 Kerry Collins	6.00	2.70	.75
☐ 162 Eddie George	12.00	5.50	1.50
☐ 163 Mark Brunell	8.00	3.60	1.00
☐ 166 Corey Dillon	3.00	1.35	.35
☐ 167 Curtis Martin	8.00	3.60	1.00
☐ 170 Kordell Stewart	6.00	2.70	.75
☐ 174 Jim Druckenmiller	8.00	3.60	1.00
☐ 180 Deion Sanders	4.00	1.80	.50
☐ 183 Barry Sanders	8.00	3.60	1.00
☐ 185 Marvin Harrison	4.00	1.80	.50
☐ 187 Terry Glenn	8.00	3.60	1.00
☐ 189 Keyshawn Johnson	4.00	1.80	.50
☐ 193 Jerry Rice	8.00	3.60	1.00
☐ 196 Eddie Kennison	4.00	1.80	.50
☐ 200 John Elway	6.00	2.70	.75

1997 Playoff Absolute Leather Quads

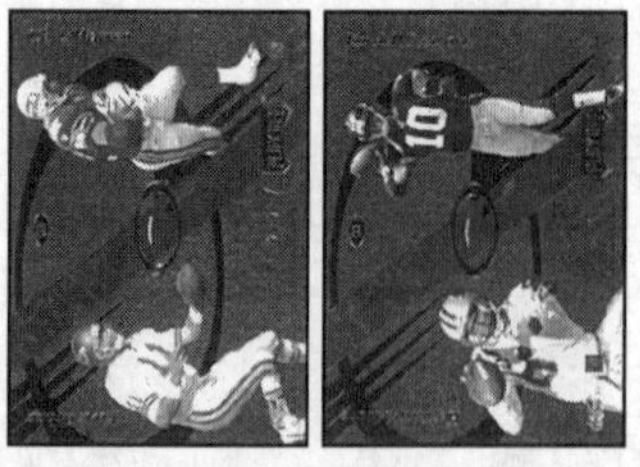

This set of 18-cards features four players per card on leather stock. Each was randomly inserted at the rate of one in 144 in 1997 Playoff Absolute packs.

	MINT	NRMT	EXC
COMPLETE SET (18)	1400.00	650.00	180.00
COMMON CARD (1-18)	30.00	13.50	3.70
☐ 1 Emmitt Smith Dan Marino Jerry Rice Brett Favre	350.00	160.00	45.00
☐ 2 Eddie George Curtis Martin Barry Sanders	200.00	90.00	25.00

Terrell Davis			
☐ 3 Herman Moore	60.00	27.00	7.50
Kordell Stewart			
Elvis Grbac			
Chris Warren			
☐ 4 Leeland McElroy	80.00	36.00	10.00
Troy Aikman			
Zach Thomas			
Cris Carter			
☐ 5 Jim Harbaugh	70.00	32.00	8.75
Michael Jackson			
Drew Bledsoe			
Jamal Anderson			
☐ 6 John Elway	70.00	32.00	8.75
Reggie White			
Warren Moon			
Terrell Owens			
☐ 7 Rashaan Salaam	70.00	32.00	8.75
Kerry Collins			
Shannon Sharpe			
Ricky Watters			
☐ 8 Larry Centers	70.00	32.00	8.75
Mario Bates			
Eric Moulds			
Mark Brunell			
☐ 9 Jerome Bettis	60.00	27.00	7.50
Carl Pickens			
Robert Brooks			
Karim Abdul-Jabbar			
☐ 10 Jeff George	60.00	27.00	7.50
Tony Martin			
Steve Young			
Tim Biakabutuka			
☐ 11 Terry Glenn	60.00	27.00	7.50
Jeff Blake			
Mike Alstott			
Curtis Conway			
☐ 12 Rick Mirer	50.00	22.00	6.25
Anthony Johnson			
Antonio Freemn			
Joey Galloway			
☐ 13 Steve McNair	50.00	22.00	6.25
Marshall Faulk			
Jimmy Smith			
Isaac Bruce			
☐ 14 Vinny Testaverde	50.00	22.00	6.25
Rodney Hampton			
Deion Sanders			
Tony Banks			
☐ 15 Chris Chandler	50.00	22.00	6.25
Thurman Thomas			
Marvin Harrison			
Lawrence Phillips			
☐ 16 Greg Hill	30.00	13.50	3.70
Gus Frerotte			
Napoleon Kaufman			
Keyshawn Johnson			
☐ 17 Terry Allen	50.00	22.00	6.25
Eddie Kennison			
Errict Rhett			
Scott Mitchell			
☐ 18 Warrick Dunn	100.00	45.00	12.50
Jim Druckenmiller			
Orlando Pace			
Darrell Russell			

1997 Playoff Absolute Pennants

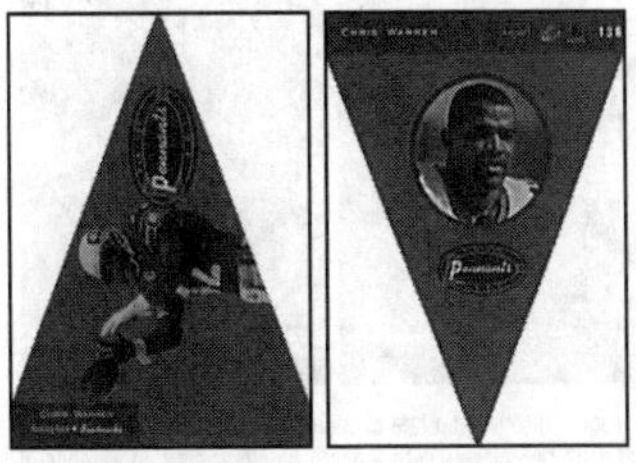

These oversized (3.5" by 5") felt pennant shaped cards were inserted one per box. Except for the different shape, they essentially form a parallel to the base set. Eight of the cards however are only included as part of the Pennant Autographs set making the total of this set 192-pennant cards.

	MINT	NRMT	EXC
COMMON CARD (1-192)	6.00	2.70	.75
SEMISTARS	10.00	4.50	1.25
UNLISTED STARS	15.00	6.75	1.85
☐ 14 Reidel Anthony	50.00	22.00	6.25
☐ 22 Sedrick Shaw	20.00	9.00	2.50
☐ 31 Warrick Dunn	70.00	32.00	8.75
☐ 38 Darnell Autry	20.00	9.00	2.50
☐ 44 Terrell Owens	50.00	22.00	6.25
☐ 46 Antowain Smith	20.00	9.00	2.50
☐ 53 Yatil Green	50.00	22.00	6.25
☐ 62 Tony Gonzalez	20.00	9.00	2.50
☐ 77 Troy Davis	40.00	18.00	5.00
☐ 81 Jerry Rice	80.00	36.00	10.00
☐ 86 Rae Carruth	25.00	11.00	3.10
☐ 101 Troy Aikman	80.00	36.00	10.00
☐ 102 Byron Hanspard	25.00	11.00	3.10
☐ 105 Drew Bledsoe	80.00	36.00	10.00
☐ 106 Eddie Kennison	40.00	18.00	5.00
☐ 107 Steve Young	50.00	22.00	6.25
☐ 110 David LaFleur	20.00	9.00	2.50
☐ 118 Ike Hilliard	50.00	22.00	6.25
☐ 120 Steve McNair	50.00	22.00	6.25
☐ 134 Danny Wuerffel	60.00	27.00	7.50
☐ 142 Jake Plummer	20.00	9.00	2.50
☐ 145 Terrell Davis	80.00	36.00	10.00
☐ 151 Brett Favre	150.00	70.00	19.00
☐ 152 Emmitt Smith	150.00	70.00	19.00
☐ 153 Dan Marino	150.00	70.00	19.00
☐ 156 Kerry Collins	60.00	27.00	7.50
☐ 163 Mark Brunell	80.00	36.00	10.00
☐ 166 Corey Dillon	25.00	11.00	3.10
☐ 167 Curtis Martin	80.00	36.00	10.00
☐ 174 Jim Druckenmiller	60.00	27.00	7.50
☐ 180 Deion Sanders	40.00	18.00	5.00
☐ 182 Shawn Springs	20.00	9.00	2.50
☐ 183 Barry Sanders	80.00	36.00	10.00
☐ 185 Marvin Harrison	40.00	18.00	5.00
☐ 187 John Elway	60.00	27.00	7.50
☐ 189 Keyshawn Johnson	40.00	18.00	5.00

1997 Playoff Absolute Pennant Autographs

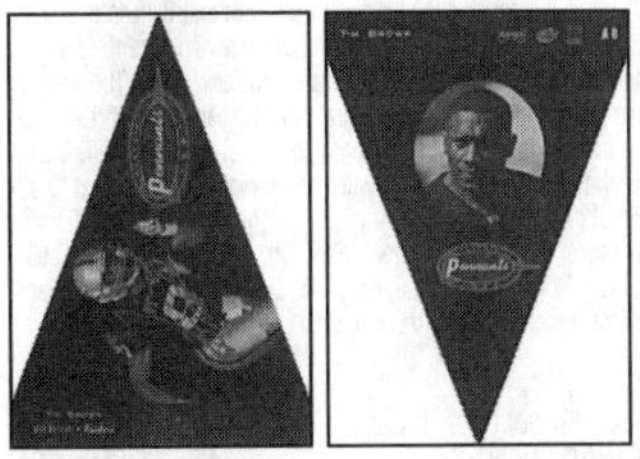

Randomly inserted at the rate of one per box, this "chip-topper" set is very similar to the Pennant Insert set except for the gold foil stamping on the side of the pennant and an autograph of one of the eight players in the set. The autographs are signed in gold ink across the photo of the player and many times onto the pennant material as well.

	MINT	NRMT	EXC
COMPLETE SET (8)	700.00	325.00	90.00
COMMON CARD (A1-A8)	50.00	22.00	6.25
☐ A1 Kordell Stewart	135.00	60.00	17.00
☐ A2 Eddie George	160.00	70.00	20.00
☐ A3 Karim Abdul-Jabbar	75.00	34.00	9.50
☐ A4 Mike Alstott	50.00	22.00	6.25
☐ A5 Terry Glenn	125.00	55.00	15.50
☐ A6 Napoleon Kaufman	50.00	22.00	6.25
☐ A7 Terry Allen	50.00	22.00	6.25
☐ A8 Tim Brown	60.00	27.00	7.50

1997 Playoff Absolute Unsung Heroes

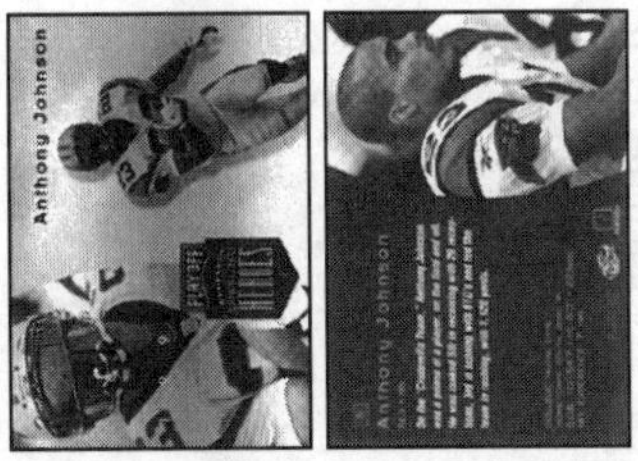

Randomly inserted in packs at the rate of one in 12, this 30 card set highlights players that are not found very often in the spotlight. The players in the set were selected by fan ballots inserted in 1996 Playoff Prime packs. Zach Thomas highlights a set full of unheralded hard workers.

	MINT	NRMT	EXC
COMPLETE SET (30)	25.00	11.00	3.10
COMMON CARD (1-30)	1.00	.45	.12
☐ 1 Larry Centers	1.50	.70	.19
☐ 2 Jessie Tuggle	1.00	.45	.12
☐ 3 Stevon Moore	1.00	.45	.12
☐ 4 Mark Pike	1.00	.45	.12
☐ 5 Anthony Johnson	1.50	.70	.19
☐ 6 Anthony Carter RB	1.00	.45	.12
☐ 7 Eric Bieniemy	1.00	.45	.12
☐ 8 Jim Schwantz	1.00	.45	.12
☐ 9 Tyrone Braxton	1.00	.45	.12
☐ 10 Bennie Blades	1.00	.45	.12
☐ 11 Don Beebe	1.50	.70	.19
☐ 12 Barron Wortham	1.00	.45	.12
☐ 13 Jason Belser	1.00	.45	.12
☐ 14 Mickey Washington	1.00	.45	.12
☐ 15 Dave Szott	1.00	.45	.12
☐ 16 Zach Thomas	4.00	1.80	.50
☐ 17 Chris Walsh	1.00	.45	.12
☐ 18 Sam Gash	1.00	.45	.12
☐ 19 Willie Roaf	1.00	.45	.12
☐ 20 Charles Way	1.00	.45	.12
☐ 21 Wayne Chrebet	2.00	.90	.25
☐ 22 Russell Maryland	1.00	.45	.12
☐ 23 Michael Zordich	1.00	.45	.12
☐ 24 Tim Lester	1.00	.45	.12
☐ 25 Harold Green	1.50	.70	.19
☐ 26 Rodney Harrison	1.00	.45	.12
☐ 27 Gary Plummer	1.00	.45	.12
☐ 28 Winston Moss	1.00	.45	.12
☐ 29 Robb Thomas	1.00	.45	.12
☐ 30 Darrick Brownlow	1.00	.45	.12

1997 Playoff Sports Cards Picks

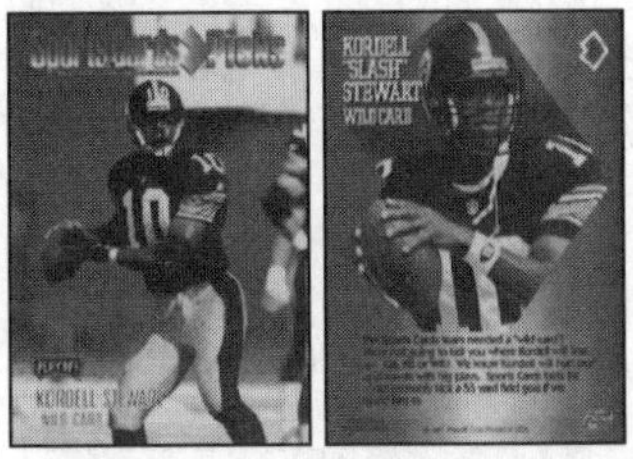

Playoff produced this set distributed by Sports Cards magazine as a subscription premium. It includes a short dream pick line-up of the staff's favorite players.

	MINT	NRMT	EXC
COMPLETE SET (6)	6.00	2.70	.75
COMMON CARD (1-6)	.75	.35	.09
☐ 1 Brett Favre	2.00	.90	.25
☐ 2 Barry Sanders	1.25	.55	.16
☐ 3 Terrell Davis	1.25	.55	.16
☐ 4 Jerry Rice	1.25	.55	.16
☐ 5 Deion Sanders	.75	.35	.09
☐ 6 Kordell Stewart	1.00	.45	.12

1997 Playoff Super Bowl Card Show

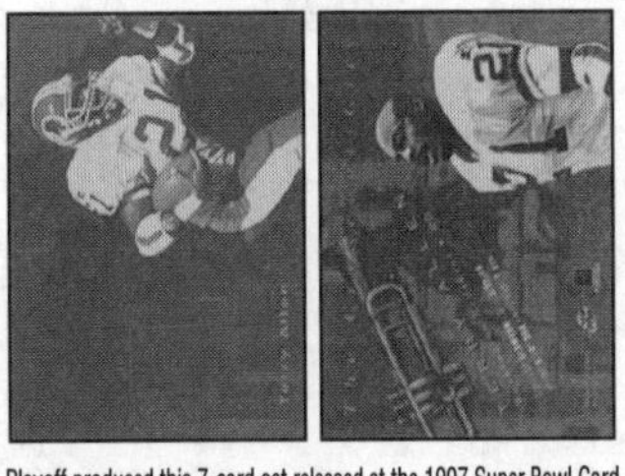

Playoff produced this 7-card set released at the 1997 Super Bowl Card Show in New Orleans. All cards, except Terrell Davis, were available each day of the show in exchange for three Playoff card wrappers opened at the Playoff booth. Two different players were made available each day Thursday through Saturday with all six available on Sunday. Terrell Davis was only available by opening and redeeming a foil box worth of wrappers for a complete 7-card set. The cards are unnumbered and listed below alphabetically.

	MINT	NRMT	EXC
COMPLETE SET (7)	20.00	9.00	2.50
COMMON CARD (1-7)	2.00	.90	.25
☐ 1 Terry Allen	2.00	.90	.25
☐ 2 Jerome Bettis	3.00	1.35	.35
☐ 3 Terrell Davis	5.00	2.20	.60
☐ 4 Marshall Faulk	3.00	1.35	.35
☐ 5 Eddie George	8.00	3.60	1.00
☐ 6 Deion Sanders	3.50	1.55	.45
☐ 7 Reggie White	3.00	1.35	.35

1993 Playoff Contenders Promos

This six-card standard-size set was issued to herald the release of the 150-card 1993 Playoff Contenders set. The fronts display borderless color action shots that have a metallic sheen. The player's name appears below the Playoff logo, both within a silver-colored box in a lower corner. The horizontal back carries a color player close-up on the left, and a broad team color-coded stripe on the right, in which appears the player's name, his team's helmet, and season highlights. The cards are numbered on the back by Roman numerals.

	MINT	NRMT	EXC
COMPLETE SET (6)	10.00	4.50	1.25
COMMON CARD (1-6)	.75	.35	.09
☐ 1 Drew Bledsoe	3.00	1.35	.35
☐ 2 Neil Smith	.75	.35	.09
☐ 3 Rick Mirer	1.25	.55	.16
☐ 4 Rodney Hampton	.75	.35	.09
☐ 5 Barry Sanders	2.00	.90	.25
☐ 6 Emmitt Smith	4.00	1.80	.50

1993 Playoff Contenders

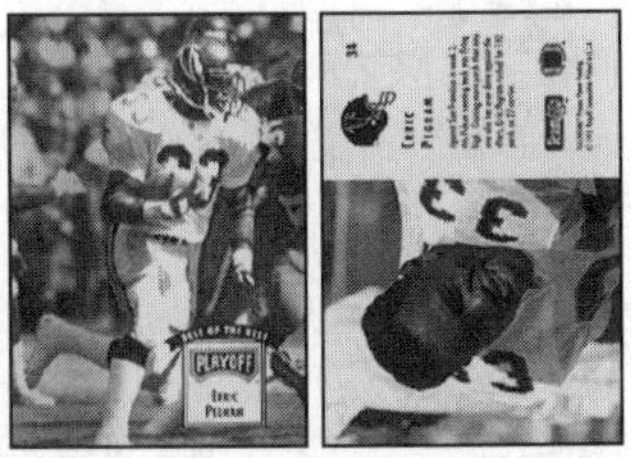

This 150-card standard-size set has fronts that display borderless color action shots that have a metallic sheen. Cards were issued in eight-card packs. The player's name appears below the Playoff logo, both within a silver-colored box usually placed in a lower corner. The horizontal back carries a color player close-up on the left, and a broad team-colored stripe on the right, in which appears the player's name, his team's helmet, and season highlights. Rookie Cards include Jerome Bettis, Drew Bledsoe, Vincent Brisby, Reggie Brooks, Curtis Conway, Garrison Hearst, Terry Kirby, Natrone Means, O.J. McDuffie, Rick Mirer, Ron Moore, Robert Smith and Kevin Williams.

	MINT	NRMT	EXC
COMPLETE SET (150)	25.00	11.00	3.10
COMMON CARD (1-150)	.10	.05	.01
☐ 1 Brett Favre	4.00	1.80	.50
☐ 2 Thurman Thomas	.40	.18	.05
☐ 3 Barry Word	.10	.05	.01
☐ 4 Herman Moore	1.50	.70	.19
☐ 5 Reggie Langhorne	.10	.05	.01
☐ 6 Wilber Marshall	.10	.05	.01
☐ 7 Ricky Watters	.40	.18	.05
☐ 8 Marcus Allen	.40	.18	.05
☐ 9 Jeff Hostetler	.20	.09	.03
☐ 10 Steve Young	1.50	.70	.19
☐ 11 Bobby Hebert	.10	.05	.01
☐ 12 David Klingler	.10	.05	.01
☐ 13 Craig Heyward	.20	.09	.03
☐ 14 Andre Reed	.20	.09	.03
☐ 15 Tommy Vardell	.10	.05	.01
☐ 16 Anthony Carter	.20	.09	.03
☐ 17 Mel Gray	.20	.09	.03
☐ 18 Dan Marino	4.00	1.80	.50
☐ 19 Haywood Jeffires	.20	.09	.03
☐ 20 Joe Montana	2.50	1.10	.30
☐ 21 Tim Brown	.40	.18	.05
☐ 22 Jim McMahon	.10	.05	.01
☐ 23 Scott Mitchell	.40	.18	.05
☐ 24 Rickey Jackson	.10	.05	.01
☐ 25 Troy Aikman	2.50	1.10	.30
☐ 26 Rodney Hampton	.40	.18	.05
☐ 27 Fred Barnett	.20	.09	.03
☐ 28 Gary Clark	.20	.09	.03
☐ 29 Barry Foster	.20	.09	.03
☐ 30 Brian Blades	.20	.09	.03
☐ 31 Tim McDonald	.10	.05	.01
☐ 32 Kelvin Martin	.10	.05	.01
☐ 33 Henry Jones	.10	.05	.01
☐ 34 Erric Pegram	.20	.09	.03
☐ 35 Don Beebe	.10	.05	.01
☐ 36 Eric Metcalf	.20	.09	.03
☐ 37 Charles Haley	.20	.09	.03
☐ 38 Robert Delpino	.10	.05	.01
☐ 39 Leonard Russell UER (Detroit Lions logo on back)	.20	.09	.03
☐ 40 Jackie Harris	.10	.05	.01
☐ 41 Ernest Givins	.20	.09	.03
☐ 42 Willie Davis	.40	.18	.05
☐ 43 Alexander Wright	.10	.05	.01
☐ 44 Keith Byars	.10	.05	.01
☐ 45 Dave Meggett	.10	.05	.01
☐ 46 Johnny Johnson	.10	.05	.01
☐ 47 Mark Bavaro	.10	.05	.01
☐ 48 Seth Joyner	.10	.05	.01
☐ 49 Junior Seau	.40	.18	.05
☐ 50 Emmitt Smith	4.00	1.80	.50
☐ 51 Shannon Sharpe	.40	.18	.05
☐ 52 Rodney Peete	.10	.05	.01
☐ 53 Andre Rison	.20	.09	.03

☐ 54 Cornelius Bennett	.20	.09	.03
☐ 55 Mark Carrier WR	.20	.09	.03
☐ 56 Mark Clayton	.10	.05	.01
☐ 57 Warren Moon	.40	.18	.05
☐ 58 J.J. Birden	.10	.05	.01
☐ 59 Howie Long	.20	.09	.03
☐ 60 Irving Fryar	.20	.09	.03
☐ 61 Mark Jackson	.10	.05	.01
☐ 62 Eric Martin	.10	.05	.01
☐ 63 Herschel Walker	.20	.09	.03
☐ 64 Cortez Kennedy	.20	.09	.03
☐ 65 Steve Beuerlein	.10	.05	.01
☐ 66 Jim Kelly	.40	.18	.05
☐ 67 Bernie Kosar	.20	.09	.03
☐ 68 Pat Swilling	.10	.05	.01
☐ 69 Michael Irvin	.40	.18	.05
☐ 70 Harvey Williams	.20	.09	.03
☐ 71 Steve Smith	.10	.05	.01
☐ 72 Wade Wilson	.10	.05	.01
☐ 73 Phil Simms	.20	.09	.03
☐ 74 Vinny Testaverde	.20	.09	.03
☐ 75 Barry Sanders	2.50	1.10	.30
☐ 76 Ken Norton Jr.	.20	.09	.03
☐ 77 Rod Woodson	.40	.18	.05
☐ 78 Webster Slaughter	.10	.05	.01
☐ 79 Derrick Thomas	.40	.18	.05
☐ 80 Mike Sherrard	.10	.05	.01
☐ 81 Calvin Williams	.20	.09	.03
☐ 82 Jay Novacek	.20	.09	.03
☐ 83 Michael Brooks	.10	.05	.01
☐ 84 Randall Cunningham	.20	.09	.03
☐ 85 Chris Warren	.20	.09	.03
☐ 86 Johnny Mitchell	.10	.05	.01
☐ 87 Jim Harbaugh	.40	.18	.05
☐ 88 Rod Bernstine	.10	.05	.01
☐ 89 John Elway	1.50	.70	.19
☐ 90 Jerry Rice	2.50	1.10	.30
☐ 91 Brent Jones	.20	.09	.03
☐ 92 Cris Carter	.40	.18	.05
☐ 93 Alvin Harper	.20	.09	.03
☐ 94 Horace Copeland	.20	.09	.03
☐ 95 Raghib Ismail	.20	.09	.03
☐ 96 Darrin Smith	.20	.09	.03
☐ 97 Reggie Brooks	.20	.09	.03
☐ 98 Demetrius DuBose	.10	.05	.01
☐ 99 Eric Curry	.10	.05	.01
☐ 100 Rick Mirer	3.00	1.35	.35
☐ 101 Carlton Gray UER (Name spelled Grey on front)	.10	.05	.01
☐ 102 Dana Stubblefield	.40	.18	.05
☐ 103 Todd Kelly	.10	.05	.01
☐ 104 Natrone Means	3.00	1.35	.35
☐ 105 Darrien Gordon	.10	.05	.01
☐ 106 Deon Figures	.20	.09	.03
☐ 107 Garrison Hearst	3.00	1.35	.35
☐ 108 Ronald Moore	.20	.09	.03
☐ 109 Leonard Renfro	.10	.05	.01
☐ 110 Lester Holmes	.10	.05	.01
☐ 111 Vaughn Hebron	.10	.05	.01
☐ 112 Marvin Jones	.10	.05	.01
☐ 113 Irv Smith	.10	.05	.01
☐ 114 Willie Roaf	.20	.09	.03
☐ 115 Derek Brown RB	.20	.09	.03
☐ 116 Vincent Brisby	.40	.18	.05
☐ 117 Drew Bledsoe	7.00	3.10	.85
☐ 118 Gino Torretta	.20	.09	.03
☐ 119 Robert Smith	2.00	.90	.25
☐ 120 Qadry Ismail	.40	.18	.05
☐ 121 O.J. McDuffie	2.00	.90	.25
☐ 122 Terry Kirby	.60	.25	.07
☐ 123 Troy Drayton	.20	.09	.03
☐ 124 Jerome Bettis	3.50	1.55	.45
☐ 125 Patrick Bates	.10	.05	.01
☐ 126 Roosevelt Potts	.10	.05	.01
☐ 127 Tom Carter	.20	.09	.03
☐ 128 Patrick Robinson	.10	.05	.01
☐ 129 Brad Hopkins	.10	.05	.01
☐ 130 George Teague	.20	.09	.03
☐ 131 Wayne Simmons	.10	.05	.01
☐ 132 Mark Brunell	7.00	3.10	.85
☐ 133 Ryan McNeil	.10	.05	.01
☐ 134 Dan Williams	.10	.05	.01
☐ 135 Glyn Milburn	.40	.18	.05
☐ 136 Kevin Williams	.60	.25	.07
☐ 137 Derrick Lassic	.10	.05	.01
☐ 138 Steve Everitt	.10	.05	.01
☐ 139 Lance Gunn	.10	.05	.01
☐ 140 John Copeland	.20	.09	.03
☐ 141 Curtis Conway	2.00	.90	.25
☐ 142 Thomas Smith	.20	.09	.03
☐ 143 Russell Copeland	.20	.09	.03
☐ 144 Lincoln Kennedy	.10	.05	.01
☐ 145 Boomer Esiason CL	.10	.05	.01
☐ 146 Neil Smith CL	.10	.05	.01
☐ 147 Jack Del Rio CL	.10	.05	.01
☐ 148 Morten Andersen CL	.10	.05	.01
☐ 149 Sterling Sharpe CL	.20	.09	.03
☐ 150 Reggie White CL	.20	.09	.03

1993 Playoff Contenders Rick Mirer

Randomly inserted in 1993 Playoff Contenders packs at an approximate rate of one in 80, these five standard-size cards feature

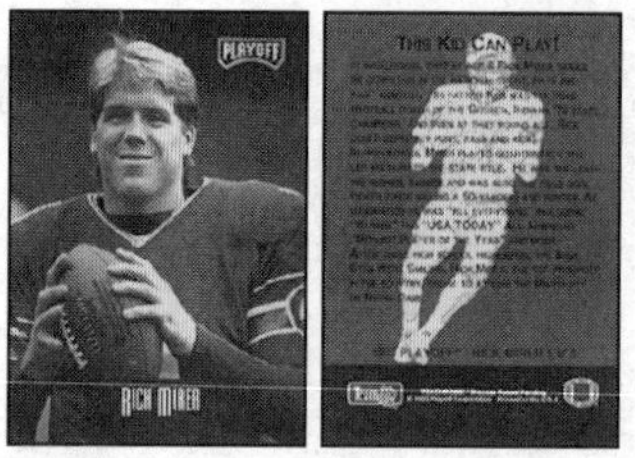

borderless fronts with color player action photos that have a metallic sheen. The player's name appears in a black box at the bottom. On a blue panel displaying a ghosted version of Mirer's photo on card number 3, the back presents career highlights. The cards are numbered on the back as "X of 5".

	MINT	NRMT	EXC
COMPLETE SET (5)	40.00	18.00	5.00
COMMON MIRER (1-5)	8.00	3.60	1.00
☐ 1 Rick Mirer This Kid Can Play	8.00	3.60	1.00
☐ 2 Rick Mirer Notre Dame All-American	8.00	3.60	1.00
☐ 3 Rick Mirer First-Round Draft Pick	8.00	3.60	1.00
☐ 4 Rick Mirer Seattle in the Hunt	8.00	3.60	1.00
☐ 5 Rick Mirer A Tough Guy	8.00	3.60	1.00

1993 Playoff Contenders Rookie Contenders

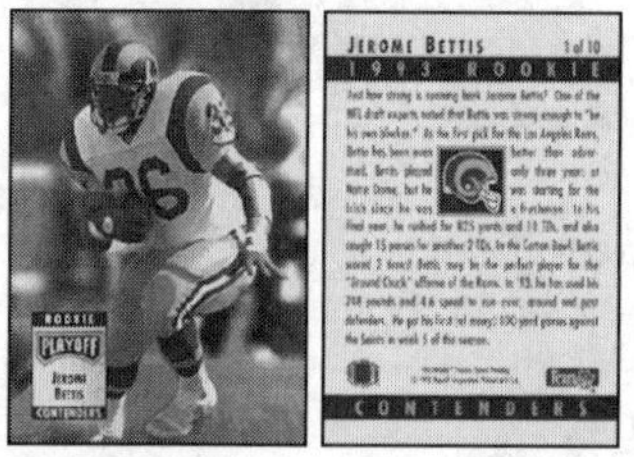

Randomly inserted in packs at an approximate rate of one in 40, these ten standard-size cards feature on their fronts borderless color player action shots that have a metallic sheen and blurred backgrounds, which serves to focus attention on the rookie. The player's name, along with the Playoff logo, appears within a gold-colored box in a lower corner. The white back carries the player's name at the top, with the set's title shown in white lettering within black stripes across the top and bottom. The player's career highlights round out the card. The cards are numbered on the back as "X of 10."

	MINT	NRMT	EXC
COMPLETE SET (10)	125.00	55.00	15.50
COMMON CARD (1-10)	4.00	1.80	.50
☐ 1 Jerome Bettis	25.00	11.00	3.10
☐ 2 Drew Bledsoe UER (Text states he played for Washington; he played for Washington St.)	50.00	22.00	6.25
☐ 3 Reggie Brooks	6.00	2.70	.75
☐ 4 Derek Brown RB	4.00	1.80	.50
☐ 5 Garrison Hearst	20.00	9.00	2.50
☐ 6 Vaughn Hebron	4.00	1.80	.50
☐ 7 Qadry Ismail	8.00	3.60	1.00
☐ 8 Derrick Lassic	4.00	1.80	.50
☐ 9 Glyn Milburn	6.00	2.70	.75
☐ 10 Dana Stubblefield	8.00	3.60	1.00

1994 Playoff Contenders Promos

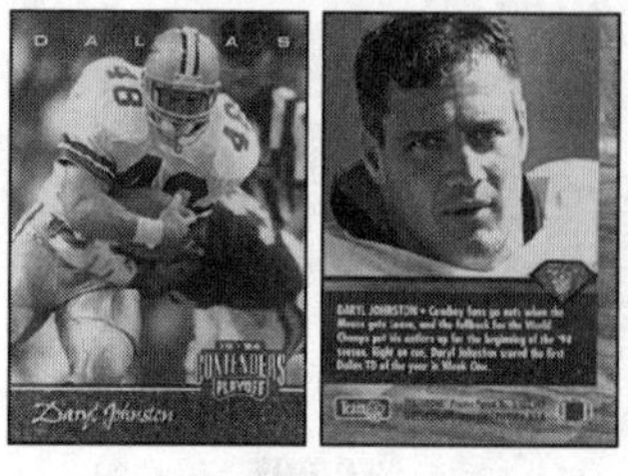

This seven-card standard-size set was issued to herald the release of the 120-card 1994 Playoff Contenders series. The fronts display borderless color action shots that have a metallic sheen. The player's name in silver foil appears in a grass border on the bottom. The team name is printed in the upper portion of the photo. The backs carry a color player close-up with season highlights. The cards are unnumbered and checklisted below in alphabetical order.

	MINT	NRMT	EXC
COMPLETE SET (7)	8.00	3.60	1.00
COMMON CARD (1-7)	.50	.23	.06
☐ 1 Qadry Ismail	3.00	1.35	.35
☐ 2 Daryl Johnston	1.00	.45	.12
☐ 3 John Jurkovic	.50	.23	.06
☐ 4 Eric Metcalf	1.50	.70	.19
☐ 5 Andre Reed	1.50	.70	.19
☐ 6 Calvin Williams	.50	.23	.06
☐ 7 Title Card	.50	.23	.06

1994 Playoff Contenders

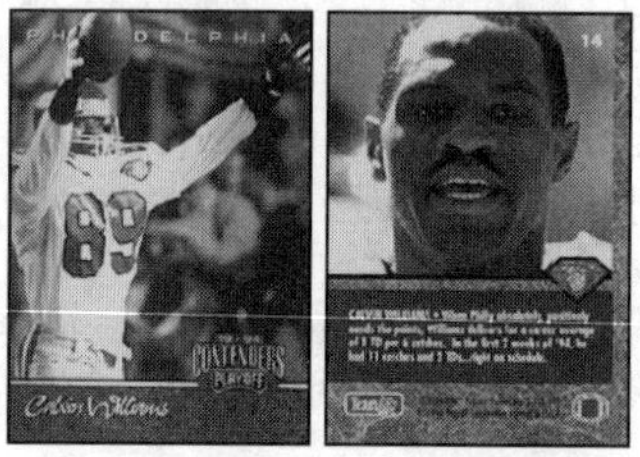

Distributed through hobby stores in the U.S. and Canada only, this 120-card set measures the standard size. The fronts display borderless color action shots that have a metallic sheen. The player's name in silver-foil appears in a grass-like border on the bottom. The team name is printed in the upper portion of the photo. The backs carry a color player close-up with season highlights. A subset "Draft Picks" (94-120) is featured in this set. Rookie Cards include Derrick Alexander, Lake Dawson, Trent Dilfer, Bert Emanuel, Marshall Faulk, William Floyd, Gus Frerotte, Greg Hill, Charles Johnson, Byron Bam Morris, Errict Rhett and Heath Shuler.

	MINT	NRMT	EXC
COMPLETE SET (120)	35.00	16.00	4.40
COMMON CARD (1-120)	.15	.07	.02
☐ 1 Drew Bledsoe	2.50	1.10	.30
☐ 2 Barry Sanders	2.50	1.10	.30
☐ 3 Jerry Rice	2.50	1.10	.30
☐ 4 Rod Woodson	.50	.23	.06
☐ 5 Irving Fryar	.30	.14	.04
☐ 6 Charles Haley	.30	.14	.04
☐ 7 Chris Warren	.30	.14	.04
☐ 8 Craig Erickson	.15	.07	.02
☐ 9 Eric Metcalf	.30	.14	.04
☐ 10 Marcus Allen	.50	.23	.06
☐ 11 Chris Miller	.15	.07	.02
☐ 12 Andre Rison	.30	.14	.04
☐ 13 Art Monk	.30	.14	.04
☐ 14 Calvin Williams	.30	.14	.04
☐ 15 Shannon Sharpe	.30	.14	.04
☐ 16 Rodney Hampton	.50	.23	.06
☐ 17 Marion Butts	.15	.07	.02
☐ 18 John Jurkovic	.30	.14	.04
☐ 19 Jim Kelly	.50	.23	.06
☐ 20 Emmitt Smith	5.00	2.20	.60
☐ 21 Jeff Hostetler	.30	.14	.04
☐ 22 Barry Foster	.15	.07	.02
☐ 23 Boomer Esiason	.30	.14	.04
☐ 24 Jim Harbaugh	.50	.23	.06
☐ 25 Joe Montana	2.50	1.10	.30
☐ 26 Jeff George	.50	.23	.06
☐ 27 Warren Moon	.50	.23	.06
☐ 28 Steve Young	2.00	.90	.25
☐ 29 Randall Cunningham	.30	.14	.04
☐ 30 Shawn Jefferson	.15	.07	.02
☐ 31 Cortez Kennedy	.30	.14	.04
☐ 32 Reggie Brooks	.30	.14	.04
☐ 33 Alvin Harper	.30	.14	.04
☐ 34 Brent Jones	.30	.14	.04
☐ 35 O.J. McDuffie	.50	.23	.06
☐ 36 Jerome Bettis	1.50	.70	.19
☐ 37 Daryl Johnston	.30	.14	.04
☐ 38 Herman Moore	1.25	.55	.16
☐ 39 Dave Meggett	.15	.07	.02
☐ 40 Reggie White	.50	.23	.06
☐ 41 Junior Seau	.50	.23	.06
☐ 42 Dan Marino	5.00	2.20	.60
☐ 43 Scott Mitchell	.50	.23	.06
☐ 44 John Elway	2.00	.90	.25
☐ 45 Troy Aikman	2.50	1.10	.30
☐ 46 Terry Allen	.30	.14	.04
☐ 47 David Klingler	.15	.07	.02
☐ 48 Stan Humphries	.50	.23	.06
☐ 49 Rick Mirer	.50	.23	.06
☐ 50 Neil O'Donnell	.50	.23	.06
☐ 51 Keith Jackson	.15	.07	.02
☐ 52 Ricky Watters	.50	.23	.06
☐ 53 Dave Brown	.30	.14	.04
☐ 54 Neil Smith	.50	.23	.06
☐ 55 Johnny Mitchell	.15	.07	.02
☐ 56 Jackie Harris	.15	.07	.02
☐ 57 Terry Kirby	.50	.23	.06
☐ 58 Willie Davis	.30	.14	.04
☐ 59 Rob Moore	.30	.14	.04
☐ 60 Nate Newton	.15	.07	.02
☐ 61 Deion Sanders	2.00	.90	.25
☐ 62 John Taylor	.30	.14	.04
☐ 63 Sterling Sharpe	.30	.14	.04
☐ 64 Natrone Means	1.25	.55	.16
☐ 65 Steve Beuerlein	.15	.07	.02
☐ 66 Erik Kramer	.30	.14	.04
☐ 67 Qadry Ismail	.50	.23	.06
☐ 68 Johnny Johnson	.15	.07	.02
☐ 69 Herschel Walker	.30	.14	.04
☐ 70 Mark Stepnoski	.15	.07	.02
☐ 71 Brett Favre	5.00	2.20	.60
☐ 72 Dana Stubblefield	.50	.23	.06
☐ 73 Bruce Smith	.50	.23	.06
☐ 74 Leroy Hoard	.15	.07	.02
☐ 75 Steve Walsh	.15	.07	.02
☐ 76 Jay Novacek	.30	.14	.04
☐ 77 Derrick Thomas	.50	.23	.06
☐ 78 Keith Byars	.15	.07	.02
☐ 79 Ben Coates	.50	.23	.06
☐ 80 Lorenzo Neal	.15	.07	.02
☐ 81 Ronnie Lott	.30	.14	.04
☐ 82 Tim Brown	.50	.23	.06
☐ 83 Michael Irvin	.50	.23	.06
☐ 84 Ronald Moore	.15	.07	.02
☐ 85 Andre Reed	.30	.14	.04
☐ 86 James Jett	.15	.07	.02
☐ 87 Curtis Conway	.50	.23	.06
☐ 88 Bernie Parmalee	.50	.23	.06
☐ 89 Keith Cash	.15	.07	.02
☐ 90 Russell Copeland	.15	.07	.02
☐ 91 Kevin Williams	.30	.14	.04
☐ 92 Gary Brown	.15	.07	.02
☐ 93 Thurman Thomas	.50	.23	.06
☐ 94 Jamir Miller	.15	.07	.02
☐ 95 Bert Emanuel	1.50	.70	.19
☐ 96 Bucky Brooks	.15	.07	.02
☐ 97 Jeff Burris	.30	.14	.04
☐ 98 Antonio Langham	.30	.14	.04
☐ 99 Derrick Alexander WR	.50	.23	.06
☐ 100 Dan Wilkinson	.30	.14	.04
☐ 101 Shante Carver	.15	.07	.02
☐ 102 Johnnie Morton	.75	.35	.09
☐ 103 LeShon Johnson	.30	.14	.04
☐ 104 Marshall Faulk	4.00	1.80	.50
☐ 105 Greg Hill	1.00	.45	.12
☐ 106 Lake Dawson	1.00	.45	.12
☐ 107 Irving Spikes	.30	.14	.04
☐ 108 David Palmer	.30	.14	.04
☐ 109 Willie McGinest	.50	.23	.06
☐ 110 Joe Johnson	.15	.07	.02
☐ 111 Aaron Glenn	.30	.14	.04
☐ 112 Charlie Garner	.30	.14	.04
☐ 113 Charles Johnson	.75	.35	.09
☐ 114 Byron Bam Morris	.50	.23	.06
☐ 115 Bryant Young	.75	.35	.09
☐ 116 William Floyd	1.50	.70	.19
☐ 117 Trent Dilfer	1.25	.55	.16
☐ 118 Errict Rhett	2.00	.90	.25
☐ 119 Heath Shuler	1.50	.70	.19
☐ 120 Gus Frerotte	3.00	1.35	.35

1994 Playoff Contenders Back-to-Back

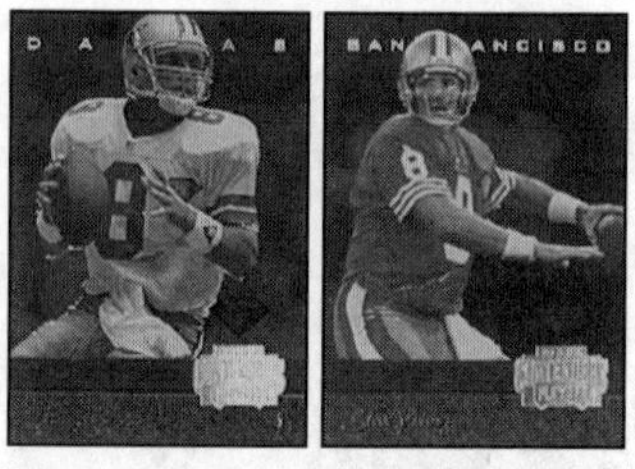

Randomly inserted at a rate of one in 24, this 60-card standard-size set pairs two players with a photo on either side. In essence, it parallels the 120-card basic Playoff Contenders set. The difference being the two photo format. Either side is metallic with an action photo that is bordered at the bottom by the player's name and a silver Playoff Contenders logo.

	MINT	NRMT	EXC
COMPLETE SET (60)	2000.00	900.00	250.00
COMMON PAIR (1-60)	15.00	6.75	1.85
☐ 1 Joe Montana Dan Marino	400.00	180.00	50.00
☐ 2 Drew Bledsoe John Elway	150.00	70.00	19.00
☐ 3 Jerry Rice Sterling Sharpe	100.00	45.00	12.50
☐ 4 Barry Sanders Emmitt Smith	250.00	110.00	31.00
☐ 5 Troy Aikman Steve Young	150.00	70.00	19.00
☐ 6 Erik Kramer	15.00	6.75	1.85

	MINT	NRMT	EXC
Steve Walsh			
☐ 7 Nate Newton	20.00	9.00	2.50
Bruce Smith			
☐ 8 Johnny Mitchell	15.00	6.75	1.85
Aaron Glenn			
☐ 9 Neil O'Donnell	15.00	6.75	1.85
Jay Novacek			
☐ 10 Herman Moore	40.00	18.00	5.00
Calvin Williams			
☐ 11 Alvin Harper	25.00	11.00	3.10
Michael Irvin			
☐ 12 Jim Harbaugh	30.00	13.50	3.70
Curtis Conway			
☐ 13 Brett Favre	150.00	70.00	19.00
LeShon Johnson			
☐ 14 Eric Metcalf	50.00	22.00	6.25
Marshall Faulk			
☐ 15 Qadry Ismail	20.00	9.00	2.50
David Palmer			
☐ 16 Deion Sanders	50.00	22.00	6.25
Andre Rison			
☐ 17 Jackie Harris	30.00	13.50	3.70
Errict Rhett			
☐ 18 Keith Jackson	15.00	6.75	1.85
Irving Spikes			
☐ 19 Dave Meggett	15.00	6.75	1.85
Jeff Burris			
☐ 20 Dana Stubblefield	20.00	9.00	2.50
William Floyd			
☐ 21 Randall Cunningham	25.00	11.00	3.10
Reggie White			
☐ 22 Shannon Sharpe	15.00	6.75	1.85
Keith Cash			
☐ 23 Marcus Allen	25.00	11.00	3.10
Derrick Thomas			
☐ 24 Irving Fryar	15.00	6.75	1.85
Russell Copeland			
☐ 25 Johnny Johnson	15.00	6.75	1.85
Ben Coates			
☐ 26 John Taylor	20.00	9.00	2.50
Brent Jones			
☐ 27 Terry Kirby	20.00	9.00	2.50
Bernie Parmalee			
☐ 28 Ricky Watters	25.00	11.00	3.10
Ronnie Lott			
☐ 29 Scott Mitchell	15.00	6.75	1.85
James Jett			
☐ 30 O.J. McDuffie	25.00	11.00	3.10
Keith Byars			
☐ 31 Shawn Jefferson	20.00	9.00	2.50
Andre Reed			
☐ 32 Rodney Hampton	20.00	9.00	2.50
Lorenzo Neal			
☐ 33 Chris Miller	15.00	6.75	1.85
Ronald Moore			
☐ 34 Charles Haley	25.00	11.00	3.10
Thurman Thomas			
☐ 35 Herschel Walker	15.00	6.75	1.85
Leroy Hoard			
☐ 36 Natrone Means	35.00	16.00	4.40
Stan Humphries			
☐ 37 Willie Davis	20.00	9.00	2.50
Kevin Williams WR			
☐ 38 Dave Brown	15.00	6.75	1.85
Gary Brown			
☐ 39 Jerome Bettis	60.00	27.00	7.50
Terry Allen			
☐ 40 Cortez Kennedy	20.00	9.00	2.50
Junior Seau			
☐ 41 David Klingler	20.00	9.00	2.50
Derrick Alexander			
☐ 42 Chris Warren	20.00	9.00	2.50
Bucky Brooks			
☐ 43 Mark Stepnoski	20.00	9.00	2.50
Greg Hill			
☐ 44 Steve Beuerlein	20.00	9.00	2.50
Johnnie Morton			
☐ 45 Rob Moore	15.00	6.75	1.85
James Jett			
☐ 46 Neil Smith	20.00	9.00	2.50
Lake Dawson			
☐ 47 Rick Mirer	25.00	11.00	3.10
Bryant Young			
☐ 48 Daryl Johnston	15.00	6.75	1.85
Charlie Garner			
☐ 49 Reggie Brooks	35.00	16.00	4.40
Gus Frerotte			
☐ 50 Barry Foster	20.00	9.00	2.50
Byron Bam Morris			
☐ 51 Art Monk	25.00	11.00	3.10
Heath Shuler			
☐ 52 Craig Erickson	20.00	9.00	2.50
Trent Dilfer			
☐ 53 Jeff George	20.00	9.00	2.50
Bert Emanuel			
☐ 54 Rod Woodson	20.00	9.00	2.50
Antonio Langham			
☐ 55 Marion Butts	15.00	6.75	1.85
Willie McGinest			
☐ 56 John Jurkovic	15.00	6.75	1.85
Dan Wilkinson			
☐ 57 Jim Kelly	25.00	11.00	3.10
Shante Carver			
☐ 58 Jeff Hostetler	15.00	6.75	1.85
Charles Johnson			
☐ 59 Boomer Esiason	15.00	6.75	1.85
Jamir Miller			
☐ 60 Warren Moon	20.00	9.00	2.50
Joe Johnson			

1994 Playoff Contenders Rookie Contenders

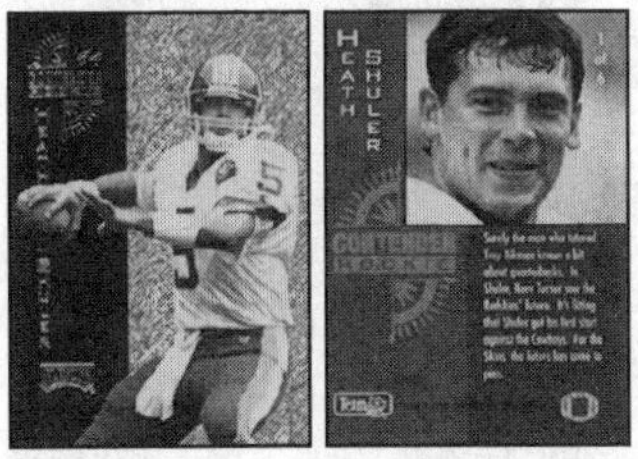

Randomly inserted in packs at a rate of one in 48, this six-card standard-size set spotlights some of the top rookies from 1994. Metallic card fronts have an action photo superimposed over a silver prismatic background with a thick deep purple left border. The backs have a small player photo and highlights.

	MINT	NRMT	EXC
COMPLETE SET (6)	120.00	55.00	15.00
COMMON CARD (1-6)	8.00	3.60	1.00
☐ 1 Heath Shuler	15.00	6.75	1.85
☐ 2 Trent Dilfer	12.00	5.50	1.50
☐ 3 David Palmer	8.00	3.60	1.00
☐ 4 Marshall Faulk	40.00	18.00	5.00
☐ 5 Charlie Garner	8.00	3.60	1.00
☐ 6 Dan Wilkinson	8.00	3.60	1.00

1994 Playoff Contenders Sophomore Contenders

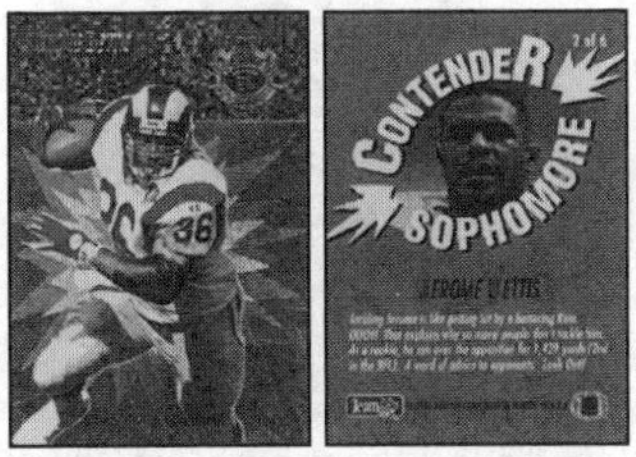

Randomly inserted at a rate of one in 48, this six-card standard-size set spotlights some of the top second year players. An action photo is superimposed over a background that consists of a prismatic silver border and a deep purple upper border. Dark blue backs have a small player photo and brief highlights.

	MINT	NRMT	EXC
COMPLETE SET (6)	90.00	40.00	11.00
COMMON CARD (1-6)	6.00	2.70	.75
☐ 1 Drew Bledsoe	50.00	22.00	6.25
☐ 2 Jerome Bettis	20.00	9.00	2.50
☐ 3 Reggie Brooks	6.00	2.70	.75
☐ 4 Rick Mirer	8.00	3.60	1.00
☐ 5 Natrone Means	12.00	5.50	1.50
☐ 6 O.J.McDuffie	8.00	3.60	1.00

1994 Playoff Contenders Throwbacks

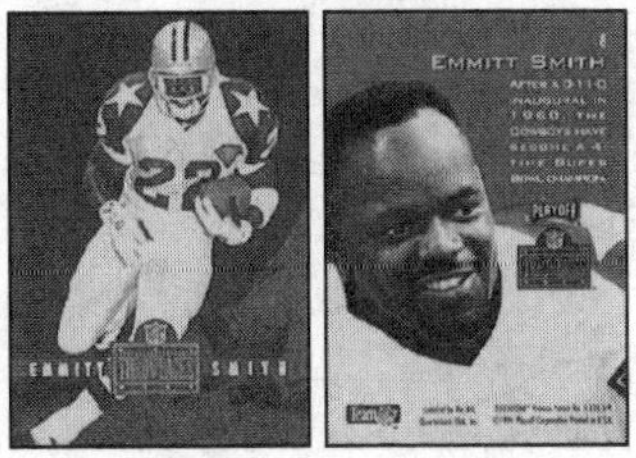

Randomly inserted in packs at a rate of one in 12, this 30-card standard-size set takes a look at Throwback uniforms that were occasionally worn by each NFL team during the 1994 campaign. This was done to help celebrate the National Football League's 75th Anniversary. Full-bleed metallic fronts with purplish backgrounds feature the player in his Throwback uniform emerging from a generic game action photo.The backs have a close-up of the player with a brief write-up.

	MINT	NRMT	EXC
COMPLETE SET (30)	175.00	80.00	22.00
COMMON CARD (1-30)	2.00	.90	.25
☐ 1 Larry Centers	4.00	1.80	.50
☐ 2 Andre Rison	4.00	1.80	.50
☐ 3 Jim Kelly	6.00	2.70	.75
☐ 4 Curtis Conway	6.00	2.70	.75
☐ 5 David Klingler	2.00	.90	.25
☐ 6 Vinny Testaverde	2.00	.90	.25
☐ 7 Troy Aikman	15.00	6.75	1.85
☐ 8 Emmitt Smith	30.00	13.50	3.70
☐ 9 John Elway	12.00	5.50	1.50
☐ 10 Barry Sanders	15.00	6.75	1.85
☐ 11 Sterling Sharpe	4.00	1.80	.50
☐ 12 Gary Brown	2.00	.90	.25
☐ 13 Jim Harbaugh	4.00	1.80	.50
☐ 14 Joe Montana	15.00	6.75	1.85
☐ 15 Tim Brown	4.00	1.80	.50
☐ 16 Chris Miller	2.00	.90	.25
☐ 17 Dan Marino	30.00	13.50	3.70
☐ 18 Terry Allen	4.00	1.80	.50
☐ 19 Marion Butts	2.00	.90	.25
☐ 20 Jim Everett	2.00	.90	.25
☐ 21 Dave Brown	2.00	.90	.25
☐ 22 Johnny Johnson	2.00	.90	.25
☐ 23 Randall Cunningham	2.00	.90	.25
☐ 24 Barry Foster	2.00	.90	.25
☐ 25 Stan Humphries	2.00	.90	.25
☐ 26 Jerry Rice	15.00	6.75	1.85
☐ 27 Steve Young	12.00	5.50	1.50
☐ 28 Chris Warren	4.00	1.80	.50
☐ 29 Errict Rhett	6.00	2.70	.75
☐ 30 John Friesz	2.00	.90	.25

1995 Playoff Contenders

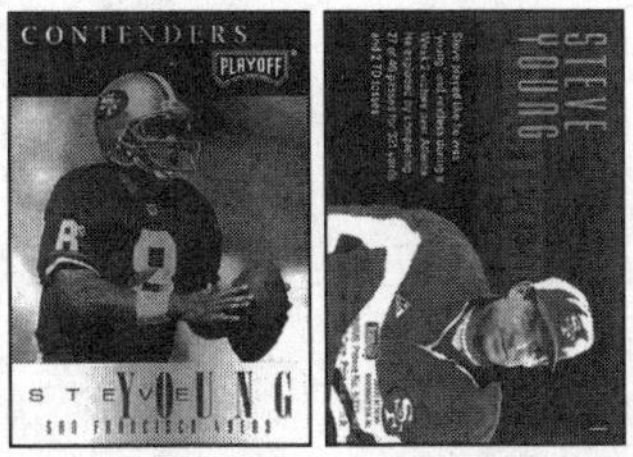

The 1995 Playoff Contenders was issued in one series totalling 150 cards. The 6-card pack retails for $3.75. Card fronts feature a navy background at the top of the card with a silver background at the bottom. Card backs feature a navy and black background with a player shot, the player's name in the upper left and a brief statistical summary at the bottom left. The set features the topical subset: Rookies (121-150). Rookie Cards include Kerry Collins, Terrell Davis, Joey Galloway, Curtis Martin, Steve McNair, Rashaan Salaam, Kordell Stewart, J.J. Stokes, Yancey Thigpen, Tamarick Vanover and Michael Westbrook.

	MINT	NRMT	EXC
COMPLETE SET (150)	25.00	11.00	3.10
COMMON CARD (1-150)	.08	.04	.01
☐ 1 Steve Young	1.00	.45	.12
☐ 2 Jeff Blake	1.25	.55	.16
☐ 3 Rick Mirer	.30	.14	.04
☐ 4 Brett Favre	2.50	1.10	.30
☐ 5 Heath Shuler	.30	.14	.04
☐ 6 Steve Bono	.15	.07	.02
☐ 7 John Elway	1.00	.45	.12
☐ 8 Troy Aikman	1.25	.55	.16
☐ 9 Rodney Peete	.08	.04	.01
☐ 10 Gus Frerotte	.60	.25	.07
☐ 11 Drew Bledsoe	1.25	.55	.16
☐ 12 Jim Kelly	.30	.14	.04
☐ 13 Dan Marino	2.50	1.10	.30
☐ 14 Errict Rhett	.30	.14	.04
☐ 15 Jeff Hostetler	.15	.07	.02
☐ 16 Erik Kramer	.08	.04	.01
☐ 17 Jim Everett	.08	.04	.01
☐ 18 Elvis Grbac	.30	.14	.04
☐ 19 Scott Mitchell	.15	.07	.02
☐ 20 Barry Sanders	1.25	.55	.16
☐ 21 Deion Sanders	.75	.35	.09
☐ 22 Emmitt Smith	2.50	1.10	.30
☐ 23 Garrison Hearst	.30	.14	.04
☐ 24 Mario Bates	.30	.14	.04
☐ 25 Mark Brunell	1.25	.55	.16
☐ 26 Robert Smith	.30	.14	.04
☐ 27 Rodney Hampton	.15	.07	.02
☐ 28 Marshall Faulk	.60	.25	.07
☐ 29 Greg Hill	.15	.07	.02
☐ 30 Bernie Parmalee	.15	.07	.02
☐ 31 Natrone Means	.30	.14	.04
☐ 32 Marcus Allen	.30	.14	.04
☐ 33 Byron Bam Morris	.15	.07	.02
☐ 34 Edgar Bennett	.15	.07	.02
☐ 35 Vincent Brisby	.08	.04	.01
☐ 36 Jerome Bettis	.50	.23	.06
☐ 37 Craig Heyward	.15	.07	.02
☐ 38 Anthony Miller	.15	.07	.02
☐ 39 Curtis Conway	.30	.14	.04
☐ 40 William Floyd	.30	.14	.04
☐ 41 Chris Warren	.15	.07	.02
☐ 42 Terry Kirby	.15	.07	.02
☐ 43 Herschel Walker	.15	.07	.02
☐ 44 Eric Metcalf	.15	.07	.02
☐ 45 Darnay Scott	.30	.14	.04
☐ 46 Jackie Harris	.08	.04	.01
☐ 47 Dana Stubblefield	.30	.14	.04
☐ 48 Daryl Johnston	.15	.07	.02
☐ 49 Dave Meggett	.08	.04	.01
☐ 50 Ricky Watters	.30	.14	.04
☐ 51 Ken Norton	.15	.07	.02
☐ 52 Boomer Esiason	.15	.07	.02
☐ 53 Lake Dawson	.15	.07	.02
☐ 54 Eric Green	.08	.04	.01
☐ 55 Junior Seau	.30	.14	.04
☐ 56 Yancey Thigpen	1.00	.45	.12
☐ 57 James Jett	.15	.07	.02
☐ 58 Leonard Russell	.08	.04	.01
☐ 59 Brent Jones	.08	.04	.01
☐ 60 Trent Dilfer	.30	.14	.04
☐ 61 Terance Mathis	.15	.07	.02
☐ 62 Jeff George	.15	.07	.02
☐ 63 Alvin Harper	.08	.04	.01
☐ 64 Terry Allen	.15	.07	.02
☐ 65 Stan Humphries	.15	.07	.02
☐ 66 Robert Green	.08	.04	.01
☐ 67 Bryce Paup	.30	.14	.04
☐ 68 Tamarick Vanover	1.25	.55	.16
☐ 69 Desmond Howard	.15	.07	.02
☐ 70 Derek Loville	.08	.04	.01
☐ 71 Dave Brown	.15	.07	.02
☐ 72 Carl Pickens	.30	.14	.04
☐ 73 Gary Clark	.08	.04	.01
☐ 74 Gary Brown	.08	.04	.01
☐ 75 Brett Perriman	.15	.07	.02
☐ 76 Charlie Garner	.15	.07	.02
☐ 77 Ben Coates	.15	.07	.02
☐ 78 Bruce Smith	.30	.14	.04
☐ 79 Eric Pegram	.15	.07	.02
☐ 80 Jerry Rice	1.25	.55	.16
☐ 81 Tim Brown	.30	.14	.04
☐ 82 John Taylor	.08	.04	.01
☐ 83 Will Moore	.08	.04	.01
☐ 84 Jay Novacek	.15	.07	.02
☐ 85 Kevin Williams	.15	.07	.02
☐ 86 Rocket Ismail	.15	.07	.02
☐ 87 Robert Brooks	.30	.14	.04
☐ 88 Michael Irvin	.30	.14	.04
☐ 89 Mark Chmura	.75	.35	.09
☐ 90 Shannon Sharpe	.15	.07	.02
☐ 91 Henry Ellard	.15	.07	.02
☐ 92 Reggie White	.30	.14	.04
☐ 93 Isaac Bruce	.60	.25	.07
☐ 94 Charles Haley	.15	.07	.02
☐ 95 Jake Reed	.15	.07	.02
☐ 96 Pete Metzelaars	.08	.04	.01
☐ 97 Dave Krieg	.08	.04	.01
☐ 98 Tony Martin	.15	.07	.02
☐ 99 Charles Jordan	.08	.04	.01
☐ 100 Bert Emanuel	.30	.14	.04
☐ 101 Andre Rison	.15	.07	.02
☐ 102 Jeff Graham	.08	.04	.01
☐ 103 O.J. McDuffie	.30	.14	.04
☐ 104 Randall Cunningham	.15	.07	.02
☐ 105 Harvey Williams	.08	.04	.01
☐ 106 Cris Carter	.30	.14	.04
☐ 107 Irving Fryar	.15	.07	.02
☐ 108 Jim Harbaugh	.15	.07	.02
☐ 109 Bernie Kosar	.08	.04	.01
☐ 110 Charles Johnson	.15	.07	.02
☐ 111 Warren Moon	.15	.07	.02
☐ 112 Neil O'Donnell	.15	.07	.02
☐ 113 Fred Barnett	.15	.07	.02
☐ 114 Herman Moore	.60	.25	.07
☐ 115 Chris Miller	.08	.04	.01
☐ 116 Vinny Testaverde	.15	.07	.02
☐ 117 Craig Erickson	.08	.04	.01
☐ 118 Qadry Ismail	.15	.07	.02
☐ 119 Willie Davis	.15	.07	.02
☐ 120 Michael Jackson	.15	.07	.02
☐ 121 Stoney Case	.08	.04	.01
☐ 122 Frank Sanders	.30	.14	.04
☐ 123 Todd Collins	.30	.14	.04
☐ 124 Kerry Collins	3.00	1.35	.35
☐ 125 Sherman Williams	.08	.04	.01
☐ 126 Terrell Davis	4.00	1.80	.50
☐ 127 Luther Elliss	.08	.04	.01
☐ 128 Steve McNair	2.50	1.10	.30
☐ 129 Chris Sanders	1.25	.55	.16
☐ 130 Ki-Jana Carter	1.00	.45	.12
☐ 131 Rodney Thomas	.30	.14	.04
☐ 132 Tony Boselli	.15	.07	.02
☐ 133 Rob Johnson	.08	.04	.01
☐ 134 James O.Stewart	.30	.14	.04
☐ 135 Chad May	.08	.04	.01
☐ 136 Eric Bjornson	.15	.07	.02
☐ 137 Tyrone Wheatley	.50	.23	.06
☐ 138 Kyle Brady	.30	.14	.04
☐ 139 Curtis Martin	4.00	1.80	.50
☐ 140 Eric Zeier	.30	.14	.04
☐ 141 Ray Zellars	.15	.07	.02
☐ 142 Napoleon Kaufman	1.00	.45	.12

☐ 143 Mike Mamula	.15	.07	.02
☐ 144 Mark Bruener	.15	.07	.02
☐ 145 Kordell Stewart	3.00	1.35	.35
☐ 146 J.J. Stokes	1.00	.45	.12
☐ 147 Joey Galloway	2.00	.90	.25
☐ 148 Warren Sapp	.15	.07	.02
☐ 149 Michael Westbrook	1.25	.55	.16
☐ 150 Rashaan Salaam	1.25	.55	.16

1995 Playoff Contenders Back-To-Back

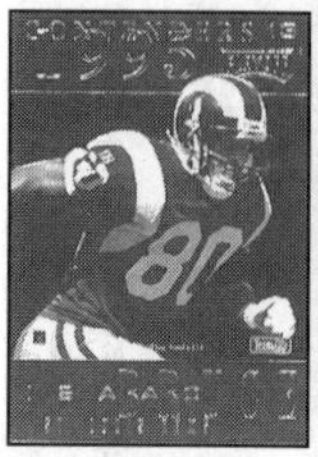

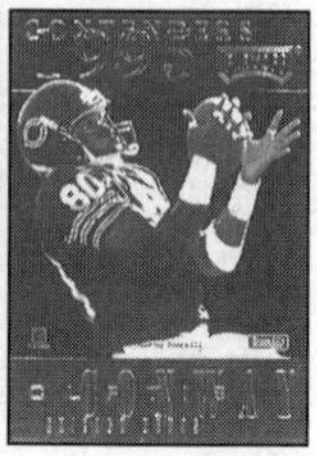

Randomly inserted in packs at a rate of one in 19, this 75 card parallel set features 150 of the regular player cards including the Rookies subset. The cards have a gold embossed bar at the top and a silver embossed bar at the bottom. The players are featured against a black background in the center.

	MINT	NRMT	EXC
COMPLETE SET (75)	1400.00	650.00	180.00
COMMON CARD (1-75)	10.00	4.50	1.25
☐ 1 Dan Marino Troy Aikman	140.00	65.00	17.50
☐ 2 Marshall Faulk Emmitt Smith	100.00	45.00	12.50
☐ 3 John Elway Brett Favre	120.00	55.00	15.00
☐ 4 Drew Bledsoe Steve Young	80.00	36.00	10.00
☐ 5 Errict Rhett Barry Sanders	70.00	32.00	8.75
☐ 6 Jerry Rice Deion Sanders	70.00	32.00	8.75
☐ 7 Rick Mirer Jeff Blake	20.00	9.00	2.50
☐ 8 Tim Brown Michael Irvin	20.00	9.00	2.50
☐ 9 Ricky Watters Chris Warren	15.00	6.75	1.85
☐ 10 Vincent Brisby Herman Moore	20.00	9.00	2.50
☐ 11 Eric Metcalf James Jett	15.00	6.75	1.85
☐ 12 Terance Mathis Henry Ellard	15.00	6.75	1.85
☐ 13 Isaac Bruce Curtis Conway	30.00	13.50	3.70
☐ 14 Jeff Hostetler Steve Bono	15.00	6.75	1.85
☐ 15 Harvey Williams Greg Hill	15.00	6.75	1.85
☐ 16 Jerome Bettis Garrison Hearst	30.00	13.50	3.70
☐ 17 Brent Jones Jay Novacek	15.00	6.75	1.85
☐ 18 Bruce Smith Reggie White	20.00	9.00	2.50
☐ 19 Shannon Sharpe Eric Green	15.00	6.75	1.85
☐ 20 Jeff George Gus Frerotte	15.00	6.75	1.85
☐ 21 Scott Mitchell Erik Kramer	10.00	4.50	1.25
☐ 22 Jim Kelly Warren Moon	20.00	9.00	2.50
☐ 23 Ben Coates Mark Chmura	15.00	6.75	1.85
☐ 24 Heath Shuler Trent Dilfer	20.00	9.00	2.50
☐ 25 Edgar Bennett Craig Heyward	15.00	6.75	1.85
☐ 26 Dave Brown Jim Everett	10.00	4.50	1.25
☐ 27 Ande Rison Bert Emanuel	10.00	4.50	1.25
☐ 28 Alvin Harper Robert Brooks	10.00	4.50	1.25
☐ 29 Tony Martin Desmond Howard	15.00	6.75	1.85
☐ 30 Fred Barnett Rodney Peete	10.00	4.50	1.25
☐ 31 William Floyd Natrone Means	15.00	6.75	1.85
☐ 32 Rocket Ismail Brett Perriman	10.00	4.50	1.25
☐ 33 Irving Fryar Cris Carter	15.00	6.75	1.85
☐ 34 Darnay Scott Tamarick Vanover	20.00	9.00	2.50
☐ 35 Dana Stubblefield Charles Haley	15.00	6.75	1.85
☐ 36 Ken Norton Bryce Paup	10.00	4.50	1.25
☐ 37 Herschel Walker Marcus Allen	20.00	9.00	2.50
☐ 38 Terry Allen Leonard Russell	10.00	4.50	1.25
☐ 39 Derek Loville Junior Seau	15.00	6.75	1.85
☐ 40 Charles Johnson Lake Dawson	15.00	6.75	1.85
☐ 41 Charles Jordan Kevin Williams	10.00	4.50	1.25
☐ 42 Carl Pickens Jeff Graham	15.00	6.75	1.85
☐ 43 O.J.McDuffie Anthony Miller	15.00	6.75	1.85
☐ 44 Jim Harbaugh Elvis Grbac	15.00	6.75	1.85
☐ 45 Terry Kirby Dave Meggett	15.00	6.75	1.85
☐ 46 Stan Humphries Dave Krieg	10.00	4.50	1.25
☐ 47 Boomer Esiason Mark Brunell	60.00	27.00	7.50
☐ 48 Vinny Testaverde Craig Erickson	10.00	4.50	1.25
☐ 49 Bernie Kosar Randall Cunningham	10.00	4.50	1.25
☐ 50 Charlie Garner Erric Pegram	10.00	4.50	1.25
☐ 51 Gary Clark Will Moore	10.00	4.50	1.25
☐ 52 Willie Davis Qadry Ismail	15.00	6.75	1.85
☐ 53 Chris Miller Neil O'Donnell	10.00	4.50	1.25
☐ 54 Robert Smith Mario Bates	15.00	6.75	1.85
☐ 55 Bernie Parmalee Rodney Hampton	15.00	6.75	1.85
☐ 56 Daryl Johnston Byron Bam Morris	15.00	6.75	1.85
☐ 57 Jake Reed Jack Harris	10.00	4.50	1.25
☐ 58 Pete Metzelaars John Taylor	10.00	4.50	1.25
☐ 59 Michael Jackson Yancey Thigpen	20.00	9.00	2.50
☐ 60 Robert Green Gary Brown	10.00	4.50	1.25
☐ 61 N.Kaufman Rashaan Salaam	20.00	9.00	2.50
☐ 62 Kyle Brady Mark Bruener	10.00	4.50	1.25
☐ 63 Rodney Thomas Ki-Jana Carter	20.00	9.00	2.50
☐ 64 Steve McNair Chad May	60.00	27.00	7.50
☐ 65 J.J.Stokes Frank Sanders	20.00	9.00	2.50
☐ 66 Warren Sapp Mike Mamula	10.00	4.50	1.25
☐ 67 Stoney Case Kordell Stewart	70.00	32.00	8.75
☐ 68 Curtis Martin Terrell Davis	100.00	45.00	12.50
☐ 69 Chris Sanders Sherman Williams	20.00	9.00	2.50
☐ 70 Eric Bjornson James O.Stewart	15.00	6.75	1.85
☐ 71 Ray Zellars Tyrone Wheatley	15.00	6.75	1.85
☐ 72 Luther Elliss Tony Boselli	15.00	6.75	1.85
☐ 73 Todd Collins Rob Johnson	15.00	6.75	1.85
☐ 74 Eric Zeier Kerry Collins	70.00	32.00	8.75
☐ 75 Michael Westbrook Joey Galloway	50.00	22.00	6.25

1995 Playoff Contenders Hog Heaven

Randomly inserted in packs at a rate of one in 48, this 30-card set features a leather-shaped football on the front with a foil branded player image and team logo. The player's name and the "Playoff" symbol are in gold at the bottom of the front. Card backs are all brown leather with the player's image in black and the player's name, position and team. Card backs are numbered with a "HH" prefix.

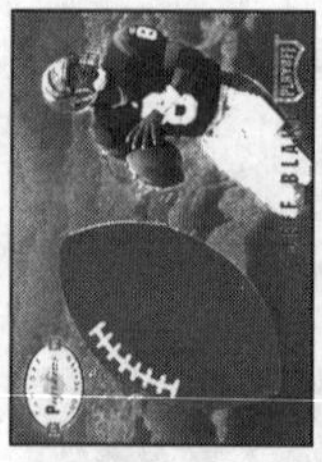

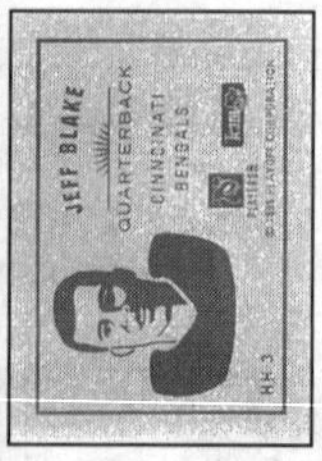

	MINT	NRMT	EXC
COMPLETE SET (30)	1200.00	550.00	150.00
COMMON CARD (HH1-HH30)	15.00	6.75	1.85
☐ HH1 Troy Aikman	80.00	36.00	10.00
☐ HH2 Marcus Allen	20.00	9.00	2.50
☐ HH3 Jeff Blake	25.00	11.00	3.10
☐ HH4 Drew Bledsoe	80.00	36.00	10.00
☐ HH5 Steve Bono	15.00	6.75	1.85
☐ HH6 Isaac Bruce	40.00	18.00	5.00
☐ HH7 Trent Dilfer	20.00	9.00	2.50
☐ HH8 John Elway	70.00	32.00	8.75
☐ HH9 Marshall Faulk	40.00	18.00	5.00
☐ HH10 Brett Favre	150.00	70.00	19.00
☐ HH11 Gus Frerotte	25.00	11.00	3.10
☐ HH12 Irving Fryar	15.00	6.75	1.85
☐ HH13 Jeff George	15.00	6.75	1.85
☐ HH14 Rodney Hampton	15.00	6.75	1.85
☐ HH15 Garrison Hearst	20.00	9.00	2.50
☐ HH16 Michael Irvin	20.00	9.00	2.50
☐ HH17 Erik Kramer	15.00	6.75	1.85
☐ HH18 Dan Marino	150.00	70.00	19.00
☐ HH19 Natrone Means	20.00	9.00	2.50
☐ HH20 Errict Rhett	20.00	9.00	2.50
☐ HH21 Jerry Rice	80.00	36.00	10.00
☐ HH22 Barry Sanders	80.00	36.00	10.00
☐ HH23 Deion Sanders	50.00	22.00	6.25
☐ HH24 Shannon Sharpe	15.00	6.75	1.85
☐ HH25 Emmitt Smith	150.00	70.00	19.00
☐ HH26 Robert Smith	15.00	6.75	1.85
☐ HH27 Chris Warren	15.00	6.75	1.85
☐ HH28 Reggie White	20.00	9.00	2.50
☐ HH29 Harvey Williams	15.00	6.75	1.85
☐ HH30 Steve Young	60.00	27.00	7.50

1995 Playoff Contenders Rookie Kickoff

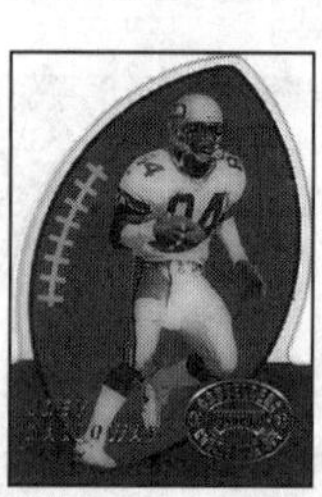

Randomly inserted in packs at a rate of one in 24, this 30-card set features a plastic die-cut football shaped top with a green background at the bottom. Card backs are blank outside of a light shading at the bottom of the card which features the card number with a "RKO" prefix.

	MINT	NRMT	EXC
COMPLETE SET (30)	400.00	180.00	50.00
COMMON CARD (RKO1-RKO30)	5.00	2.20	.60
☐ RK01 Eric Bjornson	5.00	2.20	.60
☐ RK02 Tony Boselli	5.00	2.20	.60
☐ RK03 Kyle Brady	5.00	2.20	.60
☐ RK04 Mark Bruener	5.00	2.20	.60
☐ RK05 Ki-Jana Carter	12.00	5.50	1.50
☐ RK06 Stoney Case	5.00	2.20	.60
☐ RK07 Kerry Collins	40.00	18.00	5.00
☐ RK08 Todd Collins	12.00	5.50	1.50
☐ RK09 Terrell Davis	40.00	18.00	5.00
☐ RK010 Luther Elliss	5.00	2.20	.60
☐ RK011 Joey Galloway	25.00	11.00	3.10
☐ RK012 Rob Johnson	5.00	2.20	.60
☐ RK013 Napoleon Kaufman	12.00	5.50	1.50
☐ RK014 Mike Mamula	5.00	2.20	.60
☐ RK015 Curtis Martin	40.00	18.00	5.00
☐ RK016 Chad May	5.00	2.20	.60
☐ RK017 Steve McNair	30.00	13.50	3.70
☐ RK018 Rashaan Salaam	16.00	7.25	2.00
☐ RK019 Chris Sanders	16.00	7.25	2.00
☐ RK020 Frank Sanders	8.00	3.60	1.00
☐ RK021 Warren Sapp	5.00	2.20	.60
☐ RK022 James O.Stewart	8.00	3.60	1.00
☐ RK023 Kordell Stewart	40.00	18.00	5.00
☐ RK024 J.J. Stokes	12.00	5.50	1.50
☐ RK025 Rodney Thomas	12.00	5.50	1.50
☐ RK026 Michael Westbrook	16.00	7.25	2.00
☐ RK027 Tyrone Wheatley	8.00	3.60	1.00
☐ RK028 Sherman Williams	5.00	2.20	.60
☐ RK029 Eric Zeier	8.00	3.60	1.00
☐ RK030 Ray Zellars	5.00	2.20	.60

1996 Playoff Contenders Leather

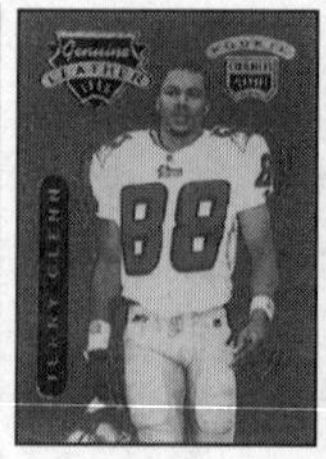

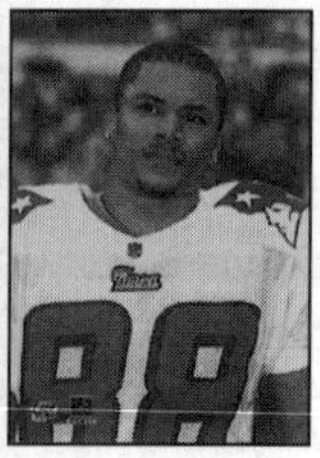

The 1996 Playoff Contenders Leather set was issued in one series totalling 100 cards. The three-card packs retail for $6.99 each, and contained one Leather, one parallel Pennant, and one parallel Open Field card. The fronts of the Leather cards feature a player image on a genuine leather background with a borderless player portrait on the backs. The set is divided into three color-coded insertion ratios: 50 "Scarce" greens which are the most common, 25 "Rare" purples with a ration of 1:11, and 25 "Ultra Rare" reds with a 1:22 ratio.

	MINT	NRMT	EXC
COMPLETE SET (100)	900.00	400.00	110.00
COMMON GREEN (1-100)	1.50	.70	.19
COMMON PURPLE (1-100)	3.00	1.35	.35
COMMON RED (1-100)	8.00	3.60	1.00
☐ 1 Brett Favre R	80.00	36.00	10.00
☐ 2 Steve Young P	16.00	7.25	2.00
☐ 3 Herman Moore P	6.00	2.70	.75
☐ 4 Jim Harbaugh P	4.00	1.80	.50
☐ 5 Curtis Martin R	40.00	18.00	5.00
☐ 6 Junior Seau G	3.00	1.35	.35
☐ 7 John Elway R	30.00	13.50	3.70
☐ 8 Troy Aikman R	40.00	18.00	5.00
☐ 9 Terry Allen G	2.00	.90	.25
☐ 10 Kordell Stewart R	35.00	16.00	4.40
☐ 11 Drew Bledsoe R	40.00	18.00	5.00
☐ 12 Jim Kelly R	18.00	8.00	2.20
☐ 13 Dan Marino R	80.00	36.00	10.00
☐ 14 Andre Rison G	2.00	.90	.25
☐ 15 Jeff Hostetler G	2.00	.90	.25
☐ 16 Scott Mitchell G	2.00	.90	.25
☐ 17 Carl Pickens G	3.00	1.35	.35
☐ 18 Larry Centers R	12.00	5.50	1.50
☐ 19 Craig Heyward G	1.50	.70	.19
☐ 20 Barry Sanders R	40.00	18.00	5.00
☐ 21 Deion Sanders P	14.00	6.25	1.75
☐ 22 Emmitt Smith R	80.00	36.00	10.00
☐ 23 Rashaan Salaam P	6.00	2.70	.75
☐ 24 Mario Bates G	2.00	.90	.25
☐ 25 Lawrence Phillips R	16.00	7.25	2.00
☐ 26 Napoleon Kaufman P	4.00	1.80	.50
☐ 27 Rodney Hampton G	2.00	.90	.25
☐ 28 Marshall Faulk R	16.00	7.25	2.00
☐ 29 Trent Dilfer G	2.00	.90	.25
☐ 30 Leeland McElroy G	3.00	1.35	.35
☐ 31 Marcus Allen G	3.00	1.35	.35
☐ 32 Ricky Watters R	12.00	5.50	1.50
☐ 33 Karim Abdul-Jabbar R	30.00	13.50	3.70
☐ 34 Herschel Walker G	2.00	.90	.25
☐ 35 Thurman Thomas G	3.00	1.35	.35
☐ 36 Jerome Bettis G	3.00	1.35	.35
☐ 37 Gus Frerotte P	6.00	2.70	.75
☐ 38 Neil O'Donnell P	4.00	1.80	.50
☐ 39 Rick Mirer G	2.00	.90	.25
☐ 40 Mike Alstott P	6.00	2.70	.75
☐ 41 Vinny Testaverde P	4.00	1.80	.50
☐ 42 Derek Loville G	1.50	.70	.19
☐ 43 Ben Coates G	2.00	.90	.25
☐ 44 Steve McNair G	5.00	2.20	.60
☐ 45 Bobby Engram G	3.00	1.35	.35
☐ 46 Yancey Thigpen G	2.00	.90	.25
☐ 47 Lake Dawson G	2.00	.90	.25
☐ 48 Terrell Davis G	8.00	3.60	1.00
☐ 49 Kerry Collins P	20.00	9.00	2.50
☐ 50 Eric Metcalf G	2.00	.90	.25
☐ 51 Stanley Pritchett P	4.00	1.80	.50
☐ 52 Robert Brooks G	3.00	1.35	.35
☐ 53 Isaac Bruce R	16.00	7.25	2.00
☐ 54 Tim Brown G	2.00	.90	.25
☐ 55 Edgar Bennett G	2.00	.90	.25
☐ 56 Warren Moon G	2.00	.90	.25
☐ 57 Jerry Rice R	40.00	18.00	5.00
☐ 58 Michael Westbrook G	3.00	1.35	.35
☐ 59 Keyshawn Johnson R	20.00	9.00	2.50
☐ 60 Steve Bono G	2.00	.90	.25
☐ 61 Derrick Mayes G	3.00	1.35	.35
☐ 62 Erik Kramer G	1.50	.70	.19
☐ 63 Rodney Peete G	1.50	.70	.19
☐ 64 Eddie Kennison P	10.00	4.50	1.25
☐ 65 Derrick Thomas G	2.00	.90	.25
☐ 66 Joey Galloway P	10.00	4.50	1.25
☐ 67 Amani Toomer G	3.00	1.35	.35
☐ 68 Reggie White P	6.00	2.70	.75
☐ 69 Heath Shuler R	16.00	7.25	2.00
☐ 70 Dave Brown R	12.00	5.50	1.50
☐ 71 Tony Banks G	3.50	1.55	.45
☐ 72 Chris Warren R	12.00	5.50	1.50
☐ 73 J.J. Stokes R	16.00	7.25	2.00
☐ 74 Rickey Dudley G	3.00	1.35	.35
☐ 75 Stan Humphries G	2.00	.90	.25
☐ 76 Jason Dunn G	2.00	.90	.25
☐ 77 Tyrone Wheatley P	4.00	1.80	.50
☐ 78 Jim Everett R	8.00	3.60	1.00
☐ 79 Cris Carter P	6.00	2.70	.75

	MINT	NRMT	EXC
□ 80 Alex Van Dyke G	2.00	.90	.25
□ 81 O.J. McDuffie G	2.00	.90	.25
□ 82 Mark Chmura G	2.00	.90	.25
□ 83 Terry Glenn G	8.00	3.60	1.00
□ 84 Boomer Esiason G	2.00	.90	.25
□ 85 Bruce Smith G	3.00	1.35	.35
□ 86 Curtis Conway P	6.00	2.70	.75
□ 87 Ki-Jana Carter G	2.00	.90	.25
□ 88 Tamarick Vanover G	3.00	1.35	.35
□ 89 Michael Jackson G	2.00	.90	.25
□ 90 Mark Brunell P	20.00	9.00	2.50
□ 91 Tim Biakabutuka P	6.00	2.70	.75
□ 92 Anthony Miller P	4.00	1.80	.50
□ 93 Marvin Harrison P	10.00	4.50	1.25
□ 94 Jeff George R	12.00	5.50	1.50
□ 95 Jeff Blake P	6.00	2.70	.75
□ 96 Eddie George R	40.00	18.00	5.00
□ 97 Eric Moulds G	3.00	1.35	.35
□ 98 Mike Tomczak P	3.00	1.35	.35
□ 99 Chris Sanders P	4.00	1.80	.50
□ 100 Chris Chandler G	2.00	.90	.25

1996 Playoff Contenders Leather Accents

Randomly inserted in packs at the rate of one in 216, this 100-card set is a parallel version of the regular Leather set and is distinguished by the word "Accent" printed on the back towards the bottom.

	MINT	NRMT	EXC
COMMON CARD (1-100)	40.00	18.00	5.00
SEMISTARS	60.00	27.00	7.50
UNLISTED STARS	80.00	36.00	10.00
□ 1 Brett Favre	600.00	275.00	75.00
□ 2 Steve Young	250.00	110.00	31.00
□ 5 Curtis Martin	350.00	160.00	45.00
□ 7 John Elway	300.00	135.00	38.00
□ 8 Troy Aikman	350.00	160.00	45.00
□ 10 Kordell Stewart	300.00	135.00	38.00
□ 11 Drew Bledsoe	350.00	160.00	45.00
□ 12 Jim Kelly	100.00	45.00	12.50
□ 13 Dan Marino	600.00	275.00	75.00
□ 20 Barry Sanders	350.00	160.00	45.00
□ 21 Deion Sanders	250.00	110.00	31.00
□ 22 Emmitt Smith	600.00	275.00	75.00
□ 31 Marcus Allen	100.00	45.00	12.50
□ 33 Karim Abdul-Jabbar	250.00	110.00	31.00
□ 44 Steve McNair	300.00	135.00	38.00
□ 48 Terrell Davis	350.00	160.00	45.00
□ 49 Kerry Collins	350.00	160.00	45.00
□ 57 Jerry Rice	350.00	160.00	45.00
□ 59 Keyshawn Johnson	200.00	90.00	25.00
□ 64 Eddie Kennison	150.00	70.00	19.00
□ 66 Joey Galloway	150.00	70.00	19.00
□ 68 Reggie White	100.00	45.00	12.50
□ 71 Tony Banks	100.00	45.00	12.50
□ 83 Terry Glenn	300.00	135.00	38.00
□ 90 Mark Brunell	350.00	160.00	45.00
□ 93 Marvin Harrison	200.00	90.00	25.00
□ 96 Eddie George	400.00	180.00	50.00

1996 Playoff Contenders Open Field Foil

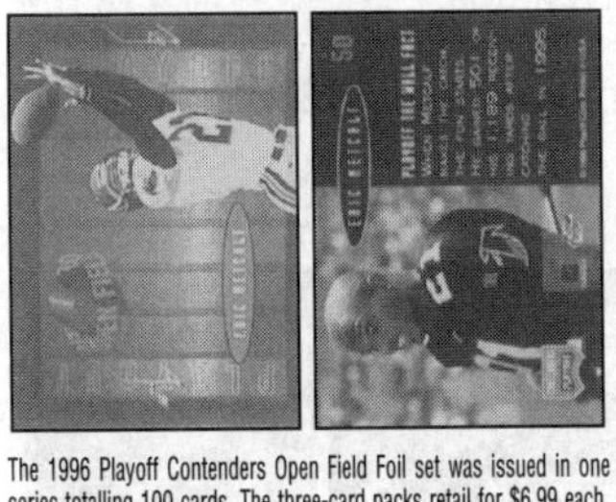

The 1996 Playoff Contenders Open Field Foil set was issued in one series totalling 100 cards. The three-card packs retail for $6.99 each, and contained one Open Field Foil, one parallel Pennant, and one parallel Leather card. This holographic mini card set features a color player image on a football field background. The set is divided into three color-coded insertion ratios: 50 "Scarce" greens which are the most common, 25 "Rare" purples with a ration of 1:11, and 25 "Ultra Rare" reds with a 1:22 ratio.

	MINT	NRMT	EXC
COMPLETE SET (100)	350.00	160.00	45.00
COMMON GREEN (1-100)	1.00	.45	.12
COMMON PURPLE (1-100)	1.50	.70	.19
COMMON RED (1-100)	4.00	1.80	.50
□ 1 Brett Favre P	18.00	8.00	2.20
□ 2 Steve Young R	15.00	6.75	1.85
□ 3 Herman Moore P	3.00	1.35	.35
□ 4 Jim Harbaugh G	1.50	.70	.19
□ 5 Curtis Martin P	12.00	5.50	1.50
□ 6 Junior Seau P	3.00	1.35	.35
□ 7 John Elway P	8.00	3.60	1.00
□ 8 Troy Aikman R	18.00	8.00	2.20
□ 9 Terry Allen G	1.50	.70	.19
□ 10 Kordell Stewart P	10.00	4.50	1.25
□ 11 Drew Bledsoe G	5.00	2.20	.60
□ 12 Jim Kelly G	2.00	.90	.25
□ 13 Dan Marino R	35.00	16.00	4.40
□ 14 Andre Rison P	2.00	.90	.25
□ 15 Jeff Hostetler G	1.50	.70	.19
□ 16 Scott Mitchell R	5.00	2.20	.60
□ 17 Carl Pickens G	2.00	.90	.25
□ 18 Larry Centers G	1.50	.70	.19
□ 19 Craig Heyward R	4.00	1.80	.50
□ 20 Barry Sanders R	18.00	8.00	2.20
□ 21 Deion Sanders P	6.00	2.70	.75
□ 22 Emmitt Smith P	18.00	8.00	2.20
□ 23 Rashaan Salaam R	7.00	3.10	.85
□ 24 Mario Bates P	1.50	.70	.19
□ 25 Lawrence Phillips P	3.00	1.35	.35
□ 26 Napoleon Kaufman G	1.50	.70	.19
□ 27 Rodney Hampton G	1.50	.70	.19
□ 28 Marshall Faulk R	7.00	3.10	.85
□ 29 Trent Dilfer G	1.50	.70	.19
□ 30 Leeland McElroy R	7.00	3.10	.85
□ 31 Marcus Allen G	2.00	.90	.25
□ 32 Ricky Watters P	2.00	.90	.25
□ 33 Karim Abdul-Jabbar P	10.00	4.50	1.25
□ 34 Herschel Walker R	5.00	2.20	.60
□ 35 Thurman Thomas G	2.00	.90	.25
□ 36 Jerome Bettis G	2.00	.90	.25
□ 37 Gus Frerotte R	7.00	3.10	.85
□ 38 Neil O'Donnell G	1.50	.70	.19
□ 39 Rick Mirer G	1.50	.70	.19
□ 40 Mike Alstott G	2.00	.90	.25
□ 41 Vinny Testaverde G	1.50	.70	.19
□ 42 Derek Loville G	1.00	.45	.12
□ 43 Ben Coates G	1.50	.70	.19
□ 44 Steve McNair G	3.00	1.35	.35
□ 45 Bobby Engram R	7.00	3.10	.85
□ 46 Yancey Thigpen G	1.50	.70	.19
□ 47 Lake Dawson P	2.00	.90	.25
□ 48 Terrell Davis G	4.00	1.80	.50
□ 49 Kerry Collins P	10.00	4.50	1.25
□ 50 Eric Metcalf G	1.50	.70	.19
□ 51 Stanley Pritchett G	1.50	.70	.19
□ 52 Robert Brooks P	3.00	1.35	.35
□ 53 Isaac Bruce P	3.00	1.35	.35
□ 54 Tim Brown P	2.00	.90	.25
□ 55 Edgar Bennett G	1.50	.70	.19
□ 56 Warren Moon P	2.00	.90	.25
□ 57 Jerry Rice P	10.00	4.50	1.25
□ 58 Michael Westbrook G	2.00	.90	.25
□ 59 Keyshawn Johnson P	6.00	2.70	.75
□ 60 Steve Bono G	1.50	.70	.19
□ 61 Derrick Mayes R	7.00	3.10	.85
□ 62 Erik Kramer G	1.00	.45	.12
□ 63 Rodney Peete G	1.00	.45	.12
□ 64 Eddie Kennison G	2.50	1.10	.30
□ 65 Derrick Thomas G	1.50	.70	.19
□ 66 Joey Galloway R	8.00	3.60	1.00
□ 67 Amani Toomer R	7.00	3.10	.85
□ 68 Reggie White R	7.00	3.10	.85
□ 69 Heath Shuler P	3.00	1.35	.35
□ 70 Dave Brown G	1.50	.70	.19
□ 71 Tony Banks R	8.00	3.60	1.00
□ 72 Chris Warren G	1.50	.70	.19
□ 73 J.J. Stokes G	2.00	.90	.25
□ 74 Rickey Dudley R	7.00	3.10	.85
□ 75 Stan Humphries G	1.50	.70	.19
□ 76 Jason Dunn R	5.00	2.20	.60
□ 77 Tyrone Wheatley G	1.50	.70	.19
□ 78 Jim Everett G	1.00	.45	.12
□ 79 Cris Carter G	2.00	.90	.25
□ 80 Alex Van Dyke R	5.00	2.20	.60
□ 81 O.J. McDuffie P	2.00	.90	.25
□ 82 Mark Chmura G	1.50	.70	.19
□ 83 Terry Glenn R	20.00	9.00	2.50
□ 84 Boomer Esiason G	1.50	.70	.19
□ 85 Bruce Smith G	2.00	.90	.25
□ 86 Curtis Conway G	2.00	.90	.25
□ 87 Ki-Jana Carter R	5.00	2.20	.60
□ 88 Tamarick Vanover P	3.00	1.35	.35
□ 89 Michael Jackson R	5.00	2.20	.60
□ 90 Mark Brunell G	5.00	2.20	.60
□ 91 Tim Biakabutuka G	2.00	.90	.25
□ 92 Anthony Miller G	1.50	.70	.19
□ 93 Marvin Harrison G	2.50	1.10	.30
□ 94 Jeff George G	1.50	.70	.19
□ 95 Jeff Blake G	2.00	.90	.25
□ 96 Eddie George P	15.00	6.75	1.85
□ 97 Eric Moulds R	7.00	3.10	.85
□ 98 Mike Tomczak R	4.00	1.80	.50
□ 99 Chris Sanders G	1.50	.70	.19
□ 100 Chris Chandler G	1.50	.70	.19

1996 Playoff Contenders Pennants

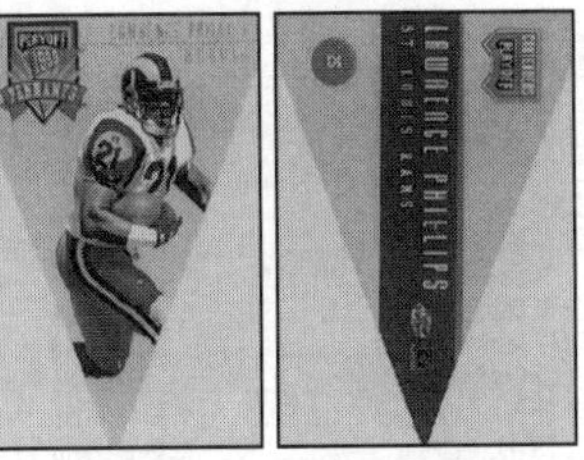

The 1996 Playoff Contenders Pennants set was issued in one series totalling 100 cards. The three-card packs retail for $6.99 each, and contained one Pennant, one parallel Open Field Foil, and one parallel Leather card. The fronts of this Pennant set feature a color player image on a felt-like pennant shapped card with the player's name and team name on the back. The set is divided into three color-coded insertion ratios: 50 "Scarce" greens which are the most common, 25 "Rare" purples with a ration of 1:11, and 25 "Ultra Rare" reds with a 1:22 ratio.

	MINT	NRMT	EXC
COMPLETE SET (100)	700.00	325.00	90.00
COMMON GREEN (1-100)	1.50	.70	.19
COMMON PURPLE (1-100)	2.50	1.10	.30
COMMON RED (1-100)	6.00	2.70	.75
□ 1 Brett Favre R	70.00	32.00	8.75
□ 2 Steve Young R	25.00	11.00	3.10
□ 3 Herman Moore R	12.00	5.50	1.50
□ 4 Jim Harbaugh R	8.00	3.60	1.00
□ 5 Curtis Martin R	30.00	13.50	3.70
□ 6 Junior Seau G	3.00	1.35	.35
□ 7 John Elway R	30.00	13.50	3.70
□ 8 Troy Aikman P	20.00	9.00	2.50
□ 9 Terry Allen G	2.00	.90	.25
□ 10 Kordell Stewart R	30.00	13.50	3.70
□ 11 Drew Bledsoe G	10.00	4.50	1.25
□ 12 Jim Kelly P	4.00	1.80	.50
□ 13 Dan Marino P	40.00	18.00	5.00
□ 14 Andre Rison G	2.00	.90	.25
□ 15 Jeff Hostetler G	2.00	.90	.25
□ 16 Scott Mitchell G	2.00	.90	.25
□ 17 Carl Pickens R	12.00	5.50	1.50
□ 18 Larry Centers P	3.00	1.35	.35
□ 19 Craig Heyward G	1.50	.70	.19
□ 20 Barry Sanders P	20.00	9.00	2.50
□ 21 Deion Sanders R	20.00	9.00	2.50
□ 22 Emmitt Smith R	70.00	32.00	8.75
□ 23 Rashaan Salaam R	12.00	5.50	1.50
□ 24 Mario Bates G	2.00	.90	.25
□ 25 Lawrence Phillips G	3.00	1.35	.35
□ 26 Napoleon Kaufman G	2.00	.90	.25
□ 27 Rodney Hampton G	2.00	.90	.25
□ 28 Marshall Faulk P	4.00	1.80	.50
□ 29 Trent Dilfer G	2.00	.90	.25
□ 30 Leeland McElroy P	4.00	1.80	.50
□ 31 Marcus Allen P	4.00	1.80	.50
□ 32 Ricky Watters G	2.00	.90	.25
□ 33 Karim Abdul-Jabbar G	8.00	3.60	1.00
□ 34 Herschel Walker P	3.00	1.35	.35
□ 35 Thurman Thomas R	12.00	5.50	1.50
□ 36 Jerome Bettis P	4.00	1.80	.50
□ 37 Gus Frerotte G	3.00	1.35	.35
□ 38 Neil O'Donnell G	2.00	.90	.25
□ 39 Rick Mirer G	2.00	.90	.25
□ 40 Mike Alstott R	12.00	5.50	1.50
□ 41 Vinny Testaverde R	6.00	2.70	.75
□ 42 Derek Loville G	1.50	.70	.19
□ 43 Ben Coates G	2.00	.90	.25
□ 44 Steve McNair R	20.00	9.00	2.50
□ 45 Bobby Engram P	4.00	1.80	.50
□ 46 Yancey Thigpen G	2.00	.90	.25
□ 47 Lake Dawson G	2.00	.90	.25
□ 48 Terrell Davis P	20.00	9.00	2.50
□ 49 Kerry Collins R	30.00	13.50	3.70
□ 50 Eric Metcalf G	2.00	.90	.25
□ 51 Stanley Pritchett R	6.00	2.70	.75
□ 52 Robert Brooks R	12.00	5.50	1.50
□ 53 Isaac Bruce G	3.00	1.35	.35
□ 54 Tim Brown G	2.00	.90	.25
□ 55 Edgar Bennett P	3.00	1.35	.35
□ 56 Warren Moon G	2.00	.90	.25
□ 57 Jerry Rice R	35.00	16.00	4.40
□ 58 Michael Westbrook G	3.00	1.35	.35
□ 59 Keyshawn Johnson G	4.00	1.80	.50
□ 60 Steve Bono R	2.00	.90	.25
□ 61 Derrick Mayes P	4.00	1.80	.50
□ 62 Erik Kramer P	2.50	1.10	.30
□ 63 Rodney Peete G	1.50	.70	.19
□ 64 Eddie Kennison G	4.00	1.80	.50
□ 65 Derrick Thomas G	2.00	.90	.25
□ 66 Joey Galloway R	12.00	5.50	1.50
□ 67 Amani Toomer P	4.00	1.80	.50
□ 68 Reggie White G	3.00	1.35	.35
□ 69 Heath Shuler G	3.00	1.35	.35
□ 70 Dave Brown G	2.00	.90	.25
□ 71 Tony Banks P	5.00	2.20	.60
□ 72 Chris Warren G	2.00	.90	.25
□ 73 J.J. Stokes G	3.00	1.35	.35
□ 74 Rickey Dudley P	4.00	1.80	.50
□ 75 Stan Humphries G	2.00	.90	.25
□ 76 Jason Dunn P	3.00	1.35	.35
□ 77 Tyrone Wheatley G	2.00	.90	.25
□ 78 Jim Everett G	1.50	.70	.19
□ 79 Cris Carter P	4.00	1.80	.50
□ 80 Alex Van Dyke P	3.00	1.35	.35
□ 81 O.J. McDuffie G	2.00	.90	.25
□ 82 Mark Chmura P	3.00	1.35	.35
□ 83 Terry Glenn P	20.00	9.00	2.50
□ 84 Boomer Esiason R	8.00	3.60	1.00
□ 85 Bruce Smith G	3.00	1.35	.35
□ 86 Curtis Conway G	3.00	1.35	.35
□ 87 Ki-Jana Carter G	2.00	.90	.25
□ 88 Tamarick Vanover G	3.00	1.35	.35
□ 89 Michael Jackson G	2.00	.90	.25
□ 90 Mark Brunell G	10.00	4.50	1.25
□ 91 Tim Biakabutuka R	12.00	5.50	1.50
□ 92 Anthony Miller G	2.00	.90	.25
□ 93 Marvin Harrison R	18.00	8.00	2.20
□ 94 Jeff George P	3.00	1.35	.35
□ 95 Jeff Blake R	12.00	5.50	1.50
□ 96 Eddie George G	12.00	5.50	1.50
□ 97 Eric Moulds P	4.00	1.80	.50
□ 98 Mike Tomczak G	1.50	.70	.19
□ 99 Chris Sanders G	2.00	.90	.25
□ 100 Chris Chandler G	2.00	.90	.25

1996 Playoff Contenders Air Command

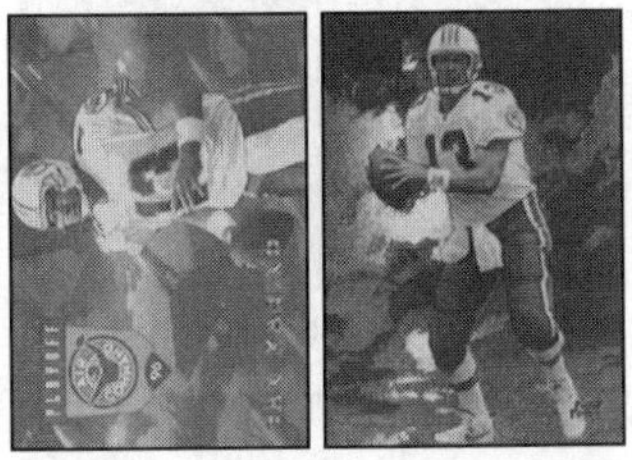

Randomly inserted in hobby packs at a rate of one in 96, this eight-card set features images of the game's hottest quarterbacks on holographic mini cards measuring approximately 2 1/4" by 3 1/8".

	MINT	NRMT	EXC
COMPLETE SET (8)	200.00	90.00	25.00
COMMON CARD (AC1-AC8)	12.00	5.50	1.50
□ AC1 Dan Marino	60.00	27.00	7.50
□ AC2 Brett Favre	60.00	27.00	7.50
□ AC3 Troy Aikman	30.00	13.50	3.70
□ AC4 Mike Tomczak	12.00	5.50	1.50
□ AC5 John Elway	25.00	11.00	3.10
□ AC6 Jeff George	15.00	6.75	1.85
□ AC7 Chris Chandler	12.00	5.50	1.50
□ AC8 Steve Bono	12.00	5.50	1.50

1996 Playoff Contenders Ground Hogs

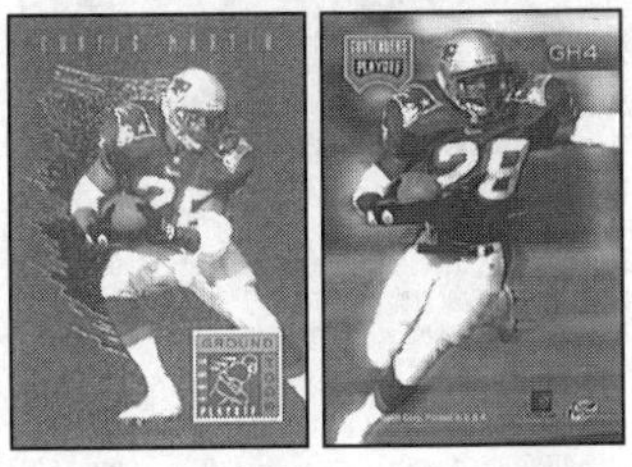

Randomly inserted in packs at a rate of one in 144, this eight-card set features color action images of football's top running backs on a leather background. The backs carry a borderless player action photo.

	MINT	NRMT	EXC
COMPLETE SET (8)	400.00	180.00	50.00
COMMON CARD (GH1-GH8)	30.00	13.50	3.70
□ GH1 Emmitt Smith	100.00	45.00	12.50
□ GH2 Barry Sanders	60.00	27.00	7.50
□ GH3 Marshall Faulk	40.00	18.00	5.00
□ GH4 Curtis Martin	50.00	22.00	6.25
□ GH5 Chris Warren	30.00	13.50	3.70
□ GH6 Ricky Watters	30.00	13.50	3.70
□ GH7 Thurman Thomas	40.00	18.00	5.00
□ GH8 Terrell Davis	50.00	22.00	6.25

1996 Playoff Contenders Honors

Randomly inserted in hobby packs at a rate of one in 7200, this three-card set is a continuation of the 1996 Playoff Prime Honors set and features color player images on a holographic design. The backs carry a borderless player photo.

	MINT	NRMT	EXC
COMPLETE SET (3)	750.00	350.00	95.00
COMMON CARD (PH4-PH6)	100.00	45.00	12.50

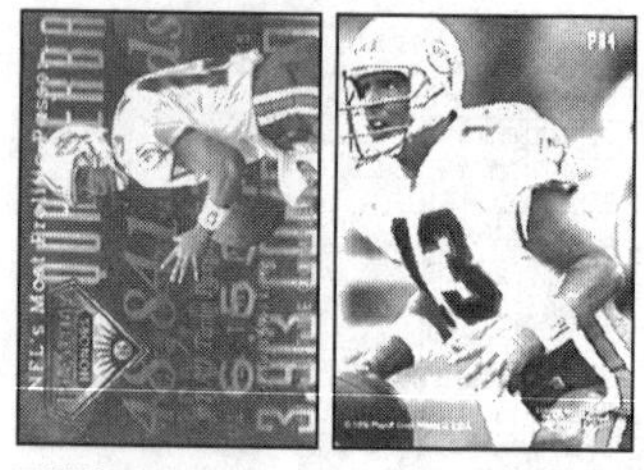

	MINT	NRMT	EXC
☐ PH4 Dan Marino	500.00	220.00	60.00
☐ PH5 Deion Sanders	175.00	80.00	22.00
☐ PH6 Marcus Allen	100.00	45.00	12.50

1996 Playoff Contenders Pennant Flyers

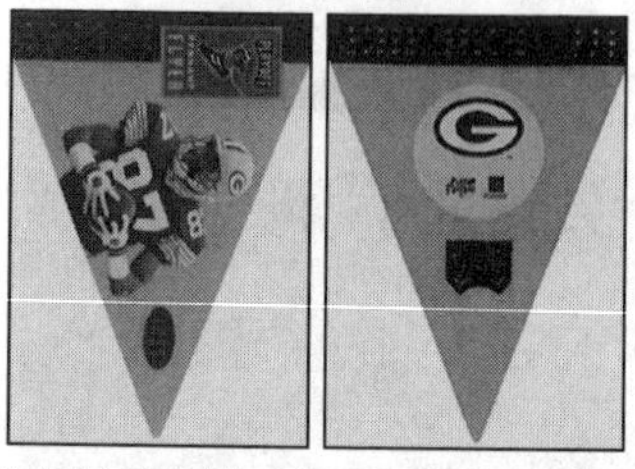

Randomly inserted in hobby packs at a rate of one in 48, this eight-card set features color images of the NFL's best receivers on a felt-like pennant shaped card. The backs carry the player's team logo.

	MINT	NRMT	EXC
COMPLETE SET (8)	120.00	55.00	15.00
COMMON CARD (PF1-PF8)	10.00	4.50	1.25
☐ PF1 Jerry Rice	40.00	18.00	5.00
☐ PF2 Joey Galloway	15.00	6.75	1.85
☐ PF3 Isaac Bruce	15.00	6.75	1.85
☐ PF4 Herman Moore	15.00	6.75	1.85
☐ PF5 Carl Pickens	10.00	4.50	1.25
☐ PF6 Yancey Thigpen	10.00	4.50	1.25
☐ PF7 Deion Sanders	20.00	9.00	2.50
☐ PF8 Robert Brooks	15.00	6.75	1.85

1996 Playoff Illusions

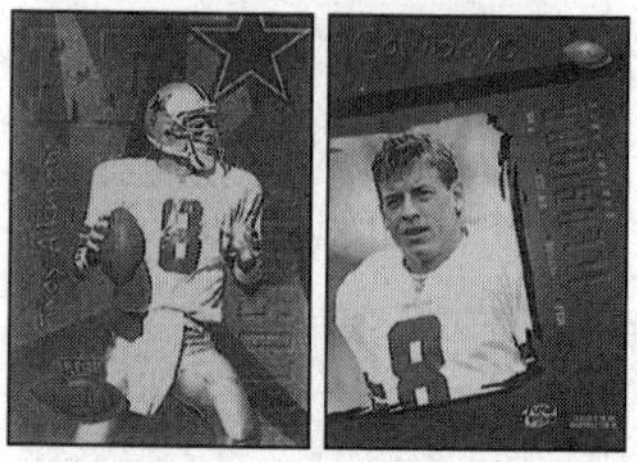

This 120-card 1996 Playoff Illusions set was distributed in five-card packs with a suggested retail price of $4.39. The set features six different designs representing the six NFL divisions. Cards 1-63 appear four cards per pack and cards 64-120 appear one per pack. The fonts display color player photos with tie-dyed color graphics.

	MINT	NRMT	EXC
COMPLETE SET (120)	140.00	65.00	17.50
COMPLETE SERIES 1 (63)	40.00	18.00	5.00
COMPLETE SERIES 2 (57)	100.00	45.00	12.50
COMMON CARD (1-63)	.25	.11	.03
COMMON CARD (64-120)	.75	.35	.09
☐ 1 Troy Aikman	2.50	1.10	.30
☐ 2 Larry Centers	.40	.18	.05
☐ 3 Terance Mathis	.25	.11	.03
☐ 4 Michael Irvin	.75	.35	.09
☐ 5 Jim Kelly	.75	.35	.09
☐ 6 Tim Biakabutuka	1.25	.55	.16
☐ 7 Rashaan Salaam	.75	.35	.09
☐ 8 Ki-Jana Carter	.40	.18	.05
☐ 9 Anthony Miller	.40	.18	.05
☐ 10 Deion Sanders	1.50	.70	.19
☐ 11 Scott Mitchell	.40	.18	.05
☐ 12 Robert Brooks	.75	.35	.09
☐ 13 Willie Davis	.40	.18	.05
☐ 14 Zack Crockett	.25	.11	.03
☐ 15 James O.Stewart	.75	.35	.09
☐ 16 Tamarick Vanover	.75	.35	.09
☐ 17 Stanley Pritchett	.40	.18	.05
☐ 18 Warren Moon	.40	.18	.05
☐ 19 Shawn Jefferson	.25	.11	.03
☐ 20 Shannon Sharpe	.40	.18	.05
☐ 21 Jim Everett	.25	.11	.03
☐ 22 Dave Brown	.40	.18	.05
☐ 23 Adrian Murrell	.40	.18	.05
☐ 24 Rickey Dudley	.40	.18	.05
☐ 25 Chris T. Jones	.75	.35	.09
☐ 26 Andre Hastings	.40	.18	.05
☐ 27 Stan Humphries	.40	.18	.05
☐ 28 Steve Young	2.00	.90	.25
☐ 29 Joey Galloway	1.00	.45	.12
☐ 30 Jim Harbaugh	.40	.18	.05
☐ 31 Eddie Kennison	1.25	.55	.16
☐ 32 Mike Alstott	.75	.35	.09
☐ 33 Michael Westbrook	.75	.35	.09
☐ 34 Leeland McElroy	.50	.23	.06
☐ 35 Erik Kramer	.25	.11	.03
☐ 36 Mark Chmura	.40	.18	.05
☐ 37 Cris Carter	.75	.35	.09
☐ 38 Ben Coates	.40	.18	.05
☐ 39 Wayne Chrebet	.40	.18	.05
☐ 40 Jerome Bettis	.75	.35	.09
☐ 41 Tim Brown	.40	.18	.05
☐ 42 Jason Dunn	.40	.18	.05
☐ 43 William Henderson	.25	.11	.03
☐ 44 Rick Mirer	.40	.18	.05
☐ 45 J.J. Stokes	.75	.35	.09
☐ 46 Rodney Peete	.25	.11	.03
☐ 47 Neil O'Donnell	.40	.18	.05
☐ 48 Tyrone Wheatley	.40	.18	.05
☐ 49 Terry Glenn	4.00	1.80	.50
☐ 50 Junior Seau	.75	.35	.09
☐ 51 Jake Reed	.40	.18	.05
☐ 52 O.J. McDuffie	.40	.18	.05
☐ 53 Steve Bono	.40	.18	.05
☐ 54 Steve McNair	2.00	.90	.25
☐ 55 Antonio Freeman	1.00	.45	.12
☐ 56 Johnnie Morton	.40	.18	.05
☐ 57 Eric Metcalf	.40	.18	.05
☐ 58 Andre Reed	.40	.18	.05
☐ 59 Bobby Engram	1.25	.55	.16
☐ 60 Gus Frerotte	.75	.35	.09
☐ 61 Jeff Blake	.75	.35	.09
☐ 62 Erric Pegram	.40	.18	.05
☐ 63 Jeff Hostetler	.40	.18	.05
☐ 64 Edgar Bennett	1.25	.55	.16
☐ 65 Eddie George	8.00	3.60	1.00
☐ 66 Marvin Harrison	4.00	1.80	.50
☐ 67 Leshon Johnson	.75	.35	.09
☐ 68 Jamal Anderson	3.00	1.35	.35
☐ 69 Thurman Thomas	2.00	.90	.25
☐ 70 Barry Sanders	5.00	2.20	.60
☐ 71 Muhsin Muhammad	3.00	1.35	.35
☐ 72 Robert Green	.75	.35	.09
☐ 73 Garrison Hearst	1.25	.55	.16
☐ 74 John Elway	4.00	1.80	.50
☐ 75 Herman Moore	2.00	.90	.25
☐ 76 Chris Chandler	1.25	.55	.16
☐ 77 Marshall Faulk	2.00	.90	.25
☐ 78 Mark Brunell	5.00	2.20	.60
☐ 79 Tony Banks	3.00	1.35	.35
☐ 80 Terrell Davis	6.00	2.70	.75
☐ 81 Marcus Allen	2.00	.90	.25
☐ 82 Dan Marino	10.00	4.50	1.25
☐ 83 Robert Smith	1.25	.55	.16
☐ 84 Curtis Martin	6.00	2.70	.75
☐ 85 Amani Toomer	2.00	.90	.25
☐ 86 Napoleon Kaufman	1.25	.55	.16
☐ 87 Ricky Watters	1.25	.55	.16
☐ 88 Kordell Stewart	5.00	2.20	.60
☐ 89 Keyshawn Johnson	4.00	1.80	.50
☐ 90 Emmitt Smith	10.00	4.50	1.25
☐ 91 Chris Warren	1.25	.55	.16
☐ 92 Isaac Bruce	2.00	.90	.25
☐ 93 Terry Allen	1.25	.55	.16
☐ 94 Trent Dilfer	1.25	.55	.16
☐ 95 Vinny Testaverde	1.25	.55	.16
☐ 96 Bruce Smith	2.00	.90	.25
☐ 97 Kerry Collins	5.00	2.20	.60
☐ 98 Curtis Conway	2.00	.90	.25
☐ 99 Karim Abdul-Jabbar	5.00	2.20	.60
☐ 100 Brett Favre	10.00	4.50	1.25
☐ 101 Carl Pickens	2.00	.90	.25
☐ 102 Brett Perriman	1.25	.55	.16
☐ 103 Keith Jackson	.75	.35	.09
☐ 104 Drew Bledsoe	5.00	2.20	.60
☐ 105 Rodney Hampton	1.25	.55	.16
☐ 106 Ray Zellars	.75	.35	.09
☐ 107 Jeff Graham	.75	.35	.09
☐ 108 Irving Fryar	1.25	.55	.16
☐ 109 Lawrence Phillips	2.50	1.10	.30
☐ 110 Jerry Rice	5.00	2.20	.60
☐ 111 Mike Tomczak	.75	.35	.09
☐ 112 Tony Martin	1.25	.55	.16
☐ 113 Brian Blades	1.25	.55	.16
☐ 114 Bill Brooks	.75	.35	.09
☐ 115 Rob Moore	.75	.35	.09
☐ 116 Quinn Early	.75	.35	.09
☐ 117 Darnay Scott	1.25	.55	.16
☐ 118 Ken Dilger	1.25	.55	.16
☐ 119 Derek Loville	.75	.35	.09
☐ 120 Reggie White	2.00	.90	.25

1996 Playoff Illusions Spectralusion Dominion

Randomly inserted in packs at the rate of one in 192, this 120-card set is a parallel version of the regular Playoff Illusions set utilizing the Illusion printing technology and a gold holographic foil background.

	MINT	NRMT	EXC
COMMON CARD (1-120)	20.00	9.00	2.50
*STARS: 10X TO 25X ELITES			
*YOUNG STARS: 6X TO 15X ELITES			

1996 Playoff Illusions Spectralusion Elite

Randomly inserted in packs at the rate of one in five, this 120-card set is parallel to the regular Playoff Illusions set utilizing the Illusion printing technology and a silver holographic foil background.

	MINT	NRMT	EXC
COMP.SPECT.ELITE SET (120)	300.00	135.00	38.00
COMMON SPECT.ELITE (1-120)	1.00	.45	.12
SEMISTARS	2.00	.90	.25
UNLISTED STARS	4.00	1.80	.50
COMMON SPECT.DOMINION	20.00	9.00	2.50
*SPECT.DOM.STARS: 10X TO 25X ELITES			
*SPECT.DOM.YOUNG STARS: 6X TO 15X ELITES			
COMP. XXXI SET (120)	600.00	275.00	75.00
COMMON XXXI CARD	2.00	.90	.25
*XXXI STARS: 1X TO 2X ELITES			
*XXXI YOUNG STARS: .75X TO 1.5X ELITES			
COMP.XXXI SPECT. (120)	1800.00	825.00	225.00
COMMON XXXI SPECT.DOM.	10.00	4.50	1.25
*XXXI SPECT.DOM.STARS: 6X TO 12X ELITES			
*XXXI SPECT.DOM.YOU.STARS:4X TO 8X ELITES			
☐ 1 Troy Aikman	10.00	4.50	1.25
☐ 10 Deion Sanders	6.00	2.70	.75
☐ 28 Steve Young	8.00	3.60	1.00
☐ 29 Joey Galloway	5.00	2.20	.60
☐ 31 Eddie Kennison	6.00	2.70	.75
☐ 49 Terry Glenn	12.00	5.50	1.50
☐ 54 Steve McNair	8.00	3.60	1.00
☐ 65 Eddie George	14.00	6.25	1.75
☐ 66 Marvin Harrison	6.00	2.70	.75
☐ 70 Barry Sanders	10.00	4.50	1.25
☐ 74 John Elway	8.00	3.60	1.00
☐ 78 Mark Brunell	10.00	4.50	1.25
☐ 79 Tony Banks	5.00	2.20	.60
☐ 80 Terrell Davis	12.00	5.50	1.50
☐ 82 Dan Marino	20.00	9.00	2.50
☐ 84 Curtis Martin	12.00	5.50	1.50
☐ 88 Kordell Stewart	10.00	4.50	1.25
☐ 89 Keyshawn Johnson	6.00	2.70	.75
☐ 90 Emmitt Smith	20.00	9.00	2.50
☐ 97 Kerry Collins	10.00	4.50	1.25
☐ 99 Karim Abdul-Jabbar	8.00	3.60	1.00
☐ 100 Brett Favre	20.00	9.00	2.50
☐ 104 Drew Bledsoe	10.00	4.50	1.25
☐ 110 Jerry Rice	10.00	4.50	1.25

1996 Playoff Illusions XXXI

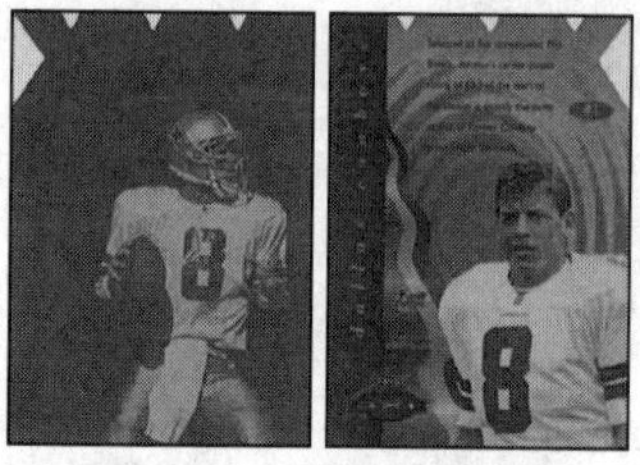

Randomly inserted in packs at the rate of one in 12, this 120-card set is a die-cut parallel version of the regular Playoff Illusions set.

	MINT	NRMT	EXC
COMPLETE SET (120)	600.00	275.00	75.00
COMMON CARD (1-120)	2.00	.90	.25
*STARS: 1X TO 2X ELITES			
*YOUNG STARS: .75X TO 1.5X ELITES			

1996 Playoff Illusions XXXI Spectralusion

Randomly inserted in packs at the rate of one in 96, this 120-card set is parallel to the Playoff Illusions XXXI set with an added gold holographic foil background.

	MINT	NRMT	EXC
COMMON CARD (1-120)	10.00	4.50	1.25
*VETERAN STARS: 6X TO 12X ELITES			
*YOUNG STARS: 4X TO 8X ELITES			

1996 Playoff Illusions Optical Illusions

Randomly inserted in packs at the rate of one in 96, this 18-card set features color player images of fantasy tandems that will never happen.

	MINT	NRMT	EXC
COMPLETE SET (18)	1000.00	450.00	125.00
COMMON CARD (1-18)	20.00	9.00	2.50
☐ 1 Brett Favre Jerry Rice	160.00	70.00	20.00

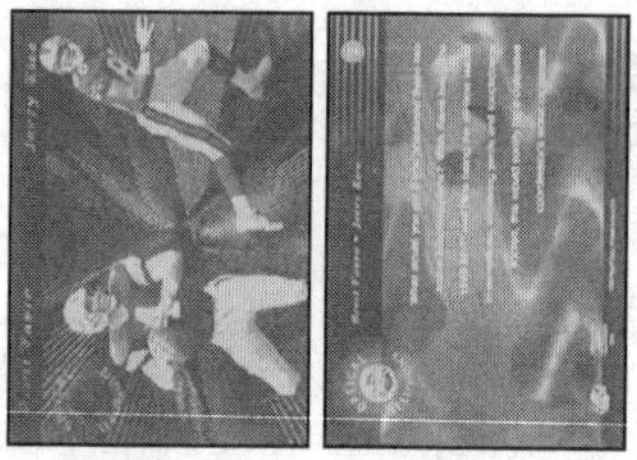

	MINT	NRMT	EXC
☐ 2 Troy Aikman Barry Sanders	120.00	55.00	15.00
☐ 3 Dan Marino Emmitt Smith	200.00	90.00	25.00
☐ 4 Warren Moon Carl Pickens	20.00	9.00	2.50
☐ 5 John Elway Herman Moore	70.00	32.00	8.75
☐ 6 Steve Young Anthony Miller	60.00	27.00	7.50
☐ 7 Jim Harbaugh Terrell Davis	50.00	22.00	6.25
☐ 8 Kordell Stewart Kordell Stewart	80.00	36.00	10.00
☐ 9 Deion Sanders Deion Sanders	50.00	22.00	6.25
☐ 10 Kerry Collins Curtis Martin	100.00	45.00	12.50
☐ 11 Scott Mitchell Robert Brooks	20.00	9.00	2.50
☐ 12 Jeff Blake Tony Martin	20.00	9.00	2.50
☐ 13 Mark Brunell Marshall Faulk	70.00	32.00	8.75
☐ 14 Drew Bledsoe Jerome Bettis	80.00	36.00	10.00
☐ 15 Gus Frerotte Karim Abdul-Jabbar	40.00	18.00	5.00
☐ 16 Steve Bono Ricky Watters	20.00	9.00	2.50
☐ 17 Chris Chandler Terry Allen	20.00	9.00	2.50
☐ 18 Tony Banks Keyshawn Johnson	35.00	16.00	4.40

1996 Playoff Prime Promos

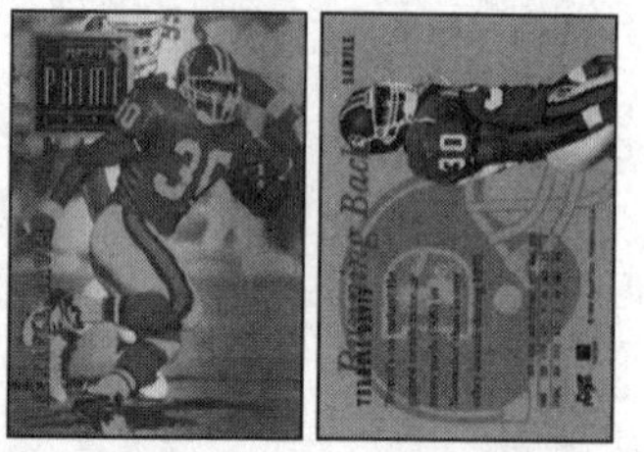

These promo cards were issued to preview the 1996 Playoff Prime release. Each is very similar to its base brand card in design, except for the word "sample" where the card number otherwise would be.

	MINT	NRMT	EXC
COMPLETE SET (2)	3.00	1.35	.37
COMMON CARD (1-2)	1.00	.45	.12
☐ 1 Terrell Davis	2.00	.90	.25
☐ 2 J.J. Stokes	1.00	.45	.12

1996 Playoff Prime

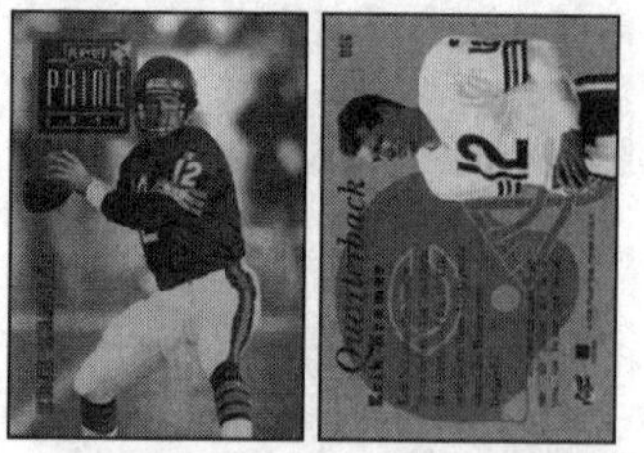

The 1996 Playoff Prime set was issued in one series totalling 200 cards. The five-card packs retail for $3.75 each and were distributed in three color-coded pack types: bronze (#1-100), silver (#101-150), and gold (#151-200). The fronts feature color player photos with player statistics on the backs.

	MINT	NRMT	EXC
COMPLETE SET (200)	200.00	90.00	25.00
COMP. BRONZE SET (100)	25.00	11.00	3.10
COMMON BRONZE CARD (1-100)	.15	.07	.02
COMP. SILVER SET (50)	75.00	34.00	9.50
COMMON SILVER (101-150)	.60	.25	.07
COMP. GOLD SET (50)	125.00	55.00	15.50
COMMON GOLD (151-200)	1.50	.70	.19

☐ 1 Brett Favre	4.00	1.80	.50
☐ 2 Jerry Rice	2.00	.90	.25
☐ 3 Troy Aikman	2.00	.90	.25
☐ 4 Bruce Smith	.30	.14	.04
☐ 5 Marshall Faulk	.30	.14	.04
☐ 6 Erik Kramer	.15	.07	.02
☐ 7 Carl Pickens	.30	.14	.04
☐ 8 Anthony Miller	.20	.09	.03
☐ 9 Cris Carter	.30	.14	.04
☐ 10 Todd Kinchen	.15	.07	.02
☐ 11 Stoney Case	.15	.07	.02
☐ 12 Chris Calloway	.15	.07	.02
☐ 13 Andre Rison	.20	.09	.03
☐ 14 Bill Brooks	.15	.07	.02
☐ 15 Shawn Jefferson	.15	.07	.02
☐ 16 Eric Zeier	.20	.09	.03
☐ 17 Yancey Thigpen	.20	.09	.03
☐ 18 Edgar Bennett	.20	.09	.03
☐ 19 Garrison Hearst	.20	.09	.03
☐ 20 Daryl Johnston	.20	.09	.03
☐ 21 Tyrone Wheatley	.20	.09	.03
☐ 22 Darick Holmes	.20	.09	.03
☐ 23 Dave Brown	.20	.09	.03
☐ 24 Leeland McElroy	.40	.18	.05
☐ 25 Craig Heyward	.15	.07	.02
☐ 26 Kevin Hardy	.60	.25	.07
☐ 27 Scott Mitchell	.20	.09	.03
☐ 28 Willie Green	.15	.07	.02
☐ 29 Vincent Brisby	.15	.07	.02
☐ 30 Mike Tomczak	.15	.07	.02
☐ 31 Luther Elliss	.15	.07	.02
☐ 32 Mike Pritchard	.15	.07	.02
☐ 33 Robert Green	.15	.07	.02
☐ 34 Jeff Graham	.15	.07	.02
☐ 35 Tamarick Vanover	.30	.14	.04
☐ 36 William Floyd	.20	.09	.03
☐ 37 Alvin Harper	.15	.07	.02
☐ 38 Stan Humphries	.20	.09	.03
☐ 39 Herman Moore	.30	.14	.04
☐ 40 Tony Martin	.20	.09	.03
☐ 41 Jonathan Ogden	.15	.07	.02
☐ 42 Randall Cunningham	.20	.09	.03
☐ 43 Chris Warren	.20	.09	.03
☐ 44 Bobby Hebert	.15	.07	.02
☐ 45 Jerome Bettis	.30	.14	.04
☐ 46 Joey Galloway	1.00	.45	.12
☐ 47 Ernie Mills	.15	.07	.02
☐ 48 Steve McNair	2.00	.90	.25
☐ 49 Karim Abdul-Jabbar	2.50	1.10	.30
☐ 50 Chad May	.15	.07	.02
☐ 51 Jim Everett	.15	.07	.02
☐ 52 Robert Smith	.20	.09	.03
☐ 53 Tony Boselli	.20	.09	.03
☐ 54 William Henderson	.15	.07	.02
☐ 55 Terry Glenn UER	3.50	1.55	.45
(Joey Galloway biography on back of card)			
☐ 56 Neil O'Donnell	.20	.09	.03
☐ 57 Chris Chandler	.20	.09	.03
☐ 58 Michael Jackson	.20	.09	.03
☐ 59 Jason Dunn	.20	.09	.03
☐ 60 James O. Stewart	.30	.14	.04
☐ 61 Greg Hill	.20	.09	.03
☐ 62 Mark Carrier WR	.20	.09	.03
☐ 63 Bernie Parmalee	.15	.07	.02
☐ 64 Chris Sanders	.20	.09	.03
☐ 65 Jeff Hostetler	.20	.09	.03
☐ 66 Eric Moulds	1.00	.45	.12
☐ 67 James Jett	.15	.07	.02
☐ 68 Henry Ellard	.20	.09	.03
☐ 69 Mario Bates	.20	.09	.03
☐ 70 Natrone Means	.30	.14	.04
☐ 71 Bobby Engram	1.00	.45	.12
☐ 72 Christian Fauria	.15	.07	.02
☐ 73 Gus Frerotte	.30	.14	.04
☐ 74 Aaron Hayden	.15	.07	.02
☐ 75 Reggie White	.30	.14	.04
☐ 76 Dave Meggett	.15	.07	.02
☐ 77 Harvey Williams	.15	.07	.02
☐ 78 Terance Mathis	.15	.07	.02
☐ 79 Byron Bam Morris	.20	.09	.03
☐ 80 Trent Dilfer	.20	.09	.03
☐ 81 Irving Fryar	.20	.09	.03
☐ 82 Quinn Early	.15	.07	.02
☐ 83 Lake Dawson	.20	.09	.03
☐ 84 Todd Collins	.20	.09	.03
☐ 85 Eric Metcalf	.20	.09	.03
☐ 86 Tim Biakabutuka	1.00	.45	.12
☐ 87 Rob Johnson	.15	.07	.02
☐ 88 Charlie Garner	.15	.07	.02
☐ 89 Mike Mamula	.15	.07	.02
☐ 90 Steve Walsh	.15	.07	.02
☐ 91 Charles Haley	.20	.09	.03
☐ 92 Mike Alstott	.50	.23	.06
☐ 93 Wayne Chrebet	.20	.09	.03
☐ 94 Vinny Testaverde	.20	.09	.03
☐ 95 Fred Barnett	.20	.09	.03
☐ 96 Boomer Esiason	.20	.09	.03
☐ 97 Zack Crockett	.15	.07	.02
☐ 98 Kevin Williams	.15	.07	.02
☐ 99 Eric Bieniemy	.15	.07	.02
☐ 100 Bryan Cox	.15	.07	.02
☐ 101 Larry Centers	1.00	.45	.12
☐ 102 Jeff George	1.00	.45	.12
☐ 103 Bryce Paup	1.00	.45	.12
☐ 104 Kerry Collins	5.00	2.20	.60
☐ 105 Derrick Moore	.60	.25	.07
☐ 106 Adrian Murrell	1.00	.45	.12
☐ 107 Harold Green	.60	.25	.07
☐ 108 Ki-Jana Carter	1.00	.45	.12
☐ 109 Sherman Williams	.60	.25	.07
☐ 110 Deion Sanders	4.00	1.80	.50
☐ 111 Emmitt Smith	10.00	4.50	1.25
☐ 112 Shannon Sharpe	1.00	.45	.12
☐ 113 Johnnie Morton	1.00	.45	.12
☐ 114 Eddie Kennison	5.00	2.20	.60
☐ 115 Marvin Harrison	5.00	2.20	.60
☐ 116 Amani Toomer	2.50	1.10	.30
☐ 117 Rickey Dudley	2.50	1.10	.30
☐ 118 Alex Van Dyke	1.00	.45	.12
☐ 119 Dorsey Levens	1.00	.45	.12
☐ 120 Antonio Freeman	3.00	1.35	.35
☐ 121 Willie Davis	1.00	.45	.12
☐ 122 Lamont Warren	.60	.25	.07
☐ 123 Sean Dawkins	.60	.25	.07
☐ 124 Willie Jackson	1.00	.45	.12
☐ 125 Kimble Anders	.60	.25	.07
☐ 126 Dan Marino	10.00	4.50	1.25
☐ 127 Terry Kirby	1.00	.45	.12
☐ 128 Amp Lee	.60	.25	.07
☐ 129 Jake Reed	1.00	.45	.12
☐ 130 Curtis Martin	6.00	2.70	.75
☐ 131 Ray Zellars	.60	.25	.07
☐ 132 Herschel Walker	1.00	.45	.12
☐ 133 Mike Sherrard	.60	.25	.07
☐ 134 Kyle Brady	1.00	.45	.12
☐ 135 Rocket Ismail	1.00	.45	.12
☐ 136 Ricky Watters	1.00	.45	.12
☐ 137 Kordell Stewart	5.00	2.20	.60
☐ 138 Andre Hastings	1.00	.45	.12
☐ 139 Ronnie Harmon	.60	.25	.07
☐ 140 Terrell Fletcher	.60	.25	.07
☐ 141 J.J. Stokes	2.00	.90	.25
☐ 142 Brent Jones	.60	.25	.07
☐ 143 Tony McGee	.60	.25	.07
☐ 144 Brian Blades	1.00	.45	.12
☐ 145 Isaac Bruce	2.00	.90	.25
☐ 146 Errict Rhett	1.00	.45	.12
☐ 147 Warren Sapp	.60	.25	.07
☐ 148 Horace Copeland	.60	.25	.07
☐ 149 Heath Shuler	2.00	.90	.25
☐ 150 Michael Westbrook	2.00	.90	.25
☐ 151 Frank Sanders	2.00	.90	.25
☐ 152 Rob Moore	1.50	.70	.19
☐ 153 Bert Emanuel	2.00	.90	.25
☐ 154 J.J. Birden	1.50	.70	.19
☐ 155 Thurman Thomas	3.00	1.35	.35
☐ 156 Jim Kelly	3.00	1.35	.35
☐ 157 Curtis Conway	3.00	1.35	.35
☐ 158 Darnay Scott	2.00	.90	.25
☐ 159 Jeff Blake	4.00	1.80	.50
☐ 160 Jay Novacek	2.00	.90	.25
☐ 161 Michael Irvin	3.00	1.35	.35
☐ 162 John Elway	10.00	4.50	1.25
☐ 163 Terrell Davis	12.00	5.50	1.50
☐ 164 Barry Sanders	12.00	5.50	1.50
☐ 165 Brett Perriman	2.00	.90	.25
☐ 166 Keyshawn Johnson	8.00	3.60	1.00
☐ 167 Eddie George	15.00	6.75	1.85
☐ 168 Derrick Mayes	3.50	1.55	.45
☐ 169 Simeon Rice	4.00	1.80	.50
☐ 170 Lawrence Phillips	4.00	1.80	.50
☐ 171 Robert Brooks	3.00	1.35	.35
☐ 172 Mark Chmura	2.00	.90	.25
☐ 173 Rodney Thomas	1.50	.70	.19
☐ 174 Jim Harbaugh	2.00	.90	.25
☐ 175 Ken Dilger	2.00	.90	.25
☐ 176 Mark Brunell	12.00	5.50	1.50
☐ 177 Steve Bono	2.00	.90	.25
☐ 178 Marcus Allen	3.00	1.35	.35
☐ 179 O.J. McDuffie	2.00	.90	.25
☐ 180 Eric Green	1.50	.70	.19
☐ 181 Warren Moon	2.00	.90	.25
☐ 182 Drew Bledsoe	12.00	5.50	1.50
☐ 183 Ben Coates	2.00	.90	.25
☐ 184 Michael Haynes	2.00	.90	.25
☐ 185 Rodney Hampton	2.00	.90	.25
☐ 186 Rashaan Salaam	3.00	1.35	.35
☐ 187 Napoleon Kaufman	2.00	.90	.25
☐ 188 Tim Brown	2.00	.90	.25
☐ 189 Rodney Peete	1.50	.70	.19
☐ 190 Calvin Williams	1.50	.70	.19
☐ 191 Erric Pegram	2.00	.90	.25
☐ 192 Mark Bruener	1.50	.70	.19
☐ 193 Junior Seau	3.00	1.35	.35
☐ 194 Steve Young	10.00	4.50	1.25
☐ 195 Derek Loville	1.50	.70	.19
☐ 196 Rick Mirer	2.00	.90	.25
☐ 197 Mark Rypien	1.50	.70	.19
☐ 198 Jackie Harris	1.50	.70	.19
☐ 199 Terry Allen	2.00	.90	.25
☐ 200 Brian Mitchell	1.50	.70	.19

1996 Playoff Prime Boss Hogs

Randomly inserted in silver inner packs of the regular Playoff Prime set at a rate of one in 96, this 18-card set features color player photos of some of the NFL's best players on all-leather fronts with black and gold foil stamping. The closely cropped back photos show full-color action printed on acetate.

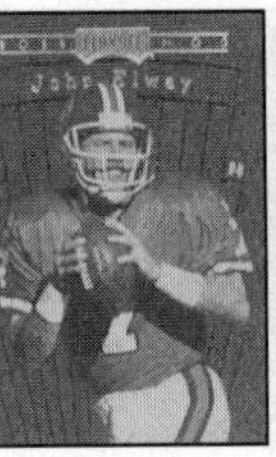

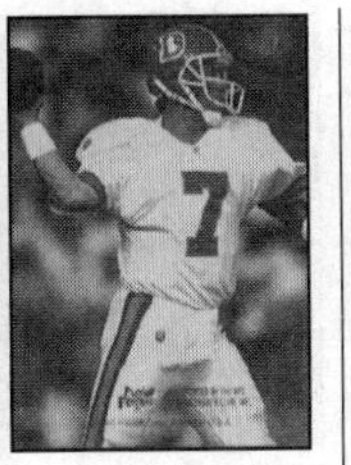

	MINT	NRMT	EXC
COMPLETE SET (18)	700.00	325.00	90.00
COMMON CARD (1-18)	20.00	9.00	2.50
☐ 1 Curtis Martin	60.00	27.00	7.50
☐ 2 Chris Warren	20.00	9.00	2.50
☐ 3 Emmitt Smith	125.00	55.00	15.50
☐ 4 Barry Sanders	60.00	27.00	7.50
☐ 5 Rashaan Salaam	25.00	11.00	3.10
☐ 6 Marshall Faulk	25.00	11.00	3.10
☐ 7 Errict Rhett	20.00	9.00	2.50
☐ 8 Thurman Thomas	25.00	11.00	3.10
☐ 9 Kerry Collins	60.00	27.00	7.50
☐ 10 Dan Marino	125.00	55.00	15.50
☐ 11 Jerry Rice	60.00	27.00	7.50
☐ 12 Troy Aikman	60.00	27.00	7.50
☐ 13 Jeff George	20.00	9.00	2.50
☐ 14 Brett Favre	125.00	55.00	15.50
☐ 15 Robert Brooks	25.00	11.00	3.10
☐ 16 John Elway	50.00	22.00	6.25
☐ 17 Deion Sanders	35.00	16.00	4.40
☐ 18 Kordell Stewart	60.00	27.00	7.50

1996 Playoff Prime Honors

Randomly inserted in packs at a rate of one in 7200, this three-card set features color player images on a leather-like embossed background. The backs carry a borderless color player action photo.

	MINT	NRMT	EXC
COMPLETE SET (3)	800.00	350.00	100.00
COMMON CARD (1-3)	200.00	90.00	25.00
☐ PH1 Emmitt Smith	350.00	160.00	45.00
☐ PH2 Curtis Martin	200.00	90.00	25.00
☐ PH3 Brett Favre	350.00	160.00	45.00

1996 Playoff Prime Surprise

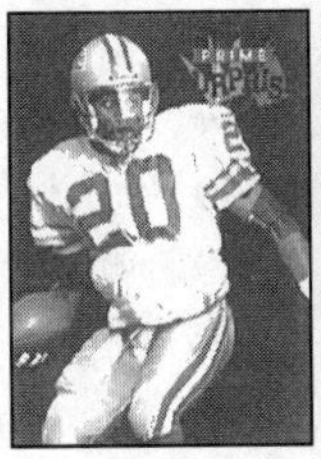

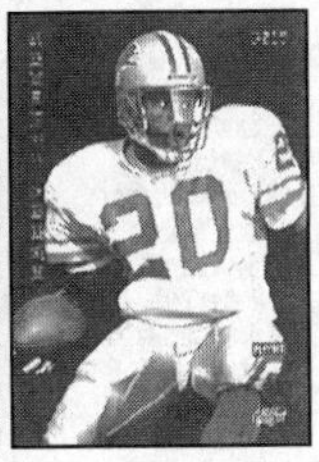

Randomly inserted in packs at a rate of one in 288, this 14-card set features color player images on colorful foil backgrounds. The backs carry another image of the same player on a different colored foil background.

	MINT	NRMT	EXC
COMPLETE SET (14)	1250.00	550.00	160.00
COMMON CARD (1-14)	20.00	9.00	2.50
☐ 1 Dan Marino	200.00	90.00	25.00
☐ 2 Brett Favre	200.00	90.00	25.00
☐ 3 Emmitt Smith	200.00	90.00	25.00
☐ 4 Kordell Stewart	70.00	32.00	8.75
☐ 5 Jerry Rice	100.00	45.00	12.50
☐ 6 Troy Aikman	100.00	45.00	12.50
☐ 7 Barry Sanders	100.00	45.00	12.50
☐ 8 Curtis Martin	90.00	40.00	11.00
☐ 9 Marshall Faulk	25.00	11.00	3.10
☐ 10 Joey Galloway	40.00	18.00	5.00
☐ 11 Robert Brooks	20.00	9.00	2.50
☐ 12 Deion Sanders	60.00	27.00	7.50
☐ 13 Reggie White	25.00	11.00	3.10
☐ 14 Marcus Allen	25.00	11.00	3.10

1996 Playoff Prime X's and O's

Randomly inserted in packs at a rate of one in 7.2, this 200-card set is parallel to the 1996 Playoff Prime regular set and silhouettes the player against his team helmet on a die cut card. The backs illustrate and detail one of the player's trademark plays.

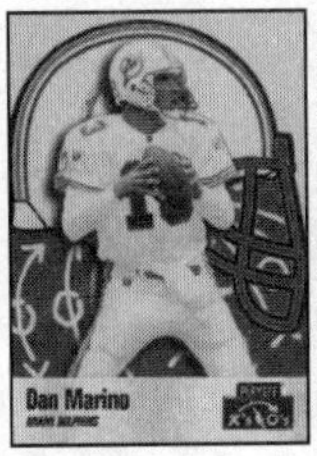

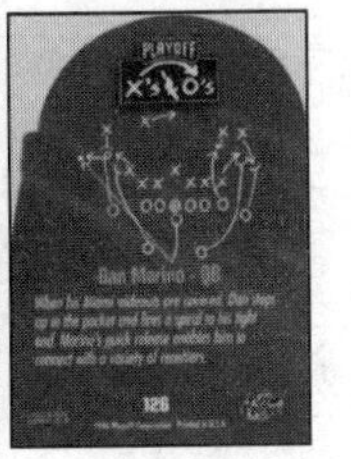

	MINT	NRMT	EXC
COMPLETE SET (200)	1000.00	450.00	125.00
COMMON CARD (1-200)	2.50	1.10	.30
SEMISTARS	4.00	1.80	.50
UNLISTED STARS	8.00	3.60	1.00
☐ 1 Brett Favre	60.00	27.00	7.50
☐ 2 Jerry Rice	35.00	16.00	4.40
☐ 3 Troy Aikman	35.00	16.00	4.40
☐ 46 Joey Galloway	15.00	6.75	1.85
☐ 48 Steve McNair	25.00	11.00	3.10
☐ 49 Karim Abdul-Jabbar	30.00	13.50	3.70
☐ 55 Terry Glenn	35.00	16.00	4.40
☐ 104 Kerry Collins	35.00	16.00	4.40
☐ 110 Deion Sanders	20.00	9.00	2.50
☐ 111 Emmitt Smith	60.00	27.00	7.50
☐ 114 Eddie Kennison	15.00	6.75	1.85
☐ 115 Marvin Harrison	15.00	6.75	1.85
☐ 120 Antonio Freeman	15.00	6.75	1.85
☐ 126 Dan Marino	60.00	27.00	7.50
☐ 130 Curtis Martin	35.00	16.00	4.40
☐ 137 Kordell Stewart	35.00	16.00	4.40
☐ 162 John Elway	30.00	13.50	3.70
☐ 163 Terrell Davis	35.00	16.00	4.40
☐ 164 Barry Sanders	35.00	16.00	4.40
☐ 166 Keyshawn Johnson	15.00	6.75	1.85
☐ 167 Eddie George	40.00	18.00	5.00
☐ 176 Mark Brunell	35.00	16.00	4.40
☐ 182 Drew Bledsoe	35.00	16.00	4.40
☐ 194 Steve Young	25.00	11.00	3.10

1996 Playoff Trophy Contenders

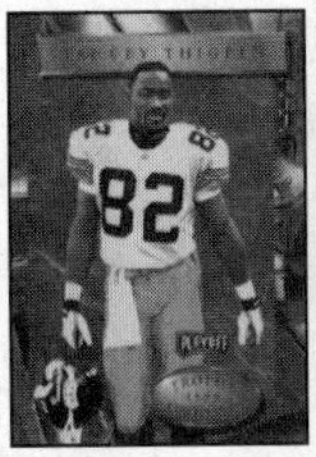

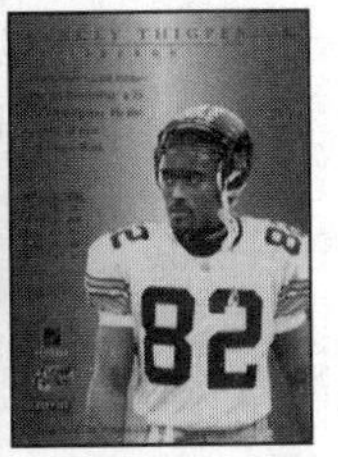

The 1996 Playoff Trophy Contenders set was issued in one series totalling 120 cards. The six-card packs retail for $3.75 each. The only Rookie Card of note in this set is Aaron Hayden.

	MINT	NRMT	EXC
COMPLETE SET (120)	25.00	11.00	3.10
COMMON CARD (1-120)	.08	.04	.01
☐ 1 Brett Favre	2.50	1.10	.30
☐ 2 Troy Aikman	1.25	.55	.16
☐ 3 Dan Marino	2.50	1.10	.30
☐ 4 Emmitt Smith	2.50	1.10	.30
☐ 5 Marshall Faulk	.30	.14	.04
☐ 6 Jeff Blake	.30	.14	.04
☐ 7 John Elway	1.00	.45	.12
☐ 8 Steve Young	1.00	.45	.12
☐ 9 Curtis Martin	2.00	.90	.25
☐ 10 Kordell Stewart	1.50	.70	.19
☐ 11 Drew Bledsoe	1.25	.55	.16
☐ 12 Jim Kelly	.30	.14	.04
☐ 13 Steve Bono	.15	.07	.02
☐ 14 Neil O'Donnell	.15	.07	.02
☐ 15 Jeff Hostetler	.15	.07	.02
☐ 16 Jim Harbaugh	.15	.07	.02
☐ 17 Jim Everett	.08	.04	.01
☐ 18 Erric Pegram	.15	.07	.02
☐ 19 Tyrone Wheatley	.15	.07	.02
☐ 20 Barry Sanders	1.25	.55	.16
☐ 21 Deion Sanders	.75	.35	.09
☐ 22 Harvey Williams	.08	.04	.01
☐ 23 Garrison Hearst	.15	.07	.02
☐ 24 Aaron Hayden	.08	.04	.01
☐ 25 Dorsey Levens	.15	.07	.02
☐ 26 Napoleon Kaufman	.15	.07	.02
☐ 27 Rodney Hampton	.15	.07	.02
☐ 28 Scott Mitchell	.15	.07	.02
☐ 29 Greg Hill	.15	.07	.02
☐ 30 Charlie Garner	.08	.04	.01
☐ 31 Rashaan Salaam	.30	.14	.04
☐ 32 Errict Rhett	.15	.07	.02
☐ 33 Byron Bam Morris	.15	.07	.02
☐ 34 Edgar Bennett	.15	.07	.02
☐ 35 Jeff George	.15	.07	.02
☐ 36 Rodney Peete	.08	.04	.01
☐ 37 Stan Humphries	.15	.07	.02

☐ 38 Kimble Anders	.08	.04	.01
☐ 39 Natrone Means	.30	.14	.04
☐ 40 Sherman Williams	.08	.04	.01
☐ 41 Eric Metcalf	.15	.07	.02
☐ 42 Chris Warren	.15	.07	.02
☐ 43 Marcus Allen	.30	.14	.04
☐ 44 Bill Brooks	.08	.04	.01
☐ 45 Wayne Chrebet	.15	.07	.02
☐ 46 Irving Fryar	.15	.07	.02
☐ 47 Tony Martin	.15	.07	.02
☐ 48 Daryl Johnston	.15	.07	.02
☐ 49 O.J. McDuffie	.15	.07	.02
☐ 50 Frank Sanders	.15	.07	.02
☐ 51 Ken Norton	.15	.07	.02
☐ 52 Jake Reed	.15	.07	.02
☐ 53 Bert Emanuel	.15	.07	.02
☐ 54 Floyd Turner	.08	.04	.01
☐ 55 Junior Seau	.30	.14	.04
☐ 56 Ernie Mills	.08	.04	.01
☐ 57 Mark Pike	.08	.04	.01
☐ 58 Warren Moon	.15	.07	.02
☐ 59 Mike Mamula	.08	.04	.01
☐ 60 Kerry Collins	1.50	.70	.19
☐ 61 Nate Newton	.08	.04	.01
☐ 62 Terry Allen	.15	.07	.02
☐ 63 Bernie Parmalee	.08	.04	.01
☐ 64 James O.Stewart	.30	.14	.04
☐ 65 Isaac Bruce	.30	.14	.04
☐ 66 Lake Dawson	.15	.07	.02
☐ 67 Terance Mathis	.08	.04	.01
☐ 68 Chris Sanders	.15	.07	.02
☐ 69 Anthony Miller	.15	.07	.02
☐ 70 Jay Novacek	.15	.07	.02
☐ 71 Sean Dawkins	.08	.04	.01
☐ 72 J.J. Birden	.08	.04	.01
☐ 73 Calvin Williams	.30	.14	.04
☐ 74 Rick Mirer	.15	.07	.02
☐ 75 Steve McNair	1.25	.55	.16
☐ 76 Lamont Warren	.08	.04	.01
☐ 77 Rod Woodson	.15	.07	.02
☐ 78 Larry Brown	.08	.04	.01
☐ 79 Zack Crockett	.08	.04	.01
☐ 80 Jerry Rice	1.25	.55	.16
☐ 81 Tim Brown	.15	.07	.02
☐ 82 Yancey Thigpen	.15	.07	.02
☐ 83 J.J. Stokes	.30	.14	.04
☐ 84 Herman Moore	.30	.14	.04
☐ 85 Kevin Williams	.08	.04	.01
☐ 86 Gus Frerotte	.30	.14	.04
☐ 87 Robert Brooks	.30	.14	.04
☐ 88 Michael Irvin	.30	.14	.04
☐ 89 Steve Tasker	.08	.04	.01
☐ 90 Joey Galloway	.75	.35	.09
☐ 91 Kevin Greene	.15	.07	.02
☐ 92 Reggie White	.30	.14	.04
☐ 93 Cris Carter	.30	.14	.04
☐ 94 Charles Haley	.15	.07	.02
☐ 95 Bryce Paup	.15	.07	.02
☐ 96 Heath Shuler	.30	.14	.04
☐ 97 Eric Zeier	.15	.07	.02
☐ 98 Antonio Freeman	.75	.35	.09
☐ 99 Erik Kramer	.08	.04	.01
☐ 100 Derek Loville	.08	.04	.01
☐ 101 Rodney Thomas	.08	.04	.01
☐ 102 Terrell Davis	2.00	.90	.25
☐ 103 Ricky Watters	.15	.07	.02
☐ 104 Craig Heyward	.08	.04	.01
☐ 105 Terry Kirby	.15	.07	.02
☐ 106 Bruce Smith	.30	.14	.04
☐ 107 Curtis Conway	.30	.14	.04
☐ 108 Charles Johnson	.15	.07	.02
☐ 109 Brett Perriman	.15	.07	.02
☐ 110 Carl Pickens	.30	.14	.04
☐ 111 Michael Westbrook	.30	.14	.04
☐ 112 Brent Jones	.08	.04	.01
☐ 113 Ken Dilger	.15	.07	.02
☐ 114 Fred Barnett	.15	.07	.02
☐ 115 Mark Bruener	.08	.04	.01
☐ 116 Tamarick Vanover	.30	.14	.04
☐ 117 Quinn Early	.08	.04	.01
☐ 118 Mark Chmura	.15	.07	.02
☐ 119 Andre Hastings	.15	.07	.02
☐ 120 Craig Newsome	.08	.04	.01

1996 Playoff Trophy Contenders Mini Back-To-Backs

Randomly inserted in packs at a rate of one in 17, this 60-card measure 2 1/4" by 3". These cards were inserted approximately one every 17 packs. The first 11 cards in the set feature Super Bowl XXX opponents: Dallas and Pittsburgh on each side.

	MINT	NRMT	EXC
COMPLETE SET (60)	800.00	350.00	100.00
COMMON CARD (1-60)	8.00	3.60	1.00
☐ 1 Troy Aikman	50.00	22.00	6.25
Neil O'Donnell			
☐ 2 Kordell Stewart	40.00	18.00	5.00
Sherman Williams			
☐ 3 Deion Sanders	30.00	13.50	3.70
Andre Hastings			
☐ 4 Emmitt Smith	80.00	36.00	10.00
Byron Bam Morris			

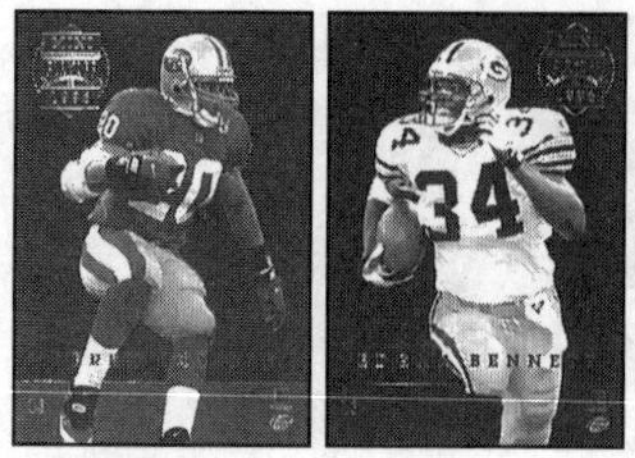

☐ 5 Daryl Johnston	8.00	3.60	1.00
Erric Pegram			
☐ 6 Nate Newton	8.00	3.60	1.00
Kevin Greene			
☐ 7 Larry Brown	8.00	3.60	1.00
Charles Johnson			
☐ 8 Jay Novacek	12.00	5.50	1.50
Mark Bruener			
☐ 9 Yancey Thigpen	12.00	5.50	1.50
Kevin Williams			
☐ 10 Michael Irvin	15.00	6.75	1.85
Ernie Mills			
☐ 11 Charles Haley	12.00	5.50	1.50
Rod Woodson			
☐ 12 Brett Favre	80.00	36.00	10.00
Steve Young			
☐ 13 Edgar Bennett	12.00	5.50	1.50
Derek Loville			
☐ 14 Reggie White	15.00	6.75	1.85
Ken Norton			
☐ 15 Jerry Rice	50.00	22.00	6.25
Robert Brooks			
☐ 16 J.J. Stokes	15.00	6.75	1.85
Dorsey Levens			
☐ 17 Mark Chmura	12.00	5.50	1.50
Brent Jones			
☐ 18 Craig Newsome	20.00	9.00	2.50
Antonio Freeman			
☐ 19 Dan Marino	80.00	36.00	10.00
Jim Kelly			
☐ 20 Bernie Parmalee	12.00	5.50	1.50
Bruce Smith			
☐ 21 Irving Fryar	8.00	3.60	1.00
Bill Brooks			
☐ 22 O.J. McDuffie	12.00	5.50	1.50
Steve Tasker			
☐ 23 Terry Kirby	12.00	5.50	1.50
Bryce Paup			
☐ 24 Jim Harbaugh	12.00	5.50	1.50
Steve Bono			
☐ 25 Marshall Faulk	15.00	6.75	1.85
Greg Hill			
☐ 26 Lamont Warren	15.00	6.75	1.85
Marcus Allen			
☐ 27 Floyd Turner	8.00	3.60	1.00
Kimble Anders			
☐ 28 Sean Dawkins	12.00	5.50	1.50
Lake Dawson			
☐ 29 Tamarick Vanover	15.00	6.75	1.85
Zack Crockett			
☐ 30 Scott Mitchell	8.00	3.60	1.00
Rodney Peete			
☐ 31 Barry Sanders	50.00	22.00	6.25
Ricky Watters			
☐ 32 Brett Perriman	12.00	5.50	1.50
Calvin Williams			
☐ 33 Herman Moore	15.00	6.75	1.85
Fred Barnett			
☐ 34 Stan Humphries	12.00	5.50	1.50
Jeff George			
☐ 35 Natrone Means	15.00	6.75	1.85
Craig Heyward			
☐ 36 Aaron Hayden	8.00	3.60	1.00
Terance Mathis			
☐ 37 Junior Seau	12.00	5.50	1.50
Bert Emanuel			
☐ 38 Tony Martin	8.00	3.60	1.00
J.J. Birden			
☐ 39 Jeff Blake	15.00	6.75	1.85
Carl Pickens			
☐ 40 Erik Kramer	12.00	5.50	1.50
Curtis Conway			
☐ 41 Frank Sanders	15.00	6.75	1.85
Garrison Hearst			
☐ 42 John Elway	40.00	18.00	5.00
Anthony Miller			
☐ 43 Steve McNair	30.00	13.50	3.70
Chris Sanders			
☐ 44 Warren Moon	12.00	5.50	1.50
Cris Carter			
☐ 45 Curtis Martin	80.00	36.00	10.00
Drew Bledsoe			
☐ 46 Jim Everett	12.00	5.50	1.50
Quinn Early			
☐ 47 Rodney Hampton	12.00	5.50	1.50
Tyrone Wheatley			
☐ 48 Jeff Hostetler	12.00	5.50	1.50
Tim Brown			
☐ 49 Joey Galloway	20.00	9.00	2.50
Rick Mirer			
☐ 50 Michael Westbrook	15.00	6.75	1.85
Gus Frerotte			
☐ 51 Heath Shuler	15.00	6.75	1.85
Terry Allen			
☐ 52 Charlie Garner	8.00	3.60	1.00
Mike Mamula			
☐ 53 Napoleon Kaufman	12.00	5.50	1.50
Harvey Williams			
☐ 54 Errict Rhett	20.00	9.00	2.50
Rashaan Salaam			
☐ 55 Kerry Collins	40.00	18.00	5.00
Mark Pike			
☐ 56 Ken Dilger	12.00	5.50	1.50
Eric Zeier			
☐ 57 Terrell Davis	50.00	22.00	6.25
Chris Warren			
☐ 58 Isaac Bruce	15.00	6.75	1.85
Jake Reed			
☐ 59 Eric Metcalf	12.00	5.50	1.50
Wayne Chrebet			
☐ 60 James O.Stewart	15.00	6.75	1.85
Rodney Thomas			

1996 Playoff Trophy Contenders Playoff Zone

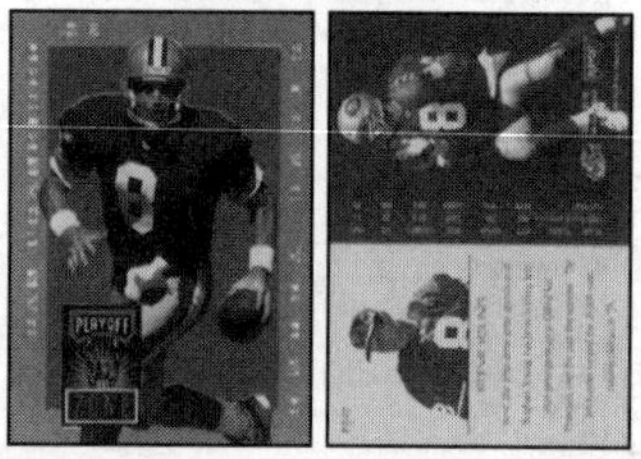

Randomly inserted in packs at a rate of one in 24, this 36-card standard-size set has some of the best NFL players. The cards feature a mix of silver and gold foil backgrounds. There are three groups of cards: Quarterbacks (1-12), Running Backs (13-24) and Receivers (25-36), within each group the cards are sequenced in alphabetical order. The cards are numbered with a "PZ" prefix.

	MINT	NRMT	EXC
COMPLETE SET (36)	350.00	160.00	45.00
COMMON CARD (1-36)	5.00	2.20	.60
☐ 1 Troy Aikman	25.00	11.00	3.10
☐ 2 Jeff Blake	8.00	3.60	1.00
☐ 3 John Elway	20.00	9.00	2.50
☐ 4 Brett Favre	50.00	22.00	6.25
☐ 5 Jeff George	8.00	3.60	1.00
☐ 6 Jim Harbaugh	8.00	3.60	1.00
☐ 7 Erik Kramer	5.00	2.20	.60
☐ 8 Dan Marino	50.00	22.00	6.25
☐ 9 Scott Mitchell	5.00	2.20	.60
☐ 10 Warren Moon	8.00	3.60	1.00
☐ 11 Neil O'Donnell	8.00	3.60	1.00
☐ 12 Steve Young	15.00	6.75	1.85
☐ 13 Marcus Allen	10.00	4.50	1.25
☐ 14 Terry Allen	8.00	3.60	1.00
☐ 15 Edgar Bennett	8.00	3.60	1.00
☐ 16 Marshall Faulk	10.00	4.50	1.25
☐ 17 Rodney Hampton	8.00	3.60	1.00
☐ 18 Craig Heyward	5.00	2.20	.60
☐ 19 Errict Rhett	10.00	4.50	1.25
☐ 20 Barry Sanders	25.00	11.00	3.10
☐ 21 Emmitt Smith	50.00	22.00	6.25
☐ 22 Chris Warren	8.00	3.60	1.00
☐ 23 Ricky Watters	8.00	3.60	1.00
☐ 24 Harvey Williams	5.00	2.20	.60
☐ 25 Robert Brooks	8.00	3.60	1.00
☐ 26 Isaac Bruce	10.00	4.50	1.25
☐ 27 Cris Carter	8.00	3.60	1.00
☐ 28 Curtis Conway	8.00	3.60	1.00
☐ 29 Michael Irvin	10.00	4.50	1.25
☐ 30 Anthony Miller	5.00	2.20	.60
☐ 31 Herman Moore	10.00	4.50	1.25
☐ 32 Brett Perriman	5.00	2.20	.60
☐ 33 Carl Pickens	8.00	3.60	1.00
☐ 34 Jerry Rice	25.00	11.00	3.10
☐ 35 Deion Sanders	15.00	6.75	1.85
☐ 36 Yancey Thigpen	8.00	3.60	1.00

1996 Playoff Trophy Contenders Rookie Stallions

Randomly inserted in packs at a rate of one in 24, this 20-card standard-size set featured leading 1995 NFL rookies. The player's photo is etched into a gold foil background of stallions. The cards are numbered with an "RS" prefix and are sequenced in alphabetical order.

	MINT	NRMT	EXC
COMPLETE SET (20)	250.00	110.00	31.00
COMMON CARD (1-20)	6.00	2.70	.75
☐ 1 Mark Bruener	6.00	2.70	.75
☐ 2 Wayne Chrebet	6.00	2.70	.75
☐ 3 Kerry Collins	25.00	11.00	3.10
☐ 4 Zack Crockett	6.00	2.70	.75

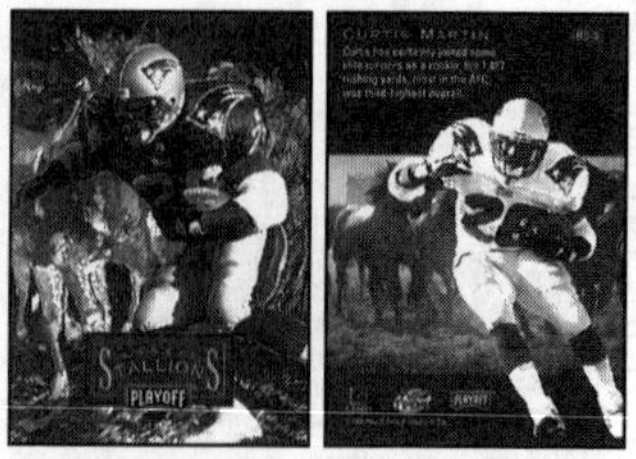

☐ 5 Terrell Davis	25.00	11.00	3.10
☐ 6 Antonio Freeman	15.00	6.75	1.85
☐ 7 Joey Galloway	12.00	5.50	1.50
☐ 8 Napoleon Kaufman	8.00	3.60	1.00
☐ 9 Curtis Martin	25.00	11.00	3.10
☐ 10 Steve McNair	20.00	9.00	2.50
☐ 11 Rashaan Salaam	10.00	4.50	1.25
☐ 12 Chris Sanders	8.00	3.60	1.00
☐ 13 Frank Sanders	8.00	3.60	1.00
☐ 14 Kordell Stewart	25.00	11.00	3.10
☐ 15 J.J. Stokes	8.00	3.60	1.00
☐ 16 Rodney Thomas	6.00	2.70	.75
☐ 17 Tamarick Vanover	8.00	3.60	1.00
☐ 18 Michael Westbrook	10.00	4.50	1.25
☐ 19 Tyrone Wheatley	6.00	2.70	.75
☐ 20 Eric Zeier	6.00	2.70	.75

1985 Police Raiders/Rams

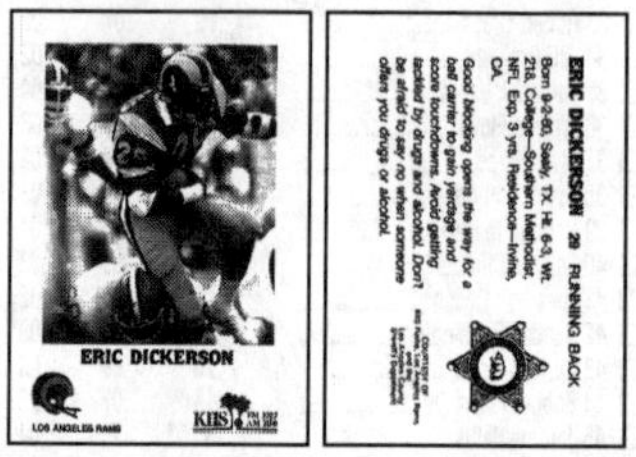

This 30-card set is actually two subsets, 15 cards featuring Los Angeles Rams and 15 cards featuring Los Angeles Raiders. The set was actually sponsored by the Sheriff's Department of Los Angeles County, KIIS Radio, and the Rams/Raiders, so technically it is a safety set but not a "police" set. The cards are unnumbered except for the uniform number listed on the card back. The list below is organized alphabetically within each team. Card backs are printed in black ink on white card stock. Cards measure approximately 2 13/16" by 4 1/8".

	MINT	NRMT	EXC
COMPLETE SET (30)	25.00	11.00	3.10
COMMON RAIDERS (1-15)	1.00	.45	.12
COMMON RAMS (16-30)	.75	.35	.09
☐ 1 Marcus Allen	8.00	3.60	1.00
☐ 2 Lyle Alzado	1.25	.55	.16
☐ 3 Todd Christensen	1.25	.55	.16
☐ 4 Dave Dalby	1.00	.45	.12
☐ 5 Mike Davis	1.00	.45	.12
☐ 6 Ray Guy	1.25	.55	.16
☐ 7 Frank Hawkins	1.00	.45	.12
☐ 8 Lester Hayes	1.25	.55	.16
☐ 9 Mike Haynes	1.25	.55	.16
☐ 10 Howie Long	2.00	.90	.25
☐ 11 Rod Martin	1.00	.45	.12
☐ 12 Mickey Marvin	1.00	.45	.12
☐ 13 Jim Plunkett	1.25	.55	.16
☐ 14 Brad Van Pelt	1.00	.45	.12
☐ 15 Dokie Williams	1.00	.45	.12
☐ 16 Bill Bain	.75	.35	.09
☐ 17 Mike Barber	.75	.35	.09
☐ 18 Dieter Brock	1.00	.45	.12
☐ 19 Nolan Cromwell	1.00	.45	.12
☐ 20 Eric Dickerson	2.00	.90	.25
☐ 21 Reggie Doss	.75	.35	.09
☐ 22 Carl Ekern	.75	.35	.09
☐ 23 Kent Hill	.75	.35	.09
☐ 24 LeRoy Irvin	1.00	.45	.12
☐ 25 Johnnie Johnson	.75	.35	.09
☐ 26 Jeff Kemp	1.00	.45	.12
☐ 27 Mike Lansford	.75	.35	.09
☐ 28 Mel Owens	.75	.35	.09
☐ 29 Barry Redden	.75	.35	.09
☐ 30 Mike Wilcher	.75	.35	.09

1986 Police Bears/Patriots

This set was supposedly not an authorized police issue as it is unclear which police department(s) truly sponsored the set. The 17 cards feature members of the Chicago Bears and New England Patriots who were in the Super Bowl in early 1986. The cards measure approximately 2 5/8" by 4 1/4". The card fronts give the player's name and uniform number under his red/blue bordered color photo. The card backs are printed in black ink on white card stock. Cards are numbered on the back in the lower right corner: the Bears (2-9) and the Patriots (10-17).

	MINT	NRMT	EXC
COMPLETE SET (17)	15.00	6.75	1.85
COMMON CARD (1-17)	.50	.23	.06

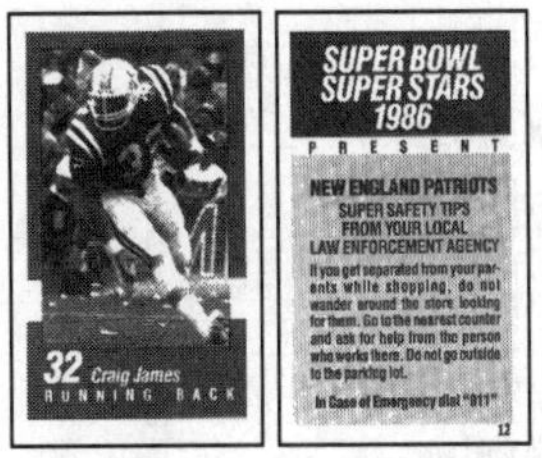

☐ 1 Title Card (Checklist on back of card)	.50	.23	.06
☐ 2 Richard Dent	2.00	.90	.25
☐ 3 Walter Payton	8.00	3.60	1.00
☐ 4 William Perry	1.00	.45	.12
☐ 5 Jim McMahon	1.00	.45	.12
☐ 6 Dave Duerson	.50	.23	.06
☐ 7 Gary Fencik	.75	.35	.09
☐ 8 Otis Wilson	.50	.23	.06
☐ 9 Willie Gault	.75	.35	.09
☐ 10 Craig James	1.50	.70	.19
☐ 11 Fred Marion	.50	.23	.06
☐ 12 Ronnie Lippett	.50	.23	.06
☐ 13 Stanley Morgan	1.00	.45	.12
☐ 14 John Hannah	1.50	.70	.19
☐ 15 Andre Tippett	.75	.35	.09
☐ 16 Tony Franklin	.50	.23	.06
☐ 17 Tony Eason	.75	.35	.09

1976 Popsicle Teams

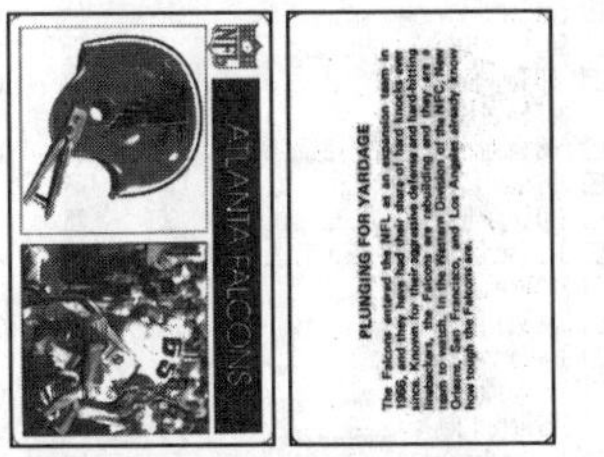

This set of 28 teams is printed on plastic material similar to that found on thin credit cards. There is a variation on the New York Giants card; one version shows the helmet logo as Giants and the other shows it as New York. The first version was apparently issued in error and the correction was issued but it is now unclear as to which version is more difficult to find. The title card reads, "Pro Quarterback, Pro Football's Leading Magazine". The cards measure approximately 3 3/8" by 2 1/8", have rounded corners, and are slightly thinner than a credit card. Below the NFL logo and the team, the front features a color helmet shot and a color action photo. The back contains a brief team history. Some consider the new expansion teams, Tampa Bay and Seattle, to be somewhat tougher to find. The cards are unnumbered and are ordered below alphabetically by team location name. The set is considered complete with just the 28 team cards.

	NRMT-MT	EXC	G-VG
COMPLETE SET (28)	80.00	36.00	10.00
COMMON TEAM (1-28)	2.50	1.10	.30
☐ 1 Atlanta Falcons	2.50	1.10	.30
☐ 2 Baltimore Colts	2.50	1.10	.30
☐ 3 Buffalo Bills	2.50	1.10	.30
☐ 4 Chicago Bears	2.50	1.10	.30
☐ 5 Cincinnati Bengals	2.50	1.10	.30
☐ 6 Cleveland Browns	2.50	1.10	.30
☐ 7 Dallas Cowboys	3.50	1.55	.45
☐ 8 Denver Broncos	2.50	1.10	.30
☐ 9 Detroit Lions	2.50	1.10	.30
☐ 10 Green Bay Packers	2.50	1.10	.30
☐ 11 Houston Oilers	2.50	1.10	.30
☐ 12 Kansas City Chiefs	2.50	1.10	.30
☐ 13 Los Angeles Rams	2.50	1.10	.30
☐ 14 Miami Dolphins	3.50	1.55	.45
☐ 15 Minnesota Vikings	2.50	1.10	.30
☐ 16 New England Patriots	2.50	1.10	.30
☐ 17 New Orleans Saints	2.50	1.10	.30
☐ 18A New York Giants (Giants on helmet)	2.50	1.10	.30
☐ 18B New York Giants (New York on helmet)	2.50	1.10	.30
☐ 19 New York Jets	2.50	1.10	.30
☐ 20 Oakland Raiders	3.50	1.55	.45
☐ 21 Philadelphia Eagles	2.50	1.10	.30
☐ 22 Pittsburgh Steelers	3.50	1.55	.45
☐ 23 St. Louis Cardinals	2.50	1.10	.30
☐ 24 San Diego Chargers	2.50	1.10	.30
☐ 25 San Francisco 49ers	3.50	1.55	.45
☐ 26 Seattle Seahawks	2.50	1.10	.30
☐ 27 Tampa Bay Buccaneers	2.50	1.10	.30
☐ 28 Washington Redskins	3.50	1.55	.45
☐ NNO Title Card SP Pro Quarterback, Pro Football's Leading Magazine	35.00	16.00	4.40

1962 Post Cereal

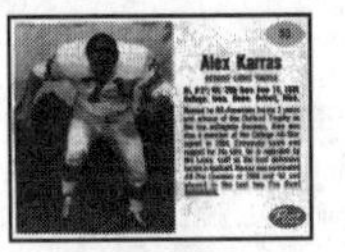

The 1962 Post Cereal set of 200 cards is Post's only American football issue. The cards were distributed on the back panels of various flavors of Post Cereals. As is typical of the Post package-back issues, the cards are blank-backed and are typically found poorly cut from the cereal box. The cards (when properly trimmed) measure 2 1/2" by 3 1/2". The cards are grouped in order of the team's 1961 season finish. The players within each team are also grouped in alphabetical order with the exception of 135 Frank Clarke of the Cowboys. Certain cards printed only on unpopular types of cereal are relatively difficult to obtain. Thirty-one such cards are known and are indicated by an SP (short printed) in the checklist. Some players who had been traded had asterisks after their positions. Jim Ninowski (57) and Sam Baker (74) can be found with either a red or black (traded) asterisk. The set price below does not include both variations. The cards of Jim Johnson, Bob Lilly, and Larry Wilson predate their Rookie Cards. Also noteworthy is the card of Fran Tarkenton, whose rookie year for cards is 1962.

	NRMT	VG-E	GOOD
COMPLETE SET (200)	4500.00	2000.00	550.00
COMMON CARD (1-200)	4.00	1.80	.50
☐ 1 Dan Currie	5.00	2.20	.60
☐ 2 Boyd Dowler	7.00	3.10	.85
☐ 3 Bill Forester	5.00	2.20	.60
☐ 4 Forrest Gregg	8.00	3.60	1.00
☐ 5 Dave Hanner	5.00	2.20	.60
☐ 6 Paul Hornung	18.00	8.00	2.20
☐ 7 Hank Jordan	7.00	3.10	.85
☐ 8 Jerry Kramer SP	35.00	16.00	4.40
☐ 9 Max McGee SP	25.00	11.00	3.10
☐ 10 Tom Moore SP	175.00	80.00	22.00
☐ 11 Jim Ringo	7.00	3.10	.85
☐ 12 Bart Starr	20.00	9.00	2.50
☐ 13 Jim Taylor	15.00	6.75	1.85
☐ 14 Fuzzy Thurston	7.00	3.10	.85
☐ 15 Jesse Whittenton	4.00	1.80	.50
☐ 16 Erich Barnes	5.00	2.20	.60
☐ 17 Roosevelt Brown	7.00	3.10	.85
☐ 18 Bob Gaiters	4.00	1.80	.50
☐ 19 Roosevelt Grier	7.00	3.10	.85
☐ 20 Sam Huff	10.00	4.50	1.25
☐ 21 Jim Katcavage	5.00	2.20	.60
☐ 22 Cliff Livingston	4.00	1.80	.50
☐ 23 Dick Lynch	4.00	1.80	.50
☐ 24 Joe Morrison SP	60.00	27.00	7.50
☐ 25 Dick Nolan SP	50.00	22.00	6.25
☐ 26 Andy Robustelli	8.00	3.60	1.00
☐ 27 Kyle Rote	7.00	3.10	.85
☐ 28 Del Shofner SP	100.00	45.00	12.50
☐ 29 Y.A. Tittle SP (Only player in set shown with helmet on)	125.00	55.00	15.50
☐ 30 Alex Webster	5.00	2.20	.60
☐ 31 Bill Barnes	4.00	1.80	.50
☐ 32 Maxie Baughan	5.00	2.20	.60
☐ 33 Chuck Bednarik	10.00	4.50	1.25
☐ 34 Tom Brookshier	7.00	3.10	.85
☐ 35 Jimmy Carr	4.00	1.80	.50
☐ 36 Ted Dean SP	50.00	22.00	6.25
☐ 37 Sonny Jurgensen	15.00	6.75	1.85
☐ 38 Tommy McDonald	5.00	2.20	.60
☐ 39 Clarence Peaks	4.00	1.80	.50
☐ 40 Pete Retzlaff	5.00	2.20	.60
☐ 41 Jesse Richardson SP	125.00	55.00	15.50
☐ 42 Leo Sugar	4.00	1.80	.50
☐ 43 Bobby Walston SP	60.00	27.00	7.50
☐ 44 Chuck Weber	10.00	4.50	1.25
☐ 45 Ed Khayat	4.00	1.80	.50
☐ 46 Howard Cassady	5.00	2.20	.60
☐ 47 Gail Cogdill	4.00	1.80	.50
☐ 48 Jim Gibbons SP	60.00	27.00	7.50
☐ 49 Bill Glass	4.00	1.80	.50
☐ 50 Alex Karras	10.00	4.50	1.25
☐ 51 Dick Lane	7.00	3.10	.85
☐ 52 Yale Lary	7.00	3.10	.85
☐ 53 Dan Lewis	4.00	1.80	.50
☐ 54 Darris McCord SP	100.00	45.00	12.50
☐ 55 Jim Martin	4.00	1.80	.50
☐ 56 Earl Morrall	5.00	2.20	.60
☐ 57A Jim Ninowski (red asterisk)	5.00	2.20	.60
☐ 57B Jim Ninowski (black asterisk)	5.00	2.20	.60
☐ 58 Nick Pietrosante	5.00	2.20	.60
☐ 59 Joe Schmidt SP	100.00	45.00	12.50
☐ 60 Harley Sewell	4.00	1.80	.50
☐ 61 Jim Brown	70.00	32.00	8.75
☐ 62 Galen Fiss SP	60.00	27.00	7.50
☐ 63 Bob Gain	4.00	1.80	.50
☐ 64 Jim Houston	4.00	1.80	.50
☐ 65 Mike McCormack	7.00	3.10	.85
☐ 66 Gene Hickerson	5.00	2.20	.60
☐ 67 Bobby Mitchell	8.00	3.60	1.00
☐ 68 John Morrow	4.00	1.80	.50
☐ 69 Bernie Parrish	4.00	1.80	.50
☐ 70 Milt Plum	5.00	2.20	.60
☐ 71 Ray Renfro	5.00	2.20	.60
☐ 72 Dick Schafrath	5.00	2.20	.60
☐ 73 Jim Ray Smith	4.00	1.80	.50
☐ 74A Sam Baker SP (red asterisk)	350.00	160.00	45.00
☐ 74B Sam Baker SP (black asterisk)	300.00	135.00	38.00
☐ 75 Paul Wiggin SP	30.00	13.50	3.70
☐ 76 Raymond Berry	10.00	4.50	1.25
☐ 77 Bob Boyd	4.00	1.80	.50
☐ 78 Ordell Braase	4.00	1.80	.50
☐ 79 Art Donovan	10.00	4.50	1.25
☐ 80 Dee Mackey	4.00	1.80	.50
☐ 81 Gino Marchetti	8.00	3.60	1.00
☐ 82 Lenny Moore	10.00	4.50	1.25
☐ 83 Jim Mutscheller	4.00	1.80	.50
☐ 84 Steve Myhra	4.00	1.80	.50
☐ 85 Jimmy Orr	5.00	2.20	.60
☐ 86 Jim Parker	8.00	3.60	1.00
☐ 87 Bill Pellington	4.00	1.80	.50
☐ 88 Alex Sandusky	4.00	1.80	.50
☐ 89 Dick Szymanski	4.00	1.80	.50
☐ 90 Johnny Unitas	30.00	13.50	3.70
☐ 91 Bruce Bosley	4.00	1.80	.50
☐ 92 John Brodie	12.00	5.50	1.50
☐ 93 Dave Baker SP	400.00	180.00	50.00
☐ 94 Tommy Davis	4.00	1.80	.50
☐ 95 Bob Harrison	4.00	1.80	.50
☐ 96 Matt Hazeltine	4.00	1.80	.50
☐ 97 Jim Johnson SP	70.00	32.00	8.75
☐ 98 Billy Kilmer	7.00	3.10	.85
☐ 99 Jerry Mertens	4.00	1.80	.50
☐ 100 Frank Morze	4.00	1.80	.50
☐ 101 R.C. Owens	5.00	2.20	.60
☐ 102 J.D. Smith	4.00	1.80	.50
☐ 103 Bob St. Clair SP	100.00	45.00	12.50
☐ 104 Monty Stickles	4.00	1.80	.50
☐ 105 Abe Woodson	4.00	1.80	.50
☐ 106 Doug Atkins	8.00	3.60	1.00
☐ 107 Ed Brown	5.00	2.20	.60
☐ 108 J.C. Caroline	4.00	1.80	.50
☐ 109 Rick Casares	5.00	2.20	.60
☐ 110 Angelo Coia SP	225.00	100.00	28.00
☐ 111 Mike Ditka SP	100.00	45.00	12.50
☐ 112 Joe Fortunato	4.00	1.80	.50
☐ 113 Willie Galimore	5.00	2.20	.60
☐ 114 Bill George	7.00	3.10	.85
☐ 115 Stan Jones	7.00	3.10	.85
☐ 116 Johnny Morris	5.00	2.20	.60
☐ 117 Larry Morris SP	60.00	27.00	7.50
☐ 118 Richie Petitbon	5.00	2.20	.60
☐ 119 Bill Wade	5.00	2.20	.60
☐ 120 Maury Youmans	4.00	1.80	.50
☐ 121 Preston Carpenter	4.00	1.80	.50
☐ 122 Buddy Dial	5.00	2.20	.60
☐ 123 Bobby Joe Green	4.00	1.80	.50
☐ 124 Mike Henry	4.00	1.80	.50
☐ 125 John Henry Johnson	8.00	3.60	1.00
☐ 126 Bobby Layne	20.00	9.00	2.50
☐ 127 Gene Lipscomb	7.00	3.10	.85
☐ 128 Lou Michaels	5.00	2.20	.60
☐ 129 John Nisby	4.00	1.80	.50
☐ 130 John Reger	4.00	1.80	.50
☐ 131 Mike Sandusky	4.00	1.80	.50
☐ 132 George Tarasovic	4.00	1.80	.50
☐ 133 Tom Tracy SP	110.00	50.00	14.00
☐ 134 Glynn Gregory	4.00	1.80	.50
☐ 135 Frank Clarke SP	75.00	34.00	9.50
☐ 136 Mike Connelly SP	60.00	27.00	7.50
☐ 137 L.G. Dupre	4.00	1.80	.50
☐ 138 Bob Fry	4.00	1.80	.50
☐ 139 Allen Green SP	125.00	55.00	15.50
☐ 140 Billy Howton	5.00	2.20	.60
☐ 141 Bob Lilly	30.00	13.50	3.70
☐ 142 Don Meredith	25.00	11.00	3.10
☐ 143 Dick Moegle	4.00	1.80	.50
☐ 144 Don Perkins	7.00	3.10	.85
☐ 145 Jerry Tubbs SP	90.00	40.00	11.00
☐ 146 J.W. Lockett	4.00	1.80	.50
☐ 147 Ed Cook	4.00	1.80	.50
☐ 148 John David Crow	5.00	2.20	.60
☐ 149 Sam Etcheverry	4.00	1.80	.50
☐ 150 Frank Fuller	4.00	1.80	.50
☐ 151 Prentice Gautt	4.00	1.80	.50
☐ 152 Jimmy Hill	4.00	1.80	.50
☐ 153 Bill Koman SP	50.00	22.00	6.25
☐ 154 Larry Wilson	15.00	6.75	1.85
☐ 155 Dale Meinert	4.00	1.80	.50
☐ 156 Ed Henke	4.00	1.80	.50
☐ 157 Sonny Randle	4.00	1.80	.50
☐ 158 Ralph Guglielmi SP	50.00	22.00	6.25
☐ 159 Joe Childress	4.00	1.80	.50
☐ 160 Jon Arnett	5.00	2.20	.60
☐ 161 Dick Bass	4.00	1.80	.50
☐ 162 Zeke Bratkowski	5.00	2.20	.60
☐ 163 Carroll Dale SP	25.00	11.00	3.10
☐ 164 Art Hunter	4.00	1.80	.50
☐ 165 John Lovetere	4.00	1.80	.50
☐ 166 Lamar Lundy	5.00	2.20	.60
☐ 167 Ollie Matson	10.00	4.50	1.25
☐ 168 Ed Meador	4.00	1.80	.50
☐ 169 Jack Pardee SP	75.00	34.00	9.50
☐ 170 Jim Phillips	4.00	1.80	.50
☐ 171 Les Richter	5.00	2.20	.60
☐ 172 Frank Ryan	5.00	2.20	.60
☐ 173 Frank Varrichione	4.00	1.80	.50
☐ 174 Grady Alderman	5.00	2.20	.60
☐ 175 Rip Hawkins	4.00	1.80	.50
☐ 176 Don Joyce SP	125.00	55.00	15.50
☐ 177 Bill Lapham	4.00	1.80	.50
☐ 178 Tommy Mason	5.00	2.20	.60
☐ 179 Hugh McElhenny	10.00	4.50	1.25
☐ 180 Dave Middleton	4.00	1.80	.50
☐ 181 Dick Pesonen SP	30.00	13.50	3.70
☐ 182 Karl Rubke	4.00	1.80	.50
☐ 183 George Shaw	4.00	1.80	.50
☐ 184 Fran Tarkenton	50.00	22.00	6.25
☐ 185 Mel Triplett	4.00	1.80	.50
☐ 186 Frank Youso SP	100.00	45.00	12.50
☐ 187 Bill Bishop	5.00	2.20	.60
☐ 188 Bill Anderson SP	75.00	34.00	9.50
☐ 189 Don Bosseler	4.00	1.80	.50
☐ 190 Fred Hageman	4.00	1.80	.50
☐ 191 Sam Horner	4.00	1.80	.50
☐ 192 Jim Kerr	4.00	1.80	.50
☐ 193 Joe Krakoski SP	225.00	100.00	28.00
☐ 194 Fred Dugan	4.00	1.80	.50
☐ 195 John Paluck	4.00	1.80	.50
☐ 196 Vince Promuto	4.00	1.80	.50
☐ 197 Joe Rutgens	4.00	1.80	.50
☐ 198 Norm Snead	7.00	3.10	.85
☐ 199 Andy Stynchula	4.00	1.80	.50
☐ 200 Bob Toneff	4.00	1.80	.50

1962 Post Booklets

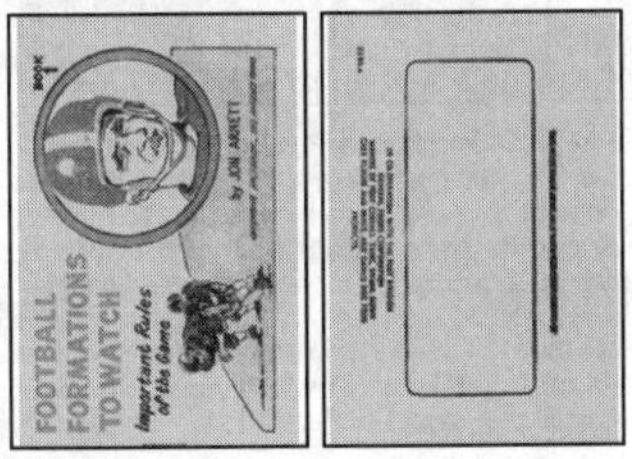

Each of these booklets measures approximately 5" by 3" and contained fifteen pages. The front cover carries the title of each booklet and a color cartoon headshot of the player inside a circle. While the first page presents biography and career summary, the remainder of each booklet consists of various tips, diagrams of basic formations and plays, officials' signals, football lingo, statistics, or team standings. The booklets are illustrated throughout by crude color drawings. These booklets are numbered on the front page in the upper right corner.

	NRMT	VG-E	GOOD
COMPLETE SET (4)	75.00	34.00	9.50
COMMON BOOK (1-4)	10.00	4.50	1.25
☐ 1 Jon Arnett Football Formations To Watch (Important Rules of the Game)	10.00	4.50	1.25
☐ 2 Paul Hornung Fundamentals of Football	35.00	16.00	4.40
☐ 3 Sonny Jurgensen How To Play On Offense (How To Call Signals And Key Plays)	20.00	9.00	2.50
☐ 4 Sam Huff How To Play Defense	15.00	6.75	1.85

1977 Pottsville Maroons

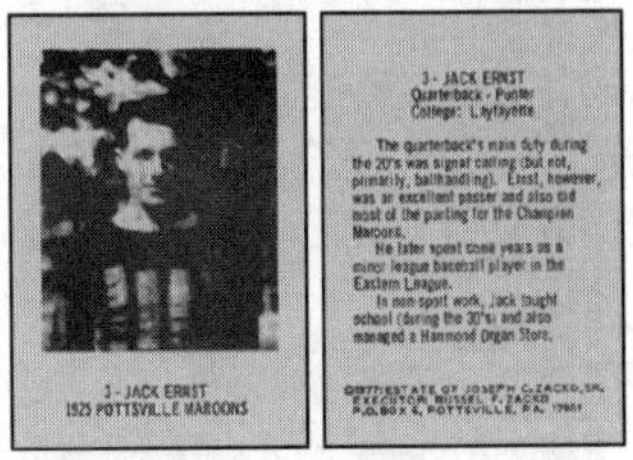

Reportedly issued in 1977, this standard-size 17-card set features helmetless player photos of the disputed 1925 NFL champion Pottsville Maroons on the card fronts. The pictures are white-bordered and red-screened, with the player's name, card number, and team name in red beneath each photo. The player's name, team, and card number appear again at the top of the card back, along with the name of the college (if any) attended previous to playing for the Maroons and brief biographical information, all in red. The set producer's name, Joseph C. Zacko Sr., appears at the bottom, along with the copyright date, 1977.

	NRMT-MT	EXC	G-VG
COMPLETE SET (17)	20.00	9.00	2.50
COMMON CARD (1-17)	1.50	.70	.19
☐ 1 Team History	2.00	.90	.25
☐ 2 The Symbolic Shoe	1.50	.70	.19

	MINT	NRMT	EXC
☐ 3 Jack Ernst	1.50	.70	.19
☐ 4 Tony Latone	1.50	.70	.19
☐ 5 Duke Osborn	1.50	.70	.19
☐ 6 Frank Bucher	1.50	.70	.19
☐ 7 Frankie Racis	1.50	.70	.19
☐ 8 Russ Hathaway	1.50	.70	.19
☐ 9 W.H.(Hoot) Flanagan	1.50	.70	.19
☐ 10 Charlie Berry	2.00	.90	.25
☐ 11 Russ Stein Herb Stein	1.50	.70	.19
☐ 12 Howard Lebengood	1.50	.70	.19
☐ 13 Denny Hughes	1.50	.70	.19
☐ 14 Barney Wentz	1.50	.70	.19
☐ 15 Eddie Doyle UER (Bio says American troops landed in Africa 1943; should be 1942)	1.50	.70	.19
☐ 16 Walter French	1.50	.70	.19
☐ 17 Dick Rauch	2.00	.90	.25

1992 Power

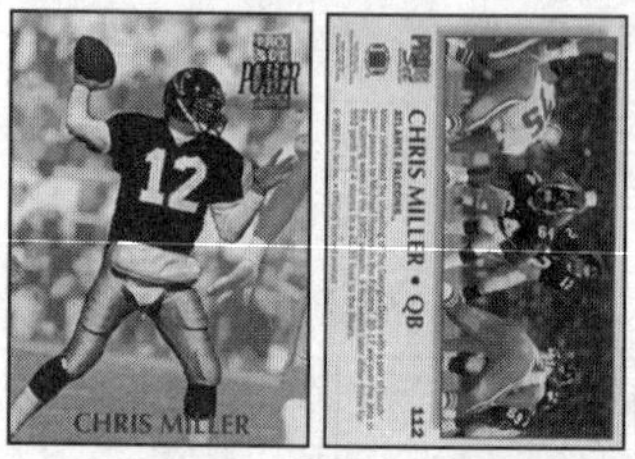

The 1992 Power set produced by Pro Set consists of 330 standard-size cards that were issued in 12-card packs. The fronts feature action player photos with the featured player in color against a semi-ghosted background. The player's name appears in brick-red lettering at the bottom. The horizontal backs have a second color player photo with a shadow border. The player's name and team name are printed in the team's colors, and a brief player profile fills out the back. Rookie Cards include Edgar Bennett, Steve Bono, Quentin Coryatt, Steve Emtman, Amp Lee, Johnny Mitchell, Carl Pickens and Tommy Vardell.

	MINT	NRMT	EXC
COMPLETE SET (330)	12.00	5.50	1.50
COMMON CARD (1-330)	.05	.02	.01

	MINT	NRMT	EXC
☐ 1 Warren Moon	.20	.09	.03
☐ 2 Mike Horan	.05	.02	.01
☐ 3 Bobby Hebert	.10	.05	.01
☐ 4 Jim Harbaugh	.20	.09	.03
☐ 5 Sean Landeta	.05	.02	.01
☐ 6 Bubby Brister	.10	.05	.01
☐ 7 John Elway	.50	.23	.06
☐ 8 Troy Aikman	.75	.35	.09
☐ 9 Rodney Peete	.10	.05	.01
☐ 10 Dan McGwire	.05	.02	.01
☐ 11 Mark Rypien	.10	.05	.01
☐ 12 Randall Cunningham	.10	.05	.01
☐ 13 Dan Marino	1.25	.55	.16
☐ 14 Vinny Testaverde	.10	.05	.01
☐ 15 Jeff Hostetler	.10	.05	.01
☐ 16 Joe Montana	.75	.35	.09
☐ 17 Dave Krieg	.10	.05	.01
☐ 18 Jeff Jaeger	.05	.02	.01
☐ 19 Bernie Kosar	.10	.05	.01
☐ 20 Barry Sanders	.75	.35	.09
☐ 21 Deion Sanders	.40	.18	.05
☐ 22 Emmitt Smith	2.00	.90	.25
☐ 23 Mel Gray	.10	.05	.01
☐ 24 Stanley Richard	.05	.02	.01
☐ 25 Brad Muster	.05	.02	.01
☐ 26 Rod Woodson	.20	.09	.03
☐ 27 Rodney Hampton	.20	.09	.03
☐ 28 Darrell Green	.05	.02	.01
☐ 29 Barry Foster	.10	.05	.01
☐ 30 Dave Meggett	.10	.05	.01
☐ 31 Lonnie Young	.05	.02	.01
☐ 32 Marcus Allen	.20	.09	.03
☐ 33 Merril Hoge	.05	.02	.01
☐ 34 Thurman Thomas	.20	.09	.03
☐ 35 Neal Anderson	.10	.05	.01
☐ 36 Bennie Blades	.05	.02	.01
☐ 37 Pat Terrell	.05	.02	.01
☐ 38 Nick Bell	.05	.02	.01
☐ 39 Johnny Johnson	.10	.05	.01
☐ 40 Bill Bates	.10	.05	.01
☐ 41 Keith Byars	.05	.02	.01
☐ 42 Ronnie Lott	.10	.05	.01
☐ 43 Elvis Patterson	.05	.02	.01
☐ 44 Lorenzo White	.10	.05	.01
☐ 45 Tony Stargell	.05	.02	.01
☐ 46 Tim McDonald	.05	.02	.01
☐ 47 Kirby Jackson	.05	.02	.01
☐ 48 Lionel Washington	.05	.02	.01
☐ 49 Dennis Smith	.05	.02	.01
☐ 50 Mike Singletary	.10	.05	.01
☐ 51 Mike Croel	.05	.02	.01
☐ 52 Pepper Johnson	.05	.02	.01
☐ 53 Vaughan Johnson	.05	.02	.01
☐ 54 Chris Spielman	.10	.05	.01
☐ 55 Junior Seau	.20	.09	.03
☐ 56 Lawrence Taylor	.20	.09	.03
☐ 57 Clay Matthews	.10	.05	.01
☐ 58 Derrick Thomas	.20	.09	.03
☐ 59 Seth Joyner	.10	.05	.01
☐ 60 Stan Thomas	.05	.02	.01
☐ 61 Nate Newton	.10	.05	.01
☐ 62 Matt Brock	.05	.02	.01
☐ 63 Gene Chilton	.05	.02	.01
☐ 64 Randall McDaniel	.05	.02	.01
☐ 65 Max Montoya	.05	.02	.01
☐ 66 Joe Jacoby	.05	.02	.01
☐ 67 Russell Maryland	.10	.05	.01
☐ 68 Ed King	.05	.02	.01
☐ 69 Mark Schlereth	.05	.02	.01
☐ 70 Charles McRae	.05	.02	.01
☐ 71 Charles Mann	.05	.02	.01
☐ 72 William Perry	.10	.05	.01
☐ 73 Simon Fletcher	.05	.02	.01
☐ 74 Paul Gruber	.05	.02	.01
☐ 75 Howie Long	.10	.05	.01
☐ 76 Steve McMichael	.05	.02	.01
☐ 77 Karl Mecklenburg	.05	.02	.01
☐ 78 Anthony Munoz	.20	.09	.03
☐ 79 Ray Childress	.10	.05	.01
☐ 80 Jerry Rice	.75	.35	.09
☐ 81 Art Monk	.10	.05	.01
☐ 82 John Taylor	.10	.05	.01
☐ 83 Andre Reed	.20	.09	.03
☐ 84 Haywood Jeffires	.10	.05	.01
☐ 85 Mark Duper	.10	.05	.01
☐ 86 Fred Barnett	.20	.09	.03
☐ 87 Tom Waddle	.05	.02	.01
☐ 88 Michael Irvin	.20	.09	.03
☐ 89 Brian Blades	.10	.05	.01
☐ 90 Neil Smith	.20	.09	.03
☐ 91 Kevin Greene	.20	.09	.03
☐ 92 Reggie White	.20	.09	.03
☐ 93 Jerry Ball	.05	.02	.01
☐ 94 Charles Haley	.10	.05	.01
☐ 95 Richard Dent	.10	.05	.01
☐ 96 Clyde Simmons	.10	.05	.01
☐ 97 Cornelius Bennett	.10	.05	.01
☐ 98 Eric Swann	.20	.09	.03
☐ 99 Doug Smith	.05	.02	.01
☐ 100 Jim Kelly	.20	.09	.03
☐ 101 Michael Jackson	.10	.05	.01
☐ 102 Steve Christie	.05	.02	.01
☐ 103 Timm Rosenbach	.05	.02	.01
☐ 104 Brett Favre	2.50	1.10	.30
☐ 105 Jeff Feagles	.05	.02	.01
☐ 106 Kevin Butler	.05	.02	.01
☐ 107 Boomer Esiason	.10	.05	.01
☐ 108 Steve Young	.50	.23	.06
☐ 109 Norm Johnson	.05	.02	.01
☐ 110 Jay Schroeder	.05	.02	.01
☐ 111 Jeff George	.20	.09	.03
☐ 112 Chris Miller	.10	.05	.01
☐ 113 Steve Bono	.20	.09	.03
☐ 114 Neil O'Donnell	.20	.09	.03
☐ 115 David Klingler	.20	.09	.03
☐ 116 Rich Gannon	.10	.05	.01
☐ 117 Chris Chandler	.10	.05	.01
☐ 118 Stan Gelbaugh	.05	.02	.01
☐ 119 Scott Mitchell	.20	.09	.03
☐ 120 Mark Carrier DB	.05	.02	.01
☐ 121 Terry Allen	.20	.09	.03
☐ 122 Tim McKyer	.05	.02	.01
☐ 123 Barry Word	.05	.02	.01
☐ 124 Freeman McNeil	.10	.05	.01
☐ 125 Louis Oliver	.05	.02	.01
☐ 126 Jarvis Williams	.05	.02	.01
☐ 127 Steve Atwater	.05	.02	.01
☐ 128 Cris Dishman	.05	.02	.01
☐ 129 Eric Dickerson	.20	.09	.03
☐ 130 Brad Baxter	.10	.05	.01
☐ 131 Frank Minnifield	.05	.02	.01
☐ 132 Ricky Watters	.20	.09	.03
☐ 133 David Fulcher	.05	.02	.01
☐ 134 Herschel Walker	.10	.05	.01
☐ 135 Christian Okoye	.10	.05	.01
☐ 136 Jerome Henderson	.05	.02	.01
☐ 137 Nate Odomes	.05	.02	.01
☐ 138 Todd Scott	.05	.02	.01
☐ 139 Robert Delpino	.05	.02	.01
☐ 140 Gary Anderson RB	.05	.02	.01
☐ 141 Todd Lyght	.05	.02	.01
☐ 142 Chris Warren	.20	.09	.03
☐ 143 Mike Brim	.05	.02	.01
☐ 144 Tom Rathman	.05	.02	.01
☐ 145 Dexter McNabb	.05	.02	.01
☐ 146 Vince Workman	.10	.05	.01
☐ 147 Anthony Johnson	.05	.02	.01
☐ 148 Brian Washington	.05	.02	.01
☐ 149 David Tate	.05	.02	.01
☐ 150 Johnny Holland	.05	.02	.01
☐ 151 Monte Coleman	.05	.02	.01
☐ 152 Keith McCants	.05	.02	.01
☐ 153 Eugene Seale	.05	.02	.01
☐ 154 Al Smith	.05	.02	.01
☐ 155 Andre Collins	.05	.02	.01
☐ 156 Pat Swilling	.10	.05	.01
☐ 157 Rickey Jackson	.05	.02	.01
☐ 158 Wilber Marshall	.05	.02	.01
☐ 159 Kyle Clifton	.05	.02	.01
☐ 160 Fred Stokes	.05	.02	.01
☐ 161 Lance Smith	.05	.02	.01
☐ 162 Guy McIntyre	.05	.02	.01
☐ 163 Bill Maas	.05	.02	.01
☐ 164 Gerald Perry	.05	.02	.01
☐ 165 Bart Oates	.05	.02	.01
☐ 166 Tony Jones	.05	.02	.01
☐ 167 Moe Gardner	.05	.02	.01
☐ 168 Joe Wolf	.05	.02	.01
☐ 169 Tim Krumrie	.05	.02	.01
☐ 170 Leonard Marshall	.05	.02	.01
☐ 171 Kevin Call	.05	.02	.01
☐ 172 Keith Kartz	.05	.02	.01
☐ 173 Ron Heller	.05	.02	.01
☐ 174 Steve Wallace	.05	.02	.01
☐ 175 Tony Casillas	.05	.02	.01
☐ 176 Tim Irwin	.05	.02	.01
☐ 177 Pat Harlow	.05	.02	.01
☐ 178 Bruce Smith	.20	.09	.03
☐ 179 Jim Lachey	.05	.02	.01
☐ 180 Andre Rison	.20	.09	.03
☐ 181 Michael Haynes	.10	.05	.01
☐ 182 Rod Bernstine	.05	.02	.01
☐ 183 Mark Clayton	.10	.05	.01
☐ 184 Jay Novacek	.20	.09	.03
☐ 185 Rob Moore	.10	.05	.01
☐ 186 Willie Green	.10	.05	.01
☐ 187 Ricky Proehl	.05	.02	.01
☐ 188 Al Toon	.10	.05	.01
☐ 189 Webster Slaughter	.05	.02	.01
☐ 190 Tony Bennett	.05	.02	.01
☐ 191 Jeff Cross	.05	.02	.01
☐ 192 Michael Dean Perry	.10	.05	.01
☐ 193 Greg Townsend	.05	.02	.01
☐ 194 Alfred Williams	.05	.02	.01
☐ 195 William Fuller	.10	.05	.01
☐ 196 Cortez Kennedy	.10	.05	.01
☐ 197 Henry Thomas	.05	.02	.01
☐ 198 Esera Tuaolo	.05	.02	.01
☐ 199 Tim Green	.05	.02	.01
☐ 200 Keith Jackson	.10	.05	.01
☐ 201 Don Majkowski	.05	.02	.01
☐ 202 Steve Beuerlein	.10	.05	.01
☐ 203 Hugh Millen	.05	.02	.01
☐ 204 Browning Nagle	.05	.02	.01
☐ 205 Chip Lohmiller	.05	.02	.01
☐ 206 Phil Simms	.10	.05	.01
☐ 207 Jim Everett	.10	.05	.01
☐ 208 Erik Kramer	.10	.05	.01
☐ 209 Todd Marinovich	.05	.02	.01
☐ 210 Henry Jones	.10	.05	.01
☐ 211 Dwight Stone	.05	.02	.01
☐ 212 Andre Waters	.05	.02	.01
☐ 213 Darryl Henley	.05	.02	.01
☐ 214 Mark Higgs	.05	.02	.01
☐ 215 Dalton Hilliard	.05	.02	.01
☐ 216 Earnest Byner	.05	.02	.01
☐ 217 Eric Metcalf	.20	.09	.03
☐ 218 Gill Byrd	.05	.02	.01
☐ 219 Robert Williams	.05	.02	.01
☐ 220 Kenneth Davis	.05	.02	.01
☐ 221 Larry Brown DB	.20	.09	.03
☐ 222 Mark Collins	.05	.02	.01
☐ 223 Vinnie Clark	.05	.02	.01
☐ 224 Patrick Hunter	.05	.02	.01
☐ 225 Gaston Green	.05	.02	.01
☐ 226 Everson Walls	.05	.02	.01
☐ 227 Harold Green	.10	.05	.01
☐ 228 Albert Lewis	.05	.02	.01
☐ 229 Don Griffin	.05	.02	.01
☐ 230 Lorenzo Lynch	.05	.02	.01
☐ 231 Brian Mitchell	.10	.05	.01
☐ 232 Thomas Everett	.05	.02	.01
☐ 233 Leonard Russell	.10	.05	.01
☐ 234 Eric Bieniemy	.05	.02	.01
☐ 235 John L. Williams	.05	.02	.01
☐ 236 Leroy Hoard	.10	.05	.01
☐ 237 Darren Lewis	.05	.02	.01
☐ 238 Reggie Cobb	.05	.02	.01
☐ 239 Steve Broussard	.05	.02	.01
☐ 240 Marion Butts	.10	.05	.01
☐ 241 Mike Pritchard	.10	.05	.01
☐ 242 Dexter Carter	.05	.02	.01
☐ 243 Aeneas Williams	.10	.05	.01
☐ 244 Bruce Pickens	.05	.02	.01
☐ 245 Harvey Williams	.20	.09	.03
☐ 246 Bobby Humphrey	.05	.02	.01
☐ 247 Duane Bickett	.05	.02	.01
☐ 248 James Francis	.05	.02	.01
☐ 249 Broderick Thomas	.05	.02	.01
☐ 250 Chip Banks	.05	.02	.01
☐ 251 Bryan Cox	.10	.05	.01
☐ 252 Sam Mills	.05	.02	.01
☐ 253 Ken Norton Jr.	.20	.09	.03
☐ 254 Jeff Herrod	.05	.02	.01
☐ 255 John Roper	.05	.02	.01
☐ 256 Darryl Talley	.05	.02	.01
☐ 257 Andre Tippett	.05	.02	.01
☐ 258 Jeff Lageman	.05	.02	.01
☐ 259 Chris Doleman	.10	.05	.01
☐ 260 Shane Conlan	.05	.02	.01
☐ 261 Jessie Tuggle	.05	.02	.01
☐ 262 Eric Hill	.05	.02	.01
☐ 263 Bruce Armstrong	.05	.02	.01
☐ 264 Bill Fralic	.05	.02	.01
☐ 265 Alvin Harper	.20	.09	.03
☐ 266 Bill Brooks	.10	.05	.01
☐ 267 Henry Ellard	.10	.05	.01
☐ 268 Cris Carter	.20	.09	.03
☐ 269 Irving Fryar	.10	.05	.01
☐ 270 Lawrence Dawsey	.10	.05	.01
☐ 271 James Lofton	.10	.05	.01
☐ 272 Ernest Givins	.10	.05	.01
☐ 273 Terance Mathis	.20	.09	.03
☐ 274 Randal Hill	.05	.02	.01
☐ 275 Eddie Brown	.05	.02	.01
☐ 276 Tim Brown	.20	.09	.03
☐ 277 Anthony Carter	.10	.05	.01
☐ 278 Wendell Davis	.05	.02	.01
☐ 279 Mark Ingram	.05	.02	.01
☐ 280 Anthony Miller	.20	.09	.03
☐ 281 Clarence Verdin	.05	.02	.01
☐ 282 Flipper Anderson	.05	.02	.01
☐ 283 Ricky Sanders	.05	.02	.01
☐ 284 Steve Jordan	.05	.02	.01
☐ 285 Gary Clark	.20	.09	.03
☐ 286 Sterling Sharpe	.20	.09	.03
☐ 287 Herman Moore	.60	.25	.07
☐ 288 Stephen Baker	.05	.02	.01
☐ 289 Marv Cook	.05	.02	.01
☐ 290 Ernie Jones	.05	.02	.01
☐ 291 Eric Green	.10	.05	.01
☐ 292 Mervyn Fernandez	.05	.02	.01
☐ 293 Greg McMurtry	.05	.02	.01
☐ 294 Quinn Early	.10	.05	.01
☐ 295 Tim Harris	.05	.02	.01
☐ 296 Will Furrer	.05	.02	.01
☐ 297 Jason Hanson	.10	.05	.01
☐ 298 Chris Hakel	.05	.02	.01
☐ 299 Ty Detmer	.50	.23	.06
☐ 300 David Klingler	.20	.09	.03
☐ 301 Amp Lee	.10	.05	.01
☐ 302 Troy Vincent	.20	.09	.03
☐ 303 Kevin Smith	.20	.09	.03
☐ 304 Terrell Buckley	.10	.05	.01
☐ 305 Dana Hall	.10	.05	.01
☐ 306 Tony Smith	.05	.02	.01
☐ 307 Steve Israel	.05	.02	.01
☐ 308 Vaughn Dunbar	.10	.05	.01
☐ 309 Ashley Ambrose	.10	.05	.01
☐ 310 Edgar Bennett	.60	.25	.07
☐ 311 Dale Carter	.20	.09	.03
☐ 312 Rodney Culver	.10	.05	.01
☐ 313 Matt Darby	.05	.02	.01
☐ 314 Tommy Vardell	.10	.05	.01
☐ 315 Quentin Coryatt	.20	.09	.03
☐ 316 Robert Jones	.10	.05	.01
☐ 317 Joe Bowden	.05	.02	.01
☐ 318 Eugene Chung	.05	.02	.01
☐ 319 Troy Auzenne	.05	.02	.01
☐ 320 Santana Dotson	.20	.09	.03
☐ 321 Greg Skrepenak	.10	.05	.01
☐ 322 Steve Emtman	.10	.05	.01
☐ 323 Carl Pickens	1.50	.70	.19
☐ 324 Johnny Mitchell	.20	.09	.03
☐ 325 Patrick Rowe	.05	.02	.01
☐ 326 Alonzo Spellman	.20	.09	.03
☐ 327 Robert Porcher	.10	.05	.01
☐ 328 Chris Mims	.20	.09	.03
☐ 329 Marc Boutte	.05	.02	.01
☐ 330 Shane Dronett	.05	.02	.01

1992 Power Combos

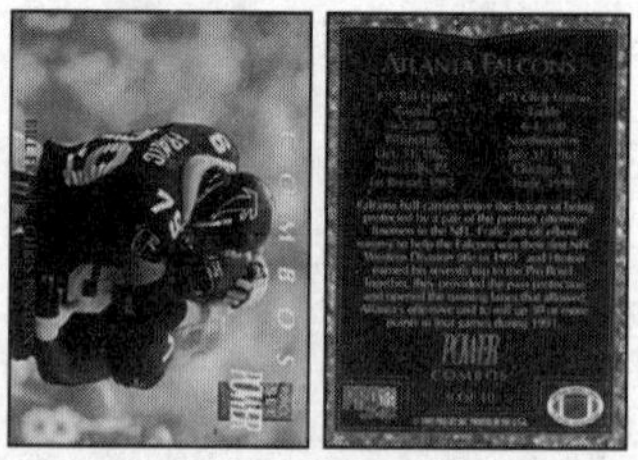

Randomly inserted into foil packs, this ten-card, standard-size set spotlights powerful offensive and defensive player combinations. The horizontal fronts feature a full-bleed color photo of both players with the background ghosted. The words "Combos" and "Power" are printed across the top in holographic lettering. On a purple panel inside marbleized borders, the backs present biography on both players and summarize their contribution to the team.

	MINT	NRMT	EXC
COMPLETE SET (10)	30.00	13.50	3.70
COMMON PAIR (1-10)	2.00	.90	.25

	MINT	NRMT	EXC
☐ 1 Steve Emtman Quentin Coryatt	3.00	1.35	.35
☐ 2 Barry Word Christian Okoye	2.00	.90	.25
☐ 3 Sam Mills Vaughan Johnson	2.00	.90	.25
☐ 4 Broderick Thomas Keith McCants	2.00	.90	.25
☐ 5 Michael Irvin Emmitt Smith	15.00	6.75	1.85
☐ 6 Jerry Ball Chris Spielman	2.00	.90	.25
☐ 7 Ricky Sanders	3.00	1.35	.35

Gary Clark			
Art Monk			
☐ 8 D.J. Johnson	3.00	1.35	.35
Rod Woodson			
☐ 9 Bill Fralic	2.00	.90	.25
Chris Hinton			
☐ 10 Irving Fryar	3.00	1.35	.35
Marv Cook			

1992-93 Power Emmitt Smith

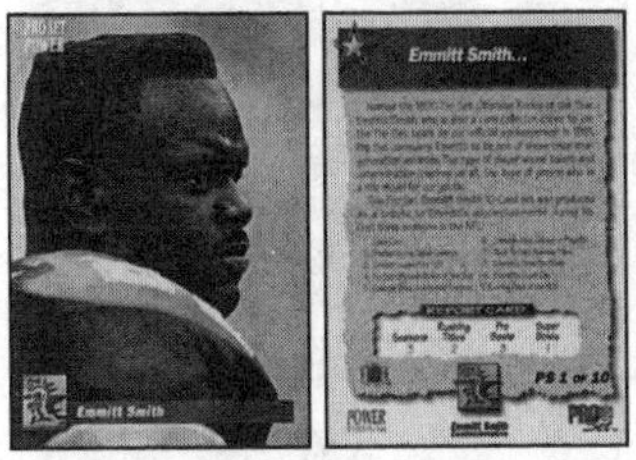

This ten-card standard size set features Emmitt Smith's career highlights. The production run was 25,000 sets. The offer for this set was found on the back of a Pro Set Emmitt Smith special card, which was randomly inserted in second series foil packs. To order the ten-card set, the collector had to mail in ten 1992 NFL Pro Set (first or second series) wrappers and ten 1992 Pro Set Power wrappers along with 7.50 for each set ordered (limit four sets per person). For an additional 20.00, the first 7,500 orders received a personally autographed uncut sheet hand numbered. The signed sheet had a limit of one per person. The fronts display full-bleed color action player photos in which the featured player is enhanced by ghosting of the background. The words "Pro Set Power" appear in holographic lettering at one of the upper corners, while a blue stripe toward the bottom carries the player's name and card subtitle. A special Emmitt Smith Commemorative emblem at the lower left corner rounds out the front. The team color-coded backs summarize Smith's career and feature a "Report Card" at the bottom. The cards are numbered on the back and have a "PS" prefix.

	MINT	NRMT	EXC
COMPLETE SET (10)	30.00	13.50	3.70
COMP.SHEET AUTO (10)	75.00	34.00	9.50
COMMON CARD (1-10)	3.00	1.35	.35
☐ 1 Emmitt Smith	3.00	1.35	.35
(Title card)			
☐ 2 Emmitt Smith	3.00	1.35	.35
Drafted by the			
☐ 3 Emmitt Smith	3.00	1.35	.35
Emmitt Scores Four Touchdowns			
☐ 4 Emmitt Smith	3.00	1.35	.35
Pro Set Offensive Rookie of the Year			
☐ 5 Emmitt Smith	3.00	1.35	.35
Cowboys Beat Undefeated Redskins			
☐ 6 Emmitt Smith	3.00	1.35	.35
Cowboys Beat Chicago In Playoffs			
☐ 7 Emmitt Smith	3.00	1.35	.35
Back-to-Back Rushing Titles			
☐ 8 Emmitt Smith	3.00	1.35	.35
Emmitt's Three Pro Bowls			
☐ 9 Emmitt Smith	3.00	1.35	.35
Emmitt's Super Day			
☐ 10 Emmitt Smith	3.00	1.35	.35
Running Back of the '90s			

1993 Power Prototypes

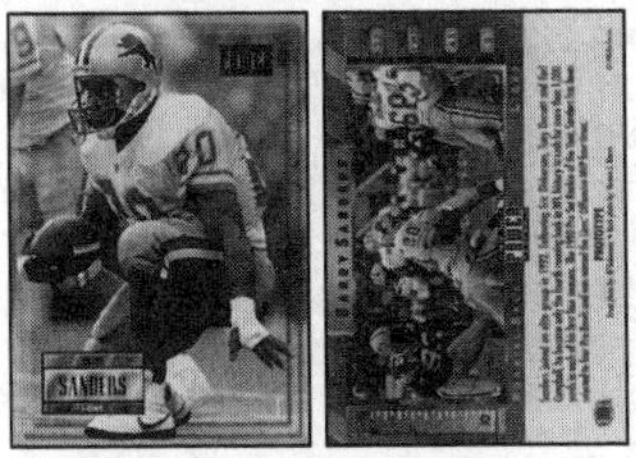

This nine-card standard-size set was issued to preview the style of the 1993 Pro Set Power football series. Pro Set sent one of these prototype cards to each dealer or wholesaler. The cards were also packaged in a cello pack with an ad card and given away at the 1993 National Sports Collectors Convention. The full-bleed color action photos on the fronts have a shadow-border effect that gives the appearance of depth to the pictures. The player's name and team name are printed in a red, gray, and blue-striped box at the lower left corner. The Pro Set Power logo is silver foil stamped on the fronts. The horizontal backs carry a color close-up photo, career summary, and a rating of players (from 1 to 10).

	MINT	NRMT	EXC
COMPLETE SET (10)	10.00	4.50	1.25
COMMON CARD	.40	.18	.05
☐ 20 Barry Sanders	2.00	.90	.25
☐ 22 Emmitt Smith	4.00	1.80	.50
☐ 26 Rod Woodson	.60	.25	.07
☐ 32 Ricky Watters	.60	.25	.07
☐ 37 Larry Centers	.60	.25	.07
☐ 71 Santana Dotson	.40	.18	.05
☐ 80 Jerry Rice	2.00	.90	.25
☐ 138 Reggie Rivers	.40	.18	.05
☐ 193 Trace Armstrong	.40	.18	.05
☐ NNO Title/Ad Card	.40	.18	.05

1993 Power

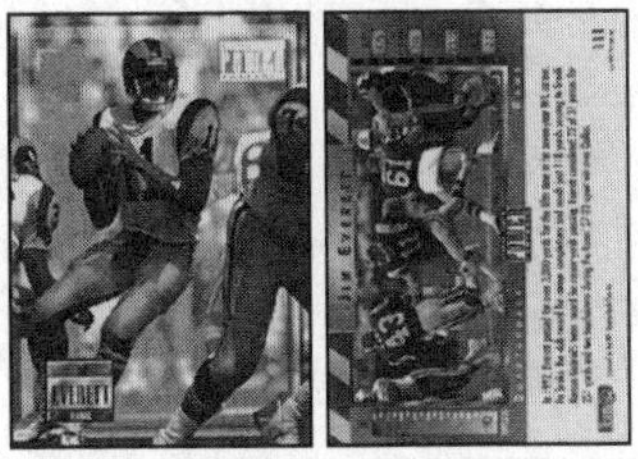

The 1993 Power set produced by Pro Set consists of 200 standard-size cards. Including foil and jumbo cases, a total of 8,000 cases were produced. Cards were issued in 12 and 25-card packs. The fronts feature borderless color player action shots, with the player's name within a red, white, and blue rectangle at the lower left. The horizontal back carries a color player action shot, which is flanked on the left by a rating scale, and on the right by 1992 stats. The player's name appears above the photo, and his position and team appear below. Season highlights from 1992 at the bottom round out the card. Randomly inserted in 1993 Power foil packs were two redemption cards entitling the collector to receive an Emmitt Smith hologram (HOLO) card through a mail-in offer. Randomly inserted in jumbo packs were seven update cards depicting traded players in their new uniforms. Except for the new player photos and "UD" suffixes on the back, the design is identical to the regular Power cards. Also one parallel gold Power card was inserted in every pack. These are distinguished by gold within the Power logo on front. Larry Centers is the only Rookie Card of note in this set.

	MINT	NRMT	EXC
COMPLETE SET (200)	8.00	3.60	1.00
COMMON CARD (1-200)	.05	.02	.01
☐ 1 Warren Moon	.20	.09	.03
☐ 2 Steve Christie	.05	.02	.01
☐ 3 Jim Breech	.05	.02	.01
☐ 4 Brett Favre	2.00	.90	.25
☐ 5 Sean Landeta	.05	.02	.01
☐ 6 Jim Arnold	.05	.02	.01
☐ 7 John Elway	.50	.23	.06
☐ 8 Troy Aikman	.75	.35	.09
☐ 9 Rodney Peete	.10	.05	.01
☐ 10 Pete Stoyanovich	.05	.02	.01
☐ 11 Mark Rypien	.10	.05	.01
☐ 12 Jim Kelly	.20	.09	.03
☐ 13 Dan Marino	1.50	.70	.19
☐ 14 Neil O'Donnell	.20	.09	.03
☐ 15 David Klingler	.10	.05	.01
☐ 16 Rich Gannon	.10	.05	.01
☐ 16UD Rich Gannon	.10	.05	.01
☐ 17 Dave Krieg	.10	.05	.01
☐ 18 Jeff Jaeger	.05	.02	.01
☐ 19 Bernie Kosar	.10	.05	.01
☐ 20 Barry Sanders	.75	.35	.09
☐ 21 Deion Sanders	.40	.18	.05
☐ 22 Emmitt Smith	1.50	.70	.19
☐ 23 Barry Word	.05	.02	.01
☐ 23UD Barry Word	.10	.05	.01
☐ 24 Stanley Richard	.05	.02	.01
☐ 25 Louis Oliver	.05	.02	.01
☐ 26 Rod Woodson	.20	.09	.03
☐ 27 Rodney Hampton	.20	.09	.03
☐ 28 Cris Dishman	.05	.02	.01
☐ 29 Barry Foster	.10	.05	.01
☐ 30 Dave Meggett	.10	.05	.01
☐ 31 Kevin Ross	.05	.02	.01
☐ 32 Ricky Watters	.20	.09	.03
☐ 33 Darren Lewis	.05	.02	.01
☐ 34 Thurman Thomas	.20	.09	.03
☐ 35 Rodney Culver	.05	.02	.01
☐ 36 Bennie Blades	.05	.02	.01
☐ 37 Larry Centers	.20	.09	.03
☐ 38 Todd Scott	.05	.02	.01
☐ 39 Darren Perry	.05	.02	.01
☐ 40 Robert Massey	.05	.02	.01
☐ 41 Keith Byars	.05	.02	.01
☐ 41UD Keith Byars UER	.10	.05	.01
(Misspelled Mimai on back)			
☐ 42 Chris Warren	.20	.09	.03
☐ 43 Cleveland Gary	.05	.02	.01
☐ 44 Lorenzo White	.10	.05	.01
☐ 45 Tony Stargell	.05	.02	.01
☐ 46 Bennie Thompson	.05	.02	.01
☐ 47 A.J. Johnson	.05	.02	.01
☐ 48 Daryl Johnston	.20	.09	.03
☐ 49 Dennis Smith	.05	.02	.01
☐ 50 Johnny Holland	.05	.02	.01
☐ 51 Ken Norton Jr.	.10	.05	.01
☐ 52 Pepper Johnson	.05	.02	.01
☐ 52UD Pepper Johnson	.10	.05	.01
☐ 53 Vaughan Johnson	.05	.02	.01
☐ 54 Chris Spielman	.10	.05	.01
☐ 55 Junior Seau	.20	.09	.03
☐ 56 Chris Doleman	.10	.05	.01
☐ 57 Rickey Jackson	.05	.02	.01
☐ 58 Derrick Thomas	.20	.09	.03
☐ 59 Seth Joyner	.10	.05	.01
☐ 60 Stan Thomas	.05	.02	.01
☐ 61 Nate Newton	.10	.05	.01
☐ 62 Matt Brock	.05	.02	.01
☐ 63 Mike Munchak	.05	.02	.01
☐ 64 Randall McDaniel	.05	.02	.01
☐ 65 Ron Hallstrom	.05	.02	.01
☐ 66 Andy Heck	.05	.02	.01
☐ 67 Russell Maryland	.10	.05	.01
☐ 68 Bruce Wilkerson	.05	.02	.01
☐ 69 Mark Schlereth	.05	.02	.01
☐ 70 John Fina	.05	.02	.01
☐ 71 Santana Dotson	.10	.05	.01
☐ 72 Don Mosebar UER	.05	.02	.01
(Listed as tackle; should be center)			
☐ 73 Simon Fletcher	.05	.02	.01
☐ 74 Paul Gruber	.05	.02	.01
☐ 75 Howard Ballard	.05	.02	.01
☐ 76 John Alt	.05	.02	.01
☐ 77 Carlton Haselrig	.05	.02	.01
☐ 78 Bruce Smith	.20	.09	.03
☐ 79 Ray Childress	.10	.05	.01
☐ 80 Jerry Rice	.75	.35	.09
☐ 81 Art Monk	.10	.05	.01
☐ 82 John Taylor	.10	.05	.01
☐ 83 Andre Reed	.20	.09	.03
☐ 84 Sterling Sharpe	.20	.09	.03
☐ 85 Sam Graddy	.05	.02	.01
☐ 86 Fred Barnett	.10	.05	.01
☐ 87 Ricky Proehl	.05	.02	.01
☐ 88 Michael Irvin	.20	.09	.03
☐ 89 Webster Slaughter	.05	.02	.01
☐ 90 Tony Bennett	.05	.02	.01
☐ 91 Leslie O'Neal	.10	.05	.01
☐ 92 Michael Dean Perry	.10	.05	.01
☐ 93 Greg Townsend	.05	.02	.01
☐ 94 Anthony Smith	.10	.05	.01
☐ 95 Richard Dent	.10	.05	.01
☐ 96 Clyde Simmons	.10	.05	.01
☐ 97 Cornelius Bennett	.10	.05	.01
☐ 98 Eric Swann	.10	.05	.01
☐ 99 Cortez Kennedy	.10	.05	.01
☐ 100 Emmitt Smith	1.00	.45	.12
☐ 101 Michael Jackson	.10	.05	.01
☐ 102 Lin Elliott	.05	.02	.01
☐ 103 Rohn Stark	.05	.02	.01
☐ 104 Jim Harbaugh	.20	.09	.03
☐ 105 Greg Davis	.05	.02	.01
☐ 106 Mike Cofer	.05	.02	.01
☐ 107 Morten Andersen	.05	.02	.01
☐ 108 Steve Young	.50	.23	.06
☐ 109 Norm Johnson	.05	.02	.01
☐ 110 Dan McGwire	.05	.02	.01
☐ 111 Jim Everett	.10	.05	.01
☐ 112 Randall Cunningham	.10	.05	.01
☐ 113 Steve Bono	.20	.09	.03
☐ 114 Cody Carlson	.05	.02	.01
☐ 115 Jeff Hostetler	.10	.05	.01
☐ 116 Rich Camarillo	.05	.02	.01
☐ 117 Chris Chandler	.10	.05	.01
☐ 118 Stan Gelbaugh	.05	.02	.01
☐ 119 Tony Sacca	.05	.02	.01
☐ 120 Henry Jones	.05	.02	.01
☐ 121 Terry Allen	.20	.09	.03
☐ 122 Amp Lee	.05	.02	.01
☐ 123 Mel Gray	.10	.05	.01
☐ 124 Jon Vaughn	.05	.02	.01
☐ 124UD Jon Vaughn UER	.10	.05	.01
(Misspelled Saehawks on front)			
☐ 125 Bubba McDowell	.05	.02	.01
☐ 126 Audray McMillian	.05	.02	.01
☐ 127 Terrell Buckley	.05	.02	.01
☐ 128 Dana Hall	.05	.02	.01
☐ 129 Eric Dickerson	.20	.09	.03
☐ 130 Martin Bayless	.05	.02	.01
☐ 131 Steve Israel	.05	.02	.01
☐ 132 Vaughn Dunbar	.05	.02	.01
☐ 133 Ronnie Harmon	.10	.05	.01
☐ 134 Dale Carter	.10	.05	.01
☐ 135 Neal Anderson	.10	.05	.01
☐ 136 Merton Hanks	.10	.05	.01
☐ 137 James Washington	.05	.02	.01
☐ 138 Reggie Rivers	.05	.02	.01
☐ 139 Bruce Pickens	.05	.02	.01
☐ 140 Gary Anderson RB	.05	.02	.01
☐ 141 Eugene Robinson	.05	.02	.01
☐ 142 Charles Mincy UER	.10	.05	.01
(Listed as running back; he is a defensive back)			
☐ 143 Matt Darby	.05	.02	.01
☐ 144 Tom Rathman	.05	.02	.01
☐ 145 Mike Prior	.05	.02	.01
☐ 146 Sean Lumpkin	.05	.02	.01
☐ 147 Greg Jackson	.05	.02	.01
☐ 148 Wes Hopkins	.05	.02	.01
☐ 149 David Tate UER	.05	.02	.01
(Listed as linebacker; should be safety)			
☐ 150 James Francis	.05	.02	.01
☐ 151 Bryan Cox	.05	.02	.01
☐ 152 Keith McCants	.05	.02	.01
☐ 152UD Keith McCants	.10	.05	.01
☐ 153 Mark Stepnoski	.05	.02	.01
☐ 154 Al Smith	.05	.02	.01
☐ 155 Robert Jones	.05	.02	.01
☐ 156 Lawrence Taylor	.20	.09	.03
☐ 157 Clay Matthews	.10	.05	.01
☐ 158 Wilber Marshall	.05	.02	.01
☐ 158UD Wilber Marshall UER	.10	.05	.01
(Misspelled Marshal on front)			
☐ 159 Mike Johnson	.05	.02	.01
☐ 160 Adam Schreiber	.05	.02	.01
☐ 161 Tim Grunhard	.05	.02	.01
☐ 162 Mark Bortz	.05	.02	.01
☐ 163 Gene Chilton	.05	.02	.01
☐ 164 Jamie Dukes	.05	.02	.01
☐ 165 Bart Oates	.05	.02	.01
☐ 166 Kevin Gogan	.05	.02	.01
☐ 167 Kent Hull	.05	.02	.01
☐ 168 Ed King	.05	.02	.01
☐ 169 Eugene Chung	.05	.02	.01
☐ 170 Troy Auzenne	.05	.02	.01
☐ 171 Charles Mann	.05	.02	.01
☐ 172 William Perry	.10	.05	.01
☐ 173 Mike Lodish	.05	.02	.01
☐ 174 Bruce Matthews	.05	.02	.01
☐ 175 Tony Casillas	.05	.02	.01
☐ 176 Steve Wisniewski	.05	.02	.01
☐ 177 Karl Mecklenburg	.05	.02	.01
☐ 178 Richmond Webb	.05	.02	.01
☐ 179 Erik Williams	.10	.05	.01
☐ 180 Andre Rison	.20	.09	.03
☐ 181 Michael Haynes	.10	.05	.01
☐ 182 Don Beebe	.05	.02	.01
☐ 183 Anthony Miller	.10	.05	.01
☐ 184 Jay Novacek	.20	.09	.03
☐ 185 Rob Moore	.10	.05	.01
☐ 186 Willie Green	.05	.02	.01
☐ 187 Tom Waddle	.05	.02	.01
☐ 188 Keith Jackson	.10	.05	.01
☐ 189 Steve Tasker	.10	.05	.01
☐ 190 Marco Coleman	.05	.02	.01
☐ 191 Jeff Wright	.05	.02	.01
☐ 192 Burt Grossman	.05	.02	.01
☐ 193 Trace Armstrong	.05	.02	.01
☐ 194 Charles Haley	.10	.05	.01
☐ 195 Greg Lloyd	.20	.09	.03
☐ 196 Marc Boutte	.05	.02	.01
☐ 197 Rufus Porter	.05	.02	.01
☐ 198 Dennis Gibson	.05	.02	.01
☐ 199 Shane Dronett	.05	.02	.01
☐ 200 Joe Montana	.75	.35	.09
☐ H1 Emmitt Smith	20.00	9.00	2.50
Hologram Redemption Back to Back			
☐ H2 Emmitt Smith	20.00	9.00	2.50
Hologram Redemption Super Day			

1993 Power Gold

This 200-card standard-size set is a parallel to the regular 1993 Power issue and were inserted one per pack. The cards are differentiated by having a "gold" Power logo on front. The gold foil is very difficult to determine and has to be held correctly for the difference to be noticed.

	MINT	NRMT	EXC
COMPLETE SET (200)	20.00	9.00	2.50
COMMON CARD (1-200)	.10	.05	.01

*GOLD CARDS: 1X TO 2X BASIC CARDS

1993 Power All-Power Defense

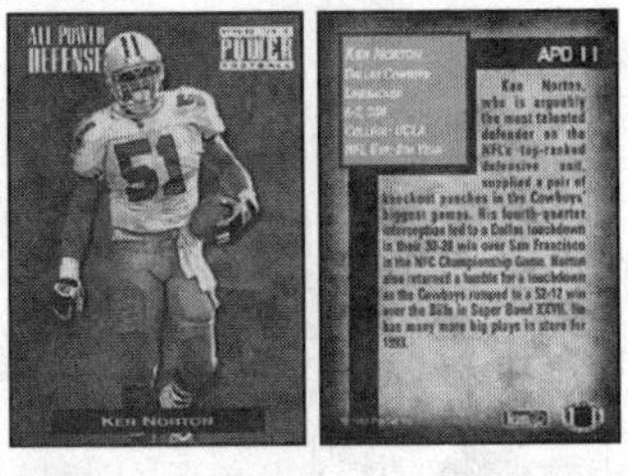

Randomly inserted at a rate of two per jumbo pack, these 25 standard-size cards feature on their fronts borderless color player photos with textured brown backgrounds. The player's name appears in yellow lettering within a black rectangle near the bottom. The textured brown background continues on the back, which carries the player's name, team, position, and biography in a yellow box at the upper left. Career highlights in red lettering follow alongside and below. The cards are numbered on the back with an "APD" prefix. Parallel gold cards were also randomly inserted in packs.

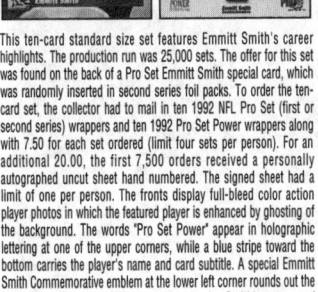

	MINT	NRMT	EXC
COMPLETE SET (25)	5.00	2.20	.60
COMMON CARD (1-25)	.20	.09	.03
COMPLETE GOLD SET (25)	10.00	4.50	1.25
*GOLD CARDS: 1X to 2X BASIC CARDS			

□ 1 Clyde Simmons	.20	.09	.03
□ 2 Anthony Smith	.20	.09	.03
□ 3 Ray Childress	.30	.14	.04
□ 4 Michael Dean Perry	.30	.14	.04
□ 5 Bruce Smith	.50	.23	.06
□ 6 Cortez Kennedy	.30	.14	.04
□ 7 Charles Haley	.30	.14	.04
□ 8 Marco Coleman	.20	.09	.03
□ 9 Alonzo Spellman	.30	.14	.04
□ 10 Junior Seau	.50	.23	.06
□ 11 Ken Norton Jr.	.30	.14	.04
□ 12 Derrick Thomas	.50	.23	.06
□ 13 Wilber Marshall	.20	.09	.03
□ 14 Chris Doleman	.20	.09	.03
□ 15 Seth Joyner	.30	.14	.04
□ 16 Al Smith	.20	.09	.03
□ 17 Deion Sanders	.75	.35	.09
□ 18 Rod Woodson	.50	.23	.06
□ 19 Audray McMillian	.20	.09	.03
□ 20 Dale Carter	.30	.14	.04
□ 21 Terrell Buckley	.20	.09	.03
□ 22 Bennie Thompson	.20	.09	.03
□ 23 Chris Spielman	.30	.14	.04
□ 24 Lawrence Taylor	.50	.23	.06
□ 25 Tony Bennett	.20	.09	.03

1993 Power Combos

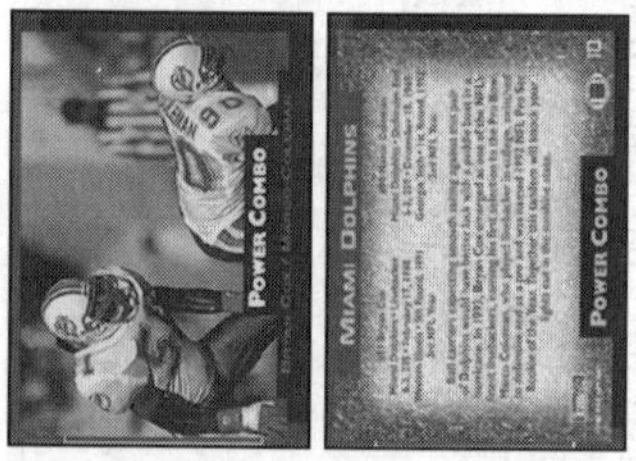

Randomly inserted in foil packs, these ten standard-size cards feature on their horizontal fronts two-player photos that are bordered in black, blue, and purple. The players' names appear in red lettering within a black bar near the bottom. The horizontal back carries the team name of the two players in yellow lettering within a purple rectangle at the top. The players' names, uniform numbers, positions, biography, and career highlights follow below. All this is on a green, grassy background bordered in the same colors as the front. Gold Combos parallel cards were also randomly inserted in packs. Also, cards from 10-card Prism Combos set were random inserts in Power Update jumbo packs.

	MINT	NRMT	EXC
COMPLETE SET (10)	5.00	2.20	.60
COMMON PAIR (1-10)	.30	.14	.04
COMPLETE GOLD SET (10)	10.00	4.50	1.25
*GOLD CARDS: 1X to 2X BASIC CARDS			
COMPLETE PRISM SET (10)	15.00	6.75	1.85
*PRISM CARDS: 1.5X to 3X BASIC CARDS			

□ 1 Emmitt Smith Barry Sanders	3.00	1.35	.35
□ 2 Terrell Buckley Sterling Sharpe	.50	.23	.06
□ 3 Junior Seau Gary Plummer	.75	.35	.09
□ 4 Deion Sanders Tim McKyer	1.00	.45	.12
□ 5 Bruce Smith Darryl Talley	.75	.35	.09
□ 6 Warren Moon Webster Slaughter	.50	.23	.06
□ 7 Chris Doleman Henry Thomas	.30	.14	.04
□ 8 Karl Mecklenburg Michael Brooks	.30	.14	.04
□ 9 Ken Norton Jr. Robert Jones	.50	.23	.06
□ 10 Marco Coleman Bryan Cox	.30	.14	.04

1993 Power Draft Picks

Randomly inserted in 1993 Power packs, these 30 standard-size cards feature on their fronts borderless color player photos with black-and-white backgrounds. The player's name appears in red lettering near the bottom. The black and horizontal back carries the player's name in red lettering near the top, followed below by his team and career highlights. The cards are numbered on the back with a "PDP" prefix. Gold parallel cards were also randomly inserted.

	MINT	NRMT	EXC
COMPLETE SET (30)	8.00	3.60	1.00
COMMON CARD (1-30)	.15	.07	.02
COMPLETE GOLD SET (30)	16.00	7.25	2.00
*GOLD CARDS: 1X to 2X BASIC CARDS			

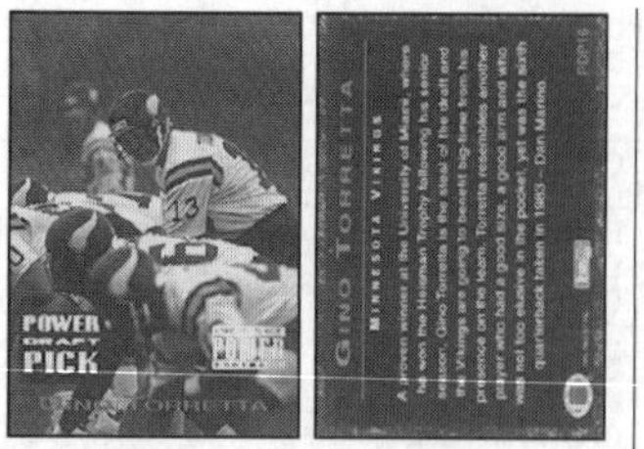

□ 1 Lincoln Kennedy UER (Misnumbered 10)	.15	.07	.02
□ 2 Thomas Smith UER (Misnumbered 20)	.25	.11	.03
□ 3 Robert Smith UER (Misnumbered 30)	.50	.23	.06
□ 4 John Copeland UER (Misnumbered 40)	.15	.07	.02
□ 5 Dan Footman UER (Misnumbered 50)	.15	.07	.02
□ 6 Darrin Smith UER (Misnumbered 60)	.25	.11	.03
□ 7 Qadry Ismail UER (Misnumbered 70)	.25	.11	.03
□ 8 Ryan McNeil UER (Misnumbered 80)	.15	.07	.02
□ 9 George Teague UER (Misnumbered 90)	.15	.07	.02
□ 10 Brad Hopkins	.15	.07	.02
□ 11 Ernest Dye	.15	.07	.02
□ 12 Jaime Fields	.15	.07	.02
□ 13 Patrick Bates	.15	.07	.02
□ 14 Jerome Bettis	1.50	.70	.19
□ 15 O.J. McDuffie	.50	.23	.06
□ 16 Gino Torretta	.25	.11	.03
□ 17 Drew Bledsoe	3.00	1.35	.35
□ 18 Irv Smith	.15	.07	.02
□ 19 Marcus Buckley	.15	.07	.02
□ 20 Coleman Rudolph	.15	.07	.02
□ 21 Leonard Renfro	.15	.07	.02
□ 22 Garrison Hearst	1.00	.45	.12
□ 23 Deon Figures	.15	.07	.02
□ 24 Natrone Means	.50	.23	.06
□ 25 Todd Kelly	.15	.07	.02
□ 26 Carlton Gray	.15	.07	.02
□ 27 Eric Curry	.25	.11	.03
□ 28 Tom Carter	.15	.07	.02
□ 29 AFC Logo CL	.15	.07	.02
□ 30 NFC Logo CL	.15	.07	.02

1993 Power Moves

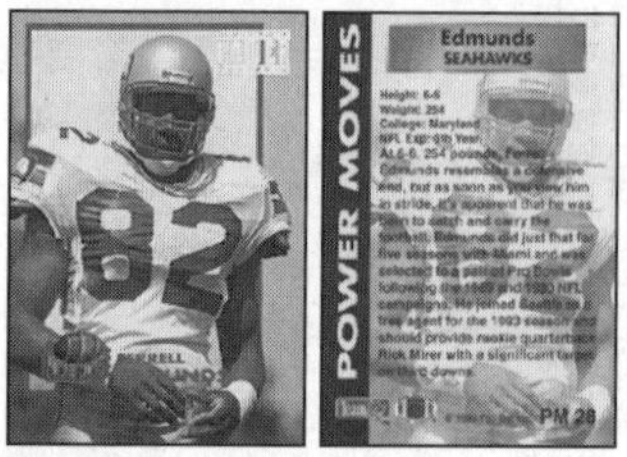

The first 30 cards of this 40-card standard-size set were randomly inserted in 1993 Power packs, the last ten were random inserts in 1993 Power jumbo packs. The cards feature on their fronts borderless color player photos framed by a red line. The player's name appears in red lettering near the bottom. The back carries a ghosted version of the photo on the front, with the player's last name and team printing in black lettering within a grayish plaque at the top. Biography and career highlights follow below. The set's title appears in vertical white lettering within a blue stripe that edges the left side. The cards are numbered on the back with a "PM" prefix. Gold parallel cards were randomly inserted in packs.

	MINT	NRMT	EXC
COMPLETE SET (40)	5.00	2.20	.60
COMPLETE SERIES 1 (30)	3.00	1.35	.35
COMPLETE SERIES 2 (10)	2.00	.90	.25
COMMON CARD (PM1-PM40)	.15	.07	.02
COMPLETE GOLD SET (40)	10.00	4.50	1.25
*GOLD CARDS: 1X to 2X BASIC CARDS			

□ PM1 Bobby Hebert	.15	.07	.02
□ PM2 Bill Brooks	.25	.11	.03
□ PM3 Vinny Testaverde	.25	.11	.03
□ PM4 Hugh Millen	.15	.07	.02
□ PM5 Rod Bernstine	.15	.07	.02
□ PM6 Robert Delpino	.15	.07	.02
□ PM7 Pat Swilling	.25	.11	.03
□ PM8 Reggie White	.50	.23	.06
□ PM9 Aaron Cox	.15	.07	.02
□ PM10 Joe Montana	2.00	.90	.25
□ PM11 Gaston Green	.15	.07	.02
□ PM12 Jeff Hostetler	.25	.11	.03
□ PM13 Shane Conlan	.15	.07	.02
□ PM14 Irv Eatman	.15	.07	.02
□ PM15 Mark Ingram	.15	.07	.02
□ PM16 Irving Fryar	.25	.11	.03
□ PM17 Don Majkowski	.15	.07	.02
□ PM18 Will Wolford	.15	.07	.02
□ PM19 Boomer Esiason	.25	.11	.03
□ PM20 Ronnie Lott	.25	.11	.03
□ PM21 Johnny Johnson	.15	.07	.02
□ PM22 Steve Beuerlein	.25	.11	.03
□ PM23 Chuck Cecil	.15	.07	.02
□ PM24 Gary Clark	.25	.11	.03
□ PM25 Kevin Greene	.50	.23	.06
□ PM26 Jerrol Williams	.15	.07	.02
□ PM27 Tim McDonald	.15	.07	.02
□ PM28 Ferrell Edmunds	.15	.07	.02
□ PM29 Kelvin Martin	.15	.07	.02
□ PM30 Hardy Nickerson	.15	.07	.02
□ PM31 Jerry Ball	.15	.07	.02
□ PM32 Jim McMahon	.25	.11	.03
□ PM33 Marcus Allen	.50	.23	.06
□ PM34 John Stephens	.15	.07	.02
□ PM35 John Booty	.15	.07	.02
□ PM36 Wade Wilson	.15	.07	.02
□ PM37 Mark Bavaro	.15	.07	.02
□ PM38 Bill Fralic	.15	.07	.02
□ PM39 Mark Clayton	.25	.11	.03
□ PM40 Mike Sherrard	.25	.11	.03

1993 Power Update Moves

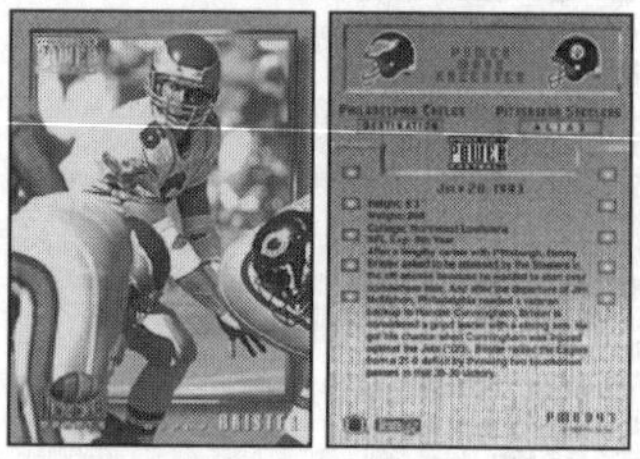

These 50 standard-size cards shared nine-card packs with 1993 Power Update Prospects cards. The fronts feature color player action shots with purplish borders and framed with red and blue lines. The player's name appears in yellow lettering within the lower margin. The back carries the player's team name and helmet from before his trade at the upper right, and the name and helmet of his new team at the upper left. Below are the date of the trade, followed by a brief biography and season highlights. The cards are numbered on the back with a "PMUD" prefix. Gold parallel versions were also inserted in packs.

	MINT	NRMT	EXC
COMPLETE SET (50)	5.00	2.20	.60
COMMON CARD (1-50)	.10	.05	.01
COMPLETE GOLD SET (50)	10.00	4.50	1.25
*GOLD CARDS: 1X to 2X BASIC CARDS			

□ 1 Bobby Hebert	.10	.05	.01
□ 2 Bill Brooks	.15	.07	.02
□ 3 Vinny Testaverde	.15	.07	.02
□ 4 Hugh Millen	.10	.05	.01
□ 5 Rod Bernstine	.10	.05	.01
□ 6 Robert Delpino	.10	.05	.01
□ 7 Pat Swilling	.15	.07	.02
□ 8 Reggie White	.25	.11	.03
□ 9 Aaron Cox	.10	.05	.01
□ 10 Joe Montana	2.00	.90	.25
□ 11 Vinnie Clark UER (Name misspelled Vinny on card)	.10	.05	.01
□ 12 Jeff Hostetler	.15	.07	.02
□ 13 Shane Conlan	.10	.05	.01
□ 14 Irv Eatman	.10	.05	.01
□ 15 Mark Ingram	.15	.07	.02
□ 16 Irving Fryar	.15	.07	.02
□ 17 Don Majkowski	.10	.05	.01
□ 18 Will Wolford	.10	.05	.01
□ 19 Boomer Esiason	.15	.07	.02
□ 20 Ronnie Lott	.15	.07	.02
□ 21 Johnny Johnson	.10	.05	.01
□ 22 Steve Beuerlein	.15	.07	.02
□ 23 Chuck Cecil	.10	.05	.01
□ 24 Gary Clark	.15	.07	.02
□ 25 Kevin Greene	.25	.11	.03
□ 26 Jerrol Williams	.10	.05	.01
□ 27 Tim McDonald	.10	.05	.01
□ 28 Ferrell Edmunds	.10	.05	.01
□ 29 Kelvin Martin	.10	.05	.01
□ 30 Hardy Nickerson	.10	.05	.01
□ 31 Jumpy Geathers	.10	.05	.01
□ 32 Craig Heyward	.15	.07	.02
□ 33 Tim McKyer	.10	.05	.01
□ 34 Mark Carrier WR	.25	.11	.03
□ 35 Gary Zimmerman	.10	.05	.01
□ 36 Jay Schroeder	.10	.05	.01
□ 37 Keith Millard	.10	.05	.01
□ 38 Vince Workman	.10	.05	.01
□ 39 Kirk Lowdermilk	.10	.05	.01
□ 40 Fred Stokes	.10	.05	.01
□ 41 Ernie Jones	.10	.05	.01
□ 42 Keith Byars	.10	.05	.01
□ 43 Carlton Bailey	.10	.05	.01
□ 44 Michael Brooks	.10	.05	.01
□ 45 Tim McGee	.10	.05	.01
□ 46 Leonard Marshall	.10	.05	.01
□ 47 Bubby Brister	.10	.05	.01
□ 48 Mike Tomczak	.15	.07	.02
□ 49 Mark Jackson	.10	.05	.01
□ 50 Wade Wilson	.10	.05	.01

1993 Power Update Prospects

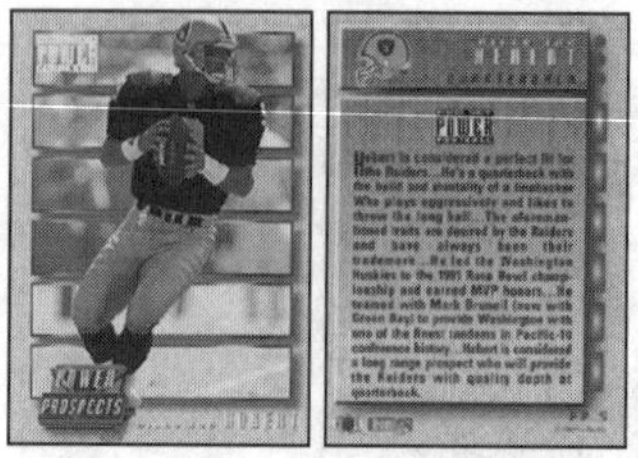

These 60 standard-size cards were issued in nine-card retail packs with the Power Update Moves cards. The fronts feature gray-bordered color player action shots with horizontally interrupted backgounds. The player's name appears in yellow lettering within the lower margin. The grayish back carries the player's name and team helmet in the upper panel followed in the lower panel by career highlights. The cards are numbered on the back with a "PP" prefix. Rookie Cards include Jerome Bettis, Drew Bledsoe, Reggie Brooks , Curtis Conway, Garrison Hearst, Rick Mirer, Ronald Moore and Kevin Williams. Gold Parallel cards were also inserted in packs.

	MINT	NRMT	EXC
COMPLETE SET (60)	10.00	4.50	1.25
COMMON CARD (1-60)	.10	.05	.01
*GOLD CARDS: 1X to 2X BASIC CARDS			

□ 1 Drew Bledsoe	3.00	1.35	.35
□ 2 Rick Mirer	.75	.35	.09
□ 3 Trent Green	.10	.05	.01
□ 4 Mark Brunell	3.00	1.35	.35
□ 5 Billy Joe Hobert UER Name spelled Hebert on back	.30	.14	.04
□ 6 Ronald Moore	.20	.09	.03
□ 7 Elvis Grbac UER (Spelled Grback on both sides)	.30	.14	.04
□ 8 Garrison Hearst	1.00	.45	.12
□ 9 Jerome Bettis	1.50	.70	.19
□ 10 Reggie Brooks	.20	.09	.03
□ 11 Robert Smith	.20	.09	.03
□ 12 Vaughn Hebron	.10	.05	.01
□ 13 Derek Brown RB	.20	.09	.03
□ 14 Roosevelt Potts	.20	.09	.03
□ 15 Terry Kirby UER (Card says wide receiver; he is a running back)	.30	.14	.04
□ 16 Glyn Milburn	.20	.09	.03
□ 17 Greg Robinson	.10	.05	.01
□ 18 Natrone Means	1.00	.45	.12
□ 19 Curtis Conway	.75	.35	.09
□ 20 James Jett	.20	.09	.03
□ 21 O.J. McDuffie	.75	.35	.09
□ 22 Rocket Ismail	.20	.09	.03
□ 23 Qadry Ismail	.30	.14	.04
□ 24 Kevin Williams	.30	.14	.04
□ 25 Victor Bailey UER (Name spelled Baily on front)	.10	.05	.01
□ 26 Vincent Brisby	.20	.09	.03
□ 27 Irv Smith	.20	.09	.03
□ 28 Troy Drayton	.20	.09	.03
□ 29 Wayne Simmons	.20	.09	.03
□ 30 Marvin Jones	.10	.05	.01
□ 31 Demetrius DuBose	.10	.05	.01
□ 32 Chad Brown	.20	.09	.03
□ 33 Micheal Barrow	.10	.05	.01
□ 34 Darrin Smith	.20	.09	.03
□ 35 Deon Figures	.20	.09	.03
□ 36 Darrien Gordon	.10	.05	.01
□ 37 Patrick Bates	.10	.05	.01
□ 38 George Teague	.10	.05	.01
□ 39 Lance Gunn	.10	.05	.01
□ 40 Tom Carter	.10	.05	.01
□ 41 Carlton Gray	.10	.05	.01
□ 42 John Copeland	.20	.09	.03
□ 43 Eric Curry	.20	.09	.03
□ 44 Dana Stubblefield	.20	.09	.03
□ 45 Leonard Renfro	.10	.05	.01
□ 46 Dan Williams	.10	.05	.01
□ 47 Todd Kelly	.10	.05	.01
□ 48 Chris Slade	.20	.09	.03
□ 49 Carl Simpson UER (Defensive Back spelled Dfensive on back)	.10	.05	.01
□ 50 Coleman Rudolph	.10	.05	.01
□ 51 Michael Strahan	.10	.05	.01
□ 52 Dan Footman	.10	.05	.01
□ 53 Steve Everitt	.10	.05	.01
□ 54 Will Shields	.10	.05	.01
□ 55 Ben Coleman	.10	.05	.01
□ 56 William Roaf	.20	.09	.03
□ 57 Lincoln Kennedy	.10	.05	.01
□ 58 Brad Hopkins	.10	.05	.01
□ 59 Ernest Dye	.10	.05	.01
□ 60 Jason Elam	.20	.09	.03

1993 Power Update Combos

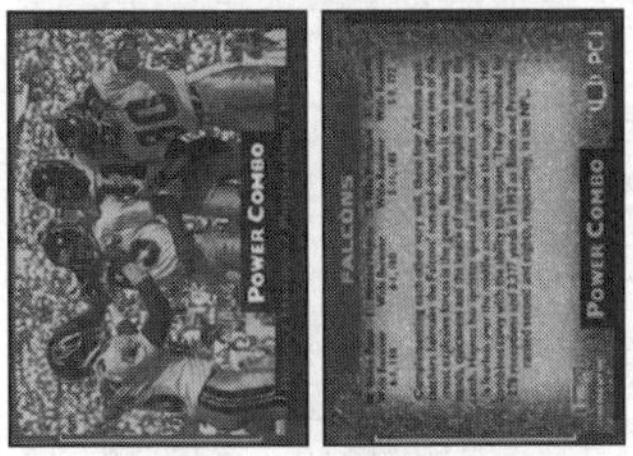

Randomly inserted in 1993 Power Update packs, these 10 standard-size multiplayer cards feature on their horizontal fronts multicolor-bordered color player action shots. The players' names appear in red lettering at the bottom. The horizontal back carries each player's name at the top, followed below by combo highlights, all on a simulated turf background. The cards are numbered on the back with a "PC" prefix. Gold parallel cards were randomly inserted in Update packs. Parallel Prism cards were also random inserts in Update packs.

	MINT	NRMT	EXC
COMPLETE SET (10)	8.00	3.60	1.00
COMMON CARD (PC1-PC10)	.50	.23	.06
COMPLETE GOLD SET (10)	12.00	5.50	1.50
*GOLD CARDS: .75X to 1.5X BASIC CARDS			
COMPLETE PRISM SET (10)	20.00	9.00	2.50
*PRISM CARDS: 1.25X to 2.5X BASIC CARDS			

☐ PC1 Andre Rison	.50	.23	.06
Michael Haynes			
Mike Pritchard			
Drew Hill			
☐ PC2 Steve Young UER	4.00	1.80	.50
Jerry Rice			
(Young's uniform number on back is 7)			
☐ PC3 Jim Kelly	1.00	.45	.12
Frank Reich			
☐ PC4 Alvin Harper	1.00	.45	.12
Michael Irvin			
☐ PC5 Rod Woodson	.75	.35	.09
Deon Figures			
☐ PC6 Bruce Smith	.75	.35	.09
Cornelius Bennett			
☐ PC7 Bryan Cox	.50	.23	.06
Marco Coleman			
☐ PC8 Troy Aikman	4.00	1.80	.50
Emmitt Smith			
☐ PC9 Tim Brown	1.00	.45	.12
Rocket Ismail			
☐ PC10 Art Monk UER	.75	.35	.09
Desmond Howard			
Ricky Sanders			
(Atlanta Falcons on back)			

1993 Power Update Impact Rookies

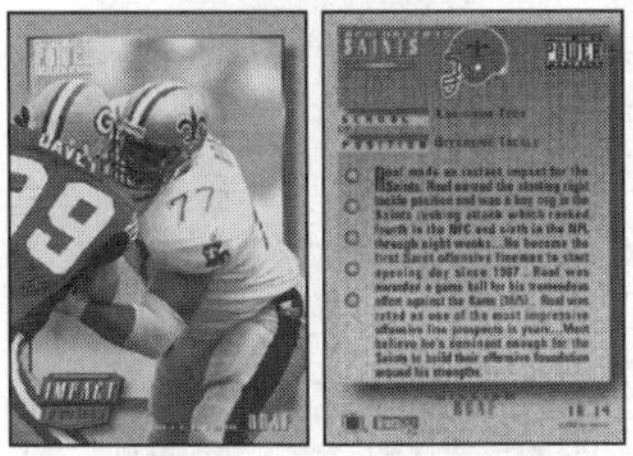

Randomly inserted in 1993 Power Update packs, these 15 standard-size cards feature gray-bordered color player action shots on their fronts. The player's name appears in yellow lettering at the bottom right. The gray back carries the player's team name and helmet at the top, followed by college, position, and career highlights. The cards are numbered on the back with an "IR" prefix.

	MINT	NRMT	EXC
COMPLETE SET (15)	8.00	3.60	1.00
COMMON CARD (IR1-IR15)	.30	.14	.04
COMPLETE GOLD SET (15)	16.00	7.25	2.00
*GOLD CARDS: 1X TO 2X BASIC CARDS			

☐ IR1 Rick Mirer	1.00	.45	.12
☐ IR2 Drew Bledsoe	4.00	1.80	.50
☐ IR3 Jerome Bettis	1.50	.70	.19
☐ IR4 Derek Brown RB	.30	.14	.04
☐ IR5 Roosevelt Potts	.30	.14	.04
☐ IR6 Glyn Milburn	.50	.23	.06
☐ IR7 Adrian Murrell	.75	.35	.09
☐ IR8 Victor Bailey	.30	.14	.04
☐ IR9 Vincent Brisby	.50	.23	.06
☐ IR10 O.J. McDuffie	.75	.35	.09
☐ IR11 James Jett	.30	.14	.04
☐ IR12 Eric Curry	.30	.14	.04
☐ IR13 Dana Stubblefield	.50	.23	.06
☐ IR14 Willie Roaf	.30	.14	.04
☐ IR15 Patrick Bates	.30	.14	.04

1994 Predators Arena Team Issue

The Orlando Predators of the Arena Football League issued this set for distribution through their consession stands and gift shop. Each card is unnumbered and measures the standard size. Reportedly, the set was limited to a production run of 2000.

	MINT	NRMT	EXC
COMPLETE SET (27)	6.00	2.70	.75
COMMON CARD (1-27)	.25	.11	.03

☐ 1 Ben Bennett	.40	.18	.05
☐ 2 Henry Brown	.25	.11	.03
☐ 3 Webbie Burnett	.25	.11	.03
☐ 4 Jorge Cimadevilla	.25	.11	.03
☐ 5 Bernard Clark	.25	.11	.03
☐ 6 Wayne Dickson	.25	.11	.03
☐ 7 Eric Drakes	.25	.11	.03
☐ 8 Chris Ford	.25	.11	.03
☐ 9 Victor Hall	.25	.11	.03
☐ 10 Paul McGowan	.25	.11	.03
☐ 11 Perry Moss CO	.40	.18	.05
☐ 12 Jerry Odom	.25	.11	.03
☐ 13 Billy Owens WR	.25	.11	.03
☐ 14 Marshall Roberts	.25	.11	.03
☐ 15 Durwood Roquemore	.25	.11	.03
☐ 16 Rusty Russell DL	.25	.11	.03
☐ 17 Tony Scott	.25	.11	.03
☐ 18 Ricky Shaw	.25	.11	.03
☐ 19 Alex Shell	.25	.11	.03
☐ 20 Bill Stewart	.25	.11	.03
☐ 21 Duke Tobin	.25	.11	.03
☐ 22 Barry Wagner	.25	.11	.03
☐ 23 Jackie Walker	.25	.11	.03
☐ 24 Herkie Walls	.25	.11	.03
☐ 25 Isaac Williams	.25	.11	.03
☐ 26 Coaches	.25	.11	.03
☐ 27 The Klaw (mascot)	.25	.11	.03

1994 Press Pass SB Photo Board

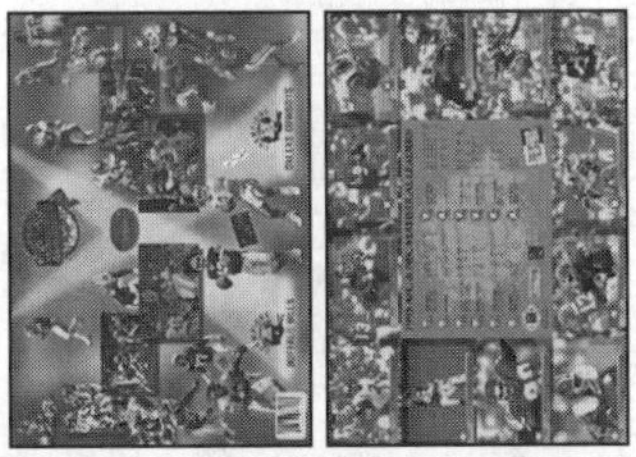

Press Pass shipped 50,000 individually numbered (approximately) 10" by 14" Photo Boards to hobby and retail outlets Jan. 24, the day after both Buffalo and Dallas earned their Super Bowl berths. The Photo Board was also available at the NFL Experience and the Super Bowl Card Show V in Atlanta. The front visually describes each team's road to the Super Bowl with color photos from NFL playoff action. The Super Bowl logo is featured on the front of each board etched in gold foil. The back carries color action photos of AFC and NFC statistical leaders and an outstanding 1993 rookie from each conference, as well as accompanying statistics. The sheet is unnumbered, and the AFC and NFC statistical leaders honored on its back are listed below.

	MINT	NRMT	EXC
COMPLETE SET (1)	10.00	4.50	1.25
COMMON PANEL	10.00	4.50	1.25

☐ 1 SB XXVIII Photo Board	10.00	4.50	1.25
John Elway			
Rick Mirer			
Reggie Langhorne			
Neil Smith			
Nate Odomes			
Thurman Thomas			
Steve Young			
Jerome Bettis			
Sterling Sharpe			
Reggie White			
Deion Sanders			
Emmitt Smith			

1993-94 Pro Athletes Outreach

This 12-card set was issued by Pro Athletes Outreach, a Christian leadership training ministry for pro athletes and their families. The tri-fold cards measure approximately 7 1/8" by 4 1/8". The right portion of the tri-fold carries a color player photo bordered in white on a light gray background. Below the picture are the player's name, position, and the PAO logo. The remainder of the card front and back contains the player's personal Christian testimony followed by an invitation to write them in care of the PAO address, for more information. With the exception of the Gill Byrd card, a second black-and-white player photo appears on the left portion of the tri-fold card. A brief career summary rounds out the card. The cards are unnumbered and checklisted below in alphabetical order.

	MINT	NRMT	EXC
COMPLETE SET (12)	10.00	4.50	1.25
COMMON CARD (1-12)	.50	.23	.06

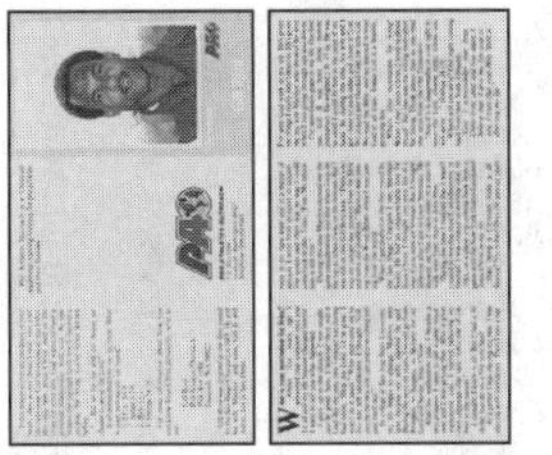

☐ 1 Mark Boyer	.50	.23	.06
☐ 2 Gill Byrd	.75	.35	.09
☐ 3 Darren Carrington	.50	.23	.06
☐ 4 Paul Coffman	.50	.23	.06
☐ 5 Burnell Dent	.50	.23	.06
☐ 6 Johnny Holland	.50	.23	.06
☐ 7 Jeff Kemp	.75	.35	.09
☐ 8 Steve Largent	4.00	1.80	.50
☐ 9 John Offerdahl	.50	.23	.06
☐ 10 Stephone Paige	.50	.23	.06
☐ 11 Doug Smith	.50	.23	.06
☐ 12 Rob Taylor	.50	.23	.06

1990-91 Pro Line Samples

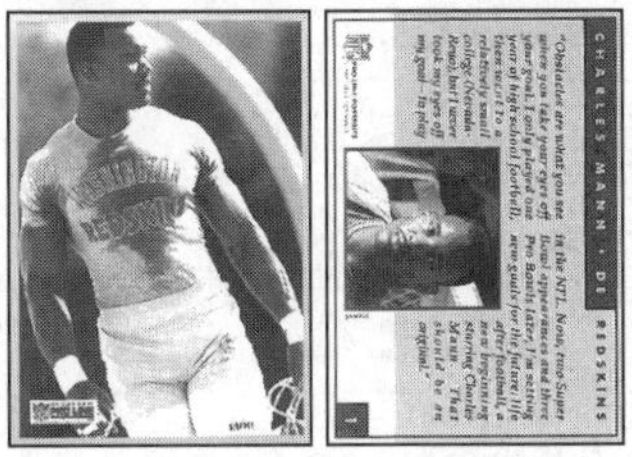

Unlike the borderless regular set, the fronts of these standard-size cards have silver borders. Many photos (both front and back) are different or are cropped differently than the corresponding regular-issue cards, and many of the quotes on the back also are different from the regular issue cards. The word "SAMPLE" is printed in small type next to the mugshots on the backs. The cards are skipnumbered on the back by odd numbers except that sample card number 15 was apparently not issued.

	MINT	NRMT	EXC
COMPLETE SET (18)	150.00	70.00	19.00
COMMON CARD	6.00	2.70	.75

☐ 1 Charles Mann	6.00	2.70	.75
☐ 3 Troy Aikman	25.00	11.00	3.10
☐ 5 Boomer Esiason	8.00	3.60	1.00
☐ 7 Warren Moon	10.00	4.50	1.25
☐ 9 Bill Fralic	6.00	2.70	.75
☐ 11 Lawrence Taylor	10.00	4.50	1.25
☐ 13 George Seifert CO	6.00	2.70	.75
☐ 17 Dan Marino	40.00	18.00	5.00
☐ 19 Jim Everett	8.00	3.60	1.00
☐ 21 John Elway	20.00	9.00	2.50
☐ 23 Jeff George	10.00	4.50	1.25
☐ 25 Lindy Infante CO	6.00	2.70	.75
☐ 27 Dan Reeves CO	8.00	3.60	1.00
☐ 29 Steve Largent	12.00	5.50	1.50
☐ 31 Roger Craig	8.00	3.60	1.00
☐ 33 Marty Schottenheimer CO	6.00	2.70	.75
☐ 35 Mike Ditka CO	10.00	4.50	1.25
☐ 37 Sam Wyche CO	6.00	2.70	.75

1991 Pro Line Portraits

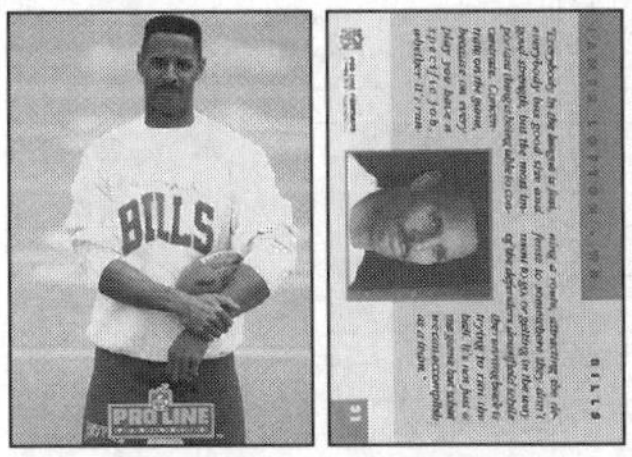

This 300-card standard-size set features some of the NFL's most popular players in non-game shots. The players and coaches are posed wearing their team's colors. The fronts are full-color borderless shots of the players, while the backs feature a quote from the player and a portrait pose of the player. The cards were available in wax packs. Essentially the whole set was available individually autographed; these certified autographed cards randomly included in packs were unnumbered. The key Rookie Cards in this set are Randal Hill, Herman Moore and Mike Pritchard. The Santa Claus card could be obtained through a mail-in offer in exchange for ten 1991 ProLine Portraits foil pack wrappers. Complete sets featuring "National 1991" embossed logos were produced and distributed to guests of an event at The National Card Collector's Convention in Anaheim. Reportedly, 250-complete sets were produced with the special logo.

	MINT	NRMT	EXC
COMPLETE SET (300)	6.00	2.70	.75
COMMON CARD (1-300)	.04	.02	.01

☐ 1 Jim Kelly	.20	.09	.03
☐ 2 Carl Banks	.04	.02	.01
☐ 3 Neal Anderson	.10	.05	.01
☐ 4 James Brooks	.04	.02	.01
☐ 5 Reggie Langhorne	.04	.02	.01
☐ 6 Robert Awalt	.04	.02	.01
☐ 7 Greg Kragen	.04	.02	.01
☐ 8 Steve Young	.75	.35	.09
☐ 9 Nick Bell	.04	.02	.01
☐ 10 Ray Childress	.10	.05	.01
☐ 11 Albert Bentley	.04	.02	.01
☐ 12 Albert Lewis	.04	.02	.01
☐ 13 Howie Long	.10	.05	.01
☐ 14 Flipper Anderson	.04	.02	.01
☐ 15 Mark Clayton	.10	.05	.01
☐ 16 Jarrod Bunch	.04	.02	.01
☐ 17 Bruce Armstrong	.04	.02	.01
☐ 18 Vinnie Clark	.04	.02	.01
☐ 19 Rob Moore	.10	.05	.01
☐ 20 Eric Allen	.04	.02	.01
☐ 21 Timm Rosenbach	.04	.02	.01
☐ 22 Gary Anderson K	.04	.02	.01
☐ 23 Martin Bayless	.04	.02	.01
☐ 24 Kevin Fagan	.04	.02	.01
☐ 25 Brian Blades	.10	.05	.01
☐ 26 Gary Anderson RB	.04	.02	.01
☐ 27 Earnest Byner	.10	.05	.01
☐ 28 O.J. Simpson RET	.20	.09	.03
☐ 29 Dan Henning CO	.04	.02	.01
☐ 30 Sean Landeta	.04	.02	.01
☐ 31 James Lofton	.10	.05	.01
☐ 32 Mike Singletary	.10	.05	.01
☐ 33 David Fulcher	.04	.02	.01
☐ 34 Mark Murphy	.04	.02	.01
☐ 35 Issiac Holt	.04	.02	.01
☐ 36 Dennis Smith	.04	.02	.01
☐ 37 Lomas Brown	.04	.02	.01
☐ 38 Ernest Givins	.10	.05	.01
☐ 39 Duane Bickett	.04	.02	.01
☐ 40 Barry Word	.04	.02	.01
☐ 41 Tony Mandarich	.04	.02	.01
☐ 42 Cleveland Gary	.04	.02	.01
☐ 43 Ferrell Edmunds	.04	.02	.01
☐ 44 Randal Hill	.10	.05	.01
☐ 45 Irving Fryar	.10	.05	.01
☐ 46 Henry Jones	.10	.05	.01
☐ 47 Blair Thomas	.04	.02	.01
☐ 48 Andre Waters	.04	.02	.01
☐ 49 J.T. Smith	.04	.02	.01
☐ 50 Thomas Everett	.04	.02	.01
☐ 51 Marion Butts	.10	.05	.01
☐ 52 Tom Rathman	.04	.02	.01
☐ 53 Vann McElroy	.04	.02	.01
☐ 54 Mark Carrier WR	.10	.05	.01
☐ 55 Jim Lachey	.04	.02	.01
☐ 56 Joe Theismann RET	.10	.05	.01
☐ 57 Jerry Glanville CO	.04	.02	.01
☐ 58 Doug Riesenberg	.04	.02	.01
☐ 59 Cornelius Bennett	.10	.05	.01
☐ 60 Mark Carrier DB	.10	.05	.01
☐ 61 Rodney Holman	.04	.02	.01
☐ 62 Leroy Hoard	.10	.05	.01
☐ 63 Michael Irvin	.20	.09	.03
☐ 64 Bobby Humphrey	.04	.02	.01
☐ 65 Mel Gray	.10	.05	.01
☐ 66 Brian Noble	.04	.02	.01
☐ 67 Al Smith	.04	.02	.01
☐ 68 Eric Dickerson	.10	.05	.01
☐ 69 Steve DeBerg	.10	.05	.01
☐ 70 Jay Schroeder	.04	.02	.01
☐ 71 Irv Pankey	.04	.02	.01
☐ 72 Reggie Roby	.04	.02	.01
☐ 73 Wade Wilson	.04	.02	.01
☐ 74 Johnny Rembert	.04	.02	.01
☐ 75 Russell Maryland	.10	.05	.01
☐ 76 Al Toon	.10	.05	.01
☐ 77 Randall Cunningham	.10	.05	.01
☐ 78 Lonnie Young	.04	.02	.01
☐ 79 Carnell Lake	.04	.02	.01
☐ 80 Burt Grossman	.04	.02	.01
☐ 81 Jim Mora CO	.04	.02	.01
☐ 82 Dave Krieg	.04	.02	.01
☐ 83 Bruce Hill	.04	.02	.01
☐ 84 Ricky Sanders	.04	.02	.01
☐ 85 Roger Staubach RET	.20	.09	.03
☐ 86 Richard Williamson CO	.04	.02	.01
☐ 87 Everson Walls	.04	.02	.01
☐ 88 Shane Conlan	.04	.02	.01
☐ 89 Mike Ditka CO	.20	.09	.03
☐ 90 Mark Bortz	.04	.02	.01
☐ 91 Tim McGee	.04	.02	.01
☐ 92 Michael Dean Perry	.10	.05	.01
☐ 93 Danny Noonan	.04	.02	.01
☐ 94 Mark Jackson	.04	.02	.01
☐ 95 Chris Miller	.10	.05	.01
☐ 96 Ed McCaffrey	.04	.02	.01
☐ 97 Lorenzo White	.10	.05	.01
☐ 98 Ray Donaldson	.04	.02	.01
☐ 99 Nick Lowery	.04	.02	.01
☐ 100 Steve Smith	.04	.02	.01
☐ 101 Jackie Slater	.04	.02	.01
☐ 102 Louis Oliver	.04	.02	.01
☐ 103 Kanavis McGhee	.04	.02	.01
☐ 104 Ray Agnew	.04	.02	.01
☐ 105 Sam Mills	.10	.05	.01

☐ 106 Bill Pickel	.04	.02	.01
☐ 107 Keith Byars	.10	.05	.01
☐ 108 Ricky Proehl	.04	.02	.01
☐ 109 Merril Hoge	.04	.02	.01
☐ 110 Rod Bernstine	.04	.02	.01
☐ 111 Andy Heck	.04	.02	.01
☐ 112 Broderick Thomas	.04	.02	.01
☐ 113 Andre Collins	.04	.02	.01
☐ 114 Paul Warfield RET	.10	.05	.01
☐ 115 Bill Belichick CO	.04	.02	.01
☐ 116 Ottis Anderson	.10	.05	.01
☐ 117 Andre Reed	.10	.05	.01
☐ 118 Andre Rison	.10	.05	.01
☐ 119 Dexter Carter	.04	.02	.01
☐ 120 Anthony Munoz	.10	.05	.01
☐ 121 Bernie Kosar	.10	.05	.01
☐ 122 Alonzo Highsmith	.04	.02	.01
☐ 123 David Treadwell	.04	.02	.01
☐ 124 Rodney Peete	.10	.05	.01
☐ 125 Haywood Jeffires	.10	.05	.01
☐ 126 Clarence Verdin	.04	.02	.01
☐ 127 Christian Okoye	.04	.02	.01
☐ 128 Greg Townsend	.04	.02	.01
☐ 129 Tom Newberry	.04	.02	.01
☐ 130 Keith Sims	.04	.02	.01
☐ 131 Myron Guyton	.04	.02	.01
☐ 132 Andre Tippett	.04	.02	.01
☐ 133 Steve Walsh	.04	.02	.01
☐ 134 Erik McMillan	.04	.02	.01
☐ 135 Jim McMahon	.10	.05	.01
☐ 136 Derek Hill	.04	.02	.01
☐ 137 D.J. Johnson	.04	.02	.01
☐ 138 Leslie O'Neal	.10	.05	.01
☐ 139 Pierce Holt	.04	.02	.01
☐ 140 Cortez Kennedy	.10	.05	.01
☐ 141 Danny Peebles	.04	.02	.01
☐ 142 Alvin Walton	.04	.02	.01
☐ 143 Drew Pearson RET	.04	.02	.01
☐ 144 Dick MacPherson CO	.04	.02	.01
☐ 145 Erik Howard	.04	.02	.01
☐ 146 Steve Tasker	.10	.05	.01
☐ 147 Bill Fralic	.04	.02	.01
☐ 148 Don Warren	.04	.02	.01
☐ 149 Eric Thomas	.04	.02	.01
☐ 150 Jack Pardee CO	.04	.02	.01
☐ 151 Gary Zimmerman	.04	.02	.01
☐ 152 Leonard Marshall	.04	.02	.01
☐ 153 Chris Spielman	.10	.05	.01
☐ 154 Sam Wyche CO	.04	.02	.01
☐ 155 Rohn Stark	.04	.02	.01
☐ 156 Stephone Paige	.04	.02	.01
☐ 157 Lionel Washington	.04	.02	.01
☐ 158 Henry Ellard	.10	.05	.01
☐ 159 Dan Marino	1.50	.70	.19
☐ 160 Lindy Infante CO	.04	.02	.01
☐ 161 Dan McGwire	.04	.02	.01
☐ 162 Ken O'Brien	.04	.02	.01
☐ 163 Tim McDonald	.04	.02	.01
☐ 164 Louis Lipps	.04	.02	.01
☐ 165 Billy Joe Tolliver	.04	.02	.01
☐ 166 Harris Barton	.04	.02	.01
☐ 167 Tony Woods	.04	.02	.01
☐ 168 Matt Millen	.10	.05	.01
☐ 169 Gale Sayers RET	.20	.09	.03
☐ 170 Ron Meyer CO	.04	.02	.01
☐ 171 William Roberts	.04	.02	.01
☐ 172 Thurman Thomas	.20	.09	.03
☐ 173 Steve McMichael	.04	.02	.01
☐ 174 Ickey Woods	.04	.02	.01
☐ 175 Eugene Lockhart	.04	.02	.01
☐ 176 George Seifert CO	.10	.05	.01
☐ 177 Keith Jones	.04	.02	.01
☐ 178 Jack Trudeau	.04	.02	.01
☐ 179 Kevin Porter	.04	.02	.01
☐ 180 Ronnie Lott	.10	.05	.01
☐ 181 Marty Schottenheimer CO	.04	.02	.01
☐ 182 Morten Andersen	.04	.02	.01
☐ 183 Anthony Thompson	.04	.02	.01
☐ 184 Tim Worley	.04	.02	.01
☐ 185 Billy Ray Smith	.04	.02	.01
☐ 186 David Whitmore	.04	.02	.01
☐ 187 Jacob Green	.04	.02	.01
☐ 188 Browning Nagle	.04	.02	.01
☐ 189 Franco Harris RET	.10	.05	.01
☐ 190 Art Shell CO	.10	.05	.01
☐ 191 Bart Oates	.04	.02	.01
☐ 192 William Perry	.10	.05	.01
☐ 193 Chuck Noll CO	.10	.05	.01
☐ 194 Troy Aikman	1.00	.45	.12
☐ 195 Jeff George	.10	.05	.01
☐ 196 Derrick Thomas	.20	.09	.03
☐ 197 Roger Craig	.10	.05	.01
☐ 198 John Fourcade	.04	.02	.01
☐ 199 Rod Woodson	.20	.09	.03
☐ 200 Anthony Miller	.10	.05	.01
☐ 201 Jerry Rice	1.00	.45	.12
☐ 202 Eugene Robinson	.04	.02	.01
☐ 203 Charles Mann	.04	.02	.01
☐ 204 Mel Blount RET	.10	.05	.01
☐ 205 Don Shula CO	.10	.05	.01
☐ 206 Jumbo Elliott	.04	.02	.01
☐ 207 Jay Hilgenberg	.04	.02	.01
☐ 208 Deron Cherry	.04	.02	.01
☐ 209 Dan Reeves CO	.10	.05	.01
☐ 210 Roman Phifer	.04	.02	.01
☐ 211 David Little	.04	.02	.01
☐ 212 Lee Williams	.04	.02	.01
☐ 213 John Taylor	.10	.05	.01
☐ 214 Monte Coleman	.04	.02	.01
☐ 215 Walter Payton RET	.20	.09	.03
☐ 216 John Robinson CO	.04	.02	.01
☐ 217 Pepper Johnson	.04	.02	.01
☐ 218 Tom Thayer	.04	.02	.01
☐ 219 Dan Saleaumua	.04	.02	.01
☐ 220 Ernest Spears	.04	.02	.01
☐ 221 Bubby Brister	.04	.02	.01
☐ 222 Junior Seau	.20	.09	.03
☐ 223 Brent Jones	.10	.05	.01
☐ 224 Rufus Porter	.04	.02	.01
☐ 225 Jack Kemp RET	.20	.09	.03
☐ 226 Wayne Fontes CO	.04	.02	.01
☐ 227 Phil Simms	.10	.05	.01
☐ 228 Shaun Gayle	.04	.02	.01
☐ 229 Bill Maas	.04	.02	.01
☐ 230 Renaldo Turnbull	.04	.02	.01
☐ 231 Bryan Hinkle	.04	.02	.01
☐ 232 Gary Plummer	.04	.02	.01
☐ 233 Jerry Burns CO	.04	.02	.01
☐ 234 Lawrence Taylor	.10	.05	.01
☐ 235 Joe Gibbs CO	.10	.05	.01
☐ 236 Neil Smith	.10	.05	.01
☐ 237 Rich Kotite CO	.04	.02	.01
☐ 238 Jim Covert	.04	.02	.01
☐ 239 Tim Grunhard	.04	.02	.01
☐ 240 Joe Bugel CO	.04	.02	.01
☐ 241 David Wyman	.04	.02	.01
☐ 242 Maury Buford	.04	.02	.01
☐ 243 Kevin Ross	.04	.02	.01
☐ 244 Jimmy Johnson CO	.10	.05	.01
☐ 245 Jim Morrissey	.04	.02	.01
☐ 246 Jeff Hostetler	.10	.05	.01
☐ 247 Andre Ware	.10	.05	.01
☐ 248 Steve Largent RET	.20	.09	.03
☐ 249 Chuck Knox CO	.04	.02	.01
☐ 250 Boomer Esiason	.10	.05	.01
☐ 251 Kevin Butler	.04	.02	.01
☐ 252 Bruce Smith	.20	.09	.03
☐ 253 Webster Slaughter	.10	.05	.01
☐ 254 Mike Sherrard	.04	.02	.01
☐ 255 Steve Broussard	.04	.02	.01
☐ 256 Warren Moon	.20	.09	.03
☐ 257 John Elway	.75	.35	.09
☐ 258 Bob Golic	.04	.02	.01
☐ 259 Jim Everett	.10	.05	.01
☐ 260 Bruce Coslet CO	.04	.02	.01
☐ 261 James Francis	.04	.02	.01
☐ 262 Eric Dorsey	.04	.02	.01
☐ 263 Marcus Dupree	.04	.02	.01
☐ 264 Hart Lee Dykes	.04	.02	.01
☐ 265 Vinny Testaverde	.10	.05	.01
☐ 266 Chip Lohmiller	.04	.02	.01
☐ 267 John Riggins RET	.10	.05	.01
☐ 268 Mike Schad	.04	.02	.01
☐ 269 Kevin Greene	.20	.09	.03
☐ 270 Dean Biasucci	.04	.02	.01
☐ 271 Mike Pritchard	.10	.05	.01
☐ 272 Ted Washington	.04	.02	.01
☐ 273 Alfred Williams	.04	.02	.01
☐ 274 Chris Zorich	.10	.05	.01
☐ 275 Reggie Barrett	.04	.02	.01
☐ 276 Chris Hinton	.04	.02	.01
☐ 277 Tracy Johnson	.04	.02	.01
☐ 278 Jim Harbaugh	.10	.05	.01
☐ 279 John Roper	.04	.02	.01
☐ 280 Mike Dumas	.04	.02	.01
☐ 281 Herman Moore	1.50	.70	.19
☐ 282 Eric Turner	.10	.05	.01
☐ 283 Steve Atwater	.04	.02	.01
☐ 284 Michael Cofer	.04	.02	.01
☐ 285 Darion Conner	.04	.02	.01
☐ 286 Darryl Talley	.04	.02	.01
☐ 287 Donnell Woolford	.04	.02	.01
☐ 288 Keith McCants	.04	.02	.01
☐ 289 Ray Handley CO	.04	.02	.01
☐ 290 Ahmad Rashad RET	.10	.05	.01
☐ 291 Eric Swann	.10	.05	.01
☐ 292 Dalton Hilliard	.04	.02	.01
☐ 293 Rickey Jackson	.10	.05	.01
☐ 294 Vaughan Johnson	.04	.02	.01
☐ 295 Eric Martin	.04	.02	.01
☐ 296 Pat Swilling	.10	.05	.01
☐ 297 Anthony Carter	.10	.05	.01
☐ 298 Guy McIntyre	.04	.02	.01
☐ 299 Bennie Blades	.04	.02	.01
☐ 300 Paul Farren	.04	.02	.01
☐ PLC1 Rashad Family	6.00	2.70	.75
☐ PLC2 Payne Stewart	6.00	2.70	.75
☐ NNO Santa Claus 1991	3.00	1.35	.35

1991 Pro Line Portraits Autographs

This 300-card standard-size set features some of the NFL's most popular players in non-game shots. These certified autographed cards were randomly included into packs as unnumbered cards. They are listed below according to the numbers assigned to them in the regular series. It has been reported by collectors that an autographed card is found with a frequency of about one per three boxes of 1991 ProLine.

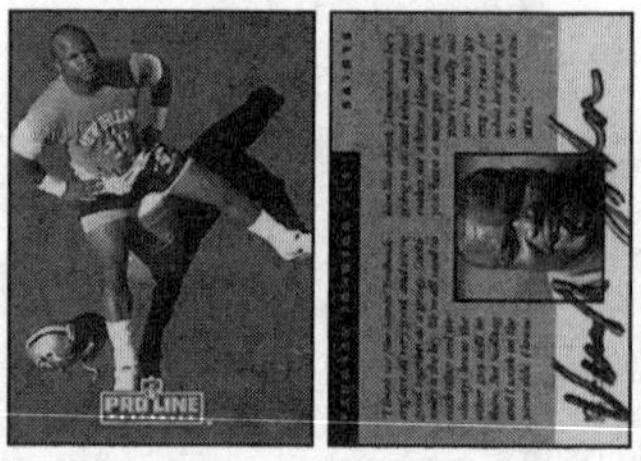

The Tim McDonald card (163) is not included in the set price as only one card is known to exist. Cards with signatures cut in half are considered to have major defects. The autographed Santa cards are not considered part of the set.

	MINT	NRMT	EXC
COMPLETE SET (301)	5500.00	2500.00	700.00
COMMON CARD (1-300)	6.00	2.70	.75
☐ 1A Jim Kelly	15.00	6.75	1.85
(Autopenned)			
☐ 1B Jim Kelly	150.00	70.00	19.00
(Real signature)			
☐ 2 Carl Banks	6.00	2.70	.75
☐ 3 Neal Anderson	8.00	3.60	1.00
☐ 4 James Brooks	8.00	3.60	1.00
☐ 5 Reggie Langhorne	50.00	22.00	6.25
☐ 6 Robert Awalt	6.00	2.70	.75
☐ 7 Greg Kragen	6.00	2.70	.75
☐ 8 Steve Young	100.00	45.00	12.50
☐ 9 Nick Bell	6.00	2.70	.75
☐ 10 Ray Childress	8.00	3.60	1.00
☐ 11 Albert Bentley	6.00	2.70	.75
☐ 12 Albert Lewis	50.00	22.00	6.25
Most signatures are cut off			
☐ 13 Howie Long	25.00	11.00	3.10
☐ 14 Flipper Anderson	8.00	3.60	1.00
☐ 15 Mark Clayton	8.00	3.60	1.00
☐ 16 Jarrod Bunch	6.00	2.70	.75
☐ 17 Bruce Armstrong	6.00	2.70	.75
☐ 18 Vinnie Clark	6.00	2.70	.75
☐ 19 Rob Moore	8.00	3.60	1.00
☐ 20 Eric Allen	8.00	3.60	1.00
☐ 21 Timm Rosenbach	6.00	2.70	.75
☐ 22 Gary Anderson K	6.00	2.70	.75
☐ 23 Martin Bayless	6.00	2.70	.75
☐ 24 Kevin Fagan	6.00	2.70	.75
☐ 25 Brian Blades	8.00	3.60	1.00
☐ 26 Gary Anderson RB	8.00	3.60	1.00
☐ 27 Earnest Byner	8.00	3.60	1.00
☐ 28 O.J. Simpson RET	250.00	110.00	31.00
☐ 29 Dan Henning CO	6.00	2.70	.75
☐ 30 Sean Landeta	6.00	2.70	.75
☐ 31 James Lofton	20.00	9.00	2.50
☐ 32 Mike Singletary	35.00	16.00	4.40
☐ 33 David Fulcher	6.00	2.70	.75
☐ 34 Mark Murphy	6.00	2.70	.75
☐ 35 Issiac Holt	6.00	2.70	.75
☐ 36 Dennis Smith	6.00	2.70	.75
☐ 37 Lomas Brown	6.00	2.70	.75
☐ 38 Ernest Givins	12.00	5.50	1.50
☐ 39 Duane Bickett	6.00	2.70	.75
☐ 40 Barry Word	6.00	2.70	.75
☐ 41 Tony Mandarich	6.00	2.70	.75
☐ 42 Cleveland Gary	6.00	2.70	.75
☐ 43 Ferrell Edmunds	6.00	2.70	.75
☐ 44 Randal Hill	8.00	3.60	1.00
☐ 45 Irving Fryar	12.00	5.50	1.50
☐ 46 Henry Jones	8.00	3.60	1.00
☐ 47 Blair Thomas	6.00	2.70	.75
☐ 48 Andre Waters	6.00	2.70	.75
☐ 49 J.T. Smith	6.00	2.70	.75
☐ 50 Thomas Everett	8.00	3.60	1.00
☐ 51 Marion Butts	8.00	3.60	1.00
☐ 52 Tom Rathman	6.00	2.70	.75
☐ 53 Vann McElroy	6.00	2.70	.75
☐ 54 Mark Carrier WR	8.00	3.60	1.00
☐ 55 Jim Lachey	8.00	3.60	1.00
☐ 56 Joe Theismann RET	20.00	9.00	2.50
☐ 57 Jerry Glanville CO	6.00	2.70	.75
☐ 58 Doug Riesenberg	6.00	2.70	.75
☐ 59 Cornelius Bennett	8.00	3.60	1.00
☐ 60 Mark Carrier DB	100.00	45.00	12.50
☐ 61 Rodney Holman	225.00	100.00	28.00
☐ 62 Leroy Hoard	8.00	3.60	1.00
☐ 63 Michael Irvin	30.00	13.50	3.70
☐ 64 Bobby Humphrey	6.00	2.70	.75
☐ 65 Mel Gray	8.00	3.60	1.00
☐ 66 Brian Noble	6.00	2.70	.75
☐ 67 Al Smith	6.00	2.70	.75
☐ 68 Eric Dickerson	30.00	13.50	3.70
☐ 69 Steve DeBerg	8.00	3.60	1.00
☐ 70 Jay Schroeder	6.00	2.70	.75
☐ 71 Irv Pankey	6.00	2.70	.75
☐ 72 Reggie Roby	6.00	2.70	.75
☐ 73 Wade Wilson	6.00	2.70	.75
☐ 74 Johnny Rembert	6.00	2.70	.75
☐ 75 Russell Maryland	8.00	3.60	1.00
☐ 76 Al Toon	8.00	3.60	1.00
☐ 77 Randall Cunningham	8.00	3.60	1.00
☐ 78 Lonnie Young	6.00	2.70	.75
☐ 79 Carnell Lake	8.00	3.60	1.00
☐ 80 Burt Grossman	6.00	2.70	.75
☐ 81 Jim Mora CO	6.00	2.70	.75
☐ 82 Dave Krieg	8.00	3.60	1.00
☐ 83 Bruce Hill	6.00	2.70	.75
☐ 84 Ricky Sanders	8.00	3.60	1.00
☐ 85 Roger Staubach RET	125.00	55.00	15.50
☐ 86 Richard Williamson CO	6.00	2.70	.75
☐ 87 Everson Walls	6.00	2.70	.75
☐ 88 Shane Conlan	8.00	3.60	1.00
☐ 89 Mike Ditka CO	30.00	13.50	3.70
☐ 90 Mark Bortz	6.00	2.70	.75
☐ 91 Tim McGee	8.00	3.60	1.00
☐ 92 Michael Dean Perry	8.00	3.60	1.00
☐ 93 Danny Noonan	6.00	2.70	.75
☐ 94 Mark Jackson	8.00	3.60	1.00
☐ 95 Chris Miller	8.00	3.60	1.00
☐ 96 Ed McCaffrey	6.00	2.70	.75
☐ 97 Lorenzo White	8.00	3.60	1.00
☐ 98 Ray Donaldson	6.00	2.70	.75
☐ 99 Nick Lowery	6.00	2.70	.75
(May be autopenned)			
☐ 100 Steve Smith	6.00	2.70	.75
☐ 101 Jackie Slater	8.00	3.60	1.00
☐ 102 Louis Oliver	6.00	2.70	.75
☐ 103 Kanavis McGhee	6.00	2.70	.75
☐ 104 Ray Agnew	6.00	2.70	.75
☐ 105 Sam Mills	8.00	3.60	1.00
☐ 106 Bill Pickel	6.00	2.70	.75
☐ 107 Keith Byars	8.00	3.60	1.00
☐ 108 Ricky Proehl	6.00	2.70	.75
☐ 109 Merril Hoge	6.00	2.70	.75
☐ 110 Rod Bernstine	6.00	2.70	.75
☐ 111 Andy Heck	6.00	2.70	.75
☐ 112 Broderick Thomas	6.00	2.70	.75
☐ 113 Andre Collins	6.00	2.70	.75
☐ 114 Paul Warfield RET	20.00	9.00	2.50
☐ 115 Bill Belichick CO	6.00	2.70	.75
☐ 116 Ottis Anderson	8.00	3.60	1.00
☐ 117 Andre Reed	20.00	9.00	2.50
☐ 118A Andre Rison	12.00	5.50	1.50
(Ball-point pen)			
☐ 118B Andre Rison	30.00	13.50	3.70
(Signed in Sharpie)			
☐ 119 Dexter Carter	6.00	2.70	.75
☐ 120 Anthony Munoz	12.00	5.50	1.50
☐ 121 Bernie Kosar	8.00	3.60	1.00
☐ 122 Alonzo Highsmith	60.00	27.00	7.50
☐ 123 David Treadwell	6.00	2.70	.75
☐ 124 Rodney Peete	8.00	3.60	1.00
☐ 125 Haywood Jeffires	8.00	3.60	1.00
☐ 126 Clarence Verdin	6.00	2.70	.75
☐ 127 Christian Okoye	8.00	3.60	1.00
☐ 128 Greg Townsend	125.00	55.00	15.50
☐ 129 Tom Newberry	6.00	2.70	.75
☐ 130 Keith Sims	6.00	2.70	.75
☐ 131 Myron Guyton	6.00	2.70	.75
☐ 132 Andre Tippett	8.00	3.60	1.00
☐ 133 Steve Walsh	6.00	2.70	.75
☐ 134 Erik McMillan	6.00	2.70	.75
☐ 135 Jim McMahon	250.00	110.00	31.00
☐ 136 Derek Hill	6.00	2.70	.75
☐ 137 D.J. Johnson	6.00	2.70	.75
☐ 138 Leslie O'Neal	8.00	3.60	1.00
☐ 139 Pierce Holt	6.00	2.70	.75
☐ 140 Cortez Kennedy	12.00	5.50	1.50
☐ 141 Danny Peebles	6.00	2.70	.75
☐ 142 Alvin Walton	6.00	2.70	.75
☐ 143 Drew Pearson RET	12.00	5.50	1.50
☐ 144 Dick MacPherson CO	6.00	2.70	.75
☐ 145 Erik Howard	6.00	2.70	.75
☐ 146 Steve Tasker	8.00	3.60	1.00
☐ 147 Bill Fralic	6.00	2.70	.75
☐ 148 Don Warren	6.00	2.70	.75
☐ 149 Eric Thomas	6.00	2.70	.75
☐ 150 Jack Pardee CO	6.00	2.70	.75
☐ 151 Gary Zimmerman	6.00	2.70	.75
☐ 152 Leonard Marshall	6.00	2.70	.75
(Frequently miscut)			
☐ 153 Chris Spielman	8.00	3.60	1.00
☐ 154 Sam Wyche CO	6.00	2.70	.75
☐ 155 Rohn Stark	6.00	2.70	.75
☐ 156 Stephone Paige	6.00	2.70	.75
☐ 157 Lionel Washington	100.00	45.00	12.50
Most signatures are cut off			
☐ 158 Henry Ellard	12.00	5.50	1.50
☐ 159 Dan Marino	175.00	80.00	22.00
☐ 160 Lindy Infante CO	6.00	2.70	.75
☐ 161 Dan McGwire	6.00	2.70	.75
☐ 162 Ken O'Brien	8.00	3.60	1.00
☐ 164 Louis Lipps	8.00	3.60	1.00
☐ 165 Billy Joe Tolliver	6.00	2.70	.75
☐ 166 Harris Barton	8.00	3.60	1.00
☐ 167 Tony Woods	6.00	2.70	.75
☐ 168 Matt Millen	8.00	3.60	1.00
☐ 169 Gale Sayers RET	40.00	18.00	5.00
☐ 170 Ron Meyer CO	6.00	2.70	.75
☐ 171 William Roberts	6.00	2.70	.75
☐ 172 Thurman Thomas	35.00	16.00	4.40
☐ 173 Steve McMichael	8.00	3.60	1.00
☐ 174 Ickey Woods	6.00	2.70	.75
☐ 175 Eugene Lockhart	6.00	2.70	.75
☐ 176 George Seifert CO	8.00	3.60	1.00
☐ 177 Keith Jones	6.00	2.70	.75
☐ 178 Jack Trudeau	6.00	2.70	.75
☐ 179 Kevin Porter	6.00	2.70	.75

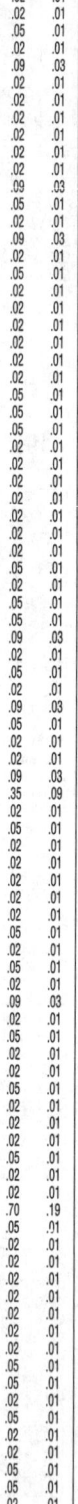

☐ 180 Ronnie Lott	20.00	9.00	2.50
☐ 181 Marty Schottenheimer CO	8.00	3.60	1.00
☐ 182 Morten Andersen	8.00	3.60	1.00
☐ 183 Anthony Thompson	6.00	2.70	.75
☐ 184 Tim Worley	6.00	2.70	.75
☐ 185 Billy Ray Smith	6.00	2.70	.75
☐ 186 David Whitmore	6.00	2.70	.75
☐ 187 Jacob Green	6.00	2.70	.75
☐ 188 Browning Nagle	6.00	2.70	.75
☐ 189 Franco Harris RET	35.00	16.00	4.40
Most signatures are cut off			
☐ 190 Art Shell CO	20.00	9.00	2.50
☐ 191 Bart Oates	6.00	2.70	.75
☐ 192 William Perry	8.00	3.60	1.00
☐ 193 Chuck Noll CO	20.00	9.00	2.50
☐ 194 Troy Aikman	125.00	55.00	15.50
☐ 195 Jeff George	12.00	5.50	1.50
☐ 196 Derrick Thomas	20.00	9.00	2.50
☐ 197 Roger Craig	12.00	5.50	1.50
☐ 198 John Fourcade	6.00	2.70	.75
☐ 199 Rod Woodson	20.00	9.00	2.50
☐ 200 Anthony Miller	12.00	5.50	1.50
☐ 201 Jerry Rice	125.00	55.00	15.50
☐ 202 Eugene Robinson	6.00	2.70	.75
☐ 203 Charles Mann	6.00	2.70	.75
☐ 204 Mel Blount RET	12.00	5.50	1.50
☐ 205 Don Shula CO	40.00	18.00	5.00
☐ 206 Jumbo Elliott	6.00	2.70	.75
☐ 207 Jay Hilgenberg	6.00	2.70	.75
☐ 208 Deron Cherry	6.00	2.70	.75
☐ 209 Dan Reeves CO	12.00	5.50	1.50
☐ 210 Roman Phifer	6.00	2.70	.75
☐ 211 David Little	6.00	2.70	.75
☐ 212 Lee Williams	6.00	2.70	.75
☐ 213 John Taylor	8.00	3.60	1.00
☐ 214 Monte Coleman	6.00	2.70	.75
☐ 215 Walter Payton RET	60.00	27.00	7.50
☐ 216 John Robinson CO	6.00	2.70	.75
☐ 217 Pepper Johnson	6.00	2.70	.75
☐ 218 Tom Thayer	6.00	2.70	.75
☐ 219 Dan Saleaumua	6.00	2.70	.75
☐ 220 Ernest Spears	6.00	2.70	.75
☐ 221 Bubby Brister	6.00	2.70	.75
(Signed Bubby 6)			
☐ 222 Junior Seau	20.00	9.00	2.50
☐ 223 Brent Jones	8.00	3.60	1.00
☐ 224 Rufus Porter	6.00	2.70	.75
☐ 225 Jack Kemp RET	30.00	13.50	3.70
(Autopenned)			
☐ 226 Wayne Fontes CO	6.00	2.70	.75
☐ 227 Phil Simms	25.00	11.00	3.10
☐ 228 Shaun Gayle	6.00	2.70	.75
☐ 229 Bill Maas	6.00	2.70	.75
☐ 230 Renaldo Turnbull	8.00	3.60	1.00
☐ 231 Bryan Hinkle	6.00	2.70	.75
☐ 232 Gary Plummer	6.00	2.70	.75
☐ 233 Jerry Burns CO	6.00	2.70	.75
☐ 234 Lawrence Taylor	35.00	16.00	4.40
☐ 235 Joe Gibbs CO	20.00	9.00	2.50
☐ 236 Neil Smith	60.00	27.00	7.50
(Most signatures are cut off)			
☐ 237 Rich Kotite CO	6.00	2.70	.75
☐ 238 Jim Covert	6.00	2.70	.75
☐ 239 Tim Grunhard	6.00	2.70	.75
(Two different signatures known for this card)			
☐ 240 Joe Bugel CO	6.00	2.70	.75
☐ 241 David Wyman	6.00	2.70	.75
☐ 242 Maury Buford	6.00	2.70	.75
☐ 243 Kevin Ross	6.00	2.70	.75
☐ 244 Jimmy Johnson CO	30.00	13.50	3.70
☐ 245 Jim Morrissey	6.00	2.70	.75
☐ 246 Jeff Hostetler	8.00	3.60	1.00
☐ 247 Andre Ware	8.00	3.60	1.00
☐ 248 Steve Largent RET	40.00	18.00	5.00
☐ 249 Chuck Knox CO	8.00	3.60	1.00
☐ 250 Boomer Esiason	12.00	5.50	1.50
☐ 251 Kevin Butler	8.00	3.60	1.00
☐ 252 Bruce Smith	20.00	9.00	2.50
☐ 253 Webster Slaughter	8.00	3.60	1.00
☐ 254 Mike Sherrard	8.00	3.60	1.00
☐ 255 Steve Broussard	6.00	2.70	.75
☐ 256 Warren Moon	35.00	16.00	4.40
☐ 257 John Elway	60.00	27.00	7.50
☐ 258 Bob Golic	6.00	2.70	.75
☐ 259 Jim Everett	8.00	3.60	1.00
☐ 260 Bruce Coslet CO	6.00	2.70	.75
☐ 261 James Francis	250.00	110.00	31.00
☐ 262 Eric Dorsey	6.00	2.70	.75
☐ 263 Marcus Dupree	6.00	2.70	.75
☐ 264 Hart Lee Dykes	6.00	2.70	.75
☐ 265 Vinny Testaverde	8.00	3.60	1.00
☐ 266 Chip Lohmiller	6.00	2.70	.75
☐ 267 John Riggins RET	20.00	9.00	2.50
☐ 268 Mike Schad	6.00	2.70	.75
☐ 269 Kevin Greene	12.00	5.50	1.50
☐ 270 Dean Biasucci	6.00	2.70	.75
☐ 271 Mike Pritchard	8.00	3.60	1.00
☐ 272 Ted Washington	6.00	2.70	.75
☐ 273 Alfred Williams	6.00	2.70	.75
☐ 274 Chris Zorich	8.00	3.60	1.00
☐ 275 Reggie Barrett	6.00	2.70	.75
☐ 276 Chris Hinton	6.00	2.70	.75
☐ 277 Tracy Johnson	6.00	2.70	.75
☐ 278 Jim Harbaugh	12.00	5.50	1.50
☐ 279 John Roper	6.00	2.70	.75
☐ 280 Mike Dumas	6.00	2.70	.75
☐ 281 Herman Moore	40.00	18.00	5.00
☐ 282 Eric Turner	8.00	3.60	1.00
☐ 283 Steve Atwater	8.00	3.60	1.00
☐ 284 Michael Cofer	6.00	2.70	.75
☐ 285 Darion Conner	6.00	2.70	.75
☐ 286 Darryl Talley	6.00	2.70	.75
☐ 287 Donnell Woolford	6.00	2.70	.75
☐ 288 Keith McCants	6.00	2.70	.75
☐ 289 Ray Handley CO	6.00	2.70	.75
☐ 290 Ahmad Rashad RET	175.00	80.00	22.00
☐ 291 Eric Swann	12.00	5.50	1.50
☐ 292 Dalton Hilliard	25.00	11.00	3.10
(Signatures usually miscut)			
☐ 293 Rickey Jackson	8.00	3.60	1.00
☐ 294 Vaughan Johnson	8.00	3.60	1.00
☐ 295 Eric Martin	8.00	3.60	1.00
☐ 296 Pat Swilling	8.00	3.60	1.00
☐ 297 Anthony Carter	25.00	11.00	3.10
(Signatures usually miscut)			
☐ 298 Guy McIntyre	60.00	27.00	7.50
☐ 299 Bennie Blades	6.00	2.70	.75
☐ 300 Paul Farren	6.00	2.70	.75
☐ PLC2 Payne Stewart	100.00	45.00	12.50
Golfer			
☐ NNO Santa Claus Sendaway	30.00	13.50	3.70
(Signed)			
☐ NNO Santa Claus Sendaway	50.00	22.00	6.25
(Signed and numbered)			

1991 Pro Line Portraits Wives

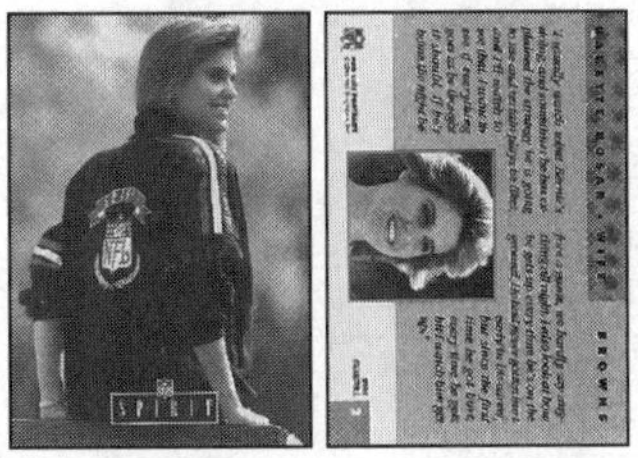

This seven-card standard size set was issued with the 1991 Pro Line Portraits set as inserts in the regular foil packs. These seven cards feature wives of some of the NFL's most popular personalities, including former television actress Jennifer Montana and star of the Cosby show, Phylicia Rashad. The cards are numbered on the back with an "SC" prefix.

	MINT	NRMT	EXC
COMPLETE SET (7)	.75	.35	.09
COMMON CARD (SC1-SC7)	.10	.05	.01
☐ SC1 Jennifer Montana	.30	.14	.04
☐ SC2 Babette Kosar	.10	.05	.01
☐ SC3 Janet Elway	.10	.05	.01
☐ SC4 Michelle Oates	.10	.05	.01
☐ SC5 Toni Lipps	.10	.05	.01
☐ SC6 Stacey O'Brien	.10	.05	.01
☐ SC7 Phylicia Rashad	.15	.07	.02

1991 Pro Line Portraits Wives Autographs

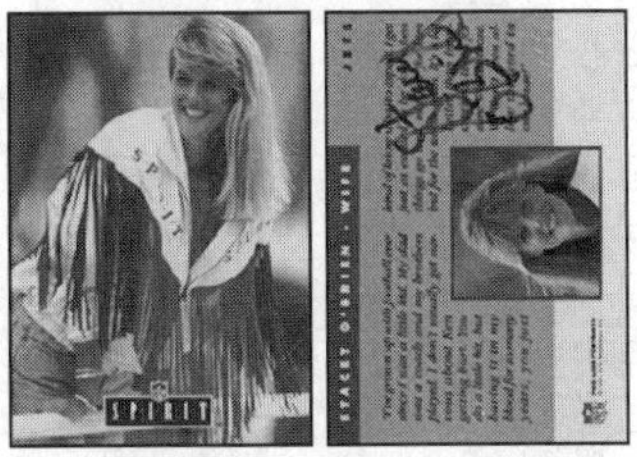

This seven-card standard-size set was included in the 1991 Pro Line Portraits set as inserts in the regular foil packs. These cards feature wives of some of the NFL's most popular personalities, including former television actress Jennifer Montana and star of the Cosby show, Phylicia Rashad. Less than 15 of Rashad's cards are currently known to exist. The cards are unnumbered but are listed below according to the numbers assigned to them in the regular series.

	MINT	NRMT	EXC
COMPLETE SET (7)	600.00	275.00	75.00
COMMON CARD (1-7)	15.00	6.75	1.85
☐ SC1 Jennifer Montana	75.00	34.00	9.50
☐ SC2 Babette Kosar	15.00	6.75	1.85
☐ SC3 Janet Elway	15.00	6.75	1.85
☐ SC4 Michelle Oates	15.00	6.75	1.85
☐ SC5 Toni Lipps	15.00	6.75	1.85
☐ SC6 Stacey O'Brien	15.00	6.75	1.85
☐ SC7 Phylicia Rashad	500.00	220.00	60.00

1991 Pro Line Punt, Pass and Kick

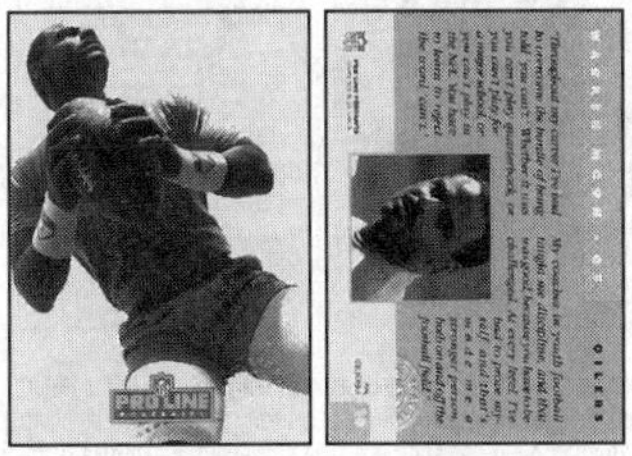

This 12-card standard-size set was issued to honor 1991 NFL quarterbacks in conjunction with the long-standing Punt, Pass, and Kick program. Cards 1-11 show each quarterback in various still-life poses. Card fronts also feature an embossed Punt, Pass, and Kick logo in the lower right corner and the NFL Pro Line Portraits logo at the bottom center. Horizontally oriented card backs have player's name printed in reverse-out fashion in a team color. The team's name in black appears in the upper right corner. A close-up head shot is centered on the lower middle section of the back and a quote from the quarterback about being successful in the NFL is printed on a silver background.

	MINT	NRMT	EXC
COMPLETE SET (12)	80.00	36.00	10.00
COMMON CARD (PPK1-PPK11)	3.00	1.35	.35
☐ PPK1 Troy Aikman	20.00	9.00	2.50
☐ PPK2 Bubby Brister	3.00	1.35	.35
☐ PPK3 Randall Cunningham	3.00	1.35	.35
☐ PPK4 John Elway	15.00	6.75	1.85
☐ PPK5 Boomer Esiason	4.00	1.80	.50
☐ PPK6 Jim Everett	4.00	1.80	.50
☐ PPK7 Jim Kelly	5.00	2.20	.60
☐ PPK8 Bernie Kosar	3.00	1.35	.35
☐ PPK9 Dan Marino	30.00	13.50	3.70
☐ PPK10 Warren Moon	5.00	2.20	.60
☐ PPK11 Phil Simms	4.00	1.80	.50
☐ SC3 Punt Pass and Kick Checklist Card	3.00	1.35	.35

1991-92 Pro Line Profiles Anthony Munoz

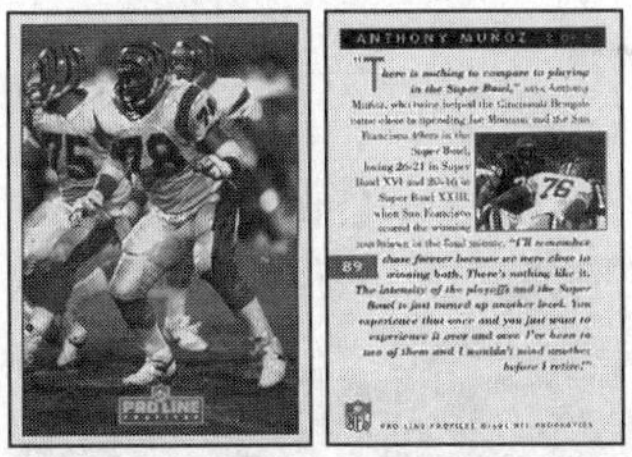

This nine-card standard-size set was inserted into the Super Bowl XXVI game program. The slick four-color cards depict different phases of the career of Munoz, and the Pro Line Profile logo is centered at the bottom of each perforated card. The back features a black bar with the player's name reversed out in white lettering, while the card numbers appear in burnt orange in the right corner of the black bar. The backs present career highlights, family life, and community service projects that Munoz promotes.

	MINT	NRMT	EXC
COMPLETE SET (9)	5.00	2.20	.60
COMMON CARD (1-9)	.60	.25	.07
☐ 1 Anthony Munoz 1991 NFL Man of Year	.60	.25	.07
☐ 2 Anthony Munoz Little League Player	.60	.25	.07
☐ 3 Anthony Munoz 1980 Rose Bowl	.60	.25	.07
☐ 4 Anthony Munoz Community Service	.60	.25	.07
☐ 5 Anthony Munoz Portrait	.60	.25	.07
☐ 6 Anthony Munoz 1981 AFC Championship Game	.60	.25	.07
☐ 7 Anthony Munoz 1992 Pro Bowl	.60	.25	.07
☐ 8 Anthony Munoz Super Bowl XVI and XXIII	.60	.25	.07
☐ 9 Anthony Munoz Physical Fitness Photo	.60	.25	.07

1992 Pro Line Draft Day

Each of these draft day collectible cards measures the standard size. The fronts feature full-bleed color photos, while the horizontally oriented backs have an head shot surrounded by an extended quote. Emtman is pictured sitting on a boat holding a fishing rod, with a

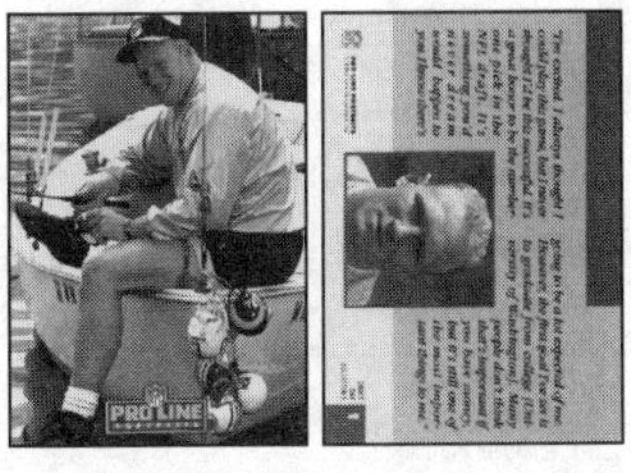

"stringer" of NFL helmets dangling from the bow. The other card features a group picture of NFL coaches on the front, while the head shot and extended quote on the back are by Chris Berman, an ESPN commentator.

	MINT	NRMT	EXC
COMPLETE SET (2)	5.00	2.20	.60
COMMON CARD (1-2)	2.50	1.10	.30
☐ 1 Steve Emtman	2.50	1.10	.30
☐ 2 Coaches Photo	2.50	1.10	.30

1992 Pro Line Mobil

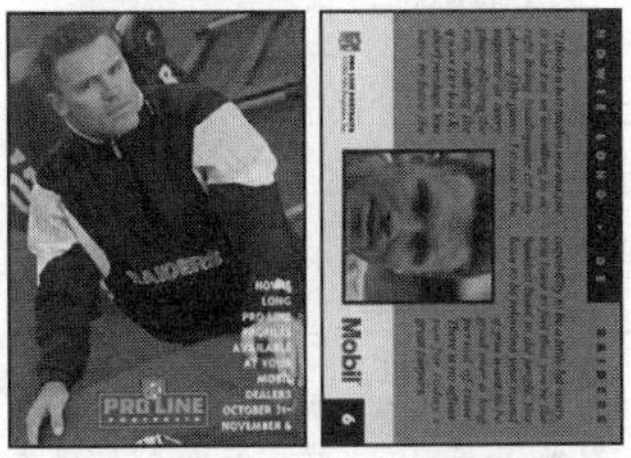

Produced by NFL Properties, this 72-card regionally distributed standard-size set consists of 1991 Portraits (1-9) and 1992 Profiles (10-72) cards. The set was part of an eight-week promotion in Southern California. Each week a nine-card pack could be obtained by purchasing at least eight gallons of Mobil Super Unleaded Plus. The nine cards available the first week were a title card, a checklist, and seven Portrait cards which have printed on their fronts the dates that nine-card packs of that player would be available. During the following seven weeks, one player was featured per week in the packs. The cards carry full-bleed posed and action color player/family photos. The Pro Line logo is at the bottom. The backs feature player information with the Mobil logo at the bottom. Card number 9 picturing Eric Dickerson in a Raiders' uniform is exclusive to the set. The cards are numbered on the back "X of 9" and arranged below chronologically according to the eight-week promotion. The week the cards were available is listed under the first card of the nine-card subsets. Each nine-card cello pack included an unperforated sheet with four coupon offers.

	MINT	NRMT	EXC
COMPLETE SET (72)	8.00	3.60	1.00
COMMON CARD (1-72)	.10	.05	.01
☐ 1 Title Card (October 3-9)	.10	.05	.01
☐ 2 Checklist	.10	.05	.01
☐ 3 Ronnie Lott	.15	.07	.02
☐ 4 Junior Seau	.30	.14	.04
☐ 5 Jim Everett	.10	.05	.01
☐ 6 Howie Long	.15	.07	.02
☐ 7 Jerry Rice	.75	.35	.09
☐ 8 Art Shell CO	.15	.07	.02
☐ 9 Eric Dickerson	.25	.11	.03
☐ 10 Ronnie Lott (October 10-16) (Making Hit)	.15	.07	.02
☐ 11 Ronnie Lott (Little Leaguer)	.15	.07	.02
☐ 12 Ronnie Lott (Playing for USC)	.15	.07	.02
☐ 13 Ronnie Lott (Exultation)	.15	.07	.02
☐ 14 Ronnie Lott (Portrait)	.15	.07	.02
☐ 15 Ronnie Lott (Behind Bar)	.15	.07	.02
☐ 16 Ronnie Lott (With Family)	.15	.07	.02
☐ 17 Ronnie Lott (Catching Ball)	.15	.07	.02
☐ 18 Ronnie Lott (Tuxedo)	.15	.07	.02
☐ 19 Junior Seau (October 17-23) (With Ball)	.25	.11	.03
☐ 20 Junior Seau (Young Junior)	.25	.11	.03
☐ 21 Junior Seau (Pointing)	.25	.11	.03
☐ 22 Junior Seau (Over Fallen Opponent)	.25	.11	.03
☐ 23 Junior Seau (Portrait)	.25	.11	.03
☐ 24 Junior Seau (With Wife)	.25	.11	.03

☐ 25 Junior Seau (Running in Surf)	.25	.11	.03
☐ 26 Junior Seau (Weightlifting)	.25	.11	.03
☐ 27 Junior Seau (Seaweed Boa)	.25	.11	.03
☐ 28 Jim Everett (October 24-30) (Looking for Receiver)	.10	.05	.01
☐ 29 Jim Everett (Young Jim)	.10	.05	.01
☐ 30 Jim Everett (Playing for Purdue)	.10	.05	.01
☐ 31 Jim Everett (With Parents, Sister)	.10	.05	.01
☐ 32 Jim Everett (Portrait)	.10	.05	.01
☐ 33 Jim Everett (Eluding Rush)	.10	.05	.01
☐ 34 Jim Everett (Fishing)	.10	.05	.01
☐ 35 Jim Everett (Handing Off)	.10	.05	.01
☐ 36 Jim Everett (Studio Photo)	.10	.05	.01
☐ 37 Howie Long (October 31-November 6) (Hand Up to Block Pass)	.15	.07	.02
☐ 38 Howie Long (High School Footballer)	.15	.07	.02
☐ 39 Howie Long (Closing in for Sack)	.15	.07	.02
☐ 40 Howie Long (With Family)	.15	.07	.02
☐ 41 Howie Long (Portrait)	.15	.07	.02
☐ 42 Howie Long (Fundraising for Kids)	.15	.07	.02
☐ 43 Howie Long (Hitting the Heavy Bag)	.15	.07	.02
☐ 44 Howie Long (Taking Swipe at Ball)	.15	.07	.02
☐ 45 Howie Long (Studio Photo)	.15	.07	.02
☐ 46 Jerry Rice (November 7-13) (With Trophy)	.40	.18	.05
☐ 47 Jerry Rice (Avoiding Block)	.40	.18	.05
☐ 48 Jerry Rice (Eluding Steeler)	.40	.18	.05
☐ 49 Jerry Rice (With Family)	.40	.18	.05
☐ 50 Jerry Rice (Portrait)	.40	.18	.05
☐ 51 Jerry Rice (With Toddler)	.40	.18	.05
☐ 52 Jerry Rice (Playing Tennis)	.40	.18	.05
☐ 53 Jerry Rice (Scoring TD)	.40	.18	.05
☐ 54 Jerry Rice (Studio Photo)	.40	.18	.05
☐ 55 Art Shell CO (November 14-20) (In Front of His Team)	.15	.07	.02
☐ 56 Art Shell CO (At Maryland State)	.15	.07	.02
☐ 57 Art Shell CO (Blocking Viking)	.15	.07	.02
☐ 58 Art Shell CO (Playing Basketball)	.15	.07	.02
☐ 59 Art Shell CO (Portrait)	.15	.07	.02
☐ 60 Art Shell CO (Talking to Player)	.15	.07	.02
☐ 61 Art Shell CO (In Front of TV)	.15	.07	.02
☐ 62 Art Shell CO (Blocking for Raiders)	.15	.07	.02
☐ 63 Art Shell CO (With Teddy Bear)	.15	.07	.02
☐ 64 Eric Dickerson (November 21-30) (Studio Suit Up)	.15	.07	.02
☐ 65 Eric Dickerson (Running for SMU)	.15	.07	.02
☐ 66 Eric Dickerson (With Mom)	.15	.07	.02
☐ 67 Eric Dickerson (49ers in Pursuit)	.15	.07	.02
☐ 68 Eric Dickerson (Portrait)	.15	.07	.02
☐ 69 Eric Dickerson (Running for Colts)	.15	.07	.02
☐ 70 Eric Dickerson (On Training Ramp)	.15	.07	.02
☐ 71 Eric Dickerson (Running Against Rams)	.15	.07	.02
☐ 72 Eric Dickerson (Posed With Football)	.15	.07	.02

1992 Pro Line Prototypes

This 13-card sample standard-size set was distributed by Pro Line to show the design of their 1992 Pro Line football card series. The cards

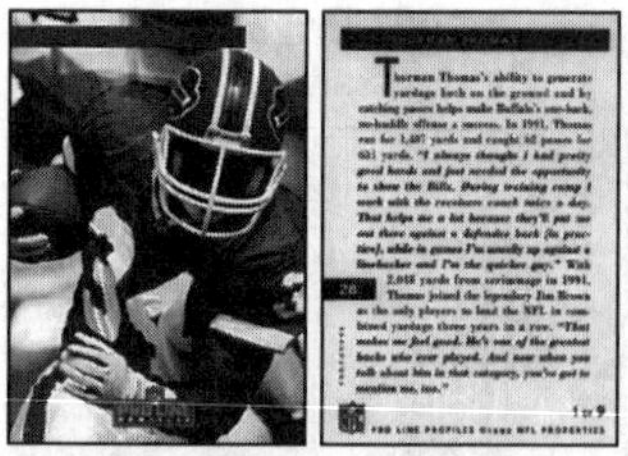

were distributed as a complete set in a cello pack. The fronts feature full-bleed color photos, while the backs carry a color close-up photo, extended quote, or statistics. The set includes samples of the following Pro Line series: Profiles (28-36), Spirit (12), and Portraits (379, 386). The cards are numbered on the back, and their numbering is the same as in the regular series. These cards were also distributed by Classic at major card and trade shows. These prototypes can be distinguished from the regular issue cards in that they are vertically marked "prototype" in the lower left corner of the Profiles reverse and or "sample" next to the picture on the Portraits reverse.

	MINT	NRMT	EXC
COMPLETE SET (13)	8.00	3.60	1.00
COMMON CARD	.50	.23	.06
☐ 12 Kathie Lee Gifford	.75	.35	.09
☐ 28 Thurman Thomas (Bills' uniform, action shot)	.75	.35	.09
☐ 29 Thurman Thomas (With his mother)	.75	.35	.09
☐ 30 Thurman Thomas (OSU Cowboy uniform, action shot)	.75	.35	.09
☐ 31 Thurman Thomas (With family)	.75	.35	.09
☐ 32 Thurman Thomas (Color portrait)	.75	.35	.09
☐ 33 Thurman Thomas (Action shot, Super Bowl XXV)	.75	.35	.09
☐ 34 Thurman Thomas (Fishing)	.75	.35	.09
☐ 35 Thurman Thomas (Stretching on track)	.75	.35	.09
☐ 36 Thurman Thomas (Close-up photo)	.75	.35	.09
☐ 379 Jessie Tuggle	.50	.23	.06
☐ 386 Neil O'Donnell	.75	.35	.09
☐ NNO Advertisement Card	.50	.23	.06

1992 Pro Line Portraits

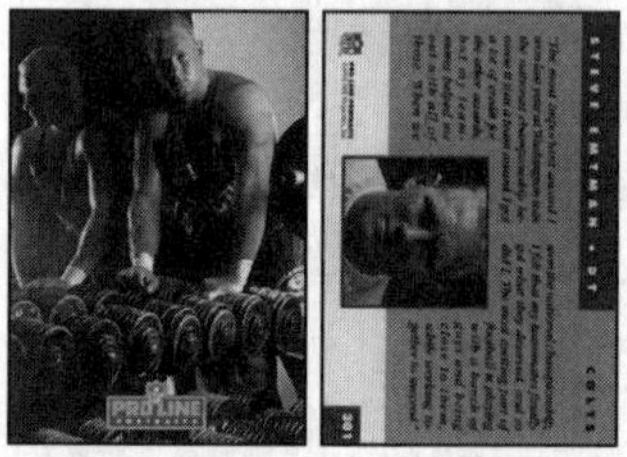

This 167-card standard-size set is numbered in continuation of the 1991 ProLine Portraits set. Each Pro Line Collection pack contained nine Profiles and three Portraits cards. Pro Line's goal was to have an autographed card in each box and, as a bonus, some 1991 ProLine Portrait autographed cards were included. Also autograph cards could be obtained through a mail-in offer in exchange for 12 1991 ProLine Portraits wrappers (black) and 12 1992 ProLine wrappers (white). The fronts display full-bleed color photos in non-game shots while the backs carry personal information. The cards are numbered on the back. A special boxed set, with the cards displayed in two notebooks, was distributed at the National. The promo cards differ from the regular series in two respects: the cards are unnumbered and are stamped with a "The National, 1992" seal. The key Rookie Cards in this set are Edgar Bennett, Terrell Buckley, Dale Carter, Marco Coleman, Quentin Coryatt, Steve Emtman, Johnny Mitchell and Tommy Vardell. The 1992 ProLine Santa Claus card could be obtained through a mail-in offer in exchange for ten 1991 Pro Line Portraits wrappers (black) and ten 1992 Pro Line Collection wrappers (white). The first 10,000 to respond to the offer received Mrs. Claus card.through a mail-in offer in exchange for ten 1991 Pro Line Portraits wrappers (black) and ten 1992 Pro Line Collection wrappers (white). The first 10,000 to respond to the offer received a Mrs. Claus card.

	MINT	NRMT	EXC
COMPLETE SET (167)	6.00	2.70	.75
COMMON CARD (301-467)	.04	.02	.01
☐ 301 Steve Emtman	.10	.05	.01
☐ 302 Al Edwards	.04	.02	.01
☐ 303 Wendell Davis	.04	.02	.01
☐ 304 Lewis Billups	.04	.02	.01
☐ 305 Brian Brennan	.04	.02	.01
☐ 306 John Gesek	.04	.02	.01
☐ 307 Terrell Buckley	.10	.05	.01
☐ 308 Johnny Mitchell	.04	.02	.01
☐ 309 LeRoy Butler	.04	.02	.01
☐ 310 William Fuller	.10	.05	.01
☐ 311 Bill Brooks	.10	.05	.01
☐ 312 Dino Hackett	.04	.02	.01
☐ 313 Willie Gault	.10	.05	.01
☐ 314 Aaron Cox	.04	.02	.01
☐ 315 Jeff Cross	.04	.02	.01
☐ 316 Emmitt Smith	2.00	.90	.25
☐ 317 Marv Cook	.04	.02	.01
☐ 318 Gill Fenerty	.04	.02	.01
☐ 319 Jeff Carlson	.04	.02	.01
☐ 320 Brad Baxter	.04	.02	.01
☐ 321 Fred Barnett	.10	.05	.01
☐ 322 Kurt Barber	.04	.02	.01
☐ 323 Eric Green	.10	.05	.01
☐ 324 Greg Clark	.04	.02	.01
☐ 325 Keith DeLong	.04	.02	.01
☐ 326 Patrick Hunter	.04	.02	.01
☐ 327 Troy Vincent	.10	.05	.01
☐ 328 Gary Clark	.10	.05	.01
☐ 329 Joe Montana	1.50	.70	.19
☐ 330 Michael Haynes	.10	.05	.01
☐ 331 Edgar Bennett	.20	.09	.03
☐ 332 Darren Lewis	.04	.02	.01
☐ 333 Derrick Fenner	.04	.02	.01
☐ 334 Rob Burnett	.04	.02	.01
☐ 335 Alvin Harper	.10	.05	.01
☐ 336 Vance Johnson	.04	.02	.01
☐ 337 William White	.04	.02	.01
☐ 338 Sterling Sharpe	.10	.05	.01
☐ 339 Sean Jones	.10	.05	.01
☐ 340 Jeff Herrod	.04	.02	.01
☐ 341 Chris Martin	.04	.02	.01
☐ 342 Ethan Horton	.04	.02	.01
☐ 343 Robert Delpino	.04	.02	.01
☐ 344 Mark Higgs	.04	.02	.01
☐ 345 Chris Doleman	.10	.05	.01
☐ 346 Tommy Hodson	.04	.02	.01
☐ 347 Craig Heyward	.10	.05	.01
☐ 348 Cary Conklin	.04	.02	.01
☐ 349 James Hasty	.04	.02	.01
☐ 350 Antone Davis	.04	.02	.01
☐ 351 Ernie Jones	.04	.02	.01
☐ 352 Greg Lloyd	.20	.09	.03
☐ 353 John Friesz	.10	.05	.01
☐ 354 Charles Haley	.10	.05	.01
☐ 355 Tracy Scroggins	.04	.02	.01
☐ 356 Paul Gruber	.04	.02	.01
☐ 357 Ricky Ervins	.04	.02	.01
☐ 358 Brad Muster	.04	.02	.01
☐ 359 Deion Sanders	.50	.23	.06
☐ 360 Mitch Frerotte	.04	.02	.01
☐ 361 Stan Thomas	.04	.02	.01
☐ 362 Harold Green	.10	.05	.01
☐ 363 Eric Metcalf	.20	.09	.03
☐ 364 Ken Norton Jr.	.10	.05	.01
☐ 365 Dave Widell Doug Widell	.04	.02	.01
☐ 366 Mike Tomczak	.04	.02	.01
☐ 367 Bubba McDowell	.04	.02	.01
☐ 368 Jessie Hester	.04	.02	.01
☐ 369 Ervin Randle	.04	.02	.01
☐ 370 Tony Smith	.04	.02	.01
☐ 371 Pat Terrell	.04	.02	.01
☐ 372 Jim C. Jensen	.04	.02	.01
☐ 373 Mike Merriweather	.04	.02	.01
☐ 374 Chris Singleton	.04	.02	.01
☐ 375 Floyd Turner	.04	.02	.01
☐ 376 Jim Sweeney	.04	.02	.01
☐ 377 Keith Jackson	.10	.05	.01
☐ 378 Walter Reeves	.04	.02	.01
☐ 379 Neil O'Donnell	.20	.09	.03
☐ 380 Nate Lewis	.04	.02	.01
☐ 381 Keith Henderson	.04	.02	.01
☐ 382 Kelly Stouffer	.04	.02	.01
☐ 383 Ricky Reynolds	.04	.02	.01
☐ 384 Joe Jacoby	.04	.02	.01
☐ 385 Fred Biletnikoff RET	.10	.05	.01
☐ 386 Jessie Tuggle	.04	.02	.01
☐ 387 Tom Waddle	.04	.02	.01
☐ 388 David Shula CO	.04	.02	.01
☐ 389 Van Waiters	.04	.02	.01
☐ 390 Jay Novacek	.10	.05	.01
☐ 391 Michael Young	.04	.02	.01
☐ 392 Mike Holmgren CO	.04	.02	.01
☐ 393 Doug Smith	.04	.02	.01
☐ 394 Mike Prior	.04	.02	.01
☐ 395 Harvey Williams	.10	.05	.01
☐ 396 Aaron Wallace	.04	.02	.01
☐ 397 Tony Zendejas	.04	.02	.01
☐ 398 Sammie Smith	.04	.02	.01
☐ 399 Henry Thomas	.04	.02	.01
☐ 400 Jon Vaughn	.04	.02	.01
☐ 401 Brian Washington	.04	.02	.01
☐ 402 Leon Searcy	.04	.02	.01
☐ 403 Lance Smith	.04	.02	.01
☐ 404 Warren Williams	.04	.02	.01
☐ 405 Bobby Ross CO	.04	.02	.01
☐ 406 Harry Sydney	.04	.02	.01
☐ 407 John L. Williams	.04	.02	.01
☐ 408 Ken Willis	.04	.02	.01
☐ 409 Brian Mitchell	.10	.05	.01
☐ 410 Dick Butkus RET	.10	.05	.01
☐ 411 Chuck Knox CO	.04	.02	.01
☐ 412 Robert Porcher	.10	.05	.01
☐ 413 Calvin Williams	.10	.05	.01
☐ 414 Bill Cowher CO	.10	.05	.01
☐ 415 Eric Moore	.04	.02	.01
☐ 416 Derek Brown TE	.04	.02	.01
☐ 417 Dennis Green CO	.04	.02	.01
☐ 418 Tom Flores CO	.04	.02	.01
☐ 419 Dale Carter	.10	.05	.01
☐ 420 Tony Dorsett RET	.10	.05	.01
☐ 421 Marco Coleman	.10	.05	.01
☐ 422 Sam Wyche CO	.04	.02	.01
☐ 423 Ray Crockett	.04	.02	.01
☐ 424 Dan Fouts RET	.10	.05	.01
☐ 425 Hugh Millen	.04	.02	.01
☐ 426 Quentin Coryatt	.20	.09	.03
☐ 427 Brian Jordan	.10	.05	.01
☐ 428 Frank Gifford RET	.10	.05	.01
☐ 429 Toby Caston	.04	.02	.01
☐ 430 Ted Marchibroda CO	.04	.02	.01
☐ 431 Cris Carter	.20	.09	.03
☐ 432 Tim Krumrie	.04	.02	.01
☐ 433 Otto Graham RET	.10	.05	.01
☐ 434 Vaughn Dunbar	.04	.02	.01
☐ 435 John Fina	.04	.02	.01
☐ 436 Sonny Jurgensen RET	.10	.05	.01
☐ 437 Robert Jones	.04	.02	.01
☐ 438 Steve DeOssie	.04	.02	.01
☐ 439 Eddie LeBaron RET	.04	.02	.01
☐ 440 Chester McGlockton	.10	.05	.01
☐ 441 Ken Stabler RET	.10	.05	.01
☐ 442 Joe DeLamielleure RET	.04	.02	.01
☐ 443 Charley Taylor RET	.04	.02	.01
☐ 444 Greg Skrepenak	.04	.02	.01
☐ 445 Y.A. Tittle RET	.10	.05	.01
☐ 446 Chuck Smith	.04	.02	.01
☐ 447 Kellen Winslow RET	.04	.02	.01
☐ 448 Kevin Smith	.10	.05	.01
☐ 449 Phillippi Sparks	.04	.02	.01
☐ 450 Alonzo Spellman	.10	.05	.01
☐ 451 Mark Rypien	.10	.05	.01
☐ 452 Darryl Williams	.04	.02	.01
☐ 453 Tommy Vardell	.10	.05	.01
☐ 454 Tommy Maddox	.04	.02	.01
☐ 455 Steve Israel	.04	.02	.01
☐ 456 Marquez Pope	.04	.02	.01
☐ 457 Eugene Chung	.04	.02	.01
☐ 458 Lynn Swann RET	.10	.05	.01
☐ 459 Sean Gilbert	.10	.05	.01
☐ 460 Chris Mims	.10	.05	.01
☐ 461 Al Davis OWN	.10	.05	.01
☐ 462 Richard Todd RET	.04	.02	.01
☐ 463 Mike Fox	.04	.02	.01
☐ 464 David Klingler	.10	.05	.01
☐ 465 Darren Woodson	.10	.05	.01
☐ 466 Jason Hanson	.10	.05	.01
☐ 467 Lem Barney RET	.04	.02	.01
☐ NNO Santa Claus Sendaway	4.00	1.80	.50
☐ NNO Mrs.Claus Sendaway	5.00	2.20	.60

1992 Pro Line Portraits Autographs

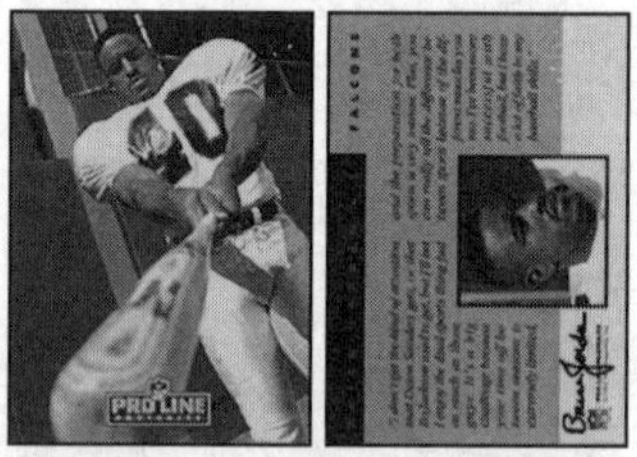

This 167-card standard-size set continues the numbering of the 1991 Pro Line Portraits set. Reportedly 35,000 ten-box cases were produced. Pro Line's goal was to have an autographed card in each box. Also autograph cards could be obtained through a mail-in offer in exchange for 12 1991 Pro Line Portraits wrappers (black) and 12 1992 Pro Line Collection wrappers (white). The fronts display full-bleed color photos in non-game shots while the backs carry personal information. The cards are unnumbered but are listed below according to the numbers assigned to them in the regular series. The following cards were not signed: 349 James Hasty, 370 Anthony Smith, 417 Dennis Green, 428 Frank Gifford, 451 Mark Rypien, 462 Richard Todd. The Santa and Mrs. Claus autographed cards are not considered part of the complete set.

	MINT	NRMT	EXC
COMPLETE SET (161)	1200.00	550.00	150.00
COMMON CARD (301-467)	4.00	1.80	.50
☐ 301 Steve Emtman	6.00	2.70	.75
☐ 302 Al Edwards	4.00	1.80	.50
☐ 303 Wendell Davis	4.00	1.80	.50
☐ 304 Lewis Billups	8.00	2.70	.75
☐ 305 Brian Brennan	4.00	1.80	.50
☐ 306 John Gesek	4.00	1.80	.50
☐ 307 Terrell Buckley	4.00	1.80	.50
☐ 308 Johnny Mitchell	4.00	1.80	.50
☐ 309 LeRoy Butler	6.00	1.80	.50
☐ 310 William Fuller	6.00	2.70	.75
☐ 311 Bill Brooks	6.00	2.70	.75
☐ 312 Dino Hackett	4.00	1.80	.50
☐ 313 Willie Gault	6.00	2.70	.75

☐ 314 Aaron Cox	4.00	1.80	.50
☐ 315 Jeff Cross	4.00	1.80	.50
☐ 316 Emmitt Smith	75.00	34.00	9.50
☐ 317 Marv Cook	4.00	1.80	.50
☐ 318 Gill Fenerty	4.00	1.80	.50
☐ 319 Jeff Carlson	4.00	1.80	.50
☐ 320 Brad Baxter	4.00	1.80	.50
☐ 321 Fred Barnett	10.00	4.50	1.25
☐ 322 Kurt Barber	4.00	1.80	.50
☐ 323 Eric Green	4.00	1.80	.50
☐ 324 Greg Clark	4.00	1.80	.50
☐ 325 Keith DeLong	4.00	1.80	.50
☐ 326 Patrick Hunter	4.00	1.80	.50
☐ 327 Troy Vincent	6.00	2.70	.75
☐ 328 Gary Clark	6.00	2.70	.75
☐ 329 Joe Montana	125.00	55.00	15.50
☐ 330 Michael Haynes	6.00	2.70	.75
☐ 331 Edgar Bennett	10.00	4.50	1.25
☐ 332 Darren Lewis	4.00	1.80	.50
☐ 333 Derrick Fenner	4.00	1.80	.50
☐ 334 Rob Burnett	4.00	1.80	.50
☐ 335 Alvin Harper	6.00	2.70	.75
☐ 336 Vance Johnson	4.00	1.80	.50
☐ 337 William White	4.00	1.80	.50
☐ 338 Sterling Sharpe	15.00	6.75	1.85
☐ 339 Sean Jones	6.00	2.70	.75
☐ 340 Jeff Herrod	4.00	1.80	.50
☐ 341 Chris Martin	4.00	1.80	.50
☐ 342 Ethan Horton	4.00	1.80	.50
☐ 343 Robert Delpino	4.00	1.80	.50
☐ 344 Mark Higgs	4.00	1.80	.50
☐ 345 Chris Doleman	6.00	2.70	.75
☐ 346 Tommy Hodson	4.00	1.80	.50
☐ 347 Craig Heyward	6.00	2.70	.75
☐ 348 Cary Conklin	4.00	1.80	.50
☐ 350 Antone Davis	4.00	1.80	.50
☐ 351 Ernie Jones	4.00	1.80	.50
☐ 352 Greg Lloyd	10.00	4.50	1.25
☐ 353 John Friesz	6.00	2.70	.75
☐ 354 Charles Haley	6.00	2.70	.75
☐ 355 Tracy Scroggins	4.00	1.80	.50
☐ 356 Paul Gruber	4.00	1.80	.50
☐ 357 Ricky Ervins	6.00	2.70	.75
☐ 358 Brad Muster	4.00	1.80	.50
☐ 359 Deion Sanders (Deion also signed and numbered 200 cards from his personal stock; these are worth double)	40.00	18.00	5.00
☐ 360 Mitch Frerotte	4.00	1.80	.50
☐ 361 Stan Thomas	4.00	1.80	.50
☐ 362 Harold Green	6.00	2.70	.75
☐ 363 Eric Metcalf	10.00	4.50	1.25
☐ 364 Ken Norton Jr.	6.00	2.70	.75
☐ 365 Dave Widell Doug Widell	6.00	2.70	.75
☐ 366 Mike Tomczak	4.00	1.80	.50
☐ 367 Bubba McDowell	4.00	1.80	.50
☐ 368 Jessie Hester (Signed in ball-point pen)	4.00	1.80	.50
☐ 369 Ervin Randle	4.00	1.80	.50
☐ 371 Pat Terrell	4.00	1.80	.50
☐ 372 Jim C. Jensen	4.00	1.80	.50
☐ 373 Mike Merriweather	4.00	1.80	.50
☐ 374 Chris Singleton	4.00	1.80	.50
☐ 375 Floyd Turner	4.00	1.80	.50
☐ 376 Jim Sweeney	4.00	1.80	.50
☐ 377 Keith Jackson	6.00	2.70	.75
☐ 378 Walter Reeves	4.00	1.80	.50
☐ 379 Neil O'Donnell	10.00	4.50	1.25
☐ 380 Nate Lewis	4.00	1.80	.50
☐ 381 Keith Henderson	4.00	1.80	.50
☐ 382 Kelly Stouffer	4.00	1.80	.50
☐ 383 Ricky Reynolds	4.00	1.80	.50
☐ 384 Joe Jacoby	4.00	1.80	.50
☐ 385 Fred Biletnikoff RET	250.00	110.00	31.00
☐ 386 Jessie Tuggle	4.00	1.80	.50
☐ 387 Tom Waddle	4.00	1.80	.50
☐ 388 David Shula CO	4.00	1.80	.50
☐ 389 Van Waiters	4.00	1.80	.50
☐ 390 Jay Novacek	6.00	2.70	.75
☐ 391 Michael Young	4.00	1.80	.50
☐ 392 Mike Holmgren CO	6.00	2.70	.75
☐ 393 Doug Smith	4.00	1.80	.50
☐ 394 Mike Prior	4.00	1.80	.50
☐ 395 Harvey Williams	6.00	2.70	.75
☐ 396 Aaron Wallace	4.00	1.80	.50
☐ 397 Tony Zendejas	4.00	1.80	.50
☐ 398 Sammie Smith	4.00	1.80	.50
☐ 399 Henry Thomas	6.00	2.70	.75
☐ 400 Jon Vaughn	4.00	1.80	.50
☐ 401 Brian Washington	4.00	1.80	.50
☐ 402 Leon Searcy	4.00	1.80	.50
☐ 403 Lance Smith	4.00	1.80	.50
☐ 404 Warren Williams	4.00	1.80	.50
☐ 405 Bobby Ross CO	4.00	1.80	.50
☐ 406 Harry Sydney	4.00	1.80	.50
☐ 407 John L. Williams	6.00	2.70	.75
☐ 408 Ken Willis	4.00	1.80	.50
☐ 409 Brian Mitchell	6.00	2.70	.75
☐ 410 Dick Butkus RET	20.00	9.00	2.50
☐ 411 Chuck Knox CO	4.00	1.80	.50
☐ 412 Robert Porcher	6.00	2.70	.75
☐ 413 Calvin Williams	6.00	2.70	.75
☐ 414 Bill Cowher CO	6.00	2.70	.75
☐ 415 Eric Moore	4.00	1.80	.50
☐ 416 Derek Brown TE	4.00	1.80	.50
☐ 418 Tom Flores CO	6.00	2.70	.75
☐ 419 Dale Carter	6.00	2.70	.75
☐ 420 Tony Dorsett RET	15.00	9.00	2.50
☐ 421 Marco Coleman	6.00	2.70	.75
☐ 422 Sam Wyche CO	4.00	1.80	.50
☐ 423 Ray Crockett	4.00	1.80	.50
☐ 424 Dan Fouts RET	15.00	6.75	1.85
☐ 425 Hugh Millen	4.00	1.80	.50
☐ 426 Quentin Coryatt	6.00	2.70	.75
☐ 427 Brian Jordan	10.00	2.70	.75
☐ 429 Toby Caston	8.00	1.80	.50
☐ 430 Ted Marchibroda CO	6.00	2.70	.75
☐ 431 Cris Carter	10.00	4.50	1.25
☐ 432 Tim Krumrie	4.00	1.80	.50
☐ 433 Otto Graham RET	25.00	11.00	3.10
☐ 434 Vaughn Dunbar	4.00	1.80	.50
☐ 435 John Fina	4.00	1.80	.50
☐ 436 Sonny Jurgensen RET	15.00	6.75	1.85
☐ 437 Robert Jones	4.00	1.80	.50
☐ 438 Steve DeOssie	4.00	1.80	.50
☐ 439 Eddie LeBaron RET	15.00	6.75	1.85
☐ 440 Chester McGlockton	6.00	2.70	.75
☐ 441 Ken Stabler RET	25.00	11.00	3.10
☐ 442 Joe DeLamielleure RET	4.00	1.80	.50
☐ 443 Charley Taylor RET	15.00	6.75	1.85
☐ 444 Greg Skrepenak	4.00	1.80	.50
☐ 445 Y.A. Tittle RET	20.00	9.00	2.50
☐ 446 Chuck Smith	4.00	1.80	.50
☐ 447 Kellen Winslow RET	10.00	4.50	1.25
☐ 448 Kevin Smith	6.00	2.70	.75
☐ 449 Phillippi Sparks	4.00	1.80	.50
☐ 450 Alonzo Spellman	6.00	2.70	.75
☐ 452 Darryl Williams	4.00	1.80	.50
☐ 453 Tommy Vardell	6.00	2.70	.75
☐ 454 Tommy Maddox	4.00	1.80	.50
☐ 455 Steve Israel	4.00	1.80	.50
☐ 456 Marquez Pope	4.00	1.80	.50
☐ 457 Eugene Chung	4.00	1.80	.50
☐ 458 Lynn Swann RET	75.00	34.00	9.50
☐ 459 Sean Gilbert	6.00	2.70	.75
☐ 460 Chris Mims	6.00	2.70	.75
☐ 461 Al Davis OWN	350.00	160.00	45.00
☐ 463 Mike Fox	4.00	1.80	.50
☐ 464 David Klingler	6.00	2.70	.75
☐ 465 Darren Woodson	6.00	2.70	.75
☐ 466 Jason Hanson	6.00	2.70	.75
☐ 467 Lem Barney RET	10.00	4.50	1.25
☐ NNO Santa Claus	20.00	9.00	2.50
☐ NNO Mrs. Santa Claus	20.00	9.00	2.50

1992 Pro Line Portraits Collectibles

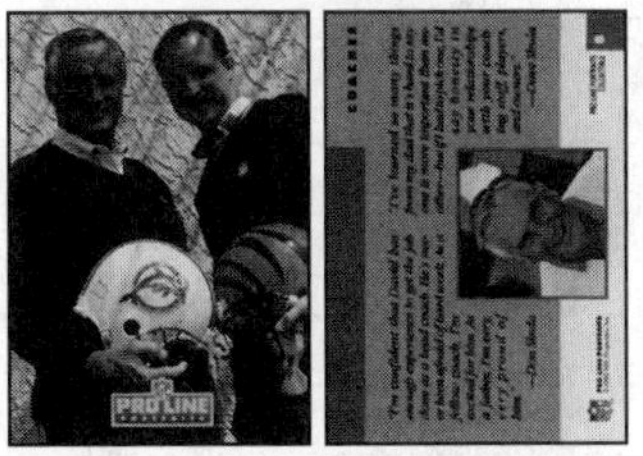

These standard-size cards were inserted in 1992 Pro Line foil packs. Their numbering picks up after the two special collectible cards issued the previous year. The fronts display full-bleed color photos, while the backs carry extended quotes on a silver panel.

	MINT	NRMT	EXC
COMPLETE SET (6)	6.00	2.70	.75
COMMON CARD (PLC3-PLC8)	1.00	.45	.12
☐ PLC3 Coaches Photo Chris Berman	1.00	.45	.12
☐ PLC4 Joe Gibbs CO (Racing)	1.00	.45	.12
☐ PLC5 Gifford Family Frank Gifford Kathie Lee Gifford Cody Gifford	1.00	.45	.12
☐ PLC6 Dale Jarrett (NASCAR driver)	1.50	.70	.19
☐ PLC7 Paul Tagliabue COM	1.00	.45	.12
☐ PLC8 Don Shula CO and David Shula CO	1.50	.70	.19

1992 Pro Line Portraits Collectibles Autographs

These standard-size cards were inserted in 1992 Pro Line foil packs. The fronts display full-bleed color photos, while the backs carry extended quotes on a silver panel. The cards are unnumbered but are listed below according to the numbers assigned to them in the regular series.

	MINT	NRMT	EXC
COMPLETE SET (4)	120.00	55.00	15.00
COMMON CARD	5.00	2.20	.60

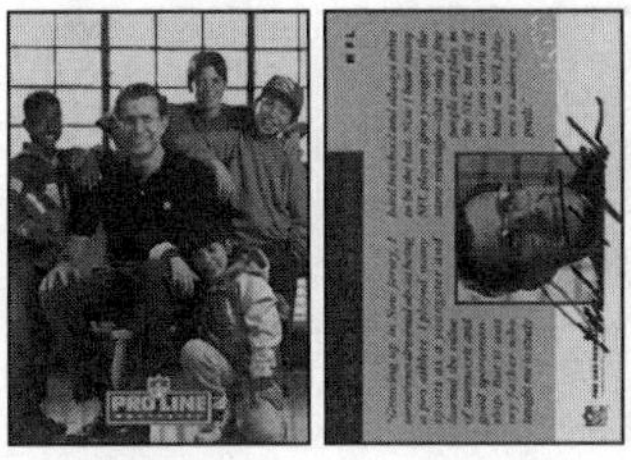

☐ PCL3 Coaches Photo Chris Berman	15.00	6.75	1.85
☐ PCL6 Dale Jarrett (NASCAR driver)	25.00	11.00	3.10
☐ PCL7 Paul Tagliabue COM (Autopenned)	5.00	2.20	.60
☐ PCL8 Don Shula CO and David Shula CO	75.00	34.00	9.50

1992 Pro Line Portraits QB Gold

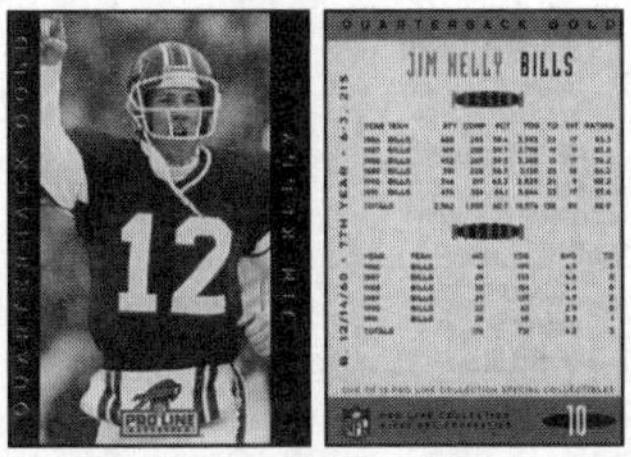

Featuring the top NFL quarterbacks, this 18-card set was randomly inserted into 1992 Pro Line foil packs at a rate of three per box. A complete set was also packed with each hobby case. Special retail packs that were later produced included a QB Gold card in each pack. The cards measure the standard size and feature posed color player photos of NFL quarterbacks of the fronts. The pictures are bordered on two sides by gold foil stripes that run the length of the card. The player's name and the words "Quarterback Gold" are printed in black on the stripes. The backs are bordered by gold stripes at the top and bottom. The background is off-white and displays passing and rushing statistics in black print. The cards are arranged in alphabetical order.

	MINT	NRMT	EXC
COMPLETE SET (18)	7.50	3.40	.95
COMMON CARD (1-18)	.25	.11	.03
☐ 1 Troy Aikman	1.25	.55	.16
☐ 2 Bubby Brister	.25	.11	.03
☐ 3 Randall Cunningham	.40	.18	.05
☐ 4 John Elway	1.00	.45	.12
☐ 5 Boomer Esiason	.40	.18	.05
☐ 6 Jim Everett	.25	.11	.03
☐ 7 Jeff George	.40	.18	.05
☐ 8 Jim Harbaugh	.40	.18	.05
☐ 9 Jeff Hostetler	.40	.18	.05
☐ 10 Jim Kelly	.60	.25	.07
☐ 11 Bernie Kosar	.25	.11	.03
☐ 12 Dan Marino	2.50	1.10	.30
☐ 13 Chris Miller UER (Birthdate incorrectly listed as 8-91-65)	.25	.11	.03
☐ 14 Joe Montana	1.25	.55	.16
☐ 15 Warren Moon	.40	.18	.05
☐ 16 Mark Rypien	.25	.11	.03
☐ 17 Phil Simms	.40	.18	.05
☐ 18 Steve Young	1.00	.45	.12

1992 Pro Line Portraits Rookie Gold

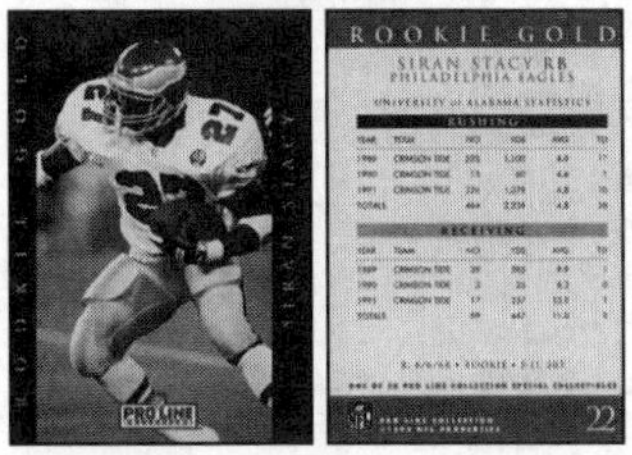

Featuring the top NFL rookies, one card of this 28-card standard-size set was inserted into each 1992 Pro Line jumbo pack. The cards feature posed color player photos on the fronts. The pictures are bordered on two sides by gold foil stripes that run the length of the card. The player's name and the words "Rookie Gold" are printed in black on the stripes. The backs are bordered by gold stripes at the top and bottom. The background is white and displays complete college statistics in black print. Production was limited to 4,000 cases of the jumbo packs. The cards are arranged in alphabetical order by team.

	MINT	NRMT	EXC
COMPLETE SET (28)	10.00	4.50	1.25
COMMON CARD (1-28)	.25	.11	.03
☐ 1 Tony Smith	.25	.11	.03
☐ 2 John Fina	.25	.11	.03
☐ 3 Alonzo Spellman	.40	.18	.05
☐ 4 David Klinger	.40	.18	.05
☐ 5 Tommy Vardell	.40	.18	.05
☐ 6 Kevin Smith	.75	.35	.09
☐ 7 Tommy Maddox	.40	.18	.05
☐ 8 Robert Porcher	.40	.18	.05
☐ 9 Terrell Buckley	.40	.18	.05
☐ 10 Eddie Robinson	.25	.11	.03
☐ 11 Steve Emtman	.40	.18	.05
☐ 12 Quentin Coryatt	.75	.35	.09
☐ 13 Dale Carter	.75	.35	.09
☐ 14 Chester McGlockton	.75	.35	.09
☐ 15 Sean Gilbert	.40	.18	.05
☐ 16 Troy Vincent	.75	.35	.09
☐ 17 Robert Harris	.25	.11	.03
☐ 18 Eugene Chung	.25	.11	.03
☐ 19 Vaughn Dunbar	.25	.11	.03
☐ 20 Derek Brown TE	.25	.11	.03
☐ 21 Johnny Mitchell	.25	.11	.03
☐ 22 Siran Stacy	.25	.11	.03
☐ 23 Tony Sacca	.25	.11	.03
☐ 24 Leon Searcy	.25	.11	.03
☐ 25 Chris Mims	.40	.18	.05
☐ 26 Dana Hall	.25	.11	.03
☐ 27 Courtney Hawkins	.40	.18	.05
☐ 28 Shane Collins	.25	.11	.03

1992 Pro Line Portraits Team NFL

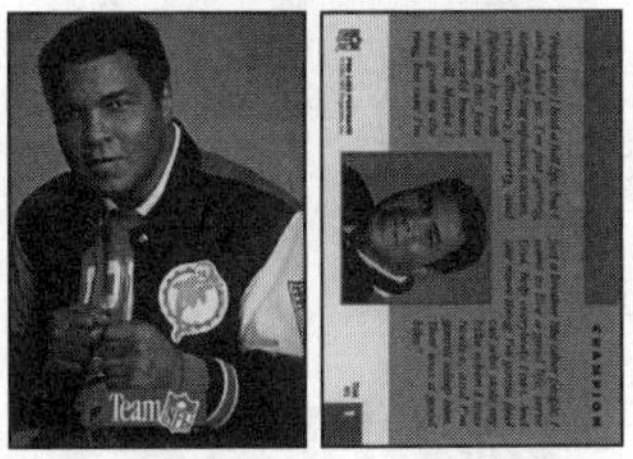

This five-card standard-size set marks the debut of Pro Line's Team NFL cards, which features stars from other sports as well as celebrities from the entertainment world. The cards were randomly inserted in 1992 Pro Line Portraits packs. On the fronts, each personality is pictured wearing attire of their favorite NFL team. The horizontal backs have team color-coded stripes at the top and an extended quote on a silver panel. In small print to the left of the card number, it reads "Team NFL."

	MINT	NRMT	EXC
COMPLETE SET (5)	6.00	2.70	.75
COMMON CARD (TNC1-TNC5)	1.00	.45	.12
☐ TNC1 Muhammad Ali	2.00	.90	.25
☐ TNC2 Milton Berle	1.00	.45	.12
☐ TNC3 Don Mattingly	1.50	.70	.19
☐ TNC4 Martin Mull	1.00	.45	.12
☐ TNC5 Isiah Thomas	1.00	.45	.12

1992 Pro Line Portraits Team NFL Autographs

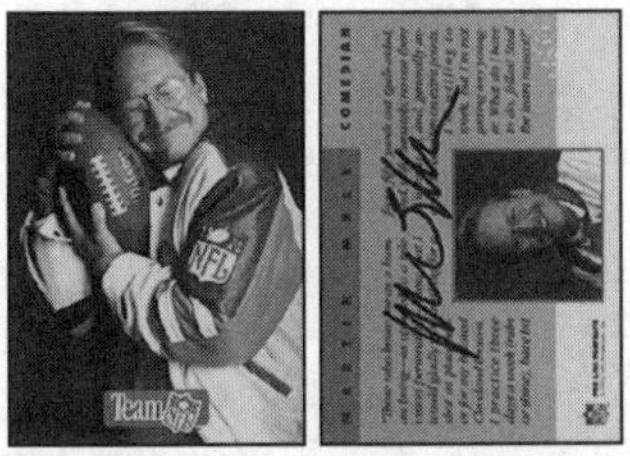

This five-card standard-size set marks the debut of Pro Line's Team NFL Collectible cards, which features stars from other sports as well as celebrities from the entertainment world. On the fronts, each personality is pictured wearing attire of their favorite NFL team. The horizontal backs have team color-coded stripes at the top and an extended quote on a silver panel. The cards are unnumbered but are listed below according to the numbers assigned to them in the regular series. Card #1B, of which Muhammad Ali signed a limited number with his birth name, Cassius Clay, is not included in the set price.

	MINT	NRMT	EXC
COMPLETE SET (5)	200.00	90.00	25.00
COMMON CARD (1-5)	10.00	4.50	1.25
☐ TNC1A Muhammad Ali	125.00	55.00	15.50
☐ TNC1B Muhammad Ali (Signed Cassius Clay)	500.00	220.00	60.00
☐ TNC2 Milton Berle	25.00	11.00	3.10
☐ TNC3 Don Mattingly	35.00	16.00	4.40
☐ TNC4 Martin Mull	10.00	4.50	1.25
☐ TNC5 Isiah Thomas (Card is signed Isiah)	15.00	6.75	1.85

1992 Pro Line Portraits Wives

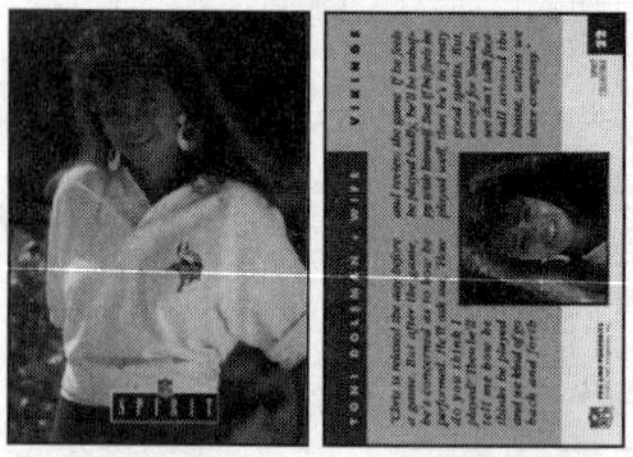

This 16-card standard-size set was issued with the 1992 Pro Line Portraits set as foil pack inserts. Its numbering is in continuation of the 1991 Pro Line Wives set. The set features full-bleed photos of wives of star NFL players and coaches. The cards are numbered on the back with an "SC" prefix.

	MINT	NRMT	EXC
COMPLETE SET (16)	1.00	.45	.12
COMMON CARD (SC8-SC23)	.10	.05	.01
☐ SC8 Ortancis Carter	.10	.05	.01
☐ SC9 Faith Cherry	.10	.05	.01
☐ SC10 Kaye Cowher	.10	.05	.01
☐ SC11 Dainnese Gault	.10	.05	.01
☐ SC12 Kathie Lee Gifford	.20	.09	.03
☐ SC13 Carole Hinton	.10	.05	.01
☐ SC14 Diane Long	.10	.05	.01
☐ SC15 Karen Lott	.10	.05	.01
☐ SC16 Felicia Moon	.10	.05	.01
☐ SC17 Cindy Noble	.10	.05	.01
☐ SC18 Linda Seifert	.10	.05	.01
☐ SC19 Mitzi Testaverde	.10	.05	.01
☐ SC20 Robin Swilling	.10	.05	.01
☐ SC21 Lesley Visser ANN	.20	.09	.03
☐ SC22 Toni Doleman	.10	.05	.01
☐ SC23 Diana Ditka (With Mike Ditka)	.40	.18	.05

1992 Pro Line Portraits Wives Autographs

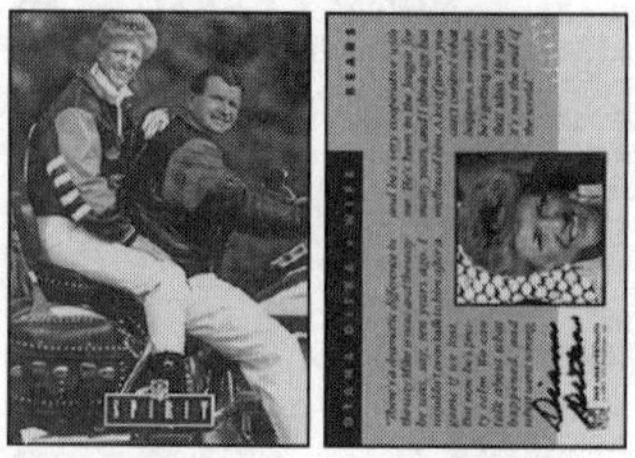

This 16-card standard-size set was included in the 1992 Pro Line Portraits set, and its numbering is in continuation of the 1991 Pro Line Wives set. The set features full-bleed photos of wives of star NFL players and coaches. The cards are unnumbered but are listed below according to the numbers assigned to them in the regular series. Kathie Lee Gifford (12) did not sign her cards.

	MINT	NRMT	EXC
COMPLETE SET (16)	90.00	40.00	11.00
COMMON CARD (8-23)	6.00	2.70	.75
☐ 8 Ortancis Carter	6.00	2.70	.75
☐ 9 Faith Cherry	6.00	2.70	.75
☐ 10 Kaye Cowher	6.00	2.70	.75
☐ 11 Dainnese Gault	6.00	2.70	.75
☐ 13 Carole Hinton	6.00	2.70	.75
☐ 14 Diane Long	6.00	2.70	.75
☐ 15 Karen Lott	6.00	2.70	.75
☐ 16 Felicia Moon	6.00	2.70	.75
☐ 17 Cindy Noble	6.00	2.70	.75
☐ 18 Linda Seifert	6.00	2.70	.75
☐ 19 Mitzi Testaverde	6.00	2.70	.75
☐ 20 Robin Swilling	6.00	2.70	.75
☐ 21 Lesley Visser ANN	12.00	5.50	1.50
☐ 22 Toni Doleman	6.00	2.70	.75
☐ 23 Diana Ditka (With Mike Ditka)	6.00	2.70	.75

1992 Pro Line Profiles

Together with the 1992 Pro Line Portraits, this 495-card standard-size set constitutes the bulk of the 1992 ProLine issue. This Profiles set consists of nine-card mini-biographies on 55 of the NFL's most well-known personalities. Each set chronicles the player's career from his days in college to the present day, including his life off of the football field. Each Pro Line pack contained nine Profiles and three Portraits cards, and Quarterback Gold cards were randomly inserted throughout the packs. The fronts display full-bleed color photos, and the fifth card in each subset features a color portrait by a noted sports artist. The text on the backs captures moments from the player's career or life, including quotes from the player himself. The set concludes with a ten-card Art Monk bonus set, which was available through a mail-in offer in exchange for ten 1991 ProLine Portraits wrappers (black) and ten 1992 ProLine wrappers (white). The cards in

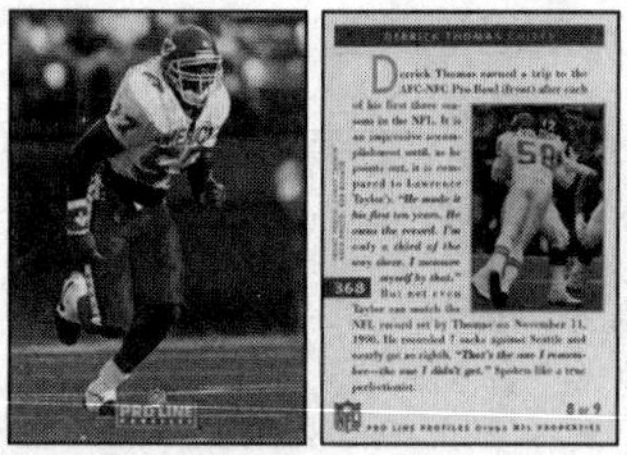

each subset are numbered "X of 9." A special boxed set, with the cards displayed in two notebooks, was distributed at the National. These cards differ from the regular series in two respects, the cards are unnumbered (except within nine-card subsets) and are stamped with a "The National, 1992" seal.

	MINT	NRMT	EXC
COMPLETE SET (495)	10.00	4.50	1.25
COMMON CARD (1-495)	.04	.02	.01
MONK SENDAWAY (496-504)	.40	.18	.05
MONK TITLE CARD (NNO)	.40	.18	.05
☐ 1 Ronnie Lott (Tackling opponent)	.10	.05	.01
☐ 2 Ronnie Lott (As youth, in baseball uniform)	.10	.05	.01
☐ 3 Ronnie Lott (Playing for USC)	.10	.05	.01
☐ 4 Ronnie Lott (Arms raised in triumph)	.10	.05	.01
☐ 5 Ronnie Lott (Portrait by Chris Hopkins)	.10	.05	.01
☐ 6 Ronnie Lott (At the Sports City Cafe)	.10	.05	.01
☐ 7 Ronnie Lott (With family)	.10	.05	.01
☐ 8 Ronnie Lott (Catching)	.10	.05	.01
☐ 9 Ronnie Lott (In tuxedo)	.10	.05	.01
☐ 10 Rodney Peete (Right arm raised)	.04	.02	.01
☐ 11 Rodney Peete (As youth, in football uniform)	.04	.02	.01
☐ 12 Rodney Peete (Playing baseball)	.04	.02	.01
☐ 13 Rodney Peete (In sweats with ball)	.04	.02	.01
☐ 14 Rodney Peete (Portrait by Merv Corning)	.04	.02	.01
☐ 15 Rodney Peete (Looking for receiver)	.04	.02	.01
☐ 16 Rodney Peete (Playing pool)	.04	.02	.01
☐ 17 Rodney Peete (Passing)	.04	.02	.01
☐ 18 Rodney Peete (Injured)	.04	.02	.01
☐ 19 Carl Banks (In action on field)	.04	.02	.01
☐ 20 Carl Banks (Playing basketball at Beecher High School)	.04	.02	.01
☐ 21 Carl Banks (In Michigan State uniform)	.04	.02	.01
☐ 22 Carl Banks (With family)	.04	.02	.01
☐ 23 Carl Banks (Portrait by Merv Corning)	.04	.02	.01
☐ 24 Carl Banks (Talking, wearing suit)	.04	.02	.01
☐ 25 Carl Banks (Tackling opponent)	.04	.02	.01
☐ 26 Carl Banks (On the air)	.04	.02	.01
☐ 27 Carl Banks (Close-up)	.04	.02	.01
☐ 28 Thurman Thomas (Running with ball, blue jersey)	.20	.09	.03
☐ 29 Thurman Thomas (With mother, Terlisha Cockrell)	.20	.09	.03
☐ 30 Thurman Thomas (At Oklahoma State)	.20	.09	.03
☐ 31 Thurman Thomas (With family)	.20	.09	.03
☐ 32 Thurman Thomas (Portrait by Gary Kelley)	.20	.09	.03
☐ 33 Thurman Thomas (Running with ball, white jersey)	.20	.09	.03
☐ 34 Thurman Thomas (Fishing)	.20	.09	.03
☐ 35 Thurman Thomas (Stretching)	.20	.09	.03
☐ 36 Thurman Thomas (Close-up)	.20	.09	.03
☐ 37 Roger Staubach RET (With Heisman Trophy)	.20	.09	.03
☐ 38 Roger Staubach RET (At Naval Academy)	.20	.09	.03
☐ 39 Roger Staubach RET (In Navy dress whites)	.20	.09	.03
☐ 40 Roger Staubach RET (Front view, running with ball)	.20	.09	.03
☐ 41 Roger Staubach RET (Portrait by John Collier)	.20	.09	.03
☐ 42 Roger Staubach RET (Passing, side view)	.20	.09	.03
☐ 43 Roger Staubach RET (With family)	.20	.09	.03
☐ 44 Roger Staubach RET (With young person at Daytop, substance abuse recovery facility)	.20	.09	.03
☐ 45 Roger Staubach RET (Calling the play)	.20	.09	.03
☐ 46 Jerry Rice (With MVP trophy)	.50	.23	.06
☐ 47 Jerry Rice (At Mississippi Valley State)	.50	.23	.06
☐ 48 Jerry Rice (Running with ball)	.50	.23	.06
☐ 49 Jerry Rice (With family)	.50	.23	.06
☐ 50 Jerry Rice (Portrait by Gary Kelley)	.50	.23	.06
☐ 51 Jerry Rice (With March of Dimes Ambassador, Ashley Johnson)	.50	.23	.06
☐ 52 Jerry Rice (Playing tennis)	.50	.23	.06
☐ 53 Jerry Rice (Arms raised in triumph)	.50	.23	.06
☐ 54 Jerry Rice (Close-up)	.50	.23	.06
☐ 55 Vinny Testaverde (Posed with Heisman)	.10	.05	.01
☐ 56 Vinny Testaverde (At Fork Union Military Academy)	.10	.05	.01
☐ 57 Vinny Testaverde (Playing for the University of Miami)	.10	.05	.01
☐ 58 Vinny Testaverde (Passing)	.10	.05	.01
☐ 59 Vinny Testaverde (Portrait by Merv Corning)	.10	.05	.01
☐ 60 Vinny Testaverde (Running with ball)	.10	.05	.01
☐ 61 Vinny Testaverde (With family)	.10	.05	.01
☐ 62 Vinny Testaverde (View from hips up, fist raised in triumph)	.10	.05	.01
☐ 63 Vinny Testaverde (With Vince Hanley)	.10	.05	.01
☐ 64 Anthony Carter (Maneuvering around opponent, with ball)	.10	.05	.01
☐ 65 Anthony Carter (In high school football game, black-and-white)	.10	.05	.01
☐ 66 Anthony Carter (At Michigan, running with ball)	.10	.05	.01
☐ 67 Anthony Carter (Fishing)	.10	.05	.01
☐ 68 Anthony Carter (Portrait by John Collier)	.10	.05	.01
☐ 69 Anthony Carter (Running, looking over shoulder)	.10	.05	.01
☐ 70 Anthony Carter (With family)	.10	.05	.01
☐ 71 Anthony Carter (Catching pass)	.10	.05	.01
☐ 72 Anthony Carter (Close-up)	.10	.05	.01
☐ 73 Sterling Sharpe (Catching)	.10	.05	.01
☐ 74 Sterling Sharpe (Passing, in high school)	.10	.05	.01
☐ 75 Sterling Sharpe (Walking on field at South Carolina)	.10	.05	.01
☐ 76 Sterling Sharpe (With books on SC campus)	.10	.05	.01
☐ 77 Sterling Sharpe (Portrait by Chris Hopkins)	.10	.05	.01
☐ 78 Sterling Sharpe (Running with ball against Rams)	.10	.05	.01
☐ 79 Sterling Sharpe (At the piano)	.10	.05	.01
☐ 80 Sterling Sharpe (Running with ball against Lions)	.10	.05	.01
☐ 81 Sterling Sharpe (In brick arch with football)	.10	.05	.01
☐ 82 Anthony Munoz (With NFL Man of the Year award)	.04	.02	.01
☐ 83 Anthony Munoz (As youth, batting)	.04	.02	.01
☐ 84 Anthony Munoz (Playing for USC)	.04	.02	.01
☐ 85 Anthony Munoz (With child at Children's Hospital)	.04	.02	.01
☐ 86 Anthony Munoz (Portrait by Merv Corning)	.04	.02	.01
☐ 87 Anthony Munoz (Blocking opponent)	.04	.02	.01
☐ 88 Anthony Munoz (Holding baby, with fellow players and children)	.04	.02	.01
☐ 89 Anthony Munoz (In action for Bengals)	.04	.02	.01
☐ 90 Anthony Munoz (Close-up)	.04	.02	.01
☐ 91 Bubby Brister (Passing, white jersey)	.04	.02	.01
☐ 92 Bubby Brister (NLU uniform)	.04	.02	.01
☐ 93 Bubby Brister (Baseball uniform)	.04	.02	.01
☐ 94 Bubby Brister (With kids at Ronald McDonald House)	.04	.02	.01
☐ 95 Bubby Brister (Portrait by Greg Spalenka)	.04	.02	.01
☐ 96 Bubby Brister (Wearing western attire)	.04	.02	.01
☐ 97 Bubby Brister (Running with ball, white jersey)	.04	.02	.01
☐ 98 Bubby Brister (Passing, black jersey)	.04	.02	.01
☐ 99 Bubby Brister (Close-up)	.04	.02	.01
☐ 100 Bernie Kosar (Passing, white jersey)	.04	.02	.01
☐ 101 Bernie Kosar (In high school)	.04	.02	.01
☐ 102 Bernie Kosar (Playing for Miami)	.04	.02	.01
☐ 103 Bernie Kosar (Being tackled)	.04	.02	.01
☐ 104 Bernie Kosar (Portrait by Greg Spalenka)	.04	.02	.01
☐ 105 Bernie Kosar (With family)	.04	.02	.01
☐ 106 Bernie Kosar (Playing golf)	.04	.02	.01
☐ 107 Bernie Kosar (Looking for receiver)	.04	.02	.01
☐ 108 Bernie Kosar (Close-up)	.04	.02	.01
☐ 109 Art Shell CO (On sidelines)	.10	.05	.01
☐ 110 Art Shell CO (At Maryland State)	.10	.05	.01
☐ 111 Art Shell CO (Playing for Raiders)	.10	.05	.01
☐ 112 Art Shell CO (Playing basketball with sons)	.10	.05	.01
☐ 113 Art Shell CO (Portrait by Chris Hopkins)	.10	.05	.01
☐ 114 Art Shell CO (Talking to player on sidelines)	.10	.05	.01
☐ 115 Art Shell CO (In front of big screen TV)	.10	.05	.01
☐ 116 Art Shell CO (In line of scrimmage)	.10	.05	.01

☐ 117 Art Shell CO (With teddy bear)	.10	.05	.01
☐ 118 Don Shula CO (With players)	.10	.05	.01
☐ 119 Don Shula CO (At John Carroll University)	.10	.05	.01
☐ 120 Don Shula CO (Coaching Baltimore Colts)	.10	.05	.01
☐ 121 Don Shula CO (With son, Mike)	.10	.05	.01
☐ 122 Don Shula CO (Portrait by Merv Corning)	.10	.05	.01
☐ 123 Don Shula CO (With daughters)	.10	.05	.01
☐ 124 Don Shula CO (With Dan Marino)	.10	.05	.01
☐ 125 Don Shula CO (With doctor at The Don Shula Foundation)	.10	.05	.01
☐ 126 Don Shula CO (With Super Bowl Trophies)	.10	.05	.01
☐ 127 Joe Gibbs CO (Writing out play)	.10	.05	.01
☐ 128 Joe Gibbs CO (Playing for San Diego State)	.10	.05	.01
☐ 129 Joe Gibbs CO (Coaching on sidelines)	.10	.05	.01
☐ 130 Joe Gibbs CO (With sons)	.10	.05	.01
☐ 131 Joe Gibbs CO (Portrait by John Collier)	.10	.05	.01
☐ 132 Joe Gibbs CO (Reading in office)	.10	.05	.01
☐ 133 Joe Gibbs CO (With Youth For Tomorrow group)	.10	.05	.01
☐ 134 Joe Gibbs CO (In front of race car)	.10	.05	.01
☐ 135 Joe Gibbs CO (In front of Church)	.10	.05	.01
☐ 136 Junior Seau (Holding ball)	.20	.09	.03
☐ 137 Junior Seau (As youth, in football uniform)	.20	.09	.03
☐ 138 Junior Seau (At USC)	.20	.09	.03
☐ 139 Junior Seau (Finger pointing up)	.20	.09	.03
☐ 140 Junior Seau (Portrait by Merv Corning)	.20	.09	.03
☐ 141 Junior Seau (With wife, Gina)	.20	.09	.03
☐ 142 Junior Seau (Running on beach)	.20	.09	.03
☐ 143 Junior Seau (Lifting weights)	.20	.09	.03
☐ 144 Junior Seau (In swim trunks with seaweed)	.20	.09	.03
☐ 145 Al Toon (Running with ball, white jersey)	.04	.02	.01
☐ 146 Al Toon (During Pee-Wee football days)	.04	.02	.01
☐ 147 Al Toon (On the field at Wisconsin)	.04	.02	.01
☐ 148 Al Toon (With family)	.04	.02	.01
☐ 149 Al Toon (Portrait by Gary Kelley)	.04	.02	.01
☐ 150 Al Toon (Catching)	.04	.02	.01
☐ 151 Al Toon (Working out)	.04	.02	.01
☐ 152 Al Toon (Running with ball, green jersey)	.04	.02	.01
☐ 153 Al Toon (Close-up)	.04	.02	.01
☐ 154 Jack Kemp RET (In office)	.20	.09	.03
☐ 155 Jack Kemp RET (Portrait from Occidental College)	.20	.09	.03
☐ 156 Jack Kemp RET (Playing for Chargers)	.20	.09	.03
☐ 157 Jack Kemp RET (With family)	.20	.09	.03
☐ 158 Jack Kemp RET (Portrait by Merv Corning)	.20	.09	.03
☐ 159 Jack Kemp RET (Playing for Buffalo)	.20	.09	.03
☐ 160 Jack Kemp RET (Passing)	.20	.09	.03
☐ 161 Jack Kemp RET (With son, Jeff)	.20	.09	.03
☐ 162 Jack Kemp RET (In Washington)	.20	.09	.03
☐ 163 Jim Harbaugh (Passing, blue jersey)	.10	.05	.01
☐ 164 Jim Harbaugh (Playing in high school)	.10	.05	.01
☐ 165 Jim Harbaugh (Playing for Michigan)	.10	.05	.01
☐ 166 Jim Harbaugh (Passing, white jersey)	.10	.05	.01
☐ 167 Jim Harbaugh (Portrait by Gary Kelley)	.10	.05	.01
☐ 168 Jim Harbaugh (With children in children's home)	.10	.05	.01
☐ 169 Jim Harbaugh (Working out)	.10	.05	.01
☐ 170 Jim Harbaugh (Calling play)	.10	.05	.01
☐ 171 Jim Harbaugh (Close-up)	.10	.05	.01
☐ 172 Dan McGwire (From waist up)	.04	.02	.01
☐ 173 Dan McGwire (At Purdue)	.04	.02	.01
☐ 174 Dan McGwire (At San Diego)	.04	.02	.01
☐ 175 Dan McGwire (From waist down)	.04	.02	.01
☐ 176 Dan McGwire (Portrait by Chris Hopkins)	.04	.02	.01
☐ 177 Dan McGwire (Passing, blue jersey)	.04	.02	.01
☐ 178 Dan McGwire (Passing, white jersey)	.04	.02	.01
☐ 179 Dan McGwire (Working out)	.04	.02	.01
☐ 180 Dan McGwire (With wife, Dana)	.04	.02	.01
☐ 181 Troy Aikman (Passing, wearing blue jersey)	.50	.23	.06
☐ 182 Troy Aikman (As youth)	.50	.23	.06
☐ 183 Troy Aikman (Passing, at UCLA)	.50	.23	.06
☐ 184 Troy Aikman (Preparing to pass, with Cowboys)	.50	.23	.06
☐ 185 Troy Aikman (Portrait by Greg Spalenka)	.50	.23	.06
☐ 186 Troy Aikman (Golfing)	.50	.23	.06
☐ 187 Troy Aikman (Looking for opening, front view)	.50	.23	.06
☐ 188 Troy Aikman (In sweats, passing)	.50	.23	.06
☐ 189 Troy Aikman (In cowboy hat)	.50	.23	.06
☐ 190 Keith Byars (With little brother)	.04	.02	.01
☐ 191 Keith Byars (Childhood picture)	.04	.02	.01
☐ 192 Keith Byars (High School football photo)	.04	.02	.01
☐ 193 Keith Byars (Ohio State photo, red jersey)	.04	.02	.01
☐ 194 Keith Byars (Portrait by Chris Hopkins)	.04	.02	.01
☐ 195 Keith Byars (Working out)	.04	.02	.01
☐ 196 Keith Byars (Running, green jersey)	.04	.02	.01
☐ 197 Keith Byars (Running, white jersey)	.04	.02	.01
☐ 198 Keith Byars (Close-up)	.04	.02	.01
☐ 199 Timm Rosenbach (Running with ball, red jersey)	.04	.02	.01
☐ 200 Timm Rosenbach (In high school football uniform)	.04	.02	.01
☐ 201 Timm Rosenbach (At Washington State)	.04	.02	.01
☐ 202 Timm Rosenbach (With wife, Kerry)	.04	.02	.01
☐ 203 Timm Rosenbach (Portrait by John Collier)	.04	.02	.01
☐ 204 Timm Rosenbach (Passing, white jersey)	.04	.02	.01
☐ 205 Timm Rosenbach (Roping a calf)	.04	.02	.01
☐ 206 Timm Rosenbach (Working out)	.04	.02	.01
☐ 207 Timm Rosenbach (Seated on hay, in western attire)	.04	.02	.01
☐ 208 Gary Clark (In the end zone)	.10	.05	.01
☐ 209 Gary Clark (Playing for James Madison Univ.)	.10	.05	.01
☐ 210 Gary Clark (Catching ball in end zone)	.10	.05	.01
☐ 211 Gary Clark (With daughter)	.10	.05	.01
☐ 212 Gary Clark (Portrait by John Collier)	.10	.05	.01
☐ 213 Gary Clark (Running, slouched position)	.10	.05	.01
☐ 214 Gary Clark (Playing basketball)	.10	.05	.01
☐ 215 Gary Clark (Lifted by teammates)	.10	.05	.01
☐ 216 Gary Clark (Close-up)	.10	.05	.01
☐ 217 Chris Doleman (Playing for Vikings, white jersey)	.04	.02	.01
☐ 218 Chris Doleman (In Pittsburgh uniform)	.04	.02	.01
☐ 219 Chris Doleman (With wife, Toni, and dog)	.04	.02	.01
☐ 220 Chris Doleman (Playing for Vikings, blue jersey)	.04	.02	.01
☐ 221 Chris Doleman (Portrait by John Collier)	.04	.02	.01
☐ 222 Chris Doleman (Working out)	.04	.02	.01
☐ 223 Chris Doleman (Leaping over opponent)	.04	.02	.01
☐ 224 Chris Doleman (Playing golf)	.04	.02	.01
☐ 225 Chris Doleman (Close-up)	.04	.02	.01
☐ 226 John Elway (Passing, orange jersey)	.40	.18	.05
☐ 227 John Elway (Playing for Stanford)	.40	.18	.05
☐ 228 John Elway (Passing, white jersey)	.40	.18	.05
☐ 229 John Elway (With family)	.40	.18	.05
☐ 230 John Elway (Portrait by Greg Spalenka)	.40	.18	.05
☐ 231 John Elway (Working out)	.40	.18	.05
☐ 232 John Elway (Sitting on car)	.40	.18	.05
☐ 233 John Elway (Running with ball)	.40	.18	.05
☐ 234 John Elway (Close-up)	.40	.18	.05
☐ 235 Boomer Esiason (Calling play)	.10	.05	.01
☐ 236 Boomer Esiason (In high school)	.10	.05	.01
☐ 237 Boomer Esiason (In Terps uniform)	.10	.05	.01
☐ 238 Boomer Esiason (Passing)	.10	.05	.01
☐ 239 Boomer Esiason (Portrait by Greg Spalenka)	.10	.05	.01
☐ 240 Boomer Esiason (With dogs)	.10	.05	.01
☐ 241 Boomer Esiason (With Kinny McQuade)	.10	.05	.01
☐ 242 Boomer Esiason (Looking for pass receiver)	.10	.05	.01
☐ 243 Boomer Esiason (Close-up)	.10	.05	.01
☐ 244 Jim Everett (Passing, white jersey)	.10	.05	.01
☐ 245 Jim Everett (In high school uniform)	.10	.05	.01
☐ 246 Jim Everett (Playing for Purdue)	.10	.05	.01
☐ 247 Jim Everett (With family)	.10	.05	.01
☐ 248 Jim Everett (Portrait by Greg Spalenka)	.10	.05	.01
☐ 249 Jim Everett (Running with ball, blue jersey)	.10	.05	.01
☐ 250 Jim Everett (Fishing)	.10	.05	.01
☐ 251 Jim Everett (Handing off ball)	.10	.05	.01
☐ 252 Jim Everett (Close-up)	.10	.05	.01
☐ 253 Eric Green (Running with ball)	.04	.02	.01
☐ 254 Eric Green (With coach Sam Rutigliano)	.04	.02	.01
☐ 255 Eric Green (Being blocked by opponent)	.04	.02	.01
☐ 256 Eric Green (Playing basketball)	.04	.02	.01
☐ 257 Eric Green (Portrait by Merv Corning)	.04	.02	.01
☐ 258 Eric Green (In locker room)	.04	.02	.01
☐ 259 Eric Green (Blocking opponent)	.04	.02	.01
☐ 260 Eric Green (Catching)	.04	.02	.01
☐ 261 Eric Green (Close-up)	.04	.02	.01
☐ 262 Jerry Glanville CO (On motorcycle)	.04	.02	.01
☐ 263 Jerry Glanville CO (With Lions coaching staff)	.04	.02	.01
☐ 264 Jerry Glanville CO (Coaching, clapping)	.04	.02	.01
☐ 265 Jerry Glanville CO (With family)	.04	.02	.01
☐ 266 Jerry Glanville CO (Portrait by Gary Kelley)	.04	.02	.01
☐ 267 Jerry Glanville CO (Coaching, with players)	.04	.02	.01
☐ 268 Jerry Glanville CO (In race car)	.04	.02	.01
☐ 269 Jerry Glanville CO (With country music stars)	.04	.02	.01
☐ 270 Jerry Glanville CO (In black western attire)	.04	.02	.01
☐ 271 Jeff Hostetler (Passing, blue jersey)	.04	.02	.01
☐ 272 Jeff Hostetler (Playing for West Virginia)	.04	.02	.01
☐ 273 Jeff Hostetler (Lifting weights)	.04	.02	.01
☐ 274 Jeff Hostetler (With family)	.04	.02	.01
☐ 275 Jeff Hostetler (Portrait by John Collier)	.04	.02	.01
☐ 276 Jeff Hostetler (Passing, white jersey)	.04	.02	.01
☐ 277 Jeff Hostetler (At Ronald McDonald house)	.04	.02	.01
☐ 278 Jeff Hostetler (With father-in-law)	.04	.02	.01
☐ 279 Jeff Hostetler (Close-up)	.04	.02	.01
☐ 280 Haywood Jeffires (Catching, Houston uniform)	.10	.05	.01
☐ 281 Haywood Jeffires (Playing for North Carolina)	.10	.05	.01
☐ 282 Haywood Jeffires (With wife, Robin)	.10	.05	.01
☐ 283 Haywood Jeffires (Pushing past opponent)	.10	.05	.01
☐ 284 Haywood Jeffires (Portrait by John Collier)	.10	.05	.01
☐ 285 Haywood Jeffires (With car)	.10	.05	.01
☐ 286 Haywood Jeffires (With Boy and Girls Club members)	.10	.05	.01
☐ 287 Haywood Jeffires (Being tackled)	.10	.05	.01

No.	Player (Description)			
☐ 288	Haywood Jeffires (Close-up)	.10	.05	.01
☐ 289	Michael Irvin (Running with ball)	.20	.09	.03
☐ 290	Michael Irvin (Playing basketball)	.20	.09	.03
☐ 291	Michael Irvin (In Miami uniform)	.20	.09	.03
☐ 292	Michael Irvin (With wife, Sandy)	.20	.09	.03
☐ 293	Michael Irvin (Portrait by Gary Kelley)	.20	.09	.03
☐ 294	Michael Irvin (Catching)	.20	.09	.03
☐ 295	Michael Irvin (With student, Nyna Sherte)	.20	.09	.03
☐ 296	Michael Irvin (Playing in Pro Bowl)	.20	.09	.03
☐ 297	Michael Irvin (Close-up)	.20	.09	.03
☐ 298	Steve Largent RET (Catching, blue jersey)	.20	.09	.03
☐ 299	Steve Largent RET (Playing for Tulsa)	.20	.09	.03
☐ 300	Steve Largent RET (With family)	.20	.09	.03
☐ 301	Steve Largent RET (At school for disabled children)	.20	.09	.03
☐ 302	Steve Largent RET (Portrait by Chris Hopkins)	.20	.09	.03
☐ 303	Steve Largent RET (Catching, white jersey)	.20	.09	.03
☐ 304	Steve Largent RET (In dress attire)	.20	.09	.03
☐ 305	Steve Largent RET (Running, white jersey)	.20	.09	.03
☐ 306	Steve Largent RET (Close-up)	.20	.09	.03
☐ 307	Ken O'Brien (Passing, side view)	.04	.02	.01
☐ 308	Ken O'Brien (With University of California-Davis)	.04	.02	.01
☐ 309	Ken O'Brien (With family)	.04	.02	.01
☐ 310	Ken O'Brien (Passing, front view)	.04	.02	.01
☐ 311	Ken O'Brien (Portrait by Chris Hopkins)	.04	.02	.01
☐ 312	Ken O'Brien (Shaking hands with Tony Eason)	.04	.02	.01
☐ 313	Ken O'Brien (Playing golf)	.04	.02	.01
☐ 314	Ken O'Brien (Handing off the ball)	.04	.02	.01
☐ 315	Ken O'Brien (Close-up)	.04	.02	.01
☐ 316	Christian Okoye (Running with ball, red jersey)	.04	.02	.01
☐ 317	Christian Okoye (Close-up at Asuza Pacific Univ.)	.04	.02	.01
☐ 318	Christian Okoye (Cooking)	.04	.02	.01
☐ 319	Christian Okoye (Running with ball, white jersey)	.04	.02	.01
☐ 320	Christian Okoye (Portrait by Chris Hopkins)	.04	.02	.01
☐ 321	Christian Okoye (In Nigerian attire)	.04	.02	.01
☐ 322	Christian Okoye (With daughter, Christiana)	.04	.02	.01
☐ 323	Christian Okoye (Withstanding an opponent)	.04	.02	.01
☐ 324	Christian Okoye (In casual attire)	.04	.02	.01
☐ 325	Michael Dean Perry (Blocking opponent, white jersey)	.10	.05	.01
☐ 326	Michael Dean Perry (Playing for Clemson)	.10	.05	.01
☐ 327	Michael Dean Perry (Blocking opponent, brown jersey)	.10	.05	.01
☐ 328	Michael Dean Perry (With family)	.10	.05	.01
☐ 329	Michael Dean Perry (Portrait by Merv Corning)	.10	.05	.01
☐ 330	Michael Dean Perry (At Children's Hospital)			
☐ 331	Michael Dean Perry (Playing basketball)	.10	.05	.01
☐ 332	Michael Dean Perry (Blocking opponent, horizontal shot)	.10	.05	.01
☐ 333	Michael Dean Perry (With AFC Player of the Year trophy)	.10	.05	.01
☐ 334	Chris Miller (Passing, black jersey)	.10	.05	.01
☐ 335	Chris Miller (As youth, fishing)	.04	.02	.01
☐ 336	Chris Miller (Playing for Oregon)	.04	.02	.01
☐ 337	Chris Miller (In baseball uniform)	.04	.02	.01
☐ 338	Chris Miller (Portrait by Greg Spalenka)	.04	.02	.01
☐ 339	Chris Miller (Running with ball)	.04	.02	.01
☐ 340	Chris Miller (With wife, Jennifer)	.04	.02	.01
☐ 341	Chris Miller (In the Pro Bowl)	.04	.02	.01
☐ 342	Chris Miller (Close-up)	.04	.02	.01
☐ 343	Phil Simms (Passing, blue jersey)	.10	.05	.01
☐ 344	Phil Simms (Calling the play)	.10	.05	.01
☐ 345	Phil Simms (With family)	.10	.05	.01
☐ 346	Phil Simms (Playing pool)	.10	.05	.01
☐ 347	Phil Simms (Portrait by Greg Spalenka)	.10	.05	.01
☐ 348	Phil Simms (Running with ball)	.10	.05	.01
☐ 349	Phil Simms (With young man from the Eastern Christian School for handicapped children)	.10	.05	.01
☐ 350	Phil Simms (Passing, white jersey)	.10	.05	.01
☐ 351	Phil Simms (Close-up)	.10	.05	.01
☐ 352	Bruce Smith (Tackling opponent, white jersey)	.20	.09	.03
☐ 353	Bruce Smith (At Virginia Tech)	.20	.09	.03
☐ 354	Bruce Smith (Close-up in game)	.20	.09	.03
☐ 355	Bruce Smith (With wife, Carmen)	.20	.09	.03
☐ 356	Bruce Smith (Portrait by John Collier)	.20	.09	.03
☐ 357	Bruce Smith (In Pro Bowl)	.20	.09	.03
☐ 358	Bruce Smith (Working out)	.20	.09	.03
☐ 359	Bruce Smith (Blocking, blue jersey)	.20	.09	.03
☐ 360	Bruce Smith (Close-up)	.20	.09	.03
☐ 361	Derrick Thomas (Running, red jersey)	.20	.09	.03
☐ 362	Derrick Thomas (At the University of Alabama)	.20	.09	.03
☐ 363	Derrick Thomas (With his father's Air Force momentos)	.20	.09	.03
☐ 364	Derrick Thomas (Seated on helmet)	.20	.09	.03
☐ 365	Derrick Thomas (Portrait by Merv Corning)	.20	.09	.03
☐ 366	Derrick Thomas (With motivational program participants)	.20	.09	.03
☐ 367	Derrick Thomas (Posed with Limo)	.20	.09	.03
☐ 368	Derrick Thomas (In Pro Bowl)	.20	.09	.03
☐ 369	Derrick Thomas (Close-up)	.20	.09	.03
☐ 370	Pat Swilling (Relaxed against tree)	.04	.02	.01
☐ 371	Pat Swilling (At Georgia Tech)	.04	.02	.01
☐ 372	Pat Swilling (With family)	.04	.02	.01
☐ 373	Pat Swilling (Running on field)	.04	.02	.01
☐ 374	Pat Swilling (Portrait by John Collier)	.04	.02	.01
☐ 375	Pat Swilling (Working out)	.04	.02	.01
☐ 376	Pat Swilling (Tackling opponent on icy field)	.04	.02	.01
☐ 377	Pat Swilling (With underprivileged children)	.04	.02	.01
☐ 378	Pat Swilling (Relaxed at home)	.04	.02	.01
☐ 379	Eric Dickerson (Close-up in Rams football gear)	.10	.05	.01
☐ 380	Eric Dickerson (Playing for SMU)	.10	.05	.01
☐ 381	Eric Dickerson (With great aunt Viola)	.10	.05	.01
☐ 382	Eric Dickerson (Running with ball, Rams uniform)	.10	.05	.01
☐ 383	Eric Dickerson (Portrait by Merv Corning)	.10	.05	.01
☐ 384	Eric Dickerson (Running with ball, Colts uniform)	.10	.05	.01
☐ 385	Eric Dickerson (Working out)	.10	.05	.01
☐ 386	Eric Dickerson (Leaping over other players, Colts uniform)	.10	.05	.01
☐ 387	Eric Dickerson (Close-up)	.10	.05	.01
☐ 388	Howie Long (Being blocked by opponent)	.10	.05	.01
☐ 389	Howie Long (At Villanova)	.10	.05	.01
☐ 390	Howie Long (Rushing Quarterback)	.10	.05	.01
☐ 391	Howie Long (With family)	.10	.05	.01
☐ 392	Howie Long (Portrait by Chris Hopkins)	.10	.05	.01
☐ 393	Howie Long (On sidelines)	.10	.05	.01
☐ 394	Howie Long (Boxing)	.10	.05	.01
☐ 395	Howie Long (Blocking pass)	.10	.05	.01
☐ 396	Howie Long (Close-up)	.10	.05	.01
☐ 397	Mike Singletary (Crouched, ready for play)	.10	.05	.01
☐ 398	Mike Singletary (At Baylor)	.10	.05	.01
☐ 399	Mike Singletary (With children)	.10	.05	.01
☐ 400	Mike Singletary (In the gym)	.10	.05	.01
☐ 401	Mike Singletary (Portrait by Gary Kelley)	.10	.05	.01
☐ 402	Mike Singletary (Rushing, white jersey)	.10	.05	.01
☐ 403	Mike Singletary (With Man of the Year Award)	.10	.05	.01
☐ 404	Mike Singletary (Tackling, blue jersey)	.10	.05	.01
☐ 405	Mike Singletary (In sweatshirt)	.10	.05	.01
☐ 406	John Taylor (Celebrating on the field)	.04	.02	.01
☐ 407	John Taylor (In high school)	.04	.02	.01
☐ 408	John Taylor (Playing for Delaware State)	.04	.02	.01
☐ 409	John Taylor (Posed with bowling ball and pins)	.04	.02	.01
☐ 410	John Taylor (Portrait by John Collier)	.04	.02	.01
☐ 411	John Taylor (With family)	.04	.02	.01
☐ 412	John Taylor (With kids from Northern Light School)	.04	.02	.01
☐ 413	John Taylor (Catching)	.04	.02	.01
☐ 414	John Taylor (Close-up)	.04	.02	.01
☐ 415	Andre Tippett (Blocking opponent, arms outspred)	.04	.02	.01
☐ 416	Andre Tippett (At Iowa State)	.04	.02	.01
☐ 417	Andre Tippett (With daughter, Janea Lynn)	.04	.02	.01
☐ 418	Andre Tippett (In Okinawa with karate masters)	.04	.02	.01
☐ 419	Andre Tippett (Portrait by Gary Kelley)	.04	.02	.01
☐ 420	Andre Tippett (Running on the field)	.04	.02	.01
☐ 421	Andre Tippett (Performing karate move)	.04	.02	.01
☐ 422	Andre Tippett (In action, from knees up)	.04	.02	.01
☐ 423	Andre Tippett (Close-up)	.04	.02	.01
☐ 424	Jim Kelly (Passing, white jersey)	.20	.09	.03
☐ 425	Jim Kelly (With Punt, Pass, and Kick trophy)	.20	.09	.03
☐ 426	Jim Kelly (Passing for Miami)	.20	.09	.03
☐ 427	Jim Kelly (With family)	.20	.09	.03
☐ 428	Jim Kelly (Portrait by Greg Spalenka)	.20	.09	.03
☐ 429	Jim Kelly (With sports jersey collection)	.20	.09	.03
☐ 430	Jim Kelly (With young cancer patients)	.20	.09	.03
☐ 431	Jim Kelly (Calling play)	.20	.09	.03
☐ 432	Jim Kelly (Close-up)	.20	.09	.03
☐ 433	Mark Rypien (Passing, horizontal shot)	.04	.02	.01
☐ 434	Mark Rypien (In high school football uniform)	.04	.02	.01
☐ 435	Mark Rypien (At Washington State)	.04	.02	.01
☐ 436	Mark Rypien (Playing golf)	.04	.02	.01
☐ 437	Mark Rypien (Portrait by Merv Corning)	.04	.02	.01
☐ 438	Mark Rypien (With family)	.04	.02	.01
☐ 439	Mark Rypien (Passing, vertical shot)	.04	.02	.01
☐ 440	Mark Rypien (With young cystic fibrosis patients)	.04	.02	.01
☐ 441	Mark Rypien (Close-up)	.04	.02	.01
☐ 442	Warren Moon (Passing, white jersey)	.10	.05	.01
☐ 443	Warren Moon (As youth, in football uniform)	.10	.05	.01
☐ 444	Warren Moon (Playing for Washington)	.10	.05	.01
☐ 445	Warren Moon (With Edmonton Eskimos)	.10	.05	.01
☐ 446	Warren Moon (Portrait by Greg Spalenka)	.10	.05	.01
☐ 447	Warren Moon (With family)	.10	.05	.01
☐ 448	Warren Moon (Calling the play)	.10	.05	.01
☐ 449	Warren Moon (In his office)	.10	.05	.01
☐ 450	Warren Moon (Posed with football and helmet)	.10	.05	.01
☐ 451	Deion Sanders (In position for a play)	.30	.14	.04
☐ 452	Deion Sanders (As youth, in football uniform)	.30	.14	.04
☐ 453	Deion Sanders (With Florida State)	.30	.14	.04
☐ 454	Deion Sanders (Playing baseball)	.30	.14	.04
☐ 455	Deion Sanders	.30	.14	.04

(Portrait by Gary Kelley)			
☐ 456 Deion Sanders (Running with ball)	.30	.14	.04
☐ 457 Deion Sanders (With family)	.30	.14	.04
☐ 458 Deion Sanders (Walking on field)	.30	.14	.04
☐ 459 Deion Sanders (Close-up)	.30	.14	.04
☐ 460 Lawrence Taylor (Facing opponent, blue jersey)	.20	.09	.03
☐ 461 Lawrence Taylor (At North Carolina State)	.20	.09	.03
☐ 462 Lawrence Taylor (Side view, white jersey)	.20	.09	.03
☐ 463 Lawrence Taylor (Playing golf on football field)	.20	.09	.03
☐ 464 Lawrence Taylor (Portrait by Chris Hopkins)	.20	.09	.03
☐ 465 Lawrence Taylor (In Honolulu)	.20	.09	.03
☐ 466 Lawrence Taylor (In front of his restaurant)	.20	.09	.03
☐ 467 Lawrence Taylor (Stepping over Jets player)	.20	.09	.03
☐ 468 Lawrence Taylor (Close-up)	.20	.09	.03
☐ 469 Randall Cunningham (Looking for receiver)	.10	.05	.01
☐ 470 Randall Cunningham (In Pop Warner team uniform)	.10	.05	.01
☐ 471 Randall Cunningham (Playing for UNLV)	.10	.05	.01
☐ 472 Randall Cunningham (Running with ball)	.10	.05	.01
☐ 473 Randall Cunningham (Portrait by Greg Spalenka)	.10	.05	.01
☐ 474 Randall Cunningham (Playing golf)	.10	.05	.01
☐ 475 Randall Cunningham (Passing)	.10	.05	.01
☐ 476 Randall Cunningham (Working out)	.10	.05	.01
☐ 477 Randall Cunningham (In dress attire)	.10	.05	.01
☐ 478 Earnest Byner (Redskins uniform, running, side view)	.04	.02	.01
☐ 479 Earnest Byner (At East Carolina, black and white)	.04	.02	.01
☐ 480 Earnest Byner (Browns, brown jersey)	.04	.02	.01
☐ 481 Earnest Byner (With family)	.04	.02	.01
☐ 482 Earnest Byner (Portrait by Chris Hopkins)	.04	.02	.01
☐ 483 Earnest Byner (Browns, white jersey)	.04	.02	.01
☐ 484 Earnest Byner (Fishing)	.04	.02	.01
☐ 485 Earnest Byner (Redskins uniform, running, front view)	.04	.02	.01
☐ 486 Earnest Byner (In workout attire)	.04	.02	.01
☐ 487 Mike Ditka CO (On sideline, in shirt and tie)	.10	.05	.01
☐ 488 Mike Ditka CO (Playing for Bears)	.10	.05	.01
☐ 489 Mike Ditka CO (With family)	.10	.05	.01
☐ 490 Mike Ditka CO (Playing for Cowboys)	.10	.05	.01
☐ 491 Mike Ditka CO (Portrait by Garry Kelley)	.10	.05	.01
☐ 492 Mike Ditka CO (With antique car)	.10	.05	.01
☐ 493 Mike Ditka CO (Playing golf)	.10	.05	.01
☐ 494 Mike Ditka CO (Eating)	.10	.05	.01
☐ 495 Mike Ditka CO (Close-up)	.10	.05	.01
☐ 496 Art Monk (Catching, close-up)	.40	.18	.05
☐ 497 Art Monk (Running hurdles in high school)	.40	.18	.05
☐ 498 Art Monk (Running with ball, front view)	.40	.18	.05
☐ 499 Art Monk (With family)	.40	.18	.05
☐ 500 Art Monk (Portrait by Gary Kelley)	.40	.18	.05
☐ 501 Art Monk (With youth at his football camp)	.40	.18	.05
☐ 502 Art Monk (Running with ball, side view)	.40	.18	.05
☐ 503 Art Monk (Working out)	.40	.18	.05
☐ 504 Art Monk (Ready to catch ball, hands extended)	.40	.18	.05
☐ NNO Art Monk Pro Line Collection Bonus Set (Title Card)	.40	.18	.05

1992 Pro Line Profiles Autographs

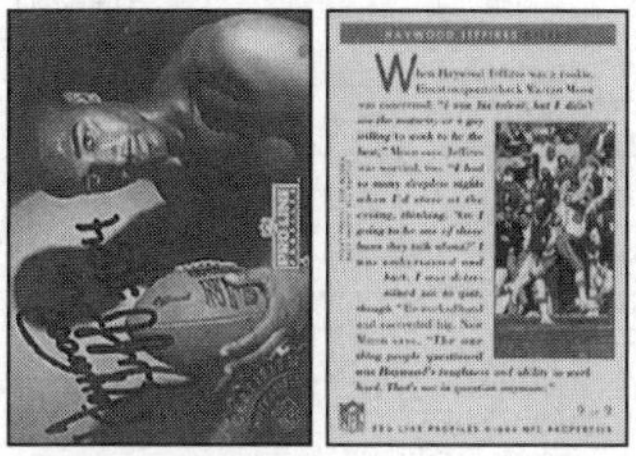

These inserts parallel the regular Profiles set. The 1992 Pro Line autographs were randomly inserted in 1992 Pro Line foil (not jumbo) packs at the rate of approximately one per box. Like the Portrait autographs, these cards are signed in black Sharpie, embossed with an NFL seal and are missing the card number to distinguish them from regular cards. The Art Monk autographs (496-504) were sent to the earliest respondents to the wrapper mail-in offer. They are not considered part of the complete set. The card numbers were not removed from the Art Monk autographs. The prices below refer to all autograph cards from the subset. However, certain types of Profile autographs are more popular than others. Cards showing the player in NFL action or in the uniform of a popular college sometimes bring a 25 to 50 percent premium above the prices listed below. Cards signed by Jack Kemp (154-162), Chris Miller (334-342), and Mark Rypien (433-441) are not known to exist. Also the following cards are not known to exist in signed form: 46-49, 56, 58, 356, 376, 383, 457-459, 504. Card #2 was not signed by Ronnie Lott but by his wife Karen.

	MINT	NRMT	EXC
COMPLETE SET (457)	3000.00	1350.00	375.00
COMMON RONNIE LOTT (1-9)	8.00	3.60	1.00
COMMON RODNEY PEETE (10-18)	4.00	1.80	.50
COMMON CARL BANKS (19-27)	4.00	1.80	.50
COMMON T. THOMAS (28-36)	15.00	6.75	1.85
COMMON R. STAUBACH (37-45)	25.00	11.00	3.10
COMMON JERRY RICE (46-54)	50.00	22.00	6.25
COMMON V. TESTAVERDE (55-63)	4.00	1.80	.50
COMMON A. CARTER (64-72)	4.00	1.80	.50
COMMON ST. SHARPE (73-81)	12.00	5.50	1.50
COMMON ANTHONY MUNOZ (82-90)	8.00	3.60	1.00
COMMON BUBBY BRISTER (91-99)	4.00	1.80	.50
COMMON B. KOSAR (100-108)	6.00	2.70	.75
COMMON ART SHELL (109-117)	8.00	3.60	1.00
COMMON DON SHULA (118-126)	25.00	11.00	3.10
COMMON JOE GIBBS (127-135)	8.00	3.60	1.00
COMMON JUNIOR SEAU (136-144)	8.00	3.60	1.00
COMMON AL TOON (145-153)	4.00	1.80	.50
COMMON JACK KEMP (154-162)	30.00	13.50	3.70
COMMON J. HARBAUGH (163-171)	6.00	2.70	.75
COMMON D. MCGWIRE (172-180)	4.00	1.80	.50
COMMON TROY AIKMAN (181-189)	50.00	22.00	6.25
COMMON KEITH BYARS (190-198)	4.00	1.80	.50
COMMON T. ROSENBACH (199-207)	4.00	1.80	.50
COMMON GARY CLARK (208-216)	6.00	2.70	.75
COMMON C. DOLEMAN (217-225)	4.00	1.80	.50
COMMON JOHN ELWAY (226-234)	30.00	13.50	3.70
COMMON B. ESIASON (235-243)	8.00	3.60	1.00
COMMON JIM EVERETT (244-252)	30.00	9.00	2.50
COMMON ERIC GREEN (253-261)	4.00	1.80	.50
COMMON J. GLANVILLE (262-270)	4.00	1.80	.50
COMMON J. HOSTETLER (271-279)	4.00	1.80	.50
COMMON H. JEFFIRES (280-288)	4.00	1.80	.50
COMMON M. IRVIN (289-297)	20.00	9.00	2.50
COMMON S. LARGENT (298-306)	25.00	11.00	3.10
COMMON KEN O'BRIEN (307-315)	4.00	1.80	.50
COMMON C. OKOYE (316-324)	4.00	1.80	.50
COMMON M.D. PERRY (325-333)	6.00	2.70	.75
COMMON PHIL SIMMS (343-351)	12.00	5.50	1.50
COMMON BRUCE SMITH (352-360)	10.00	4.50	1.25
COMMON D. THOMAS (361-369)	10.00	4.50	1.25
COMMON PAT SWILLING (370-378)	4.00	1.80	.50
COMMON E. DICKERSON (379-387)	12.00	5.50	1.50
COMMON HOWIE LONG (388-396)	8.00	3.60	1.00
COMMON M. SINGLET. (397-405)	10.00	4.50	1.25
COMMON JOHN TAYLOR (406-414)	6.00	2.70	.75
COMMON ANDRE TIPPETT (415-423)	4.00	1.80	.50
COMMON JIM KELLY (424-432)	15.00	6.75	1.85
COMMON W. MOON (442-450)	12.00	5.50	1.50
COMMON D. SANDERS (451-459)	40.00	16.00	4.40
COMMON L. TAYLOR (460-468)	12.00	5.50	1.50
COMMON R. CUNNING. (469-477)	8.00	3.60	1.00
COMMON E. BYNER (478-486)	4.00	1.80	.50
COMMON MIKE DITKA (487-495)	20.00	9.00	2.50
COMMON ART MONK (496-504)	50.00	18.00	5.00

1992-93 Pro Line SB Program

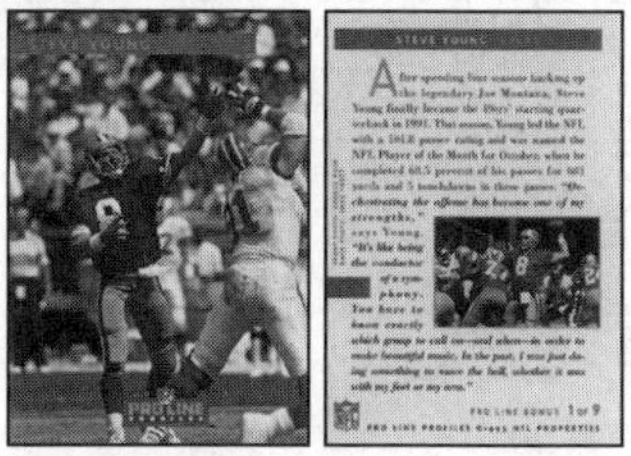

This nine-card standard-size set features Steve Young. One Steve Young promo card was inserted in each copy of the 1993 Super Bowl program. The fronts display full-bleed glossy color photos that capture Young both on and off the field. In text printed around a small color picture, the backs discuss chapters in Young's career and life and carry Young's comments as well. The cards are numbered on the back "X of 9."

	MINT	NRMT	EXC
COMPLETE SET (9)	7.50	3.40	.95
COMMON CARD (1-9)	1.00	.45	.12
☐ 1 Steve Young (Just after release of ball)	1.00	.45	.12
☐ 2 Steve Young (Posed beside statute of Brigham Young)	1.00	.45	.12
☐ 3 Steve Young (In BYU uniform)	1.00	.45	.12
☐ 4 Steve Young (In Los Angeles Express uniform USFL)	1.00	.45	.12
☐ 5 Steve Young (Portrait)	1.00	.45	.12
☐ 6 Steve Young (In Tampa Bay Buccaneers uniform)	1.00	.45	.12
☐ 7 Steve Young (Posed with children for the Children's Miracle Network)	1.00	.45	.12
☐ 8 Steve Young (In San Francisco 49ers uniform)	1.00	.45	.12
☐ 9 Steve Young (Close-up shot; posed in law library)	1.00	.45	.12

1993 Pro Line Live Draft Day NYC

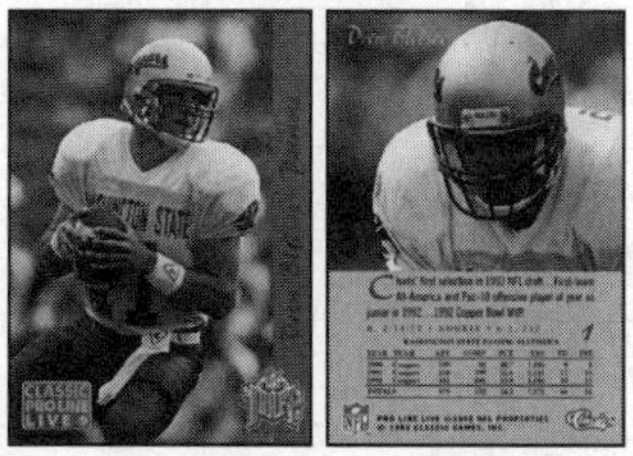

Packaged in a cello pack, this set of ten standard-size cards was passed out at the NFL Draft held April 25th in New York. The cards were created in anticipation of the draft, thus portraying the featured players with several possible teams, and to preview the 1993 Classic NFL Pro Line card design. The full-bleed color player photos on the fronts are accented on the right by a team color-coded stripe that carries the player's name and team name. The "Classic ProLine Live" and "NFL Draft 1993" logos at the lower corners round out the card face. Above a team color-coded panel presenting biography, statistics, and career highlights, the backs display a full-bleed color close-up photo. All the cards are numbered "1" on the back and are checklisted below alphabetically according to player's last name. Suffixes have been added in order to differentiate specific cards. Reportedly about 1,000 sets were distributed at the NFL Draft in New York City.

	MINT	NRMT	EXC
COMPLETE SET (10)	75.00	34.00	9.50
COMMON CARD (1A-1J)	2.50	1.10	.30
☐ 1A Drew Bledsoe Patriots	20.00	9.00	2.50
☐ 1B Drew Bledsoe Chiefs	20.00	9.00	2.50
☐ 1C Drew Bledsoe Seahawks	20.00	9.00	2.50
☐ 1D Eric Curry Cardinals	2.50	1.10	.30
☐ 1E Eric Curry Patriots	2.50	1.10	.30
☐ 1F Marvin Jones Jets	2.50	1.10	.30
☐ 1G Marvin Jones Patriots	2.50	1.10	.30
☐ 1H Rick Mirer Seahawks	8.00	3.60	1.00
☐ 1I Rick Mirer Patriots	8.00	3.60	1.00
☐ 1J Rick Mirer 49ers	8.00	3.60	1.00

1993 Pro Line Live Draft Day QVC

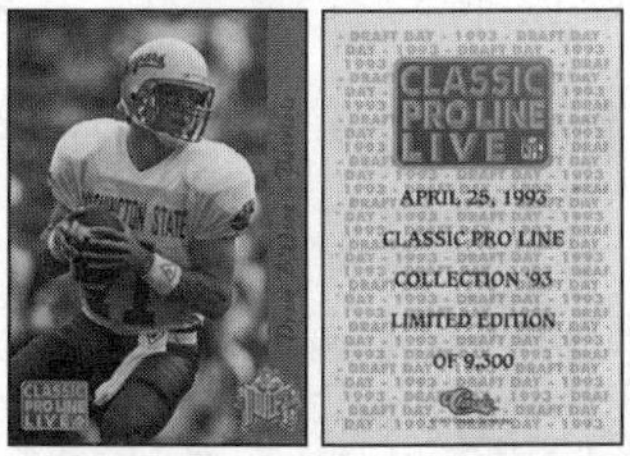

Packaged in a cello pack, this set of ten standard-size cards has the same fronts as the set passed out at the NFL Draft held April 25th in New York. The cards were created in anticipation of the draft, thus portraying the featured players with several possible teams, and to preview the 1993 Classic NFL Pro Line card design. The full-bleed color player photos on the fronts are accented on the right by a team color-coded stripe that carries the player's name and team name. The "Classic ProLine Live" and "NFL Draft 1993" logos at the lower corners round out the card face. On a white, screened back with "1993 Draft Day" in gray lettering, the QVC-version's back has an oversized version of the Classic ProLine Live logo with black lettering immediately below. Reportedly only 9,300 sets with this special back were produced for sale through QVC.

	MINT	NRMT	EXC
COMPLETE SET (10)	20.00	9.00	2.50
COMMON CARD (1A-1J)	.75	.35	.09
☐ 1A Drew Bledsoe Patriots	4.00	1.80	.50
☐ 1B Drew Bledsoe Chiefs	4.00	1.80	.50
☐ 1C Drew Bledsoe Seahawks	4.00	1.80	.50
☐ 1D Eric Curry Cardinals	.75	.35	.09
☐ 1E Eric Curry Patriots	.75	.35	.09
☐ 1F Marvin Jones Jets	.75	.35	.09
☐ 1G Marvin Jones Patriots	.75	.35	.09
☐ 1H Rick Mirer Seahawks	2.00	.90	.25
☐ 1I Rick Mirer Patriots	2.00	.90	.25
☐ 1J Rick Mirer 49ers	2.00	.90	.25

1993 Pro Line Previews

Featuring the last five number one NFL Draft Picks, these five standard-size cards were randomly inserted in 1993 Classic Football Draft Pick foil packs. Twelve Thousand of each card were produced. The fronts from the Classic Pro Line Live, Profiles and Portraits sets appear in this preview of Pro Line's main sets. The backs, however, are more or less the same, featuring the set logo, year and player who was selected the number one draft pick, all printed on a gray background of diagonal Team NFL logos. The NFL and Classic logos appear in the bottom corners. The production number is shown at the bottom.

	MINT	NRMT	EXC
COMPLETE SET (5)	35.00	16.00	4.40
COMMON CARD (PL1-PL5)	3.00	1.35	.35
☐ PL1 Troy Aikman Live	15.00	6.75	1.85
☐ PL2 Jeff George Profile	5.00	2.20	.60
☐ PL3 Russell Maryland Live	3.00	1.35	.35
☐ PL4 Steve Emtman	3.00	1.35	.35
☐ PL5 Drew Bledsoe Portrait	15.00	6.75	1.85

1993 Pro Line Live

The 1993 edition of Pro Line consists of 285 Pro Line Live cards, 48 Portraits and thirteen nine-card (117) Profiles. All three sets were distributed by Classic through 12 and 23-card packs. The fronts feature full-bleed color action photos that are bordered on the right by a team color-coded stripe that carries the player's name and team name. The top portion of the back has a second color action photo, while the bottom portion consists of a team color-coded panel overprinted with player information. A collector could also have ordered a 100-card uncut sheet - featuring better players - from Classic for $39.95 plus shipping and handling. The cards are numbered on the back and checklisted below alphabetically according to teams. Rookie Cards include Jerome Bettis, Drew Bledsoe, Reggie

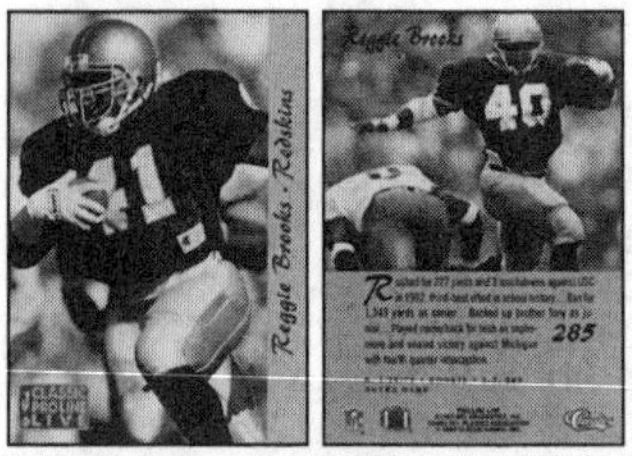

Brooks, Curtis Conway, Garrison Hearst, Billy Joe Hobert, Terry Kirby, O.J. McDuffie, Natrone Means, Glyn Milburn, Rick Mirer, Robert Smith and Kevin Williams. Troy Aikman promo cards were produced and are listed below.

	MINT	NRMT	EXC
COMPLETE SET (285)	15.00	6.75	1.85
COMMON CARD (1-285)	.05	.02	.01
□ 1 Michael Haynes	.10	.05	.01
□ 2 Chris Hinton	.05	.02	.01
□ 3 Pierce Holt	.05	.02	.01
□ 4 Chris Miller	.10	.05	.01
□ 5 Mike Pritchard	.10	.05	.01
□ 6 Andre Rison	.10	.05	.01
□ 7 Deion Sanders	.60	.25	.07
□ 8 Jessie Tuggle	.05	.02	.01
□ 9 Lincoln Kennedy	.05	.02	.01
□ 10 Roger Harper	.05	.02	.01
□ 11 Cornelius Bennett	.10	.05	.01
□ 12 Henry Jones	.05	.02	.01
□ 13 Jim Kelly	.25	.11	.03
□ 14 Bill Brooks	.05	.02	.01
□ 15 Nate Odomes	.05	.02	.01
□ 16 Andre Reed	.10	.05	.01
□ 17 Frank Reich	.10	.05	.01
□ 18 Bruce Smith	.25	.11	.03
□ 19 Steve Tasker	.10	.05	.01
□ 20 Thurman Thomas	.25	.11	.03
□ 21 Thomas Smith	.10	.05	.01
□ 22 John Parrella	.05	.02	.01
□ 23 Neal Anderson	.05	.02	.01
□ 24 Mark Carrier DB	.05	.02	.01
□ 25 Jim Harbaugh	.25	.11	.03
□ 26 Darren Lewis	.05	.02	.01
□ 27 Steve McMichael	.10	.05	.01
□ 28 Alonzo Spellman	.05	.02	.01
□ 29 Tom Waddle	.05	.02	.01
□ 30 Curtis Conway	.75	.35	.09
□ 31 Carl Simpson	.05	.02	.01
□ 32 David Fulcher	.05	.02	.01
□ 33 Harold Green	.05	.02	.01
□ 34 David Klingler	.05	.02	.01
□ 35 Tim Krumrie	.05	.02	.01
□ 36 Carl Pickens	.75	.35	.09
□ 37 Alfred Williams	.05	.02	.01
□ 38 Darryl Williams	.05	.02	.01
□ 39 John Copeland	.10	.05	.01
□ 40 Tony McGee	.10	.05	.01
□ 41 Bernie Kosar	.10	.05	.01
□ 42 Kevin Mack	.05	.02	.01
□ 43 Clay Matthews	.10	.05	.01
□ 44 Eric Metcalf	.10	.05	.01
□ 45 Michael Dean Perry	.10	.05	.01
□ 46 Vinny Testaverde	.10	.05	.01
□ 47 Jerry Ball	.05	.02	.01
□ 48 Tommy Vardell	.05	.02	.01
□ 49 Steve Everitt	.05	.02	.01
□ 50 Dan Footman	.05	.02	.01
□ 51 Troy Aikman	1.00	.45	.12
□ 52 Daryl Johnston	.25	.11	.03
□ 53 Tony Casillas	.05	.02	.01
□ 54 Charles Haley	.10	.05	.01
□ 55 Alvin Harper	.10	.05	.01
□ 56 Michael Irvin	.25	.11	.03
□ 57 Robert Jones	.05	.02	.01
□ 58 Russell Maryland	.05	.02	.01
□ 59 Nate Newton	.10	.05	.01
□ 60 Ken Norton Jr.	.10	.05	.01
□ 61 Jay Novacek	.10	.05	.01
□ 62 Emmitt Smith	2.00	.90	.25
□ 63 Kevin Smith	.10	.05	.01
□ 64 Kevin Williams	.05	.02	.01
□ 65 Darrin Smith	.10	.05	.01
□ 66 Steve Atwater	.05	.02	.01
□ 67 Rod Bernstine	.05	.02	.01
□ 68 Mike Croel	.05	.02	.01
□ 69 John Elway	.75	.35	.09
□ 70 Tommy Maddox	.05	.02	.01
□ 71 Karl Mecklenburg	.05	.02	.01
□ 72 Shannon Sharpe	.25	.11	.03
□ 73 Dennis Smith	.05	.02	.01
□ 74 Dan Williams	.05	.02	.01
□ 75 Glyn Milburn	.25	.11	.03
□ 76 Pat Swilling	.05	.02	.01
□ 77 Bennie Blades	.05	.02	.01
□ 78 Herman Moore	.75	.35	.09
□ 79 Rodney Peete	.05	.02	.01
□ 80 Brett Perriman	.25	.11	.03
□ 81 Barry Sanders	1.00	.45	.12
□ 82 Chris Spielman	.10	.05	.01
□ 83 Andre Ware	.05	.02	.01
□ 84 Ryan McNeil	.05	.02	.01
□ 85 Antonio London	.05	.02	.01
□ 86 Tony Bennett	.05	.02	.01
□ 87 Terrell Buckley	.05	.02	.01
□ 88 Brett Favre	2.00	.90	.25
□ 89 Brian Noble	.05	.02	.01
□ 90 Ken O'Brien	.05	.02	.01
□ 91 Sterling Sharpe	.25	.11	.03
□ 92 Reggie White	.25	.11	.03
□ 93 John Stephens	.05	.02	.01
□ 94 Wayne Simmons	.05	.02	.01
□ 95 George Teague	.10	.05	.01
□ 96 Ray Childress	.05	.02	.01
□ 97 Curtis Duncan	.05	.02	.01
□ 98 Ernest Givins	.10	.05	.01
□ 99 Haywood Jeffires	.10	.05	.01
□ 100 Bubba McDowell	.05	.02	.01
□ 101 Warren Moon	.25	.11	.03
□ 102 Al Smith	.05	.02	.01
□ 103 Lorenzo White	.05	.02	.01
□ 104 Brad Hopkins	.05	.02	.01
□ 105 Micheal Barrow UER (Name misspelled Michael)	.05	.02	.01
□ 106 Duane Bickett	.05	.02	.01
□ 107 Quentin Coryatt	.10	.05	.01
□ 108 Steve Emtman	.05	.02	.01
□ 109 Jeff George	.25	.11	.03
□ 110 Anthony Johnson	.10	.05	.01
□ 111 Reggie Langhorne	.05	.02	.01
□ 112 Jack Trudeau	.05	.02	.01
□ 113 Clarence Verdin	.05	.02	.01
□ 114 Jessie Hester	.05	.02	.01
□ 115 Roosevelt Potts	.05	.02	.01
□ 116 Dale Carter	.05	.02	.01
□ 117 Dave Krieg	.10	.05	.01
□ 118 Nick Lowery	.05	.02	.01
□ 119 Christian Okoye	.05	.02	.01
□ 120 Neil Smith	.25	.11	.03
□ 121 Derrick Thomas	.25	.11	.03
□ 122 Harvey Williams	.10	.05	.01
□ 123 Barry Word	.05	.02	.01
□ 124 Joe Montana	1.00	.45	.12
□ 125 Marcus Allen	.25	.11	.03
□ 126 James Lofton	.10	.05	.01
□ 127 Nick Bell	.05	.02	.01
□ 128 Tim Brown	.25	.11	.03
□ 129 Eric Dickerson	.10	.05	.01
□ 130 Jeff Hostetler	.10	.05	.01
□ 131 Howie Long	.10	.05	.01
□ 132 Todd Marinovich	.05	.02	.01
□ 133 Greg Townsend	.05	.02	.01
□ 134 Patrick Bates	.05	.02	.01
□ 135 Billy Joe Hobert	.40	.18	.05
□ 136 Flipper Anderson	.05	.02	.01
□ 137 Shane Conlan	.05	.02	.01
□ 138 Henry Ellard	.10	.05	.01
□ 139 Jim Everett	.10	.05	.01
□ 140 Cleveland Gary	.05	.02	.01
□ 141 Sean Gilbert	.10	.05	.01
□ 142 Todd Lyght	.05	.02	.01
□ 143 Jerome Bettis	1.50	.70	.19
□ 144 Troy Drayton	.10	.05	.01
□ 145 Louis Oliver	.05	.02	.01
□ 146 Marco Coleman	.05	.02	.01
□ 147 Bryan Cox	.05	.02	.01
□ 148 Mark Duper	.05	.02	.01
□ 149 Irving Fryar	.10	.05	.01
□ 150 Mark Higgs	.05	.02	.01
□ 151 Keith Jackson	.10	.05	.01
□ 152 Dan Marino	2.00	.90	.25
□ 153 Troy Vincent	.05	.02	.01
□ 154 Richmond Webb	.05	.02	.01
□ 155 O.J. McDuffie	.75	.35	.09
□ 156 Terry Kirby	.40	.18	.05
□ 157 Terry Allen	.25	.11	.03
□ 158 Anthony Carter	.10	.05	.01
□ 159 Cris Carter	.25	.11	.03
□ 160 Chris Doleman	.05	.02	.01
□ 161 Randall McDaniel	.05	.02	.01
□ 162 Audray McMillian	.05	.02	.01
□ 163 Henry Thomas	.05	.02	.01
□ 164 Gary Zimmerman	.05	.02	.01
□ 165 Robert Smith	.75	.35	.09
□ 166 Qadry Ismail	.25	.11	.03
□ 167 Vincent Brown	.05	.02	.01
□ 168 Marv Cook	.05	.02	.01
□ 169 Greg McMurtry	.05	.02	.01
□ 170 Jon Vaughn	.05	.02	.01
□ 171 Leonard Russell	.10	.05	.01
□ 172 Andre Tippett	.05	.02	.01
□ 173 Scott Zolak	.05	.02	.01
□ 174 Drew Bledsoe	3.00	1.35	.35
□ 175 Chris Slade	.10	.05	.01
□ 176 Morten Andersen	.05	.02	.01
□ 177 Vaughn Dunbar	.05	.02	.01
□ 178 Rickey Jackson	.05	.02	.01
□ 179 Vaughan Johnson	.05	.02	.01
□ 180 Eric Martin	.05	.02	.01
□ 181 Sam Mills	.05	.02	.01
□ 182 Brad Muster	.05	.02	.01
□ 183 Willie Roaf	.10	.05	.01
□ 184 Irv Smith UER (Birthdate is 7/31/61; should be 9/13/71)	.05	.02	.01
□ 185 Reggie Freeman	.05	.02	.01
□ 186 Michael Brooks	.05	.02	.01
□ 187 Dave Brown	.25	.11	.03
□ 188 Rodney Hampton	.25	.11	.03
□ 189 Pepper Johnson	.05	.02	.01
□ 190 Ed McCaffrey	.05	.02	.01
□ 191 Dave Meggett	.05	.02	.01
□ 192 Bart Oates	.05	.02	.01
□ 193 Phil Simms	.10	.05	.01
□ 194 Lawrence Taylor	.25	.11	.03
□ 195 Michael Strahan	.05	.02	.01
□ 196 Brad Baxter	.05	.02	.01
□ 197 Johnny Johnson	.05	.02	.01
□ 198 Boomer Esiason	.10	.05	.01
□ 199 Ronnie Lott	.10	.05	.01
□ 200 Johnny Mitchell	.05	.02	.01
□ 201 Rob Moore	.10	.05	.01
□ 202 Browning Nagle	.05	.02	.01
□ 203 Blair Thomas	.05	.02	.01
□ 204 Marvin Jones	.05	.02	.01
□ 205 Coleman Rudolph	.05	.02	.01
□ 206 Eric Allen	.05	.02	.01
□ 207 Fred Barnett	.10	.05	.01
□ 208 Tim Harris	.05	.02	.01
□ 209 Randall Cunningham	.10	.05	.01
□ 210 Seth Joyner	.05	.02	.01
□ 211 Clyde Simmons	.05	.02	.01
□ 212 Herschel Walker	.10	.05	.01
□ 213 Calvin Williams	.10	.05	.01
□ 214 Lester Holmes	.05	.02	.01
□ 215 Leonard Renfro	.05	.02	.01
□ 216 Chris Chandler	.10	.05	.01
□ 217 Gary Clark	.10	.05	.01
□ 218 Ken Harvey	.05	.02	.01
□ 219 Randal Hill	.05	.02	.01
□ 220 Steve Beuerlein	.05	.02	.01
□ 221 Ricky Proehl	.05	.02	.01
□ 222 Timm Rosenbach	.05	.02	.01
□ 223 Garrison Hearst	1.25	.55	.16
□ 224 Ernest Dye UER (Birthdate 7/31/61: should be 7/15/71)	.05	.02	.01
□ 225 Bubby Brister	.05	.02	.01
□ 226 Dermontti Dawson	.05	.02	.01
□ 227 Barry Foster	.10	.05	.01
□ 228 Kevin Greene	.25	.11	.03
□ 229 Merril Hoge	.05	.02	.01
□ 230 Greg Lloyd	.25	.11	.03
□ 231 Neil O'Donnell	.25	.11	.03
□ 232 Rod Woodson	.25	.11	.03
□ 233 Deon Figures	.10	.05	.01
□ 234 Chad Brown	.10	.05	.01
□ 235 Marion Butts	.05	.02	.01
□ 236 Gill Byrd	.05	.02	.01
□ 237 Ronnie Harmon	.05	.02	.01
□ 238 Stan Humphries	.25	.11	.03
□ 239 Anthony Miller	.10	.05	.01
□ 240 Leslie O'Neal	.10	.05	.01
□ 241 Stanley Richard	.05	.02	.01
□ 242 Junior Seau	.25	.11	.03
□ 243 Darrien Gordon	.05	.02	.01
□ 244 Natrone Means	1.25	.55	.16
□ 245 Dana Hall	.05	.02	.01
□ 246 Brent Jones	.10	.05	.01
□ 247 Tim McDonald	.05	.02	.01
□ 248 Steve Bono	.25	.11	.03
□ 249 Jerry Rice	1.00	.45	.12
□ 250 John Taylor	.10	.05	.01
□ 251 Ricky Watters	.25	.11	.03
□ 252 Steve Young	.75	.35	.09
□ 253 Dana Stubblefield	.25	.11	.03
□ 254 Todd Kelly	.05	.02	.01
□ 255 Brian Blades	.05	.02	.01
□ 256 Ferrell Edmunds	.05	.02	.01
□ 257 Stan Gelbaugh	.05	.02	.01
□ 258 Cortez Kennedy	.10	.05	.01
□ 259 Dan McGwire	.05	.02	.01
□ 260 Chris Warren	.10	.05	.01
□ 261 John L. Williams	.05	.02	.01
□ 262 David Wyman	.05	.02	.01
□ 263 Rick Mirer	1.25	.55	.16
□ 264 Carlton Gray	.05	.02	.01
□ 265 Marty Carter	.05	.02	.01
□ 266 Reggie Cobb	.05	.02	.01
□ 267 Lawrence Dawsey	.05	.02	.01
□ 268 Santana Dotson	.10	.05	.01
□ 269 Craig Erickson	.10	.05	.01
□ 270 Paul Gruber	.05	.02	.01
□ 271 Keith McCants	.05	.02	.01
□ 272 Broderick Thomas	.05	.02	.01
□ 273 Eric Curry	.05	.02	.01
□ 274 Demetrius DuBose	.05	.02	.01
□ 275 Earnest Byner	.05	.02	.01
□ 276 Ricky Ervins	.05	.02	.01
□ 277 Brad Edwards	.05	.02	.01
□ 278 Jim Lachey	.05	.02	.01
□ 279 Charles Mann	.05	.02	.01
□ 280 Carl Banks	.05	.02	.01
□ 281 Art Monk	.10	.05	.01
□ 282 Mark Rypien	.05	.02	.01
□ 283 Ricky Sanders	.05	.02	.01
□ 284 Tom Carter	.10	.05	.01
□ 285 Reggie Brooks	.10	.05	.01
□ P1 Troy Aikman Promo Numbered 51	3.00	1.35	.35
□ P2 Troy Aikman Promo Tri-Star Prod. Back	2.00	.90	.25

1993 Pro Line Live Autographs

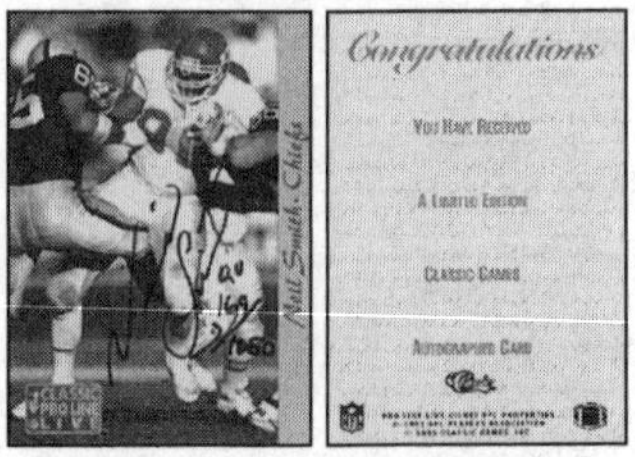

The 1993 Pro Line Live Autographs set comprises standard-size cards. Randomly inserted at an average of two per 1993 Pro Line Live 10 box case, the cards are similar in design to that issue. The fronts sport color player action photos that are bordered on the right by a team color-coded stripe that carries the player's name and team name. The player's autograph across the photo and the limited edition number round out the card front. The white backs carry a congratulatory message. The cards are unnumbered and checklisted below according to how they were numbered in the basic issue. The cards' regular-issue card number, followed by the number of autographed cards produced, are shown with each card in the checklist below. There has been speculation that Troy Aikman's cards may have been autopenned.

	MINT	NRMT	EXC
COMPLETE SET (38)	1250.00	550.00	160.00
COMMON 900 OR MORE	12.00	5.50	1.50
COMMON 750 OR 800	16.00	7.25	2.00
□ 7 Deion Sanders (900)	80.00	36.00	10.00
□ 16 Andre Reed (1050)	25.00	11.00	3.10
□ 23 Neal Anderson (1050)	20.00	9.00	2.50
□ 34 David Klingler (1200)	12.00	5.50	1.50
□ 46 Vinny Testaverde (900)	20.00	9.00	2.50
□ 51 Troy Aikman (700)	75.00	34.00	9.50
□ 67 Rod Bernstine (1000)	12.00	5.50	1.50
□ 70 Tommy Maddox (1050)	12.00	5.50	1.50
□ 76 Pat Swilling (950)	20.00	9.00	2.50
□ 79 Rodney Peete (1000)	20.00	9.00	2.50
□ 87 Terrell Buckley (1050)	12.00	5.50	1.50
□ 88 Brett Favre (650)	175.00	80.00	22.00
□ 91 Sterling Sharpe (1050)	25.00	11.00	3.10
□ 96 Ray Childress (950)	12.00	5.50	1.50
□ 99 Haywood Jeffires (950)	20.00	9.00	2.50
□ 107 Quentin Coryatt (900)	20.00	9.00	2.50
□ 108 Steve Emtman (800)	16.00	7.25	2.00
□ 109 Jeff George (1050)	20.00	9.00	2.50
□ 119 Christian Okoye (900)	12.00	5.50	1.50
□ 120 Neil Smith (1050)	25.00	11.00	3.10
□ 121 Derrick Thomas (550)	30.00	13.50	3.70
□ 124 Joe Montana (600)	175.00	80.00	22.00
□ 129 Eric Dickerson (900)	20.00	9.00	2.50
□ 131 Howie Long (950)	25.00	11.00	3.10
□ 146 Marco Coleman (1000)	12.00	5.50	1.50
□ 151 Keith Jackson (650)	16.00	7.25	2.00
□ 158 Anthony Carter (950)	20.00	9.00	2.50
□ 160 Chris Doleman (1000)	12.00	5.50	1.50
□ 188 Rodney Hampton (650)	25.00	11.00	3.10
□ 199 Ronnie Lott (1050)	20.00	9.00	2.50
□ 201 Rob Moore (950)	20.00	9.00	2.50
□ 212 Herschel Walker (400)	20.00	9.00	2.50
□ 217 Gary Clark (1050)	20.00	9.00	2.50
□ 227 Barry Foster (750)	20.00	9.00	2.50
□ 231 Neil O'Donnell (1050)	20.00	9.00	2.50

	MINT	NRMT	EXC
☐ 242 Junior Seau (900)	25.00	11.00	3.10
☐ 275 Earnest Byner (750)	16.00	7.25	2.00
☐ 281 Art Monk (750)	20.00	9.00	2.50

1993 Pro Line Live Future Stars

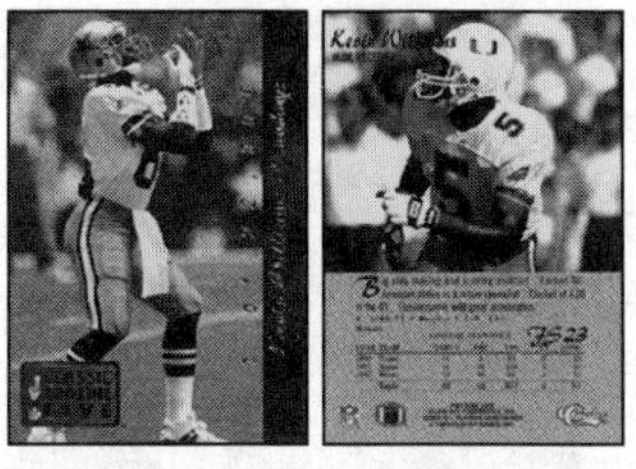

The 1993 Pro Line Live Future Stars set comprises 28 standard-size cards. The insertion rate was one per 1993 Pro Line Live jumbo pack. The fronts sport color player action shots with black-and-white backgrounds that are borderless, except on the right, where a gold foil-stamped stripe carries the player's name and team name. The gold foil-stamped production number, "1 of 22,000," also appears along the right side. Above a team color-coded panel presenting biography, statistics, and career highlights, the backs carry a full-bleed color action player shot. The cards are numbered on the back with an "FS" prefix.

	MINT	NRMT	EXC
COMPLETE SET (28)	16.00	7.25	2.00
COMMON CARD (1-28)	.25	.11	.03
☐ 1 Patrick Bates	.25	.11	.03
☐ 2 Jerome Bettis	2.50	1.10	.30
☐ 3 Drew Bledsoe	5.00	2.20	.60
☐ 4 Tom Carter	.25	.11	.03
☐ 5 Curtis Conway	1.25	.55	.16
☐ 6 Steve Everitt	.25	.11	.03
☐ 7 Deon Figures	.40	.18	.05
☐ 8 Darrien Gordon	.25	.11	.03
☐ 9 Lester Holmes	.25	.11	.03
☐ 10 Brad Hopkins	.25	.11	.03
☐ 11 Marvin Jones	.25	.11	.03
☐ 12 Lincoln Kennedy	.25	.11	.03
☐ 13 O.J. McDuffie	1.25	.55	.16
☐ 14 Rick Mirer	1.50	.70	.19
☐ 15 Willie Roaf	.40	.18	.05
☐ 16 Will Shields	.25	.11	.03
☐ 17 Wayne Simmons	.40	.18	.05
☐ 18 Robert Smith	1.25	.55	.16
☐ 19 Thomas Smith	.40	.18	.05
☐ 20 Michael Strahan	.25	.11	.03
☐ 21 Dana Stubblefield	.75	.35	.09
☐ 22 Dan Williams	.25	.11	.03
☐ 23 Kevin Williams (WR)	.75	.35	.09
☐ 24 Garrison Hearst	1.50	.70	.19
☐ 25 John Copeland	.40	.18	.05
☐ 26 Ryan McNeil	.25	.11	.03
☐ 27 Eric Curry	.40	.18	.05
☐ 28 Roosevelt Potts	.25	.11	.03

1993 Pro Line Live Illustrated

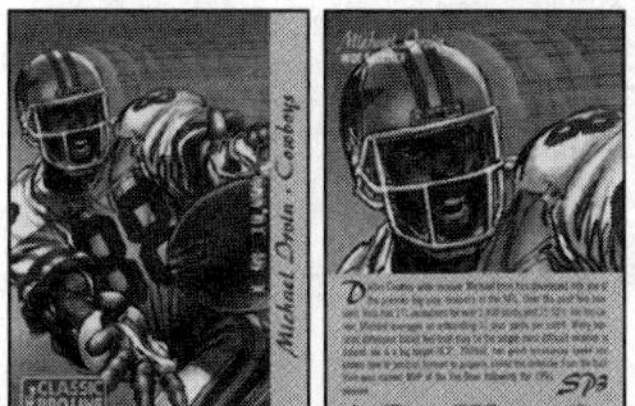

Illustrated by comic artist Neal Adams, this six-card standard-size set was randomly inserted on an average of three per case in 1993 Classic Pro Line packs. Reportedly 10,000 of each card were produced. The front of each card features Adams' colorful player action illustration, which is borderless on three sides. The right side is edged by a team-colored stripe that carries the player's name and team name. In its top half, the back carries a portion of the same player action drawing, followed below by career highlights in a team-colored area at the bottom. The cards are numbered on the back with an "SP" prefix.

	MINT	NRMT	EXC
COMPLETE SET (6)	20.00	9.00	2.50
COMMON CARD (SP1-SP6)	1.50	.70	.19
☐ SP1 Troy Aikman	6.00	2.70	.75
☐ SP2 Jerry Rice	6.00	2.70	.75
☐ SP3 Michael Irvin	2.50	1.10	.30
☐ SP4 Thurman Thomas	2.50	1.10	.30
☐ SP5 Lawrence Taylor	1.50	.70	.19
☐ SP6 Deion Sanders	4.00	1.80	.50

1993 Pro Line Live LPs

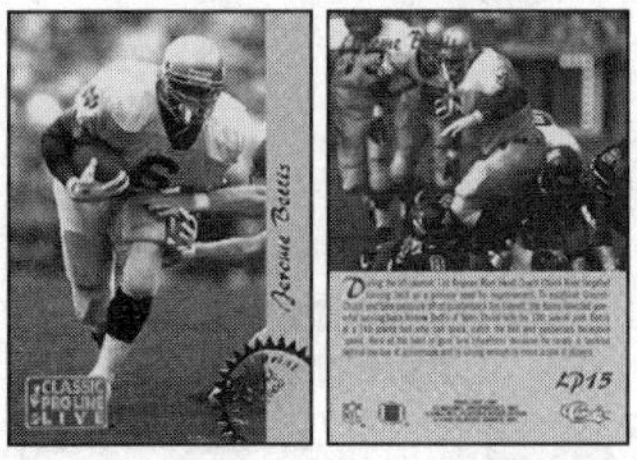

These 20 limited-print, foil-stamped standard-size cards spotlight top young NFL talent along with three top NBA draft picks. The cards were randomly inserted throughout 1993 Classic Pro Line packs on an average of four per point of purchase box. Each card front features a color player action shot that is borderless on three sides. The right side is edged by a team-colored stripe that carries the player's name in gold foil. The gold-foil limited print seal, which carries the words "One of 40,000," appears at the lower right. In its top half, the back carries another player action shot, followed below by career highlights in a team-colored area at the bottom. The cards are numbered on the back with an "LP" prefix.

	MINT	NRMT	EXC
COMPLETE SET (20)	30.00	13.50	3.70
COMMON CARD (LP1-LP20)	.75	.35	.09
☐ LP1 Chris Webber (Dunking football)	2.00	.90	.25
☐ LP2 Shaquille O'Neal (Wearing street clothes)	5.00	2.20	.60
☐ LP3 Jamal Mashburn (Wearing ProLine apparel)	1.25	.55	.16
☐ LP4 Marcus Allen	2.00	.90	.25
☐ LP5 Neal Anderson	.75	.35	.09
☐ LP6 Reggie Cobb	.75	.35	.09
☐ LP7 Rod Bernstine	.75	.35	.09
☐ LP8 Barry Word	.75	.35	.09
☐ LP9 Troy Aikman	3.00	1.35	.35
☐ LP10 Brett Favre	6.00	2.70	.75
☐ LP11 Ricky Watters	2.00	.90	.25
☐ LP12 Terry Allen	1.25	.55	.16
☐ LP13 Rodney Hampton	1.25	.55	.16
☐ LP14 Garrison Hearst	2.00	.90	.25
☐ LP15 Jerome Bettis	2.50	1.10	.30
☐ LP16 Barry Foster	.75	.35	.09
☐ LP17 Harold Green	.75	.35	.09
☐ LP18 Tommy Vardell	.75	.35	.09
☐ LP19 Lorenzo White	.75	.35	.09
☐ LP20 Marion Butts	.75	.35	.09

1993 Pro Line Live Tonx

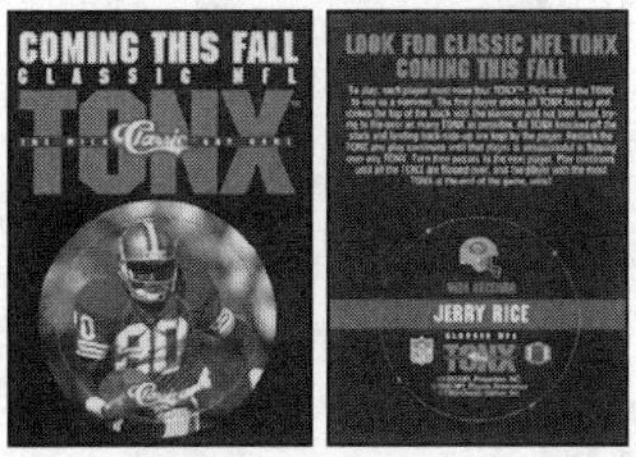

Issued to herald the release of 1993 Classic NFL Tonx in the fall, these six "milk cap" game cards were random inserts in packs of 1993 Pro Line Live. The cards included a circular piece that measures about 1 5/8" in diameter and could be popped out of its standard-size card. The front of each disc features a borderless color player action shot. The black back carries the player's team helmet at the top, followed below by his position, and name within a blue stripe. The cards are unnumbered and checklisted below in alphabetical order.

	MINT	NRMT	EXC
COMPLETE SET (6)	4.00	1.80	.50
COMMON CARD (1-6)	.25	.11	.03
☐ 1 Troy Aikman	1.50	.70	.19
☐ 2 Michael Irvin	.40	.18	.05
☐ 3 Jerry Rice	1.50	.70	.19
☐ 4 Deion Sanders	.60	.25	.07
☐ 5 Lawrence Taylor	.25	.11	.03
☐ 6 Thurman Thomas	.40	.18	.05

1993 Pro Line Portraits

As part of the 1993 Classic Pro Line issue, this 44-card standard-size set features full-bleed non-game photos on the front. The bottom center of the back has a color head shot, and a player quote on a silver panel wraps around the picture. The set closes with a Throwbacks (507-511) subset. The cards are numbered on the back in continuation of the 1992 Pro Line Portraits set. This set was the last of the Portraits series ('91-'93). Rookie Cards include Jerome Bettis, Drew Bledsoe, Garrison Hearst and Rick Mirer.

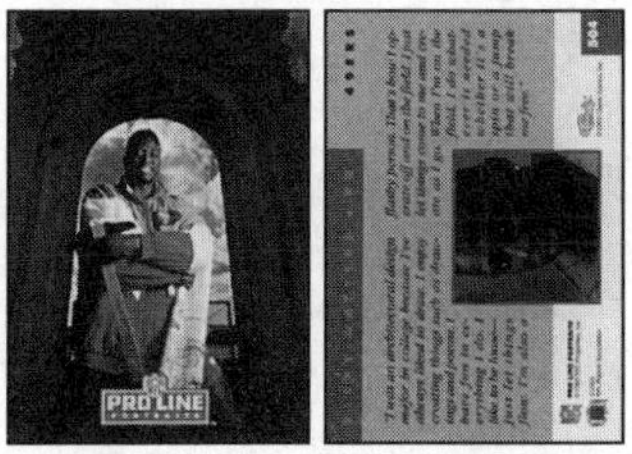

	MINT	NRMT	EXC
COMPLETE SET (44)	7.00	3.10	.85
COMMON CARD (468-511)	.04	.02	.01
☐ 468 Willie Roaf	.08	.04	.01
☐ 469 Terry Allen	.08	.04	.01
☐ 470 Jerry Ball	.04	.02	.01
☐ 471 Patrick Bates	.04	.02	.01
☐ 472 Ray Bentley	.04	.02	.01
☐ 473 Jerome Bettis	1.00	.45	.12
☐ 474 Steve Beuerlein	.04	.02	.01
☐ 475 Drew Bledsoe	2.00	.90	.25
☐ 476 Dave Brown	.08	.04	.01
☐ 477 Gill Byrd	.04	.02	.01
☐ 478 Tony Casillas	.04	.02	.01
☐ 479 Chuck Cecil	.04	.02	.01
☐ 480 Reggie Cobb	.04	.02	.01
☐ 481 Pat Harlow	.04	.02	.01
☐ 482 John Copeland	.08	.04	.01
☐ 483 Bryan Cox	.04	.02	.01
☐ 484 Eric Curry	.08	.04	.01
☐ 485 Jeff Lageman	.04	.02	.01
☐ 486 Brett Favre UER (Name spelled Bret on back)	2.00	.90	.25
☐ 487 Barry Foster	.08	.04	.01
☐ 488 Gaston Green	.04	.02	.01
☐ 489 Rodney Hampton	.15	.07	.02
☐ 490 Tim Harris	.04	.02	.01
☐ 491 Garrison Hearst	.75	.35	.09
☐ 492 Tony Smith	.04	.02	.01
☐ 493 Marvin Jones	.04	.02	.01
☐ 494 Lincoln Kennedy	.04	.02	.01
☐ 495 Wilber Marshall	.04	.02	.01
☐ 496 Terry McDaniel	.04	.02	.01
☐ 497 Rick Mirer	.75	.35	.09
☐ 498 Art Monk	.08	.04	.01
☐ 499 Mike Munchak	.04	.02	.01
☐ 500 Frank Reich	.08	.04	.01
☐ 501 Barry Sanders	1.00	.45	.12
☐ 502 Shannon Sharpe	.08	.04	.01
☐ 503 Gino Torretta	.04	.02	.01
☐ 504 Ricky Watters	.15	.07	.02
☐ 505 Richmond Webb	.04	.02	.01
☐ 506 Reggie White	.15	.07	.02
☐ 507 Bert Jones TB	.04	.02	.01
☐ 508 Billy Kilmer TB	.04	.02	.01
☐ 509 John Mackey TB	.04	.02	.01
☐ 510 Archie Manning TB	.08	.04	.01
☐ 511 Harvey Martin TB	.04	.02	.01

1993 Pro Line Portraits Autographs

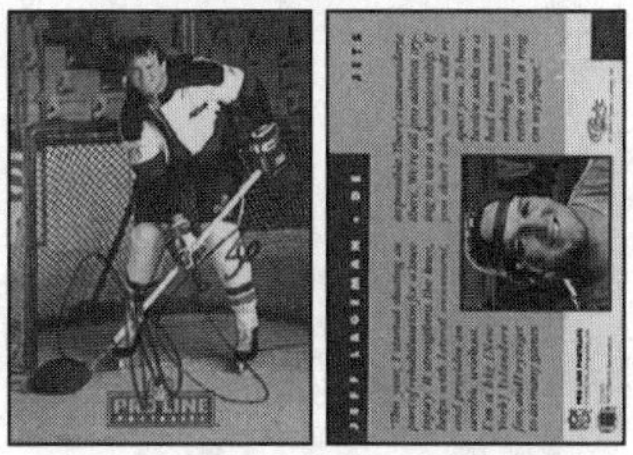

Randomly inserted in packs, the 1993 Classic Pro Line Portraits features 26 standard-size signed cards. These cards are identical to the 1993 Pro Line Portraits set except for the signatures and the Pro Line certified stamp. Out of the 44 players featured in the basic set, only 26 signed cards.

	MINT	NRMT	EXC
COMPLETE SET (26)	700.00	325.00	90.00
COMMON CARD (468-511)	20.00	9.00	2.50
☐ 468 Willie Roaf	25.00	11.00	3.10
☐ 471 Patrick Bates	20.00	9.00	2.50
☐ 473 Jerome Bettis	40.00	22.00	6.25
☐ 474 Steve Beuerlein	25.00	11.00	3.10
☐ 478 Tony Casillas	20.00	9.00	2.50
☐ 479 Chuck Cecil	20.00	9.00	2.50
☐ 480 Reggie Cobb	20.00	9.00	2.50
☐ 481 Pat Harlow	20.00	9.00	2.50
☐ 482 John Copeland	20.00	9.00	2.50
☐ 484 Eric Curry	20.00	9.00	2.50
☐ 485 Jeff Lageman	20.00	9.00	2.50
☐ 486 Brett Favre	175.00	80.00	22.00
☐ 488 Gaston Green	20.00	9.00	2.50
☐ 489 Rodney Hampton	30.00	13.50	3.70
☐ 492 Tony Smith	20.00	9.00	2.50
☐ 493 Marvin Jones	20.00	9.00	2.50
☐ 494 Lincoln Kennedy	20.00	9.00	2.50
☐ 496 Terry McDaniel	20.00	9.00	2.50
☐ 499 Mike Munchak	20.00	9.00	2.50
☐ 500 Frank Reich	20.00	9.00	2.50
☐ 502 Shannon Sharpe	35.00	13.50	3.70
☐ 503 Gino Torretta	25.00	11.00	3.10
☐ 507 Bert Jones TB	25.00	11.00	3.10
☐ 508 Billy Kilmer TB	25.00	11.00	3.10
☐ 510 Archie Manning TB	30.00	13.50	3.70
☐ 511 Harvey Martin TB	25.00	11.00	3.10

1993 Pro Line Portraits Wives

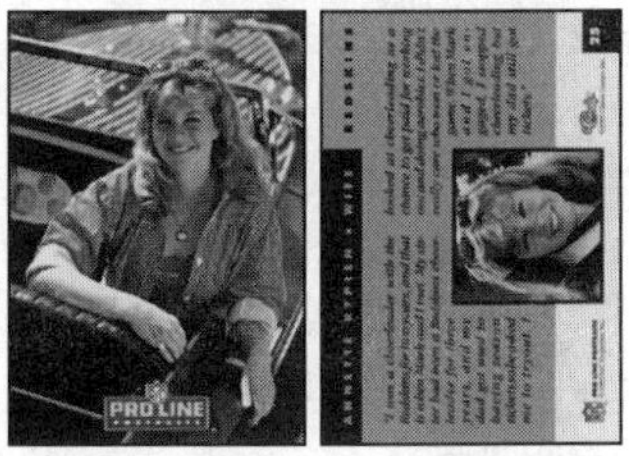

Randomly inserted in 1993 Pro Line packs, this four-card standard-size set features wives of NFL stars. The fronts feature full-bleed color action photos, while the horizontal backs carry a quote and a color close-up shot. The cards are numbered on the back in continuation of the 1992 Pro Line Wives ("Spirit") insert. Card SC24 was never produced.

	MINT	NRMT	EXC
COMPLETE SET (4)	.50	.23	.06
COMMON CARD (SC25-SC28)	.15	.07	.02
☐ SC25 Annette Rypien	.15	.07	.02
☐ SC26 Ann Stark	.15	.07	.02
☐ SC27 Cindy Walker	.15	.07	.02
☐ SC28 Cindy Reed	.15	.07	.02

1993 Pro Line Portraits Wives Autographs

Randomly inserted in packs, the 1993 Pro Line Portraits Wives features three standard-size signed cards. These cards are identical to the 1993 Pro Line Portraits Wives sets except for the signatures and the Pro Line certified stamp. Out of the four wives featured in the basic set, three signed cards. The cards are numbered on the back in continuation of the 1992 Pro Line Wives ("Spirit") subset.

	MINT	NRMT	EXC
COMPLETE SET (3)	50.00	22.00	6.25
COMMON CARD (25-28)	10.00	4.50	1.25
☐ SC25 Annette Rypien	10.00	4.50	1.25
☐ SC26 Ann Stark	20.00	9.00	2.50
☐ SC28 Cindy Reed	20.00	9.00	2.50

1993 Pro Line Profiles

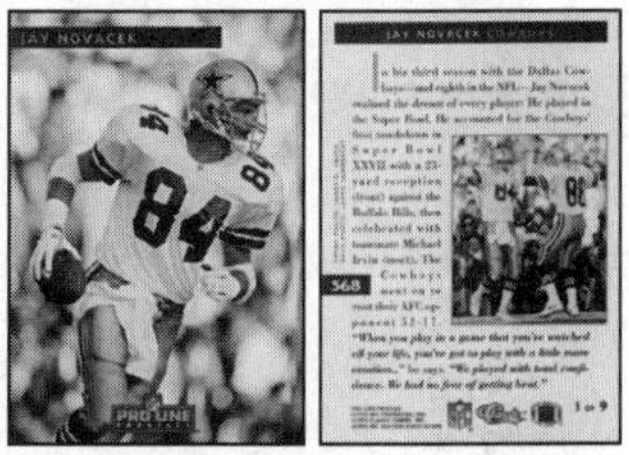

As part of the 1993 Classic Pro Line issue, this 117-card standard-size set features thirteen nine-card subsets devoted to outstanding NFL players. The fronts display full-bleed color action player photos. The lettering and the stripe carrying the player's name are team color-coded. The backs have a second color action shot, career highlights in the form of an expanded caption, and a player quote. The cards are individually numbered on the back as an extension of the 1992 Profiles issue. Each subset ("X of 9") is also numbered.

	MINT	NRMT	EXC
COMPLETE SET (117)	6.00	2.70	.75
COMMON CARD (496-612)	.04	.02	.01
☐ 496 Ray Childress (Versus Steelers)	.04	.02	.01
☐ 497 Ray Childress (Childhood Photo)	.04	.02	.01
☐ 498 Ray Childress (With Aggie trophies)	.04	.02	.01
☐ 499 Ray Childress (Versus Rams)	.04	.02	.01
☐ 500 Ray Childress (Portrait)	.04	.02	.01
☐ 501 Ray Childress (With family)	.04	.02	.01
☐ 502 Ray Childress (Lifting Weights)	.04	.02	.01
☐ 503 Ray Childress (During Pro Bowl)	.04	.02	.01
☐ 504 Ray Childress (Holding calf)	.04	.02	.01
☐ 505 Jeff George	.04	.02	.01

☐ 506 Jeff George (Childhood Photo)	.04	.02	.01
☐ 507 Jeff George (Playing billiards)	.04	.02	.01
☐ 508 Jeff George (In varsity jacket)	.04	.02	.01
☐ 509 Jeff George (Portrait)	.04	.02	.01
☐ 510 Jeff George	.04	.02	.01
☐ 511 Jeff George (With handicapped boy)	.04	.02	.01
☐ 512 Jeff George (Versus Buccaneers)	.04	.02	.01
☐ 513 Jeff George (Studio with football)	.04	.02	.01
☐ 514 Franco Harris (Bust)	.08	.04	.01
☐ 515 Franco Harris (Versus Raiders)	.08	.04	.01
☐ 516 Franco Harris (With son)	.08	.04	.01
☐ 517 Franco Harris (Versus Vikings)	.08	.04	.01
☐ 518 Franco Harris (Portrait)	.08	.04	.01
☐ 519 Franco Harris (Carrying ball)	.08	.04	.01
☐ 520 Franco Harris (Salvation Army kids)	.08	.04	.01
☐ 521 Franco Harris (With ball held aloft)	.08	.04	.01
☐ 522 Franco Harris (With bicycle)	.08	.04	.01
☐ 523 Keith Jackson (Carrying football)	.04	.02	.01
☐ 524 Keith Jackson (With family)	.04	.02	.01
☐ 525 Keith Jackson (On Sooner sideline)	.04	.02	.01
☐ 526 Keith Jackson (In recording studio)	.04	.02	.01
☐ 527 Keith Jackson (Portrait)	.04	.02	.01
☐ 528 Keith Jackson (with Eagles)	.04	.02	.01
☐ 529 Keith Jackson (Dunking Basketball)	.04	.02	.01
☐ 530 Keith Jackson (Running with Ball)	.04	.02	.01
☐ 531 Keith Jackson (Studio Closeup)	.04	.02	.01
☐ 532 Jimmy Johnson (With SB XXVII trophy)	.08	.04	.01
☐ 533 Jimmy Johnson (In Arkansas uniform)	.08	.04	.01
☐ 534 Jimmy Johnson (Smiling)	.08	.04	.01
☐ 535A Jimmy Johnson ERR (With sons) (Name spelled Johnny on back)	.15	.07	.02
☐ 535B Jimmy Johnson COR (With sons) (Name spelled Jimmy on back)	.15	.07	.02
☐ 536 Jimmy Johnson (Portrait)	.08	.04	.01
☐ 537 Jimmy Johnson (On telephone)	.08	.04	.01
☐ 538 Jimmy Johnson (Lifting Weights)	.08	.04	.01
☐ 539 Jimmy Johnson (Scuba Diving with Shark)	.08	.04	.01
☐ 540 Jimmy Johnson (with Jerry Jones)	.08	.04	.01
☐ 541 James Lofton (Catching ball)	.08	.04	.01
☐ 542 James Lofton (Childhood Photo)	.08	.04	.01
☐ 543 James Lofton (Running with Ball)	.08	.04	.01
☐ 544 James Lofton (Versus Dolphins)	.08	.04	.01
☐ 545 James Lofton (Portrait)	.08	.04	.01
☐ 546 James Lofton (On track)	.08	.04	.01
☐ 547 James Lofton (In Bills uniform)	.08	.04	.01
☐ 548 James Lofton (With family)	.08	.04	.01
☐ 549 James Lofton (Versus Rams)	.08	.04	.01
☐ 550 Dan Marino (Versus Jets)	.60	.25	.07
☐ 551 Dan Marino (U.of Pitt.)	.60	.25	.07
☐ 552 Dan Marino (Spinning football)	.60	.25	.07
☐ 553 Dan Marino (With son)	.60	.25	.07
☐ 554 Dan Marino (Portrait)	.60	.25	.07
☐ 555 Dan Marino (Dropping back)	.60	.25	.07
☐ 556 Dan Marino (Playing golf)	.60	.25	.07
☐ 557 Dan Marino (By goal post)	.60	.25	.07
☐ 558 Dan Marino (Studio closeup)	.60	.25	.07
☐ 559 Joe Montana (Helmetless with ball)	.40	.18	.05
☐ 560 Joe Montana (In high school jersey)	.40	.18	.05
☐ 561 Joe Montana (Handing off)	.40	.18	.05
☐ 562 Joe Montana (Passing, 49ers Photo)	.40	.18	.05
☐ 563 Joe Montana (Portrait)	.40	.18	.05
☐ 564 Joe Montana (Making TD gesture)	.40	.18	.05
☐ 565 Joe Montana (High-fiving Rice)	.40	.18	.05
☐ 566 Joe Montana (With wife)	.40	.18	.05
☐ 567 Joe Montana (Studio pose)	.40	.18	.05
☐ 568 Jay Novacek (Running with Ball)	.04	.02	.01
☐ 569 Jay Novacek (Young Jay with pooch)	.04	.02	.01
☐ 570 Jay Novacek (Hurling javelin)	.04	.02	.01
☐ 571 Jay Novacek (In Cardinal uniform)	.04	.02	.01
☐ 572 Jay Novacek (Portrait)	.04	.02	.01
☐ 573 Jay Novacek (With wife)	.04	.02	.01
☐ 574 Jay Novacek (Rodeo)	.04	.02	.01
☐ 575 Jay Novacek (Doing pushups)	.04	.02	.01
☐ 576 Jay Novacek (Riding horse)	.04	.02	.01
☐ 577 Gale Sayers (Bust)	.08	.04	.01
☐ 578 Gale Sayers (In Kansas jersey)	.08	.04	.01
☐ 579 Gale Sayers (Versus Lions)	.08	.04	.01
☐ 580 Gale Sayers (Carrying ball)	.08	.04	.01
☐ 581 Gale Sayers (Portrait)	.08	.04	.01
☐ 582 Gale Sayers (Versus Redskins)	.08	.04	.01
☐ 583 Gale Sayers (With wife)	.08	.04	.01
☐ 584 Gale Sayers (With disabled kids)	.08	.04	.01
☐ 585 Gale Sayers (Dressed in Suit)	.08	.04	.01
☐ 586 Emmitt Smith (Carrying Ball)	.60	.25	.07
☐ 587 Emmitt Smith (College Ball)	.60	.25	.07
☐ 588 Emmitt Smith (Florida Gators Photo)	.60	.25	.07
☐ 589 Emmitt Smith (With Family in Shop)	.60	.25	.07
☐ 590 Emmitt Smith (Portrait)	.60	.25	.07
☐ 591 Emmitt Smith (Carrying Ball)	.60	.25	.07
☐ 592 Emmitt Smith (in His Card Shop)	.60	.25	.07
☐ 593 Emmitt Smith (Running toward camera)	.60	.25	.07
☐ 594 Emmitt Smith (Close-up shot, SB ring displayed)	.60	.25	.07
☐ 595 Herschel Walker (Georgia Photo)	.08	.04	.01
☐ 596 Herschel Walker (Childhood Photo)	.08	.04	.01
☐ 597 Herschel Walker (Jumping rope)	.08	.04	.01
☐ 598 Herschel Walker (Practicing Twae Kwon-Do)	.08	.04	.01
☐ 599 Herschel Walker (Portrait)	.08	.04	.01
☐ 600 Herschel Walker (Cowboy Photo)	.08	.04	.01
☐ 601 Herschel Walker (with Wife, Cindy)	.08	.04	.01
☐ 602 Herschel Walker (Bobsled at '92 Olympics)	.08	.04	.01
☐ 603 Herschel Walker (Shirtless Photo)	.08	.04	.01
☐ 604 Steve Young (Just after passing)	.30	.14	.04
☐ 605 Steve Young (Beside statute of Brigham Young)	.30	.14	.04
☐ 606 Steve Young (BYU Photo)	.30	.14	.04
☐ 607 Steve Young (L.A.Express Photo)	.30	.14	.04
☐ 608 Steve Young (Portrait)	.30	.14	.04
☐ 609 Steve Young (Buccaneer Photo)	.30	.14	.04
☐ 610 Steve Young (With kids)	.30	.14	.04
☐ 611 Steve Young (Carrying Ball)	.30	.14	.04
☐ 612 Steve Young (Studio closeup)	.30	.14	.04

1993 Pro Line Profiles Autographs

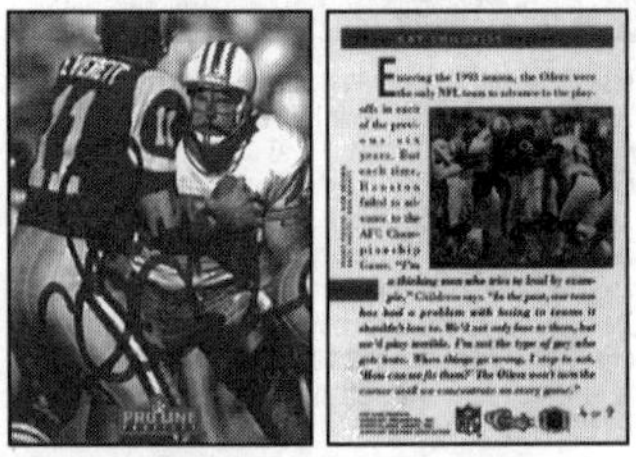

Cards from this set are identical to the 1993 Pro Line Profiles except for the signatures and the Pro Line certified stamp. The prices below refer to all autograph cards from the subset that are known to exist. However, the list is likely incomplete. The signed cards were issued sporadically in various '93 Pro Line packaging types, including hobby, jumbo, and retail packs.

	MINT	NRMT	EXC
COMMON CARD (496-612)	10.00	4.50	1.25
☐ 496 Ray Childress (Versus Steelers)	10.00	4.50	1.25
☐ 497 Ray Childress (Childhood Photo)	10.00	4.50	1.25
☐ 498 Ray Childress (With Aggie trophies)	10.00	4.50	1.25
☐ 499 Ray Childress (Versus Rams)	10.00	4.50	1.25
☐ 500 Ray Childress (Portrait)	10.00	4.50	1.25
☐ 501 Ray Childress (With family)	10.00	4.50	1.25
☐ 502 Ray Childress (Lifting Weights)	10.00	4.50	1.25
☐ 503 Ray Childress (During Pro Bowl)	10.00	4.50	1.25
☐ 504 Ray Childress (Holding calf)	10.00	4.50	1.25
☐ 505 Jeff George	15.00	6.75	1.85
☐ 506 Jeff George (Childhood Photo)	15.00	6.75	1.85
☐ 507 Jeff George (Playing billiards)	15.00	6.75	1.85
☐ 508 Jeff George (In varsity jacket)	15.00	6.75	1.85
☐ 509 Jeff George (Portrait)	15.00	6.75	1.85
☐ 510 Jeff George	15.00	6.75	1.85
☐ 511 Jeff George (With handicapped boy)	15.00	6.75	1.85
☐ 512 Jeff George (Versus Buccaneers)	15.00	6.75	1.85
☐ 513 Jeff George (Studio with football)	15.00	6.75	1.85
☐ 523 Keith Jackson (Carrying football)	15.00	6.75	1.85
☐ 524 Keith Jackson (With family)	15.00	6.75	1.85
☐ 525 Keith Jackson (On Sooner sideline)	15.00	6.75	1.85
☐ 526 Keith Jackson (In recording studio)	15.00	6.75	1.85
☐ 527 Keith Jackson (Portrait)	15.00	6.75	1.85
☐ 528 Keith Jackson (with Eagles)	15.00	6.75	1.85
☐ 529 Keith Jackson (Dunking Basketball)	15.00	6.75	1.85
☐ 530 Keith Jackson (Running with Ball)	15.00	6.75	1.85
☐ 531 Keith Jackson (Studio Closeup)	15.00	6.75	1.85
☐ 532 Jimmy Johnson (With SB XXVII trophy)	50.00	22.00	6.25
☐ 533 Jimmy Johnson (In Arkansas uniform)	15.00	6.75	1.85
☐ 534 Jimmy Johnson (Smiling)	50.00	22.00	6.25
☐ 535 Jimmy Johnson CO (With sons)	15.00	6.75	1.85
☐ 536 Jimmy Johnson (Portrait)	50.00	22.00	6.25
☐ 537 Jimmy Johnson (On telephone)	50.00	22.00	6.25
☐ 538 Jimmy Johnson (Lifting Weights)	15.00	6.75	1.85
☐ 539 Jimmy Johnson (Scuba Diving with Shark)	15.00	6.75	1.85
☐ 540 Jimmy Johnson (with Jerry Jones)	15.00	6.75	1.85
☐ 568 Jay Novacek (Running with Ball)	15.00	6.75	1.85
☐ 569 Jay Novacek (Young Jay with pooch)	15.00	6.75	1.85
☐ 570 Jay Novacek (Hurling javelin)	15.00	6.75	1.85
☐ 571 Jay Novacek (In Cardinal uniform)	15.00	6.75	1.85
☐ 572 Jay Novacek (Portrait)	15.00	6.75	1.85
☐ 573 Jay Novacek (With wife)	15.00	6.75	1.85
☐ 574 Jay Novacek (Rodeo)	15.00	6.75	1.85
☐ 575 Jay Novacek (Doing pushups)	15.00	6.75	1.85
☐ 576 Jay Novacek (Riding horse)	15.00	6.75	1.85
☐ 577 Gale Sayers (Bust)	50.00	22.00	6.25
☐ 578 Gale Sayers (In Kansas jersey)	50.00	22.00	6.25
☐ 579 Gale Sayers (Versus Lions)	50.00	22.00	6.25
☐ 580 Gale Sayers (Carrying ball)	50.00	22.00	6.25
☐ 581 Gale Sayers (Portrait)	50.00	22.00	6.25
☐ 582 Gale Sayers (Versus Redskins)	50.00	22.00	6.25
☐ 583 Gale Sayers (With wife)	50.00	22.00	6.25
☐ 584 Gale Sayers (With disabled kids)	50.00	22.00	6.25
☐ 585 Gale Sayers (Dressed in Suit)	50.00	22.00	6.25

1994 Pro Line Live Draft Day Prototypes

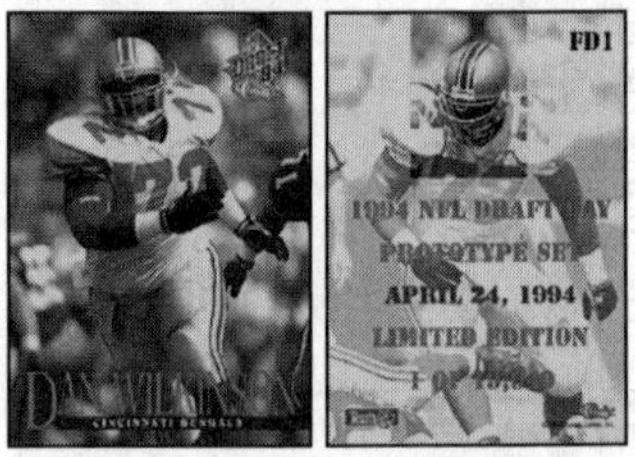

This 13-card standard-size set previews the 1994 NFL Draft by portraying the featured players with several possible teams (with the exception of Troy Aikman). The fronts feature full-bleed color action player photos. At the bottom the player's name is printed in team color-coded letters, which in turn are underscored by a team color-coded stripe. The backs have a full-bleed ghosted photo except for a square at the player's head. The set name, draft date (April 24, 1994), and production figures (1 of 19,940) are stenciled over the ghosted photo.

	MINT	NRMT	EXC
COMPLETE SET (13)	30.00	13.50	3.70
COMMON CARD (1-13)	1.00	.45	.12
☐ FD1 Dan Wilkinson Bengals	1.00	.45	.12
☐ FD2 Dan Wilkinson Patriots	1.00	.45	.12
☐ FD3 Marshall Faulk Bengals	5.00	2.20	.60
☐ FD4 Marshall Faulk Colts	5.00	2.20	.60
☐ FD5 Marshall Faulk Buccaneers	5.00	2.20	.60
☐ FD6 Troy Aikman 1989 First Pick	4.00	1.80	.50
☐ FD7 Trent Dilfer Redskins	2.00	.90	.25
☐ FD8 Trent Dilfer Colts	2.00	.90	.25
☐ FD9 Heath Shuler Redskins	2.00	.90	.25
☐ FD10 Heath Shuler Colts	2.00	.90	.25
☐ FD11 Aaron Glenn Buccaneers	1.00	.45	.12
☐ FD12 Aaron Glenn Rams	1.00	.45	.12
☐ FD13 Dan Wilkinson Cardinals	1.00	.45	.12

1994 Pro Line Live Previews

Randomly inserted in 1994 Classic NFL Draft Picks packs, the five standard-size cards comprising this set feature borderless color player action shots on their fronts. The player's name in upper case lettering, along with his team's name in a colored stripe, appears at the bottom. The back carries a color player action shot with colored borders above and on one side. The player's name and position appear in the margin above the photo; career highlights and a brief biography appear in the margin alongside. Player statistics appear

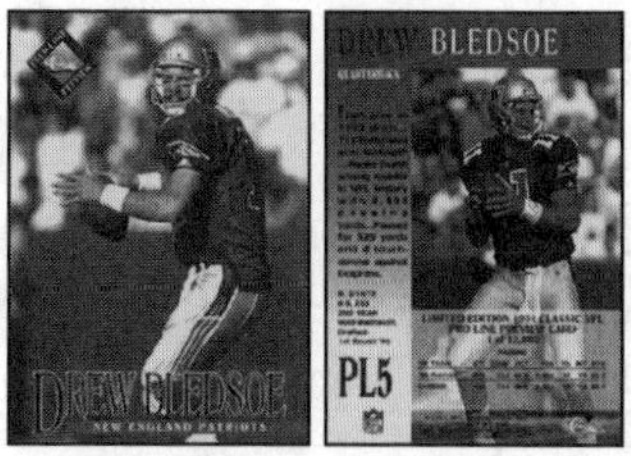

within a ghosted band near the bottom of the photo. A message in black lettering states that production was limited to 12,000 of each card. The cards are numbered on the back with a "PL" prefix.

	MINT	NRMT	EXC
COMPLETE SET (5)	40.00	18.00	5.00
COMMON CARD (PL1-PL5)	6.00	2.70	.75
☐ PL1 Troy Aikman	10.00	4.50	1.25
☐ PL2 Jerry Rice	10.00	4.50	1.25
☐ PL3 Steve Young	8.00	3.60	1.00
☐ PL4 Rick Mirer	6.00	2.70	.75
☐ PL5 Drew Bledsoe	10.00	4.50	1.25

1994 Pro Line Live

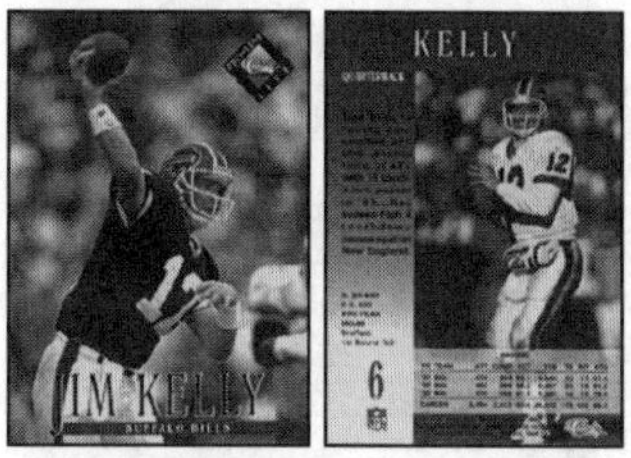

Produced by Classic, these 405 standard-size cards were issued in 10 and 16-card packs. Cards feature borderless fronts and color action shots. The player's name appears in uppercase lettering at the bottom along with his team name within a team color-coded stripe. The backs carry another color player action shot with statistics appearing within a ghosted stripe near the bottom of the photo. Career highlights and biography appear within a team color-coded band down the left side. Rookie Cards include Derrick Alexander, Isaac Bruce, Lake Dawson, Marshall Faulk, William Floyd, Greg Hill, Charles Johnson, Bam Morris, Errict Rhett, Darnay Scott and Heath Shuler.

	MINT	NRMT	EXC
COMPLETE SET (405)	20.00	9.00	2.50
COMMON CARD (1-405)	.05	.02	.01
☐ 1 Emmitt Smith	2.00	.90	.25
☐ 2 Andre Rison	.10	.05	.01
☐ 3 Deion Sanders	.60	.25	.07
☐ 4 Jeff George	.20	.09	.03
☐ 5 Cornelius Bennett	.10	.05	.01
☐ 6 Jim Kelly	.20	.09	.03
☐ 7 Andre Reed	.10	.05	.01
☐ 8 Bruce Smith	.20	.09	.03
☐ 9 Thurman Thomas	.20	.09	.03
☐ 10 Mark Carrier DB	.05	.02	.01
☐ 11 Curtis Conway	.20	.09	.03
☐ 12 Donnell Woolford	.05	.02	.01
☐ 13 Chris Zorich	.05	.02	.01
☐ 14 Erik Kramer	.10	.05	.01
☐ 15 John Copeland	.05	.02	.01
☐ 16 Harold Green	.05	.02	.01
☐ 17 David Klingler	.05	.02	.01
☐ 18 Tony McGee	.05	.02	.01
☐ 19 Carl Pickens	.50	.23	.06
☐ 20 Michael Jackson	.10	.05	.01
☐ 21 Eric Metcalf	.10	.05	.01
☐ 22 Michael Dean Perry	.10	.05	.01
☐ 23 Vinny Testaverde	.10	.05	.01
☐ 24 Eric Turner	.05	.02	.01
☐ 25 Tommy Vardell	.05	.02	.01
☐ 26 Troy Aikman	1.00	.45	.12
☐ 27 Charles Haley	.10	.05	.01
☐ 28 Michael Irvin	.20	.09	.03
☐ 29 Pierce Holt	.05	.02	.01
☐ 30 Russell Maryland	.05	.02	.01
☐ 31 Erik Williams	.05	.02	.01
☐ 32 Thomas Everett	.05	.02	.01
☐ 33 Steve Atwater	.05	.02	.01
☐ 34 John Elway	.75	.35	.09
☐ 35 Glyn Milburn	.10	.05	.01
☐ 36 Shannon Sharpe	.10	.05	.01
☐ 37 Anthony Miller	.10	.05	.01
☐ 38 Barry Sanders	1.00	.45	.12
☐ 39 Chris Spielman	.10	.05	.01
☐ 40 Pat Swilling	.05	.02	.01
☐ 41 Brett Perriman	.10	.05	.01
☐ 42 Herman Moore	.50	.23	.06
☐ 43 Scott Mitchell	.20	.09	.03
☐ 44 Edgar Bennett	.20	.09	.03
☐ 45 Terrell Buckley	.05	.02	.01
☐ 46 LeRoy Butler	.05	.02	.01
☐ 47 Brett Favre	2.00	.90	.25
☐ 48 Jackie Harris	.05	.02	.01
☐ 49 Sterling Sharpe	.10	.05	.01
☐ 50 Reggie White	.20	.09	.03
☐ 51 Gary Brown	.05	.02	.01
☐ 52 Cody Carlson	.05	.02	.01
☐ 53 Ray Childress	.05	.02	.01
☐ 54 Ernest Givins	.10	.05	.01
☐ 55 Bruce Matthews	.05	.02	.01
☐ 56 Quentin Coryatt	.05	.02	.01
☐ 57 Steve Emtman	.05	.02	.01
☐ 58 Roosevelt Potts	.05	.02	.01
☐ 59 Tony Bennett	.05	.02	.01
☐ 60 Marcus Allen	.20	.09	.03
☐ 61 Joe Montana	1.00	.45	.12
☐ 62 Neil Smith	.20	.09	.03
☐ 63 Derrick Thomas	.20	.09	.03
☐ 64 Dale Carter	.05	.02	.01
☐ 65 Tim Brown	.20	.09	.03
☐ 66 Jeff Hostetler	.10	.05	.01
☐ 67 Terry McDaniel	.05	.02	.01
☐ 68 Chester McGlockton	.05	.02	.01
☐ 69 Anthony Smith	.05	.02	.01
☐ 70 Albert Lewis	.05	.02	.01
☐ 71 Jerome Bettis	.60	.25	.07
☐ 72 Shane Conlan	.05	.02	.01
☐ 73 Troy Drayton	.05	.02	.01
☐ 74 Sean Gilbert	.05	.02	.01
☐ 75 Chris Miller	.05	.02	.01
☐ 76 Bryan Cox	.05	.02	.01
☐ 77 Irving Fryar	.10	.05	.01
☐ 78 Keith Jackson	.05	.02	.01
☐ 79 Terry Kirby	.20	.09	.03
☐ 80 Dan Marino	2.00	.90	.25
☐ 81 O.J. McDuffie	.20	.09	.03
☐ 82 Terry Allen	.10	.05	.01
☐ 83 Cris Carter	.20	.09	.03
☐ 84 Chris Doleman	.05	.02	.01
☐ 85 Randall McDaniel	.05	.02	.01
☐ 86 John Randle	.05	.02	.01
☐ 87 Robert Smith	.20	.09	.03
☐ 88 Jason Belser	.05	.02	.01
☐ 89 Jack Del Rio	.05	.02	.01
☐ 90 Vincent Brown	.05	.02	.01
☐ 91 Ben Coates	.20	.09	.03
☐ 92 Chris Slade	.05	.02	.01
☐ 93 Derek Brown RB	.05	.02	.01
☐ 94 Morten Andersen	.05	.02	.01
☐ 95 Willie Roaf	.05	.02	.01
☐ 96 Irv Smith	.05	.02	.01
☐ 97 Tyrone Hughes	.10	.05	.01
☐ 98 Michael Haynes	.10	.05	.01
☐ 99 Jim Everett	.10	.05	.01
☐ 100 Michael Brooks	.05	.02	.01
☐ 101 Leroy Thompson	.05	.02	.01
☐ 102 Rodney Hampton	.20	.09	.03
☐ 103 Dave Meggett	.05	.02	.01
☐ 104 Phil Simms	.10	.05	.01
☐ 105 Boomer Esiason	.10	.05	.01
☐ 106 Johnny Johnson	.05	.02	.01
☐ 107 Gary Anderson K	.05	.02	.01
☐ 108 Mo Lewis	.05	.02	.01
☐ 109 Ronnie Lott	.10	.05	.01
☐ 110 Johnny Mitchell	.05	.02	.01
☐ 111 Howard Cross	.05	.02	.01
☐ 112 Victor Bailey	.05	.02	.01
☐ 113 Fred Barnett	.10	.05	.01
☐ 114 Randall Cunningham	.10	.05	.01
☐ 115 Calvin Williams	.10	.05	.01
☐ 116 Steve Beuerlein	.05	.02	.01
☐ 117 Gary Clark	.10	.05	.01
☐ 118 Ronald Moore	.05	.02	.01
☐ 119 Ricky Proehl	.05	.02	.01
☐ 120 Eric Swann	.10	.05	.01
☐ 121 Barry Foster	.05	.02	.01
☐ 122 Kevin Greene	.20	.09	.03
☐ 123 Greg Lloyd	.20	.09	.03
☐ 124 Neil O'Donnell	.20	.09	.03
☐ 125 Rod Woodson	.20	.09	.03
☐ 126 Ronnie Harmon	.05	.02	.01
☐ 127 Mark Higgs	.05	.02	.01
☐ 128 Stan Humphries	.20	.09	.03
☐ 129 Leslie O'Neal	.05	.02	.01
☐ 130 Chris Mims	.05	.02	.01
☐ 131 Stanley Richard	.05	.02	.01
☐ 132 Junior Seau	.20	.09	.03
☐ 133 Brent Jones	.10	.05	.01
☐ 134 Tim McDonald	.05	.02	.01
☐ 135 Jerry Rice	1.00	.45	.12
☐ 136 Dana Stubblefield	.20	.09	.03
☐ 137 Ricky Watters	.20	.09	.03
☐ 138 Steve Young	.75	.35	.09
☐ 139 Cortez Kennedy	.10	.05	.01
☐ 140 Rick Mirer	.20	.09	.03
☐ 141 Eugene Robinson	.05	.02	.01
☐ 142 Chris Warren	.10	.05	.01
☐ 143 Nate Odomes	.05	.02	.01
☐ 144 Howard Ballard	.05	.02	.01
☐ 145 Flipper Anderson	.05	.02	.01
☐ 146 Chris Jacke	.05	.02	.01
☐ 147 Santana Dotson	.10	.05	.01
☐ 148 Craig Erickson	.05	.02	.01
☐ 149 Hardy Nickerson	.10	.05	.01
☐ 150 Lawrence Dawsey	.05	.02	.01
☐ 151 Terry Wooden	.05	.02	.01
☐ 152 Ethan Horton	.05	.02	.01
☐ 153 John Kasay	.05	.02	.01
☐ 154 Desmond Howard	.10	.05	.01
☐ 155 Ken Harvey	.05	.02	.01
☐ 156 William Fuller	.05	.02	.01
☐ 157 Clyde Simmons	.05	.02	.01
☐ 158 Randal Hill	.05	.02	.01
☐ 159 Garrison Hearst	.50	.23	.06
☐ 160 Mike Pritchard	.05	.02	.01
☐ 161 Jessie Tuggle	.05	.02	.01
☐ 162 Erric Pegram	.05	.02	.01
☐ 163 Kevin Ross	.05	.02	.01
☐ 164 Bill Brooks	.05	.02	.01
☐ 165 Darryl Talley	.05	.02	.01
☐ 166 Steve Tasker	.10	.05	.01
☐ 167 Pete Stoyanovich	.05	.02	.01
☐ 168 Dante Jones	.05	.02	.01
☐ 169 Vencie Glenn	.05	.02	.01
☐ 170 Tom Waddle	.05	.02	.01
☐ 171 Harlon Barnett	.05	.02	.01
☐ 172 Trace Armstrong	.05	.02	.01
☐ 173 Tim Worley	.05	.02	.01
☐ 174 Alfred Williams	.05	.02	.01
☐ 175 Louis Oliver	.05	.02	.01
☐ 176 Darryl Williams	.05	.02	.01
☐ 177 Clay Matthews	.05	.02	.01
☐ 178 Kyle Clifton	.05	.02	.01
☐ 179 Alvin Harper	.10	.05	.01
☐ 180 Jay Novacek	.10	.05	.01
☐ 181 Ken Norton Jr.	.10	.05	.01
☐ 182 Kevin Williams	.10	.05	.01
☐ 183 Daryl Johnston	.10	.05	.01
☐ 184 Rod Bernstine	.05	.02	.01
☐ 185 Karl Mecklenburg	.05	.02	.01
☐ 186 Dennis Smith	.05	.02	.01
☐ 187 Robert Delpino	.05	.02	.01
☐ 188 Bennie Blades	.05	.02	.01
☐ 189 Jason Hanson	.05	.02	.01
☐ 190 Derrick Moore	.05	.02	.01
☐ 191 Mark Clayton	.05	.02	.01
☐ 192 Webster Slaughter	.05	.02	.01
☐ 193 Haywood Jeffires	.10	.05	.01
☐ 194 Bubba McDowell	.05	.02	.01
☐ 195 Warren Moon	.20	.09	.03
☐ 196 Al Smith	.05	.02	.01
☐ 197 Bill Romanowski	.05	.02	.01
☐ 198 John Carney	.05	.02	.01
☐ 199 Kerry Cash	.05	.02	.01
☐ 200 Darren Carrington	.05	.02	.01
☐ 201 Jeff Lageman	.05	.02	.01
☐ 202 Tracy Simien	.05	.02	.01
☐ 203 Willie Davis	.10	.05	.01
☐ 204 Dan Saleaumua	.05	.02	.01
☐ 205 Rocket Ismail	.10	.05	.01
☐ 206 James Jett	.05	.02	.01
☐ 207 Todd Lyght	.05	.02	.01
☐ 208 Roman Phifer	.05	.02	.01
☐ 209 Jimmie Jones	.05	.02	.01
☐ 210 Jeff Cross	.05	.02	.01
☐ 211 Eric Davis	.05	.02	.01
☐ 212 Keith Byars	.05	.02	.01
☐ 213 Richmond Webb	.05	.02	.01
☐ 214 Anthony Carter	.10	.05	.01
☐ 215 Henry Thomas	.05	.02	.01
☐ 216 Andre Tippett	.05	.02	.01
☐ 217 Rickey Jackson	.05	.02	.01
☐ 218 Vaughan Johnson	.05	.02	.01
☐ 219 Eric Martin	.05	.02	.01
☐ 220 Sam Mills	.05	.02	.01
☐ 221 Renaldo Turnbull	.05	.02	.01
☐ 222 Mark Collins	.05	.02	.01
☐ 223 Mike Johnson	.05	.02	.01
☐ 224 Rob Moore	.10	.05	.01
☐ 225 Seth Joyner	.05	.02	.01
☐ 226 Herschel Walker	.10	.05	.01
☐ 227 Eric Green	.05	.02	.01
☐ 228 Marion Butts	.05	.02	.01
☐ 229 John Friesz	.10	.05	.01
☐ 230 John Taylor	.10	.05	.01
☐ 231 Dexter Carter	.05	.02	.01
☐ 232 Brian Blades	.10	.05	.01
☐ 233 Reggie Cobb	.05	.02	.01
☐ 234 Paul Gruber	.05	.02	.01
☐ 235 Ricky Reynolds	.05	.02	.01
☐ 236 Vince Workman	.05	.02	.01
☐ 237 Darrell Green	.05	.02	.01
☐ 238 Jim Lachey	.05	.02	.01
☐ 239 James Hasty	.05	.02	.01
☐ 240 Howie Long	.10	.05	.01
☐ 241 Aeneas Williams	.05	.02	.01
☐ 242 Mike Kenn	.05	.02	.01
☐ 243 Henry Jones	.05	.02	.01
☐ 244 Kenneth Davis	.05	.02	.01
☐ 245 Tim Krumrie	.05	.02	.01
☐ 246 Derrick Fenner	.05	.02	.01
☐ 247 Mark Carrier WR	.10	.05	.01
☐ 248 Robert Porcher	.05	.02	.01
☐ 249 Darren Woodson	.10	.05	.01
☐ 250 Kevin Smith	.05	.02	.01
☐ 251 Mark Stepnoski	.05	.02	.01
☐ 252 Simon Fletcher	.05	.02	.01
☐ 253 Derek Russell	.05	.02	.01
☐ 254 Mike Croel	.05	.02	.01
☐ 255 Johnny Holland	.05	.02	.01
☐ 256 Bryce Paup	.20	.09	.03
☐ 257 Cris Dishman	.05	.02	.01
☐ 258 Sean Jones	.05	.02	.01
☐ 259 Marcus Robertson	.05	.02	.01
☐ 260 Steve Jackson	.05	.02	.01
☐ 261 Jeff Herrod	.05	.02	.01
☐ 262 John Alt	.05	.02	.01
☐ 263 Nick Lowery	.05	.02	.01
☐ 264 Greg Robinson	.05	.02	.01
☐ 265 Alexander Wright	.05	.02	.01
☐ 266 Steve Wisniewski	.05	.02	.01
☐ 267 Henry Ellard	.10	.05	.01
☐ 268 Tracy Scroggins	.05	.02	.01
☐ 269 Jackie Slater	.05	.02	.01
☐ 270 Troy Vincent	.05	.02	.01
☐ 271 Qadry Ismail	.20	.09	.03
☐ 272 Steve Jordan	.05	.02	.01
☐ 273 Leonard Russell	.05	.02	.01
☐ 274 Maurice Hurst	.05	.02	.01
☐ 275 Scottie Graham	.10	.05	.01
☐ 276 Carlton Bailey	.05	.02	.01
☐ 277 John Elliott	.05	.02	.01
☐ 278 Corey Miller	.05	.02	.01
☐ 279 Brad Baxter	.05	.02	.01
☐ 280 Brian Washington	.05	.02	.01
☐ 281 Tim Harris	.05	.02	.01
☐ 282 Byron Evans	.05	.02	.01
☐ 283 Dermontti Dawson	.05	.02	.01
☐ 284 Carnell Lake	.05	.02	.01
☐ 285 Jeff Graham	.05	.02	.01
☐ 286 Merton Hanks	.10	.05	.01
☐ 287 Harris Barton	.05	.02	.01
☐ 288 Guy McIntyre	.05	.02	.01
☐ 289 Kelvin Martin	.05	.02	.01
☐ 290 John L. Williams	.05	.02	.01
☐ 291 Courtney Hawkins	.05	.02	.01
☐ 292 Vaughn Hebron	.05	.02	.01
☐ 293 Brian Mitchell	.05	.02	.01
☐ 294 Andre Collins	.05	.02	.01
☐ 295 Art Monk	.10	.05	.01
☐ 296 Mark Rypien	.05	.02	.01
☐ 297 Ricky Sanders	.05	.02	.01
☐ 298 Eric Hill	.05	.02	.01
☐ 299 Larry Centers	.20	.09	.03
☐ 300 Norm Johnson	.05	.02	.01
☐ 301 Pete Metzelaars	.05	.02	.01
☐ 302 Ricardo McDonald	.05	.02	.01
☐ 303 Stevon Moore	.05	.02	.01
☐ 304 Mike Sherrard	.05	.02	.01
☐ 305 Andy Harmon	.05	.02	.01
☐ 306 Anthony Johnson	.10	.05	.01
☐ 307 J.J. Birden	.05	.02	.01
☐ 308 Neal Anderson	.05	.02	.01
☐ 309 Lewis Tillman	.05	.02	.01
☐ 310 Richard Dent	.10	.05	.01
☐ 311 Nate Newton	.05	.02	.01
☐ 312 Sean Dawkins	.20	.09	.03
☐ 313 Lawrence Taylor	.20	.09	.03
☐ 314 Wilber Marshall	.05	.02	.01
☐ 315 Tom Carter	.05	.02	.01
☐ 316 Reggie Brooks	.10	.05	.01
☐ 317 Eric Curry	.05	.02	.01
☐ 318 Horace Copeland	.05	.02	.01
☐ 319 Natrone Means	.50	.23	.06
☐ 320 Eric Allen	.05	.02	.01
☐ 321 Marvin Jones	.05	.02	.01
☐ 322 Keith Hamilton	.05	.02	.01
☐ 323 Vincent Brisby	.20	.09	.03
☐ 324 Drew Bledsoe	1.25	.55	.16
☐ 325 Tom Rathman	.05	.02	.01
☐ 326 Ed McCaffrey	.05	.02	.01
☐ 327 Steve Israel	.05	.02	.01
☐ 328 Dan Wilkinson	.10	.05	.01
☐ 329 Marshall Faulk	3.00	1.35	.35
☐ 330 Heath Shuler	1.00	.45	.12
☐ 331 Willie McGinest	.20	.09	.03
☐ 332 Trev Alberts	.10	.05	.01
☐ 333 Trent Dilfer	.60	.25	.07
☐ 334 Bryant Young	.20	.09	.03
☐ 335 Sam Adams	.10	.05	.01
☐ 336 Antonio Langham	.10	.05	.01
☐ 337 Jamir Miller	.05	.02	.01
☐ 338 John Thierry	.05	.02	.01
☐ 339 Aaron Glenn	.10	.05	.01
☐ 340 Joe Johnson	.05	.02	.01
☐ 341 Bernard Williams	.05	.02	.01
☐ 342 Wayne Gandy	.05	.02	.01
☐ 343 Aaron Taylor	.05	.02	.01
☐ 344 Charles Johnson	.20	.09	.03
☐ 345 Dewayne Washington	.10	.05	.01
☐ 346 Todd Steussie	.10	.05	.01
☐ 347 Tim Bowens	.10	.05	.01
☐ 348 Johnnie Morton	.20	.09	.03
☐ 349 Rob Fredrickson	.10	.05	.01
☐ 350 Shante Carver	.05	.02	.01
☐ 351 Thomas Lewis	.10	.05	.01
☐ 352 Greg Hill	.20	.09	.03
☐ 353 Henry Ford	.05	.02	.01
☐ 354 Jeff Burris	.10	.05	.01
☐ 355 William Floyd	1.00	.45	.12
☐ 356 Derrick Alexander WR	.20	.09	.03
☐ 357 Darnay Scott	2.00	.90	.25
☐ 358 Isaac Bruce	3.00	1.35	.35
☐ 359 Errict Rhett	1.25	.55	.16
☐ 360 Kevin Lee	.05	.02	.01
☐ 361 Chuck Levy	.05	.02	.01
☐ 362 David Palmer	.10	.05	.01
☐ 363 Ryan Yarborough	.05	.02	.01

	MINT	NRMT	EXC
□ 364 Charlie Garner	.10	.05	.01
□ 365 Isaac Davis	.05	.02	.01
□ 366 Mario Bates	.50	.23	.06
□ 367 Bert Emanuel	1.00	.45	.12
□ 368 Thomas Randolph	.05	.02	.01
□ 369 Bucky Brooks	.05	.02	.01
□ 370 Allen Aldridge	.05	.02	.01
□ 371 Charlie Ward 1993 Heisman Trophy Winner	.20	.09	.03
□ 372 Aubrey Beavers	.05	.02	.01
□ 373 Donnell Bennett	.05	.02	.01
□ 374 Jason Sehorn	.05	.02	.01
□ 375 Lonnie Johnson	.05	.02	.01
□ 376 Tyronne Drakeford	.05	.02	.01
□ 377 Andre Coleman	.05	.02	.01
□ 378 Lamar Smith	.05	.02	.01
□ 379 Calvin Jones	.05	.02	.01
□ 380 LeShon Johnson	.10	.05	.01
□ 381 Byron Bam Morris	.20	.09	.03
□ 382 Lake Dawson	.60	.25	.07
□ 383 Corey Sawyer	.05	.02	.01
□ 384 Willie Jackson	.20	.09	.03
□ 385 Perry Klein	.05	.02	.01
□ 386 Ronnie Woolfork	.05	.02	.01
□ 387 Doug Nussmeier	.05	.02	.01
□ 388 Rob Waldrop	.05	.02	.01
□ 389 Glenn Foley	.05	.02	.01
□ 390 Troy Aikman CC Michael Irvin	.50	.23	.06
□ 391 Steve Young CC Jerry Rice	.50	.23	.06
□ 392 Brett Favre CC Sterling Sharpe	1.00	.45	.12
□ 393 Jim Kelly CC Andre Reed	.20	.09	.03
□ 394 John Elway CC Shannon Sharpe	.40	.18	.05
□ 395 Carolina Panthers	.25	.11	.03
□ 396 Jacksonville Jaguars	.25	.11	.03
□ 397 Checklist 1	.05	.02	.01
□ 398 Checklist 2	.05	.02	.01
□ 399 Checklist 3	.05	.02	.01
□ 400 Checklist 4	.05	.02	.01
□ 401 Sterling Sharpe ILL	.10	.05	.01
□ 402 Derrick Thomas ILL	.10	.05	.01
□ 403 Joe Montana ILL	.50	.23	.06
□ 404 Emmitt Smith ILL	1.00	.45	.12
□ 405 Barry Sanders ILL	.50	.23	.06
□ ES1 Emmitt Smith/15000 Super Bowl MVP	30.00	13.50	3.70
□ JB1 Jerome Bettis ROY	15.00	6.75	1.85
□ P1 Troy Aikman Promo International Sportscard Expo back	2.00	.90	.25
□ PR1 Emmitt Smith Promo numbered PR1	3.00	1.35	.35

1994 Pro Line Live Autographs

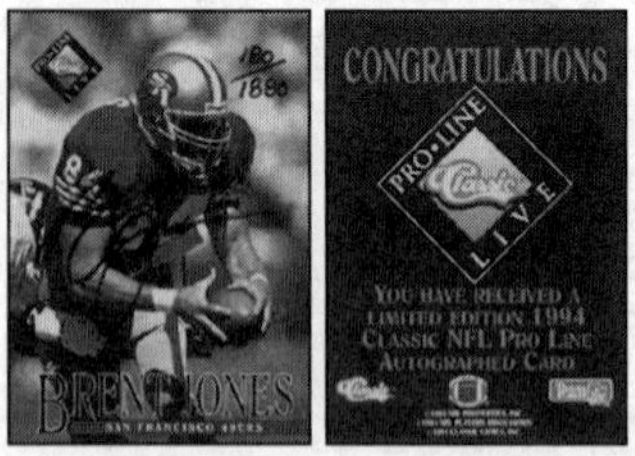

Issued one per Pro Line Live box, the 132 standard-size cards that make up this set are identical in design on front to the basic card. The individually numbered autograph appears on the front and the back offers a congratulatory message. The cards are unnumbered but have been arranged below based on the regular issue set.

	MINT	NRMT	EXC
COMPLETE SET (132)	3500.00	1600.00	450.00
COMMON AUTO	10.00	4.50	1.25
□ 1 Emmitt Smith/925	200.00	90.00	25.00
□ 4 Jeff George/2140	15.00	6.75	1.85
□ 12 Donnell Woolford/1000	10.00	4.50	1.25
□ 14 Erik Kramer/1020	15.00	6.75	1.85
□ 17 David Klingler/2140	10.00	4.50	1.25
□ 20 Michael Jackson/1490	15.00	6.75	1.85
□ 24 Eric Turner/1030	10.00	4.50	1.25
□ 25 Tommy Vardell/1000	15.00	6.75	1.85
□ 26 Troy Aikman/340	175.00	80.00	22.00
□ 28 Michael Irvin/450	50.00	22.00	6.25
□ 29 Pierce Holt/2020	10.00	4.50	1.25
□ 30 Russell Maryland/1945	10.00	4.50	1.25
□ 33 Steve Atwater/1040	10.00	4.50	1.25
□ 34 John Elway/1000	80.00	36.00	10.00
□ 35 Glyn Milburn/440	20.00	9.00	2.50
□ 36 Shannon Sharpe/1020	20.00	6.75	1.85
□ 37 Anthony Miller/2070	15.00	6.75	1.85
□ 47 Brett Favre/1130	140.00	65.00	17.50
□ 49 Sterling Sharpe/450	50.00	22.00	6.25
□ 51 Gary Brown/950	10.00	4.50	1.25
□ 53 Ray Childress/2240	10.00	4.50	1.25
□ 56 Quentin Coryatt/970	15.00	6.75	1.85
□ 57 Steve Emtman/1900	10.00	4.50	1.25
□ 61 Joe Montana/920	160.00	70.00	20.00
□ 62 Neil Smith/1000	20.00	9.00	2.50
□ 63 Derrick Thomas/1087	20.00	9.00	2.50
□ 64 Dale Carter/1031	15.00	6.75	1.85
□ 65 Tim Brown/1920	20.00	9.00	2.50
□ 66 Jeff Hostetler/955	15.00	6.75	1.85
□ 67 Terry McDaniel/1980	10.00	4.50	1.25
□ 72 Shane Conlan/1110	10.00	4.50	1.25
□ 73 Troy Drayton/450	15.00	6.75	1.85
□ 77 Irving Fryar/1040	15.00	6.75	1.85
□ 78 Keith Jackson/1020	10.00	4.50	1.25
□ 93 Derek Brown RB/449	15.00	6.75	1.85
□ 96 Irv Smith/470	15.00	6.75	1.85
□ 97 Tyrone Hughes/470	15.00	6.75	1.85
□ 99 Jim Everett/1265	15.00	6.75	1.85
□ 102 Rodney Hampton/1090	20.00	9.00	2.50
□ 105 Boomer Esiason/920	15.00	6.75	1.85
□ 109 Ronnie Lott/910	15.00	6.75	1.85
□ 112 Victor Bailey/450	15.00	6.75	1.85
□ 116 Steve Beuerlein/970	15.00	6.75	1.85
□ 119 Ricky Proehl/1020	10.00	4.50	1.25
□ 121 Barry Foster/1080	15.00	6.75	1.85
□ 127 Mark Higgs/980	10.00	4.50	1.25
□ 129 Leslie O'Neal/2050	10.00	4.50	1.25
□ 133 Brent Jones/1880	15.00	6.75	1.85
□ 134 Tim McDonald/2040	10.00	4.50	1.25
□ 138 Steve Young/925	90.00	40.00	11.00
□ 149 Hardy Nickerson/1175	10.00	4.50	1.25
□ 159 Garrison Hearst/1435	25.00	11.00	3.10
□ 162 Erric Pegram/1020	15.00	6.75	1.85
□ 164 Bill Brooks/1030	10.00	4.50	1.25
□ 177 Clay Matthews/2000	10.00	4.50	1.25
□ 184 Rod Bernstine/1010	10.00	4.50	1.25
□ 187 Robert Delpino/1030	10.00	4.50	1.25
□ 208 Roman Phifer/2140	10.00	4.50	1.25
□ 212 Keith Byars/1020	10.00	4.50	1.25
□ 213 Richmond Webb/1020	10.00	4.50	1.25
□ 214 Anthony Carter/1020	15.00	6.75	1.85
□ 216 Andre Tippett/1090	10.00	4.50	1.25
□ 220 Sam Mills/1115	15.00	6.75	1.85
□ 221 Renaldo Turnbull/945	10.00	4.50	1.25
□ 224 Rob Moore/1025	15.00	6.75	1.85
□ 228 Marion Butts/2040	10.00	4.50	1.25
□ 229 John Friesz/2150	10.00	4.50	1.25
□ 230 John Taylor/1030	10.00	4.50	1.25
□ 238 Jim Lachey/1850	10.00	4.50	1.25
□ 244 Kenneth Davis/1170	10.00	4.50	1.25
□ 266 Steve Wisniewski/2150	10.00	4.50	1.25
□ 269 Jackie Slater/1110	10.00	4.50	1.25
□ 271 Qadry Ismail/450	30.00	13.50	3.70
□ 277 John Elliott/2150	10.00	4.50	1.25
□ 279 Brad Baxter/1070	10.00	4.50	1.25
□ 284 Carnell Lake/1985	10.00	4.50	1.25
□ 287 Harris Barton/2120	10.00	4.50	1.25
□ 294 Andre Collins/1100	10.00	4.50	1.25
□ 315 Tom Carter/460	15.00	6.75	1.85
□ 316 Reggie Brooks/460	15.00	6.75	1.85
□ 318 Horace Copeland/450	15.00	6.75	1.85
□ 319 Natrone Means/445	30.00	13.50	3.70
□ 320 Eric Allen/1980	10.00	4.50	1.25
□ 324 Drew Bledsoe/1150	90.00	40.00	11.00
□ 325 Tom Rathman/2230	10.00	4.50	1.25
□ 326 Ed McCaffrey/2030	10.00	4.50	1.25
□ 327 Steve Israel/2020	10.00	4.50	1.25
□ 328 Dan Wilkinson/1960	15.00	6.75	1.85
□ 329 Marshall Faulk/2230	50.00	22.00	6.25
□ 330 Heath Shuler/2020	25.00	11.00	3.10
□ 331 Willie McGinest/3520	10.00	4.50	1.25
□ 333 Trent Dilfer/2680	20.00	9.00	2.50
□ 336 Antonio Langham/1240	15.00	6.75	1.85
□ 338 John Thierry/1150	10.00	4.50	1.25
□ 339 Aaron Glenn/1140	15.00	6.75	1.85
□ 342 Wayne Gandy/1040	10.00	4.50	1.25
□ 343 Aaron Taylor/950	10.00	4.50	1.25
□ 344 Charles Johnson/950	20.00	9.00	2.50
□ 345 Dewayne Washington/1040	15.00	6.75	1.85
□ 348 Johnnie Morton/2945	15.00	6.75	1.85
□ 349 Rob Fredrickson/1160	10.00	4.50	1.25
□ 350 Shante Carver/1160	10.00	4.50	1.25
□ 351 Thomas Lewis/1140	15.00	6.75	1.85
□ 352 Greg Hill/1145	20.00	9.00	2.50
□ 353 Henry Ford/1110	10.00	4.50	1.25
□ 354 Jeff Burris/1140	10.00	4.50	1.25
□ 355 William Floyd/950	35.00	16.00	4.40
□ 356 Derrick Alexander WR/950	20.00	9.00	2.50
□ 357 Darnay Scott/1400	40.00	18.00	5.00
□ 359 Errict Rhett/1120	30.00	13.50	3.70
□ 360 Kevin Lee/1190	10.00	4.50	1.25
□ 361 Chuck Levy/950	15.00	6.75	1.85
□ 362 David Palmer/950	15.00	6.75	1.85
□ 364 Charlie Garner/1130	15.00	6.75	1.85
□ 365 Isaac Davis/1150	10.00	4.50	1.25
□ 366 Mario Bates/1145	15.00	6.75	1.85
□ 368 Thomas Randolph/1100	10.00	4.50	1.25
□ 369 Bucky Brooks/1090	10.00	4.50	1.25
□ 372 Aubrey Beavers/1150	10.00	4.50	1.25
□ 373 Donnell Bennett/1130	10.00	4.50	1.25
□ 374 Jason Sehorn/950	10.00	4.50	1.25
□ 377 Andre Coleman/1000	10.00	4.50	1.25
□ 378 Lamar Smith/1130	10.00	4.50	1.25
□ 379 Calvin Jones/960	10.00	4.50	1.25
□ 381 Byron Bam Morris/1130	20.00	9.00	2.50
□ 382 Lake Dawson/1100	20.00	9.00	2.50
□ 384 Willie Jackson/1140	10.00	4.50	1.25
□ 385 Perry Klein/1000	10.00	4.50	1.25
□ 386 Ronnie Woolfork/360	10.00	4.50	1.25
□ 387 Doug Nussmeier/1150	10.00	4.50	1.25
□ 389 Glenn Foley/890	15.00	6.75	1.85
□ 390 Troy Aikman Combo/345 Michael Irvin	250.00	110.00	31.00
□ 391 Steve Young Combo/450 Jerry Rice	250.00	110.00	31.00

1994 Pro Line Live MVP Sweepstakes

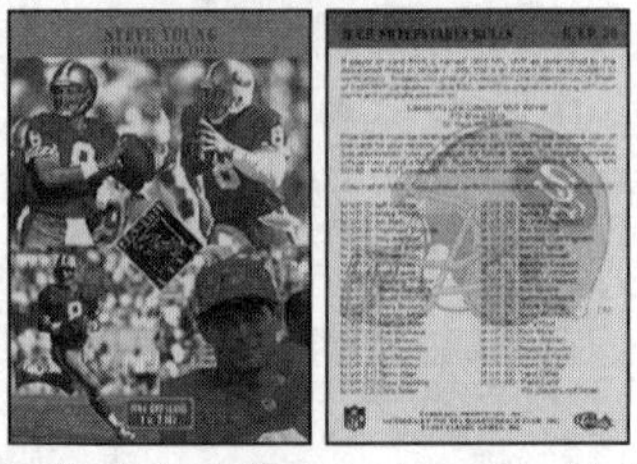

Issued in packs at a rate of five per case, collectors who also obtained one of 2,083 cards of the eventual 1994 Associated Press NFL MVP could have redeemed the card for an exclusive limited-edition uncut sheet of this set. The winner was San Francisco's Steve Young. The attractive fronts feature four color photos with the player's name at the top and the Classic Pro Line Live logo in gold in the middle. The backs offer a complete checklist and contest information. The cards are numbered with an "MVP" prefix.

	MINT	NRMT	EXC
COMPLETE SET (45)	300.00	135.00	38.00
COMMON CARD (1-45)	3.00	1.35	.35
□ 1 Jeff George	3.00	1.35	.35
□ 2 Andre Rison	5.00	2.20	.60
□ 3 Jim Kelly	7.00	3.10	.85
□ 4 Thurman Thomas	7.00	3.10	.85
□ 5 Troy Aikman	20.00	9.00	2.50
□ 6 Emmitt Smith	40.00	18.00	5.00
□ 7 Michael Irvin	7.00	3.10	.85
□ 8 John Elway	16.00	7.25	2.00
□ 9 Brett Favre	40.00	18.00	5.00
□ 10 Sterling Sharpe	5.00	2.20	.60
□ 11 Barry Sanders	20.00	9.00	2.50
□ 12 Scott Mitchell	3.00	1.35	.35
□ 13 Gary Brown	3.00	1.35	.35
□ 14 Warren Moon	5.00	2.20	.60
□ 15 Marcus Allen	7.00	3.10	.85
□ 16 Joe Montana	20.00	9.00	2.50
□ 17 Tim Brown	7.00	3.10	.85
□ 18 Jeff Hostetler	3.00	1.35	.35
□ 19 Dan Marino	40.00	18.00	5.00
□ 20 Terry Kirby	5.00	2.20	.60
□ 21 Terry Allen	5.00	2.20	.60
□ 22 Drew Bledsoe	20.00	9.00	2.50
□ 23 Chris Miller	3.00	1.35	.35
□ 24 Jerome Bettis	10.00	4.50	1.25
□ 25 Derek Brown RB	3.00	1.35	.35
□ 26 Rodney Hampton	5.00	2.20	.60
□ 27 Phil Simms	5.00	2.20	.60
□ 28 Randall Cunningham	3.00	1.35	.35
□ 29 Barry Foster	3.00	1.35	.35
□ 30 Neil O'Donnell	5.00	2.20	.60
□ 31 Boomer Esiason	5.00	2.20	.60
□ 32 Johnny Johnson	3.00	1.35	.35
□ 33 Garrison Hearst	8.00	3.60	1.00
□ 34 Ronald Moore	3.00	1.35	.35
□ 35 Natrone Means	8.00	3.60	1.00
□ 36 Steve Young	16.00	7.25	2.00
□ 37 Ricky Watters	5.00	2.20	.60
□ 38 Jerry Rice	20.00	9.00	2.50
□ 39 Rick Mirer	7.00	3.10	.85
□ 40 Chris Warren	5.00	2.20	.60
□ 41 Reggie Brooks	3.00	1.35	.35
□ 42 Marshall Faulk	16.00	7.25	2.00
□ 43 Heath Shuler	7.00	3.10	.85
□ 44 Trent Dilfer	7.00	3.10	.85
□ 45 Field Card	3.00	1.35	.35

1994 Pro Line Live Spotlight

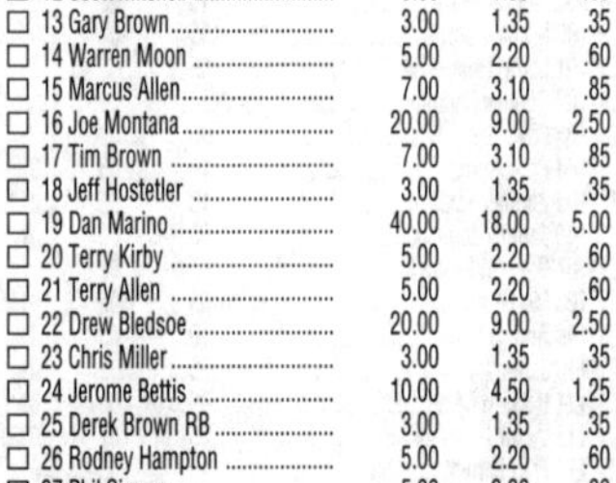

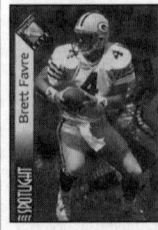

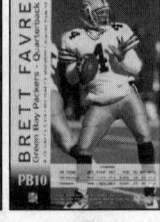

Issued one per 16-card pack, the 25-card Spotlight standard-size set showcases top players. Metallic, full-bleed fronts feature an action photo with the player's name in a stripe up the right side. The backs contain a photo, 1993 and career statistics. The cards are numbered with a "PB" prefix.

	MINT	NRMT	EXC
COMPLETE SET (25)	25.00	11.00	3.10
COMMON CARD (PB1-PB25)	.30	.14	.04
□ PB1 Trent Dilfer	.75	.35	.09
□ PB2 Heath Shuler	.75	.35	.09
□ PB3 Marshall Faulk	1.00	.45	.12
□ PB4 Troy Aikman	1.50	.70	.19
□ PB5 Emmitt Smith	3.00	1.35	.35
□ PB6 Thurman Thomas	.75	.35	.09
□ PB7 Andre Rison	.50	.23	.06
□ PB8 Jerry Rice	1.50	.70	.19
□ PB9 Sterling Sharpe	.50	.23	.06
□ PB10 Brett Favre	3.00	1.35	.35
□ PB11 Steve Young	1.25	.55	.16
□ PB12 Drew Bledsoe	1.50	.70	.19
□ PB13 Rick Mirer	.75	.35	.09
□ PB14 Barry Sanders	1.50	.70	.19
□ PB15 Joe Montana	1.50	.70	.19
□ PB16 Jerome Bettis	1.00	.45	.12
□ PB17 Ricky Watters	.50	.23	.06
□ PB18 Rodney Hampton	.50	.23	.06
□ PB19 Tim Brown	.50	.23	.06
□ PB20 Reggie Brooks	.30	.14	.04
□ PB21 Natrone Means	.75	.35	.09
□ PB22 Marcus Allen	.75	.35	.09
□ PB23 Gary Brown	.30	.14	.04
□ PB24 Barry Foster	.30	.14	.04
□ PB25 Dan Marino	3.00	1.35	.35

1995 Pro Line Previews

This five-card standard-size set was inserted in Classic Draft NFL Rookie packs at the rate of 1:36. The cards preview the 1995 ProLine GameBreakers design and feature five leading NFL players.

	MINT	NRMT	EXC
COMPLETE SET (5)	30.00	13.50	3.70
COMMON CARD (GP1-GP5)	3.00	1.35	.35
□ GP1 Dan Marino	10.00	4.50	1.25
□ GP2 Natrone Means	3.00	1.35	.35
□ GP3 Joe Montana	6.00	2.70	.75
□ GP4 Barry Sanders	6.00	2.70	.75
□ GP5 Deion Sanders	4.00	1.80	.50

1995 Pro Line Previews Phone Cards 2.00/5.00

Both 5 card sets were randomly inserted into packs of 1995 Classic Basketball Rookies. These cards previewed the $2 and $5 phone cards that were inserted into packs of 1995 ProLine.

	MINT	NRMT	EXC
COMPLETE 2.00 SET (5)	6.00	2.70	.75
COMMON CARD 2.00	1.00	.45	.12
COMPLETE 5.00 SET (5)	16.00	7.25	2.00
5.00 PHONE CARDS: 1X TO 2X BASIC CARDS			
□ 1 Troy Aikman	2.00	.90	.25
□ 2 Drew Bledsoe	2.00	.90	.25
□ 3 Ki-Jana Carter	1.00	.45	.12
□ 4 Marshall Faulk	1.25	.55	.16
□ 5 Steve Young	1.50	.70	.19

1995 Pro Line

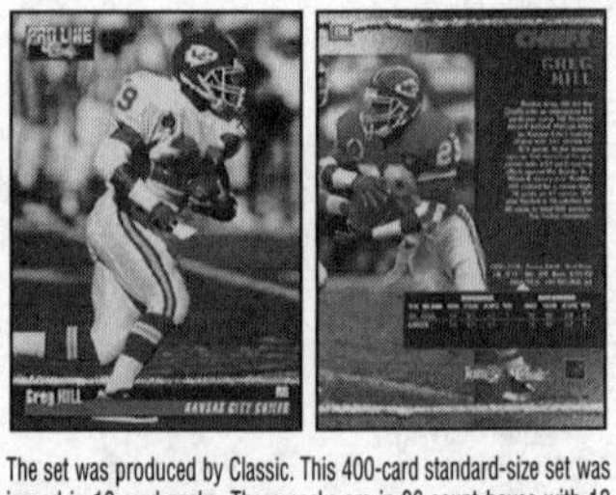

The set was produced by Classic. This 400-card standard-size set was issued in 10-card packs. These packs are in 36 count boxes with 12 boxes per case. Each box was guaranteed by the manufacturer to contain a signed card. Hot boxes (containing mostly insert cards) are inserted one in ten cases for retail and one in five for hobby. The hobby "Hot Boxes" are identified while the retail "Hot Boxes" are not explicitly identified. The full-bleed fronts feature color action photos. The player's name, position and team name are printed in white lettering near the bottom. The backs feature another color photo, biographical information, player information as well as recent and career statistics. Rookie Cards in this set include Jeff Blake, Ki-Jana Carter, Kerry Collins, Joey Galloway, Steve McNair, Kordell Stewart, J.J. Stokes, Ynacey Thigpen, Tamarick Vanover and Michael Westbrook. The basic set includes three parallels: a Silver set inserted one per hobby and retail pack, a Printer's Proof set inserted two per hobby box and a Printer's Proof Silver set inserted one per hobby box. A Marshall Faulk GameBreakers Promo card was produced for distribution at the 1995 St.Louis National Card Collectors Convention. It carries the card number NA1.

	MINT	NRMT	EXC
COMPLETE SET (400)	18.00	8.00	2.20
COMMON CARD (1-400)	.05	.02	.01
□ 1 Garrison Hearst	.20	.09	.03
□ 2 Anthony Miller	.10	.05	.01

☐ 3 Brett Favre	2.00	.90	.25
☐ 4 Jessie Hester	.05	.02	.01
☐ 5 Mike Fox	.05	.02	.01
☐ 6 Jeff Blake	1.00	.45	.12
☐ 7 J.J. Birden	.05	.02	.01
☐ 8 Greg Jackson	.05	.02	.01
☐ 9 Leon Lett	.05	.02	.01
☐ 10 Bruce Matthews	.05	.02	.01
☐ 11 Andre Reed	.10	.05	.01
☐ 12 Joe Montana	1.00	.45	.12
☐ 13 Craig Heyward	.10	.05	.01
☐ 14 Henry Ellard UER	.10	.05	.01
☐ 15 Chris Spielman	.10	.05	.01
☐ 16 Tony Woods	.05	.02	.01
☐ 17 Carl Banks	.05	.02	.01
☐ 18 Eric Zeier	.20	.09	.03
☐ 19 Michael Brooks	.05	.02	.01
☐ 20 Kevin Ross	.05	.02	.01
☐ 21 Qadry Ismail	.10	.05	.01
☐ 22 Mel Gray	.05	.02	.01
☐ 23 Ty Law	.10	.05	.01
☐ 24 Mark Collins	.05	.02	.01
☐ 25 Neil O'Donnell	.10	.05	.01
☐ 26 Ellis Johnson	.05	.02	.01
☐ 27 Rick Mirer	.20	.09	.03
☐ 28 Fred Barnett	.10	.05	.01
☐ 29 Mike Mamula	.10	.05	.01
☐ 30 Jim Jeffcoat	.05	.02	.01
☐ 31 Reggie Cobb	.05	.02	.01
☐ 32 Mark Carrier WR UER	.10	.05	.01
Mark Carrier of the Bears is on front of card			
☐ 33 Darnay Scott	.20	.09	.03
☐ 34 Michael Jackson	.10	.05	.01
☐ 35 Terrell Buckley	.05	.02	.01
☐ 36 Nolan Harrison	.05	.02	.01
☐ 37 Thurman Thomas	.20	.09	.03
☐ 38 Anthony Smith	.05	.02	.01
☐ 39 Phillippi Sparks	.05	.02	.01
☐ 40 Cornelius Bennett	.10	.05	.01
☐ 41 Robert Young	.05	.02	.01
☐ 42 Pierce Holt	.05	.02	.01
☐ 43 Greg Lloyd	.10	.05	.01
☐ 44 Chad May	.05	.02	.01
☐ 45 Darrien Gordon	.05	.02	.01
☐ 46 Bryan Cox	.05	.02	.01
☐ 47 Junior Seau	.20	.09	.03
☐ 48 Al Smith	.05	.02	.01
☐ 49 Chris Slade	.10	.05	.01
☐ 50 Hardy Nickerson	.05	.02	.01
☐ 51 Brad Baxter	.05	.02	.01
☐ 52 Darryll Lewis	.05	.02	.01
☐ 53 Bryant Young	.10	.05	.01
☐ 54 Chris Warren	.10	.05	.01
☐ 55 Darion Conner	.05	.02	.01
☐ 56 Thomas Everett	.05	.02	.01
☐ 57 Charles Haley	.10	.05	.01
☐ 58 Chris Mims	.05	.02	.01
☐ 59 Sean Jones	.05	.02	.01
☐ 60 Tamarick Vanover	1.00	.45	.12
☐ 61 Daryl Johnston	.10	.05	.01
☐ 62 Rashaan Salaam	1.00	.45	.12
☐ 63 James Hasty	.05	.02	.01
☐ 64 Dante Jones	.05	.02	.01
☐ 65 Darren Perry UER	.05	.02	.01
Card is numbered as 367			
☐ 66 Troy Drayton	.05	.02	.01
☐ 67 Mark Fields	.05	.02	.01
☐ 68 Brian Williams	.05	.02	.01
☐ 69 Steve Bono UER	.10	.05	.01
Name spelled Bond on card			
☐ 70 Eric Allen	.05	.02	.01
☐ 71 Chris Zorich	.05	.02	.01
☐ 72 Dave Brown	.10	.05	.01
☐ 73 Ken Norton Jr.	.10	.05	.01
☐ 74 Wayne Martin	.05	.02	.01
☐ 75 Mo Lewis	.05	.02	.01
☐ 76 Johnny Mitchell	.05	.02	.01
☐ 77 Todd Lyght	.05	.02	.01
☐ 78 Erric Pegram	.10	.05	.01
☐ 79 Kevin Greene	.10	.05	.01
☐ 80 Randal Hill	.05	.02	.01
☐ 81 Brett Perriman	.10	.05	.01
☐ 82 Mike Sherrard	.05	.02	.01
☐ 83 Curtis Conway	.20	.09	.03
☐ 84 Mark Tuinei	.05	.02	.01
☐ 85 Mark Seay	.10	.05	.01
☐ 86 Randy Baldwin	.05	.02	.01
☐ 87 Ricky Ervins	.05	.02	.01
☐ 88 Chester McGlockton	.10	.05	.01
☐ 89 Tyrone Wheatley	.40	.18	.05
☐ 90 Micheal Barrow UER	.05	.02	.01
☐ 91 Kenneth Davis	.05	.02	.01
☐ 92 Napoleon Kaufman	.75	.35	.09
☐ 93 Webster Slaughter	.05	.02	.01
☐ 94 Darren Woodson	.10	.05	.01
☐ 95 Pete Stoyanovich	.05	.02	.01
☐ 96 Jimmie Jones	.05	.02	.01
☐ 97 Craig Erickson	.05	.02	.01
☐ 98 Michael Westbrook	1.00	.45	.12
☐ 99 Steve McNair	2.00	.90	.25
☐ 100 Errict Rhett	.20	.09	.03
☐ 101 Devin Bush	.05	.02	.01
☐ 102 Dewayne Washington	.10	.05	.01
☐ 103 Bart Oates	.05	.02	.01

☐ 104 Aaron Pierce	.05	.02	.01
☐ 105 Warren Sapp	.10	.05	.01
☐ 106 Eric Green	.05	.02	.01
☐ 107 Glyn Milburn	.05	.02	.01
☐ 108 Johnny Johnson	.05	.02	.01
☐ 109 Marshall Faulk	.50	.23	.06
☐ 110 William Thomas	.05	.02	.01
☐ 111 George Koonce	.05	.02	.01
☐ 112 Dana Stubblefield	.20	.09	.03
☐ 113 Steve Tovar	.05	.02	.01
☐ 114 Steve Israel	.05	.02	.01
☐ 115 Brent Williams	.05	.02	.01
☐ 116 Shane Conlan	.05	.02	.01
☐ 117 Winston Moss	.05	.02	.01
☐ 118 Nate Newton	.10	.05	.01
☐ 119 Michael Irvin	.20	.09	.03
☐ 120 Jeff Lageman	.05	.02	.01
☐ 121 Ki-Jana Carter	.75	.35	.09
☐ 122 Dan Marino	2.00	.90	.25
☐ 123 Tony Casillas	.05	.02	.01
☐ 124 Kevin Carter	.20	.09	.03
☐ 125 Warren Moon	.10	.05	.01
☐ 126 Byron Bam Morris	.10	.05	.01
☐ 127 Ben Coates	.10	.05	.01
☐ 128 Michael Bankston	.05	.02	.01
☐ 129 Anthony Parker	.05	.02	.01
☐ 130 LeRoy Butler	.05	.02	.01
☐ 131 Tony Bennett	.05	.02	.01
☐ 132 Alvin Harper	.05	.02	.01
☐ 133 Tim Brown	.20	.09	.03
☐ 134 Tom Carter	.05	.02	.01
☐ 135 Lorenzo White	.05	.02	.01
☐ 136 Shane Dronett	.05	.02	.01
☐ 137 John Elliott UER	.05	.02	.01
☐ 138 Korey Stringer	.05	.02	.01
☐ 139 Jerry Rice	1.00	.45	.12
☐ 140 Sherman Williams	.05	.02	.01
☐ 141 Kevin Turner	.05	.02	.01
☐ 142 Randall Cunningham	.10	.05	.01
☐ 143 Vinny Testaverde	.10	.05	.01
☐ 144 Tim Bowens	.05	.02	.01
☐ 145 Russell Maryland	.05	.02	.01
☐ 146 Chris Miller	.05	.02	.01
☐ 147 Vince Buck	.05	.02	.01
☐ 148 Willie Clay	.05	.02	.01
☐ 149 Jeff Graham	.05	.02	.01
☐ 150 Shannon Sharpe	.10	.05	.01
☐ 151 Carnell Lake	.05	.02	.01
☐ 152 Mark Bruener	.10	.05	.01
☐ 153 James Washington	.05	.02	.01
☐ 154 Pepper Johnson	.05	.02	.01
☐ 155 Bert Emanuel	.20	.09	.03
☐ 156 Mark Stepnoski	.05	.02	.01
☐ 157 Robert Jones	.05	.02	.01
☐ 158 Cris Dishman	.05	.02	.01
☐ 159 Henry Jones	.05	.02	.01
☐ 160 Henry Thomas	.05	.02	.01
☐ 161 John L. Williams	.05	.02	.01
☐ 162 Joe Cain	.05	.02	.01
☐ 163 Mike Johnson	.05	.02	.01
☐ 164 Merton Hanks	.05	.02	.01
☐ 165 Deion Sanders	.60	.25	.07
☐ 166 William Floyd	.20	.09	.03
☐ 167 Leroy Thompson	.05	.02	.01
☐ 168 Ray Childress	.05	.02	.01
☐ 169 Donnell Woolford	.05	.02	.01
☐ 170 Tony Siragusa	.05	.02	.01
☐ 171 Chad Brown	.10	.05	.01
☐ 172 Stanley Richard	.05	.02	.01
☐ 173 Rob Johnson	.05	.02	.01
☐ 174 Derrick Brooks	.05	.02	.01
☐ 175 Drew Bledsoe	1.00	.45	.12
☐ 176 Maurice Hurst	.05	.02	.01
☐ 177 Ricky Watters	.20	.09	.03
☐ 178 Myron Guyton	.05	.02	.01
☐ 179 Ricky Proehl	.05	.02	.01
☐ 180 Haywood Jeffires	.05	.02	.01
☐ 181 Michael Strahan	.05	.02	.01
☐ 182 Charles Wilson	.05	.02	.01
☐ 183 Mark Carrier DB	.05	.02	.01
☐ 184 James O.Stewart	.20	.09	.03
☐ 185 Andy Harmon	.05	.02	.01
☐ 186 Ronnie Lott	.10	.05	.01
☐ 187 Clay Matthews	.10	.05	.01
☐ 188 John Carney	.05	.02	.01
☐ 189 Andre Rison	.10	.05	.01
☐ 190 Aeneas Williams	.05	.02	.01
☐ 191 Alexander Wright	.05	.02	.01
☐ 192 Desmond Howard	.10	.05	.01
☐ 193 Herman Moore	.50	.23	.06
☐ 194 Alfred Williams	.05	.02	.01
☐ 195 Tyrone Poole	.10	.05	.01
☐ 196 Darren Mickell	.05	.02	.01
☐ 197 Steve Young	.75	.35	.09
☐ 198 Roman Phifer	.05	.02	.01
☐ 199 Darrell Green	.05	.02	.01
☐ 200 Terry Wooden	.05	.02	.01
☐ 201 Chris Calloway	.05	.02	.01
☐ 202 Lewis Tillman	.05	.02	.01
☐ 203 Cris Carter	.20	.09	.03
☐ 204 Jim Everett	.05	.02	.01
☐ 205 Adrian Murrell	.10	.05	.01
☐ 206 Barry Sanders	1.00	.45	.12
☐ 207 Mario Bates	.20	.09	.03
☐ 208 Shawn Lee	.05	.02	.01

☐ 209 Charles Mincy	.05	.02	.01
☐ 210 Kerry Collins	2.50	1.10	.30
☐ 211 Steve Walsh	.05	.02	.01
☐ 212 Chris Chandler	.10	.05	.01
☐ 213 Bennie Blades	.05	.02	.01
☐ 214 Kevin Williams WR	.10	.05	.01
☐ 215 Jim Kelly	.20	.09	.03
☐ 216 Marion Butts	.05	.02	.01
☐ 217 Jay Novacek	.10	.05	.01
☐ 218 Shawn Jefferson	.05	.02	.01
☐ 219 O.J. McDuffie	.20	.09	.03
☐ 220 Ray Seals	.05	.02	.01
☐ 221 Arthur Marshall	.05	.02	.01
☐ 222 Karl Mecklenburg	.05	.02	.01
☐ 223 Terance Mathis	.10	.05	.01
☐ 224 David Klingler	.10	.05	.01
☐ 225 Rod Woodson	.10	.05	.01
☐ 226 Quentin Coryatt	.10	.05	.01
☐ 227 Leroy Hoard	.05	.02	.01
☐ 228 Brian Blades	.10	.05	.01
☐ 229 Rob Moore	.05	.02	.01
☐ 230 Boomer Esiason	.10	.05	.01
☐ 231 Dave Krieg	.05	.02	.01
☐ 232 Sterling Sharpe	.10	.05	.01
☐ 233 Marcus Allen	.20	.09	.03
☐ 234 John Randle	.05	.02	.01
☐ 235 Craig Powell	.05	.02	.01
☐ 236 John Elway	.75	.35	.09
☐ 237 Mark Ingram	.05	.02	.01
☐ 238 Cortez Kennedy	.10	.05	.01
☐ 239 Brent Jones	.05	.02	.01
☐ 240 Ken Harvey	.05	.02	.01
☐ 241 Keenan McCardell	.20	.09	.03
☐ 242 Dan Wilkinson	.10	.05	.01
☐ 243 Don Beebe	.05	.02	.01
☐ 244 Jack Del Rio	.05	.02	.01
☐ 245 Byron Evans	.05	.02	.01
☐ 246 Ronald Moore	.05	.02	.01
☐ 247 Edgar Bennett	.10	.05	.01
☐ 248 William Fuller	.05	.02	.01
☐ 249 James Williams	.05	.02	.01
☐ 250 Neil Smith	.10	.05	.01
☐ 251 Sam Mills	.10	.05	.01
☐ 252 Willie McGinest	.10	.05	.01
☐ 253 Howard Cross	.05	.02	.01
☐ 254 Troy Aikman	1.00	.45	.12
☐ 255 Herschel Walker	.10	.05	.01
☐ 256 Dale Carter	.10	.05	.01
☐ 257 Sean Dawkins	.10	.05	.01
☐ 258 Greg Hill	.10	.05	.01
☐ 259 Stan Humphries	.10	.05	.01
☐ 260 Erik Kramer	.05	.02	.01
☐ 261 Leslie O'Neal	.10	.05	.01
☐ 262 Trezelle Jenkins	.05	.02	.01
☐ 263 Antonio Langham	.05	.02	.01
☐ 264 Bryce Paup	.20	.09	.03
☐ 265 Jake Reed	.10	.05	.01
☐ 266 Richmond Webb	.05	.02	.01
☐ 267 Eric Davis	.05	.02	.01
☐ 268 Mark McMillian	.05	.02	.01
☐ 269 John Walsh	.05	.02	.01
☐ 270 Irving Fryar	.10	.05	.01
☐ 271 Rocket Ismail	.10	.05	.01
☐ 272 Phil Hansen	.05	.02	.01
☐ 273 J.J. Stokes	.75	.35	.09
☐ 274 Craig Newsome	.05	.02	.01
☐ 275 Leonard Russell	.05	.02	.01
☐ 276 Derrick Deese	.05	.02	.01
☐ 277 Broderick Thomas	.05	.02	.01
☐ 278 Bobby Houston	.05	.02	.01
☐ 279 Lamar Lathon	.05	.02	.01
☐ 280 Eugene Robinson	.05	.02	.01
☐ 281 Dan Saleaumua	.05	.02	.01
☐ 282 Kyle Brady	.20	.09	.03
☐ 283 John Taylor UER	.05	.02	.01
Card lists him as a Tight End			
☐ 284 Tony Boselli	.10	.05	.01
☐ 285 Seth Joyner	.05	.02	.01
☐ 286 Steve Beuerlein	.05	.02	.01
☐ 287 Sam Adams	.05	.02	.01
☐ 288 Frank Reich	.05	.02	.01
☐ 289 Patrick Hunter	.05	.02	.01
☐ 290 Sean Gilbert	.10	.05	.01
☐ 291 Dermontti Dawson UER	.10	.05	.01
☐ 292 Shaun Gayle	.05	.02	.01
☐ 293 Vincent Brown	.05	.02	.01
☐ 294 Terry Kirby	.10	.05	.01
☐ 295 Courtney Hawkins	.05	.02	.01
☐ 296 Carl Pickens	.20	.09	.03
☐ 297 Luther Elliss	.05	.02	.01
☐ 298 Steve Atwater	.05	.02	.01
☐ 299 James Francis	.05	.02	.01
☐ 300 Rob Burnett	.05	.02	.01
☐ 301 Keith Hamilton	.05	.02	.01
☐ 302 Rob Fredrickson	.05	.02	.01
☐ 303 Jerome Bettis	.30	.14	.04
☐ 304 Emmitt Smith	2.00	.90	.25
☐ 305 Clyde Simmons	.05	.02	.01
☐ 306 Reggie White	.20	.09	.03
☐ 307 Rodney Hampton	.10	.05	.01
☐ 308 Steve Emtman	.05	.02	.01
☐ 309 Hugh Douglas	.10	.05	.01
☐ 310 Bernie Parmalee	.10	.05	.01
☐ 311 Trent Dilfer	.20	.09	.03
☐ 312 Flipper Anderson	.05	.02	.01

☐ 313 Heath Shuler	.20	.09	.03
☐ 314 Rod Smith DB	.10	.05	.01
☐ 315 Ray Zellars	.10	.05	.01
☐ 316 Robert Brooks	.20	.09	.03
☐ 317 Lee Woodall	.05	.02	.01
☐ 318 Robert Porcher	.05	.02	.01
☐ 319 Todd Collins	.20	.09	.03
☐ 320 Willie Roaf	.05	.02	.01
☐ 321 Erik Williams	.05	.02	.01
☐ 322 Steve Wisniewski	.05	.02	.01
☐ 323 Derrick Alexander DE	.05	.02	.01
☐ 324 Frank Warren	.05	.02	.01
☐ 325 Kelvin Pritchett	.05	.02	.01
☐ 326 Dennis Gibson	.05	.02	.01
☐ 327 Jason Belser	.05	.02	.01
☐ 328 Vincent Brisby	.05	.02	.01
☐ 329 Calvin Williams	.10	.05	.01
☐ 330 Derek Brown RB	.05	.02	.01
☐ 331 Blake Brockermeyer	.05	.02	.01
☐ 332 Jeff Herrod	.05	.02	.01
☐ 333 Darryl Williams	.05	.02	.01
☐ 334 Aaron Glenn	.05	.02	.01
☐ 335 Eric Metcalf	.10	.05	.01
☐ 336 Billy Milner	.05	.02	.01
☐ 337 Terry McDaniel	.05	.02	.01
☐ 338 Trace Armstrong	.05	.02	.01
☐ 339 Yancey Thigpen	.75	.35	.09
☐ 340 Jackie Harris	.05	.02	.01
☐ 341 Jeff George	.10	.05	.01
☐ 342 Darryl Talley	.05	.02	.01
☐ 343 Marcus Robertson	.05	.02	.01
☐ 344 Robert Massey	.05	.02	.01
☐ 345 Jessie Tuggle	.05	.02	.01
☐ 346 Scott Mitchell	.10	.05	.01
☐ 347 Harvey Williams	.05	.02	.01
☐ 348 Jack Jackson	.05	.02	.01
☐ 349 Brian Mitchell	.05	.02	.01
☐ 350 Lawrence Dawsey	.05	.02	.01
☐ 351 Erik Howard	.05	.02	.01
☐ 352 Quinn Early	.10	.05	.01
☐ 353 Terry Allen	.10	.05	.01
☐ 354 Simon Fletcher	.05	.02	.01
☐ 355 Eric Turner	.05	.02	.01
☐ 356 Natrone Means	.20	.09	.03
☐ 357 Frank Sanders	.20	.09	.03
☐ 358 Michael Timpson	.05	.02	.01
☐ 359 Michael Haynes	.10	.05	.01
☐ 360 Ruben Brown	.05	.02	.01
☐ 361 Troy Vincent UER	.05	.02	.01
Name spelled Vicent on back			
☐ 362 Floyd Turner	.05	.02	.01
☐ 363 Larry Centers	.10	.05	.01
☐ 364 Eric Swann	.10	.05	.01
☐ 365 Albert Lewis	.05	.02	.01
☐ 366 Barry Foster	.10	.05	.01
☐ 367 Michael Dean Perry	.05	.02	.01
☐ 368 Jumpy Geathers UER	.05	.02	.01
Name spelled Jummpy on front			
☐ 369 Kordell Stewart	2.50	1.10	.30
☐ 370 Chuck Smith	.05	.02	.01
☐ 371 Lake Dawson	.10	.05	.01
☐ 372 Terry Hoage	.05	.02	.01
☐ 373 Jeff Cross	.05	.02	.01
☐ 374 Tony McGee	.05	.02	.01
☐ 375 Eric Curry	.05	.02	.01
☐ 376 Harold Green	.05	.02	.01
☐ 377 Eric Hill	.05	.02	.01
☐ 378 Ray Buchanan	.05	.02	.01
☐ 379 Willie Davis	.10	.05	.01
☐ 380 Chris T. Jones	.20	.09	.03
☐ 381 Martin Mayhew	.05	.02	.01
☐ 382 Anthony Pleasant	.05	.02	.01
☐ 383 Joey Galloway	1.50	.70	.19
☐ 384 Anthony Morgan	.05	.02	.01
☐ 385 Harlon Barnett	.05	.02	.01
☐ 386 Bruce Smith	.20	.09	.03
☐ 387 Jeff Hostetler	.10	.05	.01
☐ 388 Randall McDaniel	.05	.02	.01
☐ 389 Dave Meggett	.05	.02	.01
☐ 390 Bill Romanowski	.05	.02	.01
☐ 391 Gary Brown	.05	.02	.01
☐ 392 Charles Johnson	.10	.05	.01
☐ 393 Chris Doleman	.05	.02	.01
☐ 394 Tony Martin	.10	.05	.01
☐ 395 Raymont Harris	.05	.02	.01
☐ 396 John Copeland	.05	.02	.01
☐ 397 Emmitt Smith CL UER	.50	.23	.06
Several wrong names			
☐ 398 Steve Young CL UER	.25	.11	.03
Many wrong names			
☐ 399 Marshall Faulk CL UER	.10	.05	.01
Many wrong names			
☐ 400 Ki-Jana Carter CL UER	.10	.05	.01
Many wrong names			
☐ P1 Marshall Faulk Promo	1.00	.45	.12
GameBreakers card			
1995 National Convention back			

1995 Pro Line National Silver

This 400-card parallel set was inserted into 1995 Pro Line National version packs at a rate of one per pack. The cards are differentiated from the base brand issue by having a silver foil background and "16th National Sports Collector's Convention St.Louis 1995" blue foil logo on the cardfronts. ProLine National cases contained an assortment of base ProLine cards and inserts, along with this special

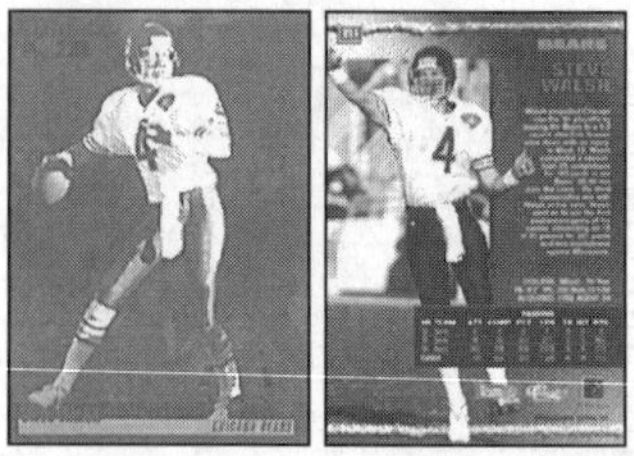

parallel and the National Attention insert set. Reportedly, 500 cases of the National version were produced with each case containing 12-boxes.

	MINT	NRMT	EXC
COMPLETE SET (400)	250.00	110.00	31.00
COMMON CARD (1-400)	.50	.23	.06

*VETERAN STARS: 5X TO 10X BASIC CARDS
*YOUNG STARS: 4X TO 8X BASIC CARDS
*RCs: 3X TO 6X BASIC CARDS

1995 Pro Line Printer's Proofs

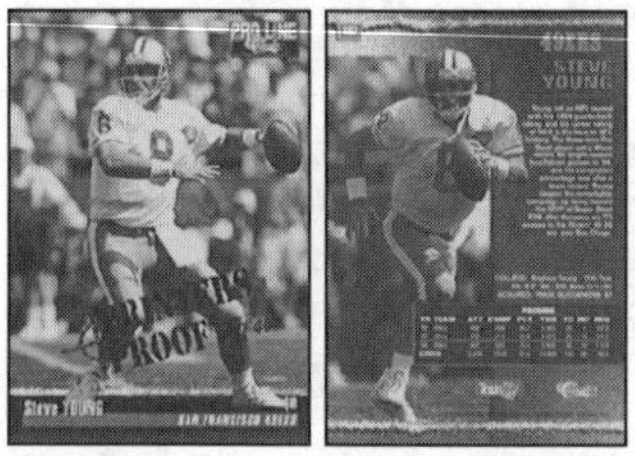

This set is a parallel to the regular ProLine set. Each hobby box contained two of these cards. 400 of each card were produced and all have the words "Printer's Proof" overprinted on the front. There is also a silver parallel version of which 175 of each card were produced. The cards are identical except for the number and the silver sheen on the card.

	MINT	NRMT	EXC
COMPLETE PRINT.PROOF (400)	600.00	275.00	75.00
COMMON PRINT.PROOF (1-400)	1.25	.55	.16

*VETERAN STARS: 20X to 35X BASIC CARDS
*YOUNG STARS: 10X to 18X BASIC CARDS
*RCS: 8X to 14X

1995 Pro Line Printer's Proof Silver

This 400 card parallel set was randomly inserted into packs at a rate of one per hobby box. 175 of these cards were produced and have the words "Printer's Proof" overprinted on the front against a silver foil background.

	MINT	NRMT	EXC
COMPLETE SET (400)	1300.00	575.00	160.00
COMMON CARD (1-400)	2.50	1.10	.30

*VETERAN STARS: 40X TO 70X BASIC CARDS
*YOUNG STARS: 20X TO 35X BASIC CARDS
*RC's: 16X TO 28X BASIC CARDS

1995 Pro Line Silver

This 400 card parallel set was randomly inserted into packs at a rate of one per hobby and retail pack. Cards are differentiated from the basic card by having a silver foil background.

	MINT	NRMT	EXC
COMPLETE SET (400)	50.00	22.00	6.25
COMMON CARD (1-400)	.15	.07	.02

*VETERAN STARS: 2X TO 4X BASIC CARDS
*YOUNG STARS/RCs: 1X TO 2X BASIC CARDS

1995 Pro Line Autographs

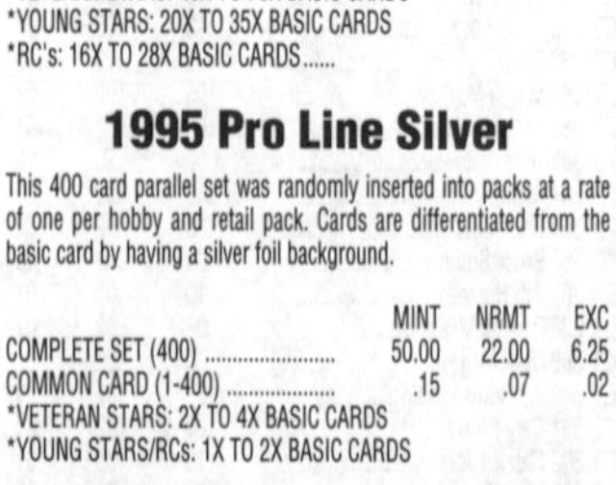

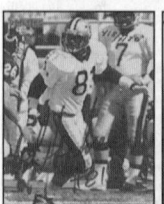

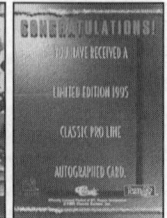

This 128 card standard-size set was inserted into packs. Classic, the producers of the set, guaranteed an autograph card in each box. No player signed more than 2500 cards and many signed fewer. The cards were inserted in either hobby or retail packs and are similar in design to the base Pro Line issue. The backs carry a congratulatory message. The unnumbered cards were assigned card numbers below based upon the base Pro Line set. The tough John Elway card and many of the numbering variation cards are not considered part of the complete set price. Elway signed 50 cards for each major card manufacturer to be inserted in one the company's card brands for 1995.

	MINT	NRMT	EXC
COMPLETE SET (128)	2400.00	1100.00	300.00
COMMON AUTO	8.00	3.60	1.00
☐ 1 Garrison Hearst/1460	20.00	9.00	2.50
☐ 2 Anthony Miller/2385	12.00	5.50	1.50
☐ 5 Mike Fox/1445	8.00	3.60	1.00
☐ 6 Jeff Blake/1200	25.00	11.00	3.10
☐ 7 J.J. Birden/775	12.00	5.50	1.50
☐ 9 Leon Lett/1550	8.00	3.60	1.00
☐ 11 Andre Reed/1440	12.00	5.50	1.50
☐ 13A Craig Heyward/1200	8.00	3.60	1.00
☐ 13B Craig Heyward/265AP	12.00	5.50	1.50
☐ 14 Henry Ellard/1440	12.00	5.50	1.50
☐ 18 Eric Zeier/500	20.00	9.00	2.50
☐ 21 Qadry Ismail/1170	12.00	5.50	1.50
☐ 23 Ty Law/1460	12.00	5.50	1.50
☐ 24 Mark Collins/1430	8.00	3.60	1.00
☐ 29 Mike Mamula/1250	8.00	3.60	1.00
☐ 34 Michael Jackson/1200	12.00	5.50	1.50
☐ 40A Cornelius Bennett/1200	12.00	5.50	1.50
☐ 40B Cornelius Bennett/255AP	12.00	5.50	1.50
☐ 42 Pierce Holt/1440	8.00	3.60	1.00
☐ 44A Chad May/1180	8.00	3.60	1.00
☐ 44B Chad May/2410AP	8.00	3.60	1.00
☐ 45 Darrien Gordon/2400	8.00	3.60	1.00
☐ 48 Al Smith/1360	8.00	3.60	1.00
☐ 49A Chris Slade/1100	8.00	3.60	1.00
☐ 49B Chris Slade/2417AP	8.00	3.60	1.00
☐ 57 Charles Haley/1420	12.00	5.50	1.50
☐ 59 Sean Jones/2385	8.00	3.60	1.00
☐ 60 Tamarick Vanover/1155	30.00	13.50	3.70
☐ 62 Rashaan Salaam/1320	30.00	13.50	3.70
☐ 66 Troy Drayton/1375	8.00	3.60	1.00
☐ 68A Brian Williams/1175	8.00	3.60	1.00
☐ 68B Brian Williams/2670AP	8.00	3.60	1.00
☐ 68C Brian Williams/865AP	8.00	3.60	1.00
☐ 70A Eric Allen/1225	8.00	3.60	1.00
☐ 70B Eric Allen/2398AP	8.00	3.60	1.00
☐ 70C Eric Allen/745AP	8.00	3.60	1.00
☐ 81A Brett Perriman/1380	12.00	5.50	1.50
☐ 81B Brett Perriman/935	12.00	5.50	1.50
☐ 82 Mike Sherrard/1450	8.00	3.60	1.00
☐ 83 Curtis Conway/1200	12.00	5.50	1.50
☐ 86A Randy Baldwin/1435	8.00	3.60	1.00
☐ 86B Randy Baldwin/2405AP	8.00	3.60	1.00
☐ 86C Randy Baldwin/760AP	8.00	3.60	1.00
☐ 88 Chester McGlockton/1280	12.00	5.50	1.50
☐ 97A Craig Erickson/630	12.00	5.50	1.50
☐ 97B Craig Erickson/890AP	8.00	3.60	1.00
☐ 99 Steve McNair/3490	35.00	16.00	4.40
☐ 100 Errict Rhett/1400	30.00	13.50	3.70
☐ 106 Eric Green/1460	8.00	3.60	1.00
☐ 109 Marshall Faulk/1030	60.00	27.00	7.50
☐ 114A Steve Israel/1200	8.00	3.60	1.00
☐ 114B Steve Israel/2413AP	8.00	3.60	1.00
☐ 114C Steve Israel/750AP	8.00	3.60	1.00
☐ 119 Michael Irvin/1490	15.00	6.75	1.85
☐ 126 Byron Bam Morris/1430	12.00	5.50	1.50
☐ 127 Ben Coates/1175	15.00	6.75	1.85
☐ 131 Tony Bennett/1475	8.00	3.60	1.00
☐ 133 Tim Brown/2410	15.00	6.75	1.85
☐ 137 John Elliott/2380	8.00	3.60	1.00
☐ 140 Sherman Williams/1460	8.00	3.60	1.00
☐ 142 R. Cunningham/470	25.00	11.00	3.10
☐ 143 Vinny Testaverde/1020	12.00	5.50	1.50
☐ 145 Russell Maryland/1250	12.00	5.50	1.50
☐ 149 Jeff Graham/1465	12.00	5.50	1.50
☐ 155 Bert Emanuel/1445	12.00	5.50	1.50
☐ 156 Mark Stepnoski/1500	8.00	3.60	1.00
☐ 160 Henry Thomas/1420	8.00	3.60	1.00
☐ 168A Ray Childress/1200	8.00	3.60	1.00
☐ 168B Ray Childress/235AP	8.00	3.60	1.00
☐ 173A Rob Johnson/2815	12.00	5.50	1.50
☐ 173B Rob Johnson/500	12.00	5.50	1.50
☐ 174 Derrick Brooks/1470	8.00	3.60	1.00
☐ 175 Drew Bledsoe/515	100.00	45.00	12.50
☐ 179 Ricky Proehl/1475	8.00	3.60	1.00
☐ 180 Haywood Jeffires/1470	12.00	5.50	1.50
☐ 185 Andy Harmon/1200	8.00	3.60	1.00
☐ 186 Ronnie Lott/1900	15.00	6.75	1.85
☐ 187 Clay Matthews/2385	12.00	5.50	1.50
☐ 193 Herman Moore/2070	15.00	6.75	1.85
☐ 197 Steve Young/500	90.00	40.00	11.00
☐ 198 Roman Phifer/2395	8.00	3.60	1.00
☐ 202 Lewis Tillman/1170	8.00	3.60	1.00
☐ 207 Mario Bates/1480	12.00	5.50	1.50
☐ 210 Kerry Collins/3300	50.00	22.00	6.25
☐ 211A Steve Walsh/1185	12.00	5.50	1.50
☐ 211B Steve Walsh/1015AP	12.00	5.50	1.50
☐ 215 Jim Kelly/470	40.00	18.00	5.00
☐ 217 Jay Novacek/1195	12.00	5.50	1.50
☐ 218A Shawn Jefferson/1200	8.00	3.60	1.00
☐ 218B Shawn Jefferson/240AP	12.00	5.50	1.50
☐ 221A Arthur Marshall/1165	8.00	3.60	1.00
☐ 221B Arthur Marshall/2400AP	8.00	3.60	1.00
☐ 221C Arthur Marshall/870AP	8.00	3.60	1.00
☐ 226 Quentin Coryatt/1400	12.00	5.50	1.50
☐ 228 Brian Blades/1465	12.00	5.50	1.50
☐ 230 Boomer Esiason/1700	12.00	5.50	1.50
☐ 231 Dave Krieg/1470	12.00	5.50	1.50
☐ 234A John Randle/1170	8.00	3.60	1.00
☐ 234B John Randle/2400AP	8.00	3.60	1.00
☐ 234C John Randle/757AP	8.00	3.60	1.00
☐ 238 Cortez Kennedy/1380	12.00	5.50	1.50
☐ 241A Keenan McCardell/1235	12.00	5.50	1.50
☐ 241B Keenan McCardell/2403AP	12.00	5.50	1.50
☐ 243A Don Beebe/1200	12.00	5.50	1.50
☐ 243B Don Beebe/275AP	12.00	5.50	1.50
☐ 244A Jack Del Rio/1480	8.00	3.60	1.00
☐ 244B Jack Del Rio/930AP	8.00	3.60	1.00
☐ 247 Edgar Bennett/1475	12.00	5.50	1.50
☐ 250 Neil Smith/1465	12.00	5.50	1.50
☐ 251 Sam Mills/1470	12.00	5.50	1.50
☐ 252A Willie McGinest/1160	12.00	5.50	1.50
☐ 252B Willie McGinest/2407AP	12.00	5.50	1.50
☐ 252C Willie McGinest/754AP	12.00	5.50	1.50
☐ 254 Troy Aikman/500	100.00	45.00	12.50
☐ 256 Dale Carter/1400	12.00	5.50	1.50
☐ 258 Greg Hill/1455	12.00	5.50	1.50
☐ 262 Trezelle Jenkins/1470	8.00	3.60	1.00
☐ 263A Antonio Langham/1200	8.00	3.60	1.00
☐ 263B Antonio Langham/1200	8.00	3.60	1.00
☐ 265 Jake Reed/1470	12.00	5.50	1.50
☐ 268A Mark McMillian/1175	8.00	3.60	1.00
☐ 268B Mark McMillian/2400AP	8.00	3.60	1.00
☐ 268C Mark McMillian/1175	8.00	3.60	1.00
☐ 269 John Walsh/3340	8.00	3.60	1.00
☐ 270 Irving Fryar/1500	12.00	5.50	1.50
☐ 273 J.J. Stokes/1435	25.00	11.00	3.10
☐ 276A Derrick Deese/1200	8.00	3.60	1.00
☐ 276B Derrick Deese/2375AP	8.00	3.60	1.00
☐ 276C Derrick Deese/735AP	8.00	3.60	1.00
☐ 285 Seth Joyner/1480	8.00	3.60	1.00
☐ 286 Steve Beuerlein/1465	12.00	5.50	1.50
☐ 289 Patrick Hunter/2375	8.00	3.60	1.00
☐ 292A Shaun Gayle/1200	8.00	3.60	1.00
☐ 292B Shaun Gayle/265AP	12.00	5.50	1.50
☐ 294 Terry Kirby/1450	12.00	5.50	1.50
☐ 295 Courtney Hawkins/1445	8.00	3.60	1.00
☐ 297 Luther Ellis/1470	8.00	3.60	1.00
☐ 304 Emmitt Smith/500	200.00	90.00	25.00
☐ 305 Clyde Simmons/735	12.00	5.50	1.50
☐ 307 Rodney Hampton/1120	12.00	5.50	1.50
☐ 308 Steve Emtman/2365	8.00	3.60	1.00
☐ 311A Trent Dilfer/2010	15.00	6.75	1.85
☐ 311B Trent Dilfer/306AP	15.00	6.75	1.85
☐ 312 Flipper Anderson/1140	8.00	3.60	1.00
☐ 313A Heath Shuler/2000	15.00	6.75	1.85
☐ 313B Heath Shuler/366AP	25.00	11.00	3.10
☐ 320A Willie Roaf/1200	12.00	5.50	1.50
☐ 320B Willie Roaf/245AP	12.00	5.50	1.50
☐ 329 Calvin Williams/1200	12.00	5.50	1.50
☐ 331A Blake Brockermeyer/1445	8.00	3.60	1.00
☐ 331B Bla.Brockermeyer/2315AP	8.00	3.60	1.00
☐ 337 Terry McDaniel/2340	8.00	3.60	1.00
☐ 341 Jeff George/1295	12.00	5.50	1.50
☐ 345A Jessie Tuggle/1200	8.00	3.60	1.00
☐ 345B Jessie Tuggle/195AP	12.00	5.50	1.50
☐ 348 Jack Jackson/1475	8.00	3.60	1.00
☐ 352 Quinn Early/1200	12.00	5.50	1.50
☐ 356 Natrone Means/1058	15.00	6.75	1.85
☐ 359 Michael Haynes/1180	12.00	5.50	1.50
☐ 361 Troy Vincent/1490	8.00	3.60	1.00
☐ 366 Barry Foster/1455	12.00	5.50	1.50
☐ 367A Michael D. Perry/1200	12.00	5.50	1.50
☐ 367B Michael Dean Perry/295AP	12.00	5.50	1.50
☐ 374 Tony McGee/1385	12.00	5.50	1.50
☐ 379 Willie Davis/1500	12.00	5.50	1.50
☐ 383 Joey Galloway/1445	40.00	18.00	5.00
☐ 390 Bill Romanowski/1450	8.00	3.60	1.00

1995 Pro Line Autograph Printer's Proofs

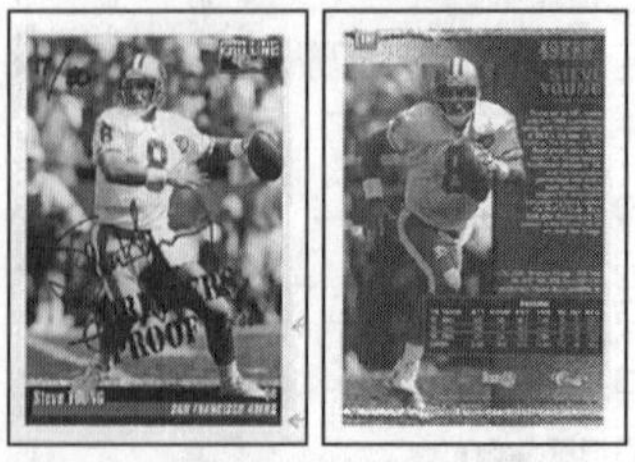

Eight players signed 50-each of their 1995 Pro Line Printer's Proof cards which were randomly inserted into packs. Each signed card was numbered of 50 signed and contains the Classic corporate seal. Reportedly, approximately 80% of the 400 total autographs were inserted into 1995 Pro Line Hot Box packs. The signed cards are virtually identical to the Printer's Proof version, on both front and back, except that the UV coating was left off so that the autograph would adhere to the card.

	MINT	NRMT	EXC
COMPLETE SET (8)	3000.00	1350.00	375.00
COMMON CARD (230/311)	200.00	90.00	25.00
☐ 99 Steve McNair	300.00	135.00	38.00
☐ 175 Drew Bledsoe	500.00	220.00	60.00
☐ 197 Steve Young	400.00	180.00	50.00
☐ 210 Kerry Collins	400.00	180.00	50.00
☐ 230 Boomer Esiason	200.00	90.00	25.00
☐ 254 Troy Aikman	500.00	220.00	60.00
☐ 304 Emmitt Smith	800.00	350.00	100.00
☐ 311 Trent Dilfer	250.00	110.00	31.00

1995 Pro Line Bonus Card Jumbos

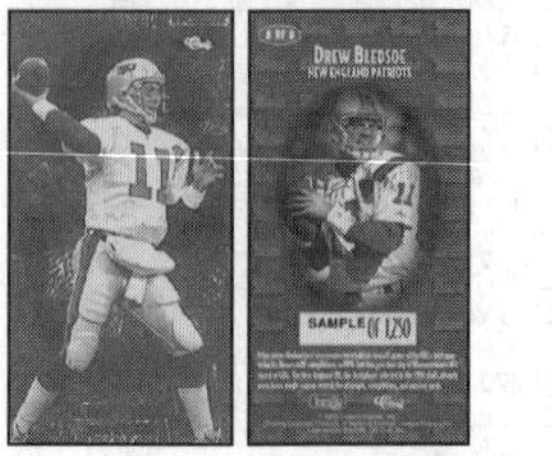

This 14 card jumbo-sized (2 1/2" by 4 3/4") set was distributed in four different modes. The first three cards, featuring top picks, were issued one per Classic NFL Rookies Hobby case. Cards 4-8 were issued one per ProLine Series 1 Hobby case. Cards 9-11 were issued one per ProLine Series 2 Hobby case. Cards 13-15 were issued one per 1996 Classic NFL Experience case. Card number 12 was never issued. There was 1,250 of each card made for cards 1-11. The fronts feature a full-color action photo with the player's name and position at the bottom. The background is silver and has the team's name or logo on it numerous times and the middle has a multi-color cloudiness to it. The backs have a small player photo in the middle with his name above it and information below or beside it. The background is gray, tan or green with the team's name or logo shown many times. Cards 13-15 have a colorful foil background with the player's name in gold script. Card backs contain an action shot of the player with information underneath.

	MINT	NRMT	EXC
COMPLETE SET (14)	100.00	45.00	12.50
COMMON CARD (1-15)	3.00	1.35	.35
☐ 1 Ki-Jana Carter	3.00	1.35	.35
☐ 2 Steve McNair	10.00	4.50	1.25
☐ 3 Kerry Collins	12.00	5.50	1.50
☐ 4 Deion Sanders	6.00	2.70	.75
☐ 5 Steve Young	8.00	3.60	1.00
☐ 6 Emmitt Smith	25.00	11.00	3.10
☐ 7 Natrone Means	4.00	1.80	.50
☐ 8 Drew Bledsoe	10.00	4.50	1.25
☐ 9 Troy Aikman	10.00	4.50	1.25
☐ 10 Marshall Faulk	4.00	1.80	.50
☐ 11 J.J.Stokes	4.00	1.80	.50
☐ 13 Emmitt Smith	20.00	9.00	2.50
☐ 14 Rashaan Salaam	4.00	1.80	.50
☐ 15 Reggie White	4.00	1.80	.50

1995 Pro Line Field Generals

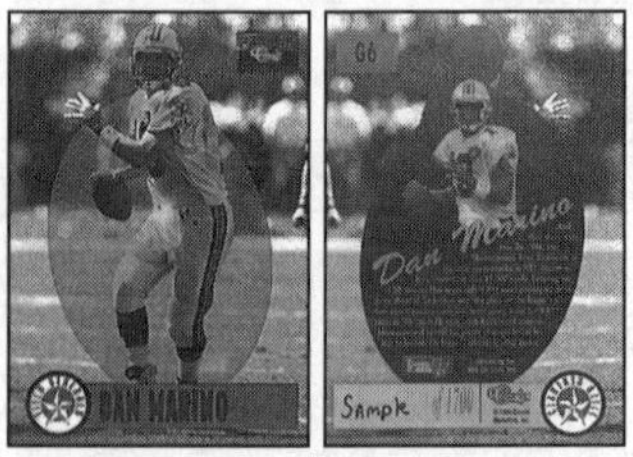

Inserted at a rate of one in 60 Series 2 packs, this 10 card set features a clear plastic stock in the background. Card fronts contain a shot of the player with his name and the "Field General" logo at the bottom of the card. Card backs contain a small shot of the player with a brief statistical summary. Cards are numbered out of 1,700 and have a "G" prefix.

	MINT	NRMT	EXC
COMPLETE SET (10)	300.00	135.00	38.00
COMMON CARD (G1-G10)	12.00	5.50	1.50
☐ G1 Marshall Faulk	15.00	6.75	1.85
☐ G2 Emmitt Smith	50.00	22.00	6.25
☐ G3 Steve Young	20.00	9.00	2.50
☐ G4 Ki-Jana Carter	12.00	5.50	1.50
☐ G5 Rashaan Salaam	12.00	5.50	1.50
☐ G6 Dan Marino	50.00	22.00	6.25
☐ G7 J.J. Stokes	12.00	5.50	1.50
☐ G8 Drew Bledsoe	25.00	11.00	3.10
☐ G9 Brett Favre	50.00	22.00	6.25
☐ G10 Barry Sanders	25.00	11.00	3.10

1995 Pro Line Game of the Week

This 60 card set was randomly inserted one per special retail packs and features a match-up of teams for different weeks of the season. Cards either contain a "H" or "V" prefix on the back to denote home or visitor. The first 1,000 participants who submitted 21-30 different game cards with the actual winner of the game received the first prize, which was a complete set of 30 NFL Pro Line winning cards printed on silver foil board with the final score of the game foil stamped on the card. The first 2,500 participants who submitted 10-20 different

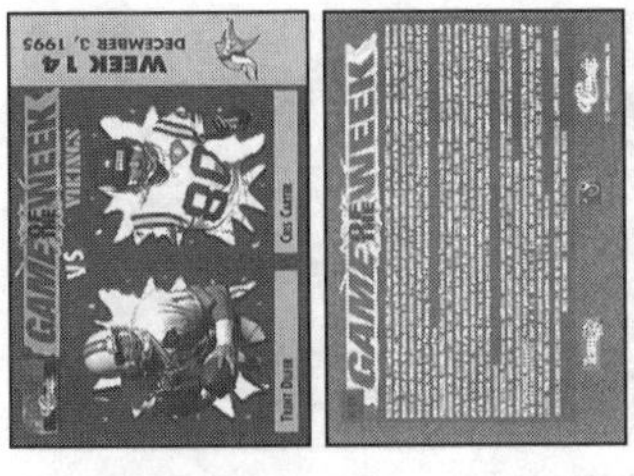

game cards with the actual winner of the game received the second prize, which was a complete set of 30 NFL Pro Line winning cards with the final score of the game foil stamped on the card. Each participant who sent in all 30 winning cards were eligble for the grand prize drawing, which was either a Steve Young or Jerry Rice game-used jersey from the 1995 season. The redemption cards expired on 3/10/96.

	MINT	NRMT	EXC
COMPLETE SET (60)	25.00	11.00	3.10
COMMON CARD (1-30)	.40	.18	.05

☐ 1 Barry Sanders Reggie White	1.50	.70	.19
☐ 2 Jeff Hostetler John Elway	1.00	.45	.12
☐ 3 Michael Westbrook Ricky Watters	.75	.35	.09
☐ 4 Jim Kelly Mo Lewis	.75	.35	.09
☐ 5 Marshall Faulk Jerome Bettis	.75	.35	.09
☐ 6 Natrone Means Byron Bam Morris	.75	.35	.09
☐ 7 Seth Joyner Michael Irvin	.75	.35	.09
☐ 8 Errict Rhett Heath Shuler	.75	.35	.09
☐ 9 Junior Seau Randall Cunningham	.60	.25	.07
☐ 10 Drew Bledsoe Steve Young	1.50	.70	.19
☐ 11 Dave Krieg Kerry Collins	1.50	.70	.19
☐ 12 Steve Beuerlein Alvin Harper	.40	.18	.05
☐ 13 Ben Coates Troy Vincent	.40	.18	.05
☐ 14 Jerry Rice Michael Irvin	1.50	.70	.19
☐ 15 Rodney Hampton Cortez Kennedy	.60	.25	.07
☐ 16 Ray Childress Leroy Hoard	.40	.18	.05
☐ 17 Thurman Thomas Irving Fryar	.75	.35	.09
☐ 18 Andre Rison Ki-Jana Carter	.60	.25	.07
☐ 19 Dan Marino Boomer Esiason	2.00	.90	.25
☐ 20 Brett Favre Warren Moon	2.00	.90	.25
☐ 21 Anthony Miller Tim Brown	.60	.25	.07
☐ 22 Chris Warren Steve Bono	.60	.25	.07
☐ 23 Shannon Sharpe Neil Smith	.40	.18	.05
☐ 24 John Randle Dana Stubblefield	.40	.18	.05
☐ 25 Jim Everett Terance Mathis	.40	.18	.05
☐ 26 Troy Aikman Mike Mamula	1.50	.70	.19
☐ 27 Trent Dilfer Cris Carter	.60	.25	.07
☐ 28 Steve Walsh Scott Mitchell	.40	.18	.05
☐ 29 Greg Lloyd Vinny Testaverde	.60	.25	.07
☐ 30 Jeff George Garrison Hearst	.75	.35	.09

1995 Pro Line GameBreakers

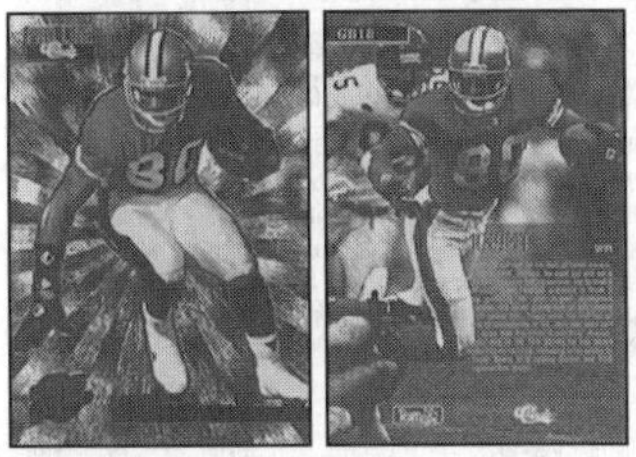

This 30-card standard-size set was randomly inserted into both retail and hobby packs. They were inserted at a ratio of one card per box. The fronts feature an action photo against a metallic background. The title "GameBreakers" as well as the player's name is located at the bottom. The backs have a full-bleed photo and player information. 175 Printer's proofs of each card were also produced and randomly inserted at a rate of one per case. Card backs are numbered with a "GB" prefix.

	MINT	NRMT	EXC
COMPLETE SET (30)	125.00	55.00	15.50
COMMON CARD (GB1-GB30)	1.50	.70	.19
COMP. GB PR.PROOF (30)	500.00	220.00	60.00

*GB PRINTER'S PROOFS: 1.5X TO 3X BASIC CARDS

☐ GB1 Troy Aikman	10.00	4.50	1.25
☐ GB2 Drew Bledsoe	10.00	4.50	1.25
☐ GB3 Tim Brown	1.50	.70	.19
☐ GB4 Cris Carter	1.50	.70	.19
☐ GB5 Ki-Jana Carter	2.50	1.10	.30
☐ GB6 Kerry Collins	10.00	4.50	1.25
☐ GB7 John Elway	8.00	3.60	1.00
☐ GB8 Marshall Faulk	5.00	2.20	.60
☐ GB9 Brett Favre	20.00	9.00	2.50
☐ GB10 Garrison Hearst	2.50	1.10	.30
☐ GB11 Michael Irvin	2.50	1.10	.30
☐ GB12 Jim Kelly	2.50	1.10	.30
☐ GB13 Dan Marino	20.00	9.00	2.50
☐ GB14 Natrone Means	1.50	.70	.19
☐ GB15 Eric Metcalf	1.50	.70	.19
☐ GB16 J.J. Stokes	2.50	1.10	.30
☐ GB17 Carl Pickens	1.50	.70	.19
☐ GB18 Jerry Rice	10.00	4.50	1.25
☐ GB19 Andre Rison	1.50	.70	.19
☐ GB20 Barry Sanders	10.00	4.50	1.25
☐ GB21 Deion Sanders	6.00	2.70	.75
☐ GB22 Junior Seau	1.50	.70	.19
☐ GB23 Emmitt Smith	20.00	9.00	2.50
☐ GB24 Thurman Thomas	2.50	1.10	.30
☐ GB25 Ricky Watters	1.50	.70	.19
☐ GB26 Reggie White	2.50	1.10	.30
☐ GB27 Rod Woodson	1.50	.70	.19
☐ GB28 Steve Young	8.00	3.60	1.00
☐ GB29 Rashaan Salaam	3.00	1.35	.35
☐ GB30 Michael Westbrook	2.50	1.10	.30

1995 Pro Line Grand Gainers

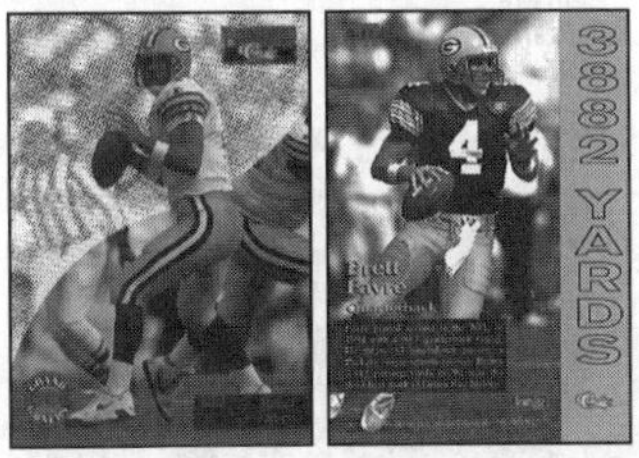

Inserted in retail packs at a rate of one per pack, this 30 card set features a white mesh card front on one half, with game action in the background on the other half. The player's name and position are located in the bottom right corner. Card backs include a particular statistic on the right side of the card with a brief commentary. Cards are numbered with a "G" prefix.

	MINT	NRMT	EXC
COMPLETE SET (30)	25.00	11.00	3.10
COMMON CARD (G1-G30)	.40	.18	.05

☐ G1 Barry Sanders	2.00	.90	.25
☐ G2 Emmitt Smith	4.00	1.80	.50
☐ G3 Natrone Means	1.00	.45	.12
☐ G4 Marshall Faulk	1.00	.45	.12
☐ G5 Errict Rhett	1.00	.45	.12
☐ G6 Jerry Rice	2.00	.90	.25
☐ G7 Tim Brown	.60	.25	.07
☐ G8 Cris Carter	.60	.25	.07
☐ G9 Irving Fryar	.40	.18	.05
☐ G10 Ben Coates	.40	.18	.05
☐ G11 Fred Barnett	.40	.18	.05
☐ G12 Andre Rison	.60	.25	.07
☐ G13 Drew Bledsoe	2.00	.90	.25
☐ G14 Dan Marino	4.00	1.80	.50
☐ G15 Warren Moon	.60	.25	.07
☐ G16 Steve Young	1.50	.70	.19
☐ G17 Brett Favre	4.00	1.80	.50
☐ G18 John Elway	1.50	.70	.19
☐ G19 Randall Cunningham	.40	.18	.05
☐ G20 Stan Humphries	.40	.18	.05
☐ G21 Jim Kelly	1.00	.45	.12
☐ G22 Ki-Jana Carter	.60	.25	.07
☐ G23 Rodney Hampton	.60	.25	.07
☐ G24 Tyrone Wheatley	.60	.25	.07
☐ G25 J.J. Stokes	1.00	.45	.12
☐ G26 Michael Irvin	1.00	.45	.12
☐ G27 Herman Moore	1.00	.45	.12
☐ G28 Kerry Collins	2.50	1.10	.30
☐ G29 Steve McNair	2.00	.90	.25
☐ G30 Rob Johnson	.60	.25	.07

1995 Pro Line Images Previews

Randomly inserted into Series 2 packs at a rate of one in 18 packs, this set previewed the 1995 Images release.

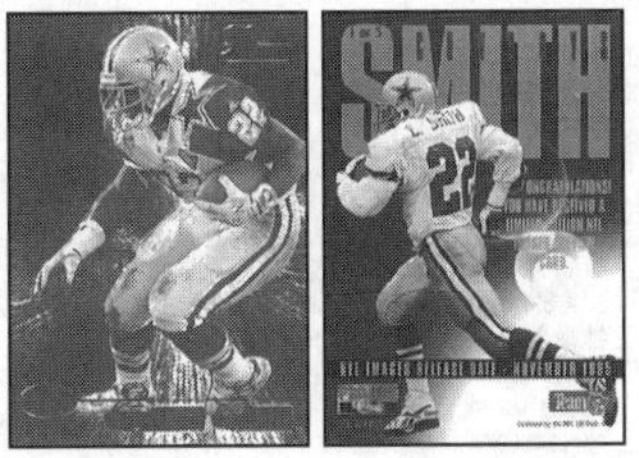

	MINT	NRMT	EXC
COMPLETE SET (5)	25.00	11.00	3.10
COMMON CARD (1-5)	3.00	1.35	.35

☐ 1 Emmitt Smith	10.00	4.50	1.25
☐ 2 Steve Young	4.00	1.80	.50
☐ 3 Drew Bledsoe	4.00	1.80	.50
☐ 4 Kerry Collins	8.00	3.60	1.00
☐ 5 Marshall Faulk	3.00	1.35	.35

1995 Pro Line Impact

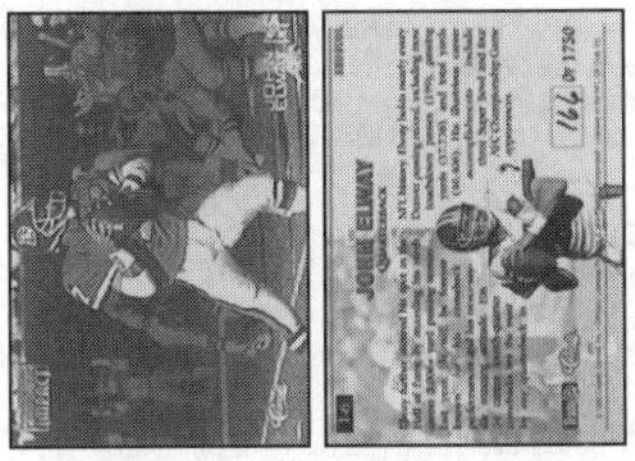

Sequentially numbered out of 4,500, these 30 standard-size cards were randomly inserted into retail packs. These cards were available at a rate of one per box. Horizontally designed, the card fronts feature a full-bleed metallic finish. The player stands out from the rest of the photo which is lightly shaded. The backs present career highlights, a small photo and are numbered with an "I" prefix. A gold parallel set, numbered out of 1,750, was also produced and randomly inserted at a rate of one in 90 retail packs.

	MINT	NRMT	EXC
COMPLETE SET (30)	125.00	55.00	15.50
COMMON CARD (1-30)	2.00	.90	.25
COMPLETE GOLD SET (30)	300.00	135.00	38.00

*GOLD CARDS: 1X TO 2X BASIC CARDS

☐ 1 Jim Kelly	3.50	1.55	.45
☐ 2 Thurman Thomas	3.50	1.55	.45
☐ 3 Troy Aikman	10.00	4.50	1.25
☐ 4 Michael Irvin	3.50	1.55	.45
☐ 5 Emmitt Smith	20.00	9.00	2.50
☐ 6 John Elway	8.00	3.60	1.00
☐ 7 Barry Sanders	10.00	4.50	1.25
☐ 8 Brett Favre	20.00	9.00	2.50
☐ 9 Reggie White	3.50	1.55	.45
☐ 10 Marshall Faulk	4.00	1.80	.50
☐ 11 Ki-Jana Carter	3.50	1.55	.45
☐ 12 Tim Brown	3.00	1.35	.35
☐ 13 Jeff Hostetler	2.00	.90	.25
☐ 14 Dan Marino	20.00	9.00	2.50
☐ 15 Drew Bledsoe	10.00	4.50	1.25
☐ 16 Ben Coates	2.00	.90	.25
☐ 17 Rodney Hampton	3.00	1.35	.35
☐ 18 Randall Cunningham	2.00	.90	.25
☐ 19 Ricky Watters	3.00	1.35	.35
☐ 20 Byron Bam Morris	3.00	1.35	.35
☐ 21 Natrone Means	3.00	1.35	.35
☐ 22 Junior Seau	3.00	1.35	.35
☐ 23 Jerry Rice	10.00	4.50	1.25
☐ 24 Steve Young	8.00	3.60	1.00
☐ 25 William Floyd	3.50	1.55	.45
☐ 26 Rick Mirer	3.50	1.55	.45
☐ 27 Chris Warren	3.00	1.35	.35
☐ 28 Jerome Bettis	3.50	1.55	.45
☐ 29 Alvin Harper	2.00	.90	.25
☐ 30 Heath Shuler	3.50	1.55	.45

1995 Pro Line MVP Redemption

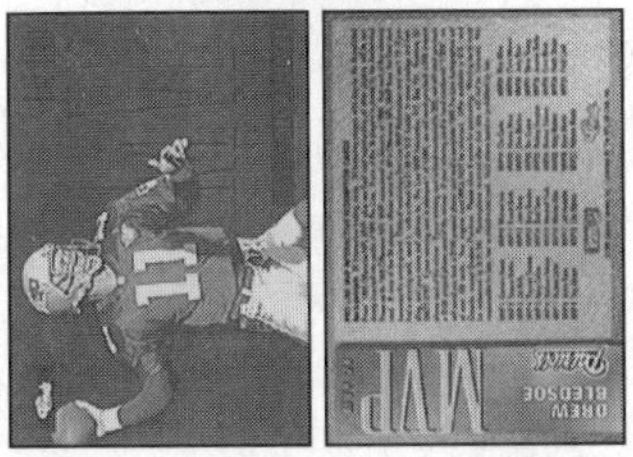

This 35-card horizontal standard-size set was randomly inserted into packs. These cards were inserted one every two boxes (Hobby or Retail). Thirty-four players as well as one field card was issued. If the player featured on the card won the 1995 Associated Press Offensive MVP award, the following prizes were issued. If the card was stamped one of 4,000 the bearer received a prepaid $50 phone card of that player. For a card hand-numbered to 200, the owner received a $100 prepaid phone card of that player. If a collector had the #1 card that was hand-numbered, he would receive not only the $100 prepaid phone card but also a complete 1995 Pro Line Live Autographed set. The redemption expiration date was 3/31/96.

	MINT	NRMT	EXC
COMPLETE SET (35)	200.00	90.00	25.00
COMMON CARD (1-35)	3.00	1.35	.35

*NUMBERED OF 200: 1.5X to 4X BASIC CARDS

☐ 1 Garrison Hearst	5.00	2.20	.60
☐ 2 Terance Mathis	3.00	1.35	.35
☐ 3 Jim Kelly	5.00	2.20	.60
☐ 4 Thurman Thomas	5.00	2.20	.60
☐ 5 Kerry Collins	12.00	5.50	1.50
☐ 6 Rashaan Salaam	5.00	2.20	.60
☐ 7 Ki-Jana Carter	5.00	2.20	.60
☐ 8 Andre Rison	3.00	1.35	.35
☐ 9 Troy Aikman	12.00	5.50	1.50
☐ 10 Michael Irvin	5.00	2.20	.60
☐ 11 Emmitt Smith	25.00	11.00	3.10
☐ 12 John Elway	10.00	4.50	1.25
☐ 13 Barry Sanders	12.00	5.50	1.50
☐ 14 Brett Favre	25.00	11.00	3.10
☐ 15 Marshall Faulk	6.00	2.70	.75
☐ 16 Marcus Allen	5.00	2.20	.60
☐ 17 Jeff Hostetler	3.00	1.35	.35
☐ 18 Dan Marino	25.00	11.00	3.10
☐ 19 Cris Carter	3.00	1.35	.35
☐ 20 Warren Moon	3.00	1.35	.35
☐ 21 Drew Bledsoe	12.00	5.50	1.50
☐ 22 Ben Coates	3.00	1.35	.35
☐ 23 Rodney Hampton	3.00	1.35	.35
☐ 24 Boomer Esiason	3.00	1.35	.35
☐ 25 Ricky Watters	3.00	1.35	.35
☐ 26 Barry Foster	3.00	1.35	.35
☐ 27 Natrone Means	3.00	1.35	.35
☐ 28 Rick Mirer	5.00	2.20	.60
☐ 29 Chris Warren	3.00	1.35	.35
☐ 30 Jerry Rice	12.00	5.50	1.50
☐ 31 Steve Young	10.00	4.50	1.25
☐ 32 Jerome Bettis	5.00	2.20	.60
☐ 33 Errict Rhett	5.00	2.20	.60
☐ 34 Heath Shuler	5.00	2.20	.60
☐ 35 Field Card	3.00	1.35	.35

1995 Pro Line National Attention

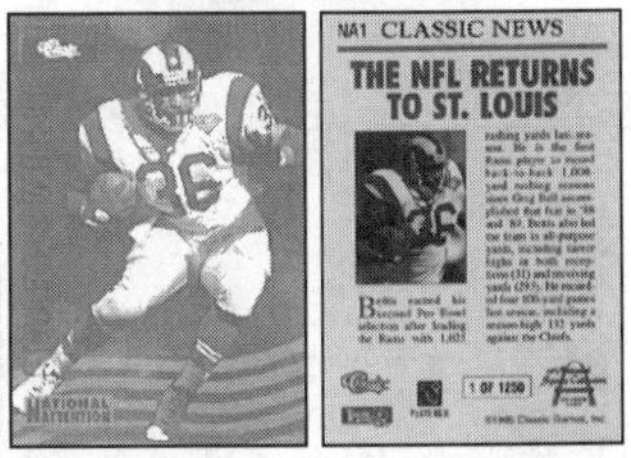

This 10 card set was inserted in 1995 ProLine National boxes that were only available to dealers who participated in the National Sports Collectors Convention show held in St. Louis, MO. Due to the relocation of the NFL Rams franchise to St. Louis, this set contains several players from the 1995 Rams team, as well as other major stars. Reportedly, 1250 of each card were produced.

	MINT	NRMT	EXC
COMPLETE SET (10)	60.00	27.00	7.50
COMMON CARD (NA1-NA10)	4.00	1.80	.50

☐ NA1 Jerome Bettis	6.00	2.70	.75
☐ NA2 Sean Gilbert	4.00	1.80	.50
☐ NA3 Chris Miller	4.00	1.80	.50
☐ NA4 Troy Aikman	10.00	4.50	1.25
☐ NA5 Kevin Carter	4.00	1.80	.50
☐ NA6 Marshall Faulk	6.00	2.70	.75
☐ NA7 Drew Bledsoe	10.00	4.50	1.25
☐ NA8 Shane Conlan	4.00	1.80	.50
☐ NA9 Emmitt Smith	20.00	9.00	2.50
☐ NA10 Steve Young	8.00	3.60	1.00

1995 Pro Line Phone Cards 1.00

Randomly inserted at a rate of at least one per series 2 pack (unless another denomination was pulled), this 30 card set is phone card sized with a full bleed shot of the player on the front. Information about using the phone card is contained on the back. The phone time expiration date is 12/31/96. A parallel Printer's Proof set was also randomly inserted at a rate of one in 44 packs.

	MINT	NRMT	EXC
COMPLETE SET (30)	16.00	7.25	2.00
COMMON CARD (1-30)	.40	.18	.05
COMP.PRINT.PROOF SET (30)	80.00	36.00	10.00

*PRINTER'S PROOFS: 2.5X TO 5X BASIC CARDS

☐ 1 Kerry Collins	1.50	.70	.19
☐ 2 Barry Foster	.40	.18	.05

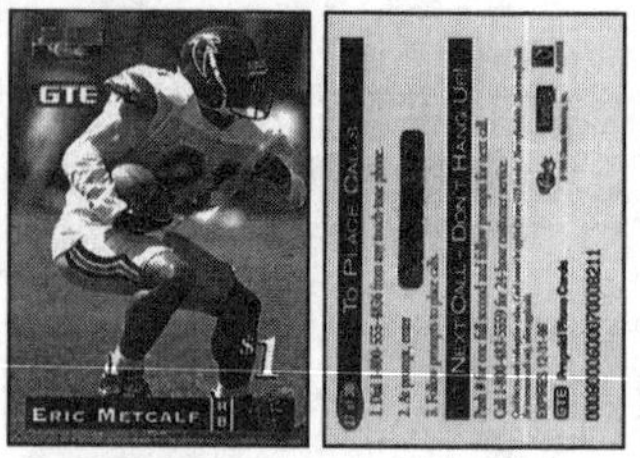

	MINT	NRMT	EXC
☐ 3 Jeff Blake	.75	.35	.09
☐ 4 Troy Aikman	1.50	.70	.19
☐ 5 Reggie White	.60	.25	.07
☐ 6 Marshall Faulk	.75	.35	.09
☐ 7 Steve Bono	.40	.18	.05
☐ 8 Drew Bledsoe	1.50	.70	.19
☐ 9 Byron Bam Morris	.40	.18	.05
☐ 10 Rodney Hampton	.40	.18	.05
☐ 11 Trent Dilfer	.60	.25	.07
☐ 12 Errict Rhett	.75	.35	.09
☐ 13 Heath Shuler	.75	.35	.09
☐ 14 Mike Mamula	.40	.18	.05
☐ 15 Ricky Watters	.40	.18	.05
☐ 16 Stan Humphries	.40	.18	.05
☐ 17 Natrone Means	.60	.25	.07
☐ 18 William Floyd	.40	.18	.05
☐ 19 Joey Galloway	.75	.35	.09
☐ 20 Ki-Jana Carter	.60	.25	.07
☐ 21 Andre Rison	.60	.25	.07
☐ 22 Steve McNair	1.25	.55	.16
☐ 23 Napoleon Kaufman	.60	.25	.07
☐ 24 Kyle Brady	.40	.18	.05
☐ 25 Steve Beuerlein	.40	.18	.05
☐ 26 Ben Coates	.40	.18	.05
☐ 27 Eric Metcalf	.40	.18	.05
☐ 28 Desmond Howard	.40	.18	.05
☐ 29 Deion Sanders	.75	.35	.09
☐ 30 J.J. Stokes	.75	.35	.09

1995 Pro Line Phone Cards 2.00

Randomly inserted at a rate of one in six Series 2 packs, this 25 card set is phone card sized with a full bleed shot of the player on the front. Information about using the phone card is contained on the back. The phone time expiration date is 12/31/96. A parallel Printer's Proof set was also randomly inserted at a rate of one in 75 packs.

	MINT	NRMT	EXC
COMPLETE SET (25)	25.00	11.00	3.10
COMMON CARD (1-25)	.75	.35	.09
COMP.PRINT.PROOF SET (25)	100.00	45.00	12.50
*PRINTER'S PROOFS: 2X TO 4X BASIC CARDS			
☐ 1 Kerry Collins	3.00	1.35	.35
☐ 2 Barry Foster	.75	.35	.09
☐ 3 Andre Rison	.75	.35	.09
☐ 4 Troy Aikman	3.00	1.35	.35
☐ 5 Steve McNair	2.50	1.10	.30
☐ 6 Marshall Faulk	1.25	.55	.16
☐ 7 J.J. Stokes	.75	.35	.09
☐ 8 Drew Bledsoe	3.00	1.35	.35
☐ 9 Byron Bam Morris	1.25	.55	.16
☐ 10 Rodney Hampton	.75	.35	.09
☐ 11 Deion Sanders	1.50	.70	.19
☐ 12 Errict Rhett	1.25	.55	.16
☐ 13 Heath Shuler	1.25	.55	.16
☐ 14 Mike Mamula	.75	.35	.09
☐ 15 Ricky Watters	.75	.35	.09
☐ 16 Stan Humphries	.75	.35	.09
☐ 17 Natrone Means	1.25	.55	.16
☐ 18 William Floyd	.75	.35	.09
☐ 19 Kyle Brady	.75	.35	.09
☐ 20 Ki-Jana Carter	1.25	.55	.16
☐ 21 Jeff Blake	1.25	.55	.16
☐ 22 Eric Metcalf	.75	.35	.09
☐ 23 Steve Bono	.75	.35	.09
☐ 24 Steve Beuerlein	.75	.35	.09
☐ 25 Eric Green	.75	.35	.09

1995 Pro Line Phone Cards 5.00

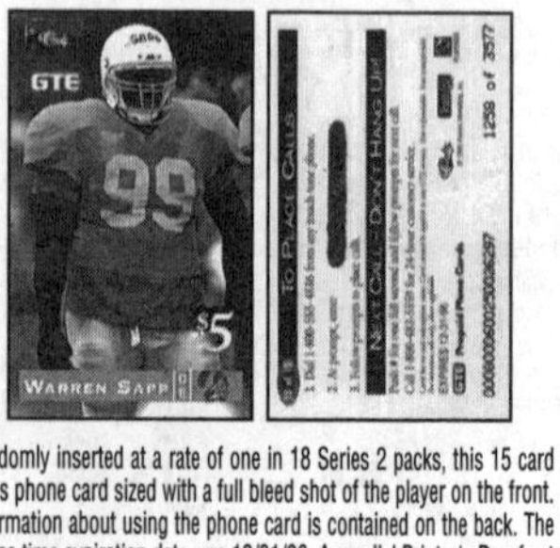

Randomly inserted at a rate of one in 18 Series 2 packs, this 15 card set is phone card sized with a full bleed shot of the player on the front. Information about using the phone card is contained on the back. The phone time expiration date was 12/31/96. A parallel Printer's Proof set was also randomly inserted at a rate of one in 210 packs.

	MINT	NRMT	EXC
COMPLETE SET (15)	50.00	22.00	6.25
COMMON CARD (1-15)	2.00	.90	.25
COMP.PRINT.PROOF SET (15)	200.00	90.00	25.00
*PRINTER'S PROOFS: 2X TO 4X BASIC CARDS			
☐ 1 Marshall Faulk	3.00	1.35	.35
☐ 2 Troy Aikman	6.00	2.70	.75
☐ 3 J.J. Stokes	3.00	1.35	.35
☐ 4 Kyle Brady	2.00	.90	.25
☐ 5 Steve McNair	5.00	2.20	.60
☐ 6 Deion Sanders	3.50	1.55	.45
☐ 7 Ki-Jana Carter	3.00	1.35	.35
☐ 8 Kerry Collins	6.00	2.70	.75
☐ 9 Drew Bledsoe	6.00	2.70	.75
☐ 10 Emmitt Smith	12.00	5.50	1.50
☐ 11 William Floyd	2.00	.90	.25
☐ 12 Ricky Watters	2.00	.90	.25
☐ 13 Reggie White	3.00	1.35	.35
☐ 14 Steve Young	5.00	2.20	.60
☐ 15 Warren Sapp	2.00	.90	.25

1995 Pro Line Phone Cards 20.00

Randomly inserted at a rate of one in 144 Series 2 packs, this 5 card set is phone card sized with a full bleed shot of the player on the front. Information about using the phone card is contained on the back. The phone time expiration date is 12/31/96.

	MINT	NRMT	EXC
COMPLETE SET (5)	80.00	36.00	10.00
COMMON CARD (1-5)	12.00	5.50	1.50
☐ 1 Steve Young	20.00	9.00	2.50
☐ 2 Drew Bledsoe	25.00	11.00	3.10
☐ 3 Marshall Faulk	15.00	6.75	1.85
☐ 4 Ki-Jana Carter	12.00	5.50	1.50
☐ 5 Kerry Collins	25.00	11.00	3.10

1995 Pro Line Phone Cards 100.00

Randomly inserted at a rate of one in 266 Series 2 packs, this 5 card set is phone card sized with a full bleed shot of the player on the front. Information about using the phone card is contained on the back. The phone time expiration date is 12/31/96.

	MINT	NRMT	EXC
COMPLETE SET (5)	350.00	160.00	45.00
COMMON CARD (1-5)	50.00	22.00	6.25
☐ 1 Emmitt Smith	125.00	55.00	15.50
☐ 2 Steve Young	60.00	27.00	7.50
☐ 3 Drew Bledsoe	75.00	34.00	9.50
☐ 4 Ki-Jana Carter	110.00	50.00	14.00
☐ 5 Troy Aikman	75.00	34.00	9.50

1995 Pro Line Phone Cards 1000.00/1500.00

Randomly inserted at a rate of one in 2,995 Series 2 packs for the $1000 cards and one in 11,980 for the $1500 card, this 5 card set is phone card sized with a full bleed shot of the player on the front. The Emmitt Smith is the only card that has a $1500 denomination and is not included in the complete set price. Information about using the phone card is contained on the back. The phone time expiration date was 12/31/96.

	MINT	NRMT	EXC
COMPLETE SET 1000 (4)	2200.00	1000.00	275.00
COMMON CARD 1000 (1-4)	400.00	180.00	50.00
☐ 1 Steve Young	600.00	275.00	75.00
☐ 1B Emmitt Smith/$1500	1200.00	550.00	150.00
☐ 2 Drew Bledsoe	600.00	275.00	75.00
☐ 3 Ki-Jana Carter	400.00	180.00	50.00
☐ 4 Troy Aikman	700.00	325.00	90.00

1995 Pro Line Pogs

Randomly inserted in retail packs, this 30-card set contains a dual player Pogs. Card fronts contain action shots with the two Pogs in the middle. Card backs are brown with each player's name on their Pog and some brief statistical summary below. Cards are numbered with a "C" prefix.

	MINT	NRMT	EXC
COMPLETE SET (30)	7.00	3.10	.85
COMMON CARD (C1-C30)	.20	.09	.03
☐ C1 Steve Walsh Rashaan Salaam	.40	.18	.05
☐ C2 Kerry Collins Barry Foster	.60	.25	.07
☐ C3 Jim Kelly Thurman Thomas	.40	.18	.05
☐ C4 Terance Mathis Jeff George	.20	.09	.03
☐ C5 Garrison Hearst Seth Joyner	.30	.14	.04
☐ C6 Barry Sanders Herman Moore	.60	.25	.07
☐ C7 John Elway Shannon Sharpe	.50	.23	.06
☐ C8 Troy Aikman Emmitt Smith	1.25	.55	.16
☐ C9 Leroy Hoard Andre Rison	.20	.09	.03
☐ C10 Jeff Blake Ki-Jana Carter	.30	.14	.04
☐ C11 Marcus Allen Steve Bono	.40	.18	.05
☐ C12 Tony Boselli Steve Beuerlein	.20	.09	.03
☐ C13 Marshall Faulk Quentin Coryatt	.40	.18	.05
☐ C14 Steve McNair Gary Brown	.40	.18	.05
☐ C15 Brett Favre Reggie White	1.00	.45	.12
☐ C16 Jim Everett Mario Bates	.20	.09	.03
☐ C17 Drew Bledsoe Ben Coates	.60	.25	.07
☐ C18 Warren Moon Chris Carter	.30	.14	.04
☐ C19 Dan Marino Irving Fryar	1.00	.45	.12
☐ C20 Jeff Hostetler Tim Brown	.30	.14	.04
☐ C21 Kevin Greene Byron Bam Morris	.20	.09	.03
☐ C22 Dave Brown Rodney Hampton	.30	.14	.04
☐ C23 Boomer Esiason Mo Lewis	.20	.09	.03
☐ C24 Randall Cunningham Ricky Watters	.30	.14	.04
☐ C25 Natrone Means Junior Seau	.30	.14	.04
☐ C26 Heath Shuler Michael Westbrook	.40	.18	.05
☐ C27 Trent Dilfer Errict Rhett	.40	.18	.05
☐ C28 Jerome Bettis Kevin Carter	.40	.18	.05
☐ C29 Steve Young Jerry Rice	.60	.25	.07
☐ C30 Rick Mirer Chris Warren	.30	.14	.04

1995 Pro Line Precision Cuts

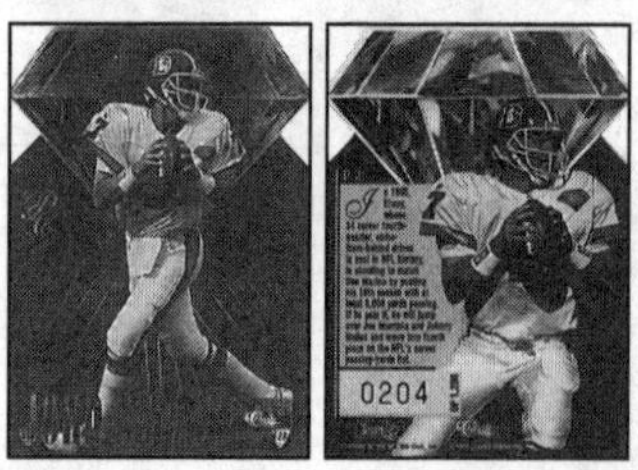

Inserted at a rate of one in 45 packs, this 20 card set was randomly inserted into Series 2 packs. Card fronts contain a blue background with a diamond-shape die cut design at the top. Card backs contain a shot of the player with a brief commentary. Card backs are numbered with a "P" prefix.

	MINT	NRMT	EXC
COMPLETE SET (20)	400.00	180.00	50.00
COMMON CARD (P1-P20)	6.00	2.70	.75
☐ P1 Jim Kelly	8.00	3.60	1.00
☐ P2 John Elway	25.00	11.00	3.10
☐ P3 Kerry Collins	30.00	13.50	3.70
☐ P4 Ki-Jana Carter	8.00	3.60	1.00
☐ P5 Andre Rison	6.00	2.70	.75
☐ P6 Troy Aikman	30.00	13.50	3.70
☐ P7 Emmitt Smith	60.00	27.00	7.50
☐ P8 Barry Sanders	30.00	13.50	3.70
☐ P9 Warren Moon	8.00	3.60	1.00
☐ P10 Jeff Hostetler	6.00	2.70	.75
☐ P11 Dan Marino	60.00	27.00	7.50
☐ P12 Drew Bledsoe	30.00	13.50	3.70
☐ P13 Rodney Hampton	6.00	2.70	.75
☐ P14 Ricky Watters	6.00	2.70	.75
☐ P15 Byron Bam Morris	6.00	2.70	.75
☐ P16 Natrone Means	8.00	3.60	1.00
☐ P17 Steve Young	20.00	9.00	2.50
☐ P18 Jerry Rice	30.00	13.50	3.70
☐ P19 J.J. Stokes	8.00	3.60	1.00
☐ P20 Errict Rhett	8.00	3.60	1.00

1995 Pro Line Pro Bowl

Randomly inserted in pre-priced ($1.99) retail packs at a rate of one per box, this 30-card set highlights players named to past and present Pro Bowls. Card fronts are die cut in the shape of a ticket stub with an all foil silver background. Each card contains the number "250392" on the top and bottom. Card backs show a game action shot with a brief commentary on the player. Cards are numbered with a "PB" prefix.

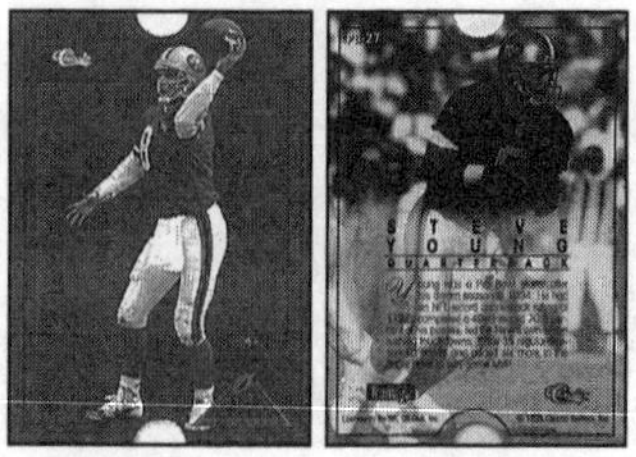

	MINT	NRMT	EXC
COMPLETE SET (30)	35.00	16.00	4.40
COMMON CARD (PB1-PB30)	.75	.35	.09
☐ PB1 Seth Joyner	.75	.35	.09
☐ PB2 Andre Reed	.75	.35	.09
☐ PB3 Bruce Smith	1.00	.45	.12
☐ PB4 Michael Irvin	1.25	.55	.16
☐ PB5 Troy Aikman	2.50	1.10	.30
☐ PB6 Emmitt Smith	5.00	2.20	.60
☐ PB7 Charles Haley	.75	.35	.09
☐ PB8 Shannon Sharpe	.75	.35	.09
☐ PB9 John Elway	2.00	.90	.25
☐ PB10 Barry Sanders	2.50	1.10	.30
☐ PB11 Reggie White	1.25	.55	.16
☐ PB12 Marshall Faulk	1.25	.55	.16
☐ PB13 Tim Brown	1.00	.45	.12
☐ PB14 Chester McGlockton	.75	.35	.09
☐ PB15 Dan Marino	5.00	2.20	.60
☐ PB16 Cris Carter	1.00	.45	.12
☐ PB17 Warren Moon	1.00	.45	.12
☐ PB18 Ben Coates	.75	.35	.09
☐ PB19 Drew Bledsoe	2.50	1.10	.30
☐ PB20 Rod Woodson	1.00	.45	.12
☐ PB21 Natrone Means	1.25	.55	.16
☐ PB22 Leslie O'Neal	.75	.35	.09
☐ PB23 Junior Seau	1.00	.45	.12
☐ PB24 Jerry Rice	2.50	1.10	.30
☐ PB25 Chris Warren	1.00	.45	.12
☐ PB26 Brent Jones	.75	.35	.09
☐ PB27 Steve Young	2.00	.90	.25
☐ PB28 Dana Stubblefield	.75	.35	.09
☐ PB29 Deion Sanders	1.50	.70	.19
☐ PB30 Jerome Bettis	1.25	.55	.16

1995 Pro Line Record Breakers

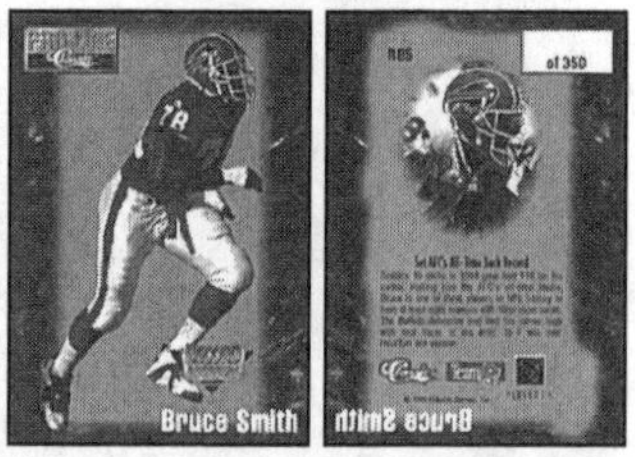

This ten card standard-size set was randomly inserted only in the "Hot Boxes" and split five in the hobby series and five in the retail. The first five cards are from hobby packs and commemorate a new NFL record. The last five are from retail packs and commemorate a new team record. The fronts of these acetate cards, have a color photo of the player on a solid orange background in the middle of the card. Surrounding that is a see through purple border. The player's name is at the bottom and is also see through. The backs have a head shot, player information and the player's name backwards, due to the see through front. The background is the same as the front. Cards numbered with a "HB" prefix were randomly inserted into Series 1 hobby hot boxes and are numbered out of 425. Cards numbered with a "RB" prefix were randomly inserted into Series 1 retail hot boxes and are numbered out of 350.

	MINT	NRMT	EXC
COMPLETE SET (10)	500.00	220.00	60.00
COMMON CARD	20.00	9.00	2.50
☐ HB1 Drew Bledsoe	80.00	36.00	10.00
☐ HB2 Cris Carter	25.00	11.00	3.10
☐ HB3 Jerry Rice	80.00	36.00	10.00
☐ HB4 Steve Young	60.00	27.00	7.50
☐ HB5 Marshall Faulk	40.00	18.00	5.00
☐ RB1 Emmitt Smith	140.00	65.00	17.50
☐ RB2 Barry Sanders	80.00	36.00	10.00
☐ RB3 Natrone Means	20.00	9.00	2.50
☐ RB4 Ben Coates	20.00	9.00	2.50
☐ RB5 Bruce Smith	25.00	11.00	3.10

1995 Pro Line Series 2

Issued by Classic, this 75 card set came in 6 card packs and included one prepaid phone card per pack. Card fronts are similar to series one, but the player's name and team are against a blue holographic background at the bottom of the card. The "ProLine" emblem at the top left also shows the card as being a series 2 card. Terrell Fletcher is the only Rookie Card of note in this set. Card backs are numbered with a "II" prefix.

	MINT	NRMT	EXC
COMPLETE SET (75)	15.00	6.75	1.85
COMMON CARD (1-75)	.05	.02	.01
☐ 1 Jim Kelly	.20	.09	.03
☐ 2 Steve Walsh	.05	.02	.01

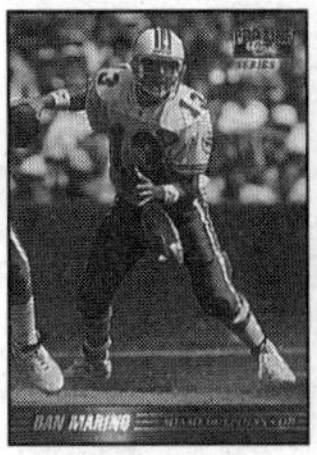

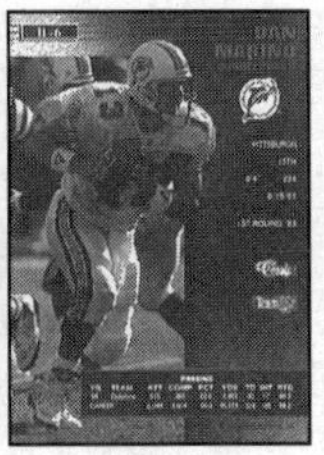
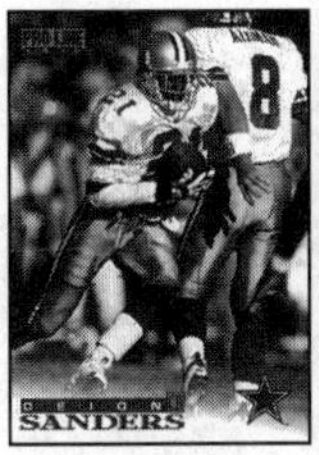

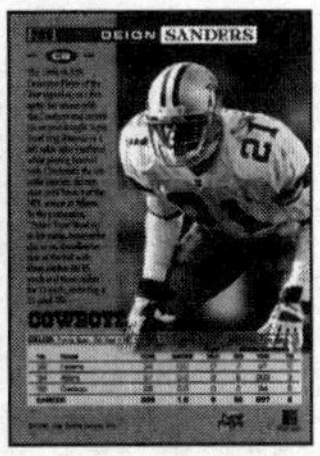

☐ 3 Jeff Blake	.60	.25	.07
☐ 4 Vinny Testaverde	.10	.05	.01
☐ 5 Jeff Hostetler	.10	.05	.01
☐ 6 Dan Marino	2.00	.90	.25
☐ 7 Cris Carter	.20	.09	.03
☐ 8 Drew Bledsoe	1.00	.45	.12
☐ 9 Jim Everett	.05	.02	.01
☐ 10 Neil O'Donnell	.10	.05	.01
☐ 11 Rodney Hampton	.10	.05	.01
☐ 12 Troy Aikman	1.00	.45	.12
☐ 13 John Elway	.75	.35	.09
☐ 14 Barry Sanders	1.00	.45	.12
☐ 15 Reggie White	.20	.09	.03
☐ 16 Marshall Faulk	.50	.23	.06
☐ 17 Marcus Allen	.20	.09	.03
☐ 18 James O.Stewart	.20	.09	.03
☐ 19 Randall Cunningham	.10	.05	.01
☐ 20 Natrone Means	.20	.09	.03
☐ 21 Rick Mirer	.20	.09	.03
☐ 22 Jerry Rice	1.00	.45	.12
☐ 23 Errict Rhett	.20	.09	.03
☐ 24 Heath Shuler	.20	.09	.03
☐ 25 Jerome Bettis	.30	.14	.04
☐ 26 Garrison Hearst	.20	.09	.03
☐ 27 Jeff George	.10	.05	.01
☐ 28 Andre Reed	.10	.05	.01
☐ 29 Warren Moon	.10	.05	.01
☐ 30 Ben Coates	.10	.05	.01
☐ 31 Mario Bates	.20	.09	.03
☐ 32 Byron Bam Morris	.10	.05	.01
☐ 33 Dave Brown	.10	.05	.01
☐ 34 Emmitt Smith	2.00	.90	.25
☐ 35 Anthony Miller	.10	.05	.01
☐ 36 Herman Moore	.50	.23	.06
☐ 37 Brett Favre	2.00	.90	.25
☐ 38 Steve Bono	.10	.05	.01
☐ 39 Stan Humphries	.10	.05	.01
☐ 40 Steve Young	.75	.35	.09
☐ 41 Trent Dilfer	.20	.09	.03
☐ 42 Chris Miller	.05	.02	.01
☐ 43 Herschel Walker	.10	.05	.01
☐ 44 Michael Irvin	.20	.09	.03
☐ 45 Junior Seau	.20	.09	.03
☐ 46 Deion Sanders	.60	.25	.07
☐ 47 William Floyd	.20	.09	.03
☐ 48 Ki-Jana Carter	.50	.23	.06
☐ 49 Kerry Collins	1.50	.70	.19
☐ 50 Steve McNair	1.25	.55	.16
☐ 51 Tony Boselli	.10	.05	.01
☐ 52 Kyle Brady	.20	.09	.03
☐ 53 Mike Mamula	.10	.05	.01
☐ 54 Warren Sapp	.10	.05	.01
☐ 55 J.J. Stokes	.50	.23	.06
☐ 56 Joey Galloway	1.00	.45	.12
☐ 57 Hugh Douglas	.10	.05	.01
☐ 58 Michael Westbrook	.60	.25	.07
☐ 59 Napoleon Kaufman	.20	.09	.03
☐ 60 Rashaan Salaam	.60	.25	.07
☐ 61 Tyrone Wheatley	.20	.09	.03
☐ 62 Terrell Fletcher	.05	.02	.01
☐ 63 Eric Metcalf	.10	.05	.01
☐ 64 Kevin Carter	.20	.09	.03
☐ 65 Andre Rison	.10	.05	.01
☐ 66 Eric Green	.05	.02	.01
☐ 67 Dave Meggett	.05	.02	.01
☐ 68 Ricky Watters	.20	.09	.03
☐ 69 Steve Beuerlein	.05	.02	.01
☐ 70 Craig Erickson	.05	.02	.01
☐ 71 Michael Dean Perry	.05	.02	.01
☐ 72 Alvin Harper	.05	.02	.01
☐ 73 Rob Moore	.05	.02	.01
☐ 74 Frank Reich	.05	.02	.01
☐ 75 Checklist	.10	.05	.01

1995 Pro Line Series 2 Printer's Proofs

This 75 card parallel set was randomly inserted into series 2 Pro Line packs at a rate of one in 18 packs. Cards are differentiated by having the Printer's Proof logo on the card front.

	MINT	NRMT	EXC
COMPLETE SET (75)	250.00	110.00	31.00
COMMON CARD (1-75)	1.00	.45	.12

*PP VET.STARS: 10X TO 18X BASIC CARDS
*PP YOUNG STARS: 7.5X TO 15X BASIC CARDS
*PP RC's: 5X TO 10X BASIC CARDS ..

1996 Pro Line

The 1996 Pro Line set was issued in one series totalling 350 standard-size cards. The set was issued in 10 card packs (suggested retail price of $1.79) with 28 packs in a box and 12 boxes in a case. There is a Rookies subset as well as checklists that feature players on the front. An unnumbered Emmitt Smith Promo card was produced and priced below.

	MINT	NRMT	EXC
COMPLETE SET (350)	30.00	13.50	3.70
COMMON CARD (1-350)	.05	.02	.01

☐ 1 Troy Aikman	1.00	.45	.12
☐ 2 Steve Young	.75	.35	.09
☐ 3 John Elway	.75	.35	.09
☐ 4 Jim Kelly	.20	.09	.03
☐ 5 Dan Marino	2.00	.90	.25
☐ 6 Brett Favre	2.00	.90	.25
☐ 7 Kerry Collins	1.00	.45	.12
☐ 8 Jeff Blake	.20	.09	.03
☐ 9 Stan Humphries	.10	.05	.01
☐ 10 Steve Bono	.10	.05	.01
☐ 11 Jeff George	.10	.05	.01
☐ 12 Mark Brunell	1.00	.45	.12
☐ 13 Scott Mitchell	.10	.05	.01
☐ 14 Steve McNair	.75	.35	.09
☐ 15 Jeff Hostetler	.10	.05	.01
☐ 16 Jim Everett	.05	.02	.01
☐ 17 Rick Mirer	.10	.05	.01
☐ 18 Boomer Esiason	.10	.05	.01
☐ 19 Neil O'Donnell	.10	.05	.01
☐ 20 Dave Brown	.10	.05	.01
☐ 21 Erik Kramer	.05	.02	.01
☐ 22 Trent Dilfer	.10	.05	.01
☐ 23 Jim Harbaugh	.10	.05	.01
☐ 24 Vinny Testaverde	.10	.05	.01
☐ 25 Thurman Thomas	.20	.09	.03
☐ 26 Rodney Peete	.05	.02	.01
☐ 27 Gus Frerotte	.20	.09	.03
☐ 28 Warren Moon	.10	.05	.01
☐ 29 Eric Zeier	.10	.05	.01
☐ 30 Randall Cunningham	.10	.05	.01
☐ 31 Heath Shuler	.20	.09	.03
☐ 32 John Friesz	.05	.02	.01
☐ 33 Tommy Maddox	.05	.02	.01
☐ 34 Glenn Foley	.05	.02	.01
☐ 35 Drew Bledsoe	1.00	.45	.12
☐ 36 Kordell Stewart	1.00	.45	.12
☐ 37 Natrone Means	.20	.09	.03
☐ 38 Errict Rhett	.10	.05	.01
☐ 39 Rashaan Salaam	.20	.09	.03
☐ 40 Emmitt Smith	2.00	.90	.25
☐ 41 Larry Centers	.10	.05	.01
☐ 42 Terrell Davis	1.25	.55	.16
☐ 43 Marshall Faulk	.20	.09	.03
☐ 44 Rodney Hampton	.10	.05	.01
☐ 45 Byron Bam Morris	.10	.05	.01
☐ 46 Chris Warren	.10	.05	.01
☐ 47 Curtis Martin	1.25	.55	.16
☐ 48 Ricky Watters	.10	.05	.01
☐ 49 Marcus Allen	.20	.09	.03
☐ 50 Barry Sanders	1.00	.45	.12
☐ 51 Edgar Bennett	.10	.05	.01
☐ 52 Adrian Murrell	.10	.05	.01
☐ 53 James O. Stewart	.20	.09	.03
☐ 54 Leroy Hoard	.05	.02	.01
☐ 55 Jerome Bettis	.20	.09	.03
☐ 56 Craig Heyward	.05	.02	.01
☐ 57 Harvey Williams	.05	.02	.01
☐ 58 Bernie Parmalee	.05	.02	.01
☐ 59 Garrison Hearst	.10	.05	.01
☐ 60 Terry Allen	.10	.05	.01
☐ 61 Charlie Garner	.05	.02	.01
☐ 62 Dorsey Levens	.10	.05	.01
☐ 63 Derek Loville	.05	.02	.01
☐ 64 Greg Hill	.10	.05	.01
☐ 65 Derrick Moore	.05	.02	.01
☐ 66 Rodney Thomas	.05	.02	.01
☐ 67 Daryl Johnston	.10	.05	.01
☐ 68 Mario Bates	.10	.05	.01
☐ 69 Aaron Hayden	.05	.02	.01
☐ 70 Napoleon Kaufman	.10	.05	.01
☐ 71 Terry Kirby	.10	.05	.01
☐ 72 Glyn Milburn	.05	.02	.01
☐ 73 Robert Smith	.10	.05	.01
☐ 74 Ki-Jana Carter	.10	.05	.01
☐ 75 Tyrone Wheatley	.10	.05	.01
☐ 76 Erric Pegram	.10	.05	.01
☐ 77 Brian Mitchell	.05	.02	.01
☐ 78 Vaughn Dunbar	.05	.02	.01
☐ 79 Dave Meggett	.05	.02	.01
☐ 80 Scottie Graham	.05	.02	.01
☐ 81 Darick Holmes	.10	.05	.01
☐ 82 Marion Butts	.05	.02	.01
☐ 83 Harold Green	.05	.02	.01
☐ 84 Zack Crockett	.05	.02	.01
☐ 85 Amp Lee	.05	.02	.01
☐ 86 Lamont Warren	.05	.02	.01
☐ 87 Mark Chmura	.10	.05	.01
☐ 88 Irving Fryar	.10	.05	.01
☐ 89 Tim Brown	.10	.05	.01
☐ 90 Michael Irvin	.20	.09	.03
☐ 91 Tony Martin	.10	.05	.01
☐ 92 Alvin Harper	.05	.02	.01
☐ 93 Darnay Scott	.10	.05	.01
☐ 94 Eric Metcalf	.10	.05	.01
☐ 95 Michael Timpson	.05	.02	.01
☐ 96 Sean Dawkins	.05	.02	.01
☐ 97 Qadry Ismail	.10	.05	.01
☐ 98 Yancey Thigpen	.10	.05	.01
☐ 99 Joey Galloway	.40	.18	.05
☐ 100 Herman Moore	.20	.09	.03
☐ 101 J.J. Stokes	.20	.09	.03
☐ 102 Wayne Chrebet	.10	.05	.01
☐ 103 Ernest Givins	.05	.02	.01
☐ 104 Michael Jackson	.10	.05	.01
☐ 105 Henry Ellard	.10	.05	.01
☐ 106 Thomas Lewis	.05	.02	.01
☐ 107 Anthony Miller	.10	.05	.01
☐ 108 Terance Mathis	.05	.02	.01
☐ 109 Horace Copeland	.05	.02	.01
☐ 110 Rocket Ismail	.10	.05	.01
☐ 111 Quinn Early	.05	.02	.01
☐ 112 Haywood Jeffires	.05	.02	.01
☐ 113 Mark Carrier WR	.10	.05	.01
☐ 114 Brent Jones	.05	.02	.01
☐ 115 Ben Coates	.10	.05	.01
☐ 116 Ken Dilger	.10	.05	.01
☐ 117 Irv Smith	.05	.02	.01
☐ 118 Jay Novacek	.10	.05	.01
☐ 119 Tony McGee	.05	.02	.01
☐ 120 Troy Drayton	.05	.02	.01
☐ 121 Johnny Mitchell	.05	.02	.01
☐ 122 Rob Moore	.05	.02	.01
☐ 123 Kevin Williams WR	.05	.02	.01
☐ 124 O.J. McDuffie	.10	.05	.01
☐ 125 Carl Pickens	.20	.09	.03
☐ 126 Curtis Conway	.20	.09	.03
☐ 127 Ed McCaffrey	.05	.02	.01
☐ 128 Arthur Marshall	.05	.02	.01
☐ 129 Ernie Mills	.05	.02	.01
☐ 130 Cris Carter	.20	.09	.03
☐ 131 Isaac Bruce	.20	.09	.03
☐ 132 Brian Blades	.10	.05	.01
☐ 133 Michael Westbrook	.20	.09	.03
☐ 134 Andre Reed	.10	.05	.01
☐ 135 Andre Rison	.10	.05	.01
☐ 136 Brett Perriman	.10	.05	.01
☐ 137 Willie Jackson	.10	.05	.01
☐ 138 Ryan Yarborough	.05	.02	.01
☐ 139 Chris T. Jones	.20	.09	.03
☐ 140 Jerry Rice	1.00	.45	.12
☐ 141 Lake Dawson	.10	.05	.01
☐ 142 Robert Brooks	.20	.09	.03
☐ 143 Vincent Brisby	.05	.02	.01
☐ 144 Desmond Howard	.10	.05	.01
☐ 145 Johnnie Morton	.10	.05	.01
☐ 146 Steve Tasker	.05	.02	.01
☐ 147 Ty Detmer	.10	.05	.01
☐ 148 Todd Kinchen	.05	.02	.01
☐ 149 Mike Sherrard	.05	.02	.01
☐ 150 Eric Green	.05	.02	.01
☐ 151 Mark Bruener	.05	.02	.01
☐ 152 Kyle Brady	.10	.05	.01
☐ 153 Frank Sanders	.10	.05	.01
☐ 154 Willie Green	.05	.02	.01
☐ 155 Jeff Graham	.05	.02	.01
☐ 156 Bert Emanuel	.10	.05	.01
☐ 157 Courtney Hawkins	.05	.02	.01
☐ 158 Mark Seay	.05	.02	.01
☐ 159 Chris Calloway	.05	.02	.01
☐ 160 John Taylor	.05	.02	.01
☐ 161 Fred Barnett	.10	.05	.01
☐ 162 Tamarick Vanover	.20	.09	.03
☐ 163 Keenan McCardell	.20	.09	.03
☐ 164 Bill Brooks	.05	.02	.01
☐ 165 Alexander Wright	.05	.02	.01
☐ 166 Jake Reed	.10	.05	.01
☐ 167 Floyd Turner	.05	.02	.01
☐ 168 Mike Pritchard	.05	.02	.01
☐ 169 Lawrence Dawsey	.05	.02	.01
☐ 170 Shawn Jefferson	.05	.02	.01
☐ 171 Michael Haynes	.10	.05	.01
☐ 172 Shannon Sharpe	.10	.05	.01
☐ 173 Jackie Harris	.05	.02	.01
☐ 174 Daryl Hobbs	.05	.02	.01
☐ 175 Chris Sanders	.10	.05	.01
☐ 176 Willie Davis	.10	.05	.01
☐ 177 Marco Coleman	.05	.02	.01
☐ 178 Pat Swilling	.05	.02	.01
☐ 179 Alonzo Spellman	.05	.02	.01
☐ 180 Simon Fletcher	.05	.02	.01
☐ 181 Sean Gilbert	.05	.02	.01
☐ 182 Tracy Scroggins	.05	.02	.01
☐ 183 Hugh Douglas	.05	.02	.01
☐ 184 Eric Swann	.10	.05	.01
☐ 185 Russell Maryland	.05	.02	.01
☐ 186 Warren Sapp	.05	.02	.01
☐ 187 Jim Flanigan	.05	.02	.01
☐ 188 Cortez Kennedy	.10	.05	.01
☐ 189 Andy Harmon	.05	.02	.01
☐ 190 Dan Saleaumua	.05	.02	.01
☐ 191 Kelvin Pritchett	.05	.02	.01
☐ 192 John Randle	.05	.02	.01
☐ 193 Dan Wilkinson	.05	.02	.01
☐ 194 Chester McGlockton	.05	.02	.01
☐ 195 Leon Lett	.05	.02	.01
☐ 196 Neil Smith	.10	.05	.01
☐ 197 Mike Mamula	.05	.02	.01
☐ 198 Mike Jones	.05	.02	.01
☐ 199 Reggie White	.20	.09	.03
☐ 200 Anthony Pleasant	.05	.02	.01
☐ 201 Phil Hansen	.05	.02	.01
☐ 202 Ray Seals	.05	.02	.01
☐ 203 Tony Bennett	.05	.02	.01
☐ 204 Leslie O'Neal	.05	.02	.01
☐ 205 Jeff Cross	.05	.02	.01
☐ 206 Anthony Cook	.05	.02	.01
☐ 207 Clyde Simmons	.05	.02	.01
☐ 208 Renaldo Turnbull	.05	.02	.01
☐ 209 Charles Haley	.10	.05	.01
☐ 210 John Copeland	.05	.02	.01
☐ 211 John Thierry	.05	.02	.01
☐ 212 Michael Strahan	.05	.02	.01
☐ 213 Jeff Lageman	.05	.02	.01
☐ 214 William Fuller	.05	.02	.01
☐ 215 Rickey Jackson	.05	.02	.01
☐ 216 Wayne Martin	.05	.02	.01
☐ 217 Steve Emtman	.05	.02	.01
☐ 218 Shawn Lee	.05	.02	.01
☐ 219 Chris Zorich	.05	.02	.01
☐ 220 Henry Thomas	.05	.02	.01
☐ 221 Dana Stubblefield	.10	.05	.01
☐ 222 D'Marco Farr	.05	.02	.01
☐ 223 Pierce Holt	.05	.02	.01
☐ 224 Sean Jones	.05	.02	.01
☐ 225 Robert Porcher	.05	.02	.01
☐ 226 Kevin Carter	.10	.05	.01
☐ 227 Chris Doleman	.05	.02	.01
☐ 228 Tony Tolbert	.05	.02	.01
☐ 229 Bruce Smith	.20	.09	.03
☐ 230 Marvin Washington	.05	.02	.01
☐ 231 Blaine Bishop	.05	.02	.01
☐ 232 Bryant Young	.10	.05	.01
☐ 233 Rob Burnett	.05	.02	.01
☐ 234 Lawrence Phillips	.40	.18	.05
☐ 235 Trev Alberts	.05	.02	.01
☐ 236 Eric Curry	.05	.02	.01
☐ 237 Anthony Smith	.05	.02	.01
☐ 238 Sam Mills	.10	.05	.01
☐ 239 Seth Joyner	.05	.02	.01
☐ 240 Quentin Coryatt	.05	.02	.01
☐ 241 Levon Kirkland	.05	.02	.01
☐ 242 Cornelius Bennett	.10	.05	.01
☐ 243 Chris Spielman	.10	.05	.01
☐ 244 Mo Lewis	.05	.02	.01
☐ 245 Lee Woodall	.05	.02	.01
☐ 246 Derrick Thomas	.10	.05	.01
☐ 247 Willie McGinest	.05	.02	.01
☐ 248 Terry Wooden	.05	.02	.01
☐ 249 Greg Lloyd	.10	.05	.01
☐ 250 Jack Del Rio	.05	.02	.01
☐ 251 Hardy Nickerson	.05	.02	.01
☐ 252 Micheal Barrow	.05	.02	.01
☐ 253 Lamar Lathon	.05	.02	.01
☐ 254 Bryan Cox	.05	.02	.01
☐ 255 Randy Kirk	.05	.02	.01
☐ 256 Jessie Tuggle	.05	.02	.01
☐ 257 Roman Phifer	.05	.02	.01
☐ 258 Ken Harvey	.05	.02	.01
☐ 259 Junior Seau	.20	.09	.03
☐ 260 Pepper Johnson	.05	.02	.01
☐ 261 Chris Slade	.05	.02	.01
☐ 262 Gary Plummer	.05	.02	.01
☐ 263 Wayne Simmons	.05	.02	.01
☐ 264 Bryce Paup	.10	.05	.01
☐ 265 William Thomas	.05	.02	.01
☐ 266 Kevin Greene	.10	.05	.01
☐ 267 Bobby Engram	.75	.35	.09
☐ 268 Ken Norton	.10	.05	.01
☐ 269 Eric Hill	.05	.02	.01
☐ 270 Darion Conner	.05	.02	.01
☐ 271 Tyrone Poole	.05	.02	.01
☐ 272 Cris Dishman	.05	.02	.01
☐ 273 Marcus Jones	.05	.02	.01
☐ 274 Rod Woodson	.10	.05	.01
☐ 275 Mark McMillian	.05	.02	.01
☐ 276 Dale Carter	.05	.02	.01
☐ 277 Darrell Green	.05	.02	.01
☐ 278 Donnell Woolford	.05	.02	.01
☐ 279 Troy Vincent	.05	.02	.01
☐ 280 Larry Brown	.05	.02	.01
☐ 281 Aeneas Williams	.05	.02	.01
☐ 282 Eric Allen	.05	.02	.01
☐ 283 Ray Buchanan	.05	.02	.01
☐ 284 Ty Law	.10	.05	.01
☐ 285 Eric Davis	.05	.02	.01
☐ 286 Todd Lyght	.10	.05	.01
☐ 287 Terry McDaniel	.05	.02	.01
☐ 288 Darryll Lewis	.05	.02	.01
☐ 289 Deion Sanders	.60	.25	.07
☐ 290 Phillippi Sparks	.05	.02	.01
☐ 291 Bobby Taylor	.10	.05	.01
☐ 292 Mark Collins	.05	.02	.01
☐ 293 Steve Atwater	.05	.02	.01

☐ 294 Stanley Richard	.05	.02	.01
☐ 295 Stevon Moore	.05	.02	.01
☐ 296 Bennie Blades	.05	.02	.01
☐ 297 Tim McDonald	.05	.02	.01
☐ 298 Shaun Gayle	.05	.02	.01
☐ 299 Darren Woodson	.10	.05	.01
☐ 300 Mark Carrier DB	.05	.02	.01
☐ 301 Carnell Lake	.05	.02	.01
☐ 302 James Washington	.05	.02	.01
☐ 303 LeRoy Butler	.05	.02	.01
☐ 304 Henry Jones	.05	.02	.01
☐ 305 Darryl Williams	.05	.02	.01
☐ 306 Darren Perry	.05	.02	.01
☐ 307 Merton Hanks	.05	.02	.01
☐ 308 Orlando Thomas	.05	.02	.01
☐ 309 Eric Turner	.05	.02	.01
☐ 310 Nate Newton	.05	.02	.01
☐ 311 Steve Wisniewski	.05	.02	.01
☐ 312 Derrick Deese	.05	.02	.01
☐ 313 Larry Allen	.05	.02	.01
☐ 314 Aaron Taylor	.05	.02	.01
☐ 315 Blake Brockermeyer	.05	.02	.01
☐ 316 William Roaf	.05	.02	.01
☐ 317 Jumbo Elliott	.05	.02	.01
☐ 318 Keyshawn Johnson	1.50	.70	.19
☐ 319 Karim Abdul-Jabbar	2.50	1.10	.30
☐ 320 Kevin Hardy	.10	.05	.01
☐ 321 Duane Clemons	.05	.02	.01
☐ 322 Jevon Langford	.05	.02	.01
☐ 323 Mike Alstott	.40	.18	.05
☐ 324 Scott Greene	.05	.02	.01
☐ 325 Derrick Mayes	.75	.35	.09
☐ 326 Chris Doering	.05	.02	.01
☐ 327 Amani Toomer	.20	.09	.03
☐ 328 Eric Moulds	.75	.35	.09
☐ 329 Alex Molden	.05	.02	.01
☐ 330 Lawyer Milloy	.10	.05	.01
☐ 331 Daryl Gardener	.10	.05	.01
☐ 332 Randall Godfrey	.10	.05	.01
☐ 333 Willie Anderson	.05	.02	.01
☐ 334 Tony Banks	.75	.35	.09
☐ 335 Jeff Lewis	.10	.05	.01
☐ 336 Roman Oben	.05	.02	.01
☐ 337 Andre Johnson	.05	.02	.01
☐ 338 Brian Roche	.05	.02	.01
☐ 339 Johnny McWilliams	.05	.02	.01
☐ 340 Alex Van Dyke	.10	.05	.01
☐ 341 Ray Mickens	.05	.02	.01
☐ 342 Marvin Harrison	1.50	.70	.19
☐ 343 Terry Glenn	3.00	1.35	.35
☐ 344 Tim Biakabutuka	.75	.35	.09
☐ 345 Simeon Rice	.20	.09	.03
☐ 346 Cedric Jones	.10	.05	.01
☐ 347 Eddie George	4.00	1.80	.50
☐ 348 Drew Bledsoe Checklist	.20	.09	.03
☐ 349 Emmitt Smith Checklist	.40	.18	.05
☐ 350 Keyshawn Johnson Checklist	.40	.18	.05

1996 Pro Line Headliners

A parallel to the 350-card base brand 1996 ProLine release, the Headliners version was inserted one per jumbo pack of 1996 ProLine. The parallel cards contained a large "Headliners" logo on the cardfronts.

	MINT	NRMT	EXC
COMPLETE SET (350)	350.00	160.00	45.00
COMMON CARD (1-350)	.60	.25	.07

*VETERAN STARS: 4X TO 8X BASIC CARDS
*YOUNG STARS: 3X TO 6X BASIC CARDS
*RCs: 3X TO 6X BASIC CARDS

1996 Pro Line National

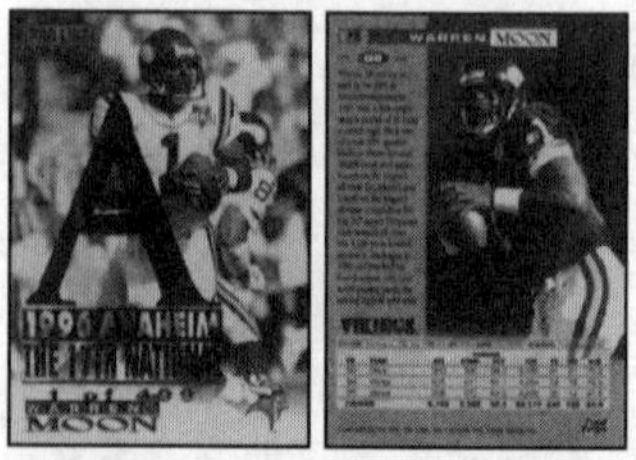

A Parallel to the 350-card base brand 1996 ProLine release, the National version was inserted one per pack into 1996 ProLine National packs. The National issue was reportedly produced in a case lot of 500 with each case containing 12-boxes, and each box 28-packs. The parallel cards were each numbered of 499 made, and contained a large silver foil "1996 Anaheim, The 17th National" logo on the cardfronts along with a very large "A."

	MINT	NRMT	EXC
COMPLETE SET (350)	350.00	160.00	45.00
COMMON CARD (1-350)	.60	.25	.07

*NATIONAL VET.STARS: 4X TO 8X BASIC CARDS
*NATIONAL YOUNG STARS: 3X TO 6X BASIC CARDS
*NATIONAL RCs: 2X TO 4X BASIC CARDS

1996 Pro Line Printer's Proof

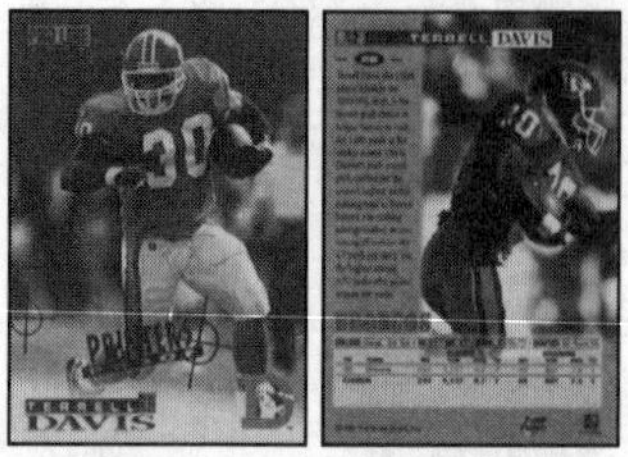

A Parallel to the 350-card base brand 1996 Pro Line release, the Printer's Proof version was randomly inserted into special retail packs at the rate of 1:10. The parallel cards each contained a red foil "Printer's Proof" logo on the cardfront.

	MINT	NRMT	EXC
COMPLETE SET (350)	600.00	275.00	75.00
COMMON CARD (1-350)	1.25	.55	.16

*PP VETERAN STARS: 7X TO 15X BASIC CARDS
*PP YOUNG STARS: 5X TO 10X BASIC CARDS
*PP RCs: 3.5X TO 7X BASIC CARDS ..

1996 Pro Line Autographs

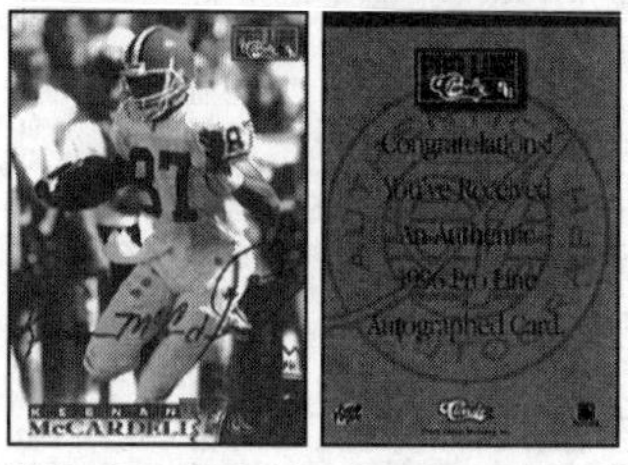

This 73-card set features borderless color action player photos with a gold foil player autograph. We have priced the gold foil versions which were inserted at a rate of every 170 packs in hobby and retail packs and one every 200 in jumbo packs. The blue foil varieties were inserted more frequently. Blue foil versions were inserted one ever 25 hobby and retail packs and one every 90 jumbo packs. Since the cards are not numbered we have sequenced them alphabetically.

	MINT	NRMT	EXC
COMP.GOLD SET (73)	2800.00	1250.00	350.00
COMMON GOLD FOIL	20.00	9.00	2.50
COMP.BLUE SET (68)	650.00	300.00	80.00
COMMON BLUE FOIL	10.00	4.50	1.25

*BLUE CARDS: .3X TO .6X GOLDS

☐ 1 Troy Aikman Emmitt Smith Gold Only	500.00	220.00	60.00
☐ 2 Eric Allen	20.00	9.00	2.50
☐ 3 Mike Alstott	35.00	16.00	4.40
☐ 4 Tony Banks	40.00	18.00	5.00
☐ 5 Blaine Bishop	20.00	9.00	2.50
☐ 6 Drew Bledsoe	150.00	70.00	19.00
☐ 7 Tim Brown	25.00	11.00	3.10
☐ 8 Marion Butts	20.00	9.00	2.50
☐ 9 Sedric Clark	20.00	9.00	2.50
☐ 10 Duane Clemons	20.00	9.00	2.50
☐ 11 Marco Coleman	20.00	9.00	2.50
☐ 12 Eric Davis	20.00	9.00	2.50
☐ 13 Derrick Deese	20.00	9.00	2.50
☐ 14 Jack Del Rio	20.00	9.00	2.50
☐ 15 Ty Detmer	25.00	11.00	3.10
☐ 16 Chris Doering	20.00	9.00	2.50
☐ 17 Jumbo Elliott	20.00	9.00	2.50
☐ 18 Marshall Faulk	60.00	27.00	7.50
☐ 19 Glenn Foley	20.00	9.00	2.50
☐ 20 John Friesz	20.00	9.00	2.50
☐ 21 Daryl Gardener	25.00	11.00	3.10
☐ 22 Randall Godfrey	20.00	9.00	2.50
☐ 23 Scott Greene	20.00	9.00	2.50
☐ 24 Rhett Hall	20.00	9.00	2.50
☐ 25 Merton Hanks	20.00	9.00	2.50
☐ 26 Kevin Hardy	20.00	9.00	2.50
☐ 27 Richard Huntley	20.00	9.00	2.50
☐ 28 Michael Jackson	20.00	9.00	2.50
☐ 29 Ron Jaworski	25.00	11.00	3.10
☐ 30 Andre Johnson	20.00	9.00	2.50
☐ 31 Keyshawn Johnson	90.00	40.00	11.00
☐ 32 Keyshawn Johnson Neil O'Donnell Gold Only	175.00	80.00	22.00
☐ 33 Mike Jones	20.00	9.00	2.50
☐ 34 Jim Kiick	20.00	9.00	2.50
☐ 35 Jeff Lewis	25.00	11.00	3.10
☐ 36 Tommy Maddox	20.00	9.00	2.50
☐ 37 Arthur Marshall	20.00	9.00	2.50
☐ 38 Russell Maryland	20.00	9.00	2.50
☐ 39 Derrick Mayes	40.00	18.00	5.00
☐ 40 Ed McCaffrey	20.00	9.00	2.50
☐ 41 Keenan McCardell	25.00	11.00	3.10
☐ 42 Terry McDaniel	20.00	9.00	2.50
☐ 43 Tim McDonald	20.00	9.00	2.50
☐ 44 Willie McGinest	20.00	9.00	2.50
☐ 45 Mark McMillian	20.00	9.00	2.50
☐ 46 Johnny McWilliams	20.00	9.00	2.50
☐ 47 Ray Mickens	20.00	9.00	2.50
☐ 48 Anthony Miller	20.00	9.00	2.50
☐ 49 Rick Mirer	20.00	9.00	2.50
☐ 50 Alex Molden	20.00	9.00	2.50
☐ 51 Johnnie Morton	25.00	11.00	3.10
☐ 52 Eric Moulds	35.00	16.00	4.40
☐ 53 Roman Oben	20.00	9.00	2.50
☐ 54 Neil O'Donnell Gold Only	60.00	27.00	7.50
☐ 55 Leslie O'Neal	20.00	9.00	2.50
☐ 56 Roman Phifer	20.00	9.00	2.50
☐ 57 Gary Plummer	20.00	9.00	2.50
☐ 58 Jim Plunkett	20.00	9.00	2.50
☐ 59 Stanley Pritchett	25.00	11.00	3.10
☐ 60 John Randle	20.00	9.00	2.50
☐ 61 Brian Roche	20.00	9.00	2.50
☐ 62 Orpheus Roye	20.00	9.00	2.50
☐ 63 Mark Seay	20.00	9.00	2.50
☐ 64 Mike Sherrard	20.00	9.00	2.50
☐ 65 Chris Slade	20.00	9.00	2.50
☐ 66 Scott Slutzker	20.00	9.00	2.50
☐ 67 Emmitt Smith Gold Only	350.00	160.00	45.00
☐ 68 Steve Taneyhill	20.00	9.00	2.50
☐ 69 Robb Thomas	20.00	9.00	2.50
☐ 70 William Thomas	20.00	9.00	2.50
☐ 71 Alex Van Dyke	20.00	9.00	2.50
☐ 72 Randy White	30.00	13.50	3.70
☐ 73 Steve Young Gold Only	150.00	70.00	19.00

1996 Pro Line Cels

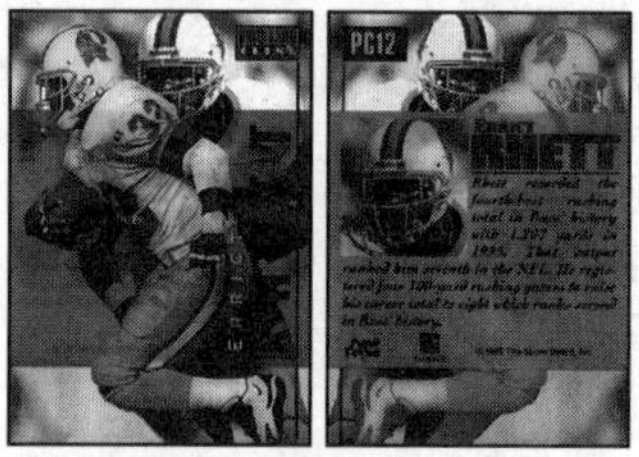

These 20 standard-size all-acetate cards are inserted approximately one every 75 hobby packs. There are two player photos on the front as well as the words "ProLine Cels 96" in the upper right corner. The backs have some text and are numbered with a "PC" prefix.

	MINT	NRMT	EXC
COMPLETE SET (20)	300.00	135.00	38.00
COMMON CARD (PC1-PC20)	6.00	2.70	.75

☐ PC1 Bryce Paup	6.00	2.70	.75
☐ PC2 Kerry Collins	25.00	11.00	3.10
☐ PC3 Troy Aikman	25.00	11.00	3.10
☐ PC4 Deion Sanders	15.00	6.75	1.85
☐ PC5 Emmitt Smith	50.00	22.00	6.25
☐ PC6 Steve McNair	20.00	9.00	2.50
☐ PC7 Drew Bledsoe	25.00	11.00	3.10
☐ PC8 Kordell Stewart	25.00	11.00	3.10
☐ PC9 Ricky Watters	10.00	4.50	1.25
☐ PC10 Jerry Rice	25.00	11.00	3.10
☐ PC11 Steve Young	20.00	9.00	2.50
☐ PC12 Errict Rhett	10.00	4.50	1.25
☐ PC13 Brett Favre	50.00	22.00	6.25
☐ PC14 Jeff Blake	10.00	4.50	1.25
☐ PC15 Joey Galloway	12.00	5.50	1.50
☐ PC16 Herman Moore	10.00	4.50	1.25
☐ PC17 Curtis Martin	25.00	11.00	3.10
☐ PC18 Keyshawn Johnson	15.00	6.75	1.85
☐ PC19 Eddie George	25.00	11.00	3.10
☐ PC20 Simeon Rice	6.00	2.70	.75

1996 Pro Line Cover Story

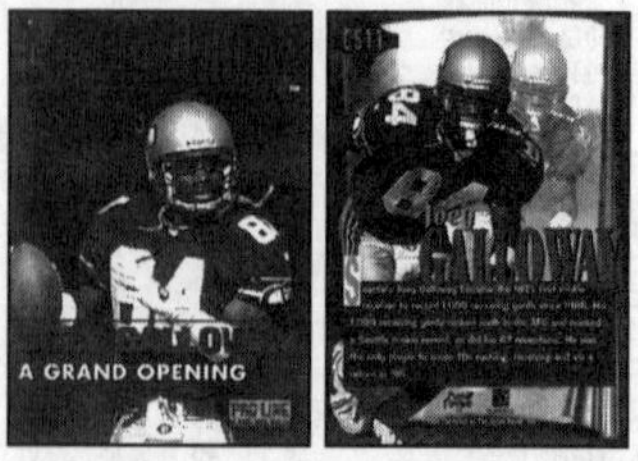

These 20 standard-size cards are randomly inserted into one of every 30 periodical packs. They feature some leading NFL players of 1995 as well as some 1996 rookies and are numbered with a "CS" prefix.

	MINT	NRMT	EXC
COMPLETE SET (20)	150.00	70.00	19.00
COMMON CARD (CS1-CS20)	3.00	1.35	.35

☐ CS1 Bryce Paup	3.00	1.35	.35
☐ CS2 Kerry Collins	16.00	7.25	2.00
☐ CS3 Rashaan Salaam	5.00	2.20	.60
☐ CS4 Troy Aikman	15.00	6.75	1.85
☐ CS5 Emmitt Smith	30.00	13.50	3.70
☐ CS6 Herman Moore	5.00	2.20	.60
☐ CS7 Curtis Martin	16.00	7.25	2.00
☐ CS8 Kordell Stewart	16.00	7.25	2.00
☐ CS9 Ricky Watters	3.00	1.35	.35
☐ CS10 Carl Pickens	3.00	1.35	.35
☐ CS11 Joey Galloway	8.00	3.60	1.00
☐ CS12 Errict Rhett	5.00	2.20	.60
☐ CS13 Deion Sanders	8.00	3.60	1.00
☐ CS14 Reggie White	5.00	2.20	.60
☐ CS15 Hugh Douglas	3.00	1.35	.35
☐ CS16 Tamarick Vanover	5.00	2.20	.60
☐ CS17 Derrick Mayes	3.00	1.35	.35
☐ CS18 Marvin Harrison	10.00	4.50	1.25
☐ CS19 Tim Biakabutuka	5.00	2.20	.60
☐ CS20 Terry Glenn	15.00	6.75	1.85

1996 Pro Line Rivalries

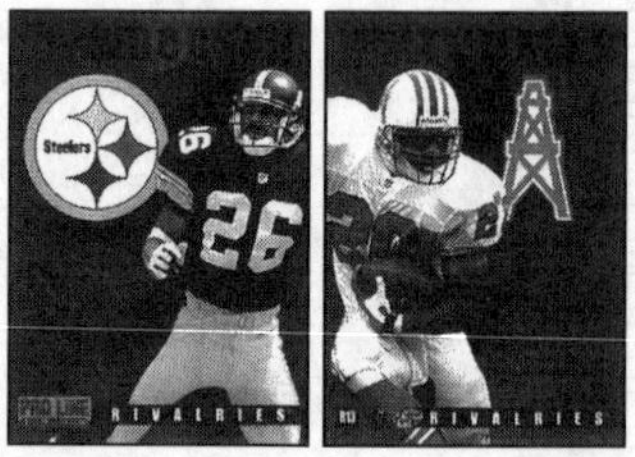

These 20 standard-size double-sided cards feature two players from the same division. Each side has a player photo, a team logo and a "Pro Line 1996 Rivalries" line on the bottom. The cards are numbered with an "R" prefix and were randomly inserted into both hobby and national packs at the rate of 1:15.

	MINT	NRMT	EXC
COMPLETE SET (20)	175.00	80.00	22.00
COMMON CARD (R1-R20)	2.00	.90	.25

☐ R1 Drew Bledsoe Jim Kelly	12.00	5.50	1.50
☐ R2 Dan Marino Greg Lloyd	20.00	9.00	2.50
☐ R3 Kordell Stewart Mark Brunell	12.00	5.50	1.50
☐ R4 Tamarick Vanover Napoleon Kaufman	4.00	1.80	.50
☐ R5 John Elway Jeff Blake	10.00	4.50	1.25
☐ R6 Emmitt Smith Ricky Watters	20.00	9.00	2.50
☐ R7 Troy Aikman Steve Young	12.00	5.50	1.50
☐ R8 Deion Sanders Gus Frerotte	8.00	3.60	1.00
☐ R9 Brett Favre Errict Rhett	20.00	9.00	2.50
☐ R10 Rashaan Salaam Warren Moon	4.00	1.80	.50
☐ R11 Kerry Collins Ken Norton Jr.	12.00	5.50	1.50
☐ R12 Jeff George Isaac Bruce	4.00	1.80	.50
☐ R13 Rod Woodson Rodney Thomas	2.00	.90	.25
☐ R14 Herman Moore Reggie White	4.00	1.80	.50
☐ R15 Marshall Faulk Curtis Martin	14.00	6.25	1.75
☐ R16 Keyshawn Johnson Marvin Harrison	10.00	4.50	1.25
☐ R17 Kevin Hardy Alex Molden	2.00	.90	.25
☐ R18 Terry Glenn Simeon Rice	15.00	6.75	1.85
☐ R19 Eddie George Tim Biakabutuka	20.00	9.00	2.50
☐ R20 Karim Abdul-Jabbar Cedric Jones	10.00	4.50	1.25

1996 Pro Line Touchdown Performers

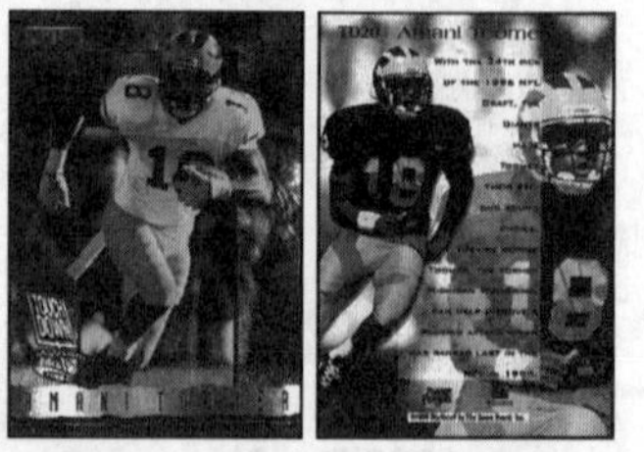

These 20 standard-size cards are randomly inserted into retail packs. They feature leading NFL players as well as some rookies and are numbered with a "TD" prefix.

	MINT	NRMT	EXC
COMPLETE SET (20)	300.00	135.00	38.00
COMMON CARD (TD1-TD20)	6.00	2.70	.75
☐ TD1 Kerry Collins	25.00	11.00	3.10
☐ TD2 Troy Aikman	25.00	11.00	3.10
☐ TD3 Deion Sanders	15.00	6.75	1.85
☐ TD4 Emmitt Smith	50.00	22.00	6.25
☐ TD5 Mark Brunell	25.00	11.00	3.10
☐ TD6 Steve McNair	20.00	9.00	2.50
☐ TD7 Marshall Faulk	10.00	4.50	1.25
☐ TD8 Dan Marino	50.00	22.00	6.25
☐ TD9 Cris Carter	6.00	2.70	.75
☐ TD10 Drew Bledsoe	25.00	11.00	3.10
☐ TD11 Yancey Thigpen	6.00	2.70	.75
☐ TD12 Jerry Rice	25.00	11.00	3.10
☐ TD13 J.J. Stokes	10.00	4.50	1.25
☐ TD14 Terrell Davis	30.00	13.50	3.70
☐ TD15 Carl Pickens	6.00	2.70	.75
☐ TD16 Joey Galloway	12.00	5.50	1.50
☐ TD17 Kordell Stewart	25.00	11.00	3.10
☐ TD18 Isaac Bruce	10.00	4.50	1.25
☐ TD19 Keyshawn Johnson	20.00	9.00	2.50
☐ TD20 Amani Toomer	6.00	2.70	.75

1996 Pro Line National Laser Promos

These 5-promo cards were distributed at the 1996 National Card Collector's Convention in Anaheim. Each card was distributed during the show at the Classic booth. Complete sets framed in a lucite holder were also produced and individually numbered of 300.

	MINT	NRMT	EXC
COMPLETE SET (5)	20.00	9.00	2.50
COMPLETE FRAMED SET (5)	30.00	13.50	3.70
COMMON CARD (1-5)	3.00	1.35	.35
☐ 1 Kordell Stewart	4.00	1.80	.50
☐ 2 Troy Aikman	4.00	1.80	.50
☐ 3 Emmitt Smith	8.00	3.60	1.00
☐ 4 Lawrence Phillips	3.00	1.35	.35
☐ 5 Keyshawn Johnson	3.00	1.35	.35

1996 Pro Line DC3

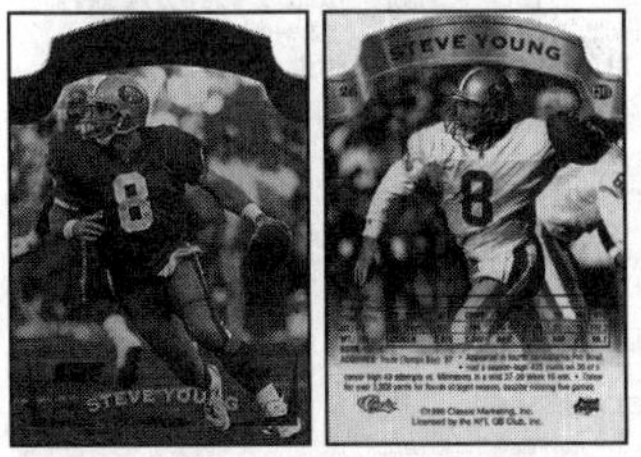

The 1996 ProLine DC3 set was issued in one series totalling 100 cards. The first all-die cut series from Classic features the top 1995 NFL veterans and rookies. There are no Rookie Cards in this set. The set was issued in five-card packs. An Emmitt Smith Sample card was produced and priced below.

	MINT	NRMT	EXC
COMPLETE SET (100)	35.00	16.00	4.40
COMMON CARD (1-100)	.10	.05	.01
☐ 1 Emmitt Smith	4.00	1.80	.50
☐ 2 Larry Centers	.20	.09	.03
☐ 3 Jeff George	.20	.09	.03
☐ 4 Jim Kelly	.40	.18	.05
☐ 5 Kerry Collins	2.50	1.10	.30
☐ 6 Erik Kramer	.10	.05	.01
☐ 7 Jeff Blake	.40	.18	.05
☐ 8 Andre Rison	.20	.09	.03
☐ 9 John Elway	1.25	.55	.16
☐ 10 Herman Moore	.40	.18	.05
☐ 11 Robert Brooks	.40	.18	.05
☐ 12 Steve McNair	2.00	.90	.25
☐ 13 Jim Harbaugh	.20	.09	.03
☐ 14 Mark Brunell	2.00	.90	.25
☐ 15 Steve Bono	.20	.09	.03
☐ 16 Dan Marino	4.00	1.80	.50
☐ 17 Warren Moon	.20	.09	.03
☐ 18 Drew Bledsoe	2.00	.90	.25
☐ 19 Jim Everett	.10	.05	.01
☐ 20 Rodney Hampton	.20	.09	.03
☐ 21 Kyle Brady	.20	.09	.03
☐ 22 Jeff Hostetler	.20	.09	.03
☐ 23 Neil O'Donnell	.20	.09	.03
☐ 24 Ricky Watters	.20	.09	.03
☐ 25 Isaac Bruce	.40	.18	.05
☐ 26 Steve Young	1.25	.55	.16
☐ 27 Stan Humphries	.20	.09	.03
☐ 28 Joey Galloway	1.00	.45	.12
☐ 29 Errict Rhett	.20	.09	.03
☐ 30 Terry Allen	.20	.09	.03
☐ 31 Eric Swann	.20	.09	.03
☐ 32 Craig Heyward	.10	.05	.01
☐ 33 Bryce Paup	.20	.09	.03
☐ 34 Sam Mills	.20	.09	.03
☐ 35 Jim Flanigan	.10	.05	.01
☐ 36 Carl Pickens	.40	.18	.05
☐ 37 Pepper Johnson	.10	.05	.01
☐ 38 Troy Aikman	2.00	.90	.25
☐ 39 Terrell Davis	3.00	1.35	.35
☐ 40 Scott Mitchell	.20	.09	.03
☐ 41 Brett Favre	4.00	1.80	.50
☐ 42 Chris Sanders	.20	.09	.03
☐ 43 Marshall Faulk	.40	.18	.05
☐ 44 James O. Stewart	.40	.18	.05
☐ 45 Marcus Allen	.40	.18	.05
☐ 46 Bernie Parmalee	.10	.05	.01
☐ 47 Cris Carter	.40	.18	.05
☐ 48 Ben Coates	.20	.09	.03
☐ 49 Quinn Early	.10	.05	.01
☐ 50 Tyrone Wheatley	.20	.09	.03
☐ 51 Adrian Murrell	.20	.09	.03
☐ 52 Tim Brown	.20	.09	.03
☐ 53 Yancey Thigpen	.20	.09	.03
☐ 54 Andy Harmon	.10	.05	.01
☐ 55 Jerome Bettis	.40	.18	.05
☐ 56 Jerry Rice	2.00	.90	.25
☐ 57 Natrone Means	.40	.18	.05
☐ 58 Chris Warren	.20	.09	.03
☐ 59 Warren Sapp	.10	.05	.01
☐ 60 Michael Westbrook	.40	.18	.05
☐ 61 Aeneas Williams	.10	.05	.01
☐ 62 Eric Metcalf	.20	.09	.03
☐ 63 Bruce Smith	.40	.18	.05
☐ 64 Rashaan Salaam	.40	.18	.05
☐ 65 Michael Irvin	.40	.18	.05
☐ 66 Anthony Miller	.20	.09	.03
☐ 67 Barry Sanders	2.00	.90	.25
☐ 68 Reggie White	.40	.18	.05
☐ 69 Rodney Thomas	.10	.05	.01
☐ 70 Zack Crockett	.10	.05	.01
☐ 71 Neil Smith	.20	.09	.03
☐ 72 Bryan Cox	.10	.05	.01
☐ 73 Curtis Martin	3.00	1.35	.35
☐ 74 Eric Allen	.10	.05	.01
☐ 75 Hugh Douglas	.10	.05	.01
☐ 76 Napoleon Kaufman	.20	.09	.03
☐ 77 Greg Lloyd	.20	.09	.03
☐ 78 Charlie Garner	.10	.05	.01
☐ 79 Lee Woodall	.10	.05	.01
☐ 80 Tony Martin	.20	.09	.03
☐ 81 Cortez Kennedy	.20	.09	.03
☐ 82 Gus Frerotte	.40	.18	.05
☐ 83 Darick Holmes	.20	.09	.03
☐ 84 Jay Novacek	.20	.09	.03
☐ 85 Brett Perriman	.20	.09	.03
☐ 86 Mark Chmura	.20	.09	.03
☐ 87 Chester McGlockton	.10	.05	.01
☐ 88 Dave Brown	.20	.09	.03
☐ 89 William Thomas	.10	.05	.01
☐ 90 Ken Norton	.20	.09	.03
☐ 91 Junior Seau	.40	.18	.05
☐ 92 Deion Sanders	1.00	.45	.12
☐ 93 J.J. Stokes	.40	.18	.05
☐ 94 Kordell Stewart	2.50	1.10	.30
☐ 95 Tamarick Vanover	.40	.18	.05
☐ 96 Ken Harvey	.10	.05	.01
☐ 97 John Randle	.10	.05	.01
☐ 98 Lamont Warren	.10	.05	.01
☐ 99 Dorsey Levens	.20	.09	.03
☐ 100 Frank Sanders	.20	.09	.03
☐ S1 Emmitt Smith Sample	2.50	1.10	.30

1996 Pro Line DC3 All-Pros

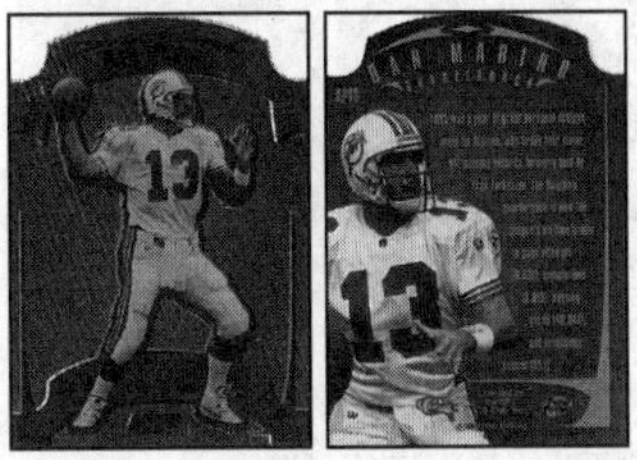

Randomly inserted in packs at a rate of one in 100, this 20-card set includes Pro Bowl and Pro Bowl-caliber players. The cards were printed on 24-point "fabric" card stock. The cards are numbered with an "AP" prefix.

	MINT	NRMT	EXC
COMPLETE SET (20)	700.00	325.00	90.00
COMMON CARD (AP1-AP20)	10.00	4.50	1.25
☐ AP1 Bryce Paup	10.00	4.50	1.25
☐ AP2 Kerry Collins	40.00	18.00	5.00
☐ AP3 Rashaan Salaam	20.00	9.00	2.50
☐ AP4 Emmitt Smith	80.00	36.00	10.00
☐ AP5 Terrell Davis	40.00	18.00	5.00
☐ AP6 Herman Moore	20.00	9.00	2.50
☐ AP7 Barry Sanders	50.00	22.00	6.25
☐ AP8 Brett Favre	80.00	36.00	10.00
☐ AP9 Marshall Faulk	20.00	9.00	2.50
☐ AP10 Dan Marino	80.00	36.00	10.00
☐ AP11 Cris Carter	15.00	6.75	1.85
☐ AP12 Curtis Martin	40.00	18.00	5.00
☐ AP13 Hugh Douglas	10.00	4.50	1.25
☐ AP14 Kordell Stewart	40.00	18.00	5.00
☐ AP15 Jerry Rice	50.00	22.00	6.25
☐ AP16 J.J. Stokes	20.00	9.00	2.50
☐ AP17 Joey Galloway	20.00	9.00	2.50
☐ AP18 Isaac Bruce	20.00	9.00	2.50
☐ AP19 Steve McNair	35.00	16.00	4.40
☐ AP20 Tim Brown	15.00	6.75	1.85

1996 Pro Line DC3 Road to the Super Bowl

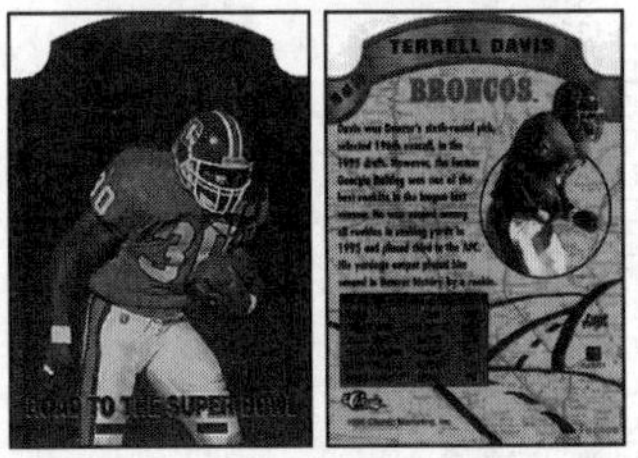

Randomly inserted in packs at a rate of one in 15, this 30-card set printed on 24-point micro-lined silver foil board includes key moments from the 1995 season. Every card back features statistics or a brief "box score" from the game, allowing collectors to relive the highlights of the game featured.

	MINT	NRMT	EXC
COMPLETE SET (30)	400.00	180.00	50.00
COMMON CARD (1-30)	5.00	2.20	.60
☐ 1 Larry Centers	5.00	2.20	.60
☐ 2 Eric Metcalf	8.00	3.60	1.00
☐ 3 Jim Kelly	10.00	4.50	1.25
☐ 4 Bryce Paup	5.00	2.20	.60
☐ 5 Kerry Collins	25.00	11.00	3.10
☐ 6 Carl Pickens	8.00	3.60	1.00
☐ 7 Emmitt Smith	50.00	22.00	6.25
☐ 8 Michael Irvin	10.00	4.50	1.25
☐ 9 Troy Aikman	25.00	11.00	3.10
☐ 10 Terrell Davis	30.00	13.50	3.70
☐ 11 Barry Sanders	25.00	11.00	3.10
☐ 12 Herman Moore	10.00	4.50	1.25
☐ 13 Brett Favre	50.00	22.00	6.25
☐ 14 Robert Brooks	10.00	4.50	1.25
☐ 15 Jim Harbaugh	8.00	3.60	1.00
☐ 16 Tony Bennett	5.00	2.20	.60
☐ 17 Steve Bono	5.00	2.20	.60
☐ 18 Dan Marino	50.00	22.00	6.25
☐ 19 Cris Carter	8.00	3.60	1.00
☐ 20 Curtis Martin	30.00	13.50	3.70
☐ 21 Tim Brown	8.00	3.60	1.00
☐ 22 Ricky Watters	8.00	3.60	1.00
☐ 23 Yancey Thigpen	8.00	3.60	1.00
☐ 24 Neil O'Donnell	5.00	2.20	.60
☐ 25 Kordell Stewart	25.00	11.00	3.10
☐ 26 Isaac Bruce	10.00	4.50	1.25
☐ 27 Tony Martin	5.00	2.20	.60
☐ 28 Steve Young	20.00	9.00	2.50
☐ 29 Jerry Rice	25.00	11.00	3.10
☐ 30 Chris Warren	8.00	3.60	1.00

1997 Pro Line DC3

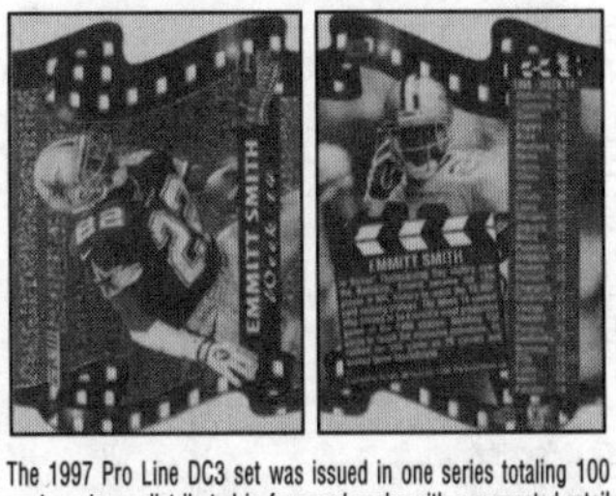

The 1997 Pro Line DC3 set was issued in one series totaling 100 cards and was distributed in four card packs with a suggested retail price of $3.99. The set features top NFL stars from the previous season on a unique die-cut design with detailed copy and statistical information that recaps the 1996 NFL season and allows the collector to accurately judge and compare the performances of offensive and defensive players. The set contains the topical subsets: DC Rewind (68-89) and DC Top Ten (90-100).

	MINT	NRMT	EXC
COMPLETE SET (100)	45.00	20.00	5.50
COMMON CARD (1-100)	.10	.05	.01
☐ 1 Emmitt Smith	4.00	1.80	.50
☐ 2 Rod Woodson	.10	.05	.01
☐ 3 Eddie George	2.50	1.10	.30
☐ 4 Ty Detmer	.20	.09	.03
☐ 5 Zach Thomas	.60	.25	.07
☐ 6 Kevin Greene	.10	.05	.01
☐ 7 Michael Jackson	.10	.05	.01
☐ 8 Isaac Bruce	.10	.05	.01
☐ 9 Joey Galloway	.60	.25	.07
☐ 10 Bryant Young	.10	.05	.01
☐ 11 Terrell Davis	2.00	.90	.25
☐ 12 Mark Brunell	2.00	.90	.25
☐ 13 Marvin Harrison	.75	.35	.09
☐ 14 Jake Reed	.10	.05	.01
☐ 15 Terry Allen	.10	.05	.01
☐ 16 Kordell Stewart	1.50	.70	.19
☐ 17 Reggie White	.10	.05	.01
☐ 18 Michael Irvin	.10	.05	.01
☐ 19 Tony Martin	.10	.05	.01
☐ 20 Barry Sanders	2.00	.90	.25
☐ 21 Tony Boselli	.10	.05	.01
☐ 22 Carl Pickens	.10	.05	.01
☐ 23 Simeon Rice	.10	.05	.01
☐ 24 Adrian Murrell	.10	.05	.01
☐ 25 Lamar Lathon	.10	.05	.01
☐ 26 Thurman Thomas	.10	.05	.01
☐ 27 Tim Brown	.10	.05	.01
☐ 28 Karim Abdul-Jabbar	1.25	.55	.16
☐ 29 Brad Johnson	.10	.05	.01
☐ 30 Keenan McCardell	.10	.05	.01
☐ 31 Keyshawn Johnson	.75	.35	.09
☐ 32 Ricky Watters	.10	.05	.01
☐ 33 Michael McCrary	.10	.05	.01
☐ 34 Brett Favre	4.00	1.80	.50
☐ 35 Steve McNair	1.25	.55	.16
☐ 36 Herman Moore	.10	.05	.01
☐ 37 Tony Banks	.60	.25	.07
☐ 38 Deion Sanders	1.00	.45	.12
☐ 39 Kerry Collins	1.50	.70	.19
☐ 40 Shannon Sharpe	.10	.05	.01
☐ 41 Drew Bledsoe	2.00	.90	.25
☐ 42 Jim Everett	.10	.05	.01
☐ 43 Jamal Anderson	.10	.05	.01
☐ 44 Irving Fryar	.10	.05	.01
☐ 45 Terry Glenn	1.50	.70	.19
☐ 46 Jerry Rice	2.00	.90	.25
☐ 47 Curtis Martin	2.00	.90	.25
☐ 48 Curtis Conway	.10	.05	.01
☐ 49 Jerome Bettis	.10	.05	.01
☐ 50 Vinny Testaverde	.10	.05	.01
☐ 51 Mike Alstott	.10	.05	.01
☐ 52 Anthony Johnson	.10	.05	.01
☐ 53 Dan Marino	4.00	1.80	.50
☐ 54 Junior Seau	.10	.05	.01
☐ 55 Steve Young	1.25	.55	.16
☐ 56 Troy Aikman	2.00	.90	.25
☐ 57 Jimmy Smith	.10	.05	.01
☐ 58 Cris Carter	.10	.05	.01
☐ 59 Gus Frerotte	.10	.05	.01
☐ 60 Marcus Allen	.10	.05	.01
☐ 61 Rodney Hampton	.10	.05	.01
☐ 62 Bruce Smith	.10	.05	.01
☐ 63 Leroy Butler	.10	.05	.01
☐ 64 Jeff Blake	.10	.05	.01
☐ 65 Antonio Freeman	.60	.25	.07
☐ 66 John Elway	1.50	.70	.19
☐ 67 Brett Favre John Michaels Andre Rison Checklist Card 1-67	.75	.35	.09
☐ 68 Barry Sanders REW	1.00	.45	.12
☐ 69 Troy Aikman REW	1.00	.45	.12
☐ 70 Jerome Bettis REW	.10	.05	.01
☐ 71 Mark Brunell REW	1.00	.45	.12
☐ 72 Junior Seau REW	.10	.05	.01
☐ 73 John Elway REW	.75	.35	.09
☐ 74 Chad Brown REW	.10	.05	.01
☐ 75 Irving Fryar REW	.10	.05	.01
☐ 76 Drew Bledsoe REW	1.00	.45	.12
☐ 77 Jerry Rice REW	1.00	.45	.12
☐ 78 Larry Centers REW	.10	.05	.01
☐ 79 Terrell Davis REW	1.25	.55	.16
☐ 80 Carl Pickens REW	.10	.05	.01
☐ 81 Emmitt Smith REW	2.00	.90	.25
☐ 82 Kerry Collins REW	1.00	.45	.12
☐ 83 Eddie Kennison REW	.75	.35	.09
☐ 84 Kordell Stewart REW	1.00	.45	.12
☐ 85 Natrone Means REW	.10	.05	.01
☐ 86 Curtis Martin REW UER back reads Curtin...	1.25	.55	.16
☐ 87 Dorsey Levens REW	.10	.05	.01
☐ 88 Desmond Howard REW	.10	.05	.01
☐ 89 Brett Favre REW Checklist Card 68-89	1.00	.45	.12
☐ 90 Brett Favre T10	2.00	.90	.25
☐ 91 Terrell Davis T10	1.25	.55	.16
☐ 92 Kevin Greene T10	.10	.05	.01
☐ 93 Terry Allen T10	.10	.05	.01
☐ 94 Barry Sanders T10	1.00	.45	.12
☐ 95 John Elway T10	.75	.35	.09
☐ 96 Ricky Watters T10	.10	.05	.01
☐ 97 Reggie White T10	.10	.05	.01
☐ 98 Jerome Bettis T10	.10	.05	.01
☐ 99 Jerry Rice T10	1.00	.45	.12
☐ 100 Brett Favre T10 Checklist Card 90-100	1.00	.45	.12

1997 Pro Line DC3 Autographs

Randomly inserted at the rate of only one per case, this six-card insert set features color player photos of six hot, up-and-coming NFL stars. Only a maximum of 300 cards were signed by each player.

	MINT	NRMT	EXC
COMPLETE SET (6)	800.00	350.00	100.00
COMMON CARD (1-6)	60.00	27.00	7.50

	MINT	NRMT	EXC
☐ 1 Kordell Stewart	160.00	70.00	20.00
☐ 2 Kerry Collins	160.00	70.00	20.00
☐ 3 Terrell Davis	175.00	80.00	22.00
☐ 4 Eddie George	175.00	80.00	22.00
☐ 5 Karim Abdul-Jabbar	100.00	45.00	12.50
☐ 6 Keyshawn Johnson	60.00	27.00	7.50

1997 Pro Line DC3 All-Pros

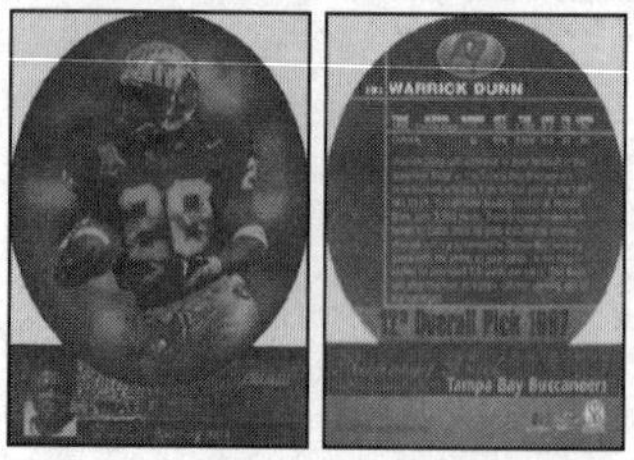

Randomly inserted in packs at a rate of one in 22, this 20-card set features color photos of perennial all-pros and future all-pro players with a unique die-cut card design with bronze foil layering.

	MINT	NRMT	EXC
COMPLETE SET (20)	350.00	160.00	45.00
COMMON CARD (1-20)	6.00	2.70	.75
☐ 1 Emmitt Smith	40.00	18.00	5.00
☐ 2 Brett Favre	40.00	18.00	5.00
☐ 3 Jerry Rice	25.00	11.00	3.10
☐ 4 Steve Young	20.00	9.00	2.50
☐ 5 Barry Sanders	25.00	11.00	3.10
☐ 6 Reggie White	10.00	4.50	1.25
☐ 7 Ricky Watters	6.00	2.70	.75
☐ 8 Lawrence Phillips	6.00	2.70	.75
☐ 9 Kerry Collins	20.00	9.00	2.50
☐ 10 Mark Brunell	25.00	11.00	3.10
☐ 11 John Elway	20.00	9.00	2.50
☐ 12 Dan Marino	40.00	18.00	5.00
☐ 13 Drew Bledsoe	25.00	11.00	3.10
☐ 14 Curtis Martin	25.00	11.00	3.10
☐ 15 Terrell Davis	25.00	11.00	3.10
☐ 16 Karim Abdul-Jabbar	15.00	6.75	1.85
☐ 17 Marvin Harrison	10.00	4.50	1.25
☐ 18 Keyshawn Johnson	6.00	2.70	.75
☐ 19 Terry Glenn	20.00	9.00	2.50
☐ 20 Eddie George	25.00	11.00	3.10

1997 Pro Line DC3 Draftnix Redemption

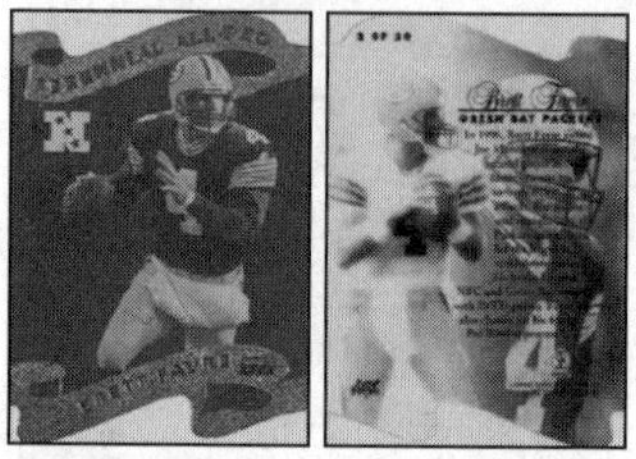

The Draftnix redemption cards were randomly seeded in 1997 Pro Line DC3 packs. The common silver version was inserted at the rate of 1:24 packs and was redeemable for a foil card of the featured player. The more difficult foil redemption card versions (bronze and gold) were redeemable for signed jerseys or complete uniforms of the featured player. A secondary market has not been set for the tougher trade cards.

	MINT	NRMT	EXC
COMPLETE SET (3)	20.00	9.00	2.50
COMMON CARD (1-3)	5.00	2.20	.60
☐ 1 Darrell Russell	5.00	2.20	.60
☐ 2 Warrick Dunn	10.00	4.50	1.25
☐ 3 Tony Gonzalez	5.00	2.20	.60

1997 Pro Line DC3 Road to the Super Bowl

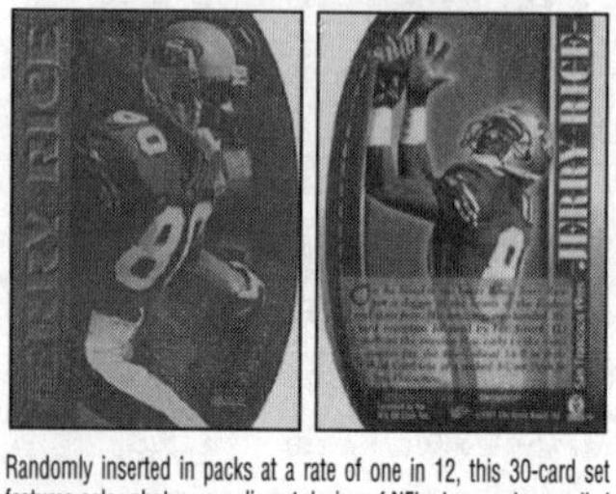

Randomly inserted in packs at a rate of one in 12, this 30-card set features color photos on a die-cut design of NFL players who excelled throughout the regular season and playoffs. The cards are numbered with an "SB" prefix.

	MINT	NRMT	EXC
COMPLETE SET (30)	300.00	135.00	38.00
COMMON CARD (SB1-SB30)	4.00	1.80	.50
☐ SB1 Ricky Watters	6.00	2.70	.75
☐ SB2 Ty Detmer	4.00	1.80	.50
☐ SB3 Emmitt Smith	30.00	13.50	3.70
☐ SB4 Troy Aikman	15.00	6.75	1.85
☐ SB5 Kerry Collins	12.00	5.50	1.50
☐ SB6 Kevin Greene	4.00	1.80	.50
☐ SB7 Steve Young	12.00	5.50	1.50
☐ SB8 Jerry Rice	15.00	6.75	1.85
☐ SB9 Brett Favre	30.00	13.50	3.70
☐ SB10 Reggie White	8.00	3.60	1.00
☐ SB11 Cris Carter	6.00	2.70	.75
☐ SB12 Brad Johnson	4.00	1.80	.50
☐ SB13 Drew Bledsoe	15.00	6.75	1.85
☐ SB14 Curtis Martin	15.00	6.75	1.85
☐ SB15 Bruce Smith	6.00	2.70	.75
☐ SB16 Thurman Thomas	8.00	3.60	1.00
☐ SB17 Jim Harbaugh	6.00	2.70	.75
☐ SB18 Marshall Faulk	8.00	3.60	1.00
☐ SB19 Mark Brunell	15.00	6.75	1.85
☐ SB20 Natrone Means	6.00	2.70	.75
☐ SB21 John Elway	12.00	5.50	1.50
☐ SB22 Terrell Davis	15.00	6.75	1.85
☐ SB23 Kordell Stewart	12.00	5.50	1.50
☐ SB24 Jerome Bettis	8.00	3.60	1.00
☐ SB25 Eddie George	20.00	9.00	2.50
☐ SB26 Dan Marino	30.00	13.50	3.70
☐ SB27 Terry Glenn	15.00	6.75	1.85
☐ SB28 Antonio Freeman	8.00	3.60	1.00
☐ SB29 Anthony Johnson	4.00	1.80	.50
☐ SB30 Kevin Hardy	4.00	1.80	.50

1996 Pro Line Intense

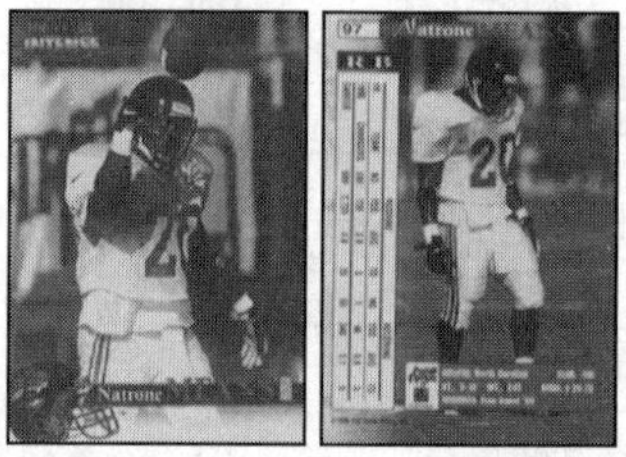

The 1996 Proline Intense set was issued in one series totalling 100 cards and was distributed in five-card packs. The fronts feature borderless color action player photos with the player's name and team helmet at the bottom. The backs carry player information and career statistics.

	MINT	NRMT	EXC
COMPLETE SET (100)	25.00	11.00	3.10
COMMON CARD (1-100)	.08	.04	.01
☐ 1 Kerry Collins	1.50	.70	.19
☐ 2 Jeff George	.15	.07	.02
☐ 3 Mark Brunell	1.25	.55	.16
☐ 4 Steve McNair	1.25	.55	.16
☐ 5 Rick Mirer	.15	.07	.02
☐ 6 Dave Brown	.15	.07	.02
☐ 7 Rashaan Salaam	.30	.14	.04
☐ 8 Marshall Faulk	.30	.14	.04
☐ 9 Erric Pegram	.15	.07	.02
☐ 10 Cris Carter	.30	.14	.04
☐ 11 Eric Allen	.08	.04	.01
☐ 12 Jim Kelly	.30	.14	.04
☐ 13 Jeff Blake	.30	.14	.04
☐ 14 Stan Humphries	.15	.07	.02
☐ 15 Scott Mitchell	.15	.07	.02
☐ 16 Jeff Hostetler	.15	.07	.02
☐ 17 Rodney Peete	.08	.04	.01
☐ 18 Warren Moon	.15	.07	.02
☐ 19 Erict Rhett	.15	.07	.02
☐ 20 Terrell Davis	2.00	.90	.25
☐ 21 J.J. Stokes	.30	.14	.04
☐ 22 Marco Coleman	.08	.04	.01
☐ 23 Heath Shuler	.30	.14	.04
☐ 24 Duane Clemons	.08	.04	.01
☐ 25 Amani Toomer	.30	.14	.04
☐ 26 Leslie O'Neal	.08	.04	.01
☐ 27 Tamarick Vanover	.30	.14	.04
☐ 28 Steve Bono	.15	.07	.02
☐ 29 Jim Everett	.08	.04	.01
☐ 30 Erik Kramer	.08	.04	.01
☐ 31 Trent Dilfer	.15	.07	.02
☐ 32 Jim Harbaugh	.15	.07	.02
☐ 33 Vinny Testaverde	.15	.07	.02
☐ 34 Rodney Hampton	.15	.07	.02
☐ 35 Chris Warren	.15	.07	.02
☐ 36 Curtis Martin	2.00	.90	.25
☐ 37 Eddie Kennison	1.50	.70	.19
☐ 38 Herman Moore	.30	.14	.04
☐ 39 Terance Mathis	.08	.04	.01
☐ 40 Carl Pickens	.30	.14	.04
☐ 41 Isaac Bruce	.30	.14	.04
☐ 42 Reggie White	.30	.14	.04
☐ 43 Junior Seau	.30	.14	.04
☐ 44 Bryce Paup	.15	.07	.02
☐ 45 Deion Sanders	.75	.35	.09
☐ 46 Thurman Thomas	.30	.14	.04
☐ 47 Gus Frerotte	.30	.14	.04
☐ 48 Tony Mandarich	.08	.04	.01
☐ 49 Michael Irvin	.30	.14	.04
☐ 50 Wayne Chrebet	.15	.07	.02
☐ 51 Bobby Engram	1.00	.45	.12
☐ 52 Marcus Jones	.08	.04	.01
☐ 53 Daryl Gardener	.15	.07	.02
☐ 54 Alex Van Dyke	.15	.07	.02
☐ 55 Andre Rison	.15	.07	.02
☐ 56 Regan Upshaw	.08	.04	.01
☐ 57 Jason Dunn	.15	.07	.02
☐ 58 Mark Chmura	.15	.07	.02
☐ 59 Ray Lewis	.08	.04	.01
☐ 60 Rickey Dudley	.30	.14	.04
☐ 61 Leeland McElroy	.30	.14	.04
☐ 62 Derrick Thomas	.15	.07	.02
☐ 63 Bobby Hoying	.30	.14	.04
☐ 64 Robert Brooks	.30	.14	.04
☐ 65 Tim Brown	.15	.07	.02
☐ 66 Michael Westbrook	.30	.14	.04
☐ 67 Jim Miller	.08	.04	.01
☐ 68 Aaron Hayden	.08	.04	.01
☐ 69 Marcus Allen	.30	.14	.04
☐ 70 Troy Aikman	1.25	.55	.16
☐ 71 Steve Young	1.00	.45	.12
☐ 72 Neil O'Donnell	.15	.07	.02
☐ 73 Drew Bledsoe	1.25	.55	.16
☐ 74 Emmitt Smith	2.50	1.10	.30
☐ 75 Ki-Jana Carter	.15	.07	.02
☐ 76 Irving Fryar	.15	.07	.02
☐ 77 Joey Galloway	.60	.25	.07
☐ 78 Russell Maryland	.08	.04	.01
☐ 79 Kordell Stewart	1.50	.70	.19
☐ 80 Barry Sanders	1.25	.55	.16
☐ 81 Bryan Cox	.08	.04	.01
☐ 82 Keyshawn Johnson	1.50	.70	.19
☐ 83 Karim Abdul-Jabbar	2.00	.90	.25
☐ 84 Kevin Hardy	.15	.07	.02
☐ 85 Rodney Thomas	.08	.04	.01
☐ 86 John Elway	1.00	.45	.12
☐ 87 Dan Marino	2.50	1.10	.30
☐ 88 Brett Favre	2.50	1.10	.30
☐ 89 Eric Metcalf	.15	.07	.02
☐ 90 Jonathan Ogden	.08	.04	.01
☐ 91 Eddie George	3.00	1.35	.35
☐ 92 Simeon Rice	.30	.14	.04
☐ 93 Tim Biakabutuka	1.00	.45	.12
☐ 94 Terry Glenn	2.50	1.10	.30
☐ 95 Marvin Harrison	1.50	.70	.19
☐ 96 Lawrence Phillips	.50	.23	.06
☐ 97 Natrone Means	.30	.14	.04
☐ 98 Jerry Rice	1.25	.55	.16
☐ 99 Ricky Watters	.15	.07	.02
☐ 100 Emmitt Smith Checklist card	.40	.18	.05

1996 Pro Line Intense Double Intensity

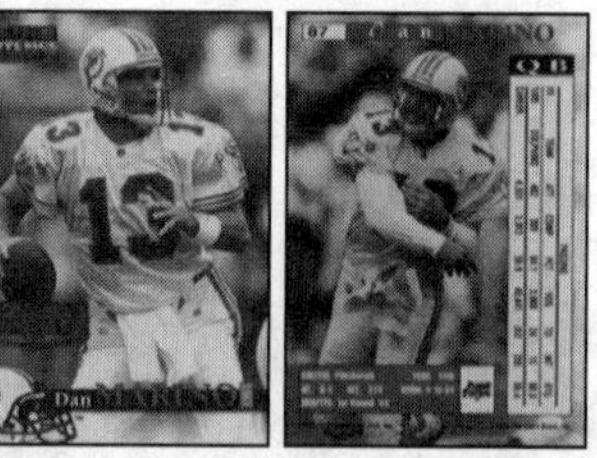

Randomly inserted in packs at a rate of one in five, this 100-card set is a foil parallel version of the regular Proline Intensity set.

	MINT	NRMT	EXC
COMPLETE SET (100)	150.00	70.00	19.00
COMMON CARD (1-100)	.50	.23	.06

*VETERAN STARS: 3X TO 6X BASIC CARDS
*YOUNG STARS: 2X TO 4X BASIC CARDS
*RCs: 1.5X TO 3X BASIC CARDS

1996 Pro Line Intense Determined

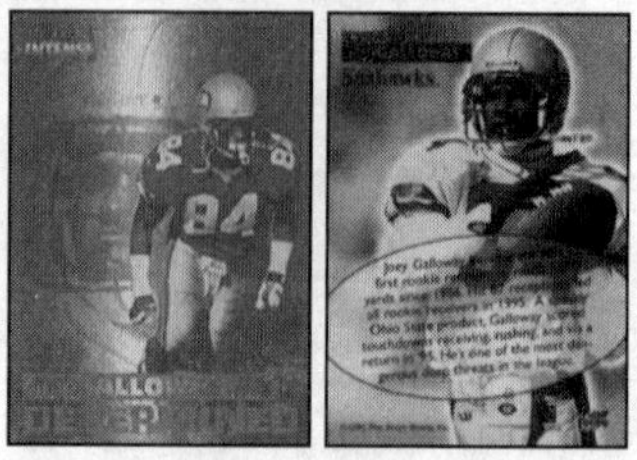

Randomly inserted in packs at a rate of one in 50, this 20-card set features color player images on a silver metallic-look background of a large head photo of the player. The backs feature another player image with a paragraph about the player.

	MINT	NRMT	EXC
COMPLETE SET (20)	300.00	135.00	38.00
COMMON CARD (1-20)	6.00	2.70	.75
☐ 1 Kerry Collins	20.00	9.00	2.50
☐ 2 Troy Aikman	20.00	9.00	2.50
☐ 3 Herman Moore	8.00	3.60	1.00
☐ 4 Mark Brunell	20.00	9.00	2.50
☐ 5 Dan Marino	40.00	18.00	5.00
☐ 6 Kordell Stewart	20.00	9.00	2.50
☐ 7 Junior Seau	6.00	2.70	.75
☐ 8 Steve Young	16.00	7.25	2.00
☐ 9 John Elway	16.00	7.25	2.00
☐ 10 Emmitt Smith	40.00	18.00	5.00
☐ 11 Steve McNair	15.00	6.75	1.85
☐ 12 Drew Bledsoe	20.00	9.00	2.50
☐ 13 Joey Galloway	10.00	4.50	1.25
☐ 14 Deion Sanders	12.00	5.50	1.50
☐ 15 Kevin Hardy	6.00	2.70	.75
☐ 16 Keyshawn Johnson	12.00	5.50	1.50
☐ 17 Marvin Harrison	12.00	5.50	1.50
☐ 18 Tim Biakabutuka	8.00	3.60	1.00
☐ 19 Eddie George	30.00	13.50	3.70
☐ 20 Terry Glenn	25.00	11.00	3.10

1996 Pro Line Intense Phone Cards 3.00

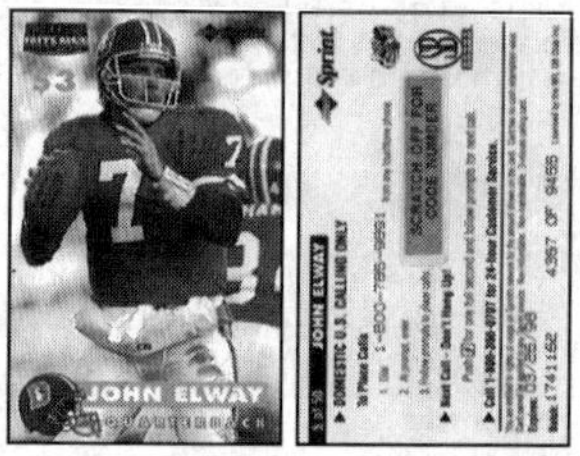

Randomly inserted in 1996 Pro Line Intense packs at a rate of one in 18, this 50-card set includes $3.00 worth of Sprint long distance per card. Two parallel sets of the $3.00 cards were also included in the Phone Card pack release. Proof cards were inserted at the rate of 1:29 and Test cards were inserted at the rate of 1:55 packs.

	MINT	NRMT	EXC
COMPLETE SET (50)	100.00	45.00	12.50
COMMON CARD (1-50)	1.50	.70	.19

*PROOF CARDS: 1X TO 2X BASIC CARDS
*TEST CARDS: 2X TO 4X BASIC CARDS

	MINT	NRMT	EXC
☐ 1 Jim Kelly	2.00	.90	.25
☐ 2 Kerry Collins	4.00	1.80	.50
☐ 3 Jeff George	1.50	.70	.19
☐ 4 Troy Aikman	4.00	1.80	.50
☐ 5 John Elway	3.00	1.35	.35
☐ 6 Herman Moore	2.00	.90	.25
☐ 7 Barry Sanders	4.00	1.80	.50
☐ 8 Brett Favre	8.00	3.60	1.00
☐ 9 Jim Harbaugh	1.50	.70	.19
☐ 10 Steve Bono	1.50	.70	.19
☐ 11 Dan Marino	8.00	3.60	1.00
☐ 12 Drew Bledsoe	4.00	1.80	.50
☐ 13 Jim Everett	1.50	.70	.19
☐ 14 Neil O'Donnell	1.50	.70	.19
☐ 15 Ricky Watters	1.50	.70	.19
☐ 16 Junior Seau	1.50	.70	.19
☐ 17 Jerry Rice	4.00	1.80	.50
☐ 18 Errict Rhett	2.00	.90	.25
☐ 19 Joey Galloway	2.00	.90	.25
☐ 20 Steve Young	3.00	1.35	.35
☐ 21 Kordell Stewart	4.00	1.80	.50
☐ 22 Rodney Hampton	1.50	.70	.19
☐ 23 Curtis Martin	5.00	2.20	.60
☐ 24 Mark Brunell	4.00	1.80	.50
☐ 25 Steve McNair	3.00	1.35	.35
☐ 26 Deion Sanders	2.50	1.10	.30
☐ 27 Carl Pickens	1.50	.70	.19
☐ 28 Michael Irvin	2.00	.90	.25
☐ 29 Tamarick Vanover	1.50	.70	.19
☐ 30 Trent Dilfer	1.50	.70	.19
☐ 31 Chris Warren	1.50	.70	.19
☐ 32 Stan Humphries	1.50	.70	.19
☐ 33 J.J. Stokes	2.00	.90	.25
☐ 34 Tim Biakabutuka	2.00	.90	.25
☐ 35 Keyshawn Johnson	2.50	1.10	.30
☐ 36 Simeon Rice	1.50	.70	.19
☐ 37 Jonathan Ogden	1.50	.70	.19
☐ 38 Rashaan Salaam	2.00	.90	.25
☐ 39 Bobby Engram	1.50	.70	.19
☐ 40 Reggie White	2.00	.90	.25
☐ 41 Isaac Bruce	2.00	.90	.25
☐ 42 Eddie George	6.00	2.70	.75
☐ 43 Marvin Harrison	2.50	1.10	.30
☐ 44 Kevin Hardy	1.50	.70	.19
☐ 45 Karim Abdul-Jabbar	4.00	1.80	.50
☐ 46 Duane Clemons	1.50	.70	.19
☐ 47 Terry Glenn	5.00	2.20	.60
☐ 48 Marcus Allen	1.50	.70	.19
☐ 49 Rickey Dudley	1.50	.70	.19
☐ 50 Lawrence Phillips	1.50	.70	.19

1996 Pro Line Intense Phone Cards 5.00

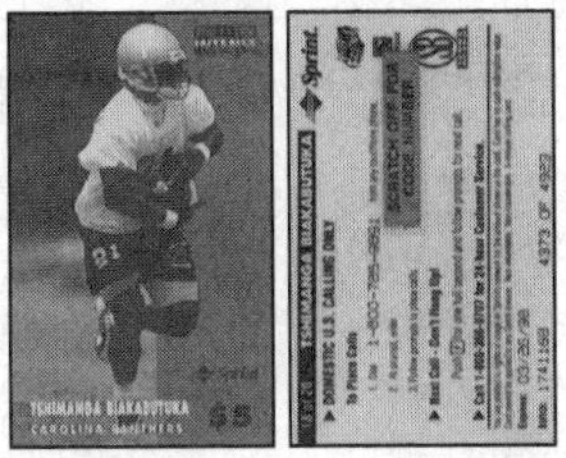

Randomly inserted in 1996 Pro Line Intense packs at a rate of one in 35, this 20-card set includes $5.00 worth of Sprint long distance phone calls per card. The expiration date for calling is March 26, 1998. The cards were released as well in 1996 Score Board NFL Phone Card packs. Two parallel sets of the $5.00 cards were included in the Phone Card pack release. Proof cards were inserted at the rate of 1:65 (numbered of 108 made) and Test cards were inserted at the rate of 1:130 packs (numbered of 52 made).

	MINT	NRMT	EXC
COMPLETE SET (20)	120.00	55.00	15.00
COMMON CARD (1-20)	2.00	.90	.25

*PROOF CARDS: 1X TO 2X BASIC CARDS
*TEST CARDS: 2X TO 4X BASIC CARDS

☐ 1 Kerry Collins	7.00	3.10	.85
☐ 2 Troy Aikman	7.00	3.10	.85
☐ 3 Reggie White	3.00	1.35	.35
☐ 4 Mark Brunell	7.00	3.10	.85
☐ 5 Dan Marino	14.00	6.25	1.75
☐ 6 Kordell Stewart	7.00	3.10	.85
☐ 7 Junior Seau	2.00	.90	.25
☐ 8 Steve Young	6.00	2.70	.75
☐ 9 John Elway	6.00	2.70	.75
☐ 10 Terrell Davis	8.00	3.60	1.00
☐ 11 Steve McNair	5.00	2.20	.60
☐ 12 Drew Bledsoe	7.00	3.10	.85
☐ 13 Joey Galloway	3.00	1.35	.35
☐ 14 Deion Sanders	5.00	2.20	.60
☐ 15 Kevin Hardy	2.00	.90	.25
☐ 16 Keyshawn Johnson	4.00	1.80	.50
☐ 17 Marvin Harrison	4.00	1.80	.50
☐ 18 Tim Biakabutuka	3.00	1.35	.35
☐ 19 Eddie George	10.00	4.50	1.25
☐ 20 Terry Glenn	8.00	3.60	1.00

1996 Pro Line Intense Phone Cards 10.00

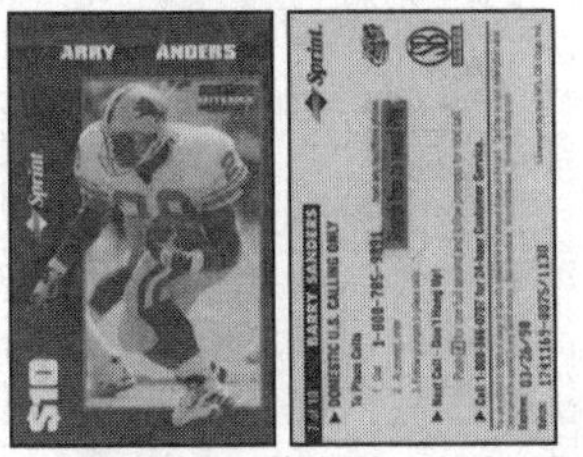

Randomly inserted in Score Board Phone Card packs at a rate of one in 12, this 10-card set features color action player photos with the Sprint calling value of the card printed on the front. The backs carry the instructions on how to use the phone cards. Only 1130 of each card was produced and each is sequentially numbered. Two parallel sets were also included in the Phone Card pack release. Proof cards were inserted at the rate of 1:400 and Test cards were inserted at the rate of 1:800 packs. The expiration date is March 26, 1998.

	MINT	NRMT	EXC
COMPLETE SET (10)	100.00	45.00	12.50
COMMON CARD (1-10)	5.00	2.20	.60

*PROOF CARDS: 1X TO 2X BASIC CARDS
*TEST CARDS: 2X TO 4X BASIC CARDS

☐ 1 Dan Marino	20.00	9.00	2.50
☐ 2 Jim Harbaugh	5.00	2.20	.60
☐ 3 Troy Aikman	12.00	5.50	1.50
☐ 4 Curtis Martin	14.00	6.25	1.75
☐ 5 Kordell Stewart	12.00	5.50	1.50
☐ 6 Steve Young	10.00	4.50	1.25
☐ 7 Barry Sanders	10.00	4.50	1.25
☐ 8 Keyshawn Johnson	7.00	3.10	.85
☐ 9 Lawrence Phillips	7.00	3.10	.85
☐ 10 Eddie George	16.00	7.25	2.00

1996 Pro Line Intense Phone Cards 25.00 Die-Cuts

Randomly inserted in 1996 Score Board Phone Card packs at a rate of one in 36, this 10-card set features color action player photos with the calling value of the card printed on the die-cut front. The backs carry the instructions on how to use the phone cards. Only 377 of each card was produced and are sequentially numbered. Two parallel sets were also included in the Phone Card pack release. Proof cards were inserted at the rate of 1:550 and Test cards were inserted at the rate of 1:1100 packs. The expiration date is March 26, 1998.

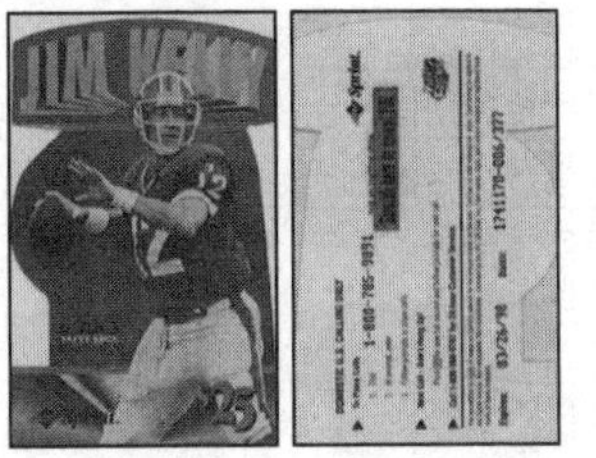

	MINT	NRMT	EXC
COMPLETE SET (10)	200.00	90.00	25.00
COMMON CARD (1-10)	12.00	5.50	1.50

*PROOF CARDS: 1X TO 2X BASIC CARDS
*TEST CARDS: 2X TO 4X BASIC CARDS

☐ 1 Jim Kelly	12.00	5.50	1.50
☐ 2 Troy Aikman	20.00	9.00	2.50
☐ 3 John Elway	18.00	8.00	2.20
☐ 4 Kerry Collins	20.00	9.00	2.50
☐ 5 Barry Sanders	20.00	9.00	2.50
☐ 6 Drew Bledsoe	20.00	9.00	2.50
☐ 7 Keyshawn Johnson	12.00	5.50	1.50
☐ 8 Deion Sanders	15.00	6.75	1.85
☐ 9 Dan Marino	40.00	18.00	5.00
☐ 10 Brett Favre	40.00	18.00	5.00

1996 Pro Line Memorabilia

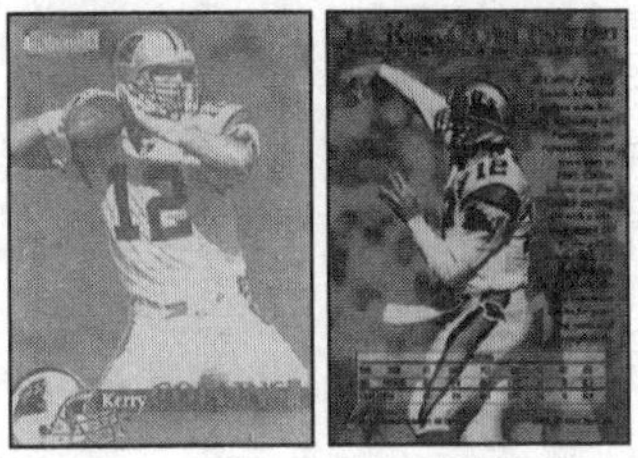

The 1996 Pro Line Memorabilia set was issued in one series totalling 100 cards and was distributed in five-card packs with a suggested retail price of $4.99. The fronts feature borderless action player photos with the player's name and team helmet at the bottom. The backs carry a paragraph about the player and statistics.

	MINT	NRMT	EXC
COMPLETE SET (100)	30.00	13.50	3.70
COMMON CARD (1-100)	.10	.05	.01

*MEMOR.CARDS: SAME PRICE AS INTENSE

1996 Pro Line Memorabilia Producers

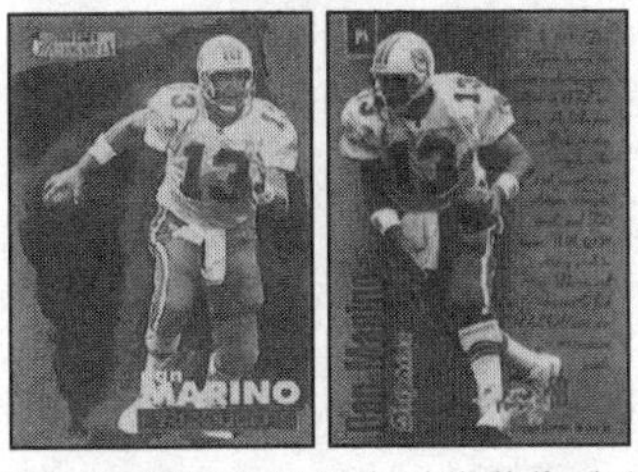

Randomly inserted in packs at a rate of one in six, this 10-card set features color player image with a silver foil shadow on a copper metallic-look background. The backs carry another player image and a paragraph about the player.

	MINT	NRMT	EXC
COMPLETE SET (10)	60.00	27.00	7.50
COMMON CARD (P1-P10)	1.25	.55	.16

*SILVER SIGNATURES: 2X TO 4X

☐ P1 Keyshawn Johnson	3.00	1.35	.35
☐ P2 Barry Sanders	6.00	2.70	.75
☐ P3 Eddie George	10.00	4.50	1.25
☐ P4 Emmitt Smith	12.00	5.50	1.50
☐ P5 Jerry Rice	6.00	2.70	.75
☐ P6 Brett Favre	12.00	5.50	1.50
☐ P7 Ricky Watters	1.25	.55	.16
☐ P8 Dan Marino	12.00	5.50	1.50
☐ P9 Deion Sanders	4.00	1.80	.50
☐ P10 Marshall Faulk	2.00	.90	.25

1996 Pro Line Memorabilia Rookie Autographs

Randomly inserted in packs at the rate of one in 12, this 15-card set features borderless color action player photos of NFL rookies with the player's autograph on the front. A limited number of each card was signed by the pictured player and are sequentially numbered. The cards are unnumbered and checklisted below alphabetically.

	MINT	NRMT	EXC
COMPLETE SET (15)	900.00	400.00	110.00
COMMON CARD	15.00	6.75	1.85

☐ 1 Tim Biakabutuka/210	70.00	32.00	8.75
☐ 2 Tim Biakabutuka/600	200.00	90.00	25.00
Eddie George			
☐ 3 Duane Clemons/1255	15.00	6.75	1.85
☐ 4 Daryl Gardener/1390	20.00	9.00	2.50
☐ 5 Eddie George/395	175.00	80.00	22.00
☐ 6 Terry Glenn/600	200.00	90.00	25.00
Keyshawn Johnson			
☐ 7 Kevin Hardy/940	20.00	9.00	2.50
☐ 8 Jeff Hartings/1370	15.00	6.75	1.85
☐ 9 Andre Johnson/1370	15.00	6.75	1.85
☐ 10 Keyshawn Johnson/195	125.00	55.00	15.50
☐ 11 Pete Kendall/1495	15.00	6.75	1.85
☐ 12 Alex Molden/1320	15.00	6.75	1.85
☐ 13 Eric Moulds/1010	35.00	16.00	4.40
☐ 14 Jamain Stephens/795	15.00	6.75	1.85
☐ 15 Jerome Woods/1375	15.00	6.75	1.85

1996 Pro Line Memorabilia Stretch Drive

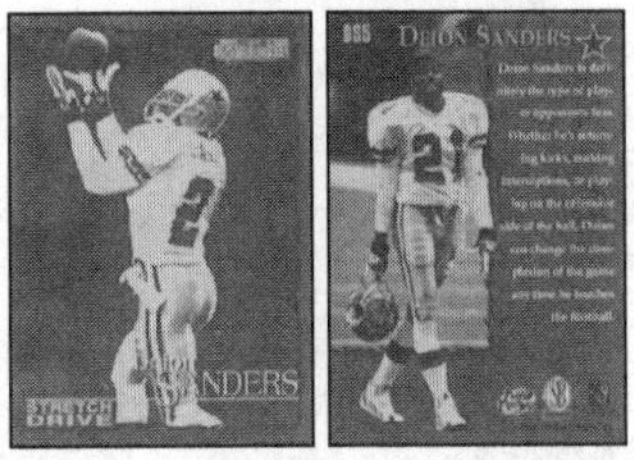

Randomly inserted in packs at a rate of one in three, this 30-card set features color player photos with a three-sided silver-tone border. The backs carry another player photo and a paragraph about the player.

	MINT	NRMT	EXC
COMPLETE SET (30)	150.00	70.00	19.00
COMMON CARD (DS1-DS30)	2.00	.90	.25

*SILVER SIGNATURES: 1X TO 2X BASIC CARDS

☐ DS1 Jim Kelly	3.00	1.35	.35
☐ DS2 Kerry Collins	8.00	3.60	1.00
☐ DS3 Rashaan Salaam	3.00	1.35	.35
☐ DS4 Jeff Blake	2.00	.90	.25
☐ DS5 Deion Sanders	5.00	2.20	.60
☐ DS6 Troy Aikman	8.00	3.60	1.00
☐ DS7 Emmitt Smith	15.00	6.75	1.85
☐ DS8 John Elway	6.00	2.70	.75
☐ DS9 Terrell Davis	10.00	4.50	1.25
☐ DS10 Barry Sanders	8.00	3.60	1.00
☐ DS11 Brett Favre	15.00	6.75	1.85
☐ DS12 Steve McNair	6.00	2.70	.75
☐ DS13 Eddie George	12.00	5.50	1.50
☐ DS14 Marshall Faulk	3.00	1.35	.35
☐ DS15 Marvin Harrison	4.00	1.80	.50
☐ DS16 Herman Moore	3.00	1.35	.35
☐ DS17 Dan Marino	15.00	6.75	1.85
☐ DS18 Curtis Martin	10.00	4.50	1.25
☐ DS19 Drew Bledsoe	8.00	3.60	1.00
☐ DS20 Terry Glenn	8.00	3.60	1.00
☐ DS21 Lawrence Phillips	2.00	.90	.25
☐ DS22 Neil O'Donnell	2.00	.90	.25
☐ DS23 Keyshawn Johnson	4.00	1.80	.50
☐ DS24 Isaac Bruce	3.00	1.35	.35
☐ DS25 Ricky Watters	2.00	.90	.25
☐ DS26 Kordell Stewart	8.00	3.60	1.00
☐ DS27 J.J. Stokes	3.00	1.35	.35
☐ DS28 Steve Young	6.00	2.70	.75
☐ DS29 Joey Galloway	4.00	1.80	.50
☐ DS30 Errict Rhett	3.00	1.35	.35

1995 ProMint Marino Promo

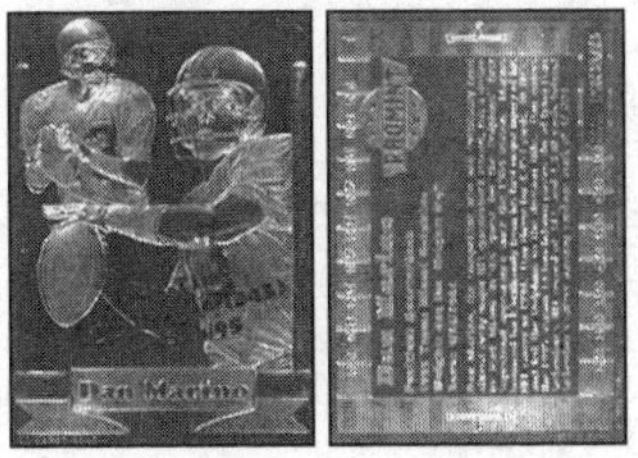

ProMint released this Dan Marino Promo "gold" card. It was printed on front and back fully in gold foil with a 22 Karat Gold notation at the bottom of the cardfront. The back includes a write-up, the card number 1, and the Promo designation.

	MINT	NRMT	EXC
COMPLETE SET (1)	5.00	2.20	.60
COMMON CARD	5.00	2.20	.60

☐ 1 Dan Marino	5.00	2.20	.60

1988 Pro Set Test Designs

These five Randall Cunningham standard-size cards are the test designs for the 1989 Pro Set football cards. As tests, they were produced in very small quantities. It seems that all cards in this five-card set were printed at the same time and in the same (small) quantities. The five variations are basically experiments with and without borders and different color combinations. Horizontally oriented backs have a close-up photograph of player, statistical and biographical information, card number, and the Pro Set logo in a box enclosed in a white border. Player's name and personal statistics appear in reverse-out lettering in a colored band across the top of the card.

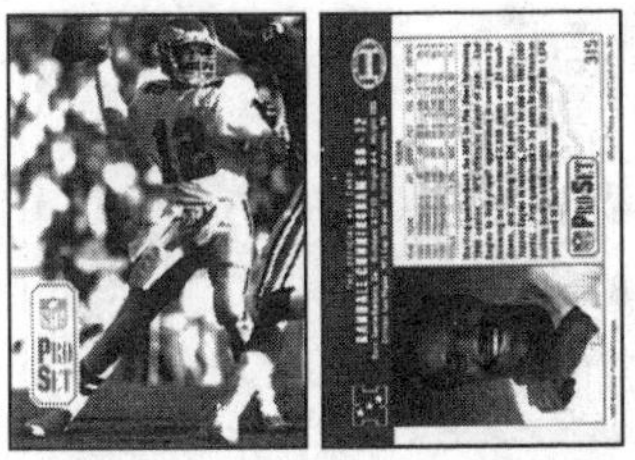

	MINT	NRMT	EXC
COMPLETE SET (5)	250.00	110.00	31.00
COMMON CARD	50.00	22.00	6.25

☐ 315A Randall Cunningham (No name or team designated on card front; borderless; vertical logo)	50.00	22.00	6.25
☐ 315B Randall Cunningham (No name or team designated on card front; silver border; vertical logo)	50.00	22.00	6.25
☐ 315C Randall Cunningham (Name and team designated on card front; borderless; horizontal logo)	50.00	22.00	6.25
☐ 315D Randall Cunningham (Name and team designated on card front; black border; horizontal logo)	50.00	22.00	6.25
☐ 315E Randall Cunningham (Name and team designated on card front; gray border; horizontal logo)	50.00	22.00	6.25

1988 Pro Set Test

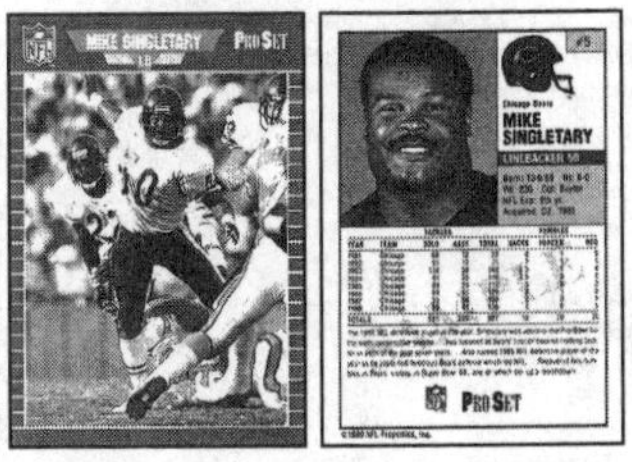

This eight-card standard-size set was reportedly produced as a give-away to show interested parties what the new "Pro Set" cards were going to be like. They were produced in limited quantities and merely given away primarily at the National Candy show in Phoenix. The only front photo that was the same in the actual set was Jerry Rice. This set is also distinguishable in that the backs are oriented vertically rather than horizontally as the regular set.

	MINT	NRMT	EXC
COMPLETE SET (8)	300.00	135.00	38.00
COMMON CARD (1-8)	15.00	6.75	1.85

☐ 1 Dan Marino	125.00	55.00	15.50
☐ 2 Jerry Rice	75.00	34.00	9.50
☐ 3 Eric Dickerson	20.00	9.00	2.50
☐ 4 Reggie White	35.00	16.00	4.40
☐ 5 Mike Singletary	20.00	9.00	2.50
☐ 6 Frank Minnifield	15.00	6.75	1.85
☐ 7 Phil Simms	20.00	9.00	2.50
☐ 8 Jim Kelly	35.00	16.00	4.40

1989 Pro Set Promos

Cards 445, 455, and 463 were planned for inclusion in the Pro Set second series but were withdrawn before mass production began. Note, however, that Thomas Sanders was included in the set but as number 446. The Santa Claus card was mailed out to dealers and NFL dignitaries in December 1989. The Super Bowl Show card was given out to attendees at the show in New Orleans in late January 1990. All of these cards are standard size and utilize the 1989 Pro Set design.

	MINT	NRMT	EXC
COMPLETE SET (5)	75.00	34.00	9.50
COMMON CARD	2.00	.90	.25

☐ 445 Thomas Sanders	10.00	4.50	1.25
☐ 455 Blair Bush	10.00	4.50	1.25

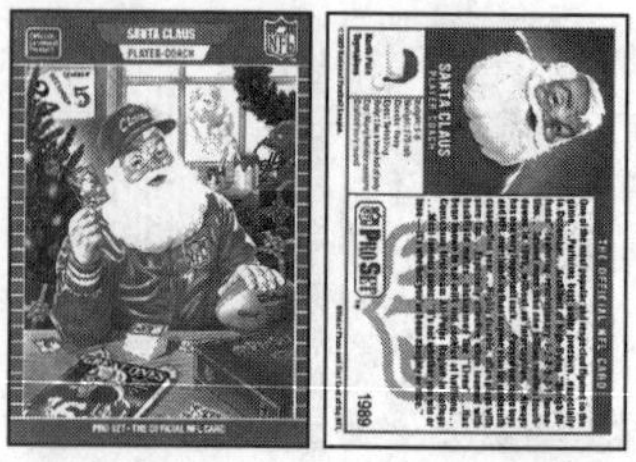

☐ 463 James Lofton	20.00	9.00	2.50
☐ 1989 Santa Claus	40.00	18.00	5.00
☐ NNO Super Bowl Card Show I	2.00	.90	.25
New Orleans Super Bowl XXIV			

1989 Pro Set

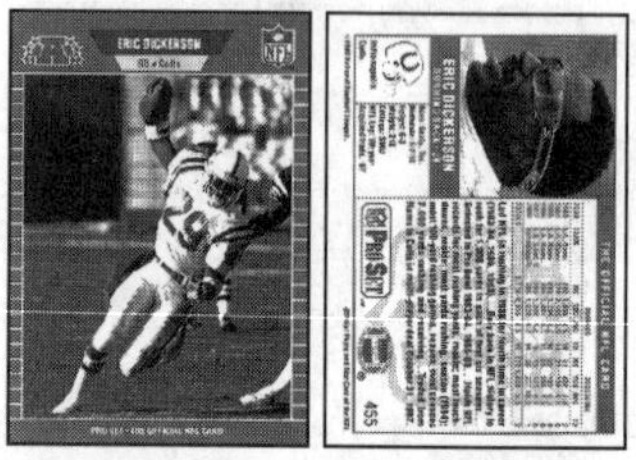

Pro Set entered the football card market with a three series offering for 1989. A first series consisted of 440 cards followed by a 100-card second series offering. A Final Update set consisted of 21 cards for a total of 561 standard-size full-color cards. The backs are horizontal with a small photo, statistics and highlights. The first series is ordered numerically by teams and alphabetically within teams. The second series, issued five cards per Series II pack, includes first-round draft picks (485-515) from the previous spring's college draft and cards numbered 516-540 are "Pro Set Prospects". The second series cards differ in design by having a red border. The Final Update set includes Pro Set Prospects (542-549) and several cards (550-561) of players that were traded since the start of the season. These cards were also part of the second series offering. Complete Final Update sets were offered direct from Pro Set for $2.00 plus 50 Pro Set Play Book points. Rookie Cards include Troy Aikman, Flipper Anderson, Don Beebe, Brian Blades, Tim Brown, Cris Carter, Michael Irvin, Keith Jackson, Dave Meggett, Eric Metcalf, Anthony Miller, Jay Novacek, Rodney Peete, Andre Rison, Mark Rypien, Barry Sanders, Deion Sanders, Sterling Sharpe, Neil Smith, Chris Spielman, John Taylor, Derrick Thomas, Thurman Thomas and Rod Woodson. Card No. 47A William Perry, was pulled early in the initial production run creating a short print. He was replaced by Ron Morris (47B). A single print by design, the Pete Rozelle commemorative card was randomly inserted in one out of every 200 first series packs. The set is considered complete without either the Perry or the Rozelle cards.

	MINT	NRMT	EXC
COMPLETE SET (561)	20.00	9.00	2.50
COMPLETE SERIES 1 (440)	6.00	2.70	.75
COMPLETE SERIES 2 (100)	12.00	5.50	1.50
COMPLETE FINAL SERIES (21)	2.00	.90	.25
COMPLETE FINAL FACT. (21)	2.00	.90	.25
COMMON CARD (1-561)	.04	.02	.01
☐ 1 Stacey Bailey	.04	.02	.01
☐ 2 Aundray Bruce	.04	.02	.01
☐ 3 Rick Bryan	.04	.02	.01
☐ 4 Bobby Butler	.04	.02	.01
☐ 5 Scott Case	.04	.02	.01
☐ 6 Tony Casillas	.04	.02	.01
☐ 7 Floyd Dixon	.04	.02	.01
☐ 8 Rick Donnelly	.04	.02	.01
☐ 9 Bill Fralic	.04	.02	.01
☐ 10 Mike Gann	.04	.02	.01
☐ 11 Mike Kenn	.04	.02	.01
☐ 12 Chris Miller	.25	.11	.03
☐ 13 John Rade	.04	.02	.01
☐ 14 Gerald Riggs UER	.10	.05	.01
(Uniform number is 42			
but 43 on back)			
☐ 15 John Settle	.04	.02	.01
☐ 16 Marion Campbell CO	.04	.02	.01
☐ 17 Cornelius Bennett	.10	.05	.01
☐ 18 Derrick Burroughs	.04	.02	.01
☐ 19 Shane Conlan	.04	.02	.01
☐ 20 Ronnie Harmon	.10	.05	.01
☐ 21 Kent Hull	.04	.02	.01
☐ 22 Jim Kelly	.40	.18	.05
☐ 23 Mark Kelso	.04	.02	.01
☐ 24 Pete Metzelaars	.04	.02	.01
☐ 25 Scott Norwood	.04	.02	.01
☐ 26 Andre Reed	.25	.11	.03
☐ 27 Fred Smerlas	.04	.02	.01
☐ 28 Bruce Smith	.25	.11	.03
☐ 29 Leonard Smith	.04	.02	.01
☐ 30 Art Still	.04	.02	.01
☐ 31 Darryl Talley	.10	.05	.01
☐ 32 Thurman Thomas	2.00	.90	.25
☐ 33 Will Wolfford	.04	.02	.01
☐ 34 Marv Levy CO	.04	.02	.01
☐ 35 Neal Anderson	.10	.05	.01
☐ 36 Kevin Butler	.04	.02	.01
☐ 37 Jim Covert	.04	.02	.01
☐ 38 Richard Dent	.10	.05	.01
☐ 39 Dave Duerson	.04	.02	.01
☐ 40 Dennis Gentry	.04	.02	.01
☐ 41 Dan Hampton	.10	.05	.01
☐ 42 Jay Hilgenberg	.04	.02	.01
☐ 43 Dennis McKinnon UER	.04	.02	.01
(Caught 20 or 21			
passes as a rookie)			
☐ 44 Jim McMahon	.10	.05	.01
☐ 45 Steve McMichael	.10	.05	.01
☐ 46 Brad Muster	.04	.02	.01
☐ 47A William Perry SP	3.00	1.35	.35
☐ 47B Ron Morris	.04	.02	.01
☐ 48 Ron Rivera	.04	.02	.01
☐ 49 Vestee Jackson	.04	.02	.01
☐ 50 Mike Singletary	.10	.05	.01
☐ 51 Mike Tomczak	.10	.05	.01
☐ 52 Keith Van Horne	.04	.02	.01
☐ 53A Mike Ditka CO	.25	.11	.03
(No HOF mention			
on card front)			
☐ 53B Mike Ditka CO	.40	.18	.05
(HOF banner on front)			
☐ 54 Lewis Billups	.04	.02	.01
☐ 55 James Brooks	.10	.05	.01
☐ 56 Eddie Brown	.04	.02	.01
☐ 57 Jason Buck	.04	.02	.01
☐ 58 Boomer Esiason	.10	.05	.01
☐ 59 David Fulcher	.10	.05	.01
☐ 60A Rodney Holman	.10	.05	.01
(BENGALS on front)			
☐ 60B Rodney Holman	.75	.35	.09
(Bengals on front)			
☐ 61 Reggie Williams	.04	.02	.01
☐ 62 Joe Kelly	.04	.02	.01
☐ 63 Tim Krumrie	.04	.02	.01
☐ 64 Tim McGee	.04	.02	.01
☐ 65 Max Montoya	.04	.02	.01
☐ 66 Anthony Munoz	.10	.05	.01
☐ 67 Jim Skow	.04	.02	.01
☐ 68 Eric Thomas	.04	.02	.01
☐ 69 Leon White	.04	.02	.01
☐ 70 Ickey Woods	.10	.05	.01
☐ 71 Carl Zander	.04	.02	.01
☐ 72 Sam Wyche CO	.04	.02	.01
☐ 73 Brian Brennan	.04	.02	.01
☐ 74 Earnest Byner	.04	.02	.01
☐ 75 Hanford Dixon	.04	.02	.01
☐ 76 Mike Pagel	.04	.02	.01
☐ 77 Bernie Kosar	.10	.05	.01
☐ 78 Reggie Langhorne	.04	.02	.01
☐ 79 Kevin Mack	.04	.02	.01
☐ 80 Clay Matthews	.10	.05	.01
☐ 81 Gerald McNeil	.04	.02	.01
☐ 82 Frank Minnifield	.04	.02	.01
☐ 83 Cody Risien	.04	.02	.01
☐ 84 Webster Slaughter	.10	.05	.01
☐ 85 Felix Wright	.04	.02	.01
☐ 86 Bud Carson CO UER	.04	.02	.01
(NFLPA logo on back)			
☐ 87 Bill Bates	.10	.05	.01
☐ 88 Kevin Brooks	.04	.02	.01
☐ 89 Michael Irvin	1.50	.70	.19
☐ 90 Jim Jeffcoat	.04	.02	.01
☐ 91 Ed Too Tall Jones	.10	.05	.01
☐ 92 Eugene Lockhart	.04	.02	.01
☐ 93 Nate Newton	.10	.05	.01
☐ 94 Danny Noonan	.04	.02	.01
☐ 95 Steve Pelluer	.04	.02	.01
☐ 96 Herschel Walker	.10	.05	.01
☐ 97 Everson Walls	.04	.02	.01
☐ 98 Jimmy Johnson CO	.10	.05	.01
☐ 99 Keith Bishop	.04	.02	.01
☐ 100A John Elway ERR	3.00	1.35	.35
(Drafted 1st Round)			
☐ 100B John Elway COR	1.00	.45	.12
(Acquired Trade)			
☐ 101 Simon Fletcher	.04	.02	.01
☐ 102 Mike Harden	.04	.02	.01
☐ 103 Mike Horan	.04	.02	.01
☐ 104 Mark Jackson	.04	.02	.01
☐ 105 Vance Johnson	.10	.05	.01
☐ 106 Rulon Jones	.04	.02	.01
☐ 107 Clarence Kay	.04	.02	.01
☐ 108 Karl Mecklenburg	.04	.02	.01
☐ 109 Ricky Nattiel	.04	.02	.01
☐ 110 Steve Sewell	.04	.02	.01
☐ 111 Dennis Smith	.10	.05	.01
☐ 112 Gerald Willhite	.04	.02	.01
☐ 113 Sammy Winder	.04	.02	.01
☐ 114 Dan Reeves CO	.04	.02	.01
☐ 115 Jim Arnold	.04	.02	.01
☐ 116 Jerry Ball	.04	.02	.01
☐ 117 Bennie Blades	.04	.02	.01
☐ 118 Lomas Brown	.04	.02	.01
☐ 119 Mike Cofer	.04	.02	.01
☐ 120 Garry James	.04	.02	.01
☐ 121 James Jones	.04	.02	.01
☐ 122 Chuck Long	.04	.02	.01
☐ 123 Pete Mandley	.04	.02	.01
☐ 124 Eddie Murray	.04	.02	.01
☐ 125 Chris Spielman	.50	.23	.06
☐ 126 Dennis Gibson	.04	.02	.01
☐ 127 Wayne Fontes CO	.04	.02	.01
☐ 128 John Anderson	.04	.02	.01
☐ 129 Brent Fullwood	.04	.02	.01
☐ 130 Mark Cannon	.04	.02	.01
☐ 131 Tim Harris	.04	.02	.01
☐ 132 Mark Lee	.04	.02	.01
☐ 133 Don Majkowski	.10	.05	.01
☐ 134 Mark Murphy	.04	.02	.01
☐ 135 Brian Noble	.04	.02	.01
☐ 136 Ken Ruettgers	.04	.02	.01
☐ 137 Johnny Holland	.04	.02	.01
☐ 138 Randy Wright	.04	.02	.01
☐ 139 Lindy Infante CO	.04	.02	.01
☐ 140 Steve Brown	.04	.02	.01
☐ 141 Ray Childress	.04	.02	.01
(Sacking Joe Montana)			
☐ 142 Jeff Donaldson	.04	.02	.01
☐ 143 Ernest Givins	.10	.05	.01
☐ 144 John Grimsley	.04	.02	.01
☐ 145 Alonzo Highsmith	.04	.02	.01
☐ 146 Drew Hill	.04	.02	.01
☐ 147 Robert Lyles	.04	.02	.01
☐ 148 Bruce Matthews	.25	.11	.03
☐ 149 Warren Moon	.25	.11	.03
☐ 150 Mike Munchak	.04	.02	.01
☐ 151 Allen Pinkett	.04	.02	.01
☐ 152 Mike Rozier	.04	.02	.01
☐ 153 Tony Zendejas	.04	.02	.01
☐ 154 Jerry Glanville CO	.04	.02	.01
☐ 155 Albert Bentley	.04	.02	.01
☐ 156 Dean Biasucci	.04	.02	.01
☐ 157 Duane Bickett	.04	.02	.01
☐ 158 Bill Brooks	.10	.05	.01
☐ 159 Chris Chandler	.50	.23	.06
☐ 160 Pat Beach	.04	.02	.01
☐ 161 Ray Donaldson	.04	.02	.01
☐ 162 Jon Hand	.04	.02	.01
☐ 163 Chris Hinton	.04	.02	.01
☐ 164 Rohn Stark	.04	.02	.01
☐ 165 Fredd Young	.04	.02	.01
☐ 166 Ron Meyer CO	.04	.02	.01
☐ 167 Lloyd Burruss	.04	.02	.01
☐ 168 Carlos Carson	.04	.02	.01
☐ 169 Deron Cherry	.10	.05	.01
☐ 170 Irv Eatman	.04	.02	.01
☐ 171 Dino Hackett	.04	.02	.01
☐ 172 Steve DeBerg	.04	.02	.01
☐ 173 Albert Lewis	.04	.02	.01
☐ 174 Nick Lowery	.04	.02	.01
☐ 175 Bill Maas	.04	.02	.01
☐ 176 Christian Okoye	.04	.02	.01
☐ 177 Stephone Paige	.04	.02	.01
☐ 178 Mark Adickes	.04	.02	.01
(Out of alphabetical			
sequence for his team)			
☐ 179 Kevin Ross	.10	.05	.01
☐ 180 Neil Smith	.50	.23	.06
☐ 181 M. Schottenheimer CO	.04	.02	.01
☐ 182 Marcus Allen	.25	.11	.03
☐ 183 Tim Brown	1.50	.70	.19
☐ 184 Willie Gault	.10	.05	.01
☐ 185 Bo Jackson	.25	.11	.03
☐ 186 Howie Long	.10	.05	.01
☐ 187 Vann McElroy	.04	.02	.01
☐ 188 Matt Millen	.10	.05	.01
☐ 189 Don Mosebar	.04	.02	.01
☐ 190 Bill Pickel	.04	.02	.01
☐ 191 Jerry Robinson UER	.04	.02	.01
(Stats show 1 TD, but			
text says 2 TD's)			
☐ 192 Jay Schroeder	.04	.02	.01
☐ 193A Stacey Toran	.04	.02	.01
(No mention of death			
on card front)			
☐ 193B Stacey Toran	.50	.23	.06
(1961-1989 banner			
on card front)			
☐ 194 Mike Shanahan CO	.04	.02	.01
☐ 195 Greg Bell	.04	.02	.01
☐ 196 Ron Brown	.04	.02	.01
☐ 197 Aaron Cox	.04	.02	.01
☐ 198 Henry Ellard	.25	.11	.03
☐ 199 Jim Everett	.10	.05	.01
☐ 200 Jerry Gray	.04	.02	.01
☐ 201 Kevin Greene	.25	.11	.03
☐ 202 Pete Holohan	.04	.02	.01
☐ 203 LeRoy Irvin	.04	.02	.01
☐ 204 Mike Lansford	.04	.02	.01
☐ 205 Tom Newberry	.04	.02	.01
☐ 206 Mel Owens	.04	.02	.01
☐ 207 Jackie Slater	.04	.02	.01
☐ 208 Doug Smith	.04	.02	.01
☐ 209 Mike Wilcher	.04	.02	.01
☐ 210 John Robinson CO	.04	.02	.01
☐ 211 John Bosa	.04	.02	.01
☐ 212 Mark Brown	.04	.02	.01
☐ 213 Mark Clayton	.10	.05	.01
☐ 214A Ferrell Edmunds ERR	.50	.23	.06
(Misspelled Edmonds			
on front and back)			
☐ 214B Ferrell Edmunds COR	.04	.02	.01
☐ 215 Roy Foster	.04	.02	.01
☐ 216 Lorenzo Hampton	.04	.02	.01
☐ 217 Jim C. Jensen UER	.04	.02	.01
(Born Albington,			
should be Abington)			
☐ 218 William Judson	.04	.02	.01
☐ 219 Eric Kumerow	.04	.02	.01
☐ 220 Dan Marino	2.00	.90	.25
☐ 221 John Offerdahl	.04	.02	.01
☐ 222 Fuad Reveiz	.04	.02	.01
☐ 223 Reggie Roby	.04	.02	.01
☐ 224 Brian Sochia	.04	.02	.01
☐ 225 Don Shula CO	.25	.11	.03
☐ 226 Alfred Anderson	.04	.02	.01
☐ 227 Joey Browner	.04	.02	.01
☐ 228 Anthony Carter	.10	.05	.01
☐ 229 Chris Doleman	.10	.05	.01
☐ 230 Hassan Jones	.04	.02	.01
☐ 231 Steve Jordan	.04	.02	.01
☐ 232 Tommy Kramer	.04	.02	.01
☐ 233 Carl Lee	.04	.02	.01
☐ 234 Kirk Lowdermilk	.04	.02	.01
☐ 235 Randall McDaniel	.10	.05	.01
☐ 236 Doug Martin	.04	.02	.01
☐ 237 Keith Millard	.04	.02	.01
☐ 238 Darrin Nelson	.04	.02	.01
☐ 239 Jesse Solomon	.04	.02	.01
☐ 240 Scott Studwell	.04	.02	.01
☐ 241 Wade Wilson	.10	.05	.01
☐ 242 Gary Zimmerman	.04	.02	.01
☐ 243 Jerry Burns CO	.04	.02	.01
☐ 244 Bruce Armstrong	.04	.02	.01
☐ 245 Raymond Clayborn	.04	.02	.01
☐ 246 Reggie Dupard	.04	.02	.01
☐ 247 Tony Eason	.04	.02	.01
☐ 248 Sean Farrell	.04	.02	.01
☐ 249 Doug Flutie	.25	.11	.03
☐ 250 Brent Williams	.04	.02	.01
☐ 251 Roland James	.04	.02	.01
☐ 252 Ronnie Lippett	.04	.02	.01
☐ 253 Fred Marion	.04	.02	.01
☐ 254 Larry McGrew	.04	.02	.01
☐ 255 Stanley Morgan	.04	.02	.01
☐ 256 Johnny Rembert	.04	.02	.01
☐ 257 John Stephens	.04	.02	.01
☐ 258 Andre Tippett	.04	.02	.01
☐ 259 Garin Veris	.04	.02	.01
☐ 260A Raymond Berry CO	.04	.02	.01
(No HOF mention			
on card front)			
☐ 260B Raymond Berry CO	.04	.02	.01
(HOF banner			
on card front)			
☐ 261 Morten Andersen	.04	.02	.01
☐ 262 Hoby Brenner	.04	.02	.01
☐ 263 Stan Brock	.04	.02	.01
☐ 264 Brad Edelman	.04	.02	.01
☐ 265 Jumpy Geathers	.04	.02	.01
☐ 266A Bobby Hebert ERR	.50	.23	.06
("passers" in 42-0)			
☐ 266B Bobby Hebert COR	.04	.02	.01
("passes" in 42-0)			
☐ 267 Craig Heyward	.25	.11	.03
☐ 268 Lonzell Hill	.04	.02	.01
☐ 269 Dalton Hilliard	.04	.02	.01
☐ 270 Rickey Jackson	.10	.05	.01
☐ 271 Steve Korte	.04	.02	.01
☐ 272 Eric Martin	.04	.02	.01
☐ 273 Rueben Mayes	.04	.02	.01
☐ 274 Sam Mills	.10	.05	.01
☐ 275 Brett Perriman	1.00	.45	.12
☐ 276 Pat Swilling	.10	.05	.01
☐ 277 John Tice	.04	.02	.01
☐ 278 Jim Mora CO	.04	.02	.01
☐ 279 Eric Moore	.04	.02	.01
☐ 280 Carl Banks	.04	.02	.01
☐ 281 Mark Bavaro	.10	.05	.01
☐ 282 Maurice Carthon	.04	.02	.01
☐ 283 Mark Collins	.04	.02	.01
☐ 284 Erik Howard	.04	.02	.01
☐ 285 Terry Kinard	.04	.02	.01
☐ 286 Sean Landeta	.04	.02	.01
☐ 287 Lionel Manuel	.04	.02	.01
☐ 288 Leonard Marshall	.04	.02	.01
☐ 289 Joe Morris	.04	.02	.01
☐ 290 Bart Oates	.04	.02	.01
☐ 291 Phil Simms	.10	.05	.01
☐ 292 Lawrence Taylor	.25	.11	.03
☐ 293 Bill Parcells CO	.10	.05	.01
☐ 294 Dave Cadigan	.04	.02	.01
☐ 295 Kyle Clifton	.04	.02	.01
☐ 296 Alex Gordon	.04	.02	.01
☐ 297 James Hasty	.04	.02	.01
☐ 298 Johnny Hector	.04	.02	.01
☐ 299 Bobby Humphery	.04	.02	.01
☐ 300 Pat Leahy	.04	.02	.01
☐ 301 Marty Lyons	.04	.02	.01
☐ 302 Reggie McElroy	.04	.02	.01
☐ 303 Erik McMillan	.04	.02	.01
☐ 304 Freeman McNeil	.04	.02	.01
☐ 305 Ken O'Brien	.04	.02	.01
☐ 306 Pat Ryan	.04	.02	.01
☐ 307 Mickey Shuler	.04	.02	.01
☐ 308 Al Toon	.10	.05	.01
☐ 309 Jo Jo Townsell	.04	.02	.01
☐ 310 Roger Vick	.04	.02	.01
☐ 311 Joe Walton CO	.04	.02	.01
☐ 312 Jerome Brown	.10	.05	.01
☐ 313 Keith Byars	.10	.05	.01
☐ 314 Cris Carter	1.50	.70	.19

☐ 315 Randall Cunningham	.10	.05	.01
☐ 316 Terry Hoage	.04	.02	.01
☐ 317 Wes Hopkins	.04	.02	.01
☐ 318 Keith Jackson	.50	.23	.06
☐ 319 Mike Quick	.04	.02	.01
☐ 320 Mike Reichenbach	.04	.02	.01
☐ 321 Dave Rimington	.04	.02	.01
☐ 322 John Teltschik	.04	.02	.01
☐ 323 Anthony Toney	.04	.02	.01
☐ 324 Andre Waters	.04	.02	.01
☐ 325 Reggie White	.25	.11	.03
☐ 326 Luis Zendejas	.04	.02	.01
☐ 327 Buddy Ryan CO	.04	.02	.01
☐ 328 Robert Awalt	.04	.02	.01
☐ 329 Tim McDonald	.10	.05	.01
☐ 330 Roy Green	.10	.05	.01
☐ 331 Neil Lomax	.04	.02	.01
☐ 332 Cedric Mack	.04	.02	.01
☐ 333 Stump Mitchell	.04	.02	.01
☐ 334 Niko Noga	.04	.02	.01
☐ 335 Jay Novacek	.50	.23	.06
☐ 336 Freddie Joe Nunn	.04	.02	.01
☐ 337 Luis Sharpe	.04	.02	.01
☐ 338 Vai Sikahema	.04	.02	.01
☐ 339 J.T. Smith	.04	.02	.01
☐ 340 Ron Wolfley	.04	.02	.01
☐ 341 Gene Stallings CO	.10	.05	.01
☐ 342 Gary Anderson K	.04	.02	.01
☐ 343 Bubby Brister	.10	.05	.01
☐ 344 Dermontti Dawson	.10	.05	.01
☐ 345 Thomas Everett	.04	.02	.01
☐ 346 Delton Hall	.04	.02	.01
☐ 347 Bryan Hinkle	.04	.02	.01
☐ 348 Merril Hoge	.04	.02	.01
☐ 349 Tunch Ilkin	.04	.02	.01
☐ 350 Aaron Jones	.04	.02	.01
☐ 351 Louis Lipps	.10	.05	.01
☐ 352 David Little	.04	.02	.01
☐ 353 Hardy Nickerson	.25	.11	.03
☐ 354 Rod Woodson	1.00	.45	.12
☐ 355A Chuck Noll CO ERR ("one of only three")	.10	.05	.01
☐ 355B Chuck Noll CO COR ("one of only two")	.10	.05	.01
☐ 356 Gary Anderson RB	.04	.02	.01
☐ 357 Rod Bernstine	.04	.02	.01
☐ 358 Gill Byrd	.04	.02	.01
☐ 359 Vencie Glenn	.04	.02	.01
☐ 360 Dennis McKnight	.04	.02	.01
☐ 361 Lionel James	.04	.02	.01
☐ 362 Mark Malone	.04	.02	.01
☐ 363A Anthony Miller ERR (TD total 14.8)	.75	.35	.09
☐ 363B Anthony Miller COR (TD total 3)	.75	.35	.09
☐ 364 Ralf Mojsiejenko	.04	.02	.01
☐ 365 Leslie O'Neal	.10	.05	.01
☐ 366 Jamie Holland	.04	.02	.01
☐ 367 Lee Williams	.04	.02	.01
☐ 368 Dan Henning CO	.04	.02	.01
☐ 369 Harris Barton	.04	.02	.01
☐ 370 Michael Carter	.04	.02	.01
☐ 371 Mike Cofer (Joe Montana holding)	.04	.02	.01
☐ 372 Roger Craig	.25	.11	.03
☐ 373 Riki Ellison	.04	.02	.01
☐ 374 Jim Fahnhorst	.04	.02	.01
☐ 375 John Frank	.04	.02	.01
☐ 376 Jeff Fuller	.04	.02	.01
☐ 377 Don Griffin	.04	.02	.01
☐ 378 Charles Haley	.25	.11	.03
☐ 379 Ronnie Lott	.10	.05	.01
☐ 380 Tim McKyer	.04	.02	.01
☐ 381 Joe Montana	1.50	.70	.19
☐ 382 Tom Rathman	.04	.02	.01
☐ 383 Jerry Rice	1.50	.70	.19
☐ 384 John Taylor	.25	.11	.03
☐ 385 Keena Turner	.04	.02	.01
☐ 386 Michael Walter	.04	.02	.01
☐ 387 Bubba Paris	.04	.02	.01
☐ 388 Steve Young	1.00	.45	.12
☐ 389 George Seifert CO UER (NFLPA logo on back)	.10	.05	.01
☐ 390 Brian Blades	.50	.23	.06
☐ 391A Brian Bosworth ERR (Seattle on front)	.30	.14	.04
☐ 391B Brian Bosworth COR (Listed by team nick-name on front)	.10	.05	.01
☐ 392 Jeff Bryant	.04	.02	.01
☐ 393 Jacob Green	.04	.02	.01
☐ 394 Norm Johnson	.04	.02	.01
☐ 395 Dave Krieg	.10	.05	.01
☐ 396 Steve Largent	.25	.11	.03
☐ 397 Bryan Millard	.04	.02	.01
☐ 398 Paul Moyer	.04	.02	.01
☐ 399 Joe Nash	.04	.02	.01
☐ 400 Rufus Porter	.04	.02	.01
☐ 401 Eugene Robinson	.04	.02	.01
☐ 402 Bruce Scholtz	.04	.02	.01
☐ 403 Kelly Stouffer	.04	.02	.01
☐ 404A Curt Warner ERR ("yards 1455")	1.25	.55	.16
☐ 404B Curt Warner COR ("yards 6074")	.10	.05	.01
☐ 405 John L. Williams	.04	.02	.01
☐ 406 Tony Woods	.04	.02	.01
☐ 407 David Wyman	.04	.02	.01
☐ 408 Chuck Knox CO	.04	.02	.01
☐ 409 Mark Carrier WR	.50	.23	.06
☐ 410 Randy Grimes	.04	.02	.01
☐ 411 Paul Gruber	.04	.02	.01
☐ 412 Harry Hamilton	.04	.02	.01
☐ 413 Ron Holmes	.04	.02	.01
☐ 414 Donald Igwebuike	.04	.02	.01
☐ 415 Dan Turk	.04	.02	.01
☐ 416 Ricky Reynolds	.04	.02	.01
☐ 417 Bruce Hill	.04	.02	.01
☐ 418 Lars Tate	.04	.02	.01
☐ 419 Vinny Testaverde	.10	.05	.01
☐ 420 James Wilder	.04	.02	.01
☐ 421 Ray Perkins CO	.04	.02	.01
☐ 422 Jeff Bostic	.04	.02	.01
☐ 423 Kelvin Bryant	.04	.02	.01
☐ 424 Gary Clark	.25	.11	.03
☐ 425 Monte Coleman	.04	.02	.01
☐ 426 Darrell Green	.10	.05	.01
☐ 427 Joe Jacoby	.04	.02	.01
☐ 428 Jim Lachey	.04	.02	.01
☐ 429 Charles Mann	.04	.02	.01
☐ 430 Dexter Manley	.04	.02	.01
☐ 431 Darryl Grant	.04	.02	.01
☐ 432 Mark May	.04	.02	.01
☐ 433 Art Monk	.10	.05	.01
☐ 434 Mark Rypien	.25	.11	.03
☐ 435 Ricky Sanders	.04	.02	.01
☐ 436 Alvin Walton	.04	.02	.01
☐ 437 Don Warren	.04	.02	.01
☐ 438 Jamie Morris	.04	.02	.01
☐ 439 Doug Williams	.10	.05	.01
☐ 440 Joe Gibbs CO	.10	.05	.01
☐ 441 Marcus Cotton	.04	.02	.01
☐ 442 Joel Williams	.04	.02	.01
☐ 443 Joe Devlin	.04	.02	.01
☐ 444 Robb Riddick	.04	.02	.01
☐ 445 William Perry	.10	.05	.01
☐ 446 Thomas Sanders	.04	.02	.01
☐ 447 Brian Blados	.04	.02	.01
☐ 448 Cris Collinsworth	.10	.05	.01
☐ 449 Stanford Jennings	.04	.02	.01
☐ 450 Barry Krauss UER (Listed as playing for Indianapolis 1979-88)	.04	.02	.01
☐ 451 Ozzie Newsome	.10	.05	.01
☐ 452 Mike Oliphant	.04	.02	.01
☐ 453 Tony Dorsett	.25	.11	.03
☐ 454 Bruce McNorton	.04	.02	.01
☐ 455 Eric Dickerson	.10	.05	.01
☐ 456 Keith Bostic	.04	.02	.01
☐ 457 Sam Clancy	.04	.02	.01
☐ 458 Jack Del Rio	.10	.05	.01
☐ 459 Mike Webster	.10	.05	.01
☐ 460 Bob Golic	.04	.02	.01
☐ 461 Otis Wilson	.04	.02	.01
☐ 462 Mike Haynes	.10	.05	.01
☐ 463 Greg Townsend	.04	.02	.01
☐ 464 Mark Duper	.10	.05	.01
☐ 465 E.J. Junior	.04	.02	.01
☐ 466 Troy Stradford	.04	.02	.01
☐ 467 Mike Merriweather	.04	.02	.01
☐ 468 Irving Fryar	.25	.11	.03
☐ 469 Vaughan Johnson	.04	.02	.01
☐ 470 Pepper Johnson	.04	.02	.01
☐ 471 Gary Reasons	.04	.02	.01
☐ 472 Perry Williams	.04	.02	.01
☐ 473 Wesley Walker	.04	.02	.01
☐ 474 Anthony Bell	.04	.02	.01
☐ 475 Earl Ferrell	.04	.02	.01
☐ 476 Craig Wolfley	.04	.02	.01
☐ 477 Billy Ray Smith	.04	.02	.01
☐ 478A Jim McMahon (No mention of trade on card front)	.10	.05	.01
☐ 478B Jim McMahon (Traded banner on card front)	.10	.05	.01
☐ 478C Jim McMahon (Traded banner on card front but no line on back saying also see card 44)	40.00	18.00	5.00
☐ 479 Eric Wright	.04	.02	.01
☐ 480A Earnest Byner (No mention of trade on card front)	.04	.02	.01
☐ 480B Earnest Byner (Traded banner on card front)	.30	.14	.04
☐ 480C Earnest Byner (Traded banner on card front but no line on back saying also see card 74)	40.00	18.00	5.00
☐ 481 Russ Grimm	.04	.02	.01
☐ 482 Wilber Marshall	.04	.02	.01
☐ 483A Gerald Riggs (No mention of trade on card front)	.10	.05	.01
☐ 483B Gerald Riggs (Traded banner on card front)	.30	.14	.04
☐ 483C Gerald Riggs (Traded banner on card front but no line on back saying also see card 14)	40.00	18.00	5.00
☐ 484 Brian Davis	.04	.02	.01
☐ 485 Shawn Collins	.04	.02	.01
☐ 486 Deion Sanders	2.00	.90	.25
☐ 487 Trace Armstrong	.04	.02	.01
☐ 488 Donnell Woolford	.10	.05	.01
☐ 489 Eric Metcalf	1.00	.45	.12
☐ 490 Troy Aikman	4.00	1.80	.50
☐ 491 Steve Walsh	.10	.05	.01
☐ 492 Steve Atwater	.25	.11	.03
☐ 493 Bobby Humphrey UER (Jersey 41 on back, should be 26)	.04	.02	.01
☐ 494 Barry Sanders	4.00	1.80	.50
☐ 495 Tony Mandarich	.04	.02	.01
☐ 496 David Williams	.04	.02	.01
☐ 497 Andre Rison UER (Jersey number not listed on back)	1.00	.45	.12
☐ 498 Derrick Thomas	1.00	.45	.12
☐ 499 Cleveland Gary	.04	.02	.01
☐ 500 Bill Hawkins	.04	.02	.01
☐ 501 Louis Oliver	.10	.05	.01
☐ 502 Sammie Smith	.04	.02	.01
☐ 503 Hart Lee Dykes	.04	.02	.01
☐ 504 Wayne Martin	.04	.02	.01
☐ 505 Brian Williams	.04	.02	.01
☐ 506 Jeff Lageman	.10	.05	.01
☐ 507 Eric Hill	.04	.02	.01
☐ 508 Joe Wolf	.04	.02	.01
☐ 509 Timm Rosenbach	.04	.02	.01
☐ 510 Tom Ricketts	.04	.02	.01
☐ 511 Tim Worley	.04	.02	.01
☐ 512 Burt Grossman	.04	.02	.01
☐ 513 Keith DeLong	.04	.02	.01
☐ 514 Andy Heck	.04	.02	.01
☐ 515 Broderick Thomas	.25	.11	.03
☐ 516 Don Beebe	.25	.11	.03
☐ 517 James Thornton	.04	.02	.01
☐ 518 Eric Kattus	.04	.02	.01
☐ 519 Bruce Kozerski	.04	.02	.01
☐ 520 Brian Washington	.04	.02	.01
☐ 521 Rodney Peete UER (Jersey 19 on back, should be 9)	.25	.11	.03
☐ 522 Erik Affholter	.04	.02	.01
☐ 523 Anthony Dilweg	.04	.02	.01
☐ 524 O'Brien Alston	.04	.02	.01
☐ 525 Mike Elkins	.04	.02	.01
☐ 526 Jonathan Hayes	.04	.02	.01
☐ 527 Terry McDaniel	.04	.02	.01
☐ 528 Frank Stams	.04	.02	.01
☐ 529 Darryl Ingram	.04	.02	.01
☐ 530 Henry Thomas	.04	.02	.01
☐ 531 Eric Coleman	.04	.02	.01
☐ 532 Sheldon White	.04	.02	.01
☐ 533 Eric Allen	.25	.11	.03
☐ 534 Robert Drummond	.04	.02	.01
☐ 535A Gizmo Williams (Without Scouting Photo on front and "Footbal" misspelled on back)	10.00	4.50	1.25
☐ 535B Gizmo Williams (Without Scouting Photo on front but "Canadian Football" on back)	.25	.11	.03
☐ 535C Gizmo Williams (With Scouting Photo on card front)	.04	.02	.01
☐ 536 Billy Joe Tolliver	.04	.02	.01
☐ 537 Daniel Stubbs	.04	.02	.01
☐ 538 Wesley Walls	.04	.02	.01
☐ 539A James Jefferson ERR (No Prospect banner on card front)	.30	.14	.04
☐ 539B James Jefferson COR (Prospect banner on card front)	.04	.02	.01
☐ 540 Tracy Rocker	.04	.02	.01
☐ 541 Art Shell CO	.10	.05	.01
☐ 542 Lemuel Stinson	.04	.02	.01
☐ 543 Tyrone Braxton UER (back photo actually Ken Bell)	.04	.02	.01
☐ 544 David Treadwell	.04	.02	.01
☐ 545 Flipper Anderson	.25	.11	.03
☐ 546 Dave Meggett	.25	.11	.03
☐ 547 Lewis Tillman	.04	.02	.01
☐ 548 Carnell Lake	.10	.05	.01
☐ 549 Marion Butts	.10	.05	.01
☐ 550 Sterling Sharpe	1.00	.45	.12
☐ 551 Ezra Johnson	.04	.02	.01
☐ 552 Clarence Verdin	.04	.02	.01
☐ 553 Mervyn Fernandez	.04	.02	.01
☐ 554 Ottis Anderson	.10	.05	.01
☐ 555 Gary Hogeboom	.04	.02	.01
☐ 556 Paul Palmer TR	.04	.02	.01
☐ 557 Jesse Solomon TR	.04	.02	.01
☐ 558 Chip Banks TR	.04	.02	.01
☐ 559 Steve Pelluer TR	.04	.02	.01
☐ 560 Darrin Nelson TR	.04	.02	.01
☐ 561 Herschel Walker TR	.10	.05	.01
☐ CC1 Pete Rozelle SP (Commissioner)	.50	.23	.06

1989 Pro Set Announcers

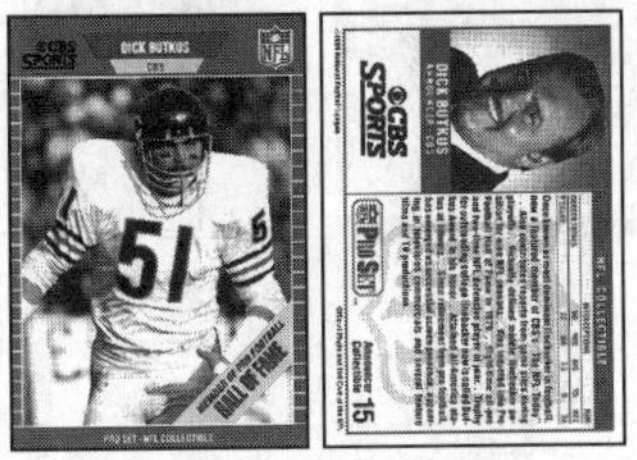

The 1989 Pro Set Announcers set contains 30 standard-size cards. The fronts have color photos bordered in red with TV network logos; otherwise, they are similar in appearance to the regular 1989 Pro Set cards. One announcer card was included in each Series II pack. Although Dan Jiggetts was listed as card number 21 on early checklists, he was replaced by Verne Lundquist when the cards were actually released. Those announcers who had previously played in the NFL were depicted with a photo from their active playing career.

	MINT	NRMT	EXC
COMPLETE SET (30)	3.00	1.35	.35
COMMON ANNOUNCER (1-30)	.10	.05	.01
☐ 1 Dan Dierdorf ABC	.20	.09	.03
☐ 2 Frank Gifford ABC	.40	.18	.05
☐ 3 Al Michaels ABC	.10	.05	.01
☐ 4 Pete Axthelm ESPN	.10	.05	.01
☐ 5 Chris Berman ESPN	.20	.09	.03
☐ 6 Tom Jackson ESPN	.20	.09	.03
☐ 7 Mike Patrick ESPN	.20	.09	.03
☐ 8 John Saunders ESPN	.10	.05	.01
☐ 9 Joe Theismann ESPN	.20	.09	.03
☐ 10 Steve Sabol NFL Films	.10	.05	.01
☐ 11 Jack Buck CBS	.10	.05	.01
☐ 12 Terry Bradshaw CBS	.60	.25	.07
☐ 13 James Brown CBS	.10	.05	.01
☐ 14 Dan Fouts CBS	.20	.09	.03
☐ 15 Dick Butkus CBS	.40	.18	.05
☐ 16 Irv Cross CBS	.10	.05	.01
☐ 17 Brent Musburger CBS	.10	.05	.01
☐ 18 Ken Stabler CBS	.30	.14	.04
☐ 19 Dick Stockton CBS	.10	.05	.01
☐ 20 Hank Stram CBS	.10	.05	.01
☐ 21 Verne Lundquist CBS	.10	.05	.01
☐ 22 Will McDonough CBS	.10	.05	.01
☐ 23 Bob Costas NBC	.10	.05	.01
☐ 24 Dick Enberg NBC	.10	.05	.01
☐ 25 Joe Namath NBC	.60	.25	.07
☐ 26 Bob Trumpy NBC	.10	.05	.01
☐ 27 Merlin Olsen NBC	.20	.09	.03
☐ 28 Ahmad Rashad NBC	.20	.09	.03
☐ 29 O.J. Simpson NBC	.30	.14	.04
☐ 30 Bill Walsh NBC	.20	.09	.03

1989 Pro Set Super Bowl Logos

This 23-card standard-size set contains a card for each Super Bowl played up through the production of the 1989 Pro Set regular set. These cards were inserted with the regular player cards in the wax packs of the 1989 Pro Set. The cards are unnumbered.

	MINT	NRMT	EXC
COMPLETE SET (23)	3.00	1.35	.35
COMMON CARD (1-23)	.20	.09	.03

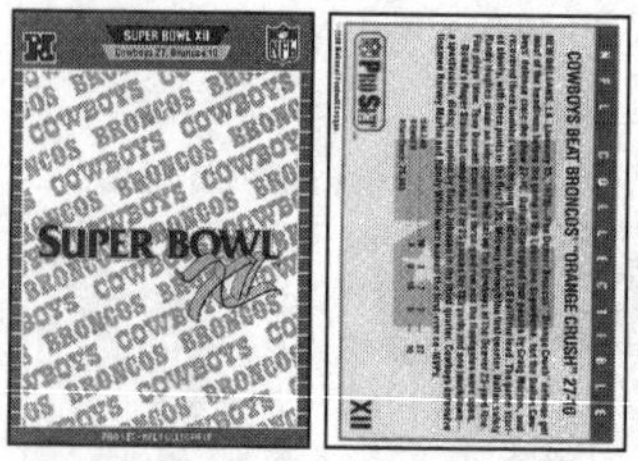

	MINT	NRMT	EXC
☐ 1 Super Bowl I	.20	.09	.03
☐ 2 Super Bowl II	.20	.09	.03
☐ 3 Super Bowl III	.20	.09	.03
☐ 4 Super Bowl IV	.20	.09	.03
☐ 5 Super Bowl V	.20	.09	.03
☐ 6 Super Bowl VI	.20	.09	.03
☐ 7 Super Bowl VII	.20	.09	.03
☐ 8 Super Bowl VIII	.20	.09	.03
☐ 9 Super Bowl IX	.20	.09	.03
☐ 10 Super Bowl X	.20	.09	.03
☐ 11 Super Bowl XI	.20	.09	.03
☐ 12 Super Bowl XII	.20	.09	.03
☐ 13 Super Bowl XIII	.20	.09	.03
☐ 14 Super Bowl XIV	.20	.09	.03
☐ 15 Super Bowl XV	.20	.09	.03
☐ 16 Super Bowl XVI	.20	.09	.03
☐ 17 Super Bowl XVII	.20	.09	.03
☐ 18 Super Bowl XVIII	.20	.09	.03
☐ 19 Super Bowl XIX	.20	.09	.03
☐ 20 Super Bowl XX	.20	.09	.03
☐ 21 Super Bowl XXI	.20	.09	.03
☐ 22 Super Bowl XXII	.20	.09	.03
☐ 23 Super Bowl XXIII	.20	.09	.03

1989-90 Pro Set GTE SB Album

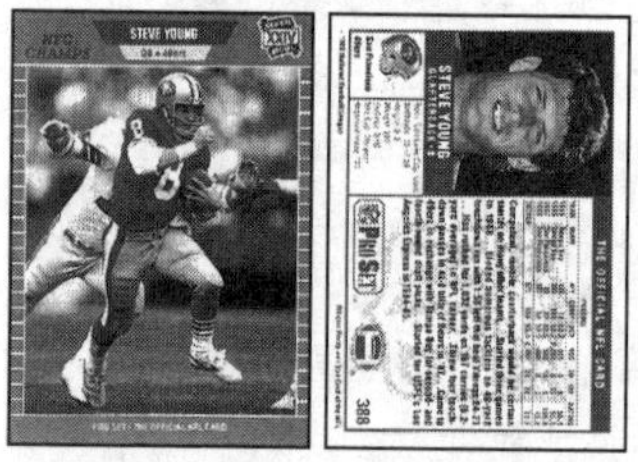

This set was produced by Pro Set for GTE and issued in a special folder inside plastic sheets. Each ticket holder at the Super Bowl game in New Orleans received a set. Later Pro Set offered their surplus of these sets to the public at 20.00 per set, one to a customer; they apparently ran out quickly. The cards are standard size and feature solely members of the San Francisco 49ers and Denver Broncos. The cards are distinguished from the regular issue Pro Set cards (even though they have the same card numbers) by their silver and gold top and bottom borders on each card front.

	MINT	NRMT	EXC
COMPLETE SET (40)	12.00	5.50	1.50
COMMON CARD	.20	.09	.03
☐ 99 Keith Bishop	.20	.09	.03
☐ 100 John Elway	2.00	.90	.25
☐ 101 Simon Fletcher	.20	.09	.03
☐ 103 Mike Horan	.20	.09	.03
☐ 104 Mark Jackson	.30	.14	.04
☐ 105 Vance Johnson	.30	.14	.04
☐ 107 Clarence Kay	.20	.09	.03
☐ 108 Karl Mecklenburg	.30	.14	.04
☐ 109 Ricky Nattiel	.20	.09	.03
☐ 110 Steve Sewell	.20	.09	.03
☐ 111 Dennis Smith	.20	.09	.03
☐ 113 Sammy Winder	.20	.09	.03
☐ 114 Dan Reeves CO	.30	.14	.04
☐ 369 Harris Barton	.20	.09	.03
☐ 370 Michael Carter	.20	.09	.03
☐ 371 Mike Cofer	.20	.09	.03
☐ 372 Roger Craig	.30	.14	.04
☐ 374 Jim Fahnhorst	.20	.09	.03
☐ 377 Don Griffin	.20	.09	.03
☐ 378 Charles Haley	.30	.14	.04
☐ 379 Ronnie Lott	.50	.23	.06
☐ 380 Tim McKyer	.20	.09	.03
☐ 381 Joe Montana	3.00	1.35	.35
☐ 382 Tom Rathman	.30	.14	.04
☐ 383 Jerry Rice	3.00	1.35	.35
☐ 384 John Taylor	.30	.14	.04
☐ 385 Keena Turner	.20	.09	.03
☐ 386 Michael Walter	.20	.09	.03
☐ 387 Bubba Paris	.20	.09	.03
☐ 388 Steve Young	2.00	.90	.25
☐ 389 George Seifert CO	.30	.14	.04
☐ 479 Eric Wright	.20	.09	.03
☐ 492 Steve Atwater	.20	.09	.03
☐ 493 Bobby Humphrey	.20	.09	.03
☐ 537 Daniel Stubbs	.20	.09	.03
☐ 543 Tyrone Braxton	.20	.09	.03
☐ 544 David Treadwell	.20	.09	.03
☐ NNO AFC Logo XXIV Collectible	.20	.09	.03
☐ NNO NFC Logo XXIV Collectible	.20	.09	.03
☐ NNO Superdome XXIV Collectible	.20	.09	.03

1990 Pro Set Draft Day

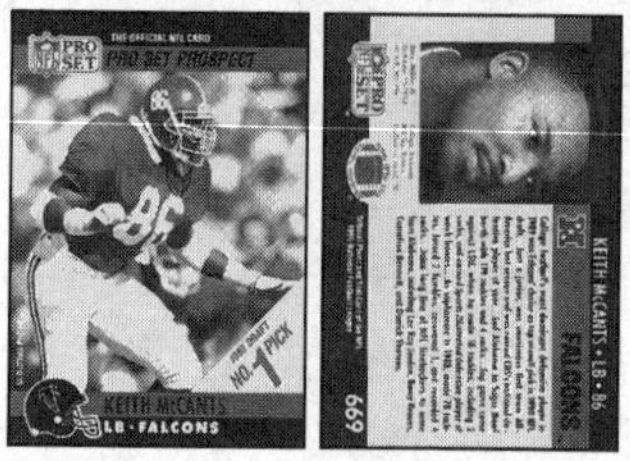

This four-card standard-size set was issued by Pro Set on the date of the 1990 NFL draft. The cards, which are all numbered 669, feature action shots in the 1990 Pro Set design of all potential number one draft picks according to Pro Set's crystal ball. The backs of the cards have a horizontal format with one half of the card being a full-color portrait of the player and the other half consisting of biographical information. The set is checklisted below in alphabetical order by subject. The fourth card in the set, not listed below but listed in with the 1990 Pro Set regular issue cards, Jeff George Colts card, was actually later issued unchanged in selected first series Pro Set packs accounting for its much lesser value.

	MINT	NRMT	EXC
COMPLETE SET (3)	12.00	5.50	1.50
COMMON CARD (669A-669C)	2.00	.90	.25
☐ 669A Jeff George	6.00	2.70	.75
☐ 669B Jeff George	6.00	2.70	.75
☐ 669C Keith McCants	2.00	.90	.25

1990 Pro Set

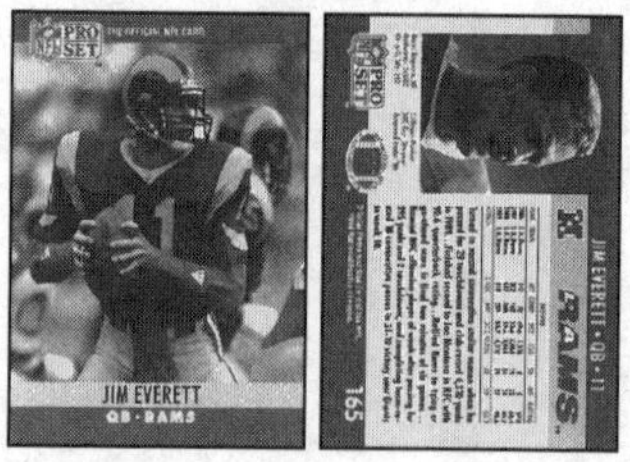

This set consists of 801 standard-size cards issued in three series. The first series contains 377 cards, the second series 392 and a 32-card Final Update. The set was issued in 14-card packs. The fronts have striking color action photos and team colored borders on the top and bottom edges. They are borderless on the sides. The horizontally oriented backs have stats, highlights and a color photo. Cards 1-29 are special selections from Pro Set commemorating events or leaders from the previous year. The cards in the set are numbered by teams. Pro Set also produced and randomly inserted 10,000 Lombardi Trophy hologram cards. Speculation is that one special Lombardi card was inserted in every tenth case. These attractive cards are hand numbered out of 10,000. Due to a contractual dispute, the Pro Bowl card of Eric Dickerson (No. 338) was withdrawn early creating a short print. The card is not included in the complete set price below. Similarly, the set price below does not include any of the tougher variation cards: 1A Barry Sanders, 72A Dexter Manley and 75A Cody Risien. The 1990 Pro Set Final Update series was issued in a special mail-away offer. The series included a special Ronnie Lott Stay in School card and the 1990 Pro Set Rookie of the Year card which introduced the 1991 Pro Set design. Rookie Cards include Fred Barnett, Jeff George, Rodney Hampton, Michael Haynes, Jeff Hostetler, Stan Humphries, Haywood Jeffires, Johnny Johnson, Brent Jones, Cortez Kennedy, Brian Mitchell, Rob Moore, Ken Norton Jr., Junior Seau, Emmitt Smith and Andre Ware.

	MINT	NRMT	EXC
COMPLETE SET (801)	15.00	6.75	1.85
COMPLETE SERIES 1 (377)	6.00	2.70	.75
COMPLETE SERIES 2 (392)	6.00	2.70	.75
COMPLETE FINAL SER. (32)	3.00	1.35	.35
COMPLETE FINAL FACT. (32)	3.00	1.35	.35
COMMON CARD (1-800/SC4)	.04	.02	.01
☐ 1A Barry Sanders ROY (Distributed to dealers at the Hawaii trade show in February 1990; distinguished from the regular card by profile head shot photo without ROY trophy on on card back)	100.00	45.00	12.50
☐ 1B Barry Sanders UER Rookie of the Year (TD total says 14, but adds up to 11)	.60	.25	.07
☐ 2A Joe Montana ERR Player of the Year (Jim Kelly's stats in text)	.50	.23	.06
☐ 2B Joe Montana COR Player of the Year (Corrected from 3521 yards to 3130)	.50	.23	.06
☐ 3 Lindy Infante UER Coach of the Year (missing Coach next to Packers)	.04	.02	.01
☐ 4 Warren Moon UER Man of the Year (missing R symbol)	.25	.11	.03
☐ 5 Keith Millard Defensive Player of the Year	.04	.02	.01
☐ 6 Derrick Thomas UER Defensive Rookie of the Year (no 1989 on front banner of card)	.25	.11	.03
☐ 7 Ottis Anderson Comeback Player of the Year	.10	.05	.01
☐ 8 Joe Montana Passing Leader	.50	.23	.06
☐ 9 Christian Okoye Rushing Leader	.04	.02	.01
☐ 10 Thurman Thomas Total Yardage Leader	.25	.11	.03
☐ 11 Mike Cofer Kick Scoring Leader	.04	.02	.01
☐ 12 Dalton Hilliard UER TD Scoring Leader (O.J. Simpson not listed in stats, but is mentioned in text)	.04	.02	.01
☐ 13 Sterling Sharpe Receiving Leader	.25	.11	.03
☐ 14 Rich Camarillo Punting Leader	.04	.02	.01
☐ 15A Walter Stanley ERR Punt Return Leader (jersey on front reads 87, back says 8 or 86)	.50	.23	.06
☐ 15B Walter Stanley COR Punt Return Leader	.04	.02	.01
☐ 16 Rod Woodson Kickoff Return Leader	.25	.11	.03
☐ 17 Felix Wright Interception Leader	.04	.02	.01
☐ 18A Chris Doleman ERR Sack Leader (Townsent, Jeffcoact)	.05	.02	.01
☐ 18B Chris Doleman COR Sack Leader (Townsend, Jeffcoat)	.05	.02	.01
☐ 19A Andre Ware Heisman Trophy (No drafted stripe on card front)	.10	.05	.01
☐ 19B Andre Ware Heisman Trophy (Drafted stripe on card front)	.10	.05	.01
☐ 20A Mo Elewonibi Outland Trophy (No drafted stripe on card front)	.04	.02	.01
☐ 20B Mo Elewonibi Outland Trophy (Drafted stripe on card front)	.04	.02	.01
☐ 21A Percy Snow Lombardi Award (No drafted stripe on card front)	.05	.02	.01
☐ 21B Percy Snow Lombardi Award (Drafted stripe on card front)	.04	.02	.01
☐ 22A Anthony Thompson Maxwell Award (No drafted stripe on card front)	.04	.02	.01
☐ 22B Anthony Thompson Maxwell Award (Drafted stripe on card front)	.04	.02	.01
☐ 23 Buck Buchanan (Sacking Bart Starr) 1990 HOF Selection	.04	.02	.01
☐ 24 Bob Griese 1990 HOF Selection	.10	.05	.01
☐ 25A Franco Harris ERR 1990 HOF Selection (Born 2/7/50)	.05	.02	.01
☐ 25B Franco Harris COR 1990 HOF Selection (Born 3/7/50)	.10	.05	.01
☐ 26 Ted Hendricks 1990 HOF Selection	.04	.02	.01
☐ 27A Jack Lambert ERR 1990 HOF Selection (Born 7/2/52)	.05	.02	.01
☐ 27B Jack Lambert COR 1990 HOF Selection (Born 7/8/52)	.05	.02	.01
☐ 28 Tom Landry 1990 HOF Selection	.10	.05	.01
☐ 29 Bob St.Clair 1990 HOF Selection	.04	.02	.01
☐ 30 Aundray Bruce UER (Stats say Falcons)	.04	.02	.01
☐ 31 Tony Casillas UER (Stats say Falcons)	.04	.02	.01
☐ 32 Shawn Collins	.04	.02	.01
☐ 33 Marcus Cotton	.04	.02	.01
☐ 34 Bill Fralic	.04	.02	.01
☐ 35 Chris Miller	.10	.05	.01
☐ 36 Deion Sanders UER (Stats say Falcons)	.50	.23	.06
☐ 37 John Settle	.04	.02	.01
☐ 38 Jerry Glanville CO	.04	.02	.01
☐ 39 Cornelius Bennett	.10	.05	.01
☐ 40 Jim Kelly	.25	.11	.03
☐ 41 Mark Kelso UER (No fumble rec. in '88; mentioned in '89)	.04	.02	.01
☐ 42 Scott Norwood	.04	.02	.01
☐ 43 Nate Odomes	.10	.05	.01
☐ 44 Scott Radecic	.04	.02	.01
☐ 45 Jim Ritcher	.04	.02	.01
☐ 46 Leonard Smith	.04	.02	.01
☐ 47 Darryl Talley	.04	.02	.01
☐ 48 Marv Levy CO	.04	.02	.01
☐ 49 Neal Anderson	.10	.05	.01
☐ 50 Kevin Butler	.04	.02	.01
☐ 51 Jim Covert	.04	.02	.01
☐ 52 Richard Dent	.10	.05	.01
☐ 53 Jay Hilgenberg	.04	.02	.01
☐ 54 Steve McMichael	.10	.05	.01
☐ 55 Ron Morris	.04	.02	.01
☐ 56 John Roper	.04	.02	.01
☐ 57 Mike Singletary	.10	.05	.01
☐ 58 Keith Van Horne	.04	.02	.01
☐ 59 Mike Ditka CO	.25	.11	.03
☐ 60 Lewis Billups	.04	.02	.01
☐ 61 Eddie Brown	.04	.02	.01
☐ 62 Jason Buck	.04	.02	.01
☐ 63A Rickey Dixon ERR (Info missing under bio notes)	.50	.23	.06
☐ 63B Rickey Dixon COR	.10	.05	.01
☐ 64 Tim McGee	.04	.02	.01
☐ 65 Eric Thomas	.04	.02	.01
☐ 66 Ickey Woods	.04	.02	.01
☐ 67 Carl Zander	.04	.02	.01
☐ 68A Sam Wyche CO ERR (Info missing under bio notes)	.50	.23	.06
☐ 68B Sam Wyche CO COR	.05	.02	.01
☐ 69 Paul Farren	.04	.02	.01
☐ 70 Thane Gash	.04	.02	.01
☐ 71 David Grayson	.04	.02	.01
☐ 72 Bernie Kosar	.10	.05	.01
☐ 73 Reggie Langhorne	.04	.02	.01
☐ 74 Eric Metcalf	.25	.11	.03
☐ 75A Ozzie Newsome ERR (Born Muscle Shoals)	.10	.05	.01
☐ 75B Ozzie Newsome COR (Born Little Rock)	.10	.05	.01
☐ 75C Cody Risien SP (withdrawn)	2.00	.90	.25
☐ 76 Felix Wright	.04	.02	.01
☐ 77 Bud Carson CO	.04	.02	.01
☐ 78 Troy Aikman	1.25	.55	.16
☐ 79 Michael Irvin	.25	.11	.03
☐ 80 Jim Jeffcoat	.04	.02	.01
☐ 81 Crawford Ker	.04	.02	.01
☐ 82 Eugene Lockhart	.04	.02	.01
☐ 83 Kelvin Martin	.04	.02	.01
☐ 84 Ken Norton	.60	.25	.07
☐ 85 Jimmy Johnson CO	.10	.05	.01
☐ 86 Steve Atwater	.04	.02	.01
☐ 87 Tyrone Braxton	.04	.02	.01
☐ 88 John Elway	.50	.23	.06
☐ 89 Simon Fletcher	.04	.02	.01
☐ 90 Ron Holmes	.04	.02	.01
☐ 91 Bobby Humphrey	.04	.02	.01
☐ 92 Vance Johnson	.04	.02	.01
☐ 93 Ricky Nattiel	.04	.02	.01
☐ 94 Dan Reeves CO	.04	.02	.01
☐ 95 Jim Arnold	.04	.02	.01
☐ 96 Jerry Ball	.04	.02	.01
☐ 97 Bennie Blades	.04	.02	.01
☐ 98 Lomas Brown	.04	.02	.01
☐ 99 Michael Cofer	.04	.02	.01
☐ 100 Richard Johnson	.04	.02	.01
☐ 101 Eddie Murray	.04	.02	.01
☐ 102 Barry Sanders	1.25	.55	.16
☐ 103 Chris Spielman	.25	.11	.03
☐ 104 William White	.04	.02	.01
☐ 105 Eric Williams	.04	.02	.01
☐ 106 Wayne Fontes CO UER (Says born in MO, actually born in MA)	.04	.02	.01
☐ 107 Brent Fullwood	.04	.02	.01
☐ 108 Ron Hallstrom	.04	.02	.01
☐ 109 Tim Harris	.04	.02	.01
☐ 110A Johnny Holland ERR (No name or position at top of reverse)	.40	.18	.05

☐ 110B Johnny Holland COR	.05	.02	.01
☐ 111A Perry Kemp ERR	.50	.23	.06
(Photo on back is actually Ken Stiles, wearing gray shirt)			
☐ 111B Perry Kemp COR	.05	.02	.01
(Wearing green shirt)			
☐ 112 Don Majkowski	.04	.02	.01
☐ 113 Mark Murphy	.04	.02	.01
☐ 114A Sterling Sharpe ERR	.25	.11	.03
(Born Glenville, Ga.)			
☐ 114B Sterling Sharpe COR	1.00	.45	.12
(Born Chicago)			
☐ 115 Ed West	.04	.02	.01
☐ 116 Lindy Infante CO	.04	.02	.01
☐ 117 Steve Brown	.04	.02	.01
☐ 118 Ray Childress	.04	.02	.01
☐ 119 Ernest Givins	.10	.05	.01
☐ 120 John Grimsley	.04	.02	.01
☐ 121 Alonzo Highsmith	.04	.02	.01
☐ 122 Drew Hill	.04	.02	.01
☐ 123 Bubba McDowell	.04	.02	.01
☐ 124 Dean Steinkuhler	.04	.02	.01
☐ 125 Lorenzo White	.10	.05	.01
☐ 126 Tony Zendejas	.04	.02	.01
☐ 127 Jack Pardee CO	.04	.02	.01
☐ 128 Albert Bentley	.04	.02	.01
☐ 129 Dean Biasucci	.04	.02	.01
☐ 130 Duane Bickett	.04	.02	.01
☐ 131 Bill Brooks	.04	.02	.01
☐ 132 Jon Hand	.04	.02	.01
☐ 133 Mike Prior	.04	.02	.01
☐ 134A Andre Rison	.25	.11	.03
(No mention of trade on card front)			
☐ 134B Andre Rison	.25	.11	.03
(Traded banner on card front; also reissued with Final Update)			
☐ 134C Andre Rison	.25	.11	.03
(Traded banner on card front; message from Lud Denny on back)			
☐ 135 Rohn Stark	.04	.02	.01
☐ 136 Donnell Thompson	.04	.02	.01
☐ 137 Clarence Verdin	.04	.02	.01
☐ 138 Fredd Young	.04	.02	.01
☐ 139 Ron Meyer CO	.04	.02	.01
☐ 140 John Alt	.04	.02	.01
☐ 141 Steve DeBerg	.04	.02	.01
☐ 142 Irv Eatman	.04	.02	.01
☐ 143 Dino Hackett	.04	.02	.01
☐ 144 Nick Lowery	.04	.02	.01
☐ 145 Bill Maas	.04	.02	.01
☐ 146 Stephone Paige	.04	.02	.01
☐ 147 Neil Smith	.25	.11	.03
☐ 148 Marty Schottenheimer CO	.04	.02	.01
☐ 149 Steve Beuerlein	.10	.05	.01
☐ 150 Tim Brown	.25	.11	.03
☐ 151 Mike Dyal	.04	.02	.01
☐ 152A Mervyn Fernandez ERR	.08	.04	.01
(Acquired: Free Agent '87)			
☐ 152B Mervyn Fernandez COR	.08	.04	.01
(Acquired: Drafted 10th Round, 1983)			
☐ 153 Willie Gault	.10	.05	.01
☐ 154 Bob Golic	.04	.02	.01
☐ 155 Bo Jackson	.25	.11	.03
☐ 156 Don Mosebar	.04	.02	.01
☐ 157 Steve Smith	.04	.02	.01
☐ 158 Greg Townsend	.04	.02	.01
☐ 159 Bruce Wilkerson	.04	.02	.01
☐ 160 Steve Wisniewski	.10	.05	.01
(Blocking for Bo Jackson)			
☐ 161A Art Shell CO ERR	.05	.02	.01
(Born 11/25/46)			
☐ 161B Art Shell CO COR	.50	.23	.06
(Born 11/26/46; large HOF print on front)			
☐ 161C Art Shell CO COR	.50	.23	.06
(Born 11/26/46; small HOF print on front)			
☐ 162 Flipper Anderson	.04	.02	.01
☐ 163 Greg Bell UER	.04	.02	.01
(Stats have 5 catches, should be 9)			
☐ 164 Henry Ellard	.10	.05	.01
☐ 165 Jim Everett	.10	.05	.01
☐ 166 Jerry Gray	.04	.02	.01
☐ 167 Kevin Greene	.25	.11	.03
☐ 168 Pete Holohan	.04	.02	.01
☐ 169 Larry Kelm	.04	.02	.01
☐ 170 Tom Newberry	.04	.02	.01
☐ 171 Vince Newsome	.04	.02	.01
☐ 172 Irv Pankey	.04	.02	.01
☐ 173 Jackie Slater	.04	.02	.01
☐ 174 Fred Strickland	.04	.02	.01
☐ 175 Mike Wilcher UER	.04	.02	.01
(Fumble rec. number different from 1989 Pro Set card)			
☐ 176 John Robinson CO UER	.04	.02	.01
(Stats say Rams, should say L.A. Rams)			
☐ 177 Mark Clayton	.10	.05	.01
☐ 178 Roy Foster	.04	.02	.01
☐ 179 Harry Galbreath	.04	.02	.01
☐ 180 Jim C. Jensen	.04	.02	.01
☐ 181 Dan Marino	1.25	.55	.16
☐ 182 Louis Oliver	.04	.02	.01
☐ 183 Sammie Smith	.04	.02	.01
☐ 184 Brian Sochia	.04	.02	.01
☐ 185 Don Shula CO	.10	.05	.01
☐ 186 Joey Browner	.04	.02	.01
☐ 187 Anthony Carter	.10	.05	.01
☐ 188 Chris Doleman	.04	.02	.01
☐ 189 Steve Jordan	.04	.02	.01
☐ 190 Carl Lee	.04	.02	.01
☐ 191 Randall McDaniel	.04	.02	.01
☐ 192 Mike Merriweather	.04	.02	.01
☐ 193 Keith Millard	.04	.02	.01
☐ 194 Al Noga	.04	.02	.01
☐ 195 Scott Studwell	.04	.02	.01
☐ 196 Henry Thomas	.04	.02	.01
☐ 197 Herschel Walker	.10	.05	.01
☐ 198 Wade Wilson	.10	.05	.01
☐ 199 Gary Zimmerman	.04	.02	.01
☐ 200 Jerry Burns CO	.04	.02	.01
☐ 201 Vincent Brown	.04	.02	.01
☐ 202 Hart Lee Dykes	.04	.02	.01
☐ 203 Sean Farrell	.04	.02	.01
☐ 204A Fred Marion	.04	.02	.01
(Belt visible on John Taylor)			
☐ 204B Fred Marion	.04	.02	.01
(Belt not visible)			
☐ 205 Stanley Morgan UER	.04	.02	.01
(Text says he reached 10,000 yards fastest; 3 players did it in 10 seasons)			
☐ 206 Eric Sievers	.04	.02	.01
☐ 207 John Stephens	.04	.02	.01
☐ 208 Andre Tippett	.04	.02	.01
☐ 209 Rod Rust CO	.04	.02	.01
☐ 210A Morten Andersen ERR	.50	.23	.06
(Card number and name on back in white)			
☐ 210B Morten Andersen COR	.05	.02	.01
(Card number and name on back in black)			
☐ 211 Brad Edelman	.04	.02	.01
☐ 212 John Fourcade	.04	.02	.01
☐ 213 Dalton Hilliard	.04	.02	.01
☐ 214 Rickey Jackson	.10	.05	.01
(Forcing Jim Kelly fumble)			
☐ 215 Vaughan Johnson	.04	.02	.01
☐ 216A Eric Martin ERR	.50	.23	.06
(Card number and name on back in white)			
☐ 216B Eric Martin COR	.05	.02	.01
(Card number and name on back in black)			
☐ 217 Sam Mills	.10	.05	.01
☐ 218 Pat Swilling UER	.10	.05	.01
(Total fumble recoveries listed as 4, should be 5)			
☐ 219 Frank Warren	.04	.02	.01
☐ 220 Jim Wilks	.04	.02	.01
☐ 221A Jim Mora CO ERR	.50	.23	.06
(Card number and name on back in white)			
☐ 221B Jim Mora CO COR	.05	.02	.01
(Card number and name on back in black)			
☐ 222 Raul Allegre	.04	.02	.01
☐ 223 Carl Banks	.04	.02	.01
☐ 224 John Elliott	.04	.02	.01
☐ 225 Erik Howard	.04	.02	.01
☐ 226 Pepper Johnson	.04	.02	.01
☐ 227 Leonard Marshall UER	.04	.02	.01
(In Super Bowl XXI, George Martin had the safety)			
☐ 228 Dave Meggett	.10	.05	.01
☐ 229 Bart Oates	.04	.02	.01
☐ 230 Phil Simms	.10	.05	.01
☐ 231 Lawrence Taylor	.25	.11	.03
☐ 232 Bill Parcells CO	.10	.05	.01
☐ 233 Troy Benson	.04	.02	.01
☐ 234 Kyle Clifton UER	.04	.02	.01
(Born: Onley, should be Olney)			
☐ 235 Johnny Hector	.04	.02	.01
☐ 236 Jeff Lageman	.04	.02	.01
☐ 237 Pat Leahy	.04	.02	.01
☐ 238 Freeman McNeil	.04	.02	.01
☐ 239 Ken O'Brien	.04	.02	.01
☐ 240 Al Toon	.10	.05	.01
☐ 241 Jo Jo Townsell	.04	.02	.01
☐ 242 Bruce Coslet CO	.04	.02	.01
☐ 243 Eric Allen	.04	.02	.01
☐ 244 Jerome Brown	.04	.02	.01
☐ 245 Keith Byars	.04	.02	.01
☐ 246 Cris Carter	.25	.11	.03
☐ 247 Randall Cunningham	.10	.05	.01
☐ 248 Keith Jackson	.10	.05	.01
☐ 249 Mike Quick	.04	.02	.01
(Darrell Green also in photo)			
☐ 250 Clyde Simmons	.04	.02	.01
☐ 251 Andre Waters	.04	.02	.01
☐ 252 Reggie White	.25	.11	.03
☐ 253 Buddy Ryan CO	.04	.02	.01
☐ 254 Rich Camarillo	.04	.02	.01
☐ 255 Earl Ferrell	.04	.02	.01
(No mention of retirement on card front)			
☐ 256 Roy Green	.10	.05	.01
☐ 257 Ken Harvey	.25	.11	.03
☐ 258 Ernie Jones	.04	.02	.01
☐ 259 Tim McDonald	.04	.02	.01
☐ 260 Timm Rosenbach UER	.04	.02	.01
(Born '67, should be '66)			
☐ 261 Luis Sharpe	.04	.02	.01
☐ 262 Vai Sikahema	.04	.02	.01
☐ 263 J.T. Smith	.04	.02	.01
☐ 264 Ron Wolfley UER	.04	.02	.01
(Born Blaisdel, should be Blasdel)			
☐ 265 Joe Bugel CO	.04	.02	.01
☐ 266 Gary Anderson K	.04	.02	.01
☐ 267 Bubby Brister	.04	.02	.01
☐ 268 Merril Hoge	.04	.02	.01
☐ 269 Carnell Lake	.04	.02	.01
☐ 270 Louis Lipps	.10	.05	.01
☐ 271 David Little	.04	.02	.01
☐ 272 Greg Lloyd	.25	.11	.03
☐ 273 Keith Willis	.04	.02	.01
☐ 274 Tim Worley	.04	.02	.01
☐ 275 Chuck Noll CO	.10	.05	.01
☐ 276 Marion Butts	.10	.05	.01
☐ 277 Gill Byrd	.04	.02	.01
☐ 278 Vencie Glenn UER	.04	.02	.01
(Sack total should be 2, not 2.5)			
☐ 279 Burt Grossman	.04	.02	.01
☐ 280 Gary Plummer	.04	.02	.01
☐ 281 Billy Ray Smith	.04	.02	.01
☐ 282 Billy Joe Tolliver	.04	.02	.01
☐ 283 Dan Henning CO	.04	.02	.01
☐ 284 Harris Barton	.04	.02	.01
☐ 285 Michael Carter	.04	.02	.01
☐ 286 Mike Cofer	.04	.02	.01
☐ 287 Roger Craig	.10	.05	.01
☐ 288 Don Griffin	.04	.02	.01
☐ 289A Charles Haley ERR	.05	.02	.01
(Fumble recoveries 1 in '86 and 4 total)			
☐ 289B Charles Haley COR	.75	.35	.09
(Fumble recoveries 2 in '86 and 5 total)			
☐ 290 Pierce Holt	.04	.02	.01
☐ 291 Ronnie Lott	.10	.05	.01
☐ 292 Guy McIntyre	.04	.02	.01
☐ 293 Joe Montana	1.00	.45	.12
☐ 294 Tom Rathman	.04	.02	.01
☐ 295 Jerry Rice	1.00	.45	.12
☐ 296 Jesse Sapolu	.04	.02	.01
☐ 297 John Taylor	.10	.05	.01
☐ 298 Michael Walter	.04	.02	.01
☐ 299 George Seifert CO	.10	.05	.01
☐ 300 Jeff Bryant	.04	.02	.01
☐ 301 Jacob Green	.04	.02	.01
☐ 302 Norm Johnson UER	.04	.02	.01
(Card shop not in Garden Grove, should say Fullerton)			
☐ 303 Bryan Millard	.04	.02	.01
☐ 304 Joe Nash	.04	.02	.01
☐ 305 Eugene Robinson	.04	.02	.01
☐ 306 John L. Williams	.04	.02	.01
☐ 307 David Wyman	.04	.02	.01
(NFL EXP is in caps, inconsistent with rest of the set)			
☐ 308 Chuck Knox CO	.04	.02	.01
☐ 309 Mark Carrier WR	.25	.11	.03
☐ 310 Paul Gruber	.04	.02	.01
☐ 311 Harry Hamilton	.04	.02	.01
☐ 312 Bruce Hill	.04	.02	.01
☐ 313 Donald Igwebuike	.04	.02	.01
☐ 314 Kevin Murphy	.04	.02	.01
☐ 315 Ervin Randle	.04	.02	.01
☐ 316 Mark Robinson	.04	.02	.01
☐ 317 Lars Tate	.04	.02	.01
☐ 318 Vinny Testaverde	.10	.05	.01
☐ 319A Ray Perkins CO ERR	.75	.35	.09
(No name or title at top of reverse)			
☐ 319B Ray Perkins CO COR	.04	.02	.01
☐ 320 Earnest Byner	.04	.02	.01
☐ 321 Gary Clark	.25	.11	.03
☐ 322 Darryl Grant	.04	.02	.01
☐ 323 Darrell Green	.10	.05	.01
☐ 324 Jim Lachey	.04	.02	.01
☐ 325 Charles Mann	.04	.02	.01
☐ 326 Wilber Marshall	.04	.02	.01
☐ 327 Ralf Mojsiejenko	.04	.02	.01
☐ 328 Art Monk	.10	.05	.01
☐ 329 Gerald Riggs	.10	.05	.01
☐ 330 Mark Rypien	.10	.05	.01
☐ 331 Ricky Sanders	.04	.02	.01
☐ 332 Alvin Walton	.04	.02	.01
☐ 333 Joe Gibbs CO	.10	.05	.01
☐ 334 Aloha Stadium	.04	.02	.01
Site of Pro Bowl			
☐ 335 Brian Blades PB	.04	.02	.01
☐ 336 James Brooks PB	.04	.02	.01
☐ 337 Shane Conlan PB	.04	.02	.01
☐ 338 Eric Dickerson PB SP	3.00	1.35	.35
(Card withdrawn)			
☐ 339 Ray Donaldson PB	.04	.02	.01
☐ 340 Ferrell Edmunds PB	.04	.02	.01
☐ 341 Boomer Esiason PB	.04	.02	.01
☐ 342 David Fulcher PB	.04	.02	.01
☐ 343A Chris Hinton PB	.50	.23	.06
(No mention of trade on card front)			
☐ 343B Chris Hinton PB	.04	.02	.01
(Traded banner on card front)			
☐ 344 Rodney Holman PB	.04	.02	.01
☐ 345 Kent Hull PB	.04	.02	.01
☐ 346 Tunch Ilkin PB	.04	.02	.01
☐ 347 Mike Johnson PB	.04	.02	.01
☐ 348 Greg Kragen PB	.04	.02	.01
☐ 349 Dave Krieg PB	.10	.05	.01
☐ 350 Albert Lewis PB	.04	.02	.01
☐ 351 Howie Long PB	.10	.05	.01
☐ 352 Bruce Matthews PB	.04	.02	.01
☐ 353 Clay Matthews PB	.04	.02	.01
☐ 354 Erik McMillan PB	.04	.02	.01
☐ 355 Karl Mecklenburg PB	.04	.02	.01
☐ 356 Anthony Miller PB	.04	.02	.01
☐ 357 Frank Minnifield PB	.04	.02	.01
☐ 358 Max Montoya PB	.04	.02	.01
☐ 359 Warren Moon PB	.25	.11	.03
☐ 360 Mike Munchak PB	.04	.02	.01
☐ 361 Anthony Munoz PB	.04	.02	.01
☐ 362 John Offerdahl PB	.04	.02	.01
☐ 363 Christian Okoye PB	.04	.02	.01
☐ 364 Leslie O'Neal PB	.04	.02	.01
☐ 365 Rufus Porter PB UER	.04	.02	.01
(TM logo missing)			
☐ 366 Andre Reed PB	.10	.05	.01
☐ 367 Johnny Rembert PB	.04	.02	.01
☐ 368 Reggie Roby PB	.04	.02	.01
☐ 369 Kevin Ross PB	.04	.02	.01
☐ 370 Webster Slaughter PB	.04	.02	.01
☐ 371 Bruce Smith PB	.10	.05	.01
☐ 372 Dennis Smith PB	.04	.02	.01
☐ 373 Derrick Thomas PB	.10	.05	.01
☐ 374 Thurman Thomas PB	.25	.11	.03
☐ 375 David Treadwell PB	.04	.02	.01
☐ 376 Lee Williams PB	.04	.02	.01
☐ 377 Rod Woodson PB	.10	.05	.01
☐ 378 Bud Carson CO PB	.04	.02	.01
☐ 379 Eric Allen PB	.04	.02	.01
☐ 380 Neal Anderson PB	.10	.05	.01
☐ 381 Jerry Ball PB	.04	.02	.01
☐ 382 Joey Browner PB	.04	.02	.01
☐ 383 Rich Camarillo PB	.04	.02	.01
☐ 384 Mark Carrier WR PB	.04	.02	.01
☐ 385 Roger Craig PB	.10	.05	.01
☐ 386A Randall Cunningham PB	.10	.05	.01
(Small print on front)			
☐ 386B Randall Cunningham PB	.10	.05	.01
(Large print on front)			
☐ 387 Chris Doleman PB	.04	.02	.01
☐ 388 Henry Ellard PB	.04	.02	.01
☐ 389 Bill Fralic PB	.04	.02	.01
☐ 390 Brent Fullwood PB	.04	.02	.01
☐ 391 Jerry Gray PB	.04	.02	.01
☐ 392 Kevin Greene PB	.10	.05	.01
☐ 393 Tim Harris PB	.04	.02	.01
☐ 394 Jay Hilgenberg PB	.04	.02	.01
☐ 395 Dalton Hilliard PB	.04	.02	.01
☐ 396 Keith Jackson PB	.10	.05	.01
☐ 397 Vaughan Johnson PB	.04	.02	.01
☐ 398 Steve Jordan PB	.04	.02	.01
☐ 399 Carl Lee PB	.04	.02	.01
☐ 400 Ronnie Lott PB	.10	.05	.01
☐ 401 Don Majkowski PB	.04	.02	.01
☐ 402 Charles Mann PB	.04	.02	.01
☐ 403 Randall McDaniel PB	.04	.02	.01
☐ 404 Tim McDonald PB	.04	.02	.01
☐ 405 Guy McIntyre PB	.04	.02	.01
☐ 406 Dave Meggett PB	.04	.02	.01
☐ 407 Keith Millard PB	.04	.02	.01
☐ 408 Joe Montana PB	.50	.23	.06
(not pictured in Pro Bowl uniform)			
☐ 409 Eddie Murray PB	.04	.02	.01
☐ 410 Tom Newberry PB	.04	.02	.01
☐ 411 Jerry Rice PB	.50	.23	.06
☐ 412 Mark Rypien PB	.04	.02	.01
☐ 413 Barry Sanders PB	.60	.25	.07
☐ 414 Luis Sharpe PB	.04	.02	.01
☐ 415 Sterling Sharpe PB	.04	.02	.01
☐ 416 Mike Singletary PB	.10	.05	.01
☐ 417 Jackie Slater PB	.04	.02	.01
☐ 418 Doug Smith PB	.04	.02	.01
☐ 419 Chris Spielman PB	.04	.02	.01
☐ 420 Pat Swilling PB	.04	.02	.01
☐ 421 John Taylor PB	.04	.02	.01
☐ 422 Lawrence Taylor PB	.10	.05	.01
☐ 423 Reggie White PB	.10	.05	.01
☐ 424 Ron Wolfley PB	.04	.02	.01
☐ 425 Gary Zimmerman PB	.04	.02	.01

□ 426 John Robinson CO PB .04 .02 .01
□ 427 Scott Case UER .04 .02 .01
(front CB, back S)
□ 428 Mike Kenn .04 .02 .01
□ 429 Mike Gann .04 .02 .01
□ 430 Tim Green .04 .02 .01
□ 431 Michael Haynes .25 .11 .03
□ 432 Jessie Tuggle UER .04 .02 .01
(Front Jesse,
back Jessie)
□ 433 John Rade .04 .02 .01
□ 434 Andre Rison .25 .11 .03
□ 435 Don Beebe .10 .05 .01
□ 436 Ray Bentley .04 .02 .01
□ 437 Shane Conlan .04 .02 .01
□ 438 Kent Hull .04 .02 .01
□ 439 Pete Metzelaars .04 .02 .01
□ 440 Andre Reed UER .25 .11 .03
(Vance Johnson also had
more catches in '85)
□ 441 Frank Reich .25 .11 .03
□ 442 Leon Seals .04 .02 .01
□ 443 Bruce Smith .25 .11 .03
□ 444 Thurman Thomas .40 .18 .05
□ 445 Will Wolford .04 .02 .01
□ 446 Trace Armstrong .04 .02 .01
□ 447 Mark Bortz .04 .02 .01
□ 448 Tom Thayer .04 .02 .01
□ 449A Dan Hampton ERR .50 .23 .06
(Card back says DE)
□ 449B Dan Hampton COR .05 .02 .01
(Card back says DT)
□ 450 Shaun Gayle .04 .02 .01
□ 451 Dennis Gentry .04 .02 .01
□ 452 Jim Harbaugh .25 .11 .03
□ 453 Vestee Jackson .04 .02 .01
□ 454 Brad Muster .04 .02 .01
□ 455 William Perry .10 .05 .01
□ 456 Ron Rivera .04 .02 .01
□ 457 James Thornton .04 .02 .01
□ 458 Mike Tomczak .10 .05 .01
□ 459 Donnell Woolford .04 .02 .01
□ 460 Eric Ball .04 .02 .01
□ 461 James Brooks .10 .05 .01
□ 462 David Fulcher .04 .02 .01
□ 463 Boomer Esiason .10 .05 .01
□ 464 Rodney Holman .04 .02 .01
□ 465 Bruce Kozerski .04 .02 .01
□ 466 Tim Krumrie .04 .02 .01
□ 467 Anthony Munoz .10 .05 .01
(Type on front smaller
compared to other cards)
□ 468 Brian Blados .04 .02 .01
□ 469 Mike Baab .04 .02 .01
□ 470 Brian Brennan .04 .02 .01
□ 471 Raymond Clayborn .04 .02 .01
□ 472 Mike Johnson .04 .02 .01
□ 473 Kevin Mack .04 .02 .01
□ 474 Clay Matthews .10 .05 .01
□ 475 Frank Minnifield .04 .02 .01
□ 476 Gregg Rakoczy .04 .02 .01
□ 477 Webster Slaughter .10 .05 .01
□ 478 James Dixon .04 .02 .01
□ 479 Robert Awalt UER .04 .02 .01
(front 89, back 46)
□ 480 Dennis McKinnon UER .04 .02 .01
(front 81, back 85)
□ 481 Danny Noonan .04 .02 .01
□ 482 Jesse Solomon .04 .02 .01
□ 483 Daniel Stubbs UER .04 .02 .01
(front 66, back 96)
□ 484 Steve Walsh .10 .05 .01
□ 485 Michael Brooks .04 .02 .01
□ 486 Mark Jackson .04 .02 .01
□ 487 Greg Kragen .04 .02 .01
□ 488 Ken Lanier .04 .02 .01
□ 489 Karl Mecklenburg .04 .02 .01
□ 490 Steve Sewell .04 .02 .01
□ 491 Dennis Smith .04 .02 .01
□ 492 David Treadwell .04 .02 .01
□ 493 Michael Young .04 .02 .01
□ 494 Robert Clark .04 .02 .01
□ 495 Dennis Gibson .04 .02 .01
□ 496A Kevin Glover ERR .20 .09 .03
(Card back says C/G)
□ 496B Kevin Glover COR .04 .02 .01
(Card back says C)
□ 497 Mel Gray .10 .05 .01
□ 498 Rodney Peete .10 .05 .01
□ 499 Dave Brown .04 .02 .01
□ 500 Jerry Holmes .04 .02 .01
□ 501 Chris Jacke .04 .02 .01
□ 502 Alan Veingrad .04 .02 .01
□ 503 Mark Lee .04 .02 .01
□ 504 Tony Mandarich .04 .02 .01
□ 505 Brian Noble .04 .02 .01
□ 506 Jeff Query .04 .02 .01
□ 507 Ken Ruettgers .04 .02 .01
□ 508 Patrick Allen .04 .02 .01
□ 509 Curtis Duncan .04 .02 .01
□ 510 William Fuller .10 .05 .01
□ 511 Haywood Jeffires .25 .11 .03
□ 512 Sean Jones .10 .05 .01
□ 513 Terry Kinard .04 .02 .01
□ 514 Bruce Matthews .10 .05 .01
□ 515 Gerald McNeil .04 .02 .01
□ 516 Greg Montgomery .04 .02 .01
□ 517 Warren Moon .25 .11 .03
□ 518 Mike Munchak .04 .02 .01
□ 519 Allen Pinkett .04 .02 .01
□ 520 Pat Beach .04 .02 .01
□ 521 Eugene Daniel .04 .02 .01
□ 522 Kevin Call .04 .02 .01
□ 523 Ray Donaldson .04 .02 .01
□ 524 Jeff Herrod .04 .02 .01
□ 525 Keith Taylor .04 .02 .01
□ 526 Jack Trudeau .04 .02 .01
□ 527 Deron Cherry .04 .02 .01
□ 528 Jeff Donaldson .04 .02 .01
□ 529 Albert Lewis .04 .02 .01
□ 530 Pete Mandley .04 .02 .01
□ 531 Chris Martin .04 .02 .01
□ 532 Christian Okoye .04 .02 .01
□ 533 Steve Pelluer .04 .02 .01
□ 534 Kevin Ross .04 .02 .01
□ 535 Dan Saleaumua .04 .02 .01
□ 536 Derrick Thomas .25 .11 .03
□ 537 Mike Webster .10 .05 .01
□ 538 Marcus Allen .25 .11 .03
□ 539 Greg Bell .04 .02 .01
□ 540 Thomas Benson .04 .02 .01
□ 541 Ron Brown .04 .02 .01
□ 542 Scott Davis .04 .02 .01
□ 543 Riki Ellison .04 .02 .01
□ 544 Jamie Holland .04 .02 .01
□ 545 Howie Long .10 .05 .01
□ 546 Terry McDaniel .04 .02 .01
□ 547 Max Montoya .04 .02 .01
□ 548 Jay Schroeder .04 .02 .01
□ 549 Lionel Washington .04 .02 .01
□ 550 Robert Delpino .04 .02 .01
□ 551 Bobby Humphery .04 .02 .01
□ 552 Mike Lansford .04 .02 .01
□ 553 Michael Stewart .04 .02 .01
□ 554 Doug Smith .04 .02 .01
□ 555 Curt Warner .04 .02 .01
□ 556 Alvin Wright .04 .02 .01
□ 557 Jeff Cross .04 .02 .01
□ 558 Jeff Dellenbach .04 .02 .01
□ 559 Mark Duper .10 .05 .01
□ 560 Ferrell Edmunds .04 .02 .01
□ 561 Tim McKyer .04 .02 .01
□ 562 John Offerdahl .04 .02 .01
□ 563 Reggie Roby .04 .02 .01
□ 564 Pete Stoyanovich .04 .02 .01
□ 565 Alfred Anderson .04 .02 .01
□ 566 Ray Berry .04 .02 .01
□ 567 Rick Fenney .04 .02 .01
□ 568 Rich Gannon .04 .02 .01
□ 569 Tim Irwin .04 .02 .01
□ 570 Hassan Jones .04 .02 .01
□ 571 Cris Carter .25 .11 .03
□ 572 Kirk Lowdermilk .04 .02 .01
□ 573 Reggie Rutland .04 .02 .01
□ 574 Ken Stills .04 .02 .01
□ 575 Bruce Armstrong .04 .02 .01
□ 576 Irving Fryar .10 .05 .01
□ 577 Roland James .04 .02 .01
□ 578 Robert Perryman .04 .02 .01
□ 579 Cedric Jones .04 .02 .01
□ 580 Steve Grogan .10 .05 .01
□ 581 Johnny Rembert .04 .02 .01
□ 582 Ed Reynolds .04 .02 .01
□ 583 Brent Williams .04 .02 .01
□ 584 Marc Wilson .04 .02 .01
□ 585 Hoby Brenner .04 .02 .01
□ 586 Stan Brock .04 .02 .01
□ 587 Jim Dombrowski .04 .02 .01
□ 588 Joel Hilgenberg .04 .02 .01
□ 589 Robert Massey .04 .02 .01
□ 590 Floyd Turner .04 .02 .01
□ 591 Ottis Anderson .10 .05 .01
□ 592 Mark Bavaro .04 .02 .01
□ 593 Maurice Carthon .04 .02 .01
□ 594 Eric Dorsey .04 .02 .01
□ 595 Myron Guyton .04 .02 .01
□ 596 Jeff Hostetler .40 .18 .05
□ 597 Sean Landeta .04 .02 .01
□ 598 Lionel Manuel .04 .02 .01
□ 599 Odessa Turner .04 .02 .01
□ 600 Perry Williams .04 .02 .01
□ 601 James Hasty .04 .02 .01
□ 602 Erik McMillan .04 .02 .01
□ 603 Alex Gordon UER .04 .02 .01
(reversed photo on back)
□ 604 Ron Stallworth .04 .02 .01
□ 605 Byron Evans .04 .02 .01
□ 606 Ron Heller .04 .02 .01
□ 607 Wes Hopkins .04 .02 .01
(Hitting Ottis Anderson)
□ 608 Mickey Shuler UER .04 .02 .01
(Reversed photo on back)
□ 609 Seth Joyner .10 .05 .01
□ 610 Jim McMahon .10 .05 .01
□ 611 Mike Pitts .04 .02 .01
□ 612 Izel Jenkins .04 .02 .01
□ 613 Anthony Bell .04 .02 .01
□ 614 David Galloway .04 .02 .01
□ 615 Eric Hill .04 .02 .01
□ 616 Cedric Mack .04 .02 .01
□ 617 Freddie Joe Nunn .04 .02 .01
□ 618 Tootie Robbins .04 .02 .01
□ 619 Tom Tupa .04 .02 .01
□ 620 Joe Wolf .04 .02 .01
□ 621 Dermontti Dawson .10 .05 .01
□ 622 Thomas Everett .04 .02 .01
□ 623 Tunch Ilkin .04 .02 .01
□ 624 Hardy Nickerson .10 .05 .01
□ 625 Gerald Williams .04 .02 .01
□ 626 Rod Woodson .25 .11 .03
□ 627A Rod Bernstine TE ERR .20 .09 .03
□ 627B Rod Bernstine RB COR .04 .02 .01
□ 628 Courtney Hall .04 .02 .01
□ 629 Ronnie Harmon .10 .05 .01
□ 630A Anthony Miller ERR .25 .11 .03
(Back says WR)
□ 630B Anthony Miller COR .10 .05 .01
(Back says WR-KR)
□ 631 Joe Phillips .04 .02 .01
□ 632A Leslie O'Neal ERR .50 .23 .06
(Listed as LB-DE on
front and back)
□ 632B Leslie O'Neal ERR .12 .05 .01
(Listed as LB-DE on
front and LB on back)
□ 632C Leslie O'Neal COR .10 .05 .01
(Listed as LB on
front and back)
□ 633A David Richards ERR .12 .05 .01
(Back says G-T)
□ 633B David Richards COR .12 .05 .01
(Back says G)
□ 634 Mark Vlasic .04 .02 .01
□ 635 Lee Williams .04 .02 .01
□ 636 Chet Brooks .04 .02 .01
□ 637 Keena Turner .04 .02 .01
□ 638 Kevin Fagan .04 .02 .01
□ 639 Brent Jones .60 .25 .07
□ 640 Matt Millen .10 .05 .01
□ 641 Bubba Paris .04 .02 .01
□ 642 Bill Romanowski .04 .02 .01
□ 643 Fred Smerlas UER .04 .02 .01
(Front 67, back 76)
□ 644 Dave Waymer .04 .02 .01
□ 645 Steve Young .50 .23 .06
□ 646 Brian Blades .10 .05 .01
□ 647 Andy Heck .04 .02 .01
□ 648 Dave Krieg .10 .05 .01
□ 649 Rufus Porter .04 .02 .01
□ 650 Kelly Stouffer .04 .02 .01
□ 651 Tony Woods .04 .02 .01
□ 652 Gary Anderson RB .04 .02 .01
□ 653 Reuben Davis .04 .02 .01
□ 654 Randy Grimes .04 .02 .01
□ 655 Ron Hall .04 .02 .01
□ 656 Eugene Marve .04 .02 .01
□ 657A Curt Jarvis ERR .50 .23 .06
(No NFL logo on
front of card)
□ 657B Curt Jarvis COR .05 .02 .01
□ 658 Ricky Reynolds .04 .02 .01
□ 659 Broderick Thomas .04 .02 .01
□ 660 Jeff Bostic .04 .02 .01
□ 661 Todd Bowles .04 .02 .01
□ 662 Ravin Caldwell .04 .02 .01
□ 663 Russ Grimm UER .04 .02 .01
(Back photo is act-
ually Jeff Bostic)
□ 664 Joe Jacoby .04 .02 .01
□ 665 Mark May .04 .02 .01
(Front G, back G/T)
□ 666 Walter Stanley .04 .02 .01
□ 667 Don Warren .04 .02 .01
□ 668 Stan Humphries 1.00 .45 .12
□ 669A Jeff George SP .75 .35 .09
(Illinois uniform;
issued in first series)
□ 669B Jeff George .75 .35 .09
(Colts uniform;
issued in second series)
□ 670 Blair Thomas .10 .05 .01
(No color stripe along
line with AFC symbol
and Jets logo)
□ 671 Cortez Kennedy UER .25 .11 .03
(No scouting photo
line on back)
□ 672 Keith McCants .04 .02 .01
□ 673 Junior Seau 1.25 .55 .16
□ 674 Mark Carrier DB .25 .11 .03
□ 675 Andre Ware .10 .05 .01
□ 676 Chris Singleton UER .04 .02 .01
(Parsippany High,
should be Parsippany
Hills High)
□ 677 Richmond Webb .04 .02 .01
□ 678 Ray Agnew .04 .02 .01
□ 679 Anthony Smith .04 .02 .01
□ 680 James Francis .04 .02 .01
□ 681 Percy Snow .04 .02 .01
□ 682 Renaldo Turnbull .04 .02 .01
□ 683 Lamar Lathon .10 .05 .01
□ 684 James Williams .04 .02 .01
□ 685 Emmitt Smith 5.00 2.20 .60
□ 686 Tony Bennett .25 .11 .03
□ 687 Darrell Thompson .04 .02 .01
□ 688 Steve Broussard .04 .02 .01
□ 689 Eric Green .10 .05 .01
□ 690 Ben Smith .04 .02 .01
□ 691 Bern Brostek UER .04 .02 .01
(Listed as Center but
is playing Guard)
□ 692 Rodney Hampton 1.00 .45 .12
□ 693 Dexter Carter .04 .02 .01
□ 694 Rob Moore .40 .18 .05
□ 695 Alexander Wright .04 .02 .01
□ 696 Darion Conner .10 .05 .01
□ 697 Reggie Rembert UER .04 .02 .01
(Missing Scouting Line
credit on the front)
□ 698A Terry Wooden ERR .20 .09 .03
(Number on back is 51)
□ 698B Terry Wooden COR .04 .02 .01
(Number on back is 90)
□ 699 Reggie Cobb .04 .02 .01
□ 700 Anthony Thompson .04 .02 .01
□ 701 Fred Washington .04 .02 .01
(Final Update version
mentions his death;
this card does not)
□ 702 Ron Cox .04 .02 .01
□ 703 Robert Blackmon .04 .02 .01
□ 704 Dan Owens .04 .02 .01
□ 705 Anthony Johnson .25 .11 .03
□ 706 Aaron Wallace .04 .02 .01
□ 707 Harold Green .25 .11 .03
□ 708 Keith Sims .04 .02 .01
□ 709 Tim Grunhard .04 .02 .01
□ 710 Jeff Alm .04 .02 .01
□ 711 Carwell Gardner .04 .02 .01
□ 712 Kenny Davidson .04 .02 .01
□ 713 Vince Buck .04 .02 .01
□ 714 Leroy Hoard .25 .11 .03
□ 715 Andre Collins .04 .02 .01
□ 716 Dennis Brown .04 .02 .01
□ 717 LeRoy Butler .25 .11 .03
□ 718A Pat Terrell 41 ERR .20 .09 .03
□ 718B Pat Terrell 37 COR .04 .02 .01
□ 719 Mike Bellamy .04 .02 .01
□ 720 Mike Fox .04 .02 .01
□ 721 Alton Montgomery .04 .02 .01
□ 722 Eric Davis .10 .05 .01
□ 723A Oliver Barnett ERR .50 .23 .06
(Front says DT)
□ 723B Oliver Barnett COR .04 .02 .01
(Front says NT)
□ 724 Houston Hoover .04 .02 .01
□ 725 Howard Ballard .04 .02 .01
□ 726 Keith McKeller .04 .02 .01
□ 727 Wendell Davis .04 .02 .01
(Pro Set Prospect in
white, not black)
□ 728 Peter Tom Willis .04 .02 .01
□ 729 Bernard Clark .04 .02 .01
□ 730 Doug Widell .04 .02 .01
□ 731 Eric Andolsek .04 .02 .01
□ 732 Jeff Campbell .04 .02 .01
□ 733 Marc Spindler .04 .02 .01
□ 734 Keith Woodside .04 .02 .01
□ 735 Willis Peguese .04 .02 .01
□ 736 Frank Stams .04 .02 .01
□ 737 Jeff Uhlenhake .04 .02 .01
□ 738 Todd Kalis .04 .02 .01
□ 739 Tommy Hodson UER .04 .02 .01
(Born Matthews,
should be Mathews)
□ 740 Greg McMurtry .04 .02 .01
□ 741 Mike Buck .04 .02 .01
□ 742 Kevin Haverdink UER .04 .02 .01
(Jersey says 70,
back says 74)
□ 743A Johnny Bailey .10 .05 .01
(Back says 46)
□ 743B Johnny Bailey .10 .05 .01
(Back says 22)
□ 744A Eric Moore .12 .05 .01
(No Pro Set Prospect
on front of card)
□ 744B Eric Moore .05 .02 .01
(Pro Set Prospect
on front of card)
□ 745 Tony Stargell .04 .02 .01
□ 746 Fred Barnett .40 .18 .05
□ 747 Walter Reeves .04 .02 .01
□ 748 Derek Hill .04 .02 .01
□ 749 Quinn Early .25 .11 .03
□ 750 Ronald Lewis .04 .02 .01
□ 751 Ken Clark .04 .02 .01
□ 752 Garry Lewis .04 .02 .01
□ 753 James Lofton .10 .05 .01
□ 754 Steve Tasker UER .04 .02 .01
(Back says photo is
against Raiders, but
front shows a Steeler)
□ 755 Jim Shofner CO .04 .02 .01
□ 756 Jimmie Jones .04 .02 .01
□ 757 Jay Novacek .25 .11 .03
□ 758 Jessie Hester .04 .02 .01
□ 759 Barry Word .04 .02 .01
□ 760 Eddie Anderson .04 .02 .01

☐ 761 Cleveland Gary	.04	.02	.01
☐ 762 Marcus Dupree	.04	.02	.01
☐ 763 David Griggs	.04	.02	.01
☐ 764 Rueben Mayes	.04	.02	.01
☐ 765 Stephen Baker	.04	.02	.01
☐ 766 Reyna Thompson UER (Front CB, back ST-CB)	.04	.02	.01
☐ 767 Everson Walls	.04	.02	.01
☐ 768 Brad Baxter	.04	.02	.01
☐ 769 Steve Walsh	.10	.05	.01
☐ 770 Heath Sherman	.04	.02	.01
☐ 771 Johnny Johnson	.10	.05	.01
☐ 772A Dexter Manley (Back mentions substance abuse violation)	30.00	13.50	3.70
☐ 772B Dexter Manley (Bio on back changed; doesn't mention substance abuse violation)	.04	.02	.01
☐ 773 Ricky Proehl	.10	.05	.01
☐ 774 Frank Cornish	.04	.02	.01
☐ 775 Tommy Kane	.04	.02	.01
☐ 776 Derrick Fenner	.04	.02	.01
☐ 777 Steve Christie	.04	.02	.01
☐ 778 Wayne Haddix	.04	.02	.01
☐ 779 Richard Williamson UER (Experience is misspelled as esperience)	.04	.02	.01
☐ 780 Brian Mitchell	.25	.11	.03
☐ 781 American Bowl/London Raiders vs. Saints	.04	.02	.01
☐ 782 American Bowl/Berlin Rams vs. Chiefs	.04	.02	.01
☐ 783 American Bowl/Tokyo Broncos vs. Seahawks	.04	.02	.01
☐ 784 American Bowl/Montreal Steelers vs. Patriots	.04	.02	.01
☐ 785A Berlin Wall Paul Tagliabue ("Peered through the Berlin Wall")	.08	.04	.01
☐ 785B Berlin Wall Paul Tagliabue ("Posed at the Berlin Wall")	.08	.04	.01
☐ 786 Raiders Stay in LA (Al Davis)	.04	.02	.01
☐ 787 Falcons Back in Black (Jerry Glanville)	.04	.02	.01
☐ 788 NFL Goes International World League Spring Debut (Number on back is black, Newsreel cards are otherwise white; only Newsreel card with silver borders)	.04	.02	.01
☐ 789 Overseas Appeal (Cheerleaders)	.04	.02	.01
☐ 790 Photo Contest (Mike Mularkey awash)	.04	.02	.01
☐ 791 Photo Contest (Gary Reasons hitting Bobby Humphrey)	.04	.02	.01
☐ 792 Photo Contest (Maurice Hurst covering Drew Hill)	.04	.02	.01
☐ 793 Photo Contest (Ronnie Lott celebrating)	.04	.02	.01
☐ 794 Photo Contest (Felix Wright grabbing Barry Sanders' jersey)	.60	.25	.07
☐ 795 Photo Contest (George Seifert in Gatorade Shower)	.04	.02	.01
☐ 796 Photo Contest (Doug Smith praying)	.04	.02	.01
☐ 797 Photo Contest (Doug Widell keeping cool)	.04	.02	.01
☐ 798 Photo Contest (Todd Bowles covering Cris Carter)	.04	.02	.01
☐ 799 Ronnie Lott School	.10	.05	.01
☐ 800D Mark Carrier DB D-ROY	.10	.05	.01
☐ 800O Emmitt Smith O-ROY	1.25	.55	.16
☐ 1990 Santa Claus SP (Second series only; No quote mark after Andre Ware)	.50	.23	.06
☐ CC2 Paul Tagliabue SP NFL Commissioner (First series only)	.40	.18	.05
☐ CC3 Joe Robbie Mem SP (Second series only)	.50	.23	.06
☐ SC Super Pro SP (Second series only)	.50	.23	.06
☐ SC4 Fred Washington UER (Memorial to his death; word patches repeated in fourth line of text)	.04	.02	.01
☐ SP1 Payne Stewart SP (First series only)	.50	.23	.06
☐ NNO Lombardi Trophy SP (Hologram: numbered out of 10,000)	90.00	40.00	11.00
☐ NNO Super Bowl XXIV Logo	.04	.02	.01

1990 Pro Set Super Bowl MVP's

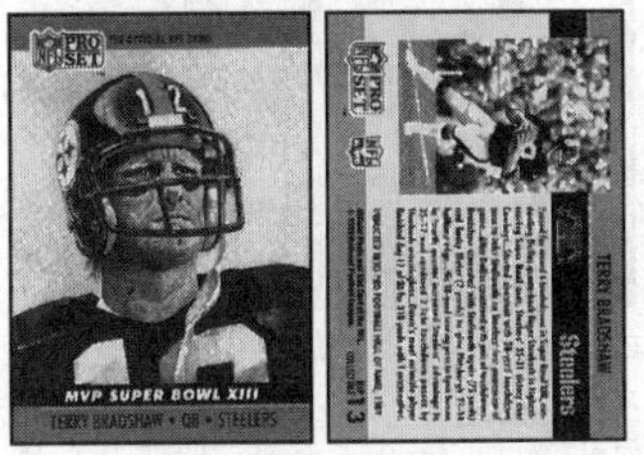

This 24-card standard size set displays color portraits of Super Bowl MVP's by noted sports artist Merv Corning. The portraits bleed to the sides of the card, and they are bordered above by a silver stripe and below by two stripes in the team's colors as well as another silver stripe. The horizontally oriented backs present a color action photo on the left portion and summary of the player's Super Bowl performance on the right portion. The cards are numbered on the back; the set numbering is in chronolgical order by Super Bowl number. These cards were included as an insert with Pro Set's second series football card packs.

	MINT	NRMT	EXC
COMPLETE SET (24)	4.00	1.80	.50
COMMON CARD (1-24)	.10	.05	.01
☐ 1 Bart Starr Super Bowl I	.25	.11	.03
☐ 2 Bart Starr Super Bowl II	.25	.11	.03
☐ 3 Joe Namath Super Bowl III	.40	.18	.05
☐ 4 Len Dawson Super Bowl IV	.10	.05	.01
☐ 5 Chuck Howley Super Bowl V	.10	.05	.01
☐ 6 Roger Staubach Super Bowl VI	.40	.18	.05
☐ 7 Jake Scott Super Bowl VII	.10	.05	.01
☐ 8 Larry Csonka Super Bowl VIII	.20	.09	.03
☐ 9 Franco Harris Super Bowl IX	.20	.09	.03
☐ 10 Lynn Swann Super Bowl X	.20	.09	.03
☐ 11 Fred Biletnikoff Super Bowl XI	.20	.09	.03
☐ 12 Harvey Martin Randy White Dallas Cowboys Super Bowl XII	.10	.05	.01
☐ 13 Terry Bradshaw Super Bowl XIII	.30	.14	.04
☐ 14 Terry Bradshaw Super Bowl XIV	.30	.14	.04
☐ 15 Jim Plunkett Super Bowl XV	.10	.05	.01
☐ 16 Joe Montana Super Bowl XVI	.60	.25	.07
☐ 17 John Riggins Super Bowl XVII	.20	.09	.03
☐ 18 Marcus Allen Super Bowl XVIII	.30	.14	.04
☐ 19 Joe Montana Super Bowl XIX	.60	.25	.07
☐ 20 Richard Dent Super Bowl XX	.10	.05	.01
☐ 21 Phil Simms Super Bowl XXI	.20	.09	.03
☐ 22 Doug Williams Super Bowl XXII	.10	.05	.01
☐ 23 Jerry Rice Super Bowl XXIII	.60	.25	.07
☐ 24 Joe Montana Super Bowl XXIV	.60	.25	.07

1990 Pro Set Theme Art

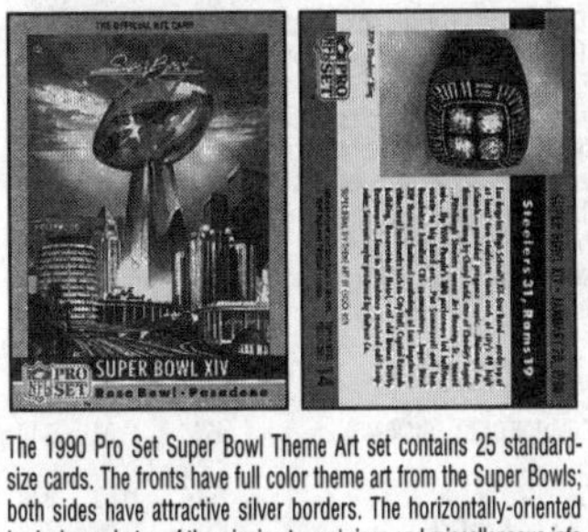

The 1990 Pro Set Super Bowl Theme Art set contains 25 standard-size cards. The fronts have full color theme art from the Super Bowls; both sides have attractive silver borders. The horizontally-oriented backs have photos of the winning teams' rings and miscellaneous info about the games. These cards were distributed one per 1990 Pro Set Series I pack.

	MINT	NRMT	EXC
COMPLETE SET (24)	3.00	1.35	.35
COMMON CARD (1-24)	.15	.07	.02
☐ 1 Super Bowl I	.15	.07	.02
☐ 2 Super Bowl II	.15	.07	.02
☐ 3 Super Bowl III	.15	.07	.02
☐ 4 Super Bowl IV	.15	.07	.02
☐ 5 Super Bowl V	.15	.07	.02
☐ 6 Super Bowl VI	.15	.07	.02
☐ 7 Super Bowl VII	.15	.07	.02
☐ 8 Super Bowl VIII	.15	.07	.02
☐ 9 Super Bowl IX	.15	.07	.02
☐ 10 Super Bowl X	.15	.07	.02
☐ 11 Super Bowl XI	.15	.07	.02
☐ 12 Super Bowl XII	.15	.07	.02
☐ 13 Super Bowl XIII UER (Colgate University 7, should be Colgate 13)	.15	.07	.02
☐ 14 Super Bowl XIV	.15	.07	.02
☐ 15 Super Bowl XV	.15	.07	.02
☐ 16 Super Bowl XVI	.15	.07	.02
☐ 17 Super Bowl XVII	.15	.07	.02
☐ 18 Super Bowl XVIII	.15	.07	.02
☐ 19 Super Bowl XIX	.15	.07	.02
☐ 20 Super Bowl XX	.15	.07	.02
☐ 21 Super Bowl XXI	.15	.07	.02
☐ 22A Super Bowl XXII ERR (Jan. 31, 1989 on back)	.50	.23	.06
☐ 22B Super Bowl XXII COR (Jan. 31, 1988 on back)	.15	.07	.02
☐ 23 Super Bowl XXIII	.15	.07	.02
☐ 24 Super Bowl XXIV Theme Art	.15	.07	.02

1990 Pro Set Collect-A-Books

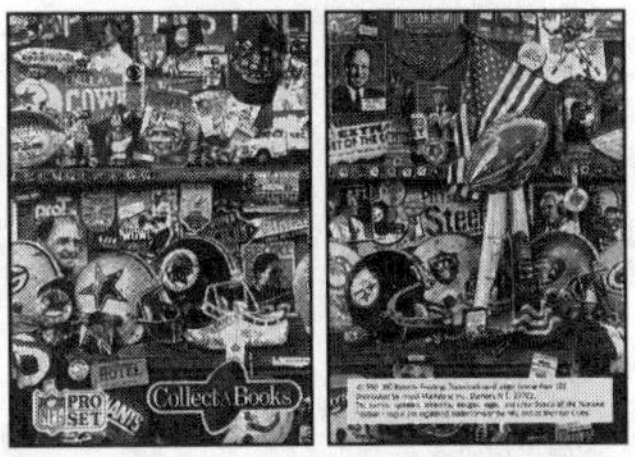

This 36-card (booklet) set, which measures the standard size, features some of the leading stars of the National Football League. The set features action photos of the players on the front of the card along with their name on the top of the front and the NFL Pro Set logo on the lower left hand corner. The cards have six pages including the outer cover photos and is interesting in that both Michael Dean Perry and Eric Dickerson have cards in this set but do not have cards in the regular Pro Set series. The set was released in three series of 12 cards each, with there being one rookie in each of the subsets. Not included in the complete set price below is a 1990-91 Pro Set Collect-A-Book Super Bowl XXV, numbered "SB" in the checklist below which presents color pictures with captions summarizing Super Bowls I-XXIV. The front and back cover form one painting of a wall and table covered with football memorabilia. This single item was apparently only available as part of the Super Bowl XXV Commemorative Tin.

	MINT	NRMT	EXC
COMPLETE SET (36)	5.00	2.20	.60
COMMON CARD (1-36)	.15	.07	.02
☐ 1 Jim Kelly	.35	.16	.04
☐ 2 Andre Ware	.15	.07	.02
☐ 3 Phil Simms	.25	.11	.03
☐ 4 Bubby Brister	.15	.07	.02
☐ 5 Bernie Kosar	.25	.11	.03
☐ 6 Eric Dickerson	.25	.11	.03
☐ 7 Barry Sanders	.75	.35	.09
☐ 8 Jerry Rice	.75	.35	.09
☐ 9 Keith Millard	.15	.07	.02
☐ 10 Erik McMillan	.15	.07	.02
☐ 11 Ickey Woods	.15	.07	.02
☐ 12 Mike Singletary	.25	.11	.03
☐ 13 Randall Cunningham	.25	.11	.03
☐ 14 Boomer Esiason	.25	.11	.03
☐ 15 John Elway	.60	.25	.07
☐ 16 Wade Wilson	.15	.07	.02
☐ 17 Troy Aikman	.75	.35	.09
☐ 18 Dan Marino	1.25	.55	.16
☐ 19 Lawrence Taylor	.25	.11	.03
☐ 20 Roger Craig	.25	.11	.03
☐ 21 Merril Hoge	.15	.07	.02
☐ 22 Christian Okoye	.15	.07	.02
☐ 23 Blair Thomas	.15	.07	.02
☐ 24 William Perry	.15	.07	.02
☐ 25 Bill Fralic	.15	.07	.02
☐ 26 Warren Moon	.25	.11	.03
☐ 27 Jim Everett	.25	.11	.03
☐ 28 Jeff George	.25	.11	.03
☐ 29 Shane Conlan	.15	.07	.02
☐ 30 Carl Banks	.15	.07	.02
☐ 31 Charles Mann	.15	.07	.02
☐ 32 Anthony Munoz	.25	.11	.03
☐ 33 Dan Hampton	.15	.07	.02
☐ 34 Michael Dean Perry	.15	.07	.02
☐ 35 Joey Browner	.15	.07	.02
☐ 36 Ken O'Brien	.15	.07	.02
☐ SB Super Bowl Story 24 Years of Champions	.25	.11	.03

1990-91 Pro Set Pro Bowl 106

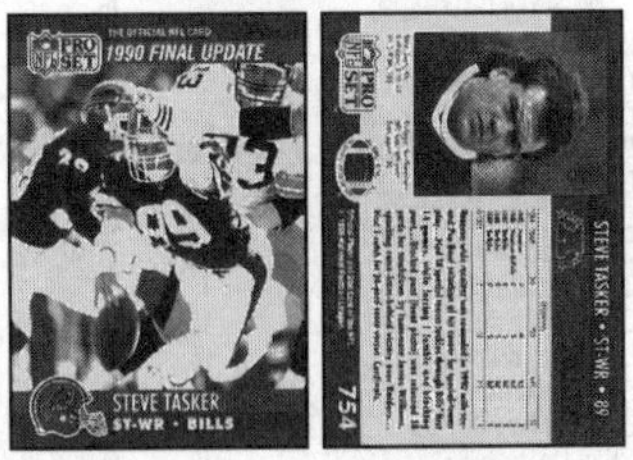

This 106 standard-size set honored the Pro Bowl squad members. The set features regular cards already issued by Pro Set with no indication that these cards were specially issued for the Pro Bowl. There are no differences on these cards. The cards in the set are 39, 40, 49, 52, 53, 57, 86, 91, 96, 98, 102, 114, 118, 119, 122, 135, 137, 144, 155, 156, 158, 160, 173, 186, 188, 189, 190, 191, 210, 215, 218, 226, 229, 231, 244, 247, 248, 252, 271, 276, 289, 291, 292, 293, 295, 320, 321, 323, 324, 334, 434, 438, 440, 443, 444, 447, 462, 464, 467, 491, 497, 514, 517, 529, 534, 536, 557, 560, 562, 575, 597, 626, 630, 632, 677, 800D. The only exception are the four players who were in Pro Set's Final Update. These Pro Bowl cards show "1990 Final Update" on the front; this notation was not used on the regular issue Final Update cards. These are obviously the key cards in the set as they are distinguishable from regular Pro Set's issue whereas the other Pro Bowl cards are not. Therefore, we are only explicitly listing these four cards. In addition to the player cards, the 1990 Super Bowl Theme Art insert set was also issued. This set is housed in an attractive white binder with the identification of the Pro Bowl game on the front of the binder.

	MINT	NRMT	EXC
COMPLETE SET (106)	12.00	5.50	1.50
COMMON CARD	.04	.02	.01
☐ 754 Steve Tasker (1990 Final Update on card front)	1.50	.70	.19
☐ 766 Reyna Thompson (1990 Final Update on card front)	1.50	.70	.19
☐ 771 Johnny Johnson (1990 Final Update on card front)	2.00	.90	.25
☐ 778 Wayne Haddix (1990 Final Update on card front)	1.50	.70	.19

1990-91 Pro Set Super Bowl 160

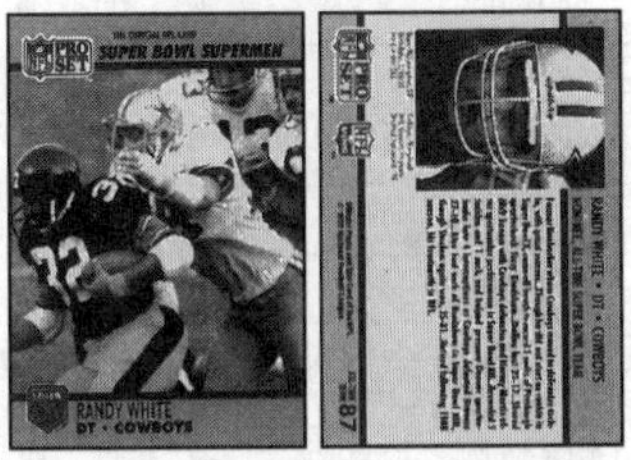

This 160-card standard-size set was issued by Pro Set as a complete set in a special commemorative box. Cards were also issued in eight-card wax packs along with six pieces of gum. The cards were introduced at the first Dallas Cowboys Pro Set Sports Collectors Show at Texas Stadium. The set features the highlights of the first 24 Super Bowls with the set being divided into the following sub-sets: Super Bowl Tickets (1-24), Super Bowl Supermen (25-135), Super Bowl Super Moments (136-151), and nine puzzle cards depicting the twenty-fifth Super Bowl Art (152-160).

	MINT	NRMT	EXC
COMPLETE SET (160)	4.00	1.80	.50
COMMON TICKET (1-24)	.03	.01	.01
COMMON CARD (25-151)	.05	.02	.01
COMMON PUZZLE (152-160)	.03	.01	.01
☐ 1 SB I Ticket	.03	.01	.01
☐ 2 SB II Ticket	.03	.01	.01
☐ 3 SB III Ticket	.03	.01	.01
☐ 4 SB IV Ticket	.03	.01	.01
☐ 5 SB V Ticket	.03	.01	.01
☐ 6 SB VI Ticket	.03	.01	.01
☐ 7 SB VII Ticket	.03	.01	.01
☐ 8 SB VIII Ticket	.03	.01	.01
☐ 9 SB IX Ticket	.03	.01	.01
☐ 10 SB X Ticket	.03	.01	.01
☐ 11 SB XI Ticket	.03	.01	.01
☐ 12 SB XII Ticket	.03	.01	.01
☐ 13 SB XIII Ticket	.03	.01	.01

14 SB XIV Ticket	.03	.01	.01
15 SB XV Ticket	.03	.01	.01
16 SB XVI Ticket	.03	.01	.01
17 SB XVII Ticket	.03	.01	.01
18 SB XVIII Ticket	.03	.01	.01
19 SB XIX Ticket	.03	.01	.01
20 SB XX Ticket	.03	.01	.01
21 SB XXI Ticket	.03	.01	.01
22 SB XXII Ticket	.03	.01	.01
23 SB XXIII Ticket	.03	.01	.01
24 SB XXIV Ticket	.03	.01	.01
25 Tom Flores CO	.05	.02	.01
26 Joe Gibbs CO	.10	.05	.01
27 Tom Landry CO	.15	.07	.02
28 Vince Lombardi CO	.20	.09	.03
29 Chuck Noll CO	.15	.07	.02
30 Don Shula CO	.15	.07	.02
31 Bill Walsh CO	.15	.07	.02
32 Terry Bradshaw	.25	.11	.03
33 Joe Montana	.75	.35	.09
34 Joe Namath	.30	.14	.04
35 Jim Plunkett	.10	.05	.01
36 Bart Starr	.20	.09	.03
37 Roger Staubach	.30	.14	.04
38 Marcus Allen	.20	.09	.03
39 Roger Craig	.10	.05	.01
40 Larry Csonka	.15	.07	.02
41 Franco Harris	.10	.05	.01
42 John Riggins	.10	.05	.01
43 Timmy Smith	.05	.02	.01
44 Matt Snell	.05	.02	.01
45 Fred Biletnikoff	.15	.07	.02
46 Cliff Branch	.10	.05	.01
47 Max McGee	.05	.02	.01
48 Jerry Rice	.40	.18	.05
49 Ricky Sanders	.05	.02	.01
50 George Sauer Jr.	.05	.02	.01
51 John Stallworth	.10	.05	.01
52 Lynn Swann	.15	.07	.02
53 Dave Casper	.05	.02	.01
54 Marv Fleming	.05	.02	.01
55 Dan Ross	.05	.02	.01
56 Forrest Gregg	.10	.05	.01
57 Winston Hill	.05	.02	.01
58 Joe Jacoby	.05	.02	.01
59 Anthony Munoz	.10	.05	.01
60 Art Shell	.10	.05	.01
61 Rayfield Wright	.05	.02	.01
62 Ron Yary	.05	.02	.01
63 Randy Cross	.05	.02	.01
64 Jerry Kramer	.10	.05	.01
65 Bob Kuechenberg	.05	.02	.01
66 Larry Little	.10	.05	.01
67 Gerry Mullins	.05	.02	.01
68 John Niland	.05	.02	.01
69 Gene Upshaw	.10	.05	.01
70 Dave Dalby	.05	.02	.01
71 Jim Langer	.05	.02	.01
72 Dwight Stephenson	.05	.02	.01
73 Mike Webster	.10	.05	.01
74 Ross Browner	.05	.02	.01
75 Willie Davis	.10	.05	.01
76 Richard Dent	.10	.05	.01
77 L.C. Greenwood	.10	.05	.01
78 Ed Too Tall Jones	.10	.05	.01
79 Harvey Martin	.10	.05	.01
80 Dwight White	.10	.05	.01
81 Buck Buchanan	.10	.05	.01
82 Curley Culp	.05	.02	.01
83 Manny Fernandez	.05	.02	.01
84 Joe Greene	.15	.07	.02
85 Bob Lilly	.15	.07	.02
86 Alan Page	.10	.05	.01
87 Randy White	.15	.07	.02
88 Nick Buoniconti	.10	.05	.01
89 Lee Roy Jordan	.10	.05	.01
90 Jack Lambert	.15	.07	.02
91 Willie Lanier	.10	.05	.01
92 Ray Nitschke	.10	.05	.01
93 Mike Singletary	.10	.05	.01
94 Carl Banks	.10	.05	.01
95 Charles Haley	.10	.05	.01
96 Jack Ham	.10	.05	.01
97 Ted Hendricks	.10	.05	.01
98 Chuck Howley	.05	.02	.01
99 Rod Martin	.05	.02	.01
100 Herb Adderley	.10	.05	.01
101 Mel Blount	.10	.05	.01
102 Willie Brown	.10	.05	.01
103 Lester Hayes	.05	.02	.01
104 Mike Haynes	.05	.02	.01
105 Ronnie Lott	.10	.05	.01
106 Mel Renfro	.10	.05	.01
107 Eric Wright	.05	.02	.01
108 Dick Anderson	.05	.02	.01
109 David Fulcher	.05	.02	.01
110 Cliff Harris	.05	.02	.01
111 Johnny Robinson	.05	.02	.01
112 Jake Scott	.05	.02	.01
113 Donnie Shell	.10	.05	.01
114 Mike Wagner	.05	.02	.01
115 Willie Wood	.10	.05	.01
116 Ray Guy	.10	.05	.01
117 Lee Johnson	.05	.02	.01
118 Larry Seiple	.05	.02	.01
119 Jerrel Wilson	.05	.02	.01
120 Kevin Butler	.05	.02	.01
121 Don Chandler	.05	.02	.01
122 Jan Stenerud	.10	.05	.01
123 Jim Turner	.05	.02	.01
124 Ray Wersching	.05	.02	.01
125 Larry Anderson	.05	.02	.01
126 Stanford Jennings	.05	.02	.01
127 Mike Nelms	.05	.02	.01
128 John Taylor	.10	.05	.01
129 Fulton Walker	.05	.02	.01
130 E.J. Holub	.05	.02	.01
131 George Siefert CO	.10	.05	.01
132 Jim Taylor	.15	.07	.02
133 Joe Theismann	.15	.07	.02
134 Johnny Unitas	.25	.11	.03
135 Reggie Williams	.05	.02	.01
136 Two Networks (Paul Christman and Frank Gifford)	.10	.05	.01
137 First Fly-Over (Military jets)	.05	.02	.01
138 Weeb Ewbank (Super Bowl Super Moment)	.05	.02	.01
139 Otis Taylor (Super Bowl Super Moment)	.10	.05	.01
140 Jim O'Brien (Super Bowl Super Moment)	.05	.02	.01
141 Garo Yepremian (Super Bowl Super Moment)	.05	.02	.01
142 Pete Rozelle and Art Rooney	.05	.02	.01
143 Percy Howard (Super Bowl Super Moment)	.05	.02	.01
144 Jackie Smith (Super Bowl Super Moment)	.10	.05	.01
145 Record Crowd (Super Bowl Super Moment)	.05	.02	.01
146 Yellow Ribbon UER (Fourth line says more than year, should say more than a year)	.05	.02	.01
147 Dan Bunz and Charles Alexander (Super Bowl Super Moment)	.05	.02	.01
148 Smurfs (Redskins) (Super Bowl Super Moment)	.05	.02	.01
149 The Fridge, William Perry Scores (Super Bowl Super Moment)	.10	.05	.01
150 Phil McConkey (Super Bowl Super Moment)	.05	.02	.01
151 Doug Williams (Super Bowl Super Moment)	.10	.05	.01
152 Top row left XXV Theme Art Puzzle	.03	.01	.01
153 Top row middle XXV Theme Art Puzzle	.03	.01	.01
154 Top row right XXV Theme Art Puzzle	.03	.01	.01
155 Center row left XXV Theme Art Puzzle	.03	.01	.01
156 Center row middle XXV Theme Art Puzzle	.03	.01	.01
157 Center row right XXV Theme Art Puzzle	.03	.01	.01
158 Bottom row left XXV Theme Art Puzzle	.03	.01	.01
159 Bottom row middle XXV Theme Art Puzzle	.03	.01	.01
160 Bottom row right XXV Theme Art Puzzle	.05	.02	.01
NNO Special Offer Card (SB Game Program direct from Pro Set)	.05	.02	.01

1990-91 Pro Set Super Bowl Binder

This set of 56 standard-size cards features members of the all-time Super Bowl team and members of the teams which competed in the 25th Super Bowl, New York Giants and Buffalo Bills. This set also included card number 799 from the 1990 Pro Set Football set: the Ronnie Lott Stay in School Card. Published reports indicated that Pro Set made 125,000 of these sets, 90,000 for distribution at the Super Bowl and 35,000 for a special mail-away offer at 30.00 per set. The set is housed in an attractive binder with special plastic pages holding four cards per. The cards of the players playing in the Super Bowl have the same number on the back as their regular issue set but the fronts acknowledge their teams as champions of their conferences.

	MINT	NRMT	EXC
COMPLETE SET (56)	22.00	10.00	2.70
COMMON CARD	.20	.09	.03

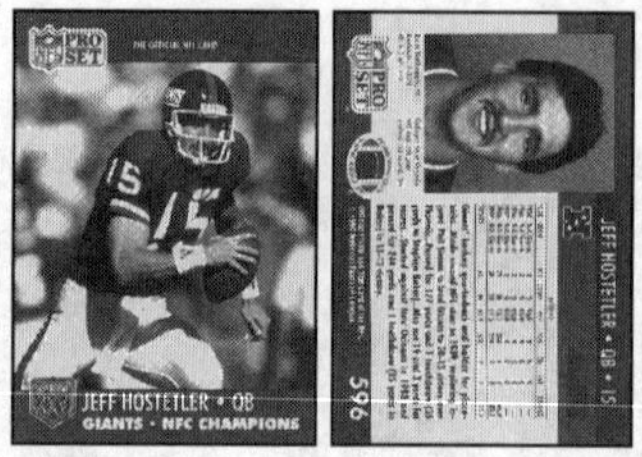

1 Vince Lombardi CO	.40	.18	.05
2 Joe Montana	5.00	2.20	.60
3 Larry Csonka	.50	.23	.06
4 Franco Harris	.50	.23	.06
5 Jerry Rice	4.00	1.80	.50
6 Lynn Swann	.50	.23	.06
7 Forrest Gregg	.30	.14	.04
8 Art Shell	.30	.14	.04
9 Jerry Kramer	.20	.09	.03
10 Gene Upshaw	.20	.09	.03
11 Mike Webster	.20	.09	.03
12 Dave Casper	.20	.09	.03
13 Jan Stenerud	.20	.09	.03
14 John Taylor	.20	.09	.03
15 L.C. Greenwood	.20	.09	.03
16 Ed Too Tall Jones	.30	.14	.04
17 Joe Greene	.50	.23	.06
18 Randy White	.50	.23	.06
19 Jack Lambert	.50	.23	.06
20 Mike Singletary	.30	.14	.04
21 Jack Ham	.30	.14	.04
22 Ted Hendricks	.30	.14	.04
23 Mel Blount	.30	.14	.04
24 Ronnie Lott	.30	.14	.04
25 Donnie Shell	.20	.09	.03
26 Willie Wood	.30	.14	.04
27 Ray Guy	.20	.09	.03
39 Cornelius Bennett	.30	.14	.04
40 Jim Kelly	1.00	.45	.12
47 Darryl Talley	.20	.09	.03
48 Marv Levy CO	.20	.09	.03
223 Carl Banks	.20	.09	.03
226 Pepper Johnson	.20	.09	.03
228 Dave Meggett	.30	.14	.04
230 Phil Simms	.30	.14	.04
231 Lawrence Taylor	.40	.18	.05
232 Bill Parcells CO	.20	.09	.03
437 Shane Conlan	.20	.09	.03
438 Kent Hull	.20	.09	.03
440 Andre Reed	.30	.14	.04
443 Bruce Smith	.30	.14	.04
444 Thurman Thomas	1.00	.45	.12
591 Ottis Anderson	.20	.09	.03
592 Mark Bavaro	.20	.09	.03
596 Jeff Hostetler	.30	.14	.04
692 Rodney Hampton	.50	.23	.06
725 Howard Ballard	.20	.09	.03
753 James Lofton	.30	.14	.04
754 Steve Tasker	.20	.09	.03
765 Stephen Baker	.20	.09	.03
766 Reyna Thompson	.20	.09	.03
799 Ronnie Lott Education	.30	.14	.04
SC1 2,000,000th Fan	.20	.09	.03
SC2 Buick Checklist Card	.20	.09	.03
SC3 Lamar Hunt Trophy	.20	.09	.03
SC4 George Halas Trophy	.20	.09	.03

1991 Pro Set Draft Day

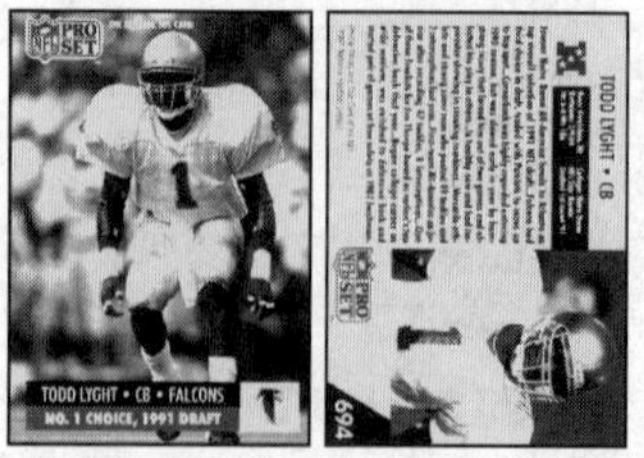

This eight-card standard-size set was issued by Pro Set on April 21, 1991 the date of the NFL draft. The cards, which are all numbered 694, feature action shots in the 1991 Pro Set design of all the potential number one draft picks. The backs of the cards have a horizontal format, with one half of the card being a full-color portrait of the player and the other half consisting of biographical information. The set is checklisted below in alphabetical order. The Russell Maryland card was eventually released (on a somewhat limited basis) with the first series of 1991 Pro Set cards and is listed there rather than here.

	MINT	NRMT	EXC
COMPLETE SET (7)	250.00	110.00	31.00
COMMON CARD (694A-694G)	25.00	11.00	3.10
694A Nick Bell	25.00	11.00	3.10
694B Mike Croel	25.00	11.00	3.10
694C Rocket Ismail Falcons	40.00	18.00	5.00
694D Rocket Ismail Cowboys	100.00	45.00	12.50
694E Rocket Ismail Patriots	40.00	18.00	5.00
694F Todd Lyght	25.00	11.00	3.10
694G Dan McGwire	25.00	11.00	3.10

1991 Pro Set Promos

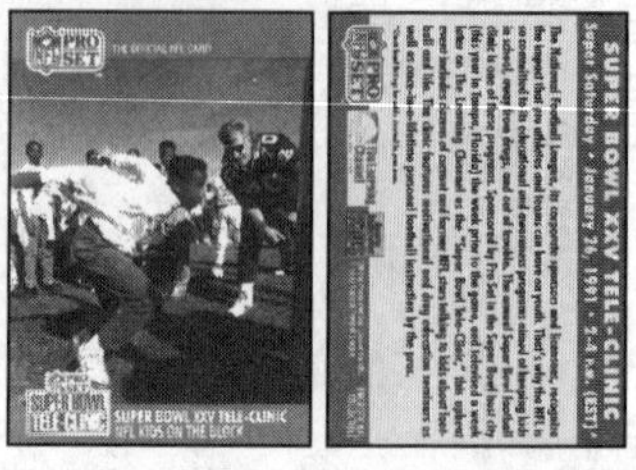

The Tele-Clinic card was given away as a promotion at Super Bowl XXV and was co-sponsored by NFL Pro Set, The Learning Channel, and Sports Illustrated for Kids. The card features a color photo on the front of an NFL player giving some football tips to a young kid. This card promotes the annual Super Bowl football clinic, in which current and former NFL stars talk to kids about football and life. The Super Bowl Card Show II card was issued in conjunction with the second annual Super Bowl show which was held in Tampa, Florida across the street from Tampa Stadium. The card is in the design on the Pro Set Super Bowl insert set from 1989 with a little inset on the bottom right hand corner of the card which states "Super Bowl Card Show II, January 24-27, 1991". The back of the card has information about the show and the other promotional activities which accompanied Super Bowl week. The Perry and Roberts cards were apparently planned but pulled from the Pro Bowl albums just prior to distribution. All of the above cards measure the standard size.

	MINT	NRMT	EXC
COMPLETE SET (6)	75.00	34.00	9.50
COMMON CARD	.50	.23	.06
NNO NFL Kids on the Block (Tele-Clinic)	.50	.23	.06
NNO Super Bowl XXV Card Show II	.50	.23	.06
NNO Michael Dean Perry Pro Bowl Special (unnumbered; without Pro Set logo)	25.00	11.00	3.10
NNO Michael Dean Perry Pro Bowl Special (unnumbered; with Pro Set logo)	25.00	11.00	3.10
NNO William Roberts Pro Bowl Special (unnumbered)	25.00	11.00	3.10
NNO Emmitt Smith Gazette (Given away with Pro Set Gazette mail-out)	2.50	1.10	.30

1991 Pro Set

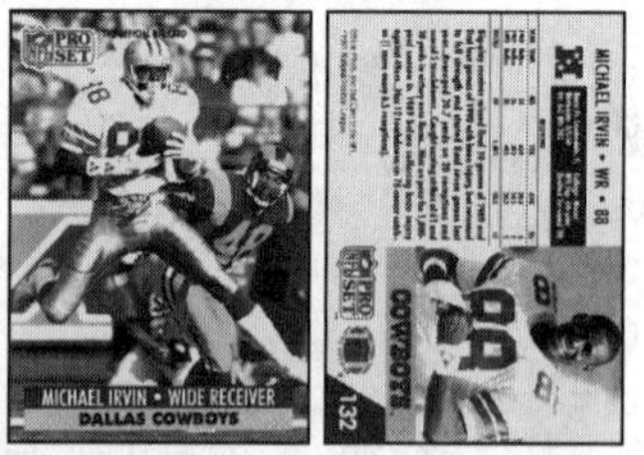

This set contains 850 standard-size cards issued in three series of 405, 407 and a 38-card Final Update set. The front design features full-bleed glossy color action photos with player, position and team name at the bottom in two stripes reflecting the team's colors. The horizontally oriented backs have a color head shot on the right side, with player profile highlights and statistics on the left. The set starts with NFL leaders (3-19), 1990 milestones (20-26), 1991 Hall of Fame inductees (27-31), college award winners (32-36), past Heisman trophy winners (37-45) and Super Bowl XXV highlights (46-54). Cards 55-324 and 433-684 are in team order. Further subsets include special games of the 1990 season (325-342), NFL officals (352-369), Stay in School (370-378) and 54 All-NFC (379-405) and All-AFC (406-432) drawings by artist Merv Corning, NFL Newsreel (685-693/813-815), Legends (694-702), World League Leaders (703-711), Hall of Fame Photo Contest (712-720), Think About It (721-729), first through third round Draft Choices (730-772) and a Super Bowl XXV Theme Art card. Rookie Cards include Terry Allen, Ty Detmer, Ricky Ervins, Brett Favre, Jeff Graham, Alvin Harper, Rocket Ismail, Erik Kramer, Herman Moore, Neil O'Donnell, Mike Pritchard, Jake Reed, Ricky Watters and Harvey Williams.

	MINT	NRMT	EXC
COMPLETE SET (850)	15.00	6.75	1.85
COMPLETE SERIES 1 (405)	6.00	2.70	.75
COMPLETE SERIES 2 (407)	6.00	2.70	.75
COMPLETE FINAL FACT. (38)	2.50	1.10	.30
COMMON CARD (1-850)	.05	.02	.01
PIONEER CARDS (SC3-SC5)	.75	.35	.09

☐ 1D Mark Carrier DB Defensive ROY	.10	.05	.01
☐ 1O Emmitt Smith Offensive ROY	1.00	.45	.12
☐ 2 Does Not Exist			
☐ 3 Joe Montana NFL Player of the Year	.40	.18	.05
☐ 4 Art Shell NFL Coach of the Year	.10	.05	.01
☐ 5 Mike Singletary NFL Man of the Year	.10	.05	.01
☐ 6 Bruce Smith NFL Defensive Player of the Year	.10	.05	.01
☐ 7 Barry Word NFL Comeback Player of the Year	.05	.02	.01
☐ 8A Jim Kelly NFL Passing Leader (NFLPA logo on back)	.25	.11	.03
☐ 8B Jim Kelly NFL Passing Leader (No NFLPA logo on back)	.25	.11	.03
☐ 8C Jim Kelly NFL Passing Leader (No NFLPA logo on back but the registered symbol remains)	6.00	2.70	.75
☐ 9 Warren Moon NFL Passing Yardage and TD Leader	.10	.05	.01
☐ 10 Barry Sanders NFL Rushing and TD Leader	.50	.23	.06
☐ 11 Jerry Rice NFL Receiving and Receiving Yardage Leader	.50	.23	.06
☐ 12 Jay Novacek Tight End Leader	.10	.05	.01
☐ 13 Thurman Thomas NFL Total Yardage Leader	.10	.05	.01
☐ 14 Nick Lowery NFL Scoring Leader, Kickers	.05	.02	.01
☐ 15 Mike Horan NFL Punting Leader	.05	.02	.01
☐ 16 Clarence Verdin NFL Punt Return Leader	.05	.02	.01
☐ 17 Kevin Clark NFL Kickoff Return Leader	.05	.02	.01
☐ 18 Mark Carrier DB NFL Interception Leader	.10	.05	.01
☐ 19A Derrick Thomas ERR NFL Sack Leader (Bills helmet on front)	12.00	5.50	1.50
☐ 19B Derrick Thomas COR NFL Sack Leader (Chiefs helmet on front)	.10	.05	.01
☐ 20 Ottis Anderson ML 10000 Career Rushing Yards	.10	.05	.01
☐ 21 Roger Craig ML Most Career Receptions by RB	.10	.05	.01
☐ 22 Art Monk ML 700 Career Receptions	.10	.05	.01
☐ 23 Chuck Noll ML 200 Victories	.10	.05	.01
☐ 24 Randall Cunningham ML Leads team in rushing, fourth straight year UER (586 rushes, should be 486; average 5.9, should be 7.1)	.10	.05	.01
☐ 25 Dan Marino ML 7th Straight 3000 yard season	.75	.35	.09
☐ 26 49ers Road Record ML 18 victories in row, still alive	.05	.02	.01
☐ 27 Earl Campbell HOF	.05	.02	.01
☐ 28 John Hannah HOF	.05	.02	.01
☐ 29 Stan Jones HOF	.05	.02	.01
☐ 30 Tex Schramm HOF	.05	.02	.01
☐ 31 Jan Stenerud HOF	.05	.02	.01
☐ 32 Russell Maryland Outland Winner	.10	.05	.01
☐ 33 Chris Zorich Lombardi Winner	.10	.05	.01
☐ 34 Darryll Lewis UER Thorpe Winner (Name misspelled Darryl on card)	.10	.05	.01
☐ 35 Alfred Williams Butkus Winner	.05	.02	.01
☐ 36 Raghib(Rocket) Ismail Walter Camp POY	.75	.35	.09
☐ 37 Ty Detmer HH	.75	.35	.09
☐ 38 Andre Ware HH	.10	.05	.01
☐ 39 Barry Sanders HH	.50	.23	.06
☐ 40 Tim Brown HH UER (No "Official Photo and Stat Card of the NFL" on card back)	.10	.05	.01
☐ 41 Vinny Testaverde HH	.10	.05	.01
☐ 42 Bo Jackson HH	.10	.05	.01
☐ 43 Mike Rozier HH	.05	.02	.01
☐ 44 Herschel Walker HH	.10	.05	.01
☐ 45 Marcus Allen HH	.10	.05	.01
☐ 46A James Lofton SB (NFLPA logo on back)	.10	.05	.01
☐ 46B James Lofton SB (No NFLPA logo on back)	.10	.05	.01
☐ 47A Bruce Smith SB (Official NFL Card in black letters)	.10	.05	.01
☐ 47B Bruce Smith SB (Official NFL Card in white letters)	.10	.05	.01
☐ 48 Myron Guyton SB	.05	.02	.01
☐ 49 Stephen Baker SB	.05	.02	.01
☐ 50 Mark Ingram SB UER (First repeated twice on back title)	.05	.02	.01
☐ 51 Ottis Anderson SB	.10	.05	.01
☐ 52 Thurman Thomas SB	.25	.11	.03
☐ 53 Matt Bahr SB	.05	.02	.01
☐ 54 Scott Norwood SB	.05	.02	.01
☐ 55 Stephen Baker	.05	.02	.01
☐ 56 Carl Banks	.05	.02	.01
☐ 57 Mark Collins	.05	.02	.01
☐ 58 Steve DeOssie	.05	.02	.01
☐ 59 Eric Dorsey	.05	.02	.01
☐ 60 John Elliott	.05	.02	.01
☐ 61 Myron Guyton	.05	.02	.01
☐ 62 Rodney Hampton	.25	.11	.03
☐ 63 Jeff Hostetler	.10	.05	.01
☐ 64 Erik Howard	.05	.02	.01
☐ 65 Mark Ingram	.10	.05	.01
☐ 66 Greg Jackson	.05	.02	.01
☐ 67 Leonard Marshall	.05	.02	.01
☐ 68 David Meggett	.10	.05	.01
☐ 69 Eric Moore	.05	.02	.01
☐ 70 Bart Oates	.05	.02	.01
☐ 71 Gary Reasons	.05	.02	.01
☐ 72 Bill Parcells CO	.10	.05	.01
☐ 73 Howard Ballard	.05	.02	.01
☐ 74A Cornelius Bennett (NFLPA logo on back)	.25	.11	.03
☐ 74B Cornelius Bennett (No NFLPA logo on back)	.05	.02	.01
☐ 75 Shane Conlan	.05	.02	.01
☐ 76 Kent Hull	.05	.02	.01
☐ 77 Kirby Jackson	.05	.02	.01
☐ 78A Jim Kelly (NFLPA logo on back)	.60	.25	.07
☐ 78B Jim Kelly (No NFLPA logo on back)	.25	.11	.03
☐ 79 Mark Kelso	.05	.02	.01
☐ 80 Nate Odomes	.05	.02	.01
☐ 81 Andre Reed	.10	.05	.01
☐ 82 Jim Ritcher	.05	.02	.01
☐ 83 Bruce Smith	.25	.11	.03
☐ 84 Darryl Talley	.05	.02	.01
☐ 85 Steve Tasker	.10	.05	.01
☐ 86 Thurman Thomas	.25	.11	.03
☐ 87 James Williams	.05	.02	.01
☐ 88 Will Wolford	.05	.02	.01
☐ 89 Jeff Wright UER (Went to Central Missouri State, not Central Missouri)	.05	.02	.01
☐ 90 Marv Levy CO	.05	.02	.01
☐ 91 Steve Broussard	.05	.02	.01
☐ 92A Darion Conner ERR (Drafted 1st round, '99)	8.00	3.60	1.00
☐ 92B Darion Conner COR (Drafted 2nd round, '90)	.15	.07	.02
☐ 93 Bill Fralic	.05	.02	.01
☐ 94 Tim Green	.05	.02	.01
☐ 95 Michael Haynes	.25	.11	.03
☐ 96 Chris Hinton	.05	.02	.01
☐ 97 Chris Miller UER (Two commas after city in his birth info)	.10	.05	.01
☐ 98 Deion Sanders UER (Career TD's 3, but only 2 in yearly stats)	.60	.25	.07
☐ 99 Jerry Glanville CO	.05	.02	.01
☐ 100 Kevin Butler	.05	.02	.01
☐ 101 Mark Carrier DB	.10	.05	.01
☐ 102 Jim Covert	.05	.02	.01
☐ 103 Richard Dent	.10	.05	.01
☐ 104 Jim Harbaugh	.25	.11	.03
☐ 105 Brad Muster	.05	.02	.01
☐ 106 Lemuel Stinson	.05	.02	.01
☐ 107 Keith Van Horne	.05	.02	.01
☐ 108 Mike Ditka CO UER (Winning percent in '87 was .733, not .753)	.25	.11	.03
☐ 109 Lewis Billups	.05	.02	.01
☐ 110 James Brooks	.10	.05	.01
☐ 111 Boomer Esiason	.10	.05	.01
☐ 112 James Francis	.05	.02	.01
☐ 113 David Fulcher	.05	.02	.01
☐ 114 Rodney Holman	.05	.02	.01
☐ 115 Tim McGee	.05	.02	.01
☐ 116 Anthony Munoz	.10	.05	.01
☐ 117 Sam Wyche CO	.05	.02	.01
☐ 118 Paul Farren	.05	.02	.01
☐ 119 Thane Gash	.05	.02	.01
☐ 120 Mike Johnson	.05	.02	.01
☐ 121A Bernie Kosar (NFLPA logo on back)	.10	.05	.01
☐ 121B Bernie Kosar (No NFLPA logo on back)	.10	.05	.01
☐ 122 Clay Matthews	.10	.05	.01
☐ 123 Eric Metcalf	.10	.05	.01
☐ 124 Frank Minnifield	.05	.02	.01
☐ 125A Webster Slaughter (NFLPA logo on back)	.08	.04	.01
☐ 125B Webster Slaughter (No NFLPA logo on back)	.05	.02	.01
☐ 126 Bill Belichick CO	.05	.02	.01
☐ 127 Tommie Agee	.05	.02	.01
☐ 128 Troy Aikman	1.00	.45	.12
☐ 129 Jack Del Rio	.05	.02	.01
☐ 130 John Gesek	.05	.02	.01
☐ 131 Issiac Holt	.05	.02	.01
☐ 132 Michael Irvin	.25	.11	.03
☐ 133 Ken Norton	.25	.11	.03
☐ 134 Daniel Stubbs	.05	.02	.01
☐ 135 Jimmy Johnson CO	.10	.05	.01
☐ 136 Steve Atwater	.05	.02	.01
☐ 137 Michael Brooks	.05	.02	.01
☐ 138 John Elway	.75	.35	.09
☐ 139 Wymon Henderson	.05	.02	.01
☐ 140 Bobby Humphrey	.05	.02	.01
☐ 141 Mark Jackson	.05	.02	.01
☐ 142 Karl Mecklenburg	.05	.02	.01
☐ 143 Doug Widell	.05	.02	.01
☐ 144 Dan Reeves CO	.05	.02	.01
☐ 145 Eric Andolsek	.05	.02	.01
☐ 146 Jerry Ball	.05	.02	.01
☐ 147 Bennie Blades	.05	.02	.01
☐ 148 Lomas Brown	.05	.02	.01
☐ 149 Robert Clark	.05	.02	.01
☐ 150 Michael Cofer	.05	.02	.01
☐ 151 Dan Owens	.05	.02	.01
☐ 152 Rodney Peete	.10	.05	.01
☐ 153 Wayne Fontes CO	.05	.02	.01
☐ 154 Tim Harris	.05	.02	.01
☐ 155 Johnny Holland	.05	.02	.01
☐ 156 Don Majkowski	.05	.02	.01
☐ 157 Tony Mandarich	.05	.02	.01
☐ 158 Mark Murphy	.05	.02	.01
☐ 159 Brian Noble	.05	.02	.01
☐ 160 Jeff Query	.05	.02	.01
☐ 161 Sterling Sharpe	.25	.11	.03
☐ 162 Lindy Infante CO	.05	.02	.01
☐ 163 Ray Childress	.05	.02	.01
☐ 164 Ernest Givins	.10	.05	.01
☐ 165 Richard Johnson	.05	.02	.01
☐ 166 Bruce Matthews	.10	.05	.01
☐ 167 Warren Moon	.25	.11	.03
☐ 168 Mike Munchak	.05	.02	.01
☐ 169 Al Smith	.05	.02	.01
☐ 170 Lorenzo White	.05	.02	.01
☐ 171 Jack Pardee CO	.05	.02	.01
☐ 172 Albert Bentley	.05	.02	.01
☐ 173 Duane Bickett	.05	.02	.01
☐ 174 Bill Brooks	.05	.02	.01
☐ 175A Eric Dickerson (NFLPA logo on back)	.40	.18	.05
☐ 175B Eric Dickerson (No NFLPA logo on back and 667 yards rushing for 1990 in text)	1.25	.55	.16
☐ 175C Eric Dickerson (No NFLPA logo on back and 677 yards rushing for 1990 in text)	.25	.11	.03
☐ 176 Ray Donaldson	.05	.02	.01
☐ 177 Jeff George	.25	.11	.03
☐ 178 Jeff Herrod	.05	.02	.01
☐ 179 Clarence Verdin	.05	.02	.01
☐ 180 Ron Meyer CO	.05	.02	.01
☐ 181 John Alt	.05	.02	.01
☐ 182 Steve DeBerg	.05	.02	.01
☐ 183 Albert Lewis	.05	.02	.01
☐ 184 Nick Lowery UER (In his 13th year, not 12th)	.05	.02	.01
☐ 185 Christian Okoye	.05	.02	.01
☐ 186 Stephone Paige	.05	.02	.01
☐ 187 Kevin Porter	.05	.02	.01
☐ 188 Derrick Thomas	.25	.11	.03
☐ 189 Marty Schottenheimer CO	.05	.02	.01
☐ 190 Willie Gault	.10	.05	.01
☐ 191 Howie Long	.10	.05	.01
☐ 192 Terry McDaniel	.05	.02	.01
☐ 193 Jay Schroeder UER (Passing total yards 13863, should be 13683)	.05	.02	.01
☐ 194 Steve Smith	.05	.02	.01
☐ 195 Greg Townsend	.05	.02	.01
☐ 196 Lionel Washington	.05	.02	.01
☐ 197 Steve Wisniewski UER (Back says drafted, should say traded to)	.05	.02	.01
☐ 198 Art Shell CO	.10	.05	.01
☐ 199 Henry Ellard	.10	.05	.01
☐ 200 Jim Everett	.10	.05	.01
☐ 201 Jerry Gray	.05	.02	.01
☐ 202 Kevin Greene	.25	.11	.03
☐ 203 Buford McGee	.05	.02	.01
☐ 204 Tom Newberry	.05	.02	.01
☐ 205 Frank Stams	.05	.02	.01
☐ 206 Alvin Wright	.05	.02	.01
☐ 207 John Robinson CO	.05	.02	.01
☐ 208 Jeff Cross	.05	.02	.01
☐ 209 Mark Duper	.10	.05	.01
☐ 210 Dan Marino	1.50	.70	.19
☐ 211A Tim McKyer (No Traded box on front)	.25	.11	.03
☐ 211B Tim McKyer (Traded box on front)	.15	.07	.02
☐ 212 John Offerdahl	.05	.02	.01
☐ 213 Sammie Smith	.05	.02	.01
☐ 214 Richmond Webb	.05	.02	.01
☐ 215 Jarvis Williams	.05	.02	.01
☐ 216 Don Shula CO	.10	.05	.01
☐ 217A Darrell Fullington ERR (No registered symbol on card back)	.08	.04	.01
☐ 217B Darrell Fullington COR (Registered symbol on card back)	.08	.04	.01
☐ 218 Tim Irwin	.05	.02	.01
☐ 219 Mike Merriweather	.05	.02	.01
☐ 220 Keith Millard	.05	.02	.01
☐ 221 Al Noga	.05	.02	.01
☐ 222 Henry Thomas	.05	.02	.01
☐ 223 Wade Wilson	.10	.05	.01
☐ 224 Gary Zimmerman	.05	.02	.01
☐ 225 Jerry Burns CO	.05	.02	.01
☐ 226 Bruce Armstrong	.05	.02	.01
☐ 227 Marv Cook	.05	.02	.01
☐ 228 Hart Lee Dykes	.05	.02	.01
☐ 229 Tommy Hodson	.05	.02	.01
☐ 230 Ronnie Lippett	.05	.02	.01
☐ 231 Ed Reynolds	.05	.02	.01
☐ 232 Chris Singleton	.05	.02	.01
☐ 233 John Stephens	.05	.02	.01
☐ 234 Dick MacPherson CO	.05	.02	.01
☐ 235 Stan Brock	.05	.02	.01
☐ 236 Craig Heyward	.10	.05	.01
☐ 237 Vaughan Johnson	.05	.02	.01
☐ 238 Robert Massey	.05	.02	.01
☐ 239 Brett Maxie	.05	.02	.01
☐ 240 Rueben Mayes	.05	.02	.01
☐ 241 Pat Swilling	.10	.05	.01
☐ 242 Renaldo Turnbull	.05	.02	.01
☐ 243 Jim Mora CO	.05	.02	.01
☐ 244 Kyle Clifton	.05	.02	.01
☐ 245 Jeff Criswell	.05	.02	.01
☐ 246 James Hasty	.05	.02	.01
☐ 247 Erik McMillan	.05	.02	.01
☐ 248 Scott Mersereau	.05	.02	.01
☐ 249 Ken O'Brien	.05	.02	.01
☐ 250A Blair Thomas (NFLPA logo on back)	.30	.14	.04
☐ 250B Blair Thomas (No NFLPA logo on back)	.10	.05	.01
☐ 251 Al Toon	.10	.05	.01
☐ 252 Bruce Coslet CO	.05	.02	.01
☐ 253 Eric Allen	.05	.02	.01
☐ 254 Fred Barnett	.25	.11	.03
☐ 255 Keith Byars	.05	.02	.01
☐ 256 Randall Cunningham	.10	.05	.01
☐ 257 Seth Joyner	.10	.05	.01
☐ 258 Clyde Simmons	.05	.02	.01
☐ 259 Jessie Small	.05	.02	.01
☐ 260 Andre Waters	.05	.02	.01
☐ 261 Rich Kotite CO	.05	.02	.01
☐ 262 Roy Green	.05	.02	.01
☐ 263 Ernie Jones	.05	.02	.01
☐ 264 Tim McDonald	.05	.02	.01
☐ 265 Timm Rosenbach	.05	.02	.01
☐ 266 Rod Saddler	.05	.02	.01
☐ 267 Luis Sharpe	.05	.02	.01
☐ 268 Anthony Thompson UER (Terra Haute should be Terre Haute)	.05	.02	.01
☐ 269 Marcus Turner	.05	.02	.01
☐ 270 Joe Bugel CO	.05	.02	.01
☐ 271 Gary Anderson K	.05	.02	.01
☐ 272 Dermontti Dawson	.05	.02	.01
☐ 273 Eric Green	.05	.02	.01
☐ 274 Merril Hoge	.05	.02	.01
☐ 275 Tunch Ilkin	.05	.02	.01
☐ 276 D.J. Johnson	.05	.02	.01
☐ 277 Louis Lipps	.05	.02	.01
☐ 278 Rod Woodson	.25	.11	.03
☐ 279 Chuck Noll CO	.10	.05	.01
☐ 280 Martin Bayless	.05	.02	.01
☐ 281 Marion Butts UER (2 years exp., should be 3)	.10	.05	.01
☐ 282 Gill Byrd	.05	.02	.01
☐ 283 Burt Grossman	.05	.02	.01
☐ 284 Courtney Hall	.05	.02	.01
☐ 285 Anthony Miller	.10	.05	.01
☐ 286 Leslie O'Neal	.10	.05	.01
☐ 287 Billy Joe Tolliver	.05	.02	.01
☐ 288 Dan Henning CO	.05	.02	.01

☐ 289 Dexter Carter	.05	.02	.01
☐ 290 Michael Carter	.05	.02	.01
☐ 291 Kevin Fagan	.05	.02	.01
☐ 292 Pierce Holt	.05	.02	.01
☐ 293 Guy McIntyre (Joe Montana also in photo)	.05	.02	.01
☐ 294 Tom Rathman	.05	.02	.01
☐ 295 John Taylor	.10	.05	.01
☐ 296 Steve Young	.75	.35	.09
☐ 297 George Seifert CO	.10	.05	.01
☐ 298 Brian Blades	.10	.05	.01
☐ 299 Jeff Bryant	.05	.02	.01
☐ 300 Norm Johnson	.05	.02	.01
☐ 301 Tommy Kane	.05	.02	.01
☐ 302 Cortez Kennedy UER (Played for Seattle in '90, not Miami)	.25	.11	.03
☐ 303 Bryan Millard	.05	.02	.01
☐ 304 John L. Williams	.05	.02	.01
☐ 305 David Wyman	.05	.02	.01
☐ 306A Chuck Knox CO ERR (Has NFLPA logo, but should not)	.05	.02	.01
☐ 306B Chuck Knox CO COR (No NFLPA logo on back)	.50	.23	.06
☐ 307 Gary Anderson RB	.05	.02	.01
☐ 308 Reggie Cobb	.05	.02	.01
☐ 309 Randy Grimes	.05	.02	.01
☐ 310 Harry Hamilton	.05	.02	.01
☐ 311 Bruce Hill	.05	.02	.01
☐ 312 Eugene Marve	.05	.02	.01
☐ 313 Ervin Randle	.05	.02	.01
☐ 314 Vinny Testaverde	.10	.05	.01
☐ 315 Richard Williamson CO UER (Coach: 1st year, should be 2nd year)	.05	.02	.01
☐ 316 Earnest Byner	.05	.02	.01
☐ 317 Gary Clark	.25	.11	.03
☐ 318A Andre Collins (NFLPA logo on back)	.08	.04	.01
☐ 318B Andre Collins (No NFLPA logo on back)	.05	.02	.01
☐ 319 Darryl Grant	.05	.02	.01
☐ 320 Chip Lohmiller	.05	.02	.01
☐ 321 Martin Mayhew	.05	.02	.01
☐ 322 Mark Rypien	.10	.05	.01
☐ 323 Alvin Walton	.05	.02	.01
☐ 324 Joe Gibbs CO UER (Has registered symbol but should not)	.10	.05	.01
☐ 325 Jerry Glanville REP	.05	.02	.01
☐ 326A John Elway REP (NFLPA logo on back)	.08	.04	.01
☐ 326B John Elway REP (No NFLPA logo on back)	.05	.02	.01
☐ 327 Boomer Esiason REP	.05	.02	.01
☐ 328A Steve Tasker REP (NFLPA logo on back)	.08	.04	.01
☐ 328B Steve Tasker REP (No NFLPA logo on back)	.05	.02	.01
☐ 329 Jerry Rice REP	.50	.23	.06
☐ 330 Jeff Rutledge REP	.05	.02	.01
☐ 331 K.C. Defense REP	.05	.02	.01
☐ 332 49ers Streak REP (Cleveland Gary)	.05	.02	.01
☐ 333 Monday Meeting REP (John Taylor)	.05	.02	.01
☐ 334A Randall Cunningham REP (NFLPA logo on back)	.05	.02	.01
☐ 334B Randall Cunningham REP (No NFLPA logo on back)	.05	.02	.01
☐ 335A Bo Jackson and Barry Sanders REP (NFLPA logo on back)	.30	.14	.04
☐ 335B Bo Jackson and Barry Sanders REP (No NFLPA logo on back)	.30	.14	.04
☐ 336 Lawrence Taylor REP	.25	.11	.03
☐ 337 Warren Moon REP	.25	.11	.03
☐ 338 Alan Grant REP	.05	.02	.01
☐ 339 Todd McNair REP	.05	.02	.01
☐ 340A Miami Dolphins REP (Mark Clayton; TM symbol on Chiefs player's shoulder)	.05	.02	.01
☐ 340B Miami Dolphins REP (Mark Clayton; TM symbol off Chiefs player's shoulder)	.05	.02	.01
☐ 341A Highest Scoring REP Jim Kelly Passing (NFLPA logo on back)	.08	.04	.01
☐ 341B Highest Scoring REP Jim Kelly Passing (No NFLPA logo on back)	.05	.02	.01
☐ 342 Matt Bahr REP	.05	.02	.01
☐ 343 Robert Tisch NEW (With Wellington Mara)	.05	.02	.01
☐ 344 Sam Jankovich NEW	.05	.02	.01
☐ 345 In-the-Grasp NEW (John Elway)	.05	.02	.01
☐ 346 Bo Jackson NEW (Career in Jeopardy)	.10	.05	.01
☐ 347 NFL Teacher of the Year Jack Williams with Paul Tagliabue	.05	.02	.01
☐ 348 Ronnie Lott NEW (Plan B Free Agent)	.10	.05	.01
☐ 349 Super Bowl XXV Teleclinic NEW (Greg Gumbel with Warren Moon, Derrick Thomas, and Wade Wilson)	.05	.02	.01
☐ 350 Whitney Houston NEW	.05	.02	.01
☐ 351 U.S. Troops in Saudia Arabia NEW (Troops watching TV with gas masks)	.05	.02	.01
☐ 352 Art McNally OFF	.05	.02	.01
☐ 353 Dick Jorgensen OFF	.05	.02	.01
☐ 354 Jerry Seeman OFF	.05	.02	.01
☐ 355 Jim Tunney OFF	.05	.02	.01
☐ 356 Gerry Austin OFF	.05	.02	.01
☐ 357 Gene Barth OFF	.05	.02	.01
☐ 358 Red Cashion OFF	.05	.02	.01
☐ 359 Tom Dooley OFF	.05	.02	.01
☐ 360 Johnny Grier OFF	.05	.02	.01
☐ 361 Pat Haggerty OFF	.05	.02	.01
☐ 362 Dale Hamer OFF	.05	.02	.01
☐ 363 Dick Hantak OFF	.05	.02	.01
☐ 364 Jerry Markbreit OFF	.05	.02	.01
☐ 365 Gordon McCarter OFF	.05	.02	.01
☐ 366 Bob McElwee OFF	.05	.02	.01
☐ 367 Howard Roe OFF (Illustrations on back smaller than other officials' cards)	.05	.02	.01
☐ 368 Tom White OFF	.05	.02	.01
☐ 369 Norm Schachter OFF	.05	.02	.01
☐ 370A Warren Moon Crack Kills (Small type on back)	.25	.11	.03
☐ 370B Warren Moon Crack Kills (Large type on back)	.25	.11	.03
☐ 371A Boomer Esiason Don't Drink (Small type on back)	.06	.03	.01
☐ 371B Boomer Esiason Don't Drink (Large type on back)	.10	.05	.01
☐ 372A Troy Aikman Play It Straight (Small type on back)	.50	.23	.06
☐ 372B Troy Aikman Play It Straight (Large type on back)	.50	.23	.06
☐ 373A Carl Banks Read (Small type on back)	.06	.03	.01
☐ 373B Carl Banks Read (Large type on back)	.05	.02	.01
☐ 374A Jim Everett Study (Small type on back)	.06	.03	.01
☐ 374B Jim Everett Study (Large type on back)	.10	.05	.01
☐ 375A Anthony Munoz Quadante en la Escuela (Dificul; small type)	.10	.05	.01
☐ 375B Anthony Munoz Quadante en la Escuela (Dificil; small type)	.10	.05	.01
☐ 375C Anthony Munoz Quadante en la Escuela (Dificil; large type)	.10	.05	.01
☐ 375D Anthony Munoz Quedate en la Escuela (Large type)	.10	.05	.01
☐ 376A Ray Childress Don't Pollute (Small type on back)	.06	.03	.01
☐ 376B Ray Childress Don't Pollute (Large type on back)	.05	.02	.01
☐ 377A Charles Mann Steroids Destroy (Small type on back)	.06	.03	.01
☐ 377B Charles Mann Steroids Destroy (Large type on back)	.05	.02	.01
☐ 378A Jackie Slater Keep the Peace (Small type on back)	.06	.03	.01
☐ 378B Jackie Slater Keep the Peace (Large type on back)	.05	.02	.01
☐ 379 Jerry Rice NFC	.50	.23	.06
☐ 380 Andre Rison NFC	.10	.05	.01
☐ 381 Jim Lachey NFC	.05	.02	.01
☐ 382 Jackie Slater NFC	.05	.02	.01
☐ 383 Randall McDaniel NFC	.05	.02	.01
☐ 384 Mark Bortz NFC	.05	.02	.01
☐ 385 Jay Hilgenberg NFC	.05	.02	.01
☐ 386 Keith Jackson NFC	.05	.02	.01
☐ 387 Joe Montana NFC	.40	.18	.05
☐ 388 Barry Sanders NFC	.50	.23	.06
☐ 389 Neal Anderson NFC	.05	.02	.01
☐ 390 Reggie White NFC	.25	.11	.03
☐ 391 Chris Doleman NFC	.05	.02	.01
☐ 392 Jerome Brown NFC	.05	.02	.01
☐ 393 Charles Haley NFC	.05	.02	.01
☐ 394 Lawrence Taylor NFC	.25	.11	.03
☐ 395 Pepper Johnson NFC	.05	.02	.01
☐ 396 Mike Singletary NFC	.10	.05	.01
☐ 397 Darrell Green NFC	.05	.02	.01
☐ 398 Carl Lee NFC	.05	.02	.01
☐ 399 Joey Browner NFC	.05	.02	.01
☐ 400 Ronnie Lott NFC	.10	.05	.01
☐ 401 Sean Landeta NFC	.05	.02	.01
☐ 402 Morten Andersen NFC	.05	.02	.01
☐ 403 Mel Gray NFC	.05	.02	.01
☐ 404 Reyna Thompson NFC	.05	.02	.01
☐ 405 Jimmy Johnson CO NFC	.10	.05	.01
☐ 406 Andre Reed AFC	.10	.05	.01
☐ 407 Anthony Miller AFC	.10	.05	.01
☐ 408 Anthony Munoz AFC	.10	.05	.01
☐ 409 Bruce Armstrong AFC	.05	.02	.01
☐ 410 Bruce Matthews AFC	.05	.02	.01
☐ 411 Mike Munchak AFC	.05	.02	.01
☐ 412 Kent Hull AFC	.05	.02	.01
☐ 413 Rodney Holman AFC	.05	.02	.01
☐ 414 Warren Moon AFC	.25	.11	.03
☐ 415 Thurman Thomas AFC	.25	.11	.03
☐ 416 Marion Butts AFC	.10	.05	.01
☐ 417 Bruce Smith AFC	.10	.05	.01
☐ 418 Greg Townsend AFC	.05	.02	.01
☐ 419 Ray Childress AFC	.05	.02	.01
☐ 420 Derrick Thomas AFC	.25	.11	.03
☐ 421 Leslie O'Neal AFC	.10	.05	.01
☐ 422 John Offerdahl AFC	.05	.02	.01
☐ 423 Shane Conlan AFC	.05	.02	.01
☐ 424 Rod Woodson AFC	.25	.11	.03
☐ 425 Albert Lewis AFC	.05	.02	.01
☐ 426 Steve Atwater AFC	.05	.02	.01
☐ 427 David Fulcher AFC	.05	.02	.01
☐ 428 Rohn Stark AFC	.05	.02	.01
☐ 429 Nick Lowery AFC	.05	.02	.01
☐ 430 Clarence Verdin AFC	.05	.02	.01
☐ 431 Steve Tasker AFC	.05	.02	.01
☐ 432 Art Shell CO AFC	.10	.05	.01
☐ 433 Scott Case	.05	.02	.01
☐ 434 Tory Epps UER (No TM next to Pro Set on card back)	.05	.02	.01
☐ 435 Mike Gann UER (Text has 2 fumble recoveries, stats say 3)	.05	.02	.01
☐ 436 Brian Jordan UER (No TM next to Pro Set on card back)	.10	.05	.01
☐ 437 Mike Kenn	.05	.02	.01
☐ 438 John Rade	.05	.02	.01
☐ 439 Andre Rison	.10	.05	.01
☐ 440 Mike Rozier	.05	.02	.01
☐ 441 Jessie Tuggle	.05	.02	.01
☐ 442 Don Beebe	.05	.02	.01
☐ 443 John Davis	.05	.02	.01
☐ 444 James Lofton	.10	.05	.01
☐ 445 Keith McKeller	.05	.02	.01
☐ 446 Jamie Mueller	.05	.02	.01
☐ 447 Scott Norwood	.05	.02	.01
☐ 448 Frank Reich	.10	.05	.01
☐ 449 Leon Seals	.05	.02	.01
☐ 450 Leonard Smith	.05	.02	.01
☐ 451 Neal Anderson	.10	.05	.01
☐ 452 Trace Armstrong	.05	.02	.01
☐ 453 Mark Bortz	.05	.02	.01
☐ 454 Wendell Davis	.05	.02	.01
☐ 455 Shaun Gayle	.05	.02	.01
☐ 456 Jay Hilgenberg	.05	.02	.01
☐ 457 Steve McMichael	.10	.05	.01
☐ 458 Mike Singletary	.10	.05	.01
☐ 459 Donnell Woolford	.05	.02	.01
☐ 460 Jim Breech	.05	.02	.01
☐ 461 Eddie Brown	.05	.02	.01
☐ 462 Barney Bussey	.05	.02	.01
☐ 463 Bruce Kozerski	.05	.02	.01
☐ 464 Tim Krumrie	.05	.02	.01
☐ 465 Bruce Reimers	.05	.02	.01
☐ 466 Kevin Walker	.05	.02	.01
☐ 467 Ickey Woods	.05	.02	.01
☐ 468 Carl Zander UER (DOB: 4/12/63, should be 3/23/63)	.05	.02	.01
☐ 469 Mike Baab	.05	.02	.01
☐ 470 Brian Brennan	.05	.02	.01
☐ 471 Rob Burnett	.05	.02	.01
☐ 472 Raymond Clayborn	.05	.02	.01
☐ 473 Reggie Langhorne	.05	.02	.01
☐ 474 Kevin Mack	.05	.02	.01
☐ 475 Anthony Pleasant	.05	.02	.01
☐ 476 Joe Morris	.05	.02	.01
☐ 477 Dan Fike	.05	.02	.01
☐ 478 Ray Horton	.05	.02	.01
☐ 479 Jim Jeffcoat	.05	.02	.01
☐ 480 Jimmie Jones	.05	.02	.01
☐ 481 Kelvin Martin	.05	.02	.01
☐ 482 Nate Newton	.10	.05	.01
☐ 483 Danny Noonan	.05	.02	.01
☐ 484 Jay Novacek	.25	.11	.03
☐ 485 Emmitt Smith	2.00	.90	.25
☐ 486 James Washington	.05	.02	.01
☐ 487 Simon Fletcher	.05	.02	.01
☐ 488 Ron Holmes	.05	.02	.01
☐ 489 Mike Horan	.05	.02	.01
☐ 490 Vance Johnson	.05	.02	.01
☐ 491 Keith Kartz	.05	.02	.01
☐ 492 Greg Kragen	.05	.02	.01
☐ 493 Ken Lanier	.05	.02	.01
☐ 494 Warren Powers	.05	.02	.01
☐ 495 Dennis Smith	.05	.02	.01
☐ 496 Jeff Campbell	.05	.02	.01
☐ 497 Ken Dallafior	.05	.02	.01
☐ 498 Dennis Gibson	.05	.02	.01
☐ 499 Kevin Glover	.05	.02	.01
☐ 500 Mel Gray	.10	.05	.01
☐ 501 Eddie Murray	.05	.02	.01
☐ 502 Barry Sanders	1.00	.45	.12
☐ 503 Chris Spielman	.10	.05	.01
☐ 504 William White	.05	.02	.01
☐ 505 Matt Brock	.05	.02	.01
☐ 506 Robert Brown	.05	.02	.01
☐ 507 LeRoy Butler	.10	.05	.01
☐ 508 James Campen	.05	.02	.01
☐ 509 Jerry Holmes	.05	.02	.01
☐ 510 Perry Kemp	.05	.02	.01
☐ 511 Ken Ruettgers	.05	.02	.01
☐ 512 Scott Stephen	.05	.02	.01
☐ 513 Ed West	.05	.02	.01
☐ 514 Cris Dishman	.05	.02	.01
☐ 515 Curtis Duncan	.05	.02	.01
☐ 516 Drew Hill UER (Text says 390 catches and 6368 yards, stats say 450 and 7715)	.05	.02	.01
☐ 517 Haywood Jeffires	.10	.05	.01
☐ 518 Sean Jones	.10	.05	.01
☐ 519 Lamar Lathon	.05	.02	.01
☐ 520 Don Maggs	.05	.02	.01
☐ 521 Bubba McDowell	.05	.02	.01
☐ 522 Johnny Meads	.05	.02	.01
☐ 523A Chip Banks ERR (No text)	.50	.23	.06
☐ 523B Chip Banks COR	.08	.04	.01
☐ 524 Pat Beach	.05	.02	.01
☐ 525 Sam Clancy	.05	.02	.01
☐ 526 Eugene Daniel	.05	.02	.01
☐ 527 Jon Hand	.05	.02	.01
☐ 528 Jessie Hester	.05	.02	.01
☐ 529A Mike Prior ERR (No textual information)	.50	.23	.06
☐ 529B Mike Prior COR	.08	.04	.01
☐ 530 Keith Taylor	.05	.02	.01
☐ 531 Donnell Thompson	.05	.02	.01
☐ 532 Dino Hackett	.05	.02	.01
☐ 533 David Lutz	.05	.02	.01
☐ 534 Chris Martin	.05	.02	.01
☐ 535 Kevin Ross	.05	.02	.01
☐ 536 Dan Saleaumua	.05	.02	.01
☐ 537 Neil Smith	.25	.11	.03
☐ 538 Percy Snow	.05	.02	.01
☐ 539 Robb Thomas	.05	.02	.01
☐ 540 Barry Word	.05	.02	.01
☐ 541 Marcus Allen	.25	.11	.03
☐ 542 Eddie Anderson	.05	.02	.01
☐ 543 Scott Davis	.05	.02	.01
☐ 544 Mervyn Fernandez	.05	.02	.01
☐ 545 Ethan Horton	.05	.02	.01
☐ 546 Ronnie Lott	.10	.05	.01
☐ 547 Don Mosebar	.05	.02	.01
☐ 548 Jerry Robinson	.05	.02	.01
☐ 549 Aaron Wallace	.05	.02	.01
☐ 550 Flipper Anderson	.05	.02	.01
☐ 551 Cleveland Gary	.05	.02	.01
☐ 552 Damone Johnson	.05	.02	.01
☐ 553 Duval Love	.05	.02	.01
☐ 554 Irv Pankey	.05	.02	.01
☐ 555 Mike Piel	.05	.02	.01
☐ 556 Jackie Slater	.05	.02	.01
☐ 557 Michael Stewart	.05	.02	.01
☐ 558 Pat Terrell	.05	.02	.01
☐ 559 J.B. Brown	.05	.02	.01
☐ 560 Mark Clayton	.10	.05	.01
☐ 561 Ferrell Edmunds	.05	.02	.01
☐ 562 Harry Galbreath	.05	.02	.01
☐ 563 David Griggs	.05	.02	.01
☐ 564 Jim C. Jensen	.05	.02	.01
☐ 565 Louis Oliver	.05	.02	.01
☐ 566 Tony Paige	.05	.02	.01
☐ 567 Keith Sims	.05	.02	.01
☐ 568 Joey Browner	.05	.02	.01
☐ 569 Anthony Carter	.10	.05	.01
☐ 570 Chris Doleman	.05	.02	.01
☐ 571 Rich Gannon UER (Acquired in '87, not '88 as in text)	.05	.02	.01
☐ 572 Hassan Jones	.05	.02	.01
☐ 573 Steve Jordan	.05	.02	.01
☐ 574 Carl Lee	.05	.02	.01
☐ 575 Randall McDaniel	.05	.02	.01
☐ 576 Herschel Walker	.10	.05	.01
☐ 577 Ray Agnew	.05	.02	.01
☐ 578 Vincent Brown	.05	.02	.01
☐ 579 Irving Fryar	.10	.05	.01

☐ 580 Tim Goad	.05	.02	.01
☐ 581 Maurice Hurst	.05	.02	.01
☐ 582 Fred Marion	.05	.02	.01
☐ 583 Johnny Rembert	.05	.02	.01
☐ 584 Andre Tippett	.05	.02	.01
☐ 585 Brent Williams	.05	.02	.01
☐ 586 Morten Andersen	.05	.02	.01
☐ 587 Toi Cook	.05	.02	.01
☐ 588 Jim Dombrowski	.05	.02	.01
☐ 589 Dalton Hilliard	.05	.02	.01
☐ 590 Rickey Jackson	.05	.02	.01
☐ 591 Eric Martin	.05	.02	.01
☐ 592 Sam Mills	.05	.02	.01
☐ 593 Bobby Hebert	.05	.02	.01
☐ 594 Steve Walsh	.05	.02	.01
☐ 595 Ottis Anderson	.10	.05	.01
☐ 596 Pepper Johnson	.05	.02	.01
☐ 597 Bob Kratch	.05	.02	.01
☐ 598 Sean Landeta	.05	.02	.01
☐ 599 Doug Riesenberg	.05	.02	.01
☐ 600 William Roberts	.05	.02	.01
☐ 601 Phil Simms	.10	.05	.01
☐ 602 Lawrence Taylor	.25	.11	.03
☐ 603 Everson Walls	.05	.02	.01
☐ 604 Brad Baxter	.05	.02	.01
☐ 605 Dennis Byrd	.05	.02	.01
☐ 606 Jeff Lageman	.05	.02	.01
☐ 607 Pat Leahy	.05	.02	.01
☐ 608 Rob Moore	.25	.11	.03
☐ 609 Joe Mott	.05	.02	.01
☐ 610 Tony Stargell	.05	.02	.01
☐ 611 Brian Washington	.05	.02	.01
☐ 612 Marvin Washington	.05	.02	.01
☐ 613 David Alexander	.05	.02	.01
☐ 614 Jerome Brown	.05	.02	.01
☐ 615 Byron Evans	.05	.02	.01
☐ 616 Ron Heller	.05	.02	.01
☐ 617 Wes Hopkins	.05	.02	.01
☐ 618 Keith Jackson	.10	.05	.01
☐ 619 Heath Sherman	.05	.02	.01
☐ 620 Reggie White	.25	.11	.03
☐ 621 Calvin Williams	.10	.05	.01
☐ 622 Ken Harvey	.10	.05	.01
☐ 623 Eric Hill	.05	.02	.01
☐ 624 Johnny Johnson	.05	.02	.01
☐ 625 Freddie Joe Nunn	.05	.02	.01
☐ 626 Ricky Proehl	.05	.02	.01
☐ 627 Tootie Robbins	.05	.02	.01
☐ 628 Jay Taylor	.05	.02	.01
☐ 629 Tom Tupa	.05	.02	.01
☐ 630 Jim Wahler	.05	.02	.01
☐ 631 Bubby Brister	.05	.02	.01
☐ 632 Thomas Everett	.05	.02	.01
☐ 633 Bryan Hinkle	.05	.02	.01
☐ 634 Carnell Lake	.05	.02	.01
☐ 635 David Little	.05	.02	.01
☐ 636 Hardy Nickerson	.10	.05	.01
☐ 637 Gerald Williams	.05	.02	.01
☐ 638 Keith Willis	.05	.02	.01
☐ 639 Tim Worley	.05	.02	.01
☐ 640 Rod Bernstine	.05	.02	.01
☐ 641 Frank Cornish	.05	.02	.01
☐ 642 Gary Plummer	.05	.02	.01
☐ 643 Henry Rolling	.05	.02	.01
☐ 644 Sam Seale	.05	.02	.01
☐ 645 Junior Seau	.40	.18	.05
☐ 646 Billy Ray Smith	.05	.02	.01
☐ 647 Broderick Thompson	.05	.02	.01
☐ 648 Derrick Walker	.05	.02	.01
☐ 649 Todd Bowles	.05	.02	.01
☐ 650 Don Griffin	.05	.02	.01
☐ 651 Charles Haley	.10	.05	.01
☐ 652 Brent Jones UER	.10	.05	.01
(Born in Santa Clara,			
not San Jose)			
☐ 653 Joe Montana	1.00	.45	.12
☐ 654 Jerry Rice	1.00	.45	.12
☐ 655 Bill Romanowski	.05	.02	.01
☐ 656 Michael Walter	.05	.02	.01
☐ 657 Dave Waymer	.05	.02	.01
☐ 658 Jeff Chadwick	.05	.02	.01
☐ 659 Derrick Fenner	.05	.02	.01
☐ 660 Nesby Glasgow	.05	.02	.01
☐ 661 Jacob Green	.05	.02	.01
☐ 662 Dwayne Harper	.05	.02	.01
☐ 663 Andy Heck	.05	.02	.01
☐ 664 Dave Krieg	.10	.05	.01
☐ 665 Rufus Porter	.05	.02	.01
☐ 666 Eugene Robinson	.05	.02	.01
☐ 667 Mark Carrier WR	.25	.11	.03
☐ 668 Steve Christie	.05	.02	.01
☐ 669 Reuben Davis	.05	.02	.01
☐ 670 Paul Gruber	.05	.02	.01
☐ 671 Wayne Haddix	.05	.02	.01
☐ 672 Ron Hall	.05	.02	.01
☐ 673 Keith McCants UER	.05	.02	.01
(Senior All-American,			
sic, left school			
after junior year)			
☐ 674 Ricky Reynolds	.05	.02	.01
☐ 675 Mark Robinson	.05	.02	.01
☐ 676 Jeff Bostic	.05	.02	.01
☐ 677 Darrell Green	.05	.02	.01
☐ 678 Markus Koch	.05	.02	.01
☐ 679 Jim Lachey	.05	.02	.01
☐ 680 Charles Mann	.05	.02	.01
☐ 681 Wilber Marshall	.05	.02	.01
☐ 682 Art Monk	.10	.05	.01
☐ 683 Gerald Riggs	.05	.02	.01
☐ 684 Ricky Sanders	.05	.02	.01
☐ 685 Ray Handley NEW	.05	.02	.01
(Replaces Bill Parcells as			
Giants head coach)			
☐ 686 NFL announces NEW	.05	.02	.01
expansion			
☐ 687 Miami gets NEW	.05	.02	.01
Super Bowl XXIX			
☐ 688 Giants' George Young NEW ..	.05	.02	.01
is named NFL Executive			
of the Year by			
The Sporting News			
☐ 689 Five-millionth fan NEW	.05	.02	.01
visits Pro Football			
Hall of Fame			
☐ 690 Sports Illustrated NEW	.05	.02	.01
poll finds pro football			
is America's Number 1			
spectator sport			
☐ 691 American Bowl NEW	.05	.02	.01
London Theme Art			
☐ 692 American Bowl NEW	.05	.02	.01
Berlin Theme Art			
☐ 693 American Bowl NEW	.05	.02	.01
Tokyo Theme Art			
☐ 694A Russell Maryland	.30	.14	.04
(Says he runs a 4.91			
40, card 32 has 4.8)			
☐ 694B Joe Ferguson LEG	.05	.02	.01
☐ 695 Carl Hairston LEG	.10	.05	.01
☐ 696 Dan Hampton LEG	.10	.05	.01
☐ 697 Mike Haynes LEG	.05	.02	.01
☐ 698 Marty Lyons LEG	.05	.02	.01
☐ 699 Ozzie Newsome LEG	.10	.05	.01
☐ 700 Scott Studwell LEG	.05	.02	.01
☐ 701 Mike Webster LEG	.05	.02	.01
☐ 702 Dwayne Woodruff LEG	.05	.02	.01
☐ 703 Larry Kennan CO	.05	.02	.01
London Monarchs			
☐ 704 Stan Gelbaugh LL	.10	.05	.01
London Monarchs			
☐ 705 John Brantley LL	.05	.02	.01
Birmingham Fire			
☐ 706 Danny Lockett LL	.05	.02	.01
London Monarchs			
☐ 707 Anthony Parker LL	.10	.05	.01
NY/NJ Knights			
☐ 708 Dan Crossman LL	.05	.02	.01
London Monarchs			
☐ 709 Eric Wilkerson LL	.05	.02	.01
NY/NJ Knights			
☐ 710 Judd Garrett LL	.05	.02	.01
London Monarchs			
☐ 711 Tony Baker LL	.05	.02	.01
Frankfurt Galaxy			
☐ 712 1st Place BW PHOTO	.05	.02	.01
Randall Cunningham			
☐ 713 2nd Place BW PHOTO	.05	.02	.01
Mark Ingram			
☐ 714 3rd Place BW PHOTO	.05	.02	.01
Pete Holohan			
Barney Bussey			
Carl Carter			
☐ 715 1st Place Color PHOTO	.05	.02	.01
Action			
Sterling Sharpe			
☐ 716 2nd Place Color PHOTO	.05	.02	.01
Action			
Jim Harbaugh			
☐ 717 3rd Place Color PHOTO	.05	.02	.01
Action			
Anthony Miller			
David Fulcher			
☐ 718 1st Place Color PHOTO	.05	.02	.01
Feature			
Bill Parcells CO			
Lawrence Taylor			
☐ 719 2nd Place Color PHOTO	.05	.02	.01
Feature			
Patriotic Crowd			
☐ 720 3rd Place Color PHOTO	.05	.02	.01
Feature			
Alfredo Roberts			
☐ 721 Ray Bentley	.05	.02	.01
Read And Study			
☐ 722 Earnest Byner	.05	.02	.01
Never Give Up			
☐ 723 Bill Fralic	.05	.02	.01
Steroids Destroy			
☐ 724 Joe Jacoby	.05	.02	.01
Don't Pollute			
☐ 725 Howie Long	.10	.05	.01
Aids Kills			
☐ 726 Dan Marino	.75	.35	.09
School's The Ticket			
☐ 727 Ron Rivera	.05	.02	.01
Leer Y Estudiar			
☐ 728 Mike Singletary	.10	.05	.01
Be The Best			
☐ 729 Cornelius Bennett	.10	.05	.01
Chill			
☐ 730 Russell Maryland	.25	.11	.03
☐ 731 Eric Turner	.10	.05	.01
☐ 732 Bruce Pickens UER	.05	.02	.01
(Wearing 38, but card			
back lists 39)			
☐ 733 Mike Croel	.05	.02	.01
☐ 734 Todd Lyght	.05	.02	.01
☐ 735 Eric Swann	.25	.11	.03
☐ 736 Charles McRae	.05	.02	.01
☐ 737 Antone Davis	.05	.02	.01
☐ 738 Stanley Richard	.05	.02	.01
☐ 739 Herman Moore	2.00	.90	.25
☐ 740 Pat Harlow	.05	.02	.01
☐ 741 Alvin Harper	.25	.11	.03
☐ 742 Mike Pritchard	.25	.11	.03
☐ 743 Leonard Russell	.25	.11	.03
☐ 744 Huey Richardson	.05	.02	.01
☐ 745 Dan McGwire	.05	.02	.01
☐ 746 Bobby Wilson	.05	.02	.01
☐ 747 Alfred Williams	.05	.02	.01
☐ 748 Vinnie Clark	.05	.02	.01
☐ 749 Kelvin Pritchett	.10	.05	.01
☐ 750 Harvey Williams	.25	.11	.03
☐ 751 Stan Thomas	.05	.02	.01
☐ 752 Randal Hill	.10	.05	.01
☐ 753 Todd Marinovich	.05	.02	.01
☐ 754 Ted Washington	.05	.02	.01
☐ 755 Henry Jones	.10	.05	.01
☐ 756 Jarrod Bunch	.05	.02	.01
☐ 757 Mike Dumas	.05	.02	.01
☐ 758 Ed King	.05	.02	.01
☐ 759 Reggie Johnson	.05	.02	.01
☐ 760 Roman Phifer	.05	.02	.01
☐ 761 Mike Jones	.05	.02	.01
☐ 762 Brett Favre	4.00	1.80	.50
☐ 763 Browning Nagle	.05	.02	.01
☐ 764 Esera Tuaolo	.05	.02	.01
☐ 765 George Thornton	.05	.02	.01
☐ 766 Dixon Edwards	.05	.02	.01
☐ 767 Darryll Lewis	.10	.05	.01
☐ 768 Eric Bieniemy	.05	.02	.01
☐ 769 Shane Curry	.05	.02	.01
☐ 770 Jerome Henderson	.05	.02	.01
☐ 771 Wesley Carroll	.05	.02	.01
☐ 772 Nick Bell	.05	.02	.01
☐ 773 John Flannery	.05	.02	.01
☐ 774 Ricky Watters	1.50	.70	.19
☐ 775 Jeff Graham	.25	.11	.03
☐ 776 Eric Moten	.05	.02	.01
☐ 777 Jesse Campbell	.05	.02	.01
☐ 778 Chris Zorich	.10	.05	.01
☐ 779 Joe Valerio	.05	.02	.01
☐ 780 Doug Thomas	.05	.02	.01
☐ 781 Lamar Rogers UER	.05	.02	.01
(No "Official Card of			
NFL" and TM on			
card front)			
☐ 782 John Johnson	.05	.02	.01
☐ 783 Phil Hansen	.05	.02	.01
☐ 784 Kanavis McGhee	.05	.02	.01
☐ 785 Calvin Stephens UER	.05	.02	.01
(Card says New England,			
others say New England			
Patriots)			
☐ 786 James Jones	.05	.02	.01
☐ 787 Reggie Barrett	.05	.02	.01
☐ 788 Aeneas Williams	.25	.11	.03
☐ 789 Aaron Craver	.05	.02	.01
☐ 790 Keith Traylor	.05	.02	.01
☐ 791 Godfrey Myles	.05	.02	.01
☐ 792 Mo Lewis	.10	.05	.01
☐ 793 James Richards	.05	.02	.01
☐ 794 Carlos Jenkins	.05	.02	.01
☐ 795 Lawrence Dawsey	.10	.05	.01
☐ 796 Don Davey	.05	.02	.01
☐ 797 Jake Reed	1.00	.45	.12
☐ 798 Dave McCloughan	.05	.02	.01
☐ 799 Erik Williams	.10	.05	.01
☐ 800 Steve Jackson	.05	.02	.01
☐ 801 Bob Dahl	.05	.02	.01
☐ 802 Ernie Mills	.10	.05	.01
☐ 803 David Daniels	.05	.02	.01
☐ 804 Rob Selby	.05	.02	.01
☐ 805 Ricky Ervins	.10	.05	.01
☐ 806 Tim Barnett	.05	.02	.01
☐ 807 Chris Gardocki	.05	.02	.01
☐ 808 Kevin Donnalley	.05	.02	.01
☐ 809 Robert Wilson	.05	.02	.01
☐ 810 Chuck Webb	.05	.02	.01
☐ 811 Darryl Wren	.05	.02	.01
☐ 812 Ed McCaffrey	.10	.05	.01
☐ 813 Shula's 300th Victory	.05	.02	.01
NEWS			
☐ 814 Raiders-49ers sell	.05	.02	.01
out Coliseum NEWS			
☐ 815 NFL International NEWS	.05	.02	.01
☐ 816 Moe Gardner	.05	.02	.01
☐ 817 Tim McKyer	.05	.02	.01
☐ 818 Tom Waddle	.05	.02	.01
☐ 819 Michael Jackson	.25	.11	.03
☐ 820 Tony Casillas	.05	.02	.01
☐ 821 Gaston Green	.05	.02	.01
☐ 822 Kenny Walker	.05	.02	.01
☐ 823 Willie Green	.05	.02	.01
☐ 824 Erik Kramer	.75	.35	.09
☐ 825 William Fuller	.10	.05	.01
☐ 826 Allen Pinkett	.05	.02	.01
☐ 827 Rick Venturi CO	.05	.02	.01
☐ 828 Bill Maas	.05	.02	.01
☐ 829 Jeff Jaeger	.05	.02	.01
☐ 830 Robert Delpino	.05	.02	.01
☐ 831 Mark Higgs	.05	.02	.01
☐ 832 Reggie Roby	.05	.02	.01
☐ 833 Terry Allen	2.00	.90	.25
☐ 834 Cris Carter	.25	.11	.03
(No indication when			
acquired on waivers)			
☐ 835 John Randle	.25	.11	.03
☐ 836 Hugh Millen	.05	.02	.01
☐ 837 Jon Vaughn	.05	.02	.01
☐ 838 Gill Fenerty	.05	.02	.01
☐ 839 Floyd Turner	.05	.02	.01
☐ 840 Irv Eatman	.05	.02	.01
☐ 841 Lonnie Young	.05	.02	.01
☐ 842 Jim McMahon	.10	.05	.01
☐ 843 Randal Hill UER	.05	.02	.01
(Traded to Phoenix,			
not drafted)			
☐ 844 Barry Foster	.10	.05	.01
☐ 845 Neil O'Donnell	.75	.35	.09
☐ 846 John Friesz UER	.25	.11	.03
(Wears 17, not 7)			
☐ 847 Broderick Thomas	.05	.02	.01
☐ 848 Brian Mitchell	.10	.05	.01
☐ 849 Mike Utley	.10	.05	.01
☐ 850 Mike Croel ROY	.05	.02	.01
☐ SC1 Super Bowl XXVI	.25	.11	.03
Theme Art UER			
(Card says SB 26,			
should be 25)			
☐ SC3 Jim Thorpe	.75	.35	.09
Pioneers of the Game			
☐ SC4 Otto Graham	.75	.35	.09
Pioneers of the Game			
☐ SC5 Paul Brown	.75	.35	.09
Pioneers of the Game			
☐ PSS1 Walter Payton	1.00	.45	.12
and Team 34			
☐ PSS2 Red Grange	.75	.35	.09
☐ MVPC25 Ottis Anderson	.25	.11	.03
MVP Super Bowl XXV			
☐ AU336 Lawrence Taylor	175.00	80.00	22.00
REP (autographed/500)			
☐ AU394 Lawrence Taylor	175.00	80.00	22.00
PB (autographed/500)			
☐ AU699 Ozzie Newsome	50.00	22.00	6.25
(Certified autograph)			
☐ AU824 Erik Kramer	50.00	22.00	6.25
(Certified autograph)			
☐ NNO Mini Pro Set Gazette	.25	.11	.03
☐ NNO Pro Set Gazette	.25	.11	.03
☐ NNO Santa Claus	.75	.35	.09
☐ NNO Super Bowl XXV Art	.25	.11	.03
☐ NNO Super Bowl XXV Logo	.25	.11	.03

1991 Pro Set WLAF Helmets

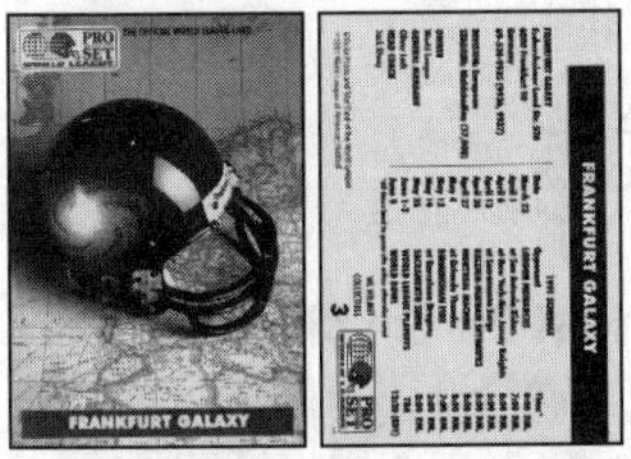

This set of ten standard size cards features (on the front of each card) a helmet of the teams of the WLAF's first season. These cards were included in the 1991 Pro Set first series wax packs. The back has information about the teams.

	MINT	NRMT	EXC
COMPLETE SET (10)	2.00	.90	.25
COMMON CARD (1-10)	.25	.11	.03
☐ 1 Barcelona Dragons	.25	.11	.03
Helmet			
☐ 2 Birmingham Fire	.25	.11	.03
Helmet			
☐ 3 Frankfurt Galaxy	.25	.11	.03
Helmet			
☐ 4 London Monarchs	.25	.11	.03
Helmet			
☐ 5 Montreal Machine	.25	.11	.03
Helmet			
☐ 6 NY-NJ Knights	.25	.11	.03
Helmet			
☐ 7 Orlando Thunder	.25	.11	.03
Helmet			
☐ 8 Ral.-Durham Skyhawks	.25	.11	.03
Helmet			
☐ 9 Sacramento Surge	.25	.11	.03
Helmet			
☐ 10 San Antonio Riders	.25	.11	.03
Helmet			

1991 Pro Set WLAF Inserts

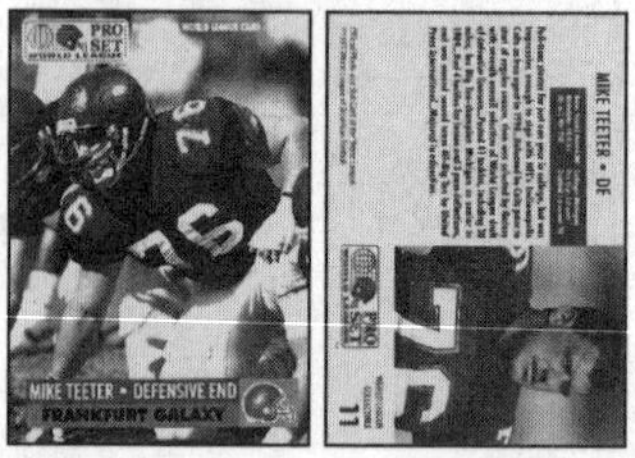

This 32-card standard size set was issued by Pro Set as an insert to the 1991 Pro Set Football first series. This set features the leading players from the WLAF. All ten WLAF teams are represented, and each team's head coach and quarterback are depicted on a card.

	MINT	NRMT	EXC
COMPLETE SET (32)	4.00	1.80	.50
COMMON CARD (WL1-WL32)	.10	.05	.01
☐ WL1 Mike Lynn (President/CEO)	.10	.05	.01
☐ WL2 London 24, Frankfurt 11; World League Opener Larry Kennan CO	.10	.05	.01
☐ WL3 Jack Bicknell CO	.10	.05	.01
☐ WL4 Scott Erney	.10	.05	.01
☐ WL5 A.J. Green (Anthony on card front)	.10	.05	.01
☐ WL6 Chan Gailey CO	.10	.05	.01
☐ WL7 Paul McGowan	.10	.05	.01
☐ WL8 Brent Pease	.10	.05	.01
☐ WL9 Jack Elway CO	.20	.09	.03
☐ WL10 Mike Perez	.10	.05	.01
☐ WL11 Mike Teeter	.10	.05	.01
☐ WL12 Larry Kennan CO UER (Coaching experience should say first year)	.10	.05	.01
☐ WL13 Corris Ervin	.10	.05	.01
☐ WL14 John Witkowski	.10	.05	.01
☐ WL15 Jacques Dussault CO	.10	.05	.01
☐ WL16 Ray Savage UER (Back should say DE, not Defensive End)	.10	.05	.01
☐ WL17 Kevin Sweeney	.10	.05	.01
☐ WL18 Mouse Davis CO	.20	.09	.03
☐ WL19 Todd Hammel UER (Missing TM on card front)	.10	.05	.01
☐ WL20 Anthony Parker	.30	.14	.04
☐ WL21 Don Matthews CO	.10	.05	.01
☐ WL22 Kerwin Bell	.20	.09	.03
☐ WL23 Wayne Davis	.10	.05	.01
☐ WL24 Roman Gabriel CO	.30	.14	.04
☐ WL25 Jon Carter	.10	.05	.01
☐ WL26 Mark Maye	.10	.05	.01
☐ WL27 Kay Stephenson CO	.10	.05	.01
☐ WL28 Ben Bennett	.10	.05	.01
☐ WL29 Shawn Knight UER (Back has NFL Exp. WLAF cards have Pro Exp.)	.10	.05	.01
☐ WL30 Mike Riley	.10	.05	.01
☐ WL31 Jason Garrett	.75	.35	.09
☐ WL32 Greg Gilbert UER (6th round choice, should say 5th)	.10	.05	.01

1991 Pro Set Cinderella Story

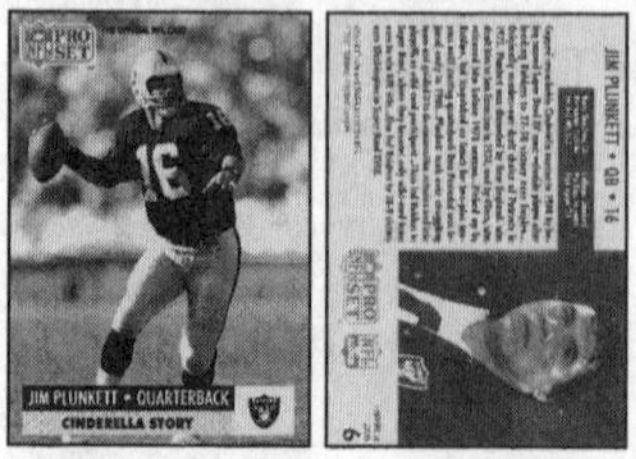

This nine-card set was issued as a perforated insert sheet in The Official NFL Pro Set Card Book, which chronicles the history of NFL Pro Set cards. The unifying theme of this set is summed up by the words "Cinderella Story" on the card fronts. The set highlights players or teams who overcame formidable obstacles to become winners. After perforation, the cards measure the standard size. The front design is similar to the 1991 regular issue, with full-bleed color photos and player (or team) identification in colored stripes traversing the bottom of the card. All the cards feature color photos, with the exception of card numbers 4-6. The back has an extended caption for the card on the left portion, and a different photo on the right portion.

	MINT	NRMT	EXC
COMPLETE SET (9)	20.00	9.00	2.50
COMMON CARD (1-9)	1.00	.45	.12
☐ 1 Rocky Bleier	1.50	.70	.19
☐ 2 Tom Dempsey	1.00	.45	.12
☐ 3 Dan Hampton	1.50	.70	.19
☐ 4 Charlie Hennigan	1.00	.45	.12
☐ 5 Dante Lavelli	1.50	.70	.19
☐ 6 Jim Plunkett	1.50	.70	.19
☐ 7 1968 New York Jets (Joe Namath handing off)	4.00	1.80	.50
☐ 8 1981 San Francisco 49ers (Joe Montana passing)	10.00	4.50	1.25
☐ 9 1979 Tampa Bay Bucs (Ricky Bell running)	1.00	.45	.12

1991 Pro Set National Banquet

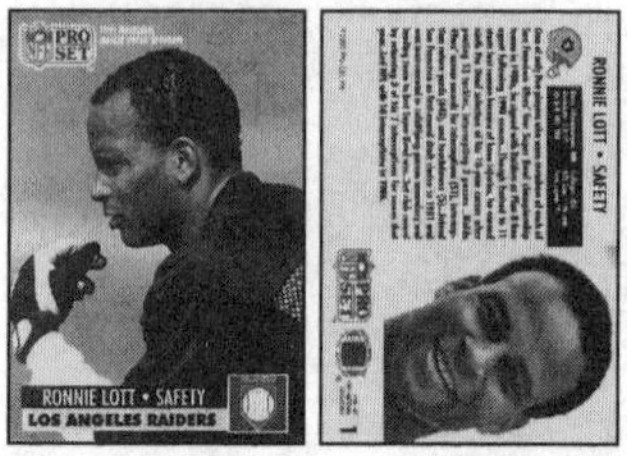

This five-card standard-size set was given away by Pro Set, one of the sponsors of the 1991 12th National Sports Collectors Convention in Anaheim, California. The cards have full-bleed color photos on the fronts. The horizontally oriented backs have other color photos and career summaries. The back of the ProFiles card has a picture of TV announcers Tim Brant and Craig James.

	MINT	NRMT	EXC
COMPLETE SET (5)	5.00	2.20	.60
COMMON CARD (1-5)	1.00	.45	.12
☐ 1 Ronnie Lott	1.25	.55	.16
☐ 2 Roy Firestone (Television celebrity)	1.00	.45	.12
☐ 3 Roger Craig	1.25	.55	.16
☐ 4 ProFiles Television show (Craig James and Tim Brant)	1.00	.45	.12
☐ 5 Title card	1.00	.45	.12

1991 Pro Set Platinum

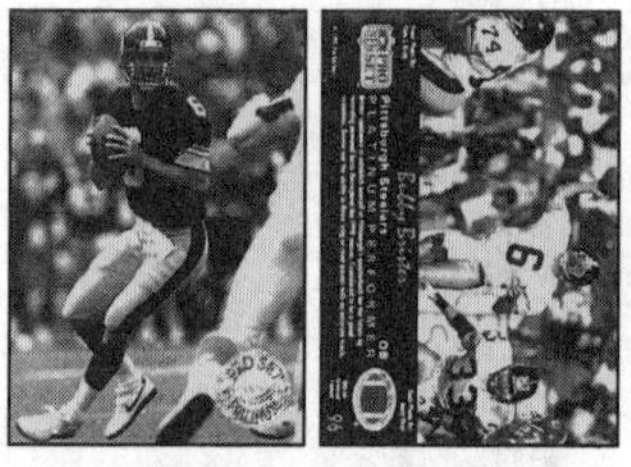

This set contains 315 standard-size cards. The cards were issued in series of 150 and 165. Cards were issued in 12-card packs for both series. The front design has full-bleed glossy color player photos capturing game action. The Pro Set Platinum icon appears in the lower left corner. The horizontally oriented backs feature other glossy color action photos. In the black rectangle below the picture, the player's name, team, and position are given, along with a "Platinum Performer" feature that highlights the player's outstanding performance. The cards are checklisted below alphabetically according to teams. Special Collectibles (PC1-PC10) cards were randomly distributed in 12-card second series foil packs. Also randomly inserted in the packs were 2,150 bonus card certificates. One thousand five hundred could be redeemed for limited edition platinum cards of Paul Brown (first series) and 650 for Emmitt Smith (second series). Rookie Cards include Ricky Ervins, Brett Favre, Mike Pritchard, Leonard Russell and Harvey Williams.

	MINT	NRMT	EXC
COMPLETE SET (315)	12.00	5.50	1.50
COMPLETE SERIES 1 (150)	6.00	2.70	.75
COMPLETE SERIES 2 (165)	6.00	2.70	.75
COMMON CARD (1-315)	.05	.02	.01
☐ 1 Chris Miller	.10	.05	.01
☐ 2 Andre Rison	.20	.09	.03
☐ 3 Tim Green	.05	.02	.01
☐ 4 Jessie Tuggle	.05	.02	.01
☐ 5 Thurman Thomas	.20	.09	.03
☐ 6 Darryl Talley	.05	.02	.01
☐ 7 Kent Hull	.05	.02	.01
☐ 8 Bruce Smith	.20	.09	.03
☐ 9 Shane Conlan	.05	.02	.01
☐ 10 Jim Harbaugh	.20	.09	.03
☐ 11 Neal Anderson	.10	.05	.01
☐ 12 Mark Bortz	.05	.02	.01
☐ 13 Richard Dent	.10	.05	.01
☐ 14 Steve McMichael	.05	.02	.01
☐ 15 James Brooks	.05	.02	.01
☐ 16 Boomer Esiason	.10	.05	.01
☐ 17 Tim Krumrie	.05	.02	.01
☐ 18 James Francis	.05	.02	.01
☐ 19 Lewis Billups	.05	.02	.01
☐ 20 Eric Metcalf	.20	.09	.03
☐ 21 Kevin Mack	.05	.02	.01
☐ 22 Clay Matthews	.10	.05	.01
☐ 23 Mike Johnson	.05	.02	.01
☐ 24 Troy Aikman	1.00	.45	.12
☐ 25 Emmitt Smith	2.00	.90	.25
☐ 26 Daniel Stubbs	.05	.02	.01
☐ 27 Ken Norton	.20	.09	.03
☐ 28 John Elway	.75	.35	.09
☐ 29 Bobby Humphrey	.05	.02	.01
☐ 30 Simon Fletcher	.05	.02	.01
☐ 31 Karl Mecklenburg	.05	.02	.01
☐ 32 Rodney Peete	.10	.05	.01
☐ 33 Barry Sanders	1.00	.45	.12
☐ 34 Michael Cofer	.05	.02	.01
☐ 35 Jerry Ball	.05	.02	.01
☐ 36 Sterling Sharpe	.20	.09	.03
☐ 37 Tony Mandarich	.05	.02	.01
☐ 38 Brian Noble	.05	.02	.01
☐ 39 Tim Harris	.05	.02	.01
☐ 40 Warren Moon	.10	.05	.01
☐ 41 Ernest Givins UER (Misspelled Givens on card back)	.10	.05	.01
☐ 42 Mike Munchak	.05	.02	.01
☐ 43 Sean Jones	.10	.05	.01
☐ 44 Ray Childress	.10	.05	.01
☐ 45 Jeff George	.20	.09	.03
☐ 46 Albert Bentley	.05	.02	.01
☐ 47 Duane Bickett	.05	.02	.01
☐ 48 Steve DeBerg	.10	.05	.01
☐ 49 Christian Okoye	.10	.05	.01
☐ 50 Neil Smith	.20	.09	.03
☐ 51 Derrick Thomas	.20	.09	.03
☐ 52 Willie Gault	.10	.05	.01
☐ 53 Don Mosebar	.05	.02	.01
☐ 54 Howie Long	.10	.05	.01
☐ 55 Greg Townsend	.05	.02	.01
☐ 56 Terry McDaniel	.10	.05	.01
☐ 57 Jackie Slater	.05	.02	.01
☐ 58 Jim Everett	.10	.05	.01
☐ 59 Cleveland Gary	.05	.02	.01
☐ 60 Mike Piel	.05	.02	.01
☐ 61 Jerry Gray	.05	.02	.01
☐ 62 Dan Marino	1.50	.70	.19
☐ 63 Sammie Smith	.05	.02	.01
☐ 64 Richmond Webb	.05	.02	.01
☐ 65 Louis Oliver	.05	.02	.01
☐ 66 Ferrell Edmunds	.05	.02	.01
☐ 67 Jeff Cross	.05	.02	.01
☐ 68 Wade Wilson	.05	.02	.01
☐ 69 Chris Doleman	.10	.05	.01
☐ 70 Joey Browner	.05	.02	.01
☐ 71 Keith Millard	.05	.02	.01
☐ 72 John Stephens	.05	.02	.01
☐ 73 Andre Tippett	.05	.02	.01
☐ 74 Brent Williams	.05	.02	.01
☐ 75 Craig Heyward	.10	.05	.01
☐ 76 Eric Martin	.05	.02	.01
☐ 77 Pat Swilling	.10	.05	.01
☐ 78 Sam Mills	.10	.05	.01
☐ 79 Jeff Hostetler	.10	.05	.01
☐ 80 Ottis Anderson	.10	.05	.01
☐ 81 Lawrence Taylor	.20	.09	.03
☐ 82 Pepper Johnson	.05	.02	.01
☐ 83 Blair Thomas	.05	.02	.01
☐ 84 Al Toon	.10	.05	.01
☐ 85 Ken O'Brien	.05	.02	.01
☐ 86 Erik McMillan	.05	.02	.01
☐ 87 Dennis Byrd	.10	.05	.01
☐ 88 Randall Cunningham	.10	.05	.01
☐ 89 Fred Barnett	.20	.09	.03
☐ 90 Seth Joyner	.10	.05	.01
☐ 91 Reggie White	.20	.09	.03
☐ 92 Timm Rosenbach	.05	.02	.01
☐ 93 Johnny Johnson	.05	.02	.01
☐ 94 Tim McDonald	.05	.02	.01
☐ 95 Freddie Joe Nunn	.05	.02	.01
☐ 96 Bubby Brister	.10	.05	.01
☐ 97 Gary Anderson K UER (Listed as RB)	.05	.02	.01
☐ 98 Merril Hoge	.05	.02	.01
☐ 99 Keith Willis	.05	.02	.01
☐ 100 Rod Woodson	.20	.09	.03
☐ 101 Billy Joe Tolliver	.05	.02	.01
☐ 102 Marion Butts	.10	.05	.01
☐ 103 Rod Bernstine	.05	.02	.01
☐ 104 Lee Williams	.05	.02	.01
☐ 105 Burt Grossman UER (Photo on back is reversed)	.05	.02	.01
☐ 106 Tom Rathman	.05	.02	.01
☐ 107 John Taylor	.10	.05	.01
☐ 108 Michael Carter	.05	.02	.01
☐ 109 Guy McIntyre	.05	.02	.01
☐ 110 Pierce Holt	.05	.02	.01
☐ 111 John L. Williams	.05	.02	.01
☐ 112 Dave Krieg	.10	.05	.01
☐ 113 Bryan Millard	.05	.02	.01
☐ 114 Cortez Kennedy	.20	.09	.03
☐ 115 Derrick Fenner	.05	.02	.01
☐ 116 Vinny Testaverde	.10	.05	.01
☐ 117 Reggie Cobb	.05	.02	.01
☐ 118 Gary Anderson RB	.05	.02	.01
☐ 119 Bruce Hill	.05	.02	.01
☐ 120 Wayne Haddix	.05	.02	.01
☐ 121 Broderick Thomas	.05	.02	.01
☐ 122 Keith McCants	.05	.02	.01
☐ 123 Andre Collins	.10	.05	.01
☐ 124 Earnest Byner	.05	.02	.01
☐ 125 Jim Lachey	.05	.02	.01
☐ 126 Mark Rypien	.10	.05	.01
☐ 127 Charles Mann	.05	.02	.01
☐ 128 Nick Lowery	.05	.02	.01
☐ 129 Chip Lohmiller	.05	.02	.01
☐ 130 Mike Horan	.05	.02	.01
☐ 131 Rohn Stark	.05	.02	.01
☐ 132 Sean Landeta	.05	.02	.01
☐ 133 Clarence Verdin	.05	.02	.01
☐ 134 Johnny Bailey	.05	.02	.01
☐ 135 Herschel Walker	.10	.05	.01
☐ 136 Bo Jackson PP	.20	.09	.03
☐ 137 Dexter Carter PP	.05	.02	.01
☐ 138 Warren Moon PP	.10	.05	.01
☐ 139 Joe Montana PP	1.00	.45	.12
☐ 140 Jerry Rice PP	1.00	.45	.12
☐ 141 Deion Sanders PP	.50	.23	.06
☐ 142 Ronnie Lippett PP	.05	.02	.01
☐ 143 Terance Mathis PP	.20	.09	.03
☐ 144 Gaston Green PP	.05	.02	.01
☐ 145 Dean Biasucci PP	.05	.02	.01
☐ 146 Charles Haley PP	.10	.05	.01
☐ 147 Derrick Thomas PP	.20	.09	.03
☐ 148 Lawrence Taylor PP	.10	.05	.01
☐ 149 Art Shell CO PP	.10	.05	.01
☐ 150 Bill Parcells CO PP	.10	.05	.01
☐ 151 Steve Broussard	.05	.02	.01
☐ 152 Darion Conner	.05	.02	.01
☐ 153 Bill Fralic	.05	.02	.01
☐ 154 Mike Gann	.05	.02	.01
☐ 155 Tim McKyer	.05	.02	.01
☐ 156 Don Beebe UER (4 TD's against Dolphins, should be against Steelers)	.05	.02	.01
☐ 157 Cornelius Bennett	.10	.05	.01
☐ 158 Andre Reed	.20	.09	.03
☐ 159 Leonard Smith	.05	.02	.01
☐ 160 Will Wolford	.05	.02	.01
☐ 161 Mark Carrier DB	.10	.05	.01
☐ 162 Wendell Davis	.05	.02	.01
☐ 163 Jay Hilgenberg	.05	.02	.01
☐ 164 Brad Muster	.05	.02	.01
☐ 165 Mike Singletary	.10	.05	.01
☐ 166 Eddie Brown	.05	.02	.01
☐ 167 David Fulcher	.05	.02	.01
☐ 168 Rodney Holman	.05	.02	.01
☐ 169 Anthony Munoz	.10	.05	.01
☐ 170 Craig Taylor	.05	.02	.01
☐ 171 Mike Baab	.05	.02	.01
☐ 172 David Grayson	.05	.02	.01
☐ 173 Reggie Langhorne	.05	.02	.01
☐ 174 Joe Morris	.05	.02	.01
☐ 175 Kevin Gogan	.05	.02	.01
☐ 176 Jack Del Rio	.05	.02	.01
☐ 177 Issiac Holt	.05	.02	.01
☐ 178 Michael Irvin	.20	.09	.03
☐ 179 Jay Novacek	.20	.09	.03
☐ 180 Steve Atwater	.05	.02	.01
☐ 181 Mark Jackson	.05	.02	.01
☐ 182 Ricky Nattiel	.05	.02	.01
☐ 183 Warren Powers	.05	.02	.01
☐ 184 Dennis Smith	.05	.02	.01
☐ 185 Bennie Blades	.05	.02	.01
☐ 186 Lomas Brown UER (Spent 6 seasons with Detroit, not 7)	.05	.02	.01
☐ 187 Robert Clark UER (Plan B acquisition in '89, not '90)	.05	.02	.01
☐ 188 Mel Gray	.10	.05	.01
☐ 189 Chris Spielman	.10	.05	.01
☐ 190 Johnny Holland	.05	.02	.01
☐ 191 Don Majkowski	.05	.02	.01
☐ 192 Bryce Paup	.20	.09	.03
☐ 193 Darrell Thompson	.05	.02	.01
☐ 194 Ed West UER (Photo on back is reversed)	.05	.02	.01
☐ 195 Cris Dishman	.10	.05	.01
☐ 196 Drew Hill	.10	.05	.01
☐ 197 Bruce Matthews	.10	.05	.01
☐ 198 Bubba McDowell	.05	.02	.01
☐ 199 Allen Pinkett	.05	.02	.01
☐ 200 Bill Brooks	.10	.05	.01
☐ 201 Jeff Herrod	.05	.02	.01
☐ 202 Anthony Johnson	.10	.05	.01
☐ 203 Mike Prior	.05	.02	.01
☐ 204 John Alt	.05	.02	.01
☐ 205 Stephone Paige	.05	.02	.01
☐ 206 Kevin Ross	.05	.02	.01
☐ 207 Dan Saleaumua	.05	.02	.01
☐ 208 Barry Word	.05	.02	.01
☐ 209 Marcus Allen	.20	.09	.03
☐ 210 Roger Craig	.10	.05	.01
☐ 211 Ronnie Lott	.10	.05	.01
☐ 212 Winston Moss	.05	.02	.01
☐ 213 Jay Schroeder	.05	.02	.01
☐ 214 Robert Delpino	.05	.02	.01

	MINT	NRMT	EXC
☐ 215 Henry Ellard	.10	.05	.01
☐ 216 Kevin Greene	.20	.09	.03
☐ 217 Tom Newberry	.05	.02	.01
☐ 218 Michael Stewart	.05	.02	.01
☐ 219 Mark Duper	.10	.05	.01
☐ 220 Mark Higgs	.05	.02	.01
☐ 221 John Offerdahl UER (2nd round pick in '86, not 6th)	.05	.02	.01
☐ 222 Keith Sims	.05	.02	.01
☐ 223 Anthony Carter	.10	.05	.01
☐ 224 Cris Carter	.20	.09	.03
☐ 225 Steve Jordan	.05	.02	.01
☐ 226 Randall McDaniel	.05	.02	.01
☐ 227 Al Noga	.05	.02	.01
☐ 228 Ray Agnew	.05	.02	.01
☐ 229 Bruce Armstrong	.05	.02	.01
☐ 230 Irving Fryar	.10	.05	.01
☐ 231 Greg McMurtry	.05	.02	.01
☐ 232 Chris Singleton	.05	.02	.01
☐ 233 Morten Andersen	.05	.02	.01
☐ 234 Vince Buck	.05	.02	.01
☐ 235 Gill Fenerty	.05	.02	.01
☐ 236 Rickey Jackson	.10	.05	.01
☐ 237 Vaughan Johnson	.05	.02	.01
☐ 238 Carl Banks	.05	.02	.01
☐ 239 Mark Collins	.05	.02	.01
☐ 240 Rodney Hampton	.20	.09	.03
☐ 241 David Meggett	.10	.05	.01
☐ 242 Bart Oates	.05	.02	.01
☐ 243 Kyle Clifton	.05	.02	.01
☐ 244 Jeff Lageman	.10	.05	.01
☐ 245 Freeman McNeil UER (Drafted in '81, not '80)	.10	.05	.01
☐ 246 Rob Moore	.20	.09	.03
☐ 247 Eric Allen	.05	.02	.01
☐ 248 Keith Byars	.10	.05	.01
☐ 249 Keith Jackson	.10	.05	.01
☐ 250 Jim McMahon	.10	.05	.01
☐ 251 Andre Waters	.05	.02	.01
☐ 252 Ken Harvey	.10	.05	.01
☐ 253 Ernie Jones	.05	.02	.01
☐ 254 Luis Sharpe	.05	.02	.01
☐ 255 Anthony Thompson	.05	.02	.01
☐ 256 Tom Tupa	.05	.02	.01
☐ 257 Eric Green	.10	.05	.01
☐ 258 Barry Foster	.10	.05	.01
☐ 259 Bryan Hinkle	.05	.02	.01
☐ 260 Tunch Ilkin	.05	.02	.01
☐ 261 Louis Lipps	.05	.02	.01
☐ 262 Gill Byrd	.05	.02	.01
☐ 263 John Friesz	.10	.05	.01
☐ 264 Anthony Miller	.10	.05	.01
☐ 265 Junior Seau	.20	.09	.03
☐ 266 Ronnie Harmon	.10	.05	.01
☐ 267 Harris Barton	.05	.02	.01
☐ 268 Todd Bowles	.05	.02	.01
☐ 269 Don Griffin	.05	.02	.01
☐ 270 Bill Romanowski	.05	.02	.01
☐ 271 Steve Young	.75	.35	.09
☐ 272 Brian Blades	.10	.05	.01
☐ 273 Jacob Green	.05	.02	.01
☐ 274 Rufus Porter	.05	.02	.01
☐ 275 Eugene Robinson	.05	.02	.01
☐ 276 Mark Carrier WR	.10	.05	.01
☐ 277 Reuben Davis	.05	.02	.01
☐ 278 Paul Gruber	.05	.02	.01
☐ 279 Gary Clark	.20	.09	.03
☐ 280 Darrell Green	.10	.05	.01
☐ 281 Wilber Marshall	.05	.02	.01
☐ 282 Matt Millen	.10	.05	.01
☐ 283 Alvin Walton	.05	.02	.01
☐ 284 Joe Gibbs CO UER (NFLPA logo on back)	.10	.05	.01
☐ 285 Don Shula CO UER (NFLPA logo on back)	.10	.05	.01
☐ 286 Larry Brown DB	.10	.05	.01
☐ 287 Mike Croel	.05	.02	.01
☐ 288 Antone Davis	.05	.02	.01
☐ 289 Ricky Ervins UER (2nd round choice, should say 3rd)	.10	.05	.01
☐ 290 Brett Favre	3.00	1.35	.35
☐ 291 Pat Harlow	.05	.02	.01
☐ 292 Michael Jackson	.20	.09	.03
☐ 293 Henry Jones	.10	.05	.01
☐ 294 Aaron Craver	.05	.02	.01
☐ 295 Nick Bell	.05	.02	.01
☐ 296 Todd Lyght	.10	.05	.01
☐ 297 Todd Marinovich	.05	.02	.01
☐ 298 Russell Maryland	.10	.05	.01
☐ 299 Kanavis McGhee	.05	.02	.01
☐ 300 Dan McGwire	.10	.05	.01
☐ 301 Charles McRae	.05	.02	.01
☐ 302 Eric Moten	.05	.02	.01
☐ 303 Jerome Henderson	.05	.02	.01
☐ 304 Browning Nagle	.05	.02	.01
☐ 305 Mike Pritchard	.20	.09	.03
☐ 306 Stanley Richard	.10	.05	.01
☐ 307 Randal Hill	.10	.05	.01
☐ 308 Leonard Russell	.10	.05	.01
☐ 309 Eric Swann	.10	.05	.01
☐ 310 Phil Hansen	.05	.02	.01
☐ 311 Moe Gardner	.05	.02	.01
☐ 312 Jon Vaughn	.05	.02	.01
☐ 313 Aeneas Williams UER (Misspelled Aaneas on card back)	.20	.09	.03
☐ 314 Alfred Williams	.05	.02	.01
☐ 315 Harvey Williams	.20	.09	.03
☐ PM1 Emmitt Smith Platinum metal card	400.00	180.00	50.00
☐ PM2 Paul Brown Platinum metal card	100.00	45.00	12.50

1991 Pro Set Platinum PC

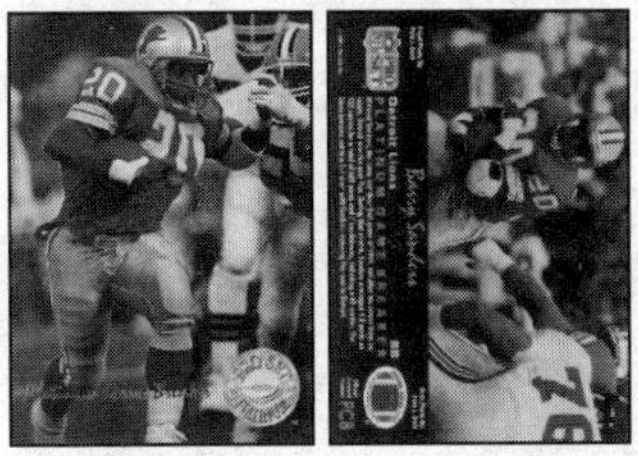

These ten Pro Set Platinum Collectible PC cards were randomly inserted in 1991 Pro Set Platinum second series foil packs. The standard-size cards feature full-bleed color player photos on the fronts, with a second color photo on the horizontally oriented backs. The set is subdivided as follows: Platinum Profile (1-3), Platinum Photo (4-5), and Platinum Game Breaker (6-10). The Platinum Game Breaker cards present in alphabetical order five standout NFL running backs. The cards are numbered on the back with a "PC" prefix.

	MINT	NRMT	EXC
COMPLETE SET (10)	10.00	4.50	1.25
COMMON CARD (PC1-PC10)	.50	.23	.06
☐ PC1 Bobby Hebert	.50	.23	.06
☐ PC2 Art Monk	.75	.35	.09
☐ PC3 Kenny Walker	.50	.23	.06
☐ PC4 Low Fives	.50	.23	.06
☐ PC5 Touchdown Kevin Mack	.50	.23	.06
☐ PC6 Neal Anderson	.75	.35	.09
☐ PC7 Gaston Green	.50	.23	.06
☐ PC8 Barry Sanders	2.50	1.10	.30
☐ PC9 Emmitt Smith	4.00	1.80	.50
☐ PC10 Thurman Thomas	1.25	.55	.16

1991 Pro Set Spanish

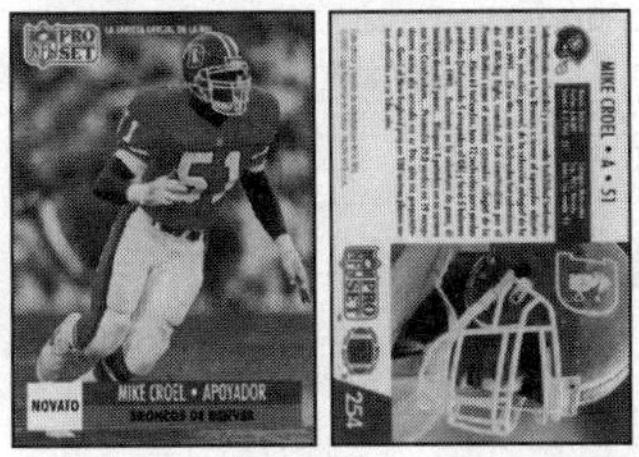

The 1991 Pro Set Spanish football card set contains 300 standard-size cards selected from 1991 Pro Set Series I and II along with five special collectibles cards. Though the cards display the same player photos, the terminology has been translated into Spanish. The cards are numbered on the back and checklisted alphabetically according to teams.

	MINT	NRMT	EXC
COMPLETE SET (305)	15.00	6.75	1.85
COMMON CARD (1-300)	.04	.02	.01
☐ 1 Steve Broussard	.04	.02	.01
☐ 2 Darion Conner	.04	.02	.01
☐ 3 Tory Epps	.04	.02	.01
☐ 4 Bill Fralic	.04	.02	.01
☐ 5 Mike Gann	.04	.02	.01
☐ 6 Chris Miller	.10	.05	.01
☐ 7 Andre Rison	.20	.09	.03
☐ 8 Deion Sanders	.40	.18	.05
☐ 9 Jessie Tuggle	.04	.02	.01
☐ 10 Cornelius Bennett	.10	.05	.01
☐ 11 Shane Conlan	.04	.02	.01
☐ 12 Kent Hull	.04	.02	.01
☐ 13 Kirby Jackson	.04	.02	.01
☐ 14 James Lofton	.10	.05	.01
☐ 15 Andre Reed	.10	.05	.01
☐ 16 Bruce Smith	.20	.09	.03
☐ 17 Darryl Talley	.04	.02	.01
☐ 18 Thurman Thomas	.20	.09	.03
☐ 19 Neal Anderson	.10	.05	.01
☐ 20 Trace Armstrong	.04	.02	.01
☐ 21 Mark Carrier DB	.10	.05	.01
☐ 22 Wendell Davis	.04	.02	.01
☐ 23 Richard Dent	.10	.05	.01
☐ 24 Jim Harbaugh	.20	.09	.03
☐ 25 Ron Rivera	.04	.02	.01
☐ 26 Mike Singletary	.10	.05	.01
☐ 27 Lemuel Stinson	.04	.02	.01
☐ 28 James Brooks	.04	.02	.01
☐ 29 Eddie Brown	.04	.02	.01
☐ 30 Boomer Esiason	.10	.05	.01
☐ 31 James Francis	.04	.02	.01
☐ 32 David Fulcher	.04	.02	.01
☐ 33 Rodney Holman	.04	.02	.01
☐ 34 Anthony Munoz	.10	.05	.01
☐ 35 Bruce Reimers	.04	.02	.01
☐ 36 Ickey Woods	.04	.02	.01
☐ 37 Mike Baab	.04	.02	.01
☐ 38 Brian Brennan	.04	.02	.01
☐ 39 Raymond Clayborn	.04	.02	.01
☐ 40 Mike Johnson	.04	.02	.01
☐ 41 Clay Matthews	.10	.05	.01
☐ 42 Eric Metcalf	.20	.09	.03
☐ 43 Frank Minnifield	.04	.02	.01
☐ 44 Joe Morris	.04	.02	.01
☐ 45 Anthony Pleasant	.04	.02	.01
☐ 46 Troy Aikman	1.00	.45	.12
☐ 47 Jack Del Rio	.04	.02	.01
☐ 48 Issiac Holt	.04	.02	.01
☐ 49 Michael Irvin	.20	.09	.03
☐ 50 Jimmie Jones	.04	.02	.01
☐ 51 Nate Newton	.10	.05	.01
☐ 52 Danny Noonan	.04	.02	.01
☐ 53 Jay Novacek	.20	.09	.03
☐ 54 Emmitt Smith	2.50	1.10	.30
☐ 55 Steve Atwater	.04	.02	.01
☐ 56 Michael Brooks	.04	.02	.01
☐ 57 John Elway	.75	.35	.09
☐ 58 Mike Horan	.04	.02	.01
☐ 59 Mark Jackson	.04	.02	.01
☐ 60 Karl Mecklenburg	.04	.02	.01
☐ 61 Warren Powers	.04	.02	.01
☐ 62 Dennis Smith	.04	.02	.01
☐ 63 Doug Widell	.04	.02	.01
☐ 64 Jerry Ball	.04	.02	.01
☐ 65 Bennie Blades	.04	.02	.01
☐ 66 Robert Clark	.04	.02	.01
☐ 67 Ken Dallafior	.04	.02	.01
☐ 68 Mel Gray	.10	.05	.01
☐ 69 Eddie Murray	.04	.02	.01
☐ 70 Rodney Peete	.10	.05	.01
☐ 71 Barry Sanders	1.00	.45	.12
☐ 72 Chris Spielman	.10	.05	.01
☐ 73 Robert Brown	.04	.02	.01
☐ 74 LeRoy Butler	.10	.05	.01
☐ 75 Perry Kemp	.04	.02	.01
☐ 76 Don Majkowski	.04	.02	.01
☐ 77 Tony Mandarich	.04	.02	.01
☐ 78 Mark Murphy	.04	.02	.01
☐ 79 Brian Noble	.04	.02	.01
☐ 80 Sterling Sharpe	.20	.09	.03
☐ 81 Ed West	.04	.02	.01
☐ 82 Ray Childress	.10	.05	.01
☐ 83 Cris Dishman	.04	.02	.01
☐ 84 Ernest Givins	.10	.05	.01
☐ 85 Drew Hill	.10	.05	.01
☐ 86 Haywood Jeffires	.10	.05	.01
☐ 87 Lamar Lathon	.04	.02	.01
☐ 88 Bruce Matthews	.10	.05	.01
☐ 89 Bubba McDowell	.04	.02	.01
☐ 90 Warren Moon	.10	.05	.01
☐ 91 Chip Banks	.04	.02	.01
☐ 92 Albert Bentley	.04	.02	.01
☐ 93 Duane Bickett	.04	.02	.01
☐ 94 Bill Brooks	.10	.05	.01
☐ 95 Sam Clancy	.04	.02	.01
☐ 96 Ray Donaldson	.04	.02	.01
☐ 97 Jeff George	.20	.09	.03
☐ 98 Mike Prior	.04	.02	.01
☐ 99 Clarence Verdin	.04	.02	.01
☐ 100 Steve DeBerg	.10	.05	.01
☐ 101 Albert Lewis	.04	.02	.01
☐ 102 Christian Okoye	.10	.05	.01
☐ 103 Kevin Ross	.04	.02	.01
☐ 104 Stephone Paige	.04	.02	.01
☐ 105 Kevin Porter	.04	.02	.01
☐ 106 Percy Snow	.04	.02	.01
☐ 107 Derrick Thomas	.20	.09	.03
☐ 108 Barry Word	.04	.02	.01
☐ 109 Marcus Allen	.20	.09	.03
☐ 110 Mervyn Fernandez	.04	.02	.01
☐ 111 Howie Long	.10	.05	.01
☐ 112 Ronnie Lott	.10	.05	.01
☐ 113 Terry McDaniel	.10	.05	.01
☐ 114 Max Montoya	.04	.02	.01
☐ 115 Don Mosebar	.04	.02	.01
☐ 116 Jay Schroeder	.04	.02	.01
☐ 117 Greg Townsend	.04	.02	.01
☐ 118 Flipper Anderson	.04	.02	.01
☐ 119 Henry Ellard	.10	.05	.01
☐ 120 Jim Everett	.10	.05	.01
☐ 121 Kevin Greene	.20	.09	.03
☐ 122 Damone Johnson	.04	.02	.01
☐ 123 Buford McGee	.04	.02	.01
☐ 124 Tom Newberry	.04	.02	.01
☐ 125 Michael Stewart	.04	.02	.01
☐ 126 Alvin Wright	.04	.02	.01
☐ 127 Mark Clayton	.10	.05	.01
☐ 128 Jeff Cross	.04	.02	.01
☐ 129 Mark Duper	.10	.05	.01
☐ 130 Ferrell Edmunds	.04	.02	.01
☐ 131 Dan Marino	2.00	.90	.25
☐ 132 Tim McKyer	.04	.02	.01
☐ 133 John Offerdahl	.04	.02	.01
☐ 134 Louis Oliver	.04	.02	.01
☐ 135 Sammie Smith	.04	.02	.01
☐ 136 Joey Browner	.04	.02	.01
☐ 137 Anthony Carter	.10	.05	.01
☐ 138 Chris Doleman	.10	.05	.01
☐ 139 Hassan Jones	.04	.02	.01
☐ 140 Steve Jordan	.04	.02	.01
☐ 141 Carl Lee	.04	.02	.01
☐ 142 Al Noga	.04	.02	.01
☐ 143 Henry Thomas	.10	.05	.01
☐ 144 Herschel Walker	.10	.05	.01
☐ 145 Ray Agnew	.04	.02	.01
☐ 146 Bruce Armstrong	.04	.02	.01
☐ 147 Marv Cook	.04	.02	.01
☐ 148 Irving Fryar	.10	.05	.01
☐ 149 Tommy Hodson	.04	.02	.01
☐ 150 Fred Marion	.04	.02	.01
☐ 151 Johnny Rembert	.04	.02	.01
☐ 152 Chris Singleton	.04	.02	.01
☐ 153 Andre Tippett	.04	.02	.01
☐ 154 Morten Andersen	.04	.02	.01
☐ 155 Toi Cook	.04	.02	.01
☐ 156 Craig Heyward	.10	.05	.01
☐ 157 Dalton Hilliard	.04	.02	.01
☐ 158 Rickey Jackson	.10	.05	.01
☐ 159 Vaughan Johnson	.04	.02	.01
☐ 160 Rueben Mayes	.04	.02	.01
☐ 161 Pat Swilling	.10	.05	.01
☐ 162 Bobby Hebert	.10	.05	.01
☐ 163 Ottis Anderson	.10	.05	.01
☐ 164 Carl Banks	.04	.02	.01
☐ 165 Rodney Hampton	.20	.09	.03
☐ 166 Jeff Hostetler	.10	.05	.01
☐ 167 Mark Ingram	.10	.05	.01
☐ 168 Leonard Marshall	.04	.02	.01
☐ 169 Dave Meggett	.10	.05	.01
☐ 170 Lawrence Taylor	.20	.09	.03
☐ 171 Everson Walls	.04	.02	.01
☐ 172 Brad Baxter	.10	.05	.01
☐ 173 Jeff Lageman	.10	.05	.01
☐ 174 Pat Leahy	.04	.02	.01
☐ 175 Erik McMillan	.04	.02	.01
☐ 176 Scott Mersereau	.04	.02	.01
☐ 177 Rob Moore	.10	.05	.01
☐ 178 Ken O'Brien	.04	.02	.01
☐ 179 Blair Thomas	.04	.02	.01
☐ 180 Al Toon	.04	.02	.01
☐ 181 Eric Allen	.04	.02	.01
☐ 182 Jerome Brown	.10	.05	.01
☐ 183 Keith Byars	.10	.05	.01
☐ 184 Randall Cunningham	.10	.05	.01
☐ 185 Byron Evans	.04	.02	.01
☐ 186 Keith Jackson	.10	.05	.01
☐ 187 Heath Sherman	.04	.02	.01
☐ 188 Clyde Simmons	.10	.05	.01
☐ 189 Reggie White	.20	.09	.03
☐ 190 Rich Camarillo	.04	.02	.01
☐ 191 Johnny Johnson	.10	.05	.01
☐ 192 Ernie Jones	.04	.02	.01
☐ 193 Tim McDonald	.04	.02	.01
☐ 194 Freddie Joe Nunn	.04	.02	.01
☐ 195 Luis Sharpe	.04	.02	.01
☐ 196 Jay Taylor	.04	.02	.01
☐ 197 Anthony Thompson	.04	.02	.01
☐ 198 Tom Tupa	.04	.02	.01
☐ 199 Gary Anderson K	.04	.02	.01
☐ 200 Bubby Brister	.10	.05	.01
☐ 201 Eric Green	.10	.05	.01
☐ 202 Bryan Hinkle	.04	.02	.01
☐ 203 Merril Hoge	.04	.02	.01
☐ 204 Carnell Lake	.10	.05	.01
☐ 205 Louis Lipps	.04	.02	.01
☐ 206 Keith Willis	.04	.02	.01
☐ 207 Rod Woodson	.20	.09	.03
☐ 208 Rod Bernstine	.04	.02	.01
☐ 209 Marion Butts	.04	.02	.01
☐ 210 Anthony Miller	.10	.05	.01
☐ 211 Leslie O'Neal	.10	.05	.01
☐ 212 Henry Rolling	.04	.02	.01
☐ 213 Junior Seau	.20	.09	.03
☐ 214 Billy Ray Smith	.04	.02	.01
☐ 215 Broderick Thompson	.04	.02	.01
☐ 216 Derrick Walker	.04	.02	.01
☐ 217 Dexter Carter	.04	.02	.01
☐ 218 Don Griffin	.04	.02	.01
☐ 219 Charles Haley	.10	.05	.01
☐ 220 Pierce Holt	.04	.02	.01
☐ 221 Joe Montana	1.00	.45	.12
☐ 222 Jerry Rice	1.00	.45	.12
☐ 223 John Taylor	.10	.05	.01
☐ 224 Michael Walter	.04	.02	.01
☐ 225 Steve Young	.75	.35	.09
☐ 226 Brian Blades	.10	.05	.01
☐ 227 Jeff Bryant	.04	.02	.01
☐ 228 Jacob Green	.04	.02	.01
☐ 229 Tommy Kane	.04	.02	.01
☐ 230 Dave Krieg	.10	.05	.01
☐ 231 Bryan Millard	.04	.02	.01
☐ 232 Rufus Porter	.04	.02	.01
☐ 233 Eugene Robinson	.04	.02	.01
☐ 234 John L. Williams	.04	.02	.01
☐ 235 Gary Anderson RB	.04	.02	.01
☐ 236 Mark Carrier WR	.10	.05	.01
☐ 237 Reggie Cobb	.04	.02	.01
☐ 238 Reuben Davis	.04	.02	.01

	MINT	NRMT	EXC
☐ 239 Paul Gruber	.04	.02	.01
☐ 240 Harry Hamilton	.04	.02	.01
☐ 241 Keith McCants	.04	.02	.01
☐ 242 Ricky Reynolds	.04	.02	.01
☐ 243 Vinny Testaverde	.10	.05	.01
☐ 244 Earnest Byner	.04	.02	.01
☐ 245 Gary Clark	.10	.05	.01
☐ 246 Andre Collins	.04	.02	.01
☐ 247 Darrell Green	.10	.05	.01
☐ 248 Jim Lachey	.04	.02	.01
☐ 249 Charles Mann	.04	.02	.01
☐ 250 Wilber Marshall	.04	.02	.01
☐ 251 Art Monk	.10	.05	.01
☐ 252 Mark Rypien	.10	.05	.01
☐ 253 Russell Maryland	.10	.05	.01
☐ 254 Mike Croel	.04	.02	.01
☐ 255 Stanley Richard	.10	.05	.01
☐ 256 Leonard Russell	.20	.09	.03
☐ 257 Dan McGwire	.04	.02	.01
☐ 258 Todd Marinovich	.04	.02	.01
☐ 259 Eric Swann	.20	.09	.03
☐ 260 Mike Pritchard	.20	.09	.03
☐ 261 Alfred Williams	.04	.02	.01
☐ 262 Brett Favre	4.00	1.80	.50
☐ 263 Browning Nagle	.04	.02	.01
☐ 264 Darryll Lewis	.10	.05	.01
☐ 265 Nick Bell	.04	.02	.01
☐ 266 Jeff Graham	.20	.09	.03
☐ 267 Eric Moten	.04	.02	.01
☐ 268 Roman Phifer	.04	.02	.01
☐ 269 Eric Bieniemy	.10	.05	.01
☐ 270 Phil Hansen	.04	.02	.01
☐ 271 Reggie Barrett	.04	.02	.01
☐ 272 Aeneas Williams	.10	.05	.01
☐ 273 Aaron Craver	.04	.02	.01
☐ 274 Lawrence Dawsey	.10	.05	.01
☐ 275 Ricky Ervins	.04	.02	.01
☐ 276 Jake Reed	.20	.09	.03
☐ 277 Erik Williams	.10	.05	.01
☐ 278 Tim Barnett	.04	.02	.01
☐ 279 Keith Traylor	.04	.02	.01
☐ 280 Jerry Rice PB UER (Back color is AFC red, instead of NFC blue)	.50	.23	.06
☐ 281 Jim Lachey	.04	.02	.01
☐ 282 Barry Sanders PB	.50	.23	.06
☐ 283 Neal Anderson	.10	.05	.01
☐ 284 Reggie White	.20	.09	.03
☐ 285 Lawrence Taylor	.20	.09	.03
☐ 286 Mike Singletary	.10	.05	.01
☐ 287 Joey Browner	.04	.02	.01
☐ 288 Morten Andersen SS	.04	.02	.01
☐ 289 Andre Reed SS	.10	.05	.01
☐ 290 Anthony Munoz SS	.10	.05	.01
☐ 291 Warren Moon SS	.20	.09	.03
☐ 292 Thurman Thomas SS	.20	.09	.03
☐ 293 Ray Childress SS	.04	.02	.01
☐ 294 Derrick Thomas SS	.20	.09	.03
☐ 295 Rod Woodson SS	.20	.09	.03
☐ 296 Steve Atwater SS	.04	.02	.01
☐ 297 David Fulcher SS	.04	.02	.01
☐ 298 Anthony Munoz Think	.10	.05	.01
☐ 299 Ron Rivera Think	.04	.02	.01
☐ 300 Cornelius Bennett Think	.10	.05	.01
☐ E1 Tom Flores	1.00	.45	.12
☐ E2 Anthony Munoz	1.00	.45	.12
☐ E3 Tony Casillas	1.00	.45	.12
☐ E4 Super Bowl XXVI Logo Minneapolis	1.00	.45	.12
☐ E5 Felicidades	1.00	.45	.12

1991 Pro Set UK Sheets

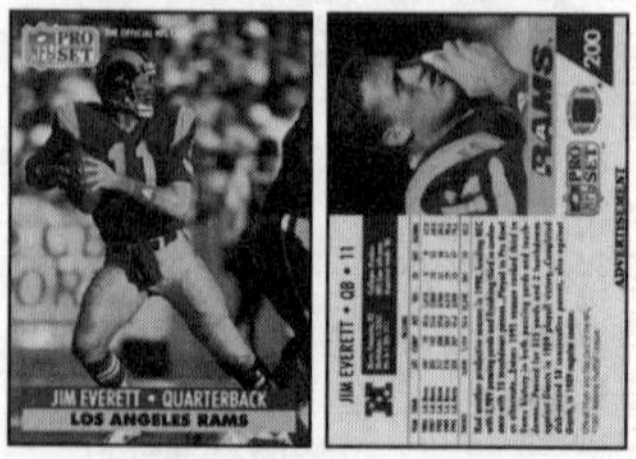

This set of five (approximately) 5 1/8" by 11 3/4" six-card strips was issued by Pro Set in England as an advertisement in Today, a newspaper in Middlesex, England. The unperforated strips are numbered 1-5, and each presents a "collection" of six player cards that measure the standard size. The sheets were issued one per week in consecutive Sunday editions of the paper during the Fall of 1991. The cards and their numbering are identical to the 1991 regular issues. They are checklisted below by strips, and within strips listed beginning from the top left card and moving to the bottom right card.

	MINT	NRMT	EXC
COMPLETE SET (5)	45.00	20.00	5.50
COMMON SHEET (1-5)	4.00	1.80	.50
☐ 1 Quarterbacks	15.00	6.75	1.85
200 Jim Everett			
167 Warren Moon			
111 Boomer Esiason			
128 Troy Aikman			
726 Dan Marino			
138 John Elway			
☐ 2 Running Backs	15.00	6.75	1.85
576 Herschel Walker			
86 Thurman Thomas			
213 Sammie Smith			
722 Earnest Byner			
123 Eric Metcalf			
485 Emmitt Smith			
☐ 3 Receivers	10.00	4.50	1.25
209 Mark Duper			
654 Jerry Rice			
251 Al Toon			
161 Sterling Sharpe			
618 Keith Jackson			
115 Tim McGee			
☐ 4 Kickers	4.00	1.80	.50
460 Jim Breech			
447 Scott Norwood			
489 Mike Horan			
300 Norm Johnson			
184 Nick Lowery			
401 Sean Landeta			
☐ 5 Defensive	6.00	2.70	.75
728 Mike Singletary			
56 Carl Banks			
98 Deion Sanders			
191 Howie Long			
131 Issiac Holt			
241 Pat Swilling			

1991 Pro Set WLAF 150

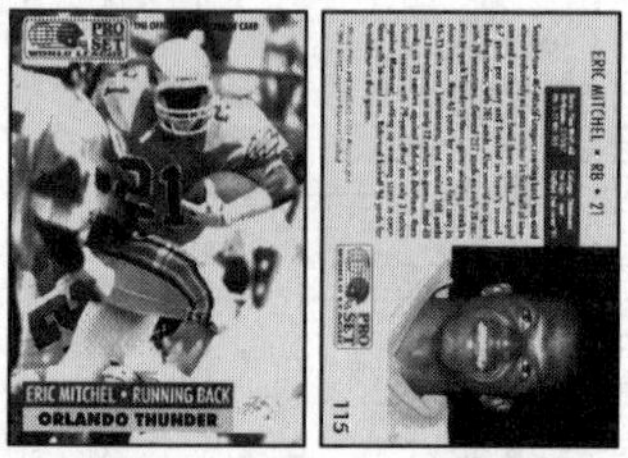

The premier edition of the 1991 Pro Set World League of American Football set contains 150 standard-size cards. The front features a borderless color action player photo, with the player's name, position, and team appearing in various color stripes at the bottom of the card face. The horizontally oriented backs have a color head shot on the right portion, while the left portion has a biography and career summary. The first 29 cards of the set are subdivided as follows: League Overview (1-3), World Bowl (4-9), Helmet Collectibles (10-19), and 1991 Statistical Leaders (20-29). The player cards are numbered 30-150, and they are checklisted below alphabetically within and according to teams.

	MINT	NRMT	EXC
COMPLETE SET (150)	4.00	1.80	.50
COMMON CARD (1-150)	.05	.02	.01
☐ 1 World League Logo	.05	.02	.01
☐ 2 Mike Lynn PRES	.05	.02	.01
☐ 3 First Weekend	.05	.02	.01
☐ 4 World Bowl Trophy	.05	.02	.01
☐ 5 Jon Horton	.05	.02	.01
☐ 6 Stan Gelbaugh	.20	.09	.03
☐ 7 Dan Crossman	.05	.02	.01
☐ 8 Marlon Brown	.05	.02	.01
☐ 9 Judd Garrett	.10	.05	.01
☐ 10 Barcelona Dragons Helmet	.10	.05	.01
☐ 11 Birmingham Fire Helmet	.10	.05	.01
☐ 12 Frankfurt Galaxy Helmet	.10	.05	.01
☐ 13 London Monarchs Helmet	.10	.05	.01
☐ 14 Montreal Machine Helmet	.10	.05	.01
☐ 15 NY-NJ Knights Helmet	.10	.05	.01
☐ 16 Orlando Thunder Helmet	.10	.05	.01
☐ 17 Raleigh-Durham Skyhawks Helmet	.10	.05	.01
☐ 18 Sacramento Surge Helmet	.10	.05	.01
☐ 19 San Antonio Riders Helmet	.10	.05	.01
☐ 20 Eric Wilkerson SL	.05	.02	.01
☐ 21 Stan Gelbaugh SL	.20	.09	.03
☐ 22 Judd Garrett SL	.05	.02	.01
☐ 23 Tony Baker SL	.05	.02	.01
☐ 24 Byron Williams SL	.05	.02	.01
☐ 25 Chris Mohr SL	.05	.02	.01
☐ 26 Errol Tucker SL	.05	.02	.01
☐ 27 Carl Painter SL	.05	.02	.01
☐ 28 Anthony Parker SL	.10	.05	.01
☐ 29 Danny Lockett SL	.05	.02	.01
☐ 30 Scott Adams	.05	.02	.01
☐ 31 Jim Bell	.05	.02	.01
☐ 32 Lydell Carr	.10	.05	.01
☐ 33 Bruce Clark	.05	.02	.01
☐ 34 Demetrius Davis	.10	.05	.01
☐ 35 Scott Erney	.05	.02	.01
☐ 36 Ron Goetz	.05	.02	.01
☐ 37 Xisco Marcos	.05	.02	.01
☐ 38 Paul Palmer	.05	.02	.01
☐ 39 Tony Rice	.20	.09	.03
☐ 40 Bobby Sign	.05	.02	.01
☐ 41 Gene Taylor	.05	.02	.01
☐ 42 Barry Voorhees	.05	.02	.01
☐ 43 Jack Bicknell CO	.05	.02	.01
☐ 44 Ken Bell	.05	.02	.01
☐ 45 Willie Bouyer	.05	.02	.01
☐ 46 John Brantley	.05	.02	.01
☐ 47 Elroy Harris	.05	.02	.01
☐ 48 James Henry	.05	.02	.01
☐ 49 John Holland	.05	.02	.01
☐ 50 Arthur Hunter	.05	.02	.01
☐ 51 Eric Jones	.05	.02	.01
☐ 52 Kirk Maggio	.05	.02	.01
☐ 53 Paul McGowan	.05	.02	.01
☐ 54 John Miller	.05	.02	.01
☐ 55 Maurice Oliver	.05	.02	.01
☐ 56 Darrell Phillips	.05	.02	.01
☐ 57 Chan Gailey CO	.05	.02	.01
☐ 58 Tony Baker	.10	.05	.01
☐ 59 Tim Broady	.05	.02	.01
☐ 60 Garry Frank	.05	.02	.01
☐ 61 Jason Johnson	.05	.02	.01
☐ 62 Stefan Maslo	.05	.02	.01
☐ 63 Mark Mraz	.05	.02	.01
☐ 64 Yepi Pau'u	.05	.02	.01
☐ 65 Mike Perez	.05	.02	.01
☐ 66 Mike Teeter	.05	.02	.01
☐ 67 Chris Williams	.05	.02	.01
☐ 68 Jack Elway CO	.10	.05	.01
☐ 69 Theo Adams	.05	.02	.01
☐ 70 Jeff Alexander	.05	.02	.01
☐ 71 Phil Alexander	.05	.02	.01
☐ 72 Paul Berardelli	.05	.02	.01
☐ 73 Dana Brinson	.05	.02	.01
☐ 74 Marlon Brown	.05	.02	.01
☐ 75 Dedrick Dodge	.05	.02	.01
☐ 76 Victor Ebubedike	.05	.02	.01
☐ 77 Corris Ervin	.05	.02	.01
☐ 78 Steve Gabbard	.05	.02	.01
☐ 79 Judd Garrett	.10	.05	.01
☐ 80 Stan Gelbaugh	.20	.09	.03
☐ 81 Roy Hart	.05	.02	.01
☐ 82 Jon Horton	.05	.02	.01
☐ 83 Danny Lockett	.05	.02	.01
☐ 84 Doug Marrone	.05	.02	.01
☐ 85 Ken Sale	.05	.02	.01
☐ 86 Larry Kennan CO	.05	.02	.01
☐ 87 Mike Cadore	.05	.02	.01
☐ 88 K.D. Dunn	.05	.02	.01
☐ 89 Ricky Johnson	.05	.02	.01
☐ 90 Chris Mohr	.10	.05	.01
☐ 91 Bjorn Nittmo	.05	.02	.01
☐ 92 Michael Proctor	.05	.02	.01
☐ 93 Richard Shelton	.05	.02	.01
☐ 94 Tracy Simien	.20	.09	.03
☐ 95 Jacques Dussault CO	.05	.02	.01
☐ 96 Cornell Burbage	.05	.02	.01
☐ 97 Joe Campbell	.05	.02	.01
☐ 98 Monty Gilbreath	.05	.02	.01
☐ 99 Jeff Graham	.75	.35	.09
☐ 100 Kip Lewis	.05	.02	.01
☐ 101 Bobby Lilljedahl	.05	.02	.01
☐ 102 Falanda Newton	.05	.02	.01
☐ 103 Anthony Parker	.20	.09	.03
☐ 104 Caesar Rentie	.05	.02	.01
☐ 105 Ron Sancho	.05	.02	.01
☐ 106 Craig Schlicting	.05	.02	.01
☐ 107 Lonnie Turner	.05	.02	.01
☐ 108 Eric Wilkerson	.05	.02	.01
☐ 109 Tony Woods	.10	.05	.01
☐ 110 Darrell(Mouse) Davis CO	.10	.05	.01
☐ 111 Kerwin Bell	.10	.05	.01
☐ 112 Wayne Davis	.05	.02	.01
☐ 113 John Guerrero	.05	.02	.01
☐ 114 Myron Jones	.05	.02	.01
☐ 115 Eric Mitchel	.05	.02	.01
☐ 116 Billy Owens	.05	.02	.01
☐ 117 Carl Painter	.05	.02	.01
☐ 118 Rob Sterling	.05	.02	.01
☐ 119 Errol Tucker	.05	.02	.01
☐ 120 Byron Williams	.05	.02	.01
☐ 121 Mike Withycombe	.05	.02	.01
☐ 122 Don Matthews CO	.05	.02	.01
☐ 123 Jon Carter	.05	.02	.01
☐ 124 Marvin Hargrove	.05	.02	.01
☐ 125 Clarkston Hines	.05	.02	.01
☐ 126 Ray Jackson	.05	.02	.01
☐ 127 Bobby McAllister	.05	.02	.01
☐ 128 Darryl McGill	.05	.02	.01
☐ 129 Pat McGuirk	.05	.02	.01
☐ 130 Shawn Woodson	.05	.02	.01
☐ 131 Roman Gabriel CO	.20	.09	.03
☐ 132 Greg Coauette	.05	.02	.01
☐ 133 Mike Elkins	.05	.02	.01
☐ 134 Victor Floyd	.05	.02	.01
☐ 135 Shawn Knight	.05	.02	.01
☐ 136 Pete Najarian	.05	.02	.01
☐ 137 Carl Parker	.05	.02	.01
☐ 138 Richard Stephens	.05	.02	.01
☐ 139 Curtis Wilson	.05	.02	.01
☐ 140 Kay Stephenson CO	.05	.02	.01
☐ 141 Ricky Blake	.10	.05	.01
☐ 142 Donnie Gardner	.05	.02	.01
☐ 143 Jason Garrett	.20	.09	.03
☐ 144 Mike Johnson	.05	.02	.01
☐ 145 Undra Johnson	.05	.02	.01
☐ 146 John Layfield	.05	.02	.01
☐ 147 Mark Ledbetter	.05	.02	.01
☐ 148 Gary Richard	.05	.02	.01
☐ 149 Tim Walton	.05	.02	.01
☐ 150 Mike Riley CO	.05	.02	.01

1991 Pro Set WLAF World Bowl Combo 43

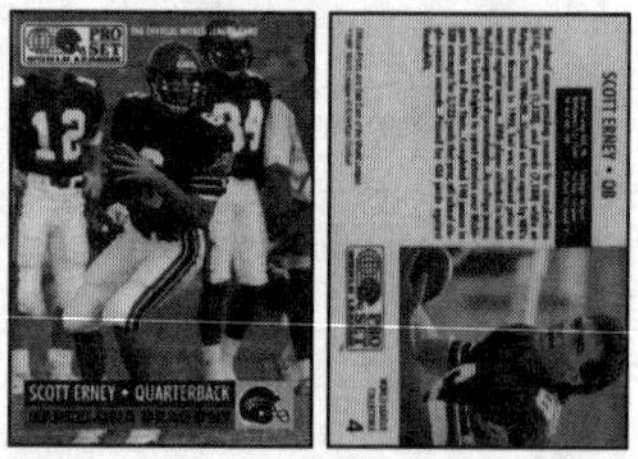

With a few subtle changes, this 43-card standard-size set is a reissue of the 1991 Pro Set WLAF Helmet and 1991 Pro Set WLAF sets. The cards have been renumbered on the back. As with the previous sets, the front designs have borderless color player photos, while the backs have color head and shoulders shots and player information in a horizontal format. The cards are checklisted below alphabetically according to teams. The helmet cards can also be distinguished on the back by the presence of Chronology narrative instead of Schedule. The set was passed out to attendees of the World Bowl Game in Wembley Stadium, London, England.

	MINT	NRMT	EXC
COMPLETE SET (43)	40.00	18.00	5.00
COMMON CARD (1-32)	.75	.35	.09
COMMON HELMET (34-43)	1.00	.45	.12
☐ 1 Mike Lynn PRES	.75	.35	.09
☐ 2 World League Opener London 24, Frankfurt 11	.75	.35	.09
☐ 3 Jack Bicknell CO	.75	.35	.09
☐ 4 Scott Erney	.75	.35	.09
☐ 5 Anthony Greene	.75	.35	.09
☐ 6 Chan Gailey CO	.75	.35	.09
☐ 7 Paul McGowan	.75	.35	.09
☐ 8 Brent Pease	.75	.35	.09
☐ 9 Jack Elway CO	.75	.35	.09
☐ 10 Mike Perez	.75	.35	.09
☐ 11 Mike Teeter	.75	.35	.09
☐ 12 Larry Kennan CO	.75	.35	.09
☐ 13 Corris Ervin	.75	.35	.09
☐ 14 John Witkowski	.75	.35	.09
☐ 15 Jacques Dussault CO	.75	.35	.09
☐ 16 Ray Savage	.75	.35	.09
☐ 17 Kevin Sweeney	.75	.35	.09
☐ 18 Mouse Davis CO	.75	.35	.09
☐ 19 Todd Hammel	.75	.35	.09
☐ 20 Anthony Parker	1.00	.45	.12
☐ 21 Don Matthews CO	.75	.35	.09
☐ 22 Kerwin Bell	1.25	.55	.16
☐ 23 Wayne Davis	.75	.35	.09
☐ 24 Roman Gabriel CO	1.50	.70	.19
☐ 25 Jon Carter	.75	.35	.09
☐ 26 Bobby McAllister	.75	.35	.09
☐ 27 Kay Stephenson CO	.75	.35	.09
☐ 28 Mike Elkins	.75	.35	.09
☐ 29 Shawn Knight	.75	.35	.09
☐ 30 Mike Riley CO	.75	.35	.09
☐ 31 Jason Garrett	5.00	2.20	.60
☐ 32 Greg Gilbert	.75	.35	.09
☐ 33 World Bowl Trophy	1.25	.55	.16
☐ 34 Barcelona Dragons Helmet	1.00	.45	.12
☐ 35 Birmingham Fire Helmet	1.00	.45	.12
☐ 36 Frankfurt Galaxy Helmet	1.00	.45	.12
☐ 37 London Monarchs Helmet	1.00	.45	.12
☐ 38 Montreal Machine Helmet	1.00	.45	.12
☐ 39 NY-NJ Knights Helmet	1.00	.45	.12
☐ 40 Orlando Thunder Helmet	1.00	.45	.12
☐ 41 Ral.-Durham Skyhawks Helmet	1.00	.45	.12
☐ 42 Sacramento Surge Helmet	1.00	.45	.12
☐ 43 San Antonio Riders Helmet	1.00	.45	.12

1991-92 Pro Set Super Bowl Binder

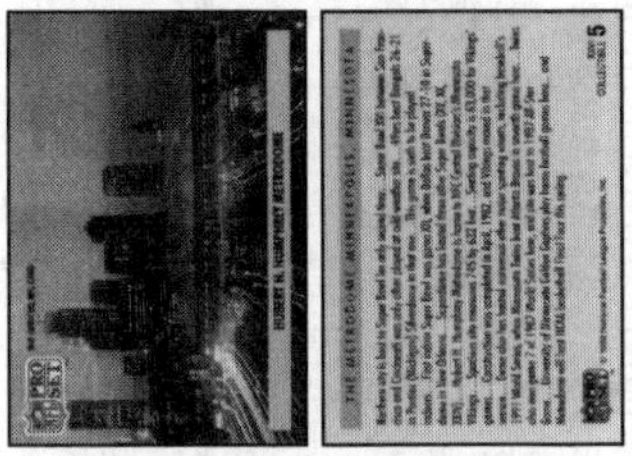

This 49-card standard-size set was sponsored by American Express and produced by Pro Set to commemorate Super Bowl XXVI. The set was sold in a white binder that housed four cards per page. It includes five new cards (1-5), four Think About It cards (300, 370, 725-726), as well as player cards for the Buffalo Bills (73-77, 79-84, 86, 88-90, 444-445, 449-450) and Washington Redskins (316-318, 320-324, 676-684, 746, 805, 848). The player cards are the same as the regular issue (including numbering), except that the Bills' cards have a "1991 AFC Champs" logo on the front, while the Redskins' cards carry a "1991 NFC Champs" logo on their fronts. A Jim Kelly card was apparently produced separately (individually cellophane wrapped and unnumbered) and was only available at the Super Bowl with the seat-cushion sets. Kelly was not included in sets sent out as as part of the mail-away offer advertised after the Super Bowl. The Kelly card does not include the Pro Set logo on the back.

	MINT	NRMT	EXC
COMPLETE SET (49)	20.00	9.00	2.50
COMMON CARD	.20	.09	.03
☐ 1 The NFL Experience	.50	.23	.06
☐ 2 Super Bowl XXVI	.20	.09	.03
☐ 3 AFC Standings	.20	.09	.03
☐ 4 NFC Standings	.20	.09	.03
☐ 5 The Metrodome	.20	.09	.03
☐ 73 Howard Ballard	.20	.09	.03
☐ 74 Cornelius Bennett	.50	.23	.06
☐ 75 Shane Conlan	.20	.09	.03
☐ 76 Kent Hull	.20	.09	.03
☐ 77 Kirby Jackson	.20	.09	.03
☐ 79 Mark Kelso	.20	.09	.03
☐ 80 Nate Odomes	.30	.14	.04
☐ 81 Andre Reed	.50	.23	.06
☐ 82 Jim Ritcher	.20	.09	.03
☐ 83 Bruce Smith	.50	.23	.06
☐ 84 Darryl Talley	.20	.09	.03
☐ 86 Thurman Thomas	.75	.35	.09
☐ 88 Will Wolford	.20	.09	.03
☐ 89 Jeff Wright	.20	.09	.03
☐ 90 Marv Levy CO	.20	.09	.03
☐ 300 Cornelius Bennett	.30	.14	.04
Piensalo			
☐ 316 Earnest Byner	.30	.14	.04
☐ 317 Gary Clark	.50	.23	.06
☐ 318 Andre Collins	.30	.14	.04
☐ 320 Chip Lohmiller	.20	.09	.03
☐ 321 Martin Mayhew	.20	.09	.03
☐ 322 Mark Rypien	.30	.14	.04
☐ 323 Alvin Walton	.20	.09	.03
☐ 324 Joe Gibbs CO	.50	.23	.06
☐ 370 Warren Moon	.40	.18	.05
Think About It			
☐ 444 James Lofton	.50	.23	.06
☐ 445 Keith McKeller	.20	.09	.03
☐ 449 Leon Seals	.20	.09	.03
☐ 450 Leonard Smith	.20	.09	.03
☐ 676 Jeff Bostic	.20	.09	.03
☐ 677 Darrell Green	.30	.14	.04
☐ 678 Markus Koch	.20	.09	.03
☐ 679 Jim Lachey	.30	.14	.04
☐ 680 Charles Mann	.30	.14	.04
☐ 681 Wilber Marshall	.30	.14	.04
☐ 682 Art Monk	.40	.18	.05
☐ 683 Gerald Riggs	.20	.09	.03
☐ 684 Ricky Sanders	.30	.14	.04
☐ 725 Howie Long	.50	.23	.06
Think About It			
☐ 726 Dan Marino	2.00	.90	.25
Think About It			
☐ 746 Bobby Wilson	.20	.09	.03
☐ 805 Ricky Ervins	.30	.14	.04
☐ 848 Brian Mitchell	.50	.23	.06
☐ NNO Jim Kelly SP	15.00	6.75	1.85

1992 Pro Set

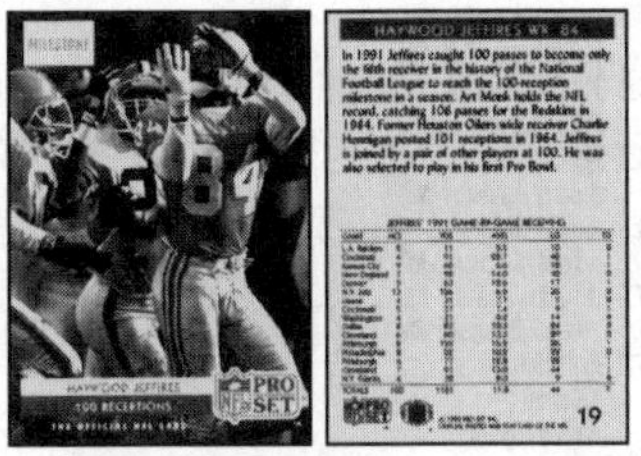

This standard-size set contains 700 cards issued in two differently designed series of 400 and 300. Cards for either series were issued in 15-card packs. First series fronts feature full-bleed color player photos with the player's name in a stripe at the bottom. The NFL Pro Set logo in the lower right corner. In a horizontal format, the backs have a close-up color player photo, biography, career highlights and complete statistical information. Second series cards are full-bleed on the right side with the players name running up the left border. A team logo is at the bottom left. Vertical backs have stats from the last three years, highlights and a small photo. Gray backgrounds contain all NFL team logos in white. The set opens with the following subsets: League Leaders (1-18), Milestones (19-27), Draft Day (28-33), Innovators (34-36), 1991 Replays (37-63), and Super Bowl XXVI Replays (64-72). Other than Washington and Buffalo leading off the first series, player cards are in team order by series. A number of subsets include Pro Set Newsreel (343-346), Magic Numbers (347-351), Play Smart (352-360), NFC Spirit of the Game (361-374), AFC Pro Bowl Stars (375-400), NFC Pro Bowl (401-427), Spirit of the Game (680-693) cards and some miscellaneous special cards (694-700). The key Rookie Cards in the set are Edgar Bennett, Steve Bono, Quentin Coryatt, Amp Lee and Carl Pickens. Randomly inserted in packs and listed at the end of the checklist below were Emmitt Smith and Erik Kramer autograph cards. Each player signed 1,000 cards that are individually numbered. Also inserted were a Smith Power Preview card, a Santa Claus card and Super Bowl XXVI logo card.

	MINT	NRMT	EXC
COMPLETE SET (700)	18.00	8.00	2.20
COMPLETE SERIES 1 (400)	8.00	3.60	1.00
COMPLETE SERIES 2 (300)	10.00	4.50	1.25
COMMON CARD (1-700)	.04	.02	.01
☐ 1 Mike Croel LL	.04	.02	.01
Rookie of the Year			
☐ 2 Thurman Thomas LL	.25	.11	.03
Player of the Year			
☐ 3 Wayne Fontes CO LL	.04	.02	.01
Coach of the Year			
☐ 4 Anthony Munoz LL	.10	.05	.01
Man of the Year			
☐ 5 Steve Young LL	.30	.14	.04
Passing Leader			
☐ 6 Warren Moon LL	.10	.05	.01
Passing Yardage Leader			
☐ 7 Emmitt Smith LL	1.00	.45	.12
Rushing Leader			
☐ 8 Haywood Jeffires LL	.04	.02	.01
Receiving Leader			
☐ 9 Marv Cook LL	.04	.02	.01
Receiving Leader/TE			
☐ 10 Michael Irvin LL	.25	.11	.03
Receiving Yardage Leader			
☐ 11 Thurman Thomas LL UER	.25	.11	.03
Total Yardage Leader			
(Total combined yards			
should be 2,038)			
☐ 12 Chip Lohmiller LL UER	.04	.02	.01
Scoring Leader			
(FG Attempt Totals			
are off by one)			
☐ 13 Barry Sanders LL	.50	.23	.06
Scoring Leader TD's			
☐ 14 Reggie Roby LL	.04	.02	.01
Punting Leader			
☐ 15 Mel Gray LL	.04	.02	.01
Kickoff/Punt Return			
Leader			
☐ 16 Ronnie Lott LL	.10	.05	.01
Interception Leader			
☐ 17 Pat Swilling LL	.04	.02	.01
Sack Leader			
☐ 18 Reggie White LL	.10	.05	.01
Defensive MVP			
☐ 19 Haywood Jeffires MILE	.04	.02	.01
100 Receptions			
☐ 20 Pat Leahy MILE	.04	.02	.01
300 Field Goals			
☐ 21 James Lofton MILE	.10	.05	.01
13,000 Yards			
☐ 22 Art Monk MILE	.10	.05	.01
800 Receptions			
☐ 23 Don Shula MILE	.10	.05	.01
300 Wins			
☐ 24A Nick Lowery MILE ERR	.04	.02	.01
9th 100-Point Season			
(Says he wears 9)			
☐ 24B Nick Lowery MILE COR	.04	.02	.01
9th 100-Point Season			
(Says he wears 8)			
☐ 25 John Elway MILE	.30	.14	.04
2,000 Completed Passes			
☐ 26 Chicago Bears MILE	.04	.02	.01
8 Straight Opening Wins			
☐ 27 Marcus Allen MILE	.10	.05	.01
2,000 Rushing Attempts			
☐ 28 Terrell Buckley DD	.04	.02	.01
☐ 29 Amp Lee DD	.04	.02	.01
☐ 30 Chris Mims DD	.10	.05	.01
☐ 31 Leon Searcy DD	.10	.05	.01
☐ 32 Jimmy Smith DD	.25	.11	.03
☐ 33 Siran Stacy DD	.04	.02	.01
☐ 34 Pete Gogolak INN	.04	.02	.01
☐ 35 Cheerleaders INN	.04	.02	.01
☐ 36 Houston Astrodome INN	.04	.02	.01
☐ 37 Week 1 REPLAY	.04	.02	.01
Chiefs 14, Falcons 3			
(Christian Okoye)			
☐ 38 Week 2 REPLAY	.04	.02	.01
Bills 52, Steelers 34			
(Don Beebe)			
☐ 39 Week 3 REPLAY	.04	.02	.01
Bears 20, Giants 17			
(Wendell Davis)			
☐ 40 Week 4 REPLAY	.04	.02	.01
Dolphins 16, Packers 13			
(Don Shula CO)			
☐ 41 Week 5 REPLAY	.04	.02	.01
Raiders 12 49ers 6			
(Ronnie Lott)			
☐ 42 Week 6 REPLAY	.04	.02	.01
Redskins 20, Bears 7			
(Art Monk)			
☐ 43 Week 7 REPLAY	.10	.05	.01
Bills 42, Colts 6			
(Thurman Thomas)			
☐ 44 Week 8 REPLAY	.04	.02	.01
Patriots 26 Vikings 23			
(John Stephens)			
☐ 45 Week 9 REPLAY UER	.04	.02	.01
Vikings 28, Cardinals 0			
(Herschel Walker;			
misspelled Hershel			
on card back)			
☐ 46 Week 10 REPLAY	.04	.02	.01
Jets 19 Packers 16			
(Chris Burkett)			
☐ 47 Week 11 REPLAY	.04	.02	.01
Colts 28 Jets 27			
(Line play)			
☐ 48 Week 12 REPLAY	.04	.02	.01
Falcons 43 Buccaneers 7			
(Andre Rison)			
☐ 49 Week 13 REPLAY	.04	.02	.01
Cowboys 24 Redskins 21			
(Steve Beuerlein			
and Michael Irvin)			
☐ 50 Week 14 REPLAY	.04	.02	.01
Broncos 20 Patriots 3			
(Irving Fryar)			
☐ 51 Week 15 REPLAY	.04	.02	.01
Bills 30 Raiders 27			
(Bills' Defense)			
☐ 52 Week 16 REPLAY	.04	.02	.01
Cowboys 25 Eagles 13			
(Kelvin Martin)			
☐ 53 Week 17 REPLAY	.04	.02	.01
Jets 23 Dolphins 20			
(Bruce Coslet CO)			
☐ 54 AFC Wild Card REPLAY	.04	.02	.01
Chiefs 10 Raiders 6			
(Fred Jones)			
☐ 55 AFC Wild Card REPLAY	.04	.02	.01
Oilers 17 Jets 10			
(Oilers' Run-and-Shoot)			
☐ 56 NFC Wild Card REPLAY	.04	.02	.01
Cowboys 17 Bears 13			
(Bill Bates)			
☐ 57 NFC Wild Card REPLAY	.04	.02	.01
Falcons 27 Saints 20			
(Michael Haynes)			
☐ 58 AFC Divis. Playoff REPLAY	.04	.02	.01
Broncos 26 Oilers 24			
(Bronco interception)			
☐ 59 AFC Divis. Playoff REPLAY	.10	.05	.01
Bills 37 Chiefs 14			
(Thurman Thomas)			
☐ 60 NFC Divis. Playoff REPLAY	.04	.02	.01
Lions 38 Cowboys 6			
(Eric Kramer)			
☐ 61 NFC Divis. Playoff REPLAY	.04	.02	.01
Redskins 24 Falcons 7			
(Darrell Green)			
☐ 62 AFC Championship REPLAY	.04	.02	.01
Bills 10 Broncos 7			
(Carlton Bailey)			
☐ 63 NFC Championship REPLAY	.04	.02	.01
Redskins 41 Lions 10			
(Mark Rypien)			
☐ 64 Super Bowl XXVI REPLAY	.04	.02	.01
TD Reversed, FG Botched			
☐ 65 Super Bowl XXVI REPLAY	.04	.02	.01
(Brad) Edwards Picks Off			
First of Two			
☐ 66 Super Bowl XXVI REPLAY	.04	.02	.01
Rypien to Byner, 10-0			
☐ 67 Super Bowl XXVI REPLAY	.04	.02	.01
Riggs Puts Redskins Up 17-10			
☐ 68 Super Bowl XXVI REPLAY	.04	.02	.01
Gouveia Interception Buries Bills			
☐ 69 Super Bowl XXVI REPLAY	.10	.05	.01
Thomas Scores Bills' First TD			
☐ 70 Super Bowl XXVI REPLAY	.04	.02	.01
Clark Catches Rypien's Second TD			
☐ 71 Super Bowl XXVI REPLAY	.04	.02	.01
Bills Convert Late Break			
☐ 72 Super Bowl XXVI REPLAY	.04	.02	.01
Redskins Run Out the Clock			
☐ 73 Jeff Bostic	.04	.02	.01
☐ 74 Earnest Byner	.04	.02	.01
☐ 75 Gary Clark	.25	.11	.03
☐ 76 Andre Collins	.04	.02	.01
☐ 77 Darrell Green	.04	.02	.01
☐ 78 Joe Jacoby	.04	.02	.01
☐ 79 Jim Lachey	.04	.02	.01
☐ 80 Chip Lohmiller	.04	.02	.01
☐ 81 Charles Mann	.04	.02	.01
☐ 82 Martin Mayhew	.04	.02	.01
☐ 83 Matt Millen	.10	.05	.01
☐ 84 Brian Mitchell	.10	.05	.01
☐ 85 Art Monk	.10	.05	.01
☐ 86 Gerald Riggs	.04	.02	.01
☐ 87 Mark Rypien	.04	.02	.01
☐ 88 Fred Stokes	.04	.02	.01
☐ 89 Bobby Wilson	.04	.02	.01
☐ 90 Joe Gibbs CO	.10	.05	.01
☐ 91 Howard Ballard	.04	.02	.01
☐ 92 Cornelius Bennett UER	.10	.05	.01
(Interception total reads 0;			
he had 4)			
☐ 93 Kenneth Davis	.04	.02	.01
☐ 94 Al Edwards	.04	.02	.01
☐ 95 Kent Hull	.04	.02	.01
☐ 96 Kirby Jackson	.04	.02	.01
☐ 97 Mark Kelso	.04	.02	.01
☐ 98 James Lofton UER	.10	.05	.01
(Says he played in '75			
Pro Bowl, but he wasn't			
in NFL until 1978)			
☐ 99 Keith McKeller	.04	.02	.01
☐ 100 Nate Odomes	.04	.02	.01
☐ 101 Jim Ritcher	.04	.02	.01
☐ 102 Leon Seals	.04	.02	.01
☐ 103 Steve Tasker	.10	.05	.01
☐ 104 Darryl Talley	.04	.02	.01
☐ 105 Thurman Thomas	.25	.11	.03
☐ 106 Will Wolford	.04	.02	.01
☐ 107 Jeff Wright	.04	.02	.01
☐ 108 Marv Levy CO	.04	.02	.01
☐ 109 Darion Conner	.04	.02	.01
☐ 110 Bill Fralic	.04	.02	.01
☐ 111 Moe Gardner	.04	.02	.01
☐ 112 Michael Haynes	.10	.05	.01
☐ 113 Chris Miller	.10	.05	.01
☐ 114 Erric Pegram	.10	.05	.01
☐ 115 Bruce Pickens	.04	.02	.01
☐ 116 Andre Rison	.10	.05	.01
☐ 117 Jerry Glanville CO	.04	.02	.01
☐ 118 Neal Anderson	.04	.02	.01
☐ 119 Trace Armstrong	.04	.02	.01
☐ 120 Wendell Davis	.04	.02	.01
☐ 121 Richard Dent	.10	.05	.01
☐ 122 Jay Hilgenberg	.04	.02	.01
☐ 123 Lemuel Stinson	.04	.02	.01
☐ 124 Stan Thomas	.04	.02	.01
☐ 125 Tom Waddle	.04	.02	.01
☐ 126 Mike Ditka CO	.25	.11	.03
☐ 127 James Brooks	.10	.05	.01
☐ 128 Eddie Brown	.04	.02	.01
☐ 129 David Fulcher	.04	.02	.01
☐ 130 Harold Green	.04	.02	.01
☐ 131 Tim Krumrie UER	.04	.02	.01
(Misspelled Krumerie			
on card front)			
☐ 132 Anthony Munoz	.10	.05	.01
☐ 133 Craig Taylor	.04	.02	.01
☐ 134 Eric Thomas	.04	.02	.01
☐ 135 David Shula CO	.04	.02	.01
☐ 136 Mike Baab	.04	.02	.01
☐ 137 Brian Brennan	.04	.02	.01
☐ 138 Michael Jackson	.10	.05	.01
☐ 139 James Jones UER	.04	.02	.01
(DL on front, DT on back)			
☐ 140 Ed King	.04	.02	.01
☐ 141 Clay Matthews	.10	.05	.01
☐ 142 Eric Metcalf	.10	.05	.01
☐ 143 Joe Morris	.04	.02	.01
☐ 144A Bill Belichick CO ERR	.10	.05	.01
(No HC next to name			
on back)			
☐ 144B Bill Belichick CO COR	.10	.05	.01
(HC next to name			
on back)			
☐ 145 Steve Beuerlein	.04	.02	.01
☐ 146 Larry Brown DB	.04	.02	.01
☐ 147 Ray Horton	.04	.02	.01
☐ 148 Ken Norton	.25	.11	.03
☐ 149 Mike Saxon	.04	.02	.01
☐ 150 Emmitt Smith	2.00	.90	.25
☐ 151 Mark Stepnoski	.10	.05	.01
☐ 152 Alexander Wright	.04	.02	.01
☐ 153 Jimmy Johnson CO	.10	.05	.01
☐ 154 Mike Croel	.04	.02	.01
☐ 155 John Elway	.60	.25	.07
☐ 156 Gaston Green UER	.04	.02	.01
(Lists 1991 team as			
Rams, but was Broncos)			
☐ 157 Wymon Henderson	.04	.02	.01
☐ 158 Karl Mecklenburg UER	.04	.02	.01
(Card back repeats			
Super Bowl XXI)			
☐ 159 Warren Powers	.04	.02	.01
☐ 160 Steve Sewell UER	.04	.02	.01
(Card back repeats			
Super Bowl XXI)			
☐ 161 Doug Widell	.04	.02	.01
☐ 162 Dan Reeves CO	.04	.02	.01

☐ 163 Eric Andolsek	.04	.02	.01
☐ 164 Jerry Ball	.04	.02	.01
☐ 165 Bennie Blades	.04	.02	.01
☐ 166 Ray Crockett	.04	.02	.01
☐ 167 Willie Green UER	.04	.02	.01
(Card back repeats			
and in last sentence)			
☐ 168 Erik Kramer	.10	.05	.01
☐ 169 Barry Sanders	1.00	.45	.12
☐ 170 Chris Spielman UER	.04	.02	.01
(Card says named to			
Pro Bowl 1989-90,			
should say 1989-91)			
☐ 171 Wayne Fontes CO	.04	.02	.01
☐ 172 Vinnie Clark	.04	.02	.01
☐ 173 Tony Mandarich	.04	.02	.01
☐ 174 Brian Noble	.04	.02	.01
☐ 175 Bryce Paup	.25	.11	.03
☐ 176 Sterling Sharpe	.25	.11	.03
☐ 177 Darrell Thompson	.04	.02	.01
☐ 178 Esera Tuaolo UER	.04	.02	.01
(Text has 1 TD via			
interception, stats do not)			
☐ 179 Ed West	.04	.02	.01
☐ 180 Mike Holmgren CO	.10	.05	.01
☐ 181 Ray Childress	.04	.02	.01
☐ 182 Cris Dishman	.04	.02	.01
☐ 183 Curtis Duncan	.04	.02	.01
☐ 184 William Fuller	.10	.05	.01
☐ 185 Lamar Lathon	.04	.02	.01
☐ 186 Warren Moon	.25	.11	.03
☐ 187 Bo Orlando	.04	.02	.01
☐ 188 Lorenzo White	.04	.02	.01
☐ 189 Jack Pardee CO	.04	.02	.01
☐ 190 Chip Banks	.04	.02	.01
☐ 191 Dean Biasucci UER	.04	.02	.01
(PK on front, K on back)			
☐ 192 Bill Brooks	.04	.02	.01
☐ 193 Ray Donaldson	.04	.02	.01
☐ 194 Jeff Herrod	.04	.02	.01
☐ 195 Mike Prior	.04	.02	.01
☐ 196 Mark Vander Poel	.04	.02	.01
☐ 197 Clarence Verdin	.04	.02	.01
☐ 198 Ted Marchibroda CO	.04	.02	.01
☐ 199 John Alt	.04	.02	.01
☐ 200 Deron Cherry	.04	.02	.01
☐ 201 Steve DeBerg	.04	.02	.01
☐ 202 Nick Lowery	.04	.02	.01
☐ 203 Neil Smith	.25	.11	.03
☐ 204 Derrick Thomas	.25	.11	.03
☐ 205 Joe Valerio	.04	.02	.01
☐ 206 Barry Word	.04	.02	.01
☐ 207 Marty Schottenheimer CO	.04	.02	.01
☐ 208 Marcus Allen	.25	.11	.03
☐ 209 Nick Bell	.04	.02	.01
☐ 210 Tim Brown	.25	.11	.03
☐ 211 Howie Long	.10	.05	.01
☐ 212 Ronnie Lott	.10	.05	.01
☐ 213 Todd Marinovich	.04	.02	.01
☐ 214 Greg Townsend	.04	.02	.01
☐ 215 Steve Wright	.04	.02	.01
☐ 216 Art Shell CO	.10	.05	.01
☐ 217 Flipper Anderson	.04	.02	.01
☐ 218 Robert Delpino	.04	.02	.01
☐ 219 Henry Ellard	.10	.05	.01
☐ 220 Kevin Greene	.25	.11	.03
☐ 221 Todd Lyght	.04	.02	.01
☐ 222 Tom Newberry	.04	.02	.01
☐ 223 Roman Phifer	.04	.02	.01
☐ 224 Michael Stewart	.04	.02	.01
☐ 225 Chuck Knox CO	.04	.02	.01
☐ 226 Aaron Craver	.04	.02	.01
☐ 227 Jeff Cross	.04	.02	.01
☐ 228 Mark Duper	.04	.02	.01
☐ 229 Ferrell Edmunds	.04	.02	.01
☐ 230 Jim C. Jensen	.04	.02	.01
☐ 231 Louis Oliver UER	.04	.02	.01
(Card has 215 tackles,			
but he only had 88)			
☐ 232 Reggie Roby	.04	.02	.01
☐ 233 Sammie Smith	.04	.02	.01
☐ 234 Don Shula CO	.10	.05	.01
☐ 235 Joey Browner	.04	.02	.01
☐ 236 Anthony Carter	.10	.05	.01
☐ 237 Chris Doleman	.04	.02	.01
☐ 238 Steve Jordan	.04	.02	.01
☐ 239 Kirk Lowdermilk	.04	.02	.01
☐ 240 Henry Thomas	.04	.02	.01
☐ 241 Herschel Walker	.10	.05	.01
☐ 242 Felix Wright	.04	.02	.01
☐ 243 Dennis Green CO	.04	.02	.01
☐ 244 Ray Agnew	.04	.02	.01
☐ 245 Marv Cook	.04	.02	.01
☐ 246 Irving Fryar UER	.10	.05	.01
(WR/KR on front,			
WR on back)			
☐ 247 Pat Harlow	.04	.02	.01
☐ 248 Hugh Millen	.04	.02	.01
☐ 249 Leonard Russell	.10	.05	.01
☐ 250 Andre Tippett	.04	.02	.01
☐ 251 Jon Vaughn	.04	.02	.01
☐ 252 Dick MacPherson CO	.04	.02	.01
☐ 253 Morten Andersen	.04	.02	.01
☐ 254 Bobby Hebert	.04	.02	.01
☐ 255 Joel Hilgenberg	.04	.02	.01
☐ 256 Vaughan Johnson	.04	.02	.01
☐ 257 Sam Mills	.04	.02	.01
☐ 258 Pat Swilling	.10	.05	.01
☐ 259 Floyd Turner	.04	.02	.01
☐ 260 Steve Walsh	.04	.02	.01
☐ 261 Jim Mora CO UER	.04	.02	.01
(No TM by Pro Set logo)			
☐ 262 Stephen Baker	.04	.02	.01
☐ 263 Mark Collins	.04	.02	.01
☐ 264 Rodney Hampton	.25	.11	.03
☐ 265 Jeff Hostetler	.10	.05	.01
☐ 266 Erik Howard	.04	.02	.01
☐ 267 Sean Landeta	.04	.02	.01
☐ 268 Gary Reasons UER	.04	.02	.01
(Fumble recovery noted			
on card, but not in stats)			
☐ 269 Everson Walls	.04	.02	.01
☐ 270 Ray Handley CO	.04	.02	.01
☐ 271 Louis Aguiar	.04	.02	.01
☐ 272 Brad Baxter	.04	.02	.01
☐ 273 Chris Burkett	.04	.02	.01
☐ 274 Irv Eatman	.04	.02	.01
☐ 275 Jeff Lageman	.04	.02	.01
☐ 276 Freeman McNeil	.04	.02	.01
☐ 277 Rob Moore	.10	.05	.01
☐ 278 Lonnie Young	.04	.02	.01
☐ 279 Bruce Coslet CO	.04	.02	.01
☐ 280 Jerome Brown	.04	.02	.01
☐ 281 Keith Byars	.04	.02	.01
☐ 282 Bruce Collie UER	.04	.02	.01
(No stats on back)			
☐ 283 Keith Jackson	.10	.05	.01
☐ 284 James Joseph	.04	.02	.01
☐ 285 Seth Joyner	.10	.05	.01
☐ 286 Andre Waters	.04	.02	.01
☐ 287 Reggie White	.25	.11	.03
☐ 288 Rich Kotite CO	.04	.02	.01
☐ 289 Rich Camarillo	.04	.02	.01
☐ 290 Garth Jax	.04	.02	.01
☐ 291 Ernie Jones	.04	.02	.01
☐ 292 Tim McDonald	.04	.02	.01
☐ 293 Rod Saddler	.04	.02	.01
☐ 294 Anthony Thompson UER	.04	.02	.01
(NO TD stats for			
1991 receiving)			
☐ 295 Tom Tupa UER	.04	.02	.01
(QB/P on front,			
QB on back)			
☐ 296 Ron Wolfley	.04	.02	.01
☐ 297 Joe Bugel CO	.04	.02	.01
☐ 298 Gary Anderson K	.04	.02	.01
☐ 299 Jeff Graham	.25	.11	.03
☐ 300 Eric Green	.04	.02	.01
☐ 301 Bryan Hinkle	.04	.02	.01
☐ 302 Tunch Ilkin	.04	.02	.01
☐ 303 Louis Lipps	.04	.02	.01
☐ 304 Neil O'Donnell	.25	.11	.03
☐ 305 Rod Woodson	.25	.11	.03
☐ 306 Bill Cowher CO	.10	.05	.01
☐ 307 Eric Bieniemy	.04	.02	.01
☐ 308 Marion Butts	.04	.02	.01
☐ 309 John Friesz	.10	.05	.01
☐ 310 Courtney Hall	.04	.02	.01
☐ 311 Ronnie Harmon	.04	.02	.01
☐ 312 Henry Rolling	.04	.02	.01
☐ 313 Billy Ray Smith	.04	.02	.01
☐ 314 George Thornton	.04	.02	.01
☐ 315 Bobby Ross CO	.04	.02	.01
☐ 316 Todd Bowles	.04	.02	.01
☐ 317 Michael Carter	.04	.02	.01
☐ 318 Don Griffin	.04	.02	.01
☐ 319 Charles Haley	.10	.05	.01
☐ 320 Brent Jones	.10	.05	.01
☐ 321 John Taylor	.10	.05	.01
☐ 322 Ted Washington	.04	.02	.01
☐ 323 Steve Young	.60	.25	.07
☐ 324 George Seifert CO	.10	.05	.01
☐ 325 Brian Blades	.10	.05	.01
☐ 326 Jacob Green	.04	.02	.01
☐ 327 Patrick Hunter	.04	.02	.01
☐ 328 Tommy Kane	.04	.02	.01
☐ 329 Cortez Kennedy	.10	.05	.01
☐ 330 Dave Krieg	.10	.05	.01
☐ 331 Rufus Porter	.04	.02	.01
☐ 332 John L. Williams	.04	.02	.01
☐ 333 Tom Flores CO	.04	.02	.01
☐ 334 Gary Anderson RB	.04	.02	.01
☐ 335 Mark Carrier WR	.10	.05	.01
☐ 336 Reuben Davis	.04	.02	.01
☐ 337 Lawrence Dawsey	.10	.05	.01
☐ 338 Keith McCants UER	.04	.02	.01
(LB on front, DE on back)			
☐ 339 Vinny Testaverde	.10	.05	.01
☐ 340 Broderick Thomas	.04	.02	.01
☐ 341 Robert Wilson	.04	.02	.01
☐ 342 Sam Wyche CO	.04	.02	.01
☐ 343 1991 Teacher of	.04	.02	.01
the Year NEWS			
☐ 344 Owners Reject Instant	.04	.02	.01
Replay NEWS			
☐ 345 NFL Experience	.04	.02	.01
Unveiled NEWS			
☐ 346 Chuck Noll Retires	.10	.05	.01
Tosses Coin NEWS			
☐ 347 Isaac Curtis	.04	.02	.01
and Tim McGee MN UER			
(Birthdates switched)			
☐ 348 Drew Pearson	.10	.05	.01
Michael Irvin MN			
☐ 349 Billy Sims	.40	.18	.05
Barry Sanders MN			
☐ 350 Ken Stabler	.04	.02	.01
Todd Marinovich MN			
☐ 351 Craig James	.10	.05	.01
Leonard Russell MN			
☐ 352 Bob Golic	.04	.02	.01
Graffiti			
It's a Sign of			
Ignorance			
☐ 353 Pat Harlow	.04	.02	.01
Vote, Let			
Your Choice Be Heard			
☐ 354 Esera Tuaolo	.04	.02	.01
Stand Tall, Be Proud			
of Your Heritage			
☐ 355 Mark Schlereth	.04	.02	.01
Save The Environment			
Be a Team Player			
☐ 356 Trace Armstrong	.04	.02	.01
Drug Abuse			
Stay in Control			
☐ 357 Eric Bieniemy	.04	.02	.01
Save a Life			
Buckle Up			
☐ 358 Bill Romanowski	.04	.02	.01
Education			
Stay In School			
☐ 359 Irv Eatman	.04	.02	.01
Exercise			
Be Active			
☐ 360 Jonathan Hayes	.04	.02	.01
Diabetes			
Be Your Best			
☐ 361 Atlanta Falcons	.04	.02	.01
Spirit of the Game			
(Helmet)			
☐ 362 Chicago Bears	.04	.02	.01
Spirit of the Game			
(Vintage game photo)			
☐ 363 Dallas Cowboys	.04	.02	.01
Spirit of the Game			
(Mascot)			
☐ 364 Detroit Lions	.04	.02	.01
Spirit of the Game			
(Overhead game photo)			
☐ 365 Green Bay Packers	.04	.02	.01
Spirit of the Game			
(60's huddle)			
☐ 366 Los Angeles Rams	.04	.02	.01
Spirit of the Game			
(Fans)			
☐ 367 Minnesota Vikings	.04	.02	.01
Spirit of the Game			
(Vintage game photo)			
☐ 368 New Orleans Saints UER	.04	.02	.01
Spirit of the Game			
(Fans; Post-season record			
was 0-3, not 0-2)			
☐ 369 New York Giants	.04	.02	.01
Spirit of the Game			
(Fan's banner)			
☐ 370 Philadelphia Eagles	.04	.02	.01
Spirit of the Game			
(Eric Allen)			
☐ 371 Phoenix Cardinals	.04	.02	.01
Spirit of the Game			
(Fan)			
☐ 372 San Francisco 49ers	.04	.02	.01
Spirit of the Game			
(Tom Rathman)			
☐ 373 Tampa Bay Buccaneers	.04	.02	.01
Spirit of the Game			
(Mascot)			
☐ 374 Washington Redskins	.04	.02	.01
Spirit of the Game			
(Fans)			
☐ 375 Steve Atwater PB UER	.04	.02	.01
(Photo shows regular			
game instead of Pro Bowl)			
☐ 376 Cornelius Bennett PB	.10	.05	.01
☐ 377 Tim Brown PB	.10	.05	.01
☐ 378 Marion Butts PB	.04	.02	.01
☐ 379 Ray Childress PB	.04	.02	.01
(Photo shows regular			
game instead of Pro Bowl)			
☐ 380 Mark Clayton PB	.04	.02	.01
☐ 381 Marv Cook PB	.04	.02	.01
☐ 382 Cris Dishman PB	.04	.02	.01
☐ 383 William Fuller PB	.04	.02	.01
☐ 384 Gaston Green PB	.04	.02	.01
☐ 385 Jeff Jaeger PB	.04	.02	.01
☐ 386 Haywood Jeffires PB	.10	.05	.01
☐ 387 James Lofton PB	.10	.05	.01
☐ 388 Ronnie Lott PB	.10	.05	.01
☐ 389 Karl Mecklenburg PB UER	.04	.02	.01
(Back and front read ...berg)			
☐ 390 Warren Moon PB	.10	.05	.01
☐ 391 Anthony Munoz PB	.04	.02	.01
☐ 392 Dennis Smith PB	.04	.02	.01
☐ 393 Neil Smith PB	.10	.05	.01
☐ 394 Darryl Talley PB	.04	.02	.01
☐ 395 Derrick Thomas PB	.10	.05	.01
☐ 396 Thurman Thomas PB	.10	.05	.01
☐ 397 Greg Townsend PB	.04	.02	.01
☐ 398 Richmond Webb PB	.04	.02	.01
☐ 399 Rod Woodson PB	.10	.05	.01
☐ 400 Dan Reeves CO PB	.04	.02	.01
☐ 401 Troy Aikman PB	.50	.23	.06
☐ 402 Eric Allen PB	.04	.02	.01
☐ 403 Bennie Blades PB	.04	.02	.01
☐ 404 Lomas Brown PB	.04	.02	.01
☐ 405 Mark Carrier DB PB	.04	.02	.01
☐ 406 Gary Clark PB	.10	.05	.01
☐ 407 Mel Gray PB	.04	.02	.01
☐ 408 Darrell Green PB	.04	.02	.01
☐ 409 Michael Irvin PB	.25	.11	.03
☐ 410 Vaughan Johnson PB	.04	.02	.01
☐ 411 Seth Joyner PB	.04	.02	.01
☐ 412 Jim Lachey PB	.04	.02	.01
☐ 413 Chip Lohmiller PB	.04	.02	.01
☐ 414 Charles Mann PB	.04	.02	.01
☐ 415 Chris Miller PB	.10	.05	.01
☐ 416 Sam Mills PB	.04	.02	.01
☐ 417 Bart Oates PB	.04	.02	.01
☐ 418 Jerry Rice PB	.40	.18	.05
☐ 419 Andre Rison PB	.10	.05	.01
☐ 420 Mark Rypien PB	.04	.02	.01
☐ 421 Barry Sanders PB	.50	.23	.06
☐ 422 Deion Sanders PB	.25	.11	.03
☐ 423 Mark Schlereth PB	.04	.02	.01
☐ 424 Mike Singletary PB	.04	.02	.01
☐ 425 Emmitt Smith PB	1.00	.45	.12
☐ 426 Pat Swilling PB	.04	.02	.01
☐ 427 Reggie White PB	.10	.05	.01
☐ 428 Rick Bryan	.04	.02	.01
☐ 429 Tim Green	.04	.02	.01
☐ 430 Drew Hill	.04	.02	.01
☐ 431 Norm Johnson	.04	.02	.01
☐ 432 Keith Jones	.04	.02	.01
☐ 433 Mike Pritchard	.10	.05	.01
☐ 434 Deion Sanders	.50	.23	.06
☐ 435 Tony Smith	.04	.02	.01
☐ 436 Jessie Tuggle	.04	.02	.01
☐ 437 Steve Christie	.04	.02	.01
☐ 438 Shane Conlan	.04	.02	.01
☐ 439 Matt Darby	.04	.02	.01
☐ 440 John Fina	.04	.02	.01
☐ 441 Henry Jones	.04	.02	.01
☐ 442 Jim Kelly	.25	.11	.03
☐ 443 Pete Metzelaars	.04	.02	.01
☐ 444 Andre Reed	.10	.05	.01
☐ 445 Bruce Smith	.25	.11	.03
☐ 446 Troy Auzenne	.04	.02	.01
☐ 447 Mark Carrier DB	.04	.02	.01
☐ 448 Will Furrer	.04	.02	.01
☐ 449 Jim Harbaugh	.25	.11	.03
☐ 450 Brad Muster	.04	.02	.01
☐ 451 Darren Lewis	.04	.02	.01
☐ 452 Mike Singletary	.10	.05	.01
☐ 453 Alonzo Spellman	.10	.05	.01
☐ 454 Chris Zorich	.10	.05	.01
☐ 455 Jim Breech	.04	.02	.01
☐ 456 Boomer Esiason	.10	.05	.01
☐ 457 Derrick Fenner	.04	.02	.01
☐ 458 James Francis	.04	.02	.01
☐ 459 David Klingler	.10	.05	.01
☐ 460 Tim McGee	.04	.02	.01
☐ 461 Carl Pickens	2.00	.90	.25
☐ 462 Alfred Williams	.04	.02	.01
☐ 463 Darryl Williams	.04	.02	.01
☐ 464 Mark Bavaro	.04	.02	.01
☐ 465 Jay Hilgenberg	.04	.02	.01
☐ 466 Leroy Hoard	.10	.05	.01
☐ 467 Bernie Kosar	.10	.05	.01
☐ 468 Michael Dean Perry	.10	.05	.01
☐ 469 Todd Philcox	.04	.02	.01
☐ 470 Patrick Rowe	.04	.02	.01
☐ 471 Tommy Vardell	.10	.05	.01
☐ 472 Everson Walls	.04	.02	.01
☐ 473 Troy Aikman	1.00	.45	.12
☐ 474 Kenneth Gant	.04	.02	.01
☐ 475 Charles Haley	.10	.05	.01
☐ 476 Michael Irvin	.25	.11	.03
☐ 477 Robert Jones	.04	.02	.01
☐ 478 Russell Maryland	.10	.05	.01
☐ 479 Jay Novacek	.10	.05	.01
☐ 480 Kevin Smith	.25	.11	.03
☐ 481 Tony Tolbert	.04	.02	.01
☐ 482 Steve Atwater	.04	.02	.01
☐ 483 Shane Dronett	.04	.02	.01
☐ 484 Simon Fletcher	.04	.02	.01
☐ 485 Greg Lewis	.04	.02	.01
☐ 486 Tommy Maddox	.04	.02	.01
☐ 487 Shannon Sharpe	.25	.11	.03
☐ 488 Dennis Smith	.04	.02	.01
☐ 489 Sammie Smith	.04	.02	.01
☐ 490 Kenny Walker	.04	.02	.01
☐ 491 Lomas Brown	.04	.02	.01
☐ 492 Mike Farr	.04	.02	.01
☐ 493 Mel Gray	.10	.05	.01
☐ 494 Jason Hanson	.10	.05	.01
☐ 495 Herman Moore	.75	.35	.09
☐ 496 Rodney Peete	.10	.05	.01
☐ 497 Robert Porcher	.10	.05	.01
☐ 498 Kelvin Pritchett	.04	.02	.01
☐ 499 Andre Ware	.04	.02	.01

☐ 500 Sanjay Beach	.04	.02	.01
☐ 501 Edgar Bennett	.75	.35	.09
☐ 502 Lewis Billups	.04	.02	.01
☐ 503 Terrell Buckley	.04	.02	.01
☐ 504 Ty Detmer	.40	.18	.05
☐ 505 Brett Favre	2.50	1.10	.30
☐ 506 Johnny Holland	.04	.02	.01
☐ 507 Dexter McNabb	.04	.02	.01
☐ 508 Vince Workman	.10	.05	.01
☐ 509 Cody Carlson	.04	.02	.01
☐ 510 Ernest Givins	.10	.05	.01
☐ 511 Jerry Gray	.04	.02	.01
☐ 512 Haywood Jeffires	.10	.05	.01
☐ 513 Bruce Matthews	.04	.02	.01
☐ 514 Bubba McDowell	.04	.02	.01
☐ 515 Bucky Richardson	.04	.02	.01
☐ 516 Webster Slaughter	.04	.02	.01
☐ 517 Al Smith	.04	.02	.01
☐ 518 Mel Agee	.04	.02	.01
☐ 519 Ashley Ambrose	.10	.05	.01
☐ 520 Kevin Call	.04	.02	.01
☐ 521 Ken Clark	.04	.02	.01
☐ 522 Quentin Coryatt	.25	.11	.03
☐ 523 Steve Emtman	.04	.02	.01
☐ 524 Jeff George	.25	.11	.03
☐ 525 Jessie Hester	.04	.02	.01
☐ 526 Anthony Johnson	.10	.05	.01
☐ 527 Tim Barnett	.04	.02	.01
☐ 528 Martin Bayless	.04	.02	.01
☐ 529 J.J. Birden	.04	.02	.01
☐ 530 Dale Carter	.25	.11	.03
☐ 531 Dave Krieg	.10	.05	.01
☐ 532 Albert Lewis	.04	.02	.01
☐ 533 Nick Lowery	.04	.02	.01
☐ 534 Christian Okoye	.04	.02	.01
☐ 535 Harvey Williams	.25	.11	.03
☐ 536 Aundray Bruce	.04	.02	.01
☐ 537 Eric Dickerson	.10	.05	.01
☐ 538 Willie Gault	.10	.05	.01
☐ 539 Ethan Horton	.04	.02	.01
☐ 540 Jeff Jaeger	.04	.02	.01
☐ 541 Napoleon McCallum	.04	.02	.01
☐ 542 Chester McGlockton	.25	.11	.03
☐ 543 Steve Smith	.04	.02	.01
☐ 544 Steve Wisniewski	.04	.02	.01
☐ 545 Marc Boutte	.04	.02	.01
☐ 546 Pat Carter	.04	.02	.01
☐ 547 Jim Everett	.10	.05	.01
☐ 548 Cleveland Gary	.04	.02	.01
☐ 549 Sean Gilbert	.25	.11	.03
☐ 550 Steve Israel	.04	.02	.01
☐ 551 Todd Kinchen	.04	.02	.01
☐ 552 Jackie Slater	.04	.02	.01
☐ 553 Tony Zendejas	.04	.02	.01
☐ 554 Robert Clark	.04	.02	.01
☐ 555 Mark Clayton	.10	.05	.01
☐ 556 Marco Coleman	.10	.05	.01
☐ 557 Bryan Cox	.10	.05	.01
☐ 558 Keith Jackson UER	.10	.05	.01
(Card says drafted in			
'88, but acquired as			
free agent in '92)			
☐ 559 Dan Marino	1.50	.70	.19
☐ 560 John Offerdahl	.04	.02	.01
☐ 561 Troy Vincent	.10	.05	.01
☐ 562 Richmond Webb	.04	.02	.01
☐ 563 Terry Allen	.40	.18	.05
☐ 564 Cris Carter	.25	.11	.03
☐ 565 Roger Craig	.10	.05	.01
☐ 566 Rich Gannon	.04	.02	.01
☐ 567 Hassan Jones	.04	.02	.01
☐ 568 Randall McDaniel	.04	.02	.01
☐ 569 Al Noga	.04	.02	.01
☐ 570 Todd Scott	.04	.02	.01
☐ 571 Van Waiters	.04	.02	.01
☐ 572 Bruce Armstrong	.04	.02	.01
☐ 573 Gene Chilton	.04	.02	.01
☐ 574 Eugene Chung	.04	.02	.01
☐ 575 Todd Collins	.04	.02	.01
☐ 576 Hart Lee Dykes	.04	.02	.01
☐ 577 David Howard	.04	.02	.01
☐ 578 Eugene Lockhart	.04	.02	.01
☐ 579 Greg McMurtry	.04	.02	.01
☐ 580 Rod Smith DB	.04	.02	.01
☐ 581 Gene Atkins	.04	.02	.01
☐ 582 Vince Buck	.04	.02	.01
☐ 583 Wesley Carroll	.04	.02	.01
☐ 584 Jim Dombrowski	.04	.02	.01
☐ 585 Vaughn Dunbar	.04	.02	.01
☐ 586 Craig Heyward	.10	.05	.01
☐ 587 Dalton Hilliard	.04	.02	.01
☐ 588 Wayne Martin	.04	.02	.01
☐ 589 Renaldo Turnbull	.04	.02	.01
☐ 590 Carl Banks	.04	.02	.01
☐ 591 Derek Brown TE	.04	.02	.01
☐ 592 Jarrod Bunch	.04	.02	.01
☐ 593 Mark Ingram	.04	.02	.01
☐ 594 Ed McCaffrey	.04	.02	.01
☐ 595 Phil Simms	.10	.05	.01
☐ 596 Phillippi Sparks	.04	.02	.01
☐ 597 Lawrence Taylor	.25	.11	.03
☐ 598 Lewis Tillman	.04	.02	.01
☐ 599 Kyle Clifton	.04	.02	.01
☐ 600 Mo Lewis	.04	.02	.01
☐ 601 Terance Mathis	.10	.05	.01
☐ 602 Scott Mersereau	.04	.02	.01
☐ 603 Johnny Mitchell	.04	.02	.01
☐ 604 Browning Nagle	.04	.02	.01
☐ 605 Ken O'Brien	.04	.02	.01
☐ 606 Al Toon	.10	.05	.01
☐ 607 Marvin Washington	.04	.02	.01
☐ 608 Eric Allen	.04	.02	.01
☐ 609 Fred Barnett	.25	.11	.03
☐ 610 John Booty	.04	.02	.01
☐ 611 Randall Cunningham	.10	.05	.01
☐ 612 Rich Miano	.04	.02	.01
☐ 613 Clyde Simmons	.04	.02	.01
☐ 614 Siran Stacy	.04	.02	.01
☐ 615 Herschel Walker	.10	.05	.01
☐ 616 Calvin Williams	.10	.05	.01
☐ 617 Chris Chandler	.10	.05	.01
☐ 618 Randal Hill	.04	.02	.01
☐ 619 Johnny Johnson	.04	.02	.01
☐ 620 Lorenzo Lynch	.04	.02	.01
☐ 621 Robert Massey	.04	.02	.01
☐ 622 Ricky Proehl	.04	.02	.01
☐ 623 Timm Rosenbach	.04	.02	.01
☐ 624 Tony Sacca	.04	.02	.01
☐ 625 Aeneas Williams UER	.10	.05	.01
(Name misspelled			
Aaneas)			
☐ 626 Bubby Brister	.04	.02	.01
☐ 627 Barry Foster	.10	.05	.01
☐ 628 Merril Hoge	.04	.02	.01
☐ 629 D.J. Johnson	.04	.02	.01
☐ 630 David Little	.04	.02	.01
☐ 631 Greg Lloyd	.25	.11	.03
☐ 632 Ernie Mills	.04	.02	.01
☐ 633 Leon Searcy	.10	.05	.01
☐ 634 Dwight Stone	.04	.02	.01
☐ 635 Sam Anno	.04	.02	.01
☐ 636 Burt Grossman	.04	.02	.01
☐ 637 Stan Humphries	.25	.11	.03
☐ 638 Nate Lewis	.04	.02	.01
☐ 639 Anthony Miller	.10	.05	.01
☐ 640 Chris Mims	.25	.11	.03
☐ 641 Marquez Pope	.04	.02	.01
☐ 642 Stanley Richard	.04	.02	.01
☐ 643 Junior Seau	.25	.11	.03
☐ 644 Brian Bollinger	.04	.02	.01
☐ 645 Steve Bono	.25	.11	.03
☐ 646 Dexter Carter	.04	.02	.01
☐ 647 Dana Hall	.10	.05	.01
☐ 648 Amp Lee	.04	.02	.01
☐ 649 Joe Montana	1.00	.45	.12
☐ 650 Tom Rathman	.04	.02	.01
☐ 651 Jerry Rice	1.00	.45	.12
☐ 652 Ricky Watters	.50	.23	.06
☐ 653 Robert Blackmon	.04	.02	.01
☐ 654 John Kasay	.04	.02	.01
☐ 655 Ronnie Lee	.04	.02	.01
☐ 656 Dan McGwire	.04	.02	.01
☐ 657 Ray Roberts	.04	.02	.01
☐ 658 Kelly Stouffer	.04	.02	.01
☐ 659 Chris Warren	.25	.11	.03
☐ 660 Tony Woods	.04	.02	.01
☐ 661 David Wyman	.04	.02	.01
☐ 662 Reggie Cobb	.04	.02	.01
☐ 663A Steve DeBerg ERR	.10	.05	.01
(Career yardage 1455;			
found in foil packs)			
☐ 663B Steve DeBerg COR	.10	.05	.01
(Career yardage 31,455;			
found in jumbo packs)			
☐ 664 Santana Dotson	.25	.11	.03
☐ 665 Willie Drewery	.04	.02	.01
☐ 666 Paul Gruber	.04	.02	.01
☐ 667 Ron Hall	.04	.02	.01
☐ 668 Courtney Hawkins	.10	.05	.01
☐ 669 Charles McRae	.04	.02	.01
☐ 670 Ricky Reynolds	.04	.02	.01
☐ 671 Monte Coleman	.04	.02	.01
☐ 672 Brad Edwards	.04	.02	.01
☐ 673 Jumpy Geathers UER	.04	.02	.01
(Card says played in			
New Orleans in '89;			
should say Washington)			
☐ 674 Kelly Goodburn	.04	.02	.01
☐ 675 Kurt Gouveia	.04	.02	.01
☐ 676 Chris Hakel	.04	.02	.01
☐ 677 Wilber Marshall	.04	.02	.01
☐ 678 Ricky Sanders	.04	.02	.01
☐ 679 Mark Schlereth	.04	.02	.01
☐ 680 Buffalo Bills	.04	.02	.01
Spirit of the Game			
Rich Stadium			
☐ 681 Cincinnati Bengals	.04	.02	.01
Spirit of the Game			
Boomer Esiason			
(with tiger cub)			
☐ 682 Cleveland Browns	.04	.02	.01
Spirit of the Game			
The Dog Pound			
☐ 683 Denver Broncos	.04	.02	.01
Spirit of the Game			
Bronco Statue			
☐ 684 Houston Oilers	.04	.02	.01
Spirit of the Game			
"Luv Ya Blue"			
☐ 685 Indianapolis Colts	.04	.02	.01
Spirit of the Game			
Hoosier Dome			
☐ 686 Kansas City Chiefs	.04	.02	.01
Spirit of the Game			
Mack Lee Hill Award			
Mack Lee Hill			
Tracy Simien			
☐ 687 Los Angeles Raiders	.04	.02	.01
Spirit of the Game			
The Team of the Decades			
☐ 688 Miami Dolphins	.04	.02	.01
Spirit of the Game			
Dolphins' helmet			
☐ 689 New England Patriots	.04	.02	.01
Spirit of the Game			
Francis J. Kilroy VP			
☐ 690 New York Jets	.04	.02	.01
Spirit of the Game			
Team mascot			
☐ 691 Pittsburgh Steelers	.04	.02	.01
Spirit of the Game			
Steelers' helmet			
☐ 692 San Diego Chargers	.04	.02	.01
Spirit of the Game			
Charger in parachute			
☐ 693 Seattle Seahawks	.04	.02	.01
Spirit of the Game			
Kingdome			
☐ 694 Play Smart	.04	.02	.01
Stephen Baker			
☐ 695 Hank Williams Jr. NEWS	.04	.02	.01
☐ 696 3 Brothers in NFL NEWS	.04	.02	.01
Brian Baldinger			
Gary Baldinger			
Rich Baldinger			
☐ 697 Japan Bowl NEWS	.04	.02	.01
August 2, 1992			
☐ 698 Georgia Dome NEWS	.04	.02	.01
☐ 699 Theme Art NEWS	.04	.02	.01
Super Bowl XXVII			
☐ 700 Mark Rypien NEWS	.04	.02	.01
Super Bowl XXVI MVP			
☐ AU150 Emmitt Smith AU	200.00	90.00	25.00
(Certified autograph)			
☐ AU168 Erik Kramer AU	35.00	16.00	4.40
(Certified autograph)			
☐ NNO Emmitt Smith	1.00	.45	.12
Power Preview Card			
☐ NNO Santa Claus	.50	.23	.06
Spirit of the Season			
☐ SC5 Super Bowl XXVI	.20	.09	.03
Logo card			
☐ P1 Cover Card Promo	3.00	1.35	.35
Hologram, numbered of 2000			

1992 Pro Set Emmitt Smith Holograms

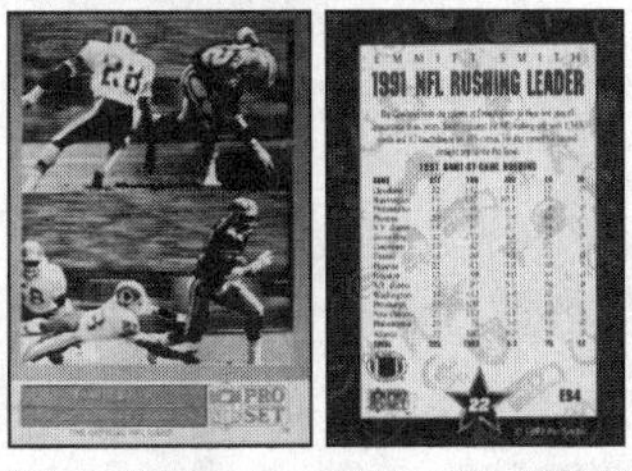

This four-card hologram set was randomly inserted into 1992 Pro Set I foil packs. The ES1 card was the least difficult to find, while the ES4 card was the most difficult. The holograms on the fronts capture different moments in Smith's career, while the red, white, and blue backs present player profile, statistics (1991 and projected), or career summary.

	MINT	NRMT	EXC
COMPLETE SET (4)	60.00	27.00	7.50
COMMON SMITH (ES1-ES4)	6.00	2.70	.75
☐ ES1 Emmitt Smith	6.00	2.70	.75
Stats 1990-1999			
☐ ES2 Emmitt Smith	10.00	4.50	1.25
Drafted by Cowboys			
☐ ES3 Emmitt Smith	20.00	9.00	2.50
'90 Pro Set Offensive			
Rookie of the Year			
☐ ES4 Emmitt Smith	30.00	13.50	3.70
'91 NFL Rushing Leader			

1992 Pro Set Gold MVPs

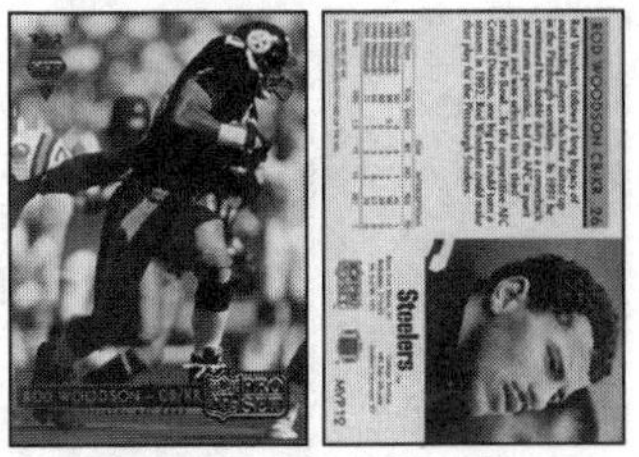

This 30-card standard-size insert set features the most valuable player for each of the 28 NFL teams plus two outstanding coaches. Card numbers 1-15 were offered one per series I jumbo pack, while card numbers 16-30 were inserted one per series II jumbo pack. Series II jumbo pack production was limited to 4,000 numbered cases. The cards differ in design according to series. Series I inserts have full-bleed color action player photos. A diamond-shaped "'92 MVP" emblem appears at the upper right corner, while a gold-foil stamped bar (carrying the player's name) and NFL/Pro Set logo cuts across the bottom. The horizontal backs have career summary, statistics, biography, and a color head shot. Series II inserts have full-bleed color action photos edged on the left by a two-toned stripe. A gray block at the lower left corner carries "MVP" in gold foil. On a screened background, the backs have a color close-up shot and career summary. The set is arranged as follows: AFC "Team MVPs" (1-14), a coach card of Don Shula (15), 14 NFC "Team MVPs" (16-29), and a coach card of Jimmy Johnson (30). All cards are numbered on the back with an "MVP" prefix.

	MINT	NRMT	EXC
COMPLETE SET (30)	15.00	6.75	1.85
COMPLETE SERIES 1 (15)	5.00	2.20	.60
COMPLETE SERIES 2 (15)	10.00	4.50	1.25
COMMON CARD (1-30)	.25	.11	.03
☐ 1 Thurman Thomas	.75	.35	.09
☐ 2 Anthony Munoz	.40	.18	.05
☐ 3 Clay Matthews	.40	.18	.05
☐ 4 John Elway	1.50	.70	.19
☐ 5 Warren Moon	.40	.18	.05
☐ 6 Bill Brooks	.40	.18	.05
☐ 7 Derrick Thomas	.75	.35	.09
☐ 8 Todd Marinovich	.25	.11	.03
☐ 9 Mark Higgs	.25	.11	.03
☐ 10 Leonard Russell	.25	.11	.03
☐ 11 Rob Moore	.40	.18	.05
☐ 12 Rod Woodson	.75	.35	.09
☐ 13 Marion Butts	.25	.11	.03
☐ 14 Brian Blades	.40	.18	.05
☐ 15 Don Shula CO	.40	.18	.05
☐ 16 Deion Sanders	1.25	.55	.16
☐ 17 Neal Anderson	.25	.11	.03
☐ 18 Emmitt Smith	3.00	1.35	.35
☐ 19 Barry Sanders	2.00	.90	.25
☐ 20 Brett Favre	4.00	1.80	.50
☐ 21 Kevin Greene	.75	.35	.09
☐ 22 Terry Allen	.75	.35	.09
☐ 23 Pat Swilling	.25	.11	.03
☐ 24 Rodney Hampton	.75	.35	.09
☐ 25 Randall Cunningham	.40	.18	.05
☐ 26 Randal Hill	.25	.11	.03
☐ 27 Jerry Rice	2.00	.90	.25
☐ 28 Vinny Testaverde	.25	.11	.03
☐ 29 Mark Rypien	.25	.11	.03
☐ 30 Jimmy Johnson CO	.40	.18	.05

1992 Pro Set Ground Force

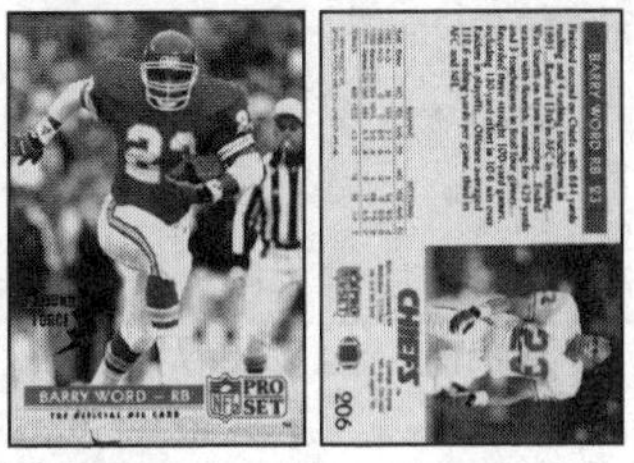

These six standard-size cards were randomly inserted only in foil packs of numbered hobby cases. They are identical in design and numbering to their regular issue counterparts, except that these insert cards are stamped with a gold foil "Ground Force" logo.

	MINT	NRMT	EXC
COMPLETE SET (6)	55.00	25.00	7.00
COMMON (86/118/206/249)	3.00	1.35	.35
☐ 86 Gerald Riggs	3.00	1.35	.35
☐ 105 Thurman Thomas	8.00	3.60	1.00
☐ 118 Neal Anderson	4.00	1.80	.50
☐ 150 Emmitt Smith	40.00	18.00	5.00
☐ 206 Barry Word	3.00	1.35	.35
☐ 249 Leonard Russell	4.00	1.80	.50

1992 Pro Set HOF Inductees

This "Special Collectibles" subset was issued as a random insert with 1992 Pro Set first series packs. These standard-size cards are numbered with an "SC" prefix and feature the 1992 Pro Football Hall of Fame induction class.

	MINT	NRMT	EXC
COMPLETE SET (4)	1.50	.70	.19
COMMON CARD (SC1-SC4)	.40	.18	.05
☐ SC1 Lem Barney	.40	.18	.05
☐ SC2 Al Davis	.40	.18	.05

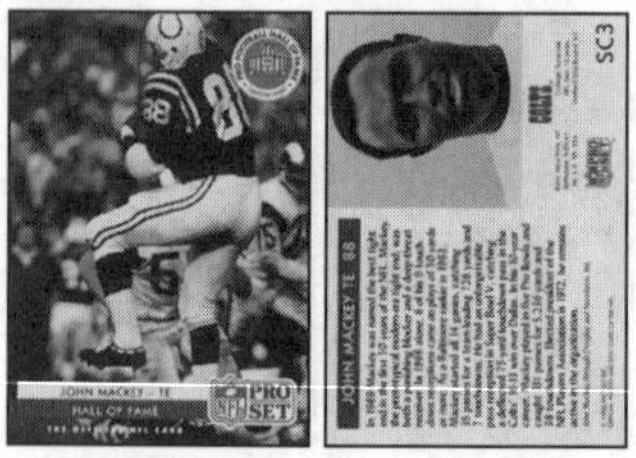

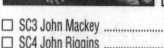

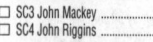

	MINT	NRMT	EXC
☐ SC3 John Mackey	.40	.18	.05
☐ SC4 John Riggins	.60	.25	.07

1992 Pro Set HOF 2000

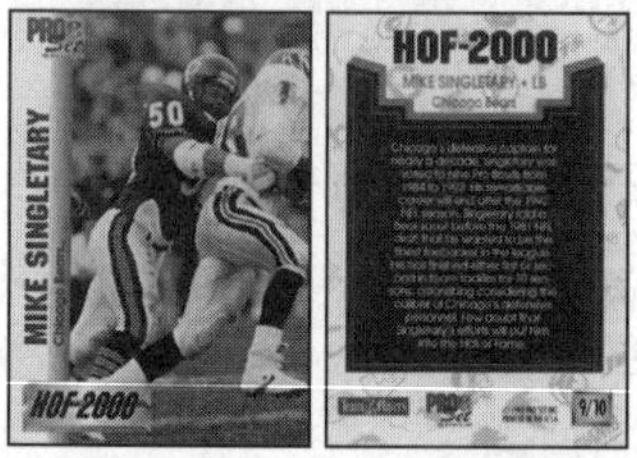

This ten-card standard size set features ten of the NFL's all-time top players whom Pro Set predicts are worthy candidates for the Hall of Fame in the beginning of the next century. The cards were randomly inserted in series II foil packs. The fronts are like the regular issue Pro Set series, with full-bleed color action photos edged on the left a two-toned stripe, except that "HOF-2000" is gold-foil stamped on two horizontal bars at the lower left corner. On the backs, a purple panel on a screened background summarizes the player's career. The cards are numbered on the back "X/10."

	MINT	NRMT	EXC
COMPLETE SET (10)	20.00	9.00	2.50
COMMON CARD (1-10)	1.50	.70	.19
☐ 1 Marcus Allen	4.00	1.80	.50
☐ 2 Richard Dent	1.50	.70	.19
☐ 3 Eric Dickerson	2.00	.90	.25
☐ 4 Ronnie Lott	3.00	1.35	.35
☐ 5 Art Monk	2.00	.90	.25
☐ 6 Joe Montana	8.00	3.60	1.00
☐ 7 Warren Moon	2.00	.90	.25
☐ 8 Anthony Munoz	1.50	.70	.19
☐ 9 Mike Singletary	2.00	.90	.25
☐ 10 Lawrence Taylor	3.00	1.35	.35

1992 Pro Set Club

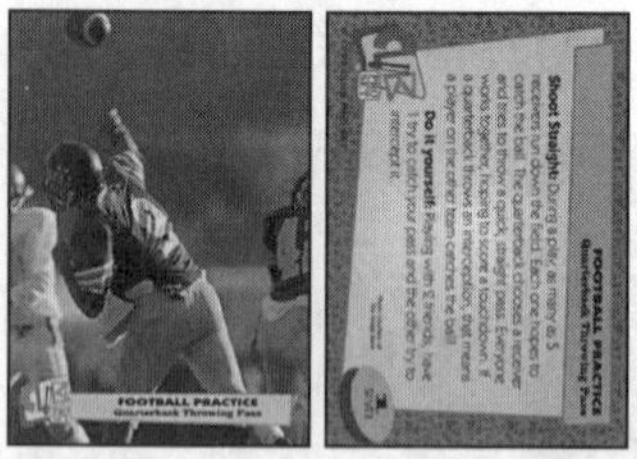

The theme of the 1992 Pro Set Club set is "Football Practice." Each of the nine cards measures the standard-size. The full-bleed color photos on the fronts illustrate various aspects of the game. The card subtitle appears in a pastel purple bar superimposed over the picture toward the bottom. At the left end of the bar is the Pro Set Club logo. On a yellow panel inside a turquoise bordered speckled with green, the backs discuss how to play football and challenge the reader to "do it yourself," "think about it," "check it out," or "take a look."

	MINT	NRMT	EXC
COMPLETE SET (9)	6.00	2.70	.75
COMMON CARD (1-9)	.75	.35	.09
☐ 1 Quarterback Throwing	1.00	.45	.12
Pass			
☐ 2 Coach Reviewing Play	.75	.35	.09
Strategy			
☐ 3 Team Stretching	.75	.35	.09
☐ 4 Offensive Play	.75	.35	.09
☐ 5 Kickoff	.75	.35	.09
☐ 6 Player's Stance	.75	.35	.09
☐ 7 Football Is a	.75	.35	.09
Spectator Sport			
☐ 8 Defensive Practice	.75	.35	.09
☐ 9 Play in Motion	.75	.35	.09

1992 Pro Set Emmitt Smith Promo Sheet

Pro Set produced this 5-card sheet to announce Emmitt Smith as the company spokesman for Pro Set. The sheet features reprints of Smith's past Pro Set cards up to that time: 1990, 1991, 1991

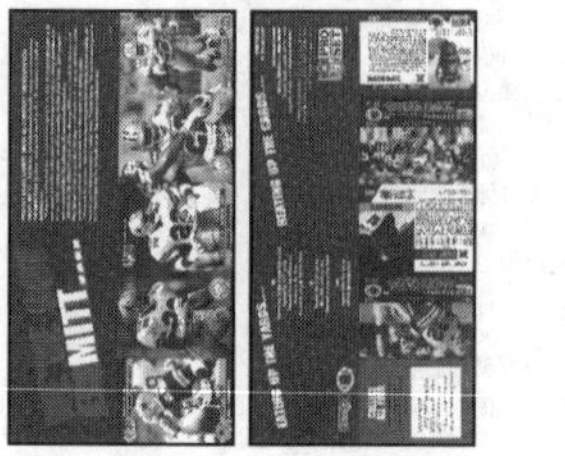

Platinum, 1991 Platinum Game Breaker, and 1992 with a checklist back. Each sheet is numbered of 2000 produced and measures approximately 7" by 13."

	MINT	NRMT	EXC
COMPLETE SET (1)	10.00	4.50	1.25
COMMON SHEET	10.00	4.50	1.25
☐ NNO Emmitt Smith Sheet	10.00	4.50	1.25
five cards featured			
numbered of 2000			

1992-93 Pro Set Super Bowl XXVII

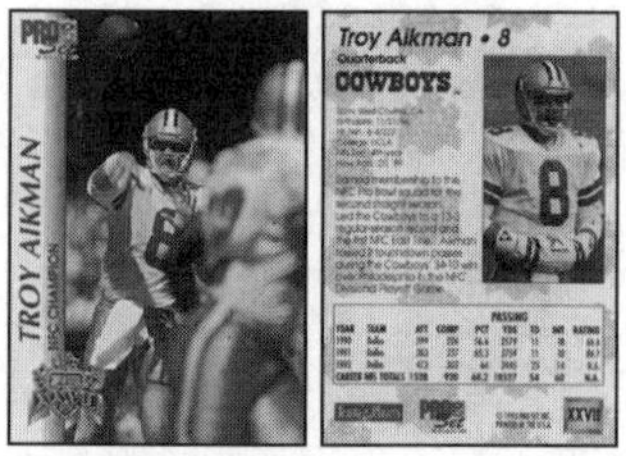

Produced by Pro Set to commemorate Super Bowl XXVII, this 38-card standard-size set was packaged in two cello packs. For those who paid admission to Super Bowl XXVII, January 31, 1993, in Pasadena, a set was inserted into the GTE seat cushion. The set was also available through mail-order for 22.00 plus either a Dallas Cowboys or Buffalo Bills mini-binder. Just 7,000 sets were produced for the mail-away offer. The cards have the same design as the regular issue except for the following differences: 1) all cards have a Super Bowl XXVII emblem on their fronts; 2) the Bills' and the Cowboys' cards have AFC Champion and NFC Champion respectively printed beneath the player's name; and 3) all the backs have a screened background of Super Bowl XXVII emblems. The set includes an AFL Conference logo card (1), Buffalo Bills (2-18), an NFL Conference logo card (19), Dallas Cowboys (20-36), a Newsreel card (37), and a card of Marco Coleman (701), the 1992 Pro Set Rookie of the Year. With the exception of the Coleman, all the cards are numbered on the back "XXVII" and checklisted below in alphabetical order within teams.

	MINT	NRMT	EXC
COMPLETE SET (38)	12.00	5.50	1.50
COMMON CARD (1-37)	.20	.09	.03
☐ 1 AFC Logo	.20	.09	.03
☐ 2 Cornelius Bennett	.30	.14	.04
☐ 3 Steve Christie	.20	.09	.03
☐ 4 Shane Conlan	.20	.09	.03
☐ 5 Matt Darby	.20	.09	.03
☐ 6 Kenneth Davis	.20	.09	.03
☐ 7 John Fina	.20	.09	.03
☐ 8 Henry Jones	.20	.09	.03
☐ 9 Jim Kelly	.75	.35	.09
☐ 10 Marv Levy CO	.20	.09	.03
☐ 11 James Lofton	.30	.14	.04
☐ 12 Pete Metzelaars	.20	.09	.03
☐ 13 Nate Odomes	.20	.09	.03
☐ 14 Andre Reed	.50	.23	.06
☐ 15 Bruce Smith	.50	.23	.06
☐ 16 Darryl Talley	.20	.09	.03
☐ 17 Steve Tasker	.20	.09	.03
☐ 18 Thurman Thomas	.75	.35	.09
☐ 19 NFC Logo	.20	.09	.03
☐ 20 Troy Aikman	2.50	1.10	.30
☐ 21 Steve Beuerlein	.20	.09	.03
☐ 22 Tony Casillas	.20	.09	.03
☐ 23 Kenneth Gant	.20	.09	.03
☐ 24 Charles Haley	.30	.14	.04
☐ 25 Alvin Harper	.20	.09	.03
☐ 26 Michael Irvin	.75	.35	.09
☐ 27 Jimmy Johnson CO	.30	.14	.04
☐ 28 Robert Jones	.20	.09	.03
☐ 29 Russell Maryland	.20	.09	.03
☐ 30 Nate Newton	.20	.09	.03
☐ 31 Ken Norton Jr.	.30	.14	.04
☐ 32 Jay Novacek	.30	.14	.04
☐ 33 Emmitt Smith	5.00	2.20	.60
☐ 34 Kevin Smith	.20	.09	.03
☐ 35 Mark Stepnoski	.20	.09	.03
☐ 36 Tony Tolbert	.20	.09	.03
☐ 37 Newsreel Art	.20	.09	.03
Super Bowl XXVII			
☐ 701 Marco Coleman PS-ROY	.20	.09	.03

1993 Pro Set Promos

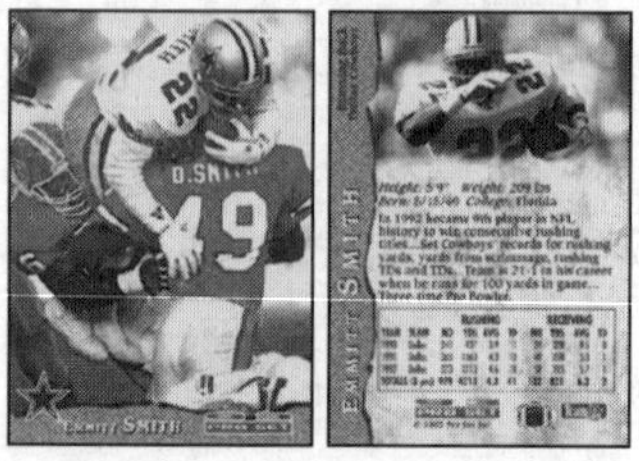

These six standard-size cards were distributed to dealers, promoters, and card show attendees to promote the release of the 1993 Pro Set issue. The six cards were also issued in an uncut ten-card 8" by 13 1/2" sheet, the bottom row of which consisted of five copies of the Emmitt Smith card. The fronts feature color player action shots that are borderless, except at the bottom, where the photo appears to be torn away, revealing an irregular gray stripe that carries the player's name in team color-coded lettering. On the regular series cards, the color of this stripe varies, reflecting the team's primary color. The back appears to be torn away on the left edge, revealing a gray stripe that carries the player's name in vertical team color-coded lettering, and his position and team in black lettering. A color player action photo is displayed at the top, which blends into a grayish background that carries the player's biography, career highlights, and stats. On the regular cards, the stat box has a white background rather than a grayish one. The cards are unnumbered and checklisted below in alphabetical order.

	MINT	NRMT	EXC
COMPLETE SET (6)	7.00	3.10	.85
COMMON CARD (1-6)	.75	.35	.09
☐ 1 Jerome Bettis	1.50	.70	.19
☐ 2 Reggie Brooks	1.00	.45	.12
☐ 3 Cortez Kennedy	.75	.35	.09
☐ 4 Junior Seau	1.00	.45	.12
☐ 5 Emmitt Smith	3.00	1.35	.35
☐ 6 Wade Wilson	.75	.35	.09

1993 Pro Set

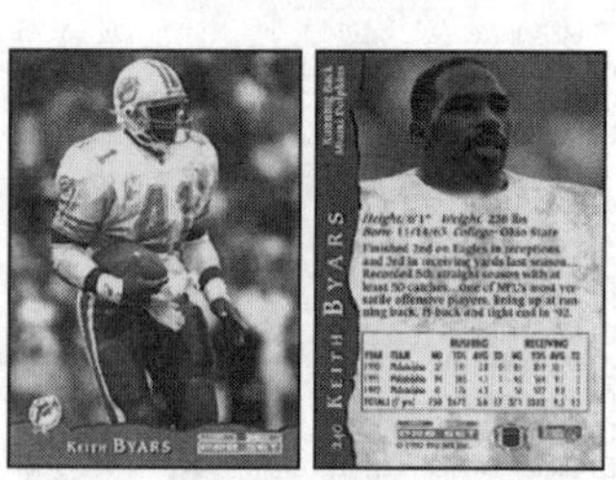

The 1993 Pro Set football set was issued in one series of 449 standard-size cards. Including foil and jumbo cases, a total of 15,000 cases were reportedly produced. Cards were issued in 15-card foil packs and 32-card jumbo packs. The fronts feature color player action shots that are borderless, except at the bottom, where the photo appears to be torn away, revealing an irregular team color-coded stripe that carries the player's name in white lettering. The back appears to be torn away on the left edge, revealing a team color-coded stripe that carries the player's name, position, and team in vertical white lettering. A color player action photo is displayed at the top, which blends into a grayish background that carries his biography, career highlights, and stats. After an 18-card Stat Leader subset (1-18) and an 11-card Replay 1992 subset (19-29), the cards are checklisted below according to teams. Rookie Cards include Jerome Bettis, Drew Bledsoe, Vincent Brisby, Reggie Brooks, Derek Brown, Mark Brunell, Curtis Conway, Garrison Hearst, Billy Joe Hobert, Qadry Ismail, Terry Kirby, O.J. McDuffie, Rick Mirer, Natrone Means, Glyn Milburn, Ronald Moore, Robert Smith, Dana Stubblefield and Kevin Williams.

	MINT	NRMT	EXC
COMPLETE SET (449)	14.00	6.25	1.75
COMMON CARD (1-449)	.05	.02	.01
☐ 1 Marco Coleman	.05	.02	.01
Rookie of the Year			
☐ 2 Steve Young	.30	.14	.04
Player of the Year			
☐ 3 Mike Holmgren	.10	.05	.01
Coach of the Year			
☐ 4 John Elway	.30	.14	.04
Man of the Year			
☐ 5 Steve Young	.30	.14	.04
Passing Leader			
☐ 6 Dan Marino	1.00	.45	.12
Passing Yardage			
☐ 7 Emmitt Smith	1.00	.45	.12
Rushing Leader			
☐ 8 Sterling Sharpe	.10	.05	.01
Receiving Leader			
☐ 9 Jay Novacek	.10	.05	.01
Receiving TE			
☐ 10 Sterling Sharpe	.10	.05	.01
Receiving Yardage			
☐ 11 Thurman Thomas	.10	.05	.01
Total Yardage			
☐ 12 Pete Stoyanovich	.05	.02	.01
Scoring Leader			
☐ 13 Greg Montgomery	.05	.02	.01
Punting Leader			
☐ 14 Johnny Bailey	.05	.02	.01
Punt Return			
☐ 15 Jon Vaughn	.05	.02	.01
Kickoff Return			
☐ 16 Audray McMillian	.05	.02	.01
Henry Jones UER			
Interception			
(Name spelled McMillan on back)			
☐ 17 Clyde Simmons	.05	.02	.01
Sack Leader			
☐ 18 Cortez Kennedy	.05	.02	.01
Defensive MVP			
☐ 19 AFC Wildcard	.05	.02	.01
(Stan Humphries)			
☐ 20 AFC Wildcard	.05	.02	.01
(Don Beebe)			
☐ 21 NFC Wildcard	.05	.02	.01
(Eric Allen)			
☐ 22 NFC Wildcard	.05	.02	.01
(Brian Mitchell)			
☐ 23 AFC Divisional	.05	.02	.01
(Frank Reich)			
☐ 24 AFC Divisional	1.00	.45	.12
(Dan Marino)			
☐ 25 NFC Divisional	.50	.23	.06
(Troy Aikman)			
☐ 26 NFC Divisional	.10	.05	.01
(Ricky Watters)			
☐ 27 AFC Championship	.05	.02	.01
(Bruce Smith sacking			
(Dan Marino)			
☐ 28 NFC Championship	.05	.02	.01
(Tony Casillas sacking			
(Steve Young)			
☐ 29 Super Bowl XXVIII Logo	.05	.02	.01
☐ 30 Troy Aikman	1.00	.45	.12
☐ 31 Thomas Everett	.05	.02	.01
☐ 32 Charles Haley	.10	.05	.01
☐ 33 Alvin Harper	.10	.05	.01
☐ 34 Michael Irvin	.25	.11	.03
☐ 35 Robert Jones	.05	.02	.01
☐ 36 Russell Maryland	.05	.02	.01
☐ 37 Ken Norton	.10	.05	.01
☐ 38 Jay Novacek	.10	.05	.01
☐ 39 Emmitt Smith	2.00	.90	.25
☐ 40 Darrin Smith	.10	.05	.01
☐ 41 Mark Stepnoski	.05	.02	.01
☐ 42 Kevin Williams	.25	.11	.03
☐ 43 Daryl Johnston	.25	.11	.03
☐ 44 Derrick Lassic	.05	.02	.01
☐ 45 Don Beebe	.05	.02	.01
☐ 46 Cornelius Bennett	.10	.05	.01
☐ 47 Bill Brooks	.05	.02	.01
☐ 48 Kenneth Davis	.05	.02	.01
☐ 49 Jim Kelly	.25	.11	.03
☐ 50 Andre Reed	.10	.05	.01
☐ 51 Bruce Smith	.25	.11	.03
☐ 52 Thomas Smith	.10	.05	.01
☐ 53 Darryl Talley	.05	.02	.01
☐ 54 Thurman Thomas	.25	.11	.03
☐ 55 Russell Copeland	.10	.05	.01
☐ 56 Steve Christie	.05	.02	.01
☐ 57 Pete Metzelaars	.05	.02	.01
☐ 58 Frank Reich	.10	.05	.01
☐ 59 Henry Jones	.05	.02	.01
☐ 60 Vinnie Clark	.05	.02	.01
☐ 61 Eric Dickerson	.10	.05	.01
☐ 62 Jumpy Geathers	.05	.02	.01
☐ 63 Roger Harper	.05	.02	.01
☐ 64 Michael Haynes	.10	.05	.01
☐ 65 Bobby Hebert	.05	.02	.01
☐ 66 Lincoln Kennedy	.05	.02	.01
☐ 67 Chris Miller	.10	.05	.01
☐ 68 Andre Rison	.10	.05	.01
☐ 69 Deion Sanders	.60	.25	.07
☐ 70 Jessie Tuggle	.05	.02	.01
☐ 71 Ron George	.05	.02	.01
☐ 72 Erric Pegram	.10	.05	.01
☐ 73 Melvin Jenkins	.05	.02	.01
☐ 74 Pierce Holt	.05	.02	.01
☐ 75 Neal Anderson	.05	.02	.01
☐ 76 Mark Carrier DB	.05	.02	.01
☐ 77 Curtis Conway	.75	.35	.09
☐ 78 Richard Dent	.10	.05	.01
☐ 79 Jim Harbaugh	.25	.11	.03
☐ 80 Craig Heyward	.10	.05	.01
☐ 81 Darren Lewis	.05	.02	.01
☐ 82 Alonzo Spellman	.05	.02	.01
☐ 83 Tom Waddle	.05	.02	.01
☐ 84 Wendell Davis	.05	.02	.01
☐ 85 Chris Zorich	.05	.02	.01
☐ 86 Carl Simpson	.05	.02	.01
☐ 87 Chris Gedney	.05	.02	.01
☐ 88 Trace Armstrong	.05	.02	.01
☐ 89 Peter Tom Willis	.05	.02	.01
☐ 90 John Copeland	.10	.05	.01
☐ 91 Derrick Fenner	.05	.02	.01
☐ 92 James Francis	.05	.02	.01
☐ 93 Harold Green	.05	.02	.01

☐ 94 David Klingler	.05	.02	.01
☐ 95 Tim Krumrie	.05	.02	.01
☐ 96 Tony McGee	.10	.05	.01
☐ 97 Carl Pickens	.75	.35	.09
☐ 98 Alfred Williams	.05	.02	.01
☐ 99 Doug Pelfrey	.05	.02	.01
☐ 100 Lance Gunn	.05	.02	.01
☐ 101 Jay Schroeder	.05	.02	.01
☐ 102 Steve Tovar	.05	.02	.01
☐ 103 Jeff Query	.05	.02	.01
☐ 104 Ty Parten	.05	.02	.01
☐ 105 Jerry Ball	.05	.02	.01
☐ 106 Mark Carrier WR	.10	.05	.01
☐ 107 Rob Burnett	.05	.02	.01
☐ 108 Michael Jackson	.10	.05	.01
☐ 109 Mike Johnson	.05	.02	.01
☐ 110 Bernie Kosar	.10	.05	.01
☐ 111 Clay Matthews	.10	.05	.01
☐ 112 Eric Metcalf	.10	.05	.01
☐ 113 Michael Dean Perry	.10	.05	.01
☐ 114 Vinny Testaverde	.10	.05	.01
☐ 115 Eric Turner	.05	.02	.01
☐ 116 Tommy Vardell	.05	.02	.01
☐ 117 Leroy Hoard	.10	.05	.01
☐ 118 Steve Everitt	.05	.02	.01
☐ 119 Everson Walls	.05	.02	.01
☐ 120 Steve Atwater	.05	.02	.01
☐ 121 Rod Bernstine	.05	.02	.01
☐ 122 Mike Croel	.05	.02	.01
☐ 123 John Elway	.75	.35	.09
☐ 124 Simon Fletcher	.05	.02	.01
☐ 125 Glyn Milburn	.25	.11	.03
☐ 126 Reggie Rivers	.05	.02	.01
☐ 127 Shannon Sharpe	.25	.11	.03
☐ 128 Dennis Smith	.05	.02	.01
☐ 129 Dan Williams	.05	.02	.01
☐ 130 Rondell Jones	.05	.02	.01
☐ 131 Jason Elam	.05	.02	.01
☐ 132 Arthur Marshall	.05	.02	.01
☐ 133 Gary Zimmerman	.05	.02	.01
☐ 134 Karl Mecklenburg	.05	.02	.01
☐ 135 Bennie Blades	.05	.02	.01
☐ 136 Lomas Brown	.05	.02	.01
☐ 137 Bill Fralic	.05	.02	.01
☐ 138 Mel Gray	.10	.05	.01
☐ 139 Willie Green	.05	.02	.01
☐ 140 Ryan McNeil	.05	.02	.01
☐ 141 Rodney Peete	.05	.02	.01
☐ 142 Barry Sanders	1.00	.45	.12
☐ 143 Chris Spielman	.10	.05	.01
☐ 144 Pat Swilling	.05	.02	.01
☐ 145 Andre Ware	.05	.02	.01
☐ 146 Herman Moore	.75	.35	.09
☐ 147 Tim McKyer	.05	.02	.01
☐ 148 Brett Perriman	.25	.11	.03
☐ 149 Antonio London	.05	.02	.01
☐ 150 Edgar Bennett	.25	.11	.03
☐ 151 Terrell Buckley	.05	.02	.01
☐ 152 Brett Favre	2.00	.90	.25
☐ 153 Jackie Harris	.05	.02	.01
☐ 154 Johnny Holland	.05	.02	.01
☐ 155 Sterling Sharpe	.25	.11	.03
☐ 156 Tim Hauck	.05	.02	.01
☐ 157 George Teague	.10	.05	.01
☐ 158 Reggie White	.25	.11	.03
☐ 159 Mark Clayton	.05	.02	.01
☐ 160 Ty Detmer	.25	.11	.03
☐ 161 Wayne Simmons	.05	.02	.01
☐ 162 Mark Brunell	3.00	1.35	.35
☐ 163 Tony Bennett	.05	.02	.01
☐ 164 Brian Noble	.05	.02	.01
☐ 165 Cody Carlson	.05	.02	.01
☐ 166 Ray Childress	.05	.02	.01
☐ 167 Cris Dishman	.05	.02	.01
☐ 168 Curtis Duncan	.05	.02	.01
☐ 169 Brad Hopkins	.05	.02	.01
☐ 170 Haywood Jeffires	.10	.05	.01
☐ 171 Wilber Marshall	.05	.02	.01
☐ 172 Micheal Barrow UER	.05	.02	.01
(Name spelled Michael on both sided)			
☐ 173 Bubba McDowell	.05	.02	.01
☐ 174 Warren Moon	.25	.11	.03
☐ 175 Webster Slaughter	.05	.02	.01
☐ 176 Travis Hannah	.05	.02	.01
☐ 177 Lorenzo White	.05	.02	.01
☐ 178 Ernest Givins UER	.10	.05	.01
(Name spelled Givens on front)			
☐ 179 Keith McCants	.05	.02	.01
☐ 180 Kerry Cash	.05	.02	.01
☐ 181 Quentin Coryatt	.10	.05	.01
☐ 182 Kirk Lowdermilk	.05	.02	.01
☐ 183 Rodney Culver	.05	.02	.01
☐ 184 Rohn Stark	.05	.02	.01
☐ 185 Steve Emtman	.05	.02	.01
☐ 186 Jeff George	.25	.11	.03
☐ 187 Jeff Herrod	.05	.02	.01
☐ 188 Reggie Langhorne	.05	.02	.01
☐ 189 Roosevelt Potts	.05	.02	.01
☐ 190 Jack Trudeau	.05	.02	.01
☐ 191 Will Wolford	.05	.02	.01
☐ 192 Jessie Hester	.05	.02	.01
☐ 193 Anthony Johnson	.10	.05	.01
☐ 194 Ray Buchanan	.05	.02	.01
☐ 195 Dale Carter	.05	.02	.01
☐ 196 Willie Davis	.25	.11	.03
☐ 197 John Alt	.05	.02	.01
☐ 198 Joe Montana	1.00	.45	.12
☐ 199 Will Shields	.05	.02	.01
☐ 200 Neil Smith	.25	.11	.03
☐ 201 Derrick Thomas	.25	.11	.03
☐ 202 Harvey Williams	.10	.05	.01
☐ 203 Marcus Allen	.25	.11	.03
☐ 204 J.J. Birden	.05	.02	.01
☐ 205 Tim Barnett	.05	.02	.01
☐ 206 Albert Lewis	.05	.02	.01
☐ 207 Nick Lowery	.05	.02	.01
☐ 208 Dave Krieg	.10	.05	.01
☐ 209 Keith Cash	.05	.02	.01
☐ 210 Patrick Bates	.05	.02	.01
☐ 211 Nick Bell	.05	.02	.01
☐ 212 Tim Brown	.25	.11	.03
☐ 213 Willie Gault	.05	.02	.01
☐ 214 Ethan Horton	.05	.02	.01
☐ 215 Jeff Hostetler	.10	.05	.01
☐ 216 Howie Long	.10	.05	.01
☐ 217 Greg Townsend	.05	.02	.01
☐ 218 Raghib Ismail	.10	.05	.01
☐ 219 Alexander Wright	.05	.02	.01
☐ 220 Greg Robinson	.05	.02	.01
☐ 221 Billy Joe Hobert	.40	.18	.05
☐ 222 Steve Wisniewski	.05	.02	.01
☐ 223 Steve Smith	.05	.02	.01
☐ 224 Vince Evans	.05	.02	.01
☐ 225 Flipper Anderson	.05	.02	.01
☐ 226 Jerome Bettis	1.50	.70	.19
☐ 227 Troy Drayton	.10	.05	.01
☐ 228 Henry Ellard	.10	.05	.01
☐ 229 Jim Everett	.10	.05	.01
☐ 230 Tony Zendejas	.05	.02	.01
☐ 231 Todd Lyght	.05	.02	.01
☐ 232 Todd Kinchen	.05	.02	.01
☐ 233 Jackie Slater	.05	.02	.01
☐ 234 Fred Stokes	.05	.02	.01
☐ 235 Russell White	.10	.05	.01
☐ 236 Cleveland Gary	.05	.02	.01
☐ 237 Sean LaChapelle	.05	.02	.01
☐ 238 Steve Israel	.05	.02	.01
☐ 239 Shane Conlan	.05	.02	.01
☐ 240 Keith Byars	.05	.02	.01
☐ 241 Marco Coleman	.05	.02	.01
☐ 242 Bryan Cox	.05	.02	.01
☐ 243 Irving Fryar	.10	.05	.01
☐ 244 Richmond Webb	.05	.02	.01
☐ 245 Mark Higgs	.05	.02	.01
☐ 246 Terry Kirby	.40	.18	.05
☐ 247 Mark Ingram	.05	.02	.01
☐ 248 John Offerdahl	.05	.02	.01
☐ 249 Keith Jackson	.10	.05	.01
☐ 250 Dan Marino	2.00	.90	.25
☐ 251 O.J. McDuffie	.75	.35	.09
☐ 252 Louis Oliver	.05	.02	.01
☐ 253 Pete Stoyanovich	.05	.02	.01
☐ 254 Troy Vincent	.05	.02	.01
☐ 255 Anthony Carter	.10	.05	.01
☐ 256 Cris Carter	.25	.11	.03
☐ 257 Roger Craig	.10	.05	.01
☐ 258 Jack Del Rio	.05	.02	.01
☐ 259 Chris Doleman	.05	.02	.01
☐ 260 Barry Word	.05	.02	.01
☐ 261 Qadry Ismail	.25	.11	.03
☐ 262 Jim McMahon	.05	.02	.01
☐ 263 Robert Smith	.75	.35	.09
☐ 264 Fred Strickland	.05	.02	.01
☐ 265 Randall McDaniel	.05	.02	.01
☐ 266 Carl Lee	.05	.02	.01
☐ 267 Olanda Truitt UER	.05	.02	.01
(Name spelled Olanda on front)			
☐ 268 Terry Allen	.25	.11	.03
☐ 269 Audray McMillian	.05	.02	.01
☐ 270 Drew Bledsoe	3.00	1.35	.35
☐ 271 Eugene Chung	.05	.02	.01
☐ 272 Marv Cook	.05	.02	.01
☐ 273 Pat Harlow	.05	.02	.01
☐ 274 Greg McMurtry	.05	.02	.01
☐ 275 Leonard Russell	.10	.05	.01
☐ 276 Chris Slade	.10	.05	.01
☐ 277 Andre Tippett	.05	.02	.01
☐ 278 Vincent Brisby	.25	.11	.03
☐ 279 Ben Coates	.50	.23	.06
☐ 280 Sam Gash	.05	.02	.01
☐ 281 Bruce Armstrong	.05	.02	.01
☐ 282 Rod Smith DB	.05	.02	.01
☐ 283 Michael Timpson	.05	.02	.01
☐ 284 Scott Sisson	.05	.02	.01
☐ 285 Morten Andersen	.05	.02	.01
☐ 286 Reggie Freeman	.05	.02	.01
☐ 287 Dalton Hilliard	.05	.02	.01
☐ 288 Rickey Jackson	.05	.02	.01
☐ 289 Vaughan Johnson	.05	.02	.01
☐ 290 Eric Martin	.05	.02	.01
☐ 291 Sam Mills	.05	.02	.01
☐ 292 Brad Muster	.05	.02	.01
☐ 293 William Roaf	.10	.05	.01
☐ 294 Irv Smith	.05	.02	.01
☐ 295 Wade Wilson	.05	.02	.01
☐ 296 Derek Brown RB	.10	.05	.01
☐ 297 Quinn Early	.10	.05	.01
☐ 298 Steve Walsh	.05	.02	.01
☐ 299 Renaldo Turnbull	.05	.02	.01
☐ 300 Jessie Armstead	.05	.02	.01
☐ 301 Carlton Bailey	.05	.02	.01
☐ 302 Michael Brooks	.05	.02	.01
☐ 303 Rodney Hampton	.25	.11	.03
☐ 304 Ed McCaffrey	.05	.02	.01
☐ 305 Dave Meggett	.05	.02	.01
☐ 306 Bart Oates	.05	.02	.01
☐ 307 Mike Sherrard	.05	.02	.01
☐ 308 Phil Simms	.10	.05	.01
☐ 309 Lawrence Taylor	.25	.11	.03
☐ 310 Mark Jackson	.05	.02	.01
☐ 311 Jarrod Bunch	.05	.02	.01
☐ 312 Howard Cross	.05	.02	.01
☐ 313 Michael Strahan	.05	.02	.01
☐ 314 Marcus Buckley	.05	.02	.01
☐ 315 Brad Baxter	.05	.02	.01
☐ 316 Adrian Murrell	.75	.35	.09
☐ 317 Boomer Esiason	.10	.05	.01
☐ 318 Johnny Johnson	.05	.02	.01
☐ 319 Marvin Jones	.05	.02	.01
☐ 320 Jeff Lageman	.05	.02	.01
☐ 321 Ronnie Lott	.10	.05	.01
☐ 322 Leonard Marshall	.05	.02	.01
☐ 323 Johnny Mitchell	.05	.02	.01
☐ 324 Rob Moore	.10	.05	.01
☐ 325 Browning Nagle	.05	.02	.01
☐ 326 Blair Thomas	.05	.02	.01
☐ 327 Brian Washington	.05	.02	.01
☐ 328 Terance Mathis	.10	.05	.01
☐ 329 Kyle Clifton	.05	.02	.01
☐ 330 Eric Allen	.05	.02	.01
☐ 331 Victor Bailey	.05	.02	.01
☐ 332 Fred Barnett	.10	.05	.01
☐ 333 Mark Bavaro	.05	.02	.01
☐ 334 Randall Cunningham	.10	.05	.01
☐ 335 Ken O'Brien	.05	.02	.01
☐ 336 Seth Joyner	.05	.02	.01
☐ 337 Leonard Renfro	.05	.02	.01
☐ 338 Heath Sherman	.05	.02	.01
☐ 339 Clyde Simmons	.05	.02	.01
☐ 340 Herschel Walker	.10	.05	.01
☐ 341 Calvin Williams	.10	.05	.01
☐ 342 Bubby Brister	.05	.02	.01
☐ 343 Vaughn Hebron	.05	.02	.01
☐ 344 Keith Millard	.05	.02	.01
☐ 345 Johnny Bailey	.05	.02	.01
☐ 346 Steve Beuerlein	.05	.02	.01
☐ 347 Chuck Cecil	.05	.02	.01
☐ 348 Larry Centers	.40	.18	.05
☐ 349 Chris Chandler	.10	.05	.01
☐ 350 Ernest Dye	.05	.02	.01
☐ 351 Garrison Hearst	1.00	.45	.12
☐ 352 Randal Hill	.05	.02	.01
☐ 353 John Booty	.05	.02	.01
☐ 354 Gary Clark	.10	.05	.01
☐ 355 Ronald Moore	.10	.05	.01
☐ 356 Ricky Proehl	.05	.02	.01
☐ 357 Eric Swann	.10	.05	.01
☐ 358 Ken Harvey	.05	.02	.01
☐ 359 Ben Coleman	.05	.02	.01
☐ 360 Deon Figures	.10	.05	.01
☐ 361 Barry Foster	.10	.05	.01
☐ 362 Jeff Graham	.10	.05	.01
☐ 363 Eric Green	.05	.02	.01
☐ 364 Kevin Greene	.25	.11	.03
☐ 365 Andre Hastings	.25	.11	.03
☐ 366 Greg Lloyd	.25	.11	.03
☐ 367 Neil O'Donnell	.25	.11	.03
☐ 368 Dwight Stone	.05	.02	.01
☐ 369 Mike Tomczak	.05	.02	.01
☐ 370 Rod Woodson	.25	.11	.03
☐ 371 Chad Brown	.10	.05	.01
☐ 372 Ernie Mills	.05	.02	.01
☐ 373 Darren Perry	.05	.02	.01
☐ 374 Leon Searcy	.05	.02	.01
☐ 375 Marion Butts	.05	.02	.01
☐ 376 John Carney	.05	.02	.01
☐ 377 Ronnie Harmon	.05	.02	.01
☐ 378 Stan Humphries	.25	.11	.03
☐ 379 Nate Lewis	.05	.02	.01
☐ 380 Natrone Means	1.00	.45	.12
☐ 381 Anthony Miller	.10	.05	.01
☐ 382 Chris Mims	.05	.02	.01
☐ 383 Leslie O'Neal	.10	.05	.01
☐ 384 Joe Cocozzo	.05	.02	.01
☐ 385 Junior Seau	.25	.11	.03
☐ 386 Jerrol Williams	.05	.02	.01
☐ 387 John Friesz	.10	.05	.01
☐ 388 Darrien Gordon	.05	.02	.01
☐ 389 Derrick Walker	.05	.02	.01
☐ 390 Dana Hall	.05	.02	.01
☐ 391 Brent Jones	.10	.05	.01
☐ 392 Todd Kelly	.05	.02	.01
☐ 393 Amp Lee	.05	.02	.01
☐ 394 Tim McDonald	.05	.02	.01
☐ 395 Jerry Rice	1.00	.45	.12
☐ 396 Dana Stubblefield	.25	.11	.03
☐ 397 John Taylor	.10	.05	.01
☐ 398 Ricky Watters	.25	.11	.03
☐ 399 Steve Young	.75	.35	.09
☐ 400 Steve Bono	.25	.11	.03
☐ 401 Adrian Hardy	.05	.02	.01
☐ 402 Tom Rathman	.05	.02	.01
☐ 403 Elvis Grbac UER	1.00	.45	.12
(Name spelled Grabac on front)			
☐ 404 Bill Romanowski	.05	.02	.01
☐ 405 Brian Blades	.10	.05	.01
☐ 406 Ferrell Edmunds	.05	.02	.01
☐ 407 Carlton Gray	.05	.02	.01
☐ 408 Cortez Kennedy	.10	.05	.01
☐ 409 Kelvin Martin	.05	.02	.01
☐ 410 Dan McGwire	.05	.02	.01
☐ 411 Rick Mirer	1.00	.45	.12
☐ 412 Rufus Porter	.05	.02	.01
☐ 413 Chris Warren	.10	.05	.01
☐ 414 Jon Vaughn	.05	.02	.01
☐ 415 John L. Williams	.05	.02	.01
☐ 416 Eugene Robinson	.05	.02	.01
☐ 417 Michael McCrary	.05	.02	.01
☐ 418 Michael Bates	.05	.02	.01
☐ 419 Stan Gelbaugh	.05	.02	.01
☐ 420 Reggie Cobb	.05	.02	.01
☐ 421 Eric Curry	.05	.02	.01
☐ 422 Lawrence Dawsey	.05	.02	.01
☐ 423 Santana Dotson	.10	.05	.01
☐ 424 Craig Erickson	.10	.05	.01
☐ 425 Ron Hall	.05	.02	.01
☐ 426 Courtney Hawkins	.05	.02	.01
☐ 427 Broderick Thomas	.05	.02	.01
☐ 428 Vince Workman	.05	.02	.01
☐ 429 Demetrius DuBose	.05	.02	.01
☐ 430 Lamar Thomas	.05	.02	.01
☐ 431 John Lynch	.05	.02	.01
☐ 432 Hardy Nickerson	.10	.05	.01
☐ 433 Horace Copeland	.10	.05	.01
☐ 434 Steve DeBerg	.05	.02	.01
☐ 435 Joe Jacoby	.05	.02	.01
☐ 436 Tom Carter	.10	.05	.01
☐ 437 Andre Collins	.05	.02	.01
☐ 438 Darrell Green	.05	.02	.01
☐ 439 Desmond Howard	.10	.05	.01
☐ 440 Chip Lohmiller	.05	.02	.01
☐ 441 Charles Mann	.05	.02	.01
☐ 442 Tim McGee	.05	.02	.01
☐ 443 Art Monk	.10	.05	.01
☐ 444 Mark Rypien	.05	.02	.01
☐ 445 Ricky Sanders	.05	.02	.01
☐ 446 Brian Mitchell	.10	.05	.01
☐ 447 Reggie Brooks	.10	.05	.01
☐ 448 Carl Banks	.05	.02	.01
☐ 449 Cary Conklin	.05	.02	.01
☐ NNO Santa Card	1.50	.70	.19

1993 Pro Set All-Rookies

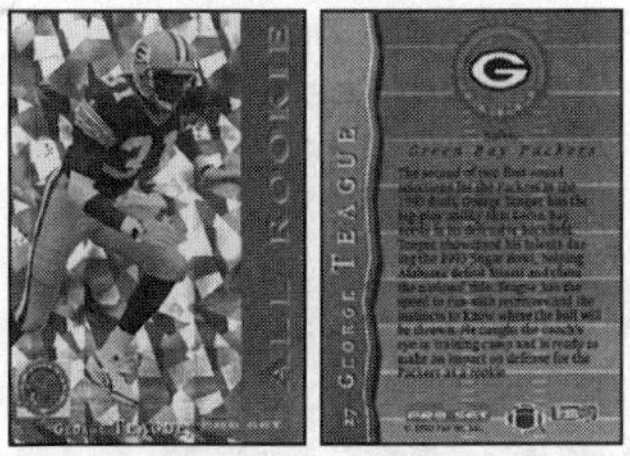

The 1993 Pro Set All-Rookies set comprises 27 standard-size cards, randomly inserted in 1993 Pro Set foil packs. The fronts display color action player cut-outs on prismatic backgrounds. The player's name appears at the bottom of the picture, and the set title appears within a brown lithic stripe edging the right side. The green back has a ghosted football field design with player profile and team logo. An irregular gray stripe along the left side carries the player's name and the card's number.

	MINT	NRMT	EXC
COMPLETE SET (27)	8.00	3.60	1.00
COMMON CARD (1-27)	.20	.09	.03
☐ 1 Rick Mirer	1.50	.70	.19
☐ 2 Garrison Hearst	1.50	.70	.19
☐ 3 Jerome Bettis	2.00	.90	.25
☐ 4 Vincent Brisby	.60	.25	.07
☐ 5 O.J. McDuffie	1.00	.45	.12
☐ 6 Curtis Conway	1.00	.45	.12
☐ 7 Rocket Ismail	.40	.18	.05
☐ 8 Steve Everitt	.20	.09	.03
☐ 9 Ernest Dye	.20	.09	.03
☐ 10 Todd Rucci	.20	.09	.03
☐ 11 Willie Roaf	.40	.18	.05
☐ 12 Lincoln Kennedy	.20	.09	.03
☐ 13 Irv Smith	.20	.09	.03
☐ 14 Jason Elam	.40	.18	.05
☐ 15 Harold Alexander	.20	.09	.03
☐ 16 John Copeland	.40	.18	.05
☐ 17 Eric Curry	.20	.09	.03
☐ 18 Dana Stubblefield	.60	.25	.07
☐ 19 Leonard Renfro	.20	.09	.03
☐ 20 Marvin Jones	.20	.09	.03
☐ 21 Demetrius DuBose	.20	.09	.03
☐ 22 Chris Slade	.40	.18	.05
☐ 23 Darrin Smith	.40	.18	.05
☐ 24 Deon Figures	.40	.18	.05
☐ 25 Darrien Gordon	.40	.18	.05
☐ 26 Patrick Bates	.20	.09	.03
☐ 27 George Teague	.20	.09	.03

1993 Pro Set College Connections

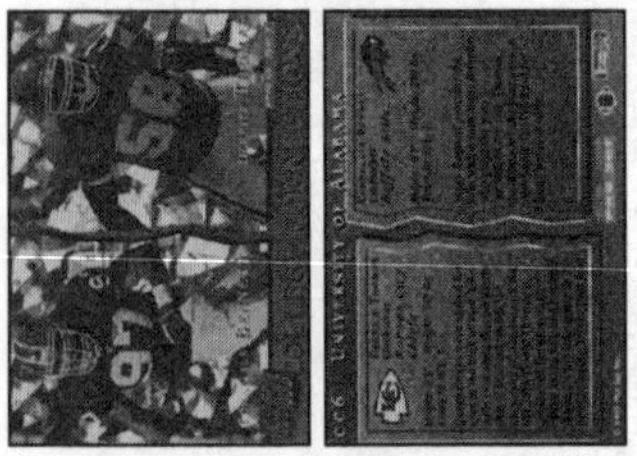

Randomly inserted in 32-card jumbo packs, this 10-card, standard size set spotlights NFL stars who came from the same college. The horizontal fronts feature two color action player cutouts alongside one another on a silver prismatic background. The set title is displayed on a gray stripe at the bottom. On two granite panels, the back presents biographical information and player comparisons. The cards are numbered with a "CC" prefix.

	MINT	NRMT	EXC
COMPLETE SET (10)	30.00	13.50	3.70
COMMON PAIR (CC1-CC10)	1.00	.45	.12
☐ CC1 Barry Sanders / Thurman Thomas	5.00	2.20	.60
☐ CC2 Jerome Bettis / Reggie Brooks	1.25	.55	.16
☐ CC3 Neal Anderson / Cedric Smith	8.00	3.60	1.00
☐ CC4 Rocket Ismail / Tim Brown	1.25	.55	.16
☐ CC5 Rodney Hampton / Garrison Hearst UER (Hearst listed with Lions instead of Cardinals)	2.00	.90	.25
☐ CC6 Derrick Thomas / Cornelius Bennett	1.00	.45	.12
☐ CC7 Jim McMahon / Steve Young	3.00	1.35	.35
☐ CC8 Rick Mirer / Joe Montana	5.00	2.20	.60
☐ CC9 Terrell Buckley / Deion Sanders	3.00	1.35	.35
☐ CC10 Mark Rypien / Drew Bledsoe	5.00	2.20	.60

1993 Pro Set Rookie Quarterbacks

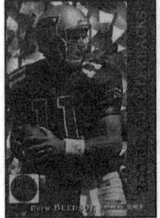

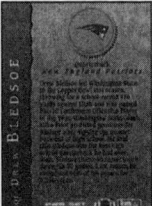

The 1993 Pro Set Rookie Quarterbacks set comprises six standard-size cards, randomly inserted in 1993 Pro Set jumbo packs. The fronts display color action player cut-outs on prismatic backgrounds. The player's name appears at the bottom of the picture, and the set title appears within a gray lithic stripe edging right side. The back sports a textured pinkish background that carries the player's career highlights and the team logo. The player's name appears on an irregular purple stripe edging the left side. The cards are numbered on the back with an "RQ" prefix.

	MINT	NRMT	EXC
COMPLETE SET (6)	12.00	5.50	1.50
COMMON CARD (RQ1-RQ6)	.75	.35	.09
☐ RQ1 Drew Bledsoe	5.00	2.20	.60
☐ RQ2 Rick Mirer	2.00	.90	.25
☐ RQ3 Mark Brunell	5.00	2.20	.60
☐ RQ4 Billy Joe Hobert	1.00	.45	.12
☐ RQ5 Trent Green	.75	.35	.09
☐ RQ6 Elvis Grbac	2.00	.90	.25

1993 Pro Set Rookie Running Backs

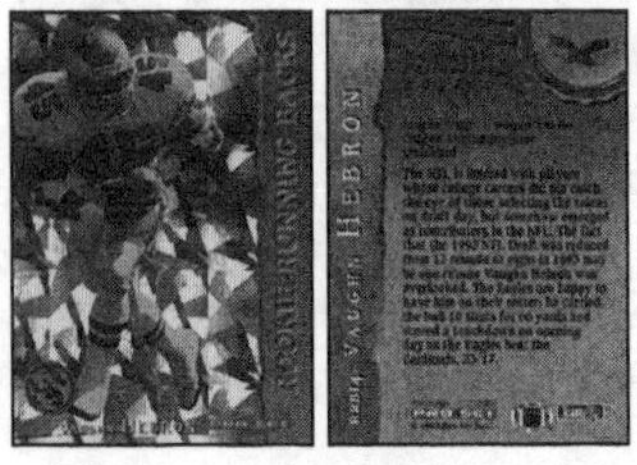

The 1993 Pro Set Rookie Running Backs set comprises 14 standard-size cards, randomly inserted in 1993 Pro Set foil packs. The fronts display color action player cut-outs on prismatic backgrounds. The player's name appears at the bottom of the picture, and the set's title appears within a brown lithic stripe edging right side. The back sports a textured gray background that carries the player's position, team, biography, and career highlights. The player's name appears within an irregular light brown stripe edging the left side. The cards are numbered on the back with an "RRB" prefix.

	MINT	NRMT	EXC
COMPLETE SET (14)	14.00	6.25	1.75
COMMON CARD (1-14)	.75	.35	.09
☐ 1 Derrick Lassic	.75	.35	.09
☐ 2 Reggie Brooks	.75	.35	.09
☐ 3 Garrison Hearst	2.00	.90	.25
☐ 4 Ronald Moore	1.25	.55	.16
☐ 5 Robert Smith	1.50	.70	.19
☐ 6 Jerome Bettis	3.00	1.35	.35
☐ 7 Russell White	.75	.35	.09
☐ 8 Derek Brown RB	.75	.35	.09
☐ 9 Roosevelt Potts	.75	.35	.09
☐ 10 Terry Kirby	1.50	.70	.19
☐ 11 Glyn Milburn	1.25	.55	.16
☐ 12 Greg Robinson	.75	.35	.09
☐ 13 Natrone Means	2.00	.90	.25
☐ 14 Vaughn Hebron	.75	.35	.09

1994 Pro Set National Promos *

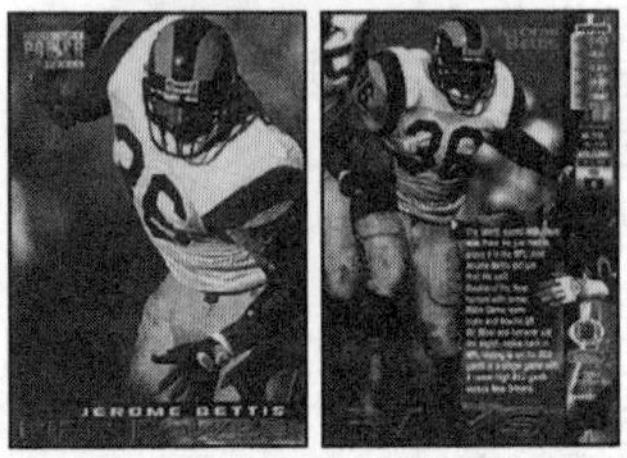

Distributed during the 1994 National Sports Collectors Convention, cards 1-5 and the letter-numbered cards feature prototype cards from Pro Set football, Power football, and Power racing. Cards 6 and 7 were inserted in Tuff Stuff and bear gold foil "Tuff Stuff" emblem; they are part of a 5-card set made for that magazine and inserted one per month. Cards of Darrien Gordon and Joe Montana/Marcus Allen were also produced; licensing problems prevented their release and distribution. The cards are identical to the regular issue except for a black diagonal "proto" stripe cutting across the lower right corner. The front of the title card has the convention logo on a blue screened background with the words Pro Set faintly detectible. The title card also carries the serial number "X" out of 10,000. The football cards are unnumbered and checklisted below in alphabetical order.

	MINT	NRMT	EXC
COMPLETE SET (8)	18.00	8.00	2.20
COMMON CARD	1.00	.45	.12
☐ 1 Jerome Bettis / Fire Power	2.00	.90	.25
☐ 2 Drew Bledsoe	4.00	1.80	.50
☐ 3 Brett Favre / Sterling Sharpe / Air Power	8.00	3.60	1.00
☐ 4 Ronald Moore	1.00	.45	.12
☐ 5 Willie Roaf / Power Line	1.00	.45	.12
☐ 6 Garrison Hearst	1.50	.70	.19
☐ 7 Richmond Webb	1.00	.45	.12
☐ NNO Title Card (1994 National)	1.00	.45	.12

1991 Quarterback Legends

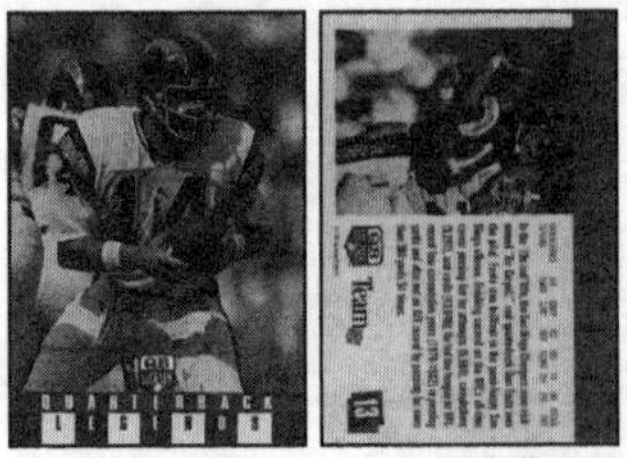

This 50-card set, measuring the standard size was produced by NFL Quarterback Legends and issued on high-quality card stock. The set is packaged in a red, white, and blue box. Card fronts feature a color action shot of the player. At the bottom of the card appears a red stripe and a blue and white checker board stripe, with the words "Quarterback Legends" reversed out in white and blue lettering. Card backs, printed horizontally, feature a full-bleed red stripe at the top with player's name in blue, another action photo, and statistical and biographical information. Sponsors' (QB Legends and Team NFL) logos and card number appear to the bottom right of card. The cards are numbered on the back. The first 46 cards in the set are ordered alphabetically by name. The last four cards depict legendary feats. The team name listed in the checklist below corresponds to uniform on front of cards; the photo on back of cards sometimes has player in a different team uniform. This set was introduced and distributed at the Quarterback Legends Show in Nashville, Tennessee in January, 1992.

	MINT	NRMT	EXC
COMPLETE SET (50)	15.00	6.75	1.85
COMMON CARD (1-50)	.25	.11	.03
☐ 1 Ken Anderson	.75	.35	.09
☐ 2 Steve Bartkowski	.35	.16	.04
☐ 3 George Blanda	.75	.35	.09
☐ 4 Terry Bradshaw	2.00	.90	.25
☐ 5 Zeke Bratkowski	.25	.11	.03
☐ 6 John Brodie	.50	.23	.06
☐ 7 Charley Conerly	.35	.16	.04
☐ 8 Len Dawson	.50	.23	.06
☐ 9 Lynn Dickey	.25	.11	.03
☐ 10 Joe Ferguson	.25	.11	.03
☐ 11 Vince Ferragamo	.25	.11	.03
☐ 12 Tom Flores	.35	.16	.04
☐ 13 Dan Fouts	.75	.35	.09
☐ 14 Roman Gabriel	.35	.16	.04
☐ 15 Otto Graham	1.00	.45	.12
☐ 16 Bob Griese	1.00	.45	.12
☐ 17 Steve Grogan	.35	.16	.04
☐ 18 John Hadl	.35	.16	.04
☐ 19 James Harris	.25	.11	.03
☐ 20 Jim Hart	.25	.11	.03
☐ 21 Ron Jaworski	.25	.11	.03
☐ 22 Charlie Johnson	.25	.11	.03
☐ 23 Bert Jones	.35	.16	.04
☐ 24 Sonny Jurgensen	.50	.23	.06
☐ 25 Joe Kapp	.25	.11	.03
☐ 26 Billy Kilmer	.35	.16	.04
☐ 27 Daryle Lamonica	.35	.16	.04
☐ 28 Greg Landry	.25	.11	.03
☐ 29 Neil Lomax	.25	.11	.03
☐ 30 Archie Manning	.35	.16	.04
☐ 31 Earl Morrall	.25	.11	.03
☐ 32 Craig Morton	.35	.16	.04
☐ 33 Gifford Nielsen	.25	.11	.03
☐ 34 Dan Pastorini	.25	.11	.03
☐ 35 Jim Plunkett	.35	.16	.04
☐ 36 Norm Snead	.25	.11	.03
☐ 37 Ken Stabler	1.00	.45	.12
☐ 38 Bart Starr	1.25	.55	.16
☐ 39 Roger Staubach	2.50	1.10	.30
☐ 40 Joe Theismann	.75	.35	.09
☐ 41 Y.A. Tittle	1.00	.45	.12
☐ 42 Johnny Unitas	1.50	.70	.19
☐ 43 Bill Wade	.25	.11	.03
☐ 44 Danny White	.35	.16	.04
☐ 45 Doug Williams	.25	.11	.03
☐ 46 Jim Zorn	.35	.16	.04
☐ 47 Otto Graham / Legendary Feats	1.00	.45	.12
☐ 48 Johnny Unitas / Legendary Feats	1.50	.70	.19
☐ 49 Bart Starr / Legendary Feats	1.25	.55	.16
☐ 50 Terry Bradshaw / Legendary Feats	2.00	.90	.25

1992 Quarterback Greats GE

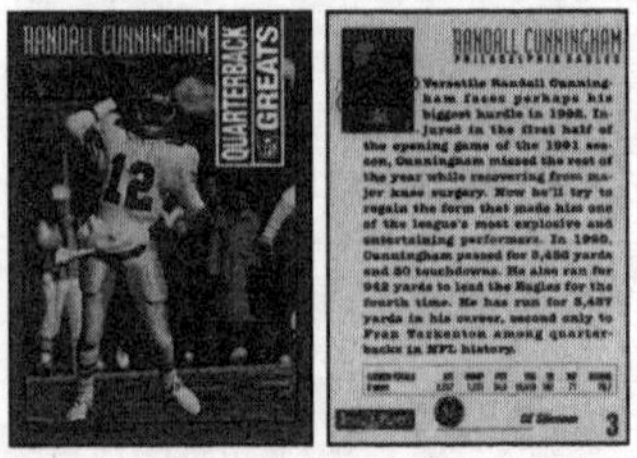

Produced by NFL Properties, this 12-card standard-size set was prepared for General Electric Silicones and features members of the Quarterback Club. The cards could be obtained by sending in proofs of purchase. The fronts carry action color player photos on a red face. The player's name is printed in white lettering above the picture. A blue and red bar icon containing the words "Quarterback Greats" runs horizontally from the top right and overlaps the picture. The backs carry statistics and career highlights. The GE logo and NFL Team Players logo appear at the bottom. The Quarterback Club icon (a black box with a brightly colored football player outline) is in the upper left corner.

	MINT	NRMT	EXC
COMPLETE SET (12)	18.00	8.00	2.20
COMMON CARD (1-11)	.50	.23	.06
☐ 1 Troy Aikman	4.00	1.80	.50
☐ 2 Bubby Brister	.50	.23	.06
☐ 3 Randall Cunningham	.75	.35	.09
☐ 4 John Elway	3.00	1.35	.35
☐ 5 Boomer Esiason	.75	.35	.09
☐ 6 Jim Everett	.50	.23	.06
☐ 7 Jim Kelly	1.25	.55	.16
☐ 8 Bernie Kosar	.50	.23	.06
☐ 9 Dan Marino	8.00	3.60	1.00
☐ 10 Warren Moon	.75	.35	.09
☐ 11 Phil Simms	.75	.35	.09
☐ NNO Title Card (Checklist)	.50	.23	.06

1993 Quarterback Legends

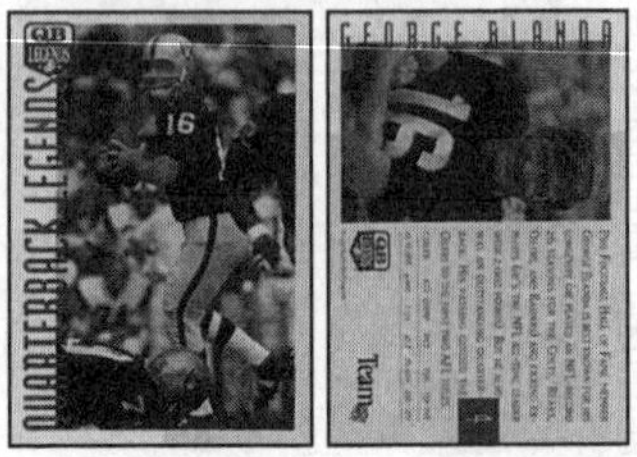

This 50-card standard-size set showcases outstanding quarterbacks throughout NFL history. The fronts feature action player photos in which the player appears in color against a sepia-toned background. The borders shade from white to pastel yellow as one moves from left to right, and the set title "Quarterback Legends" is printed vertically on the left edge in bronze lettering. The horizontal backs carry a close-up color player photo and career summary. The set closes with a Legendary Feats (48-50) subset.

	MINT	NRMT	EXC
COMPLETE SET (50)	12.00	5.50	1.50
COMMON CARD (1-50)	.25	.11	.03
☐ 1 Checklist Card	.35	.16	.04
☐ 2 Ken Anderson	.60	.25	.07
☐ 3 Steve Bartkowski	.35	.16	.04
☐ 4 George Blanda	.60	.25	.07
☐ 5 Terry Bradshaw	1.50	.70	.19
☐ 6 Zeke Bratkowski	.25	.11	.03
☐ 7 John Brodie	.50	.23	.06
☐ 8 Charley Conerly	.35	.16	.04
☐ 9 Len Dawson	.50	.23	.06
☐ 10 Lynn Dickey	.25	.11	.03
☐ 11 Joe Ferguson	.25	.11	.03
☐ 12 Vince Ferragamo	.25	.11	.03
☐ 13 Tom Flores	.35	.16	.04
☐ 14 Dan Fouts	.75	.35	.09
☐ 15 Roman Gabriel	.35	.16	.04
☐ 16 Otto Graham	.75	.35	.09
☐ 17 Bob Griese	1.00	.45	.12
☐ 18 Steve Grogan	.35	.16	.04
☐ 19 John Hadl	.35	.16	.04
☐ 20 James Harris	.25	.11	.03
☐ 21 Jim Hart	.25	.11	.03
☐ 22 Ron Jaworski	.25	.11	.03
☐ 23 Charlie Johnson	.25	.11	.03
☐ 24 Bert Jones	.35	.16	.04
☐ 25 Sonny Jurgensen	.50	.23	.06
☐ 26 Joe Kapp	.25	.11	.03
☐ 27 Billy Kilmer	.35	.16	.04
☐ 28 Daryle Lamonica	.35	.16	.04
☐ 29 Greg Landry	.25	.11	.03
☐ 30 Neil Lomax	.25	.11	.03
☐ 31 Archie Manning	.50	.23	.06
☐ 32 Earl Morrall	.25	.11	.03
☐ 33 Craig Morton	.35	.16	.04
☐ 34 Gifford Nielsen	.25	.11	.03
☐ 35 Dan Pastorini	.25	.11	.03
☐ 36 Jim Plunkett	.35	.16	.04
☐ 37 Norm Snead	.25	.11	.03
☐ 38 Ken Stabler	.75	.35	.09
☐ 39 Bart Starr	1.00	.45	.12
☐ 40 Roger Staubach	2.00	.90	.25
☐ 41 Joe Theismann	.60	.25	.07
☐ 42 Y.A. Tittle	.75	.35	.09
☐ 43 Johnny Unitas	1.00	.45	.12
☐ 44 Bill Wade	.25	.11	.03
☐ 45 Danny White	.35	.16	.04
☐ 46 Doug Williams	.25	.11	.03
☐ 47 Jim Zorn	.25	.11	.03
☐ 48 George Blanda / Miracle Streak	.60	.25	.07
☐ 49 Bob Griese / Earl Morrall / Perfect Season	.50	.23	.06
☐ 50 Doug Williams / Record-setting Super Bowl XXII	.25	.11	.03

1935 R311-2 Premium Photos

The R311-2 (as referenced in the American Card Catalog) Football Stars and Scenes set consists of 17 glossy, unnumbered, 6" by 8" photos. Both professional and collegiate players are pictured on these photos. These blank-back photos have been numbered in the checklist below alphabetically by the player's name or title. These premium photos were available from National Chicle with one premium given for every 20 wrappers turned in to the retailer.

	EX-MT	VG-E	GOOD
COMPLETE SET (17)	3500.00	1600.00	450.00
COMMON PHOTO (1-17)	150.00	70.00	19.00

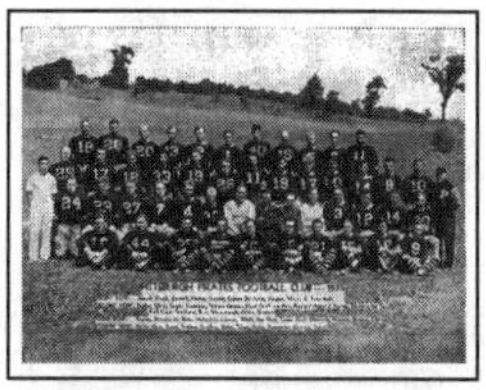

☐ 1 Joe Bach	150.00	70.00	19.00
☐ 2 Eddie Casey	150.00	70.00	19.00
☐ 3 George Christensen	150.00	70.00	19.00
☐ 4 Red Grange	600.00	275.00	75.00
☐ 5 Stan Kostka TD Next Stop	150.00	70.00	19.00
☐ 6 Joe Maniaci Fordham Back (26 with ball, shown trying to gain around left end)	150.00	70.00	19.00
☐ 7 Harry Newman	150.00	70.00	19.00
☐ 8 Walter Switzer Cornell quarterback	150.00	70.00	19.00
☐ 9 Chicago Bears 1934 Western Champs	350.00	160.00	45.00
☐ 10 New York Giants 1934 World's Champs	350.00	160.00	45.00
☐ 11 Notre Dame's Quick Kick Against Army, 1934	200.00	90.00	25.00
☐ 12 Pittsburgh in Rough Going Against the Navy 1934	150.00	70.00	19.00
☐ 13 Pittsburgh Pirates 1935 Football Club	250.00	110.00	31.00
☐ 14 Touchdown: Morton of Yale	150.00	70.00	19.00
☐ 15 A Tight Spot	150.00	70.00	19.00
☐ 16 Cotton (Warburton) Goes Places	150.00	70.00	19.00
☐ 17 Ace Gutowky Steve Hokuf The Greatest Tackle Picture Ever Photographed	200.00	90.00	25.00

1962 Raiders Team Issue

The Raiders likely released these photos over a number of seasons. Each measures approximately 8" by 10" and includes a black and white photo on the cardfront with a blank cardback. The team name, player's name, and position (abbreviated) appear below the photo from left to right. The checklist is thought to be incomplete. Any additions to this list are appreciated.

	NRMT	VG-E	GOOD
COMPLETE SET (4)	12.00	5.50	1.50
COMMON CARD (1-4)	3.00	1.35	.35
☐ 1 Wayne Hawkins	4.00	1.80	.50
☐ 2 Jon Jelacic	3.00	1.35	.35
☐ 3 Pete Nicklas	3.00	1.35	.35
☐ 4 Chuck McMurtry	3.00	1.35	.35

1964 Raiders Team Issue

The Raiders likely released these photos over a number of seasons. Each measures approximately 8" by 10" and includes a black and white photo on the cardfront with a blank cardback. The player's name, position and team name appear below the photo. The text style and size varies slightly from photo to photo and the checklist is thought to be incomplete. Any additions to this list are appreciated.

	NRMT	VG-E	GOOD
COMPLETE SET (13)	35.00	16.00	4.40
COMMON CARD (1-13)	3.00	1.35	.35
☐ 1 Bill Budness	3.00	1.35	.35
☐ 2 Claude Gibson	3.00	1.35	.35
☐ 3 Wayne Hawkins	4.00	1.80	.50
☐ 4 Ken Herock	3.00	1.35	.35
☐ 5 Jon Jelacic	3.00	1.35	.35
☐ 6 Dick Klein	3.00	1.35	.35
☐ 7 Joe Krakoski	3.00	1.35	.35
☐ 8 Mike Mercer	3.00	1.35	.35
☐ 9 Tommy Morrow	3.00	1.35	.35
☐ 10 Clancy Osborne	3.00	1.35	.35
☐ 11 Ken Rice	4.00	1.80	.50
☐ 12 Bo Roberson	3.00	1.35	.35
☐ 13 Howie Williams	3.00	1.35	.35

1985 Raiders Shell Oil Posters

Available only at participating Southern California Shell stations during the 1985 season, these five posters measure approximately 11 5/8" by 18" and feature an artist's color renderings of the Raiders in action. The unnumbered posters are blank-backed, except for number 1 below, the back of which carries the Raiders and Shell logos along with the month in which each subsequent poster was released. The posters are listed below accordingly.

	MINT	NRMT	EXC
COMPLETE SET (5)	25.00	11.00	3.10
COMMON POSTER (1-5)	5.00	2.20	.60

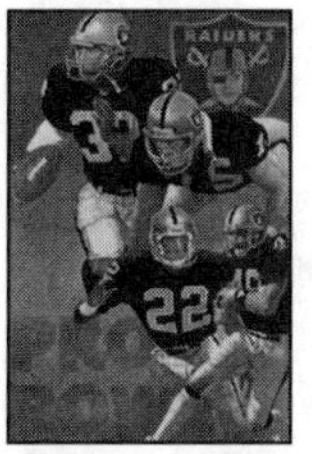

☐ 1 Pro Bowl (No release date)	5.00	2.20	.60
☐ 2 Defensive Front (September)	5.00	2.20	.60
☐ 3 Deep Secondary (October)	5.00	2.20	.60
☐ 4 Big Offensive Line (November)	5.00	2.20	.60
☐ 5 Scores (December)	5.00	2.20	.60

1985 Raiders Smokey

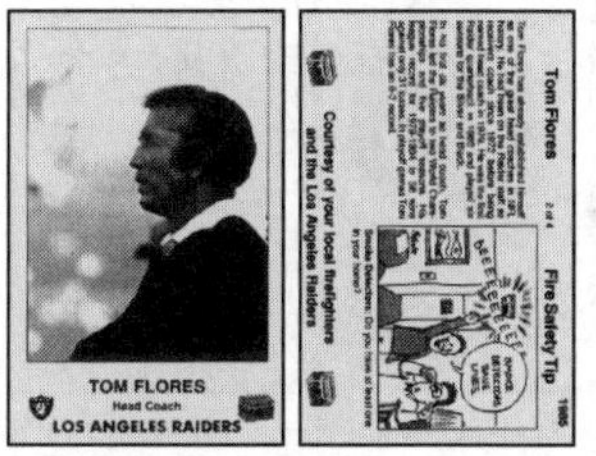

This four-card set of Los Angeles Raiders was also sponsored by Kodak. The cards measure approximately 2 5/8" by 4 1/8". It is technically a "fire safety" set as Smokey is not mentioned anywhere on the cards. The cards are numbered (and dated) on the back. The fire safety tip on the back is in the form of a cartoon. There are also two or three paragraphs of biographical information about the player on the card backs. The card fronts show a full-color photo inside a white border. The player's name, team, position, height, and weight are given at the bottom of the card front.

	MINT	NRMT	EXC
COMPLETE SET (4)	3.50	1.55	.45
COMMON CARD (1-4)	.35	.16	.04
☐ 1 Marcus Allen	2.00	.90	.25
☐ 2 Tom Flores CO	.35	.16	.04
☐ 3 Howie Long	1.00	.45	.12
☐ 4 Rod Martin	.35	.16	.04

1987 Raiders Smokey Color-Grams

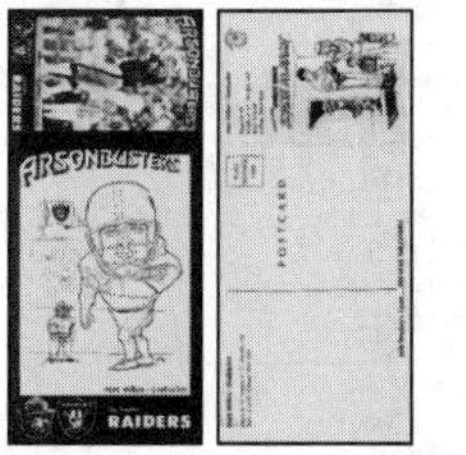

This set is actually a 14-page booklet featuring 13 player caricatures (all from the Los Angeles Raiders) and one of Smokey and Huddles. Each page includes a 5 5/8" by 3 11/16" postcard perforated with a card measuring 2 1/2" by 3 11/16". The booklet itself is approximately 8 1/8" by 3 11/16". The set is headlined as "Arsonbusters" in white over a black frame. The backs offer a fire prevention tip from Smokey. The cards are unnumbered, but are listed below according to booklet page number.

	MINT	NRMT	EXC
COMPLETE SET (14)	30.00	13.50	3.70
COMMON CARD (1-14)	1.25	.55	.16
☐ 1 Smokey and Huddles	1.25	.55	.16
☐ 2 Matt Millen	1.50	.70	.19
☐ 3 Rod Martin	1.50	.70	.19
☐ 4 Sean Jones	2.50	1.10	.30
☐ 5 Dokie Williams	1.25	.55	.16
☐ 6 Don Mosebar	1.50	.70	.19
☐ 7 Todd Christensen	1.50	.70	.19
☐ 8 Bill Pickel	1.25	.55	.16
☐ 9 Marcus Allen	10.00	4.50	1.25
☐ 10 Charley Hannah	1.25	.55	.16
☐ 11 Howie Long	4.00	1.80	.50
☐ 12 Vann McElroy	1.25	.55	.16
☐ 13 Reggie McKenzie	1.25	.55	.16
☐ 14 Mike Haynes	2.50	1.10	.30

1988 Raiders Police

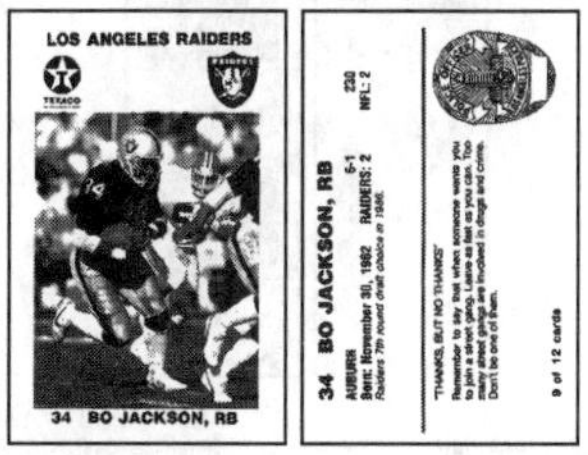

The 1988 Police Los Angeles Raiders set contains 12 numbered cards measuring approximately 2 3/4" by 4 1/8". There are 11 player cards and one coach card. The backs have biographical information and safety tips. The set was sponsored by Texaco and the Los Angeles Raiders.

	MINT	NRMT	EXC
COMPLETE SET (12)	7.00	3.10	.85
COMMON CARD (1-12)	.40	.18	.05
☐ 1 Vann McElroy	.40	.18	.05
☐ 2 Bill Pickel	.40	.18	.05
☐ 3 Marcus Allen	3.00	1.35	.35
☐ 4 Rod Martin	.50	.23	.06
☐ 5 Lionel Washington	.50	.23	.06
☐ 6 Don Mosebar	.50	.23	.06
☐ 7 Reggie McKenzie	.40	.18	.05
☐ 8 Todd Christensen	.75	.35	.09
☐ 9 Bo Jackson	1.50	.70	.19
☐ 10 James Lofton	1.00	.45	.12
☐ 11 Howie Long	1.00	.45	.12
☐ 12 Mike Shanahan CO	.75	.35	.09

1988 Raiders Smokey

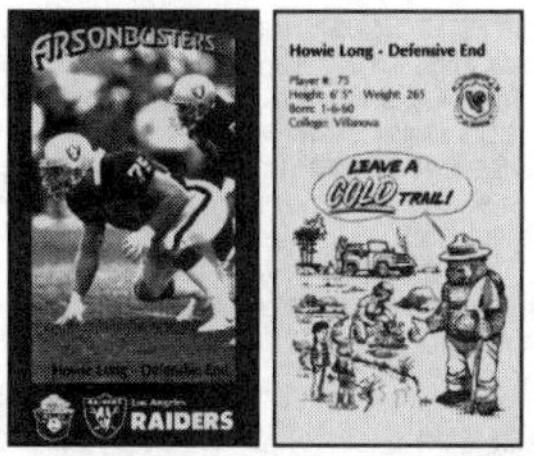

This 14-card set is distinguished by its thick black border on the front of every card as well as the presence of "Arsonbusters" in orange as a subtitle. The cards measure approximately 3" by 5". The set is not numbered although the players' uniform numbers are in small print on the back; the list below has been ordered alphabetically. Each card back features a different fire safety cartoon starring Smokey.

	MINT	NRMT	EXC
COMPLETE SET (14)	15.00	6.75	1.85
COMMON CARD (1-14)	.75	.35	.09
☐ 1 Marcus Allen	6.00	2.70	.75
☐ 2 Todd Christensen	1.25	.55	.16
☐ 3 Bo Jackson	3.00	1.35	.35
☐ 4 James Lofton	1.50	.70	.19
☐ 5 Howie Long	1.50	.70	.19
☐ 6 Rod Martin	1.00	.45	.12
☐ 7 Vann McElroy	.75	.35	.09
☐ 8 Don Mosebar	1.00	.45	.12
☐ 9 Bill Pickel	.75	.35	.09
☐ 10 Jerry Robinson	.75	.35	.09
☐ 11 Mike Shanahan CO	1.25	.55	.16
☐ 12 Smokey Bear	.75	.35	.09
☐ 13 Stacey Toran	.75	.35	.09
☐ 14 Greg Townsend	1.00	.45	.12

1989 Raiders Swanson

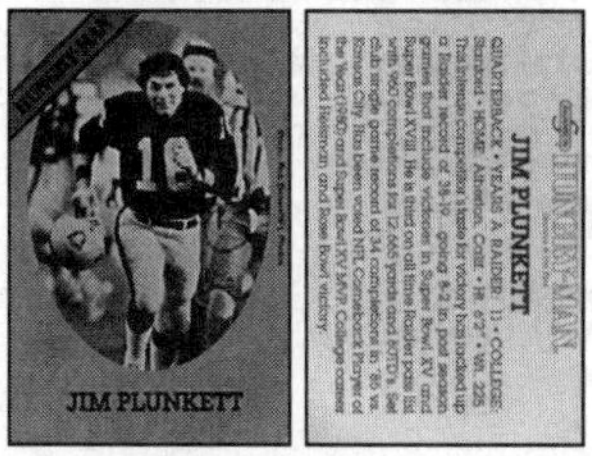

This three-card set was issued in a perforated strip containing five card slots; after perforation, the cards measure approximately 2 1/2" by 3 3/4". The first two slots consist of manufacturer's coupons to save 25 cents on the purchase of any variety of Swanson Hungry-Man dinners. The player cards feature an oval-shamped black and white player photo on a silver card face. A red diagonal with the words "Hungry-Man" cuts across the upper left corner, and the player's name appears in black lettering below the picture. The horizontal backs present biographical information and player profile. The cards are unnumbered and checklisted below in alphabetical order.

	MINT	NRMT	EXC
COMPLETE SET (3)	10.00	4.50	1.25
COMMON CARD (1-3)	2.50	1.10	.30
☐ 1 Marcus Allen	6.00	2.70	.75
☐ 2 Howie Long	3.00	1.35	.35
☐ 3 Jim Plunkett	2.50	1.10	.30

1990 Raiders Smokey

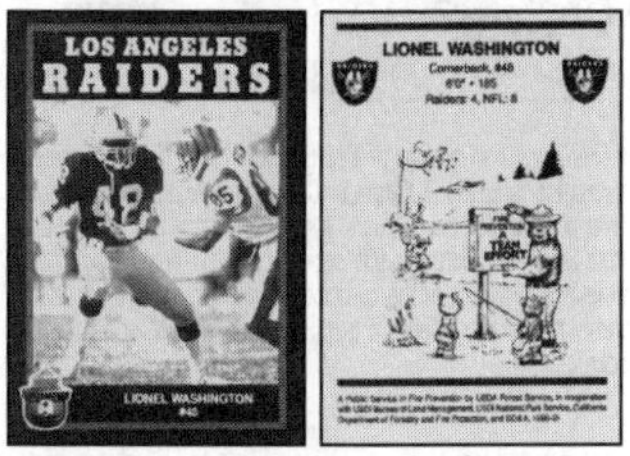

This 16-card standard size set was issued by the USDA Forest Service in conjuction with the USDI Bureau of Land Management, USDI National Park Service, California Department of Forestry and Fire Prevention, and BDA. The set features solid black borders framing a full-color action shot with the Los Angeles Raiders team name in white. The player's name and uniform number is directly underneath the photo and there is a photo of the Smokey the Bear mascot in the lower left hand corner of the card. The back of the card has only the basic biographical information, as well as a fire safety tip. Surprisingly, there is no card of either Bo Jackson or Marcus Allen in this set. The set has been checklisted below in alphabetical order.

	MINT	NRMT	EXC
COMPLETE SET (16)	12.00	5.50	1.50
COMMON CARD (1-16)	.75	.35	.09
☐ 1 Eddie Anderson	1.00	.45	.12
☐ 2 Thomas Benson	.75	.35	.09
☐ 3 Mervyn Fernandez	1.25	.55	.16
☐ 4 Bob Golic	1.00	.45	.12
☐ 5 Jeff Gossett	.75	.35	.09
☐ 6 Rory Graves	.75	.35	.09
☐ 7 Jeff Jaeger	.75	.35	.09
☐ 8 Howie Long	2.50	1.10	.30
☐ 9 Don Mosebar	1.00	.45	.12
☐ 10 Jay Schroeder	1.25	.55	.16
☐ 11 Art Shell CO	2.00	.90	.25
☐ 12 Greg Townsend	1.25	.55	.16
☐ 13 Lionel Washington	1.00	.45	.12
☐ 14 Steve Wisniewski	1.25	.55	.16
☐ 15 Commitment to Excellence (Helmet and Super Bowl trophies)	.75	.35	.09
☐ 16 Denise Franzen Cheerleader	.75	.35	.09

1990-91 Raiders Main Street Dairy

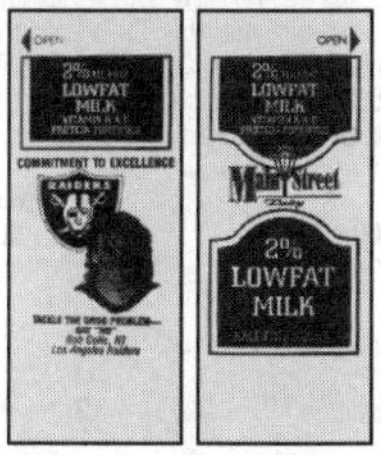

This set of six half-pint milk cartons features the Raiders' team patch, a head shot of a player, and a safety tip to youngsters on one of its panels. When collapsed, the cartons measure approximately 4 1/2" by 6". The cartons were issued in the Los Angeles area and were printed in three colors, brown (chocolate lowfat), red (vitamin D), and blue (2 percent low fat). The primary color of the carton is given on the continuation line below.

	MINT	NRMT	EXC
COMPLETE SET (6)	20.00	9.00	2.50
COMMON CARD (1-6)	3.00	1.35	.35
☐ 1 Bob Golic (Blue)	4.00	1.80	.50
☐ 2 Terry McDaniel (Brown)	3.00	1.35	.35
☐ 3 Don Mosebar (Red)	3.00	1.35	.35
☐ 4 Jay Schroeder (Blue)	4.00	1.80	.50
☐ 5 Art Shell CO (Red)	5.00	2.20	.60
☐ 6 Steve Wisniewski (Brown)	3.00	1.35	.35

1991 Raiders Police

This 12-card standard-size set was sponsored by Clovis Police Department, REHCO Heating and Air Conditioning, and the Los Angeles Raiders. Five thousand sets were distributed throughout the

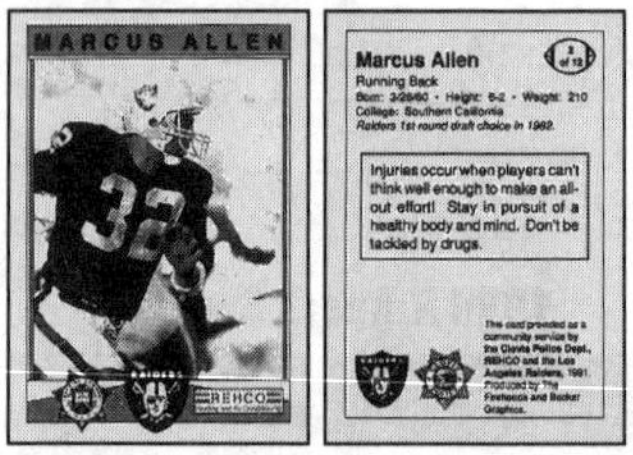

Fresno/Clovis area as part of a sixth grade DARE (Drug Awareness Resistance Education) program. Card fronts feature color action player photos with white borders. The player's name appears in a gray stripe above the picture, while sponsor logos overlay another gray stripe at the bottom of the card face. The backs have biographical information and a safety tip printed in black lettering on a white background.

	MINT	NRMT	EXC
COMPLETE SET (12)	15.00	6.75	1.85
COMMON CARD (1-12)	1.00	.45	.12
☐ 1 Art Shell CO	2.50	1.10	.30
☐ 2 Marcus Allen	5.00	2.20	.60
☐ 3 Mervyn Fernandez	1.50	.70	.19
☐ 4 Willie Gault	1.50	.70	.19
☐ 5 Howie Long	2.00	.90	.25
☐ 6 Don Mosebar	1.25	.55	.16
☐ 7 Winston Moss	1.00	.45	.12
☐ 8 Jay Schroeder	1.50	.70	.19
☐ 9 Steve Wisniewski	1.25	.55	.16
☐ 10 Ethan Horton	1.00	.45	.12
☐ 11 Lionel Washington	1.25	.55	.16
☐ 12 Greg Townsend	1.50	.70	.19

1991-92 Raiders Adohr Farms Dairy

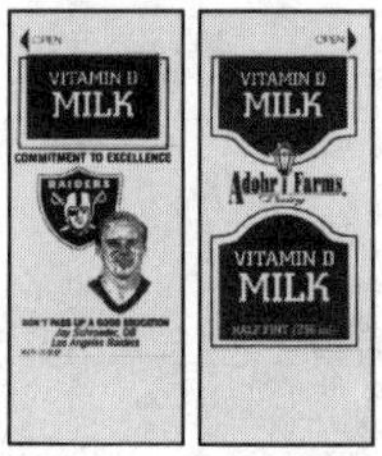

This set of ten half-pint milk cartons features the Raiders' team patch, a head shot of a player, and a safety message on one of its panels. When collapsed, the cartons measure approximately 4 1/2" by 6". The cartons were issued in the Los Angeles area and were printed in red (vitamin D) and blue (2 percent lowfat). Apparently only the Greg Townsend carton was issued in two varieties. The primary color of the carton is given on the continuation line. The cartons are unnumbered and checklisted below in alphabetical order. Apparently Adohr Farms Dairy bought out Main Street Dairy and with the buyout, obtained the rights to produce the selected Raiders.

	MINT	NRMT	EXC
COMPLETE SET (10)	40.00	18.00	5.00
COMMON CARD (1-10)	3.00	1.35	.35
☐ 1 Jeff Gossett (Red)	3.00	1.35	.35
☐ 2 Ethan Horton (Blue)	3.00	1.35	.35
☐ 3 Jeff Jaeger (Red)	3.00	1.35	.35
☐ 4 Ronnie Lott (Blue)	8.00	3.60	1.00
☐ 5 Terry McDaniel (Red)	4.00	1.80	.50
☐ 6 Don Mosebar (Red)	3.00	1.35	.35
☐ 7 Jay Schroeder (Red)	3.00	1.35	.35
☐ 8 Art Shell CO (Red)	6.00	2.70	.75
☐ 9 Greg Townsend (Red or blue)	4.00	1.80	.50
☐ 10 Steve Wisniewski (Red)	3.00	1.35	.35

1993-94 Raiders Adohr Farms Dairy

This set of six half-pint vitamin D milk cartons features the Raiders team patch, a head shot of a player, and a message about education or crime prevention, all printed in red. When collapsed, the cartons measure approximately 4 1/2" by 6". Two million milk cartons were distributed only to Los Angeles area schools and hospitals in a two-week period during the season. Reportedly only 1,400 were produced flat and undistributed. The cartons are unnumbered and checklisted below in alphabetical order.

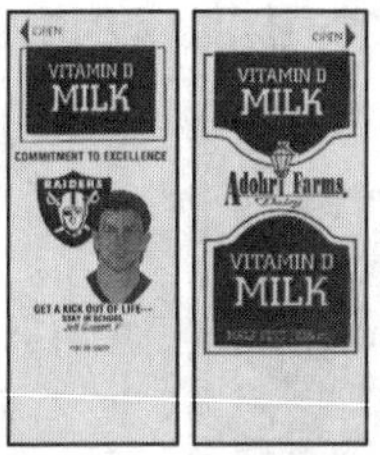

	MINT	NRMT	EXC
COMPLETE SET (6)	20.00	9.00	2.50
COMMON CARD (1-6)	3.00	1.35	.35
☐ 1 Jeff Gossett	3.00	1.35	.35
☐ 2 Ethan Horton	3.00	1.35	.35
☐ 3 Terry McDaniel	3.00	1.35	.35
☐ 4 Don Mosebar	3.00	1.35	.35
☐ 5 Art Shell CO	5.00	2.20	.60
☐ 6 Steve Wisniewski	3.00	1.35	.35

1994-95 Raiders Adohr Farms Dairy

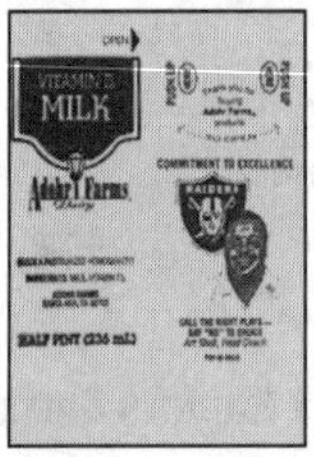

This set of four half-pint Vitamin D milk cartons features the Raiders' team patch, a head shot of the player, and a safety tip on one of its panels. When collapsed, the cartons measure approximately 4 1/2" by 6". All cartons are printed in red with some black lettering. It was reported that 20,000,000 cartons (or five million sets) were issued in a three-week period. Ninety percent were distributed to hospitals, schools, and airlines, while ten percent were sold to the general public. Reportedly, 800 cartons (or 200 sets) were left flat and undistributed. The cartons are unnumbered and checklisted below in alphabetical order.

	MINT	NRMT	EXC
COMPLETE SET (4)	18.00	8.00	2.20
COMMON CARD (1-4)	4.00	1.80	.50
☐ 1 Jeff Jaeger	4.00	1.80	.50
☐ 2 Terry McDaniel	4.00	1.80	.50
☐ 3 Art Shell CO	6.00	2.70	.75
☐ 4 Steve Wisniewski	4.00	1.80	.50

1950 Rams Admiral

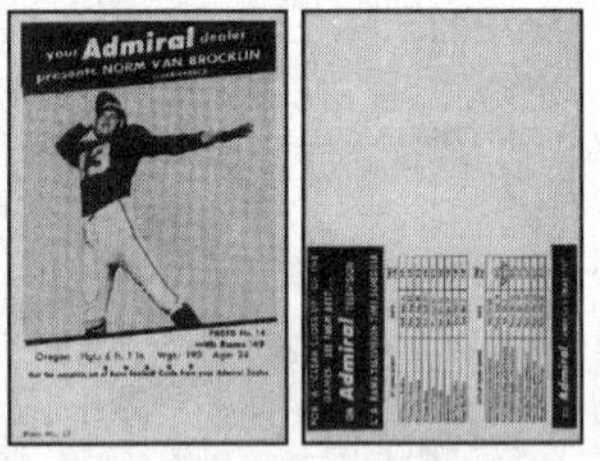

This 35-card set was sponsored by Admiral and features cards measuring approximately 3 1/2" by 5 1/2". The front design has a black and white action pose of the player, without borders on the sides of the picture. The words "Your Admiral dealer presents" followed by the player's name and position appear in the black stripe at the top of each card. A black border separates the bottom of the picture from the biographical information below. In a horizontal format, the backs are blank on the right half, and have a season schedule as well as Admiral advertisements on the left half. The cards are numbered on the front by the photos. Card numbers 26-35 are slightly smaller and have blank backs. Norm Van Brocklin appears in his Rookie Card year.

	NRMT	VG-E	GOOD
COMPLETE SET (35)	1600.00	700.00	200.00
COMMON CARD (1-35)	25.00	11.00	3.10
☐ 1 Joe Stydahar CO	40.00	18.00	5.00
☐ 2 Hampton Pool CO	25.00	11.00	3.10
☐ 3 Fred Naumetz	25.00	11.00	3.10
☐ 4 Jack Finlay	25.00	11.00	3.10
☐ 5 Gil Bouley	25.00	11.00	3.10
☐ 6 Bob Reinhard	25.00	11.00	3.10
☐ 7 Bob Boyd	30.00	13.50	3.70
☐ 8 Bob Waterfield	200.00	90.00	25.00
☐ 9 Mel Hein CO	50.00	22.00	6.25
☐ 10 Howard(Red) Hickey CO	25.00	11.00	3.10
☐ 11 Ralph Pasquariello	25.00	11.00	3.10
☐ 12 Jack Zilly	25.00	11.00	3.10
☐ 13 Tom Kalmanir	25.00	11.00	3.10
☐ 14 Norm Van Brocklin	250.00	110.00	31.00
☐ 15 Woodley Lewis	30.00	13.50	3.70
☐ 16 Glenn Davis	90.00	40.00	11.00
☐ 17 Dick Hoerner	25.00	11.00	3.10
☐ 18 Bob Kelley ANN	25.00	11.00	3.10
☐ 19 Paul(Tank) Younger	40.00	18.00	5.00
☐ 20 George Sims	25.00	11.00	3.10
☐ 21 Dick Huffman	25.00	11.00	3.10
☐ 22 Tom Fears	90.00	40.00	11.00
☐ 23 Vitamin T. Smith	30.00	13.50	3.70
☐ 24 Elroy Hirsch	200.00	90.00	25.00
☐ 25 Don Paul	30.00	13.50	3.70
☐ 26 Bill Lange	25.00	11.00	3.10
☐ 27 Paul Barry	25.00	11.00	3.10
☐ 28 Deacon Dan Towler	40.00	18.00	5.00
☐ 29 Vic Vasicek	25.00	11.00	3.10
☐ 30 Bill Smyth	25.00	11.00	3.10
☐ 31 Larry Brink	25.00	11.00	3.10
☐ 32 Jerry Williams	25.00	11.00	3.10
☐ 33 Stan West	25.00	11.00	3.10
☐ 34 Art Statuto	25.00	11.00	3.10
☐ 35 Ed Champagne	25.00	11.00	3.10

1953 Rams Team Issue

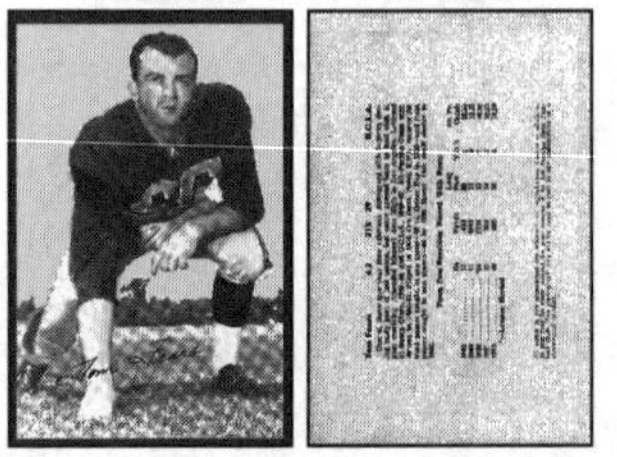

This 36-card unnumbered set measures approximately 4 1/4" by 6 3/8" and was issued by the Los Angeles Rams for their fans. This set has black borders on the front framing posed action shots with the player's signature across the bottom portion of the picture. Biographical information on the back relating to the player pictured listing the player's name, height, weight, age, and college is also included. Among the interesting cards in this set are early cards of Dick "Night-Train" Lane and Andy Robustelli. The cards were available directly from the team as a complete set. We have checklisted this set in alphabetical order. Many cards from the 1953-1955 and 1957 Rams Team Issue Black Border sets are identical except for text differences on the card backs. Player stat lines are also helpful in identifying year of issue; the year of issue is typically the next year after the last year on the stats. The first few words of the first line of text is listed for players without stat lines.

	NRMT	VG-E	GOOD
COMPLETE SET (36)	350.00	160.00	45.00
COMMON CARD (1-36)	5.00	2.20	.60
☐ 1 Ben Agajanian	6.00	2.70	.75
☐ 2 Bob Boyd (Born in Riverside ...)	6.00	2.70	.75
☐ 3 Larry Brink	5.00	2.20	.60
☐ 4 Rudy Bukich	8.00	3.60	1.00
☐ 5 Tom Dahms (4 text lines)	5.00	2.20	.60
☐ 6 Dick Daugherty (Regular Ram ...)	5.00	2.20	.60
☐ 7 Jack Dwyer (Played 1951 ...)	5.00	2.20	.60
☐ 8 Tom Fears (1952 stats)	25.00	11.00	3.10
☐ 9 Bob Fry (Was sprinter ...)	5.00	2.20	.60
☐ 10 Frank Fuller (Attended ...)	5.00	2.20	.60
☐ 11 Norbert Hecker	5.00	2.20	.60
☐ 12 Elroy Hirsch (1952 stats)	40.00	18.00	5.00
☐ 13 John Hock (Just completed ...)	5.00	2.20	.60
☐ 14 Bob Kelley ANN (Signature in upper left of photo)	5.00	2.20	.60
☐ 15 Dick Lane	25.00	11.00	3.10
☐ 16 Woodley Lewis (Ram utility ...)	6.00	2.70	.75
☐ 17 Tom McCormick (Set three ...)	5.00	2.20	.60
☐ 18 Lewis(Bud) McFadin (Came to Rams ...)	5.00	2.20	.60
☐ 19 Leon McLaughlin (Played every ...)	5.00	2.20	.60
☐ 20 Brad Myers	5.00	2.20	.60
☐ 21 Don Paul (A five year ...)	6.00	2.70	.75
☐ 22 Hampton Pool CO (Hampton Pool ...)	5.00	2.20	.60
☐ 23 Duane Putnam (As rookie ...)	6.00	2.70	.75
☐ 24 Volney Quinlan (Nickname ...)	6.00	2.70	.75
☐ 25 Herb Rich	5.00	2.20	.60
☐ 26 Andy Robustelli (Rams' regular ...)	35.00	16.00	4.40
☐ 27 Vitamin T. Smith	6.00	2.70	.75
☐ 28 Harland Svare (Attended ...)	5.00	2.20	.60
☐ 29 Len Teeuws	5.00	2.20	.60
☐ 30 Harry Thompson (Used at ...)	5.00	2.20	.60
☐ 31 Charley Toogood (Been defensive ...)	5.00	2.20	.60
☐ 32 Deacon Dan Towler (National football ...)	10.00	4.50	1.25
☐ 33 Norm Van Brocklin (1952 stats)	50.00	22.00	6.25
☐ 34 Stan West (Rams' regular ...)	5.00	2.20	.60
☐ 35 Paul(Tank) Younger (1952 stats)	10.00	4.50	1.25
☐ 36 Coaches: John Sauer, William Battles, and Howard(Red) Hickey	6.00	2.70	.75

1954 Rams Team Issue

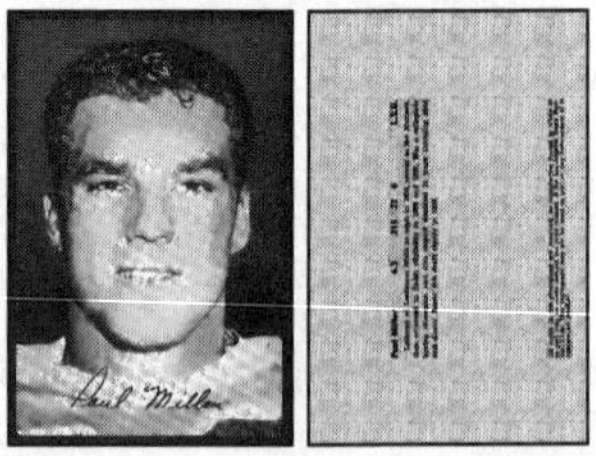

This 36-card set measures approximately 4 1/4" by 6 3/8". The front features a black and white posed action photo enclosed by a black border, with the player's signature across the bottom portion of the picture. The back lists the player's name, height, weight, age, and college, along with basic biographical information. The set was available direct from the team as part of a package for their fans. The cards are listed alphabetically below since they are unnumbered. Many cards from the 1953-1955 and 1957 Rams Team Issue Black Border sets are identical except for text differences on the card backs. Player stat lines are also helpful in identifying year of issue; the year of issue is typically the next year after the last year on the stats. The first few words of the first line of text is listed for players without stat lines. The set features the first card appearance of Gene "Big Daddy" Lipscomb.

	NRMT	VG-E	GOOD
COMPLETE SET (36)	275.00	125.00	34.00
COMMON CARD (1-36)	4.00	1.80	.50
☐ 1 Bob Boyd (One of fastest ...)	5.00	2.20	.60
☐ 2 Bob Carey	4.00	1.80	.50
☐ 3 Bobby Cross	4.00	1.80	.50
☐ 4 Tom Dahms (5 text lines)	4.00	1.80	.50
☐ 5 Don Doll	4.00	1.80	.50
☐ 6 Jack Dwyer (Regular defensive ...)	4.00	1.80	.50
☐ 7 Tom Fears (1953 stats)	20.00	9.00	2.50
☐ 8 Bob Griffin (All American ...)	4.00	1.80	.50
☐ 9 Art Hauser (Was fastest ...)	4.00	1.80	.50
☐ 10 Hall Haynes	4.00	1.80	.50
☐ 11 Elroy Hirsch (1953 stats)	35.00	16.00	4.40
☐ 12 Ed Hughes	4.00	1.80	.50
☐ 13 Bob Kelley ANN (Signature across photo)	4.00	1.80	.50
☐ 14 Woodley Lewis (Established ...)	5.00	2.20	.60
☐ 15 Gene Lipscomb	20.00	9.00	2.50
☐ 16 Tom McCormick (Rams' regular ...)	4.00	1.80	.50
☐ 17 Bud McFadin (Although ...)	4.00	1.80	.50
☐ 18 Leon McLaughlin (Started every ...)	4.00	1.80	.50
☐ 19 Paul Miller (Lettered at ...)	4.00	1.80	.50
☐ 20 Don Paul (One of two ...)	5.00	2.20	.60
☐ 21 Hampton Pool CO (Since taking ...)	4.00	1.80	.50
☐ 22 Duane Putnam (Offensive guard ...)	5.00	2.20	.60
☐ 23 Volney Quinlan (Had best ...)	5.00	2.20	.60
☐ 24 Les Richter (Rated one ...)	5.00	2.20	.60
☐ 25 Andy Robustelli (L.A.'s regular ...)	25.00	11.00	3.10
☐ 26 Willard Sherman (Played at ...)	5.00	2.20	.60
☐ 27 Harland Svare (An outside ...)	4.00	1.80	.50
☐ 28 Harry Thompson (Played offensive ...)	4.00	1.80	.50
☐ 29 Charley Toogood	4.00	1.80	.50

	NRMT	VG-E	GOOD
☐ 30 Deacon Dan Towler	8.00	3.60	1.00
(Since becoming ...)			
☐ 31 Norm Van Brocklin	40.00	18.00	5.00
(1953 stats)			
☐ 32 Bill Wade	12.00	5.50	1.50
(Selected as ...)			
☐ 33 Duane Wardlow	4.00	1.80	.50
☐ 34 Stan West	4.00	1.80	.50
(Virtually ...)			
☐ 35 Paul(Tank) Younger	8.00	3.60	1.00
(1953 stats)			
☐ 36 Coaches Card	5.00	2.20	.60
Bill Battles			
Howard(Red) Hickey			
John Sauer			
Dick Voris			
Buck Weaver			
Hampton Pool			

1955 Rams Team Issue

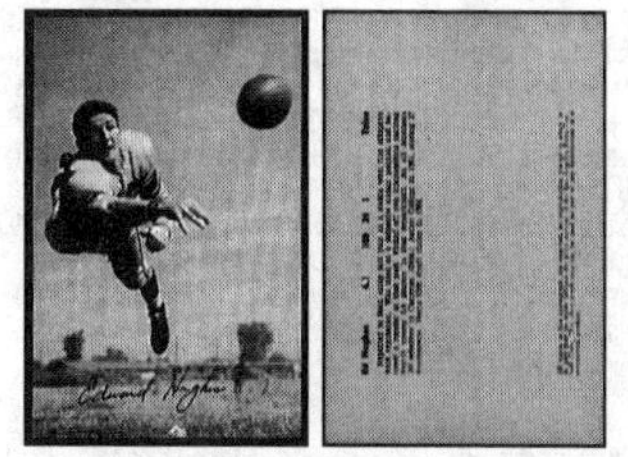

This 37-card set measures approximately 4 1/4" by 6 3/8". The front features a black and white posed action photo enclosed by a black border, with the player's signature across the bottom portion of the picture. The back lists the player's name, height, weight, age, and college, along with basic biographical information. The set was available direct from the team as part of a package for their fans. The cards are listed alphabetically below since they are unnumbered. Many cards from the 1953-1955 and 1957 Rams Team Issue Black Border sets are identical except for text differences on the card backs. Player stat lines are also helpful in identifying year of issue; the year of issue is typically the next year after the last year on the stats. The first few words of the first line of text is listed for players without stat lines.

	NRMT	VG-E	GOOD
COMPLETE SET (37)	250.00	110.00	31.00
COMMON CARD (1-37)	4.00	1.80	.50
☐ 1 Jack Bighead	4.00	1.80	.50
☐ 2 Bob Boyd	5.00	2.20	.60
☐ 3 Don Burroughs	4.00	1.80	.50
☐ 4 Jim Cason	4.00	1.80	.50
☐ 5 Bobby Cross	4.00	1.80	.50
☐ 6 Jack Ellena	4.00	1.80	.50
☐ 7 Tom Fears	15.00	6.75	1.85
☐ 8 Sid Fournet	4.00	1.80	.50
☐ 9 Frank Fuller	5.00	2.20	.60
☐ 10 Sid Gillman and staff	12.00	5.50	1.50
☐ 11 Bob Griffin	4.00	1.80	.50
☐ 12 Art Hauser	4.00	1.80	.50
☐ 13 Hall Haynes	4.00	1.80	.50
☐ 14 Elroy Hirsch	25.00	11.00	3.10
☐ 15 John Hock	4.00	1.80	.50
☐ 16 Glenn Holtzman	4.00	1.80	.50
☐ 17 Ed Hughes	4.00	1.80	.50
☐ 18 Woodley Lewis	5.00	2.20	.60
☐ 19 Gene Lipscomb	12.00	5.50	1.50
☐ 20 Tom McCormick	4.00	1.80	.50
☐ 21 Bud McFadin	4.00	1.80	.50
☐ 22 Leon McLaughlin	4.00	1.80	.50
☐ 23 Paul Miller	4.00	1.80	.50
☐ 24 Larry Morris	4.00	1.80	.50
☐ 25 Don Paul	5.00	2.20	.60
☐ 26 Duane Putnam	5.00	2.20	.60
☐ 27 Volney Quinlan	4.00	1.80	.50
☐ 28 Les Richter	5.00	2.20	.60
☐ 29 Andy Robustelli	15.00	6.75	1.85
☐ 30 Willard Sherman	5.00	2.20	.60
☐ 31 Corky Taylor	4.00	1.80	.50
☐ 32 Charley Toogood	4.00	1.80	.50
☐ 33 Deacon Dan Towler	8.00	3.60	1.00
☐ 34 Norm Van Brocklin	30.00	13.50	3.70
☐ 35 Bill Wade	8.00	3.60	1.00
☐ 36 Ron Waller	4.00	1.80	.50
☐ 37 Paul(Tank) Younger	7.00	3.10	.85

1956 Rams Team Issue

This 37-card team-issued set measures approximately 4 1/4" by 6 3/8" and features members of the Los Angeles Rams. The set has posed action shots on the front framed by a white border with the player's signature across the picture, while the back has biographical information about the player listing the player's name, height, weight, age, number of years in NFL, and college. We have checklisted this (unnumbered) set in alphabetical order. The set was available direct from the team as part of a package for their fans.

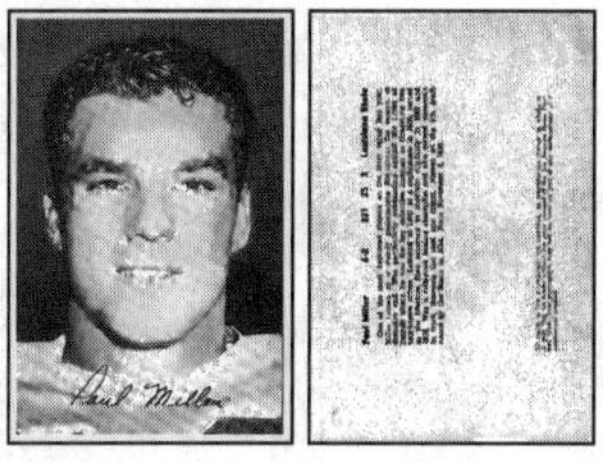

	NRMT	VG-E	GOOD
COMPLETE SET (37)	225.00	100.00	28.00
COMMON CARD (1-37)	4.00	1.80	.50
☐ 1 Bob Boyd	5.00	2.20	.60
☐ 2 Rudy Bukich	5.00	2.20	.60
☐ 3 Don Burroughs	4.00	1.80	.50
☐ 4 Jim Cason	4.00	1.80	.50
☐ 5 Leon Clarke	5.00	2.20	.60
☐ 6 Dick Daugherty	4.00	1.80	.50
☐ 7 Jack Ellena	4.00	1.80	.50
☐ 8 Tom Fears	15.00	6.75	1.85
☐ 9 Sid Fournet	4.00	1.80	.50
☐ 10 Bob Fry	4.00	1.80	.50
☐ 11 Sid Gillman and	10.00	4.50	1.25
Coaches: Joe Madro,			
Jack Faulkner,			
Joe Thomas, and			
Lowell Storm			
☐ 12 Bob Griffin	4.00	1.80	.50
☐ 13 Art Hauser	4.00	1.80	.50
☐ 14 Elroy Hirsch	25.00	11.00	3.10
☐ 15 John Hock	4.00	1.80	.50
☐ 16 Bob Holladay	4.00	1.80	.50
☐ 17 Glenn Holtzman	4.00	1.80	.50
☐ 18 Bob Kelley ANN	4.00	1.80	.50
☐ 19 Joe Marconi	5.00	2.20	.60
☐ 20 Bud McFadin	4.00	1.80	.50
☐ 21 Paul Miller	4.00	1.80	.50
☐ 22 Ron Miller	4.00	1.80	.50
☐ 23 Larry Morris	4.00	1.80	.50
☐ 24 John Morrow	4.00	1.80	.50
☐ 25 Brad Myers	4.00	1.80	.50
☐ 26 Hugh Pitts	4.00	1.80	.50
☐ 27 Duane Putnam	5.00	2.20	.60
☐ 28 Les Richter	5.00	2.20	.60
☐ 29 Willard Sherman	5.00	2.20	.60
☐ 30 Charley Toogood	4.00	1.80	.50
☐ 31 Norm Van Brocklin	30.00	13.50	3.70
☐ 32 Bill Wade	8.00	3.60	1.00
☐ 33 Ron Waller	5.00	2.20	.60
☐ 34 Duane Wardlow	4.00	1.80	.50
☐ 35 Jesse Whittenton	5.00	2.20	.60
☐ 36 Tom Wilson	5.00	2.20	.60
☐ 37 Paul(Tank) Younger	7.00	3.10	.85

1957 Rams Team Issue

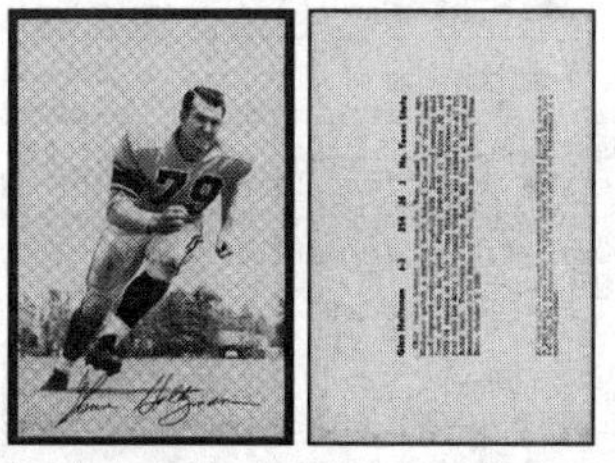

This 38-card team-issued set measures approximately 4 1/4" by 6 3/8" and features posed action shots on the front surrounded by black borders with the player's signature across the picture. The card backs contain biographical information about the player listing the player's name, height, weight, age, number of years in NFL, and college. We have checklisted this (unnumbered) set in alphabetical order. The set was available direct from the team as part of a package for their fans. Many cards from the 1953-1955 and 1957 Rams Team Issue Black Border sets are identical except for text differences on the card backs. Player stat lines are also helpful in identifying year of issue; the year of issue is typically the next year after the last year on the stats. The first few words of the first line of text is listed for players without stat lines. The set features the first card appearance of Jack Pardee.

	NRMT	VG-E	GOOD
COMPLETE SET (38)	225.00	100.00	28.00
COMMON CARD (1-38)	4.00	1.80	.50
☐ 1 Jon Arnett	8.00	3.60	1.00
☐ 2 Bob Boyd	5.00	2.20	.60
(Frequently called ...)			
☐ 3 Alex Bravo	4.00	1.80	.50
☐ 4 Bill Brundige ANN	4.00	1.80	.50
☐ 5 Don Burroughs	4.00	1.80	.50
☐ 6 Jerry Castete	4.00	1.80	.50
☐ 7 Leon Clarke	5.00	2.20	.60
☐ 8 Paige Cothren	4.00	1.80	.50
☐ 9 Dick Daugherty	4.00	1.80	.50
(Has the ...)			
☐ 10 Bob Dougherty	4.00	1.80	.50
☐ 11 Bob Fry	4.00	1.80	.50
(One of the ...)			
☐ 12 Frank Fuller	4.00	1.80	.50
(One of the ...)			
☐ 13 Sid Gillman and	25.00	11.00	3.10
Coaches: Joe Madro,			
George Allen,			
Jack Faulkner, and			
Lowell Storm			
☐ 14 Bob Griffin	4.00	1.80	.50
(After four ...)			
☐ 15 Art Hauser	4.00	1.80	.50
(One of the ...)			
☐ 16 Elroy Hirsch	25.00	11.00	3.10
(A legendary ...)			
☐ 17 John Hock	4.00	1.80	.50
(Teamed with ...)			
☐ 18 Glenn Holtzman	4.00	1.80	.50
☐ 19 John Houser	4.00	1.80	.50
☐ 20 Bob Kelley ANN	4.00	1.80	.50
(Signature near right			
border of photo)			
☐ 21 Lamar Lundy	8.00	3.60	1.00
☐ 22 Joe Marconi	4.00	1.80	.50
☐ 23 Paul Miller	4.00	1.80	.50
(From a ...)			
☐ 24 Larry Morris	4.00	1.80	.50
☐ 25 Ken Panfil	4.00	1.80	.50
☐ 26 Jack Pardee	12.00	5.50	1.50
☐ 27 Duane Putnam	5.00	2.20	.60
(Named to a ...)			
☐ 28 Les Richter	5.00	2.20	.60
(One of the ...)			
☐ 29 Willard Sherman	5.00	2.20	.60
(One of the ...)			
☐ 30 Del Shofner	8.00	3.60	1.00
☐ 31 Billy Ray Smith	6.00	2.70	.75
☐ 32 George Strugar	4.00	1.80	.50
☐ 33 Norm Van Brocklin	30.00	13.50	3.70
(When Van Brocklin ...)			
☐ 34 Bill Wade	8.00	3.60	1.00
(In the first ...)			
☐ 35 Ron Waller	4.00	1.80	.50
☐ 36 Jesse Whittenton	5.00	2.20	.60
☐ 37 Tom Wilson	5.00	2.20	.60
☐ 38 Paul(Tank) Younger	7.00	3.10	.85
(One of a ...)			

1959 Rams Bell Brand

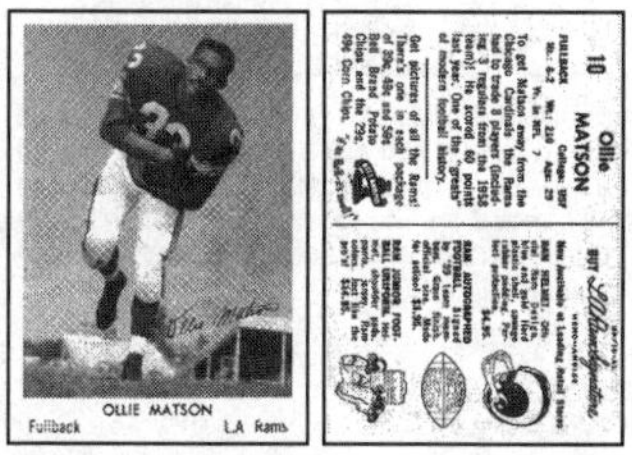

The 1959 Bell Brand Los Angeles Rams set contains 40 numbered standard-size cards. The catalog designation for this set is F387-1. The obverses contain white-bordered color photos of the player with a facsimile autograph. The backs contain the card number, a short biography and vital statistics of the player, a Bell Brand ad, and advertisements for Los Angeles Rams' merchandise. These cards were issued as inserts in potato chip and corn chip bags in the Los Angeles area and are frequently found with oil stains from the chips. The set features the first card appearance of Frank Ryan.

	NRMT	VG-E	GOOD
COMPLETE SET (40)	1500.00	700.00	190.00
COMMON CARD (1-40)	35.00	16.00	4.40
☐ 1 Bill Wade	45.00	20.00	5.50
☐ 2 Buddy Humphrey	35.00	16.00	4.40
☐ 3 Frank Ryan	50.00	22.00	6.25
☐ 4 Ed Meador	40.00	18.00	5.00
☐ 5 Tom Wilson	35.00	16.00	4.40
☐ 6 Don Burroughs	35.00	16.00	4.40
☐ 7 Jon Arnett	45.00	20.00	5.50
☐ 8 Del Shofner	45.00	20.00	5.50
☐ 9 Jack Pardee	50.00	22.00	6.25
☐ 10 Ollie Matson	75.00	34.00	9.50
☐ 11 Joe Marconi	35.00	16.00	4.40
☐ 12 Jim Jones	35.00	16.00	4.40
☐ 13 Jack Morris	35.00	16.00	4.40
☐ 14 Willard Sherman	40.00	18.00	5.00
☐ 15 Clendon Thomas	40.00	18.00	5.00
☐ 16 Les Richter	40.00	18.00	5.00
☐ 17 John Morrow	35.00	16.00	4.40
☐ 18 Lou Michaels	40.00	18.00	5.00
☐ 19 Bob Reifsnyder	35.00	16.00	4.40
☐ 20 John Guzik	35.00	16.00	4.40
☐ 21 Duane Putnam	35.00	16.00	4.40
☐ 22 John Houser	35.00	16.00	4.40
☐ 23 Buck Lansford	35.00	16.00	4.40
☐ 24 Gene Selawski	35.00	16.00	4.40
☐ 25 John Baker	35.00	16.00	4.40
☐ 26 Bob Fry	35.00	16.00	4.40
☐ 27 John Lovetere	35.00	16.00	4.40
☐ 28 George Strugar	35.00	16.00	4.40
☐ 29 Roy Wilkins	35.00	16.00	4.40
☐ 30 Charley Bradshaw	35.00	16.00	4.40
☐ 31 Gene Brito	40.00	18.00	5.00
☐ 32 Jim Phillips	40.00	18.00	5.00
☐ 33 Leon Clarke	40.00	18.00	5.00
☐ 34 Lamar Lundy	45.00	20.00	5.50
☐ 35 Sam Williams	35.00	16.00	4.40
☐ 36 Sid Gillman CO	60.00	27.00	7.50
☐ 37 Jack Faulkner CO	35.00	16.00	4.40
☐ 38 Joe Madro CO	35.00	16.00	4.40
☐ 39 Don Paul CO	35.00	16.00	4.40
☐ 40 Lou Rymkus CO	40.00	18.00	5.00

1960 Rams Bell Brand

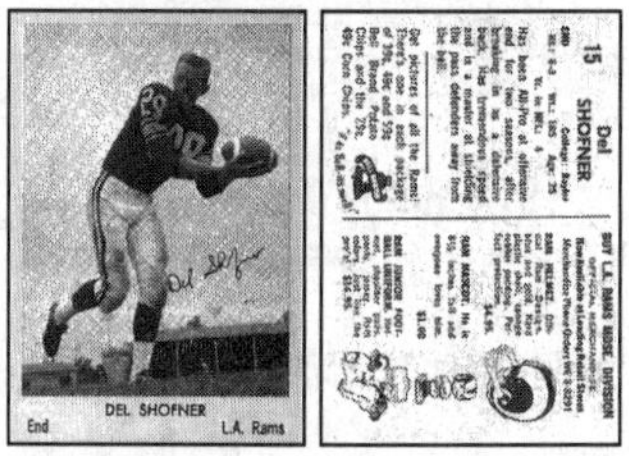

The 1960 Bell Brand Los Angeles Rams Football set contains 39 standard-size cards in a format similar to the 1959 Bell Brand set. The fronts of the cards have distinctive yellow borders. The catalog designation for this set is F387-2. Card numbers 1-18, except number 2, are repeated photos from the 1959 set and were available throughout the season. Numbers 19-39 were available later in the 1960 season. These cards were issued as inserts in potato chip and corn chip bags in the Los Angeles area and are frequently found with oil stains from the chips. Card number 2 Selawski was withdrawn early in the year (after he was cut from the team) and was available only upon request from the company; therefore he is not included in the complete set price below.

	NRMT	VG-E	GOOD
COMPLETE SET (38)	1800.00	800.00	220.00
COMMON CARD (1-18)	25.00	11.00	3.10
COMMON CARD (19-39)	50.00	22.00	6.25
☐ 1 Joe Marconi	25.00	11.00	3.10
☐ 2 Gene Selawski SP	1200.00	550.00	150.00
☐ 3 Frank Ryan	40.00	18.00	5.00
☐ 4 Ed Meador	30.00	13.50	3.70
☐ 5 Tom Wilson	25.00	11.00	3.10
☐ 6 Gene Brito	30.00	13.50	3.70
☐ 7 Jon Arnett	35.00	16.00	4.40
☐ 8 Buck Lansford	25.00	11.00	3.10
☐ 9 Jack Pardee	45.00	20.00	5.50
☐ 10 Ollie Matson	65.00	29.00	8.00
☐ 11 John Lovetere	25.00	11.00	3.10
☐ 12 Bill Jolko	25.00	11.00	3.10
☐ 13 Jim Phillips	30.00	13.50	3.70
☐ 14 Lamar Lundy	35.00	16.00	4.40
☐ 15 Del Shofner	40.00	18.00	5.00
☐ 16 Les Richter	30.00	13.50	3.70
☐ 17 Bill Wade	35.00	16.00	4.40
☐ 18 Lou Michaels	30.00	13.50	3.70
☐ 19 Dick Bass	60.00	27.00	7.50
☐ 20 Charley Britt	50.00	22.00	6.25
☐ 21 Willard Sherman	60.00	27.00	7.50
☐ 22 George Strugar	50.00	22.00	6.25
☐ 23 Bob Long	50.00	22.00	6.25
☐ 24 Danny Villanueva	60.00	27.00	7.50
☐ 25 Jim Boeke	50.00	22.00	6.25
☐ 26 Clendon Thomas	50.00	22.00	6.25
☐ 27 Art Hunter	50.00	22.00	6.25
☐ 28 Carl Karilivacz	50.00	22.00	6.25
☐ 29 John Baker	50.00	22.00	6.25
☐ 30 Charley Bradshaw	50.00	22.00	6.25
☐ 31 John Guzik	50.00	22.00	6.25
☐ 32 Buddy Humphrey	50.00	22.00	6.25
☐ 33 Carroll Dale	60.00	27.00	7.50
☐ 34 Don Ellersick	50.00	22.00	6.25
☐ 35 Ray Hord	50.00	22.00	6.25
☐ 36 Charlie Janerette	50.00	22.00	6.25
☐ 37 John Kenerson	50.00	22.00	6.25
☐ 38 Jerry Stalcup	50.00	22.00	6.25
☐ 39 Bob Waterfield CO	125.00	55.00	15.50

1967 Rams Team Issue

The Los Angeles Rams issued these black and white player photos. Each measures roughly 8" by 10" and is blank backed. The checklist below is thought to be incomplete.

	NRMT	VG-E	GOOD
COMPLETE SET (9)	60.00	27.00	7.50
COMMON CARD (1-9)	3.00	1.35	.35
☐ 1 George Allen CO	10.00	4.50	1.25
☐ 2 Dick Bass	3.00	1.35	.35
☐ 3 Bernie Casey	3.00	1.35	.35
☐ 4 Lamar Lundy	4.00	1.80	.50
☐ 5 Deacon Jones	10.00	4.50	1.25
☐ 6 Les Josephson	3.00	1.35	.35
☐ 7 Merlin Olsen	12.00	5.50	1.50
☐ 8 Jack Snow	4.00	1.80	.50
☐ 9 Team Photo	10.00	4.50	1.25

1973 Rams Team Issue

These approximately 7" by 8 3/4" sheets feature close-up color photos of Los Angeles Rams players. The pictures have white borders with

the player's name and team printed in the bottom border. The backs are blank. The cards are unnumbered and checklisted below in alphabetical order.

	NRMT-MT	EXC	G-VG
COMPLETE SET (6)	30.00	13.50	3.70
COMMON CARD (1-6)	2.50	1.10	.30
☐ 1 Jim Bertelsen	2.50	1.10	.30
☐ 2 John Hadl	7.00	3.10	.85
☐ 3 Harold Jackson	5.00	2.20	.60
☐ 4 Merlin Olsen	10.00	4.50	1.25
☐ 5 Isiah Robertson	3.50	1.55	.45
☐ 6 Jack Snow	3.50	1.55	.45

1974 Rams Team Issue

The Rams issued this group of photos around 1974. Each measures roughly 5" by 7 1/4" and features a black and white player photo on blankbacked paper stock. The player's name and position are included in the border below the photo as is the Rams' helmet logo.

	NRMT-MT	EXC	G-VG
COMPLETE SET (10)	25.00	11.00	3.10
COMMON CARD (1-10)	2.50	1.10	.30
☐ 1 Al Clark	2.50	1.10	.30
☐ 2 Bill Curry	2.50	1.10	.30
☐ 3 Chuck Knox CO	4.00	1.80	.50
☐ 4 Willie McGee	2.50	1.10	.30
☐ 5 Phil Olsen	2.50	1.10	.30
☐ 6 Tony Plummer	2.50	1.10	.30
☐ 7 Steve Preece	2.50	1.10	.30
☐ 8 David Ray	2.50	1.10	.30
☐ 9 Isiah Robertson	3.50	1.55	.45
☐ 10 Charlie Stukes	2.50	1.10	.30

1980 Rams Police

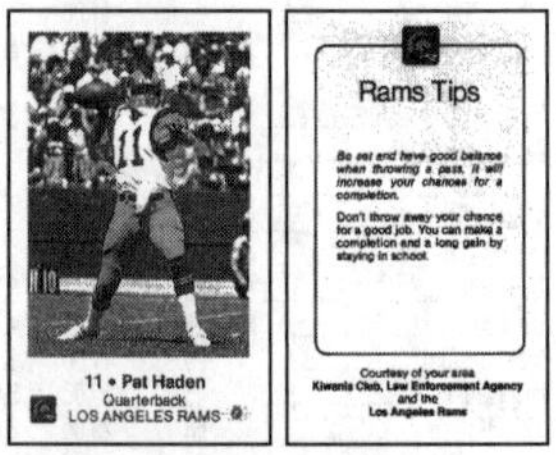

This unnumbered, 14-card set has been listed in the checklist below by uniform number, which appears on the fronts of the cards. The cards measure approximately 2 5/8" by 4 1/8". The Kiwanis Club, who sponsored this set along with the local law enforcement agency and the Rams, has their logo on the fronts of the cards. These cards, which contain "Rams Tips" on the backs, were distributed by police officers, one per week over a 14-week period.

	MINT	NRMT	EXC
COMPLETE SET (14)	20.00	9.00	2.50
COMMON CARD	1.00	.45	.12
☐ 11 Pat Haden	3.50	1.55	.45
☐ 15 Vince Ferragamo	2.50	1.10	.30
☐ 21 Nolan Cromwell	2.50	1.10	.30
☐ 26 Wendell Tyler	2.00	.90	.25
☐ 32 Cullen Bryant	1.25	.55	.16
☐ 53 Jim Youngblood	1.25	.55	.16
☐ 59 Bob Brudzinski	1.00	.45	.12
☐ 61 Rich Saul	1.00	.45	.12
☐ 77 Doug France	1.00	.45	.12
☐ 82 Willie Miller	1.00	.45	.12
☐ 85 Jack Youngblood	4.00	1.80	.50
☐ 88 Preston Dennard	1.00	.45	.12
☐ 90 Larry Brooks	1.00	.45	.12
☐ NNO Ray Malavasi CO	1.00	.45	.12

1985 Rams Smokey

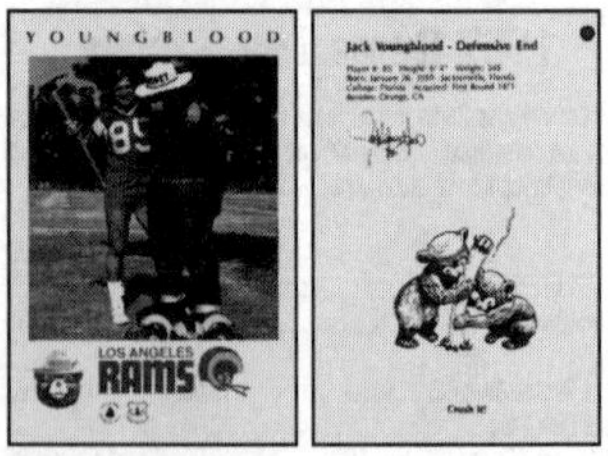

This set of 24 cards was issued in the Summer of 1985 and features players of the Los Angeles Rams. The cards measure approximately 4" by 6". Each card photo also features Smokey Bear. The cards are numbered on the back essentially in alphabetical order; there are a few exceptions and two Smokey cards are unnumbered (listed at the end of the checklist below). Supposedly, LeRoy Irvin is more difficult to find than the other cards in the set.

	MINT	NRMT	EXC
COMPLETE SET (24)	25.00	11.00	3.10
COMMON CARD (1-24)	.75	.35	.09
☐ 1 George Andrews	.75	.35	.09
☐ 2 Bill Bain	.75	.35	.09
☐ 3 Russ Bolinger	.75	.35	.09
☐ 4 Jim Collins	.75	.35	.09
☐ 5 Nolan Cromwell	1.50	.70	.19
☐ 6 Reggie Doss	.75	.35	.09
☐ 7 Carl Ekern	.75	.35	.09
☐ 8 Vince Ferragamo	1.50	.70	.19
☐ 9 Gary Green	.75	.35	.09
☐ 10 Mike Guman	.75	.35	.09
☐ 11 David Hill	.75	.35	.09
☐ 12 LeRoy Irvin SP	6.00	2.70	.75
☐ 13 Mark Jerue	.75	.35	.09
☐ 14 Johnnie Johnson	.75	.35	.09
☐ 15 Jeff Kemp	1.50	.70	.19
☐ 16 Mel Owens	.75	.35	.09
☐ 17 Irv Pankey	.75	.35	.09
☐ 18 Doug Smith	1.00	.45	.12
☐ 19 Ivory Sully	.75	.35	.09
☐ 20 Jack Youngblood	2.00	.90	.25
☐ 21 Mike McDonald	.75	.35	.09
☐ 22 Norwood Vann	.75	.35	.09
☐ 23 Smokey Bear (Unnumbered)	.75	.35	.09
☐ 24 Smokey Bear with Reggie Doss, Gary Green, Johnnie Johnson, and Carl Ekern (Unnumbered)	1.00	.45	.12

1986 Rams Smokey Flipbooks

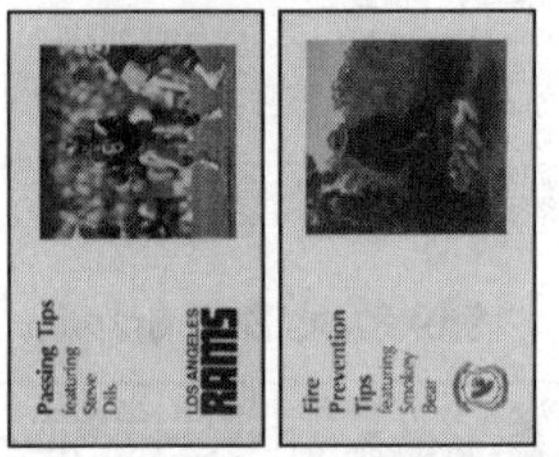

In conjunction with California Fire Prevention, the Rams issued these flipbooks in 1986. The books contain a black and white flip movie of the player on one side and a movie of Smokey on the other side, along with fire prevention tips. The books measure approximately 2 3/4" by 4 1/2" and are unnumbered. We have assigned card numbers to them alphabetically.

	MINT	NRMT	EXC
COMPLETE SET (2)	8.00	3.60	1.00
COMMON BOOK	4.00	1.80	.50
☐ 1 Steve Dils	4.00	1.80	.50
☐ 2 Mike Lansford	4.00	1.80	.50

1987 Rams Jello/General Foods

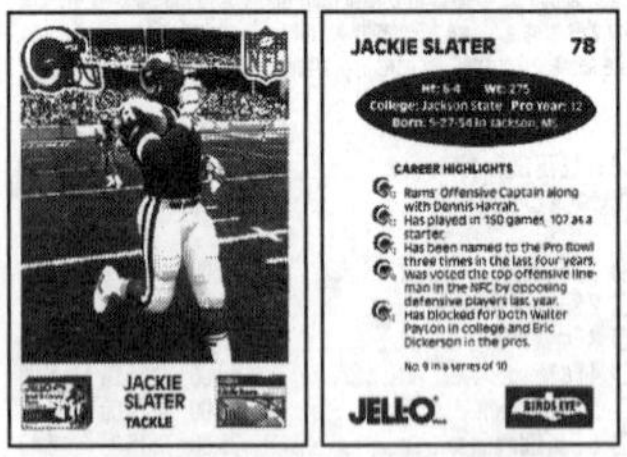

This ten-card standard-size set was sponsored by Jello and Birds Eye and features players of the Los Angeles Rams. The cards are numbered on the back; card backs are printed in black ink on heavy white card stock. The set comes as a perforated sheet including a coupon each for Birds Eye Cob Corn and any Jello product. This unnumbered set is listed below alphabetically.

	MINT	NRMT	EXC
COMPLETE SET (10)	6.00	2.70	.75
COMMON CARD (1-10)	.35	.16	.04
☐ 1 Ron Brown	.50	.23	.06
☐ 2 Nolan Cromwell	.60	.25	.07
☐ 3 Eric Dickerson	2.00	.90	.25
☐ 4 Carl Ekern	.35	.16	.04
☐ 5 Jim Everett	2.00	.90	.25
☐ 6 Dennis Harrah	.35	.16	.04
☐ 7 LeRoy Irvin	.50	.23	.06
☐ 8 Mike Lansford	.35	.16	.04
☐ 9 Jackie Slater	.60	.25	.07
☐ 10 Doug Smith	.50	.23	.06

1987 Rams Oscar Mayer

This 19-card standard-size set was sponsored by Oscar Mayer to honor the Special Teams Player of the Week. On a light blue background, the front features a color head shot inside a bullet hole

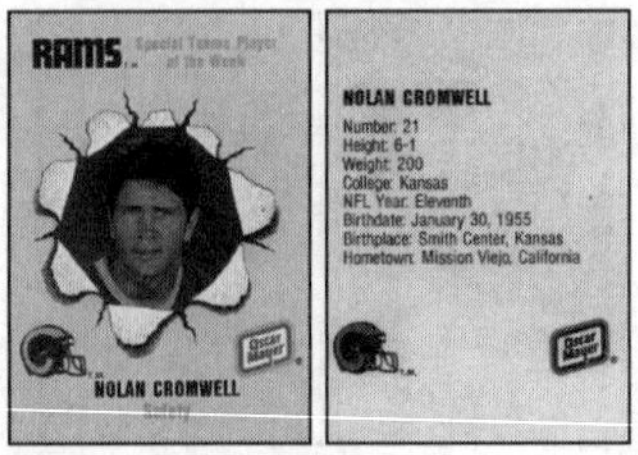

design, with the jagged edges of the paper turned out. The team helmet and sponsor logo appear below the head shot. In dark blue print on white, the backs have biographical information as well as the Rams' helmet and the sponsor logo. The cards are unnumbered and checklisted below in alphabetical order.

	MINT	NRMT	EXC
COMPLETE SET (19)	15.00	6.75	1.85
COMMON CARD (1-19)	.75	.35	.09
☐ 1 Sam Anno	.75	.35	.09
☐ 2 Ron Brown	1.00	.45	.12
☐ 3 Nolan Cromwell	1.25	.55	.16
☐ 4 Henry Ellard	1.50	.70	.19
☐ 5 Jerry Gray	1.00	.45	.12
☐ 6 Kevin Greene	4.00	1.80	.50
☐ 7 Mike Guman	.75	.35	.09
☐ 8 Dale Hatcher	.75	.35	.09
☐ 9 Clifford Hicks	.75	.35	.09
☐ 10 Mark Jerue	.75	.35	.09
☐ 11 Johnnie Johnson	.75	.35	.09
☐ 12 Larry Kelm	.75	.35	.09
☐ 13 Mike Lansford	.75	.35	.09
☐ 14 Vince Newsome	.75	.35	.09
☐ 15 Michael Stewart	.75	.35	.09
☐ 16 Mickey Sutton	.75	.35	.09
☐ 17 Tim Tyrrell	.75	.35	.09
☐ 18 Norwood Vann	.75	.35	.09
☐ 19 Charles White	1.25	.55	.16

1989 Rams Police

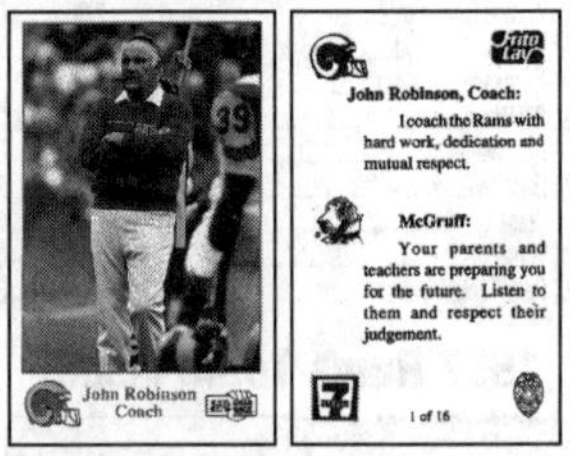

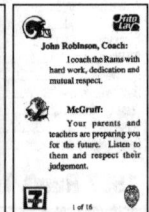

This 16-card standard size set was issued in an uncut (perforated) sheet of 16 numbered cards which feature an action photo of various members of the 1989 Rams on the front and a football tip along with a safety tip on the back of the card. The safety tip features the popular anti-crime mascot McGruff. There was also a coupon for Frito-Lay products on the bottom of the sheet. The set was also sponsored by 7-Eleven stores.

	MINT	NRMT	EXC
COMPLETE SET (16)	12.00	5.50	1.50
COMMON CARD (1-16)	1.00	.45	.12
☐ 1 John Robinson CO	1.50	.70	.19
☐ 2 Jim Everett	2.00	.90	.25
☐ 3 Doug Smith	1.25	.55	.16
☐ 4 Duval Love	1.00	.45	.12
☐ 5 Henry Ellard	2.50	1.10	.30
☐ 6 Mel Owens	1.00	.45	.12
☐ 7 Jerry Gray	1.25	.55	.16
☐ 8 Kevin Greene	3.00	1.35	.35
☐ 9 Vince Newsome	1.00	.45	.12
☐ 10 Irv Pankey	1.00	.45	.12
☐ 11 Tom Newberry	1.25	.55	.16
☐ 12 Pete Holohan	1.00	.45	.12
☐ 13 Mike Lansford	1.00	.45	.12
☐ 14 Greg Bell	1.25	.55	.16
☐ 15 Jackie Slater	1.25	.55	.16
☐ 16 Dale Hatcher	1.00	.45	.12

1990 Rams Smokey

This 12-card set features members of the 1990 Rams and was sponsored by local Fire Departments. Borderless cardfronts feature a color player photo with backs including a small black and white photo and player bio. The cards measure approximately 3 3/4" by 5 3/4" and are unnumbered.

	MINT	NRMT	EXC
COMPLETE SET (12)	10.00	4.50	1.25
COMMON CARD	.75	.35	.09
☐ 1 Aaron Cox	.75	.35	.09
☐ 2 Henry Ellard	1.50	.70	.19
☐ 3 Jim Everett	1.25	.55	.16
☐ 4 Jerry Gray	1.00	.45	.12
☐ 5 Kevin Greene	2.00	.90	.25
☐ 6 Pete Holohan	.75	.35	.09
☐ 7 Mike Lansford	.75	.35	.09
☐ 8 Vince Newsome	.75	.35	.09
☐ 9 Doug Reed	.75	.35	.09
☐ 10 Jackie Slater	1.00	.45	.12
☐ 11 Fred Strickland	.75	.35	.09
☐ 12 Mike Wilcher	.75	.35	.09

1992 Rams Carl's Jr.

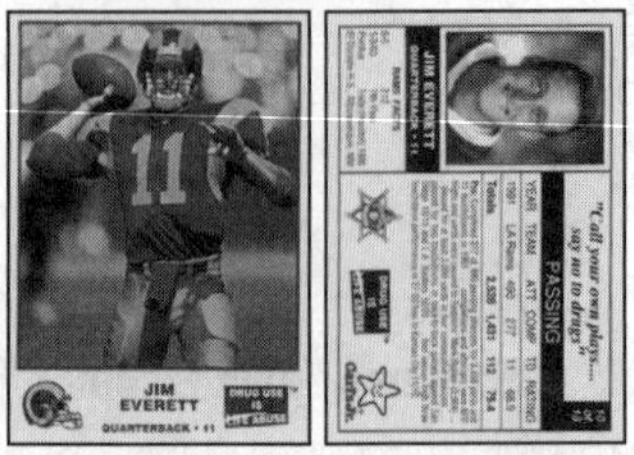

This 21-card safety standard-size set was sponsored by Carl's Jr. restaurants and distributed by the Orange County Sheriff's Department. It was reported that 80,000 sets were produced. Eleven Rams players participated in the program with autograph sessions at six Carl's Junior restaurants in Southern California. The fronts feature color action player photos inside a blue picture frame on a white card face. Player information appears below the photo between a Rams' helmet and a "Drug Use is Life Abuse" warning. Printed in black on white, the horizontal backs have a black-and-white headshot, biography, player profile, and an anti-drug or alcohol slogan.

	MINT	NRMT	EXC
COMPLETE SET (21)	12.00	5.50	1.50
COMMON CARD (1-18)	.60	.25	.07
☐ 1 Carl Karcher (Founder)	.60	.25	.07
☐ 2 Happy Star (Carl's Jr. symbol)	.75	.35	.09
☐ 3 Tony Zendejas	.60	.25	.07
☐ 4 Henry Ellard	1.50	.70	.19
☐ 5 Jackie Slater	.75	.35	.09
☐ 6 Bern Brostek	.60	.25	.07
☐ 7 Cleveland Gary	.75	.35	.09
☐ 8 Larry Kelm	.60	.25	.07
☐ 9 Roman Phifer	.75	.35	.09
☐ 10 Jim Everett	1.25	.55	.16
☐ 11 Anthony Newman	.60	.25	.07
☐ 12 Steve Israel	.60	.25	.07
☐ 13 Marc Boutte	.75	.35	.09
☐ 14 Darryl Henley	.60	.25	.07
☐ 15 Michael Stewart	.60	.25	.07
☐ 16 Flipper Anderson	.75	.35	.09
☐ 17 Kevin Greene	2.00	.90	.25
☐ 18 Sean Gilbert	1.25	.55	.16
☐ NNO Skippy Be Drug Free	.75	.35	.09
☐ NNO Spike Be Drug Free	.75	.35	.09
☐ NNO Wise Owl Mike Be Drug Free	.75	.35	.09

1994 Rams L.A. Times

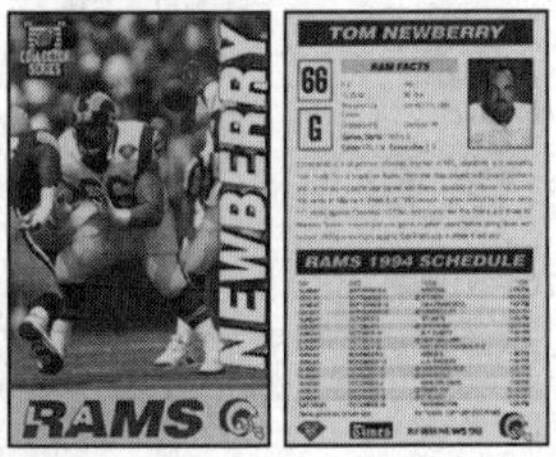

These 32 collector sheets were issued by the Los Angeles Times, were printed on semi-gloss paper, and measure approximately 5 1/2" by 8 1/2". The fronts feature color player action shots that are borderless, except at the bottom, where a yellow border carries the team name and helmet logo. The player's last name appears in large white vertical lettering near the right edge. The white back carries the player's name at the top, followed below by his uniform number, position, biography, head shot, career highlights and Rams 1994 game schedule. The sheets are numbered on the front as "X of 32." These sheets were distributed as inserts in weekend issues of the paper. Cleveland Gary and Marc Boutte were pulled from the set and not distributed since they were no longer with the Rams at the inception of the promotion.

	MINT	NRMT	EXC
COMPLETE SET (32)	12.00	5.50	1.50
COMMON CARD (1-32)	.40	.18	.05
☐ 1 Toby Wright	.40	.18	.05
☐ 2 Tim Lester	.40	.18	.05
☐ 3 Shane Conlan	.50	.23	.06
☐ 4 Troy Drayton	.50	.23	.06
☐ 5 Fred Stokes	.40	.18	.05
☐ 6 Jerome Bettis	2.50	1.10	.30
☐ 7 Jimmie Jones	.40	.18	.05
☐ 8 Henry Rolling	.40	.18	.05

	MINT	NRMT	EXC
☐ 9 Anthony Newman	.40	.18	.05
☐ 10 Flipper Anderson	.75	.35	.09
☐ 11 Steve Israel	.40	.18	.05
☐ 12 Johnny Bailey	.40	.18	.05
☐ 13 Jackie Slater	.50	.23	.06
☐ 14 Chris Chandler	.50	.23	.06
☐ 15 Sean Landeta	.40	.18	.05
☐ 16 Bern Brostek	.40	.18	.05
☐ 17 Roman Phifer	.40	.18	.05
☐ 18 Robert Young	.50	.23	.06
☐ 19 Leo Goeas	.40	.18	.05
☐ 20 Chris Miller	.75	.35	.09
☐ 21 Darryl Ashmore	.40	.18	.05
☐ 22 Joe Kelly	.40	.18	.05
☐ 23 Wayne Gandy	.50	.23	.06
☐ 24 Tony Zendejas	.40	.18	.05
☐ 25 Tom Newberry	.40	.18	.05
☐ 26 David Lang	.40	.18	.05
☐ 27 Sean Gilbert	.50	.23	.06
☐ 28 Chris Martin	.40	.18	.05
☐ 29 Thomas Homco	.40	.18	.05
☐ 30 Chuck Knox CO	.50	.23	.06
☐ 31 Todd Lyght	.50	.23	.06
☐ 32 Jerome Bettis Sean Gilbert	1.00	.45	.12

1995 Rams Upper Deck McDonalds

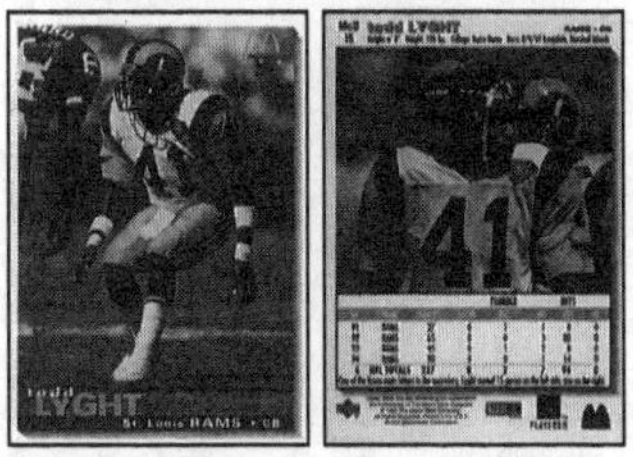

Upper Deck produced this set for distribution through McDonald's restaurants in the St.Louis area. The cards were sold in five-card packs for 79 cents per pack with the purchase of any McDonald's Value Meal. The cards were primarily available in the month of October and all royalties for the promotion were donated to Ronald McDonald Children's Charities. The phrases "Special Edition" and "Premiere Season" are printed in gold lettering running up the edge of the front, and the McDonald's logo appears in the upper right corner. The backs present biography, a second color photo, and a table displaying season-by-season statistics.

	MINT	NRMT	EXC
COMPLETE SET (26)	8.00	3.60	1.00
COMMON CARD (MCD1-MCD25)	.25	.11	.03
☐ MCD1 Johnny Bailey	.25	.11	.03
☐ MCD2 Jerome Bettis	1.25	.55	.16
☐ MCD3 Isaac Bruce	2.00	.90	.25
☐ MCD4 Kevin Carter	.40	.18	.05
☐ MCD5 Shane Conlan	.25	.11	.03
☐ MCD6 Troy Drayton	.40	.18	.05
☐ MCD7 Wayne Gandy	.40	.18	.05
☐ MCD8 Sean Gilbert	.40	.18	.05
☐ MCD9 Jessie Hester	.25	.11	.03
☐ MCD10 Bern Brostek	.25	.11	.03
☐ MCD11 Jimmie Jones	.25	.11	.03
☐ MCD12 Todd Kinchen	.40	.18	.05
☐ MCD13 Sean Landeta	.25	.11	.03
☐ MCD14 Thomas Homco	.25	.11	.03
☐ MCD15 Todd Lyght	.25	.11	.03
☐ MCD16 Keith Lyle	.25	.11	.03
☐ MCD17 Chris Miller	.40	.18	.05
☐ MCD18 Toby Wright	.25	.11	.03
☐ MCD19 Anthony Parker	.25	.11	.03
☐ MCD20 Roman Phifer	.25	.11	.03
☐ MCD21 Leonard Russell	.25	.11	.03
☐ MCD22 Jackie Slater	.40	.18	.05
☐ MCD23 Fred Stokes	.25	.11	.03
☐ MCD24 Alexander Wright	.25	.11	.03
☐ MCD25 Robert Young	.40	.18	.05
☐ NNO Checklist Card	.40	.18	.05

1996 Ravens Score Board/Exxon

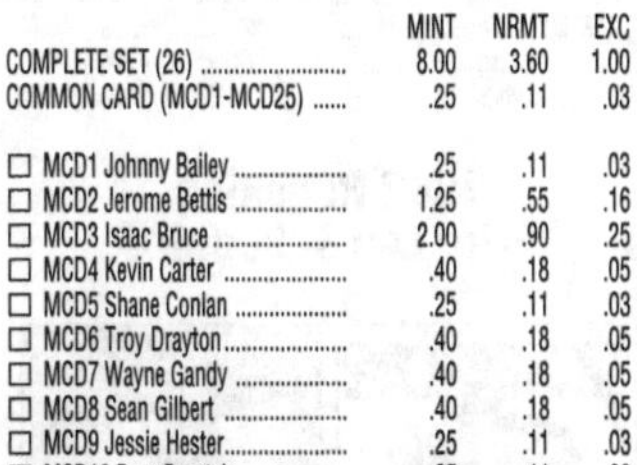

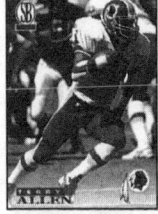

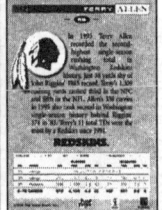

Score Board produced this team set for distribution by the Baltimore area Exxon stations. Each card appears similar to a 1996 Pro Line card, but contains the Score Board logo at the top. The Exxon sponsor logo appears only on the checklist card. Packs could be obtained, with the appropriate gasoline purchase, for 49-cents each and contained three-player cards and a checklist card.

	MINT	NRMT	EXC
COMPLETE SET (9)	2.50	1.10	.30
COMMON CARD (BR1-BR9)	.25	.11	.03
☐ BR1 Vinny Testaverde	.40	.18	.05
☐ BR2 Eric Zeier	.40	.18	.05
☐ BR3 Earnest Byner	.25	.11	.03
☐ BR4 Derrick Alexander WR	.75	.35	.09
☐ BR5 Michael Jackson	.40	.18	.05
☐ BR6 Jonathan Ogden	.25	.11	.03
☐ BR7 Ray Lewis	.25	.11	.03
☐ BR8 Eric Turner	.25	.11	.03
☐ BR9 Ravens Checklist	.25	.11	.03

1939 Redskins Matchbooks

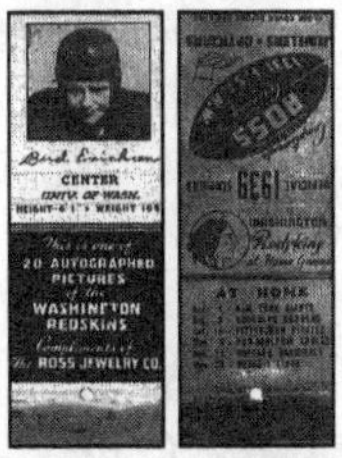

Sponsored by Ross Jewelers, these 20 matchbooks measure approximately 1 1/2" by 4 1/2" (when completely folded out) and feature black-and-white photos of the 1939 Washington Redskins, with simulated autographs on the inside panel. The player's position and college, along with his height and weight, appear below the photo. The bottom half of the inside panel reads "This is one of 20 autographed pictures of the Washington Redskins compliments of the Ross Jewelry Co." In maroon lettering upon a gold background, the top half of the outside of the matchbook carries on its front the Ross Company name and address within a drawing of a football. the Redskins 1939 home game schedule is shown on the bottom half. This is the only distinguishing characteristic between the 1939 and 1940 issues. The covers of Jim Barber and Steve Slivinski are considered scarce. The matchbooks are unnumbered and checklisted below in alphabetical order. The prices given are for full covers (with strikers) missing the actual matches. This is the form in which the matchbooks are most commonly found. Complete books with matches typically carry a 50% premium. Books missing the striker are considered VG at best.

	EX-MT	VG-E	GOOD
COMPLETE SET (20)	600.00	275.00	75.00
COMMON MATCHBOOK (1-20)	15.00	6.75	1.85
☐ 1 Jim Barber SP	135.00	60.00	17.00
☐ 2 Sammy Baugh	90.00	40.00	11.00
☐ 3 Hal Bradley	15.00	6.75	1.85
☐ 4 Vic Carroll	15.00	6.75	1.85
☐ 5 Bud Erickson	15.00	6.75	1.85
☐ 6 Andy Farkas	15.00	6.75	1.85
☐ 7 Frank Filchock	15.00	6.75	1.85
☐ 8 Ray Flaherty CO	18.00	8.00	2.20
☐ 9 Don Irwin	15.00	6.75	1.85
☐ 10 Ed Justice	15.00	6.75	1.85
☐ 11 Jim Karcher	15.00	6.75	1.85
☐ 12 Max Krause	15.00	6.75	1.85
☐ 13 Charley Malone	15.00	6.75	1.85
☐ 14 Bob Masterson	15.00	6.75	1.85
☐ 15 Wayne Millner	20.00	9.00	2.50
☐ 16 Mickey Parks	15.00	6.75	1.85
☐ 17 Erny Pinckert	15.00	6.75	1.85
☐ 18 Steve Slivinski SP	135.00	60.00	17.00
☐ 19 Clem Stralka	15.00	6.75	1.85
☐ 20 Jay Turner	15.00	6.75	1.85

1940 Redskins Matchbooks

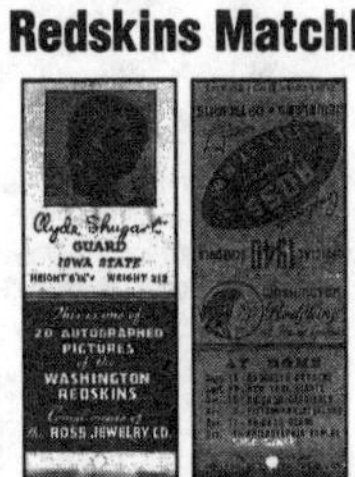

Made for Ross Jewelers by the Universal Match Corp. of Philadelphia, these 20 matchbooks measure approximately 1 1/2" by 4 1/2" (when completely folded out) and feature black-and-white photos of the 1940 Washington Redskins, with simulated autographs on the inside panel. The player's position and college, along with his height and weight, appear below the photo. The bottom half of the inside panel reads "This is one of 20 autographed pictures of the Washington Redskins compliments of Ross Jewelry Co." In maroon lettering upon a gold background, the top half of the outside of the matchbook carries on its front the Ross Company name and address within a drawing of a football. On the bottom half is shown the Redskins 1940 home game schedule. This is the only distinguishing characteristic between the 1939 and 1940 issues. The matchbooks are unnumbered and checklisted below in alphabetical order. The prices given are for full covers (with strikers) missing the actual matches. This is the form in which the matchbooks are most commonly found. Complete books with matches typically carry a 50% premium. Books missing the striker are considered VG at best.

	EX-MT	VG-E	GOOD
COMPLETE SET (20)	300.00	135.00	38.00
COMMON MATCHBOOK (1-20)	12.00	5.50	1.50
☐ 1 Jim Barber	12.00	5.50	1.50
☐ 2 Sammy Baugh	75.00	34.00	9.50
☐ 3 Vic Carroll	12.00	5.50	1.50
☐ 4 Turk Edwards	30.00	13.50	3.70
☐ 5 Andy Farkas	12.00	5.50	1.50
☐ 6 Dick Farman	12.00	5.50	1.50
☐ 7 Bob Hoffman	12.00	5.50	1.50
☐ 8 Don Irwin	12.00	5.50	1.50
☐ 9 Charley Malone	12.00	5.50	1.50
☐ 10 Bob Masterson	12.00	5.50	1.50
☐ 11 Wayne Millner	20.00	9.00	2.50
☐ 12 Mickey Parks	12.00	5.50	1.50
☐ 13 Erny Pinckert	12.00	5.50	1.50
☐ 14 Bo Russell	12.00	5.50	1.50
☐ 15 Clyde Shugart	12.00	5.50	1.50
☐ 16 Steve Slivinski	12.00	5.50	1.50
☐ 17 Clem Stralka	12.00	5.50	1.50
☐ 18 Dick Todd	12.00	5.50	1.50
☐ 19 Bill Young	12.00	5.50	1.50
☐ 20 Roy Zimmerman	12.00	5.50	1.50

1941 Redskins Matchbooks

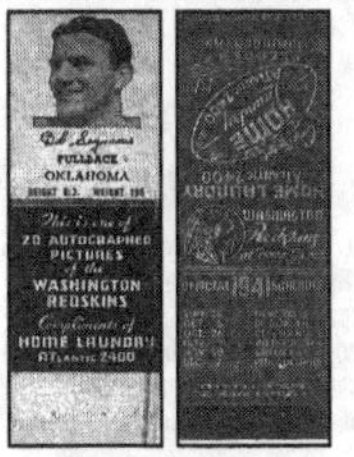

Made for Home Laundry by the Maryland Match Co. of Baltimore, these 20 matchbooks measure approximately 1 1/2" by 4 1/2" (when completely folded out) and feature black-and-white photos of the 1941 Washington Redskins, with simulated autographs on the inside panel. The player's position and college, along with his height and weight, appear below the photo. The bottom half of the inside panel reads "This is one of 20 autographed pictures of the Washington Redskins compliments of Home Laundry," followed by the business's 1941 six-digit phone number, ATlantic 2400. In gold lettering upon a maroon background, the outside of the matchbook carries on its front the Home Laundry name and telephone number within a drawing of a football. On the back is shown the Redskins 1941 home game schedule, which ended with a game against Philadelphia, on Sunday, Dec. 7, 1941. The matchbooks are unnumbered and checklisted below in alphabetical order. The prices given are for full covers (with strikers) missing the actual matches. This is the form in which the matchbooks are most commonly found. Complete books with matches typically carry a 50% premium. Books missing the striker are considered VG at best.

	EX-MT	VG-E	GOOD
COMPLETE SET (20)	225.00	100.00	28.00
COMMON MATCHBOOK (1-20)	10.00	4.50	1.25
☐ 1 Ki Aldrich	10.00	4.50	1.25
☐ 2 Jim Barber	10.00	4.50	1.25
☐ 3 Sammy Baugh	60.00	27.00	7.50
☐ 4 Vic Carroll	10.00	4.50	1.25
☐ 5 Fred Davis	10.00	4.50	1.25
☐ 6 Andy Farkas	10.00	4.50	1.25
☐ 7 Dick Farman	10.00	4.50	1.25
☐ 8 Frank Filchock	10.00	4.50	1.25
☐ 9 Ray Flaherty CO	15.00	6.75	1.85
☐ 10 Bob Masterson	10.00	4.50	1.25
☐ 11 Bob McChesney	10.00	4.50	1.25
☐ 12 Wayne Millner	15.00	6.75	1.85
☐ 13 Wilbur Moore	10.00	4.50	1.25
☐ 14 Bob Seymour	10.00	4.50	1.25
☐ 15 Clyde Shugart	10.00	4.50	1.25
☐ 16 Clem Stralka	10.00	4.50	1.25
☐ 17 Robert Titchenal	10.00	4.50	1.25
☐ 18 Dick Todd	10.00	4.50	1.25
☐ 19 Bill Young	10.00	4.50	1.25
☐ 20 Roy Zimmerman	10.00	4.50	1.25

1942 Redskins Matchbooks

Made for Home Laundry by the Maryland Match Co. of Baltimore, these 20 matchbooks measure approximately 1 1/2" by 4 1/2" (when completely folded out) and feature black-and-white photos of the 1942 Washington Redskins, with simulated autographs, on the inside panel. The player's position and college, along with his height and weight, appear below the photo. The bottom half of the inside panel reads "This is one of 20 autographed pictures of the Washington Redskins compliments of Home Laundry," followed by the business's 1942 six-digit phone number, ATlantic 2400. In maroon lettering upon a yellow-orange background, the outside of the matchbook carries on its front the Home Laundry name and telephone number within a drawing of a football. On the back is shown the Redskins 1942 home game schedule. The matchbooks are unnumbered and checklisted below in alphabetical order. The prices given are for full covers (with strikers) missing the actual matches. This is the form in which the matchbooks are most commonly found. Complete books with matches typically carry a 50% premium. Books missing the striker are considered VG at best.

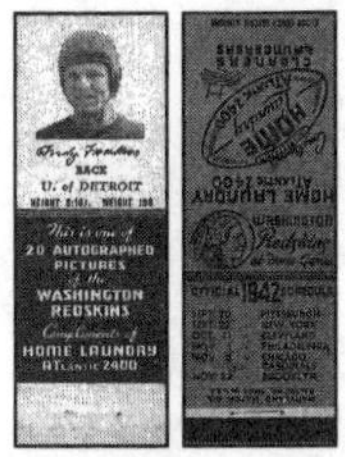

	EX-MT	VG-E	GOOD
COMPLETE SET (20)	225.00	100.00	28.00
COMMON MATCHBOOK (1-20)	10.00	4.50	1.25
☐ 1 Ki Aldrich	10.00	4.50	1.25
☐ 2 Sammy Baugh	60.00	27.00	7.50
☐ 3 Joe Beinor	10.00	4.50	1.25
☐ 4 Vic Carroll	10.00	4.50	1.25
☐ 5 Ed Cifers	10.00	4.50	1.25
☐ 6 Fred Davis	10.00	4.50	1.25
☐ 7 Turk Edwards	20.00	9.00	2.50
☐ 8 Andy Farkas	10.00	4.50	1.25
☐ 9 Dick Farman	10.00	4.50	1.25
☐ 10 Ray Flaherty CO	15.00	6.75	1.85
☐ 11 Al Krueger	10.00	4.50	1.25
☐ 12 Bob Masterson	10.00	4.50	1.25
☐ 13 Bob McChesney	10.00	4.50	1.25
☐ 14 Wilbur Moore	10.00	4.50	1.25
☐ 15 Bob Seymour	10.00	4.50	1.25
☐ 16 Clyde Shugart	10.00	4.50	1.25
☐ 17 Clem Stralka	10.00	4.50	1.25
☐ 18 Dick Todd	10.00	4.50	1.25
☐ 19 Willie Wilkin	10.00	4.50	1.25
☐ 20 Bill Young	10.00	4.50	1.25

1951-52 Redskins Matchbooks

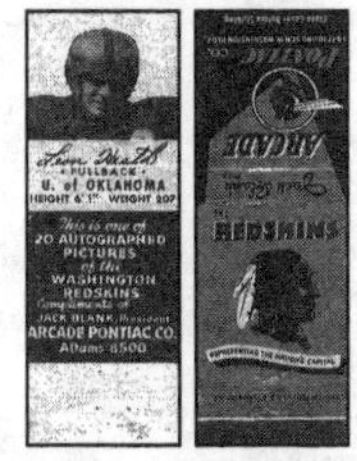

Sponsored by Arcade Pontiac and produced by the Universal Match Corp.,Washington D.C., these 20 matchbooks measure approximately 1 1/2" by 4 1/2" (when completely folded out) and feature small black-and-white photos of the 1951 and 1952 Washington Redskins, with simulated autographs on the inside panel. The player's position and college, along with his height and weight, appear below the photo. The bottom half of the inside panel reads "This is one of 20 autographed pictures of the Washington Redskins compliments of Jack Blank, President Arcade Pontiac Co.," followed by the business' 1950s six-digit phone number, ADams 8500. The outside of the matchbook carries on its top half the Arcade Pontiac name along with a logo on a black and gold background. On the bottom half is shown the Redskins logo on a gold background. The matchbooks are unnumbered and checklisted below in alphabetical order. Most of the 20-matchbooks were released in both 1951 and 1952 with a few containing very minor differences in the photo cropping. Major variations between the two years and covers issued only one year are listed below as such. The prices given are for full covers (with strikers) missing the actual matches. This is the form in which the matchbooks are most commonly found. Complete books with matches typically carry a 50% premium. Books missing the striker are considered VG at best.

	NRMT	VG-E	GOOD
COMPLETE SET (25)	250.00	110.00	31.00
COMMON MATCHBOOK (1-25)	8.00	3.60	1.00
☐ 1 John Badaczewski	8.00	3.60	1.00
☐ 2A Herman Ball CO Head Coach	10.00	4.50	1.25
☐ 2B Herman Ball CO Assistant Coach	10.00	4.50	1.25
☐ 3 Sammy Baugh	50.00	22.00	6.25
☐ 4 Ed Berrang 1951	10.00	4.50	1.25
☐ 5 Dan Brown 1951	10.00	4.50	1.25
☐ 6 Al DeMao	8.00	3.60	1.00
☐ 7 Harry Dowda 1952	10.00	4.50	1.25
☐ 8 Chuck Drazenovich	8.00	3.60	1.00
☐ 9 Bill Dudley 1951	20.00	9.00	2.50
☐ 10 Harry Gilmer	12.00	5.50	1.50
☐ 11 Bob Goode 1951	10.00	4.50	1.25
☐ 12 Leon Heath 1952	10.00	4.50	1.25
☐ 13 Charlie Justice 1952	15.00	6.75	1.85

☐ 14 Lou Karras	8.00	3.60	1.00
☐ 15 Eddie LeBaron 1952	15.00	6.75	1.85
☐ 16 Paul Lipscomb	8.00	3.60	1.00
☐ 17 Laurie Niemi	8.00	3.60	1.00
☐ 18 Johnny Papit 1952	10.00	4.50	1.25
☐ 19 James Peebles 1951	10.00	4.50	1.25
☐ 20 Ed Quirk	8.00	3.60	1.00
☐ 21 Jim Ricca 1952	10.00	4.50	1.25
☐ 22 James Staton 1951	10.00	4.50	1.25
☐ 23 Hugh Taylor	10.00	4.50	1.25
☐ 24 Joe Tereshinski	8.00	3.60	1.00
☐ 25 Dick Todd CO 1952	10.00	4.50	1.25

1958-59 Redskins Matchbooks

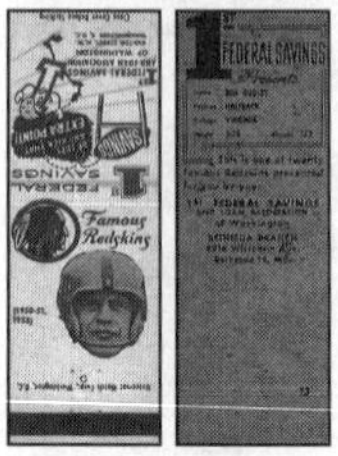

Sponsored by First Federal Savings and produced by Universal Match Corp., Washington D.C., these 20 matchcovers measure approximately 1 1/2" by 4 1/2" (when completely folded out). Each front cover features a small black-and-white photo of a popular Washington Redskins player with the Redskins logo and the title "Famous Redskins" on the bottom half and a First Federal Savings advertisement on the top half. A player profile is given at the top of the matchcover back along with the words "This is one of twenty famous Redskins presented for you by your 1st Federal Savings and Loan Association of Washington, Bethesda Branch," followed by the address. The matchbooks are unnumbered and checklisted below in alphabetical order. It is most commonly thought that the set was issued in two ten-cover series over a two-year period. We've included the presumed year of issue after each cover. The matchbooks are very similar to the 1960-61 issue, but can be distinguished by their light gray colored paper stock instead of off-white. The prices given are for full covers (with strikers) missing the actual matches. This is the form in which the matchbooks are most commonly found. Complete books with matches typically carry a 50% premium. Books missing the striker are considered VG at best.

	NRMT	VG-E	GOOD
COMPLETE SET (20)	200.00	90.00	25.00
COMMON MATCHBOOK (1-20)	8.00	3.60	1.00
☐ 1 Steve Bagarus 58	8.00	3.60	1.00
☐ 2 Cliff Battles 58	16.00	7.25	2.00
☐ 3 Sammy Baugh 58	40.00	18.00	5.00
☐ 4 Gene Brito 58	8.00	3.60	1.00
☐ 5 Jim Castiglia 58	8.00	3.60	1.00
☐ 6 Al DeMao 58	8.00	3.60	1.00
☐ 7 Chuck Drazenovich 59	8.00	3.60	1.00
☐ 8 Bill Dudley 59	18.00	8.00	2.20
☐ 9 Al Fiorentino 59	8.00	3.60	1.00
☐ 10 Don Irwin 59	8.00	3.60	1.00
☐ 11 Eddie LeBaron 58	14.00	6.25	1.75
☐ 12 Wayne Millner 58	14.00	6.25	1.75
☐ 13 Wilbur Moore 58	10.00	4.50	1.25
☐ 14 Jim Schrader 59	8.00	3.60	1.00
☐ 15 Riley Smith 59	8.00	3.60	1.00
☐ 16 Mike Sommer 59	8.00	3.60	1.00
☐ 17 Joe Tereshinski 58	8.00	3.60	1.00
☐ 18 Dick Todd 59	8.00	3.60	1.00
☐ 19 Willie Wilkin 59	8.00	3.60	1.00
☐ 20 Casimir Witucki 59	8.00	3.60	1.00

1960-61 Redskins Matchbooks

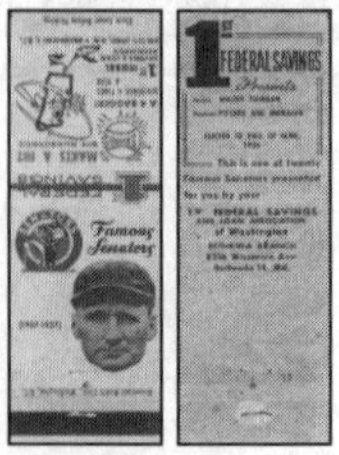

Sponsored by First Federal Savings and produced by Universal Match Corp., Washington D.C., these 20 matchcovers measure approximately 1 1/2" by 4 1/2" (when completely folded out). Each front cover features a small black-and-white photo of a popular Washington Redskins player with the Redskins logo and the title "Famous Redskins" on the bottom half and a First Federal Savings advertisement on the top half. A player profile is given at the top of the matchcover back along with the words "This is one of twenty famous Redskins presented for you by your 1st Federal Savings and Loan Association of Washington, Bethesda Branch," followed by the address and a Universal Match Corporation company logo. The matchbooks are unnumbered and checklisted below in alphabetical order. It is most commonly thought that the set was issued in two ten-cover series over a two-year period. We've included the presumed year of issue after each cover. The matchbooks are very similar to the 1958-59 issue, but can be distinguished by their off-white colored paper stock instead of light gray. The prices given are for full covers (with strikers) missing the actual matches. This is the form in which the matchbooks are most commonly found. Complete books with matches typically carry a 50% premium. Books missing the striker are considered VG at best.

	NRMT	VG-E	GOOD
COMPLETE SET (20)	175.00	80.00	22.00
COMMON MATCHBOOK (1-20)	8.00	3.60	1.00
☐ 1 Bill Anderson 61	10.00	4.50	1.25
☐ 2 Don Bosseler 60	10.00	4.50	1.25
☐ 3 Turk Edwards 60	18.00	8.00	2.20
☐ 4 Ralph Guglielmi 61	10.00	4.50	1.25
☐ 5 Bill Hartman 60	8.00	3.60	1.00
☐ 6 Norb Hecker 61	8.00	3.60	1.00
☐ 7 Dick James 61	10.00	4.50	1.25
☐ 8 Charlie Justice 60	14.00	6.25	1.75
☐ 9 Ray Krouse 61	8.00	3.60	1.00
☐ 10 Ray Lemek 61	8.00	3.60	1.00
☐ 11 Tommy Mont 60	8.00	3.60	1.00
☐ 12 John Olszewski 61	10.00	4.50	1.25
☐ 13 John Paluck 61	8.00	3.60	1.00
☐ 14 Jim Peebles 60	8.00	3.60	1.00
☐ 15 Bo Russell 60	8.00	3.60	1.00
☐ 16 Jim Schrader 61	8.00	3.60	1.00
☐ 17 Louis Stephens 61	8.00	3.60	1.00
☐ 18 Ed Sutton 60	8.00	3.60	1.00
☐ 19 Bob Toneff 60	10.00	4.50	1.25
☐ 20 Lavern Torgeson 60	10.00	4.50	1.25

1960 Redskins Jay Publishing

This 12-card set features (approximately) 5" by 7" black-and-white player photos. The photos show players in traditional poses with the quarterback preparing to throw, the runner heading downfield, and the defenseman ready for the tackle. These cards were packaged 12 to a packet and originally sold for 25 cents. The backs are blank. The cards are unnumbered and checklisted below in alphabetical order.

	NRMT	VG-E	GOOD
COMPLETE SET (12)	75.00	34.00	9.50
COMMON CARD (1-12)	6.00	2.70	.75
☐ 1 Sam Baker	7.00	3.10	.85
☐ 2 Don Bosseler	7.00	3.10	.85
☐ 3 Gene Brito	6.00	2.70	.75
☐ 4 Johnny Carson	6.00	2.70	.75
☐ 5 Chuck Drazenovich	7.00	3.10	.85
☐ 6 Ralph Guglielmi	7.00	3.10	.85
☐ 7 Dick James	7.00	3.10	.85
☐ 8 Eddie LeBaron	12.00	5.50	1.50
☐ 9 Jim Podoley	6.00	2.70	.75
☐ 10 Jim Schrader	6.00	2.70	.75
☐ 11 Ed Sutton	6.00	2.70	.75
☐ 12 Albert Zagers	6.00	2.70	.75

1961 Redskins Jay Publishing

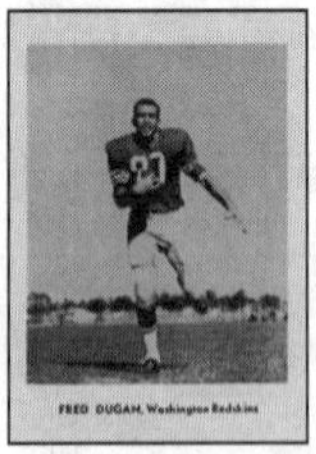

This 12-card set features 5" by 7" black-and-white player photos. The photos show players in traditional poses with the quarterback preparing to throw, the runner heading downfield, and the defenseman ready for the tackle. These cards were packaged 12 to a packet and originally sold for 25 cents through Jay Publishing's annual football magazine. The backs are blank. The cards are unnumbered and checklisted below in alphabetical order.

	NRMT	VG-E	GOOD
COMPLETE SET (12)	75.00	34.00	9.50
COMMON CARD	6.00	2.70	.75
☐ 1 Don Bosseler	7.00	3.10	.85
☐ 2 Eagle Day	6.00	2.70	.75
☐ 3 Fred Dugan	6.00	2.70	.75
☐ 4 Gary Glick	6.00	2.70	.75
☐ 5 Sam Horner	6.00	2.70	.75
☐ 6 Dick James	7.00	3.10	.85
☐ 7 Bob Khayat	6.00	2.70	.75
☐ 8 Bill McPeak CO	6.00	2.70	.75
☐ 9 Jim Schrader	6.00	2.70	.75
☐ 10 Norm Snead	12.00	5.50	1.50
☐ 11 Bob Toneff	6.00	2.70	.75
☐ 12 Ed Vereb	6.00	2.70	.75

1965 Redskins Volpe Tumblers

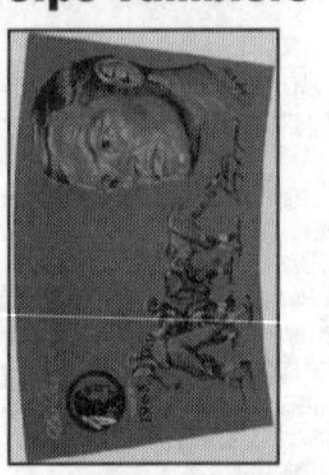

These Redskins artist's renderings were part of a plastic cup tumbler produced in 1965. The noted sports artist Volpe created the artwork which includes an action scene and a player portrait. The "cards" are unnumbered, each measures approximately 5" by 8 1/2" and is curved in the shape required to fit inside a plastic cup. There is only one known card at this time. Any additions to this list are welcomed.

	NRMT	VG-E	GOOD
COMPLETE SET (1)	40.00	18.00	5.00
COMMON CARD (1)	40.00	18.00	5.00
☐ 1 Sonny Jurgensen	40.00	18.00	5.00

1969 Redskins High's Dairy

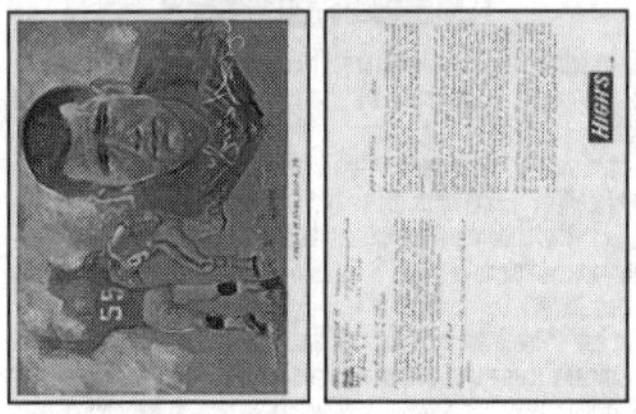

This eight-card set was sponsored by High's Dairy Stores and measures approximately 8" by 10". The front has white borders and a full color painting of the player by Alex Fournier, with the player's signature near the bottom of the portrait. The plain white back gives biographical and statistical information on the player on its left side, and information about Fournier on the right. Reportedly 70,000 of each card was produced. Collectors could receive a free card for each two half gallons of milk they purchased or could buy them singlely from High's Dairy Stores. The cards are unnumbered and checklisted below in alphabetical order.

	NRMT-MT	EXC	G-VG
COMPLETE SET (8)	100.00	45.00	12.50
COMMON CARD (1-8)	8.00	3.60	1.00
☐ 1 Chris Hanburger	10.00	4.50	1.25
☐ 2 Len Hauss	10.00	4.50	1.25
☐ 3 Sam Huff	15.00	6.75	1.85
☐ 4 Sonny Jurgensen	25.00	11.00	3.10
☐ 5 Carl Kammerer	8.00	3.60	1.00
☐ 6 Brig Owens	8.00	3.60	1.00
☐ 7 Pat Richter	10.00	4.50	1.25
☐ 8 Charley Taylor	20.00	9.00	2.50

1972 Redskins Characatures

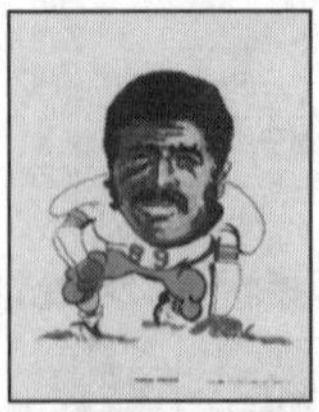

This set was produced by Dick Shuman and Compu-Set, Inc. in 1972 and features players of the Washington Redskins. Each card measures approximatley 8" by 10" and features a characature drawing of the player with his name printed below. The cards are unnumbered and blankbacked.

	NRMT-MT	EXC	G-VG
COMPLETE SET (16)	125.00	55.00	15.50
COMMON CARD (1-16)	8.00	3.60	1.00
☐ 1 Mike Bass	10.00	4.50	1.25
☐ 2 Verlon Biggs	8.00	3.60	1.00
☐ 3 Mike Bragg	8.00	3.60	1.00
☐ 4 Speedy Duncan	10.00	4.50	1.25
☐ 5 Pat Fischer	10.00	4.50	1.25
☐ 6 Chris Hanburger	10.00	4.50	1.25
☐ 7 Curt Knight	8.00	3.60	1.00
☐ 8 Ron McDole	8.00	3.60	1.00
☐ 9 Brig Owens	8.00	3.60	1.00
☐ 10 Jack Pardee	10.00	4.50	1.25
☐ 11 Richie Petitbon	10.00	4.50	1.25
☐ 12 Myron Pottios	8.00	3.60	1.00
☐ 13 Manny Sistrunk	8.00	3.60	1.00
☐ 14 Diron Talbert	8.00	3.60	1.00
☐ 15 Ted Vactor	8.00	3.60	1.00
☐ 16 Cover Card Jack Pardee Mike Bass Manny Sistrunk Chris Hanburger	10.00	4.50	1.25

1981 Redskins Frito Lay Schedules

This 30-card bi-fold schedule set sponsored by Frito Lay measures approximately standard card size when folded and opens to measure 3-1/2" by 7-1/2." Each schedule features a color action shot of a Washington Redskins player inside with sponsor logos on the back. When completely opened, the left panel contains the 1981 schedule. The center panel features a color action player shot with the player's name, biography, and profile appearing on another fold. The regular season schedule is printed on the right inside panel. The schedules are unnumbered and checklisted below in alphabetical order.

	MINT	NRMT	EXC
COMPLETE SET (30)	18.00	8.00	2.20
COMMON CARD	.50	.23	.06
☐ 1 Coy Bacon	.75	.35	.09
☐ 2 Perry Brooks	.50	.23	.06
☐ 3 Dave Butz	.75	.35	.09
☐ 4 Rickey Claitt	.50	.23	.06
☐ 5 Monte Coleman	.75	.35	.09
☐ 6 Mike Connell	.50	.23	.06
☐ 7 Brad Dusek	.75	.35	.09
☐ 8 Ike Forte	.50	.23	.06
☐ 9 Clarence Harmon	.50	.23	.06
☐ 10 Terry Hermeling	.50	.23	.06
☐ 11 Wilbur Jackson	.50	.23	.06
☐ 12 Mike Kruczek	.50	.23	.06
☐ 13 Bob Kuziel	.50	.23	.06
☐ 14 Joe Lavender	.75	.35	.09
☐ 15 Karl Lorch	.50	.23	.06
☐ 16 LeCharls McDaniel	.50	.23	.06
☐ 17 Rich Milot	.50	.23	.06
☐ 18 Art Monk	2.50	1.10	.30
☐ 19 Mark Moseley	1.00	.45	.12
☐ 20 Mark Murphy	.75	.35	.09
☐ 21 Mike Nelms	.50	.23	.06
☐ 22 Neal Olkewicz	.50	.23	.06
☐ 23 Lemar Parrish	.75	.35	.09
☐ 24 Tony Peters	.50	.23	.06
☐ 25 Ron Saul	.50	.23	.06
☐ 26 George Starke	.50	.23	.06
☐ 27 Joe Theismann	2.00	.90	.25
☐ 28 Ricky Thompson	.50	.23	.06
☐ 29 Don Warren	.75	.35	.09
☐ 30 Jeris White	.50	.23	.06

1982 Redskins Frito Lay Schedules

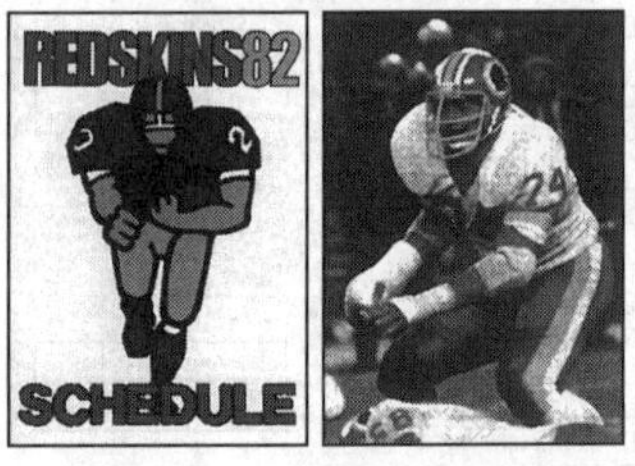

This 15-card bi-fold schedule set measures the standard card size when folded and opens to measure 3-1/2" by 7-1/2." Each schedule features a color action shot of a Washington Redskins player inside with sponsor logos on the back. When completely opened, the left panel contains the preseason and postseason schedules. The center panel features a color action player shot with the player's name, biography, and profile appearing on another fold. The regular season schedule is printed on the right inside panel. The schedules are unnumbered and checklisted below in alphabetical order.

	MINT	NRMT	EXC
COMPLETE SET (15)	12.00	5.50	1.50
COMMON CARD (1-15)	.50	.23	.06
☐ 1 Dave Butz	.75	.35	.09
☐ 2 Monte Coleman	.75	.35	.09
☐ 3 Brad Dusek	.50	.23	.06
☐ 4 Joe Lavender	.75	.35	.09
☐ 5 Art Monk	2.00	.90	.25
☐ 6 Mark Moseley	.75	.35	.09
☐ 7 Mark Murphy	.75	.35	.09
☐ 8 Mike Nelms	.50	.23	.06
☐ 9 Neal Olkewicz	.50	.23	.06
☐ 10 Tony Peters	.50	.23	.06
☐ 11 John Riggins	2.50	1.10	.30
☐ 12 George Starke	.50	.23	.06
☐ 13 Joe Theismann	2.00	.90	.25
☐ 14 Don Warren	.75	.35	.09
☐ 15 Joe Washington	1.00	.45	.12

1982 Redskins Police

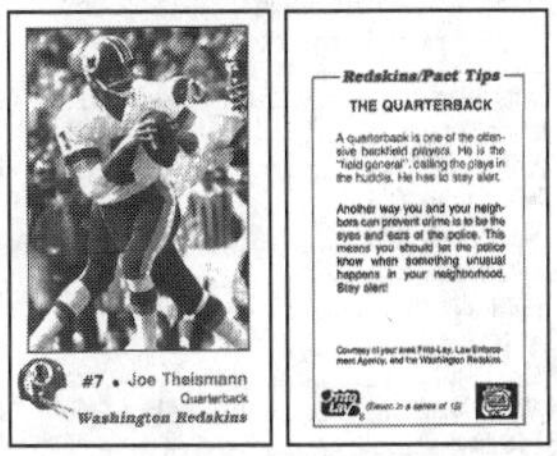

The 1982 Washington Redskins set contains 15 numbered (in very small print on the card backs) full-color cards. The cards measure approximately 2 5/8" by 4 1/8". The set was sponsored by Frito-Lay, the local law enforcement agency, the Washington Redskins, and an organization known as PACT (Police and Citizens Together). Logos of Frito-Lay and PACT appear on the backs of the cards as do "Redskins PACT Tips". A Redskins helmet appears on the fronts of the cards.

	MINT	NRMT	EXC
COMPLETE SET (15)	10.00	4.50	1.25
COMMON CARD (1-15)	.50	.23	.06
☐ 1 Dave Butz	.75	.35	.09
☐ 2 Art Monk	2.50	1.10	.30
☐ 3 Mark Murphy	.50	.23	.06
☐ 4 Monte Coleman	.75	.35	.09
☐ 5 Mark Moseley	.75	.35	.09
☐ 6 George Starke	.50	.23	.06
☐ 7 Perry Brooks	.50	.23	.06
☐ 8 Joe Washington	.75	.35	.09
☐ 9 Don Warren	.75	.35	.09
☐ 10 Joe Lavender	.50	.23	.06
☐ 11 Joe Theismann	2.00	.90	.25
☐ 12 Tony Peters	.50	.23	.06
☐ 13 Neal Olkewicz	.50	.23	.06
☐ 14 Mike Nelms	.50	.23	.06
☐ 15 John Riggins	2.00	.90	.25

1983 Redskins Frito Lay Schedules

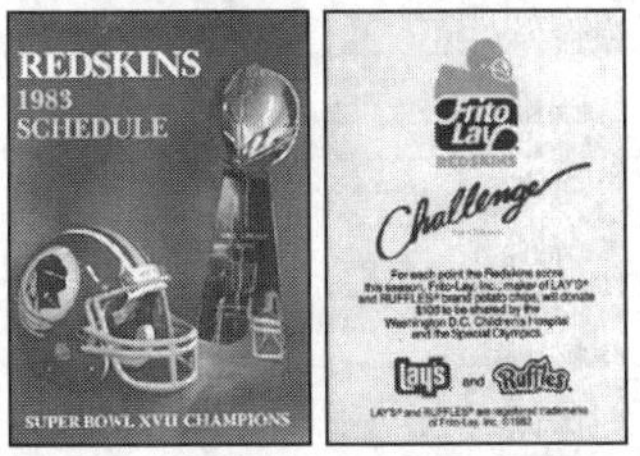

This 15-card bi-fold schedule set measures 2 1/2" by 3 1/2" when folded and features the Super Bowl trophy and a Redskins helmet on front with sponsor logos on the back. When completely opened, the left panel contains the preseason and post season schedules. The center panel features a color action player shot with the player's name, biography, and profile appearing on another fold. The regular season schedule is printed on the right inside panel. The schedules are unnumbered and checklisted below in alphabetical order.

	MINT	NRMT	EXC
COMPLETE SET (15)	10.00	4.50	1.25
COMMON CARD	.50	.23	.06
☐ 1 Charlie Brown	.75	.35	.09
☐ 2 Dave Butz	.75	.35	.09
☐ 3 The Hogs	.75	.35	.09
☐ 4 Dexter Manley	.75	.35	.09
☐ 5 Rich Milot	.50	.23	.06
☐ 6 Art Monk	1.50	.70	.19
☐ 7 Mark Moseley	.75	.35	.09
☐ 8 Mark Murphy	.50	.23	.06
☐ 9 Mike Nelms	.50	.23	.06
☐ 10 Neal Olkewicz	.50	.23	.06
☐ 11 Tony Peters	.50	.23	.06
☐ 12 John Riggins	2.00	.90	.25
☐ 13 Joe Theismann	2.00	.90	.25
☐ 14 Joe Washington	.75	.35	.09
☐ 15 Jeris White	.50	.23	.06

1983 Redskins Police

The 1983 Washington Redskins Police set consists of 16 numbered cards sponsored by Frito-Lay, the local law enforcement agency, PACT, and the Redskins. The cards measure 2 5/8" by 4 1/8" and were given out one per week (and are numbered according to that order) by the police department, except for week number 10, whose card featured Jeris White. White sat out the season and his card was not distributed; hence, it is available in lesser quantity than other cards in the set. Interestingly enough, the seventh week featured the issuance of Joe Theisman's card, who coincidentally, wears uniform number 7. The final card in this set, issued the 16th week, featured John Riggins. Logos of Frito-Lay and PACT appear on the back along with "Redskins/PACT Tips". The backs are printed in black with red accent on white card stock. There were some cards produced with a maroon color back. Although these maroon backs are more difficult to find, they are valued essentially the same.

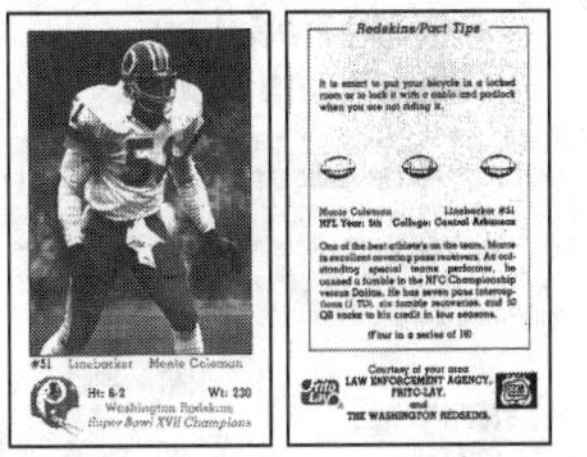

	MINT	NRMT	EXC
COMPLETE SET (16)	10.00	4.50	1.25
COMMON CARD (1-16)	.50	.23	.06
☐ 1 Joe Washington	1.00	.45	.12
☐ 2 The Hogs (Offensive Line)	.75	.35	.09
☐ 3 Mark Moseley	1.00	.45	.12
☐ 4 Monte Coleman	.50	.23	.06
☐ 5 Mike Nelms	.50	.23	.06
☐ 6 Neal Olkewicz	.50	.23	.06
☐ 7 Joe Theismann	2.50	1.10	.30
☐ 8 Charlie Brown	.75	.35	.09
☐ 9 Dave Butz	.75	.35	.09
☐ 10 Jeris White SP	1.50	.70	.19
☐ 11 Mark Murphy	.50	.23	.06
☐ 12 Dexter Manley	.75	.35	.09
☐ 13 Art Monk	2.50	1.10	.30
☐ 14 Rich Milot	.50	.23	.06
☐ 15 Vernon Dean	.50	.23	.06
☐ 16 John Riggins	2.00	.90	.25

1984 Redskins Frito Lay Schedules

This 15-card bi-fold schedule set measures the standard card size when folded and opens to measure 3-1/2" by 7-1/2." Each schedule features a color action shot of a Washington Redskins player inside with sponsor logos on the back. When completely opened, the left panel contains the preseason and postseason schedules. The center panel features a color action player shot with the player's name, biography, and profile appearing on another fold. The regular season schedule is printed on the right inside panel. The schedules are unnumbered and checklisted below in alphabetical order.

	MINT	NRMT	EXC
COMPLETE SET (15)	10.00	4.50	1.25
COMMON CARD	.50	.23	.06
☐ 1 Charlie Brown	.75	.35	.09
☐ 2 Dave Butz	.75	.35	.09
☐ 3 Ken Coffey	.50	.23	.06
☐ 4 Clint Didier	.50	.23	.06
☐ 5 Darryl Grant	.50	.23	.06
☐ 6 Darrell Green	1.00	.45	.12
☐ 7 Jeff Hayes	.50	.23	.06
☐ 8 The Hogs	.75	.35	.09
☐ 9 Rich Milot	.50	.23	.06
☐ 10 Art Monk	1.50	.70	.19
☐ 11 Mark Murphy	.50	.23	.06
☐ 12 John Riggins	1.50	.70	.19
☐ 13 Joe Theismann	1.50	.70	.19
☐ 14 Don Warren	.75	.35	.09
☐ 15 Joe Washington	.75	.35	.09

1984 Redskins Police

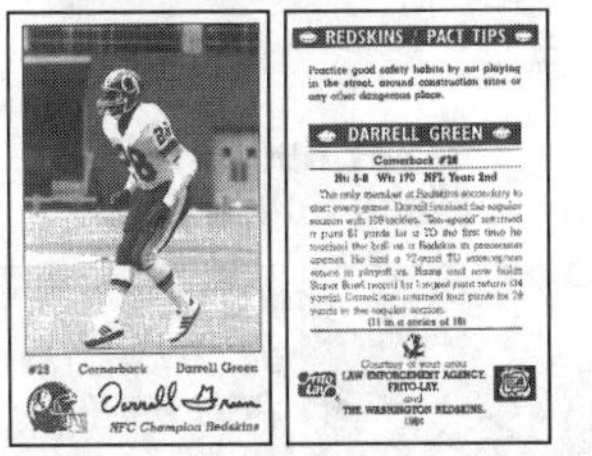

This numbered (on back) set of 16 cards features the Washington Redskins. Cards measure approximately 2 5/8" by 4 1/8". Backs are printed in black ink with a maroon accent. The set was sponsored by Frito-Lay, the local law enforcement agency, and the Washington Redskins.

	MINT	NRMT	EXC
COMPLETE SET (16)	7.00	3.10	.85
COMMON CARD (1-16)	.35	.16	.04
☐ 1 John Riggins	1.25	.55	.16
☐ 2 Darryl Grant	.35	.16	.04
☐ 3 Art Monk	1.50	.70	.19
☐ 4 Neal Olkewicz	.35	.16	.04
☐ 5 The Hogs	.50	.23	.06
☐ 6 Jeff Hayes	.35	.16	.04
☐ 7 Joe Theismann	1.25	.55	.16
☐ 8 Clint Didier	.35	.16	.04
☐ 9 Mark Murphy	.35	.16	.04
☐ 10 Don Warren	.50	.23	.06
☐ 11 Darrell Green	1.00	.45	.12
☐ 12 Dave Butz	.50	.23	.06
☐ 13 Ken Coffey	.35	.16	.04
☐ 14 Rich Milot	.35	.16	.04
☐ 15 Charlie Brown	.50	.23	.06
☐ 16 Joe Washington	.50	.23	.06

1985 Redskins Frito Lay Schedules

This 16-card bi-fold schedule set sponsored by Frito Lay measures approximately standard card size when folded and opens to measure 3-1/2" by 7-1/2." Each schedule features a photo of an all-time great Washington Redskins player inside with sponsor logos on the back. When completely opened, the inside contains the season schedule. The schedules are unnumbered and checklisted below in alphabetical order.

	MINT	NRMT	EXC
COMPLETE SET (16)	10.00	4.50	1.25
COMMON CARD	.50	.23	.06
☐ 1 Cliff Battles	.75	.35	.09
☐ 2 Sammy Baugh	1.50	.70	.19
☐ 3 Larry Brown	.75	.35	.09
☐ 4 Bill Dudley	.75	.35	.09
☐ 5 Turk Edwards	.75	.35	.09
☐ 6 Pat Fischer	.50	.23	.06
☐ 7 Chris Hanburger	.50	.23	.06
☐ 8 Len Hauss	.50	.23	.06
☐ 9 Ken Houston	.75	.35	.09
☐ 10 Sam Huff	1.00	.45	.12
☐ 11 Sonny Jurgensen	1.25	.55	.16
☐ 12 Bill Kilmer	.50	.23	.06
☐ 13 Wayne Millner	.50	.23	.06
☐ 14 Bobby Mitchell	.75	.35	.09
☐ 15 Brig Owens	.50	.23	.06
☐ 16 Charley Taylor	1.00	.45	.12

1985 Redskins Police

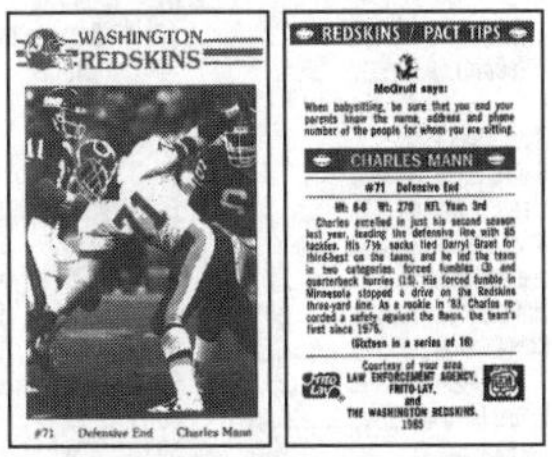

This 16-card set of Washington Redskins is numbered on the back. Cards measure approximately 2 5/8" by 4 1/8" and the backs contain a "McGruff Says". Each player's uniform number is given on the card front. The set was sponsored by Frito-Lay, the Redskins, and local law enforcement agencies. Card backs are written in maroon and black on white card stock.

	MINT	NRMT	EXC
COMPLETE SET (16)	6.00	2.70	.75
COMMON CARD (1-16)	.35	.16	.04
☐ 1 Darrell Green	.75	.35	.09
☐ 2 Clint Didier	.35	.16	.04
☐ 3 Neal Olkewicz	.35	.16	.04
☐ 4 Darryl Grant	.35	.16	.04
☐ 5 Joe Jacoby	.50	.23	.06
☐ 6 Vernon Dean	.35	.16	.04
☐ 7 Joe Theismann	1.00	.45	.12
☐ 8 Mel Kaufman	.35	.16	.04
☐ 9 Calvin Muhammad	.35	.16	.04
☐ 10 Dexter Manley	.50	.23	.06
☐ 11 John Riggins	1.00	.45	.12
☐ 12 Mark May	.50	.23	.06
☐ 13 Dave Butz	.50	.23	.06
☐ 14 Art Monk	1.25	.55	.16
☐ 15 Russ Grimm	.50	.23	.06
☐ 16 Charles Mann	.50	.23	.06

1986 Redskins Frito Lay Schedules

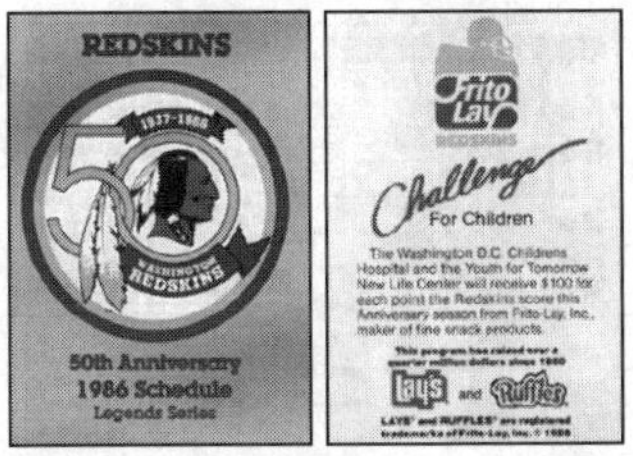

These schedules feature all-time great members of the Redskins in celebration of the team's 50th anniversary in Washington. They are standard schedule size and were sponsored by Frito Lay. The schedules measure 2 1/2" by 3 1/2" when folded and opens to approximately 3 1/2" by 7 1/2." The schedules feature the Redskins' 50th Anniversary logo against a yellow background on the front with Frito-Lay's sponsor logos on the back. When completely opened the left panel contains the preseason and post season schedules with the center panel featuring the player's photo. The regular season schedule is printed on the right inside panel with the player's profile featured on the other side. Each schedule is unnumbered and checklisted below in alphabetical order.

	MINT	NRMT	EXC
COMPLETE SET (16)	20.00	9.00	2.50
COMMON CARD	1.00	.45	.12
☐ 1 Cliff Battles	1.50	.70	.19
☐ 2 Sammy Baugh	2.00	.90	.25
☐ 3 Larry Brown	1.00	.45	.12
☐ 4 Bill Dudley	1.50	.70	.19
☐ 5 Turk Edwards	1.00	.45	.12
☐ 6 Pat Fischer	1.00	.45	.12
☐ 7 Chris Hanburger	1.00	.45	.12
☐ 8 Len Hauss	1.00	.45	.12
☐ 9 Sam Huff	2.00	.90	.25
☐ 10 Ken Houston	1.50	.70	.19
☐ 11 Sonny Jurgensen	2.00	.90	.25
☐ 12 Billy Kilmer	1.50	.70	.19
☐ 13 Wayne Millner	1.50	.70	.19
☐ 14 Bobby Mitchell	2.00	.90	.25
☐ 15 Brig Owens	1.00	.45	.12
☐ 16 Charley Taylor	2.00	.90	.25

1986 Redskins Police

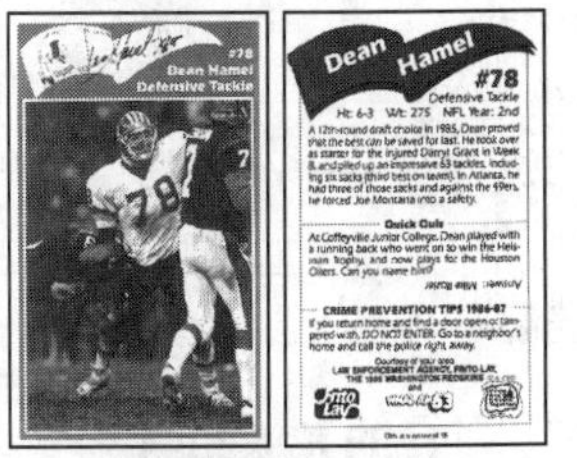

This 16-card set of Washington Redskins is numbered on the back. Cards measure approximately 2 5/8" by 4 1/8" and the backs contain a "Crime Prevention Tip". Each player's uniform number is given on the card front. The set was sponsored by Frito Lay, the Redskins, WMAL-AM63, and local law enforcement agencies. Card backs are printed in maroon and black on white card stock. The set commemorates the Redskins 50th Anniversary as a team.

	MINT	NRMT	EXC
COMPLETE SET (16)	6.00	2.70	.75
COMMON CARD (1-16)	.35	.16	.04
☐ 1 Darrell Green	.75	.35	.09
☐ 2 Joe Jacoby	.50	.23	.06
☐ 3 Charles Mann	.50	.23	.06
☐ 4 Jay Schroeder	.50	.23	.06
☐ 5 Raphel Cherry	.35	.16	.04
☐ 6 Russ Grimm	.50	.23	.06
☐ 7 Mel Kaufman	.35	.16	.04
☐ 8 Gary Clark	1.25	.55	.16
☐ 9 Vernon Dean	.35	.16	.04
☐ 10 Mark May	.50	.23	.06
☐ 11 Dave Butz	.50	.23	.06
☐ 12 Jeff Bostic	.50	.23	.06
☐ 13 Dean Hamel	.35	.16	.04
☐ 14 Dexter Manley	.50	.23	.06
☐ 15 George Rogers	.50	.23	.06
☐ 16 Art Monk	1.00	.45	.12

1987 Redskins Frito Lay Schedules

This 16-card bi-fold schedule set measures the standard card size when folded and opens to measure 3-1/2" by 7-1/2." Each schedule features a color action shot of a Washington Redskins player with sponsor logos on the back. When completely opened, the inside contains the season schedule. The schedules are unnumbered and checklisted below in alphabetical order.

	MINT	NRMT	EXC
COMPLETE SET (16)	10.00	4.50	1.25
COMMON CARD	.50	.23	.06
☐ 1 Jeff Bostic	.75	.35	.09
☐ 2 Kelvin Bryant	.75	.35	.09
☐ 3 Dave Butz	.75	.35	.09
☐ 4 Gary Clark	1.00	.45	.12
☐ 5 Steve Cox	.50	.23	.06
☐ 6 Clint Didier	.50	.23	.06
☐ 7 Darryl Grant	.50	.23	.06
☐ 8 Darrell Green	.75	.35	.09
☐ 9 Joe Jacoby	.75	.35	.09
☐ 10 Dexter Manley	.75	.35	.09
☐ 11 Charles Mann	.75	.35	.09
☐ 12 Mark May	.75	.35	.09
☐ 13 Art Monk	1.00	.45	.12
☐ 14 Jay Schroeder	.75	.35	.09
☐ 15 Alvin Walton	.50	.23	.06
☐ 16 Don Warren	.75	.35	.09

1987 Redskins Police

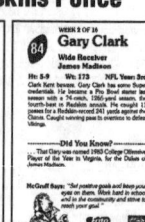

GARY CLARK

This 16-card set of Washington Redskins is numbered on the back. The cards measure approximately 2 5/8" by 4 1/8" and the backs contain a 'McGruff Says' crime prevention tip. The set was sponsored by Frito Lay and PACT (Police and Citizens Together). Card backs are written in red and black on white card stock. The cards were given out one per week in the greater Washington metropolitan area.

	MINT	NRMT	EXC
COMPLETE SET (16)	5.00	2.20	.60
COMMON CARD (1-16)	.30	.14	.04
☐ 1 Joe Jacoby	.40	.18	.05
☐ 2 Gary Clark	.75	.35	.09
☐ 3 Dexter Manley	.40	.18	.05
☐ 4 Darrell Green	.40	.18	.05
☐ 5 Alvin Walton	.30	.14	.04
☐ 6 Clint Didier	.30	.14	.04
☐ 7 Art Monk	1.00	.45	.12
☐ 8 Darryl Grant	.30	.14	.04
☐ 9 Kelvin Bryant	.40	.18	.05
☐ 10 Jay Schroeder	.40	.18	.05
☐ 11 Don Warren	.40	.18	.05
☐ 12 Steve Cox	.30	.14	.04
☐ 13 Mark May	.40	.18	.05
☐ 14 Jeff Bostic	.40	.18	.05
☐ 15 Charles Mann	.40	.18	.05
☐ 16 Dave Butz	.40	.18	.05

1988 Redskins Frito Lay Schedules

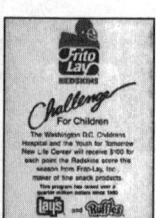

1988 SCHEDULE

This 16-card bi-fold schedule set measures 2 1/2" by 3 1/2" when folded and opens to approximately 3 1/2" by 7 1/2." The schedules feature the Super Bowl trophy on front against a maroon background with Frito-Lay sponsor logos on the back. When completely opened the left panel contains the preseason schedule and the center panel features a color action player shot with the player's name, biography, and profile appearing on another fold. The regular season schedule is printed on the right inside panel. Each schedule is unnumbered and checklisted below in alphabetical order.

	MINT	NRMT	EXC
COMPLETE SET (16)	10.00	4.50	1.25
COMMON CARD	.50	.23	.06
☐ 1 Jeff Bostic	.75	.35	.09
☐ 2 Dave Butz	.75	.35	.09
☐ 3 Gary Clark	1.00	.45	.12
☐ 4 Brian Davis	.50	.23	.06
☐ 5 Joe Jacoby	.75	.35	.09
☐ 6 Markus Koch	.50	.23	.06
☐ 7 Charles Mann	.75	.35	.09
☐ 8 Wilber Marshall	.75	.35	.09
☐ 9 Mark May	.75	.35	.09
☐ 10 Raleigh McKenzie	.50	.23	.06
☐ 11 Art Monk	1.00	.45	.12
☐ 12 Ricky Sanders	.75	.35	.09
☐ 13 Alvin Walton	.50	.23	.06
☐ 14 Don Warren	.75	.35	.09
☐ 15 Barry Wilburn	.50	.23	.06
☐ 16 Doug Williams	1.00	.45	.12

1988 Redskins Police

The 1988 Police Washington Redskins set contains 16 player cards measuring approximately 2 5/8" by 4 1/8". The fronts feature color action photos. The backs feature career highlights and safety tips. The Redskins team name appearing above the photo on the card front differentiates this set from other similar-looking Police Redskins sets.

	MINT	NRMT	EXC
COMPLETE SET (16)	5.00	2.20	.60
COMMON CARD (1-16)	.30	.14	.04

☐ 1 Jeff Bostic	.40	.18	.05
☐ 2 Dave Butz	.40	.18	.05
☐ 3 Gary Clark	.75	.35	.09
☐ 4 Brian Davis	.30	.14	.04
☐ 5 Joe Jacoby	.40	.18	.05
☐ 6 Markus Koch	.30	.14	.04
☐ 7 Charles Mann	.40	.18	.05
☐ 8 Wilber Marshall	.40	.18	.05
☐ 9 Mark May	.40	.18	.05
☐ 10 Raleigh McKenzie	.30	.14	.04
☐ 11 Art Monk	1.00	.45	.12
☐ 12 Ricky Sanders	.75	.35	.09
☐ 13 Alvin Walton	.30	.14	.04
☐ 14 Don Warren	.40	.18	.05
☐ 15 Barry Wilburn	.30	.14	.04
☐ 16 Doug Williams	.75	.35	.09

1989 Redskins Mobil Schedules

This 16-card bi-fold schedule set sponsored by Mobil Oil measures the standard card size when folded and opens to measure 3-1/2" by 7-1/2." Each schedule features a color action shot of a Washington Redskins player with sponsor logos on back. When completely opened, the inside contains the season schedule. The schedules are unnumbered and checklisted below in alphabetical order.

	MINT	NRMT	EXC
COMPLETE SET (16)	8.00	3.60	1.00
COMMON CARD	.40	.18	.05
☐ 1 Ravin Caldwell	.40	.18	.05
☐ 2 Gary Clark	1.00	.45	.12
☐ 3 Monte Coleman	.60	.25	.07
☐ 4 Brian Davis	.40	.18	.05
☐ 5 Joe Jacoby	.60	.25	.07
☐ 6 Jim Lachey	.60	.25	.07
☐ 7 Chip Lohmiller	.60	.25	.07
☐ 8 Charles Mann	.60	.25	.07
☐ 9 Wilber Marshall	.60	.25	.07
☐ 10 Mark May	.40	.18	.05
☐ 11 Raleigh McKenzie	.40	.18	.05
☐ 12 Art Monk	1.00	.45	.12
☐ 13 Mark Rypien	.60	.25	.07
☐ 14 Ricky Sanders	.60	.25	.07
☐ 15 Don Warren	.60	.25	.07
☐ 16 Doug Williams	.75	.35	.09

1989 Redskins Police

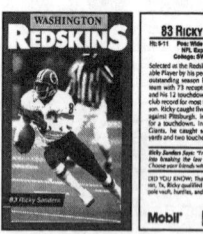

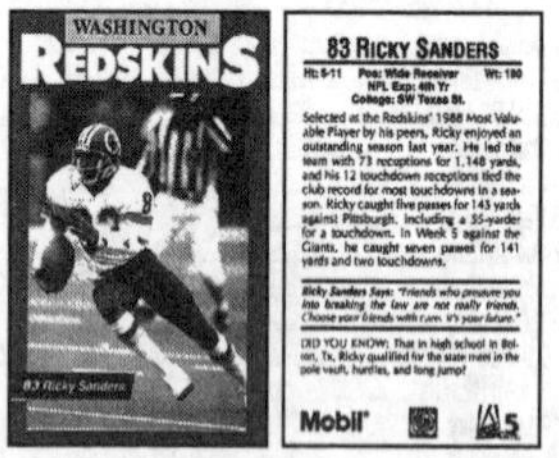

The 1989 Police Washington Redskins set contains 16 cards measuring approximately 2 5/8" by 4 1/8". The fronts have maroon borders and color action photos; the vertically oriented backs have safety tips, bios, and career highlights. These cards were printed on very thin stock. The cards are unnumbered, so therefore are listed below according to uniform number.

	MINT	NRMT	EXC
COMPLETE SET (16)	5.00	2.20	.60
COMMON CARD	.30	.14	.04
☐ 11 Mark Rypien	.60	.25	.07
☐ 17 Doug Williams	.60	.25	.07
☐ 21 Earnest Byner	.40	.18	.05
☐ 22 Jamie Morris	.30	.14	.04
☐ 28 Darrell Green	.40	.18	.05
☐ 34 Brian Davis	.30	.14	.04
☐ 37 Gerald Riggs	.40	.18	.05
☐ 50 Ravin Caldwell	.30	.14	.04
☐ 52 Neal Olkewicz	.30	.14	.04
☐ 58 Wilber Marshall	.40	.18	.05
☐ 73 Mark May	.30	.14	.04
☐ 74 Markus Koch	.30	.14	.04
☐ 81 Art Monk	1.00	.45	.12
☐ 83 Ricky Sanders	.60	.25	.07
☐ 84 Gary Clark	.75	.35	.09
☐ 85 Don Warren	.40	.18	.05

1990 Redskins Mobil Schedules

This 16-card bi-fold schedule set sponsored by Mobil Oil measures the standard card size when folded and opens to measure 3-1/2" by 7-1/2." Each schedule features a color action shot of a Washington Redskins player with sponsor logos on the back. When completely opened, the inside contains the season schedule. The schedules are unnumbered and checklisted below in alphabetical order.

	MINT	NRMT	EXC
COMPLETE SET (16)	8.00	3.60	1.00
COMMON CARD	.40	.18	.05
☐ 1 Jeff Bostic	.60	.25	.07
☐ 2 Earnest Byner	.60	.25	.07
☐ 3 Gary Clark	.75	.35	.09
☐ 4 Darryl Grant	.40	.18	.05
☐ 5 Darrell Green	.60	.25	.07
☐ 6 Jim Lachey	.60	.25	.07
☐ 7 Chip Lohmiller	.60	.25	.07
☐ 8 Charles Mann	.60	.25	.07
☐ 9 Wilber Marshall	.60	.25	.07
☐ 10 Ralf Mojsiejenko	.40	.18	.05
☐ 11 Art Monk	1.00	.45	.12
☐ 12 Gerald Riggs	.60	.25	.07
☐ 13 Mark Rypien	.60	.25	.07
☐ 14 Ricky Sanders	.60	.25	.07
☐ 15 Alvin Walton	.40	.18	.05
☐ 16 Don Warren	.60	.25	.07

1990 Redskins Police

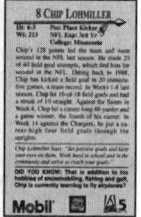

This 16-card set, which measures approximately 2 5/8" by 4 1/8", features members of the 1990 Washington Redskins. This set features white borders surrounding full-color photos on the front and biographical information on the back along with a safety tip. The set was sponsored by Mobil Oil, PACT (Police and Citizens Together), and Fox-5 of Washington WTIC. We have checklisted this set alphabetically.

	MINT	NRMT	EXC
COMPLETE SET (16)	5.00	2.20	.60
COMMON CARD (1-16)	.25	.11	.03
☐ 1 Todd Bowles	.25	.11	.03
☐ 2 Earnest Byner	.35	.16	.04
☐ 3 Ravin Caldwell	.25	.11	.03
☐ 4 Gary Clark	.60	.25	.07
☐ 5 Darrell Green	.35	.16	.04
☐ 6 Jimmie Johnson	.25	.11	.03
☐ 7 Jim Lachey	.35	.16	.04
☐ 8 Chip Lohmiller	.35	.16	.04
☐ 9 Charles Mann	.35	.16	.04
☐ 10 Greg Manusky	.25	.11	.03
☐ 11 Wilber Marshall	.35	.16	.04
☐ 12 Art Monk	.75	.35	.09
☐ 13 Gerald Riggs	.35	.16	.04
☐ 14 Mark Rypien	.35	.16	.04
☐ 15 Alvin Walton	.25	.11	.03
☐ 16 Don Warren	.35	.16	.04

1991 Redskins Mobil Schedules

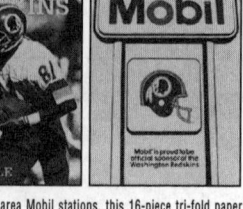

Distributed at area Mobil stations, this 16-piece tri-fold paper schedule set measures 2 1/2" by 3 1/2" when folded and features a color action shot of Art Monk on the front with the Mobil logo on the back. When completely opened, the left panel contains the preseason and postseason schedule while the right panel presents the regular season schedule. The center panel features a full color action player shot. The player's name, biography, and profile appear on the following fold. The schedules are unnumbered and checklisted below in alphabetical order.

	MINT	NRMT	EXC
COMPLETE SET (16)	7.50	3.40	.95
COMMON CARD	.40	.18	.05

☐ 1 Earnest Byner	.60	.25	.07
☐ 2 Gary Clark	.75	.35	.09
☐ 3 Andre Collins	.60	.25	.07
☐ 4 Kurt Gouveia	.40	.18	.05
☐ 5 Darrell Green	.60	.25	.07
☐ 6 Jimmie Johnson	.40	.18	.05
☐ 7 Markus Koch	.40	.18	.05
☐ 8 Jim Lachey	.60	.25	.07
☐ 9 Chip Lohmiller	.40	.18	.05
☐ 10 Charles Mann	.60	.25	.07
☐ 11 Martin Mayhew	.40	.18	.05
☐ 12 Art Monk	1.00	.45	.12
☐ 13 Mark Rypien	.60	.25	.07
☐ 14 Mark Schlereth	.40	.18	.05
☐ 15 Ed Simmons	.40	.18	.05
☐ 16 Eric Williams	.40	.18	.05

1991 Redskins Police

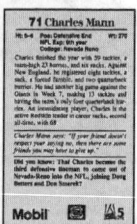

This 16-card set was jointly sponsored by Mobil, PACT (Police and Citizens Together), and WTTG Channel 5 TV. The set was released in the Washington area during the 1991 season. The cards measure approximately 2 5/8" by 4 1/8" and are printed on thin card stock. Card fronts carry a full-color player action shot on a white background. The word "Washington" is printed in black in a gold bar at top of card while the team name appears in large red print up the left side. Player's name is reversed out in a black stripe at bottom, while player's number appears in a gold circle to the left. Vertically printed backs present biographical information, player profile, an anti-drug message, and trivia question. Sponsors' logos appear at bottom. The cards are unnumbered and checklisted below in alphabetical order.

	MINT	NRMT	EXC
COMPLETE SET (16)	5.00	2.20	.60
COMMON CARD (1-16)	.25	.11	.03
☐ 1 John Brandes	.25	.11	.03
☐ 2 Earnest Byner	.35	.16	.04
☐ 3 Gary Clark	.60	.25	.07
☐ 4 Andre Collins	.35	.16	.04
☐ 5 Darrell Green	.35	.16	.04
☐ 6 Joe Howard	.25	.11	.03
☐ 7 Tim Johnson	.25	.11	.03
☐ 8 Jim Lachey	.35	.16	.04
☐ 9 Chip Lohmiller	.25	.11	.03
☐ 10 Charles Mann	.35	.16	.04
☐ 11 Art Monk	.75	.35	.09
☐ 12 Mark Rypien	.35	.16	.04
☐ 13 Mark Schlereth	.25	.11	.03
☐ 14 Fred Stokes	.25	.11	.03
☐ 15 Don Warren	.35	.16	.04
☐ 16 Eric Williams	.25	.11	.03

1992 Redskins Mobil Schedules

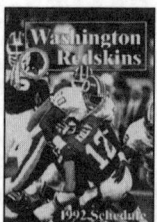

Distributed at area Mobil stations, this 16-piece bi-fold paper schedule set measures 2 1/2" by 3 1/2" when folded and features a color action shot of Fred Stokes sacking Jim Kelly on the front with the Mobil logo on the back. When completely opened, the left panel contains the preseason and postseason schedule while the right panel contains the regular season schedule. The center panel features a full color action player shot. The player's name, biography, and profile appear on the following fold. The schedules are unnumbered and checklisted below in alphabetical order.

	MINT	NRMT	EXC
COMPLETE SET (16)	7.50	3.40	.95
COMMON CARD	.40	.18	.05
☐ 1 Gary Clark	.75	.35	.09
☐ 2 Brad Edwards	.40	.18	.05
☐ 3 Ricky Ervins	.75	.35	.09
☐ 4 Jumpy Geathers	.40	.18	.05
☐ 5 Darrell Green	.60	.25	.07
☐ 6 Joe Jacoby	.60	.25	.07
☐ 7 Tim Johnson	.40	.18	.05
☐ 8 Charles Mann	.60	.25	.07

☐ 9 Wilber Marshall	.60	.25	.07
☐ 10 Ron Middleton	.40	.18	.05
☐ 11 Brian Mitchell	.75	.35	.09
☐ 12 Art Monk	1.00	.45	.12
☐ 13 Jim Lachey	.60	.25	.07
☐ 14 Chip Lohmiller	.40	.18	.05
☐ 15 Mark Rypien	.60	.25	.07
☐ 16 Fred Stokes	.40	.18	.05

1992 Redskins Police

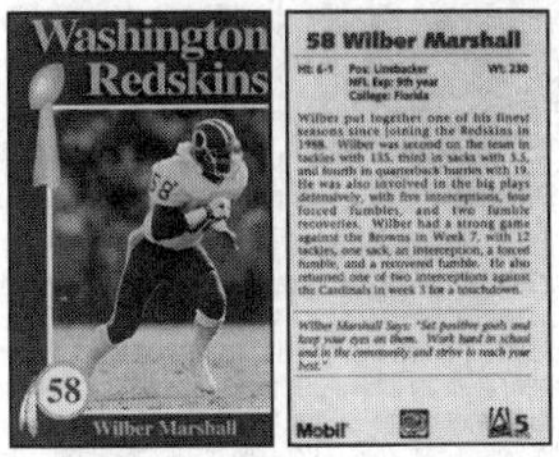

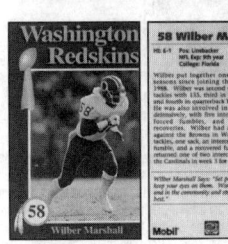

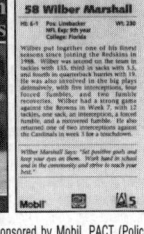

This 16-card set was jointly sponsored by Mobil, PACT (Police and Citizens Together), and Fox WTTG Channel 5. The cards measure approximately 2 1/2" by 4 1/8" and features action color player photos on a brick-red background. The pictures are offset, bleeding off the right edge of the card, and are framed on the other three sides in white. At the upper left corner of the picture is the Vince Lombardi trophy, and at the lower left corner is the uniform number in a circle. The team name appears at the top in mustard. The white backs feature biographical information, career highlights, and anti-drug and crime prevention tips in the form of player quotes. The cards are unnumbered and checklisted below in alphabetical order.

	MINT	NRMT	EXC
COMPLETE SET (16)	5.00	2.20	.60
COMMON CARD (1-16)	.30	.14	.04
☐ 1 Jeff Bostic	.40	.18	.05
☐ 2 Earnest Byner	.40	.18	.05
☐ 3 Gary Clark	.60	.25	.07
☐ 4 Monte Coleman	.40	.18	.05
☐ 5 Andre Collins	.40	.18	.05
☐ 6 Danny Copeland	.30	.14	.04
☐ 7 Kurt Gouveia	.30	.14	.04
☐ 8 Darrell Green	.40	.18	.05
☐ 9 Jim Lachey	.40	.18	.05
☐ 10 Charles Mann	.40	.18	.05
☐ 11 Wilber Marshall	.40	.18	.05
☐ 12 Raleigh McKenzie	.30	.14	.04
☐ 13 Art Monk	1.00	.45	.12
☐ 14 Mark Rypien	.40	.18	.05
☐ 15 Mark Schlereth	.30	.14	.04
☐ 16 Eric Williams	.30	.14	.04

1993 Redskins Mobil Schedules

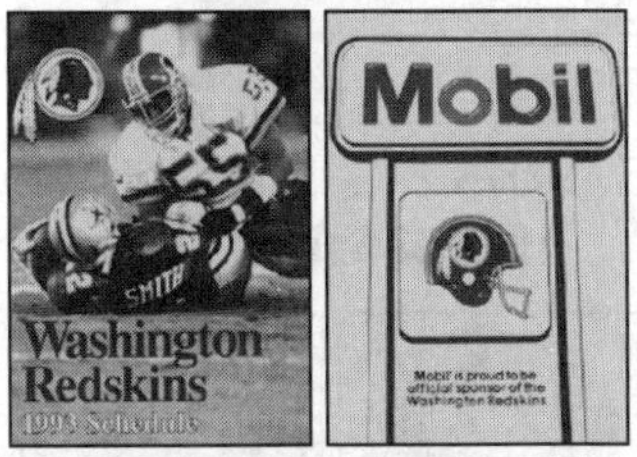

Distributed at area Mobil stations, this 16-piece tri-fold paper schedule set measures 2 1/2" by 3 1/2" when folded and features a color action shot of Andre Collins tackling Emmitt Smith on the front with the Mobil logo on the back. When completely opened, the left panel contains the preseason and postseason schedule while the right panel contains the regular season schedule. The center panel features a full color action player shot. The player's name, biography, and profile appear on the following fold. The schedules are unnumbered and checklisted below in alphabetical order.

	MINT	NRMT	EXC
COMPLETE SET (16)	7.50	3.40	.95
COMMON CARD	.40	.18	.05
☐ 1 Todd Bowles	.40	.18	.05
☐ 2 Earnest Byner	.60	.25	.07
☐ 3 Monte Coleman	.60	.25	.07
☐ 4 Andre Collins	.60	.25	.07
☐ 5 Shane Collins	.40	.18	.05
☐ 6 Danny Copeland	.40	.18	.05
☐ 7 Kurt Gouveia	.40	.18	.05
☐ 8 Darrell Green	.60	.25	.07
☐ 9 A.J. Johnson	.40	.18	.05
☐ 10 Jim Lachey	.40	.18	.05
☐ 11 Ron Middleton	.40	.18	.05
☐ 12 Brian Mitchell	.75	.35	.09
☐ 13 Mark Rypien	.60	.25	.07
☐ 14 Ricky Sanders	.60	.25	.07
☐ 15 Mark Schlereth	.40	.18	.05
☐ 16 Ed Simmons	.40	.18	.05

1993 Redskins Police

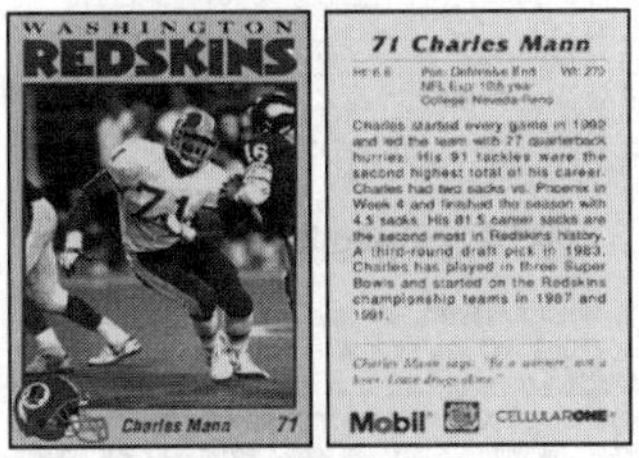

These 16 cards measure approximately 2 3/4" by 4 1/8" and feature on their fronts yellow-bordered color player action shots. The player's name, team helmet, and uniform number rest within the bottom yellow margin. The white back carries the player's name and uniform number at the top, followed below by biography, career highlights, and safety message. The logos for Mobil, Cellular One, and Police and Citizens Together (PACT) at the bottom round out the card. The cards are unnumbered and checklisted below in alphabetical order.

	MINT	NRMT	EXC
COMPLETE SET (16)	5.00	2.20	.60
COMMON CARD (1-16)	.30	.14	.04
☐ 1 Ray Brown	.30	.14	.04
☐ 2 Andre Collins	.40	.18	.05
☐ 3 Brad Edwards	.30	.14	.04
☐ 4 Matt Elliott	.30	.14	.04
☐ 5 Ricky Ervins	.40	.18	.05
☐ 6 Darrell Green	.40	.18	.05
☐ 7 Desmond Howard	.75	.35	.09
☐ 8 Joe Jacoby	.40	.18	.05
☐ 9 Tim Johnson	.30	.14	.04
☐ 10 Jim Lachey	.40	.18	.05
☐ 11 Chip Lohmiller	.30	.14	.04
☐ 12 Charles Mann	.40	.18	.05
☐ 13 Raleigh McKenzie	.30	.14	.04
☐ 14 Brian Mitchell	.50	.23	.06
☐ 15 Terry Orr	.30	.14	.04
☐ 16 Mark Rypien	.40	.18	.05

1994 Redskins Mobil Schedules

Distributed at area Mobil stations, this 16-piece bi-fold paper schedule set measures 2 1/2" by 3 1/2" when folded and features a color action shot on the front with the Mobil logo on the back. When completely opened, the left panel contains the preseason and postseason schedule while the right panel contains the regular season schedule. The center panel features a full color action player shot. The player's name, biography, and profile appear on the following fold. The schedules are unnumbered and checklisted below in alphabetical order.

	MINT	NRMT	EXC
COMPLETE SET (16)	7.50	3.40	.95
COMMON CARD	.40	.18	.05
☐ 1 Reggie Brooks	.60	.25	.07
☐ 2 Ray Brown	.40	.18	.05
☐ 3 Tom Carter	.60	.25	.07
☐ 4 Shane Collins	.40	.18	.05
☐ 5 Darrell Green	.60	.25	.07
☐ 6 Ken Harvey	.60	.25	.07
☐ 7 Lamont Hollinquest	.40	.18	.05
☐ 8 Desmond Howard	.60	.25	.07
☐ 9 Tim Johnson	.40	.18	.05
☐ 10 Jim Lachey	.60	.25	.07
☐ 11 Chip Lohmiller	.40	.18	.05
☐ 12 Brian Mitchell	.60	.25	.07
☐ 13 Sterling Palmer	.40	.18	.05
☐ 14 Heath Shuler	1.50	.70	.19
☐ 15 Bobby Wilson	.40	.18	.05
☐ 16 Frank Wycheck	.40	.18	.05

1995 Redskins Program Sheets

These eight sheets measure approximately 8" by 10" and appeared in regular-season issues of the Redskins' GameDay program. The set features panoramic stadium photographs at which championship games involving the Washington Redskins were played. The sheets are listed below in chronological order.

	MINT	NRMT	EXC
COMPLETE SET (8)	25.00	11.00	3.10
COMMON CARD (1-8)	3.50	1.55	.45
☐ 1 9/3/95 vs. Cardinals Wrigley Field Redskins vs Bears 1937, 1943	3.50	1.55	.45
☐ 2 9/10/95 vs. Raiders Griffith Stadium Redskins vs Bears, 1940, 1942	3.50	1.55	.45
☐ 3 10/1/95 vs. Cowboys Cleveland Stadium Redskins vs Rams, 1945	3.50	1.55	.45
☐ 4 10/22/95 vs. Lions L.A. Coliseum Redskins vs Dolphins, S.B. VII	3.50	1.55	.45
☐ 5 10/29/95 vs. Giants Rose Bowl Redskins vs Dolphins, S.B. XVII	3.50	1.55	.45
☐ 6 11/19/95 vs. Seahawks Tampa Stadium Redskins vs Raiders, S.B. XVIII	3.50	1.55	.45
☐ 7 11/26/95 vs. Eagles Jack Murphy Stadium Skins vs Broncos, S.B. XXII	3.50	1.55	.45
☐ 8 12/24/95 vs. Panthers H.H.H. Metrodome Redskins vs Bills, S.B. XXVI	3.50	1.55	.45

1996 Redskins Score Board/Exxon

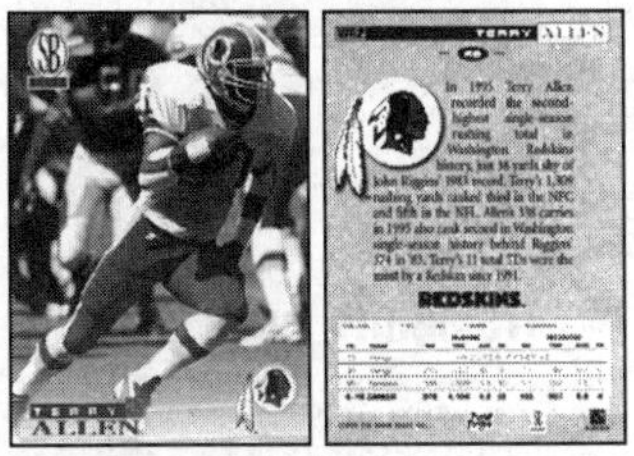

Score Board produced this team set for distribution by the Washington D.C. area Exxon stations. Each card appears similar to a 1996 Pro Line card, but contains the Score Board logo at the top. The Exxon sponsor logo appears only on the checklist card. Packs could be obtained, with the appropriate gasoline purchase, for 49-cents each and contained three-player cards and a checklist card.

	MINT	NRMT	EXC
COMPLETE SET (9)	3.50	1.55	.45
COMMON CARD (WR1-WR9)	.25	.11	.03
☐ WR1 Gus Frerotte	.75	.35	.09
☐ WR2 Terry Allen	.40	.18	.05
☐ WR3 Henry Ellard	.40	.18	.05
☐ WR4 Michael Westbrook	1.25	.55	.16
☐ WR5 Brian Mitchell	.25	.11	.03
☐ WR6 Sean Gilbert	.25	.11	.03
☐ WR7 Ken Harvey	.25	.11	.03
☐ WR8 Darrell Green	.40	.18	.05
☐ WR9 Redskins Checklist	.25	.11	.03

1993 Rice Council *

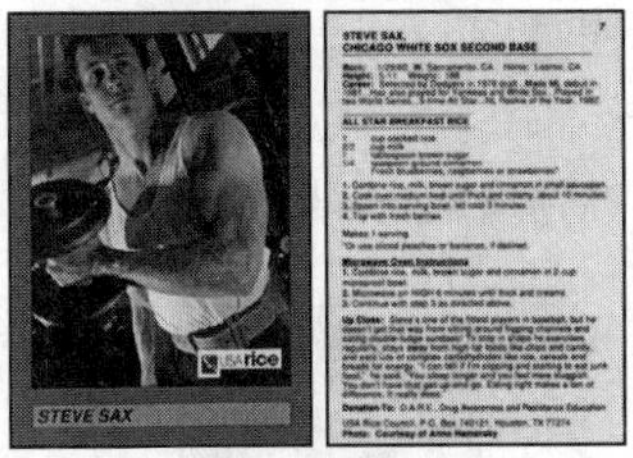

Sponsored by the USA Rice Council (Houston, Texas), this ten-card standard-size set of recipe trading cards was issued to promote the consumption of rice. These sets were originally available from the Rice Council for 2.00. The fronts feature color photos with either blue or red borders. The player's name appears in black lettering in an orange stripe beneath the picture. The backs present biographical information, career summary, a favorite rice recipe, an up-close trivia fact, and the athlete's favorite charity to which the profits generated from the sale of the cards will be donated. The sports represented in this set are baseball (1, 3, 7), football (2, 5), tennis (4), swimming (6), and bobsledding (8).

	MINT	NRMT	EXC
COMPLETE SET (10)	10.00	4.50	1.25
COMMON CARD (1-10)	.25	.11	.03
☐ 1 Steve Sax	.50	.23	.06
☐ 2 Troy Aikman	4.00	1.80	.50
☐ 3 Roger Clemens	2.50	1.10	.30
☐ 4 Zina Garrison	.50	.23	.06
☐ 5 Warren Moon	1.25	.55	.16
☐ 6 Summer Sanders	.50	.23	.06
☐ 7 Steve Sax	.50	.23	.06
☐ 8 Brian Shimer	.25	.11	.03
☐ 9 Food Guide Pyramid	.25	.11	.03
☐ 10 Ten Tips to Healthy Eating for Kids	.25	.11	.03

1976 Saga Discs

These cards parallel the 1976 Crane Disc Set. They feature the "SAGA" sponsor logo on back and are more difficult to find than their Crane counterparts.

	NRMT-MT	EXC	G-VG
COMPLETE SET (30)	1000.00	450.00	125.00
COMMON CARD (1-30)	10.00	4.50	1.25
☐ 1 Ken Anderson	40.00	18.00	5.00
☐ 2 Otis Armstrong	12.00	5.50	1.50
☐ 3 Steve Bartkowski	15.00	6.75	1.85
☐ 4 Terry Bradshaw	200.00	90.00	25.00
☐ 5 John Brockington	10.00	4.50	1.25
☐ 6 Doug Buffone	10.00	4.50	1.25
☐ 7 Wally Chambers	10.00	4.50	1.25
☐ 8 Isaac Curtis	10.00	4.50	1.25
☐ 9 Chuck Foreman	12.00	5.50	1.50
☐ 10 Roman Gabriel	15.00	6.75	1.85
☐ 11 Mel Gray	12.00	5.50	1.50
☐ 12 Joe Greene	100.00	45.00	12.50
☐ 13 James Harris	10.00	4.50	1.25
☐ 14 Jim Hart	12.00	5.50	1.50
☐ 15 Billy Kilmer	15.00	6.75	1.85
☐ 16 Greg Landry	12.00	5.50	1.50
☐ 17 Ed Marinaro	12.00	5.50	1.50
☐ 18 Lawrence McCutcheon	12.00	5.50	1.50
☐ 19 Terry Metcalf	12.00	5.50	1.50
☐ 20 Lydell Mitchell	10.00	4.50	1.25
☐ 21 Jim Otis	10.00	4.50	1.25
☐ 22 Alan Page	30.00	13.50	3.70
☐ 23 Walter Payton	350.00	160.00	45.00
☐ 24 Greg Pruitt	12.00	5.50	1.50
☐ 25 Charlie Sanders	10.00	4.50	1.25
☐ 26 Ron Shanklin	10.00	4.50	1.25
☐ 27 Roger Staubach	250.00	110.00	31.00
☐ 28 Jan Stenerud	15.00	6.75	1.85
☐ 29 Charley Taylor	50.00	22.00	6.25
☐ 30 Roger Wehrli	10.00	4.50	1.25

1967-68 Saints Team Issue 5X7 Bordered

The Saints issued two different sets of 5" by 7" photos, presumably over a period of years. The photographs of the same players in both sets are identical except for the white border or lack of a border. The text size and style varies from photo to photo as does the player information below the picture. All are head and chest shots instead of action. The two groups were likely issued together but have been separated for ease in cataloging. Each is unnumbered and blankbacked.

	NRMT	VG-E	GOOD
COMPLETE SET (20)	40.00	18.00	5.00
COMMON CARD (1-20)	2.00	.90	.25
☐ 1 Tom Barrington	2.00	.90	.25
☐ 2 Bo Burris	2.00	.90	.25
☐ 3 Bill Cody	2.00	.90	.25
☐ 4 Lou Cordileone	2.00	.90	.25
☐ 5 Ted Davis	2.00	.90	.25
☐ 6 Charles Durkee	2.00	.90	.25
☐ 7 Jim Hester	2.00	.90	.25
☐ 8 Kent Kramer	2.00	.90	.25
☐ 9 Jake Kupp	3.00	1.35	.35
☐ 10 Obert Logan	2.00	.90	.25
☐ 11 Don McCall	2.00	.90	.25
☐ 12 Thomas McNeill	2.00	.90	.25
☐ 13 Ray Ogden	2.00	.90	.25
☐ 14 Ray Rissmiller	2.00	.90	.25
☐ 15 Walter Roberts	2.00	.90	.25
☐ 16 George Rose	2.00	.90	.25
☐ 17 Randy Schultz	2.00	.90	.25
☐ 18 Joe Wendryhoski	2.00	.90	.25
☐ 19 Dave Whitsell	3.00	1.35	.35
☐ 20 Gary Wood	3.00	1.35	.35

1967-68 Saints Team Issue 5X7 Borderless

The Saints issued two different sets of 5" by 7" photos, presumably over a period of years. The photographs of the same players in both sets are identical except for the white border or lack of a border. The text size and style varies from photo to photo as does the player information below the picture. All are head and chest shots instead of action. The two groups were likely issued together but have been separated for ease in cataloging. Each is unnumbered and blankbacked.

	NRMT	VG-E	GOOD
COMPLETE SET (22)	40.00	18.00	5.00
COMMON CARD (1-22)	2.00	.90	.25
☐ 1 Charlie Brown	2.00	.90	.25
☐ 2 Vern Burke	2.00	.90	.25
☐ 3 Jackie Burkett	2.00	.90	.25
☐ 4 Bill Cody	2.00	.90	.25
☐ 5 Jim Garcia	2.00	.90	.25
☐ 6 Tom Hall	2.00	.90	.25
☐ 7 Jimmy Heidel	2.00	.90	.25
☐ 8 Les Kelley	2.00	.90	.25
☐ 9 Jake Kupp	3.00	1.35	.35
☐ 10 Ray Ogden	2.00	.90	.25
☐ 11 Ray Rissmiller	2.00	.90	.25
☐ 12 Bill Sandeman	2.00	.90	.25
☐ 13 Brian Schweda	2.00	.90	.25
☐ 14 Roy Schmidt	2.00	.90	.25
☐ 15 Dave Simmons	2.00	.90	.25
☐ 16 Jerry Simmons	2.00	.90	.25
☐ 17 Mike Tilleman	2.00	.90	.25
☐ 18 Joe Wendryhoski	2.00	.90	.25
☐ 19 Ernie Wheelwright UER misspelled Wheelright	3.00	1.35	.35
☐ 20 Fred Whittingham	2.00	.90	.25
☐ 21 Del Williams	3.00	1.35	.35
☐ 22 Bo Wood	2.00	.90	.25

1967-68 Saints Team Issue 8X10

The Saints released these posed action photos primarily for fans and to fulfill autograph reguests. Each measures roughly 8" by 10" and features a black and white player photo with information in the border below the picture. They were likely released over a period of years as the type style and size used varies from photo to photo. There appear to be four distinct groups issued with text as follows reading left to right: (1) player's name in all caps, position initials only, and team name in all caps, (2) player's name, position spelled out completely and team in all capital letters, (3) player's name in caps, position spelled out in upper and lower case letters, and team in upper and lower case letters, and (4) player's name in all caps (no position) and team name in all caps. Any additions to this list are appreciated.

	NRMT	VG-E	GOOD
COMPLETE SET (30)	80.00	36.00	10.00
COMMON CARD (1-30)	3.00	1.35	.35
☐ 1 Dan Abramowicz	5.00	2.20	.60
☐ 2 Doug Atkins	7.50	3.40	.95
☐ 3 Tom Barrington	3.00	1.35	.35
☐ 4 Jim Boeke	3.00	1.35	.35
☐ 5 Johnny Brewer	3.00	1.35	.35
☐ 6 Bo Burris	3.00	1.35	.35
☐ 7 Bill Cody	3.00	1.35	.35
☐ 8 Ted Davis	3.00	1.35	.35
☐ 9 John Douglas	3.00	1.35	.35
☐ 10 John Gilliam	4.00	1.80	.50
☐ 11 Jim Hester	3.00	1.35	.35
☐ 12 Gene Howard	3.00	1.35	.35
☐ 13 Les Kelley	3.00	1.35	.35
☐ 14 Billy Kilmer	7.50	3.40	.95
☐ 15 Jake Kupp	4.00	1.80	.50
☐ 16 Earl Leggett	3.00	1.35	.35
☐ 17 Don McCall	3.00	1.35	.35
☐ 18 Tom McNeill	3.00	1.35	.35
☐ 19 Ray Poage	3.00	1.35	.35
☐ 20 David Rowe	3.00	1.35	.35
☐ 21 Roy Schmidt	3.00	1.35	.35
☐ 22 Randy Schultz	3.00	1.35	.35
☐ 23 Brian Schweda	3.00	1.35	.35
☐ 24 Monty Stickles	3.00	1.35	.35
☐ 25 Steve Stonebreaker	3.00	1.35	.35
☐ 26 Mike Tilleman	3.00	1.35	.35
☐ 27 Joe Wendryhoski	3.00	1.35	.35
☐ 28 Ernie Wheelwright UER misspelled Wheelright	4.00	1.80	.50
☐ 29 Fred Whittingham	3.00	1.35	.35
☐ 30 Del Williams	3.00	1.35	.35

1968 Saints Doubloons

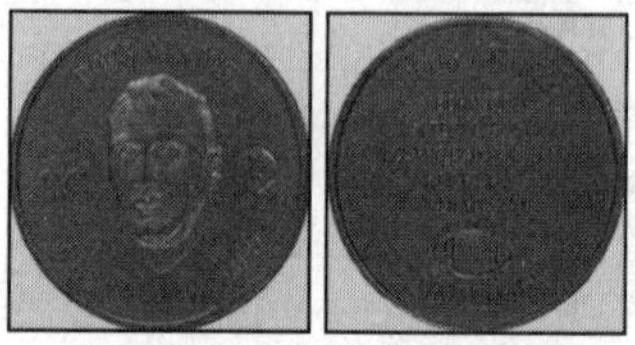

These coins were produced by Pro Players Doubloons, Inc. and distributed by the New Orleans Saints at games during the 1968 season. Each coin is unnumbered and measures approximately 1 1/2" in diameter. They are gold colored and feature a player bust on front with a short player bio and copyright information on back.

	NRMT-MT	EXC	G-VG
COMPLETE SET (23)	120.00	55.00	15.00
COMMON COIN (1-23)	5.00	2.20	.60
☐ 1 Dan Abramowicz	6.00	2.70	.75
☐ 2 Doug Atkins	10.00	4.50	1.25
☐ 3 Tom Barrington	5.00	2.20	.60
☐ 4 Johnny Brewer	5.00	2.20	.60
☐ 5 Bo Burris	5.00	2.20	.60
☐ 6 Ted Davis	5.00	2.20	.60
☐ 7 John Douglas	5.00	2.20	.60
☐ 8 Charlie Durkee	5.00	2.20	.60
☐ 9 Gene Howard	5.00	2.20	.60
☐ 10 Billy Kilmer	10.00	4.50	1.25
☐ 11 Jake Kupp	5.00	2.20	.60
☐ 12 Errol Linden	5.00	2.20	.60
☐ 13 Tony Lorick	5.00	2.20	.60
☐ 14 Don McCall	5.00	2.20	.60
☐ 15 Dave Parks	6.00	2.70	.75
☐ 16 Dave Rowe	5.00	2.20	.60
☐ 17 Brian Schweda	5.00	2.20	.60
☐ 18 Monte Stickles	5.00	2.20	.60
☐ 19 Jerry Sturm	5.00	2.20	.60
☐ 20 Mike Tilleman	5.00	2.20	.60
☐ 21 Joe Wendryhoski	5.00	2.20	.60
☐ 22 Dave Whitsell	6.00	2.70	.75
☐ 23 Fred Whittingham	5.00	2.20	.60

1971-72 Saints Team Issue

The Saints issued several very similar photo series in the early 1970s. This set was likely issued between 1971 and 1972. Each black and white portrait (no action) photo measures approximately 4" by 5" and carries the player's name and team in the border below the picture. Most include the player's name in large capital letters with the team name abbreviated "N.O. Saints." We've also included a few photos that feature the player's name and team in bold block letters. Any additions to this list are appreciated.

	NRMT-MT	EXC	G-VG
COMPLETE SET (14)	25.00	11.00	3.10
COMMON CARD (1-14)	2.00	.90	.25
☐ 1 Carl Cunningham	2.00	.90	.25
☐ 2 Al Dodd	2.00	.90	.25
☐ 3 Julian Fagan	2.00	.90	.25
☐ 4 Edd Hargett	3.00	1.35	.35
☐ 5 Glen Ray Hines	2.00	.90	.25
☐ 6 Jake Kupp	3.00	1.35	.35
☐ 7 Bivian Lee	2.00	.90	.25
☐ 8 D'Artagnan Martin	2.00	.90	.25
☐ 9 Reynaud Moore	2.00	.90	.25
☐ 10 Don Morrison	2.00	.90	.25
☐ 11 Joe Owens	2.00	.90	.25
☐ 12 Dave Parks	3.00	1.35	.35
☐ 13 John Shinners	2.00	.90	.25
☐ 14 Doug Wyatt UER	2.00	.90	.25

1973 Saints Team Issue

The Saints issued several very similar photo series in the early 1970s. This set was most likely issued in 1973. Each black and white portrait (no action) photo measures approximately 4" by 5" and carries the player's name, postion (initials) and team in the border below the picture. The type style used was small (all caps) block lettering with the team name spelled out completely.

	NRMT-MT	EXC	G-VG
COMPLETE SET (17)	30.00	13.50	3.70
COMMON CARD (1-17)	2.00	.90	.25
☐ 1 Bill Butler	2.00	.90	.25
☐ 2 Drew Buie	2.00	.90	.25
☐ 3 Bob Davis	2.00	.90	.25
☐ 4 Ernie Jackson facing right	2.00	.90	.25
☐ 5 Ernie Jackson facing left	2.00	.90	.25
☐ 6 Mike Kelly	2.00	.90	.25
☐ 7 Jake Kupp	3.00	1.35	.35
☐ 8 Jim Merlo	2.00	.90	.25
☐ 9 Don Morrison	2.00	.90	.25
☐ 10 Bob Newland	2.00	.90	.25
☐ 11 Joe Owens	2.00	.90	.25
☐ 12 Dick Palmer	2.00	.90	.25
☐ 13 Elex Price	2.00	.90	.25
☐ 14 Preston Riley	2.00	.90	.25
☐ 15 Bobby Scott	3.00	1.35	.35
☐ 16 Royce Smith	2.00	.90	.25
☐ 17 Howard Stevens	2.00	.90	.25

1974 Saints Circle Inset

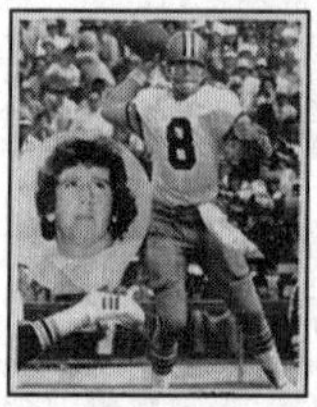

Each of these 22 photos measures approximately 10" by 8". The fronts feature black-and-white action player photos with white borders. In one of the upper corners, a black-and-white headshot appears in a circle. The player's name, position, and team name are printed in the lower border. The backs are blank. The photos are unnumbered and checklisted below in alphabetical order. The year of issue for this set is clearly determined by the fact that Jack DeGrenier's only year with the Saints was 1974; in addition 1974 was the first year with the Saints for Tom Blanchard, Larry Cipa, Don Coleman, Phil LaPorta, Alvin Maxson, Rod McNeill, Rick Middleton, Joel Parker, Terry Schmidt, Paul Seal, and Dave Thompson and the last year with the Saints for John Beasley, Odell Lawson, Jerry Moore, and Jess Phillips. The cards in the set may actually have been issued over a period of years.

	NRMT-MT	EXC	G-VG
COMPLETE SET (22)	125.00	55.00	15.50
COMMON CARD (1-22)	5.00	2.20	.60
☐ 1 John Beasley	5.00	2.20	.60
☐ 2 Tom Blanchard	6.00	2.70	.75
☐ 3 Larry Cipa	5.00	2.20	.60
☐ 4 Don Coleman	5.00	2.20	.60
☐ 5 Wayne Colman	5.00	2.20	.60
☐ 6 Jack DeGrenier	5.00	2.20	.60
☐ 7 Rick Kingrea	5.00	2.20	.60
☐ 8 Phil LaPorta	5.00	2.20	.60
☐ 9 Odell Lawson	5.00	2.20	.60
☐ 10 Archie Manning	25.00	11.00	3.10
☐ 11 Alvin Maxson	6.00	2.70	.75
☐ 12 Bill McClard	5.00	2.20	.60
☐ 13 Rod McNeill	5.00	2.20	.60
☐ 14 Jim Merlo	5.00	2.20	.60
☐ 15 Rick Middleton	5.00	2.20	.60
☐ 16 Derland Moore	5.00	2.20	.60
☐ 17 Jerry Moore	5.00	2.20	.60
☐ 18 Joel Parker	5.00	2.20	.60
☐ 19 Jess Phillips	5.00	2.20	.60
☐ 20 Terry Schmidt	5.00	2.20	.60
☐ 21 Paul Seal	5.00	2.20	.60
☐ 22 Dave Thompson	5.00	2.20	.60

1974 Saints Team Issue

The Saints issued several very similar photo series in the early 1970s. This set was most likely issued in 1974. Each black and white portrait (no action) photo measures approximately 4" by 5" and carries the player's name, postion (initials) and team in the border below the picture. The type style used was small italicized block lettering with the team name spelled out completely.

	NRMT-MT	EXC	G-VG
COMPLETE SET (13)	25.00	11.00	3.10
COMMON CARD (1-13)	2.00	.90	.25
☐ 1 Andy Dorris	2.00	.90	.25
☐ 2 Paul Fersen	2.00	.90	.25
☐ 3 Len Garrett	2.00	.90	.25
☐ 4 Rick Kingrea	2.00	.90	.25
☐ 5 Odell Lawson	2.00	.90	.25
☐ 6 Jim Merlo	2.00	.90	.25
☐ 7 Jerry Moore	2.00	.90	.25
☐ 8 Don Morrison	2.00	.90	.25
☐ 9 Bob Newland	2.00	.90	.25
☐ 10 Joe Owens	2.00	.90	.25
☐ 11 Elex Price	2.00	.90	.25
☐ 12 Bobby Scott	3.00	1.35	.35
☐ 13 Howard Stevens	2.00	.90	.25

1979 Saints Coke

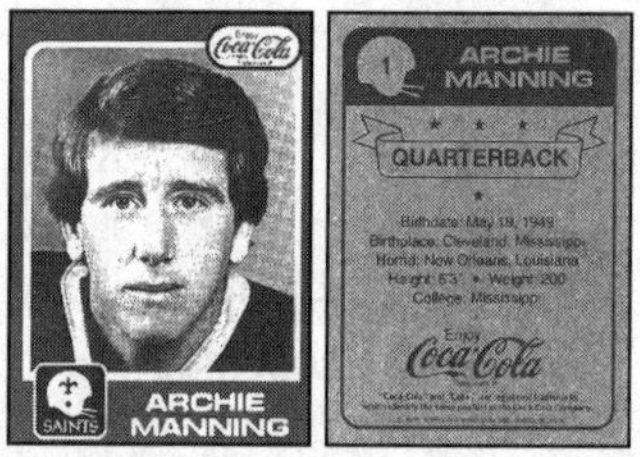

The 1979 Coca-Cola New Orleans Saints set contains 45 black and white standard-size cards with red borders. The Coca-Cola logo appears in the upper right hand corner while a New Orleans Saints helmet appears in the lower left. The backs of this gray stock card contain minimal biographical data, the card number and the Coke logo. The cards were produced in conjunction with Topps. There were also unnumbered ad cards for Coke, Mr. Pibb, and Sprite, one of which was included in each pack of cards.

	NRMT-MT	EXC	G-VG
COMPLETE SET (45)	60.00	27.00	7.50
COMMON CARD (1-45)	1.50	.70	.19
☐ 1 Archie Manning	8.00	3.60	1.00
☐ 2 Ed Burns	1.50	.70	.19
☐ 3 Bobby Scott	2.00	.90	.25
☐ 4 Russell Erxleben	2.00	.90	.25
☐ 5 Eric Felton	1.50	.70	.19
☐ 6 David Gray	1.50	.70	.19
☐ 7 Ricky Ray	1.50	.70	.19
☐ 8 Clarence Chapman	1.50	.70	.19
☐ 9 Kim Jones	1.50	.70	.19
☐ 10 Mike Strachan	1.50	.70	.19
☐ 11 Tony Galbreath	2.00	.90	.25
☐ 12 Tom Myers	1.50	.70	.19
☐ 13 Chuck Muncie	3.50	1.55	.45
☐ 14 Jack Holmes	1.50	.70	.19
☐ 15 Don Schwartz	1.50	.70	.19
☐ 16 Ralph McGill	1.50	.70	.19
☐ 17 Ken Bordelon	1.50	.70	.19
☐ 18 Jim Kovach	1.50	.70	.19
☐ 19 Pat Hughes	1.50	.70	.19
☐ 20 Reggie Mathis	1.50	.70	.19
☐ 21 Jim Merlo	1.50	.70	.19
☐ 22 Joe Federspiel	1.50	.70	.19
☐ 23 Don Reese	1.50	.70	.19
☐ 24 Roger Finnie	1.50	.70	.19
☐ 25 John Hill	1.50	.70	.19
☐ 26 Barry Bennett	1.50	.70	.19
☐ 27 Dave Lafary	1.50	.70	.19
☐ 28 Robert Woods	1.50	.70	.19
☐ 29 Conrad Dobler	2.00	.90	.25
☐ 30 John Watson	1.50	.70	.19
☐ 31 Fred Sturt	1.50	.70	.19
☐ 32 J.T. Taylor	1.50	.70	.19
☐ 33 Mike Fultz	1.50	.70	.19
☐ 34 Joe Campbell	1.50	.70	.19
☐ 35 Derland Moore	1.50	.70	.19
☐ 36 Elex Price	1.50	.70	.19
☐ 37 Elois Grooms	1.50	.70	.19
☐ 38 Emanuel Zanders	1.50	.70	.19
☐ 39 Ike Harris	1.50	.70	.19
☐ 40 Tinker Owens	2.00	.90	.25
☐ 41 Rich Mauti	1.50	.70	.19
☐ 42 Henry Childs	2.00	.90	.25
☐ 43 Larry Hardy	1.50	.70	.19
☐ 44 Brooks Williams	1.50	.70	.19
☐ 45 Wes Chandler	4.00	1.80	.50

1992 Saints McDag

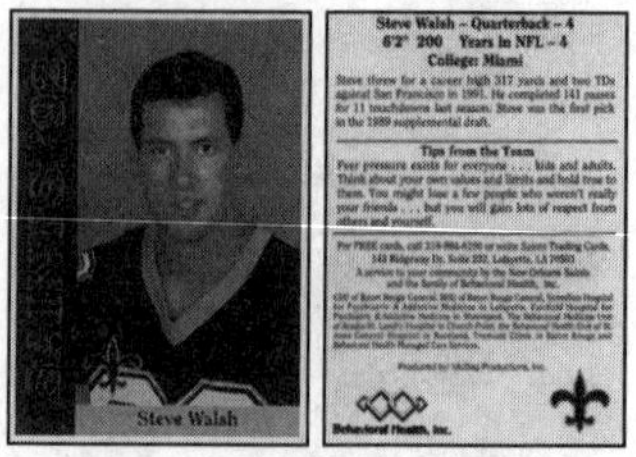

This 32-card safety standard-size set was produced by McDag Productions Inc. for the New Orleans Saints and Behavioral Health Inc. The cards feature posed color player photos with white borders. The pictures are studio shots with a blue background. Running horizontally down the left is a wide brown stripe with the team name and year in yellow outline lettering. A mustard stripe at the bottom of the photo intersects the brown stripe and contains the player's name. The backs are white with black print and carry biographical information, career highlights, and "Tips from the Team" in the form of public service messages. There is also an address and phone number for obtaining free cards. The cards are unnumbered and checklisted below in alphabetical order.

	MINT	NRMT	EXC
COMPLETE SET (32)	10.00	4.50	1.25
COMMON CARD (1-32)	.25	.11	.03
☐ 1 Morten Andersen	.50	.23	.06
☐ 2 Gene Atkins	.40	.18	.05
☐ 3 Toi Cook	.25	.11	.03
☐ 4 Tommy Barnhardt	.25	.11	.03
☐ 5 Hoby Brenner	.25	.11	.03
☐ 6 Stan Brock	.25	.11	.03
☐ 7 Vince Buck	.25	.11	.03
☐ 8 Wesley Carroll	.40	.18	.05
☐ 9 Jim Dombrowski	.25	.11	.03
☐ 10 Vaughn Dunbar	.40	.18	.05
☐ 11 Quinn Early	.75	.35	.09
☐ 12 Bobby Hebert	.40	.18	.05
☐ 13 Craig Heyward	.60	.25	.07
☐ 14 Joel Hilgenberg	.25	.11	.03
☐ 15 Dalton Hilliard	.25	.11	.03
☐ 16 Rickey Jackson	.40	.18	.05
☐ 17 Vaughan Johnson	.40	.18	.05
☐ 18 Reginald Jones	.25	.11	.03
☐ 19 Eric Martin	.40	.18	.05
☐ 20 Wayne Martin	.40	.18	.05
☐ 21 Brett Maxie	.25	.11	.03
☐ 22 Fred McAfee	.25	.11	.03
☐ 23 Sam Mills	.50	.23	.06
☐ 24 Jim Mora CO	.40	.18	.05
☐ 25 Pat Swilling	.40	.18	.05
☐ 26 John Tice	.25	.11	.03
☐ 27 Renaldo Turnbull	.40	.18	.05
☐ 28 Floyd Turner	.40	.18	.05
☐ 29 Steve Walsh	.40	.18	.05
☐ 30 Frank Warren	.25	.11	.03
☐ 31 Jim Wilks	.25	.11	.03
☐ 32 Saints Cheerleaders	.25	.11	.03

1962-63 Salada Coins

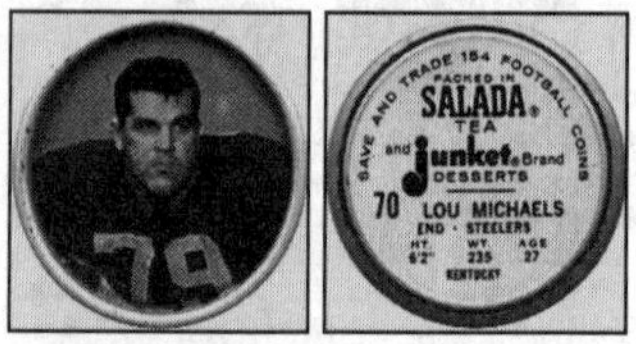

This 154-coin set features popular NFL and AFL players from selected teams. Each team had a specific rim color. The numbering of the coins is essentially by teams, i.e., Colts (1-11 blue), Packers (12-22 green), 49ers (23-33 salmon), Bears (34-44 black), Rams (45-55 yellow), Browns (56-66 black), Steelers (67-77 yellow), Lions (78-88 blue), Redskins (89-99 yellow), Eagles (100-110 green), Giants (111-121 blue), Patriots (122-132 salmon), Titans (133-143 blue), and Bills (144-154 salmon). All players are pictured without their helmets. The coins measure approximately 1 1/2" in diameter. The coin backs give the player's name, position, pro team, college, height, and weight. The coins were originally produced on sheets measuring 31 1/2" by 25"; the 255 coins on the sheet included the complete set as well as duplicates and triplicates. Double prints (DP) and triple prints (TP) are listed below. The double-printed coins are generally from certain teams, i.e., Packers, Bears, Browns, Lions, Eagles, Giants, Patriots, Titans, and Bills. Those coins below not listed explicitly as to the frequency of printing are in fact single printed (SP) and hence more difficult to find. The set is sometimes found intact as a presentation set in its own custom box; such a set would be valued 25 percent higher than the complete set price below.

	NRMT	VG-E	GOOD
COMPLETE SET (154)	2750.00	1250.00	350.00
COMMON COIN DP	5.00	2.20	.60
COMMON COIN SP	25.00	11.00	3.10

☐ 1 Johnny Unitas	160.00	70.00	20.00
☐ 2 Lenny Moore	80.00	36.00	10.00
☐ 3 Jim Parker	50.00	22.00	6.25
☐ 4 Gino Marchetti	60.00	27.00	7.50
☐ 5 Dick Szymanski	25.00	11.00	3.10
☐ 6 Alex Sandusky	25.00	11.00	3.10
☐ 7 Raymond Berry	80.00	36.00	10.00
☐ 8 Jimmy Orr	25.00	11.00	3.10
☐ 9 Ordell Braase	25.00	11.00	3.10
☐ 10 Bill Pellington	25.00	11.00	3.10
☐ 11 Bob Boyd	25.00	11.00	3.10
☐ 12 Paul Hornung DP	30.00	13.50	3.70
☐ 13 Jim Taylor DP	25.00	11.00	3.10
☐ 14 Hank Jordan DP	10.00	4.50	1.25
☐ 15 Dan Currie DP	5.00	2.20	.60
☐ 16 Bill Forester DP	6.00	2.70	.75
☐ 17 Dave Hanner DP	6.00	2.70	.75
☐ 18 Bart Starr DP	35.00	16.00	4.40
☐ 19 Max McGee DP	6.00	2.70	.75
☐ 20 Jerry Kramer DP	10.00	4.50	1.25
☐ 21 Forrest Gregg DP	12.00	5.50	1.50
☐ 22 Jim Ringo DP	12.00	5.50	1.50
☐ 23 Billy Kilmer	50.00	22.00	6.25
☐ 24 Charlie Krueger	25.00	11.00	3.10
☐ 25 Bob St. Clair	50.00	22.00	6.25
☐ 26 Abe Woodson	25.00	11.00	3.10
☐ 27 Jim Johnson	50.00	22.00	6.25
☐ 28 Matt Hazeltine	25.00	11.00	3.10
☐ 29 Bruce Bosley	25.00	11.00	3.10
☐ 30 Clyde Conner	25.00	11.00	3.10
☐ 31 John Brodie	75.00	34.00	9.50
☐ 32 J.D. Smith	25.00	11.00	3.10
☐ 33 Monty Stickles	25.00	11.00	3.10
☐ 34 Johnny Morris DP	6.00	2.70	.75
☐ 35 Stan Jones DP	10.00	4.50	1.25
☐ 36 J.C. Caroline DP	5.00	2.20	.60
☐ 37 Richie Petitbon DP	6.00	2.70	.75
☐ 38 Joe Fortunato DP	6.00	2.70	.75
☐ 39 Larry Morris DP	5.00	2.20	.60
☐ 40 Doug Atkins DP	12.00	5.50	1.50
☐ 41 Bill Wade DP	6.00	2.70	.75
☐ 42 Rick Casares DP	6.00	2.70	.75
☐ 43 Willie Galimore DP	6.00	2.70	.75
☐ 44 Angelo Coia DP	5.00	2.20	.60
☐ 45 Ollie Matson	65.00	29.00	8.00
☐ 46 Carroll Dale	30.00	13.50	3.70
☐ 47 Ed Meador	30.00	13.50	3.70
☐ 48 Jon Arnett	30.00	13.50	3.70
☐ 49 Joe Marconi	25.00	11.00	3.10
☐ 50 John LoVetere	25.00	11.00	3.10
☐ 51 Red Phillips	25.00	11.00	3.10
☐ 52 Zeke Bratkowski	30.00	13.50	3.70
☐ 53 Dick Bass	30.00	13.50	3.70
☐ 54 Les Richter	30.00	13.50	3.70
☐ 55 Art Hunter DP	5.00	2.20	.60
☐ 56 Jim Brown TP	60.00	27.00	7.50
☐ 57 Mike McCormack DP	10.00	4.50	1.25
☐ 58 Bob Gain DP	5.00	2.20	.60
☐ 59 Paul Wiggin DP	5.00	2.20	.60
☐ 60 Jim Houston DP	5.00	2.20	.60
☐ 61 Ray Renfro DP	6.00	2.70	.75
☐ 62 Galen Fiss DP	5.00	2.20	.60
☐ 63 J.R. Smith DP	5.00	2.20	.60
☐ 64 John Morrow DP	5.00	2.20	.60
☐ 65 Gene Hickerson DP	5.00	2.20	.60
☐ 66 Jim Ninowski DP	5.00	2.20	.60
☐ 67 Tom Tracy	30.00	13.50	3.70
☐ 68 Buddy Dial	30.00	13.50	3.70
☐ 69 Mike Sandusky	25.00	11.00	3.10
☐ 70 Lou Michaels	30.00	13.50	3.70
☐ 71 Preston Carpenter	25.00	11.00	3.10
☐ 72 John Reger	25.00	11.00	3.10
☐ 73 John Henry Johnson	60.00	27.00	7.50
☐ 74 Gene Lipscomb	35.00	16.00	4.40
☐ 75 Mike Henry	25.00	11.00	3.10
☐ 76 George Tarasovic	25.00	11.00	3.10
☐ 77 Bobby Layne	75.00	34.00	9.50
☐ 78 Harley Sewell DP	5.00	2.20	.60
☐ 79 Darris McCord DP	5.00	2.20	.60
☐ 80 Yale Lary DP	10.00	4.50	1.25
☐ 81 Jim Gibbons DP	6.00	2.70	.75
☐ 82 Gail Cogdill DP	5.00	2.20	.60
☐ 83 Nick Pietrosante DP	5.00	2.20	.60
☐ 84 Alex Karras DP	15.00	6.75	1.85
☐ 85 Dick Lane DP	10.00	4.50	1.25
☐ 86 Joe Schmidt DP	12.00	5.50	1.50
☐ 87 John Gordy DP	5.00	2.20	.60
☐ 88 Milt Plum DP	6.00	2.70	.75
☐ 89 Andy Stynchula	25.00	11.00	3.10
☐ 90 Bob Toneff	25.00	11.00	3.10
☐ 91 Bill Anderson	25.00	11.00	3.10
☐ 92 Sam Horner	25.00	11.00	3.10
☐ 93 Norm Snead	35.00	16.00	4.40
☐ 94 Bobby Mitchell	60.00	27.00	7.50
☐ 95 Bill Barnes	25.00	11.00	3.10
☐ 96 Rod Breedlove	25.00	11.00	3.10
☐ 97 Fred Hageman	25.00	11.00	3.10
☐ 98 Vince Promuto	25.00	11.00	3.10
☐ 99 Joe Rutgens	25.00	11.00	3.10
☐ 100 Maxie Baughan DP	5.00	2.20	.60
☐ 101 Pete Retzlaff DP	6.00	2.70	.75
☐ 102 Tom Brookshier DP	6.00	2.70	.75
☐ 103 Sonny Jurgensen DP	18.00	8.00	2.20
☐ 104 Ed Khayat DP	5.00	2.20	.60
☐ 105 Chuck Bednarik DP	15.00	6.75	1.85
☐ 106 Tommy McDonald DP	6.00	2.70	.75
☐ 107 Bobby Walston DP	5.00	2.20	.60
☐ 108 Ted Dean DP	5.00	2.20	.60
☐ 109 Clarence Peaks DP	6.00	2.70	.75
☐ 110 Jimmy Carr DP	5.00	2.20	.60
☐ 111 Sam Huff DP	15.00	6.75	1.85
☐ 112 Erich Barnes DP	5.00	2.20	.60
☐ 113 Del Shofner DP	6.00	2.70	.75
☐ 114 Bob Gaiters DP	5.00	2.20	.60
☐ 115 Alex Webster DP	6.00	2.70	.75
☐ 116 Dick Modzelewski DP	5.00	2.20	.60
☐ 117 Jim Katcavage DP	6.00	2.70	.75
☐ 118 Roosevelt Brown DP	10.00	4.50	1.25
☐ 119 Y.A. Tittle DP	25.00	11.00	3.10
☐ 120 Andy Robustelli DP	12.00	5.50	1.50
☐ 121 Dick Lynch DP	5.00	2.20	.60
☐ 122 Don Webb DP	5.00	2.20	.60
☐ 123 Larry Eisenhauer DP	5.00	2.20	.60
☐ 124 Babe Parilli DP	6.00	2.70	.75
☐ 125 Charles Long DP	5.00	2.20	.60
☐ 126 Billy Lott DP	5.00	2.20	.60
☐ 127 Harry Jacobs DP	5.00	2.20	.60
☐ 128 Bob Dee DP	5.00	2.20	.60
☐ 129 Ron Burton DP	6.00	2.70	.75
☐ 130 Jim Colclough TP	3.00	1.35	.35
☐ 131 Gino Cappelletti DP	6.00	2.70	.75
☐ 132 Tommy Addison DP	5.00	2.20	.60
☐ 133 Larry Grantham DP	5.00	2.20	.60
☐ 134 Dick Christy DP	5.00	2.20	.60
☐ 135 Bill Mathis DP	6.00	2.70	.75
☐ 136 Butch Songin DP	5.00	2.20	.60
☐ 137 Dainard Paulson DP	5.00	2.20	.60
☐ 138 Roger Ellis DP	5.00	2.20	.60
☐ 139 Mike Hudock DP	5.00	2.20	.60
☐ 140 Don Maynard DP	20.00	9.00	2.50
☐ 141 Al Dorow DP	5.00	2.20	.60
☐ 142 Jack Klotz DP	5.00	2.20	.60
☐ 143 Lee Riley DP	5.00	2.20	.60
☐ 144 Bill Atkins DP	5.00	2.20	.60
☐ 145 Art Baker DP	5.00	2.20	.60
☐ 146 Stew Barber DP	5.00	2.20	.60
☐ 147 Glenn Bass DP	5.00	2.20	.60
☐ 148 Al Bemiller DP	5.00	2.20	.60
☐ 149 Richie Lucas DP	5.00	2.20	.60
☐ 150 Archie Matsos DP	5.00	2.20	.60
☐ 151 Warren Rabb DP	5.00	2.20	.60
☐ 152 Ken Rice DP	5.00	2.20	.60
☐ 153 Billy Shaw DP	6.00	2.70	.75
☐ 154 Lavern Torczon DP	5.00	2.20	.60

1959 San Giorgio Flipbooks

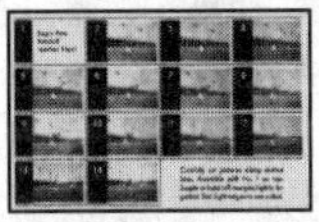

This 17-card set features members of the NFL in an action sequence. The set is sometimes referenced as the San Giorgio Macaroni Football Flipbooks. The set features only members of the Philadelphia Eagles, Pittsburgh Steelers, and Washington Redskins. When the flipbooks are still in the uncut form (which is most desirable), they measure approximately 5 3/4" by 3 9/16". The sheets are blank backed, in black and white, and provide 14 small numbered pages when cut apart.

	NRMT	VG-E	GOOD
COMPLETE SET (17)	2800.00	1250.00	350.00
COMMON CARD (1-17)	150.00	70.00	19.00
☐ 1 Sam Baker	175.00	80.00	22.00
☐ 2 Bill Barnes	150.00	70.00	19.00
☐ 3 Chuck Bednarik	400.00	180.00	50.00
☐ 4 Don Bosseler	150.00	70.00	19.00
☐ 5 Darrell Pete Brewster	150.00	70.00	19.00
☐ 6 Jack Butler	150.00	70.00	19.00
☐ 7 Proverb Jacobs	150.00	70.00	19.00
☐ 8 Eddie LeBaron	250.00	110.00	31.00
☐ 9 Tommy McDonald	175.00	80.00	22.00
☐ 10 Ed Meadows	150.00	70.00	19.00
☐ 11 Gern Nagler	150.00	70.00	19.00
☐ 12 Clarence Peaks	150.00	70.00	19.00
☐ 13 Pete Retzlaff	175.00	80.00	22.00
☐ 14 Mike Sommer	150.00	70.00	19.00
☐ 15 Tom Tracy	175.00	80.00	22.00
☐ 16 Bobby Walston	150.00	70.00	19.00
☐ 17 Chuck Weber	150.00	70.00	19.00

1989 Score Promos

This set of six football standard-size full-color cards was intended as a preview of Score's first football set, after two years of baseball card issues. The cards were sent out to prospective dealers along with the ordering forms for Score's debut football set. The cards are distinguishable from the regular issue cards of the same numbers as indicated in the checklist below. One good way to recognize these promos is that the stats on the promo card backs are carried out to only one decimal place instead of two. In addition, the promo cards show a registered symbol (R with circle around it) rather than a trademark (TM) symbol.

	MINT	NRMT	EXC
COMPLETE SET (6)	100.00	45.00	12.50
COMMON CARD (1-6)	6.00	2.70	.75

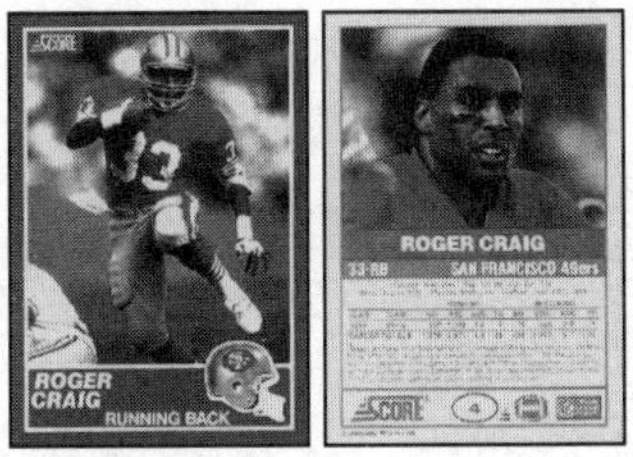

☐ 1 Joe Montana	60.00	27.00	7.50
☐ 2 Bo Jackson	15.00	6.75	1.85
☐ 3 Boomer Esiason	10.00	4.50	1.25
☐ 4 Roger Craig (Born: Preston, Mississippi, should be Davenport, Iowa)	10.00	4.50	1.25
☐ 5 Ed Too Tall Jones (Registered seven sacks, regular card issue has registered 7.0 sacks)	6.00	2.70	.75
☐ 6 Phil Simms (Moorehead State, should say Morehead State; front photo cropped so that Score logo blocks part of the ball)	10.00	4.50	1.25

1989 Score

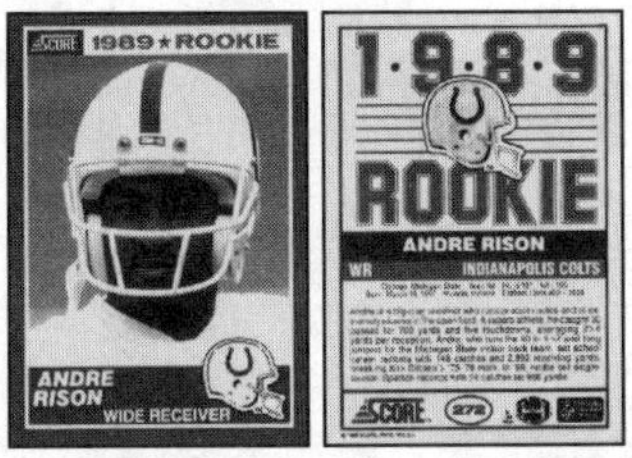

This set of 330 standard-size full-color cards marks Score's entry into the football card market. The set was issued in 15-card packs along with a trivia card. The front has a player photo surrounded by a color border that differs according to team. The player's name and team helmet are at the bottom. The backs contain a photo, statistics and highlights. The first 244 cards in the set are regular player cards. Cards 245-272 are rookie cards of players selected in the '89 NFL draft. Other subsets are post-season action (273-275), combo cards (277-284), All-Pro selections (285-309), Speedburners (310-317), Predators (318-325) and Record Breakers (326-329). The last card in the set is a tribute to Tom Landry. Rookie Cards include Troy Aikman, Steve Atwater, Don Beebe, Steve Beuerlein, Brian Blades, Bubby Brister, Tim Brown, Mark (WR) Carrier, Cris Carter, Gaston Green, Michael Irvin, Keith Jackson, Eric Metcalf, Anthony Miller, Chris Miller, Andre Rison, Mark Rypien, Barry Sanders, Deion Sanders, Chris Spielman, John Taylor, Broderick Thomas, Derrick Thomas, Thurman Thomas, and Rod Woodson.

	MINT	NRMT	EXC
COMPLETE SET (330)	140.00	65.00	17.50
COMPLETE FACT.SET (330)	150.00	70.00	19.00
COMMON CARD (1-330)	.10	.05	.01
☐ 1 Joe Montana	3.00	1.35	.35
☐ 2 Bo Jackson	.50	.23	.06
☐ 3 Boomer Esiason	.15	.07	.02
☐ 4 Roger Craig	.50	.23	.06
☐ 5 Ed Too Tall Jones	.15	.07	.02
☐ 6 Phil Simms	.15	.07	.02
☐ 7 Dan Hampton	.15	.07	.02
☐ 8 John Settle	.10	.05	.01
☐ 9 Bernie Kosar	.15	.07	.02
☐ 10 Al Toon	.15	.07	.02
☐ 11 Bubby Brister	.15	.07	.02
☐ 12 Mark Clayton	.15	.07	.02
☐ 13 Dan Marino	4.00	1.80	.50
☐ 14 Joe Morris	.10	.05	.01
☐ 15 Warren Moon	.50	.23	.06
☐ 16 Chuck Long	.10	.05	.01
☐ 17 Mark Jackson	.10	.05	.01
☐ 18 Michael Irvin	7.00	3.10	.85
☐ 19 Bruce Smith	.50	.23	.06
☐ 20 Anthony Carter	.15	.07	.02
☐ 21 Charles Haley	.50	.23	.06
☐ 22 Dave Duerson	.10	.05	.01
☐ 23 Troy Stradford	.10	.05	.01
☐ 24 Freeman McNeil	.10	.05	.01
☐ 25 Jerry Gray	.10	.05	.01
☐ 26 Bill Maas	.10	.05	.01
☐ 27 Chris Chandler	2.00	.90	.25
☐ 28 Tom Newberry	.10	.05	.01
☐ 29 Albert Lewis	.10	.05	.01
☐ 30 Jay Schroeder	.10	.05	.01
☐ 31 Dalton Hilliard	.10	.05	.01
☐ 32 Tony Eason	.10	.05	.01
☐ 33 Rick Donnelly UER (229.11 yards per punt)	.10	.05	.01
☐ 34 Herschel Walker	.15	.07	.02
☐ 35 Wesley Walker	.10	.05	.01
☐ 36 Chris Doleman	.15	.07	.02
☐ 37 Pat Swilling	.15	.07	.02
☐ 38 Joey Browner	.10	.05	.01
☐ 39 Shane Conlan	.10	.05	.01
☐ 40 Mike Tomczak	.15	.07	.02
☐ 41 Webster Slaughter	.15	.07	.02
☐ 42 Ray Donaldson	.10	.05	.01
☐ 43 Christian Okoye	.10	.05	.01
☐ 44 John Bosa	.10	.05	.01
☐ 45 Aaron Cox	.10	.05	.01
☐ 46 Bobby Hebert	.15	.07	.02
☐ 47 Carl Banks	.10	.05	.01
☐ 48 Jeff Fuller	.10	.05	.01
☐ 49 Gerald Willhite	.10	.05	.01
☐ 50 Mike Singletary	.15	.07	.02
☐ 51 Stanley Morgan	.10	.05	.01
☐ 52 Mark Bavaro	.15	.07	.02
☐ 53 Mickey Shuler	.10	.05	.01
☐ 54 Keith Millard	.10	.05	.01
☐ 55 Andre Tippett	.10	.05	.01
☐ 56 Vance Johnson	.15	.07	.02
☐ 57 Bennie Blades	.10	.05	.01
☐ 58 Tim Harris	.10	.05	.01
☐ 59 Hanford Dixon	.10	.05	.01
☐ 60 Chris Miller	.50	.23	.06
☐ 61 Cornelius Bennett	.50	.23	.06
☐ 62 Neal Anderson	.15	.07	.02
☐ 63 Ickey Woods UER (Jersey is 31 but listed as 30 on card back)	.15	.07	.02
☐ 64 Gary Anderson RB	.10	.05	.01
☐ 65 Vaughan Johnson	.10	.05	.01
☐ 66 Ronnie Lippett	.10	.05	.01
☐ 67 Mike Quick	.10	.05	.01
☐ 68 Roy Green	.15	.07	.02
☐ 69 Tim Krumrie	.10	.05	.01
☐ 70 Mark Malone	.10	.05	.01
☐ 71 James Jones	.10	.05	.01
☐ 72 Cris Carter	6.00	2.70	.75
☐ 73 Ricky Nattiel	.10	.05	.01
☐ 74 Jim Arnold UER (238.83 yards per punt)	.10	.05	.01
☐ 75 Randall Cunningham	.15	.07	.02
☐ 76 John L. Williams	.10	.05	.01
☐ 77 Paul Gruber	.10	.05	.01
☐ 78 Rod Woodson	4.00	1.80	.50
☐ 79 Ray Childress	.10	.05	.01
☐ 80 Doug Williams	.15	.07	.02
☐ 81 Deron Cherry	.15	.07	.02
☐ 82 John Offerdahl	.10	.05	.01
☐ 83 Louis Lipps	.15	.07	.02
☐ 84 Neil Lomax	.10	.05	.01
☐ 85 Wade Wilson	.15	.07	.02
☐ 86 Tim Brown	6.00	2.70	.75
☐ 87 Chris Hinton	.10	.05	.01
☐ 88 Stump Mitchell	.10	.05	.01
☐ 89 Tunch Ilkin	.10	.05	.01
☐ 90 Steve Pelluer	.10	.05	.01
☐ 91 Brian Noble	.10	.05	.01
☐ 92 Reggie White	.75	.35	.09
☐ 93 Aundray Bruce	.10	.05	.01
☐ 94 Garry James	.10	.05	.01
☐ 95 Drew Hill	.10	.05	.01
☐ 96 Anthony Munoz	.15	.07	.02
☐ 97 James Wilder	.10	.05	.01
☐ 98 Dexter Manley	.10	.05	.01
☐ 99 Lee Williams	.10	.05	.01
☐ 100 Dave Krieg	.15	.07	.02
☐ 101A Keith Jackson ERR (Listed as 84 on card back)	2.00	.90	.25
☐ 101B Keith Jackson COR (Listed as 88 on card back)	2.00	.90	.25
☐ 102 Luis Sharpe	.10	.05	.01
☐ 103 Kevin Greene	.50	.23	.06
☐ 104 Duane Bickett	.10	.05	.01
☐ 105 Mark Rypien	.50	.23	.06
☐ 106 Curt Warner	.10	.05	.01
☐ 107 Jacob Green	.10	.05	.01
☐ 108 Gary Clark	.50	.23	.06
☐ 109 Bruce Matthews	.50	.23	.06
☐ 110 Bill Fralic	.10	.05	.01
☐ 111 Bill Bates	.15	.07	.02
☐ 112 Jeff Bryant	.10	.05	.01
☐ 113 Charles Mann	.10	.05	.01
☐ 114 Richard Dent	.15	.07	.02
☐ 115 Bruce Hill	.10	.05	.01
☐ 116 Mark May	.10	.05	.01
☐ 117 Mark Collins	.10	.05	.01
☐ 118 Ron Holmes	.10	.05	.01
☐ 119 Scott Case	.10	.05	.01
☐ 120 Tom Rathman	.10	.05	.01
☐ 121 Dennis McKinnon	.10	.05	.01
☐ 122A Ricky Sanders ERR (Listed as 46 on card back)	.25	.11	.03
☐ 122B Ricky Sanders COR (Listed as 83 on card back)	.50	.23	.06
☐ 123 Michael Carter	.10	.05	.01
☐ 124 Ozzie Newsome	.15	.07	.02
☐ 125 Irving Fryar UER ('wide reveiver')	.15	.07	.02

☐ 126A Ron Hall ERR
(wrong photos on card)
☐ 126B Ron Hall COR .50 .23 .06
(correct photos used)
☐ 127 Clay Matthews .15 .07 .02
☐ 128 Leonard Marshall .10 .05 .01
☐ 129 Kevin Mack .10 .05 .01
☐ 130 Art Monk .15 .07 .02
☐ 131 Garin Veris .10 .05 .01
☐ 132 Steve Jordan .10 .05 .01
☐ 133 Frank Minnifield .10 .05 .01
☐ 134 Eddie Brown .10 .05 .01
☐ 135 Stacey Bailey .10 .05 .01
☐ 136 Rickey Jackson .15 .07 .02
☐ 137 Henry Ellard .15 .07 .02
☐ 138 Jim Burt .10 .05 .01
☐ 139 Jerome Brown .15 .07 .02
☐ 140 Rodney Holman .10 .05 .01
☐ 141 Sammy Winder .10 .05 .01
☐ 142 Marcus Cotton .10 .05 .01
☐ 143 Jim Jeffcoat .10 .05 .01
☐ 144 Rueben Mayes .10 .05 .01
☐ 145 Jim McMahon .15 .07 .02
☐ 146 Reggie Williams .10 .05 .01
☐ 147 John Anderson .10 .05 .01
☐ 148 Harris Barton .10 .05 .01
☐ 149 Phillip Epps .10 .05 .01
☐ 150 Jay Hilgenberg .10 .05 .01
☐ 151 Earl Ferrell .10 .05 .01
☐ 152 Andre Reed .50 .23 .06
☐ 153 Dennis Gentry .10 .05 .01
☐ 154 Max Montoya .10 .05 .01
☐ 155 Darrin Nelson .10 .05 .01
☐ 156 Jeff Chadwick .10 .05 .01
☐ 157 James Brooks .15 .07 .02
☐ 158 Keith Bishop .10 .05 .01
☐ 159 Robert Awalt .10 .05 .01
☐ 160 Marty Lyons .10 .05 .01
☐ 161 Johnny Hector .10 .05 .01
☐ 162 Tony Casillas .10 .05 .01
☐ 163 Kyle Clifton .10 .05 .01
☐ 164 Cody Risien .10 .05 .01
☐ 165 Jamie Holland .10 .05 .01
☐ 166 Merril Hoge .10 .05 .01
☐ 167 Chris Spielman 2.00 .90 .25
☐ 168 Carlos Carson .10 .05 .01
☐ 169 Jerry Ball .10 .05 .01
☐ 170 Don Majkowski .15 .07 .02
☐ 171 Everson Walls .10 .05 .01
☐ 172 Mike Rozier .10 .05 .01
☐ 173 Matt Millen .15 .07 .02
☐ 174 Karl Mecklenburg .10 .05 .01
☐ 175 Paul Palmer .10 .05 .01
☐ 176 Brian Blades UER 2.50 1.10 .30
(Photo on back is
reversed negative)
☐ 177 Brent Fullwood .10 .05 .01
☐ 178 Anthony Miller 3.00 1.35 .35
☐ 179 Brian Sochia .10 .05 .01
☐ 180 Stephen Baker .15 .07 .02
☐ 181 Jesse Solomon .10 .05 .01
☐ 182 John Grimsley .10 .05 .01
☐ 183 Timmy Newsome .10 .05 .01
☐ 184 Steve Sewell .10 .05 .01
☐ 185 Dean Biasucci .10 .05 .01
☐ 186 Alonzo Highsmith .10 .05 .01
☐ 187 Randy Grimes .10 .05 .01
☐ 188A Mark Carrier WR ERR 2.00 .90 .25
(Photo on back is
actually Bruce Hill)
☐ 188B Mark Carrier WR COR 2.00 .90 .25
(Wearing helmet in
photo on back)
☐ 189 Vann McElroy .10 .05 .01
☐ 190 Greg Bell .10 .05 .01
☐ 191 Quinn Early 3.00 1.35 .35
☐ 192 Lawrence Taylor .50 .23 .06
☐ 193 Albert Bentley .10 .05 .01
☐ 194 Ernest Givins .15 .07 .02
☐ 195 Jackie Slater .10 .05 .01
☐ 196 Jim Sweeney .10 .05 .01
☐ 197 Freddie Joe Nunn .10 .05 .01
☐ 198 Keith Byars .15 .07 .02
☐ 199 Hardy Nickerson .50 .23 .06
☐ 200 Steve Beuerlein .50 .23 .06
☐ 201 Bruce Armstrong .10 .05 .01
☐ 202 Lionel Manuel .10 .05 .01
☐ 203 J.T. Smith .10 .05 .01
☐ 204 Mark Ingram .50 .23 .06
☐ 205 Fred Smerlas .10 .05 .01
☐ 206 Bryan Hinkle .10 .05 .01
☐ 207 Steve McMichael .15 .07 .02
☐ 208 Nick Lowery .10 .05 .01
☐ 209 Jack Trudeau .10 .05 .01
☐ 210 Lorenzo Hampton .10 .05 .01
☐ 211 Thurman Thomas 8.00 3.60 1.00
☐ 212 Steve Young 1.50 .70 .19
☐ 213 James Lofton .50 .23 .06
☐ 214 Jim Covert .10 .05 .01
☐ 215 Ronnie Lott .15 .07 .02
☐ 216 Stephone Paige .10 .05 .01
☐ 217 Mark Duper .15 .07 .02
☐ 218A Willie Gault ERR
(Front photo actually
93 Greg Townsend)
☐ 218B Willie Gault COR .50 .23 .06
(83 clearly visible)
☐ 219 Ken Ruettgers .10 .05 .01
☐ 220 Kevin Ross .15 .07 .02
☐ 221 Jerry Rice 3.00 1.35 .35
☐ 222 Billy Ray Smith .10 .05 .01
☐ 223 Jim Kelly 1.00 .45 .12
☐ 224 Vinny Testaverde .50 .23 .06
☐ 225 Steve Largent .75 .35 .09
☐ 226 Warren Williams .10 .05 .01
☐ 227 Morten Andersen .10 .05 .01
☐ 228 Bill Brooks .15 .07 .02
☐ 229 Reggie Langhorne .10 .05 .01
☐ 230 Pepper Johnson .10 .05 .01
☐ 231 Pat Leahy .10 .05 .01
☐ 232 Fred Marion .10 .05 .01
☐ 233 Gary Zimmerman .10 .05 .01
☐ 234 Marcus Allen .50 .23 .06
☐ 235 Gaston Green .10 .05 .01
☐ 236 John Stephens .10 .05 .01
☐ 237 Terry Kinard .10 .05 .01
☐ 238 John Taylor .50 .23 .06
☐ 239 Brian Bosworth .15 .07 .02
☐ 240 Anthony Toney .10 .05 .01
☐ 241 Ken O'Brien .10 .05 .01
☐ 242 Howie Long .15 .07 .02
☐ 243 Doug Flutie .50 .23 .06
☐ 244 Jim Everett .50 .23 .06
☐ 245 Broderick Thomas .50 .23 .06
☐ 246 Deion Sanders 20.00 9.00 2.50
☐ 247 Donnell Woolford .15 .07 .02
☐ 248 Wayne Martin .10 .05 .01
☐ 249 David Williams .10 .05 .01
☐ 250 Bill Hawkins .10 .05 .01
☐ 251 Eric Hill .10 .05 .01
☐ 252 Burt Grossman .10 .05 .01
☐ 253 Tracy Rocker .10 .05 .01
☐ 254 Steve Wisniewski .15 .07 .02
☐ 255 Jessie Small .10 .05 .01
☐ 256 David Braxton .10 .05 .01
☐ 257 Barry Sanders 55.00 25.00 7.00
☐ 258 Derrick Thomas 4.00 1.80 .50
☐ 259 Eric Metcalf 4.00 1.80 .50
☐ 260 Keith DeLong .10 .05 .01
☐ 261 Hart Lee Dykes .10 .05 .01
☐ 262 Sammie Smith .10 .05 .01
☐ 263 Steve Atwater .50 .23 .06
☐ 264 Eric Ball .10 .05 .01
☐ 265 Don Beebe .50 .23 .06
☐ 266 Brian Williams .10 .05 .01
☐ 267 Jeff Lageman .15 .07 .02
☐ 268 Tim Worley .10 .05 .01
☐ 269 Tony Mandarich .10 .05 .01
☐ 270 Troy Aikman 50.00 22.00 6.25
☐ 271 Andy Heck .10 .05 .01
☐ 272 Andre Rison 4.00 1.80 .50
☐ 273 AFC Championship .10 .05 .01
Bengals over Bills
(Ickey Woods and
Boomer Esiason)
☐ 274 NFC Championship 1.00 .45 .12
49ers over Bears
(Joe Montana)
☐ 275 Super Bowl XXIII 2.00 .90 .25
49ers over Bengals
(Joe Montana and
Jerry Rice)
☐ 276 Rodney Carter .10 .05 .01
☐ 277 Mark Jackson, .10 .05 .01
Vance Johnson,
and Ricky Nattiel
☐ 278 John L. Williams .10 .05 .01
and Curt Warner
☐ 279 Joe Montana and 2.00 .90 .25
Jerry Rice
☐ 280 Roy Green and .10 .05 .01
Neil Lomax
☐ 281 Randall Cunningham .10 .05 .01
and Keith Jackson
☐ 282 Chris Doleman and .10 .05 .01
Keith Millard
☐ 283 Mark Duper and .10 .05 .01
Mark Clayton
☐ 284 Marcus Allen and .50 .23 .06
Bo Jackson
☐ 285 Frank Minnifield AP .10 .05 .01
☐ 286 Bruce Matthews AP .15 .07 .02
☐ 287 Joey Browner AP .10 .05 .01
☐ 288 Jay Hilgenberg AP .10 .05 .01
☐ 289 Carl Lee AP .10 .05 .01
☐ 290 Scott Norwood AP .10 .05 .01
☐ 291 John Taylor AP .50 .23 .06
☐ 292 Jerry Rice AP 1.50 .70 .19
☐ 293A Keith Jackson AP ERR .75 .35 .09
(Listed as 84
on card back)
☐ 293B Keith Jackson AP COR .75 .35 .09
(Listed as 88
on card back)
☐ 294 Gary Zimmerman AP .10 .05 .01
☐ 295 Lawrence Taylor AP .50 .23 .06
☐ 296 Reggie White AP .50 .23 .06
☐ 297 Roger Craig AP .15 .07 .02
☐ 298 Boomer Esiason AP .15 .07 .02
☐ 299 Cornelius Bennett AP .15 .07 .02
☐ 300 Mike Horan AP .10 .05 .01
☐ 301 Deron Cherry AP .10 .05 .01
☐ 302 Tom Newberry AP .10 .05 .01
☐ 303 Mike Singletary AP .15 .07 .02
☐ 304 Shane Conlan AP .10 .05 .01
☐ 305A Tim Brown ERR AP 2.00 .90 .25
(Photo on front act-
ually 80 James Lofton)
☐ 305B Tim Brown COR AP 2.00 .90 .25
(Dark jersey 81)
☐ 306 Henry Ellard AP .15 .07 .02
☐ 307 Bruce Smith AP .15 .07 .02
☐ 308 Tim Krumrie AP .10 .05 .01
☐ 309 Anthony Munoz AP .15 .07 .02
☐ 310 Darrell Green SPEED .10 .05 .01
☐ 311 Anthony Miller SPEED 1.00 .45 .12
☐ 312 Wesley Walker SPEED .10 .05 .01
☐ 313 Ron Brown SPEED .10 .05 .01
☐ 314 Bo Jackson SPEED .50 .23 .06
☐ 315 Phillip Epps SPEED .10 .05 .01
☐ 316A Eric Thomas ERR SPEED
(Listed as 31
on card back)
☐ 316B Eric Thomas COR SPEED .50 .23 .06
(Listed as 22
on card back)
☐ 317 Herschel Walker SPEED .15 .07 .02
☐ 318 Jacob Green PRED .10 .05 .01
☐ 319 Andre Tippett PRED .10 .05 .01
☐ 320 Freddie Joe Nunn PRED .10 .05 .01
☐ 321 Reggie White PRED .50 .23 .06
☐ 322 Lawrence Taylor PRED .50 .23 .06
☐ 323 Greg Townsend PRED .10 .05 .01
☐ 324 Tim Harris PRED .10 .05 .01
☐ 325 Bruce Smith PRED .15 .07 .02
☐ 326 Tony Dorsett RB .50 .23 .06
☐ 327 Steve Largent RB .50 .23 .06
☐ 328 Tim Brown RB 2.00 .90 .25
☐ 329 Joe Montana RB 1.50 .70 .19
☐ 330 Tom Landry Tribute 1.00 .45 .12

1989 Score Supplemental

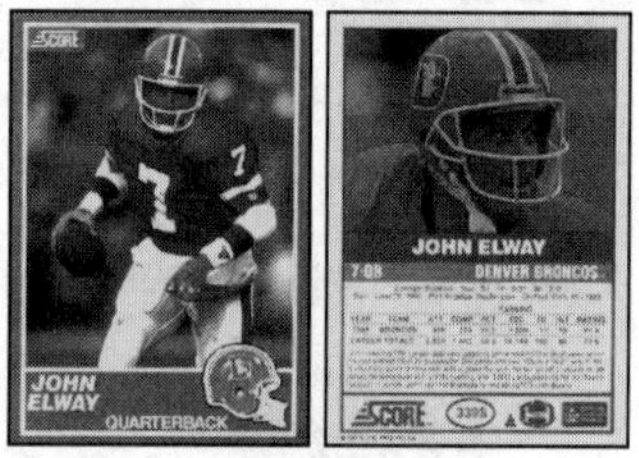

The 1989 Score Supplemental set contains 110 standard-size cards that were issued as a complete set through hobby dealers. The card numbering is a continuation of the basic set except for an "S" suffix. The fronts have purple borders, otherwise, the cards are identical to the regular issue 1989 Score football cards. There is a card of Bo Jackson in baseball regalia. Rookie Cards include Eric Allen, Jack Del Rio, Simon Fletcher, Dave Meggett, Rodney Peete, Frank Reich, Sterling Sharpe, Neil Smith, Steve Walsh and Lorenzo White.

	MINT	NRMT	EXC
COMPLETE FACT.SET (110)	12.00	5.50	1.50
COMMON CARD (331S-440S)	.05	.02	.01

☐ 331S Herschel Walker .30 .14 .04
☐ 332S Allen Pinkett .05 .02 .01
☐ 333S Sterling Sharpe 5.00 2.20 .60
☐ 334S Alvin Walton .05 .02 .01
☐ 335S Frank Reich .30 .14 .04
☐ 336S Jim Thornton .05 .02 .01
☐ 337S David Fulcher .10 .05 .01
☐ 338S Raul Allegre .05 .02 .01
☐ 339S John Elway 3.00 1.35 .35
☐ 340S Michael Cofer .05 .02 .01
☐ 341S Jim Skow .05 .02 .01
☐ 342S Steve DeBerg .05 .02 .01
☐ 343S Mervyn Fernandez .05 .02 .01
☐ 344S Mike Lansford .05 .02 .01
☐ 345S Reggie Roby .05 .02 .01
☐ 346S Raymond Clayborn .05 .02 .01
☐ 347S Lonzell Hill .05 .02 .01
☐ 348S Ottis Anderson .10 .05 .01
☐ 349S Erik McMillan .05 .02 .01
☐ 350S Al Harris .05 .02 .01
☐ 351S Jack Del Rio .10 .05 .01
☐ 352S Gary Anderson K .05 .02 .01
☐ 353S Jim McMahon .10 .05 .01
☐ 354S Keena Turner .05 .02 .01
☐ 355S Tony Woods .05 .02 .01
☐ 356S Donald Igwebuike .05 .02 .01
☐ 357S Gerald Riggs .10 .05 .01
☐ 358S Eddie Murray .05 .02 .01
☐ 359S Dino Hackett .05 .02 .01
☐ 360S Brad Muster .05 .02 .01
☐ 361S Paul Palmer .05 .02 .01
☐ 362S Jerry Robinson .05 .02 .01
☐ 363S Simon Fletcher .10 .05 .01
☐ 364S Tommy Kramer .05 .02 .01
☐ 365S Jim C. Jensen .05 .02 .01
☐ 366S Lorenzo White .30 .14 .04
☐ 367S Fredd Young .05 .02 .01
☐ 368S Ron Jaworski .05 .02 .01
☐ 369S Mel Owens .05 .02 .01
☐ 370S Dave Waymer .05 .02 .01
☐ 371S Sean Landeta .05 .02 .01
☐ 372S Sam Mills .10 .05 .01
☐ 373S Todd Blackledge .05 .02 .01
☐ 374S Jo Jo Townsell .05 .02 .01
☐ 375S Ron Wolfley .05 .02 .01
☐ 376S Ralf Mojsiejenko .05 .02 .01
☐ 377S Eric Wright .05 .02 .01
☐ 378S Nesby Glasgow .05 .02 .01
☐ 379S Darryl Talley .10 .05 .01
☐ 380S Eric Allen .30 .14 .04
☐ 381S Dennis Smith .10 .05 .01
☐ 382S John Tice .05 .02 .01
☐ 383S Jesse Solomon .05 .02 .01
☐ 384S Bo Jackson 1.00 .45 .12
(FB/BB Pose)
☐ 385S Mike Merriweather .05 .02 .01
☐ 386S Maurice Carthon .05 .02 .01
☐ 387S David Grayson .05 .02 .01
☐ 388S Wilber Marshall .05 .02 .01
☐ 389S David Wyman .05 .02 .01
☐ 390S Thomas Everett .05 .02 .01
☐ 391S Alex Gordon .05 .02 .01
☐ 392S D.J. Dozier .05 .02 .01
☐ 393S Scott Radecic .05 .02 .01
☐ 394S Eric Thomas .05 .02 .01
☐ 395S Mike Gann .05 .02 .01
☐ 396S William Perry .10 .05 .01
☐ 397S Carl Hairston .05 .02 .01
☐ 398S Billy Ard .05 .02 .01
☐ 399S Donnell Thompson .05 .02 .01
☐ 400S Mike Webster .10 .05 .01
☐ 401S Scott Davis .05 .02 .01
☐ 402S Sean Farrell .05 .02 .01
☐ 403S Mike Golic .05 .02 .01
☐ 404S Mike Kenn .05 .02 .01
☐ 405S Keith Van Horne .05 .02 .01
☐ 406S Bob Golic .05 .02 .01
☐ 407S Neil Smith 2.50 1.10 .30
☐ 408S Dermontti Dawson .10 .05 .01
☐ 409S Leslie O'Neal .10 .05 .01
☐ 410S Matt Bahr .05 .02 .01
☐ 411S Guy McIntyre .05 .02 .01
☐ 412S Bryan Millard .05 .02 .01
☐ 413S Joe Jacoby .05 .02 .01
☐ 414S Rob Taylor .05 .02 .01
☐ 415S Tony Zendejas .05 .02 .01
☐ 416S Vai Sikahema .05 .02 .01
☐ 417S Gary Reasons .05 .02 .01
☐ 418S Shawn Collins .05 .02 .01
☐ 419S Mark Green .05 .02 .01
☐ 420S Courtney Hall .05 .02 .01
☐ 421S Bobby Humphrey .05 .02 .01
☐ 422S Myron Guyton .05 .02 .01
☐ 423S Darryl Ingram .05 .02 .01
☐ 424S Chris Jacke .05 .02 .01
☐ 425S Keith Jones .05 .02 .01
☐ 426S Robert Massey .05 .02 .01
☐ 427S Bubba McDowell .30 .14 .04
☐ 428S Dave Meggett .75 .35 .09
☐ 429S Louis Oliver .10 .05 .01
☐ 430S Danny Peebles .05 .02 .01
☐ 431S Rodney Peete .50 .23 .06
☐ 432S Jeff Query .05 .02 .01
☐ 433S Timm Rosenbach UER .05 .02 .01
(Photo actually
Gary Hogeboom)
☐ 434S Frank Stams .05 .02 .01
☐ 435S Lawyer Tillman .05 .02 .01
☐ 436S Billy Joe Tolliver .05 .02 .01
☐ 437S Floyd Turner .10 .05 .01
☐ 438S Steve Walsh .10 .05 .01
☐ 439S Joe Wolf .05 .02 .01
☐ 440S Trace Armstrong .05 .02 .01

1989-90 Score Franco Harris

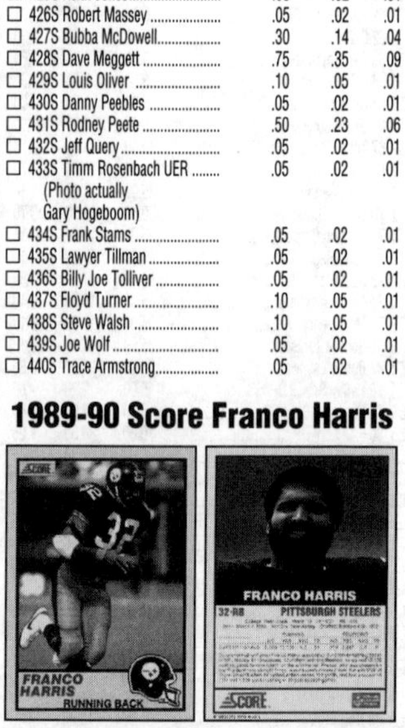

These standard size cards were given away to all persons at the Super Bowl Show I in New Orleans who acquired Franco Harris' autograph while at the show. However, there were two different backs prepared and distributed since Franco's "Sure-shot" election was announced during the course of the show, after which time the "Hall of Famer" variety was passed out. The card fronts are exactly the same. The only difference in the two varieties on the back is essentially the presence of "Sure-shot" at the beginning of the narrative. The cards are unnumbered. The card fronts are in the style of the popular 1989 Score regular issue football cards. Although both varieties were produced on a limited basis, it is thought that the "Sure-shot" variety is the tougher of the two.

	MINT	NRMT	EXC
COMPLETE SET (2)	150.00	70.00	19.00
COMMON CARD (1A-1B)	60.00	27.00	7.50
☐ 1A Franco Harris (Sure-shot)	85.00	38.00	10.50
☐ 1B Franco Harris (Hall of Famer)	75.00	34.00	9.50

1990 Score Promos

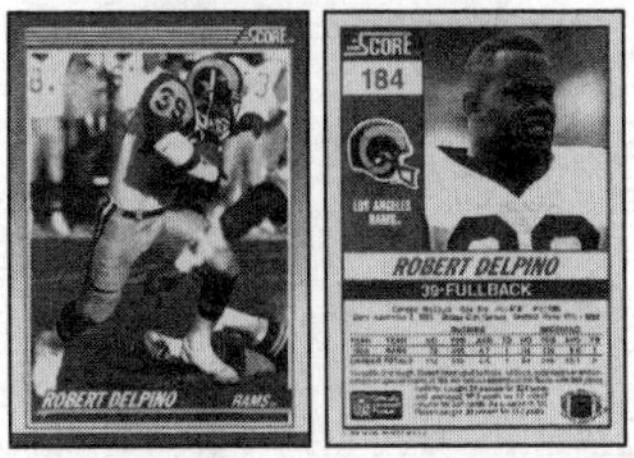

This set of three football standard-size full-color cards was intended as a preview of Score's football set. The cards were sent out to prospective dealers along with the ordering forms for Score's 1990 football set. The cards are distinguishable from the regular issue cards of the same numbers as indicated in the checklist below. The promo cards show a registered symbol (R with circle around it) rather than a trademark (TM) symbol as on the regular cards. In addition, these promos are cropped tighter than the regular issue cards.

	MINT	NRMT	EXC
COMPLETE SET (3)	15.00	6.75	1.85
COMMON CARD	2.00	.90	.25
☐ 20 Barry Sanders	10.00	4.50	1.25
☐ 184 Robert Delpino	2.00	.90	.25
☐ 256 Cornelius Bennett	3.00	1.35	.35

1990 Score

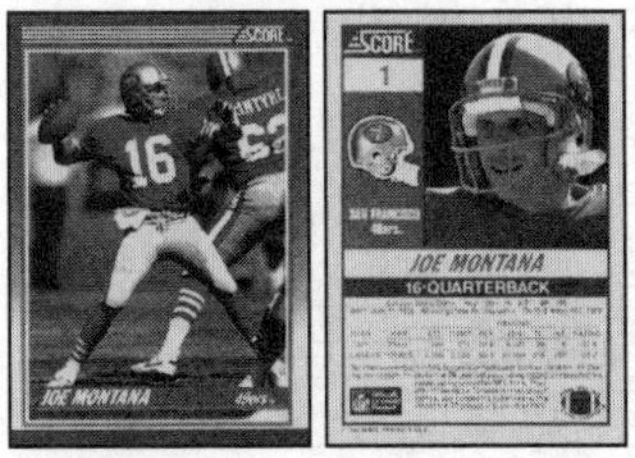

The 1990 Score football set consists of 660 standard-size cards issued in two series of 330. The set was issued in 16-card packs along with a trivia card. The fronts have sharp color action photos and multicolored borders. The vertically oriented backs have color photos, stats and highlights. There are numerous subsets including Draft Picks (289-310/618-657), Hot Guns (311-320/563/564), Ground Force (321-330/561/562), Crunch Crew (551-555), Rocket Man (556-560), All-Pros (565-590), Record Breakers (591-594), Hall of Famers (595-601) and Class of '90 (606-617). Rookie Cards include Mark (DB) Carrier, Barry Foster, Barry Foster, Jeff George, Eric Green, Rodney Hampton, Haywood Jeffires, Cortez Kennedy, Scott Mitchell, Junior Seau and Andre Ware. The five-card "Final Five" set was a special insert in factory sets. These cards honor the final five picks of the 1990 National Football League Draft and are numbered with a "B" prefix. These cards have a "Final Five" logo on the front along with the photo of the player, while the back has a brief biographical description of the player.

	MINT	NRMT	EXC
COMPLETE SET (660)	7.50	3.40	.95
COMPLETE FACT.SET (665)	8.00	3.60	1.00
COMMON CARD (1-660)	.04	.02	.01
COMMON CARD (B1-B5)	.05	.02	.01
☐ 1 Joe Montana	1.00	.45	.12
☐ 2 Christian Okoye	.04	.02	.01
☐ 3 Mike Singletary UER (Text says 146 tackles in '89, should be 151)	.10	.05	.01
☐ 4 Jim Everett UER (Text says 415 yards against Saints, should be 454)	.10	.05	.01
☐ 5 Phil Simms	.10	.05	.01
☐ 6 Brent Fullwood	.04	.02	.01
☐ 7 Bill Fralic	.04	.02	.01
☐ 8 Leslie O'Neal	.10	.05	.01
☐ 9 John Taylor	.25	.11	.03
☐ 10 Bo Jackson	.25	.11	.03
☐ 11 John Stephens	.04	.02	.01
☐ 12 Art Monk	.10	.05	.01
☐ 13 Dan Marino	1.25	.55	.16
☐ 14 John Settle	.04	.02	.01
☐ 15 Don Majkowski	.04	.02	.01
☐ 16 Bruce Smith	.25	.11	.03
☐ 17 Brad Muster	.04	.02	.01
☐ 18 Jason Buck	.04	.02	.01
☐ 19 James Brooks	.10	.05	.01
☐ 20 Barry Sanders	1.25	.55	.16
☐ 21 Troy Aikman	1.25	.55	.16
☐ 22 Allen Pinkett	.04	.02	.01
☐ 23 Duane Bickett	.04	.02	.01
☐ 24 Kevin Ross	.04	.02	.01
☐ 25 John Elway	.50	.23	.06
☐ 26 Jeff Query	.04	.02	.01
☐ 27 Eddie Murray	.04	.02	.01
☐ 28 Richard Dent	.10	.05	.01
☐ 29 Lorenzo White	.04	.02	.01
☐ 30 Eric Metcalf	.25	.11	.03
☐ 31 Jeff Dellenbach	.04	.02	.01
☐ 32 Leon White	.04	.02	.01
☐ 33 Jim Jeffcoat	.04	.02	.01
☐ 34 Herschel Walker	.10	.05	.01
☐ 35 Mike Johnson UER (Front photo actually 51 Eddie Johnson)	.04	.02	.01
☐ 36 Joe Phillips	.04	.02	.01
☐ 37 Willie Gault	.10	.05	.01
☐ 38 Keith Millard	.04	.02	.01
☐ 39 Fred Marion	.04	.02	.01
☐ 40 Boomer Esiason	.10	.05	.01
☐ 41 Dermontti Dawson	.10	.05	.01
☐ 42 Dino Hackett	.04	.02	.01
☐ 43 Reggie Roby	.04	.02	.01
☐ 44 Roger Vick	.04	.02	.01
☐ 45 Bobby Hebert	.04	.02	.01
☐ 46 Don Beebe	.10	.05	.01
☐ 47 Neal Anderson	.10	.05	.01
☐ 48 Johnny Holland	.04	.02	.01
☐ 49 Bobby Humphery	.04	.02	.01
☐ 50 Lawrence Taylor	.25	.11	.03
☐ 51 Billy Ray Smith	.04	.02	.01
☐ 52 Robert Perryman	.04	.02	.01
☐ 53 Gary Anderson K	.04	.02	.01
☐ 54 Raul Allegre	.04	.02	.01
☐ 55 Pat Swilling	.10	.05	.01
☐ 56 Chris Doleman	.04	.02	.01
☐ 57 Andre Reed	.25	.11	.03
☐ 58 Seth Joyner	.10	.05	.01
☐ 59 Bart Oates	.04	.02	.01
☐ 60 Bernie Kosar	.10	.05	.01
☐ 61 Dave Krieg	.10	.05	.01
☐ 62 Lars Tate	.04	.02	.01
☐ 63 Scott Norwood	.04	.02	.01
☐ 64 Kyle Clifton	.04	.02	.01
☐ 65 Alan Veingrad	.04	.02	.01
☐ 66 Gerald Riggs UER (Text begins Depite, should be Despite)	.10	.05	.01
☐ 67 Tim Worley	.04	.02	.01
☐ 68 Rodney Holman	.04	.02	.01
☐ 69 Tony Zendejas	.04	.02	.01
☐ 70 Chris Miller	.25	.11	.03
☐ 71 Wilber Marshall	.04	.02	.01
☐ 72 Skip McClendon	.04	.02	.01
☐ 73 Jim Covert	.04	.02	.01
☐ 74 Sam Mills	.10	.05	.01
☐ 75 Chris Hinton	.04	.02	.01
☐ 76 Irv Eatman	.04	.02	.01
☐ 77 Bubba Paris UER (No draft team mentioned)	.04	.02	.01
☐ 78 John Elliott UER (No draft team mentioned; missing Team/FA status)	.04	.02	.01
☐ 79 Thomas Everett	.04	.02	.01
☐ 80 Steve Smith	.04	.02	.01
☐ 81 Jackie Slater	.04	.02	.01
☐ 82 Kelvin Martin	.04	.02	.01
☐ 83 Jo Jo Townsell	.04	.02	.01
☐ 84 Jim C. Jensen	.04	.02	.01
☐ 85 Bobby Humphrey	.04	.02	.01
☐ 86 Mike Dyal	.04	.02	.01
☐ 87 Andre Rison UER (Front 87, back 85)	.25	.11	.03
☐ 88 Brian Sochia	.04	.02	.01
☐ 89 Greg Bell	.04	.02	.01
☐ 90 Dalton Hilliard	.04	.02	.01
☐ 91 Carl Banks	.04	.02	.01
☐ 92 Dennis Smith	.04	.02	.01
☐ 93 Bruce Matthews	.10	.05	.01
☐ 94 Charles Haley	.10	.05	.01
☐ 95 Deion Sanders UER (Reversed photo on back)	.50	.23	.06
☐ 96 Stephone Paige	.04	.02	.01
☐ 97 Marion Butts	.10	.05	.01
☐ 98 Howie Long	.10	.05	.01
☐ 99 Donald Igwebuike	.04	.02	.01
☐ 100 Roger Craig UER (Text says 2 TD's in SB XXIV, should be 1; everything misspelled)	.10	.05	.01
☐ 101 Charles Mann	.04	.02	.01
☐ 102 Fredd Young	.04	.02	.01
☐ 103 Chris Jacke	.04	.02	.01
☐ 104 Scott Case	.04	.02	.01
☐ 105 Warren Moon	.25	.11	.03
☐ 106 Clyde Simmons	.04	.02	.01
☐ 107 Steve Atwater	.04	.02	.01
☐ 108 Morten Andersen	.04	.02	.01
☐ 109 Eugene Marve	.04	.02	.01
☐ 110 Thurman Thomas	.40	.18	.05
☐ 111 Carnell Lake	.04	.02	.01
☐ 112 Jim Kelly	.25	.11	.03
☐ 113 Stanford Jennings	.04	.02	.01
☐ 114 Jacob Green	.04	.02	.01
☐ 115 Karl Mecklenburg	.04	.02	.01
☐ 116 Ray Childress	.04	.02	.01
☐ 117 Erik McMillan	.04	.02	.01
☐ 118 Harry Newsome	.04	.02	.01
☐ 119 James Dixon	.04	.02	.01
☐ 120 Hassan Jones	.04	.02	.01
☐ 121 Eric Allen	.04	.02	.01
☐ 122 Felix Wright	.04	.02	.01
☐ 123 Merril Hoge	.04	.02	.01
☐ 124 Eric Ball	.04	.02	.01
☐ 125 Flipper Anderson	.04	.02	.01
☐ 126 James Jefferson	.04	.02	.01
☐ 127 Tim McDonald	.04	.02	.01
☐ 128 Larry Kinnebrew	.04	.02	.01
☐ 129 Mark Collins	.04	.02	.01
☐ 130 Ickey Woods	.04	.02	.01
☐ 131 Jeff Donaldson UER (Stats say 0 int. and 0 fumble rec., text says 4 and 1)	.04	.02	.01
☐ 132 Rich Camarillo	.04	.02	.01
☐ 133 Melvin Bratton	.04	.02	.01
☐ 134A Kevin Butler (Photo on back has helmet on)	.35	.16	.04
☐ 134B Kevin Butler (Photo on back has no helmet on)	.05	.02	.01
☐ 135 Albert Bentley	.04	.02	.01
☐ 136A Vai Sikahema (Photo on back has helmet on)	.35	.16	.04
☐ 136B Vai Sikahema (Photo on back has no helmet on)	.05	.02	.01
☐ 137 Todd McNair	.04	.02	.01
☐ 138 Alonzo Highsmith	.04	.02	.01
☐ 139 Brian Blades	.10	.05	.01
☐ 140 Jeff Lageman	.04	.02	.01
☐ 141 Eric Thomas	.04	.02	.01
☐ 142 Derek Hill	.04	.02	.01
☐ 143 Rick Fenney	.04	.02	.01
☐ 144 Herman Heard	.04	.02	.01
☐ 145 Steve Young	.50	.23	.06
☐ 146 Kent Hull	.04	.02	.01
☐ 147A Joey Browner (Photo on back looking to side)	.35	.16	.04
☐ 147B Joey Browner (Photo on back looking up)	.05	.02	.01
☐ 148 Frank Minnifield	.04	.02	.01
☐ 149 Robert Massey	.04	.02	.01
☐ 150 Dave Meggett	.10	.05	.01
☐ 151 Bubba McDowell	.04	.02	.01
☐ 152 Rickey Dixon	.04	.02	.01
☐ 153 Ray Donaldson	.04	.02	.01
☐ 154 Alvin Walton	.04	.02	.01
☐ 155 Mike Cofer	.04	.02	.01
☐ 156 Darryl Talley	.04	.02	.01
☐ 157 A.J. Johnson	.04	.02	.01
☐ 158 Jerry Gray	.04	.02	.01
☐ 159 Keith Byars	.04	.02	.01
☐ 160 Andy Heck	.04	.02	.01
☐ 161 Mike Munchak	.04	.02	.01
☐ 162 Dennis Gentry	.04	.02	.01
☐ 163 Timm Rosenbach UER (Born 1967 in Everett, Wa., should be 1966 in Missoula, Mont.)	.04	.02	.01
☐ 164 Randall McDaniel	.04	.02	.01
☐ 165 Pat Leahy	.04	.02	.01
☐ 166 Bubby Brister	.04	.02	.01
☐ 167 Aundray Bruce	.04	.02	.01
☐ 168 Bill Brooks	.04	.02	.01
☐ 169 Eddie Anderson	.04	.02	.01
☐ 170 Ronnie Lott	.10	.05	.01
☐ 171 Jay Hilgenberg	.04	.02	.01
☐ 172 Joe Nash	.04	.02	.01
☐ 173 Simon Fletcher	.04	.02	.01
☐ 174 Shane Conlan	.04	.02	.01
☐ 175 Sean Landeta	.04	.02	.01
☐ 176 John Alt	.04	.02	.01
☐ 177 Clay Matthews	.10	.05	.01
☐ 178 Anthony Munoz	.10	.05	.01
☐ 179 Pete Holohan	.04	.02	.01
☐ 180 Robert Awalt	.04	.02	.01
☐ 181 Rohn Stark	.04	.02	.01
☐ 182 Vance Johnson	.04	.02	.01
☐ 183 David Fulcher	.04	.02	.01
☐ 184 Robert Delpino	.04	.02	.01
☐ 185 Drew Hill	.04	.02	.01
☐ 186 Reggie Langhorne UER (Stats read 1988, not 1989)	.04	.02	.01
☐ 187 Lonzell Hill	.04	.02	.01
☐ 188 Tom Rathman UER (On back, blocker misspelled)	.04	.02	.01
☐ 189 Greg Montgomery	.04	.02	.01
☐ 190 Leonard Smith	.04	.02	.01
☐ 191 Chris Spielman	.25	.11	.03
☐ 192 Tom Newberry	.04	.02	.01
☐ 193 Cris Carter	.25	.11	.03
☐ 194 Kevin Porter	.04	.02	.01
☐ 195 Donnell Thompson	.04	.02	.01
☐ 196 Vaughan Johnson	.04	.02	.01
☐ 197 Steve McMichael	.10	.05	.01
☐ 198 Jim Sweeney	.04	.02	.01
☐ 199 Rich Karlis UER (No comma between day and year in birth data)	.04	.02	.01
☐ 200 Jerry Rice	1.00	.45	.12
☐ 201 Dan Hampton UER (Card says he's a DE, should be DT)	.10	.05	.01
☐ 202 Jim Lachey	.04	.02	.01
☐ 203 Reggie White	.25	.11	.03
☐ 204 Jerry Ball	.04	.02	.01
☐ 205 Russ Grimm	.04	.02	.01
☐ 206 Tim Green	.04	.02	.01
☐ 207 Shawn Collins	.04	.02	.01
☐ 208A Ralf Mojsiejenko ERR (Chargers stats)	.15	.07	.02
☐ 208B Ralf Mojsiejenko COR (Redskins stats)	.05	.02	.01
☐ 209 Trace Armstrong	.04	.02	.01
☐ 210 Keith Jackson	.10	.05	.01
☐ 211 Jamie Holland	.04	.02	.01
☐ 212 Mark Clayton	.10	.05	.01
☐ 213 Jeff Cross	.04	.02	.01
☐ 214 Bob Gagliano	.04	.02	.01
☐ 215 Louis Oliver UER (Text says played at Miami, should be Florida as in bio)	.04	.02	.01
☐ 216 Jim Arnold	.04	.02	.01
☐ 217 Robert Clark	.04	.02	.01
☐ 218 Gill Byrd	.04	.02	.01
☐ 219 Rodney Peete	.10	.05	.01
☐ 220 Anthony Miller	.25	.11	.03
☐ 221 Steve Grogan	.10	.05	.01
☐ 222 Vince Newsome	.04	.02	.01
☐ 223 Thomas Benson	.04	.02	.01
☐ 224 Kevin Murphy	.04	.02	.01
☐ 225 Henry Ellard	.10	.05	.01
☐ 226 Richard Johnson	.04	.02	.01
☐ 227 Jim Skow	.04	.02	.01
☐ 228 Keith Jones	.04	.02	.01
☐ 229 Dave Brown	.04	.02	.01
☐ 230 Marcus Allen	.25	.11	.03
☐ 231 Steve Walsh	.10	.05	.01
☐ 232 Jim Harbaugh	.25	.11	.03
☐ 233 Mel Gray	.10	.05	.01
☐ 234 David Treadwell	.04	.02	.01
☐ 235 John Offerdahl	.04	.02	.01
☐ 236 Gary Reasons	.04	.02	.01
☐ 237 Tim Krumrie	.04	.02	.01
☐ 238 Dave Duerson	.04	.02	.01
☐ 239 Gary Clark UER (Stats read 1988, not 1989)	.25	.11	.03
☐ 240 Mark Jackson	.04	.02	.01
☐ 241 Mark Murphy	.04	.02	.01
☐ 242 Jerry Holmes	.04	.02	.01
☐ 243 Tim McGee	.04	.02	.01
☐ 244 Mike Tomczak	.10	.05	.01
☐ 245 Sterling Sharpe UER (Broke 47-yard-old record, should be year)	.25	.11	.03
☐ 246 Bennie Blades	.04	.02	.01
☐ 247 Ken Harvey UER (Sacks and fumble recovery listings are switched; disappointing misspelled)	.25	.11	.03
☐ 248 Ron Heller	.04	.02	.01
☐ 249 Louis Lipps	.10	.05	.01
☐ 250 Wade Wilson	.10	.05	.01
☐ 251 Freddie Joe Nunn	.04	.02	.01
☐ 252 Jerome Brown UER ('89 stats show 2 fumble rec., should be 1)	.04	.02	.01
☐ 253 Myron Guyton	.04	.02	.01
☐ 254 Nate Odomes	.10	.05	.01
☐ 255 Rod Woodson	.25	.11	.03
☐ 256 Cornelius Bennett	.10	.05	.01
☐ 257 Keith Woodside	.04	.02	.01
☐ 258 Jeff Uhlenhake UER (Text calls him Ron)	.04	.02	.01
☐ 259 Harry Hamilton	.04	.02	.01
☐ 260 Mark Bavaro	.04	.02	.01
☐ 261 Vinny Testaverde	.10	.05	.01
☐ 262 Steve DeBerg	.04	.02	.01
☐ 263 Steve Wisniewski UER (Drafted by Dallas, not the Raiders)	.10	.05	.01
☐ 264 Pete Mandley	.04	.02	.01
☐ 265 Tim Harris	.04	.02	.01
☐ 266 Jack Trudeau	.04	.02	.01
☐ 267 Mark Kelso	.04	.02	.01
☐ 268 Brian Noble	.04	.02	.01
☐ 269 Jessie Tuggle	.04	.02	.01
☐ 270 Ken O'Brien	.04	.02	.01
☐ 271 David Little	.04	.02	.01
☐ 272 Pete Stoyanovich	.04	.02	.01
☐ 273 Odessa Turner	.04	.02	.01
☐ 274 Anthony Toney	.04	.02	.01
☐ 275 Tunch Ilkin	.04	.02	.01

☐ 276 Carl Lee	.04	.02	.01
☐ 277 Hart Lee Dykes	.04	.02	.01
☐ 278 Al Noga	.04	.02	.01
☐ 279 Greg Lloyd	.25	.11	.03
☐ 280 Billy Joe Tolliver	.04	.02	.01
☐ 281 Kirk Lowdermilk	.04	.02	.01
☐ 282 Earl Ferrell	.04	.02	.01
☐ 283 Eric Sievers	.04	.02	.01
☐ 284 Steve Jordan	.04	.02	.01
☐ 285 Burt Grossman	.04	.02	.01
☐ 286 Johnny Rembert	.04	.02	.01
☐ 287 Jeff Jaeger	.04	.02	.01
☐ 288 James Hasty	.04	.02	.01
☐ 289 Tony Mandarich DRAFT	.04	.02	.01
☐ 290 Chris Singleton DRAFT	.04	.02	.01
☐ 291 Lynn James DRAFT	.04	.02	.01
☐ 292 Andre Ware DRAFT	.25	.11	.03
☐ 293 Ray Agnew DRAFT	.04	.02	.01
☐ 294 Joel Smeenge DRAFT	.04	.02	.01
☐ 295 Marc Spindler DRAFT	.04	.02	.01
☐ 296 Renaldo Turnbull DRAFT	.04	.02	.01
☐ 297 Reggie Rembert DRAFT	.04	.02	.01
☐ 298 Jeff Alm DRAFT	.04	.02	.01
☐ 299 Cortez Kennedy DRAFT	.25	.11	.03
☐ 300 Blair Thomas DRAFT	.10	.05	.01
☐ 301 Pat Terrell DRAFT	.04	.02	.01
☐ 302 Junior Seau DRAFT	1.25	.55	.16
☐ 303 Mo Elewonibi DRAFT	.04	.02	.01
☐ 304 Tony Bennett DRAFT	.25	.11	.03
☐ 305 Percy Snow DRAFT	.04	.02	.01
☐ 306 Richmond Webb DRAFT	.04	.02	.01
☐ 307 Rodney Hampton DRAFT	1.00	.45	.12
☐ 308 Barry Foster DRAFT	.25	.11	.03
☐ 309 John Friesz DRAFT	.25	.11	.03
☐ 310 Ben Smith DRAFT	.04	.02	.01
☐ 311 Joe Montana HG	.50	.23	.06
☐ 312 Jim Everett HG	.10	.05	.01
☐ 313 Mark Rypien HG	.10	.05	.01
☐ 314 Phil Simms HG UER (Lists him as playing in the AFC)	.10	.05	.01
☐ 315 Don Majkowski HG	.04	.02	.01
☐ 316 Boomer Esiason HG	.04	.02	.01
☐ 317 Warren Moon HG (Moon on card)	.25	.11	.03
☐ 318 Jim Kelly HG	.25	.11	.03
☐ 319 Bernie Kosar HG UER (Word just is mis-spelled as justs)	.10	.05	.01
☐ 320 Dan Marino HG UER (Text says 378 completions in 1984, should be 1986)	.60	.25	.07
☐ 321 Christian Okoye GF	.04	.02	.01
☐ 322 Thurman Thomas GF	.25	.11	.03
☐ 323 James Brooks GF	.10	.05	.01
☐ 324 Bobby Humphrey GF	.04	.02	.01
☐ 325 Barry Sanders GF	.60	.25	.07
☐ 326 Neal Anderson GF	.04	.02	.01
☐ 327 Dalton Hilliard GF	.04	.02	.01
☐ 328 Greg Bell GF	.04	.02	.01
☐ 329 Roger Craig GF UER (Text says 2 TD's in SB XXIV, should be 1)	.10	.05	.01
☐ 330 Bo Jackson GF	.25	.11	.03
☐ 331 Don Warren	.04	.02	.01
☐ 332 Rufus Porter	.04	.02	.01
☐ 333 Sammie Smith	.04	.02	.01
☐ 334 Lewis Tillman UER (Born 4/16/67, should be 1966)	.04	.02	.01
☐ 335 Michael Walter	.04	.02	.01
☐ 336 Marc Logan	.04	.02	.01
☐ 337 Ron Hallstrom	.04	.02	.01
☐ 338 Stanley Morgan	.04	.02	.01
☐ 339 Mark Robinson	.04	.02	.01
☐ 340 Frank Reich	.25	.11	.03
☐ 341 Chip Lohmiller	.04	.02	.01
☐ 342 Steve Beuerlein	.10	.05	.01
☐ 343 John L. Williams	.04	.02	.01
☐ 344 Irving Fryar	.25	.11	.03
☐ 345 Anthony Carter	.10	.05	.01
☐ 346 Al Toon	.10	.05	.01
☐ 347 J.T. Smith	.04	.02	.01
☐ 348 Pierce Holt	.04	.02	.01
☐ 349 Ferrell Edmunds	.04	.02	.01
☐ 350 Mark Rypien	.10	.05	.01
☐ 351 Paul Gruber	.04	.02	.01
☐ 352 Ernest Givins	.10	.05	.01
☐ 353 Ervin Randle	.04	.02	.01
☐ 354 Guy McIntyre	.04	.02	.01
☐ 355 Webster Slaughter	.10	.05	.01
☐ 356 Reuben Davis	.04	.02	.01
☐ 357 Rickey Jackson	.10	.05	.01
☐ 358 Earnest Byner	.04	.02	.01
☐ 359 Eddie Brown	.04	.02	.01
☐ 360 Troy Stradford	.04	.02	.01
☐ 361 Pepper Johnson	.04	.02	.01
☐ 362 Ravin Caldwell	.04	.02	.01
☐ 363 Chris Mohr	.04	.02	.01
☐ 364 Jeff Bryant	.04	.02	.01
☐ 365 Bruce Collie	.04	.02	.01
☐ 366 Courtney Hall	.04	.02	.01
☐ 367 Jerry Olsavsky	.04	.02	.01
☐ 368 David Galloway	.04	.02	.01
☐ 369 Wes Hopkins	.04	.02	.01
☐ 370 Johnny Hector	.04	.02	.01
☐ 371 Clarence Verdin	.04	.02	.01
☐ 372 Nick Lowery	.04	.02	.01
☐ 373 Tim Brown	.25	.11	.03
☐ 374 Kevin Greene	.25	.11	.03
☐ 375 Leonard Marshall	.04	.02	.01
☐ 376 Roland James	.04	.02	.01
☐ 377 Scott Studwell	.04	.02	.01
☐ 378 Jarvis Williams	.04	.02	.01
☐ 379 Mike Saxon	.04	.02	.01
☐ 380 Kevin Mack	.04	.02	.01
☐ 381 Joe Kelly	.04	.02	.01
☐ 382 Tom Thayer	.04	.02	.01
☐ 383 Roy Green	.10	.05	.01
☐ 384 Michael Brooks	.04	.02	.01
☐ 385 Michael Cofer	.04	.02	.01
☐ 386 Ken Ruettgers	.04	.02	.01
☐ 387 Dean Steinkuhler	.04	.02	.01
☐ 388 Maurice Carthon	.04	.02	.01
☐ 389 Ricky Sanders	.04	.02	.01
☐ 390 Winston Moss	.04	.02	.01
☐ 391 Tony Woods	.04	.02	.01
☐ 392 Keith DeLong	.04	.02	.01
☐ 393 David Wyman	.04	.02	.01
☐ 394 Vencie Glenn	.04	.02	.01
☐ 395 Harris Barton	.04	.02	.01
☐ 396 Bryan Hinkle	.04	.02	.01
☐ 397 Derek Kennard	.04	.02	.01
☐ 398 Heath Sherman	.04	.02	.01
☐ 399 Troy Benson	.04	.02	.01
☐ 400 Gary Zimmerman	.04	.02	.01
☐ 401 Mark Duper	.10	.05	.01
☐ 402 Eugene Lockhart	.04	.02	.01
☐ 403 Tim Manoa	.04	.02	.01
☐ 404 Reggie Williams	.04	.02	.01
☐ 405 Mark Bortz	.04	.02	.01
☐ 406 Mike Kenn	.04	.02	.01
☐ 407 John Grimsley	.04	.02	.01
☐ 408 Bill Romanowski	.04	.02	.01
☐ 409 Perry Kemp	.04	.02	.01
☐ 410 Norm Johnson	.04	.02	.01
☐ 411 Broderick Thomas	.04	.02	.01
☐ 412 Joe Wolf	.04	.02	.01
☐ 413 Andre Waters	.04	.02	.01
☐ 414 Jason Staurovsky	.04	.02	.01
☐ 415 Eric Martin	.04	.02	.01
☐ 416 Joe Prokop	.04	.02	.01
☐ 417 Steve Sewell	.04	.02	.01
☐ 418 Cedric Jones	.04	.02	.01
☐ 419 Alphonso Carreker	.04	.02	.01
☐ 420 Keith Willis	.04	.02	.01
☐ 421 Bobby Butler	.04	.02	.01
☐ 422 John Roper	.04	.02	.01
☐ 423 Tim Spencer	.04	.02	.01
☐ 424 Jesse Sapolu	.04	.02	.01
☐ 425 Ron Wolfley	.04	.02	.01
☐ 426 Doug Smith	.04	.02	.01
☐ 427 William Howard	.04	.02	.01
☐ 428 Keith Van Horne	.04	.02	.01
☐ 429 Tony Jordan	.04	.02	.01
☐ 430 Mervyn Fernandez	.04	.02	.01
☐ 431 Shaun Gayle	.04	.02	.01
☐ 432 Ricky Nattiel	.04	.02	.01
☐ 433 Albert Lewis	.04	.02	.01
☐ 434 Fred Banks	.04	.02	.01
☐ 435 Henry Thomas	.04	.02	.01
☐ 436 Chet Brooks	.04	.02	.01
☐ 437 Mark Ingram	.10	.05	.01
☐ 438 Jeff Gossett	.04	.02	.01
☐ 439 Mike Wilcher	.04	.02	.01
☐ 440 Deron Cherry UER (Text says 7 cons. Pro Bowls, but he didn't play in 1989 Pro Bowl)	.04	.02	.01
☐ 441 Mike Rozier	.04	.02	.01
☐ 442 Jon Hand	.04	.02	.01
☐ 443 Ozzie Newsome	.10	.05	.01
☐ 444 Sammy Martin	.04	.02	.01
☐ 445 Luis Sharpe	.04	.02	.01
☐ 446 Lee Williams	.04	.02	.01
☐ 447 Chris Martin	.04	.02	.01
☐ 448 Kevin Fagan	.04	.02	.01
☐ 449 Gene Lang	.04	.02	.01
☐ 450 Greg Townsend	.04	.02	.01
☐ 451 Robert Lyles	.04	.02	.01
☐ 452 Eric Hill	.04	.02	.01
☐ 453 John Teltschik	.04	.02	.01
☐ 454 Vestee Jackson	.04	.02	.01
☐ 455 Bruce Reimers	.04	.02	.01
☐ 456 Butch Rolle	.04	.02	.01
☐ 457 Lawyer Tillman	.04	.02	.01
☐ 458 Andre Tippett	.04	.02	.01
☐ 459 James Thornton	.04	.02	.01
☐ 460 Randy Grimes	.04	.02	.01
☐ 461 Larry Roberts	.04	.02	.01
☐ 462 Ron Holmes	.04	.02	.01
☐ 463 Mike Wise	.04	.02	.01
☐ 464 Danny Copeland	.04	.02	.01
☐ 465 Bruce Wilkerson	.04	.02	.01
☐ 466 Mike Quick	.04	.02	.01
☐ 467 Mickey Shuler	.04	.02	.01
☐ 468 Mike Prior	.04	.02	.01
☐ 469 Ron Rivera	.04	.02	.01
☐ 470 Dean Biasucci	.04	.02	.01
☐ 471 Perry Williams	.04	.02	.01
☐ 472 Darren Comeaux UER (Front 53, back 52)	.04	.02	.01
☐ 473 Freeman McNeil	.04	.02	.01
☐ 474 Tyrone Braxton	.04	.02	.01
☐ 475 Jay Schroeder	.04	.02	.01
☐ 476 Naz Worthen	.04	.02	.01
☐ 477 Lionel Washington	.04	.02	.01
☐ 478 Carl Zander	.04	.02	.01
☐ 479 Al(Bubba) Baker	.10	.05	.01
☐ 480 Mike Merriweather	.04	.02	.01
☐ 481 Mike Gann	.04	.02	.01
☐ 482 Brent Williams	.04	.02	.01
☐ 483 Eugene Robinson	.04	.02	.01
☐ 484 Ray Horton	.04	.02	.01
☐ 485 Bruce Armstrong	.04	.02	.01
☐ 486 John Fourcade	.04	.02	.01
☐ 487 Lewis Billups	.04	.02	.01
☐ 488 Scott Davis	.04	.02	.01
☐ 489 Kenneth Sims	.04	.02	.01
☐ 490 Chris Chandler	.25	.11	.03
☐ 491 Mark Lee	.04	.02	.01
☐ 492 Johnny Meads	.04	.02	.01
☐ 493 Tim Irwin	.04	.02	.01
☐ 494 E.J. Junior	.04	.02	.01
☐ 495 Hardy Nickerson	.10	.05	.01
☐ 496 Rob McGovern	.04	.02	.01
☐ 497 Fred Strickland	.04	.02	.01
☐ 498 Reggie Rutland	.04	.02	.01
☐ 499 Mel Owens	.04	.02	.01
☐ 500 Derrick Thomas	.25	.11	.03
☐ 501 Jerrol Williams	.04	.02	.01
☐ 502 Maurice Hurst	.04	.02	.01
☐ 503 Larry Kelm	.04	.02	.01
☐ 504 Herman Fontenot	.04	.02	.01
☐ 505 Pat Beach	.04	.02	.01
☐ 506 Haywood Jeffires	.25	.11	.03
☐ 507 Neil Smith	.25	.11	.03
☐ 508 Cleveland Gary	.04	.02	.01
☐ 509 William Perry	.10	.05	.01
☐ 510 Michael Carter	.04	.02	.01
☐ 511 Walker Lee Ashley	.04	.02	.01
☐ 512 Bob Golic	.04	.02	.01
☐ 513 Danny Villa	.04	.02	.01
☐ 514 Matt Millen	.10	.05	.01
☐ 515 Don Griffin	.04	.02	.01
☐ 516 Jonathan Hayes	.04	.02	.01
☐ 517 Gerald Williams	.04	.02	.01
☐ 518 Scott Fulhage	.04	.02	.01
☐ 519 Irv Pankey	.04	.02	.01
☐ 520 Randy Dixon	.04	.02	.01
☐ 521 Terry McDaniel	.04	.02	.01
☐ 522 Dan Saleaumua	.04	.02	.01
☐ 523 Darrin Nelson	.04	.02	.01
☐ 524 Leonard Griffin	.04	.02	.01
☐ 525 Michael Ball	.04	.02	.01
☐ 526 Ernie Jones	.04	.02	.01
☐ 527 Tony Eason UER (Drafted in 1963, should be 1983)	.04	.02	.01
☐ 528 Ed Reynolds	.04	.02	.01
☐ 529 Gary Hogeboom	.04	.02	.01
☐ 530 Don Mosebar	.04	.02	.01
☐ 531 Ottis Anderson	.10	.05	.01
☐ 532 Bucky Scribner	.04	.02	.01
☐ 533 Aaron Cox	.04	.02	.01
☐ 534 Sean Jones	.10	.05	.01
☐ 535 Doug Flutie	.25	.11	.03
☐ 536 Leo Lewis	.04	.02	.01
☐ 537 Art Still	.04	.02	.01
☐ 538 Matt Bahr	.04	.02	.01
☐ 539 Keena Turner	.04	.02	.01
☐ 540 Sammy Winder	.04	.02	.01
☐ 541 Mike Webster	.10	.05	.01
☐ 542 Doug Riesenberg	.04	.02	.01
☐ 543 Dan Fike	.04	.02	.01
☐ 544 Clarence Kay	.04	.02	.01
☐ 545 Jim Burt	.04	.02	.01
☐ 546 Mike Horan	.04	.02	.01
☐ 547 Al Harris	.04	.02	.01
☐ 548 Maury Buford	.04	.02	.01
☐ 549 Jerry Robinson	.04	.02	.01
☐ 550 Tracy Rocker	.04	.02	.01
☐ 551 Karl Mecklenburg CC	.04	.02	.01
☐ 552 Lawrence Taylor CC	.25	.11	.03
☐ 553 Derrick Thomas CC	.25	.11	.03
☐ 554 Mike Singletary CC	.10	.05	.01
☐ 555 Tim Harris CC	.04	.02	.01
☐ 556 Jerry Rice RM	.50	.23	.06
☐ 557 Art Monk RM	.10	.05	.01
☐ 558 Mark Carrier WR RM	.10	.05	.01
☐ 559 Andre Reed RM	.10	.05	.01
☐ 560 Sterling Sharpe RM	.25	.11	.03
☐ 561 Herschel Walker GF	.10	.05	.01
☐ 562 Ottis Anderson GF	.10	.05	.01
☐ 563 Randall Cunningham HG	.10	.05	.01
☐ 564 John Elway HG	.30	.14	.04
☐ 565 David Fulcher AP	.04	.02	.01
☐ 566 Ronnie Lott AP	.10	.05	.01
☐ 567 Jerry Gray AP	.04	.02	.01
☐ 568 Albert Lewis AP	.04	.02	.01
☐ 569 Karl Mecklenburg AP	.04	.02	.01
☐ 570 Mike Singletary AP	.10	.05	.01
☐ 571 Lawrence Taylor AP	.25	.11	.03
☐ 572 Tim Harris AP	.04	.02	.01
☐ 573 Keith Millard AP	.04	.02	.01
☐ 574 Reggie White AP	.25	.11	.03
☐ 575 Chris Doleman AP	.04	.02	.01
☐ 576 Dave Meggett AP	.10	.05	.01
☐ 577 Rod Woodson AP	.25	.11	.03
☐ 578 Sean Landeta AP	.04	.02	.01
☐ 579 Eddie Murray AP	.04	.02	.01
☐ 580 Barry Sanders AP	.60	.25	.07
☐ 581 Christian Okoye AP	.04	.02	.01
☐ 582 Joe Montana AP	.50	.23	.06
☐ 583 Jay Hilgenberg AP	.04	.02	.01
☐ 584 Bruce Matthews AP	.10	.05	.01
☐ 585 Tom Newberry AP	.04	.02	.01
☐ 586 Gary Zimmerman AP	.04	.02	.01
☐ 587 Anthony Munoz AP	.10	.05	.01
☐ 588 Keith Jackson AP	.10	.05	.01
☐ 589 Sterling Sharpe AP	.25	.11	.03
☐ 590 Jerry Rice AP	.50	.23	.06
☐ 591 Bo Jackson RB	.25	.11	.03
☐ 592 Steve Largent RB	.25	.11	.03
☐ 593 Flipper Anderson RB	.04	.02	.01
☐ 594 Joe Montana RB	.50	.23	.06
☐ 595 Franco Harris HOF	.10	.05	.01
☐ 596 Bob St. Clair HOF	.04	.02	.01
☐ 597 Tom Landry HOF	.10	.05	.01
☐ 598 Jack Lambert HOF	.10	.05	.01
☐ 599 Ted Hendricks HOF UER (Int. avg. says 12.8, should be 8.9)	.04	.02	.01
☐ 600A Buck Buchanan HOF UER (Drafted in 1983)	.08	.04	.01
☐ 600B Buck Buchanan HOF COR (Drafted in 1963)	.08	.04	.01
☐ 601 Bob Griese HOF	.10	.05	.01
☐ 602 Super Bowl Wrap	.04	.02	.01
☐ 603A Vince Lombardi UER Lombardi Legend (Disciplinarian mis-spelled; no logo for Curtis Mgt. at bottom)	.20	.09	.03
☐ 603B Vince Lombardi UER Lombardi Legend (Disciplinarian mis-spelled; logo for Curtis Mgt. at bottom)	.20	.09	.03
☐ 604 Mark Carrier UER (Front 88, back 89)	.10	.05	.01
☐ 605 Randall Cunningham	.10	.05	.01
☐ 606 Percy Snow C90	.04	.02	.01
☐ 607 Andre Ware C90	.25	.11	.03
☐ 608 Blair Thomas C90	.10	.05	.01
☐ 609 Eric Green C90	.04	.02	.01
☐ 610 Reggie Rembert C90	.04	.02	.01
☐ 611 Richmond Webb C90	.04	.02	.01
☐ 612 Bern Brostek C90	.04	.02	.01
☐ 613 James Williams C90	.04	.02	.01
☐ 614 Mark Carrier DB C90	.10	.05	.01
☐ 615 Renaldo Turnbull C90	.04	.02	.01
☐ 616 Cortez Kennedy C90	.10	.05	.01
☐ 617 Keith McCants C90	.04	.02	.01
☐ 618 Anthony Thompson DRAFT	.04	.02	.01
☐ 619 LeRoy Butler DRAFT	.25	.11	.03
☐ 620 Aaron Wallace DRAFT	.04	.02	.01
☐ 621 Alexander Wright DRAFT	.04	.02	.01
☐ 622 Keith McCants DRAFT	.04	.02	.01
☐ 623 Jimmie Jones UER DRAFT (January misspelled)	.04	.02	.01
☐ 624 Anthony Johnson DRAFT	.25	.11	.03
☐ 625 Fred Washington DRAFT	.04	.02	.01
☐ 626 Mike Bellamy DRAFT	.04	.02	.01
☐ 627 Mark Carrier DB DRAFT	.25	.11	.03
☐ 628 Harold Green DRAFT	.25	.11	.03
☐ 629 Eric Green DRAFT	.10	.05	.01
☐ 630 Andre Collins DRAFT	.04	.02	.01
☐ 631 Lamar Lathon DRAFT	.10	.05	.01
☐ 632 Terry Wooden DRAFT	.04	.02	.01
☐ 633 Jesse Anderson DRAFT	.04	.02	.01
☐ 634 Jeff George DRAFT	.75	.35	.09
☐ 635 Carwell Gardner DRAFT	.04	.02	.01
☐ 636 Darrell Thompson DRAFT	.04	.02	.01
☐ 637 Vince Buck DRAFT	.04	.02	.01
☐ 638 Mike Jones DRAFT	.04	.02	.01
☐ 639 Charles Arbuckle DRAFT	.04	.02	.01
☐ 640 Dennis Brown DRAFT	.04	.02	.01
☐ 641 James Williams DRAFT	.04	.02	.01
☐ 642 Bern Brostek DRAFT	.04	.02	.01
☐ 643 Darion Conner DRAFT	.10	.05	.01
☐ 644 Mike Fox DRAFT	.04	.02	.01
☐ 645 Cary Conklin DRAFT	.04	.02	.01
☐ 646 Tim Grunhard DRAFT	.04	.02	.01
☐ 647 Ron Cox DRAFT	.04	.02	.01
☐ 648 Keith Sims DRAFT	.04	.02	.01
☐ 649 Alton Montgomery DRAFT	.04	.02	.01
☐ 650 Greg McMurtry DRAFT	.04	.02	.01
☐ 651 Scott Mitchell DRAFT	1.00	.45	.12
☐ 652 Tim Ryan DRAFT	.04	.02	.01
☐ 653 Jeff Mills DRAFT	.04	.02	.01
☐ 654 Ricky Proehl DRAFT	.10	.05	.01
☐ 655 Steve Broussard DRAFT	.04	.02	.01
☐ 656 Peter Tom Willis DRAFT	.04	.02	.01
☐ 657 Dexter Carter DRAFT	.04	.02	.01
☐ 658 Tony Casillas	.04	.02	.01

	MINT	NRMT	EXC
□ 659 Joe Morris	.04	.02	.01
□ 660 Greg Kragen	.04	.02	.01
□ B1 Matt Stover	.05	.02	.01
□ B2 Demetrius Davis	.05	.02	.01
□ B3 Ken McMichel	.05	.02	.01
□ B4 Judd Garrett	.05	.02	.01
□ B5 Elliott Searcy	.05	.02	.01

1990 Score Hot Cards

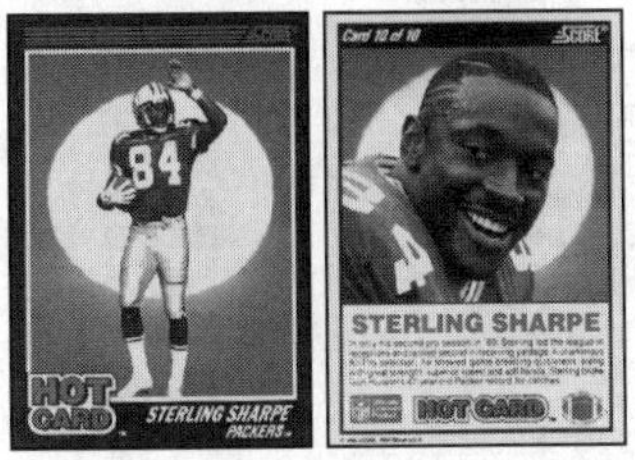

This ten-card standard size set was issued by Score as an insert (one per) in their 100-card blister packs, which feature Score cards from both Series 1 and Series 2. The cards have black borders which surround the player's photo set against the sun. The back of the card features a large color photo of the player on the top 2/3 of the card and brief biographical identification on the bottom.

	MINT	NRMT	EXC
COMPLETE SET (10)	25.00	11.00	3.10
COMMON CARD (1-10)	1.00	.45	.12
□ 1 Joe Montana	5.00	2.20	.60
□ 2 Bo Jackson	2.00	.90	.25
□ 3 Barry Sanders	5.00	2.20	.60
□ 4 Jerry Rice	5.00	2.20	.60
□ 5 Eric Metcalf	2.00	.90	.25
□ 6 Don Majkowski	1.00	.45	.12
□ 7 Christian Okoye	1.00	.45	.12
□ 8 Bobby Humphrey	1.00	.45	.12
□ 9 Dan Marino	10.00	4.50	1.25
□ 10 Sterling Sharpe	2.00	.90	.25

1990 Score Supplemental

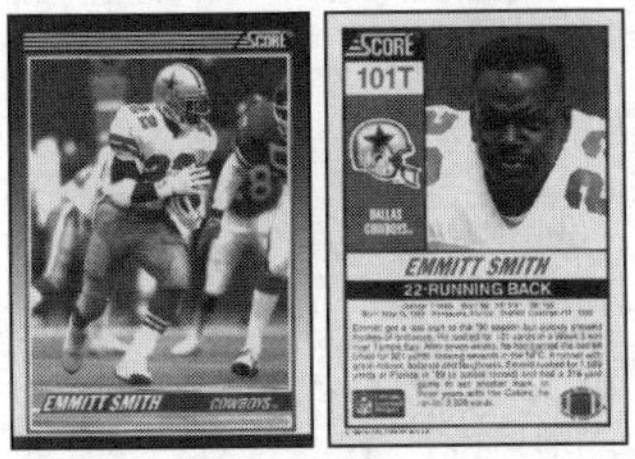

This 110-card standard size set was issued in the same design as the regular Score issue, but with blue and purple borders. The set included cards of rookies and cards of players who switched teams during the off-season. The set was released through Score's dealer outlets and was available only in complete set form. The key Rookie Card is Emmitt Smith. Other Rookie Cards include Reggie Cobb, Derrick Fenner, Stan Humphries, Johnny Johnson and Rob Moore. The cards are numbered on the back with a "T" suffix.

	MINT	NRMT	EXC
COMPLETE FACT.SET (110)	110.00	50.00	14.00
COMMON CARD (1T-110T)	.15	.07	.02
□ 1T Marcus Dupree	.15	.07	.02
□ 2T Jerry Kauric	.15	.07	.02
□ 3T Everson Walls	.15	.07	.02
□ 4T Elliott Smith	.15	.07	.02
□ 5T Donald Evans UER (Misspelled Pittsburg on card back)	.30	.14	.04
□ 6T Jerry Holmes	.15	.07	.02
□ 7T Dan Stryzinski	.15	.07	.02
□ 8T Gerald McNeil	.15	.07	.02
□ 9T Rick Tuten	.15	.07	.02
□ 10T Mickey Shuler	.15	.07	.02
□ 11T Jay Novacek	1.00	.45	.12
□ 12T Eric Williams	.15	.07	.02
□ 13T Stanley Morgan	.15	.07	.02
□ 14T Wayne Haddix	.15	.07	.02
□ 15T Gary Anderson RB	.15	.07	.02
□ 16T Stan Humphries	3.00	1.35	.35
□ 17T Raymond Clayborn	.15	.07	.02
□ 18T Mark Boyer	.15	.07	.02
□ 19T Dave Waymer	.15	.07	.02
□ 20T Andre Rison	.60	.25	.07
□ 21T Daniel Stubbs	.15	.07	.02
□ 22T Mike Rozier	.15	.07	.02
□ 23T Damian Johnson	.15	.07	.02
□ 24T Don Smith	.15	.07	.02
□ 25T Max Montoya	.15	.07	.02
□ 26T Terry Kinard	.15	.07	.02
□ 27T Herb Welch	.15	.07	.02
□ 28T Cliff Odom	.15	.07	.02
□ 29T John Kidd	.15	.07	.02
□ 30T Barry Word	.15	.07	.02
□ 31T Rich Karlis	.15	.07	.02
□ 32T Mike Baab	.15	.07	.02
□ 33T Ronnie Harmon	.30	.14	.04
□ 34T Jeff Donaldson	.15	.07	.02
□ 35T Riki Ellison	.15	.07	.02
□ 36T Steve Walsh	.30	.14	.04
□ 37T Bill Lewis	.15	.07	.02
□ 38T Tim McKyer	.15	.07	.02
□ 39T James Wilder	.15	.07	.02
□ 40T Tony Paige	.15	.07	.02
□ 41T Derrick Fenner	.15	.07	.02
□ 42T Thane Gash	.15	.07	.02
□ 43T Dave Duerson	.15	.07	.02
□ 44T Clarence Weathers	.15	.07	.02
□ 45T Matt Bahr	.15	.07	.02
□ 46T Alonzo Highsmith	.15	.07	.02
□ 47T Joe Kelly	.15	.07	.02
□ 48T Chris Hinton	.15	.07	.02
□ 49T Bobby Humphery	.15	.07	.02
□ 50T Greg Bell	.15	.07	.02
□ 51T Fred Smerlas	.15	.07	.02
□ 52T Walter Stanley	.15	.07	.02
□ 53T Jim Skow	.15	.07	.02
□ 54T Renaldo Turnbull	.15	.07	.02
□ 55T Bern Brostek	.15	.07	.02
□ 56T Charles Wilson	.15	.07	.02
□ 57T Keith McCants	.15	.07	.02
□ 58T Alexander Wright	.30	.14	.04
□ 59T Ian Beckles	.15	.07	.02
□ 60T Eric Davis	.30	.14	.04
□ 61T Chris Singleton	.15	.07	.02
□ 62T Rob Moore	2.00	.90	.25
□ 63T Darion Conner	.30	.14	.04
□ 64T Tim Grunhard	.15	.07	.02
□ 65T Junior Seau	4.00	1.80	.50
□ 66T Tony Stargell	.15	.07	.02
□ 67T Anthony Thompson	.15	.07	.02
□ 68T Cortez Kennedy	.60	.25	.07
□ 69T Darrell Thompson	.15	.07	.02
□ 70T Calvin Williams	.60	.25	.07
□ 71T Rodney Hampton	3.00	1.35	.35
□ 72T Terry Wooden	.15	.07	.02
□ 73T Leo Goeas	.15	.07	.02
□ 74T Ken Willis	.15	.07	.02
□ 75T Ricky Proehl	.30	.14	.04
□ 76T Steve Christie	.15	.07	.02
□ 77T Andre Ware	.60	.25	.07
□ 78T Jeff George	3.00	1.35	.35
□ 79T Walter Wilson	.15	.07	.02
□ 80T Johnny Bailey	.15	.07	.02
□ 81T Harold Green	.30	.14	.04
□ 82T Mark Carrier	.60	.25	.07
□ 83T Frank Cornish	.15	.07	.02
□ 84T James Williams	.15	.07	.02
□ 85T James Francis	.15	.07	.02
□ 86T Percy Snow	.15	.07	.02
□ 87T Anthony Johnson	.75	.35	.09
□ 88T Tim Ryan	.15	.07	.02
□ 89T Dan Owens	.15	.07	.02
□ 90T Aaron Wallace	.15	.07	.02
□ 91T Steve Broussard	.15	.07	.02
□ 92T Eric Green	.15	.07	.02
□ 93T Blair Thomas	.30	.14	.04
□ 94T Robert Blackmon	.15	.07	.02
□ 95T Alan Grant	.15	.07	.02
□ 96T Andre Collins	.15	.07	.02
□ 97T Dexter Carter	.15	.07	.02
□ 98T Reggie Cobb	.15	.07	.02
□ 99T Dennis Brown	.15	.07	.02
□ 100T Kenny Davidson	.15	.07	.02
□ 101T Emmitt Smith	100.00	45.00	12.50
□ 102T Jeff Alm	.15	.07	.02
□ 103T Alton Montgomery	.15	.07	.02
□ 104T Tony Bennett	.60	.25	.07
□ 105T Johnny Johnson	.30	.14	.04
□ 106T Leroy Hoard	.60	.25	.07
□ 107T Ray Agnew	.15	.07	.02
□ 108T Richmond Webb	.15	.07	.02
□ 109T Keith Sims	.15	.07	.02
□ 110T Barry Foster	.60	.25	.07

1990 Score 100 Hottest

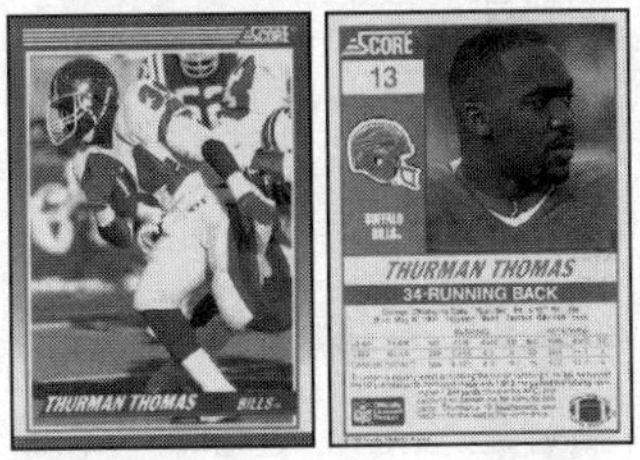

This 100-card standard size set, featuring some of the most popular football stars of 1990, was issued by Score in conjunction with Publications International, which issued an attractive magazine-style publication giving more biographical information about the players featured on the front. These cards have the same photos on the front as the regular issue Score Football cards with the only difference being the numbering on the back of the card.

	MINT	NRMT	EXC
COMPLETE SET (100)	12.00	5.50	1.50
COMMON CARD (1-100)	.10	.05	.01
□ 1 Bo Jackson	.40	.18	.05
□ 2 Joe Montana	2.00	.90	.25
□ 3 Deion Sanders	.75	.35	.09
□ 4 Dan Marino	2.50	1.10	.30
□ 5 Barry Sanders	1.50	.70	.19
□ 6 Neal Anderson	.15	.07	.02
□ 7 Phil Simms	.15	.07	.02
□ 8 Bobby Humphrey	.10	.05	.01
□ 9 Roger Craig	.15	.07	.02
□ 10 John Elway	.60	.25	.07
□ 11 James Brooks	.15	.07	.02
□ 12 Ken O'Brien	.10	.05	.01
□ 13 Thurman Thomas	.75	.35	.09
□ 14 Troy Aikman	1.50	.70	.19
□ 15 Karl Mecklenburg	.15	.07	.02
□ 16 Dave Krieg	.15	.07	.02
□ 17 Chris Spielman	.15	.07	.02
□ 18 Tim Harris	.10	.05	.01
□ 19 Tim Worley	.10	.05	.01
□ 20 Clay Matthews	.15	.07	.02
□ 21 Lars Tate	.10	.05	.01
□ 22 Hart Lee Dykes	.10	.05	.01
□ 23 Cornelius Bennett	.15	.07	.02
□ 24 Anthony Miller	.15	.07	.02
□ 25 Lawrence Taylor	.15	.07	.02
□ 26 Jay Hilgenberg	.10	.05	.01
□ 27 Tom Rathman	.15	.07	.02
□ 28 Brian Blades	.15	.07	.02
□ 29 David Fulcher	.10	.05	.01
□ 30 Cris Carter	.40	.18	.05
□ 31 Marcus Allen	.40	.18	.05
□ 32 Eric Metcalf	.30	.14	.04
□ 33 Bruce Smith	.30	.14	.04
□ 34 Jim Kelly	.50	.23	.06
□ 35 Wade Wilson	.10	.05	.01
□ 36 Rich Camarillo	.10	.05	.01
□ 37 Boomer Esiason	.15	.07	.02
□ 38 John Offerdahl	.10	.05	.01
□ 39 Vance Johnson	.10	.05	.01
□ 40 Ronnie Lott	.15	.07	.02
□ 41 Kevin Ross	.10	.05	.01
□ 42 Greg Bell	.15	.07	.02
□ 43 Erik McMillan	.10	.05	.01
□ 44 Mike Singletary	.15	.07	.02
□ 45 Roger Vick	.10	.05	.01
□ 46 Keith Jackson	.30	.14	.04
□ 47 Henry Ellard	.15	.07	.02
□ 48 Gary Anderson RB	.15	.07	.02
□ 49 Art Monk	.15	.07	.02
□ 50 Jim Everett	.15	.07	.02
□ 51 Anthony Munoz	.15	.07	.02
□ 52 Ray Childress	.15	.07	.02
□ 53 Howie Long	.15	.07	.02
□ 54 Chris Hinton	.10	.05	.01
□ 55 John Stephens	.10	.05	.01
□ 56 Reggie White	.30	.14	.04
□ 57 Rodney Peete	.15	.07	.02
□ 58 Don Majkowski	.10	.05	.01
□ 59 Michael Cofer	.10	.05	.01
□ 60 Bubby Brister	.10	.05	.01
□ 61 Jerry Gray	.10	.05	.01
□ 62 Rodney Holman	.10	.05	.01
□ 63 Vinny Testaverde	.15	.07	.02
□ 64 Sterling Sharpe	.40	.18	.05
□ 65 Keith Millard	.10	.05	.01
□ 66 Jim Lachey	.10	.05	.01
□ 67 Dave Meggett	.15	.07	.02
□ 68 Brent Fullwood	.10	.05	.01
□ 69 Bobby Hebert	.15	.07	.02
□ 70 Joey Browner	.10	.05	.01
□ 71 Flipper Anderson	.15	.07	.02
□ 72 Tim McGee	.10	.05	.01
□ 73 Eric Allen	.15	.07	.02
□ 74 Charles Haley	.15	.07	.02
□ 75 Christian Okoye	.10	.05	.01
□ 76 Herschel Walker	.15	.07	.02
□ 77 Kelvin Martin	.10	.05	.01
□ 78 Bill Fralic	.10	.05	.01
□ 79 Leslie O'Neal	.15	.07	.02
□ 80 Bernie Kosar	.15	.07	.02
□ 81 Eric Sievers	.10	.05	.01
□ 82 Timm Rosenbach	.10	.05	.01
□ 83 Steve DeBerg	.15	.07	.02
□ 84 Duane Bickett	.10	.05	.01
□ 85 Chris Doleman	.15	.07	.02
□ 86 Carl Banks	.15	.07	.02
□ 87 Vaughan Johnson	.10	.05	.01
□ 88 Dennis Smith	.10	.05	.01
□ 89 Billy Joe Tolliver	.10	.05	.01
□ 90 Dalton Hilliard	.10	.05	.01
□ 91 John Taylor	.15	.07	.02
□ 92 Mark Rypien	.15	.07	.02
□ 93 Chris Miller	.15	.07	.02
□ 94 Mark Clayton	.15	.07	.02
□ 95 Andre Reed	.30	.14	.04
□ 96 Warren Moon	.30	.14	.04
□ 97 Bruce Matthews	.10	.05	.01
□ 98 Rod Woodson	.30	.14	.04
□ 99 Pat Swilling	.15	.07	.02
□ 100 Jerry Rice	1.50	.70	.19

1990 Score Young Superstars

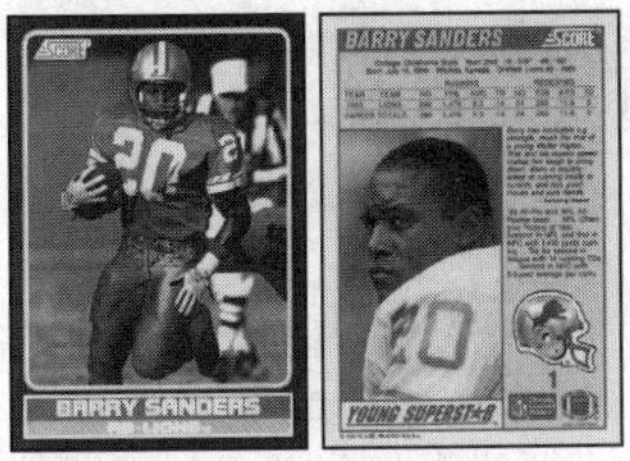

This 40-card standard size set was issued by Score in 1990 (via a mail-in offer), featuring forty of the leading young football players. This set features a glossy front with the player's photo being surrounded by black borders on the front of the card. The back, meanwhile, features a full color photo of the player along with seasonal and career statistics about the player.

	MINT	NRMT	EXC
COMPLETE SET (40)	6.00	2.70	.75
COMMON CARD (1-40)	.05	.02	.01
□ 1 Barry Sanders	1.50	.70	.19
□ 2 Bobby Humphrey	.05	.02	.01
□ 3 Ickey Woods	.05	.02	.01
□ 4 Shawn Collins	.05	.02	.01
□ 5 Dave Meggett	.10	.05	.01
□ 6 Keith Jackson	.10	.05	.01
□ 7 Sterling Sharpe	.20	.09	.03
□ 8 Troy Aikman	1.50	.70	.19
□ 9 Tim McDonald	.05	.02	.01
□ 10 Tim Brown	.20	.09	.03
□ 11 Trace Armstrong	.05	.02	.01
□ 12 Eric Metcalf UER (Led Bears in rushing, should be Browns)	.20	.09	.03
□ 13 Derrick Thomas	.20	.09	.03
□ 14 Eric Hill	.05	.02	.01
□ 15 Deion Sanders	.60	.25	.07
□ 16 Steve Atwater	.05	.02	.01
□ 17 Carnell Lake	.10	.05	.01
□ 18 Andre Reed	.10	.05	.01
□ 19 Chris Spielman	.10	.05	.01
□ 20 Eric Allen	.10	.05	.01
□ 21 Erik McMillan	.05	.02	.01
□ 22 Louis Oliver	.05	.02	.01
□ 23 Robert Massey	.05	.02	.01
□ 24 John Roper	.05	.02	.01
□ 25 Burt Grossman	.05	.02	.01
□ 26 Chris Jacke	.05	.02	.01
□ 27 Steve Wisniewski	.05	.02	.01
□ 28 Alonzo Highsmith	.05	.02	.01
□ 29 Mark Carrier WR	.10	.05	.01
□ 30 Bruce Armstrong	.05	.02	.01
□ 31 Jerome Brown	.10	.05	.01
□ 32 Cornelius Bennett	.10	.05	.01
□ 33 Flipper Anderson	.10	.05	.01
□ 34 Brian Blades	.10	.05	.01
□ 35 Anthony Miller	.10	.05	.01
□ 36 Thurman Thomas	.50	.23	.06
□ 37 Chris Miller	.10	.05	.01
□ 38 Aundray Bruce	.05	.02	.01
□ 39 Robert Clark	.05	.02	.01
□ 40 Robert Delpino	.05	.02	.01

1990-91 Score Franco Harris

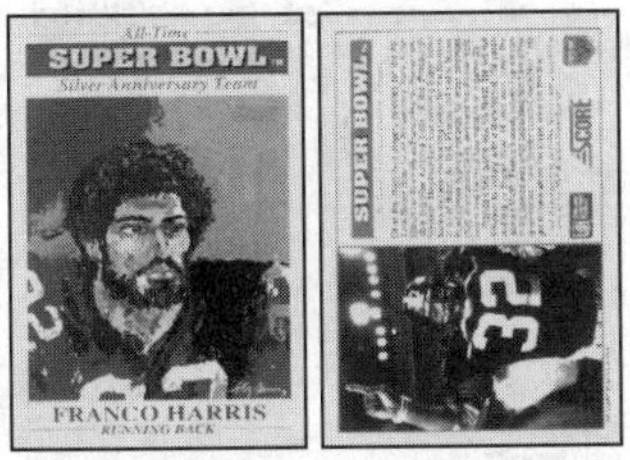

This standard-size card was given away to all persons at the Super Bowl Card Show II in Tampa who acquired Franco Harris' autograph while at the show. It was estimated that between 1500 and 5000 cards were printed. The card features a Leroy Nieman painting of Harris on the front which has the words "All-Time Super Bowl Silver Anniversary Team" on top of the portrait and Franco Harris' name and position underneath the drawing. The back of the card is split horizontally between a shot of Harris celebrating a Super Bowl victory and a brief Super Bowl history of Harris on the back. The card is unnumbered.

	MINT	NRMT	EXC
COMPLETE SET (1)	20.00	9.00	2.50
COMMON CARD	20.00	9.00	2.50
□ 1 Franco Harris (Leroy Nieman's artistic rendition)	20.00	9.00	2.50

1991 Score Prototypes

This six-card prototype standard-size set was issued to show the design of the 1991 Score regular series. As with the regular issue, the fronts display color action player photos with borders that shade from white to a solid color, while the horizontal backs carry biographical and statistical information on the left half and a color close-up photo on the right. The prototypes may be distinguished from the regular issues by noting the following minor differences: 1) the prototypes omit the tiny trademark symbol next to the Team NFL logo; 2) the shading of the borders on the front has been reversed on the Singletary and Cunningham cards; 3) statistics are printed in bluish-green on the prototypes rather than green as on the regular issues (except for Taylor, whose statistics are printed in red on his regular card); 4) on the Taylor prototype, his name appears in a blue (rather than a black) stripe on the back; and 5) the Montana, Esiason, and Thomas cards are cropped slightly differently. All cards are numbered on the back; the numbering of the prototype cards corresponds to their regular issue counterparts except for the Taylor card, who is card number 529 in the regular issue.

	MINT	NRMT	EXC
COMPLETE SET (6)	10.00	4.50	1.25
COMMON CARD	1.00	.45	.12

		MINT	NRMT	EXC
☐	1 Joe Montana	5.00	2.20	.60
☐	4 Lawrence Taylor	1.00	.45	.12
☐	5 Derrick Thomas	1.25	.55	.16
☐	6 Mike Singletary	1.00	.45	.12
☐	7 Boomer Esiason	1.00	.45	.12
☐	12 Randall Cunningham	1.00	.45	.12

1991 Score

The 1991 Score set consists of two series of 345 and 341 for a total of 686 standard size cards. Factory sets include four Super Bowl cards (B1-B4) for a total of 690. Cards were issued in 16-card packs. The cards feature full-color photographs on the front with the player's name and team logo at the bottom. Horizontal backs contain a small photo, statistics and highlights. Subsets include 1991 Rookies (311-319/564-589/591-596/598-612/ 614-616), the players who had plays which resulted in 90 or more yards (320-328), Top Leaders (329-330/662-669), Dream Team (331-345/676-686), Team MVP's (620-647), Crunch Crew (648-654), Sack Attack (655-661), 1991 Hall of Fame (670-674). As part of a promotion, the 11 offensive Dream Team members each signed 500 of their cards. Of this total, 5,478 were randomly inserted in second series packs and 22 were given away in a mail-in sweepstakes. Rookie Cards include Mike Croel, Ricky Ervins, Brett Favre, Alvin Harper, Herman Moore, Mike Pritchard, Jake Reed, Ricky Watters and Harvey Williams.

	MINT	NRMT	EXC
COMPLETE SET (686)	8.00	3.60	1.00
COMPLETE FACT.SET (690)	8.00	3.60	1.00
COMMON CARD (1-686)	.04	.02	.01
COMMON BONUS (B1-B4)	.06	.03	.01

		MINT	NRMT	EXC
☐	1 Joe Montana	1.00	.45	.12
☐	2 Eric Allen	.04	.02	.01
☐	3 Rohn Stark	.04	.02	.01
☐	4 Frank Reich	.10	.05	.01
☐	5 Derrick Thomas	.25	.11	.03
☐	6 Mike Singletary	.10	.05	.01
☐	7 Boomer Esiason	.10	.05	.01
☐	8 Matt Millen	.10	.05	.01
☐	9 Chris Spielman	.10	.05	.01
☐	10 Gerald McNeil	.04	.02	.01
☐	11 Nick Lowery	.04	.02	.01
☐	12 Randall Cunningham	.10	.05	.01
☐	13 Marion Butts	.10	.05	.01
☐	14 Tim Brown	.25	.11	.03
☐	15 Emmitt Smith	2.00	.90	.25
☐	16 Rich Camarillo	.04	.02	.01
☐	17 Mike Merriweather	.04	.02	.01
☐	18 Derrick Fenner	.04	.02	.01
☐	19 Clay Matthews	.10	.05	.01
☐	20 Barry Sanders	1.00	.45	.12
☐	21 James Brooks	.10	.05	.01
☐	22 Alton Montgomery	.04	.02	.01
☐	23 Steve Atwater	.04	.02	.01
☐	24 Ron Morris	.04	.02	.01
☐	25 Brad Muster	.04	.02	.01
☐	26 Andre Rison	.10	.05	.01
☐	27 Brian Brennan	.04	.02	.01
☐	28 Leonard Smith	.04	.02	.01
☐	29 Kevin Butler	.04	.02	.01
☐	30 Tim Harris	.04	.02	.01
☐	31 Jay Novacek	.25	.11	.03
☐	32 Eddie Murray	.04	.02	.01
☐	33 Keith Woodside	.04	.02	.01
☐	34 Ray Crockett	.04	.02	.01
☐	35 Eugene Lockhart	.04	.02	.01
☐	36 Bill Romanowski	.04	.02	.01
☐	37 Eddie Brown	.04	.02	.01
☐	38 Eugene Daniel	.04	.02	.01
☐	39 Scott Fulhage	.04	.02	.01
☐	40 Harold Green	.10	.05	.01
☐	41 Mark Jackson	.04	.02	.01
☐	42 Sterling Sharpe	.25	.11	.03
☐	43 Mel Gray	.10	.05	.01
☐	44 Jerry Holmes	.04	.02	.01
☐	45 Allen Pinkett	.04	.02	.01
☐	46 Warren Powers	.04	.02	.01
☐	47 Rodney Peete	.10	.05	.01
☐	48 Lorenzo White	.04	.02	.01
☐	49 Dan Owens	.04	.02	.01
☐	50 James Francis	.04	.02	.01
☐	51 Ken Norton	.25	.11	.03
☐	52 Ed West	.04	.02	.01
☐	53 Andre Reed	.10	.05	.01
☐	54 John Grimsley	.04	.02	.01
☐	55 Michael Cofer	.04	.02	.01
☐	56 Chris Doleman	.04	.02	.01
☐	57 Pat Swilling	.10	.05	.01
☐	58 Jessie Tuggle	.04	.02	.01
☐	59 Mike Johnson	.04	.02	.01
☐	60 Steve Walsh	.04	.02	.01
☐	61 Sam Mills	.04	.02	.01
☐	62 Don Mosebar	.04	.02	.01
☐	63 Jay Hilgenberg	.04	.02	.01
☐	64 Cleveland Gary	.04	.02	.01
☐	65 Andre Tippett	.04	.02	.01
☐	66 Tom Newberry	.04	.02	.01
☐	67 Maurice Hurst	.04	.02	.01
☐	68 Louis Oliver	.04	.02	.01
☐	69 Fred Marion	.04	.02	.01
☐	70 Christian Okoye	.04	.02	.01
☐	71 Marv Cook	.04	.02	.01
☐	72 Darryl Talley	.04	.02	.01
☐	73 Rick Fenney	.04	.02	.01
☐	74 Kelvin Martin	.04	.02	.01
☐	75 Howie Long	.10	.05	.01
☐	76 Steve Wisniewski	.04	.02	.01
☐	77 Karl Mecklenburg	.04	.02	.01
☐	78 Dan Saleaumua	.04	.02	.01
☐	79 Ray Childress	.04	.02	.01
☐	80 Henry Ellard	.10	.05	.01
☐	81 Ernest Givins UER	.10	.05	.01
	(3rd on Oilers in			
	receiving, not 4th)			
☐	82 Ferrell Edmunds	.04	.02	.01
☐	83 Steve Jordan	.04	.02	.01
☐	84 Tony Mandarich	.04	.02	.01
☐	85 Eric Martin	.04	.02	.01
☐	86 Rich Gannon	.04	.02	.01
☐	87 Irving Fryar	.10	.05	.01
☐	88 Tom Rathman	.04	.02	.01
☐	89 Dan Hampton	.10	.05	.01
☐	90 Barry Word	.04	.02	.01
☐	91 Kevin Greene	.25	.11	.03
☐	92 Sean Landeta	.04	.02	.01
☐	93 Trace Armstrong	.04	.02	.01
☐	94 Dennis Byrd	.04	.02	.01
☐	95 Timm Rosenbach	.04	.02	.01
☐	96 Anthony Toney	.04	.02	.01
☐	97 Tim Krumrie	.04	.02	.01
☐	98 Jerry Ball	.04	.02	.01
☐	99 Tim Green	.04	.02	.01
☐	100 Bo Jackson	.10	.05	.01
☐	101 Myron Guyton	.04	.02	.01
☐	102 Mike Mularkey	.04	.02	.01
☐	103 Jerry Gray	.04	.02	.01
☐	104 Scott Stephen	.04	.02	.01
☐	105 Anthony Bell	.04	.02	.01
☐	106 Lomas Brown	.04	.02	.01
☐	107 David Little	.04	.02	.01
☐	108 Brad Baxter	.04	.02	.01
☐	109 Freddie Joe Nunn	.04	.02	.01
☐	110 Dave Meggett	.10	.05	.01
☐	111 Mark Rypien	.10	.05	.01
☐	112 Warren Williams	.04	.02	.01
☐	113 Ron Rivera	.04	.02	.01
☐	114 Terance Mathis	.10	.05	.01
☐	115 Anthony Munoz	.10	.05	.01
☐	116 Jeff Bryant	.04	.02	.01
☐	117 Issiac Holt	.04	.02	.01
☐	118 Steve Sewell	.04	.02	.01
☐	119 Tim Newton	.04	.02	.01
☐	120 Emile Harry	.04	.02	.01
☐	121 Gary Anderson K	.04	.02	.01
☐	122 Mark Lee	.04	.02	.01
☐	123 Alfred Anderson	.04	.02	.01
☐	124 Anthony Blaylock	.04	.02	.01
☐	125 Earnest Byner	.04	.02	.01
☐	126 Bill Maas	.04	.02	.01
☐	127 Keith Taylor	.04	.02	.01
☐	128 Cliff Odom	.04	.02	.01
☐	129 Bob Golic	.04	.02	.01
☐	130 Bart Oates	.04	.02	.01
☐	131 Jim Arnold	.04	.02	.01
☐	132 Jeff Herrod	.04	.02	.01
☐	133 Bruce Armstrong	.04	.02	.01
☐	134 Craig Heyward	.10	.05	.01
☐	135 Joey Browner	.04	.02	.01
☐	136 Darren Comeaux	.04	.02	.01
☐	137 Pat Beach	.04	.02	.01
☐	138 Dalton Hilliard	.04	.02	.01
☐	139 David Treadwell	.04	.02	.01
☐	140 Gary Anderson RB	.04	.02	.01
☐	141 Eugene Robinson	.04	.02	.01
☐	142 Scott Case	.04	.02	.01
☐	143 Paul Farren	.04	.02	.01
☐	144 Gill Fenerty	.04	.02	.01
☐	145 Tim Irwin	.04	.02	.01
☐	146 Norm Johnson	.04	.02	.01
☐	147 Willie Gault	.10	.05	.01
☐	148 Clarence Verdin	.04	.02	.01
☐	149 Jeff Uhlenhake	.04	.02	.01
☐	150 Erik McMillan	.04	.02	.01
☐	151 Kevin Ross	.04	.02	.01
☐	152 Pepper Johnson	.04	.02	.01
☐	153 Bryan Hinkle	.04	.02	.01
☐	154 Gary Clark	.25	.11	.03
☐	155 Robert Delpino	.04	.02	.01
☐	156 Doug Smith	.04	.02	.01
☐	157 Chris Martin	.04	.02	.01
☐	158 Ray Berry	.04	.02	.01
☐	159 Steve Christie	.04	.02	.01
☐	160 Don Smith	.04	.02	.01
☐	161 Greg McMurtry	.04	.02	.01
☐	162 Jack Del Rio	.04	.02	.01
☐	163 Floyd Dixon	.04	.02	.01
☐	164 Buford McGee	.04	.02	.01
☐	165 Brett Maxie	.04	.02	.01
☐	166 Morten Andersen	.04	.02	.01
☐	167 Kent Hull	.04	.02	.01
☐	168 Skip McClendon	.04	.02	.01
☐	169 Keith Sims	.04	.02	.01
☐	170 Leonard Marshall	.04	.02	.01
☐	171 Tony Woods	.04	.02	.01
☐	172 Byron Evans	.04	.02	.01
☐	173 Rob Burnett	.04	.02	.01
☐	174 Tory Epps	.04	.02	.01
☐	175 Toi Cook	.04	.02	.01
☐	176 John Elliott	.04	.02	.01
☐	177 Tommie Agee	.04	.02	.01
☐	178 Keith Van Horne	.04	.02	.01
☐	179 Dennis Smith	.04	.02	.01
☐	180 James Lofton	.10	.05	.01
☐	181 Art Monk	.10	.05	.01
☐	182 Anthony Carter	.10	.05	.01
☐	183 Louis Lipps	.04	.02	.01
☐	184 Bruce Hill	.04	.02	.01
☐	185 Michael Young	.04	.02	.01
☐	186 Eric Green	.04	.02	.01
☐	187 Barney Bussey	.04	.02	.01
☐	188 Curtis Duncan	.04	.02	.01
☐	189 Robert Awalt	.04	.02	.01
☐	190 Johnny Johnson	.04	.02	.01
☐	191 Jeff Cross	.04	.02	.01
☐	192 Keith McKeller	.04	.02	.01
☐	193 Robert Brown	.04	.02	.01
☐	194 Vincent Brown	.04	.02	.01
☐	195 Calvin Williams	.10	.05	.01
☐	196 Sean Jones	.04	.02	.01
☐	197 Willie Drewrey	.04	.02	.01
☐	198 Bubba McDowell	.04	.02	.01
☐	199 Al Noga	.04	.02	.01
☐	200 Ronnie Lott	.10	.05	.01
☐	201 Warren Moon	.25	.11	.03
☐	202 Chris Hinton	.04	.02	.01
☐	203 Jim Sweeney	.04	.02	.01
☐	204 Wayne Haddix	.04	.02	.01
☐	205 Tim Jorden	.04	.02	.01
☐	206 Marvin Allen	.04	.02	.01
☐	207 Jim Morrissey	.04	.02	.01
☐	208 Ben Smith	.04	.02	.01
☐	209 William White	.04	.02	.01
☐	210 Jim C. Jensen	.04	.02	.01
☐	211 Doug Reed	.04	.02	.01
☐	212 Ethan Horton	.04	.02	.01
☐	213 Chris Jacke	.04	.02	.01
☐	214 Johnny Hector	.04	.02	.01
☐	215 Drew Hill UER	.04	.02	.01
	(Tied for the NFC lead,			
	should say AFC)			
☐	216 Roy Green	.04	.02	.01
☐	217 Dean Steinkuhler	.04	.02	.01
☐	218 Cedric Mack	.04	.02	.01
☐	219 Chris Miller	.10	.05	.01
☐	220 Keith Byars	.04	.02	.01
☐	221 Lewis Billups	.04	.02	.01
☐	222 Roger Craig	.10	.05	.01
☐	223 Shaun Gayle	.04	.02	.01
☐	224 Mike Rozier	.04	.02	.01
☐	225 Troy Aikman	1.00	.45	.12
☐	226 Bobby Humphrey	.04	.02	.01
☐	227 Eugene Marve	.04	.02	.01
☐	228 Michael Carter	.04	.02	.01
☐	229 Richard Johnson	.04	.02	.01
☐	230 Billy Joe Tolliver	.04	.02	.01
☐	231 Mark Murphy	.04	.02	.01
☐	232 John L. Williams	.04	.02	.01
☐	233 Ronnie Harmon	.04	.02	.01
☐	234 Thurman Thomas	.25	.11	.03
☐	235 Martin Mayhew	.04	.02	.01
☐	236 Richmond Webb	.04	.02	.01
☐	237 Gerald Riggs UER	.10	.05	.01
	(Earnest Byner mis-			
	spelled as Ernest)			
☐	238 Mike Prior	.04	.02	.01
☐	239 Mike Gann	.04	.02	.01
☐	240 Alvin Walton	.04	.02	.01
☐	241 Tim McGee	.04	.02	.01
☐	242 Bruce Matthews	.10	.05	.01
☐	243 Johnny Holland	.04	.02	.01
☐	244 Martin Bayless	.04	.02	.01
☐	245 Eric Metcalf	.10	.05	.01
☐	246 John Alt	.04	.02	.01
☐	247 Max Montoya	.04	.02	.01
☐	248 Rod Bernstine	.04	.02	.01
☐	249 Paul Gruber	.04	.02	.01
☐	250 Charles Haley	.10	.05	.01
☐	251 Scott Norwood	.04	.02	.01
☐	252 Michael Haddix	.04	.02	.01
☐	253 Ricky Sanders	.04	.02	.01
☐	254 Ervin Randle	.04	.02	.01
☐	255 Duane Bickett	.04	.02	.01
☐	256 Mike Munchak	.04	.02	.01
☐	257 Keith Jones	.04	.02	.01
☐	258 Riki Ellison	.04	.02	.01
☐	259 Vince Newsome	.04	.02	.01
☐	260 Lee Williams	.04	.02	.01
☐	261 Steve Smith	.04	.02	.01
☐	262 Sam Clancy	.04	.02	.01
☐	263 Pierce Holt	.04	.02	.01
☐	264 Jim Harbaugh	.25	.11	.03
☐	265 Dino Hackett	.04	.02	.01
☐	266 Andy Heck	.04	.02	.01
☐	267 Leo Goeas	.04	.02	.01
☐	268 Russ Grimm	.04	.02	.01
☐	269 Gill Byrd	.04	.02	.01
☐	270 Neal Anderson	.10	.05	.01
☐	271 Jackie Slater	.04	.02	.01
☐	272 Joe Nash	.04	.02	.01
☐	273 Todd Bowles	.04	.02	.01
☐	274 D.J. Dozier	.04	.02	.01
☐	275 Kevin Fagan	.04	.02	.01
☐	276 Don Warren	.04	.02	.01
☐	277 Jim Jeffcoat	.04	.02	.01
☐	278 Bruce Smith	.25	.11	.03
☐	279 Cortez Kennedy	.25	.11	.03
☐	280 Thane Gash	.04	.02	.01
☐	281 Perry Kemp	.04	.02	.01
☐	282 John Taylor	.10	.05	.01
☐	283 Stephone Paige	.04	.02	.01
☐	284 Paul Skansi	.04	.02	.01
☐	285 Shawn Collins	.04	.02	.01
☐	286 Mervyn Fernandez	.04	.02	.01
☐	287 Daniel Stubbs	.04	.02	.01
☐	288 Chip Lohmiller	.04	.02	.01
☐	289 Brian Blades	.10	.05	.01
☐	290 Mark Carrier WR	.25	.11	.03
☐	291 Carl Zander	.04	.02	.01
☐	292 David Wyman	.04	.02	.01
☐	293 Jeff Bostic	.04	.02	.01
☐	294 Irv Pankey	.04	.02	.01
☐	295 Keith Millard	.04	.02	.01
☐	296 Jamie Mueller	.04	.02	.01
☐	297 Bill Fralic	.04	.02	.01
☐	298 Wendell Davis	.04	.02	.01
☐	299 Ken Clarke	.04	.02	.01
☐	300 Wymon Henderson	.04	.02	.01
☐	301 Jeff Campbell	.04	.02	.01
☐	302 Cody Carlson	.04	.02	.01
☐	303 Matt Brock	.04	.02	.01
☐	304 Maurice Carthon	.04	.02	.01
☐	305 Scott Mersereau	.04	.02	.01
☐	306 Steve Wright	.04	.02	.01
☐	307 J.B. Brown	.04	.02	.01
☐	308 Ricky Reynolds	.04	.02	.01
☐	309 Darryl Pollard	.04	.02	.01
☐	310 Donald Evans	.04	.02	.01
☐	311 Nick Bell	.04	.02	.01
☐	312 Pat Harlow	.04	.02	.01
☐	313 Dan McGwire	.04	.02	.01
☐	314 Mike Dumas	.04	.02	.01
☐	315 Mike Croel	.04	.02	.01
☐	316 Chris Smith	.04	.02	.01
☐	317 Kenny Walker	.04	.02	.01
☐	318 Todd Lyght	.04	.02	.01
☐	319 Mike Stonebreaker	.04	.02	.01
☐	320 Randall Cunningham 90	.10	.05	.01
☐	321 Terance Mathis 90	.25	.11	.03
☐	322 Gaston Green 90	.04	.02	.01
☐	323 Johnny Bailey 90	.04	.02	.01
☐	324 Donnie Elder 90	.04	.02	.01
☐	325 Dwight Stone 90 UER	.04	.02	.01
	(No '91 copyright			
	on card back)			
☐	326 J.J. Birden 90	.10	.05	.01
☐	327 Alexander Wright 90	.04	.02	.01
☐	328 Eric Metcalf 90	.10	.05	.01
☐	329 Andre Rison TL	.10	.05	.01

☐ 330 Warren Moon TL UER (Not Blanda's record, should be Van Brocklin)	.10	.05	.01
☐ 331 Steve Tasker DT	.04	.02	.01
☐ 332 Mel Gray DT	.10	.05	.01
☐ 333 Nick Lowery DT	.04	.02	.01
☐ 334 Sean Landeta DT	.04	.02	.01
☐ 335 David Fulcher DT	.04	.02	.01
☐ 336 Joey Browner DT	.04	.02	.01
☐ 337 Albert Lewis DT	.04	.02	.01
☐ 338 Rod Woodson DT	.10	.05	.01
☐ 339 Shane Conlan DT	.04	.02	.01
☐ 340 Pepper Johnson DT	.04	.02	.01
☐ 341 Chris Spielman DT	.04	.02	.01
☐ 342 Derrick Thomas DT	.10	.05	.01
☐ 343 Ray Childress DT	.04	.02	.01
☐ 344 Reggie White DT	.10	.05	.01
☐ 345 Bruce Smith DT	.10	.05	.01
☐ 346 Darrell Green	.04	.02	.01
☐ 347 Ray Bentley	.04	.02	.01
☐ 348 Herschel Walker	.10	.05	.01
☐ 349 Rodney Holman	.04	.02	.01
☐ 350 Al Toon	.10	.05	.01
☐ 351 Harry Hamilton	.04	.02	.01
☐ 352 Albert Lewis	.04	.02	.01
☐ 353 Renaldo Turnbull	.04	.02	.01
☐ 354 Junior Seau	.40	.18	.05
☐ 355 Merril Hoge	.04	.02	.01
☐ 356 Shane Conlan	.04	.02	.01
☐ 357 Jay Schroeder	.04	.02	.01
☐ 358 Steve Broussard	.04	.02	.01
☐ 359 Mark Bavaro	.04	.02	.01
☐ 360 Jim Lachey	.04	.02	.01
☐ 361 Greg Townsend	.04	.02	.01
☐ 362 Dave Krieg	.10	.05	.01
☐ 363 Jessie Hester	.04	.02	.01
☐ 364 Steve Tasker	.10	.05	.01
☐ 365 Ron Hall	.04	.02	.01
☐ 366 Pat Leahy	.04	.02	.01
☐ 367 Jim Everett	.10	.05	.01
☐ 368 Felix Wright	.04	.02	.01
☐ 369 Ricky Proehl	.04	.02	.01
☐ 370 Anthony Miller	.10	.05	.01
☐ 371 Keith Jackson	.10	.05	.01
☐ 372 Pete Stoyanovich	.04	.02	.01
☐ 373 Tommy Kane	.04	.02	.01
☐ 374 Richard Johnson	.04	.02	.01
☐ 375 Randall McDaniel	.04	.02	.01
☐ 376 John Stephens	.04	.02	.01
☐ 377 Haywood Jeffires	.10	.05	.01
☐ 378 Rodney Hampton	.25	.11	.03
☐ 379 Tim Grunhard	.04	.02	.01
☐ 380 Jerry Rice	1.00	.45	.12
☐ 381 Ken Harvey	.10	.05	.01
☐ 382 Vaughan Johnson	.04	.02	.01
☐ 383 J.T. Smith	.04	.02	.01
☐ 384 Carnell Lake	.04	.02	.01
☐ 385 Dan Marino	1.50	.70	.19
☐ 386 Kyle Clifton	.04	.02	.01
☐ 387 Wilber Marshall	.04	.02	.01
☐ 388 Pete Holohan	.04	.02	.01
☐ 389 Gary Plummer	.04	.02	.01
☐ 390 William Perry	.10	.05	.01
☐ 391 Mark Robinson	.04	.02	.01
☐ 392 Nate Odomes	.04	.02	.01
☐ 393 Ickey Woods	.04	.02	.01
☐ 394 Reyna Thompson	.04	.02	.01
☐ 395 Deion Sanders	.60	.25	.07
☐ 396 Harris Barton	.04	.02	.01
☐ 397 Sammie Smith	.04	.02	.01
☐ 398 Vinny Testaverde	.10	.05	.01
☐ 399 Ray Donaldson	.04	.02	.01
☐ 400 Tim McKyer	.04	.02	.01
☐ 401 Nesby Glasgow	.04	.02	.01
☐ 402 Brent Williams	.04	.02	.01
☐ 403 Rob Moore	.25	.11	.03
☐ 404 Bubby Brister	.04	.02	.01
☐ 405 David Fulcher	.04	.02	.01
☐ 406 Reggie Cobb	.04	.02	.01
☐ 407 Jerome Brown	.04	.02	.01
☐ 408 Erik Howard	.04	.02	.01
☐ 409 Tony Paige	.04	.02	.01
☐ 410 John Elway	.75	.35	.09
☐ 411 Charles Mann	.04	.02	.01
☐ 412 Luis Sharpe	.04	.02	.01
☐ 413 Hassan Jones	.04	.02	.01
☐ 414 Frank Minnifield	.04	.02	.01
☐ 415 Steve DeBerg	.04	.02	.01
☐ 416 Mark Carrier DB	.10	.05	.01
☐ 417 Brian Jordan	.10	.05	.01
☐ 418 Reggie Langhorne	.04	.02	.01
☐ 419 Don Majkowski	.04	.02	.01
☐ 420 Marcus Allen	.25	.11	.03
☐ 421 Michael Brooks	.04	.02	.01
☐ 422 Vai Sikahema	.04	.02	.01
☐ 423 Dermontti Dawson	.04	.02	.01
☐ 424 Jacob Green	.04	.02	.01
☐ 425 Flipper Anderson	.04	.02	.01
☐ 426 Bill Brooks	.04	.02	.01
☐ 427 Keith McCants	.04	.02	.01
☐ 428 Ken O'Brien	.04	.02	.01
☐ 429 Fred Barnett	.25	.11	.03
☐ 430 Mark Duper	.10	.05	.01
☐ 431 Mark Kelso	.04	.02	.01
☐ 432 Leslie O'Neal	.10	.05	.01

☐ 433 Ottis Anderson	.10	.05	.01
☐ 434 Jesse Sapolu	.04	.02	.01
☐ 435 Gary Zimmerman	.04	.02	.01
☐ 436 Kevin Porter	.04	.02	.01
☐ 437 Anthony Thompson	.04	.02	.01
☐ 438 Robert Clark	.04	.02	.01
☐ 439 Chris Warren	.40	.18	.05
☐ 440 Gerald Williams	.04	.02	.01
☐ 441 Jim Skow	.04	.02	.01
☐ 442 Rick Donnelly	.04	.02	.01
☐ 443 Guy McIntyre	.04	.02	.01
☐ 444 Jeff Lageman	.04	.02	.01
☐ 445 John Offerdahl	.04	.02	.01
☐ 446 Clyde Simmons	.04	.02	.01
☐ 447 John Kidd	.04	.02	.01
☐ 448 Chip Banks	.04	.02	.01
☐ 449 Johnny Meads	.04	.02	.01
☐ 450 Rickey Jackson	.04	.02	.01
☐ 451 Lee Johnson	.04	.02	.01
☐ 452 Michael Irvin	.25	.11	.03
☐ 453 Leon Seals	.04	.02	.01
☐ 454 Darrell Thompson	.04	.02	.01
☐ 455 Everson Walls	.04	.02	.01
☐ 456 LeRoy Butler	.10	.05	.01
☐ 457 Marcus Dupree	.04	.02	.01
☐ 458 Kirk Lowdermilk	.04	.02	.01
☐ 459 Chris Singleton	.04	.02	.01
☐ 460 Seth Joyner	.10	.05	.01
☐ 461 Rueben Mayes UER (Hayes in bio should be Heyward)	.04	.02	.01
☐ 462 Ernie Jones	.04	.02	.01
☐ 463 Greg Kragen	.04	.02	.01
☐ 464 Bennie Blades	.04	.02	.01
☐ 465 Mark Bortz	.04	.02	.01
☐ 466 Tony Stargell	.04	.02	.01
☐ 467 Mike Cofer	.04	.02	.01
☐ 468 Randy Grimes	.04	.02	.01
☐ 469 Tim Worley	.04	.02	.01
☐ 470 Kevin Mack	.04	.02	.01
☐ 471 Wes Hopkins	.04	.02	.01
☐ 472 Will Wolford	.04	.02	.01
☐ 473 Sam Seale	.04	.02	.01
☐ 474 Jim Ritcher	.04	.02	.01
☐ 475 Jeff Hostetler	.25	.11	.03
☐ 476 Mitchell Price	.04	.02	.01
☐ 477 Ken Lanier	.04	.02	.01
☐ 478 Naz Worthen	.04	.02	.01
☐ 479 Ed Reynolds	.04	.02	.01
☐ 480 Mark Clayton	.10	.05	.01
☐ 481 Matt Bahr	.04	.02	.01
☐ 482 Gary Reasons	.04	.02	.01
☐ 483 David Szott	.04	.02	.01
☐ 484 Barry Foster	.10	.05	.01
☐ 485 Bruce Reimers	.04	.02	.01
☐ 486 Dean Biasucci	.04	.02	.01
☐ 487 Cris Carter	.25	.11	.03
☐ 488 Albert Bentley	.04	.02	.01
☐ 489 Robert Massey	.04	.02	.01
☐ 490 Al Smith	.04	.02	.01
☐ 491 Greg Lloyd	.25	.11	.03
☐ 492 Steve McMichael UER (Photo on back actually Dan Hampton)	.10	.05	.01
☐ 493 Jeff Wright	.04	.02	.01
☐ 494 Scott Davis	.04	.02	.01
☐ 495 Freeman McNeil	.04	.02	.01
☐ 496 Simon Fletcher	.04	.02	.01
☐ 497 Terry McDaniel	.04	.02	.01
☐ 498 Heath Sherman	.04	.02	.01
☐ 499 Jeff Jaeger	.04	.02	.01
☐ 500 Mark Collins	.04	.02	.01
☐ 501 Tim Goad	.04	.02	.01
☐ 502 Jeff George	.25	.11	.03
☐ 503 Jimmie Jones	.04	.02	.01
☐ 504 Henry Thomas	.04	.02	.01
☐ 505 Steve Young	.75	.35	.09
☐ 506 William Roberts	.04	.02	.01
☐ 507 Neil Smith	.25	.11	.03
☐ 508 Mike Saxon	.04	.02	.01
☐ 509 Johnny Bailey	.04	.02	.01
☐ 510 Broderick Thomas	.04	.02	.01
☐ 511 Wade Wilson	.10	.05	.01
☐ 512 Hart Lee Dykes	.04	.02	.01
☐ 513 Hardy Nickerson	.10	.05	.01
☐ 514 Tim McDonald	.04	.02	.01
☐ 515 Frank Cornish	.04	.02	.01
☐ 516 Jarvis Williams	.04	.02	.01
☐ 517 Carl Lee	.04	.02	.01
☐ 518 Carl Banks	.04	.02	.01
☐ 519 Mike Golic	.04	.02	.01
☐ 520 Brian Noble	.04	.02	.01
☐ 521 James Hasty	.04	.02	.01
☐ 522 Bubba Paris	.04	.02	.01
☐ 523 Kevin Walker	.04	.02	.01
☐ 524 William Fuller	.10	.05	.01
☐ 525 Eddie Anderson	.04	.02	.01
☐ 526 Roger Ruzek	.04	.02	.01
☐ 527 Robert Blackmon	.04	.02	.01
☐ 528 Vince Buck	.04	.02	.01
☐ 529 Lawrence Taylor	.25	.11	.03
☐ 530 Reggie Roby	.04	.02	.01
☐ 531 Doug Riesenberg	.04	.02	.01
☐ 532 Joe Jacoby	.04	.02	.01
☐ 533 Kirby Jackson	.04	.02	.01

☐ 534 Robb Thomas	.04	.02	.01
☐ 535 Don Griffin	.04	.02	.01
☐ 536 Andre Waters	.04	.02	.01
☐ 537 Marc Logan	.04	.02	.01
☐ 538 James Thornton	.04	.02	.01
☐ 539 Ray Agnew	.04	.02	.01
☐ 540 Frank Stams	.04	.02	.01
☐ 541 Brett Perriman	.25	.11	.03
☐ 542 Andre Ware	.10	.05	.01
☐ 543 Kevin Haverdink	.04	.02	.01
☐ 544 Greg Jackson	.04	.02	.01
☐ 545 Tunch Ilkin	.04	.02	.01
☐ 546 Dexter Carter	.04	.02	.01
☐ 547 Rod Woodson	.25	.11	.03
☐ 548 Donnell Woolford	.04	.02	.01
☐ 549 Mark Boyer	.04	.02	.01
☐ 550 Jeff Query	.04	.02	.01
☐ 551 Burt Grossman	.04	.02	.01
☐ 552 Mike Kenn	.04	.02	.01
☐ 553 Richard Dent	.10	.05	.01
☐ 554 Gaston Green	.04	.02	.01
☐ 555 Phil Simms	.10	.05	.01
☐ 556 Brent Jones	.25	.11	.03
☐ 557 Ronnie Lippett	.04	.02	.01
☐ 558 Mike Horan	.04	.02	.01
☐ 559 Danny Noonan	.04	.02	.01
☐ 560 Reggie White	.25	.11	.03
☐ 561 Rufus Porter	.04	.02	.01
☐ 562 Aaron Wallace	.04	.02	.01
☐ 563 Vance Johnson	.04	.02	.01
☐ 564A Aaron Craver ERR (No copyright line on back)	.04	.02	.01
☐ 564B Aaron Craver COR	.04	.02	.01
☐ 565A Russell Maryland ERR (No copyright line on back)	.25	.11	.03
☐ 565B Russell Maryland COR	.25	.11	.03
☐ 566 Paul Justin	.04	.02	.01
☐ 567 Walter Dean	.04	.02	.01
☐ 568 Herman Moore	2.00	.90	.25
☐ 569 Bill Musgrave	.04	.02	.01
☐ 570 Rob Carpenter	.04	.02	.01
☐ 571 Greg Lewis	.04	.02	.01
☐ 572 Ed King	.04	.02	.01
☐ 573 Ernie Mills	.10	.05	.01
☐ 574 Jake Reed	1.00	.45	.12
☐ 575 Ricky Watters	1.50	.70	.19
☐ 576 Derek Russell	.04	.02	.01
☐ 577 Shawn Moore	.04	.02	.01
☐ 578 Eric Bieniemy	.04	.02	.01
☐ 579 Chris Zorich	.25	.11	.03
☐ 580 Scott Miller	.04	.02	.01
☐ 581 Jarrod Bunch	.04	.02	.01
☐ 582 Ricky Ervins	.10	.05	.01
☐ 583 Browning Nagle	.04	.02	.01
☐ 584 Eric Turner	.10	.05	.01
☐ 585 William Thomas	.04	.02	.01
☐ 586 Stanley Richard	.04	.02	.01
☐ 587 Adrian Cooper	.04	.02	.01
☐ 588 Harvey Williams	.25	.11	.03
☐ 589 Alvin Harper	.25	.11	.03
☐ 590 John Carney	.04	.02	.01
☐ 591 Mark Vander Poel	.04	.02	.01
☐ 592 Mike Pritchard	.25	.11	.03
☐ 593 Eric Moten	.04	.02	.01
☐ 594 Moe Gardner	.04	.02	.01
☐ 595 Wesley Carroll	.04	.02	.01
☐ 596 Eric Swann	.25	.11	.03
☐ 597 Joe Kelly	.04	.02	.01
☐ 598 Steve Jackson	.04	.02	.01
☐ 599 Kelvin Pritchett	.10	.05	.01
☐ 600 Jesse Campbell	.04	.02	.01
☐ 601 Darryll Lewis UER (Name misspelled Darryl)	.10	.05	.01
☐ 602 Howard Griffith	.04	.02	.01
☐ 603 Blaise Bryant	.04	.02	.01
☐ 604 Vinnie Clark	.04	.02	.01
☐ 605 Mel Agee	.04	.02	.01
☐ 606 Bobby Wilson	.04	.02	.01
☐ 607 Kevin Donnalley	.04	.02	.01
☐ 608 Randal Hill	.10	.05	.01
☐ 609 Stan Thomas	.04	.02	.01
☐ 610 Mike Heldt	.04	.02	.01
☐ 611 Brett Favre	4.00	1.80	.50
☐ 612 Lawrence Dawsey UER (Went to Florida State, not Florida)	.10	.05	.01
☐ 613 Dennis Gibson	.04	.02	.01
☐ 614 Dean Dingman	.04	.02	.01
☐ 615 Bruce Pickens	.04	.02	.01
☐ 616 Todd Marinovich	.04	.02	.01
☐ 617 Gene Atkins	.04	.02	.01
☐ 618 Marcus Dupree (Comeback Player)	.04	.02	.01
☐ 619 Warren Moon (Man of the Year)	.10	.05	.01
☐ 620 Joe Montana MVP	.40	.18	.05
☐ 621 Neal Anderson MVP	.04	.02	.01
☐ 622 James Brooks MVP	.10	.05	.01
☐ 623 Thurman Thomas MVP	.10	.05	.01
☐ 624 Bobby Humphrey MVP	.04	.02	.01
☐ 625 Kevin Mack MVP	.04	.02	.01
☐ 626 Mark Carrier WR MVP	.04	.02	.01
☐ 627 Johnny Johnson MVP	.04	.02	.01

☐ 628 Marion Butts MVP	.10	.05	.01
☐ 629 Steve DeBerg MVP	.04	.02	.01
☐ 630 Jeff George MVP	.10	.05	.01
☐ 631 Troy Aikman MVP	.50	.23	.06
☐ 632 Dan Marino MVP	.75	.35	.09
☐ 633 Randall Cunningham MVP	.10	.05	.01
☐ 634 Andre Rison MVP	.10	.05	.01
☐ 635 Pepper Johnson MVP	.04	.02	.01
☐ 636 Pat Leahy MVP	.04	.02	.01
☐ 637 Barry Sanders MVP	.50	.23	.06
☐ 638 Warren Moon MVP	.10	.05	.01
☐ 639 Sterling Sharpe MVP	.04	.02	.01
☐ 640 Bruce Armstrong MVP	.04	.02	.01
☐ 641 Bo Jackson MVP	.10	.05	.01
☐ 642 Henry Ellard MVP	.10	.05	.01
☐ 643 Earnest Byner MVP	.04	.02	.01
☐ 644 Pat Swilling MVP	.04	.02	.01
☐ 645 John L. Williams MVP	.04	.02	.01
☐ 646 Rod Woodson MVP	.10	.05	.01
☐ 647 Chris Doleman MVP	.04	.02	.01
☐ 648 Joey Browner CC	.04	.02	.01
☐ 649 Erik McMillan CC	.04	.02	.01
☐ 650 David Fulcher CC	.04	.02	.01
☐ 651A Ronnie Lott CC ERR (Front 47, back 42)	.10	.05	.01
☐ 651B Ronnie Lott CC COR (Front 47, back 42 is now blacked out)	.10	.05	.01
☐ 652 Louis Oliver CC	.04	.02	.01
☐ 653 Mark Robinson CC	.04	.02	.01
☐ 654 Dennis Smith CC	.04	.02	.01
☐ 655 Reggie White SA	.10	.05	.01
☐ 656 Charles Haley SA	.04	.02	.01
☐ 657 Leslie O'Neal SA	.10	.05	.01
☐ 658 Kevin Greene SA	.10	.05	.01
☐ 659 Dennis Byrd SA	.04	.02	.01
☐ 660 Bruce Smith SA	.10	.05	.01
☐ 661 Derrick Thomas SA	.10	.05	.01
☐ 662 Steve DeBerg TL	.04	.02	.01
☐ 663 Barry Sanders TL	.50	.23	.06
☐ 664 Thurman Thomas TL	.10	.05	.01
☐ 665 Jerry Rice TL	.50	.23	.06
☐ 666 Derrick Thomas TL	.10	.05	.01
☐ 667 Bruce Smith TL	.10	.05	.01
☐ 668 Mark Carrier DB TL	.04	.02	.01
☐ 669 Richard Johnson TL	.04	.02	.01
☐ 670 Jan Stenerud HOF	.04	.02	.01
☐ 671 Stan Jones HOF	.04	.02	.01
☐ 672 John Hannah HOF	.04	.02	.01
☐ 673 Tex Schramm HOF	.04	.02	.01
☐ 674 Earl Campbell HOF	.25	.11	.03
☐ 675 Mark Carrier and Emmitt Smith (Rookies of the Year)	.50	.23	.06
☐ 676 Warren Moon DT	.10	.05	.01
☐ 677 Barry Sanders DT	.50	.23	.06
☐ 678 Thurman Thomas DT	.25	.11	.03
☐ 679 Andre Reed DT	.10	.05	.01
☐ 680 Andre Rison DT	.10	.05	.01
☐ 681 Keith Jackson DT	.04	.02	.01
☐ 682 Bruce Armstrong DT	.04	.02	.01
☐ 683 Jim Lachey DT	.04	.02	.01
☐ 684 Bruce Matthews DT	.04	.02	.01
☐ 685 Mike Munchak DT	.04	.02	.01
☐ 686 Don Mosebar DT	.04	.02	.01
☐ B1 Jeff Hostetler SB	.30	.14	.04
☐ B2 Matt Bahr SB	.06	.03	.01
☐ B3 Ottis Anderson SB	.10	.05	.01
☐ B4 Ottis Anderson SB	.10	.05	.01

1991 Score Dream Team Autographs

This 11-card standard-size set was randomly inserted in second series packs. The odds of receiving them according to Score is not less than 1 in 5,000 packs. These cards are distinguishable from regular Dream Team cards (which carry facsimile autographs on the backs) because the facsimile autographs are replaced by actual player autographs. Players used a variety of inks and some signed on the card fronts. According to Score's press releases only 500 of each player were autographed.

	MINT	NRMT	EXC
COMPLETE SET (11)	850.00	375.00	105.00
COMMON CARD (676-686)	30.00	13.50	3.70
☐ 676 Warren Moon	100.00	45.00	12.50
☐ 677 Barry Sanders	300.00	135.00	38.00
☐ 678 Thurman Thomas	125.00	55.00	15.50
☐ 679 Andre Reed	75.00	34.00	9.50
☐ 680 Andre Rison	75.00	34.00	9.50
☐ 681 Keith Jackson	40.00	18.00	5.00
☐ 682 Bruce Armstrong	30.00	13.50	3.70
☐ 683 Jim Lachey	30.00	13.50	3.70
☐ 684 Bruce Matthews	30.00	13.50	3.70
☐ 685 Mike Munchak	30.00	13.50	3.70
☐ 686 Don Mosebar	30.00	13.50	3.70

1991 Score Hot Rookies

The 1991 Score Hot Rookie 10-card standard-size set was inserted in blister packs. The front design has color action shots of the players (in college uniforms) lifted from their real-life background and superimposed on a hot pink and yellow geometric design. The black borders provide a sharp contrast. The back has a color head shot of the player and a brief player profile.

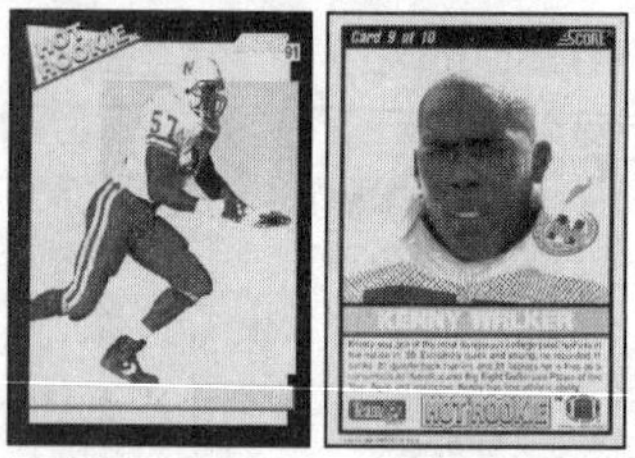

	MINT	NRMT	EXC
COMPLETE SET (10)	12.00	5.50	1.50
COMMON CARD (1-10)	1.25	.55	.16
☐ 1 Dan McGwire	1.25	.55	.16
☐ 2 Todd Lyght	1.50	.70	.19
☐ 3 Mike Dumas	1.25	.55	.16
☐ 4 Pat Harlow	1.25	.55	.16
☐ 5 Nick Bell	1.50	.70	.19
☐ 6 Chris Smith	1.25	.55	.16
☐ 7 Mike Stonebreaker	1.25	.55	.16
☐ 8 Mike Croel	1.50	.70	.19
☐ 9 Kenny Walker	1.25	.55	.16
☐ 10 Rob Carpenter	1.25	.55	.16

1991 Score Supplemental

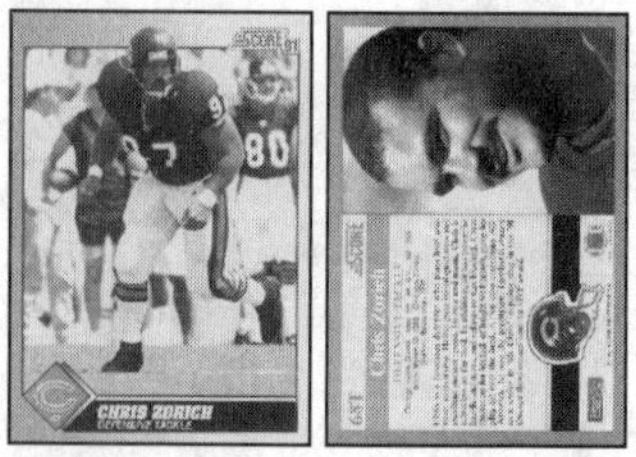

This 110-card standard size set features rookies and players who switched teams during the off-season. The set was issued only as a complete set. The front design is the same as the regular Score issue, but with borders that shade from blue-green to white. Within gold borders, the horizontally oriented backs have player information and a color head shot. The cards are numbered on the back with a "T" suffix. Rookie Cards include Bryan Cox, Merton Hanks, Michael Jackson, Erric Pegram and Leonard Russell.

	MINT	NRMT	EXC
COMPLETE FACT.SET (110)	4.00	1.80	.50
COMMON CARD (1T-110T)	.04	.02	.01
☐ 1T Ronnie Lott	.10	.05	.01
☐ 2T Matt Millen	.10	.05	.01
☐ 3T Tim McKyer	.04	.02	.01
☐ 4T Vince Newsome	.04	.02	.01
☐ 5T Gaston Green	.04	.02	.01
☐ 6T Brett Perriman	.25	.11	.03
☐ 7T Roger Craig	.10	.05	.01
☐ 8T Pete Holohan	.04	.02	.01
☐ 9T Tony Zendejas	.04	.02	.01
☐ 10T Lee Williams	.04	.02	.01
☐ 11T Mike Stonebreaker	.04	.02	.01
☐ 12T Felix Wright	.04	.02	.01
☐ 13T Lonnie Young	.04	.02	.01
☐ 14T Hugh Millen	.04	.02	.01
☐ 15T Roy Green	.04	.02	.01
☐ 16T Greg Davis	.04	.02	.01
☐ 17T Dexter Manley	.04	.02	.01
☐ 18T Ted Washington	.04	.02	.01
☐ 19T Norm Johnson	.04	.02	.01
☐ 20T Joe Morris	.04	.02	.01
☐ 21T Robert Perryman	.04	.02	.01
☐ 22T Mike Iaquaniello UER (Free agent in '91, not '87)	.04	.02	.01
☐ 23T Gerald Perry UER (School should be Southern University A and M)	.04	.02	.01
☐ 24T Zeke Mowatt	.04	.02	.01
☐ 25T Rich Miano	.04	.02	.01
☐ 26T Nick Bell	.04	.02	.01
☐ 27T Terry Orr	.04	.02	.01
☐ 28T Matt Stover	.10	.05	.01
☐ 29T Bubba Paris	.04	.02	.01
☐ 30T Ron Brown	.04	.02	.01
☐ 31T Don Davey	.04	.02	.01
☐ 32T Lee Rouson	.04	.02	.01
☐ 33T Terry Hoage UER (Eagles, sic)	.04	.02	.01
☐ 34T Tony Covington	.04	.02	.01
☐ 35T John Rienstra	.04	.02	.01
☐ 36T Charles Dimry	.04	.02	.01
☐ 37T Todd Marinovich	.04	.02	.01
☐ 38T Winston Moss	.04	.02	.01
☐ 39T Vestee Jackson	.04	.02	.01
☐ 40T Brian Hansen	.04	.02	.01
☐ 41T Irv Eatman	.04	.02	.01
☐ 42T Jarrod Bunch	.04	.02	.01
☐ 43T Kanavis McGhee	.04	.02	.01
☐ 44T Vai Sikahema	.04	.02	.01
☐ 45T Charles McRae	.04	.02	.01
☐ 46T Quinn Early	.10	.05	.01
☐ 47T Jeff Faulkner	.04	.02	.01
☐ 48T William Frizzell	.04	.02	.01
☐ 49T John Booty	.04	.02	.01
☐ 50T Tim Harris	.04	.02	.01
☐ 51T Derek Russell	.04	.02	.01
☐ 52T John Flannery	.04	.02	.01
☐ 53T Tim Barnett	.04	.02	.01
☐ 54T Alfred Williams	.04	.02	.01
☐ 55T Dan McGwire	.04	.02	.01
☐ 56T Ernie Mills	.04	.02	.01
☐ 57T Stanley Richard	.04	.02	.01
☐ 58T Huey Richardson	.04	.02	.01
☐ 59T Jerome Henderson	.04	.02	.01
☐ 60T Bryan Cox	.25	.11	.03
☐ 61T Russell Maryland	.10	.05	.01
☐ 62T Reginald Jones	.04	.02	.01
☐ 63T Mo Lewis	.10	.05	.01
☐ 64T Moe Gardner	.04	.02	.01
☐ 65T Wesley Carroll	.04	.02	.01
☐ 66T Michael Jackson	.25	.11	.03
☐ 67T Shawn Jefferson	.10	.05	.01
☐ 68T Chris Zorich	.10	.05	.01
☐ 69T Kenny Walker	.04	.02	.01
☐ 70T Erric Pegram	.25	.11	.03
☐ 71T Alvin Harper	.25	.11	.03
☐ 72T Harry Colon	.04	.02	.01
☐ 73T Scott Miller	.04	.02	.01
☐ 74T Lawrence Dawsey	.10	.05	.01
☐ 75T Phil Hansen	.04	.02	.01
☐ 76T Roman Phifer	.04	.02	.01
☐ 77T Greg Lewis	.04	.02	.01
☐ 78T Merton Hanks	.25	.11	.03
☐ 79T James Jones	.04	.02	.01
☐ 80T Vinnie Clark	.04	.02	.01
☐ 81T R.J. Kors	.04	.02	.01
☐ 82T Mike Pritchard	.25	.11	.03
☐ 83T Stan Thomas	.04	.02	.01
☐ 84T Lamar Rogers	.04	.02	.01
☐ 85T Erik Williams	.10	.05	.01
☐ 86T Keith Traylor	.04	.02	.01
☐ 87T Mike Dumas	.04	.02	.01
☐ 88T Mel Agee	.04	.02	.01
☐ 89T Harvey Williams	.25	.11	.03
☐ 90T Todd Lyght	.04	.02	.01
☐ 91T Jake Reed	.60	.25	.07
☐ 92T Pat Harlow	.04	.02	.01
☐ 93T Antone Davis	.04	.02	.01
☐ 94T Aeneas Williams	.25	.11	.03
☐ 95T Eric Bieniemy	.04	.02	.01
☐ 96T John Kasay	.10	.05	.01
☐ 97T Robert Wilson	.04	.02	.01
☐ 98T Ricky Ervins	.10	.05	.01
☐ 99T Mike Croel	.04	.02	.01
☐ 100T David Lang	.04	.02	.01
☐ 101T Esera Tuaolo	.04	.02	.01
☐ 102T Randal Hill	.10	.05	.01
☐ 103T Jon Vaughn	.04	.02	.01
☐ 104T Dave McCloughan	.04	.02	.01
☐ 105T David Daniels	.04	.02	.01
☐ 106T Eric Moten	.04	.02	.01
☐ 107T Anthony Morgan	.04	.02	.01
☐ 108T Ed King	.04	.02	.01
☐ 109T Leonard Russell	.10	.05	.01
☐ 110T Aaron Craver	.04	.02	.01

1991 Score National 10

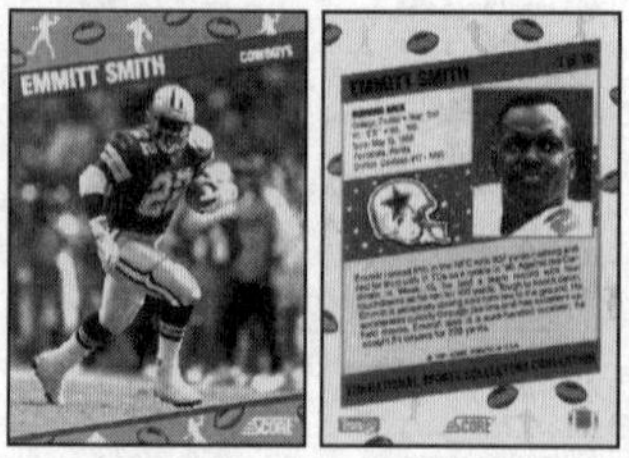

This set contains ten standard-size cards. The front design is distinctively colorful at the top and bottom of the obverse. In the middle of the back the cards are labeled as 12th National Sports Collectors Convention. The cards were given away as a complete set wrapped in its own cello wrapper.

	MINT	NRMT	EXC
COMPLETE SET (10)	8.00	3.60	1.00
COMMON CARD (1-10)	.50	.23	.06
☐ 1 Emmitt Smith	4.00	1.80	.50
☐ 2 Mark Carrier DB	.75	.35	.09
☐ 3 Steve Broussard	.50	.23	.06
☐ 4 Johnny Johnson	.50	.23	.06
☐ 5 Steve Christie	.50	.23	.06
☐ 6 Richmond Webb	.50	.23	.06
☐ 7 James Francis	.50	.23	.06
☐ 8 Jeff George	1.00	.45	.12
☐ 9 Rodney Hampton	1.25	.55	.16
☐ 10 Calvin Williams	.75	.35	.09

1991 Score Young Superstars

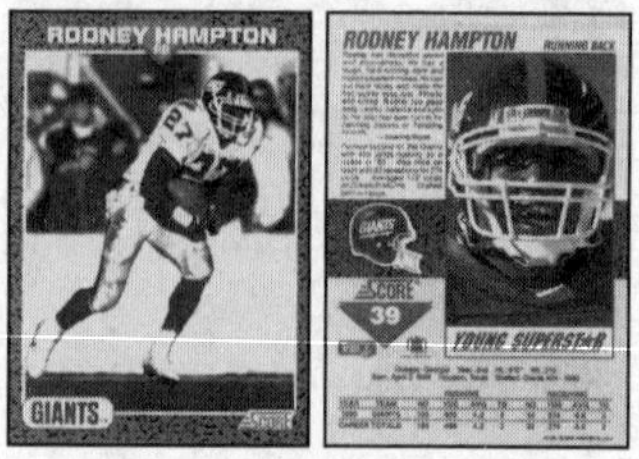

This 40-card standard-size set features some of the leading young players in football. The key player in the set is Emmitt Smith. The front has a color action player photo, with a white border on a purple and black background. The player's name appears in yellow lettering above the picture, while the team name is given in the lower left corner. The back has a color head shot, a scouting report, career summary, biography, and statistics. The predominant color on the back is yellow, and the card number appears in a red triangle. This set was available from a mail-away offer on 1991 Score Football wax packs.

	MINT	NRMT	EXC
COMPLETE SET (40)	5.00	2.20	.60
COMMON CARD (1-40)	.05	.02	.01
☐ 1 Johnny Bailey	.05	.02	.01
☐ 2 Johnny Johnson	.05	.02	.01
☐ 3 Fred Barnett	.20	.09	.03
☐ 4 Keith McCants	.05	.02	.01
☐ 5 Brad Baxter	.05	.02	.01
☐ 6 Dan Owens	.05	.02	.01
☐ 7 Steve Broussard	.05	.02	.01
☐ 8 Ricky Proehl	.10	.05	.01
☐ 9 Marion Butts	.10	.05	.01
☐ 10 Reggie Cobb	.05	.02	.01
☐ 11 Dennis Byrd	.10	.05	.01
☐ 12 Emmitt Smith	3.50	1.55	.45
☐ 13 Mark Carrier DB	.10	.05	.01
☐ 14 Keith Sims	.05	.02	.01
☐ 15 Dexter Carter	.05	.02	.01
☐ 16 Chris Singleton	.05	.02	.01
☐ 17 Steve Christie	.10	.05	.01
☐ 18 Frank Cornish	.05	.02	.01
☐ 19 Timm Rosenbach	.05	.02	.01
☐ 20 Sammie Smith	.05	.02	.01
☐ 21 Calvin Williams UER (Listed as WR on front, but back says FB)	.10	.05	.01
☐ 22 Merril Hoge	.05	.02	.01
☐ 23 Hart Lee Dykes	.05	.02	.01
☐ 24 Darrell Thompson	.05	.02	.01
☐ 25 James Francis	.10	.05	.01
☐ 26 John Elliott	.05	.02	.01
☐ 27 Jeff George	.30	.14	.04
☐ 28 Broderick Thomas	.05	.02	.01
☐ 29 Eric Green	.10	.05	.01
☐ 30 Steve Walsh	.10	.05	.01
☐ 31 Harold Green	.10	.05	.01
☐ 32 Andre Ware	.10	.05	.01
☐ 33 Richmond Webb	.05	.02	.01
☐ 34 Junior Seau	.50	.23	.06
☐ 35 Tim Grunhard	.05	.02	.01
☐ 36 Tim Worley	.05	.02	.01
☐ 37 Haywood Jeffires	.10	.05	.01
☐ 38 Rod Woodson	.20	.09	.03
☐ 39 Rodney Hampton	.50	.23	.06
☐ 40 David Szott	.05	.02	.01

1992 Score

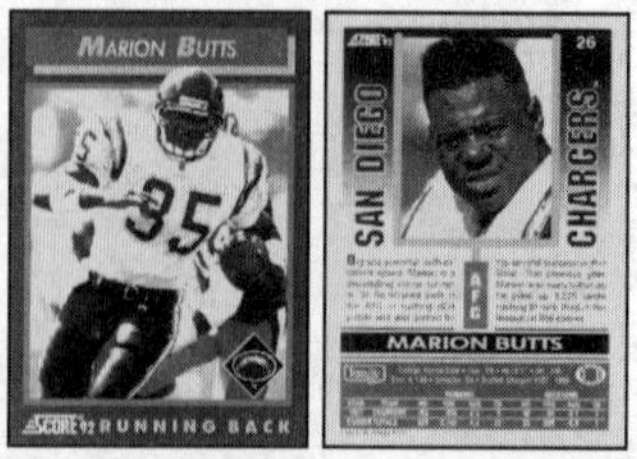

The 1992 Score football set contains 550 standard-size cards. Cards were issued in 16 and 35-card packs. The fronts display color action player photos enclosed by a solid colored border. The player's name appears in a green stripe at the top, while his position is printed in the bottom dark blue border. The backs have a close-up photo (with goal posts serving as the borders) and player profile; biography and statistics (1991 and career) appear in a green box at the card bottom. Topical subsets featured include Draft Pick (476-514), Crunch Crew (515-519), Rookie of the Year (520-523), Little Big Men (524-528), Sack Attack (529-533), Hall of Fame (535-537), and 90 Plus Club (538-547). Rookie Cards include Edgar Bennett, Steve Bono, Terrell Buckley, Amp Lee, Derrick Moore, Michael Timpson and Tommy Vardell.

	MINT	NRMT	EXC
COMPLETE SET (550)	25.00	11.00	3.10
COMMON CARD (1-550)	.08	.04	.01
☐ 1 Barry Sanders	2.00	.90	.25
☐ 2 Pat Swilling	.15	.07	.02
☐ 3 Moe Gardner	.08	.04	.01
☐ 4 Steve Young	.75	.35	.09
☐ 5 Chris Spielman	.15	.07	.02
☐ 6 Richard Dent	.15	.07	.02
☐ 7 Anthony Munoz	.15	.07	.02
☐ 8 Martin Mayhew	.08	.04	.01
☐ 9 Terry McDaniel	.08	.04	.01
☐ 10 Thurman Thomas	.30	.14	.04
☐ 11 Ricky Sanders	.08	.04	.01
☐ 12 Steve Atwater	.08	.04	.01
☐ 13 Tony Tolbert	.08	.04	.01
☐ 14 Vince Workman	.15	.07	.02
☐ 15 Haywood Jeffires	.15	.07	.02
☐ 16 Duane Bickett	.08	.04	.01
☐ 17 Jeff Uhlenhake	.08	.04	.01
☐ 18 Tim McDonald	.08	.04	.01
☐ 19 Cris Carter	.30	.14	.04
☐ 20 Derrick Thomas	.30	.14	.04
☐ 21 Hugh Millen	.08	.04	.01
☐ 22 Bart Oates	.08	.04	.01
☐ 23 Eugene Robinson	.08	.04	.01
☐ 24 Jerrol Williams	.08	.04	.01
☐ 25 Reggie White	.30	.14	.04
☐ 26 Marion Butts	.08	.04	.01
☐ 27 Jim Sweeney	.08	.04	.01
☐ 28 Tom Newberry	.08	.04	.01
☐ 29 Pete Stoyanovich	.08	.04	.01
☐ 30 Ronnie Lott	.15	.07	.02
☐ 31 Simon Fletcher	.08	.04	.01
☐ 32 Dino Hackett	.08	.04	.01
☐ 33 Morten Andersen	.08	.04	.01
☐ 34 Clyde Simmons	.08	.04	.01
☐ 35 Mark Rypien	.08	.04	.01
☐ 36 Greg Montgomery	.08	.04	.01
☐ 37 Nate Lewis	.08	.04	.01
☐ 38 Henry Ellard	.15	.07	.02
☐ 39 Luis Sharpe	.08	.04	.01
☐ 40 Michael Irvin	.30	.14	.04
☐ 41 Louis Lipps	.08	.04	.01
☐ 42 John L. Williams	.08	.04	.01
☐ 43 Broderick Thomas	.08	.04	.01
☐ 44 Michael Haynes	.15	.07	.02
☐ 45 Don Majkowski	.08	.04	.01
☐ 46 William Perry	.15	.07	.02
☐ 47 David Fulcher	.08	.04	.01
☐ 48 Tony Bennett	.08	.04	.01
☐ 49 Clay Matthews	.15	.07	.02
☐ 50 Warren Moon	.30	.14	.04
☐ 51 Bruce Armstrong	.08	.04	.01
☐ 52 Harry Newsome	.08	.04	.01
☐ 53 Bill Brooks	.08	.04	.01
☐ 54 Greg Townsend	.08	.04	.01
☐ 55 Tom Rathman	.08	.04	.01
☐ 56 Sean Landeta	.08	.04	.01
☐ 57 Kyle Clifton	.08	.04	.01
☐ 58 Steve Broussard	.08	.04	.01
☐ 59 Mark Carrier WR	.15	.07	.02
☐ 60 Mel Gray	.15	.07	.02
☐ 61 Tim Krumrie	.08	.04	.01
☐ 62 Rufus Porter	.08	.04	.01
☐ 63 Kevin Mack	.08	.04	.01
☐ 64 Todd Bowles	.08	.04	.01
☐ 65 Emmitt Smith	3.00	1.35	.35
☐ 66 Mike Croel	.08	.04	.01
☐ 67 Brian Mitchell	.15	.07	.02
☐ 68 Bennie Blades	.08	.04	.01
☐ 69 Carnell Lake	.08	.04	.01
☐ 70 Cornelius Bennett	.15	.07	.02
☐ 71 Darrell Thompson	.08	.04	.01
☐ 72 Wes Hopkins	.08	.04	.01
☐ 73 Jessie Hester	.08	.04	.01
☐ 74 Irv Eatman	.08	.04	.01
☐ 75 Marv Cook	.08	.04	.01
☐ 76 Tim Brown	.30	.14	.04
☐ 77 Pepper Johnson	.08	.04	.01
☐ 78 Mark Duper	.08	.04	.01
☐ 79 Robert Delpino	.08	.04	.01
☐ 80 Charles Mann	.08	.04	.01
☐ 81 Brian Jordan	.15	.07	.02
☐ 82 Wendell Davis	.08	.04	.01
☐ 83 Lee Johnson	.08	.04	.01
☐ 84 Ricky Reynolds	.08	.04	.01
☐ 85 Vaughan Johnson	.08	.04	.01
☐ 86 Brian Blades	.15	.07	.02
☐ 87 Sam Seale	.08	.04	.01
☐ 88 Ed King	.08	.04	.01
☐ 89 Gaston Green	.08	.04	.01
☐ 90 Christian Okoye	.08	.04	.01
☐ 91 Chris Jacke	.08	.04	.01
☐ 92 Rohn Stark	.08	.04	.01
☐ 93 Kevin Greene	.30	.14	.04
☐ 94 Jay Novacek	.15	.07	.02
☐ 95 Chip Lohmiller	.08	.04	.01
☐ 96 Cris Dishman	.08	.04	.01
☐ 97 Ethan Horton	.08	.04	.01
☐ 98 Pat Harlow	.08	.04	.01
☐ 99 Mark Ingram	.08	.04	.01
☐ 100 Mark Carrier DB	.08	.04	.01
☐ 101 Deron Cherry	.08	.04	.01
☐ 102 Sam Mills	.08	.04	.01
☐ 103 Mark Higgs	.08	.04	.01
☐ 104 Keith Jackson	.15	.07	.02
☐ 105 Steve Tasker	.15	.07	.02

☐ 106 Ken Harvey	.08	.04	.01
☐ 107 Bryan Hinkle	.08	.04	.01
☐ 108 Anthony Carter	.15	.07	.02
☐ 109 Johnny Hector	.08	.04	.01
☐ 110 Randall McDaniel	.08	.04	.01
☐ 111 Johnny Johnson	.08	.04	.01
☐ 112 Shane Conlan	.08	.04	.01
☐ 113 Ray Horton	.08	.04	.01
☐ 114 Sterling Sharpe	.30	.14	.04
☐ 115 Guy McIntyre	.08	.04	.01
☐ 116 Tom Waddle	.08	.04	.01
☐ 117 Albert Lewis	.08	.04	.01
☐ 118 Riki Ellison	.08	.04	.01
☐ 119 Chris Doleman	.08	.04	.01
☐ 120 Andre Rison	.15	.07	.02
☐ 121 Bobby Hebert	.08	.04	.01
☐ 122 Dan Owens	.08	.04	.01
☐ 123 Rodney Hampton	.30	.14	.04
☐ 124 Ron Holmes	.08	.04	.01
☐ 125 Ernie Jones	.08	.04	.01
☐ 126 Michael Carter	.08	.04	.01
☐ 127 Reggie Cobb	.08	.04	.01
☐ 128 Esera Tuaolo	.08	.04	.01
☐ 129 Wilber Marshall	.08	.04	.01
☐ 130 Mike Munchak	.08	.04	.01
☐ 131 Cortez Kennedy	.15	.07	.02
☐ 132 Lamar Lathon	.08	.04	.01
☐ 133 Todd Lyght	.08	.04	.01
☐ 134 Jeff Feagles	.08	.04	.01
☐ 135 Burt Grossman	.08	.04	.01
☐ 136 Mike Cofer	.08	.04	.01
☐ 137 Frank Warren	.08	.04	.01
☐ 138 Jarvis Williams	.08	.04	.01
☐ 139 Eddie Brown	.08	.04	.01
☐ 140 John Elliott	.08	.04	.01
☐ 141 Jim Everett	.15	.07	.02
☐ 142 Hardy Nickerson	.15	.07	.02
☐ 143 Eddie Murray	.08	.04	.01
☐ 144 Andre Tippett	.08	.04	.01
☐ 145 Heath Sherman	.08	.04	.01
☐ 146 Ronnie Harmon	.08	.04	.01
☐ 147 Eric Metcalf	.15	.07	.02
☐ 148 Tony Martin	.30	.14	.04
☐ 149 Chris Burkett	.08	.04	.01
☐ 150 Andre Waters	.08	.04	.01
☐ 151 Ray Donaldson	.08	.04	.01
☐ 152 Paul Gruber	.08	.04	.01
☐ 153 Chris Singleton	.08	.04	.01
☐ 154 Clarence Kay	.08	.04	.01
☐ 155 Ernest Givins	.15	.07	.02
☐ 156 Eric Hill	.08	.04	.01
☐ 157 Jesse Sapolu	.08	.04	.01
☐ 158 Jack Del Rio	.08	.04	.01
☐ 159 Eric Pegram	.15	.07	.02
☐ 160 Joey Browner	.08	.04	.01
☐ 161 Marcus Allen	.30	.14	.04
☐ 162 Eric Moten	.08	.04	.01
☐ 163 Donnell Thompson	.08	.04	.01
☐ 164 Chuck Cecil	.08	.04	.01
☐ 165 Matt Millen	.15	.07	.02
☐ 166 Barry Foster	.15	.07	.02
☐ 167 Kent Hull	.08	.04	.01
☐ 168 Tony Jones	.08	.04	.01
☐ 169 Mike Prior	.08	.04	.01
☐ 170 Neal Anderson	.08	.04	.01
☐ 171 Roger Craig	.15	.07	.02
☐ 172 Felix Wright	.08	.04	.01
☐ 173 James Francis	.08	.04	.01
☐ 174 Eugene Lockhart	.08	.04	.01
☐ 175 Dalton Hilliard	.08	.04	.01
☐ 176 Nick Lowery	.08	.04	.01
☐ 177 Tim McKyer	.08	.04	.01
☐ 178 Lorenzo White	.08	.04	.01
☐ 179 Jeff Hostetler	.15	.07	.02
☐ 180 Jackie Harris	.15	.07	.02
☐ 181 Ken Norton	.30	.14	.04
☐ 182 Flipper Anderson	.08	.04	.01
☐ 183 Don Warren	.08	.04	.01
☐ 184 Brad Baxter	.08	.04	.01
☐ 185 John Taylor	.15	.07	.02
☐ 186 Harold Green	.08	.04	.01
☐ 187 James Washington	.08	.04	.01
☐ 188 Aaron Craver	.08	.04	.01
☐ 189 Mike Merriweather	.08	.04	.01
☐ 190 Gary Clark	.30	.14	.04
☐ 191 Vince Buck	.08	.04	.01
☐ 192 Cleveland Gary	.08	.04	.01
☐ 193 Dan Saleaumua	.08	.04	.01
☐ 194 Gary Zimmerman	.08	.04	.01
☐ 195 Richmond Webb	.08	.04	.01
☐ 196 Gary Plummer	.08	.04	.01
☐ 197 Willie Green	.08	.04	.01
☐ 198 Chris Warren	.30	.14	.04
☐ 199 Mike Pritchard	.15	.07	.02
☐ 200 Art Monk	.15	.07	.02
☐ 201 Matt Stover	.08	.04	.01
☐ 202 Tim Grunhard	.08	.04	.01
☐ 203 Mervyn Fernandez	.08	.04	.01
☐ 204 Mark Jackson	.08	.04	.01
☐ 205 Freddie Joe Nunn	.08	.04	.01
☐ 206 Stan Thomas	.08	.04	.01
☐ 207 Keith McKeller	.08	.04	.01
☐ 208 Jeff Lageman	.08	.04	.01
☐ 209 Kenny Walker	.08	.04	.01
☐ 210 Dave Krieg	.15	.07	.02
☐ 211 Dean Biasucci	.08	.04	.01
☐ 212 Herman Moore	1.25	.55	.16
☐ 213 Jon Vaughn	.08	.04	.01
☐ 214 Howard Cross	.08	.04	.01
☐ 215 Greg Davis	.08	.04	.01
☐ 216 Bubby Brister	.08	.04	.01
☐ 217 John Kasay	.08	.04	.01
☐ 218 Ron Hall	.08	.04	.01
☐ 219 Mo Lewis	.08	.04	.01
☐ 220 Eric Green	.08	.04	.01
☐ 221 Scott Case	.08	.04	.01
☐ 222 Sean Jones	.15	.07	.02
☐ 223 Winston Moss	.08	.04	.01
☐ 224 Reggie Langhorne	.08	.04	.01
☐ 225 Greg Lewis	.08	.04	.01
☐ 226 Todd McNair	.08	.04	.01
☐ 227 Rod Bernstine	.08	.04	.01
☐ 228 Joe Jacoby	.08	.04	.01
☐ 229 Brad Muster	.08	.04	.01
☐ 230 Nick Bell	.08	.04	.01
☐ 231 Terry Allen	.75	.35	.09
☐ 232 Cliff Odom	.08	.04	.01
☐ 233 Brian Hansen	.08	.04	.01
☐ 234 William Fuller	.15	.07	.02
☐ 235 Issiac Holt	.08	.04	.01
☐ 236 Dexter Carter	.08	.04	.01
☐ 237 Gene Atkins	.08	.04	.01
☐ 238 Pat Beach	.08	.04	.01
☐ 239 Tim McGee	.08	.04	.01
☐ 240 Dermontti Dawson	.08	.04	.01
☐ 241 Dan Fike	.08	.04	.01
☐ 242 Don Beebe	.08	.04	.01
☐ 243 Jeff Bostic	.08	.04	.01
☐ 244 Mark Collins	.08	.04	.01
☐ 245 Steve Sewell	.08	.04	.01
☐ 246 Steve Walsh	.08	.04	.01
☐ 247 Erik Kramer	.15	.07	.02
☐ 248 Scott Norwood	.08	.04	.01
☐ 249 Jesse Solomon	.08	.04	.01
☐ 250 Jerry Ball	.08	.04	.01
☐ 251 Eugene Daniel	.08	.04	.01
☐ 252 Michael Stewart	.08	.04	.01
☐ 253 Fred Barnett	.30	.14	.04
☐ 254 Rodney Holman	.08	.04	.01
☐ 255 Stephen Baker	.08	.04	.01
☐ 256 Don Griffin	.08	.04	.01
☐ 257 Will Wolford	.08	.04	.01
☐ 258 Perry Kemp	.08	.04	.01
☐ 259 Leonard Russell	.15	.07	.02
☐ 260 Jeff Gossett	.08	.04	.01
☐ 261 Dwayne Harper	.08	.04	.01
☐ 262 Vinny Testaverde	.15	.07	.02
☐ 263 Maurice Hurst	.08	.04	.01
☐ 264 Tony Casillas	.08	.04	.01
☐ 265 Louis Oliver	.08	.04	.01
☐ 266 Jim Morrissey	.08	.04	.01
☐ 267 Kenneth Davis	.08	.04	.01
☐ 268 John Alt	.08	.04	.01
☐ 269 Michael Zordich	.08	.04	.01
☐ 270 Brian Brennan	.08	.04	.01
☐ 271 Greg Kragen	.08	.04	.01
☐ 272 Andre Collins	.08	.04	.01
☐ 273 Dave Meggett	.15	.07	.02
☐ 274 Scott Fulhage	.08	.04	.01
☐ 275 Tony Zendejas	.08	.04	.01
☐ 276 Herschel Walker	.15	.07	.02
☐ 277 Keith Henderson	.08	.04	.01
☐ 278 Johnny Bailey	.08	.04	.01
☐ 279 Vince Newsome	.08	.04	.01
☐ 280 Chris Hinton	.08	.04	.01
☐ 281 Robert Blackmon	.08	.04	.01
☐ 282 James Hasty	.08	.04	.01
☐ 283 John Offerdahl	.08	.04	.01
☐ 284 Wesley Carroll	.08	.04	.01
☐ 285 Lomas Brown	.08	.04	.01
☐ 286 Neil O'Donnell	.30	.14	.04
☐ 287 Kevin Porter	.08	.04	.01
☐ 288 Lionel Washington	.08	.04	.01
☐ 289 Carlton Bailey	.15	.07	.02
☐ 290 Leonard Marshall	.08	.04	.01
☐ 291 John Carney	.08	.04	.01
☐ 292 Bubba McDowell	.08	.04	.01
☐ 293 Nate Newton	.15	.07	.02
☐ 294 Dave Waymer	.08	.04	.01
☐ 295 Rob Moore	.15	.07	.02
☐ 296 Earnest Byner	.08	.04	.01
☐ 297 Jason Staurovsky	.08	.04	.01
☐ 298 Keith McCants	.08	.04	.01
☐ 299 Floyd Turner	.08	.04	.01
☐ 300 Steve Jordan	.08	.04	.01
☐ 301 Nate Odomes	.08	.04	.01
☐ 302 Gerald Riggs	.08	.04	.01
☐ 303 Marvin Washington	.08	.04	.01
☐ 304 Anthony Thompson	.08	.04	.01
☐ 305 Steve DeBerg	.08	.04	.01
☐ 306 Jim Harbaugh	.30	.14	.04
☐ 307 Larry Brown DB	.08	.04	.01
☐ 308 Roger Ruzek	.08	.04	.01
☐ 309 Jessie Tuggle	.08	.04	.01
☐ 310 Al Smith	.08	.04	.01
☐ 311 Mark Kelso	.08	.04	.01
☐ 312 Lawrence Dawsey	.15	.07	.02
☐ 313 Steve Bono	.40	.18	.05
☐ 314 Greg Lloyd	.30	.14	.04
☐ 315 Steve Wisniewski	.08	.04	.01
☐ 316 Gill Fenerty	.08	.04	.01
☐ 317 Mark Stepnoski	.15	.07	.02
☐ 318 Derek Russell	.08	.04	.01
☐ 319 Chris Martin	.08	.04	.01
☐ 320 Shaun Gayle	.08	.04	.01
☐ 321 Bob Golic	.08	.04	.01
☐ 322 Larry Kelm	.08	.04	.01
☐ 323 Mike Brim	.08	.04	.01
☐ 324 Tommy Kane	.08	.04	.01
☐ 325 Mark Schlereth	.08	.04	.01
☐ 326 Ray Childress	.08	.04	.01
☐ 327 Richard Brown	.08	.04	.01
☐ 328 Vincent Brown	.08	.04	.01
☐ 329 Mike Farr UER (Back of card refers to him as Mel)	.08	.04	.01
☐ 330 Eric Swann	.15	.07	.02
☐ 331 Bill Fralic	.08	.04	.01
☐ 332 Rodney Peete	.15	.07	.02
☐ 333 Jerry Gray	.08	.04	.01
☐ 334 Ray Berry	.08	.04	.01
☐ 335 Dennis Smith	.08	.04	.01
☐ 336 Jeff Herrod	.08	.04	.01
☐ 337 Tony Mandarich	.08	.04	.01
☐ 338 Matt Bahr	.08	.04	.01
☐ 339 Mike Saxon	.08	.04	.01
☐ 340 Bruce Matthews	.08	.04	.01
☐ 341 Rickey Jackson	.08	.04	.01
☐ 342 Eric Allen	.08	.04	.01
☐ 343 Lonnie Young	.08	.04	.01
☐ 344 Steve McMichael	.15	.07	.02
☐ 345 Willie Gault	.15	.07	.02
☐ 346 Barry Word	.08	.04	.01
☐ 347 Rich Camarillo	.08	.04	.01
☐ 348 Bill Romanowski	.08	.04	.01
☐ 349 Jim Lachey	.08	.04	.01
☐ 350 Jim Ritcher	.08	.04	.01
☐ 351 Irving Fryar	.15	.07	.02
☐ 352 Gary Anderson K	.08	.04	.01
☐ 353 Henry Rolling	.08	.04	.01
☐ 354 Mark Bortz	.08	.04	.01
☐ 355 Mark Clayton	.15	.07	.02
☐ 356 Keith Woodside	.08	.04	.01
☐ 357 Jonathan Hayes	.08	.04	.01
☐ 358 Derrick Fenner	.08	.04	.01
☐ 359 Keith Byars	.08	.04	.01
☐ 360 Drew Hill	.08	.04	.01
☐ 361 Harris Barton	.08	.04	.01
☐ 362 John Kidd	.08	.04	.01
☐ 363 Aeneas Williams	.15	.07	.02
☐ 364 Brian Washington	.08	.04	.01
☐ 365 John Stephens	.08	.04	.01
☐ 366 Norm Johnson	.08	.04	.01
☐ 367 Darryl Henley	.08	.04	.01
☐ 368 William White	.08	.04	.01
☐ 369 Mark Murphy	.08	.04	.01
☐ 370 Myron Guyton	.08	.04	.01
☐ 371 Leon Seals	.08	.04	.01
☐ 372 Rich Gannon	.08	.04	.01
☐ 373 Toi Cook	.08	.04	.01
☐ 374 Anthony Johnson	.15	.07	.02
☐ 375 Rod Woodson	.30	.14	.04
☐ 376 Alexander Wright	.08	.04	.01
☐ 377 Kevin Butler	.08	.04	.01
☐ 378 Neil Smith	.30	.14	.04
☐ 379 Gary Anderson RB	.08	.04	.01
☐ 380 Reggie Roby	.08	.04	.01
☐ 381 Jeff Bryant	.08	.04	.01
☐ 382 Ray Crockett	.08	.04	.01
☐ 383 Richard Johnson	.08	.04	.01
☐ 384 Hassan Jones	.08	.04	.01
☐ 385 Karl Mecklenburg	.08	.04	.01
☐ 386 Jeff Jaeger	.08	.04	.01
☐ 387 Keith Willis	.08	.04	.01
☐ 388 Phil Simms	.15	.07	.02
☐ 389 Kevin Ross	.08	.04	.01
☐ 390 Chris Miller	.15	.07	.02
☐ 391 Brian Noble	.08	.04	.01
☐ 392 Jamie Dukes	.08	.04	.01
☐ 393 George Jamison	.08	.04	.01
☐ 394 Rickey Dixon	.08	.04	.01
☐ 395 Carl Lee	.08	.04	.01
☐ 396 Jon Hand	.08	.04	.01
☐ 397 Kirby Jackson	.08	.04	.01
☐ 398 Pat Terrell	.08	.04	.01
☐ 399 Howie Long	.15	.07	.02
☐ 400 Michael Young	.08	.04	.01
☐ 401 Keith Sims	.08	.04	.01
☐ 402 Tommy Barnhardt	.08	.04	.01
☐ 403 Greg McMurtry	.08	.04	.01
☐ 404 Keith Van Horne	.08	.04	.01
☐ 405 Seth Joyner	.15	.07	.02
☐ 406 Jim Jeffcoat	.08	.04	.01
☐ 407 Courtney Hall	.08	.04	.01
☐ 408 Tony Covington	.08	.04	.01
☐ 409 Jacob Green	.08	.04	.01
☐ 410 Charles Haley	.15	.07	.02
☐ 411 Darryl Talley	.08	.04	.01
☐ 412 Jeff Cross	.08	.04	.01
☐ 413 John Elway	.75	.35	.09
☐ 414 Donald Evans	.08	.04	.01
☐ 415 Jackie Slater	.08	.04	.01
☐ 416 John Friesz	.15	.07	.02
☐ 417 Anthony Smith	.08	.04	.01
☐ 418 Gill Byrd	.08	.04	.01
☐ 419 Willie Drewrey	.08	.04	.01
☐ 420 Jay Hilgenberg	.08	.04	.01
☐ 421 David Treadwell	.08	.04	.01
☐ 422 Curtis Duncan	.08	.04	.01
☐ 423 Sammie Smith	.08	.04	.01
☐ 424 Henry Thomas	.08	.04	.01
☐ 425 James Lofton	.15	.07	.02
☐ 426 Fred Marion	.08	.04	.01
☐ 427 Bryce Paup	.30	.14	.04
☐ 428 Michael Timpson	.15	.07	.02
☐ 429 Reyna Thompson	.08	.04	.01
☐ 430 Mike Kenn	.08	.04	.01
☐ 431 Bill Maas	.08	.04	.01
☐ 432 Quinn Early	.15	.07	.02
☐ 433 Everson Walls	.08	.04	.01
☐ 434 Jimmie Jones	.08	.04	.01
☐ 435 Dwight Stone	.08	.04	.01
☐ 436 Harry Colon	.08	.04	.01
☐ 437 Don Mosebar	.08	.04	.01
☐ 438 Calvin Williams	.15	.07	.02
☐ 439 Tom Tupa	.08	.04	.01
☐ 440 Darrell Green	.08	.04	.01
☐ 441 Eric Thomas	.08	.04	.01
☐ 442 Terry Wooden	.08	.04	.01
☐ 443 Brett Perriman	.30	.14	.04
☐ 444 Todd Marinovich	.08	.04	.01
☐ 445 Jim Breech	.08	.04	.01
☐ 446 Eddie Anderson	.08	.04	.01
☐ 447 Jay Schroeder	.08	.04	.01
☐ 448 William Roberts	.08	.04	.01
☐ 449 Brad Edwards	.08	.04	.01
☐ 450 Tunch Ilkin	.08	.04	.01
☐ 451 Ivy Joe Hunter	.08	.04	.01
☐ 452 Robert Clark	.08	.04	.01
☐ 453 Tim Barnett	.08	.04	.01
☐ 454 Jarrod Bunch	.08	.04	.01
☐ 455 Tim Harris	.08	.04	.01
☐ 456 James Brooks	.15	.07	.02
☐ 457 Trace Armstrong	.08	.04	.01
☐ 458 Michael Brooks	.08	.04	.01
☐ 459 Andy Heck	.08	.04	.01
☐ 460 Greg Jackson	.08	.04	.01
☐ 461 Vance Johnson	.08	.04	.01
☐ 462 Kirk Lowdermilk	.08	.04	.01
☐ 463 Erik McMillan	.08	.04	.01
☐ 464 Scott Mersereau	.08	.04	.01
☐ 465 Jeff Wright	.08	.04	.01
☐ 466 Mike Tomczak	.08	.04	.01
☐ 467 David Alexander	.08	.04	.01
☐ 468 Bryan Millard	.08	.04	.01
☐ 469 John Randle	.15	.07	.02
☐ 470 Joel Hilgenberg	.08	.04	.01
☐ 471 Bennie Thompson	.08	.04	.01
☐ 472 Freeman McNeil	.08	.04	.01
☐ 473 Terry Orr	.08	.04	.01
☐ 474 Mike Horan	.08	.04	.01
☐ 475 Leroy Hoard	.15	.07	.02
☐ 476 Patrick Rowe DRAFT	.08	.04	.01
☐ 477 Siran Stacy DRAFT	.08	.04	.01
☐ 478 Amp Lee DRAFT	.08	.04	.01
☐ 479 Eddie Blake DRAFT	.08	.04	.01
☐ 480 Joe Bowden DRAFT	.08	.04	.01
☐ 481 Rod Milstead DRAFT	.08	.04	.01
☐ 482 Keith Hamilton DRAFT	.08	.04	.01
☐ 483 Darryl Williams DRAFT	.08	.04	.01
☐ 484 Robert Porcher DRAFT	.15	.07	.02
☐ 485 Ed Cunningham DRAFT	.08	.04	.01
☐ 486 Chris Mims DRAFT	.15	.07	.02
☐ 487 Chris Hakel DRAFT	.08	.04	.01
☐ 488 Jimmy Smith DRAFT	.30	.14	.04
☐ 489 Todd Harrison DRAFT	.08	.04	.01
☐ 490 Edgar Bennett DRAFT	1.25	.55	.16
☐ 491 Dexter McNabb DRAFT	.08	.04	.01
☐ 492 Leon Searcy DRAFT	.15	.07	.02
☐ 493 Tommy Vardell DRAFT	.15	.07	.02
☐ 494 Terrell Buckley DRAFT	.08	.04	.01
☐ 495 Kevin Turner DRAFT	.08	.04	.01
☐ 496 Russ Campbell DRAFT	.08	.04	.01
☐ 497 Torrance Small DRAFT	.15	.07	.02
☐ 498 Nate Turner DRAFT	.08	.04	.01
☐ 499 Cornelius Benton DRAFT	.15	.07	.02
☐ 500 Matt Elliott DRAFT	.08	.04	.01
☐ 501 Robert Stewart DRAFT	.08	.04	.01
☐ 502 Muhammad Shamsid-Deen DRAFT	.08	.04	.01
☐ 503 George Williams DRAFT	.08	.04	.01
☐ 504 Pumpy Tudors DRAFT	.08	.04	.01
☐ 505 Matt LaBounty DRAFT	.08	.04	.01
☐ 506 Darryl Hardy DRAFT	.08	.04	.01
☐ 507 Derrick Moore DRAFT	.15	.07	.02
☐ 508 Willie Clay DRAFT	.08	.04	.01
☐ 509 Bob Whitfield DRAFT	.08	.04	.01
☐ 510 Ricardo McDonald DRAFT	.08	.04	.01
☐ 511 Carlos Huerta DRAFT	.08	.04	.01
☐ 512 Selwyn Jones DRAFT	.08	.04	.01
☐ 513 Steve Gordon DRAFT	.08	.04	.01
☐ 514 Bob Meeks DRAFT	.08	.04	.01
☐ 515 Bennie Blades CC	.08	.04	.01
☐ 516 Andre Waters CC	.08	.04	.01
☐ 517 Bubba McDowell CC	.08	.04	.01
☐ 518 Kevin Porter CC	.08	.04	.01
☐ 519 Carnell Lake CC	.08	.04	.01
☐ 520 Leonard Russell ROY	.15	.07	.02
☐ 521 Mike Croel ROY	.08	.04	.01
☐ 522 Lawrence Dawsey ROY	.08	.04	.01

	MINT	NRMT	EXC
☐ 523 Moe Gardner ROY	.08	.04	.01
☐ 524 Steve Broussard LBM	.08	.04	.01
☐ 525 Dave Meggett LBM	.08	.04	.01
☐ 526 Darrell Green LBM	.08	.04	.01
☐ 527 Tony Jones LBM	.08	.04	.01
☐ 528 Barry Sanders LBM	.50	.23	.06
☐ 529 Pat Swilling SA	.08	.04	.01
☐ 530 Reggie White SA	.15	.07	.02
☐ 531 William Fuller SA	.08	.04	.01
☐ 532 Simon Fletcher SA	.08	.04	.01
☐ 533 Derrick Thomas SA	.15	.07	.02
☐ 534 Mark Rypien MOY	.08	.04	.01
☐ 535 John Mackey HOF	.08	.04	.01
☐ 536 John Riggins HOF	.15	.07	.02
☐ 537 Lem Barney HOF	.08	.04	.01
☐ 538 Shawn McCarthy 90	.08	.04	.01
☐ 539 Al Edwards 90	.08	.04	.01
☐ 540 Alexander Wright 90	.08	.04	.01
☐ 541 Ray Crockett 90	.08	.04	.01
☐ 542 Steve Young 90 and John Taylor 90	.30	.14	.04
☐ 543 Nate Lewis 90	.08	.04	.01
☐ 544 Dexter Carter 90	.08	.04	.01
☐ 545 Reggie Rutland 90	.08	.04	.01
☐ 546 Jon Vaughn 90	.08	.04	.01
☐ 547 Chris Martin 90	.08	.04	.01
☐ 548 Warren Moon HL	.15	.07	.02
☐ 549 Super Bowl Highlights	.08	.04	.01
☐ 550 Robb Thomas	.08	.04	.01

1992 Score Dream Team

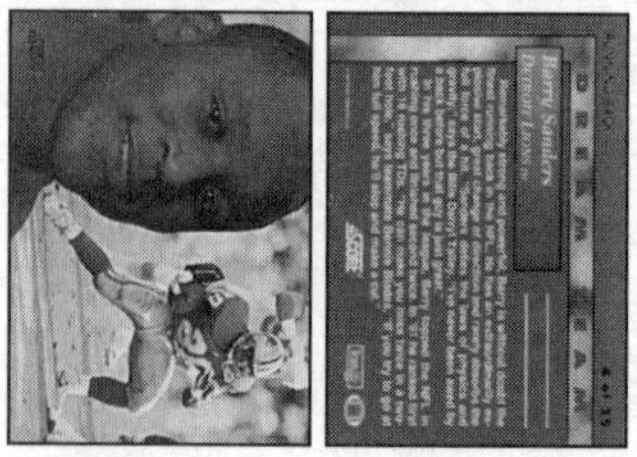

Randomly inserted in 1992 Score foil packs, this 25-card standard-size set pays tribute to some of the NFL's best offensive and defensive players as chosen by Score. The horizontal fronts are full-bleed and display on the left a close-up color head shot and on the right a color player action photo which stands out against a background shot with a yellowish tint. The Score logo is gold-foil stamped at the lower left corner. On the back, a player profile is printed on a background that shades from tan to purple as one moves down the card face.

	MINT	NRMT	EXC
COMPLETE SET (25)	125.00	55.00	15.50
COMMON CARD (1-25)	3.00	1.35	.35
☐ 1 Michael Irvin	8.00	3.60	1.00
☐ 2 Haywood Jeffires	5.00	2.20	.60
☐ 3 Emmitt Smith	40.00	18.00	5.00
☐ 4 Barry Sanders	25.00	11.00	3.10
☐ 5 Marv Cook	3.00	1.35	.35
☐ 6 Bart Oates	3.00	1.35	.35
☐ 7 Steve Wisniewski	3.00	1.35	.35
☐ 8 Randall McDaniel	3.00	1.35	.35
☐ 9 Jim Lachey	3.00	1.35	.35
☐ 10 Lomas Brown	3.00	1.35	.35
☐ 11 Reggie White	8.00	3.60	1.00
☐ 12 Clyde Simmons	3.00	1.35	.35
☐ 13 Jerome Brown	3.00	1.35	.35
☐ 14 Seth Joyner	5.00	2.20	.60
☐ 15 Darryl Talley	3.00	1.35	.35
☐ 16 Karl Mecklenburg	3.00	1.35	.35
☐ 17 Sam Mills	5.00	2.20	.60
☐ 18 Darrell Green	5.00	2.20	.60
☐ 19 Steve Atwater	3.00	1.35	.35
☐ 20 Mark Carrier DB	5.00	2.20	.60
☐ 21 Jeff Gossett UER (Card says Rams, should say Raiders)	3.00	1.35	.35
☐ 22 Chip Lohmiller	3.00	1.35	.35
☐ 23 Mel Gray	5.00	2.20	.60
☐ 24 Steve Tasker	3.00	1.35	.35
☐ 25 Mark Rypien	3.00	1.35	.35

1992 Score Gridiron Stars

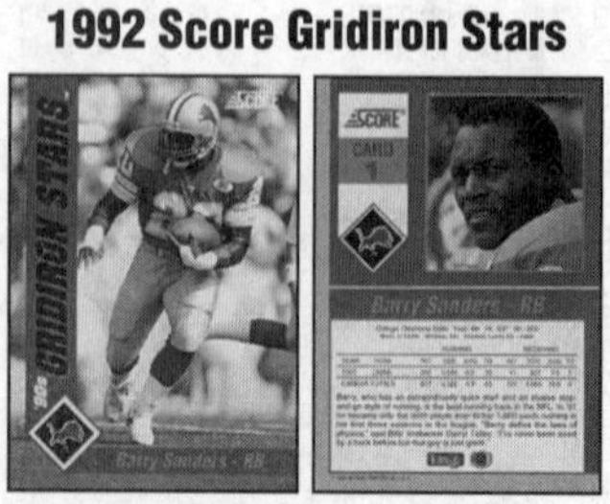

Three of these standard-size cards were inserted in each 1992 Score jumbo pack. The fronts feature full-bleed color action player photos. Team color-coded stripes intersect a diamond carrying the team logo in the lower left corner. The vertical stripe has "Gridiron Stars" gold-foil stamped on it, while the player's name and position are printed in the horizontal stripe. On the backs, the team logo and color close-up photo appear on the top half, while on the bottom half a white panel presents biography, statistics, and player profile.

	MINT	NRMT	EXC
COMPLETE SET (45)	12.00	5.50	1.50
COMMON CARD (1-45)	.25	.11	.03
☐ 1 Barry Sanders	5.00	2.20	.60
☐ 2 Mike Croel	.25	.11	.03
☐ 3 Thurman Thomas	.75	.35	.09
☐ 4 Lawrence Dawsey	.40	.18	.05
☐ 5 Brad Baxter	.25	.11	.03
☐ 6 Moe Gardner	.25	.11	.03
☐ 7 Emmitt Smith	7.00	3.10	.85
☐ 8 Sammie Smith	.25	.11	.03
☐ 9 Rodney Hampton	.75	.35	.09
☐ 10 Mark Carrier DB	.25	.11	.03
☐ 11 Mo Lewis	.40	.18	.05
☐ 12 Andre Rison	.75	.35	.09
☐ 13 Eric Green	.40	.18	.05
☐ 14 Richmond Webb	.25	.11	.03
☐ 15 Johnny Bailey	.25	.11	.03
☐ 16 Mike Pritchard	.40	.18	.05
☐ 17 John Friesz	.25	.11	.03
☐ 18 Leonard Russell	.40	.18	.05
☐ 19 Derrick Thomas	.75	.35	.09
☐ 20 Ken Harvey	.40	.18	.05
☐ 21 Fred Barnett	.40	.18	.05
☐ 22 Aeneas Williams	.40	.18	.05
☐ 23 Marion Butts	.25	.11	.03
☐ 24 Harold Green	.40	.18	.05
☐ 25 Michael Irvin	.75	.35	.09
☐ 26 Dan Owens	.25	.11	.03
☐ 27 Curtis Duncan	.25	.11	.03
☐ 28 Rodney Peete	.40	.18	.05
☐ 29 Brian Blades	.40	.18	.05
☐ 30 Marv Cook	.25	.11	.03
☐ 31 Burt Grossman	.25	.11	.03
☐ 32 Michael Haynes	.40	.18	.05
☐ 33 Bennie Blades	.25	.11	.03
☐ 34 Cornelius Bennett	.40	.18	.05
☐ 35 Louis Oliver	.25	.11	.03
☐ 36 Rod Woodson	.75	.35	.09
☐ 37 Steve Wisniewski	.25	.11	.03
☐ 38 Neil Smith	.40	.18	.05
☐ 39 Gaston Green	.25	.11	.03
☐ 40 Jeff Lageman	.25	.11	.03
☐ 41 Chip Lohmiller	.25	.11	.03
☐ 42 Tim McDonald	.25	.11	.03
☐ 43 John Elliott	.25	.11	.03
☐ 44 Steve Atwater	.25	.11	.03
☐ 45 Flipper Anderson	.25	.11	.03

1992 Score Young Superstars

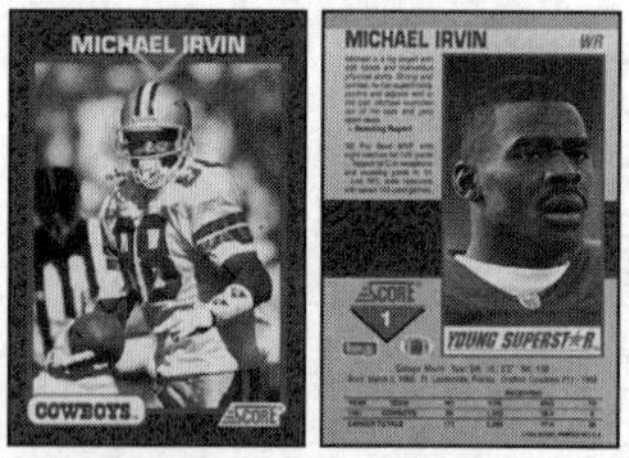

This 40-card boxed standard-size set features some of the young stars in the NFL. The fronts feature glossy color action player photos inside a green inner border and a purple outer border speckled with black. The player's name appears in white lettering at the top, while the team name is printed at the lower left corner. On a gradated yellow background, the backs carry a color close-up photo, a scouting report feature, career highlights, biography, and statistics.

	MINT	NRMT	EXC
COMPLETE SET (40)	4.00	1.80	.50
COMMON CARD (1-40)	.10	.05	.01
☐ 1 Michael Irvin	.50	.23	.06
☐ 2 Cortez Kennedy	.25	.11	.03
☐ 3 Ken Harvey	.15	.07	.02
☐ 4 Bubba McDowell	.10	.05	.01
☐ 5 Mark Higgs	.10	.05	.01
☐ 6 Andre Rison	.40	.18	.05
☐ 7 Lamar Lathon	.10	.05	.01
☐ 8 Bennie Blades	.10	.05	.01
☐ 9 Anthony Johnson	.10	.05	.01
☐ 10 Vince Buck	.10	.05	.01
☐ 11 Pat Harlow	.10	.05	.01
☐ 12 Mike Croel	.10	.05	.01
☐ 13 Myron Guyton	.10	.05	.01
☐ 14 Curtis Duncan	.10	.05	.01
☐ 15 Michael Haynes	.25	.11	.03
☐ 16 Alexander Wright	.10	.05	.01
☐ 17 Greg Lewis	.10	.05	.01
☐ 18 Chip Lohmiller	.10	.05	.01
☐ 19 Nate Lewis	.15	.07	.02
☐ 20 Rodney Peete	.15	.07	.02
☐ 21 Marv Cook	.10	.05	.01
☐ 22 Lawrence Dawsey	.15	.07	.02
☐ 23 Pat Terrell	.10	.05	.01
☐ 24 John Friesz	.15	.07	.02
☐ 25 Tony Bennett	.15	.07	.02
☐ 26 Gaston Green	.10	.05	.01
☐ 27 Kevin Porter	.10	.05	.01
☐ 28 Mike Pritchard	.25	.11	.03
☐ 29 Keith Henderson	.10	.05	.01
☐ 30 Mo Lewis	.10	.05	.01
☐ 31 John Randle	.10	.05	.01
☐ 32 Aeneas Williams	.15	.07	.02
☐ 33 Floyd Turner	.15	.07	.02
☐ 34 Neil Smith	.25	.11	.03
☐ 35 Tom Waddle	.15	.07	.02
☐ 36 Jeff Lageman	.10	.05	.01
☐ 37 Cris Carter	.25	.11	.03
☐ 38 Leonard Russell	.15	.07	.02
☐ 39 Terry McDaniel	.10	.05	.01
☐ 40 Moe Gardner	.10	.05	.01

1993 Score Samples

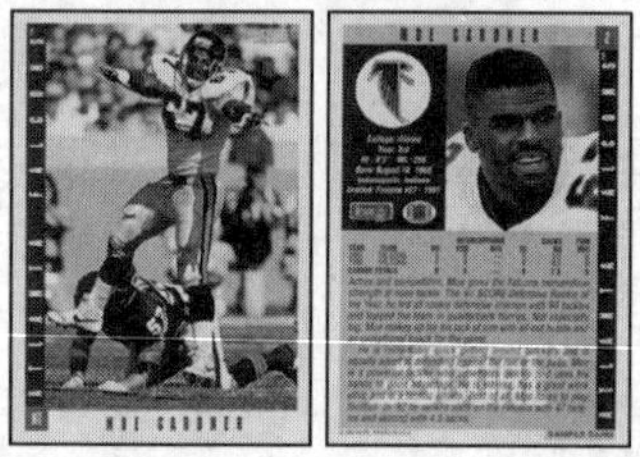

This six-card standard-size set was issued to preview the 1993 Score regular series. The fronts feature color action player photos bordered in white. The player's name appears in the bottom white border, while the team name is printed vertically in a team color-coded bar that edges the left side of the picture. On team color-coded and pastel panels, the backs present a color head shot, biography, statistics, and player profile. These cards are also issued as an uncut sheet. In a short yellow bar at the lower right corner, the cards are marked "sample card."

	MINT	NRMT	EXC
COMPLETE SET (6)	6.00	2.70	.75
COMMON CARD (1-6)	.50	.23	.06
☐ 1 Barry Sanders	3.00	1.35	.35
☐ 2 Moe Gardner	.50	.23	.06
☐ 3 Ricky Watters	1.25	.55	.16
☐ 4 Todd Lyght	.50	.23	.06
☐ 5 Rodney Hampton	.75	.35	.09
☐ 6 Curtis Duncan	.50	.23	.06

1993 Score

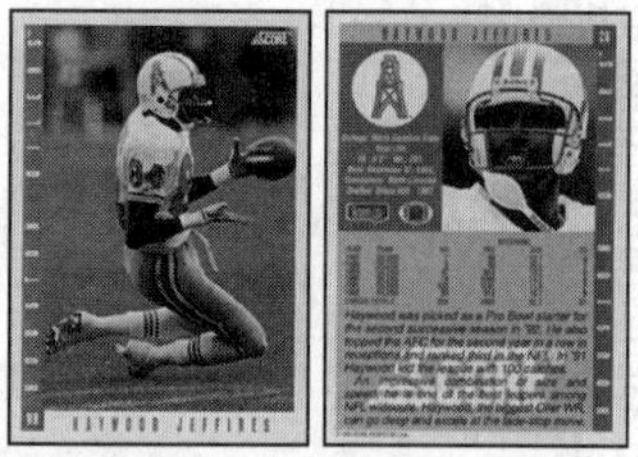

The 1993 Score football set consists of 440 standard-size cards. Cards were issued in 16 and 35-card packs. The fronts have color photos with the player's name at the bottom and tean name in a color stripe running up the right border. The backs have a small color player photo with statistics and highlights. Subsets featured are Rookies (306-315), Super Bowl Highlights (411-412), Double Trouble (413-416), Rookie of the Year (417-420), 90 Plus Club (421-430), Highlights (431-434), and Hall of Fame (436-439). The set concludes with a Man of the Year card (440), honoring Steve Young. Each 16-card pack included one Pinnacle card from a 55-card "Men of Autumn" set not found in regular Pinnacle packs. Dealers could receive one of 3,000 limited-edition autographed Dick Butkus cards for each order of 20 foil boxes. Rookie Cards include Jerome Bettis, Drew Bledsoe, Curtis Conway and Garrison Hearst.

	MINT	NRMT	EXC
COMPLETE SET (440)	16.00	7.25	2.00
COMMON CARD (1-440)	.05	.02	.01
☐ 1 Barry Sanders	1.00	.45	.12
☐ 2 Moe Gardner	.05	.02	.01
☐ 3 Ricky Watters	.25	.11	.03
☐ 4 Todd Lyght	.05	.02	.01
☐ 5 Rodney Hampton	.25	.11	.03
☐ 6 Curtis Duncan	.05	.02	.01
☐ 7 Barry Word	.05	.02	.01
☐ 8 Reggie Cobb	.05	.02	.01
☐ 9 Mike Kenn	.05	.02	.01
☐ 10 Michael Irvin	.25	.11	.03
☐ 11 Bryan Cox	.05	.02	.01
☐ 12 Chris Doleman	.05	.02	.01
☐ 13 Rod Woodson	.25	.11	.03
☐ 14 Emmitt Smith	2.00	.90	.25
☐ 15 Pete Stoyanovich	.05	.02	.01
☐ 16 Steve Young	.75	.35	.09
☐ 17 Randall McDaniel	.05	.02	.01
☐ 18 Cortez Kennedy	.10	.05	.01
☐ 19 Mel Gray	.10	.05	.01
☐ 20 Barry Foster	.10	.05	.01
☐ 21 Tim Brown	.25	.11	.03
☐ 22 Todd McNair	.05	.02	.01
☐ 23 Anthony Johnson	.10	.05	.01
☐ 24 Nate Odomes	.05	.02	.01
☐ 25 Brett Favre	2.00	.90	.25
☐ 26 Jack Del Rio	.05	.02	.01
☐ 27 Terry McDaniel	.05	.02	.01
☐ 28 Haywood Jeffires	.10	.05	.01
☐ 29 Jay Novacek	.10	.05	.01
☐ 30 Wilber Marshall	.05	.02	.01
☐ 31 Richmond Webb	.05	.02	.01
☐ 32 Steve Atwater	.05	.02	.01
☐ 33 James Lofton	.10	.05	.01
☐ 34 Harold Green	.05	.02	.01
☐ 35 Eric Metcalf	.10	.05	.01
☐ 36 Bruce Matthews	.05	.02	.01
☐ 37 Albert Lewis	.05	.02	.01
☐ 38 Jeff Herrod	.05	.02	.01
☐ 39 Vince Workman	.05	.02	.01
☐ 40 John Elway	.75	.35	.09
☐ 41 Brett Perriman	.25	.11	.03
☐ 42 Jon Vaughn	.05	.02	.01
☐ 43 Terry Allen	.25	.11	.03
☐ 44 Clyde Simmons	.05	.02	.01
☐ 45 Bennie Thompson	.05	.02	.01
☐ 46 Wendell Davis	.05	.02	.01
☐ 47 Bobby Hebert	.05	.02	.01
☐ 48 John Offerdahl	.05	.02	.01
☐ 49 Jeff Graham	.10	.05	.01
☐ 50 Steve Wisniewski	.05	.02	.01
☐ 51 Louis Oliver	.05	.02	.01
☐ 52 Rohn Stark	.05	.02	.01
☐ 53 Cleveland Gary	.05	.02	.01
☐ 54 John Randle	.05	.02	.01
☐ 55 Jim Everett	.10	.05	.01
☐ 56 Donnell Woolford	.05	.02	.01
☐ 57 Pepper Johnson	.05	.02	.01
☐ 58 Irving Fryar	.10	.05	.01
☐ 59 Greg Townsend	.05	.02	.01
☐ 60 Chris Burkett	.05	.02	.01
☐ 61 Johnny Johnson	.05	.02	.01
☐ 62 Ronnie Harmon	.05	.02	.01
☐ 63 Don Griffin	.05	.02	.01
☐ 64 Wayne Martin	.05	.02	.01
☐ 65 John L. Williams	.05	.02	.01
☐ 66 Brad Edwards	.05	.02	.01
☐ 67 Toi Cook	.05	.02	.01
☐ 68 Lawrence Dawsey	.05	.02	.01
☐ 69 Johnny Bailey	.05	.02	.01
☐ 70 Mike Brim	.05	.02	.01
☐ 71 Andre Rison	.10	.05	.01
☐ 72 Cornelius Bennett	.10	.05	.01
☐ 73 Brad Muster	.05	.02	.01
☐ 74 Broderick Thomas	.05	.02	.01
☐ 75 Tom Waddle	.05	.02	.01
☐ 76 Paul Gruber	.05	.02	.01
☐ 77 Jackie Harris	.05	.02	.01
☐ 78 Kenneth Davis	.05	.02	.01
☐ 79 Norm Johnson	.05	.02	.01
☐ 80 Jim Jeffcoat	.05	.02	.01
☐ 81 Chris Warren	.10	.05	.01
☐ 82 Greg Kragen	.05	.02	.01
☐ 83 Ricky Reynolds	.05	.02	.01
☐ 84 Hardy Nickerson	.10	.05	.01
☐ 85 Brian Mitchell	.10	.05	.01
☐ 86 Rufus Porter	.05	.02	.01
☐ 87 Greg Jackson	.05	.02	.01
☐ 88 Seth Joyner	.05	.02	.01
☐ 89 Tim Grunhard	.05	.02	.01
☐ 90 Tim Harris	.05	.02	.01
☐ 91 Sterling Sharpe	.25	.11	.03
☐ 92 Daniel Stubbs	.05	.02	.01
☐ 93 Rob Burnett	.05	.02	.01
☐ 94 Rich Camarillo	.05	.02	.01
☐ 95 Al Smith	.05	.02	.01
☐ 96 Thurman Thomas	.25	.11	.03
☐ 97 Morten Andersen	.05	.02	.01
☐ 98 Reggie White	.25	.11	.03
☐ 99 Gill Byrd	.05	.02	.01
☐ 100 Pierce Holt	.05	.02	.01
☐ 101 Tim McGee	.05	.02	.01
☐ 102 Rickey Jackson	.05	.02	.01
☐ 103 Vince Newsome	.05	.02	.01
☐ 104 Chris Spielman	.10	.05	.01
☐ 105 Tim McDonald	.05	.02	.01
☐ 106 James Francis	.05	.02	.01
☐ 107 Andre Tippett	.05	.02	.01
☐ 108 Sam Mills	.05	.02	.01
☐ 109 Hugh Millen	.05	.02	.01
☐ 110 Brad Baxter	.05	.02	.01
☐ 111 Ricky Sanders	.05	.02	.01
☐ 112 Marion Butts	.05	.02	.01
☐ 113 Fred Barnett	.10	.05	.01
☐ 114 Wade Wilson	.05	.02	.01
☐ 115 Dave Meggett	.05	.02	.01
☐ 116 Kevin Greene	.25	.11	.03
☐ 117 Reggie Langhorne	.05	.02	.01
☐ 118 Simon Fletcher	.05	.02	.01
☐ 119 Tommy Vardell	.05	.02	.01
☐ 120 Darion Conner	.05	.02	.01
☐ 121 Darren Lewis	.05	.02	.01
☐ 122 Charles Mann	.05	.02	.01

□ 123 David Fulcher	.05	.02	.01
□ 124 Tommy Kane	.05	.02	.01
□ 125 Richard Brown	.05	.02	.01
□ 126 Nate Lewis	.05	.02	.01
□ 127 Tony Tolbert	.05	.02	.01
□ 128 Greg Lloyd	.25	.11	.03
□ 129 Herman Moore	.75	.35	.09
□ 130 Robert Massey	.05	.02	.01
□ 131 Chris Jacke	.05	.02	.01
□ 132 Keith Byars	.05	.02	.01
□ 133 William Fuller	.05	.02	.01
□ 134 Rob Moore	.10	.05	.01
□ 135 Duane Bickett	.05	.02	.01
□ 136 Jarrod Bunch	.05	.02	.01
□ 137 Ethan Horton	.05	.02	.01
□ 138 Leonard Russell	.10	.05	.01
□ 139 Darryl Henley	.05	.02	.01
□ 140 Tony Bennett	.05	.02	.01
□ 141 Harry Newsome	.05	.02	.01
□ 142 Kelvin Martin	.05	.02	.01
□ 143 Audray McMillian	.05	.02	.01
□ 144 Chip Lohmiller	.05	.02	.01
□ 145 Henry Jones	.05	.02	.01
□ 146 Rod Bernstine	.05	.02	.01
□ 147 Darryl Talley	.05	.02	.01
□ 148 Clarence Verdin	.05	.02	.01
□ 149 Derrick Thomas	.25	.11	.03
□ 150 Raleigh McKenzie	.05	.02	.01
□ 151 Phil Hansen	.05	.02	.01
□ 152 Lin Elliott	.05	.02	.01
□ 153 Chip Banks	.05	.02	.01
□ 154 Shannon Sharpe	.25	.11	.03
□ 155 David Williams	.05	.02	.01
□ 156 Gaston Green	.05	.02	.01
□ 157 Trace Armstrong	.05	.02	.01
□ 158 Todd Scott	.05	.02	.01
□ 159 Stan Humphries	.25	.11	.03
□ 160 Christian Okoye	.05	.02	.01
□ 161 Dennis Smith	.05	.02	.01
□ 162 Derek Kennard	.05	.02	.01
□ 163 Melvin Jenkins	.05	.02	.01
□ 164 Tommy Barnhardt	.05	.02	.01
□ 165 Eugene Robinson	.05	.02	.01
□ 166 Tom Rathman	.05	.02	.01
□ 167 Chris Chandler	.10	.05	.01
□ 168 Steve Broussard	.05	.02	.01
□ 169 Wymon Henderson	.05	.02	.01
□ 170 Bryce Paup	.25	.11	.03
□ 171 Kent Hull	.05	.02	.01
□ 172 Willie Davis	.25	.11	.03
□ 173 Richard Dent	.10	.05	.01
□ 174 Rodney Peete	.05	.02	.01
□ 175 Clay Matthews	.10	.05	.01
□ 176 Erik Williams	.05	.02	.01
□ 177 Mike Cofer	.05	.02	.01
□ 178 Mark Kelso	.05	.02	.01
□ 179 Kurt Gouveia	.05	.02	.01
□ 180 Keith McCants	.05	.02	.01
□ 181 Jim Arnold	.05	.02	.01
□ 182 Sean Jones	.05	.02	.01
□ 183 Chuck Cecil	.05	.02	.01
□ 184 Mark Rypien	.05	.02	.01
□ 185 William Perry	.10	.05	.01
□ 186 Mark Jackson	.05	.02	.01
□ 187 Jim Dombrowski	.05	.02	.01
□ 188 Heath Sherman	.05	.02	.01
□ 189 Bubba McDowell	.05	.02	.01
□ 190 Fuad Reveiz	.05	.02	.01
□ 191 Darren Perry	.05	.02	.01
□ 192 Karl Mecklenburg	.05	.02	.01
□ 193 Frank Reich	.10	.05	.01
□ 194 Tony Casillas	.05	.02	.01
□ 195 Jerry Ball	.05	.02	.01
□ 196 Jessie Hester	.05	.02	.01
□ 197 David Lang	.05	.02	.01
□ 198 Sean Landeta	.05	.02	.01
□ 199 Jerry Gray	.05	.02	.01
□ 200 Mark Higgs	.05	.02	.01
□ 201 Bruce Armstrong	.05	.02	.01
□ 202 Vaughan Johnson	.05	.02	.01
□ 203 Calvin Williams	.10	.05	.01
□ 204 Leonard Marshall	.05	.02	.01
□ 205 Mike Munchak	.05	.02	.01
□ 206 Kevin Ross	.05	.02	.01
□ 207 Daryl Johnston	.25	.11	.03
□ 208 Jay Schroeder	.05	.02	.01
□ 209 Mo Lewis	.05	.02	.01
□ 210 Carlton Haselrig	.05	.02	.01
□ 211 Cris Carter	.25	.11	.03
□ 212 Marv Cook	.05	.02	.01
□ 213 Mark Duper	.05	.02	.01
□ 214 Jackie Slater	.05	.02	.01
□ 215 Mike Prior	.05	.02	.01
□ 216 Warren Moon	.25	.11	.03
□ 217 Mike Saxon	.05	.02	.01
□ 218 Derrick Fenner	.05	.02	.01
□ 219 Brian Washington	.05	.02	.01
□ 220 Jessie Tuggle	.05	.02	.01
□ 221 Jeff Hostetler	.10	.05	.01
□ 222 Deion Sanders	.60	.25	.07
□ 223 Neal Anderson	.05	.02	.01
□ 224 Kevin Mack	.05	.02	.01
□ 225 Tommy Maddox	.05	.02	.01
□ 226 Neil Smith	.25	.11	.03
□ 227 Ronnie Lott	.10	.05	.01
□ 228 Flipper Anderson	.05	.02	.01
□ 229 Keith Jackson	.10	.05	.01
□ 230 Pat Swilling	.05	.02	.01
□ 231 Carl Banks	.05	.02	.01
□ 232 Eric Allen	.05	.02	.01
□ 233 Randal Hill	.05	.02	.01
□ 234 Burt Grossman	.05	.02	.01
□ 235 Jerry Rice	1.00	.45	.12
□ 236 Santana Dotson	.10	.05	.01
□ 237 Andre Reed	.10	.05	.01
□ 238 Troy Aikman	1.00	.45	.12
□ 239 Ray Childress	.05	.02	.01
□ 240 Phil Simms	.10	.05	.01
□ 241 Steve McMichael	.10	.05	.01
□ 242 Browning Nagle	.05	.02	.01
□ 243 Anthony Miller	.10	.05	.01
□ 244 Earnest Byner	.05	.02	.01
□ 245 Jay Hilgenberg	.05	.02	.01
□ 246 Jeff George	.25	.11	.03
□ 247 Marco Coleman	.05	.02	.01
□ 248 Mark Carrier DB	.05	.02	.01
□ 249 Howie Long	.10	.05	.01
□ 250 Ed McCaffrey	.05	.02	.01
□ 251 Jim Kelly	.25	.11	.03
□ 252 Henry Ellard	.10	.05	.01
□ 253 Joe Montana	1.00	.45	.12
□ 254 Dale Carter	.05	.02	.01
□ 255 Boomer Esiason	.10	.05	.01
□ 256 Gary Clark	.10	.05	.01
□ 257 Carl Pickens	.75	.35	.09
□ 258 Dave Krieg	.10	.05	.01
□ 259 Russell Maryland	.05	.02	.01
□ 260 Randall Cunningham	.10	.05	.01
□ 261 Leslie O'Neal	.10	.05	.01
□ 262 Vinny Testaverde	.10	.05	.01
□ 263 Ricky Ervins	.05	.02	.01
□ 264 Chris Mims	.05	.02	.01
□ 265 Dan Marino	2.00	.90	.25
□ 266 Eric Martin	.05	.02	.01
□ 267 Bruce Smith	.25	.11	.03
□ 268 Jim Harbaugh	.25	.11	.03
□ 269 Steve Emtman	.05	.02	.01
□ 270 Ricky Proehl	.05	.02	.01
□ 271 Vaughn Dunbar	.05	.02	.01
□ 272 Junior Seau	.25	.11	.03
□ 273 Sean Gilbert	.10	.05	.01
□ 274 Jim Lachey	.05	.02	.01
□ 275 Dalton Hilliard	.05	.02	.01
□ 276 David Klingler	.05	.02	.01
□ 277 Robert Jones	.05	.02	.01
□ 278 David Treadwell	.05	.02	.01
□ 279 Tracy Scroggins	.05	.02	.01
□ 280 Terrell Buckley	.05	.02	.01
□ 281 Quentin Coryatt	.10	.05	.01
□ 282 Jason Hanson	.05	.02	.01
□ 283 Shane Conlan	.05	.02	.01
□ 284 Guy McIntyre	.05	.02	.01
□ 285 Gary Zimmerman	.05	.02	.01
□ 286 Marty Carter	.05	.02	.01
□ 287 Jim Sweeney	.05	.02	.01
□ 288 Arthur Marshall	.05	.02	.01
□ 289 Eugene Chung	.05	.02	.01
□ 290 Mike Pritchard	.10	.05	.01
□ 291 Jim Ritcher	.05	.02	.01
□ 292 Todd Marinovich	.05	.02	.01
□ 293 Courtney Hall	.05	.02	.01
□ 294 Mark Collins	.05	.02	.01
□ 295 Troy Auzenne	.05	.02	.01
□ 296 Aeneas Williams	.05	.02	.01
□ 297 Andy Heck	.05	.02	.01
□ 298 Shaun Gayle	.05	.02	.01
□ 299 Kevin Fagan	.05	.02	.01
□ 300 Carnell Lake	.05	.02	.01
□ 301 Bernie Kosar	.10	.05	.01
□ 302 Maurice Hurst	.05	.02	.01
□ 303 Mike Merriweather	.05	.02	.01
□ 304 Reggie Roby	.05	.02	.01
□ 305 Darryl Williams	.05	.02	.01
□ 306 Jerome Bettis	1.50	.70	.19
□ 307 Curtis Conway	.75	.35	.09
□ 308 Drew Bledsoe	3.00	1.35	.35
□ 309 John Copeland	.10	.05	.01
□ 310 Eric Curry	.05	.02	.01
□ 311 Lincoln Kennedy	.05	.02	.01
□ 312 Dan Williams	.05	.02	.01
□ 313 Patrick Bates	.05	.02	.01
□ 314 Tom Carter	.10	.05	.01
□ 315 Garrison Hearst	1.25	.55	.16
□ 316 Joel Hilgenberg	.05	.02	.01
□ 317 Harris Barton	.05	.02	.01
□ 318 Jeff Lageman	.05	.02	.01
□ 319 Charles Mincy	.05	.02	.01
□ 320 Ricardo McDonald	.05	.02	.01
□ 321 Lorenzo White	.05	.02	.01
□ 322 Troy Vincent	.05	.02	.01
□ 323 Bennie Blades	.05	.02	.01
□ 324 Dana Hall	.05	.02	.01
□ 325 Ken Norton Jr.	.10	.05	.01
□ 326 Will Wolford	.05	.02	.01
□ 327 Neil O'Donnell	.25	.11	.03
□ 328 Tracy Simien	.05	.02	.01
□ 329 Darrell Green	.05	.02	.01
□ 330 Kyle Clifton	.05	.02	.01
□ 331 Elbert Shelley	.05	.02	.01
□ 332 Jeff Wright	.05	.02	.01
□ 333 Mike Johnson	.05	.02	.01
□ 334 John Gesek	.05	.02	.01
□ 335 Michael Brooks	.05	.02	.01
□ 336 George Jamison	.05	.02	.01
□ 337 Johnny Holland	.05	.02	.01
□ 338 Lamar Lathon	.05	.02	.01
□ 339 Bern Brostek	.05	.02	.01
□ 340 Steve Jordan	.05	.02	.01
□ 341 Gene Atkins	.05	.02	.01
□ 342 Aaron Wallace	.05	.02	.01
□ 343 Adrian Cooper	.05	.02	.01
□ 344 Amp Lee	.05	.02	.01
□ 345 Vincent Brown	.05	.02	.01
□ 346 James Hasty	.05	.02	.01
□ 347 Ron Hall	.05	.02	.01
□ 348 Matt Elliott	.05	.02	.01
□ 349 Tim Krumrie	.05	.02	.01
□ 350 Mark Stepnoski	.05	.02	.01
□ 351 Matt Stover	.05	.02	.01
□ 352 James Washington	.05	.02	.01
□ 353 Marc Spindler	.05	.02	.01
□ 354 Frank Warren	.05	.02	.01
□ 355 Vai Sikahema	.05	.02	.01
□ 356 Dan Saleaumua	.05	.02	.01
□ 357 Mark Clayton	.05	.02	.01
□ 358 Brent Jones	.10	.05	.01
□ 359 Andy Harmon	.10	.05	.01
□ 360 Anthony Parker	.05	.02	.01
□ 361 Chris Hinton	.05	.02	.01
□ 362 Greg Montgomery	.05	.02	.01
□ 363 Greg McMurtry	.05	.02	.01
□ 364 Craig Heyward	.10	.05	.01
□ 365 D.J. Johnson	.05	.02	.01
□ 366 Bill Romanowski	.05	.02	.01
□ 367 Steve Christie	.05	.02	.01
□ 368 Art Monk	.10	.05	.01
□ 369 Howard Ballard	.05	.02	.01
□ 370 Andre Collins	.05	.02	.01
□ 371 Alvin Harper	.10	.05	.01
□ 372 Blaise Winter	.05	.02	.01
□ 373 Al Del Greco	.05	.02	.01
□ 374 Eric Green	.05	.02	.01
□ 375 Chris Mohr	.05	.02	.01
□ 376 Tom Newberry	.05	.02	.01
□ 377 Cris Dishman	.05	.02	.01
□ 378 Jumpy Geathers	.05	.02	.01
□ 379 Don Mosebar	.05	.02	.01
□ 380 Andre Ware	.05	.02	.01
□ 381 Marvin Washington	.05	.02	.01
□ 382 Bobby Humphrey	.05	.02	.01
□ 383 Marc Logan	.05	.02	.01
□ 384 Lomas Brown	.05	.02	.01
□ 385 Steve Tasker	.10	.05	.01
□ 386 Chris Miller	.10	.05	.01
□ 387 Tony Paige	.05	.02	.01
□ 388 Charles Haley	.10	.05	.01
□ 389 Rich Moran	.05	.02	.01
□ 390 Mike Sherrard	.05	.02	.01
□ 391 Nick Lowery	.05	.02	.01
□ 392 Henry Thomas	.05	.02	.01
□ 393 Keith Sims	.05	.02	.01
□ 394 Thomas Everett	.05	.02	.01
□ 395 Steve Wallace	.05	.02	.01
□ 396 John Carney	.05	.02	.01
□ 397 Tim Johnson	.05	.02	.01
□ 398 Jeff Gossett	.05	.02	.01
□ 399 Anthony Smith	.05	.02	.01
□ 400 Kelvin Pritchett	.05	.02	.01
□ 401 Dermontti Dawson	.05	.02	.01
□ 402 Alfred Williams	.05	.02	.01
□ 403 Michael Haynes	.10	.05	.01
□ 404 Bart Oates	.05	.02	.01
□ 405 Ken Lanier	.05	.02	.01
□ 406 Vencie Glenn	.05	.02	.01
□ 407 John Taylor	.10	.05	.01
□ 408 Nate Newton	.10	.05	.01
□ 409 Mark Carrier WR	.10	.05	.01
□ 410 Ken Harvey	.05	.02	.01
□ 411 Troy Aikman SB	.50	.23	.06
□ 412 Charles Haley SB	.05	.02	.01
□ 413 Warren Moon DT Haywood Jeffires	.10	.05	.01
□ 414 Henry Jones DT Mark Kelso	.05	.02	.01
□ 415 Rickey Jackson DT Sam Mills	.05	.02	.01
□ 416 Clyde Simmons DT Reggie White	.05	.02	.01
□ 417 Dale Carter ROY	.05	.02	.01
□ 418 Carl Pickens ROY	.40	.18	.05
□ 419 Vaughn Dunbar ROY	.05	.02	.01
□ 420 Santana Dotson ROY	.05	.02	.01
□ 421 Steve Emtman 90	.05	.02	.01
□ 422 Louis Oliver 90	.05	.02	.01
□ 423 Carl Pickens 90	.40	.18	.05
□ 424 Eddie Anderson 90	.05	.02	.01
□ 425 Deion Sanders 90	.30	.14	.04
□ 426 Jon Vaughn 90	.05	.02	.01
□ 427 Darren Lewis 90	.05	.02	.01
□ 428 Kevin Ross 90	.05	.02	.01
□ 429 David Brandon 90	.05	.02	.01
□ 430 Dave Meggett 90	.05	.02	.01
□ 431 Jerry Rice HL	.50	.23	.06
□ 432 Sterling Sharpe HL	.10	.05	.01
□ 433 Art Monk HL	.05	.02	.01
□ 434 James Lofton HL	.05	.02	.01
□ 435 Lawrence Taylor	.10	.05	.01
□ 436 Bill Walsh HOF	.10	.05	.01
□ 437 Chuck Noll HOF	.10	.05	.01
□ 438 Dan Fouts HOF	.05	.02	.01
□ 439 Larry Little HOF	.05	.02	.01
□ 440 Steve Young MOY	.40	.18	.05
□ NNO Dick Butkus AUTO/3000	30.00	13.50	3.70

1993 Score Dream Team

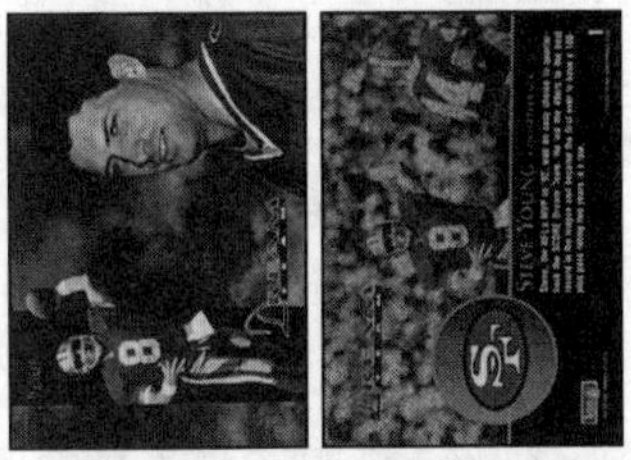

Issued one per 1993 Score 35-card jumbo packs, this 26-card standard-size set features the best offensive (1-13) and defensive (14-26) players by position as selected by Score. On a background consisting of a cloudy sky with a dark brown tint, the horizontal fronts have a color player cut-out emerging out of a black stripe on the left portion while the right portion displays a close-up color player cut-out. On the backs, the upper portion displays a larger, fuzzy version of the same player cut-out on the front left portion. The lower portion is a thick black stripe featuring a brief player profile. The team logo in a circle straddles the two portions.

	MINT	NRMT	EXC
COMPLETE SET (26)	25.00	11.00	3.10
COMMON CARD (1-26)	.60	.25	.07
□ 1 Steve Young	5.00	2.20	.60
□ 2 Emmitt Smith	12.00	5.50	1.50
□ 3 Barry Foster	.75	.35	.09
□ 4 Sterling Sharpe	1.25	.55	.16
□ 5 Jerry Rice	6.00	2.70	.75
□ 6 Keith Jackson	.75	.35	.09
□ 7 Steve Wallace	.60	.25	.07
□ 8 Richmond Webb	.60	.25	.07
□ 9 Guy McIntyre	.60	.25	.07
□ 10 Carlton Haselrig	.60	.25	.07
□ 11 Bruce Matthews	.60	.25	.07
□ 12 Morten Andersen	.60	.25	.07
□ 13 Rich Camarillo	.60	.25	.07
□ 14 Deion Sanders	4.00	1.80	.50
□ 15 Steve Tasker	.75	.35	.09
□ 16 Clyde Simmons	.75	.35	.09
□ 17 Reggie White	1.25	.55	.16
□ 18 Cortez Kennedy	.75	.35	.09
□ 19 Rod Woodson	1.25	.55	.16
□ 20 Terry McDaniel	.60	.25	.07
□ 21 Chuck Cecil	.60	.25	.07
□ 22 Steve Atwater	.60	.25	.07
□ 23 Bryan Cox	.60	.25	.07
□ 24 Derrick Thomas	1.25	.55	.16
□ 25 Wilber Marshall	.60	.25	.07
□ 26 Sam Mills	.75	.35	.09

1993 Score Franchise

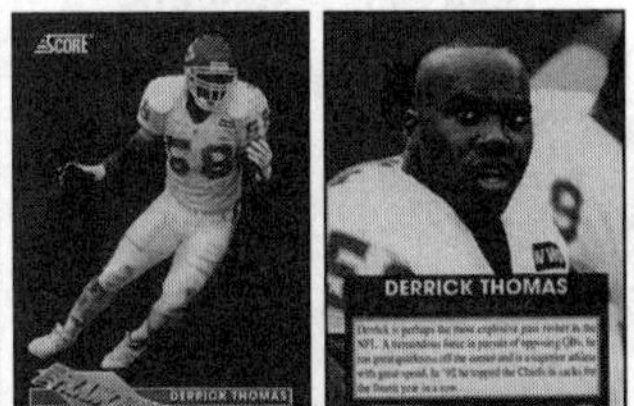

Randomly inserted in 1993 Score foil packs at a rate of approximately one in 24, this 28-card standard-size set features a top player from each NFL team. Fronts feature a player photo that stands out from a dark shaded background. The background contain a greyscaled player photo. Backs have a small write-up and a close-up shot of the player. The cards are arranged in alphabetical order by team.

	MINT	NRMT	EXC
COMPLETE SET (28)	175.00	80.00	22.00
COMMON CARD (1-28)	2.50	1.10	.30
□ 1 Andre Rison	4.00	1.80	.50
□ 2 Thurman Thomas	6.00	2.70	.75
□ 3 Richard Dent	2.50	1.10	.30
□ 4 Harold Green	2.50	1.10	.30
□ 5 Eric Metcalf	4.00	1.80	.50
□ 6 Emmitt Smith	40.00	18.00	5.00
□ 7 John Elway	20.00	9.00	2.50
□ 8 Barry Sanders	25.00	11.00	3.10
□ 9 Sterling Sharpe	6.00	2.70	.75
□ 10 Warren Moon	4.00	1.80	.50
□ 11 Jeff Herrod	2.50	1.10	.30
□ 12 Derrick Thomas	6.00	2.70	.75
□ 13 Steve Wisniewski	2.50	1.10	.30

☐ 14 Cleveland Gary	2.50	1.10	.30
☐ 15 Dan Marino	40.00	18.00	5.00
☐ 16 Chris Doleman	2.50	1.10	.30
☐ 17 Marv Cook	2.50	1.10	.30
☐ 18 Rickey Jackson	2.50	1.10	.30
☐ 19 Rodney Hampton	4.00	1.80	.50
☐ 20 Jeff Lageman	2.50	1.10	.30
☐ 21 Clyde Simmons	2.50	1.10	.30
☐ 22 Rich Camarillo	2.50	1.10	.30
☐ 23 Rod Woodson	4.00	1.80	.50
☐ 24 Ronnie Harmon	2.50	1.10	.30
☐ 25 Steve Young	20.00	9.00	2.50
☐ 26 Cortez Kennedy	2.50	1.10	.30
☐ 27 Reggie Cobb	2.50	1.10	.30
☐ 28 Mark Rypien	2.50	1.10	.30

1993 Score Ore-Ida QB Club

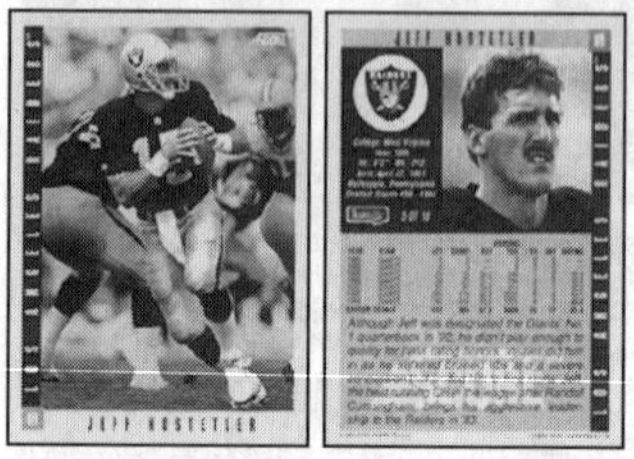

This set of 18 standard-size cards could be obtained by the purchase of specially marked Ore-Ida products (Bagel Bites, Twice Baked, or Topped Baked Potatoes), filling out the order form on one of the packages, and mailing it plus six proofs-of-purchase and 1.50. Collectors would then receive two nine-card packs. For three proofs-of-purchase and 1.00, collectors could receive one nine-card set. The packs are sequentially numbered, with the first pack containing cards 1-9 and the second containing cards 10-18. Aside from sporting different color player action photos on their fronts (Hostetler and Esiason are pictured in their new Raiders and Jets uniforms, respectively), and the different numbering on the backs, the cards are identical in design to the regular 1993 Score issue.

	MINT	NRMT	EXC
COMPLETE SET (18)	35.00	16.00	4.40
COMMON CARD (1-18)	.75	.35	.09
☐ 1 John Elway	4.00	1.80	.50
☐ 2 Steve Young	4.00	1.80	.50
☐ 3 Warren Moon	1.00	.45	.12
☐ 4 Randall Cunningham	.75	.35	.09
☐ 5 Jeff Hostetler	.75	.35	.09
☐ 6 Phil Simms	1.00	.45	.12
☐ 7 Jim Everett	.75	.35	.09
☐ 8 David Klingler	.75	.35	.09
☐ 9 Brett Favre	10.00	4.50	1.25
☐ 10 Troy Aikman	5.00	2.20	.60
☐ 11 Dan Marino	10.00	4.50	1.25
☐ 12 Mark Rypien	.75	.35	.09
☐ 13 Jim Kelly	2.00	.90	.25
☐ 14 Jim Harbaugh	1.00	.45	.12
☐ 15 Bernie Kosar	.75	.35	.09
☐ 16 Boomer Esiason	.75	.35	.09
☐ 17 Chris Miller	.75	.35	.09
☐ 18 Neil O'Donnell	.75	.35	.09

1994 Score Samples

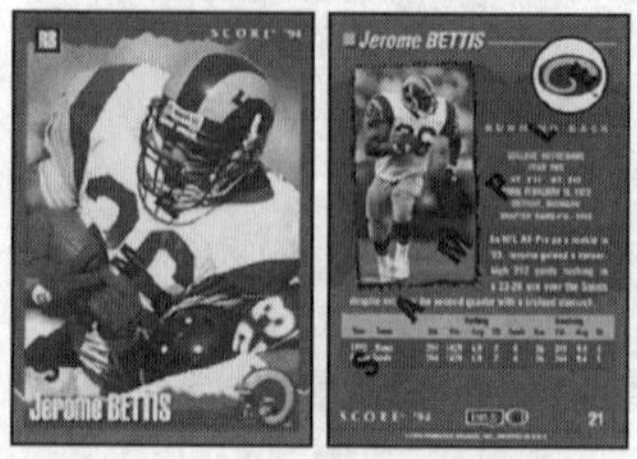

These nine sample standard-size cards were issued to herald the August release of the 1994 Score football set. The cards feature on their fronts color player action shots with irregular purple and teal borders, except for the Glyn Milburn card (112), which is a sample foil card from the parallel Gold Zone set. The player's name appears in white lettering below the photo; his position appears in white lettering within a black box at the upper left. The multicolored back carries the player's name and team logo at the top, followed below by his position, biography, profile, and statistics.

	MINT	NRMT	EXC
COMPLETE SET (9)	4.00	1.80	.50
COMMON CARD	.25	.11	.03
☐ 21 Jerome Bettis	2.00	.90	.25
☐ 25 Steve Jordan	.40	.18	.05
☐ 50 Shannon Sharpe	.40	.18	.05
☐ 112 Glyn Milburn FOIL	.40	.18	.05
☐ 161 Ronnie Lott	.40	.18	.05
☐ 257 Derrick Thomas	.75	.35	.09
☐ 0 Generic Rookie Card	.25	.11	.03
☐ NNO Sample Redemption Card	.25	.11	.03
☐ NNO Score Ad Card	.25	.11	.03

1994 Score

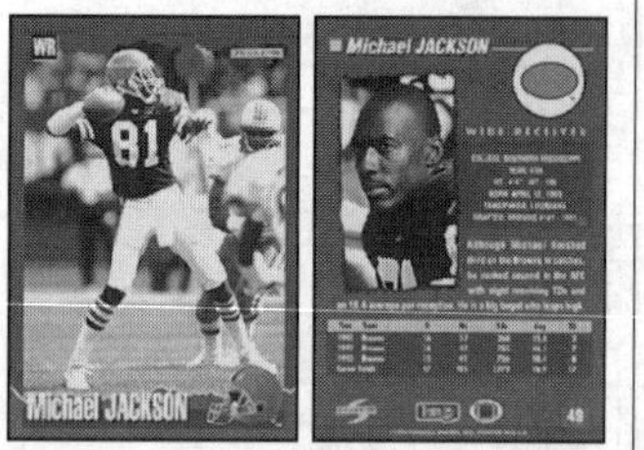

The 1994 Score football set consists of 330 standard-size cards. Cards were issued in 14-card foil packs as well as in jumbo packs. The fronts feature color action player photos with bright borders. The photos appear to be torn at the top and bottom. The player's name, position and team helmet also appear on the front. On a very colorful background, the backs contain a headshot, along with his name, biography and stats. Topical subsets featured are Rookies (276-305) and Team Checklists (306-319). Cards of players that were named All-Pro, have an All-Pro (AP) notation on front. A 330-card parallel set "Gold Zone" was inserted one card per pack. Randomly inserted redemption cards gave collectors an opportunity to receive ten cards of top rookie players in their NFL uniforms. Rookie Cards include Derrick Alexander, Marshall Faulk, William Floyd, Greg Hill, Charles Johnson, Errict Rhett, Darnay Scott and Heath Shuler.

	MINT	NRMT	EXC
COMPLETE SET (330)	15.00	6.75	1.85
COMMON CARD (1-330)	.05	.02	.01
☐ 1 Barry Sanders	.75	.35	.09
☐ 2 Troy Aikman	.75	.35	.09
☐ 3 Sterling Sharpe	.10	.05	.01
☐ 4 Deion Sanders	.60	.25	.07
☐ 5 Bruce Smith	.20	.09	.03
☐ 6 Eric Metcalf	.10	.05	.01
☐ 7 John Elway	.60	.25	.07
☐ 8 Bruce Matthews	.05	.02	.01
☐ 9 Rickey Jackson	.05	.02	.01
☐ 10 Cortez Kennedy	.10	.05	.01
☐ 11 Jerry Rice	.75	.35	.09
☐ 12 Stanley Richard	.05	.02	.01
☐ 13 Rod Woodson	.10	.05	.01
☐ 14 Eric Swann	.10	.05	.01
☐ 15 Eric Allen	.05	.02	.01
☐ 16 Richard Dent	.10	.05	.01
☐ 17 Carl Pickens	.40	.18	.05
☐ 18 Rohn Stark	.05	.02	.01
☐ 19 Marcus Allen	.20	.09	.03
☐ 20 Steve Wisniewski	.05	.02	.01
☐ 21 Jerome Bettis	.60	.25	.07
☐ 22 Darrell Green	.05	.02	.01
☐ 23 Lawrence Dawsey	.05	.02	.01
☐ 24 Larry Centers	.20	.09	.03
☐ 25 Steve Jordan	.05	.02	.01
☐ 26 Johnny Johnson	.05	.02	.01
☐ 27 Phil Simms	.10	.05	.01
☐ 28 Bruce Armstrong	.05	.02	.01
☐ 29 Willie Roaf	.05	.02	.01
☐ 30 Andre Rison	.10	.05	.01
☐ 31 Henry Jones	.05	.02	.01
☐ 32 Warren Moon	.20	.09	.03
☐ 33 Sean Gilbert	.05	.02	.01
☐ 34 Ben Coates	.20	.09	.03
☐ 35 Seth Joyner	.05	.02	.01
☐ 36 Ronnie Harmon	.05	.02	.01
☐ 37 Quentin Coryatt	.05	.02	.01
☐ 38 Ricky Sanders	.05	.02	.01
☐ 39 Gerald Williams	.05	.02	.01
☐ 40 Emmitt Smith	1.50	.70	.19
☐ 41 Jason Hanson	.05	.02	.01
☐ 42 Kevin Smith	.05	.02	.01
☐ 43 Irving Fryar	.10	.05	.01
☐ 44 Boomer Esiason	.10	.05	.01
☐ 45 Darryl Talley	.05	.02	.01
☐ 46 Paul Gruber	.05	.02	.01
☐ 47 Anthony Smith	.05	.02	.01
☐ 48 John Copeland	.05	.02	.01
☐ 49 Michael Jackson	.10	.05	.01
☐ 50 Shannon Sharpe	.10	.05	.01
☐ 51 Reggie White	.20	.09	.03
☐ 52 Andre Collins	.05	.02	.01
☐ 53 Jack Del Rio	.05	.02	.01
☐ 54 John Elliott	.05	.02	.01
☐ 55 Kevin Greene	.20	.09	.03
☐ 56 Steve Young	.60	.25	.07
☐ 57 Erric Pegram	.05	.02	.01
☐ 58 Donnell Woolford	.05	.02	.01
☐ 59 Darryl Williams	.05	.02	.01
☐ 60 Michael Irvin	.20	.09	.03
☐ 61 Mel Gray	.05	.02	.01
☐ 62 Greg Montgomery	.05	.02	.01
☐ 63 Neil Smith	.10	.05	.01
☐ 64 Andy Harmon	.05	.02	.01
☐ 65 Dan Marino	1.50	.70	.19
☐ 66 Leonard Russell	.05	.02	.01
☐ 67 Joe Montana	.75	.35	.09
☐ 68 John Taylor	.10	.05	.01
☐ 69 Cris Dishman	.05	.02	.01
☐ 70 Cornelius Bennett	.10	.05	.01
☐ 71 Harold Green	.05	.02	.01
☐ 72 Anthony Pleasant	.05	.02	.01
☐ 73 Dennis Smith	.05	.02	.01
☐ 74 Bryce Paup	.20	.09	.03
☐ 75 Jeff George	.20	.09	.03
☐ 76 Henry Ellard	.10	.05	.01
☐ 77 Randall McDaniel	.05	.02	.01
☐ 78 Derek Brown RB	.05	.02	.01
☐ 79 Johnny Mitchell	.05	.02	.01
☐ 80 Leroy Thompson	.05	.02	.01
☐ 81 Junior Seau	.10	.05	.01
☐ 82 Kelvin Martin	.05	.02	.01
☐ 83 Guy McIntyre	.05	.02	.01
☐ 84 Elbert Shelley	.05	.02	.01
☐ 85 Louis Oliver	.05	.02	.01
☐ 86 Tommy Vardell	.05	.02	.01
☐ 87 Jeff Herrod	.05	.02	.01
☐ 88 Edgar Bennett	.20	.09	.03
☐ 89 Reggie Langhorne	.05	.02	.01
☐ 90 Terry Kirby	.20	.09	.03
☐ 91 Marcus Robertson	.05	.02	.01
☐ 92 Mark Collins	.05	.02	.01
☐ 93 Calvin Williams	.10	.05	.01
☐ 94 Barry Foster	.05	.02	.01
☐ 95 Brent Jones	.10	.05	.01
☐ 96 Reggie Cobb	.05	.02	.01
☐ 97 Ray Childress	.05	.02	.01
☐ 98 Chris Miller	.05	.02	.01
☐ 99 John Carney	.05	.02	.01
☐ 100 Ricky Proehl	.05	.02	.01
☐ 101 Renaldo Turnbull	.05	.02	.01
☐ 102 John Randle	.05	.02	.01
☐ 103 Flipper Anderson	.05	.02	.01
☐ 104 Scottie Graham	.10	.05	.01
☐ 105 Webster Slaughter	.05	.02	.01
☐ 106 Tyrone Hughes	.10	.05	.01
☐ 107 Ken Norton Jr.	.10	.05	.01
☐ 108 Jim Kelly	.20	.09	.03
☐ 109 Michael Haynes	.10	.05	.01
☐ 110 Mark Carrier DB	.05	.02	.01
☐ 111 Eddie Murray	.05	.02	.01
☐ 112 Glyn Milburn	.10	.05	.01
☐ 113 Jackie Harris	.05	.02	.01
☐ 114 Dean Biasucci	.05	.02	.01
☐ 115 Tim Brown	.20	.09	.03
☐ 116 Mark Higgs	.05	.02	.01
☐ 117 Steve Emtman	.05	.02	.01
☐ 118 Clay Matthews	.05	.02	.01
☐ 119 Clyde Simmons	.05	.02	.01
☐ 120 Howard Ballard	.05	.02	.01
☐ 121 Ricky Watters	.20	.09	.03
☐ 122 William Fuller	.05	.02	.01
☐ 123 Robert Brooks	.30	.14	.04
☐ 124 Brian Blades	.10	.05	.01
☐ 125 Leslie O'Neal	.05	.02	.01
☐ 126 Gary Clark	.10	.05	.01
☐ 127 Jim Sweeney	.05	.02	.01
☐ 128 Vaughan Johnson	.05	.02	.01
☐ 129 Gary Brown	.05	.02	.01
☐ 130 Todd Lyght	.05	.02	.01
☐ 131 Nick Lowery	.05	.02	.01
☐ 132 Ernest Givins	.10	.05	.01
☐ 133 Lomas Brown	.05	.02	.01
☐ 134 Craig Erickson	.05	.02	.01
☐ 135 James Francis	.05	.02	.01
☐ 136 Andre Reed	.10	.05	.01
☐ 137 Jim Everett	.10	.05	.01
☐ 138 Nate Odomes	.05	.02	.01
☐ 139 Tom Waddle	.05	.02	.01
☐ 140 Stevon Moore	.05	.02	.01
☐ 141 Rod Bernstine	.05	.02	.01
☐ 142 Brett Favre	1.50	.70	.19
☐ 143 Roosevelt Potts	.05	.02	.01
☐ 144 Chester McGlockton	.05	.02	.01
☐ 145 LeRoy Butler	.05	.02	.01
☐ 146 Charles Haley	.10	.05	.01
☐ 147 Rodney Hampton	.20	.09	.03
☐ 148 George Teague	.05	.02	.01
☐ 149 Gary Anderson K	.05	.02	.01
☐ 150 Mark Stepnoski	.05	.02	.01
☐ 151 Courtney Hawkins	.05	.02	.01
☐ 152 Tim Grunhard	.05	.02	.01
☐ 153 David Klingler	.05	.02	.01
☐ 154 Erik Williams	.05	.02	.01
☐ 155 Herman Moore	.40	.18	.05
☐ 156 Daryl Johnston	.10	.05	.01
☐ 157 Chris Zorich	.05	.02	.01
☐ 158 Shane Conlan	.05	.02	.01
☐ 159 Santana Dotson	.10	.05	.01
☐ 160 Sam Mills	.05	.02	.01
☐ 161 Ronnie Lott	.10	.05	.01
☐ 162 Jesse Sapolu	.05	.02	.01
☐ 163 Marion Butts	.05	.02	.01
☐ 164 Eugene Robinson	.05	.02	.01
☐ 165 Mark Schlereth	.05	.02	.01
☐ 166 John L. Williams	.05	.02	.01
☐ 167 Anthony Miller	.10	.05	.01
☐ 168 Rich Camarillo	.05	.02	.01
☐ 169 Jeff Lageman	.05	.02	.01
☐ 170 Michael Brooks	.05	.02	.01
☐ 171 Scott Mitchell	.20	.09	.03
☐ 172 Duane Bickett	.05	.02	.01
☐ 173 Willie Davis	.10	.05	.01
☐ 174 Maurice Hurst	.05	.02	.01
☐ 175 Brett Perriman	.10	.05	.01
☐ 176 Jay Novacek	.10	.05	.01
☐ 177 Terry Allen	.10	.05	.01
☐ 178 Pete Metzelaars	.05	.02	.01
☐ 179 Erik Kramer	.10	.05	.01
☐ 180 Neal Anderson	.05	.02	.01
☐ 181 Ethan Horton	.05	.02	.01
☐ 182 Tony Bennett	.05	.02	.01
☐ 183 Gary Zimmerman	.05	.02	.01
☐ 184 Jeff Hostetler	.10	.05	.01
☐ 185 Jeff Cross	.05	.02	.01
☐ 186 Vincent Brown	.05	.02	.01
☐ 187 Herschel Walker	.10	.05	.01
☐ 188 Courtney Hall	.05	.02	.01
☐ 189 Norm Johnson	.05	.02	.01
☐ 190 Hardy Nickerson	.10	.05	.01
☐ 191 Greg Townsend	.05	.02	.01
☐ 192 Mike Munchak	.05	.02	.01
☐ 193 Dante Jones	.05	.02	.01
☐ 194 Vinny Testaverde	.10	.05	.01
☐ 195 Vance Johnson	.05	.02	.01
☐ 196 Chris Jacke	.05	.02	.01
☐ 197 Will Wolford	.05	.02	.01
☐ 198 Terry McDaniel	.05	.02	.01
☐ 199 Bryan Cox	.05	.02	.01
☐ 200 Nate Newton	.05	.02	.01
☐ 201 Keith Byars	.05	.02	.01
☐ 202 Neil O'Donnell	.20	.09	.03
☐ 203 Harris Barton	.05	.02	.01
☐ 204 Thurman Thomas	.20	.09	.03
☐ 205 Jeff Query	.05	.02	.01
☐ 206 Russell Maryland	.05	.02	.01
☐ 207 Pat Swilling	.05	.02	.01
☐ 208 Haywood Jeffires	.10	.05	.01
☐ 209 John Alt	.05	.02	.01
☐ 210 O.J. McDuffie	.20	.09	.03
☐ 211 Keith Sims	.05	.02	.01
☐ 212 Eric Martin	.05	.02	.01
☐ 213 Kyle Clifton	.05	.02	.01
☐ 214 Luis Sharpe	.05	.02	.01
☐ 215 Thomas Everett	.05	.02	.01
☐ 216 Chris Warren	.10	.05	.01
☐ 217 Chris Doleman	.05	.02	.01
☐ 218 Tony Jones	.05	.02	.01
☐ 219 Karl Mecklenburg	.05	.02	.01
☐ 220 Rob Moore	.10	.05	.01
☐ 221 Jessie Hester	.05	.02	.01
☐ 222 Jeff Jaeger	.05	.02	.01
☐ 223 Keith Jackson	.05	.02	.01
☐ 224 Mo Lewis	.05	.02	.01
☐ 225 Mike Horan	.05	.02	.01
☐ 226 Eric Green	.05	.02	.01
☐ 227 Jim Ritcher	.05	.02	.01
☐ 228 Eric Curry	.05	.02	.01
☐ 229 Stan Humphries	.20	.09	.03
☐ 230 Mike Johnson	.05	.02	.01
☐ 231 Alvin Harper	.10	.05	.01
☐ 232 Bennie Blades	.05	.02	.01
☐ 233 Cris Carter	.20	.09	.03
☐ 234 Morten Andersen	.05	.02	.01
☐ 235 Brian Washington	.05	.02	.01
☐ 236 Eric Hill	.05	.02	.01
☐ 237 Natrone Means	.40	.18	.05
☐ 238 Carlton Bailey	.05	.02	.01
☐ 239 Anthony Carter	.10	.05	.01
☐ 240 Jessie Tuggle	.05	.02	.01
☐ 241 Tim Irwin	.05	.02	.01
☐ 242 Mark Carrier WR	.10	.05	.01
☐ 243 Steve Atwater	.05	.02	.01
☐ 244 Sean Jones	.05	.02	.01
☐ 245 Bernie Kosar	.10	.05	.01
☐ 246 Richmond Webb	.05	.02	.01
☐ 247 Dave Meggett	.05	.02	.01
☐ 248 Vincent Brisby	.20	.09	.03
☐ 249 Fred Barnett	.10	.05	.01
☐ 250 Greg Lloyd	.20	.09	.03
☐ 251 Tim McDonald	.05	.02	.01
☐ 252 Mike Pritchard	.05	.02	.01
☐ 253 Greg Robinson	.05	.02	.01
☐ 254 Tony McGee	.05	.02	.01
☐ 255 Chris Spielman	.10	.05	.01
☐ 256 Keith Loneker	.05	.02	.01
☐ 257 Derrick Thomas	.20	.09	.03
☐ 258 Wayne Martin	.05	.02	.01
☐ 259 Art Monk	.10	.05	.01
☐ 260 Andy Heck	.05	.02	.01
☐ 261 Chip Lohmiller	.05	.02	.01
☐ 262 Simon Fletcher	.05	.02	.01
☐ 263 Ricky Reynolds	.05	.02	.01
☐ 264 Chris Hinton	.05	.02	.01
☐ 265 Ronald Moore	.05	.02	.01
☐ 266 Rocket Ismail	.10	.05	.01
☐ 267 Pete Stoyanovich	.05	.02	.01
☐ 268 Mark Jackson	.05	.02	.01
☐ 269 Randall Cunningham	.10	.05	.01
☐ 270 Dermontti Dawson	.05	.02	.01
☐ 271 Bill Romanowski	.05	.02	.01
☐ 272 Tim Johnson	.05	.02	.01
☐ 273 Steve Tasker	.05	.02	.01
☐ 274 Keith Hamilton	.05	.02	.01
☐ 275 Pierce Holt	.05	.02	.01
☐ 276 Heath Shuler	1.00	.45	.12
☐ 277 Marshall Faulk	3.00	1.35	.35
☐ 278 Charles Johnson	.20	.09	.03
☐ 279 Sam Adams	.10	.05	.01
☐ 280 Trev Alberts	.10	.05	.01
☐ 281 Derrick Alexander WR	.20	.09	.03

□ 282 Bryant Young	.20	.09	.03
□ 283 Greg Hill	.20	.09	.03
□ 284 Darnay Scott	2.00	.90	.25
□ 285 Willie McGinest	.20	.09	.03
□ 286 Thomas Randolph	.05	.02	.01
□ 287 Errict Rhett	1.25	.55	.16
□ 288 Lamar Smith	.05	.02	.01
□ 289 William Floyd	1.00	.45	.12
□ 290 Johnnie Morton	.20	.09	.03
□ 291 Jamir Miller	.05	.02	.01
□ 292 David Palmer	.10	.05	.01
□ 293 Dan Wilkinson	.10	.05	.01
□ 294 Trent Dilfer	.60	.25	.07
□ 295 Antonio Langham	.10	.05	.01
□ 296 Chuck Levy	.05	.02	.01
□ 297 John Thierry	.05	.02	.01
□ 298 Kevin Lee	.05	.02	.01
□ 299 Aaron Glenn	.10	.05	.01
□ 300 Charlie Garner	.10	.05	.01
□ 301 Lonnie Johnson	.05	.02	.01
□ 302 LeShon Johnson	.10	.05	.01
□ 303 Thomas Lewis	.10	.05	.01
□ 304 Ryan Yarborough	.05	.02	.01
□ 305 Mario Bates	.50	.23	.06
□ 306 Buffalo Bills TC	.05	.02	.01
□ 307 Cincinnati Bengals TC	.05	.02	.01
□ 308 Cleveland Browns TC	.05	.02	.01
□ 309 Denver Broncos TC	.05	.02	.01
□ 310 Houston Oilers TC	.05	.02	.01
□ 311 Indianapolis Colts TC	.05	.02	.01
□ 312 Kansas City Chiefs TC	.05	.02	.01
□ 313 Los Angeles Raiders TC	.05	.02	.01
□ 314 Miami Dolphins TC	.05	.02	.01
□ 315 New England Patriots TC	.05	.02	.01
□ 316 New York Jets TC	.05	.02	.01
□ 317 Pittsburgh Steelers TC	.05	.02	.01
□ 318 San Diego Charges TC	.05	.02	.01
□ 319 Seattle Seahawks TC	.05	.02	.01
□ 320 Garrison Hearst FF	.20	.09	.03
□ 321 Drew Bledsoe FF	1.00	.45	.12
□ 322 Tyrone Hughes FF	.10	.05	.01
□ 323 James Jett FF	.05	.02	.01
□ 324 Tom Carter FF	.05	.02	.01
□ 325 Reggie Brooks FF	.05	.02	.01
□ 326 Dana Stubblefield FF	.20	.09	.03
□ 327 Jerome Bettis FF	.30	.14	.04
□ 328 Chris Slade FF	.05	.02	.01
□ 329 Rick Mirer FF	.20	.09	.03
□ 330 Emmitt Smith NFL MVP	1.00	.45	.12

1994 Score Gold Zone

Inserted one card per pack, this 330-card standard size set is a parallel to the basic 1994 Score set. The major difference is that the fronts have a metallic gold sheen.

	MINT	NRMT	EXC
COMPLETE SET (330)	100.00	45.00	12.50
COMMON CARD (1-330)	.30	.14	.04
*STARS: 3X TO 6X BASIC CARDS			
*RCs: 1.5X TO 3X BASIC CARDS			

1994 Score Dream Team

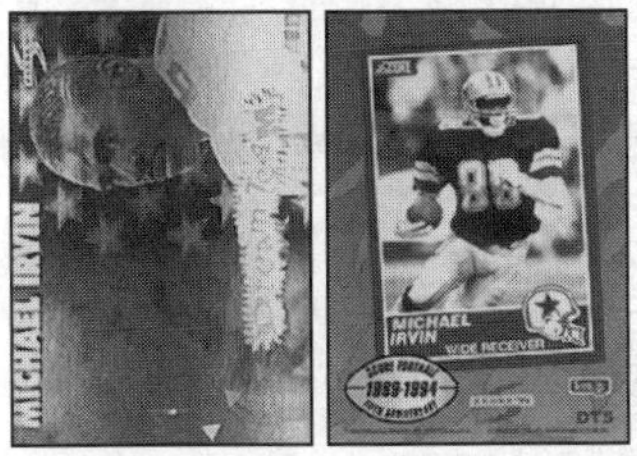

Randomly inserted in '94 Score packs, these 18 standard-size cards feature on their horizontal borderless fronts multiple holographic player images. A replica of the player's 1989 Score card appears on a colorful and borderless mottled background on the back. The cards are numbered on the back with a "DT" prefix.

	MINT	NRMT	EXC
COMPLETE SET (18)	175.00	80.00	22.00
COMMON CARD (DT1-DT18)	6.00	2.70	.75
□ DT1 Troy Aikman	30.00	13.50	3.70
□ DT2 Steve Atwater	6.00	2.70	.75
□ DT3 Cornelius Bennett	6.00	2.70	.75
□ DT4 Tim Brown	8.00	3.60	1.00
□ DT5 Michael Irvin	10.00	4.50	1.25
□ DT6 Bruce Matthews	6.00	2.70	.75
□ DT7 Eric Metcalf	8.00	3.60	1.00
□ DT8 Anthony Miller	8.00	3.60	1.00
□ DT9 Jerry Rice	30.00	13.50	3.70
□ DT10 Andre Rison	8.00	3.60	1.00
□ DT11 Barry Sanders	30.00	13.50	3.70
□ DT12 Deion Sanders	15.00	6.75	1.85
□ DT13 Sterling Sharpe	8.00	3.60	1.00
□ DT14 Neil Smith	6.00	2.70	.75
□ DT15 Derrick Thomas	8.00	3.60	1.00
□ DT16 Thurman Thomas	10.00	4.50	1.25
□ DT17 Rod Woodson	8.00	3.60	1.00
□ DT18 Steve Young	20.00	9.00	2.50

1994 Score Rookie Redemption

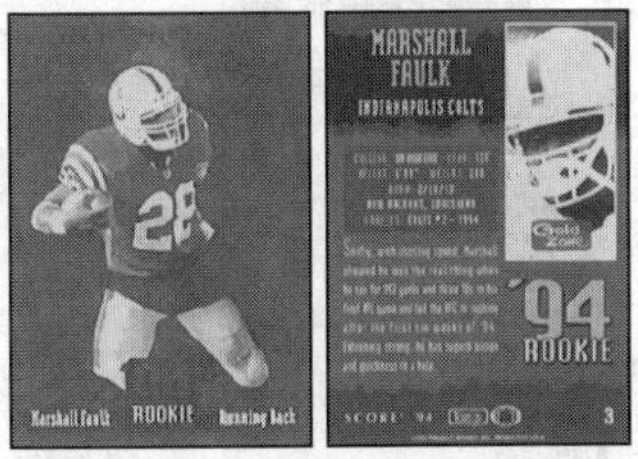

Randomly inserted in packs at a rate of one in 72, were 10 Rookie Redemption cards that could be exchanged for the player indicated on the card. The player cards feature the rookie in his NFL uniform. Referred to as "Gold Zone" technology, the player photo stands out on a metallic card with gold borders at the top and bottom. The backs have a small up-close photo and highlights from early in the 1994 season.

	MINT	NRMT	EXC
COMPLETE SET (10)	175.00	80.00	22.00
COMMON CARD (1-10)	10.00	4.50	1.25
□ 1 Heath Shuler	25.00	11.00	3.10
□ 2 Trent Dilfer	15.00	6.75	1.85
□ 3 Marshall Faulk	50.00	22.00	6.25
□ 4 Charlie Garner	10.00	4.50	1.25
□ 5 LeShon Johnson	10.00	4.50	1.25
□ 6 Charles Johnson	12.00	5.50	1.50
□ 7 Errict Rhett	30.00	13.50	3.70
□ 8 Lake Dawson	15.00	6.75	1.85
□ 9 Bert Emanuel	25.00	11.00	3.10
□ 10 Greg Hill	12.00	5.50	1.50

1994 Score Sophomore Showcase

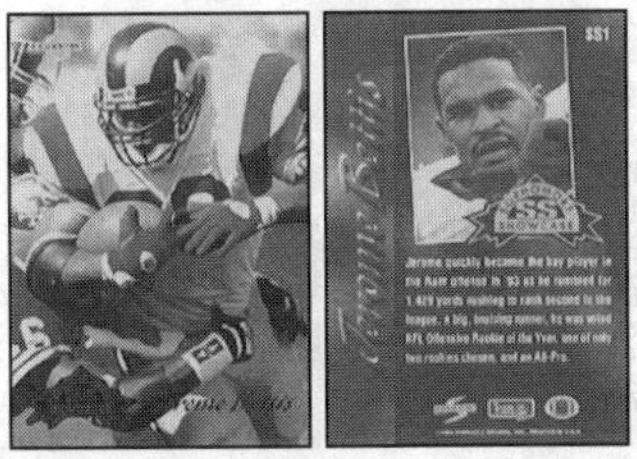

Randomly inserted in jumbo packs at a rate of one in four, this 18-card standard-size set highlights top second year players. Full-bleed fronts have a player photo over a blurred background. The Sophomore Showcase logo is at bottom left. The backs contain a small photo and a brief write-up. The cards are numbered with an SS prefix.

	MINT	NRMT	EXC
COMPLETE SET (18)	60.00	27.00	7.50
COMMON CARD (SS1-SS18)	2.00	.90	.25
□ SS1 Jerome Bettis	10.00	4.50	1.25
□ SS2 Rick Mirer	4.00	1.80	.50
□ SS3 Reggie Brooks	2.00	.90	.25
□ SS4 Drew Bledsoe	20.00	9.00	2.50
□ SS5 Ronald Moore	3.00	1.35	.35
□ SS6 Derek Brown RB	2.00	.90	.25
□ SS7 Roosevelt Potts	2.00	.90	.25
□ SS8 Terry Kirby	4.00	1.80	.50
□ SS9 James Jett	2.00	.90	.25
□ SS10 Vincent Brisby	3.00	1.35	.35
□ SS11 Tyrone Hughes	3.00	1.35	.35
□ SS12 Rocket Ismail	3.00	1.35	.35
□ SS13 Tony McGee	3.00	1.35	.35
□ SS14 Garrison Hearst	6.00	2.70	.75
□ SS15 Eric Curry	2.00	.90	.25
□ SS16 Dana Stubblefield	4.00	1.80	.50
□ SS17 Tom Carter	2.00	.90	.25
□ SS18 Chris Slade	2.00	.90	.25

1995 Score Promos

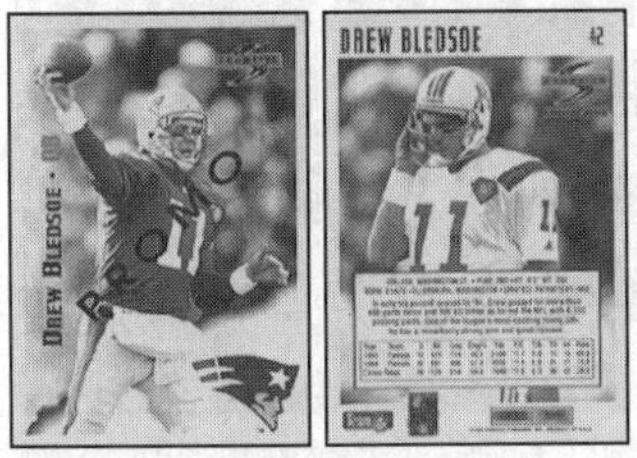

These cards were issued to preview the 1995 Score series. Four cards were packaged together in a cello wrapper. The pack included the Drew Bledsoe, Jerry Rice Star Struck, Troy Aikman Dream Team, and title cards. These four Promo cards can easily be distinguished from their regular issue counterparts by the disclaimer "PROMO" stamped in black across their fronts. The other two Promo cards were issued separately and include the word "Promotional" across the cardbacks.

	MINT	NRMT	EXC
COMPLETE SET (6)	10.00	4.50	1.25
COMMON CARD	.50	.23	.06
□ 42 Drew Bledsoe	3.00	1.35	.35
□ 47 Barry Foster	.50	.23	.06
□ 58 Steve Broussard	.50	.23	.06
□ 211 Jerry Rice Star Struck card	3.00	1.35	.35
□ DT2 Troy Aikman Dream Team card	4.00	1.80	.50
□ NNO Title Card	.50	.23	.06

1995 Score

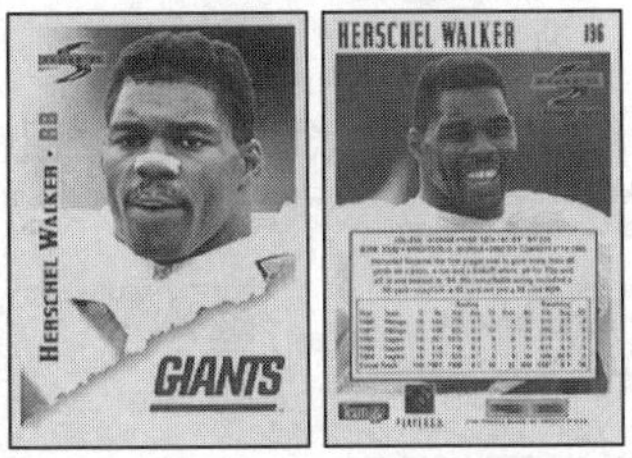

This 275-card standard-size set is issued in 12 card foil-packs (suggested retail price of 99 cents per pack) and 20-card jumbo packs. The fronts have white borders with the player identified in black lettering and his position in red up the left side. The action photo fades to solid white and a team logo at the bottom. The "Score 95" logo is in the upper right corner. The backs feature the player's name and card number in black lettering across the top. Also on the back is a player photo with biographical information, some personal history, and recent seasonal and career statistics superimposed. Parallel cards to this set include Red Siege Cards (one in three packs) and Red Siege Artist Proof Cards (one in 36 packs), both of which were randomly inserted. Rookie Cards in this set include Jeff Blake, Ki-Jana Carter, Kerry Collins, Joey Galloway, Steve McNair, Rashaan Salaam, Kordell Stewart, J.J Stokes and Michael Westbrook. A foil Steve Young card was distributed to collectors who correctly identified intentional errors from a Pinnacle print ad run throughout the season. The contest was the third part following two baseball ads, thus the AD3 card numbering.

	MINT	NRMT	EXC
COMPLETE SET (275)	15.00	6.75	1.85
COMMON CARD (1-275)	.05	.02	.01
□ 1 Steve Young	.60	.25	.07
□ 2 Barry Sanders	.75	.35	.09
□ 3 Jerry Rice	.75	.35	.09
□ 4 Marshall Faulk	.40	.18	.05
□ 5 Terance Mathis	.10	.05	.01
□ 6 Rod Woodson	.10	.05	.01
□ 7 Seth Joyner	.05	.02	.01
□ 8 Michael Timpson	.05	.02	.01
□ 9 Deion Sanders	.50	.23	.06
□ 10 Emmitt Smith	1.50	.70	.19
□ 11 Cris Carter	.20	.09	.03
□ 12 Jake Reed	.10	.05	.01
□ 13 Reggie White	.20	.09	.03
□ 14 Shannon Sharpe	.10	.05	.01
□ 15 Troy Aikman	.75	.35	.09
□ 16 Andre Reed	.10	.05	.01
□ 17 Tyrone Hughes	.10	.05	.01
□ 18 Sterling Sharpe	.10	.05	.01
□ 19 Jerome Bettis	.30	.14	.04
□ 20 Irving Fryar	.10	.05	.01
□ 21 Warren Moon	.10	.05	.01
□ 22 Ben Coates	.10	.05	.01
□ 23 Frank Reich	.05	.02	.01
□ 24 Henry Ellard	.10	.05	.01
□ 25 Steve Atwater	.05	.02	.01
□ 26 Willie Davis	.10	.05	.01
□ 27 Michael Irvin	.20	.09	.03
□ 28 Harvey Williams	.05	.02	.01
□ 29 Aeneas Williams	.05	.02	.01
□ 30 Errict Rhett	.20	.09	.03
□ 31 Lorenzo White	.05	.02	.01
□ 32 John Elway	.60	.25	.07
□ 33 Rodney Hampton	.10	.05	.01
□ 34 Webster Slaughter	.05	.02	.01
□ 35 Eric Turner	.05	.02	.01
□ 36 Dan Marino	1.50	.70	.19
□ 37 Daryl Johnston	.10	.05	.01
□ 38 Bruce Smith	.20	.09	.03
□ 39 Ronald Moore	.05	.02	.01
□ 40 Larry Centers	.10	.05	.01
□ 41 Curtis Conway	.20	.09	.03
□ 42 Drew Bledsoe	.75	.35	.09
□ 43 Quinn Early	.10	.05	.01
□ 44 Marcus Allen	.20	.09	.03
□ 45 Andre Rison	.10	.05	.01
□ 46 Jeff Blake	1.00	.45	.12
□ 47 Barry Foster	.10	.05	.01
□ 48 Antonio Langham	.05	.02	.01
□ 49 Herman Moore	.40	.18	.05
□ 50 Flipper Anderson	.05	.02	.01
□ 51 Rick Mirer	.20	.09	.03
□ 52 Jay Novacek	.10	.05	.01
□ 53 Tim Bowens	.05	.02	.01
□ 54 Carl Pickens	.20	.09	.03
□ 55 Lewis Tillman	.05	.02	.01
□ 56 Lawrence Dawsey	.05	.02	.01
□ 57 Leroy Hoard	.05	.02	.01
□ 58 Steve Broussard	.05	.02	.01
□ 59 Dave Krieg	.05	.02	.01
□ 60 John Taylor	.05	.02	.01
□ 61 Johnny Mitchell	.05	.02	.01
□ 62 Jessie Hester	.05	.02	.01
□ 63 Johnny Bailey	.05	.02	.01
□ 64 Brett Favre	1.50	.70	.19
□ 65 Bryce Paup	.20	.09	.03
□ 66 J.J. Birden	.05	.02	.01
□ 67 Steve Tasker	.10	.05	.01
□ 68 Edgar Bennett	.10	.05	.01
□ 69 Ray Buchanan	.05	.02	.01
□ 70 Brent Jones	.05	.02	.01
□ 71 Dave Meggett	.05	.02	.01
□ 72 Jeff Graham	.05	.02	.01
□ 73 Michael Brooks	.05	.02	.01
□ 74 Ricky Ervins	.05	.02	.01
□ 75 Chris Warren	.10	.05	.01
□ 76 Natrone Means	.20	.09	.03
□ 77 Tim Brown	.20	.09	.03
□ 78 Jim Everett	.05	.02	.01
□ 79 Chris Calloway	.05	.02	.01
□ 80 John L. Williams	.05	.02	.01
□ 81 Chris Chandler	.10	.05	.01
□ 82 Tim McDonald	.05	.02	.01
□ 83 Calvin Williams	.10	.05	.01
□ 84 Tony McGee	.05	.02	.01
□ 85 Erik Kramer	.05	.02	.01
□ 86 Eric Green	.05	.02	.01
□ 87 Nate Newton	.10	.05	.01
□ 88 Leonard Russell	.05	.02	.01
□ 89 Jeff George	.10	.05	.01
□ 90 Raymont Harris	.05	.02	.01
□ 91 Darnay Scott	.20	.09	.03
□ 92 Brian Mitchell	.05	.02	.01
□ 93 Craig Erickson	.05	.02	.01
□ 94 Cortez Kennedy	.10	.05	.01
□ 95 Derrick Alexander WR	.20	.09	.03
□ 96 Charles Haley	.10	.05	.01
□ 97 Randall Cunningham	.10	.05	.01
□ 98 Haywood Jeffires	.05	.02	.01
□ 99 Ronnie Harmon	.05	.02	.01
□ 100 Dale Carter	.10	.05	.01
□ 101 Dave Brown	.10	.05	.01
□ 102 Michael Haynes	.10	.05	.01
□ 103 Johnny Johnson	.05	.02	.01
□ 104 William Floyd	.20	.09	.03
□ 105 Jeff Hostetler	.10	.05	.01
□ 106 Bernie Parmalee	.10	.05	.01
□ 107 Mo Lewis	.05	.02	.01
□ 108 Byron Bam Morris	.10	.05	.01
□ 109 Vincent Brisby	.05	.02	.01
□ 110 John Randle	.05	.02	.01
□ 111 Steve Walsh	.05	.02	.01
□ 112 Terry Allen	.10	.05	.01
□ 113 Greg Lloyd	.10	.05	.01
□ 114 Merton Hanks	.05	.02	.01
□ 115 Mel Gray	.05	.02	.01
□ 116 Jim Kelly	.20	.09	.03
□ 117 Don Beebe	.05	.02	.01
□ 118 Floyd Turner	.05	.02	.01
□ 119 Neil Smith	.10	.05	.01
□ 120 Keith Byars	.05	.02	.01
□ 121 Rocket Ismail	.10	.05	.01
□ 122 Leslie O'Neal	.10	.05	.01
□ 123 Mike Sherrard	.05	.02	.01
□ 124 Marion Butts	.05	.02	.01
□ 125 Andre Coleman	.05	.02	.01
□ 126 Charles Johnson	.10	.05	.01
□ 127 Derrick Fenner	.05	.02	.01
□ 128 Vinny Testaverde	.10	.05	.01
□ 129 Chris Spielman	.10	.05	.01
□ 130 Bert Emanuel	.20	.09	.03
□ 131 Craig Heyward	.10	.05	.01
□ 132 Anthony Miller	.10	.05	.01
□ 133 Rob Moore	.05	.02	.01
□ 134 Gary Brown	.05	.02	.01
□ 135 David Klingler UER Photo on back is Erik Wilhelm	.10	.05	.01
□ 136 Sean Dawkins	.10	.05	.01
□ 137 Terry McDaniel	.05	.02	.01
□ 138 Fred Barnett	.10	.05	.01
□ 139 Bryan Cox	.05	.02	.01
□ 140 Andrew Jordan	.05	.02	.01
□ 141 Leroy Thompson	.05	.02	.01
□ 142 Richmond Webb	.05	.02	.01
□ 143 Kimble Anders	.10	.05	.01
□ 144 Mario Bates	.20	.09	.03
□ 145 Irv Smith	.05	.02	.01
□ 146 Carnell Lake	.05	.02	.01
□ 147 Mark Seay	.10	.05	.01
□ 148 Dana Stubblefield	.20	.09	.03
□ 149 Kelvin Martin	.05	.02	.01
□ 150 Pete Metzelaars	.05	.02	.01
□ 151 Roosevelt Potts	.05	.02	.01
□ 152 Bubby Brister	.05	.02	.01
□ 153 Trent Dilfer	.20	.09	.03
□ 154 Ricky Proehl	.05	.02	.01

	MINT	NRMT	EXC
☐ 155 Aaron Glenn	.05	.02	.01
☐ 156 Eric Metcalf	.10	.05	.01
☐ 157 Kevin Williams WR	.10	.05	.01
☐ 158 Charlie Garner	.10	.05	.01
☐ 159 Glyn Milburn	.05	.02	.01
☐ 160 Fuad Reveiz	.05	.02	.01
☐ 161 Brett Perriman	.10	.05	.01
☐ 162 Neil O'Donnell	.10	.05	.01
☐ 163 Tony Martin	.10	.05	.01
☐ 164 Sam Adams	.05	.02	.01
☐ 165 John Friesz	.10	.05	.01
☐ 166 Bryant Young	.10	.05	.01
☐ 167 Junior Seau	.20	.09	.03
☐ 168 Ken Harvey	.05	.02	.01
☐ 169 Bill Brooks	.05	.02	.01
☐ 170 Eugene Robinson	.05	.02	.01
☐ 171 Ricky Sanders	.10	.05	.01
☐ 172 Rodney Peete	.05	.02	.01
☐ 173 Boomer Esiason	.10	.05	.01
☐ 174 Reggie Roby	.05	.02	.01
☐ 175 Michael Jackson	.10	.05	.01
☐ 176 Gus Frerotte	.40	.18	.05
☐ 177 Terry Kirby	.10	.05	.01
☐ 178 Jessie Tuggle	.05	.02	.01
☐ 179 Courtney Hawkins	.05	.02	.01
☐ 180 Heath Shuler	.20	.09	.03
☐ 181 Jack Del Rio	.05	.02	.01
☐ 182 O.J. McDuffie	.20	.09	.03
☐ 183 Ricky Watters	.20	.09	.03
☐ 184 Willie Roaf	.05	.02	.01
☐ 185 Glenn Foley	.05	.02	.01
☐ 186 Blair Thomas	.05	.02	.01
☐ 187 Darren Woodson	.05	.02	.01
☐ 188 Kevin Greene	.10	.05	.01
☐ 189 Jeff Burris	.05	.02	.01
☐ 190 Jay Schroeder	.05	.02	.01
☐ 191 Stan Humphries	.10	.05	.01
☐ 192 Irving Spikes	.10	.05	.01
☐ 193 Jim Harbaugh	.10	.05	.01
☐ 194 Robert Brooks	.20	.09	.03
☐ 195 Greg Hill	.10	.05	.01
☐ 196 Herschel Walker	.10	.05	.01
☐ 197 Brian Blades	.10	.05	.01
☐ 198 Mark Ingram	.05	.02	.01
☐ 199 Kevin Turner	.05	.02	.01
☐ 200 Lake Dawson	.10	.05	.01
☐ 201 Alvin Harper	.05	.02	.01
☐ 202 Derek Brown RB	.05	.02	.01
☐ 203 Qadry Ismail	.10	.05	.01
☐ 204 Reggie Brooks	.10	.05	.01
☐ 205 Steve Young SS	.30	.14	.04
☐ 206 Emmitt Smith SS	1.00	.45	.12
☐ 207 Stan Humphries SS	.05	.02	.01
☐ 208 Barry Sanders SS	.40	.18	.05
☐ 209 Marshall Faulk SS	.20	.09	.03
☐ 210 Drew Bledsoe SS	.40	.18	.05
☐ 211 Jerry Rice SS	.40	.18	.05
☐ 212 Tim Brown SS	.10	.05	.01
☐ 213 Cris Carter SS	.20	.09	.03
☐ 214 Dan Marino SS	1.00	.45	.12
☐ 215 Troy Aikman SS	.40	.18	.05
☐ 216 Jerome Bettis SS	.10	.05	.01
☐ 217 Deion Sanders SS	.20	.09	.03
☐ 218 Junior Seau SS	.10	.05	.01
☐ 219 John Elway SS	.30	.14	.04
☐ 220 Warren Moon SS	.05	.02	.01
☐ 221 Sterling Sharpe SS	.10	.05	.01
☐ 222 Marcus Allen SS	.20	.09	.03
☐ 223 Michael Irvin SS	.10	.05	.01
☐ 224 Brett Favre SS	1.00	.45	.12
☐ 225 Rodney Hampton SS	.05	.02	.01
☐ 226 Dave Brown SS	.10	.05	.01
☐ 227 Ben Coates SS	.10	.05	.01
☐ 228 Jim Kelly SS	.20	.09	.03
☐ 229 Heath Shuler SS	.20	.09	.03
☐ 230 Herman Moore SS	.20	.09	.03
☐ 231 Jeff Hostetler SS	.10	.05	.01
☐ 232 Rick Mirer SS	.10	.05	.01
☐ 233 Byron Bam Morris SS	.10	.05	.01
☐ 234 Terance Mathis SS	.05	.02	.01
☐ 235 John Elway CL Barry Sanders CL	.25	.11	.03
☐ 236 Troy Aikman CL	.25	.11	.03
☐ 237 Jerry Rice CL	.25	.11	.03
☐ 238 Emmitt Smith CL	.40	.18	.05
☐ 239 Steve Young CL	.20	.09	.03
☐ 240 Drew Bledsoe CL	.25	.11	.03
☐ 241 Marshall Faulk CL	.20	.09	.03
☐ 242 Dan Marino CL	.40	.18	.05
☐ 243 Junior Seau CL	.10	.05	.01
☐ 244 Ray Zellars	.10	.05	.01
☐ 245 Rob Johnson	.05	.02	.01
☐ 246 Tony Boselli	.10	.05	.01
☐ 247 Kevin Carter	.20	.09	.03
☐ 248 Steve McNair	2.00	.90	.25
☐ 249 Tyrone Wheatley	.40	.18	.05
☐ 250 Steve Stenstrom	.05	.02	.01
☐ 251 Stoney Case	.05	.02	.01
☐ 252 Rodney Thomas	.20	.09	.03
☐ 253 Michael Westbrook	1.00	.45	.12
☐ 254 Derrick Alexander DE	.05	.02	.01
☐ 255 Kyle Brady	.20	.09	.03
☐ 256 Kerry Collins	2.50	1.10	.30
☐ 257 Rashaan Salaam	1.00	.45	.12
☐ 258 Frank Sanders	.20	.09	.03
☐ 259 John Walsh	.05	.02	.01
☐ 260 Sherman Williams	.05	.02	.01
☐ 261 Ki-Jana Carter	.75	.35	.09
☐ 262 Jack Jackson	.05	.02	.01
☐ 263 J.J. Stokes	.75	.35	.09
☐ 264 Kordell Stewart	2.50	1.10	.30
☐ 265 Dave Barr	.05	.02	.01
☐ 266 Eddie Goines	.05	.02	.01
☐ 267 Warren Sapp	.10	.05	.01
☐ 268 James O.Stewart	.20	.09	.03
☐ 269 Joey Galloway	1.50	.70	.19
☐ 270 Tyrone Davis	.05	.02	.01
☐ 271 Napoleon Kaufman	.75	.35	.09
☐ 272 Mark Bruener	.10	.05	.01
☐ 273 Todd Collins	.20	.09	.03
☐ 274 Billy Williams	.05	.02	.01
☐ 275 James A.Stewart	.05	.02	.01
☐ AD3 Steve Young Ad Contest Redemption	3.00	1.35	.35

1995 Score Red Siege

This 275 card parallel set was randomly inserted into packs at a rate of one in three packs. Card fronts are differentiated by having a silver foil background rather than the standard white. A "Red Siege" logo also appears in the background of the card backs.

	MINT	NRMT	EXC
COMPLETE SET (275)	200.00	90.00	25.00
COMMON CARD (1-275)	.30	.14	.04

*VETERAN STARS: 5X TO 10X BASIC CARDS
*YOUNG STARS: 4X TO 8X BASIC CARDS
*RCs: 2.5X TO 5X BASIC CARDS

1995 Score Red Siege Artist's Proofs

This 275 card parallel set was randomly inserted into packs at a rate of one in 36 packs. Card fronts are differentiated by having a silver foil background and red "Artist's Proof" stamp on the card front.

	MINT	NRMT	EXC
COMPLETE SET (275)	900.00	400.00	110.00
COMMON CARD (1-275)	3.00	1.35	.35

*VETERAN STARS: 30X TO 50X BASIC CARDS
*YOUNG STARS: 20X TO 40X BASIC CARDS
*RCs: 12X TO 25X BASIC CARDS

1995 Score Dream Team

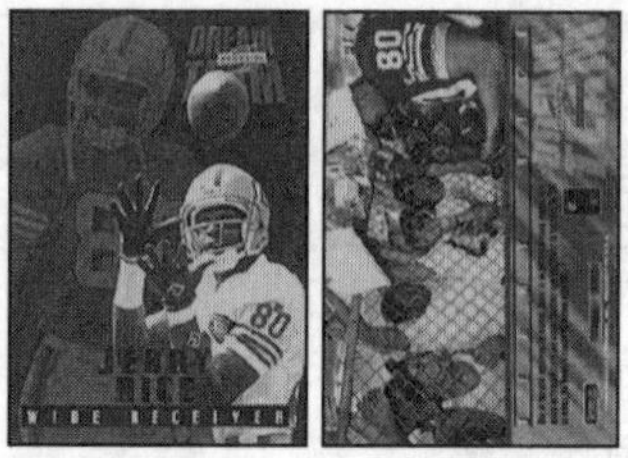

Randomly inserted into packs at a rate of one in 72, this 10-card standard-size set features some of the leading NFL players. Against a gold metallic background, the fronts feature two photos. One photo is a full color shot while the other is a shaded picture. The horizontal backs feature another photo on the top half with some player information underneath. The cards are numbered in the upper right corner with a "DT" prefix.

	MINT	NRMT	EXC
COMPLETE SET (10)	100.00	45.00	12.50
COMMON CARD (DT1-DT10)	6.00	2.70	.75
☐ DT1 Steve Young	10.00	4.50	1.25
☐ DT2 Troy Aikman	12.00	5.50	1.50
☐ DT3 Dan Marino	20.00	9.00	2.50
☐ DT4 Drew Bledsoe	12.00	5.50	1.50
☐ DT5 Emmitt Smith	20.00	9.00	2.50
☐ DT6 Barry Sanders	12.00	5.50	1.50
☐ DT7 Jerry Rice	12.00	5.50	1.50
☐ DT8 Marshall Faulk	6.00	2.70	.75
☐ DT9 Deion Sanders	8.00	3.60	1.00
☐ DT10 John Elway	10.00	4.50	1.25

1995 Score Offense Inc.

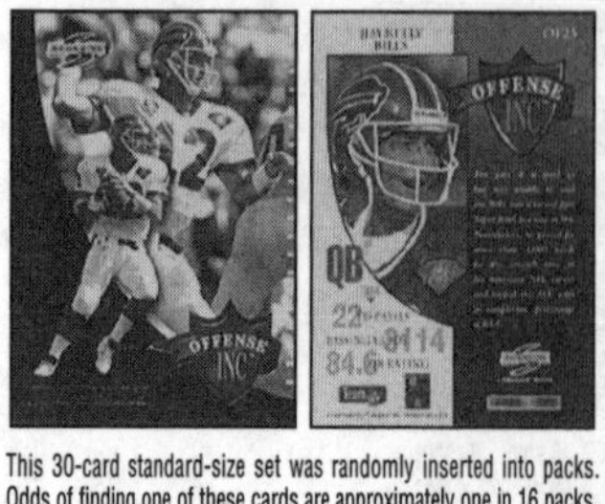

This 30-card standard-size set was randomly inserted into packs. Odds of finding one of these cards are approximately one in 16 packs. The set features leading NFL offensive players. Card fronts feature two player shots with the player's name and the border on the logo "Offense Inc." in gold foil. The background on the left side of the card is in black. Card backs contain a headshot with a summary to the right. Cards are numbered with an "OF" prefix.

	MINT	NRMT	EXC
COMPLETE SET (30)	80.00	36.00	10.00
COMMON CARD (OF1-OF30)	1.50	.70	.19
☐ 1 Steve Young	4.00	1.80	.50
☐ 2 Emmitt Smith	12.00	5.50	1.50
☐ 3 Dan Marino	12.00	5.50	1.50
☐ 4 Barry Sanders	5.00	2.20	.60
☐ 5 Jeff Blake	3.00	1.35	.35
☐ 6 Jerry Rice	5.00	2.20	.60
☐ 7 Troy Aikman	5.00	2.20	.60
☐ 8 Brett Favre	12.00	5.50	1.50
☐ 9 Marshall Faulk	3.00	1.35	.35
☐ 10 Drew Bledsoe	5.00	2.20	.60
☐ 11 Natrone Means	3.00	1.35	.35
☐ 12 John Elway	4.00	1.80	.50
☐ 13 Chris Warren	1.50	.70	.19
☐ 14 Michael Irvin	3.00	1.35	.35
☐ 15 Mario Bates	1.50	.70	.19
☐ 16 Warren Moon	2.00	.90	.25
☐ 17 Jerome Bettis	3.00	1.35	.35
☐ 18 Herman Moore	3.00	1.35	.35
☐ 19 Barry Foster	1.50	.70	.19
☐ 20 Jeff George	1.50	.70	.19
☐ 21 Cris Carter	1.50	.70	.19
☐ 22 Sterling Sharpe	1.50	.70	.19
☐ 23 Jim Kelly	3.00	1.35	.35
☐ 24 Heath Shuler	2.00	.90	.25
☐ 25 Marcus Allen	2.00	.90	.25
☐ 26 Dave Brown	1.50	.70	.19
☐ 27 Rick Mirer	3.00	1.35	.35
☐ 28 Rodney Hampton	1.50	.70	.19
☐ 29 Errict Rhett	3.00	1.35	.35
☐ 30 Ben Coates	1.50	.70	.19

1995 Score Pass Time

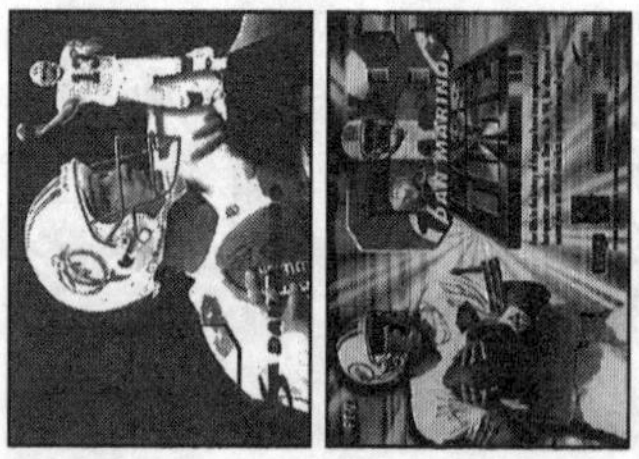

Randomly inserted into jumbo packs at a rate of one in 18, this 18 card set focuses on the "hottest arms" in the NFL Quarterback Club. Card fronts include two player shots against an all-foil gold background. Card backs have a yellow and white background with two player shots and a brief commentary. Cards are numbered with a "PT" prefix.

	MINT	NRMT	EXC
COMPLETE SET (18)	175.00	80.00	22.00
COMMON CARD (PT1-PT18)	4.00	1.80	.50
☐ PT1 Steve Young	16.00	7.25	2.00
☐ PT2 Dan Marino	35.00	16.00	4.40
☐ PT3 Drew Bledsoe	20.00	9.00	2.50
☐ PT4 Troy Aikman	20.00	9.00	2.50
☐ PT5 Glenn Foley	4.00	1.80	.50
☐ PT6 John Elway	16.00	7.25	2.00
☐ PT7 Brett Favre	35.00	16.00	4.40
☐ PT8 Heath Shuler	6.00	2.70	.75
☐ PT9 Warren Moon	6.00	2.70	.75
☐ PT10 Rick Mirer	6.00	2.70	.75
☐ PT11 Stan Humphries	4.00	1.80	.50
☐ PT12 Jeff Hostetler	4.00	1.80	.50
☐ PT13 Jim Kelly	6.00	2.70	.75
☐ PT14 Randall Cunningham	4.00	1.80	.50
☐ PT15 Jeff Blake	10.00	4.50	1.25
☐ PT16 Trent Dilfer	6.00	2.70	.75
☐ PT17 Jeff George	6.00	2.70	.75
☐ PT18 Dave Brown	4.00	1.80	.50

1995 Score Reflextions

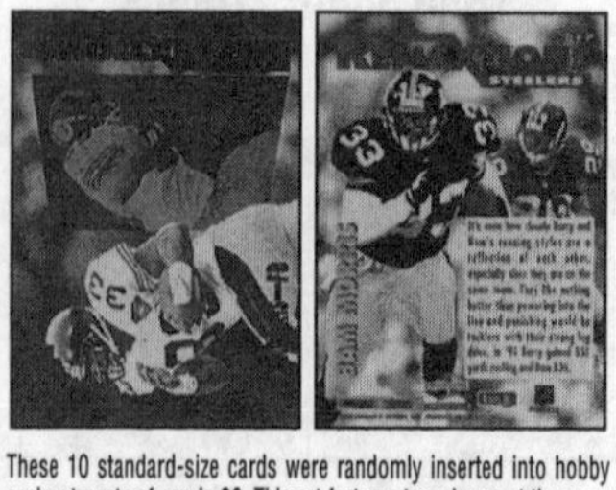

These 10 standard-size cards were randomly inserted into hobby packs at a rate of one in 36. This set features two players at the same position. One of the players is an established star while the other one is a younger player. The cards feature a mirror effect on the front with the "Reflextions" title on the right. Card backs are vertical with "Reflextions" in red at the top and shots of both players with a brief comparison commentary. Cards are numbered with a "RF" prefix.

	MINT	NRMT	EXC
COMPLETE SET (10)	150.00	70.00	19.00
COMMON CARD (RF1-RF10)	6.00	2.70	.75
☐ RF1 Drew Bledsoe Dan Marino	35.00	16.00	4.40
☐ RF2 Charlie Garner Barry Sanders	15.00	6.75	1.85
☐ RF3 Rick Mirer Warren Moon	8.00	3.60	1.00
☐ RF4 Heath Shuler Steve Young	10.00	4.50	1.25
☐ RF5 Marshall Faulk Emmitt Smith	30.00	13.50	3.70
☐ RF6 Derrick Alexander WR Jerry Rice	15.00	6.75	1.85
☐ RF7 Barry Foster Byron Bam Morris	6.00	2.70	.75
☐ RF8 Natrone Means Chris Warren	8.00	3.60	1.00
☐ RF9 Tim Brown Lake Dawson	8.00	3.60	1.00
☐ RF10 Mario Bates Rodney Hampton	6.00	2.70	.75

1995 Score Pin-Cards

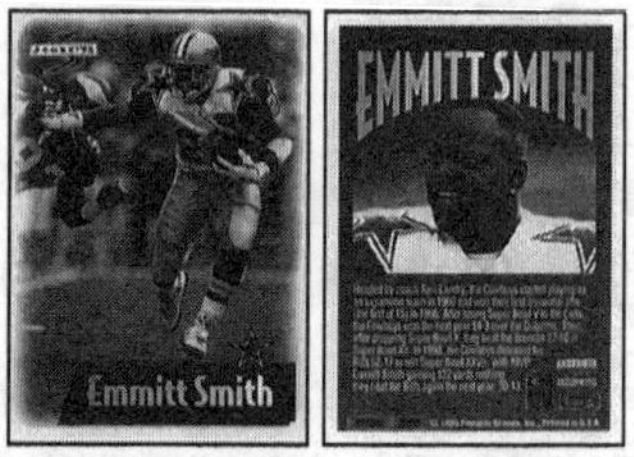

Sold in blister packs, each NFL team is represented by either one standard-size card depicting an NFL Quarterback Club member or a team helmet and a pin depicting the team logo. There are also 3 card sets in addition to regular cards for both expansion teams and the relocated St. Louis Rams, as well as a Super Bowl XXX card. The expansion and relocated team cards are black bordered with the team name repeated in the background on the front, and have copy relating to the teams' history, stadium, and logo lore on the back.These cards are also numbered 1-9. The other cards have fronts that feature color action photos of players or team helmets that fade to the surrounding white borders and are unnumbered. The player's or team's name appears on a rusty brown bar at the bottom. On a color panel, the backs present a color closeup photo and a brief player or team history. The cards are listed below by expansion and relocated teams, then alphabetically by player, and alphabetically by helmet. The prices below are for the trading cards only.

	MINT	NRMT	EXC
COMPLETE SET (40)	35.00	16.00	4.40
COMMON HELMET CARD	.40	.18	.05
COMMON PLAYER CARD	.60	.25	.07
☐ 1 Jacksonville Jaguars-History	.75	.35	.09
☐ 2 Jacksonville Jaguars-Stadium	.75	.35	.09
☐ 3 Jacksonville Jaguars-Logo Lore	.75	.35	.09
☐ 4 Carolina Panthers-History	.75	.35	.09
☐ 5 Carolina Panthers-Stadium	.75	.35	.09
☐ 6 Carolina Panthers-Logo Lore	.75	.35	.09
☐ 7 St. Louis Rams-History	.75	.35	.09
☐ 8 St. Louis Rams-Stadium	.40	.18	.05
☐ 9 St. Louis Rams-Logo Lore	.40	.18	.05
☐ 10 Drew Bledsoe	2.00	.90	.25
☐ 11 Dave Brown	.60	.25	.07
☐ 12 Randall Cunningham	.60	.25	.07
☐ 13 John Elway	1.50	.70	.19
☐ 14 Jim Everett	.60	.25	.07
☐ 15 Boomer Esiason	.60	.25	.07
☐ 16 Brett Favre	4.00	1.80	.50
☐ 17 Jeff Hostetler	.60	.25	.07
☐ 18 Jim Kelly	1.00	.45	.12
☐ 19 David Klingler	.60	.25	.07
☐ 20 Dan Marino	4.00	1.80	.50
☐ 21 Chris Miller	.60	.25	.07
☐ 22 Rick Mirer	.75	.35	.09
☐ 23 Warren Moon	.75	.35	.09
☐ 24 Neil O'Donnell	.75	.35	.09
☐ 25 Jerry Rice	2.00	.90	.25
☐ 26 Barry Sanders	2.00	.90	.25
☐ 27 Junior Seau	.75	.35	.09
☐ 28 Heath Shuler	1.00	.45	.12
☐ 29 Emmitt Smith	4.00	1.80	.50
☐ 30 Arizona Cardinals	.40	.18	.05
☐ 31 Atlanta Falcons	.40	.18	.05
☐ 32 Carolina Panthers	.75	.35	.09
☐ 33 Chicago Bears	.40	.18	.05
☐ 34 Cleveland Browns	.75	.35	.09
☐ 35 Houston Oilers	.40	.18	.05
☐ 36 Indianapolis Colts	.40	.18	.05
☐ 37 Jacksonville Jaguars	.75	.35	.09
☐ 38 Kansas City Chiefs	.40	.18	.05
☐ 39 Tampa Bay Buccaneers	.40	.18	.05
☐ 40 Super Bowl XXX logo	.40	.18	.05

1995 Score Young Stars

These standard-size cards were available at the 1995 NFL Experience Super Bowl Card Show in exchange for three or five Pinnacle brand wrappers. Each day Pinnacle exchanged a Gold Zone or Platinum card of a different NFL star. Two thousand Gold Zone and one thousand Platinum cards were produced for each of the players listed below. We've included individual prices for the Gold Zone version. The Platinum version is valued using the multiplier line below.

	MINT	NRMT	EXC
COMPLETE SET (4)	30.00	13.50	3.70
COMMON CARD (YSG1-YSG4)	5.00	2.20	.60
*PLATINUM CARDS: 1X TO 2X GOLDS			
☐ YSG1 Marshall Faulk	8.00	3.60	1.00
☐ YSG2 Jeff Blake	8.00	3.60	1.00
☐ YSG3 Drew Bledsoe	12.00	5.50	1.50
☐ YSG4 Natrone Means	5.00	2.20	.60

1996 Score

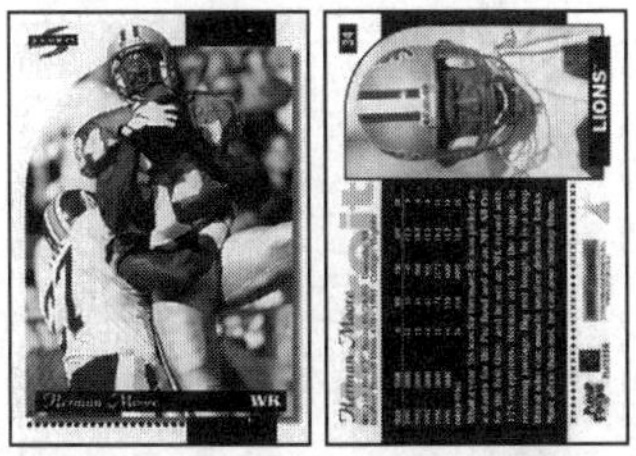

The 1996 Score set was issued in one series totalling 275 standard-size cards. The set was issued in three different pack types: Hobby, Retail and Jumbo. The Hobby and Retail packs had a suggested retail price of .99 per pack and were packed with 10 cards in each pack, 36 packs in a box and 20 boxes in a case. Subsets include: Rookies 214-243, Second Effort 244-268, and Checklists 269-275. A Barry Sanders Dream Team Promo card was produced and priced below.

	MINT	NRMT	EXC
COMPLETE SET (275)	16.00	7.25	2.00
COMMON CARD (1-275)	.05	.02	.01
☐ 1 Emmitt Smith	1.50	.70	.19
☐ 2 Flipper Anderson	.05	.02	.01
☐ 3 Kordell Stewart	.75	.35	.09
☐ 4 Bruce Smith	.20	.09	.03
☐ 5 Marshall Faulk	.20	.09	.03
☐ 6 William Floyd	.10	.05	.01
☐ 7 Darren Woodson	.10	.05	.01
☐ 8 Lake Dawson	.10	.05	.01
☐ 9 Terry Allen	.10	.05	.01
☐ 10 Ki-Jana Carter	.10	.05	.01
☐ 11 Tony Boselli	.10	.05	.01
☐ 12 Christian Fauria	.05	.02	.01
☐ 13 Jeff George	.10	.05	.01
☐ 14 Dan Marino	1.50	.70	.19
☐ 15 Rodney Thomas	.05	.02	.01
☐ 16 Anthony Miller	.10	.05	.01
☐ 17 Chris Sanders	.10	.05	.01
☐ 18 Natrone Means	.20	.09	.03
☐ 19 Curtis Conway	.20	.09	.03
☐ 20 Ben Coates	.10	.05	.01
☐ 21 Alvin Harper	.05	.02	.01
☐ 22 Frank Sanders	.10	.05	.01
☐ 23 Boomer Esiason	.10	.05	.01
☐ 24 Lovell Pinkney	.05	.02	.01
☐ 25 Troy Aikman	.75	.35	.09
☐ 26 Quinn Early	.05	.02	.01
☐ 27 Adrian Murrell	.10	.05	.01
☐ 28 Chris Spielman	.10	.05	.01
☐ 29 Tyrone Wheatley	.10	.05	.01
☐ 30 Tim Brown	.10	.05	.01
☐ 31 Erik Kramer	.05	.02	.01
☐ 32 Warren Moon	.10	.05	.01
☐ 33 Jimmy Oliver	.05	.02	.01
☐ 34 Herman Moore	.20	.09	.03
☐ 35 Quentin Coryatt	.05	.02	.01
☐ 36 Heath Shuler	.20	.09	.03
☐ 37 Jim Kelly	.20	.09	.03
☐ 38 Mike Morris	.05	.02	.01
☐ 39 Harvey Williams	.05	.02	.01
☐ 40 Vinny Testaverde	.10	.05	.01
☐ 41 Steve McNair	.50	.23	.06
☐ 42 Jerry Rice	.75	.35	.09
☐ 43 Darick Holmes	.10	.05	.01
☐ 44 Kyle Brady	.10	.05	.01
☐ 45 Greg Lloyd	.10	.05	.01
☐ 46 Kerry Collins	.75	.35	.09
☐ 47 Willie McGinest	.05	.02	.01
☐ 48 Isaac Bruce	.20	.09	.03
☐ 49 Carnell Lake	.05	.02	.01
☐ 50 Charles Haley	.10	.05	.01
☐ 51 Troy Vincent	.05	.02	.01
☐ 52 Randall Cunningham	.10	.05	.01
☐ 53 Rashaan Salaam	.20	.09	.03
☐ 54 Willie Jackson	.10	.05	.01
☐ 55 Chris Warren	.10	.05	.01
☐ 56 Michael Irvin	.20	.09	.03
☐ 57 Mario Bates	.10	.05	.01
☐ 58 Warren Sapp	.05	.02	.01
☐ 59 John Elway	.60	.25	.07
☐ 60 Shannon Sharpe	.10	.05	.01
☐ 61 Cornelius Bennett	.10	.05	.01
☐ 62 Robert Brooks	.20	.09	.03
☐ 63 Rodney Hampton	.10	.05	.01
☐ 64 Ken Norton Jr.	.10	.05	.01
☐ 65 Bryce Paup	.10	.05	.01
☐ 66 Eric Swann	.10	.05	.01
☐ 67 Rodney Peete	.05	.02	.01
☐ 68 Larry Centers	.10	.05	.01
☐ 69 Lamont Warren	.05	.02	.01
☐ 70 Jay Novacek	.10	.05	.01
☐ 71 Cris Carter	.20	.09	.03
☐ 72 Terrell Fletcher	.05	.02	.01
☐ 73 Andre Rison	.10	.05	.01
☐ 74 Ricky Watters	.10	.05	.01
☐ 75 Napoleon Kaufman	.10	.05	.01
☐ 76 Reggie White	.20	.09	.03
☐ 77 Yancey Thigpen	.10	.05	.01
☐ 78 Terry Kirby	.10	.05	.01
☐ 79 Deion Sanders	.40	.18	.05
☐ 80 Irving Fryar	.10	.05	.01
☐ 81 Marcus Allen	.20	.09	.03
☐ 82 Carl Pickens	.20	.09	.03
☐ 83 Drew Bledsoe	.75	.35	.09
☐ 84 Eric Metcalf	.10	.05	.01
☐ 85 Robert Smith	.10	.05	.01
☐ 86 Tamarick Vanover	.20	.09	.03
☐ 87 Henry Ellard	.10	.05	.01
☐ 88 Kevin Greene	.10	.05	.01
☐ 89 Mark Brunell	.75	.35	.09
☐ 90 Terrell Davis	1.00	.45	.12
☐ 91 Brian Mitchell	.05	.02	.01
☐ 92 Aaron Bailey	.05	.02	.01
☐ 93 Rocket Ismail	.10	.05	.01
☐ 94 Dave Brown	.10	.05	.01
☐ 95 Rod Woodson	.10	.05	.01
☐ 96 Sean Gilbert	.05	.02	.01
☐ 97 Mark Seay	.05	.02	.01
☐ 98 Zack Crockett	.05	.02	.01
☐ 99 Scott Mitchell	.10	.05	.01
☐ 100 Eric Pegram	.10	.05	.01
☐ 101 David Palmer	.10	.05	.01
☐ 102 Vincent Brisby	.05	.02	.01
☐ 103 Brett Perriman	.10	.05	.01
☐ 104 Jim Everett	.05	.02	.01
☐ 105 Tony Martin	.10	.05	.01
☐ 106 Desmond Howard	.10	.05	.01
☐ 107 Stan Humphries	.10	.05	.01
☐ 108 Bill Brooks	.05	.02	.01
☐ 109 Neil Smith	.10	.05	.01
☐ 110 Michael Westbrook	.20	.09	.03
☐ 111 Herschel Walker	.10	.05	.01
☐ 112 Andre Coleman	.05	.02	.01
☐ 113 Derrick Alexander WR	.10	.05	.01
☐ 114 Jeff Blake	.20	.09	.03
☐ 115 Sherman Williams	.05	.02	.01
☐ 116 James O.Stewart	.20	.09	.03
☐ 117 Hardy Nickerson	.05	.02	.01
☐ 118 Elvis Grbac	.20	.09	.03
☐ 119 Brett Favre	1.50	.70	.19
☐ 120 Mike Sherrard	.05	.02	.01
☐ 121 Edgar Bennett	.10	.05	.01
☐ 122 Calvin Williams	.20	.09	.03
☐ 123 Brian Blades	.10	.05	.01
☐ 124 Jeff Graham	.05	.02	.01
☐ 125 Gary Brown	.05	.02	.01
☐ 126 Bernie Parmalee	.05	.02	.01
☐ 127 Kimble Anders	.05	.02	.01
☐ 128 Hugh Douglas	.05	.02	.01
☐ 129 James A.Stewart	.05	.02	.01
☐ 130 Eric Bjornson	.05	.02	.01
☐ 131 Ken Dilger	.10	.05	.01
☐ 132 Jerome Bettis	.20	.09	.03
☐ 133 Cortez Kennedy	.10	.05	.01
☐ 134 Bryan Cox	.05	.02	.01
☐ 135 Darnay Scott	.10	.05	.01
☐ 136 Bert Emanuel	.10	.05	.01
☐ 137 Steve Bono	.10	.05	.01
☐ 138 Charles Johnson	.10	.05	.01
☐ 139 Glyn Milburn	.05	.02	.01
☐ 140 Derrick Alexander DE	.05	.02	.01
☐ 141 Dave Meggett	.05	.02	.01
☐ 142 Trent Dilfer	.10	.05	.01
☐ 143 Eric Zeier	.10	.05	.01
☐ 144 Jim Harbaugh	.10	.05	.01
☐ 145 Antonio Freeman	.30	.14	.04
☐ 146 Orlando Thomas	.05	.02	.01
☐ 147 Russell Maryland	.05	.02	.01
☐ 148 Chad May	.05	.02	.01
☐ 149 Craig Heyward	.05	.02	.01
☐ 150 Aeneas Williams	.05	.02	.01
☐ 151 Kevin Williams WR	.05	.02	.01
☐ 152 Charlie Garner	.05	.02	.01
☐ 153 J.J. Stokes	.20	.09	.03
☐ 154 Stoney Case	.05	.02	.01
☐ 155 Mark Chmura	.10	.05	.01
☐ 156 Mark Bruener	.05	.02	.01
☐ 157 Derek Loville	.05	.02	.01
☐ 158 Justin Armour	.05	.02	.01
☐ 159 Brent Jones	.05	.02	.01
☐ 160 Aaron Craver	.05	.02	.01
☐ 161 Terance Mathis	.05	.02	.01
☐ 162 Chris Zorich	.05	.02	.01
☐ 163 Glenn Foley	.05	.02	.01
☐ 164 Johnny Mitchell	.05	.02	.01
☐ 165 Junior Seau	.20	.09	.03
☐ 166 Willie Davis	.10	.05	.01
☐ 167 Rick Mirer	.10	.05	.01
☐ 168 Mike Jones	.05	.02	.01
☐ 169 Greg Hill	.10	.05	.01
☐ 170 Steve Tasker	.05	.02	.01
☐ 171 Tony Bennett	.05	.02	.01
☐ 172 Jeff Hostetler	.10	.05	.01
☐ 173 Dave Krieg	.05	.02	.01
☐ 174 Mark Carrier WR	.10	.05	.01
☐ 175 Michael Haynes	.10	.05	.01
☐ 176 Chris Chandler	.10	.05	.01
☐ 177 Ernie Mills	.05	.02	.01
☐ 178 Jake Reed	.10	.05	.01
☐ 179 Erric Rhett	.10	.05	.01
☐ 180 Garrison Hearst	.10	.05	.01
☐ 181 Derrick Thomas	.10	.05	.01
☐ 182 Aaron Hayden	.20	.09	.03
☐ 183 Jackie Harris	.05	.02	.01
☐ 184 Curtis Martin	1.00	.45	.12
☐ 185 Neil O'Donnell	.10	.05	.01
☐ 186 Derrick Moore	.05	.02	.01
☐ 187 Steve Young	.60	.25	.07
☐ 188 Pat Swilling	.05	.02	.01
☐ 189 Amp Lee	.05	.02	.01
☐ 190 Rob Johnson	.05	.02	.01
☐ 191 Todd Collins	.10	.05	.01
☐ 192 J.J. Birden	.05	.02	.01
☐ 193 O.J. McDuffie	.10	.05	.01
☐ 194 Shawn Jefferson	.05	.02	.01
☐ 195 Sean Dawkins	.05	.02	.01
☐ 196 Fred Barnett	.10	.05	.01
☐ 197 Roosevelt Potts	.05	.02	.01
☐ 198 Rob Moore	.05	.02	.01
☐ 199 Kevin Miniefield	.05	.02	.01
☐ 200 Barry Sanders	.75	.35	.09
☐ 201 Floyd Turner	.05	.02	.01
☐ 202 Wayne Chrebet	.10	.05	.01
☐ 203 Andre Reed	.10	.05	.01
☐ 204 Tyrone Hughes	.05	.02	.01
☐ 205 Keenan McCardell	.20	.09	.03
☐ 206 Gus Frerotte	.20	.09	.03
☐ 207 Daryl Johnston	.10	.05	.01
☐ 208 Steve Broussard	.05	.02	.01
☐ 209 Steve Atwater	.05	.02	.01
☐ 210 Thurman Thomas	.20	.09	.03
☐ 211 Andre Hastings	.10	.05	.01
☐ 212 Joey Galloway	.30	.14	.04
☐ 213 Kevin Carter	.10	.05	.01
☐ 214 Keyshawn Johnson	1.00	.45	.12
☐ 215 Tony Brackens	.10	.05	.01
☐ 216 Stepfret Williams	.05	.02	.01
☐ 217 Mike Alstott	.40	.18	.05
☐ 218 Terry Glenn	2.00	.90	.25
☐ 219 Tim Biakabutuka	.50	.23	.06
☐ 220 Eric Moulds	.50	.23	.06
☐ 221 Jeff Lewis	.10	.05	.01
☐ 222 Bobby Engram	.50	.23	.06
☐ 223 Cedric Jones	.10	.05	.01
☐ 224 Stanley Pritchett	.10	.05	.01
☐ 225 Kevin Hardy	.10	.05	.01
☐ 226 Alex Van Dyke	.10	.05	.01
☐ 227 Willie Anderson	.05	.02	.01
☐ 228 Regan Upshaw	.05	.02	.01
☐ 229 Leeland McElroy	.20	.09	.03
☐ 230 Marvin Harrison	1.00	.45	.12
☐ 231 Eddie George	2.50	1.10	.30
☐ 232 Lawrence Phillips	.40	.18	.05
☐ 233 Daryl Gardener	.10	.05	.01
☐ 234 Alex Molden	.05	.02	.01
☐ 235 Derrick Mayes	.50	.23	.06
☐ 236 John Mobley	.05	.02	.01
☐ 237 Israel Ifeanyi	.10	.05	.01
☐ 238 Pete Kendall	.05	.02	.01
☐ 239 Danny Kanell	.20	.09	.03
☐ 240 Jonathan Ogden	.05	.02	.01
☐ 241 Reggie Brown LB	.05	.02	.01
☐ 242 Marcus Jones	.05	.02	.01
☐ 243 Jon Stark	.05	.02	.01
☐ 244 Barry Sanders SE	.40	.18	.05
☐ 245 Brett Favre SE	.75	.35	.09
☐ 246 John Elway SE	.30	.14	.04
☐ 247 Dan Marino SE	.75	.35	.09
☐ 248 Drew Bledsoe SE	.40	.18	.05
☐ 249 Michael Irvin SE	.10	.05	.01
☐ 250 Troy Aikman SE	.40	.18	.05
☐ 251 Emmitt Smith SE	.75	.35	.09
☐ 252 Steve Young SE	.30	.14	.04
☐ 253 Jerry Rice SE	.40	.18	.05
☐ 254 Jeff Blake SE	.10	.05	.01
☐ 255 Tim Brown SE	.10	.05	.01
☐ 256 Eric Metcalf SE	.10	.05	.01
☐ 257 Rodney Hampton SE	.05	.02	.01
☐ 258 Scott Mitchell SE	.05	.02	.01
☐ 259 Garrison Hearst SE	.10	.05	.01
☐ 260 Larry Centers SE	.10	.05	.01
☐ 261 Neil O'Donnell SE	.10	.05	.01
☐ 262 Orlando Thomas SE	.05	.02	.01
☐ 263 Hugh Douglas SE	.05	.02	.01
☐ 264 Bill Brooks SE	.05	.02	.01
☐ 265 Harvey Williams SE	.05	.02	.01
☐ 266 Charles Haley SE	.10	.05	.01
☐ 267 Greg Lloyd SE	.10	.05	.01
☐ 268 Daryl Johnston SE	.10	.05	.01
☐ 269 Dan Marino CL	.30	.14	.04
☐ 270 Jeff Blake CL	.10	.05	.01
☐ 271 John Elway CL	.20	.09	.03
☐ 272 Emmitt Smith CL	.30	.14	.04
☐ 273 Brett Favre CL	.30	.14	.04
☐ 274 Jerry Rice CL	.25	.11	.03
☐ 275 Dan Marino Jeff Blake John Elway Emmitt Smith Brett Favre Jerry Rice Checklist	.20	.09	.03
☐ P1 Barry Sanders Promo Dream Team card	2.00	.90	.25

1996 Score Artist's Proofs

A parallel to the regular issue 1996 Score cards, these feature an "Artist's Proof" logo on the cardfront. The cards were randomly inserted in hobby and retail packs at the rate of 1:36. Jumbo packs included the cards at the rate of 1:18.

	MINT	NRMT	EXC
COMP.AP SET (275)	1000.00	450.00	125.00
COMMON CARD (1-275)	3.00	1.35	.35
*AP STARS: 30X TO 50X BASIC CARDS			
*AP YOUNG STARS: 20X TO 40X BASIC CARDS			
*AP RCs: 12X TO 25X BASIC CARDS			

1996 Score Field Force

A parallel to the regular issue 1996 Score cards, these feature a matte finish to the cardfront as opposed to the high gloss surface of the base brand. The cards were random inserted in hobby and retail packs at the rate of 1:6. Jumbo packs included the cards at the rate of 1:3.

	MINT	NRMT	EXC
COMPLETE SET (275)	300.00	135.00	38.00
COMMON CARD (1-275)	.40	.18	.05
*VETERAN STARS: 5X TO 10X BASIC CARDS			
*YOUNG STARS: 4X TO 8X BASIC CARDS			
*RCs: 3X TO 6X BASIC CARDS			

1996 Score Dream Team

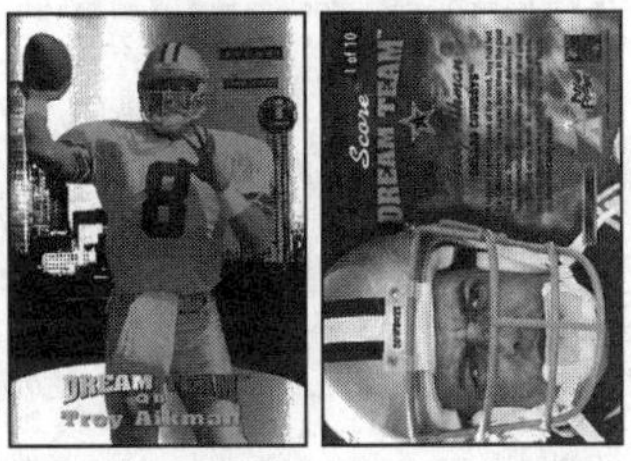

Randomly inserted in packs at a rate of one in 72 retail and hobby packs, these 10 standard-size cards feature a full-bleed, rainbow all gold-foil design. The cards are numbered as "X" of 10.

	MINT	NRMT	EXC
COMPLETE SET (10)	125.00	55.00	15.50
COMMON CARD (1-10)	4.00	1.80	.50
☐ 1 Troy Aikman	15.00	6.75	1.85
☐ 2 Michael Irvin	4.00	1.80	.50
☐ 3 Emmitt Smith	25.00	11.00	3.10
☐ 4 John Elway	12.00	5.50	1.50
☐ 5 Barry Sanders	15.00	6.75	1.85
☐ 6 Brett Favre	25.00	11.00	3.10
☐ 7 Dan Marino	25.00	11.00	3.10
☐ 8 Drew Bledsoe	15.00	6.75	1.85
☐ 9 Jerry Rice	15.00	6.75	1.85
☐ 10 Steve Young	12.00	5.50	1.50

1996 Score Footsteps

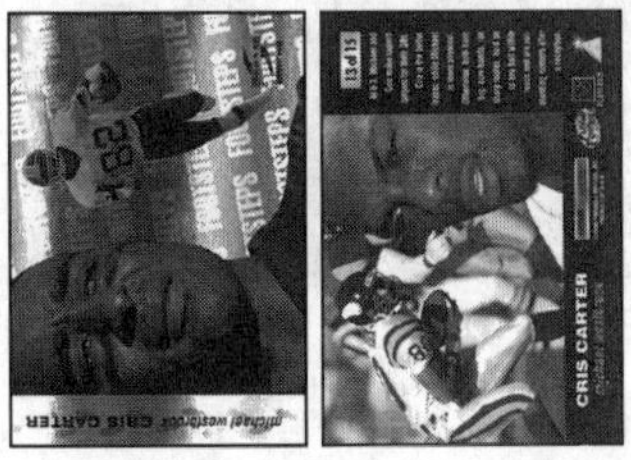

Randomly inserted in hobby packs only at a rate of one in 36, this 15-card horizontal standard-size set features an established player as well as a young player at the same position. The cards are numbered as "X" of 15.

	MINT	NRMT	EXC
COMPLETE SET (15)	120.00	55.00	15.00
COMMON CARD (1-15)	2.50	1.10	.30
☐ 1 Darick Holmes Erric Rhett	4.00	1.80	.50
☐ 2 Rashaan Salaam	5.00	2.20	.60

Natrone Means			
☐ 3 Ki-Jana Carter	12.00	5.50	1.50
Barry Sanders			
☐ 4 Terrell Davis	15.00	6.75	1.85
Marshall Faulk			
☐ 5 Rodney Thomas	2.50	1.10	.30
Chris Warren			
☐ 6 Curtis Martin	25.00	11.00	3.10
Emmitt Smith			
☐ 7 Kerry Collins	20.00	9.00	2.50
Troy Aikman			
☐ 8 Eric Zeier	12.00	5.50	1.50
Drew Bledsoe			
☐ 9 Steve McNair	25.00	11.00	3.10
Brett Favre			
☐ 10 Steve Young	15.00	6.75	1.85
Kordell Stewart			
☐ 11 J.J.Stokes	12.00	5.50	1.50
Jerry Rice			
☐ 12 Joey Galloway	5.00	2.20	.60
Michael Irvin			
☐ 13 Michael Westbrook	5.00	2.20	.60
Cris Carter			
☐ 14 Tamarick Vanover	4.00	1.80	.50
Isaac Bruce			
☐ 15 Orlando Thomas	6.00	2.70	.75
Deion Sanders			

1996 Score In The Zone

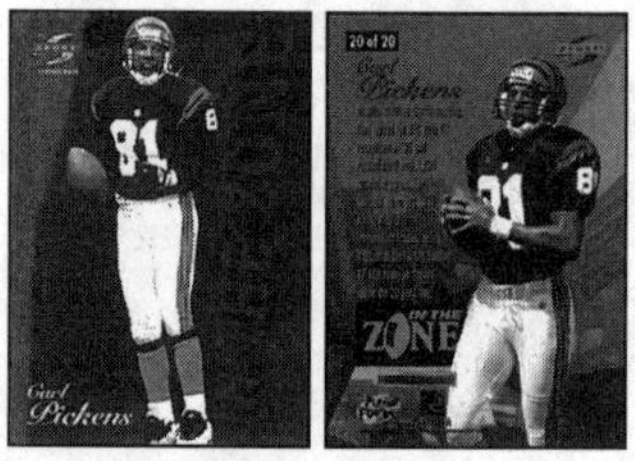

Randomly inserted in retail packs only at a rate of one in 33, this 20-card standard-size set features leading offensive threats. The player's photo is in the middle with his name in the lower left and the words "In the Zone" on the right. The cards are numbered "X" of 20.

	MINT	NRMT	EXC
COMPLETE SET (20)	175.00	80.00	22.00
COMMON CARD (1-20)	4.00	1.80	.50
☐ 1 Brett Favre	30.00	13.50	3.70
☐ 2 Warren Moon	6.00	2.70	.75
☐ 3 Erik Kramer	4.00	1.80	.50
☐ 4 Scott Mitchell	4.00	1.80	.50
☐ 5 Jeff Blake	8.00	3.60	1.00
☐ 6 Steve Bono	4.00	1.80	.50
☐ 7 Dan Marino	30.00	13.50	3.70
☐ 8 Troy Aikman	15.00	6.75	1.85
☐ 9 Emmitt Smith	30.00	13.50	3.70
☐ 10 Curtis Martin	20.00	9.00	2.50
☐ 11 Errict Rhett	8.00	3.60	1.00
☐ 12 Terrell Davis	20.00	9.00	2.50
☐ 13 Derek Loville	4.00	1.80	.50
☐ 14 Rodney Hampton	4.00	1.80	.50
☐ 15 Cris Carter	6.00	2.70	.75
☐ 16 Herman Moore	8.00	3.60	1.00
☐ 17 Jerry Rice	15.00	6.75	1.85
☐ 18 Ben Coates	4.00	1.80	.50
☐ 19 Michael Irvin	8.00	3.60	1.00
☐ 20 Carl Pickens	6.00	2.70	.75

1996 Score Numbers Game

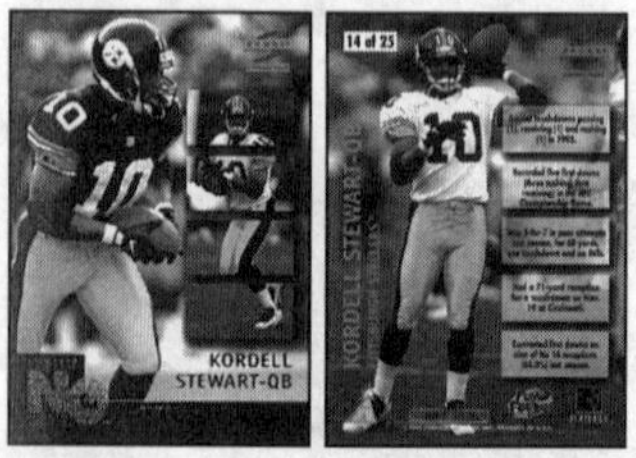

Randomly inserted in packs at a rate of one in 17, this 25-card standard-size set features leading players. Jumbo pack ratio was 1:9 packs. The backs have various blurbs which feature player's significant numbers. The cards are numbered "X"of 25 on the back.

	MINT	NRMT	EXC
COMPLETE SET (25)	80.00	36.00	10.00
COMMON CARD (1-25)	1.25	.55	.16
☐ 1 Barry Sanders	5.00	2.20	.60
☐ 2 Drew Bledsoe	5.00	2.20	.60
☐ 3 Brett Favre	10.00	4.50	1.25
☐ 4 John Elway	4.00	1.80	.50
☐ 5 Dan Marino	10.00	4.50	1.25
☐ 6 Michael Irvin	3.00	1.35	.35
☐ 7 Troy Aikman	5.00	2.20	.60
☐ 8 Emmitt Smith	10.00	4.50	1.25
☐ 9 Steve Young	4.00	1.80	.50
☐ 10 Jerry Rice	5.00	2.20	.60
☐ 11 Chris Sanders	2.00	.90	.25
☐ 12 Herman Moore	3.00	1.35	.35
☐ 13 Frank Sanders	2.00	.90	.25
☐ 14 Kordell Stewart	5.00	2.20	.60
☐ 15 Jeff Blake	3.00	1.35	.35
☐ 16 Robert Brooks	1.25	.55	.16
☐ 17 Marshall Faulk	3.00	1.35	.35
☐ 18 Carl Pickens	2.00	.90	.25
☐ 19 Greg Lloyd	1.25	.55	.16
☐ 20 Curtis Conway	1.25	.55	.16
☐ 21 Chris Warren	2.00	.90	.25
☐ 22 Natrone Means	2.00	.90	.25
☐ 23 Deion Sanders	3.00	1.35	.35
☐ 24 Neil O'Donnell	1.25	.55	.16
☐ 25 Ricky Watters	2.00	.90	.25

1996 Score Settle the Score

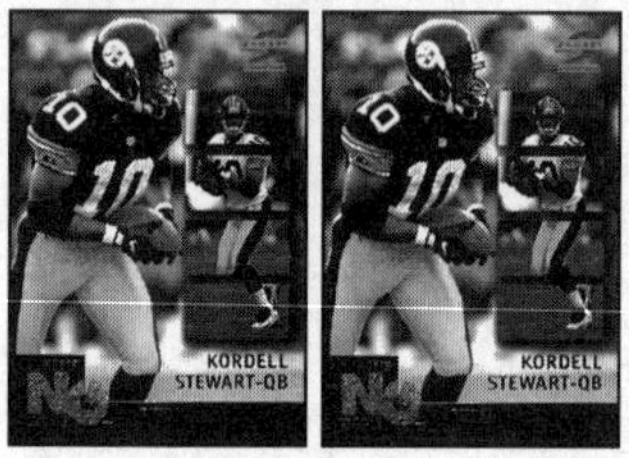

Randomly inserted in packs at a rate of one in 35 jumbo packs, this 30-card standard-size horizontal set features two players who were on opposing teams during 1995 NFL games. The fronts have the players names on the left with each player against a prismatic background. The backs have another player photo of each player as well as a description of how the player performed in each game. The cards are numbered as "X" of 30.

	MINT	NRMT	EXC
COMPLETE SET (30)	550.00	250.00	70.00
COMMON CARD (1-30)	5.00	2.20	.60
☐ 1 Frank Sanders	5.00	2.20	.60
Charlie Garner			
☐ 2 Drew Bledsoe	20.00	9.00	2.50
Neil O'Donnell			
☐ 3 Jerry Rice	20.00	9.00	2.50
Craig Heyward			
☐ 4 Emmitt Smith	40.00	18.00	5.00
Rod Woodson			
☐ 5 Derrick Holmes	40.00	18.00	5.00
Dan Marino			
☐ 6 Kerry Collins	20.00	9.00	2.50
Steve Young			
☐ 7 Rashaan Salaam	40.00	18.00	5.00
Brett Favre			
☐ 8 Curtis Conway	20.00	9.00	2.50
Barry Sanders			
☐ 9 Troy Aikman	50.00	22.00	6.25
Dan Marino			
☐ 10 Dan Marino	40.00	18.00	5.00
Neil O'Donnell			
☐ 11 Eric Zeier	12.00	5.50	1.50
Steve McNair			
☐ 12 Jeff Blake	20.00	9.00	2.50
Kordell Stewart			
☐ 13 Troy Aikman	20.00	9.00	2.50
Heath Shuler			
☐ 14 Michael Irvin	20.00	9.00	2.50
Jerry Rice			
☐ 15 Emmitt Smith	40.00	18.00	5.00
Ricky Watters			
☐ 16 John Elway	15.00	6.75	1.85
Steve Bono			
☐ 17 John Elway	15.00	6.75	1.85
Rick Mirer			
☐ 18 John Elway	15.00	6.75	1.85
Tim Brown			
☐ 19 Barry Sanders	50.00	22.00	6.25
Brett Favre			
☐ 20 Barry Sanders	20.00	9.00	2.50
Warren Moon			
☐ 21 Trent Dilfer	40.00	18.00	5.00
Brett Favre			
☐ 22 Rodney Thomas	5.00	2.20	.60
James O.Stewart			
☐ 23 Jim Harbaugh	20.00	9.00	2.50
Drew Bledsoe			
☐ 24 Marcus Allen	8.00	3.60	1.00
Harvey Williams			
☐ 25 Tamarick Vanover	8.00	3.60	1.00
Joey Galloway			
☐ 26 Dan Marino	50.00	22.00	6.25
Drew Bledsoe			
☐ 27 Mario Bates	20.00	9.00	2.50
Jerry Rice			
☐ 28 Tyrone Wheatley	8.00	3.60	1.00
Michael Westbrook			
☐ 29 Napoleon Kaufman	5.00	2.20	.60
Junior Seau			
☐ 30 J.J.Stokes	8.00	3.60	1.00

1962 Tang Team Photos

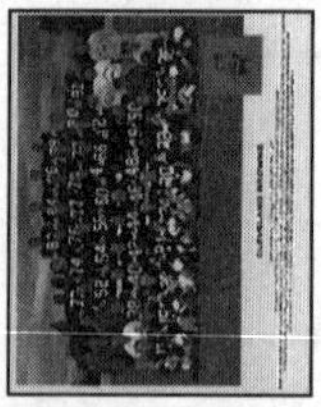

Each team in the NFL is represented in this set of 10" by 8" white-bordered color team photos. The team logo is superimposed over the picture at the lower right, and all the players and team personnel are identified by rows in wider white border. The backs are completely blank and the paper stock is thin. While Tang is not specifically identified as the sponsor on the photos, advertising pieces exist to verify this fact. Originally, complete sets were available via mail for 50-cents each with one innerseal from a Tang drink mix jar. The team photos are listed below in alphabetical order. Beware reprints.

	NRMT	VG-E	GOOD
COMPLETE SET (14)	175.00	80.00	22.00
COMMON TEAM (1-14)	12.00	5.50	1.50
☐ 1 Baltimore Colts	12.00	5.50	1.50
☐ 2 Chicago Bears	12.00	5.50	1.50
☐ 3 Cleveland Browns	12.00	5.50	1.50
☐ 4 Dallas Cowboys	20.00	9.00	2.50
☐ 5 Detroit Lions	12.00	5.50	1.50
☐ 6 Green Bay Packers	20.00	9.00	2.50
☐ 7 Los Angeles Rams	12.00	5.50	1.50
☐ 8 Minnesota Vikings	12.00	5.50	1.50
☐ 9 New York Giants	12.00	5.50	1.50
☐ 10 Philadelphia Eagles	12.00	5.50	1.50
☐ 11 Pittsburgh Steelers	12.00	5.50	1.50
☐ 12 St. Louis Cardinals	12.00	5.50	1.50
☐ 13 San Francisco 49ers	15.00	6.75	1.85
☐ 14 Washington Redskins	15.00	6.75	1.85

1981 TCMA Greats

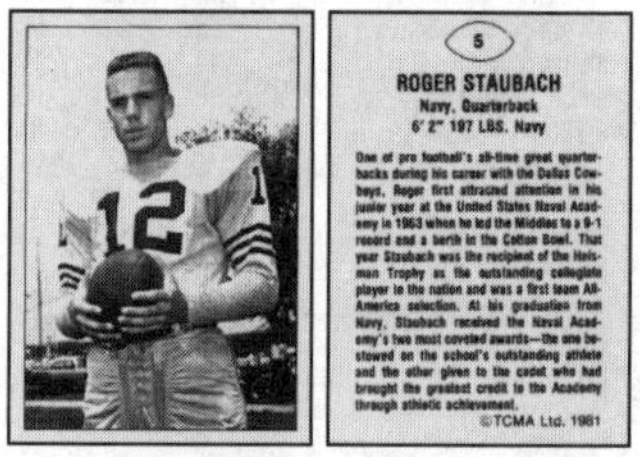

This 78-card standard-size set was put out by TCMA in 1981. The set features retired football players from the '50s and '60s. The cards are in the popular "pure card" format where there is nothing on the card front except the color photo of the subject inside a simple white border. The card backs provide a short narrative printed in black ink on white card stock. The TCMA copyright is located in the lower right corner. The cards are numbered on the back at the top inside a football; however, some cards can be found without the card number inside the football. The unnumbered versions are valued at one and a half times the prices listed below.

	MINT	NRMT	EXC
COMPLETE SET (78)	30.00	13.50	3.70
COMMON CARD (1-78)	.25	.11	.03
☐ 1 Alex Karras	.75	.35	.09
☐ 2 Fran Tarkenton	2.00	.90	.25
☐ 3 Johnny Unitas	3.00	1.35	.35
☐ 4 Bobby Layne	1.50	.70	.19
☐ 5 Roger Staubach	4.00	1.80	.50
☐ 6 Joe Namath	5.00	2.20	.60
☐ 7 1954 New York Giants Offense	.40	.18	.05
☐ 8 Jim Brown	5.00	2.20	.60
☐ 9 Ray Wietecha	.25	.11	.03
☐ 10 R.C. Owens	.25	.11	.03
☐ 11 Alex Webster	.25	.11	.03
☐ 12 Jim Otto UER (College was Miami, not Minnesota)	.60	.25	.07
☐ 13 Jim Taylor	1.50	.70	.19
☐ 14 Kyle Rote	.40	.18	.05
☐ 15 Roger Ellis	.25	.11	.03
☐ 16 Nick Pietrosante	.25	.11	.03
☐ 17 Milt Plum	.25	.11	.03
☐ 18 Eddie LeBaron	.40	.18	.05
☐ 19 Jimmy Patton	.25	.11	.03
☐ 20 Yale Lary	.40	.18	.05
☐ 21 Leo Nomellini	.60	.25	.07
☐ 22 John Olszewski	.25	.11	.03
☐ 23 Ernie Koy	.25	.11	.03
☐ 24 Bill Wade	.25	.11	.03
☐ 25 Billy Wells	.25	.11	.03
☐ 26 Ron Waller	.25	.11	.03
☐ 27 Pat Summerall	.60	.25	.07
☐ 28 Joe Schmidt	.60	.25	.07
☐ 29 Bob St.Clair	.40	.18	.05
☐ 30 Dick Lynch	.25	.11	.03
☐ 31 Tommy McDonald	.25	.11	.03
☐ 32 Earl Morrall	.25	.11	.03
☐ 33 Jim Martin	.25	.11	.03
☐ 34 Dick Modzelewski	.25	.11	.03
☐ 35 Dick LeBeau	.25	.11	.03
☐ 36 Dick Post	.25	.11	.03
☐ 37 Les Richter	.25	.11	.03
☐ 38 Andy Robustelli	.60	.25	.07
☐ 39 Pete Retzlaff	.25	.11	.03
☐ 40 Fred Biletnikoff	1.50	.70	.19
☐ 41 Timmy Brown	.25	.11	.03
☐ 42 Babe Parilli	.25	.11	.03
☐ 43 Lance Alworth	1.50	.70	.19
☐ 44 Sammy Baugh	2.00	.90	.25
☐ 45 Paul(Tank) Younger	.25	.11	.03
☐ 46 Chuck Bednarik	1.25	.55	.16
☐ 47 Art Donovan	1.25	.55	.16
☐ 48 Len Dawson	1.50	.70	.19
☐ 49 Don Maynard	1.25	.55	.16
☐ 50 Joe Morrison	.25	.11	.03
☐ 51 John Elliott	.25	.11	.03
☐ 52 Jim Ringo	.60	.25	.07
☐ 53 Max McGee	.25	.11	.03
☐ 54 Art Powell	.25	.11	.03
☐ 55 Galen Fiss	.25	.11	.03
☐ 56 Jack Stroud	.25	.11	.03
☐ 57 Bake Turner	.25	.11	.03
☐ 58 Mike McCormack	.40	.18	.05
☐ 59 L.G. Dupre	.25	.11	.03
☐ 60 Bill McPeak	.25	.11	.03
☐ 61 Art Spinney	.25	.11	.03
☐ 62 Fran Rogel	.25	.11	.03
☐ 63 Ollie Matson	1.25	.55	.16
☐ 64 Doak Walker	.75	.35	.09
☐ 65 Lenny Moore	1.25	.55	.16
☐ 66 George Shaw and Bert Rechichar	.25	.11	.03
☐ 67 Kyle Rote, Jim Lee Howell, Ray Krause	.40	.18	.05
☐ 68 Andy Robustelli, Roosevelt Grier, Dick Modzelewski, and Jim Katcavage	.60	.25	.07
☐ 69 Tucker Frederickson and Ernie Koy	.25	.11	.03
☐ 70 Gino Marchetti	.60	.25	.07
☐ 71 Earl Morrall and Allie Sherman	.25	.11	.03
☐ 72 Roosevelt Brown	.40	.18	.05
☐ 73 Howard Cassady (Hopalong)	.25	.11	.03
☐ 74 Don Chandler	.25	.11	.03
☐ 75 Joe Childress	.25	.11	.03
☐ 76 Rick Casares	.25	.11	.03
☐ 77 Charley Conerly	.75	.35	.09
☐ 78 1958 Giants QB's (Don Heinrich, Tom Dublinski, and Charley Conerly)	.40	.18	.05

1987 TCMA Update CMC

In 1987 CMC (the successor to TCMA) produced this 12-card standard-size set updating the 1981 TCMA issue. In fact the first 78 numbered cards were reissued at this time as part of a 90-card set; only the new-issue cards are listed below. Instead of copyright TCMA 1981, these 12 cards indicate copyright CMC 1987.

	MINT	NRMT	EXC
COMPLETE SET (12)	40.00	18.00	5.00
COMMON CARD (79-90)	3.00	1.35	.35
☐ 79 Fred Dryer	3.00	1.35	.35
☐ 80 Ed Marinaro	3.00	1.35	.35
☐ 81 O.J. Simpson	12.00	5.50	1.50
☐ 82 Joe Theismann	8.00	3.60	1.00
☐ 83 Roman Gabriel	3.00	1.35	.35
☐ 84 Terry Metcalf	3.00	1.35	.35
☐ 85 Lyle Alzado	4.00	1.80	.50
☐ 86 Jake Scott	3.00	1.35	.35
☐ 87 Cliff Branch	4.00	1.80	.50
☐ 88 Rocky Bleier	5.00	2.20	.60
☐ 89 Cliff Harris	3.00	1.35	.35
☐ 90 Archie Manning	5.00	2.20	.60

1960 Texans 7-Eleven

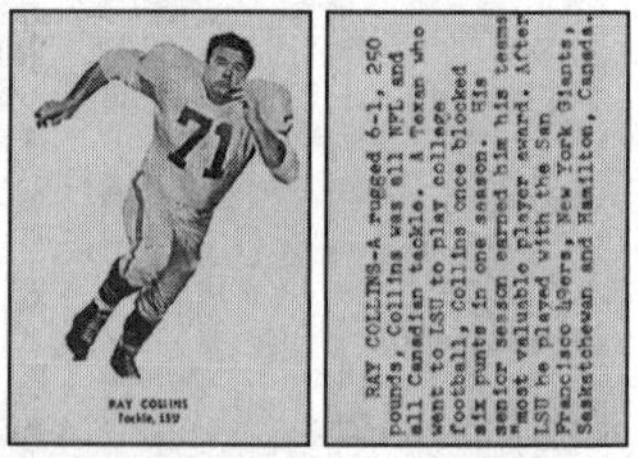

The cards measure the standard size 2 1/2" by 3 1/2" and are unnumbered. The front has a posed black and white photo of the player with no frame, with the player's name, position, and school

listed below the picture. On many of the cards the team name is written from bottom to top on the right hand side. The back has biographical information running the length of the card in typewriter script. Since the cards are unnumbered, they are listed below alphabetically. Any additional cards that can be verifiably added to this list would be appreciated.

	NRMT	VG-E	GOOD
COMPLETE SET (11)	475.00	210.00	60.00
COMMON CARD (1-11)	40.00	18.00	5.00
☐ 1 Max Boydston	40.00	18.00	5.00
☐ 2 Mel Branch	40.00	18.00	5.00
☐ 3 Chris Burford	40.00	18.00	5.00
☐ 4 Ray Collins UER (No team name on front)	40.00	18.00	5.00
☐ 5 Cotton Davidson	40.00	18.00	5.00
☐ 6 Abner Haynes	80.00	36.00	10.00
☐ 7 Sherrill Headrick	40.00	18.00	5.00
☐ 8 Bill Krisher	40.00	18.00	5.00
☐ 9 Paul Miller	40.00	18.00	5.00
☐ 10 Johnny Robinson	55.00	25.00	7.00
☐ 11 Jack Spikes	40.00	18.00	5.00

1992 Thunderbolts Arena

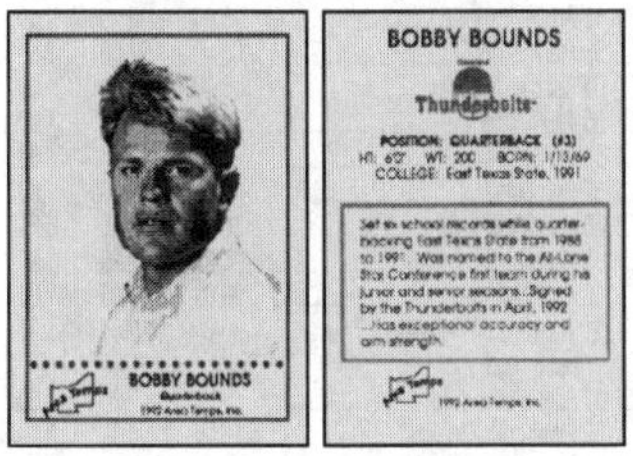

Printed on plain white card stock, these 24 cards are irregularly cut and so vary in size, but are close to standard size. Framed by a purple line, the fronts feature coarsely screened posed black-and-white player photos of the Arena Football League's (AFL) Cleveland Thunderbolts. The player's name and position, along with the logo of the sponsor, Area Temps, appear below the photo. The backs carry the player's name at the top, followed by the team logo, position, jersey number, biography, and career highlights. The cards are unnumbered and checklisted below in alphabetical order.

	MINT	NRMT	EXC
COMPLETE SET (24)	15.00	6.75	1.85
COMMON CARD (1-24)	.60	.25	.07
☐ 1 Eric Anderson	.60	.25	.07
☐ 2 Robert Banks	.60	.25	.07
☐ 3 Bobby Bounds	.60	.25	.07
☐ 4 Marvin Bowman	.60	.25	.07
☐ 5 George Cooper	.60	.25	.07
☐ 6 Michael Denbrock ACO	.60	.25	.07
☐ 7 Chris Drennan	.60	.25	.07
☐ 8 Dennis Fitzgerald ACO	.60	.25	.07
☐ 9 John Fletcher	.60	.25	.07
☐ 10 Andre Giles	.60	.25	.07
☐ 11 Chris Harkness	.60	.25	.07
☐ 12 Major Harris	5.00	2.20	.60
☐ 13 Luther Johnson	.60	.25	.07
☐ 14 Marvin Mattox	.60	.25	.07
☐ 15 Cedric McKinnon	.60	.25	.07
☐ 16 Cleo Miller ACO	.75	.35	.09
☐ 17 Tony Missick	.60	.25	.07
☐ 18 Anthony Newsom	.60	.25	.07
☐ 19 Phil Poirier	.60	.25	.07
☐ 20 Alvin Powell	.60	.25	.07
☐ 21 Ray Puryear	.60	.25	.07
☐ 22 Dave Whinham CO	.60	.25	.07
☐ 23 Brian Williams	.60	.25	.07
☐ 24 Kennedy Wilson	.60	.25	.07

1961 Titans Jay Publishing

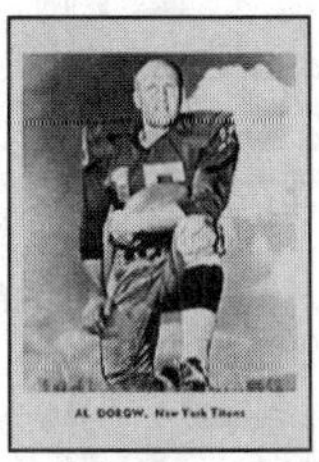

This 12-card set features (approximately) 5" by 7" black-and-white player photos of the New York Titans, one of the original AFL teams who later became the New York Jets. The photos show players in traditional poses with the quarterback preparing to throw, the runner heading downfield, and the defenseman ready for the tackle. The player's name and the team name appear in the wider bottom border. These cards were packaged 12 to a packet and originally sold for 25 cents. The backs are blank. The cards are unnumbered and checklisted below in alphabetical order.

	NRMT	VG-E	GOOD
COMPLETE SET (12)	100.00	45.00	12.50
COMMON CARD (1-12)	6.00	2.70	.75
☐ 1 Al Dorow	7.50	3.40	.95
☐ 2 Larry Grantham	7.50	3.40	.95
☐ 3 Mike Hagler	6.00	2.70	.75
☐ 4 Mike Hudock	6.00	2.70	.75
☐ 5 Bob Jewett	6.00	2.70	.75
☐ 6 Jack Klotz	6.00	2.70	.75
☐ 7 Don Maynard	30.00	13.50	3.70
☐ 8 John McMullan	6.00	2.70	.75
☐ 9 Bob Mischak	6.00	2.70	.75
☐ 10 Art Powell	10.00	4.50	1.25
☐ 11 Bob Reifsnyder	7.50	3.40	.95
☐ 12 Sid Youngelman	7.50	3.40	.95

1995 Tombstone Pizza

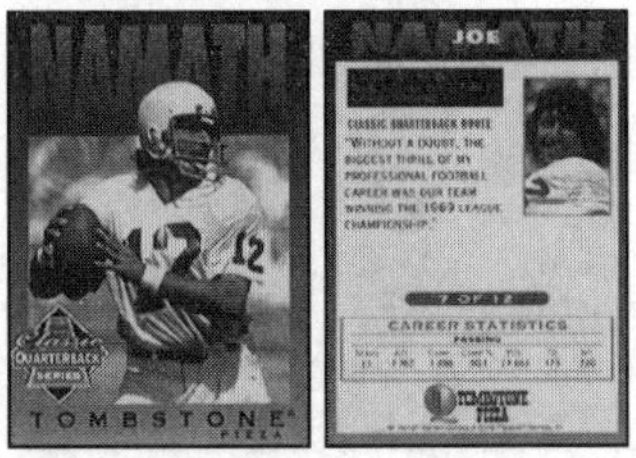

Titled "Classic Quarterback Series," one card from this 12-card standard-size set was inserted in specially-marked packages of Tombstone Pizza. Each of the quarterbacks autographed 10,000 cards for random insertion. The entire set was available through a mail-in offer for three Tombstone pizza logos plus 1.00. The fronts display color action cutouts framed by borders that fade from dark brown to orange. The player's last name is printed in large block lettering across the top. In addition to biography, career statistics, and a color headshot, the backs carry a "Classic Quarterback Quote."

	MINT	NRMT	EXC
COMPLETE SET (12)	20.00	9.00	2.50
COMMON CARD (1-12)	1.00	.45	.12
☐ 1 Ken Anderson	1.00	.45	.12
☐ 2 Terry Bradshaw	4.00	1.80	.50
☐ 3 Len Dawson	1.50	.70	.19
☐ 4 Dan Fouts	1.50	.70	.19
☐ 5 Bob Griese	2.00	.90	.25
☐ 6 Billy Kilmer	1.00	.45	.12
☐ 7 Joe Namath	5.00	2.20	.60
☐ 8 Jim Plunkett	1.00	.45	.12
☐ 9 Ken Stabler	2.50	1.10	.30
☐ 10 Bart Starr	2.00	.90	.25
☐ 11 Joe Theismann	1.00	.45	.12
☐ 12 Johnny Unitas	2.50	1.10	.30

1995 Tombstone Pizza Autographs

Titled "Classic Quarterback Series," one card from this 12-card standard-size set was inserted in specially-marked packages of Tombstone Pizza. Each quarterback autographed 10,000 cards for random insertion.

	MINT	NRMT	EXC
COMPLETE SET (12)	325.00	145.00	40.00
COMMON CARD (1-12)	15.00	6.75	1.85
☐ 1 Ken Anderson	15.00	6.75	1.85
☐ 2 Terry Bradshaw	50.00	22.00	6.25
☐ 3 Len Dawson	25.00	11.00	3.10
☐ 4 Dan Fouts	25.00	11.00	3.10
☐ 5 Bob Griese	25.00	11.00	3.10
☐ 6 Billy Kilmer	15.00	6.75	1.85
☐ 7 Joe Namath	60.00	27.00	7.50
☐ 8 Jim Plunkett	15.00	6.75	1.85
☐ 9 Ken Stabler	40.00	18.00	5.00
☐ 10 Bart Starr	30.00	13.50	3.70
☐ 11 Joe Theismann	15.00	6.75	1.85
☐ 12 Johnny Unitas	40.00	18.00	5.00

1996 Tombstone Pizza Quarterback Club Caps

This "milk cap" set was produced for Tombstone Pizza by Pinnacle Brands. The caps were distributed as a complete player set of 14 in a punch-out type board measuring approximately 8-1/2" by 11" and as two-cap packs in selected Tombstone Pizza packages. The two-cap packs included one player cap and the team logo cap. Each cap has a 1-5/8" diameter and features a player in the Quarterback Club. A black plastic "slammer" was also included with the set.

	MINT	NRMT	EXC
COMPLETE SET (14)	20.00	9.00	2.50
COMMON CAP (1-14)	.50	.23	.06
☐ 1 Steve Young	1.25	.55	.16
☐ 2 Emmitt Smith	3.00	1.35	.35
☐ 3 Junior Seau	.50	.23	.06
☐ 4 Barry Sanders	1.50	.70	.19
☐ 5 Jerry Rice	1.50	.70	.19
☐ 6 Dan Marino	3.00	1.35	.35
☐ 7 Jim Kelly	.75	.35	.09
☐ 8 Michael Irvin	.75	.35	.09
☐ 9 Brett Favre	3.00	1.35	.35
☐ 10 Marshall Faulk	1.00	.45	.12
☐ 11 John Elway	1.25	.55	.16
☐ 12 Randall Cunningham	.50	.23	.06
☐ 13 Drew Bledsoe	1.50	.70	.19
☐ 14 Troy Aikman	1.50	.70	.19

1950 Topps Felt Backs

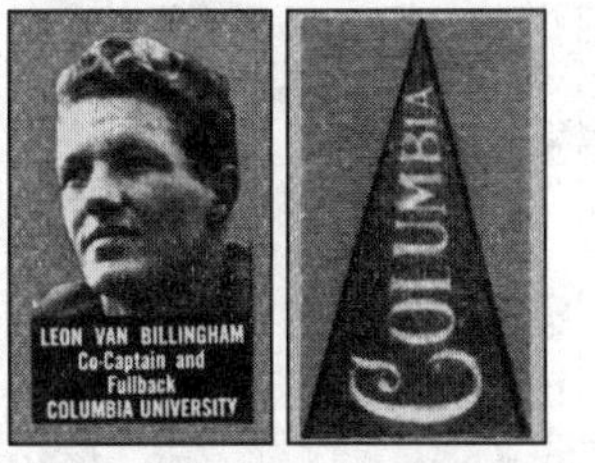

The 1950 Topps felt-back set contains 100 cards, each measuring approximately 7/8" by 1 7/16". The cards are arranged in alphabetical order. Sheets of 25 cards with the same color background are often found. The backs are made of felt and depict a college pennant. Twenty-five of the cards have either a brown or yellow background. The yellow version is more difficult to find. The following players come with either brown or yellow (B variations) backgrounds: Boldin, Botula, Burnett, Cecconi, Gitschier, Hart, Hester, Jensen, Lee, Malekoff, Martin, Mathews, McKissack, J. Miller, Nagel, Perini, Royal, Shaw, Sitko, Stalloni, Teninga, Towler, Turek, Walker, and Zinaich. The key Rookie Cards in this set are Lou Creekmur, Joe Paterno, Darrell Royal, and Ernie Stautner.

	NRMT	VG-E	GOOD
COMPLETE SET (100)	5000.00	2200.00	600.00
COMMON CARD (1-100)	40.00	18.00	5.00
COMMON YELLOW BORDER	65.00	29.00	8.00
WRAPPER (1-CENT)	500.00	220.00	60.00
☐ 1 Lou Allen	40.00	18.00	5.00
☐ 2 Morris Bailey	40.00	18.00	5.00
☐ 3 George Bell	40.00	18.00	5.00
☐ 4 Lindy Berry HOR	40.00	18.00	5.00
☐ 5A Mike Boldin	40.00	18.00	5.00
☐ 5B Mike Boldin	65.00	29.00	8.00
☐ 6A Bernie Botula	40.00	18.00	5.00
☐ 6B Bernie Botula	65.00	29.00	8.00
☐ 7 Bob Bowlby	40.00	18.00	5.00
☐ 8 Bob Bucher	40.00	18.00	5.00
☐ 9A Al Burnett	40.00	18.00	5.00
☐ 9B Al Burnett	65.00	29.00	8.00
☐ 10 Don Burson	40.00	18.00	5.00
☐ 11 Paul Campbell	40.00	18.00	5.00
☐ 12 Herb Carey	40.00	18.00	5.00
☐ 13A Bimbo Cecconi	40.00	18.00	5.00
☐ 13B Bimbo Cecconi	65.00	29.00	8.00
☐ 14 Bill Chauncey	40.00	18.00	5.00
☐ 15 Dick Clark	40.00	18.00	5.00
☐ 16 Tom Coleman	40.00	18.00	5.00
☐ 17 Billy Conn	40.00	18.00	5.00
☐ 18 John Cox	40.00	18.00	5.00
☐ 19 Lou Creekmur	80.00	36.00	10.00
☐ 20 Glen Davis	50.00	22.00	6.25
☐ 21 Warren Davis	40.00	18.00	5.00
☐ 22 Bob Deuber	40.00	18.00	5.00
☐ 23 Ray Dooney	40.00	18.00	5.00
☐ 24 Tom Dublinski	40.00	18.00	5.00
☐ 25 Jeff Fleischman	40.00	18.00	5.00
☐ 26 Jack Friedland	40.00	18.00	5.00
☐ 27 Bob Fuchs	40.00	18.00	5.00
☐ 28 Arnold Galiffa	50.00	22.00	6.25
☐ 29 Dick Gilman	40.00	18.00	5.00
☐ 30A Frank Gitschier	40.00	18.00	5.00
☐ 30B Frank Gitschier	65.00	29.00	8.00
☐ 31 Gene Glick	40.00	18.00	5.00
☐ 32 Bill Gregus	40.00	18.00	5.00
☐ 33 Harold Hagan	40.00	18.00	5.00
☐ 34 Charles Hall	40.00	18.00	5.00
☐ 35A Leon Hart	80.00	36.00	10.00
☐ 35B Leon Hart	140.00	65.00	17.50
☐ 36A Bob Hester	40.00	18.00	5.00
☐ 36B Bob Hester	65.00	29.00	8.00
☐ 37 George Hughes	40.00	18.00	5.00
☐ 38 Levi Jackson	50.00	22.00	6.25
☐ 39A Jackie Jensen	140.00	65.00	17.50
☐ 39B Jackie Jensen	250.00	110.00	31.00
☐ 40 Charlie Justice	125.00	55.00	15.50
☐ 41 Gary Kerkorian	40.00	18.00	5.00
☐ 42 Bernie Krueger	40.00	18.00	5.00
☐ 43 Bill Kuhn	40.00	18.00	5.00
☐ 44 Dean Laun	40.00	18.00	5.00
☐ 45 Chet Leach	40.00	18.00	5.00
☐ 46A Bobby Lee	40.00	18.00	5.00
☐ 46B Bobby Lee	65.00	29.00	8.00
☐ 47 Roger Lehew	40.00	18.00	5.00
☐ 48 Glenn Lippman	40.00	18.00	5.00
☐ 49 Melvin Lyle	40.00	18.00	5.00
☐ 50 Len Makowski	40.00	18.00	5.00
☐ 51A Al Malekoff	40.00	18.00	5.00
☐ 51B Al Malekoff	65.00	29.00	8.00
☐ 52A Jim Martin	50.00	22.00	6.25
☐ 52B Jim Martin	90.00	40.00	11.00
☐ 53 Frank Mataya	40.00	18.00	5.00
☐ 54A Ray Mathews	50.00	22.00	6.25
☐ 54B Ray Mathews	90.00	40.00	11.00
☐ 55A Dick McKissack	40.00	18.00	5.00
☐ 55B Dick McKissack	65.00	29.00	8.00
☐ 56 Frank Miller	40.00	18.00	5.00
☐ 57A John Miller	40.00	18.00	5.00
☐ 57B John Miller	65.00	29.00	8.00
☐ 58 Ed Modzelewski	50.00	22.00	6.25
☐ 59 Don Mouser	40.00	18.00	5.00
☐ 60 James Murphy	40.00	18.00	5.00
☐ 61A Ray Nagle	40.00	18.00	5.00
☐ 61B Ray Nagle	65.00	29.00	8.00
☐ 62 Leo Nomellini	175.00	80.00	22.00
☐ 63 James O'Day	40.00	18.00	5.00
☐ 64 Joe Paterno	950.00	425.00	120.00
☐ 65 Andy Pavich	40.00	18.00	5.00
☐ 66A Pete Perini	40.00	18.00	5.00
☐ 66B Pete Perini	65.00	29.00	8.00
☐ 67 Jim Powers	40.00	18.00	5.00
☐ 68 Dave Rakestraw	40.00	18.00	5.00
☐ 69 Herb Rich	40.00	18.00	5.00
☐ 70 Fran Rogel	40.00	18.00	5.00
☐ 71A Darrell Royal	120.00	55.00	15.00
☐ 71B Darrell Royal	225.00	100.00	28.00
☐ 72 Steve Sawle	40.00	18.00	5.00
☐ 73 Nick Sebek	40.00	18.00	5.00
☐ 74 Herb Seidell	40.00	18.00	5.00
☐ 75A Charles Shaw	40.00	18.00	5.00
☐ 75B Charles Shaw	65.00	29.00	8.00
☐ 76A Emil Sitko	50.00	22.00	6.25
☐ 76B Emil Sitko	90.00	40.00	11.00
☐ 77 Ed(Butch) Songin	50.00	22.00	6.25
☐ 78A Mariano Stalloni	40.00	18.00	5.00
☐ 78B Mariano Stalloni	65.00	29.00	8.00
☐ 79 Ernie Stautner	175.00	80.00	22.00
☐ 80 Don Stehley	40.00	18.00	5.00
☐ 81 Gil Stevenson	40.00	18.00	5.00
☐ 82 Bishop Strickland	40.00	18.00	5.00
☐ 83 Harry Szulborski	40.00	18.00	5.00
☐ 84A Wally Teninga	40.00	18.00	5.00
☐ 84B Wally Teninga	65.00	29.00	8.00
☐ 85 Clayton Tonnemaker	40.00	18.00	5.00
☐ 86A Deacon Dan Towler	75.00	34.00	9.50
☐ 86B Deacon Dan Towler	130.00	57.50	16.00
☐ 87A Bert Turek	40.00	18.00	5.00
☐ 87B Bert Turek	65.00	29.00	8.00
☐ 88 Harry Ulinski	40.00	18.00	5.00
☐ 89 Leon Van Billingham	40.00	18.00	5.00
☐ 90 Langdon Viracola	40.00	18.00	5.00
☐ 91 Leo Wagner	40.00	18.00	5.00
☐ 92A Doak Walker	200.00	90.00	25.00
☐ 92B Doak Walker	350.00	160.00	45.00
☐ 93 Jim Ward	40.00	18.00	5.00
☐ 94 Art Weiner	40.00	18.00	5.00
☐ 95 Dick Weiss	40.00	18.00	5.00
☐ 96 Froggie Williams	40.00	18.00	5.00
☐ 97 Robert Red Wilson	40.00	18.00	5.00
☐ 98 Roger Red Wilson	40.00	18.00	5.00
☐ 99 Carl Wren	40.00	18.00	5.00
☐ 100A Pete Zinaich	40.00	18.00	5.00
☐ 100B Pete Zinaich	65.00	29.00	8.00

1951 Topps Magic

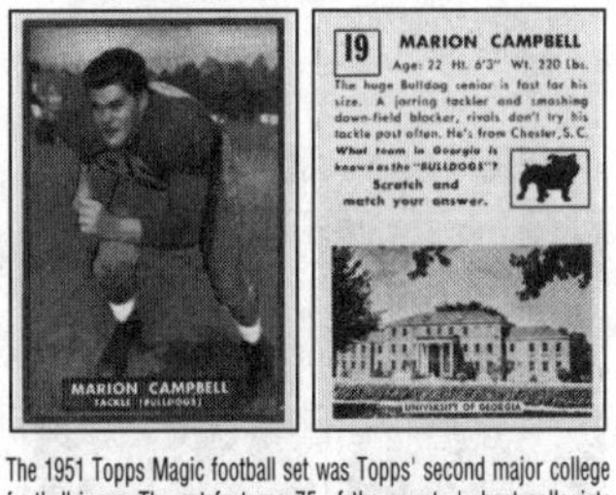

The 1951 Topps Magic football set was Topps' second major college football issue. The set features 75 of the country's best collegiate players. The cards measure approximately 2 1/16" by 2 15/16". The fronts contain color portraits with the player's name, position and team nickname in a black box at the bottom. The backs contain a brief write-up, a black and white photo of the player's college or university and scratch-off section which gives the answer to a football quiz. Cards with the scratch-off back intact are valued at 50 percent more than the prices listed below. Rookie Cards in this set include Marion Campbell, Vic Janowicz, Babe Parilli, Bert Rechichar, Bill Wade and George Young. The player's college nicknames are provided as they are listed physically on the card fronts.

	NRMT	VG-E	GOOD
COMPLETE SET (75)	1100.00	500.00	140.00
COMMON CARD (1-75)	18.00	8.00	2.20
*BACK UNSCRATCHED: 1.5X TO 2.5X BASIC CARDS			
WRAPPER (1-CENT)	200.00	90.00	25.00
WRAPPER (5-CENT)	300.00	135.00	38.00
☐ 1 Jimmy Monahan	30.00	13.50	3.70
☐ 2 Bill Wade	50.00	22.00	6.25
☐ 3 Bill Reichardt	18.00	8.00	2.20
☐ 4 Babe Parilli	55.00	25.00	7.00
☐ 5 Billie Burkhalter	18.00	8.00	2.20

6 Ed Weber	18.00	8.00	2.20
7 Tom Scott	25.00	11.00	3.10
8 Frank Guthridge	18.00	8.00	2.20
9 John Karras	18.00	8.00	2.20
10 Vic Janowicz	150.00	70.00	19.00
11 Lloyd Hill	18.00	8.00	2.20
12 Jim Weatherall	25.00	11.00	3.10
13 Howard Hansen	18.00	8.00	2.20
14 Lou D'Achille	18.00	8.00	2.20
15 Johnny Turco	18.00	8.00	2.20
16 Jerrell Price	18.00	8.00	2.20
17 John Coatta	18.00	8.00	2.20
18 Bruce Patton	18.00	8.00	2.20
19 Marion Campbell	35.00	16.00	4.40
20 Blaine Earon	18.00	8.00	2.20
21 Dewey McConnell	18.00	8.00	2.20
22 Ray Beck	18.00	8.00	2.20
23 Jim Prewett	18.00	8.00	2.20
24 Bob Steele	18.00	8.00	2.20
25 Art Betts	18.00	8.00	2.20
26 Walt Trillhaase	18.00	8.00	2.20
27 Gil Bartosh	18.00	8.00	2.20
28 Bob Bestwick	18.00	8.00	2.20
29 Tom Rushing	18.00	8.00	2.20
30 Bert Rechichar	35.00	16.00	4.40
31 Bill Owens	18.00	8.00	2.20
32 Mike Goggins	18.00	8.00	2.20
33 John Petitbon	18.00	8.00	2.20
34 Byron Townsend	18.00	8.00	2.20
35 Ed Rotticci	18.00	8.00	2.20
36 Steve Wadiak	18.00	8.00	2.20
37 Bobby Marlow	25.00	11.00	3.10
38 Bill Fuchs	18.00	8.00	2.20
39 Ralph Staub	18.00	8.00	2.20
40 Bill Vesprini	18.00	8.00	2.20
41 Zack Jordan	18.00	8.00	2.20
42 Bob Smith	25.00	11.00	3.10
43 Charles Hanson	18.00	8.00	2.20
44 Glenn Smith	18.00	8.00	2.20
45 Armand Kitto	18.00	8.00	2.20
46 Vinnie Drake	18.00	8.00	2.20
47 Bill Putich	18.00	8.00	2.20
48 George Young	40.00	18.00	5.00
49 Don McRae	18.00	8.00	2.20
50 Frank Smith	18.00	8.00	2.20
51 Dick Hightower	18.00	8.00	2.20
52 Clyde Pickard	18.00	8.00	2.20
53 Bob Reynolds	18.00	8.00	2.20
54 Dick Gregory	18.00	8.00	2.20
55 Dale Samuels	18.00	8.00	2.20
56 Gale Galloway	18.00	8.00	2.20
57 Vic Pujo	18.00	8.00	2.20
58 Dave Waters	18.00	8.00	2.20
59 Joe Ernest	18.00	8.00	2.20
60 Elmer Costa	18.00	8.00	2.20
61 Nick Liotta	18.00	8.00	2.20
62 John Dottley	18.00	8.00	2.20
63 Hi Faubion	18.00	8.00	2.20
64 David Harr	18.00	8.00	2.20
65 Bill Matthews	18.00	8.00	2.20
66 Carroll McDonald	18.00	8.00	2.20
67 Dick Dewing	18.00	8.00	2.20
68 Joe Johnson	18.00	8.00	2.20
69 Arnold Burwitz	18.00	8.00	2.20
70 Ed Dobrowolski	18.00	8.00	2.20
71 Joe Dudeck	18.00	8.00	2.20
72 Johnny Bright	25.00	11.00	3.10
73 Harold Loehlein	18.00	8.00	2.20
74 Lawrence Hairston	18.00	8.00	2.20
75 Bob Carey	25.00	11.00	3.10

1955 Topps All-American

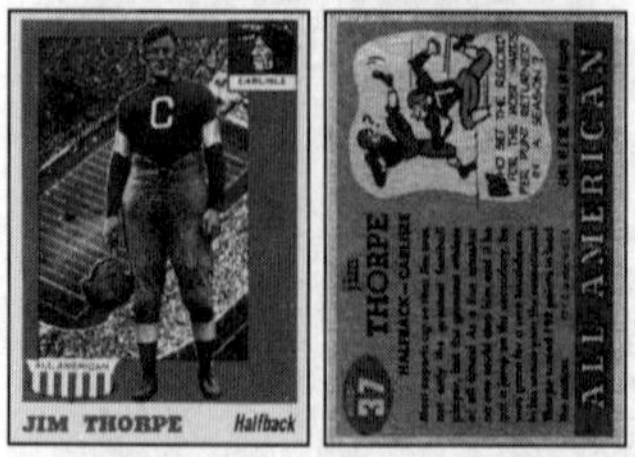

Issued in one-card penny packs, nine-card nickel packs as well as 22-card cello packs, the 1955 Topps All-American set features 100 cards of college football greats from years past. The cards measure approximately 2 5/8" by 3 5/8". Card fronts contain a color player photo superimposed over a black and white action photo. The player's college logo is in one upper corner and an All-American logo is at the bottom with the player's name and position. The backs contain collegiate highlights and a cartoon. There are many numbers which were printed in lesser supply. These short-printed cards are denoted in the checklist below by SP. The key Rookie Cards in this set are Doc Blanchard, Tommy Harmon, Don Hutson, Ernie Nevers and Amos Alonzo Stagg. The Four Horsemen (Notre Dame backfield in 1924), Knute Rockne, Jim Thorpe, Red Grange and former Supreme Court Justice Whizzer White are also key cards.

	NRMT	VG-E	GOOD
COMPLETE SET (100)	3600.00	1600.00	450.00
COMMON CARD (1-92)	16.00	7.25	2.00
COMMON CARD SP (93-100)	40.00	18.00	5.00
WRAPPER (1-CENT)	250.00	110.00	31.00
WRAPPER (5-CENT)	150.00	70.00	19.00

1 Herman Hickman	125.00	31.00	12.50
2 John Kimbrough	16.00	7.25	2.00
3 Ed Weir	16.00	7.25	2.00
4 Erny Pinckert	16.00	7.25	2.00
5 Bobby Grayson	16.00	7.25	2.00
6 Nile Kinnick UER Spelled Niles	80.00	36.00	10.00
7 Andy Bershak	16.00	7.25	2.00
8 George Cafego	16.00	7.25	2.00
9 Tom Hamilton SP	30.00	13.50	3.70
10 Bill Dudley	35.00	16.00	4.40
11 Bobby Dodd SP	30.00	13.50	3.70
12 Otto Graham	200.00	90.00	25.00
13 Aaron Rosenberg	16.00	7.25	2.00
14A Gaynell Tinsley ERR Wrong back 21 with Whizzer White bio	100.00	45.00	12.50
14B Gaynell Tinsley COR	25.00	11.00	3.10
15 Ed Kaw SP	30.00	13.50	3.70
16 Knute Rockne	325.00	145.00	40.00
17 Bob Reynolds	16.00	7.25	2.00
18 Pudge Heffelfinger SP	40.00	18.00	5.00
19 Bruce Smith	30.00	13.50	3.70
20 Sammy Baugh	200.00	90.00	25.00
21A Whizzer White ERR SP Wrong back 14 with Gaynell Tinsley bio	150.00	70.00	19.00
21B Whizzer White COR SP	75.00	34.00	9.50
22 Brick Muller	16.00	7.25	2.00
23 Dick Kazmaier	16.00	7.25	2.00
24 Ken Strong	35.00	16.00	4.40
25 Casimir Myslinski SP	30.00	13.50	3.70
26 Larry Kelley SP	40.00	18.00	5.00
27 Red Grange UER Card says he was QB should say halfback	350.00	160.00	45.00
28 Mel Hein SP	40.00	18.00	5.00
29 Leo Nomellini SP	60.00	27.00	7.50
30 Wes Fesler	16.00	7.25	2.00
31 George Sauer Sr.	20.00	9.00	2.50
32 Hank Foldberg	16.00	7.25	2.00
33 Bob Higgins	16.00	7.25	2.00
34 Davey O'Brien	35.00	16.00	4.40
35 Tom Harmon SP	50.00	22.00	6.25
36 Turk Edwards SP	40.00	18.00	5.00
37 Jim Thorpe	375.00	170.00	47.50
38A Amos Alonzo Stagg ERR Wrong back 19	100.00	45.00	12.50
38B Amos Alonzo Stagg COR	60.00	27.00	7.50
39 Jerome Holland	20.00	9.00	2.50
40 Donn Moomaw	16.00	7.25	2.00
41 Joseph Alexander SP	30.00	13.50	3.70
42 Eddie Tryon SP	40.00	18.00	5.00
43 George Savitsky	16.00	7.25	2.00
44 Ed Garbisch	16.00	7.25	2.00
45 Elmer Oliphant	16.00	7.25	2.00
46 Arnold Lassman	16.00	7.25	2.00
47 Bo McMillin	20.00	9.00	2.50
48 Ed Widseth	16.00	7.25	2.00
49 Don Zimmerman	16.00	7.25	2.00
50 Ken Kavanaugh	20.00	9.00	2.50
51 Duane Purvis SP	30.00	13.50	3.70
52 John Lujack	50.00	22.00	6.25
53 John F. Green	16.00	7.25	2.00
54 Edwin Dooley SP	30.00	13.50	3.70
55 Frank Merritt SP	30.00	13.50	3.70
56 Ernie Nevers	65.00	29.00	8.00
57 Vic Hanson SP	30.00	13.50	3.70
58 Ed Franco	16.00	7.25	2.00
59 Doc Blanchard	55.00	25.00	7.00
60 Dan Hill	16.00	7.25	2.00
61 Charles Brickley SP	40.00	18.00	5.00
62 Harry Newman	16.00	7.25	2.00
63 Charlie Justice	35.00	16.00	4.40
64 Benny Friedman	20.00	9.00	2.50
65 Joe Donchess SP	30.00	13.50	3.70
66 Bruiser Kinard	25.00	11.00	3.10
67 Frankie Albert	20.00	9.00	2.50
68 Four Horsemen SP Jim Crowley Elmer Layden Creighton Miller Harry Stuhldreher	500.00	220.00	60.00
69 Frank Sinkwich	20.00	9.00	2.50
70 Bill Daddio	16.00	7.25	2.00
71 Bob Wilson	16.00	7.25	2.00
72 Chub Peabody	16.00	7.25	2.00
73 Paul Governali	20.00	9.00	2.50
74 Gene McEver	16.00	7.25	2.00
75 Hugh Gallarneau	16.00	7.25	2.00
76 Angelo Bertelli	20.00	9.00	2.50
77 Bowden Wyatt SP	30.00	13.50	3.70
78 Jay Berwanger	35.00	16.00	4.40
79 Pug Lund	16.00	7.25	2.00
80 Bennie Oosterbaan	16.00	7.25	2.00
81 Cotton Warburton	16.00	7.25	2.00
82 Alex Wojciechowicz	25.00	11.00	3.10
83 Ted Coy SP	30.00	13.50	3.70
84 Ace Parker SP	40.00	18.00	5.00
85 Sid Luckman	100.00	45.00	12.50
86 Albie Booth SP	30.00	13.50	3.70
87 Adolph Schultz SP	30.00	13.50	3.70
88 Ralph G. Kercheval	16.00	7.25	2.00
89 Marshall Goldberg	20.00	9.00	2.50
90 Charlie O'Rourke	16.00	7.25	2.00
91 Bob Odell UER Photo actually Howard Odell	16.00	7.25	2.00
92 Biggie Munn	16.00	7.25	2.00
93 Willie Heston SP	40.00	18.00	5.00
94 Joe Bernard SP	40.00	18.00	5.00
95 Chris(Red) Cagle SP	40.00	18.00	5.00
96 Bill Hollenback SP	40.00	18.00	5.00
97 Don Hutson SP	225.00	100.00	28.00
98 Beattie Feathers SP	45.00	20.00	5.50
99 Don Whitmire SP	40.00	18.00	5.00
100 Fats Henry SP	160.00	40.00	16.00

1956 Topps

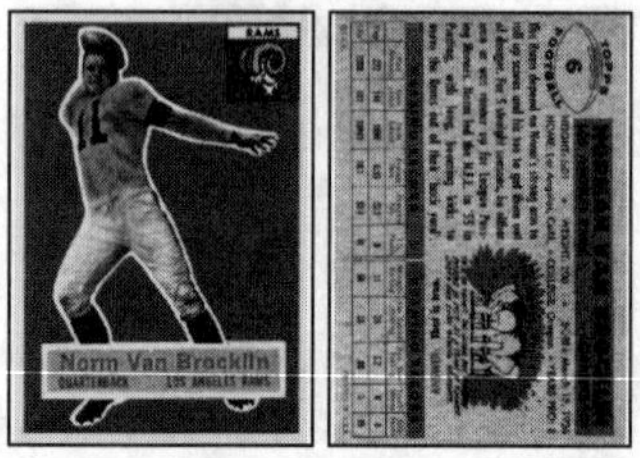

The 1956 set of 120 player cards marks Topps' first standard NFL football card set since acquiring Bowman. The cards measure 2 5/8" by 3 5/8" and were issued in one-card penny packs, nickel packs and 15-card cello packs. The card fronts have a player photo superimposed over a solid color background. The team logo is an upper corner with the player's name, team name and position grouped in a box toward the bottom of the photo. The card backs were printed in red and black on gray card stock. Statistical information from the immediate past season and career totals are given at the bottom. Players from the Washington Redskins and the Chicago Cardinals were apparently produced in lesser quantities, as they are more difficult to find compared to the other teams. Some veteran collectors believe that cards of members of the Baltimore Colts, Chicago Bears, and Cleveland Browns may also be slightly more difficult to find as well. An unnumbered checklist card and six contest cards were also issued along with this set, although in much lesser quantities. The contest cards have advertisements on both sides for Bazooka Bubble Gum. Both sides have orange-red and blue type on an off-white background. The fronts of the contest cards feature an offer to win one of three prizes (basketball, football, or autographed baseball glove) in the Bazooka Bubble Gum football contest, and the rules governing the contest are listed on the back. Any eligible contestant (not over 15 years old) who mailed in (before November 19th) the correct scores to the two NFL football games listed on the front of that particular card and includes five one-cent Bazooka Bubble Gum wrappers or one nickel Bazooka wrapper with the entry received a choice of one of the three above-mentioned prizes. The cards are either numbered (1-3) or lettered (A-C). Some dealers have doubted the existence of Contest Card C. Any proof of this card would be greatly appreciated. There also exists a three-card advertising panel consisting of the card fronts of Lou Groza, Don Colo, and Darrell Brewster with ad copy on the back. The key Rookie Cards in this set are Roosevelt Brown, Bill George, Rosey Grier, Stan Jones, Lenny Moore, and Joe Schmidt.

	NRMT	VG-E	GOOD
COMPLETE SET (120)	1300.00	575.00	160.00
COMMON CARD (1-120)	5.00	2.20	.60
WRAPPER (1-CENT)	300.00	135.00	38.00
WRAPPER (5-CENT)	50.00	22.00	6.25

1 Johnny Carson SP	75.00	19.00	7.50
2 Gordy Soltau	5.00	2.20	.60
3 Frank Varrichione	5.00	2.20	.60
4 Eddie Bell	5.00	2.20	.60
5 Alex Webster	12.00	5.50	1.50
6 Norm Van Brocklin	30.00	13.50	3.70
7 Green Bay Packers Team Card	18.00	8.00	2.20
8 Lou Creekmur	15.00	6.75	1.85
9 Lou Groza	25.00	11.00	3.10
10 Tom Bienemann SP	25.00	11.00	3.10
11 George Blanda	45.00	20.00	5.50
12 Alan Ameche	15.00	6.75	1.85
13 Vic Janowicz SP	45.00	20.00	5.50
14 Dick Moegle	8.00	3.60	1.00
15 Fran Rogel	5.00	2.20	.60
16 Harold Giancanelli	5.00	2.20	.60
17 Emlen Tunnell	15.00	6.75	1.85
18 Tank Younger	8.00	3.60	1.00
19 Billy Howton	8.00	3.60	1.00
20 Jack Christiansen	15.00	6.75	1.85
21 Darrell Brewster	5.00	2.20	.60
22 Chicago Cardinals SP Team Card	100.00	45.00	12.50
23 Ed Brown	8.00	3.60	1.00
24 Joe Campanella	5.00	2.20	.60
25 Leon Heath SP	22.00	10.00	2.70
26 San Francisco 49ers Team Card	18.00	8.00	2.20
27 Dick Flanagan	5.00	2.20	.60
28 Chuck Bednarik	25.00	11.00	3.10
29 Kyle Rote	14.00	6.25	1.75
30 Les Richter	8.00	3.60	1.00
31 Howard Ferguson	5.00	2.20	.60
32 Dorne Dibble	5.00	2.20	.60
33 Kenny Konz	5.00	2.20	.60
34 Dave Mann SP	25.00	11.00	3.10
35 Rick Casares	8.00	3.60	1.00
36 Art Donovan	30.00	13.50	3.70
37 Chuck Drazenovich SP	22.00	10.00	2.70
38 Joe Arenas	5.00	2.20	.60
39 Lynn Chandnois	5.00	2.20	.60
40 Philadelphia Eagles Team Card	18.00	8.00	2.20
41 Roosevelt Brown	35.00	16.00	4.40
42 Tom Fears	16.00	7.25	2.00
43 Gary Knafelc	5.00	2.20	.60
44 Joe Schmidt	45.00	20.00	5.50
45 Cleveland Browns Team Card UER (Card back does not credit the Browns with being Champs in 1955)	18.00	8.00	2.20
46 Len Teeuws SP	25.00	11.00	3.10
47 Bill George	30.00	13.50	3.70
48 Baltimore Colts Team Card	18.00	8.00	2.20
49 Eddie LeBaron SP	35.00	16.00	4.40
50 Hugh McElhenny	25.00	11.00	3.10
51 Ted Marchibroda	8.00	3.60	1.00
52 Adrian Burk	5.00	2.20	.60
53 Frank Gifford	60.00	27.00	7.50
54 Charley Toogood	5.00	2.20	.60
55 Tobin Rote	8.00	3.60	1.00
56 Bill Stits	5.00	2.20	.60
57 Don Colo	5.00	2.20	.60
58 Ollie Matson SP	70.00	32.00	8.75
59 Harlon Hill	5.00	2.20	.60
60 Lenny Moore	90.00	40.00	11.00
61 Washington Redskins SP Team Card	90.00	40.00	11.00
62 Billy Wilson	5.00	2.20	.60
63 Pittsburgh Steelers Team Card	18.00	8.00	2.20
64 Bob Pellegrini	5.00	2.20	.60
65 Ken MacAfee	5.00	2.20	.60
66 Willard Sherman	5.00	2.20	.60
67 Roger Zatkoff	5.00	2.20	.60
68 Dave Middleton	5.00	2.20	.60
69 Ray Renfro	8.00	3.60	1.00
70 Don Stonesifer SP	25.00	11.00	3.10
71 Stan Jones	30.00	13.50	3.70
72 Jim Mutscheller	5.00	2.20	.60
73 Volney Peters SP	22.00	10.00	2.70
74 Leo Nomellini	18.00	8.00	2.20
75 Ray Mathews	5.00	2.20	.60
76 Dick Bielski	5.00	2.20	.60
77 Charley Conerly	22.00	10.00	2.70
78 Elroy Hirsch	25.00	11.00	3.10
79 Bill Forester	8.00	3.60	1.00
80 Jim Doran	5.00	2.20	.60
81 Fred Morrison	5.00	2.20	.60
82 Jack Simmons SP	25.00	11.00	3.10
83 Bill McColl	5.00	2.20	.60
84 Bert Rechichar	5.00	2.20	.60
85 Joe Scudero SP	22.00	10.00	2.70
86 Y.A. Tittle	45.00	20.00	5.50
87 Ernie Stautner	18.00	8.00	2.20
88 Norm Willey	5.00	2.20	.60
89 Bob Schnelker	5.00	2.20	.60
90 Dan Towler	8.00	3.60	1.00
91 John Martinkovic	5.00	2.20	.60
92 Detroit Lions Team Card	18.00	8.00	2.20
93 George Ratterman	8.00	3.60	1.00
94 Chuck Ulrich SP	25.00	11.00	3.10
95 Bobby Watkins	5.00	2.20	.60
96 Buddy Young	8.00	3.60	1.00
97 Billy Wells SP	22.00	10.00	2.70
98 Bob Toneff	5.00	2.20	.60
99 Bill McPeak	5.00	2.20	.60
100 Bobby Thomason	5.00	2.20	.60
101 Roosevelt Grier	35.00	16.00	4.40
102 Ron Waller	5.00	2.20	.60
103 Bobby Dillon	5.00	2.20	.60
104 Leon Hart	8.00	3.60	1.00
105 Mike McCormack	15.00	6.75	1.85
106 John Olszewski SP	25.00	11.00	3.10
107 Bill Wightkin	5.00	2.20	.60
108 George Shaw	5.00	2.20	.60
109 Dale Atkeson SP	22.00	10.00	2.70
110 Joe Perry	25.00	11.00	3.10
111 Dale Dodrill	5.00	2.20	.60
112 Tom Scott	5.00	2.20	.60
113 New York Giants Team Card	18.00	8.00	2.20
114 Los Angeles Rams Team Card UER (back incorrect, Rams were not 1955 champs)	18.00	8.00	2.20
115 Al Carmichael	5.00	2.20	.60
116 Bobby Layne	45.00	20.00	5.50
117 Ed Modzelewski	5.00	2.20	.60
118 Lamar McHan SP	25.00	11.00	3.10
119 Chicago Bears Team Card	18.00	8.00	2.20
120 Billy Vessels	35.00	8.75	3.50

	NRMT	VG-E	GOOD
☐ C1 Sunday, October 14th Colts vs. Packers Cards vs. Redskins (Numbered as 1)	80.00	36.00	10.00
☐ C2 Sunday, October 14th Rams vs. Lions Giants vs. Browns (Numbered as 2)	80.00	36.00	10.00
☐ C3 Sunday, October 14th Eagles vs. Steelers 49ers vs. Bears (Numbered as 3)	80.00	36.00	10.00
☐ CA Sunday, November 25th Bears vs. Giants Rams vs. Colts (Numbered as A)	90.00	40.00	11.00
☐ CB Sunday, November 25th Steelers vs. Cards 49ers vs. Eagles (Numbered as B)	110.00	50.00	14.00
☐ NNO Checklist Card (unnumbered)	350.00	90.00	35.00

1957 Topps

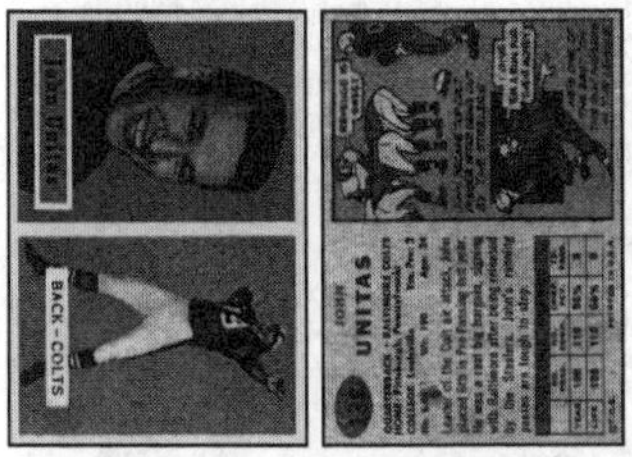

The 1957 Topps football set contains 154 standard-size cards of NFL players. Cards were issued in penny, nickel and cello packs. Horizontally designed fronts have a close-up photo (with player name) on the left and an in-action pose (with position and team name) to the right. Both have solid color backgrounds. The card backs were printed in red and black on gray card stock. Backs are also divided in two with statistical information on one side and a cartoon on the other. The Rookie Cards of Johnny Unitas, Bart Starr, and Paul Hornung are included in this set. Other notable Rookie Cards in this set are Raymond Berry, Dick "Night Train" Lane, Tommy McDonald and Earl Morrall. The second series (89-154) is generally more difficult to obtain than the first series. A number of cards (22) from the second series are much easier to find than the other 44, making those double prints (DP). It's thought that the John Unitas Rookie card is among the 22-DPs. An unnumbered checklist card was also issued with this set. The checklist card was printed in red, yellow, and blue or in red, white, and blue; neither variety currently is recognized as having any additional premium value above the price listed below. There also were produced several three-card advertising panels consisting of the card fronts of three players with ad copy on the reverse of the top two cards and a player's cardback at the bottom. The complete set price below refers to the 154 numbered cards minus the unnumbered checklist card.

	NRMT	VG-E	GOOD
COMPLETE SET (154)	2200.00	1000.00	275.00
COMMON CARD (1-88)	4.00	1.80	.50
COMMON CARD (89-154)	10.00	4.50	1.25
WRAPPER (1-CENT)	50.00	22.00	6.25
WRAPPER (5-CENT)	60.00	27.00	7.50

	NRMT	VG-E	GOOD
☐ 1 Eddie LeBaron	35.00	8.75	3.50
☐ 2 Pete Retzlaff	14.00	6.25	1.75
☐ 3 Mike McCormack	12.00	5.50	1.50
☐ 4 Lou Baldacci	4.00	1.80	.50
☐ 5 Gino Marchetti	16.00	7.25	2.00
☐ 6 Leo Nomellini	16.00	7.25	2.00
☐ 7 Bobby Watkins	4.00	1.80	.50
☐ 8 Dave Middleton	4.00	1.80	.50
☐ 9 Bobby Dillon	4.00	1.80	.50
☐ 10 Les Richter	6.00	2.70	.75
☐ 11 Roosevelt Brown	15.00	6.75	1.85
☐ 12 Lavern Torgeson	4.00	1.80	.50
☐ 13 Dick Bielski	4.00	1.80	.50
☐ 14 Pat Summerall	16.00	7.25	2.00
☐ 15 Jack Butler	6.00	2.70	.75
☐ 16 John Henry Johnson	15.00	6.75	1.85
☐ 17 Art Spinney	4.00	1.80	.50
☐ 18 Bob St. Clair	12.00	5.50	1.50
☐ 19 Perry Jeter	4.00	1.80	.50
☐ 20 Lou Creekmur	10.00	4.50	1.25
☐ 21 Dave Hanner	4.00	1.80	.50
☐ 22 Norm Van Brocklin	25.00	11.00	3.10
☐ 23 Don Chandler	8.00	3.60	1.00
☐ 24 Al Dorow	4.00	1.80	.50
☐ 25 Tom Scott	4.00	1.80	.50
☐ 26 Ollie Matson	18.00	8.00	2.20
☐ 27 Fran Rogel	4.00	1.80	.50
☐ 28 Lou Groza	18.00	8.00	2.20
☐ 29 Billy Vessels	6.00	2.70	.75
☐ 30 Y.A. Tittle	35.00	16.00	4.40
☐ 31 George Blanda	35.00	16.00	4.40
☐ 32 Bobby Layne	40.00	18.00	5.00
☐ 33 Billy Howton	6.00	2.70	.75
☐ 34 Bill Wade	6.00	2.70	.75
☐ 35 Emlen Tunnell	12.00	5.50	1.50
☐ 36 Leo Elter	4.00	1.80	.50
☐ 37 Clarence Peaks	6.00	2.70	.75
☐ 38 Don Stonesifer	4.00	1.80	.50
☐ 39 George Tarasovic	4.00	1.80	.50
☐ 40 Darrell Brewster	4.00	1.80	.50
☐ 41 Bert Rechichar	4.00	1.80	.50
☐ 42 Billy Wilson	4.00	1.80	.50
☐ 43 Ed Brown	6.00	2.70	.75
☐ 44 Gene Gedman	4.00	1.80	.50
☐ 45 Gary Knafelc	4.00	1.80	.50
☐ 46 Elroy Hirsch	20.00	9.00	2.50
☐ 47 Don Heinrich	6.00	2.70	.75
☐ 48 Gene Brito	4.00	1.80	.50
☐ 49 Chuck Bednarik	20.00	9.00	2.50
☐ 50 Dave Mann	4.00	1.80	.50
☐ 51 Bill McPeak	4.00	1.80	.50
☐ 52 Kenny Konz	4.00	1.80	.50
☐ 53 Alan Ameche	10.00	4.50	1.25
☐ 54 Gordy Soltau	4.00	1.80	.50
☐ 55 Rick Casares	6.00	2.70	.75
☐ 56 Charlie Ane	4.00	1.80	.50
☐ 57 Al Carmichael	4.00	1.80	.50
☐ 58A Willard Sherman ERR (no team on front)	325.00	145.00	40.00
☐ 58B Willard Sherman COR	4.00	1.80	.50
☐ 59 Kyle Rote	10.00	4.50	1.25
☐ 60 Chuck Drazenovich	4.00	1.80	.50
☐ 61 Bobby Walston	4.00	1.80	.50
☐ 62 John Olszewski	4.00	1.80	.50
☐ 63 Ray Mathews	4.00	1.80	.50
☐ 64 Maurice Bassett	4.00	1.80	.50
☐ 65 Art Donovan	25.00	11.00	3.10
☐ 66 Joe Arenas	4.00	1.80	.50
☐ 67 Harlon Hill	6.00	2.70	.75
☐ 68 Yale Lary	10.00	4.50	1.25
☐ 69 Bill Forester	6.00	2.70	.75
☐ 70 Bob Boyd	4.00	1.80	.50
☐ 71 Andy Robustelli	16.00	7.25	2.00
☐ 72 Sam Baker	6.00	2.70	.75
☐ 73 Bob Pellegrini	4.00	1.80	.50
☐ 74 Leo Sanford	4.00	1.80	.50
☐ 75 Sid Watson	4.00	1.80	.50
☐ 76 Ray Renfro	6.00	2.70	.75
☐ 77 Carl Taseff	4.00	1.80	.50
☐ 78 Clyde Conner	4.00	1.80	.50
☐ 79 J.C. Caroline	4.00	1.80	.50
☐ 80 Howard Cassady	14.00	6.25	1.75
☐ 81 Tobin Rote	6.00	2.70	.75
☐ 82 Ron Waller	4.00	1.80	.50
☐ 83 Jim Patton	6.00	2.70	.75
☐ 84 Volney Peters	4.00	1.80	.50
☐ 85 Dick Lane	40.00	18.00	5.00
☐ 86 Royce Womble	4.00	1.80	.50
☐ 87 Duane Putnam	6.00	2.70	.75
☐ 88 Frank Gifford	60.00	27.00	7.50
☐ 89 Steve Meilinger	10.00	4.50	1.25
☐ 90 Buck Lansford	10.00	4.50	1.25
☐ 91 Lindon Crow DP	8.00	3.60	1.00
☐ 92 Ernie Stautner DP	18.00	8.00	2.20
☐ 93 Preston Carpenter DP	8.00	3.60	1.00
☐ 94 Raymond Berry	125.00	55.00	15.50
☐ 95 Hugh McElhenny	25.00	11.00	3.10
☐ 96 Stan Jones	15.00	6.75	1.85
☐ 97 Dorne Dibble	10.00	4.50	1.25
☐ 98 Joe Scudero DP	8.00	3.60	1.00
☐ 99 Eddie Bell	10.00	4.50	1.25
☐ 100 Joe Childress DP	8.00	3.60	1.00
☐ 101 Elbert Nickel	12.00	5.50	1.50
☐ 102 Walt Michaels	12.00	5.50	1.50
☐ 103 Jim Mutscheller DP	8.00	3.60	1.00
☐ 104 Earl Morrall	40.00	18.00	5.00
☐ 105 Larry Strickland	10.00	4.50	1.25
☐ 106 Jack Christiansen	16.00	7.25	2.00
☐ 107 Fred Cone DP	8.00	3.60	1.00
☐ 108 Bud McFadin	12.00	5.50	1.50
☐ 109 Charley Conerly	25.00	11.00	3.10
☐ 110 Tom Runnels DP	8.00	3.60	1.00
☐ 111 Ken Keller DP	8.00	3.60	1.00
☐ 112 James Root	10.00	4.50	1.25
☐ 113 Ted Marchibroda DP	10.00	4.50	1.25
☐ 114 Don Paul	10.00	4.50	1.25
☐ 115 George Shaw	12.00	5.50	1.50
☐ 116 Dick Moegle	12.00	5.50	1.50
☐ 117 Don Bingham	10.00	4.50	1.25
☐ 118 Leon Hart	12.00	5.50	1.50
☐ 119 Bart Starr	450.00	200.00	55.00
☐ 120 Paul Miller DP	8.00	3.60	1.00
☐ 121 Alex Webster	12.00	5.50	1.50
☐ 122 Ray Wietecha DP	8.00	3.60	1.00
☐ 123 Johnny Carson	10.00	4.50	1.25
☐ 124 Tommy McDonald DP	15.00	6.75	1.85
☐ 125 Jerry Tubbs	12.00	5.50	1.50
☐ 126 Jack Scarbath	10.00	4.50	1.25
☐ 127 Ed Modzelewski DP	8.00	3.60	1.00
☐ 128 Lenny Moore	50.00	22.00	6.25
☐ 129 Joe Perry DP	25.00	11.00	3.10
☐ 130 Bill Wightkin	10.00	4.50	1.25
☐ 131 Jim Doran	10.00	4.50	1.25
☐ 132 Howard Ferguson UER (Name misspelled Furgeson on front)	10.00	4.50	1.25
☐ 133 Tom Wilson	10.00	4.50	1.25
☐ 134 Dick James	10.00	4.50	1.25
☐ 135 Jimmy Harris	10.00	4.50	1.25
☐ 136 Chuck Ulrich	10.00	4.50	1.25
☐ 137 Lynn Chandnois	10.00	4.50	1.25
☐ 138 John Unitas DP	450.00	200.00	55.00
☐ 139 Jim Ridlon DP	8.00	3.60	1.00
☐ 140 Zeke Bratkowski DP	10.00	4.50	1.25
☐ 141 Ray Krouse	10.00	4.50	1.25
☐ 142 John Martinkovic	10.00	4.50	1.25
☐ 143 Jim Cason DP	8.00	3.60	1.00
☐ 144 Ken MacAfee	10.00	4.50	1.25
☐ 145 Sid Youngelman	12.00	5.50	1.50
☐ 146 Paul Larson	10.00	4.50	1.25
☐ 147 Len Ford	25.00	11.00	3.10
☐ 148 Bob Toneff DP	8.00	3.60	1.00
☐ 149 Ronnie Knox DP	8.00	3.60	1.00
☐ 150 Jim David	12.00	5.50	1.50
☐ 151 Paul Hornung	450.00	200.00	55.00
☐ 152 Tank Younger	12.00	5.50	1.50
☐ 153 Bill Svoboda DP	8.00	3.60	1.00
☐ 154 Fred Morrison	70.00	17.50	7.00
☐ NNO Checklist Card SP	750.00	190.00	75.00

1958 Topps

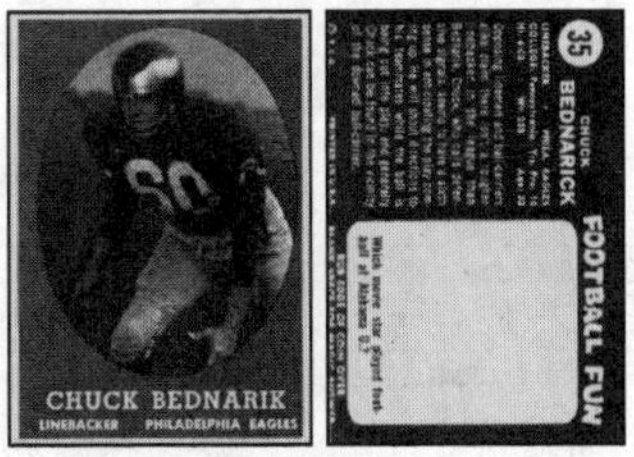

The 1958 Topps set of 132 standard-size cards contains NFL players. After a one-year interruption, team cards returned to the Topps lineup. The cards were issued in penny, nickel and cello packs. Card fronts have an oval player photo surrounded by a solid color that varies according to team. The player's name, position and team are at the bottom. The backs are easily distinguished from other years, as they are printed in bright red ink on white stock. The right-hand side has a trivia question with which the answer could be obtained by rubbing with a coin over the blank space. The left side has stats and highlights. The key Rookie Cards in this set are Jim Brown and Sonny Jurgensen. Topps also randomly inserted in packs a card with the words "Free Felt Initial" across the top. The horizontally oriented front pictures a boy in a red shirt and a girl in a blue shirt, with a large yellow "L" and "A" respectively on each of their shirts. The card back indicates an initial could be obtained by sending in three Bazooka or Blony wrappers and a self-addressed stamped envelope with the initial of choice printed on the front and back of the envelope.

	NRMT	VG-E	GOOD
COMPLETE SET (132)	1250.00	550.00	160.00
COMMON CARD (1-132)	3.50	1.55	.45
WRAPPER (1-CENT)	25.00	11.00	3.10
WRAPPER (5-CENT)	50.00	22.00	6.25

	NRMT	VG-E	GOOD
☐ 1 Gene Filipski	14.00	3.50	1.40
☐ 2 Bobby Layne	30.00	13.50	3.70
☐ 3 Joe Schmidt	10.00	4.50	1.25
☐ 4 Bill Barnes	3.50	1.55	.45
☐ 5 Milt Plum	8.00	3.60	1.00
☐ 6 Billy Howton UER (Misspelled Billie on card front)	5.00	2.20	.60
☐ 7 Howard Cassady	5.00	2.20	.60
☐ 8 Jim Dooley	3.50	1.55	.45
☐ 9 Cleveland Browns Team Card	6.00	2.70	.75
☐ 10 Lenny Moore	20.00	9.00	2.50
☐ 11 Darrell Brewster UER (Misspelled Darrel on card back)	3.50	1.55	.45
☐ 12 Alan Ameche	8.00	3.60	1.00
☐ 13 Jim David	3.50	1.55	.45
☐ 14 Jim Mutscheller	3.50	1.55	.45
☐ 15 Andy Robustelli UER (Never played for San Francisco)	8.00	3.60	1.00
☐ 16 Gino Marchetti	10.00	4.50	1.25
☐ 17 Ray Renfro	5.00	2.20	.60
☐ 18 Yale Lary	8.00	3.60	1.00
☐ 19 Gary Glick	3.50	1.55	.45
☐ 20 Jon Arnett	8.00	3.60	1.00
☐ 21 Bob Boyd	3.50	1.55	.45
☐ 22 John Unitas UER (College: Pittsburgh should be Louisville)	100.00	45.00	12.50
☐ 23 Zeke Bratkowski	5.00	2.20	.60
☐ 24 Sid Youngelman UER (Misspelled Youngleman on card back)	3.50	1.55	.45
☐ 25 Leo Elter	3.50	1.55	.45
☐ 26 Kenny Konz	3.50	1.55	.45
☐ 27 Washington Redskins Team Card	6.00	2.70	.75
☐ 28 Carl Brettschneider UER (Misspelled on back as Brettschnieder)	3.50	1.55	.45
☐ 29 Chicago Bears Team Card	6.00	2.70	.75
☐ 30 Alex Webster	5.00	2.20	.60
☐ 31 Al Carmichael	3.50	1.55	.45
☐ 32 Bobby Dillon	3.50	1.55	.45
☐ 33 Steve Meilinger	3.50	1.55	.45
☐ 34 Sam Baker	3.50	1.55	.45
☐ 35 Chuck Bednarik UER (Misspelled Bednarick on card back)	16.00	7.25	2.00
☐ 36 Bert Vic Zucco	3.50	1.55	.45
☐ 37 George Tarasovic	3.50	1.55	.45
☐ 38 Bill Wade	5.00	2.20	.60
☐ 39 Dick Stanfel	5.00	2.20	.60
☐ 40 Jerry Norton	3.50	1.55	.45
☐ 41 San Francisco 49ers Team Card	6.00	2.70	.75
☐ 42 Emlen Tunnell	10.00	4.50	1.25
☐ 43 Jim Doran	3.50	1.55	.45
☐ 44 Ted Marchibroda	5.00	2.20	.60
☐ 45 Chet Hanulak	3.50	1.55	.45
☐ 46 Dale Dodrill	3.50	1.55	.45
☐ 47 Johnny Carson	3.50	1.55	.45
☐ 48 Dick Deschaine	3.50	1.55	.45
☐ 49 Billy Wells UER (College should be Michigan State)	3.50	1.55	.45
☐ 50 Larry Morris	3.50	1.55	.45
☐ 51 Jack McClairen	3.50	1.55	.45
☐ 52 Lou Groza	15.00	6.75	1.85
☐ 53 Rick Casares	5.00	2.20	.60
☐ 54 Don Chandler	5.00	2.20	.60
☐ 55 Duane Putnam	3.50	1.55	.45
☐ 56 Gary Knafelc	3.50	1.55	.45
☐ 57 Earl Morrall UER (Misspelled Morall on card back)	10.00	4.50	1.25
☐ 58 Ron Kramer	5.00	2.20	.60
☐ 59 Mike McCormack	8.00	3.60	1.00
☐ 60 Gern Nagler	3.50	1.55	.45
☐ 61 New York Giants Team Card	6.00	2.70	.75
☐ 62 Jim Brown	450.00	200.00	55.00
☐ 63 Joe Marconi UER (Avg. gain should be 4.4)	3.50	1.55	.45
☐ 64 R.C. Owens UER (Photo actually Don Owens)	5.00	2.20	.60
☐ 65 Jimmy Carr	5.00	2.20	.60
☐ 66 Bart Starr UER (Life and year stats reversed)	100.00	45.00	12.50
☐ 67 Tom Wilson	3.50	1.55	.45
☐ 68 Lamar McHan	3.50	1.55	.45
☐ 69 Chicago Cardinals Team Card	6.00	2.70	.75
☐ 70 Jack Christiansen	8.00	3.60	1.00
☐ 71 Don McIlhenny	3.50	1.55	.45
☐ 72 Ron Waller	3.50	1.55	.45
☐ 73 Frank Gifford	50.00	22.00	6.25
☐ 74 Bert Rechichar	3.50	1.55	.45
☐ 75 John Henry Johnson	8.00	3.60	1.00
☐ 76 Jack Butler	5.00	2.20	.60
☐ 77 Frank Varrichione	3.50	1.55	.45
☐ 78 Ray Mathews	3.50	1.55	.45
☐ 79 Marv Matuszak UER (Misspelled Matuzsak on card front)	3.50	1.55	.45
☐ 80 Harlon Hill UER (Lifetime yards and Avg. gain incorrect)	3.50	1.55	.45
☐ 81 Lou Creekmur	8.00	3.60	1.00
☐ 82 Woodley Lewis UER (misspelled Woodly on front; end on front and halfback on back)	3.50	1.55	.45
☐ 83 Don Heinrich	3.50	1.55	.45
☐ 84 Charley Conerly UER (Misspelled Charlie on card back)	16.00	7.25	2.00
☐ 85 Los Angeles Rams Team Card	6.00	2.70	.75
☐ 86 Y.A. Tittle	30.00	13.50	3.70
☐ 87 Bobby Walston	3.50	1.55	.45
☐ 88 Earl Putman	3.50	1.55	.45
☐ 89 Leo Nomellini	12.00	5.50	1.50
☐ 90 Sonny Jurgensen	100.00	45.00	12.50
☐ 91 Don Paul	3.50	1.55	.45
☐ 92 Paige Cothren	3.50	1.55	.45
☐ 93 Joe Perry	15.00	6.75	1.85
☐ 94 Tobin Rote	5.00	2.20	.60
☐ 95 Billy Wilson	3.50	1.55	.45
☐ 96 Green Bay Packers Team Card	6.00	2.70	.75
☐ 97 Lavern Torgeson	3.50	1.55	.45
☐ 98 Milt Davis	3.50	1.55	.45
☐ 99 Larry Strickland	3.50	1.55	.45
☐ 100 Matt Hazeltine	5.00	2.20	.60
☐ 101 Walt Yowarsky	3.50	1.55	.45
☐ 102 Roosevelt Brown	8.00	3.60	1.00
☐ 103 Jim Ringo	8.00	3.60	1.00
☐ 104 Joe Krupa	3.50	1.55	.45
☐ 105 Les Richter	5.00	2.20	.60
☐ 106 Art Donovan	18.00	8.00	2.20
☐ 107 John Olszewski	3.50	1.55	.45
☐ 108 Ken Keller	3.50	1.55	.45
☐ 109 Philadelphia Eagles Team Card	6.00	2.70	.75
☐ 110 Baltimore Colts Team Card	6.00	2.70	.75
☐ 111 Dick Bielski	3.50	1.55	.45

Card	NRMT	VG-E	GOOD
☐ 112 Eddie LeBaron	5.00	2.20	.60
☐ 113 Gene Brito	3.50	1.55	.45
☐ 114 Willie Galimore	8.00	3.60	1.00
☐ 115 Detroit Lions Team Card	6.00	2.70	.75
☐ 116 Pittsburgh Steelers Team Card	6.00	2.70	.75
☐ 117 L.G. Dupre	3.50	1.55	.45
☐ 118 Babe Parilli	5.00	2.20	.60
☐ 119 Bill George	8.00	3.60	1.00
☐ 120 Raymond Berry	40.00	18.00	5.00
☐ 121 Jim Podoley UER (Photo actually Volney Peters; Podoly in cartoon)	3.50	1.55	.45
☐ 122 Hugh McElhenny	16.00	7.25	2.00
☐ 123 Ed Brown	5.00	2.20	.60
☐ 124 Dick Moegle	5.00	2.20	.60
☐ 125 Tom Scott	3.50	1.55	.45
☐ 126 Tommy McDonald	5.00	2.20	.60
☐ 127 Ollie Matson	14.00	6.25	1.75
☐ 128 Preston Carpenter	3.50	1.55	.45
☐ 129 George Blanda	30.00	13.50	3.70
☐ 130 Gordy Soltau	3.50	1.55	.45
☐ 131 Dick Nolan	5.00	2.20	.60
☐ 132 Don Bosseler	18.00	4.50	1.80
☐ NNO Free Felt Initial Card	20.00	9.00	2.50

1959 Topps

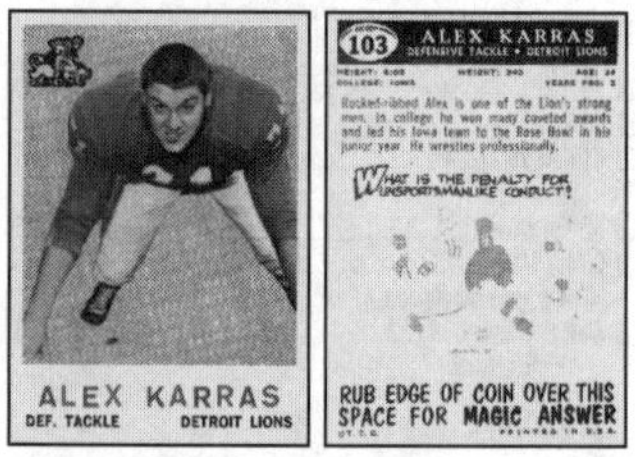

The 1959 Topps football set contains 176 standard-size cards which were issued in two series of 88. The cards were issued in penny, nickel and cello packs. Card fronts contain a player photo over a solid background. Beneath the photo, is the player's name in red and blue letters. Beneath the name are the player's position and team. The card backs were printed in gray on white card stock. Statistical information from the immediate past season and career totals are given on the reverse. Card backs include a scratch-off quiz. Team cards (with checklist backs) as well as team pennant cards are included in the set. The key Rookie Cards in this set are Sam Huff, Alex Karras, Jerry Kramer, Bobby Mitchell, Jim Parker and Jim Taylor. The Taylor card was supposed to portray the great Packers running back. Instead, the card depicts the Cardinals linebacker.

	NRMT	VG-E	GOOD
COMPLETE SET (176)	900.00	400.00	110.00
COMMON CARD (1-88)	3.00	1.35	.35
COMMON CARD (89-176)	2.00	.90	.25
WRAPPER (1-CENT)	35.00	16.00	4.40
WRAPPER (1-CENT, REPEAT)	50.00	22.00	6.25
WRAPPER (5-CENT)	50.00	22.00	6.25

Card	NRMT	VG-E	GOOD
☐ 1 Johnny Unitas	100.00	25.00	10.00
☐ 2 Gene Brito	3.00	1.35	.35
☐ 3 Detroit Lions Team Card (checklist back)	6.00	2.70	.75
☐ 4 Max McGee	16.00	7.25	2.00
☐ 5 Hugh McElhenny	15.00	6.75	1.85
☐ 6 Joe Schmidt	8.00	3.60	1.00
☐ 7 Kyle Rote	5.00	2.20	.60
☐ 8 Clarence Peaks	3.00	1.35	.35
☐ 9 Pittsburgh Steelers Pennant Card	3.50	1.55	.45
☐ 10 Jim Brown	150.00	70.00	19.00
☐ 11 Ray Mathews	3.00	1.35	.35
☐ 12 Bobby Dillon	3.00	1.35	.35
☐ 13 Joe Childress	3.00	1.35	.35
☐ 14 Terry Barr	3.00	1.35	.35
☐ 15 Del Shofner	4.00	1.80	.50
☐ 16 Bob Pellegrini UER (Misspelled Pellagrini on card back)	3.00	1.35	.35
☐ 17 Baltimore Colts Team Card (checklist back)	6.00	2.70	.75
☐ 18 Preston Carpenter	3.00	1.35	.35
☐ 19 Leo Nomellini	10.00	4.50	1.25
☐ 20 Frank Gifford	45.00	20.00	5.50
☐ 21 Charlie Ane	3.00	1.35	.35
☐ 22 Jack Butler	3.00	1.35	.35
☐ 23 Bart Starr	55.00	25.00	7.00
☐ 24 Chicago Cardinals Pennant Card	3.50	1.55	.45
☐ 25 Bill Barnes	3.00	1.35	.35
☐ 26 Walt Michaels	4.00	1.80	.50
☐ 27 Clyde Conner UER (Misspelled Connor on card back)	3.00	1.35	.35
☐ 28 Paige Cothren	3.00	1.35	.35
☐ 29 Roosevelt Grier	6.00	2.70	.75
☐ 30 Alan Ameche	6.00	2.70	.75
☐ 31 Philadelphia Eagles Team Card (checklist back)	6.00	2.70	.75
☐ 32 Dick Nolan	4.00	1.80	.50
☐ 33 R.C. Owens	4.00	1.80	.50
☐ 34 Dale Dodrill	3.00	1.35	.35
☐ 35 Gene Gedman	3.00	1.35	.35
☐ 36 Gene Lipscomb	10.00	4.50	1.25
☐ 37 Ray Renfro	4.00	1.80	.50
☐ 38 Cleveland Browns Pennant Card	3.50	1.55	.45
☐ 39 Bill Forester	4.00	1.80	.50
☐ 40 Bobby Layne	25.00	11.00	3.10
☐ 41 Pat Summerall	10.00	4.50	1.25
☐ 42 Jerry Mertens	3.00	1.35	.35
☐ 43 Steve Myhra	3.00	1.35	.35
☐ 44 John Henry Johnson	6.00	2.70	.75
☐ 45 Woodley Lewis UER (misspelled Woody)	3.00	1.35	.35
☐ 46 Green Bay Packers Team Card (checklist back)	7.00	3.10	.85
☐ 47 Don Owens UER (Def.Tackle on front, Linebacker on back)	3.00	1.35	.35
☐ 48 Ed Beatty	3.00	1.35	.35
☐ 49 Don Chandler	3.00	1.35	.35
☐ 50 Ollie Matson	12.00	5.50	1.50
☐ 51 Sam Huff	45.00	20.00	5.50
☐ 52 Tom Miner	3.00	1.35	.35
☐ 53 New York Giants Pennant Card	3.50	1.55	.45
☐ 54 Kenny Konz	3.00	1.35	.35
☐ 55 Raymond Berry	20.00	9.00	2.50
☐ 56 Howard Ferguson UER (Misspelled Fergeson on card back)	3.00	1.35	.35
☐ 57 Chuck Ulrich	3.00	1.35	.35
☐ 58 Bob St. Clair	5.00	2.20	.60
☐ 59 Don Burroughs	3.00	1.35	.35
☐ 60 Lou Groza	12.00	5.50	1.50
☐ 61 San Francisco 49ers Team Card (checklist back)	6.00	2.70	.75
☐ 62 Andy Nelson	3.00	1.35	.35
☐ 63 Harold Bradley	3.00	1.35	.35
☐ 64 Dave Hanner	3.00	1.35	.35
☐ 65 Charley Conerly	10.00	4.50	1.25
☐ 66 Gene Cronin	3.00	1.35	.35
☐ 67 Duane Putnam	3.00	1.35	.35
☐ 68 Baltimore Colts Pennant Card	3.50	1.55	.45
☐ 69 Ernie Stautner	8.00	3.60	1.00
☐ 70 Jon Arnett	4.00	1.80	.50
☐ 71 Ken Panfil	3.00	1.35	.35
☐ 72 Matt Hazeltine	3.00	1.35	.35
☐ 73 Harley Sewell	3.00	1.35	.35
☐ 74 Mike McCormack	6.00	2.70	.75
☐ 75 Jim Ringo	7.00	3.10	.85
☐ 76 Los Angeles Rams Team Card (checklist back)	6.00	2.70	.75
☐ 77 Bob Gain	3.00	1.35	.35
☐ 78 Buzz Nutter	3.00	1.35	.35
☐ 79 Jerry Norton	3.00	1.35	.35
☐ 80 Joe Perry	10.00	4.50	1.25
☐ 81 Carl Brettschneider	3.00	1.35	.35
☐ 82 Paul Hornung	65.00	29.00	8.00
☐ 83 Philadelphia Eagles Pennant Card	3.50	1.55	.45
☐ 84 Les Richter	4.00	1.80	.50
☐ 85 Howard Cassady	4.00	1.80	.50
☐ 86 Art Donovan	15.00	6.75	1.85
☐ 87 Jim Patton	4.00	1.80	.50
☐ 88 Pete Retzlaff	4.00	1.80	.50
☐ 89 Jim Mutscheller	2.00	.90	.25
☐ 90 Zeke Bratkowski	3.00	1.35	.35
☐ 91 Washington Redskins Team Card (Checklist back)	4.00	1.80	.50
☐ 92 Art Hunter	2.00	.90	.25
☐ 93 Gern Nagler	2.00	.90	.25
☐ 94 Chuck Weber	2.00	.90	.25
☐ 95 Lew Carpenter	2.00	.90	.25
☐ 96 Stan Jones	5.00	2.20	.60
☐ 97 Ralph Guglielmi UER (Misspelled Gugliemi on card front)	3.00	1.35	.35
☐ 98 Green Bay Packers Pennant Card	3.00	1.35	.35
☐ 99 Ray Wietecha	2.00	.90	.25
☐ 100 Lenny Moore	12.00	5.50	1.50
☐ 101 Jim Ray Smith UER (Lions logo on front)	3.00	1.35	.35
☐ 102 Abe Woodson	3.00	1.35	.35
☐ 103 Alex Karras	40.00	18.00	5.00
☐ 104 Chicago Bears Team Card (checklist back)	4.00	1.80	.50
☐ 105 John David Crow	10.00	4.50	1.25
☐ 106 Joe Fortunato	2.00	.90	.25
☐ 107 Babe Parilli	3.00	1.35	.35
☐ 108 Proverb Jacobs	2.00	.90	.25
☐ 109 Gino Marchetti	8.00	3.60	1.00
☐ 110 Bill Wade	3.00	1.35	.35
☐ 111 San Francisco 49ers Pennant Card	3.00	1.35	.35
☐ 112 Karl Rubke	2.00	.90	.25
☐ 113 Dave Middleton UER (Browns logo in upper left corner)	2.00	.90	.25
☐ 114 Roosevelt Brown	5.00	2.20	.60
☐ 115 John Olszewski	2.00	.90	.25
☐ 116 Jerry Kramer	30.00	13.50	3.70
☐ 117 King Hill	3.00	1.35	.35
☐ 118 Chicago Cardinals Team Card (Checklist back)	4.00	1.80	.50
☐ 119 Frank Varrichione	2.00	.90	.25
☐ 120 Rick Casares	3.00	1.35	.35
☐ 121 George Strugar	2.00	.90	.25
☐ 122 Bill Glass UER (Center on front, tackle on back)	3.00	1.35	.35
☐ 123 Don Bosseler	2.00	.90	.25
☐ 124 John Reger	2.00	.90	.25
☐ 125 Jim Ninowski	2.00	.90	.25
☐ 126 Los Angeles Rams Pennant Card	3.00	1.35	.35
☐ 127 Willard Sherman	2.00	.90	.25
☐ 128 Bob Schnelker	2.00	.90	.25
☐ 129 Ollie Spencer	2.00	.90	.25
☐ 130 Y.A. Tittle	25.00	11.00	3.10
☐ 131 Yale Lary	6.00	2.70	.75
☐ 132 Jim Parker	20.00	9.00	2.50
☐ 133 New York Giants Team Card (Checklist back)	4.00	1.80	.50
☐ 134 Jim Schrader	2.00	.90	.25
☐ 135 M.C. Reynolds	2.00	.90	.25
☐ 136 Mike Sandusky	2.00	.90	.25
☐ 137 Ed Brown	3.00	1.35	.35
☐ 138 Al Barry	2.00	.90	.25
☐ 139 Detroit Lions Pennant Card	3.00	1.35	.35
☐ 140 Bobby Mitchell	35.00	16.00	4.40
☐ 141 Larry Morris	2.00	.90	.25
☐ 142 Jim Phillips	3.00	1.35	.35
☐ 143 Jim David	2.00	.90	.25
☐ 144 Joe Krupa	2.00	.90	.25
☐ 145 Willie Galimore	3.00	1.35	.35
☐ 146 Pittsburgh Steelers Team Card (Checklist back)	4.00	1.80	.50
☐ 147 Andy Robustelli	6.00	2.70	.75
☐ 148 Billy Wilson	2.00	.90	.25
☐ 149 Leo Sanford	2.00	.90	.25
☐ 150 Eddie LeBaron	4.00	1.80	.50
☐ 151 Bill McColl	2.00	.90	.25
☐ 152 Buck Lansford UER (Tackle on front, guard on back)	2.00	.90	.25
☐ 153 Chicago Bears Pennant Card	3.00	1.35	.35
☐ 154 Leo Sugar	2.00	.90	.25
☐ 155 Jim Taylor UER (Photo actually other Jim Taylor, Cardinal LB)	20.00	9.00	2.50
☐ 156 Lindon Crow	2.00	.90	.25
☐ 157 Jack McClairen	2.00	.90	.25
☐ 158 Vince Costello UER (Linebacker on front, Guard on back)	2.00	.90	.25
☐ 159 Stan Wallace	2.00	.90	.25
☐ 160 Mel Triplett	2.00	.90	.25
☐ 161 Cleveland Browns Team Card (Checklist back)	4.00	1.80	.50
☐ 162 Dan Currie	3.00	1.35	.35
☐ 163 L.G. Dupre UER (Misspelled DuPre on back)	3.00	1.35	.35
☐ 164 John Morrow UER (Center on front, Linebacker on back)	2.00	.90	.25
☐ 165 Jim Podoley	2.00	.90	.25
☐ 166 Bruce Bosley	2.00	.90	.25
☐ 167 Harlon Hill	2.00	.90	.25
☐ 168 Washington Redskins Pennant Card	3.00	1.35	.35
☐ 169 Junior Wren	2.00	.90	.25
☐ 170 Tobin Rote	3.00	1.35	.35
☐ 171 Art Spinney	2.00	.90	.25
☐ 172 Chuck Drazenovich UER (Linebacker on front, Defensive Back on back)	2.00	.90	.25
☐ 173 Bobby Joe Conrad	3.00	1.35	.35
☐ 174 Jesse Richardson	2.00	.90	.25
☐ 175 Sam Baker	2.00	.90	.25
☐ 176 Tom Tracy	8.00	2.00	.80

1960 Topps

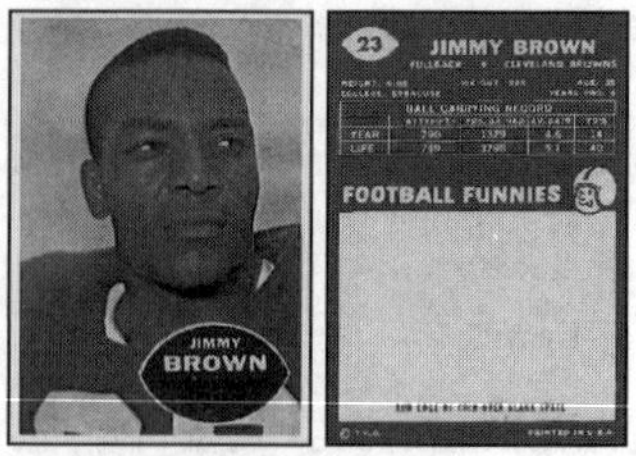

The 1960 Topps football set contains 132 standard-size cards. Card fronts have a "pure card" effect in that the player photo dominates the card. The only design on front is the player's name, team name and position within a football-shaped icon toward the bottom of the file. The card backs are printed in green on white card stock. Statistical information from the immediate past season and career totals are given on the reverse. The set marks the debut of the Dallas Cowboys into the National Football League. The backs feature a "Football Funnies" scratch-off quiz; answer was revealed by rubbing with an edge of a coin. The set marks the debut of the Dallas Cowboys into the National Football League. The team cards feature numerical checklist backs. The team cards that have the 67-132 checklist backs (card Nos. 60, 102, 112, 122, 132) all misspell 124 Don Bosseler as Bossler along with a number of other like errors. The cards are numbered in team order. The set is sequenced in this order: Baltimore Colts (1-11), Chicago Bears (12-21), Cleveland Browns (22-31), Dallas Cowboys (32-40), Detroit Lions (41-50), Green Bay Packers (51-60), Los Angeles Rams (61-71), New York Giants (72-82), Philadelphia Eagles (83-92), Pittsburgh Steelers (93-102), St. Louis Cardinals (103-112), San Francisco 49ers (113-122) and Washington Redskins (123-132). The set marks the first apprearance of the St. Louis Cardinals after their move from Chicago. The key Rookie Card in this set is Forrest Gregg.

	NRMT	VG-E	GOOD
COMPLETE SET (132)	600.00	275.00	75.00
COMMON CARD (1-132)	2.00	.90	.25
WRAPPER (1-CENT)	40.00	18.00	5.00
WRAPPER (1-CENT, REPEAT)	150.00	70.00	19.00
WRAPPER (5-CENT)	40.00	18.00	5.00

Card	NRMT	VG-E	GOOD
☐ 1 John Unitas	80.00	20.00	8.00
☐ 2 Alan Ameche	4.00	1.80	.50
☐ 3 Lenny Moore	10.00	4.50	1.25
☐ 4 Raymond Berry	12.00	5.50	1.50
☐ 5 Jim Parker	8.00	3.60	1.00
☐ 6 George Preas	2.00	.90	.25
☐ 7 Art Spinney	2.00	.90	.25
☐ 8 Bill Pellington	3.00	1.35	.35
☐ 9 John Sample	3.00	1.35	.35
☐ 10 Gene Lipscomb UER (Def. Tackle on front, Tackle on back)	3.00	1.35	.35
☐ 11 Baltimore Colts Team Card (Checklist 67-132)	4.00	1.80	.50
☐ 12 Ed Brown	3.00	1.35	.35
☐ 13 Rick Casares	3.00	1.35	.35
☐ 14 Willie Galimore	3.00	1.35	.35
☐ 15 Jim Dooley	2.00	.90	.25
☐ 16 Harlon Hill UER (Lifetime yards and Avg. gain incorrect)	2.00	.90	.25
☐ 17 Stan Jones UER (Defensive ... All-Star Team, should be Offensive)	4.00	1.80	.50
☐ 18 Bill George	4.00	1.80	.50
☐ 19 Erich Barnes	2.00	.90	.25
☐ 20 Doug Atkins UER (reversed negative)	6.00	2.70	.75
☐ 21 Chicago Bears Team Card (Checklist 1-66)	4.00	1.80	.50
☐ 22 Milt Plum	3.00	1.35	.35
☐ 23 Jim Brown	100.00	45.00	12.50
☐ 24 Sam Baker	2.00	.90	.25
☐ 25 Bobby Mitchell	10.00	4.50	1.25
☐ 26 Ray Renfro	3.00	1.35	.35
☐ 27 Billy Howton	3.00	1.35	.35
☐ 28 Jim Ray Smith	2.00	.90	.25
☐ 29 Jim Shofner	3.00	1.35	.35
☐ 30 Bob Gain	2.00	.90	.25
☐ 31 Cleveland Browns Team Card (Checklist 1-66)	4.00	1.80	.50
☐ 32 Don Heinrich	2.00	.90	.25
☐ 33 Ed Modzelewski UER (Lifetime yards and Avg. gain incorrect)	2.00	.90	.25
☐ 34 Fred Cone	2.00	.90	.25
☐ 35 L.G. Dupre	3.00	1.35	.35
☐ 36 Dick Bielski	2.00	.90	.25
☐ 37 Charlie Ane UER (Misspelled Charley)	2.00	.90	.25
☐ 38 Jerry Tubbs	3.00	1.35	.35
☐ 39 Doyle Nix	2.00	.90	.25
☐ 40 Ray Krouse	2.00	.90	.25
☐ 41 Earl Morrall	5.00	2.20	.60
☐ 42 Howard Cassady	3.00	1.35	.35
☐ 43 Dave Middleton	2.00	.90	.25
☐ 44 Jim Gibbons	3.00	1.35	.35
☐ 45 Darris McCord	2.00	.90	.25
☐ 46 Joe Schmidt	6.00	2.70	.75
☐ 47 Terry Barr	2.00	.90	.25
☐ 48 Yale Lary UER (Def.back on front, halfback on back)	4.00	1.80	.50
☐ 49 Gil Mains	2.00	.90	.25

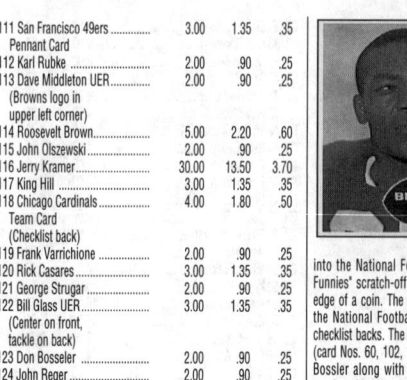

□ 50 Detroit Lions Team Card (Checklist 1-66)	4.00	1.80	.50
□ 51 Bart Starr	40.00	18.00	5.00
□ 52 Jim Taylor UER (photo actually Jim Taylor, Cardinal LB)	8.00	3.60	1.00
□ 53 Lew Carpenter	3.00	1.35	.35
□ 54 Paul Hornung UER (Halfback on front, fullback on back)	35.00	16.00	4.40
□ 55 Max McGee	4.00	1.80	.50
□ 56 Forrest Gregg	25.00	11.00	3.10
□ 57 Jim Ringo	5.00	2.20	.60
□ 58 Bill Forester	3.00	1.35	.35
□ 59 Dave Hanner	3.00	1.35	.35
□ 60 Green Bay Packers Team Card (Checklist 67-132)	6.00	2.70	.75
□ 61 Bill Wade	3.00	1.35	.35
□ 62 Frank Ryan	6.00	2.70	.75
□ 63 Ollie Matson	7.00	3.10	.85
□ 64 Jon Arnett	3.00	1.35	.35
□ 65 Del Shofner	3.00	1.35	.35
□ 66 Jim Phillips	2.00	.90	.25
□ 67 Art Hunter	2.00	.90	.25
□ 68 Les Richter	3.00	1.35	.35
□ 69 Lou Michaels	3.00	1.35	.35
□ 70 John Baker	2.00	.90	.25
□ 71 Los Angeles Rams Team Card (Checklist 1-66)	4.00	1.80	.50
□ 72 Charley Conerly	8.00	3.60	1.00
□ 73 Mel Triplett	2.00	.90	.25
□ 74 Frank Gifford	35.00	16.00	4.40
□ 75 Alex Webster	3.00	1.35	.35
□ 76 Bob Schnelker	2.00	.90	.25
□ 77 Pat Summerall	8.00	3.60	1.00
□ 78 Roosevelt Brown	5.00	2.20	.60
□ 79 Jim Patton	2.00	.90	.25
□ 80 Sam Huff UER (Def.tackle on front, linebacker on back)	15.00	6.75	1.85
□ 81 Andy Robustelli	6.00	2.70	.75
□ 82 New York Giants Team Card (Checklist 1-66)	4.00	1.80	.50
□ 83 Clarence Peaks	2.00	.90	.25
□ 84 Bill Barnes	2.00	.90	.25
□ 85 Pete Retzlaff	3.00	1.35	.35
□ 86 Bobby Walston	2.00	.90	.25
□ 87 Chuck Bednarik UER (Misspelled Bednarick on both sides of card)	8.00	3.60	1.00
□ 88 Bob Pellegrini (Misspelled Pellagrini on both sides)	2.00	.90	.25
□ 89 Tom Brookshier	3.00	1.35	.35
□ 90 Marion Campbell	3.00	1.35	.35
□ 91 Jesse Richardson	2.00	.90	.25
□ 92 Philadelphia Eagles Team Card (Checklist 1-66)	4.00	1.80	.50
□ 93 Bobby Layne	25.00	11.00	3.10
□ 94 John Henry Johnson	5.00	2.20	.60
□ 95 Tom Tracy UER (Halfback on front, fullback on back)	3.00	1.35	.35
□ 96 Preston Carpenter	2.00	.90	.25
□ 97 Frank Varrichione UER (Reversed negative)	2.00	.90	.25
□ 98 John Nisby	2.00	.90	.25
□ 99 Dean Derby	2.00	.90	.25
□ 100 George Tarasovic	2.00	.90	.25
□ 101 Ernie Stautner	5.00	2.20	.60
□ 102 Pittsburgh Steelers Team Card (Checklist 67-132)	4.00	1.80	.50
□ 103 King Hill	3.00	1.35	.35
□ 104 Mal Hammack	2.00	.90	.25
□ 105 John David Crow	3.00	1.35	.35
□ 106 Bobby Joe Conrad	3.00	1.35	.35
□ 107 Woodley Lewis	2.00	.90	.25
□ 108 Don Gillis	2.00	.90	.25
□ 109 Carl Brettschneider	2.00	.90	.25
□ 110 Leo Sugar	2.00	.90	.25
□ 111 Frank Fuller	2.00	.90	.25
□ 112 St. Louis Cardinals Team Card (Checklist 67-132)	4.00	1.80	.50
□ 113 Y.A. Tittle	20.00	9.00	2.50
□ 114 Joe Perry	8.00	3.60	1.00
□ 115 J.D. Smith	3.00	1.35	.35
□ 116 Hugh McElhenny	8.00	3.60	1.00
□ 117 Billy Wilson	2.00	.90	.25
□ 118 Bob St. Clair	4.00	1.80	.50
□ 119 Matt Hazeltine	2.00	.90	.25
□ 120 Abe Woodson	2.00	.90	.25
□ 121 Leo Nomellini	6.00	2.70	.75
□ 122 San Francisco 49ers Team Card (Checklist 67-132)	4.00	1.80	.50
□ 123 Ralph Guglielmi UER (Misspelled Gugliemi on card front)	2.00	.90	.25
□ 124 Don Bosseler	2.00	.90	.25
□ 125 John Olszewski	2.00	.90	.25
□ 126 Bill Anderson UER (Walt on back)	2.00	.90	.25
□ 127 Joe Walton	3.00	1.35	.35
□ 128 Jim Schrader	2.00	.90	.25
□ 129 Ralph Felton	2.00	.90	.25
□ 130 Gary Glick	2.00	.90	.25
□ 131 Bob Toneff	2.00	.90	.25
□ 132 Washington Redskins Team Card (Checklist 67-132)	30.00	7.50	3.00

1960 Topps Metallic Inserts

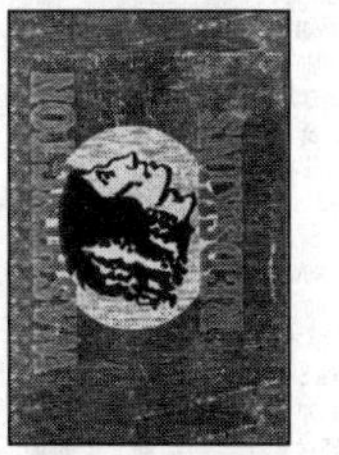

This set of 33 metallic team emblem stickers was inserted with the 1960 Topps regular issue football set. The stickers are unnumbered and are ordered below alphabetically within type. NFL teams are listed first (1-13) followed by college teams (14-33). The stickers measure approximately 2 1/8" by 3 1/16". The sticker fronts are either silver, gold, or blue with a black border.

	NRMT	VG-E	GOOD
COMPLETE SET (33)	400.00	180.00	50.00
COMMON CARD (1-13)	15.00	6.75	1.85
COMMON CARD (14-33)	10.00	4.50	1.25

□ 1 Baltimore Colts	15.00	6.75	1.85
□ 2 Chicago Bears	15.00	6.75	1.85
□ 3 Cleveland Browns	15.00	6.75	1.85
□ 4 Dallas Cowboys	25.00	11.00	3.10
□ 5 Detroit Lions	15.00	6.75	1.85
□ 6 Green Bay Packers	20.00	9.00	2.50
□ 7 Los Angeles Rams	15.00	6.75	1.85
□ 8 New York Giants	15.00	6.75	1.85
□ 9 Philadelphia Eagles	15.00	6.75	1.85
□ 10 Pittsburgh Steelers	15.00	6.75	1.85
□ 11 St. Louis Cardinals	15.00	6.75	1.85
□ 12 San Francisco 49ers	20.00	9.00	2.50
□ 13 Washington Redskins	20.00	9.00	2.50
□ 14 Air Force Academy Falcons	10.00	4.50	1.25
□ 15 Army	10.00	4.50	1.25
□ 16 California Golden Bears	10.00	4.50	1.25
□ 17 Dartmouth	10.00	4.50	1.25
□ 18 Duke Blue Devils	10.00	4.50	1.25
□ 19 LSU	12.00	5.50	1.50
□ 20 Michigan Wolverines	20.00	9.00	2.50
□ 21 Minnesota	10.00	4.50	1.25
□ 22 Mississippi Rebels	10.00	4.50	1.25
□ 23 Navy	10.00	4.50	1.25
□ 24 Notre Dame	25.00	11.00	3.10
□ 25 SMU Mustangs	10.00	4.50	1.25
□ 26 Southern California	12.00	5.50	1.50
□ 27 Syracuse Orange Men	10.00	4.50	1.25
□ 28 Tennessee Volunteers	12.00	5.50	1.50
□ 29 Texas Longhorns	12.00	5.50	1.50
□ 30 UCLA Bruins	12.00	5.50	1.50
□ 31 Washington Huskies	10.00	4.50	1.25
□ 32 Wisconsin Badgers	10.00	4.50	1.25
□ 33 Yale Bulldogs	10.00	4.50	1.25

1961 Topps

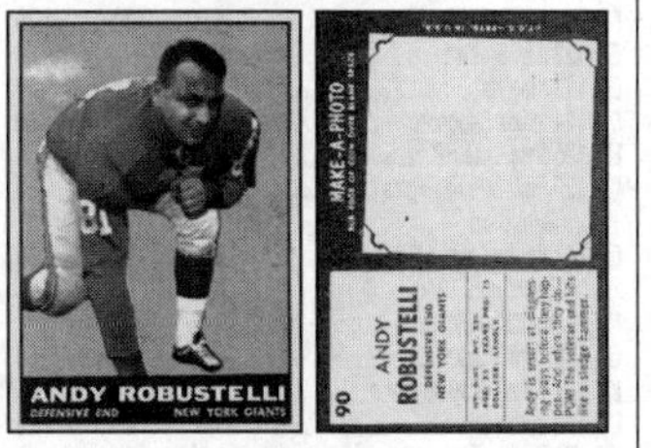

The 1961 Topps football set of 198 standard-size cards contains NFL players (1-132) and AFL players (133-197). The fronts are very similar to the Topps 1961 baseball issue with the player's name, team and position at beneath posed player photos. The card backs are printed in light blue on white card stock. Statistical information from the immediate past season and career totals are given on the reverse. A "coin-rub" picture was featured on the right of the reverse. Cards are essentially numbered in team order by league. There are three checklist cards in the set, numbers 67, 122, and 198. The key Rookie Cards in this set are John Brodie, Tom Flores, Henry Jordan, Don Maynard, and Jim Otto.

	NRMT	VG-E	GOOD
COMPLETE SET (198)	1000.00	450.00	125.00
COMMON CARD (1-132)	2.50	1.10	.30
COMMON CARD (133-198)	3.00	1.35	.35
WRAPPER (1-CENT)	275.00	125.00	34.00
WRAPPER (1-CENT, REPEAT)	225.00	100.00	28.00
WRAPPER (5-CENT)	50.00	22.00	6.25

□ 1 Johnny Unitas	100.00	25.00	10.00
□ 2 Lenny Moore	12.00	5.50	1.50
□ 3 Alan Ameche	4.00	1.80	.50
□ 4 Raymond Berry	12.00	5.50	1.50
□ 5 Jim Mutscheller	2.50	1.10	.30
□ 6 Jim Parker	5.00	2.20	.60
□ 7 Gino Marchetti	6.00	2.70	.75
□ 8 Gene Lipscomb	3.00	1.35	.35
□ 9 Baltimore Colts Team Card	4.00	1.80	.50
□ 10 Bill Wade	3.00	1.35	.35
□ 11 Johnny Morris UER (Years pro and return averages wrong)	6.00	2.70	.75
□ 12 Rick Casares	3.00	1.35	.35
□ 13 Harlon Hill	2.50	1.10	.30
□ 14 Stan Jones	4.00	1.80	.50
□ 15 Doug Atkins	5.00	2.20	.60
□ 16 Bill George	4.00	1.80	.50
□ 17 J.C. Caroline	2.50	1.10	.30
□ 18 Chicago Bears Team Card	4.00	1.80	.50
□ 19 Big Time Football Comes to Texas (Eddie LeBaron)	3.00	1.35	.35
□ 20 Eddie LeBaron	3.00	1.35	.35
□ 21 Don McIlhenny	2.50	1.10	.30
□ 22 L.G. Dupre	3.00	1.35	.35
□ 23 Jim Doran	2.50	1.10	.30
□ 24 Billy Howton	3.00	1.35	.35
□ 25 Buzz Guy	2.50	1.10	.30
□ 26 Jack Patera	2.50	1.10	.30
□ 27 Tom Frankhauser	2.50	1.10	.30
□ 28 Dallas Cowboys Team Card	14.00	6.25	1.75
□ 29 Jim Ninowski	2.50	1.10	.30
□ 30 Dan Lewis	2.50	1.10	.30
□ 31 Nick Pietrosante	3.00	1.35	.35
□ 32 Gail Cogdill	3.00	1.35	.35
□ 33 Jim Gibbons	2.50	1.10	.30
□ 34 Jim Martin	2.50	1.10	.30
□ 35 Alex Karras	14.00	6.25	1.75
□ 36 Joe Schmidt	5.00	2.20	.60
□ 37 Detroit Lions Team Card	4.00	1.80	.50
□ 38 Packers' Hornung Sets NFL Scoring Record	16.00	7.25	2.00
□ 39 Bart Starr	45.00	20.00	5.50
□ 40 Paul Hornung	40.00	18.00	5.00
□ 41 Jim Taylor	30.00	13.50	3.70
□ 42 Max McGee	4.00	1.80	.50
□ 43 Boyd Dowler	8.00	3.60	1.00
□ 44 Jim Ringo	5.00	2.20	.60
□ 45 Hank Jordan	20.00	9.00	2.50
□ 46 Bill Forester	3.00	1.35	.35
□ 47 Green Bay Packers Team Card	8.00	3.60	1.00
□ 48 Frank Ryan	3.00	1.35	.35
□ 49 Jon Arnett	3.00	1.35	.35
□ 50 Ollie Matson	6.00	2.70	.75
□ 51 Jim Phillips	2.50	1.10	.30
□ 52 Del Shofner	3.00	1.35	.35
□ 53 Art Hunter	2.50	1.10	.30
□ 54 Gene Brito	2.50	1.10	.30
□ 55 Lindon Crow	2.50	1.10	.30
□ 56 Los Angeles Rams Team Card	4.00	1.80	.50
□ 57 Colts' Unitas 25 TD Passes	18.00	8.00	2.20
□ 58 Y.A. Tittle	25.00	11.00	3.10
□ 59 John Brodie	35.00	16.00	4.40
□ 60 J.D. Smith	2.50	1.10	.30
□ 61 R.C. Owens	3.00	1.35	.35
□ 62 Clyde Conner	2.50	1.10	.30
□ 63 Bob St. Clair	4.00	1.80	.50
□ 64 Leo Nomellini	6.00	2.70	.75
□ 65 Abe Woodson	2.50	1.10	.30
□ 66 San Francisco 49ers Team Card	4.00	1.80	.50
□ 67 Checklist Card	40.00	10.00	4.00
□ 68 Milt Plum	3.00	1.35	.35
□ 69 Ray Renfro	3.00	1.35	.35
□ 70 Bobby Mitchell	7.00	3.10	.85
□ 71 Jim Brown	90.00	40.00	11.00
□ 72 Mike McCormack	4.00	1.80	.50
□ 73 Jim Ray Smith	2.50	1.10	.30
□ 74 Sam Baker	2.50	1.10	.30
□ 75 Walt Michaels	3.00	1.35	.35
□ 76 Cleveland Browns Team Card	4.00	1.80	.50
□ 77 Jimmy Brown Gains 1257 Yards	35.00	16.00	4.40
□ 78 George Shaw	2.50	1.10	.30
□ 79 Hugh McElhenny	8.00	3.60	1.00
□ 80 Clancy Osborne	2.50	1.10	.30
□ 81 Dave Middleton	2.50	1.10	.30
□ 82 Frank Youso	2.50	1.10	.30
□ 83 Don Joyce	2.50	1.10	.30
□ 84 Ed Culpepper	2.50	1.10	.30
□ 85 Charley Conerly	8.00	3.60	1.00
□ 86 Mel Triplett	2.50	1.10	.30
□ 87 Kyle Rote	3.00	1.35	.35
□ 88 Roosevelt Brown	4.00	1.80	.50
□ 89 Ray Wietecha	2.50	1.10	.30
□ 90 Andy Robustelli	5.00	2.20	.60
□ 91 Sam Huff	8.00	3.60	1.00
□ 92 Jim Patton	2.50	1.10	.30
□ 93 New York Giants Team Card	4.00	1.80	.50
□ 94 Charley Conerly UER Leads Giants for 13th Year (Misspelled Charlie on card)	6.00	2.70	.75
□ 95 Sonny Jurgensen	20.00	9.00	2.50
□ 96 Tommy McDonald	3.00	1.35	.35
□ 97 Bill Barnes	2.50	1.10	.30
□ 98 Bobby Walston	2.50	1.10	.30
□ 99 Pete Retzlaff	3.00	1.35	.35
□ 100 Jim McCusker	2.50	1.10	.30
□ 101 Chuck Bednarik	8.00	3.60	1.00
□ 102 Tom Brookshier	3.00	1.35	.35
□ 103 Philadelphia Eagles Team Card	4.00	1.80	.50
□ 104 Bobby Layne	25.00	11.00	3.10
□ 105 John Henry Johnson	5.00	2.20	.60
□ 106 Tom Tracy	3.00	1.35	.35
□ 107 Buddy Dial	2.50	1.10	.30
□ 108 Jimmy Orr	6.00	2.70	.75
□ 109 Mike Sandusky	2.50	1.10	.30
□ 110 John Reger	2.50	1.10	.30
□ 111 Junior Wren	2.50	1.10	.30
□ 112 Pittsburgh Steelers Team Card	4.00	1.80	.50
□ 113 Bobby Layne Sets New Passing Record	10.00	4.50	1.25
□ 114 John Roach	2.50	1.10	.30
□ 115 Sam Etcheverry	3.00	1.35	.35
□ 116 John David Crow	3.00	1.35	.35
□ 117 Mal Hammack	2.50	1.10	.30
□ 118 Sonny Randle	3.00	1.35	.35
□ 119 Leo Sugar	2.50	1.10	.30
□ 120 Jerry Norton	2.50	1.10	.30
□ 121 St. Louis Cardinals Team Card	4.00	1.80	.50
□ 122 Checklist Card	40.00	10.00	4.00
□ 123 Ralph Guglielmi	2.50	1.10	.30
□ 124 Dick James	2.50	1.10	.30
□ 125 Don Bosseler	2.50	1.10	.30
□ 126 Joe Walton	2.50	1.10	.30
□ 127 Bill Anderson	2.50	1.10	.30
□ 128 Vince Promuto	3.00	1.35	.35
□ 129 Bob Toneff	2.50	1.10	.30
□ 130 John Paluck	2.50	1.10	.30
□ 131 Washington Redskins Team Card	4.00	1.80	.50
□ 132 Browns' Plum Wins NFL Passing Title	3.00	1.35	.35
□ 133 Abner Haynes	7.00	3.10	.85
□ 134 Mel Branch UER (Def. Tackle on front, Def. End on back)	4.00	1.80	.50
□ 135 Jerry Cornelison UER (Misspelled Cornielson)	3.00	1.35	.35
□ 136 Bill Krisher	3.00	1.35	.35
□ 137 Paul Miller	3.00	1.35	.35
□ 138 Jack Spikes	4.00	1.80	.50
□ 139 Johnny Robinson	8.00	3.60	1.00
□ 140 Cotton Davidson	4.00	1.80	.50
□ 141 Dave Smith	3.00	1.35	.35
□ 142 Bill Groman	3.00	1.35	.35
□ 143 Rich Michael	3.00	1.35	.35
□ 144 Mike Dukes	3.00	1.35	.35
□ 145 George Blanda	25.00	11.00	3.10
□ 146 Billy Cannon	6.00	2.70	.75
□ 147 Dennit Morris	3.00	1.35	.35
□ 148 Jacky Lee UER (Misspelled Jackie on card back)	4.00	1.80	.50
□ 149 Al Dorow	3.00	1.35	.35
□ 150 Don Maynard	65.00	29.00	8.00
□ 151 Art Powell	8.00	3.60	1.00
□ 152 Sid Youngelman	3.00	1.35	.35
□ 153 Bob Mischak	3.00	1.35	.35
□ 154 Larry Grantham	3.00	1.35	.35
□ 155 Tom Saidock	3.00	1.35	.35
□ 156 Roger Donnahoo	3.00	1.35	.35
□ 157 Lavern Torczon	3.00	1.35	.35
□ 158 Archie Matsos	4.00	1.80	.50
□ 159 Elbert Dubenion	4.00	1.80	.50
□ 160 Wray Carlton	4.00	1.80	.50
□ 161 Rich McCabe	3.00	1.35	.35
□ 162 Ken Rice	3.00	1.35	.35
□ 163 Art Baker	3.00	1.35	.35
□ 164 Tom Rychlec	3.00	1.35	.35
□ 165 Mack Yoho	3.00	1.35	.35
□ 166 Jack Kemp	150.00	70.00	19.00
□ 167 Paul Lowe	5.00	2.20	.60
□ 168 Ron Mix	10.00	4.50	1.25
□ 169 Paul Maguire	6.00	2.70	.75
□ 170 Volney Peters	3.00	1.35	.35
□ 171 Ernie Wright	5.00	2.20	.60
□ 172 Ron Nery	3.00	1.35	.35
□ 173 Dave Kocourek	4.00	1.80	.50
□ 174 Jim Colclough	3.00	1.35	.35

□ 175 Babe Parilli	4.00	1.80	.50
□ 176 Billy Lott	3.00	1.35	.35
□ 177 Fred Bruney	3.00	1.35	.35
□ 178 Ross O'Hanley	3.00	1.35	.35
□ 179 Walt Cudzik	3.00	1.35	.35
□ 180 Charley Leo	3.00	1.35	.35
□ 181 Bob Dee	3.00	1.35	.35
□ 182 Jim Otto	50.00	22.00	6.25
□ 183 Eddie Macon	3.00	1.35	.35
□ 184 Dick Christy	3.00	1.35	.35
□ 185 Alan Miller	3.00	1.35	.35
□ 186 Tom Flores	20.00	9.00	2.50
□ 187 Joe Cannavino	3.00	1.35	.35
□ 188 Don Manoukian	3.00	1.35	.35
□ 189 Bob Coolbaugh	3.00	1.35	.35
□ 190 Lionel Taylor	8.00	3.60	1.00
□ 191 Bud McFadin	3.00	1.35	.35
□ 192 Goose Gonsoulin	7.00	3.10	.85
□ 193 Frank Tripucka	4.00	1.80	.50
□ 194 Gene Mingo	4.00	1.80	.50
□ 195 Eldon Danenhauer	3.00	1.35	.35
□ 196 Bob McNamara	3.00	1.35	.35
□ 197 Dave Rolle UER (End on front, Fullback on back)	3.00	1.35	.35
□ 198 Checklist Card UER (135 Cornielson)	90.00	22.00	9.00

1961 Topps Flocked Stickers

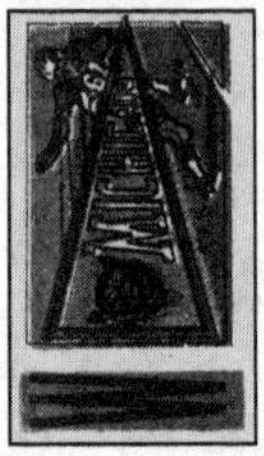

This set of 48 flocked stickers was inserted with the 1961 Topps regular issue football set. The stickers are unnumbered and are ordered below alphabetically within type. NFL teams are listed first (1-15), followed by AFL teams (16-24), and college teams (25-48). The capital letters in the listing below signify the letter on the detachable tab. The stickers measure approximately 2" by 2 3/4" without the letter tab and 2" by 3 3/8" with the letter tab. The prices below are for the stickers with tabs intact; stickers without tabs would be considered VG-E at best. There are letter tab variations on 12 of the stickers as noted by the double letters below. The complete set price below considers the set complete with the 48 different distinct teams, i.e., not including all 60 different tab combinations.

	NRMT	VG-E	GOOD
COMPLETE SET (48)	650.00	300.00	80.00
COMMON NFL (1-15)	15.00	6.75	1.85
COMMON AFL (16-24)	15.00	6.75	1.85
COMMON COLLEGE (25-48)	12.00	5.50	1.50
□ 1 NFL Emblem N	15.00	6.75	1.85
□ 2 Baltimore Colts U	15.00	6.75	1.85
□ 3 Chicago Bears H	15.00	6.75	1.85
□ 4 Cleveland Browns I	15.00	6.75	1.85
□ 5 Dallas Cowboys K	25.00	11.00	3.10
□ 6 Detroit Lions E	15.00	6.75	1.85
□ 7 Green Bay Packers A	20.00	9.00	2.50
□ 8 Los Angeles Rams M	15.00	6.75	1.85
□ 9 Minnesota Vikings R	15.00	6.75	1.85
□ 10 New York Giants D	15.00	6.75	1.85
□ 11 Philadelphia Eagles O	15.00	6.75	1.85
□ 12 Pittsburgh Steelers S	15.00	6.75	1.85
□ 13 San Francisco 49ers P	20.00	9.00	2.50
□ 14 St. Louis Cardinals L	15.00	6.75	1.85
□ 15 Washington Redskins J	20.00	9.00	2.50
□ 16 AFL Emblem A/G	15.00	6.75	1.85
□ 17 Boston Patriots F/T	15.00	6.75	1.85
□ 18 Buffalo Bills I/M	15.00	6.75	1.85
□ 19 Dallas Texans P/R	20.00	9.00	2.50
□ 20 Denver Broncos G/I	15.00	6.75	1.85
□ 21 Houston Oilers A/H	15.00	6.75	1.85
□ 22 Oakland Raiders B/O	25.00	11.00	3.10
□ 23 San Diego Chargers E/K	15.00	6.75	1.85
□ 24 New York Titans D/E	18.00	8.00	2.20
□ 25 Air Force V	12.00	5.50	1.50
□ 26 Alabama L	15.00	6.75	1.85
□ 27 Arkansas A	15.00	6.75	1.85
□ 28 Army Cadets G	12.00	5.50	1.50
□ 29 Baylor Bears E	12.00	5.50	1.50
□ 30 California T	12.00	5.50	1.50
□ 31 Georgia Tech F	12.00	5.50	1.50
□ 32 Illinois Fighting Illini C	12.00	5.50	1.50
□ 33 Kansas J	12.00	5.50	1.50
□ 34 Kentucky R	12.00	5.50	1.50
□ 35 Miami H	15.00	6.75	1.85
□ 36 Michigan W	18.00	8.00	2.20
□ 37 Missouri B	12.00	5.50	1.50
□ 38 Navy Midshipmen J/S	12.00	5.50	1.50
□ 39 Oregon C/N	12.00	5.50	1.50
□ 40 Penn State Z	15.00	6.75	1.85
□ 41 Pittsburgh G	12.00	5.50	1.50
□ 42 Purdue Boilermakers B	12.00	5.50	1.50
□ 43 Southern California Y	15.00	6.75	1.85
□ 44 Stanford Indians L/O	12.00	5.50	1.50
□ 45 TCU Horned Frogs C	12.00	5.50	1.50
□ 46 Virginia Cavilers S	12.00	5.50	1.50
□ 47 Washington Huskies D	12.00	5.50	1.50
□ 48 Washington State Cougers M	12.00	5.50	1.50

1962 Topps

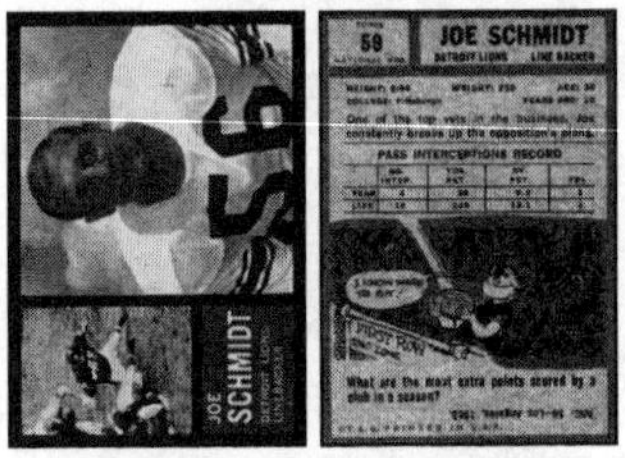

The 1962 Topps football set contains 176 black-bordered standard-size cards. In designing the 1962 set, Topps chose a horizontally oriented card front for the first time since 1957. Two photos include a small action photo to the left that is joined by the player's name, team name and position. An up-close photo to the right covers majority of the card. Black borders, which are prone to chipping, make it quite difficult to put together a set in top grades. The short-printed (SP) cards are indicated in the checklist below. The shortage is probably attributable to the fact that the set size is not the standard 132-card, single-sheet size; hence all cards were not printed in equal amounts. Cards are again organized numerically in team order. The last card within each team grouping was a "rookie prospect" for that team. Many of the black and white inset photos on the card fronts (especially those of the rookie prospects) are not the player pictured and described on the card. The key Rookie Cards in this set are Ernie Davis, Mike Ditka, Roman Gabriel, Bill Kilmer, Norm Snead and Fran Tarkenton.

	NRMT	VG-E	GOOD
COMPLETE SET (176)	1800.00	800.00	220.00
COMMON CARD (1-176)	4.00	1.80	.50
WRAPPER (1-CENT)	250.00	110.00	31.00
WRAPPER (5-CENT)	25.00	11.00	3.10
WRAPPER (5-CENT, BUCKS)	30.00	13.50	3.70
□ 1 John Unitas	135.00	34.00	13.50
□ 2 Lenny Moore	12.00	5.50	1.50
□ 3 Alex Hawkins SP	10.00	4.50	1.25
□ 4 Joe Perry	10.00	4.50	1.25
□ 5 Raymond Berry SP	30.00	13.50	3.70
□ 6 Steve Myhra	4.00	1.80	.50
□ 7 Tom Gilburg SP	8.00	3.60	1.00
□ 8 Gino Marchetti	8.00	3.60	1.00
□ 9 Bill Pellington	4.00	1.80	.50
□ 10 Andy Nelson	4.00	1.80	.50
□ 11 Wendell Harris SP	8.00	3.60	1.00
□ 12 Baltimore Colts Team Card	6.00	2.70	.75
□ 13 Bill Wade SP	10.00	4.50	1.25
□ 14 Willie Galimore	5.00	2.20	.60
□ 15 Johnny Morris SP	8.00	3.60	1.00
□ 16 Rick Casares	5.00	2.20	.60
□ 17 Mike Ditka	225.00	100.00	28.00
□ 18 Stan Jones	6.00	2.70	.75
□ 19 Roger LeClerc	4.00	1.80	.50
□ 20 Angelo Coia	4.00	1.80	.50
□ 21 Doug Atkins	7.00	3.10	.85
□ 22 Bill George	6.00	2.70	.75
□ 23 Richie Petitbon	5.00	2.20	.60
□ 24 Ron Bull SP	8.00	3.60	1.00
□ 25 Chicago Bears Team Card	6.00	2.70	.75
□ 26 Howard Cassady	5.00	2.20	.60
□ 27 Ray Renfro SP	10.00	4.50	1.25
□ 28 Jim Brown	135.00	60.00	17.00
□ 29 Rich Kreitling	4.00	1.80	.50
□ 30 Jim Ray Smith	4.00	1.80	.50
□ 31 John Morrow	4.00	1.80	.50
□ 32 Lou Groza	10.00	4.50	1.25
□ 33 Bob Gain	4.00	1.80	.50
□ 34 Bernie Parrish	4.00	1.80	.50
□ 35 Jim Shofner	4.00	1.80	.50
□ 36 Ernie Davis SP	140.00	65.00	17.50
□ 37 Cleveland Browns Team Card	6.00	2.70	.75
□ 38 Eddie LeBaron	5.00	2.20	.60
□ 39 Don Meredith SP	90.00	40.00	11.00
□ 40 J.W. Lockett SP	8.00	3.60	1.00
□ 41 Don Perkins	8.00	3.60	1.00
□ 42 Billy Howton	5.00	2.20	.60
□ 43 Dick Bielski	4.00	1.80	.50
□ 44 Mike Connelly	4.00	1.80	.50
□ 45 Jerry Tubbs SP	8.00	3.60	1.00
□ 46 Don Bishop SP	8.00	3.60	1.00
□ 47 Dick Moegle	4.00	1.80	.50
□ 48 Bobby Plummer SP	8.00	3.60	1.00
□ 49 Dallas Cowboys Team Card	15.00	6.75	1.85
□ 50 Milt Plum	5.00	2.20	.60
□ 51 Dan Lewis	4.00	1.80	.50
□ 52 Nick Pietrosante SP	8.00	3.60	1.00
□ 53 Gail Cogdill	4.00	1.80	.50
□ 54 Jim Gibbons	4.00	1.80	.50
□ 55 Jim Martin	4.00	1.80	.50
□ 56 Yale Lary	6.00	2.70	.75
□ 57 Darris McCord	4.00	1.80	.50
□ 58 Alex Karras	14.00	6.25	1.75
□ 59 Joe Schmidt	6.00	2.70	.75
□ 60 Dick Lane	6.00	2.70	.75
□ 61 John Lomakoski SP	8.00	3.60	1.00
□ 62 Detroit Lions SP Team Card	18.00	8.00	2.20
□ 63 Bart Starr SP	70.00	32.00	8.75
□ 64 Paul Hornung SP	65.00	29.00	8.00
□ 65 Tom Moore SP	12.00	5.50	1.50
□ 66 Jim Taylor SP	45.00	20.00	5.50
□ 67 Max McGee SP	12.00	5.50	1.50
□ 68 Jim Ringo SP	15.00	6.75	1.85
□ 69 Fuzzy Thurston SP	20.00	9.00	2.50
□ 70 Forrest Gregg	7.00	3.10	.85
□ 71 Boyd Dowler	6.00	2.70	.75
□ 72 Hank Jordan SP	15.00	6.75	1.85
□ 73 Bill Forester SP	8.00	3.60	1.00
□ 74 Earl Gros SP	8.00	3.60	1.00
□ 75 Green Bay Packers SP Team Card	35.00	16.00	4.40
□ 76 Checklist SP	80.00	20.00	8.00
□ 77 Zeke Bratkowski SP (Inset photo is Johnny Unitas)	10.00	4.50	1.25
□ 78 Jon Arnett SP	10.00	4.50	1.25
□ 79 Ollie Matson SP	25.00	11.00	3.10
□ 80 Dick Bass SP	10.00	4.50	1.25
□ 81 Jim Phillips	4.00	1.80	.50
□ 82 Carroll Dale	5.00	2.20	.60
□ 83 Frank Varrichione	4.00	1.80	.50
□ 84 Art Hunter	4.00	1.80	.50
□ 85 Danny Villanueva	4.00	1.80	.50
□ 86 Les Richter SP	8.00	3.60	1.00
□ 87 Lindon Crow	4.00	1.80	.50
□ 88 Roman Gabriel SP (Inset photo is Y.A. Tittle)	65.00	29.00	8.00
□ 89 Los Angeles Rams SP Team Card	18.00	8.00	2.20
□ 90 Fran Tarkenton SP UER (Small photo actually Jurgensen with air-brushed jersey)	175.00	80.00	22.00
□ 91 Jerry Reichow SP	8.00	3.60	1.00
□ 92 Hugh McElhenny SP	25.00	11.00	3.10
□ 93 Mel Triplett SP	8.00	3.60	1.00
□ 94 Tommy Mason SP	10.00	4.50	1.25
□ 95 Dave Middleton SP	8.00	3.60	1.00
□ 96 Frank Youso SP	8.00	3.60	1.00
□ 97 Mike Mercer SP	8.00	3.60	1.00
□ 98 Rip Hawkins SP	8.00	3.60	1.00
□ 99 Cliff Livingston SP	8.00	3.60	1.00
□ 100 Roy Winston SP	8.00	3.60	1.00
□ 101 Minnesota Vikings SP Team Card	25.00	11.00	3.10
□ 102 Y.A. Tittle	30.00	13.50	3.70
□ 103 Joe Walton	4.00	1.80	.50
□ 104 Frank Gifford	35.00	16.00	4.40
□ 105 Alex Webster	5.00	2.20	.60
□ 106 Del Shofner	5.00	2.20	.60
□ 107 Don Chandler	4.00	1.80	.50
□ 108 Andy Robustelli	7.00	3.10	.85
□ 109 Jim Katcavage	5.00	2.20	.60
□ 110 Sam Huff SP	25.00	11.00	3.10
□ 111 Erich Barnes	4.00	1.80	.50
□ 112 Jim Patton	4.00	1.80	.50
□ 113 Jerry Hillebrand SP	8.00	3.60	1.00
□ 114 New York Giants Team Card	6.00	2.70	.75
□ 115 Sonny Jurgensen	18.00	8.00	2.20
□ 116 Tommy McDonald	5.00	2.20	.60
□ 117 Ted Dean SP	8.00	3.60	1.00
□ 118 Clarence Peaks	4.00	1.80	.50
□ 119 Bobby Walston	4.00	1.80	.50
□ 120 Pete Retzlaff SP	10.00	4.50	1.25
□ 121 Jim Schrader SP	8.00	3.60	1.00
□ 122 J.D. Smith T	4.00	1.80	.50
□ 123 King Hill	5.00	2.20	.60
□ 124 Maxie Baughan	5.00	2.20	.60
□ 125 Pete Case SP	8.00	3.60	1.00
□ 126 Philadelphia Eagles Team Card	6.00	2.70	.75
□ 127 Bobby Layne UER (Bears until 1958, should be Lions)	25.00	11.00	3.10
□ 128 Tom Tracy	5.00	2.20	.60
□ 129 John Henry Johnson	7.00	3.10	.85
□ 130 Buddy Dial SP	10.00	4.50	1.25
□ 131 Preston Carpenter	4.00	1.80	.50
□ 132 Lou Michaels SP	8.00	3.60	1.00
□ 133 Gene Lipscomb SP	10.00	4.50	1.25
□ 134 Ernie Stautner SP	16.00	7.25	2.00
□ 135 John Reger SP	8.00	3.60	1.00
□ 136 Myron Pottios	4.00	1.80	.50
□ 137 Bob Ferguson SP	8.00	3.60	1.00
□ 138 Pittsburgh Steelers Team Card SP	18.00	8.00	2.20
□ 139 Sam Etcheverry	5.00	2.20	.60
□ 140 John David Crow SP	10.00	4.50	1.25
□ 141 Bobby Joe Conrad SP	10.00	4.50	1.25
□ 142 Prentice Gautt SP	8.00	3.60	1.00
□ 143 Frank Mestnick	4.00	1.80	.50
□ 144 Sonny Randle	5.00	2.20	.60
□ 145 Gerry Perry UER (T-K on both sides, but Def. End in bio)	4.00	1.80	.50
□ 146 Jerry Norton	4.00	1.80	.50
□ 147 Jimmy Hill	4.00	1.80	.50
□ 148 Bill Stacy	4.00	1.80	.50
□ 149 Fate Echols SP	8.00	3.60	1.00
□ 150 St. Louis Cardinals Team Card	6.00	2.70	.75
□ 151 Bill Kilmer	25.00	11.00	3.10
□ 152 John Brodie	15.00	6.75	1.85
□ 153 J.D. Smith RB	5.00	2.20	.60
□ 154 C.R. Roberts SP	8.00	3.60	1.00
□ 155 Monty Stickles	4.00	1.80	.50
□ 156 Clyde Conner UER (Misspelled Connor on card back)	4.00	1.80	.50
□ 157 Bob St. Clair	6.00	2.70	.75
□ 158 Tommy Davis	4.00	1.80	.50
□ 159 Leo Nomellini	7.00	3.10	.85
□ 160 Matt Hazeltine	4.00	1.80	.50
□ 161 Abe Woodson	4.00	1.80	.50
□ 162 Dave Baker	4.00	1.80	.50
□ 163 San Francisco 49ers Team Card	6.00	2.70	.75
□ 164 Norm Snead SP	25.00	11.00	3.10
□ 165 Dick James (Inset photo is Don Bosseler)	8.00	3.60	1.00
□ 166 Bobby Mitchell	8.00	3.60	1.00
□ 167 Sam Horner	4.00	1.80	.50
□ 168 Bill Barnes	4.00	1.80	.50
□ 169 Bill Anderson	4.00	1.80	.50
□ 170 Fred Dugan	4.00	1.80	.50
□ 171 John Aveni SP	8.00	3.60	1.00
□ 172 Bob Toneff	4.00	1.80	.50
□ 173 Jim Kerr	4.00	1.80	.50
□ 174 Leroy Jackson SP	8.00	3.60	1.00
□ 175 Washington Redskins Team Card	6.00	2.70	.75
□ 176 Checklist	100.00	25.00	10.00

1962 Topps Bucks

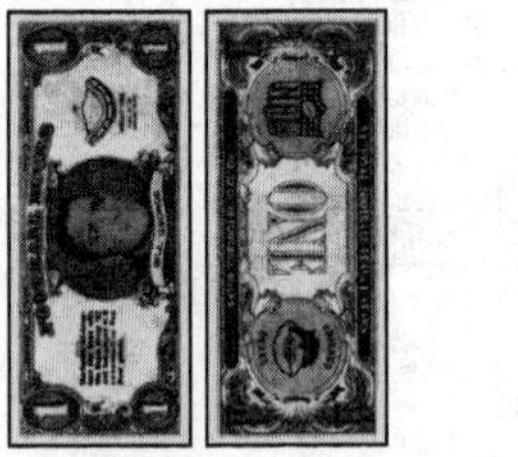

The 1962 Topps Football Bucks set contains 48 cards and was issued as an insert into wax packs of the 1962 Topps regular issue of football cards. Printing was done with black and green ink on off-white (very thin) paper stock. Bucks are typically found with a fold crease in the middle as they were inserted in packs in that manner. These "football bucks" measure approximately 1 1/4" by 4 1/4". Mike Ditka and Fran Tarkenton appear in their Rookie Card year.

	NRMT	VG-E	GOOD
COMPLETE SET (48)	450.00	200.00	55.00
COMMON CARD (1-48)	4.00	1.80	.50
□ 1 J.D. Smith	4.00	1.80	.50
□ 2 Bart Starr	20.00	9.00	2.50
□ 3 Dick James	4.00	1.80	.50
□ 4 Alex Webster	5.00	2.20	.60
□ 5 Paul Hornung	20.00	9.00	2.50
□ 6 John David Crow	5.00	2.20	.60
□ 7 Jimmy Brown	50.00	22.00	6.25
□ 8 Don Perkins	5.00	2.20	.60
□ 9 Bobby Walston	4.00	1.80	.50
□ 10 Jim Phillips	4.00	1.80	.50
□ 11 Y.A. Tittle	15.00	6.75	1.85
□ 12 Sonny Randle	4.00	1.80	.50
□ 13 Jerry Reichow	4.00	1.80	.50
□ 14 Yale Lary	6.00	2.70	.75
□ 15 Buddy Dial	5.00	2.20	.60
□ 16 Ray Renfro	4.00	1.80	.50
□ 17 Norm Snead	6.00	2.70	.75
□ 18 Leo Nomellini	6.00	2.70	.75
□ 19 Hugh McElhenny	10.00	4.50	1.25
□ 20 Eddie LeBaron	5.00	2.20	.60
□ 21 Billy Howton	5.00	2.20	.60
□ 22 Bobby Mitchell	7.50	3.40	.95
□ 23 Nick Pietrosante	4.00	1.80	.50
□ 24 Johnny Unitas	30.00	13.50	3.70
□ 25 Raymond Berry	10.00	4.50	1.25
□ 26 Billy Kilmer	7.50	3.40	.95
□ 27 Lenny Moore	10.00	4.50	1.25
□ 28 Tommy McDonald	5.00	2.20	.60
□ 29 Del Shofner	4.00	1.80	.50
□ 30 Jim Taylor	15.00	6.75	1.85
□ 31 Joe Schmidt	7.50	3.40	.95
□ 32 Bill George	6.00	2.70	.75
□ 33 Fran Tarkenton	50.00	22.00	6.25
□ 34 Willie Galimore	5.00	2.20	.60
□ 35 Bobby Layne	15.00	6.75	1.85
□ 36 Max McGee	5.00	2.20	.60

Card	NRMT	VG-E	GOOD
☐ 37 Jon Arnett	5.00	2.20	.60
☐ 38 Lou Groza	12.00	5.50	1.50
☐ 39 Frank Varrichione	4.00	1.80	.50
☐ 40 Milt Plum	5.00	2.20	.60
☐ 41 Prentice Gautt	4.00	1.80	.50
☐ 42 Bill Wade	5.00	2.20	.60
☐ 43 Gino Marchetti	7.50	3.40	.95
☐ 44 John Brodie	10.00	4.50	1.25
☐ 45 Sonny Jurgensen UER (Misspelled Jurgenson)	10.00	4.50	1.25
☐ 46 Clarence Peaks	5.00	2.20	.60
☐ 47 Mike Ditka	45.00	20.00	5.50
☐ 48 John Henry Johnson	6.00	2.70	.75

1963 Topps

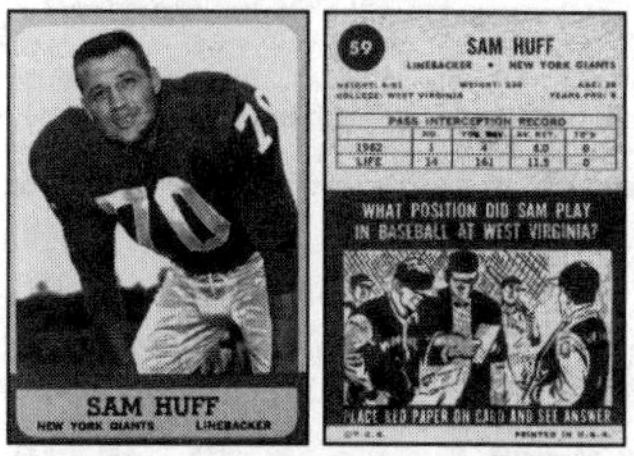

The 1963 Topps set contains 170 standard-size cards of NFL players grouped together by teams. The card backs are printed in light orange ink on white card stock. Statistical information from the immediate past season and career totals are given on the reverse. The illustrated trivia question on the reverse (of each card) could be answered by placing red cellophane paper (which was inserted into wax packs) over the card. The 76 cards indicated by SP below are in shorter supply than the others because the set size is not the standard 132-card, single-sheet size; hence, all cards were not printed in equal amounts. There also exists a three-card advertising panel consisting of card fronts of Charlie Johnson, John David Crow and Bobby Joe Conrad. The back of the latter two players contains ad copy and a Y.A. Tittle card back on Johnson. The key Rookie Cards in this set are defensive stalwarts Deacon Jones, Bob Lilly, Jim Marshall, Ray Nitschke, Larry Wilson, and Willie Wood.

	NRMT	VG-E	GOOD
COMPLETE SET (170)	1350.00	600.00	170.00
COMMON CARD (1-170)	2.50	1.10	.30
WRAPPER (1-CENT)	400.00	180.00	50.00
WRAPPER (5-CENT)	50.00	22.00	6.25

Card	NRMT	VG-E	GOOD
☐ 1 John Unitas	100.00	25.00	10.00
☐ 2 Lenny Moore	8.00	3.60	1.00
☐ 3 Jimmy Orr	2.50	1.10	.30
☐ 4 Raymond Berry	8.00	3.60	1.00
☐ 5 Jim Parker	5.00	2.20	.60
☐ 6 Alex Sandusky	2.50	1.10	.30
☐ 7 Dick Szymanski	2.50	1.10	.30
☐ 8 Gino Marchetti	6.00	2.70	.75
☐ 9 Billy Ray Smith	3.50	1.55	.45
☐ 10 Bill Pellington	2.50	1.10	.30
☐ 11 Bob Boyd	2.50	1.10	.30
☐ 12 Baltimore Colts SP Team Card	10.00	4.50	1.25
☐ 13 Frank Ryan SP	8.00	3.60	1.00
☐ 14 Jim Brown SP	200.00	90.00	25.00
☐ 15 Ray Renfro SP	6.00	2.70	.75
☐ 16 Rich Kreitling SP	6.00	2.70	.75
☐ 17 Mike McCormack SP	10.00	4.50	1.25
☐ 18 Jim Ray Smith SP	6.00	2.70	.75
☐ 19 Lou Groza SP	18.00	8.00	2.20
☐ 20 Bill Glass SP	6.00	2.70	.75
☐ 21 Galen Fiss SP	6.00	2.70	.75
☐ 22 Don Fleming SP	8.00	3.60	1.00
☐ 23 Bob Gain SP	6.00	2.70	.75
☐ 24 Cleveland Browns SP Team Card	10.00	4.50	1.25
☐ 25 Milt Plum	3.50	1.55	.45
☐ 26 Dan Lewis	2.50	1.10	.30
☐ 27 Nick Pietrosante	2.50	1.10	.30
☐ 28 Gail Cogdill	2.50	1.10	.30
☐ 29 Harley Sewell	2.50	1.10	.30
☐ 30 Jim Gibbons	2.50	1.10	.30
☐ 31 Carl Brettschneider	2.50	1.10	.30
☐ 32 Dick Lane	5.00	2.20	.60
☐ 33 Yale Lary	5.00	2.20	.60
☐ 34 Roger Brown	3.50	1.55	.45
☐ 35 Joe Schmidt	6.00	2.70	.75
☐ 36 Detroit Lions SP Team Card	10.00	4.50	1.25
☐ 37 Roman Gabriel	8.00	3.60	1.00
☐ 38 Zeke Bratkowski	3.50	1.55	.45
☐ 39 Dick Bass	3.50	1.55	.45
☐ 40 Jon Arnett	3.50	1.55	.45
☐ 41 Jim Phillips	2.50	1.10	.30
☐ 42 Frank Varrichione	2.50	1.10	.30
☐ 43 Danny Villanueva	2.50	1.10	.30
☐ 44 Deacon Jones	50.00	22.00	6.25
☐ 45 Lindon Crow	2.50	1.10	.30
☐ 46 Marlin McKeever	2.50	1.10	.30
☐ 47 Ed Meador	2.50	1.10	.30
☐ 48 Los Angeles Rams Team Card	4.00	1.80	.50
☐ 49 Y.A. Tittle SP	45.00	20.00	5.50
☐ 50 Del Shofner SP	6.00	2.70	.75
☐ 51 Alex Webster SP	8.00	3.60	1.00
☐ 52 Phil King SP	6.00	2.70	.75
☐ 53 Jack Stroud SP	6.00	2.70	.75
☐ 54 Darrell Dess SP	6.00	2.70	.75
☐ 55 Jim Katcavage SP	6.00	2.70	.75
☐ 56 Roosevelt Grier SP	10.00	4.50	1.25
☐ 57 Erich Barnes SP	6.00	2.70	.75
☐ 58 Jim Patton SP	6.00	2.70	.75
☐ 59 Sam Huff SP	18.00	8.00	2.20
☐ 60 New York Giants Team Card	4.00	1.80	.50
☐ 61 Bill Wade	3.50	1.55	.45
☐ 62 Mike Ditka	65.00	29.00	8.00
☐ 63 Johnny Morris	2.50	1.10	.30
☐ 64 Roger LeClerc	2.50	1.10	.30
☐ 65 Roger Davis	2.50	1.10	.30
☐ 66 Joe Marconi	2.50	1.10	.30
☐ 67 Herman Lee	2.50	1.10	.30
☐ 68 Doug Atkins	6.00	2.70	.75
☐ 69 Joe Fortunato	2.50	1.10	.30
☐ 70 Bill George	5.00	2.20	.60
☐ 71 Richie Petitbon	3.50	1.55	.45
☐ 72 Chicago Bears SP Team Card	10.00	4.50	1.25
☐ 73 Eddie LeBaron SP	8.00	3.60	1.00
☐ 74 Don Meredith SP	60.00	27.00	7.50
☐ 75 Don Perkins SP	8.00	3.60	1.00
☐ 76 Amos Marsh SP	6.00	2.70	.75
☐ 77 Billy Howton SP	8.00	3.60	1.00
☐ 78 Andy Cvercko SP	6.00	2.70	.75
☐ 79 Sam Baker SP	6.00	2.70	.75
☐ 80 Jerry Tubbs SP	6.00	2.70	.75
☐ 81 Don Bishop SP	6.00	2.70	.75
☐ 82 Bob Lilly SP	160.00	70.00	20.00
☐ 83 Jerry Norton SP	6.00	2.70	.75
☐ 84 Dallas Cowboys SP Team Card	20.00	9.00	2.50
☐ 85 Checklist Card	25.00	6.25	2.50
☐ 86 Bart Starr	45.00	20.00	5.50
☐ 87 Jim Taylor	20.00	9.00	2.50
☐ 88 Boyd Dowler	5.00	2.20	.60
☐ 89 Forrest Gregg	6.00	2.70	.75
☐ 90 Fuzzy Thurston	6.00	2.70	.75
☐ 91 Jim Ringo	6.00	2.70	.75
☐ 92 Ron Kramer	2.50	1.10	.30
☐ 93 Hank Jordan	6.00	2.70	.75
☐ 94 Bill Forester	3.50	1.55	.45
☐ 95 Willie Wood	30.00	13.50	3.70
☐ 96 Ray Nitschke	90.00	40.00	11.00
☐ 97 Green Bay Packers Team Card	6.00	2.70	.75
☐ 98 Fran Tarkenton	40.00	18.00	5.00
☐ 99 Tommy Mason	3.50	1.55	.45
☐ 100 Mel Triplett	2.50	1.10	.30
☐ 101 Jerry Reichow	2.50	1.10	.30
☐ 102 Frank Youso	2.50	1.10	.30
☐ 103 Hugh McElhenny	8.00	3.60	1.00
☐ 104 Gerald Huth	2.50	1.10	.30
☐ 105 Ed Sharockman	2.50	1.10	.30
☐ 106 Rip Hawkins	2.50	1.10	.30
☐ 107 Jim Marshall	30.00	13.50	3.70
☐ 108 Jim Prestel	2.50	1.10	.30
☐ 109 Minnesota Vikings Team Card	4.00	1.80	.50
☐ 110 Sonny Jurgensen SP	25.00	11.00	3.10
☐ 111 Tim Brown SP	10.00	4.50	1.25
☐ 112 Tommy McDonald SP	8.00	3.60	1.00
☐ 113 Clarence Peaks SP	6.00	2.70	.75
☐ 114 Pete Retzlaff SP	8.00	3.60	1.00
☐ 115 Jim Schrader SP	6.00	2.70	.75
☐ 116 Jim McCusker SP	6.00	2.70	.75
☐ 117 Don Burroughs SP	6.00	2.70	.75
☐ 118 Maxie Baughan SP	6.00	2.70	.75
☐ 119 Riley Gunnels SP	6.00	2.70	.75
☐ 120 Jimmy Carr SP	6.00	2.70	.75
☐ 121 Philadelphia Eagles Team Card SP	10.00	4.50	1.25
☐ 122 Ed Brown SP	8.00	3.60	1.00
☐ 123 John Henry Johnson SP	14.00	6.25	1.75
☐ 124 Buddy Dial SP	6.00	2.70	.75
☐ 125 Bill Red Mack SP	6.00	2.70	.75
☐ 126 Preston Carpenter SP	6.00	2.70	.75
☐ 127 Ray Lemek SP	6.00	2.70	.75
☐ 128 Buzz Nutter SP	6.00	2.70	.75
☐ 129 Ernie Stautner SP	15.00	6.75	1.85
☐ 130 Lou Michaels SP	6.00	2.70	.75
☐ 131 Clendon Thomas SP	6.00	2.70	.75
☐ 132 Tom Bettis SP	6.00	2.70	.75
☐ 133 Pittsburgh Steelers Team Card SP	10.00	4.50	1.25
☐ 134 John Brodie	8.00	3.60	1.00
☐ 135 J.D. Smith	2.50	1.10	.30
☐ 136 Bill Kilmer UER (College listed as San Francisco 49ers)	6.00	2.70	.75
☐ 137 Bernie Casey	3.50	1.55	.45
☐ 138 Tommy Davis	2.50	1.10	.30
☐ 139 Ted Connolly	2.50	1.10	.30
☐ 140 Bob St. Clair	5.00	2.20	.60
☐ 141 Abe Woodson	2.50	1.10	.30
☐ 142 Matt Hazeltine	2.50	1.10	.30
☐ 143 Leo Nomellini	6.00	2.70	.75
☐ 144 Dan Colchico	2.50	1.10	.30
☐ 145 San Francisco 49ers Team Card SP	10.00	4.50	1.25
☐ 146 Charlie Johnson	8.00	3.60	1.00
☐ 147 John David Crow	3.50	1.55	.45
☐ 148 Bobby Joe Conrad	3.50	1.55	.45
☐ 149 Sonny Randle	2.50	1.10	.30
☐ 150 Prentice Gautt	2.50	1.10	.30
☐ 151 Taz Anderson	2.50	1.10	.30
☐ 152 Ernie McMillan	3.50	1.55	.45
☐ 153 Jimmy Hill	2.50	1.10	.30
☐ 154 Bill Koman	2.50	1.10	.30
☐ 155 Larry Wilson	20.00	9.00	2.50
☐ 156 Don Owens	2.50	1.10	.30
☐ 157 St. Louis Cardinals Team Card SP	10.00	4.50	1.25
☐ 158 Norm Snead SP	12.00	5.50	1.50
☐ 159 Bobby Mitchell SP	15.00	6.75	1.85
☐ 160 Bill Barnes SP	6.00	2.70	.75
☐ 161 Fred Dugan SP	6.00	2.70	.75
☐ 162 Don Bosseler SP	6.00	2.70	.75
☐ 163 John Nisby SP	6.00	2.70	.75
☐ 164 Riley Mattson SP	6.00	2.70	.75
☐ 165 Bob Toneff SP	6.00	2.70	.75
☐ 166 Rod Breedlove SP	6.00	2.70	.75
☐ 167 Dick James SP	6.00	2.70	.75
☐ 168 Claude Crabb SP UER (Claud on front)	6.00	2.70	.75
☐ 169 Washington Redskins Team Card SP	10.00	4.50	1.25
☐ 170 Checklist Card UER (108 Jim Prestal)	60.00	15.00	6.00

1964 Topps

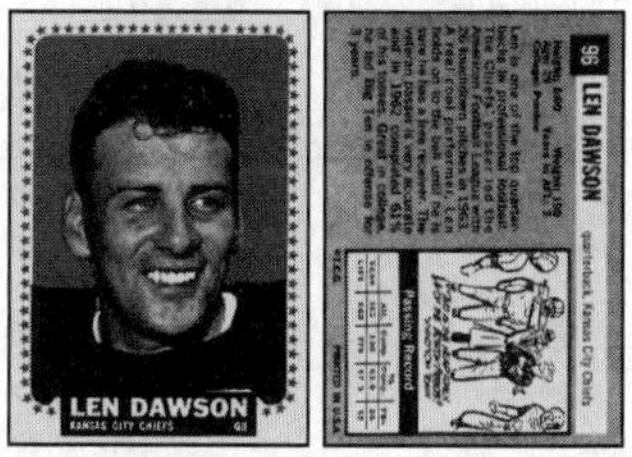

The 1964 Topps football set begins a run of four straight years that Topps issued cards of American Football League (AFL) player cards. The cards in this 176-card set measure the standard size and are grouped by teams. Because the cards were not printed on a standard 132-card sheet, some cards are printed in lesser quantities than others. These cards are marked in the checklist with SP for short print. Cards fronts feature white boders with tiny red stars outlining the photo. The player's name, team and position are in a black box beneath the photo. The backs of the cards contain the card number, vital statistics, a short biography, the player's record for the past year and his career, and a cartoon-illustrated question and answer section. The cards are organized alphabetically within teams. The key Rookie Cards in this set are Bobby Bell, Buck Buchanan, John Hadl, and Daryle Lamonica.

	NRMT	VG-E	GOOD
COMPLETE SET (176)	1500.00	700.00	190.00
COMMON CARD (1-176)	4.00	1.80	.50
WRAPPER (1-CENT)	40.00	18.00	5.00
WRAPPER (5-CENT)	40.00	18.00	5.00
WRAPPER (5-CENT, 8-CARD)	75.00	34.00	9.50

Card	NRMT	VG-E	GOOD
☐ 1 Tommy Addison SP	30.00	7.50	3.00
☐ 2 Houston Antwine	4.00	1.80	.50
☐ 3 Nick Buoniconti	14.00	6.25	1.75
☐ 4 Ron Burton SP	10.00	4.50	1.25
☐ 5 Gino Cappelletti UER (Misspelled Cappalletti on card front)	5.00	2.20	.60
☐ 6 Jim Colclough SP	6.00	2.70	.75
☐ 7 Bob Dee SP	6.00	2.70	.75
☐ 8 Larry Eisenhauer	4.00	1.80	.50
☐ 9 Dick Felt SP	6.00	2.70	.75
☐ 10 Larry Garron	4.00	1.80	.50
☐ 11 Art Graham	4.00	1.80	.50
☐ 12 Ron Hall	4.00	1.80	.50
☐ 13 Charles Long	4.00	1.80	.50
☐ 14 Don McKinnon	4.00	1.80	.50
☐ 15 Don Oakes SP	6.00	2.70	.75
☐ 16 Ross O'Hanley SP	6.00	2.70	.75
☐ 17 Babe Parilli SP	10.00	4.50	1.25
☐ 18 Jesse Richardson SP	6.00	2.70	.75
☐ 19 Jack Rudolph SP	6.00	2.70	.75
☐ 20 Don Webb	4.00	1.80	.50
☐ 21 Boston Patriots Team Card	9.00	4.00	1.15
☐ 22 Ray Abruzzese	4.00	1.80	.50
☐ 23 Stew Barber	4.00	1.80	.50
☐ 24 Dave Behrman	4.00	1.80	.50
☐ 25 Al Bemiller	4.00	1.80	.50
☐ 26 Elbert Dubenion SP	10.00	4.50	1.25
☐ 27 Jim Dunaway SP	6.00	2.70	.75
☐ 28 Booker Edgerson SP	6.00	2.70	.75
☐ 29 Cookie Gilchrist SP	20.00	9.00	2.50
☐ 30 Jack Kemp SP	200.00	90.00	25.00
☐ 31 Daryle Lamonica	70.00	32.00	8.75
☐ 32 Bill Miller	4.00	1.80	.50
☐ 33 Herb Paterra	4.00	1.80	.50
☐ 34 Ken Rice SP	6.00	2.70	.75
☐ 35 Ed Rutkowski	4.00	1.80	.50
☐ 36 George Saimes	4.00	1.80	.50
☐ 37 Tom Sestak	4.00	1.80	.50
☐ 38 Billy Shaw SP	6.00	2.70	.75
☐ 39 Mike Stratton	5.00	2.20	.60
☐ 40 Gene Sykes	4.00	1.80	.50
☐ 41 John Tracey SP	6.00	2.70	.75
☐ 42 Sid Youngelman SP	6.00	2.70	.75
☐ 43 Buffalo Bills Team Card	9.00	4.00	1.15
☐ 44 Eldon Danenhauer SP	6.00	2.70	.75
☐ 45 Jim Fraser SP	6.00	2.70	.75
☐ 46 Chuck Gavin SP	6.00	2.70	.75
☐ 47 Goose Gonsoulin SP	10.00	4.50	1.25
☐ 48 Ernie Barnes	4.00	1.80	.50
☐ 49 Tom Janik	4.00	1.80	.50
☐ 50 Billy Joe	5.00	2.20	.60
☐ 51 Ike Lassiter	4.00	1.80	.50
☐ 52 John McCormick SP	6.00	2.70	.75
☐ 53 Bud McFadin SP	6.00	2.70	.75
☐ 54 Gene Mingo SP	6.00	2.70	.75
☐ 55 Charlie Mitchell	4.00	1.80	.50
☐ 56 John Nocera SP	6.00	2.70	.75
☐ 57 Tom Nomina	4.00	1.80	.50
☐ 58 Harold Olson SP	6.00	2.70	.75
☐ 59 Bob Scarpitto	4.00	1.80	.50
☐ 60 John Sklopan	4.00	1.80	.50
☐ 61 Mickey Slaughter	4.00	1.80	.50
☐ 62 Don Stone	4.00	1.80	.50
☐ 63 Jerry Sturm	4.00	1.80	.50
☐ 64 Lionel Taylor SP	12.00	5.50	1.50
☐ 65 Denver Broncos SP Team Card	15.00	6.75	1.85
☐ 66 Scott Appleton	4.00	1.80	.50
☐ 67 Tony Banfield SP	6.00	2.70	.75
☐ 68 George Blanda SP	60.00	27.00	7.50
☐ 69 Billy Cannon	7.00	3.10	.85
☐ 70 Doug Cline SP	6.00	2.70	.75
☐ 71 Gary Cutsinger SP	6.00	2.70	.75
☐ 72 Willard Dewveall SP	6.00	2.70	.75
☐ 73 Don Floyd SP	6.00	2.70	.75
☐ 74 Freddy Glick SP	6.00	2.70	.75
☐ 75 Charlie Hennigan SP	10.00	4.50	1.25
☐ 76 Ed Husmann SP	6.00	2.70	.75
☐ 77 Bobby Jancik SP	6.00	2.70	.75
☐ 78 Jacky Lee SP	10.00	4.50	1.25
☐ 79 Bob McLeod SP	6.00	2.70	.75
☐ 80 Rich Michael SP	6.00	2.70	.75
☐ 81 Larry Onesti	4.00	1.80	.50
☐ 82 Checklist Card UER (16 Ross O'Hanldy)	60.00	15.00	6.00
☐ 83 Bob Schmidt SP	6.00	2.70	.75
☐ 84 Walt Suggs SP	6.00	2.70	.75
☐ 85 Bob Talamini SP	6.00	2.70	.75
☐ 86 Charley Tolar SP	6.00	2.70	.75
☐ 87 Don Trull	4.00	1.80	.50
☐ 88 Houston Oilers Team Card	9.00	4.00	1.15
☐ 89 Fred Arbanas	4.00	1.80	.50
☐ 90 Bobby Bell	40.00	18.00	5.00
☐ 91 Mel Branch SP	10.00	4.50	1.25
☐ 92 Buck Buchanan	40.00	18.00	5.00
☐ 93 Ed Budde	4.00	1.80	.50
☐ 94 Chris Burford SP	10.00	4.50	1.25
☐ 95 Walt Corey	5.00	2.20	.60
☐ 96 Len Dawson SP	80.00	36.00	10.00
☐ 97 Dave Grayson	4.00	1.80	.50
☐ 98 Abner Haynes	6.00	2.70	.75
☐ 99 Sherrill Headrick SP	10.00	4.50	1.25
☐ 100 E.J. Holub	4.00	1.80	.50
☐ 101 Bobby Hunt	4.00	1.80	.50
☐ 102 Frank Jackson SP	6.00	2.70	.75
☐ 103 Curtis McClinton	5.00	2.20	.60
☐ 104 Jerry Mays SP	10.00	4.50	1.25
☐ 105 Johnny Robinson SP	10.00	4.50	1.25
☐ 106 Jack Spikes SP	6.00	2.70	.75
☐ 107 Smokey Stover SP	6.00	2.70	.75
☐ 108 Jim Tyrer	8.00	3.60	1.00
☐ 109 Duane Wood SP	6.00	2.70	.75
☐ 110 Kansas City Chiefs Team Card	9.00	4.00	1.15
☐ 111 Dick Christy SP	6.00	2.70	.75
☐ 112 Dan Ficca SP	6.00	2.70	.75
☐ 113 Larry Grantham	4.00	1.80	.50
☐ 114 Curley Johnson SP	6.00	2.70	.75
☐ 115 Gene Heeter	4.00	1.80	.50
☐ 116 Jack Klotz	4.00	1.80	.50
☐ 117 Pete Liske	5.00	2.20	.60
☐ 118 Bob McAdam	4.00	1.80	.50
☐ 119 Dee Mackey SP	6.00	2.70	.75
☐ 120 Bill Mathis SP	10.00	4.50	1.25
☐ 121 Don Maynard	35.00	16.00	4.40
☐ 122 Dainard Paulson SP	6.00	2.70	.75
☐ 123 Gerry Philbin	5.00	2.20	.60
☐ 124 Mark Smolinski SP	6.00	2.70	.75
☐ 125 Matt Snell	20.00	9.00	2.50
☐ 126 Mike Taliaferro	4.00	1.80	.50
☐ 127 Bake Turner SP	12.00	5.50	1.50
☐ 128 Jeff Ware	4.00	1.80	.50
☐ 129 Clyde Washington	4.00	1.80	.50
☐ 130 Dick Wood	4.00	1.80	.50
☐ 131 New York Jets Team Card	9.00	4.00	1.15
☐ 132 Dalva Allen SP	6.00	2.70	.75
☐ 133 Dan Birdwell	4.00	1.80	.50
☐ 134 Dave Costa	4.00	1.80	.50

☐ 135 Dobie Craig	4.00	1.80	.50
☐ 136 Clem Daniels	5.00	2.20	.60
☐ 137 Cotton Davidson SP	10.00	4.50	1.25
☐ 138 Claude Gibson	4.00	1.80	.50
☐ 139 Tom Flores SP	16.00	7.25	2.00
☐ 140 Wayne Hawkins SP	6.00	2.70	.75
☐ 141 Ken Herock	4.00	1.80	.50
☐ 142 Jon Jelacic SP	6.00	2.70	.75
☐ 143 Joe Krakoski	4.00	1.80	.50
☐ 144 Archie Matsos SP	6.00	2.70	.75
☐ 145 Mike Mercer	4.00	1.80	.50
☐ 146 Alan Miller SP	6.00	2.70	.75
☐ 147 Bob Mischak SP	6.00	2.70	.75
☐ 148 Jim Otto SP	30.00	13.50	3.70
☐ 149 Clancy Osborne SP	6.00	2.70	.75
☐ 150 Art Powell SP	12.00	5.50	1.50
☐ 151 Bo Roberson (Raider helmet placed over his foot)	4.00	1.80	.50
☐ 152 Fred Williamson SP	15.00	6.75	1.85
☐ 153 Oakland Raiders Team Card	9.00	4.00	1.15
☐ 154 Chuck Allen SP	10.00	4.50	1.25
☐ 155 Lance Alworth	50.00	22.00	6.25
☐ 156 George Blair	4.00	1.80	.50
☐ 157 Earl Faison	4.00	1.80	.50
☐ 158 Sam Gruneisen	4.00	1.80	.50
☐ 159 John Hadl	35.00	16.00	4.40
☐ 160 Dick Harris SP	6.00	2.70	.75
☐ 161 Emil Karas SP	6.00	2.70	.75
☐ 162 Dave Kocourek SP	6.00	2.70	.75
☐ 163 Ernie Ladd	6.00	2.70	.75
☐ 164 Keith Lincoln	6.00	2.70	.75
☐ 165 Paul Lowe SP	12.00	5.50	1.50
☐ 166 Charley McNeil	4.00	1.80	.50
☐ 167 Jacque MacKinnon SP	6.00	2.70	.75
☐ 168 Ron Mix SP	18.00	8.00	2.20
☐ 169 Don Norton SP	6.00	2.70	.75
☐ 170 Don Rogers SP	6.00	2.70	.75
☐ 171 Tobin Rote SP	10.00	4.50	1.25
☐ 172 Henry Schmidt SP	6.00	2.70	.75
☐ 173 Bud Whitehead	4.00	1.80	.50
☐ 174 Ernie Wright SP	10.00	4.50	1.25
☐ 175 San Diego Chargers Team Card	9.00	4.00	1.15
☐ 176 Checklist SP UER (155 Lance Allworth)	160.00	40.00	16.00

1964 Topps Pennant Stickers

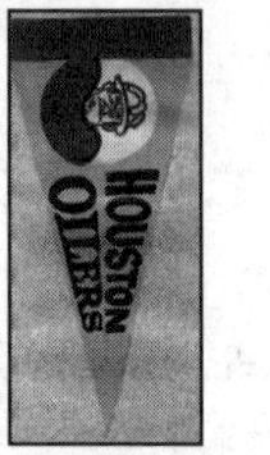

This set of 24 pennant stickers was inserted into the 1964 Topps regular issue AFL set. These inserts are actually 2 1/8" by 4 1/2" glassine type peel-offs on gray backing. The pennants are unnumbered and are ordered below alphabetically within type. The stickers were folded in order to fit into the 1964 Topps wax packs, so they are virtually always found with a crease or fold.

	NRMT	VG-E	GOOD
COMPLETE SET (24)	1200.00	550.00	150.00
COMMON AFL (1-8)	65.00	29.00	8.00
COMMON COLLEGE (9-24)	40.00	18.00	5.00
☐ 1 Boston Patriots	65.00	29.00	8.00
☐ 2 Buffalo Bills	65.00	29.00	8.00
☐ 3 Denver Broncos	65.00	29.00	8.00
☐ 4 Houston Oilers	65.00	29.00	8.00
☐ 5 Kansas City Chiefs	65.00	29.00	8.00
☐ 6 New York Jets	65.00	29.00	8.00
☐ 7 Oakland Raiders	90.00	40.00	11.00
☐ 8 San Diego Chargers	65.00	29.00	8.00
☐ 9 Air Force Academy	40.00	18.00	5.00
☐ 10 Army	40.00	18.00	5.00
☐ 11 Dartmouth Indians	40.00	18.00	5.00
☐ 12 Duke	40.00	18.00	5.00
☐ 13 Michigan	60.00	27.00	7.50
☐ 14 Minnesota	40.00	18.00	5.00
☐ 15 Mississippi Rebels	40.00	18.00	5.00
☐ 16 Navy	40.00	18.00	5.00
☐ 17 Notre Dame	125.00	55.00	15.50
☐ 18 SMU	40.00	18.00	5.00
☐ 19 Southern California	50.00	22.00	6.25
☐ 20 Syracuse	40.00	18.00	5.00
☐ 21 Texas	50.00	22.00	6.25
☐ 22 Washington	40.00	18.00	5.00
☐ 23 Wisconsin	40.00	18.00	5.00
☐ 24 Yale Bulldogs	40.00	18.00	5.00

1965 Topps

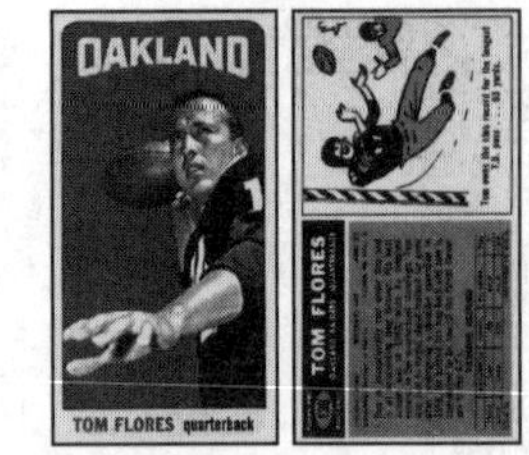

The 1965 Topps football card set contains 176 oversized (2 1/2" by 4 11/16") cards of American Football League players. Colorful card fronts have a player photo over a solid color background. The team name is at the top with the player's name and position at the bottom. Horizontal backs contain highlights and statistics to the left with a cartoon pertaining to the player to the right. The cards are grouped together and numbered in basic alphabetical order by teams. Since this set was not printed in the standard fashion, many of the cards were printed in lesser quantities than others. These cards are marked in the checklist with SP for short print. This set is somewhat significant in that it contains the Rookie Card of Joe Namath. Other notable Rookie Cards in this set of Oakland Raiders stars Fred Biletnikoff, Willie Brown and Ben Davidson.

	NRMT	VG-E	GOOD
COMPLETE SET (176)	4000.00	1800.00	500.00
COMMON CARD (1-176)	7.00	3.10	.85
WRAPPER (5-CENT)	25.00	11.00	3.10
☐ 1 Tommy Addison SP	35.00	8.75	3.50
☐ 2 Houston Antwine SP	12.00	5.50	1.50
☐ 3 Nick Buoniconti SP	25.00	11.00	3.10
☐ 4 Ron Burton SP	16.00	7.25	2.00
☐ 5 Gino Cappelletti SP	16.00	7.25	2.00
☐ 6 Jim Colclough	7.00	3.10	.85
☐ 7 Bob Dee SP	12.00	5.50	1.50
☐ 8 Larry Eisenhauer	7.00	3.10	.85
☐ 9 J.D. Garrett	7.00	3.10	.85
☐ 10 Larry Garron	7.00	3.10	.85
☐ 11 Art Graham SP	12.00	5.50	1.50
☐ 12 Ron Hall	7.00	3.10	.85
☐ 13 Charles Long	7.00	3.10	.85
☐ 14 Jon Morris	10.00	4.50	1.25
☐ 15 Billy Neighbors SP	12.00	5.50	1.50
☐ 16 Ross O'Hanley	7.00	3.10	.85
☐ 17 Babe Parilli SP	16.00	7.25	2.00
☐ 18 Tony Romeo SP	12.00	5.50	1.50
☐ 19 Jack Rudolph SP	12.00	5.50	1.50
☐ 20 Bob Schmidt	7.00	3.10	.85
☐ 21 Don Webb SP	12.00	5.50	1.50
☐ 22 Jim Whalen SP	12.00	5.50	1.50
☐ 23 Stew Barber	7.00	3.10	.85
☐ 24 Glenn Bass SP	12.00	5.50	1.50
☐ 25 Al Bemiller SP	12.00	5.50	1.50
☐ 26 Wray Carlton SP	12.00	5.50	1.50
☐ 27 Tom Day	7.00	3.10	.85
☐ 28 Elbert Dubenion SP	16.00	7.25	2.00
☐ 29 Jim Dunaway	7.00	3.10	.85
☐ 30 Pete Gogolak SP	18.00	8.00	2.20
☐ 31 Dick Hudson SP	12.00	5.50	1.50
☐ 32 Harry Jacobs SP	12.00	5.50	1.50
☐ 33 Billy Joe SP	16.00	7.25	2.00
☐ 34 Tom Keating SP	12.00	5.50	1.50
☐ 35 Jack Kemp SP	200.00	90.00	25.00
☐ 36 Daryle Lamonica SP	35.00	16.00	4.40
☐ 37 Paul Maguire SP	16.00	7.25	2.00
☐ 38 Ron McDole SP	12.00	5.50	1.50
☐ 39 George Saimes SP	12.00	5.50	1.50
☐ 40 Tom Sestak SP	12.00	5.50	1.50
☐ 41 Billy Shaw SP	12.00	5.50	1.50
☐ 42 Mike Stratton SP	12.00	5.50	1.50
☐ 43 John Tracey SP	12.00	5.50	1.50
☐ 44 Ernie Warlick	7.00	3.10	.85
☐ 45 Odell Barry	7.00	3.10	.85
☐ 46 Willie Brown SP	90.00	40.00	11.00
☐ 47 Gerry Bussell SP	12.00	5.50	1.50
☐ 48 Eldon Danenhauer SP	12.00	5.50	1.50
☐ 49 Al Denson SP	12.00	5.50	1.50
☐ 50 Hewritt Dixon SP	16.00	7.25	2.00
☐ 51 Cookie Gilchrist SP	30.00	13.50	3.70
☐ 52 Goose Gonsoulin SP	16.00	7.25	2.00
☐ 53 Abner Haynes SP	22.00	10.00	2.70
☐ 54 Jerry Hopkins	7.00	3.10	.85
☐ 55 Ray Jacobs SP	12.00	5.50	1.50
☐ 56 Jacky Lee SP	16.00	7.25	2.00
☐ 57 John McCormick	7.00	3.10	.85
☐ 58 Bob McCullough SP	12.00	5.50	1.50
☐ 59 John McGeever	7.00	3.10	.85
☐ 60 Charlie Mitchell SP	12.00	5.50	1.50
☐ 61 Jim Perkins SP	12.00	5.50	1.50
☐ 62 Bob Scarpitto SP	12.00	5.50	1.50
☐ 63 Mickey Slaughter SP	12.00	5.50	1.50
☐ 64 Jerry Sturm SP	12.00	5.50	1.50
☐ 65 Lionel Taylor SP	20.00	9.00	2.50
☐ 66 Scott Appleton SP	12.00	5.50	1.50
☐ 67 Johnny Baker SP	12.00	5.50	1.50
☐ 68 Sonny Bishop SP	12.00	5.50	1.50
☐ 69 George Blanda SP	100.00	45.00	12.50
☐ 70 Sid Blanks SP	12.00	5.50	1.50
☐ 71 Ode Burrell SP	12.00	5.50	1.50
☐ 72 Doug Cline SP	12.00	5.50	1.50
☐ 73 Willard Dewveall	7.00	3.10	.85
☐ 74 Larry Elkins	7.00	3.10	.85
☐ 75 Don Floyd SP	12.00	5.50	1.50
☐ 76 Freddy Glick	7.00	3.10	.85
☐ 77 Tom Goode SP	12.00	5.50	1.50
☐ 78 Charlie Hennigan SP	16.00	7.25	2.00
☐ 79 Ed Husmann	7.00	3.10	.85
☐ 80 Bobby Jancik SP	12.00	5.50	1.50
☐ 81 Bud McFadin SP	12.00	5.50	1.50
☐ 82 Bob McLeod SP	12.00	5.50	1.50
☐ 83 Jim Norton SP	12.00	5.50	1.50
☐ 84 Walt Suggs	7.00	3.10	.85
☐ 85 Bob Talamini	7.00	3.10	.85
☐ 86 Charley Tolar SP	12.00	5.50	1.50
☐ 87 Checklist 1-88 SP	150.00	38.00	15.00
☐ 88 Don Trull SP	12.00	5.50	1.50
☐ 89 Fred Arbanas SP	12.00	5.50	1.50
☐ 90 Pete Beathard SP	7.00	3.10	.85
☐ 91 Bobby Bell SP	35.00	16.00	4.40
☐ 92 Mel Branch SP	12.00	5.50	1.50
☐ 93 Tommy Brooker SP	12.00	5.50	1.50
☐ 94 Buck Buchanan SP	35.00	16.00	4.40
☐ 95 Ed Budde SP	12.00	5.50	1.50
☐ 96 Chris Burford SP	12.00	5.50	1.50
☐ 97 Walt Corey	7.00	3.10	.85
☐ 98 Jerry Cornelison	7.00	3.10	.85
☐ 99 Len Dawson SP	100.00	45.00	12.50
☐ 100 Jon Gilliam SP	12.00	5.50	1.50
☐ 101 Sherrill Headrick SP UER (Name spelled Sherill on front)	12.00	5.50	1.50
☐ 102 Dave Hill SP	12.00	5.50	1.50
☐ 103 E.J. Holub SP	12.00	5.50	1.50
☐ 104 Bobby Hunt SP	12.00	5.50	1.50
☐ 105 Frank Jackson SP	12.00	5.50	1.50
☐ 106 Jerry Mays	10.00	4.50	1.25
☐ 107 Curtis McClinton SP	16.00	7.25	2.00
☐ 108 Bobby Ply SP	12.00	5.50	1.50
☐ 109 Johnny Robinson SP	16.00	7.25	2.00
☐ 110 Jim Tyrer SP	12.00	5.50	1.50
☐ 111 Bill Baird SP	12.00	5.50	1.50
☐ 112 Ralph Baker SP	12.00	5.50	1.50
☐ 113 Sam DeLuca SP	12.00	5.50	1.50
☐ 114 Larry Grantham SP	16.00	7.25	2.00
☐ 115 Gene Heeter SP	12.00	5.50	1.50
☐ 116 Winston Hill SP	16.00	7.25	2.00
☐ 117 John Huarte SP	30.00	13.50	3.70
☐ 118 Cosmo Iacavazzi SP	12.00	5.50	1.50
☐ 119 Curley Johnson SP	12.00	5.50	1.50
☐ 120 Dee Mackey UER (College WVU, should be East Texas State)	7.00	3.10	.85
☐ 121 Don Maynard	50.00	22.00	6.25
☐ 122 Joe Namath SP	1500.00	700.00	190.00
☐ 123 Dainard Paulson	7.00	3.10	.85
☐ 124 Gerry Philbin SP	12.00	5.50	1.50
☐ 125 Sherman Plunkett SP	16.00	7.25	2.00
☐ 126 Mark Smolinski	7.00	3.10	.85
☐ 127 Matt Snell SP	30.00	13.50	3.70
☐ 128 Mike Taliaferro SP	12.00	5.50	1.50
☐ 129 Bake Turner SP	7.00	3.10	.85
☐ 130 Clyde Washington SP	12.00	5.50	1.50
☐ 131 Verlon Biggs SP	12.00	5.50	1.50
☐ 132 Dalva Allen	7.00	3.10	.85
☐ 133 Fred Biletnikoff SP	225.00	100.00	28.00
☐ 134 Billy Cannon SP	22.00	10.00	2.70
☐ 135 Dave Costa SP	12.00	5.50	1.50
☐ 136 Clem Daniels SP	16.00	7.25	2.00
☐ 137 Ben Davidson SP	55.00	25.00	7.00
☐ 138 Cotton Davidson SP	16.00	7.25	2.00
☐ 139 Tom Flores SP	22.00	10.00	2.70
☐ 140 Claude Gibson	7.00	3.10	.85
☐ 141 Wayne Hawkins	7.00	3.10	.85
☐ 142 Archie Matsos SP	12.00	5.50	1.50
☐ 143 Mike Mercer SP	12.00	5.50	1.50
☐ 144 Bob Mischak SP	12.00	5.50	1.50
☐ 145 Jim Otto	25.00	11.00	3.10
☐ 146 Art Powell UER (Photo actually Clem Daniels)	12.00	5.50	1.50
☐ 147 Warren Powers SP	12.00	5.50	1.50
☐ 148 Ken Rice SP	12.00	5.50	1.50
☐ 149 Bo Roberson SP	12.00	5.50	1.50
☐ 150 Harry Schuh	7.00	3.10	.85
☐ 151 Larry Todd SP	12.00	5.50	1.50
☐ 152 Fred Williamson SP	20.00	9.00	2.50
☐ 153 J.R. Williamson	7.00	3.10	.85
☐ 154 Chuck Allen	10.00	4.50	1.25
☐ 155 Lance Alworth	70.00	32.00	8.75
☐ 156 Frank Buncom	7.00	3.10	.85
☐ 157 Steve DeLong SP	12.00	5.50	1.50
☐ 158 Earl Faison SP	16.00	7.25	2.00
☐ 159 Kenny Graham SP	12.00	5.50	1.50
☐ 160 George Gross SP	12.00	5.50	1.50
☐ 161 John Hadl SP	30.00	13.50	3.70
☐ 162 Emil Karas SP	12.00	5.50	1.50
☐ 163 Dave Kocourek SP	12.00	5.50	1.50
☐ 164 Ernie Ladd SP	20.00	9.00	2.50
☐ 165 Keith Lincoln SP	20.00	9.00	2.50
☐ 166 Paul Lowe SP	20.00	9.00	2.50
☐ 167 Jacque MacKinnon	7.00	3.10	.85
☐ 168 Ron Mix	20.00	9.00	2.50
☐ 169 Don Norton SP	12.00	5.50	1.50
☐ 170 Bob Petrich	7.00	3.10	.85
☐ 171 Rick Redman SP	12.00	5.50	1.50
☐ 172 Pat Shea	7.00	3.10	.85
☐ 173 Walt Sweeney SP	16.00	7.25	2.00
☐ 174 Dick Westmoreland	7.00	3.10	.85
☐ 175 Ernie Wright SP	16.00	7.25	2.00
☐ 176 Checklist 89-176 SP	225.00	55.00	22.00

1965 Topps Magic Rub-Off Inserts

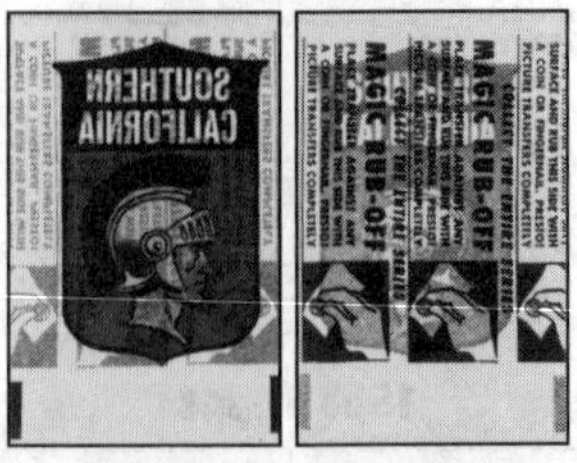

This set of 36 rub-off team emblems was inserted into packs of the 1965 Topps AFL regular football issue. They are very similar to the 1961 Topps Baseball Magic Rub-Offs. Each rub-off measures 2" by 3"; eight AFL teams and 28 college teams are featured. The rub-offs are unnumbered and, hence, are numbered below alphabetically within type, i.e., AFL teams 1-8 and college teams 9-36.

	NRMT	VG-E	GOOD
COMPLETE SET (36)	500.00	220.00	60.00
COMMON CARD (1-8)	20.00	9.00	2.50
COMMON CARD (9-36)	12.00	5.50	1.50
☐ 1 Boston Patriots	20.00	9.00	2.50
☐ 2 Buffalo Bills	20.00	9.00	2.50
☐ 3 Denver Broncos	20.00	9.00	2.50
☐ 4 Houston Oilers	20.00	9.00	2.50
☐ 5 Kansas City Chiefs	20.00	9.00	2.50
☐ 6 New York Jets	20.00	9.00	2.50
☐ 7 Oakland Raiders	30.00	13.50	3.70
☐ 8 San Diego Chargers	20.00	9.00	2.50
☐ 9 Alabama	15.00	6.75	1.85
☐ 10 Air Force Academy	12.00	5.50	1.50
☐ 11 Arkansas	12.00	5.50	1.50
☐ 12 Army	12.00	5.50	1.50
☐ 13 Boston College	12.00	5.50	1.50
☐ 14 Duke	12.00	5.50	1.50
☐ 15 Illinois	12.00	5.50	1.50
☐ 16 Kansas	12.00	5.50	1.50
☐ 17 Kentucky	12.00	5.50	1.50
☐ 18 Maryland	12.00	5.50	1.50
☐ 19 Miami	15.00	6.75	1.85
☐ 20 Minnesota	12.00	5.50	1.50
☐ 21 Mississippi Rebels	12.00	5.50	1.50
☐ 22 Navy	12.00	5.50	1.50
☐ 23 Nebraska	15.00	6.75	1.85
☐ 24 Notre Dame	35.00	16.00	4.40
☐ 25 Penn State	15.00	6.75	1.85
☐ 26 Purdue	12.00	5.50	1.50
☐ 27 SMU	12.00	5.50	1.50
☐ 28 Southern California	15.00	6.75	1.85
☐ 29 Stanford	12.00	5.50	1.50
☐ 30 Syracuse	12.00	5.50	1.50
☐ 31 TCU	12.00	5.50	1.50
☐ 32 Texas	15.00	6.75	1.85
☐ 33 Virginia	12.00	5.50	1.50
☐ 34 Washington	12.00	5.50	1.50
☐ 35 Wisconsin	12.00	5.50	1.50
☐ 36 Yale Bulldogs	12.00	5.50	1.50

1966 Topps

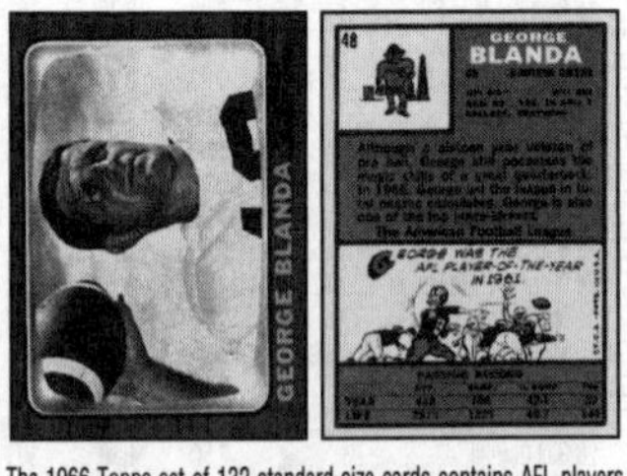

The 1966 Topps set of 132 standard-size cards contains AFL players grouped together and numbered alphabetically within teams. The set marks the debut into the AFL of the Miami Dolphins. Card fronts are horizontal with woodgrain borders. Such a border offers a challenge to locate cards in top grades. The player's name, team and position are within the border below the photo. The card backs are printed in black and pink on white card stock. In actuality, card number 15 is not a football card at all but a "Funny Ring" checklist card; nevertheless, it is considered part of the set and is now regarded as the toughest card in the set to find in mint condition. Funny Ring cards were inserted one per pack but measure only 2 1/2" by 3 3/8". Notable Rookie Cards in this set include Wendell Hayes, George Sauer Jr., Otis Taylor, and Jim Turner.

	NRMT	VG-E	GOOD
COMPLETE SET (132)	1500.00	700.00	190.00
COMMON CARD (1-132)	5.00	2.20	.60
WRAPPER (5-CENT)	20.00	9.00	2.50
☐ 1 Tommy Addison	18.00	4.50	1.80
☐ 2 Houston Antwine	5.00	2.20	.60
☐ 3 Nick Buoniconti	10.00	4.50	1.25
☐ 4 Gino Cappelletti	7.00	3.10	.85
☐ 5 Bob Dee	5.00	2.20	.60
☐ 6 Larry Garron	5.00	2.20	.60

☐ 7 Art Graham	5.00	2.20	.60
☐ 8 Ron Hall	5.00	2.20	.60
☐ 9 Charles Long	5.00	2.20	.60
☐ 10 Jon Morris	5.00	2.20	.60
☐ 11 Don Oakes	5.00	2.20	.60
☐ 12 Babe Parilli	7.00	3.10	.85
☐ 13 Don Webb	5.00	2.20	.60
☐ 14 Jim Whalen	5.00	2.20	.60
☐ 15 Funny Ring Checklist	300.00	75.00	30.00
☐ 16 Stew Barber	5.00	2.20	.60
☐ 17 Glenn Bass	5.00	2.20	.60
☐ 18 Dave Behrman	5.00	2.20	.60
☐ 19 Al Bemiller	5.00	2.20	.60
☐ 20 George Butch Byrd	7.00	3.10	.85
☐ 21 Wray Carlton	5.00	2.20	.60
☐ 22 Tom Day	5.00	2.20	.60
☐ 23 Elbert Dubenion	7.00	3.10	.85
☐ 24 Jim Dunaway	5.00	2.20	.60
☐ 25 Dick Hudson	5.00	2.20	.60
☐ 26 Jack Kemp	175.00	80.00	22.00
☐ 27 Daryle Lamonica	16.00	7.25	2.00
☐ 28 Tom Sestak	5.00	2.20	.60
☐ 29 Billy Shaw	5.00	2.20	.60
☐ 30 Mike Stratton	5.00	2.20	.60
☐ 31 Eldon Danenhauer	5.00	2.20	.60
☐ 32 Cookie Gilchrist	10.00	4.50	1.25
☐ 33 Goose Gonsoulin	7.00	3.10	.85
☐ 34 Wendell Hayes	10.00	4.50	1.25
☐ 35 Abner Haynes	7.00	3.10	.85
☐ 36 Jerry Hopkins	5.00	2.20	.60
☐ 37 Ray Jacobs	5.00	2.20	.60
☐ 38 Charlie Janerette	5.00	2.20	.60
☐ 39 Ray Kubala	5.00	2.20	.60
☐ 40 John McCormick	5.00	2.20	.60
☐ 41 Leroy Moore	5.00	2.20	.60
☐ 42 Bob Scarpitto	5.00	2.20	.60
☐ 43 Mickey Slaughter	5.00	2.20	.60
☐ 44 Jerry Sturm	5.00	2.20	.60
☐ 45 Lionel Taylor	7.00	3.10	.85
☐ 46 Scott Appleton	5.00	2.20	.60
☐ 47 Johnny Baker	5.00	2.20	.60
☐ 48 George Blanda	30.00	13.50	3.70
☐ 49 Sid Blanks	5.00	2.20	.60
☐ 50 Danny Brabham	5.00	2.20	.60
☐ 51 Ode Burrell	5.00	2.20	.60
☐ 52 Gary Cutsinger	5.00	2.20	.60
☐ 53 Larry Elkins	5.00	2.20	.60
☐ 54 Don Floyd	5.00	2.20	.60
☐ 55 Willie Frazier	7.00	3.10	.85
☐ 56 Freddy Glick	5.00	2.20	.60
☐ 57 Charlie Hennigan	7.00	3.10	.85
☐ 58 Bobby Jancik	5.00	2.20	.60
☐ 59 Rich Michael	5.00	2.20	.60
☐ 60 Don Trull	5.00	2.20	.60
☐ 61 Checklist Card	55.00	14.00	5.50
☐ 62 Fred Arbanas	5.00	2.20	.60
☐ 63 Pete Beathard	5.00	2.20	.60
☐ 64 Bobby Bell	10.00	4.50	1.25
☐ 65 Ed Budde	5.00	2.20	.60
☐ 66 Chris Burford	5.00	2.20	.60
☐ 67 Len Dawson	40.00	18.00	5.00
☐ 68 Jon Gilliam	5.00	2.20	.60
☐ 69 Sherrill Headrick	5.00	2.20	.60
☐ 70 E.J. Holub UER (College: TCU, should be Texas Tech)	5.00	2.20	.60
☐ 71 Bobby Hunt	5.00	2.20	.60
☐ 72 Curtis McClinton	7.00	3.10	.85
☐ 73 Jerry Mays	5.00	2.20	.60
☐ 74 Johnny Robinson	7.00	3.10	.85
☐ 75 Otis Taylor	25.00	11.00	3.10
☐ 76 Tom Erlandson	7.00	3.10	.85
☐ 77 Norm Evans UER (Flanker on front, tackle on back)	8.00	3.60	1.00
☐ 78 Tom Goode	7.00	3.10	.85
☐ 79 Mike Hudock	7.00	3.10	.85
☐ 80 Frank Jackson	7.00	3.10	.85
☐ 81 Billy Joe	7.00	3.10	.85
☐ 82 Dave Kocourek	7.00	3.10	.85
☐ 83 Bo Roberson	7.00	3.10	.85
☐ 84 Jack Spikes	7.00	3.10	.85
☐ 85 Jim Warren	7.00	3.10	.85
☐ 86 Willie West	7.00	3.10	.85
☐ 87 Dick Westmoreland	7.00	3.10	.85
☐ 88 Eddie Wilson	7.00	3.10	.85
☐ 89 Dick Wood	7.00	3.10	.85
☐ 90 Verlon Biggs	7.00	3.10	.85
☐ 91 Sam DeLuca	5.00	2.20	.60
☐ 92 Winston Hill	5.00	2.20	.60
☐ 93 Dee Mackey	5.00	2.20	.60
☐ 94 Bill Mathis	5.00	2.20	.60
☐ 95 Don Maynard	30.00	13.50	3.70
☐ 96 Joe Namath	350.00	160.00	45.00
☐ 97 Dainard Paulson	5.00	2.20	.60
☐ 98 Gerry Philbin	7.00	3.10	.85
☐ 99 Sherman Plunkett	5.00	2.20	.60
☐ 100 Paul Rochester	5.00	2.20	.60
☐ 101 George Sauer Jr.	14.00	6.25	1.75
☐ 102 Matt Snell	8.00	3.60	1.00
☐ 103 Jim Turner	8.00	3.60	1.00
☐ 104 Fred Biletnikoff UER (Misspelled on back as Bilentnikoff)	50.00	22.00	6.25
☐ 105 Bill Budness	5.00	2.20	.60
☐ 106 Billy Cannon	7.00	3.10	.85
☐ 107 Clem Daniels	7.00	3.10	.85
☐ 108 Ben Davidson	16.00	7.25	2.00
☐ 109 Cotton Davidson	7.00	3.10	.85
☐ 110 Claude Gibson	5.00	2.20	.60
☐ 111 Wayne Hawkins	5.00	2.20	.60
☐ 112 Ken Herock	5.00	2.20	.60
☐ 113 Bob Mischak	5.00	2.20	.60
☐ 114 Gus Otto	5.00	2.20	.60
☐ 115 Jim Otto	18.00	8.00	2.20
☐ 116 Art Powell	7.00	3.10	.85
☐ 117 Harry Schuh	5.00	2.20	.60
☐ 118 Chuck Allen	5.00	2.20	.60
☐ 119 Lance Alworth	40.00	18.00	5.00
☐ 120 Frank Buncom	5.00	2.20	.60
☐ 121 Steve DeLong	5.00	2.20	.60
☐ 122 John Farris	5.00	2.20	.60
☐ 123 Kenny Graham	5.00	2.20	.60
☐ 124 Sam Gruneisen	5.00	2.20	.60
☐ 125 John Hadl	8.00	3.60	1.00
☐ 126 Walt Sweeney	5.00	2.20	.60
☐ 127 Keith Lincoln	7.00	3.10	.85
☐ 128 Ron Mix	8.00	3.60	1.00
☐ 129 Don Norton	5.00	2.20	.60
☐ 130 Pat Shea	5.00	2.20	.60
☐ 131 Ernie Wright	7.00	3.10	.85
☐ 132 Checklist Card	95.00	24.00	9.50

1966 Topps Funny Rings

This 24-card set was inserted one per pack in football packs. They measure approximately 1 1/4" by 3". The fronts feature a "ring" that can be punched out of the card and folded to make the ring. The backs are blank. The ring titles are listed below.

	NRMT	VG-E	GOOD
COMPLETE SET (24)	500.00	220.00	60.00
COMMON CARD (1-24)	25.00	11.00	3.10
☐ 1 Funny Ring Kiss Me	25.00	11.00	3.10
☐ 2 Funny Ring Bloodshot Eye	25.00	11.00	3.10
☐ 3 Funny Ring Big Mouth	25.00	11.00	3.10
☐ 4 Funny Ring Tooth-ache	25.00	11.00	3.10
☐ 5 Funny Ring Fish eats Fish	25.00	11.00	3.10
☐ 6 Funny Ring Mrs. Skull	25.00	11.00	3.10
☐ 7 Funny Ring Hot Dog	25.00	11.00	3.10
☐ 8 Funny Ring Head with Nail	25.00	11.00	3.10
☐ 9 Funny Ring Ah	25.00	11.00	3.10
☐ 10 Funny Ring Apple With Worm	25.00	11.00	3.10
☐ 11 Funny Ring Snake	25.00	11.00	3.10
☐ 12 Funny Ring Yicch	25.00	11.00	3.10
☐ 13 Funny Ring If You Can Read This	25.00	11.00	3.10
☐ 14 Funny Ring Nuts to You	25.00	11.00	3.10
☐ 15 Funny Ring Get Lost	25.00	11.00	3.10
☐ 16 Funny Ring You Fink	25.00	11.00	3.10
☐ 17 Funny Ring Hole in Shoe	25.00	11.00	3.10
☐ 18 Funny Ring Head With One Eye	25.00	11.00	3.10
☐ 19 Funny Ring Mr. Ugly	25.00	11.00	3.10
☐ 20 Funny Ring Mr. Fang	25.00	11.00	3.10
☐ 21 Funny Ring Mr. Fright	25.00	11.00	3.10
☐ 22 Funny Ring Mr. Boo	25.00	11.00	3.10
☐ 23 Funny Ring Mr. Glug	25.00	11.00	3.10
☐ 24 Funny Ring Mr. Blech	25.00	11.00	3.10

1967 Topps

The 1967 Topps set of 132 standard-size cards contains AFL players only, with players grouped together and numbered by teams. Card fronts contain an oval player photo surrounded by a team color. The player's name and position are at the bottom. The card backs are printed in gold and black on white card stock and contain statistics and highlights. A question (with upside-down answer) is given on the bottom of the reverse. The only notable Rookie Card in this set is Wahoo McDaniel, who later gained greater fame as a professional wrestler.

	NRMT	VG-E	GOOD
COMPLETE SET (132)	700.00	325.00	90.00
COMMON CARD (1-132)	3.00	1.35	.35
WRAPPER (5-CENT)	20.00	9.00	2.50

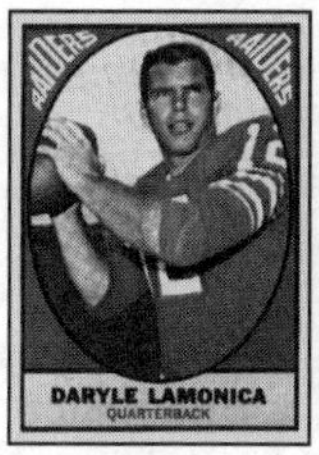

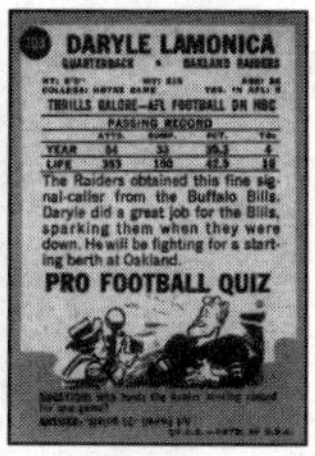

☐ 1 John Huarte	16.00	4.00	1.60
☐ 2 Babe Parilli	4.00	1.80	.50
☐ 3 Gino Cappelletti	4.00	1.80	.50
☐ 4 Larry Garron	3.00	1.35	.35
☐ 5 Tommy Addison	3.00	1.35	.35
☐ 6 Jon Morris	3.00	1.35	.35
☐ 7 Houston Antwine	3.00	1.35	.35
☐ 8 Don Oakes	3.00	1.35	.35
☐ 9 Larry Eisenhauer	3.00	1.35	.35
☐ 10 Jim Hunt	3.00	1.35	.35
☐ 11 Jim Whalen	3.00	1.35	.35
☐ 12 Art Graham	3.00	1.35	.35
☐ 13 Nick Buoniconti	6.00	2.70	.75
☐ 14 Bob Dee	3.00	1.35	.35
☐ 15 Keith Lincoln	4.00	1.80	.50
☐ 16 Tom Flores	5.00	2.20	.60
☐ 17 Art Powell	4.00	1.80	.50
☐ 18 Stew Barber	3.00	1.35	.35
☐ 19 Wray Carlton	3.00	1.35	.35
☐ 20 Elbert Dubenion	4.00	1.80	.50
☐ 21 Jim Dunaway	3.00	1.35	.35
☐ 22 Dick Hudson	3.00	1.35	.35
☐ 23 Harry Jacobs	3.00	1.35	.35
☐ 24 Jack Kemp	100.00	45.00	12.50
☐ 25 Ron McDole	3.00	1.35	.35
☐ 26 George Saimes	3.00	1.35	.35
☐ 27 Tom Sestak	3.00	1.35	.35
☐ 28 Billy Shaw	3.00	1.35	.35
☐ 29 Mike Stratton	3.00	1.35	.35
☐ 30 Nemiah Wilson	3.00	1.35	.35
☐ 31 John McCormick	3.00	1.35	.35
☐ 32 Rex Mirich	3.00	1.35	.35
☐ 33 Dave Costa	3.00	1.35	.35
☐ 34 Goose Gonsoulin	4.00	1.80	.50
☐ 35 Abner Haynes	4.00	1.80	.50
☐ 36 Wendell Hayes	4.00	1.80	.50
☐ 37 Archie Matsos	3.00	1.35	.35
☐ 38 John Bramlett	3.00	1.35	.35
☐ 39 Jerry Sturm	3.00	1.35	.35
☐ 40 Max Leetzow	3.00	1.35	.35
☐ 41 Bob Scarpitto	3.00	1.35	.35
☐ 42 Lionel Taylor	4.00	1.80	.50
☐ 43 Al Denson	3.00	1.35	.35
☐ 44 Miller Farr	3.00	1.35	.35
☐ 45 Don Trull	3.00	1.35	.35
☐ 46 Jacky Lee	4.00	1.80	.50
☐ 47 Bobby Jancik	3.00	1.35	.35
☐ 48 Ode Burrell	3.00	1.35	.35
☐ 49 Larry Elkins	3.00	1.35	.35
☐ 50 W.K. Hicks	3.00	1.35	.35
☐ 51 Sid Blanks	3.00	1.35	.35
☐ 52 Jim Norton	3.00	1.35	.35
☐ 53 Bobby Maples	3.00	1.35	.35
☐ 54 Bob Talamini	3.00	1.35	.35
☐ 55 Walt Suggs	3.00	1.35	.35
☐ 56 Gary Cutsinger	3.00	1.35	.35
☐ 57 Danny Brabham	3.00	1.35	.35
☐ 58 Ernie Ladd	6.00	2.70	.75
☐ 59 Checklist Card	45.00	20.00	5.50
☐ 60 Pete Beathard	3.00	1.35	.35
☐ 61 Len Dawson	30.00	13.50	3.70
☐ 62 Bobby Hunt	3.00	1.35	.35
☐ 63 Bert Coan	3.00	1.35	.35
☐ 64 Curtis McClinton	4.00	1.80	.50
☐ 65 Johnny Robinson	4.00	1.80	.50
☐ 66 E.J. Holub	3.00	1.35	.35
☐ 67 Jerry Mays	3.00	1.35	.35
☐ 68 Jim Tyrer	4.00	1.80	.50
☐ 69 Bobby Bell	6.00	2.70	.75
☐ 70 Fred Arbanas	3.00	1.35	.35
☐ 71 Buck Buchanan	6.00	2.70	.75
☐ 72 Chris Burford	3.00	1.35	.35
☐ 73 Otis Taylor	6.00	2.70	.75
☐ 74 Cookie Gilchrist	8.00	3.60	1.00
☐ 75 Earl Faison	3.00	1.35	.35
☐ 76 George Wilson Jr.	4.00	1.80	.50
☐ 77 Rick Norton	3.00	1.35	.35
☐ 78 Frank Jackson	4.00	1.80	.50
☐ 79 Joe Auer	3.00	1.35	.35
☐ 80 Willie West	3.00	1.35	.35
☐ 81 Jim Warren	3.00	1.35	.35
☐ 82 Wahoo McDaniel	40.00	18.00	5.00
☐ 83 Ernie Park	3.00	1.35	.35
☐ 84 Billy Neighbors	3.00	1.35	.35
☐ 85 Norm Evans	4.00	1.80	.50
☐ 86 Tom Nomina	3.00	1.35	.35
☐ 87 Rich Zecher	3.00	1.35	.35
☐ 88 Dave Kocourek	3.00	1.35	.35
☐ 89 Bill Baird	3.00	1.35	.35
☐ 90 Ralph Baker	3.00	1.35	.35
☐ 91 Verlon Biggs	3.00	1.35	.35
☐ 92 Sam DeLuca	3.00	1.35	.35
☐ 93 Larry Grantham	4.00	1.80	.50
☐ 94 Jim Harris	3.00	1.35	.35
☐ 95 Winston Hill	3.00	1.35	.35
☐ 96 Bill Mathis	3.00	1.35	.35
☐ 97 Don Maynard	20.00	9.00	2.50
☐ 98 Joe Namath	175.00	80.00	22.00
☐ 99 Gerry Philbin	4.00	1.80	.50
☐ 100 Paul Rochester	3.00	1.35	.35
☐ 101 George Sauer Jr.	4.00	1.80	.50
☐ 102 Matt Snell	6.00	2.70	.75
☐ 103 Daryle Lamonica	8.00	3.60	1.00
☐ 104 Glenn Bass	3.00	1.35	.35
☐ 105 Jim Otto	6.00	2.70	.75
☐ 106 Fred Biletnikoff	30.00	13.50	3.70
☐ 107 Cotton Davidson	4.00	1.80	.50
☐ 108 Larry Todd	3.00	1.35	.35
☐ 109 Billy Cannon	4.00	1.80	.50
☐ 110 Clem Daniels	4.00	1.80	.50
☐ 111 Dave Grayson	3.00	1.35	.35
☐ 112 Kent McCloughan	3.00	1.35	.35
☐ 113 Bob Svihus	3.00	1.35	.35
☐ 114 Ike Lassiter	3.00	1.35	.35
☐ 115 Harry Schuh	3.00	1.35	.35
☐ 116 Ben Davidson	8.00	3.60	1.00
☐ 117 Tom Day	3.00	1.35	.35
☐ 118 Scott Appleton	3.00	1.35	.35
☐ 119 Steve Tensi	3.00	1.35	.35
☐ 120 John Hadl	6.00	2.70	.75
☐ 121 Paul Lowe	4.00	1.80	.50
☐ 122 Jim Allison	3.00	1.35	.35
☐ 123 Lance Alworth	30.00	13.50	3.70
☐ 124 Jacque MacKinnon	3.00	1.35	.35
☐ 125 Ron Mix	6.00	2.70	.75
☐ 126 Bob Petrich	3.00	1.35	.35
☐ 127 Howard Kindig	3.00	1.35	.35
☐ 128 Steve DeLong	3.00	1.35	.35
☐ 129 Chuck Allen	3.00	1.35	.35
☐ 130 Frank Buncom	3.00	1.35	.35
☐ 131 Speedy Duncan	4.00	1.80	.50
☐ 132 Checklist Card	70.00	17.50	7.00

1967 Topps Comic Pennants

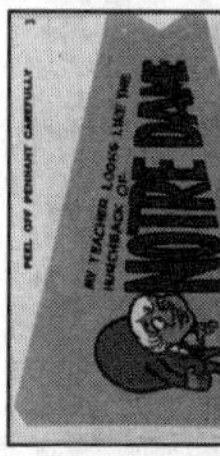

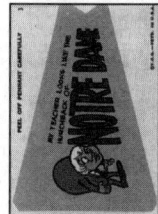

This set was issued as an insert with the 1967 Topps regular issue football cards as well as being issued separately. The stickers are standard size, and the backs are blank. The set can also be found in adhesive form with the pennant merely printed on card stock. They are numbered in the upper right corner, although reportedly they can also occasionally be found without numbers. Many of the cards feature sayings or depictions that are in poor taste, i.e., sick humor. Perhaps they were discontinued or recalled before the end of the season, which would explain their relative scarcity.

	NRMT	VG-E	GOOD
COMPLETE SET (31)	600.00	275.00	75.00
COMMON CARD (1-31)	20.00	9.00	2.50
☐ 1 Navel Academy	20.00	9.00	2.50
☐ 2 City College of Useless Knowledge	20.00	9.00	2.50
☐ 3 Notre Dame (Hunchback of)	40.00	18.00	5.00
☐ 4 Psychedelic State	20.00	9.00	2.50
☐ 5 Minneapolis Mini-skirts	20.00	9.00	2.50
☐ 6 School of Art Go, Van Gogh	20.00	9.00	2.50
☐ 7 Washington Is Dead	25.00	11.00	3.10
☐ 8 School of Hard Knocks	20.00	9.00	2.50
☐ 9 Alaska (If I See Her ...)	20.00	9.00	2.50
☐ 10 Confused State	20.00	9.00	2.50
☐ 11 Yale Locks Are Tough to Pick	20.00	9.00	2.50
☐ 12 University of Transylvania	20.00	9.00	2.50
☐ 13 Down With Teachers	20.00	9.00	2.50
☐ 14 Cornell Caught Me Cheating	20.00	9.00	2.50
☐ 15 Houston Oilers (You're a Fink)	25.00	11.00	3.10
☐ 16 Harvard (Flunked Out)	20.00	9.00	2.50
☐ 17 Diskotech	20.00	9.00	2.50
☐ 18 Dropout U.	20.00	9.00	2.50
☐ 19 Air Force (Gas Masks)	20.00	9.00	2.50
☐ 20 Nutstu U.	20.00	9.00	2.50
☐ 21 Michigan State Pen	20.00	9.00	2.50
☐ 22 Denver Broncos (Girls Look Like)	25.00	11.00	3.10
☐ 23 Buffalo Bills	25.00	11.00	3.10

(Without Paying My)			
☐ 24 Army of Dropouts	20.00	9.00	2.50
☐ 25 Miami Dolphins (Bitten by Two)	30.00	13.50	3.70
☐ 26 Kansas City (Has Too Few Workers And Too Many) Chiefs	20.00	9.00	2.50
☐ 27 Boston Patriots (Banned In)	20.00	9.00	2.50
☐ 28 (Fat People In) Oakland (Are Usually Icebox) Raiders	30.00	13.50	3.70
☐ 29 (I'd Go) West (If You'd Just) Point (In The Right Direction)	20.00	9.00	2.50
☐ 30 New York Jets (Skies Are Crowded With)	25.00	11.00	3.10
☐ 31 San Diego Chargers (Police Will Press)	20.00	9.00	2.50

1968 Topps

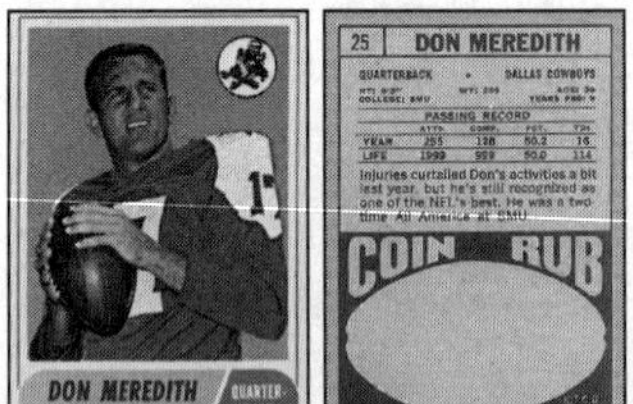

The 1968 set marks the beginning of a 21-year run of Topps being the only major producer of football cards. The two-series set of 219 standard-size cards is Topps' first set in seven years (since 1961) to contain players from both leagues. The set marks the AFL debut of the Cincinnati Bengals. Card fronts feature the player photo over a solid background. A team logo is in an upper corner. The player's name, team name and position are in a colored cicular box at the bottom. Cards for players from the previous year's Super Bowl teams, the Green Bay Packers and the Oakland Raiders, are the only cards to contain horizontally designed fronts. In addition, these cards also have color boders at top and bottom and the player photo is superimposed over yellow tinted game action artwork. The backs have statistics and highlights as well as a rub-off cartoon at the bottom. The cards in the second series have blue printing on the back whereas the cards in the first series had green printing on the back. Card backs of some of the cards in the second series can be used to form a ten-card puzzle of Bart Starr (141, 148, 153, 155, 168, 172, 186, 197, 201, and 213) or Len Dawson (145, 146, 151, 152, 163, 166, 170, 195, 199, and 200). The set features the Rookie Cards of quarterbacks Bob Griese, Jim Hart, and Craig Morton, and (ex-Syracuse) running backs Floyd Little and Jim Nance. The second series (132-219) is slightly more difficult to obtain than the first series.

	NRMT-MT	EXC	G-VG
COMPLETE SET (219)	550.00	250.00	70.00
COMMON CARD (1-131)	1.50	.70	.19
COMMON CARD (132-219)	2.00	.90	.25
WRAPPER (5-CENT, SERIES I)	15.00	6.75	1.85
WRAPPER (5-CENT, SERIES II)	25.00	11.00	3.10

☐ 1 Bart Starr	30.00	7.50	3.00
☐ 2 Dick Bass	2.00	.90	.25
☐ 3 Grady Alderman	1.50	.70	.19
☐ 4 Obert Logan	1.50	.70	.19
☐ 5 Ernie Koy	2.00	.90	.25
☐ 6 Don Hultz	1.50	.70	.19
☐ 7 Earl Gros	2.00	.90	.25
☐ 8 Jim Bakken	1.50	.70	.19
☐ 9 George Mira	2.00	.90	.25
☐ 10 Carl Kammerer	1.50	.70	.19
☐ 11 Willie Frazier	1.50	.70	.19
☐ 12 Kent McCloughan UER (McCloughlan on card back)	1.50	.70	.19
☐ 13 George Sauer Jr.	2.00	.90	.25
☐ 14 Jack Clancy	1.50	.70	.19
☐ 15 Jim Tyrer	2.00	.90	.25
☐ 16 Bobby Maples	1.50	.70	.19
☐ 17 Bo Hickey	1.50	.70	.19
☐ 18 Frank Buncom	1.50	.70	.19
☐ 19 Keith Lincoln	2.00	.90	.25
☐ 20 Jim Whalen	1.50	.70	.19
☐ 21 Junior Coffey	1.50	.70	.19
☐ 22 Billy Ray Smith	1.50	.70	.19
☐ 23 Johnny Morris	1.50	.70	.19
☐ 24 Ernie Green	2.00	.90	.25
☐ 25 Don Meredith	20.00	9.00	2.50
☐ 26 Wayne Walker	1.50	.70	.19
☐ 27 Carroll Dale	2.50	1.10	.30
☐ 28 Bernie Casey	2.00	.90	.25
☐ 29 Dave Osborn	2.00	.90	.25
☐ 30 Ray Poage	1.50	.70	.19
☐ 31 Homer Jones	1.50	.70	.19
☐ 32 Sam Baker	1.50	.70	.19
☐ 33 Bill Saul	1.50	.70	.19
☐ 34 Ken Willard	2.00	.90	.25
☐ 35 Bobby Mitchell	4.00	1.80	.50
☐ 36 Gary Garrison	2.00	.90	.25
☐ 37 Billy Cannon	2.00	.90	.25
☐ 38 Ralph Baker	1.50	.70	.19
☐ 39 Howard Twilley	4.00	1.80	.50
☐ 40 Wendell Hayes	2.00	.90	.25
☐ 41 Jim Norton	1.50	.70	.19
☐ 42 Tom Beer	1.50	.70	.19
☐ 43 Chris Burford	1.50	.70	.19
☐ 44 Stew Barber	1.50	.70	.19
☐ 45 Leroy Mitchell UER (Lifetime Int. should be 3, not 2)	1.50	.70	.19
☐ 46 Dan Grimm	1.50	.70	.19
☐ 47 Jerry Logan	1.50	.70	.19
☐ 48 Andy Livingston	1.50	.70	.19
☐ 49 Paul Warfield	10.00	4.50	1.25
☐ 50 Don Perkins	2.00	.90	.25
☐ 51 Ron Kramer	1.50	.70	.19
☐ 52 Bob Jeter	2.00	.90	.25
☐ 53 Les Josephson	1.50	.70	.19
☐ 54 Bobby Walden	1.50	.70	.19
☐ 55 Checklist Card	15.00	3.70	1.50
☐ 56 Walter Roberts	1.50	.70	.19
☐ 57 Henry Carr	1.50	.70	.19
☐ 58 Gary Ballman	1.50	.70	.19
☐ 59 J.R. Wilburn	1.50	.70	.19
☐ 60 Jim Hart	10.00	4.50	1.25
☐ 61 Jim Johnson	3.00	1.35	.35
☐ 62 Chris Hanburger	2.00	.90	.25
☐ 63 John Hadl	3.00	1.35	.35
☐ 64 Hewritt Dixon	2.00	.90	.25
☐ 65 Joe Namath	85.00	38.00	10.50
☐ 66 Jim Warren	1.50	.70	.19
☐ 67 Curtis McClinton	2.00	.90	.25
☐ 68 Bob Talamini	1.50	.70	.19
☐ 69 Steve Tensi	1.50	.70	.19
☐ 70 Dick Van Raaphorst UER (Van Raap Horst on card back)	1.50	.70	.19
☐ 71 Art Powell	2.00	.90	.25
☐ 72 Jim Nance	4.00	1.80	.50
☐ 73 Bob Riggle	1.50	.70	.19
☐ 74 John Mackey	4.00	1.80	.50
☐ 75 Gale Sayers	40.00	18.00	5.00
☐ 76 Gene Hickerson	2.00	.90	.25
☐ 77 Dan Reeves	10.00	4.50	1.25
☐ 78 Tom Nowatzke	1.50	.70	.19
☐ 79 Elijah Pitts	3.00	1.35	.35
☐ 80 Lamar Lundy	2.00	.90	.25
☐ 81 Paul Flatley	1.50	.70	.19
☐ 82 Dave Whitsell	1.50	.70	.19
☐ 83 Spider Lockhart	2.00	.90	.25
☐ 84 Dave Lloyd	1.50	.70	.19
☐ 85 Roy Jefferson	2.00	.90	.25
☐ 86 Jackie Smith	6.00	2.70	.75
☐ 87 John David Crow	2.00	.90	.25
☐ 88 Sonny Jurgensen	6.00	2.70	.75
☐ 89 Ron Mix	3.00	1.35	.35
☐ 90 Clem Daniels	2.00	.90	.25
☐ 91 Cornell Gordon	1.50	.70	.19
☐ 92 Tom Goode	1.50	.70	.19
☐ 93 Bobby Bell	3.00	1.35	.35
☐ 94 Walt Suggs	1.50	.70	.19
☐ 95 Eric Crabtree	1.50	.70	.19
☐ 96 Sherrill Headrick	1.50	.70	.19
☐ 97 Wray Carlton	1.50	.70	.19
☐ 98 Gino Cappelletti	2.00	.90	.25
☐ 99 Tommy McDonald	2.00	.90	.25
☐ 100 John Unitas	25.00	11.00	3.10
☐ 101 Richie Petitbon	2.00	.90	.25
☐ 102 Erich Barnes	1.50	.70	.19
☐ 103 Bob Hayes	6.00	2.70	.75
☐ 104 Milt Plum	2.00	.90	.25
☐ 105 Boyd Dowler	2.00	.90	.25
☐ 106 Ed Meador	1.50	.70	.19
☐ 107 Fred Cox	2.00	.90	.25
☐ 108 Steve Stonebreaker	1.50	.70	.19
☐ 109 Aaron Thomas	1.50	.70	.19
☐ 110 Norm Snead	2.00	.90	.25
☐ 111 Paul Martha	1.50	.70	.19
☐ 112 Jerry Stovall	1.50	.70	.19
☐ 113 Kay McFarland	1.50	.70	.19
☐ 114 Pat Richter	1.50	.70	.19
☐ 115 Rick Redman	1.50	.70	.19
☐ 116 Tom Keating	1.50	.70	.19
☐ 117 Matt Snell	2.00	.90	.25
☐ 118 Dick Westmoreland	1.50	.70	.19
☐ 119 Jerry Mays	1.50	.70	.19
☐ 120 Sid Blanks	1.50	.70	.19
☐ 121 Al Denson	1.50	.70	.19
☐ 122 Bobby Hunt	1.50	.70	.19
☐ 123 Mike Mercer	1.50	.70	.19
☐ 124 Nick Buoniconti	3.00	1.35	.35
☐ 125 Ron Vanderkelen	1.50	.70	.19
☐ 126 Ordell Braase	1.50	.70	.19
☐ 127 Dick Butkus	45.00	20.00	5.50
☐ 128 Gary Collins	2.00	.90	.25
☐ 129 Mel Renfro	5.00	2.20	.60
☐ 130 Alex Karras	5.00	2.20	.60
☐ 131 Herb Adderley	4.00	1.80	.50
☐ 132 Roman Gabriel	3.50	1.55	.45
☐ 133 Bill Brown	2.50	1.10	.30
☐ 134 Kent Kramer	2.00	.90	.25
☐ 135 Tucker Frederickson	2.50	1.10	.30
☐ 136 Nate Ramsey	2.00	.90	.25
☐ 137 Marv Woodson	2.00	.90	.25
☐ 138 Ken Gray	2.00	.90	.25
☐ 139 John Brodie	5.00	2.20	.60
☐ 140 Jerry Smith	2.00	.90	.25
☐ 141 Brad Hubbert	2.00	.90	.25
☐ 142 George Blanda	18.00	8.00	2.20
☐ 143 Pete Lammons	2.00	.90	.25
☐ 144 Doug Moreau	2.00	.90	.25
☐ 145 E.J. Holub	2.00	.90	.25
☐ 146 Ode Burrell	2.00	.90	.25
☐ 147 Bob Scarpitto	2.00	.90	.25
☐ 148 Andre White	2.00	.90	.25
☐ 149 Jack Kemp	60.00	27.00	7.50
☐ 150 Art Graham	2.00	.90	.25
☐ 151 Tommy Nobis	6.00	2.70	.75
☐ 152 Willie Richardson	2.50	1.10	.30
☐ 153 Jack Concannon	2.50	1.10	.30
☐ 154 Bill Glass	2.00	.90	.25
☐ 155 Craig Morton	10.00	4.50	1.25
☐ 156 Pat Studstill	2.00	.90	.25
☐ 157 Ray Nitschke	7.00	3.10	.85
☐ 158 Roger Brown	2.00	.90	.25
☐ 159 Joe Kapp	5.00	2.20	.60
☐ 160 Jim Taylor (Shown in uniform of Green Bay Packers)	12.00	5.50	1.50
☐ 161 Fran Tarkenton	16.00	7.25	2.00
☐ 162 Mike Ditka	25.00	11.00	3.10
☐ 163 Andy Russell	6.00	2.70	.75
☐ 164 Larry Wilson	3.00	1.35	.35
☐ 165 Tommy Davis	2.00	.90	.25
☐ 166 Paul Krause	3.50	1.55	.45
☐ 167 Speedy Duncan	2.00	.90	.25
☐ 168 Fred Biletnikoff	12.00	5.50	1.50
☐ 169 Don Maynard	10.00	4.50	1.25
☐ 170 Frank Emanuel	2.00	.90	.25
☐ 171 Len Dawson	14.00	6.25	1.75
☐ 172 Miller Farr	2.00	.90	.25
☐ 173 Floyd Little	20.00	9.00	2.50
☐ 174 Lonnie Wright	2.00	.90	.25
☐ 175 Paul Costa	2.00	.90	.25
☐ 176 Don Trull	2.00	.90	.25
☐ 177 Jerry Simmons	2.00	.90	.25
☐ 178 Tom Matte	2.50	1.10	.30
☐ 179 Bennie McRae	2.00	.90	.25
☐ 180 Jim Kanicki	2.00	.90	.25
☐ 181 Bob Lilly	10.00	4.50	1.25
☐ 182 Tom Watkins	2.00	.90	.25
☐ 183 Jim Grabowski	4.00	1.80	.50
☐ 184 Jack Snow	4.00	1.80	.50
☐ 185 Gary Cuozzo	2.50	1.10	.30
☐ 186 Bill Kilmer	3.00	1.35	.35
☐ 187 Jim Katcavage	2.50	1.10	.30
☐ 188 Floyd Peters	2.00	.90	.25
☐ 189 Bill Nelsen	2.50	1.10	.30
☐ 190 Bobby Joe Conrad	2.50	1.10	.30
☐ 191 Kermit Alexander	2.00	.90	.25
☐ 192 Charley Taylor UER (Called Charley and Charlie on back)	6.00	2.70	.75
☐ 193 Lance Alworth	14.00	6.25	1.75
☐ 194 Daryle Lamonica	3.50	1.55	.45
☐ 195 Al Atkinson	2.00	.90	.25
☐ 196 Bob Griese	80.00	36.00	10.00
☐ 197 Buck Buchanan	3.50	1.55	.45
☐ 198 Pete Beathard	2.00	.90	.25
☐ 199 Nemiah Wilson	2.00	.90	.25
☐ 200 Ernie Wright	2.00	.90	.25
☐ 201 George Saimes	2.00	.90	.25
☐ 202 John Charles	2.00	.90	.25
☐ 203 Randy Johnson	2.00	.90	.25
☐ 204 Tony Lorick	2.00	.90	.25
☐ 205 Dick Evey	2.00	.90	.25
☐ 206 Leroy Kelly	10.00	4.50	1.25
☐ 207 Lee Roy Jordan	6.00	2.70	.75
☐ 208 Jim Gibbons	2.00	.90	.25
☐ 209 Donny Anderson	5.00	2.20	.60
☐ 210 Maxie Baughan	2.00	.90	.25
☐ 211 Joe Morrison	2.50	1.10	.30
☐ 212 Jim Snowden	2.00	.90	.25
☐ 213 Lenny Lyles	2.00	.90	.25
☐ 214 Bobby Joe Green	2.00	.90	.25
☐ 215 Frank Ryan	2.50	1.10	.30
☐ 216 Cornell Green	2.50	1.10	.30
☐ 217 Karl Sweetan	2.00	.90	.25
☐ 218 Dave Williams	2.00	.90	.25
☐ 219A Checklist 132-218 (green print on back)	18.00	4.50	1.80
☐ 219B Checklist 132-218 (blue print on back)	20.00	5.00	2.00

1968 Topps Posters

The 1968 Topps Football Posters set contains 16 NFL and AFL players on paper stock; the cards (posters) measure approximately 5" by 7". The posters, folded twice for insertion into first series wax packs, are numbered on the obverse at the lower left hand corner. The backs of these posters are blank. Fold marks are normal and do not detract from the poster's condition. These posters are the same style as the 1967 Topps baseball

	NRMT-MT	EXC	G-VG
COMPLETE SET (16)	75.00	34.00	9.50
COMMON CARD (1-16)	3.00	1.35	.35

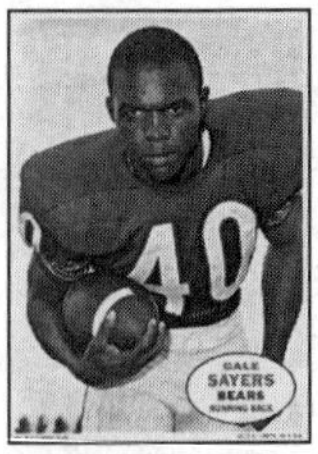

☐ 1 Johnny Unitas	16.00	7.25	2.00
☐ 2 Leroy Kelly	5.00	2.20	.60
☐ 3 Bob Hayes	5.00	2.20	.60
☐ 4 Bart Starr	12.00	5.50	1.50
☐ 5 Charley Taylor	5.00	2.20	.60
☐ 6 Fran Tarkenton	10.00	4.50	1.25
☐ 7 Jim Bakken	3.00	1.35	.35
☐ 8 Gale Sayers	12.00	5.50	1.50
☐ 9 Gary Cuozzo	3.00	1.35	.35
☐ 10 Les Josephson	3.00	1.35	.35
☐ 11 Jim Nance	3.00	1.35	.35
☐ 12 Brad Hubbert	3.00	1.35	.35
☐ 13 Keith Lincoln	3.00	1.35	.35
☐ 14 Don Maynard	6.00	2.70	.75
☐ 15 Len Dawson	7.00	3.10	.85
☐ 16 Jack Clancy	3.00	1.35	.35

1968 Topps Stand-Ups

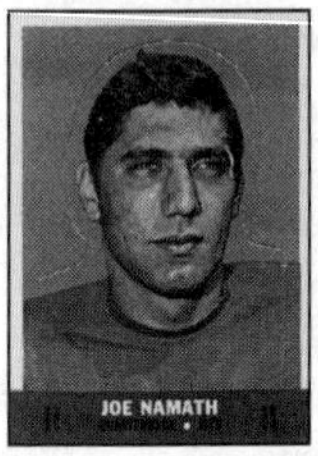

The 22-card 1968 Topps Football Stand-Ups standard-size set is unnumbered but has been numbered alphabetically in the checklist below for your convenience. Values listed below are for complete cards; the value is greatly reduced if the backs are detached, and such a card can be considered fair to good at best. The cards were issued as an insert in second series packs of 1968 Topps football cards, one per pack.

	NRMT-MT	EXC	G-VG
COMPLETE SET (22)	250.00	110.00	31.00
COMMON CARD (1-22)	6.00	2.70	.75

☐ 1 Sid Blanks	6.00	2.70	.75
☐ 2 John Brodie	12.00	5.50	1.50
☐ 3 Jack Concannon	6.00	2.70	.75
☐ 4 Roman Gabriel	8.00	3.60	1.00
☐ 5 Art Graham	6.00	2.70	.75
☐ 6 Jim Grabowski	6.00	2.70	.75
☐ 7 John Hadl	8.00	3.60	1.00
☐ 8 Jim Hart	8.00	3.60	1.00
☐ 9 Homer Jones	6.00	2.70	.75
☐ 10 Sonny Jurgensen	12.00	5.50	1.50
☐ 11 Alex Karras	10.00	4.50	1.25
☐ 12 Billy Kilmer	8.00	3.60	1.00
☐ 13 Daryle Lamonica	8.00	3.60	1.00
☐ 14 Floyd Little	8.00	3.60	1.00
☐ 15 Curtis McClinton	6.00	2.70	.75
☐ 16 Don Meredith	40.00	18.00	5.00
☐ 17 Joe Namath	90.00	40.00	11.00
☐ 18 Bill Nelsen	7.00	3.10	.85
☐ 19 Dave Osborn	6.00	2.70	.75
☐ 20 Willie Richardson	6.00	2.70	.75
☐ 21 Frank Ryan	7.00	3.10	.85
☐ 22 Norm Snead	7.00	3.10	.85

1968 Topps Test Teams

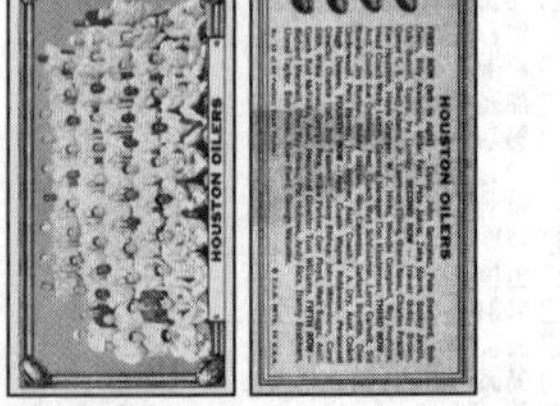

The 25-card set of team cards was a limited production by Topps. The obverse provides a black and white picture of the team, whereas the reverse gives the names of the players in the picture in red print on vanilla card stock. Due to their positioning within the pack, these test team cards are typically found with gum stains on the card backs. The cards measure approximately 2 1/2" by 4 11/16" and are numbered on the back.

	NRMT-MT	EXC	G-VG
COMPLETE SET (25)	2800.00	1250.00	350.00
COMMON TEAM (1-25)	100.00	45.00	12.50

☐ 1 Green Bay Packers	135.00	60.00	17.00
☐ 2 New Orleans Saints	100.00	45.00	12.50
☐ 3 New York Jets	150.00	70.00	19.00
☐ 4 Miami Dolphins	175.00	80.00	22.00
☐ 5 Pittsburgh Steelers	125.00	55.00	15.50
☐ 6 Detroit Lions	100.00	45.00	12.50
☐ 7 Los Angeles Rams	100.00	45.00	12.50
☐ 8 Atlanta Falcons	100.00	45.00	12.50
☐ 9 New York Giants	125.00	55.00	15.50
☐ 10 Denver Broncos	300.00	135.00	38.00
☐ 11 Dallas Cowboys	250.00	110.00	31.00
☐ 12 Buffalo Bills	125.00	55.00	15.50
☐ 13 Cleveland Browns	125.00	55.00	15.50
☐ 14 San Francisco 49ers	125.00	55.00	15.50
☐ 15 Baltimore Colts	100.00	45.00	12.50
☐ 16 San Diego Chargers	100.00	45.00	12.50
☐ 17 Oakland Raiders	200.00	90.00	25.00
☐ 18 Houston Oilers	100.00	45.00	12.50
☐ 19 Minnesota Vikings	125.00	55.00	15.50
☐ 20 Washington Redskins	175.00	80.00	22.00
☐ 21 St. Louis Cardinals	100.00	45.00	12.50
☐ 22 Kansas City Chiefs	100.00	45.00	12.50
☐ 23 Boston Patriots	100.00	45.00	12.50
☐ 24 Chicago Bears	135.00	60.00	17.00
☐ 25 Philadelphia Eagles	100.00	45.00	12.50

1968 Topps Test Team Patches

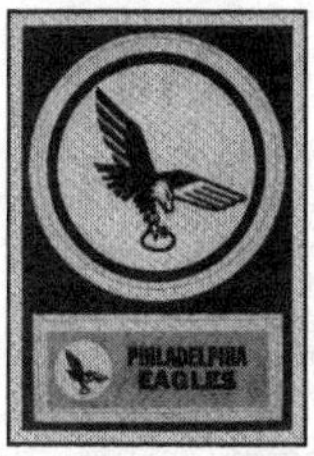

These team emblem cloth patches/stickers were distributed as an insert with the 1968 Topps Test Teams: one sticker per pack along with one test team. In fact according to the wrapper, these stickers were the featured item; however the hobby has deemed the team cards to be more collectible and hence more valuable than these rather bland, but scarce, logo stickers. The complete set of 44 patches consisted of team emblems, the letters A through Z, and the numbers 0 through 9. The letters and number patches contained two letters or numbers on each patch. The number patches are printed in black on a blue background, the letter patches are white on a red background, and the team emblems were done in the team colors. The stickers measure 2 1/2" by 3 1/2". The backs are blank.

	NRMT-MT	EXC	G-VG
COMPLETE SET (44)	2500.00	1100.00	300.00
COMMON NUMBER/LETTER	10.00	4.50	1.25
COMMON TEAM	75.00	34.00	9.50
☐ 1 1 and 2	10.00	4.50	1.25
☐ 2 3 and 4	10.00	4.50	1.25
☐ 3 5 and 6	10.00	4.50	1.25
☐ 4 7 and 8	10.00	4.50	1.25
☐ 5 9 and 0	10.00	4.50	1.25
☐ 6 A and B	10.00	4.50	1.25
☐ 7 C and D	10.00	4.50	1.25
☐ 8 E and F	10.00	4.50	1.25
☐ 9 G and H	10.00	4.50	1.25
☐ 10 I and W	10.00	4.50	1.25
☐ 11 J and X	10.00	4.50	1.25
☐ 12 Atlanta Falcons	75.00	34.00	9.50
☐ 13 Baltimore Colts	75.00	34.00	9.50
☐ 14 Chicago Bears	90.00	40.00	11.00
☐ 15 Cleveland Browns	75.00	34.00	9.50
☐ 16 Dallas Cowboys	175.00	80.00	22.00
☐ 17 Detroit Lions	75.00	34.00	9.50
☐ 18 Green Bay Packers	100.00	45.00	12.50
☐ 19 Los Angeles Rams	75.00	34.00	9.50
☐ 20 Minnesota Vikings	100.00	45.00	12.50
☐ 21 New Orleans Saints	75.00	34.00	9.50
☐ 22 New York Giants	90.00	40.00	11.00
☐ 23 K and L	10.00	4.50	1.25
☐ 24 M and O	10.00	4.50	1.25
☐ 25 N and P	10.00	4.50	1.25
☐ 26 Q and R	10.00	4.50	1.25
☐ 27 S and T	10.00	4.50	1.25
☐ 28 U and V	10.00	4.50	1.25
☐ 29 Y and Z	10.00	4.50	1.25
☐ 30 Philadelphia Eagles	75.00	34.00	9.50
☐ 31 Pittsburgh Steelers	100.00	45.00	12.50
☐ 32 St. Louis Cardinals	75.00	34.00	9.50
☐ 33 San Francisco 49ers	90.00	40.00	11.00
☐ 34 Washington Redskins	100.00	45.00	12.50
☐ 35 Boston Patriots	75.00	34.00	9.50
☐ 36 Buffalo Bills	75.00	34.00	9.50
☐ 37 Denver Broncos	135.00	60.00	17.00
☐ 38 Houston Oilers	75.00	34.00	9.50
☐ 39 Kansas City Chiefs	75.00	34.00	9.50
☐ 40 Miami Dolphins	150.00	70.00	19.00
☐ 41 New York Jets	75.00	34.00	9.50
☐ 42 Oakland Raiders	150.00	70.00	19.00
☐ 43 San Diego Chargers	75.00	34.00	9.50
☐ 44 Cincinnati Bengals	75.00	34.00	9.50

1969 Topps

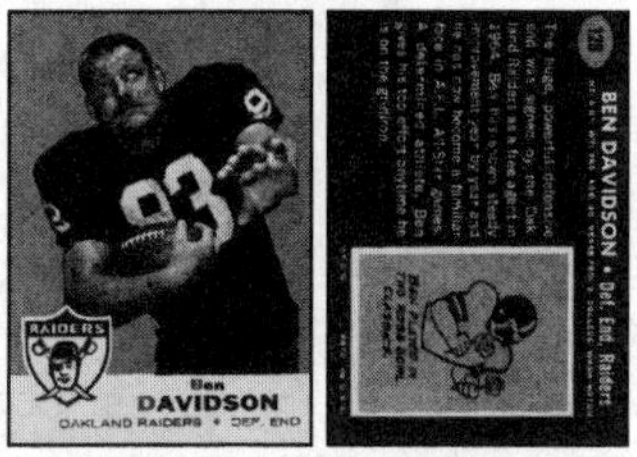

The 1969 Topps set of 263 standard-size cards was issued in two series. First series cards (1-132) are borderless whereas the second series (133-263) cards have white borders. The lack of borders makes the first series especially difficult to find in mint condition. The checklist card (132) was obviously printed with each series as it is found in both styles (with and without borders). The set was issued in 12-card 10-cent packs. Though the borders differ, the fronts have otherwise consistent designs. A player photo is superimposed over a solid color background with the team logo, player's name, team name and position at the bottom. The backs of the cards are predominantly black, but with a green and white accent. Card backs of some of the cards in the second series can be used to form a ten-card puzzle of Fran Tarkenton (137, 145, 168, 174, 177, 194, 211, 219, 224, and 256). This set is distinctive in that it contains the late Brian Piccolo's only regular issue card. Another notable Rookie Card in this set is Larry Csonka.

	NRMT-MT	EXC	G-VG
COMPLETE SET (263)	550.00	250.00	70.00
COMMON CARD (1-132)	1.50	.70	.19
COMMON CARD (133-263)	2.00	.90	.25
☐ 1 Leroy Kelly	16.00	4.00	1.60
☐ 2 Paul Flatley	1.50	.70	.19
☐ 3 Jim Cadile	1.50	.70	.19
☐ 4 Erich Barnes	1.50	.70	.19
☐ 5 Willie Richardson	2.00	.90	.25
☐ 6 Bob Hayes	5.00	2.20	.60
☐ 7 Bob Jeter	2.00	.90	.25
☐ 8 Jim Colclough	1.50	.70	.19
☐ 9 Sherrill Headrick	1.50	.70	.19
☐ 10 Jim Dunaway	1.50	.70	.19
☐ 11 Bill Munson	2.00	.90	.25
☐ 12 Jack Pardee	2.00	.90	.25
☐ 13 Jim Lindsey	1.50	.70	.19
☐ 14 Dave Whitsell	1.50	.70	.19
☐ 15 Tucker Frederickson	2.00	.90	.25
☐ 16 Alvin Haymond	2.00	.90	.25
☐ 17 Andy Russell	2.00	.90	.25
☐ 18 Tom Beer	1.50	.70	.19
☐ 19 Bobby Maples	1.50	.70	.19
☐ 20 Len Dawson	8.00	3.60	1.00
☐ 21 Willis Crenshaw	1.50	.70	.19
☐ 22 Tommy Davis	1.50	.70	.19
☐ 23 Rickie Harris	1.50	.70	.19
☐ 24 Jerry Simmons	1.50	.70	.19
☐ 25 John Unitas	25.00	11.00	3.10
☐ 26 Brian Piccolo UER (Misspelled Bryon on front and Bryan on back)	90.00	40.00	11.00
☐ 27 Bob Matheson	1.50	.70	.19
☐ 28 Howard Twilley	2.00	.90	.25
☐ 29 Jim Turner	2.00	.90	.25
☐ 30 Pete Banaszak	2.00	.90	.25
☐ 31 Lance Rentzel	2.00	.90	.25
☐ 32 Bill Triplett	1.50	.70	.19
☐ 33 Boyd Dowler	2.00	.90	.25
☐ 34 Merlin Olsen	4.00	1.80	.50
☐ 35 Joe Kapp	2.50	1.10	.30
☐ 36 Dan Abramowicz	4.00	1.80	.50
☐ 37 Spider Lockhart	2.00	.90	.25
☐ 38 Tom Day	1.50	.70	.19
☐ 39 Art Graham	1.50	.70	.19
☐ 40 Bob Cappadona	1.50	.70	.19
☐ 41 Gary Ballman	1.50	.70	.19
☐ 42 Clendon Thomas	1.50	.70	.19
☐ 43 Jackie Smith	4.00	1.80	.50
☐ 44 Dave Wilcox	2.00	.90	.25
☐ 45 Jerry Smith	1.50	.70	.19
☐ 46 Dan Grimm	1.50	.70	.19
☐ 47 Tom Matte	2.00	.90	.25
☐ 48 John Stofa	1.50	.70	.19
☐ 49 Rex Mirich	1.50	.70	.19
☐ 50 Miller Farr	1.50	.70	.19
☐ 51 Gale Sayers	35.00	16.00	4.40
☐ 52 Bill Nelsen	2.00	.90	.25
☐ 53 Bob Lilly	6.00	2.70	.75
☐ 54 Wayne Walker	1.50	.70	.19
☐ 55 Ray Nitschke	5.00	2.20	.60
☐ 56 Ed Meador	1.50	.70	.19
☐ 57 Lonnie Warwick	1.50	.70	.19
☐ 58 Wendell Hayes	1.50	.70	.19
☐ 59 Dick Anderson	5.00	2.20	.60
☐ 60 Don Maynard	7.00	3.10	.85
☐ 61 Tony Lorick	1.50	.70	.19
☐ 62 Pete Gogolak	1.50	.70	.19
☐ 63 Nate Ramsey	1.50	.70	.19
☐ 64 Dick Shiner	1.50	.70	.19
☐ 65 Larry Wilson	2.50	1.10	.30
☐ 66 Ken Willard	2.00	.90	.25
☐ 67 Charley Taylor UER (Led Redskins in pass interceptions)	5.00	2.20	.60
☐ 68 Billy Cannon	2.00	.90	.25
☐ 69 Lance Alworth	8.00	3.60	1.00
☐ 70 Jim Nance	2.00	.90	.25
☐ 71 Nick Rassas	1.50	.70	.19
☐ 72 Lenny Lyles	1.50	.70	.19
☐ 73 Bennie McRae	1.50	.70	.19
☐ 74 Bill Glass	1.50	.70	.19
☐ 75 Don Meredith	22.00	10.00	2.70
☐ 76 Dick LeBeau	1.50	.70	.19
☐ 77 Carroll Dale	2.00	.90	.25
☐ 78 Ron McDole	1.50	.70	.19
☐ 79 Charley King	1.50	.70	.19
☐ 80 Checklist 1-132 UER (26 Bryon Piccolo)	16.00	4.00	1.60
☐ 81 Dick Bass	2.00	.90	.25
☐ 82 Roy Winston	1.50	.70	.19
☐ 83 Don McCall	1.50	.70	.19
☐ 84 Jim Katcavage	2.00	.90	.25
☐ 85 Norm Snead	2.00	.90	.25
☐ 86 Earl Gros	1.50	.70	.19
☐ 87 Don Brumm	1.50	.70	.19
☐ 88 Sonny Bishop	1.50	.70	.19
☐ 89 Fred Arbanas	1.50	.70	.19
☐ 90 Karl Noonan	1.50	.70	.19
☐ 91 Dick Witcher	1.50	.70	.19
☐ 92 Vince Promuto	1.50	.70	.19
☐ 93 Tommy Nobis	4.00	1.80	.50
☐ 94 Jerry Hill	1.50	.70	.19
☐ 95 Ed O'Bradovich	1.50	.70	.19
☐ 96 Ernie Kellerman	2.00	.90	.25
☐ 97 Chuck Howley	2.00	.90	.25
☐ 98 Hewritt Dixon	1.50	.70	.19
☐ 99 Ron Mix	3.00	1.35	.35
☐ 100 Joe Namath	75.00	34.00	9.50
☐ 101 Billy Gambrell	1.50	.70	.19
☐ 102 Elijah Pitts	2.00	.90	.25
☐ 103 Billy Truax	2.00	.90	.25
☐ 104 Ed Sharockman	1.50	.70	.19
☐ 105 Doug Atkins	3.00	1.35	.35
☐ 106 Greg Larson	1.50	.70	.19
☐ 107 Israel Lang	1.50	.70	.19
☐ 108 Houston Antwine	1.50	.70	.19
☐ 109 Paul Guidry	1.50	.70	.19
☐ 110 Al Denson	1.50	.70	.19
☐ 111 Roy Jefferson	2.00	.90	.25
☐ 112 Chuck Latourette	1.50	.70	.19
☐ 113 Jim Johnson	3.00	1.35	.35
☐ 114 Bobby Mitchell	3.50	1.55	.45
☐ 115 Randy Johnson	1.50	.70	.19
☐ 116 Lou Michaels	1.50	.70	.19
☐ 117 Rudy Kuechenberg	1.50	.70	.19
☐ 118 Walt Suggs	1.50	.70	.19
☐ 119 Goldie Sellers	1.50	.70	.19
☐ 120 Larry Csonka	75.00	34.00	9.50
☐ 121 Jim Houston	1.50	.70	.19
☐ 122 Craig Baynham	1.50	.70	.19
☐ 123 Alex Karras	5.00	2.20	.60
☐ 124 Jim Grabowski	2.00	.90	.25
☐ 125 Roman Gabriel	3.50	1.55	.45
☐ 126 Larry Bowie	1.50	.70	.19
☐ 127 Dave Parks	2.00	.90	.25
☐ 128 Ben Davidson	4.00	1.80	.50
☐ 129 Steve DeLong	1.50	.70	.19
☐ 130 Fred Hill	1.50	.70	.19
☐ 131 Ernie Koy	2.00	.90	.25
☐ 132A Checklist 133-263 (no border)	16.00	4.00	1.60
☐ 132B Checklist 133-263 (thin white border like second series)	18.00	4.50	1.80
☐ 133 Dick Hoak	2.00	.90	.25
☐ 134 Larry Stallings	2.50	1.10	.30
☐ 135 Clifton McNeil	2.00	.90	.25
☐ 136 Walter Rock	2.00	.90	.25
☐ 137 Billy Lothridge	2.00	.90	.25
☐ 138 Bob Vogel	2.00	.90	.25
☐ 139 Dick Butkus	40.00	18.00	5.00
☐ 140 Frank Ryan	2.50	1.10	.30
☐ 141 Larry Garron	2.00	.90	.25
☐ 142 George Saimes	2.00	.90	.25
☐ 143 Frank Buncom	2.00	.90	.25
☐ 144 Don Perkins	2.50	1.10	.30
☐ 145 Johnnie Robinson UER (Misspelled Johnny)	2.00	.90	.25
☐ 146 Lee Roy Caffey	2.50	1.10	.30
☐ 147 Bernie Casey	2.50	1.10	.30
☐ 148 Billy Martin	2.00	.90	.25
☐ 149 Gene Howard	2.00	.90	.25
☐ 150 Fran Tarkenton	16.00	7.25	2.00
☐ 151 Eric Crabtree	2.00	.90	.25
☐ 152 W.K. Hicks	2.00	.90	.25
☐ 153 Bobby Bell	3.50	1.55	.45
☐ 154 Sam Baker	2.00	.90	.25
☐ 155 Marv Woodson	2.00	.90	.25
☐ 156 Dave Williams	2.00	.90	.25
☐ 157 Bruce Bosley UER (Considered one of the three centers in all of pro football)	2.00	.90	.25
☐ 158 Carl Kammerer	2.00	.90	.25
☐ 159 Jim Burson	2.00	.90	.25
☐ 160 Roy Hilton	2.00	.90	.25
☐ 161 Bob Griese	25.00	11.00	3.10
☐ 162 Bob Talamini	2.00	.90	.25
☐ 163 Jim Otto	4.00	1.80	.50
☐ 164 Ron Bull	2.00	.90	.25
☐ 165 Walter Johnson	2.00	.90	.25
☐ 166 Lee Roy Jordan	4.00	1.80	.50
☐ 167 Mike Lucci	2.00	.90	.25
☐ 168 Willie Wood	3.50	1.55	.45
☐ 169 Maxie Baughan	2.00	.90	.25
☐ 170 Bill Brown	2.50	1.10	.30
☐ 171 John Hadl	3.00	1.35	.35
☐ 172 Gino Cappelletti	2.50	1.10	.30
☐ 173 George Butch Byrd	2.50	1.10	.30
☐ 174 Steve Stonebreaker	2.00	.90	.25
☐ 175 Joe Morrison	2.50	1.10	.30
☐ 176 Joe Scarpati	2.00	.90	.25
☐ 177 Bobby Walden	2.00	.90	.25
☐ 178 Roy Shivers	2.00	.90	.25
☐ 179 Kermit Alexander	2.00	.90	.25
☐ 180 Pat Richter	2.00	.90	.25
☐ 181 Pete Perreault	2.00	.90	.25
☐ 182 Pete Duranko	2.00	.90	.25
☐ 183 Leroy Mitchell	2.00	.90	.25
☐ 184 Jim Simon	2.00	.90	.25
☐ 185 Billy Ray Smith	2.00	.90	.25
☐ 186 Jack Concannon	2.00	.90	.25
☐ 187 Ben Davis	2.00	.90	.25
☐ 188 Mike Clark	2.00	.90	.25
☐ 189 Jim Gibbons	2.00	.90	.25
☐ 190 Dave Robinson	2.50	1.10	.30
☐ 191 Otis Taylor	2.50	1.10	.30
☐ 192 Nick Buoniconti	3.00	1.35	.35
☐ 193 Matt Snell	2.50	1.10	.30
☐ 194 Bruce Gossett	2.00	.90	.25
☐ 195 Mick Tingelhoff	2.50	1.10	.30
☐ 196 Earl Leggett	2.00	.90	.25
☐ 197 Pete Case	2.00	.90	.25
☐ 198 Tom Woodeshick	2.00	.90	.25
☐ 199 Ken Kortas	2.00	.90	.25
☐ 200 Jim Hart	3.00	1.35	.35
☐ 201 Fred Biletnikoff	10.00	4.50	1.25
☐ 202 Jacque MacKinnon	2.00	.90	.25
☐ 203 Jim Whalen	2.00	.90	.25
☐ 204 Matt Hazeltine	2.00	.90	.25
☐ 205 Charlie Gogolak	2.00	.90	.25
☐ 206 Ray Ogden	2.00	.90	.25
☐ 207 John Mackey	4.00	1.80	.50
☐ 208 Roosevelt Taylor	2.00	.90	.25
☐ 209 Gene Hickerson	2.00	.90	.25
☐ 210 Dave Edwards	2.50	1.10	.30
☐ 211 Tom Sestak	2.00	.90	.25
☐ 212 Ernie Wright	2.00	.90	.25
☐ 213 Dave Costa	2.00	.90	.25
☐ 214 Tom Vaughn	2.00	.90	.25
☐ 215 Bart Starr	25.00	11.00	3.10
☐ 216 Les Josephson	2.50	1.10	.30
☐ 217 Fred Cox	2.50	1.10	.30
☐ 218 Mike Tilleman	2.00	.90	.25
☐ 219 Darrell Dess	2.00	.90	.25
☐ 220 Dave Lloyd	2.00	.90	.25
☐ 221 Pete Beathard	2.00	.90	.25
☐ 222 Buck Buchanan	3.50	1.55	.45
☐ 223 Frank Emanuel	2.00	.90	.25
☐ 224 Paul Martha	2.00	.90	.25
☐ 225 Johnny Roland	2.00	.90	.25
☐ 226 Gary Lewis	2.00	.90	.25
☐ 227 Sonny Jurgensen UER (Chiefs logo)	6.00	2.70	.75
☐ 228 Jim Butler	2.00	.90	.25
☐ 229 Mike Curtis	6.00	2.70	.75
☐ 230 Richie Petitbon	2.50	1.10	.30
☐ 231 George Sauer Jr.	2.50	1.10	.30
☐ 232 George Blanda	18.00	8.00	2.20
☐ 233 Gary Garrison	2.00	.90	.25
☐ 234 Gary Collins	2.50	1.10	.30
☐ 235 Craig Morton	3.50	1.55	.45
☐ 236 Tom Nowatzke	2.00	.90	.25
☐ 237 Donny Anderson	2.50	1.10	.30
☐ 238 Deacon Jones	4.00	1.80	.50
☐ 239 Grady Alderman	2.00	.90	.25
☐ 240 Bill Kilmer	3.00	1.35	.35
☐ 241 Mike Taliaferro	2.00	.90	.25
☐ 242 Stew Barber	2.00	.90	.25
☐ 243 Bobby Hunt	2.00	.90	.25
☐ 244 Homer Jones	2.00	.90	.25
☐ 245 Bob Brown OT	2.50	1.10	.30
☐ 246 Bill Asbury	2.00	.90	.25
☐ 247 Charlie Johnson UER (Misspelled Charley on both sides)	2.50	1.10	.30
☐ 248 Chris Hanburger	2.50	1.10	.30
☐ 249 John Brodie	6.00	2.70	.75
☐ 250 Earl Morrall	2.50	1.10	.30
☐ 251 Floyd Little	5.00	2.20	.60
☐ 252 Jerrel Wilson	2.00	.90	.25
☐ 253 Jim Keyes	2.00	.90	.25
☐ 254 Mel Renfro	4.00	1.80	.50
☐ 255 Herb Adderley	4.00	1.80	.50
☐ 256 Jack Snow	2.50	1.10	.30
☐ 257 Charlie Durkee	2.00	.90	.25
☐ 258 Charlie Harper	2.00	.90	.25
☐ 259 J.R. Wilburn	2.00	.90	.25
☐ 260 Charlie Krueger	2.00	.90	.25
☐ 261 Pete Jacques	2.00	.90	.25
☐ 262 Gerry Philbin	2.00	.90	.25
☐ 263 Daryle Lamonica	10.00	2.50	1.00

1969 Topps Four-in-One

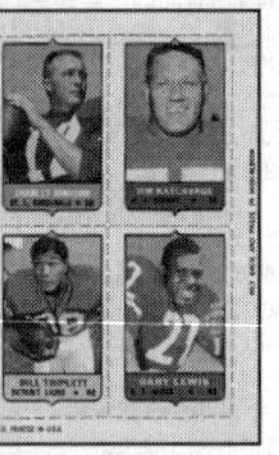

The 1969 Topps Four-in-One set contains 66 cards (each measuring the standard size) with each card having four small (1" by 1 1/2") cardboard stamps on the front. Cards 27 and 28 are the same except for colors. The cards were issued as inserts to the 1969 Topps regular football card set. The cards are unnumbered, but have been numbered in the checklist below for convenience in alphabetical order by the player in the northwest quadrant of the card. Prices below are for complete cards; individual stamps are not priced. An album exists to house the stamps on these cards (see 1969 Topps Mini Albums). It is interesting to note that not all the players appearing in this set also appear in the 1969 Topps regular issue set especially since there are almost the same number of players in each set. Jack Kemp is included in this set but not in the regular 1969 Topps set. Bryan Piccolo also appears in his only Topps appearance other than the 1969 Topps regular issue set. There are 19 players in this set who do not appear in the regular issue 1969 Topps set; they are marked by asterisks in the list below.

	NRMT-MT	EXC	G-VG
COMPLETE SET (66)	300.00	135.00	38.00
COMMON CARD (1-66)	3.50	1.55	.45
☐ 1 Grady Alderman	12.00	5.50	1.50
Jerry Smith			
Gale Sayers			
Dick LeBeau			
☐ 2 Jim Allison *	3.50	1.55	.45
Frank Buncom			
Frank Emanuel			
George Sauer Jr.			
☐ 3 Lance Alworth	8.00	3.60	1.00
Don Maynard			
Ron McDole			
Billy Cannon			
☐ 4 Dick Anderson	5.00	2.20	.60
Mike Taliaferro			
Fred Biletnikoff			
Otis Taylor			
☐ 5 Ralph Baker	5.00	2.20	.60
Speedy Duncan			
Eric Crabtree			
Bobby Bell			
☐ 6 Gary Ballman	3.50	1.55	.45
Jerry Hill			
Roy Jefferson			
Boyd Dowler			
☐ 7 Tom Beer	3.50	1.55	.45
Miller Farr			
Jim Colclough			
Steve DeLong			
☐ 8 Sonny Bishop	3.50	1.55	.45
Pete Banaszak			
Paul Guidry			
Tom Day			
☐ 9 Bruce Bosley	3.50	1.55	.45
J.R. Wilburn			
Tom Nowatzke			
Jim Simon			
☐ 10 Larry Bowie	3.50	1.55	.45
Willis Crenshaw			
Tommy Davis			
Paul Flatley			
☐ 11 Nick Buoniconti	5.00	2.20	.60
George Saimes			
Jacque MacKinnon			
Pete Duranko			
☐ 12 Jim Burson	3.50	1.55	.45
Dan Abramowicz			
Ed O'Bradovich			
Dick Witcher			
☐ 13 Reg Carolan *	3.50	1.55	.45
Larry Garron			
W.K. Hicks			
Pete Jacques			
☐ 14 Bert Coan *	5.00	2.20	.60
John Hadl			
Dan Birdwell *			
Sam Brunelli *			
☐ 15 Hewritt Dixon	30.00	13.50	3.70
Goldie Sellers			
Joe Namath			
Howard Twilley			
☐ 16 Charlie Durkee	10.00	4.50	1.25
Clifton McNeil			
Maxie Baughan			
Fran Tarkenton			
☐ 17 Pete Gogolak	3.50	1.55	.45
Ron Bull			
Chuck Latourette			
Willie Richardson			
☐ 18 Bob Griese	10.00	4.50	1.25
Jim LeMoine *			
Dave Grayson			
Walt Sweeney			
☐ 19 Jim Hart	3.50	1.55	.45
Darrell Dess			
Kermit Alexander			
Mick Tingelhoff			
☐ 20 Alvin Haymond	3.50	1.55	.45
Elijah Pitts			
Billy Ray Smith			
Ken Willard			
☐ 21 Gene Hickerson	12.00	5.50	1.50
Donny Anderson			
Dick Butkus			
Mike Lucci			
☐ 22 Fred Hill	5.00	2.20	.60
Ernie Koy			
Tommy Nobis			
Bennie McRae			
☐ 23 Dick Hoak	5.00	2.20	.60
Roman Gabriel			
Ed Sharockman			
Dave Williams			
☐ 24 Jim Houston	3.50	1.55	.45
Roy Shivers			
Carroll Dale			
Bill Asbury			
☐ 25 Gene Howard	3.50	1.55	.45
Joe Morrison			
Billy Martin			
Ben Davis			
☐ 26 Chuck Howley	25.00	11.00	3.10
Brian Piccolo UER			
Chris Hanburger			
Erich Barnes			
☐ 27 Charlie Johnson (red)	3.50	1.55	.45
Jim Katcavage			
Gary Lewis			
Bill Triplett			
(white)			
☐ 28 Charlie Johnson	3.50	1.55	.45
(white)			
Jim Katcavage			
Gary Lewis			
Bill Triplett (red)			
☐ 29 Walter Johnson	3.50	1.55	.45
Tucker Frederickson			
Dave Lloyd			
Bobby Walden			
☐ 30 Sonny Jurgensen	8.00	3.60	1.00
Dick Bass			
Paul Martha			
Dave Parks			
☐ 31 Leroy Kelly	12.00	5.50	1.50
Ed Meador			
Bart Starr			
Ray Ogden			
☐ 32 Charley King	3.50	1.55	.45
Bob Cappadona			
Fred Arbanas			
Ben Davidson			
☐ 33 Daryle Lamonica	5.00	2.20	.60
Carl Cunningham *			
Bobby Hunt			
Stew Barber			
☐ 34 Israel Lang	6.00	2.70	.75
Bob Lilly			
Jim Butler			
John Brodie			
☐ 35 Jim Lindsey	5.00	2.20	.60
Ray Nitschke			
Rickie Harris			
Bob Vogel			
☐ 36 Billy Lothridge	5.00	2.20	.60
Herb Adderley			
Charlie Gogolak			
John Mackey			
☐ 37 Bobby Maples	3.50	1.55	.45
Karl Noonan			
Houston Antwine			
Wendell Hayes			
☐ 38 Don Meredith	10.00	4.50	1.25
Gary Collins			
Homer Jones			
Marv Woodson			
☐ 39 Rex Mirich	3.50	1.55	.45
Art Graham			
Jim Turner			
John Stofa			
☐ 40 Leroy Mitchell	3.50	1.55	.45
Sid Blanks *			
Paul Rochester *			
Pete Perreault			
☐ 41 Jim Nance	12.00	5.50	1.50
Jim Dunaway			
Larry Csonka			
Ron Mix			
☐ 42 Bill Nelsen	3.50	1.55	.45
Bill Munson			
Nate Ramsey			
Mike Curtis			
☐ 43 Jim Otto	5.00	2.20	.60
Dave Herman *			
Dave Costa			
Dennis Randall *			
☐ 44 Jack Pardee	3.50	1.55	.45
Norm Snead			
Craig Baynham			
Bob Jeter			
☐ 45 Richie Petitbon	3.50	1.55	.45
Johnny Robinson			
Mike Clark			
Jack Snow			
☐ 46 Nick Rassas	5.00	2.20	.60
Tom Matte			
Lance Rentzel			
Bobby Mitchell			
☐ 47 Pat Richter	3.50	1.55	.45
Dave Whitsell			
Joe Kapp			
Bill Glass			
☐ 48 Johnny Roland	3.50	1.55	.45
Craig Morton			
Bill Brown			
Sam Baker			
☐ 49 Andy Russell	5.00	2.20	.60
Randy Johnson			
Bob Matheson			
Alex Karras			
☐ 50 Joe Scarpati	3.50	1.55	.45
Walter Rock			
Jack Concannon			
Bernie Casey			
☐ 51 Tom Sestak	3.50	1.55	.45
Ernie Wright			
Doug Moreau *			
Matt Snell			
☐ 52 Jerry Simmons	5.00	2.20	.60
Bob Hayes			
Doug Atkins			
Spider Lockhart			
☐ 53 Jackie Smith	6.00	2.70	.75
Jim Grabowski			
Jim Johnson			
Charley Taylor			
☐ 54 Larry Stallings	3.50	1.55	.45
Roosevelt Taylor			
Jim Gibbons			
Bob Brown OT			
☐ 55 Mike Stratton *	3.50	1.55	.45
Marion Rushing *			
Solomon Brannan *			
Jim Keyes			
☐ 56 Walt Suggs	6.00	2.70	.75
Len Dawson			
Sherrill Headrick			
Al Denson			
☐ 57 Bob Talamini	30.00	13.50	3.70
George Blanda			
Jim Whalen			
Jack Kemp *			
☐ 58 Clendon Thomas	3.50	1.55	.45
Don McCall			
Earl Morrall			
Lonnie Warwick			
☐ 59 Don Trull *	5.00	2.20	.60
Gerry Philbin			
Gary Garrison			
Buck Buchanan			
☐ 60 Johnny Unitas	15.00	6.75	1.85
Les Josephson			
Fred Cox			
Mel Renfro			
☐ 61 Wayne Walker	5.00	2.20	.60
Tony Lorick			
Dave Wilcox			
Merlin Olsen			
☐ 62 Willie West *	3.50	1.55	.45
Ken Herock *			
George Byrd			
Gino Cappelletti			
☐ 63 Jerrel Wilson	3.50	1.55	.45
John Bramlett *			
Pete Beathard			
Floyd Little			
☐ 64 Larry Wilson	5.00	2.20	.60
Lou Michaels			
Billy Gambrell			
Earl Gros			
☐ 65 Willie Wood	5.00	2.20	.60
Steve Stonebreaker			
Vince Promuto			
Jim Cadile			
☐ 66 Tom Woodeshick	5.00	2.20	.60
Greg Larson			
Billy Kilmer			
Don Perkins			

1969 Topps Mini-Albums

The 1969 Topps Mini-Card Team Albums is a set of 26 small (2 1/2" by 3 1/2") booklets which were issued in conjunction with the 1969 Four-in-One inserts. Each of these booklets has eight pages and a game action photo on the front. Many of the cover photos were from games from the early 1960s. We've included the player's names when known. A picture of each player is contained in the album, over which the stamps from the Four-in-One inserts were to be pasted. In order to be mint, the album must have no stamps pasted in it. The booklets

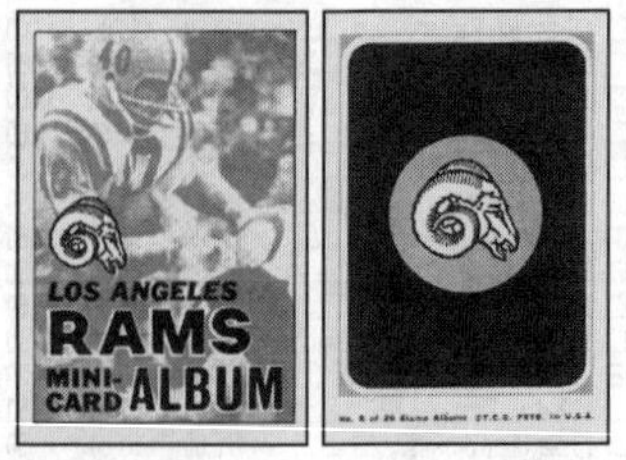

are printed in blue and black ink on thick white paper and are numbered on the last page of the album. The card numbering coresponds to an alphabetical listing by team name within each league.

	NRMT-MT	EXC	G-VG
COMPLETE SET (26)	75.00	34.00	9.50
COMMON ALBUM (1-26)	3.00	1.35	.35
☐ 1 Atlanta Falcons	3.00	1.35	.35
☐ 2 Baltimore Colts	6.00	2.70	.75
(John Unitas pictured on front)			
☐ 3 Chicago Bears	3.00	1.35	.35
(Bob Gaiters pictured)			
☐ 4 Cleveland Browns	4.00	1.80	.50
(Bill George and Bill Wade pictured)			
☐ 5 Dallas Cowboys	5.00	2.20	.60
Jimmy Patton and Joe Morrison pictured)			
☐ 6 Detroit Lions	3.00	1.35	.35
(college teams pictured)			
☐ 7 Green Bay Packers	5.00	2.20	.60
(Bart Starr pictured)			
☐ 8 Los Angeles Rams	3.00	1.35	.35
(college teams pictured)			
☐ 9 Minnesota Vikings	3.00	1.35	.35
(J.D.Smith pictured)			
☐ 10 New Orleans Saints	3.00	1.35	.35
(Mel Triplett pictured)			
☐ 11 New York Giants	3.00	1.35	.35
(Dick Modzelewski and Norm Snead pictured)			
☐ 12 Philadelphia Eagles	4.00	1.80	.50
(Ray Nitschke pictured)			
☐ 13 Pittsburgh Steelers	4.00	1.80	.50
(Kyle Rote pictured)			
☐ 14 St. Louis Cardinals	3.00	1.35	.35
(Tom Brookshier pictured)			
☐ 15 San Francisco 49ers	3.00	1.35	.35
(Joe Walton pictured)			
☐ 16 Washington Redskins	3.00	1.35	.35
(Dick James pictured)			
☐ 17 Boston Patriots	3.00	1.35	.35
(Jim Katcavage, Andy Robustelli and Timmy Brown pictured)			
☐ 18 Buffalo Bills	4.00	1.80	.50
(Roosevelt Grier and Tom Scott pictured)			
☐ 19 Cincinnati Bengals	4.00	1.80	.50
(Norm Van Brocklin and J.D.Smith pictured)			
☐ 20 Denver Broncos	3.00	1.35	.35
(college teams pictured)			
☐ 21 Houston Oilers	3.00	1.35	.35
(Billy Ray Smith Sr. and Carl Taseff pictured)			
☐ 22 Kansas City Chiefs	6.00	2.70	.75
(Jim Brown and Bobby Freeman pictured)			
☐ 23 Miami Dolphins	4.00	1.80	.50
(Roosevelt Grier and Frank Budd pictured)			
☐ 24 New York Jets	4.00	1.80	.50
Bobby Layne pictured)			
☐ 25 Oakland Raiders	5.00	2.20	.60
(Jim Taylor and Linden Crow pictured)			
☐ 26 San Diego Chargers	3.00	1.35	.35
(Rich Kreitling and Steeler defender pictured)			

1970 Topps

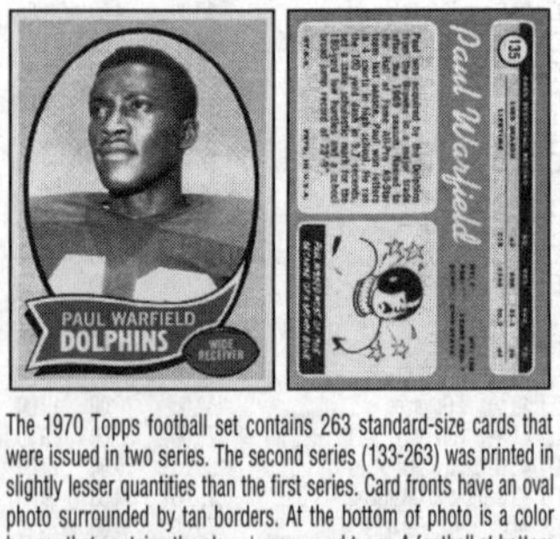

The 1970 Topps football set contains 263 standard-size cards that were issued in two series. The second series (133-263) was printed in slightly lesser quantities than the first series. Card fronts have an oval photo surrounded by tan borders. At the bottom of photo is a color banner that contains the player's name and team. A football at bottom

right contain the player's position. The card backs are done in orange, purple, and white and are horizontally designed. Statistics, highlights and a player cartoon adorn the backs. In the second series, card backs of offensive and defensive linemen have a coin rub-off cartoon rather than a printed cartoon as seen on all the other cards in the set. O.J. Simpson's Rookie Card appears in this set. Other notable Rookie Cards in this set are Lem Barney, Bill Bergey, Larry Brown, Fred Dryer, Mike Garrett, Calvin Hill, Harold Jackson, Tom Mack, Alan Page, Bubba Smith, Jan Stenerud, Bob Trumpy, and both Gene Washingtons.

	NRMT-MT	EXC	G-VG
COMPLETE SET (263)	450.00	200.00	55.00
COMMON CARD (1-132)	1.00	.45	.12
COMMON CARD (133-263)	1.25	.55	.16
☐ 1 Len Dawson UER (Cartoon caption says, "AFL AN NFL")	16.00	4.00	1.60
☐ 2 Doug Hart	1.00	.45	.12
☐ 3 Verlon Biggs	1.00	.45	.12
☐ 4 Ralph Neely	1.50	.70	.19
☐ 5 Harmon Wages	1.00	.45	.12
☐ 6 Dan Conners	1.00	.45	.12
☐ 7 Gino Cappelletti	1.50	.70	.19
☐ 8 Erich Barnes	1.00	.45	.12
☐ 9 Checklist 1-132	10.00	2.50	1.00
☐ 10 Bob Griese	16.00	7.25	2.00
☐ 11 Ed Flanagan	1.00	.45	.12
☐ 12 George Seals	1.00	.45	.12
☐ 13 Harry Jacobs	1.00	.45	.12
☐ 14 Mike Haffner	1.00	.45	.12
☐ 15 Bob Vogel	1.00	.45	.12
☐ 16 Bill Peterson	1.00	.45	.12
☐ 17 Spider Lockhart	1.50	.70	.19
☐ 18 Billy Truax	1.50	.70	.19
☐ 19 Jim Beirne	1.00	.45	.12
☐ 20 Leroy Kelly	6.00	2.70	.75
☐ 21 Dave Lloyd	1.00	.45	.12
☐ 22 Mike Tilleman	1.00	.45	.12
☐ 23 Gary Garrison	1.50	.70	.19
☐ 24 Larry Brown	8.00	3.60	1.00
☐ 25 Jan Stenerud	12.00	5.50	1.50
☐ 26 Rolf Krueger	1.00	.45	.12
☐ 27 Roland Lakes	1.00	.45	.12
☐ 28 Dick Hoak	1.00	.45	.12
☐ 29 Gene Washington	2.00	.90	.25
☐ 30 Bart Starr	20.00	9.00	2.50
☐ 31 Dave Grayson	1.00	.45	.12
☐ 32 Jerry Rush	1.00	.45	.12
☐ 33 Len St. Jean	1.00	.45	.12
☐ 34 Randy Edmunds	1.00	.45	.12
☐ 35 Matt Snell	1.50	.70	.19
☐ 36 Paul Costa	1.00	.45	.12
☐ 37 Mike Pyle	1.00	.45	.12
☐ 38 Roy Hilton	1.00	.45	.12
☐ 39 Steve Tensi	1.00	.45	.12
☐ 40 Tommy Nobis	2.50	1.10	.30
☐ 41 Pete Case	1.00	.45	.12
☐ 42 Andy Rice	1.00	.45	.12
☐ 43 Elvin Bethea	2.50	1.10	.30
☐ 44 Jack Snow	1.50	.70	.19
☐ 45 Mel Renfro	3.00	1.35	.35
☐ 46 Andy Livingston	1.00	.45	.12
☐ 47 Gary Ballman	1.00	.45	.12
☐ 48 Bob DeMarco	1.00	.45	.12
☐ 49 Steve DeLong	1.00	.45	.12
☐ 50 Daryle Lamonica	3.50	1.55	.45
☐ 51 Jim Lynch	1.00	.45	.12
☐ 52 Mel Farr	1.50	.70	.19
☐ 53 Bob Long	1.00	.45	.12
☐ 54 John Elliott	1.00	.45	.12
☐ 55 Ray Nitschke	5.00	2.20	.60
☐ 56 Jim Shorter	1.00	.45	.12
☐ 57 Dave Wilcox	1.50	.70	.19
☐ 58 Eric Crabtree	1.00	.45	.12
☐ 59 Alan Page	40.00	18.00	5.00
☐ 60 Jim Nance	1.50	.70	.19
☐ 61 Glen Ray Hines	1.00	.45	.12
☐ 62 John Mackey	3.00	1.35	.35
☐ 63 Ron McDole	1.00	.45	.12
☐ 64 Tom Beier	1.00	.45	.12
☐ 65 Bill Nelsen	1.50	.70	.19
☐ 66 Paul Flatley	1.00	.45	.12
☐ 67 Sam Brunelli	1.00	.45	.12
☐ 68 Jack Pardee	1.50	.70	.19
☐ 69 Brig Owens	1.00	.45	.12
☐ 70 Gale Sayers	25.00	11.00	3.10
☐ 71 Lee Roy Jordan	2.50	1.10	.30
☐ 72 Harold Jackson	5.00	2.20	.60
☐ 73 John Hadl	2.00	.90	.25
☐ 74 Dave Parks	1.50	.70	.19
☐ 75 Lem Barney	14.00	6.25	1.75
☐ 76 Johnny Roland	1.00	.45	.12
☐ 77 Ed Budde	1.00	.45	.12
☐ 78 Ben McGee	1.00	.45	.12
☐ 79 Ken Bowman	1.00	.45	.12
☐ 80 Fran Tarkenton	14.00	6.25	1.75
☐ 81 Gene Washington	5.00	2.20	.60
☐ 82 Larry Grantham	1.00	.45	.12
☐ 83 Bill Brown	1.50	.70	.19
☐ 84 John Charles	1.00	.45	.12
☐ 85 Fred Biletnikoff	7.00	3.10	.85
☐ 86 Royce Berry	1.00	.45	.12
☐ 87 Bob Lilly	5.00	2.20	.60
☐ 88 Earl Morrall	1.50	.70	.19
☐ 89 Jerry LeVias	1.50	.70	.19
☐ 90 O.J. Simpson	75.00	34.00	9.50
☐ 91 Mike Howell	1.00	.45	.12
☐ 92 Ken Gray	1.00	.45	.12
☐ 93 Chris Hanburger	1.50	.70	.19
☐ 94 Larry Seiple	1.50	.70	.19
☐ 95 Rich Jackson	1.00	.45	.12
☐ 96 Rockne Freitas	1.00	.45	.12
☐ 97 Dick Post	1.50	.70	.19
☐ 98 Ben Hawkins	1.00	.45	.12
☐ 99 Ken Reaves	1.00	.45	.12
☐ 100 Roman Gabriel	2.50	1.10	.30
☐ 101 Dave Rowe	1.00	.45	.12
☐ 102 Dave Robinson	1.50	.70	.19
☐ 103 Otis Taylor	1.50	.70	.19
☐ 104 Jim Turner	1.00	.45	.12
☐ 105 Joe Morrison	1.50	.70	.19
☐ 106 Dick Evey	1.00	.45	.12
☐ 107 Ray Mansfield	1.00	.45	.12
☐ 108 Grady Alderman	1.00	.45	.12
☐ 109 Bruce Gossett	1.00	.45	.12
☐ 110 Bob Trumpy	4.00	1.80	.50
☐ 111 Jim Hunt	1.00	.45	.12
☐ 112 Larry Stallings	1.00	.45	.12
☐ 113A Lance Rentzel (name in red)	1.50	.70	.19
☐ 113B Lance Rentzel (name in black)	1.50	.70	.19
☐ 114 Bubba Smith	25.00	11.00	3.10
☐ 115 Norm Snead	1.50	.70	.19
☐ 116 Jim Otto	3.00	1.35	.35
☐ 117 Bo Scott	1.00	.45	.12
☐ 118 Rick Redman	1.00	.45	.12
☐ 119 George Butch Byrd	1.00	.45	.12
☐ 120 George Webster	1.50	.70	.19
☐ 121 Chuck Walton	1.00	.45	.12
☐ 122 Dave Costa	1.00	.45	.12
☐ 123 Al Dodd	1.00	.45	.12
☐ 124 Len Hauss	1.50	.70	.19
☐ 125 Deacon Jones	3.00	1.35	.35
☐ 126 Randy Johnson	1.00	.45	.12
☐ 127 Ralph Heck	1.00	.45	.12
☐ 128 Emerson Boozer	1.50	.70	.19
☐ 129 Johnny Robinson	1.50	.70	.19
☐ 130 John Brodie	5.00	2.20	.60
☐ 131 Gale Gillingham	1.00	.45	.12
☐ 132 Checklist 133-263 DP UER (145 Charley Taylor misspelled Charlie)	6.00	1.50	.60
☐ 133 Chuck Walker	1.25	.55	.16
☐ 134 Bennie McRae	1.25	.55	.16
☐ 135 Paul Warfield	7.00	3.10	.85
☐ 136 Dan Darragh	1.25	.55	.16
☐ 137 Paul Robinson	1.25	.55	.16
☐ 138 Ed Philpott	1.25	.55	.16
☐ 139 Craig Morton	2.50	1.10	.30
☐ 140 Tom Dempsey	2.00	.90	.25
☐ 141 Al Nelson	1.25	.55	.16
☐ 142 Tom Matte	2.00	.90	.25
☐ 143 Dick Schafrath	1.25	.55	.16
☐ 144 Willie Brown	4.00	1.80	.50
☐ 145 Charley Taylor UER (Misspelled Charlie on both sides)	5.00	2.20	.60
☐ 146 John Huard	1.25	.55	.16
☐ 147 Dave Osborn	2.00	.90	.25
☐ 148 Gene Mingo	1.25	.55	.16
☐ 149 Larry Hand	1.25	.55	.16
☐ 150 Joe Namath	65.00	29.00	8.00
☐ 151 Tom Mack	7.00	3.10	.85
☐ 152 Kenny Graham	1.25	.55	.16
☐ 153 Don Herrmann	1.25	.55	.16
☐ 154 Bobby Bell	2.50	1.10	.30
☐ 155 Hoyle Granger	1.25	.55	.16
☐ 156 Claude Humphrey	2.00	.90	.25
☐ 157 Clifton McNeil	1.25	.55	.16
☐ 158 Mick Tingelhoff	2.00	.90	.25
☐ 159 Don Horn	2.00	.90	.25
☐ 160 Larry Wilson	2.50	1.10	.30
☐ 161 Tom Neville	1.25	.55	.16
☐ 162 Larry Csonka	20.00	9.00	2.50
☐ 163 Doug Buffone	2.00	.90	.25
☐ 164 Cornell Green	2.00	.90	.25
☐ 165 Haven Moses	2.00	.90	.25
☐ 166 Bill Kilmer	2.50	1.10	.30
☐ 167 Tim Rossovich	1.25	.55	.16
☐ 168 Bill Bergey	4.00	1.80	.50
☐ 169 Gary Collins	2.00	.90	.25
☐ 170 Floyd Little	3.00	1.35	.35
☐ 171 Tom Keating	1.25	.55	.16
☐ 172 Pat Fischer	2.00	.90	.25
☐ 173 Walt Sweeney	1.25	.55	.16
☐ 174 Greg Larson	1.25	.55	.16
☐ 175 Carl Eller	2.00	.90	.25
☐ 176 George Sauer Jr.	2.00	.90	.25
☐ 177 Jim Hart	2.50	1.10	.30
☐ 178 Bob Brown OT	2.00	.90	.25
☐ 179 Mike Garrett	2.50	1.10	.30
☐ 180 John Unitas	25.00	11.00	3.10
☐ 181 Tom Regner	1.25	.55	.16
☐ 182 Bob Jeter	1.25	.55	.16
☐ 183 Gail Cogdill	1.25	.55	.16
☐ 184 Earl Gros	2.00	.90	.25
☐ 185 Dennis Partee	1.25	.55	.16
☐ 186 Charlie Krueger	1.25	.55	.16
☐ 187 Martin Baccaglio	1.25	.55	.16
☐ 188 Charles Long	1.25	.55	.16
☐ 189 Bob Hayes	4.00	1.80	.50
☐ 190 Dick Butkus	25.00	11.00	3.10
☐ 191 Al Bemiller	1.25	.55	.16
☐ 192 Dick Westmoreland	1.25	.55	.16
☐ 193 Joe Scarpati	1.25	.55	.16
☐ 194 Ron Snidow	1.25	.55	.16
☐ 195 Earl McCullouch	2.00	.90	.25
☐ 196 Jake Kupp	1.25	.55	.16
☐ 197 Bob Lurtsema	1.25	.55	.16
☐ 198 Mike Current	1.25	.55	.16
☐ 199 Charlie Smith	1.25	.55	.16
☐ 200 Sonny Jurgensen	6.00	2.70	.75
☐ 201 Mike Curtis	2.00	.90	.25
☐ 202 Aaron Brown	1.25	.55	.16
☐ 203 Richie Petitbon	2.00	.90	.25
☐ 204 Walt Suggs	1.25	.55	.16
☐ 205 Roy Jefferson	2.00	.90	.25
☐ 206 Russ Washington	1.25	.55	.16
☐ 207 Woody Peoples	1.25	.55	.16
☐ 208 Dave Williams	1.25	.55	.16
☐ 209 John Zook	1.25	.55	.16
☐ 210 Tom Woodeshick	1.25	.55	.16
☐ 211 Howard Fest	1.25	.55	.16
☐ 212 Jack Concannon	1.25	.55	.16
☐ 213 Jim Marshall	2.50	1.10	.30
☐ 214 Jon Morris	1.25	.55	.16
☐ 215 Dan Abramowicz	2.00	.90	.25
☐ 216 Paul Martha	1.25	.55	.16
☐ 217 Ken Willard	2.00	.90	.25
☐ 218 Walter Rock	1.25	.55	.16
☐ 219 Garland Boyette	1.25	.55	.16
☐ 220 Buck Buchanan	2.50	1.10	.30
☐ 221 Bill Munson	2.00	.90	.25
☐ 222 David Lee	1.25	.55	.16
☐ 223 Karl Noonan	1.25	.55	.16
☐ 224 Harry Schuh	1.25	.55	.16
☐ 225 Jackie Smith	2.50	1.10	.30
☐ 226 Gerry Philbin	1.25	.55	.16
☐ 227 Ernie Koy	1.25	.55	.16
☐ 228 Chuck Howley	2.00	.90	.25
☐ 229 Billy Shaw	1.25	.55	.16
☐ 230 Jerry Hillebrand	1.25	.55	.16
☐ 231 Bill Thompson	2.00	.90	.25
☐ 232 Carroll Dale	2.00	.90	.25
☐ 233 Gene Hickerson	1.25	.55	.16
☐ 234 Jim Butler	1.25	.55	.16
☐ 235 Greg Cook	2.00	.90	.25
☐ 236 Lee Roy Caffey	1.25	.55	.16
☐ 237 Merlin Olsen	3.50	1.55	.45
☐ 238 Fred Cox	2.00	.90	.25
☐ 239 Nate Ramsey	1.25	.55	.16
☐ 240 Lance Alworth	7.00	3.10	.85
☐ 241 Chuck Hinton	1.25	.55	.16
☐ 242 Jerry Smith	1.25	.55	.16
☐ 243 Tony Baker	1.25	.55	.16
☐ 244 Nick Buoniconti	2.00	.90	.25
☐ 245 Jim Johnson	2.50	1.10	.30
☐ 246 Willie Richardson	1.25	.55	.16
☐ 247 Fred Dryer	10.00	4.50	1.25
☐ 248 Bobby Maples	1.25	.55	.16
☐ 249 Alex Karras	3.50	1.55	.45
☐ 250 Joe Kapp	2.00	.90	.25
☐ 251 Ben Davidson	2.50	1.10	.30
☐ 252 Mike Stratton	1.25	.55	.16
☐ 253 Les Josephson	1.25	.55	.16
☐ 254 Don Maynard	6.00	2.70	.75
☐ 255 Houston Antwine	1.25	.55	.16
☐ 256 Mac Percival	1.25	.55	.16
☐ 257 George Goeddeke	1.25	.55	.16
☐ 258 Homer Jones	1.25	.55	.16
☐ 259 Bob Berry	1.25	.55	.16
☐ 260A Calvin Hill (Name in red)	12.00	5.50	1.50
☐ 260B Calvin Hill (Name in black)	16.00	7.25	2.00
☐ 261 Willie Wood	2.50	1.10	.30
☐ 262 Ed Weisacosky	1.25	.55	.16
☐ 263 Jim Tyrer	3.50	.85	.35

1970 Topps Glossy

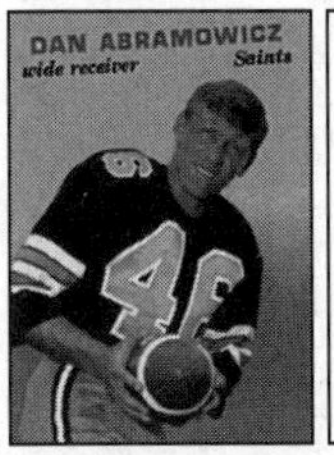

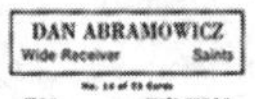

The 1970 Topps Super Glossy football set features 33 full-color, thick-stock, glossy cards each measuring 2 1/4" by 3 1/4". The corners are rounded and the backs contain only the player's name, his position, his team and the card number. The set numbering follows the player's team location within league (NFC 1-20 and AFC 21-33). The cards are quite attractive and a favorite with collectors. The cards were inserted in 1970 Topps first series football wax packs. The key cards in the set are Joe Namath and O.J. Simpson, appearing in his Rookie Card year.

	NRMT-MT	EXC	G-VG
COMPLETE SET (33)	250.00	110.00	31.00
COMMON CARD (1-33)	3.00	1.35	.35
☐ 1 Tommy Nobis	5.00	2.20	.60
☐ 2 Johnny Unitas	25.00	11.00	3.10
☐ 3 Tom Matte	4.00	1.80	.50
☐ 4 Mac Percival	3.00	1.35	.35
☐ 5 Leroy Kelly	6.00	2.70	.75
☐ 6 Mel Renfro	5.00	2.20	.60
☐ 7 Bob Hayes	4.00	1.80	.50
☐ 8 Earl McCullouch	3.00	1.35	.35
☐ 9 Bart Starr	20.00	9.00	2.50
☐ 10 Willie Wood	6.00	2.70	.75
☐ 11 Jack Snow	3.00	1.35	.35
☐ 12 Joe Kapp	3.00	1.35	.35
☐ 13 Dave Osborn	3.00	1.35	.35
☐ 14 Dan Abramowicz	3.00	1.35	.35
☐ 15 Fran Tarkenton	18.00	8.00	2.20
☐ 16 Tom Woodeshick	3.00	1.35	.35
☐ 17 Roy Jefferson	3.00	1.35	.35
☐ 18 Jackie Smith	5.00	2.20	.60
☐ 19 Jim Johnson	5.00	2.20	.60
☐ 20 Sonny Jurgensen	10.00	4.50	1.25
☐ 21 Houston Antwine	3.00	1.35	.35
☐ 22 O.J. Simpson	55.00	25.00	7.00
☐ 23 Greg Cook	3.00	1.35	.35
☐ 24 Floyd Little	4.00	1.80	.50
☐ 25 Rich Jackson	3.00	1.35	.35
☐ 26 George Webster	3.00	1.35	.35
☐ 27 Len Dawson	10.00	4.50	1.25
☐ 28 Bob Griese	15.00	6.75	1.85
☐ 29 Joe Namath	65.00	29.00	8.00
☐ 30 Matt Snell	4.00	1.80	.50
☐ 31 Daryle Lamonica	4.00	1.80	.50
☐ 32 Fred Biletnikoff	7.50	3.40	.95
☐ 33 Dick Post	3.00	1.35	.35

1970 Topps Poster Inserts

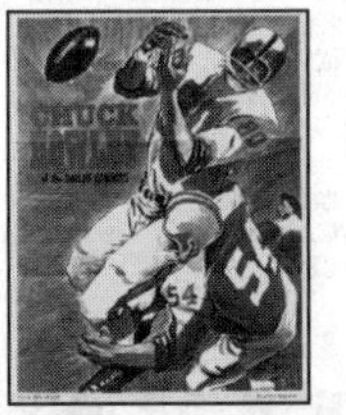

This insert set of 24 folded thin paper posters was issued with the 1970 Topps regular football card issue. The posters are approximately 8" by 10" and were inserted in wax packs along with the 1970 Topps regular issue (second series) football cards. The posters are blank backed.

	NRMT-MT	EXC	G-VG
COMPLETE SET (24)	90.00	40.00	11.00
COMMON CARD (1-24)	2.50	1.10	.30
☐ 1 Gale Sayers	15.00	6.75	1.85
☐ 2 Bobby Bell	4.00	1.80	.50
☐ 3 Roman Gabriel	3.00	1.35	.35
☐ 4 Jim Tyrer	2.50	1.10	.30
☐ 5 Willie Brown	4.00	1.80	.50
☐ 6 Carl Eller	3.00	1.35	.35
☐ 7 Tom Mack	2.50	1.10	.30
☐ 8 Deacon Jones	4.00	1.80	.50
☐ 9 Johnny Robinson	2.50	1.10	.30
☐ 10 Jan Stenerud	3.00	1.35	.35
☐ 11 Dick Butkus	15.00	6.75	1.85
☐ 12 Lem Barney	4.00	1.80	.50
☐ 13 David Lee	2.50	1.10	.30
☐ 14 Larry Wilson	3.00	1.35	.35
☐ 15 Gene Hickerson	2.50	1.10	.30
☐ 16 Lance Alworth	6.00	2.70	.75
☐ 17 Merlin Olsen	5.00	2.20	.60
☐ 18 Bob Trumpy	3.00	1.35	.35
☐ 19 Bob Lilly	6.00	2.70	.75
☐ 20 Mick Tingelhoff	2.50	1.10	.30
☐ 21 Calvin Hill	3.00	1.35	.35
☐ 22 Paul Warfield	7.50	3.40	.95
☐ 23 Chuck Howley	3.00	1.35	.35
☐ 24 Bob Brown OT	2.50	1.10	.30

1970 Topps Super

The 1970 Topps Super set contains 35 cards. The cards measure approximately 3 1/8" by 5 1/4". The backs of the cards are identical in format to the regular football issue of 1970. The cards were sold in packs of three with a stick of gum for a dime and are on very thick card stock. The last seven cards in the set were printed in smaller quantities, i.e., short printed; these seven are designated SP in the checklist below. The cards were printed in sheets of seven rows and nine columns or 63 cards; thus 28 cards were double printed and seven cards were single printed. The key cards in the set are Joe Namath and O.J. Simpson, appearing in his Rookie Card year.

	NRMT-MT	EXC	G-VG
COMPLETE SET (35)	250.00	110.00	31.00
COMMON CARD (1-28)	2.50	1.10	.30
COMMON CARD SP (29-35)	4.00	1.80	.50

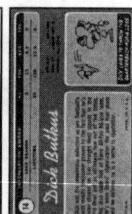

362 • 1970 Topps Super

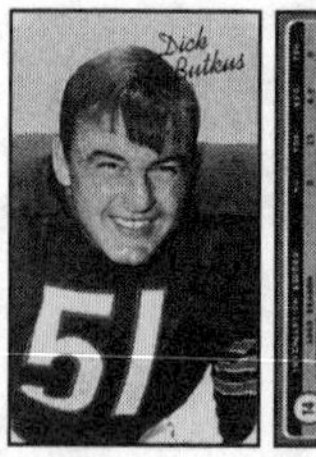

☐ 1 Fran Tarkenton	10.00	4.50	1.25
☐ 2 Floyd Little	3.00	1.35	.35
☐ 3 Bart Starr	12.00	5.50	1.50
☐ 4 Len Dawson	7.50	3.40	.95
☐ 5 Dick Post	2.50	1.10	.30
☐ 6 Sonny Jurgensen	7.50	3.40	.95
☐ 7 Deacon Jones	5.00	2.20	.60
☐ 8 Leroy Kelly	5.00	2.20	.60
☐ 9 Larry Wilson	3.50	1.55	.45
☐ 10 Greg Cook	2.50	1.10	.30
☐ 11 Carl Eller	3.00	1.35	.35
☐ 12 Lem Barney	5.00	2.20	.60
☐ 13 Lance Alworth	7.50	3.40	.95
☐ 14 Dick Butkus	15.00	6.75	1.85
☐ 15 Johnny Unitas	20.00	9.00	2.50
☐ 16 Roy Jefferson	2.50	1.10	.30
☐ 17 Bobby Bell	4.00	1.80	.50
☐ 18 John Brodie	6.00	2.70	.75
☐ 19 Dan Abramowicz	2.50	1.10	.30
☐ 20 Matt Snell	3.00	1.35	.35
☐ 21 Tom Matte	2.50	1.10	.30
☐ 22 Gale Sayers	15.00	6.75	1.85
☐ 23 Tom Woodeshick	2.50	1.10	.30
☐ 24 O.J. Simpson	50.00	22.00	6.25
☐ 25 Roman Gabriel	3.00	1.35	.35
☐ 26 Jim Nance	2.50	1.10	.30
☐ 27 Joe Morrison	2.50	1.10	.30
☐ 28 Calvin Hill	3.00	1.35	.35
☐ 29 Tommy Nobis SP	6.00	2.70	.75
☐ 30 Bob Hayes SP	6.00	2.70	.75
☐ 31 Joe Kapp SP	4.00	1.80	.50
☐ 32 Daryle Lamonica SP	5.00	2.20	.60
☐ 33 Joe Namath SP	60.00	27.00	7.50
☐ 34 George Webster SP	4.00	1.80	.50
☐ 35 Bob Griese SP	15.00	6.75	1.85

1971 Topps

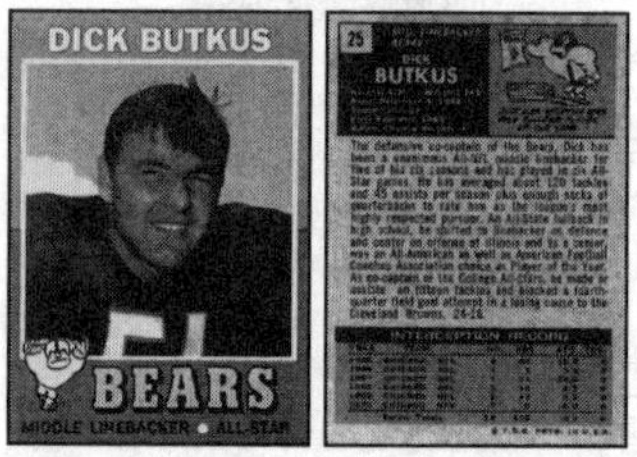

The 1971 Topps set contains 263 standard-size cards issued in two series. The second series (133-263) was printed in slightly lesser quantities than the first series. Card have a player photo surrounded by either a red (AFC), blue (NFC) or blue and red (All-Pros) border. The player's name, team name, position and conference are within the bottom border. An animated cartoon-like player icon appears by the position listing at the bottom. The card backs are printed in black ink with a gold accent on gray card stock. The content includes highlights and, a first for Topps football cards, yearly statistics. A player cartoon is at the top. The first cards of two Steeler greats, Terry Bradshaw and Mean Joe Greene, appear in this set. Other notable Rookie Cards in this set are Hall of Famers Ken Houston and Willie Lanier.

	NRMT-MT	EXC	G-VG
COMPLETE SET (263)	450.00	200.00	55.00
COMMON CARD (1-132)	.75	.35	.09
COMMON CARD (133-263)	1.00	.45	.12
☐ 1 John Unitas	30.00	7.50	3.00
☐ 2 Jim Butler	.75	.35	.09
☐ 3 Marty Schottenheimer	14.00	6.25	1.75
☐ 4 Joe O'Donnell	.75	.35	.09
☐ 5 Tom Dempsey	1.25	.55	.16
☐ 6 Chuck Allen	.75	.35	.09
☐ 7 Ernie Kellerman	.75	.35	.09
☐ 8 Walt Garrison	2.00	.90	.25
☐ 9 Bill Van Heusen	.75	.35	.09
☐ 10 Lance Alworth	7.00	3.10	.85
☐ 11 Greg Landry	3.00	1.35	.35
☐ 12 Larry Krause	.75	.35	.09
☐ 13 Buck Buchanan	2.00	.90	.25
☐ 14 Roy Gerela	1.25	.55	.16
☐ 15 Clifton McNeil	.75	.35	.09
☐ 16 Bob Brown OT	1.25	.55	.16
☐ 17 Lloyd Mumphord	.75	.35	.09
☐ 18 Gary Cuozzo	1.25	.55	.16
☐ 19 Don Maynard	5.00	2.20	.60
☐ 20 Larry Wilson	2.00	.90	.25
☐ 21 Charlie Smith	.75	.35	.09
☐ 22 Ken Avery	.75	.35	.09
☐ 23 Billy Walik	.75	.35	.09
☐ 24 Jim Johnson	2.00	.90	.25
☐ 25 Dick Butkus	25.00	11.00	3.10
☐ 26 Charley Taylor UER (Misspelled Charlie on both sides)	4.00	1.80	.50
☐ 27 Checklist 1-132 UER (26 Charlie Taylor should be Charley)	8.00	2.00	.80
☐ 28 Lionel Aldridge	1.25	.55	.16
☐ 29 Billy Lothridge	.75	.35	.09
☐ 30 Terry Hanratty	1.25	.55	.16
☐ 31 Lee Roy Jordan	2.00	.90	.25
☐ 32 Rick Volk	.75	.35	.09
☐ 33 Howard Kindig	.75	.35	.09
☐ 34 Carl Garrett	1.25	.55	.16
☐ 35 Bobby Bell	2.00	.90	.25
☐ 36 Gene Hickerson	.75	.35	.09
☐ 37 Dave Parks	.75	.35	.09
☐ 38 Paul Martha	.75	.35	.09
☐ 39 George Blanda	16.00	7.25	2.00
☐ 40 Tom Woodeshick	.75	.35	.09
☐ 41 Alex Karras	3.00	1.35	.35
☐ 42 Rick Redman	.75	.35	.09
☐ 43 Zeke Moore	.75	.35	.09
☐ 44 Jack Snow	1.25	.55	.16
☐ 45 Larry Csonka	12.00	5.50	1.50
☐ 46 Karl Kassulke	.75	.35	.09
☐ 47 Jim Hart	1.50	.70	.19
☐ 48 Al Atkinson	.75	.35	.09
☐ 49 Horst Muhlmann	.75	.35	.09
☐ 50 Sonny Jurgensen	5.00	2.20	.60
☐ 51 Ron Johnson	1.25	.55	.16
☐ 52 Cas Banaszek	.75	.35	.09
☐ 53 Bubba Smith	8.00	3.60	1.00
☐ 54 Bobby Douglass	1.25	.55	.16
☐ 55 Willie Wood	2.00	.90	.25
☐ 56 Bake Turner	.75	.35	.09
☐ 57 Mike Morgan	.75	.35	.09
☐ 58 George Butch Byrd	1.25	.55	.16
☐ 59 Don Horn	1.25	.55	.16
☐ 60 Tommy Nobis	2.00	.90	.25
☐ 61 Jan Stenerud	4.00	1.80	.50
☐ 62 Altie Taylor	1.25	.55	.16
☐ 63 Gary Pettigrew	.75	.35	.09
☐ 64 Spike Jones	.75	.35	.09
☐ 65 Duane Thomas	1.25	.55	.16
☐ 66 Marty Domres	1.25	.55	.16
☐ 67 Dick Anderson	1.25	.55	.16
☐ 68 Ken Iman	.75	.35	.09
☐ 69 Miller Farr	.75	.35	.09
☐ 70 Daryle Lamonica	3.00	1.35	.35
☐ 71 Alan Page	12.00	5.50	1.50
☐ 72 Pat Matson	.75	.35	.09
☐ 73 Emerson Boozer	1.25	.55	.16
☐ 74 Pat Fischer	1.25	.55	.16
☐ 75 Gary Collins	1.25	.55	.16
☐ 76 John Fuqua	1.25	.55	.16
☐ 77 Bruce Gossett	.75	.35	.09
☐ 78 Ed O'Bradovich	.75	.35	.09
☐ 79 Bob Tucker	1.25	.55	.16
☐ 80 Mike Curtis	1.25	.55	.16
☐ 81 Rich Jackson	.75	.35	.09
☐ 82 Tom Janik	.75	.35	.09
☐ 83 Gale Gillingham	.75	.35	.09
☐ 84 Jim Mitchell	.75	.35	.09
☐ 85 Charlie Johnson	1.25	.55	.16
☐ 86 Edgar Chandler	.75	.35	.09
☐ 87 Cyril Pinder	.75	.35	.09
☐ 88 Johnny Robinson	1.25	.55	.16
☐ 89 Ralph Neely	1.25	.55	.16
☐ 90 Dan Abramowicz	1.25	.55	.16
☐ 91 Mercury Morris	5.00	2.20	.60
☐ 92 Steve DeLong	.75	.35	.09
☐ 93 Larry Stallings	.75	.35	.09
☐ 94 Tom Mack	2.50	1.10	.30
☐ 95 Hewritt Dixon	.75	.35	.09
☐ 96 Fred Cox	.75	.35	.09
☐ 97 Chris Hanburger	1.25	.55	.16
☐ 98 Gerry Philbin	.75	.35	.09
☐ 99 Ernie Wright	.75	.35	.09
☐ 100 John Brodie	4.00	1.80	.50
☐ 101 Tucker Frederickson	1.25	.55	.16
☐ 102 Bobby Walden	.75	.35	.09
☐ 103 Dick Gordon	1.25	.55	.16
☐ 104 Walter Johnson	.75	.35	.09
☐ 105 Mike Lucci	.75	.35	.09
☐ 106 Checklist 133-263 DP	6.00	1.50	.60
☐ 107 Ron Berger	.75	.35	.09
☐ 108 Dan Sullivan	.75	.35	.09
☐ 109 George Kunz	.75	.35	.09
☐ 110 Floyd Little	2.00	.90	.25
☐ 111 Zeke Bratkowski	1.25	.55	.16
☐ 112 Haven Moses	1.25	.55	.16
☐ 113 Ken Houston	20.00	9.00	2.50
☐ 114 Willie Lanier	20.00	9.00	2.50
☐ 115 Larry Brown	2.00	.90	.25
☐ 116 Tim Rossovich	.75	.35	.09
☐ 117 Errol Linden	.75	.35	.09
☐ 118 Mel Renfro	2.50	1.10	.30
☐ 119 Mike Garrett	1.25	.55	.16
☐ 120 Fran Tarkenton	14.00	6.25	1.75
☐ 121 Garo Yepremian	2.50	1.10	.30
☐ 122 Glen Condren	.75	.35	.09
☐ 123 Johnny Roland	.75	.35	.09
☐ 124 Dave Herman	.75	.35	.09
☐ 125 Merlin Olsen	3.00	1.35	.35
☐ 126 Doug Buffone	.75	.35	.09
☐ 127 Earl McCullouch	.75	.35	.09
☐ 128 Spider Lockhart	1.25	.55	.16
☐ 129 Ken Willard	1.25	.55	.16
☐ 130 Gene Washington	1.25	.55	.16
☐ 131 Mike Phipps	1.25	.55	.16
☐ 132 Andy Russell	1.25	.55	.16
☐ 133 Ray Nitschke	4.00	1.80	.50
☐ 134 Jerry Logan	1.00	.45	.12
☐ 135 MacArthur Lane	1.50	.70	.19
☐ 136 Jim Turner	1.00	.45	.12
☐ 137 Kent McCloughan	1.00	.45	.12
☐ 138 Paul Guidry	1.00	.45	.12
☐ 139 Otis Taylor	1.50	.70	.19
☐ 140 Virgil Carter	1.00	.45	.12
☐ 141 Joe Dawkins	1.00	.45	.12
☐ 142 Steve Preece	1.00	.45	.12
☐ 143 Mike Bragg	1.00	.45	.12
☐ 144 Bob Lilly	5.00	2.20	.60
☐ 145 Joe Kapp	1.50	.70	.19
☐ 146 Al Dodd	1.00	.45	.12
☐ 147 Nick Buoniconti	2.00	.90	.25
☐ 148 Speedy Duncan (Back mentions his trade to Redskins)	1.00	.45	.12
☐ 149 Cedrick Hardman	1.50	.70	.19
☐ 150 Gale Sayers	25.00	11.00	3.10
☐ 151 Jim Otto	2.50	1.10	.30
☐ 152 Billy Truax	1.50	.70	.19
☐ 153 John Elliott	1.00	.45	.12
☐ 154 Dick LeBeau	1.50	.70	.19
☐ 155 Bill Bergey	1.50	.70	.19
☐ 156 Terry Bradshaw	180.00	80.00	22.00
☐ 157 Leroy Kelly	6.00	2.70	.75
☐ 158 Paul Krause	2.00	.90	.25
☐ 159 Ted Vactor	1.00	.45	.12
☐ 160 Bob Griese	16.00	7.25	2.00
☐ 161 Ernie McMillan	1.00	.45	.12
☐ 162 Donny Anderson	1.50	.70	.19
☐ 163 John Pitts	1.00	.45	.12
☐ 164 Dave Costa	1.00	.45	.12
☐ 165 Gene Washington	1.50	.70	.19
☐ 166 John Zook	1.00	.45	.12
☐ 167 Pete Gogolak	1.00	.45	.12
☐ 168 Erich Barnes	1.00	.45	.12
☐ 169 Alvin Reed	1.00	.45	.12
☐ 170 Jim Nance	1.50	.70	.19
☐ 171 Craig Morton	2.00	.90	.25
☐ 172 Gary Garrison	1.50	.70	.19
☐ 173 Joe Scarpati	1.00	.45	.12
☐ 174 Adrian Young UER (Photo actually Rick Duncan)	1.00	.45	.12
☐ 175 John Mackey	3.00	1.35	.35
☐ 176 Mac Percival	1.00	.45	.12
☐ 177 Preston Pearson	5.00	2.20	.60
☐ 178 Fred Biletnikoff	7.00	3.10	.85
☐ 179 Mike Battle	1.00	.45	.12
☐ 180 Len Dawson	8.00	3.60	1.00
☐ 181 Les Josephson	1.50	.70	.19
☐ 182 Royce Berry	1.00	.45	.12
☐ 183 Herman Weaver	1.00	.45	.12
☐ 184 Norm Snead	1.50	.70	.19
☐ 185 Sam Brunelli	1.00	.45	.12
☐ 186 Jim Kiick	5.00	2.20	.60
☐ 187 Austin Denney	1.00	.45	.12
☐ 188 Roger Wehrli	1.50	.70	.19
☐ 189 Dave Wilcox	1.50	.70	.19
☐ 190 Bob Hayes	3.50	1.55	.45
☐ 191 Joe Morrison	1.50	.70	.19
☐ 192 Manny Sistrunk	1.50	.70	.19
☐ 193 Don Cockroft	1.50	.70	.19
☐ 194 Lee Bouggess	1.00	.45	.12
☐ 195 Bob Berry	1.00	.45	.12
☐ 196 Ron Sellers	1.00	.45	.12
☐ 197 George Webster	1.50	.70	.19
☐ 198 Hoyle Granger	1.00	.45	.12
☐ 199 Bob Vogel	1.00	.45	.12
☐ 200 Bart Starr	20.00	9.00	2.50
☐ 201 Mike Mercer	1.00	.45	.12
☐ 202 Dave Smith	1.00	.45	.12
☐ 203 Lee Roy Caffey	1.00	.45	.12
☐ 204 Mick Tingelhoff	1.50	.70	.19
☐ 205 Matt Snell	1.50	.70	.19
☐ 206 Jim Tyrer	1.00	.45	.12
☐ 207 Willie Brown	3.00	1.35	.35
☐ 208 Bob Johnson	1.00	.45	.12
☐ 209 Deacon Jones	3.00	1.35	.35
☐ 210 Charlie Sanders	1.50	.70	.19
☐ 211 Jake Scott	6.00	2.70	.75
☐ 212 Bob Anderson	1.00	.45	.12
☐ 213 Charlie Krueger	1.50	.70	.19
☐ 214 Jim Bakken	1.00	.45	.12
☐ 215 Harold Jackson	1.50	.70	.19
☐ 216 Bill Brundige	1.00	.45	.12
☐ 217 Calvin Hill	5.00	2.20	.60
☐ 218 Claude Humphrey	1.50	.70	.19
☐ 219 Glen Ray Hines	1.00	.45	.12
☐ 220 Bill Nelsen	1.50	.70	.19
☐ 221 Roy Hilton	1.00	.45	.12
☐ 222 Don Herrmann	1.00	.45	.12
☐ 223 John Bramlett	1.00	.45	.12
☐ 224 Ken Ellis	1.00	.45	.12
☐ 225 Dave Osborn	1.50	.70	.19
☐ 226 Edd Hargett	1.50	.70	.19
☐ 227 Gene Mingo	1.00	.45	.12
☐ 228 Larry Grantham	1.00	.45	.12
☐ 229 Dick Post	1.50	.70	.19
☐ 230 Roman Gabriel	2.00	.90	.25
☐ 231 Mike Eischeid	1.00	.45	.12
☐ 232 Jim Lynch	1.50	.70	.19
☐ 233 Lemar Parrish	1.50	.70	.19
☐ 234 Cecil Turner	1.00	.45	.12
☐ 235 Dennis Shaw	1.50	.70	.19
☐ 236 Mel Farr	1.50	.70	.19
☐ 237 Curt Knight	1.00	.45	.12
☐ 238 Chuck Howley	1.50	.70	.19
☐ 239 Bruce Taylor	1.00	.45	.12
☐ 240 Jerry LeVias	1.50	.70	.19
☐ 241 Bob Lurtsema	1.00	.45	.12
☐ 242 Earl Morrall	1.50	.70	.19
☐ 243 Kermit Alexander	1.00	.45	.12
☐ 244 Jackie Smith	2.00	.90	.25
☐ 245 Joe Greene	55.00	25.00	7.00
☐ 246 Harmon Wages	1.00	.45	.12
☐ 247 Errol Mann	1.50	.70	.19
☐ 248 Mike McCoy	1.00	.45	.12
☐ 249 Milt Morin	1.00	.45	.12
☐ 250 Joe Namath UER (In 9th line, Joe is spelled in small letters)	65.00	29.00	8.00
☐ 251 Jackie Burkett	1.00	.45	.12
☐ 252 Steve Chomyszak	1.00	.45	.12
☐ 253 Ed Sharockman	1.00	.45	.12
☐ 254 Robert Holmes	1.00	.45	.12
☐ 255 John Hadl	2.00	.90	.25
☐ 256 Cornell Gordon	1.00	.45	.12
☐ 257 Mark Moseley	2.50	1.10	.30
☐ 258 Gus Otto	1.00	.45	.12
☐ 259 Mike Taliaferro	1.00	.45	.12
☐ 260 O.J. Simpson	25.00	11.00	3.10
☐ 261 Paul Warfield	8.00	3.60	1.00
☐ 262 Jack Concannon	1.00	.45	.12
☐ 263 Tom Matte	3.00	.75	.30

1971 Topps Game

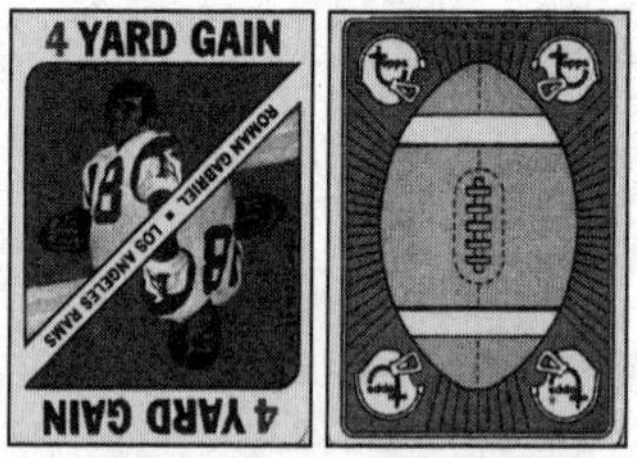

The 1971 Topps Game cards were issued as inserts with the 1971 regular issue football cards. The cards measure 2 1/4" by 3 1/4" with rounded corners. The cards can be used for a table game of football. The 52 player cards in the set are numbered and have light blue backs. The 53rd card (actually unnumbered) is a field position/first down marker which is used in the table game. Six of the cards in the set were double printed and are marked as DP in the checklist below. The key card in the set is Terry Bradshaw, appearing in his Rookie Card year.

	NRMT-MT	EXC	G-VG
COMPLETE SET (53)	125.00	55.00	15.50
COMMON CARD (1-53)	.60	.25	.07
☐ 1 Dick Butkus DP	10.00	4.50	1.25
☐ 2 Bob Berry DP	.60	.25	.07
☐ 3 Joe Namath DP	15.00	6.75	1.85
☐ 4 Mike Curtis	.60	.25	.07
☐ 5 Jim Nance	.60	.25	.07
☐ 6 Ron Berger	.60	.25	.07
☐ 7 O.J. Simpson	18.00	8.00	2.20
☐ 8 Haven Moses	.60	.25	.07
☐ 9 Tommy Nobis	1.25	.55	.16
☐ 10 Gale Sayers	12.00	5.50	1.50
☐ 11 Virgil Carter	.60	.25	.07
☐ 12 Andy Russell DP	.60	.25	.07
☐ 13 Bill Nelsen	.60	.25	.07
☐ 14 Gary Collins	.60	.25	.07
☐ 15 Duane Thomas	1.00	.45	.12
☐ 16 Bob Hayes	1.50	.70	.19
☐ 17 Floyd Little	1.25	.55	.16
☐ 18 Sam Brunelli	.60	.25	.07
☐ 19 Charlie Sanders	.60	.25	.07
☐ 20 Mike Lucci	.60	.25	.07
☐ 21 Gene Washington	1.00	.45	.12
☐ 22 Willie Wood	2.00	.90	.25
☐ 23 Jerry LeVias	.60	.25	.07
☐ 24 Charlie Johnson	.60	.25	.07
☐ 25 Len Dawson	4.00	1.80	.50
☐ 26 Bobby Bell	2.00	.90	.25
☐ 27 Merlin Olsen	2.50	1.10	.30
☐ 28 Roman Gabriel	1.50	.70	.19
☐ 29 Bob Griese	5.00	2.20	.60
☐ 30 Larry Csonka	5.00	2.20	.60
☐ 31 Dave Osborn	.60	.25	.07
☐ 32 Gene Washington	.60	.25	.07
☐ 33 Dan Abramowicz	.60	.25	.07
☐ 34 Tom Dempsey	.60	.25	.07
☐ 35 Fran Tarkenton	8.00	3.60	1.00

☐ 36 Clifton McNeil	.60	.25	.07
☐ 37 Johnny Unitas	15.00	6.75	1.85
☐ 38 Matt Snell	1.00	.45	.12
☐ 39 Daryle Lamonica	1.25	.55	.16
☐ 40 Hewritt Dixon	.60	.25	.07
☐ 41 Tom Woodeshick DP	.60	.25	.07
☐ 42 Harold Jackson	1.00	.45	.12
☐ 43 Terry Bradshaw	25.00	11.00	3.10
☐ 44 Ken Avery	.60	.25	.07
☐ 45 MacArthur Lane	.60	.25	.07
☐ 46 Larry Wilson	1.50	.70	.19
☐ 47 John Hadl	1.25	.55	.16
☐ 48 Lance Alworth	4.00	1.80	.50
☐ 49 John Brodie	2.50	1.10	.30
☐ 50 Bart Starr DP	8.00	3.60	1.00
☐ 51 Sonny Jurgensen	5.00	2.20	.60
☐ 52 Larry Brown	1.00	.45	.12
☐ NNO Field Marker	.60	.25	.07

1971 Topps Posters

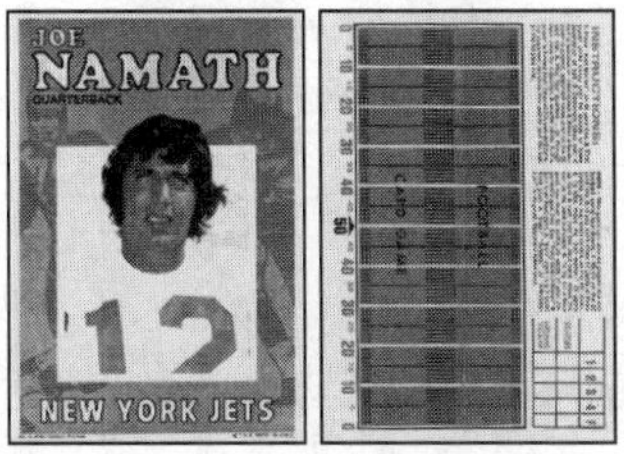

The 1971 Topps Football pin-up posters are a set of 32 paper inserts each folded twice for insertion into gum packs. The cards (small posters) measure 4 7/8" by 6 7/8". The lower left hand corner of the obverse contains the pin-up number while the back features a green simulated football field upon which a football card game could be played as well as the instructions to accompany the card insert game. Inexplicably the second half of the set seems to be somewhat more difficult to find.

	NRMT-MT	EXC	G-VG
COMPLETE SET (32)	100.00	45.00	12.50
COMMON CARD (1-16)	1.00	.45	.12
COMMON CARD (17-32)	2.00	.90	.25
☐ 1 Gene Washington	1.50	.70	.19
☐ 2 Andy Russell	1.50	.70	.19
☐ 3 Harold Jackson	1.50	.70	.19
☐ 4 Joe Namath	15.00	6.75	1.85
☐ 5 Fran Tarkenton	4.00	1.80	.50
☐ 6 Dave Osborn	1.00	.45	.12
☐ 7 Bob Griese	4.00	1.80	.50
☐ 8 Roman Gabriel	2.00	.90	.25
☐ 9 Jerry LeVias	1.00	.45	.12
☐ 10 Bart Starr	5.00	2.20	.60
☐ 11 Bob Hayes	2.00	.90	.25
☐ 12 Gale Sayers	6.00	2.70	.75
☐ 13 O.J. Simpson	10.00	4.50	1.25
☐ 14 Sam Brunelli	1.00	.45	.12
☐ 15 Jim Nance	1.50	.70	.19
☐ 16 Bill Nelsen	1.00	.45	.12
☐ 17 Sonny Jurgensen	5.00	2.20	.60
☐ 18 John Brodie	4.00	1.80	.50
☐ 19 Lance Alworth	5.00	2.20	.60
☐ 20 Larry Wilson	4.00	1.80	.50
☐ 21 Daryle Lamonica	3.00	1.35	.35
☐ 22 Dan Abramowicz	2.00	.90	.25
☐ 23 Gene Washington	2.00	.90	.25
☐ 24 Bobby Bell	4.00	1.80	.50
☐ 25 Merlin Olsen	4.00	1.80	.50
☐ 26 Charlie Sanders	2.00	.90	.25
☐ 27 Virgil Carter	2.00	.90	.25
☐ 28 Dick Butkus	8.00	3.60	1.00
☐ 29 Johnny Unitas	12.00	5.50	1.50
☐ 30 Tommy Nobis	3.00	1.35	.35
☐ 31 Floyd Little	3.00	1.35	.35
☐ 32 Larry Brown	2.00	.90	.25

1972 Topps

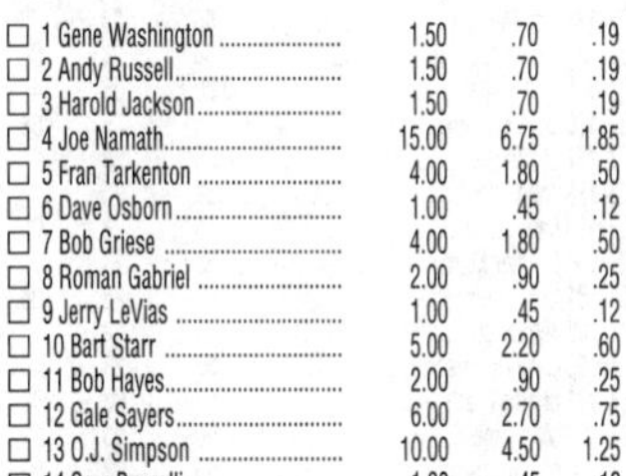

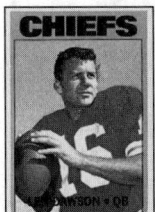

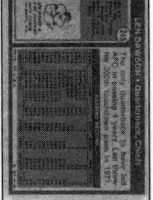

The 1972 Topps set contains 351 standard size cards that were issued in three series. The third series (264-351) is considerably more difficult to obtain than cards in the first two series. Card fronts are either horizontal and vertical and contain player photos that are bordered by a color that, for the most part, is part of the player's team color scheme. Vertical photos have team names at the top and horizontal photos have team names to the left. In either case, the player's name and position are at the bottom of the photo. The card backs are printed in blue and green on gray card stock. The backs have yearly statistics and a cartoon. Subsets include league leaders (1-8), In-Action cards (119-132, 250-263, 338-351), 1971 Playoffs (133-139) and All-Pro (264-287). The key Rookie Cards in this set are Lyle Alzado, L.C. Greenwood, Ted Hendricks, Charlie Joiner, Larry Little, Archie Manning, Jim Plunkett, John Riggins, Steve Spurrier, Roger Staubach, and Gene Upshaw.

	NRMT-MT	EXC	G-VG
COMPLETE SET (351)	2500.00	1100.00	300.00
COMMON CARD (1-132)	.50	.23	.06
COMMON CARD (133-263)	.60	.25	.07
COMMON CARD (264-351)	20.00	9.00	2.50
☐ 1 AFC Rushing Leaders	4.00	1.80	.50
Floyd Little			
Larry Csonka			
Marv Hubbard			
☐ 2 NFC Rushing Leaders	.75	.35	.09
John Brockington			
Steve Owens			
Willie Ellison			
☐ 3 AFC Passing Leaders	2.00	.90	.25
Bob Griese			
Len Dawson			
Virgil Carter			
☐ 4 NFC Passing Leaders	5.00	2.20	.60
Roger Staubach			
Greg Landry			
Bill Kilmer			
☐ 5 AFC Receiving Leaders	1.00	.45	.12
Fred Biletnikoff			
Otis Taylor			
Randy Vataha			
☐ 6 NFC Receiving Leaders	.75	.35	.09
Bob Tucker			
Ted Kwalick			
Harold Jackson			
Roy Jefferson			
☐ 7 AFC Scoring Leaders	.75	.35	.09
Garo Yepremian			
Jan Stenerud			
Jim O'Brien			
☐ 8 NFC Scoring Leaders	.75	.35	.09
Curt Knight			
Errol Mann			
Bruce Gossett			
☐ 9 Jim Kiick	1.50	.70	.19
☐ 10 Otis Taylor	1.00	.45	.12
☐ 11 Bobby Joe Green	.50	.23	.06
☐ 12 Ken Ellis	.50	.23	.06
☐ 13 John Riggins	20.00	9.00	2.50
☐ 14 Dave Parks	1.00	.45	.12
☐ 15 John Hadl	1.00	.45	.12
☐ 16 Ron Hornsby	.50	.23	.06
☐ 17 Chip Myers	.50	.23	.06
☐ 18 Bill Kilmer	1.00	.45	.12
☐ 19 Fred Hoaglin	.50	.23	.06
☐ 20 Carl Eller	1.25	.55	.16
☐ 21 Steve Zabel	.50	.23	.06
☐ 22 Vic Washington	.50	.23	.06
☐ 23 Len St. Jean	.50	.23	.06
☐ 24 Bill Thompson	1.00	.45	.12
☐ 25 Steve Owens	2.50	1.10	.30
☐ 26 Ken Burrough	1.00	.45	.12
☐ 27 Mike Clark	.50	.23	.06
☐ 28 Willie Brown	2.50	1.10	.30
☐ 29 Checklist 1-132	7.00	1.75	.70
☐ 30 Marlin Briscoe	.50	.23	.06
☐ 31 Jerry Logan	.50	.23	.06
☐ 32 Donny Anderson	1.00	.45	.12
☐ 33 Rich McGeorge	.50	.23	.06
☐ 34 Charlie Durkee	.50	.23	.06
☐ 35 Willie Lanier	4.00	1.80	.50
☐ 36 Chris Farasopoulos	.50	.23	.06
☐ 37 Ron Shanklin	.50	.23	.06
☐ 38 Forrest Blue	.50	.23	.06
☐ 39 Ken Reaves	.50	.23	.06
☐ 40 Roman Gabriel	1.50	.70	.19
☐ 41 Mac Percival	.50	.23	.06
☐ 42 Lem Barney	3.00	1.35	.35
☐ 43 Nick Buoniconti	1.50	.70	.19
☐ 44 Charlie Gogolak	.50	.23	.06
☐ 45 Bill Bradley	1.00	.45	.12
☐ 46 Joe Jones	.50	.23	.06
☐ 47 Dave Williams	.50	.23	.06
☐ 48 Pete Athas	.50	.23	.06
☐ 49 Virgil Carter	.50	.23	.06
☐ 50 Floyd Little	2.00	.90	.25
☐ 51 Curt Knight	.50	.23	.06
☐ 52 Bobby Maples	.50	.23	.06
☐ 53 Charlie West	.50	.23	.06
☐ 54 Marv Hubbard	1.00	.45	.12
☐ 55 Archie Manning	18.00	8.00	2.20
☐ 56 Jim O'Brien	1.00	.45	.12
☐ 57 Wayne Patrick	.50	.23	.06
☐ 58 Ken Bowman	.50	.23	.06
☐ 59 Roger Wehrli	1.00	.45	.12
☐ 60 Charlie Sanders UER	1.00	.45	.12
(Front WR, back TE)			
☐ 61 Jan Stenerud	2.00	.90	.25
☐ 62 Willie Ellison	.50	.23	.06
☐ 63 Walt Sweeney	.50	.23	.06
☐ 64 Ron Smith	.50	.23	.06
☐ 65 Jim Plunkett	16.00	7.25	2.00
☐ 66 Herb Adderley UER	2.00	.90	.25
(misspelled Adderly)			
☐ 67 Mike Reid	3.00	1.35	.35
☐ 68 Richard Caster	1.00	.45	.12
☐ 69 Dave Wilcox	1.00	.45	.12
☐ 70 Leroy Kelly	3.00	1.35	.35
☐ 71 Bob Lee	1.00	.45	.12
☐ 72 Verlon Biggs	.50	.23	.06
☐ 73 Henry Allison	.50	.23	.06
☐ 74 Steve Ramsey	.50	.23	.06
☐ 75 Claude Humphrey	1.00	.45	.12
☐ 76 Bob Grim	.50	.23	.06
☐ 77 John Fuqua	1.00	.45	.12
☐ 78 Ken Houston	4.00	1.80	.50
☐ 79 Checklist 133-263 DP	5.00	1.25	.50
☐ 80 Bob Griese	8.00	3.60	1.00
☐ 81 Lance Rentzel	1.00	.45	.12
☐ 82 Ed Podolak	1.00	.45	.12
☐ 83 Ike Hill	.50	.23	.06
☐ 84 George Farmer	.50	.23	.06
☐ 85 John Brockington	2.00	.90	.25
☐ 86 Jim Otto	2.00	.90	.25
☐ 87 Richard Neal	.50	.23	.06
☐ 88 Jim Hart	1.00	.45	.12
☐ 89 Bob Babich	.50	.23	.06
☐ 90 Gene Washington	1.00	.45	.12
☐ 91 John Zook	.50	.23	.06
☐ 92 Bobby Duhon	.50	.23	.06
☐ 93 Ted Hendricks	16.00	7.25	2.00
☐ 94 Rockne Freitas	.50	.23	.06
☐ 95 Larry Brown	2.00	.90	.25
☐ 96 Mike Phipps	1.00	.45	.12
☐ 97 Julius Adams	.50	.23	.06
☐ 98 Dick Anderson	1.00	.45	.12
☐ 99 Fred Willis	.50	.23	.06
☐ 100 Joe Namath	35.00	16.00	4.40
☐ 101 L.C. Greenwood	15.00	6.75	1.85
☐ 102 Mark Nordquist	.50	.23	.06
☐ 103 Robert Holmes	.50	.23	.06
☐ 104 Ron Yary	2.50	1.10	.30
☐ 105 Bob Hayes	2.00	.90	.25
☐ 106 Lyle Alzado	16.00	7.25	2.00
☐ 107 Bob Berry	.50	.23	.06
☐ 108 Phil Villapiano	1.00	.45	.12
☐ 109 Dave Elmendorf	.50	.23	.06
☐ 110 Gale Sayers	15.00	6.75	1.85
☐ 111 Jim Tyrer	1.00	.45	.12
☐ 112 Mel Gray	2.00	.90	.25
☐ 113 Gerry Philbin	.50	.23	.06
☐ 114 Bob James	.50	.23	.06
☐ 115 Garo Yepremian	1.00	.45	.12
☐ 116 Dave Robinson	1.00	.45	.12
☐ 117 Jeff Queen	.50	.23	.06
☐ 118 Norm Snead	1.00	.45	.12
☐ 119 Jim Nance IA	1.00	.45	.12
☐ 120 Terry Bradshaw IA	16.00	7.25	2.00
☐ 121 Jim Kiick IA	1.00	.45	.12
☐ 122 Roger Staubach IA	20.00	9.00	2.50
☐ 123 Bo Scott IA	1.00	.45	.12
☐ 124 John Brodie IA	1.50	.70	.19
☐ 125 Rick Volk IA	.50	.23	.06
☐ 126 John Riggins IA	6.00	2.70	.75
☐ 127 Bubba Smith IA	1.50	.70	.19
☐ 128 Roman Gabriel IA	1.00	.45	.12
☐ 129 Calvin Hill IA	1.00	.45	.12
☐ 130 Bill Nelsen IA	1.00	.45	.12
☐ 131 Tom Matte IA	1.00	.45	.12
☐ 132 Bob Griese IA	4.00	1.80	.50
☐ 133 AFC Semi-Final	1.00	.45	.12
Dolphins 27,			
Chiefs 24			
☐ 134 NFC Semi-Final	1.00	.45	.12
Cowboys 20,			
Vikings 12			
(Duane Thomas			
getting tackled)			
☐ 135 AFC Semi-Final	1.00	.45	.12
Colts 20,			
Browns 3			
(Don Nottingham)			
☐ 136 NFC Semi-Final	1.00	.45	.12
49ers 24,			
Redskins 20			
☐ 137 AFC Title Game	2.50	1.10	.30
Dolphins 21,			
Colts 0			
(Johnny Unitas			
getting tackled)			
☐ 138 NFC Title Game	2.00	.90	.25
Cowboys 14,			
49ers 3			
(Bob Lilly			
making tackle)			
☐ 139 Super Bowl	5.00	2.20	.60
Cowboys 24,			
Dolphins 3			
(Roger Staubach			
rolling out)			
☐ 140 Larry Csonka	8.00	3.60	1.00
☐ 141 Rick Volk	.60	.25	.07
☐ 142 Roy Jefferson	1.00	.45	.12
☐ 143 Raymond Chester	1.00	.45	.12
☐ 144 Bobby Douglass	1.00	.45	.12
☐ 145 Bob Lilly	4.00	1.80	.50
☐ 146 Harold Jackson	1.25	.55	.16
☐ 147 Pete Gogolak	.60	.25	.07
☐ 148 Art Malone	.60	.25	.07
☐ 149 Ed Flanagan	.60	.25	.07
☐ 150 Terry Bradshaw	50.00	22.00	6.25
☐ 151 MacArthur Lane	1.00	.45	.12
☐ 152 Jack Snow	1.00	.45	.12
☐ 153 Al Beauchamp	.60	.25	.07
☐ 154 Bob Anderson	.60	.25	.07
☐ 155 Ted Kwalick	1.00	.45	.12
☐ 156 Dan Pastorini	2.50	1.10	.30
☐ 157 Emmitt Thomas	1.00	.45	.12
☐ 158 Randy Vataha	1.00	.45	.12
☐ 159 Al Atkinson	.60	.25	.07
☐ 160 O.J. Simpson	16.00	7.25	2.00
☐ 161 Jackie Smith	1.50	.70	.19
☐ 162 Ernie Kellerman	.60	.25	.07
☐ 163 Dennis Partee	.60	.25	.07
☐ 164 Jake Kupp	.60	.25	.07
☐ 165 John Unitas	20.00	9.00	2.50
☐ 166 Clint Jones	.60	.25	.07
☐ 167 Paul Warfield	6.00	2.70	.75
☐ 168 Roland McDole	.60	.25	.07
☐ 169 Daryle Lamonica	2.00	.90	.25
☐ 170 Dick Butkus	16.00	7.25	2.00
☐ 171 Jim Butler	.60	.25	.07
☐ 172 Mike McCoy	.60	.25	.07
☐ 173 Dave Smith	.60	.25	.07
☐ 174 Greg Landry	1.50	.70	.19
☐ 175 Tom Dempsey	1.00	.45	.12
☐ 176 John Charles	.60	.25	.07
☐ 177 Bobby Bell	1.50	.70	.19
☐ 178 Don Horn	.60	.25	.07
☐ 179 Bob Trumpy	2.00	.90	.25
☐ 180 Duane Thomas	1.00	.45	.12
☐ 181 Merlin Olsen	2.50	1.10	.30
☐ 182 Dave Herman	.60	.25	.07
☐ 183 Jim Nance	1.00	.45	.12
☐ 184 Pete Beathard	.60	.25	.07
☐ 185 Bob Tucker	1.00	.45	.12
☐ 186 Gene Upshaw	15.00	6.75	1.85
☐ 187 Bo Scott	.60	.25	.07
☐ 188 J.D. Hill	1.00	.45	.12
☐ 189 Bruce Gossett	.60	.25	.07
☐ 190 Bubba Smith	4.00	1.80	.50
☐ 191 Edd Hargett	1.00	.45	.12
☐ 192 Gary Garrison	.60	.25	.07
☐ 193 Jake Scott	1.50	.70	.19
☐ 194 Fred Cox	.60	.25	.07
☐ 195 Sonny Jurgensen	4.00	1.80	.50
☐ 196 Greg Brezina	1.00	.45	.12
☐ 197 Ed O'Bradovich	.60	.25	.07
☐ 198 John Rowser	.60	.25	.07
☐ 199 Altie Taylor UER	.60	.25	.07
(Taylor misspelled as			
Tayor on front)			
☐ 200 Roger Staubach	180.00	80.00	22.00
☐ 201 Leroy Keyes	.60	.25	.07
☐ 202 Garland Boyette	.60	.25	.07
☐ 203 Tom Beer	.60	.25	.07
☐ 204 Buck Buchanan	1.50	.70	.19
☐ 205 Larry Wilson	1.50	.70	.19
☐ 206 Scott Hunter	1.00	.45	.12
☐ 207 Ron Johnson	1.00	.45	.12
☐ 208 Sam Brunelli	.60	.25	.07
☐ 209 Deacon Jones	2.50	1.10	.30
☐ 210 Fred Biletnikoff	6.00	2.70	.75
☐ 211 Bill Nelsen	1.00	.45	.12
☐ 212 George Nock	.60	.25	.07
☐ 213 Dan Abramowicz	1.00	.45	.12
☐ 214 Irv Goode	.60	.25	.07
☐ 215 Isiah Robertson	1.00	.45	.12
☐ 216 Tom Matte	1.00	.45	.12
☐ 217 Pat Fischer	1.00	.45	.12
☐ 218 Gene Washington	1.00	.45	.12
☐ 219 Paul Robinson	.60	.25	.07
☐ 220 John Brodie	3.50	1.55	.45
☐ 221 Manny Fernandez	1.50	.70	.19
☐ 222 Errol Mann	.60	.25	.07
☐ 223 Dick Gordon	.60	.25	.07
☐ 224 Calvin Hill	3.00	1.35	.35
☐ 225 Fran Tarkenton UER	12.00	5.50	1.50
(Plays in the Masters			
each spring)			
☐ 226 Jim Turner	.60	.25	.07
☐ 227 Jim Mitchell	1.00	.45	.12
☐ 228 Pete Liske	.60	.25	.07
☐ 229 Carl Garrett	1.00	.45	.12
☐ 230 Joe Greene	18.00	8.00	2.20
☐ 231 Gale Gillingham	.60	.25	.07
☐ 232 Norm Bulaich	.60	.25	.07
☐ 233 Spider Lockhart	1.00	.45	.12
☐ 234 Ken Willard	1.00	.45	.12
☐ 235 George Blanda	12.00	5.50	1.50
☐ 236 Wayne Mulligan	.60	.25	.07
☐ 237 Dave Lewis	.60	.25	.07
☐ 238 Dennis Shaw	.60	.25	.07
☐ 239 Fair Hooker	1.00	.45	.12
☐ 240 Larry Little	14.00	6.25	1.75
☐ 241 Mike Garrett	1.00	.45	.12
☐ 242 Glen Ray Hines	.60	.25	.07
☐ 243 Myron Pottios	.60	.25	.07
☐ 244 Charlie Joiner	20.00	9.00	2.50
☐ 245 Len Dawson	6.00	2.70	.75
☐ 246 W.K. Hicks	.60	.25	.07
☐ 247 Les Josephson	1.00	.45	.12
☐ 248 Lance Alworth UER	6.00	2.70	.75
(Front TE, back WR)			

249 Frank Nunley	.60	.25	.07
250 Mel Farr IA	.60	.25	.07
251 Johnny Unitas IA	8.00	3.60	1.00
252 George Farmer IA	.60	.25	.07
253 Duane Thomas IA	1.00	.45	.12
254 John Hadl IA	1.00	.45	.12
255 Vic Washington IA	.60	.25	.07
256 Don Horn IA	.60	.25	.07
257 L.C. Greenwood IA	3.00	1.35	.35
258 Bob Lee IA	.60	.25	.07
259 Larry Csonka IA	4.00	1.80	.50
260 Mike McCoy IA	.60	.25	.07
261 Greg Landry IA	1.00	.45	.12
262 Ray May IA	.60	.25	.07
263 Bobby Douglass IA	1.00	.45	.12
264 Charlie Sanders AP	30.00	13.50	3.70
265 Ron Yary AP	30.00	13.50	3.70
266 Rayfield Wright AP	30.00	13.50	3.70
267 Larry Little AP	35.00	16.00	4.40
268 John Niland AP	30.00	13.50	3.70
269 Forrest Blue AP	30.00	13.50	3.70
270 Otis Taylor AP	30.00	13.50	3.70
271 Paul Warfield AP	75.00	34.00	9.50
272 Bob Griese AP	80.00	36.00	10.00
273 John Brockington AP	30.00	13.50	3.70
274 Floyd Little AP	30.00	13.50	3.70
275 Garo Yepremian AP	30.00	13.50	3.70
276 Jerrel Wilson AP	20.00	9.00	2.50
277 Carl Eller AP	30.00	13.50	3.70
278 Bubba Smith AP	45.00	20.00	5.50
279 Alan Page AP	45.00	20.00	5.50
280 Bob Lilly AP	65.00	29.00	8.00
281 Ted Hendricks AP	55.00	25.00	7.00
282 Dave Wilcox AP	30.00	13.50	3.70
283 Willie Lanier AP	35.00	16.00	4.40
284 Jim Johnson AP	30.00	13.50	3.70
285 Willie Brown AP	35.00	16.00	4.40
286 Bill Bradley AP	30.00	13.50	3.70
287 Ken Houston AP	35.00	16.00	4.40
288 Mel Farr	25.00	11.00	3.10
289 Kermit Alexander	20.00	9.00	2.50
290 John Gilliam	25.00	11.00	3.10
291 Steve Spurrier	150.00	70.00	19.00
292 Walter Johnson	20.00	9.00	2.50
293 Jack Pardee	25.00	11.00	3.10
294 Checklist 264-351 UER (334 Charlie Taylor should be Charley)	90.00	22.00	9.00
295 Winston Hill	20.00	9.00	2.50
296 Hugo Hollas	20.00	9.00	2.50
297 Ray May	20.00	9.00	2.50
298 Jim Bakken	25.00	11.00	3.10
299 Larry Carwell	20.00	9.00	2.50
300 Alan Page	55.00	25.00	7.00
301 Walt Garrison	25.00	11.00	3.10
302 Mike Lucci	25.00	11.00	3.10
303 Nemiah Wilson	20.00	9.00	2.50
304 Carroll Dale	25.00	11.00	3.10
305 Jim Kanicki	20.00	9.00	2.50
306 Preston Pearson	30.00	13.50	3.70
307 Lemar Parrish	25.00	11.00	3.10
308 Earl Morrall	25.00	11.00	3.10
309 Tommy Nobis	25.00	11.00	3.10
310 Rich Jackson	20.00	9.00	2.50
311 Doug Cunningham	20.00	9.00	2.50
312 Jim Marsalis	20.00	9.00	2.50
313 Jim Beirne	20.00	9.00	2.50
314 Tom McNeill	20.00	9.00	2.50
315 Milt Morin	20.00	9.00	2.50
316 Rayfield Wright	25.00	11.00	3.10
317 Jerry LeVias	25.00	11.00	3.10
318 Travis Williams	25.00	11.00	3.10
319 Edgar Chandler	20.00	9.00	2.50
320 Bob Wallace	20.00	9.00	2.50
321 Delles Howell	20.00	9.00	2.50
322 Emerson Boozer	25.00	11.00	3.10
323 George Atkinson	25.00	11.00	3.10
324 Mike Montler	20.00	9.00	2.50
325 Randy Johnson	25.00	11.00	3.10
326 Mike Curtis UER (Text on back states he was named Super Bowl MVP in 1972. Chuck Howley won the award)	25.00	11.00	3.10
327 Miller Farr	20.00	9.00	2.50
328 Horst Muhlmann	20.00	9.00	2.50
329 John Niland	25.00	11.00	3.10
330 Andy Russell	25.00	11.00	3.10
331 Mercury Morris	35.00	16.00	4.40
332 Jim Johnson	30.00	13.50	3.70
333 Jerrel Wilson	20.00	9.00	2.50
334 Charley Taylor UER (Misspelled Charlie on both sides)	40.00	18.00	5.00
335 Dick LeBeau	25.00	11.00	3.10
336 Jim Marshall	30.00	13.50	3.70
337 Tom Mack	25.00	11.00	3.10
338 Steve Spurrier IA	80.00	36.00	10.00
339 Floyd Little IA	25.00	11.00	3.10
340 Len Dawson IA	45.00	20.00	5.50
341 Dick Butkus IA	80.00	36.00	10.00
342 Larry Brown IA	25.00	11.00	3.10
343 Joe Namath IA	350.00	160.00	45.00
344 Jim Turner IA	20.00	9.00	2.50
345 Doug Cunningham IA	20.00	9.00	2.50
346 Edd Hargett IA	20.00	9.00	2.50
347 Steve Owens IA	20.00	9.00	2.50
348 George Blanda IA	50.00	22.00	6.25
349 Ed Podolak IA	20.00	9.00	2.50
350 Rich Jackson IA	20.00	9.00	2.50
351 Ken Willard IA	35.00	16.00	4.40

1973 Topps

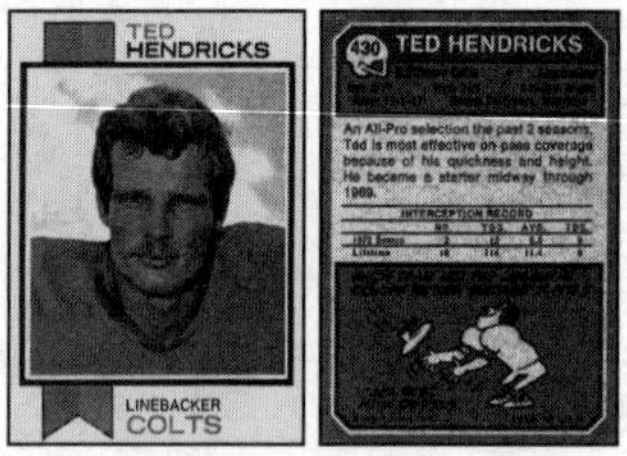

The 1973 set marks the first of ten years in a row that Topps produced a 528-card football standard-size set issued in a single series. The fronts have the players name at the top and position and team name at the bottom. The player's first name and team name are in a color that corresponds to one of the colors in a small banner-like design that emanates from the photo. The card backs are printed in blue ink with a red background on gray card stock. Highlights and statistics are accompanied by a cartoon and trivia question and answer. The first six cards in the set are statistical league leader cards. Cards 133-139 show the results of the previous season's playoff games. Cards 265-267 are Kid Pictures (KP) showing the player in a boyhood photo. Rookie Cards include this set are Ken Anderson, Al Cowlings, Dan Dierdorf, Jack Ham, Franco Harris, Jim Langer, Art Shell, Ken Stabler, and Jack Youngblood. An uncut sheet of team checklist cards was also available via a mail-in offer on wax pack wrappers.

	NRMT-MT	EXC	G-VG
COMPLETE SET (528)	400.00	180.00	50.00
COMMON CARD (1-528)	.50	.23	.06
1 Rushing Leaders Larry Brown O.J. Simpson	6.00	1.50	.60
2 Passing Leaders Norm Snead Earl Morrall	.75	.35	.09
3 Receiving Leaders UER Harold Jackson Fred Biletnikoff (Charley Taylor mis- spelled as Charlie)	.75	.35	.09
4 Scoring Leaders Chester Marcol Bobby Howfield	.75	.35	.09
5 Interception Leaders Bill Bradley Mike Sensibaugh	.75	.35	.09
6 Punting Leaders Dave Chapple Jerrel Wilson	.75	.35	.09
7 Bob Trumpy	1.00	.45	.12
8 Mel Tom	.50	.23	.06
9 Clarence Ellis	.50	.23	.06
10 John Niland	.50	.23	.06
11 Randy Jackson	.50	.23	.06
12 Greg Landry	1.00	.45	.12
13 Cid Edwards	.50	.23	.06
14 Phil Olsen	.50	.23	.06
15 Terry Bradshaw	25.00	11.00	3.10
16 Al Cowlings	1.00	.45	.12
17 Walker Gillette	.50	.23	.06
18 Bob Atkins	.50	.23	.06
19 Diron Talbert	.50	.23	.06
20 Jim Johnson	1.00	.45	.12
21 Howard Twilley	.75	.35	.09
22 Dick Enderle	.50	.23	.06
23 Wayne Colman	.50	.23	.06
24 John Schmitt	.50	.23	.06
25 George Blanda	10.00	4.50	1.25
26 Milt Morin	.50	.23	.06
27 Mike Current	.50	.23	.06
28 Rex Kern	.50	.23	.06
29 MacArthur Lane	.75	.35	.09
30 Alan Page	3.00	1.35	.35
31 Randy Vataha	.50	.23	.06
32 Jim Kearney	.50	.23	.06
33 Steve Smith	.50	.23	.06
34 Ken Anderson	16.00	7.25	2.00
35 Calvin Hill	2.00	.90	.25
36 Andy Maurer	.50	.23	.06
37 Joe Taylor	.50	.23	.06
38 Deacon Jones	2.00	.90	.25
39 Mike Weger	.50	.23	.06
40 Roy Gerela	.75	.35	.09
41 Les Josephson	.50	.23	.06
42 Dave Washington	.50	.23	.06
43 Bill Curry	.75	.35	.09
44 Fred Heron	.50	.23	.06
45 John Brodie	3.50	1.55	.45
46 Roy Winston	.50	.23	.06
47 Mike Bragg	.50	.23	.06
48 Mercury Morris	1.50	.70	.19
49 Jim Files	.50	.23	.06
50 Gene Upshaw	3.00	1.35	.35
51 Hugo Hollas	.50	.23	.06
52 Rod Sherman	.50	.23	.06
53 Ron Snidow	.50	.23	.06
54 Steve Tannen	.50	.23	.06
55 Jim Carter	.50	.23	.06
56 Lydell Mitchell	1.50	.70	.19
57 Jack Rudnay	.50	.23	.06
58 Halvor Hagen	.50	.23	.06
59 Tom Dempsey	.75	.35	.09
60 Fran Tarkenton	10.00	4.50	1.25
61 Lance Alworth	5.00	2.20	.60
62 Vern Holland	.50	.23	.06
63 Steve DeLong	.50	.23	.06
64 Art Malone	.50	.23	.06
65 Isiah Robertson	.75	.35	.09
66 Jerry Rush	.50	.23	.06
67 Bryant Salter	.50	.23	.06
68 Checklist 1-132	5.00	1.25	.50
69 J.D. Hill	.50	.23	.06
70 Forrest Blue	.50	.23	.06
71 Myron Pottios	.50	.23	.06
72 Norm Thompson	.50	.23	.06
73 Paul Robinson	.50	.23	.06
74 Larry Grantham	.50	.23	.06
75 Manny Fernandez	.75	.35	.09
76 Kent Nix	.50	.23	.06
77 Art Shell	16.00	7.25	2.00
78 George Saimes	.50	.23	.06
79 Don Cockroft	.50	.23	.06
80 Bob Tucker	.75	.35	.09
81 Don McCauley	.50	.23	.06
82 Bob Brown DT	.50	.23	.06
83 Larry Carwell	.50	.23	.06
84 Mo Moorman	.50	.23	.06
85 John Gilliam	.75	.35	.09
86 Wade Key	.50	.23	.06
87 Ross Brupbacher	.50	.23	.06
88 Dave Lewis	.50	.23	.06
89 Franco Harris	50.00	22.00	6.25
90 Tom Mack	1.00	.45	.12
91 Mike Tilleman	.50	.23	.06
92 Carl Mauck	.50	.23	.06
93 Larry Hand	.50	.23	.06
94 Dave Foley	.50	.23	.06
95 Frank Nunley	.50	.23	.06
96 John Charles	.50	.23	.06
97 Jim Bakken	.50	.23	.06
98 Pat Fischer	.75	.35	.09
99 Randy Rasmussen	.50	.23	.06
100 Larry Csonka	5.00	2.20	.60
101 Mike Siani	.50	.23	.06
102 Tom Roussel	.50	.23	.06
103 Clarence Scott	.75	.35	.09
104 Charlie Johnson	.75	.35	.09
105 Rick Volk	.50	.23	.06
106 Willie Young	.50	.23	.06
107 Emmitt Thomas	.75	.35	.09
108 Jon Morris	.50	.23	.06
109 Clarence Williams	.50	.23	.06
110 Rayfield Wright	.75	.35	.09
111 Norm Bulaich	.50	.23	.06
112 Mike Eischeid	.50	.23	.06
113 Speedy Thomas	.50	.23	.06
114 Glen Holloway	.50	.23	.06
115 Jack Ham	30.00	13.50	3.70
116 Jim Nettles	.50	.23	.06
117 Errol Mann	.50	.23	.06
118 John Mackey	2.00	.90	.25
119 George Kunz	.50	.23	.06
120 Bob James	.50	.23	.06
121 Garland Boyette	.50	.23	.06
122 Mel Phillips	.50	.23	.06
123 Johnny Roland	.50	.23	.06
124 Doug Swift	.50	.23	.06
125 Archie Manning	4.00	1.80	.50
126 Dave Herman	.50	.23	.06
127 Carleton Oats	.50	.23	.06
128 Bill Van Heusen	.50	.23	.06
129 Rich Jackson	.50	.23	.06
130 Len Hauss	.75	.35	.09
131 Billy Parks	.50	.23	.06
132 Ray May	.50	.23	.06
133 NFC Semi-Final Cowboys 30, 49ers 28 (Roger Staubach dropping back)	3.50	1.55	.45
134 AFC Semi-Final Steelers 13, Raiders 7 (line play)	.75	.35	.09
135 NFC Semi-Final Redskins 16, Packers 3 (Redskins defense)	.75	.35	.09
136 AFC Semi-Final Dolphins 20, Browns 14 (Bob Griese handing off to Larry Csonka)	2.00	.90	.25
137 NFC Title Game Redskins 26, Cowboys 3 (Bill Kilmer handing off to Larry Brown)	1.50	.70	.19
138 AFC Title Game Dolphins 21, Steelers 17 (Miami defense stops John Fuqua)	.75	.35	.09
139 Super Bowl Dolphins 14, Redskins 7 (Miami defense)	1.50	.70	.19
140 Dwight White UER (College North Texas State, should be East Texas State)	2.00	.90	.25
141 Jim Marsalis	.50	.23	.06
142 Doug Van Horn	.50	.23	.06
143 Al Matthews	.50	.23	.06
144 Bob Windsor	.50	.23	.06
145 Dave Hampton	.50	.23	.06
146 Horst Muhlmann	.50	.23	.06
147 Wally Hilgenberg	.50	.23	.06
148 Ron Smith	.50	.23	.06
149 Coy Bacon	.75	.35	.09
150 Winston Hill	.50	.23	.06
151 Ron Jessie	.75	.35	.09
152 Ken Iman	.50	.23	.06
153 Ron Saul	.50	.23	.06
154 Jim Braxton	.75	.35	.09
155 Bubba Smith	2.50	1.10	.30
156 Gary Cuozzo	.75	.35	.09
157 Charlie Krueger	.75	.35	.09
158 Tim Foley	.75	.35	.09
159 Lee Roy Jordan	1.50	.70	.19
160 Bob Brown OT	.75	.35	.09
161 Margene Adkins	.50	.23	.06
162 Ron Widby	.50	.23	.06
163 Jim Houston	.50	.23	.06
164 Joe Dawkins	.50	.23	.06
165 L.C. Greenwood	4.00	1.80	.50
166 Richmond Flowers	.50	.23	.06
167 Curley Culp	1.00	.45	.12
168 Len St. Jean	.50	.23	.06
169 Walter Rock	.50	.23	.06
170 Bill Bradley	.75	.35	.09
171 Ken Riley	1.50	.70	.19
172 Rich Coady	.50	.23	.06
173 Don Hansen	.50	.23	.06
174 Lionel Aldridge	.50	.23	.06
175 Don Maynard	3.50	1.55	.45
176 Dave Osborn	.75	.35	.09
177 Jim Bailey	.50	.23	.06
178 John Pitts	.50	.23	.06
179 Dave Parks	.50	.23	.06
180 Chester Marcol	.50	.23	.06
181 Len Rohde	.50	.23	.06
182 Jeff Staggs	.50	.23	.06
183 Gene Hickerson	.50	.23	.06
184 Charlie Evans	.50	.23	.06
185 Mel Renfro	2.00	.90	.25
186 Marvin Upshaw	.50	.23	.06
187 George Atkinson	.75	.35	.09
188 Norm Evans	.75	.35	.09
189 Steve Ramsey	.50	.23	.06
190 Dave Chapple	.50	.23	.06
191 Gerry Mullins	.50	.23	.06
192 John Didion	.50	.23	.06
193 Bob Gladieux	.50	.23	.06
194 Don Hultz	.50	.23	.06
195 Mike Lucci	.50	.23	.06
196 John Wilbur	.50	.23	.06
197 George Farmer	.50	.23	.06
198 Tommy Casanova	.75	.35	.09
199 Russ Washington	.50	.23	.06
200 Claude Humphrey Tackling Roger Staubach	1.00	.45	.12
201 Pat Hughes	.50	.23	.06
202 Zeke Moore	.50	.23	.06
203 Chip Glass	.50	.23	.06
204 Glenn Ressler	.50	.23	.06
205 Willie Ellison	.75	.35	.09
206 John Leypoldt	.50	.23	.06
207 Johnny Fuller	.50	.23	.06
208 Bill Hayhoe	.50	.23	.06
209 Ed Bell	.50	.23	.06
210 Willie Brown	2.00	.90	.25
211 Carl Eller	1.00	.45	.12
212 Mark Nordquist	.50	.23	.06
213 Larry Willingham	.50	.23	.06
214 Nick Buoniconti	1.00	.45	.12
215 John Hadl	1.00	.45	.12
216 Jethro Pugh	1.00	.45	.12
217 Leroy Mitchell	.50	.23	.06
218 Billy Newsome	.50	.23	.06
219 John McMakin	.50	.23	.06
220 Larry Brown	1.00	.45	.12
221 Clarence Scott	.50	.23	.06
222 Paul Naumoff	.50	.23	.06
223 Ted Fritsch Jr.	.50	.23	.06
224 Checklist 133-264	5.00	1.25	.50
225 Dan Pastorini	1.00	.45	.12
226 Joe Beauchamp UER (Safety on front, Cornerback on back)	.50	.23	.06
227 Pat Matson	.50	.23	.06

□ 228 Tony McGee	.50	.23	.06
□ 229 Mike Phipps	.75	.35	.09
□ 230 Harold Jackson	1.00	.45	.12
□ 231 Willie Williams	.50	.23	.06
□ 232 Spike Jones	.50	.23	.06
□ 233 Jim Tyrer	.50	.23	.06
□ 234 Roy Hilton	.50	.23	.06
□ 235 Phil Villapiano	.75	.35	.09
□ 236 Charley Taylor UER (Misspelled Charlie on both sides)	3.50	1.55	.45
□ 237 Malcolm Snider	.50	.23	.06
□ 238 Vic Washington	.50	.23	.06
□ 239 Grady Alderman	.50	.23	.06
□ 240 Dick Anderson	.75	.35	.09
□ 241 Ron Yankowski	.50	.23	.06
□ 242 Billy Masters	.50	.23	.06
□ 243 Herb Adderley	2.00	.90	.25
□ 244 David Ray	.50	.23	.06
□ 245 John Riggins	8.00	3.60	1.00
□ 246 Mike Wagner	1.50	.70	.19
□ 247 Don Morrison	.50	.23	.06
□ 248 Earl McCullouch	.50	.23	.06
□ 249 Dennis Wirgowski	.50	.23	.06
□ 250 Chris Hanburger	.75	.35	.09
□ 251 Pat Sullivan	1.50	.70	.19
□ 252 Walt Sweeney	.50	.23	.06
□ 253 Willie Alexander	.50	.23	.06
□ 254 Doug Dressler	.50	.23	.06
□ 255 Walter Johnson	.50	.23	.06
□ 256 Ron Hornsby	.50	.23	.06
□ 257 Ben Hawkins	.50	.23	.06
□ 258 Donnie Green	.50	.23	.06
□ 259 Fred Hoaglin	.50	.23	.06
□ 260 Jerrel Wilson	.50	.23	.06
□ 261 Horace Jones	.50	.23	.06
□ 262 Woody Peoples	.50	.23	.06
□ 263 Jim Hill	.50	.23	.06
□ 264 John Fuqua	.50	.23	.06
□ 265 Donny Anderson KP	.75	.35	.09
□ 266 Roman Gabriel KP	1.00	.45	.12
□ 267 Mike Garrett KP	.75	.35	.09
□ 268 Rufus Mayes	.50	.23	.06
□ 269 Chip Myrtle	.50	.23	.06
□ 270 Bill Stanfill	.75	.35	.09
□ 271 Clint Jones	.50	.23	.06
□ 272 Miller Farr	.50	.23	.06
□ 273 Harry Schuh	.50	.23	.06
□ 274 Bob Hayes	2.00	.90	.25
□ 275 Bobby Douglass	.75	.35	.09
□ 276 Gus Hollomon	.50	.23	.06
□ 277 Del Williams	.50	.23	.06
□ 278 Julius Adams	.50	.23	.06
□ 279 Herman Weaver	.50	.23	.06
□ 280 Joe Greene	8.00	3.60	1.00
□ 281 Wes Chesson	.50	.23	.06
□ 282 Charlie Harraway	.50	.23	.06
□ 283 Paul Guidry	.50	.23	.06
□ 284 Terry Owens	.50	.23	.06
□ 285 Jan Stenerud	1.00	.45	.12
□ 286 Pete Athas	.50	.23	.06
□ 287 Dale Lindsey	.50	.23	.06
□ 288 Jack Tatum	8.00	3.60	1.00
□ 289 Floyd Little	2.00	.90	.25
□ 290 Bob Johnson	.50	.23	.06
□ 291 Tommy Hart	.50	.23	.06
□ 292 Tom Mitchell	.50	.23	.06
□ 293 Walt Patulski	.50	.23	.06
□ 294 Jim Skaggs	.50	.23	.06
□ 295 Bob Griese	6.00	2.70	.75
□ 296 Mike McCoy	.50	.23	.06
□ 297 Mel Gray	.75	.35	.09
□ 298 Bobby Bryant	.50	.23	.06
□ 299 Blaine Nye	.50	.23	.06
□ 300 Dick Butkus	12.00	5.50	1.50
□ 301 Charlie Cowan	.50	.23	.06
□ 302 Mark Lomas	.50	.23	.06
□ 303 Josh Ashton	.50	.23	.06
□ 304 Happy Feller	.50	.23	.06
□ 305 Ron Shanklin	.50	.23	.06
□ 306 Wayne Rasmussen	.50	.23	.06
□ 307 Jerry Smith	.50	.23	.06
□ 308 Ken Reaves	.50	.23	.06
□ 309 Ron East	.50	.23	.06
□ 310 Otis Taylor	1.00	.45	.12
□ 311 John Garlington	.50	.23	.06
□ 312 Lyle Alzado	4.00	1.80	.50
□ 313 Remi Prudhomme	.50	.23	.06
□ 314 Cornelius Johnson	.50	.23	.06
□ 315 Lemar Parrish	.75	.35	.09
□ 316 Jim Kiick	1.00	.45	.12
□ 317 Steve Zabel	.50	.23	.06
□ 318 Alden Roche	.50	.23	.06
□ 319 Tom Blanchard	.50	.23	.06
□ 320 Fred Biletnikoff	4.00	1.80	.50
□ 321 Ralph Neely	.75	.35	.09
□ 322 Dan Dierdorf	20.00	9.00	2.50
□ 323 Richard Caster	.75	.35	.09
□ 324 Gene Howard	.50	.23	.06
□ 325 Elvin Bethea	.75	.35	.09
□ 326 Carl Garrett	.75	.35	.09
□ 327 Ron Billingsley	.50	.23	.06
□ 328 Charlie West	.50	.23	.06
□ 329 Tom Neville	.50	.23	.06
□ 330 Ted Kwalick	.75	.35	.09
□ 331 Rudy Redmond	.50	.23	.06
□ 332 Henry Davis	.50	.23	.06
□ 333 John Zook	.50	.23	.06
□ 334 Jim Turner	.50	.23	.06
□ 335 Len Dawson	5.00	2.20	.60
□ 336 Bob Chandler	.75	.35	.09
□ 337 Al Beauchamp	.50	.23	.06
□ 338 Tom Matte	.75	.35	.09
□ 339 Paul Laaveg	.50	.23	.06
□ 340 Ken Ellis	.50	.23	.06
□ 341 Jim Langer	10.00	4.50	1.25
□ 342 Ron Porter	.50	.23	.06
□ 343 Jack Youngblood	12.00	5.50	1.50
□ 344 Cornell Green	1.00	.45	.12
□ 345 Marv Hubbard	.75	.35	.09
□ 346 Bruce Taylor	.50	.23	.06
□ 347 Sam Havrilak	.50	.23	.06
□ 348 Walt Sumner	.50	.23	.06
□ 349 Steve O'Neal	.50	.23	.06
□ 350 Ron Johnson	.75	.35	.09
□ 351 Rockne Freitas	.50	.23	.06
□ 352 Larry Stallings	.50	.23	.06
□ 353 Jim Cadile	.50	.23	.06
□ 354 Ken Burrough	.75	.35	.09
□ 355 Jim Plunkett	4.00	1.80	.50
□ 356 Dave Long	.50	.23	.06
□ 357 Ralph Anderson	.50	.23	.06
□ 358 Checklist 265-396	5.00	1.25	.50
□ 359 Gene Washington	.75	.35	.09
□ 360 Dave Wilcox	.75	.35	.09
□ 361 Paul Smith	.50	.23	.06
□ 362 Alvin Wyatt	.50	.23	.06
□ 363 Charlie Smith	.50	.23	.06
□ 364 Royce Berry	.50	.23	.06
□ 365 Dave Elmendorf	.50	.23	.06
□ 366 Scott Hunter	.75	.35	.09
□ 367 Bob Kuechenberg	2.00	.90	.25
□ 368 Pete Gogolak	.50	.23	.06
□ 369 Dave Edwards	.50	.23	.06
□ 370 Lem Barney	2.50	1.10	.30
□ 371 Verlon Biggs	.50	.23	.06
□ 372 John Reaves	.50	.23	.06
□ 373 Ed Podolak	.75	.35	.09
□ 374 Chris Farasopoulos	.50	.23	.06
□ 375 Gary Garrison	.50	.23	.06
□ 376 Tom Funchess	.50	.23	.06
□ 377 Bobby Joe Green	.50	.23	.06
□ 378 Don Brumm	.50	.23	.06
□ 379 Jim O'Brien	.50	.23	.06
□ 380 Paul Krause	1.00	.45	.12
□ 381 Leroy Kelly	2.50	1.10	.30
□ 382 Ray Mansfield	.50	.23	.06
□ 383 Dan Abramowicz	.75	.35	.09
□ 384 John Outlaw	.50	.23	.06
□ 385 Tommy Nobis	1.50	.70	.19
□ 386 Tom Domres	.50	.23	.06
□ 387 Ken Willard	.75	.35	.09
□ 388 Mike Stratton	.50	.23	.06
□ 389 Fred Dryer	2.50	1.10	.30
□ 390 Jake Scott	1.00	.45	.12
□ 391 Rich Houston	.50	.23	.06
□ 392 Virgil Carter	.50	.23	.06
□ 393 Tody Smith	.50	.23	.06
□ 394 Ernie Calloway	.50	.23	.06
□ 395 Charlie Sanders	.75	.35	.09
□ 396 Fred Willis	.50	.23	.06
□ 397 Curt Knight	.50	.23	.06
□ 398 Nemiah Wilson	.50	.23	.06
□ 399 Carroll Dale	.75	.35	.09
□ 400 Joe Namath	25.00	11.00	3.10
□ 401 Wayne Mulligan	.50	.23	.06
□ 402 Jim Harrison	.50	.23	.06
□ 403 Tim Rossovich	.50	.23	.06
□ 404 David Lee	.50	.23	.06
□ 405 Frank Pitts	.50	.23	.06
□ 406 Jim Marshall	1.25	.55	.16
□ 407 Bob Brown TE	.50	.23	.06
□ 408 John Rowser	.50	.23	.06
□ 409 Mike Montler	.50	.23	.06
□ 410 Willie Lanier	2.00	.90	.25
□ 411 Bill Bell	.50	.23	.06
□ 412 Cedrick Hardman	.50	.23	.06
□ 413 Bob Anderson	.50	.23	.06
□ 414 Earl Morrall	1.00	.45	.12
□ 415 Ken Houston	2.00	.90	.25
□ 416 Jack Snow	.75	.35	.09
□ 417 Dick Cunningham	.50	.23	.06
□ 418 Greg Larson	.50	.23	.06
□ 419 Mike Bass	.75	.35	.09
□ 420 Mike Reid	1.50	.70	.19
□ 421 Walt Garrison	1.00	.45	.12
□ 422 Pete Liske	.50	.23	.06
□ 423 Jim Yarbrough	.50	.23	.06
□ 424 Rich McGeorge	.50	.23	.06
□ 425 Bobby Howfield	.50	.23	.06
□ 426 Pete Banaszak	.75	.35	.09
□ 427 Willie Holman	.50	.23	.06
□ 428 Dale Hackbart	.50	.23	.06
□ 429 Fair Hooker	.50	.23	.06
□ 430 Ted Hendricks	5.00	2.20	.60
□ 431 Mike Garrett	.75	.35	.09
□ 432 Glen Ray Hines	.50	.23	.06
□ 433 Fred Cox	.50	.23	.06
□ 434 Bobby Walden	.50	.23	.06
□ 435 Bobby Bell	1.25	.55	.16
□ 436 Dave Rowe	.50	.23	.06
□ 437 Bob Berry	.50	.23	.06
□ 438 Bill Thompson	.50	.23	.06
□ 439 Jim Beirne	.50	.23	.06
□ 440 Larry Little	3.00	1.35	.35
□ 441 Rocky Thompson	.50	.23	.06
□ 442 Brig Owens	.50	.23	.06
□ 443 Richard Neal	.50	.23	.06
□ 444 Al Nelson	.50	.23	.06
□ 445 Chip Myers	.50	.23	.06
□ 446 Ken Bowman	.50	.23	.06
□ 447 Jim Purnell	.50	.23	.06
□ 448 Altie Taylor	.50	.23	.06
□ 449 Linzy Cole	.50	.23	.06
□ 450 Bob Lilly	4.00	1.80	.50
□ 451 Charlie Ford	.50	.23	.06
□ 452 Milt Sunde	.50	.23	.06
□ 453 Doug Wyatt	.50	.23	.06
□ 454 Don Nottingham	.75	.35	.09
□ 455 John Unitas	16.00	7.25	2.00
□ 456 Frank Lewis	.75	.35	.09
□ 457 Roger Wehrli	.75	.35	.09
□ 458 Jim Cheyunski	.50	.23	.06
□ 459 Jerry Sherk	.75	.35	.09
□ 460 Gene Washington	.75	.35	.09
□ 461 Jim Otto	1.50	.70	.19
□ 462 Ed Budde	.50	.23	.06
□ 463 Jim Mitchell	.75	.35	.09
□ 464 Emerson Boozer	.75	.35	.09
□ 465 Garo Yepremian	1.00	.45	.12
□ 466 Pete Duranko	.50	.23	.06
□ 467 Charlie Joiner	8.00	3.60	1.00
□ 468 Spider Lockhart	.75	.35	.09
□ 469 Marty Domres	.50	.23	.06
□ 470 John Brockington	1.00	.45	.12
□ 471 Ed Flanagan	.50	.23	.06
□ 472 Roy Jefferson	.75	.35	.09
□ 473 Julian Fagan	.50	.23	.06
□ 474 Bill Brown	.75	.35	.09
□ 475 Roger Staubach	40.00	18.00	5.00
□ 476 Jan White	.50	.23	.06
□ 477 Pat Holmes	.50	.23	.06
□ 478 Bob DeMarco	.50	.23	.06
□ 479 Merlin Olsen	2.50	1.10	.30
□ 480 Andy Russell	1.00	.45	.12
□ 481 Steve Spurrier	15.00	6.75	1.85
□ 482 Nate Ramsey	.50	.23	.06
□ 483 Dennis Partee	.50	.23	.06
□ 484 Jerry Simmons	.50	.23	.06
□ 485 Donny Anderson	1.00	.45	.12
□ 486 Ralph Baker	.50	.23	.06
□ 487 Ken Stabler	65.00	29.00	8.00
□ 488 Ernie McMillan	.50	.23	.06
□ 489 Ken Burrow	.50	.23	.06
□ 490 Jack Gregory	.50	.23	.06
□ 491 Larry Seiple	.75	.35	.09
□ 492 Mick Tingelhoff	.75	.35	.09
□ 493 Craig Morton	1.25	.55	.16
□ 494 Cecil Turner	.50	.23	.06
□ 495 Steve Owens	1.00	.45	.12
□ 496 Rickie Harris	.50	.23	.06
□ 497 Buck Buchanan	1.25	.55	.16
□ 498 Checklist 397-528	5.00	1.25	.50
□ 499 Billy Kilmer	1.00	.45	.12
□ 500 O.J. Simpson	15.00	6.75	1.85
□ 501 Bruce Gossett	.50	.23	.06
□ 502 Art Thoms	.50	.23	.06
□ 503 Larry Kaminski	.50	.23	.06
□ 504 Larry Smith	.50	.23	.06
□ 505 Bruce Van Dyke	.50	.23	.06
□ 506 Alvin Reed	.50	.23	.06
□ 507 Delles Howell	.50	.23	.06
□ 508 Leroy Keyes	.50	.23	.06
□ 509 Bo Scott	.75	.35	.09
□ 510 Ron Yary	.75	.35	.09
□ 511 Paul Warfield	5.00	2.20	.60
□ 512 Mac Percival	.50	.23	.06
□ 513 Essex Johnson	.50	.23	.06
□ 514 Jackie Smith	1.25	.55	.16
□ 515 Norm Snead	1.00	.45	.12
□ 516 Charlie Stukes	.50	.23	.06
□ 517 Reggie Rucker	.75	.35	.09
□ 518 Bill Sandeman UER (Should be a period between run and he instead of a comma)	.50	.23	.06
□ 519 Mel Farr	.75	.35	.09
□ 520 Raymond Chester	.75	.35	.09
□ 521 Fred Carr	.75	.35	.09
□ 522 Jerry LeVias	.75	.35	.09
□ 523 Jim Strong	.50	.23	.06
□ 524 Roland McDole	.50	.23	.06
□ 525 Dennis Shaw	.50	.23	.06
□ 526 Dave Manders	.50	.23	.06
□ 527 Skip Vanderbundt	.50	.23	.06
□ 528 Mike Sensibaugh	1.50	.35	.15

1973 Topps Team Checklists

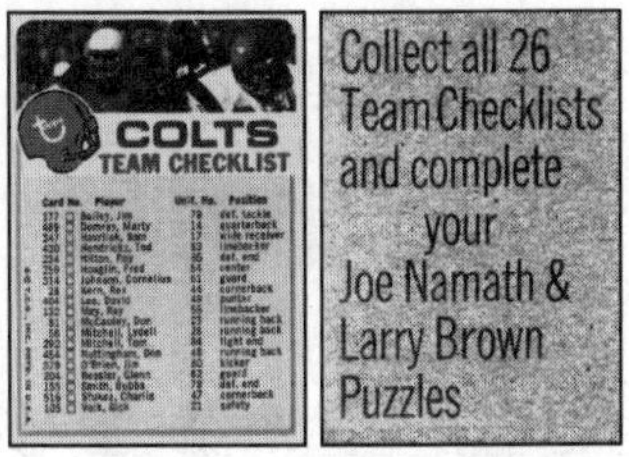

The 1973 Topps Team Checklist set contains 26 checklist cards, one for each of the 26 NFL teams. The cards measure 2 1/2" by 3 1/2" and were inserted into regular issue 1973 Topps football wax packs. The fronts show action scenes at the top of the card and a Topps helmet with the team name at its immediate right. The bottom portion of the card contains the checklist, complete with boxes in which to place check marks. Uniform numbers and positions are also given with the player's name. The backs of the cards form puzzles of Joe Namath and Larry Brown. These unnumbered cards are numbered below for convenience in alphabetical order by team name. The cards can all be found with one or two asterisks on the front.

	NRMT-MT	EXC	G-VG
COMPLETE SET (26)	75.00	19.00	7.50
COMMON TEAM (1-26)	3.00	.75	.30
□ 1 Atlanta Falcons	3.00	.75	.30
□ 2 Baltimore Colts	3.00	.75	.30
□ 3 Buffalo Bills	3.00	.75	.30
□ 4 Chicago Bears	3.00	.75	.30
□ 5 Cincinnati Bengals	3.00	.75	.30
□ 6 Cleveland Browns	3.00	.75	.30
□ 7 Dallas Cowboys	5.00	1.25	.50
□ 8 Denver Broncos	3.00	.75	.30
□ 9 Detroit Lions	3.00	.75	.30
□ 10 Green Bay Packers	4.00	1.00	.40
□ 11 Houston Oilers	3.00	.75	.30
□ 12 Kansas City Chiefs	3.00	.75	.30
□ 13 Los Angeles Rams	3.00	.75	.30
□ 14 Miami Dolphins	4.00	1.00	.40
□ 15 Minnesota Vikings	3.00	.75	.30
□ 16 New England Patriots	3.00	.75	.30
□ 17 New Orleans Saints	3.00	.75	.30
□ 18 New York Giants	3.00	.75	.30
□ 19 New York Jets	3.00	.75	.30
□ 20 Oakland Raiders	5.00	1.25	.50
□ 21 Philadelphia Eagles	3.00	.75	.30
□ 22 Pittsburgh Steelers	4.00	1.00	.40
□ 23 St. Louis Cardinals	3.00	.75	.30
□ 24 San Diego Chargers	3.00	.75	.30
□ 25 San Francisco 49ers	4.00	1.00	.40
□ 26 Washington Redskins	4.00	1.00	.40

1974 Topps

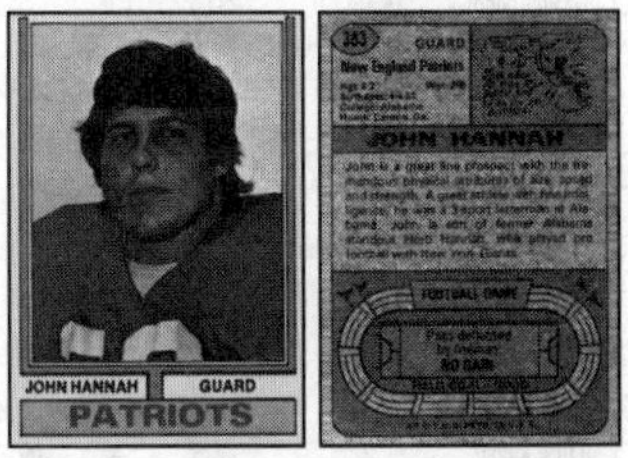

The 1974 Topps set contains 528 standard-size cards. Card fronts have photos that are bordered on either side by uprights of a goal post. The goal post has a different color depending upon the player's team. The team name is in a color bar at the bottom. The player's name and position are beneath the crossbar. The card backs are printed in blue and yellow on gray card stock and include statistics and highlights. The bottom of the back provides part of a simulated football game which could be played by drawing cards. Subsets inlcude All-Pro (121-144), league leaders (328-333) and post-season action (460-463). This set contains the Rookie Cards of Harold Carmichael, Chuck Foreman, Ray Guy, John Hannah, Bert Jones, Ed Marinaro, John Matuszak and Ahmad Rashad. An uncut sheet of team checklist cards was also available via a mail-in offer on wax pack wrappers. There are a number of cards with copyright variations. On cards 26, 129, 130, 156, 162, 219, 265-364, 367-422, and 424-528, there are two asterisks with the copyright line. The rest of the cards have one asterisk. Topps also printed a very similar (and very confusing) 50-card set for Parker Brothers in early 1974 as part of its Pro Draft football board game. The only players in this set (game) were offensive players (with an emphasis on the skill positions) that were among the first 132 cards in the 1974 Topps set. There are several notable differences between these Parker Brothers Pro Draft cards and the basic issue. Those cards ending with 1972 statistics on the back (unlike the basic issue which go through 1973) are Parker Brothers cards. Parker Brothers game cards can also be distinguished by the presence of two asterisks rather than one on the copyright line. However, as noted above, there are cards in the regular 1974 Topps set that do have two asterisks but are not Parker Brothers Pro Draft cards. In fact, variations 23A, 49A, 116A, 124A, 126A, and 127A listed in the checklist below were issued with a later version of the Pro Draft game creating two variations of the set. The backs of the latter issued 50 cards were updated to include 1973 statistics.

	NRMT-MT	EXC	G-VG
COMPLETE SET (528)	300.00	135.00	38.00
COMMON CARD (1-528)	.40	.18	.05
□ 1 O.J. Simpson RB UER (Text on back says 100 years, should say 100 yards)	20.00	5.00	2.00

☐ 2 Blaine Nye	.40	.18	.05
☐ 3 Don Hansen	.40	.18	.05
☐ 4 Ken Bowman	.40	.18	.05
☐ 5 Carl Eller	.75	.35	.09
☐ 6 Jerry Smith	.40	.18	.05
☐ 7 Ed Podolak	.40	.18	.05
☐ 8 Mel Gray	.75	.35	.09
☐ 9 Pat Matson	.40	.18	.05
☐ 10 Floyd Little	1.50	.70	.19
☐ 11 Frank Pitts	.40	.18	.05
☐ 12 Vern Den Herder	.60	.25	.07
☐ 13 John Fuqua	.60	.25	.07
☐ 14 Jack Tatum	2.00	.90	.25
☐ 15 Winston Hill	.40	.18	.05
☐ 16 John Beasley	.40	.18	.05
☐ 17 David Lee	.40	.18	.05
☐ 18 Rich Coady	.40	.18	.05
☐ 19 Ken Willard	.40	.18	.05
☐ 20 Coy Bacon	.60	.25	.07
☐ 21 Ben Hawkins	.40	.18	.05
☐ 22 Paul Guidry	.40	.18	.05
☐ 23A Norm Snead	5.00	2.20	.60
(Vertical pose; 1973			
stats; one asterisk			
before TCG on back)			
☐ 23B Norm Snead HOR	.60	.25	.07
☐ 24 Jim Yarbrough	.40	.18	.05
☐ 25 Jack Reynolds	2.50	1.10	.30
☐ 26 Josh Ashton	.40	.18	.05
☐ 27 Donnie Green	.40	.18	.05
☐ 28 Bob Hayes	1.50	.70	.19
☐ 29 John Zook	.40	.18	.05
☐ 30 Bobby Bryant	.40	.18	.05
☐ 31 Scott Hunter	.60	.25	.07
☐ 32 Dan Dierdorf	6.00	2.70	.75
☐ 33 Curt Knight	.40	.18	.05
☐ 34 Elmo Wright	.40	.18	.05
☐ 35 Essex Johnson	.40	.18	.05
☐ 36 Walt Sumner	.40	.18	.05
☐ 37 Marv Montgomery	.40	.18	.05
☐ 38 Tim Foley	.60	.25	.07
☐ 39 Mike Siani	.40	.18	.05
☐ 40 Joe Greene	6.00	2.70	.75
☐ 41 Bobby Howfield	.40	.18	.05
☐ 42 Del Williams	.40	.18	.05
☐ 43 Don McCauley	.40	.18	.05
☐ 44 Randy Jackson	.40	.18	.05
☐ 45 Ron Smith	.40	.18	.05
☐ 46 Gene Washington	.60	.25	.07
☐ 47 Po James	.40	.18	.05
☐ 48 Solomon Freelon	.40	.18	.05
☐ 49A Bob Windsor	3.00	1.35	.35
(Vertical pose; 1973			
stats; one asterisk			
before TCG on back)			
☐ 49B Bob Windsor HOR	.40	.18	.05
☐ 50 John Hadl	.75	.35	.09
☐ 51 Greg Larson	.40	.18	.05
☐ 52 Steve Owens	.60	.25	.07
☐ 53 Jim Cheyunski	.40	.18	.05
☐ 54 Rayfield Wright	.60	.25	.07
☐ 55 Dave Hampton	.40	.18	.05
☐ 56 Ron Widby	.40	.18	.05
☐ 57 Milt Sunde	.40	.18	.05
☐ 58 Billy Kilmer	.75	.35	.09
☐ 59 Bobby Bell	1.00	.45	.12
☐ 60 Jim Bakken	.40	.18	.05
☐ 61 Rufus Mayes	.40	.18	.05
☐ 62 Vic Washington	.40	.18	.05
☐ 63 Gene Washington	.60	.25	.07
☐ 64 Clarence Scott	.40	.18	.05
☐ 65 Gene Upshaw	2.00	.90	.25
☐ 66 Larry Seiple	.60	.25	.07
☐ 67 John McMakin	.40	.18	.05
☐ 68 Ralph Baker	.40	.18	.05
☐ 69 Lydell Mitchell	.60	.25	.07
☐ 70 Archie Manning	2.50	1.10	.30
☐ 71 George Farmer	.40	.18	.05
☐ 72 Ron East	.40	.18	.05
☐ 73 Al Nelson	.40	.18	.05
☐ 74 Pat Hughes	.40	.18	.05
☐ 75 Fred Willis	.40	.18	.05
☐ 76 Larry Walton	.40	.18	.05
☐ 77 Tom Neville	.40	.18	.05
☐ 78 Ted Kwalick	.40	.18	.05
☐ 79 Walt Patulski	.40	.18	.05
☐ 80 John Niland	.40	.18	.05
☐ 81 Ted Fritsch Jr.	.40	.18	.05
☐ 82 Paul Krause	.75	.35	.09
☐ 83 Jack Snow	.60	.25	.07
☐ 84 Mike Bass	.40	.18	.05
☐ 85 Jim Tyrer	.40	.18	.05
☐ 86 Ron Yankowski	.40	.18	.05
☐ 87 Mike Phipps	.60	.25	.07
☐ 88 Al Beauchamp	.40	.18	.05
☐ 89 Riley Odoms	.75	.35	.09
☐ 90 MacArthur Lane	.40	.18	.05
☐ 91 Art Thoms	.40	.18	.05
☐ 92 Marlin Briscoe	.40	.18	.05
☐ 93 Bruce Van Dyke	.40	.18	.05
☐ 94 Tom Myers	.40	.18	.05
☐ 95 Calvin Hill	.75	.35	.09
☐ 96 Bruce Laird	.40	.18	.05
☐ 97 Tony McGee	.40	.18	.05
☐ 98 Len Rohde	.40	.18	.05
☐ 99 Tom McNeill	.40	.18	.05
☐ 100 Delles Howell	.40	.18	.05
☐ 101 Gary Garrison	.40	.18	.05
☐ 102 Dan Goich	.40	.18	.05
☐ 103 Len St. Jean	.40	.18	.05
☐ 104 Zeke Moore	.40	.18	.05
☐ 105 Ahmad Rashad	14.00	6.25	1.75
☐ 106 Mel Renfro	1.50	.70	.19
☐ 107 Jim Mitchell	.40	.18	.05
☐ 108 Ed Budde	.40	.18	.05
☐ 109 Harry Schuh	.40	.18	.05
☐ 110 Greg Pruitt	4.00	1.80	.50
☐ 111 Ed Flanagan	.40	.18	.05
☐ 112 Larry Stallings	.40	.18	.05
☐ 113 Chuck Foreman	4.00	1.80	.50
☐ 114 Royce Berry	.40	.18	.05
☐ 115 Gale Gillingham	.40	.18	.05
☐ 116A Charlie Johnson	5.00	2.20	.60
(Vertical pose; 1973			
stats; one asterisk			
before TCG on back)			
☐ 116B Charlie Johnson HOR	1.25	.55	.16
☐ 117 Checklist 1-132 UER	4.00	1.00	.40
(345 Hamburger)			
☐ 118 Bill Butler	.40	.18	.05
☐ 119 Roy Jefferson	.60	.25	.07
☐ 120 Bobby Douglass	.60	.25	.07
☐ 121 Harold Carmichael AP	12.00	5.50	1.50
☐ 122 George Kunz AP	.40	.18	.05
☐ 123 Larry Little AP	2.00	.90	.25
☐ 124A Forrest Blue AP	3.00	1.35	.35
(Not All-Pro style; 1973			
stats; one asterisk			
before TCG on back)			
☐ 124B Forrest Blue AP	.40	.18	.05
☐ 125 Ron Yary AP	.60	.25	.07
☐ 126A Tom Mack	3.00	1.35	.35
(Not All-Pro style; 1973			
stats; one asterisk			
before TCG on back)			
☐ 126B Tom Mack AP	.75	.35	.09
☐ 127A Bob Tucker	3.00	1.35	.35
(Not All-Pro style; 1973			
stats; one asterisk			
before TCG on back)			
☐ 127B Bob Tucker AP	.60	.25	.07
☐ 128 Paul Warfield AP	4.00	1.80	.50
☐ 129 Fran Tarkenton AP	10.00	4.50	1.25
☐ 130 O.J. Simpson AP	14.00	6.25	1.75
☐ 131 Larry Csonka AP	5.00	2.20	.60
☐ 132 Bruce Gossett AP	.40	.18	.05
☐ 133 Bill Stanfill AP	.60	.25	.07
☐ 134 Alan Page AP	2.50	1.10	.30
☐ 135 Paul Smith AP	.40	.18	.05
☐ 136 Claude Humphrey AP	.60	.25	.07
☐ 137 Jack Ham AP	10.00	4.50	1.25
☐ 138 Lee Roy Jordan AP	1.25	.55	.16
☐ 139 Phil Villapiano AP	.60	.25	.07
☐ 140 Ken Ellis AP	.40	.18	.05
☐ 141 Willie Brown AP	1.25	.55	.16
☐ 142 Dick Anderson AP	.60	.25	.07
☐ 143 Bill Bradley AP	.60	.25	.07
☐ 144 Jerrel Wilson AP	.40	.18	.05
☐ 145 Reggie Rucker	.60	.25	.07
☐ 146 Marty Domres	.40	.18	.05
☐ 147 Bob Kowalkowski	.40	.18	.05
☐ 148 John Matuszak	3.00	1.35	.35
☐ 149 Mike Adamle	.60	.25	.07
☐ 150 John Unitas	15.00	6.75	1.85
☐ 151 Charlie Ford	.40	.18	.05
☐ 152 Bob Klein	.40	.18	.05
☐ 153 Jim Merlo	.40	.18	.05
☐ 154 Willie Young	.40	.18	.05
☐ 155 Donny Anderson	.60	.25	.07
☐ 156 Brig Owens	.40	.18	.05
☐ 157 Bruce Jarvis	.40	.18	.05
☐ 158 Ron Carpenter	.40	.18	.05
☐ 159 Don Cockroft	.40	.18	.05
☐ 160 Tommy Nobis	1.00	.45	.12
☐ 161 Craig Morton	.75	.35	.09
☐ 162 Jon Staggers	.40	.18	.05
☐ 163 Mike Eischeid	.40	.18	.05
☐ 164 Jerry Sisemore	.40	.18	.05
☐ 165 Cedrick Hardman	.40	.18	.05
☐ 166 Bill Thompson	.60	.25	.07
☐ 167 Jim Lynch	.60	.25	.07
☐ 168 Bob Moore	.40	.18	.05
☐ 169 Glen Edwards	.40	.18	.05
☐ 170 Mercury Morris	.75	.35	.09
☐ 171 Julius Adams	.40	.18	.05
☐ 172 Cotton Speyrer	.40	.18	.05
☐ 173 Bill Munson	.60	.25	.07
☐ 174 Benny Johnson	.40	.18	.05
☐ 175 Burgess Owens	.40	.18	.05
☐ 176 Cid Edwards	.40	.18	.05
☐ 177 Doug Buffone	.40	.18	.05
☐ 178 Charlie Cowan	.40	.18	.05
☐ 179 Bob Newland	.40	.18	.05
☐ 180 Ron Johnson	.60	.25	.07
☐ 181 Bob Rowe	.40	.18	.05
☐ 182 Len Hauss	.40	.18	.05
☐ 183 Joe DeLamielleure	.75	.35	.09
☐ 184 Sherman White	.40	.18	.05
☐ 185 Fair Hooker	.40	.18	.05
☐ 186 Nick Mike-Mayer	.40	.18	.05
☐ 187 Ralph Neely	.40	.18	.05
☐ 188 Rich McGeorge	.40	.18	.05
☐ 189 Ed Marinaro	3.00	1.35	.35
☐ 190 Dave Wilcox	.60	.25	.07
☐ 191 Joe Owens	.40	.18	.05
☐ 192 Bill Van Heusen	.40	.18	.05
☐ 193 Jim Kearney	.40	.18	.05
☐ 194 Otis Sistrunk	2.00	.90	.25
☐ 195 Ron Shanklin	.40	.18	.05
☐ 196 Bill Lenkaitis	.40	.18	.05
☐ 197 Tom Drougas	.40	.18	.05
☐ 198 Larry Hand	.40	.18	.05
☐ 199 Mack Alston	.40	.18	.05
☐ 200 Bob Griese	6.00	2.70	.75
☐ 201 Earlie Thomas	.40	.18	.05
☐ 202 Carl Gersbach	.40	.18	.05
☐ 203 Jim Harrison	.40	.18	.05
☐ 204 Jake Kupp	.40	.18	.05
☐ 205 Merlin Olsen	2.00	.90	.25
☐ 206 Spider Lockhart	.60	.25	.07
☐ 207 Walker Gillette	.40	.18	.05
☐ 208 Verlon Biggs	.40	.18	.05
☐ 209 Bob James	.40	.18	.05
☐ 210 Bob Trumpy	.75	.35	.09
☐ 211 Jerry Sherk HOR	.40	.18	.05
☐ 212 Andy Maurer	.40	.18	.05
☐ 213 Fred Carr	.40	.18	.05
☐ 214 Mick Tingelhoff	.60	.25	.07
☐ 215 Steve Spurrier	10.00	4.50	1.25
☐ 216 Richard Harris	.40	.18	.05
☐ 217 Charlie Greer	.40	.18	.05
☐ 218 Buck Buchanan	1.00	.45	.12
☐ 219 Ray Guy	10.00	4.50	1.25
☐ 220 Franco Harris	16.00	7.25	2.00
☐ 221 Darryl Stingley	2.00	.90	.25
☐ 222 Rex Kern	.40	.18	.05
☐ 223 Toni Fritsch	.60	.25	.07
☐ 224 Levi Johnson	.40	.18	.05
☐ 225 Bob Kuechenberg	.60	.25	.07
☐ 226 Elvin Bethea	.60	.25	.07
☐ 227 Al Woodall	.60	.25	.07
☐ 228 Terry Owens	.40	.18	.05
☐ 229 Bivian Lee	.40	.18	.05
☐ 230 Dick Butkus	8.00	3.60	1.00
☐ 231 Jim Bertelsen	.60	.25	.07
☐ 232 John Mendenhall	.40	.18	.05
☐ 233 Conrad Dobler	.75	.35	.09
☐ 234 J.D. Hill	.60	.25	.07
☐ 235 Ken Houston	1.25	.55	.16
☐ 236 Dave Lewis	.40	.18	.05
☐ 237 John Garlington	.40	.18	.05
☐ 238 Bill Sandeman	.40	.18	.05
☐ 239 Alden Roche	.40	.18	.05
☐ 240 John Gilliam	.60	.25	.07
☐ 241 Bruce Taylor	.40	.18	.05
☐ 242 Vern Winfield	.40	.18	.05
☐ 243 Bobby Maples	.40	.18	.05
☐ 244 Wendell Hayes	.40	.18	.05
☐ 245 George Blanda	8.00	3.60	1.00
☐ 246 Dwight White	.60	.25	.07
☐ 247 Sandy Durko	.40	.18	.05
☐ 248 Tom Mitchell	.40	.18	.05
☐ 249 Chuck Walton	.40	.18	.05
☐ 250 Bob Lilly	3.00	1.35	.35
☐ 251 Doug Swift	.40	.18	.05
☐ 252 Lynn Dickey	.75	.35	.09
☐ 253 Jerome Barkum	.40	.18	.05
☐ 254 Clint Jones	.40	.18	.05
☐ 255 Billy Newsome	.40	.18	.05
☐ 256 Bob Asher	.40	.18	.05
☐ 257 Joe Scibelli	.40	.18	.05
☐ 258 Tom Blanchard	.40	.18	.05
☐ 259 Norm Thompson	.40	.18	.05
☐ 260 Larry Brown	.75	.35	.09
☐ 261 Paul Seymour	.40	.18	.05
☐ 262 Checklist 133-264	4.00	1.00	.40
☐ 263 Doug Dieken	.40	.18	.05
☐ 264 Lemar Parrish	.60	.25	.07
☐ 265 Bob Lee UER	.40	.18	.05
(listed as Atlanta			
Hawks on card back)			
☐ 266 Bob Brown DT	.40	.18	.05
☐ 267 Roy Winston	.40	.18	.05
☐ 268 Randy Beisler	.40	.18	.05
☐ 269 Joe Dawkins	.40	.18	.05
☐ 270 Tom Dempsey	.60	.25	.07
☐ 271 Jack Rudnay	.40	.18	.05
☐ 272 Art Shell	5.00	2.20	.60
☐ 273 Mike Wagner	.60	.25	.07
☐ 274 Rick Cash	.40	.18	.05
☐ 275 Greg Landry	.75	.35	.09
☐ 276 Glenn Ressler	.40	.18	.05
☐ 277 Billy Joe DuPree	2.00	.90	.25
☐ 278 Norm Evans	.40	.18	.05
☐ 279 Billy Parks	.40	.18	.05
☐ 280 John Riggins	6.00	2.70	.75
☐ 281 Lionel Aldridge	.40	.18	.05
☐ 282 Steve O'Neal	.40	.18	.05
☐ 283 Craig Clemons	.40	.18	.05
☐ 284 Willie Williams	.40	.18	.05
☐ 285 Isiah Robertson	.60	.25	.07
☐ 286 Dennis Shaw	.40	.18	.05
☐ 287 Bill Brundige	.40	.18	.05
☐ 288 John Leypoldt	.40	.18	.05
☐ 289 John DeMarie	.40	.18	.05
☐ 290 Mike Reid	1.50	.70	.19
☐ 291 Greg Brezina	.40	.18	.05
☐ 292 Willie Buchanon	.40	.18	.05
☐ 293 Dave Osborn	.60	.25	.07
☐ 294 Mel Phillips	.40	.18	.05
☐ 295 Haven Moses	.60	.25	.07
☐ 296 Wade Key	.40	.18	.05
☐ 297 Marvin Upshaw	.40	.18	.05
☐ 298 Ray Mansfield	.40	.18	.05
☐ 299 Edgar Chandler	.40	.18	.05
☐ 300 Marv Hubbard	.60	.25	.07
☐ 301 Herman Weaver	.40	.18	.05
☐ 302 Jim Bailey	.40	.18	.05
☐ 303 D.D. Lewis	.75	.35	.09
☐ 304 Ken Burrough	.60	.25	.07
☐ 305 Jake Scott	.75	.35	.09
☐ 306 Randy Rasmussen	.40	.18	.05
☐ 307 Pettis Norman	.40	.18	.05
☐ 308 Carl Johnson	.40	.18	.05
☐ 309 Joe Taylor	.40	.18	.05
☐ 310 Pete Gogolak	.40	.18	.05
☐ 311 Tony Baker	.40	.18	.05
☐ 312 John Richardson	.40	.18	.05
☐ 313 Dave Robinson	.60	.25	.07
☐ 314 Reggie McKenzie	.75	.35	.09
☐ 315 Isaac Curtis	1.50	.70	.19
☐ 316 Thom Darden	.40	.18	.05
☐ 317 Ken Reaves	.40	.18	.05
☐ 318 Malcolm Snider	.40	.18	.05
☐ 319 Jeff Siemon	.60	.25	.07
☐ 320 Dan Abramowicz	.60	.25	.07
☐ 321 Lyle Alzado	2.00	.90	.25
☐ 322 John Reaves	.40	.18	.05
☐ 323 Morris Stroud	.40	.18	.05
☐ 324 Bobby Walden	.40	.18	.05
☐ 325 Randy Vataha	.40	.18	.05
☐ 326 Nemiah Wilson	.40	.18	.05
☐ 327 Paul Naumoff	.40	.18	.05
☐ 328 Rushing Leaders	3.00	1.35	.35
O.J. Simpson			
John Brockington			
☐ 329 Passing Leaders	5.00	2.20	.60
Ken Stabler			
Roger Staubach			
☐ 330 Receiving Leaders	1.25	.55	.16
Fred Willis			
Harold Carmichael			
☐ 331 Scoring Leaders	.60	.25	.07
Roy Gerela			
David Ray			
☐ 332 Interception Leaders	.60	.25	.07
Dick Anderson			
Mike Wagner			
Bobby Bryant			
☐ 333 Punting Leaders	.60	.25	.07
Jerrel Wilson			
Tom Wittum			
☐ 334 Dennis Nelson	.40	.18	.05
☐ 335 Walt Garrison	.60	.25	.07
☐ 336 Tody Smith	.40	.18	.05
☐ 337 Ed Bell	.40	.18	.05
☐ 338 Bryant Salter	.40	.18	.05
☐ 339 Wayne Colman	.40	.18	.05
☐ 340 Garo Yepremian	.60	.25	.07
☐ 341 Bob Newton	.40	.18	.05
☐ 342 Vince Clements	.40	.18	.05
☐ 343 Ken Iman	.40	.18	.05
☐ 344 Jim Tolbert	.40	.18	.05
☐ 345 Chris Hanburger	.60	.25	.07
☐ 346 Dave Foley	.40	.18	.05
☐ 347 Tommy Casanova	.60	.25	.07
☐ 348 John James	.40	.18	.05
☐ 349 Clarence Williams	.40	.18	.05
☐ 350 Leroy Kelly	1.25	.55	.16
☐ 351 Stu Voigt	.60	.25	.07
☐ 352 Skip Vanderbundt	.40	.18	.05
☐ 353 Pete Duranko	.40	.18	.05
☐ 354 John Outlaw	.40	.18	.05
☐ 355 Jan Stenerud	.75	.35	.09
☐ 356 Barry Pearson	.40	.18	.05
☐ 357 Brian Dowling	.40	.18	.05
☐ 358 Dan Conners	.40	.18	.05
☐ 359 Bob Bell	.40	.18	.05
☐ 360 Rick Volk	.40	.18	.05
☐ 361 Pat Toomay	.60	.25	.07
☐ 362 Bob Gresham	.40	.18	.05
☐ 363 John Schmitt	.40	.18	.05
☐ 364 Mel Rogers	.40	.18	.05
☐ 365 Manny Fernandez	.60	.25	.07
☐ 366 Ernie Jackson	.40	.18	.05
☐ 367 Gary Huff	.60	.25	.07
☐ 368 Bob Grim	.40	.18	.05
☐ 369 Ernie McMillan	.40	.18	.05
☐ 370 Dave Elmendorf	.40	.18	.05
☐ 371 Mike Bragg	.40	.18	.05
☐ 372 John Skorupan	.40	.18	.05
☐ 373 Howard Fest	.40	.18	.05
☐ 374 Jerry Tagge	.60	.25	.07
☐ 375 Art Malone	.40	.18	.05
☐ 376 Bob Babich	.40	.18	.05
☐ 377 Jim Marshall	1.00	.45	.12
☐ 378 Bob Hoskins	.40	.18	.05
☐ 379 Don Zimmerman	.40	.18	.05
☐ 380 Ray May	.40	.18	.05
☐ 381 Emmitt Thomas	.60	.25	.07

☐ 382 Terry Hanratty	.60	.25	.07
☐ 383 John Hannah	12.00	5.50	1.50
☐ 384 George Atkinson	.40	.18	.05
☐ 385 Ted Hendricks	3.00	1.35	.35
☐ 386 Jim O'Brien	.40	.18	.05
☐ 387 Jethro Pugh	.60	.25	.07
☐ 388 Elbert Drungo	.40	.18	.05
☐ 389 Richard Caster	.60	.25	.07
☐ 390 Deacon Jones	2.00	.90	.25
☐ 391 Checklist 265-396	4.00	1.00	.40
☐ 392 Jess Phillips	.40	.18	.05
☐ 393 Garry Lyle UER	.40	.18	.05
(Misspelled Gary on card front)			
☐ 394 Jim Files	.40	.18	.05
☐ 395 Jim Hart	.75	.35	.09
☐ 396 Dave Chapple	.40	.18	.05
☐ 397 Jim Langer	2.00	.90	.25
☐ 398 John Wilbur	.40	.18	.05
☐ 399 Dwight Harrison	.40	.18	.05
☐ 400 John Brockington	.60	.25	.07
☐ 401 Ken Anderson	6.00	2.70	.75
☐ 402 Mike Tilleman	.40	.18	.05
☐ 403 Charlie Hall	.40	.18	.05
☐ 404 Tommy Hart	.40	.18	.05
☐ 405 Norm Bulaich	.60	.25	.07
☐ 406 Jim Turner	.40	.18	.05
☐ 407 Mo Moorman	.40	.18	.05
☐ 408 Ralph Anderson	.40	.18	.05
☐ 409 Jim Otto	1.25	.55	.16
☐ 410 Andy Russell	.75	.35	.09
☐ 411 Glenn Doughty	.40	.18	.05
☐ 412 Altie Taylor	.40	.18	.05
☐ 413 Marv Bateman	.40	.18	.05
☐ 414 Willie Alexander	.40	.18	.05
☐ 415 Bill Zapalac	.40	.18	.05
☐ 416 Russ Washington	.40	.18	.05
☐ 417 Joe Federspiel	.40	.18	.05
☐ 418 Craig Cotton	.40	.18	.05
☐ 419 Randy Johnson	.40	.18	.05
☐ 420 Harold Jackson	.75	.35	.09
☐ 421 Roger Wehrli	.60	.25	.07
☐ 422 Charlie Harraway	.40	.18	.05
☐ 423 Spike Jones	.40	.18	.05
☐ 424 Bob Johnson	.40	.18	.05
☐ 425 Mike McCoy	.40	.18	.05
☐ 426 Dennis Havig HOR	.40	.18	.05
☐ 427 Bob McKay	.40	.18	.05
☐ 428 Steve Zabel	.40	.18	.05
☐ 429 Horace Jones	.40	.18	.05
☐ 430 Jim Johnson	.75	.35	.09
☐ 431 Roy Gerela	.60	.25	.07
☐ 432 Tom Graham	.40	.18	.05
☐ 433 Curley Culp	.60	.25	.07
☐ 434 Ken Mendenhall	.40	.18	.05
☐ 435 Jim Plunkett	2.50	1.10	.30
☐ 436 Julian Fagan	.40	.18	.05
☐ 437 Mike Garrett	.60	.25	.07
☐ 438 Bobby Joe Green	.40	.18	.05
☐ 439 Jack Gregory HOR	.40	.18	.05
☐ 440 Charlie Sanders	.60	.25	.07
☐ 441 Bill Curry	.60	.25	.07
☐ 442 Bob Pollard	.40	.18	.05
☐ 443 David Ray	.40	.18	.05
☐ 444 Terry Metcalf	3.00	1.35	.35
☐ 445 Pat Fischer	.60	.25	.07
☐ 446 Bob Chandler	.60	.25	.07
☐ 447 Bill Bergey	.60	.25	.07
☐ 448 Walter Johnson	.40	.18	.05
☐ 449 Charley Young	.75	.35	.09
☐ 450 Chester Marcol	.40	.18	.05
☐ 451 Ken Stabler	25.00	11.00	3.10
☐ 452 Preston Pearson	.75	.35	.09
☐ 453 Mike Current	.40	.18	.05
☐ 454 Ron Bolton	.40	.18	.05
☐ 455 Mark Lomas	.40	.18	.05
☐ 456 Raymond Chester	.60	.25	.07
☐ 457 Jerry LeVias	.60	.25	.07
☐ 458 Skip Butler	.40	.18	.05
☐ 459 Mike Livingston	.40	.18	.05
☐ 460 AFC Semi-Finals	.75	.35	.09
Raiders 33, Steelers 14 and Dolphins 34, Bengals 16			
☐ 461 NFC Semi-Finals	4.00	1.80	.50
Vikings 27, Redskins 20 and Cowboys 27, Rams 16 (Staubach)			
☐ 462 Playoff Championship	3.00	1.35	.35
Dolphins 27, Raiders 10 and Vikings 27, Cowboys 10 (Ken Stabler and Fran Tarkenton)			
☐ 463 Super Bowl	2.00	.90	.25
Dolphins 24, Vikings 7			
☐ 464 Wayne Mulligan	.40	.18	.05
☐ 465 Horst Muhlmann	.40	.18	.05
☐ 466 Milt Morin	.40	.18	.05
☐ 467 Don Parish	.40	.18	.05
☐ 468 Richard Neal	.40	.18	.05
☐ 469 Ron Jessie	.60	.25	.07
☐ 470 Terry Bradshaw	22.00	10.00	2.70
☐ 471 Fred Dryer	2.00	.90	.25
☐ 472 Jim Carter	.40	.18	.05
☐ 473 Ken Burrow	.40	.18	.05
☐ 474 Wally Chambers	.60	.25	.07
☐ 475 Dan Pastorini	.75	.35	.09
☐ 476 Don Morrison	.40	.18	.05
☐ 477 Carl Mauck	.40	.18	.05
☐ 478 Larry Cole	.60	.25	.07
☐ 479 Jim Kiick	.75	.35	.09
☐ 480 Willie Lanier	1.00	.45	.12
☐ 481 Don Herrmann	.60	.25	.07
☐ 482 George Hunt	.40	.18	.05
☐ 483 Bob Howard	.40	.18	.05
☐ 484 Myron Pottios	.40	.18	.05
☐ 485 Jackie Smith	1.00	.45	.12
☐ 486 Vern Holland	.40	.18	.05
☐ 487 Jim Braxton	.40	.18	.05
☐ 488 Joe Reed	.40	.18	.05
☐ 489 Wally Hilgenberg	.40	.18	.05
☐ 490 Fred Biletnikoff	3.50	1.55	.45
☐ 491 Bob DeMarco HOR	.40	.18	.05
☐ 492 Mark Nordquist	.40	.18	.05
☐ 493 Larry Brooks	.40	.18	.05
☐ 494 Pete Athas	.40	.18	.05
☐ 495 Emerson Boozer	.60	.25	.07
☐ 496 L.C. Greenwood	2.00	.90	.25
☐ 497 Rockne Freitas	.40	.18	.05
☐ 498 Checklist 397-528 UER	4.00	1.00	.40
(510 Charlie Taylor should be Charley)			
☐ 499 Joe Schmiesing	.40	.18	.05
☐ 500 Roger Staubach	25.00	11.00	3.10
☐ 501 Al Cowlings UER	.60	.25	.07
(Def. tackle on front, Def. End on back)			
☐ 502 Sam Cunningham	.75	.35	.09
☐ 503 Dennis Partee	.40	.18	.05
☐ 504 John Didion	.40	.18	.05
☐ 505 Nick Buoniconti	.75	.35	.09
☐ 506 Carl Garrett	.60	.25	.07
☐ 507 Doug Van Horn	.40	.18	.05
☐ 508 Jamie Rivers	.40	.18	.05
☐ 509 Jack Youngblood	4.00	1.80	.50
☐ 510 Charley Taylor UER	2.50	1.10	.30
(Misspelled Charlie on both sides)			
☐ 511 Ken Riley	.75	.35	.09
☐ 512 Joe Ferguson	2.00	.90	.25
☐ 513 Bill Lueck	.40	.18	.05
☐ 514 Ray Brown	.40	.18	.05
☐ 515 Fred Cox	.40	.18	.05
☐ 516 Joe Jones	.40	.18	.05
☐ 517 Larry Schreiber	.40	.18	.05
☐ 518 Dennis Wirgowski	.40	.18	.05
☐ 519 Leroy Mitchell	.40	.18	.05
☐ 520 Otis Taylor	.75	.35	.09
☐ 521 Henry Davis	.40	.18	.05
☐ 522 Bruce Barnes	.40	.18	.05
☐ 523 Charlie Smith	.40	.18	.05
☐ 524 Bert Jones	4.00	1.80	.50
☐ 525 Lem Barney	2.00	.90	.25
☐ 526 John Fitzgerald	.60	.25	.07
☐ 527 Tom Funchess	.40	.18	.05
☐ 528 Steve Tannen	.75	.35	.09

1974 Topps Team Checklists

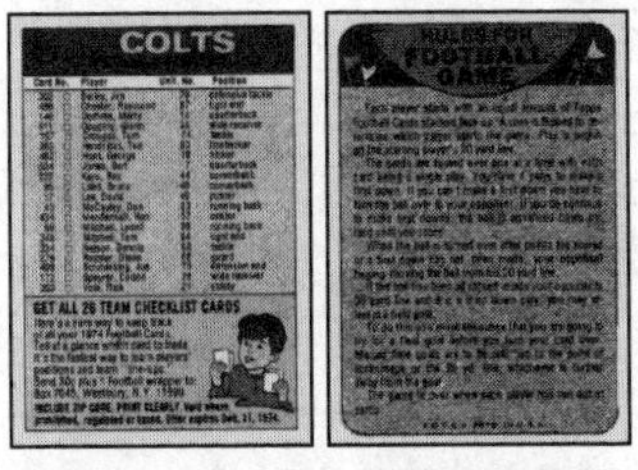

The 1974 Topps Team Checklist set contains 26 standard-size cards. The cards were inserted into regular issue 1974 Topps football wax packs. The Topps logo and team name appear at the top of the card, while the mid-portion of the card contains the actual checklist giving each player's card number, check-off box, name, uniform number, and position. The lower portion of the card contains an ad to obtain all 26 team checklists. A picture of a boy collector is shown in the lower right corner. The back of the card contains rules for a football game to be played with the 1974 Topps football cards. These unnumbered cards are numbered below for convenience in alphabetical order by team name. Twenty of the 26 checklist cards show players out of alphabetical order on the card front. The cards can all be found with one or two asterisks on the front. The set was also available directly from Topps as a mail-away offer as a pair of unperforated uncut sheets, which had blank backs. Measuring approximately 13 1/2" by 10 1/2", each sheet featured thirteen team checklist cards and an offer for a football action poster.

	NRMT-MT	EXC	G-VG
COMPLETE SET (26)	75.00	19.00	7.50
COMMON TEAM (1-26)	3.00	.75	.30
☐ 1 Atlanta Falcons	3.00	.75	.30
☐ 2 Baltimore Colts	3.00	.75	.30
☐ 3 Buffalo Bills	3.00	.75	.30
☐ 4 Chicago Bears	3.00	.75	.30
☐ 5 Cincinnati Bengals	3.00	.75	.30
☐ 6 Cleveland Browns UER	3.00	.75	.30
(Reggie Rucher)			
☐ 7 Dallas Cowboys	5.00	1.25	.50
☐ 8 Denver Broncos	3.00	.75	.30
☐ 9 Detroit Lions	3.00	.75	.30
☐ 10 Green Bay Packers	4.00	1.00	.40
☐ 11 Houston Oilers	3.00	.75	.30
☐ 12 Kansas City Chiefs	3.00	.75	.30
☐ 13 Los Angeles Rams	3.00	.75	.30
☐ 14 Miami Dolphins	4.00	1.00	.40
☐ 15 Minnesota Vikings	3.00	.75	.30
☐ 16 New England Patriots	3.00	.75	.30
☐ 17 New Orleans Saints	3.00	.75	.30
☐ 18 New York Giants	3.00	.75	.30
☐ 19 New York Jets	3.00	.75	.30
☐ 20 Oakland Raiders	5.00	1.25	.50
☐ 21 Philadelphia Eagles	3.00	.75	.30
☐ 22 Pittsburgh Steelers	4.00	1.00	.40
☐ 23 St. Louis Cardinals	3.00	.75	.30
☐ 24 San Diego Chargers	3.00	.75	.30
☐ 25 San Francisco 49ers	4.00	1.00	.40
☐ 26 Washington Redskins UER	4.00	1.00	.40
(Charley Taylor misspelled as Charlie)			

1975 Topps

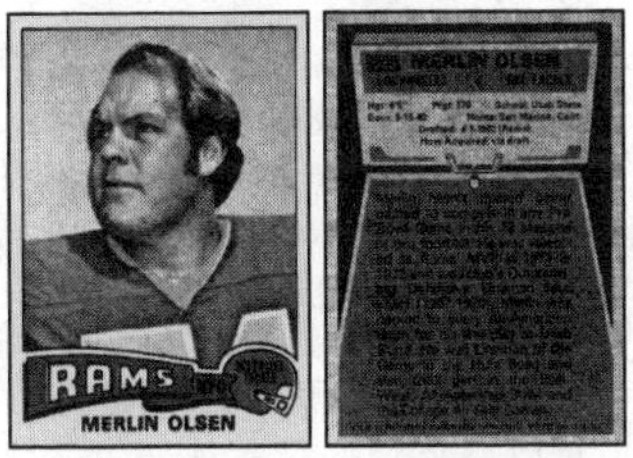

The 1975 Topps football set contains 528 standard-size cards. Beneath a color photo, card fronts contain a banner with the team name. Both were done in a team color. To the right of the banner is a football helmet the includes the player's position. The player's name is at the bottom. Subsets include leaders (1-6), All-Pro (201-225), Record Breakers (351-356), Highlights (452-460) and playoffs (526-528). The card backs are printed in black ink with a green background on gray card stock and contain statistics and highlights. The key Rookie Cards in this set are Otis Armstrong, Rocky Bleier, Mel Blount, Cliff Branch, Dan Fouts, Cliff Harris, Drew Pearson, Lynn Swann and Charlie Waters. The set also includes Joe Theismann's first NFL card after having performed in the Canadian Football League. An uncut sheet of team checklist cards was also available via a mail-in offer wax pack wrappers.

	NRMT-MT	EXC	G-VG
COMPLETE SET (528)	300.00	135.00	38.00
COMMON CARD (1-528)	.30	.14	.04
☐ 1 Rushing Leaders	1.50	.35	.15
Lawrence McCutcheon, Otis Armstrong			
☐ 2 Passing Leaders	1.25	.55	.16
Sonny Jurgensen, Ken Anderson			
☐ 3 Receiving Leaders	.60	.25	.07
Charley Young, Lydell Mitchell			
☐ 4 Scoring Leaders	.60	.25	.07
Chester Marcol, Roy Gerela			
☐ 5 Interception Leaders	.60	.25	.07
Ray Brown, Emmitt Thomas			
☐ 6 Punting Leaders	.60	.25	.07
Tom Blanchard, Ray Guy			
☐ 7 George Blanda	5.00	2.20	.60
(Black jersey; highlights on back)			
☐ 8 George Blanda	5.00	2.20	.60
(White jersey; career record on back)			
☐ 9 Ralph Baker	.30	.14	.04
☐ 10 Don Woods	.30	.14	.04
☐ 11 Bob Asher	.30	.14	.04
☐ 12 Mel Blount	20.00	9.00	2.50
☐ 13 Sam Cunningham	.50	.23	.06
☐ 14 Jackie Smith	.75	.35	.09
☐ 15 Greg Landry	.50	.23	.06
☐ 16 Buck Buchanan	1.00	.45	.12
☐ 17 Haven Moses	.50	.23	.06
☐ 18 Clarence Ellis	.30	.14	.04
☐ 19 Jim Carter	.30	.14	.04
☐ 20 Charley Taylor UER	2.00	.90	.25
(Misspelled Charlie on card front)			
☐ 21 Jess Phillips	.30	.14	.04
☐ 22 Larry Seiple	.30	.14	.04
☐ 23 Doug Dieken	.30	.14	.04
☐ 24 Ron Saul	.30	.14	.04
☐ 25 Isaac Curtis UER	.75	.35	.09
(Misspelled Issac on card front)			
☐ 26 Gary Larsen	.30	.14	.04
☐ 27 Bruce Jarvis	.30	.14	.04
☐ 28 Steve Zabel	.30	.14	.04
☐ 29 John Mendenhall	.30	.14	.04
☐ 30 Rick Volk	.30	.14	.04
☐ 31 Checklist 1-132	3.50	.85	.35
☐ 32 Dan Abramowicz	.50	.23	.06
☐ 33 Bubba Smith	1.50	.70	.19
☐ 34 David Ray	.30	.14	.04
☐ 35 Dan Dierdorf	4.00	1.80	.50
☐ 36 Randy Rasmussen	.30	.14	.04
☐ 37 Bob Howard	.30	.14	.04
☐ 38 Gary Huff	.50	.23	.06
☐ 39 Rocky Bleier	20.00	9.00	2.50
☐ 40 Mel Gray	.50	.23	.06
☐ 41 Tony McGee	.30	.14	.04
☐ 42 Larry Hand	.30	.14	.04
☐ 43 Wendell Hayes	.30	.14	.04
☐ 44 Doug Wilkerson	.30	.14	.04
☐ 45 Paul Smith	.30	.14	.04
☐ 46 Dave Robinson	.50	.23	.06
☐ 47 Bivian Lee	.30	.14	.04
☐ 48 Jim Mandich	.50	.23	.06
☐ 49 Greg Pruitt	.75	.35	.09
☐ 50 Dan Pastorini UER	.75	.35	.09
(5/26/39 birthdate incorrect)			
☐ 51 Ron Pritchard	.30	.14	.04
☐ 52 Dan Conners	.30	.14	.04
☐ 53 Fred Cox	.30	.14	.04
☐ 54 Tony Greene	.30	.14	.04
☐ 55 Craig Morton	.75	.35	.09
☐ 56 Jim Sisemore	.30	.14	.04
☐ 57 Glenn Doughty	.30	.14	.04
☐ 58 Larry Schreiber	.30	.14	.04
☐ 59 Charlie Waters	4.00	1.80	.50
☐ 60 Jack Youngblood	1.50	.70	.19
☐ 61 Bill Lenkaitis	.30	.14	.04
☐ 62 Greg Brezina	.30	.14	.04
☐ 63 Bob Pollard	.30	.14	.04
☐ 64 Mack Alston	.30	.14	.04
☐ 65 Drew Pearson	12.00	5.50	1.50
☐ 66 Charlie Stukes	.30	.14	.04
☐ 67 Emerson Boozer	.50	.23	.06
☐ 68 Dennis Partee	.30	.14	.04
☐ 69 Bob Newton	.30	.14	.04
☐ 70 Jack Tatum	.75	.35	.09
☐ 71 Frank Lewis	.30	.14	.04
☐ 72 Bob Young	.30	.14	.04
☐ 73 Julius Adams	.30	.14	.04
☐ 74 Paul Naumoff	.30	.14	.04
☐ 75 Otis Taylor	.75	.35	.09
☐ 76 Dave Hampton	.30	.14	.04
☐ 77 Mike Current	.30	.14	.04
☐ 78 Brig Owens	.30	.14	.04
☐ 79 Bobby Scott	.30	.14	.04
☐ 80 Harold Carmichael	3.00	1.35	.35
☐ 81 Bill Stanfill	.30	.14	.04
☐ 82 Bob Babich	.30	.14	.04
☐ 83 Vic Washington	.30	.14	.04
☐ 84 Mick Tingelhoff	.50	.23	.06
☐ 85 Bob Trumpy	.75	.35	.09
☐ 86 Earl Edwards	.30	.14	.04
☐ 87 Ron Hornsby	.30	.14	.04
☐ 88 Don McCauley	.30	.14	.04
☐ 89 Jim Johnson	.75	.35	.09
☐ 90 Andy Russell	.50	.23	.06
☐ 91 Cornell Green	.75	.35	.09
☐ 92 Charlie Cowan	.30	.14	.04
☐ 93 Jon Staggers	.30	.14	.04
☐ 94 Billy Newsome	.30	.14	.04
☐ 95 Willie Brown	1.00	.45	.12
☐ 96 Carl Mauck	.30	.14	.04
☐ 97 Doug Buffone	.30	.14	.04
☐ 98 Preston Pearson	.50	.23	.06
☐ 99 Jim Bakken	.30	.14	.04
☐ 100 Bob Griese	5.00	2.20	.60
☐ 101 Bob Windsor	.30	.14	.04
☐ 102 Rockne Freitas	.30	.14	.04
☐ 103 Jim Marsalis	.30	.14	.04
☐ 104 Bill Thompson	.50	.23	.06
☐ 105 Ken Burrow	.30	.14	.04
☐ 106 Diron Talbert	.30	.14	.04
☐ 107 Joe Federspiel	.30	.14	.04
☐ 108 Norm Bulaich	.50	.23	.06
☐ 109 Bob DeMarco	.30	.14	.04
☐ 110 Tom Wittum	.30	.14	.04
☐ 111 Larry Hefner	.30	.14	.04
☐ 112 Tody Smith	.30	.14	.04
☐ 113 Stu Voigt	.30	.14	.04
☐ 114 Horst Muhlmann	.30	.14	.04
☐ 115 Ahmad Rashad	5.00	2.20	.60
☐ 116 Joe Dawkins	.30	.14	.04
☐ 117 George Kunz	.30	.14	.04
☐ 118 D.D. Lewis	.50	.23	.06
☐ 119 Levi Johnson	.30	.14	.04
☐ 120 Len Dawson	4.00	1.80	.50
☐ 121 Jim Bertelsen	.30	.14	.04
☐ 122 Ed Bell	.30	.14	.04
☐ 123 Art Thoms	.30	.14	.04
☐ 124 Joe Beauchamp	.30	.14	.04

☐ 125 Jack Ham	6.00	2.70	.75
☐ 126 Carl Garrett	.50	.23	.06
☐ 127 Roger Finnie	.30	.14	.04
☐ 128 Howard Twilley	.50	.23	.06
☐ 129 Bruce Barnes	.30	.14	.04
☐ 130 Nate Wright	.30	.14	.04
☐ 131 Jerry Tagge	.30	.14	.04
☐ 132 Floyd Little	.75	.35	.09
☐ 133 John Zook	.30	.14	.04
☐ 134 Len Hauss	.30	.14	.04
☐ 135 Archie Manning	1.50	.70	.19
☐ 136 Po James	.30	.14	.04
☐ 137 Walt Sumner	.30	.14	.04
☐ 138 Randy Beisler	.30	.14	.04
☐ 139 Willie Alexander	.30	.14	.04
☐ 140 Garo Yepremian	.50	.23	.06
☐ 141 Chip Myers	.30	.14	.04
☐ 142 Jim Braxton	.30	.14	.04
☐ 143 Doug Van Horn	.30	.14	.04
☐ 144 Stan White	.30	.14	.04
☐ 145 Roger Staubach	25.00	11.00	3.10
☐ 146 Herman Weaver	.30	.14	.04
☐ 147 Marvin Upshaw	.30	.14	.04
☐ 148 Bob Klein	.30	.14	.04
☐ 149 Earlie Thomas	.30	.14	.04
☐ 150 John Brockington	.50	.23	.06
☐ 151 Mike Siani	.30	.14	.04
☐ 152 Sam Davis	.30	.14	.04
☐ 153 Mike Wagner	.50	.23	.06
☐ 154 Larry Stallings	.30	.14	.04
☐ 155 Wally Chambers	.30	.14	.04
☐ 156 Randy Vataha	.30	.14	.04
☐ 157 Jim Marshall	.75	.35	.09
☐ 158 Jim Turner	.30	.14	.04
☐ 159 Walt Sweeney	.30	.14	.04
☐ 160 Ken Anderson	4.00	1.80	.50
☐ 161 Ray Brown	.30	.14	.04
☐ 162 John Didion	.30	.14	.04
☐ 163 Tom Dempsey	.30	.14	.04
☐ 164 Clarence Scott	.30	.14	.04
☐ 165 Gene Washington	.50	.23	.06
☐ 166 Willie Rogers	.30	.14	.04
☐ 167 Doug Swift	.30	.14	.04
☐ 168 Rufus Mayes	.30	.14	.04
☐ 169 Marv Bateman	.30	.14	.04
☐ 170 Lydell Mitchell	.50	.23	.06
☐ 171 Ron Smith	.30	.14	.04
☐ 172 Bill Munson	.50	.23	.06
☐ 173 Bob Grim	.30	.14	.04
☐ 174 Ed Budde	.30	.14	.04
☐ 175 Bob Lilly UER	3.00	1.35	.35
(Was first draft,			
not first player)			
☐ 176 Jim Youngblood	.75	.35	.09
☐ 177 Steve Tannen	.30	.14	.04
☐ 178 Rich McGeorge	.30	.14	.04
☐ 179 Jim Tyrer	.30	.14	.04
☐ 180 Forrest Blue	.30	.14	.04
☐ 181 Jerry LeVias	.50	.23	.06
☐ 182 Joe Gilliam	.30	.14	.04
☐ 183 Jim Otis	.50	.23	.06
☐ 184 Mel Tom	.30	.14	.04
☐ 185 Paul Seymour	.30	.14	.04
☐ 186 George Webster	.30	.14	.04
☐ 187 Pete Duranko	.30	.14	.04
☐ 188 Essex Johnson	.30	.14	.04
☐ 189 Bob Lee	.50	.23	.06
☐ 190 Gene Upshaw	1.25	.55	.16
☐ 191 Tom Myers	.30	.14	.04
☐ 192 Don Zimmerman	.30	.14	.04
☐ 193 John Garlington	.30	.14	.04
☐ 194 Skip Butler	.30	.14	.04
☐ 195 Tom Mitchell	.30	.14	.04
☐ 196 Jim Langer	.75	.35	.09
☐ 197 Ron Carpenter	.30	.14	.04
☐ 198 Dave Foley	.30	.14	.04
☐ 199 Bert Jones	1.50	.70	.19
☐ 200 Larry Brown	.50	.23	.06
☐ 201 All Pro Receivers	2.00	.90	.25
Charley Taylor			
Fred Biletnikoff			
☐ 202 All Pro Tackles	.75	.35	.09
Rayfield Wright			
Russ Washington			
☐ 203 All Pro Guards	.75	.35	.09
Tom Mack			
Larry Little			
☐ 204 All Pro Centers	.50	.23	.06
Jeff Van Note			
Jack Rudnay			
☐ 205 All Pro Guards	.75	.35	.09
Gale Gillingham			
John Hannah			
☐ 206 All Pro Tackles	.75	.35	.09
Dan Dierdorf			
Winston Hill			
☐ 207 All Pro Tight Ends	.50	.23	.06
Charley Young			
Riley Odoms			
☐ 208 All Pro Quarterbacks	4.00	1.80	.50
Fran Tarkenton			
Ken Stabler			
☐ 209 All Pro Backs	3.50	1.55	.45
Lawrence McCutcheon			
O.J. Simpson			
☐ 210 All Pro Backs	.75	.35	.09
Terry Metcalf			
Otis Armstrong			
☐ 211 All Pro Receivers	.50	.23	.06
Mel Gray			
Isaac Curtis			
☐ 212 All Pro Kickers	.50	.23	.06
Chester Marcol			
Roy Gerela			
☐ 213 All Pro Ends	.75	.35	.09
Jack Youngblood			
Elvin Bethea			
☐ 214 All Pro Tackles	.50	.23	.06
Alan Page			
Otis Sistrunk			
☐ 215 All Pro Tackles	.75	.35	.09
Merlin Olsen			
Mike Reid			
☐ 216 All Pro Ends	.75	.35	.09
Carl Eller			
Lyle Alzado			
☐ 217 All Pro Linebackers	.75	.35	.09
Ted Hendricks			
Phil Villapiano			
☐ 218 All Pro Linebackers	.75	.35	.09
Lee Roy Jordan			
Willie Lanier			
☐ 219 All Pro Linebackers	.50	.23	.06
Isiah Robertson			
Andy Russell			
☐ 220 All Pro Cornerbacks	.50	.23	.06
Nate Wright			
Emmitt Thomas			
☐ 221 All Pro Cornerbacks	.50	.23	.06
Willie Buchanon			
Lemar Parrish			
☐ 222 All Pro Safeties	.50	.23	.06
Ken Houston			
Dick Anderson			
☐ 223 All Pro Safeties	.75	.35	.09
Cliff Harris			
Jack Tatum			
☐ 224 All Pro Punters	.50	.23	.06
Tom Wittum			
Ray Guy			
☐ 225 All Pro Returners	.50	.23	.06
Terry Metcalf			
Greg Pruitt			
☐ 226 Ted Kwalick	.30	.14	.04
☐ 227 Spider Lockhart	.50	.23	.06
☐ 228 Mike Livingston	.30	.14	.04
☐ 229 Larry Cole	.30	.14	.04
☐ 230 Gary Garrison	.30	.14	.04
☐ 231 Larry Brooks	.30	.14	.04
☐ 232 Bobby Howfield	.30	.14	.04
☐ 233 Fred Carr	.30	.14	.04
☐ 234 Norm Evans	.30	.14	.04
☐ 235 Dwight White	.50	.23	.06
☐ 236 Conrad Dobler	.50	.23	.06
☐ 237 Garry Lyle	.30	.14	.04
☐ 238 Darryl Stingley	.75	.35	.09
☐ 239 Tom Graham	.30	.14	.04
☐ 240 Chuck Foreman	1.25	.55	.16
☐ 241 Ken Riley	.50	.23	.06
☐ 242 Don Morrison	.30	.14	.04
☐ 243 Lynn Dickey	.50	.23	.06
☐ 244 Don Cockroft	.30	.14	.04
☐ 245 Claude Humphrey	.50	.23	.06
☐ 246 John Skorupan	.30	.14	.04
☐ 247 Raymond Chester	.50	.23	.06
☐ 248 Cas Banaszek	.30	.14	.04
☐ 249 Art Malone	.30	.14	.04
☐ 250 Ed Flanagan	.30	.14	.04
☐ 251 Checklist 133-264	3.50	.85	.35
☐ 252 Nemiah Wilson	.30	.14	.04
☐ 253 Ron Jessie	.30	.14	.04
☐ 254 Jim Lynch	.30	.14	.04
☐ 255 Bob Tucker	.50	.23	.06
☐ 256 Terry Owens	.30	.14	.04
☐ 257 John Fitzgerald	.30	.14	.04
☐ 258 Jack Snow	.50	.23	.06
☐ 259 Garry Puetz	.30	.14	.04
☐ 260 Mike Phipps	.50	.23	.06
☐ 261 Al Matthews	.30	.14	.04
☐ 262 Bob Kuechenberg	.30	.14	.04
☐ 263 Ron Yankowski	.30	.14	.04
☐ 264 Ron Shanklin	.30	.14	.04
☐ 265 Bobby Douglass	.50	.23	.06
☐ 266 Josh Ashton	.30	.14	.04
☐ 267 Bill Van Heusen	.30	.14	.04
☐ 268 Jeff Siemon	.30	.14	.04
☐ 269 Bob Newland	.30	.14	.04
☐ 270 Gale Gillingham	.30	.14	.04
☐ 271 Zeke Moore	.30	.14	.04
☐ 272 Mike Tilleman	.30	.14	.04
☐ 273 John Leypoldt	.30	.14	.04
☐ 274 Ken Mendenhall	.30	.14	.04
☐ 275 Norm Snead	.50	.23	.06
☐ 276 Bill Bradley	.50	.23	.06
☐ 277 Jerry Smith	.30	.14	.04
☐ 278 Clarence Davis	.30	.14	.04
☐ 279 Jim Yarbrough	.30	.14	.04
☐ 280 Lemar Parrish	.30	.14	.04
☐ 281 Bobby Bell	1.00	.45	.12
☐ 282 Lynn Swann UER	55.00	25.00	7.00
(Wide Reciever on front)			
☐ 283 John Hicks	.30	.14	.04
☐ 284 Coy Bacon	.50	.23	.06
☐ 285 Lee Roy Jordan	1.00	.45	.12
☐ 286 Willie Buchanon	.30	.14	.04
☐ 287 Al Woodall	.30	.14	.04
☐ 288 Reggie Rucker	.50	.23	.06
☐ 289 John Schmitt	.30	.14	.04
☐ 290 Carl Eller	.75	.35	.09
☐ 291 Jake Scott	.50	.23	.06
☐ 292 Donny Anderson	.50	.23	.06
☐ 293 Charley Wade	.30	.14	.04
☐ 294 John Tanner	.30	.14	.04
☐ 295 Charlie Johnson	.50	.23	.06
(Misspelled Charley			
on both sides)			
☐ 296 Tom Blanchard	.30	.14	.04
☐ 297 Curley Culp	.50	.23	.06
☐ 298 Jeff Van Note	.50	.23	.06
☐ 299 Bob James	.30	.14	.04
☐ 300 Franco Harris	8.00	3.60	1.00
☐ 301 Tim Berra	.50	.23	.06
☐ 302 Bruce Gossett	.30	.14	.04
☐ 303 Verlon Biggs	.30	.14	.04
☐ 304 Bob Kowalkowski	.30	.14	.04
☐ 305 Marv Hubbard	.30	.14	.04
☐ 306 Ken Avery	.30	.14	.04
☐ 307 Mike Adamle	.30	.14	.04
☐ 308 Don Herrmann	.30	.14	.04
☐ 309 Chris Fletcher	.30	.14	.04
☐ 310 Roman Gabriel	1.25	.55	.16
☐ 311 Billy Joe DuPree	.75	.35	.09
☐ 312 Fred Dryer	1.25	.55	.16
☐ 313 John Riggins	5.00	2.20	.60
☐ 314 Bob McKay	.30	.14	.04
☐ 315 Ted Hendricks	2.00	.90	.25
☐ 316 Bobby Bryant	.30	.14	.04
☐ 317 Don Nottingham	.30	.14	.04
☐ 318 John Hannah	4.00	1.80	.50
☐ 319 Rich Coady	.30	.14	.04
☐ 320 Phil Villapiano	.50	.23	.06
☐ 321 Jim Plunkett	1.50	.70	.19
☐ 322 Lyle Alzado	1.25	.55	.16
☐ 323 Ernie Jackson	.30	.14	.04
☐ 324 Billy Parks	.30	.14	.04
☐ 325 Willie Lanier	1.00	.45	.12
☐ 326 John James	.30	.14	.04
☐ 327 Joe Ferguson	.50	.23	.06
☐ 328 Ernie Holmes	.75	.35	.09
☐ 329 Bruce Laird	.30	.14	.04
☐ 330 Chester Marcol	.30	.14	.04
☐ 331 Dave Wilcox	.50	.23	.06
☐ 332 Pat Fischer	.50	.23	.06
☐ 333 Steve Owens	.50	.23	.06
☐ 334 Royce Berry	.30	.14	.04
☐ 335 Russ Washington	.30	.14	.04
☐ 336 Walker Gillette	.30	.14	.04
☐ 337 Mark Nordquist	.30	.14	.04
☐ 338 James Harris	.75	.35	.09
☐ 339 Warren Koegel	.30	.14	.04
☐ 340 Emmitt Thomas	.50	.23	.06
☐ 341 Walt Garrison	.50	.23	.06
☐ 342 Thom Darden	.30	.14	.04
☐ 343 Mike Eischeid	.30	.14	.04
☐ 344 Ernie McMillan	.30	.14	.04
☐ 345 Nick Buoniconti	.75	.35	.09
☐ 346 George Farmer	.30	.14	.04
☐ 347 Sam Adams	.30	.14	.04
☐ 348 Larry Cipa	.30	.14	.04
☐ 349 Bob Moore	.30	.14	.04
☐ 350 Otis Armstrong	1.50	.70	.19
☐ 351 George Blanda RB	3.00	1.35	.35
All Time Scoring			
Leader			
☐ 352 Fred Cox RB	.60	.25	.07
151 Straight PAT's			
☐ 353 Tom Dempsey RB	.60	.25	.07
63 Yard FG			
☐ 354 Ken Houston RB	.75	.35	.09
9th Int. for TD			
(Shown as Oiler,			
should be Redskin)			
☐ 355 O.J. Simpson RB	5.00	2.20	.60
2003 Yard Season			
☐ 356 Ron Smith RB	.60	.25	.07
All Time Return			
Yardage Mark			
☐ 357 Bob Atkins	.30	.14	.04
☐ 358 Pat Sullivan	.50	.23	.06
☐ 359 Joe DeLamielleure	.50	.23	.06
☐ 360 Lawrence McCutcheon	1.50	.70	.19
☐ 361 David Lee	.30	.14	.04
☐ 362 Mike McCoy	.30	.14	.04
☐ 363 Skip Vanderbundt	.30	.14	.04
☐ 364 Mark Moseley	.50	.23	.06
☐ 365 Lem Barney	1.25	.55	.16
☐ 366 Doug Dressler	.30	.14	.04
☐ 367 Dan Fouts	45.00	20.00	5.50
☐ 368 Bob Hyland	.30	.14	.04
☐ 369 John Outlaw	.30	.14	.04
☐ 370 Roy Gerela	.30	.14	.04
☐ 371 Isiah Robertson	.50	.23	.06
☐ 372 Jerome Barkum	.30	.14	.04
☐ 373 Ed Podolak	.30	.14	.04
☐ 374 Milt Morin	.30	.14	.04
☐ 375 John Niland	.30	.14	.04
☐ 376 Checklist 265-396 UER	3.50	.85	.35
(295 Charlie Johnson			
missppelled as Charley)			
☐ 377 Ken Iman	.30	.14	.04
☐ 378 Manny Fernandez	.50	.23	.06
☐ 379 Dave Gallagher	.30	.14	.04
☐ 380 Ken Stabler	18.00	8.00	2.20
☐ 381 Mack Herron	.30	.14	.04
☐ 382 Bill McClard	.30	.14	.04
☐ 383 Ray May	.30	.14	.04
☐ 384 Don Hansen	.30	.14	.04
☐ 385 Elvin Bethea	.50	.23	.06
☐ 386 Joe Scibelli	.30	.14	.04
☐ 387 Neal Craig	.30	.14	.04
☐ 388 Marty Domres	.30	.14	.04
☐ 389 Ken Ellis	.30	.14	.04
☐ 390 Charley Young	.50	.23	.06
☐ 391 Tommy Hart	.30	.14	.04
☐ 392 Moses Denson	.30	.14	.04
☐ 393 Larry Walton	.30	.14	.04
☐ 394 Dave Green	.30	.14	.04
☐ 395 Ron Johnson	.50	.23	.06
☐ 396 Ed Bradley	.30	.14	.04
☐ 397 J.T. Thomas	.30	.14	.04
☐ 398 Jim Bailey	.30	.14	.04
☐ 399 Barry Pearson	.30	.14	.04
☐ 400 Fran Tarkenton	8.00	3.60	1.00
☐ 401 Jack Rudnay	.30	.14	.04
☐ 402 Rayfield Wright	.50	.23	.06
☐ 403 Roger Wehrli	.50	.23	.06
☐ 404 Vern Den Herder	.30	.14	.04
☐ 405 Fred Biletnikoff	3.50	1.55	.45
☐ 406 Ken Grandberry	.30	.14	.04
☐ 407 Bob Adams	.30	.14	.04
☐ 408 Jim Merlo	.30	.14	.04
☐ 409 John Pitts	.30	.14	.04
☐ 410 Dave Osborn	.50	.23	.06
☐ 411 Dennis Havig	.30	.14	.04
☐ 412 Bob Johnson	.30	.14	.04
☐ 413 Ken Burrough UER	.50	.23	.06
(Misspelled Burrow			
on card front)			
☐ 414 Jim Cheyunski	.30	.14	.04
☐ 415 MacArthur Lane	.30	.14	.04
☐ 416 Joe Theismann	25.00	11.00	3.10
☐ 417 Mike Boryla	.30	.14	.04
☐ 418 Bruce Taylor	.30	.14	.04
☐ 419 Chris Hanburger	.50	.23	.06
☐ 420 Tom Mack	.50	.23	.06
☐ 421 Errol Mann	.30	.14	.04
☐ 422 Jack Gregory	.30	.14	.04
☐ 423 Harrison Davis	.30	.14	.04
☐ 424 Burgess Owens	.30	.14	.04
☐ 425 Joe Greene	5.00	2.20	.60
☐ 426 Morris Stroud	.30	.14	.04
☐ 427 John DeMarie	.30	.14	.04
☐ 428 Mel Renfro	1.25	.55	.16
☐ 429 Cid Edwards	.30	.14	.04
☐ 430 Mike Reid	.75	.35	.09
☐ 431 Jack Mildren	.30	.14	.04
☐ 432 Jerry Simmons	.30	.14	.04
☐ 433 Ron Yary	.50	.23	.06
☐ 434 Howard Stevens	.30	.14	.04
☐ 435 Ray Guy	2.00	.90	.25
☐ 436 Tommy Nobis	.75	.35	.09
☐ 437 Solomon Freelon	.30	.14	.04
☐ 438 J.D. Hill	.50	.23	.06
☐ 439 Toni Linhart	.30	.14	.04
☐ 440 Dick Anderson	.50	.23	.06
☐ 441 Guy Morriss	.30	.14	.04
☐ 442 Bob Hoskins	.30	.14	.04
☐ 443 John Hadl	.75	.35	.09
☐ 444 Roy Jefferson	.30	.14	.04
☐ 445 Charlie Sanders	.50	.23	.06
☐ 446 Pat Curran	.30	.14	.04
☐ 447 David Knight	.30	.14	.04
☐ 448 Bob Brown DT	.30	.14	.04
☐ 449 Pete Gogolak	.30	.14	.04
☐ 450 Terry Metcalf	.75	.35	.09
☐ 451 Bill Bergey	.75	.35	.09
☐ 452 Dan Abramowicz HL	.50	.23	.06
105 Straight Games			
☐ 453 Otis Armstrong HL	.75	.35	.09
183 Yard Game			
☐ 454 Cliff Branch HL	1.50	.70	.19
13 TD Passes			
☐ 455 John James HL	.50	.23	.06
Record 96 Punts			
☐ 456 Lydell Mitchell HL	.50	.23	.06
13 Passes in Game			
☐ 457 Lemar Parrish HL	.50	.23	.06
3 TD Punt Returns			
☐ 458 Ken Stabler HL	5.00	2.20	.60
26 TD Passes			
in One Season			
☐ 459 Lynn Swann HL	8.00	3.60	1.00
577 Yards in			
Punt Returns			
☐ 460 Emmitt Thomas HL	.50	.23	.06
73 Yd. Interception			
☐ 461 Terry Bradshaw	20.00	9.00	2.50
☐ 462 Jerrel Wilson	.30	.14	.04
☐ 463 Walter Johnson	.30	.14	.04
☐ 464 Golden Richards	.50	.23	.06
☐ 465 Tommy Casanova	.50	.23	.06

466 Randy Jackson	.30	.14	.04
467 Ron Bolton	.30	.14	.04
468 Joe Owens	.30	.14	.04
469 Wally Hilgenberg	.30	.14	.04
470 Riley Odoms	.50	.23	.06
471 Otis Sistrunk	.50	.23	.06
472 Eddie Ray	.30	.14	.04
473 Reggie McKenzie	.50	.23	.06
474 Elbert Drungo	.30	.14	.04
475 Mercury Morris	.75	.35	.09
476 Dan Dickel	.30	.14	.04
477 Merritt Kersey	.30	.14	.04
478 Mike Holmes	.30	.14	.04
479 Clarence Williams	.30	.14	.04
480 Billy Kilmer	.75	.35	.09
481 Altie Taylor	.30	.14	.04
482 Dave Elmendorf	.30	.14	.04
483 Bob Rowe	.30	.14	.04
484 Pete Athas	.30	.14	.04
485 Winston Hill	.30	.14	.04
486 Bo Matthews	.30	.14	.04
487 Earl Thomas	.30	.14	.04
488 Jan Stenerud	.75	.35	.09
489 Steve Holden	.30	.14	.04
490 Cliff Harris	4.00	1.80	.50
491 Boobie Clark	.50	.23	.06
492 Joe Taylor	.30	.14	.04
493 Tom Neville	.30	.14	.04
494 Wayne Colman	.30	.14	.04
495 Jim Mitchell	.30	.14	.04
496 Paul Krause	.75	.35	.09
497 Jim Otto	1.00	.45	.12
498 John Rowser	.30	.14	.04
499 Larry Little	1.25	.55	.16
500 O.J. Simpson	10.00	4.50	1.25
501 John Dutton	.75	.35	.09
502 Pat Hughes	.30	.14	.04
503 Malcolm Snider	.30	.14	.04
504 Fred Willis	.30	.14	.04
505 Harold Jackson	.75	.35	.09
506 Mike Bragg	.30	.14	.04
507 Jerry Sherk	.50	.23	.06
508 Mirro Roder	.30	.14	.04
509 Tom Sullivan	.30	.14	.04
510 Jim Hart	.75	.35	.09
511 Cedrick Hardman	.30	.14	.04
512 Blaine Nye	.30	.14	.04
513 Elmo Wright	.30	.14	.04
514 Herb Orvis	.30	.14	.04
515 Richard Caster	.50	.23	.06
516 Doug Kotar	.30	.14	.04
517 Checklist 397-528	3.50	.85	.35
518 Jesse Freitas	.30	.14	.04
519 Ken Houston	.75	.35	.09
520 Alan Page	2.00	.90	.25
521 Tim Foley	.50	.23	.06
522 Bill Olds	.30	.14	.04
523 Bobby Maples	.30	.14	.04
524 Cliff Branch	12.00	5.50	1.50
525 Merlin Olsen	1.50	.70	.19
526 AFC Champs Pittsburgh 24, Oakland 13 (Bradshaw and Franco Harris)	3.50	1.55	.45
527 NFC Champs Minnesota 14, Los Angeles 10 (C.Foreman tackled)	1.00	.45	.12
528 Super Bowl IX Steelers 16, Vikings 6 (Bradshaw watching pass)	5.00	1.25	.50

1975 Topps Team Checklists

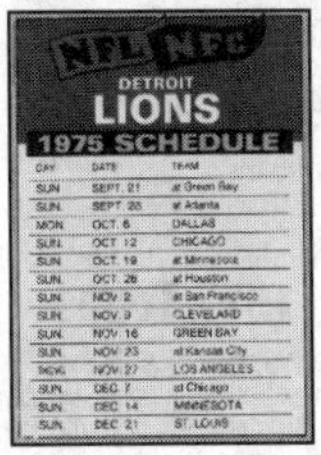

The 1975 Topps Team Checklist set contains 26 standard-size cards, one for each of the 26 NFL teams. The front of the card has the 1975 schedule, while the back of the card contains the checklist, complete with boxes in which to place check marks. The player's position is also listed with his name. The set was only available directly from Topps as a send-off offer as an uncut sheet; the prices below apply equally to uncut sheets as they are frequently found in their original uncut condition. As for individual cards, thin card stock mkaes it a challenge to find these cards in top grades. These unnumbered cards are numbered below for convenience in alphabetical order by team name.

	NRMT-MT	EXC	G-VG
COMPLETE SET (26)	200.00	50.00	20.00
COMMON CARD (1-26)	10.00	2.50	1.00
1 Atlanta Falcons	10.00	2.50	1.00
2 Baltimore Colts	10.00	2.50	1.00
3 Buffalo Bills	10.00	2.50	1.00
4 Chicago Bears	10.00	2.50	1.00
5 Cincinnati Bengals	10.00	2.50	1.00
6 Cleveland Browns	10.00	2.50	1.00
7 Dallas Cowboys	20.00	5.00	2.00
8 Denver Broncos	10.00	2.50	1.00
9 Detroit Lions	10.00	2.50	1.00
10 Green Bay Packers	15.00	3.70	1.50
11 Houston Oilers	10.00	2.50	1.00
12 Kansas City Chiefs	10.00	2.50	1.00
13 Los Angeles Rams	10.00	2.50	1.00
14 Miami Dolphins	15.00	3.70	1.50
15 Minnesota Vikings	10.00	2.50	1.00
16 New England Patriots	10.00	2.50	1.00
17 New York Giants	10.00	2.50	1.00
18 New York Jets	10.00	2.50	1.00
19 New Orleans Saints	10.00	2.50	1.00
20 Oakland Raiders	20.00	5.00	2.00
21 Philadelphia Eagles	10.00	2.50	1.00
22 Pittsburgh Steelers	15.00	3.70	1.50
23 St. Louis Cardinals	10.00	2.50	1.00
24 San Diego Chargers	10.00	2.50	1.00
25 San Francisco 49ers	15.00	3.70	1.50
26 Washington Redskins	15.00	3.70	1.50

1976 Topps

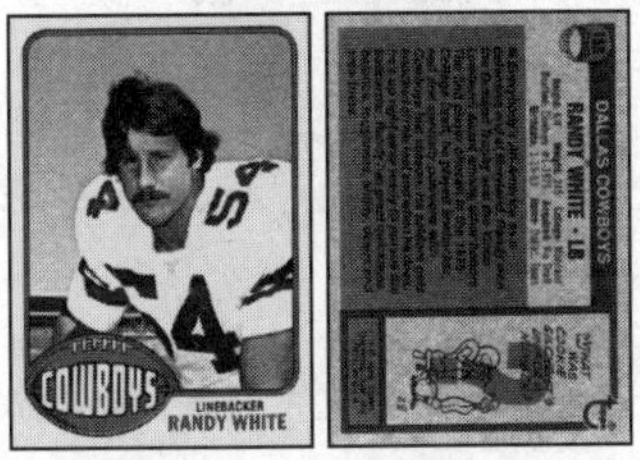

The 1976 Topps football set contains 528 standard-size cards including the first year cards of Seattle Seahwaks and Tampa Bay Buccaneers. Underneath photos that are bordered by a team color, card fronts contain a team colored football at bottom left with the team name within. The player's name and position are also at the bottom. The card backs are printed in orange and blue on gray card stock and are horizontally designed. The content includes statistics, highlights and a trivia question with answer. Subsets include Record Breakers (1-6), league leaders (201-206), playoffs (331-333) and team checklist (451-478) cards. The key Rookie Card belongs to all-time rushing leader Walter Payton. Other Rookie Cards include Randy Gradishar, Ed Too Tall Jones, Jack Lambert, Harvey Martin, and Randy White. An uncut sheet of team checklist cards was also available via a mail-in offer on wax packs.

	NRMT-MT	EXC	G-VG
COMPLETE SET (528)	325.00	145.00	40.00
COMMON CARD (1-528)	.30	.14	.04
1 George Blanda RB First to Score 2000 Points	5.00	1.25	.50
2 Neal Colzie RB Punt Returns	.50	.23	.06
3 Chuck Foreman RB Catches 73 Passes	.75	.35	.09
4 Jim Marshall RB 26th Fumble Recovery	.50	.23	.06
5 Terry Metcalf RB Most all-purpose yards; season	.75	.35	.09
6 O.J. Simpson RB 23 Touchdowns	3.00	1.35	.35
7 Fran Tarkenton RB Most Attempts;Season	3.00	1.35	.35
8 Charley Taylor RB Career Receptions	1.00	.45	.12
9 Ernie Holmes	.50	.23	.06
10 Ken Anderson AP	1.50	.70	.19
11 Bobby Bryant	.30	.14	.04
12 Jerry Smith	.50	.23	.06
13 David Lee	.30	.14	.04
14 Robert Newhouse	.75	.35	.09
15 Vern Den Herder	.30	.14	.04
16 John Hannah	1.50	.70	.19
17 J.D. Hill	.50	.23	.06
18 James Harris	.50	.23	.06
19 Willie Buchanon	.30	.14	.04
20 Charley Young AP	.50	.23	.06
21 Jim Yarbrough	.30	.14	.04
22 Ronnie Coleman	.30	.14	.04
23 Don Cockroft	.30	.14	.04
24 Willie Lanier	.75	.35	.09
25 Fred Biletnikoff	3.00	1.35	.35
26 Ron Yankowski	.30	.14	.04
27 Spider Lockhart	.30	.14	.04
28 Bob Johnson	.30	.14	.04
29 J.T. Thomas	.30	.14	.04
30 Ron Yary AP	.50	.23	.06
31 Brad Dusek	.30	.14	.04
32 Raymond Chester	.50	.23	.06
33 Larry Little	.75	.35	.09
34 Pat Leahy	.75	.35	.09
35 Steve Bartkowski	2.50	1.10	.30
36 Tom Myers	.30	.14	.04
37 Bill Van Heusen	.30	.14	.04
38 Russ Washington	.30	.14	.04
39 Tom Sullivan	.30	.14	.04
40 Curley Culp AP	.50	.23	.06
41 Johnnie Gray	.30	.14	.04
42 Bob Klein	.30	.14	.04
43 Lem Barney	1.00	.45	.12
44 Harvey Martin	4.00	1.80	.50
45 Reggie Rucker	.50	.23	.06
46 Neil Clabo	.30	.14	.04
47 Ray Hamilton	.30	.14	.04
48 Joe Ferguson	.50	.23	.06
49 Ed Podolak	.30	.14	.04
50 Ray Guy AP	2.00	.90	.25
51 Glen Edwards	.30	.14	.04
52 Jim LeClair	.30	.14	.04
53 Mike Barnes	.30	.14	.04
54 Nat Moore	.75	.35	.09
55 Billy Kilmer	.75	.35	.09
56 Larry Stallings	.30	.14	.04
57 Jack Gregory	.30	.14	.04
58 Steve Mike-Mayer	.30	.14	.04
59 Virgil Livers	.30	.14	.04
60 Jerry Sherk AP	.50	.23	.06
61 Guy Morriss	.30	.14	.04
62 Barty Smith	.30	.14	.04
63 Jerome Barkum	.30	.14	.04
64 Ira Gordon	.30	.14	.04
65 Paul Krause	.75	.35	.09
66 John McMakin	.30	.14	.04
67 Checklist 1-132	3.00	.75	.30
68 Charlie Johnson UER (Misspelled Charley on both sides)	.50	.23	.06
69 Tommy Nobis	.75	.35	.09
70 Lydell Mitchell	.50	.23	.06
71 Vern Holland	.30	.14	.04
72 Tim Foley	.50	.23	.06
73 Golden Richards	.50	.23	.06
74 Bryant Salter	.30	.14	.04
75 Terry Bradshaw	16.00	7.25	2.00
76 Ted Hendricks	1.25	.55	.16
77 Rich Saul	.30	.14	.04
78 John Smith	.30	.14	.04
79 Altie Taylor	.30	.14	.04
80 Cedrick Hardman AP	.30	.14	.04
81 Ken Payne	.30	.14	.04
82 Zeke Moore	.30	.14	.04
83 Alvin Maxson	.30	.14	.04
84 Wally Hilgenberg	.30	.14	.04
85 John Niland	.30	.14	.04
86 Mike Sensibaugh	.30	.14	.04
87 Ron Johnson	.50	.23	.06
88 Winston Hill	.30	.14	.04
89 Charlie Joiner	4.00	1.80	.50
90 Roger Wehrli AP	.50	.23	.06
91 Mike Bragg	.30	.14	.04
92 Dan Dickel	.30	.14	.04
93 Earl Morrall	.50	.23	.06
94 Pat Toomay	.30	.14	.04
95 Gary Garrison	.30	.14	.04
96 Ken Geddes	.30	.14	.04
97 Mike Current	.30	.14	.04
98 Bob Avellini	.50	.23	.06
99 Dave Pureifory	.30	.14	.04
100 Franco Harris AP	8.00	3.60	1.00
101 Randy Logan	.30	.14	.04
102 John Fitzgerald	.30	.14	.04
103 Gregg Bingham	.50	.23	.06
104 Jim Plunkett	1.00	.45	.12
105 Carl Eller	.75	.35	.09
106 Larry Walton	.30	.14	.04
107 Clarence Scott	.30	.14	.04
108 Skip Vanderbundt	.30	.14	.04
109 Boobie Clark	.50	.23	.06
110 Tom Mack AP	.50	.23	.06
111 Bruce Laird	.30	.14	.04
112 Dave Dalby	.30	.14	.04
113 John Leypoldt	.30	.14	.04
114 Barry Pearson	.30	.14	.04
115 Larry Brown	.50	.23	.06
116 Jackie Smith	.75	.35	.09
117 Pat Hughes	.30	.14	.04
118 Al Woodall	.30	.14	.04
119 John Zook	.30	.14	.04
120 Jake Scott AP	.50	.23	.06
121 Rich Glover	.30	.14	.04
122 Ernie Jackson	.30	.14	.04
123 Otis Armstrong	.75	.35	.09
124 Bob Grim	.30	.14	.04
125 Jeff Siemon	.50	.23	.06
126 Harold Hart	.30	.14	.04
127 John DeMarie	.30	.14	.04
128 Dan Fouts	12.00	5.50	1.50
129 Jim Kearney	.30	.14	.04
130 John Dutton AP	.50	.23	.06
131 Calvin Hill	.75	.35	.09
132 Toni Fritsch	.30	.14	.04
133 Ron Jessie	.30	.14	.04
134 Don Nottingham	.30	.14	.04
135 Lemar Parrish	.30	.14	.04
136 Russ Francis	1.50	.70	.19
137 Joe Reed	.30	.14	.04
138 C.L. Whittington	.30	.14	.04
139 Otis Sistrunk	.50	.23	.06
140 Lynn Swann AP	18.00	8.00	2.20
141 Jim Carter	.30	.14	.04
142 Mike Montler	.30	.14	.04
143 Walter Johnson	.30	.14	.04
144 Doug Kotar	.30	.14	.04
145 Roman Gabriel	.75	.35	.09
146 Billy Newsome	.30	.14	.04
147 Ed Bradley	.30	.14	.04
148 Walter Payton	160.00	70.00	20.00
149 Johnny Fuller	.30	.14	.04
150 Alan Page AP	1.25	.55	.16
151 Frank Grant	.30	.14	.04
152 Dave Green	.30	.14	.04
153 Nelson Munsey	.30	.14	.04
154 Jim Mandich	.30	.14	.04
155 Lawrence McCutcheon	.75	.35	.09
156 Steve Ramsey	.30	.14	.04
157 Ed Flanagan	.30	.14	.04
158 Randy White	25.00	11.00	3.10
159 Gerry Mullins	.30	.14	.04
160 Jan Stenerud AP	.75	.35	.09
161 Steve Odom	.30	.14	.04
162 Roger Finnie	.30	.14	.04
163 Norm Snead	.50	.23	.06
164 Jeff Van Note	.50	.23	.06
165 Bill Bergey	.75	.35	.09
166 Allen Carter	.30	.14	.04
167 Steve Holden	.30	.14	.04
168 Sherman White	.30	.14	.04
169 Bob Berry	.30	.14	.04
170 Ken Houston AP	.75	.35	.09
171 Bill Olds	.30	.14	.04
172 Larry Seiple	.30	.14	.04
173 Cliff Branch	4.00	1.80	.50
174 Reggie McKenzie	.50	.23	.06
175 Dan Pastorini	.75	.35	.09
176 Paul Naumoff	.30	.14	.04
177 Checklist 133-264	3.00	.75	.30
178 Durwood Keeton	.30	.14	.04
179 Earl Thomas	.30	.14	.04
180 L.C. Greenwood AP	1.00	.45	.12
181 John Outlaw	.30	.14	.04
182 Frank Nunley	.30	.14	.04
183 Dave Jennings	.50	.23	.06
184 MacArthur Lane	.30	.14	.04
185 Chester Marcol	.30	.14	.04
186 J.J. Jones	.30	.14	.04
187 Tom DeLeone	.30	.14	.04
188 Steve Zabel	.30	.14	.04
189 Ken Johnson	.30	.14	.04
190 Rayfield Wright AP	.50	.23	.06
191 Brent McClanahan	.30	.14	.04
192 Pat Fischer	.50	.23	.06
193 Roger Carr	.50	.23	.06
194 Manny Fernandez	.50	.23	.06
195 Roy Gerela	.30	.14	.04
196 Dave Elmendorf	.30	.14	.04
197 Bob Kowalkowski	.30	.14	.04
198 Phil Villapiano	.50	.23	.06
199 Will Wynn	.30	.14	.04
200 Terry Metcalf	.75	.35	.09
201 Passing Leaders Ken Anderson Fran Tarkenton	2.00	.90	.25
202 Receiving Leaders Reggie Rucker Lydell Mitchell Chuck Foreman	.50	.23	.06
203 Rushing Leaders O.J. Simpson Jim Otis	2.50	1.10	.30
204 Scoring Leaders O.J. Simpson Chuck Foreman	2.50	1.10	.30
205 Interception Leaders Mel Blount Paul Krause	.75	.35	.09
206 Punting Leaders Ray Guy Herman Weaver	.50	.23	.06
207 Ken Ellis	.30	.14	.04
208 Ron Saul	.30	.14	.04
209 Toni Linhart	.30	.14	.04
210 Jim Langer AP	.75	.35	.09
211 Jeff Wright	.30	.14	.04
212 Moses Denson	.30	.14	.04
213 Earl Edwards	.30	.14	.04
214 Walker Gillette	.30	.14	.04
215 Bob Trumpy	.50	.23	.06
216 Emmitt Thomas	.50	.23	.06
217 Lyle Alzado	.75	.35	.09
218 Carl Garrett	.50	.23	.06
219 Van Green	.30	.14	.04
220 Jack Lambert AP	25.00	11.00	3.10
221 Spike Jones	.30	.14	.04
222 John Hadl	.75	.35	.09
223 Billy Johnson	1.50	.70	.19
224 Tony McGee	.30	.14	.04
225 Preston Pearson	.50	.23	.06
226 Isiah Robertson	.50	.23	.06
227 Errol Mann	.30	.14	.04
228 Paul Seal	.30	.14	.04
229 Roland Harper	.30	.14	.04

☐ 230 Ed White AP	.50	.23	.06
☐ 231 Joe Theismann	6.00	2.70	.75
☐ 232 Jim Cheyunski	.30	.14	.04
☐ 233 Bill Stanfill	.50	.23	.06
☐ 234 Marv Hubbard	.30	.14	.04
☐ 235 Tommy Casanova	.50	.23	.06
☐ 236 Bob Hyland	.30	.14	.04
☐ 237 Jesse Freitas	.30	.14	.04
☐ 238 Norm Thompson	.30	.14	.04
☐ 239 Charlie Smith	.30	.14	.04
☐ 240 John James AP	.30	.14	.04
☐ 241 Alden Roche	.30	.14	.04
☐ 242 Gordon Jolley	.30	.14	.04
☐ 243 Larry Ely	.30	.14	.04
☐ 244 Richard Caster	.30	.14	.04
☐ 245 Joe Greene	4.00	1.80	.50
☐ 246 Larry Schreiber	.30	.14	.04
☐ 247 Terry Schmidt	.30	.14	.04
☐ 248 Jerrel Wilson	.30	.14	.04
☐ 249 Marty Domres	.30	.14	.04
☐ 250 Isaac Curtis AP	.50	.23	.06
☐ 251 Harold McLinton	.30	.14	.04
☐ 252 Fred Dryer	.75	.35	.09
☐ 253 Bill Lenkaitis	.30	.14	.04
☐ 254 Don Hardeman	.30	.14	.04
☐ 255 Bob Griese	5.00	2.20	.60
☐ 256 Oscar Roan	.30	.14	.04
☐ 257 Randy Gradishar	2.50	1.10	.30
☐ 258 Bob Thomas	.30	.14	.04
☐ 259 Joe Owens	.30	.14	.04
☐ 260 Cliff Harris AP	1.25	.55	.16
☐ 261 Frank Lewis	.30	.14	.04
☐ 262 Mike McCoy	.30	.14	.04
☐ 263 Rickey Young	.30	.14	.04
☐ 264 Brian Kelley	.30	.14	.04
☐ 265 Charlie Sanders	.50	.23	.06
☐ 266 Jim Hart	.75	.35	.09
☐ 267 Greg Gantt	.30	.14	.04
☐ 268 John Ward	.30	.14	.04
☐ 269 Al Beauchamp	.30	.14	.04
☐ 270 Jack Tatum AP	.75	.35	.09
☐ 271 Jim Lash	.30	.14	.04
☐ 272 Diron Talbert	.30	.14	.04
☐ 273 Checklist 265-396	3.00	.75	.30
☐ 274 Steve Spurrier	7.00	3.10	.85
☐ 275 Greg Pruitt	.75	.35	.09
☐ 276 Jim Mitchell	.30	.14	.04
☐ 277 Jack Rudnay	.30	.14	.04
☐ 278 Freddie Solomon	.50	.23	.06
☐ 279 Frank LeMaster	.30	.14	.04
☐ 280 Wally Chambers AP	.30	.14	.04
☐ 281 Mike Collier	.30	.14	.04
☐ 282 Clarence Williams	.30	.14	.04
☐ 283 Mitch Hoopes	.30	.14	.04
☐ 284 Ron Bolton	.30	.14	.04
☐ 285 Harold Jackson	.75	.35	.09
☐ 286 Greg Landry	.50	.23	.06
☐ 287 Tony Greene	.30	.14	.04
☐ 288 Howard Stevens	.30	.14	.04
☐ 289 Roy Jefferson	.30	.14	.04
☐ 290 Jim Bakken AP	.30	.14	.04
☐ 291 Doug Sutherland	.30	.14	.04
☐ 292 Marvin Cobb	.30	.14	.04
☐ 293 Mack Alston	.30	.14	.04
☐ 294 Rod McNeill	.30	.14	.04
☐ 295 Gene Upshaw	.75	.35	.09
☐ 296 Dave Gallagher	.30	.14	.04
☐ 297 Larry Ball	.30	.14	.04
☐ 298 Ron Howard	.30	.14	.04
☐ 299 Don Strock	.75	.35	.09
☐ 300 O.J. Simpson AP	8.00	3.60	1.00
☐ 301 Ray Mansfield	.30	.14	.04
☐ 302 Larry Marshall	.30	.14	.04
☐ 303 Dick Himes	.30	.14	.04
☐ 304 Ray Wersching	.30	.14	.04
☐ 305 John Riggins	4.00	1.80	.50
☐ 306 Bob Parsons	.30	.14	.04
☐ 307 Ray Brown	.30	.14	.04
☐ 308 Len Dawson	3.00	1.35	.35
☐ 309 Andy Maurer	.30	.14	.04
☐ 310 Jack Youngblood AP	.75	.35	.09
☐ 311 Essex Johnson	.30	.14	.04
☐ 312 Stan White	.30	.14	.04
☐ 313 Drew Pearson	4.00	1.80	.50
☐ 314 Rockne Freitas	.30	.14	.04
☐ 315 Mercury Morris	.75	.35	.09
☐ 316 Willie Alexander	.30	.14	.04
☐ 317 Paul Warfield	3.00	1.35	.35
☐ 318 Bob Chandler	.50	.23	.06
☐ 319 Bobby Walden	.30	.14	.04
☐ 320 Riley Odoms AP	.50	.23	.06
☐ 321 Mike Boryla	.30	.14	.04
☐ 322 Bruce Van Dyke	.30	.14	.04
☐ 323 Pete Banaszak	.30	.14	.04
☐ 324 Darryl Stingley	.75	.35	.09
☐ 325 John Mendenhall	.30	.14	.04
☐ 326 Dan Dierdorf	2.00	.90	.25
☐ 327 Bruce Taylor	.30	.14	.04
☐ 328 Don McCauley	.30	.14	.04
☐ 329 John Reaves UER (24 attempts in '72; should be 224)	.30	.14	.04
☐ 330 Chris Hanburger AP	.50	.23	.06
☐ 331 NFC Champions Cowboys 37, Rams 7 (Roger Staubach)	3.00	1.35	.35
☐ 332 AFC Champions Steelers 16, Raiders 10 (Franco Harris)	2.00	.90	.25
☐ 333 Super Bowl X Steelers 21, Cowboys 17 (Terry Bradshaw)	2.50	1.10	.30
☐ 334 Godwin Turk	.30	.14	.04
☐ 335 Dick Anderson	.50	.23	.06
☐ 336 Woody Green	.30	.14	.04
☐ 337 Pat Curran	.30	.14	.04
☐ 338 Council Rudolph	.30	.14	.04
☐ 339 Joe Lavender	.30	.14	.04
☐ 340 John Gilliam AP	.50	.23	.06
☐ 341 Steve Furness	.50	.23	.06
☐ 342 D.D. Lewis	.50	.23	.06
☐ 343 Duane Carrell	.30	.14	.04
☐ 344 Jon Morris	.30	.14	.04
☐ 345 John Brockington	.50	.23	.06
☐ 346 Mike Phipps	.50	.23	.06
☐ 347 Lyle Blackwood	.30	.14	.04
☐ 348 Julius Adams	.30	.14	.04
☐ 349 Terry Hermeling	.30	.14	.04
☐ 350 Rolland Lawrence AP	.30	.14	.04
☐ 351 Glenn Doughty	.30	.14	.04
☐ 352 Doug Swift	.30	.14	.04
☐ 353 Mike Strachan	.30	.14	.04
☐ 354 Craig Morton	.75	.35	.09
☐ 355 George Blanda	5.00	2.20	.60
☐ 356 Garry Puetz	.30	.14	.04
☐ 357 Carl Mauck	.30	.14	.04
☐ 358 Walt Patulski	.30	.14	.04
☐ 359 Stu Voigt	.30	.14	.04
☐ 360 Fred Carr AP	.30	.14	.04
☐ 361 Po James	.30	.14	.04
☐ 362 Otis Taylor	.75	.35	.09
☐ 363 Jeff West	.30	.14	.04
☐ 364 Gary Huff	.50	.23	.06
☐ 365 Dwight White	.50	.23	.06
☐ 366 Dan Ryczek	.30	.14	.04
☐ 367 Jon Keyworth	.30	.14	.04
☐ 368 Mel Renfro	1.25	.55	.16
☐ 369 Bruce Coslet	.50	.23	.06
☐ 370 Len Hauss AP	.30	.14	.04
☐ 371 Rick Volk	.30	.14	.04
☐ 372 Howard Twilley	.50	.23	.06
☐ 373 Cullen Bryant	.50	.23	.06
☐ 374 Bob Babich	.30	.14	.04
☐ 375 Herman Weaver	.30	.14	.04
☐ 376 Steve Grogan	2.50	1.10	.30
☐ 377 Bubba Smith	1.00	.45	.12
☐ 378 Burgess Owens	.30	.14	.04
☐ 379 Al Matthews	.30	.14	.04
☐ 380 Art Shell	1.50	.70	.19
☐ 381 Larry Brown	.30	.14	.04
☐ 382 Horst Muhlmann	.30	.14	.04
☐ 383 Ahmad Rashad	2.50	1.10	.30
☐ 384 Bobby Maples	.30	.14	.04
☐ 385 Jim Marshall	.75	.35	.09
☐ 386 Joe Dawkins	.30	.14	.04
☐ 387 Dennis Partee	.30	.14	.04
☐ 388 Eddie McMillan	.30	.14	.04
☐ 389 Randy Johnson	.30	.14	.04
☐ 390 Bob Kuechenberg AP	.30	.14	.04
☐ 391 Rufus Mayes	.30	.14	.04
☐ 392 Lloyd Mumphord	.30	.14	.04
☐ 393 Ike Harris	.30	.14	.04
☐ 394 Dave Hampton	.30	.14	.04
☐ 395 Roger Staubach	18.00	8.00	2.20
☐ 396 Doug Buffone	.30	.14	.04
☐ 397 Howard Fest	.30	.14	.04
☐ 398 Wayne Mulligan	.30	.14	.04
☐ 399 Bill Bradley	.50	.23	.06
☐ 400 Chuck Foreman AP	.75	.35	.09
☐ 401 Jack Snow	.50	.23	.06
☐ 402 Bob Howard	.30	.14	.04
☐ 403 John Matuszak	.75	.35	.09
☐ 404 Bill Munson	.50	.23	.06
☐ 405 Andy Russell	.50	.23	.06
☐ 406 Skip Butler	.30	.14	.04
☐ 407 Hugh McKinnis	.30	.14	.04
☐ 408 Bob Penchion	.30	.14	.04
☐ 409 Mike Bass	.30	.14	.04
☐ 410 George Kunz AP	.30	.14	.04
☐ 411 Ron Pritchard	.30	.14	.04
☐ 412 Barry Smith	.30	.14	.04
☐ 413 Norm Bulaich	.30	.14	.04
☐ 414 Marv Bateman	.30	.14	.04
☐ 415 Ken Stabler	12.00	5.50	1.50
☐ 416 Conrad Dobler	.50	.23	.06
☐ 417 Bob Tucker	.50	.23	.06
☐ 418 Gene Washington	.50	.23	.06
☐ 419 Ed Marinaro	.75	.35	.09
☐ 420 Jack Ham AP	4.00	1.80	.50
☐ 421 Jim Turner	.30	.14	.04
☐ 422 Chris Fletcher	.30	.14	.04
☐ 423 Carl Barzilauskas	.30	.14	.04
☐ 424 Robert Brazile	.75	.35	.09
☐ 425 Harold Carmichael	2.00	.90	.25
☐ 426 Ron Jaworski	4.00	1.80	.50
☐ 427 Ed Too Tall Jones	20.00	9.00	2.50
☐ 428 Larry McCarren	.30	.14	.04
☐ 429 Mike Thomas	.30	.14	.04
☐ 430 Joe DeLamielleure AP	.30	.14	.04
☐ 431 Tom Blanchard	.30	.14	.04
☐ 432 Ron Carpenter	.30	.14	.04
☐ 433 Levi Johnson	.30	.14	.04
☐ 434 Sam Cunningham	.50	.23	.06
☐ 435 Garo Yepremian	.50	.23	.06
☐ 436 Mike Livingston	.30	.14	.04
☐ 437 Larry Csonka	3.00	1.35	.35
☐ 438 Doug Dieken	.50	.23	.06
☐ 439 Bill Lueck	.30	.14	.04
☐ 440 Tom MacLeod AP	.30	.14	.04
☐ 441 Mick Tingelhoff	.50	.23	.06
☐ 442 Terry Hanratty	.50	.23	.06
☐ 443 Mike Siani	.30	.14	.04
☐ 444 Dwight Harrison	.30	.14	.04
☐ 445 Jim Otis	.50	.23	.06
☐ 446 Jack Reynolds	.50	.23	.06
☐ 447 Jean Fugett	.50	.23	.06
☐ 448 Dave Beverly	.30	.14	.04
☐ 449 Bernard Jackson	.30	.14	.04
☐ 450 Charley Taylor	2.00	.90	.25
☐ 451 Atlanta Falcons Team Checklist	2.00	.50	.20
☐ 452 Baltimore Colts Team Checklist	2.00	.50	.20
☐ 453 Buffalo Bills Team Checklist	2.00	.50	.20
☐ 454 Chicago Bears Team Checklist	2.00	.50	.20
☐ 455 Cincinnati Bengals Team Checklist	2.00	.50	.20
☐ 456 Cleveland Browns Team Checklist	2.00	.50	.20
☐ 457 Dallas Cowboys Team Checklist	2.00	.50	.20
☐ 458 Denver Broncos UER Team Checklist (Charlie Johnson spelled Charley)	2.00	.50	.20
☐ 459 Detroit Lions Team Checklist	2.00	.50	.20
☐ 460 Green Bay Packers Team Checklist	2.00	.50	.20
☐ 461 Houston Oilers Team Checklist	2.00	.50	.20
☐ 462 Kansas City Chiefs Team Checklist	2.00	.50	.20
☐ 463 Los Angeles Rams Team Checklist	2.00	.50	.20
☐ 464 Miami Dolphins Team Checklist	2.00	.50	.20
☐ 465 Minnesota Vikings Team Checklist	2.00	.50	.20
☐ 466 New England Patriots Team Checklist	2.00	.50	.20
☐ 467 New Orleans Saints Team Checklist	2.00	.50	.20
☐ 468 New York Giants Team Checklist	2.00	.50	.20
☐ 469 New York Jets Team Checklist	2.00	.50	.20
☐ 470 Oakland Raiders Team Checklist	2.00	.50	.20
☐ 471 Philadelphia Eagles Team Checklist	2.00	.50	.20
☐ 472 Pittsburgh Steelers Team Checklist	2.00	.50	.20
☐ 473 St. Louis Cardinals Team Checklist	2.00	.50	.20
☐ 474 San Diego Chargers Team Checklist	2.00	.50	.20
☐ 475 San Francisco 49ers Team Checklist	2.00	.50	.20
☐ 476 Seattle Seahawks Team Checklist	2.00	.50	.20
☐ 477 Tampa Bay Buccaneers Team Checklist	2.00	.50	.20
☐ 478 Washington Redskins Team Checklist	2.00	.50	.20
☐ 479 Fred Cox	.30	.14	.04
☐ 480 Mel Blount AP	6.00	2.70	.75
☐ 481 John Bunting	.30	.14	.04
☐ 482 Ken Mendenhall	.30	.14	.04
☐ 483 Will Harrell	.30	.14	.04
☐ 484 Marlin Briscoe	.30	.14	.04
☐ 485 Archie Manning	1.00	.45	.12
☐ 486 Tody Smith	.30	.14	.04
☐ 487 George Hunt	.30	.14	.04
☐ 488 Roscoe Word	.30	.14	.04
☐ 489 Paul Seymour	.30	.14	.04
☐ 490 Lee Roy Jordan AP	.75	.35	.09
☐ 491 Chip Myers	.30	.14	.04
☐ 492 Norm Evans	.30	.14	.04
☐ 493 Jim Bertelsen	.30	.14	.04
☐ 494 Mark Moseley	.50	.23	.06
☐ 495 George Buehler	.30	.14	.04
☐ 496 Charlie Hall	.30	.14	.04
☐ 497 Marvin Upshaw	.30	.14	.04
☐ 498 Tom Banks	.30	.14	.04
☐ 499 Randy Vataha	.30	.14	.04
☐ 500 Fran Tarkenton AP	6.00	2.70	.75
☐ 501 Mike Wagner	.50	.23	.06
☐ 502 Art Malone	.30	.14	.04
☐ 503 Fred Cook	.30	.14	.04
☐ 504 Rich McGeorge	.30	.14	.04
☐ 505 Ken Burrough	.50	.23	.06
☐ 506 Nick Mike-Mayer	.30	.14	.04
☐ 507 Checklist 397-528	3.00	.75	.30
☐ 508 Steve Owens	.50	.23	.06
☐ 509 Brad Van Pelt	.30	.14	.04
☐ 510 Ken Riley AP	.50	.23	.06
☐ 511 Art Thoms	.30	.14	.04
☐ 512 Ed Bell	.30	.14	.04
☐ 513 Tom Wittum	.30	.14	.04
☐ 514 Jim Braxton	.30	.14	.04
☐ 515 Nick Buoniconti	.75	.35	.09
☐ 516 Brian Sipe	2.00	.90	.25
☐ 517 Jim Lynch	.30	.14	.04
☐ 518 Prentice McCray	.30	.14	.04
☐ 519 Tom Dempsey	.30	.14	.04
☐ 520 Mel Gray AP	.50	.23	.06
☐ 521 Nate Wright	.30	.14	.04
☐ 522 Rocky Bleier	6.00	2.70	.75
☐ 523 Dennis Johnson	.30	.14	.04
☐ 524 Jerry Sisemore	.30	.14	.04
☐ 525 Bert Jones	.30	.14	.04
☐ 526 Perry Smith	.30	.14	.04
☐ 527 Blaine Nye	.30	.14	.04
☐ 528 Bob Moore	1.00	.25	.10

1976 Topps Team Checklists

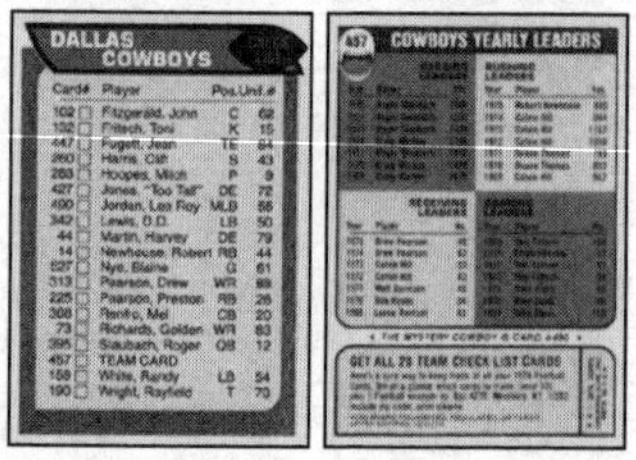

The 1976 Topps Team Checklist set contains 30 standard-size cards, one for each of the 28 NFL teams plus two checklist cards. The front of the card has the 1976 Topps checklist for that particular team, complete with boxes in which to place check marks. The set was only available directly from Topps as a send-off offer as an uncut sheet; the prices below apply equally to uncut sheets as they are frequently found in their original uncut condition. As for individual cards, thin card stock makes it a challenge to obtain singles in top grades. These unnumbered cards are numbered below for convenience in alphabetical order by team name.

	NRMT-MT	EXC	G-VG
COMPLETE SET (30)	125.00	31.00	12.50
COMMON CARD (1-30)	5.00	2.20	.50

☐ 1 Atlanta Falcons	5.00	1.25	.50
☐ 2 Baltimore Colts	5.00	1.25	.50
☐ 3 Buffalo Bills	5.00	1.25	.50
☐ 4 Chicago Bears	5.00	1.25	.50
☐ 5 Cincinnati Bengals	5.00	1.25	.50
☐ 6 Cleveland Browns	5.00	1.25	.50
☐ 7 Dallas Cowboys	10.00	2.50	1.00
☐ 8 Denver Broncos	5.00	1.25	.50
☐ 9 Detroit Lions	5.00	1.25	.50
☐ 10 Green Bay Packers	7.50	1.85	.75
☐ 11 Houston Oilers	5.00	1.25	.50
☐ 12 Kansas City Chiefs	5.00	1.25	.50
☐ 13 Los Angeles Rams	5.00	1.25	.50
☐ 14 Miami Dolphins	7.50	1.85	.75
☐ 15 Minnesota Vikings	5.00	1.25	.50
☐ 16 New England Patriots	5.00	1.25	.50
☐ 17 New York Giants	5.00	1.25	.50
☐ 18 New York Jets	5.00	1.25	.50
☐ 19 New Orleans Saints	5.00	1.25	.50
☐ 20 Oakland Raiders	10.00	2.50	1.00
☐ 21 Philadelphia Eagles	5.00	1.25	.50
☐ 22 Pittsburgh Steelers	7.50	1.85	.75
☐ 23 St. Louis Cardinals	5.00	1.25	.50
☐ 24 San Diego Chargers	5.00	1.25	.50
☐ 25 San Francisco 49ers	7.50	1.85	.75
☐ 26 Seattle Seahawks	5.00	1.25	.50
☐ 27 Tampa Bay Buccaneers	5.00	1.25	.50
☐ 28 Washington Redskins	7.50	1.85	.75
☐ 29 Checklist 1-132	5.00	1.25	.50
☐ 30 Checklist 133-264	5.00	1.25	.50

1977 Topps

The 1977 Topps football set contains 528 standard-size cards. Card fronts have a banner (with team name), the player's name and position at the top. Backs that rushed for 1,000 yards have a "1,000 Yarder" football logo on front. The card backs are printed in purple and black on gray card stock. The backs contain yearly statistics, highlights and a note on the player's college career. Subsets include league leaders (1-6), team checklist cards (201-208), Record Breakers (451-455) and playoffs (526-528). The key Rookie Card is Steve Largent. Other Rookie Cards include Harry Carson, Dave Casper, Archie Griffin, Mike Haynes, Ray Rhodes, Lee Roy Selmon, Mike Webster, Danny White and Jim Zorn. An uncut sheet of team checklist cards was also available via a mail-in offer on wax pack wrappers. A Mexican version of this set was produced. All text is in Spanish (front and back) and is quite a bit tougher to find than the basic issue.

	NRMT-MT	EXC	G-VG
COMPLETE SET (528)	225.00	100.00	28.00
COMMON CARD (1-528)	.25	.11	.03

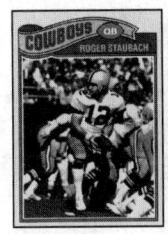
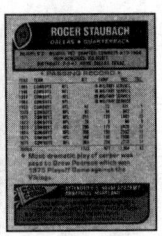

☐ 1 Passing Leaders	2.50	.60	.25
James Harris			
Ken Stabler			
☐ 2 Receiving Leaders	.40	.18	.05
Drew Pearson			
MacArthur Lane			
☐ 3 Rushing Leaders	10.00	4.50	1.25
Walter Payton			
O.J. Simpson			
☐ 4 Scoring Leaders	.40	.18	.05
Mark Moseley			
Toni Linhart			
☐ 5 Interception Leaders	.40	.18	.05
Monte Jackson			
Ken Riley			
☐ 6 Punting Leaders	.40	.18	.05
John James			
Marv Bateman			
☐ 7 Mike Phipps	.40	.18	.05
☐ 8 Rick Volk	.25	.11	.03
☐ 9 Steve Furness	.40	.18	.05
☐ 10 Isaac Curtis	.40	.18	.05
☐ 11 Nate Wright	.40	.18	.05
☐ 12 Jean Fugett	.25	.11	.03
☐ 13 Ken Mendenhall	.25	.11	.03
☐ 14 Sam Adams	.25	.11	.03
☐ 15 Charlie Waters	.60	.25	.07
☐ 16 Bill Stanfill	.25	.11	.03
☐ 17 John Holland	.25	.11	.03
☐ 18 Pat Haden	2.50	1.10	.30
☐ 19 Bob Young	.25	.11	.03
☐ 20 Wally Chambers AP	.25	.11	.03
☐ 21 Lawrence Gaines	.25	.11	.03
☐ 22 Larry McCarren	.25	.11	.03
☐ 23 Horst Muhlmann	.25	.11	.03
☐ 24 Phil Villapiano	.40	.18	.05
☐ 25 Greg Pruitt	.40	.18	.05
☐ 26 Ron Howard	.25	.11	.03
☐ 27 Craig Morton	.60	.25	.07
☐ 28 Rufus Mayes	.25	.11	.03
☐ 29 Lee Roy Selmon UER	10.00	4.50	1.25
Misspelled Leroy			
☐ 30 Ed White AP	.40	.18	.05
☐ 31 Harold McLinton	.25	.11	.03
☐ 32 Glenn Doughty	.25	.11	.03
☐ 33 Bob Kuechenberg	.60	.25	.07
☐ 34 Duane Carrell	.25	.11	.03
☐ 35 Riley Odoms	.25	.11	.03
☐ 36 Bobby Scott	.25	.11	.03
☐ 37 Nick Mike-Mayer	.25	.11	.03
☐ 38 Bill Lenkaitis	.25	.11	.03
☐ 39 Roland Harper	.40	.18	.05
☐ 40 Tommy Hart AP	.25	.11	.03
☐ 41 Mike Sensibaugh	.25	.11	.03
☐ 42 Rusty Jackson	.25	.11	.03
☐ 43 Levi Johnson	.25	.11	.03
☐ 44 Mike McCoy	.25	.11	.03
☐ 45 Roger Staubach	15.00	6.75	1.85
☐ 46 Fred Cox	.25	.11	.03
☐ 47 Bob Babich	.25	.11	.03
☐ 48 Reggie McKenzie	.40	.18	.05
☐ 49 Dave Jennings	.25	.11	.03
☐ 50 Mike Haynes AP	5.00	2.20	.60
☐ 51 Larry Brown	.40	.18	.05
☐ 52 Marvin Cobb	.25	.11	.03
☐ 53 Fred Cook	.25	.11	.03
☐ 54 Freddie Solomon	.40	.18	.05
☐ 55 John Riggins	2.50	1.10	.30
☐ 56 John Bunting	.25	.11	.03
☐ 57 Ray Wersching	.40	.18	.05
☐ 58 Mike Livingston	.25	.11	.03
☐ 59 Billy Johnson	.40	.18	.05
☐ 60 Mike Wagner AP	.25	.11	.03
☐ 61 Waymond Bryant	.25	.11	.03
☐ 62 Jim Otis	.40	.18	.05
☐ 63 Ed Galigher	.25	.11	.03
☐ 64 Randy Vataha	.25	.11	.03
☐ 65 Jim Zorn	3.00	1.35	.35
☐ 66 Jon Keyworth	.25	.11	.03
☐ 67 Checklist 1-132	2.00	.50	.20
☐ 68 Henry Childs	.25	.11	.03
☐ 69 Thom Darden	.25	.11	.03
☐ 70 George Kunz AP	.25	.11	.03
☐ 71 Lenvil Elliott	.25	.11	.03
☐ 72 Curtis Johnson	.25	.11	.03
☐ 73 Doug Van Horn	.25	.11	.03
☐ 74 Joe Theismann	4.00	1.80	.50
☐ 75 Dwight White	.40	.18	.05
☐ 76 Scott Laidlaw	.25	.11	.03
☐ 77 Monte Johnson	.25	.11	.03
☐ 78 Dave Beverly	.25	.11	.03
☐ 79 Jim Mitchell	.25	.11	.03

☐ 80 Jack Youngblood AP	.60	.25	.07
☐ 81 Mel Gray	.40	.18	.05
☐ 82 Dwight Harrison	.25	.11	.03
☐ 83 John Hadl	.40	.18	.05
☐ 84 Matt Blair	.60	.25	.07
☐ 85 Charlie Sanders	.25	.11	.03
☐ 86 Noah Jackson	.25	.11	.03
☐ 87 Ed Marinaro	.40	.18	.05
☐ 88 Bob Howard	.25	.11	.03
☐ 89 John McDaniel	.25	.11	.03
☐ 90 Dan Dierdorf AP	1.50	.70	.19
☐ 91 Mark Moseley	.40	.18	.05
☐ 92 Cleo Miller	.25	.11	.03
☐ 93 Andre Tillman	.25	.11	.03
☐ 94 Bruce Taylor	.25	.11	.03
☐ 95 Bert Jones	1.00	.45	.12
☐ 96 Anthony Davis	.75	.35	.09
☐ 97 Don Goode	.25	.11	.03
☐ 98 Ray Rhodes	6.00	2.70	.75
☐ 99 Mike Webster	10.00	4.50	1.25
☐ 100 O.J. Simpson AP	5.00	2.20	.60
☐ 101 Doug Plank	.25	.11	.03
☐ 102 Efren Herrera	.40	.18	.05
☐ 103 Charlie Smith	.25	.11	.03
☐ 104 Carlos Brown	.25	.11	.03
☐ 105 Jim Marshall	.60	.25	.07
☐ 106 Paul Naumoff	.25	.11	.03
☐ 107 Walter White	.25	.11	.03
☐ 108 John Cappelletti	2.00	.90	.25
☐ 109 Chip Myers	.25	.11	.03
☐ 110 Ken Stabler AP	10.00	4.50	1.25
☐ 111 Joe Ehrmann	.25	.11	.03
☐ 112 Rick Engles	.25	.11	.03
☐ 113 Jack Dolbin	.25	.11	.03
☐ 114 Ron Bolton	.25	.11	.03
☐ 115 Mike Thomas	.25	.11	.03
☐ 116 Mike Fuller	.25	.11	.03
☐ 117 John Hill	.25	.11	.03
☐ 118 Richard Todd	.60	.25	.07
☐ 119 Duriel Harris	.40	.18	.05
☐ 120 John James AP	.25	.11	.03
☐ 121 Lionel Antoine	.25	.11	.03
☐ 122 John Skorupan	.25	.11	.03
☐ 123 Skip Butler	.25	.11	.03
☐ 124 Bob Tucker	.25	.11	.03
☐ 125 Paul Krause	.40	.18	.05
☐ 126 Dave Hampton	.25	.11	.03
☐ 127 Tom Wittum	.25	.11	.03
☐ 128 Gary Huff	.40	.18	.05
☐ 129 Emmitt Thomas	.25	.11	.03
☐ 130 Drew Pearson AP	2.00	.90	.25
☐ 131 Ron Saul	.25	.11	.03
☐ 132 Steve Niehaus	.25	.11	.03
☐ 133 Fred Carr	.60	.25	.07
☐ 134 Norm Bulaich	.25	.11	.03
☐ 135 Bob Trumpy	.40	.18	.05
☐ 136 Greg Landry	.40	.18	.05
☐ 137 George Buehler	.25	.11	.03
☐ 138 Reggie Rucker	.40	.18	.05
☐ 139 Julius Adams	.25	.11	.03
☐ 140 Jack Ham AP	2.50	1.10	.30
☐ 141 Wayne Morris	.25	.11	.03
☐ 142 Marv Bateman	.25	.11	.03
☐ 143 Bobby Maples	.25	.11	.03
☐ 144 Harold Carmichael	1.25	.55	.16
☐ 145 Bob Avellini	.40	.18	.05
☐ 146 Harry Carson	3.00	1.35	.35
☐ 147 Lawrence Pillers	.25	.11	.03
☐ 148 Ed Williams	.25	.11	.03
☐ 149 Dan Pastorini	.40	.18	.05
☐ 150 Ron Yary AP	.40	.18	.05
☐ 151 Joe Lavender	.25	.11	.03
☐ 152 Pat McInally	.40	.18	.05
☐ 153 Lloyd Mumphord	.25	.11	.03
☐ 154 Cullen Bryant	.40	.18	.05
☐ 155 Willie Lanier	.60	.25	.07
☐ 156 Gene Washington	.40	.18	.05
☐ 157 Scott Hunter	.25	.11	.03
☐ 158 Jim Merlo	.25	.11	.03
☐ 159 Randy Grossman	.40	.18	.05
☐ 160 Blaine Nye AP	.25	.11	.03
☐ 161 Ike Harris	.25	.11	.03
☐ 162 Doug Dieken	.25	.11	.03
☐ 163 Guy Morriss	.25	.11	.03
☐ 164 Bob Parsons	.25	.11	.03
☐ 165 Steve Grogan	1.00	.45	.12
☐ 166 John Brockington	.40	.18	.05
☐ 167 Charlie Joiner	2.50	1.10	.30
☐ 168 Ron Carpenter	.25	.11	.03
☐ 169 Jeff Wright	.25	.11	.03
☐ 170 Chris Hanburger AP	.25	.11	.03
☐ 171 Roosevelt Leaks	.40	.18	.05
☐ 172 Larry Little	.60	.25	.07
☐ 173 John Matuszak	.40	.18	.05
☐ 174 Joe Ferguson	.40	.18	.05
☐ 175 Brad Van Pelt	.40	.18	.05
☐ 176 Dexter Bussey	.25	.11	.03
☐ 177 Steve Largent	50.00	22.00	6.25
☐ 178 Dewey Selmon	.40	.18	.05
☐ 179 Randy Gradishar	1.00	.45	.12
☐ 180 Mel Blount AP	3.00	1.35	.35
☐ 181 Dan Neal	.25	.11	.03
☐ 182 Rich Szaro	.25	.11	.03
☐ 183 Mike Boryla	.25	.11	.03
☐ 184 Steve Jones	.25	.11	.03

☐ 185 Paul Warfield	2.50	1.10	.30
☐ 186 Greg Buttle	.25	.11	.03
☐ 187 Rich McGeorge	.25	.11	.03
☐ 188 Leon Gray	.40	.18	.05
☐ 189 John Shinners	.25	.11	.03
☐ 190 Toni Linhart AP	.25	.11	.03
☐ 191 Robert Miller	.25	.11	.03
☐ 192 Jake Scott	.25	.11	.03
☐ 193 Jon Morris	.25	.11	.03
☐ 194 Randy Crowder	.25	.11	.03
☐ 195 Lynn Swann UER	16.00	7.25	2.00
(Interception Record			
on card back)			
☐ 196 Marsh White	.25	.11	.03
☐ 197 Rod Perry	.25	.11	.03
☐ 198 Willie Hall	.25	.11	.03
☐ 199 Mike Hartenstine	.25	.11	.03
☐ 200 Jim Bakken AP	.25	.11	.03
☐ 201 Atlanta Falcons UER	1.25	.30	.12
(79 Jim Mitchell			
is not listed)			
Team Checklist			
☐ 202 Baltimore Colts	1.25	.30	.12
Team Checklist			
☐ 203 Buffalo Bills	1.25	.30	.12
Team Checklist			
☐ 204 Chicago Bears	1.25	.30	.12
Team Checklist			
☐ 205 Cincinnati Bengals	1.25	.30	.12
Team Checklist			
☐ 206 Cleveland Browns	1.25	.30	.12
Team Checklist			
☐ 207 Dallas Cowboys	1.25	.30	.12
Team Checklist			
☐ 208 Denver Broncos	1.25	.30	.12
Team Checklist			
☐ 209 Detroit Lions	1.25	.30	.12
Team Checklist			
☐ 210 Green Bay Packers	1.25	.30	.12
Team Checklist			
☐ 211 Houston Oilers	1.25	.30	.12
Team Checklist			
☐ 212 Kansas City Chiefs	1.25	.30	.12
Team Checklist			
☐ 213 Los Angeles Rams	1.25	.30	.12
Team Checklist			
☐ 214 Miami Dolphins	1.25	.30	.12
Team Checklist			
☐ 215 Minnesota Vikings	1.25	.30	.12
Team Checklist			
☐ 216 New England Patriots	1.25	.30	.12
Team Checklist			
☐ 217 New Orleans Saints	1.25	.30	.12
Team Checklist			
☐ 218 New York Giants	1.25	.30	.12
Team Checklist			
☐ 219 New York Jets	1.25	.30	.12
Team Checklist			
☐ 220 Oakland Raiders	1.25	.30	.12
Team Checklist			
☐ 221 Philadelphia Eagles	1.25	.30	.12
Team Checklist			
☐ 222 Pittsburgh Steelers	1.25	.30	.12
Team Checklist			
☐ 223 St. Louis Cardinals	1.25	.30	.12
Team Checklist			
☐ 224 San Diego Chargers	1.25	.30	.12
Team Checklist			
☐ 225 San Francisco 49ers	1.25	.30	.12
Team Checklist			
☐ 226 Seattle Seahawks	1.25	.30	.12
Team Checklist			
☐ 227 Tampa Bay Buccaneers	1.25	.30	.12
Team Checklist UER			
(Lee Roy Selmon mis-			
spelled as Leroy)			
☐ 228 Washington Redskins	1.25	.30	.12
Team Checklist			
☐ 229 Sam Cunningham	.40	.18	.05
☐ 230 Alan Page AP	1.00	.45	.12
☐ 231 Eddie Brown	.25	.11	.03
☐ 232 Stan White	.25	.11	.03
☐ 233 Vern Den Herder	.25	.11	.03
☐ 234 Clarence Davis	.25	.11	.03
☐ 235 Ken Anderson	1.50	.70	.19
☐ 236 Karl Chandler	.25	.11	.03
☐ 237 Will Harrell	.25	.11	.03
☐ 238 Clarence Scott	.25	.11	.03
☐ 239 Bo Rather	.25	.11	.03
☐ 240 Robert Brazile AP	.40	.18	.05
☐ 241 Bob Bell	.25	.11	.03
☐ 242 Rolland Lawrence	.25	.11	.03
☐ 243 Tom Sullivan	.25	.11	.03
☐ 244 Larry Brunson	.25	.11	.03
☐ 245 Terry Bradshaw	12.00	5.50	1.50
☐ 246 Rich Saul	.25	.11	.03
☐ 247 Cleveland Elam	.25	.11	.03
☐ 248 Don Woods	.25	.11	.03
☐ 249 Bruce Laird	.25	.11	.03
☐ 250 Coy Bacon AP	.25	.11	.03
☐ 251 Russ Francis	.60	.25	.07
☐ 252 Jim Braxton	.25	.11	.03
☐ 253 Perry Smith	.25	.11	.03
☐ 254 Jerome Barkum	.25	.11	.03
☐ 255 Garo Yepremian	.40	.18	.05

☐ 256 Checklist 133-264	2.00	.50	.20
☐ 257 Tony Galbreath	.40	.18	.05
☐ 258 Troy Archer	.25	.11	.03
☐ 259 Brian Sipe	.75	.35	.09
☐ 260 Billy Joe DuPree AP	.40	.18	.05
☐ 261 Bobby Walden	.25	.11	.03
☐ 262 Larry Marshall	.25	.11	.03
☐ 263 Ted Fritsch Jr.	.25	.11	.03
☐ 264 Larry Hand	.25	.11	.03
☐ 265 Tom Mack	.40	.18	.05
☐ 266 Ed Bradley	.25	.11	.03
☐ 267 Pat Leahy	.40	.18	.05
☐ 268 Louis Carter	.25	.11	.03
☐ 269 Archie Griffin	4.00	1.80	.50
☐ 270 Art Shell AP	1.00	.45	.12
☐ 271 Stu Voigt	.25	.11	.03
☐ 272 Prentice McCray	.25	.11	.03
☐ 273 MacArthur Lane	.25	.11	.03
☐ 274 Dan Fouts	6.00	2.70	.75
☐ 275 Charley Young	.40	.18	.05
☐ 276 Wilbur Jackson	.25	.11	.03
☐ 277 John Hicks	.25	.11	.03
☐ 278 Nat Moore	.60	.25	.07
☐ 279 Virgil Livers	.25	.11	.03
☐ 280 Curley Culp AP	.40	.18	.05
☐ 281 Rocky Bleier	2.50	1.10	.30
☐ 282 John Zook	.25	.11	.03
☐ 283 Tom DeLeone	.25	.11	.03
☐ 284 Danny White	5.00	2.20	.60
☐ 285 Otis Armstrong	.40	.18	.05
☐ 286 Larry Walton	.25	.11	.03
☐ 287 Jim Carter	.25	.11	.03
☐ 288 Don McCauley	.25	.11	.03
☐ 289 Frank Grant	.25	.11	.03
☐ 290 Roger Wehrli AP	.40	.18	.05
☐ 291 Mick Tingelhoff	.40	.18	.05
☐ 292 Bernard Jackson	.25	.11	.03
☐ 293 Tom Owen	.25	.11	.03
☐ 294 Mike Esposito	.25	.11	.03
☐ 295 Fred Biletnikoff	2.50	1.10	.30
☐ 296 Revie Sorey	.25	.11	.03
☐ 297 John McMakin	.25	.11	.03
☐ 298 Dan Ryczek	.25	.11	.03
☐ 299 Wayne Moore	.25	.11	.03
☐ 300 Franco Harris AP	4.00	1.80	.50
☐ 301 Rick Upchurch	.60	.25	.07
☐ 302 Jim Stienke	.25	.11	.03
☐ 303 Charlie Davis	.25	.11	.03
☐ 304 Don Cockroft	.25	.11	.03
☐ 305 Ken Burrough	.40	.18	.05
☐ 306 Clark Gaines	.25	.11	.03
☐ 307 Bobby Douglass	.25	.11	.03
☐ 308 Ralph Perretta	.25	.11	.03
☐ 309 Wally Hilgenberg	.25	.11	.03
☐ 310 Monte Jackson AP	.40	.18	.05
☐ 311 Chris Bahr	.40	.18	.05
☐ 312 Jim Cheyunski	.25	.11	.03
☐ 313 Mike Patrick	.25	.11	.03
☐ 314 Ed Too Tall Jones	5.00	2.20	.60
☐ 315 Bill Bradley	.25	.11	.03
☐ 316 Benny Malone	.25	.11	.03
☐ 317 Paul Seymour	.25	.11	.03
☐ 318 Jim Laslavic	.25	.11	.03
☐ 319 Frank Lewis	.40	.18	.05
☐ 320 Ray Guy AP	.60	.25	.07
☐ 321 Allan Ellis	.25	.11	.03
☐ 322 Conrad Dobler	.40	.18	.05
☐ 323 Chester Marcol	.25	.11	.03
☐ 324 Doug Kotar	.25	.11	.03
☐ 325 Lemar Parrish	.40	.18	.05
☐ 326 Steve Holden	.25	.11	.03
☐ 327 Jeff Van Note	.40	.18	.05
☐ 328 Howard Stevens	.25	.11	.03
☐ 329 Brad Dusek	.40	.18	.05
☐ 330 Joe DeLamielleure AP	.25	.11	.03
☐ 331 Jim Plunkett	.60	.25	.07
☐ 332 Checklist 265-396	2.00	.50	.20
☐ 333 Lou Piccone	.25	.11	.03
☐ 334 Ray Hamilton	.25	.11	.03
☐ 335 Jan Stenerud	.40	.18	.05
☐ 336 Jeris White	.25	.11	.03
☐ 337 Sherman Smith	.25	.11	.03
☐ 338 Dave Green	.25	.11	.03
☐ 339 Terry Schmidt	.25	.11	.03
☐ 340 Sammie White AP	1.00	.45	.12
☐ 341 Jon Kolb	.25	.11	.03
☐ 342 Randy White	8.00	3.60	1.00
☐ 343 Bob Klein	.25	.11	.03
☐ 344 Bob Kowalkowski	.25	.11	.03
☐ 345 Terry Metcalf	.40	.18	.05
☐ 346 Joe Danelo	.25	.11	.03
☐ 347 Ken Payne	.25	.11	.03
☐ 348 Neal Craig	.25	.11	.03
☐ 349 Dennis Johnson	.25	.11	.03
☐ 350 Bill Bergey AP	.40	.18	.05
☐ 351 Raymond Chester	.25	.11	.03
☐ 352 Bob Matheson	.25	.11	.03
☐ 353 Mike Kadish	.25	.11	.03
☐ 354 Mark Van Eeghen	.60	.25	.07
☐ 355 L.C. Greenwood	.75	.35	.09
☐ 356 Sam Hunt	.25	.11	.03
☐ 357 Darrell Austin	.25	.11	.03
☐ 358 Jim Turner	.25	.11	.03
☐ 359 Ahmad Rashad	2.00	.90	.25
☐ 360 Walter Payton AP	30.00	13.50	3.70

361 Mark Arneson	.25	.11	.03
362 Jerrel Wilson	.25	.11	.03
363 Steve Bartkowski	1.00	.45	.12
364 John Watson	.25	.11	.03
365 Ken Riley	.40	.18	.05
366 Gregg Bingham	.25	.11	.03
367 Golden Richards	.40	.18	.05
368 Clyde Powers	.25	.11	.03
369 Diron Talbert	.25	.11	.03
370 Lydell Mitchell	.40	.18	.05
371 Bob Jackson	.25	.11	.03
372 Jim Mandich	.25	.11	.03
373 Frank LeMaster	.25	.11	.03
374 Benny Ricardo	.25	.11	.03
375 Lawrence McCutcheon	.40	.18	.05
376 Lynn Dickey	.40	.18	.05
377 Phil Wise	.25	.11	.03
378 Tony McGee	.25	.11	.03
379 Norm Thompson	.25	.11	.03
380 Dave Casper AP	1.50	.70	.19
381 Glen Edwards	.25	.11	.03
382 Bob Thomas	.25	.11	.03
383 Bob Chandler	.40	.18	.05
384 Rickey Young	.40	.18	.05
385 Carl Eller	.60	.25	.07
386 Lyle Alzado	.60	.25	.07
387 John Leypoldt	.25	.11	.03
388 Gordon Bell	.25	.11	.03
389 Mike Bragg	.25	.11	.03
390 Jim Langer AP	.60	.25	.07
391 Vern Holland	.25	.11	.03
392 Nelson Munsey	.25	.11	.03
393 Mack Mitchell	.25	.11	.03
394 Tony Adams	.25	.11	.03
395 Preston Pearson	.40	.18	.05
396 Emanuel Zanders	.25	.11	.03
397 Vince Papale	.25	.11	.03
398 Joe Fields	.40	.18	.05
399 Craig Clemons	.25	.11	.03
400 Fran Tarkenton AP	5.00	2.20	.60
401 Andy Johnson	.25	.11	.03
402 Willie Buchanon	.25	.11	.03
403 Pat Curran	.25	.11	.03
404 Ray Jarvis	.25	.11	.03
405 Joe Greene	2.50	1.10	.30
406 Bill Simpson	.25	.11	.03
407 Ronnie Coleman	.25	.11	.03
408 J.K. McKay	.40	.18	.05
409 Pat Fischer	.40	.18	.05
410 John Dutton AP	.40	.18	.05
411 Boobie Clark	.25	.11	.03
412 Pat Tilley	.60	.25	.07
413 Don Strock	.40	.18	.05
414 Brian Kelley	.25	.11	.03
415 Gene Upshaw	.60	.25	.07
416 Mike Montler	.25	.11	.03
417 Checklist 397-528	2.00	.50	.20
418 John Gilliam	.25	.11	.03
419 Brent McClanahan	.25	.11	.03
420 Jerry Sherk AP	.25	.11	.03
421 Roy Gerela	.25	.11	.03
422 Tim Fox	.40	.18	.05
423 John Ebersole	.25	.11	.03
424 James Scott	.25	.11	.03
425 Delvin Williams	.40	.18	.05
426 Spike Jones	.25	.11	.03
427 Harvey Martin	1.25	.55	.16
428 Don Herrmann	.25	.11	.03
429 Calvin Hill	.40	.18	.05
430 Isiah Robertson AP	.25	.11	.03
431 Tony Greene	.25	.11	.03
432 Bob Johnson	.25	.11	.03
433 Lem Barney	.60	.25	.07
434 Eric Torkelson	.25	.11	.03
435 John Mendenhall	.25	.11	.03
436 Larry Seiple	.40	.18	.05
437 Art Kuehn	.25	.11	.03
438 John Vella	.25	.11	.03
439 Greg Latta	.25	.11	.03
440 Roger Carr AP	.40	.18	.05
441 Doug Sutherland	.25	.11	.03
442 Mike Kruczek	.25	.11	.03
443 Steve Zabel	.25	.11	.03
444 Mike Pruitt	.60	.25	.07
445 Harold Jackson	.40	.18	.05
446 George Jakowenko	.25	.11	.03
447 John Fitzgerald	.25	.11	.03
448 Carey Joyce	.25	.11	.03
449 Jim LeClair	.25	.11	.03
450 Ken Houston AP	.60	.25	.07
451 Steve Grogan RB Most Touchdowns Rushing by QB, Season	.50	.23	.06
452 Jim Marshall RB Most Games Played, Lifetime	.50	.23	.06
453 O.J. Simpson RB Most Yardage, Rushing, Game	2.50	1.10	.30
454 Fran Tarkenton RB Most Yardage, Passing, Lifetime	3.00	1.35	.35
455 Jim Zorn RB Most Passing Yards Season, Rookie	.50	.23	.06
456 Robert Pratt	.25	.11	.03
457 Walker Gillette	.25	.11	.03
458 Charlie Hall	.25	.11	.03
459 Robert Newhouse	.40	.18	.05
460 John Hannah AP	.60	.25	.07
461 Ken Reaves	.25	.11	.03
462 Herman Weaver	.25	.11	.03
463 James Harris	.40	.18	.05
464 Howard Twilley	.40	.18	.05
465 Jeff Siemon	.40	.18	.05
466 John Outlaw	.25	.11	.03
467 Chuck Muncie	1.00	.45	.12
468 Bob Moore	.25	.11	.03
469 Robert Woods	.25	.11	.03
470 Cliff Branch AP	2.00	.90	.25
471 Johnnie Gray	.25	.11	.03
472 Don Hardeman	.25	.11	.03
473 Steve Ramsey	.25	.11	.03
474 Steve Mike-Mayer	.25	.11	.03
475 Gary Garrison	.25	.11	.03
476 Walter Johnson	.25	.11	.03
477 Neil Clabo	.25	.11	.03
478 Len Hauss	.25	.11	.03
479 Darryl Stingley	.40	.18	.05
480 Jack Lambert AP	8.00	3.60	1.00
481 Mike Adamle	.40	.18	.05
482 David Lee	.25	.11	.03
483 Tom Mullen	.25	.11	.03
484 Claude Humphrey	.25	.11	.03
485 Jim Hart	.60	.25	.07
486 Bobby Thompson RB	.25	.11	.03
487 Jack Rudnay	.25	.11	.03
488 Rich Sowells	.25	.11	.03
489 Reuben Gant	.25	.11	.03
490 Cliff Harris AP	.60	.25	.07
491 Bob Brown DT	.25	.11	.03
492 Don Nottingham	.25	.11	.03
493 Ron Jessie	.25	.11	.03
494 Otis Sistrunk	.40	.18	.05
495 Billy Kilmer	.40	.18	.05
496 Oscar Roan	.25	.11	.03
497 Bill Van Heusen	.25	.11	.03
498 Randy Logan	.25	.11	.03
499 John Smith	.25	.11	.03
500 Chuck Foreman AP	.40	.18	.05
501 J.T. Thomas	.25	.11	.03
502 Steve Schubert	.25	.11	.03
503 Mike Barnes	.25	.11	.03
504 J.V. Cain	.25	.11	.03
505 Larry Csonka	2.50	1.10	.30
506 Elvin Bethea	.40	.18	.05
507 Ray Easterling	.25	.11	.03
508 Joe Reed	.25	.11	.03
509 Steve Odom	.25	.11	.03
510 Tommy Casanova AP	.25	.11	.03
511 Dave Dalby	.25	.11	.03
512 Richard Caster	.25	.11	.03
513 Fred Dryer	.60	.25	.07
514 Jeff Kinney	.25	.11	.03
515 Bob Griese	4.00	1.80	.50
516 Butch Johnson	.60	.25	.07
517 Gerald Irons	.25	.11	.03
518 Don Calhoun	.25	.11	.03
519 Jack Gregory	.25	.11	.03
520 Tom Banks AP	.25	.11	.03
521 Bobby Bryant	.25	.11	.03
522 Reggie Harrison	.25	.11	.03
523 Terry Hermeling	.25	.11	.03
524 David Taylor	.25	.11	.03
525 Brian Baschnagel	.40	.18	.05
526 AFC Championship Raiders 24, Steelers 7 (Stabler)	.50	.23	.06
527 NFC Championship Vikings 24, Rams 13	.50	.23	.06
528 Super Bowl XI Raiders 32, Vikings 14 (line play)	1.00	.25	.10

1977 Topps Holsum Packers/Vikings

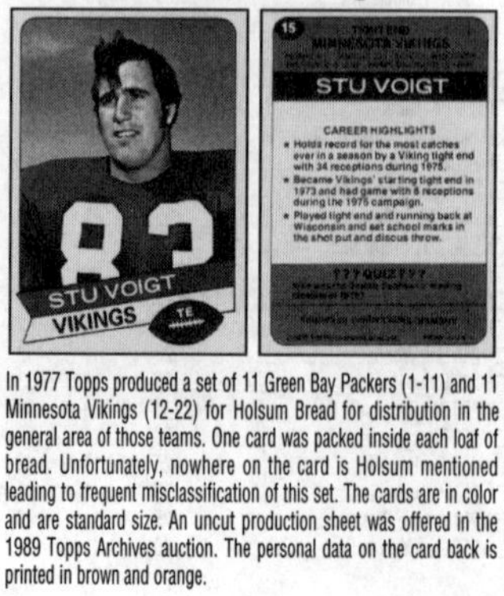

In 1977 Topps produced a set of 11 Green Bay Packers (1-11) and 11 Minnesota Vikings (12-22) for Holsum Bread for distribution in the general area of those teams. One card was packed inside each loaf of bread. Unfortunately, nowhere on the card is Holsum mentioned leading to frequent misclassification of this set. The cards are in color and are standard size. An uncut production sheet was offered in the 1989 Topps Archives auction. The personal data on the card back is printed in brown and orange.

	NRMT-MT	EXC	G-VG
COMPLETE SET (22)	40.00	18.00	5.00
COMMON CARD (1-22)	1.25	.55	.16
1 Lynn Dickey	3.00	1.35	.35
2 John Brockington	2.00	.90	.25
3 Will Harrell	1.25	.55	.16
4 Ken Payne	1.25	.55	.16
5 Rich McGeorge	1.25	.55	.16
6 Steve Odom	1.25	.55	.16
7 Jim Carter	1.25	.55	.16
8 Fred Carr	1.25	.55	.16
9 Willie Buchanon	2.00	.90	.25
10 Mike McCoy	1.25	.55	.16
11 Chester Marcol	1.25	.55	.16
12 Chuck Foreman	4.00	1.80	.50
13 Ahmad Rashad	6.00	2.70	.75
14 Sammie White	3.00	1.35	.35
15 Stu Voigt	1.25	.55	.16
16 Fred Cox	1.25	.55	.16
17 Carl Eller	4.00	1.80	.50
18 Alan Page	6.00	2.70	.75
19 Jeff Siemon	1.25	.55	.16
20 Bobby Bryant	1.25	.55	.16
21 Paul Krause	3.00	1.35	.35
22 Ron Yary	2.00	.90	.25

1977 Topps Mexican

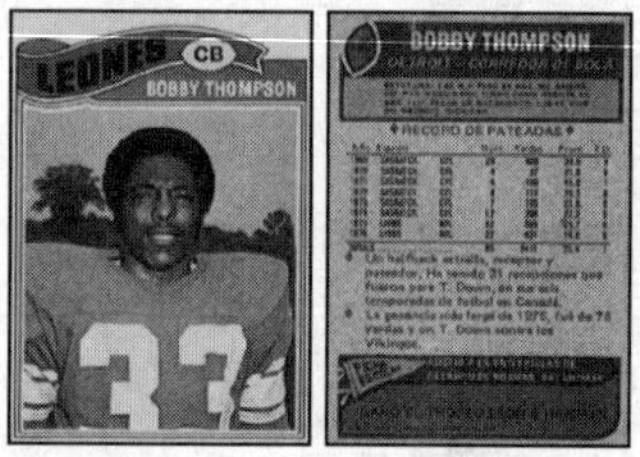

The Mexican version of the 1977 Topps football series contains the same 528 players as the American issue. The cards were issued in 2-card packs with a stick of gum, or in scarcer 4-card packs without gum. All text is in Spanish (front and back). All cards have been discovered, however, some cards are considered to be tougher to obtain and could vary in price depending on the outlet. Some collectors also pursue the wrappers, which feature various NFL stars on them.

	NRMT-MT	EXC	G-VG
COMPLETE SET (528)	7500.00	3400.00	950.00
COMMON CARD (1-528)	8.00	3.60	1.00
COMMON CHECKLIST	12.00	5.50	1.50
SEMISTARS	10.00	4.50	1.25
UNLISTED STARS	15.00	6.75	1.85
1 Passing Leaders James Harris Ken Stabler	110.00	50.00	14.00
3 Rushing Leaders Walter Payton O.J. Simpson	200.00	90.00	25.00
4 Scoring Leaders Mark Moseley Toni Linhart	30.00	13.50	3.70
18 Pat Haden	40.00	18.00	5.00
29 Lee Roy Selmon UER Misspelled Leroy	80.00	36.00	10.00
45 Roger Staubach	135.00	60.00	17.00
50 Mike Haynes AP	25.00	11.00	3.10
55 John Riggins	30.00	13.50	3.70
65 Jim Zorn	30.00	13.50	3.70
74 Joe Theismann	40.00	18.00	5.00
90 Dan Dierdorf AP	18.00	8.00	2.20
96 Anthony Davis	20.00	9.00	2.50
98 Ray Rhodes	25.00	11.00	3.10
99 Mike Webster	60.00	27.00	7.50
100 O.J. Simpson AP	90.00	40.00	11.00
108 John Cappelletti	20.00	9.00	2.50
110 Ken Stabler AP	125.00	55.00	15.50
130 Drew Pearson AP	25.00	11.00	3.10
140 Jack Ham AP	30.00	13.50	3.70
146 Harry Carson	40.00	18.00	5.00
165 Steve Grogan	20.00	9.00	2.50
167 Charlie Joiner	20.00	9.00	2.50
173 John Matuszak	18.00	8.00	2.20
177 Steve Largent	600.00	275.00	75.00
180 Mel Blount AP	35.00	16.00	4.40
185 Paul Warfield	35.00	16.00	4.40
195 Lynn Swann	110.00	50.00	14.00
230 Alan Page AP	20.00	9.00	2.50
235 Ken Anderson	20.00	9.00	2.50
245 Terry Bradshaw	120.00	55.00	15.00
269 Archie Griffin	60.00	27.00	7.50
274 Dan Fouts	70.00	32.00	8.75
281 Rocky Bleier	30.00	13.50	3.70
284 Danny White	50.00	22.00	6.25
295 Fred Biletnikoff	35.00	16.00	4.40
300 Franco Harris AP	50.00	22.00	6.25
314 Ed Too Tall Jones	70.00	32.00	8.75
320 Ray Guy AP	20.00	9.00	2.50
331 Jim Plunkett	20.00	9.00	2.50
342 Randy White	60.00	27.00	7.50
359 Ahmad Rashad	20.00	9.00	2.50
360 Walter Payton AP	375.00	170.00	47.50
380 Dave Casper AP	40.00	18.00	5.00
400 Fran Tarkenton AP	60.00	27.00	7.50
405 Joe Greene	30.00	13.50	3.70
412 Pat Tilley	8.00	3.60	1.00
415 Gene Upshaw	18.00	8.00	2.20
427 Harvey Martin	20.00	9.00	2.50
444 Mike Pruitt	20.00	9.00	2.50
453 O.J. Simpson RB	60.00	27.00	7.50
454 Fran Tarkenton RB Most Yardage, Passing, Lifetime	35.00	16.00	4.40
455 Jim Zorn RB Most Passing Yards Season, Rookie	25.00	11.00	3.10
470 Cliff Branch AP	35.00	16.00	4.40
480 Jack Lambert AP	60.00	27.00	7.50
505 Larry Csonka	50.00	22.00	6.25
515 Bob Griese	50.00	22.00	6.25
526 AFC Championship (Ken Stabler)	75.00	34.00	9.50
527 NFC Championship	75.00	34.00	9.50
528 Super Bowl XI	200.00	90.00	25.00

1977 Topps Team Checklists

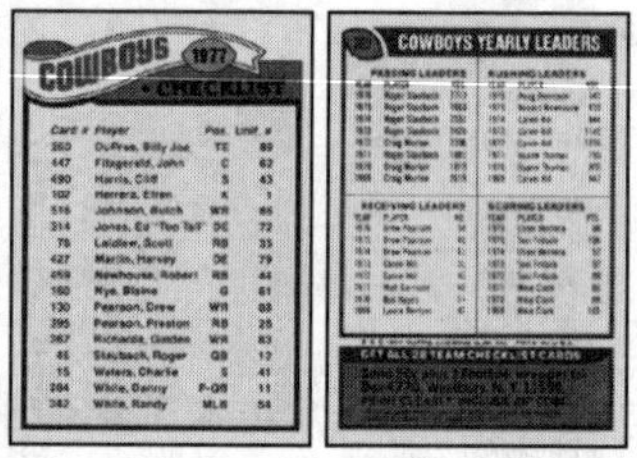

The 1977 Topps Team Checklist set contains 30 standard-size cards. The 28 NFL teams as well as 2 regular checklists were printed in this set. The front of the card has the 1977 Topps checklist for that particular team, complete with boxes in which to place check marks. The set was only available directly from Topps as a send-off offer as an uncut sheet; the prices below apply equally to uncut sheets as they are frequently found in their original uncut condition. As for individual cards, thin white card (almost paper-thin) stock makes it a challenge to find singles in top grades. These unnumbered cards are numbered below for convenience in alphabetical order by team name.

	NRMT-MT	EXC	G-VG
COMPLETE SET (30)	110.00	28.00	11.00
COMMON CARD (1-30)	5.00	1.25	.50
1 Atlanta Falcons	5.00	1.25	.50
2 Baltimore Colts	5.00	1.25	.50
3 Buffalo Bills	5.00	1.25	.50
4 Chicago Bears	7.50	1.85	.75
5 Cincinnati Bengals	5.00	1.25	.50
6 Cleveland Browns	5.00	1.25	.50
7 Dallas Cowboys	10.00	2.50	1.00
8 Denver Broncos	5.00	1.25	.50
9 Detroit Lions	5.00	1.25	.50
10 Green Bay Packers	7.50	1.85	.75
11 Houston Oilers	5.00	1.25	.50
12 Kansas City Chiefs	5.00	1.25	.50
13 Los Angeles Rams	5.00	1.25	.50
14 Miami Dolphins	7.50	1.85	.75
15 Minnesota Vikings	5.00	1.25	.50
16 New England Patriots	5.00	1.25	.50
17 New York Giants	5.00	1.25	.50
18 New York Jets	5.00	1.25	.50
19 New Orleans Saints	5.00	1.25	.50
20 Oakland Raiders	7.50	1.85	.75
21 Philadelphia Eagles	5.00	1.25	.50
22 Pittsburgh Steelers	7.50	1.85	.75
23 St. Louis Cardinals	5.00	1.25	.50
24 San Diego Chargers	5.00	1.25	.50
25 San Francisco 49ers	7.50	1.85	.75
26 Seattle Seahawks	5.00	1.25	.50
27 Tampa Bay Buccaneers	5.00	1.25	.50
28 Washington Redskins	7.50	1.85	.75
NNO1 Checklist 1-132	5.00	1.25	.50
NNO2 Checklist 133-264	5.00	1.25	.50

1978 Topps

The 1978 Topps football set contains 528 standard-size cards. Card fronts have a color border that runs up the left side and contains the team name. The player's name is at the top and his position is within a football at the bottom right of the photo. The card backs are printed in black and green on gray card stock and are horizontally designed. Statistics, highlights and a player fact cartton are inlcuded. Subsets include Highlights (1-6), playoffs (166-168), league leaders (331-336) and team leaders (501-528). Rookie Cards include Tony Dorsett, Randy Cross, Tom Jackson, Joe Klecko, Stanley Morgan, John Stallworth, Wesley Walker and Reggie Williams.

	NRMT-MT	EXC	G-VG
COMPLETE SET (528)	140.00	65.00	17.50
COMMON CARD (1-528)	.20	.09	.03

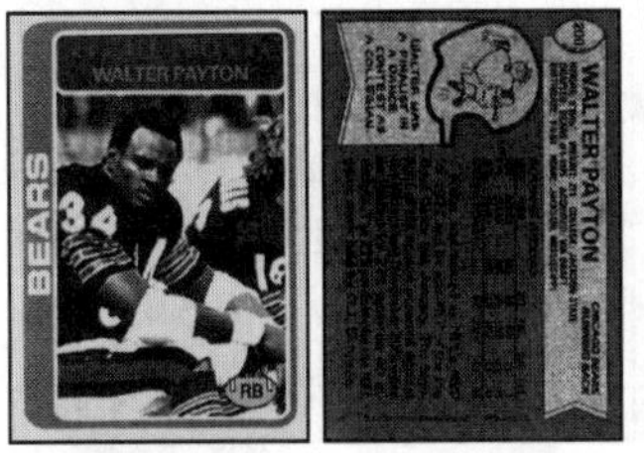

☐ 1 Gary Huff HL	.60	.15	.06
Huff Leads Bucs			
to First Win			
☐ 2 Craig Morton HL	.30	.14	.04
Morton Passes Broncos			
to Super Bowl			
☐ 3 Walter Payton HL	8.00	3.60	1.00
Rushes for 275 Yards			
☐ 4 O.J. Simpson HL	2.00	.90	.25
Reaches 10,000 Yards			
☐ 5 Fran Tarkenton HL	2.00	.90	.25
Completes 17 of 18			
☐ 6 Bob Thomas HL	.30	.14	.04
Thomas' FG Sends			
Bears to Playoffs			
☐ 7 Joe Pisarcik	.30	.14	.04
☐ 8 Skip Thomas	.20	.09	.03
☐ 9 Roosevelt Leaks	.20	.09	.03
☐ 10 Ken Houston AP	.50	.23	.06
☐ 11 Tom Blanchard	.20	.09	.03
☐ 12 Jim Turner	.20	.09	.03
☐ 13 Tom DeLeone	.20	.09	.03
☐ 14 Jim LeClair	.20	.09	.03
☐ 15 Bob Avellini	.30	.14	.04
☐ 16 Tony McGee	.20	.09	.03
☐ 17 James Harris	.30	.14	.04
☐ 18 Terry Nelson	.20	.09	.03
☐ 19 Rocky Bleier	2.00	.90	.25
☐ 20 Joe DeLamielleure AP	.30	.14	.04
☐ 21 Richard Caster	.20	.09	.03
☐ 22 A.J. Duhe	.50	.23	.06
☐ 23 John Outlaw	.20	.09	.03
☐ 24 Danny White	1.25	.55	.16
☐ 25 Larry Csonka	2.00	.90	.25
☐ 26 David Hill	.30	.14	.04
☐ 27 Mark Arneson	.20	.09	.03
☐ 28 Jack Tatum	.30	.14	.04
☐ 29 Norm Thompson	.20	.09	.03
☐ 30 Sammie White	.30	.14	.04
☐ 31 Dennis Johnson	.20	.09	.03
☐ 32 Robin Earl	.20	.09	.03
☐ 33 Don Cockroft	.20	.09	.03
☐ 34 Bob Johnson	.20	.09	.03
☐ 35 John Hannah	.50	.23	.06
☐ 36 Scott Hunter	.20	.09	.03
☐ 37 Ken Burrough	.30	.14	.04
☐ 38 Wilbur Jackson	.30	.14	.04
☐ 39 Rich McGeorge	.20	.09	.03
☐ 40 Lyle Alzado AP	.50	.23	.06
☐ 41 John Ebersole	.20	.09	.03
☐ 42 Gary Green	.20	.09	.03
☐ 43 Art Kuehn	.20	.09	.03
☐ 44 Glen Edwards	.30	.14	.04
☐ 45 Lawrence McCutcheon	.30	.14	.04
☐ 46 Duriel Harris	.20	.09	.03
☐ 47 Rich Szaro	.20	.09	.03
☐ 48 Mike Washington	.20	.09	.03
☐ 49 Stan White	.20	.09	.03
☐ 50 Dave Casper AP	1.00	.45	.12
☐ 51 Len Hauss	.20	.09	.03
☐ 52 James Scott	.20	.09	.03
☐ 53 Brian Sipe	.50	.23	.06
☐ 54 Gary Shirk	.20	.09	.03
☐ 55 Archie Griffin	1.00	.45	.12
☐ 56 Mike Patrick	.20	.09	.03
☐ 57 Mario Clark	.20	.09	.03
☐ 58 Jeff Siemon	.20	.09	.03
☐ 59 Steve Mike-Mayer	.20	.09	.03
☐ 60 Randy White AP	4.00	1.80	.50
☐ 61 Darrell Austin	.20	.09	.03
☐ 62 Tom Sullivan	.20	.09	.03
☐ 63 Johnny Rodgers	1.25	.55	.16
☐ 64 Ken Reaves	.20	.09	.03
☐ 65 Terry Bradshaw	10.00	4.50	1.25
☐ 66 Fred Steinfort	.20	.09	.03
☐ 67 Curley Culp	.30	.14	.04
☐ 68 Ted Hendricks	.75	.35	.09
☐ 69 Raymond Chester	.20	.09	.03
☐ 70 Jim Langer AP	.50	.23	.06
☐ 71 Calvin Hill	.30	.14	.04
☐ 72 Mike Hartenstine	.20	.09	.03
☐ 73 Gerald Irons	.20	.09	.03
☐ 74 Billy Brooks	.30	.14	.04
☐ 75 John Mendenhall	.20	.09	.03
☐ 76 Andy Johnson	.20	.09	.03
☐ 77 Tom Wittum	.20	.09	.03
☐ 78 Lynn Dickey	.30	.14	.04
☐ 79 Carl Eller	.50	.23	.06
☐ 80 Tom Mack	.30	.14	.04
☐ 81 Clark Gaines	.20	.09	.03
☐ 82 Lem Barney	.50	.23	.06
☐ 83 Mike Montler	.20	.09	.03

☐ 84 Jon Kolb	.20	.09	.03
☐ 85 Bob Chandler	.30	.14	.04
☐ 86 Robert Newhouse	.30	.14	.04
☐ 87 Frank LeMaster	.20	.09	.03
☐ 88 Jeff West	.20	.09	.03
☐ 89 Lyle Blackwood	.30	.14	.04
☐ 90 Gene Upshaw AP	.50	.23	.06
☐ 91 Frank Grant	.20	.09	.03
☐ 92 Tom Hicks	.20	.09	.03
☐ 93 Mike Pruitt	.30	.14	.04
☐ 94 Chris Bahr	.20	.09	.03
☐ 95 Russ Francis	.30	.14	.04
☐ 96 Norris Thomas	.20	.09	.03
☐ 97 Gary Barbaro	.30	.14	.04
☐ 98 Jim Merlo	.20	.09	.03
☐ 99 Karl Chandler	.20	.09	.03
☐ 100 Fran Tarkenton	3.50	1.55	.45
☐ 101 Abdul Salaam	.20	.09	.03
☐ 102 Marv Kellum	.20	.09	.03
☐ 103 Herman Weaver	.20	.09	.03
☐ 104 Roy Gerela	.20	.09	.03
☐ 105 Harold Jackson	.30	.14	.04
☐ 106 Dewey Selmon	.30	.14	.04
☐ 107 Checklist 1-132	1.00	.25	.10
☐ 108 Clarence Davis	.20	.09	.03
☐ 109 Robert Pratt	.20	.09	.03
☐ 110 Harvey Martin AP	.50	.23	.06
☐ 111 Brad Dusek	.20	.09	.03
☐ 112 Greg Latta	.20	.09	.03
☐ 113 Tony Peters	.20	.09	.03
☐ 114 Jim Braxton	.20	.09	.03
☐ 115 Ken Riley	.30	.14	.04
☐ 116 Steve Nelson	.20	.09	.03
☐ 117 Rick Upchurch	.30	.14	.04
☐ 118 Spike Jones	.20	.09	.03
☐ 119 Doug Kotar	.20	.09	.03
☐ 120 Bob Griese AP	3.50	1.55	.45
☐ 121 Burgess Owens	.20	.09	.03
☐ 122 Rolf Benirschke	.30	.14	.04
☐ 123 Haskel Stanback	.20	.09	.03
☐ 124 J.T. Thomas	.20	.09	.03
☐ 125 Ahmad Rashad	1.50	.70	.19
☐ 126 Rick Kane	.20	.09	.03
☐ 127 Elvin Bethea	.20	.09	.03
☐ 128 Dave Dalby	.20	.09	.03
☐ 129 Mike Barnes	.20	.09	.03
☐ 130 Isiah Robertson	.20	.09	.03
☐ 131 Jim Plunkett	.50	.23	.06
☐ 132 Allan Ellis	.20	.09	.03
☐ 133 Mike Bragg	.20	.09	.03
☐ 134 Bob Jackson	.20	.09	.03
☐ 135 Coy Bacon	.20	.09	.03
☐ 136 John Smith	.20	.09	.03
☐ 137 Chuck Muncie	.30	.14	.04
☐ 138 Johnnie Gray	.20	.09	.03
☐ 139 Jimmy Robinson	.20	.09	.03
☐ 140 Tom Banks	.20	.09	.03
☐ 141 Marvin Powell	.20	.09	.03
☐ 142 Jerrel Wilson	.20	.09	.03
☐ 143 Ron Howard	.20	.09	.03
☐ 144 Rob Lytle	.30	.14	.04
☐ 145 L.C. Greenwood	.60	.25	.07
☐ 146 Morris Owens	.20	.09	.03
☐ 147 Joe Reed	.20	.09	.03
☐ 148 Mike Kadish	.20	.09	.03
☐ 149 Phil Villapiano	.30	.14	.04
☐ 150 Lydell Mitchell	.30	.14	.04
☐ 151 Randy Logan	.20	.09	.03
☐ 152 Mike Williams	.20	.09	.03
☐ 153 Jeff Van Note	.30	.14	.04
☐ 154 Steve Schubert	.20	.09	.03
☐ 155 Billy Kilmer	.30	.14	.04
☐ 156 Boobie Clark	.20	.09	.03
☐ 157 Charlie Hall	.20	.09	.03
☐ 158 Raymond Clayborn	.50	.23	.06
☐ 159 Jack Gregory	.20	.09	.03
☐ 160 Cliff Harris AP	.50	.23	.06
☐ 161 Joe Fields	.20	.09	.03
☐ 162 Don Nottingham	.20	.09	.03
☐ 163 Ed White	.30	.14	.04
☐ 164 Toni Fritsch	.20	.09	.03
☐ 165 Jack Lambert	4.00	1.80	.50
☐ 166 NFC Champions	1.50	.70	.19
Cowboys 23,			
Vikings 6			
(Roger Staubach)			
☐ 167 AFC Champions	.30	.14	.04
Broncos 20,			
Raiders 17			
(Lytle running)			
☐ 168 Super Bowl XII	3.00	1.35	.35
Cowboys 27,			
Broncos 10			
(Tony Dorsett)			
☐ 169 Neal Colzie	.20	.09	.03
☐ 170 Cleveland Elam AP	.20	.09	.03
☐ 171 David Lee	.20	.09	.03
☐ 172 Jim Otis	.20	.09	.03
☐ 173 Archie Manning	.50	.23	.06
☐ 174 Jim Carter	.20	.09	.03
☐ 175 Jean Fugett	.20	.09	.03
☐ 176 Willie Parker	.20	.09	.03
☐ 177 Haven Moses	.30	.14	.04
☐ 178 Horace King	.20	.09	.03
☐ 179 Bob Thomas	.20	.09	.03

☐ 180 Monte Jackson	.20	.09	.03
☐ 181 Steve Zabel	.20	.09	.03
☐ 182 John Fitzgerald	.20	.09	.03
☐ 183 Mike Livingston	.20	.09	.03
☐ 184 Larry Poole	.20	.09	.03
☐ 185 Isaac Curtis	.30	.14	.04
☐ 186 Chuck Ramsey	.20	.09	.03
☐ 187 Bob Klein	.20	.09	.03
☐ 188 Ray Rhodes	.50	.23	.06
☐ 189 Otis Sistrunk	.30	.14	.04
☐ 190 Bill Bergey	.30	.14	.04
☐ 191 Sherman Smith	.30	.14	.04
☐ 192 Dave Green	.20	.09	.03
☐ 193 Carl Mauck	.20	.09	.03
☐ 194 Reggie Harrison	.20	.09	.03
☐ 195 Roger Carr	.30	.14	.04
☐ 196 Steve Bartkowski	.50	.23	.06
☐ 197 Ray Wersching	.20	.09	.03
☐ 198 Willie Buchanon	.20	.09	.03
☐ 199 Neil Clabo	.20	.09	.03
☐ 200 Walter Payton AP	18.00	8.00	2.20
UER (Born 7/5/54,			
should be 7/25/54)			
☐ 201 Sam Adams	.20	.09	.03
☐ 202 Larry Gordon	.20	.09	.03
☐ 203 Pat Tilley	.30	.14	.04
☐ 204 Mack Mitchell	.20	.09	.03
☐ 205 Ken Anderson	1.25	.55	.16
☐ 206 Scott Dierking	.20	.09	.03
☐ 207 Jack Rudnay	.20	.09	.03
☐ 208 Jim Stienke	.20	.09	.03
☐ 209 Bill Simpson	.20	.09	.03
☐ 210 Errol Mann	.20	.09	.03
☐ 211 Bucky Dilts	.20	.09	.03
☐ 212 Reuben Gant	.20	.09	.03
☐ 213 Thomas Henderson	.50	.23	.06
☐ 214 Steve Furness	.30	.14	.04
☐ 215 John Riggins	2.00	.90	.25
☐ 216 Keith Krepfle	.20	.09	.03
☐ 217 Fred Dean	.30	.14	.04
☐ 218 Emanuel Zanders	.20	.09	.03
☐ 219 Don Testerman	.20	.09	.03
☐ 220 George Kunz	.20	.09	.03
☐ 221 Darryl Stingley	.30	.14	.04
☐ 222 Ken Sanders	.20	.09	.03
☐ 223 Gary Huff	.20	.09	.03
☐ 224 Gregg Bingham	.20	.09	.03
☐ 225 Jerry Sherk	.20	.09	.03
☐ 226 Doug Plank	.20	.09	.03
☐ 227 Ed Taylor	.20	.09	.03
☐ 228 Emery Moorehead	.20	.09	.03
☐ 229 Reggie Williams	.50	.23	.06
☐ 230 Claude Humphrey	.20	.09	.03
☐ 231 Randy Cross	2.00	.90	.25
☐ 232 Jim Hart	.50	.23	.06
☐ 233 Bobby Bryant	.20	.09	.03
☐ 234 Larry Brown	.20	.09	.03
☐ 235 Mark Van Eeghen	.30	.14	.04
☐ 236 Terry Hermeling	.20	.09	.03
☐ 237 Steve Odom	.20	.09	.03
☐ 238 Jan Stenerud	.50	.23	.06
☐ 239 Andre Tillman	.20	.09	.03
☐ 240 Tom Jackson AP	4.00	1.80	.50
☐ 241 Ken Mendenhall	.20	.09	.03
☐ 242 Tim Fox	.20	.09	.03
☐ 243 Don Herrmann	.20	.09	.03
☐ 244 Eddie McMillan	.20	.09	.03
☐ 245 Greg Pruitt	.30	.14	.04
☐ 246 J.K. McKay	.20	.09	.03
☐ 247 Larry Keller	.20	.09	.03
☐ 248 Dave Jennings	.30	.14	.04
☐ 249 Bo Harris	.20	.09	.03
☐ 250 Revie Sorey	.20	.09	.03
☐ 251 Tony Greene	.20	.09	.03
☐ 252 Butch Johnson	.30	.14	.04
☐ 253 Paul Naumoff	.20	.09	.03
☐ 254 Rickey Young	.30	.14	.04
☐ 255 Dwight White	.30	.14	.04
☐ 256 Joe Lavender	.20	.09	.03
☐ 257 Checklist 133-264	1.00	.25	.10
☐ 258 Ronnie Coleman	.20	.09	.03
☐ 259 Charlie Smith	.20	.09	.03
☐ 260 Ray Guy AP	.50	.23	.06
☐ 261 David Taylor	.20	.09	.03
☐ 262 Bill Lenkaitis	.20	.09	.03
☐ 263 Jim Mitchell	.20	.09	.03
☐ 264 Delvin Williams	.20	.09	.03
☐ 265 Jack Youngblood	.50	.23	.06
☐ 266 Chuck Crist	.20	.09	.03
☐ 267 Richard Todd	.30	.14	.04
☐ 268 Dave Logan	.30	.14	.04
☐ 269 Rufus Mayes	.20	.09	.03
☐ 270 Brad Van Pelt	.20	.09	.03
☐ 271 Chester Marcol	.20	.09	.03
☐ 272 J.V. Cain	.20	.09	.03
☐ 273 Larry Seiple	.20	.09	.03
☐ 274 Brent McClanahan	.20	.09	.03
☐ 275 Mike Wagner	.20	.09	.03
☐ 276 Diron Talbert	.20	.09	.03
☐ 277 Brian Baschnagel	.20	.09	.03
☐ 278 Ed Podolak	.20	.09	.03
☐ 279 Don Goode	.20	.09	.03
☐ 280 John Dutton	.30	.14	.04
☐ 281 Don Calhoun	.20	.09	.03
☐ 282 Monte Johnson	.20	.09	.03

☐ 283 Ron Jessie	.20	.09	.03
☐ 284 Jon Morris	.20	.09	.03
☐ 285 Riley Odoms	.20	.09	.03
☐ 286 Marv Bateman	.20	.09	.03
☐ 287 Joe Klecko	.50	.23	.06
☐ 288 Oliver Davis	.20	.09	.03
☐ 289 John McDaniel	.20	.09	.03
☐ 290 Roger Staubach	12.00	5.50	1.50
☐ 291 Brian Kelley	.20	.09	.03
☐ 292 Mike Hogan	.20	.09	.03
☐ 293 John Leypoldt	.20	.09	.03
☐ 294 Jack Novak	.20	.09	.03
☐ 295 Joe Greene	2.00	.90	.25
☐ 296 John Hill	.20	.09	.03
☐ 297 Danny Buggs	.20	.09	.03
☐ 298 Ted Albrecht	.20	.09	.03
☐ 299 Nelson Munsey	.20	.09	.03
☐ 300 Chuck Foreman	.30	.14	.04
☐ 301 Dan Pastorini	.30	.14	.04
☐ 302 Tommy Hart	.20	.09	.03
☐ 303 Dave Beverly	.20	.09	.03
☐ 304 Tony Reed	.30	.14	.04
☐ 305 Cliff Branch	1.50	.70	.19
☐ 306 Clarence Duren	.20	.09	.03
☐ 307 Randy Rasmussen	.20	.09	.03
☐ 308 Oscar Roan	.20	.09	.03
☐ 309 Lenvil Elliott	.20	.09	.03
☐ 310 Dan Dierdorf AP	1.00	.45	.12
☐ 311 Johnny Perkins	.20	.09	.03
☐ 312 Rafael Septien	.30	.14	.04
☐ 313 Terry Beeson	.20	.09	.03
☐ 314 Lee Roy Selmon	2.00	.90	.25
☐ 315 Tony Dorsett	30.00	13.50	3.70
☐ 316 Greg Landry	.30	.14	.04
☐ 317 Jake Scott	.20	.09	.03
☐ 318 Dan Peiffer	.20	.09	.03
☐ 319 John Bunting	.20	.09	.03
☐ 320 John Stallworth	20.00	9.00	2.50
☐ 321 Bob Howard	.20	.09	.03
☐ 322 Larry Little	.50	.23	.06
☐ 323 Reggie McKenzie	.30	.14	.04
☐ 324 Duane Carrell	.20	.09	.03
☐ 325 Ed Simonini	.20	.09	.03
☐ 326 John Vella	.20	.09	.03
☐ 327 Wesley Walker	3.00	1.35	.35
☐ 328 Jon Keyworth	.20	.09	.03
☐ 329 Ron Bolton	.20	.09	.03
☐ 330 Tommy Casanova	.20	.09	.03
☐ 331 Passing Leaders	4.00	1.80	.50
Bob Griese			
Roger Staubach			
☐ 332 Receiving Leaders	.50	.23	.06
Lydell Mitchell			
Ahmad Rashad			
☐ 333 Rushing Leaders	3.00	1.35	.35
Mark Van Eeghen			
Walter Payton			
☐ 334 Scoring Leaders	3.00	1.35	.35
Errol Mann			
Walter Payton			
☐ 335 Interception Leaders	.30	.14	.04
Lyle Blackwood			
Rolland Lawrence			
☐ 336 Punting Leaders	.30	.14	.04
Ray Guy			
Tom Blanchard			
☐ 337 Robert Brazile	.30	.14	.04
☐ 338 Charlie Joiner	1.50	.70	.19
☐ 339 Joe Ferguson	.30	.14	.04
☐ 340 Bill Thompson	.20	.09	.03
☐ 341 Sam Cunningham	.30	.14	.04
☐ 342 Curtis Johnson	.20	.09	.03
☐ 343 Jim Marshall	.50	.23	.06
☐ 344 Charlie Sanders	.20	.09	.03
☐ 345 Willie Hall	.20	.09	.03
☐ 346 Pat Haden	.50	.23	.06
☐ 347 Jim Bakken	.20	.09	.03
☐ 348 Bruce Taylor	.20	.09	.03
☐ 349 Barty Smith	.20	.09	.03
☐ 350 Drew Pearson AP	1.50	.70	.19
☐ 351 Mike Webster	2.50	1.10	.30
☐ 352 Bobby Hammond	.20	.09	.03
☐ 353 Dave Mays	.20	.09	.03
☐ 354 Pat McInally	.20	.09	.03
☐ 355 Toni Linhart	.20	.09	.03
☐ 356 Larry Hand	.20	.09	.03
☐ 357 Ted Fritsch Jr.	.20	.09	.03
☐ 358 Larry Marshall	.20	.09	.03
☐ 359 Waymond Bryant	.20	.09	.03
☐ 360 Louie Kelcher	.30	.14	.04
☐ 361 Stanley Morgan	2.00	.90	.25
☐ 362 Bruce Harper	.30	.14	.04
☐ 363 Bernard Jackson	.20	.09	.03
☐ 364 Walter White	.20	.09	.03
☐ 365 Ken Stabler	8.00	3.60	1.00
☐ 366 Fred Dryer	.50	.23	.06
☐ 367 Ike Harris	.20	.09	.03
☐ 368 Norm Bulaich	.20	.09	.03
☐ 369 Merv Krakau	.20	.09	.03
☐ 370 John James	.20	.09	.03
☐ 371 Bennie Cunningham	.20	.09	.03
☐ 372 Doug Van Horn	.20	.09	.03
☐ 373 Thom Darden	.20	.09	.03
☐ 374 Eddie Edwards	.20	.09	.03
☐ 375 Mike Thomas	.20	.09	.03

☐ 376 Fred Cook	.20	.09	.03
☐ 377 Mike Phipps	.30	.14	.04
☐ 378 Paul Krause	.50	.23	.06
☐ 379 Harold Carmichael	1.00	.45	.12
☐ 380 Mike Haynes AP	1.25	.55	.16
☐ 381 Wayne Morris	.20	.09	.03
☐ 382 Greg Buttle	.20	.09	.03
☐ 383 Jim Zorn	1.00	.45	.12
☐ 384 Jack Dolbin	.20	.09	.03
☐ 385 Charlie Waters	.50	.23	.06
☐ 386 Dan Ryczek	.20	.09	.03
☐ 387 Joe Washington	.50	.23	.06
☐ 388 Checklist 265-396	1.00	.25	.10
☐ 389 James Hunter	.20	.09	.03
☐ 390 Billy Johnson	.30	.14	.04
☐ 391 Jim Allen	.20	.09	.03
☐ 392 George Buehler	.20	.09	.03
☐ 393 Harry Carson	.20	.09	.03
☐ 394 Cleo Miller	.20	.09	.03
☐ 395 Gary Burley	.20	.09	.03
☐ 396 Mark Moseley	.30	.14	.04
☐ 397 Virgil Livers	.20	.09	.03
☐ 398 Joe Ehrmann	.20	.09	.03
☐ 399 Freddie Solomon	.20	.09	.03
☐ 400 O.J. Simpson	4.00	1.80	.50
☐ 401 Julius Adams	.20	.09	.03
☐ 402 Artimus Parker	.20	.09	.03
☐ 403 Gene Washington	.30	.14	.04
☐ 404 Herman Edwards	.20	.09	.03
☐ 405 Craig Morton	.50	.23	.06
☐ 406 Alan Page	.75	.35	.09
☐ 407 Larry McCarren	.20	.09	.03
☐ 408 Tony Galbreath	.30	.14	.04
☐ 409 Roman Gabriel	.50	.23	.06
☐ 410 Efren Herrera AP	.20	.09	.03
☐ 411 Jim Smith	.50	.23	.06
☐ 412 Bill Bryant	.20	.09	.03
☐ 413 Doug Dieken	.20	.09	.03
☐ 414 Marvin Cobb	.20	.09	.03
☐ 415 Fred Biletnikoff	2.00	.90	.25
☐ 416 Joe Theismann	2.50	1.10	.30
☐ 417 Roland Harper	.20	.09	.03
☐ 418 Derrel Luce	.20	.09	.03
☐ 419 Ralph Perretta	.20	.09	.03
☐ 420 Louis Wright	.50	.23	.06
☐ 421 Prentice McCray	.20	.09	.03
☐ 422 Garry Puetz	.20	.09	.03
☐ 423 Alfred Jenkins	.50	.23	.06
☐ 424 Paul Seymour	.20	.09	.03
☐ 425 Garo Yepremian	.30	.14	.04
☐ 426 Emmitt Thomas	.20	.09	.03
☐ 427 Dexter Bussey	.20	.09	.03
☐ 428 John Sanders	.20	.09	.03
☐ 429 Ed Too Tall Jones	2.00	.90	.25
☐ 430 Ron Yary	.30	.14	.04
☐ 431 Frank Lewis	.30	.14	.04
☐ 432 Jerry Golsteyn	.20	.09	.03
☐ 433 Clarence Scott	.20	.09	.03
☐ 434 Pete Johnson	.50	.23	.06
☐ 435 Charley Young	.30	.14	.04
☐ 436 Harold McLinton	.20	.09	.03
☐ 437 Noah Jackson	.20	.09	.03
☐ 438 Bruce Laird	.20	.09	.03
☐ 439 John Matuszak	.30	.14	.04
☐ 440 Nat Moore AP	.30	.14	.04
☐ 441 Leon Gray	.20	.09	.03
☐ 442 Jerome Barkum	.20	.09	.03
☐ 443 Steve Largent	14.00	6.25	1.75
☐ 444 John Zook	.20	.09	.03
☐ 445 Preston Pearson	.30	.14	.04
☐ 446 Conrad Dobler	.30	.14	.04
☐ 447 Wilbur Summers	.20	.09	.03
☐ 448 Lou Piccone	.20	.09	.03
☐ 449 Ron Jaworski	1.00	.45	.12
☐ 450 Jack Ham AP	1.50	.70	.19
☐ 451 Mick Tingelhoff	.30	.14	.04
☐ 452 Clyde Powers	.20	.09	.03
☐ 453 John Cappelletti	.50	.23	.06
☐ 454 Dick Ambrose	.20	.09	.03
☐ 455 Lemar Parrish	.20	.09	.03
☐ 456 Ron Saul	.20	.09	.03
☐ 457 Bob Parsons	.20	.09	.03
☐ 458 Glenn Doughty	.20	.09	.03
☐ 459 Don Woods	.20	.09	.03
☐ 460 Art Shell AP	.75	.35	.09
☐ 461 Sam Hunt	.20	.09	.03
☐ 462 Lawrence Pillers	.20	.09	.03
☐ 463 Henry Childs	.20	.09	.03
☐ 464 Roger Wehrli	.20	.09	.03
☐ 465 Otis Armstrong	.30	.14	.04
☐ 466 Bob Baumhower	.75	.35	.09
☐ 467 Ray Jarvis	.20	.09	.03
☐ 468 Guy Morriss	.20	.09	.03
☐ 469 Matt Blair	.30	.14	.04
☐ 470 Billy Joe DuPree	.30	.14	.04
☐ 471 Roland Hooks	.20	.09	.03
☐ 472 Joe Danelo	.20	.09	.03
☐ 473 Reggie Rucker	.30	.14	.04
☐ 474 Vern Holland	.20	.09	.03
☐ 475 Mel Blount	1.50	.70	.19
☐ 476 Eddie Brown	.20	.09	.03
☐ 477 Bo Rather	.20	.09	.03
☐ 478 Don McCauley	.20	.09	.03
☐ 479 Glen Walker	.20	.09	.03
☐ 480 Randy Gradishar AP	.50	.23	.06
☐ 481 Dave Rowe	.20	.09	.03
☐ 482 Pat Leahy	.30	.14	.04
☐ 483 Mike Fuller	.20	.09	.03
☐ 484 David Lewis	.20	.09	.03
☐ 485 Steve Grogan	.50	.23	.06
☐ 486 Mel Gray	.30	.14	.04
☐ 487 Eddie Payton	.30	.14	.04
☐ 488 Checklist 397-528	1.00	.25	.10
☐ 489 Stu Voigt	.20	.09	.03
☐ 490 Rolland Lawrence AP	.20	.09	.03
☐ 491 Nick Mike-Mayer	.20	.09	.03
☐ 492 Troy Archer	.20	.09	.03
☐ 493 Benny Malone	.20	.09	.03
☐ 494 Golden Richards	.30	.14	.04
☐ 495 Chris Hanburger	.20	.09	.03
☐ 496 Dwight Harrison	.20	.09	.03
☐ 497 Gary Fencik	.50	.23	.06
☐ 498 Rich Saul	.20	.09	.03
☐ 499 Dan Fouts	4.00	1.80	.50
☐ 500 Franco Harris AP	3.50	1.55	.45
☐ 501 Atlanta Falcons TL Haskel Stanback Alfred Jenkins Claude Humphrey Jeff Merrow Rolland Lawrence (checklist back)	.60	.15	.06
☐ 502 Baltimore Colts TL Lydell Mitchell Lydell Mitchell Lyle Blackwood Fred Cook (checklist back)	.60	.15	.06
☐ 503 Buffalo Bills TL O.J. Simpson Bob Chandler Tony Greene Sherman White (checklist back)	1.00	.25	.10
☐ 504 Chicago Bears TL Walter Payton James Scott Allan Ellis Ron Rydalch (checklist back)	2.00	.50	.20
☐ 505 Cincinnati Bengals TL Pete Johnson Billy Brooks Lemar Parrish Reggie Williams Gary Burley (checklist back)	.60	.15	.06
☐ 506 Cleveland Browns TL Greg Pruitt Reggie Rucker Thom Darden Mack Mitchell (checklist back)	.60	.15	.06
☐ 507 Dallas Cowboys TL Tony Dorsett Drew Pearson Cliff Harris Harvey Martin (checklist back)	2.50	.60	.25
☐ 508 Denver Broncos TL Otis Armstrong Haven Moses Bill Thompson Rick Upchurch (checklist back)	.60	.15	.06
☐ 509 Detroit Lions TL Horace King David Hill James Hunter Ken Sanders (checklist back)	.60	.15	.06
☐ 510 Green Bay Packers TL Barty Smith Steve Odom Steve Luke Mike C. McCoy Dave Pureifory Dave Roller (checklist back)	.60	.15	.06
☐ 511 Houston Oilers TL Ronnie Coleman Ken Burrough Mike Reinfeldt James Young (checklist back)	.60	.15	.06
☐ 512 Kansas City Chiefs TL Ed Podolak Walter White Gary Barbaro Wilbur Young (checklist back)	.60	.15	.06
☐ 513 Los Angeles Rams TL Lawrence McCutcheon Harold Jackson Bill Simpson Jack Youngblood (checklist back)	.60	.15	.06
☐ 514 Miami Dolphins TL Benny Malone Nat Moore Curtis Johnson A.J. Duhe (checklist back)	.60	.15	.06
☐ 515 Minnesota Vikings TL Chuck Foreman Sammie White Bobby Bryant Carl Eller (checklist back)	.60	.15	.06
☐ 516 New England Patriots TL Sam Cunningham Darryl Stingley Mike Haynes Tony McGee (checklist back)	.60	.15	.06
☐ 517 New Orleans Saints TL Chuck Muncie Don Herrmann Chuck Crist Elois Grooms (checklist back)	.60	.15	.06
☐ 518 New York Giants TL Bobby Hammond Jimmy Robinson Bill Bryant John Mendenhall (checklist back)	.60	.15	.06
☐ 519 New York Jets TL Clark Gaines Wesley Walker Burgess Owens Joe Klecko (checklist back)	.60	.15	.06
☐ 520 Oakland Raiders TL Mark Van Eeghen Dave Casper Jack Tatum Neal Colzie (checklist back)	.60	.15	.06
☐ 521 Philadelphia Eagles TL Mike Hogan Harold Carmichael Herman Edwards John Sanders Lem Burnham (checklist back)	.60	.15	.06
☐ 522 Pittsburgh Steelers TL Franco Harris Jim Smith Mel Blount Steve Furness (checklist back)	1.25	.30	.12
☐ 523 St.Louis Cardinals TL Terry Metcalf Mel Gray Roger Wehrli Mike Dawson (checklist back)	.60	.15	.06
☐ 524 San Diego Chargers TL Rickey Young Charlie Joiner Mike Fuller Gary Johnson (checklist back)	.60	.15	.06
☐ 525 San Francisco 49ers TL Delvin Williams Gene Washington Mel Phillips Dave Washington Cleveland Elam (checklist back)	.60	.15	.06
☐ 526 Seattle Seahawks TL Sherman Smith Steve Largent Autry Beamon Walter Packer (checklist back)	1.50	.35	.15
☐ 527 Tampa Bay Bucs TL Morris Owens Isaac Hagins Mike Washington Lee Roy Selmon (checklist back)	.60	.15	.06
☐ 528 Wash. Redskins TL Mike Thomas Jean Fugett Ken Houston Dennis Johnson (checklist back)	1.00	.25	.10

1978 Topps Holsum

In 1978, Topps produced a set of 33 NFL full-color standard-size cards for Holsum Bread. One card was packed inside each loaf of bread. Unfortunately, nowhere on the card is Holsum mentioned, leading to frequent misclassification of this set. An uncut production sheet was offered in the 1989 Topps Archives auction. The personal data on the card back is printed in yellow and green. Each card can be found with either one or two asterisks on the copyright line.

	NRMT-MT	EXC	G-VG
COMPLETE SET (33)	275.00	125.00	34.00
COMMON CARD (1-33)	3.00	1.35	.35

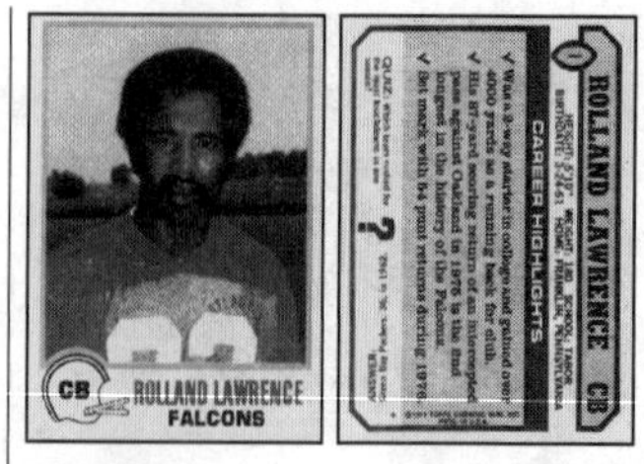

☐ 1 Rolland Lawrence	3.00	1.35	.35
☐ 2 Walter Payton	75.00	34.00	9.50
☐ 3 Lydell Mitchell	4.00	1.80	.50
☐ 4 Joe DeLamielleure	3.00	1.35	.35
☐ 5 Ken Anderson	10.00	4.50	1.25
☐ 6 Greg Pruitt	4.00	1.80	.50
☐ 7 Harvey Martin	5.00	2.20	.60
☐ 8 Tom Jackson	5.00	2.20	.60
☐ 9 Chester Marcol	3.00	1.35	.35
☐ 10 Jim Carter	3.00	1.35	.35
☐ 11 Will Harrell	3.00	1.35	.35
☐ 12 Greg Landry	4.00	1.80	.50
☐ 13 Billy Johnson	4.00	1.80	.50
☐ 14 Jan Stenerud	5.00	2.20	.60
☐ 15 Lawrence McCutcheon	4.00	1.80	.50
☐ 16 Bob Griese	25.00	11.00	3.10
☐ 17 Chuck Foreman	4.00	1.80	.50
☐ 18 Sammie White	4.00	1.80	.50
☐ 19 Jeff Siemon	3.00	1.35	.35
☐ 20 Mike Haynes	5.00	2.20	.60
☐ 21 Archie Manning	6.00	2.70	.75
☐ 22 Brad Van Pelt	3.00	1.35	.35
☐ 23 Richard Todd	4.00	1.80	.50
☐ 24 Dave Casper	4.00	1.80	.50
☐ 25 Bill Bergey	4.00	1.80	.50
☐ 26 Franco Harris	20.00	9.00	2.50
☐ 27 Mel Gray	4.00	1.80	.50
☐ 28 Louie Kelcher	3.00	1.35	.35
☐ 29 O.J. Simpson	30.00	13.50	3.70
☐ 30 Jim Zorn	4.00	1.80	.50
☐ 31 Lee Roy Selmon	6.00	2.70	.75
☐ 32 Ken Houston	6.00	2.70	.75
☐ 33 Checklist Card	12.00	3.00	1.20

1979 Topps

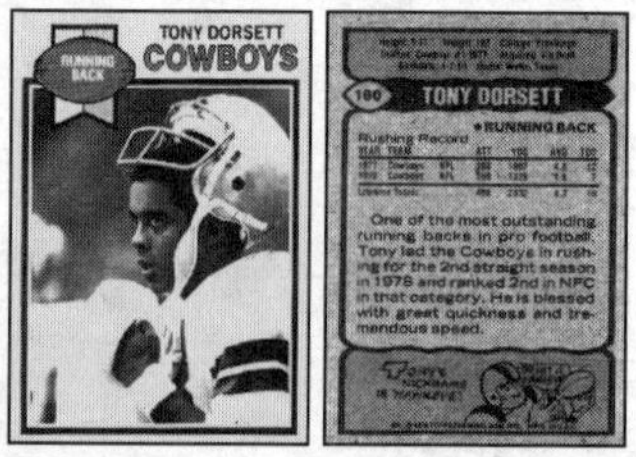

The 1979 Topps football set contains 528 standard-size cards. Card fronts have the player's name, team name and position at he top. The position is within a football that is part of a banner-like design. The backs contain yearly statistics, highlights and a player cartoon. Subsets include league leaders (1-6), playoffs (166-168) and Record Breakers (331-336). Team Leaders (TL) depict team leaders in various categories on front and a team checklist on back. An uncut sheet of the 28-Team Leaders cards along with two checklists was available via a wrapper mail order offer. The set features the first and only major issue cards of Earl Campbell. Other Rookie Cards include Steve DeBerg, James Lofton, Ozzie Newsome and Doug Williams.

	NRMT-MT	EXC	G-VG
COMPLETE SET (528)	140.00	65.00	17.50
COMMON CARD (1-528)	.20	.09	.03

☐ 1 Passing Leaders Roger Staubach Terry Bradshaw	8.00	2.00	.80
☐ 2 Receiving Leaders Rickey Young Steve Largent	1.00	.45	.12
☐ 3 Rushing Leaders Walter Payton Earl Campbell	8.00	3.60	1.00
☐ 4 Scoring Leaders Frank Corral Pat Leahy	.30	.14	.04
☐ 5 Interception Leaders Willie Buchanon Ken Stone Thom Darden	.30	.14	.04
☐ 6 Punting Leaders Tom Skladany Pat McInally	.30	.14	.04
☐ 7 Johnny Perkins	.20	.09	.03
☐ 8 Charles Phillips	.20	.09	.03
☐ 9 Derrel Luce	.20	.09	.03
☐ 10 John Riggins	1.25	.55	.16
☐ 11 Chester Marcol	.20	.09	.03
☐ 12 Bernard Jackson	.20	.09	.03
☐ 13 Dave Logan	.20	.09	.03
☐ 14 Bo Harris	.20	.09	.03
☐ 15 Alan Page	.60	.25	.07
☐ 16 John Smith	.20	.09	.03

☐ 17 Dwight McDonald	.20	.09	.03
☐ 18 John Cappelletti	.30	.14	.04
☐ 19 Pittsburgh Steelers TL	1.00	.45	.12
Franco Harris			
Larry Anderson			
Tony Dungy			
L.C. Greenwood			
(checklist back)			
☐ 20 Bill Bergey AP	.30	.14	.04
☐ 21 Jerome Barkum	.20	.09	.03
☐ 22 Larry Csonka	2.00	.90	.25
☐ 23 Joe Ferguson	.30	.14	.04
☐ 24 Ed Too Tall Jones	1.25	.55	.16
☐ 25 Dave Jennings	.30	.14	.04
☐ 26 Horace King	.20	.09	.03
☐ 27 Steve Little	.30	.14	.04
☐ 28 Morris Bradshaw	.20	.09	.03
☐ 29 Joe Ehrmann	.20	.09	.03
☐ 30 Ahmad Rashad AP	1.00	.45	.12
☐ 31 Joe Lavender	.20	.09	.03
☐ 32 Dan Neal	.20	.09	.03
☐ 33 Johnny Evans	.20	.09	.03
☐ 34 Pete Johnson	.30	.14	.04
☐ 35 Mike Haynes AP	.75	.35	.09
☐ 36 Tim Mazzetti	.20	.09	.03
☐ 37 Mike Barber	.20	.09	.03
☐ 38 San Francisco 49ers TL	1.00	.45	.12
O.J. Simpson			
Freddie Solomon			
Chuck Crist			
Cedrick Hardman			
(checklist back)			
☐ 39 Bill Gregory	.20	.09	.03
☐ 40 Randy Gradishar AP	.50	.23	.06
☐ 41 Richard Todd	.30	.14	.04
☐ 42 Henry Marshall	.20	.09	.03
☐ 43 John Hill	.20	.09	.03
☐ 44 Sidney Thornton	.20	.09	.03
☐ 45 Ron Jessie	.20	.09	.03
☐ 46 Bob Baumhower	.30	.14	.04
☐ 47 Johnnie Gray	.20	.09	.03
☐ 48 Doug Williams	2.00	.90	.25
☐ 49 Don McCauley	.20	.09	.03
☐ 50 Ray Guy AP	.30	.14	.04
☐ 51 Bob Klein	.20	.09	.03
☐ 52 Golden Richards	.20	.09	.03
☐ 53 Mark Miller	.20	.09	.03
☐ 54 John Sanders	.20	.09	.03
☐ 55 Gary Burley	.20	.09	.03
☐ 56 Steve Nelson	.20	.09	.03
☐ 57 Buffalo Bills TL	.75	.35	.09
Terry Miller			
Frank Lewis			
Mario Clark			
Lucius Sanford			
(checklist back)			
☐ 58 Bobby Bryant	.20	.09	.03
☐ 59 Rick Kane	.20	.09	.03
☐ 60 Larry Little	.50	.23	.06
☐ 61 Ted Fritsch Jr.	.20	.09	.03
☐ 62 Larry Mallory	.20	.09	.03
☐ 63 Marvin Powell	.20	.09	.03
☐ 64 Jim Hart	.50	.23	.06
☐ 65 Joe Greene AP	1.50	.70	.19
☐ 66 Walter White	.20	.09	.03
☐ 67 Gregg Bingham	.20	.09	.03
☐ 68 Errol Mann	.20	.09	.03
☐ 69 Bruce Laird	.20	.09	.03
☐ 70 Drew Pearson	1.00	.45	.12
☐ 71 Steve Bartkowski	.50	.23	.06
☐ 72 Ted Albrecht	.20	.09	.03
☐ 73 Charlie Hall	.20	.09	.03
☐ 74 Pat McInally	.20	.09	.03
☐ 75 Al(Bubba) Baker AP	.75	.35	.09
☐ 76 New England Pats TL	.75	.35	.09
Sam Cunningham			
Stanley Morgan			
Mike Haynes			
Tony McGee			
(checklist back)			
☐ 77 Steve DeBerg	1.50	.70	.19
☐ 78 John Yarno	.20	.09	.03
☐ 79 Stu Voigt	.20	.09	.03
☐ 80 Frank Corral AP	.20	.09	.03
☐ 81 Troy Archer	.20	.09	.03
☐ 82 Bruce Harper	.20	.09	.03
☐ 83 Tom Jackson	1.00	.45	.12
☐ 84 Larry Brown	.30	.14	.04
☐ 85 Wilbert Montgomery AP	1.00	.45	.12
☐ 86 Butch Johnson	.30	.14	.04
☐ 87 Mike Kadish	.20	.09	.03
☐ 88 Ralph Perretta	.20	.09	.03
☐ 89 David Lee	.20	.09	.03
☐ 90 Mark Van Eeghen	.30	.14	.04
☐ 91 John McDaniel	.20	.09	.03
☐ 92 Gary Fencik	.30	.14	.04
☐ 93 Mack Mitchell	.20	.09	.03
☐ 94 Cincinnati Bengals TL	.75	.35	.09
Pete Johnson			
Isaac Curtis			
Dick Jauron			
Ross Browner			
(checklist back)			
☐ 95 Steve Grogan	.50	.23	.06
☐ 96 Garo Yepremian	.30	.14	.04

☐ 97 Barty Smith	.20	.09	.03
☐ 98 Frank Reed	.20	.09	.03
☐ 99 Jim Clack	.20	.09	.03
☐ 100 Chuck Foreman	.30	.14	.04
☐ 101 Joe Klecko	.50	.23	.06
☐ 102 Pat Tilley	.30	.14	.04
☐ 103 Conrad Dobler	.30	.14	.04
☐ 104 Craig Colquitt	.20	.09	.03
☐ 105 Dan Pastorini	.30	.14	.04
☐ 106 Rod Perry AP	.20	.09	.03
☐ 107 Nick Mike-Mayer	.20	.09	.03
☐ 108 John Matuszak	.30	.14	.04
☐ 109 David Taylor	.20	.09	.03
☐ 110 Billy Joe DuPree AP	.30	.14	.04
☐ 111 Harold McLinton	.20	.09	.03
☐ 112 Virgil Livers	.20	.09	.03
☐ 113 Cleveland Browns TL	.75	.35	.09
Greg Pruitt			
Reggie Rucker			
Thom Darden			
Mack Mitchell			
(checklist back)			
☐ 114 Checklist 1-132	1.00	.25	.10
☐ 115 Ken Anderson	1.00	.45	.12
☐ 116 Bill Lenkaitis	.20	.09	.03
☐ 117 Bucky Dilts	.20	.09	.03
☐ 118 Tony Greene	.20	.09	.03
☐ 119 Bobby Hammond	.20	.09	.03
☐ 120 Nat Moore	.30	.14	.04
☐ 121 Pat Leahy AP	.30	.14	.04
☐ 122 James Harris	.30	.14	.04
☐ 123 Lee Roy Selmon	1.25	.55	.16
☐ 124 Bennie Cunningham	.30	.14	.04
☐ 125 Matt Blair AP	.30	.14	.04
☐ 126 Jim Allen	.20	.09	.03
☐ 127 Alfred Jenkins	.30	.14	.04
☐ 128 Arthur Whittington	.20	.09	.03
☐ 129 Norm Thompson	.20	.09	.03
☐ 130 Pat Haden	.50	.23	.06
☐ 131 Freddie Solomon	.20	.09	.03
☐ 132 Chicago Bears TL	2.00	.90	.25
Walter Payton			
James Scott			
Gary Fencik			
Alan Page			
(checklist back)			
☐ 133 Mark Moseley	.20	.09	.03
☐ 134 Cleo Miller	.20	.09	.03
☐ 135 Ross Browner	.30	.14	.04
☐ 136 Don Calhoun	.20	.09	.03
☐ 137 David Whitehurst	.20	.09	.03
☐ 138 Terry Beeson	.20	.09	.03
☐ 139 Ken Stone	.20	.09	.03
☐ 140 Brad Van Pelt AP	.20	.09	.03
☐ 141 Wesley Walker AP	.75	.35	.09
☐ 142 Jan Stenerud	.50	.23	.06
☐ 143 Henry Childs	.20	.09	.03
☐ 144 Otis Armstrong	.50	.23	.06
☐ 145 Dwight White	.30	.14	.04
☐ 146 Steve Wilson	.20	.09	.03
☐ 147 Tom Skladany AP	.20	.09	.03
☐ 148 Lou Piccone	.20	.09	.03
☐ 149 Monte Johnson	.20	.09	.03
☐ 150 Joe Washington	.30	.14	.04
☐ 151 Philadelphia Eagles TL	.75	.35	.09
Wilbert Montgomery			
Harold Carmichael			
Herman Edwards			
Dennis Harrison			
(checklist back)			
☐ 152 Fred Dean	.20	.09	.03
☐ 153 Rolland Lawrence	.20	.09	.03
☐ 154 Brian Baschnagel	.20	.09	.03
☐ 155 Joe Theismann	2.00	.90	.25
☐ 156 Marvin Cobb	.20	.09	.03
☐ 157 Dick Ambrose	.20	.09	.03
☐ 158 Mike Patrick	.20	.09	.03
☐ 159 Gary Shirk	.20	.09	.03
☐ 160 Tony Dorsett	10.00	4.50	1.25
☐ 161 Greg Buttle	.20	.09	.03
☐ 162 A.J. Duhe	.30	.14	.04
☐ 163 Mick Tingelhoff	.30	.14	.04
☐ 164 Ken Burrough	.30	.14	.04
☐ 165 Mike Wagner	.20	.09	.03
☐ 166 AFC Championship	1.00	.45	.12
Steelers 34,			
Oilers 5			
(Franco Harris)			
☐ 167 NFC Championship	.30	.14	.04
Cowboys 28,			
Rams 0			
(line of scrimmage)			
☐ 168 Super Bowl XIII	1.25	.55	.16
Steelers 35,			
Cowboys 31			
(Franco Harris)			
☐ 169 Oakland Raiders TL	.75	.35	.09
Mark Van Eeghen			
Dave Casper			
Charles Phillips			
Ted Hendricks			
(checklist back)			
☐ 170 O.J. Simpson	3.00	1.35	.35
☐ 171 Doug Nettles	.20	.09	.03
☐ 172 Dan Dierdorf AP	.75	.35	.09

☐ 173 Dave Beverly	.20	.09	.03
☐ 174 Jim Zorn	.50	.23	.06
☐ 175 Mike Thomas	.20	.09	.03
☐ 176 John Outlaw	.20	.09	.03
☐ 177 Jim Turner	.20	.09	.03
☐ 178 Freddie Scott	.20	.09	.03
☐ 179 Mike Phipps	.30	.14	.04
☐ 180 Jack Youngblood AP	.50	.23	.06
☐ 181 Sam Hunt	.20	.09	.03
☐ 182 Tony Hill	.50	.23	.06
☐ 183 Gary Barbaro	.20	.09	.03
☐ 184 Archie Griffin	.30	.14	.04
☐ 185 Jerry Sherk	.20	.09	.03
☐ 186 Bobby Jackson	.20	.09	.03
☐ 187 Don Woods	.20	.09	.03
☐ 188 New York Giants TL	.75	.35	.09
Doug Kotar			
Jimmy Robinson			
Terry Jackson			
George Martin			
(checklist back)			
☐ 189 Raymond Chester	.20	.09	.03
☐ 190 Joe DeLamielleure AP	.20	.09	.03
☐ 191 Tony Galbreath	.30	.14	.04
☐ 192 Robert Brazile AP	.30	.14	.04
☐ 193 Neil O'Donoghue	.20	.09	.03
☐ 194 Mike Webster AP	1.00	.45	.12
☐ 195 Ed Simonini	.20	.09	.03
☐ 196 Benny Malone	.20	.09	.03
☐ 197 Tom Wittum	.20	.09	.03
☐ 198 Steve Largent AP	8.00	3.60	1.00
☐ 199 Tommy Hart	.20	.09	.03
☐ 200 Fran Tarkenton	3.00	1.35	.35
☐ 201 Leon Gray AP	.20	.09	.03
☐ 202 Leroy Harris	.20	.09	.03
☐ 203 Eric Williams	.20	.09	.03
☐ 204 Thom Darden AP	.20	.09	.03
☐ 205 Ken Riley	.30	.14	.04
☐ 206 Clark Gaines	.20	.09	.03
☐ 207 Kansas City Chiefs TL	.75	.35	.09
Tony Reed			
Tony Reed			
Tim Gray			
Art Still			
(checklist back)			
☐ 208 Joe Danelo	.20	.09	.03
☐ 209 Glen Walker	.20	.09	.03
☐ 210 Art Shell	.60	.25	.07
☐ 211 Jon Keyworth	.20	.09	.03
☐ 212 Herman Edwards	.20	.09	.03
☐ 213 John Fitzgerald	.20	.09	.03
☐ 214 Jim Smith	.30	.14	.04
☐ 215 Coy Bacon	.30	.14	.04
☐ 216 Dennis Johnson	.20	.09	.03
☐ 217 John Jefferson	2.00	.90	.25
(Charlie Joiner			
in background)			
☐ 218 Gary Weaver	.20	.09	.03
☐ 219 Tom Blanchard	.20	.09	.03
☐ 220 Bert Jones	.50	.23	.06
☐ 221 Stanley Morgan	1.00	.45	.12
☐ 222 James Hunter	.20	.09	.03
☐ 223 Jim O'Bradovich	.20	.09	.03
☐ 224 Carl Mauck	.20	.09	.03
☐ 225 Chris Bahr	.20	.09	.03
☐ 226 New York Jets TL	.75	.35	.09
Kevin Long			
Wesley Walker			
Bobby Jackson			
Burgess Owens			
Joe Klecko			
(checklist back)			
☐ 227 Roland Harper	.20	.09	.03
☐ 228 Randy Dean	.20	.09	.03
☐ 229 Bob Jackson	.20	.09	.03
☐ 230 Sammie White	.30	.14	.04
☐ 231 Mike Dawson	.20	.09	.03
☐ 232 Checklist 133-264	1.00	.25	.10
☐ 233 Ken MacAfee	.20	.09	.03
☐ 234 Jon Kolb AP	.20	.09	.03
☐ 235 Willie Hall	.20	.09	.03
☐ 236 Ron Saul AP	.20	.09	.03
☐ 237 Haskel Stanback	.20	.09	.03
☐ 238 Zenon Andrusyshyn	.20	.09	.03
☐ 239 Norris Thomas	.20	.09	.03
☐ 240 Rick Upchurch	.30	.14	.04
☐ 241 Robert Pratt	.20	.09	.03
☐ 242 Julius Adams	.20	.09	.03
☐ 243 Rich McGeorge	.20	.09	.03
☐ 244 Seattle Seahawks TL	1.25	.55	.16
Sherman Smith			
Steve Largent			
Cornell Webster			
Bill Gregory			
(checklist back)			
☐ 245 Blair Bush	.20	.09	.03
☐ 246 Billy Johnson	.30	.14	.04
☐ 247 Randy Rasmussen	.20	.09	.03
☐ 248 Brian Kelley	.20	.09	.03
☐ 249 Mike Pruitt	.30	.14	.04
☐ 250 Harold Carmichael AP	.75	.35	.09
☐ 251 Mike Hartenstine	.20	.09	.03
☐ 252 Robert Newhouse	.30	.14	.04
☐ 253 Gary Danielson	.50	.23	.06
☐ 254 Mike Fuller	.20	.09	.03

☐ 255 L.C. Greenwood AP	.50	.23	.06
☐ 256 Lemar Parrish	.20	.09	.03
☐ 257 Ike Harris	.20	.09	.03
☐ 258 Ricky Bell	1.00	.45	.12
☐ 259 Willie Parker	.20	.09	.03
☐ 260 Gene Upshaw	.50	.23	.06
☐ 261 Glenn Doughty	.20	.09	.03
☐ 262 Steve Zabel	.20	.09	.03
☐ 263 Atlanta Falcons TL	.75	.35	.09
Bubba Bean			
Wallace Francis			
Rolland Lawrence			
Greg Brezina			
(checklist back)			
☐ 264 Ray Wersching	.20	.09	.03
☐ 265 Lawrence McCutcheon	.30	.14	.04
☐ 266 Willie Buchanon AP	.20	.09	.03
☐ 267 Matt Robinson	.20	.09	.03
☐ 268 Reggie Rucker	.30	.14	.04
☐ 269 Doug Van Horn	.20	.09	.03
☐ 270 Lydell Mitchell	.30	.14	.04
☐ 271 Vern Holland	.20	.09	.03
☐ 272 Eason Ramson	.20	.09	.03
☐ 273 Steve Towle	.20	.09	.03
☐ 274 Jim Marshall	.50	.23	.06
☐ 275 Mel Blount	1.25	.55	.16
☐ 276 Bob Kuziel	.20	.09	.03
☐ 277 James Scott	.20	.09	.03
☐ 278 Tony Reed	.20	.09	.03
☐ 279 Dave Green	.20	.09	.03
☐ 280 Toni Linhart	.20	.09	.03
☐ 281 Andy Johnson	.20	.09	.03
☐ 282 Los Angeles Rams TL	.75	.35	.09
Cullen Bryant			
Willie Miller			
Rod Perry			
Pat Thomas			
Larry Brooks			
(checklist back)			
☐ 283 Phil Villapiano	.30	.14	.04
☐ 284 Dexter Bussey	.20	.09	.03
☐ 285 Craig Morton	.50	.23	.06
☐ 286 Guy Morriss	.20	.09	.03
☐ 287 Lawrence Pillers	.20	.09	.03
☐ 288 Gerald Irons	.20	.09	.03
☐ 289 Scott Perry	.20	.09	.03
☐ 290 Randy White AP	2.00	.90	.25
☐ 291 Jack Gregory	.20	.09	.03
☐ 292 Bob Chandler	.20	.09	.03
☐ 293 Rich Szaro	.20	.09	.03
☐ 294 Sherman Smith	.20	.09	.03
☐ 295 Tom Banks AP	.20	.09	.03
☐ 296 Revie Sorey AP	.20	.09	.03
☐ 297 Ricky Thompson	.20	.09	.03
☐ 298 Ron Yary	.30	.14	.04
☐ 299 Lyle Blackwood	.20	.09	.03
☐ 300 Franco Harris	2.50	1.10	.30
☐ 301 Houston Oilers TL	3.00	1.35	.35
Earl Campbell			
Ken Burrough			
Willie Alexander			
Elvin Bethea			
(checklist back)			
☐ 302 Scott Bull	.20	.09	.03
☐ 303 Dewey Selmon	.30	.14	.04
☐ 304 Jack Rudnay	.20	.09	.03
☐ 305 Fred Biletnikoff	2.00	.90	.25
☐ 306 Jeff West	.20	.09	.03
☐ 307 Shafer Suggs	.20	.09	.03
☐ 308 Ozzie Newsome	12.00	5.50	1.50
☐ 309 Boobie Clark	.20	.09	.03
☐ 310 James Lofton	12.00	5.50	1.50
☐ 311 Joe Pisarcik	.20	.09	.03
☐ 312 Bill Simpson AP	.20	.09	.03
☐ 313 Haven Moses	.30	.14	.04
☐ 314 Jim Merlo	.20	.09	.03
☐ 315 Preston Pearson	.30	.14	.04
☐ 316 Larry Tearry	.20	.09	.03
☐ 317 Tom Dempsey	.20	.09	.03
☐ 318 Greg Latta	.20	.09	.03
☐ 319 Wash. Redskins TL	.75	.35	.09
John Riggins			
John McDaniel			
Jake Scott			
Coy Bacon			
(checklist back)			
☐ 320 Jack Ham AP	1.25	.55	.16
☐ 321 Harold Jackson	.30	.14	.04
☐ 322 George Roberts	.20	.09	.03
☐ 323 Ron Jaworski	.50	.23	.06
☐ 324 Jim Otis	.20	.09	.03
☐ 325 Roger Carr	.30	.14	.04
☐ 326 Jack Tatum	.30	.14	.04
☐ 327 Derrick Gaffney	.20	.09	.03
☐ 328 Reggie Williams	.50	.23	.06
☐ 329 Doug Dieken	.20	.09	.03
☐ 330 Efren Herrera	.20	.09	.03
☐ 331 Earl Campbell RB	6.00	2.70	.75
Most Yards			
Rushing, Rookie			
☐ 332 Tony Galbreath RB	.30	.14	.04
Most Receptions,			
Running Back, Game			
☐ 333 Bruce Harper RB	.30	.14	.04
Most Combined Kick			

Return Yards, Season
334 John James RB .30 .14 .04
  Most Punts, Season
335 Walter Payton RB 4.00 1.80 .50
  Most Combined Attempts, Season
336 Rickey Young RB .30 .14 .04
  Most Receptions, Running Back, Season
337 Jeff Van Note .30 .14 .04
338 San Diego Chargers TL .75 .35 .09
  Lydell Mitchell
  John Jefferson
  Mike Fuller
  Fred Dean
  (checklist back)
339 Stan Walters AP .20 .09 .03
340 Louis Wright AP .30 .14 .04
341 Horace Ivory .20 .09 .03
342 Andre Tillman .20 .09 .03
343 Greg Coleman .20 .09 .03
344 Doug English AP .50 .23 .06
345 Ted Hendricks .50 .23 .06
346 Rich Saul .20 .09 .03
347 Mel Gray .30 .14 .04
348 Toni Fritsch .20 .09 .03
349 Cornell Webster .20 .09 .03
350 Ken Houston .50 .23 .06
351 Ron Johnson .30 .14 .04
352 Doug Kotar .20 .09 .03
353 Brian Sipe .50 .23 .06
354 Billy Brooks .20 .09 .03
355 John Dutton .30 .14 .04
356 Don Goode .20 .09 .03
357 Detroit Lions TL .75 .35 .09
  Dexter Bussey
  David Hill
  Jim Allen
  Al(Bubba) Baker
  (checklist back)
358 Reuben Gant .20 .09 .03
359 Bob Parsons .20 .09 .03
360 Cliff Harris AP .50 .23 .06
361 Raymond Clayborn .30 .14 .04
362 Scott Dierking .20 .09 .03
363 Bill Bryan .20 .09 .03
364 Mike Livingston .20 .09 .03
365 Otis Sistrunk .30 .14 .04
366 Charley Young .30 .14 .04
367 Keith Wortman .20 .09 .03
368 Checklist 265-396 1.00 .45 .10
369 Mike Michel .20 .09 .03
370 Delvin Williams AP .20 .09 .03
371 Steve Furness .30 .14 .04
372 Emery Moorehead .20 .09 .03
373 Clarence Scott .20 .09 .03
374 Rufus Mayes .20 .09 .03
375 Chris Hanburger .20 .09 .03
376 Baltimore Colts TL .75 .35 .09
  Joe Washington
  Roger Carr
  Norm Thompson
  John Dutton
  (checklist back)
377 Bob Avellini .30 .14 .04
378 Jeff Siemon .20 .09 .03
379 Roland Hooks .20 .09 .03
380 Russ Francis .30 .14 .04
381 Roger Wehrli .20 .09 .03
382 Joe Fields .20 .09 .03
383 Archie Manning .50 .23 .06
384 Rob Lytle .20 .09 .03
385 Thomas Henderson .30 .14 .04
386 Morris Owens .20 .09 .03
387 Dan Fouts 3.00 1.35 .35
388 Chuck Crist .20 .09 .03
389 Ed O'Neil .20 .09 .03
390 Earl Campbell AP 30.00 13.50 3.70
391 Randy Grossman .20 .09 .03
392 Monte Jackson .20 .09 .03
393 John Mendenhall .20 .09 .03
394 Miami Dolphins TL .75 .35 .09
  Delvin Williams
  Duriel Harris
  Tim Foley
  Vern Den Herder
  (checklist back)
395 Isaac Curtis .30 .14 .04
396 Mike Bragg .20 .09 .03
397 Doug Plank .20 .09 .03
398 Mike Barnes .20 .09 .03
399 Calvin Hill .30 .14 .04
400 Roger Staubach AP 10.00 4.50 1.25
401 Doug Beaudoin .20 .09 .03
402 Chuck Ramsey .20 .09 .03
403 Mike Hogan .20 .09 .03
404 Mario Clark .20 .09 .03
405 Riley Odoms .20 .09 .03
406 Carl Eller .30 .14 .04
407 Green Bay Packers TL 2.00 .90 .25
  Terdell Middleton
  James Lofton
  Willie Buchanon
  Ezra Johnson
  (checklist back)
408 Mark Arneson .20 .09 .03

409 Vince Ferragamo .50 .23 .06
410 Cleveland Elam .20 .09 .03
411 Donnie Shell 2.50 1.10 .30
412 Ray Rhodes .50 .23 .06
413 Don Cockroft .20 .09 .03
414 Don Bass .30 .14 .04
415 Cliff Branch 1.00 .45 .12
416 Diron Talbert .20 .09 .03
417 Tom Hicks .20 .09 .03
418 Roosevelt Leaks .20 .09 .03
419 Charlie Joiner 1.00 .45 .12
420 Lyle Alzado AP .50 .23 .06
421 Sam Cunningham .30 .14 .04
422 Larry Keller .20 .09 .03
423 Jim Mitchell .20 .09 .03
424 Randy Logan .20 .09 .03
425 Jim Langer .50 .23 .06
426 Gary Green .20 .09 .03
427 Luther Blue .20 .09 .03
428 Dennis Johnson .20 .09 .03
429 Danny White .75 .35 .09
430 Roy Gerela .20 .09 .03
431 Jimmy Robinson .20 .09 .03
432 Minnesota Vikings TL .75 .35 .09
  Chuck Foreman
  Ahmad Rashad
  Bobby Bryant
  Mark Mullaney
  (checklist back)
433 Oliver Davis .20 .09 .03
434 Lenvil Elliott .20 .09 .03
435 Willie Miller .20 .09 .03
436 Brad Dusek .20 .09 .03
437 Bob Thomas .20 .09 .03
438 Ken Mendenhall .20 .09 .03
439 Clarence Davis .20 .09 .03
440 Bob Griese 3.00 1.35 .35
441 Tony McGee .20 .09 .03
442 Ed Taylor .20 .09 .03
443 Ron Howard .20 .09 .03
444 Wayne Morris .20 .09 .03
445 Charlie Waters .50 .23 .06
446 Rick Danmeier .20 .09 .03
447 Paul Naumoff .20 .09 .03
448 Keith Krepfle .20 .09 .03
449 Rusty Jackson .20 .09 .03
450 John Stallworth 4.00 1.80 .50
451 New Orleans Saints TL .75 .35 .09
  Tony Galbreath
  Henry Childs
  Tom Myers
  Elex Price
  (checklist back)
452 Ron Mikolajczyk .20 .09 .03
453 Fred Dryer .50 .23 .06
454 Jim LeClair .20 .09 .03
455 Greg Pruitt .30 .14 .04
456 Jake Scott .20 .09 .03
457 Steve Schubert .20 .09 .03
458 George Kunz .20 .09 .03
459 Mike Williams .20 .09 .03
460 Dave Casper AP .30 .14 .04
461 Sam Adams .20 .09 .03
462 Abdul Salaam .20 .09 .03
463 Terdell Middleton .30 .14 .04
464 Mike Wood .20 .09 .03
465 Bill Thompson AP .20 .09 .03
466 Larry Gordon .20 .09 .03
467 Benny Ricardo .20 .09 .03
468 Reggie McKenzie .30 .14 .04
469 Dallas Cowboys TL 1.25 .55 .16
  Tony Dorsett
  Tony Hill
  Benny Barnes
  Harvey Martin
  Randy White
  (checklist back)
470 Rickey Young .30 .14 .04
471 Charlie Smith .20 .09 .03
472 Al Dixon .20 .09 .03
473 Tom DeLeone .20 .09 .03
474 Louis Breeden .30 .14 .04
475 Jack Lambert 2.00 .90 .25
476 Terry Hermeling .20 .09 .03
477 J.K. McKay .20 .09 .03
478 Stan White .20 .09 .03
479 Terry Nelson .20 .09 .03
480 Walter Payton AP 14.00 6.25 1.75
481 Dave Dalby .20 .09 .03
482 Burgess Owens .20 .09 .03
483 Rolf Benirschke .20 .09 .03
484 Jack Dolbin .20 .09 .03
485 John Hannah AP .50 .23 .06
486 Checklist 397-528 1.00 .25 .10
487 Greg Landry .30 .14 .04
488 St. Louis Cardinals TL .75 .35 .09
  Jim Otis
  Pat Tilley
  Ken Stone
  Mike Dawson
  (checklist back)
489 Paul Krause .30 .14 .04
490 John James .20 .09 .03
491 Merv Krakau .20 .09 .03
492 Dan Doornink .20 .09 .03

493 Curtis Johnson .20 .09 .03
494 Rafael Septien .20 .09 .03
495 Jean Fugett .20 .09 .03
496 Frank LeMaster .20 .09 .03
497 Allan Ellis .20 .09 .03
498 Billy Waddy .30 .14 .04
499 Hank Bauer .20 .09 .03
500 Terry Bradshaw AP UER 8.00 3.60 1.00
  (Stat headers on back are for a runner)
501 Larry McCarren .20 .09 .03
502 Fred Cook .20 .09 .03
503 Chuck Muncie .30 .14 .04
504 Herman Weaver .20 .09 .03
505 Eddie Edwards .20 .09 .03
506 Tony Peters .20 .09 .03
507 Denver Broncos TL .75 .35 .09
  Lonnie Perrin
  Riley Odoms
  Steve Foley
  Bernard Jackson
  Lyle Alzado
  (checklist back)
508 Jimbo Elrod .20 .09 .03
509 David Hill .20 .09 .03
510 Harvey Martin .50 .23 .06
511 Terry Miller .30 .14 .04
512 June Jones .30 .14 .04
513 Randy Cross .50 .23 .06
514 Duriel Harris .20 .09 .03
515 Harry Carson .50 .23 .06
516 Tim Fox .20 .09 .03
517 John Zook .20 .09 .03
518 Bob Tucker .20 .09 .03
519 Kevin Long .20 .09 .03
520 Ken Stabler 6.00 2.70 .75
521 John Bunting .20 .09 .03
522 Rocky Bleier 1.25 .55 .16
523 Noah Jackson .20 .09 .03
524 Cliff Parsley .20 .09 .03
525 Louie Kelcher AP .30 .14 .04
526 Tampa Bay Bucs TL .75 .35 .09
  Ricky Bell
  Morris Owens
  Cedric Brown
  Lee Roy Selmon
  (checklist back)
527 Bob Brudzinski .20 .09 .03
528 Danny Buggs .20 .09 .03

1980 Topps

The 1980 Topps football card set contains 528 standard-size cards of NFL players. The set was issued in 12-card packs along with a bubble gum slab. The fronts feature a football at the bottom of the photo. Within the football is the player's team and position. A bar with the player's name runs through the center of the football. The backs of the cards contain year-by-year and career statistics and a cartoon-illustrated fact section. Subsets include Record-Breakers (1-6), league leaders (331-336) and playoffs (492-494). Team Leader (TL) cards depict team statistical leaders on the front and a team checklist on the back. The key Rookie Cards in this set are Ottis Anderson, Clay Matthews, and Phil Simms.

	MINT	NRMT	EXC
COMPLETE SET (528)	60.00	27.00	7.50
COMMON CARD (1-528)	.12	.05	.01

1 Ottis Anderson RB 1.00 .45 .12
  Most Yardage, Rushing, Rookie
2 Harold Carmichael RB .40 .18 .05
  Most Consec. Games, One or More Receptions
3 Dan Fouts RB 1.00 .45 .12
  Most Yardage, Passing, Season
4 Paul Krause RB .25 .11 .03
  Most Interceptions, Lifetime
5 Rick Upchurch RB .12 .05 .01
  Most Punt Return Yards, Lifetime
6 Garo Yepremian RB .12 .05 .01
  Most Consecutive Field Goals
7 Harold Jackson .25 .11 .03
8 Mike Williams .12 .05 .01
9 Calvin Hill .25 .11 .03
10 Jack Ham AP 1.00 .45 .12
11 Dan Melville .12 .05 .01
12 Matt Robinson .12 .05 .01

13 Billy Campfield .12 .05 .01
14 Phil Tabor .12 .05 .01
15 Randy Hughes UER .12 .05 .01
  (Cowboys didn't play in SB VII)
16 Andre Tillman .12 .05 .01
17 Isaac Curtis .25 .11 .03
18 Charley Hannah .12 .05 .01
19 Wash. Redskins TL .30 .14 .04
  John Riggins
  Danny Buggs
  Joe Lavender
  Coy Bacon
  (checklist back)
20 Jim Zorn .25 .11 .03
21 Brian Baschnagel .12 .05 .01
22 Jon Keyworth .12 .05 .01
23 Phil Villapiano .12 .05 .01
24 Richard Osborne .12 .05 .01
25 Rich Saul AP .12 .05 .01
26 Doug Beaudoin .12 .05 .01
27 Cleveland Elam .12 .05 .01
28 Charlie Joiner .75 .35 .09
29 Dick Ambrose .12 .05 .01
30 Mike Reinfeldt AP .12 .05 .01
31 Matt Bahr .40 .18 .05
32 Keith Krepfle .12 .05 .01
33 Herb Scott .12 .05 .01
34 Doug Kotar .12 .05 .01
35 Bob Griese 2.00 .90 .25
36 Jerry Butler .12 .05 .01
37 Rolland Lawrence .12 .05 .01
38 Gary Weaver .12 .05 .01
39 Kansas City Chiefs TL .30 .14 .04
  Ted McKnight
  J.T. Smith
  Gary Barbaro
  Art Still
  (checklist back)
40 Chuck Muncie .25 .11 .03
41 Mike Hartenstine .12 .05 .01
42 Sammie White .25 .11 .03
43 Ken Clark .12 .05 .01
44 Clarence Harmon .12 .05 .01
45 Bert Jones .40 .18 .05
46 Mike Washington .12 .05 .01
47 Joe Fields .12 .05 .01
48 Mike Wood .12 .05 .01
49 Oliver Davis .12 .05 .01
50 Stan Walters AP .12 .05 .01
51 Riley Odoms .12 .05 .01
52 Steve Pisarkiewicz .12 .05 .01
53 Tony Hill .40 .18 .05
54 Scott Perry .12 .05 .01
55 George Martin .12 .05 .01
56 George Roberts .12 .05 .01
57 Seattle Seahawks TL 1.00 .45 .12
  Sherman Smith
  Steve Largent
  Dave Brown
  Manu Tuiasosopo
  (checklist back)
58 Billy Johnson .25 .11 .03
59 Reuben Gant .12 .05 .01
60 Dennis Harrah AP .12 .05 .01
61 Rocky Bleier .75 .35 .09
62 Sam Hunt .12 .05 .01
63 Allan Ellis .12 .05 .01
64 Ricky Thompson .12 .05 .01
65 Ken Stabler 3.50 1.55 .45
66 Dexter Bussey .12 .05 .01
67 Ken Mendenhall .12 .05 .01
68 Woodrow Lowe .12 .05 .01
69 Thom Darden .12 .05 .01
70 Randy White AP 1.50 .70 .19
71 Ken MacAfee .12 .05 .01
72 Ron Jaworski .40 .18 .05
73 William Andrews .75 .35 .09
74 Jimmy Robinson .12 .05 .01
75 Roger Wehrli AP .12 .05 .01
76 Miami Dolphins TL .50 .23 .06
  Larry Csonka
  Nat Moore
  Neal Colzie
  Gerald Small
  Vern Den Herder
  (checklist back)
77 Jack Rudnay .12 .05 .01
78 James Lofton 2.00 .90 .25
79 Robert Brazile .25 .11 .03
80 Russ Francis .25 .11 .03
81 Ricky Bell .40 .18 .05
82 Bob Avellini .25 .11 .03
83 Bobby Jackson .12 .05 .01
84 Mike Bragg .12 .05 .01
85 Cliff Branch .40 .18 .05
86 Blair Bush .12 .05 .01
87 Sherman Smith .12 .05 .01
88 Glen Edwards .12 .05 .01
89 Don Cockroft .12 .05 .01
90 Louis Wright AP .25 .11 .03
91 Randy Grossman .12 .05 .01
92 Carl Hairston .40 .18 .05
93 Archie Manning .50 .23 .06
94 New York Giants TL .30 .14 .04

Billy Taylor			
Earnest Gray			
George Martin			
(checklist back)			
☐ 95 Preston Pearson	.25	.11	.03
☐ 96 Rusty Chambers	.12	.05	.01
☐ 97 Greg Coleman	.12	.05	.01
☐ 98 Charley Young	.12	.05	.01
☐ 99 Matt Cavanaugh	.25	.11	.03
☐ 100 Jesse Baker	.12	.05	.01
☐ 101 Doug Plank	.12	.05	.01
☐ 102 Checklist 1-132	.60	.15	.06
☐ 103 Luther Bradley	.12	.05	.01
☐ 104 Bob Kuziel	.12	.05	.01
☐ 105 Craig Morton	.25	.11	.03
☐ 106 Sherman White	.12	.05	.01
☐ 107 Jim Breech	.25	.11	.03
☐ 108 Hank Bauer	.12	.05	.01
☐ 109 Tom Blanchard	.12	.05	.01
☐ 110 Ozzie Newsome AP	2.00	.90	.25
☐ 111 Steve Furness	.12	.05	.01
☐ 112 Frank LeMaster	.12	.05	.01
☐ 113 Dallas Cowboys TL	1.00	.45	.12
Tony Dorsett			
Tony Hill			
Harvey Martin			
(checklist back)			
☐ 114 Doug Van Horn	.12	.05	.01
☐ 115 Delvin Williams	.12	.05	.01
☐ 116 Lyle Blackwood	.12	.05	.01
☐ 117 Derrick Gaffney	.12	.05	.01
☐ 118 Cornell Webster	.12	.05	.01
☐ 119 Sam Cunningham	.25	.11	.03
☐ 120 Jim Youngblood AP	.25	.11	.03
☐ 121 Bob Thomas	.12	.05	.01
☐ 122 Jack Thompson	.25	.11	.03
☐ 123 Randy Cross	.40	.18	.05
☐ 124 Karl Lorch	.12	.05	.01
☐ 125 Mel Gray	.12	.05	.01
☐ 126 John James	.12	.05	.01
☐ 127 Terdell Middleton	.12	.05	.01
☐ 128 Leroy Jones	.12	.05	.01
☐ 129 Tom DeLeone	.12	.05	.01
☐ 130 John Stallworth AP	1.50	.70	.19
☐ 131 Jimmie Giles	.25	.11	.03
☐ 132 Philadelphia Eagles TL	.30	.14	.04
Wilbert Montgomery			
Harold Carmichael			
Brenard Wilson			
Carl Hairston			
(checklist back)			
☐ 133 Gary Green	.12	.05	.01
☐ 134 John Dutton	.25	.11	.03
☐ 135 Harry Carson AP	.40	.18	.05
☐ 136 Bob Kuechenberg	.25	.11	.03
☐ 137 Ike Harris	.12	.05	.01
☐ 138 Tommy Kramer	.40	.18	.05
☐ 139 Sam Adams	.12	.05	.01
☐ 140 Doug English AP	.25	.11	.03
☐ 141 Steve Schubert	.12	.05	.01
☐ 142 Rusty Jackson	.12	.05	.01
☐ 143 Reese McCall	.12	.05	.01
☐ 144 Scott Dierking	.12	.05	.01
☐ 145 Ken Houston AP	.40	.18	.05
☐ 146 Bob Martin	.12	.05	.01
☐ 147 Sam McCullum	.12	.05	.01
☐ 148 Tom Banks	.12	.05	.01
☐ 149 Willie Buchanon	.12	.05	.01
☐ 150 Greg Pruitt	.25	.11	.03
☐ 151 Denver Broncos TL	.30	.14	.04
Otis Armstrong			
Rick Upchurch			
Steve Foley			
Brison Manor			
(checklist back)			
☐ 152 Don Smith	.12	.05	.01
☐ 153 Pete Johnson	.25	.11	.03
☐ 154 Charlie Smith	.12	.05	.01
☐ 155 Mel Blount	.75	.35	.09
☐ 156 John Mendenhall	.12	.05	.01
☐ 157 Danny White	.50	.23	.06
☐ 158 Jimmy Cefalo	.25	.11	.03
☐ 159 Richard Bishop AP	.12	.05	.01
☐ 160 Walter Payton AP	8.00	3.60	1.00
☐ 161 Dave Dalby	.12	.05	.01
☐ 162 Preston Dennard	.12	.05	.01
☐ 163 Johnnie Gray	.12	.05	.01
☐ 164 Russell Erxleben	.12	.05	.01
☐ 165 Toni Fritsch AP	.12	.05	.01
☐ 166 Terry Hermeling	.12	.05	.01
☐ 167 Roland Hooks	.12	.05	.01
☐ 168 Roger Carr	.12	.05	.01
☐ 169 San Diego Chargers TL	.30	.14	.04
Clarence Williams			
John Jefferson			
Woodrow Lowe			
Ray Preston			
Wilbur Young			
(checklist back)			
☐ 170 Ottis Anderson AP	4.00	1.80	.50
☐ 171 Brian Sipe	.40	.18	.05
☐ 172 Leonard Thompson	.12	.05	.01
☐ 173 Tony Reed	.12	.05	.01
☐ 174 Bob Tucker	.12	.05	.01
☐ 175 Joe Greene	1.00	.45	.12
☐ 176 Jack Dolbin	.12	.05	.01
☐ 177 Chuck Ramsey	.12	.05	.01
☐ 178 Paul Hofer	.12	.05	.01
☐ 179 Randy Logan	.12	.05	.01
☐ 180 David Lewis AP	.12	.05	.01
☐ 181 Duriel Harris	.12	.05	.01
☐ 182 June Jones	.25	.11	.03
☐ 183 Larry McCarren	.12	.05	.01
☐ 184 Ken Johnson	.12	.05	.01
☐ 185 Charlie Waters	.40	.18	.05
☐ 186 Noah Jackson	.12	.05	.01
☐ 187 Reggie Williams	.25	.11	.03
☐ 188 New England Patriots TL	.30	.14	.04
Sam Cunningham			
Harold Jackson			
Raymond Clayborn			
Tony McGee			
(checklist back)			
☐ 189 Carl Eller	.25	.11	.03
☐ 190 Ed White AP	.12	.05	.01
☐ 191 Mario Clark	.12	.05	.01
☐ 192 Roosevelt Leaks	.12	.05	.01
☐ 193 Ted McKnight	.12	.05	.01
☐ 194 Danny Buggs	.12	.05	.01
☐ 195 Lester Hayes	1.00	.45	.12
☐ 196 Clarence Scott	.12	.05	.01
☐ 197 New Orleans Saints TL	.30	.14	.04
Chuck Muncie			
Wes Chandler			
Tom Myers			
Elois Grooms			
Don Reese			
(checklist back)			
☐ 198 Richard Caster	.12	.05	.01
☐ 199 Louie Giammona	.12	.05	.01
☐ 200 Terry Bradshaw	5.00	2.20	.60
☐ 201 Ed Newman	.12	.05	.01
☐ 202 Fred Dryer	.40	.18	.05
☐ 203 Dennis Franks	.12	.05	.01
☐ 204 Bob Breunig	.25	.11	.03
☐ 205 Alan Page	.40	.18	.05
☐ 206 Earnest Gray	.12	.05	.01
☐ 207 Minnesota Vikings TL	.30	.14	.04
Rickey Young			
Ahmad Rashad			
Tom Hannon			
Nate Wright			
Mark Mullaney			
(checklist back)			
☐ 208 Horace Ivory	.12	.05	.01
☐ 209 Isaac Hagins	.12	.05	.01
☐ 210 Gary Johnson AP	.12	.05	.01
☐ 211 Kevin Long	.12	.05	.01
☐ 212 Bill Thompson	.12	.05	.01
☐ 213 Don Bass	.12	.05	.01
☐ 214 George Starke	.12	.05	.01
☐ 215 Efren Herrera	.12	.05	.01
☐ 216 Theo Bell	.12	.05	.01
☐ 217 Monte Jackson	.12	.05	.01
☐ 218 Reggie McKenzie	.12	.05	.01
☐ 219 Bucky Dilts	.12	.05	.01
☐ 220 Lyle Alzado	.40	.18	.05
☐ 221 Tim Foley	.12	.05	.01
☐ 222 Mark Arneson	.12	.05	.01
☐ 223 Fred Quillan	.12	.05	.01
☐ 224 Benny Ricardo	.12	.05	.01
☐ 225 Phil Simms	20.00	9.00	2.50
☐ 226 Chicago Bears TL	1.25	.55	.16
Walter Payton			
Brian Baschnagel			
Gary Fencik			
Terry Schmidt			
Jim Osborne			
(checklist back)			
☐ 227 Max Runager	.12	.05	.01
☐ 228 Barty Smith	.12	.05	.01
☐ 229 Jay Saldi	.25	.11	.03
☐ 230 John Hannah AP	.40	.18	.05
☐ 231 Tim Wilson	.12	.05	.01
☐ 232 Jeff Van Note	.12	.05	.01
☐ 233 Henry Marshall	.12	.05	.01
☐ 234 Diron Talbert	.12	.05	.01
☐ 235 Garo Yepremian	.25	.11	.03
☐ 236 Larry Brown	.12	.05	.01
☐ 237 Clarence Williams	.12	.05	.01
☐ 238 Burgess Owens	.12	.05	.01
☐ 239 Vince Ferragamo	.25	.11	.03
☐ 240 Rickey Young	.12	.05	.01
☐ 241 Dave Logan	.12	.05	.01
☐ 242 Larry Gordon	.12	.05	.01
☐ 243 Terry Miller	.12	.05	.01
☐ 244 Baltimore Colts TL	.30	.14	.04
Joe Washington			
Joe Washington			
Fred Cook			
(checklist back)			
☐ 245 Steve DeBerg	.40	.18	.05
☐ 246 Checklist 133-264	.60	.15	.06
☐ 247 Greg Latta	.12	.05	.01
☐ 248 Raymond Clayborn	.25	.11	.03
☐ 249 Jim Clack	.12	.05	.01
☐ 250 Drew Pearson	.40	.18	.05
☐ 251 John Bunting	.12	.05	.01
☐ 252 Rob Lytle	.12	.05	.01
☐ 253 Jim Hart	.40	.18	.05
☐ 254 John McDaniel	.12	.05	.01
☐ 255 Dave Pear AP	.12	.05	.01
☐ 256 Donnie Shell	.75	.35	.09
☐ 257 Dan Doornink	.12	.05	.01
☐ 258 Wallace Francis	.40	.18	.05
☐ 259 Dave Beverly	.12	.05	.01
☐ 260 Lee Roy Selmon AP	.75	.35	.09
☐ 261 Doug Dieken	.12	.05	.01
☐ 262 Gary Davis	.12	.05	.01
☐ 263 Bob Rush	.12	.05	.01
☐ 264 Buffalo Bills TL	.30	.14	.04
Curtis Brown			
Frank Lewis			
Keith Moody			
Sherman White			
(checklist back)			
☐ 265 Greg Landry	.25	.11	.03
☐ 266 Jan Stenerud	.25	.11	.03
☐ 267 Tom Hicks	.12	.05	.01
☐ 268 Pat McInally	.12	.05	.01
☐ 269 Tim Fox	.12	.05	.01
☐ 270 Harvey Martin	.40	.18	.05
☐ 271 Dan Lloyd	.12	.05	.01
☐ 272 Mike Barber	.12	.05	.01
☐ 273 Wendell Tyler	.40	.18	.05
☐ 274 Jeff Komlo	.12	.05	.01
☐ 275 Wes Chandler	1.00	.45	.12
☐ 276 Brad Dusek	.12	.05	.01
☐ 277 Charlie Johnson	.12	.05	.01
☐ 278 Dennis Swilley	.12	.05	.01
☐ 279 Johnny Evans	.12	.05	.01
☐ 280 Jack Lambert AP	1.50	.70	.19
☐ 281 Vern Den Herder	.12	.05	.01
☐ 282 Tampa Bay Bucs TL	.30	.14	.04
Ricky Bell			
Isaac Hagins			
Lee Roy Selmon			
(checklist back)			
☐ 283 Bob Klein	.12	.05	.01
☐ 284 Jim Turner	.12	.05	.01
☐ 285 Marvin Powell AP	.25	.11	.03
☐ 286 Aaron Kyle	.12	.05	.01
☐ 287 Dan Neal	.12	.05	.01
☐ 288 Wayne Morris	.12	.05	.01
☐ 289 Steve Bartkowski	.25	.11	.03
☐ 290 Dave Jennings AP	.25	.11	.03
☐ 291 John Smith	.12	.05	.01
☐ 292 Bill Gregory	.12	.05	.01
☐ 293 Frank Lewis	.12	.05	.01
☐ 294 Fred Cook	.12	.05	.01
☐ 295 David Hill AP	.12	.05	.01
☐ 296 Wade Key	.12	.05	.01
☐ 297 Sidney Thornton	.12	.05	.01
☐ 298 Charlie Hall	.12	.05	.01
☐ 299 Joe Lavender	.12	.05	.01
☐ 300 Tom Rafferty	.12	.05	.01
☐ 301 Mike Renfro	.25	.11	.03
☐ 302 Wilbur Jackson	.25	.11	.03
☐ 303 Green Bay Packers TL	.40	.18	.05
Terdell Middleton			
James Lofton			
Johnnie Gray			
Robert Barber			
Ezra Johnson			
(checklist back)			
☐ 304 Henry Childs	.12	.05	.01
☐ 305 Russ Washington AP	.12	.05	.01
☐ 306 Jim LeClair	.12	.05	.01
☐ 307 Tommy Hart	.12	.05	.01
☐ 308 Gary Barbaro	.12	.05	.01
☐ 309 Billy Taylor	.12	.05	.01
☐ 310 Ray Guy	.25	.11	.03
☐ 311 Don Hasselbeck	.12	.05	.01
☐ 312 Doug Williams	.60	.25	.07
☐ 313 Nick Mike-Mayer	.12	.05	.01
☐ 314 Don McCauley	.12	.05	.01
☐ 315 Wesley Walker	.40	.18	.05
☐ 316 Dan Dierdorf	1.00	.45	.12
☐ 317 Dave Brown	.25	.11	.03
☐ 318 Leroy Harris	.12	.05	.01
☐ 319 Pittsburgh Steelers TL	.75	.35	.09
Franco Harris			
John Stallworth			
Jack Lambert			
Steve Furness			
L.C. Greenwood			
(checklist back)			
☐ 320 Mark Moseley AP UER	.12	.05	.01
(Bio on back refers			
to him as Mike)			
☐ 321 Mark Dennard	.12	.05	.01
☐ 322 Terry Nelson	.12	.05	.01
☐ 323 Tom Jackson	.40	.18	.05
☐ 324 Rick Kane	.12	.05	.01
☐ 325 Jerry Sherk	.12	.05	.01
☐ 326 Ray Preston	.12	.05	.01
☐ 327 Golden Richards	.12	.05	.01
☐ 328 Randy Dean	.12	.05	.01
☐ 329 Rick Danmeier	.12	.05	.01
☐ 330 Tony Dorsett	6.00	2.70	.75
☐ 331 Passing Leaders	3.00	1.35	.35
Dan Fouts			
Roger Staubach			
☐ 332 Receiving Leaders	.25	.11	.03
Joe Washington			
Ahmad Rashad			
☐ 333 Sacks Leaders	.12	.05	.01
Jesse Baker			
Al(Bubba) Baker			
Jack Youngblood			
☐ 334 Scoring Leaders	.12	.05	.01
John Smith			
Mark Moseley			
☐ 335 Interception Leaders	.12	.05	.01
Mike Reinfeldt			
Lemar Parrish			
☐ 336 Punting Leaders	.12	.05	.01
Bob Grupp			
Dave Jennings			
☐ 337 Freddie Solomon	.12	.05	.01
☐ 338 Cincinnati Bengals TL	.30	.14	.04
Pete Johnson			
Don Bass			
Dick Jauron			
Gary Burley			
(checklist back)			
☐ 339 Ken Stone	.12	.05	.01
☐ 340 Greg Buttle AP	.12	.05	.01
☐ 341 Bob Baumhower	.25	.11	.03
☐ 342 Billy Waddy	.12	.05	.01
☐ 343 Cliff Parsley	.12	.05	.01
☐ 344 Walter White	.12	.05	.01
☐ 345 Mike Thomas	.12	.05	.01
☐ 346 Neil O'Donoghue	.12	.05	.01
☐ 347 Freddie Scott	.12	.05	.01
☐ 348 Joe Ferguson	.25	.11	.03
☐ 349 Doug Nettles	.12	.05	.01
☐ 350 Mike Webster AP	.40	.18	.05
☐ 351 Ron Saul	.12	.05	.01
☐ 352 Julius Adams	.12	.05	.01
☐ 353 Rafael Septien	.12	.05	.01
☐ 354 Cleo Miller	.12	.05	.01
☐ 355 Keith Simpson AP	.12	.05	.01
☐ 356 Johnny Perkins	.12	.05	.01
☐ 357 Jerry Sisemore	.12	.05	.01
☐ 358 Arthur Whittington	.12	.05	.01
☐ 359 St. Louis Cardinals TL	.30	.14	.04
Ottis Anderson			
Pat Tilley			
Ken Stone			
Bob Pollard			
(checklist back)			
☐ 360 Rick Upchurch	.25	.11	.03
☐ 361 Kim Bokamper	.12	.05	.01
☐ 362 Roland Harper	.12	.05	.01
☐ 363 Pat Leahy	.12	.05	.01
☐ 364 Louis Breeden	.12	.05	.01
☐ 365 John Jefferson	.60	.25	.07
☐ 366 Jerry Eckwood	.12	.05	.01
☐ 367 David Whitehurst	.12	.05	.01
☐ 368 Willie Parker	.12	.05	.01
☐ 369 Ed Simonini	.12	.05	.01
☐ 370 Jack Youngblood AP	.40	.18	.05
☐ 371 Don Warren	.40	.18	.05
☐ 372 Andy Johnson	.12	.05	.01
☐ 373 D.D. Lewis	.25	.11	.03
☐ 374A Beasley Reece ERR	.40	.18	.05
(No S in position			
on front of card)			
☐ 374B Beasley Reece COR	.25	.11	.03
☐ 375 L.C. Greenwood	.40	.18	.05
☐ 376 Cleveland Browns TL	.30	.14	.04
Mike Pruitt			
Dave Logan			
Thom Darden			
Jerry Sherk			
(checklist back)			
☐ 377 Herman Edwards	.12	.05	.01
☐ 378 Rob Carpenter	.12	.05	.01
☐ 379 Herman Weaver	.12	.05	.01
☐ 380 Gary Fencik AP	.12	.05	.01
☐ 381 Don Strock	.25	.11	.03
☐ 382 Art Shell	.50	.23	.06
☐ 383 Tim Mazzetti	.12	.05	.01
☐ 384 Bruce Harper	.12	.05	.01
☐ 385 Al(Bubba) Baker	.25	.11	.03
☐ 386 Conrad Dobler	.12	.05	.01
☐ 387 Stu Voigt	.12	.05	.01
☐ 388 Ken Anderson	1.00	.45	.12
☐ 389 Pat Tilley	.12	.05	.01
☐ 390 John Riggins	.75	.35	.09
☐ 391 Checklist 265-396	.60	.15	.06
☐ 392 Fred Dean AP	.12	.05	.01
☐ 393 Benny Barnes	.12	.05	.01
☐ 394 Los Angeles Rams TL	.30	.14	.04
Wendell Tyler			
Preston Dennard			
Nolan Cromwell			
Jim Youngblood			
Jack Youngblood			
(checklist back)			
☐ 395 Brad Van Pelt	.12	.05	.01
☐ 396 Eddie Hare	.12	.05	.01
☐ 397 John Sciarra	.12	.05	.01
☐ 398 Bob Jackson	.12	.05	.01
☐ 399 John Yarno	.12	.05	.01
☐ 400 Franco Harris AP	2.00	.90	.25
☐ 401 Ray Wersching	.12	.05	.01
☐ 402 Virgil Livers	.12	.05	.01
☐ 403 Raymond Chester	.12	.05	.01
☐ 404 Leon Gray	.12	.05	.01

☐ 405 Richard Todd	.25	.11	.03
☐ 406 Larry Little	.40	.18	.05
☐ 407 Ted Fritsch Jr.	.12	.05	.01
☐ 408 Larry Mucker	.12	.05	.01
☐ 409 Jim Allen	.12	.05	.01
☐ 410 Randy Gradishar	.40	.18	.05
☐ 411 Atlanta Falcons TL	.30	.14	.04
William Andrews			
Wallace Francis			
Rolland Lawrence			
Don Smith			
(checklist back)			
☐ 412 Louie Kelcher	.25	.11	.03
☐ 413 Robert Newhouse	.25	.11	.03
☐ 414 Gary Shirk	.12	.05	.01
☐ 415 Mike Haynes AP	.40	.18	.05
☐ 416 Craig Colquitt	.12	.05	.01
☐ 417 Lou Piccone	.12	.05	.01
☐ 418 Clay Matthews	2.50	1.10	.30
☐ 419 Marvin Cobb	.12	.05	.01
☐ 420 Harold Carmichael AP	.40	.18	.05
☐ 421 Uwe Von Schamann	.25	.11	.03
☐ 422 Mike Phipps	.25	.11	.03
☐ 423 Nolan Cromwell	.40	.18	.05
☐ 424 Glenn Doughty	.12	.05	.01
☐ 425 Bob Young AP	.12	.05	.01
☐ 426 Tony Galbreath	.12	.05	.01
☐ 427 Luke Prestridge	.12	.05	.01
☐ 428 Terry Beeson	.12	.05	.01
☐ 429 Jack Tatum	.25	.11	.03
☐ 430 Lemar Parrish AP	.12	.05	.01
☐ 431 Chester Marcol	.12	.05	.01
☐ 432 Houston Oilers TL	.30	.14	.04
Dan Pastorini			
Ken Burrough			
Mike Reinfeldt			
Jesse Baker			
(checklist back)			
☐ 433 John Fitzgerald	.12	.05	.01
☐ 434 Gary Jeter	.25	.11	.03
☐ 435 Steve Grogan	.40	.18	.05
☐ 436 Jon Kolb UER	.12	.05	.01
John on front			
☐ 437 Jim O'Bradovich UER	.12	.05	.01
(Neil O'Donoghue's bio)			
☐ 438 Gerald Irons	.12	.05	.01
☐ 439 Jeff West	.12	.05	.01
☐ 440 Wilbert Montgomery	.25	.11	.03
☐ 441 Norris Thomas	.12	.05	.01
☐ 442 James Scott	.12	.05	.01
☐ 443 Curtis Brown	.12	.05	.01
☐ 444 Ken Fantetti	.12	.05	.01
☐ 445 Pat Haden	.40	.18	.05
☐ 446 Carl Mauck	.12	.05	.01
☐ 447 Bruce Laird	.12	.05	.01
☐ 448 Otis Armstrong	.12	.05	.01
☐ 449 Gene Upshaw	.40	.18	.05
☐ 450 Steve Largent AP	6.00	2.70	.75
☐ 451 Benny Malone	.12	.05	.01
☐ 452 Steve Nelson	.12	.05	.01
☐ 453 Mark Cotney	.12	.05	.01
☐ 454 Joe Danelo	.12	.05	.01
☐ 455 Billy Joe DuPree	.25	.11	.03
☐ 456 Ron Johnson	.12	.05	.01
☐ 457 Archie Griffin	.25	.11	.03
☐ 458 Reggie Rucker	.12	.05	.01
☐ 459 Claude Humphrey	.12	.05	.01
☐ 460 Lydell Mitchell	.25	.11	.03
☐ 461 Steve Towle	.12	.05	.01
☐ 462 Revie Sorey	.12	.05	.01
☐ 463 Tom Skladany	.12	.05	.01
☐ 464 Clark Gaines	.12	.05	.01
☐ 465 Frank Corral	.12	.05	.01
☐ 466 Steve Fuller	.25	.11	.03
☐ 467 Ahmad Rashad AP	.40	.18	.05
☐ 468 Oakland Raiders TL	.30	.14	.04
Mark Van Eeghen			
Cliff Branch			
Lester Hayes			
Willie Jones			
(checklist back)			
☐ 469 Brian Peets	.12	.05	.01
☐ 470 Pat Donovan AP	.25	.11	.03
☐ 471 Ken Burrough	.12	.05	.01
☐ 472 Don Calhoun	.12	.05	.01
☐ 473 Bill Bryan	.12	.05	.01
☐ 474 Terry Jackson	.12	.05	.01
☐ 475 Joe Theismann	1.25	.55	.16
☐ 476 Jim Smith	.25	.11	.03
☐ 477 Joe DeLamielleure	.12	.05	.01
☐ 478 Mike Pruitt AP	.25	.11	.03
☐ 479 Steve Mike-Mayer	.12	.05	.01
☐ 480 Bill Bergey	.25	.11	.03
☐ 481 Mike Fuller	.12	.05	.01
☐ 482 Bob Parsons	.12	.05	.01
☐ 483 Billy Brooks	.12	.05	.01
☐ 484 Jerome Barkum	.12	.05	.01
☐ 485 Larry Csonka	1.50	.70	.19
☐ 486 John Hill	.12	.05	.01
☐ 487 Mike Dawson	.12	.05	.01
☐ 488 Detroit Lions TL	.30	.14	.04
Dexter Bussey			
Freddie Scott			
Jim Allen			
Luther Bradley			
Al(Bubba) Baker			
(checklist back)			
☐ 489 Ted Hendricks	.40	.18	.05
☐ 490 Dan Pastorini	.25	.11	.03
☐ 491 Stanley Morgan	.40	.18	.05
☐ 492 AFC Championship	.20	.09	.03
Steelers 27,			
Oilers 13			
(Rocky Bleier running)			
☐ 493 NFC Championship	.20	.09	.03
Rams 9,			
Buccaneers 0			
(Vince Ferragamo)			
☐ 494 Super Bowl XIV	.40	.18	.05
Steelers 31,			
Rams 19			
(line play)			
☐ 495 Dwight White	.25	.11	.03
☐ 496 Haven Moses	.12	.05	.01
☐ 497 Guy Morriss	.12	.05	.01
☐ 498 Dewey Selmon	.25	.11	.03
☐ 499 Dave Butz	.40	.18	.05
☐ 500 Chuck Foreman	.25	.11	.03
☐ 501 Chris Bahr	.12	.05	.01
☐ 502 Mark Miller	.12	.05	.01
☐ 503 Tony Greene	.12	.05	.01
☐ 504 Brian Kelley	.12	.05	.01
☐ 505 Joe Washington	.25	.11	.03
☐ 506 Butch Johnson	.25	.11	.03
☐ 507 New York Jets TL	.30	.14	.04
Clark Gaines			
Wesley Walker			
Burgess Owens			
Joe Klecko			
(checklist back0			
☐ 508 Steve Little	.12	.05	.01
☐ 509 Checklist 397-528	.60	.15	.06
☐ 510 Mark Van Eeghen	.12	.05	.01
☐ 511 Gary Danielson	.25	.11	.03
☐ 512 Manu Tuiasosopo	.12	.05	.01
☐ 513 Paul Coffman	.25	.11	.03
☐ 514 Cullen Bryant	.12	.05	.01
☐ 515 Nat Moore	.25	.11	.03
☐ 516 Bill Lenkaitis	.12	.05	.01
☐ 517 Lynn Cain	.12	.05	.01
☐ 518 Gregg Bingham	.12	.05	.01
☐ 519 Ted Albrecht	.12	.05	.01
☐ 520 Dan Fouts AP	2.00	.90	.25
☐ 521 Bernard Jackson	.12	.05	.01
☐ 522 Coy Bacon	.12	.05	.01
☐ 523 Tony Franklin	.25	.11	.03
☐ 524 Bo Harris	.12	.05	.01
☐ 525 Bob Grupp AP	.12	.05	.01
☐ 526 San Francisco 49ers TL	.30	.14	.04
Paul Hofer			
Freddie Solomon			
James Owens			
Dwaine Board			
(checklist back)			
☐ 527 Steve Wilson	.12	.05	.01
☐ 528 Bennie Cunningham	.25	.11	.03

1980 Topps Super

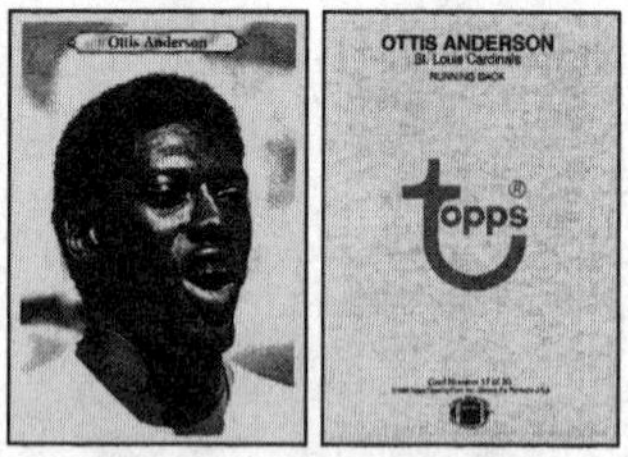

The 1980 Topps Superstar Photo Football set features 30 large (approximately 4 7/8" by 6 7/8") and very colorful cards. This set, a football counterpart to Topps' Superstar Photo Baseball set of the same year, is numbered and is printed on white stock. The cards in this set, sold over the counter without gum at retail establishments, could be individually chosen by the buyer.

	MINT	NRMT	EXC
COMPLETE SET (30)	15.00	6.75	1.85
COMMON CARD (1-30)	.35	.16	.04
☐ 1 Franco Harris	2.00	.90	.25
☐ 2 Bob Griese	2.00	.90	.25
☐ 3 Archie Manning	.50	.23	.06
☐ 4 Harold Carmichael	.50	.23	.06
☐ 5 Wesley Walker	.50	.23	.06
☐ 6 Richard Todd	.35	.16	.04
☐ 7 Dan Fouts	1.50	.70	.19
☐ 8 Ken Stabler	3.00	1.35	.35
☐ 9 Jack Youngblood	.50	.23	.06
☐ 10 Jim Zorn	.50	.23	.06
☐ 11 Tony Dorsett	3.00	1.35	.35
☐ 12 Lee Roy Selmon	.75	.35	.09
☐ 13 Russ Francis	.35	.16	.04
☐ 14 John Stallworth	.75	.35	.09
☐ 15 Terry Bradshaw	3.50	1.55	.45
☐ 16 Joe Theismann	1.25	.55	.16
☐ 17 Ottis Anderson	1.25	.55	.16
☐ 18 John Jefferson	.75	.35	.09
☐ 19 Jack Ham	.75	.35	.09
☐ 20 Joe Greene	1.00	.45	.12
☐ 21 Chuck Muncie	.35	.16	.04
☐ 22 Ron Jaworski	.50	.23	.06
☐ 23 John Hannah	.50	.23	.06
☐ 24 Randy Gradishar	.35	.16	.04
☐ 25 Jack Lambert	1.00	.45	.12
☐ 26 Ricky Bell	.35	.16	.04
☐ 27 Drew Pearson	.75	.35	.09
☐ 28 Rick Upchurch	.35	.16	.04
☐ 29 Brad Van Pelt	.35	.16	.04
☐ 30 Walter Payton	5.00	2.20	.60

1981 Topps

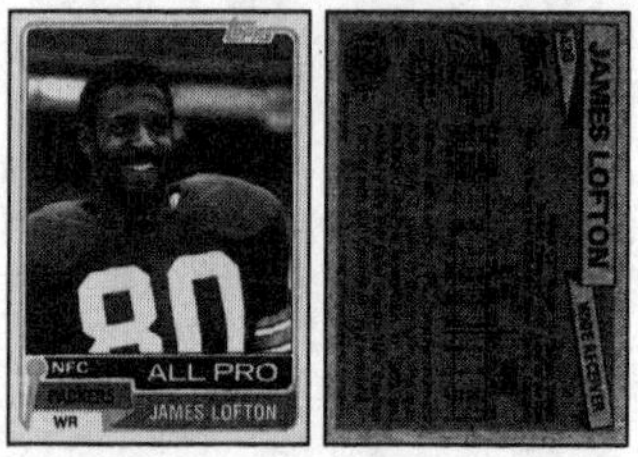

The 1981 Topps football card set contains 528 standard-size cards. This set was issued in 15-card wax packs as well as rack packs and cello packs. The fronts have a pennant-like design at the bottom. This design includes the team name and the player's name. The player's position is also at the bottom. Horizontally designed backs contain year-by-year records, highlights and a cartoon. Super Action (SA) cards of top players are scattered throughout the set. Subsets include league leaders (1-6), Record Breakers (331-336) and playoffs (492-494). Team Leader (TL) cards feature statistical leaders on the front and a team checklist on the back. The key Rookie Card in this set is Joe Montana. Other Rookie Cards include Dwight Clark, Vince Evans, Dan Hampton, Art Monk, Eddie Murray, Billy Sims and Kellen Winslow.

	MINT	NRMT	EXC
COMPLETE SET (528)	200.00	90.00	25.00
COMMON CARD (1-528)	.10	.05	.01
☐ 1 Passing Leaders	.50	.23	.06
Ron Jaworski			
Brian Sipe			
☐ 2 Receiving Leaders	.60	.25	.07
Earl Cooper			
Kellen Winslow			
☐ 3 Sack Leaders	.15	.07	.02
Al(Bubba) Baker			
Gary Johnson			
☐ 4 Scoring Leaders	.15	.07	.02
Eddie Murray			
John Smith			
☐ 5 Interception Leaders	.15	.07	.02
Nolan Cromwell			
Lester Hayes			
☐ 6 Punting Leaders	.15	.07	.02
Dave Jennings			
Luke Prestridge			
☐ 7 Don Calhoun	.10	.05	.01
☐ 8 Jack Tatum	.20	.09	.03
☐ 9 Reggie Rucker	.10	.05	.01
☐ 10 Mike Webster AP	.40	.18	.05
☐ 11 Vince Evans	.40	.18	.05
☐ 12 Ottis Anderson SA	.40	.18	.05
☐ 13 Leroy Harris	.10	.05	.01
☐ 14 Gordon King	.10	.05	.01
☐ 15 Harvey Martin	.40	.18	.05
☐ 16 Johnny Lam Jones	.20	.09	.03
☐ 17 Ken Greene	.10	.05	.01
☐ 18 Frank Lewis	.10	.05	.01
☐ 19 Seattle Seahawks TL	.60	.25	.07
Jim Jodat			
Dave Brown			
John Harris			
Steve Largent			
Jacob Green			
(checklist back)			
☐ 20 Lester Hayes AP	.40	.18	.05
☐ 21 Uwe Von Schamann	.10	.05	.01
☐ 22 Joe Washington	.10	.05	.01
☐ 23 Louie Kelcher	.10	.05	.01
☐ 24 Willie Miller	.10	.05	.01
☐ 25 Steve Grogan	.40	.18	.05
☐ 26 John Hill	.10	.05	.01
☐ 27 Stan White	.10	.05	.01
☐ 28 William Andrews SA	.20	.09	.03
☐ 29 Clarence Scott	.10	.05	.01
☐ 30 Leon Gray AP	.10	.05	.01
☐ 31 Craig Colquitt	.10	.05	.01
☐ 32 Doug Williams	.40	.18	.05
☐ 33 Bob Breunig	.20	.09	.03
☐ 34 Billy Taylor	.10	.05	.01
☐ 35 Harold Carmichael	.40	.18	.05
☐ 36 Ray Wersching	.10	.05	.01
☐ 37 Dennis Johnson	.10	.05	.01
☐ 38 Archie Griffin	.20	.09	.03
☐ 39 Los Angeles Rams TL	.30	.14	.04
Cullen Bryant			
Billy Waddy			
Nolan Cromwell			
Jack Youngblood			
(checklist back)			
☐ 40 Gary Fencik AP	.20	.09	.03
☐ 41 Lynn Dickey	.10	.05	.01
☐ 42 Steve Bartkowski SA	.20	.09	.03
☐ 43 Art Shell	.50	.23	.06
☐ 44 Wilbur Jackson	.10	.05	.01
☐ 45 Frank Corral	.10	.05	.01
☐ 46 Ted McKnight	.10	.05	.01
☐ 47 Joe Klecko	.20	.09	.03
☐ 48 Dan Doornink	.10	.05	.01
☐ 49 Doug Dieken	.10	.05	.01
☐ 50 Jerry Robinson AP	.20	.09	.03
☐ 51 Wallace Francis	.10	.05	.01
☐ 52 Dave Preston	.10	.05	.01
☐ 53 Jay Saldi	.10	.05	.01
☐ 54 Rush Brown	.10	.05	.01
☐ 55 Phil Simms	3.00	1.35	.35
☐ 56 Nick Mike-Mayer	.10	.05	.01
☐ 57 Wash. Redskins TL	2.00	.90	.25
Wilbur Jackson			
Art Monk			
Lemar Parrish			
Coy Bacon			
(checklist back)			
☐ 58 Mike Renfro	.10	.05	.01
☐ 59 Ted Brown SA	.10	.05	.01
☐ 60 Steve Nelson AP	.10	.05	.01
☐ 61 Sidney Thornton	.10	.05	.01
☐ 62 Kent Hill	.10	.05	.01
☐ 63 Don Bessillieu	.10	.05	.01
☐ 64 Fred Cook	.10	.05	.01
☐ 65 Raymond Chester	.10	.05	.01
☐ 66 Rick Kane	.10	.05	.01
☐ 67 Mike Fuller	.10	.05	.01
☐ 68 Dewey Selmon	.20	.09	.03
☐ 69 Charles White	.75	.35	.09
☐ 70 Jeff Van Note AP	.10	.05	.01
☐ 71 Robert Newhouse	.20	.09	.03
☐ 72 Roynell Young	.10	.05	.01
☐ 73 Lynn Cain SA	.10	.05	.01
☐ 74 Mike Friede	.10	.05	.01
☐ 75 Earl Cooper	.10	.05	.01
☐ 76 New Orleans Saints TL	.30	.14	.04
Jimmy Rogers			
Wes Chandler			
Tom Myers			
Elois Grooms			
Derland Moore			
(checklist back)			
☐ 77 Rick Danmeier	.10	.05	.01
☐ 78 Darrol Ray	.10	.05	.01
☐ 79 Gregg Bingham	.10	.05	.01
☐ 80 John Hannah AP	.40	.18	.05
☐ 81 Jack Thompson	.20	.09	.03
☐ 82 Rick Upchurch	.20	.09	.03
☐ 83 Mike Butler	.10	.05	.01
☐ 84 Don Warren	.10	.05	.01
☐ 85 Mark Van Eeghen	.10	.05	.01
☐ 86 J.T. Smith	.40	.18	.05
☐ 87 Herman Weaver	.10	.05	.01
☐ 88 Terry Bradshaw SA	2.00	.90	.25
☐ 89 Charlie Hall	.10	.05	.01
☐ 90 Donnie Shell	.40	.18	.05
☐ 91 Ike Harris	.10	.05	.01
☐ 92 Charlie Johnson	.10	.05	.01
☐ 93 Rickey Watts	.10	.05	.01
☐ 94 New England Patriots TL	.30	.14	.04
Vagas Ferguson			
Stanley Morgan			
Raymond Clayborn			
Julius Adams			
(checklist back)			
☐ 95 Drew Pearson	.40	.18	.05
☐ 96 Neil O'Donoghue	.10	.05	.01
☐ 97 Conrad Dobler	.10	.05	.01
☐ 98 Jewerl Thomas	.10	.05	.01
☐ 99 Mike Barber	.10	.05	.01
☐ 100 Billy Sims AP	1.25	.55	.16
☐ 101 Vern Den Herder	.10	.05	.01
☐ 102 Greg Landry	.20	.09	.03
☐ 103 Joe Cribbs SA	.20	.09	.03
☐ 104 Mark Murphy	.10	.05	.01
☐ 105 Chuck Muncie	.20	.09	.03
☐ 106 Alfred Jackson	.20	.09	.03
☐ 107 Chris Bahr	.10	.05	.01
☐ 108 Gordon Jones	.10	.05	.01
☐ 109 Willie Harper	.10	.05	.01
☐ 110 Dave Jennings AP	.10	.05	.01
☐ 111 Bennie Cunningham	.10	.05	.01
☐ 112 Jerry Sisemore	.10	.05	.01
☐ 113 Cleveland Browns TL	.30	.14	.04
Mike Pruitt			
Dave Logan			
Ron Bolton			
Lyle Alzado			
(checklist back)			
☐ 114 Rickey Young	.10	.05	.01
☐ 115 Ken Anderson	.75	.35	.09
☐ 116 Randy Gradishar	.40	.18	.05
☐ 117 Eddie Lee Ivery	.10	.05	.01
☐ 118 Wesley Walker	.40	.18	.05
☐ 119 Chuck Foreman	.20	.09	.03
☐ 120 Nolan Cromwell AP	.20	.09	.03

UER (Rushing TD's added wrong)			
☐ 121 Curtis Dickey SA	.10	.05	.01
☐ 122 Wayne Morris	.10	.05	.01
☐ 123 Greg Stemrick	.10	.05	.01
☐ 124 Coy Bacon	.10	.05	.01
☐ 125 Jim Zorn	.20	.09	.03
(Steve Largent in background)			
☐ 126 Henry Childs	.10	.05	.01
☐ 127 Checklist 1-132	.50	.23	.06
☐ 128 Len Walterscheid	.10	.05	.01
☐ 129 Johnny Evans	.10	.05	.01
☐ 130 Gary Barbaro AP	.10	.05	.01
☐ 131 Jim Smith	.10	.05	.01
☐ 132 New York Jets TL	.30	.14	.04
Scott Dierking			
Bruce Harper			
Ken Schroy			
Mark Gastineau			
(checklist back)			
☐ 133 Curtis Brown	.10	.05	.01
☐ 134 D.D. Lewis	.10	.05	.01
☐ 135 Jim Plunkett	.50	.23	.06
☐ 136 Nat Moore	.20	.09	.03
☐ 137 Don McCauley	.10	.05	.01
☐ 138 Tony Dorsett SA	.75	.35	.09
☐ 139 Julius Adams	.10	.05	.01
☐ 140 Ahmad Rashad AP	.40	.18	.05
☐ 141 Rich Saul	.10	.05	.01
☐ 142 Ken Fantetti	.10	.05	.01
☐ 143 Kenny Johnson	.10	.05	.01
☐ 144 Clark Gaines	.10	.05	.01
☐ 145 Mark Moseley	.10	.05	.01
☐ 146 Vernon Perry	.10	.05	.01
☐ 147 Jerry Eckwood	.10	.05	.01
☐ 148 Freddie Solomon	.10	.05	.01
☐ 149 Jerry Sherk	.10	.05	.01
☐ 150 Kellen Winslow AP	8.00	3.60	1.00
☐ 151 Green Bay Packers TL	.30	.14	.04
Eddie Lee Ivery			
James Lofton			
Johnnie Gray			
Mike Butler			
(checklist back)			
☐ 152 Ross Browner	.10	.05	.01
☐ 153 Dan Fouts SA	.75	.35	.09
☐ 154 Woody Peoples	.10	.05	.01
☐ 155 Jack Lambert	1.00	.45	.12
☐ 156 Mike Dennis	.10	.05	.01
☐ 157 Rafael Septien	.10	.05	.01
☐ 158 Archie Manning	.40	.18	.05
☐ 159 Don Hasselbeck	.10	.05	.01
☐ 160 Alan Page AP	.40	.18	.05
☐ 161 Arthur Whittington	.10	.05	.01
☐ 162 Billy Waddy	.10	.05	.01
☐ 163 Horace Belton	.10	.05	.01
☐ 164 Luke Prestridge	.10	.05	.01
☐ 165 Joe Theismann	.75	.35	.09
☐ 166 Morris Towns	.10	.05	.01
☐ 167 Dave Brown	.10	.05	.01
☐ 168 Ezra Johnson	.10	.05	.01
☐ 169 Tampa Bay Buccaneers TL	.30	.14	.04
Ricky Bell			
Gordon Jones			
Mike Washington			
Lee Roy Selmon			
(checklist back)			
☐ 170 Joe DeLamielleure AP	.10	.05	.01
☐ 171 Earnest Gray SA	.10	.05	.01
☐ 172 Mike Thomas	.10	.05	.01
☐ 173 Jim Haslett	.10	.05	.01
☐ 174 David Woodley	.20	.09	.03
☐ 175 Al(Bubba) Baker	.20	.09	.03
☐ 176 Nesby Glasgow	.10	.05	.01
☐ 177 Pat Leahy	.10	.05	.01
☐ 178 Tom Brahaney	.10	.05	.01
☐ 179 Herman Edwards	.10	.05	.01
☐ 180 Junior Miller AP	.10	.05	.01
☐ 181 Richard Wood	.10	.05	.01
☐ 182 Lenvil Elliott	.10	.05	.01
☐ 183 Sammie White	.20	.09	.03
☐ 184 Russell Erxleben	.10	.05	.01
☐ 185 Ed Too Tall Jones	.75	.35	.09
☐ 186 Ray Guy SA	.20	.09	.03
☐ 187 Haven Moses	.10	.05	.01
☐ 188 New York Giants TL	.30	.14	.04
Billy Taylor			
Earnest Gray			
Mike Dennis			
Gary Jeter			
(checklist back)			
☐ 189 David Whitehurst	.10	.05	.01
☐ 190 John Jefferson AP	.40	.18	.05
☐ 191 Terry Beeson	.10	.05	.01
☐ 192 Dan Ross	.20	.09	.03
☐ 193 Dave Williams	.10	.05	.01
☐ 194 Art Monk	14.00	6.25	1.75
☐ 195 Roger Wehrli	.10	.05	.01
☐ 196 Ricky Feacher	.10	.05	.01
☐ 197 Miami Dolphins TL	.30	.14	.04
Delvin Williams			
Tony Nathan			
Gerald Small			
Kim Bokamper			
A.J. Duhe			
(checklist back)			
☐ 198 Carl Roaches	.10	.05	.01
☐ 199 Billy Campfield	.10	.05	.01
☐ 200 Ted Hendricks AP	.40	.18	.05
☐ 201 Fred Smerlas	.40	.18	.05
☐ 202 Walter Payton SA	2.50	1.10	.30
☐ 203 Luther Bradley	.10	.05	.01
☐ 204 Herb Scott	.10	.05	.01
☐ 205 Jack Youngblood	.40	.18	.05
☐ 206 Danny Pittman	.10	.05	.01
☐ 207 Houston Oilers TL	.30	.14	.04
Carl Roaches			
Mike Barber			
Jack Tatum			
Jesse Baker			
Robert Brazile			
(checklist back)			
☐ 208 Vagas Ferguson	.20	.09	.03
☐ 209 Mark Dennard	.10	.05	.01
☐ 210 Lemar Parrish AP	.10	.05	.01
☐ 211 Bruce Harper	.10	.05	.01
☐ 212 Ed Simonini	.10	.05	.01
☐ 213 Nick Lowery	.40	.18	.05
☐ 214 Kevin House	.20	.09	.03
☐ 215 Mike Kenn	.40	.18	.05
☐ 216 Joe Montana	180.00	80.00	22.00
☐ 217 Joe Senser	.10	.05	.01
☐ 218 Lester Hayes SA	.20	.09	.03
☐ 219 Gene Upshaw	.40	.18	.05
☐ 220 Franco Harris	1.25	.55	.16
☐ 221 Ron Bolton	.10	.05	.01
☐ 222 Charles Alexander	.20	.09	.03
☐ 223 Matt Robinson	.10	.05	.01
☐ 224 Ray Oldham	.10	.05	.01
☐ 225 George Martin	.10	.05	.01
☐ 226 Buffalo Bills TL	.30	.14	.04
Joe Cribbs			
Jerry Butler			
Steve Freeman			
Ben Williams			
(checklist back)			
☐ 227 Tony Franklin	.10	.05	.01
☐ 228 George Cumby	.10	.05	.01
☐ 229 Butch Johnson	.20	.09	.03
☐ 230 Mike Haynes AP	.40	.18	.05
☐ 231 Rob Carpenter	.20	.09	.03
☐ 232 Steve Fuller	.20	.09	.03
☐ 233 John Sawyer	.10	.05	.01
☐ 234 Kenny King SA	.10	.05	.01
☐ 235 Jack Ham	.75	.35	.09
☐ 236 Jimmy Rogers	.10	.05	.01
☐ 237 Bob Parsons	.10	.05	.01
☐ 238 Marty Lyons	.40	.18	.05
☐ 239 Pat Tilley	.10	.05	.01
☐ 240 Dennis Harrah AP	.10	.05	.01
☐ 241 Thom Darden	.10	.05	.01
☐ 242 Rolf Benirschke	.10	.05	.01
☐ 243 Gerald Small	.10	.05	.01
☐ 244 Atlanta Falcons TL	.30	.14	.04
William Andrews			
Alfred Jenkins			
Al Richardson			
Joel Williams			
(checklist back)			
☐ 245 Roger Carr	.10	.05	.01
☐ 246 Sherman White	.10	.05	.01
☐ 247 Ted Brown	.10	.05	.01
☐ 248 Matt Cavanaugh	.20	.09	.03
☐ 249 John Dutton	.10	.05	.01
☐ 250 Bill Bergey AP	.20	.09	.03
☐ 251 Jim Allen	.10	.05	.01
☐ 252 Mike Nelms SA	.10	.05	.01
☐ 253 Tom Blanchard	.10	.05	.01
☐ 254 Ricky Thompson	.10	.05	.01
☐ 255 John Matuszak	.20	.09	.03
☐ 256 Randy Grossman	.10	.05	.01
☐ 257 Ray Griffin	.10	.05	.01
☐ 258 Lynn Cain	.10	.05	.01
☐ 259 Checklist 133-264	.50	.23	.06
☐ 260 Mike Pruitt AP	.20	.09	.03
☐ 261 Chris Ward	.10	.05	.01
☐ 262 Fred Steinfort	.10	.05	.01
☐ 263 James Owens	.10	.05	.01
☐ 264 Chicago Bears TL	1.50	.70	.19
Walter Payton			
James Scott			
Len Walterscheid			
Dan Hampton			
(checklist back)			
☐ 265 Dan Fouts	1.50	.70	.19
☐ 266 Arnold Morgado	.10	.05	.01
☐ 267 John Jefferson SA	.40	.18	.05
☐ 268 Bill Lenkaitis	.10	.05	.01
☐ 269 James Jones	.10	.05	.01
☐ 270 Brad Van Pelt	.10	.05	.01
☐ 271 Steve Largent	2.50	1.10	.30
☐ 272 Elvin Bethea	.10	.05	.01
☐ 273 Cullen Bryant	.10	.05	.01
☐ 274 Gary Danielson	.20	.09	.03
☐ 275 Tony Galbreath	.10	.05	.01
☐ 276 Dave Butz	.10	.05	.01
☐ 277 Steve Mike-Mayer	.10	.05	.01
☐ 278 Ron Johnson	.10	.05	.01
☐ 279 Tom DeLeone	.10	.05	.01
☐ 280 Ron Jaworski	.40	.18	.05
☐ 281 Mel Gray	.10	.05	.01
☐ 282 San Diego Chargers TL	.30	.14	.04
Chuck Muncie			
John Jefferson			
Glen Edwards			
Gary Johnson			
(checklist back)			
☐ 283 Mark Brammer	.10	.05	.01
☐ 284 Alfred Jenkins SA	.20	.09	.03
☐ 285 Greg Buttle	.10	.05	.01
☐ 286 Randy Hughes	.10	.05	.01
☐ 287 Delvin Williams	.10	.05	.01
☐ 288 Brian Baschnagel	.10	.05	.01
☐ 289 Gary Jeter	.10	.05	.01
☐ 290 Stanley Morgan AP	.40	.18	.05
☐ 291 Gerry Ellis	.10	.05	.01
☐ 292 Al Richardson	.10	.05	.01
☐ 293 Jimmie Giles	.20	.09	.03
☐ 294 Dave Jennings SA	.10	.05	.01
☐ 295 Wilbert Montgomery	.20	.09	.03
☐ 296 Dave Pureifory	.10	.05	.01
☐ 297 Greg Hawthorne	.10	.05	.01
☐ 298 Dick Ambrose	.10	.05	.01
☐ 299 Terry Hermeling	.10	.05	.01
☐ 300 Danny White	.50	.23	.06
☐ 301 Ken Burrough	.10	.05	.01
☐ 302 Paul Hofer	.10	.05	.01
☐ 303 Denver Broncos TL	.30	.14	.04
Jim Jensen			
Haven Moses			
Steve Foley			
Rulon Jones			
(checklist back)			
☐ 304 Eddie Payton	.20	.09	.03
☐ 305 Isaac Curtis	.20	.09	.03
☐ 306 Benny Ricardo	.10	.05	.01
☐ 307 Riley Odoms	.10	.05	.01
☐ 308 Bob Chandler	.10	.05	.01
☐ 309 Larry Heater	.10	.05	.01
☐ 310 Art Still AP	.40	.18	.05
☐ 311 Harold Jackson	.20	.09	.03
☐ 312 Charlie Joiner SA	.40	.18	.05
☐ 313 Jeff Nixon	.10	.05	.01
☐ 314 Aundra Thompson	.10	.05	.01
☐ 315 Richard Todd	.20	.09	.03
☐ 316 Dan Hampton	2.50	1.10	.30
☐ 317 Doug Marsh	.10	.05	.01
☐ 318 Louie Giammona	.10	.05	.01
☐ 319 San Francisco 49ers TL	.30	.14	.04
Earl Cooper			
Dwight Clark			
Ricky Churchman			
Dwight Hicks			
Jim Stuckey			
(checklist back)			
☐ 320 Manu Tuiasosopo	.10	.05	.01
☐ 321 Rich Milot	.10	.05	.01
☐ 322 Mike Guman	.10	.05	.01
☐ 323 Bob Kuechenberg	.20	.09	.03
☐ 324 Tom Skladany	.10	.05	.01
☐ 325 Dave Logan	.10	.05	.01
☐ 326 Bruce Laird	.10	.05	.01
☐ 327 James Jones SA	.10	.05	.01
☐ 328 Joe Danelo	.10	.05	.01
☐ 329 Kenny King	.20	.09	.03
☐ 330 Pat Donovan AP	.10	.05	.01
☐ 331 Earl Cooper RB	.15	.07	.02
Most Receptions,			
Running Back,			
Season, Rookie			
☐ 332 John Jefferson RB	.40	.18	.05
Most Cons. Seasons,			
1000 Yards Receiving,			
Start of Career			
☐ 333 Kenny King RB	.15	.07	.02
Longest Pass Caught,			
Super Bowl History			
☐ 334 Rod Martin RB	.15	.07	.02
Most Interceptions			
Super Bowl Game			
☐ 335 Jim Plunkett RB	.40	.18	.05
Longest Pass,			
Super Bowl History			
☐ 336 Bill Thompson RB	.15	.07	.02
Most Touchdowns,			
Fumble Recoveries,			
Lifetime			
☐ 337 John Cappelletti	.20	.09	.03
☐ 338 Detroit Lions TL	.30	.14	.04
Billy Sims			
Freddie Scott			
Jim Allen			
James Hunter			
Al(Bubba) Baker			
(checklist back)			
☐ 339 Don Smith	.10	.05	.01
☐ 340 Rod Perry AP	.10	.05	.01
☐ 341 David Lewis	.10	.05	.01
☐ 342 Mark Gastineau	.40	.18	.05
☐ 343 Steve Largent SA	.75	.35	.09
☐ 344 Charley Young	.10	.05	.01
☐ 345 Toni Fritsch	.10	.05	.01
☐ 346 Matt Blair	.20	.09	.03
☐ 347 Don Bass	.10	.05	.01
☐ 348 Jim Jensen	.20	.09	.03
☐ 349 Karl Lorch	.10	.05	.01
☐ 350 Brian Sipe AP	.20	.09	.03
☐ 351 Theo Bell	.10	.05	.01
☐ 352 Sam Adams	.10	.05	.01
☐ 353 Paul Coffman	.10	.05	.01
☐ 354 Eric Harris	.10	.05	.01
☐ 355 Tony Hill	.20	.09	.03
☐ 356 J.T. Turner	.10	.05	.01
☐ 357 Frank LeMaster	.10	.05	.01
☐ 358 Jim Jodat	.10	.05	.01
☐ 359 Oakland Raiders TL	.30	.14	.04
Mark Van Eeghen			
Cliff Branch			
Lester Hayes			
Cedrick Hardman			
Ted Hendricks			
(checklist back)			
☐ 360 Joe Cribbs AP	.40	.18	.05
☐ 361 James Lofton SA	.75	.35	.09
☐ 362 Dexter Bussey	.10	.05	.01
☐ 363 Bobby Jackson	.10	.05	.01
☐ 364 Steve DeBerg	.40	.18	.05
☐ 365 Ottis Anderson	1.00	.45	.12
☐ 366 Tom Myers	.10	.05	.01
☐ 367 John James	.10	.05	.01
☐ 368 Reese McCall	.10	.05	.01
☐ 369 Jack Reynolds	.20	.09	.03
☐ 370 Gary Johnson AP	.10	.05	.01
☐ 371 Jimmy Cefalo	.10	.05	.01
☐ 372 Horace Ivory	.10	.05	.01
☐ 373 Garo Yepremian	.10	.05	.01
☐ 374 Brian Kelley	.10	.05	.01
☐ 375 Terry Bradshaw	4.00	1.80	.50
☐ 376 Dallas Cowboys TL	.75	.35	.09
Tony Dorsett			
Tony Hill			
Dennis Thurman			
Charlie Waters			
Harvey Martin			
(checklist back)			
☐ 377 Randy Logan	.10	.05	.01
☐ 378 Tim Wilson	.10	.05	.01
☐ 379 Archie Manning SA	.40	.18	.05
☐ 380 Revie Sorey AP	.10	.05	.01
☐ 381 Randy Holloway	.10	.05	.01
☐ 382 Henry Lawrence	.10	.05	.01
☐ 383 Pat McInally	.10	.05	.01
☐ 384 Kevin Long	.10	.05	.01
☐ 385 Louis Wright	.20	.09	.03
☐ 386 Leonard Thompson	.10	.05	.01
☐ 387 Jan Stenerud	.20	.09	.03
☐ 388 Raymond Butler	.10	.05	.01
☐ 389 Checklist 265-396	.50	.23	.06
☐ 390 Steve Bartkowski AP	.20	.09	.03
☐ 391 Clarence Harmon	.10	.05	.01
☐ 392 Wilbert Montgomery SA	.20	.09	.03
☐ 393 Billy Joe DuPree	.20	.09	.03
☐ 394 Kansas City Chiefs TL	.30	.14	.04
Ted McKnight			
Henry Marshall			
Gary Barbaro			
Art Still			
(checklist back)			
☐ 395 Earnest Gray	.10	.05	.01
☐ 396 Ray Hamilton	.10	.05	.01
☐ 397 Brenard Wilson	.10	.05	.01
☐ 398 Calvin Hill	.40	.18	.05
☐ 399 Robin Cole	.10	.05	.01
☐ 400 Walter Payton AP	6.00	2.70	.75
☐ 401 Jim Hart	.40	.18	.05
☐ 402 Ron Yary	.20	.09	.03
☐ 403 Cliff Branch	.40	.18	.05
☐ 404 Roland Hooks	.10	.05	.01
☐ 405 Ken Stabler	2.50	1.10	.30
☐ 406 Chuck Ramsey	.10	.05	.01
☐ 407 Mike Nelms	.10	.05	.01
☐ 408 Ron Jaworski SA	.20	.09	.03
☐ 409 James Hunter	.10	.05	.01
☐ 410 Lee Roy Selmon AP	.75	.35	.09
☐ 411 Baltimore Colts TL	.30	.14	.04
Curtis Dickey			
Roger Carr			
Bruce Laird			
Mike Barnes			
(checklist back)			
☐ 412 Henry Marshall	.10	.05	.01
☐ 413 Preston Pearson	.20	.09	.03
☐ 414 Richard Bishop	.10	.05	.01
☐ 415 Greg Pruitt	.20	.09	.03
☐ 416 Matt Bahr	.20	.09	.03
☐ 417 Tom Mullady	.10	.05	.01
☐ 418 Glen Edwards	.10	.05	.01
☐ 419 Sam McCullum	.10	.05	.01
☐ 420 Stan Walters AP	.10	.05	.01
☐ 421 George Roberts	.10	.05	.01
☐ 422 Dwight Clark	4.00	1.80	.50
☐ 423 Pat Thomas	.10	.05	.01
☐ 424 Bruce Harper SA	.10	.05	.01
☐ 425 Craig Morton	.20	.09	.03
☐ 426 Derrick Gaffney	.10	.05	.01
☐ 427 Pete Johnson	.10	.05	.01
☐ 428 Wes Chandler	.40	.18	.05
☐ 429 Burgess Owens	.10	.05	.01
☐ 430 James Lofton AP	2.00	.90	.25
☐ 431 Tony Reed	.10	.05	.01
☐ 432 Minnesota Vikings TL	.30	.14	.04

Ted Brown
Ahmad Rashad
John Turner
Doug Sutherland
(checklist back)

- ☐ 433 Ron Springs .20 .09 .03
- ☐ 434 Tim Fox .10 .05 .01
- ☐ 435 Ozzie Newsome 2.00 .90 .25
- ☐ 436 Steve Furness .10 .05 .01
- ☐ 437 Will Lewis .10 .05 .01
- ☐ 438 Mike Hartenstine .10 .05 .01
- ☐ 439 John Bunting .10 .05 .01
- ☐ 440 Eddie Murray .40 .18 .05
- ☐ 441 Mike Pruitt SA .20 .09 .03
- ☐ 442 Larry Swider .10 .05 .01
- ☐ 443 Steve Freeman .10 .05 .01
- ☐ 444 Bruce Hardy .10 .05 .01
- ☐ 445 Pat Haden .20 .09 .03
- ☐ 446 Curtis Dickey .10 .05 .01
- ☐ 447 Doug Wilkerson .10 .05 .01
- ☐ 448 Alfred Jenkins .20 .09 .03
- ☐ 449 Dave Dalby .10 .05 .01
- ☐ 450 Robert Brazile AP .10 .05 .01
- ☐ 451 Bobby Hammond .10 .05 .01
- ☐ 452 Raymond Clayborn .10 .05 .01
- ☐ 453 Jim Miller .10 .05 .01
- ☐ 454 Roy Simmons .10 .05 .01
- ☐ 455 Charlie Waters .40 .18 .05
- ☐ 456 Ricky Bell .40 .18 .05
- ☐ 457 Ahmad Rashad SA .40 .18 .05
- ☐ 458 Don Cockroft .10 .05 .01
- ☐ 459 Keith Krepfle .10 .05 .01
- ☐ 460 Marvin Powell AP .10 .05 .01
- ☐ 461 Tommy Kramer .40 .18 .05
- ☐ 462 Jim LeClair .10 .05 .01
- ☐ 463 Freddie Scott .10 .05 .01
- ☐ 464 Rob Lytle .10 .05 .01
- ☐ 465 Johnnie Gray .10 .05 .01
- ☐ 466 Doug France .10 .05 .01
- ☐ 467 Carlos Carson .20 .09 .03
- ☐ 468 St. Louis Cardinals TL .30 .14 .04
  Ottis Anderson
  Pat Tilley
  Ken Stone
  Curtis Greer
  Steve Neils
  (checklist back)
- ☐ 469 Efren Herrera .10 .05 .01
- ☐ 470 Randy White AP 1.00 .45 .12
- ☐ 471 Richard Caster .10 .05 .01
- ☐ 472 Andy Johnson .10 .05 .01
- ☐ 473 Billy Sims SA .50 .23 .06
- ☐ 474 Joe Lavender .10 .05 .01
- ☐ 475 Harry Carson .20 .09 .03
- ☐ 476 John Stallworth 1.00 .45 .12
- ☐ 477 Bob Thomas .10 .05 .01
- ☐ 478 Keith Wright .10 .05 .01
- ☐ 479 Ken Stone .10 .05 .01
- ☐ 480 Carl Hairston AP .20 .09 .03
- ☐ 481 Reggie McKenzie .10 .05 .01
- ☐ 482 Bob Griese 1.50 .70 .19
- ☐ 483 Mike Bragg .10 .05 .01
- ☐ 484 Scott Dierking .10 .05 .01
- ☐ 485 David Hill .10 .05 .01
- ☐ 486 Brian Sipe SA .20 .09 .03
- ☐ 487 Rod Martin .20 .09 .03
- ☐ 488 Cincinnati Bengals TL .30 .14 .04
  Pete Johnson
  Dan Ross
  Louis Breeden
  Eddie Edwards
  (checklist back)
- ☐ 489 Preston Dennard .10 .05 .01
- ☐ 490 John Smith AP .10 .05 .01
- ☐ 491 Mike Reinfeldt .10 .05 .01
- ☐ 492 1980 NFC Champions .15 .07 .02
  Eagles 20,
  Cowboys 7
  (Ron Jaworski)
- ☐ 493 1980 AFC Champions .40 .18 .05
  Raiders 34,
  Chargers 27
  (Jim Plunkett)
- ☐ 494 Super Bowl XV .75 .35 .09
  Raiders 27,
  Eagles 10
  (Plunkett handing
  off to Kenny King)
- ☐ 495 Joe Greene .75 .35 .09
- ☐ 496 Charlie Joiner .75 .35 .09
- ☐ 497 Rolland Lawrence .10 .05 .01
- ☐ 498 Al(Bubba) Baker SA .20 .09 .03
- ☐ 499 Brad Dusek .10 .05 .01
- ☐ 500 Tony Dorsett 4.00 1.80 .50
- ☐ 501 Robin Earl .10 .05 .01
- ☐ 502 Theotis Brown .10 .05 .01
- ☐ 503 Joe Ferguson .20 .09 .03
- ☐ 504 Beasley Reece .10 .05 .01
- ☐ 505 Lyle Alzado .40 .18 .05
- ☐ 506 Tony Nathan .40 .18 .05
- ☐ 507 Philadelphia Eagles TL .30 .14 .04
  Wilbert Montgomery
  Charlie Smith
  Brenard Wilson
  Claude Humphrey
  (checklist back)
- ☐ 508 Herb Orvis .10 .05 .01
- ☐ 509 Clarence Williams .10 .05 .01
- ☐ 510 Ray Guy AP .20 .09 .03
- ☐ 511 Jeff Komlo .10 .05 .01
- ☐ 512 Freddie Solomon SA .10 .05 .01
- ☐ 513 Tim Mazzetti .10 .05 .01
- ☐ 514 Elvis Peacock .10 .05 .01
- ☐ 515 Russ Francis .20 .09 .03
- ☐ 516 Roland Harper .10 .05 .01
- ☐ 517 Checklist 397-528 .50 .23 .06
- ☐ 518 Billy Johnson .20 .09 .03
- ☐ 519 Dan Dierdorf .50 .23 .06
- ☐ 520 Fred Dean AP .10 .05 .01
- ☐ 521 Jerry Butler .10 .05 .01
- ☐ 522 Ron Saul .10 .05 .01
- ☐ 523 Charlie Smith .10 .05 .01
- ☐ 524 Kellen Winslow SA 3.00 1.35 .35
- ☐ 525 Bert Jones .40 .18 .05
- ☐ 526 Pittsburgh Steelers TL .60 .25 .07
  Franco Harris
  Theo Bell
  Donnie Shell
  L.C. Greenwood
  (checklist back)
- ☐ 527 Duriel Harris .10 .05 .01
- ☐ 528 William Andrews .40 .18 .05

1982 Topps

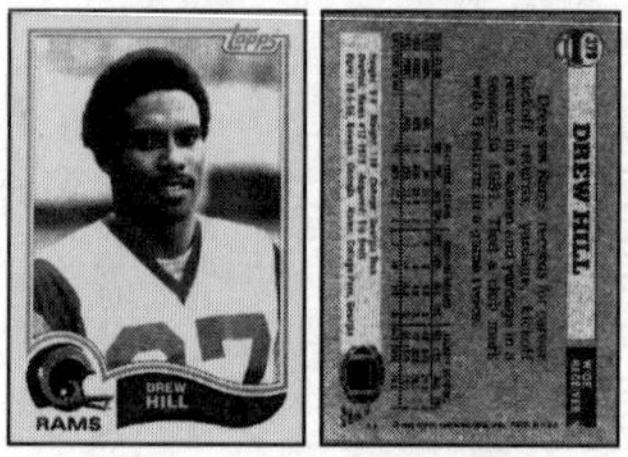

The 1982 Topps football set features 528 standard-size cards and marked a breakthrough of sorts. Wax packs contained 15 cards. Licensed by NFL Properties for the first time, Topps was able to use team logos within its photos. Previously, logos on helmets were airbrushed. Card fronts contained a team helmet at bottom left and the player's name and position within a color banner at bottom right. Horizontally designed backs featured yearly statistics and highlights. Subsets include Record Breakers (1-6), playoffs (7-9), league leaders (257-262) and brothers (263-270). In-Action (IA) cards of top players are scattered throughout the set. Team Leader (TL) cards feature statistical leaders on the front as well as a team checklist on the back. The set is organized in team order alphabetically by team within conference (and with players within teams in alphabetical order). Rookie Cards include James Brooks, Cris Collinsworth, Drew Hill, Ronnie Lott, Freeman McNeil, Anthony Munoz and Lawrence Taylor.

	MINT	NRMT	EXC
COMPLETE SET (528)	90.00	40.00	11.00
COMMON CARD (1-528)	.10	.05	.01

- ☐ 1 Ken Anderson RB .40 .18 .05
  Most Completions,
  Super Bowl Game
- ☐ 2 Dan Fouts RB .40 .18 .05
  Most Passing Yards,
  Playoff Game
- ☐ 3 LeRoy Irvin RB .15 .07 .02
  Most Punt Return
  Yardage, Game
- ☐ 4 Stump Mitchell RB .15 .07 .02
  Most Return
  Yardage, Season
- ☐ 5 George Rogers RB .40 .18 .05
  Most Rushing Yards,
  Rookie Season
- ☐ 6 Dan Ross RB .15 .07 .02
  Most Receptions,
  Super Bowl Game
- ☐ 7 AFC Championship .15 .07 .02
  Bengals 27,
  Chargers 7
  (Ken Anderson
  handing off to
  Pete Johnson)
- ☐ 8 NFC Championship .15 .07 .02
  49ers 28,
  Cowboys 27
  (Earl Cooper)
- ☐ 9 Super Bowl XVI .75 .35 .09
  49ers 26,
  Bengals 7
  (Anthony Munoz
  blocking)
- ☐ 10 Baltimore Colts TL .15 .07 .02
  Curtis Dickey
  Raymond Butler
  Larry Braziel
  Bruce Laird
- ☐ 11 Raymond Butler .10 .05 .01
- ☐ 12 Roger Carr .10 .05 .01
- ☐ 13 Curtis Dickey .20 .09 .03
- ☐ 14 Zachary Dixon .10 .05 .01
- ☐ 15 Nesby Glasgow .10 .05 .01
- ☐ 16 Bert Jones .40 .18 .05
- ☐ 17 Bruce Laird .10 .05 .01
- ☐ 18 Reese McCall .10 .05 .01
- ☐ 19 Randy McMillan .10 .05 .01
- ☐ 20 Ed Simonini .10 .05 .01
- ☐ 21 Buffalo Bills TL .15 .07 .02
  Joe Cribbs
  Frank Lewis
  Mario Clark
  Fred Smerlas
- ☐ 22 Mark Brammer .10 .05 .01
- ☐ 23 Curtis Brown .10 .05 .01
- ☐ 24 Jerry Butler .10 .05 .01
- ☐ 25 Mario Clark .10 .05 .01
- ☐ 26 Joe Cribbs .20 .09 .03
- ☐ 27 Joe Cribbs IA .20 .09 .03
- ☐ 28 Joe Ferguson .20 .09 .03
- ☐ 29 Jim Haslett .10 .05 .01
- ☐ 30 Frank Lewis AP .10 .05 .01
- ☐ 31 Frank Lewis IA .10 .05 .01
- ☐ 32 Shane Nelson .10 .05 .01
- ☐ 33 Charles Romes .10 .05 .01
- ☐ 34 Bill Simpson .10 .05 .01
- ☐ 35 Fred Smerlas .10 .05 .01
- ☐ 36 Cincinnati Bengals TL .15 .07 .02
  Pete Johnson
  Cris Collinsworth
  Ken Riley
  Reggie Williams
- ☐ 37 Charles Alexander .10 .05 .01
- ☐ 38 Ken Anderson AP .50 .23 .06
- ☐ 39 Ken Anderson IA .40 .18 .05
- ☐ 40 Jim Breech .10 .05 .01
- ☐ 41 Jim Breech IA .10 .05 .01
- ☐ 42 Louis Breeden .10 .05 .01
- ☐ 43 Ross Browner .10 .05 .01
- ☐ 44 Cris Collinsworth 1.00 .45 .12
- ☐ 45 Cris Collinsworth IA .40 .18 .05
- ☐ 46 Isaac Curtis .10 .05 .01
- ☐ 47 Pete Johnson .10 .05 .01
- ☐ 48 Pete Johnson IA .10 .05 .01
- ☐ 49 Steve Kreider .10 .05 .01
- ☐ 50 Pat McInally AP .10 .05 .01
- ☐ 51 Anthony Munoz AP 5.00 2.20 .60
- ☐ 52 Dan Ross .10 .05 .01
- ☐ 53 David Verser .10 .05 .01
- ☐ 54 Reggie Williams .20 .09 .03
- ☐ 55 Cleveland Browns TL .15 .07 .02
  Mike Pruitt
  Ozzie Newsome
  Clarence Scott
  Lyle Alzado
- ☐ 56 Lyle Alzado .40 .18 .05
- ☐ 57 Dick Ambrose .10 .05 .01
- ☐ 58 Ron Bolton .10 .05 .01
- ☐ 59 Steve Cox .10 .05 .01
- ☐ 60 Joe DeLamielleure .10 .05 .01
- ☐ 61 Tom DeLeone .10 .05 .01
- ☐ 62 Doug Dieken .10 .05 .01
- ☐ 63 Ricky Feacher .10 .05 .01
- ☐ 64 Don Goode .10 .05 .01
- ☐ 65 Robert L. Jackson .10 .05 .01
- ☐ 66 Dave Logan .10 .05 .01
- ☐ 67 Ozzie Newsome 1.00 .45 .12
- ☐ 68 Ozzie Newsome IA .40 .18 .05
- ☐ 69 Greg Pruitt .20 .09 .03
- ☐ 70 Mike Pruitt .20 .09 .03
- ☐ 71 Mike Pruitt IA .20 .09 .03
- ☐ 72 Reggie Rucker .10 .05 .01
- ☐ 73 Clarence Scott .10 .05 .01
- ☐ 74 Brian Sipe .20 .09 .03
- ☐ 75 Charles White .20 .09 .03
- ☐ 76 Denver Broncos TL .15 .07 .02
  Rick Parros
  Steve Watson
  Steve Foley
  Rulon Jones
- ☐ 77 Rubin Carter .10 .05 .01
- ☐ 78 Steve Foley .10 .05 .01
- ☐ 79 Randy Gradishar .20 .09 .03
- ☐ 80 Tom Jackson .40 .18 .05
- ☐ 81 Craig Morton .20 .09 .03
- ☐ 82 Craig Morton IA .20 .09 .03
- ☐ 83 Riley Odoms .10 .05 .01
- ☐ 84 Rick Parros .10 .05 .01
- ☐ 85 Dave Preston .10 .05 .01
- ☐ 86 Tony Reed .10 .05 .01
- ☐ 87 Bob Swenson .10 .05 .01
- ☐ 88 Bill Thompson .10 .05 .01
- ☐ 89 Rick Upchurch .20 .09 .03
- ☐ 90 Steve Watson AP .20 .09 .03
- ☐ 91 Steve Watson IA .10 .05 .01
- ☐ 92 Houston Oilers TL .15 .07 .02
  Carl Roaches
  Ken Burrough
  Carter Hartwig
  Greg Stemrick
  Jesse Baker
- ☐ 93 Mike Barber .10 .05 .01
- ☐ 94 Elvin Bethea .10 .05 .01
- ☐ 95 Gregg Bingham .10 .05 .01
- ☐ 96 Robert Brazile AP .10 .05 .01
- ☐ 97 Ken Burrough .10 .05 .01
- ☐ 98 Toni Fritsch .10 .05 .01
- ☐ 99 Leon Gray .10 .05 .01
- ☐ 100 Gifford Nielsen .20 .09 .03
- ☐ 101 Vernon Perry .10 .05 .01
- ☐ 102 Mike Reinfeldt .10 .05 .01
- ☐ 103 Mike Renfro .10 .05 .01
- ☐ 104 Carl Roaches AP .10 .05 .01
- ☐ 105 Ken Stabler 2.00 .90 .25
- ☐ 106 Greg Stemrick .10 .05 .01
- ☐ 107 J.C. Wilson .10 .05 .01
- ☐ 108 Tim Wilson .10 .05 .01
- ☐ 109 Kansas City Chiefs TL .15 .07 .02
  Joe Delaney
  J.T. Smith
  Eric Harris
  Ken Kremer
- ☐ 110 Gary Barbaro AP .10 .05 .01
- ☐ 111 Brad Budde .10 .05 .01
- ☐ 112 Joe Delaney AP .40 .18 .05
- ☐ 113 Joe Delaney IA .20 .09 .03
- ☐ 114 Steve Fuller .10 .05 .01
- ☐ 115 Gary Green .10 .05 .01
- ☐ 116 James Hadnot .10 .05 .01
- ☐ 117 Eric Harris .10 .05 .01
- ☐ 118 Billy Jackson .10 .05 .01
- ☐ 119 Bill Kenney .10 .05 .01
- ☐ 120 Nick Lowery AP .40 .18 .05
- ☐ 121 Nick Lowery IA .20 .09 .03
- ☐ 122 Henry Marshall .10 .05 .01
- ☐ 123 J.T. Smith .20 .09 .03
- ☐ 124 Art Still .10 .05 .01
- ☐ 125 Miami Dolphins TL .15 .07 .02
  Tony Nathan
  Duriel Harris
  Glenn Blackwood
  Bob Baumhower
- ☐ 126 Bob Baumhower AP .20 .09 .03
- ☐ 127 Glenn Blackwood .10 .05 .01
- ☐ 128 Jimmy Cefalo .10 .05 .01
- ☐ 129 A.J. Duhe .20 .09 .03
- ☐ 130 Andra Franklin .10 .05 .01
- ☐ 131 Duriel Harris .10 .05 .01
- ☐ 132 Nat Moore .20 .09 .03
- ☐ 133 Tony Nathan .20 .09 .03
- ☐ 134 Ed Newman .10 .05 .01
- ☐ 135 Earnie Rhone .10 .05 .01
- ☐ 136 Don Strock .10 .05 .01
- ☐ 137 Tommy Vigorito .10 .05 .01
- ☐ 138 Uwe Von Schamann .10 .05 .01
- ☐ 139 Uwe Von Schamann IA .10 .05 .01
- ☐ 140 David Woodley .20 .09 .03
- ☐ 141 New England Pats TL .15 .07 .02
  Tony Collins
  Stanley Morgan
  Tim Fox
  Rick Sanford
  Tony McGee
- ☐ 142 Julius Adams .10 .05 .01
- ☐ 143 Richard Bishop .10 .05 .01
- ☐ 144 Matt Cavanaugh .10 .05 .01
- ☐ 145 Raymond Clayborn .10 .05 .01
- ☐ 146 Tony Collins .10 .05 .01
- ☐ 147 Vagas Ferguson .10 .05 .01
- ☐ 148 Tim Fox .10 .05 .01
- ☐ 149 Steve Grogan .20 .09 .03
- ☐ 150 John Hannah AP .40 .18 .05
- ☐ 151 John Hannah IA .20 .09 .03
- ☐ 152 Don Hasselbeck .10 .05 .01
- ☐ 153 Mike Haynes .20 .09 .03
- ☐ 154 Harold Jackson .20 .09 .03
- ☐ 155 Andy Johnson .10 .05 .01
- ☐ 156 Stanley Morgan .20 .09 .03
- ☐ 157 Stanley Morgan IA .20 .09 .03
- ☐ 158 Steve Nelson .10 .05 .01
- ☐ 159 Rod Shoate .10 .05 .01
- ☐ 160 New York Jets TL .15 .07 .02
  Freeman McNeil
  Wesley Walker
  Darrol Ray
  Joe Klecko
- ☐ 161 Dan Alexander .10 .05 .01
- ☐ 162 Mike Augustyniak .10 .05 .01
- ☐ 163 Jerome Barkum .10 .05 .01
- ☐ 164 Greg Buttle .10 .05 .01
- ☐ 165 Scott Dierking .10 .05 .01
- ☐ 166 Joe Fields .10 .05 .01
- ☐ 167 Mark Gastineau AP .20 .09 .03
- ☐ 168 Mark Gastineau IA .20 .09 .03
- ☐ 169 Bruce Harper .10 .05 .01
- ☐ 170 Johnny Lam Jones .10 .05 .01
- ☐ 171 Joe Klecko AP .20 .09 .03
- ☐ 172 Joe Klecko IA .20 .09 .03
- ☐ 173 Pat Leahy .20 .09 .03
- ☐ 174 Pat Leahy IA .10 .05 .01
- ☐ 175 Marty Lyons .20 .09 .03
- ☐ 176 Freeman McNeil .60 .25 .07
- ☐ 177 Marvin Powell AP .10 .05 .01
- ☐ 178 Chuck Ramsey .10 .05 .01
- ☐ 179 Darrol Ray .10 .05 .01
- ☐ 180 Abdul Salaam .10 .05 .01
- ☐ 181 Richard Todd .20 .09 .03
- ☐ 182 Richard Todd IA .20 .09 .03
- ☐ 183 Wesley Walker .20 .09 .03
- ☐ 184 Chris Ward .10 .05 .01
- ☐ 185 Oakland Raiders TL .15 .07 .02
  Kenny King
  Derrick Ramsey

Lester Hayes			
Odis McKinney			
Rod Martin			
☐ 186 Cliff Branch	.40	.18	.05
☐ 187 Bob Chandler	.10	.05	.01
☐ 188 Ray Guy	.20	.09	.03
☐ 189 Lester Hayes AP	.20	.09	.03
☐ 190 Ted Hendricks AP	.40	.18	.05
☐ 191 Monte Jackson	.10	.05	.01
☐ 192 Derrick Jensen	.10	.05	.01
☐ 193 Kenny King	.10	.05	.01
☐ 194 Rod Martin	.10	.05	.01
☐ 195 John Matuszak	.20	.09	.03
☐ 196 Matt Millen	1.50	.70	.19
☐ 197 Derrick Ramsey	.10	.05	.01
☐ 198 Art Shell	.40	.18	.05
☐ 199 Mark Van Eeghen	.10	.05	.01
☐ 200 Arthur Whittington	.10	.05	.01
☐ 201 Marc Wilson	.20	.09	.03
☐ 202 Pittsburgh Steelers TL	.50	.23	.06
Franco Harris			
John Stallworth			
Mel Blount			
Jack Lambert			
Gary Dunn			
☐ 203 Mel Blount AP	.60	.25	.07
☐ 204 Terry Bradshaw	3.00	1.35	.35
☐ 205 Terry Bradshaw IA	1.25	.55	.16
☐ 206 Craig Colquitt	.10	.05	.01
☐ 207 Bennie Cunningham	.10	.05	.01
☐ 208 Russell Davis	.10	.05	.01
☐ 209 Gary Dunn	.10	.05	.01
☐ 210 Jack Ham	.60	.25	.07
☐ 211 Franco Harris	1.00	.45	.12
☐ 212 Franco Harris IA	.50	.23	.06
☐ 213 Jack Lambert AP	.75	.35	.09
☐ 214 Jack Lambert IA	.50	.23	.06
☐ 215 Mark Malone	.40	.18	.05
☐ 216 Frank Pollard	.10	.05	.01
☐ 217 Donnie Shell AP	.40	.18	.05
☐ 218 Jim Smith	.10	.05	.01
☐ 219 John Stallworth	.50	.23	.06
☐ 220 John Stallworth IA	.40	.18	.05
☐ 221 David Trout	.10	.05	.01
☐ 222 Mike Webster AP	.40	.18	.05
☐ 223 San Diego Chargers TL	.15	.07	.02
Chuck Muncie			
Charlie Joiner			
Willie Buchanon			
Gary Johnson			
☐ 224 Rolf Benirschke	.10	.05	.01
☐ 225 Rolf Benirschke IA	.10	.05	.01
☐ 226 James Brooks	.75	.35	.09
☐ 227 Willie Buchanon	.10	.05	.01
☐ 228 Wes Chandler	.40	.18	.05
☐ 229 Wes Chandler IA	.20	.09	.03
☐ 230 Dan Fouts	1.00	.45	.12
☐ 231 Dan Fouts IA	.50	.23	.06
☐ 232 Gary Johnson AP	.10	.05	.01
☐ 233 Charlie Joiner	.50	.23	.06
☐ 234 Charlie Joiner IA	.40	.18	.05
☐ 235 Louie Kelcher	.10	.05	.01
☐ 236 Chuck Muncie AP	.20	.09	.03
☐ 237 Chuck Muncie IA	.10	.05	.01
☐ 238 George Roberts	.10	.05	.01
☐ 239 Ed White	.10	.05	.01
☐ 240 Doug Wilkerson AP	.10	.05	.01
☐ 241 Kellen Winslow AP	2.00	.90	.25
☐ 242 Kellen Winslow IA	1.00	.45	.12
☐ 243 Seattle Seahawks TL	.50	.23	.06
Theotis Brown			
Steve Largent			
John Harris			
Jacob Green			
☐ 244 Theotis Brown	.10	.05	.01
☐ 245 Dan Doornink	.10	.05	.01
☐ 246 John Harris	.10	.05	.01
☐ 247 Efren Herrera	.10	.05	.01
☐ 248 David Hughes	.10	.05	.01
☐ 249 Steve Largent	2.00	.90	.25
☐ 250 Steve Largent IA	1.00	.45	.12
☐ 251 Sam McCullum	.10	.05	.01
☐ 252 Sherman Smith	.10	.05	.01
☐ 253 Manu Tuiasosopo	.10	.05	.01
☐ 254 John Yarno	.10	.05	.01
☐ 255 Jim Zorn	.20	.09	.03
(Sitting with Dave Krieg)			
☐ 256 Jim Zorn IA	.20	.09	.03
☐ 257 Passing Leaders	3.50	1.55	.45
Ken Anderson			
Joe Montana			
☐ 258 Receiving Leaders	.40	.18	.05
Kellen Winslow			
Dwight Clark			
☐ 259 QB Sack Leaders	.15	.07	.02
Joe Klecko			
Curtis Greer			
☐ 260 Scoring Leaders	.15	.07	.02
Jim Breech			
Nick Lowery			
Eddie Murray			
Rafael Septien			
☐ 261 Interception Leaders	.20	.09	.03
John Harris			
Everson Walls			
☐ 262 Punting Leaders	.15	.07	.02
Pat McInally			
Tom Skladany			
☐ 263 Brothers: Bahr	.15	.07	.02
Chris and Matt			
☐ 264 Brothers: Blackwood	.15	.07	.02
Lyle and Glenn			
☐ 265 Brothers: Brock	.15	.07	.02
Pete and Stan			
☐ 266 Brothers: Griffin	.15	.07	.02
Archie and Ray			
☐ 267 Brothers: Hannah	.15	.07	.02
John and Charley			
☐ 268 Brothers: Jackson	.15	.07	.02
Monte and Terry			
☐ 269 Brothers: Payton	1.00	.45	.12
Eddie and Walter			
☐ 270 Brothers: Selmon	.40	.18	.05
Dewey and Lee Roy			
☐ 271 Atlanta Falcons TL	.15	.07	.02
William Andrews			
Alfred Jenkins			
Tom Pridemore			
Al Richardson			
☐ 272 William Andrews	.20	.09	.03
☐ 273 William Andrews IA	.20	.09	.03
☐ 274 Steve Bartkowski	.20	.09	.03
☐ 275 Steve Bartkowski IA	.20	.09	.03
☐ 276 Bobby Butler	.10	.05	.01
☐ 277 Lynn Cain	.10	.05	.01
☐ 278 Wallace Francis	.10	.05	.01
☐ 279 Alfred Jackson	.10	.05	.01
☐ 280 John James	.10	.05	.01
☐ 281 Alfred Jenkins AP	.10	.05	.01
☐ 282 Alfred Jenkins IA	.10	.05	.01
☐ 283 Kenny Johnson	.10	.05	.01
☐ 284 Mike Kenn AP	.40	.18	.05
☐ 285 Fulton Kuykendall	.10	.05	.01
☐ 286 Mick Luckhurst	.10	.05	.01
☐ 287 Mick Luckhurst IA	.10	.05	.01
☐ 288 Junior Miller	.10	.05	.01
☐ 289 Al Richardson	.10	.05	.01
☐ 290 R.C. Thielemann	.10	.05	.01
☐ 291 Jeff Van Note	.10	.05	.01
☐ 292 Chicago Bears TL	.75	.35	.09
Walter Payton			
Ken Margerum			
Gary Fencik			
Dan Hampton			
Alan Page			
☐ 293 Brian Baschnagel	.10	.05	.01
☐ 294 Robin Earl	.10	.05	.01
☐ 295 Vince Evans	.20	.09	.03
☐ 296 Gary Fencik AP	.10	.05	.01
☐ 297 Dan Hampton	.50	.23	.06
☐ 298 Noah Jackson	.10	.05	.01
☐ 299 Ken Margerum	.10	.05	.01
☐ 300 Jim Osborne	.10	.05	.01
☐ 301 Bob Parsons	.10	.05	.01
☐ 302 Walter Payton	5.00	2.20	.60
☐ 303 Walter Payton IA	2.50	1.10	.30
☐ 304 Revie Sorey	.10	.05	.01
☐ 305 Matt Suhey	.40	.18	.05
(Walter Payton			
in background)			
☐ 306 Rickey Watts	.10	.05	.01
☐ 307 Dallas Cowboys TL	.50	.23	.06
Tony Dorsett			
Tony Hill			
Everson Walls			
Harvey Martin			
☐ 308 Bob Breunig	.10	.05	.01
☐ 309 Doug Cosbie	.10	.05	.01
☐ 310 Pat Donovan AP	.10	.05	.01
☐ 311 Tony Dorsett AP	1.50	.70	.19
☐ 312 Tony Dorsett IA	.75	.35	.09
☐ 313 Michael Downs	.10	.05	.01
☐ 314 Billy Joe DuPree	.20	.09	.03
☐ 315 John Dutton	.10	.05	.01
☐ 316 Tony Hill	.20	.09	.03
☐ 317 Butch Johnson	.20	.09	.03
☐ 318 Ed Too Tall Jones AP	.50	.23	.06
☐ 319 James Jones	.10	.05	.01
☐ 320 Harvey Martin	.40	.18	.05
☐ 321 Drew Pearson	.40	.18	.05
☐ 322 Herb Scott AP	.10	.05	.01
☐ 323 Rafael Septien AP	.10	.05	.01
☐ 324 Rafael Septien IA	.10	.05	.01
☐ 325 Ron Springs	.20	.09	.03
☐ 326 Dennis Thurman	.10	.05	.01
☐ 327 Everson Walls	.40	.18	.05
☐ 328 Everson Walls IA	.40	.18	.05
☐ 329 Danny White	.40	.18	.05
☐ 330 Danny White IA	.20	.09	.03
☐ 331 Randy White AP	.75	.35	.09
☐ 332 Randy White IA	.50	.23	.06
☐ 333 Detroit Lions TL	.15	.07	.02
Billy Sims			
Freddie Scott			
Jim Allen			
Dave Pureifory			
☐ 334 Jim Allen	.10	.05	.01
☐ 335 Al(Bubba) Baker	.20	.09	.03
☐ 336 Dexter Bussey	.10	.05	.01
☐ 337 Doug English AP	.20	.09	.03
☐ 338 Ken Fantetti	.10	.05	.01
☐ 339 William Gay	.10	.05	.01
☐ 340 David Hill	.10	.05	.01
☐ 341 Eric Hipple	.10	.05	.01
☐ 342 Rick Kane	.10	.05	.01
☐ 343 Ed Murray	.40	.18	.05
☐ 344 Ed Murray IA	.20	.09	.03
☐ 345 Ray Oldham	.10	.05	.01
☐ 346 Dave Pureifory	.10	.05	.01
☐ 347 Freddie Scott	.10	.05	.01
☐ 348 Freddie Scott IA	.10	.05	.01
☐ 349 Billy Sims AP	.40	.18	.05
☐ 350 Billy Sims IA	.40	.18	.05
☐ 351 Tom Skladany AP	.10	.05	.01
☐ 352 Leonard Thompson	.10	.05	.01
☐ 353 Stan White	.10	.05	.01
☐ 354 Green Bay Packers TL	.15	.07	.02
Gerry Ellis			
James Lofton			
Maurice Harvey			
Mark Lee			
Mike Butler			
☐ 355 Paul Coffman	.10	.05	.01
☐ 356 George Cumby	.10	.05	.01
☐ 357 Lynn Dickey	.10	.05	.01
☐ 358 Lynn Dickey IA	.10	.05	.01
☐ 359 Gerry Ellis	.10	.05	.01
☐ 360 Maurice Harvey	.10	.05	.01
☐ 361 Harlan Huckleby	.10	.05	.01
☐ 362 John Jefferson	.40	.18	.05
☐ 363 Mark Lee	.10	.05	.01
☐ 364 James Lofton AP	1.00	.45	.12
☐ 365 James Lofton IA	.60	.25	.07
☐ 366 Jan Stenerud	.20	.09	.03
☐ 367 Jan Stenerud IA	.20	.09	.03
☐ 368 Rich Wingo	.10	.05	.01
☐ 369 Los Angeles Rams TL	.15	.07	.02
Wendell Tyler			
Preston Dennard			
Nolan Cromwell			
Jack Youngblood			
☐ 370 Frank Corral	.10	.05	.01
☐ 371 Nolan Cromwell AP	.20	.09	.03
☐ 372 Nolan Cromwell IA	.20	.09	.03
☐ 373 Preston Dennard	.10	.05	.01
☐ 374 Mike Fanning	.10	.05	.01
☐ 375 Doug France	.10	.05	.01
☐ 376 Mike Guman	.10	.05	.01
☐ 377 Pat Haden	.20	.09	.03
☐ 378 Dennis Harrah	.10	.05	.01
☐ 379 Drew Hill	.40	.18	.05
☐ 380 LeRoy Irvin	.10	.05	.01
☐ 381 Cody Jones	.10	.05	.01
☐ 382 Rod Perry	.10	.05	.01
☐ 383 Rich Saul AP	.10	.05	.01
☐ 384 Pat Thomas	.10	.05	.01
☐ 385 Wendell Tyler	.20	.09	.03
☐ 386 Wendell Tyler IA	.20	.09	.03
☐ 387 Billy Waddy	.10	.05	.01
☐ 388 Jack Youngblood	.40	.18	.05
☐ 389 Minnesota Vikings TL	.15	.07	.02
Ted Brown			
Joe Senser			
Tom Hannon			
Willie Teal			
Matt Blair			
☐ 390 Matt Blair AP	.10	.05	.01
☐ 391 Ted Brown	.10	.05	.01
☐ 392 Ted Brown IA	.10	.05	.01
☐ 393 Rick Danmeier	.10	.05	.01
☐ 394 Tommy Kramer	.20	.09	.03
☐ 395 Mark Mullaney	.10	.05	.01
☐ 396 Eddie Payton	.10	.05	.01
☐ 397 Ahmad Rashad	.40	.18	.05
☐ 398 Joe Senser	.10	.05	.01
☐ 399 Joe Senser IA	.10	.05	.01
☐ 400 Sammie White	.20	.09	.03
☐ 401 Sammie White IA	.10	.05	.01
☐ 402 Ron Yary	.10	.05	.01
☐ 403 Rickey Young	.10	.05	.01
☐ 404 New Orleans Saints TL	.15	.07	.02
George Rogers			
Guido Merkens			
Dave Waymer			
Rickey Jackson			
☐ 405 Russell Erxleben	.10	.05	.01
☐ 406 Elois Grooms	.10	.05	.01
☐ 407 Jack Holmes	.10	.05	.01
☐ 408 Archie Manning	.40	.18	.05
☐ 409 Derland Moore	.10	.05	.01
☐ 410 George Rogers	.50	.23	.06
☐ 411 George Rogers IA	.40	.18	.05
☐ 412 Toussaint Tyler	.10	.05	.01
☐ 413 Dave Waymer	.10	.05	.01
☐ 414 Wayne Wilson	.10	.05	.01
☐ 415 New York Giants TL	.15	.07	.02
Rob Carpenter			
Johnny Perkins			
Beasley Reece			
George Martin			
☐ 416 Scott Brunner	.10	.05	.01
☐ 417 Rob Carpenter	.10	.05	.01
☐ 418 Harry Carson AP	.20	.09	.03
☐ 419 Bill Currier	.10	.05	.01
☐ 420 Joe Danelo	.10	.05	.01
☐ 421 Joe Danelo IA	.10	.05	.01
☐ 422 Mark Haynes	.10	.05	.01
☐ 423 Terry Jackson	.10	.05	.01
☐ 424 Dave Jennings	.10	.05	.01
☐ 425 Gary Jeter	.10	.05	.01
☐ 426 Brian Kelley	.10	.05	.01
☐ 427 George Martin	.10	.05	.01
☐ 428 Curtis McGriff	.10	.05	.01
☐ 429 Bill Neill	.10	.05	.01
☐ 430 Johnny Perkins	.10	.05	.01
☐ 431 Beasley Reece	.10	.05	.01
☐ 432 Gary Shirk	.10	.05	.01
☐ 433 Phil Simms	2.00	.90	.25
☐ 434 Lawrence Taylor AP	30.00	13.50	3.70
☐ 435 Lawrence Taylor IA	10.00	4.50	1.25
☐ 436 Brad Van Pelt	.10	.05	.01
☐ 437 Philadelphia Eagles TL	.15	.07	.02
Wilbert Montgomery			
Harold Carmichael			
Brenard Wilson			
Carl Hairston			
☐ 438 John Bunting	.10	.05	.01
☐ 439 Billy Campfield	.10	.05	.01
☐ 440 Harold Carmichael	.40	.18	.05
☐ 441 Harold Carmichael IA	.40	.18	.05
☐ 442 Herman Edwards	.10	.05	.01
☐ 443 Tony Franklin	.10	.05	.01
☐ 444 Tony Franklin IA	.10	.05	.01
☐ 445 Carl Hairston	.10	.05	.01
☐ 446 Dennis Harrison	.10	.05	.01
☐ 447 Ron Jaworski	.40	.18	.05
☐ 448 Charlie Johnson	.10	.05	.01
☐ 449 Keith Krepfle	.10	.05	.01
☐ 450 Frank LeMaster	.10	.05	.01
☐ 451 Randy Logan	.10	.05	.01
☐ 452 Wilbert Montgomery	.20	.09	.03
☐ 453 Wilbert Montgomery IA	.20	.09	.03
☐ 454 Hubie Oliver	.10	.05	.01
☐ 455 Jerry Robinson	.10	.05	.01
☐ 456 Jerry Robinson IA	.10	.05	.01
☐ 457 Jerry Sisemore	.10	.05	.01
☐ 458 Charlie Smith	.10	.05	.01
☐ 459 Stan Walters	.10	.05	.01
☐ 460 Brenard Wilson	.10	.05	.01
☐ 461 Roynell Young AP	.10	.05	.01
☐ 462 St. Louis Cardinals TL	.15	.07	.02
Ottis Anderson			
Pat Tilley			
Ken Greene			
Curtis Greer			
☐ 463 Ottis Anderson	.60	.25	.07
☐ 464 Ottis Anderson IA	.40	.18	.05
☐ 465 Carl Birdsong	.10	.05	.01
☐ 466 Rush Brown	.10	.05	.01
☐ 467 Mel Gray	.20	.09	.03
☐ 468 Ken Greene	.10	.05	.01
☐ 469 Jim Hart	.40	.18	.05
☐ 470 E.J. Junior	.20	.09	.03
☐ 471 Neil Lomax	.40	.18	.05
☐ 472 Stump Mitchell	.40	.18	.05
☐ 473 Wayne Morris	.10	.05	.01
☐ 474 Neil O'Donoghue	.10	.05	.01
☐ 475 Pat Tilley	.10	.05	.01
☐ 476 Pat Tilley IA	.10	.05	.01
☐ 477 San Francisco 49ers TL	.15	.07	.02
Ricky Patton			
Dwight Clark			
Dwight Hicks			
Fred Dean			
☐ 478 Dwight Clark	.75	.35	.09
☐ 479 Dwight Clark IA	.40	.18	.05
☐ 480 Earl Cooper	.10	.05	.01
☐ 481 Randy Cross AP	.20	.09	.03
☐ 482 Johnny Davis	.10	.05	.01
☐ 483 Fred Dean	.10	.05	.01
☐ 484 Fred Dean IA	.10	.05	.01
☐ 485 Dwight Hicks	.40	.18	.05
☐ 486 Ronnie Lott AP	18.00	8.00	2.20
☐ 487 Ronnie Lott IA	5.00	2.20	.60
☐ 488 Joe Montana AP	30.00	13.50	3.70
☐ 489 Joe Montana IA	12.00	5.50	1.50
☐ 490 Ricky Patton	.10	.05	.01
☐ 491 Jack Reynolds	.20	.09	.03
☐ 492 Freddie Solomon	.10	.05	.01
☐ 493 Ray Wersching	.10	.05	.01
☐ 494 Charley Young	.10	.05	.01
☐ 495 Tampa Bay Bucs TL	.15	.07	.02
Jerry Eckwood			
Kevin House			
Cedric Brown			
Lee Roy Selmon			
☐ 496 Cedric Brown	.10	.05	.01
☐ 497 Neal Colzie	.10	.05	.01
☐ 498 Jerry Eckwood	.10	.05	.01
☐ 499 Jimmie Giles AP	.20	.09	.03
☐ 500 Hugh Green	.40	.18	.05
☐ 501 Kevin House	.10	.05	.01
☐ 502 Kevin House IA	.10	.05	.01
☐ 503 Cecil Johnson	.10	.05	.01
☐ 504 James Owens	.10	.05	.01
☐ 505 Lee Roy Selmon AP	.40	.18	.05
☐ 506 Mike Washington	.10	.05	.01
☐ 507 James Wilder	.20	.09	.03
☐ 508 Doug Williams	.20	.09	.03
☐ 509 Wash. Redskins TL	.75	.35	.09
Joe Washington			
Art Monk			

Mark Murphy			
Perry Brooks			
☐ 510 Perry Brooks	.10	.05	.01
☐ 511 Dave Butz	.20	.09	.03
☐ 512 Wilbur Jackson	.10	.05	.01
☐ 513 Joe Lavender	.10	.05	.01
☐ 514 Terry Metcalf	.20	.09	.03
☐ 515 Art Monk	3.50	1.55	.45
☐ 516 Mark Moseley	.10	.05	.01
☐ 517 Mark Murphy	.10	.05	.01
☐ 518 Mike Nelms AP	.10	.05	.01
☐ 519 Lemar Parrish	.10	.05	.01
☐ 520 John Riggins	.75	.35	.09
☐ 521 Joe Theismann	.60	.25	.07
☐ 522 Ricky Thompson	.10	.05	.01
☐ 523 Don Warren UER	.10	.05	.01
(photo actually			
Ricky Thompson)			
☐ 524 Joe Washington	.20	.09	.03
☐ 525 Checklist 1-132	.40	.18	.05
☐ 526 Checklist 133-264	.40	.18	.05
☐ 527 Checklist 265-396	.40	.18	.05
☐ 528 Checklist 397-528	.40	.18	.05

1983 Topps

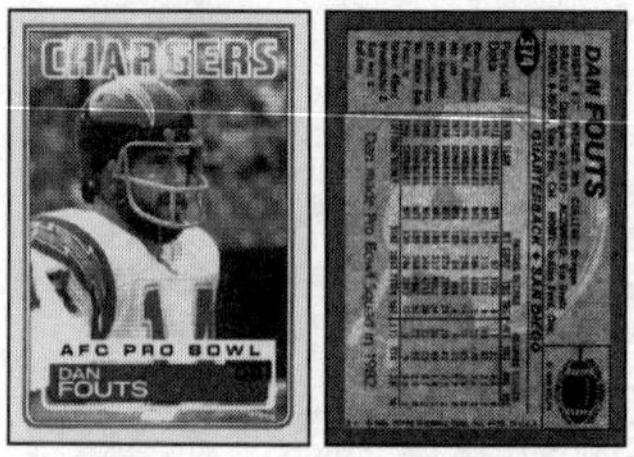

After issuing 528-card sets since 1973, Topps dropped to 396 standard-size cards for 1983. The set was printed on four sheets. As a result, there are 132 double-printed cards which are noted in the checklist below by DP. The card fronts contain the player's name and position at the bottom in a rectangular area that differs in color according to team. Team names are in block letters at the top of the cards. The backs of the cards contain yearly statistics and a "Personal Facts" section. All the text is printed over a faint white team helmet. Subsets include Record Breakers (1-9), playoffs (10-12) and league leaders (202-207). The Team Leader (TL) cards are distributed throughout the set as the first card of the team sequence. The design of these cards differs from previous years in that only one leader (usually the team's rushing leader) is pictured. The backs contain team scoring information from the previous season. The team numbering is arranged alphabetically within each conference (with players ordered alphabetically within team). Rookie Cards include Marcus Allen, Gary Anderson (K), Todd Christensen, Roy Green, Jim McMahon, and Mike Singletary.

	MINT	NRMT	EXC
COMPLETE SET (396)	55.00	25.00	7.00
COMMON CARD (1-396)	.08	.04	.01
☐ 1 Ken Anderson RB	.40	.18	.05
20 Consecutive			
Pass Completions			
☐ 2 Tony Dorsett RB	.40	.18	.05
99 Yard Run			
☐ 3 Dan Fouts RB	.30	.14	.04
30 Games Over			
300 Yards Passing			
☐ 4 Joe Montana RB	3.00	1.35	.35
Five Straight			
300 Yard Games			
☐ 5 Mark Moseley RB	.10	.05	.01
21 Straight			
Field Goals			
☐ 6 Mike Nelms RB	.10	.05	.01
Most Yards,			
Punt Returns,			
Super Bowl Game			
☐ 7 Darrol Ray RB	.10	.05	.01
Longest Interception			
Return, Playoff Game			
☐ 8 John Riggins RB	.30	.14	.04
Most Yards Rushing,			
Super Bowl Game			
☐ 9 Fulton Walker RB	.10	.05	.01
Most Yards,			
Kickoff Returns,			
Super Bowl Game			
☐ 10 NFC Championship	.10	.05	.01
Redskins 31,			
Cowboys 17			
(John Riggins tackled)			
☐ 11 AFC Championship	.10	.05	.01
Dolphins 14,			
Jets 0			
☐ 12 Super Bowl XVII	.40	.18	.05
Redskins 27,			
Dolphins 17			
(John Riggins running)			
☐ 13 Atlanta Falcons TL	.10	.05	.01
William Andrews			
☐ 14 William Andrews DP PB	.15	.07	.02
☐ 15 Steve Bartkowski	.15	.07	.02
☐ 16 Bobby Butler	.08	.04	.01
☐ 17 Buddy Curry	.08	.04	.01
☐ 18 Alfred Jackson DP	.08	.04	.01
☐ 19 Alfred Jenkins	.08	.04	.01
☐ 20 Kenny Johnson	.08	.04	.01
☐ 21 Mike Kenn PB	.08	.04	.01
☐ 22 Mick Luckhurst	.08	.04	.01
☐ 23 Junior Miller	.08	.04	.01
☐ 24 Al Richardson	.08	.04	.01
☐ 25 Gerald Riggs DP	.30	.14	.04
☐ 26 R.C. Thielemann PB	.08	.04	.01
☐ 27 Jeff Van Note PB	.08	.04	.01
☐ 28 Chicago Bears TL	1.00	.45	.12
Walter Payton			
☐ 29 Brian Baschnagel	.08	.04	.01
☐ 30 Dan Hampton PB	.30	.14	.04
☐ 31 Mike Hartenstine	.08	.04	.01
☐ 32 Noah Jackson	.08	.04	.01
☐ 33 Jim McMahon	2.50	1.10	.30
☐ 34 Emery Moorehead DP	.08	.04	.01
☐ 35 Bob Parsons	.08	.04	.01
☐ 36 Walter Payton	4.00	1.80	.50
☐ 37 Terry Schmidt	.08	.04	.01
☐ 38 Mike Singletary	5.00	2.20	.60
☐ 39 Matt Suhey DP	.15	.07	.02
☐ 40 Rickey Watts DP	.08	.04	.01
☐ 41 Otis Wilson DP	.15	.07	.02
☐ 42 Dallas Cowboys TL	.40	.18	.05
Tony Dorsett			
☐ 43 Bob Breunig PB	.15	.07	.02
☐ 44 Doug Cosbie	.08	.04	.01
☐ 45 Pat Donovan PB	.08	.04	.01
☐ 46 Tony Dorsett DP PB	1.00	.45	.12
☐ 47 Tony Hill	.15	.07	.02
☐ 48 Butch Johnson DP	.15	.07	.02
☐ 49 Ed Jones DP PB	.30	.14	.04
☐ 50 Harvey Martin DP	.15	.07	.02
☐ 51 Drew Pearson	.30	.14	.04
☐ 52 Rafael Septien	.08	.04	.01
☐ 53 Ron Springs DP	.08	.04	.01
☐ 54 Dennis Thurman	.08	.04	.01
☐ 55 Everson Walls PB	.15	.07	.02
☐ 56 Danny White DP PB	.30	.14	.04
☐ 57 Randy White PB	.50	.23	.06
☐ 58 Detroit Lions TL	.15	.07	.02
Billy Sims			
☐ 59 Al(Bubba) Baker DP	.15	.07	.02
☐ 60 Dexter Bussey DP	.08	.04	.01
☐ 61 Gary Danielson DP	.08	.04	.01
☐ 62 Keith Dorney DP PB	.08	.04	.01
☐ 63 Doug English PB	.08	.04	.01
☐ 64 Ken Fantetti DP	.08	.04	.01
☐ 65 Alvin Hall DP	.08	.04	.01
☐ 66 David Hill DP	.08	.04	.01
☐ 67 Eric Hipple	.08	.04	.01
☐ 68 Ed Murray DP	.15	.07	.02
☐ 69 Freddie Scott	.08	.04	.01
☐ 70 Billy Sims DP PB	.15	.07	.02
☐ 71 Tom Skladany DP	.08	.04	.01
☐ 72 Leonard Thompson DP	.08	.04	.01
☐ 73 Bobby Watkins	.08	.04	.01
☐ 74 Green Bay Packers TL	.10	.05	.01
Eddie Lee Ivery			
☐ 75 John Anderson	.08	.04	.01
☐ 76 Paul Coffman PB	.08	.04	.01
☐ 77 Lynn Dickey	.08	.04	.01
☐ 78 Mike Douglass DP	.08	.04	.01
☐ 79 Eddie Lee Ivery	.08	.04	.01
☐ 80 John Jefferson DP PB	.30	.14	.04
☐ 81 Ezra Johnson	.08	.04	.01
☐ 82 Mark Lee	.08	.04	.01
☐ 83 James Lofton PB	.60	.25	.07
☐ 84 Larry McCarren PB	.08	.04	.01
☐ 85 Jan Stenerud DP	.15	.07	.02
☐ 86 Los Angeles Rams TL	.10	.05	.01
Wendell Tyler			
☐ 87 Bill Bain DP	.08	.04	.01
☐ 88 Nolan Cromwell PB	.15	.07	.02
☐ 89 Preston Dennard	.08	.04	.01
☐ 90 Vince Ferragamo DP	.15	.07	.02
☐ 91 Mike Guman	.08	.04	.01
☐ 92 Kent Hill PB	.08	.04	.01
☐ 93 Mike Lansford DP	.08	.04	.01
☐ 94 Rod Perry	.08	.04	.01
☐ 95 Pat Thomas DP	.08	.04	.01
☐ 96 Jack Youngblood	.30	.14	.04
☐ 97 Minnesota Vikings TL	.10	.05	.01
Ted Brown			
☐ 98 Matt Blair PB	.08	.04	.01
☐ 99 Ted Brown	.08	.04	.01
☐ 100 Greg Coleman	.08	.04	.01
☐ 101 Randy Holloway	.08	.04	.01
☐ 102 Tommy Kramer	.15	.07	.02
☐ 103 Doug Martin DP	.08	.04	.01
☐ 104 Mark Mullaney	.08	.04	.01
☐ 105 Joe Senser	.08	.04	.01
☐ 106 Willie Teal DP	.08	.04	.01
☐ 107 Sammie White	.15	.07	.02
☐ 108 Rickey Young	.08	.04	.01
☐ 109 New Orleans Saints TL	.10	.05	.01
George Rogers			
☐ 110 Stan Brock	.08	.04	.01
☐ 111 Bruce Clark	.08	.04	.01
☐ 112 Russell Erxleben DP	.08	.04	.01
☐ 113 Russell Gary	.08	.04	.01
☐ 114 Jeff Groth DP	.08	.04	.01
☐ 115 John Hill DP	.08	.04	.01
☐ 116 Derland Moore	.08	.04	.01
☐ 117 George Rogers PB	.15	.07	.02
☐ 118 Ken Stabler	1.50	.70	.19
☐ 119 Wayne Wilson	.08	.04	.01
☐ 120 New York Giants TL	.10	.05	.01
Butch Woolfolk			
☐ 121 Scott Brunner	.08	.04	.01
☐ 122 Rob Carpenter	.08	.04	.01
☐ 123 Harry Carson PB	.15	.07	.02
☐ 124 Joe Danelo DP	.08	.04	.01
☐ 125 Earnest Gray	.08	.04	.01
☐ 126 Mark Haynes DP PB	.15	.07	.02
☐ 127 Terry Jackson	.08	.04	.01
☐ 128 Dave Jennings PB	.08	.04	.01
☐ 129 Brian Kelley	.08	.04	.01
☐ 130 George Martin	.08	.04	.01
☐ 131 Tom Mullady	.08	.04	.01
☐ 132 Johnny Perkins	.08	.04	.01
☐ 133 Lawrence Taylor PB	5.00	2.20	.60
☐ 134 Brad Van Pelt	.08	.04	.01
☐ 135 Butch Woolfolk DP	.08	.04	.01
☐ 136 Philadelphia Eagles TL	.10	.05	.01
Wilbert Montgomery			
☐ 137 Harold Carmichael	.30	.14	.04
☐ 138 Herman Edwards	.08	.04	.01
☐ 139 Tony Franklin DP	.08	.04	.01
☐ 140 Carl Hairston DP	.08	.04	.01
☐ 141 Dennis Harrison DP PB	.08	.04	.01
☐ 142 Ron Jaworski DP	.15	.07	.02
☐ 143 Frank LeMaster	.08	.04	.01
☐ 144 Wilbert Montgomery DP	.15	.07	.02
☐ 145 Guy Morriss	.08	.04	.01
☐ 146 Jerry Robinson	.08	.04	.01
☐ 147 Max Runager	.08	.04	.01
☐ 148 Ron Smith DP	.08	.04	.01
☐ 149 John Spagnola	.08	.04	.01
☐ 150 Stan Walters DP	.08	.04	.01
☐ 151 Roynell Young DP	.08	.04	.01
☐ 152 St. Louis Cardinals TL	.15	.07	.02
Ottis Anderson			
☐ 153 Ottis Anderson	.30	.14	.04
☐ 154 Carl Birdsong	.08	.04	.01
☐ 155 Dan Dierdorf DP	.30	.14	.04
☐ 156 Roy Green	.30	.14	.04
☐ 157 Elois Grooms	.08	.04	.01
☐ 158 Neil Lomax DP	.15	.07	.02
☐ 159 Wayne Morris	.08	.04	.01
☐ 160 Tootie Robbins	.08	.04	.01
☐ 161 Luis Sharpe	.08	.04	.01
☐ 162 Pat Tilley	.08	.04	.01
☐ 163 San Francisco 49ers TL	.10	.05	.01
Jeff Moore			
☐ 164 Dwight Clark PB	.40	.18	.05
☐ 165 Randy Cross PB	.15	.07	.02
☐ 166 Russ Francis	.15	.07	.02
☐ 167 Dwight Hicks PB	.08	.04	.01
☐ 168 Ronnie Lott PB	2.50	1.10	.30
☐ 169 Joe Montana DP	10.00	4.50	1.25
☐ 170 Jeff Moore	.08	.04	.01
☐ 171 Renaldo Nehemiah DP	.30	.14	.04
☐ 172 Freddie Solomon	.08	.04	.01
☐ 173 Ray Wersching DP	.08	.04	.01
☐ 174 Tampa Bay Bucs TL	.10	.05	.01
James Wilder			
☐ 175 Cedric Brown	.08	.04	.01
☐ 176 Bill Capece	.08	.04	.01
☐ 177 Neal Colzie	.08	.04	.01
☐ 178 Jimmie Giles PB	.08	.04	.01
☐ 179 Hugh Green PB	.15	.07	.02
☐ 180 Kevin House DP	.08	.04	.01
☐ 181 James Owens	.08	.04	.01
☐ 182 Lee Roy Selmon PB	.30	.14	.04
☐ 183 Mike Washington	.08	.04	.01
☐ 184 James Wilder	.08	.04	.01
☐ 185 Doug Williams DP	.15	.07	.02
☐ 186 Wash. Redskins TL	.30	.14	.04
John Riggins			
☐ 187 Jeff Bostic DP	.30	.14	.04
☐ 188 Charlie Brown PB	.15	.07	.02
☐ 189 Vernon Dean DP	.08	.04	.01
☐ 190 Joe Jacoby	.30	.14	.04
☐ 191 Dexter Manley	.15	.07	.02
☐ 192 Rich Milot	.08	.04	.01
☐ 193 Art Monk DP	1.00	.45	.12
☐ 194 Mark Moseley DP PB	.08	.04	.01
☐ 195 Mike Nelms PB	.08	.04	.01
☐ 196 Neal Olkewicz DP	.08	.04	.01
☐ 197 Tony Peters PB	.08	.04	.01
☐ 198 John Riggins DP	.50	.23	.06
☐ 199 Joe Theismann PB	.50	.23	.06
☐ 200 Don Warren	.08	.04	.01
☐ 201 Jeris White DP	.08	.04	.01
☐ 202 Passing Leaders	.30	.14	.04
Joe Theismann			
Ken Anderson			
☐ 203 Receiving Leaders	.15	.07	.02
Dwight Clark			
Kellen Winslow			
☐ 204 Rushing Leaders	.75	.35	.09
Tony Dorsett			
Freeman McNeil			
☐ 205 Scoring Leaders	1.25	.55	.16
Wendell Tyler			
Marcus Allen			
☐ 206 Interception Leaders	.10	.05	.01
Everson Walls			
AFC Tie (Four)			
☐ 207 Punting Leaders	.10	.05	.01
Carl Birdsong			
Luke Prestridge			
☐ 208 Baltimore Colts TL	.10	.05	.01
Randy McMillan			
☐ 209 Matt Bouza	.08	.04	.01
☐ 210 Johnie Cooks DP	.08	.04	.01
☐ 211 Curtis Dickey	.08	.04	.01
☐ 212 Nesby Glasgow DP	.08	.04	.01
☐ 213 Derrick Hatchett	.08	.04	.01
☐ 214 Randy McMillan	.08	.04	.01
☐ 215 Mike Pagel	.15	.07	.02
☐ 216 Rohn Stark DP	.15	.07	.02
☐ 217 Donnell Thompson DP	.08	.04	.01
☐ 218 Leo Wisniewski DP	.08	.04	.01
☐ 219 Buffalo Bills TL	.10	.05	.01
Joe Cribbs			
☐ 220 Curtis Brown	.08	.04	.01
☐ 221 Jerry Butler	.08	.04	.01
☐ 222 Greg Cater DP	.08	.04	.01
☐ 223 Joe Cribbs	.15	.07	.02
☐ 224 Joe Ferguson	.15	.07	.02
☐ 225 Roosevelt Leaks	.08	.04	.01
☐ 226 Frank Lewis	.08	.04	.01
☐ 227 Eugene Marve	.08	.04	.01
☐ 228 Fred Smerlas DP PB	.08	.04	.01
☐ 229 Ben Williams DP PB	.08	.04	.01
☐ 230 Cincinnati Bengals TL	.10	.05	.01
Pete Johnson			
☐ 231 Charles Alexander	.08	.04	.01
☐ 232 Ken Anderson DP PB	.30	.14	.04
☐ 233 Jim Breech DP	.08	.04	.01
☐ 234 Ross Browner	.08	.04	.01
☐ 235 Cris Collinsworth	.30	.14	.04
DP PB			
☐ 236 Isaac Curtis	.08	.04	.01
☐ 237 Pete Johnson	.08	.04	.01
☐ 238 Steve Kreider DP	.08	.04	.01
☐ 239 Max Montoya DP	.08	.04	.01
☐ 240 Anthony Munoz PB	1.00	.45	.12
☐ 241 Ken Riley	.08	.04	.01
☐ 242 Dan Ross PB	.08	.04	.01
☐ 243 Reggie Williams	.15	.07	.02
☐ 244 Cleveland Browns TL	.10	.05	.01
Mike Pruitt			
☐ 245 Chip Banks DP PB	.15	.07	.02
☐ 246 Tom Cousineau DP	.15	.07	.02
☐ 247 Joe DeLamielleure DP	.08	.04	.01
☐ 248 Doug Dieken DP	.08	.04	.01
☐ 249 Hanford Dixon	.08	.04	.01
☐ 250 Ricky Feacher DP	.08	.04	.01
☐ 251 Lawrence Johnson DP	.08	.04	.01
☐ 252 Dave Logan DP	.08	.04	.01
☐ 253 Paul McDonald DP	.08	.04	.01
☐ 254 Ozzie Newsome DP	.40	.18	.05
☐ 255 Mike Pruitt	.15	.07	.02
☐ 256 Clarence Scott DP	.08	.04	.01
☐ 257 Brian Sipe DP	.15	.07	.02
☐ 258 Dwight Walker DP	.08	.04	.01
☐ 259 Charles White	.15	.07	.02
☐ 260 Denver Broncos TL	.10	.05	.01
Gerald Willhite			
☐ 261 Steve DeBerg DP	.15	.07	.02
☐ 262 Randy Gradishar DP PB	.15	.07	.02
☐ 263 Rulon Jones DP	.08	.04	.01
☐ 264 Rich Karlis DP	.08	.04	.01
☐ 265 Don Latimer	.08	.04	.01
☐ 266 Rick Parros DP	.08	.04	.01
☐ 267 Luke Prestridge PB	.08	.04	.01
☐ 268 Rick Upchurch PB	.15	.07	.02
☐ 269 Steve Watson DP	.08	.04	.01
☐ 270 Gerald Willhite DP	.08	.04	.01
☐ 271 Houston Oilers TL	.10	.05	.01
Gifford Nielsen			
☐ 272 Harold Bailey	.08	.04	.01
☐ 273 Jesse Baker DP	.08	.04	.01
☐ 274 Gregg Bingham DP	.08	.04	.01
☐ 275 Robert Brazile DP PB	.08	.04	.01
☐ 276 Donnie Craft	.08	.04	.01
☐ 277 Daryl Hunt	.08	.04	.01
☐ 278 Archie Manning DP	.15	.07	.02
☐ 279 Gifford Nielsen	.08	.04	.01
☐ 280 Mike Renfro	.08	.04	.01
☐ 281 Carl Roaches DP	.08	.04	.01
☐ 282 Kansas City Chiefs TL	.10	.05	.01
Joe Delaney			
☐ 283 Gary Barbaro PB	.08	.04	.01
☐ 284 Joe Delaney	.08	.04	.01
☐ 285 Jeff Gossett	.30	.14	.04
☐ 286 Gary Green DP PB	.08	.04	.01
☐ 287 Eric Harris DP	.08	.04	.01
☐ 288 Billy Jackson DP	.08	.04	.01
☐ 289 Bill Kenney DP	.08	.04	.01
☐ 290 Nick Lowery	.30	.14	.04
☐ 291 Henry Marshall	.08	.04	.01
☐ 292 Art Still DP PB	.08	.04	.01
☐ 293 Los Angeles Raiders TL	2.00	.90	.25
Marcus Allen			
☐ 294 Marcus Allen DP PB	30.00	13.50	3.70
☐ 295 Lyle Alzado	.30	.14	.04
☐ 296 Chris Bahr DP	.08	.04	.01
☐ 297 Cliff Branch	.30	.14	.04

	MINT	NRMT	EXC
☐ 298 Todd Christensen	.75	.35	.09
☐ 299 Ray Guy	.15	.07	.02
☐ 300 Frank Hawkins DP	.08	.04	.01
☐ 301 Lester Hayes DP PB	.08	.04	.01
☐ 302 Ted Hendricks DP PB	.30	.14	.04
☐ 303 Kenny King DP	.08	.04	.01
☐ 304 Rod Martin	.08	.04	.01
☐ 305 Matt Millen DP	.30	.14	.04
☐ 306 Burgess Owens	.08	.04	.01
☐ 307 Jim Plunkett	.30	.14	.04
☐ 308 Miami Dolphins TL	.10	.05	.01
Andra Franklin			
☐ 309 Bob Baumhower PB	.08	.04	.01
☐ 310 Glenn Blackwood	.08	.04	.01
☐ 311 Lyle Blackwood DP	.08	.04	.01
☐ 312 A.J. Duhe	.08	.04	.01
☐ 313 Andra Franklin PB	.08	.04	.01
☐ 314 Duriel Harris	.08	.04	.01
☐ 315 Bob Kuechenberg DP PB	.15	.07	.02
☐ 316 Don McNeal	.08	.04	.01
☐ 317 Tony Nathan	.15	.07	.02
☐ 318 Ed Newman PB	.08	.04	.01
☐ 319 Earnie Rhone DP	.08	.04	.01
☐ 320 Joe Rose DP	.08	.04	.01
☐ 321 Don Strock DP	.08	.04	.01
☐ 322 Uwe Von Schamann	.08	.04	.01
☐ 323 David Woodley DP	.15	.07	.02
☐ 324 New England Pats TL	.10	.05	.01
Tony Collins			
☐ 325 Julius Adams	.08	.04	.01
☐ 326 Pete Brock	.08	.04	.01
☐ 327 Rich Camarillo DP	.08	.04	.01
☐ 328 Tony Collins DP	.08	.04	.01
☐ 329 Steve Grogan	.15	.07	.02
☐ 330 John Hannah PB	.30	.14	.04
☐ 331 Don Hasselbeck	.08	.04	.01
☐ 332 Mike Haynes PB	.15	.07	.02
☐ 333 Roland James	.08	.04	.01
☐ 334A Stanley Morgan ERR	.30	.14	.04
("Inside Linebacker"			
printed upside down			
on card back)			
☐ 334B Stanley Morgan COR	.15	.07	.02
☐ 335 Steve Nelson	.08	.04	.01
☐ 336 Kenneth Sims DP	.08	.04	.01
☐ 337 Mark Van Eeghen	.15	.07	.02
☐ 338 New York Jets TL	.10	.05	.01
Freeman McNeil			
☐ 339 Greg Buttle	.08	.04	.01
☐ 340 Joe Fields PB	.08	.04	.01
☐ 341 Mark Gastineau DP PB	.15	.07	.02
☐ 342 Bruce Harper	.08	.04	.01
☐ 343 Bobby Jackson	.08	.04	.01
☐ 344 Bobby Jones	.08	.04	.01
☐ 345 Johnny Lam Jones DP	.08	.04	.01
☐ 346 Joe Klecko	.15	.07	.02
☐ 347 Marty Lyons	.08	.04	.01
☐ 348 Freeman McNeil PB	.30	.14	.04
☐ 349 Lance Mehl	.08	.04	.01
☐ 350 Marvin Powell DP PB	.08	.04	.01
☐ 351 Darrol Ray DP	.08	.04	.01
☐ 352 Abdul Salaam	.08	.04	.01
☐ 353 Richard Todd	.15	.07	.02
☐ 354 Wesley Walker PB	.15	.07	.02
☐ 355 Pittsburgh Steelers TL	.10	.05	.01
Franco Harris			
☐ 356 Gary Anderson K DP	.30	.14	.04
☐ 357 Mel Blount DP	.30	.14	.04
☐ 358 Terry Bradshaw DP	1.25	.55	.16
☐ 359 Larry Brown PB	.08	.04	.01
☐ 360 Bennie Cunningham	.08	.04	.01
☐ 361 Gary Dunn	.08	.04	.01
☐ 362 Franco Harris	.75	.35	.09
☐ 363 Jack Lambert PB	.50	.23	.06
☐ 364 Frank Pollard	.08	.04	.01
☐ 365 Donnie Shell PB	.15	.07	.02
☐ 366 John Stallworth PB	.30	.14	.04
☐ 367 Loren Toews	.08	.04	.01
☐ 368 Mike Webster DP PB	.30	.14	.04
☐ 369 Dwayne Woodruff	.08	.04	.01
☐ 370 San Diego Chargers TL	.10	.05	.01
Chuck Muncie			
☐ 371 Rolf Benirschke DP PB	.08	.04	.01
☐ 372 James Brooks	.30	.14	.04
☐ 373 Wes Chandler PB	.15	.07	.02
☐ 374 Dan Fouts DP PB	.60	.25	.07
☐ 375 Tim Fox	.08	.04	.01
☐ 376 Gary Johnson PB	.08	.04	.01
☐ 377 Charlie Joiner DP	.40	.18	.05
☐ 378 Louie Kelcher	.08	.04	.01
☐ 379 Chuck Muncie PB	.08	.04	.01
☐ 380 Cliff Thrift	.08	.04	.01
☐ 381 Doug Wilkerson PB	.08	.04	.01
☐ 382 Kellen Winslow PB	.75	.35	.09
☐ 383 Seattle Seahawks TL	.10	.05	.01
Sherman Smith			
☐ 384 Kenny Easley PB	.30	.14	.04
☐ 385 Jacob Green	.15	.07	.02
☐ 386 John Harris	.08	.04	.01
☐ 387 Michael Jackson	.08	.04	.01
☐ 388 Norm Johnson	.08	.04	.01
☐ 389 Steve Largent	1.25	.55	.16
☐ 390 Keith Simpson	.08	.04	.01
☐ 391 Sherman Smith	.08	.04	.01
☐ 392 Jeff West DP	.08	.04	.01
☐ 393 Jim Zorn DP	.15	.07	.02
☐ 394 Checklist 1-132	.20	.09	.03
☐ 395 Checklist 133-264	.20	.09	.03
☐ 396 Checklist 265-396	.20	.09	.03

1983 Topps Sticker Inserts

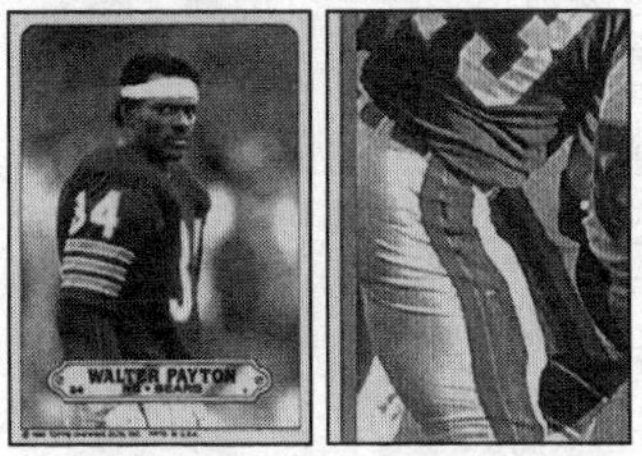

The 1983 Topps Football Sticker Inserts come as a set of 33 full-sized cards and were issued as inserts to the 1983 Topps wax packs. They were printed in the USA, whereas the smaller stickers of the previous two years were printed in Italy. The player's name, number, position, and team are included in a plaque at the bottom of the front of the card. The backs are parts of three puzzles, distinguished by either a red (A), blue (B), or green (C) border, each showing a different action scene from the previous year's Super Bowl between the Washington Redskins and Miami Dolphins. The actual set numbering is alphabetical by player's name.

	MINT	NRMT	EXC
COMPLETE SET (33)	15.00	6.75	1.85
COMMON CARD (1-33)	.25	.11	.03
☐ 1 Marcus Allen	4.00	1.80	.50
(Completed red border			
puzzle on back)			
☐ 2 Ken Anderson	.50	.23	.06
(Completed red border			
puzzle on back)			
☐ 3 Ottis Anderson	.40	.18	.05
☐ 4 William Andrews	.40	.18	.05
☐ 5 Terry Bradshaw	1.25	.55	.16
☐ 6 Wes Chandler	.25	.11	.03
☐ 7 Dwight Clark	.40	.18	.05
☐ 8 Cris Collinsworth	.40	.18	.05
☐ 9 Joe Cribbs	.25	.11	.03
☐ 10 Nolan Cromwell	.25	.11	.03
☐ 11 Tony Dorsett	1.25	.55	.16
☐ 12 Dan Fouts	.75	.35	.09
☐ 13 Mark Gastineau	.25	.11	.03
☐ 14 Jimmie Giles	.25	.11	.03
☐ 15 Franco Harris	.75	.35	.09
(Completed green border			
puzzle on back)			
☐ 16 Ted Hendricks	.40	.18	.05
☐ 17 Tony Hill	.25	.11	.03
☐ 18 John Jefferson	.40	.18	.05
(Completed red border			
puzzle on back)			
☐ 19 James Lofton	.75	.35	.09
☐ 20 Freeman McNeil	.25	.11	.03
(Completed red border			
puzzle on back)			
☐ 21 Joe Montana	6.00	2.70	.75
☐ 22 Mark Moseley	.25	.11	.03
☐ 23 Ozzie Newsome	.50	.23	.06
☐ 24 Walter Payton	2.00	.90	.25
☐ 25 John Riggins	.75	.35	.09
☐ 26 Billy Sims	.40	.18	.05
☐ 27 John Stallworth	.50	.23	.06
☐ 28 Lawrence Taylor	1.00	.45	.12
☐ 29 Joe Theismann	.60	.25	.07
☐ 30 Richard Todd	.25	.11	.03
(Completed green border			
puzzle on back)			
☐ 31 Wesley Walker	.25	.11	.03
☐ 32 Danny White	.40	.18	.05
☐ 33 Kellen Winslow	.50	.23	.06

1984 Topps

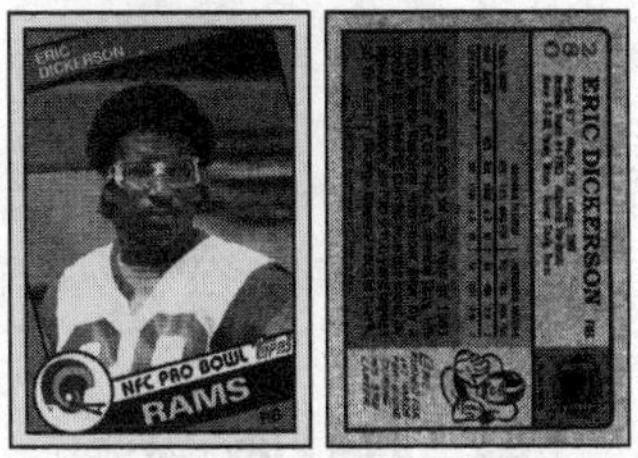

The 1984 Topps football card set contains 396 standard-size cards. Wax packs have 15 cards inside. Card photos are bordered in different colors depending on the player's team. The team logo and team name are at the bottom with the player's name in a red bar at the top. Horizontally designed green tinted backs have yearly statistics, highlights and a cartoon. Subsets include Record Breakers (1-6), playoffs (7-9) and league leaders (202-207). Team Leader (TL) cards primarily feature the team's rushing leader. The backs contain team scoring information from the previous year. Instant Replay (IR) cards of top players are scattered throughout the set. Cards are numbered and alphabetically arranged within teams except for the Colts which moved from Baltimore to Indianapolis. The set features the Rookie Cards of Morten Andersen, Roger Craig, Eric Dickerson, John Elway, Willie Gault, Darrell Green, Rickey Jackson, Dave Krieg, Howie Long, Dan Marino, Andre Tippett and Curt Warner.

	MINT	NRMT	EXC
COMPLETE SET (396)	200.00	90.00	25.00
COMMON CARD (1-396)	.08	.04	.01
☐ 1 Eric Dickerson RB	.50	.23	.06
Sets Rookie Mark			
With 1808 Yards			
☐ 2 Ali Haji-Sheikh RB	.10	.05	.01
Sets Field Goal			
Mark as a Rookie			
☐ 3 Franco Harris RB	.30	.14	.04
Records Eighth			
1000 Yard Year			
☐ 4 Mark Moseley RB	.15	.07	.02
161 Points Sets			
Mark for Kickers			
☐ 5 John Riggins RB	.30	.14	.04
24 Rushing TD's			
☐ 6 Jan Stenerud RB	.15	.07	.02
338th Career FG			
☐ 7 AFC Championship	.10	.05	.01
Raiders 30,			
Seahawks 14			
(Marcus Allen running)			
☐ 8 NFC Championship	.15	.07	.02
Redskins 24,			
49ers 21			
(John Riggins running)			
☐ 9 Super Bowl XVIII UER	.50	.23	.06
Raiders 38,			
Redskins 9			
(hand-off to Marcus			
Allen; score wrong,			
28-9 on card front)			
☐ 10 Indianapolis Colts TL	.10	.05	.01
Curtis Dickey			
☐ 11 Raul Allegre	.08	.04	.01
☐ 12 Curtis Dickey	.15	.07	.02
☐ 13 Ray Donaldson	.15	.07	.02
☐ 14 Nesby Glasgow	.08	.04	.01
☐ 15 Chris Hinton PB	.30	.14	.04
☐ 16 Vernon Maxwell	.08	.04	.01
☐ 17 Randy McMillan	.08	.04	.01
☐ 18 Mike Pagel	.15	.07	.02
☐ 19 Rohn Stark	.15	.07	.02
☐ 20 Leo Wisniewski	.08	.04	.01
☐ 21 Buffalo Bills TL	.10	.05	.01
Joe Cribbs			
☐ 22 Jerry Butler	.08	.04	.01
☐ 23 Joe Danelo	.08	.04	.01
☐ 24 Joe Ferguson	.15	.07	.02
☐ 25 Steve Freeman	.08	.04	.01
☐ 26 Roosevelt Leaks	.15	.07	.02
☐ 27 Frank Lewis	.08	.04	.01
☐ 28 Eugene Marve	.08	.04	.01
☐ 29 Booker Moore	.08	.04	.01
☐ 30 Fred Smerlas PB	.08	.04	.01
☐ 31 Ben Williams	.15	.07	.02
☐ 32 Cincinnati Bengals TL	.10	.05	.01
Cris Collinsworth			
☐ 33 Charles Alexander	.08	.04	.01
☐ 34 Ken Anderson	.30	.14	.04
☐ 35 Ken Anderson IR	.30	.14	.04
☐ 36 Jim Breech	.08	.04	.01
☐ 37 Cris Collinsworth PB	.30	.14	.04
☐ 38 Cris Collinsworth IR	.30	.14	.04
☐ 39 Isaac Curtis	.15	.07	.02
☐ 40 Eddie Edwards	.08	.04	.01
☐ 41 Ray Horton	.08	.04	.01
☐ 42 Pete Johnson	.15	.07	.02
☐ 43 Steve Kreider	.08	.04	.01
☐ 44 Max Montoya	.08	.04	.01
☐ 45 Anthony Munoz PB	.40	.18	.05
☐ 46 Reggie Williams	.15	.07	.02
☐ 47 Cleveland Browns TL	.10	.05	.01
Mike Pruitt			
☐ 48 Matt Bahr	.15	.07	.02
☐ 49 Chip Banks PB	.08	.04	.01
☐ 50 Tom Cousineau	.08	.04	.01
☐ 51 Joe DeLamielleure	.08	.04	.01
☐ 52 Doug Dieken	.08	.04	.01
☐ 53 Bob Golic	.30	.14	.04
☐ 54 Bobby Jones	.08	.04	.01
☐ 55 Dave Logan	.08	.04	.01
☐ 56 Clay Matthews	.60	.25	.07
☐ 57 Paul McDonald	.08	.04	.01
☐ 58 Ozzie Newsome	.50	.23	.06
☐ 59 Ozzie Newsome IR	.30	.14	.04
☐ 60 Mike Pruitt	.15	.07	.02
☐ 61 Denver Broncos TL	.10	.05	.01
Steve Watson			
☐ 62 Barney Chavous	.08	.04	.01
☐ 63 John Elway	55.00	25.00	7.00
☐ 64 Steve Foley	.08	.04	.01
☐ 65 Tom Jackson	.30	.14	.04
☐ 66 Rich Karlis	.08	.04	.01
☐ 67 Luke Prestridge	.08	.04	.01
☐ 68 Zach Thomas	.08	.04	.01
☐ 69 Rick Upchurch	.15	.07	.02
☐ 70 Steve Watson	.15	.07	.02
☐ 71 Sammy Winder	.15	.07	.02
☐ 72 Louis Wright PB	.15	.07	.02
☐ 73 Houston Oilers TL	.10	.05	.01
Tim Smith			
☐ 74 Jesse Baker	.08	.04	.01
☐ 75 Gregg Bingham	.08	.04	.01
☐ 76 Robert Brazile	.15	.07	.02
☐ 77 Steve Brown	.08	.04	.01
☐ 78 Chris Dressel	.08	.04	.01
☐ 79 Doug France	.08	.04	.01
☐ 80 Florian Kempf	.08	.04	.01
☐ 81 Carl Roaches	.15	.07	.02
☐ 82 Tim Smith	.15	.07	.02
☐ 83 Willie Tullis	.08	.04	.01
☐ 84 Kansas City Chiefs TL	.10	.05	.01
Carlos Carson			
☐ 85 Mike Bell	.08	.04	.01
☐ 86 Theotis Brown	.08	.04	.01
☐ 87 Carlos Carson PB	.30	.14	.04
☐ 88 Carlos Carson IR	.15	.07	.02
☐ 89 Deron Cherry PB	.15	.07	.02
☐ 90 Gary Green PB	.08	.04	.01
☐ 91 Billy Jackson	.08	.04	.01
☐ 92 Bill Kenney	.15	.07	.02
☐ 93 Bill Kenney IR	.15	.07	.02
☐ 94 Nick Lowery	.30	.14	.04
☐ 95 Henry Marshall	.08	.04	.01
☐ 96 Art Still	.08	.04	.01
☐ 97 Los Angeles Raiders TL	.10	.05	.01
Todd Christensen			
☐ 98 Marcus Allen	5.00	2.20	.60
☐ 99 Marcus Allen IR	2.50	1.10	.30
☐ 100 Lyle Alzado	.15	.07	.02
☐ 101 Lyle Alzado IR	.15	.07	.02
☐ 102 Chris Bahr	.08	.04	.01
☐ 103 Malcolm Barnwell	.08	.04	.01
☐ 104 Cliff Branch	.30	.14	.04
☐ 105 Todd Christensen PB	.30	.14	.04
☐ 106 Todd Christensen IR	.30	.14	.04
☐ 107 Ray Guy	.30	.14	.04
☐ 108 Frank Hawkins	.08	.04	.01
☐ 109 Lester Hayes PB	.15	.07	.02
☐ 110 Ted Hendricks PB	.30	.14	.04
☐ 111 Howie Long PB	8.00	3.60	1.00
☐ 112 Rod Martin PB	.15	.07	.02
☐ 113 Vann McElroy PB	.08	.04	.01
☐ 114 Jim Plunkett	.30	.14	.04
☐ 115 Greg Pruitt PB	.15	.07	.02
☐ 116 Miami Dolphins TL	.30	.14	.04
Mark Duper			
☐ 117 Bob Baumhower PB	.08	.04	.01
☐ 118 Doug Betters PB	.08	.04	.01
☐ 119 A.J. Duhe	.08	.04	.01
☐ 120 Mark Duper PB	.50	.23	.06
☐ 121 Andra Franklin	.08	.04	.01
☐ 122 William Judson	.08	.04	.01
☐ 123 Dan Marino PB UER	140.00	65.00	17.50
(Quaterback on back)			
☐ 124 Dan Marino IR	15.00	6.75	1.85
☐ 125 Nat Moore	.15	.07	.02
☐ 126 Ed Newman PB	.08	.04	.01
☐ 127 Reggie Roby	.15	.07	.02
☐ 128 Gerald Small	.08	.04	.01
☐ 129 Dwight Stephenson PB	.15	.07	.02
☐ 130 Uwe Von Schamann	.08	.04	.01
☐ 131 New England Pats TL	.10	.05	.01
Tony Collins			
☐ 132 Rich Camarillo PB	.15	.07	.02
☐ 133 Tony Collins PB	.15	.07	.02
☐ 134 Tony Collins IR	.08	.04	.01
☐ 135 Bob Cryder	.08	.04	.01
☐ 136 Steve Grogan	.15	.07	.02
☐ 137 John Hannah PB	.30	.14	.04
☐ 138 Brian Holloway PB	.08	.04	.01
☐ 139 Roland James	.08	.04	.01
☐ 140 Stanley Morgan	.15	.07	.02
☐ 141 Rick Sanford	.08	.04	.01
☐ 142 Mosi Tatupu	.08	.04	.01
☐ 143 Andre Tippett	.30	.14	.04
☐ 144 New York Jets TL	.10	.05	.01
Wesley Walker			
☐ 145 Jerome Barkum	.08	.04	.01
☐ 146 Mark Gastineau PB	.15	.07	.02
☐ 147 Mark Gastineau IR	.15	.07	.02
☐ 148 Bruce Harper	.08	.04	.01
☐ 149 Johnny Lam Jones	.08	.04	.01
☐ 150 Joe Klecko PB	.15	.07	.02
☐ 151 Pat Leahy	.08	.04	.01
☐ 152 Freeman McNeil	.15	.07	.02
☐ 153 Lance Mehl	.08	.04	.01
☐ 154 Marvin Powell PB	.15	.07	.02
☐ 155 Darrol Ray	.08	.04	.01
☐ 156 Pat Ryan	.08	.04	.01
☐ 157 Kirk Springs	.08	.04	.01
☐ 158 Wesley Walker	.15	.07	.02
☐ 159 Pittsburgh Steelers TL	.30	.14	.04
Franco Harris			
☐ 160 Walter Abercrombie	.15	.07	.02
☐ 161 Gary Anderson PB	.30	.14	.04
☐ 162 Terry Bradshaw	1.50	.70	.19
☐ 163 Craig Colquitt	.08	.04	.01
☐ 164 Bennie Cunningham	.08	.04	.01
☐ 165 Franco Harris	.50	.23	.06
☐ 166 Franco Harris IR	.30	.14	.04

☐ 167 Jack Lambert PB	.50	.23	.06
☐ 168 Jack Lambert IR	.30	.14	.04
☐ 169 Frank Pollard	.08	.04	.01
☐ 170 Donnie Shell	.15	.07	.02
☐ 171 Mike Webster PB	.15	.07	.02
☐ 172 Keith Willis	.08	.04	.01
☐ 173 Rick Woods	.08	.04	.01
☐ 174 San Diego Chargers TL Kellen Winslow	.30	.14	.04
☐ 175 Rolf Benirschke	.08	.04	.01
☐ 176 James Brooks	.15	.07	.02
☐ 177 Maury Buford	.08	.04	.01
☐ 178 Wes Chandler PB	.15	.07	.02
☐ 179 Dan Fouts PB	.60	.25	.07
☐ 180 Dan Fouts IR	.30	.14	.04
☐ 181 Charlie Joiner	.40	.18	.05
☐ 182 Linden King	.08	.04	.01
☐ 183 Chuck Muncie	.15	.07	.02
☐ 184 Billy Ray Smith	.30	.14	.04
☐ 185 Danny Walters	.08	.04	.01
☐ 186 Kellen Winslow PB	.60	.25	.07
☐ 187 Kellen Winslow IR	.30	.14	.04
☐ 188 Seattle Seahawks TL Curt Warner	.10	.05	.01
☐ 189 Steve August	.08	.04	.01
☐ 190 Dave Brown	.08	.04	.01
☐ 191 Zachary Dixon	.08	.04	.01
☐ 192 Kenny Easley	.15	.07	.02
☐ 193 Jacob Green	.08	.04	.01
☐ 194 Norm Johnson	.15	.07	.02
☐ 195 Dave Krieg	1.50	.70	.19
☐ 196 Steve Largent	1.25	.55	.16
☐ 197 Steve Largent IR	.60	.25	.07
☐ 198 Curt Warner PB	.50	.23	.06
☐ 199 Curt Warner IR	.30	.14	.04
☐ 200 Jeff West	.08	.04	.01
☐ 201 Charley Young	.08	.04	.01
☐ 202 Passing Leaders Dan Marino Steve Bartkowski	6.00	2.70	.75
☐ 203 Receiving Leaders Todd Christensen Charlie Brown Earnest Gray Roy Green	.10	.05	.01
☐ 204 Rushing Leaders Curt Warner Eric Dickerson	.50	.23	.06
☐ 205 Scoring Leaders Gary Anderson K Mark Moseley	.10	.05	.01
☐ 206 Interception Leaders Vann McElroy Ken Riley Mark Murphy	.10	.05	.01
☐ 207 Punting Leaders Rich Camarillo Greg Coleman	.10	.05	.01
☐ 208 Atlanta Falcons TL William Andrews	.10	.05	.01
☐ 209 William Andrews PB	.15	.07	.02
☐ 210 William Andrews IR	.15	.07	.02
☐ 211 Stacey Bailey	.08	.04	.01
☐ 212 Steve Bartkowski	.30	.14	.04
☐ 213 Steve Bartkowski IR	.15	.07	.02
☐ 214 Ralph Giacomarro	.08	.04	.01
☐ 215 Billy Johnson PB	.15	.07	.02
☐ 216 Mike Kenn PB	.15	.07	.02
☐ 217 Mick Luckhurst	.08	.04	.01
☐ 218 Gerald Riggs	.30	.14	.04
☐ 219 R.C. Thielemann PB	.08	.04	.01
☐ 220 Jeff Van Note	.15	.07	.02
☐ 221 Chicago Bears TL Walter Payton	.75	.35	.09
☐ 222 Jim Covert	.30	.14	.04
☐ 223 Leslie Frazier	.08	.04	.01
☐ 224 Willie Gault	.30	.14	.04
☐ 225 Mike Hartenstine	.08	.04	.01
☐ 226 Noah Jackson UER (photo actually Jim Osborne)	.08	.04	.01
☐ 227 Jim McMahon	.75	.35	.09
☐ 228 Walter Payton PB	2.00	.90	.25
☐ 229 Walter Payton IR	1.00	.45	.12
☐ 230 Mike Richardson	.08	.04	.01
☐ 231 Terry Schmidt	.08	.04	.01
☐ 232 Mike Singletary PB	1.00	.45	.12
☐ 233 Matt Suhey	.15	.07	.02
☐ 234 Bob Thomas	.08	.04	.01
☐ 235 Dallas Cowboys TL Tony Dorsett	.30	.14	.04
☐ 236 Bob Breunig	.08	.04	.01
☐ 237 Doug Cosbie PB	.15	.07	.02
☐ 238 Tony Dorsett PB	1.00	.45	.12
☐ 239 Tony Dorsett IR	.50	.23	.06
☐ 240 John Dutton	.08	.04	.01
☐ 241 Tony Hill	.15	.07	.02
☐ 242 Ed Jones PB	.30	.14	.04
☐ 243 Drew Pearson	.30	.14	.04
☐ 244 Rafael Septien	.08	.04	.01
☐ 245 Ron Springs	.15	.07	.02
☐ 246 Dennis Thurman	.08	.04	.01
☐ 247 Everson Walls PB	.08	.04	.01
☐ 248 Danny White	.30	.14	.04
☐ 249 Randy White PB	.50	.23	.06
☐ 250 Detroit Lions TL Billy Sims	.15	.07	.02
☐ 251 Jeff Chadwick	.15	.07	.02
☐ 252 Garry Cobb	.08	.04	.01
☐ 253 Doug English PB	.15	.07	.02
☐ 254 William Gay	.08	.04	.01
☐ 255 Eric Hipple	.15	.07	.02
☐ 256 James Jones	.15	.07	.02
☐ 257 Bruce McNorton	.08	.04	.01
☐ 258 Eddie Murray	.15	.07	.02
☐ 259 Ulysses Norris	.08	.04	.01
☐ 260 Billy Sims	.30	.14	.04
☐ 261 Billy Sims IR	.15	.07	.02
☐ 262 Leonard Thompson	.08	.04	.01
☐ 263 Green Bay Packers TL James Lofton	.30	.14	.04
☐ 264 John Anderson	.08	.04	.01
☐ 265 Paul Coffman PB	.15	.07	.02
☐ 266 Lynn Dickey	.15	.07	.02
☐ 267 Gerry Ellis	.08	.04	.01
☐ 268 John Jefferson	.30	.14	.04
☐ 269 John Jefferson IR	.30	.14	.04
☐ 270 Ezra Johnson	.08	.04	.01
☐ 271 Tim Lewis	.08	.04	.01
☐ 272 James Lofton PB	.50	.23	.06
☐ 273 James Lofton IR	.30	.14	.04
☐ 274 Larry McCarren PB	.08	.04	.01
☐ 275 Jan Stenerud	.15	.07	.02
☐ 276 Los Angeles Rams TL Eric Dickerson	.50	.23	.06
☐ 277 Mike Barber	.08	.04	.01
☐ 278 Jim Collins	.08	.04	.01
☐ 279 Nolan Cromwell PB	.15	.07	.02
☐ 280 Eric Dickerson PB	5.00	2.20	.60
☐ 281 Eric Dickerson IR	1.50	.70	.19
☐ 282 George Farmer	.08	.04	.01
☐ 283 Vince Ferragamo	.15	.07	.02
☐ 284 Kent Hill PB	.08	.04	.01
☐ 285 John Misko	.08	.04	.01
☐ 286 Jackie Slater PB	.30	.14	.04
☐ 287 Jack Youngblood	.15	.07	.02
☐ 288 Minnesota Vikings TL Darrin Nelson	.10	.05	.01
☐ 289 Ted Brown	.15	.07	.02
☐ 290 Greg Coleman	.08	.04	.01
☐ 291 Steve Dils	.08	.04	.01
☐ 292 Tony Galbreath	.08	.04	.01
☐ 293 Tommy Kramer	.15	.07	.02
☐ 294 Doug Martin	.08	.04	.01
☐ 295 Darrin Nelson	.15	.07	.02
☐ 296 Benny Ricardo	.08	.04	.01
☐ 297 John Swain	.08	.04	.01
☐ 298 John Turner	.08	.04	.01
☐ 299 New Orleans Saints TL George Rogers	.10	.05	.01
☐ 300 Morten Andersen	1.50	.70	.19
☐ 301 Russell Erxleben	.08	.04	.01
☐ 302 Jeff Groth	.08	.04	.01
☐ 303 Rickey Jackson PB	.75	.35	.09
☐ 304 Johnnie Poe	.08	.04	.01
☐ 305 George Rogers	.15	.07	.02
☐ 306 Richard Todd	.15	.07	.02
☐ 307 Jim Wilks	.08	.04	.01
☐ 308 Dave Wilson	.08	.04	.01
☐ 309 Wayne Wilson	.08	.04	.01
☐ 310 New York Giants TL Earnest Gray	.10	.05	.01
☐ 311 Leon Bright	.08	.04	.01
☐ 312 Scott Brunner	.08	.04	.01
☐ 313 Rob Carpenter	.08	.04	.01
☐ 314 Harry Carson PB	.15	.07	.02
☐ 315 Earnest Gray	.08	.04	.01
☐ 316 Ali Haji-Sheikh PB	.08	.04	.01
☐ 317 Mark Haynes PB	.15	.07	.02
☐ 318 Dave Jennings	.08	.04	.01
☐ 319 Brian Kelley	.08	.04	.01
☐ 320 Phil Simms	.75	.35	.09
☐ 321 Lawrence Taylor PB	3.00	1.35	.35
☐ 322 Lawrence Taylor IR	1.50	.70	.19
☐ 323 Brad Van Pelt	.08	.04	.01
☐ 324 Butch Woolfolk	.08	.04	.01
☐ 325 Philadelphia Eagles TL Mike Quick	.10	.05	.01
☐ 326 Harold Carmichael	.15	.07	.02
☐ 327 Herman Edwards	.08	.04	.01
☐ 328 Michael Haddix	.08	.04	.01
☐ 329 Dennis Harrison	.08	.04	.01
☐ 330 Ron Jaworski	.15	.07	.02
☐ 331 Wilbert Montgomery	.15	.07	.02
☐ 332 Hubie Oliver	.08	.04	.01
☐ 333 Mike Quick PB	.30	.14	.04
☐ 334 Jerry Robinson	.08	.04	.01
☐ 335 Max Runager	.08	.04	.01
☐ 336 Michael Williams	.08	.04	.01
☐ 337 St. Louis Cardinals TL Ottis Anderson	.10	.05	.01
☐ 338 Ottis Anderson	.30	.14	.04
☐ 339 Al(Bubba) Baker	.15	.07	.02
☐ 340 Carl Birdsong PB	.08	.04	.01
☐ 341 David Galloway	.08	.04	.01
☐ 342 Roy Green PB	.15	.07	.02
☐ 343 Roy Green IR	.15	.07	.02
☐ 344 Curtis Greer	.08	.04	.01
☐ 345 Neil Lomax	.15	.07	.02
☐ 346 Doug Marsh	.08	.04	.01
☐ 347 Stump Mitchell	.15	.07	.02
☐ 348 Lionel Washington	.15	.07	.02
☐ 349 San Francisco 49ers TL Dwight Clark	.10	.05	.01
☐ 350 Dwaine Board	.08	.04	.01
☐ 351 Dwight Clark	.30	.14	.04
☐ 352 Dwight Clark IR	.15	.07	.02
☐ 353 Roger Craig	2.50	1.10	.30
☐ 354 Fred Dean	.15	.07	.02
☐ 355 Fred Dean IR Marino in background	.50	.23	.06
☐ 356 Dwight Hicks PB	.15	.07	.02
☐ 357 Ronnie Lott PB	1.00	.45	.12
☐ 358 Joe Montana PB	8.00	3.60	1.00
☐ 359 Joe Montana IR	3.00	1.35	.35
☐ 360 Freddie Solomon	.08	.04	.01
☐ 361 Wendell Tyler	.08	.04	.01
☐ 362 Ray Wersching	.08	.04	.01
☐ 363 Eric Wright	.15	.07	.02
☐ 364 Tampa Bay Bucs TL Kevin House	.10	.05	.01
☐ 365 Gerald Carter	.08	.04	.01
☐ 366 Hugh Green PB	.15	.07	.02
☐ 367 Kevin House	.15	.07	.02
☐ 368 Michael Morton	.08	.04	.01
☐ 369 James Owens	.08	.04	.01
☐ 370 Booker Reese	.08	.04	.01
☐ 371 Lee Roy Selmon PB	.30	.14	.04
☐ 372 Jack Thompson	.15	.07	.02
☐ 373 James Wilder	.15	.07	.02
☐ 374 Steve Wilson	.08	.04	.01
☐ 375 Wash. Redskins TL John Riggins	.30	.14	.04
☐ 376 Jeff Bostic PB	.08	.04	.01
☐ 377 Charlie Brown PB	.30	.14	.04
☐ 378 Charlie Brown IR	.15	.07	.02
☐ 379 Dave Butz PB	.15	.07	.02
☐ 380 Darrell Green	1.00	.45	.12
☐ 381 Russ Grimm PB	.30	.14	.04
☐ 382 Joe Jacoby PB	.15	.07	.02
☐ 383 Dexter Manley	.15	.07	.02
☐ 384 Art Monk	1.00	.45	.12
☐ 385 Mark Moseley	.15	.07	.02
☐ 386 Mark Murphy PB	.08	.04	.01
☐ 387 Mike Nelms	.08	.04	.01
☐ 388 John Riggins	.50	.23	.06
☐ 389 John Riggins IR	.30	.14	.04
☐ 390 Joe Theismann PB	.40	.18	.05
☐ 391 Joe Theismann IR	.30	.14	.04
☐ 392 Don Warren	.15	.07	.02
☐ 393 Joe Washington	.15	.07	.02
☐ 394 Checklist 1-132	.20	.09	.03
☐ 395 Checklist 133-264	.20	.09	.03
☐ 396 Checklist 265-396	.20	.09	.03

1984 Topps Glossy Inserts

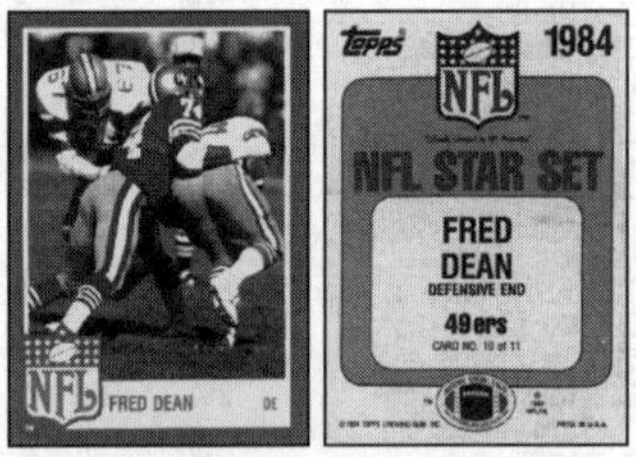

The 1984 Topps Glossy Inserts set contains 11 standard-size cards featuring an attractive blue border. They were issued as an insert with the 1984 Topps football regular issue rack packs. The player selection appears to be based on conference-leading performers from the previous season in the categories of rushing, passing, receiving, and sacks. The key card in the set is Dan Marino appearing in his Rookie Card year.

	MINT	NRMT	EXC
COMPLETE SET (11)	25.00	11.00	3.10
COMMON CARD (1-11)	.50	.23	.06
☐ 1 Curt Warner	.75	.35	.09
☐ 2 Eric Dickerson	2.00	.90	.25
☐ 3 Dan Marino	20.00	9.00	2.50
☐ 4 Steve Bartkowski	.75	.35	.09
☐ 5 Todd Christensen	.75	.35	.09
☐ 6 Roy Green	.75	.35	.09
☐ 7 Charlie Brown	.50	.23	.06
☐ 8 Earnest Gray	.50	.23	.06
☐ 9 Mark Gastineau	.50	.23	.06
☐ 10 Fred Dean	.50	.23	.06
☐ 11 Lawrence Taylor	1.50	.70	.19

1984 Topps Play Cards

Inserted one per 1984 Topps pack, this 27-card set measures the standard size. On a yellow background, the fronts describe what collectors could win and how to play the game. A team name and a number of yards gained appears on the fronts. Collectors needed to accumulate a total of 25 yards to trade for a group of five 1984 Topps Glossy Send-In cards. The backs carry the official rules. The cards are numbered on the front as "Play x of 27".

	MINT	NRMT	EXC
COMPLETE SET (27)	20.00	9.00	2.50
COMMON CARD (1-27)	.75	.35	.09
☐ 1 Houston Oilers 2 yards gained	.75	.35	.09
☐ 2 Houston Oilers 3 yards gained	.75	.35	.09
☐ 3 Cleveland Browns 4 yards gained	.75	.35	.09
☐ 4 Cleveland Browns 5 yards gained	.75	.35	.09
☐ 5 Cincinnati Bengals 6 yards gained	.75	.35	.09
☐ 6 Pittsburgh Steelers 7 yards gained	1.00	.45	.12
☐ 7 New Orleans Saints 8 yards gained	1.00	.45	.12
☐ 8 New York Giants 2 yards gained	.75	.35	.09
☐ 9 Washington Redskins 3 yards gained	1.00	.45	.12
☐ 10 Green Bay Packers 4 yards gained	.75	.35	.09
☐ 11 Atlanta Falcons 5 yards gained	.75	.35	.09
☐ 12 Detroit Lions 6 yards gained	.75	.35	.09
☐ 13 New England Patriots 7 yards gained	.75	.35	.09
☐ 14 New York Jets 8 yards gained	1.00	.45	.12
☐ 15 Buffalo Bills 2 yards gained	.75	.35	.09
☐ 16 Kansas City Chiefs 3 yards gained	.75	.35	.09
☐ 17 Miami Dolphins 4 yards gained	1.00	.45	.12
☐ 18 San Diego Chargers 5 yards gained	.75	.35	.09
☐ 19 Seattle Seahawks 6 yards gained	.75	.35	.09
☐ 20 Seattle Seahawks 7 yards gained	.75	.35	.09
☐ 21 Dallas Cowboys 8 yards gained	1.50	.70	.19
☐ 22 St. Louis Cardinals 2 yards gained	.75	.35	.09
☐ 23 Chicago Bears 3 yards gained	.75	.35	.09
☐ 24 San Francisco 49ers 4 yards gained	1.50	.70	.19
☐ 25 Philadelphia Eagles 5 yards gained	.75	.35	.09
☐ 26 Minnesota Vikings 6 yards gained	.75	.35	.09
☐ 27 Los Angeles Rams 7 yards gained	1.00	.45	.12

1984 Topps Glossy Send-In

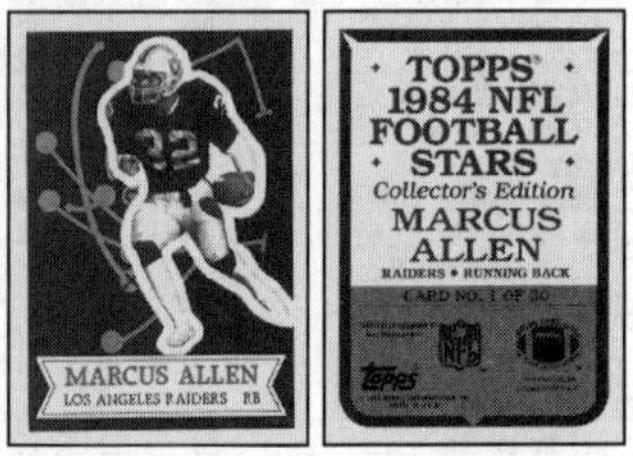

The 1984 Topps Glossy Send-In set contains 30 cards with each measuring approximately 2 1/2" by 3 1/2." Complete sets were available via a mail-away offer from Topps involving the 1984 Play cards.

	MINT	NRMT	EXC
COMPLETE SET (30)	12.00	5.50	1.50
COMMON CARD (1-30)	.25	.11	.03
☐ 1 Marcus Allen	2.00	.90	.25
☐ 2 John Riggins	.75	.35	.09
☐ 3 Walter Payton	2.00	.90	.25
☐ 4 Tony Dorsett	1.25	.55	.16
☐ 5 Franco Harris	.75	.35	.09
☐ 6 Curt Warner	.25	.11	.03
☐ 7 Eric Dickerson	1.25	.55	.16
☐ 8 Mike Pruitt	.25	.11	.03
☐ 9 Ken Anderson	.60	.25	.07
☐ 10 Dan Fouts	.75	.35	.09
☐ 11 Terry Bradshaw	1.25	.55	.16
☐ 12 Joe Theismann	.75	.35	.09
☐ 13 Joe Montana	5.00	2.20	.60
☐ 14 Danny White	.40	.18	.05
☐ 15 Kellen Winslow	.60	.25	.07
☐ 16 Wesley Walker	.25	.11	.03
☐ 17 Drew Pearson	.60	.25	.07
☐ 18 James Lofton	.75	.35	.09
☐ 19 Cris Collinsworth	.25	.11	.03
☐ 20 Dwight Clark	.40	.18	.05
☐ 21 Mark Gastineau	.25	.11	.03
☐ 22 Lawrence Taylor	1.00	.45	.12

☐ 23 Randy White	1.00	.45	.12
☐ 24 Ed Too Tall Jones	.75	.35	.09
☐ 25 Jack Lambert	1.00	.45	.12
☐ 26 Fred Dean	.25	.11	.03
☐ 27 Jan Stenerud	.40	.18	.05
☐ 28 Bruce Harper	.25	.11	.03
☐ 29 Todd Christensen	.25	.11	.03
☐ 30 Greg Pruitt	.25	.11	.03

1984 Topps USFL

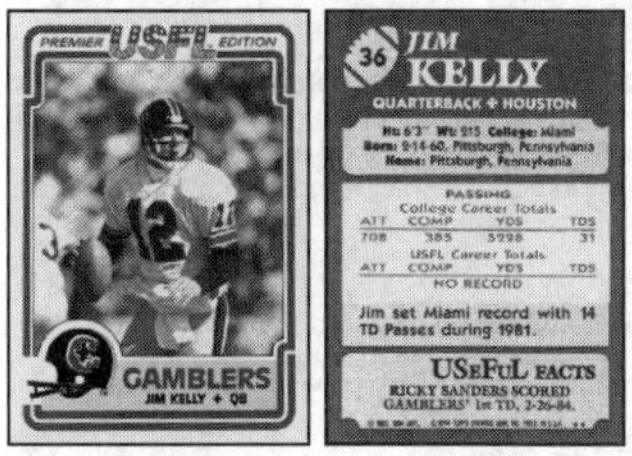

The 1984 Topps USFL set contains 132 standard-size cards, which were available as a complete set housed in its own specially made box. Card fronts have the "Premier USFL Edition" logo at the top border. Beneath the player photo is the team helmet and the player's name, team and position in a yellow box. The backs have NFL and USFL statistics (rookies have collecge stats) and a team fact. The cards in the set are numbered in alphabetical team order (with players arranged alphabetically within teams). Popular Extended Rookie Cards are quarterbacks Jim Kelly and Steve Young. Herschel Walker and Reggie White are other notable XRC's. More players making their first professional card appearence include Gary Anderson, Anthony Carter, Bobby Hebert, Craig James, Vaughan Johnson, Gary Plummer and Ricky Sanders.

	MINT	NRMT	EXC
COMPLETE FACT.SET (132)	350.00	160.00	45.00
COMMON CARD (1-132)	1.50	.70	.19
☐ 1 Luther Bradley	1.50	.70	.19
☐ 2 Frank Corral	1.50	.70	.19
☐ 3 Trumaine Johnson	1.50	.70	.19
☐ 4 Greg Landry	2.50	1.10	.30
☐ 5 Kit Lathrop	1.50	.70	.19
☐ 6 Kevin Long	1.50	.70	.19
☐ 7 Tim Spencer	1.50	.70	.19
☐ 8 Stan White	1.50	.70	.19
☐ 9 Buddy Aydelette	1.50	.70	.19
☐ 10 Tom Banks	1.50	.70	.19
☐ 11 Fred Bohannon	1.50	.70	.19
☐ 12 Joe Cribbs	4.00	1.80	.50
☐ 13 Joey Jones	1.50	.70	.19
☐ 14 Scott Norwood	2.50	1.10	.30
☐ 15 Jim Smith	2.50	1.10	.30
☐ 16 Cliff Stoudt	4.00	1.80	.50
☐ 17 Vince Evans	4.00	1.80	.50
☐ 18 Vagas Ferguson	1.50	.70	.19
☐ 19 John Gillen	1.50	.70	.19
☐ 20 Kris Haines	1.50	.70	.19
☐ 21 Glenn Hyde	1.50	.70	.19
☐ 22 Mark Keel	1.50	.70	.19
☐ 23 Gary Lewis	1.50	.70	.19
☐ 24 Doug Plank	1.50	.70	.19
☐ 25 Neil Balholm	1.50	.70	.19
☐ 26 David Dumars	1.50	.70	.19
☐ 27 David Martin	1.50	.70	.19
☐ 28 Craig Penrose	1.50	.70	.19
☐ 29 Dave Stalls	1.50	.70	.19
☐ 30 Harry Sydney	1.50	.70	.19
☐ 31 Vincent White	1.50	.70	.19
☐ 32 George Yarno	1.50	.70	.19
☐ 33 Kiki DeAyala	1.50	.70	.19
☐ 34 Sam Harrell	1.50	.70	.19
☐ 35 Mike Hawkins	1.50	.70	.19
☐ 36 Jim Kelly	90.00	40.00	11.00
☐ 37 Mark Rush	1.50	.70	.19
☐ 38 Ricky Sanders	6.00	2.70	.75
☐ 39 Paul Bergmann	1.50	.70	.19
☐ 40 Tom Dinkel	1.50	.70	.19
☐ 41 Wyatt Henderson	1.50	.70	.19
☐ 42 Vaughan Johnson	2.50	1.10	.30
☐ 43 Willie McClendon	1.50	.70	.19
☐ 44 Matt Robinson	1.50	.70	.19
☐ 45 George Achica	1.50	.70	.19
☐ 46 Mark Adickes	1.50	.70	.19
☐ 47 Howard Carson	1.50	.70	.19
☐ 48 Kevin Nelson	1.50	.70	.19
☐ 49 Jeff Partridge	1.50	.70	.19
☐ 50 Jo Jo Townsell	2.50	1.10	.30
☐ 51 Eddie Weaver	1.50	.70	.19
☐ 52 Steve Young	160.00	70.00	20.00
☐ 53 Derrick Crawford	1.50	.70	.19
☐ 54 Walter Lewis	1.50	.70	.19
☐ 55 Phil McKinnely	1.50	.70	.19
☐ 56 Vic Minore	1.50	.70	.19
☐ 57 Gary Shirk	1.50	.70	.19
☐ 58 Reggie White	100.00	45.00	12.50
☐ 59 Anthony Carter UER College stats are wrong	12.00	5.50	1.50
☐ 60 John Corker	1.50	.70	.19
☐ 61 David Greenwood	1.50	.70	.19
☐ 62 Bobby Hebert	4.00	1.80	.50
☐ 63 Derek Holloway	1.50	.70	.19
☐ 64 Ken Lacy	1.50	.70	.19
☐ 65 Tyrone McGriff	1.50	.70	.19
☐ 66 Ray Pinney	1.50	.70	.19
☐ 67 Gary Barbaro	1.50	.70	.19
☐ 68 Sam Bowers	1.50	.70	.19
☐ 69 Clarence Collins	1.50	.70	.19
☐ 70 Willie Harper	1.50	.70	.19
☐ 71 Jim LeClair	1.50	.70	.19
☐ 72 Bobby Leopold	1.50	.70	.19
☐ 73 Brian Sipe	4.00	1.80	.50
☐ 74 Herschel Walker	25.00	11.00	3.10
☐ 75 Junior Ah You	1.50	.70	.19
☐ 76 Marcus Dupree	4.00	1.80	.50
☐ 77 Marcus Marek	1.50	.70	.19
☐ 78 Tim Mazzetti	1.50	.70	.19
☐ 79 Mike Robinson	1.50	.70	.19
☐ 80 Dan Ross	4.00	1.80	.50
☐ 81 Mark Schellen	1.50	.70	.19
☐ 82 Johnnie Walton	1.50	.70	.19
☐ 83 Gordon Banks	1.50	.70	.19
☐ 84 Fred Besana	1.50	.70	.19
☐ 85 Dave Browning	1.50	.70	.19
☐ 86 Eric Jordan	1.50	.70	.19
☐ 87 Frank Manumaleuga	1.50	.70	.19
☐ 88 Gary Plummer	7.00	3.10	.85
☐ 89 Stan Talley	1.50	.70	.19
☐ 90 Arthur Whittington	1.50	.70	.19
☐ 91 Terry Beeson	1.50	.70	.19
☐ 92 Mel Gray	4.00	1.80	.50
☐ 93 Mike Katolin	1.50	.70	.19
☐ 94 Dewey McClain	1.50	.70	.19
☐ 95 Sidney Thornton	1.50	.70	.19
☐ 96 Doug Williams	4.00	1.80	.50
☐ 97 Kelvin Bryant	4.00	1.80	.50
☐ 98 John Bunting	1.50	.70	.19
☐ 99 Irv Eatman	2.50	1.10	.30
☐ 100 Scott Fitzkee	1.50	.70	.19
☐ 101 Chuck Fusina	1.50	.70	.19
☐ 102 Sean Landeta	2.50	1.10	.30
☐ 103 David Trout	1.50	.70	.19
☐ 104 Scott Woerner	1.50	.70	.19
☐ 105 Glenn Carano	1.50	.70	.19
☐ 106 Ron Crosby	1.50	.70	.19
☐ 107 Jerry Holmes	1.50	.70	.19
☐ 108 Bruce Huther	1.50	.70	.19
☐ 109 Mike Rozier	2.50	1.10	.30
☐ 110 Larry Swider	1.50	.70	.19
☐ 111 Danny Buggs	1.50	.70	.19
☐ 112 Putt Choate	1.50	.70	.19
☐ 113 Rich Garza	1.50	.70	.19
☐ 114 Joey Hackett	1.50	.70	.19
☐ 115 Rick Neuheisel	5.00	2.20	.60
☐ 116 Mike St. Clair	1.50	.70	.19
☐ 117 Gary Anderson	4.00	1.80	.50
☐ 118 Zenon Andrusyshyn	1.50	.70	.19
☐ 119 Doug Beaudoin	1.50	.70	.19
☐ 120 Mike Butler	1.50	.70	.19
☐ 121 Willie Gillespie	1.50	.70	.19
☐ 122 Fred Nordgren	1.50	.70	.19
☐ 123 John Reaves	1.50	.70	.19
☐ 124 Eric Truvillion	1.50	.70	.19
☐ 125 Reggie Collier	1.50	.70	.19
☐ 126 Mike Guess	1.50	.70	.19
☐ 127 Mike Hohensee	1.50	.70	.19
☐ 128 Craig James	6.00	2.70	.75
☐ 129 Eric Robinson	1.50	.70	.19
☐ 130 Billy Taylor	1.50	.70	.19
☐ 131 Joey Walters	1.50	.70	.19
☐ 132 Checklist 1-132	1.50	.70	.19

1985 Topps

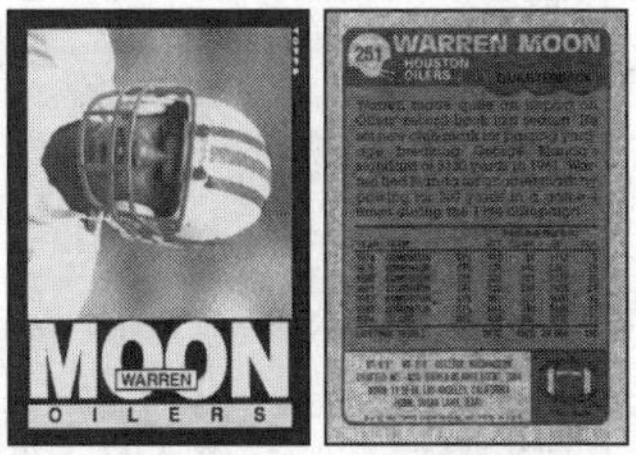

The 1985 Topps set contains 396 standard-size cards. Wax packs contained 15-cards. Horizontal card fronts have black borders that are prone to chipping. To the right is the player's name and team name. Vertical backs have highlights and statistics. Subsets include Record Breakers (1-6), playoffs (7-9) and league leaders (192-197). Team Leader (TL) cards feature an action photo on the front with a caption. The backs contain team scoring information from the previous year. The order of teams (alphabetically arranged by conference with players themselves alphabetically ordered within each team). The key Rookie Card in this set is Warren Moon (although he had already appeared in several JOGO CFL card issues). Other Rookie Cards include Carl Banks, Mark Clayton, Richard Dent, Henry Ellard, Irving Fryar, Louis Lipps, Steve McMichael, Mike Munchak and Darryl Talley.

	MINT	NRMT	EXC
COMPLETE SET (396)	70.00	32.00	8.75
COMMON CARD (1-396)	.08	.04	.01
☐ 1 Mark Clayton RB Most Touchdown Receptions, Season	.30	.14	.04
☐ 2 Eric Dickerson RB Most Yards Rushing, Season	.40	.18	.05
☐ 3 Charlie Joiner RB Most Receptions, Career	.20	.09	.03
☐ 4 Dan Marino RB UER Most Touchdown Passes, Season (Dolphins misspelled as Dophins)	8.00	3.60	1.00
☐ 5 Art Monk RB Most Receptions, Season	.20	.09	.03
☐ 6 Walter Payton RB Most Yards Rushing, Career	1.00	.45	.12
☐ 7 NFC Championship 49ers 23, Bears 0 (Matt Suhey tackled)	.10	.05	.01
☐ 8 AFC Championship Dolphins 45, Steelers 28 (Woody Bennett over)	.10	.05	.01
☐ 9 Super Bowl XIX 49ers 38, Dolphins 16 (Wendell Tyler)	.30	.14	.04
☐ 10 Atlanta Falcons TL Stretching For The First Down (Gerald Riggs)	.10	.05	.01
☐ 11 William Andrews	.15	.07	.02
☐ 12 Stacey Bailey	.08	.04	.01
☐ 13 Steve Bartkowski	.30	.14	.04
☐ 14 Rick Bryan	.08	.04	.01
☐ 15 Alfred Jackson	.08	.04	.01
☐ 16 Kenny Johnson	.08	.04	.01
☐ 17 Mike Kenn AP	.08	.04	.01
☐ 18 Mike Pitts	.08	.04	.01
☐ 19 Gerald Riggs	.15	.07	.02
☐ 20 Sylvester Stamps	.08	.04	.01
☐ 21 R.C. Thielemann	.08	.04	.01
☐ 22 Chicago Bears TL Sweetness Sets Record Straight (Walter Payton)	.75	.35	.09
☐ 23 Todd Bell AP	.08	.04	.01
☐ 24 Richard Dent AP	3.00	1.35	.35
☐ 25 Gary Fencik	.15	.07	.02
☐ 26 Dave Finzer	.08	.04	.01
☐ 27 Leslie Frazier	.08	.04	.01
☐ 28 Steve Fuller	.15	.07	.02
☐ 29 Willie Gault	.30	.14	.04
☐ 30 Dan Hampton AP	.30	.14	.04
☐ 31 Jim McMahon	.50	.23	.06
☐ 32 Steve McMichael	.50	.23	.06
☐ 33 Walter Payton AP	2.00	.90	.25
☐ 34 Mike Singletary	.75	.35	.09
☐ 35 Matt Suhey	.08	.04	.01
☐ 36 Bob Thomas	.08	.04	.01
☐ 37 Dallas Cowboys TL Busting Through The Defense (Tony Dorsett)	.35	.16	.04
☐ 38 Bill Bates	1.00	.45	.12
☐ 39 Doug Cosbie	.15	.07	.02
☐ 40 Tony Dorsett	.75	.35	.09
☐ 41 Michael Downs	.08	.04	.01
☐ 42 Mike Hegman UER (reference to SB VIII, should be SB XIII)	.08	.04	.01
☐ 43 Tony Hill	.15	.07	.02
☐ 44 Gary Hogeboom	.08	.04	.01
☐ 45 Jim Jeffcoat	.30	.14	.04
☐ 46 Ed Too Tall Jones	.30	.14	.04
☐ 47 Mike Renfro	.08	.04	.01
☐ 48 Rafael Septien	.08	.04	.01
☐ 49 Dennis Thurman	.08	.04	.01
☐ 50 Everson Walls	.15	.07	.02
☐ 51 Danny White	.30	.14	.04
☐ 52 Randy White	.40	.18	.05
☐ 53 Detroit Lions TL Popping One Loose (Lions' Defense)	.10	.05	.01
☐ 54 Jeff Chadwick	.08	.04	.01
☐ 55 Mike Cofer	.08	.04	.01
☐ 56 Gary Danielson	.08	.04	.01
☐ 57 Keith Dorney	.08	.04	.01
☐ 58 Doug English	.15	.07	.02
☐ 59 William Gay	.08	.04	.01
☐ 60 Ken Jenkins	.08	.04	.01
☐ 61 James Jones	.15	.07	.02
☐ 62 Eddie Murray	.15	.07	.02
☐ 63 Billy Sims	.30	.14	.04
☐ 64 Leonard Thompson	.08	.04	.01
☐ 65 Bobby Watkins	.08	.04	.01
☐ 66 Green Bay Packers TL Spotting His Deep Receiver (Lynn Dickey)	.10	.05	.01
☐ 67 Paul Coffman	.08	.04	.01
☐ 68 Lynn Dickey	.15	.07	.02
☐ 69 Mike Douglass	.08	.04	.01
☐ 70 Tom Flynn	.08	.04	.01
☐ 71 Eddie Lee Ivery	.08	.04	.01
☐ 72 Ezra Johnson	.08	.04	.01
☐ 73 Mark Lee	.08	.04	.01
☐ 74 Tim Lewis	.08	.04	.01
☐ 75 James Lofton	.30	.14	.04
☐ 76 Bucky Scribner	.08	.04	.01
☐ 77 Los Angeles Rams TL Record-Setting Ground Attack (Eric Dickerson)	.40	.18	.05
☐ 78 Nolan Cromwell	.15	.07	.02
☐ 79 Eric Dickerson AP	1.00	.45	.12
☐ 80 Henry Ellard	4.00	1.80	.50
☐ 81 Kent Hill	.08	.04	.01
☐ 82 LeRoy Irvin	.15	.07	.02
☐ 83 Jeff Kemp	.15	.07	.02
☐ 84 Mike Lansford	.08	.04	.01
☐ 85 Barry Redden	.08	.04	.01
☐ 86 Jackie Slater	.30	.14	.04
☐ 87 Doug Smith	.15	.07	.02
☐ 88 Jack Youngblood	.15	.07	.02
☐ 89 Minnesota Vikings TL Smothering The Opposition (Vikings' Defense)	.10	.05	.01
☐ 90 Alfred Anderson	.08	.04	.01
☐ 91 Ted Brown	.15	.07	.02
☐ 92 Greg Coleman	.08	.04	.01
☐ 93 Tommy Hannon	.08	.04	.01
☐ 94 Tommy Kramer	.15	.07	.02
☐ 95 Leo Lewis	.15	.07	.02
☐ 96 Doug Martin	.08	.04	.01
☐ 97 Darrin Nelson	.15	.07	.02
☐ 98 Jan Stenerud AP	.15	.07	.02
☐ 99 Sammie White	.15	.07	.02
☐ 100 New Orleans Saints TL Hurdling Over Front Line	.10	.05	.01
☐ 101 Morten Andersen	.30	.14	.04
☐ 102 Hoby Brenner	.15	.07	.02
☐ 103 Bruce Clark	.08	.04	.01
☐ 104 Hokie Gajan	.08	.04	.01
☐ 105 Brian Hansen	.08	.04	.01
☐ 106 Rickey Jackson	.30	.14	.04
☐ 107 George Rogers	.15	.07	.02
☐ 108 Dave Wilson	.08	.04	.01
☐ 109 Tyrone Young	.08	.04	.01
☐ 110 New York Giants TL Engulfing The Quarterback (Giants' Defense)	.10	.05	.01
☐ 111 Carl Banks	.30	.14	.04
☐ 112 Jim Burt	.15	.07	.02
☐ 113 Rob Carpenter	.08	.04	.01
☐ 114 Harry Carson	.15	.07	.02
☐ 115 Earnest Gray	.08	.04	.01
☐ 116 Ali Haji-Sheikh	.08	.04	.01
☐ 117 Mark Haynes AP	.15	.07	.02
☐ 118 Bobby Johnson	.08	.04	.01
☐ 119 Lionel Manuel	.15	.07	.02
☐ 120 Joe Morris	.30	.14	.04
☐ 121 Zeke Mowatt	.15	.07	.02
☐ 122 Jeff Rutledge	.08	.04	.01
☐ 123 Phil Simms	.50	.23	.06
☐ 124 Lawrence Taylor AP	1.50	.70	.19
☐ 125 Philadelphia Eagles TL Finding The Wide Open Spaces (Wilbert Montgomery)	.10	.05	.01
☐ 126 Greg Brown	.08	.04	.01
☐ 127 Ray Ellis	.08	.04	.01
☐ 128 Dennis Harrison	.08	.04	.01
☐ 129 Wes Hopkins	.15	.07	.02
☐ 130 Mike Horan	.08	.04	.01
☐ 131 Kenny Jackson	.08	.04	.01
☐ 132 Ron Jaworski	.15	.07	.02
☐ 133 Paul McFadden	.08	.04	.01
☐ 134 Wilbert Montgomery	.15	.07	.02
☐ 135 Mike Quick	.30	.14	.04
☐ 136 John Spagnola	.08	.04	.01
☐ 137 St.Louis Cardinals TL Exploiting The Air Route (Neil Lomax)	.10	.05	.01
☐ 138 Ottis Anderson	.30	.14	.04
☐ 139 Al(Bubba) Baker	.15	.07	.02
☐ 140 Roy Green	.15	.07	.02
☐ 141 Curtis Greer	.08	.04	.01
☐ 142 E.J. Junior AP	.08	.04	.01
☐ 143 Neil Lomax	.15	.07	.02
☐ 144 Stump Mitchell	.15	.07	.02
☐ 145 Neil O'Donoghue	.08	.04	.01
☐ 146 Pat Tilley	.08	.04	.01
☐ 147 Lionel Washington	.08	.04	.01
☐ 148 San Francisco 49ers TL The Road To Super Bowl XIX (Joe Montana)	1.25	.55	.16
☐ 149 Dwaine Board	.08	.04	.01
☐ 150 Dwight Clark	.30	.14	.04
☐ 151 Roger Craig	1.00	.45	.12
☐ 152 Randy Cross AP	.15	.07	.02

☐ 153 Fred Dean	.15	.07	.02
☐ 154 Keith Fahnhorst	.08	.04	.01
☐ 155 Dwight Hicks	.08	.04	.01
☐ 156 Ronnie Lott	.50	.23	.06
☐ 157 Joe Montana	8.00	3.60	1.00
☐ 158 Renaldo Nehemiah	.15	.07	.02
☐ 159 Fred Quillan	.08	.04	.01
☐ 160 Jack Reynolds	.08	.04	.01
☐ 161 Freddie Solomon	.08	.04	.01
☐ 162 Keena Turner	.08	.04	.01
☐ 163 Wendell Tyler	.08	.04	.01
☐ 164 Ray Wersching	.08	.04	.01
☐ 165 Carlton Williamson	.08	.04	.01
☐ 166 Tampa Bay Bucs TL	.10	.05	.01
Protecting The			
Quarterback			
(Steve DeBerg)			
☐ 167 Gerald Carter	.08	.04	.01
☐ 168 Mark Cotney	.08	.04	.01
☐ 169 Steve DeBerg	.30	.14	.04
☐ 170 Sean Farrell	.08	.04	.01
☐ 171 Hugh Green	.15	.07	.02
☐ 172 Kevin House	.15	.07	.02
☐ 173 David Logan	.08	.04	.01
☐ 174 Michael Morton	.08	.04	.01
☐ 175 Lee Roy Selmon	.30	.14	.04
☐ 176 James Wilder	.08	.04	.01
☐ 177 Wash. Redskins TL	.10	.05	.01
Diesel Named Desire			
(John Riggins)			
☐ 178 Charlie Brown	.08	.04	.01
☐ 179 Monte Coleman	.15	.07	.02
☐ 180 Vernon Dean	.08	.04	.01
☐ 181 Darrell Green	.30	.14	.04
☐ 182 Russ Grimm	.15	.07	.02
☐ 183 Joe Jacoby	.15	.07	.02
☐ 184 Dexter Manley	.15	.07	.02
☐ 185 Art Monk AP	.60	.25	.07
☐ 186 Mark Moseley	.15	.07	.02
☐ 187 Calvin Muhammad	.08	.04	.01
☐ 188 Mike Nelms	.08	.04	.01
☐ 189 John Riggins	.40	.18	.05
☐ 190 Joe Theismann	.40	.18	.05
☐ 191 Joe Washington	.15	.07	.02
☐ 192 Passing Leaders	15.00	6.75	1.85
Dan Marino			
Joe Montana			
☐ 193 Receiving Leaders	.15	.07	.02
Ozzie Newsome			
Art Monk			
☐ 194 Rushing Leaders	.30	.14	.04
Earnest Jackson			
Eric Dickerson			
☐ 195 Scoring Leaders	.10	.05	.01
Gary Anderson K			
Ray Wersching			
☐ 196 Interception Leaders	.10	.05	.01
Kenny Easley			
Tom Flynn			
☐ 197 Punting Leaders	.10	.05	.01
Jim Arnold			
Brian Hansen			
☐ 198 Buffalo Bills TL	.10	.05	.01
Rushing Toward			
Rookie Stardom			
(Greg Bell)			
☐ 199 Greg Bell	.15	.07	.02
☐ 200 Preston Dennard	.08	.04	.01
☐ 201 Joe Ferguson	.15	.07	.02
☐ 202 Byron Franklin	.08	.04	.01
☐ 203 Steve Freeman	.08	.04	.01
☐ 204 Jim Haslett	.08	.04	.01
☐ 205 Charles Romes	.08	.04	.01
☐ 206 Fred Smerlas	.08	.04	.01
☐ 207 Darryl Talley	.30	.14	.04
☐ 208 Van Williams	.08	.04	.01
☐ 209 Cincinnati Bengals TL	.10	.05	.01
Advancing The			
Ball Downfield			
(Ken Anderson and			
Larry Kinnebrew)			
☐ 210 Ken Anderson	.30	.14	.04
☐ 211 Jim Breech	.08	.04	.01
☐ 212 Louis Breeden	.08	.04	.01
☐ 213 James Brooks	.15	.07	.02
☐ 214 Ross Browner	.15	.07	.02
☐ 215 Eddie Edwards	.08	.04	.01
☐ 216 M.L. Harris	.08	.04	.01
☐ 217 Bobby Kemp	.08	.04	.01
☐ 218 Larry Kinnebrew	.08	.04	.01
☐ 219 Anthony Munoz AP	.50	.23	.06
☐ 220 Reggie Williams	.15	.07	.02
☐ 221 Cleveland Browns TL	.10	.05	.01
Evading The			
Defensive Pursuit			
(Boyce Green)			
☐ 222 Matt Bahr	.15	.07	.02
☐ 223 Chip Banks	.08	.04	.01
☐ 224 Reggie Camp	.08	.04	.01
☐ 225 Tom Cousineau	.08	.04	.01
☐ 226 Joe DeLamielleure	.08	.04	.01
☐ 227 Ricky Feacher	.08	.04	.01
☐ 228 Boyce Green	.08	.04	.01
☐ 229 Al Gross	.08	.04	.01
☐ 230 Clay Matthews	.50	.23	.06
☐ 231 Paul McDonald	.08	.04	.01
☐ 232 Ozzie Newsome AP	.30	.14	.04
☐ 233 Mike Pruitt	.15	.07	.02
☐ 234 Don Rogers	.08	.04	.01
☐ 235 Denver Broncos TL	.75	.35	.09
Thousand Yarder			
Gets The Ball			
(Sammy Winder and			
John Elway)			
☐ 236 Rubin Carter	.08	.04	.01
☐ 237 Barney Chavous	.08	.04	.01
☐ 238 John Elway	10.00	4.50	1.25
☐ 239 Steve Foley	.08	.04	.01
☐ 240 Mike Harden	.08	.04	.01
☐ 241 Tom Jackson	.30	.14	.04
☐ 242 Butch Johnson	.08	.04	.01
☐ 243 Rulon Jones	.08	.04	.01
☐ 244 Rich Karlis	.08	.04	.01
☐ 245 Steve Watson	.15	.07	.02
☐ 246 Gerald Willhite	.08	.04	.01
☐ 247 Sammy Winder	.15	.07	.02
☐ 248 Houston Oilers TL	.10	.05	.01
Eluding A			
Traffic Jam			
(Larry Moriarty)			
☐ 249 Jesse Baker	.08	.04	.01
☐ 250 Carter Hartwig	.08	.04	.01
☐ 251 Warren Moon	15.00	6.75	1.85
☐ 252 Larry Moriarty	.08	.04	.01
☐ 253 Mike Munchak	.30	.14	.04
☐ 254 Carl Roaches	.08	.04	.01
☐ 255 Tim Smith	.15	.07	.02
☐ 256 Willie Tullis	.08	.04	.01
☐ 257 Jamie Williams	.08	.04	.01
☐ 258 Indianapolis Colts TL	.10	.05	.01
Start Of A			
Long Gainer			
(Art Schlichter)			
☐ 259 Raymond Butler	.08	.04	.01
☐ 260 Johnie Cooks	.08	.04	.01
☐ 261 Eugene Daniel	.08	.04	.01
☐ 262 Curtis Dickey	.15	.07	.02
☐ 263 Chris Hinton	.15	.07	.02
☐ 264 Vernon Maxwell	.08	.04	.01
☐ 265 Randy McMillan	.08	.04	.01
☐ 266 Art Schlichter	.15	.07	.02
☐ 267 Rohn Stark	.15	.07	.02
☐ 268 Leo Wisniewski	.08	.04	.01
☐ 269 Kansas City Chiefs TL	.10	.05	.01
Pigskin About To			
Soar Upward			
(Bill Kenney)			
☐ 270 Jim Arnold	.08	.04	.01
☐ 271 Mike Bell	.08	.04	.01
☐ 272 Todd Blackledge	.15	.07	.02
☐ 273 Carlos Carson	.15	.07	.02
☐ 274 Deron Cherry	.15	.07	.02
☐ 275 Herman Heard	.08	.04	.01
☐ 276 Bill Kenney	.15	.07	.02
☐ 277 Nick Lowery	.30	.14	.04
☐ 278 Bill Maas	.08	.04	.01
☐ 279 Henry Marshall	.08	.04	.01
☐ 280 Art Still	.08	.04	.01
☐ 281 Los Angeles Raiders TL	.40	.18	.05
Diving For The			
Goal Line			
(Marcus Allen)			
☐ 282 Marcus Allen	2.50	1.10	.30
☐ 283 Lyle Alzado	.15	.07	.02
☐ 284 Chris Bahr	.08	.04	.01
☐ 285 Malcolm Barnwell	.08	.04	.01
☐ 286 Cliff Branch	.30	.14	.04
☐ 287 Todd Christensen	.30	.14	.04
☐ 288 Ray Guy	.30	.14	.04
☐ 289 Lester Hayes	.15	.07	.02
☐ 290 Mike Haynes AP	.15	.07	.02
☐ 291 Henry Lawrence	.08	.04	.01
☐ 292 Howie Long	2.00	.90	.25
☐ 293 Rod Martin AP	.15	.07	.02
☐ 294 Vann McElroy	.08	.04	.01
☐ 295 Matt Millen	.15	.07	.02
☐ 296 Bill Pickel	.08	.04	.01
☐ 297 Jim Plunkett	.30	.14	.04
☐ 298 Dokie Williams	.08	.04	.01
☐ 299 Marc Wilson	.15	.07	.02
☐ 300 Miami Dolphins TL	.10	.05	.01
Super Duper			
Performance			
(Mark Duper)			
☐ 301 Bob Baumhower	.08	.04	.01
☐ 302 Doug Betters	.08	.04	.01
☐ 303 Glenn Blackwood	.15	.07	.02
☐ 304 Lyle Blackwood	.15	.07	.02
☐ 305 Kim Bokamper	.08	.04	.01
☐ 306 Charles Bowser	.08	.04	.01
☐ 307 Jimmy Cefalo	.08	.04	.01
☐ 308 Mark Clayton AP	.75	.35	.09
☐ 309 A.J. Duhe	.08	.04	.01
☐ 310 Mark Duper	.30	.14	.04
☐ 311 Andra Franklin	.08	.04	.01
☐ 312 Bruce Hardy	.08	.04	.01
☐ 313 Pete Johnson	.15	.07	.02
☐ 314 Dan Marino AP UER	25.00	11.00	3.10
(Fouts 4802 yards in			
1981, should be 4082)			
☐ 315 Tony Nathan	.15	.07	.02
☐ 316 Ed Newman	.08	.04	.01
☐ 317 Reggie Roby AP	.30	.14	.04
☐ 318 Dwight Stephenson AP	.15	.07	.02
☐ 319 Uwe Von Schamann	.08	.04	.01
☐ 320 New England Pats TL	.10	.05	.01
Refusing To			
Be Denied			
(Tony Collins)			
☐ 321 Raymond Clayborn	.15	.07	.02
☐ 322 Tony Collins	.15	.07	.02
☐ 323 Tony Eason	.30	.14	.04
☐ 324 Tony Franklin	.08	.04	.01
☐ 325 Irving Fryar	5.00	2.20	.60
☐ 326 John Hannah AP	.30	.14	.04
☐ 327 Brian Holloway	.08	.04	.01
☐ 328 Craig James	.75	.35	.09
☐ 329 Stanley Morgan	.15	.07	.02
☐ 330 Steve Nelson AP	.08	.04	.01
☐ 331 Derrick Ramsey	.08	.04	.01
☐ 332 Stephen Starring	.15	.07	.02
☐ 333 Mosi Tatupu	.08	.04	.01
☐ 334 Andre Tippett	.30	.14	.04
☐ 335 New York Jets TL	.10	.05	.01
Thwarting The			
Passing Game			
(Mark Gastineau			
and Joe Ferguson)			
☐ 336 Russell Carter	.08	.04	.01
☐ 337 Mark Gastineau AP	.15	.07	.02
☐ 338 Bruce Harper	.08	.04	.01
☐ 339 Bobby Humphery	.08	.04	.01
☐ 340 Johnny Lam Jones	.08	.04	.01
☐ 341 Joe Klecko	.15	.07	.02
☐ 342 Pat Leahy	.08	.04	.01
☐ 343 Marty Lyons	.15	.07	.02
☐ 344 Freeman McNeil	.15	.07	.02
☐ 345 Lance Mehl	.08	.04	.01
☐ 346 Ken O'Brien	.30	.14	.04
☐ 347 Marvin Powell	.08	.04	.01
☐ 348 Pat Ryan	.08	.04	.01
☐ 349 Mickey Shuler	.08	.04	.01
☐ 350 Wesley Walker	.15	.07	.02
☐ 351 Pittsburgh Steelers TL	.10	.05	.01
Testing Defensive			
Pass Coverage			
(Mark Malone)			
☐ 352 Walter Abercrombie	.08	.04	.01
☐ 353 Gary Anderson K	.15	.07	.02
☐ 354 Robin Cole	.08	.04	.01
☐ 355 Bennie Cunningham	.08	.04	.01
☐ 356 Rich Erenberg	.08	.04	.01
☐ 357 Jack Lambert	.40	.18	.05
☐ 358 Louis Lipps	.30	.14	.04
☐ 359 Mark Malone	.15	.07	.02
☐ 360 Mike Merriweather	.08	.04	.01
☐ 361 Frank Pollard	.08	.04	.01
☐ 362 Donnie Shell	.15	.07	.02
☐ 363 John Stallworth	.30	.14	.04
☐ 364 Sam Washington	.08	.04	.01
☐ 365 Mike Webster	.15	.07	.02
☐ 366 Dwayne Woodruff	.08	.04	.01
☐ 367 San Diego Chargers TL	.10	.05	.01
Jarring The			
Ball Loose			
(Chargers' Defense)			
☐ 368 Rolf Benirschke	.08	.04	.01
☐ 369 Gill Byrd	.30	.14	.04
☐ 370 Wes Chandler	.15	.07	.02
☐ 371 Bobby Duckworth	.08	.04	.01
☐ 372 Dan Fouts	.50	.23	.06
☐ 373 Mike Green	.08	.04	.01
☐ 374 Pete Holohan	.08	.04	.01
☐ 375 Earnest Jackson	.15	.07	.02
☐ 376 Lionel James	.15	.07	.02
☐ 377 Charlie Joiner	.40	.18	.05
☐ 378 Billy Ray Smith	.15	.07	.02
☐ 379 Kellen Winslow	.40	.18	.05
☐ 380 Seattle Seahawks TL	.10	.05	.01
Setting Up For			
The Air Attack			
(Dave Krieg)			
☐ 381 Dave Brown	.08	.04	.01
☐ 382 Jeff Bryant	.08	.04	.01
☐ 383 Dan Doornink	.08	.04	.01
☐ 384 Kenny Easley AP	.15	.07	.02
☐ 385 Jacob Green	.15	.07	.02
☐ 386 David Hughes	.08	.04	.01
☐ 387 Norm Johnson	.08	.04	.01
☐ 388 Dave Krieg	.50	.23	.06
☐ 389 Steve Largent	1.00	.45	.12
☐ 390 Joe Nash	.08	.04	.01
☐ 391 Daryl Turner	.08	.04	.01
☐ 392 Curt Warner	.30	.14	.04
☐ 393 Fredd Young	.15	.07	.02
☐ 394 Checklist 1-132	.15	.07	.02
☐ 395 Checklist 133-264	.15	.07	.02
☐ 396 Checklist 265-396	.15	.07	.02

1985 Topps Box Bottoms

This 16-card set, which measures 2 1/2" by 3 1/2", was issued on the bottom of 1985 Topps wax pack boxes. The cards are in the same design as the 1985 Topps regular issues except they are bordered in red and have the words "Topps Superstars" printed in very small letters above the players' photos. Similar to the regular issue, these cards have a horizontal orientation. The backs of the cards are just like the regular card in that they have biographical and complete statistical information. The cards are arranged in alphabetical order and include such stars as Joe Montana and Walter Payton.

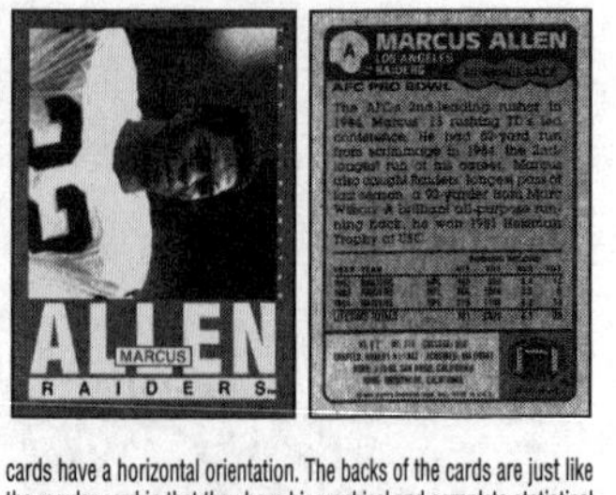

	MINT	NRMT	EXC
COMPLETE SET (16)	25.00	11.00	3.10
COMMON CARD (A-P)	.50	.23	.06
☐ A Marcus Allen	2.50	1.10	.30
☐ B Ottis Anderson	.50	.23	.06
☐ C Mark Clayton	.75	.35	.09
☐ D Eric Dickerson	.75	.35	.09
☐ E Tony Dorsett	1.00	.45	.12
☐ F Dan Fouts	.75	.35	.09
☐ G Mark Gastineau	.50	.23	.06
☐ H Charlie Joiner	.75	.35	.09
☐ I James Lofton	.75	.35	.09
☐ J Neil Lomax	.50	.23	.06
☐ K Dan Marino	12.00	5.50	1.50
☐ L Art Monk	.75	.35	.09
☐ M Joe Montana	8.00	3.60	1.00
☐ N Walter Payton	2.00	.90	.25
☐ O John Stallworth	.50	.23	.06
☐ P Lawrence Taylor	1.00	.45	.12

1985 Topps Glossy Inserts

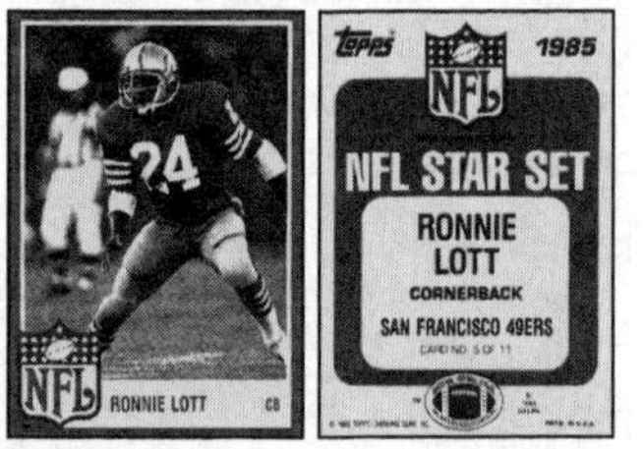

This red-bordered glossy insert set was distributed with rack packs of the 1985 Topps football regular issue. The backs of the cards are printed in red and blue on white card stock but provide very little about the player other than the most basic information.

	MINT	NRMT	EXC
COMPLETE SET (11)	20.00	9.00	2.50
COMMON CARD (1-11)	.50	.23	.06
☐ 1 Mark Clayton	.50	.23	.06
☐ 2 Eric Dickerson	.75	.35	.09
☐ 3 John Elway	5.00	2.20	.60
☐ 4 Mark Gastineau	.50	.23	.06
☐ 5 Ronnie Lott UER	.75	.35	.09
(Shown wearing 24)			
☐ 6 Dan Marino	8.00	3.60	1.00
☐ 7 Joe Montana	5.00	2.20	.60
☐ 8 Walter Payton	1.50	.70	.19
☐ 9 John Riggins	.75	.35	.09
☐ 10 John Stallworth	.50	.23	.06
☐ 11 Lawrence Taylor	.75	.35	.09

1985 Topps USFL

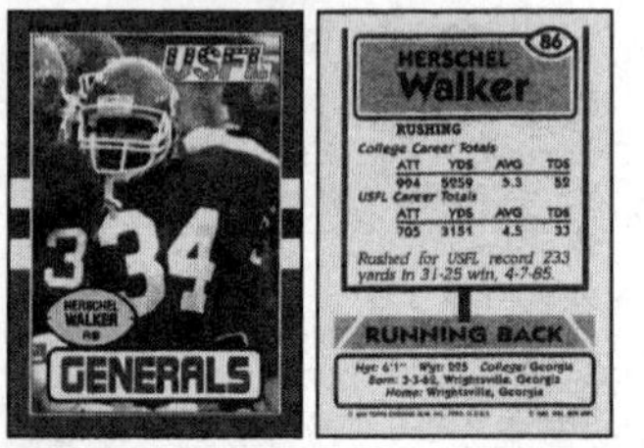

The 1985 Topps USFL set contains 132 football standard-size cards, which were available as a complete set housed in its own specially made box. The card fronts have a red border with a blue and white stripe in the middle. The USFL logo is at the top of the photo with the team name in red block letters in a white box at the bottom of the photo. Also toward the bottom of the photo, is the player's name and position within a yellow football. The card backs are printed in red and blue on white card stock. Card backs describe each player's highlights of the previous USFL season and have NFL and USFL statistics. The cards in the set are ordered numerically by team with players within teams also ordered alphabetically. The key Extended Rookie Cards in this set are Gary Clark, Doug Flutie, William Fuller and Sam Mills. Other key cards in the set include the second USFL cards of Jim Kelly, Herschel Walker, Reggie White, and Steve Young.

	MINT	NRMT	EXC
COMPLETE FACT.SET (132)	120.00	55.00	15.00
COMMON CARD (1-132)	.50	.23	.06
☐ 1 Case DeBruijn	.50	.23	.06
☐ 2 Mike Katolin	.50	.23	.06
☐ 3 Bruce Laird	.50	.23	.06
☐ 4 Kit Lathrop	.50	.23	.06
☐ 5 Kevin Long	.50	.23	.06
☐ 6 Karl Lorch	.50	.23	.06
☐ 7 Dave Tipton	.50	.23	.06
☐ 8 Doug Williams	2.00	.90	.25
☐ 9 Luis Zendejas	.50	.23	.06
☐ 10 Kelvin Bryant	1.00	.45	.12
☐ 11 Willie Collier	.50	.23	.06
☐ 12 Irv Eatman	.50	.23	.06
☐ 13 Scott Fitzkee	.50	.23	.06
☐ 14 William Fuller	6.00	2.70	.75
☐ 15 Chuck Fusina	.50	.23	.06
☐ 16 Pete Kugler	.50	.23	.06
☐ 17 Garcia Lane	.50	.23	.06
☐ 18 Mike Lush	.50	.23	.06
☐ 19 Sam Mills	7.00	3.10	.85
☐ 20 Buddy Aydelette	.50	.23	.06
☐ 21 Joe Cribbs	2.00	.90	.25
☐ 22 David Dumars	.50	.23	.06
☐ 23 Robin Earl	.50	.23	.06
☐ 24 Joey Jones	.50	.23	.06
☐ 25 Leon Perry	.50	.23	.06
☐ 26 Dave Pureifory	.50	.23	.06
☐ 27 Bill Roe	.50	.23	.06
☐ 28 Doug Smith DT	2.00	.90	.25
☐ 29 Cliff Stoudt	1.00	.45	.12
☐ 30 Jeff Delaney	.50	.23	.06
☐ 31 Vince Evans	1.00	.45	.12
☐ 32 Leonard Harris	.50	.23	.06
☐ 33 Bill Johnson	.50	.23	.06
☐ 34 Marc Lewis	.50	.23	.06
☐ 35 David Martin	.50	.23	.06
☐ 36 Bruce Thornton	.50	.23	.06
☐ 37 Craig Walls	.50	.23	.06
☐ 38 Vincent White	.50	.23	.06
☐ 39 Luther Bradley	.50	.23	.06
☐ 40 Pete Catan	.50	.23	.06
☐ 41 Kiki DeAyala	.50	.23	.06
☐ 42 Toni Fritsch	.50	.23	.06
☐ 43 Sam Harrell	.50	.23	.06
☐ 44 Richard Johnson	1.00	.45	.12
☐ 45 Jim Kelly	25.00	11.00	3.10
☐ 46 Gerald McNeil	.50	.23	.06
☐ 47 Clarence Verdin	2.00	.90	.25
☐ 48 Dale Walters	.50	.23	.06
☐ 49 Gary Clark	15.00	6.75	1.85
☐ 50 Tom Dinkel	.50	.23	.06
☐ 51 Mike Edwards	.50	.23	.06
☐ 52 Brian Franco	.50	.23	.06
☐ 53 Bob Gruber	.50	.23	.06
☐ 54 Robbie Mahfouz	.50	.23	.06
☐ 55 Mike Rozier	1.00	.45	.12
☐ 56 Brian Sipe	1.00	.45	.12
☐ 57 J.T. Turner	.50	.23	.06
☐ 58 Howard Carson	.50	.23	.06
☐ 59 Wymon Henderson	.50	.23	.06
☐ 60 Kevin Nelson	.50	.23	.06
☐ 61 Jeff Partridge	.50	.23	.06
☐ 62 Ben Rudolph	.50	.23	.06
☐ 63 Jo Jo Townsell	1.00	.45	.12
☐ 64 Eddie Weaver	.50	.23	.06
☐ 65 Steve Young	60.00	27.00	7.50
☐ 66 Tony Zendejas	1.00	.45	.12
☐ 67 Mossy Cade	.50	.23	.06
☐ 68 Leonard Coleman	.50	.23	.06
☐ 69 John Corker	.50	.23	.06
☐ 70 Derrick Crawford	.50	.23	.06
☐ 71 Art Kuehn	.50	.23	.06
☐ 72 Walter Lewis	.50	.23	.06
☐ 73 Tyrone McGriff	.50	.23	.06
☐ 74 Tim Spencer	1.00	.45	.12
☐ 75 Reggie White	30.00	13.50	3.70
☐ 76 Gizmo Williams	2.00	.90	.25
☐ 77 Sam Bowers	.50	.23	.06
☐ 78 Maurice Carthon	1.00	.45	.12
☐ 79 Clarence Collins	.50	.23	.06
☐ 80 Doug Flutie	16.00	7.25	2.00
☐ 81 Freddie Gilbert	.50	.23	.06
☐ 82 Kerry Justin	.50	.23	.06
☐ 83 Dave Lapham	.50	.23	.06
☐ 84 Rick Partridge	.50	.23	.06
☐ 85 Roger Ruzek	1.00	.45	.12
☐ 86 Herschel Walker	8.00	3.60	1.00
☐ 87 Gordon Banks	.50	.23	.06
☐ 88 Monte Bennett	.50	.23	.06
☐ 89 Albert Bentley	1.00	.45	.12
☐ 90 Novo Bojovic	.50	.23	.06
☐ 91 Dave Browning	.50	.23	.06
☐ 92 Anthony Carter	3.00	1.35	.35
☐ 93 Bobby Hebert	2.00	.90	.25
☐ 94 Ray Pinney	.50	.23	.06
☐ 95 Stan Talley	.50	.23	.06
☐ 96 Ruben Vaughan	.50	.23	.06
☐ 97 Curtis Bledsoe	.50	.23	.06
☐ 98 Reggie Collier	.50	.23	.06
☐ 99 Jerry Doerger	.50	.23	.06
☐ 100 Jerry Golsteyn	.50	.23	.06
☐ 101 Bob Niziolek	.50	.23	.06
☐ 102 Joel Patten	.50	.23	.06
☐ 103 Ricky Simmons	.50	.23	.06
☐ 104 Joey Walters	.50	.23	.06
☐ 105 Marcus Dupree	1.00	.45	.12
☐ 106 Jeff Gossett	1.00	.45	.12
☐ 107 Frank Lockett	.50	.23	.06
☐ 108 Marcus Marek	.50	.23	.06
☐ 109 Kenny Neil	.50	.23	.06
☐ 110 Robert Pennywell	.50	.23	.06
☐ 111 Matt Robinson	.50	.23	.06
☐ 112 Dan Ross	1.00	.45	.12
☐ 113 Doug Woodward	.50	.23	.06
☐ 114 Danny Buggs	.50	.23	.06
☐ 115 Putt Choate	.50	.23	.06
☐ 116 Greg Fields	.50	.23	.06
☐ 117 Ken Hartley	.50	.23	.06
☐ 118 Nick Mike-Mayer	.50	.23	.06
☐ 119 Rick Neuheisel	2.00	.90	.25
☐ 120 Peter Raeford	.50	.23	.06
☐ 121 Gary Worthy	.50	.23	.06
☐ 122 Gary Anderson RB	1.00	.45	.12
☐ 123 Zenon Andrusyshyn	.50	.23	.06
☐ 124 Greg Boone	.50	.23	.06
☐ 125 Mike Butler	.50	.23	.06
☐ 126 Mike Clark	.50	.23	.06
☐ 127 Willie Gillespie	.50	.23	.06
☐ 128 James Harrell	.50	.23	.06
☐ 129 Marvin Harvey	.50	.23	.06
☐ 130 John Reaves	1.00	.45	.12
☐ 131 Eric Truvillion	.50	.23	.06
☐ 132 Checklist 1-132	.50	.23	.06

1985 Topps USFL Generals

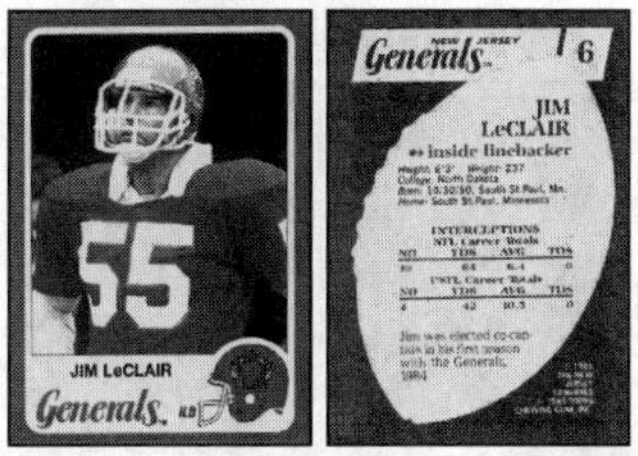

Topps produced this nine-card panel for the New Jersey Generals of the USFL. The entire panel measures approximately 7 1/2" by 10 1/2" and the individual cards, when cut, measure the standard size. Card backs are printed in yellow and red on gray card stock. The panels were supposedly distributed to members of the Generals' Infantry Club, which was a fan club for youngsters. The values below are applicable also for uncut sheets as that is the most common way this set is seen.

	MINT	NRMT	EXC
COMPLETE SET (9)	25.00	11.00	3.10
COMMON CARD (1-9)	1.25	.55	.16
☐ 1 Walt Michaels CO	2.00	.90	.25
☐ 2 Sam Bowers	1.25	.55	.16
☐ 3 Clarence Collins	1.25	.55	.16
☐ 4 Doug Flutie	8.00	3.60	1.00
☐ 5 Gregory Johnson	1.25	.55	.16
☐ 6 Jim LeClair	1.25	.55	.16
☐ 7 Bobby Leopold	1.25	.55	.16
☐ 8 Herschel Walker	12.00	5.50	1.50
☐ 9 Membership card (Schedule on back)	1.25	.55	.16

1986 Topps

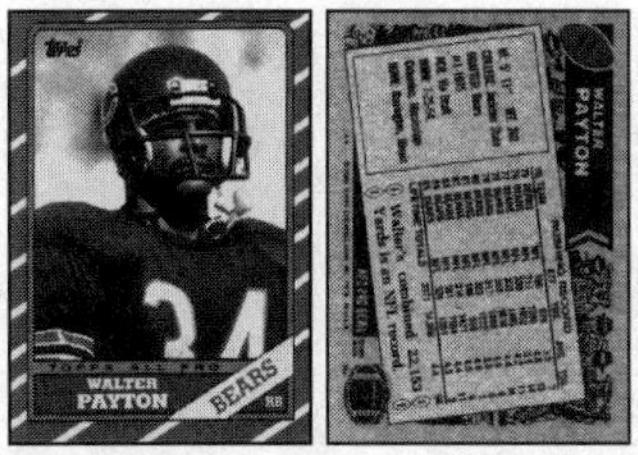

The 1986 Topps football card set contains 396 standard-size cards. As if to resemble a football field, player photos are surrounded by green borders with white lines. The player's name, team name and position are at the bottom. Horizontally designed backs have yearly statistics and highlights. The upper border has a sketching of football fans. Subsets include Record Breakers (1-7) and league leaders (225-229). Team cards feature a distinctive yellow border on the front with the team's results and leaders (from the previous season) listed on the back. The set numbering is in order of 1984 finish. Rookie Cards in this set include Mark Bavaro, Eddie Brown, Kevin Butler, Earnest Byner, Ray Childress, Boomer Esiason, Jay Hilgenberg, Bernie Kosar, Wilber Marshall, Karl Mecklenburg, William Perry, Andre Reed, Jerry Rice, Bruce Smith and Al Toon. In addition, Anthony Carter, Gary Clark, Bobby Hebert, Reggie White and Steve Young are Rookie Cards, although they had each appeared in a previous Topps USFL set.

	MINT	NRMT	EXC
COMPLETE SET (396)	180.00	80.00	22.00
COMMON CARD (1-396)	.08	.04	.01

☐ 1 Marcus Allen RB Most Yards From Scrimmage, Season	.75	.35	.09
☐ 2 Eric Dickerson RB Most Yards Rushing, Playoff Game	.30	.14	.04
☐ 3 Lionel James RB Most All-Purpose Yards, Season	.10	.05	.01
☐ 4 Steve Largent RB Most Seasons, 50 or More Receptions	.30	.14	.04
☐ 5 George Martin RB Most Touchdowns, Def. Lineman, Career	.10	.05	.01
☐ 6 Stephone Paige RB Most Yards Receiving, Game	.10	.05	.01
☐ 7 Walter Payton RB Most Consecutive Games, 100 or More Yards Rushing	.75	.35	.09
☐ 8 Super Bowl XX Bears 46, Patriots 10 (Jim McMahon handing off)	.30	.14	.04
☐ 9 Bears TL (Walter Payton in Motion)	.60	.25	.07
☐ 10 Jim McMahon	.30	.14	.04
☐ 11 Walter Payton AP	2.00	.90	.25
☐ 12 Matt Suhey	.08	.04	.01
☐ 13 Willie Gault	.15	.07	.02
☐ 14 Dennis McKinnon	.08	.04	.01
☐ 15 Emery Moorehead	.08	.04	.01
☐ 16 Jim Covert AP	.15	.07	.02
☐ 17 Jay Hilgenberg AP	.30	.14	.04
☐ 18 Kevin Butler	.15	.07	.02
☐ 19 Richard Dent AP	.75	.35	.09
☐ 20 William Perry	.50	.23	.06
☐ 21 Steve McMichael	.30	.14	.04
☐ 22 Dan Hampton	.30	.14	.04
☐ 23 Otis Wilson	.08	.04	.01
☐ 24 Mike Singletary	.60	.25	.07
☐ 25 Wilber Marshall	.30	.14	.04
☐ 26 Leslie Frazier	.08	.04	.01
☐ 27 Dave Duerson	.08	.04	.01
☐ 28 Gary Fencik	.08	.04	.01
☐ 29 Patriots TL (Craig James on the Run)	.30	.14	.04
☐ 30 Tony Eason	.08	.04	.01
☐ 31 Steve Grogan	.15	.07	.02
☐ 32 Craig James	.30	.14	.04
☐ 33 Tony Collins	.08	.04	.01
☐ 34 Irving Fryar	1.25	.55	.16
☐ 35 Brian Holloway AP	.08	.04	.01
☐ 36 John Hannah AP	.30	.14	.04
☐ 37 Tony Franklin	.08	.04	.01
☐ 38 Garin Veris	.08	.04	.01
☐ 39 Andre Tippett AP	.15	.07	.02
☐ 40 Steve Nelson	.08	.04	.01
☐ 41 Raymond Clayborn	.08	.04	.01
☐ 42 Fred Marion	.08	.04	.01
☐ 43 Rich Camarillo	.08	.04	.01
☐ 44 Dolphins TL (Dan Marino Sets Up)	3.00	1.35	.35
☐ 45 Dan Marino AP	20.00	9.00	2.50
☐ 46 Tony Nathan	.15	.07	.02
☐ 47 Ron Davenport	.08	.04	.01
☐ 48 Mark Duper	.30	.14	.04
☐ 49 Mark Clayton	.30	.14	.04
☐ 50 Nat Moore	.15	.07	.02
☐ 51 Bruce Hardy	.08	.04	.01
☐ 52 Roy Foster	.08	.04	.01
☐ 53 Dwight Stephenson	.15	.07	.02
☐ 54 Fuad Reveiz	.15	.07	.02
☐ 55 Bob Baumhower	.08	.04	.01
☐ 56 Mike Charles	.08	.04	.01
☐ 57 Hugh Green	.15	.07	.02
☐ 58 Glenn Blackwood	.08	.04	.01
☐ 59 Reggie Roby	.15	.07	.02
☐ 60 Raiders TL (Marcus Allen Cuts Upfield)	.30	.14	.04
☐ 61 Marc Wilson	.08	.04	.01
☐ 62 Marcus Allen AP	1.50	.70	.19
☐ 63 Dokie Williams	.08	.04	.01
☐ 64 Todd Christensen	.30	.14	.04
☐ 65 Chris Bahr	.08	.04	.01
☐ 66 Fulton Walker	.08	.04	.01
☐ 67 Howie Long	1.25	.55	.16
☐ 68 Bill Pickel	.08	.04	.01
☐ 69 Ray Guy	.30	.14	.04
☐ 70 Greg Townsend	.30	.14	.04
☐ 71 Rod Martin	.15	.07	.02
☐ 72 Matt Millen	.15	.07	.02
☐ 73 Mike Haynes AP	.15	.07	.02
☐ 74 Lester Hayes	.15	.07	.02
☐ 75 Vann McElroy	.08	.04	.01
☐ 76 Rams TL (Eric Dickerson Stiff-Arm)	.30	.14	.04
☐ 77 Dieter Brock	.15	.07	.02
☐ 78 Eric Dickerson	.75	.35	.09
☐ 79 Henry Ellard	1.00	.45	.12
☐ 80 Ron Brown	.15	.07	.02
☐ 81 Tony Hunter	.08	.04	.01
☐ 82 Kent Hill AP	.08	.04	.01
☐ 83 Doug Smith	.08	.04	.01
☐ 84 Dennis Harrah	.08	.04	.01
☐ 85 Jackie Slater	.30	.14	.04
☐ 86 Mike Lansford	.08	.04	.01
☐ 87 Gary Jeter	.08	.04	.01
☐ 88 Mike Wilcher	.08	.04	.01
☐ 89 Jim Collins	.08	.04	.01
☐ 90 LeRoy Irvin	.15	.07	.02
☐ 91 Gary Green	.08	.04	.01
☐ 92 Nolan Cromwell	.15	.07	.02
☐ 93 Dale Hatcher	.08	.04	.01
☐ 94 Jets TL (Freeman McNeil Powers)	.10	.05	.01
☐ 95 Ken O'Brien	.30	.14	.04
☐ 96 Freeman McNeil	.15	.07	.02
☐ 97 Tony Paige	.08	.04	.01
☐ 98 Johnny Lam Jones	.08	.04	.01
☐ 99 Wesley Walker	.15	.07	.02
☐ 100 Kurt Sohn	.08	.04	.01
☐ 101 Al Toon	.30	.14	.04
☐ 102 Mickey Shuler	.08	.04	.01
☐ 103 Marvin Powell	.08	.04	.01
☐ 104 Pat Leahy	.08	.04	.01
☐ 105 Mark Gastineau	.15	.07	.02
☐ 106 Joe Klecko AP	.15	.07	.02
☐ 107 Marty Lyons	.08	.04	.01
☐ 108 Lance Mehl	.08	.04	.01
☐ 109 Bobby Jackson	.08	.04	.01
☐ 110 Dave Jennings	.08	.04	.01
☐ 111 Broncos TL (Sammy Winder Up Middle)	.10	.05	.01
☐ 112 John Elway	8.00	3.60	1.00
☐ 113 Sammy Winder	.15	.07	.02
☐ 114 Gerald Willhite	.08	.04	.01
☐ 115 Steve Watson	.08	.04	.01
☐ 116 Vance Johnson	.30	.14	.04
☐ 117 Rich Karlis	.08	.04	.01
☐ 118 Rulon Jones	.08	.04	.01
☐ 119 Karl Mecklenburg AP	.50	.23	.06
☐ 120 Louis Wright	.08	.04	.01
☐ 121 Mike Harden	.08	.04	.01
☐ 122 Dennis Smith	.30	.14	.04
☐ 123 Steve Foley	.08	.04	.01
☐ 124 Cowboys TL (Tony Hill Evades Defender)	.10	.05	.01
☐ 125 Danny White	.30	.14	.04
☐ 126 Tony Dorsett	.60	.25	.07
☐ 127 Timmy Newsome	.08	.04	.01
☐ 128 Mike Renfro	.08	.04	.01
☐ 129 Tony Hill	.15	.07	.02
☐ 130 Doug Cosbie AP	.15	.07	.02
☐ 131 Rafael Septien	.08	.04	.01
☐ 132 Ed Too Tall Jones	.30	.14	.04
☐ 133 Randy White	.30	.14	.04
☐ 134 Jim Jeffcoat	.30	.14	.04
☐ 135 Everson Walls AP	.15	.07	.02
☐ 136 Dennis Thurman	.08	.04	.01
☐ 137 Giants TL (Joe Morris Opening)	.10	.05	.01
☐ 138 Phil Simms	.50	.23	.06
☐ 139 Joe Morris	.30	.14	.04
☐ 140 George Adams	.08	.04	.01
☐ 141 Lionel Manuel	.15	.07	.02
☐ 142 Bobby Johnson	.08	.04	.01
☐ 143 Phil McConkey	.15	.07	.02
☐ 144 Mark Bavaro	.30	.14	.04
☐ 145 Zeke Mowatt	.08	.04	.01
☐ 146 Brad Benson	.08	.04	.01
☐ 147 Bart Oates	.15	.07	.02
☐ 148 Leonard Marshall AP	.30	.14	.04
☐ 149 Jim Burt	.15	.07	.02
☐ 150 George Martin	.08	.04	.01
☐ 151 Lawrence Taylor AP	1.25	.55	.16
☐ 152 Harry Carson AP	.15	.07	.02
☐ 153 Elvis Patterson	.08	.04	.01
☐ 154 Sean Landeta	.15	.07	.02
☐ 155 49ers TL (Roger Craig Scampers)	.30	.14	.04
☐ 156 Joe Montana	6.00	2.70	.75
☐ 157 Roger Craig	.30	.14	.04
☐ 158 Wendell Tyler	.08	.04	.01
☐ 159 Carl Monroe	.08	.04	.01
☐ 160 Dwight Clark	.15	.07	.02
☐ 161 Jerry Rice	110.00	50.00	14.00
☐ 162 Randy Cross	.15	.07	.02
☐ 163 Keith Fahnhorst	.08	.04	.01
☐ 164 Jeff Stover	.08	.04	.01
☐ 165 Michael Carter	.08	.04	.01
☐ 166 Dwaine Board	.08	.04	.01
☐ 167 Eric Wright	.15	.07	.02
☐ 168 Ronnie Lott	.75	.35	.09
☐ 169 Carlton Williamson	.08	.04	.01
☐ 170 Redskins TL (Dave Butz Gets His Man)	.10	.05	.01
☐ 171 Joe Theismann	.30	.14	.04
☐ 172 Jay Schroeder	.30	.14	.04
☐ 173 George Rogers	.15	.07	.02
☐ 174 Ken Jenkins	.08	.04	.01
☐ 175 Art Monk AP	.50	.23	.06
☐ 176 Gary Clark	2.00	.90	.25
☐ 177 Joe Jacoby	.15	.07	.02
☐ 178 Russ Grimm	.15	.07	.02
☐ 179 Mark Moseley	.08	.04	.01
☐ 180 Dexter Manley	.15	.07	.02
☐ 181 Charles Mann	.30	.14	.04

#	Player	MINT	NRMT	EXC
182	Vernon Dean	.08	.04	.01
183	Raphel Cherry	.08	.04	.01
184	Curtis Jordan	.08	.04	.01
185	Browns TL	.30	.14	.04
	(Bernie Kosar Fakes Handoff)			
186	Gary Danielson	.15	.07	.02
187	Bernie Kosar	1.00	.45	.12
188	Kevin Mack	.30	.14	.04
189	Earnest Byner	.75	.35	.09
190	Glen Young	.08	.04	.01
191	Ozzie Newsome	.30	.14	.04
192	Mike Baab	.08	.04	.01
193	Cody Risien	.15	.07	.02
194	Bob Golic	.15	.07	.02
195	Reggie Camp	.08	.04	.01
196	Chip Banks	.15	.07	.02
197	Tom Cousineau	.08	.04	.01
198	Frank Minnifield	.08	.04	.01
199	Al Gross	.08	.04	.01
200	Seahawks TL	.10	.05	.01
	(Curt Warner Breaks Free)			
201	Dave Krieg	.30	.14	.04
202	Curt Warner	.15	.07	.02
203	Steve Largent AP	.60	.25	.07
204	Norm Johnson	.08	.04	.01
205	Daryl Turner	.08	.04	.01
206	Jacob Green	.08	.04	.01
207	Joe Nash	.08	.04	.01
208	Jeff Bryant	.08	.04	.01
209	Randy Edwards	.08	.04	.01
210	Fredd Young	.08	.04	.01
211	Kenny Easley	.08	.04	.01
212	John Harris	.08	.04	.01
213	Packers TL	.10	.05	.01
	(Paul Coffman Conquers)			
214	Lynn Dickey	.15	.07	.02
215	Gerry Ellis	.08	.04	.01
216	Eddie Lee Ivery	.08	.04	.01
217	Jessie Clark	.08	.04	.01
218	James Lofton	.30	.14	.04
219	Paul Coffman	.08	.04	.01
220	Alphonso Carreker	.08	.04	.01
221	Ezra Johnson	.08	.04	.01
222	Mike Douglass	.08	.04	.01
223	Tim Lewis	.08	.04	.01
224	Mark Murphy	.08	.04	.01
225	Passing Leaders:	1.00	.45	.12
	Ken O'Brien AFC			
	Joe Montana NFC			
226	Receiving Leaders:	.10	.05	.01
	Lionel James AFC			
	Roger Craig NFC			
227	Rushing Leaders:	.30	.14	.04
	Marcus Allen AFC			
	Gerald Riggs NFC			
228	Scoring Leaders:	.10	.05	.01
	Gary Anderson K AFC			
	Kevin Butler NFC			
229	Interception Leaders:	.10	.05	.01
	Eugene Daniel AFC#Albert Lewis AFC			
	Everson Walls NFC			
230	Chargers TL	.30	.14	.04
	(Dan Fouts Over Top)			
231	Dan Fouts	.50	.23	.06
232	Lionel James	.08	.04	.01
233	Gary Anderson RB	.30	.14	.04
234	Tim Spencer	.15	.07	.02
235	Wes Chandler	.15	.07	.02
236	Charlie Joiner	.30	.14	.04
237	Kellen Winslow	.30	.14	.04
238	Jim Lachey	.30	.14	.04
239	Bob Thomas	.08	.04	.01
240	Jeffery Dale	.08	.04	.01
241	Ralf Mojsiejenko	.08	.04	.01
242	Lions TL	.10	.05	.01
	(Eric Hipple Spots Receiver)			
243	Eric Hipple	.08	.04	.01
244	Billy Sims	.15	.07	.02
245	James Jones	.08	.04	.01
246	Pete Mandley	.08	.04	.01
247	Leonard Thompson	.08	.04	.01
248	Lomas Brown	.15	.07	.02
249	Eddie Murray	.15	.07	.02
250	Curtis Green	.08	.04	.01
251	William Gay	.08	.04	.01
252	Jimmy Williams	.08	.04	.01
253	Bobby Watkins	.08	.04	.01
254	Bengals TL	.30	.14	.04
	(Boomer Esiason Zeroes In)			
255	Boomer Esiason	2.00	.90	.25
256	James Brooks	.15	.07	.02
257	Larry Kinnebrew	.08	.04	.01
258	Cris Collinsworth	.15	.07	.02
259	Mike Martin	.08	.04	.01
260	Eddie Brown	.30	.14	.04
261	Anthony Munoz	.30	.14	.04
262	Jim Breech	.08	.04	.01
263	Ross Browner	.15	.07	.02
264	Carl Zander	.08	.04	.01
265	James Griffin	.08	.04	.01
266	Robert Jackson	.08	.04	.01
267	Pat McInally	.10	.05	.01
268	Eagles TL	.30	.14	.04
	(Ron Jaworski Surveys)			
269	Ron Jaworski	.15	.07	.02
270	Earnest Jackson	.15	.07	.02
271	Mike Quick	.15	.07	.02
272	John Spagnola	.08	.04	.01
273	Mark Dennard	.08	.04	.01
274	Paul McFadden	.08	.04	.01
275	Reggie White	10.00	4.50	1.25
276	Greg Brown	.08	.04	.01
277	Herman Edwards	.08	.04	.01
278	Roynell Young	.08	.04	.01
279	Wes Hopkins AP	.08	.04	.01
280	Steelers TL	.10	.05	.01
	(Walter Abercrombie Inches)			
281	Mark Malone	.15	.07	.02
282	Frank Pollard	.08	.04	.01
283	Walter Abercrombie	.08	.04	.01
284	Louis Lipps	.30	.14	.04
285	John Stallworth	.30	.14	.04
286	Mike Webster	.15	.07	.02
287	Gary Anderson K AP	.15	.07	.02
288	Keith Willis	.08	.04	.01
289	Mike Merriweather	.08	.04	.01
290	Dwayne Woodruff	.08	.04	.01
291	Donnie Shell	.15	.07	.02
292	Vikings TL	.10	.05	.01
	(Tommy Kramer Audible)			
293	Tommy Kramer	.15	.07	.02
294	Darrin Nelson	.08	.04	.01
295	Ted Brown	.15	.07	.02
296	Buster Rhymes	.08	.04	.01
297	Anthony Carter	1.00	.45	.12
298	Steve Jordan	.30	.14	.04
299	Keith Millard	.30	.14	.04
300	Joey Browner	.30	.14	.04
301	John Turner	.08	.04	.01
302	Greg Coleman	.08	.04	.01
303	Chiefs TL	.10	.05	.01
	(Todd Blackledge)			
304	Bill Kenney	.08	.04	.01
305	Herman Heard	.08	.04	.01
306	Stephone Paige	.30	.14	.04
307	Carlos Carson	.15	.07	.02
308	Nick Lowery	.15	.07	.02
309	Mike Bell	.08	.04	.01
310	Bill Maas	.08	.04	.01
311	Art Still	.08	.04	.01
312	Albert Lewis	.30	.14	.04
313	Deron Cherry AP	.15	.07	.02
314	Colts TL	.10	.05	.01
	(Rohn Stark Booms It)			
315	Mike Pagel	.08	.04	.01
316	Randy McMillan	.08	.04	.01
317	Albert Bentley	.15	.07	.02
318	George Wonsley	.08	.04	.01
319	Robbie Martin	.08	.04	.01
320	Pat Beach	.08	.04	.01
321	Chris Hinton	.15	.07	.02
322	Duane Bickett	.30	.14	.04
323	Eugene Daniel	.08	.04	.01
324	Cliff Odom	.08	.04	.01
325	Rohn Stark AP	.15	.07	.02
326	Cardinals TL	.10	.05	.01
	(Stump Mitchell Outside)			
327	Neil Lomax	.15	.07	.02
328	Stump Mitchell	.15	.07	.02
329	Ottis Anderson	.30	.14	.04
330	J.T. Smith	.15	.07	.02
331	Pat Tilley	.15	.07	.02
332	Roy Green	.15	.07	.02
333	Lance Smith	.08	.04	.01
334	Curtis Greer	.08	.04	.01
335	Freddie Joe Nunn	.15	.07	.02
336	E.J. Junior	.15	.07	.02
337	Lonnie Young	.08	.04	.01
338	Saints TL	.10	.05	.01
	(Wayne Wilson running)			
339	Bobby Hebert	.30	.14	.04
340	Dave Wilson	.08	.04	.01
341	Wayne Wilson	.08	.04	.01
342	Hoby Brenner	.08	.04	.01
343	Stan Brock	.15	.07	.02
344	Morten Andersen	.30	.14	.04
345	Bruce Clark	.08	.04	.01
346	Rickey Jackson	.30	.14	.04
347	Dave Waymer	.08	.04	.01
348	Brian Hansen	.08	.04	.01
349	Oilers TL	.60	.25	.07
	(Warren Moon Throws Bomb)			
350	Warren Moon	3.00	1.35	.35
351	Mike Rozier	.30	.14	.04
352	Butch Woolfolk	.08	.04	.01
353	Drew Hill	.30	.14	.04
354	Willie Drewrey	.08	.04	.01
355	Tim Smith	.15	.07	.02
356	Mike Munchak	.15	.07	.02
357	Ray Childress	.30	.14	.04
358	Frank Bush	.08	.04	.01
359	Steve Brown	.08	.04	.01
360	Falcons TL	.10	.05	.01
	(Gerald Riggs Around End)			
361	David Archer	.30	.14	.04
362	Gerald Riggs	.15	.07	.02
363	William Andrews	.15	.07	.02
364	Billy Johnson	.15	.07	.02
365	Arthur Cox	.08	.04	.01
366	Mike Kenn	.08	.04	.01
367	Bill Fralic	.15	.07	.02
368	Mick Luckhurst	.08	.04	.01
369	Rick Bryan	.08	.04	.01
370	Bobby Butler	.08	.04	.01
371	Rick Donnelly	.08	.04	.01
372	Buccaneers TL	.10	.05	.01
	(James Wilder Sweeps Left)			
373	Steve DeBerg	.30	.14	.04
374	Steve Young	25.00	11.00	3.10
375	James Wilder	.08	.04	.01
376	Kevin House	.08	.04	.01
377	Gerald Carter	.08	.04	.01
378	Jimmie Giles	.15	.07	.02
379	Sean Farrell	.08	.04	.01
380	Donald Igwebuike	.08	.04	.01
381	David Logan	.08	.04	.01
382	Jeremiah Castille	.08	.04	.01
383	Bills TL	.10	.05	.01
	(Greg Bell Sees Daylight)			
384	Bruce Mathison	.08	.04	.01
385	Joe Cribbs	.15	.07	.02
386	Greg Bell	.15	.07	.02
387	Jerry Butler	.08	.04	.01
388	Andre Reed	4.00	1.80	.50
389	Bruce Smith	6.00	2.70	.75
390	Fred Smerlas	.08	.04	.01
391	Darryl Talley	.30	.14	.04
392	Jim Haslett	.08	.04	.01
393	Charles Romes	.08	.04	.01
394	Checklist 1-132	.08	.04	.01
395	Checklist 133-264	.08	.04	.01
396	Checklist 265-396	.08	.04	.01

1986 Topps Box Bottoms

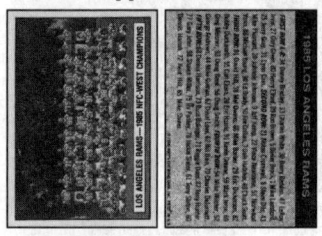

This four-card set, which measures 2 1/2" by 3 1/2", features the four teams which participated in the Super Bowl and in the Conference Championships. This set is arranged in order of how the teams finished, with the Super Bowl Champion Bears being the first team listed. The fronts of the card feature a team photo and identification of all those players is pictured on the back of the card. The cards were issued one per wax box as the side panel of the box, not on the box bottom as was typical of similar sets.

		MINT	NRMT	EXC
	COMPLETE SET (4)	8.00	3.60	1.00
	COMMON CARD (A-D)	1.50	.70	.19
A	Chicago Bears	2.50	1.10	.30
	NFL Champions			
B	New England Patriots	1.50	.70	.19
	AFC Champions			
C	Los Angeles Rams	1.50	.70	.19
	NFC West Champions			
D	Miami Dolphins	4.00	1.80	.50
	AFC East Champions			

1986 Topps 1000 Yard Club

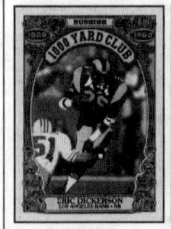 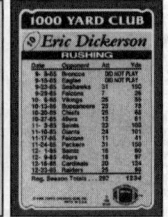

This 26-card standard-size set was distributed as an insert with the 1986 Topps regular issue football wax packs. Players featured are all members of the 1000-yard club, having gained over 1000 yards rushing or receiving during the previous season. The cards are numbered on back according to decreasing order of yardage gained. Roger Craig (22) actually gained over 1000 yards both rushing and receiving. Card backs have orange and red printing on white card stock. The obverses have an ornate border design of green and yellow.

		MINT	NRMT	EXC
	COMPLETE SET (26)	6.00	2.70	.75
	COMMON CARD (1-26)	.25	.11	.03
1	Marcus Allen	2.00	.90	.25
2	Gerald Riggs	.25	.11	.03
3	Walter Payton	1.50	.70	.19
4	Joe Morris	.25	.11	.03
5	Freeman McNeil	.25	.11	.03
6	Tony Dorsett	.75	.35	.09
7	James Wilder	.25	.11	.03
8	Steve Largent	1.00	.45	.12
9	Mike Quick	.25	.11	.03
10	Eric Dickerson	.60	.25	.07
11	Craig James	.40	.18	.05
12	Art Monk	.60	.25	.07
13	Wes Chandler	.25	.11	.03
14	Drew Hill	.25	.11	.03
15	James Lofton	.60	.25	.07
16	Louis Lipps	.25	.11	.03
17	Cris Collinsworth	.25	.11	.03
18	Tony Hill	.25	.11	.03
19	Kevin Mack	.25	.11	.03
20	Curt Warner	.25	.11	.03
21	George Rogers	.25	.11	.03
22	Roger Craig	.40	.18	.05
23	Earnest Jackson	.25	.11	.03
24	Lionel James	.25	.11	.03
25	Stump Mitchell	.25	.11	.03
26	Earnest Byner	.25	.11	.03

1987 Topps

 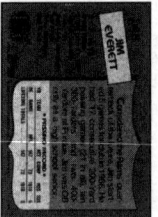

The 1987 Topps set consists of 396 standard-size cards. Wax packs contained 15 cards as well as a 1,000 yard club card. For the first time, hobby factory sets were issued. Card fronts have the team and player name in banners at the top above the player photo. These banners are in the colors of the player's team. The backs have highlights and statistics within an outline of the NFL shield. To the left is biographical information. Subsets include Record Breakers (2-8) and league leaders (227-231). The set numbering is ordered by teams. Team cards feature an action photo on the front with the team's statistical leaders and week-by-week game results from the previous season on back. Rookie Cards include Bill Brooks, Keith Byars, Randall Cunningham, Kenneth Davis, Jim Everett, Doug Flutie, Ernest Givins, Charles Haley, Sean Jones, Eric Martin and Jim Kelly. Kelly and Flutie previously appeared in a USFL set.

		MINT	NRMT	EXC
	COMPLETE SET (396)	30.00	13.50	3.70
	COMPLETE FACT.SET (396)	30.00	13.50	3.70
	COMMON CARD (1-396)	.05	.02	.01
1	Super Bowl XXI	.25	.11	.03
	Giants 39,			
	Broncos 20			
	(Line play shown)			
2	Todd Christensen RB	.05	.02	.01
	Most Seasons,			
	80 or More Receptions			
3	Dave Jennings RB	.05	.02	.01
	Most Punts, Career			
4	Charlie Joiner RB	.10	.05	.01
	Most Receiving			
	Yards, Career			
5	Steve Largent RB	.25	.11	.03
	Most Cons. Games			
	With a Reception			
6	Dan Marino RB	3.00	1.35	.35
	Most Cons. Seasons,			
	30 or More TD Passes			
7	Donnie Shell RB	.10	.05	.01
	Most Interceptions,			
	Strong Safety, Career			
8	Phil Simms RB	.10	.05	.01
	Highest Completion			
	Percentage, Super Bowl			
9	New York Giants	.10	.05	.01
	Team Card			
	(Mark Bavaro Pulls Free)			
10	Phil Simms	.25	.11	.03
11	Joe Morris AP	.10	.05	.01
12	Maurice Carthon	.05	.02	.01
13	Lee Rouson	.05	.02	.01
14	Bobby Johnson	.05	.02	.01
15	Lionel Manuel	.05	.02	.01
16	Phil McConkey	.05	.02	.01
17	Mark Bavaro AP	.25	.11	.03
18	Zeke Mowatt	.05	.02	.01
19	Raul Allegre	.05	.02	.01
20	Sean Landeta	.05	.02	.01
21	Brad Benson	.05	.02	.01
22	Jim Burt	.05	.02	.01
23	Leonard Marshall	.25	.11	.03
24	Carl Banks	.25	.11	.03
25	Harry Carson	.25	.11	.03
26	Lawrence Taylor AP	.75	.35	.09
27	Terry Kinard	.05	.02	.01
28	Pepper Johnson	.25	.11	.03
29	Erik Howard	.05	.02	.01
30	Broncos TL	.05	.02	.01
	(Gerald Willhite Dives)			
31	John Elway	4.00	1.80	.50

☐ 32 Gerald Willhite	.05	.02	.01
☐ 33 Sammy Winder	.10	.05	.01
☐ 34 Ken Bell	.05	.02	.01
☐ 35 Steve Watson	.05	.02	.01
☐ 36 Rich Karlis	.05	.02	.01
☐ 37 Keith Bishop	.05	.02	.01
☐ 38 Rulon Jones	.05	.02	.01
☐ 39 Karl Mecklenburg AP	.25	.11	.03
☐ 40 Louis Wright	.05	.02	.01
☐ 41 Mike Harden	.05	.02	.01
☐ 42 Dennis Smith	.10	.05	.01
☐ 43 Bears TL	.50	.23	.06
(Walter Payton Barrels)			
☐ 44 Jim McMahon	.25	.11	.03
☐ 45 Doug Flutie	2.00	.90	.25
☐ 46 Walter Payton	1.25	.55	.16
☐ 47 Matt Suhey	.05	.02	.01
☐ 48 Willie Gault	.10	.05	.01
☐ 49 Dennis Gentry	.05	.02	.01
☐ 50 Kevin Butler	.05	.02	.01
☐ 51 Jim Covert AP	.05	.02	.01
☐ 52 Jay Hilgenberg	.10	.05	.01
☐ 53 Dan Hampton	.10	.05	.01
☐ 54 Steve McMichael	.25	.11	.03
☐ 55 William Perry	.25	.11	.03
☐ 56 Richard Dent	.25	.11	.03
☐ 57 Otis Wilson	.05	.02	.01
☐ 58 Mike Singletary AP	.25	.11	.03
☐ 59 Wilber Marshall	.25	.11	.03
☐ 60 Mike Richardson	.05	.02	.01
☐ 61 Dave Duerson	.05	.02	.01
☐ 62 Gary Fencik	.05	.02	.01
☐ 63 Redskins TL	.10	.05	.01
(George Rogers Plunges)			
☐ 64 Jay Schroeder	.10	.05	.01
☐ 65 George Rogers	.10	.05	.01
☐ 66 Kelvin Bryant	.10	.05	.01
☐ 67 Ken Jenkins	.05	.02	.01
☐ 68 Gary Clark	.50	.23	.06
☐ 69 Art Monk	.25	.11	.03
☐ 70 Clint Didier	.05	.02	.01
☐ 71 Steve Cox	.05	.02	.01
☐ 72 Joe Jacoby	.05	.02	.01
☐ 73 Russ Grimm	.05	.02	.01
☐ 74 Charles Mann	.10	.05	.01
☐ 75 Dave Butz	.05	.02	.01
☐ 76 Dexter Manley AP	.10	.05	.01
☐ 77 Darrell Green AP	.25	.11	.03
☐ 78 Curtis Jordan	.05	.02	.01
☐ 79 Browns TL	.05	.02	.01
(Harry Holt Sees Daylight)			
☐ 80 Bernie Kosar	.25	.11	.03
☐ 81 Curtis Dickey	.05	.02	.01
☐ 82 Kevin Mack	.10	.05	.01
☐ 83 Herman Fontenot	.05	.02	.01
☐ 84 Brian Brennan	.05	.02	.01
☐ 85 Ozzie Newsome	.25	.11	.03
☐ 86 Jeff Gossett	.10	.05	.01
☐ 87 Cody Risien AP	.05	.02	.01
☐ 88 Reggie Camp	.05	.02	.01
☐ 89 Bob Golic	.05	.02	.01
☐ 90 Carl Hairston	.05	.02	.01
☐ 91 Chip Banks	.05	.02	.01
☐ 92 Frank Minnifield	.05	.02	.01
☐ 93 Hanford Dixon AP	.05	.02	.01
☐ 94 Gerald McNeil	.05	.02	.01
☐ 95 Dave Puzzuoli	.05	.02	.01
☐ 96 Patriots TL	.05	.02	.01
(Andre Tippett Gets			
His Man (Marcus Allen))			
☐ 97 Tony Eason	.10	.05	.01
☐ 98 Craig James	.10	.05	.01
☐ 99 Tony Collins	.10	.05	.01
☐ 100 Mosi Tatupu	.05	.02	.01
☐ 101 Stanley Morgan	.10	.05	.01
☐ 102 Irving Fryar	.50	.23	.06
☐ 103 Stephen Starring	.05	.02	.01
☐ 104 Tony Franklin AP	.05	.02	.01
☐ 105 Rich Camarillo	.05	.02	.01
☐ 106 Garin Veris	.05	.02	.01
☐ 107 Andre Tippett AP	.10	.05	.01
☐ 108 Don Blackmon	.05	.02	.01
☐ 109 Ronnie Lippett	.05	.02	.01
☐ 110 Raymond Clayborn	.05	.02	.01
☐ 111 49ers TL	.10	.05	.01
(Roger Craig Up the Middle)			
☐ 112 Joe Montana	5.00	2.20	.60
☐ 113 Roger Craig	.25	.11	.03
☐ 114 Joe Cribbs	.10	.05	.01
☐ 115 Jerry Rice AP	12.00	5.50	1.50
☐ 116 Dwight Clark	.10	.05	.01
☐ 117 Ray Wersching	.05	.02	.01
☐ 118 Max Runager	.05	.02	.01
☐ 119 Jeff Stover	.05	.02	.01
☐ 120 Dwaine Board	.05	.02	.01
☐ 121 Tim McKyer	.10	.05	.01
☐ 122 Don Griffin	.10	.05	.01
☐ 123 Ronnie Lott AP	.40	.18	.05
☐ 124 Tom Holmoe	.05	.02	.01
☐ 125 Charles Haley	1.50	.70	.19
☐ 126 Jets TL	.05	.02	.01
(Mark Gastineau Seeks)			
☐ 127 Ken O'Brien	.10	.05	.01
☐ 128 Pat Ryan	.05	.02	.01
☐ 129 Freeman McNeil	.10	.05	.01
☐ 130 Johnny Hector	.05	.02	.01
☐ 131 Al Toon AP	.25	.11	.03
☐ 132 Wesley Walker	.10	.05	.01
☐ 133 Mickey Shuler	.05	.02	.01
☐ 134 Pat Leahy	.05	.02	.01
☐ 135 Mark Gastineau	.10	.05	.01
☐ 136 Joe Klecko	.10	.05	.01
☐ 137 Marty Lyons	.05	.02	.01
☐ 138 Bob Crable	.05	.02	.01
☐ 139 Lance Mehl	.05	.02	.01
☐ 140 Dave Jennings	.05	.02	.01
☐ 141 Harry Hamilton	.05	.02	.01
☐ 142 Lester Lyles	.05	.02	.01
☐ 143 Bobby Humphery UER	.05	.02	.01
(Misspelled Humphrey			
on card front)			
☐ 144 Rams TL	.25	.11	.03
(Eric Dickerson			
Through the Line)			
☐ 145 Jim Everett	2.00	.90	.25
☐ 146 Eric Dickerson AP	.25	.11	.03
☐ 147 Barry Redden	.05	.02	.01
☐ 148 Ron Brown	.10	.05	.01
☐ 149 Kevin House	.05	.02	.01
☐ 150 Henry Ellard	.40	.18	.05
☐ 151 Doug Smith	.05	.02	.01
☐ 152 Dennis Harrah AP	.05	.02	.01
☐ 153 Jackie Slater	.10	.05	.01
☐ 154 Gary Jeter	.05	.02	.01
☐ 155 Carl Ekern	.05	.02	.01
☐ 156 Mike Wilcher	.05	.02	.01
☐ 157 Jerry Gray	.05	.02	.01
☐ 158 LeRoy Irvin	.05	.02	.01
☐ 159 Nolan Cromwell	.10	.05	.01
☐ 160 Chiefs TL	.05	.02	.01
(Todd Blackledge Hands Off)			
☐ 161 Bill Kenney	.05	.02	.01
☐ 162 Stephone Paige	.10	.05	.01
☐ 163 Henry Marshall	.05	.02	.01
☐ 164 Carlos Carson	.05	.02	.01
☐ 165 Nick Lowery	.10	.05	.01
☐ 166 Irv Eatman	.05	.02	.01
☐ 167 Brad Budde	.05	.02	.01
☐ 168 Art Still	.05	.02	.01
☐ 169 Bill Maas AP	.05	.02	.01
☐ 170 Lloyd Burruss	.05	.02	.01
☐ 171 Deron Cherry AP	.05	.02	.01
☐ 172 Seahawks TL	.10	.05	.01
(Curt Warner Finds Opening)			
☐ 173 Dave Krieg	.25	.11	.03
☐ 174 Curt Warner	.10	.05	.01
☐ 175 John L. Williams	.25	.11	.03
☐ 176 Bobby Joe Edmonds	.10	.05	.01
☐ 177 Steve Largent	.60	.25	.07
☐ 178 Bruce Scholtz	.05	.02	.01
☐ 179 Norm Johnson	.05	.02	.01
☐ 180 Jacob Green	.05	.02	.01
☐ 181 Fredd Young	.05	.02	.01
☐ 182 Dave Brown	.05	.02	.01
☐ 183 Kenny Easley	.05	.02	.01
☐ 184 Bengals TL	.10	.05	.01
(James Brooks Stiff-Arm)			
☐ 185 Boomer Esiason	.50	.23	.06
☐ 186 James Brooks	.10	.05	.01
☐ 187 Larry Kinnebrew	.05	.02	.01
☐ 188 Cris Collinsworth	.10	.05	.01
☐ 189 Eddie Brown	.25	.11	.03
☐ 190 Tim McGee	.25	.11	.03
☐ 191 Jim Breech	.05	.02	.01
☐ 192 Anthony Munoz	.25	.11	.03
☐ 193 Max Montoya	.05	.02	.01
☐ 194 Eddie Edwards	.05	.02	.01
☐ 195 Ross Browner	.10	.05	.01
☐ 196 Emanuel King	.05	.02	.01
☐ 197 Louis Breeden	.05	.02	.01
☐ 198 Vikings TL	.05	.02	.01
(Darrin Nelson In Motion)			
☐ 199 Tommy Kramer	.10	.05	.01
☐ 200 Darrin Nelson	.05	.02	.01
☐ 201 Allen Rice	.05	.02	.01
☐ 202 Anthony Carter	.25	.11	.03
☐ 203 Leo Lewis	.05	.02	.01
☐ 204 Steve Jordan	.25	.11	.03
☐ 205 Chuck Nelson	.05	.02	.01
☐ 206 Greg Coleman	.05	.02	.01
☐ 207 Gary Zimmerman	.10	.05	.01
☐ 208 Doug Martin	.05	.02	.01
☐ 209 Keith Millard	.05	.02	.01
☐ 210 Issiac Holt	.05	.02	.01
☐ 211 Joey Browner	.10	.05	.01
☐ 212 Rufus Bess	.05	.02	.01
☐ 213 Raiders TL	.25	.11	.03
(Marcus Allen Quick Feet)			
☐ 214 Jim Plunkett	.25	.11	.03
☐ 215 Marcus Allen	1.00	.45	.12
☐ 216 Napoleon McCallum	.10	.05	.01
☐ 217 Dokie Williams	.05	.02	.01
☐ 218 Todd Christensen	.25	.11	.03
☐ 219 Chris Bahr	.05	.02	.01
☐ 220 Howie Long	.60	.25	.07
☐ 221 Bill Pickel	.05	.02	.01
☐ 222 Sean Jones	.75	.35	.09
☐ 223 Lester Hayes	.10	.05	.01
☐ 224 Mike Haynes	.10	.05	.01
☐ 225 Vann McElroy	.05	.02	.01
☐ 226 Fulton Walker	.05	.02	.01
☐ 227 Passing Leaders	1.50	.70	.19
Tommy Kramer,			
Minnesota Vikings			
Dan Marino,			
☐ 228 Receiving Leaders	1.25	.55	.16
Jerry Rice,			
San Francisco 49ers			
Todd Christensen,			
☐ 229 Rushing Leaders	.25	.11	.03
Eric Dickerson,			
Los Angeles Rams			
Curt Warner,			
☐ 230 Scoring Leaders	.05	.02	.01
Kevin Butler,			
Chicago Bears			
Tony Franklin,			
☐ 231 Interception Leaders	.10	.05	.01
Ronnie Lott,			
San Francisco 49ers			
Deron Cherry,			
☐ 232 Dolphins TL	.05	.02	.01
(Reggie Roby Booms It)			
☐ 233 Dan Marino AP	8.00	3.60	1.00
☐ 234 Lorenzo Hampton	.05	.02	.01
☐ 235 Tony Nathan	.10	.05	.01
☐ 236 Mark Duper	.25	.11	.03
☐ 237 Mark Clayton	.25	.11	.03
☐ 238 Nat Moore	.10	.05	.01
☐ 239 Bruce Hardy	.05	.02	.01
☐ 240 Reggie Roby	.10	.05	.01
☐ 241 Roy Foster	.05	.02	.01
☐ 242 Dwight Stephenson AP	.10	.05	.01
☐ 243 Hugh Green	.05	.02	.01
☐ 244 John Offerdahl	.25	.11	.03
☐ 245 Mark Brown	.05	.02	.01
☐ 246 Doug Betters	.05	.02	.01
☐ 247 Bob Baumhower	.05	.02	.01
☐ 248 Falcons TL	.10	.05	.01
(Gerald Riggs Uses Blockers)			
☐ 249 David Archer	.25	.11	.03
☐ 250 Gerald Riggs	.10	.05	.01
☐ 251 William Andrews	.10	.05	.01
☐ 252 Charlie Brown	.05	.02	.01
☐ 253 Arthur Cox	.05	.02	.01
☐ 254 Rick Donnelly	.05	.02	.01
☐ 255 Bill Fralic AP	.05	.02	.01
☐ 256 Mike Gann	.05	.02	.01
☐ 257 Rick Bryan	.05	.02	.01
☐ 258 Bret Clark	.05	.02	.01
☐ 259 Mike Pitts	.05	.02	.01
☐ 260 Cowboys TL	.25	.11	.03
(Tony Dorsett Cuts)			
☐ 261 Danny White	.25	.11	.03
☐ 262 Steve Pelluer	.05	.02	.01
☐ 263 Tony Dorsett	.50	.23	.06
☐ 264 Herschel Walker UER	2.00	.90	.25
(Stats show 12 TD's			
in '86, text says 14)			
☐ 265 Timmy Newsome	.05	.02	.01
☐ 266 Tony Hill	.10	.05	.01
☐ 267 Mike Sherrard	.25	.11	.03
☐ 268 Jim Jeffcoat	.25	.11	.03
☐ 269 Ron Fellows	.05	.02	.01
☐ 270 Bill Bates	.25	.11	.03
☐ 271 Michael Downs	.05	.02	.01
☐ 272 Saints TL	.10	.05	.01
(Bobby Hebert Fakes)			
☐ 273 Dave Wilson	.05	.02	.01
☐ 274 Rueben Mayes UER	.05	.02	.01
(Stats show 1353 comple-			
tions, should be yards)			
☐ 275 Hoby Brenner	.05	.02	.01
☐ 276 Eric Martin	.25	.11	.03
☐ 277 Morten Andersen	.10	.05	.01
☐ 278 Brian Hansen	.05	.02	.01
☐ 279 Rickey Jackson	.25	.11	.03
☐ 280 Dave Waymer	.05	.02	.01
☐ 281 Bruce Clark	.05	.02	.01
☐ 282 James Geathers	.10	.05	.01
☐ 283 Steelers TL	.05	.02	.01
(Walter Abercrombie Resists)			
☐ 284 Mark Malone	.10	.05	.01
☐ 285 Earnest Jackson	.05	.02	.01
☐ 286 Walter Abercrombie	.05	.02	.01
☐ 287 Louis Lipps	.10	.05	.01
☐ 288 John Stallworth UER	.25	.11	.03
(Stats only go up			
through 1981)			
☐ 289 Gary Anderson K	.05	.02	.01
☐ 290 Keith Willis	.05	.02	.01
☐ 291 Mike Merriweather	.05	.02	.01
☐ 292 Lupe Sanchez	.05	.02	.01
☐ 293 Donnie Shell	.10	.05	.01
☐ 294 Eagles TL	.25	.11	.03
(Keith Byars Inches Ahead)			
☐ 295 Mike Reichenbach	.05	.02	.01
☐ 296 Randall Cunningham	2.50	1.10	.30
☐ 297 Keith Byars	.75	.35	.09
☐ 298 Mike Quick	.10	.05	.01
☐ 299 Kenny Jackson	.05	.02	.01
☐ 300 John Teltschik	.05	.02	.01
☐ 301 Reggie White AP	3.00	1.35	.35
☐ 302 Ken Clarke	.05	.02	.01
☐ 303 Greg Brown	.05	.02	.01
☐ 304 Roynell Young	.05	.02	.01
☐ 305 Andre Waters	.25	.11	.03
☐ 306 Oilers TL	.40	.18	.05
(Warren Moon Plots Play)			
☐ 307 Warren Moon	1.50	.70	.19
☐ 308 Mike Rozier	.10	.05	.01
☐ 309 Drew Hill	.10	.05	.01
☐ 310 Ernest Givins	.50	.23	.06
☐ 311 Lee Johnson	.05	.02	.01
☐ 312 Kent Hill	.05	.02	.01
☐ 313 Dean Steinkuhler	.10	.05	.01
☐ 314 Ray Childress	.25	.11	.03
☐ 315 John Grimsley	.05	.02	.01
☐ 316 Jesse Baker	.05	.02	.01
☐ 317 Lions TL	.05	.02	.01
(Eric Hipple Surveys)			
☐ 318 Chuck Long	.10	.05	.01
☐ 319 James Jones	.05	.02	.01
☐ 320 Garry James	.05	.02	.01
☐ 321 Jeff Chadwick	.05	.02	.01
☐ 322 Leonard Thompson	.05	.02	.01
☐ 323 Pete Mandley	.05	.02	.01
☐ 324 Jimmie Giles	.10	.05	.01
☐ 325 Herman Hunter	.05	.02	.01
☐ 326 Keith Ferguson	.05	.02	.01
☐ 327 Devon Mitchell	.05	.02	.01
☐ 328 Cardinals TL	.10	.05	.01
(Neil Lomax Audible)			
☐ 329 Neil Lomax	.10	.05	.01
☐ 330 Stump Mitchell	.05	.02	.01
☐ 331 Earl Ferrell	.05	.02	.01
☐ 332 Vai Sikahema	.10	.05	.01
☐ 333 Ron Wolfley	.05	.02	.01
☐ 334 J.T. Smith	.10	.05	.01
☐ 335 Roy Green	.10	.05	.01
☐ 336 Al(Bubba) Baker	.05	.02	.01
☐ 337 Freddie Joe Nunn	.05	.02	.01
☐ 338 Cedric Mack	.05	.02	.01
☐ 339 Chargers TL	.10	.05	.01
(Gary Anderson Evades)			
☐ 340 Dan Fouts	.50	.23	.06
☐ 341 Gary Anderson UER	.25	.11	.03
(Two Topps logos			
on card front)			
☐ 342 Wes Chandler	.10	.05	.01
☐ 343 Kellen Winslow	.25	.11	.03
☐ 344 Ralf Mojsiejenko	.05	.02	.01
☐ 345 Rolf Benirschke	.05	.02	.01
☐ 346 Lee Williams	.10	.05	.01
☐ 347 Leslie O'Neal	1.00	.45	.12
☐ 348 Billy Ray Smith	.10	.05	.01
☐ 349 Gill Byrd	.10	.05	.01
☐ 350 Packers TL	.05	.02	.01
(Paul Ott Carruth Around End)			
☐ 351 Randy Wright	.05	.02	.01
☐ 352 Kenneth Davis	.25	.11	.03
☐ 353 Gerry Ellis	.05	.02	.01
☐ 354 James Lofton	.25	.11	.03
☐ 355 Phillip Epps	.05	.02	.01
☐ 356 Walter Stanley	.05	.02	.01
☐ 357 Eddie Lee Ivery	.05	.02	.01
☐ 358 Tim Harris	.25	.11	.03
☐ 359 Mark Lee UER	.05	.02	.01
(Red flag, rest of			
Packers have yellow)			
☐ 360 Mossy Cade	.05	.02	.01
☐ 361 Bills TL	1.00	.45	.12
(Jim Kelly Works Ground)			
☐ 362 Jim Kelly	6.00	2.70	.75
☐ 363 Robb Riddick	.05	.02	.01
☐ 364 Greg Bell	.05	.02	.01
☐ 365 Andre Reed	1.25	.55	.16
☐ 366 Pete Metzelaars	.25	.11	.03
☐ 367 Sean McNanie	.05	.02	.01
☐ 368 Fred Smerlas	.05	.02	.01
☐ 369 Bruce Smith	2.00	.90	.25
☐ 370 Darryl Talley	.10	.05	.01
☐ 371 Charles Romes	.05	.02	.01
☐ 372 Colts TL	.05	.02	.01
(Rohn Stark High and Far)			
☐ 373 Jack Trudeau	.10	.05	.01
☐ 374 Gary Hogeboom	.05	.02	.01
☐ 375 Randy McMillan	.05	.02	.01
☐ 376 Albert Bentley	.05	.02	.01
☐ 377 Matt Bouza	.05	.02	.01
☐ 378 Bill Brooks	1.50	.70	.19
☐ 379 Rohn Stark AP	.05	.02	.01
☐ 380 Chris Hinton	.05	.02	.01
☐ 381 Ray Donaldson	.05	.02	.01
☐ 382 Jon Hand	.05	.02	.01
☐ 383 Buccaneers TL	.05	.02	.01
(James Wilder Braces)			
☐ 384 Steve Young	6.00	2.70	.75
☐ 385 James Wilder	.05	.02	.01
☐ 386 Frank Garcia	.05	.02	.01
☐ 387 Gerald Carter	.05	.02	.01
☐ 388 Phil Freeman	.05	.02	.01
☐ 389 Calvin Magee	.05	.02	.01
☐ 390 Donald Igwebuike	.05	.02	.01
☐ 391 David Logan	.05	.02	.01
☐ 392 Jeff Davis	.05	.02	.01
☐ 393 Chris Washington	.05	.02	.01
☐ 394 Checklist 1-132	.05	.02	.01
☐ 395 Checklist 133-264	.05	.02	.01
☐ 396 Checklist 265-396	.05	.02	.01

1987 Topps Box Bottoms

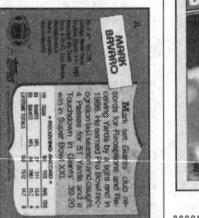

This 16-card set, which measures the standard size, was issued on the bottom of 1987 Topps wax pack boxes. The cards are in the same design as the 1987 Topps regular issues except they are bordered in yellow. The backs of the cards are just like the regular card in that they have biographical and complete statistical information. The cards are arranged in alphabetical order and include such stars as Joe Montana, Walter Payton, and Jerry Rice.

	MINT	NRMT	EXC
COMPLETE SET (16)	18.00	8.00	2.20
COMMON CARD (A-P)	.25	.11	.03

		MINT	NRMT	EXC
☐ A	Mark Bavaro	.40	.18	.05
☐ B	Todd Christensen	.40	.18	.05
☐ C	Eric Dickerson	.40	.18	.05
☐ D	John Elway	2.50	1.10	.30
☐ E	Rulon Jones	.25	.11	.03
☐ F	Dan Marino	6.00	2.70	.75
☐ G	Karl Mecklenburg	.25	.11	.03
☐ H	Joe Montana	4.00	1.80	.50
☐ I	Joe Morris	.25	.11	.03
☐ J	Walter Payton	1.00	.45	.12
☐ K	Jerry Rice	5.00	2.20	.60
☐ L	Phil Simms	.40	.18	.05
☐ M	Lawrence Taylor	.60	.25	.07
☐ N	Al Toon	.40	.18	.05
☐ O	Curt Warner	.40	.18	.05
☐ P	Reggie White	1.25	.55	.16

1987 Topps 1000 Yard Club

This glossy insert set was included one per wax pack with the regular issue 1987 Topps football cards. The set features, in order of yards gained, all players achieving 1000 yards gained either rushing or receiving. Cards have a light blue border on front; backs are blue and black print on white card stock. The cards are standard size. Card backs detail statistically the game by game performance of the player in terms of yards gained against each opponent.

	MINT	NRMT	EXC
COMPLETE SET (24)	6.00	2.70	.75
COMMON CARD (1-24)	.25	.11	.03

		MINT	NRMT	EXC
☐ 1	Eric Dickerson	.60	.25	.07
☐ 2	Jerry Rice	3.00	1.35	.35
☐ 3	Joe Morris	.25	.11	.03
☐ 4	Stanley Morgan	.25	.11	.03
☐ 5	Curt Warner	.40	.18	.05
☐ 6	Rueben Mayes	.25	.11	.03
☐ 7	Walter Payton	1.25	.55	.16
☐ 8	Gerald Riggs	.25	.11	.03
☐ 9	Mark Duper	.40	.18	.05
☐ 10	Gary Clark	.40	.18	.05
☐ 11	George Rogers	.25	.11	.03
☐ 12	Al Toon	.40	.18	.05
☐ 13	Todd Christensen	.25	.11	.03
☐ 14	Mark Clayton	.40	.18	.05
☐ 15	Bill Brooks	.40	.18	.05
☐ 16	Drew Hill	.25	.11	.03
☐ 17	James Brooks	.25	.11	.03
☐ 18	Steve Largent	1.00	.45	.12
☐ 19	Art Monk	.40	.18	.05
☐ 20	Ernest Givins	.60	.25	.07
☐ 21	Cris Collinsworth	.40	.18	.05
☐ 22	Wesley Walker	.25	.11	.03
☐ 23	J.T. Smith	.25	.11	.03
☐ 24	Mark Bavaro	.25	.11	.03

1987 Topps American/UK

This mini-size version of 1987 football cards was distributed in the United Kingdom for British fans of American football. Cards measure only 2 1/8" by 3". The photos used are different from the regular issue Topps football cards, although the style is essentially the same. The card backs are colorful and feature a "Talking Football" section where a football term is explained. A collector box (with a complete set checklist on the side) is also available. The cards are arranged

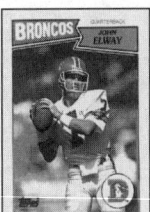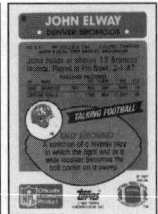

according to teams. Cards 76 through 87 are puzzle pieces, combining to show team action photos on their fronts and William "The Refrigerator" Perry on their backs.

	MINT	NRMT	EXC
COMPLETE SET (88)	60.00	27.00	7.50
COMMON CARD (1-88)	.15	.07	.02

		MINT	NRMT	EXC
☐ 1	Phil Simms	.50	.23	.06
☐ 2	Joe Morris	.30	.14	.04
☐ 3	Mark Bavaro	.30	.14	.04
☐ 4	Sean Landeta	.15	.07	.02
☐ 5	Lawrence Taylor	.75	.35	.09
☐ 6	John Elway	8.00	3.60	1.00
☐ 7	Sammy Winder	.15	.07	.02
☐ 8	Rulon Jones	.15	.07	.02
☐ 9	Karl Mecklenburg	.30	.14	.04
☐ 10	Walter Payton	4.00	1.80	.50
☐ 11	Dennis Gentry	.15	.07	.02
☐ 12	Kevin Butler	.15	.07	.02
☐ 13	Jim Covert	.15	.07	.02
☐ 14	Richard Dent	.30	.14	.04
☐ 15	Mike Singletary	.50	.23	.06
☐ 16	Jay Schroeder	.15	.07	.02
☐ 17	George Rogers	.30	.14	.04
☐ 18	Gary Clark	.50	.23	.06
☐ 19	Art Monk	.50	.23	.06
☐ 20	Dexter Manley	.15	.07	.02
☐ 21	Darrell Green	.30	.14	.04
☐ 22	Bernie Kosar	.30	.14	.04
☐ 23	Cody Risien	.15	.07	.02
☐ 24	Hanford Dixon	.15	.07	.02
☐ 25	Tony Eason	.30	.14	.04
☐ 26	Stanley Morgan	.30	.14	.04
☐ 27	Tony Franklin	.15	.07	.02
☐ 28	Andre Tippett	.30	.14	.04
☐ 29	Joe Montana	12.00	5.50	1.50
☐ 30	Jerry Rice	16.00	7.25	2.00
☐ 31	Ronnie Lott	.50	.23	.06
☐ 32	Ken O'Brien	.30	.14	.04
☐ 33	Freeman McNeil	.30	.14	.04
☐ 34	Al Toon	.30	.14	.04
☐ 35	Wesley Walker	.30	.14	.04
☐ 36	Eric Dickerson	.50	.23	.06
☐ 37	Dennis Harrah	.15	.07	.02
☐ 38	Bill Maas	.15	.07	.02
☐ 39	Deron Cherry	.15	.07	.02
☐ 40	Curt Warner	.30	.14	.04
☐ 41	Bobby Joe Edmonds	.15	.07	.02
☐ 42	Steve Largent	1.50	.70	.19
☐ 43	Boomer Esiason	1.00	.45	.12
☐ 44	James Brooks	.30	.14	.04
☐ 45	Cris Collinsworth	.30	.14	.04
☐ 46	Tim McGee	.30	.14	.04
☐ 47	Tommy Kramer	.30	.14	.04
☐ 48	Marcus Allen	2.00	.90	.25
☐ 49	Todd Christensen	.30	.14	.04
☐ 50	Sean Jones	.30	.14	.04
☐ 51	Dan Marino	16.00	7.25	2.00
☐ 52	Mark Duper	.30	.14	.04
☐ 53	Mark Clayton	.30	.14	.04
☐ 54	Dwight Stephenson	.15	.07	.02
☐ 55	Gerald Riggs	.30	.14	.04
☐ 56	Bill Fralic	.15	.07	.02
☐ 57	Tony Dorsett	1.00	.45	.12
☐ 58	Herschel Walker	.75	.35	.09
☐ 59	Rueben Mayes	.15	.07	.02
☐ 60	Lupe Sanchez	.15	.07	.02
☐ 61	Reggie White	4.00	1.80	.50
☐ 62	Warren Moon	1.50	.70	.19
☐ 63	Ernest Givins	.50	.23	.06
☐ 64	Drew Hill	.30	.14	.04
☐ 65	Jeff Chadwick	.30	.14	.04
☐ 66	Herman Hunter	.15	.07	.02
☐ 67	Vai Sikahema	.15	.07	.02
☐ 68	J.T. Smith	.30	.14	.04
☐ 69	Dan Fouts	.75	.35	.09
☐ 70	Lee Williams	.15	.07	.02
☐ 71	Randy Wright	.15	.07	.02
☐ 72	Jim Kelly	6.00	2.70	.75
☐ 73	Bruce Smith	1.00	.45	.12
☐ 74	Bill Brooks	.30	.14	.04
☐ 75	Rohn Stark	.15	.07	.02
☐ 76	Team Action	.15	.07	.02
☐ 77	Team Action	.15	.07	.02
☐ 78	Team Action	.15	.07	.02
☐ 79	Team Action	.15	.07	.02
☐ 80	Team Action	.15	.07	.02
☐ 81	Team Action	.15	.07	.02
☐ 82	Team Action	.15	.07	.02
☐ 83	Team Action	.15	.07	.02
☐ 84	Team Action	.15	.07	.02
☐ 85	Team Action	.15	.07	.02
☐ 86	Team Action	.15	.07	.02
☐ 87	Team Action	.15	.07	.02
☐ 88	Checklist Card	.15	.07	.02

1988 Topps

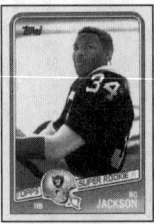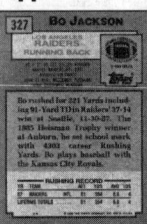

This 396-card, standard-size set was issued in 15-card wax packs as well as in factory sets. The wax packs also included an 1,000 yard club card. Card fronts feature a team helmet, player's name and position beneath the player photo. The borders surrounding the photo are in the colors of the team. The backs have highlights and yearly statistics. The set is ordered by how the teams finished. The Team Leader (TL) cards show an action scene for each team. Potential young stars are also designated by Topps as "Super Rookies" (SR). Rookie Cards include Neal Anderson, Cornelius Bennett, Jerome Brown, Shane Conlan, Chris Doleman, Mel Gray, Kevin Greene, Bo Jackson, Mark Jackson, Seth Joyner, Tom Rathman, Clyde Simmons, Webster Slaughter, Pat Swilling and Vinny Testaverde.

	MINT	NRMT	EXC
COMPLETE SET (396)	10.00	4.50	1.25
COMPLETE FACT.SET (396)	12.00	5.50	1.50
COMMON CARD (1-396)	.05	.02	.01

		MINT	NRMT	EXC
☐ 1	Super Bowl XXII Redskins 42, Broncos 10 (Redskins celebrating)	.10	.05	.01
☐ 2	Vencie Glenn RB Longest Interception Return	.05	.02	.01
☐ 3	Steve Largent RB Most Receptions, Career	.25	.11	.03
☐ 4	Joe Montana RB Most Consecutive Pass Completions	.75	.35	.09
☐ 5	Walter Payton RB Most Rushing Touchdowns, Career	.40	.18	.05
☐ 6	Jerry Rice RB Most Touchdown Receptions, Season	.75	.35	.09
☐ 7	Redskins TL (Kelvin Bryant Sees Daylight)	.05	.02	.01
☐ 8	Doug Williams	.10	.05	.01
☐ 9	George Rogers	.10	.05	.01
☐ 10	Kelvin Bryant	.10	.05	.01
☐ 11	Timmy Smith SR	.10	.05	.01
☐ 12	Art Monk	.25	.11	.03
☐ 13	Gary Clark	.25	.11	.03
☐ 14	Ricky Sanders	.25	.11	.03
☐ 15	Steve Cox	.05	.02	.01
☐ 16	Joe Jacoby	.05	.02	.01
☐ 17	Charles Mann	.10	.05	.01
☐ 18	Dave Butz	.05	.02	.01
☐ 19	Darrell Green AP	.10	.05	.01
☐ 20	Dexter Manley	.05	.02	.01
☐ 21	Barry Wilburn	.05	.02	.01
☐ 22	Broncos TL (Sammy Winder Winds Through)	.05	.02	.01
☐ 23	John Elway AP	1.00	.45	.12
☐ 24	Sammy Winder	.05	.02	.01
☐ 25	Vance Johnson	.10	.05	.01
☐ 26	Mark Jackson	.25	.11	.03
☐ 27	Ricky Nattiel SR	.05	.02	.01
☐ 28	Clarence Kay	.05	.02	.01
☐ 29	Rich Karlis	.05	.02	.01
☐ 30	Keith Bishop	.05	.02	.01
☐ 31	Mike Horan	.05	.02	.01
☐ 32	Rulon Jones	.05	.02	.01
☐ 33	Karl Mecklenburg	.10	.05	.01
☐ 34	Jim Ryan	.05	.02	.01
☐ 35	Mark Haynes	.10	.05	.01
☐ 36	Mike Harden	.05	.02	.01
☐ 37	49ers TL (Roger Craig Gallops For Yardage)	.25	.11	.03
☐ 38	Joe Montana	1.50	.70	.19
☐ 39	Steve Young	1.00	.45	.12
☐ 40	Roger Craig	.10	.05	.01
☐ 41	Tom Rathman	.25	.11	.03
☐ 42	Joe Cribbs	.10	.05	.01
☐ 43	Jerry Rice AP	2.00	.90	.25
☐ 44	Mike Wilson	.05	.02	.01
☐ 45	Ron Heller	.05	.02	.01
☐ 46	Ray Wersching	.05	.02	.01
☐ 47	Michael Carter	.05	.02	.01
☐ 48	Dwaine Board	.05	.02	.01
☐ 49	Michael Walter	.05	.02	.01
☐ 50	Don Griffin	.05	.02	.01
☐ 51	Ronnie Lott	.25	.11	.03
☐ 52	Charles Haley	.25	.11	.03
☐ 53	Dana McLemore	.05	.02	.01
☐ 54	Saints TL (Bobby Hebert Hands Off)	.10	.05	.01
☐ 55	Bobby Hebert	.10	.05	.01
☐ 56	Rueben Mayes	.05	.02	.01
☐ 57	Dalton Hilliard	.05	.02	.01
☐ 58	Eric Martin	.10	.05	.01
☐ 59	John Tice	.05	.02	.01
☐ 60	Brad Edelman	.05	.02	.01
☐ 61	Morten Andersen AP	.10	.05	.01
☐ 62	Brian Hansen	.05	.02	.01
☐ 63	Mel Gray	.25	.11	.03
☐ 64	Rickey Jackson	.10	.05	.01
☐ 65	Sam Mills	.25	.11	.03
☐ 66	Pat Swilling	.40	.18	.05
☐ 67	Dave Waymer	.05	.02	.01
☐ 68	Bears TL (Willie Gault Powers Forward)	.10	.05	.01
☐ 69	Jim McMahon	.25	.11	.03
☐ 70	Mike Tomczak	.05	.02	.01
☐ 71	Neal Anderson	.25	.11	.03
☐ 72	Willie Gault	.10	.05	.01
☐ 73	Dennis Gentry	.05	.02	.01
☐ 74	Dennis McKinnon	.05	.02	.01
☐ 75	Kevin Butler	.05	.02	.01
☐ 76	Jim Covert	.05	.02	.01
☐ 77	Jay Hilgenberg	.05	.02	.01
☐ 78	Steve McMichael	.10	.05	.01
☐ 79	William Perry	.10	.05	.01
☐ 80	Richard Dent	.25	.11	.03
☐ 81	Ron Rivera	.05	.02	.01
☐ 82	Mike Singletary AP	.25	.11	.03
☐ 83	Dan Hampton	.10	.05	.01
☐ 84	Dave Duerson	.05	.02	.01
☐ 85	Browns TL (Bernie Kosar Lets It Go)	.10	.05	.01
☐ 86	Bernie Kosar	.25	.11	.03
☐ 87	Earnest Byner	.25	.11	.03
☐ 88	Kevin Mack	.10	.05	.01
☐ 89	Webster Slaughter	.25	.11	.03
☐ 90	Gerald McNeil	.05	.02	.01
☐ 91	Brian Brennan	.05	.02	.01
☐ 92	Ozzie Newsome	.25	.11	.03
☐ 93	Cody Risien	.05	.02	.01
☐ 94	Bob Golic	.05	.02	.01
☐ 95	Carl Hairston	.05	.02	.01
☐ 96	Mike Johnson	.05	.02	.01
☐ 97	Clay Matthews	.10	.05	.01
☐ 98	Frank Minnifield	.05	.02	.01
☐ 99	Hanford Dixon AP	.05	.02	.01
☐ 100	Dave Puzzuoli	.05	.02	.01
☐ 101	Felix Wright	.05	.02	.01
☐ 102	Oilers TL (Warren Moon Over The Top)	.25	.11	.03
☐ 103	Warren Moon	.50	.23	.06
☐ 104	Mike Rozier	.05	.02	.01
☐ 105	Alonzo Highsmith SR	.10	.05	.01
☐ 106	Drew Hill	.10	.05	.01
☐ 107	Ernest Givins	.25	.11	.03
☐ 108	Curtis Duncan	.25	.11	.03
☐ 109	Tony Zendejas	.05	.02	.01
☐ 110	Mike Munchak AP	.10	.05	.01
☐ 111	Kent Hill	.05	.02	.01
☐ 112	Ray Childress	.10	.05	.01
☐ 113	Al Smith	.10	.05	.01
☐ 114	Keith Bostic	.05	.02	.01
☐ 115	Jeff Donaldson	.05	.02	.01
☐ 116	Colts TL (Eric Dickerson Finds Opening)	.25	.11	.03
☐ 117	Jack Trudeau	.05	.02	.01
☐ 118	Eric Dickerson AP	.25	.11	.03
☐ 119	Albert Bentley	.05	.02	.01
☐ 120	Matt Bouza	.05	.02	.01
☐ 121	Bill Brooks	.25	.11	.03
☐ 122	Dean Biasucci	.05	.02	.01
☐ 123	Chris Hinton	.05	.02	.01
☐ 124	Ray Donaldson	.05	.02	.01
☐ 125	Ron Solt	.05	.02	.01
☐ 126	Donnell Thompson	.05	.02	.01
☐ 127	Barry Krauss	.05	.02	.01
☐ 128	Duane Bickett	.05	.02	.01
☐ 129	Mike Prior	.05	.02	.01
☐ 130	Seahawks TL (Curt Warner Follows Blocking)	.10	.05	.01
☐ 131	Dave Krieg	.10	.05	.01
☐ 132	Curt Warner	.10	.05	.01
☐ 133	John L. Williams	.25	.11	.03
☐ 134	Bobby Joe Edmonds	.05	.02	.01
☐ 135	Steve Largent	.40	.18	.05
☐ 136	Raymond Butler	.05	.02	.01
☐ 137	Norm Johnson	.05	.02	.01
☐ 138	Ruben Rodriguez	.05	.02	.01
☐ 139	Blair Bush	.05	.02	.01
☐ 140	Jacob Green	.05	.02	.01
☐ 141	Joe Nash	.05	.02	.01
☐ 142	Jeff Bryant	.05	.02	.01
☐ 143	Fredd Young AP	.05	.02	.01
☐ 144	Brian Bosworth SR	.25	.11	.03
☐ 145	Kenny Easley AP	.05	.02	.01

☐ 146 Vikings TL	.10	.05	.01
(Tommy Kramer Spots His Man)			
☐ 147 Wade Wilson	.25	.11	.03
☐ 148 Tommy Kramer	.10	.05	.01
☐ 149 Darrin Nelson	.05	.02	.01
☐ 150 D.J. Dozier SR	.10	.05	.01
☐ 151 Anthony Carter	.10	.05	.01
☐ 152 Leo Lewis	.05	.02	.01
☐ 153 Steve Jordan	.10	.05	.01
☐ 154 Gary Zimmerman	.05	.02	.01
☐ 155 Chuck Nelson	.05	.02	.01
☐ 156 Henry Thomas SR	.25	.11	.03
☐ 157 Chris Doleman	.50	.23	.06
☐ 158 Scott Studwell	.05	.02	.01
☐ 159 Jesse Solomon	.05	.02	.01
☐ 160 Joey Browner AP	.05	.02	.01
☐ 161 Neal Guggemos	.05	.02	.01
☐ 162 Steelers TL	.10	.05	.01
(Louis Lipps In a Crowd)			
☐ 163 Mark Malone	.05	.02	.01
☐ 164 Walter Abercrombie	.05	.02	.01
☐ 165 Earnest Jackson	.05	.02	.01
☐ 166 Frank Pollard	.05	.02	.01
☐ 167 Dwight Stone	.10	.05	.01
☐ 168 Gary Anderson K	.05	.02	.01
☐ 169 Harry Newsome	.05	.02	.01
☐ 170 Keith Willis	.05	.02	.01
☐ 171 Keith Gary	.05	.02	.01
☐ 172 David Little	.05	.02	.01
☐ 173 Mike Merriweather	.05	.02	.01
☐ 174 Dwayne Woodruff	.05	.02	.01
☐ 175 Patriots TL	.25	.11	.03
(Irving Fryar One on One)			
☐ 176 Steve Grogan	.10	.05	.01
☐ 177 Tony Eason	.10	.05	.01
☐ 178 Tony Collins	.10	.05	.01
☐ 179 Mosi Tatupu	.05	.02	.01
☐ 180 Stanley Morgan	.10	.05	.01
☐ 181 Irving Fryar	.25	.11	.03
☐ 182 Stephen Starring	.05	.02	.01
☐ 183 Tony Franklin	.05	.02	.01
☐ 184 Rich Camarillo	.05	.02	.01
☐ 185 Garin Veris	.05	.02	.01
☐ 186 Andre Tippett AP	.10	.05	.01
☐ 187 Ronnie Lippett	.05	.02	.01
☐ 188 Fred Marion	.05	.02	.01
☐ 189 Dolphins TL	.75	.35	.09
(Dan Marino Play-Action Pass)			
☐ 190 Dan Marino	2.00	.90	.25
☐ 191 Troy Stradford SR	.05	.02	.01
☐ 192 Lorenzo Hampton	.05	.02	.01
☐ 193 Mark Duper	.10	.05	.01
☐ 194 Mark Clayton	.10	.05	.01
☐ 195 Reggie Roby	.10	.05	.01
☐ 196 Dwight Stephenson AP	.05	.02	.01
☐ 197 T.J. Turner	.05	.02	.01
☐ 198 John Bosa SR	.05	.02	.01
☐ 199 Jackie Shipp	.05	.02	.01
☐ 200 John Offerdahl	.10	.05	.01
☐ 201 Mark Brown	.05	.02	.01
☐ 202 Paul Lankford	.05	.02	.01
☐ 203 Chargers TL	.25	.11	.03
(Kellen Winslow Sure Hands)			
☐ 204 Tim Spencer	.05	.02	.01
☐ 205 Gary Anderson RB	.10	.05	.01
☐ 206 Curtis Adams	.05	.02	.01
☐ 207 Lionel James	.05	.02	.01
☐ 208 Chip Banks	.05	.02	.01
☐ 209 Kellen Winslow	.25	.11	.03
☐ 210 Ralf Mojsiejenko	.05	.02	.01
☐ 211 Jim Lachey	.10	.05	.01
☐ 212 Lee Williams	.05	.02	.01
☐ 213 Billy Ray Smith	.05	.02	.01
☐ 214 Vencie Glenn	.10	.05	.01
☐ 215 Passing Leaders	.50	.23	.06
Bernie Kosar			
Joe Montana			
☐ 216 Receiving Leaders	.10	.05	.01
Al Toon			
J.T. Smith			
☐ 217 Rushing Leaders	.10	.05	.01
Charles White			
Eric Dickerson			
☐ 218 Scoring Leaders	.40	.18	.05
Jim Breech			
Jerry Rice			
☐ 219 Interception Leaders	.05	.02	.01
Keith Bostic			
Mark Kelso			
Mike Prior			
Barry Wilburn			
☐ 220 Bills TL	.25	.11	.03
(Jim Kelly Plots His Course)			
☐ 221 Jim Kelly	.75	.35	.09
☐ 222 Ronnie Harmon	.25	.11	.03
☐ 223 Robb Riddick	.05	.02	.01
☐ 224 Andre Reed	.40	.18	.05
☐ 225 Chris Burkett	.05	.02	.01
☐ 226 Pete Metzelaars	.25	.11	.03
☐ 227 Bruce Smith AP	.50	.23	.06
☐ 228 Darryl Talley	.10	.05	.01
☐ 229 Eugene Marve	.05	.02	.01
☐ 230 Cornelius Bennett SR	.75	.35	.09
☐ 231 Mark Kelso	.05	.02	.01
☐ 232 Shane Conlan SR	.25	.11	.03
☐ 233 Eagles TL	.25	.11	.03
(Randall Cunningham QB Keeper)			
☐ 234 Randall Cunningham	.25	.11	.03
☐ 235 Keith Byars	.25	.11	.03
☐ 236 Anthony Toney	.05	.02	.01
☐ 237 Mike Quick	.10	.05	.01
☐ 238 Kenny Jackson	.05	.02	.01
☐ 239 John Spagnola	.05	.02	.01
☐ 240 Paul McFadden	.05	.02	.01
☐ 241 Reggie White AP	.60	.25	.07
☐ 242 Ken Clarke	.05	.02	.01
☐ 243 Mike Pitts	.05	.02	.01
☐ 244 Clyde Simmons	.25	.11	.03
☐ 245 Seth Joyner	.50	.23	.06
☐ 246 Andre Waters	.25	.11	.03
☐ 247 Jerome Brown SR	.25	.11	.03
☐ 248 Cardinals TL	.05	.02	.01
(Stump Mitchell On the Run)			
☐ 249 Neil Lomax	.10	.05	.01
☐ 250 Stump Mitchell	.05	.02	.01
☐ 251 Earl Ferrell	.05	.02	.01
☐ 252 Vai Sikahema	.05	.02	.01
☐ 253 J.T. Smith AP	.10	.05	.01
☐ 254 Roy Green	.10	.05	.01
☐ 255 Robert Awalt SR	.10	.05	.01
☐ 256 Freddie Joe Nunn	.05	.02	.01
☐ 257 Leonard Smith	.05	.02	.01
☐ 258 Travis Curtis	.05	.02	.01
☐ 259 Cowboys TL	.25	.11	.03
(Herschel Walker Around End)			
☐ 260 Danny White	.25	.11	.03
☐ 261 Herschel Walker	.25	.11	.03
☐ 262 Tony Dorsett	.25	.11	.03
☐ 263 Doug Cosbie	.05	.02	.01
☐ 264 Roger Ruzek	.10	.05	.01
☐ 265 Darryl Clack	.05	.02	.01
☐ 266 Ed Too Tall Jones	.25	.11	.03
☐ 267 Jim Jeffcoat	.05	.02	.01
☐ 268 Everson Walls	.05	.02	.01
☐ 269 Bill Bates	.10	.05	.01
☐ 270 Michael Downs	.05	.02	.01
☐ 271 Giants TL	.10	.05	.01
(Mark Bavaro Drives Ahead)			
☐ 272 Phil Simms	.25	.11	.03
☐ 273 Joe Morris	.10	.05	.01
☐ 274 Lee Rouson	.05	.02	.01
☐ 275 George Adams	.05	.02	.01
☐ 276 Lionel Manuel	.05	.02	.01
☐ 277 Mark Bavaro AP	.10	.05	.01
☐ 278 Raul Allegre	.05	.02	.01
☐ 279 Sean Landeta	.05	.02	.01
☐ 280 Erik Howard	.05	.02	.01
☐ 281 Leonard Marshall	.10	.05	.01
☐ 282 Carl Banks AP	.10	.05	.01
☐ 283 Pepper Johnson	.10	.05	.01
☐ 284 Harry Carson	.10	.05	.01
☐ 285 Lawrence Taylor	.25	.11	.03
☐ 286 Terry Kinard	.05	.02	.01
☐ 287 Rams TL	.25	.11	.03
(Jim Everett Races Downfield)			
☐ 288 Jim Everett	.25	.11	.03
☐ 289 Charles White AP	.10	.05	.01
☐ 290 Ron Brown	.10	.05	.01
☐ 291 Henry Ellard	.25	.11	.03
☐ 292 Mike Lansford	.05	.02	.01
☐ 293 Dale Hatcher	.05	.02	.01
☐ 294 Doug Smith	.05	.02	.01
☐ 295 Jackie Slater AP	.10	.05	.01
☐ 296 Jim Collins	.05	.02	.01
☐ 297 Jerry Gray	.05	.02	.01
☐ 298 LeRoy Irvin	.05	.02	.01
☐ 299 Nolan Cromwell	.10	.05	.01
☐ 300 Kevin Greene	1.50	.70	.19
☐ 301 Jets TL	.05	.02	.01
(Ken O'Brien Reads Defense)			
☐ 302 Ken O'Brien	.10	.05	.01
☐ 303 Freeman McNeil	.10	.05	.01
☐ 304 Johnny Hector	.05	.02	.01
☐ 305 Al Toon	.10	.05	.01
☐ 306 Jo Jo Townsell	.10	.05	.01
☐ 307 Mickey Shuler	.05	.02	.01
☐ 308 Pat Leahy	.05	.02	.01
☐ 309 Roger Vick	.05	.02	.01
☐ 310 Alex Gordon	.05	.02	.01
☐ 311 Troy Benson	.05	.02	.01
☐ 312 Bob Crable	.05	.02	.01
☐ 313 Harry Hamilton	.05	.02	.01
☐ 314 Packers TL	.05	.02	.01
(Phillip Epps Ready for Contact)			
☐ 315 Randy Wright	.05	.02	.01
☐ 316 Kenneth Davis	.10	.05	.01
☐ 317 Phillip Epps	.05	.02	.01
☐ 318 Walter Stanley	.05	.02	.01
☐ 319 Frankie Neal	.05	.02	.01
☐ 320 Don Bracken	.05	.02	.01
☐ 321 Brian Noble	.10	.05	.01
☐ 322 Johnny Holland SR	.10	.05	.01
☐ 323 Tim Harris	.10	.05	.01
☐ 324 Mark Murphy	.05	.02	.01
☐ 325 Raiders TL	.25	.11	.03
(Bo Jackson All Alone)			
☐ 326 Marc Wilson	.05	.02	.01
☐ 327 Bo Jackson SR	.75	.35	.09
☐ 328 Marcus Allen	.40	.18	.05
☐ 329 James Lofton	.25	.11	.03
☐ 330 Todd Christensen	.10	.05	.01
☐ 331 Chris Bahr	.05	.02	.01
☐ 332 Stan Talley	.05	.02	.01
☐ 333 Howie Long	.25	.11	.03
☐ 334 Sean Jones	.25	.11	.03
☐ 335 Matt Millen	.10	.05	.01
☐ 336 Stacey Toran	.05	.02	.01
☐ 337 Vann McElroy	.05	.02	.01
☐ 338 Greg Townsend	.10	.05	.01
☐ 339 Bengals TL	.10	.05	.01
(Boomer Esiason Calls Signals)			
☐ 340 Boomer Esiason	.25	.11	.03
☐ 341 Larry Kinnebrew	.05	.02	.01
☐ 342 Stanford Jennings	.05	.02	.01
☐ 343 Eddie Brown	.10	.05	.01
☐ 344 Jim Breech	.05	.02	.01
☐ 345 Anthony Munoz AP	.25	.11	.03
☐ 346 Scott Fulhage	.05	.02	.01
☐ 347 Tim Krumrie	.05	.02	.01
☐ 348 Reggie Williams	.10	.05	.01
☐ 349 David Fulcher	.05	.02	.01
☐ 350 Buccaneers TL	.05	.02	.01
(James Wilder Free and Clear)			
☐ 351 Frank Garcia	.05	.02	.01
☐ 352 Vinny Testaverde SR	1.50	.70	.19
☐ 353 James Wilder	.05	.02	.01
☐ 354 Jeff Smith	.05	.02	.01
☐ 355 Gerald Carter	.05	.02	.01
☐ 356 Calvin Magee	.05	.02	.01
☐ 357 Donald Igwebuike	.05	.02	.01
☐ 358 Ron Holmes	.05	.02	.01
☐ 359 Chris Washington	.05	.02	.01
☐ 360 Ervin Randle	.05	.02	.01
☐ 361 Chiefs TL	.05	.02	.01
(Bill Kenney Ground Attack)			
☐ 362 Bill Kenney	.05	.02	.01
☐ 363 Christian Okoye SR	.25	.11	.03
☐ 364 Paul Palmer	.05	.02	.01
☐ 365 Stephone Paige	.10	.05	.01
☐ 366 Carlos Carson	.05	.02	.01
☐ 367 Kelly Goodburn	.05	.02	.01
☐ 368 Bill Maas AP	.05	.02	.01
☐ 369 Mike Bell	.05	.02	.01
☐ 370 Dino Hackett	.05	.02	.01
☐ 371 Deron Cherry	.05	.02	.01
☐ 372 Lions TL	.05	.02	.01
(James Jones Stretches For More)			
☐ 373 Chuck Long	.10	.05	.01
☐ 374 Garry James	.05	.02	.01
☐ 375 James Jones	.05	.02	.01
☐ 376 Pete Mandley	.05	.02	.01
☐ 377 Gary Lee SR	.05	.02	.01
☐ 378 Eddie Murray	.05	.02	.01
☐ 379 Jim Arnold	.05	.02	.01
☐ 380 Dennis Gibson SR	.05	.02	.01
☐ 381 Mike Cofer	.05	.02	.01
☐ 382 James Griffin	.05	.02	.01
☐ 383 Falcons TL	.05	.02	.01
(Gerald Riggs Carries Heavy Load)			
☐ 384 Scott Campbell	.05	.02	.01
☐ 385 Gerald Riggs	.10	.05	.01
☐ 386 Floyd Dixon	.05	.02	.01
☐ 387 Rick Donnelly AP	.05	.02	.01
☐ 388 Bill Fralic AP	.10	.05	.01
☐ 389 Major Everett	.05	.02	.01
☐ 390 Mike Gann	.05	.02	.01
☐ 391 Tony Casillas	.10	.05	.01
☐ 392 Rick Bryan	.05	.02	.01
☐ 393 John Rade	.05	.02	.01
☐ 394 Checklist 1-132	.05	.02	.01
☐ 395 Checklist 133-264	.05	.02	.01
☐ 396 Checklist 265-396	.05	.02	.01

1988 Topps Box Bottoms

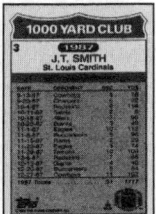

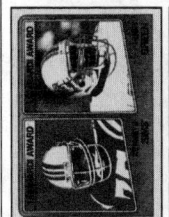

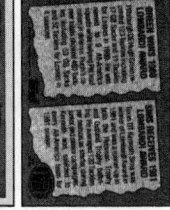

This 16-card standard-size set was issued on the bottom of 1988 Topps wax pack boxes. These cards feature NFL players who had won major awards while in college and they are displayed two players per card. The back of the card features brief biographical blurbs about how the players won the awards while they were in school. The set includes cards of Cornelius Bennett, Bo Jackson, and Vinny Testaverde during their rookie years for cards.

	MINT	NRMT	EXC
COMPLETE SET (16)	6.00	2.70	.75
COMMON CARD (A-P)	.25	.11	.03

☐ A Vinny Testaverde	.50	.23	.06
Jason Buck			
☐ B Dean Steinkuhler	.25	.11	.03
Dave Rimington			
☐ C George Rogers	.25	.11	.03
Mark May			
Washington Redskins			
☐ D Kenneth Sims	.25	.11	.03
Hugh Green			
☐ E Cornelius Bennett	.50	.23	.06
Tony Casillas			
☐ F Bo Jackson	.75	.35	.09
Mike Ruth			
☐ G Ross Browner	.35	.16	.04
Randy White			
☐ H Doug Flutie	1.00	.45	.12
Bruce Smith			
☐ I Herschel Walker	.50	.23	.06
Dave Rimington			
☐ J Jim Plunkett	.50	.23	.06
Randy White			
☐ K Charles White	.25	.11	.03
Jim Ritcher			
☐ L Brad Budde	.25	.11	.03
Bruce Clark			
☐ M Marcus Allen	1.00	.45	.12
Dave Rimington			
☐ N Mike Rozier	.25	.11	.03
Dean Steinkuhler			
Houston Oilers			
☐ O Tony Dorsett	.50	.23	.06
Ross Browner			
☐ P Checklist	.25	.11	.03

1988 Topps 1000 Yard Club

This glossy insert set was included one per wax pack with the regular issue 1988 Topps football cards. The set typically features, in order of yards gained, all players achieving 1000 yards gained either rushing or receiving. However, this year, due to the players' strike which shortened the 1987 season, Topps projected 1,000 yard seasons for those players selected as noted in the checklist below. Cards have a green inner border on the front; backs are red and black print on white card stock. The cards are standard size. Card backs detail statistically the game by game performance of the player in terms of yards gained against each opponent.

	MINT	NRMT	EXC
COMPLETE SET (28)	4.00	1.80	.50
COMMON CARD (1-28)	.15	.07	.02

☐ 1 Charles White	.15	.07	.02
☐ 2 Eric Dickerson	.25	.11	.03
☐ 3 J.T. Smith	.15	.07	.02
☐ 4 Jerry Rice	2.00	.90	.25
☐ 5 Gary Clark	.25	.11	.03
☐ 6 Carlos Carson	.15	.07	.02
☐ 7 Drew Hill	.15	.07	.02
☐ 8 Curt Warner UER	.25	.11	.03
(Reversed negative)			
☐ 9 Al Toon	.25	.11	.03
☐ 10 Mike Rozier	.15	.07	.02
☐ 11 Ernest Givins	.25	.11	.03
☐ 12 Anthony Carter	.25	.11	.03
☐ 13 Rueben Mayes	.15	.07	.02
☐ 14 Steve Largent	.50	.23	.06
☐ 15 Herschel Walker	.25	.11	.03
☐ 16 James Lofton	.40	.18	.05
☐ 17 Gerald Riggs	.15	.07	.02
☐ 18 Mark Bavaro	.15	.07	.02
☐ 19 Roger Craig	.25	.11	.03
☐ 20 Webster Slaughter	.25	.11	.03
☐ 21 Henry Ellard	.25	.11	.03
☐ 22 Mike Quick	.15	.07	.02
☐ 23 Stump Mitchell	.15	.07	.02
☐ 24 Eric Martin	.25	.11	.03
☐ 25 Mark Clayton	.25	.11	.03
☐ 26 Chris Burkett	.15	.07	.02
☐ 27 Marcus Allen	.75	.35	.09
☐ 28 Andre Reed	.40	.18	.05

1989 Topps

This 396-card standard-size set was issued in 15-card wax packs as well as in factory set form. The 15-card wax packs also included an 1,000 yard club card. Card fronts have color stripes across the border one-quarter of the way down the card. The player's name, team name and position are toward the bottom of the photo. Horizontally designed backs have yearly statistics and highlights. The card are team order according to their finish in 1988. The Team Leader cards have an action scene on the front and a recap of the team's previous season on the back. Rookie Cards include Eric Allen, Steve Beuerlein,

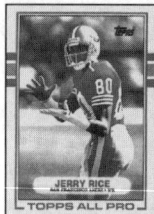

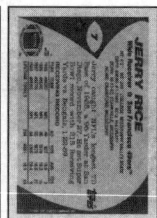

Brian Blades, Tim Brown, Mark Carrier (WR), Cris Carter, Michael Irvin, Keith Jackson, Anthony Miller, Chris Miller, Jay Novacek, Michael Dean Perry, Mark Rypien, Sterling Sharpe, Chris Spielman, John Taylor, Thurman Thomas and Rod Woodson.

	MINT	NRMT	EXC
COMPLETE SET (396)	12.00	5.50	1.50
COMPLETE FACT.SET (396)	15.00	6.75	1.85
COMMON CARD (1-396)	.05	.02	.01

□ 1 Super Bowl XXIII	.40	.18	.05
(Joe Montana back to pass)			
□ 2 Tim Brown RB	.50	.23	.06
Most Combined Net Yards Gained, Rookie Season			
□ 3 Eric Dickerson RB	.10	.05	.01
Most Consecutive Seasons, Start of Career, 1000 or More Yards Rushing			
□ 4 Steve Largent RB	.25	.11	.03
Most Yards Receiving, Career			
□ 5 Dan Marino RB	.75	.35	.09
Most Seasons 4000 or More Yards Passing			
□ 6 49ers Team	.30	.14	.04
Joe Montana On The Run			
□ 7 Jerry Rice	1.50	.70	.19
□ 8 Roger Craig	.25	.11	.03
□ 9 Ronnie Lott	.10	.05	.01
□ 10 Michael Carter	.05	.02	.01
□ 11 Charles Haley	.25	.11	.03
□ 12 Joe Montana	1.50	.70	.19
□ 13 John Taylor	.10	.05	.01
□ 14 Michael Walter	.05	.02	.01
□ 15 Mike Cofer K	.05	.02	.01
□ 16 Tom Rathman	.05	.02	.01
□ 17 Daniel Stubbs	.05	.02	.01
□ 18 Keena Turner	.05	.02	.01
□ 19 Tim McKyer	.05	.02	.01
□ 20 Larry Roberts	.05	.02	.01
□ 21 Jeff Fuller	.05	.02	.01
□ 22 Bubba Paris	.05	.02	.01
□ 23 Bengals Team UER	.05	.02	.01
Boomer Esiason Measures Up (Should be versus Steelers in week three)			
□ 24 Eddie Brown	.05	.02	.01
□ 25 Boomer Esiason	.10	.05	.01
□ 26 Tim Krumrie	.05	.02	.01
□ 27 Ickey Woods	.10	.05	.01
□ 28 Anthony Munoz	.10	.05	.01
□ 29 Tim McGee	.05	.02	.01
□ 30 Max Montoya	.05	.02	.01
□ 31 David Grant	.05	.02	.01
□ 32 Rodney Holman	.05	.02	.01
(Cincinnati Bengals on card front is subject to various printing errors)			
□ 33 David Fulcher	.10	.05	.01
□ 34 Jim Skow	.05	.02	.01
□ 35 James Brooks	.10	.05	.01
□ 36 Reggie Williams	.05	.02	.01
□ 37 Eric Thomas	.05	.02	.01
□ 38 Stanford Jennings	.05	.02	.01
□ 39 Jim Breech	.05	.02	.01
□ 40 Bills Team	.10	.05	.01
Jim Kelly Reads Defense			
□ 41 Shane Conlan	.05	.02	.01
□ 42 Scott Norwood	.05	.02	.01
□ 43 Cornelius Bennett	.10	.05	.01
□ 44 Bruce Smith	.25	.11	.03
□ 45 Thurman Thomas	2.00	.90	.25
□ 46 Jim Kelly	.40	.18	.05
□ 47 John Kidd	.05	.02	.01
□ 48 Kent Hull	.05	.02	.01
□ 49 Art Still	.05	.02	.01
□ 50 Fred Smerlas	.05	.02	.01
□ 51A Derrick Burroughs	.05	.02	.01
(White name plate)			
□ 51B Derrick Burroughs	.05	.02	.01
(Yellow name plate)			
□ 52 Andre Reed	.25	.11	.03
□ 53 Robb Riddick	.05	.02	.01
□ 54 Chris Burkett	.05	.02	.01
□ 55 Ronnie Harmon	.10	.05	.01
□ 56 Mark Kelso UER	.05	.02	.01
(team shown as "Buffalo Bill")			
□ 57 Bears Team	.05	.02	.01
Thomas Sanders Changes Pace			
□ 58 Mike Singletary	.10	.05	.01
□ 59 Jay Hilgenberg UER	.05	.02	.01
(letter "g" is missing from Chicago)			
□ 60 Richard Dent	.10	.05	.01
□ 61 Ron Rivera	.05	.02	.01
□ 62 Jim McMahon	.10	.05	.01
□ 63 Mike Tomczak	.10	.05	.01
□ 64 Neal Anderson	.10	.05	.01
□ 65 Dennis Gentry	.05	.02	.01
□ 66 Dan Hampton	.10	.05	.01
□ 67 David Tate	.05	.02	.01
□ 68 Thomas Sanders	.05	.02	.01
□ 69 Steve McMichael	.10	.05	.01
□ 70 Dennis McKinnon	.05	.02	.01
□ 71 Brad Muster	.05	.02	.01
□ 72 Vestee Jackson	.05	.02	.01
□ 73 Dave Duerson	.05	.02	.01
□ 74 Vikings Team	.05	.02	.01
Millard Gets His Man			
□ 75 Joey Browner	.05	.02	.01
□ 76 Carl Lee	.05	.02	.01
□ 77 Gary Zimmerman	.05	.02	.01
□ 78 Hassan Jones	.05	.02	.01
□ 79 Anthony Carter	.10	.05	.01
□ 80 Ray Berry	.05	.02	.01
□ 81 Steve Jordan	.05	.02	.01
□ 82 Issiac Holt	.05	.02	.01
□ 83 Wade Wilson	.10	.05	.01
□ 84 Chris Doleman	.10	.05	.01
□ 85 Alfred Anderson	.05	.02	.01
□ 86 Keith Millard	.05	.02	.01
□ 87 Darrin Nelson	.05	.02	.01
□ 88 D.J. Dozier	.05	.02	.01
□ 89 Scott Studwell	.05	.02	.01
□ 90 Oilers Team	.05	.02	.01
Tony Zendejas Big Boot			
□ 91 Bruce Matthews	.25	.11	.03
□ 92 Curtis Duncan	.05	.02	.01
□ 93 Warren Moon	.25	.11	.03
□ 94 Johnny Meads	.05	.02	.01
□ 95 Drew Hill	.05	.02	.01
□ 96 Alonzo Highsmith	.05	.02	.01
□ 97 Mike Munchak	.05	.02	.01
□ 98 Mike Rozier	.05	.02	.01
□ 99 Tony Zendejas	.05	.02	.01
□ 100 Jeff Donaldson	.05	.02	.01
□ 101 Ray Childress	.05	.02	.01
□ 102 Sean Jones	.10	.05	.01
□ 103 Ernest Givins	.10	.05	.01
□ 104 William Fuller	.25	.11	.03
□ 105 Allen Pinkett	.05	.02	.01
□ 106 Eagles Team	.05	.02	.01
Randall Cunningham Fakes Field			
□ 107 Keith Jackson	.50	.23	.06
□ 108 Reggie White	.25	.11	.03
□ 109 Clyde Simmons	.10	.05	.01
□ 110 John Teltschik	.05	.02	.01
□ 111 Wes Hopkins	.05	.02	.01
□ 112 Keith Byars	.10	.05	.01
□ 113 Jerome Brown	.10	.05	.01
□ 114 Mike Quick	.05	.02	.01
□ 115 Randall Cunningham	.10	.05	.01
□ 116 Anthony Toney	.05	.02	.01
□ 117 Ron Johnson	.05	.02	.01
□ 118 Terry Hoage	.05	.02	.01
□ 119 Seth Joyner	.10	.05	.01
□ 120 Eric Allen	.25	.11	.03
□ 121 Cris Carter	1.50	.70	.19
□ 122 Rams Team	.05	.02	.01
Greg Bell Runs To Glory			
□ 123 Tom Newberry	.05	.02	.01
□ 124 Pete Holohan	.05	.02	.01
□ 125 Robert Delpino UER	.05	.02	.01
(Listed as Raider on card back)			
□ 126 Carl Ekern	.05	.02	.01
□ 127 Greg Bell	.05	.02	.01
□ 128 Mike Lansford	.05	.02	.01
□ 129 Jim Everett	.10	.05	.01
□ 130 Mike Wilcher	.05	.02	.01
□ 131 Jerry Gray	.05	.02	.01
□ 132 Dale Hatcher	.05	.02	.01
□ 133 Doug Smith	.05	.02	.01
□ 134 Kevin Greene	.25	.11	.03
□ 135 Jackie Slater	.05	.02	.01
□ 136 Aaron Cox	.05	.02	.01
□ 137 Henry Ellard	.25	.11	.03
□ 138 Browns Team	.05	.02	.01
Bernie Kosar Quick Release			
□ 139 Frank Minnifield	.05	.02	.01
□ 140 Webster Slaughter	.10	.05	.01
□ 141 Bernie Kosar	.10	.05	.01
□ 142 Charles Buchanan	.05	.02	.01
□ 143 Clay Matthews	.10	.05	.01
□ 144 Reggie Langhorne	.05	.02	.01
□ 145 Hanford Dixon	.05	.02	.01
□ 146 Brian Brennan	.05	.02	.01
□ 147 Earnest Byner	.05	.02	.01
□ 148 Michael Dean Perry	.10	.05	.01
□ 149 Kevin Mack	.05	.02	.01
□ 150 Matt Bahr	.05	.02	.01
□ 151 Ozzie Newsome	.10	.05	.01
□ 152 Saints Team	.05	.02	.01
Craig Heyward Motors Forward			
□ 153 Morten Andersen	.05	.02	.01
□ 154 Pat Swilling	.10	.05	.01
□ 155 Sam Mills	.10	.05	.01
□ 156 Lonzell Hill	.05	.02	.01
□ 157 Dalton Hilliard	.05	.02	.01
□ 158 Craig Heyward	.10	.05	.01
□ 159 Vaughan Johnson	.05	.02	.01
□ 160 Rueben Mayes	.05	.02	.01
□ 161 Gene Atkins	.05	.02	.01
□ 162 Bobby Hebert	.10	.05	.01
□ 163 Rickey Jackson	.10	.05	.01
□ 164 Eric Martin	.05	.02	.01
□ 165 Giants Team	.05	.02	.01
Joe Morris Up The Middle			
□ 166 Lawrence Taylor	.25	.11	.03
□ 167 Bart Oates	.05	.02	.01
□ 168 Carl Banks	.05	.02	.01
□ 169 Eric Moore	.05	.02	.01
□ 170 Sheldon White	.05	.02	.01
□ 171 Mark Collins	.05	.02	.01
□ 172 Phil Simms	.10	.05	.01
□ 173 Jim Burt	.05	.02	.01
□ 174 Stephen Baker	.10	.05	.01
□ 175 Mark Bavaro	.10	.05	.01
□ 176 Pepper Johnson	.05	.02	.01
□ 177 Lionel Manuel	.05	.02	.01
□ 178 Joe Morris	.05	.02	.01
□ 179 John Elliott	.05	.02	.01
□ 180 Gary Reasons	.05	.02	.01
□ 181 Seahawks Team	.05	.02	.01
Dave Krieg Winds Up			
□ 182 Brian Blades	.50	.23	.06
□ 183 Steve Largent	.25	.11	.03
□ 184 Rufus Porter	.05	.02	.01
□ 185 Ruben Rodriguez	.05	.02	.01
□ 186 Curt Warner	.05	.02	.01
□ 187 Paul Moyer	.05	.02	.01
□ 188 Dave Krieg	.10	.05	.01
□ 189 Jacob Green	.05	.02	.01
□ 190 John L. Williams	.05	.02	.01
□ 191 Eugene Robinson	.05	.02	.01
□ 192 Brian Bosworth	.10	.05	.01
□ 193 Patriots Team	.05	.02	.01
Tony Eason Behind Blocking			
□ 194 John Stephens	.05	.02	.01
□ 195 Robert Perryman	.05	.02	.01
□ 196 Andre Tippett	.05	.02	.01
□ 197 Fred Marion	.05	.02	.01
□ 198 Doug Flutie	.25	.11	.03
□ 199 Stanley Morgan	.05	.02	.01
□ 200 Johnny Rembert	.05	.02	.01
□ 201 Tony Eason	.05	.02	.01
□ 202 Marvin Allen	.05	.02	.01
□ 203 Raymond Clayborn	.05	.02	.01
□ 204 Irving Fryar	.25	.11	.03
□ 205 Colts Team	.05	.02	.01
Chris Chandler All Alone			
□ 206 Eric Dickerson	.10	.05	.01
□ 207 Chris Hinton	.05	.02	.01
□ 208 Duane Bickett	.05	.02	.01
□ 209 Chris Chandler	.50	.23	.06
□ 210 Jon Hand	.05	.02	.01
□ 211 Ray Donaldson	.05	.02	.01
□ 212 Dean Biasucci	.05	.02	.01
□ 213 Bill Brooks	.10	.05	.01
□ 214 Chris Goode	.05	.02	.01
□ 215 Clarence Verdin	.05	.02	.01
□ 216 Albert Bentley	.05	.02	.01
□ 217 Passing Leaders	.05	.02	.01
Wade Wilson			
Boomer Esiason			
□ 218 Receiving Leaders	.05	.02	.01
Henry Ellard			
Al Toon			
□ 219 Rushing Leaders	.05	.02	.01
Herschel Walker			
Eric Dickerson			
□ 220 Scoring Leaders	.05	.02	.01
Mike Cofer			
Scott Norwood			
□ 221 Intercept Leaders	.05	.02	.01
Scott Case			
Erik McMillan			
□ 222 Jets Team	.05	.02	.01
Ken O'Brien Surveys Scene			
□ 223 Erik McMillan	.05	.02	.01
□ 224 James Hasty	.05	.02	.01
□ 225 Al Toon	.10	.05	.01
□ 226 John Booty	.05	.02	.01
□ 227 Johnny Hector	.05	.02	.01
□ 228 Ken O'Brien	.05	.02	.01
□ 229 Marty Lyons	.05	.02	.01
□ 230 Mickey Shuler	.05	.02	.01
□ 231 Robin Cole	.05	.02	.01
□ 232 Freeman McNeil	.05	.02	.01
□ 233 Marion Barber	.05	.02	.01
□ 234 Jo Jo Townsell	.05	.02	.01
□ 235 Wesley Walker	.05	.02	.01
□ 236 Roger Vick	.05	.02	.01
□ 237 Pat Leahy	.05	.02	.01
□ 238 Broncos Team UER	.30	.14	.04
John Elway Ground Attack (Score of week 15 says 42-21, should be 42-14)			
□ 239 Mike Horan	.05	.02	.01
□ 240 Tony Dorsett	.25	.11	.03
□ 241 John Elway	1.00	.45	.12
□ 242 Mark Jackson	.05	.02	.01
□ 243 Sammy Winder	.05	.02	.01
□ 244 Rich Karlis	.05	.02	.01
□ 245 Vance Johnson	.10	.05	.01
□ 246 Steve Sewell	.05	.02	.01
□ 247 Karl Mecklenburg UER	.05	.02	.01
(Drafted 2, should be 12)			
□ 248 Rulon Jones	.05	.02	.01
□ 249 Simon Fletcher	.05	.02	.01
□ 250 Redskins Team	.05	.02	.01
Doug Williams Sets Up			
□ 251 Chip Lohmiller	.05	.02	.01
□ 252 Jamie Morris	.05	.02	.01
□ 253 Mark Rypien UER	.10	.05	.01
(14 1988 completions, should be 114)			
□ 254 Barry Wilburn	.05	.02	.01
□ 255 Mark May	.05	.02	.01
□ 256 Wilber Marshall	.05	.02	.01
□ 257 Charles Mann	.05	.02	.01
□ 258 Gary Clark	.25	.11	.03
□ 259 Doug Williams	.10	.05	.01
□ 260 Art Monk	.10	.05	.01
□ 261 Kelvin Bryant	.05	.02	.01
□ 262 Dexter Manley	.05	.02	.01
□ 263 Ricky Sanders	.05	.02	.01
□ 264 Raiders Team	.25	.11	.03
Marcus Allen Through the Line			
□ 265 Tim Brown	1.50	.70	.19
□ 266 Jay Schroeder	.05	.02	.01
□ 267 Marcus Allen	.25	.11	.03
□ 268 Mike Haynes	.10	.05	.01
□ 269 Bo Jackson	.25	.11	.03
□ 270 Steve Beuerlein	.25	.11	.03
□ 271 Vann McElroy	.05	.02	.01
□ 272 Willie Gault	.10	.05	.01
□ 273 Howie Long	.10	.05	.01
□ 274 Greg Townsend	.05	.02	.01
□ 275 Mike Wise	.05	.02	.01
□ 276 Cardinals Team	.05	.02	.01
Neil Lomax Looks Long			
□ 277 Luis Sharpe	.05	.02	.01
□ 278 Scott Dill	.05	.02	.01
□ 279 Vai Sikahema	.05	.02	.01
□ 280 Ron Wolfley	.05	.02	.01
□ 281 David Galloway	.05	.02	.01
□ 282 Jay Novacek	.50	.23	.06
□ 283 Neil Lomax	.05	.02	.01
□ 284 Robert Awalt	.05	.02	.01
□ 285 Cedric Mack	.05	.02	.01
□ 286 Freddie Joe Nunn	.05	.02	.01
□ 287 J.T. Smith	.05	.02	.01
□ 288 Stump Mitchell	.05	.02	.01
□ 289 Roy Green	.10	.05	.01
□ 290 Dolphins Team	.60	.25	.07
Dan Marino High and Far			
□ 291 Jarvis Williams	.05	.02	.01
□ 292 Troy Stradford	.05	.02	.01
□ 293 Dan Marino	2.00	.90	.25
□ 294 T.J. Turner	.05	.02	.01
□ 295 John Offerdahl	.05	.02	.01
□ 296 Ferrell Edmunds	.05	.02	.01
□ 297 Scott Schwedes	.05	.02	.01
□ 298 Lorenzo Hampton	.05	.02	.01
□ 299 Jim C.Jensen	.05	.02	.01
□ 300 Brian Sochia	.05	.02	.01
□ 301 Reggie Roby	.05	.02	.01
□ 302 Mark Clayton	.10	.05	.01
□ 303 Chargers Team	.05	.02	.01
Tim Spencer Leads the Way			
□ 304 Lee Williams	.05	.02	.01
□ 305 Gary Plummer	.05	.02	.01
□ 306 Gary Anderson RB	.05	.02	.01
□ 307 Gill Byrd	.05	.02	.01
□ 308 Jamie Holland	.05	.02	.01
□ 309 Billy Ray Smith	.05	.02	.01
□ 310 Lionel James	.05	.02	.01
□ 311 Mark Vlasic	.05	.02	.01
□ 312 Curtis Adams	.05	.02	.01
□ 313 Anthony Miller	.75	.35	.09
□ 314 Steelers Team	.05	.02	.01
Frank Pollard Set for Action			
□ 315 Bubby Brister	.10	.05	.01
□ 316 David Little	.05	.02	.01
□ 317 Tunch Ilkin	.05	.02	.01
□ 318 Louis Lipps	.10	.05	.01
□ 319 Warren Williams	.05	.02	.01
□ 320 Dwight Stone	.10	.05	.01
□ 321 Merril Hoge	.05	.02	.01
□ 322 Thomas Everett	.05	.02	.01

	MINT	NRMT	EXC
☐ 323 Rod Woodson	1.00	.45	.12
☐ 324 Gary Anderson K	.05	.02	.01
☐ 325 Buccaneers Team Ron Hall in Pursuit	.05	.02	.01
☐ 326 Donnie Elder	.05	.02	.01
☐ 327 Vinny Testaverde	.10	.05	.01
☐ 328 Harry Hamilton	.05	.02	.01
☐ 329 James Wilder	.05	.02	.01
☐ 330 Lars Tate	.05	.02	.01
☐ 331 Mark Carrier WR	.50	.23	.06
☐ 332 Bruce Hill	.05	.02	.01
☐ 333 Paul Gruber	.05	.02	.01
☐ 334 Ricky Reynolds	.05	.02	.01
☐ 335 Eugene Marve	.05	.02	.01
☐ 336 Falcons Team Joel Williams Holds On	.05	.02	.01
☐ 337 Aundray Bruce	.05	.02	.01
☐ 338 John Rade	.05	.02	.01
☐ 339 Scott Case	.05	.02	.01
☐ 340 Robert Moore	.05	.02	.01
☐ 341 Chris Miller	.25	.11	.03
☐ 342 Gerald Riggs	.10	.05	.01
☐ 343 Gene Lang	.05	.02	.01
☐ 344 Marcus Cotton	.05	.02	.01
☐ 345 Rick Donnelly	.05	.02	.01
☐ 346 John Settle	.05	.02	.01
☐ 347 Bill Fralic	.05	.02	.01
☐ 348 Chiefs Team Dino Hackett Zeros In	.05	.02	.01
☐ 349 Steve DeBerg	.05	.02	.01
☐ 350 Mike Stensrud	.05	.02	.01
☐ 351 Dino Hackett	.05	.02	.01
☐ 352 Deron Cherry	.10	.05	.01
☐ 353 Christian Okoye	.05	.02	.01
☐ 354 Bill Maas	.05	.02	.01
☐ 355 Carlos Carson	.05	.02	.01
☐ 356 Albert Lewis	.05	.02	.01
☐ 357 Paul Palmer	.05	.02	.01
☐ 358 Nick Lowery	.05	.02	.01
☐ 359 Stephone Paige	.05	.02	.01
☐ 360 Lions Team Chuck Long Gets the Snap	.05	.02	.01
☐ 361 Chris Spielman	.50	.23	.06
☐ 362 Jim Arnold	.05	.02	.01
☐ 363 Devon Mitchell	.05	.02	.01
☐ 364 Mike Cofer	.05	.02	.01
☐ 365 Bennie Blades	.05	.02	.01
☐ 366 James Jones	.05	.02	.01
☐ 367 Garry James	.05	.02	.01
☐ 368 Pete Mandley	.05	.02	.01
☐ 369 Keith Ferguson	.05	.02	.01
☐ 370 Dennis Gibson	.05	.02	.01
☐ 371 Packers Team UER Johnny Holland Over the Top (Week 16 has vs. Vikings, but they played Bears)	.05	.02	.01
☐ 372 Brent Fullwood	.05	.02	.01
☐ 373 Don Majkowski UER (3 TD's in 1987, should be 5)	.10	.05	.01
☐ 374 Tim Harris	.05	.02	.01
☐ 375 Keith Woodside	.05	.02	.01
☐ 376 Mark Murphy	.05	.02	.01
☐ 377 Dave Brown	.05	.02	.01
☐ 378 Perry Kemp	.05	.02	.01
☐ 379 Sterling Sharpe	1.00	.45	.12
☐ 380 Chuck Cecil	.05	.02	.01
☐ 381 Walter Stanley	.05	.02	.01
☐ 382 Cowboys Team Steve Pelluer Lets It Go	.05	.02	.01
☐ 383 Michael Irvin	1.50	.70	.19
☐ 384 Bill Bates	.10	.05	.01
☐ 385 Herschel Walker	.25	.11	.03
☐ 386 Darryl Clack	.05	.02	.01
☐ 387 Danny Noonan	.05	.02	.01
☐ 388 Eugene Lockhart	.05	.02	.01
☐ 389 Ed Too Tall Jones	.10	.05	.01
☐ 390 Steve Pelluer	.05	.02	.01
☐ 391 Ray Alexander	.05	.02	.01
☐ 392 Nate Newton	.10	.05	.01
☐ 393 Garry Cobb	.05	.02	.01
☐ 394 Checklist 1-132	.05	.02	.01
☐ 395 Checklist 133-264	.05	.02	.01
☐ 396 Checklist 265-396	.05	.02	.01

1989 Topps Box Bottoms

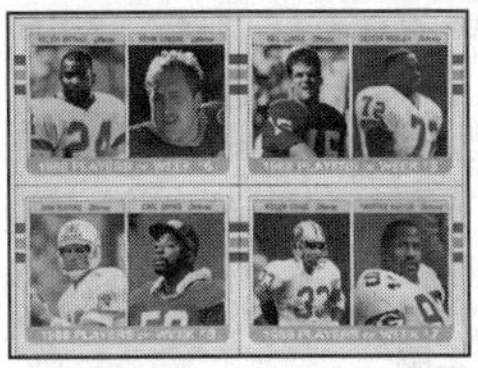

These cards were printed on the bottom of 1989 Topps wax pack boxes. This 16-card standard-size set features the NFL's offensive and defensive players of the week for each week in the 1989 season. Each card features two players on the front.

	MINT	NRMT	EXC
COMPLETE SET (16)	6.00	2.70	.75
COMMON CARD (A-P)	.25	.11	.03
☐ A Neal Anderson Terry Hoage	.25	.11	.03
☐ B Boomer Esiason Jacob Green	.50	.23	.06
☐ C Wesley Walker Gary Jeter	.35	.16	.04
☐ D Jim Everett Danny Noonan	.35	.16	.04
☐ E Neil Lomax Dexter Manley	.25	.11	.03
☐ F Kelvin Bryant Kevin Greene	.25	.11	.03
☐ G Roger Craig Tim Harris	.50	.23	.06
☐ H Dan Marino Carl Banks	3.00	1.35	.35
☐ I Drew Hill Robin Cole	.25	.11	.03
☐ J Neil Lomax Lawrence Taylor	.50	.23	.06
☐ K Roy Green Tim Krumrie	.25	.11	.03
☐ L Bobby Hebert Aundray Bruce	.25	.11	.03
☐ M Ickey Woods Lawrence Taylor	.50	.23	.06
☐ N Louis Lipps Greg Townsend	.25	.11	.03
☐ O Curt Warner Tim Harris	.35	.16	.04
☐ P Dave Krieg Kevin Greene	.75	.35	.09

1989 Topps 1000 Yard Club

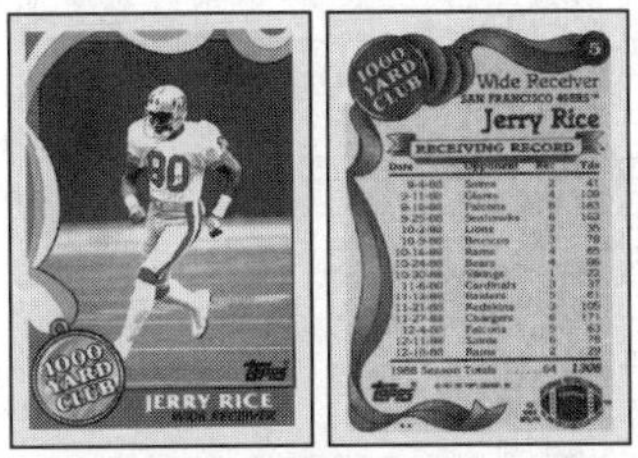

This glossy insert set was included one per wax pack with the regular issue 1989 Topps football cards. The set features, in order of yards gained, all players achieving 1000 yards gained either rushing or receiving. The cards are standard size. The card numbers are actually a ranking of each player's standing with respect to total yards gained in 1988. Card backs detail statistically the game by game performance of the player in terms of yards gained against each opponent.

	MINT	NRMT	EXC
COMPLETE SET (24)	4.00	1.80	.50
COMMON CARD (1-24)	.15	.07	.02
☐ 1 Eric Dickerson	.40	.18	.05
☐ 2 Herschel Walker	.40	.18	.05
☐ 3 Roger Craig	.40	.18	.05
☐ 4 Henry Ellard	.25	.11	.03
☐ 5 Jerry Rice	2.00	.90	.25
☐ 6 Eddie Brown	.15	.07	.02
☐ 7 Anthony Carter	.25	.11	.03
☐ 8 Greg Bell	.15	.07	.02
☐ 9 John Stephens	.15	.07	.02
☐ 10 Ricky Sanders	.15	.07	.02
☐ 11 Drew Hill	.15	.07	.02
☐ 12 Mark Clayton	.25	.11	.03
☐ 13 Gary Anderson RB	.15	.07	.02
☐ 14 Neal Anderson	.25	.11	.03
☐ 15 Roy Green	.25	.11	.03
☐ 16 Eric Martin	.25	.11	.03
☐ 17 Joe Morris	.15	.07	.02
☐ 18 Al Toon	.25	.11	.03
☐ 19 Ickey Woods	.15	.07	.02
☐ 20 Bruce Hill	.15	.07	.02
☐ 21 Lionel Manuel	.15	.07	.02
☐ 22 Curt Warner	.25	.11	.03
☐ 23 John Settle	.15	.07	.02
☐ 24 Mike Rozier	.25	.11	.03

1989 Topps Traded

The 1989 Topps Traded set contains 132 standard-size cards featuring rookies and traded players in their new uniforms. The cards are nearly identical to the 1989 Topps regular issue football set, except this traded series was printed on white stock and was distributed only as a boxed set. The card are numbered with a "T" suffix. Rookie Cards include Troy Aikman, Marion Butts, Jim Harbaugh, Greg Lloyd, Dave Meggett, Eric Metcalf, Frank Reich, Andre Rison, Barry Sanders, Deion Sanders, Derrick Thomas, Steve Walsh and Lorenzo White.

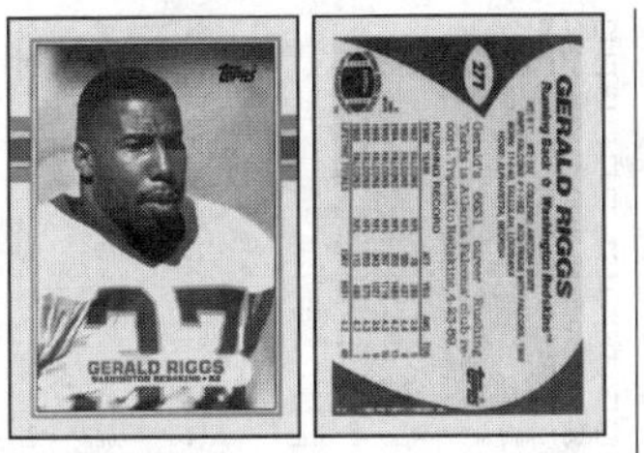

	MINT	NRMT	EXC
COMPLETE FACT.SET (132)	6.00	2.70	.75
COMMON CARD (1T-132T)	.05	.02	.01
☐ 1T Eric Ball	.05	.02	.01
☐ 2T Tony Mandarich	.05	.02	.01
☐ 3T Shawn Collins	.05	.02	.01
☐ 4T Ray Bentley	.05	.02	.01
☐ 5T Tony Casillas	.05	.02	.01
☐ 6T Al Del Greco	.05	.02	.01
☐ 7T Dan Saleaumua	.10	.05	.01
☐ 8T Keith Bishop	.05	.02	.01
☐ 9T Rodney Peete	.25	.11	.03
☐ 10T Lorenzo White	.25	.11	.03
☐ 11T Steve Smith	.10	.05	.01
☐ 12T Pete Mandley	.05	.02	.01
☐ 13T Mervyn Fernandez	.05	.02	.01
☐ 14T Flipper Anderson	.25	.11	.03
☐ 15T Louis Oliver	.10	.05	.01
☐ 16T Rick Fenney	.05	.02	.01
☐ 17T Gary Jeter	.05	.02	.01
☐ 18T Greg Cox	.05	.02	.01
☐ 19T Bubba McDowell	.10	.05	.01
☐ 20T Ron Heller	.05	.02	.01
☐ 21T Tim McDonald	.05	.02	.01
☐ 22T Jerrol Williams	.05	.02	.01
☐ 23T Marion Butts	.10	.05	.01
☐ 24T Steve Young	.75	.35	.09
☐ 25T Mike Merriweather	.05	.02	.01
☐ 26T Richard Johnson	.05	.02	.01
☐ 27T Gerald Riggs	.10	.05	.01
☐ 28T Dave Waymer	.05	.02	.01
☐ 29T Issiac Holt	.05	.02	.01
☐ 30T Deion Sanders	1.00	.45	.12
☐ 31T Todd Blackledge	.05	.02	.01
☐ 32T Jeff Cross	.05	.02	.01
☐ 33T Steve Wisniewski	.10	.05	.01
☐ 34T Ron Brown	.10	.05	.01
☐ 35T Rod Bernstine	.05	.02	.01
☐ 36T Jeff Uhlenhake	.05	.02	.01
☐ 37T Donnell Woolford	.25	.11	.03
☐ 38T Bob Gagliano	.05	.02	.01
☐ 39T Ezra Johnson	.05	.02	.01
☐ 40T Ron Jaworski	.05	.02	.01
☐ 41T Lawyer Tillman	.05	.02	.01
☐ 42T Lorenzo Lynch	.05	.02	.01
☐ 43T Mike Alexander	.05	.02	.01
☐ 44T Tim Worley	.05	.02	.01
☐ 45T Guy Bingham	.05	.02	.01
☐ 46T Cleveland Gary	.05	.02	.01
☐ 47T Danny Peebles	.05	.02	.01
☐ 48T Clarence Weathers	.05	.02	.01
☐ 49T Jeff Lageman	.25	.11	.03
☐ 50T Eric Metcalf	.40	.18	.05
☐ 51T Myron Guyton	.05	.02	.01
☐ 52T Steve Atwater	.05	.02	.01
☐ 53T John Fourcade	.05	.02	.01
☐ 54T Randall McDaniel	.10	.05	.01
☐ 55T Al Noga	.05	.02	.01
☐ 56T Sammie Smith	.10	.05	.01
☐ 57T Jesse Solomon	.05	.02	.01
☐ 58T Greg Kragen	.05	.02	.01
☐ 59T Don Beebe	.25	.11	.03
☐ 60T Hart Lee Dykes	.10	.05	.01
☐ 61T Trace Armstrong	.10	.05	.01
☐ 62T Steve Pelluer	.05	.02	.01
☐ 63T Barry Krauss	.05	.02	.01
☐ 64T Kevin Murphy	.05	.02	.01
☐ 65T Steve Tasker	.05	.02	.01
☐ 66T Jessie Small	.05	.02	.01
☐ 67T Dave Meggett	.25	.11	.03
☐ 68T Dean Hamel	.05	.02	.01
☐ 69T Jim Covert	.05	.02	.01
☐ 70T Troy Aikman	2.50	1.10	.30
☐ 71T Raul Allegre	.05	.02	.01
☐ 72T Chris Jacke	.10	.05	.01
☐ 73T Leslie O'Neal	.10	.05	.01
☐ 74T Keith Taylor	.05	.02	.01
☐ 75T Steve Walsh	.25	.11	.03
☐ 76T Tracy Rocker	.05	.02	.01
☐ 77T Robert Massey	.10	.05	.01
☐ 78T Bryan Wagner	.05	.02	.01
☐ 79T Steve DeOssie	.05	.02	.01
☐ 80T Carnell Lake	.10	.05	.01
☐ 81T Frank Reich	.25	.11	.03
☐ 82T Tyrone Braxton	.05	.02	.01
☐ 83T Barry Sanders	2.50	1.10	.30
☐ 84T Pete Stoyanovich	.10	.05	.01
☐ 85T Paul Palmer	.05	.02	.01
☐ 86T Billy Joe Tolliver	.05	.02	.01
☐ 87T Eric Hill	.10	.05	.01
☐ 88T Gerald McNeil	.05	.02	.01
☐ 89T Bill Hawkins	.05	.02	.01
☐ 90T Derrick Thomas	.40	.18	.05
☐ 91T Jim Harbaugh	1.00	.45	.12
☐ 92T Brian Williams	.05	.02	.01
☐ 93T Jack Trudeau	.05	.02	.01
☐ 94T Leonard Smith	.05	.02	.01
☐ 95T Gary Hogeboom	.05	.02	.01
☐ 96T A.J. Johnson	.05	.02	.01
☐ 97T Jim McMahon	.10	.05	.01
☐ 98T David Williams	.05	.02	.01
☐ 99T Rohn Stark	.05	.02	.01
☐ 100T Sean Landeta	.05	.02	.01
☐ 101T Tim Johnson	.05	.02	.01
☐ 102T Andre Rison	.40	.18	.05
☐ 103T Earnest Byner	.10	.05	.01
☐ 104T Don McPherson	.05	.02	.01
☐ 105T Zefross Moss	.05	.02	.01
☐ 106T Frank Stams	.05	.02	.01
☐ 107T Courtney Hall	.10	.05	.01
☐ 108T Marc Logan	.05	.02	.01
☐ 109T James Lofton	.25	.11	.03
☐ 110T Lewis Tillman	.10	.05	.01
☐ 111T Irv Pankey	.05	.02	.01
☐ 112T Ralf Mojsiejenko	.05	.02	.01
☐ 113T Bobby Humphrey	.05	.02	.01
☐ 114T Chris Burkett	.05	.02	.01
☐ 115T Greg Lloyd	.60	.25	.07
☐ 116T Matt Millen	.10	.05	.01
☐ 117T Carl Zander	.05	.02	.01
☐ 118T Wayne Martin	.25	.11	.03
☐ 119T Mike Saxon	.05	.02	.01
☐ 120T Herschel Walker	.10	.05	.01
☐ 121T Andy Heck	.05	.02	.01
☐ 122T Mark Robinson	.05	.02	.01
☐ 123T Keith Van Horne	.05	.02	.01
☐ 124T Ricky Hunley	.05	.02	.01
☐ 125T Timm Rosenbach	.10	.05	.01
☐ 126T Steve Grogan	.10	.05	.01
☐ 127T Stephen Braggs	.05	.02	.01
☐ 128T Terry Long	.05	.02	.01
☐ 129T Evan Cooper	.05	.02	.01
☐ 130T Robert Lyles	.05	.02	.01
☐ 131T Mike Webster	.10	.05	.01
☐ 132T Checklist 1-132	.05	.02	.01

1989 Topps American/UK

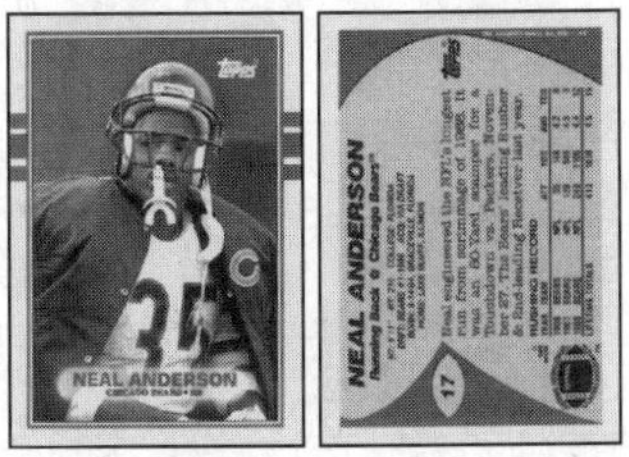

This 33-card standard-size set was sold in the United Kingdom as a boxed set. The style of the cards is very similar to the 1989 Topps regular issue set. The backs are different as this set was printed on white card stock. The checklist for the set is on the back of the box. The set is populated with name players that, presumably, would be recognizable in England.

	MINT	NRMT	EXC
COMPLETE SET (33)	25.00	11.00	3.10
COMMON CARD (1-33)	.50	.23	.06
☐ 1 Anthony Carter	.75	.35	.09
☐ 2 Jim Kelly	2.00	.90	.25
☐ 3 Bernie Kosar	.75	.35	.09
☐ 4 John Elway	4.00	1.80	.50
☐ 5 Andre Tippett	.50	.23	.06
☐ 6 Henry Ellard	.75	.35	.09
☐ 7 Eddie Brown	.50	.23	.06
☐ 8 Gary Anderson RB	.50	.23	.06
☐ 9 Eric Martin	.50	.23	.06
☐ 10 Ickey Woods	.50	.23	.06
☐ 11 Mike Singletary	.75	.35	.09
☐ 12 Phil Simms	1.00	.45	.12
☐ 13 Brian Bosworth	.50	.23	.06
☐ 14 Mark Clayton	.75	.35	.09
☐ 15 Eric Dickerson	.75	.35	.09
☐ 16 John Stephens	.50	.23	.06
☐ 17 Neal Anderson	.75	.35	.09
☐ 18 Al Toon	.50	.23	.06
☐ 19 Lionel Manuel	.50	.23	.06
☐ 20 Joe Montana	5.00	2.20	.60
☐ 21 Reggie White	2.00	.90	.25
☐ 22 Randall Cunningham	.75	.35	.09
☐ 23 Lawrence Taylor	1.25	.55	.16
☐ 24 Jim Everett	.75	.35	.09
☐ 25 Neil Lomax	.50	.23	.06
☐ 26 Herschel Walker	.75	.35	.09
☐ 27 Roger Craig	1.00	.45	.12
☐ 28 Greg Bell	.50	.23	.06
☐ 29 Ricky Sanders	.50	.23	.06
☐ 30 Joe Morris	.50	.23	.06
☐ 31 Curt Warner	.50	.23	.06
☐ 32 Boomer Esiason	.75	.35	.09
☐ 33 Dan Marino	7.50	3.40	.95

1990 Topps

Returning to 528 cards for the first time since 1982, these standard size cards were available in factory sets. Fifteen card wax packs which

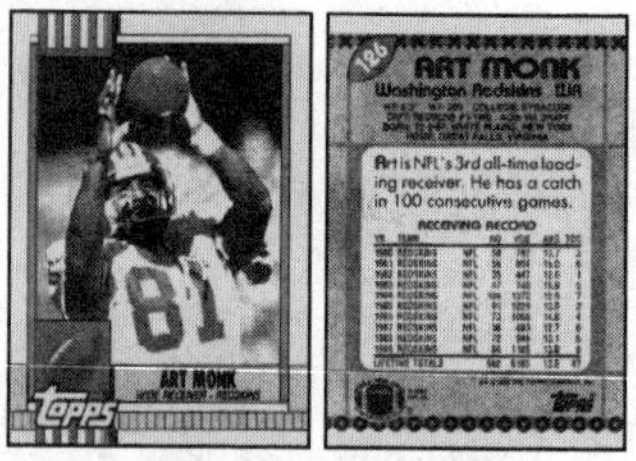

included an 1,000 yard club card were also issued. The fronts have hashmark border designs at top and bottom including and a football at bottom left. The player's name, team and position are beneath the photo. The backs, which can be found with variations, have yearly statistics and highlights. The NFL Properties disclaimer is either present or absent from the back each card. The cards are arranged in team order and the teams themselves are ordered according to their finish in the 1989 standings. Subsets include Record Breakers (1-5) and Team Action (501-528) cards. League leader cards are scattered throughout the set. A few leader cards (28, 193, 229, and 431) as well as all of the Team Action cards can be found with or without the hashmarks on the bottom of the card. Topps also produced a Tiffany or glossy edition of the set. Tiffany values are approximately five times the values listed below. Rookie Cards include Barry Foster, Jeff George, Rodney Hampton, Michael Haynes, Haywood Jeffires, Daryl Johnston, Brent Jones, Cortez Kennedy, Ken Norton Jr., Junior Seau and Blair Thomas.

	MINT	NRMT	EXC
COMPLETE SET (528)	8.00	3.60	1.00
COMPLETE FACT.SET (528)	10.00	4.50	1.25
COMMON CARD (1-528)	.04	.02	.01
☐ 1 Joe Montana RB	.50	.23	.06
Most TD Passes,			
Super Bowl			
☐ 2 Flipper Anderson RB	.04	.02	.01
Most Receiving			
Yards, Game			
☐ 3 Troy Aikman RB	.60	.25	.07
Most Passing Yards,			
Game, Rookie			
☐ 4 Kevin Butler RB	.04	.02	.01
Most Consecutive			
Field Goals			
☐ 5 Super Bowl XXIV	.04	.02	.01
49ers 55			
Broncos 10			
(line of scrimmage)			
☐ 6 Dexter Carter	.04	.02	.01
☐ 7 Matt Millen	.10	.05	.01
☐ 8 Jerry Rice	1.00	.45	.12
☐ 9 Ronnie Lott	.10	.05	.01
☐ 10 John Taylor	.10	.05	.01
☐ 11 Guy McIntyre	.04	.02	.01
☐ 12 Roger Craig	.10	.05	.01
☐ 13 Joe Montana	1.00	.45	.12
☐ 14 Brent Jones	.60	.25	.07
☐ 15 Tom Rathman	.04	.02	.01
☐ 16 Harris Barton	.04	.02	.01
☐ 17 Charles Haley	.10	.05	.01
☐ 18 Pierce Holt	.04	.02	.01
☐ 19 Michael Carter	.04	.02	.01
☐ 20 Chet Brooks	.04	.02	.01
☐ 21 Eric Wright	.04	.02	.01
☐ 22 Mike Cofer	.04	.02	.01
☐ 23 Jim Fahnhorst	.04	.02	.01
☐ 24 Keena Turner	.04	.02	.01
☐ 25 Don Griffin	.04	.02	.01
☐ 26 Kevin Fagan	.04	.02	.01
☐ 27 Bubba Paris	.04	.02	.01
☐ 28 Rushing Leaders	.30	.14	.04
Barry Sanders			
Christian Okoye			
☐ 29 Steve Atwater	.04	.02	.01
☐ 30 Tyrone Braxton	.04	.02	.01
☐ 31 Ron Holmes	.04	.02	.01
☐ 32 Bobby Humphrey	.04	.02	.01
☐ 33 Greg Kragen	.04	.02	.01
☐ 34 David Treadwell	.04	.02	.01
☐ 35 Karl Mecklenburg	.04	.02	.01
☐ 36 Dennis Smith	.04	.02	.01
☐ 37 John Elway	.50	.23	.06
☐ 38 Vance Johnson	.04	.02	.01
☐ 39 Simon Fletcher UER	.04	.02	.01
(Front DL, back LB)			
☐ 40 Jim Juriga	.04	.02	.01
☐ 41 Mark Jackson	.04	.02	.01
☐ 42 Melvin Bratton	.04	.02	.01
☐ 43 Wymon Henderson	.04	.02	.01
☐ 44 Ken Bell	.04	.02	.01
☐ 45 Sammy Winder	.04	.02	.01
☐ 46 Alphonso Carreker	.04	.02	.01
☐ 47 Orson Mobley	.04	.02	.01
☐ 48 Rodney Hampton	1.00	.45	.12
☐ 49 Dave Meggett	.10	.05	.01
☐ 50 Myron Guyton	.04	.02	.01
☐ 51 Phil Simms	.10	.05	.01
☐ 52 Lawrence Taylor	.25	.11	.03
☐ 53 Carl Banks	.04	.02	.01
☐ 54 Pepper Johnson	.04	.02	.01
☐ 55 Leonard Marshall	.04	.02	.01
☐ 56 Mark Collins	.04	.02	.01
☐ 57 Erik Howard	.04	.02	.01
☐ 58 Eric Dorsey	.04	.02	.01
☐ 59 Ottis Anderson	.10	.05	.01
☐ 60 Mark Bavaro	.04	.02	.01
☐ 61 Odessa Turner	.04	.02	.01
☐ 62 Gary Reasons	.04	.02	.01
☐ 63 Maurice Carthon	.04	.02	.01
☐ 64 Lionel Manuel	.04	.02	.01
☐ 65 Sean Landeta	.04	.02	.01
☐ 66 Perry Williams	.04	.02	.01
☐ 67 Pat Terrell	.04	.02	.01
☐ 68 Flipper Anderson	.04	.02	.01
☐ 69 Jackie Slater	.04	.02	.01
☐ 70 Tom Newberry	.04	.02	.01
☐ 71 Jerry Gray	.04	.02	.01
☐ 72 Henry Ellard	.10	.05	.01
☐ 73 Doug Smith	.04	.02	.01
☐ 74 Kevin Greene	.25	.11	.03
☐ 75 Jim Everett	.10	.05	.01
☐ 76 Mike Lansford	.04	.02	.01
☐ 77 Greg Bell	.04	.02	.01
☐ 78 Pete Holohan	.04	.02	.01
☐ 79 Robert Delpino	.04	.02	.01
☐ 80 Mike Wilcher	.04	.02	.01
☐ 81 Mike Piel	.04	.02	.01
☐ 82 Mel Owens	.04	.02	.01
☐ 83 Michael Stewart	.04	.02	.01
☐ 84 Ben Smith	.04	.02	.01
☐ 85 Keith Jackson	.10	.05	.01
☐ 86 Reggie White	.25	.11	.03
☐ 87 Eric Allen	.04	.02	.01
☐ 88 Jerome Brown	.04	.02	.01
☐ 89 Robert Drummond	.04	.02	.01
☐ 90 Anthony Toney	.04	.02	.01
☐ 91 Keith Byars	.04	.02	.01
☐ 92 Cris Carter	.25	.11	.03
☐ 93 Randall Cunningham	.10	.05	.01
☐ 94 Ron Johnson	.04	.02	.01
☐ 95 Mike Quick	.04	.02	.01
☐ 96 Clyde Simmons	.04	.02	.01
☐ 97 Mike Pitts	.04	.02	.01
☐ 98 Izel Jenkins	.04	.02	.01
☐ 99 Seth Joyner	.10	.05	.01
☐ 100 Mike Schad	.04	.02	.01
☐ 101 Wes Hopkins	.04	.02	.01
☐ 102 Kirk Lowdermilk	.04	.02	.01
☐ 103 Rick Fenney	.04	.02	.01
☐ 104 Randall McDaniel	.04	.02	.01
☐ 105 Herschel Walker	.10	.05	.01
☐ 106 Al Noga	.04	.02	.01
☐ 107 Gary Zimmerman	.04	.02	.01
☐ 108 Chris Doleman	.04	.02	.01
☐ 109 Keith Millard	.04	.02	.01
☐ 110 Carl Lee	.04	.02	.01
☐ 111 Joey Browner	.04	.02	.01
☐ 112 Steve Jordan	.04	.02	.01
☐ 113 Reggie Rutland	.04	.02	.01
☐ 114 Wade Wilson	.10	.05	.01
☐ 115 Anthony Carter	.10	.05	.01
☐ 116 Rich Karlis	.04	.02	.01
☐ 117 Hassan Jones	.04	.02	.01
☐ 118 Henry Thomas	.04	.02	.01
☐ 119 Scott Studwell	.04	.02	.01
☐ 120 Ralf Mojsiejenko	.04	.02	.01
☐ 121 Earnest Byner	.04	.02	.01
☐ 122 Gerald Riggs	.10	.05	.01
☐ 123 Tracy Rocker	.04	.02	.01
☐ 124 A.J. Johnson	.04	.02	.01
☐ 125 Charles Mann	.04	.02	.01
☐ 126 Art Monk	.10	.05	.01
☐ 127 Ricky Sanders	.04	.02	.01
☐ 128 Gary Clark	.25	.11	.03
☐ 129 Jim Lachey	.04	.02	.01
☐ 130 Martin Mayhew	.04	.02	.01
☐ 131 Ravin Caldwell	.04	.02	.01
☐ 132 Don Warren	.04	.02	.01
☐ 133 Mark Rypien	.10	.05	.01
☐ 134 Ed Simmons	.04	.02	.01
☐ 135 Darryl Grant	.04	.02	.01
☐ 136 Darrell Green	.10	.05	.01
☐ 137 Chip Lohmiller	.04	.02	.01
☐ 138 Tony Bennett	.25	.11	.03
☐ 139 Tony Mandarich	.04	.02	.01
☐ 140 Sterling Sharpe	.25	.11	.03
☐ 141 Tim Harris	.04	.02	.01
☐ 142 Don Majkowski	.04	.02	.01
☐ 143 Rich Moran	.04	.02	.01
☐ 144 Jeff Query	.04	.02	.01
☐ 145 Brent Fullwood	.04	.02	.01
☐ 146 Chris Jacke	.04	.02	.01
☐ 147 Keith Woodside	.04	.02	.01
☐ 148 Perry Kemp	.04	.02	.01
☐ 149 Herman Fontenot	.04	.02	.01
☐ 150 Dave Brown	.04	.02	.01
☐ 151 Brian Noble	.04	.02	.01
☐ 152 Johnny Holland	.04	.02	.01
☐ 153 Mark Murphy	.04	.02	.01
☐ 154 Bob Nelson	.04	.02	.01
☐ 155 Darrell Thompson	.04	.02	.01
☐ 156 Lawyer Tillman	.04	.02	.01
☐ 157 Eric Metcalf	.25	.11	.03
☐ 158 Webster Slaughter	.10	.05	.01
☐ 159 Frank Minnifield	.04	.02	.01
☐ 160 Brian Brennan	.04	.02	.01
☐ 161 Thane Gash	.04	.02	.01
☐ 162 Robert Banks	.04	.02	.01
☐ 163 Bernie Kosar	.10	.05	.01
☐ 164 David Grayson	.04	.02	.01
☐ 165 Kevin Mack	.04	.02	.01
☐ 166 Mike Johnson	.04	.02	.01
☐ 167 Tim Manoa	.04	.02	.01
☐ 168 Ozzie Newsome	.10	.05	.01
☐ 169 Felix Wright	.04	.02	.01
☐ 170 Al(Bubba) Baker	.10	.05	.01
☐ 171 Reggie Langhorne	.04	.02	.01
☐ 172 Clay Matthews	.10	.05	.01
☐ 173 Andrew Stewart	.04	.02	.01
☐ 174 Barry Foster	.25	.11	.03
☐ 175 Tim Worley	.04	.02	.01
☐ 176 Tim Johnson	.04	.02	.01
☐ 177 Carnell Lake	.04	.02	.01
☐ 178 Greg Lloyd	.25	.11	.03
☐ 179 Rod Woodson	.25	.11	.03
☐ 180 Tunch Ilkin	.04	.02	.01
☐ 181 Dermontti Dawson	.10	.05	.01
☐ 182 Gary Anderson K	.04	.02	.01
☐ 183 Bubby Brister	.04	.02	.01
☐ 184 Louis Lipps	.10	.05	.01
☐ 185 Merril Hoge	.04	.02	.01
☐ 186 Mike Mularkey	.04	.02	.01
☐ 187 Derek Hill	.04	.02	.01
☐ 188 Rodney Carter	.04	.02	.01
☐ 189 Dwayne Woodruff	.04	.02	.01
☐ 190 Keith Willis	.04	.02	.01
☐ 191 Jerry Olsavsky	.04	.02	.01
☐ 192 Mark Stock	.04	.02	.01
☐ 193 Sacks Leaders	.04	.02	.01
Chris Doleman			
Lee Williams			
☐ 194 Leonard Smith	.04	.02	.01
☐ 195 Darryl Talley	.04	.02	.01
☐ 196 Mark Kelso	.04	.02	.01
☐ 197 Kent Hull	.04	.02	.01
☐ 198 Nate Odomes	.10	.05	.01
☐ 199 Pete Metzelaars	.04	.02	.01
☐ 200 Don Beebe	.10	.05	.01
☐ 201 Ray Bentley	.04	.02	.01
☐ 202 Steve Tasker	.10	.05	.01
☐ 203 Scott Norwood	.04	.02	.01
☐ 204 Andre Reed	.25	.11	.03
☐ 205 Bruce Smith	.25	.11	.03
☐ 206 Thurman Thomas	.40	.18	.05
☐ 207 Jim Kelly	.25	.11	.03
☐ 208 Cornelius Bennett	.10	.05	.01
☐ 209 Shane Conlan	.04	.02	.01
☐ 210 Larry Kinnebrew	.04	.02	.01
☐ 211 Jeff Alm	.04	.02	.01
☐ 212 Robert Lyles	.04	.02	.01
☐ 213 Bubba McDowell	.04	.02	.01
☐ 214 Mike Munchak	.04	.02	.01
☐ 215 Bruce Matthews	.10	.05	.01
☐ 216 Warren Moon	.25	.11	.03
☐ 217 Drew Hill	.04	.02	.01
☐ 218 Ray Childress	.04	.02	.01
☐ 219 Steve Brown	.04	.02	.01
☐ 220 Alonzo Highsmith	.04	.02	.01
☐ 221 Allen Pinkett	.04	.02	.01
☐ 222 Sean Jones	.10	.05	.01
☐ 223 Johnny Meads	.04	.02	.01
☐ 224 John Grimsley	.04	.02	.01
☐ 225 Haywood Jeffires	.25	.11	.03
☐ 226 Curtis Duncan	.04	.02	.01
☐ 227 Greg Montgomery	.04	.02	.01
☐ 228 Ernest Givins	.10	.05	.01
☐ 229 Passing Leaders	.30	.14	.04
Joe Montana			
Boomer Esiason			
☐ 230 Robert Massey	.04	.02	.01
☐ 231 John Fourcade	.04	.02	.01
☐ 232 Dalton Hilliard	.04	.02	.01
☐ 233 Vaughan Johnson	.04	.02	.01
☐ 234 Hoby Brenner	.04	.02	.01
☐ 235 Pat Swilling	.10	.05	.01
☐ 236 Kevin Haverdink	.04	.02	.01
☐ 237 Bobby Hebert	.04	.02	.01
☐ 238 Sam Mills	.10	.05	.01
☐ 239 Eric Martin	.04	.02	.01
☐ 240 Lonzell Hill	.04	.02	.01
☐ 241 Steve Trapilo	.04	.02	.01
☐ 242 Rickey Jackson	.10	.05	.01
☐ 243 Craig Heyward	.10	.05	.01
☐ 244 Rueben Mayes	.04	.02	.01
☐ 245 Morten Andersen	.04	.02	.01
☐ 246 Percy Snow	.04	.02	.01
☐ 247 Pete Mandley	.04	.02	.01
☐ 248 Derrick Thomas	.25	.11	.03
☐ 249 Dan Saleaumua	.04	.02	.01
☐ 250 Todd McNair	.04	.02	.01
☐ 251 Leonard Griffin	.04	.02	.01
☐ 252 Jonathan Hayes	.04	.02	.01
☐ 253 Christian Okoye	.04	.02	.01
☐ 254 Albert Lewis	.04	.02	.01
☐ 255 Nick Lowery	.04	.02	.01
☐ 256 Kevin Ross	.04	.02	.01
☐ 257 Steve DeBerg UER	.04	.02	.01
(Total 45,046,			
should be 25,046)			
☐ 258 Stephone Paige	.04	.02	.01
☐ 259 James Saxon	.04	.02	.01
☐ 260 Herman Heard	.04	.02	.01
☐ 261 Deron Cherry	.04	.02	.01
☐ 262 Dino Hackett	.04	.02	.01
☐ 263 Neil Smith	.25	.11	.03
☐ 264 Steve Pelluer	.04	.02	.01
☐ 265 Eric Thomas	.04	.02	.01
☐ 266 Eric Ball	.04	.02	.01
☐ 267 Leon White	.04	.02	.01
☐ 268 Tim Krumrie	.04	.02	.01
☐ 269 Jason Buck	.04	.02	.01
☐ 270 Boomer Esiason	.10	.05	.01
☐ 271 Carl Zander	.04	.02	.01
☐ 272 Eddie Brown	.04	.02	.01
☐ 273 David Fulcher	.04	.02	.01
☐ 274 Tim McGee	.04	.02	.01
☐ 275 James Brooks	.10	.05	.01
☐ 276 Rickey Dixon	.04	.02	.01
☐ 277 Ickey Woods	.04	.02	.01
☐ 278 Anthony Munoz	.10	.05	.01
☐ 279 Rodney Holman	.04	.02	.01
☐ 280 Mike Alexander	.04	.02	.01
☐ 281 Mervyn Fernandez	.04	.02	.01
☐ 282 Steve Wisniewski	.10	.05	.01
☐ 283 Steve Smith	.04	.02	.01
☐ 284 Howie Long	.10	.05	.01
☐ 285 Bo Jackson	.25	.11	.03
☐ 286 Mike Dyal	.04	.02	.01
☐ 287 Thomas Benson	.04	.02	.01
☐ 288 Willie Gault	.10	.05	.01
☐ 289 Marcus Allen	.25	.11	.03
☐ 290 Greg Townsend	.04	.02	.01
☐ 291 Steve Beuerlein	.10	.05	.01
☐ 292 Scott Davis	.04	.02	.01
☐ 293 Eddie Anderson	.04	.02	.01
☐ 294 Terry McDaniel	.04	.02	.01
☐ 295 Tim Brown	.25	.11	.03
☐ 296 Bob Golic	.04	.02	.01
☐ 297 Jeff Jaeger	.04	.02	.01
☐ 298 Jeff George	.75	.35	.09
☐ 299 Chip Banks	.04	.02	.01
☐ 300 Andre Rison UER	.25	.11	.03
(Photo actually			
Clarence Weathers)			
☐ 301 Rohn Stark	.04	.02	.01
☐ 302 Keith Taylor	.04	.02	.01
☐ 303 Jack Trudeau	.04	.02	.01
☐ 304 Chris Hinton	.04	.02	.01
☐ 305 Ray Donaldson	.04	.02	.01
☐ 306 Jeff Herrod	.04	.02	.01
☐ 307 Clarence Verdin	.04	.02	.01
☐ 308 Jon Hand	.04	.02	.01
☐ 309 Bill Brooks	.04	.02	.01
☐ 310 Albert Bentley	.04	.02	.01
☐ 311 Mike Prior	.04	.02	.01
☐ 312 Pat Beach	.04	.02	.01
☐ 313 Eugene Daniel	.04	.02	.01
☐ 314 Duane Bickett	.04	.02	.01
☐ 315 Dean Biasucci	.04	.02	.01
☐ 316 Richmond Webb	.04	.02	.01
☐ 317 Jeff Cross	.04	.02	.01
☐ 318 Louis Oliver	.04	.02	.01
☐ 319 Sammie Smith	.04	.02	.01
☐ 320 Pete Stoyanovich	.04	.02	.01
☐ 321 John Offerdahl	.04	.02	.01
☐ 322 Ferrell Edmunds	.04	.02	.01
☐ 323 Dan Marino	1.25	.55	.16
☐ 324 Andre Brown	.04	.02	.01
☐ 325 Reggie Roby	.04	.02	.01
☐ 326 Jarvis Williams	.04	.02	.01
☐ 327 Roy Foster	.04	.02	.01
☐ 328 Mark Clayton	.10	.05	.01
☐ 329 Brian Sochia	.04	.02	.01
☐ 330 Mark Duper	.10	.05	.01
☐ 331 T.J. Turner	.04	.02	.01
☐ 332 Jeff Uhlenhake	.04	.02	.01
☐ 333 Jim C.Jensen	.04	.02	.01
☐ 334 Cortez Kennedy	.25	.11	.03
☐ 335 Andy Heck	.04	.02	.01
☐ 336 Rufus Porter	.04	.02	.01
☐ 337 Brian Blades	.10	.05	.01
☐ 338 Dave Krieg	.10	.05	.01
☐ 339 John L. Williams	.04	.02	.01
☐ 340 David Wyman	.04	.02	.01
☐ 341 Paul Skansi	.04	.02	.01
☐ 342 Eugene Robinson	.04	.02	.01
☐ 343 Joe Nash	.04	.02	.01
☐ 344 Jacob Green	.04	.02	.01
☐ 345 Jeff Bryant	.04	.02	.01
☐ 346 Ruben Rodriguez	.04	.02	.01
☐ 347 Norm Johnson	.04	.02	.01
☐ 348 Darren Comeaux	.04	.02	.01
☐ 349 Andre Ware	.10	.05	.01
☐ 350 Richard Johnson	.04	.02	.01
☐ 351 Rodney Peete	.10	.05	.01
☐ 352 Barry Sanders	1.25	.55	.16
☐ 353 Chris Spielman	.25	.11	.03
☐ 354 Eddie Murray	.04	.02	.01
☐ 355 Jerry Ball	.04	.02	.01
☐ 356 Mel Gray	.10	.05	.01
☐ 357 Eric Williams	.04	.02	.01
☐ 358 Robert Clark	.04	.02	.01
☐ 359 Jason Phillips	.04	.02	.01
☐ 360 Terry Taylor	.04	.02	.01
☐ 361 Bennie Blades	.04	.02	.01
☐ 362 Michael Cofer	.04	.02	.01

☐ 363 Jim Arnold .04 .02 .01
☐ 364 Marc Spindler .04 .02 .01
☐ 365 Jim Covert .04 .02 .01
☐ 366 Jim Harbaugh .25 .11 .03
☐ 367 Neal Anderson .10 .05 .01
☐ 368 Mike Singletary .10 .05 .01
☐ 369 John Roper .04 .02 .01
☐ 370 Steve McMichael .10 .05 .01
☐ 371 Dennis Gentry .04 .02 .01
☐ 372 Brad Muster .04 .02 .01
☐ 373 Ron Morris .04 .02 .01
☐ 374 James Thornton .04 .02 .01
☐ 375 Kevin Butler .04 .02 .01
☐ 376 Richard Dent .10 .05 .01
☐ 377 Dan Hampton .10 .05 .01
☐ 378 Jay Hilgenberg .04 .02 .01
☐ 379 Donnell Woolford .04 .02 .01
☐ 380 Trace Armstrong .04 .02 .01
☐ 381 Junior Seau 1.25 .55 .16
☐ 382 Rod Bernstine .04 .02 .01
☐ 383 Marion Butts .10 .05 .01
☐ 384 Burt Grossman .04 .02 .01
☐ 385 Darrin Nelson .04 .02 .01
☐ 386 Leslie O'Neal .10 .05 .01
☐ 387 Billy Joe Tolliver .04 .02 .01
☐ 388 Courtney Hall .04 .02 .01
☐ 389 Lee Williams .04 .02 .01
☐ 390 Anthony Miller .25 .11 .03
☐ 391 Gill Byrd .04 .02 .01
☐ 392 Wayne Walker .04 .02 .01
☐ 393 Billy Ray Smith .04 .02 .01
☐ 394 Vencie Glenn .04 .02 .01
☐ 395 Tim Spencer .04 .02 .01
☐ 396 Gary Plummer .04 .02 .01
☐ 397 Arthur Cox .04 .02 .01
☐ 398 Jamie Holland .04 .02 .01
☐ 399 Keith McCants .04 .02 .01
☐ 400 Kevin Murphy .04 .02 .01
☐ 401 Danny Peebles .04 .02 .01
☐ 402 Mark Robinson .04 .02 .01
☐ 403 Broderick Thomas .04 .02 .01
☐ 404 Ron Hall .04 .02 .01
☐ 405 Mark Carrier WR .25 .11 .03
☐ 406 Paul Gruber .04 .02 .01
☐ 407 Vinny Testaverde .10 .05 .01
☐ 408 Bruce Hill .04 .02 .01
☐ 409 Lars Tate .04 .02 .01
☐ 410 Harry Hamilton .04 .02 .01
☐ 411 Ricky Reynolds .04 .02 .01
☐ 412 Donald Igwebuike .04 .02 .01
☐ 413 Reuben Davis .04 .02 .01
☐ 414 William Howard .04 .02 .01
☐ 415 Winston Moss .04 .02 .01
☐ 416 Chris Singleton .04 .02 .01
☐ 417 Hart Lee Dykes .04 .02 .01
☐ 418 Steve Grogan .10 .05 .01
☐ 419 Bruce Armstrong .04 .02 .01
☐ 420 Robert Perryman .04 .02 .01
☐ 421 Andre Tippett .04 .02 .01
☐ 422 Sammy Martin .04 .02 .01
☐ 423 Stanley Morgan .04 .02 .01
☐ 424 Cedric Jones .04 .02 .01
☐ 425 Sean Farrell .04 .02 .01
☐ 426 Marc Wilson .04 .02 .01
☐ 427 John Stephens .04 .02 .01
☐ 428 Eric Sievers .04 .02 .01
☐ 429 Maurice Hurst .04 .02 .01
☐ 430 Johnny Rembert .04 .02 .01
☐ 431 Receiving Leaders .30 .14 .04
Jerry Rice
Andre Reed
☐ 432 Eric Hill .04 .02 .01
☐ 433 Gary Hogeboom .04 .02 .01
☐ 434 Timm Rosenbach UER .04 .02 .01
(Born 1967 in Everett,
Wa., should be 1966
in Missoula, Mont.)
☐ 435 Tim McDonald .04 .02 .01
☐ 436 Rich Camarillo .04 .02 .01
☐ 437 Luis Sharpe .04 .02 .01
☐ 438 J.T. Smith .04 .02 .01
☐ 439 Roy Green .10 .05 .01
☐ 440 Ernie Jones .04 .02 .01
☐ 441 Robert Awalt .04 .02 .01
☐ 442 Vai Sikahema .04 .02 .01
☐ 443 Joe Wolf .04 .02 .01
☐ 444 Stump Mitchell .04 .02 .01
☐ 445 David Galloway .04 .02 .01
☐ 446 Ron Wolfley .04 .02 .01
☐ 447 Freddie Joe Nunn .04 .02 .01
☐ 448 Blair Thomas .10 .05 .01
☐ 449 Jeff Lageman .04 .02 .01
☐ 450 Tony Eason .04 .02 .01
☐ 451 Erik McMillan .04 .02 .01
☐ 452 Jim Sweeney .04 .02 .01
☐ 453 Ken O'Brien .04 .02 .01
☐ 454 Johnny Hector .04 .02 .01
☐ 455 Jo Jo Townsell .04 .02 .01
☐ 456 Roger Vick .04 .02 .01
☐ 457 James Hasty .04 .02 .01
☐ 458 Dennis Byrd .10 .05 .01
☐ 459 Ron Stallworth .04 .02 .01
☐ 460 Mickey Shuler .04 .02 .01
☐ 461 Bobby Humphery .04 .02 .01
☐ 462 Kyle Clifton .04 .02 .01
☐ 463 Al Toon .10 .05 .01
☐ 464 Freeman McNeil .04 .02 .01
☐ 465 Pat Leahy .04 .02 .01
☐ 466 Scott Case .04 .02 .01
☐ 467 Shawn Collins .04 .02 .01
☐ 468 Floyd Dixon .04 .02 .01
☐ 469 Deion Sanders .50 .23 .06
☐ 470 Tony Casillas .04 .02 .01
☐ 471 Michael Haynes .25 .11 .03
☐ 472 Chris Miller .25 .11 .03
☐ 473 John Settle .04 .02 .01
☐ 474 Aundray Bruce .04 .02 .01
☐ 475 Gene Lang .04 .02 .01
☐ 476 Tim Gordon .04 .02 .01
☐ 477 Scott Fulhage .04 .02 .01
☐ 478 Bill Fralic .04 .02 .01
☐ 479 Jessie Tuggle .04 .02 .01
☐ 480 Marcus Cotton .04 .02 .01
☐ 481 Steve Walsh .10 .05 .01
☐ 482 Troy Aikman 1.25 .55 .16
☐ 483 Ray Horton .04 .02 .01
☐ 484 Tony Tolbert .10 .05 .01
☐ 485 Steve Folsom .04 .02 .01
☐ 486 Ken Norton .60 .25 .07
☐ 487 Kelvin Martin .04 .02 .01
☐ 488 Jack Del Rio .04 .02 .01
☐ 489 Daryl Johnston 1.00 .45 .12
☐ 490 Bill Bates .10 .05 .01
☐ 491 Jim Jeffcoat .04 .02 .01
☐ 492 Vince Albritton .04 .02 .01
☐ 493 Eugene Lockhart .04 .02 .01
☐ 494 Mike Saxon .04 .02 .01
☐ 495 James Dixon .04 .02 .01
☐ 496 Willie Broughton .04 .02 .01
☐ 497 Checklist 1-132 .04 .02 .01
☐ 498 Checklist 133-264 .04 .02 .01
☐ 499 Checklist 265-396 .04 .02 .01
☐ 500 Checklist 397-528 .04 .02 .01
☐ 501 Bears Team .10 .05 .01
(Jim) Harbaugh
Eludes the Pursuit
☐ 502 Bengals Team .04 .02 .01
Boomer (Esiason)
Studies the Defense
☐ 503 Bills Team .04 .02 .01
(Shane) Conlan Calls
Defensive Scheme
☐ 504 Broncos Team .04 .02 .01
(Melvin) Bratton
Breaks Away
☐ 505 Browns Team .04 .02 .01
(Bernie) Kosar
Calls the Play
☐ 506 Buccaneers Team .04 .02 .01
(Winston) Moss Assists
in Squeeze Play
☐ 507 Cardinals Team .04 .02 .01
(Michael) Zordich
Saves the Day
☐ 508 Chargers Team .04 .02 .01
(Lee) Williams
Plugs the Hole
☐ 509 Chiefs Team .04 .02 .01
(Deron) Cherry
Applies The "D"
☐ 510 Colts Team .04 .02 .01
(Jack) Trudeau
Begins a Reverse
☐ 511 Cowboys Team .50 .23 .06
(Troy) Aikman Directs
Ground Attack
☐ 512 Dolphins Team .04 .02 .01
Double-Decker By
(Louis) Oliver
and (Jarvis) Williams
☐ 513 Eagles Team .04 .02 .01
(Anthony) Toney
Bangs into the Line
☐ 514 Falcons Team .04 .02 .01
(Jessie) Tuggle
Falls on Fumble
☐ 515 49ers Team .25 .11 .03
(Joe) Montana To
(Roger) Craig,
A Winning Duo
☐ 516 Giants Team .04 .02 .01
(Phil) Simms Likes
His O.J. (Anderson)
☐ 517 Jets Team .04 .02 .01
A (James) Hasty Return
☐ 518 Lions Team .04 .02 .01
(Bob) Gagliano Orchestrates
The Offense
☐ 519 Oilers Team .10 .05 .01
(Warren) Moon
Scrambles to Daylight
☐ 520 Packers Team .04 .02 .01
A Bit Of Packer "Majik"
☐ 521 Patriots Team .04 .02 .01
(John) Stephens
Steams Ahead
☐ 522 Raiders Team .10 .05 .01
Bo (Jackson)
Knows Yardage
☐ 523 Rams Team .04 .02 .01
(Jim) Everett
Rolls Right
☐ 524 Redskins Team .04 .02 .01
(Gerald) Riggs
Rumbles Downfield
☐ 525 Saints Team .04 .02 .01
(Sam) Mills
Takes A Stand
☐ 526 Seahawks Team .04 .02 .01
(Grant) Feasel
Sets To Snap
☐ 527 Steelers Team .04 .02 .01
(Bubby) Brister
Has a Clear Lane
☐ 528 Vikings Team .04 .02 .01
(Rick) Fenney
Spots Opening

1990 Topps Box Bottoms

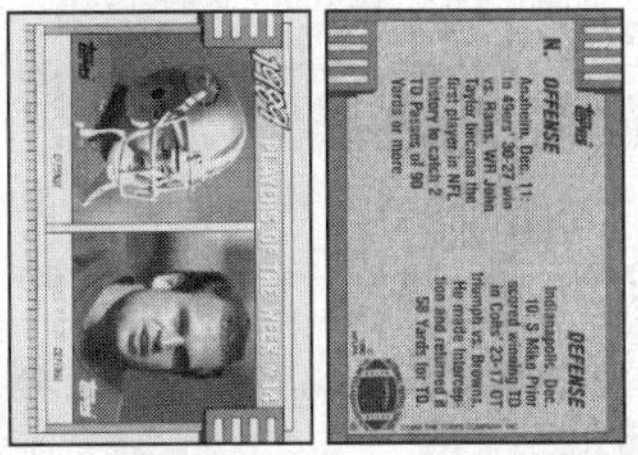

These cards were printed on the bottom of the 1990 Topps Wax Boxes. This 16-card standard-size set features the NFL's offensive and defensive player of the week for each week of the 1989 season. Each card features two players on the front and the back explains why they were the player of the week and what they did to earn the title. The cards are lettered rather than numbered. The set includes cards of Jim Kelly, Dan Marino, and Warren Moon. The set is checklisted in order of weeks of the season and is arranged alphabetically.

	MINT	NRMT	EXC
COMPLETE SET (16)	6.00	2.70	.75
COMMON CARD (A-P)	.25	.11	.03

☐ A Jim Kelly and .60 .25 .07
David Grayson
☐ B Henry Ellard and .40 .18 .05
Derrick Thomas
☐ C Joe Montana and 2.00 .90 .25
Vince Newsome
☐ D Bubby Brister and .25 .11 .03
Tim Harris
☐ E Christian Okoye and .25 .11 .03
Keith Millard
☐ F Warren Moon and .40 .18 .05
Jerome Brown
☐ G John Elway and 1.00 .45 .12
Mike Merriweather
☐ H Webster Slaughter and .25 .11 .03
Pat Swilling
☐ I Rich Karlis and .40 .18 .05
Lawrence Taylor
☐ J Dan Marino and 2.00 .90 .25
Greg Kragen
☐ K Boomer Esiason and .25 .11 .03
Brent Williams
☐ L Flipper Anderson and .25 .11 .03
Pierce Holt
☐ M Richard Johnson and .25 .11 .03
David Fulcher
☐ N John Taylor and .25 .11 .03
Mike Prior
☐ O Mark Rypien and .25 .11 .03
Brett Faryniarz
☐ P Greg Bell and .25 .11 .03
Chris Doleman

1990 Topps 1000 Yard Club

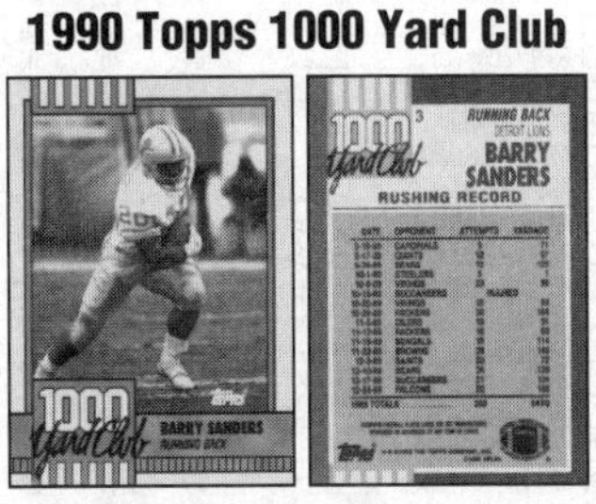

Topps once again in 1990 issued a card set which honored the players in the NFL who gained more than 1,000 yards in the 1989 season. These cards were included in every 1990 wax pack. The set consists of 30 standard size cards. The front features an attractive action photo of the player while the back has a game by game rundown of how the player achieved the 1,000 yard milestone. The set is arranged by Topps in order of number of yards gained in 1989. The cards in this set were released in two distinct varieties; the NFL Properties disclaimer is either present or absent from the back of each card.

	MINT	NRMT	EXC
COMPLETE SET (30)	5.00	2.20	.60
COMMON CARD (1-30)	.15	.07	.02

☐ 1 Jerry Rice 1.25 .55 .16
☐ 2 Christian Okoye .15 .07 .02
☐ 3 Barry Sanders 2.00 .90 .25
☐ 4 Sterling Sharpe .40 .18 .05
☐ 5 Mark Carrier WR .25 .11 .03
☐ 6 Henry Ellard .25 .11 .03
☐ 7 Andre Reed .40 .18 .05
☐ 8 Neal Anderson .15 .07 .02
☐ 9 Dalton Hilliard .15 .07 .02
☐ 10 Anthony Miller .40 .18 .05
☐ 11 Thurman Thomas .75 .35 .09
☐ 12 James Brooks .15 .07 .02
☐ 13 Webster Slaughter .15 .07 .02
☐ 14 Gary Clark .25 .11 .03
☐ 15 Tim McGee .15 .07 .02
☐ 16 Art Monk .25 .11 .03
☐ 17 Bobby Humphrey .15 .07 .02
☐ 18 Flipper Anderson .25 .11 .03
☐ 19 Ricky Sanders .15 .07 .02
☐ 20 Greg Bell .15 .07 .02
☐ 21 Vance Johnson .15 .07 .02
☐ 22 Richard Johnson UER .15 .07 .02
(Topps logo in upper
right corner)
☐ 23 Eric Martin .15 .07 .02
☐ 24 John Taylor .25 .11 .03
☐ 25 Mervyn Fernandez .15 .07 .02
☐ 26 Anthony Carter .25 .11 .03
☐ 27 Brian Blades .25 .11 .03
☐ 28 Roger Craig .25 .11 .03
☐ 29 Ottis Anderson .15 .07 .02
☐ 30 Mark Clayton .15 .07 .02

1990 Topps Traded

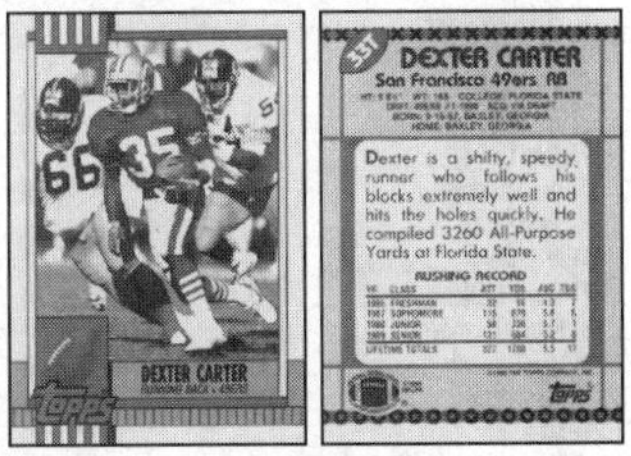

This 132-card standard-size set was released by Topps as an update to their regular issue set. The set features players who were traded after Topps printed their regular set and rookies who were not in the 1990 Topps football set. The set was issued in its own custom box and was distributed through the Topps hobby distribution system. The cards were printed on white card stock and are numbered on the back with a "T" suffix. Rookie Cards in the set inlcude Fred Barnett, Reggie Cobb, Harold Green, Stan Humphries, Johnny Johnson, Tony Martin, Terance Mathis, Rob Moore, Emmitt Smith and Calvin Williams.

	MINT	NRMT	EXC
COMPLETE FACT.SET (132)	8.00	3.60	1.00
COMMON CARD (1T-132T)	.05	.02	.01

☐ 1T Gerald McNeil .05 .02 .01
☐ 2T Andre Rison .25 .11 .03
☐ 3T Steve Walsh .25 .11 .03
☐ 4T Lorenzo White .10 .05 .01
☐ 5T Max Montoya .05 .02 .01
☐ 6T William Roberts .05 .02 .01
☐ 7T Alonzo Highsmith .05 .02 .01
☐ 8T Chris Hinton .10 .05 .01
☐ 9T Stanley Morgan .10 .05 .01
☐ 10T Mickey Shuler .05 .02 .01
☐ 11T Bobby Humphery .05 .02 .01
☐ 12T Gary Anderson RB .05 .02 .01
☐ 13T Mike Tomczak .10 .05 .01
☐ 14T Anthony Pleasant .10 .05 .01
☐ 15T Walter Stanley .05 .02 .01
☐ 16T Greg Bell .05 .02 .01
☐ 17T Tony Martin 1.00 .45 .12
☐ 18T Terry Kinard .05 .02 .01
☐ 19T Cris Carter .25 .11 .03
☐ 20T James Wilder .05 .02 .01
☐ 21T Jerry Kauric .05 .02 .01
☐ 22T Irving Fryar .25 .11 .03
☐ 23T Ken Harvey .25 .11 .03
☐ 24T James Williams .05 .02 .01
☐ 25T Ron Cox .05 .02 .01
☐ 26T Andre Ware .25 .11 .03
☐ 27T Emmitt Smith 7.00 3.10 .85
☐ 28T Junior Seau .75 .35 .09
☐ 29T Mark Carrier .25 .11 .03
☐ 30T Rodney Hampton .60 .25 .07
☐ 31T Rob Moore .40 .18 .05
☐ 32T Bern Brostek .05 .02 .01
☐ 33T Dexter Carter .10 .05 .01
☐ 34T Blair Thomas .10 .05 .01
☐ 35T Harold Green .25 .11 .03
☐ 36T Darrell Thompson .05 .02 .01
☐ 37T Eric Green .25 .11 .03
☐ 38T Renaldo Turnbull .25 .11 .03
☐ 39T Leroy Hoard .25 .11 .03

☐ 40T Anthony Thompson	.10	.05	.01
☐ 41T Jeff George	.50	.23	.06
☐ 42T Alexander Wright	.05	.02	.01
☐ 43T Richmond Webb	.05	.02	.01
☐ 44T Cortez Kennedy	.25	.11	.03
☐ 45T Ray Agnew	.05	.02	.01
☐ 46T Percy Snow	.05	.02	.01
☐ 47T Chris Singleton	.05	.02	.01
☐ 48T James Francis	.10	.05	.01
☐ 49T Tony Bennett	.10	.05	.01
☐ 50T Reggie Cobb	.10	.05	.01
☐ 51T Barry Foster	.25	.11	.03
☐ 52T Ben Smith	.05	.02	.01
☐ 53T Anthony Smith	.25	.11	.03
☐ 54T Steve Christie	.05	.02	.01
☐ 55T Johnny Bailey	.10	.05	.01
☐ 56T Alan Grant	.05	.02	.01
☐ 57T Eric Floyd	.05	.02	.01
☐ 58T Robert Blackmon	.05	.02	.01
☐ 59T Brent Williams	.05	.02	.01
☐ 60T Raymond Clayborn	.05	.02	.01
☐ 61T Dave Duerson	.05	.02	.01
☐ 62T Derrick Fenner	.10	.05	.01
☐ 63T Ken Willis	.05	.02	.01
☐ 64T Brad Baxter	.10	.05	.01
☐ 65T Tony Paige	.05	.02	.01
☐ 66T Jay Schroeder	.05	.02	.01
☐ 67T Jim Breech	.05	.02	.01
☐ 68T Barry Word	.10	.05	.01
☐ 69T Anthony Dilweg	.05	.02	.01
☐ 70T Rich Gannon	.10	.05	.01
☐ 71T Stan Humphries	.60	.25	.07
☐ 72T Jay Novacek	.25	.11	.03
☐ 73T Tommy Kane	.05	.02	.01
☐ 74T Everson Walls	.05	.02	.01
☐ 75T Mike Rozier	.10	.05	.01
☐ 76T Robb Thomas	.05	.02	.01
☐ 77T Terance Mathis	.25	.11	.03
☐ 78T LeRoy Irvin	.05	.02	.01
☐ 79T Jeff Donaldson	.05	.02	.01
☐ 80T Ethan Horton	.10	.05	.01
☐ 81T J.B. Brown	.05	.02	.01
☐ 82T Joe Kelly	.05	.02	.01
☐ 83T John Carney	.05	.02	.01
☐ 84T Dan Stryzinski	.05	.02	.01
☐ 85T John Kidd	.05	.02	.01
☐ 86T Al Smith	.10	.05	.01
☐ 87T Travis McNeal	.05	.02	.01
☐ 88T Reyna Thompson	.05	.02	.01
☐ 89T Rick Donnelly	.05	.02	.01
☐ 90T Marv Cook	.10	.05	.01
☐ 91T Mike Farr	.05	.02	.01
☐ 92T Daniel Stubbs	.05	.02	.01
☐ 93T Jeff Campbell	.05	.02	.01
☐ 94T Tim McKyer	.05	.02	.01
☐ 95T Ian Beckles	.05	.02	.01
☐ 96T Lemuel Stinson	.05	.02	.01
☐ 97T Frank Cornish	.05	.02	.01
☐ 98T Riki Ellison	.05	.02	.01
☐ 99T Jamie Mueller	.05	.02	.01
☐ 100T Brian Hansen	.05	.02	.01
☐ 101T Warren Powers	.05	.02	.01
☐ 102T Howard Cross	.05	.02	.01
☐ 103T Tim Grunhard	.05	.02	.01
☐ 104T Johnny Johnson	.25	.11	.03
☐ 105T Calvin Williams	.25	.11	.03
☐ 106T Keith McCants	.05	.02	.01
☐ 107T Lamar Lathon	.10	.05	.01
☐ 108T Steve Broussard	.10	.05	.01
☐ 109T Glenn Parker	.05	.02	.01
☐ 110T Alton Montgomery	.05	.02	.01
☐ 111T Jim McMahon	.10	.05	.01
☐ 112T Aaron Wallace	.05	.02	.01
☐ 113T Keith Sims	.05	.02	.01
☐ 114T Ervin Randle	.05	.02	.01
☐ 115T Walter Wilson	.05	.02	.01
☐ 116T Terry Wooden	.05	.02	.01
☐ 117T Bernard Clark	.05	.02	.01
☐ 118T Tony Stargell	.05	.02	.01
☐ 119T Jimmie Jones	.05	.02	.01
☐ 120T Andre Collins	.10	.05	.01
☐ 121T Ricky Proehl	.10	.05	.01
☐ 122T Darion Conner	.10	.05	.01
☐ 123T Jeff Rutledge	.05	.02	.01
☐ 124T Heath Sherman	.10	.05	.01
☐ 125T Tommie Agee	.05	.02	.01
☐ 126T Tory Epps	.05	.02	.01
☐ 127T Tommy Hodson	.05	.02	.01
☐ 128T Jessie Hester	.05	.02	.01
☐ 129T Alfred Oglesby	.05	.02	.01
☐ 130T Chris Chandler	.25	.11	.03
☐ 131T Fred Barnett	.40	.18	.05
☐ 132T Checklist 1-132	.05	.02	.01

1990 Topps Tiffany

This 528 card standard-size set parallels the regular 1990 Topps issue. These cards were printed in Ireland and feature glossy fronts and easy to read backs on white paper stock. They were issued in factory set form only.

	MINT	NRMT	EXC
COMPLETE FACT. SET (528)	50.00	22.00	6.25
COMMON CARD (1-528)	.25	.11	.03

*TIFFANY STARS: 3X TO 5X BASIC CARDS
*YOUNG STARS/RCs: 2.5X TO 4X BASIC CARDS

1991 Topps

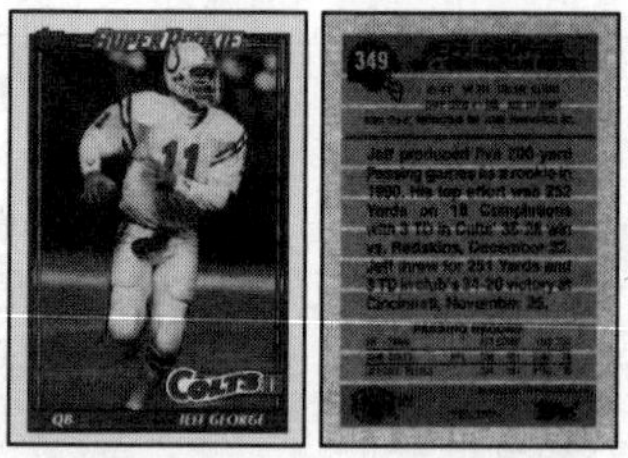

This 660-card standard size set marked Topps' largest football card set to date. Factory sets were issued once again. The design of the card front was the same as the football and hockey sets of that year. A team-colored border outlines the photo with the player's name and position appearing in the bottom border. The team name is at the bottom right of the photo. The backs contain highlights and statistics. Subsets include Highlights (2-7), league leaders (8-12) and team cards (628-655). The cards are arranged by team in order of 1991 finish. Rookie Cards include Ricky Ervins, Alvin Harper, Russell Maryland, Herman Moore, Eric Turner and Harvey Williams.

	MINT	NRMT	EXC
COMPLETE SET (660)	14.00	6.25	1.75
COMPLETE FACT.SET (660)	16.00	7.25	2.00
COMMON CARD (1-660)	.04	.02	.01

☐ 1 Super Bowl XXV	.04	.02	.01
☐ 2 Roger Craig HL	.10	.05	.01
☐ 3 Derrick Thomas HL	.10	.05	.01
☐ 4 Pete Stoyanovich HL	.04	.02	.01
☐ 5 Ottis Anderson HL	.10	.05	.01
☐ 6 Jerry Rice HL	.50	.23	.06
☐ 7 Warren Moon HL	.10	.05	.01
☐ 8 Leaders Passing Yards	.10	.05	.01
Warren Moon			
Jim Everett			
☐ 9 Leaders Rushing	.40	.18	.05
Barry Sanders			
Thurman Thomas			
☐ 10 Leaders Receiving	.30	.14	.04
Jerry Rice			
Haywood Jeffires			
☐ 11 Leaders Interceptions	.04	.02	.01
Mark Carrier DB			
Richard Johnson			
☐ 12 Leaders Sacks	.10	.05	.01
Derrick Thomas			
Charles Haley			
☐ 13 Jumbo Elliott	.04	.02	.01
☐ 14 Leonard Marshall	.04	.02	.01
☐ 15 William Roberts	.04	.02	.01
☐ 16 Lawrence Taylor	.25	.11	.03
☐ 17 Mark Ingram	.10	.05	.01
☐ 18 Rodney Hampton	.25	.11	.03
☐ 19 Carl Banks	.04	.02	.01
☐ 20 Ottis Anderson	.10	.05	.01
☐ 21 Mark Collins	.04	.02	.01
☐ 22 Pepper Johnson	.04	.02	.01
☐ 23 Dave Meggett	.10	.05	.01
☐ 24 Reyna Thompson	.04	.02	.01
☐ 25 Stephen Baker	.04	.02	.01
☐ 26 Mike Fox	.04	.02	.01
☐ 27 Maurice Carthon UER	.04	.02	.01
(Herschel Walker mis-			
spelled as Herschell)			
☐ 28 Jeff Hostetler	.25	.11	.03
☐ 29 Greg Jackson	.04	.02	.01
☐ 30 Sean Landeta	.04	.02	.01
☐ 31 Bart Oates	.04	.02	.01
☐ 32 Phil Simms	.10	.05	.01
☐ 33 Erik Howard	.04	.02	.01
☐ 34 Myron Guyton	.04	.02	.01
☐ 35 Mark Bavaro	.04	.02	.01
☐ 36 Jarrod Bunch	.04	.02	.01
☐ 37 Will Wolford	.04	.02	.01
☐ 38 Ray Bentley	.04	.02	.01
☐ 39 Nate Odomes	.04	.02	.01
☐ 40 Scott Norwood	.04	.02	.01
☐ 41 Darryl Talley	.04	.02	.01
☐ 42 Carwell Gardner	.04	.02	.01
☐ 43 James Lofton	.10	.05	.01
☐ 44 Shane Conlan	.04	.02	.01
☐ 45 Steve Tasker	.10	.05	.01
☐ 46 James Williams	.04	.02	.01
☐ 47 Kent Hull	.04	.02	.01
☐ 48 Al Edwards	.04	.02	.01
☐ 49 Frank Reich	.10	.05	.01
☐ 50 Leon Seals	.04	.02	.01
☐ 51 Keith McKeller	.04	.02	.01
☐ 52 Thurman Thomas	.25	.11	.03
☐ 53 Leonard Smith	.04	.02	.01
☐ 54 Andre Reed	.10	.05	.01
☐ 55 Kenneth Davis	.04	.02	.01
☐ 56 Jeff Wright	.04	.02	.01
☐ 57 Jamie Mueller	.04	.02	.01
☐ 58 Jim Ritcher	.04	.02	.01
☐ 59 Bruce Smith	.25	.11	.03
☐ 60 Ted Washington	.04	.02	.01
☐ 61 Guy McIntyre	.04	.02	.01
☐ 62 Michael Carter	.04	.02	.01
☐ 63 Pierce Holt	.04	.02	.01
☐ 64 Darryl Pollard	.04	.02	.01
☐ 65 Mike Sherrard	.04	.02	.01
☐ 66 Dexter Carter	.04	.02	.01
☐ 67 Bubba Paris	.04	.02	.01
☐ 68 Harry Sydney	.04	.02	.01
☐ 69 Tom Rathman	.04	.02	.01
☐ 70 Jesse Sapolu	.04	.02	.01
☐ 71 Mike Cofer	.04	.02	.01
☐ 72 Keith DeLong	.04	.02	.01
☐ 73 Joe Montana	1.00	.45	.12
☐ 74 Bill Romanowski	.04	.02	.01
☐ 75 John Taylor	.10	.05	.01
☐ 76 Brent Jones	.25	.11	.03
☐ 77 Harris Barton	.04	.02	.01
☐ 78 Charles Haley	.10	.05	.01
☐ 79 Eric Davis	.04	.02	.01
☐ 80 Kevin Fagan	.04	.02	.01
☐ 81 Jerry Rice	1.00	.45	.12
☐ 82 Dave Waymer	.04	.02	.01
☐ 83 Todd Marinovich	.04	.02	.01
☐ 84 Steve Smith	.04	.02	.01
☐ 85 Tim Brown	.25	.11	.03
☐ 86 Ethan Horton	.04	.02	.01
☐ 87 Marcus Allen	.25	.11	.03
☐ 88 Terry McDaniel	.04	.02	.01
☐ 89 Thomas Benson	.04	.02	.01
☐ 90 Roger Craig	.10	.05	.01
☐ 91 Don Mosebar	.04	.02	.01
☐ 92 Aaron Wallace	.04	.02	.01
☐ 93 Eddie Anderson	.04	.02	.01
☐ 94 Willie Gault	.10	.05	.01
☐ 95 Howie Long	.10	.05	.01
☐ 96 Jay Schroeder	.04	.02	.01
☐ 97 Ronnie Lott	.10	.05	.01
☐ 98 Bob Golic	.04	.02	.01
☐ 99 Bo Jackson	.10	.05	.01
☐ 100 Max Montoya	.04	.02	.01
☐ 101 Scott Davis	.04	.02	.01
☐ 102 Greg Townsend	.04	.02	.01
☐ 103 Garry Lewis	.04	.02	.01
☐ 104 Mervyn Fernandez	.04	.02	.01
☐ 105 Steve Wisniewski UER	.04	.02	.01
(Back has drafted,			
should be traded to)			
☐ 106 Jeff Jaeger	.04	.02	.01
☐ 107 Nick Bell	.04	.02	.01
☐ 108 Mark Dennis	.04	.02	.01
☐ 109 Jarvis Williams	.04	.02	.01
☐ 110 Mark Clayton	.10	.05	.01
☐ 111 Harry Galbreath	.04	.02	.01
☐ 112 Dan Marino	1.50	.70	.19
☐ 113 Louis Oliver	.04	.02	.01
☐ 114 Pete Stoyanovich	.04	.02	.01
☐ 115 Ferrell Edmunds	.04	.02	.01
☐ 116 Jeff Cross	.04	.02	.01
☐ 117 Richmond Webb	.04	.02	.01
☐ 118 Jim C. Jensen	.04	.02	.01
☐ 119 Keith Sims	.04	.02	.01
☐ 120 Mark Duper	.10	.05	.01
☐ 121 Shawn Lee	.04	.02	.01
☐ 122 Reggie Roby	.04	.02	.01
☐ 123 Jeff Uhlenhake	.04	.02	.01
☐ 124 Sammie Smith	.04	.02	.01
☐ 125 John Offerdahl	.04	.02	.01
☐ 126 Hugh Green	.04	.02	.01
☐ 127 Tony Paige	.04	.02	.01
☐ 128 David Griggs	.04	.02	.01
☐ 129 J.B. Brown	.04	.02	.01
☐ 130 Harvey Williams	.25	.11	.03
☐ 131 John Alt	.04	.02	.01
☐ 132 Albert Lewis	.04	.02	.01
☐ 133 Robb Thomas	.04	.02	.01
☐ 134 Neil Smith	.25	.11	.03
☐ 135 Stephone Paige	.04	.02	.01
☐ 136 Nick Lowery	.04	.02	.01
☐ 137 Steve DeBerg	.04	.02	.01
☐ 138 Rich Baldinger	.04	.02	.01
☐ 139 Percy Snow	.04	.02	.01
☐ 140 Kevin Porter	.04	.02	.01
☐ 141 Chris Martin	.04	.02	.01
☐ 142 Deron Cherry	.04	.02	.01
☐ 143 Derrick Thomas	.25	.11	.03
☐ 144 Tim Grunhard	.04	.02	.01
☐ 145 Todd McNair	.04	.02	.01
☐ 146 David Szott	.04	.02	.01
☐ 147 Dan Saleaumua	.04	.02	.01
☐ 148 Jonathan Hayes	.04	.02	.01
☐ 149 Christian Okoye	.04	.02	.01
☐ 150 Dino Hackett	.04	.02	.01
☐ 151 Bryan Barker	.04	.02	.01
☐ 152 Kevin Ross	.04	.02	.01
☐ 153 Barry Word	.04	.02	.01
☐ 154 Stan Thomas	.04	.02	.01
☐ 155 Brad Muster	.04	.02	.01
☐ 156 Donnell Woolford	.04	.02	.01
☐ 157 Neal Anderson	.10	.05	.01
☐ 158 Jim Covert	.04	.02	.01
☐ 159 Jim Harbaugh	.25	.11	.03
☐ 160 Shaun Gayle	.04	.02	.01
☐ 161 William Perry	.10	.05	.01
☐ 162 Ron Morris	.04	.02	.01
☐ 163 Mark Bortz	.04	.02	.01
☐ 164 James Thornton	.04	.02	.01
☐ 165 Ron Rivera	.04	.02	.01
☐ 166 Kevin Butler	.04	.02	.01
☐ 167 Jay Hilgenberg	.04	.02	.01
☐ 168 Peter Tom Willis	.04	.02	.01
☐ 169 Johnny Bailey	.04	.02	.01
☐ 170 Ron Cox	.04	.02	.01
☐ 171 Keith Van Horne	.04	.02	.01
☐ 172 Mark Carrier DB	.10	.05	.01
☐ 173 Richard Dent	.10	.05	.01
☐ 174 Wendell Davis	.04	.02	.01
☐ 175 Trace Armstrong	.04	.02	.01
☐ 176 Mike Singletary	.10	.05	.01
☐ 177 Chris Zorich	.25	.11	.03
☐ 178 Gerald Riggs	.04	.02	.01
☐ 179 Jeff Bostic	.04	.02	.01
☐ 180 Kurt Gouveia	.04	.02	.01
☐ 181 Stan Humphries	.25	.11	.03
☐ 182 Chip Lohmiller	.04	.02	.01
☐ 183 Raleigh McKenzie	.04	.02	.01
☐ 184 Alvin Walton	.04	.02	.01
☐ 185 Earnest Byner	.04	.02	.01
☐ 186 Markus Koch	.04	.02	.01
☐ 187 Art Monk	.10	.05	.01
☐ 188 Ed Simmons	.04	.02	.01
☐ 189 Bobby Wilson	.04	.02	.01
☐ 190 Charles Mann	.04	.02	.01
☐ 191 Darrell Green	.04	.02	.01
☐ 192 Mark Rypien	.10	.05	.01
☐ 193 Ricky Sanders	.04	.02	.01
☐ 194 Jim Lachey	.04	.02	.01
☐ 195 Martin Mayhew	.04	.02	.01
☐ 196 Gary Clark	.25	.11	.03
☐ 197 Wilber Marshall	.04	.02	.01
☐ 198 Darryl Grant	.04	.02	.01
☐ 199 Don Warren	.04	.02	.01
☐ 200 Ricky Ervins UER	.10	.05	.01
(Front has Chiefs,			
back has Redskins)			
☐ 201 Eric Allen	.04	.02	.01
☐ 202 Anthony Toney	.04	.02	.01
☐ 203 Ben Smith UER	.04	.02	.01
(Front CB, back S)			
☐ 204 David Alexander	.04	.02	.01
☐ 205 Jerome Brown	.04	.02	.01
☐ 206 Mike Golic	.04	.02	.01
☐ 207 Roger Ruzek	.04	.02	.01
☐ 208 Andre Waters	.04	.02	.01
☐ 209 Fred Barnett	.25	.11	.03
☐ 210 Randall Cunningham	.10	.05	.01
☐ 211 Mike Schad	.04	.02	.01
☐ 212 Reggie White	.25	.11	.03
☐ 213 Mike Bellamy	.04	.02	.01
☐ 214 Jeff Feagles	.04	.02	.01
☐ 215 Wes Hopkins	.04	.02	.01
☐ 216 Clyde Simmons	.04	.02	.01
☐ 217 Keith Byars	.04	.02	.01
☐ 218 Seth Joyner	.10	.05	.01
☐ 219 Byron Evans	.04	.02	.01
☐ 220 Keith Jackson	.10	.05	.01
☐ 221 Calvin Williams	.10	.05	.01
☐ 222 Mike Dumas	.04	.02	.01
☐ 223 Ray Childress	.04	.02	.01
☐ 224 Ernest Givins	.10	.05	.01
☐ 225 Lamar Lathon	.04	.02	.01
☐ 226 Greg Montgomery	.04	.02	.01
☐ 227 Mike Munchak	.04	.02	.01
☐ 228 Al Smith	.04	.02	.01
☐ 229 Bubba McDowell	.04	.02	.01
☐ 230 Haywood Jeffires	.10	.05	.01
☐ 231 Drew Hill	.04	.02	.01
☐ 232 William Fuller	.10	.05	.01
☐ 233 Warren Moon	.25	.11	.03
☐ 234 Doug Smith	.04	.02	.01
☐ 235 Cris Dishman	.04	.02	.01
☐ 236 Teddy Garcia	.04	.02	.01
☐ 237 Richard Johnson	.04	.02	.01
☐ 238 Bruce Matthews	.10	.05	.01
☐ 239 Gerald McNeil	.04	.02	.01
☐ 240 Johnny Meads	.04	.02	.01
☐ 241 Curtis Duncan	.04	.02	.01
☐ 242 Sean Jones	.10	.05	.01
☐ 243 Lorenzo White	.04	.02	.01
☐ 244 Rob Carpenter	.04	.02	.01
☐ 245 Bruce Reimers	.04	.02	.01
☐ 246 Ickey Woods	.04	.02	.01
☐ 247 Lewis Billups	.04	.02	.01
☐ 248 Boomer Esiason	.10	.05	.01
☐ 249 Tim Krumrie	.04	.02	.01
☐ 250 David Fulcher	.04	.02	.01
☐ 251 Jim Breech	.04	.02	.01
☐ 252 Mitchell Price	.04	.02	.01
☐ 253 Carl Zander	.04	.02	.01
☐ 254 Barney Bussey	.04	.02	.01
☐ 255 Leon White	.04	.02	.01
☐ 256 Eddie Brown	.04	.02	.01
☐ 257 James Francis	.04	.02	.01
☐ 258 Harold Green	.10	.05	.01
☐ 259 Anthony Munoz	.10	.05	.01
☐ 260 James Brooks	.10	.05	.01
☐ 261 Kevin Walker UER	.04	.02	.01
(Hometown should be			
West Milford Township)			
☐ 262 Bruce Kozerski	.04	.02	.01
☐ 263 David Grant	.04	.02	.01
☐ 264 Tim McGee	.04	.02	.01
☐ 265 Rodney Holman	.04	.02	.01

☐ 266 Dan McGwire	.04	.02	.01
☐ 267 Andy Heck	.04	.02	.01
☐ 268 Dave Krieg	.10	.05	.01
☐ 269 David Wyman	.04	.02	.01
☐ 270 Robert Blackmon	.04	.02	.01
☐ 271 Grant Feasel	.04	.02	.01
☐ 272 Patrick Hunter	.04	.02	.01
☐ 273 Travis McNeal	.04	.02	.01
☐ 274 John L. Williams	.04	.02	.01
☐ 275 Tony Woods	.04	.02	.01
☐ 276 Derrick Fenner	.04	.02	.01
☐ 277 Jacob Green	.04	.02	.01
☐ 278 Brian Blades	.10	.05	.01
☐ 279 Eugene Robinson	.04	.02	.01
☐ 280 Terry Wooden	.04	.02	.01
☐ 281 Jeff Bryant	.04	.02	.01
☐ 282 Norm Johnson	.04	.02	.01
☐ 283 Joe Nash UER	.04	.02	.01
Front DT, Back NT)			
☐ 284 Rick Donnelly	.04	.02	.01
☐ 285 Chris Warren	.40	.18	.05
☐ 286 Tommy Kane	.04	.02	.01
☐ 287 Cortez Kennedy	.25	.11	.03
☐ 288 Ernie Mills	.10	.05	.01
☐ 289 Dermontti Dawson	.04	.02	.01
☐ 290 Tunch Ilkin	.04	.02	.01
☐ 291 Tim Worley	.04	.02	.01
☐ 292 David Little	.04	.02	.01
☐ 293 Gary Anderson K	.04	.02	.01
☐ 294 Chris Calloway	.04	.02	.01
☐ 295 Carnell Lake	.04	.02	.01
☐ 296 Dan Stryzinski	.04	.02	.01
☐ 297 Rod Woodson	.25	.11	.03
☐ 298 John Jackson	.04	.02	.01
☐ 299 Bubby Brister	.04	.02	.01
☐ 300 Thomas Everett	.04	.02	.01
☐ 301 Merril Hoge	.04	.02	.01
☐ 302 Eric Green	.04	.02	.01
☐ 303 Greg Lloyd	.25	.11	.03
☐ 304 Gerald Williams	.04	.02	.01
☐ 305 Bryan Hinkle	.04	.02	.01
☐ 306 Keith Willis	.04	.02	.01
☐ 307 Louis Lipps	.04	.02	.01
☐ 308 Donald Evans	.04	.02	.01
☐ 309 D.J. Johnson	.04	.02	.01
☐ 310 Wesley Carroll	.04	.02	.01
☐ 311 Eric Martin	.04	.02	.01
☐ 312 Brett Maxie	.04	.02	.01
☐ 313 Rickey Jackson	.04	.02	.01
☐ 314 Robert Massey	.04	.02	.01
☐ 315 Pat Swilling	.10	.05	.01
☐ 316 Morten Andersen	.04	.02	.01
☐ 317 Toi Cook	.04	.02	.01
☐ 318 Sam Mills	.04	.02	.01
☐ 319 Steve Walsh	.04	.02	.01
☐ 320 Tommy Barnhardt	.04	.02	.01
☐ 321 Vince Buck	.04	.02	.01
☐ 322 Joel Hilgenberg	.04	.02	.01
☐ 323 Rueben Mayes	.04	.02	.01
☐ 324 Renaldo Turnbull	.04	.02	.01
☐ 325 Brett Perriman	.25	.11	.03
☐ 326 Vaughan Johnson	.04	.02	.01
☐ 327 Gill Fenerty	.04	.02	.01
☐ 328 Stan Brock	.04	.02	.01
☐ 329 Dalton Hilliard	.04	.02	.01
☐ 330 Hoby Brenner	.04	.02	.01
☐ 331 Craig Heyward	.10	.05	.01
☐ 332 Jon Hand	.04	.02	.01
☐ 333 Duane Bickett	.04	.02	.01
☐ 334 Jessie Hester	.04	.02	.01
☐ 335 Rohn Stark	.04	.02	.01
☐ 336 Zefross Moss	.04	.02	.01
☐ 337 Bill Brooks	.04	.02	.01
☐ 338 Clarence Verdin	.04	.02	.01
☐ 339 Mike Prior	.04	.02	.01
☐ 340 Chip Banks	.04	.02	.01
☐ 341 Dean Biasucci	.04	.02	.01
☐ 342 Ray Donaldson	.04	.02	.01
☐ 343 Jeff Herrod	.04	.02	.01
☐ 344 Donnell Thompson	.04	.02	.01
☐ 345 Chris Goode	.04	.02	.01
☐ 346 Eugene Daniel	.04	.02	.01
☐ 347 Pat Beach	.04	.02	.01
☐ 348 Keith Taylor	.04	.02	.01
☐ 349 Jeff George	.25	.11	.03
☐ 350 Tony Siragusa	.04	.02	.01
☐ 351 Randy Dixon	.04	.02	.01
☐ 352 Albert Bentley	.04	.02	.01
☐ 353 Russell Maryland	.25	.11	.03
☐ 354 Mike Saxon	.04	.02	.01
☐ 355 Godfrey Myles UER	.04	.02	.01
(Misspelled Miles			
on card front)			
☐ 356 Mark Stepnoski	.10	.05	.01
☐ 357 James Washington	.04	.02	.01
☐ 358 Jay Novacek	.25	.11	.03
☐ 359 Kelvin Martin	.04	.02	.01
☐ 360 Emmitt Smith UER	2.00	.90	.25
(Played for Florida,			
not Florida State)			
☐ 361 Jim Jeffcoat	.04	.02	.01
☐ 362 Alexander Wright	.04	.02	.01
☐ 363 James Dixon UER	.04	.02	.01
(Photo is not Dixon			
on card front)			
☐ 364 Alonzo Highsmith	.04	.02	.01
☐ 365 Daniel Stubbs	.04	.02	.01
☐ 366 Jack Del Rio	.04	.02	.01
☐ 367 Mark Tuinei	.04	.02	.01
☐ 368 Michael Irvin	.25	.11	.03
☐ 369 John Gesek	.04	.02	.01
☐ 370 Ken Willis	.04	.02	.01
☐ 371 Troy Aikman	1.00	.45	.12
☐ 372 Jimmie Jones	.04	.02	.01
☐ 373 Nate Newton	.10	.05	.01
☐ 374 Issiac Holt	.04	.02	.01
☐ 375 Alvin Harper	.25	.11	.03
☐ 376 Todd Kalis	.04	.02	.01
☐ 377 Wade Wilson	.10	.05	.01
☐ 378 Joey Browner	.04	.02	.01
☐ 379 Chris Doleman	.04	.02	.01
☐ 380 Hassan Jones	.04	.02	.01
☐ 381 Henry Thomas	.04	.02	.01
☐ 382 Darrell Fullington	.04	.02	.01
☐ 383 Steve Jordan	.04	.02	.01
☐ 384 Gary Zimmerman	.04	.02	.01
☐ 385 Ray Berry	.04	.02	.01
☐ 386 Cris Carter	.25	.11	.03
☐ 387 Mike Merriweather	.04	.02	.01
☐ 388 Carl Lee	.04	.02	.01
☐ 389 Keith Millard	.04	.02	.01
☐ 390 Reggie Rutland	.04	.02	.01
☐ 391 Anthony Carter	.10	.05	.01
☐ 392 Mark Dusbabek	.04	.02	.01
☐ 393 Kirk Lowdermilk	.04	.02	.01
☐ 394 Al Noga UER	.04	.02	.01
(Card says DT,			
should be DE)			
☐ 395 Herschel Walker	.10	.05	.01
☐ 396 Randall McDaniel	.04	.02	.01
☐ 397 Herman Moore	2.00	.90	.25
☐ 398 Eddie Murray	.04	.02	.01
☐ 399 Lomas Brown	.04	.02	.01
☐ 400 Marc Spindler	.04	.02	.01
☐ 401 Bennie Blades	.04	.02	.01
☐ 402 Kevin Glover	.04	.02	.01
☐ 403 Aubrey Matthews	.04	.02	.01
☐ 404 Michael Cofer	.04	.02	.01
☐ 405 Robert Clark	.04	.02	.01
☐ 406 Eric Andolsek	.04	.02	.01
☐ 407 William White	.04	.02	.01
☐ 408 Rodney Peete	.10	.05	.01
☐ 409 Mel Gray	.10	.05	.01
☐ 410 Jim Arnold	.04	.02	.01
☐ 411 Jeff Campbell	.04	.02	.01
☐ 412 Chris Spielman	.10	.05	.01
☐ 413 Jerry Ball	.04	.02	.01
☐ 414 Dan Owens	.04	.02	.01
☐ 415 Barry Sanders	1.00	.45	.12
☐ 416 Andre Ware	.10	.05	.01
☐ 417 Stanley Richard	.04	.02	.01
☐ 418 Gill Byrd	.04	.02	.01
☐ 419 John Kidd	.04	.02	.01
☐ 420 Sam Seale	.04	.02	.01
☐ 421 Gary Plummer	.04	.02	.01
☐ 422 Anthony Miller	.10	.05	.01
☐ 423 Ronnie Harmon	.04	.02	.01
☐ 424 Frank Cornish	.04	.02	.01
☐ 425 Marion Butts	.10	.05	.01
☐ 426 Leo Goeas	.04	.02	.01
☐ 427 Junior Seau	.40	.18	.05
☐ 428 Courtney Hall	.04	.02	.01
☐ 429 Leslie O'Neal	.10	.05	.01
☐ 430 Martin Bayless	.04	.02	.01
☐ 431 John Carney	.04	.02	.01
☐ 432 Lee Williams	.04	.02	.01
☐ 433 Arthur Cox	.04	.02	.01
☐ 434 Burt Grossman	.04	.02	.01
☐ 435 Nate Lewis	.04	.02	.01
☐ 436 Rod Bernstine	.04	.02	.01
☐ 437 Henry Rolling	.04	.02	.01
☐ 438 Billy Joe Tolliver	.04	.02	.01
☐ 439 Vinnie Clark	.04	.02	.01
☐ 440 Brian Noble	.04	.02	.01
☐ 441 Charles Wilson	.04	.02	.01
☐ 442 Don Majkowski	.04	.02	.01
☐ 443 Tim Harris	.04	.02	.01
☐ 444 Scott Stephen	.04	.02	.01
☐ 445 Perry Kemp	.04	.02	.01
☐ 446 Darrell Thompson	.04	.02	.01
☐ 447 Chris Jacke	.04	.02	.01
☐ 448 Mark Murphy	.04	.02	.01
☐ 449 Ed West	.04	.02	.01
☐ 450 LeRoy Butler	.10	.05	.01
☐ 451 Keith Woodside	.04	.02	.01
☐ 452 Tony Bennett	.10	.05	.01
☐ 453 Mark Lee	.04	.02	.01
☐ 454 James Campen	.04	.02	.01
☐ 455 Robert Brown	.04	.02	.01
☐ 456 Sterling Sharpe	.25	.11	.03
☐ 457A Tony Mandarich ERR	2.50	1.10	.30
Broncos listed as team			
☐ 457B Tony Mandarich COR	.04	.02	.01
Packers listed as team			
☐ 458 Johnny Holland	.04	.02	.01
☐ 459 Matt Brock	.04	.02	.01
☐ 460A Esera Tuaolo ERR	.04	.02	.01
(See also 462; no 1991			
NFL Draft Pick logo)			
☐ 460B Esera Tuaolo COR	.04	.02	.01
(See also 462; 1991 NFL			
Draft Pick logo on front)			
☐ 461 Freeman McNeil	.04	.02	.01
☐ 462 Terance Mathis UER	.25	.11	.03
(Card numbered in-			
correctly as 460)			
☐ 463 Rob Moore	.25	.11	.03
☐ 464 Darrell Davis	.04	.02	.01
☐ 465 Chris Burkett	.04	.02	.01
☐ 466 Jeff Criswell	.04	.02	.01
☐ 467 Tony Stargell	.04	.02	.01
☐ 468 Ken O'Brien	.04	.02	.01
☐ 469 Erik McMillan	.04	.02	.01
☐ 470 Jeff Lageman UER	.04	.02	.01
(Front DE, back LB)			
☐ 471 Pat Leahy	.04	.02	.01
☐ 472 Dennis Byrd	.04	.02	.01
☐ 473 Jim Sweeney	.04	.02	.01
☐ 474 Brad Baxter	.04	.02	.01
☐ 475 Joe Kelly	.04	.02	.01
☐ 476 Al Toon	.10	.05	.01
☐ 477 Joe Prokop	.04	.02	.01
☐ 478 Mark Boyer	.04	.02	.01
☐ 479 Kyle Clifton	.04	.02	.01
☐ 480 James Hasty	.04	.02	.01
☐ 481 Browning Nagle	.04	.02	.01
☐ 482 Gary Anderson RB	.04	.02	.01
☐ 483 Mark Carrier WR	.25	.11	.03
☐ 484 Ricky Reynolds	.04	.02	.01
☐ 485 Bruce Hill	.04	.02	.01
☐ 486 Steve Christie	.04	.02	.01
☐ 487 Paul Gruber	.04	.02	.01
☐ 488 Jesse Anderson	.04	.02	.01
☐ 489 Reggie Cobb	.04	.02	.01
☐ 490 Harry Hamilton	.04	.02	.01
☐ 491 Vinny Testaverde	.10	.05	.01
☐ 492 Mark Royals	.04	.02	.01
☐ 493 Keith McCants	.04	.02	.01
☐ 494 Ron Hall	.04	.02	.01
☐ 495 Ian Beckles	.04	.02	.01
☐ 496 Mark Robinson	.04	.02	.01
☐ 497 Reuben Davis	.04	.02	.01
☐ 498 Wayne Haddix	.04	.02	.01
☐ 499 Kevin Murphy	.04	.02	.01
☐ 500 Eugene Marve	.04	.02	.01
☐ 501 Broderick Thomas	.04	.02	.01
☐ 502 Eric Swann UER	.25	.11	.03
(Draft pick logo miss-			
ing from card front)			
☐ 503 Ernie Jones	.04	.02	.01
☐ 504 Rich Camarillo	.04	.02	.01
☐ 505 Tim McDonald	.04	.02	.01
☐ 506 Freddie Joe Nunn	.04	.02	.01
☐ 507 Tim Jorden	.04	.02	.01
☐ 508 Johnny Johnson	.04	.02	.01
☐ 509 Eric Hill	.04	.02	.01
☐ 510 Derek Kennard	.04	.02	.01
☐ 511 Ricky Proehl	.04	.02	.01
☐ 512 Bill Lewis	.04	.02	.01
☐ 513 Roy Green	.04	.02	.01
☐ 514 Anthony Bell	.04	.02	.01
☐ 515 Timm Rosenbach	.04	.02	.01
☐ 516 Jim Wahler	.04	.02	.01
☐ 517 Anthony Thompson	.04	.02	.01
☐ 518 Ken Harvey	.10	.05	.01
☐ 519 Luis Sharpe	.04	.02	.01
☐ 520 Walter Reeves	.04	.02	.01
☐ 521 Lonnie Young	.04	.02	.01
☐ 522 Rod Saddler	.04	.02	.01
☐ 523 Todd Lyght	.04	.02	.01
☐ 524 Alvin Wright	.04	.02	.01
☐ 525 Flipper Anderson	.04	.02	.01
☐ 526 Jackie Slater	.04	.02	.01
☐ 527 Damone Johnson	.04	.02	.01
☐ 528 Cleveland Gary	.04	.02	.01
☐ 529 Mike Piel	.04	.02	.01
☐ 530 Buford McGee	.04	.02	.01
☐ 531 Michael Stewart	.04	.02	.01
☐ 532 Jim Everett	.10	.05	.01
☐ 533 Mike Wilcher	.04	.02	.01
☐ 534 Irv Pankey	.04	.02	.01
☐ 535 Bern Brostek	.04	.02	.01
☐ 536 Henry Ellard	.10	.05	.01
☐ 537 Doug Smith	.04	.02	.01
☐ 538 Larry Kelm	.04	.02	.01
☐ 539 Pat Terrell	.04	.02	.01
☐ 540 Tom Newberry	.04	.02	.01
☐ 541 Jerry Gray	.04	.02	.01
☐ 542 Kevin Greene	.25	.11	.03
☐ 543 Duval Love	.04	.02	.01
☐ 544 Frank Stams	.04	.02	.01
☐ 545 Mike Croel	.04	.02	.01
☐ 546 Mark Jackson	.04	.02	.01
☐ 547 Greg Kragen	.04	.02	.01
☐ 548 Karl Mecklenburg	.04	.02	.01
☐ 549 Simon Fletcher	.04	.02	.01
☐ 550 Bobby Humphrey	.04	.02	.01
☐ 551 Ken Lanier	.04	.02	.01
☐ 552 Vance Johnson	.04	.02	.01
☐ 553 Ron Holmes	.04	.02	.01
☐ 554 John Elway	.75	.35	.09
☐ 555 Melvin Bratton	.04	.02	.01
☐ 556 Dennis Smith	.04	.02	.01
☐ 557 Ricky Nattiel	.04	.02	.01
☐ 558 Clarence Kay	.04	.02	.01
☐ 559 Michael Brooks	.04	.02	.01
☐ 560 Mike Horan	.04	.02	.01
☐ 561 Warren Powers	.04	.02	.01
☐ 562 Keith Kartz	.04	.02	.01
☐ 563 Shannon Sharpe	.50	.23	.06
☐ 564 Wymon Henderson	.04	.02	.01
☐ 565 Steve Atwater	.04	.02	.01
☐ 566 David Treadwell	.04	.02	.01
☐ 567 Bruce Pickens	.04	.02	.01
☐ 568 Jessie Tuggle	.04	.02	.01
☐ 569 Chris Hinton	.04	.02	.01
☐ 570 Keith Jones	.04	.02	.01
☐ 571 Bill Fralic	.04	.02	.01
☐ 572 Mike Rozier	.04	.02	.01
☐ 573 Scott Fulhage	.04	.02	.01
☐ 574 Floyd Dixon	.04	.02	.01
☐ 575 Andre Rison	.10	.05	.01
☐ 576 Darion Conner	.04	.02	.01
☐ 577 Brian Jordan	.10	.05	.01
☐ 578 Michael Haynes	.25	.11	.03
☐ 579 Oliver Barnett	.04	.02	.01
☐ 580 Shawn Collins	.04	.02	.01
☐ 581 Tim Green	.04	.02	.01
☐ 582 Deion Sanders	.60	.25	.07
☐ 583 Mike Kenn	.04	.02	.01
☐ 584 Mike Gann	.04	.02	.01
☐ 585 Chris Miller	.10	.05	.01
☐ 586 Tory Epps	.04	.02	.01
☐ 587 Steve Broussard	.04	.02	.01
☐ 588 Gary Wilkins	.04	.02	.01
☐ 589 Eric Turner	.10	.05	.01
☐ 590 Thane Gash	.04	.02	.01
☐ 591 Clay Matthews	.10	.05	.01
☐ 592 Mike Johnson	.04	.02	.01
☐ 593 Raymond Clayborn	.04	.02	.01
☐ 594 Leroy Hoard	.10	.05	.01
☐ 595 Reggie Langhorne	.04	.02	.01
☐ 596 Mike Baab	.04	.02	.01
☐ 597 Anthony Pleasant	.04	.02	.01
☐ 598 David Grayson	.04	.02	.01
☐ 599 Rob Burnett	.04	.02	.01
☐ 600 Frank Minnifield	.04	.02	.01
☐ 601 Gregg Rakoczy	.04	.02	.01
☐ 602 Eric Metcalf UER	.25	.11	.03
(1989 stats given twice)			
☐ 603 Paul Farren	.04	.02	.01
☐ 604 Brian Brennan	.04	.02	.01
☐ 605 Tony Jones	.04	.02	.01
☐ 606 Stephen Braggs	.04	.02	.01
☐ 607 Kevin Mack	.04	.02	.01
☐ 608 Pat Harlow	.04	.02	.01
☐ 609 Marv Cook	.04	.02	.01
☐ 610 John Stephens	.04	.02	.01
☐ 611 Ed Reynolds	.04	.02	.01
☐ 612 Tim Goad	.04	.02	.01
☐ 613 Chris Singleton	.04	.02	.01
☐ 614 Bruce Armstrong	.04	.02	.01
☐ 615 Tommy Hodson	.04	.02	.01
☐ 616 Sammy Martin	.04	.02	.01
☐ 617 Andre Tippett	.04	.02	.01
☐ 618 Johnny Rembert	.04	.02	.01
☐ 619 Maurice Hurst	.04	.02	.01
☐ 620 Vincent Brown	.04	.02	.01
☐ 621 Ray Agnew	.04	.02	.01
☐ 622 Ronnie Lippett	.04	.02	.01
☐ 623 Greg McMurtry	.04	.02	.01
☐ 624 Brent Williams	.04	.02	.01
☐ 625 Jason Staurovsky	.04	.02	.01
☐ 626 Marvin Allen	.04	.02	.01
☐ 627 Hart Lee Dykes	.04	.02	.01
☐ 628 Atlanta Falcons	.04	.02	.01
Team: (Keith) Jones			
Jumps for Yardage			
☐ 629 Buffalo Bills	.04	.02	.01
Team: (Jeff) Wright			
Goes for a Block			
☐ 630 Chicago Bears	.10	.05	.01
Team: (Jim) Harbaugh			
Makes Like a Halfback			
☐ 631 Cincinnati Bengals	.04	.02	.01
Team: (Stanford) Jennings			
Cuts Through Hole			
☐ 632 Cleveland Browns	.04	.02	.01
Team: (Eric) Metcalf			
Makes a Return			
☐ 633 Dallas Cowboys	.04	.02	.01
Team: (Kelvin) Martin			
Makes a Move			
☐ 634 Denver Broncos	.04	.02	.01
Team: (Shannon) Sharpe			
Into the Wedge			
☐ 635 Detroit Lions	.04	.02	.01
Team: (Rodney) Peete			
Hunted by a Bear			
(Mike Singletary)			
☐ 636 Green Bay Packers	.04	.02	.01
Team: (Don) Majkowski			
Orchestrates Some Magic			
☐ 637 Houston Oilers	.10	.05	.01
Team: (Warren) Moon			
Monitors the Action			
☐ 638 Indianapolis Colts	.04	.02	.01
Team: (Jeff) George			
Releases Just in Time			
☐ 639 Kansas City Chiefs	.04	.02	.01
Team: (Christian) Okoye			

Powers Ahead
- ☐ 640 Los Angeles Raiders .... .10 .05 .01
  Team: (Marcus) Allen
  Crosses the Plane
- ☐ 641 Los Angeles Rams .... .04 .02 .01
  Team: (Jim) Everett
  Connects With Soft Touch
- ☐ 642 Miami Dolphins.............. .04 .02 .01
  Team: (Pete) Stoyanovich
  Kicks It Through
- ☐ 643 Minnesota Vikings.............. .04 .02 .01
  Team: (Rich) Gannon
  Loads Cannon
- ☐ 644 New Eng. Patriots .... .04 .02 .01
  Team: (John) Stephens
  Gets Stood Up
- ☐ 645 New Orleans Saints.............. .04 .02 .01
  Team: (Gill) Fenerty
  Finds Opening
- ☐ 646 New York Giants.............. .04 .02 .01
  Team: (Maurice) Carthon
  Inches Ahead
- ☐ 647 New York Jets.............. .04 .02 .01
  Team: (Pat) Leahy
  Perfect on Extra Point
- ☐ 648 Philadelphia Eagles.............. .04 .02 .01
  Team: (Randall) Cunningham
  Calls Own Play for TD
- ☐ 649 Phoenix Cardinals .... .04 .02 .01
  Team: (Bill) Lewis
  Provides the Protection
- ☐ 650 Pittsburgh Steelers .... .04 .02 .01
  Team: (Bubby) Brister
  Eyes Downfield Attack
- ☐ 651 San Diego Chargers .... .04 .02 .01
  Team: (John) Friesz
  Finds the Passing Lane
- ☐ 652 San Francisco 49ers.............. .04 .02 .01
  Team: (Dexter) Carter
  Follows Rathman's Block
- ☐ 653 Seattle Seahawks .... .04 .02 .01
  Team: (Derrick) Fenner
  With Fancy Footwork
- ☐ 654 Tampa Bay Buccaneers.............. .04 .02 .01
  Team: (Reggie) Cobb
  Hurdles His Way
  to First Down
- ☐ 655 Washington Redskins.............. .04 .02 .01
  Team: (Earnest) Byner
  Cuts Back to
  Follow Block
- ☐ 656 Checklist 1-132.............. .04 .02 .01
- ☐ 657 Checklist 132-264.............. .04 .02 .01
- ☐ 658 Checklist 265-396.............. .04 .02 .01
- ☐ 659 Checklist 397-528.............. .04 .02 .01
- ☐ 660 Checklist 529-660.............. .04 .02 .01

1991 Topps 1000 Yard Club

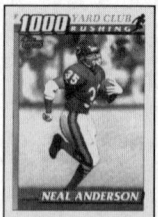

This 18-card standard-size set was issued by Topps to celebrate rushers and receivers who compiled 1000 yards or more in a season. The words "1000 Yard Club" appear at the top of the card. The color action player photo has a top red border, a red and purple left border, and no borders on the right and bottom. The player's name is given in an orange stripe toward the bottom of the picture. In blue and pink on white, the backs feature the rushing or receiving record of the player. The cards were inserted one per wax pack.

	MINT	NRMT	EXC
COMPLETE SET (18)	5.00	2.20	.60
COMMON CARD (1-18)	.15	.07	.02

- ☐ 1 Jerry Rice.............. 1.50 .70 .19
- ☐ 2 Barry Sanders.............. 1.50 .70 .19
- ☐ 3 Thurman Thomas.............. .60 .25 .07
- ☐ 4 Henry Ellard.............. .35 .16 .04
- ☐ 5 Marion Butts.............. .15 .07 .02
- ☐ 6 Earnest Byner.............. .15 .07 .02
- ☐ 7 Andre Rison.............. .35 .16 .04
- ☐ 8 Bobby Humphrey.............. .15 .07 .02
- ☐ 9 Gary Clark.............. .25 .11 .03
- ☐ 10 Sterling Sharpe.............. .35 .16 .04
- ☐ 11 Flipper Anderson.............. .15 .07 .02
- ☐ 12 Neal Anderson.............. .15 .07 .02
- ☐ 13 Haywood Jeffires.............. .25 .11 .03
- ☐ 14 Stephone Paige.............. .15 .07 .02
- ☐ 15 Drew Hill.............. .15 .07 .02
- ☐ 16 Barry Word.............. .15 .07 .02
- ☐ 17 Anthony Carter.............. .25 .11 .03
- ☐ 18 James Brooks.............. .15 .07 .02

1992 Topps

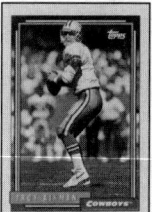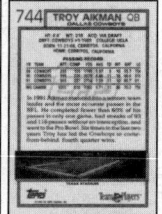

The 1992 Topps football set was issued in three series and totaled 759 standard-size cards. The first and second series consisted of 330 cards and a high series of 99 cards was released late in the season. A factory set was issued for the first 660 cards and it included 20 Topps Gold cards. A separate high series factory set of 113 cards was issued. It included 10 Topps Gold cards and one four-card No. 1 Draft Picks set. The fronts feature color action player photos inside a team color-coded picture frame and white outer borders. The player's name and team name appear in two color bars toward the bottom of the photo. The backs carry biography, statistics, a photo of the team's stadium and, where space permits, a player profile. The key Rookie Cards in the set are Edgar Bennett, Steve Bono, Robert Brooks, Terrell Buckley, Quentin Coryatt, Steve Emtman, Amp Lee, Tommy Maddox, Carl Pickens and Tommy Vardell. Members of both NFL Properties and the NFL Players Association are included in the third series.

	MINT	NRMT	EXC
COMPLETE SET (759)	30.00	13.50	3.70
COMPLETE FACT.SET (680)	32.00	14.50	4.00
COMPLETE SERIES 1 (330)	14.00	6.25	1.75
COMPLETE SERIES 2 (330)	10.00	4.50	1.25
COMPLETE HIGH SER.(99)	6.00	2.70	.75
COMP.FACT.HIGH SET (113)	8.00	3.60	1.00
COMMON CARD (1-759)	.05	.02	.01

- ☐ 1 Tim McGee.............. .05 .02 .01
- ☐ 2 Rich Camarillo.............. .05 .02 .01
- ☐ 3 Anthony Johnson.............. .10 .05 .01
- ☐ 4 Larry Kelm.............. .05 .02 .01
- ☐ 5 Irving Fryar.............. .10 .05 .01
- ☐ 6 Joey Browner.............. .05 .02 .01
- ☐ 7 Michael Walter.............. .05 .02 .01
- ☐ 8 Cortez Kennedy.............. .10 .05 .01
- ☐ 9 Reyna Thompson.............. .05 .02 .01
- ☐ 10 John Friesz.............. .10 .05 .01
- ☐ 11 Leroy Hoard.............. .10 .05 .01
- ☐ 12 Steve McMichael.............. .10 .05 .01
- ☐ 13 Marvin Washington.............. .05 .02 .01
- ☐ 14 Clyde Simmons.............. .05 .02 .01
- ☐ 15 Stephone Paige.............. .05 .02 .01
- ☐ 16 Mike Utley.............. .10 .05 .01
- ☐ 17 Tunch Ilkin.............. .05 .02 .01
- ☐ 18 Lawrence Dawsey.............. .10 .05 .01
- ☐ 19 Vance Johnson.............. .05 .02 .01
- ☐ 20 Bryce Paup.............. .25 .11 .03
- ☐ 21 Jeff Wright.............. .05 .02 .01
- ☐ 22 Gill Fenerty.............. .05 .02 .01
- ☐ 23 Lamar Lathon.............. .05 .02 .01
- ☐ 24 Danny Copeland.............. .05 .02 .01
- ☐ 25 Marcus Allen.............. .25 .11 .03
- ☐ 26 Tim Green.............. .05 .02 .01
- ☐ 27 Pete Stoyanovich.............. .05 .02 .01
- ☐ 28 Alvin Harper.............. .10 .05 .01
- ☐ 29 Roy Foster.............. .05 .02 .01
- ☐ 30 Eugene Daniel.............. .05 .02 .01
- ☐ 31 Luis Sharpe.............. .05 .02 .01
- ☐ 32 Terry Wooden.............. .05 .02 .01
- ☐ 33 Jim Breech.............. .05 .02 .01
- ☐ 34 Randy Hilliard.............. .05 .02 .01
- ☐ 35 Roman Phifer.............. .05 .02 .01
- ☐ 36 Erik Howard.............. .05 .02 .01
- ☐ 37 Chris Singleton.............. .05 .02 .01
- ☐ 38 Matt Stover.............. .05 .02 .01
- ☐ 39 Tim Irwin.............. .05 .02 .01
- ☐ 40 Karl Mecklenburg.............. .05 .02 .01
- ☐ 41 Joe Phillips.............. .05 .02 .01
- ☐ 42 Bill Jones.............. .05 .02 .01
- ☐ 43 Mark Carrier DB.............. .05 .02 .01
- ☐ 44 George Jamison.............. .05 .02 .01
- ☐ 45 Rob Taylor.............. .05 .02 .01
- ☐ 46 Jeff Jaeger.............. .05 .02 .01
- ☐ 47 Don Majkowski.............. .05 .02 .01
- ☐ 48 Al Edwards.............. .05 .02 .01
- ☐ 49 Curtis Duncan.............. .05 .02 .01
- ☐ 50 Sam Mills.............. .05 .02 .01
- ☐ 51 Terance Mathis.............. .10 .05 .01
- ☐ 52 Brian Mitchell.............. .10 .05 .01
- ☐ 53 Mike Pritchard.............. .10 .05 .01
- ☐ 54 Calvin Williams.............. .10 .05 .01
- ☐ 55 Hardy Nickerson.............. .10 .05 .01
- ☐ 56 Nate Newton.............. .10 .05 .01
- ☐ 57 Steve Wallace.............. .05 .02 .01
- ☐ 58 John Offerdahl.............. .05 .02 .01
- ☐ 59 Aeneas Williams.............. .10 .05 .01
- ☐ 60 Lee Johnson.............. .05 .02 .01
- ☐ 61 Ricardo McDonald.............. .05 .02 .01
- ☐ 62 David Richards.............. .05 .02 .01
- ☐ 63 Paul Gruber.............. .05 .02 .01
- ☐ 64 Greg McMurtry.............. .05 .02 .01
- ☐ 65 Jay Hilgenberg.............. .05 .02 .01

- ☐ 66 Tim Grunhard.............. .05 .02 .01
- ☐ 67 Dwayne White.............. .05 .02 .01
- ☐ 68 Don Beebe.............. .05 .02 .01
- ☐ 69 Simon Fletcher.............. .05 .02 .01
- ☐ 70 Warren Moon.............. .25 .11 .03
- ☐ 71 Chris Jacke.............. .05 .02 .01
- ☐ 72 Steve Wisniewski UER.............. .05 .02 .01
  (Traded to Raiders,
  not drafted by them)
- ☐ 73 Mike Cofer.............. .05 .02 .01
- ☐ 74 Tim Johnson UER.............. .05 .02 .01
  (No position listed
  on back)
- ☐ 75 T.J. Turner.............. .05 .02 .01
- ☐ 76 Scott Case.............. .05 .02 .01
- ☐ 77 Michael Jackson.............. .10 .05 .01
- ☐ 78 Jon Hand.............. .05 .02 .01
- ☐ 79 Stan Brock.............. .05 .02 .01
- ☐ 80 Robert Blackmon.............. .05 .02 .01
- ☐ 81 D.J. Johnson.............. .05 .02 .01
- ☐ 82 Damone Johnson.............. .05 .02 .01
- ☐ 83 Marc Spindler.............. .05 .02 .01
- ☐ 84 Larry Brown DB.............. .05 .02 .01
- ☐ 85 Ray Berry.............. .05 .02 .01
- ☐ 86 Andre Waters.............. .05 .02 .01
- ☐ 87 Carlos Huerta.............. .05 .02 .01
- ☐ 88 Brad Muster.............. .05 .02 .01
- ☐ 89 Chuck Cecil.............. .05 .02 .01
- ☐ 90 Nick Lowery.............. .05 .02 .01
- ☐ 91 Cornelius Bennett.............. .10 .05 .01
- ☐ 92 Jessie Tuggle.............. .05 .02 .01
- ☐ 93 Mark Schlereth.............. .05 .02 .01
- ☐ 94 Vestee Jackson.............. .05 .02 .01
- ☐ 95 Eric Bieniemy.............. .05 .02 .01
- ☐ 96 Jeff Hostetler.............. .10 .05 .01
- ☐ 97 Ken Lanier.............. .05 .02 .01
- ☐ 98 Wayne Haddix.............. .05 .02 .01
- ☐ 99 Lorenzo White.............. .05 .02 .01
- ☐ 100 Mervyn Fernandez.............. .05 .02 .01
- ☐ 101 Brent Williams.............. .05 .02 .01
- ☐ 102 Ian Beckles.............. .05 .02 .01
- ☐ 103 Harris Barton.............. .05 .02 .01
- ☐ 104 Edgar Bennett.............. .75 .35 .09
- ☐ 105 Mike Pitts.............. .05 .02 .01
- ☐ 106 Fuad Reveiz.............. .05 .02 .01
- ☐ 107 Vernon Turner.............. .05 .02 .01
- ☐ 108 Tracy Hayworth.............. .05 .02 .01
- ☐ 109 Checklist 1-110.............. .05 .02 .01
- ☐ 110 Tom Waddle.............. .05 .02 .01
- ☐ 111 Fred Stokes.............. .05 .02 .01
- ☐ 112 Howard Ballard.............. .05 .02 .01
- ☐ 113 David Szott.............. .05 .02 .01
- ☐ 114 Tim McKyer.............. .05 .02 .01
- ☐ 115 Kyle Clifton.............. .05 .02 .01
- ☐ 116 Tony Bennett.............. .05 .02 .01
- ☐ 117 Joel Hilgenberg.............. .05 .02 .01
- ☐ 118 Dwayne Harper.............. .05 .02 .01
- ☐ 119 Mike Baab.............. .05 .02 .01
- ☐ 120 Mark Clayton.............. .10 .05 .01
- ☐ 121 Eric Swann.............. .10 .05 .01
- ☐ 122 Neil O'Donnell.............. .25 .11 .03
- ☐ 123 Mike Munchak.............. .05 .02 .01
- ☐ 124 Howie Long.............. .10 .05 .01
- ☐ 125 John Elway UER.............. .60 .25 .07
  (Card says 6-year
  vet, should be 9)
- ☐ 126 Joe Prokop.............. .05 .02 .01
- ☐ 127 Pepper Johnson.............. .05 .02 .01
- ☐ 128 Richard Dent.............. .10 .05 .01
- ☐ 129 Robert Porcher.............. .10 .05 .01
- ☐ 130 Earnest Byner.............. .05 .02 .01
- ☐ 131 Kent Hull.............. .05 .02 .01
- ☐ 132 Mike Merriweather.............. .05 .02 .01
- ☐ 133 Scott Fulhage.............. .05 .02 .01
- ☐ 134 Kevin Porter.............. .05 .02 .01
- ☐ 135 Tony Casillas.............. .05 .02 .01
- ☐ 136 Dean Biasucci.............. .05 .02 .01
- ☐ 137 Ben Smith.............. .05 .02 .01
- ☐ 138 Bruce Kozerski.............. .05 .02 .01
- ☐ 139 Jeff Campbell.............. .05 .02 .01
- ☐ 140 Kevin Greene.............. .25 .11 .03
- ☐ 141 Gary Plummer.............. .05 .02 .01
- ☐ 142 Vincent Brown.............. .05 .02 .01
- ☐ 143 Ron Hall.............. .05 .02 .01
- ☐ 144 Louie Aguiar.............. .05 .02 .01
- ☐ 145 Mark Duper.............. .05 .02 .01
- ☐ 146 Jesse Sapolu.............. .05 .02 .01
- ☐ 147 Jeff Gossett.............. .05 .02 .01
- ☐ 148 Brian Noble.............. .05 .02 .01
- ☐ 149 Derek Russell.............. .05 .02 .01
- ☐ 150 Carlton Bailey.............. .10 .05 .01
- ☐ 151 Kelly Goodburn.............. .05 .02 .01
- ☐ 152 Audray McMillian UER.............. .05 .02 .01
  (Misspelled Audrey)
- ☐ 153 Neal Anderson.............. .05 .02 .01
- ☐ 154 Bill Maas.............. .05 .02 .01
- ☐ 155 Rickey Jackson.............. .05 .02 .01
- ☐ 156 Chris Miller.............. .10 .05 .01
- ☐ 157 Darren Comeaux.............. .05 .02 .01
- ☐ 158 David Williams.............. .05 .02 .01
- ☐ 159 Rich Gannon.............. .05 .02 .01
- ☐ 160 Kevin Mack.............. .05 .02 .01
- ☐ 161 Jim Arnold.............. .05 .02 .01
- ☐ 162 Reggie White.............. .25 .11 .03
- ☐ 163 Leonard Russell.............. .10 .05 .01

- ☐ 164 Doug Smith.............. .05 .02 .01
- ☐ 165 Tony Mandarich.............. .05 .02 .01
- ☐ 166 Greg Lloyd.............. .25 .11 .03
- ☐ 167 Jumbo Elliott.............. .05 .02 .01
- ☐ 168 Jonathan Hayes.............. .05 .02 .01
- ☐ 169 Jim Ritcher.............. .05 .02 .01
- ☐ 170 Mike Kenn.............. .05 .02 .01
- ☐ 171 James Washington.............. .05 .02 .01
- ☐ 172 Tim Harris.............. .05 .02 .01
- ☐ 173 James Thornton.............. .05 .02 .01
- ☐ 174 John Brandes.............. .05 .02 .01
- ☐ 175 Fred McAfee.............. .05 .02 .01
- ☐ 176 Henry Rolling.............. .05 .02 .01
- ☐ 177 Tony Paige.............. .05 .02 .01
- ☐ 178 Jay Schroeder.............. .05 .02 .01
- ☐ 179 Jeff Herrod.............. .05 .02 .01
- ☐ 180 Emmitt Smith.............. 2.00 .90 .25
- ☐ 181 Wymon Henderson.............. .05 .02 .01
- ☐ 182 Rob Moore.............. .10 .05 .01
- ☐ 183 Robert Wilson.............. .05 .02 .01
- ☐ 184 Michael Zordich.............. .05 .02 .01
- ☐ 185 Jim Harbaugh.............. .25 .11 .03
- ☐ 186 Vince Workman.............. .10 .05 .01
- ☐ 187 Ernest Givins.............. .10 .05 .01
- ☐ 188 Herschel Walker.............. .10 .05 .01
- ☐ 189 Dan Fike.............. .05 .02 .01
- ☐ 190 Seth Joyner.............. .10 .05 .01
- ☐ 191 Steve Young.............. .60 .25 .07
- ☐ 192 Dennis Gibson.............. .05 .02 .01
- ☐ 193 Darryl Talley.............. .05 .02 .01
- ☐ 194 Emile Harry.............. .05 .02 .01
- ☐ 195 Bill Fralic.............. .05 .02 .01
- ☐ 196 Michael Stewart.............. .05 .02 .01
- ☐ 197 James Francis.............. .05 .02 .01
- ☐ 198 Jerome Henderson.............. .05 .02 .01
- ☐ 199 John L. Williams.............. .05 .02 .01
- ☐ 200 Rod Woodson.............. .25 .11 .03
- ☐ 201 Mike Farr.............. .05 .02 .01
- ☐ 202 Greg Montgomery.............. .05 .02 .01
- ☐ 203 Andre Collins.............. .05 .02 .01
- ☐ 204 Scott Miller.............. .05 .02 .01
- ☐ 205 Clay Matthews.............. .10 .05 .01
- ☐ 206 Ethan Horton.............. .05 .02 .01
- ☐ 207 Rich Miano.............. .05 .02 .01
- ☐ 208 Chris Mims.............. .10 .05 .01
- ☐ 209 Anthony Morgan.............. .05 .02 .01
- ☐ 210 Rodney Hampton.............. .25 .11 .03
- ☐ 211 Chris Hinton.............. .05 .02 .01
- ☐ 212 Esera Tuaolo.............. .05 .02 .01
- ☐ 213 Shane Conlan.............. .05 .02 .01
- ☐ 214 John Carney.............. .05 .02 .01
- ☐ 215 Kenny Walker.............. .05 .02 .01
- ☐ 216 Scott Radecic.............. .05 .02 .01
- ☐ 217 Chris Martin.............. .05 .02 .01
- ☐ 218 Checklist 111-220 UER.............. .05 .02 .01
  (152 Audray McMillian
  misspelled Audrey)
- ☐ 219 Wesley Carroll UER.............. .05 .02 .01
  (Stats say 1st round
  pick, bio correctly
  has 2nd)
- ☐ 220 Bill Romanowski.............. .05 .02 .01
- ☐ 221 Reggie Cobb.............. .05 .02 .01
- ☐ 222 Alfred Anderson.............. .05 .02 .01
- ☐ 223 Cleveland Gary.............. .05 .02 .01
- ☐ 224 Eddie Blake.............. .05 .02 .01
- ☐ 225 Chris Spielman.............. .10 .05 .01
- ☐ 226 John Roper.............. .05 .02 .01
- ☐ 227 George Thomas.............. .05 .02 .01
- ☐ 228 Jeff Faulkner.............. .05 .02 .01
- ☐ 229 Chip Lohmiller UER.............. .05 .02 .01
  (RFK Stadium not
  identified on back)
- ☐ 230 Hugh Millen.............. .05 .02 .01
- ☐ 231 Ray Horton.............. .05 .02 .01
- ☐ 232 James Campen.............. .05 .02 .01
- ☐ 233 Howard Cross.............. .05 .02 .01
- ☐ 234 Keith McKeller.............. .05 .02 .01
- ☐ 235 Dino Hackett.............. .05 .02 .01
- ☐ 236 Jerome Brown.............. .05 .02 .01
- ☐ 237 Andy Heck.............. .05 .02 .01
- ☐ 238 Rodney Holman.............. .05 .02 .01
- ☐ 239 Bruce Matthews.............. .05 .02 .01
- ☐ 240 Jeff Lageman.............. .05 .02 .01
- ☐ 241 Bobby Hebert.............. .05 .02 .01
- ☐ 242 Gary Anderson K.............. .05 .02 .01
- ☐ 243 Mark Bortz.............. .05 .02 .01
- ☐ 244 Rich Moran.............. .05 .02 .01
- ☐ 245 Jeff Uhlenhake.............. .05 .02 .01
- ☐ 246 Ricky Sanders.............. .05 .02 .01
- ☐ 247 Clarence Kay.............. .05 .02 .01
- ☐ 248 Ed King.............. .05 .02 .01
- ☐ 249 Eddie Anderson.............. .05 .02 .01
- ☐ 250 Amp Lee.............. .05 .02 .01
- ☐ 251 Norm Johnson.............. .05 .02 .01
- ☐ 252 Michael Carter.............. .05 .02 .01
- ☐ 253 Felix Wright.............. .05 .02 .01
- ☐ 254 Leon Seals.............. .05 .02 .01
- ☐ 255 Nate Lewis.............. .05 .02 .01
- ☐ 256 Kevin Call.............. .05 .02 .01
- ☐ 257 Darryl Henley.............. .05 .02 .01
- ☐ 258 Jon Vaughn.............. .05 .02 .01
- ☐ 259 Matt Bahr.............. .05 .02 .01
- ☐ 260 Johnny Johnson.............. .05 .02 .01
- ☐ 261 Ken Norton.............. .25 .11 .03

☐ 262 Wendell Davis .05 .02 .01
☐ 263 Eugene Robinson .05 .02 .01
☐ 264 David Treadwell .05 .02 .01
☐ 265 Michael Haynes .10 .05 .01
☐ 266 Robb Thomas .05 .02 .01
☐ 267 Nate Odomes .05 .02 .01
☐ 268 Martin Mayhew .05 .02 .01
☐ 269 Perry Kemp .05 .02 .01
☐ 270 Jerry Ball .05 .02 .01
☐ 271 Tommy Vardell .10 .05 .01
☐ 272 Ernie Mills .05 .02 .01
☐ 273 Mo Lewis .05 .02 .01
☐ 274 Roger Ruzek .05 .02 .01
☐ 275 Steve Smith .05 .02 .01
☐ 276 Bo Orlando .05 .02 .01
☐ 277 Louis Oliver .05 .02 .01
☐ 278 Toi Cook .05 .02 .01
☐ 279 Eddie Brown .05 .02 .01
☐ 280 Keith McCants .05 .02 .01
☐ 281 Rob Burnett .05 .02 .01
☐ 282 Keith DeLong .05 .02 .01
☐ 283 Stan Thomas UER .05 .02 .01
(9th line bio notes, the word of is in caps)
☐ 284 Robert Brown .05 .02 .01
☐ 285 John Alt .05 .02 .01
☐ 286 Randy Dixon .05 .02 .01
☐ 287 Siran Stacy .05 .02 .01
☐ 288 Ray Agnew .05 .02 .01
☐ 289 Darion Conner .05 .02 .01
☐ 290 Kirk Lowdermilk .05 .02 .01
☐ 291 Greg Jackson .05 .02 .01
☐ 292 Ken Harvey .05 .02 .01
☐ 293 Jacob Green .05 .02 .01
☐ 294 Mark Tuinei .05 .02 .01
☐ 295 Mark Rypien .05 .02 .01
☐ 296 Gerald Robinson .05 .02 .01
☐ 297 Broderick Thompson .05 .02 .01
☐ 298 Doug Widell .05 .02 .01
☐ 299 Carwell Gardner .05 .02 .01
☐ 300 Barry Sanders 1.00 .45 .12
☐ 301 Eric Metcalf .10 .05 .01
☐ 302 Eric Thomas .05 .02 .01
☐ 303 Terrell Buckley .05 .02 .01
☐ 304 Byron Evans .05 .02 .01
☐ 305 Johnny Hector .05 .02 .01
☐ 306 Steve Broussard .05 .02 .01
☐ 307 Gene Atkins .05 .02 .01
☐ 308 Terry McDaniel .05 .02 .01
☐ 309 Charles McRae .05 .02 .01
☐ 310 Jim Lachey .05 .02 .01
☐ 311 Pat Harlow .05 .02 .01
☐ 312 Kevin Butler .05 .02 .01
☐ 313 Scott Stephen .05 .02 .01
☐ 314 Dermontti Dawson .05 .02 .01
☐ 315 Johnny Meads .05 .02 .01
☐ 316 Checklist 221-330 .05 .02 .01
☐ 317 Aaron Craver .05 .02 .01
☐ 318 Michael Brooks .05 .02 .01
☐ 319 Guy McIntyre .05 .02 .01
☐ 320 Thurman Thomas .25 .11 .03
☐ 321 Courtney Hall .05 .02 .01
☐ 322 Dan Saleaumua .05 .02 .01
☐ 323 Vinson Smith .05 .02 .01
☐ 324 Steve Jordan .05 .02 .01
☐ 325 Walter Reeves .05 .02 .01
☐ 326 Erik Kramer .10 .05 .01
☐ 327 Duane Bickett .05 .02 .01
☐ 328 Tom Newberry .05 .02 .01
☐ 329 John Kasay .05 .02 .01
☐ 330 Dave Meggett .10 .05 .01
☐ 331 Kevin Ross .05 .02 .01
☐ 332 Keith Hamilton .05 .02 .01
☐ 333 Dwight Stone .05 .02 .01
☐ 334 Mel Gray .10 .05 .01
☐ 335 Harry Galbreath .05 .02 .01
☐ 336 William Perry .10 .05 .01
☐ 337 Brian Blades .10 .05 .01
☐ 338 Randall McDaniel .05 .02 .01
☐ 339 Pat Coleman .05 .02 .01
☐ 340 Michael Irvin .25 .11 .03
☐ 341 Checklist 331-440 .05 .02 .01
☐ 342 Chris Mohr .05 .02 .01
☐ 343 Greg Davis .05 .02 .01
☐ 344 Dave Cadigan .05 .02 .01
☐ 345 Art Monk .10 .05 .01
☐ 346 Tim Goad .05 .02 .01
☐ 347 Vinnie Clark .05 .02 .01
☐ 348 David Fulcher .05 .02 .01
☐ 349 Craig Heyward .10 .05 .01
☐ 350 Ronnie Lott .10 .05 .01
☐ 351 Dexter Carter .05 .02 .01
☐ 352 Mark Jackson .05 .02 .01
☐ 353 Brian Jordan .10 .05 .01
☐ 354 Ray Donaldson .05 .02 .01
☐ 355 Jim Price .05 .02 .01
☐ 356 Rod Bernstine .05 .02 .01
☐ 357 Tony Mayberry .05 .02 .01
☐ 358 Richard Brown .05 .02 .01
☐ 359 David Alexander .05 .02 .01
☐ 360 Haywood Jeffires .10 .05 .01
☐ 361 Henry Thomas .05 .02 .01
☐ 362 Jeff Graham .25 .11 .03
☐ 363 Don Warren .05 .02 .01
☐ 364 Scott Davis .05 .02 .01
☐ 365 Harlon Barnett .05 .02 .01
☐ 366 Mark Collins .05 .02 .01
☐ 367 Rick Tuten .05 .02 .01
☐ 368 Lonnie Marts UER .05 .02 .01
(Injured Reserved should be Reserve)
☐ 369 Dennis Smith .05 .02 .01
☐ 370 Steve Tasker .10 .05 .01
☐ 371 Robert Massey .05 .02 .01
☐ 372 Ricky Reynolds .05 .02 .01
☐ 373 Alvin Wright .05 .02 .01
☐ 374 Kelvin Martin .05 .02 .01
☐ 375 Vince Buck .05 .02 .01
☐ 376 John Kidd .05 .02 .01
☐ 377 William White .05 .02 .01
☐ 378 Bryan Cox .10 .05 .01
☐ 379 Jamie Dukes .05 .02 .01
☐ 380 Anthony Munoz .10 .05 .01
☐ 381 Mark Gunn .05 .02 .01
☐ 382 Keith Henderson .05 .02 .01
☐ 383 Charles Wilson .05 .02 .01
☐ 384 Shawn McCarthy .05 .02 .01
☐ 385 Ernie Jones .05 .02 .01
☐ 386 Nick Bell .05 .02 .01
☐ 387 Derrick Walker .05 .02 .01
☐ 388 Mark Stepnoski .10 .05 .01
☐ 389 Broderick Thomas .05 .02 .01
☐ 390 Reggie Roby .05 .02 .01
☐ 391 Bubba McDowell .05 .02 .01
☐ 392 Eric Martin .05 .02 .01
☐ 393 Toby Caston .05 .02 .01
☐ 394 Bern Brostek .05 .02 .01
☐ 395 Christian Okoye .05 .02 .01
☐ 396 Frank Minnifield .05 .02 .01
☐ 397 Mike Golic .05 .02 .01
☐ 398 Grant Feasel .05 .02 .01
☐ 399 Michael Ball .05 .02 .01
☐ 400 Mike Croel .05 .02 .01
☐ 401 Maury Buford .05 .02 .01
☐ 402 Jeff Bostic UER .05 .02 .01
(Signed as free agent in 1980, not 1984)
☐ 403 Sean Landeta .05 .02 .01
☐ 404 Terry Allen .40 .18 .05
☐ 405 Donald Evans .05 .02 .01
☐ 406 Don Mosebar .05 .02 .01
☐ 407 D.J. Dozier .05 .02 .01
☐ 408 Bruce Pickens .05 .02 .01
☐ 409 Jim Dombrowski .05 .02 .01
☐ 410 Deron Cherry .05 .02 .01
☐ 411 Richard Johnson .05 .02 .01
☐ 412 Alexander Wright .05 .02 .01
☐ 413 Tom Rathman .05 .02 .01
☐ 414 Mark Dennis .05 .02 .01
☐ 415 Phil Hansen .05 .02 .01
☐ 416 Lonnie Young .05 .02 .01
☐ 417 Burt Grossman .05 .02 .01
☐ 418 Tony Covington .05 .02 .01
☐ 419 John Stephens .05 .02 .01
☐ 420 Jim Everett .10 .05 .01
☐ 421 Johnny Holland .05 .02 .01
☐ 422 Mike Barber .05 .02 .01
☐ 423 Carl Lee .05 .02 .01
☐ 424 Craig Patterson .05 .02 .01
☐ 425 Greg Townsend .05 .02 .01
☐ 426 Brett Perriman .25 .11 .03
☐ 427 Morten Andersen .05 .02 .01
☐ 428 John Gesek .05 .02 .01
☐ 429 Bryan Barker .05 .02 .01
☐ 430 John Taylor .10 .05 .01
☐ 431 Donnell Woolford .05 .02 .01
☐ 432 Ron Holmes .05 .02 .01
☐ 433 Lee Williams .05 .02 .01
☐ 434 Alfred Oglesby .05 .02 .01
☐ 435 Jarrod Bunch .05 .02 .01
☐ 436 Carlton Haselrig .05 .02 .01
☐ 437 Rufus Porter .05 .02 .01
☐ 438 Rohn Stark .05 .02 .01
☐ 439 Tony Jones .05 .02 .01
☐ 440 Andre Rison .10 .05 .01
☐ 441 Eric Hill .05 .02 .01
☐ 442 Jesse Solomon .05 .02 .01
☐ 443 Jackie Slater .05 .02 .01
☐ 444 Donnie Elder .05 .02 .01
☐ 445 Brett Maxie .05 .02 .01
☐ 446 Max Montoya .05 .02 .01
☐ 447 Will Wolford .05 .02 .01
☐ 448 Craig Taylor .05 .02 .01
☐ 449 Jimmie Jones .05 .02 .01
☐ 450 Anthony Carter .10 .05 .01
☐ 451 Brian Bollinger .05 .02 .01
☐ 452 Checklist 441-550 .05 .02 .01
☐ 453 Brad Edwards .05 .02 .01
☐ 454 Gene Chilton .05 .02 .01
☐ 455 Eric Allen .05 .02 .01
☐ 456 William Roberts .05 .02 .01
☐ 457 Eric Green .05 .02 .01
☐ 458 Irv Eatman .05 .02 .01
☐ 459 Derrick Thomas .25 .11 .03
☐ 460 Tommy Kane .05 .02 .01
☐ 461 LeRoy Butler .05 .02 .01
☐ 462 Oliver Barnett .05 .02 .01
☐ 463 Anthony Smith .05 .02 .01
☐ 464 Cris Dishman .05 .02 .01
☐ 465 Pat Terrell .05 .02 .01
☐ 466 Greg Kragen .05 .02 .01
☐ 467 Rodney Peete .10 .05 .01
☐ 468 Willie Drewrey .05 .02 .01
☐ 469 Jim Wilks .05 .02 .01
☐ 470 Vince Newsome .05 .02 .01
☐ 471 Chris Gardocki .05 .02 .01
☐ 472 Chris Chandler .10 .05 .01
☐ 473 George Thornton .05 .02 .01
☐ 474 Albert Lewis .05 .02 .01
☐ 475 Kevin Glover .05 .02 .01
☐ 476 Joe Bowden .05 .02 .01
☐ 477 Harry Sydney .05 .02 .01
☐ 478 Bob Golic .05 .02 .01
☐ 479 Tony Zendejas .05 .02 .01
☐ 480 Brad Baxter .05 .02 .01
☐ 481 Steve Beuerlein .05 .02 .01
☐ 482 Mark Higgs .05 .02 .01
☐ 483 Drew Hill .05 .02 .01
☐ 484 Bryan Millard .05 .02 .01
☐ 485 Mark Kelso .05 .02 .01
☐ 486 David Grant .05 .02 .01
☐ 487 Gary Zimmerman .05 .02 .01
☐ 488 Leonard Marshall .05 .02 .01
☐ 489 Keith Jackson .10 .05 .01
☐ 490 Sterling Sharpe .25 .11 .03
☐ 491 Ferrell Edmunds .05 .02 .01
☐ 492 Wilber Marshall .05 .02 .01
☐ 493 Charles Haley .10 .05 .01
☐ 494 Riki Ellison .05 .02 .01
☐ 495 Bill Brooks .05 .02 .01
☐ 496 Bill Hawkins .05 .02 .01
☐ 497 Erik Williams .05 .02 .01
☐ 498 Leon Searcy .10 .05 .01
☐ 499 Mike Horan .05 .02 .01
☐ 500 Pat Swilling .10 .05 .01
☐ 501 Maurice Hurst .05 .02 .01
☐ 502 William Fuller .10 .05 .01
☐ 503 Tim Newton .05 .02 .01
☐ 504 Lorenzo Lynch .05 .02 .01
☐ 505 Tim Barnett .05 .02 .01
☐ 506 Tom Thayer .05 .02 .01
☐ 507 Chris Burkett .05 .02 .01
☐ 508 Ronnie Harmon .05 .02 .01
☐ 509 James Brooks .10 .05 .01
☐ 510 Bennie Blades .05 .02 .01
☐ 511 Roger Craig .10 .05 .01
☐ 512 Tony Woods .05 .02 .01
☐ 513 Greg Lewis .05 .02 .01
☐ 514 Eric Pegram .10 .05 .01
☐ 515 Elvis Patterson .05 .02 .01
☐ 516 Jeff Cross .05 .02 .01
☐ 517 Myron Guyton .05 .02 .01
☐ 518 Jay Novacek .10 .05 .01
☐ 519 Leo Barker .05 .02 .01
☐ 520 Keith Byars .05 .02 .01
☐ 521 Dalton Hilliard .05 .02 .01
☐ 522 Ted Washington .05 .02 .01
☐ 523 Dexter McNabb .05 .02 .01
☐ 524 Frank Reich .10 .05 .01
☐ 525 Henry Ellard .10 .05 .01
☐ 526 Barry Foster .10 .05 .01
☐ 527 Barry Word .05 .02 .01
☐ 528 Gary Anderson RB .05 .02 .01
☐ 529 Reggie Rutland .05 .02 .01
☐ 530 Stephen Baker .05 .02 .01
☐ 531 John Flannery .05 .02 .01
☐ 532 Steve Wright .05 .02 .01
☐ 533 Eric Sanders .05 .02 .01
☐ 534 Bob Whitfield .05 .02 .01
☐ 535 Gaston Green .05 .02 .01
☐ 536 Anthony Pleasant .05 .02 .01
☐ 537 Jeff Bryant .05 .02 .01
☐ 538 Jarvis Williams .05 .02 .01
☐ 539 Jim Morrissey .05 .02 .01
☐ 540 Andre Tippett .05 .02 .01
☐ 541 Gill Byrd .05 .02 .01
☐ 542 Raleigh McKenzie .05 .02 .01
☐ 543 Jim Sweeney .05 .02 .01
☐ 544 David Lutz .05 .02 .01
☐ 545 Wayne Martin .05 .02 .01
☐ 546 Karl Wilson .05 .02 .01
☐ 547 Pierce Holt .05 .02 .01
☐ 548 Doug Smith .05 .02 .01
☐ 549 Nolan Harrison .05 .02 .01
☐ 550 Freddie Joe Nunn .05 .02 .01
☐ 551 Eric Moore .05 .02 .01
☐ 552 Cris Carter .25 .11 .03
☐ 553 Kevin Gogan .05 .02 .01
☐ 554 Harold Green .05 .02 .01
☐ 555 Kenneth Davis .05 .02 .01
☐ 556 Travis McNeal .05 .02 .01
☐ 557 Jim C. Jensen .05 .02 .01
☐ 558 Willie Green .05 .02 .01
☐ 559 Scott Galbraith UER .05 .02 .01
(Drafted in 1990, not 1989)
☐ 560 Louis Lipps .05 .02 .01
☐ 561 Matt Brock .05 .02 .01
☐ 562 Mike Prior .05 .02 .01
☐ 563 Checklist 551-660 .05 .02 .01
☐ 564 Robert Delpino .05 .02 .01
☐ 565 Vinny Testaverde .10 .05 .01
☐ 566 Willie Gault .10 .05 .01
☐ 567 Quinn Early .10 .05 .01
☐ 568 Eric Moten .05 .02 .01
☐ 569 Lance Smith .05 .02 .01
☐ 570 Darrell Green .05 .02 .01
☐ 571 Moe Gardner .05 .02 .01
☐ 572 Steve Atwater .05 .02 .01
☐ 573 Ray Childress .05 .02 .01
☐ 574 Dave Krieg .10 .05 .01
☐ 575 Bruce Armstrong .05 .02 .01
☐ 576 Fred Barnett .25 .11 .03
☐ 577 Don Griffin .05 .02 .01
☐ 578 David Brandon .05 .02 .01
☐ 579 Robert Young .05 .02 .01
☐ 580 Keith Van Horne .05 .02 .01
☐ 581 Jeff Criswell .05 .02 .01
☐ 582 Lewis Tillman .05 .02 .01
☐ 583 Bubby Brister .05 .02 .01
☐ 584 Aaron Wallace .05 .02 .01
☐ 585 Chris Doleman .05 .02 .01
☐ 586 Marty Carter .05 .02 .01
☐ 587 Chris Warren .25 .11 .03
☐ 588 David Griggs .05 .02 .01
☐ 589 Darrell Thompson .05 .02 .01
☐ 590 Marion Butts .05 .02 .01
☐ 591 Scott Norwood .05 .02 .01
☐ 592 Lomas Brown .05 .02 .01
☐ 593 Daryl Johnston .25 .11 .03
☐ 594 Alonzo Mitz .05 .02 .01
☐ 595 Tommy Barnhardt .05 .02 .01
☐ 596 Tim Jorden .05 .02 .01
☐ 597 Neil Smith .25 .11 .03
☐ 598 Todd Marinovich .05 .02 .01
☐ 599 Sean Jones .10 .05 .01
☐ 600 Clarence Verdin .05 .02 .01
☐ 601 Trace Armstrong .05 .02 .01
☐ 602 Steve Bono .25 .11 .03
☐ 603 Mark Ingram .05 .02 .01
☐ 604 Flipper Anderson .05 .02 .01
☐ 605 James Jones .05 .02 .01
☐ 606 Al Noga .05 .02 .01
☐ 607 Rick Bryan .05 .02 .01
☐ 608 Eugene Lockhart .05 .02 .01
☐ 609 Charles Mann .05 .02 .01
☐ 610 James Hasty .05 .02 .01
☐ 611 Jeff Feagles .05 .02 .01
☐ 612 Tim Brown .25 .11 .03
☐ 613 David Little .05 .02 .01
☐ 614 Keith Sims .05 .02 .01
☐ 615 Kevin Murphy .05 .02 .01
☐ 616 Ray Crockett .05 .02 .01
☐ 617 Jim Jeffcoat .05 .02 .01
☐ 618 Patrick Hunter .05 .02 .01
☐ 619 Keith Kartz .05 .02 .01
☐ 620 Peter Tom Willis .05 .02 .01
☐ 621 Vaughan Johnson .05 .02 .01
☐ 622 Shawn Jefferson .05 .02 .01
☐ 623 Anthony Thompson .05 .02 .01
☐ 624 John Rienstra .05 .02 .01
☐ 625 Don Maggs .05 .02 .01
☐ 626 Todd Lyght .05 .02 .01
☐ 627 Brent Jones .10 .05 .01
☐ 628 Todd McNair .05 .02 .01
☐ 629 Winston Moss .05 .02 .01
☐ 630 Mark Carrier WR .10 .05 .01
☐ 631 Dan Owens .05 .02 .01
☐ 632 Sammie Smith UER .05 .02 .01
(Old team front, correct new team back; acquired via trade, not draft)
☐ 633 James Lofton .10 .05 .01
☐ 634 Paul McJulien .05 .02 .01
☐ 635 Tony Tolbert .05 .02 .01
☐ 636 Carnell Lake .05 .02 .01
☐ 637 Gary Clark .25 .11 .03
☐ 638 Brian Washington .05 .02 .01
☐ 639 Jessie Hester .05 .02 .01
☐ 640 Doug Riesenberg .05 .02 .01
☐ 641 Joe Walter .05 .02 .01
☐ 642 John Rade .05 .02 .01
☐ 643 Wes Hopkins .05 .02 .01
☐ 644 Kelly Stouffer .05 .02 .01
☐ 645 Marv Cook .05 .02 .01
☐ 646 Ken Clarke .05 .02 .01
☐ 647 Bobby Humphrey UER .05 .02 .01
(Old team front, correct new team back; acquired via trade, not draft)
☐ 648 Tim McDonald .05 .02 .01
☐ 649 Donald Frank .05 .02 .01
☐ 650 Richmond Webb .05 .02 .01
☐ 651 Lemuel Stinson .05 .02 .01
☐ 652 Merton Hanks .10 .05 .01
☐ 653 Frank Warren .05 .02 .01
☐ 654 Thomas Benson .05 .02 .01
☐ 655 Al Smith .05 .02 .01
☐ 656 Steve DeBerg .05 .02 .01
☐ 657 Jayice Pearson .05 .02 .01
☐ 658 Joe Morris .05 .02 .01
☐ 659 Fred Strickland .05 .02 .01
☐ 660 Kelvin Pritchett .05 .02 .01
☐ 661 Lewis Billups .05 .02 .01
☐ 662 Todd Collins .05 .02 .01
☐ 663 Corey Miller .05 .02 .01
☐ 664 Levon Kirkland .05 .02 .01
☐ 665 Jerry Rice 1.00 .45 .12

☐ 666 Mike Lodish	.05	.02	.01
☐ 667 Chuck Smith	.05	.02	.01
☐ 668 Lance Olberding	.05	.02	.01
☐ 669 Kevin Smith	.25	.11	.03
☐ 670 Dale Carter	.25	.11	.03
☐ 671 Sean Gilbert	.25	.11	.03
☐ 672 Ken O'Brien	.05	.02	.01
☐ 673 Ricky Proehl	.05	.02	.01
☐ 674 Junior Seau	.25	.11	.03
☐ 675 Courtney Hawkins	.10	.05	.01
☐ 676 Eddie Robinson	.05	.02	.01
☐ 677 Tom Jeter	.05	.02	.01
☐ 678 Jeff George	.25	.11	.03
☐ 679 Cary Conklin	.05	.02	.01
☐ 680 Rueben Mayes	.05	.02	.01
☐ 681 Sean Lumpkin	.05	.02	.01
☐ 682 Dan Marino	1.50	.70	.19
☐ 683 Ed McDaniel	.05	.02	.01
☐ 684 Greg Skrepenak	.05	.02	.01
☐ 685 Tracy Scroggins	.05	.02	.01
☐ 686 Tommy Maddox	.05	.02	.01
☐ 687 Mike Singletary	.10	.05	.01
☐ 688 Patrick Rowe	.05	.02	.01
☐ 689 Phillippi Sparks	.05	.02	.01
☐ 690 Joel Steed	.05	.02	.01
☐ 691 Kevin Fagan	.05	.02	.01
☐ 692 Deion Sanders	.50	.23	.06
☐ 693 Bruce Smith	.25	.11	.03
☐ 694 David Klingler	.10	.05	.01
☐ 695 Clayton Holmes	.05	.02	.01
☐ 696 Brett Favre	2.50	1.10	.30
☐ 697 Marc Boutte	.05	.02	.01
☐ 698 Dwayne Sabb	.05	.02	.01
☐ 699 Ed McCaffrey	.05	.02	.01
☐ 700 Randall Cunningham	.10	.05	.01
☐ 701 Quentin Coryatt	.25	.11	.03
☐ 702 Bernie Kosar	.10	.05	.01
☐ 703 Vaughn Dunbar	.05	.02	.01
☐ 704 Browning Nagle	.05	.02	.01
☐ 705 Mark Wheeler	.05	.02	.01
☐ 706 Paul Siever	.05	.02	.01
☐ 707 Anthony Miller	.10	.05	.01
☐ 708 Corey Widmer	.05	.02	.01
☐ 709 Eric Dickerson	.10	.05	.01
☐ 710 Martin Bayless	.05	.02	.01
☐ 711 Jason Hanson	.10	.05	.01
☐ 712 Michael Dean Perry	.10	.05	.01
☐ 713 Billy Joe Tolliver UER (Stats say 1991 Chargers, should be Falcons)	.05	.02	.01
☐ 714 Chad Hennings	.10	.05	.01
☐ 715 Bucky Richardson	.05	.02	.01
☐ 716 Steve Israel	.05	.02	.01
☐ 717 Robert Harris	.05	.02	.01
☐ 718 Timm Rosenbach	.05	.02	.01
☐ 719 Joe Montana	1.00	.45	.12
☐ 720 Derek Brown TE	.05	.02	.01
☐ 721 Robert Brooks	1.50	.70	.19
☐ 722 Boomer Esiason	.10	.05	.01
☐ 723 Troy Auzenne	.05	.02	.01
☐ 724 John Fina	.05	.02	.01
☐ 725 Chris Crooms	.05	.02	.01
☐ 726 Eugene Chung	.05	.02	.01
☐ 727 Darren Woodson	.25	.11	.03
☐ 728 Leslie O'Neal	.10	.05	.01
☐ 729 Dan McGwire	.05	.02	.01
☐ 730 Al Toon	.10	.05	.01
☐ 731 Michael Brandon	.05	.02	.01
☐ 732 Steve DeOssie	.05	.02	.01
☐ 733 Jim Kelly	.25	.11	.03
☐ 734 Webster Slaughter	.05	.02	.01
☐ 735 Tony Smith	.05	.02	.01
☐ 736 Shane Collins	.05	.02	.01
☐ 737 Randal Hill	.05	.02	.01
☐ 738 Chris Holder	.05	.02	.01
☐ 739 Russell Maryland	.10	.05	.01
☐ 740 Carl Pickens	2.00	.90	.25
☐ 741 Andre Reed	.10	.05	.01
☐ 742 Steve Emtman	.05	.02	.01
☐ 743 Carl Banks	.05	.02	.01
☐ 744 Troy Aikman	1.00	.45	.12
☐ 745 Mark Royals	.05	.02	.01
☐ 746 J.J. Birden	.05	.02	.01
☐ 747 Michael Cofer	.05	.02	.01
☐ 748 Darryl Ashmore	.05	.02	.01
☐ 749 Dion Lambert	.05	.02	.01
☐ 750 Phil Simms	.10	.05	.01
☐ 751 Reggie E. White	.05	.02	.01
☐ 752 Harvey Williams	.25	.11	.03
☐ 753 Ty Detmer	.40	.18	.05
☐ 754 Tony Brooks	.05	.02	.01
☐ 755 Steve Christie	.05	.02	.01
☐ 756 Lawrence Taylor	.25	.11	.03
☐ 757 Merril Hoge	.05	.02	.01
☐ 758 Robert Jones	.05	.02	.01
☐ 759 Checklist 661-759	.05	.02	.01

1992 Topps Gold

Topps issued all three series of football cards in a gold version. In addition, all checklist cards were replaced by new player cards as listed below. The cards are standard size and are distinguished from the regular cards by the gold embossing of the player's name and team on the card front. The gold versions are valued approximately four to ten times the regular card values. The gold cards were issued in several ways: one per wax pack, three per rack pack, 20 per 660-card factory set, and ten per 99-card high-number factory set.

	MINT	NRMT	EXC
COMPLETE SET (759)	130.00	57.50	16.00
COMPLETE SERIES 1 (330)	60.00	27.00	7.50
COMPLETE SERIES 2 (330)	50.00	22.00	6.25
COMPLETE HI SERIES (99)	20.00	9.00	2.50
COMMON CARD (1-759)	.15	.07	.02
*STARS: 1.5X TO 3X BASIC CARDS			
*RC's: 1.25X TO 2.5X BASIC CARDS			

☐ 109 Freeman McNeil	.60	.25	.07
☐ 218 David Daniels	.60	.25	.07
☐ 316 Chris Hakel	.60	.25	.07
☐ 341 Ottis Anderson	.60	.25	.07
☐ 452 Shawn Moore	.60	.25	.07
☐ 563 Mike Mooney	.60	.25	.07
☐ 759 Curtis Whitley	.60	.25	.07

1992 Topps No.1 Draft Picks

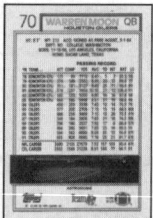

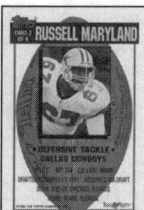

In addition to being individually inserted randomly in 1992 Topps high series packs, this four-card standard-size insert set was included in each 1992 Topps "High Series" factory set. It features the No. 1 draft pick for 1990, 1991 and 1992 as well as a card for Raghib "Rocket" Ismail, who many experts feel could have been the number 1 pick if he had entered the NFL draft. Inside white borders, the fronts display color action player photos. The words "No. 1 Draft Pick of the 90's" are printed above the picture, while the player's name and team name appear respectively in two short color bars at the bottom. On a football design, the backs carry a color close-up photo and biographical information.

	MINT	NRMT	EXC
COMPLETE SET (4)	4.00	1.80	.50
COMMON CARD (1-4)	1.00	.45	.12

☐ 1 Jeff George	1.50	.70	.19
☐ 2 Russell Maryland	1.00	.45	.12
☐ 3 Steve Emtman	1.00	.45	.12
☐ 4 Rocket Ismail	1.25	.55	.16

1992 Topps 1000 Yard Club

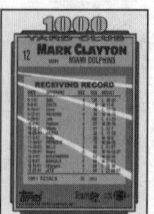

This 20-card standard-size set was issued to celebrate rushers and receivers who compiled 1000 yards or more in the 1991 season. These cards were issued three per jumbo pack. The fronts display color action player photos with white borders. A two-color picture frame overlays the picture; the words "1000 Yard Club" lay on the top crossbar of this frame. The player's name appears in a green-and-white striped bar that overlays the bottom crossbar. The design of the card fronts is enhanced by the use of red foil lettering for the number "1000" and the player's name. Receiving or rushing statistics for 1991 appear in a lime green panel against the background of a football field with white yard lines.

	MINT	NRMT	EXC
COMPLETE SET (20)	20.00	9.00	2.50
COMMON CARD (1-20)	.50	.23	.06

☐ 1 Emmitt Smith	6.00	2.70	.75
☐ 2 Barry Sanders	3.00	1.35	.35
☐ 3 Michael Irvin	1.25	.55	.16
☐ 4 Thurman Thomas	1.25	.55	.16
☐ 5 Gary Clark	.75	.35	.09
☐ 6 Haywood Jeffires	.75	.35	.09
☐ 7 Michael Haynes	.75	.35	.09
☐ 8 Drew Hill	.50	.23	.06
☐ 9 Mark Duper	.50	.23	.06
☐ 10 James Lofton	.75	.35	.09
☐ 11 Rodney Hampton	1.25	.55	.16
☐ 12 Mark Clayton	.50	.23	.06
☐ 13 Henry Ellard	.75	.35	.09
☐ 14 Art Monk	.75	.35	.09
☐ 15 Earnest Byner	.50	.23	.06
☐ 16 Gaston Green	.50	.23	.06
☐ 17 Christian Okoye	.50	.23	.06
☐ 18 Irving Fryar	.75	.35	.09
☐ 19 John Taylor	.50	.23	.06
☐ 20 Brian Blades	.75	.35	.09

1993 Topps

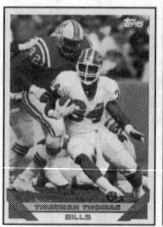

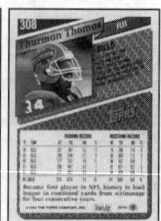

The 1993 Topps football set consists of 660 standard-size cards that were issued in two series of 330. Each pack contained 14 cards plus one Topps Gold card. Factory sets of 673 cards contain 10 Topps Gold cards and three Topps Black Gold cards. Standard card fronts feature color action player photos bordered in white. The player's name and team affiliation appear below the picture. Team color-coded diagonal bars accent the bottom corners of the photo. On team color-coded diagonal panels, the backs carry a color close-up photo, biography, and statistics, and career highlights. Subsets featured are Record Breakers (1-2), Franchise Players (82-90), Team Leaders (171-184, 261-274), League Leaders (216-220) and Field Generals (291-300). Thirty Draft Pick cards are scattered throughout the set. Rookie Cards include Jerome Bettis, Drew Bledsoe, Reggie Brooks, Dave Brown, Curtis Conway, Garrison Hearst, Qadry Ismail, O.J. McDuffie, Natrone Means, Rick Mirer, Ronald Moore, Robert Smith and Dana Stubblefield.

	MINT	NRMT	EXC
COMPLETE SET (660)	24.00	11.00	3.00
COMPLETE FACT.SET (673)	40.00	18.00	5.00
COMPLETE SERIES 1 (330)	14.00	6.25	1.75
COMPLETE SERIES 2 (330)	10.00	4.50	1.25
COMMON CARD (1-660)	.05	.02	.01

☐ 1 Art Monk RB	.05	.02	.01
☐ 2 Jerry Rice RB	.50	.23	.06
☐ 3 Stanley Richard	.05	.02	.01
☐ 4 Ron Hall	.05	.02	.01
☐ 5 Daryl Johnston	.25	.11	.03
☐ 6 Wendell Davis	.05	.02	.01
☐ 7 Vaughn Dunbar	.05	.02	.01
☐ 8 Mike Jones	.05	.02	.01
☐ 9 Anthony Johnson	.10	.05	.01
☐ 10 Chris Miller	.10	.05	.01
☐ 11 Kyle Clifton	.05	.02	.01
☐ 12 Curtis Conway	.75	.35	.09
☐ 13 Lionel Washington	.05	.02	.01
☐ 14 Reggie Johnson	.05	.02	.01
☐ 15 David Little	.05	.02	.01
☐ 16 Nick Lowery	.05	.02	.01
☐ 17 Darryl Williams	.05	.02	.01
☐ 18 Brent Jones	.10	.05	.01
☐ 19 Bruce Matthews	.05	.02	.01
☐ 20 Heath Sherman	.05	.02	.01
☐ 21 John Kasay UER (Text on back states he did not attempt any FG's over 50 yds. but made 8)	.05	.02	.01
☐ 22 Troy Drayton	.10	.05	.01
☐ 23 Eric Metcalf	.10	.05	.01
☐ 24 Andre Tippett	.05	.02	.01
☐ 25 Rodney Hampton	.25	.11	.03
☐ 26 Henry Jones	.05	.02	.01
☐ 27 Jim Everett	.10	.05	.01
☐ 28 Steve Jordan	.05	.02	.01
☐ 29 LeRoy Butler	.05	.02	.01
☐ 30 Troy Vincent	.05	.02	.01
☐ 31 Nate Lewis	.05	.02	.01
☐ 32 Rickey Jackson	.05	.02	.01
☐ 33 Darion Conner	.05	.02	.01
☐ 34 Tom Carter	.10	.05	.01
☐ 35 Jeff George	.25	.11	.03
☐ 36 Larry Centers	.40	.18	.05
☐ 37 Reggie Cobb	.05	.02	.01
☐ 38 Mike Saxon	.05	.02	.01
☐ 39 Brad Baxter	.05	.02	.01
☐ 40 Reggie White	.25	.11	.03
☐ 41 Haywood Jeffires	.10	.05	.01
☐ 42 Alfred Williams	.05	.02	.01
☐ 43 Aaron Wallace	.05	.02	.01
☐ 44 Tracy Simien	.05	.02	.01
☐ 45 Pat Harlow	.05	.02	.01
☐ 46 D.J. Johnson	.05	.02	.01
☐ 47 Don Griffin	.05	.02	.01
☐ 48 Flipper Anderson	.05	.02	.01
☐ 49 Keith Kartz	.05	.02	.01
☐ 50 Bernie Kosar	.10	.05	.01
☐ 51 Kent Hull	.05	.02	.01
☐ 52 Erik Howard	.05	.02	.01
☐ 53 Pierce Holt	.05	.02	.01
☐ 54 Dwayne Harper	.05	.02	.01
☐ 55 Bennie Blades	.05	.02	.01
☐ 56 Mark Duper	.05	.02	.01
☐ 57 Brian Noble	.05	.02	.01
☐ 58 Jeff Feagles	.05	.02	.01
☐ 59 Michael Haynes	.10	.05	.01
☐ 60 Junior Seau	.25	.11	.03
☐ 61 Gary Anderson RB	.05	.02	.01
☐ 62 Jon Hand	.05	.02	.01
☐ 63 Lin Elliott	.05	.02	.01
☐ 64 Dana Stubblefield	.25	.11	.03
☐ 65 Vaughan Johnson	.05	.02	.01
☐ 66 Mo Lewis	.05	.02	.01
☐ 67 Aeneas Williams	.05	.02	.01
☐ 68 David Fulcher	.05	.02	.01
☐ 69 Chip Lohmiller	.05	.02	.01
☐ 70 Greg Townsend	.05	.02	.01
☐ 71 Simon Fletcher	.05	.02	.01
☐ 72 Sean Salisbury	.05	.02	.01
☐ 73 Christian Okoye	.05	.02	.01
☐ 74 Jim Arnold	.05	.02	.01
☐ 75 Bruce Smith	.25	.11	.03
☐ 76 Fred Barnett	.10	.05	.01
☐ 77 Bill Romanowski	.05	.02	.01
☐ 78 Dermontti Dawson	.05	.02	.01
☐ 79 Bern Brostek	.05	.02	.01
☐ 80 Warren Moon	.25	.11	.03
☐ 81 Bill Fralic	.05	.02	.01
☐ 82 Lomas Brown FP	.05	.02	.01
☐ 83 Duane Bickett FP	.05	.02	.01
☐ 84 Neil Smith FP	.10	.05	.01
☐ 85 Reggie White FP	.10	.05	.01
☐ 86 Tim McDonald FP	.05	.02	.01
☐ 87 Leslie O'Neal FP	.05	.02	.01
☐ 88 Steve Young FP	.40	.18	.05
☐ 89 Paul Gruber FP	.05	.02	.01
☐ 90 Wilber Marshall FP	.05	.02	.01
☐ 91 Trace Armstrong	.05	.02	.01
☐ 92 Bobby Houston	.05	.02	.01
☐ 93 George Thornton	.05	.02	.01
☐ 94 Keith McCants	.05	.02	.01
☐ 95 Ricky Sanders	.05	.02	.01
☐ 96 Jackie Harris	.05	.02	.01
☐ 97 Todd Marinovich	.05	.02	.01
☐ 98 Henry Thomas	.05	.02	.01
☐ 99 Jeff Wright	.05	.02	.01
☐ 100 John Elway	.75	.35	.09
☐ 101 Garrison Hearst	1.25	.55	.16
☐ 102 Roy Foster	.05	.02	.01
☐ 103 David Lang	.05	.02	.01
☐ 104 Matt Stover	.05	.02	.01
☐ 105 Lawrence Taylor	.25	.11	.03
☐ 106 Pete Stoyanovich	.05	.02	.01
☐ 107 Jessie Tuggle	.05	.02	.01
☐ 108 William White	.05	.02	.01
☐ 109 Andy Harmon	.10	.05	.01
☐ 110 John L. Williams	.05	.02	.01
☐ 111 Jon Vaughn	.05	.02	.01
☐ 112 John Alt	.05	.02	.01
☐ 113 Chris Jacke	.05	.02	.01
☐ 114 Jim Breech	.05	.02	.01
☐ 115 Eric Martin	.05	.02	.01
☐ 116 Derrick Walker	.05	.02	.01
☐ 117 Ricky Ervins	.05	.02	.01
☐ 118 Roger Craig	.10	.05	.01
☐ 119 Jeff Gossett	.05	.02	.01
☐ 120 Emmitt Smith	2.00	.90	.25
☐ 121 Bob Whitfield	.05	.02	.01
☐ 122 Alonzo Spellman	.05	.02	.01
☐ 123 David Klingler	.05	.02	.01
☐ 124 Tommy Maddox	.05	.02	.01
☐ 125 Robert Porcher	.05	.02	.01
☐ 126 Edgar Bennett	.25	.11	.03
☐ 127 Harvey Williams	.10	.05	.01
☐ 128 Dave Brown	.25	.11	.03
☐ 129 Johnny Mitchell	.05	.02	.01
☐ 130 Drew Bledsoe	3.00	1.35	.35
☐ 131 Zefross Moss	.05	.02	.01
☐ 132 Nate Odomes	.05	.02	.01
☐ 133 Rufus Porter	.05	.02	.01
☐ 134 Jackie Slater	.05	.02	.01
☐ 135 Steve Young	.75	.35	.09
☐ 136 Chris Calloway	.05	.02	.01
☐ 137 Steve Atwater	.05	.02	.01
☐ 138 Mark Carrier DB	.05	.02	.01
☐ 139 Marvin Washington	.05	.02	.01
☐ 140 Barry Foster	.10	.05	.01
☐ 141 Ricky Reynolds	.05	.02	.01
☐ 142 Bubba McDowell	.05	.02	.01
☐ 143 Dan Footman	.05	.02	.01
☐ 144 Richmond Webb	.05	.02	.01
☐ 145 Mike Pritchard	.10	.05	.01
☐ 146 Chris Spielman	.10	.05	.01
☐ 147 Dave Krieg	.10	.05	.01
☐ 148 Nick Bell	.05	.02	.01
☐ 149 Vincent Brown	.05	.02	.01
☐ 150 Seth Joyner	.05	.02	.01

☐ 151 Tommy Kane .05 .02 .01
☐ 152 Carlton Gray .05 .02 .01
☐ 153 Harry Newsome .05 .02 .01
☐ 154 Rohn Stark .05 .02 .01
☐ 155 Shannon Sharpe .25 .11 .03
☐ 156 Charles Haley .10 .05 .01
☐ 157 Cornelius Bennett .10 .05 .01
☐ 158 Doug Riesenberg .05 .02 .01
☐ 159 Amp Lee .05 .02 .01
☐ 160 Sterling Sharpe UER .25 .11 .03
(Card front pictures
Edgar Bennett)
☐ 161 Alonzo Mitz .05 .02 .01
☐ 162 Pat Terrell .05 .02 .01
☐ 163 Mark Schlereth .05 .02 .01
☐ 164 Gary Anderson K .05 .02 .01
☐ 165 Quinn Early .10 .05 .01
☐ 166 Jerome Bettis 1.50 .70 .19
☐ 167 Lawrence Dawsey .05 .02 .01
☐ 168 Derrick Thomas .25 .11 .03
☐ 169 Rodney Peete .05 .02 .01
☐ 170 Jim Kelly .25 .11 .03
☐ 171 Deion Sanders TL .30 .14 .04
☐ 172 Richard Dent TL .05 .02 .01
☐ 173 Emmitt Smith TL 1.00 .45 .12
☐ 174 Barry Sanders TL .50 .23 .06
☐ 175 Sterling Sharpe TL .05 .02 .01
☐ 176 Cleveland Gary TL .05 .02 .01
☐ 177 Terry Allen TL .10 .05 .01
☐ 178 Vaughan Johnson TL .05 .02 .01
☐ 179 Rodney Hampton TL .05 .02 .01
☐ 180 Randall Cunningham TL .05 .02 .01
☐ 181 Ricky Proehl TL .05 .02 .01
☐ 182 Jerry Rice TL .50 .23 .06
☐ 183 Reggie Cobb TL .05 .02 .01
☐ 184 Earnest Byner TL .05 .02 .01
☐ 185 Jeff Lageman .05 .02 .01
☐ 186 Carlos Jenkins .05 .02 .01
☐ 187 Cardinals Draft Picks .40 .18 .05
Ernest Dye
Ronald Moore
Garrison Hearst
Ben Coleman
☐ 188 Todd Lyght .05 .02 .01
☐ 189 Carl Simpson .05 .02 .01
☐ 190 Barry Sanders 1.00 .45 .12
☐ 191 Jim Harbaugh .25 .11 .03
☐ 192 Roger Ruzek .05 .02 .01
☐ 193 Brent Williams .05 .02 .01
☐ 194 Chip Banks .05 .02 .01
☐ 195 Mike Croel .05 .02 .01
☐ 196 Marion Butts .05 .02 .01
☐ 197 James Washington .05 .02 .01
☐ 198 John Offerdahl .05 .02 .01
☐ 199 Tom Rathman .05 .02 .01
☐ 200 Joe Montana 1.00 .45 .12
☐ 201 Pepper Johnson .05 .02 .01
☐ 202 Cris Dishman .05 .02 .01
☐ 203 Adrian White .05 .02 .01
☐ 204 Reggie Brooks .10 .05 .01
☐ 205 Cortez Kennedy .10 .05 .01
☐ 206 Robert Massey .05 .02 .01
☐ 207 Toi Cook .05 .02 .01
☐ 208 Harry Sydney .05 .02 .01
☐ 209 Lincoln Kennedy .05 .02 .01
☐ 210 Randall McDaniel .05 .02 .01
☐ 211 Eugene Daniel .05 .02 .01
☐ 212 Rob Burnett .05 .02 .01
☐ 213 Steve Broussard .05 .02 .01
☐ 214 Brian Washington .05 .02 .01
☐ 215 Leonard Renfro .05 .02 .01
☐ 216 Audray McMillian LL .05 .02 .01
Henry Jones
☐ 217 Sterling Sharpe LL .05 .02 .01
Anthony Miller
☐ 218 Clyde Simmons LL .05 .02 .01
Leslie O'Neal
☐ 219 Emmitt Smith LL .50 .23 .06
Barry Foster
☐ 220 Steve Young LL .25 .11 .03
Warren Moon
☐ 221 Mel Gray .10 .05 .01
☐ 222 Luis Sharpe .05 .02 .01
☐ 223 Eric Moten .05 .02 .01
☐ 224 Albert Lewis .05 .02 .01
☐ 225 Alvin Harper .10 .05 .01
☐ 226 Steve Wallace .05 .02 .01
☐ 227 Mark Higgs .05 .02 .01
☐ 228 Eugene Lockhart .05 .02 .01
☐ 229 Sean Jones .05 .02 .01
☐ 230 Buccaneers Draft Picks .05 .02 .01
Eric Curry
Lamar Thomas
Demetrious DuBose
John Lynch
☐ 231 Jimmy Williams .05 .02 .01
(Text states drafted in 1992;
he was drafted in 1982)
☐ 232 Demetrius DuBose .05 .02 .01
☐ 233 John Roper .05 .02 .01
☐ 234 Keith Hamilton .05 .02 .01
☐ 235 Donald Evans .05 .02 .01
☐ 236 Kenneth Davis .05 .02 .01
☐ 237 John Copeland .10 .05 .01
☐ 238 Leonard Russell .10 .05 .01
☐ 239 Ken Harvey .05 .02 .01
☐ 240 Dale Carter .05 .02 .01
☐ 241 Anthony Pleasant .05 .02 .01
☐ 242 Darrell Green .05 .02 .01
☐ 243 Natrone Means 1.25 .55 .16
☐ 244 Rob Moore .10 .05 .01
☐ 245 Chris Doleman .05 .02 .01
☐ 246 J.B. Brown .05 .02 .01
☐ 247 Ray Crockett .05 .02 .01
☐ 248 John Taylor .10 .05 .01
☐ 249 Russell Maryland .05 .02 .01
☐ 250 Brett Favre 2.00 .90 .25
☐ 251 Carl Pickens .75 .35 .09
☐ 252 Andy Heck .05 .02 .01
☐ 253 Jerome Henderson .05 .02 .01
☐ 254 Deion Sanders .60 .25 .07
☐ 255 Steve Emtman .05 .02 .01
☐ 256 Calvin Williams .10 .05 .01
☐ 257 Sean Gilbert .10 .05 .01
☐ 258 Don Beebe .05 .02 .01
☐ 259 Robert Smith .75 .35 .09
☐ 260 Robert Blackmon .05 .02 .01
☐ 261 Jim Kelly TL .10 .05 .01
☐ 262 Harold Green TL UER .05 .02 .01
(Harold Green is identified as
Gaston Green)
☐ 263 Clay Matthews TL .05 .02 .01
☐ 264 John Elway TL .40 .18 .05
☐ 265 Warren Moon TL .10 .05 .01
☐ 266 Jeff George TL .10 .05 .01
☐ 267 Derrick Thomas TL .05 .02 .01
☐ 268 Howie Long TL .05 .02 .01
☐ 269 Dan Marino TL 1.00 .45 .12
☐ 270 Jon Vaughn TL .05 .02 .01
☐ 271 Chris Burkett TL .05 .02 .01
☐ 272 Barry Foster TL .05 .02 .01
☐ 273 Marion Butts TL .05 .02 .01
☐ 274 Chris Warren TL .05 .02 .01
☐ 275 Michael Strahan and .05 .02 .01
Marcus Buckley
Giants Draft Picks
☐ 276 Tony Casillas .05 .02 .01
☐ 277 Jarrod Bunch .05 .02 .01
☐ 278 Eric Green .05 .02 .01
☐ 279 Stan Brock .05 .02 .01
☐ 280 Chester McGlockton .10 .05 .01
☐ 281 Ricky Watters .25 .11 .03
☐ 282 Dan Saleaumua .05 .02 .01
☐ 283 Rich Camarillo .05 .02 .01
☐ 284 Cris Carter .25 .11 .03
☐ 285 Rick Mirer 1.25 .55 .16
☐ 286 Matt Brock .05 .02 .01
☐ 287 Burt Grossman .05 .02 .01
☐ 288 Andre Collins .05 .02 .01
☐ 289 Mark Jackson .05 .02 .01
☐ 290 Dan Marino 2.00 .90 .25
☐ 291 Cornelius Bennett FG .05 .02 .01
☐ 292 Steve Atwater FG .05 .02 .01
☐ 293 Bryan Cox FG .05 .02 .01
☐ 294 Sam Mills FG .05 .02 .01
☐ 295 Pepper Johnson FG .05 .02 .01
☐ 296 Seth Joyner FG .05 .02 .01
☐ 297 Chris Spielman FG .05 .02 .01
☐ 298 Junior Seau FG .10 .05 .01
☐ 299 Cortez Kennedy FG .05 .02 .01
☐ 300 Broderick Thomas FG .05 .02 .01
☐ 301 Todd McNair .05 .02 .01
☐ 302 Nate Newton .10 .05 .01
☐ 303 Michael Walter .05 .02 .01
☐ 304 Clyde Simmons .05 .02 .01
☐ 305 Ernie Mills .05 .02 .01
☐ 306 Steve Wisniewski .05 .02 .01
☐ 307 Coleman Rudolph .05 .02 .01
☐ 308 Thurman Thomas .25 .11 .03
☐ 309 Reggie Roby .05 .02 .01
☐ 310 Eric Swann .10 .05 .01
☐ 311 Mark Wheeler .05 .02 .01
☐ 312 Jeff Herrod .05 .02 .01
☐ 313 Leroy Hoard .10 .05 .01
☐ 314 Patrick Bates .05 .02 .01
☐ 315 Earnest Byner .05 .02 .01
☐ 316 Dave Meggett .05 .02 .01
☐ 317 George Teague .10 .05 .01
☐ 318 Ray Childress .05 .02 .01
☐ 319 Mike Kenn .05 .02 .01
☐ 320 Jason Hanson .05 .02 .01
☐ 321 Gary Clark .10 .05 .01
☐ 322 Chris Gardocki .05 .02 .01
☐ 323 Ken Norton .10 .05 .01
☐ 324 Eric Curry .05 .02 .01
☐ 325 Byron Evans .05 .02 .01
☐ 326 O.J. McDuffie .75 .35 .09
☐ 327 Dwight Stone .05 .02 .01
☐ 328 Tommy Barnhardt .05 .02 .01
☐ 329 Checklist 1-165 .05 .02 .01
☐ 330 Checklist 166-329 .05 .02 .01
☐ 331 Erik Williams .05 .02 .01
☐ 332 Phil Hansen .05 .02 .01
☐ 333 Martin Harrison .05 .02 .01
☐ 334 Mark Ingram .05 .02 .01
☐ 335 Mark Rypien .05 .02 .01
☐ 336 Anthony Miller .10 .05 .01
☐ 337 Antone Davis .05 .02 .01
☐ 338 Mike Munchak .05 .02 .01
☐ 339 Wayne Martin .05 .02 .01
☐ 340 Joe Montana 1.00 .45 .12
☐ 341 Deon Figures .10 .05 .01
☐ 342 Ed McDaniel .05 .02 .01
☐ 343 Chris Burkett .05 .02 .01
☐ 344 Tony Smith .05 .02 .01
☐ 345 James Lofton .10 .05 .01
☐ 346 Courtney Hawkins .05 .02 .01
☐ 347 Dennis Smith .05 .02 .01
☐ 348 Anthony Morgan .05 .02 .01
☐ 349 Chris Goode .05 .02 .01
☐ 350 Phil Simms .10 .05 .01
☐ 351 Patrick Hunter .05 .02 .01
☐ 352 Brett Perriman .25 .11 .03
☐ 353 Corey Miller .05 .02 .01
☐ 354 Harry Galbreath .05 .02 .01
☐ 355 Mark Carrier WR .10 .05 .01
☐ 356 Troy Drayton .10 .05 .01
☐ 357 Greg Davis .05 .02 .01
☐ 358 Tim Krumrie .05 .02 .01
☐ 359 Tim McDonald .05 .02 .01
☐ 360 Webster Slaughter .05 .02 .01
☐ 361 Steve Christie .05 .02 .01
☐ 362 Courtney Hall .05 .02 .01
☐ 363 Charles Mann .05 .02 .01
☐ 364 Vestee Jackson .05 .02 .01
☐ 365 Robert Jones .05 .02 .01
☐ 366 Rich Miano .05 .02 .01
☐ 367 Morten Andersen .05 .02 .01
☐ 368 Jeff Graham .10 .05 .01
☐ 369 Martin Mayhew .05 .02 .01
☐ 370 Anthony Carter .10 .05 .01
☐ 371 Greg Kragen .05 .02 .01
☐ 372 Ron Cox .05 .02 .01
☐ 373 Perry Williams .05 .02 .01
☐ 374 Willie Gault .05 .02 .01
☐ 375 Chris Warren .10 .05 .01
☐ 376 Reyna Thompson .05 .02 .01
☐ 377 Bennie Thompson .05 .02 .01
☐ 378 Kevin Mack .05 .02 .01
☐ 379 Clarence Verdin .05 .02 .01
☐ 380 Marc Boutte .05 .02 .01
☐ 381 Marvin Jones .05 .02 .01
☐ 382 Greg Jackson .05 .02 .01
☐ 383 Steve Bono .25 .11 .03
☐ 384 Terrell Buckley .05 .02 .01
☐ 385 Garrison Hearst .60 .25 .07
☐ 386 Mike Brim .05 .02 .01
☐ 387 Jesse Sapolu .05 .02 .01
☐ 388 Carl Lee .05 .02 .01
☐ 389 Jeff Cross .05 .02 .01
☐ 390 Karl Mecklenburg .05 .02 .01
☐ 391 Chad Hennings .05 .02 .01
☐ 392 Oliver Barnett .05 .02 .01
☐ 393 Dalton Hilliard .05 .02 .01
☐ 394 Broderick Thompson .05 .02 .01
☐ 395 Raghib Ismail .10 .05 .01
☐ 396 John Kidd .05 .02 .01
☐ 397 Eddie Anderson .05 .02 .01
☐ 398 Lamar Lathon .05 .02 .01
☐ 399 Darren Perry .05 .02 .01
☐ 400 Drew Bledsoe 1.50 .70 .19
☐ 401 Ferrell Edmunds .05 .02 .01
☐ 402 Lomas Brown .05 .02 .01
☐ 403 Drew Hill .05 .02 .01
☐ 404 David Whitmore .05 .02 .01
☐ 405 Mike Johnson .05 .02 .01
☐ 406 Paul Gruber .05 .02 .01
☐ 407 Kirk Lowdermilk .05 .02 .01
☐ 408 Curtis Conway .40 .18 .05
☐ 409 Bryce Paup .25 .11 .03
☐ 410 Boomer Esiason .10 .05 .01
☐ 411 Jay Schroeder .05 .02 .01
☐ 412 Anthony Newman .05 .02 .01
☐ 413 Ernie Jones .05 .02 .01
☐ 414 Carlton Bailey .05 .02 .01
☐ 415 Kenneth Gant .05 .02 .01
☐ 416 Todd Scott .05 .02 .01
☐ 417 Anthony Smith .05 .02 .01
☐ 418 Erik McMillan .05 .02 .01
☐ 419 Ronnie Harmon .05 .02 .01
☐ 420 Andre Reed .10 .05 .01
☐ 421 Wymon Henderson .05 .02 .01
☐ 422 Carnell Lake .05 .02 .01
☐ 423 Al Noga .05 .02 .01
☐ 424 Curtis Duncan .05 .02 .01
☐ 425 Mike Gann .05 .02 .01
☐ 426 Eugene Robinson .05 .02 .01
☐ 427 Scott Mersereau .05 .02 .01
☐ 428 Chris Singleton .05 .02 .01
☐ 429 Gerald Robinson .05 .02 .01
☐ 430 Pat Swilling .05 .02 .01
☐ 431 Ed McCaffrey .05 .02 .01
☐ 432 Neal Anderson .05 .02 .01
☐ 433 Joe Phillips .05 .02 .01
☐ 434 Jerry Ball .05 .02 .01
☐ 435 Tyronne Stowe .05 .02 .01
☐ 436 Dana Stubblefield .25 .11 .03
☐ 437 Eric Curry .05 .02 .01
☐ 438 Derrick Fenner .05 .02 .01
☐ 439 Mark Clayton .05 .02 .01
☐ 440 Quentin Coryatt .10 .05 .01
☐ 441 Willie Roaf .10 .05 .01
☐ 442 Ernest Dye .05 .02 .01
☐ 443 Jeff Jaeger .05 .02 .01
☐ 444 Stan Humphries .25 .11 .03
☐ 445 Johnny Johnson .05 .02 .01
☐ 446 Larry Brown DB .05 .02 .01
☐ 447 Kurt Gouveia .05 .02 .01
☐ 448 Qadry Ismail .25 .11 .03
☐ 449 Dan Footman .05 .02 .01
☐ 450 Tom Waddle .05 .02 .01
☐ 451 Kelvin Martin .05 .02 .01
☐ 452 Kanavis McGhee .05 .02 .01
☐ 453 Herman Moore .75 .35 .09
☐ 454 Jesse Solomon .05 .02 .01
☐ 455 Shane Conlan .05 .02 .01
☐ 456 Joel Steed .05 .02 .01
☐ 457 Charles Arbuckle .05 .02 .01
☐ 458 Shane Dronett .05 .02 .01
☐ 459 Steve Tasker .10 .05 .01
☐ 460 Herschel Walker .10 .05 .01
☐ 461 Willie Davis .25 .11 .03
☐ 462 Al Smith .05 .02 .01
☐ 463 O.J. McDuffie .40 .18 .05
☐ 464 Kevin Fagan .05 .02 .01
☐ 465 Hardy Nickerson .10 .05 .01
☐ 466 Leonard Marshall .05 .02 .01
☐ 467 John Baylor .05 .02 .01
☐ 468 Jay Novacek .10 .05 .01
☐ 469 Wayne Simmons .05 .02 .01
☐ 470 Tommy Vardell .05 .02 .01
☐ 471 Cleveland Gary .05 .02 .01
☐ 472 Mark Collins .05 .02 .01
☐ 473 Craig Heyward .10 .05 .01
☐ 474 John Copeland UER .10 .05 .01
(Bio states he was born 0-29-70
instead of 9-29-70)
☐ 475 Jeff Hostetler .10 .05 .01
☐ 476 Brian Mitchell .10 .05 .01
☐ 477 Natrone Means .60 .25 .07
☐ 478 Brad Muster .05 .02 .01
☐ 479 David Lutz .05 .02 .01
☐ 480 Andre Rison .10 .05 .01
☐ 481 Michael Zordich .05 .02 .01
☐ 482 Jim McMahon .05 .02 .01
☐ 483 Carlton Gray .05 .02 .01
☐ 484 Chris Mohr .05 .02 .01
☐ 485 Ernest Givins .10 .05 .01
☐ 486 Tony Tolbert .05 .02 .01
☐ 487 Vai Sikahema .05 .02 .01
☐ 488 Larry Webster .05 .02 .01
☐ 489 James Hasty .05 .02 .01
☐ 490 Reggie White .25 .11 .03
☐ 491 Reggie Rivers .05 .02 .01
☐ 492 Roman Phifer .05 .02 .01
☐ 493 Levon Kirkland .05 .02 .01
☐ 494 Demetrius DuBose .05 .02 .01
☐ 495 William Perry .10 .05 .01
☐ 496 Clay Matthews .10 .05 .01
☐ 497 Aaron Jones .05 .02 .01
☐ 498 Jack Trudeau .05 .02 .01
☐ 499 Michael Brooks .05 .02 .01
☐ 500 Jerry Rice 1.00 .45 .12
☐ 501 Lonnie Marts .05 .02 .01
☐ 502 Tim McGee .05 .02 .01
☐ 503 Kelvin Pritchett .05 .02 .01
☐ 504 Bobby Hebert .05 .02 .01
☐ 505 Audray McMillian .05 .02 .01
☐ 506 Chuck Cecil .05 .02 .01
☐ 507 Leonard Renfro .05 .02 .01
☐ 508 Ethan Horton .05 .02 .01
☐ 509 Kevin Smith .10 .05 .01
☐ 510 Louis Oliver .05 .02 .01
☐ 511 John Stephens .05 .02 .01
☐ 512 Browning Nagle .05 .02 .01
☐ 513 Ricardo McDonald .05 .02 .01
☐ 514 Leslie O'Neal .10 .05 .01
☐ 515 Lorenzo White .05 .02 .01
☐ 516 Thomas Smith .10 .05 .01
☐ 517 Tony Woods .05 .02 .01
☐ 518 Darryl Henley .05 .02 .01
☐ 519 Robert Delpino .05 .02 .01
☐ 520 Rod Woodson .25 .11 .03
☐ 521 Phillippi Sparks .05 .02 .01
☐ 522 Jessie Hester .05 .02 .01
☐ 523 Shaun Gayle .05 .02 .01
☐ 524 Brad Edwards .05 .02 .01
☐ 525 Randall Cunningham .10 .05 .01
☐ 526 Marv Cook .05 .02 .01
☐ 527 Dennis Gibson .05 .02 .01
☐ 528 Eric Pegram .10 .05 .01
☐ 529 Terry McDaniel .05 .02 .01
☐ 530 Troy Aikman 1.00 .45 .12
☐ 531 Irving Fryar .10 .05 .01
☐ 532 Blair Thomas .05 .02 .01
☐ 533 Jim Wilks .05 .02 .01
☐ 534 Michael Jackson .10 .05 .01
☐ 535 Eric Davis .05 .02 .01
☐ 536 James Campen .05 .02 .01
☐ 537 Steve Beuerlein .05 .02 .01
☐ 538 Robert Smith .40 .18 .05
☐ 539 J.J. Birden .05 .02 .01
☐ 540 Broderick Thomas .05 .02 .01
☐ 541 Darryl Talley .05 .02 .01
☐ 542 Russell Freeman .05 .02 .01
☐ 543 David Alexander .05 .02 .01
☐ 544 Chris Mims .05 .02 .01
☐ 545 Coleman Rudolph .05 .02 .01
☐ 546 Steve McMichael .10 .05 .01
☐ 547 David Williams .05 .02 .01

□ 548 Chris Hinton	.05	.02	.01
□ 549 Jim Jeffcoat	.05	.02	.01
□ 550 Howie Long	.10	.05	.01
□ 551 Roosevelt Potts	.05	.02	.01
□ 552 Bryan Cox	.05	.02	.01
□ 553 David Richards UER (Photo on front is Stanley Richards)	.05	.02	.01
□ 554 Reggie Brooks	.10	.05	.01
□ 555 Neil O'Donnell	.25	.11	.03
□ 556 Irv Smith	.05	.02	.01
□ 557 Henry Ellard	.10	.05	.01
□ 558 Steve DeBerg	.05	.02	.01
□ 559 Jim Sweeney	.05	.02	.01
□ 560 Harold Green	.05	.02	.01
□ 561 Darrell Thompson	.05	.02	.01
□ 562 Vinny Testaverde	.10	.05	.01
□ 563 Bubby Brister	.05	.02	.01
□ 564 Sean Landeta	.05	.02	.01
□ 565 Neil Smith	.25	.11	.03
□ 566 Craig Erickson	.10	.05	.01
□ 567 Jim Ritcher	.05	.02	.01
□ 568 Don Mosebar	.05	.02	.01
□ 569 John Gesek	.05	.02	.01
□ 570 Gary Plummer	.05	.02	.01
□ 571 Norm Johnson	.05	.02	.01
□ 572 Ron Heller	.05	.02	.01
□ 573 Carl Simpson	.05	.02	.01
□ 574 Greg Montgomery	.05	.02	.01
□ 575 Dana Hall	.05	.02	.01
□ 576 Vencie Glenn	.05	.02	.01
□ 577 Dean Biasucci	.05	.02	.01
□ 578 Rod Bernstine UER (Name spelled Berstein on front)	.05	.02	.01
□ 579 Randal Hill	.05	.02	.01
□ 580 Sam Mills	.05	.02	.01
□ 581 Santana Dotson	.10	.05	.01
□ 582 Greg Lloyd	.25	.11	.03
□ 583 Eric Thomas	.05	.02	.01
□ 584 Henry Rolling	.05	.02	.01
□ 585 Tony Bennett	.05	.02	.01
□ 586 Sheldon White	.05	.02	.01
□ 587 Mark Kelso	.05	.02	.01
□ 588 Marc Spindler	.05	.02	.01
□ 589 Greg McMurtry	.05	.02	.01
□ 590 Art Monk	.10	.05	.01
□ 591 Marco Coleman	.05	.02	.01
□ 592 Tony Jones	.05	.02	.01
□ 593 Melvin Jenkins	.05	.02	.01
□ 594 Kevin Ross	.05	.02	.01
□ 595 William Fuller	.05	.02	.01
□ 596 James Joseph	.05	.02	.01
□ 597 Lamar McGriggs	.05	.02	.01
□ 598 Gill Byrd	.05	.02	.01
□ 599 Alexander Wright	.05	.02	.01
□ 600 Rick Mirer	.60	.25	.07
□ 601 Richard Dent	.10	.05	.01
□ 602 Thomas Everett	.05	.02	.01
□ 603 Jack Del Rio	.05	.02	.01
□ 604 Jerome Bettis	.75	.35	.09
□ 605 Ronnie Lott	.10	.05	.01
□ 606 Marty Carter	.05	.02	.01
□ 607 Arthur Marshall	.05	.02	.01
□ 608 Lee Johnson	.05	.02	.01
□ 609 Bruce Armstrong	.05	.02	.01
□ 610 Ricky Proehl	.05	.02	.01
□ 611 Will Wolford	.05	.02	.01
□ 612 Mike Prior	.05	.02	.01
□ 613 George Jamison	.05	.02	.01
□ 614 Gene Atkins	.05	.02	.01
□ 615 Merril Hoge	.05	.02	.01
□ 616 Desmond Howard UER (Stats indicate 8 TD's receiving; he had 0)	.10	.05	.01
□ 617 Jarvis Williams	.05	.02	.01
□ 618 Marcus Allen	.25	.11	.03
□ 619 Gary Brown	.05	.02	.01
□ 620 Bill Brooks	.05	.02	.01
□ 621 Eric Allen	.05	.02	.01
□ 622 Todd Kelly	.05	.02	.01
□ 623 Michael Dean Perry	.10	.05	.01
□ 624 David Braxton	.05	.02	.01
□ 625 Mike Sherrard	.05	.02	.01
□ 626 Jeff Bryant	.05	.02	.01
□ 627 Eric Bieniemy	.05	.02	.01
□ 628 Tim Brown	.25	.11	.03
□ 629 Troy Auzenne	.05	.02	.01
□ 630 Michael Irvin	.25	.11	.03
□ 631 Maurice Hurst	.05	.02	.01
□ 632 Duane Bickett	.05	.02	.01
□ 633 George Teague	.10	.05	.01
□ 634 Vince Workman	.05	.02	.01
□ 635 Renaldo Turnbull	.05	.02	.01
□ 636 Johnny Bailey	.05	.02	.01
□ 637 Dan Williams	.05	.02	.01
□ 638 James Thornton	.05	.02	.01
□ 639 Terry Allen	.25	.11	.03
□ 640 Kevin Greene	.25	.11	.03
□ 641 Tony Zendejas	.05	.02	.01
□ 642 Scott Kowalkowski	.05	.02	.01
□ 643 Jeff Query UER (Text states he played for Packers in '92; he played for Bengals)	.05	.02	.01
□ 644 Brian Blades	.10	.05	.01
□ 645 Keith Jackson	.10	.05	.01
□ 646 Monte Coleman	.05	.02	.01
□ 647 Guy McIntyre	.05	.02	.01
□ 648 Barry Word	.05	.02	.01
□ 649 Steve Everitt	.05	.02	.01
□ 650 Patrick Bates	.05	.02	.01
□ 651 Marcus Robertson	.05	.02	.01
□ 652 John Carney	.05	.02	.01
□ 653 Derek Brown TE	.05	.02	.01
□ 654 Carwell Gardner	.05	.02	.01
□ 655 Moe Gardner	.05	.02	.01
□ 656 Andre Ware	.05	.02	.01
□ 657 Keith Van Horne	.05	.02	.01
□ 658 Hugh Millen	.05	.02	.01
□ 659 Checklist 330-495	.05	.02	.01
□ 660 Checklist 496-660	.05	.02	.01

1993 Topps Gold

The 1993 Topps Gold set consists of 660 standard-size cards. The cards were inserted one per foil pack, three per rack pack, and five per jumbo pack. In design, the cards are identical to the regular issue cards, except that the color-coded stripes carrying player information are replaced by gold foil stripes. The cards are numbered on the back. The checklist cards in the regular set were replaced by the player cards 329, 330, 659, and 660, listed below.

	MINT	NRMT	EXC
COMPLETE SET (660)	90.00	40.00	11.00
COMPLETE SERIES 1 SET (330)	50.00	22.00	6.25
COMPLETE SERIES 2 SET (330)	40.00	18.00	5.00
COMMON CARD (1-660)	.15	.07	.02
STARS: 1.5X TO 3X BASIC CARDS			
RC's:1.25X TO 2.5X BASIC CARDS			
□ 329 Terance Mathis	1.00	.45	.12
□ 330 John Wojciechowski	.50	.23	.06
□ 659 Pat Chaffey	.50	.23	.06
□ 660 Milton Mack	.50	.23	.06

1993 Topps Black Gold

One Topps Black Gold card was inserted in approximately every 48 packs of 1993 Topps football. Card numbers 1-22 were randomly inserted in first series wax packs while card numbers 23-44 were featured in second series packs. Collectors could obtain the set by collecting individual random insert cards or receive 11, 22, or 44 Black Gold cards through the mail by sending in special "You've Just Won" cards, entitling the holder to receive Group A (1-11), Group B (12-22), or Groups A and B (1-22) in series one. Likewise, four "You've Just Won" cards were inserted in second series packs and entitled the holder to receive Group C (23-33), Group D (34-44), Groups C and D (23-44), or Groups A-D (1-44). As a bonus for mailing in the special cards, the collector received a special "You've Just Won" and a congratulatory letter notifying the collector that his/her name has been entered into a drawing for one of 500 uncut sheets of all 44 Topps Black Gold cards in a leatherette frame. Inside a white border, the fronts feature color action player photos that are edged above and below by a gold foil screened background. Each of these gold foil areas is curved, and in the bottom one appears a black stripe carrying the player's name. Showing a black-and-white pinstripe background inside a white border, the horizontal backs carry a color close-up cut-out and, on a greenish-blue panel, career summary.

	MINT	NRMT	EXC
COMPLETE SET (44)	30.00	13.50	3.70
COMPLETE SERIES 1 (22)	12.00	5.50	1.50
COMPLETE SERIES 2 (22)	18.00	8.00	2.20
COMMON CARD (1-44)	.50	.23	.06
□ 1 Kelvin Martin	.50	.23	.06
□ 2 Audray McMillian	.50	.23	.06
□ 3 Terry Allen	1.50	.70	.19
□ 4 Vai Sikahema	.50	.23	.06
□ 5 Clyde Simmons	1.00	.45	.12
□ 6 Lorenzo White	1.00	.45	.12
□ 7 Michael Irvin	1.50	.70	.19
□ 8 Troy Aikman	3.50	1.55	.45
□ 9 Mark Kelso	.50	.23	.06
□ 10 Cleveland Gary	.50	.23	.06
□ 11 Greg Montgomery	.50	.23	.06
□ 12 Jerry Rice	3.50	1.55	.45
□ 13 Rod Woodson	1.50	.70	.19
□ 14 Leslie O'Neal	1.00	.45	.12
□ 15 Harold Green	.50	.23	.06
□ 16 Randall Cunningham	1.00	.45	.12
□ 17 Ricky Watters	1.50	.70	.19
□ 18 Andre Rison	1.50	.70	.19
□ 19 Eugene Robinson	.50	.23	.06
□ 20 Wayne Martin	1.00	.45	.12
□ 21 Chris Warren	1.50	.70	.19
□ 22 Anthony Miller	1.00	.45	.12
□ 23 Steve Young	2.50	1.10	.30
□ 24 Tim Harris	.50	.23	.06
□ 25 Emmitt Smith	6.00	2.70	.75
□ 26 Sterling Sharpe	1.50	.70	.19
□ 27 Henry Jones	.50	.23	.06
□ 28 Warren Moon	1.50	.70	.19
□ 29 Barry Foster	1.00	.45	.12
□ 30 Dale Carter	1.00	.45	.12
□ 31 Mel Gray	1.00	.45	.12
□ 32 Barry Sanders	3.50	1.55	.45
□ 33 Dan Marino	6.00	2.70	.75
□ 34 Fred Barnett	1.00	.45	.12
□ 35 Deion Sanders	2.00	.90	.25
□ 36 Simon Fletcher	.50	.23	.06
□ 37 Donnell Woolford	.50	.23	.06
□ 38 Reggie Cobb	.50	.23	.06
□ 39 Brett Favre	6.00	2.70	.75
□ 40 Thurman Thomas	1.50	.70	.19
□ 41 Rodney Hampton	1.50	.70	.19
□ 42 Eric Martin	.50	.23	.06
□ 43 Pete Stoyanovich	.50	.23	.06
□ 44 Herschel Walker	1.00	.45	.12
□ A Winner A 1-11 Expired	.75	.35	.09
□ B Winner B 12-22 UER Exp. (Card No. 17 listed as Herschel Walker instead of Ricky Watters)	.75	.35	.09
□ C Winner C 23-33 Expired	.75	.35	.09
□ D Winner D 34-44 Expired	.75	.35	.09
□ AB Winner AB 1-22 Expired	.75	.35	.09
□ CD Winner C/D 23-44 Exp.	.75	.35	.09

1993 Topps FantaSports

According to Topps, this was the first interactive Fantasy game that incorporated trading cards as a key playing element. The set of 200 cards was provided that featured key players. The card backs carried graphs of the players' three-year performances on all FantaSports criteria, comparisons with other players in that position, and scouting reports. The cards were used by contestants to make draft choices and trades throughout the season. The cost of playing the game was 159.00. Included were the cards, entry into the league, stat book, worksheets, and instructions. The person who earned the best 18-game NFL fantasy score won four tickets to Super Bowl XXVIII. The game was test-marketed in four cities (Houston, Kansas City, Buffalo, and Washington D.C.) and the cards were not offered at retail in those cities. The black-bordered 3" by 5" cards feature color player action shots on their fronts. The player's name and team appears in black lettering within gold-foil stripes at the bottom. The set's title appears in gold foil within the upper margin. The horizontal white back carries a color action player photo on the right, with the player's name, position, team, three-year performance graphs, and scouting report shown on the left. The cards are numbered on the back arranged by position, quarterbacks (1-30), running backs (31-89), wide receivers (90-137), tight ends (138-150), kickers (151-162), punters (163-172), and defensive players (173-200).

	MINT	NRMT	EXC
COMPLETE SET (200)	125.00	55.00	15.50
COMMON CARD (1-200)	.25	.11	.03
□ 1 Chris Miller	.50	.23	.06
□ 2 Jim Kelly	1.00	.45	.12
□ 3 Jim Harbaugh	.75	.35	.09
□ 4 David Klingler	.50	.23	.06
□ 5 Bernie Kosar	.50	.23	.06
□ 6 Troy Aikman	10.00	4.50	1.25
□ 7 John Elway	8.00	3.60	1.00
□ 8 Tommy Maddox	.25	.11	.03
□ 9 Rodney Peete	.50	.23	.06
□ 10 Andre Ware	.25	.11	.03
□ 11 Brett Favre	20.00	9.00	2.50
□ 12 Warren Moon	.75	.35	.09
□ 13 Jeff George	1.25	.55	.16
□ 14 Dave Krieg	.50	.23	.06
□ 15 Joe Montana	12.00	5.50	1.50
□ 16 Todd Marinovich	.25	.11	.03
□ 17 Jim Everett	.50	.23	.06
□ 18 Dan Marino	25.00	11.00	3.10
□ 19 Sean Salisbury	.25	.11	.03
□ 20 Drew Bledsoe	12.00	5.50	1.50
□ 21 Dave Brown	1.00	.45	.12
□ 22 Phil Simms	.50	.23	.06
□ 23 Boomer Esiason	.50	.23	.06
□ 24 Browning Nagle	.25	.11	.03
□ 25 Randall Cunningham	.50	.23	.06
□ 26 Neil O'Donnell	.50	.23	.06
□ 27 Stan Humphries	1.00	.45	.12
□ 28 Steve Young	8.00	3.60	1.00
□ 29 Rick Mirer	4.00	1.80	.50
□ 30 Mark Rypien	.50	.23	.06
□ 31 Kenneth Davis	.25	.11	.03
□ 32 Thurman Thomas	2.00	.90	.25
□ 33 Steve Broussard	.25	.11	.03
□ 34 Neal Anderson	.50	.23	.06
□ 35 Craig Heyward	.25	.11	.03
□ 36 Derrick Fenner	.25	.11	.03
□ 37 Harold Green	.25	.11	.03
□ 38 Leroy Hoard	.25	.11	.03
□ 39 Kevin Mack	.25	.11	.03
□ 40 Eric Metcalf	.75	.35	.09
□ 41 Tommy Vardell	.25	.11	.03
□ 42 Daryl Johnston	.50	.23	.06
□ 43 Emmitt Smith	20.00	9.00	2.50
□ 44 Barry Sanders	10.00	4.50	1.25
□ 45 Edgar Bennett	.75	.35	.09
□ 46 Lorenzo White	.50	.23	.06
□ 47 Anthony Johnson	.50	.23	.06
□ 48 Todd McNair	.25	.11	.03
□ 49 Christian Okoye	.25	.11	.03
□ 50 Harvey Williams	.50	.23	.06
□ 51 Barry Word	.25	.11	.03
□ 52 Nick Bell	.25	.11	.03
□ 53 Eric Dickerson	.50	.23	.06
□ 54 Jerome Bettis	6.00	2.70	.75
□ 55 Cleveland Gary	.25	.11	.03
□ 56 Mark Higgs	.25	.11	.03
□ 57 Tony Paige	.25	.11	.03
□ 58 Terry Allen	.50	.23	.06
□ 59 Roger Craig	.50	.23	.06
□ 60 Robert Smith	3.00	1.35	.35
□ 61 Leonard Russell	.50	.23	.06
□ 62 Jon Vaughn	.25	.11	.03
□ 63 Vaughn Dunbar	.25	.11	.03
□ 64 Dalton Hilliard	.25	.11	.03
□ 65 Jarrod Bunch	.25	.11	.03
□ 66 Rodney Hampton	.75	.35	.09
□ 67 Dave Meggett	.50	.23	.06
□ 68 Brad Baxter	.25	.11	.03
□ 69 Heath Sherman	.25	.11	.03
□ 70 Vai Sikahema	.25	.11	.03
□ 71 Johnny Bailey	.25	.11	.03
□ 72 Larry Centers	.75	.35	.09
□ 73 Garrison Hearst	5.00	2.20	.60
□ 74 Barry Foster	.50	.23	.06
□ 75 Eric Bieniemy	.25	.11	.03
□ 76 Marion Butts	.25	.11	.03
□ 77 Ronnie Harmon	.25	.11	.03
□ 78 Natrone Means	4.00	1.80	.50
□ 79 Amp Lee	.25	.11	.03
□ 80 Tom Rathman	.25	.11	.03
□ 81 Ricky Watters	1.25	.55	.16
□ 82 Chris Warren	.75	.35	.09
□ 83 John L. Williams	.25	.11	.03
□ 84 Gary Anderson RB	.25	.11	.03
□ 85 Reggie Cobb	.25	.11	.03
□ 86 Vince Workman	.25	.11	.03
□ 87 Reggie Brooks	.75	.35	.09
□ 88 Earnest Byner	.25	.11	.03
□ 89 Ricky Ervins	.25	.11	.03
□ 90 Michael Haynes	.50	.23	.06
□ 91 Mike Pritchard	.50	.23	.06
□ 92 Andre Rison	.75	.35	.09
□ 93 Don Beebe	.25	.11	.03
□ 94 Andre Reed	.50	.23	.06
□ 95 Curtis Conway	3.00	1.35	.35
□ 96 Wendell Davis	.25	.11	.03
□ 97 Tom Waddle	.25	.11	.03
□ 98 Carl Pickens	1.25	.55	.16
□ 99 Michael Jackson	.50	.23	.06
□ 100 Alvin Harper	.50	.23	.06
□ 101 Michael Irvin	2.00	.90	.25
□ 102 Vance Johnson	.25	.11	.03
□ 103 Mel Gray	.50	.23	.06
□ 104 Sterling Sharpe	.75	.35	.09
□ 105 Curtis Duncan	.25	.11	.03
□ 106 Ernest Givins	.50	.23	.06
□ 107 Haywood Jeffires	.50	.23	.06
□ 108 Tim Brown	1.00	.45	.12
□ 109 Willie Gault	.25	.11	.03
□ 110 Flipper Anderson	.25	.11	.03
□ 111 Henry Ellard	.50	.23	.06
□ 112 Mark Duper	.50	.23	.06
□ 113 O.J. McDuffie	3.00	1.35	.35
□ 114 Anthony Carter	.50	.23	.06
□ 115 Cris Carter	.75	.35	.09
□ 116 Mike Farr	.25	.11	.03
□ 117 Quinn Early	.50	.23	.06
□ 118 Eric Martin	.25	.11	.03
□ 119 Chris Calloway	.25	.11	.03
□ 120 Mark Jackson	.25	.11	.03
□ 121 Rob Moore	.50	.23	.06
□ 122 Fred Barnett	.50	.23	.06
□ 123 Calvin Williams	.50	.23	.06
□ 124 Gary Clark	.50	.23	.06
□ 125 Randal Hill	.25	.11	.03
□ 126 Ricky Proehl	.25	.11	.03
□ 127 Jeff Graham	.50	.23	.06
□ 128 Ernie Mills	.50	.23	.06
□ 129 Dwight Stone	.25	.11	.03
□ 130 Nate Lewis	.25	.11	.03
□ 131 Jerry Rice	10.00	4.50	1.25
□ 132 John Taylor	.50	.23	.06
□ 133 Tommy Kane	.25	.11	.03
□ 134 Kelvin Martin	.25	.11	.03
□ 135 Lawrence Dawsey	.50	.23	.06
□ 136 Courtney Hawkins	.50	.23	.06
□ 137 Art Monk	.50	.23	.06
□ 138 Pete Metzelaars	.25	.11	.03

☐ 139 Jay Novacek	.50	.23	.06
☐ 140 Reggie Johnson	.25	.11	.03
☐ 141 Shannon Sharpe	.50	.23	.06
☐ 142 Jackie Harris	.25	.11	.03
☐ 143 Troy Drayton	.50	.23	.06
☐ 144 Keith Jackson	.50	.23	.06
☐ 145 Steve Jordan	.25	.11	.03
☐ 146 Johnny Mitchell	.25	.11	.03
☐ 147 Eric Green	.50	.23	.06
☐ 148 Derrick Walker	.25	.11	.03
☐ 149 Brent Jones	.50	.23	.06
☐ 150 Ron Hall	.25	.11	.03
☐ 151 Norm Johnson	.25	.11	.03
☐ 152 Jim Breech	.25	.11	.03
☐ 153 Matt Stover	.25	.11	.03
☐ 154 Lin Elliott	.25	.11	.03
☐ 155 Jason Hanson	.25	.11	.03
☐ 156 Chris Jacke	.25	.11	.03
☐ 157 Nick Lowery	.25	.11	.03
☐ 158 Pete Stoyanovich	.25	.11	.03
☐ 159 Roger Ruzek	.25	.11	.03
☐ 160 Gary Anderson K	.25	.11	.03
☐ 161 John Kasay	.25	.11	.03
☐ 162 Chip Lohmiller	.25	.11	.03
☐ 163 Chris Gardocki	.25	.11	.03
☐ 164 Mike Saxon	.25	.11	.03
☐ 165 Jim Arnold	.25	.11	.03
☐ 166 Rohn Stark	.25	.11	.03
☐ 167 Jeff Gossett	.25	.11	.03
☐ 168 Reggie Roby	.25	.11	.03
☐ 169 Harry Newsome	.25	.11	.03
☐ 170 Tommy Barnhardt	.25	.11	.03
☐ 171 Jeff Feagles	.25	.11	.03
☐ 172 Rich Camarillo	.25	.11	.03
☐ 173 Deion Sanders Falcons Defense	6.00	2.70	.75
☐ 174 Cornelius Bennett Bills Defense	.50	.23	.06
☐ 175 Mark Carrier DB Bears Defense	.50	.23	.06
☐ 176 Darryl Williams Bengals Defense	.25	.11	.03
☐ 177 Michael Dean Perry Browns Defense	.50	.23	.06
☐ 178 Russell Maryland Cowboys Defense	.50	.23	.06
☐ 179 Steve Atwater Broncos Defense	.25	.11	.03
☐ 180 Bennie Blades Lions Defense	.25	.11	.03
☐ 181 Reggie White Packers Defense	1.00	.45	.12
☐ 182 Cris Dishman Oilers Defense	.25	.11	.03
☐ 183 Steve Emtman Colts Defense	.25	.11	.03
☐ 184 Derrick Thomas Chiefs Defense	1.00	.45	.12
☐ 185 Howie Long Raiders Defense	.50	.23	.06
☐ 186 Sean Gilbert Rams Defense	.50	.23	.06
☐ 187 John Offerdahl Dolphins Defense	.25	.11	.03
☐ 188 Chris Doleman Vikings Defense	.25	.11	.03
☐ 189 Andre Tippett Patriots Defense	.25	.11	.03
☐ 190 Sam Mills Saints Defense	.25	.11	.03
☐ 191 Lawrence Taylor Giants Defense	.75	.35	.09
☐ 192 James Hasty Jets Defense	.25	.11	.03
☐ 193 Clyde Simmons Eagles Defense	.25	.11	.03
☐ 194 Eric Swann Cardinals Defense	.50	.23	.06
☐ 195 Greg Lloyd Steelers Defense	.75	.35	.09
☐ 196 Junior Seau Chargers Defense	1.00	.45	.12
☐ 197 Kevin Fagan 49ers Defense	.25	.11	.03
☐ 198 Cortez Kennedy Seahawks Defense	.50	.23	.06
☐ 199 Broderick Thomas Buccaneers Defense	.25	.11	.03
☐ 200 Darrell Green Redskins Defense	.50	.23	.06

1994 Topps

The 1994 Topps football set consists of 660 standard-size cards issued in two series of 330. The fronts feature white-bordered, football-shaped color action player photos highlighted by gold-foil borders and placed on a pebble grain football background. The player's name in gold foil appears at the bottom, along with the team name and the player's position. The horizontal white-bordered backs carry a color action player photo on the right, with the player's name, biography, stats, and career highlights next to the photo. Subsets include League Leaders (116-120), Tools of the Game (196-205/542-556), Career Active Leaders (272-275/470-476) and Measure of Greatness (316-319/611-615). Rookie Cards include Trent Dilfer, Bert Emanuel, Marshall Faulk, William Floyd, Greg Hill, Charles Johnson,

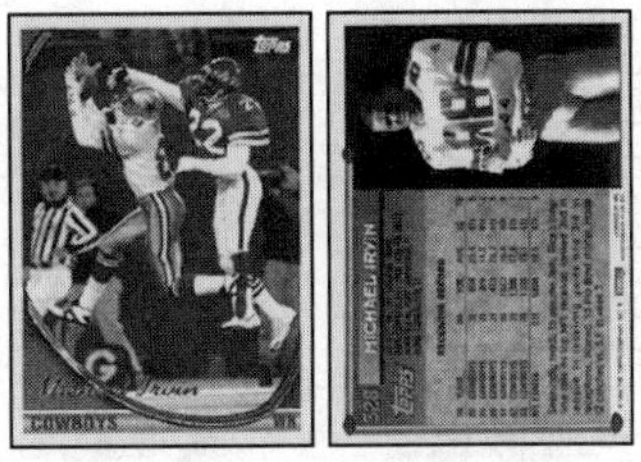

Willie McGinest, Errict Rhett, Darnay Scott, Heath Shuler and Bryant Young. A nine-card promo sheet was produced to promote the set as was a three-card Special Effects promo sheet.

	MINT	NRMT	EXC
COMPLETE SET (660)	50.00	22.00	6.25
COMPLETE FACT.SET	55.00	25.00	7.00
COMPLETE SERIES 1 (330)	25.00	11.00	3.10
COMPLETE SERIES 2 (330)	25.00	11.00	3.10
COMMON CARD (1-660)	.05	.02	.01

☐ 1 Emmitt Smith	2.00	.90	.25
☐ 2 Russell Copeland	.05	.02	.01
☐ 3 Jesse Sapolu	.05	.02	.01
☐ 4 David Szott	.05	.02	.01
☐ 5 Rodney Hampton	.20	.09	.03
☐ 6 Bubba McDowell	.05	.02	.01
☐ 7 Bryce Paup	.20	.09	.03
☐ 8 Winston Moss	.05	.02	.01
☐ 9 Brett Perriman	.10	.05	.01
☐ 10 Rod Woodson	.20	.09	.03
☐ 11 John Randle	.05	.02	.01
☐ 12 David Wyman	.05	.02	.01
☐ 13 Jeff Cross	.05	.02	.01
☐ 14 Richard Cooper	.05	.02	.01
☐ 15 Johnny Mitchell	.05	.02	.01
☐ 16 David Alexander	.05	.02	.01
☐ 17 Ronnie Harmon	.05	.02	.01
☐ 18 Tyronne Stowe UER (Tyrone on both sides)	.05	.02	.01
☐ 19 Chris Zorich	.05	.02	.01
☐ 20 Rob Burnett	.05	.02	.01
☐ 21 Harold Alexander	.05	.02	.01
☐ 22 Rod Stephens	.05	.02	.01
☐ 23 Mark Wheeler	.05	.02	.01
☐ 24 Dwayne Sabb	.05	.02	.01
☐ 25 Troy Drayton	.05	.02	.01
☐ 26 Kurt Gouveia	.05	.02	.01
☐ 27 Warren Moon	.20	.09	.03
☐ 28 Jeff Query	.05	.02	.01
☐ 29 Chuck Levy	.05	.02	.01
☐ 30 Bruce Smith	.20	.09	.03
☐ 31 Doug Riesenberg	.05	.02	.01
☐ 32 Willie Drewrey	.05	.02	.01
☐ 33 Nate Newton UER (Listed as Defensive End; should be guard)	.05	.02	.01
☐ 34 James Jett	.05	.02	.01
☐ 35 George Teague	.05	.02	.01
☐ 36 Marc Spindler	.05	.02	.01
☐ 37 Jack Del Rio	.05	.02	.01
☐ 38 Dale Carter	.05	.02	.01
☐ 39 Steve Atwater	.05	.02	.01
☐ 40 Herschel Walker	.10	.05	.01
☐ 41 James Hasty	.05	.02	.01
☐ 42 Seth Joyner	.05	.02	.01
☐ 43 Keith Jackson	.05	.02	.01
☐ 44 Tommy Vardell	.05	.02	.01
☐ 45 Antonio Langham	.10	.05	.01
☐ 46 Derek Brown RB	.05	.02	.01
☐ 47 John Wojciechowski	.05	.02	.01
☐ 48 Horace Copeland	.05	.02	.01
☐ 49 Luis Sharpe	.05	.02	.01
☐ 50 Pat Harlow	.05	.02	.01
☐ 51 David Palmer	.10	.05	.01
☐ 52 Tony Smith	.05	.02	.01
☐ 53 Tim Johnson	.05	.02	.01
☐ 54 Anthony Newman	.05	.02	.01
☐ 55 Terry Wooden	.05	.02	.01
☐ 56 Derrick Fenner	.05	.02	.01
☐ 57 Mike Fox	.05	.02	.01
☐ 58 Brad Hopkins	.05	.02	.01
☐ 59 Daryl Johnston UER (Johnson on front)	.10	.05	.01
☐ 60 Steve Young	.75	.35	.09
☐ 61 Scottie Graham	.10	.05	.01
☐ 62 Nolan Harrison	.05	.02	.01
☐ 63 David Richards	.05	.02	.01
☐ 64 Chris Mohr	.05	.02	.01
☐ 65 Hardy Nickerson	.10	.05	.01
☐ 66 Heath Sherman	.05	.02	.01
☐ 67 Irving Fryar	.10	.05	.01
☐ 68 Ray Buchanan UER (Buchannan on front)	.05	.02	.01
☐ 69 Jay Taylor	.05	.02	.01
☐ 70 Shannon Sharpe	.10	.05	.01
☐ 71 Vinny Testaverde	.10	.05	.01
☐ 72 Renaldo Turnbull	.05	.02	.01
☐ 73 Dwight Stone	.05	.02	.01
☐ 74 Willie McGinest	.20	.09	.03
☐ 75 Darrell Green	.05	.02	.01
☐ 76 Kyle Clifton	.05	.02	.01
☐ 77 Leo Goeas	.05	.02	.01
☐ 78 Ken Ruettgers	.05	.02	.01
☐ 79 Craig Heyward	.10	.05	.01
☐ 80 Andre Rison	.10	.05	.01
☐ 81 Chris Mims	.05	.02	.01
☐ 82 Gary Clark	.10	.05	.01
☐ 83 Ricardo McDonald	.05	.02	.01
☐ 84 Patrick Hunter	.05	.02	.01
☐ 85 Bruce Matthews	.05	.02	.01
☐ 86 Russell Maryland	.05	.02	.01
☐ 87 Gary Anderson K	.05	.02	.01
☐ 88 Brad Edwards	.05	.02	.01
☐ 89 Carlton Bailey	.05	.02	.01
☐ 90 Qadry Ismail	.20	.09	.03
☐ 91 Terry McDaniel	.05	.02	.01
☐ 92 Willie Green	.05	.02	.01
☐ 93 Cornelius Bennett	.10	.05	.01
☐ 94 Paul Gruber	.05	.02	.01
☐ 95 Pete Stoyanovich	.05	.02	.01
☐ 96 Merton Hanks	.10	.05	.01
☐ 97 Tre Johnson	.05	.02	.01
☐ 98 Jonathan Hayes	.05	.02	.01
☐ 99 Jason Elam	.05	.02	.01
☐ 100 Jerome Bettis	.60	.25	.07
☐ 101 Ronnie Lott	.10	.05	.01
☐ 102 Maurice Hurst	.05	.02	.01
☐ 103 Kirk Lowdermilk	.05	.02	.01
☐ 104 Tony Jones	.05	.02	.01
☐ 105 Steve Beuerlein	.05	.02	.01
☐ 106 Isaac Davis	.05	.02	.01
☐ 107 Vaughan Johnson	.05	.02	.01
☐ 108 Terrell Buckley	.05	.02	.01
☐ 109 Pierce Holt	.05	.02	.01
☐ 110 Alonzo Spellman	.05	.02	.01
☐ 111 Patrick Robinson	.05	.02	.01
☐ 112 Cortez Kennedy	.10	.05	.01
☐ 113 Kevin Williams	.10	.05	.01
☐ 114 Danny Copeland	.05	.02	.01
☐ 115 Chris Doleman	.05	.02	.01
☐ 116 Jerry Rice LL	.50	.23	.06
☐ 117 Neil Smith LL	.10	.05	.01
☐ 118 Emmitt Smith LL	1.00	.45	.12
☐ 119 Eugene Robinson LL Nate Odomes	.05	.02	.01
☐ 120 Steve Young LL	.20	.09	.03
☐ 121 Carnell Lake	.05	.02	.01
☐ 122 Ernest Givins UER (Givens on front)	.10	.05	.01
☐ 123 Henry Jones	.05	.02	.01
☐ 124 Michael Brooks	.05	.02	.01
☐ 125 Jason Hanson	.05	.02	.01
☐ 126 Andy Harmon	.05	.02	.01
☐ 127 Errict Rhett	1.25	.55	.16
☐ 128 Harris Barton	.05	.02	.01
☐ 129 Greg Robinson	.05	.02	.01
☐ 130 Derrick Thomas	.20	.09	.03
☐ 131 Keith Kartz	.05	.02	.01
☐ 132 Lincoln Kennedy	.05	.02	.01
☐ 133 Leslie O'Neal	.05	.02	.01
☐ 134 Tim Goad	.05	.02	.01
☐ 135 Rohn Stark	.05	.02	.01
☐ 136 O.J. McDuffie	.20	.09	.03
☐ 137 Donnell Woolford	.05	.02	.01
☐ 138 Jamir Miller	.05	.02	.01
☐ 139 Eric Thomas UER (Listed as tight end; he is a cornerback)	.05	.02	.01
☐ 140 Willie Roaf	.05	.02	.01
☐ 141 Wayne Gandy	.05	.02	.01
☐ 142 Mike Brim	.05	.02	.01
☐ 143 Kelvin Martin	.05	.02	.01
☐ 144 Edgar Bennett	.20	.09	.03
☐ 145 Michael Dean Perry	.10	.05	.01
☐ 146 Shante Carver	.05	.02	.01
☐ 147 Jessie Armstead UER (Jesse on both sides)	.05	.02	.01
☐ 148 Mo Elewonibi	.05	.02	.01
☐ 149 Dana Stubblefield	.20	.09	.03
☐ 150 Cody Carlson	.05	.02	.01
☐ 151 Vencie Glenn	.05	.02	.01
☐ 152 Levon Kirkland	.05	.02	.01
☐ 153 Derrick Moore	.05	.02	.01
☐ 154 John Fina	.05	.02	.01
☐ 155 Jeff Hostetler	.10	.05	.01
☐ 156 Courtney Hawkins	.05	.02	.01
☐ 157 Todd Collins	.05	.02	.01
☐ 158 Neil Smith	.20	.09	.03
☐ 159 Simon Fletcher	.05	.02	.01
☐ 160 Dan Marino	2.00	.90	.25
☐ 161 Sam Adams	.10	.05	.01
☐ 162 Marvin Washington	.05	.02	.01
☐ 163 John Copeland	.05	.02	.01
☐ 164 Eugene Robinson	.05	.02	.01
☐ 165 Mark Carrier DB	.05	.02	.01
☐ 166 Mike Kenn	.05	.02	.01
☐ 167 Tyrone Hughes	.10	.05	.01
☐ 168 Darren Carrington	.05	.02	.01
☐ 169 Shane Conlan	.05	.02	.01
☐ 170 Ricky Proehl	.05	.02	.01
☐ 171 Jeff Herrod	.05	.02	.01
☐ 172 Mark Carrier WR	.10	.05	.01
☐ 173 George Koonce	.05	.02	.01
☐ 174 Desmond Howard	.10	.05	.01
☐ 175 Dave Meggett	.05	.02	.01
☐ 176 Charles Haley	.10	.05	.01
☐ 177 Steve Wisniewski	.05	.02	.01
☐ 178 Dermontti Dawson	.05	.02	.01
☐ 179 Tim McDonald	.05	.02	.01
☐ 180 Broderick Thomas	.05	.02	.01
☐ 181 Bernard Dafney	.05	.02	.01
☐ 182 Bo Orlando	.05	.02	.01
☐ 183 Andre Reed	.10	.05	.01
☐ 184 Randall Cunningham	.10	.05	.01
☐ 185 Chris Spielman	.10	.05	.01
☐ 186 Keith Byars	.05	.02	.01
☐ 187 Ben Coates	.20	.09	.03
☐ 188 Tracy Simien	.05	.02	.01
☐ 189 Carl Pickens	.50	.23	.06
☐ 190 Reggie White	.20	.09	.03
☐ 191 Norm Johnson	.05	.02	.01
☐ 192 Brian Washington	.05	.02	.01
☐ 193 Stan Humphries	.20	.09	.03
☐ 194 Fred Stokes	.05	.02	.01
☐ 195 Dan Williams	.05	.02	.01
☐ 196 John Elway TOG	.40	.18	.05
☐ 197 Eric Allen TOG	.05	.02	.01
☐ 198 Hardy Nickerson TOG	.10	.05	.01
☐ 199 Jerome Bettis TOG	.30	.14	.04
☐ 200 Troy Aikman TOG	.50	.23	.06
☐ 201 Thurman Thomas TOG	.10	.05	.01
☐ 202 Cornelius Bennett TOG	.10	.05	.01
☐ 203 Michael Irvin TOG	.10	.05	.01
☐ 204 Jim Kelly TOG	.10	.05	.01
☐ 205 Junior Seau TOG	.10	.05	.01
☐ 206 Heath Shuler UER (Rifle spelled rife on back)	1.00	.45	.12
☐ 207 Howard Cross UER (Listed as linebacker; he plays tight end)	.05	.02	.01
☐ 208 Pat Swilling	.05	.02	.01
☐ 209 Pete Metzelaars	.05	.02	.01
☐ 210 Tony McGee	.05	.02	.01
☐ 211 Neil O'Donnell	.20	.09	.03
☐ 212 Eugene Chung	.05	.02	.01
☐ 213 J.B. Brown	.05	.02	.01
☐ 214 Marcus Allen	.20	.09	.03
☐ 215 Harry Newsome	.05	.02	.01
☐ 216 Greg Hill	.20	.09	.03
☐ 217 Ryan Yarborough	.05	.02	.01
☐ 218 Marty Carter	.05	.02	.01
☐ 219 Bern Brostek	.05	.02	.01
☐ 220 Boomer Esiason	.10	.05	.01
☐ 221 Vince Buck	.05	.02	.01
☐ 222 Jim Jeffcoat	.05	.02	.01
☐ 223 Bob Dahl	.05	.02	.01
☐ 224 Marion Butts	.05	.02	.01
☐ 225 Ronald Moore	.05	.02	.01
☐ 226 Robert Blackmon	.05	.02	.01
☐ 227 Curtis Conway	.20	.09	.03
☐ 228 Jon Hand	.05	.02	.01
☐ 229 Shane Dronett	.05	.02	.01
☐ 230 Erik Williams UER (Misspelled Eric on front)	.05	.02	.01
☐ 231 Dennis Brown	.05	.02	.01
☐ 232 Ray Childress	.05	.02	.01
☐ 233 Johnnie Morton	.20	.09	.03
☐ 234 Kent Hull	.05	.02	.01
☐ 235 John Elliott	.05	.02	.01
☐ 236 Ron Heller	.05	.02	.01
☐ 237 J.J. Birden	.05	.02	.01
☐ 238 Thomas Randolph	.05	.02	.01
☐ 239 Chip Lohmiller	.05	.02	.01
☐ 240 Tim Brown	.20	.09	.03
☐ 241 Steve Tovar	.05	.02	.01
☐ 242 Moe Gardner	.05	.02	.01
☐ 243 Vincent Brown	.05	.02	.01
☐ 244 Tony Zendejas	.05	.02	.01
☐ 245 Eric Allen	.05	.02	.01
☐ 246 Joe King	.05	.02	.01
☐ 247 Mo Lewis	.05	.02	.01
☐ 248 Rod Bernstine	.05	.02	.01
☐ 249 Tom Waddle	.05	.02	.01
☐ 250 Junior Seau	.20	.09	.03
☐ 251 Eric Metcalf	.10	.05	.01
☐ 252 Cris Carter	.20	.09	.03
☐ 253 Bill Hitchcock	.05	.02	.01
☐ 254 Zefross Moss	.05	.02	.01
☐ 255 Morten Andersen	.05	.02	.01
☐ 256 Keith Rucker	.05	.02	.01
☐ 257 Chris Jacke	.05	.02	.01
☐ 258 Richmond Webb	.05	.02	.01
☐ 259 Herman Moore	.50	.23	.06
☐ 260 Phil Simms	.10	.05	.01
☐ 261 Mark Tuinei	.05	.02	.01
☐ 262 Don Beebe	.05	.02	.01
☐ 263 Marc Logan	.05	.02	.01
☐ 264 Willie Davis	.10	.05	.01
☐ 265 David Klingler	.05	.02	.01
☐ 266 Martin Mayhew UER (Listed as wide receiver; he is a cornerback)	.05	.02	.01
☐ 267 Mark Bavaro	.05	.02	.01
☐ 268 Greg Lloyd	.20	.09	.03
☐ 269 Al Del Greco	.05	.02	.01
☐ 270 Reggie Brooks	.10	.05	.01
☐ 271 Greg Townsend	.05	.02	.01
☐ 272 Rohn Stark CAL	.05	.02	.01
☐ 273 Marcus Allen CAL	.10	.05	.01
☐ 274 Ronnie Lott CAL	.10	.05	.01
☐ 275 Dan Marino CAL	1.00	.45	.12

□ 276 Sean Gilbert	.05	.02	.01
□ 277 LeRoy Butler	.05	.02	.01
□ 278 Troy Auzenne	.05	.02	.01
□ 279 Eric Swann	.10	.05	.01
□ 280 Quentin Coryatt	.05	.02	.01
□ 281 Anthony Pleasant	.05	.02	.01
□ 282 Brad Baxter	.05	.02	.01
□ 283 Carl Lee	.05	.02	.01
□ 284 Courtney Hall	.05	.02	.01
□ 285 Quinn Early	.10	.05	.01
□ 286 Eddie Robinson	.05	.02	.01
□ 287 Marco Coleman	.05	.02	.01
□ 288 Harold Green	.05	.02	.01
□ 289 Santana Dotson	.10	.05	.01
□ 290 Robert Porcher	.05	.02	.01
□ 291 Joe Phillips	.05	.02	.01
□ 292 Mark McMillian	.05	.02	.01
□ 293 Eric Davis	.05	.02	.01
□ 294 Mark Jackson	.05	.02	.01
□ 295 Darryl Talley	.05	.02	.01
□ 296 Curtis Duncan	.05	.02	.01
□ 297 Bruce Armstrong	.05	.02	.01
□ 298 Eric Hill	.05	.02	.01
□ 299 Andre Collins	.05	.02	.01
□ 300 Jay Novacek	.10	.05	.01
□ 301 Roosevelt Potts	.05	.02	.01
□ 302 Eric Martin	.05	.02	.01
□ 303 Chris Warren	.10	.05	.01
□ 304 Deral Boykin	.05	.02	.01
□ 305 Jessie Tuggle	.05	.02	.01
□ 306 Glyn Milburn	.10	.05	.01
□ 307 Terry Obee	.05	.02	.01
□ 308 Eric Turner	.05	.02	.01
□ 309 Dewayne Washington	.10	.05	.01
□ 310 Sterling Sharpe	.10	.05	.01
□ 311 Jeff Gossett	.05	.02	.01
□ 312 John Carney	.05	.02	.01
□ 313 Aaron Glenn	.10	.05	.01
□ 314 Nick Lowery	.05	.02	.01
□ 315 Thurman Thomas	.20	.09	.03
□ 316 Troy Aikman MG	.50	.23	.06
□ 317 Thurman Thomas MG	.10	.05	.01
□ 318 Michael Irvin MG	.10	.05	.01
□ 319 Steve Beuerlein MG	.05	.02	.01
□ 320 Jerry Rice	1.00	.45	.12
□ 321 Alexander Wright	.05	.02	.01
□ 322 Michael Bates	.05	.02	.01
□ 323 Greg Davis	.05	.02	.01
□ 324 Mark Bortz	.05	.02	.01
□ 325 Kevin Greene	.20	.09	.03
□ 326 Wayne Simmons	.05	.02	.01
□ 327 Wayne Martin	.05	.02	.01
□ 328 Michael Irvin UER	.20	.09	.03
(Stats on back have three career touchdowns; should be 34)			
□ 329 Checklist 1-165	.05	.02	.01
□ 330 Checklist 166-330	.05	.02	.01
□ 331 Doug Pelfrey	.05	.02	.01
□ 332 Myron Guyton	.05	.02	.01
□ 333 Howard Ballard	.05	.02	.01
□ 334 Ricky Ervins	.05	.02	.01
□ 335 Steve Emtman	.05	.02	.01
□ 336 Eric Curry	.05	.02	.01
□ 337 Bert Emanuel	1.00	.45	.12
□ 338 Darryl Ashmore	.05	.02	.01
□ 339 Stevon Moore	.05	.02	.01
□ 340 Garrison Hearst	.50	.23	.06
□ 341 Vance Johnson	.05	.02	.01
□ 342 Anthony Johnson	.10	.05	.01
□ 343 Merril Hoge	.05	.02	.01
□ 344 William Thomas	.05	.02	.01
□ 345 Scott Mitchell	.20	.09	.03
□ 346 Jim Everett	.10	.05	.01
□ 347 Ray Crockett	.05	.02	.01
□ 348 Bryan Cox	.05	.02	.01
□ 349 Charles Johnson	.20	.09	.03
□ 350 Randall McDaniel	.05	.02	.01
□ 351 Micheal Barrow	.05	.02	.01
□ 352 Darrell Thompson	.05	.02	.01
□ 353 Kevin Gogan	.05	.02	.01
□ 354 Brad Daluiso	.05	.02	.01
□ 355 Mark Collins	.05	.02	.01
□ 356 Bryant Young	.20	.09	.03
□ 357 Steve Christie	.05	.02	.01
□ 358 Derek Kennard	.05	.02	.01
□ 359 Jon Vaughn	.05	.02	.01
□ 360 Drew Bledsoe	1.25	.55	.16
□ 361 Randy Baldwin	.05	.02	.01
□ 362 Kevin Ross	.05	.02	.01
□ 363 Reuben Davis	.05	.02	.01
□ 364 Chris Miller	.05	.02	.01
□ 365 Tim McGee	.05	.02	.01
□ 366 Tony Woods	.05	.02	.01
□ 367 Dean Biasucci	.05	.02	.01
□ 368 George Jamison	.05	.02	.01
□ 369 Lorenzo Lynch	.05	.02	.01
□ 370 Johnny Johnson	.05	.02	.01
□ 371 Greg Kragen	.05	.02	.01
□ 372 Vinson Smith	.05	.02	.01
□ 373 Vince Workman	.05	.02	.01
□ 374 Allen Aldridge	.05	.02	.01
□ 375 Terry Kirby	.20	.09	.03
□ 376 Mario Bates	.60	.25	.07
□ 377 Dixon Edwards	.05	.02	.01
□ 378 Leon Searcy	.05	.02	.01

□ 379 Eric Guliford	.05	.02	.01
□ 380 Gary Brown	.05	.02	.01
□ 381 Phil Hansen	.05	.02	.01
□ 382 Keith Hamilton	.05	.02	.01
□ 383 John Alt	.05	.02	.01
□ 384 John Taylor	.10	.05	.01
□ 385 Reggie Cobb	.05	.02	.01
□ 386 Rob Fredrickson	.10	.05	.01
□ 387 Pepper Johnson	.05	.02	.01
□ 388 Kevin Lee	.05	.02	.01
□ 389 Stanley Richard	.05	.02	.01
□ 390 Jackie Slater	.05	.02	.01
□ 391 Darrick Brilz	.05	.02	.01
□ 392 John Gesek	.05	.02	.01
□ 393 Kelvin Pritchett	.05	.02	.01
□ 394 Aeneas Williams	.05	.02	.01
□ 395 Henry Ford	.05	.02	.01
□ 396 Eric Mahlum	.05	.02	.01
□ 397 Tom Rouen	.05	.02	.01
□ 398 Vinnie Clark	.05	.02	.01
□ 399 Jim Sweeney	.05	.02	.01
□ 400 Troy Aikman UER	1.00	.45	.12
Threw for 56 TD's in 1993			
□ 401 Toi Cook	.05	.02	.01
□ 402 Dan Saleaumua	.05	.02	.01
□ 403 Andy Heck	.05	.02	.01
□ 404 Deon Figures	.05	.02	.01
□ 405 Henry Thomas	.05	.02	.01
□ 406 Glenn Montgomery	.05	.02	.01
□ 407 Trent Dilfer	.60	.25	.07
□ 408 Eddie Murray	.05	.02	.01
□ 409 Gene Atkins	.05	.02	.01
□ 410 Mike Sherrard	.05	.02	.01
□ 411 Don Mosebar	.05	.02	.01
□ 412 Thomas Smith	.05	.02	.01
□ 413 Ken Norton Jr.	.10	.05	.01
□ 414 Robert Brooks	.40	.18	.05
□ 415 Jeff Lageman	.05	.02	.01
□ 416 Tony Siragusa	.05	.02	.01
□ 417 Brian Blades	.10	.05	.01
□ 418 Matt Stover	.05	.02	.01
□ 419 Jesse Solomon	.05	.02	.01
□ 420 Reggie Roby	.05	.02	.01
□ 421 Shawn Jefferson	.05	.02	.01
□ 422 Marc Boutte	.05	.02	.01
□ 423 William White	.05	.02	.01
□ 424 Clyde Simmons	.05	.02	.01
□ 425 Anthony Miller	.10	.05	.01
□ 426 Brent Jones	.10	.05	.01
□ 427 Tim Grunhard	.05	.02	.01
□ 428 Alfred Williams	.05	.02	.01
□ 429 Roy Barker	.05	.02	.01
□ 430 Dante Jones	.05	.02	.01
□ 431 Leroy Thompson	.05	.02	.01
□ 432 Marcus Robertson	.05	.02	.01
□ 433 Thomas Lewis	.10	.05	.01
□ 434 Sean Jones	.05	.02	.01
□ 435 Michael Haynes	.10	.05	.01
□ 436 Albert Lewis	.05	.02	.01
□ 437 Tim Bowens	.10	.05	.01
□ 438 Marvcus Patton	.05	.02	.01
□ 439 Rich Miano	.05	.02	.01
□ 440 Craig Erickson	.05	.02	.01
□ 441 Larry Allen	.10	.05	.01
□ 442 Fernando Smith	.05	.02	.01
□ 443 D.J. Johnson	.05	.02	.01
□ 444 Leonard Russell	.05	.02	.01
□ 445 Marshall Faulk	3.00	1.35	.35
□ 446 Najee Mustafaa	.05	.02	.01
□ 447 Brian Hansen	.05	.02	.01
□ 448 Isaac Bruce	3.00	1.35	.35
□ 449 Kevin Scott	.05	.02	.01
□ 450 Natrone Means	.50	.23	.06
□ 451 Tracy Rogers	.05	.02	.01
□ 452 Mike Croel	.05	.02	.01
□ 453 Anthony Edwards	.05	.02	.01
□ 454 Brenston Buckner	.05	.02	.01
□ 455 Tom Carter	.05	.02	.01
□ 456 Burt Grossman	.05	.02	.01
□ 457 Jimmy Spencer	.05	.02	.01
□ 458 Rocket Ismail	.10	.05	.01
□ 459 Fred Strickland	.05	.02	.01
□ 460 Jeff Burris	.10	.05	.01
□ 461 Adrian Hardy	.05	.02	.01
□ 462 Lamar McGriggs	.05	.02	.01
□ 463 Webster Slaughter	.05	.02	.01
□ 464 Demetrius DuBose	.05	.02	.01
□ 465 Dave Brown	.10	.05	.01
□ 466 Kenneth Gant	.05	.02	.01
□ 467 Erik Kramer	.10	.05	.01
□ 468 Mark Ingram	.05	.02	.01
□ 469 Roman Phifer	.05	.02	.01
□ 470 Steve Young	.50	.23	.06
□ 471 Nick Lowery	.05	.02	.01
□ 472 Irving Fryar	.10	.05	.01
□ 473 Art Monk	.10	.05	.01
□ 474 Mel Gray	.05	.02	.01
□ 475 Reggie White	.20	.09	.03
□ 476 Eric Ball	.05	.02	.01
□ 477 Dwayne Harper	.05	.02	.01
□ 478 Will Shields	.05	.02	.01
□ 479 Roger Harper	.05	.02	.01
□ 480 Rick Mirer	.20	.09	.03
□ 481 Vincent Brisby	.20	.09	.03
□ 482 John Jurkovic	.10	.05	.01

□ 483 Michael Jackson	.10	.05	.01
□ 484 Ed Cunningham	.05	.02	.01
□ 485 Brad Ottis	.05	.02	.01
□ 486 Sterling Palmer	.05	.02	.01
□ 487 Tony Bennett	.05	.02	.01
□ 488 Mike Pritchard	.05	.02	.01
□ 489 Bucky Brooks	.05	.02	.01
□ 490 Troy Vincent	.05	.02	.01
□ 491 Eric Green	.05	.02	.01
□ 492 Van Malone	.05	.02	.01
□ 493 Marcus Spears	.05	.02	.01
□ 494 Brian Williams	.05	.02	.01
□ 495 Robert Smith	.20	.09	.03
□ 496 Haywood Jeffires	.10	.05	.01
□ 497 Darrin Smith	.05	.02	.01
□ 498 Tommy Barnhardt	.05	.02	.01
□ 499 Anthony Smith	.05	.02	.01
□ 500 Ricky Watters	.20	.09	.03
□ 501 Antone Davis	.05	.02	.01
□ 502 David Braxton	.05	.02	.01
□ 503 Donnell Bennett	.05	.02	.01
□ 504 Donald Evans	.05	.02	.01
□ 505 Lewis Tillman	.05	.02	.01
□ 506 Lance Smith	.05	.02	.01
□ 507 Aaron Taylor	.05	.02	.01
□ 508 Ricky Sanders	.05	.02	.01
□ 509 Dennis Smith	.05	.02	.01
□ 510 Barry Foster	.05	.02	.01
□ 511 Stan Brock	.05	.02	.01
□ 512 Henry Rolling	.05	.02	.01
□ 513 Walter Reeves	.05	.02	.01
□ 514 John Booty	.05	.02	.01
□ 515 Kenneth Davis	.05	.02	.01
□ 516 Cris Dishman	.05	.02	.01
□ 517 Bill Lewis	.05	.02	.01
□ 518 Jeff Bryant	.05	.02	.01
□ 519 Brian Mitchell	.05	.02	.01
□ 520 Joe Montana	1.00	.45	.12
□ 521 Keith Sims	.05	.02	.01
□ 522 Harry Colon	.05	.02	.01
□ 523 Leon Lett	.05	.02	.01
□ 524 Carlos Jenkins	.05	.02	.01
□ 525 Victor Bailey	.05	.02	.01
□ 526 Harvey Williams	.10	.05	.01
□ 527 Irv Smith	.05	.02	.01
□ 528 Jason Sehorn	.05	.02	.01
□ 529 John Thierry	.05	.02	.01
□ 530 Brett Favre	2.00	.90	.25
□ 531 Sean Dawkins	.20	.09	.03
□ 532 Erric Pegram	.05	.02	.01
□ 533 Jimmy Williams	.05	.02	.01
□ 534 Michael Timpson	.05	.02	.01
□ 535 Flipper Anderson	.05	.02	.01
□ 536 John Parrella	.05	.02	.01
□ 537 Freddie Joe Nunn	.05	.02	.01
□ 538 Doug Dawson	.05	.02	.01
□ 539 Michael Stewart	.05	.02	.01
□ 540 John Elway	.75	.35	.09
□ 541 Ronnie Lott	.10	.05	.01
□ 542 Barry Sanders	.50	.23	.06
□ 543 Andre Reed	.10	.05	.01
□ 544 Deion Sanders	.30	.14	.04
□ 545 Dan Marino	1.00	.45	.12
□ 546 Carlton Bailey	.05	.02	.01
□ 547 Emmitt Smith	1.00	.45	.12
□ 548 Alvin Harper	.10	.05	.01
□ 549 Eric Metcalf	.10	.05	.01
□ 550 Jerry Rice	.50	.23	.06
□ 551 Derrick Thomas	.20	.09	.03
□ 552 Mark Collins	.05	.02	.01
□ 553 Eric Turner	.05	.02	.01
□ 554 Sterling Sharpe	.20	.09	.03
□ 555 Steve Young	.40	.18	.05
□ 556 Darnay Scott	2.00	.90	.25
□ 557 Joel Steed	.05	.02	.01
□ 558 Dennis Gibson	.05	.02	.01
□ 559 Charles Mincy	.05	.02	.01
□ 560 Rickey Jackson	.05	.02	.01
□ 561 Dave Cadigan	.05	.02	.01
□ 562 Rick Tuten	.05	.02	.01
□ 563 Mike Caldwell	.05	.02	.01
□ 564 Todd Steussie	.10	.05	.01
□ 565 Kevin Smith	.05	.02	.01
□ 566 Arthur Marshall	.05	.02	.01
□ 567 Aaron Wallace	.05	.02	.01
□ 568 Calvin Williams	.10	.05	.01
□ 569 Todd Kelly	.05	.02	.01
□ 570 Barry Sanders	1.00	.45	.12
□ 571 Shaun Gayle	.05	.02	.01
□ 572 Will Wolford	.05	.02	.01
□ 573 Ethan Horton	.05	.02	.01
□ 574 Chris Slade	.05	.02	.01
□ 575 Jeff Wright	.05	.02	.01
□ 576 Toby Wright	.05	.02	.01
□ 577 Lamar Thomas	.05	.02	.01
□ 578 Chris Singleton	.05	.02	.01
□ 579 Ed West	.05	.02	.01
□ 580 Jeff George	.20	.09	.03
□ 581 Kevin Mitchell	.05	.02	.01
□ 582 Chad Brown	.05	.02	.01
□ 583 Rich Camarillo	.05	.02	.01
□ 584 Gary Zimmerman	.05	.02	.01
□ 585 Randal Hill	.05	.02	.01
□ 586 Keith Cash	.05	.02	.01
□ 587 Sam Mills	.05	.02	.01

□ 588 Shawn Lee	.05	.02	.01
□ 589 Kent Graham	.10	.05	.01
□ 590 Steve Everitt	.05	.02	.01
□ 591 Rob Moore	.10	.05	.01
□ 592 Kevin Mawae	.05	.02	.01
□ 593 Jerry Ball	.05	.02	.01
□ 594 Larry Brown DB	.05	.02	.01
□ 595 Tim Krumrie	.05	.02	.01
□ 596 Aubrey Beavers	.05	.02	.01
□ 597 Chris Hinton	.05	.02	.01
□ 598 Greg Montgomery	.05	.02	.01
□ 599 Jimmie Jones	.05	.02	.01
□ 600 Jim Kelly	.20	.09	.03
□ 601 Joe Johnson	.05	.02	.01
□ 602 Tim Irwin	.05	.02	.01
□ 603 Steve Jackson	.05	.02	.01
□ 604 James Williams	.05	.02	.01
□ 605 Blair Thomas	.05	.02	.01
□ 606 Danan Hughes	.05	.02	.01
□ 607 Russell Freeman	.05	.02	.01
□ 608 Andre Hastings	.10	.05	.01
□ 609 Ken Harvey	.05	.02	.01
□ 610 Jim Harbaugh	.20	.09	.03
□ 611 Emmitt Smith MG	1.00	.45	.12
□ 612 Andre Rison MG	.10	.05	.01
□ 613 Steve Young MG	.40	.18	.05
□ 614 Anthony Miller MG	.05	.02	.01
□ 615 Barry Sanders MG	.50	.23	.06
□ 616 Bernie Kosar	.10	.05	.01
□ 617 Chris Gardocki	.05	.02	.01
□ 618 William Floyd	1.00	.45	.12
□ 619 Matt Brock	.05	.02	.01
□ 620 Dan Wilkinson	.10	.05	.01
□ 621 Tony Meola	.10	.05	.01
□ 622 Tony Tolbert	.05	.02	.01
□ 623 Mike Zandofsky	.05	.02	.01
□ 624 William Fuller	.05	.02	.01
□ 625 Steve Jordan	.05	.02	.01
□ 626 Mike Johnson	.05	.02	.01
□ 627 Ferrell Edmunds	.05	.02	.01
□ 628 Gene Williams	.05	.02	.01
□ 629 Willie Beamon	.05	.02	.01
□ 630 Gerald Perry	.05	.02	.01
□ 631 John Baylor	.05	.02	.01
□ 632 Carwell Gardner	.05	.02	.01
□ 633 Thomas Everett	.05	.02	.01
□ 634 Lamar Lathon	.05	.02	.01
□ 635 Michael Bankston	.05	.02	.01
□ 636 Ray Crittenden	.05	.02	.01
□ 637 Kimble Anders	.10	.05	.01
□ 638 Robert Delpino	.05	.02	.01
□ 639 Darren Perry	.05	.02	.01
□ 640 Byron Evans	.05	.02	.01
□ 641 Mark Higgs	.05	.02	.01
□ 642 Lorenzo Neal	.05	.02	.01
□ 643 Henry Ellard	.10	.05	.01
□ 644 Trace Armstrong	.05	.02	.01
□ 645 Greg McMurtry	.05	.02	.01
□ 646 Steve McMichael	.10	.05	.01
□ 647 Terance Mathis	.10	.05	.01
□ 648 Eric Bieniemy	.05	.02	.01
□ 649 Bobby Houston	.05	.02	.01
□ 650 Alvin Harper	.10	.05	.01
□ 651 James Folston	.05	.02	.01
□ 652 Mel Gray	.05	.02	.01
□ 653 Adrian Cooper	.05	.02	.01
□ 654 Dexter Carter	.05	.02	.01
□ 655 Don Griffin	.05	.02	.01
□ 656 Corey Widmer	.05	.02	.01
□ 657 Lee Johnson	.05	.02	.01
□ 658 Nate Odomes	.05	.02	.01
□ 659 Checklist	.05	.02	.01
□ 660 Checklist	.05	.02	.01
□ P1 Promo Sheet	5.00	2.20	.60
Stan Humphries			
Darryl Talley			
Rodney Hampton			
Jerome Bettis			
Chris Zorich			
Harry Newsome			
Tyrone Hughes			
Rod Woodson			
Chris Spielman			
□ P2 Promo Sheet Special Effects	4.00	1.80	.50
Jerome Bettis			
Chris Zorich			
Harry Newsome			

1994 Topps Special Effects

These parallel cards were randomly inserted in foil packs at a rate of one in two and in rack packs at a rate of two per pack. The 660

standard-size cards are identical to the regular 1994 Topps set except that the photos feature a clear plastic prismatic overcoating with a holographic stripe.

	MINT	NRMT	EXC
COMPLETE SET (660)	350.00	160.00	45.00
COMPLETE SERIES 1 (330)	175.00	80.00	22.00
COMPLETE SERIES 2 (330)	175.00	80.00	22.00
COMMON CARD (1-660)	.30	.14	.04
*STARS: 3.5X TO 7X BASIC CARDS			
*RCs: 2X TO 4X BASIC CARDS			

1994 Topps All-Pro

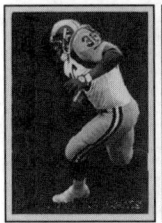

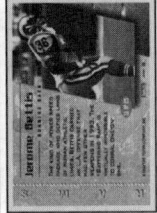

This 25-card standard-size set features NFL stars and introduces Topps "Spectralight Foil Cards," which are foil-backed, foil-stamped cards. All-Pro cards are randomly inserted at a rate of one in every 36 packs. The front has the player photo superimposed over a football field background. Horizontal backs have a player photo to the right and highlights to the left.

	MINT	NRMT	EXC
COMPLETE SET (25)	40.00	18.00	5.00
COMMON CARD (1-25)	1.00	.45	.12
☐ 1 Michael Irvin	2.50	1.10	.30
☐ 2 Erik Williams	1.50	.70	.19
☐ 3 Steve Wisniewski	1.00	.45	.12
☐ 4 Dermontti Dawson	1.00	.45	.12
☐ 5 Nate Newton	1.50	.70	.19
☐ 6 Harris Barton	1.00	.45	.12
☐ 7 Shannon Sharpe	1.50	.70	.19
☐ 8 Jerry Rice	10.00	4.50	1.25
☐ 9 Troy Aikman	10.00	4.50	1.25
☐ 10 Barry Sanders	10.00	4.50	1.25
☐ 11 Jerome Bettis	4.00	1.80	.50
☐ 12 Jason Hanson	1.00	.45	.12
☐ 13 Eric Metcalf	2.50	1.10	.30
☐ 14 Reggie White	2.50	1.10	.30
☐ 15 Cortez Kennedy	1.50	.70	.19
☐ 16 Michael Dean Perry	1.50	.70	.19
☐ 17 Bruce Smith	2.50	1.10	.30
☐ 18 Darryl Talley	1.00	.45	.12
☐ 19 Hardy Nickerson	1.50	.70	.19
☐ 20 Derrick Thomas	2.50	1.10	.30
☐ 21 Mark Collins	1.00	.45	.12
☐ 22 Eric Allen	1.00	.45	.12
☐ 23 Tim McDonald	1.00	.45	.12
☐ 24 Marcus Robertson	1.00	.45	.12
☐ 25 Greg Montgomery	1.00	.45	.12

1994 Topps 1000/3000

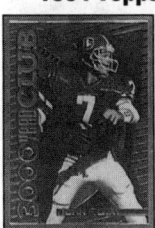

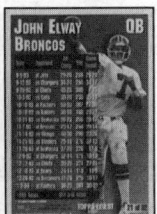

Randomly inserted in first series packs at an approximate rate of one in 36, these 32 standard-size cards feature metallic fronts with color player action cutouts set on silver-bordered multicolored designs. The player's name appears near the bottom in a colored bar. The white-bordered backs carry a color action photo on one side. The player's name, position and team name appear at the top, followed below by statistics. The cards are numbered on the back as "X of 32." The first 20 cards are of running backs and wide receivers; the last 12 are quarterbacks.

	MINT	NRMT	EXC
COMPLETE SET (32)	70.00	32.00	8.75
COMMON CARD (1-32)	1.00	.45	.12
☐ 1 Jerry Rice	6.00	2.70	.75
☐ 2 Chris Warren	2.00	.90	.25
☐ 3 Leonard Russell	1.00	.45	.12
☐ 4 Gary Brown	1.00	.45	.12
☐ 5 Tim Brown	2.00	.90	.25
☐ 6 Erric Pegram	1.50	.70	.19
☐ 7 Irving Fryar	1.50	.70	.19
☐ 8 Anthony Miller	1.50	.70	.19
☐ 9 Reggie Langhorne	1.00	.45	.12
☐ 10 Thurman Thomas	2.00	.90	.25
☐ 11 Reggie Brooks	1.00	.45	.12
☐ 12 Andre Rison	2.00	.90	.25
☐ 13 Ronald Moore	1.50	.70	.19
☐ 14 Michael Irvin	2.00	.90	.25
☐ 15 Barry Sanders	6.00	2.70	.75
☐ 16 Cris Carter	2.00	.90	.25
☐ 17 Rodney Hampton	2.00	.90	.25
☐ 18 Jerome Bettis	3.00	1.35	.35
☐ 19 Sterling Sharpe	2.00	.90	.25
☐ 20 Emmitt Smith	12.00	5.50	1.50
☐ 21 John Elway	5.00	2.20	.60
☐ 22 Brett Favre	12.00	5.50	1.50
☐ 23 Jim Kelly	2.00	.90	.25
☐ 24 Warren Moon	2.00	.90	.25
☐ 25 Phil Simms	1.50	.70	.19
☐ 26 Craig Erickson	1.50	.70	.19
☐ 27 Neil O'Donnell	2.00	.90	.25
☐ 28 Steve Young	5.00	2.20	.60
☐ 29 Steve Beuerlein	1.50	.70	.19
☐ 30 Troy Aikman	6.00	2.70	.75
☐ 31 Jeff Hostetler	1.50	.70	.19
☐ 32 Boomer Esiason	1.50	.70	.19

1994 Topps Archives 1956

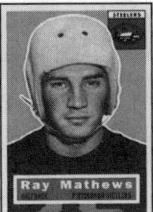

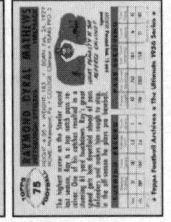

Topps reprinted all 274 standard-size cards in the original 1956 and 1957 sets. The 1956 reprint set contained 120 standard-siez cards, not including the unnumbered checklist card which was not reprinted. The suggested retail for a 12-card pack was 2.00. Factual and grammatical errors in the original cards were not changed in reprints. The fronts feature action player cutouts on bright color backgrounds. The backs were printed in red and black on gray card stock.

	MINT	NRMT	EXC
COMPLETE SET (120)	20.00	9.00	2.50
COMMON CARD (1-120)	.10	.05	.01
☐ 1 Johnny Carson	.10	.05	.01
☐ 2 Gordy Soltau	.10	.05	.01
☐ 3 Frank Varrichione	.10	.05	.01
☐ 4 Eddie Bell	.10	.05	.01
☐ 5 Alex Webster	.20	.09	.03
☐ 6 Norm Van Brocklin	2.00	.90	.25
☐ 7 Green Bay Packers Team Card	.30	.14	.04
☐ 8 Lou Creekmur	.20	.09	.03
☐ 9 Lou Groza	1.50	.70	.19
☐ 10 Tom Bienemann	.10	.05	.01
☐ 11 George Blanda	1.25	.55	.16
☐ 12 Alan Ameche	.40	.18	.05
☐ 13 Vic Janowicz	.40	.18	.05
☐ 14 Dick Moegle	.20	.09	.03
☐ 15 Fran Rogel	.10	.05	.01
☐ 16 Harold Giancanelli	.10	.05	.01
☐ 17 Emlen Tunnell	.60	.25	.07
☐ 18 Paul(Tank) Younger	.30	.14	.04
☐ 19 Billy Howton	.20	.09	.03
☐ 20 Jack Christiansen	.75	.35	.09
☐ 21 Darrell Brewster	.10	.05	.01
☐ 22 Chicago Cardinals Team Card	.30	.14	.04
☐ 23 Ed Brown	.20	.09	.03
☐ 24 Joe Campanella	.10	.05	.01
☐ 25 Leon Heath	.10	.05	.01
☐ 26 San Francisco 49ers Team Card	.30	.14	.04
☐ 27 Dick Flanagan	.10	.05	.01
☐ 28 Chuck Bednarik	1.25	.55	.16
☐ 29 Kyle Rote	.60	.25	.07
☐ 30 Les Richter	.20	.09	.03
☐ 31 Howard Ferguson	.10	.05	.01
☐ 32 Dorne Dibble	.10	.05	.01
☐ 33 Kenny Konz	.10	.05	.01
☐ 34 Dave Mann	.10	.05	.01
☐ 35 Rick Casares	.20	.09	.03
☐ 36 Art Donovan	1.00	.45	.12
☐ 37 Chuck Drazenovich	.10	.05	.01
☐ 38 Joe Arenas	.10	.05	.01
☐ 39 Lynn Chandnois	.10	.05	.01
☐ 40 Philadelphia Eagles Team Card	.30	.14	.04
☐ 41 Roosevelt Brown	.60	.25	.07
☐ 42 Tom Fears	.75	.35	.09
☐ 43 Gary Knafelc	.10	.05	.01
☐ 44 Joe Schmidt	1.00	.45	.12
☐ 45 Cleveland Browns Team Card UER (Card back does not credit the Browns with being Champs in 1955)	.60	.25	.07
☐ 46 Len Teeuws	.10	.05	.01
☐ 47 Bill George	.60	.25	.07
☐ 48 Baltimore Colts Team Card	.30	.14	.04
☐ 49 Eddie LeBaron	.40	.18	.05
☐ 50 Hugh McElhenny	1.25	.55	.16
☐ 51 Ted Marchibroda	.20	.09	.03
☐ 52 Adrian Burk	.10	.05	.01
☐ 53 Frank Gifford	3.00	1.35	.35
☐ 54 Charley Toogood	.10	.05	.01
☐ 55 Tobin Rote	.20	.09	.03
☐ 56 Bill Stits	.10	.05	.01
☐ 57 Don Colo	.10	.05	.01
☐ 58 Ollie Matson	1.25	.55	.16
☐ 59 Harlon Hill	.10	.05	.01
☐ 60 Lenny Moore	2.00	.90	.25
☐ 61 Washington Redskins Team Card	.30	.14	.04
☐ 62 Billy Wilson	.20	.09	.03
☐ 63 Pittsburgh Steelers Team Card	.30	.14	.04
☐ 64 Bob Pellegrini	.10	.05	.01
☐ 65 Ken MacAfee	.20	.09	.03
☐ 66 Willard Sherman	.10	.05	.01
☐ 67 Roger Zatkoff	.10	.05	.01
☐ 68 Dave Middleton	.10	.05	.01
☐ 69 Ray Renfro	.20	.09	.03
☐ 70 Don Stonesifer	.10	.05	.01
☐ 71 Stan Jones	.60	.25	.07
☐ 72 Jim Mutscheller	.10	.05	.01
☐ 73 Volney Peters	.10	.05	.01
☐ 74 Leo Nomellini	.75	.35	.09
☐ 75 Ray Mathews	.10	.05	.01
☐ 76 Dick Bielski	.10	.05	.01
☐ 77 Charley Conerly	1.25	.55	.16
☐ 78 Elroy Hirsch	1.25	.55	.16
☐ 79 Bill Forester	.20	.09	.03
☐ 80 Jim Doran	.10	.05	.01
☐ 81 Fred Morrison	.10	.05	.01
☐ 82 Jack Simmons	.10	.05	.01
☐ 83 Bill McColl	.10	.05	.01
☐ 84 Bert Rechichar	.10	.05	.01
☐ 85 Joe Scudero	.10	.05	.01
☐ 86 Y.A. Tittle	2.50	1.10	.30
☐ 87 Ernie Stautner	1.00	.45	.12
☐ 88 Norm Willey	.10	.05	.01
☐ 89 Bob Schnelker	.10	.05	.01
☐ 90 Dan Towler	.30	.14	.04
☐ 91 John Martinkovic	.10	.05	.01
☐ 92 Detroit Lions Team Card	.30	.14	.04
☐ 93 George Ratterman	.10	.05	.01
☐ 94 Chuck Ulrich	.10	.05	.01
☐ 95 Bobby Watkins	.10	.05	.01
☐ 96 Buddy Young	.30	.14	.04
☐ 97 Billy Wells	.10	.05	.01
☐ 98 Bob Toneff	.10	.05	.01
☐ 99 Bill McPeak	.10	.05	.01
☐ 100 Bobby Thomason	.10	.05	.01
☐ 101 Roosevelt Grier	.60	.25	.07
☐ 102 Ron Waller	.10	.05	.01
☐ 103 Bobby Dillon	.10	.05	.01
☐ 104 Leon Hart	.30	.14	.04
☐ 105 Mike McCormack	.60	.25	.07
☐ 106 John Olszewski	.10	.05	.01
☐ 107 Bill Wightkin	.10	.05	.01
☐ 108 George Shaw	.20	.09	.03
☐ 109 Dale Atkeson	.10	.05	.01
☐ 110 Joe Perry	1.25	.55	.16
☐ 111 Dale Dodrill	.10	.05	.01
☐ 112 Tom Scott	.10	.05	.01
☐ 113 New York Giants Team Card	.30	.14	.04
☐ 114 Los Angeles Rams Team Card UER (Back incorrect, Rams were not 1955 champs)	.30	.14	.04
☐ 115 Al Carmichael	.10	.05	.01
☐ 116 Bobby Layne	2.50	1.10	.30
☐ 117 Ed Modzelewski	.20	.09	.03
☐ 118 Lamar McHan	.10	.05	.01
☐ 119 Chicago Bears Team Card	.30	.14	.04
☐ 120 Billy Vessels	.50	.23	.06

1994 Topps Archives 1956 Gold

This 120-card standard-size set is a parallel to the regular Topps Archives 1956 set. These cards were inserted into 1956/57 Archives packs.

	MINT	NRMT	EXC
COMPLETE SET (120)	50.00	22.00	6.25
COMMON CARD (1-120)	.25	.11	.03
*GOLD CARDS: 1.25X TO 2X BASIC CARDS			

1994 Topps Archives 1957

Topps reprinted all 274 cards in the original 1956 and 1957 sets. The 1957 reprint set contained 154 standard-size cards, not including the unnumbered checklist card which was not reprinted. The suggested retail for a 12-card pack was 2.00. Factual and grammatical errors in the original cards were not changed in reprints. The fronts feature action player cutouts on bright color backgrounds. The backs were printed in red and black on gray card stock.

	MINT	NRMT	EXC
COMPLETE SET (154)	20.00	9.00	2.50
COMMON CARD (1-154)	.10	.05	.01
☐ 1 Eddie LeBaron	.30	.14	.04
☐ 2 Pete Retzlaff	.20	.09	.03
☐ 3 Mike McCormack	.50	.23	.06
☐ 4 Lou Baldacci	.10	.05	.01
☐ 5 Gino Marchetti	1.00	.45	.12
☐ 6 Leo Nomellini	.75	.35	.09
☐ 7 Bobby Watkins	.10	.05	.01
☐ 8 Dave Middleton	.10	.05	.01
☐ 9 Bobby Dillon	.10	.05	.01
☐ 10 Les Richter	.20	.09	.03
☐ 11 Roosevelt Brown	.50	.23	.06
☐ 12 Lavern Torgeson	.10	.05	.01
☐ 13 Dick Bielski	.10	.05	.01
☐ 14 Pat Summerall	1.00	.45	.12
☐ 15 Jack Butler	.10	.05	.01
☐ 16 John Henry Johnson	.75	.35	.09
☐ 17 Art Spinney	.10	.05	.01
☐ 18 Bob St. Clair	.50	.23	.06
☐ 19 Perry Jeter	.10	.05	.01
☐ 20 Lou Creekmur	.30	.14	.04
☐ 21 Dave Hanner	.10	.05	.01
☐ 22 Norm Van Brocklin	1.50	.70	.19
☐ 23 Don Chandler	.10	.05	.01
☐ 24 Al Dorow	.10	.05	.01
☐ 25 Tom Scott	.10	.05	.01
☐ 26 Ollie Matson	1.25	.55	.16
☐ 27 Fran Rogel	.10	.05	.01
☐ 28 Lou Groza	1.50	.70	.19
☐ 29 Billy Vessels	.20	.09	.03
☐ 30 Y.A. Tittle	2.00	.90	.25
☐ 31 George Blanda	1.50	.70	.19
☐ 32 Bobby Layne	2.00	.90	.25
☐ 33 Billy Howton	.20	.09	.03
☐ 34 Bill Wade	.20	.09	.03
☐ 35 Emlen Tunnell	.75	.35	.09
☐ 36 Leo Elter	.10	.05	.01
☐ 37 Clarence Peaks	.20	.09	.03
☐ 38 Don Stonesifer	.10	.05	.01
☐ 39 George Tarasovic	.10	.05	.01
☐ 40 Darrell Brewster	.10	.05	.01
☐ 41 Bert Rechichar	.10	.05	.01
☐ 42 Billy Wilson	.20	.09	.03
☐ 43 Ed Brown	.20	.09	.03
☐ 44 Gene Gedman	.10	.05	.01
☐ 45 Gary Knafelc	.10	.05	.01
☐ 46 Elroy Hirsch	1.25	.55	.16
☐ 47 Don Heinrich	.10	.05	.01
☐ 48 Gene Brito	.10	.05	.01
☐ 49 Chuck Bednarik	1.00	.45	.12
☐ 50 Dave Mann	.10	.05	.01
☐ 51 Bill McPeak	.10	.05	.01
☐ 52 Kenny Konz	.10	.05	.01
☐ 53 Alan Ameche	.40	.18	.05
☐ 54 Gordy Soltau	.10	.05	.01
☐ 55 Rick Casares	.30	.14	.04
☐ 56 Charlie Ane	.10	.05	.01
☐ 57 Al Carmichael	.10	.05	.01
☐ 58 Willard Sherman	.10	.05	.01
☐ 59 Kyle Rote	.50	.23	.06
☐ 60 Chuck Drazenovich	.10	.05	.01
☐ 61 Bobby Walston	.10	.05	.01
☐ 62 John Olszewski	.10	.05	.01
☐ 63 Ray Mathews	.10	.05	.01
☐ 64 Maurice Bassett	.10	.05	.01
☐ 65 Art Donovan	1.00	.45	.12
☐ 66 Joe Arenas	.10	.05	.01
☐ 67 Harlon Hill	.10	.05	.01
☐ 68 Yale Lary	.60	.25	.07
☐ 69 Bill Forester	.20	.09	.03
☐ 70 Bob Boyd	.10	.05	.01
☐ 71 Andy Robustelli	1.00	.45	.12
☐ 72 Sam Baker	.20	.09	.03
☐ 73 Bob Pellegrini	.10	.05	.01
☐ 74 Leo Sanford	.10	.05	.01
☐ 75 Sid Watson	.10	.05	.01
☐ 76 Ray Renfro	.20	.09	.03
☐ 77 Carl Taseff	.10	.05	.01
☐ 78 Clyde Conner	.10	.05	.01
☐ 79 J.C. Caroline	.10	.05	.01
☐ 80 Howard Cassady	.30	.14	.04
☐ 81 Tobin Rote	.20	.09	.03
☐ 82 Ron Waller	.10	.05	.01
☐ 83 Jim Patton	.20	.09	.03
☐ 84 Volney Peters	.10	.05	.01
☐ 85 Dick Lane	.60	.25	.07
☐ 86 Royce Womble	.10	.05	.01
☐ 87 Duane Putnam	.10	.05	.01
☐ 88 Frank Gifford	2.50	1.10	.30

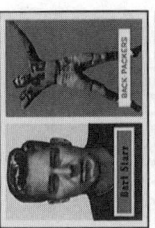

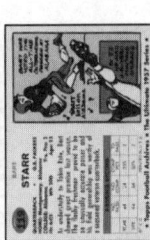

	MINT	NRMT	EXC
□ 89 Steve Meilinger	.10	.05	.01
□ 90 Buck Lansford	.10	.05	.01
□ 91 Lindon Crow	.10	.05	.01
□ 92 Ernie Stautner	.75	.35	.09
□ 93 Preston Carpenter	.20	.09	.03
□ 94 Raymond Berry	1.50	.70	.19
□ 95 Hugh McElhenny	1.25	.55	.16
□ 96 Stan Jones	.50	.23	.06
□ 97 Dorne Dibble	.10	.05	.01
□ 98 Joe Scudero	.10	.05	.01
□ 99 Eddie Bell	.10	.05	.01
□ 100 Joe Childress	.10	.05	.01
□ 101 Elbert Nickel	.10	.05	.01
□ 102 Walt Michaels	.20	.09	.03
□ 103 Jim Mutscheller	.10	.05	.01
□ 104 Earl Morrall	.40	.18	.05
□ 105 Larry Strickland	.10	.05	.01
□ 106 Jack Christiansen	.75	.35	.09
□ 107 Fred Cone	.10	.05	.01
□ 108 Bud McFadin	.10	.05	.01
□ 109 Charley Conerly	1.25	.55	.16
□ 110 Tom Runnels	.10	.05	.01
□ 111 Ken Keller	.10	.05	.01
□ 112 James Root	.10	.05	.01
□ 113 Ted Marchibroda	.30	.14	.04
□ 114 Don Paul	.10	.05	.01
□ 115 George Shaw	.20	.09	.03
□ 116 Dick Moegle	.20	.09	.03
□ 117 Don Bingham	.10	.05	.01
□ 118 Leon Hart	.20	.09	.03
□ 119 Bart Starr	4.00	1.80	.50
□ 120 Paul Miller	.10	.05	.01
□ 121 Alex Webster	.20	.09	.03
□ 122 Ray Wietecha	.10	.05	.01
□ 123 Johnny Carson	.10	.05	.01
□ 124 Tommy McDonald	.30	.14	.04
□ 125 Jerry Tubbs	.10	.05	.01
□ 126 Jack Scarbath	.10	.05	.01
□ 127 Ed Modzelewski	.10	.05	.01
□ 128 Lenny Moore	1.25	.55	.16
□ 129 Joe Perry	1.25	.55	.16
□ 130 Bill Wightkin	.10	.05	.01
□ 131 Jim Doran	.10	.05	.01
□ 132 Howard Ferguson UER (Name misspelled Furgeson on front)	.10	.05	.01
□ 133 Tom Wilson	.10	.05	.01
□ 134 Dick James	.10	.05	.01
□ 135 Jimmy Harris	.10	.05	.01
□ 136 Chuck Ulrich	.10	.05	.01
□ 137 Lynn Chandnois	.10	.05	.01
□ 138 Johnny Unitas	4.00	1.80	.50
□ 139 Jim Ridlon	.10	.05	.01
□ 140 Zeke Bratkowski	.20	.09	.03
□ 141 Ray Krouse	.10	.05	.01
□ 142 John Martinkovic	.10	.05	.01
□ 143 Jim Cason	.10	.05	.01
□ 144 Ken MacAfee	.20	.09	.03
□ 145 Sid Youngelman	.10	.05	.01
□ 146 Paul Larson	.10	.05	.01
□ 147 Len Ford	1.00	.45	.12
□ 148 Bob Toneff	.10	.05	.01
□ 149 Ronnie Knox	.10	.05	.01
□ 150 Jim David	.10	.05	.01
□ 151 Paul Hornung	4.00	1.80	.50
□ 152 Paul(Tank) Younger	.30	.14	.04
□ 153 Bill Svoboda	.10	.05	.01
□ 154 Fred Morrison	.30	.14	.04

1994 Topps Archives 1957 Gold

These 154 standard-size cards were inserted into 1956/57 Topps Archives packs. These cards are a parallel to the regular Topps Archives 1957 issue.

	MINT	NRMT	EXC
COMPLETE SET (154)	50.00	22.00	6.25
COMMON CARD (1-154)	.25	.11	.03

*GOLD CARDS: 1.25X TO 2X BASIC CARDS

1995 Topps

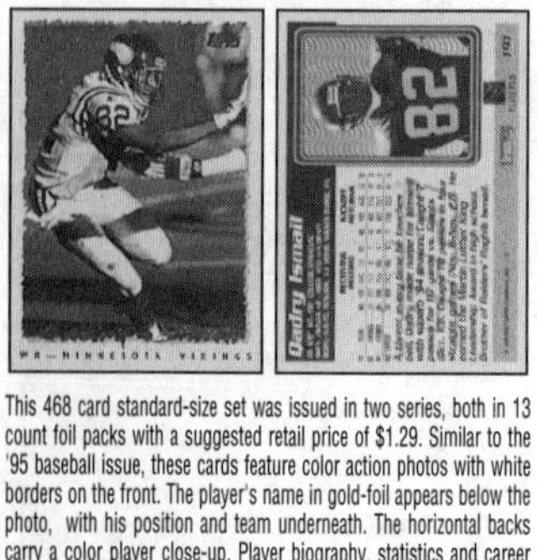

This 468 card standard-size set was issued in two series, both in 13 count foil packs with a suggested retail price of $1.29. Similar to the '95 baseball issue, these cards feature color action photos with white borders on the front. The player's name in gold-foil appears below the photo, with his position and team underneath. The horizontal backs carry a color player close-up. Player biography, statistics and career highlights complete the backs. Two subsets are included in this set: 1,000 Yard Club (1-29) and 3,000 Yard Club (30-41). Rookie Cards in this set include Ki-Jana Carter, Kerry Collins, Rashaan Salaam, J.J. Stokes and Michael Westbrook.

	MINT	NRMT	EXC
COMPLETE SET (468)	40.00	18.00	5.00
COMPLETE FACT.SET (478)	40.00	18.00	5.00
COMPLETE SERIES 1 (248)	20.00	9.00	2.50
COMPLETE SERIES 2 (220)	20.00	9.00	2.50
COMMON CARD (1-468)	.05	.02	.01

	MINT	NRMT	EXC
□ 1 Barry Sanders	.50	.23	.06
□ 2 Chris Warren	.10	.05	.01
□ 3 Jerry Rice	.50	.23	.06
□ 4 Emmitt Smith	1.00	.45	.12
□ 5 Henry Ellard	.10	.05	.01
□ 6 Natrone Means TYC	.20	.09	.03
□ 7 Terance Mathis	.10	.05	.01
□ 8 Tim Brown TYC	.10	.05	.01
□ 9 Andre Reed	.10	.05	.01
□ 10 Marshall Faulk	.20	.09	.03
□ 11 Irving Fryar	.10	.05	.01
□ 12 Cris Carter	.20	.09	.03
□ 13 Michael Irvin	.20	.09	.03
□ 14 Jake Reed	.10	.05	.01
□ 15 Ben Coates	.10	.05	.01
□ 16 Herman Moore	.20	.09	.03
□ 17 Carl Pickens	.20	.09	.03
□ 18 Fred Barnett	.10	.05	.01
□ 19 Sterling Sharpe	.10	.05	.01
□ 20 Anthony Miller	.10	.05	.01
□ 21 Thurman Thomas	.20	.09	.03
□ 22 Andre Rison	.10	.05	.01
□ 23 Brian Blades	.10	.05	.01
□ 24 Rodney Hampton	.10	.05	.01
□ 25 Terry Allen	.10	.05	.01
□ 26 Jerome Bettis	.20	.09	.03
□ 27 Errict Rhett	.20	.09	.03
□ 28 Rob Moore	.05	.02	.01
□ 29 Shannon Sharpe	.10	.05	.01
□ 30 Drew Bledsoe	.50	.23	.06
□ 31 Dan Marino	1.00	.45	.12
□ 32 Warren Moon	.10	.05	.01
□ 33 Steve Young	.40	.18	.05
□ 34 Brett Favre	1.00	.45	.12
□ 35 Jim Everett	.05	.02	.01
□ 36 Jeff George	.10	.05	.01
□ 37 John Elway	.40	.18	.05
□ 38 Jeff Hostetler	.10	.05	.01
□ 39 Randall Cunningham	.10	.05	.01
□ 40 Stan Humphries	.10	.05	.01
□ 41 Jim Kelly	.20	.09	.03
□ 42 Tommy Barnhardt	.05	.02	.01
□ 43 Bob Whitfield	.05	.02	.01
□ 44 William Thomas	.05	.02	.01
□ 45 Glyn Milburn	.05	.02	.01
□ 46 Steve Christie	.05	.02	.01
□ 47 Kevin Mawae	.05	.02	.01
□ 48 Vencie Glenn	.05	.02	.01
□ 49 Eric Curry	.05	.02	.01
□ 50 Jeff Hostetler	.10	.05	.01
□ 51 Tyronne Stowe	.05	.02	.01
□ 52 Steve Jackson	.05	.02	.01
□ 53 Ben Coleman	.05	.02	.01
□ 54 Brad Baxter	.05	.02	.01
□ 55 Darryl Williams	.05	.02	.01
□ 56 Troy Drayton	.05	.02	.01
□ 57 George Teague	.05	.02	.01
□ 58 Calvin Williams	.10	.05	.01
□ 59 Jeff Cross	.05	.02	.01
□ 60 Leroy Hoard	.05	.02	.01
□ 61 John Carney	.05	.02	.01
□ 62 Daryl Johnston	.10	.05	.01
□ 63 Jim Jeffcoat	.05	.02	.01
□ 64 Matt Stover	.05	.02	.01
□ 65 LeRoy Butler	.05	.02	.01
□ 66 Curtis Conway	.20	.09	.03
□ 67 O.J. McDuffie	.20	.09	.03
□ 68 Robert Massey	.05	.02	.01
□ 69 Ed McDaniel	.05	.02	.01
□ 70 William Floyd	.20	.09	.03
□ 71 Willie Davis	.10	.05	.01
□ 72 William Roberts	.05	.02	.01
□ 73 Chester McGlockton	.10	.05	.01
□ 74 D.J. Johnson	.05	.02	.01
□ 75 Rondell Jones	.05	.02	.01
□ 76 Morten Andersen	.05	.02	.01
□ 77 Glenn Parker	.05	.02	.01
□ 78 William Fuller	.05	.02	.01
□ 79 Ray Buchanan	.05	.02	.01
□ 80 Maurice Hurst	.05	.02	.01
□ 81 Wayne Gandy	.05	.02	.01
□ 82 Marcus Turner	.05	.02	.01
□ 83 Greg Davis	.05	.02	.01
□ 84 Terry Wooden	.05	.02	.01
□ 85 Thomas Everett	.05	.02	.01
□ 86 Steve Broussard	.05	.02	.01
□ 87 Tom Carter	.05	.02	.01
□ 88 Glenn Montgomery	.05	.02	.01
□ 89 Larry Allen	.10	.05	.01
□ 90 Donnell Woolford	.05	.02	.01
□ 91 John Alt	.05	.02	.01
□ 92 Phil Hansen	.05	.02	.01
□ 93 Seth Joyner	.05	.02	.01
□ 94 Michael Brooks	.05	.02	.01
□ 95 Randall McDaniel	.05	.02	.01
□ 96 Tydus Winans	.05	.02	.01
□ 97 Rob Fredrickson	.05	.02	.01
□ 98 Ray Crockett	.05	.02	.01
□ 99 Courtney Hall	.05	.02	.01
□ 100 Merton Hanks	.05	.02	.01
□ 101 Aaron Glenn	.05	.02	.01
□ 102 Roosevelt Potts	.05	.02	.01
□ 103 Leon Lett	.05	.02	.01
□ 104 Jessie Tuggle	.05	.02	.01
□ 105 Martin Mayhew	.05	.02	.01
□ 106 Willie Roaf	.05	.02	.01
□ 107 Todd Lyght	.05	.02	.01
□ 108 Ernest Givins	.05	.02	.01
□ 109 Tony McGee	.05	.02	.01
□ 110 Barry Sanders	1.00	.45	.12
□ 111 Dermontti Dawson	.10	.05	.01
□ 112 Rick Tuten	.05	.02	.01
□ 113 Vincent Brisby	.05	.02	.01
□ 114 Charlie Garner	.10	.05	.01
□ 115 Irving Fryar	.10	.05	.01
□ 116 Stevon Moore	.05	.02	.01
□ 117 Matt Darby	.05	.02	.01
□ 118 Howard Cross	.05	.02	.01
□ 119 John Gesek	.05	.02	.01
□ 120 Jack Del Rio	.05	.02	.01
□ 121 Marcus Allen	.20	.09	.03
□ 122 Torrance Small	.05	.02	.01
□ 123 Chris Mims	.05	.02	.01
□ 124 Don Mosebar	.05	.02	.01
□ 125 Carl Pickens	.20	.09	.03
□ 126 Tom Rouen	.05	.02	.01
□ 127 Garrison Hearst	.20	.09	.03
□ 128 Charles Johnson	.10	.05	.01
□ 129 Derek Brown RB	.05	.02	.01
□ 130 Troy Aikman	1.00	.45	.12
□ 131 Troy Vincent	.05	.02	.01
□ 132 Ken Ruettgers	.05	.02	.01
□ 133 Michael Jackson	.10	.05	.01
□ 134 Dennis Gibson	.05	.02	.01
□ 135 Brett Perriman	.10	.05	.01
□ 136 Jeff Graham	.05	.02	.01
□ 137 Chad Brown	.10	.05	.01
□ 138 Ken Norton Jr.	.10	.05	.01
□ 139 Chris Slade	.10	.05	.01
□ 140 Dave Brown	.10	.05	.01
□ 141 Bert Emanuel	.20	.09	.03
□ 142 Renaldo Turnbull	.05	.02	.01
□ 143 Jim Harbaugh	.10	.05	.01
□ 144 Micheal Barrow	.05	.02	.01
□ 145 Vincent Brown	.05	.02	.01
□ 146 Bryant Young	.10	.05	.01
□ 147 Boomer Esiason	.10	.05	.01
□ 148 Sean Gilbert	.10	.05	.01
□ 149 Greg Truitt	.05	.02	.01
□ 150 Rod Woodson	.10	.05	.01
□ 151 Robert Porcher	.05	.02	.01
□ 152 Joe Phillips	.05	.02	.01
□ 153 Gary Zimmerman	.05	.02	.01
□ 154 Bruce Smith	.20	.09	.03
□ 155 Randall Cunningham	.10	.05	.01
□ 156 Fred Strickland	.05	.02	.01
□ 157 Derrick Alexander WR	.20	.09	.03
□ 158 James Williams	.05	.02	.01
□ 159 Scott Dill	.05	.02	.01
□ 160 Tim Bowens	.05	.02	.01
□ 161 Floyd Turner	.05	.02	.01
□ 162 Ronnie Harmon	.05	.02	.01
□ 163 Wayne Martin	.05	.02	.01
□ 164 John Randle	.05	.02	.01
□ 165 Larry Centers	.10	.05	.01
□ 166 Larry Brown DB	.05	.02	.01
□ 167 Albert Lewis	.05	.02	.01
□ 168 Michael Strahan	.05	.02	.01
□ 169 Reggie Brooks	.10	.05	.01
□ 170 Craig Heyward	.10	.05	.01
□ 171 Pat Harlow	.05	.02	.01
□ 172 Eugene Robinson	.05	.02	.01
□ 173 Shane Conlan	.05	.02	.01
□ 174 Bennie Blades	.05	.02	.01
□ 175 Neil O'Donnell	.10	.05	.01
□ 176 Steve Tovar	.05	.02	.01
□ 177 Donald Evans	.05	.02	.01
□ 178 Brent Jones	.05	.02	.01
□ 179 Ray Childress	.05	.02	.01
□ 180 Reggie White	.20	.09	.03
□ 181 David Alexander	.05	.02	.01
□ 182 Greg Hill	.10	.05	.01
□ 183 Vinny Testaverde	.10	.05	.01
□ 184 Jeff Burris	.05	.02	.01
□ 185 Hardy Nickerson	.05	.02	.01
□ 186 Terry Kirby	.10	.05	.01
□ 187 Kirk Lowdermilk	.05	.02	.01
□ 188 Eric Swann	.10	.05	.01
□ 189 Chris Zorich	.05	.02	.01
□ 190 Simon Fletcher	.05	.02	.01
□ 191 Qadry Ismail	.10	.05	.01
□ 192 Heath Shuler	.20	.09	.03
□ 193 Michael Haynes	.10	.05	.01
□ 194 Mike Sherrard	.05	.02	.01
□ 195 Nolan Harrison	.05	.02	.01
□ 196 Marcus Robertson	.05	.02	.01
□ 197 Kevin Williams WR	.10	.05	.01
□ 198 Moe Gardner	.05	.02	.01
□ 199 Rick Mirer	.20	.09	.03
□ 200 Junior Seau	.20	.09	.03
□ 201 Byron Bam Morris	.10	.05	.01
□ 202 Willie McGinest	.10	.05	.01
□ 203 Chris Spielman	.10	.05	.01
□ 204 Darnay Scott	.20	.09	.03
□ 205 Jesse Sapolu	.05	.02	.01
□ 206 Marvin Washington	.05	.02	.01
□ 207 Anthony Newman	.05	.02	.01
□ 208 Cortez Kennedy	.10	.05	.01
□ 209 Quentin Coryatt	.10	.05	.01
□ 210 Neil Smith	.10	.05	.01
□ 211 Keith Sims	.05	.02	.01
□ 212 Sean Jones	.05	.02	.01
□ 213 Tony Jones	.05	.02	.01
□ 214 Lewis Tillman	.05	.02	.01
□ 215 Darren Woodson	.10	.05	.01
□ 216 Jason Hanson	.05	.02	.01
□ 217 John Taylor	.05	.02	.01
□ 218 Shawn Lee	.05	.02	.01
□ 219 Kevin Greene	.10	.05	.01
□ 220 Jerry Rice	1.00	.45	.12
□ 221 Ki-Jana Carter	1.00	.45	.12
□ 222 Tony Boselli	.10	.05	.01
□ 223 Michael Westbrook	1.25	.55	.16
□ 224 Kerry Collins	3.00	1.35	.35
□ 225 Kevin Carter	.20	.09	.03
□ 226 Kyle Brady	.20	.09	.03
□ 227 J.J. Stokes	1.00	.45	.12
□ 228 Derrick Alexander DE	.05	.02	.01
□ 229 Warren Sapp	.10	.05	.01
□ 230 Ruben Brown	.05	.02	.01
□ 231 Hugh Douglas	.10	.05	.01
□ 232 Luther Elliss	.05	.02	.01
□ 233 Rashaan Salaam	1.25	.55	.16
□ 234 Tyrone Poole	.10	.05	.01
□ 235 Korey Stringer	.05	.02	.01
□ 236 Devin Bush	.05	.02	.01
□ 237 Cory Raymer	.05	.02	.01
□ 238 Zach Wiegert	.05	.02	.01
□ 239 Ron Davis	.05	.02	.01
□ 240 Todd Collins QB	.20	.09	.03
□ 241 Bobby Taylor	.10	.05	.01
□ 242 Patrick Riley	.05	.02	.01
□ 243 Scott Gragg	.05	.02	.01
□ 244 Marvcus Patton	.05	.02	.01
□ 245 Alvin Harper	.05	.02	.01
□ 246 Ricky Watters	.20	.09	.03
□ 247 Checklist 1	.05	.02	.01
□ 248 Checklist 2	.05	.02	.01
□ 249 Terance Mathis	.10	.05	.01
□ 250 Mark Carrier DB	.05	.02	.01
□ 251 Elijah Alexander	.05	.02	.01
□ 252 George Koonce	.05	.02	.01
□ 253 Tony Bennett	.05	.02	.01
□ 254 Steve Wisniewski	.05	.02	.01
□ 255 Bernie Parmalee	.10	.05	.01
□ 256 Dwayne Sabb	.05	.02	.01
□ 257 Lorenzo Neal	.05	.02	.01
□ 258 Corey Miller	.05	.02	.01
□ 259 Fred Barnett	.10	.05	.01
□ 260 Greg Lloyd	.10	.05	.01
□ 261 Robert Blackmon	.05	.02	.01
□ 262 Ken Harvey	.05	.02	.01
□ 263 Eric Hill	.05	.02	.01
□ 264 Russell Copeland	.05	.02	.01
□ 265 Jeff Blake	1.25	.55	.16
□ 266 Carl Banks	.05	.02	.01
□ 267 Jay Novacek	.10	.05	.01
□ 268 Mel Gray	.05	.02	.01
□ 269 Kimble Anders	.10	.05	.01
□ 270 Cris Carter	.20	.09	.03
□ 271 Johnny Mitchell	.05	.02	.01
□ 272 Shawn Jefferson	.05	.02	.01
□ 273 Doug Brien	.05	.02	.01
□ 274 Sean Landeta	.05	.02	.01
□ 275 Scott Mitchell	.10	.05	.01
□ 276 Charles Wilson	.05	.02	.01
□ 277 Anthony Smith	.05	.02	.01
□ 278 Anthony Miller	.10	.05	.01
□ 279 Steve Walsh	.05	.02	.01
□ 280 Drew Bledsoe	1.00	.45	.12
□ 281 Jamir Miller	.05	.02	.01
□ 282 Robert Brooks UER Rushing and receiving totals are reversed	.20	.09	.03
□ 283 Sean Lumpkin	.05	.02	.01
□ 284 Bryan Cox	.05	.02	.01
□ 285 Byron Evans	.05	.02	.01
□ 286 Chris Doleman	.05	.02	.01
□ 287 Anthony Pleasant	.05	.02	.01
□ 288 Stephen Grant	.05	.02	.01
□ 289 Doug Riesenberg	.05	.02	.01
□ 290 Natrone Means	.20	.09	.03
□ 291 Henry Thomas	.05	.02	.01
□ 292 Mike Pritchard	.05	.02	.01
□ 293 Courtney Hawkins	.05	.02	.01
□ 294 Bill Bates	.10	.05	.01
□ 295 Jerome Bettis	.30	.14	.04
□ 296 Russell Maryland	.05	.02	.01
□ 297 Stanley Richard	.05	.02	.01
□ 298 William White	.05	.02	.01
□ 299 Dan Wilkinson	.10	.05	.01
□ 300 Steve Young	.75	.35	.09
□ 301 Gary Brown	.05	.02	.01
□ 302 Jake Reed	.10	.05	.01
□ 303 Carlton Gray	.05	.02	.01

☐ 304 Levon Kirkland	.05	.02	.01
☐ 305 Shannon Sharpe	.10	.05	.01
☐ 306 Luis Sharpe	.05	.02	.01
☐ 307 Marshall Faulk	.50	.23	.06
☐ 308 Stan Humphries	.10	.05	.01
☐ 309 Chris Calloway	.05	.02	.01
☐ 310 Tim Brown	.20	.09	.03
☐ 311 Steve Everitt	.05	.02	.01
☐ 312 Raymont Harris	.05	.02	.01
☐ 313 Tim McDonald	.05	.02	.01
☐ 314 Trent Dilfer	.20	.09	.03
☐ 315 Jim Everett	.05	.02	.01
☐ 316 Ray Crittenden	.05	.02	.01
☐ 317 Jim Kelly	.20	.09	.03
☐ 318 Andre Reed	.10	.05	.01
☐ 319 Chris Miller	.05	.02	.01
☐ 320 Bobby Houston	.05	.02	.01
☐ 321 Charles Haley	.10	.05	.01
☐ 322 James Francis	.05	.02	.01
☐ 323 Bernard Williams	.05	.02	.01
☐ 324 Michael Bates	.05	.02	.01
☐ 325 Brian Mitchell	.05	.02	.01
☐ 326 Mike Johnson	.05	.02	.01
☐ 327 Eric Bieniemy	.05	.02	.01
☐ 328 Aubrey Beavers	.05	.02	.01
☐ 329 Dale Carter	.10	.05	.01
☐ 330 Emmitt Smith	2.00	.90	.25
☐ 331 Darren Perry	.05	.02	.01
☐ 332 Marquez Pope	.05	.02	.01
☐ 333 Clyde Simmons	.05	.02	.01
☐ 334 Corey Croom	.05	.02	.01
☐ 335 Thomas Randolph	.05	.02	.01
☐ 336 Harvey Williams	.05	.02	.01
☐ 337 Michael Timpson	.05	.02	.01
☐ 338 Eugene Daniel	.05	.02	.01
☐ 339 Shane Dronett	.05	.02	.01
☐ 340 Eric Turner	.05	.02	.01
☐ 341 Eric Metcalf	.10	.05	.01
☐ 342 Leslie O'Neal	.10	.05	.01
☐ 343 Mark Wheeler	.05	.02	.01
☐ 344 Mark Pike	.05	.02	.01
☐ 345 Brett Favre	2.00	.90	.25
☐ 346 Johnny Bailey	.05	.02	.01
☐ 347 Henry Ellard	.10	.05	.01
☐ 348 Chris Gardocki	.05	.02	.01
☐ 349 Henry Jones	.05	.02	.01
☐ 350 Dan Marino	2.00	.90	.25
☐ 351 Lake Dawson	.10	.05	.01
☐ 352 Mark McMillian	.05	.02	.01
☐ 353 Deion Sanders	.60	.25	.07
☐ 354 Antonio London	.05	.02	.01
☐ 355 Cris Dishman	.05	.02	.01
☐ 356 Ricardo McDonald	.05	.02	.01
☐ 357 Dexter Carter	.05	.02	.01
☐ 358 Kevin Smith	.05	.02	.01
☐ 359 Yancey Thigpen	1.00	.45	.12
☐ 360 Chris Warren	.10	.05	.01
☐ 361 Quinn Early	.10	.05	.01
☐ 362 John Mangum	.05	.02	.01
☐ 363 Santana Dotson	.05	.02	.01
☐ 364 Rocket Ismail	.10	.05	.01
☐ 365 Aeneas Williams	.05	.02	.01
☐ 366 Dan Williams	.05	.02	.01
☐ 367 Sean Dawkins	.10	.05	.01
☐ 368 Pepper Johnson	.05	.02	.01
☐ 369 Roman Phifer	.05	.02	.01
☐ 370 Rodney Hampton	.10	.05	.01
☐ 371 Darrell Green	.05	.02	.01
☐ 372 Michael Zordich	.05	.02	.01
☐ 373 Andre Coleman	.05	.02	.01
☐ 374 Wayne Simmons	.05	.02	.01
☐ 375 Michael Irvin	.20	.09	.03
☐ 376 Clay Matthews	.10	.05	.01
☐ 377 Dewayne Washington	.10	.05	.01
☐ 378 Keith Byars	.05	.02	.01
☐ 379 Todd Collins LB	.20	.09	.03
☐ 380 Mark Collins	.05	.02	.01
☐ 381 Joel Steed	.05	.02	.01
☐ 382 Bart Oates	.05	.02	.01
☐ 383 Al Smith	.05	.02	.01
☐ 384 Rafael Robinson	.05	.02	.01
☐ 385 Mo Lewis	.05	.02	.01
☐ 386 Aubrey Matthews	.05	.02	.01
☐ 387 Corey Sawyer	.05	.02	.01
☐ 388 Bucky Brooks	.05	.02	.01
☐ 389 Erik Kramer	.05	.02	.01
☐ 390 Tyrone Hughes	.10	.05	.01
☐ 391 Terry McDaniel	.05	.02	.01
☐ 392 Craig Erickson	.05	.02	.01
☐ 393 Mike Flores	.05	.02	.01
☐ 394 Harry Swayne	.05	.02	.01
☐ 395 Irving Spikes	.10	.05	.01
☐ 396 Lorenzo Lynch	.05	.02	.01
☐ 397 Antonio Langham	.05	.02	.01
☐ 398 Edgar Bennett	.10	.05	.01
☐ 399 Thomas Lewis	.10	.05	.01
☐ 400 John Elway	.75	.35	.09
☐ 401 Jeff George	.10	.05	.01
☐ 402 Errict Rhett	.20	.09	.03
☐ 403 Bill Romanowski	.05	.02	.01
☐ 404 Alexander Wright	.05	.02	.01
☐ 405 Warren Moon	.10	.05	.01
☐ 406 Eddie Robinson	.05	.02	.01
☐ 407 John Copeland	.05	.02	.01
☐ 408 Robert Jones	.05	.02	.01
☐ 409 Steve Bono	.10	.05	.01
☐ 410 Cornelius Bennett	.10	.05	.01
☐ 411 Ben Coates	.10	.05	.01
☐ 412 Dana Stubblefield	.20	.09	.03
☐ 413 Darryl Talley	.05	.02	.01
☐ 414 Brian Blades	.10	.05	.01
☐ 415 Herman Moore	.50	.23	.06
☐ 416 Nick Lowery	.05	.02	.01
☐ 417 Donnell Bennett	.05	.02	.01
☐ 418 Van Malone	.05	.02	.01
☐ 419 Pete Stoyanovich	.05	.02	.01
☐ 420 Joe Montana	1.00	.45	.12
☐ 421 Steve Young Super Bowl XXIX MVP	.50	.23	.06
☐ 422 Steve Young Quarterback Rating Leaders	.50	.23	.06
☐ 423 Steve Young Super Bowl Touchdown Record	.50	.23	.06
☐ 424 Steve Young NFL League MVP	.50	.23	.06
☐ 425 Steve Young Pro Bowl	.50	.23	.06
☐ 426 Rod Stephens	.05	.02	.01
☐ 427 Ellis Johnson UER Card is numbered 436	.05	.02	.01
☐ 428 Kordell Stewart	3.00	1.35	.35
☐ 429 James O.Stewart	.10	.05	.01
☐ 430 Steve McNair	2.50	1.10	.30
☐ 431 Brian DeMarco	.10	.05	.01
☐ 432 Matt O'Dwyer	.05	.02	.01
☐ 433 Lorenzo Styles	.05	.02	.01
☐ 434 Anthony Cook	.05	.02	.01
☐ 435 Jesse James	.05	.02	.01
☐ 436 Darryl Pounds	.05	.02	.01
☐ 437 Derrick Graham	.05	.02	.01
☐ 438 Vernon Turner	.05	.02	.01
☐ 439 Carlton Bailey	.05	.02	.01
☐ 440 Darion Conner	.05	.02	.01
☐ 441 Randy Baldwin	.05	.02	.01
☐ 442 Tim McKyer	.05	.02	.01
☐ 443 Sam Mills	.10	.05	.01
☐ 444 Bob Christian	.05	.02	.01
☐ 445 Steve Lofton	.05	.02	.01
☐ 446 Lamar Lathon	.05	.02	.01
☐ 447 Tony Smith	.05	.02	.01
☐ 448 Don Beebe	.05	.02	.01
☐ 449 Barry Foster	.10	.05	.01
☐ 450 Frank Reich	.05	.02	.01
☐ 451 Pete Metzelaars	.05	.02	.01
☐ 452 Reggie Cobb	.05	.02	.01
☐ 453 Jeff Lageman	.05	.02	.01
☐ 454 Derek Brown TE	.05	.02	.01
☐ 455 Desmond Howard	.10	.05	.01
☐ 456 Vinnie Clark	.05	.02	.01
☐ 457 Keith Goganious	.05	.02	.01
☐ 458 Shawn Bouwens	.05	.02	.01
☐ 459 Rob Johnson	.05	.02	.01
☐ 460 Steve Beuerlein	.05	.02	.01
☐ 461 Mark Brunell	1.00	.45	.12
☐ 462 Harry Colon	.05	.02	.01
☐ 463 Chris Hudson	.05	.02	.01
☐ 464 Darren Carrington	.05	.02	.01
☐ 465 Ernest Givins	.05	.02	.01
☐ 466 Kelvin Pritchett	.05	.02	.01
☐ 467 Checklist (249-358)	.05	.02	.01
☐ 468 Checklist (358-468)	.05	.02	.01

1995 Topps Air Raid

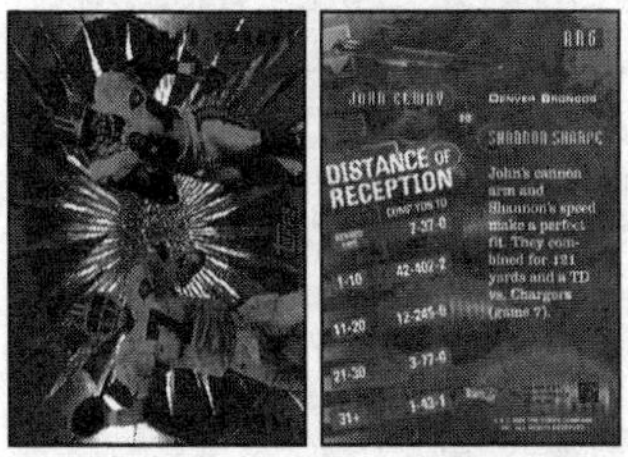

This 10 card set was randomly inserted in series two retail packs at a rate of one in 24 packs and feature some of the NFL's best quarterback/wide receiver combinations. Card fronts feature the holographic "Power Matrix" technology with the title "Air Raid" in gold along the top of the card and a foil etched football shape in the background. Card backs are vertical with commentary and statistics on the two players. The are numbered with an "AR" prefix.

	MINT	NRMT	EXC
COMPLETE SET (10)	70.00	32.00	8.75
COMMON CARD (1-10)	3.00	1.35	.35
☐ 1 Steve Young Jerry Rice	10.00	4.50	1.25
☐ 2 Cris Carter Warren Moon	5.00	2.20	.60
☐ 3 Terance Mathis Jeff George	3.00	1.35	.35
☐ 4 Dave Brown Michael Sherrard	3.00	1.35	.35
☐ 5 Drew Bledsoe Ben Coates	10.00	4.50	1.25
☐ 6 John Elway Shannon Sharpe	8.00	3.60	1.00
☐ 7 Jeff Blake Carl Pickens	6.00	2.70	.75
☐ 8 Dan Marino Irving Fryar	20.00	9.00	2.50
☐ 9 Fred Barnett Randall Cunningham	3.00	1.35	.35
☐ 10 Troy Aikman Michael Irvin	10.00	4.50	1.25

1995 Topps All-Pros

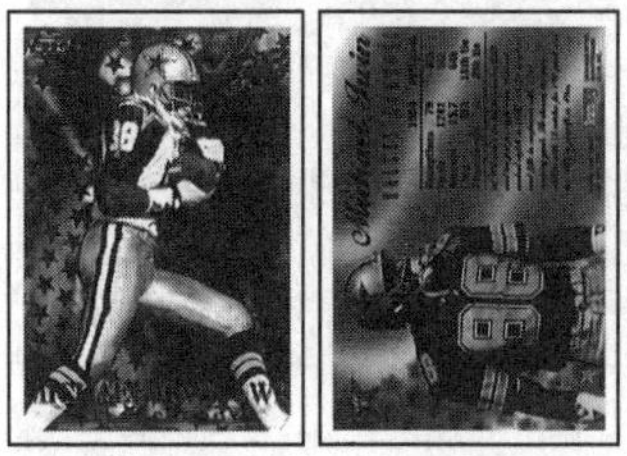

Randomly inserted at a rate of one in eight series two hobby packs, this 22 card set features some the the games best. Card fronts have an all silver foil background with stars and feature a shot of the player with his name, position and team at the bottom. Card backs are horizontal with the player's name and team and some statistical summary. Cards are numbered with an "AP" prefix.

	MINT	NRMT	EXC
COMPLETE SET (22)	30.00	13.50	3.70
COMMON CARD (1-22)	1.00	.45	.12
☐ 1 Jerry Rice	5.00	2.20	.60
☐ 2 Lomas Brown	1.00	.45	.12
☐ 3 Nate Newton	1.00	.45	.12
☐ 4 Dermontti Dawson	1.00	.45	.12
☐ 5 Keith Sims	1.00	.45	.12
☐ 6 Richmond Webb	1.00	.45	.12
☐ 7 Shannon Sharpe	1.50	.70	.19
☐ 8 Michael Irvin	1.50	.70	.19
☐ 9 Steve Young	3.00	1.35	.35
☐ 10 Barry Sanders	5.00	2.20	.60
☐ 11 Marshall Faulk	2.00	.90	.25
☐ 12 Bruce Smith	1.50	.70	.19
☐ 13 Dana Stubblefield	1.00	.45	.12
☐ 14 John Randle	1.00	.45	.12
☐ 15 Reggie White	1.50	.70	.19
☐ 16 Greg Lloyd	1.50	.70	.19
☐ 17 Junior Seau	1.50	.70	.19
☐ 18 Cornelius Bennett	1.00	.45	.12
☐ 19 Rod Woodson	1.50	.70	.19
☐ 20 Deion Sanders	2.50	1.10	.30
☐ 21 Darren Woodson	1.00	.45	.12
☐ 22 Merton Hanks	1.00	.45	.12

1995 Topps Expansion Team Boosters

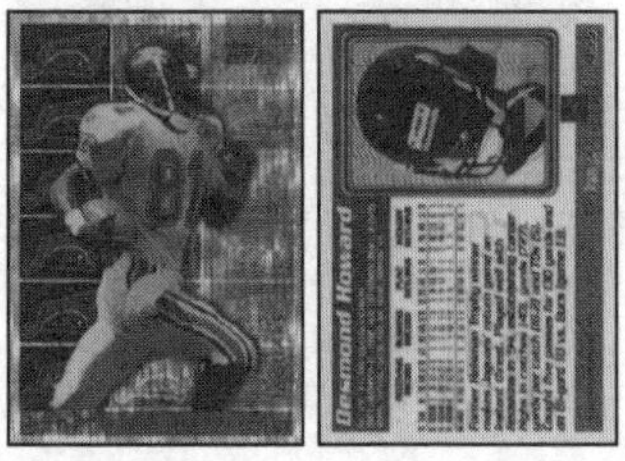

This 20 card set was randomly inserted in series two packs at a rate of one in 36 and is a parallel version of the expansion team subset in series two. The cards are printed on 28-point stock and feature a diffraction foil front.

	MINT	NRMT	EXC
COMPLETE SET (30)	80.00	36.00	10.00
COMMON CARD (437-466)	2.00	.90	.25
☐ 437 Derrick Graham	2.00	.90	.25
☐ 438 Vernon Turner	2.00	.90	.25
☐ 439 Carlton Bailey	2.00	.90	.25
☐ 440 Darion Conner	2.00	.90	.25
☐ 441 Randy Baldwin	2.00	.90	.25
☐ 442 Tim McKyer	2.00	.90	.25
☐ 443 Sam Mills	5.00	2.20	.60
☐ 444 Bob Christian	3.50	1.55	.45
☐ 445 Steve Lofton	2.00	.90	.25
☐ 446 Lamar Lathon	2.00	.90	.25
☐ 447 Tony Smith RB	2.00	.90	.25
☐ 448 Don Beebe	3.50	1.55	.45
☐ 449 Barry Foster	3.50	1.55	.45
☐ 450 Frank Reich	3.50	1.55	.45
☐ 451 Pete Metzelaars	2.00	.90	.25
☐ 452 Reggie Cobb	2.00	.90	.25
☐ 453 Jeff Lageman	2.00	.90	.25
☐ 454 Derek Brown TE	2.00	.90	.25
☐ 455 Desmond Howard	5.00	2.20	.60
☐ 456 Vinnie Clark	2.00	.90	.25
☐ 457 Keith Goganious	2.00	.90	.25
☐ 458 Shawn Bowens	2.00	.90	.25
☐ 459 Rob Johnson	3.50	1.55	.45
☐ 460 Steve Beuerlein	3.50	1.55	.45
☐ 461 Mark Brunell	20.00	9.00	2.50
☐ 462 Harry Colon	2.00	.90	.25
☐ 463 Chris Hudson	2.00	.90	.25
☐ 464 Darren Carrington	2.00	.90	.25
☐ 465 Ernest Givins	3.50	1.55	.45
☐ 466 Kelvin Pritchett	2.00	.90	.25

1995 Topps Finest Boosters

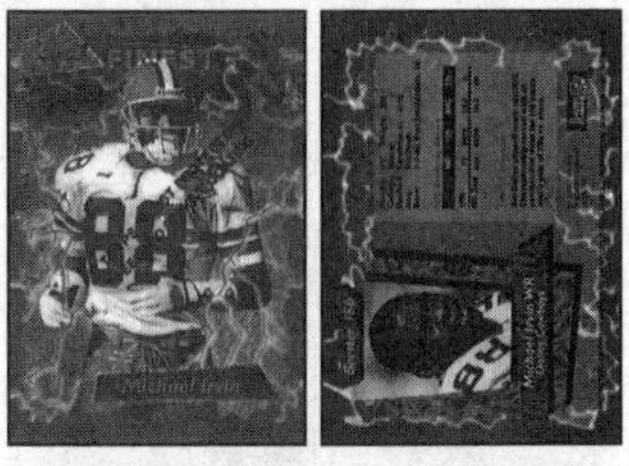

This 22 card set was randomly inserted into series two packs at a rate of one in 36 and utilizes the same design as the 1995 Finest set with players not found in series 1. Card fronts feature a blue background with white lightning. Card backs feature a headshot with biographical and statistical information. Cards are numbered with a "Booster" prefix. The set also has a refractor parallel, randomly inserted into packs at a rate of one in 36 hobby packs and one in 432 retail packs. These cards have a refractive foil front and the letter "R" located in black in the lower left corner.

	MINT	NRMT	EXC
COMPLETE SET (22)	100.00	45.00	12.50
COMMON CARD (B166-B187)	2.00	.90	.25
COMP.REFRACTOR SET (22)	200.00	90.00	25.00
*REFRACTORS: 1.25X to 2X BASIC CARDS			
☐ B166 Barry Sanders	10.00	4.50	1.25
☐ B167 Bryant Young	2.00	.90	.25
☐ B168 Boomer Esiason	2.00	.90	.25
☐ B169 Terance Mathis	2.00	.90	.25
☐ B170 Troy Aikman	10.00	4.50	1.25
☐ B171 Junior Seau	3.00	1.35	.35
☐ B172 Rodney Hampton	2.00	.90	.25
☐ B173 Jim Everett	2.00	.90	.25
☐ B174 Dan Marino	20.00	9.00	2.50
☐ B175 Steve Young	8.00	3.60	1.00
☐ B176 Cris Carter	3.00	1.35	.35
☐ B177 Eric Swann	2.00	.90	.25
☐ B178 Rick Mirer	3.00	1.35	.35
☐ B179 Jerome Bettis	3.00	1.35	.35
☐ B180 Emmitt Smith	20.00	9.00	2.50
☐ B181 Jim Kelly	3.00	1.35	.35
☐ B182 John Elway	8.00	3.60	1.00
☐ B183 Dana Stubblefield	3.00	1.35	.35
☐ B184 Drew Bledsoe	10.00	4.50	1.25
☐ B185 Jerry Rice	10.00	4.50	1.25
☐ B186 Michael Irvin	3.00	1.35	.35
☐ B187 Bruce Smith	3.00	1.35	.35

1995 Topps Finest Inserts

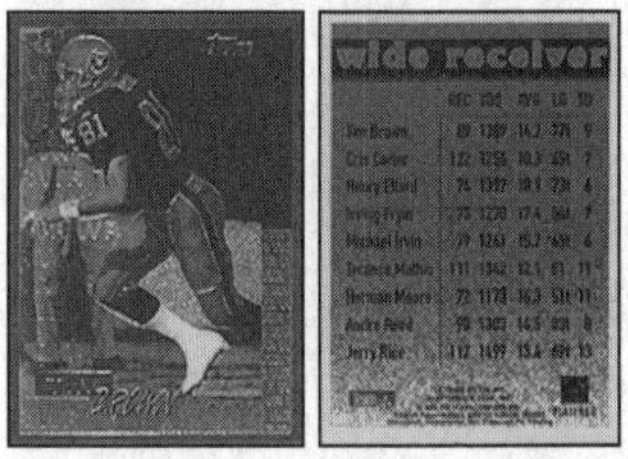

This 27 card standard-size set features leading NFL players. These cards were inserted at the rate of one in 36. A new twist to these cards is that to identify the player, the collector needs to peel off the protector to see what player they obtained out of the pack. This set features nine quarterbacks, running backs and receivers. An instant winner card for the complete set along with clear Finest protectors are included one in 1980 packs. There is a refractor parallel to this set. These cards are also included one in 36 hobby packs, but only one in 432 retail packs.

	MINT	NRMT	EXC
COMPLETE SET (27)	80.00	36.00	10.00
COMMON CARD (1-27)	1.25	.55	.16
COMP.REFRACTOR SET (27)	250.00	110.00	31.00
*REFRACTORS: 1.25X to 2.5X BASIC CARDS			
☐ 1 Troy Aikman	7.00	3.10	.85
☐ 2 Jerome Bettis	2.00	.90	.25
☐ 3 Drew Bledsoe	7.00	3.10	.85
☐ 4 Tim Brown	1.25	.55	.16
☐ 5 Cris Carter	1.25	.55	.16
☐ 6 Henry Ellard	1.25	.55	.16
☐ 7 John Elway	5.00	2.20	.60
☐ 8 Marshall Faulk	3.00	1.35	.35
☐ 9 Brett Favre	14.00	6.25	1.75
☐ 10 Irving Fryar	1.25	.55	.16

	MINT	NRMT	EXC
☐ 11 Rodney Hampton	1.25	.55	.16
☐ 12 Stan Humphries	1.25	.55	.16
☐ 13 Michael Irvin	2.00	.90	.25
☐ 14 Jim Kelly	2.00	.90	.25
☐ 15 Dan Marino	14.00	6.25	1.75
☐ 16 Terance Mathis	1.25	.55	.16
☐ 17 Natrone Means	2.00	.90	.25
☐ 18 Warren Moon	1.25	.55	.16
☐ 19 Herman Moore	3.00	1.35	.35
☐ 20 Andre Reed	1.25	.55	.16
☐ 21 Errict Rhett	2.00	.90	.25
☐ 22 Jerry Rice	7.00	3.10	.85
☐ 23 Barry Sanders	7.00	3.10	.85
☐ 24 Emmitt Smith	14.00	6.25	1.75
☐ 25 Chris Warren	1.25	.55	.16
☐ 26 Ricky Watters	1.25	.55	.16
☐ 27 Steve Young	5.00	2.20	.60
☐ NNO Set Redemption	.25	.11	.03

1995 Topps Florida Hot Bed

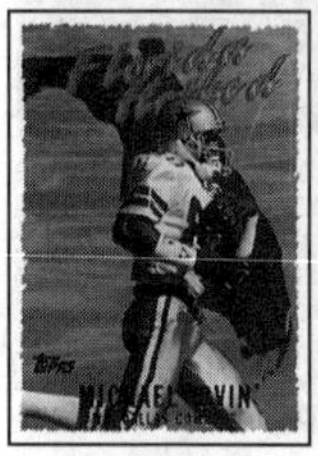
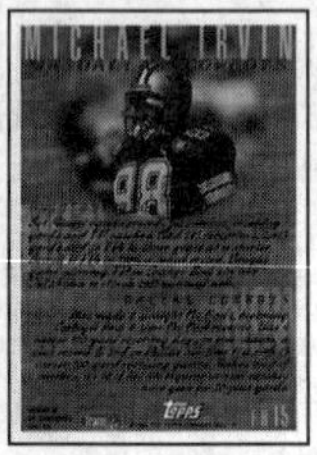

This 15 card set was randomly inserted into special retail packs at one per pack and features NFL stars who played for a college in the state of Florida. Card fronts feature a map shot of Florida in the background with the card name "Florida Hotbed" in orange at the top. The player's name and team are in gold foil at the bottom. Card backs feature a blue water background with a headshot and a brief commentary on the player's college and NFL information. Card backs are numbered with a "FH" prefix.

	MINT	NRMT	EXC
COMPLETE SET (15)	30.00	13.50	3.70
COMMON CARD (FH1-FH15)	1.25	.55	.16
☐ FH1 Deion Sanders	4.00	1.80	.50
☐ FH2 Brian Blades	1.25	.55	.16
☐ FH3 Errict Rhett	2.00	.90	.25
☐ FH4 Kevin Williams	1.25	.55	.16
☐ FH5 Cortez Kennedy	1.25	.55	.16
☐ FH6 Corey Sawyer	1.25	.55	.16
☐ FH7 Russell Maryland	1.25	.55	.16
☐ FH8 Emmitt Smith	10.00	4.50	1.25
☐ FH9 Vinny Testaverde	1.25	.55	.16
☐ FH10 William Floyd	2.00	.90	.25
☐ FH11 Brett Perriman	1.25	.55	.16
☐ FH12 Nate Newton	1.25	.55	.16
☐ FH13 Jim Kelly	2.00	.90	.25
☐ FH14 LeRoy Butler	1.25	.55	.16
☐ FH15 Michael Irvin	2.00	.90	.25

1995 Topps Hit List

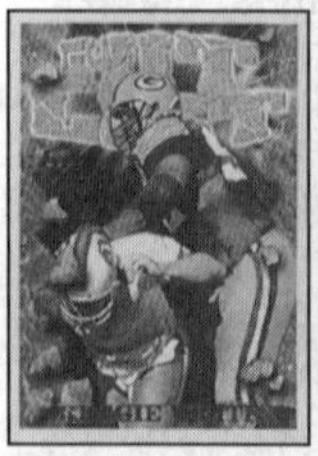
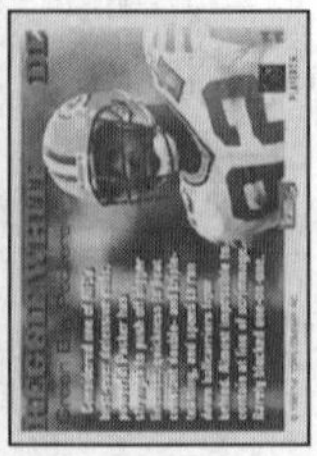

This 20-card standard-size set was randomly inserted one in four foil packs. Leading defensive players are featured in this set. The fronts feature an action player photo. The words "Hit List" are in yellow lettering on the top while the player is identified in gold foil on the bottom of the card. The horizontal backs contain player information as well as a photo.

	MINT	NRMT	EXC
COMPLETE SET (20)	6.00	2.70	.75
COMMON CARD (1-20)	.20	.09	.03
☐ 1 Pepper Johnson	.20	.09	.03
☐ 2 Elijah Alexander	.20	.09	.03
☐ 3 Joe Cain	.20	.09	.03
☐ 4 Andre Collins	.20	.09	.03
☐ 5 Chris Spielman	.40	.18	.05
☐ 6 Bryan Cox	.20	.09	.03
☐ 7 Ed McDaniel	.20	.09	.03
☐ 8 Jack Del Rio	.20	.09	.03
☐ 9 Jeff Herrod	.20	.09	.03
☐ 10 Greg Lloyd	.75	.35	.09
☐ 11 Reggie White	.75	.35	.09
☐ 12 Robert Jones	.20	.09	.03
☐ 13 Eric Turner	.40	.18	.05
☐ 14 Vincent Brown	.20	.09	.03
☐ 15 Kevin Greene	.75	.35	.09
☐ 16 Bruce Smith	.75	.35	.09
☐ 17 Hardy Nickerson UER	.40	.18	.05
☐ 18 Seth Joyner	.20	.09	.03
☐ 19 Darryl Talley	.20	.09	.03
☐ 20 Junior Seau	.75	.35	.09

1995 Topps 1000/3000 Boosters

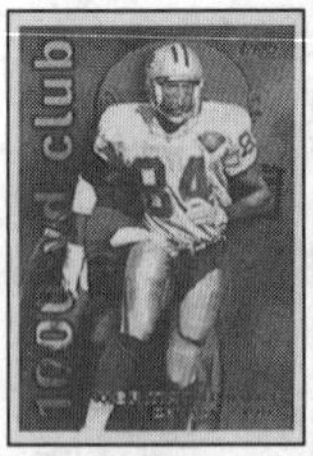
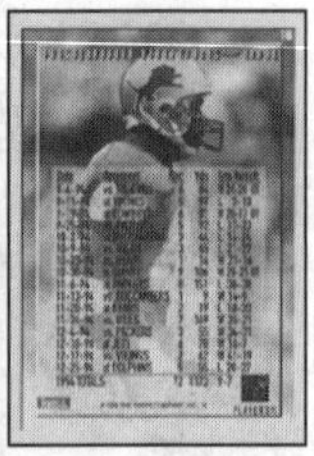

This 41 card standard-size set was randomly inserted into packs at a rate of one in 36. This set is a parallel to the first 41 cards in the 1995 Topps set which features players who ran or caught passes for 1,000 yards or threw for 3,000 yards in the 1994 season. These cards are printed on thicker stock than the regular issue cards and feature prismatic foil printing.

	MINT	NRMT	EXC
COMPLETE SET (41)	150.00	70.00	19.00
COMMON CARD (1-41)	2.00	.90	.25
☐ 1 Barry Sanders	10.00	4.50	1.25
☐ 2 Chris Warren	3.00	1.35	.35
☐ 3 Jerry Rice	10.00	4.50	1.25
☐ 4 Emmitt Smith	20.00	9.00	2.50
☐ 5 Henry Ellard	2.00	.90	.25
☐ 6 Natrone Means	3.00	1.35	.35
☐ 7 Terance Mathis	2.00	.90	.25
☐ 8 Tim Brown	3.00	1.35	.35
☐ 9 Andre Reed	2.00	.90	.25
☐ 10 Marshall Faulk	5.00	2.20	.60
☐ 11 Irving Fryar	2.00	.90	.25
☐ 12 Cris Carter	3.00	1.35	.35
☐ 13 Michael Irvin	3.50	1.55	.45
☐ 14 Jake Reed	2.00	.90	.25
☐ 15 Ben Coates	3.00	1.35	.35
☐ 16 Herman Moore	4.00	1.80	.50
☐ 17 Carl Pickens	3.00	1.35	.35
☐ 18 Fred Barnett	2.00	.90	.25
☐ 19 Sterling Sharpe	2.00	.90	.25
☐ 20 Anthony Miller	2.00	.90	.25
☐ 21 Thurman Thomas	3.50	1.55	.45
☐ 22 Andre Rison	2.00	.90	.25
☐ 23 Brian Blades	2.00	.90	.25
☐ 24 Rodney Hampton	2.00	.90	.25
☐ 25 Terry Allen	3.00	1.35	.35
☐ 26 Jerome Bettis	3.50	1.55	.45
☐ 27 Errict Rhett	3.00	1.35	.35
☐ 28 Rob Moore	2.00	.90	.25
☐ 29 Shannon Sharpe	3.00	1.35	.35
☐ 30 Drew Bledsoe	10.00	4.50	1.25
☐ 31 Dan Marino	20.00	9.00	2.50
☐ 32 Warren Moon	3.00	1.35	.35
☐ 33 Steve Young	8.00	3.60	1.00
☐ 34 Brett Favre	20.00	9.00	2.50
☐ 35 Jim Everett	2.00	.90	.25
☐ 36 Jeff George	2.00	.90	.25
☐ 37 John Elway	8.00	3.60	1.00
☐ 38 Jeff Hostetler	2.00	.90	.25
☐ 39 Randall Cunningham	2.00	.90	.25
☐ 40 Stan Humphries	2.00	.90	.25
☐ 41 Jim Kelly	3.50	1.55	.45

1995 Topps Profiles

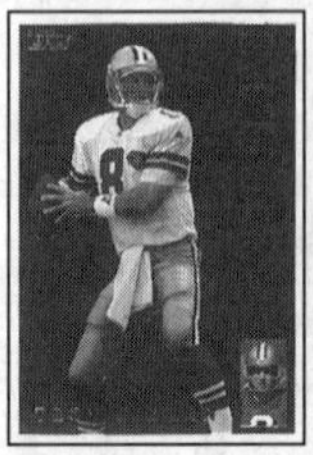
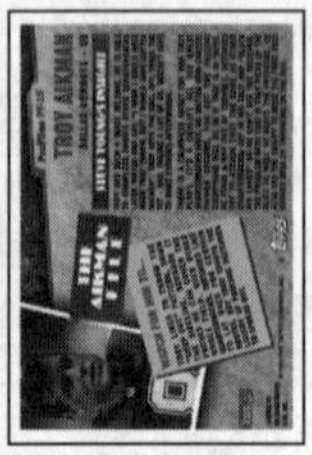

Randomly inserted into series 2 packs at a rate of one in 12, this 15 card set features a bordered silver foil background. Card fronts feature a shot of the player with his name in gold foil at the bottom and the card title "Profiles" running along the right. A headshot of Steve Young is also featured on the lower right side of each card. Card backs are horizontal with a headshot and a commentary on the player by Steve Young. Cards are numbered with a "PF" prefix.

	MINT	NRMT	EXC
COMPLETE SET (15)	40.00	18.00	5.00
COMMON CARD (1-15)	1.25	.55	.16
☐ 1 Emmitt Smith	10.00	4.50	1.25
☐ 2 Chris Spielman	1.25	.55	.16
☐ 3 Rod Woodson	2.00	.90	.25
☐ 4 Deion Sanders	4.00	1.80	.50
☐ 5 Junior Seau	2.00	.90	.25
☐ 6 Byron Evans	1.25	.55	.16
☐ 7 Jerome Bettis	2.00	.90	.25
☐ 8 Charles Haley	1.25	.55	.16
☐ 9 Jerry Rice	6.00	2.70	.75
☐ 10 Barry Sanders	6.00	2.70	.75
☐ 11 Hardy Nickerson	1.25	.55	.16
☐ 12 Natrone Means	2.00	.90	.25
☐ 13 Darren Woodson	1.25	.55	.16
☐ 14 Reggie White	2.00	.90	.25
☐ 15 Troy Aikman	6.00	2.70	.75

1995 Topps Sensational Sophomores

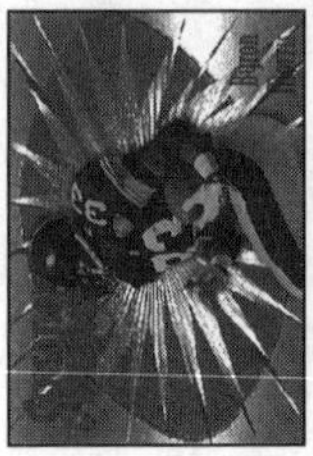
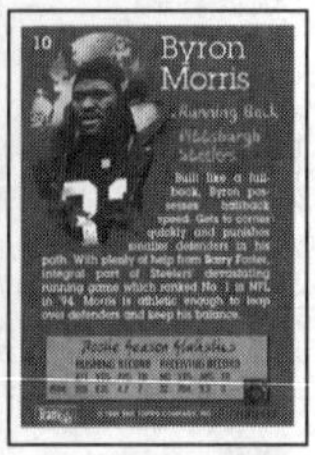

This 10 card standard-size set was randomly inserted in retail packs at a rate of one in 24 and feature 10 of the hottest 1994 rookies. Using Dot Matrix technology, card fronts have a etched football along a blue foil background. The card title "Sensational Sophomores" is in red at the top left of the card and the player's name is in purple at the lower right. Card backs are vertical with a red background and a commentary on the player. Rookie season statistics are located at the bottom of the card.

	MINT	NRMT	EXC
COMPLETE SET (10)	18.00	8.00	2.20
COMMON CARD (1-10)	1.50	.70	.19
☐ 1 Marshall Faulk	5.00	2.20	.60
☐ 2 Heath Shuler	2.50	1.10	.30
☐ 3 Tim Bowens	1.50	.70	.19
☐ 4 Bryant Young	1.50	.70	.19
☐ 5 Dan Wilkinson	1.50	.70	.19
☐ 6 Errict Rhett	2.50	1.10	.30
☐ 7 Andre Coleman	1.50	.70	.19
☐ 8 Aaron Glenn	1.50	.70	.19
☐ 9 Trent Dilfer	2.50	1.10	.30
☐ 10 Byron Bam Morris	2.50	1.10	.30

1995 Topps Yesteryear

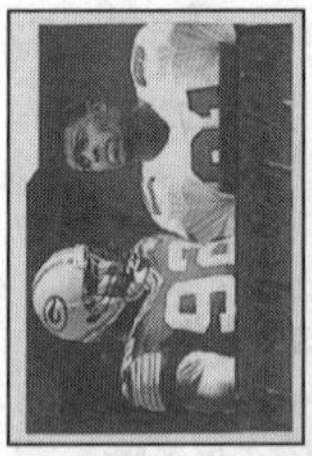
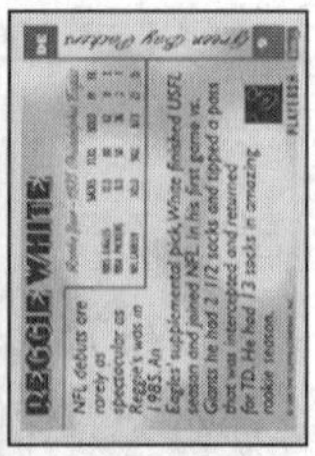

This 15-card standard-size set features leading NFL players and were inserted at a rate of one in 72 hobby packs. These cards, featuring both early career and current photos, were printed using the "Finest" technology. Card backs feature a statistical summary that compares the players rookie year to the past season and a brief commentary.

	MINT	NRMT	EXC
COMPLETE SET (15)	60.00	27.00	7.50
COMMON CARD (1-15)	1.50	.70	.19
☐ 1 Stan Humphries	1.50	.70	.19
☐ 2 Dan Marino	16.00	7.25	2.00
☐ 3 Irving Fryar	1.50	.70	.19
☐ 4 Warren Moon	3.00	1.35	.35
☐ 5 Steve Young	6.00	2.70	.75
☐ 6 Kevin Greene	1.50	.70	.19
☐ 7 Jeff Hostetler	1.50	.70	.19
☐ 8 Jack Del Rio	1.50	.70	.19
☐ 9 Reggie White	3.00	1.35	.35
☐ 10 Jerry Rice	8.00	3.60	1.00
☐ 11 Bruce Smith	3.00	1.35	.35
☐ 12 Rod Woodson	3.00	1.35	.35
☐ 13 Deion Sanders	5.00	2.20	.60
☐ 14 Barry Sanders	8.00	3.60	1.00
☐ 15 Brett Favre	16.00	7.25	2.00

1995 Topps Factory Jaguars

Topps released to the hobby complete factory sets as a parallel of its regualr issue 1995 Topps cards featuring a Jacksonville Jaguars foil stamped logo on every card. The factory set also included five random Jaguars Expansion Team Booster inserts. A Carolina Panthers version was produced in the same fashion. Reportedly, the cards were limited to 4000 sets for each expansion team.

	MINT	NRMT	EXC
COMPLETE FACT.SET (473)	50.00	22.00	6.25
COMMON CARD (1-468)	.10	.05	.01

*VETERAN STARS: .75X TO 1.5X BASIC CARDS
*YOUNG STARS/RCs: .6X TO 1.25X BASIC CARDS

1995 Topps Factory Panthers

Topps released to the hobby complete factory sets as a parallel of its regualr issue 1995 Topps cards featuring a Carolina Panthers foil stamped logo on every card. The factory set also included five random Panthers Expansion Team Booster inserts. A Jacksonville Jaguars version was produced in the same fashion. Reportedly, the sets were limited to 4000 sets for each expansion team.

	MINT	NRMT	EXC
COMPLETE FACT.SET (473)	50.00	22.00	6.25
COMMON CARD (1-468)	.10	.05	.01

*VETERAN STARS: .75X TO 1.5X BASIC CARDS
*YOUNG STARS/RCs: .6X TO 1.25X BASIC CARDS

1996 Topps

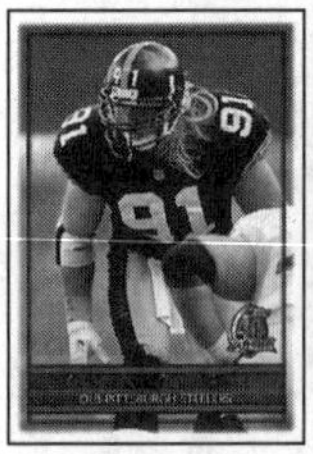
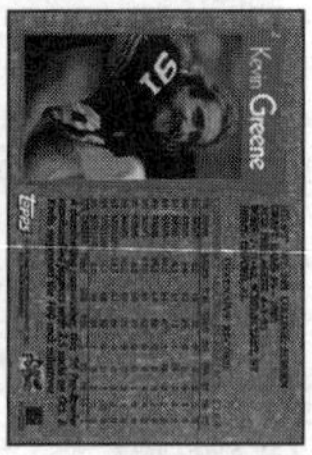

The 1996 Topps set was issued in one series totaling 440 standard-size cards. The 11-card hobby and retail foil packs carried a suggested retail price of $1.29 each. The packs were issued in 12-box foil cases which contained 36 packs in a box. Jumbo packs were also issued, these packs were in 8 box cases with 12 boxes per case and 39 cards per pack. The set contained the topical subsets: 1000 Yard Club (121-136/241-263) and 3000 Yard Club (371-386). Rookie Cards include Tim Biakabutuka, Eddie George, Marvin Harrison, Keyshawn Johnson, Leeland McLeroy, Eric Moulds and Lawrence Phillips. Topps produced a special promo card for the 1996 National Sports Collector's Convention. It featured Joe Namath and Steve Young printed in Finest technology.

	MINT	NRMT	EXC
COMPLETE SET (440)	35.00	16.00	4.40
COMP.FACT.SET (448)	40.00	18.00	5.00
COMP.CEREAL FACT.SET (445)	40.00	18.00	5.00
COMMON CARD (1-440)	.05	.02	.01
☐ 1 Troy Aikman	1.00	.45	.12
☐ 2 Kevin Greene	.10	.05	.01
☐ 3 Robert Brooks	.20	.09	.03
☐ 4 Eugene Daniel	.05	.02	.01
☐ 5 Rodney Peete	.05	.02	.01
☐ 6 James Hasty	.05	.02	.01
☐ 7 Tim McDonald	.05	.02	.01
☐ 8 Darick Holmes	.10	.05	.01
☐ 9 Morten Andersen	.05	.02	.01
☐ 10 Junior Seau	.20	.09	.03
☐ 11 Brett Perriman	.10	.05	.01
☐ 12 Eric Green	.05	.02	.01
☐ 13 Jim Flanigan	.05	.02	.01
☐ 14 Cortez Kennedy	.10	.05	.01
☐ 15 Orlando Thomas	.05	.02	.01
☐ 16 Anthony Miller	.10	.05	.01
☐ 17 Sean Gilbert	.05	.02	.01
☐ 18 Rob Fredrickson	.05	.02	.01
☐ 19 Willie Green	.05	.02	.01
☐ 20 Jeff Blake	.20	.09	.03
☐ 21 Trent Dilfer	.10	.05	.01
☐ 22 Chris Chandler	.10	.05	.01
☐ 23 Renaldo Turnbull	.05	.02	.01
☐ 24 Dave Meggett	.05	.02	.01
☐ 25 Heath Shuler	.20	.09	.03
☐ 26 Michael Jackson	.10	.05	.01
☐ 27 Thomas Randolph	.05	.02	.01
☐ 28 Keith Goganious	.05	.02	.01
☐ 29 Seth Joyner	.05	.02	.01
☐ 30 Wayne Chrebet	.10	.05	.01
☐ 31 Craig Newsome	.05	.02	.01
☐ 32 William Fuller	.05	.02	.01
☐ 33 Merton Hanks	.05	.02	.01
☐ 34 Dale Carter	.05	.02	.01
☐ 35 Quentin Coryatt	.05	.02	.01
☐ 36 Robert Jones	.05	.02	.01
☐ 37 Eric Metcalf	.10	.05	.01
☐ 38 Byron Bam Morris	.10	.05	.01
☐ 39 Bill Brooks	.05	.02	.01
☐ 40 Barry Sanders	1.00	.45	.12
☐ 41 Michael Haynes	.10	.05	.01
☐ 42 Joey Galloway	.40	.18	.05
☐ 43 Robert Smith	.10	.05	.01
☐ 44 John Thierry	.05	.02	.01
☐ 45 Bryan Cox	.05	.02	.01
☐ 46 Anthony Parker	.05	.02	.01
☐ 47 Harvey Williams	.05	.02	.01
☐ 48 Terrell Davis	1.50	.70	.19
☐ 49 Darnay Scott	.10	.05	.01
☐ 50 Kerry Collins	1.25	.55	.16
☐ 51 Cris Dishman	.05	.02	.01

□ 52 Dwayne Harper	.05	.02	.01
□ 53 Warren Sapp	.05	.02	.01
□ 54 Will Moore	.05	.02	.01
□ 55 Earnest Byner	.05	.02	.01
□ 56 Aaron Glenn	.05	.02	.01
□ 57 Michael Westbrook	.20	.09	.03
□ 58 Vencie Glenn	.05	.02	.01
□ 59 Rob Moore	.05	.02	.01
□ 60 Mark Brunell	1.00	.45	.12
□ 61 Craig Heyward	.05	.02	.01
□ 62 Eric Allen	.05	.02	.01
□ 63 Bill Romanowski	.05	.02	.01
□ 64 Dana Stubblefield	.10	.05	.01
□ 65 Steve Bono	.10	.05	.01
□ 66 George Koonce	.05	.02	.01
□ 67 Larry Brown	.05	.02	.01
□ 68 Warren Moon	.10	.05	.01
□ 69 Erric Pegram	.10	.05	.01
□ 70 Jim Kelly	.20	.09	.03
□ 71 Jason Belser	.05	.02	.01
□ 72 Henry Thomas	.05	.02	.01
□ 73 Mark Carrier	.05	.02	.01
□ 74 Terry Wooden	.05	.02	.01
□ 75 Terry McDaniel	.05	.02	.01
□ 76 O.J. McDuffie	.10	.05	.01
□ 77 Dan Wilkinson	.05	.02	.01
□ 78 Blake Brockermeyer	.05	.02	.01
□ 79 Micheal Barrow	.05	.02	.01
□ 80 Dave Brown	.10	.05	.01
□ 81 Todd Lyght	.05	.02	.01
□ 82 Henry Ellard	.10	.05	.01
□ 83 Jeff Lageman	.05	.02	.01
□ 84 Anthony Pleasant	.05	.02	.01
□ 85 Aeneas Williams	.05	.02	.01
□ 86 Vincent Brisby	.05	.02	.01
□ 87 Terrell Fletcher	.05	.02	.01
□ 88 Brad Baxter	.05	.02	.01
□ 89 Shannon Sharpe	.10	.05	.01
□ 90 Errict Rhett	.10	.05	.01
□ 91 Michael Zordich	.05	.02	.01
□ 92 Dan Saleaumua	.05	.02	.01
□ 93 Devin Bush	.05	.02	.01
□ 94 Wayne Simmons	.05	.02	.01
□ 95 Tyrone Hughes	.05	.02	.01
□ 96 John Randle	.05	.02	.01
□ 97 Tony Tolbert	.05	.02	.01
□ 98 Yancey Thigpen	.10	.05	.01
□ 99 J.J. Stokes	.20	.09	.03
□ 100 Marshall Faulk	.20	.09	.03
□ 101 Barry Minter	.05	.02	.01
□ 102 Glenn Foley	.05	.02	.01
□ 103 Chester McGlockton	.05	.02	.01
□ 104 Carlton Gray	.05	.02	.01
□ 105 Terry Kirby	.10	.05	.01
□ 106 Darryll Lewis	.05	.02	.01
□ 107 Thomas Smith	.05	.02	.01
□ 108 Mike Fox	.05	.02	.01
□ 109 Antonio Langham	.05	.02	.01
□ 110 Drew Bledsoe	1.00	.45	.12
□ 111 Troy Drayton	.05	.02	.01
□ 112 Marvcus Patton	.05	.02	.01
□ 113 Tyrone Wheatley	.10	.05	.01
□ 114 Desmond Howard	.10	.05	.01
□ 115 Johnny Mitchell	.05	.02	.01
□ 116 Dave Krieg	.05	.02	.01
□ 117 Natrone Means	.20	.09	.03
□ 118 Herman Moore	.20	.09	.03
□ 119 Darren Woodson	.10	.05	.01
□ 120 Ricky Watters	.10	.05	.01
□ 121 Emmitt Smith TYC	1.00	.45	.12
□ 122 Barry Sanders TYC	.50	.23	.06
□ 123 Curtis Martin TYC	.75	.35	.09
□ 124 Chris Warren TYC	.10	.05	.01
□ 125 Terry Allen TYC	.10	.05	.01
□ 126 Ricky Watters TYC	.10	.05	.01
□ 127 Errict Rhett TYC	.10	.05	.01
□ 128 Rodney Hampton TYC	.05	.02	.01
□ 129 Terrell Davis TYC	.75	.35	.09
□ 130 Harvey Williams TYC	.05	.02	.01
□ 131 Craig Heyward TYC	.05	.02	.01
□ 132 Marshall Faulk TYC	.10	.05	.01
□ 133 Rashaan Salaam TYC	.20	.09	.03
□ 134 Garrison Hearst TYC	.10	.05	.01
□ 135 Edgar Bennett TYC	.10	.05	.01
□ 136 Thurman Thomas TYC	.10	.05	.01
□ 137 Brian Washington	.05	.02	.01
□ 138 Derek Loville	.05	.02	.01
□ 139 Curtis Conway	.20	.09	.03
□ 140 Isaac Bruce	.20	.09	.03
□ 141 Ricardo McDonald	.05	.02	.01
□ 142 Bruce Armstrong	.05	.02	.01
□ 143 Will Wolford	.05	.02	.01
□ 144 Thurman Thomas	.20	.09	.03
□ 145 Mel Gray	.05	.02	.01
□ 146 Napoleon Kaufman	.10	.05	.01
□ 147 Terry Allen	.10	.05	.01
□ 148 Chris Calloway	.05	.02	.01
□ 149 Harry Colon	.05	.02	.01
□ 150 Pepper Johnson	.05	.02	.01
□ 151 Marco Coleman	.05	.02	.01
□ 152 Shawn Jefferson	.05	.02	.01
□ 153 Larry Centers	.10	.05	.01
□ 154 Lamar Lathon	.05	.02	.01
□ 155 Mark Chmura	.10	.05	.01
□ 156 Dermontti Dawson	.05	.02	.01
□ 157 Alvin Harper	.05	.02	.01
□ 158 Randall McDaniel	.05	.02	.01
□ 159 Allen Aldridge	.05	.02	.01
□ 160 Chris Warren	.10	.05	.01
□ 161 Jessie Tuggle	.05	.02	.01
□ 162 Sean Lumpkin	.05	.02	.01
□ 163 Bobby Houston	.05	.02	.01
□ 164 Dexter Carter	.05	.02	.01
□ 165 Erik Kramer	.05	.02	.01
□ 166 Brock Marion	.05	.02	.01
□ 167 Toby Wright	.05	.02	.01
□ 168 John Copeland	.05	.02	.01
□ 169 Sean Dawkins	.05	.02	.01
□ 170 Tim Brown	.10	.05	.01
□ 171 Darion Conner	.05	.02	.01
□ 172 Aaron Hayden	.10	.05	.01
□ 173 Charlie Garner	.05	.02	.01
□ 174 Anthony Cook	.05	.02	.01
□ 175 Derrick Thomas	.10	.05	.01
□ 176 Willie McGinest	.05	.02	.01
□ 177 Thomas Lewis	.05	.02	.01
□ 178 Sherman Williams	.05	.02	.01
□ 179 Cornelius Bennett	.10	.05	.01
□ 180 Frank Sanders	.10	.05	.01
□ 181 Leroy Hoard	.05	.02	.01
□ 182 Bernie Parmalee	.05	.02	.01
□ 183 Sterling Palmer	.05	.02	.01
□ 184 Kelvin Pritchett	.05	.02	.01
□ 185 Kordell Stewart	1.25	.55	.16
□ 186 Brent Jones	.05	.02	.01
□ 187 Robert Blackmon	.05	.02	.01
□ 188 Adrian Murrell	.10	.05	.01
□ 189 Edgar Bennett	.10	.05	.01
□ 190 Rashaan Salaam	.20	.09	.03
□ 191 Ellis Johnson	.05	.02	.01
□ 192 Andre Coleman	.05	.02	.01
□ 193 Will Shields	.05	.02	.01
□ 194 Derrick Brooks	.05	.02	.01
□ 195 Carl Pickens	.20	.09	.03
□ 196 Carlton Bailey	.05	.02	.01
□ 197 Terance Mathis	.05	.02	.01
□ 198 Carlos Jenkins	.05	.02	.01
□ 199 Derrick Alexander DE	.20	.09	.03
□ 200 Deion Sanders	.60	.25	.07
□ 201 Glyn Milburn	.05	.02	.01
□ 202 Chris Sanders	.10	.05	.01
□ 203 Rocket Ismail	.10	.05	.01
□ 204 Fred Barnett	.10	.05	.01
□ 205 Quinn Early	.05	.02	.01
□ 206 Henry Jones	.05	.02	.01
□ 207 Herschel Walker	.10	.05	.01
□ 208 James Washington	.05	.02	.01
□ 209 Lee Woodall	.05	.02	.01
□ 210 Neil Smith	.10	.05	.01
□ 211 Tony Bennett	.05	.02	.01
□ 212 Ernie Mills	.05	.02	.01
□ 213 Clyde Simmons	.05	.02	.01
□ 214 Chris Slade	.05	.02	.01
□ 215 Tony Boselli	.10	.05	.01
□ 216 Ryan McNeil	.05	.02	.01
□ 217 Rob Burnett	.05	.02	.01
□ 218 Stan Humphries	.10	.05	.01
□ 219 Rick Mirer	.10	.05	.01
□ 220 Troy Vincent	.05	.02	.01
□ 221 Sean Jones	.05	.02	.01
□ 222 Marty Carter	.05	.02	.01
□ 223 Boomer Esiason	.10	.05	.01
□ 224 Charles Haley	.10	.05	.01
□ 225 Sam Mills	.10	.05	.01
□ 226 Greg Biekert	.05	.02	.01
□ 227 Bryant Young	.10	.05	.01
□ 228 Ken Dilger	.10	.05	.01
□ 229 Levon Kirkland	.05	.02	.01
□ 230 Brian Mitchell	.05	.02	.01
□ 231 Hardy Nickerson	.05	.02	.01
□ 232 Elvis Grbac	.20	.09	.03
□ 233 Kurt Schulz	.05	.02	.01
□ 234 Chris Doleman	.05	.02	.01
□ 235 Tamarick Vanover	.20	.09	.03
□ 236 Jesse Campbell	.05	.02	.01
□ 237 William Thomas	.05	.02	.01
□ 238 Shane Conlan	.05	.02	.01
□ 239 Jason Elam	.05	.02	.01
□ 240 Steve McNair	1.00	.45	.12
□ 241 Jerry Rice TYC	.50	.23	.06
□ 242 Isaac Bruce TYC	.20	.09	.03
□ 243 Herman Moore TYC	.20	.09	.03
□ 244 Michael Irvin TYC	.10	.05	.01
□ 245 Robert Brooks TYC	.20	.09	.03
□ 246 Brett Perriman TYC	.10	.05	.01
□ 247 Cris Carter TYC	.20	.09	.03
□ 248 Tim Brown TYC	.10	.05	.01
□ 249 Yancey Thigpen TYC	.10	.05	.01
□ 250 Jeff Graham TYC	.05	.02	.01
□ 251 Carl Pickens TYC	.20	.09	.03
□ 252 Tony Martin TYC	.05	.02	.01
□ 253 Eric Metcalf TYC	.10	.05	.01
□ 254 Jake Reed TYC	.10	.05	.01
□ 255 Quinn Early TYC	.05	.02	.01
□ 256 Anthony Miller TYC	.10	.05	.01
□ 257 Joey Galloway TYC	.20	.09	.03
□ 258 Bert Emanuel TYC	.10	.05	.01
□ 259 Terance Mathis TYC	.05	.02	.01
□ 260 Curtis Conway TYC	.20	.09	.03
□ 261 Henry Ellard TYC	.10	.05	.01
□ 262 Mark Carrier WR TYC	.10	.05	.01
□ 263 Brian Blades TYC	.10	.05	.01
□ 264 William Roaf	.05	.02	.01
□ 265 Ed McDaniel	.05	.02	.01
□ 266 Nate Newton	.05	.02	.01
□ 267 Brett Maxie	.05	.02	.01
□ 268 Anthony Smith	.05	.02	.01
□ 269 Mickey Washington	.05	.02	.01
□ 270 Jerry Rice	1.00	.45	.12
□ 271 Shaun Gayle	.05	.02	.01
□ 272 Gilbert Brown	.10	.05	.01
□ 273 Mark Bruener	.05	.02	.01
□ 274 Eugene Robinson	.05	.02	.01
□ 275 Marvin Washington	.05	.02	.01
□ 276 Keith Sims	.05	.02	.01
□ 277 Ashley Ambrose	.05	.02	.01
□ 278 Garrison Hearst	.10	.05	.01
□ 279 Donnell Woolford	.05	.02	.01
□ 280 Cris Carter	.20	.09	.03
□ 281 Curtis Martin	1.50	.70	.19
□ 282 Scott Mitchell	.10	.05	.01
□ 283 Stevon Moore	.05	.02	.01
□ 284 Roman Phifer	.05	.02	.01
□ 285 Ken Harvey	.05	.02	.01
□ 286 Rodney Hampton	.10	.05	.01
□ 287 Willie Davis	.10	.05	.01
□ 288 Yonel Jourdain	.05	.02	.01
□ 289 Brian DeMarco	.10	.05	.01
□ 290 Reggie White	.20	.09	.03
□ 291 Kevin Williams	.05	.02	.01
□ 292 Gary Plummer	.05	.02	.01
□ 293 Terrance Shaw	.05	.02	.01
□ 294 Calvin Williams	.20	.09	.03
□ 295 Eddie Robinson	.05	.02	.01
□ 296 Tony McGee	.05	.02	.01
□ 297 Clay Matthews	.10	.05	.01
□ 298 Joe Cain	.05	.02	.01
□ 299 Tim McKyer	.05	.02	.01
□ 300 Greg Lloyd	.10	.05	.01
□ 301 Steve Wisniewski	.05	.02	.01
□ 302 Ray Buchanan	.05	.02	.01
□ 303 Lake Dawson	.10	.05	.01
□ 304 Kevin Carter	.10	.05	.01
□ 305 Phillippi Sparks	.05	.02	.01
□ 306 Emmitt Smith	2.00	.90	.25
□ 307 Ruben Brown	.05	.02	.01
□ 308 Tom Carter	.05	.02	.01
□ 309 William Floyd	.10	.05	.01
□ 310 Jim Everett	.05	.02	.01
□ 311 Vincent Brown	.05	.02	.01
□ 312 Dennis Gibson	.05	.02	.01
□ 313 Lorenzo Lynch	.05	.02	.01
□ 314 Corey Harris	.05	.02	.01
□ 315 James O.Stewart	.10	.05	.01
□ 316 Kyle Brady	.10	.05	.01
□ 317 Irving Fryar	.10	.05	.01
□ 318 Jake Reed	.10	.05	.01
□ 319 Vinny Testaverde	.10	.05	.01
□ 320 John Elway	.75	.35	.09
□ 321 Tracy Scroggins	.05	.02	.01
□ 322 Chris Spielman	.10	.05	.01
□ 323 Horace Copeland	.05	.02	.01
□ 324 Chris Zorich	.05	.02	.01
□ 325 Mike Mamula	.05	.02	.01
□ 326 Henry Ford	.05	.02	.01
□ 327 Steve Walsh	.05	.02	.01
□ 328 Stanley Richard	.05	.02	.01
□ 329 Mike Jones	.05	.02	.01
□ 330 Jim Harbaugh	.10	.05	.01
□ 331 Darren Perry	.05	.02	.01
□ 332 Ken Norton	.10	.05	.01
□ 333 Kimble Anders	.05	.02	.01
□ 334 Harold Green	.05	.02	.01
□ 335 Tyrone Poole	.05	.02	.01
□ 336 Mark Fields	.05	.02	.01
□ 337 Darren Bennett	.10	.05	.01
□ 338 Mike Sherrard	.05	.02	.01
□ 339 Terry Ray	.05	.02	.01
□ 340 Bruce Smith	.20	.09	.03
□ 341 Daryl Johnston	.10	.05	.01
□ 342 Vinnie Clark	.05	.02	.01
□ 343 Mike Caldwell	.05	.02	.01
□ 344 Vinson Smith	.05	.02	.01
□ 345 Mo Lewis	.05	.02	.01
□ 346 Brian Blades	.10	.05	.01
□ 347 Rod Stephens	.05	.02	.01
□ 348 David Palmer	.10	.05	.01
□ 349 Blaine Bishop	.05	.02	.01
□ 350 Jeff George	.10	.05	.01
□ 351 George Teague	.05	.02	.01
□ 352 Jeff Hostetler	.10	.05	.01
□ 353 Michael Strahan	.05	.02	.01
□ 354 Eric Davis	.05	.02	.01
□ 355 Jerome Bettis	.20	.09	.03
□ 356 Irv Smith	.05	.02	.01
□ 357 Jeff Herrod	.05	.02	.01
□ 358 Jay Novacek	.10	.05	.01
□ 359 Bryce Paup	.10	.05	.01
□ 360 Neil O'Donnell	.10	.05	.01
□ 361 Eric Swann	.10	.05	.01
□ 362 Corey Sawyer	.05	.02	.01
□ 363 Ty Law	.05	.02	.01
□ 364 Bo Orlando	.05	.02	.01
□ 365 Marcus Allen	.20	.09	.03
□ 366 Mark McMillian	.05	.02	.01
□ 367 Mark Carrier	.05	.02	.01
□ 368 Jackie Harris	.05	.02	.01
□ 369 Steve Atwater	.05	.02	.01
□ 370 Steve Young	.75	.35	.09
□ 371 Brett Favre TYC	1.00	.45	.12
□ 372 Scott Mitchell TYC	.05	.02	.01
□ 373 Warren Moon TYC	.05	.02	.01
□ 374 Jeff George TYC	.10	.05	.01
□ 375 Jim Everett TYC	.05	.02	.01
□ 376 John Elway TYC	.35	.16	.04
□ 377 Erik Kramer TYC	.05	.02	.01
□ 378 Jeff Blake TYC	.10	.05	.01
□ 379 Dan Marino TYC	1.00	.45	.12
□ 380 Dave Krieg TYC	.05	.02	.01
□ 381 Drew Bledsoe TYC	.50	.23	.06
□ 382 Stan Humphries TYC	.05	.02	.01
□ 383 Troy Aikman TYC	.50	.23	.06
□ 384 Steve Young TYC	.35	.16	.04
□ 385 Jim Kelly TYC	.20	.09	.03
□ 386 Steve Bono TYC	.05	.02	.01
□ 387 David Sloan	.10	.05	.01
□ 388 Jeff Graham	.05	.02	.01
□ 389 Hugh Douglas	.05	.02	.01
□ 390 Dan Marino	2.00	.90	.25
□ 391 Winston Moss	.05	.02	.01
□ 392 Darrell Green	.05	.02	.01
□ 393 Mark Stepnoski	.05	.02	.01
□ 394 Bert Emanuel	.10	.05	.01
□ 395 Eric Zeier	.10	.05	.01
□ 396 Willie Jackson	.10	.05	.01
□ 397 Qadry Ismail	.10	.05	.01
□ 398 Michael Brooks	.05	.02	.01
□ 399 D'Marco Farr	.05	.02	.01
□ 400 Brett Favre	2.00	.90	.25
□ 401 Carnell Lake	.05	.02	.01
□ 402 Pat Swilling	.05	.02	.01
□ 403 Stephen Grant	.05	.02	.01
□ 404 Steve Tasker	.05	.02	.01
□ 405 Ben Coates	.10	.05	.01
□ 406 Steve Tovar	.05	.02	.01
□ 407 Tony Martin	.10	.05	.01
□ 408 Greg Hill	.10	.05	.01
□ 409 Eric Guliford	.05	.02	.01
□ 410 Michael Irvin	.20	.09	.03
□ 411 Eric Hill	.05	.02	.01
□ 412 Mario Bates	.10	.05	.01
□ 413 Brian Stablein	.05	.02	.01
□ 414 Marcus Jones	.05	.02	.01
□ 415 Reggie Brown LB	.05	.02	.01
□ 416 Lawrence Phillips	.40	.18	.05
□ 417 Alex Van Dyke	.10	.05	.01
□ 418 Daryl Gardener	.10	.05	.01
□ 419 Mike Alstott	.40	.18	.05
□ 420 Kevin Hardy	.10	.05	.01
□ 421 Rickey Dudley	.20	.09	.03
□ 422 Jerome Woods	.05	.02	.01
□ 423 Eric Moulds	.75	.35	.09
□ 424 Cedric Jones	.10	.05	.01
□ 425 Simeon Rice	.20	.09	.03
□ 426 Marvin Harrison	1.25	.55	.16
□ 427 Tim Biakabutuka	.75	.35	.09
□ 428 Duane Clemons	.05	.02	.01
□ 429 Alex Molden	.05	.02	.01
□ 430 Keyshawn Johnson	1.25	.55	.16
□ 431 Willie Anderson	.05	.02	.01
□ 432 John Mobley	.05	.02	.01
□ 433 Leeland McElroy	.20	.09	.03
□ 434 Regan Upshaw	.05	.02	.01
□ 435 Eddie George	3.00	1.35	.35
□ 436 Jonathan Ogden	.05	.02	.01
□ 437 Eddie Kennison	1.25	.55	.16
□ 438 Jermane Mayberry	.05	.02	.01
□ 439 Checklist 1 of 2	.10	.05	.01
□ 440 Checklist 2 of 2	.10	.05	.01
□ P1 Joe Namath Promo Steve Young Promo	15.00	6.75	1.85

1996 Topps Broadway's Reviews

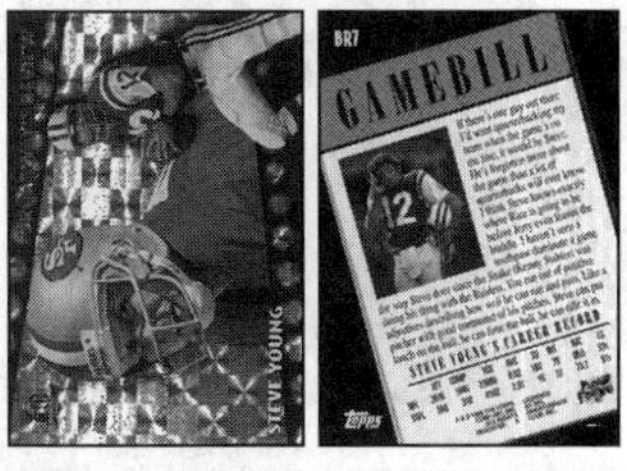

Randomly inserted in packs at a rate of one in 12 hobby foil packs, one in 8 retail, one in 6 special retail, or one in three jumbo packs, this 10-card standard-size horizontal set features Joe Namath comments about the leading active NFL quarterbacks. The cards are numbered with a "BR" prefix.

	MINT	NRMT	EXC
COMPLETE SET (10)	25.00	11.00	3.10
COMMON CARD (BR1-BR10)	1.00	.45	.12
□ BR1 Kerry Collins	3.00	1.35	.35
□ BR2 Drew Bledsoe	3.00	1.35	.35

	MINT	NRMT	EXC
☐ BR3 Jeff Blake	2.00	.90	.25
☐ BR4 Brett Favre	5.00	2.20	.60
☐ BR5 Scott Mitchell	1.00	.45	.12
☐ BR6 Troy Aikman	3.00	1.35	.35
☐ BR7 Steve Young	2.50	1.10	.30
☐ BR8 Jim Harbaugh	1.50	.70	.19
☐ BR9 John Elway	2.50	1.10	.30
☐ BR10 Dan Marino	5.00	2.20	.60

1996 Topps 40th Anniversary Retros

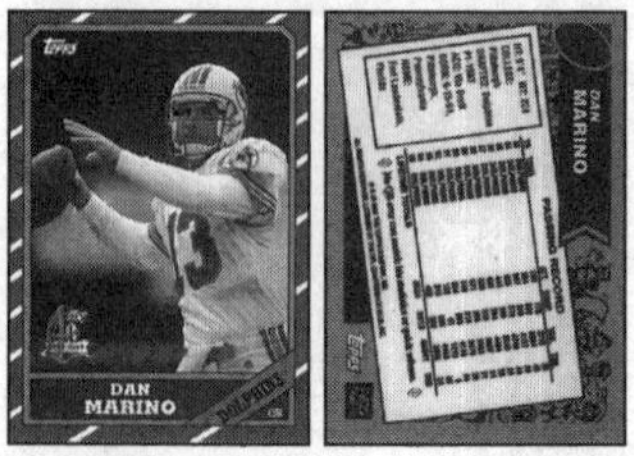

Randomly inserted in packs at a rate of one in 6 foil packs, one in 4 retail and special retail packs, and one per jumbo pack, this 40-card standard-size set has today's players featured in card designs used by Topps over their 40 years of producing professional football cards. The set is sequenced in order of the design used with the design year after the player's name.

	MINT	NRMT	EXC
COMPLETE SET (40)	75.00	34.00	9.50
COMMON CARD (1-40)	.75	.35	.09
☐ 1 Jim Harbaugh 1956	1.25	.55	.16
☐ 2 Greg Lloyd 1957	1.25	.55	.16
☐ 3 Barry Sanders 1958	4.00	1.80	.50
☐ 4 Merton Hanks 1959	.75	.35	.09
☐ 5 Herman Moore 1960	1.50	.70	.19
☐ 6 Tim Brown 1961	1.25	.55	.16
☐ 7 Brett Favre 1962	7.00	3.10	.85
☐ 8 Cris Carter 1963	1.25	.55	.16
☐ 9 Curtis Martin 1964	6.00	2.70	.75
☐ 10 Bryce Paup 1965	.75	.35	.09
☐ 11 Steve Bono 1966	.75	.35	.09
☐ 12 Blaine Bishop 1967	.75	.35	.09
☐ 13 Emmitt Smith 1968	7.00	3.10	.85
☐ 14 Carnell Lake 1969	.75	.35	.09
☐ 15 Marshall Faulk 1970	1.50	.70	.19
☐ 16 Mike Morris 1971	.75	.35	.09
☐ 17 Shannon Sharpe 1972	.75	.35	.09
☐ 18 Steve Young 1973	3.00	1.35	.35
☐ 19 Jeff George 1974	1.25	.55	.16
☐ 20 Junior Seau 1975	1.25	.55	.16
☐ 21 Chris Warren 1976	1.25	.55	.16
☐ 22 Heath Shuler 1977	1.25	.55	.16
☐ 23 Jeff Blake 1978	1.50	.70	.19
☐ 24 Reggie White 1979	1.50	.70	.19
☐ 25 Jeff Hostetler 1980	.75	.35	.09
☐ 26 Errict Rhett 1981	1.25	.55	.16
☐ 27 Rodney Hampton 1982	1.25	.55	.16
☐ 28 Jerry Rice 1983	4.00	1.80	.50
☐ 29 Jim Everett 1984	.75	.35	.09
☐ 30 Isaac Bruce 1985	1.50	.70	.19
☐ 31 Dan Marino 1986	7.00	3.10	.85
☐ 32 Marcus Allen 1987	1.50	.70	.19
☐ 33 Erik Kramer 1988	.75	.35	.09
☐ 34 John Elway 1989	3.00	1.35	.35
☐ 35 Ricky Watters 1990	1.25	.55	.16
☐ 36 Troy Aikman 1991	4.00	1.80	.50
☐ 37 Drew Bledsoe 1992	4.00	1.80	.50
☐ 38 Scott Mitchell 1993	.75	.35	.09
☐ 39 Rashaan Salaam 1994	1.50	.70	.19
☐ 40 Kerry Collins 1995	5.00	2.20	.60

1996 Topps Hobby Masters

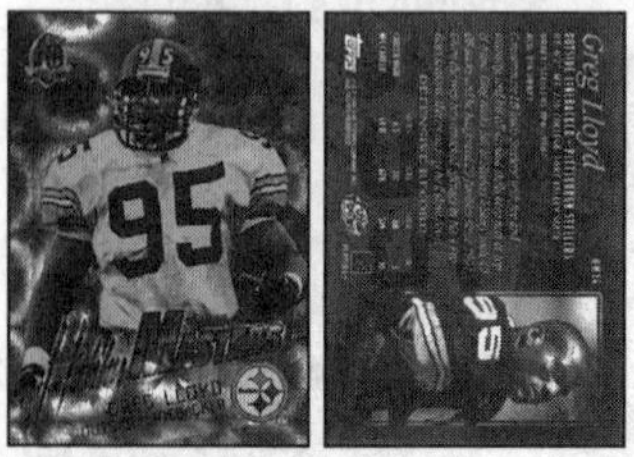

Randomly inserted in hobby foil packs at a rate of one in 36 or in hobby jumbo packs at a rate of one in ten packs, this 20-card standard-size set features players voted by hobby dealers as guys they would like to see in a set. These cards are printed on 28-point full diffraction foil stock with a prismatic background. The cards are numbered with an "HM" prefix.

	MINT	NRMT	EXC
COMPLETE SET (20)	175.00	80.00	22.00
COMMON CARD (HM1-HM20)	3.00	1.35	.35
☐ HM1 Brett Favre	25.00	11.00	3.10
☐ HM2 Emmitt Smith	25.00	11.00	3.10
☐ HM3 Drew Bledsoe	12.00	5.50	1.50
☐ HM4 Marshall Faulk	6.00	2.70	.75
☐ HM5 Steve Young	10.00	4.50	1.25
☐ HM6 Barry Sanders	12.00	5.50	1.50
☐ HM7 Troy Aikman	12.00	5.50	1.50
☐ HM8 Jerry Rice	12.00	5.50	1.50
☐ HM9 Michael Irvin	6.00	2.70	.75
☐ HM10 Dan Marino	25.00	11.00	3.10
☐ HM11 Chris Warren	3.00	1.35	.35
☐ HM12 Reggie White	6.00	2.70	.75
☐ HM13 Jeff Blake	6.00	2.70	.75
☐ HM14 Greg Lloyd	3.00	1.35	.35
☐ HM15 Curtis Martin	15.00	6.75	1.85
☐ HM16 Junior Seau	5.00	2.20	.60
☐ HM17 Kerry Collins	12.00	5.50	1.50
☐ HM18 Deion Sanders	8.00	3.60	1.00
☐ HM19 Joey Galloway	6.00	2.70	.75
☐ HM20 John Elway	10.00	4.50	1.25

1996 Topps Namath Reprint

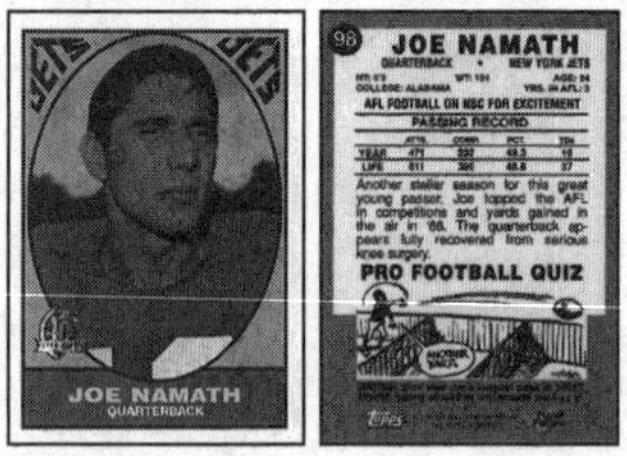

Randomly inserted in foil packs at a rate of one in 18, this 10-card standard-size set features reprints from Joe Namath's nine-year Topps card career. The cards are the same as the original cards except for the UV coating, the "Topps 40th anniversary" logo on front and 1996 copyright information on the back. Jumbo packs included the cards at 1:5.

	MINT	NRMT	EXC
COMPLETE SET (10)	50.00	22.00	6.25
COMMON NAMATH (1-10)	6.00	2.70	.75
☐ 1 Joe Namath 1965	8.00	3.60	1.00
☐ 2 Joe Namath 1966	6.00	2.70	.75
☐ 3 Joe Namath 1967	6.00	2.70	.75
☐ 4 Joe Namath 1968	6.00	2.70	.75
☐ 5 Joe Namath 1969	6.00	2.70	.75
☐ 6 Joe Namath 1970	6.00	2.70	.75
☐ 7 Joe Namath 1971	6.00	2.70	.75
☐ 8 Joe Namath 1972	6.00	2.70	.75
☐ 9 Joe Namath 1972	6.00	2.70	.75
☐ 10 Joe Namath 1973	6.00	2.70	.75

1996 Topps Turf Warriors

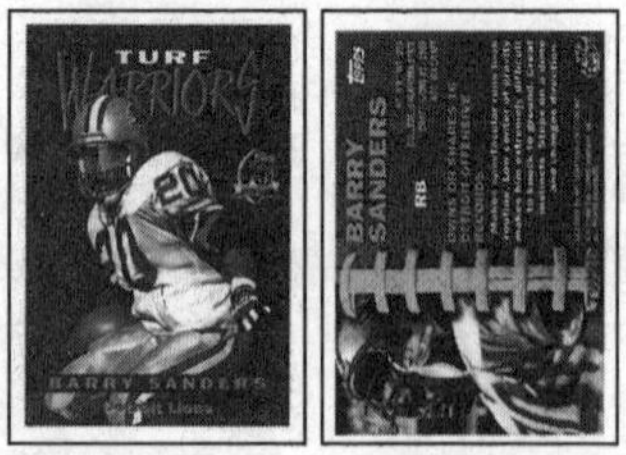

This insert set features top players with a felt "turf" finish to the cardfront. The cards were randomly inserted in hobby at 1:36, and retail packs at 1:24, and special 16-card retail packs at the rate of 1:18 packs.

	MINT	NRMT	EXC
COMPLETE SET (22)	125.00	55.00	15.50
COMMON CARD (TW1-TW22)	3.00	1.35	.35
☐ TW1 Bryce Paup	3.00	1.35	.35
☐ TW2 Ben Coates	3.00	1.35	.35
☐ TW3 Jim Harbaugh	5.00	2.20	.60
☐ TW4 Brian Mitchell	3.00	1.35	.35
☐ TW5 Brett Favre	20.00	9.00	2.50
☐ TW6 Junior Seau	5.00	2.20	.60
☐ TW7 Michael Irvin	5.00	2.20	.60
☐ TW8 Steve Young	8.00	3.60	1.00
☐ TW9 Terry McDaniel	3.00	1.35	.35
☐ TW10 Curtis Martin	15.00	6.75	1.85
☐ TW11 Greg Lloyd	3.00	1.35	.35
☐ TW12 Cris Carter	3.00	1.35	.35
☐ TW13 Emmitt Smith	20.00	9.00	2.50
☐ TW14 Reggie White	5.00	2.20	.60
☐ TW15 Marshall Faulk	5.00	2.20	.60
☐ TW16 Jerry Rice	12.00	5.50	1.50
☐ TW17 Shannon Sharpe	3.00	1.35	.35
☐ TW18 Dan Marino	20.00	9.00	2.50
☐ TW19 Ken Norton	3.00	1.35	.35
☐ TW20 Barry Sanders	12.00	5.50	1.50
☐ TW21 Neil Smith	3.00	1.35	.35
☐ TW22 Troy Aikman	12.00	5.50	1.50

1996 Topps Chrome

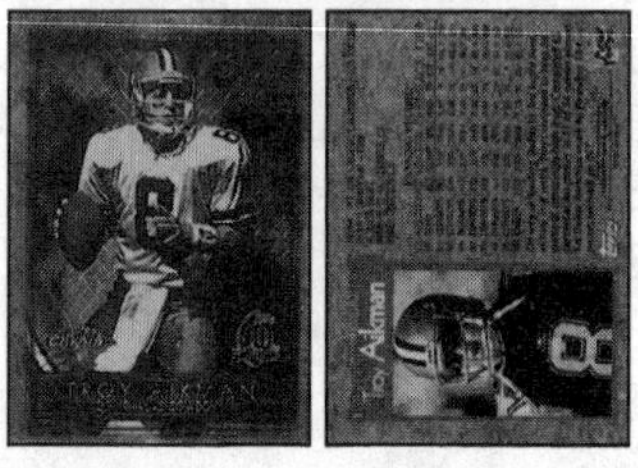

The 1996 Topps Chrome set was issued in one series totalling 165 cards. The 4-card packs had a suggested retail of $3.00 each. These standard-sized cards are the same as the regular 1996 set except for numbering and the chrome foil treatment.

	MINT	NRMT	EXC
COMPLETE SET (165)	75.00	34.00	9.50
COMMON CARD (1-165)	.15	.07	.02
☐ 1 Troy Aikman	3.00	1.35	.35
☐ 2 Kevin Greene	.30	.14	.04
☐ 3 Robert Brooks	.50	.23	.06
☐ 4 Junior Seau	.50	.23	.06
☐ 5 Brett Perriman	.30	.14	.04
☐ 6 Cortez Kennedy	.30	.14	.04
☐ 7 Orlando Thomas	.15	.07	.02
☐ 8 Anthony Miller	.30	.14	.04
☐ 9 Jeff Blake	.50	.23	.06
☐ 10 Trent Dilfer	.30	.14	.04
☐ 11 Heath Shuler	.50	.23	.06
☐ 12 Michael Jackson	.30	.14	.04
☐ 13 Merton Hanks	.15	.07	.02
☐ 14 Dale Carter	.15	.07	.02
☐ 15 Eric Metcalf	.30	.14	.04
☐ 16 Barry Sanders	3.00	1.35	.35
☐ 17 Joey Galloway	1.00	.45	.12
☐ 18 Bryan Cox	.15	.07	.02
☐ 19 Harvey Williams	.15	.07	.02
☐ 20 Terrell Davis	3.00	1.35	.35
☐ 21 Darnay Scott	.30	.14	.04
☐ 22 Kerry Collins	2.50	1.10	.30
☐ 23 Warren Sapp	.15	.07	.02
☐ 24 Michael Westbrook	.50	.23	.06
☐ 25 Mark Brunell	3.00	1.35	.35
☐ 26 Craig Heyward	.15	.07	.02
☐ 27 Eric Allen	.15	.07	.02
☐ 28 Dana Stubblefield	.30	.14	.04
☐ 29 Steve Bono	.30	.14	.04
☐ 30 Larry Brown	.15	.07	.02
☐ 31 Warren Moon	.30	.14	.04
☐ 32 Jim Kelly	.50	.23	.06
☐ 33 Terry McDaniel	.15	.07	.02
☐ 34 Dan Wilkinson	.15	.07	.02
☐ 35 Dave Brown	.30	.14	.04
☐ 36 Todd Lyght	.15	.07	.02
☐ 37 Aeneas Williams	.15	.07	.02
☐ 38 Shannon Sharpe	.30	.14	.04
☐ 39 Errict Rhett	.30	.14	.04
☐ 40 Yancey Thigpen	.30	.14	.04
☐ 41 J.J. Stokes	.50	.23	.06
☐ 42 Marshall Faulk	.50	.23	.06
☐ 43 Chester McGlockton	.15	.07	.02
☐ 44 Darryll Lewis	.15	.07	.02
☐ 45 Drew Bledsoe	3.00	1.35	.35
☐ 46 Tyrone Wheatley	.30	.14	.04
☐ 47 Herman Moore	.50	.23	.06
☐ 48 Darren Woodson	.30	.14	.04
☐ 49 Ricky Watters	.30	.14	.04
☐ 50 Emmitt Smith TYC	2.50	1.10	.30
☐ 51 Barry Sanders TYC	1.25	.55	.16
☐ 52 Curtis Martin TYC	1.50	.70	.19
☐ 53 Chris Warren TYC	.30	.14	.04
☐ 54 Errict Rhett TYC	.30	.14	.04
☐ 55 Rodney Hampton TYC	.15	.07	.02
☐ 56 Terrell Davis TYC	1.50	.70	.19
☐ 57 Marshall Faulk TYC	.30	.14	.04
☐ 58 Rashaan Salaam TYC	.50	.23	.06
☐ 59 Curtis Conway	.50	.23	.06
☐ 60 Isaac Bruce	.50	.23	.06
☐ 61 Thurman Thomas	.50	.23	.06
☐ 62 Terry Allen	.30	.14	.04
☐ 63 Lamar Lathon	.15	.07	.02
☐ 64 Mark Chmura	.30	.14	.04
☐ 65 Chris Warren	.30	.14	.04
☐ 66 Jessie Tuggle	.15	.07	.02
☐ 67 Erik Kramer	.15	.07	.02
☐ 68 Tim Brown	.30	.14	.04
☐ 69 Derrick Thomas	.30	.14	.04
☐ 70 Willie McGinest	.15	.07	.02
☐ 71 Frank Sanders	.30	.14	.04
☐ 72 Bernie Parmalee	.15	.07	.02
☐ 73 Kordell Stewart	2.50	1.10	.30
☐ 74 Brent Jones	.15	.07	.02
☐ 75 Edgar Bennett	.30	.14	.04
☐ 76 Rashaan Salaam	.50	.23	.06
☐ 77 Carl Pickens	.50	.23	.06
☐ 78 Terance Mathis	.15	.07	.02
☐ 79 Deion Sanders	1.50	.70	.19
☐ 80 Glyn Milburn	.15	.07	.02
☐ 81 Lee Woodall	.15	.07	.02
☐ 82 Neil Smith	.30	.14	.04
☐ 83 Stan Humphries	.30	.14	.04
☐ 84 Rick Mirer	.30	.14	.04
☐ 85 Troy Vincent	.15	.07	.02
☐ 86 Sam Mills	.30	.14	.04
☐ 87 Brian Mitchell	.15	.07	.02
☐ 88 Hardy Nickerson	.15	.07	.02
☐ 89 Tamarick Vanover	.50	.23	.06
☐ 90 Steve McNair	2.00	.90	.25
☐ 91 Jerry Rice TYC	1.25	.55	.16
☐ 92 Isaac Bruce TYC	.50	.23	.06
☐ 93 Herman Moore TYC	.50	.23	.06
☐ 94 Cris Carter TYC	.50	.23	.06
☐ 95 Tim Brown TYC	.30	.14	.04
☐ 96 Carl Pickens TYC	.50	.23	.06
☐ 97 Joey Galloway TYC	.50	.23	.06
☐ 98 Jerry Rice	3.00	1.35	.35
☐ 99 Cris Carter	.50	.23	.06
☐ 100 Curtis Martin	3.00	1.35	.35
☐ 101 Scott Mitchell	.30	.14	.04
☐ 102 Ken Harvey	.15	.07	.02
☐ 103 Rodney Hampton	.30	.14	.04
☐ 104 Reggie White	.50	.23	.06
☐ 105 Eddie Robinson	.15	.07	.02
☐ 106 Greg Lloyd	.30	.14	.04
☐ 107 Phillippi Sparks	.15	.07	.02
☐ 108 Emmitt Smith	6.00	2.70	.75
☐ 109 Tom Carter	.15	.07	.02
☐ 110 Jim Everett	.15	.07	.02
☐ 111 James O.Stewart	.30	.14	.04
☐ 112 Kyle Brady	.30	.14	.04
☐ 113 Irving Fryar	.30	.14	.04
☐ 114 Vinny Testaverde	.30	.14	.04
☐ 115 John Elway	2.50	1.10	.30
☐ 116 Chris Spielman	.30	.14	.04
☐ 117 Mike Mamula	.15	.07	.02
☐ 118 Jim Harbaugh	.30	.14	.04
☐ 119 Ken Norton	.30	.14	.04
☐ 120 Bruce Smith	.50	.23	.06
☐ 121 Daryl Johnston	.30	.14	.04
☐ 122 Blaine Bishop	.15	.07	.02
☐ 123 Jeff George	.30	.14	.04
☐ 124 Jeff Hostetler	.30	.14	.04
☐ 125 Jerome Bettis	.50	.23	.06
☐ 126 Jay Novacek	.30	.14	.04
☐ 127 Bryce Paup	.30	.14	.04
☐ 128 Neil O'Donnell	.30	.14	.04
☐ 129 Marcus Allen	.50	.23	.06
☐ 130 Steve Young	2.00	.90	.25
☐ 131 Brett Favre TYC	2.50	1.10	.30
☐ 132 Scott Mitchell TYC	.15	.07	.02
☐ 133 John Elway TYC	1.00	.45	.12
☐ 134 Jeff Blake TYC	.30	.14	.04
☐ 135 Dan Marino TYC	2.50	1.10	.30
☐ 136 Drew Bledsoe TYC	1.25	.55	.16
☐ 137 Troy Aikman TYC	1.25	.55	.16
☐ 138 Steve Young TYC	1.00	.45	.12
☐ 139 Jim Kelly TYC	.50	.23	.06
☐ 140 Jeff Graham	.15	.07	.02
☐ 141 Hugh Douglas	.15	.07	.02
☐ 142 Dan Marino	6.00	2.70	.75
☐ 143 Darrell Green	.15	.07	.02
☐ 144 Eric Zeier	.30	.14	.04
☐ 145 Brett Favre	6.00	2.70	.75
☐ 146 Carnell Lake	.15	.07	.02
☐ 147 Ben Coates	.30	.14	.04
☐ 148 Tony Martin	.30	.14	.04
☐ 149 Michael Irvin	.50	.23	.06
☐ 150 Lawrence Phillips	.75	.35	.09
☐ 151 Alex Van Dyke	.30	.14	.04
☐ 152 Kevin Hardy	.30	.14	.04
☐ 153 Rickey Dudley	.50	.23	.06
☐ 154 Eric Moulds	1.50	.70	.19
☐ 155 Simeon Rice	.50	.23	.06
☐ 156 Marvin Harrison	3.00	1.35	.35
☐ 157 Tim Biakabutuka	1.50	.70	.19
☐ 158 Duane Clemons	.15	.07	.02
☐ 159 Keyshawn Johnson	3.00	1.35	.35
☐ 160 John Mobley	.15	.07	.02
☐ 161 Leeland McElroy	.50	.23	.06
☐ 162 Eddie George	8.00	3.60	1.00
☐ 163 Jonathan Ogden	.15	.07	.02
☐ 164 Eddie Kennison	3.00	1.35	.35
☐ 165 Checklist	.15	.07	.02

1996 Topps Chrome Refractors

Randomly inserted in packs at a rate of one in 12, this parallel refractor set is identical to the regular issue other than the refractive sheen on the card and the small word "refractor" on the back of the card..

	MINT	NRMT	EXC
COMPLETE SET (165)	1500.00	700.00	190.00
COMMON CARD (1-165)	4.00	1.80	.50

*REFRACTOR STARS: 10X TO 18X			
*REF.YOUNG STARS: 6X TO 12X........			

☐ 1 Troy Aikman	60.00	27.00	7.50
☐ 16 Barry Sanders	60.00	27.00	7.50
☐ 17 Joey Galloway	20.00	9.00	2.50
☐ 20 Terrell Davis	50.00	22.00	6.25
☐ 22 Kerry Collins	50.00	22.00	6.25
☐ 25 Mark Brunell	60.00	27.00	7.50
☐ 45 Drew Bledsoe	60.00	27.00	7.50
☐ 50 Emmitt Smith TYC	40.00	18.00	5.00
☐ 51 Barry Sanders TYC	25.00	11.00	3.10
☐ 52 Curtis Martin TYC	25.00	11.00	3.10
☐ 56 Terrell Davis TYC	25.00	11.00	3.10
☐ 73 Kordell Stewart	40.00	18.00	5.00
☐ 79 Deion Sanders	25.00	11.00	3.10
☐ 90 Steve McNair	35.00	16.00	4.40
☐ 91 Jerry Rice TYC	25.00	11.00	3.10
☐ 98 Jerry Rice	60.00	27.00	7.50
☐ 100 Curtis Martin	50.00	22.00	6.25
☐ 108 Emmitt Smith	90.00	40.00	11.00
☐ 115 John Elway	40.00	18.00	5.00
☐ 130 Steve Young	35.00	16.00	4.40
☐ 131 Brett Favre TYC	40.00	18.00	5.00
☐ 135 Dan Marino TYC	40.00	18.00	5.00
☐ 136 Drew Bledsoe TYC	25.00	11.00	3.10
☐ 137 Troy Aikman TYC	25.00	11.00	3.10
☐ 142 Dan Marino	90.00	40.00	11.00
☐ 145 Brett Favre	100.00	45.00	12.50
☐ 156 Marvin Harrison	30.00	13.50	3.70
☐ 159 Keyshawn Johnson	30.00	13.50	3.70
☐ 162 Eddie George	90.00	40.00	11.00
☐ 164 Eddie Kennison	30.00	13.50	3.70

1996 Topps Chrome 40th Anniversary Retros

Randomly inserted in packs at a rate of one in 8, this 40-card standard-sized chrome foil set has a current player set in the design of an earlier Topps football issue. The year of the design is listed after the player below.

	MINT	NRMT	EXC
COMPLETE SET (40)	150.00	70.00	19.00
COMMON CARD (1-40)	1.50	.70	.19
COMP.REFRACT.SET (40)	450.00	200.00	55.00
COMMON REFRACTOR	5.00	2.20	.60
REFRACTORS: 1.5X TO 3X			

☐ 1 Jim Harbaugh 1956	2.50	1.10	.30
☐ 2 Greg Lloyd 1957	2.50	1.10	.30
☐ 3 Barry Sanders 1958	10.00	4.50	1.25
☐ 4 Merton Hanks 1959	1.50	.70	.19
☐ 5 Herman Moore 1960	4.00	1.80	.50
☐ 6 Tim Brown 1961	2.50	1.10	.30
☐ 7 Brett Favre 1962	18.00	8.00	2.20
☐ 8 Cris Carter 1963	2.50	1.10	.30
☐ 9 Curtis Martin 1964	12.00	5.50	1.50
☐ 10 Bryce Paup 1965	1.50	.70	.19
☐ 11 Steve Bono 1966	1.50	.70	.19
☐ 12 Blaine Bishop 1967	1.50	.70	.19
☐ 13 Emmitt Smith 1968	18.00	8.00	2.20
☐ 14 Carnell Lake 1969	1.50	.70	.19
☐ 15 Marshall Faulk 1970	4.00	1.80	.50
☐ 16 Mike Morris 1971	1.50	.70	.19
☐ 17 Shannon Sharpe 1972	1.50	.70	.19
☐ 18 Steve Young 1973	8.00	3.60	1.00
☐ 19 Jeff George 1974	2.50	1.10	.30
☐ 20 Junior Seau 1975	2.50	1.10	.30
☐ 21 Chris Warren 1976	2.50	1.10	.30
☐ 22 Heath Shuler 1977	2.50	1.10	.30
☐ 23 Jeff Blake 1978	4.00	1.80	.50
☐ 24 Reggie White 1979	4.00	1.80	.50
☐ 25 Jeff Hostetler 1980	1.50	.70	.19
☐ 26 Errict Rhett 1981	2.50	1.10	.30
☐ 27 Rodney Hampton 1982	1.50	.70	.19
☐ 28 Jerry Rice 1983	10.00	4.50	1.25
☐ 29 Jim Everett 1984	1.50	.70	.19
☐ 30 Isaac Bruce 1985	4.00	1.80	.50
☐ 31 Dan Marino 1986	18.00	8.00	2.20
☐ 32 Marcus Allen 1987	4.00	1.80	.50
☐ 33 Erik Kramer 1988	1.50	.70	.19
☐ 34 John Elway 1989	8.00	3.60	1.00
☐ 35 Ricky Watters 1990	2.50	1.10	.30
☐ 36 Troy Aikman 1991	10.00	4.50	1.25
☐ 37 Drew Bledsoe 1992	10.00	4.50	1.25
☐ 38 Scott Mitchell 1993	1.50	.70	.19
☐ 39 Rashaan Salaam 1994	4.00	1.80	.50
☐ 40 Kerry Collins 1995	10.00	4.50	1.25

1996 Topps Chrome Tide Turners

Randomly inserted in packs at a rate of one in 12, this 15-card standard-sized chrome foil set features players whose exploits can turn the tide of a game. The front of the cards have a wave over which the player is superimposed with his name and the insert name at the bottom of the card.

	MINT	NRMT	EXC
COMPLETE SET (15)	80.00	36.00	10.00
COMMON CARD (TT1-TT15)	2.00	.90	.25
COMP.REFRACT.SET (15)	300.00	135.00	38.00
COMMON REFRACTOR	6.00	2.70	.75
REFRACTORS: 1.5X TO 3X			

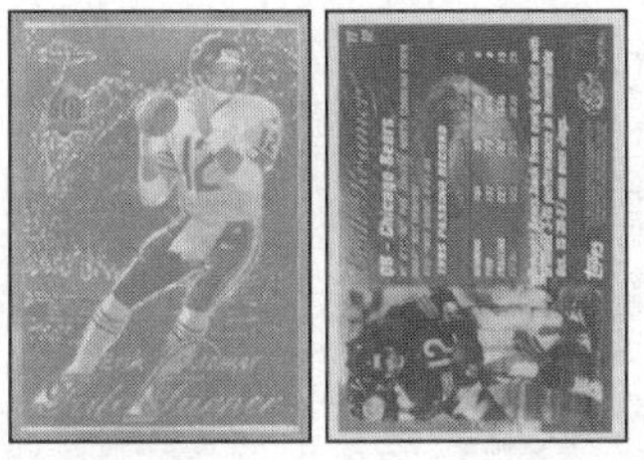

☐ TT1 Rashaan Salaam	3.00	1.35	.35
☐ TT2 Warren Moon	2.00	.90	.25
☐ TT3 Marshall Faulk	3.00	1.35	.35
☐ TT4 Jeff Blake	2.00	.90	.25
☐ TT5 Curtis Martin	14.00	6.25	1.75
☐ TT6 Eric Metcalf	2.00	.90	.25
☐ TT7 Errict Rhett	3.00	1.35	.35
☐ TT8 Scott Mitchell	2.00	.90	.25
☐ TT9 Ricky Watters	2.00	.90	.25
☐ TT10 Jerry Rice	12.00	5.50	1.50
☐ TT11 Emmitt Smith	20.00	9.00	2.50
☐ TT12 Erik Kramer	2.00	.90	.25
☐ TT13 Jim Harbaugh	2.00	.90	.25
☐ TT14 Barry Sanders	12.00	5.50	1.50
☐ TT15 John Elway	10.00	4.50	1.25

1996 Topps Gilt Edge

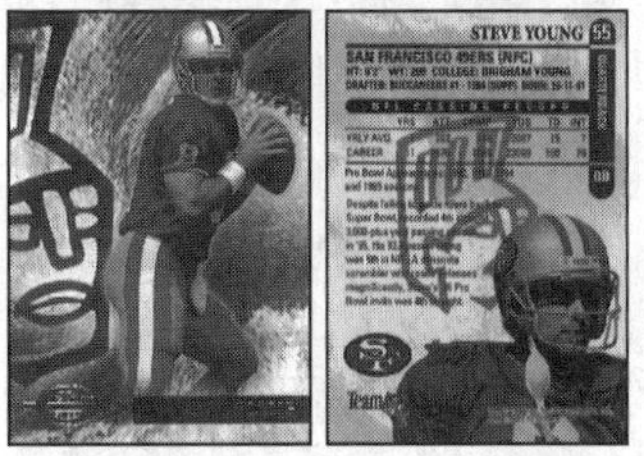

The 1996 Topps Gilt Edge set was issued in one series. This 90-card standard-size set was released in April 1996 and features the 84 members of the 1996 Pro Bowl roster, plus five players who had Pro Bowl-caliber seasons and one checklist card. Each card features Topps' new "gilt-edge" technology, placing gold foil edging around every card. The cards were issued in nine-card packs with a suggested retail price of $3.50 which included seven regular cards, a platinum card as well as a definitive edge card. Each case consisted of six boxes with 20 packs in each box. There are no Rookie Cards in this set.

	MINT	NRMT	EXC
COMPLETE SET (90)	20.00	9.00	2.50
COMMON CARD (1-90)	.10	.05	.01

☐ 1 Brett Favre	4.00	1.80	.50
☐ 2 Kevin Glover	.10	.05	.01
☐ 3 Nate Newton	.10	.05	.01
☐ 4 Randall McDaniel	.10	.05	.01
☐ 5 William Roaf	.10	.05	.01
☐ 6 Lomas Brown	.10	.05	.01
☐ 7 Jay Novacek	.20	.09	.03
☐ 8 Emmitt Smith	4.00	1.80	.50
☐ 9 Barry Sanders	2.00	.90	.25
☐ 10 Jerry Rice	2.00	.90	.25
☐ 11 Herman Moore	.40	.18	.05
☐ 12 Larry Centers	.20	.09	.03
☐ 13 Chester McGlockton	.10	.05	.01
☐ 14 Dan Saleaumua	.10	.05	.01
☐ 15 Bruce Smith	.40	.18	.05
☐ 16 Neil Smith	.20	.09	.03
☐ 17 Junior Seau	.40	.18	.05
☐ 18 Bryce Paup	.20	.09	.03
☐ 19 Greg Lloyd	.20	.09	.03
☐ 20 Terry McDaniel	.10	.05	.01
☐ 21 Dale Carter	.10	.05	.01
☐ 22 Carnell Lake	.10	.05	.01
☐ 23 Steve Atwater	.10	.05	.01
☐ 24 Elbert Shelley	.10	.05	.01
☐ 25 Brian Mitchell	.10	.05	.01
☐ 26 Jeff Feagles	.10	.05	.01
☐ 27 Morten Andersen	.10	.05	.01
☐ 28 Dan Marino	4.00	1.80	.50
☐ 29 Dermontti Dawson	.10	.05	.01
☐ 30 Steve Wisniewski	.10	.05	.01
☐ 31 Bruce Matthews	.10	.05	.01
☐ 32 Bruce Armstrong	.10	.05	.01
☐ 33 Richmond Webb	.10	.05	.01
☐ 34 Ben Coates	.20	.09	.03
☐ 35 Marshall Faulk	.40	.18	.05
☐ 36 Chris Warren	.20	.09	.03
☐ 37 Carl Pickens	.40	.18	.05
☐ 38 Tim Brown	.20	.09	.03
☐ 39 Kimble Anders	.10	.05	.01
☐ 40 John Randle	.10	.05	.01
☐ 41 Eric Swann	.20	.09	.03
☐ 42 Reggie White	.40	.18	.05
☐ 43 Charles Haley	.20	.09	.03
☐ 44 Ken Norton	.20	.09	.03
☐ 45 Lee Woodall	.10	.05	.01
☐ 46 Ken Harvey	.10	.05	.01
☐ 47 Aeneas Williams	.10	.05	.01
☐ 48 Eric Davis	.10	.05	.01
☐ 49 Darren Woodson	.20	.09	.03
☐ 50 Merton Hanks	.10	.05	.01
☐ 51 Steve Tasker	.10	.05	.01
☐ 52 Glyn Milburn	.10	.05	.01
☐ 53 Jason Elam	.10	.05	.01
☐ 54 Darren Bennett	.20	.09	.03
☐ 55 Steve Young	1.50	.70	.19
☐ 56 Bart Oates	.10	.05	.01
☐ 57 Larry Allen	.10	.05	.01
☐ 58 Mark Tuinei	.10	.05	.01
☐ 59 Mark Chmura	.20	.09	.03
☐ 60 Michael Irvin	.40	.18	.05
☐ 61 Ricky Watters	.20	.09	.03
☐ 62 Cortez Kennedy	.20	.09	.03
☐ 63 Leslie O'Neal	.10	.05	.01
☐ 64 Bryan Cox	.10	.05	.01
☐ 65 Derrick Thomas	.20	.09	.03
☐ 66 Darryll Lewis	.10	.05	.01
☐ 67 Blaine Bishop	.10	.05	.01
☐ 68 Dana Stubblefield	.20	.09	.03
☐ 69 William Fuller	.10	.05	.01
☐ 70 Jessie Tuggle	.10	.05	.01
☐ 71 William Thomas	.10	.05	.01
☐ 72 Eric Allen	.10	.05	.01
☐ 73 Tim McDonald	.10	.05	.01
☐ 74 Jim Harbaugh	.20	.09	.03
☐ 75 Mark Stepnoski	.10	.05	.01
☐ 76 Keith Sims	.10	.05	.01
☐ 77 Gary Zimmerman	.10	.05	.01
☐ 78 Shannon Sharpe	.20	.09	.03
☐ 79 Anthony Miller	.20	.09	.03
☐ 80 Curtis Martin	3.00	1.35	.35
☐ 81 Troy Aikman	2.00	.90	.25
☐ 82 Cris Carter	.40	.18	.05
☐ 83 Jeff Blake	.40	.18	.05
☐ 84 Yancey Thigpen	.20	.09	.03
☐ 85 Isaac Bruce	.40	.18	.05
☐ 86 Sam Mills	.20	.09	.03
☐ 87 Terrell Davis	3.00	1.35	.35
☐ 88 Larry Brown	.10	.05	.01
☐ 89 Joey Galloway	1.50	.70	.19
☐ 90 Checklist	.20	.09	.03

1996 Topps Gilt Edge Platinum

The 1996 Topps Gilt Edge Platinum set was issued in one per pack as a parallel to the regular set. The difference in these cards is that they feature Topps' gilt-edge technology, placing a platinum gilt edging (rather than gold) around every card.

	MINT	NRMT	EXC
COMPLETE SET (90)	90.00	40.00	11.00
COMMON CARD (1-90)	.40	.18	.05
*STARS: 1.5X TO 3X			
*YOUNG STARS: 1.25X TO 2.5X			

1996 Topps Gilt Edge Definitive Edge

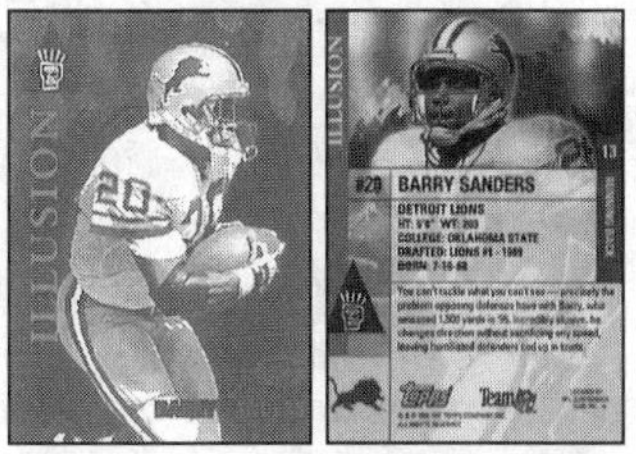

Definitive Edge cards were randomly inserted in Gilt Edge packs at the approximate rate of 1:4 packs. This 15-card set features top players with a different theme for each card. There were five card designs with each used to cover three different themes.

	MINT	NRMT	EXC
COMPLETE SET (15)	30.00	13.50	3.70
COMMON CARD (1-15)	.75	.35	.09

☐ 1 Bruce Smith	1.50	.70	.19
☐ 2 Brett Favre	8.00	3.60	1.00
☐ 3 Marcus Allen	2.00	.90	.25
☐ 4 Junior Seau	1.50	.70	.19
☐ 5 Deion Sanders	2.50	1.10	.30
☐ 6 Jerry Rice	4.00	1.80	.50
☐ 7 Steve Young	3.00	1.35	.35
☐ 8 Drew Bledsoe	4.00	1.80	.50
☐ 9 Michael Irvin	2.00	.90	.25
☐ 10 Reggie White	2.00	.90	.25
☐ 11 Dan Marino	8.00	3.60	1.00
☐ 12 John Alt	.75	.35	.09
☐ 13 Barry Sanders	4.00	1.80	.50
☐ 14 Orlanda Thomas	.75	.35	.09
☐ 15 Kordell Stewart	4.00	1.80	.50

1996 Topps Laser

The 1996 Topps Laser set was issued in one series totalling 128 cards. The 4-card packs carried a suggested retail of $5.00 each. The cards are all etch foil stamped, die-cut and UV coated.

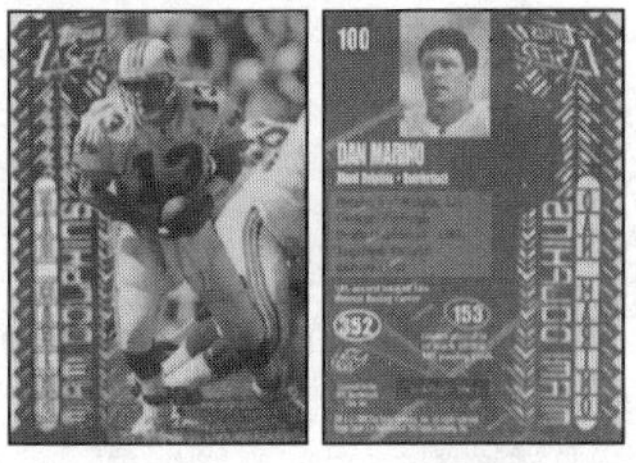

	MINT	NRMT	EXC
COMPLETE SET (128)	60.00	27.00	7.50
COMMON CARD (1-128)	.20	.09	.03

☐ 1 Marshall Faulk	.60	.25	.07
☐ 2 Alonzo Spellman	.20	.09	.03
☐ 3 Frank Sanders	.35	.16	.04
☐ 4 Anthony Pleasant	.20	.09	.03
☐ 5 Scott Mitchell	.35	.16	.04
☐ 6 Robert Brooks	.60	.25	.07
☐ 7 Robert Jones	.20	.09	.03
☐ 8 Phillippi Sparks	.20	.09	.03
☐ 9 Rodney Peete	.20	.09	.03
☐ 10 Kordell Stewart	3.00	1.35	.35
☐ 11 Ken Norton	.35	.16	.04
☐ 12 Brian Mitchell	.20	.09	.03
☐ 13 Ben Coates	.35	.16	.04
☐ 14 Quinn Early	.20	.09	.03
☐ 15 Emmitt Smith	5.00	2.20	.60
☐ 16 Steve Bono	.35	.16	.04
☐ 17 Anthony Miller	.35	.16	.04
☐ 18 Mel Gray	.20	.09	.03
☐ 19 Neil O'Donnell	.35	.16	.04
☐ 20 Tim Brown	.35	.16	.04
☐ 21 Terrell Fletcher	.20	.09	.03
☐ 22 John Randle	.20	.09	.03
☐ 23 Fred Barnett	.35	.16	.04
☐ 24 Craig Heyward	.20	.09	.03
☐ 25 Ki-Jana Carter	.35	.16	.04
☐ 26 Eric Allen	.20	.09	.03
☐ 27 Warren Sapp	.20	.09	.03
☐ 28 Terry Wooden	.20	.09	.03
☐ 29 Darion Conner	.20	.09	.03
☐ 30 Mark Brunell	3.00	1.35	.35
☐ 31 Vinny Testaverde	.35	.16	.04
☐ 32 Chris Calloway	.20	.09	.03
☐ 33 Steve Walsh	.20	.09	.03
☐ 34 Ken Dilger	.35	.16	.04
☐ 35 Bryan Cox	.20	.09	.03
☐ 36 Rob Moore	.20	.09	.03
☐ 37 Henry Thomas	.20	.09	.03
☐ 38 Henry Ellard	.35	.16	.04
☐ 39 Mark Chmura	.35	.16	.04
☐ 40 Jerry Rice	3.00	1.35	.35
☐ 41 Michael Irvin	.60	.25	.07
☐ 42 Willie McGinest	.20	.09	.03
☐ 43 Steve McNair	2.50	1.10	.30
☐ 44 Tamarick Vanover	.60	.25	.07
☐ 45 Cris Carter	.60	.25	.07
☐ 46 Levon Kirkland	.20	.09	.03
☐ 47 Terry McDaniel	.20	.09	.03
☐ 48 Jessie Tuggle	.20	.09	.03
☐ 49 O.J. McDuffie	.35	.16	.04
☐ 50 Bruce Smith	.60	.25	.07
☐ 51 Tyrone Hughes	.20	.09	.03
☐ 52 Tony Martin	.35	.16	.04
☐ 53 Hardy Nickerson	.20	.09	.03
☐ 54 Garrison Hearst	.35	.16	.04
☐ 55 Sam Mills	.35	.16	.04
☐ 56 Mark Carrier DB	.20	.09	.03
☐ 57 Quentin Coryatt	.20	.09	.03
☐ 58 Neil Smith	.35	.16	.04
☐ 59 Michael Westbrook	.60	.25	.07
☐ 60 Greg Lloyd	.35	.16	.04
☐ 61 Jeff Hostetler	.35	.16	.04
☐ 62 Wayne Chrebet	.35	.16	.04
☐ 63 Herschel Walker	.35	.16	.04
☐ 64 Pepper Johnson	.20	.09	.03
☐ 65 John Elway	2.50	1.10	.30
☐ 66 Reggie White	.60	.25	.07
☐ 67 James O.Stewart	.35	.16	.04
☐ 68 Bernie Parmalee	.20	.09	.03
☐ 69 Robert Smith	.35	.16	.04
☐ 70 Drew Bledsoe	3.00	1.35	.35
☐ 71 Marvcus Patton	.20	.09	.03
☐ 72 Stan Humphries	.35	.16	.04
☐ 73 Darnay Scott	.35	.16	.04
☐ 74 Jim Kelly	.60	.25	.07
☐ 75 Terance Mathis	.20	.09	.03
☐ 76 Erik Kramer	.20	.09	.03
☐ 77 Marcus Allen	.60	.25	.07
☐ 78 Ernie Mills	.20	.09	.03
☐ 79 Harvey Williams	.20	.09	.03
☐ 80 Brett Favre	5.00	2.20	.60
☐ 81 Seth Joyner	.20	.09	.03
☐ 82 Tyrone Poole	.20	.09	.03
☐ 83 Troy Aikman	3.00	1.35	.35
☐ 84 Warren Moon	.35	.16	.04
☐ 85 Isaac Bruce	.60	.25	.07
☐ 86 Errict Rhett	.35	.16	.04
☐ 87 Rick Mirer	.35	.16	.04
☐ 88 Anthony Smith	.20	.09	.03

☐ 89 Bert Emanuel	.35	.16	.04
☐ 90 Junior Seau	.60	.25	.07
☐ 91 Terry Allen	.35	.16	.04
☐ 92 Brent Jones	.20	.09	.03
☐ 93 Adrian Murrell	.35	.16	.04
☐ 94 Dave Brown	.35	.16	.04
☐ 95 Bryce Paup	.35	.16	.04
☐ 96 Jim Everett	.20	.09	.03
☐ 97 Brian Washington	.20	.09	.03
☐ 98 Jim Harbaugh	.35	.16	.04
☐ 99 Shannon Sharpe	.35	.16	.04
☐ 100 Dan Marino	5.00	2.20	.60
☐ 101 Curtis Martin	4.00	1.80	.50
☐ 102 Ricky Watters	.35	.16	.04
☐ 103 Yancey Thigpen	.35	.16	.04
☐ 104 Trent Dilfer	.35	.16	.04
☐ 105 Joey Galloway	1.50	.70	.19
☐ 106 Edgar Bennett	.35	.16	.04
☐ 107 Willie Jackson	.35	.16	.04
☐ 108 Mark Collins	.20	.09	.03
☐ 109 Rashaan Salaam	.60	.25	.07
☐ 110 Eric Metcalf	.35	.16	.04
☐ 111 Terrell Davis	4.00	1.80	.50
☐ 112 Darryll Lewis	.20	.09	.03
☐ 113 Ken Harvey	.20	.09	.03
☐ 114 Rob Fredrickson	.20	.09	.03
☐ 115 Rodney Hampton	.35	.16	.04
☐ 116 Chris Slade	.20	.09	.03
☐ 117 Jeff George	.35	.16	.04
☐ 118 Lamar Lathon	.20	.09	.03
☐ 119 Curtis Conway	.60	.25	.07
☐ 120 Barry Sanders	3.00	1.35	.35
☐ 121 Eric Zeier	.35	.16	.04
☐ 122 Jeff Blake	.60	.25	.07
☐ 123 Derrick Thomas	.35	.16	.04
☐ 124 Tyrone Wheatley	.35	.16	.04
☐ 125 Steve Young	2.00	.90	.25
☐ 126 Napoleon Kaufman	.35	.16	.04
☐ 127 Dave Meggett	.20	.09	.03
☐ 128 Kerry Collins	3.00	1.35	.35

1996 Topps Laser Bright Spots

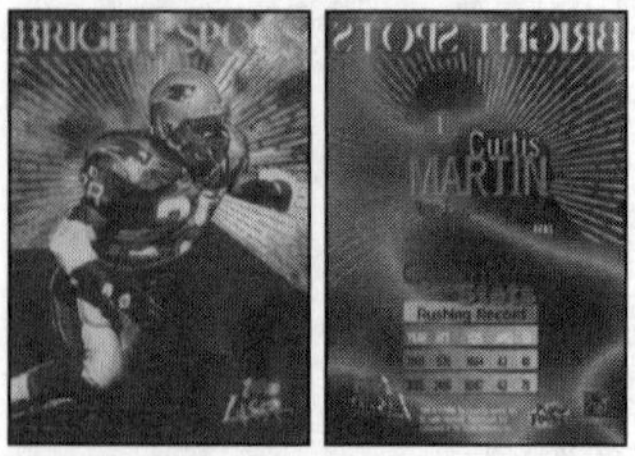

Randomly inserted in packs at a rate of one in every 24, this 16-standard-sized card set features players considered to be the "bright spots" on their team. The card fronts feature laser die-cutting technology on a gold foil board with the player photo in color and the player's name in a bronze foil. The back of the card has the player's name and statistics.

	MINT	NRMT	EXC
COMPLETE SET (16)	150.00	70.00	19.00
COMMON CARD (1-16)	5.00	2.20	.60
☐ 1 Curtis Martin	20.00	9.00	2.50
☐ 2 Tom Carter	5.00	2.20	.60
☐ 3 Dave Brown	5.00	2.20	.60
☐ 4 Wayne Chrebet	5.00	2.20	.60
☐ 5 Rashaan Salaam	8.00	3.60	1.00
☐ 6 Mark Brunell	20.00	9.00	2.50
☐ 7 Elvis Grbac	5.00	2.20	.60
☐ 8 Errict Rhett	8.00	3.60	1.00
☐ 9 Isaac Bruce	8.00	3.60	1.00
☐ 10 Kerry Collins	20.00	9.00	2.50
☐ 11 Mario Bates	5.00	2.20	.60
☐ 12 Joey Galloway	10.00	4.50	1.25
☐ 13 Napoleon Kaufman	5.00	2.20	.60
☐ 14 Tamarick Vanover	8.00	3.60	1.00
☐ 15 Marshall Faulk	8.00	3.60	1.00
☐ 16 Terrell Davis	20.00	9.00	2.50

1996 Topps Laser Draft Picks

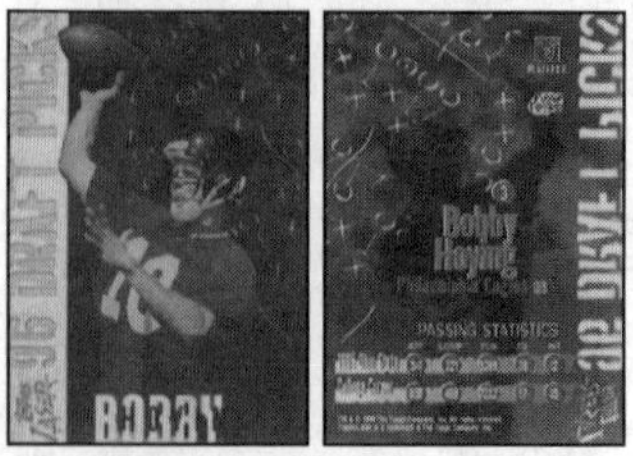

Randomly inserted in packs at a rate of one in 12, this 16-card standard-sized set contains rookies from the Class of 1996. The cards feature laser cutting and a holographic strip down the side of the card in which '96 Draft Picks" is laser cut into. The cards also feature a color player photo on the front, with the name at the bottom of the card. The backs feature a ghosted reverse of the front of the card, with the players name and college statistics listed.

	MINT	NRMT	EXC
COMPLETE SET (16)	80.00	36.00	10.00
COMMON CARD (1-16)	4.00	1.80	.50
☐ 1 Keyshawn Johnson	15.00	6.75	1.85
☐ 2 Lawrence Phillips	8.00	3.60	1.00
☐ 3 Bobby Hoying	6.00	2.70	.75
☐ 4 Marco Battaglia	4.00	1.80	.50
☐ 5 Kevin Hardy	6.00	2.70	.75
☐ 6 Jerome Woods	4.00	1.80	.50
☐ 7 Ray Mickens	4.00	1.80	.50
☐ 8 John Mobley	4.00	1.80	.50
☐ 9 Marvin Harrison	15.00	6.75	1.85
☐ 10 Walt Harris	4.00	1.80	.50
☐ 11 Duane Clemons	4.00	1.80	.50
☐ 12 Regan Upshaw	4.00	1.80	.50
☐ 13 Brian Dawkins	4.00	1.80	.50
☐ 14 Bobby Engram	10.00	4.50	1.25
☐ 15 Eddie Kennison	15.00	6.75	1.85
☐ 16 Jeff Lewis	6.00	2.70	.75

1996 Topps Laser Stadium Stars

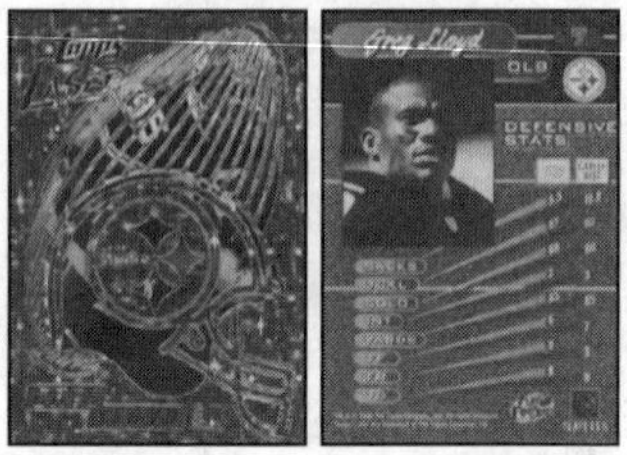

Randomly inserted in packs at a rate of one in 48, this 16-card standard-sized set when unfolded, is actually the size of two cards, as the laser sculpted holographic foil outside shows a team logo for the player on the inside of the card. The interior photo is a full bleed color photo with foil enhancements, while the back of the card has a color snapshot of the player and statistics comparing 1995 with career bests..

	MINT	NRMT	EXC
COMPLETE SET (16)	400.00	180.00	50.00
COMMON CARD (1-16)	10.00	4.50	1.25
☐ 1 Barry Sanders	40.00	18.00	5.00
☐ 2 Jim Harbaugh	15.00	6.75	1.85
☐ 3 Tim Brown	15.00	6.75	1.85
☐ 4 Jim Everett	10.00	4.50	1.25
☐ 5 Brett Favre	75.00	34.00	9.50
☐ 6 Junior Seau	15.00	6.75	1.85
☐ 7 Greg Lloyd	10.00	4.50	1.25
☐ 8 Cris Carter	10.00	4.50	1.25
☐ 9 Emmitt Smith	75.00	34.00	9.50
☐ 10 Dan Marino	75.00	34.00	9.50
☐ 11 Jeff Blake	20.00	9.00	2.50
☐ 12 Darrell Green	10.00	4.50	1.25
☐ 13 John Elway	35.00	16.00	4.40
☐ 14 Marcus Allen	15.00	6.75	1.85
☐ 15 Steve Young	30.00	13.50	3.70
☐ 16 Drew Bledsoe	40.00	18.00	5.00

1981 Topps Red Border Stickers

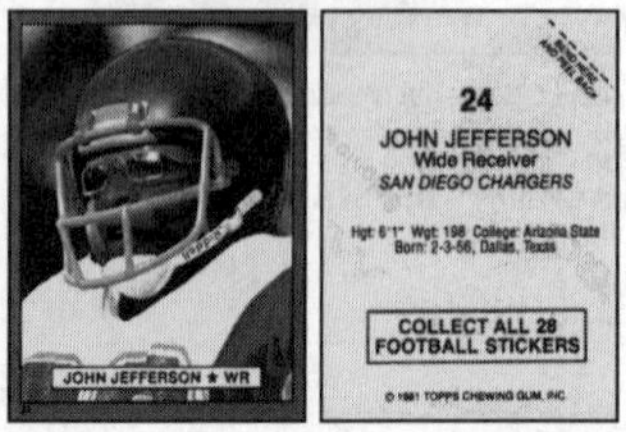

This set of 28 red-bordered stickers was distributed as a separate issue (inside a football capsule) unlike the "Coming Soon" subsets, which were inserted in with the regular football card wax packs. The stickers were actually sold in vending machines for 25 cents a sticker. They are the same size as the regular Topps stickers (1 15/16" by 2 9/16") and tougher to find than the other "Coming Soon" sticker subsets distributed in later years. The numbering in this set is completely different from the sticker numbering in the 1981 Topps 262-sticker set. There was one sticker issued for each team.

	MINT	NRMT	EXC
COMPLETE SET (28)	25.00	11.00	3.10
COMMON CARD (1-28)	.35	.16	.04
☐ 1 Steve Bartkowski	.75	.35	.09
☐ 2 Bert Jones	.75	.35	.09
☐ 3 Joe Cribbs	.60	.25	.07
☐ 4 Walter Payton	6.00	2.70	.75
☐ 5 Ross Browner	.35	.16	.04
☐ 6 Brian Sipe	.50	.23	.06
☐ 7 Tony Dorsett	3.00	1.35	.35
☐ 8 Randy Gradishar	.60	.25	.07
☐ 9 Billy Sims	1.00	.45	.12
☐ 10 James Lofton	2.00	.90	.25
☐ 11 Mike Barber	.35	.16	.04
☐ 12 Art Still	.50	.23	.06
☐ 13 Jack Youngblood	.75	.35	.09
☐ 14 David Woodley	.50	.23	.06
☐ 15 Ahmad Rashad	1.25	.55	.16
☐ 16 Russ Francis	.50	.23	.06
☐ 17 Archie Manning	.75	.35	.09
☐ 18 Dave Jennings	.35	.16	.04
☐ 19 Richard Todd	.50	.23	.06
☐ 20 Lester Hayes	.50	.23	.06
☐ 21 Ron Jaworski	.50	.23	.06
☐ 22 Franco Harris	2.00	.90	.25
☐ 23 Ottis Anderson	1.00	.45	.12
☐ 24 John Jefferson	.50	.23	.06
☐ 25 Freddie Solomon	.50	.23	.06
☐ 26 Steve Largent	3.50	1.55	.45
☐ 27 Lee Roy Selmon	1.50	.70	.19
☐ 28 Art Monk	7.50	3.40	.95

1981 Topps Stickers

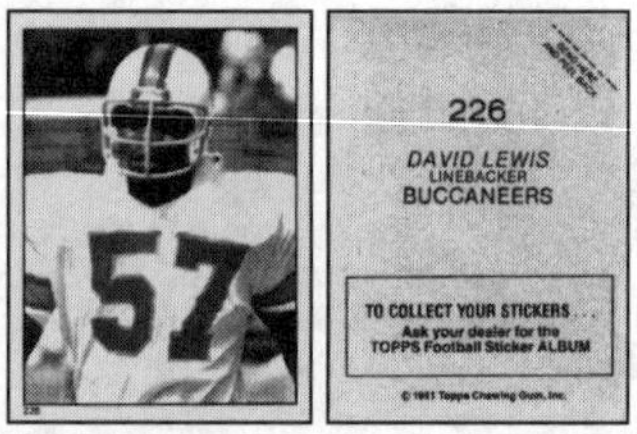

Like the 1981 baseball stickers, the 1981 Topps football stickers were also printed in Italy, each sticker measuring 1 15/16" by 2 9/16". The 262-card (sticker) set contains 22 All-Pro foil cards (numbers 121-142). The foil cards are somewhat more difficult to obtain, and a premium price is placed upon them. The card numbers begin with players from the AFC East teams and continue through the AFC Central and West divisions with teams within each division listed alphabetically. Card number 151 begins the NFC East teams, and a similar progression through the NFC divisions completes the remaining cards of the set. The backs contain a 1981 copyright date. On the inside back cover of the sticker album the company offered (via direct mail-order) any ten different stickers (but no more than two foil) of your choice for 1.00; this is one reason why the values of the most popular players in these sticker sets are somewhat depressed compared to traditional card set prices. The front cover of the sticker album features a Buffalo Bills player. The following players are shown in their Rookie Card year or earlier: Dwight Clark, Jacob Green (two years early), Dan Hampton, Art Monk, Anthony Munoz (one year early), and Kellen Winslow.

	MINT	NRMT	EXC
COMPLETE SET (262)	25.00	11.00	3.10
COMMON CARD (1-120/143-262)	.05	.02	.01
COMMON FOIL (121-142)	.20	.09	.03
☐ 1 Brian Sipe AFC Passing Leader	.10	.05	.01
☐ 2 Dan Fouts AFC Passing Yardage Leader	.30	.14	.04
☐ 3 John Jefferson AFC Receiving Yardage Leader	.10	.05	.01
☐ 4 Bruce Harper AFC Kickoff Return Yardage Leader	.05	.02	.01
☐ 5 J.T. Smith AFC Punt Return Yardage Leader	.05	.02	.01
☐ 6 Luke Prestridge AFC Punting Leader	.05	.02	.01
☐ 7 Lester Hayes AFC Interceptions Leader	.05	.02	.01
☐ 8 Gary Johnson AFC Sacks Leader	.05	.02	.01
☐ 9 Bert Jones	.20	.09	.03
☐ 10 Fred Cook	.05	.02	.01
☐ 11 Roger Carr	.05	.02	.01
☐ 12 Greg Landry	.10	.05	.01
☐ 13 Raymond Butler	.05	.02	.01
☐ 14 Bruce Laird	.05	.02	.01
☐ 15 Ed Simonini	.05	.02	.01
☐ 16 Curtis Dickey	.05	.02	.01
☐ 17 Joe Cribbs	.10	.05	.01
☐ 18 Joe Ferguson	.10	.05	.01
☐ 19 Ben Williams	.05	.02	.01
☐ 20 Jerry Butler	.05	.02	.01
☐ 21 Roland Hooks	.05	.02	.01
☐ 22 Fred Smerlas	.05	.02	.01
☐ 23 Frank Lewis	.05	.02	.01
☐ 24 Mark Brammer	.05	.02	.01
☐ 25 David Woodley	.05	.02	.01
☐ 26 Nat Moore	.10	.05	.01
☐ 27 Uwe Von Schamann	.05	.02	.01
☐ 28 Vern Den Herder	.05	.02	.01
☐ 29 Tony Nathan	.10	.05	.01
☐ 30 Duriel Harris	.05	.02	.01
☐ 31 Don McNeal	.05	.02	.01
☐ 32 Delvin Williams	.05	.02	.01
☐ 33 Stanley Morgan	.10	.05	.01
☐ 34 John Hannah	.20	.09	.03
☐ 35 Horace Ivory	.05	.02	.01
☐ 36 Steve Nelson	.05	.02	.01
☐ 37 Steve Grogan	.20	.09	.03
☐ 38 Vagas Ferguson	.05	.02	.01
☐ 39 John Smith	.05	.02	.01
☐ 40 Mike Haynes	.10	.05	.01
☐ 41 Mark Gastineau	.10	.05	.01
☐ 42 Wesley Walker	.10	.05	.01
☐ 43 Joe Klecko	.10	.05	.01
☐ 44 Chris Ward	.05	.02	.01
☐ 45 Johnny Lam Jones	.05	.02	.01
☐ 46 Marvin Powell	.05	.02	.01
☐ 47 Richard Todd	.10	.05	.01
☐ 48 Greg Buttle	.05	.02	.01
☐ 49 Eddie Edwards	.05	.02	.01
☐ 50 Dan Ross	.05	.02	.01
☐ 51 Ken Anderson	.30	.14	.04
☐ 52 Ross Browner	.05	.02	.01
☐ 53 Don Bass	.05	.02	.01
☐ 54 Jim LeClair	.05	.02	.01
☐ 55 Pete Johnson	.05	.02	.01
☐ 56 Anthony Munoz	1.00	.45	.12
☐ 57 Brian Sipe	.10	.05	.01
☐ 58 Mike Pruitt	.10	.05	.01
☐ 59 Greg Pruitt	.10	.05	.01
☐ 60 Thom Darden	.05	.02	.01
☐ 61 Ozzie Newsome	.30	.14	.04
☐ 62 Dave Logan	.05	.02	.01
☐ 63 Lyle Alzado	.20	.09	.03
☐ 64 Reggie Rucker	.05	.02	.01
☐ 65 Robert Brazile	.05	.02	.01
☐ 66 Mike Barber	.05	.02	.01
☐ 67 Carl Roaches	.05	.02	.01
☐ 68 Ken Stabler	.75	.35	.09
☐ 69 Gregg Bingham	.05	.02	.01
☐ 70 Mike Renfro	.05	.02	.01
☐ 71 Leon Gray	.05	.02	.01
☐ 72 Rob Carpenter	.05	.02	.01
☐ 73 Franco Harris	.35	.16	.04
☐ 74 Jack Lambert	.30	.14	.04
☐ 75 Jim Smith	.05	.02	.01
☐ 76 Mike Webster	.20	.09	.03
☐ 77 Sidney Thornton	.05	.02	.01
☐ 78 Joe Greene	.30	.14	.04
☐ 79 John Stallworth	.20	.09	.03
☐ 80 Tyrone McGriff	.05	.02	.01
☐ 81 Randy Gradishar	.10	.05	.01
☐ 82 Haven Moses	.05	.02	.01
☐ 83 Riley Odoms	.05	.02	.01
☐ 84 Matt Robinson	.05	.02	.01
☐ 85 Craig Morton	.10	.05	.01
☐ 86 Rulon Jones	.05	.02	.01
☐ 87 Rick Upchurch	.10	.05	.01
☐ 88 Jim Jensen	.05	.02	.01
☐ 89 Art Still	.05	.02	.01
☐ 90 J.T. Smith	.10	.05	.01
☐ 91 Steve Fuller	.05	.02	.01
☐ 92 Gary Barbaro	.05	.02	.01
☐ 93 Ted McKnight	.05	.02	.01
☐ 94 Bob Grupp	.05	.02	.01
☐ 95 Henry Marshall	.05	.02	.01
☐ 96 Mike Williams	.05	.02	.01
☐ 97 Jim Plunkett	.20	.09	.03
☐ 98 Lester Hayes	.10	.05	.01
☐ 99 Cliff Branch	.20	.09	.03
☐ 100 John Matuszak	.10	.05	.01
☐ 101 Matt Millen	.10	.05	.01
☐ 102 Kenny King	.05	.02	.01
☐ 103 Ray Guy	.10	.05	.01
☐ 104 Ted Hendricks	.20	.09	.03
☐ 105 John Jefferson	.20	.09	.03
☐ 106 Fred Dean	.05	.02	.01
☐ 107 Dan Fouts	.35	.16	.04
☐ 108 Charlie Joiner	.30	.14	.04
☐ 109 Kellen Winslow	1.50	.70	.19
☐ 110 Gary Johnson	.05	.02	.01
☐ 111 Mike Thomas	.05	.02	.01
☐ 112 Louie Kelcher	.05	.02	.01
☐ 113 Jim Zorn	.10	.05	.01
☐ 114 Terry Beeson	.05	.02	.01
☐ 115 Jacob Green	.20	.09	.03
☐ 116 Steve Largent	1.00	.45	.12
☐ 117 Dan Doornink	.05	.02	.01
☐ 118 Manu Tuiasosopo	.05	.02	.01
☐ 119 John Sawyer	.05	.02	.01
☐ 120 Jim Jodat	.05	.02	.01
☐ 121 Walter Payton All-Pro FOIL	1.50	.70	.19
☐ 122 Brian Sipe All-Pro FOIL	.30	.14	.04
☐ 123 Joe Cribbs All-Pro FOIL	.30	.14	.04
☐ 124 James Lofton All-Pro FOIL	.50	.23	.06
☐ 125 John Jefferson All-Pro FOIL	.30	.14	.04
☐ 126 Leon Gray All-Pro FOIL	.20	.09	.03
☐ 127 Joe DeLamielleure All-Pro FOIL	.20	.09	.03

☐ 128 Mike Webster All-Pro FOIL	.30	.14	.04
☐ 129 John Hannah All-Pro FOIL	.30	.14	.04
☐ 130 Mike Kenn All-Pro FOIL	.20	.09	.03
☐ 131 Kellen Winslow All-Pro FOIL	2.00	.90	.25
☐ 132 Lee Roy Selmon All-Pro FOIL	.50	.23	.06
☐ 133 Randy White All-Pro FOIL	.50	.23	.06
☐ 134 Gary Johnson All-Pro FOIL	.20	.09	.03
☐ 135 Art Still All-Pro FOIL	.20	.09	.03
☐ 136 Robert Brazile All-Pro FOIL	.20	.09	.03
☐ 137 Nolan Cromwell All-Pro FOIL	.20	.09	.03
☐ 138 Ted Hendricks All-Pro FOIL	.30	.14	.04
☐ 139 Lester Hayes All-Pro FOIL	.30	.14	.04
☐ 140 Randy Gradishar All-Pro FOIL	.30	.14	.04
☐ 141 Lemar Parrish All-Pro FOIL	.20	.09	.03
☐ 142 Donnie Shell All-Pro FOIL	.30	.14	.04
☐ 143 Ron Jaworski NFC Passing Leader	.10	.05	.01
☐ 144 Archie Manning NFC Passing Yardage Leader	.10	.05	.01
☐ 145 Walter Payton NFC Rushing Yardage Leader	.60	.25	.07
☐ 146 Billy Sims NFC Rushing Touchdowns Leader	.20	.09	.03
☐ 147 James Lofton NFC Receiving Yardage Leader	.25	.11	.03
☐ 148 Dave Jennings NFC Punting Leader	.05	.02	.01
☐ 149 Nolan Cromwell NFC Interceptions Leader	.05	.02	.01
☐ 150 Al(Bubba) Baker NFC Sacks Leader	.10	.05	.01
☐ 151 Tony Dorsett	.75	.35	.09
☐ 152 Harvey Martin	.10	.05	.01
☐ 153 Danny White	.20	.09	.03
☐ 154 Pat Donovan	.05	.02	.01
☐ 155 Drew Pearson	.20	.09	.03
☐ 156 Robert Newhouse	.10	.05	.01
☐ 157 Randy White	.30	.14	.04
☐ 158 Butch Johnson	.10	.05	.01
☐ 159 Dave Jennings	.05	.02	.01
☐ 160 Brad Van Pelt	.05	.02	.01
☐ 161 Phil Simms	.40	.18	.05
☐ 162 Mike Friede	.05	.02	.01
☐ 163 Billy Taylor	.05	.02	.01
☐ 164 Gary Jeter	.05	.02	.01
☐ 165 George Martin	.05	.02	.01
☐ 166 Earnest Gray	.05	.02	.01
☐ 167 Ron Jaworski	.20	.09	.03
☐ 168 Bill Bergey	.10	.05	.01
☐ 169 Wilbert Montgomery	.10	.05	.01
☐ 170 Charlie Smith	.05	.02	.01
☐ 171 Jerry Robinson	.05	.02	.01
☐ 172 Herman Edwards	.05	.02	.01
☐ 173 Harold Carmichael	.20	.09	.03
☐ 174 Claude Humphrey	.05	.02	.01
☐ 175 Ottis Anderson	.25	.11	.03
☐ 176 Jim Hart	.10	.05	.01
☐ 177 Pat Tilley	.05	.02	.01
☐ 178 Rush Brown	.05	.02	.01
☐ 179 Tom Brahaney	.05	.02	.01
☐ 180 Dan Dierdorf	.25	.11	.03
☐ 181 Wayne Morris	.05	.02	.01
☐ 182 Doug Marsh	.05	.02	.01
☐ 183 Art Monk	2.00	.90	.25
☐ 184 Clarence Harmon	.05	.02	.01
☐ 185 Lemar Parrish	.05	.02	.01
☐ 186 Joe Theismann	.35	.16	.04
☐ 187 Joe Lavender	.05	.02	.01
☐ 188 Wilbur Jackson	.05	.02	.01
☐ 189 Dave Butz	.10	.05	.01
☐ 190 Coy Bacon	.05	.02	.01
☐ 191 Walter Payton	1.25	.55	.16
☐ 192 Alan Page	.20	.09	.03
☐ 193 Vince Evans	.20	.09	.03
☐ 194 Roland Harper	.05	.02	.01
☐ 195 Dan Hampton	.60	.25	.07
☐ 196 Gary Fencik	.10	.05	.01
☐ 197 Mike Hartenstine	.05	.02	.01
☐ 198 Robin Earl	.05	.02	.01
☐ 199 Billy Sims	.25	.11	.03
☐ 200 Leonard Thompson	.05	.02	.01
☐ 201 Jeff Komlo	.05	.02	.01
☐ 202 Al(Bubba) Baker	.10	.05	.01
☐ 203 Eddie Murray	.10	.05	.01
☐ 204 Dexter Bussey	.05	.02	.01
☐ 205 Tom Ginn	.05	.02	.01
☐ 206 Freddie Scott	.05	.02	.01
☐ 207 James Lofton	.40	.18	.05
☐ 208 Mike Butler	.05	.02	.01
☐ 209 Lynn Dickey	.10	.05	.01
☐ 210 Gerry Ellis	.05	.02	.01
☐ 211 Eddie Lee Ivery	.10	.05	.01
☐ 212 Ezra Johnson	.05	.02	.01
☐ 213 Paul Coffman	.05	.02	.01
☐ 214 Aundra Thompson	.05	.02	.01
☐ 215 Ahmad Rashad	.20	.09	.03
☐ 216 Tommy Kramer	.10	.05	.01
☐ 217 Matt Blair	.05	.02	.01
☐ 218 Sammie White	.10	.05	.01
☐ 219 Ted Brown	.05	.02	.01
☐ 220 Joe Senser	.05	.02	.01
☐ 221 Rickey Young	.05	.02	.01
☐ 222 Randy Holloway	.05	.02	.01
☐ 223 Lee Roy Selmon	.30	.14	.04
☐ 224 Doug Williams	.10	.05	.01
☐ 225 Ricky Bell	.10	.05	.01
☐ 226 David Lewis	.05	.02	.01
☐ 227 Gordon Jones	.05	.02	.01
☐ 228 Dewey Selmon	.10	.05	.01
☐ 229 Jimmie Giles	.10	.05	.01
☐ 230 Mike Washington	.05	.02	.01
☐ 231 William Andrews	.10	.05	.01
☐ 232 Jeff Van Note	.05	.02	.01
☐ 233 Steve Bartkowski	.10	.05	.01
☐ 234 Junior Miller	.05	.02	.01
☐ 235 Lynn Cain	.05	.02	.01
☐ 236 Joel Williams	.05	.02	.01
☐ 237 Alfred Jenkins	.10	.05	.01
☐ 238 Kenny Johnson	.05	.02	.01
☐ 239 Jack Youngblood	.20	.09	.03
☐ 240 Elvis Peacock	.05	.02	.01
☐ 241 Cullen Bryant	.05	.02	.01
☐ 242 Dennis Harrah	.05	.02	.01
☐ 243 Billy Waddy	.05	.02	.01
☐ 244 Nolan Cromwell	.10	.05	.01
☐ 245 Doug France	.05	.02	.01
☐ 246 Johnnie Johnson	.05	.02	.01
☐ 247 Archie Manning	.20	.09	.03
☐ 248 Tony Galbreath	.05	.02	.01
☐ 249 Wes Chandler	.10	.05	.01
☐ 250 Stan Brock	.05	.02	.01
☐ 251 Ike Harris	.05	.02	.01
☐ 252 Russell Erxleben	.05	.02	.01
☐ 253 Jimmy Rogers	.05	.02	.01
☐ 254 Tom Myers	.05	.02	.01
☐ 255 Dwight Clark	.75	.35	.09
☐ 256 Earl Cooper	.05	.02	.01
☐ 257 Steve DeBerg	.20	.09	.03
☐ 258 Randy Cross	.10	.05	.01
☐ 259 Freddie Solomon	.05	.02	.01
☐ 260 Jim Miller	.05	.02	.01
☐ 261 Charley Young	.05	.02	.01
☐ 262 Bobby Leopold	.05	.02	.01
☐ NNO Sticker Album	2.00	.90	.25

1982 Topps Coming Soon Stickers

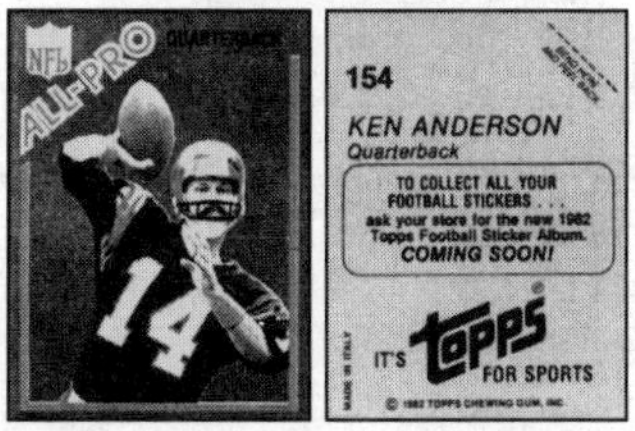

This 16-sticker set advertises "Coming Soon" on the sticker backs. All stickers in this small set were gold bordered foil stickers; these "Coming Soon" stickers were inserted in the regular issue 1982 Topps football card wax packs. They are the same size as the regular Topps stickers with the same sticker numbers as well; hence the set is skip-numbered.

	MINT	NRMT	EXC
COMPLETE SET (16)	6.00	2.70	.75
COMMON CARD	.20	.09	.03
☐ 5 MVP Super Bowl XVI (Joe Montana)	2.50	1.10	.30
☐ 6 NFC Championship	.20	.09	.03
☐ 9 Super Bowl XVI (Joe Montana handing off)	2.00	.90	.25
☐ 71 Tommy Kramer	.20	.09	.03
☐ 73 George Rogers	.30	.14	.04
☐ 75 Tom Skladany	.20	.09	.03
☐ 139 Nolan Cromwell AP	.20	.09	.03
☐ 143 Jack Lambert AP	.50	.23	.06
☐ 144 Lawrence Taylor AP	1.50	.70	.19
☐ 150 Billy Sims AP	.40	.18	.05
☐ 154 Ken Anderson AP	.50	.23	.06
☐ 159 John Hannah AP	.40	.18	.05
☐ 160 Anthony Munoz AP	1.00	.45	.12
☐ 220 Ken Anderson	.50	.23	.06
☐ 221 Dan Fouts	.50	.23	.06
☐ 222 Frank Lewis	.20	.09	.03

1982 Topps Stickers

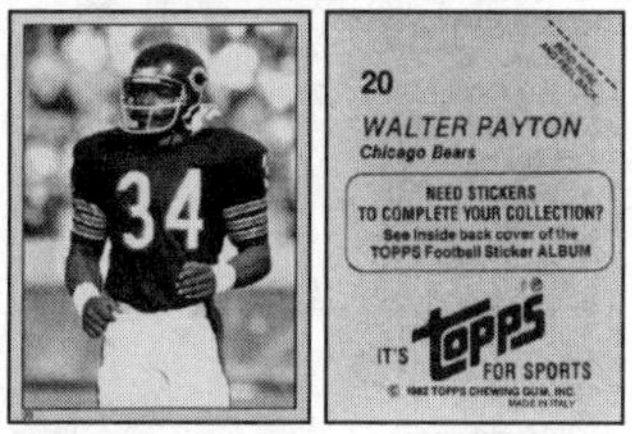

The 1982 Topps football sticker set contains 288 stickers and is similar in format to the 1981 sticker set. The stickers measure 1 15/16" by 2 9/16". This year's stickers have yellow borders compared to the white borders of the previous year. Stickers numbered 1-10, 70-77, 139-160, and 220-227 are foils. Stickers numbered 1 and 2 combine to portray the San Francisco 49ers, Super Bowl XVI Champions. Sticker numbers 3 and 4 combine to form the Super Bowl XVI theme art trophy. Stickers are numbered essentially in team order, with the teams themselves ordered alphabetically by team name within conference. Those stickers that are asterisked in the checklist below are those that were also included in the "Coming Soon" sticker set inserted in early 1982 football wax packs. The backs contain a 1982 copyright date. On the inside back cover of the sticker album the company offered (via direct mail-order) any ten different stickers (but no more than two foil) of your choice for 1.00; this is one reason why the values of the most popular players in these sticker sets are somewhat depressed compared to traditional card set prices. The front cover of the sticker album features Joe Montana. The following players are shown in their Rookie Card year: James Brooks, Cris Collinsworth, Ronnie Lott, Anthony Munoz, Lawrence Taylor, and Everson Walls.

	MINT	NRMT	EXC
COMPLETE SET (288)	30.00	13.50	3.70
COMMON CARD (1-288)	.05	.02	.01
COMMON FOIL	.15	.07	.02
☐ 1 Super Bowl XVI Champs, San Francisco 49ers Team (L) FOIL	.35	.16	.04
☐ 2 Super Bowl XVI Champs, San Francisco 49ers Team (R) FOIL	.20	.09	.03
☐ 3 Super Bowl XVI Theme Art trophy (top) FOIL	.20	.09	.03
☐ 4 Super Bowl XVI Theme Art trophy (bottom) FOIL	.20	.09	.03
☐ 5 MVP Joe Montana Super Bowl XVI * FOIL	4.00	1.80	.50
☐ 6 1981 NFC Champions 49'ers * FOIL	.10	.05	.01
☐ 7 1981 AFC Champions (Ken Anderson handing off) FOIL	.25	.11	.03
☐ 8 Super Bowl XVI (Ken Anderson dropping back) FOIL	.25	.11	.03
☐ 9 Super Bowl XVI (Joe Montana handing off) * FOIL	3.00	1.35	.35
☐ 10 Super Bowl XVI (line blocking) FOIL	.10	.05	.01
☐ 11 Steve Bartkowski	.10	.05	.01
☐ 12 William Andrews	.05	.02	.01
☐ 13 Lynn Cain	.05	.02	.01
☐ 14 Wallace Francis	.05	.02	.01
☐ 15 Alfred Jackson	.05	.02	.01
☐ 16 Alfred Jenkins	.05	.02	.01
☐ 17 Mike Kenn	.05	.02	.01
☐ 18 Junior Miller	.05	.02	.01
☐ 19 Vince Evans	.10	.05	.01
☐ 20 Walter Payton	1.00	.45	.12
☐ 21 Dave Williams	.05	.02	.01
☐ 22 Brian Baschnagel	.05	.02	.01
☐ 23 Rickey Watts	.05	.02	.01
☐ 24 Ken Margerum	.05	.02	.01
☐ 25 Revie Sorey	.05	.02	.01
☐ 26 Gary Fencik	.05	.02	.01
☐ 27 Matt Suhey	.10	.05	.01
☐ 28 Danny White	.20	.09	.03
☐ 29 Tony Dorsett	.40	.18	.05
☐ 30 Drew Pearson	.20	.09	.03
☐ 31 Rafael Septien	.05	.02	.01
☐ 32 Pat Donovan	.05	.02	.01
☐ 33 Herb Scott	.05	.02	.01
☐ 34 Ed Too Tall Jones	.20	.09	.03
☐ 35 Randy White	.25	.11	.03
☐ 36 Tony Hill	.10	.05	.01
☐ 37 Eric Hipple	.05	.02	.01
☐ 38 Billy Sims	.20	.09	.03
☐ 39 Dexter Bussey	.05	.02	.01
☐ 40 Freddie Scott	.05	.02	.01
☐ 41 David Hill	.05	.02	.01
☐ 42 Eddie Murray	.05	.02	.01
☐ 43 Tom Skladany	.05	.02	.01
☐ 44 Doug English	.05	.02	.01
☐ 45 Al(Bubba) Baker	.10	.05	.01
☐ 46 Lynn Dickey	.10	.05	.01
☐ 47 Gerry Ellis	.05	.02	.01
☐ 48 Harlan Huckleby	.05	.02	.01
☐ 49 James Lofton	.35	.16	.04
☐ 50 John Jefferson	.10	.05	.01
☐ 51 Paul Coffman	.05	.02	.01
☐ 52 Jan Stenerud	.10	.05	.01
☐ 53 Rich Wingo	.05	.02	.01
☐ 54 Wendell Tyler	.05	.02	.01
☐ 55 Preston Dennard	.05	.02	.01
☐ 56 Billy Waddy	.05	.02	.01
☐ 57 Frank Corral	.05	.02	.01
☐ 58 Jack Youngblood	.10	.05	.01
☐ 59 Pat Thomas	.05	.02	.01
☐ 60 Rod Perry	.05	.02	.01
☐ 61 Nolan Cromwell	.05	.02	.01
☐ 62 Tommy Kramer	.10	.05	.01
☐ 63 Rickey Young	.05	.02	.01
☐ 64 Ted Brown	.05	.02	.01
☐ 65 Ahmad Rashad	.25	.11	.03
☐ 66 Sammie White	.05	.02	.01
☐ 67 Joe Senser	.05	.02	.01
☐ 68 Ron Yary	.05	.02	.01
☐ 69 Matt Blair	.05	.02	.01
☐ 70 Joe Montana FOIL NFC Passing Leader	4.00	1.80	.50
☐ 71 Tommy Kramer * FOIL NFC Passing Yardage Leader	.15	.07	.02
☐ 72 Alfred Jenkins FOIL NFC Receiving Yardage Leader	.15	.07	.02
☐ 73 George Rogers * FOIL NFC Rushing Yardage Leader	.15	.07	.02
☐ 74 Wendell Tyler FOIL NFC Rushing Touchdowns Leader	.15	.07	.02
☐ 75 Tom Skladany * FOIL NFC Punting Leader	.15	.07	.02
☐ 76 Everson Walls FOIL NFC Interceptions Leader	.25	.11	.03
☐ 77 Curtis Greer FOIL NFC Sacks Leader	.15	.07	.02
☐ 78 Archie Manning	.20	.09	.03
☐ 79 Dave Waymer	.05	.02	.01
☐ 80 George Rogers	.20	.09	.03
☐ 81 Jack Holmes	.05	.02	.01
☐ 82 Toussaint Tyler	.05	.02	.01
☐ 83 Wayne Wilson	.05	.02	.01
☐ 84 Russell Erxleben	.05	.02	.01
☐ 85 Elois Grooms	.05	.02	.01
☐ 86 Phil Simms	.20	.09	.03
☐ 87 Scott Brunner	.05	.02	.01
☐ 88 Rob Carpenter	.05	.02	.01
☐ 89 Johnny Perkins	.05	.02	.01
☐ 90 Dave Jennings	.05	.02	.01
☐ 91 Harry Carson	.10	.05	.01
☐ 92 Lawrence Taylor	1.50	.70	.19
☐ 93 Beasley Reece	.05	.02	.01
☐ 94 Mark Haynes	.10	.05	.01
☐ 95 Ron Jaworski	.10	.05	.01
☐ 96 Wilbert Montgomery	.10	.05	.01
☐ 97 Hubie Oliver	.05	.02	.01
☐ 98 Harold Carmichael	.10	.05	.01
☐ 99 Jerry Robinson	.05	.02	.01
☐ 100 Stan Walters	.05	.02	.01
☐ 101 Charlie Johnson	.05	.02	.01
☐ 102 Roynell Young	.05	.02	.01
☐ 103 Tony Franklin	.05	.02	.01
☐ 104 Neil Lomax	.20	.09	.03
☐ 105 Jim Hart	.10	.05	.01
☐ 106 Ottis Anderson	.20	.09	.03
☐ 107 Stump Mitchell	.10	.05	.01
☐ 108 Pat Tilley	.05	.02	.01
☐ 109 Rush Brown	.05	.02	.01
☐ 110 E.J. Junior	.05	.02	.01
☐ 111 Ken Greene	.05	.02	.01
☐ 112 Mel Gray	.05	.02	.01
☐ 113 Joe Montana	3.00	1.35	.35
☐ 114 Ricky Patton	.05	.02	.01
☐ 115 Earl Cooper	.05	.02	.01
☐ 116 Dwight Clark	.25	.11	.03
☐ 117 Freddie Solomon	.05	.02	.01
☐ 118 Randy Cross	.05	.02	.01
☐ 119 Fred Dean	.05	.02	.01
☐ 120 Ronnie Lott	1.00	.45	.12
☐ 121 Dwight Hicks	.05	.02	.01
☐ 122 Doug Williams	.10	.05	.01
☐ 123 Jerry Eckwood	.05	.02	.01
☐ 124 James Owens	.05	.02	.01
☐ 125 Kevin House	.05	.02	.01
☐ 126 Jimmie Giles	.10	.05	.01
☐ 127 Charley Hannah	.05	.02	.01
☐ 128 Lee Roy Selmon	.25	.11	.03
☐ 129 Hugh Green	.10	.05	.01
☐ 130 Joe Theismann	.30	.14	.04
☐ 131 Joe Washington	.05	.02	.01
☐ 132 John Riggins	.25	.11	.03
☐ 133 Art Monk	.50	.23	.06
☐ 134 Ricky Thompson	.05	.02	.01
☐ 135 Don Warren	.05	.02	.01
☐ 136 Perry Brooks	.05	.02	.01
☐ 137 Mike Nelms	.05	.02	.01
☐ 138 Mark Moseley	.05	.02	.01
☐ 139 Nolan Cromwell * AP FOIL	.15	.07	.02

☐ 140 Dwight Hicks AP FOIL	.15	.07	.02
☐ 141 Ronnie Lott AP FOIL	1.50	.70	.19
☐ 142 Harry Carson AP FOIL	.25	.11	.03
☐ 143 Jack Lambert * AP FOIL	.35	.16	.04
☐ 144 Lawrence Taylor * AP FOIL	2.00	.90	.25
☐ 145 Mel Blount AP FOIL	.30	.14	.04
☐ 146 Joe Klecko AP FOIL	.15	.07	.02
☐ 147 Randy White AP FOIL	.35	.16	.04
☐ 148 Doug English AP FOIL	.15	.07	.02
☐ 149 Fred Dean AP FOIL	.15	.07	.02
☐ 150 Billy Sims * AP FOIL	.30	.14	.04
☐ 151 Tony Dorsett AP FOIL	.75	.35	.09
☐ 152 James Lofton AP FOIL	.60	.25	.07
☐ 153 Alfred Jenkins AP FOIL	.25	.11	.03
☐ 154 Ken Anderson * AP FOIL	.40	.18	.05
☐ 155 Kellen Winslow AP FOIL	.60	.25	.07
☐ 156 Marvin Powell AP FOIL	.15	.07	.02
☐ 157 Randy Cross AP FOIL	.15	.07	.02
☐ 158 Mike Webster AP FOIL	.25	.11	.03
☐ 159 John Hannah * AP FOIL	.30	.14	.04
☐ 160 Anthony Munoz * AP FOIL	1.00	.45	.12
☐ 161 Curtis Dickey	.05	.02	.01
☐ 162 Randy McMillan	.05	.02	.01
☐ 163 Roger Carr	.05	.02	.01
☐ 164 Raymond Butler	.05	.02	.01
☐ 165 Reese McCall	.05	.02	.01
☐ 166 Ed Simonini	.05	.02	.01
☐ 167 Herb Orvis	.05	.02	.01
☐ 168 Nesby Glasgow	.05	.02	.01
☐ 169 Joe Ferguson	.10	.05	.01
☐ 170 Joe Cribbs	.10	.05	.01
☐ 171 Jerry Butler	.05	.02	.01
☐ 172 Frank Lewis	.05	.02	.01
☐ 173 Mark Brammer	.05	.02	.01
☐ 174 Fred Smerlas	.05	.02	.01
☐ 175 Jim Haslett	.05	.02	.01
☐ 176 Charles Romes	.05	.02	.01
☐ 177 Bill Simpson	.05	.02	.01
☐ 178 Ken Anderson	.25	.11	.03
☐ 179 Charles Alexander	.05	.02	.01
☐ 180 Pete Johnson	.05	.02	.01
☐ 181 Isaac Curtis	.05	.02	.01
☐ 182 Cris Collinsworth	.50	.23	.06
☐ 183 Pat McInally	.05	.02	.01
☐ 184 Anthony Munoz	.50	.23	.06
☐ 185 Louis Breeden	.05	.02	.01
☐ 186 Jim Breech	.05	.02	.01
☐ 187 Brian Sipe	.10	.05	.01
☐ 188 Charles White	.10	.05	.01
☐ 189 Mike Pruitt	.05	.02	.01
☐ 190 Reggie Rucker	.05	.02	.01
☐ 191 Dave Logan	.05	.02	.01
☐ 192 Ozzie Newsome	.25	.11	.03
☐ 193 Dick Ambrose	.05	.02	.01
☐ 194 Joe DeLamielleure	.05	.02	.01
☐ 195 Ricky Feacher	.05	.02	.01
☐ 196 Craig Morton	.10	.05	.01
☐ 197 Dave Preston	.05	.02	.01
☐ 198 Rick Parros	.05	.02	.01
☐ 199 Rick Upchurch	.05	.02	.01
☐ 200 Steve Watson	.05	.02	.01
☐ 201 Riley Odoms	.05	.02	.01
☐ 202 Randy Gradishar	.10	.05	.01
☐ 203 Steve Foley	.05	.02	.01
☐ 204 Ken Stabler	.40	.18	.05
☐ 205 Gifford Nielsen	.05	.02	.01
☐ 206 Tim Wilson	.05	.02	.01
☐ 207 Ken Burrough	.05	.02	.01
☐ 208 Mike Renfro	.05	.02	.01
☐ 209 Greg Stemrick	.05	.02	.01
☐ 210 Robert Brazile	.05	.02	.01
☐ 211 Gregg Bingham	.05	.02	.01
☐ 212 Steve Fuller	.05	.02	.01
☐ 213 Bill Kenney	.05	.02	.01
☐ 214 Joe Delaney	.10	.05	.01
☐ 215 Henry Marshall	.05	.02	.01
☐ 216 Nick Lowery	.10	.05	.01
☐ 217 Art Still	.05	.02	.01
☐ 218 Gary Green	.05	.02	.01
☐ 219 Gary Barbaro	.05	.02	.01
☐ 220 Ken Anderson * FOIL AFC Passing Leader	.40	.18	.05
☐ 221 Dan Fouts * FOIL AFC Passing Yardage Leader	.50	.23	.06
☐ 222 Frank Lewis * FOIL AFC Receiving Yardage Leader	.15	.07	.02
☐ 222 Steve Watson FOIL AFC Receiving Yardage Leader	.15	.07	.02
☐ 223 James Brooks FOIL AFC Kickoff Return Yardage Leader	.60	.25	.07
☐ 224 Chuck Muncie FOIL AFC Rushing Touchdowns Leader	.15	.07	.02
☐ 225 Pat McInally FOIL AFC Punting Leader	.15	.07	.02
☐ 226 John Harris FOIL AFC Interceptions Leader	.15	.07	.02
☐ 227 Joe Klecko FOIL AFC Sacks Leader	.15	.07	.02
☐ 228 David Woodley	.10	.05	.01
☐ 229 Tony Nathan	.10	.05	.01
☐ 230 Andra Franklin	.05	.02	.01
☐ 231 Nat Moore	.10	.05	.01
☐ 232 Duriel Harris	.05	.02	.01
☐ 233 Uwe Von Schamann	.05	.02	.01
☐ 234 Bob Baumhower	.05	.02	.01
☐ 235 Glenn Blackwood	.05	.02	.01
☐ 236 Tommy Vigorito	.05	.02	.01
☐ 237 Steve Grogan	.10	.05	.01
☐ 238 Matt Cavanaugh	.05	.02	.01
☐ 239 Tony Collins	.05	.02	.01
☐ 240 Vagas Ferguson	.05	.02	.01
☐ 241 John Smith	.05	.02	.01
☐ 242 Stanley Morgan	.10	.05	.01
☐ 243 John Hannah	.10	.05	.01
☐ 244 Steve Nelson	.05	.02	.01
☐ 245 Don Hasselbeck	.05	.02	.01
☐ 246 Richard Todd	.10	.05	.01
☐ 247 Bruce Harper	.05	.02	.01
☐ 248 Wesley Walker	.10	.05	.01
☐ 249 Jerome Barkum	.05	.02	.01
☐ 250 Marvin Powell	.05	.02	.01
☐ 251 Mark Gastineau	.10	.05	.01
☐ 252 Joe Klecko	.10	.05	.01
☐ 253 Darrol Ray	.05	.02	.01
☐ 254 Marty Lyons	.05	.02	.01
☐ 255 Marc Wilson	.10	.05	.01
☐ 256 Kenny King	.05	.02	.01
☐ 257 Mark Van Eeghen	.05	.02	.01
☐ 258 Cliff Branch	.10	.05	.01
☐ 259 Bob Chandler	.05	.02	.01
☐ 260 Ray Guy	.10	.05	.01
☐ 261 Ted Hendricks	.20	.09	.03
☐ 262 Lester Hayes	.10	.05	.01
☐ 263 Terry Bradshaw	.75	.35	.09
☐ 264 Franco Harris	.40	.18	.05
☐ 265 John Stallworth	.20	.09	.03
☐ 266 Jim Smith	.05	.02	.01
☐ 267 Mike Webster	.10	.05	.01
☐ 268 Jack Lambert	.25	.11	.03
☐ 269 Mel Blount	.20	.09	.03
☐ 270 Donnie Shell	.05	.02	.01
☐ 271 Bennie Cunningham	.05	.02	.01
☐ 272 Dan Fouts	.30	.14	.04
☐ 273 Chuck Muncie	.10	.05	.01
☐ 274 James Brooks	.30	.14	.04
☐ 275 Charlie Joiner	.20	.09	.03
☐ 276 Wes Chandler	.10	.05	.01
☐ 277 Kellen Winslow	.35	.16	.04
☐ 278 Doug Wilkerson	.05	.02	.01
☐ 279 Gary Johnson	.05	.02	.01
☐ 280 Rolf Benirschke	.05	.02	.01
☐ 281 Jim Zorn	.10	.05	.01
☐ 282 Theotis Brown	.05	.02	.01
☐ 283 Dan Doornink	.05	.02	.01
☐ 284 Steve Largent	1.00	.45	.12
☐ 285 Sam McCullum	.05	.02	.01
☐ 286 Efren Herrera	.05	.02	.01
☐ 287 Manu Tuiasosopo	.05	.02	.01
☐ 288 John Harris	.05	.02	.01
☐ 288 Sticker Album (Joe Montana)	3.00	1.35	.35

1983 Topps Stickers

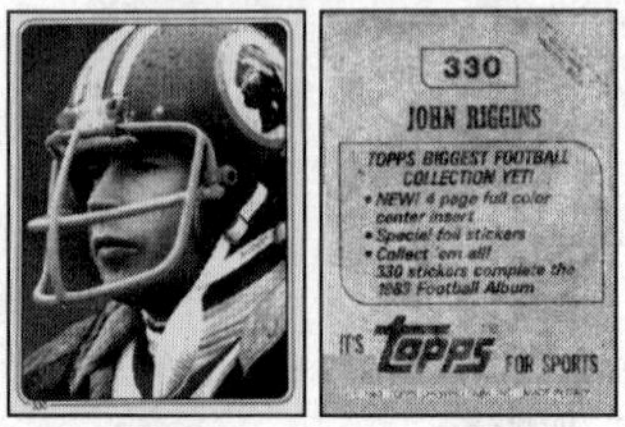

The 1983 Topps football sticker set (330) is similar to the previous years in that it contains stickers, foil stickers, and an accompanying album to house one's sticker collection. The foil stickers are noted in the checklist below by "FOIL"; foils are numbers 1-4, 73-80, 143-152, and 264-271. On the inside back cover of the sticker album the company offered (via direct mail-order) any ten different stickers (but no more than two foil) of your choice for 1.00; this is one reason why the values of the most popular players in these sticker sets are somewhat depressed compared to traditional card set prices. The following players are shown in their Rookie Card year: Marcus Allen, Jim McMahon, and Mike Singletary.

	MINT	NRMT	EXC
COMPLETE SET (330)	30.00	13.50	3.70
COMMON STICKER (1-330)	.05	.02	.01
COMMON FOIL	.10	.05	.01

☐ 1 Franco Harris (Left half) FOIL	.50	.23	.06
☐ 2 Franco Harris (Right half) FOIL	.35	.16	.04
☐ 3 Walter Payton (Left half) FOIL	1.00	.45	.12
☐ 4 Walter Payton (Right half) FOIL	1.00	.45	.12
☐ 5 John Riggins	.30	.14	.04
☐ 6 Tony Dorsett	.30	.14	.04
☐ 7 Mark Van Eeghen	.05	.02	.01
☐ 8 Chuck Muncie	.05	.02	.01
☐ 9 Wilbert Montgomery	.10	.05	.01
☐ 10 Greg Pruitt	.10	.05	.01
☐ 11 Sam Cunningham	.05	.02	.01
☐ 12 Ottis Anderson	.20	.09	.03
☐ 13 Mike Pruitt	.10	.05	.01
☐ 14 Dexter Bussey	.05	.02	.01
☐ 15 Mike Pagel	.05	.02	.01
☐ 16 Curtis Dickey	.05	.02	.01
☐ 17 Randy McMillan	.05	.02	.01
☐ 18 Raymond Butler	.05	.02	.01
☐ 19 Nesby Glasgow	.05	.02	.01
☐ 20 Zachary Dixon	.05	.02	.01
☐ 21 Matt Bouza	.05	.02	.01
☐ 22 Johnie Cooks	.05	.02	.01
☐ 23 Curtis Brown	.05	.02	.01
☐ 24 Joe Cribbs	.10	.05	.01
☐ 25 Roosevelt Leaks	.05	.02	.01
☐ 26 Jerry Butler	.05	.02	.01
☐ 27 Frank Lewis	.05	.02	.01
☐ 28 Fred Smerlas	.05	.02	.01
☐ 29 Ben Williams	.05	.02	.01
☐ 30 Joe Ferguson	.10	.05	.01
☐ 31 Isaac Curtis	.05	.02	.01
☐ 32 Cris Collinsworth	.20	.09	.03
☐ 33 Anthony Munoz	.20	.09	.03
☐ 34 Max Montoya	.10	.05	.01
☐ 35 Ross Browner	.05	.02	.01
☐ 36 Reggie Williams	.10	.05	.01
☐ 37 Ken Riley	.05	.02	.01
☐ 38 Pete Johnson	.05	.02	.01
☐ 39 Ken Anderson	.25	.11	.03
☐ 40 Charles White	.10	.05	.01
☐ 41 Dave Logan	.05	.02	.01
☐ 42 Doug Dieken	.05	.02	.01
☐ 43 Ozzie Newsome	.20	.09	.03
☐ 44 Tom Cousineau	.05	.02	.01
☐ 45 Bob Golic	.05	.02	.01
☐ 46 Brian Sipe	.10	.05	.01
☐ 47 Paul McDonald	.05	.02	.01
☐ 48 Mike Pruitt	.10	.05	.01
☐ 49 Luke Prestridge	.05	.02	.01
☐ 50 Randy Gradishar	.10	.05	.01
☐ 51 Rulon Jones	.05	.02	.01
☐ 52 Rick Parros	.05	.02	.01
☐ 53 Steve DeBerg	.05	.02	.01
☐ 54 Tom Jackson	.10	.05	.01
☐ 55 Rick Upchurch	.05	.02	.01
☐ 56 Steve Watson	.05	.02	.01
☐ 57 Robert Brazile	.05	.02	.01
☐ 58 Willie Tullis	.05	.02	.01
☐ 59 Archie Manning	.20	.09	.03
☐ 60 Gifford Nielsen	.05	.02	.01
☐ 61 Harold Bailey	.05	.02	.01
☐ 62 Carl Roaches	.05	.02	.01
☐ 63 Gregg Bingham	.05	.02	.01
☐ 64 Daryl Hunt	.05	.02	.01
☐ 65 Gary Green	.05	.02	.01
☐ 66 Gary Barbaro	.05	.02	.01
☐ 67 Bill Kenney	.05	.02	.01
☐ 68 Joe Delaney	.05	.02	.01
☐ 69 Henry Marshall	.05	.02	.01
☐ 70 Nick Lowery	.05	.02	.01
☐ 71 Jeff Gossett	.05	.02	.01
☐ 72 Art Still	.05	.02	.01
☐ 73 Ken Anderson FOIL AFC Passing Leader	.25	.11	.03
☐ 74 Dan Fouts FOIL AFC Passing Yardage Leader	.40	.18	.05
☐ 75 Wes Chandler FOIL AFC Receiving Yardage Leader	.25	.11	.03
☐ 76 James Brooks FOIL AFC Kickoff Return Yardage Leader	.30	.14	.04
☐ 77 Rick Upchurch FOIL AFC Punt Return Yardage Leader	.10	.05	.01
☐ 78 Luke Prestridge FOIL AFC Punting Leader	.10	.05	.01
☐ 79 Jesse Baker FOIL AFC Sacks Leader	.10	.05	.01
☐ 80 Freeman McNeil FOIL AFC Rushing Yardage Leader	.35	.16	.04
☐ 81 Ray Guy	.10	.05	.01
☐ 82 Jim Plunkett	.20	.09	.03
☐ 83 Lester Hayes	.05	.02	.01
☐ 84 Kenny King	.05	.02	.01
☐ 85 Cliff Branch	.20	.09	.03
☐ 86 Todd Christensen	.10	.05	.01
☐ 87 Lyle Alzado	.20	.09	.03
☐ 88 Ted Hendricks	.20	.09	.03
☐ 89 Rod Martin	.05	.02	.01
☐ 90 David Woodley	.10	.05	.01
☐ 91 Ed Newman	.05	.02	.01
☐ 92 Earnie Rhone	.05	.02	.01
☐ 93 Don McNeal	.05	.02	.01
☐ 94 Glenn Blackwood	.05	.02	.01
☐ 95 Andra Franklin	.05	.02	.01
☐ 96 Nat Moore	.10	.05	.01
☐ 97 Lyle Blackwood	.05	.02	.01
☐ 98 A.J. Duhe	.05	.02	.01
☐ 99 Tony Collins	.05	.02	.01
☐ 100 Stanley Morgan	.10	.05	.01
☐ 101 Pete Brock	.05	.02	.01
☐ 102 Steve Nelson	.05	.02	.01
☐ 103 Steve Grogan	.10	.05	.01
☐ 104 Mark Van Eeghen	.05	.02	.01
☐ 105 Don Hasselbeck	.05	.02	.01
☐ 106 John Hannah	.20	.09	.03
☐ 107 Mike Haynes	.10	.05	.01
☐ 108 Wesley Walker	.10	.05	.01
☐ 109 Marvin Powell	.05	.02	.01
☐ 110 Joe Klecko	.05	.02	.01
☐ 111 Bobby Jackson	.05	.02	.01
☐ 112 Richard Todd	.10	.05	.01
☐ 113 Lance Mehl	.05	.02	.01
☐ 114 Johnny Lam Jones	.05	.02	.01
☐ 115 Mark Gastineau	.05	.02	.01
☐ 116 Freeman McNeil	.10	.05	.01
☐ 117 Franco Harris	.35	.16	.04
☐ 118 Mike Webster	.20	.09	.03
☐ 119 Mel Blount	.20	.09	.03
☐ 120 Donnie Shell	.05	.02	.01
☐ 121 Terry Bradshaw	.50	.23	.06
☐ 122 John Stallworth	.20	.09	.03
☐ 123 Jack Lambert	.25	.11	.03
☐ 124 Dwayne Woodruff	.05	.02	.01
☐ 125 Bennie Cunningham	.05	.02	.01
☐ 126 Charlie Joiner	.20	.09	.03
☐ 127 Kellen Winslow	.30	.14	.04
☐ 128 Rolf Benirschke	.05	.02	.01
☐ 129 Louie Kelcher	.05	.02	.01
☐ 130 Chuck Muncie	.05	.02	.01
☐ 131 Wes Chandler	.10	.05	.01
☐ 132 Gary Johnson	.05	.02	.01
☐ 133 James Brooks	.20	.09	.03
☐ 134 Dan Fouts	.35	.16	.04
☐ 135 Jacob Green	.10	.05	.01
☐ 136 Michael Jackson	.05	.02	.01
☐ 137 Jim Zorn	.10	.05	.01
☐ 138 Sherman Smith	.05	.02	.01
☐ 139 Keith Simpson	.05	.02	.01
☐ 140 Steve Largent	1.00	.45	.12
☐ 141 John Harris	.05	.02	.01
☐ 142 Jeff West	.05	.02	.01
☐ 143 Ken Anderson (top) FOIL	.25	.11	.03
☐ 144 Ken Anderson (bottom) FOIL	.25	.11	.03
☐ 145 Tony Dorsett (top) FOIL	.40	.18	.05
☐ 146 Tony Dorsett (bottom) FOIL	.40	.18	.05
☐ 147 Dan Fouts (top) FOIL	.40	.18	.05
☐ 148 Dan Fouts (bottom) FOIL	.40	.18	.05
☐ 149 Joe Montana (top) FOIL	2.50	1.10	.30
☐ 150 Joe Montana (bottom) FOIL	2.50	1.10	.30
☐ 151 Mark Moseley (top) FOIL	.10	.05	.01
☐ 152 Mark Moseley (bottom) FOIL	.10	.05	.01
☐ 153 Richard Todd	.10	.05	.01
☐ 154 Butch Johnson	.05	.02	.01
☐ 155 Gary Hogeboom UER (Bill on back)	.05	.02	.01
☐ 156 A.J. Duhe	.05	.02	.01
☐ 157 Kurt Sohn	.05	.02	.01
☐ 158 Drew Pearson	.20	.09	.03
☐ 159 John Riggins	.25	.11	.03
☐ 160 Pat Donovan	.05	.02	.01
☐ 161 John Hannah	.20	.09	.03
☐ 162 Jeff Van Note	.05	.02	.01
☐ 163 Randy Cross	.10	.05	.01
☐ 164 Marvin Powell	.05	.02	.01
☐ 165 Kellen Winslow	.25	.11	.03
☐ 166 Dwight Clark	.20	.09	.03
☐ 167 Wes Chandler	.10	.05	.01
☐ 168 Tony Dorsett	.30	.14	.04
☐ 169 Freeman McNeil	.10	.05	.01
☐ 170 Ken Anderson	.20	.09	.03
☐ 171 Mark Moseley	.05	.02	.01
☐ 172 Mark Gastineau	.05	.02	.01
☐ 173 Gary Johnson	.05	.02	.01
☐ 174 Randy White	.25	.11	.03

175 Ed Too Tall Jones	.20	.09	.03
176 Hugh Green	.05	.02	.01
177 Harry Carson	.10	.05	.01
178 Lawrence Taylor	.35	.16	.04
179 Lester Hayes	.05	.02	.01
180 Mark Haynes	.10	.05	.01
181 Dave Jennings	.05	.02	.01
182 Nolan Cromwell	.05	.02	.01
183 Tony Peters	.05	.02	.01
184 Jimmy Cefalo	.05	.02	.01
185 A.J. Duhe	.05	.02	.01
186 John Riggins	.25	.11	.03
187 Charlie Brown	.05	.02	.01
188 Mike Nelms	.05	.02	.01
189 Mark Murphy	.05	.02	.01
190 Fulton Walker	.05	.02	.01
191 Marcus Allen	4.00	1.80	.50
192 Chip Banks	.05	.02	.01
193 Charlie Brown	.05	.02	.01
194 Bob Crable	.05	.02	.01
195 Vernon Dean	.05	.02	.01
196 Jim McMahon	.50	.23	.06
197 Tootie Robbins	.05	.02	.01
198 Luis Sharpe	.05	.02	.01
199 Rohn Stark	.05	.02	.01
200 Lester Williams	.05	.02	.01
201 Leo Wisniewski	.05	.02	.01
202 Butch Woolfolk	.05	.02	.01
203 Mike Kenn	.05	.02	.01
204 R.C. Thielemann	.05	.02	.01
205 Buddy Curry	.05	.02	.01
206 Steve Bartkowski	.10	.05	.01
207 Alfred Jackson	.05	.02	.01
208 Don Smith	.05	.02	.01
209 Alfred Jenkins	.05	.02	.01
210 Fulton Kuykendall	.05	.02	.01
211 William Andrews	.10	.05	.01
212 Gary Fencik	.05	.02	.01
213 Walter Payton	1.00	.45	.12
214 Mike Singletary	1.00	.45	.12
215 Otis Wilson	.05	.02	.01
216 Matt Suhey	.05	.02	.01
217 Dan Hampton	.25	.11	.03
218 Emery Moorehead	.05	.02	.01
219 Mike Hartenstine	.05	.02	.01
220 Danny White	.20	.09	.03
221 Drew Pearson	.20	.09	.03
222 Rafael Septien	.05	.02	.01
223 Ed Too Tall Jones	.20	.09	.03
224 Everson Walls	.10	.05	.01
225 Randy White	.25	.11	.03
226 Harvey Martin	.10	.05	.01
227 Tony Hill	.10	.05	.01
228 Tony Dorsett	.30	.14	.04
229 Billy Sims	.20	.09	.03
230 Leonard Thompson	.05	.02	.01
231 Eddie Murray	.05	.02	.01
232 Doug English	.05	.02	.01
233 Ken Fantetti	.05	.02	.01
234 Tom Skladany	.05	.02	.01
235 Freddie Scott	.05	.02	.01
236 Eric Hipple	.05	.02	.01
237 David Hill	.05	.02	.01
238 John Jefferson	.10	.05	.01
239 Paul Coffman	.05	.02	.01
240 Ezra Johnson	.05	.02	.01
241 Mike Douglass	.05	.02	.01
242 Mark Lee	.05	.02	.01
243 John Anderson	.05	.02	.01
244 Jan Stenerud	.20	.09	.03
245 Lynn Dickey	.10	.05	.01
246 James Lofton	.30	.14	.04
247 Vince Ferragamo	.10	.05	.01
248 Preston Dennard	.05	.02	.01
249 Jack Youngblood	.20	.09	.03
250 Mike Guman	.05	.02	.01
251 LeRoy Irvin	.05	.02	.01
252 Mike Lansford	.05	.02	.01
253 Kent Hill	.05	.02	.01
254 Nolan Cromwell	.05	.02	.01
255 Doug Martin	.05	.02	.01
256 Greg Coleman	.05	.02	.01
257 Ted Brown	.05	.02	.01
258 Mark Mullaney	.05	.02	.01
259 Joe Senser	.05	.02	.01
260 Randy Holloway	.05	.02	.01
261 Matt Blair	.05	.02	.01
262 Sammie White	.05	.02	.01
263 Tommy Kramer	.10	.05	.01
264 Joe Theismann FOIL NFC Passing Leader	.40	.18	.05
265 Joe Montana FOIL NFC Passing Yardage Leader	3.00	1.35	.35
266 Dwight Clark FOIL NFC Receiving Yardage Leader	.25	.11	.03
267 Mike Nelms FOIL NFC Kickoff Return Yardage Leader	.10	.05	.01
268 Carl Birdsong FOIL NFC Punting Leader	.10	.05	.01
269 Everson Walls FOIL NFC Interceptions Leader	.10	.05	.01
270 Doug Martin FOIL NFC Sacks Leader	.10	.05	.01
271 Tony Dorsett FOIL NFC Rushing Yardage Leader	.40	.18	.05
272 Russell Erxleben	.05	.02	.01
273 Stan Brock	.05	.02	.01
274 Jeff Groth	.05	.02	.01
275 Bruce Clark	.05	.02	.01
276 Ken Stabler	.40	.18	.05
277 George Rogers	.10	.05	.01
278 Derland Moore	.05	.02	.01
279 Wayne Wilson	.05	.02	.01
280 Lawrence Taylor	.35	.16	.04
281 Harry Carson	.10	.05	.01
282 Brian Kelley	.05	.02	.01
283 Brad Van Pelt	.05	.02	.01
284 Earnest Gray	.05	.02	.01
285 Dave Jennings	.05	.02	.01
286 Rob Carpenter	.05	.02	.01
287 Scott Brunner	.05	.02	.01
288 Ron Jaworski	.10	.05	.01
289 Jerry Robinson	.05	.02	.01
290 Frank LeMaster	.05	.02	.01
291 Wilbert Montgomery	.10	.05	.01
292 Tony Franklin	.05	.02	.01
293 Harold Carmichael	.20	.09	.03
294 John Spagnola	.05	.02	.01
295 Herman Edwards	.05	.02	.01
296 Ottis Anderson	.10	.05	.01
297 Carl Birdsong	.05	.02	.01
298 Doug Marsh	.05	.02	.01
299 Neil Lomax	.10	.05	.01
300 Rush Brown	.05	.02	.01
301 Pat Tilley	.05	.02	.01
302 Wayne Morris	.05	.02	.01
303 Dan Dierdorf	.20	.09	.03
304 Roy Green	.20	.09	.03
305 Joe Montana	2.00	.90	.25
306 Randy Cross	.10	.05	.01
307 Freddie Solomon	.05	.02	.01
308 Jack Reynolds	.10	.05	.01
309 Ronnie Lott	.40	.18	.05
310 Renaldo Nehemiah	.10	.05	.01
311 Russ Francis	.05	.02	.01
312 Dwight Clark	.20	.09	.03
313 Doug Williams	.10	.05	.01
314 Bill Capece	.05	.02	.01
315 Mike Washington	.05	.02	.01
316 Hugh Green	.10	.05	.01
317 Kevin House	.05	.02	.01
318 Lee Roy Selmon	.25	.11	.03
319 Neal Colzie	.05	.02	.01
320 Jimmie Giles	.05	.02	.01
321 Cedric Brown	.05	.02	.01
322 Tony Peters	.05	.02	.01
323 Neal Olkewicz	.05	.02	.01
324 Dexter Manley	.05	.02	.01
325 Joe Theismann	.30	.14	.04
326 Rich Milot	.05	.02	.01
327 Mark Moseley	.05	.02	.01
328 Art Monk	.35	.16	.04
329 Mike Nelms	.05	.02	.01
330 John Riggins	.25	.11	.03
NNO Sticker Album	2.00	.90	.25

1983 Topps Sticker Boxes

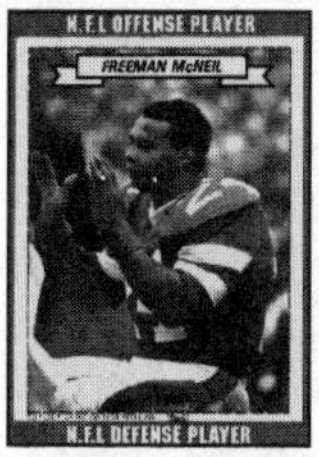

The 1983 Topps Sticker Box set contains 12 boxes each containing two large cards (24 cards total) on the side of the box itself and 35 stickers inside. Cards, when cut, measure approximately 2 1/2" by 3 1/2". These blank-backed cards are unnumbered but each box is numbered on a white box tab. The player on top is offense and the lower player is defense. Number 10 was not issued. Prices below reflect the value of the uncut boxes not including the stickers inside the box.

	MINT	NRMT	EXC
COMPLETE SET (12)	12.00	5.50	1.50
COMMON PAIR (1-13)	1.00	.45	.12
1 Pat Donovan and Mark Gastineau	1.00	.45	.12
2 Wes Chandler and Nolan Cromwell	1.00	.45	.12
3 Marvin Powell and Ed Too Tall Jones	1.25	.55	.16
4 Ken Anderson and Tony Peters	1.25	.55	.16
5 Freeman McNeil and Lawrence Taylor	2.00	.90	.25
6 Mark Moseley and Dave Jennings	1.00	.45	.12
7 Dwight Clark and Mike Haynes	1.25	.55	.16
8 Jeff Van Note and Harry Carson	1.00	.45	.12
9 Tony Dorsett and Hugh Green	2.50	1.10	.30
11 Randy Cross and Gary Johnson	1.00	.45	.12
12 Kellen Winslow and Lester Hayes	1.50	.70	.19
13 John Hannah and Randy White	2.00	.90	.25

1984 Topps Stickers

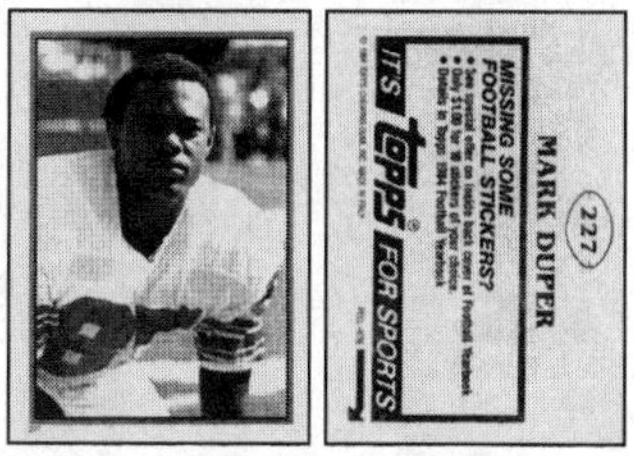

The 1984 Topps Football sticker set (283) is similar to the previous years in that it contains stickers, foil stickers, and an accompanying album to house one's sticker collection. Many of these stickers came two to a card. In the checklist below the other player on these two player stickers is listed parenthetically by number; players listed without any parenthetical number have the whole sticker card to themselves. The foil stickers are noted by "FOIL" in the checklist below. Numbers within the set are organized by subset and team. On the inside back cover of the sticker album the company offered (via direct mail-order) any 10 different stickers of your choice for 1.00; this is one reason why the values of the most popular players in these sticker sets are somewhat depressed compared to traditional card set prices. The sticker album features Charlie Joiner on the front cover and Dan Fouts on the back cover. The following players are shown in their Rookie Card year: Deron Cherry, Roger Craig, Eric Dickerson, Mark Duper, John Elway, Chris Hinton, Howie Long, Dan Marino, and Jackie Slater.

	MINT	NRMT	EXC
COMPLETE SET (283)	30.00	13.50	3.70
COMMON STICKER (1-283)	.05	.02	.01
COMMON HALF STICKER	.03	.01	.01
COMMON FOILS	.15	.07	.02
1 Super Bowl XVIII FOIL Plunkett/Allen UL	.25	.11	.03
2 Super Bowl XVIII FOIL Plunkett/Allen UR	.15	.07	.02
3 Super Bowl XVIII FOIL Plunkett/Allen LL	.15	.07	.02
4 Super Bowl XVIII FOIL Plunkett/Allen LR	.15	.07	.02
5 Marcus Allen FOIL (Super Bowl MVP)	1.00	.45	.12
6 Walter Payton	1.00	.45	.12
7 Mike Richardson (157)	.03	.01	.01
8 Jim McMahon (158)	.10	.05	.01
9 Mike Hartenstine (159)	.03	.01	.01
10 Mike Singletary	.20	.09	.03
11 Willie Gault	.10	.05	.01
12 Terry Schmidt (162)	.03	.01	.01
13 Emery Moorehead (163)	.03	.01	.01
14 Leslie Frazier (164)	.03	.01	.01
15 Jack Thompson (165)	.03	.01	.01
16 Booker Reese (166)	.03	.01	.01
17 James Wilder (167)	.10	.05	.01
18 Lee Roy Selmon	.20	.09	.03
19 Hugh Green	.10	.05	.01
20 Gerald Carter (170)	.03	.01	.01
21 Steve Wilson (171)	.03	.01	.01
22 Michael Morton (172)	.03	.01	.01
23 Kevin House	.05	.02	.01
24 Ottis Anderson	.10	.05	.01
25 Lionel Washington (175)	.10	.05	.01
26 Pat Tilley (176)	.03	.01	.01
27 Curtis Greer (177)	.03	.01	.01
28 Roy Green	.10	.05	.01
29 Carl Birdsong	.05	.02	.01
30 Neil Lomax (180)	.10	.05	.01
31 Lee Nelson (181)	.03	.01	.01
32 Stump Mitchell (182)	.03	.01	.01
33 Tony Hill (183)	.10	.05	.01
34 Everson Walls (184)	.10	.05	.01
35 Danny White (185)	.10	.05	.01
36 Tony Dorsett	.35	.16	.04
37 Ed Too Tall Jones	.20	.09	.03
38 Rafael Septien (188)	.03	.01	.01
39 Doug Cosbie (189)	.03	.01	.01
40 Drew Pearson (190)	.10	.05	.01
41 Randy White	.20	.09	.03
42 Ron Jaworski	.10	.05	.01
43 Anthony Griggs (193)	.03	.01	.01
44 Hubie Oliver (194)	.03	.01	.01
45 Wilbert Montgomery (195)	.10	.05	.01
46 Dennis Harrison	.05	.02	.01
47 Mike Quick	.10	.05	.01
48 Jerry Robinson (198)	.03	.01	.01
49 Michael Williams (199)	.03	.01	.01
50 Herman Edwards (200)	.03	.01	.01
51 Steve Bartkowski (201)	.10	.05	.01
52 Mick Luckhurst (202)	.03	.01	.01
53 Mike Pitts (203)	.03	.01	.01
54 William Andrews	.10	.05	.01
55 R.C. Thielemann	.05	.02	.01
56 Buddy Curry (206)	.03	.01	.01
57 Billy Johnson (207)	.03	.01	.01
58 Ralph Giacomarro (208)	.03	.01	.01
59 Mike Kenn	.10	.05	.01
60 Joe Montana	2.00	.90	.25
61 Fred Dean (211)	.03	.01	.01
62 Dwight Clark (212)	.10	.05	.01
63 Wendell Tyler (213)	.03	.01	.01
64 Dwight Hicks	.05	.02	.01
65 Ronnie Lott	.30	.14	.04
66 Roger Craig (216)	.30	.14	.04
67 Fred Solomon (217)	.03	.01	.01
68 Ray Wersching (218)	.03	.01	.01
69 Brad Van Pelt (219)	.03	.01	.01
70 Butch Woolfolk (220)	.03	.01	.01
71 Terry Kinard (221)	.03	.01	.01
72 Lawrence Taylor	.35	.16	.04
73 Ali Haji-Sheikh	.05	.02	.01
74 Mark Haynes (224)	.03	.01	.01
75 Rob Carpenter (225)	.03	.01	.01
76 Earnest Gray (226)	.03	.01	.01
77 Harry Carson	.10	.05	.01
78 Billy Sims	.20	.09	.03
79 Eddie Murray (229)	.03	.01	.01
80 William Gay (230)	.03	.01	.01
81 Leonard Thompson (231)	.03	.01	.01
82 Doug English	.10	.05	.01
83 Eric Hipple	.10	.05	.01
84 Ken Fantetti (234)	.03	.01	.01
85 Bruce McNorton (235)	.03	.01	.01
86 James Jones (236)	.03	.01	.01
87 Lynn Dickey (237)	.10	.05	.01
88 Ezra Johnson (238)	.03	.01	.01
89 Jan Stenerud (239)	.10	.05	.01
90 James Lofton	.20	.09	.03
91 Larry McCarren	.05	.02	.01
92 John Jefferson (242)	.10	.05	.01
93 Mike Douglass (243)	.03	.01	.01
94 Gerry Ellis (244)	.03	.01	.01
95 Paul Coffman	.10	.05	.01
96 Eric Dickerson	.75	.35	.09
97 Jackie Slater (247)	.20	.09	.03
98 Carl Ekern (248)	.03	.01	.01
99 Vince Ferragamo (249)	.10	.05	.01
100 Kent Hill	.05	.02	.01
101 Nolan Cromwell	.10	.05	.01
102 Jack Youngblood (252)	.10	.05	.01
103 John Misko (253)	.03	.01	.01
104 Mike Barber (254)	.03	.01	.01
105 Jeff Bostic (255)	.03	.01	.01
106 Mark Murphy (256)	.03	.01	.01
107 Joe Jacoby (257)	.10	.05	.01
108 John Riggins	.25	.11	.03
109 Joe Theismann	.30	.14	.04
110 Russ Grimm (260)	.03	.01	.01
111 Neal Olkewicz (261)	.03	.01	.01
112 Charlie Brown (262)	.03	.01	.01
113 Dave Butz	.10	.05	.01
114 George Rogers	.10	.05	.01
115 Jim Kovach (265)	.03	.01	.01
116 Dave Wilson (266)	.03	.01	.01
117 Johnnie Poe (267)	.03	.01	.01
118 Russell Erxleben	.05	.02	.01
119 Rickey Jackson	.50	.23	.06
120 Jeff Groth (270)	.03	.01	.01
121 Richard Todd (271)	.10	.05	.01
122 Wayne Wilson (272)	.03	.01	.01
123 Steve Dils (273)	.03	.01	.01
124 Benny Ricardo (274)	.03	.01	.01
125 John Turner (275)	.03	.01	.01
126 Ted Brown	.05	.02	.01
127 Greg Coleman	.05	.02	.01
128 Darrin Nelson (278)	.10	.05	.01
129 Scott Studwell (279)	.03	.01	.01
130 Tommy Kramer (280)	.10	.05	.01
131 Doug Martin	.05	.02	.01
132 Nolan Cromwell (144) All-Pro FOIL	.10	.05	.01
133 Carl Birdsong (145) All-Pro FOIL	.10	.05	.01
134 Deron Cherry (146) All-Pro FOIL	.20	.09	.03
135 Ronnie Lott (147) All-Pro FOIL	.30	.14	.04
136 Lester Hayes (148) All-Pro FOIL	.10	.05	.01
137 Lawrence Taylor (149) All-Pro FOIL	.35	.16	.04
138 Jack Lambert (150)	.25	.11	.03

	MINT	NRMT	EXC
All-Pro FOIL			
☐ 139 Chip Banks (151) All-Pro FOIL	.10	.05	.01
☐ 140 Lee Roy Selmon (152) All-Pro FOIL	.20	.09	.03
☐ 141 Fred Smerlas (153) All-Pro FOIL	.10	.05	.01
☐ 142 Doug English (154) All-Pro FOIL	.10	.05	.01
☐ 143 Doug Betters (155) All-Pro FOIL	.10	.05	.01
☐ 144 Dan Marino (132) All-Pro FOIL	8.00	3.60	1.00
☐ 145 Ali Haji-Sheikh (133) All-Pro FOIL	.10	.05	.01
☐ 146 Eric Dickerson (134) All-Pro FOIL	.75	.35	.09
☐ 147 Curt Warner (135) All-Pro FOIL	.15	.07	.02
☐ 148 James Lofton (136) All-Pro FOIL	.25	.11	.03
☐ 149 Todd Christensen (137) All-Pro FOIL	.15	.07	.02
☐ 150 Cris Collinsworth (138) All-Pro FOIL	.15	.07	.02
☐ 151 Mike Kenn (139) All-Pro FOIL	.10	.05	.01
☐ 152 Russ Grimm (140) All-Pro FOIL	.20	.09	.03
☐ 153 Jeff Bostic (141) All-Pro FOIL	.10	.05	.01
☐ 154 John Hannah (142) All-Pro FOIL	.20	.09	.03
☐ 155 Anthony Munoz (143) All-Pro FOIL	.20	.09	.03
☐ 156 Ken Anderson	.25	.11	.03
☐ 157 Pete Johnson (7)	.03	.01	.01
☐ 158 Reggie Williams (8)	.10	.05	.01
☐ 159 Isaac Curtis (9)	.03	.01	.01
☐ 160 Anthony Munoz	.20	.09	.03
☐ 161 Cris Collinsworth	.10	.05	.01
☐ 162 Charles Alexander(12)	.03	.01	.01
☐ 163 Ray Horton (13)	.03	.01	.01
☐ 164 Steve Kreider (14)	.03	.01	.01
☐ 165 Ben Williams (15)	.03	.01	.01
☐ 166 Frank Lewis (16)	.03	.01	.01
☐ 167 Roosevelt Leaks (17)	.03	.01	.01
☐ 168 Joe Ferguson	.10	.05	.01
☐ 169 Fred Smerlas	.10	.05	.01
☐ 170 Joe Danelo (20)	.03	.01	.01
☐ 171 Chris Keating (21)	.03	.01	.01
☐ 172 Jerry Butler (22)	.03	.01	.01
☐ 173 Eugene Marve	.05	.02	.01
☐ 174 Louis Wright	.10	.05	.01
☐ 175 Barney Chavous (25)	.03	.01	.01
☐ 176 Zach Thomas (26)	.03	.01	.01
☐ 177 Luke Prestridge (27)	.03	.01	.01
☐ 178 Steve Watson	.10	.05	.01
☐ 179 John Elway	4.00	1.80	.50
☐ 180 Steve Foley (30)	.03	.01	.01
☐ 181 Sammy Winder (31)	.03	.01	.01
☐ 182 Rick Upchurch (32)	.03	.01	.01
☐ 183 Bobby Jones (33)	.03	.01	.01
☐ 184 Matt Bahr (34)	.03	.01	.01
☐ 185 Doug Dieken (35)	.03	.01	.01
☐ 186 Mike Pruitt	.10	.05	.01
☐ 187 Chip Banks	.10	.05	.01
☐ 188 Tom Cousineau (38)	.03	.01	.01
☐ 189 Paul McDonald (39)	.03	.01	.01
☐ 190 Clay Matthews (40)	.10	.05	.01
☐ 191 Ozzie Newsome	.20	.09	.03
☐ 192 Dan Fouts	.30	.14	.04
☐ 193 Chuck Muncie (43)	.10	.05	.01
☐ 194 Linden King (44)	.03	.01	.01
☐ 195 Charlie Joiner (45)	.20	.09	.03
☐ 196 Wes Chandler	.10	.05	.01
☐ 197 Kellen Winslow	.20	.09	.03
☐ 198 James Brooks (48)	.10	.05	.01
☐ 199 Mike Green (49)	.03	.01	.01
☐ 200 Rolf Benirschke (58)	.03	.01	.01
☐ 201 Henry Marshall (51)	.03	.01	.01
☐ 202 Nick Lowery (52)	.03	.01	.01
☐ 203 Jerry Blanton (53)	.03	.01	.01
☐ 204 Bill Kenney	.10	.05	.01
☐ 205 Carlos Carson	.10	.05	.01
☐ 206 Billy Jackson (56)	.03	.01	.01
☐ 207 Art Still (57)	.03	.01	.01
☐ 208 Theotis Brown (58)	.03	.01	.01
☐ 209 Deron Cherry	.20	.09	.03
☐ 210 Curtis Dickey	.10	.05	.01
☐ 211 Nesby Glasgow (61)	.03	.01	.01
☐ 212 Mike Pagel (62)	.03	.01	.01
☐ 213 Ray Donaldson (63)	.03	.01	.01
☐ 214 Raul Allegre	.05	.02	.01
☐ 215 Chris Hinton	.10	.05	.01
☐ 216 Rohn Stark (66)	.03	.01	.01
☐ 217 Randy McMillan (67)	.03	.01	.01
☐ 218 Vernon Maxwell (68)	.03	.01	.01
☐ 219 A.J. Duhe (69)	.03	.01	.01
☐ 220 Andra Franklin (70)	.03	.01	.01
☐ 221 Ed Newman (71)	.03	.01	.01
☐ 222 Dan Marino	8.00	3.60	1.00
☐ 223 Doug Betters	.05	.02	.01
☐ 224 Bob Baumhower (74)	.03	.01	.01
☐ 225 Reggie Roby (75)	.10	.05	.01
☐ 226 Dwight Stephenson (76)	.03	.01	.01
☐ 227 Mark Duper	.35	.16	.04
☐ 228 Mark Gastineau	.10	.05	.01
☐ 229 Freeman McNeil (79)	.10	.05	.01
☐ 230 Bruce Harper (80)	.03	.01	.01
☐ 231 Wesley Walker (81)	.10	.05	.01
☐ 232 Marvin Powell	.10	.05	.01
☐ 233 Joe Klecko	.10	.05	.01
☐ 234 Johnny Lam Jones (84)	.03	.01	.01
☐ 235 Lance Mehl (85)	.03	.01	.01
☐ 236 Pat Ryan (86)	.03	.01	.01
☐ 237 Florian Kempf (87)	.03	.01	.01
☐ 238 Carl Roaches (88)	.03	.01	.01
☐ 239 Gregg Bingham (89)	.03	.01	.01
☐ 240 Tim Smith	.05	.02	.01
☐ 241 Jesse Baker	.05	.02	.01
☐ 242 Doug France (92)	.03	.01	.01
☐ 243 Chris Dressel (93)	.03	.01	.01
☐ 244 Willie Tullis (94)	.03	.01	.01
☐ 245 Robert Brazile	.10	.05	.01
☐ 246 Tony Collins	.10	.05	.01
☐ 247 Brian Holloway (97)	.03	.01	.01
☐ 248 Stanley Morgan (98)	.10	.05	.01
☐ 249 Rick Sanford (99)	.03	.01	.01
☐ 250 John Hannah	.20	.09	.03
☐ 251 Rich Camarillo	.05	.02	.01
☐ 252 Andre Tippett (102)	.10	.05	.01
☐ 253 Steve Grogan (103)	.10	.05	.01
☐ 254 Clayton Weishuhn (104)	.03	.01	.01
☐ 255 Jim Plunkett (105)	.10	.05	.01
☐ 256 Rod Martin (106)	.03	.01	.01
☐ 257 Lester Hayes (107)	.03	.01	.01
☐ 258 Marcus Allen	.75	.35	.09
☐ 259 Todd Christensen	.10	.05	.01
☐ 260 Ted Hendricks (110)	.10	.05	.01
☐ 261 Greg Pruitt (111)	.03	.01	.01
☐ 262 Howie Long (112)	.50	.23	.06
☐ 263 Vann McElroy	.05	.02	.01
☐ 264 Curt Warner	.20	.09	.03
☐ 265 Jacob Green (115)	.10	.05	.01
☐ 266 Bruce Scholtz (116)	.03	.01	.01
☐ 267 Steve Largent (117)	.50	.23	.06
☐ 268 Kenny Easley	.10	.05	.01
☐ 269 Dave Krieg	.40	.18	.05
☐ 270 Dave Brown (120)	.03	.01	.01
☐ 271 Zachary Dixon (121)	.03	.01	.01
☐ 272 Norm Johnson (122)	.10	.05	.01
☐ 273 Terry Bradshaw (123)	.35	.16	.04
☐ 274 Keith Willis (124)	.03	.01	.01
☐ 275 Gary Anderson (125)	.03	.01	.01
☐ 276 Franco Harris	.35	.16	.04
☐ 277 Mike Webster	.10	.05	.01
☐ 278 Calvin Sweeney (128)	.03	.01	.01
☐ 279 Rick Woods (129)	.03	.01	.01
☐ 280 Bennie Cunningham (130)	.03	.01	.01
☐ 281 Jack Lambert	.20	.09	.03
☐ 282 Curt Warner (283) FOIL	.30	.14	.04
☐ 283 Todd Christensen (282) FOIL	.10	.05	.01
☐ NNO Sticker Album (Charlie Joiner and Dan Fouts)	2.00	.90	.25

1985 Topps Coming Soon Stickers

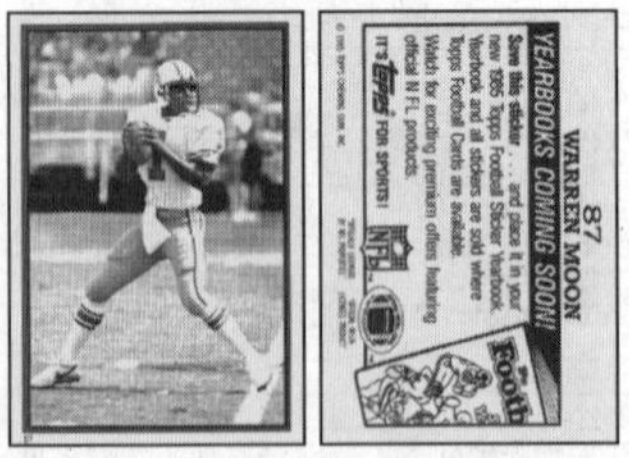

This set of 30 white-bordered stickers are usually referred to as the "Coming Soon" stickers as they were inserted in the regular issue 1985 Topps football card wax packs and prominently mention "Coming Soon" on the sticker backs. They are the same size as the regular Topps stickers (approximately 2 1/8" by 3") and were not very difficult to find. Unlike many of the sticker cards in the regular set, this subset only contains one player per sticker. This is a skip-numbered set due to the fact that these stickers have the same numbers as the regular sticker issue.

	MINT	NRMT	EXC
COMPLETE SET (30)	10.00	4.50	1.25
COMMON CARD	.10	.05	.01
☐ 6 Ken Anderson	.20	.09	.03
☐ 15 Greg Bell	.10	.05	.01
☐ 24 John Elway	1.50	.70	.19
☐ 33 Ozzie Newsome	.20	.09	.03
☐ 42 Charlie Joiner	.25	.11	.03
☐ 51 Bill Kenney	.15	.07	.02
☐ 60 Randy McMillan	.10	.05	.01
☐ 69 Dan Marino	4.00	1.80	.50
☐ 77 Mark Clayton	.20	.09	.03
☐ 78 Mark Gastineau	.15	.07	.02
☐ 87 Warren Moon	1.00	.45	.12
☐ 96 Tony Eason	.10	.05	.01
☐ 105 Marcus Allen	.60	.25	.07
☐ 114 Steve Largent	.50	.23	.06
☐ 123 John Stallworth	.15	.07	.02
☐ 156 Walter Payton	.75	.35	.09
☐ 165 James Wilder	.10	.05	.01
☐ 174 Neil Lomax	.15	.07	.02
☐ 183 Tony Dorsett	.30	.14	.04
☐ 192 Mike Quick	.10	.05	.01
☐ 201 William Andrews	.15	.07	.02
☐ 210 Joe Montana	2.50	1.10	.30
☐ 214 Dwight Clark	.20	.09	.03
☐ 219 Lawrence Taylor	.30	.14	.04
☐ 228 Billy Sims	.15	.07	.02
☐ 237 James Lofton	.30	.14	.04
☐ 246 Eric Dickerson	.30	.14	.04
☐ 255 John Riggins	.25	.11	.03
☐ 268 George Rogers	.15	.07	.02
☐ 281 Tommy Kramer	.15	.07	.02

1985 Topps Stickers

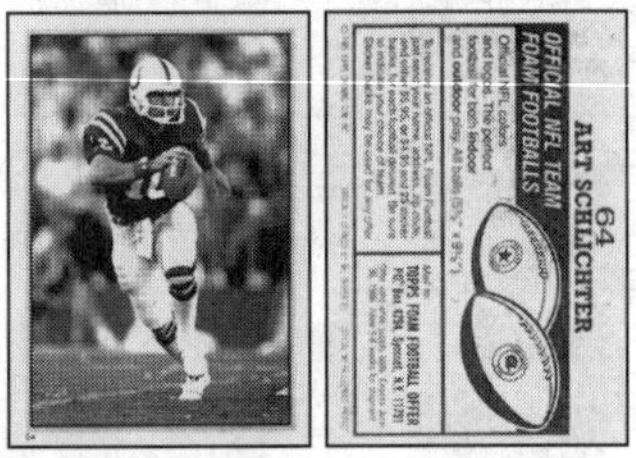

The 1985 Topps Football sticker set is similar to the previous years in that it contains stickers and an accompanying album to house one's sticker collection. However, there are no foil stickers in this set. Some of the stickers are half the size of others; those paired stickers sharing a card with another player are indicated parenthetically by the other player's sticker number in the checklist below. On the inside back cover of the sticker album the company offered (via direct mail-order) any ten different stickers of your choice for 1.00; this is one reason why the values of the most popular players in these sticker sets are somewhat depressed compared to traditional card set prices. The front cover of the sticker album features Dan Marino, Joe Montana, Walter Payton, Eric Dickerson, Art Monk, and Charlie Joiner; the back cover shows a team photo of the San Francisco 49ers. The stickers are checklisted below according to special subsets and teams. The following players are shown in their Rookie Card year or earlier: Mark Clayton, Richard Dent, Henry Ellard, Boomer Esiason (one year early), Craig James, Louis Lipps, Warren Moon, Ken O'Brien, and Darryl Talley.

	MINT	NRMT	EXC
COMPLETE SET (285)	25.00	11.00	3.10
COMMON CARD (1-285)	.05	.02	.01
COMMON HALF STICKER	.03	.01	.01
☐ 1 Super Bowl XIX Joe Montana LH	1.50	.70	.19
☐ 2 Super Bowl XIX Joe Montana RH	1.00	.45	.12
☐ 3 Super Bowl XIX Roger Craig LH	.10	.05	.01
☐ 4 Super Bowl XIX Roger Craig RH	.10	.05	.01
☐ 5 Super Bowl XIX Wendell Tyler	.10	.05	.01
☐ 6 Ken Anderson	.20	.09	.03
☐ 7 M.L. Harris (157)	.03	.01	.01
☐ 8 Eddie Edwards (157)	.03	.01	.01
☐ 9 Louis Breeden (159)	.03	.01	.01
☐ 10 Larry Kinnebrew	.05	.02	.01
☐ 11 Isaac Curtis (161)	.06	.03	.01
☐ 12 James Brooks (162)	.06	.03	.01
☐ 13 Jim Breech (163)	.03	.01	.01
☐ 14 Boomer Esiason (164)	.50	.23	.06
☐ 15 Greg Bell	.10	.05	.01
☐ 16 Fred Smerlas (166)	.03	.01	.01
☐ 17 Joe Ferguson (167)	.06	.03	.01
☐ 18 Ken Johnson (168)	.03	.01	.01
☐ 19 Darryl Talley (169)	.15	.07	.02
☐ 20 Preston Dennard (170)	.03	.01	.01
☐ 21 Charles Romes (171)	.03	.01	.01
☐ 22 Jim Haslett (172)	.03	.01	.01
☐ 23 Byron Franklin	.05	.02	.01
☐ 24 John Elway	2.00	.90	.25
☐ 25 Rulon Jones (175)	.03	.01	.01
☐ 26 Butch Johnson (176)	.03	.01	.01
☐ 27 Rich Karlis (177)	.03	.01	.01
☐ 28 Sammy Winder	.05	.02	.01
☐ 29 Tom Jackson (179)	.06	.03	.01
☐ 30 Mike Harden (180)	.03	.01	.01
☐ 31 Steve Watson (181)	.03	.01	.01
☐ 32 Steve Foley (182)	.03	.01	.01
☐ 33 Ozzie Newsome	.20	.09	.03
☐ 34 Al Gross (184)	.03	.01	.01
☐ 35 Paul McDonald (185)	.03	.01	.01
☐ 36 Matt Bahr (186)	.03	.01	.01
☐ 37 Charles White (187)	.06	.03	.01
☐ 38 Don Rogers (188)	.03	.01	.01
☐ 39 Mike Pruitt (189)	.06	.03	.01
☐ 40 Reggie Camp (190)	.03	.01	.01
☐ 41 Boyce Green	.05	.02	.01
☐ 42 Charlie Joiner	.10	.05	.01
☐ 43 Dan Fouts (193)	.15	.07	.02
☐ 44 Keith Ferguson (194)	.03	.01	.01
☐ 45 Pete Holohan (195)	.03	.01	.01
☐ 46 Earnest Jackson	.10	.05	.01
☐ 47 Wes Chandler (197)	.06	.03	.01
☐ 48 Gill Byrd (198)	.15	.07	.02
☐ 49 Kellen Winslow (199)	.15	.07	.02
☐ 50 Billy Ray Smith (200)	.06	.03	.01
☐ 51 Bill Kenney	.10	.05	.01
☐ 52 Herman Heard (202)	.03	.01	.01
☐ 53 Art Still (203)	.03	.01	.01
☐ 54 Nick Lowery (204)	.06	.03	.01
☐ 55 Deron Cherry (205)	.06	.03	.01
☐ 56 Henry Marshall (206)	.03	.01	.01
☐ 57 Mike Bell (207)	.03	.01	.01
☐ 58 Todd Blackledge (208)	.06	.03	.01
☐ 59 Carlos Carson	.10	.05	.01
☐ 60 Randy McMillan	.05	.02	.01
☐ 61 Donnell Thompson (211)	.03	.01	.01
☐ 62 Raymond Butler (212)	.03	.01	.01
☐ 63 Ray Donaldson (213)	.03	.01	.01
☐ 64 Art Schlichter	.10	.05	.01
☐ 65 Rohn Stark (215)	.06	.03	.01
☐ 66 Johnie Cooks (216)	.03	.01	.01
☐ 67 Mike Pagel (217)	.03	.01	.01
☐ 68 Eugene Daniel (218)	.03	.01	.01
☐ 69 Dan Marino	4.00	1.80	.50
☐ 70 Pete Johnson (220)	.06	.03	.01
☐ 71 Tony Nathan (221)	.06	.03	.01
☐ 72 Glenn Blackwood (222)	.03	.01	.01
☐ 73 Woody Bennett (223)	.03	.01	.01
☐ 74 Dwight Stephenson (224)	.03	.01	.01
☐ 75 Mark Duper (225)	.06	.03	.01
☐ 76 Doug Betters (226)	.03	.01	.01
☐ 77 Mark Clayton	.30	.14	.04
☐ 78 Mark Gastineau	.10	.05	.01
☐ 79 Johnny Lam Jones (229)	.03	.01	.01
☐ 80 Mickey Shuler (230)	.03	.01	.01
☐ 81 Tony Paige (231)	.15	.07	.02
☐ 82 Freeman McNeil	.10	.05	.01
☐ 83 Russell Carter (233)	.05	.02	.01
☐ 84 Wesley Walker (234)	.06	.03	.01
☐ 85 Bruce Harper (235)	.03	.01	.01
☐ 86 Ken O'Brien (236)	.15	.07	.02
☐ 87 Warren Moon	1.00	.45	.12
☐ 88 Jesse Baker (238)	.03	.01	.01
☐ 89 Carl Roaches (239)	.03	.01	.01
☐ 90 Carter Hartwig (240)	.03	.01	.01
☐ 91 Larry Moriarty (241)	.03	.01	.01
☐ 92 Robert Brazile (242)	.06	.03	.01
☐ 93 Oliver Luck (243)	.03	.01	.01
☐ 94 Willie Tullis (244)	.03	.01	.01
☐ 95 Tim Smith	.05	.02	.01
☐ 96 Tony Eason	.10	.05	.01
☐ 97 Stanley Morgan (247)	.06	.03	.01
☐ 98 Mosi Tatupu (248)	.03	.01	.01
☐ 99 Raymond Clayborn (249)	.03	.01	.01
☐ 100 Andre Tippett	.10	.05	.01
☐ 101 Craig James (251)	.15	.07	.02
☐ 102 Derrick Ramsey (252)	.03	.01	.01
☐ 103 Tony Collins (253)	.03	.01	.01
☐ 104 Tony Franklin (254)	.03	.01	.01
☐ 105 Marcus Allen	.50	.23	.06
☐ 106 Chris Bahr (256)	.03	.01	.01
☐ 107 Marc Wilson (257)	.06	.03	.01
☐ 108 Howie Long (258)	.06	.03	.01
☐ 109 Bill Pickel (259)	.03	.01	.01
☐ 110 Mike Haynes (260)	.06	.03	.01
☐ 111 Malcolm Barnwell (261)	.03	.01	.01
☐ 112 Rod Martin (262)	.03	.01	.01
☐ 113 Todd Christensen	.10	.05	.01
☐ 114 Steve Largent	.50	.23	.06
☐ 115 Curt Warner (265)	.06	.03	.01
☐ 116 Kenny Easley (266)	.03	.01	.01
☐ 117 Jacob Green (267)	.03	.01	.01
☐ 118 Daryl Turner	.05	.02	.01
☐ 119 Norm Johnson (269)	.03	.01	.01
☐ 120 Dave Krieg (270)	.15	.07	.02
☐ 121 Eric Lane (271)	.03	.01	.01
☐ 122 Jeff Bryant (272)	.03	.01	.01
☐ 123 John Stallworth	.10	.05	.01
☐ 124 Donnie Shell (274)	.03	.01	.01
☐ 125 Gary Anderson (275)	.03	.01	.01
☐ 126 Mark Malone (276)	.03	.01	.01
☐ 127 Sam Washington (277)	.03	.01	.01
☐ 128 Frank Pollard (278)	.03	.01	.01
☐ 129 Mike Merriweather (279)	.06	.03	.01
☐ 130 Walter Abercrombie (280)	.03	.01	.01
☐ 131 Louis Lipps	.25	.11	.03
☐ 132 Mark Clayton (144)	.20	.09	.03
☐ 133 Randy Cross (145)	.06	.03	.01
☐ 134 Eric Dickerson (146)	.30	.14	.04

☐ 135 John Hannah (147)	.06	.03	.01
☐ 136 Mike Kenn (148)	.03	.01	.01
☐ 137 Dan Marino (149)	1.50	.70	.19
☐ 138 Art Monk (150)	.15	.07	.02
☐ 139 Anthony Munoz (151)	.06	.03	.01
☐ 140 Ozzie Newsome (152)	.06	.03	.01
☐ 141 Walter Payton (153)	.40	.18	.05
☐ 142 Jan Stenerud (154)	.06	.03	.01
☐ 143 Dwight Stephenson (155)	.06	.03	.01
☐ 144 Todd Bell (132)	.03	.01	.01
☐ 145 Richard Dent (133)	.35	.16	.04
☐ 146 Kenny Easley (134)	.03	.01	.01
☐ 147 Mark Gastineau (135)	.06	.03	.01
☐ 148 Dan Hampton (136)	.06	.03	.01
☐ 149 Mark Haynes (137)	.06	.03	.01
☐ 150 Mike Haynes (138)	.06	.03	.01
☐ 151 E.J. Junior (139)	.03	.01	.01
☐ 152 Rod Martin (140)	.03	.01	.01
☐ 153 Steve Nelson (141)	.03	.01	.01
☐ 154 Reggie Roby (142)	.03	.01	.01
☐ 155 Lawrence Taylor (143)	.15	.07	.02
☐ 156 Walter Payton	.60	.25	.07
☐ 157 Dan Hampton (7)	.06	.03	.01
☐ 158 Willie Gault (8)	.06	.03	.01
☐ 159 Matt Suhey (9)	.03	.01	.01
☐ 160 Richard Dent	.50	.23	.06
☐ 161 Mike Singletary (11)	.06	.03	.01
☐ 162 Gary Fencik (12)	.03	.01	.01
☐ 163 Jim McMahon (13)	.15	.07	.02
☐ 164 Bob Thomas (14)	.03	.01	.01
☐ 165 James Wilder	.05	.02	.01
☐ 166 Steve DeBerg (16)	.06	.03	.01
☐ 167 Mark Cotney (17)	.03	.01	.01
☐ 168 Adger Armstrong (18)	.03	.01	.01
☐ 169 Gerald Carter (19)	.03	.01	.01
☐ 170 David Logan (20)	.03	.01	.01
☐ 171 Hugh Green (21)	.06	.03	.01
☐ 172 Lee Roy Selmon (22)	.15	.07	.02
☐ 173 Kevin House	.05	.02	.01
☐ 174 Neil Lomax	.10	.05	.01
☐ 175 Ottis Anderson (25)	.06	.03	.01
☐ 176 Al(Bubba) Baker (26)	.06	.03	.01
☐ 177 E.J. Junior (27)	.03	.01	.01
☐ 178 Roy Green	.10	.05	.01
☐ 179 Pat Tilley (29)	.03	.01	.01
☐ 180 Stump Mitchell (30)	.03	.01	.01
☐ 181 Lionel Washington (31)	.03	.01	.01
☐ 182 Curtis Greer (32)	.03	.01	.01
☐ 183 Tony Dorsett	.30	.14	.04
☐ 184 Gary Hogeboom (34)	.06	.03	.01
☐ 185 Jim Jeffcoat (35)	.06	.03	.01
☐ 186 Danny White (36)	.10	.05	.01
☐ 187 Michael Downs (37)	.03	.01	.01
☐ 188 Doug Cosbie (38)	.03	.01	.01
☐ 189 Tony Hill (39)	.06	.03	.01
☐ 190 Rafael Septien (40)	.03	.01	.01
☐ 191 Randy White	.20	.09	.03
☐ 192 Mike Quick	.10	.05	.01
☐ 193 Ray Ellis (43)	.03	.01	.01
☐ 194 John Spagnola (44)	.03	.01	.01
☐ 195 Dennis Harrison (45)	.03	.01	.01
☐ 196 Wilbert Montgomery	.10	.05	.01
☐ 197 Greg Brown (47)	.03	.01	.01
☐ 198 Ron Jaworski (48)	.10	.05	.01
☐ 199 Paul McFadden (49)	.03	.01	.01
☐ 200 Wes Hopkins (50)	.03	.01	.01
☐ 201 William Andrews	.10	.05	.01
☐ 202 Mike Pitts (52)	.03	.01	.01
☐ 203 Steve Bartkowski (53)	.06	.03	.01
☐ 204 Gerald Riggs (54)	.06	.03	.01
☐ 205 Alfred Jackson (55)	.06	.03	.01
☐ 206 Don Smith (56)	.03	.01	.01
☐ 207 Mike Kenn (57)	.03	.01	.01
☐ 208 Kenny Johnson (58)	.03	.01	.01
☐ 209 Stacey Bailey	.05	.02	.01
☐ 210 Joe Montana	2.00	.90	.25
☐ 211 Wendell Tyler (61)	.06	.03	.01
☐ 212 Keena Turner (62)	.03	.01	.01
☐ 213 Ray Wersching (63)	.03	.01	.01
☐ 214 Dwight Clark	.10	.05	.01
☐ 215 Dwaine Board (65)	.03	.01	.01
☐ 216 Roger Craig (66)	.15	.07	.02
☐ 217 Ronnie Lott (67)	.15	.07	.02
☐ 218 Freddie Solomon (68)	.03	.01	.01
☐ 219 Lawrence Taylor	.30	.14	.04
☐ 220 Zeke Mowatt (70)	.03	.01	.01
☐ 221 Harry Carson (71)	.06	.03	.01
☐ 222 Rob Carpenter (72)	.03	.01	.01
☐ 223 Bobby Johnson (73)	.03	.01	.01
☐ 224 Joe Morris (74)	.06	.03	.01
☐ 225 Mark Haynes (75)	.03	.01	.01
☐ 226 Lionel Manuel (76)	.03	.01	.01
☐ 227 Phil Simms	.20	.09	.03
☐ 228 Billy Sims	.10	.05	.01
☐ 229 Leonard Thompson (79)	.03	.01	.01
☐ 230 James Jones (80)	.06	.03	.01
☐ 231 Eddie Murray (81)	.03	.01	.01
☐ 232 William Gay	.05	.02	.01
☐ 233 Gary Danielson (83)	.03	.01	.01
☐ 234 Curtis Green (84)	.03	.01	.01
☐ 235 Bobby Watkins (85)	.03	.01	.01
☐ 236 Doug English (86)	.03	.01	.01
☐ 237 James Lofton	.20	.09	.03
☐ 238 Eddie Lee Ivery (88)	.03	.01	.01
☐ 239 Mike Douglass (89)	.03	.01	.01
☐ 240 Gerry Ellis (90)	.03	.01	.01
☐ 241 Tim Lewis (91)	.03	.01	.01
☐ 242 Paul Coffman (92)	.05	.02	.01
☐ 243 Tom Flynn (93)	.03	.01	.01
☐ 244 Ezra Johnson (94)	.03	.01	.01
☐ 245 Lynn Dickey	.10	.05	.01
☐ 246 Eric Dickerson	.30	.14	.04
☐ 247 Jack Youngblood (97)	.06	.03	.01
☐ 248 Doug Smith (98)	.06	.03	.01
☐ 249 Jeff Kemp (99)	.05	.02	.01
☐ 250 Kent Hill	.05	.02	.01
☐ 251 Mike Lansford (101)	.03	.01	.01
☐ 252 Henry Ellard (102)	.35	.16	.04
☐ 253 LeRoy Irvin (103)	.03	.01	.01
☐ 254 Ron Brown (104)	.06	.03	.01
☐ 255 John Riggins	.20	.09	.03
☐ 256 Dexter Manley (106)	.06	.03	.01
☐ 257 Darrell Green (107)	.06	.03	.01
☐ 258 Joe Theismann (108)	.15	.07	.02
☐ 259 Mark Moseley (109)	.03	.01	.01
☐ 260 Clint Didier (110)	.03	.01	.01
☐ 261 Vernon Dean (111)	.03	.01	.01
☐ 262 Calvin Muhammad (112)	.03	.01	.01
☐ 263 Art Monk	.20	.09	.03
☐ 264 Bruce Clark	.05	.02	.01
☐ 265 Hoby Brenner (115)	.03	.01	.01
☐ 266 Dave Wilson (116)	.03	.01	.01
☐ 267 Hokie Gajan (117)	.03	.01	.01
☐ 268 George Rogers	.10	.05	.01
☐ 269 Rickey Jackson (119)	.06	.03	.01
☐ 270 Brian Hansen (120)	.03	.01	.01
☐ 271 Dave Waymer (121)	.03	.01	.01
☐ 272 Richard Todd (122)	.06	.03	.01
☐ 273 Jan Stenerud	.10	.05	.01
☐ 274 Ted Brown (124)	.03	.01	.01
☐ 275 Leo Lewis (125)	.06	.03	.01
☐ 276 Scott Studwell (126)	.03	.01	.01
☐ 277 Alfred Anderson (127)	.03	.01	.01
☐ 278 Rufus Bess (128)	.03	.01	.01
☐ 279 Darrin Nelson (129)	.06	.03	.01
☐ 280 Greg Coleman (130)	.03	.01	.01
☐ 281 Tommy Kramer	.10	.05	.01
☐ 282 Joe Montana (283)	1.50	.70	.19
☐ 283 Dan Marino (282)	2.50	1.10	.30
☐ 284 Brian Hansen (285)	.03	.01	.01
☐ 285 Jim Arnold (284)	.03	.01	.01
☐ NNO Sticker Album	2.00	.90	.25

1986 Topps Stickers

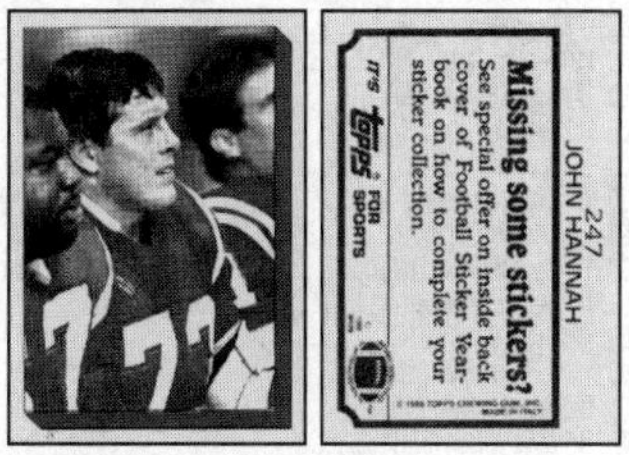

The 1986 Topps Football sticker set is similar to the previous years in that it contains stickers, foil stickers, and an accompanying album to house one's sticker collection. The stickers measure approximately 2 1/8" by 3". The sticker design shows an inverted L-shaped border in an accent color. The stickers are numbered on the front and on the back. The sticker backs are printed in brown ink on white stock. Sticker pairs are identified below by parenthetically listing the other member of the pair. On the inside back cover of the sticker album the company offered (via direct mail-order) any ten different stickers of your choice for 1.00; this is one reason why the values of the most popular players in these sticker sets are somewhat depressed compared to traditional card set prices. The front cover of the sticker album features Walter Payton and several other Chicago Bears players; the back cover shows a team photo of the Chicago Bears. The stickers are checklisted below according to special subsets and teams. The following players are shown in their Rookie Card year: Anthony Carter, Gary Clark, Bernie Kosar, Andre Reed, Bruce Smith, Al Toon, Reggie White, and Steve Young.

	MINT	NRMT	EXC
COMPLETE SET (285)	20.00	9.00	2.50
COMMON CARD (1-285)	.05	.02	.01
COMMON HALF STICKER	.03	.01	.01
COMMON FOILS	.10	.05	.01
☐ 1 Walter Payton LH	.50	.23	.06
☐ 2 Walter Payton RH	.40	.18	.05
☐ 3 Richard Dent LH	.10	.05	.01
☐ 4 Richard Dent RH	.10	.05	.01
☐ 5 Richard Dent FOIL Super Bowl MVP	.40	.18	.05
☐ 6 Walter Payton	.60	.25	.07
☐ 7 William Perry	.10	.05	.01
☐ 8 Jim McMahon (158)	.10	.05	.01
☐ 9 Richard Dent (159)	.10	.05	.01
☐ 10 Jim Covert (160)	.06	.03	.01
☐ 11 Dan Hampton (161)	.06	.03	.01
☐ 12 Mike Singletary (162)	.10	.05	.01
☐ 13 Jay Hilgenberg (163)	.06	.03	.01
☐ 14 Otis Wilson (164)	.03	.01	.01
☐ 15 Jimmie Giles	.05	.02	.01
☐ 16 Kevin House (166)	.03	.01	.01
☐ 17 Jeremiah Castille (167)	.03	.01	.01
☐ 18 James Wilder	.05	.02	.01
☐ 19 Donald Igwebuike (169)	.03	.01	.01
☐ 20 David Logan (170)	.03	.01	.01
☐ 21 Jeff Davis (171)	.03	.01	.01
☐ 22 Frank Garcia (172)	.03	.01	.01
☐ 23 Steve Young (173)	2.00	.90	.25
☐ 24 Stump Mitchell	.05	.02	.01
☐ 25 E.J. Junior	.05	.02	.01
☐ 26 J.T. Smith (176)	.06	.03	.01
☐ 27 Pat Tilley (177)	.03	.01	.01
☐ 28 Neil Lomax (178)	.06	.03	.01
☐ 29 Leonard Smith (179)	.03	.01	.01
☐ 30 Ottis Anderson (180)	.06	.03	.01
☐ 31 Curtis Greer (181)	.03	.01	.01
☐ 32 Roy Green (182)	.06	.03	.01
☐ 33 Tony Dorsett	.30	.14	.04
☐ 34 Tony Hill (184)	.06	.03	.01
☐ 35 Doug Cosbie (185)	.03	.01	.01
☐ 36 Everson Walls	.05	.02	.01
☐ 37 Randy White (187)	.10	.05	.01
☐ 38 Rafael Septien (188)	.03	.01	.01
☐ 39 Mike Renfro (189)	.03	.01	.01
☐ 40 Danny White (190)	.06	.03	.01
☐ 41 Ed Too Tall Jones (191)	.10	.05	.01
☐ 42 Earnest Jackson	.05	.02	.01
☐ 43 Mike Quick	.10	.05	.01
☐ 44 Wes Hopkins (194)	.03	.01	.01
☐ 45 Reggie White (195)	1.00	.45	.12
☐ 46 Greg Brown (196)	.03	.01	.01
☐ 47 Paul McFadden (197)	.03	.01	.01
☐ 48 John Spagnola (198)	.03	.01	.01
☐ 49 Ron Jaworski (199)	.06	.03	.01
☐ 50 Herman Hunter (200)	.03	.01	.01
☐ 51 Gerald Riggs	.10	.05	.01
☐ 52 Mike Pitts (202)	.03	.01	.01
☐ 53 Buddy Curry (203)	.03	.01	.01
☐ 54 Billy Johnson	.05	.02	.01
☐ 55 Rick Donnelly (205)	.03	.01	.01
☐ 56 Rick Bryan (206)	.03	.01	.01
☐ 57 Bobby Butler (207)	.03	.01	.01
☐ 58 Mick Luckhurst (208)	.03	.01	.01
☐ 59 Mike Kenn (209)	.03	.01	.01
☐ 60 Roger Craig	.25	.11	.03
☐ 61 Joe Montana	1.50	.70	.19
☐ 62 Michael Carter (212)	.06	.03	.01
☐ 63 Eric Wright (213)	.03	.01	.01
☐ 64 Dwight Clark (214)	.10	.05	.01
☐ 65 Ronnie Lott (215)	.10	.05	.01
☐ 66 Carlton Williamson (216)	.03	.01	.01
☐ 67 Wendell Tyler (217)	.03	.01	.01
☐ 68 Dwaine Board (218)	.03	.01	.01
☐ 69 Joe Morris	.10	.05	.01
☐ 70 Leonard Marshall (220)	.03	.01	.01
☐ 71 Lionel Manuel (221)	.03	.01	.01
☐ 72 Harry Carson	.10	.05	.01
☐ 73 Phil Simms (223)	.10	.05	.01
☐ 74 Sean Landeta (224)	.03	.01	.01
☐ 75 Lawrence Taylor (225)	.20	.09	.03
☐ 76 Elvis Patterson (226)	.03	.01	.01
☐ 77 George Adams (227)	.03	.01	.01
☐ 78 James Jones	.05	.02	.01
☐ 79 Leonard Thompson	.05	.02	.01
☐ 80 William Graham (230)	.03	.01	.01
☐ 81 Mark Nichols (231)	.03	.01	.01
☐ 82 William Gay (232)	.03	.01	.01
☐ 83 Jimmy Williams (233)	.03	.01	.01
☐ 84 Billy Sims (234)	.10	.05	.01
☐ 85 Bobby Watkins (235)	.03	.01	.01
☐ 86 Eddie Murray (236)	.03	.01	.01
☐ 87 James Lofton	.25	.11	.03
☐ 88 Jessie Clark (238)	.03	.01	.01
☐ 89 Tim Lewis (239)	.03	.01	.01
☐ 90 Eddie Lee Ivery	.05	.02	.01
☐ 91 Phillip Epps (241)	.03	.01	.01
☐ 92 Ezra Johnson (242)	.03	.01	.01
☐ 93 Mike Douglass (243)	.03	.01	.01
☐ 94 Paul Coffman (244)	.03	.01	.01
☐ 95 Randy Scott (245)	.03	.01	.01
☐ 96 Eric Dickerson	.25	.11	.03
☐ 97 Dale Hatcher	.05	.02	.01
☐ 98 Ron Brown (248)	.06	.03	.01
☐ 99 LeRoy Irvin (249)	.03	.01	.01
☐ 100 Kent Hill (250)	.03	.01	.01
☐ 101 Dennis Harrah (251)	.03	.01	.01
☐ 102 Jackie Slater (252)	.06	.03	.01
☐ 103 Mike Wilcher (253)	.03	.01	.01
☐ 104 Doug Smith (254)	.03	.01	.01
☐ 105 Art Monk	.25	.11	.03
☐ 106 Joe Jacoby (256)	.03	.01	.01
☐ 107 Russ Grimm (257)	.03	.01	.01
☐ 108 George Rogers	.05	.02	.01
☐ 109 Dexter Manley (259)	.03	.01	.01
☐ 110 Jay Schroeder (260)	.10	.05	.01
☐ 111 Gary Clark (261)	.35	.16	.04
☐ 112 Curtis Jordan (262)	.03	.01	.01
☐ 113 Charles Mann (263)	.06	.03	.01
☐ 114 Morten Andersen	.10	.05	.01
☐ 115 Rickey Jackson	.10	.05	.01
☐ 116 Glen Redd (266)	.03	.01	.01
☐ 117 Bobby Hebert (267)	.20	.09	.03
☐ 118 Hoby Brenner (268)	.03	.01	.01
☐ 119 Brian Hansen (269)	.03	.01	.01
☐ 120 Dave Waymer (270)	.03	.01	.01
☐ 121 Bruce Clark (271)	.03	.01	.01
☐ 122 Wayne Wilson (272)	.03	.01	.01
☐ 123 Joey Browner	.20	.09	.03
☐ 124 Darrin Nelson (274)	.03	.01	.01
☐ 125 Keith Millard (275)	.10	.05	.01
☐ 126 Anthony Carter	.30	.14	.04
☐ 127 Buster Rhymes (277)	.03	.01	.01
☐ 128 Steve Jordan (278)	.20	.09	.03
☐ 129 Greg Coleman (279)	.03	.01	.01
☐ 130 Ted Brown (280)	.03	.01	.01
☐ 131 John Turner (281)	.03	.01	.01
☐ 132 Harry Carson (144) AP FOIL	.10	.05	.01
☐ 133 Deron Cherry (145) AP FOIL	.10	.05	.01
☐ 134 Richard Dent (146) AP FOIL	.20	.09	.03
☐ 135 Mike Haynes (147) AP FOIL	.20	.09	.03
☐ 136 Wes Hopkins (148) AP FOIL	.10	.05	.01
☐ 137 Joe Klecko (149) AP FOIL	.10	.05	.01
☐ 138 Leonard Marshall (150) AP FOIL	.10	.05	.01
☐ 139 Karl Mecklenburg (151) AP FOIL	.10	.05	.01
☐ 140 Rohn Stark (152) AP FOIL	.10	.05	.01
☐ 141 Lawrence Taylor (153) AP FOIL	.25	.11	.03
☐ 142 Andre Tippett (154) AP FOIL	.10	.05	.01
☐ 143 Everson Walls (155) AP FOIL	.10	.05	.01
☐ 144 Marcus Allen (132) AP FOIL	.40	.18	.05
☐ 145 Gary Anderson (133) AP FOIL	.10	.05	.01
☐ 146 Doug Cosbie (134) AP FOIL	.10	.05	.01
☐ 147 Jim Covert (135) AP FOIL	.10	.05	.01
☐ 148 John Hannah (136) AP FOIL	.10	.05	.01
☐ 149 Jay Hilgenberg (137) AP FOIL	.10	.05	.01
☐ 150 Kent Hill (138) AP FOIL	.10	.05	.01
☐ 151 Brian Holloway (139) AP FOIL	.10	.05	.01
☐ 152 Steve Largent (140) AP FOIL	.60	.25	.07
☐ 153 Dan Marino (141) AP FOIL	2.00	.90	.25
☐ 154 Art Monk (142) AP FOIL	.25	.11	.03
☐ 155 Walter Payton (143) AP FOIL	.60	.25	.07
☐ 156 Anthony Munoz	.20	.09	.03
☐ 157 Boomer Esiason	.30	.14	.04
☐ 158 Cris Collinsworth (8)	.06	.03	.01
☐ 159 Eddie Edwards (9)	.03	.01	.01
☐ 160 James Griffin (10)	.03	.01	.01
☐ 161 Jim Breech (11)	.03	.01	.01
☐ 162 Eddie Brown (12)	.06	.03	.01
☐ 163 Ross Browner (13)	.03	.01	.01
☐ 164 James Brooks (14)	.06	.03	.01
☐ 165 Greg Bell	.05	.02	.01
☐ 166 Jerry Butler (16)	.03	.01	.01
☐ 167 Don Wilson (17)	.03	.01	.01
☐ 168 Andre Reed	.75	.35	.09
☐ 169 Jim Haslett (19)	.03	.01	.01
☐ 170 Bruce Mathison (20)	.03	.01	.01
☐ 171 Bruce Smith (21)	.40	.18	.05
☐ 172 Joe Cribbs (22)	.06	.03	.01
☐ 173 Charles Romes (23)	.03	.01	.01
☐ 174 Karl Mecklenburg	.10	.05	.01
☐ 175 Rulon Jones	.05	.02	.01
☐ 176 John Elway (26)	.60	.25	.07
☐ 177 Sammy Winder (27)	.03	.01	.01
☐ 178 Louis Wright (28)	.10	.05	.01
☐ 179 Steve Watson (29)	.03	.01	.01
☐ 180 Dennis Smith (30)	.03	.01	.01
☐ 181 Mike Harden (31)	.03	.01	.01
☐ 182 Vance Johnson (32)	.06	.03	.01
☐ 183 Kevin Mack	.10	.05	.01
☐ 184 Chip Banks (34)	.06	.03	.01
☐ 185 Bob Golic (35)	.06	.03	.01
☐ 186 Earnest Byner	.20	.09	.03
☐ 187 Ozzie Newsome (37)	.10	.05	.01
☐ 188 Bernie Kosar (38)	.30	.14	.04
☐ 189 Don Rogers (39)	.03	.01	.01
☐ 190 Al Gross (40)	.03	.01	.01
☐ 191 Clarence Weathers	.03	.01	.01

(41)			
□ 192 Lionel James	.05	.02	.01
□ 193 Dan Fouts	.30	.14	.04
□ 194 Wes Chandler (44)	.06	.03	.01
□ 195 Kellen Winslow (45)	.10	.05	.01
□ 196 Gary Anderson (46)	.06	.03	.01
□ 197 Charlie Joiner (47)	.06	.03	.01
□ 198 Ralf Mojsiejenko (48)	.03	.01	.01
□ 199 Bob Thomas (49)	.03	.01	.01
□ 200 Tim Spencer (50)	.03	.01	.01
□ 201 Deron Cherry	.10	.05	.01
□ 202 Bill Maas (52)	.03	.01	.01
□ 203 Herman Heard (53)	.03	.01	.01
□ 204 Carlos Carson	.05	.02	.01
□ 205 Nick Lowery (55)	.06	.03	.01
□ 206 Bill Kenney (56)	.03	.01	.01
□ 207 Albert Lewis (57)	.15	.07	.02
□ 208 Art Still (58)	.03	.01	.01
□ 209 Stephone Paige (59)	.20	.09	.03
□ 210 Rohn Stark	.05	.02	.01
□ 211 Chris Hinton	.10	.05	.01
□ 212 Albert Bentley (62)	.10	.05	.01
□ 213 Eugene Daniel (63)	.03	.01	.01
□ 214 Pat Beach (64)	.03	.01	.01
□ 215 Cliff Odom (65)	.03	.01	.01
□ 216 Duane Bickett (66)	.20	.09	.03
□ 217 George Wonsley (67)	.03	.01	.01
□ 218 Randy McMillan (68)	.03	.01	.01
□ 219 Dan Marino	3.00	1.35	.35
□ 220 Dwight Stephenson (70)	.03	.01	.01
□ 221 Roy Foster (71)	.03	.01	.01
□ 222 Mark Clayton	.20	.09	.03
□ 223 Mark Duper (73)	.06	.03	.01
□ 224 Fuad Reveiz (74)	.06	.03	.01
□ 225 Reggie Roby (75)	.06	.03	.01
□ 226 Tony Nathan (76)	.03	.01	.01
□ 227 Ron Davenport (77)	.03	.01	.01
□ 228 Freeman McNeil	.10	.05	.01
□ 229 Joe Klecko	.05	.02	.01
□ 230 Mark Gastineau (80)	.06	.03	.01
□ 231 Ken O'Brien (81)	.06	.03	.01
□ 232 Lance Mehl (82)	.03	.01	.01
□ 233 Al Toon (83)	.25	.11	.03
□ 234 Mickey Shuler (84)	.03	.01	.01
□ 235 Pat Leahy (85)	.03	.01	.01
□ 236 Wesley Walker (86)	.06	.03	.01
□ 237 Drew Hill	.10	.05	.01
□ 238 Warren Moon (88)	.30	.14	.04
□ 239 Mike Rozier (89)	.10	.05	.01
□ 240 Mike Munchak	.10	.05	.01
□ 241 Tim Smith (91)	.03	.01	.01
□ 242 Butch Woolfolk (92)	.03	.01	.01
□ 243 Willie Drewrey (93)	.03	.01	.01
□ 244 Keith Bostic (94)	.03	.01	.01
□ 245 Jesse Baker (95)	.03	.01	.01
□ 246 Craig James	.20	.09	.03
□ 247 John Hannah	.20	.09	.03
□ 248 Tony Eason (98)	.06	.03	.01
□ 249 Andre Tippett (99)	.06	.03	.01
□ 250 Tony Collins (100)	.03	.01	.01
□ 251 Brian Holloway (101)	.03	.01	.01
□ 252 Irving Fryar (102)	.10	.05	.01
□ 253 Raymond Clayborn (103)	.03	.01	.01
□ 254 Steve Nelson (104)	.03	.01	.01
□ 255 Marcus Allen	.40	.18	.05
□ 256 Mike Haynes (106)	.06	.03	.01
□ 257 Todd Christensen (107)	.06	.03	.01
□ 258 Howie Long	.20	.09	.03
□ 259 Lester Hayes (109)	.06	.03	.01
□ 260 Rod Martin (110)	.03	.01	.01
□ 261 Dokie Williams (111)	.03	.01	.01
□ 262 Chris Bahr (112)	.03	.01	.01
□ 263 Bill Pickel (113)	.03	.01	.01
□ 264 Curt Warner	.10	.05	.01
□ 265 Steve Largent	.50	.23	.06
□ 266 Fredd Young (116)	.06	.03	.01
□ 267 Dave Krieg (117)	.10	.05	.01
□ 268 Daryl Turner (118)	.03	.01	.01
□ 269 John Harris (119)	.03	.01	.01
□ 270 Randy Edwards (120)	.03	.01	.01
□ 271 Kenny Easley (121)	.03	.01	.01
□ 272 Jacob Green (122)	.03	.01	.01
□ 273 Gary Anderson K	.05	.02	.01
□ 274 Mike Webster (124)	.06	.03	.01
□ 275 Walter Abercrombie (125)	.03	.01	.01
□ 276 Louis Lipps	.10	.05	.01
□ 277 Frank Pollard (127)	.03	.01	.01
□ 278 Mike Merriweather (128)	.03	.01	.01
□ 279 Mark Malone (129)	.06	.03	.01
□ 280 Donnie Shell (130)	.03	.01	.01
□ 281 John Stallworth (131)	.06	.03	.01
□ 282 Marcus Allen (284) FOIL	.50	.23	.06
□ 283 Ken O'Brien (285) FOIL	.15	.07	.02
□ 284 Kevin Butler (282) FOIL	.10	.05	.01
□ 285 Roger Craig (283) FOIL	.30	.14	.04
□ NNO Sticker Album	2.00	.90	.25

1987 Topps Stickers

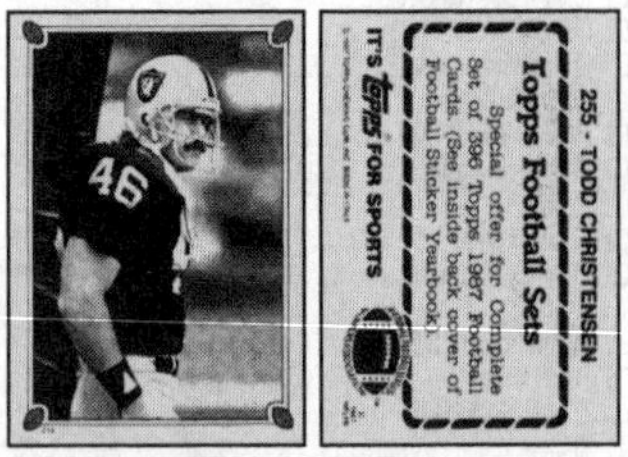

The 1987 Topps Football sticker set is similar to the previous years in that it contains stickers, foil stickers, and an accompanying album to house one's sticker collection. The stickers are approximately 2 1/8" by 3" and are in full-color with a white border with little footballs in each corner. The stickers are numbered on the front in the lower left hand border. Several of the stickers are two players per sticker card; they are designated in the checklist below with the number of the paired player in parentheses. The sticker backs are printed in red on white stock. There are 14 foil stickers, individual (half-size) player stickers numbered 132-155 and 282-285. On the inside back cover of the sticker album the company offered (via direct mail-order) any ten different stickers of your choice for 1.00; this is one reason why the values of the most popular players in these sticker sets are somewhat depressed compared to traditional card set prices. The front cover of the sticker album shows New York Giants art. The stickers are checklisted below according to special subsets and teams. The following players are shown in their Rookie Card year: Keith Byars, Randall Cunningham, Kenneth Davis, Jim Everett, Doug Flutie, Ernest Givins, Jim Kelly, Leslie O'Neal and Herschel Walker.

	MINT	NRMT	EXC
COMPLETE SET (285)	15.00	6.75	1.85
COMMON CARD (1-285)	.05	.02	.01
□ 1 Phil Simms Super Bowl MVP	.25	.11	.03
□ 2 Super Bowl XXI Phil Simms UL	.10	.05	.01
□ 3 Super Bowl XXI Phil Simms UR	.10	.05	.01
□ 4 Super Bowl XXI Phil Simms LL	.10	.05	.01
□ 5 Super Bowl XXI Phil Simms LR	.10	.05	.01
□ 6 Mike Singletary	.20	.09	.03
□ 7 Jim Covert (156)	.03	.01	.01
□ 8 Willie Gault (157)	.06	.03	.01
□ 9 Jim McMahon (158)	.10	.05	.01
□ 10 Doug Flutie (159)	.40	.18	.05
□ 11 Richard Dent (160)	.06	.03	.01
□ 12 Kevin Butler (161)	.03	.01	.01
□ 13 Wilber Marshall (162)	.06	.03	.01
□ 14 Walter Payton	.60	.25	.07
□ 15 Calvin Magee	.05	.02	.01
□ 16 David Logan (165)	.03	.01	.01
□ 17 Jeff Davis (166)	.03	.01	.01
□ 18 Gerald Carter (167)	.03	.01	.01
□ 19 James Wilder	.05	.02	.01
□ 20 Chris Washington (168)	.03	.01	.01
□ 21 Phil Freeman (169)	.03	.01	.01
□ 22 Frank Garcia (170)	.03	.01	.01
□ 23 Donald Igwebuike (171)	.03	.01	.01
□ 24 Al(Bubba) Baker (175)	.06	.03	.01
□ 25 Vai Sikahema (176)	.03	.01	.01
□ 26 Leonard Smith (177)	.03	.01	.01
□ 27 Ron Wolfley (178)	.03	.01	.01
□ 28 J.T. Smith	.10	.05	.01
□ 29 Roy Green (179)	.06	.03	.01
□ 30 Cedric Mack (180)	.03	.01	.01
□ 31 Neil Lomax (181)	.06	.03	.01
□ 32 Stump Mitchell	.05	.02	.01
□ 33 Herschel Walker	.40	.18	.05
□ 34 Danny White (184)	.06	.03	.01
□ 35 Michael Downs (185)	.03	.01	.01
□ 36 Randy White (186)	.10	.05	.01
□ 37 Eugene Lockhart (188)	.03	.01	.01
□ 38 Mike Sherrard (189)	.10	.05	.01
□ 39 Jim Jeffcoat (190)	.03	.01	.01
□ 40 Tony Hill (191)	.06	.03	.01
□ 41 Tony Dorsett	.30	.14	.04
□ 42 Keith Byars (192)	.20	.09	.03
□ 43 Andre Waters (193)	.06	.03	.01
□ 44 Kenny Jackson (194)	.03	.01	.01
□ 45 John Teltschik (195)	.03	.01	.01
□ 46 Roynell Young (196)	.03	.01	.01
□ 47 Randall Cunningham (197)	.30	.14	.04
□ 48 Mike Reichenbach (198)	.03	.01	.01
□ 49 Reggie White	.50	.23	.06
□ 50 Mike Quick	.10	.05	.01
□ 51 Bill Fralic (201)	.03	.01	.01
□ 52 Sylvester Stamps (202)	.03	.01	.01
□ 53 Bret Clark (203)	.03	.01	.01
□ 54 William Andrews (204)	.03	.01	.01
□ 55 Buddy Curry (205)	.03	.01	.01
□ 56 David Archer (206)	.06	.03	.01
□ 57 Rick Bryan (207)	.03	.01	.01
□ 58 Gerald Riggs	.10	.05	.01
□ 59 Charlie Brown	.05	.02	.01
□ 60 Joe Montana	1.25	.55	.16
□ 61 Jerry Rice	2.00	.90	.25
□ 62 Carlton Williamson (212)	.03	.01	.01
□ 63 Roger Craig (213)	.10	.05	.01
□ 64 Ronnie Lott (214)	.20	.09	.03
□ 65 Dwight Clark (215)	.10	.05	.01
□ 66 Jeff Stover (216)	.03	.01	.01
□ 67 Charles Haley (217)	.20	.09	.03
□ 68 Ray Wersching (218)	.03	.01	.01
□ 69 Lawrence Taylor	.30	.14	.04
□ 70 Joe Morris	.10	.05	.01
□ 71 Carl Banks (221)	.06	.03	.01
□ 72 Mark Bavaro (222)	.06	.03	.01
□ 73 Harry Carson (223)	.06	.03	.01
□ 74 Phil Simms (224)	.10	.05	.01
□ 75 Jim Burt (225)	.03	.01	.01
□ 76 Brad Benson (226)	.03	.01	.01
□ 77 Leonard Marshall (227)	.06	.03	.01
□ 78 Jeff Chadwick	.05	.02	.01
□ 79 Devon Mitchell (228)	.03	.01	.01
□ 80 Chuck Long (229)	.05	.02	.01
□ 81 Demetrious Johnson (230)	.03	.01	.01
□ 82 Herman Hunter (231)	.03	.01	.01
□ 83 Keith Ferguson (232)	.03	.01	.01
□ 84 Garry James (233)	.03	.01	.01
□ 85 Leonard Thompson (234)	.03	.01	.01
□ 86 James Jones	.05	.02	.01
□ 87 Kenneth Davis	.20	.09	.03
□ 88 Brian Noble (237)	.03	.01	.01
□ 89 Al Del Greco (238)	.03	.01	.01
□ 90 Mark Lee (239)	.03	.01	.01
□ 91 Randy Wright	.05	.02	.01
□ 92 Tim Harris (240)	.20	.09	.03
□ 93 Phillip Epps (241)	.03	.01	.01
□ 94 Walter Stanley (242)	.05	.02	.01
□ 95 Eddie Lee Ivery (243)	.03	.01	.01
□ 96 Doug Smith (247)	.03	.01	.01
□ 97 Jerry Gray (248)	.03	.01	.01
□ 98 Dennis Harrah (249)	.03	.01	.01
□ 99 Jim Everett (250)	.30	.14	.04
□ 100 Jackie Slater (251)	.06	.03	.01
□ 101 Vince Newsome (252)	.03	.01	.01
□ 102 LeRoy Irvin (253)	.03	.01	.01
□ 103 Henry Ellard	.10	.05	.01
□ 104 Eric Dickerson	.30	.14	.04
□ 105 George Rogers (256)	.06	.03	.01
□ 106 Darrell Green (257)	.06	.03	.01
□ 107 Art Monk (258)	.10	.05	.01
□ 108 Neal Olkewicz (260)	.03	.01	.01
□ 109 Russ Grimm (261)	.03	.01	.01
□ 110 Dexter Manley (262)	.03	.01	.01
□ 111 Kelvin Bryant (263)	.06	.03	.01
□ 112 Jay Schroeder	.10	.05	.01
□ 113 Gary Clark	.20	.09	.03
□ 114 Rickey Jackson	.10	.05	.01
□ 115 Eric Martin (264)	.06	.03	.01
□ 116 Dave Waymer (265)	.03	.01	.01
□ 117 Morten Andersen (266)	.06	.03	.01
□ 118 Bruce Clark (267)	.03	.01	.01
□ 119 Hoby Brenner (269)	.03	.01	.01
□ 120 Brian Hansen (270)	.03	.01	.01
□ 121 Dave Wilson (271)	.03	.01	.01
□ 122 Rueben Mayes	.05	.02	.01
□ 123 Tommy Kramer	.10	.05	.01
□ 124 Mark Malone (274)	.06	.03	.01
□ 125 Anthony Carter (275)	.10	.05	.01
□ 126 Keith Millard (276)	.03	.01	.01
□ 127 Steve Jordan	.10	.05	.01
□ 128 Chuck Nelson (277)	.03	.01	.01
□ 129 Issiac Holt (278)	.03	.01	.01
□ 130 Darrin Nelson (279)	.06	.03	.01
□ 131 Gary Zimmerman (280)	.06	.03	.01
□ 132 Mark Bavaro (146) All-Pro FOIL	.10	.05	.01
□ 133 Jim Covert (147) All-Pro FOIL	.10	.05	.01
□ 134 Eric Dickerson (148) All-Pro FOIL	.30	.14	.04
□ 135 Bill Fralic (149) All-Pro FOIL	.10	.05	.01
□ 136 Tony Franklin (150) All-Pro FOIL	.10	.05	.01
□ 137 Dennis Harrah (151) All-Pro FOIL	.10	.05	.01
□ 138 Dan Marino (152) All-Pro FOIL	1.50	.70	.19
□ 139 Joe Morris (153) All-Pro FOIL	.10	.05	.01
□ 140 Jerry Rice (154) All-Pro FOIL	1.50	.70	.19
□ 141 Cody Risien (155) All-Pro FOIL	.10	.05	.01
□ 142 Dwight Stephenson (282) All-Pro FOIL	.10	.05	.01
□ 143 Al Toon (283) All-Pro FOIL	.10	.05	.01
□ 144 Deron Cherry (284) All-Pro FOIL	.10	.05	.01
□ 145 Hanford Dixon (285) All-Pro FOIL	.10	.05	.01
□ 146 Darrell Green (132) All-Pro FOIL	.20	.09	.03
□ 147 Ronnie Lott (133) All-Pro FOIL	.20	.09	.03
□ 148 Bill Maas (134) All-Pro FOIL	.10	.05	.01
□ 149 Dexter Manley (135) All-Pro FOIL	.10	.05	.01
□ 150 Karl Mecklenburg (136) All-Pro FOIL	.10	.05	.01
□ 151 Mike Singletary (137) All-Pro FOIL	.20	.09	.03
□ 152 Rohn Stark (138) All-Pro FOIL	.10	.05	.01
□ 153 Lawrence Taylor (139) All-Pro FOIL	.25	.11	.03
□ 154 Andre Tippett (140) All-Pro FOIL	.10	.05	.01
□ 155 Reggie White (141) All-Pro FOIL	.40	.18	.05
□ 156 Boomer Esiason (7)	.20	.09	.03
□ 157 Anthony Munoz (8)	.10	.05	.01
□ 158 Tim McGee (9)	.10	.05	.01
□ 159 Max Montoya (10)	.06	.03	.01
□ 160 Jim Breech (11)	.03	.01	.01
□ 161 Tim Krumrie (12)	.03	.01	.01
□ 162 Eddie Brown (13)	.06	.03	.01
□ 163 James Brooks	.10	.05	.01
□ 164 Cris Collinsworth	.10	.05	.01
□ 165 Charles Romes (16)	.03	.01	.01
□ 166 Robb Riddick (17)	.03	.01	.01
□ 167 Eugene Marve (18)	.03	.01	.01
□ 168 Chris Burkett (20)	.03	.01	.01
□ 169 Bruce Smith (21)	.10	.05	.01
□ 170 Greg Bell (22)	.03	.01	.01
□ 171 Pete Metzelaars (23)	.06	.03	.01
□ 172 Jim Kelly	1.00	.45	.12
□ 173 Andre Reed	.35	.16	.04
□ 174 John Elway	1.00	.45	.12
□ 175 Mike Harden (24)	.03	.01	.01
□ 176 Gerald Willhite (25)	.03	.01	.01
□ 177 Rulon Jones (26)	.03	.01	.01
□ 178 Ricky Hunley (27)	.03	.01	.01
□ 179 Mark Jackson (29)	.03	.01	.01
□ 180 Rich Karlis (30)	.03	.01	.01
□ 181 Sammy Winder (31)	.03	.01	.01
□ 182 Karl Mecklenburg	.05	.02	.01
□ 183 Bernie Kosar	.20	.09	.03
□ 184 Kevin Mack (34)	.06	.03	.01
□ 185 Bob Golic (35)	.03	.01	.01
□ 186 Ozzie Newsome (36)	.10	.05	.01
□ 187 Brian Brennan	.05	.02	.01
□ 188 Gerald McNeil (37)	.03	.01	.01
□ 189 Hanford Dixon (38)	.03	.01	.01
□ 190 Cody Risien (39)	.03	.01	.01
□ 191 Chris Rockins (40)	.03	.01	.01
□ 192 Gill Byrd (42)	.06	.03	.01
□ 193 Kellen Winslow (43)	.10	.05	.01
□ 194 Billy Ray Smith (44)	.03	.01	.01
□ 195 Wes Chandler (45)	.06	.03	.01
□ 196 Leslie O'Neal (46)	.20	.09	.03
□ 197 Ralf Mojsiejenko (47)	.03	.01	.01
□ 198 Lee Williams (48)	.10	.05	.01
□ 199 Gary Anderson RB	.10	.05	.01
□ 200 Dan Fouts	.30	.14	.04
□ 201 Stephone Paige (51)	.06	.03	.01
□ 202 Irv Eatman (52)	.03	.01	.01
□ 203 Bill Kenney (53)	.03	.01	.01
□ 204 Dino Hackett (54)	.03	.01	.01
□ 205 Carlos Carson (55)	.06	.03	.01
□ 206 Art Still (56)	.03	.01	.01
□ 207 Lloyd Burruss (57)	.03	.01	.01
□ 208 Deron Cherry	.05	.02	.01
□ 209 Bill Maas	.05	.02	.01
□ 210 Gary Hogeboom	.05	.02	.01
□ 211 Rohn Stark	.05	.02	.01
□ 212 Cliff Odom (62)	.03	.01	.01
□ 213 Randy McMillan (63)	.03	.01	.01
□ 214 Chris Hinton (64)	.03	.01	.01
□ 215 Matt Bouza (65)	.03	.01	.01
□ 216 Ray Donaldson (66)	.03	.01	.01
□ 217 Bill Brooks (67)	.06	.03	.01
□ 218 Jack Trudeau (68)	.06	.03	.01
□ 219 Mark Duper	.10	.05	.01
□ 220 Dan Marino	2.00	.90	.25
□ 221 Dwight Stephenson (71)	.03	.01	.01
□ 222 Mark Clayton (72)	.10	.05	.01
□ 223 Roy Foster (73)	.03	.01	.01
□ 224 John Offerdahl (74)	.10	.05	.01
□ 225 Lorenzo Hampton (75)	.03	.01	.01
□ 226 Reggie Roby (76)	.03	.01	.01
□ 227 Tony Nathan (77)	.06	.03	.01
□ 228 Johnny Hector (79)	.03	.01	.01
□ 229 Wesley Walker (80)	.06	.03	.01
□ 230 Mark Gastineau (81)	.06	.03	.01
□ 231 Ken O'Brien (82)	.06	.03	.01
□ 232 Dave Jennings (83)	.03	.01	.01
□ 233 Mickey Shuler (84)	.03	.01	.01
□ 234 Joe Klecko (85)	.06	.03	.01
□ 235 Freeman McNeil	.10	.05	.01
□ 236 Al Toon	.05	.02	.01
□ 237 Warren Moon (88)	.25	.11	.03

☐ 238 Dean Steinkuhler (89)	.06	.03	.01
☐ 239 Mike Rozier (90)	.06	.03	.01
☐ 240 Ray Childress (92)	.06	.03	.01
☐ 241 Tony Zendejas (93)	.03	.01	.01
☐ 242 John Grimsley (94)	.03	.01	.01
☐ 243 Jesse Baker (95)	.03	.01	.01
☐ 244 Ernest Givins	.25	.11	.03
☐ 245 Drew Hill	.10	.05	.01
☐ 246 Tony Franklin	.05	.02	.01
☐ 247 Steve Grogan (96)	.06	.03	.01
☐ 248 Garin Veris (97)	.03	.01	.01
☐ 249 Stanley Morgan (98)	.06	.03	.01
☐ 250 Fred Marion (99)	.03	.01	.01
☐ 251 Raymond Clayborn (100)	.03	.01	.01
☐ 252 Mosi Tatupu (101)	.03	.01	.01
☐ 253 Tony Eason (102)	.03	.01	.01
☐ 254 Andre Tippett	.10	.05	.01
☐ 255 Todd Christensen	.10	.05	.01
☐ 256 Howie Long (105)	.10	.05	.01
☐ 257 Marcus Allen (106)	.10	.05	.01
☐ 258 Vann McElroy (107)	.03	.01	.01
☐ 259 Dokie Williams	.05	.02	.01
☐ 260 Mike Haynes (108)	.06	.03	.01
☐ 261 Sean Jones (109)	.06	.03	.01
☐ 262 Jim Plunkett (110)	.10	.05	.01
☐ 263 Chris Bahr (111)	.03	.01	.01
☐ 264 Dave Krieg (115)	.10	.05	.01
☐ 265 Jacob Green (116)	.03	.01	.01
☐ 266 Norm Johnson (117)	.03	.01	.01
☐ 267 Fredd Young (118)	.03	.01	.01
☐ 268 Steve Largent	.50	.23	.06
☐ 269 Dave Brown (119)	.03	.01	.01
☐ 270 Kenny Easley (120)	.03	.01	.01
☐ 271 Bobby Joe Edmonds (121)	.03	.01	.01
☐ 272 Curt Warner	.10	.05	.01
☐ 273 Mike Merriweather	.05	.02	.01
☐ 274 Mark Malone (124)	.06	.03	.01
☐ 275 Bryan Hinkle (125)	.03	.01	.01
☐ 276 Earnest Jackson (126)	.03	.01	.01
☐ 277 Keith Willis (128)	.03	.01	.01
☐ 278 Walter Abercrombie (129)	.03	.01	.01
☐ 279 Donnie Shell (130)	.03	.01	.01
☐ 280 John Stallworth (131)	.10	.05	.01
☐ 281 Louis Lipps	.10	.05	.01
☐ 282 Eric Dickerson (142) FOIL	.25	.11	.03
☐ 283 Dan Marino (143) FOIL	1.50	.70	.19
☐ 284 Tony Franklin (144) FOIL	.10	.05	.01
☐ 285 Todd Christensen (145) FOIL	.10	.05	.01
☐ NNO Sticker Album	2.00	.90	.25

1988 Topps Stickers

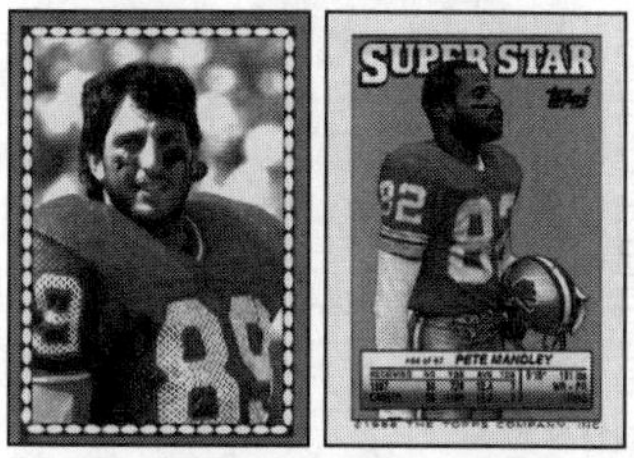

The 1988 Topps Football sticker set is very similar to the previous years in that it contains stickers, foil stickers, and an accompanying album to house one's sticker collection. The stickers measure approximately 2 1/8" by 3" and have a distinctive red border with an inner frame of small yellow footballs. The stickers are numbered on the front. The sticker backs are actually part of a different set. Sticker pairs are identified below by parenthetically listing the other member of the pair. The foil stickers are pairs of All-Pros (AP) and are so indicated in the checklist below on stickers. Stickers 2-5 are actually a large four-part action photo of Super Bowl XXII action with Doug Williams handing off to Timmy Smith. On the inside back cover of the sticker album the company offered (via direct mail-order) any ten different stickers of your choice for 1.00; this is one reason why the values of the most popular players in these sticker sets are somewhat depressed compared to traditional card set prices. The front cover of the sticker album features an action photo of the Washington Redskins; the back cover depicts Doug Williams artwork. The stickers are checklisted below according to special subsets and teams. The following players are shown in their Rookie Card year: Neal Anderson, Cornelius Bennett, Brian Bosworth, Ronnie Harmon, Bo Jackson, Clyde Simmons, Webster Slaughter, Pat Swilling, Vinny Testaverde, and Wade Wilson.

	MINT	NRMT	EXC
COMPLETE SET (285)	10.00	4.50	1.25
COMMON CARD (1-131/156-285)	.05	.02	.01
COMMON HALF STICKER	.03	.01	.01
COMMON HALF FOIL	.10	.05	.01

☐ 1 Super Bowl XXII MVP Doug Williams	.10	.05	.01
☐ 2 Super Bowl XXII Redskins vs. Broncos Doug Williams UL	.03	.01	.01
☐ 3 Super Bowl XXII Redskins vs. Broncos Doug Williams UR	.03	.01	.01
☐ 4 Super Bowl XXII Redskins vs. Broncos Doug Williams LL	.03	.01	.01
☐ 5 Super Bowl XXII Redskins vs. Broncos Doug Williams LR	.03	.01	.01
☐ 6 Neal Anderson (234)	.10	.05	.01
☐ 7 Willie Gault (224)	.03	.01	.01
☐ 8 Dennis Gentry (219)	.03	.01	.01
☐ 9 Dave Duerson (197)	.03	.01	.01
☐ 10 Steve McMichael (266)	.06	.03	.01
☐ 11 Dennis McKinnon (230)	.03	.01	.01
☐ 12 Mike Singletary (209)	.10	.05	.01
☐ 13 Jim McMahon	.10	.05	.01
☐ 14 Richard Dent	.10	.05	.01
☐ 15 Vinny Testaverde (167)	.10	.05	.01
☐ 16 Gerald Carter (187)	.03	.01	.01
☐ 17 Jeff Smith (185)	.03	.01	.01
☐ 18 Chris Washington (212)	.03	.01	.01
☐ 19 Bobby Futrell (231)	.03	.01	.01
☐ 20 Calvin Magee (182)	.03	.01	.01
☐ 21 Ron Holmes (169)	.03	.01	.01
☐ 22 Ervin Randle	.05	.02	.01
☐ 23 James Wilder	.05	.02	.01
☐ 24 Neil Lomax	.06	.03	.01
☐ 25 Robert Awalt (161)	.03	.01	.01
☐ 26 Leonard Smith (177)	.03	.01	.01
☐ 27 Stump Mitchell (178)	.03	.01	.01
☐ 28 Vai Sikahema (280)	.03	.01	.01
☐ 29 Freddie Joe Nunn (222)	.03	.01	.01
☐ 30 Earl Ferrell (223)	.03	.01	.01
☐ 31 Roy Green (157)	.06	.03	.01
☐ 32 J.T. Smith	.06	.03	.01
☐ 33 Michael Downs	.05	.02	.01
☐ 34 Herschel Walker	.25	.11	.03
☐ 35 Roger Ruzek (269)	.03	.01	.01
☐ 36 Ed Too Tall Jones (245)	.06	.03	.01
☐ 37 Everson Walls (252)	.06	.03	.01
☐ 38 Bill Bates (213)	.06	.03	.01
☐ 39 Doug Cosbie (179)	.03	.01	.01
☐ 40 Eugene Lockhart (186)	.03	.01	.01
☐ 41 Danny White (205)	.06	.03	.01
☐ 42 Randall Cunningham	.20	.09	.03
☐ 43 Reggie White	.50	.23	.06
☐ 44 Anthony Toney (256)	.03	.01	.01
☐ 45 Mike Quick (248)	.06	.03	.01
☐ 46 John Spagnola (235)	.03	.01	.01
☐ 47 Clyde Simmons (275)	.10	.05	.01
☐ 48 Andre Waters (261)	.06	.03	.01
☐ 49 Keith Byars (265)	.06	.03	.01
☐ 50 Jerome Brown (240)	.10	.05	.01
☐ 51 John Rade	.05	.02	.01
☐ 52 Rick Donnelly	.05	.02	.01
☐ 53 Scott Campbell (160)	.03	.01	.01
☐ 54 Floyd Dixon (246)	.03	.01	.01
☐ 55 Gerald Riggs (236)	.03	.01	.01
☐ 56 Bill Fralic (267)	.03	.01	.01
☐ 57 Mike Gann (165)	.03	.01	.01
☐ 58 Tony Casillas (168)	.10	.05	.01
☐ 59 Rick Bryan (257)	.03	.01	.01
☐ 60 Jerry Rice	1.25	.55	.16
☐ 61 Ronnie Lott	.15	.07	.02
☐ 62 Ray Wersching (220)	.03	.01	.01
☐ 63 Charles Haley (281)	.10	.05	.01
☐ 64 Joe Montana (190)	.75	.35	.09
☐ 65 Joe Cribbs (221)	.06	.03	.01
☐ 66 Mike Wilson (203)	.03	.01	.01
☐ 67 Roger Craig (251)	.10	.05	.01
☐ 68 Michael Walter (162)	.03	.01	.01
☐ 69 Mark Bavaro	.06	.03	.01
☐ 70 Carl Banks	.06	.03	.01
☐ 71 George Adams (274)	.03	.01	.01
☐ 72 Phil Simms (216)	.10	.05	.01
☐ 73 Lawrence Taylor (181)	.15	.07	.02
☐ 74 Joe Morris (198)	.06	.03	.01
☐ 75 Lionel Manuel (204)	.03	.01	.01
☐ 76 Sean Landeta (210)	.03	.01	.01
☐ 77 Harry Carson (159)	.03	.01	.01
☐ 78 Chuck Long (166)	.06	.03	.01
☐ 79 James Jones (259)	.03	.01	.01
☐ 80 Garry James (158)	.03	.01	.01
☐ 81 Gary Lee (176)	.03	.01	.01
☐ 82 Jim Arnold (260)	.03	.01	.01
☐ 83 Dennis Gibson (232)	.03	.01	.01
☐ 84 Mike Cofer (242)	.03	.01	.01
☐ 85 Pete Mandley	.05	.02	.01
☐ 86 James Griffin	.05	.02	.01
☐ 87 Randy Wright (206)	.03	.01	.01
☐ 88 Phillip Epps (191)	.03	.01	.01
☐ 89 Brian Noble (249)	.03	.01	.01
☐ 90 Johnny Holland (258)	.10	.05	.01
☐ 91 Dave Brown (156)	.03	.01	.01
☐ 92 Brent Fullwood (207)	.03	.01	.01
☐ 93 Kenneth Davis (194)	.06	.03	.01
☐ 94 Tim Harris	.10	.05	.01
☐ 95 Walter Stanley	.05	.02	.01
☐ 96 Charles White	.06	.03	.01
☐ 97 Jackie Slater	.10	.05	.01
☐ 98 Jim Everett (271)	.10	.05	.01
☐ 99 Mike Lansford (200)	.03	.01	.01
☐ 100 Henry Ellard (199)	.06	.03	.01
☐ 101 Dale Hatcher (170)	.03	.01	.01
☐ 102 Jim Collins (268)	.03	.01	.01
☐ 103 Jerry Gray (214)	.03	.01	.01
☐ 104 LeRoy Irvin (276)	.03	.01	.01
☐ 105 Darrell Green	.10	.05	.01
☐ 106 Doug Williams	.10	.05	.01
☐ 107 Gary Clark (247)	.10	.05	.01
☐ 108 Charles Mann (171)	.06	.03	.01
☐ 109 Art Monk (270)	.20	.09	.03
☐ 110 Barry Wilburn (196)	.03	.01	.01
☐ 111 Alvin Walton (188)	.03	.01	.01
☐ 112 Dexter Manley (233)	.03	.01	.01
☐ 113 Kelvin Bryant (180)	.03	.01	.01
☐ 114 Morten Andersen	.06	.03	.01
☐ 115 Rueben Mayes (244)	.03	.01	.01
☐ 116 Brian Hansen (279)	.03	.01	.01
☐ 117 Dalton Hilliard (241)	.03	.01	.01
☐ 118 Rickey Jackson (195)	.06	.03	.01
☐ 119 Eric Martin (189)	.06	.03	.01
☐ 120 Mel Gray (278)	.06	.03	.01
☐ 121 Bobby Hebert (215)	.06	.03	.01
☐ 122 Pat Swilling	.25	.11	.03
☐ 123 Anthony Carter	.10	.05	.01
☐ 124 Wade Wilson (225)	.10	.05	.01
☐ 125 Darrin Nelson (250)	.03	.01	.01
☐ 126 D.J. Dozier (239)	.03	.01	.01
☐ 127 Chris Doleman	.20	.09	.03
☐ 128 Henry Thomas (255)	.05	.02	.01
☐ 129 Jesse Solomon (211)	.03	.01	.01
☐ 130 Neal Guggemos (243)	.03	.01	.01
☐ 131 Joey Browner (208)	.03	.01	.01
☐ 132 Carl Banks AP (152) FOIL	.10	.05	.01
☐ 133 Joey Browner AP (145) FOIL	.10	.05	.01
☐ 134 Hanford Dixon AP (147) FOIL	.10	.05	.01
☐ 135 Rick Donnelly AP (149) FOIL	.10	.05	.01
☐ 136 Kenny Easley AP (155) FOIL	.10	.05	.01
☐ 137 Darrell Green AP (151) FOIL	.10	.05	.01
☐ 138 Bill Maas AP (148) FOIL	.10	.05	.01
☐ 139 Mike Singletary AP (153) FOIL	.20	.09	.03
☐ 140 Bruce Smith AP (154) FOIL	.20	.09	.03
☐ 141 Andre Tippett AP (146) FOIL	.10	.05	.01
☐ 142 Reggie White AP (150) FOIL	.35	.16	.04
☐ 143 Fredd Young AP (144) FOIL	.10	.05	.01
☐ 144 Morten Andersen AP (143) FOIL	.10	.05	.01
☐ 145 Mark Bavaro AP (133) FOIL	.10	.05	.01
☐ 146 Eric Dickerson AP (141) FOIL	.25	.11	.03
☐ 147 John Elway AP (134) FOIL	.75	.35	.09
☐ 148 Bill Fralic AP (138) FOIL	.10	.05	.01
☐ 149 Mike Munchak AP (135) FOIL	.10	.05	.01
☐ 150 Anthony Munoz AP (142) FOIL	.15	.07	.02
☐ 151 Jerry Rice AP (137) FOIL	1.00	.45	.12
☐ 152 Jackie Slater AP (132) FOIL	.10	.05	.01
☐ 153 J.T. Smith AP (139) FOIL	.10	.05	.01
☐ 154 Dwight Stephenson AP (140) FOIL	.10	.05	.01
☐ 155 Charles White AP (136) FOIL	.10	.05	.01
☐ 156 Larry Kinnebrew (91)	.03	.01	.01
☐ 157 Stanford Jennings (31)	.03	.01	.01
☐ 158 Eddie Brown (80)	.06	.03	.01
☐ 159 Scott Fulhage (77)	.03	.01	.01
☐ 160 Boomer Esiason (53)	.10	.05	.01
☐ 161 Tim Krumrie (25)	.03	.01	.01
☐ 162 Anthony Munoz (68)	.10	.05	.01
☐ 163 Jim Breech	.05	.02	.01
☐ 164 Reggie Williams	.05	.02	.01
☐ 165 Andre Reed (57)	.10	.05	.01
☐ 166 Cornelius Bennett (78)	.30	.14	.04
☐ 167 Ronnie Harmon (15)	.10	.05	.01
☐ 168 Shane Conlan (58)	.10	.05	.01
☐ 169 Chris Burkett (21)	.03	.01	.01
☐ 170 Mark Kelso (101)	.03	.01	.01
☐ 171 Robb Riddick (108)	.03	.01	.01
☐ 172 Bruce Smith	.20	.09	.03
☐ 173 Jim Kelly	.50	.23	.06
☐ 174 Jim Ryan	.03	.01	.01
☐ 175 John Elway	1.00	.45	.12
☐ 176 Sammy Winder (81)	.03	.01	.01
☐ 177 Karl Mecklenburg (26)	.06	.03	.01
☐ 178 Mark Haynes (27)	.03	.01	.01
☐ 179 Rulon Jones (39)	.03	.01	.01
☐ 180 Ricky Nattiel (113)	.03	.01	.01
☐ 181 Vance Johnson (73)	.03	.01	.01
☐ 182 Mike Harden (20)	.03	.01	.01
☐ 183 Frank Minnifield	.05	.02	.01
☐ 184 Bernie Kosar	.10	.05	.01
☐ 185 Earnest Byner (17)	.06	.03	.01
☐ 186 Webster Slaughter (40)	.15	.07	.02
☐ 187 Brian Brennan (16)	.03	.01	.01
☐ 188 Carl Hairston (111)	.03	.01	.01
☐ 189 Mike Johnson (119)	.03	.01	.01
☐ 190 Clay Matthews (64)	.06	.03	.01
☐ 191 Kevin Mack (88)	.06	.03	.01
☐ 192 Kellen Winslow	.10	.05	.01
☐ 193 Billy Ray Smith	.05	.02	.01
☐ 194 Gary Anderson (93)	.03	.01	.01
☐ 195 Chip Banks (118)	.03	.01	.01
☐ 196 Elvis Patterson (110)	.03	.01	.01
☐ 197 Lee Williams (9)	.03	.01	.01
☐ 198 Curtis Adams (74)	.03	.01	.01
☐ 199 Vencie Glenn (100)	.03	.01	.01
☐ 200 Ralf Mojsiejenko (99)	.03	.01	.01
☐ 201 Carlos Carson	.05	.02	.01
☐ 202 Bill Maas	.05	.02	.01
☐ 203 Christian Okoye (66)	.10	.05	.01
☐ 204 Deron Cherry (75)	.03	.01	.01
☐ 205 Dino Hackett (41)	.03	.01	.01
☐ 206 Mike Bell (87)	.03	.01	.01
☐ 207 Stephone Paige (92)	.03	.01	.01
☐ 208 Bill Kenney (131)	.03	.01	.01
☐ 209 Paul Palmer (12)	.03	.01	.01
☐ 210 Jack Trudeau (76)	.03	.01	.01
☐ 211 Albert Bentley (129)	.03	.01	.01
☐ 212 Bill Brooks (18)	.06	.03	.01
☐ 213 Dean Biasucci (38)	.03	.01	.01
☐ 214 Cliff Odom (103)	.03	.01	.01
☐ 215 Barry Krauss (121)	.03	.01	.01
☐ 216 Mike Prior (72)	.03	.01	.01
☐ 217 Eric Dickerson	.20	.09	.03
☐ 218 Duane Bickett	.10	.05	.01
☐ 219 Dwight Stephenson (8)	.03	.01	.01
☐ 220 John Offerdahl (62)	.06	.03	.01
☐ 221 Troy Stradford (65)	.03	.01	.01
☐ 222 John Bosa (29)	.03	.01	.01
☐ 223 Jackie Shipp (30)	.03	.01	.01
☐ 224 Paul Lankford (7)	.03	.01	.01
☐ 225 Mark Duper (124)	.06	.03	.01
☐ 226 Dan Marino	2.00	.90	.25
☐ 227 Mark Clayton	.10	.05	.01
☐ 228 Bob Crable	.05	.02	.01
☐ 229 Al Toon	.05	.02	.01
☐ 230 Freeman McNeil (11)	.03	.01	.01
☐ 231 Johnny Hector (19)	.03	.01	.01
☐ 232 Pat Leahy (83)	.03	.01	.01
☐ 233 Ken O'Brien (112)	.06	.03	.01
☐ 234 Alex Gordon (6)	.03	.01	.01
☐ 235 Harry Hamilton (46)	.03	.01	.01
☐ 236 Mickey Shuler (55)	.03	.01	.01
☐ 237 Mike Rozier	.05	.02	.01
☐ 238 Al Smith	.10	.05	.01
☐ 239 Ernest Givins (126)	.10	.05	.01
☐ 240 Warren Moon (50)	.20	.09	.03
☐ 241 Drew Hill (117)	.06	.03	.01
☐ 242 Alonzo Highsmith (84)	.06	.03	.01
☐ 243 Mike Munchak (130)	.03	.01	.01
☐ 244 Keith Bostic (115)	.03	.01	.01
☐ 245 Sean Jones (36)	.06	.03	.01
☐ 246 Stanley Morgan (54)	.06	.03	.01
☐ 247 Garin Veris (107)	.03	.01	.01
☐ 248 Stephen Starring (45)	.03	.01	.01
☐ 249 Steve Grogan (89)	.06	.03	.01
☐ 250 Irving Fryar (125)	.06	.03	.01
☐ 251 Rich Camarillo (67)	.03	.01	.01
☐ 252 Ronnie Lippett (37)	.03	.01	.01
☐ 253 Andre Tippett	.06	.03	.01
☐ 254 Fred Marion	.05	.02	.01
☐ 255 Howie Long (128)	.06	.03	.01
☐ 256 James Lofton (44)	.20	.09	.03
☐ 257 Vance Mueller (59)	.03	.01	.01
☐ 258 Jerry Robinson (90)	.03	.01	.01
☐ 259 Todd Christensen (79)	.06	.03	.01
☐ 260 Vann McElroy (82)	.03	.01	.01
☐ 261 Greg Townsend (48)	.06	.03	.01
☐ 262 Bo Jackson	.40	.18	.05
☐ 263 Marcus Allen	.40	.18	.05
☐ 264 Curt Warner	.06	.03	.01
☐ 265 Jacob Green (49)	.03	.01	.01
☐ 266 Norm Johnson (10)	.03	.01	.01
☐ 267 Brian Bosworth (56)	.10	.05	.01
☐ 268 Bobby Joe Edmonds (102)	.03	.01	.01
☐ 269 Dave Krieg (35)	.06	.03	.01
☐ 270 Kenny Easley (109)	.03	.01	.01
☐ 271 Steve Largent (98)	.30	.14	.04
☐ 272 Fredd Young	.05	.02	.01
☐ 273 David Little	.05	.02	.01
☐ 274 Frank Pollard (71)	.03	.01	.01
☐ 275 Dwight Stone (47)	.06	.03	.01
☐ 276 Mike Merriweather (104)	.03	.01	.01
☐ 277 Earnest Jackson	.05	.02	.01

☐ 278 Delton Hall (120)	.03	.01	.01
☐ 279 Gary Anderson (116)	.03	.01	.01
☐ 280 Harry Newsome (28)	.03	.01	.01
☐ 281 Dwayne Woodruff (63)	.03	.01	.01
☐ 282 J.T. Smith (283)	.03	.01	.01
☐ 283 Charles White (282)	.03	.01	.01
☐ 284 Reggie White (285)	.20	.09	.03
☐ 285 Morten Andersen (284)	.06	.03	.01
☐ NNO Sticker Album	2.00	.90	.25

1988 Topps Sticker Backs

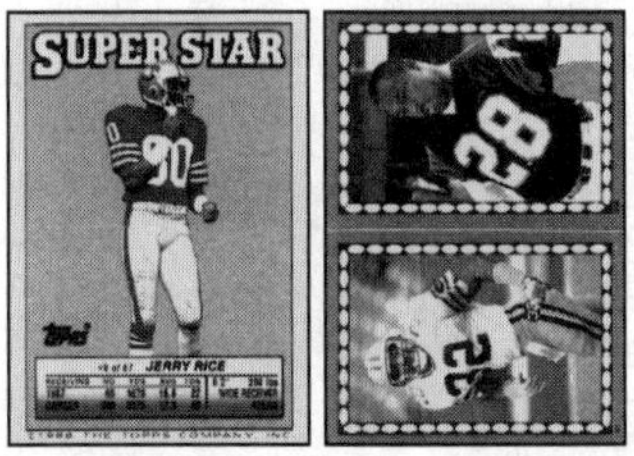

These cards are actually the backs of the Topps stickers. These cards are numbered in fine print in the statistical section of the card. The 67 cards in the set are generally a selection of popular players with all of them being quarterbacks, running backs, or receivers. The cards measure approximately 2 1/8" by 3". The cards are checklisted below alphabetically according to teams.

	MINT	NRMT	EXC
COMPLETE SET (67)	5.00	2.20	.60
COMMON CARD (1-67)	.07	.03	.01
☐ 1 Doug Williams	.10	.05	.01
☐ 2 Gary Clark	.10	.05	.01
☐ 3 John Elway	.75	.35	.09
☐ 4 Sammy Winder	.07	.03	.01
☐ 5 Vance Johnson	.10	.05	.01
☐ 6 Joe Montana	1.00	.45	.12
☐ 7 Roger Craig	.10	.05	.01
☐ 8 Jerry Rice	1.00	.45	.12
☐ 9 Rueben Mayes	.07	.03	.01
☐ 10 Eric Martin	.10	.05	.01
☐ 11 Neal Anderson	.10	.05	.01
☐ 12 Willie Gault	.10	.05	.01
☐ 13 Bernie Kosar	.10	.05	.01
☐ 14 Kevin Mack	.07	.03	.01
☐ 15 Webster Slaughter	.20	.09	.03
☐ 16 Warren Moon	.30	.14	.04
☐ 17 Mike Rozier	.07	.03	.01
☐ 18 Drew Hill	.10	.05	.01
☐ 19 Eric Dickerson	.20	.09	.03
☐ 20 Bill Brooks	.07	.03	.01
☐ 21 Curt Warner	.10	.05	.01
☐ 22 Steve Largent	.30	.14	.04
☐ 23 Darrin Nelson	.07	.03	.01
☐ 24 Anthony Carter	.10	.05	.01
☐ 25 Earnest Jackson	.07	.03	.01
☐ 26 Weegie Thompson	.07	.03	.01
☐ 27 Stephen Starring	.07	.03	.01
☐ 28 Stanley Morgan	.07	.03	.01
☐ 29 Dan Marino	1.25	.55	.16
☐ 30 Troy Stradford	.07	.03	.01
☐ 31 Mark Clayton	.10	.05	.01
☐ 32 Curtis Adams	.07	.03	.01
☐ 33 Kellen Winslow	.20	.09	.03
☐ 34 Jim Kelly	.50	.23	.06
☐ 35 Ronnie Harmon	.10	.05	.01
☐ 36 Chris Burkett	.07	.03	.01
☐ 37 Randall Cunningham	.20	.09	.03
☐ 38 Anthony Toney	.07	.03	.01
☐ 39 Mike Quick	.10	.05	.01
☐ 40 Neil Lomax	.10	.05	.01
☐ 41 Stump Mitchell	.07	.03	.01
☐ 42 J.T. Smith	.07	.03	.01
☐ 43 Herschel Walker	.20	.09	.03
☐ 44 Herschel Walker	.20	.09	.03
☐ 45 Joe Morris	.10	.05	.01
☐ 46 Mark Bavaro	.10	.05	.01
☐ 47 Charles White	.07	.03	.01
☐ 48 Henry Ellard	.20	.09	.03
☐ 49 Ken O'Brien	.10	.05	.01
☐ 50 Freeman McNeil	.10	.05	.01
☐ 51 Al Toon	.10	.05	.01
☐ 52 Kenneth Davis	.10	.05	.01
☐ 53 Walter Stanley	.07	.03	.01
☐ 54 Marcus Allen	.40	.18	.05
☐ 55 James Lofton	.20	.09	.03
☐ 56 Boomer Esiason	.20	.09	.03
☐ 57 Larry Kinnebrew	.07	.03	.01
☐ 58 Eddie Brown	.10	.05	.01
☐ 59 James Wilder	.07	.03	.01
☐ 60 Gerald Carter	.07	.03	.01
☐ 61 Christian Okoye	.10	.05	.01
☐ 62 Carlos Carson	.07	.03	.01
☐ 63 James Jones	.07	.03	.01
☐ 64 Pete Mandley	.07	.03	.01
☐ 65 Gerald Riggs	.10	.05	.01
☐ 66 Floyd Dixon	.07	.03	.01
☐ 67 Checklist Card	.07	.03	.01

1977 Touchdown Club

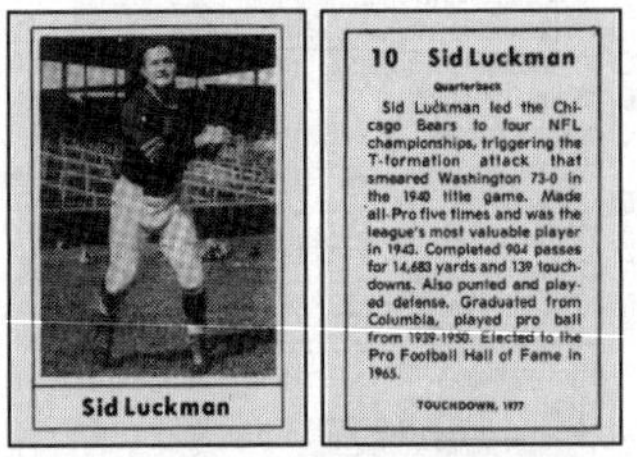

This 50-card set was initially targeted toward football autograph collectors as the set featured only living (at the time) ex-football players many of whom were or are now in the Pro Football Hall of Fame in Canton, Ohio. The set was originally sold as a complete set along with a printed address list for the players in the set. The cards are black and white (typically showing the player in his prime) and are numbered on the back. The cards measure approximately 2 1/4" by 3 1/4". Card backs list career honors the player received.

	NRMT-MT	EXC	G-VG
COMPLETE SET (50)	80.00	36.00	10.00
COMMON CARD (1-50)	1.50	.70	.19
☐ 1 Red Grange	7.50	3.40	.95
☐ 2 George Halas	5.00	2.20	.60
☐ 3 Benny Friedman	1.50	.70	.19
☐ 4 Cliff Battles	2.00	.90	.25
☐ 5 Mike Michalske	2.00	.90	.25
☐ 6 George McAfee	2.50	1.10	.30
☐ 7 Beattie Feathers	2.00	.90	.25
☐ 8 Ernie Caddel	1.50	.70	.19
☐ 9 George Musso	2.00	.90	.25
☐ 10 Sid Luckman	5.00	2.20	.60
☐ 11 Cecil Isbell	2.00	.90	.25
☐ 12 Bronko Nagurski	5.00	2.20	.60
☐ 13 Hunk Anderson	1.50	.70	.19
☐ 14 Dick Farman	1.50	.70	.19
☐ 15 Aldo Forte	1.50	.70	.19
☐ 16 Ki Aldrich	1.50	.70	.19
☐ 17 Jim Lee Howell	1.50	.70	.19
☐ 18 Ray Flaherty	2.00	.90	.25
☐ 19 Hampton Pool	1.50	.70	.19
☐ 20 Alex Wojciechowicz	2.00	.90	.25
☐ 21 Bill Osmanski	1.50	.70	.19
☐ 22 Hank Soar	1.50	.70	.19
☐ 23 Dutch Clark	2.50	1.10	.30
☐ 24 Joe Muha	1.50	.70	.19
☐ 25 Don Hutson	2.50	1.10	.30
☐ 26 Jim Poole	1.50	.70	.19
☐ 27 Charley Malone	1.50	.70	.19
☐ 28 Charley Trippi	2.50	1.10	.30
☐ 29 Andy Farkas	1.50	.70	.19
☐ 30 Clarke Hinkle	2.00	.90	.25
☐ 31 Gary Famiglietti	1.50	.70	.19
☐ 32 Bulldog Turner	2.50	1.10	.30
☐ 33 Sammy Baugh	7.50	3.40	.95
☐ 34 Pat Harder	2.00	.90	.25
☐ 35 Tuffy Leemans	2.00	.90	.25
☐ 36 Ken Strong	2.50	1.10	.30
☐ 37 Barney Poole	1.50	.70	.19
☐ 38 Frank(Bruiser) Kinard	2.00	.90	.25
☐ 39 Buford Ray	1.50	.70	.19
☐ 40 Clarence(Ace) Parker	2.00	.90	.25
☐ 41 Buddy Parker	1.50	.70	.19
☐ 42 Mel Hein	2.00	.90	.25
☐ 43 Ed Danowski	1.50	.70	.19
☐ 44 Bill Dudley	2.50	1.10	.30
☐ 45 Paul Stenn	1.50	.70	.19
☐ 46 George Connor	2.00	.90	.25
☐ 47 George Sauer Sr.	1.50	.70	.19
☐ 48 Armand Niccolai	1.50	.70	.19
☐ 49 Tony Canadeo	2.00	.90	.25
☐ 50 Bill Willis	2.50	1.10	.30

1983 Tudor Figurines

Produced by Tudor Games, these figurines were produced for each NFL team's quarterback. Although the statues are not specifically identified, they were designed to represent that team's 1983 quarterback. The pieces were rather crudely done with each appearing to by exact in design save for the team uniform. They are listed below by the product code number on the package (also in team alphabetical order) and are priced as opened statues. Complete sealed packages are valued at double the prices below.

	MINT	NRMT	EXC
COMPLETE SET (28)	500.00	220.00	60.00
COMMON FIGURINE	15.00	6.75	1.85
☐ 2001 Jim McMahon	20.00	9.00	2.50
☐ 2002 Ken Anderson	20.00	9.00	2.50
☐ 2003 Joe Ferguson	15.00	6.75	1.85
☐ 2004 John Elway	50.00	22.00	6.25
☐ 2005 Brian Sipe	15.00	6.75	1.85
☐ 2006 Doug Williams	15.00	6.75	1.85
☐ 2007 Neil Lomax	15.00	6.75	1.85
☐ 2008 Dan Fouts	25.00	11.00	3.10
☐ 2009 Bill Kenney	15.00	6.75	1.85
☐ 2010 Bert Jones	20.00	9.00	2.50
☐ 2011 Danny White	20.00	9.00	2.50
☐ 2012 David Woodley	15.00	6.75	1.85
☐ 2013 Ron Jaworski	15.00	6.75	1.85
☐ 2014 Steve Bartkowski	20.00	9.00	2.50
☐ 2015 Joe Montana	75.00	34.00	9.50
☐ 2016 Phil Simms	20.00	9.00	2.50
☐ 2017 Richard Todd	15.00	6.75	1.85
☐ 2018 Eric Hipple	15.00	6.75	1.85
☐ 2019 Archie Manning	20.00	9.00	2.50
☐ 2020 Lynn Dickey	15.00	6.75	1.85
☐ 2021 Steve Grogan	20.00	9.00	2.50
☐ 2022 Jim Plunkett	20.00	9.00	2.50
☐ 2023 Vince Ferragamo	15.00	6.75	1.85
☐ 2024 Joe Theismann	20.00	9.00	2.50
☐ 2025 Ken Stabler	30.00	13.50	3.70
☐ 2026 Jim Zorn	15.00	6.75	1.85
☐ 2027 Terry Bradshaw	30.00	13.50	3.70
☐ 2028 Tommy Kramer	15.00	6.75	1.85

1989 TV-4 NFL Quarterbacks

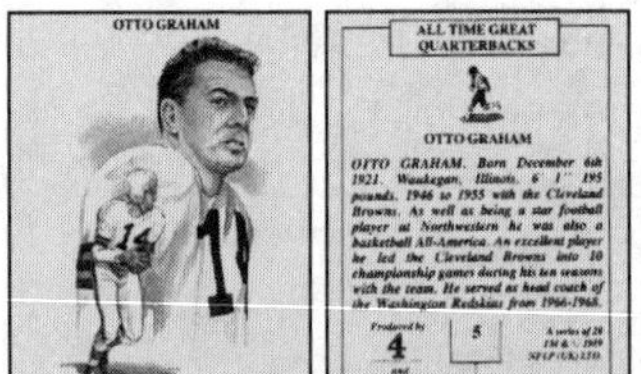

The 1989 TV-4 NFL Quarterbacks set features 20 cards measuring approximately 2 7/16" by 3 1/8". The fronts are borderless and show attractive color action and portrait drawings of each quarterback. The drawings were performed by artist J.C. Ford. The vertically oriented backs list career highlights. The TV-4 refers to a London (England) television station, which distributed the cards. The cards were distributed in England and were intended to promote the National Football League, which had begun playing pre-season games there.

	MINT	NRMT	EXC
COMPLETE SET (20)	25.00	11.00	3.10
COMMON CARD (1-20)	1.00	.45	.12
☐ 1 Dutch Clark	1.00	.45	.12
☐ 2 Sammy Baugh	1.50	.70	.19
☐ 3 Bob Waterfield	1.00	.45	.12
☐ 4 Sid Luckman	1.50	.70	.19
☐ 5 Otto Graham	1.50	.70	.19
☐ 6 Bobby Layne	1.50	.70	.19
☐ 7 Norm Van Brocklin	1.00	.45	.12
☐ 8 George Blanda	1.00	.45	.12
☐ 9 Y.A. Tittle	1.00	.45	.12
☐ 10 Johnny Unitas	2.00	.90	.25
☐ 11 Bart Starr	1.50	.70	.19
☐ 12 Sonny Jurgensen	1.00	.45	.12
☐ 13 Joe Namath	3.00	1.35	.35
☐ 14 Fran Tarkenton	1.50	.70	.19
☐ 15 Roger Staubach	2.50	1.10	.30
☐ 16 Terry Bradshaw	2.00	.90	.25
☐ 17 Dan Fouts	1.00	.45	.12
☐ 18 Joe Montana	7.00	3.10	.85
☐ 19 John Elway	5.00	2.20	.60
☐ 20 Dan Marino	10.00	4.50	1.25

1992 Ultimate WLAF

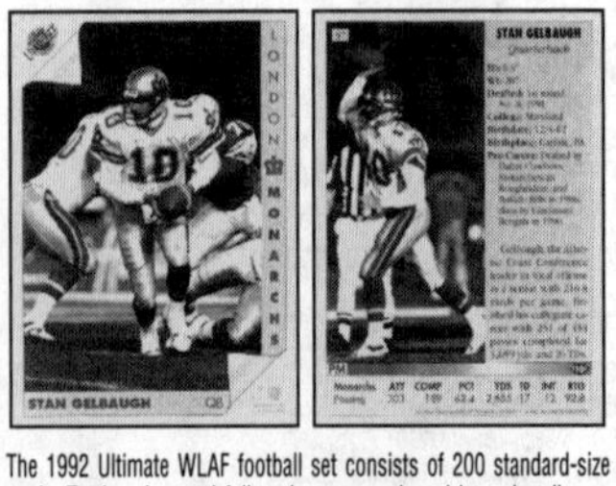

The 1992 Ultimate WLAF football set consists of 200 standard-size cards. Twelve nine-card foil packs were packaged in each coliseum display box, and each box came with a mini-poster and one hologram card. There were ten different hologram cards produced, one for each WLAF team logo. In addition, each foil pack contained a giveaway game card, and the individual who collected all five letters to spell W-O-R-L-D would win one million dollars. On a white card face, the fronts display color action player photos accented on the right and bottom by borders in the team's color. The team name, player's name, and position appear in these borders. The top left and bottom right corners of the picture are peeled back to create space for the Ultimate and World League logos. The backs feature another color photo, with biography, player profile, and a trivia note on a silver background. Some cards have a "Power Meter" for measuring each player's skills. The cards are numbered on the back and checklisted below alphabetically according to teams. The set closes with two topical subsets: How to Play the Game (180-192) and How To Collect Cards (193-200).

	MINT	NRMT	EXC
COMPLETE SET (200)	6.00	2.70	.75
COMMON CARD (1-200)	.05	.02	.01
☐ 1 Barcelona Dragons '91 Team Statistics Thomas Woods	.10	.05	.01
☐ 2 Demetrius Davis	.10	.05	.01
☐ 3 Tim Egerton	.05	.02	.01
☐ 4 Scott Erney	.05	.02	.01
☐ 5 Tony Baker '91 Rushing Attempt Leader	.20	.09	.03
☐ 6 Anthony Greene	.05	.02	.01
☐ 7 Mike Hinnant UER (No position on front)	.05	.02	.01
☐ 8 Erik Naposki	.05	.02	.01
☐ 9 Paul Palmer	.20	.09	.03
☐ 10 Gene Taylor	.05	.02	.01
☐ 11 Thomas Woods	.05	.02	.01
☐ 12 Tony Rice	.30	.14	.04
☐ 13 Terry O'Shea	.05	.02	.01
☐ 14 Brett Wiese	.05	.02	.01
☐ 15 Phil Alexander Kicking Leader	.05	.02	.01
☐ 16 Eric Wilkerson Rushing/Scoring Leader	.05	.02	.01
☐ 17 Barcelona Dragons Team Picture	.05	.02	.01
☐ 18 Barcelona Dragons Checklist	.05	.02	.01
☐ 19 Birmingham Fire '91 Team Statistics	.05	.02	.01
☐ 20 Eric Jones	.05	.02	.01
☐ 21 Steven Avery	.05	.02	.01
☐ 22 Willie Bouyer	.05	.02	.01
☐ 23 Anthony Parker '91 Interception Leader	.20	.09	.03
☐ 24 Elroy Harris	.05	.02	.01
☐ 25 James Henry	.05	.02	.01
☐ 26 John Holland	.10	.05	.01
☐ 27 Mark Hopkins	.05	.02	.01
☐ 28 Arthur Hunter	.05	.02	.01
☐ 29 Danny Lockett '91 Sacking Leader	.05	.02	.01
☐ 30 Kirk Maggio	.05	.02	.01
☐ 31 John Miller	.05	.02	.01
☐ 32 Ricky Shaw	.05	.02	.01
☐ 33 Phil Ross	.05	.02	.01
☐ 34 Mike Norseth	.05	.02	.01
☐ 35 Birmingham Fire Checklist	.05	.02	.01
☐ 36 Frankfurt Galaxy '91 Team Statistics	.05	.02	.01
☐ 37 Anthony Wallace	.05	.02	.01
☐ 38 Lew Barnes	.05	.02	.01
☐ 39 Richard Buchanan	.05	.02	.01
☐ 40 Yepi Pau'u	.05	.02	.01
☐ 41 Pat McGuirk UER (Played for Raleigh-Durham in 1991)	.05	.02	.01
☐ 42 Tony Baker	.20	.09	.03
☐ 43 1992 TV Schedule 1	.05	.02	.01
☐ 44 Tim Broady	.05	.02	.01
☐ 45 Lonnie Finch	.05	.02	.01
☐ 46 Chad Fortune	.05	.02	.01
☐ 47 Harry Jackson	.05	.02	.01
☐ 48 Jason Johnson	.05	.02	.01
☐ 49 Pat Moorer	.05	.02	.01
☐ 50 Mike Perez	.10	.05	.01
☐ 51 Mark Seals	.05	.02	.01
☐ 52 Cedric Stallworth	.05	.02	.01
☐ 53 Tom Whelihan	.05	.02	.01
☐ 54 Joe Johnson	.30	.14	.04
☐ 55 Frankfurt Galaxy Checklist	.05	.02	.01
☐ 56 London Monarchs '91 Team Statistics Stan Gelbaugh	.10	.05	.01
☐ 57 Stan Gelbaugh	.35	.16	.04
☐ 58 Jeff Alexander	.05	.02	.01
☐ 59 Dana Brinson	.05	.02	.01
☐ 60 Marlon Brown	.05	.02	.01
☐ 61 Dedrick Dodge	.05	.02	.01
☐ 62 Judd Garrett	.10	.05	.01
☐ 63 Greg Horne	.05	.02	.01
☐ 64 Jon Horton	.05	.02	.01
☐ 65 Danny Lockett	.05	.02	.01
☐ 66 Andre Riley	.05	.02	.01
☐ 67 Charlie Young	.05	.02	.01
☐ 68 David Smith	.05	.02	.01
☐ 69 Irvin Smith	.05	.02	.01
☐ 70 Rickey Williams	.05	.02	.01
☐ 71 Roland Smith	.05	.02	.01
☐ 72 William Kirksey	.05	.02	.01
☐ 73 Phil Alexander	.05	.02	.01
☐ 74 London Monarchs Team Picture	.10	.05	.01
☐ 75 London Monarchs Checklist	.05	.02	.01
☐ 76 Montreal Machine '91 Team Statistics	.05	.02	.01
☐ 77 Rollin Putzier	.05	.02	.01
☐ 78 Adam Bob	.05	.02	.01
☐ 79 K.D. Dunn	.05	.02	.01
☐ 80 Darryl Holmes	.05	.02	.01
☐ 81 Ricky Johnson	.05	.02	.01
☐ 82 Michael Finn	.05	.02	.01
☐ 83 Chris Mohr	.10	.05	.01

□ 84 Don Murray .05 .02 .01
□ 85 Bjorn Nittmo .05 .02 .01
□ 86 Michael Proctor .05 .02 .01
□ 87 Broderick Sargent .05 .02 .01
□ 88 Richard Shelton .05 .02 .01
□ 89 Emanuel King .10 .05 .01
□ 90 Pete Mandley .10 .05 .01
□ 91 Kris McCall .05 .02 .01
□ 92 1992 TV Schedule 2 .05 .02 .01
□ 93 Montreal Machine .05 .02 .01
Checklist
□ 94 NY/NJ Knights .05 .02 .01
'91 Team Statistics
□ 95 Andre Alexander .05 .02 .01
□ 96 Pat Marlatt .05 .02 .01
□ 97 Cecil Fletcher .05 .02 .01
□ 98 Lonnie Turner .05 .02 .01
□ 99 Monty Gilbreath .05 .02 .01
□ 100 Tony Jones UER .05 .02 .01
(Should be DB, not WR)
□ 101 Kip Lewis .05 .02 .01
□ 102 Bobby Lilljedahl .05 .02 .01
□ 103 Mark Moore .05 .02 .01
□ 104 Falanda Newton .05 .02 .01
□ 105 Anthony Parker UER .20 .09 .03
(Played for Chiefs in 1991, not Bears; was released by the Bears)
□ 106 Kendall Trainor .05 .02 .01
□ 107 Eric Wilkerson .05 .02 .01
□ 108 Tony Woods .20 .09 .03
□ 109 Reggie Slack .05 .02 .01
□ 110 Joey Banes .05 .02 .01
□ 111 Ron Sancho .05 .02 .01
□ 112 Mike Husar .05 .02 .01
□ 113 NY/NJ Knights .05 .02 .01
Checklist
□ 114 Orlando Thunder .05 .02 .01
'91 Team Statistics
□ 115 Byron Williams UER .05 .02 .01
(Waived by Orlando and picked up by NY-NJ)
□ 116 Charlie Baumann .10 .05 .01
□ 117 Kerwin Bell .10 .05 .01
□ 118 Rodney Lossow .05 .02 .01
□ 119 Myron Jones .05 .02 .01
□ 120 Bruce Lasane .05 .02 .01
□ 121 Eric Mitchel .05 .02 .01
□ 122 Billy Owens .05 .02 .01
□ 123 1992 TV Schedule 3 .05 .02 .01
□ 124 Chris Roscoe .05 .02 .01
□ 125 Tommie Stowers .05 .02 .01
□ 126 Wayne Dickson UER .05 .02 .01
(Not a rookie, he played for Orlando in 1991)
□ 127 Scott Mitchell 2.00 .90 .25
□ 128 Karl Dunbar .05 .02 .01
□ 129 Dana Brinson .05 .02 .01
'91 Punt Return Leader
□ 130 Orlando Thunder .05 .02 .01
Checklist
□ 131 Sacramento Surge .05 .02 .01
Team Statistics
□ 132 1992 TV Schedule 4 .05 .02 .01
□ 133 Mike Adams .05 .02 .01
□ 134 Greg Coauette .05 .02 .01
□ 135 Mel Farr Jr. .10 .05 .01
(Should be TE, not FB)
□ 136 Victor Floyd .05 .02 .01
□ 137 Paul Frazier .05 .02 .01
□ 138 Tom Gerhart .05 .02 .01
□ 139 Pete Najarian .05 .02 .01
□ 140 John Nies .05 .02 .01
□ 141 Carl Parker .05 .02 .01
□ 142 Saute Sapolu .05 .02 .01
□ 143 George Bethune .05 .02 .01
□ 144 David Archer .75 .35 .09
□ 145 John Buddenberg .05 .02 .01
□ 146 Jon Horton UER .05 .02 .01
(Incorrect stats on back)
'91 Receiving Yardage Leader
□ 147 Sacramento Surge .05 .02 .01
Checklist
□ 148 San Antonio Riders .05 .02 .01
'91 Team Statistics
□ 149 Ricky Blake .10 .05 .01
□ 150 Jim Gallery .05 .02 .01
□ 151 Jason Garrett .75 .35 .09
□ 152 John Garrett .05 .02 .01
□ 153 Broderick Graves .05 .02 .01
□ 154 Bill Hess .05 .02 .01
□ 155 Mike Johnson .10 .05 .01
□ 156 Lee Morris .05 .02 .01
□ 157 Dwight Pickens .05 .02 .01
□ 158 Kent Sullivan .05 .02 .01
□ 159 Ken Watson .05 .02 .01
□ 160 Ronnie Williams .05 .02 .01
□ 161 Titus Dixon .05 .02 .01
□ 162 Mike Kiselak .05 .02 .01
□ 163 Greg Lee .05 .02 .01
□ 164 Judd Garrett UER .10 .05 .01
'91 Receiving Leader
(Had 71 receptions in 1991, not 18; game high was 12, not 13)
□ 165 San Antonio Riders .05 .02 .01
Checklist
□ 166 Tenth Week Summaries .05 .02 .01
□ 167 Randy Bethel .05 .02 .01
□ 168 Melvin Patterson .05 .02 .01
□ 169 Eric Harmon .05 .02 .01
□ 170 Patrick Jackson .05 .02 .01
□ 171 Tim James .05 .02 .01
□ 172 George Koonce .20 .09 .03
□ 173 Babe Laufenberg .20 .09 .03
□ 174 Amir Rasul .05 .02 .01
□ 175 Stan Gelbaugh .25 .11 .03
'91 Passing Leader
□ 176 Jason Wallace .05 .02 .01
□ 177 Walter Wilson .05 .02 .01
□ 178 Power Meter Info .10 .05 .01
□ 179 Ohio Glory Checklist .05 .02 .01
□ 180 The Football Field .20 .09 .03
Jim Kelly
□ 181 Moving the Ball .20 .09 .03
Jim Kelly
□ 182 Defense/Back Field .20 .09 .03
Cornerbacks and Safeties
Lawrence Taylor
□ 183 Defense/Linebackers .20 .09 .03
Lawrence Taylor
□ 184 Defense/Defensive Line .20 .09 .03
Defensive Tackles and Ends
Lawrence Taylor
□ 185 Offense/Offensive Line .05 .02 .01
Centers, Guards, Tackles and Tight Ends
Jim Kelly
□ 186 Offense/Receivers .20 .09 .03
Lawrence Taylor
□ 187 Offense/Running Backs .20 .09 .03
Jim Kelly
□ 188 Offensive/Quarterback .20 .09 .03
Jim Kelly
□ 189 Special Teams .05 .02 .01
□ 190 Rules and Regulations .05 .02 .01
WL Rules that differ from NFL 1990 Rules
□ 191 Defensive Overview .05 .02 .01
Scoring Touchdowns and Extra Points
□ 192 Offensive Overview .05 .02 .01
Scoring, Field Goals and Safeties
□ 193 How to Collect .20 .09 .03
What is a Set
Lawrence Taylor
□ 194 How to Collect .20 .09 .03
What is a Wax Pack
Lawrence Taylor
□ 195 How to Collect .20 .09 .03
Premier Editions
Lawrence Taylor
□ 196 How to Collect .20 .09 .03
What Creates Value
Lawrence Taylor
□ 197 How to Collect .20 .09 .03
Rookie Cards
Jim Kelly
□ 198 How to Collect .20 .09 .03
Grading Your Cards
Jim Kelly
□ 199 How to Collect .20 .09 .03
Storing Your Cards
Jim Kelly
□ 200 How to Collect .20 .09 .03
Trading Your Cards
Jim Kelly

1992 Ultimate WLAF Logo Holograms

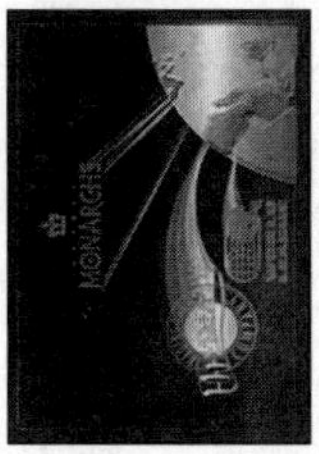

The 1992 Ultimate WLAF Team Logo Hologram set consists of ten standard-size cards. Twelve nine-card foil packs were packaged in each coliseum display box, and each box came with a mini-poster and one hologram card. There were ten different hologram cards produced, one for each WLAF team logo.

	MINT	NRMT	EXC
COMPLETE SET (10)	6.00	2.70	.75
COMMON CARD (1-10)	.75	.35	.09

□ 1 Barcelona Dragons .75 .35 .09
□ 2 Birmingham Fire .75 .35 .09
□ 3 Frankfurt Galaxy .75 .35 .09
□ 4 London Monarchs .75 .35 .09
□ 5 Montreal Machine .75 .35 .09
□ 6 NY/NJ Knights .75 .35 .09
□ 7 Ohio Glory .75 .35 .09
□ 8 Orlando Thunder .75 .35 .09
□ 9 Sacramento Surge .75 .35 .09
□ 10 San Antonio Riders .75 .35 .09

1991 Ultra

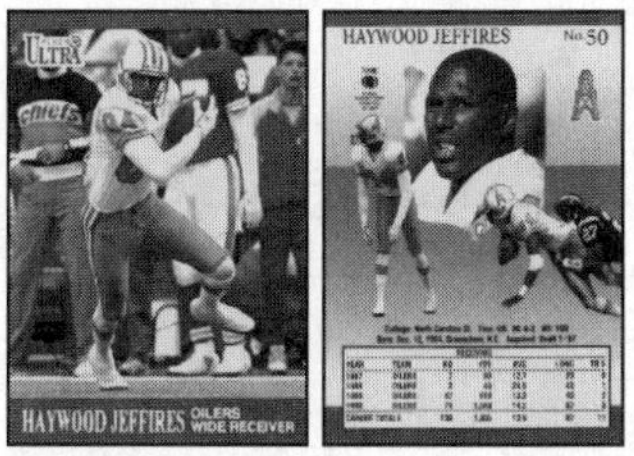

The 1991 Ultra football set contains 300 standard-size cards. Cards were issued in 14-card packs. The front design has a color action player photo, bleeding to the card sides but with silver borders above and beneath the picture. Player information is given in white lettering in the bottom silver border. The backs have a yellow fading to orange and green background, with the same silver borders as on the fronts. A color head shot of the player in a shield format is sandwiched between two smaller action shots of the player. Brief biographical information and statistics appear at the bottom of the back. The cards are numbered on the back and checklisted below alphabetically within and according to teams. The last subset included in this set was Rookie Prospects (279-298). Rookie Cards in this set include Mike Croel, Brett Favre, Randal Hill, Russell Maryland, Herman Moore, Mike Pritchard and Ricky Watters.

	MINT	NRMT	EXC
COMPLETE SET (300)	12.00	5.50	1.50
COMMON CARD (1-300)	.05	.02	.01

□ 1 Don Beebe .05 .02 .01
□ 2 Shane Conlan .05 .02 .01
□ 3 Pete Metzelaars .05 .02 .01
□ 4 Jamie Mueller .05 .02 .01
□ 5 Scott Norwood .05 .02 .01
□ 6 Andre Reed .10 .05 .01
□ 7 Leon Seals .05 .02 .01
□ 8 Bruce Smith .25 .11 .03
□ 9 Leonard Smith .05 .02 .01
□ 10 Thurman Thomas .25 .11 .03
□ 11 Lewis Billups .05 .02 .01
□ 12 Jim Breech .05 .02 .01
□ 13 James Brooks .10 .05 .01
□ 14 Eddie Brown .05 .02 .01
□ 15 Boomer Esiason .10 .05 .01
□ 16 David Fulcher .05 .02 .01
□ 17 Rodney Holman .05 .02 .01
□ 18 Bruce Kozerski .05 .02 .01
□ 19 Tim Krumrie .05 .02 .01
□ 20 Tim McGee .05 .02 .01
□ 21 Anthony Munoz .10 .05 .01
□ 22 Leon White .05 .02 .01
□ 23 Ickey Woods .05 .02 .01
□ 24 Carl Zander .05 .02 .01
□ 25 Brian Brennan .05 .02 .01
□ 26 Thane Gash .05 .02 .01
□ 27 Leroy Hoard .10 .05 .01
□ 28 Mike Johnson .05 .02 .01
□ 29 Reggie Langhorne .05 .02 .01
□ 30 Kevin Mack .05 .02 .01
□ 31 Clay Matthews .10 .05 .01
□ 32 Eric Metcalf .10 .05 .01
□ 33 Steve Atwater .05 .02 .01
□ 34 Melvin Bratton .05 .02 .01
□ 35 John Elway .75 .35 .09
□ 36 Bobby Humphrey .05 .02 .01
□ 37 Mark Jackson .05 .02 .01
□ 38 Vance Johnson .05 .02 .01
□ 39 Ricky Nattiel .05 .02 .01
□ 40 Steve Sewell .05 .02 .01
□ 41 Dennis Smith .05 .02 .01
□ 42 David Treadwell .05 .02 .01
□ 43 Michael Young .05 .02 .01
□ 44 Ray Childress .05 .02 .01
□ 45 Cris Dishman .05 .02 .01
□ 46 William Fuller .10 .05 .01
□ 47 Ernest Givins .10 .05 .01
□ 48 John Grimsley UER .05 .02 .01
(Acquired line should be Trade '91, not Draft 6-'84)
□ 49 Drew Hill .05 .02 .01
□ 50 Haywood Jeffires .10 .05 .01
□ 51 Sean Jones .10 .05 .01
□ 52 Johnny Meads .05 .02 .01
□ 53 Warren Moon .25 .11 .03
□ 54 Al Smith .05 .02 .01
□ 55 Lorenzo White .05 .02 .01
□ 56 Albert Bentley .05 .02 .01
□ 57 Duane Bickett .05 .02 .01
□ 58 Bill Brooks .05 .02 .01
□ 59 Jeff George .25 .11 .03
□ 60 Mike Prior .05 .02 .01
□ 61 Rohn Stark .05 .02 .01
□ 62 Jack Trudeau .05 .02 .01
□ 63 Clarence Verdin .05 .02 .01
□ 64 Steve DeBerg .05 .02 .01
□ 65 Emile Harry .05 .02 .01
□ 66 Albert Lewis .05 .02 .01
□ 67 Nick Lowery UER .05 .02 .01
(NFL Exp. has 12 years, should be 13)
□ 68 Todd McNair .05 .02 .01
□ 69 Christian Okoye .05 .02 .01
□ 70 Stephone Paige .05 .02 .01
□ 71 Kevin Porter UER .05 .02 .01
(Front has traded logo, but he has been a Chief all career)
□ 72 Derrick Thomas .25 .11 .03
□ 73 Robb Thomas .05 .02 .01
□ 74 Barry Word .05 .02 .01
□ 75 Marcus Allen .25 .11 .03
□ 76 Eddie Anderson .05 .02 .01
□ 77 Tim Brown .25 .11 .03
□ 78 Mervyn Fernandez .05 .02 .01
□ 79 Willie Gault .10 .05 .01
□ 80 Ethan Horton .05 .02 .01
□ 81 Howie Long .10 .05 .01
□ 82 Vance Mueller .05 .02 .01
□ 83 Jay Schroeder .05 .02 .01
□ 84 Steve Smith .05 .02 .01
□ 85 Greg Townsend .05 .02 .01
□ 86 Mark Clayton .10 .05 .01
□ 87 Jim C. Jensen .05 .02 .01
□ 88 Dan Marino 1.50 .70 .19
□ 89 Tim McKyer UER .05 .02 .01
(Acquired line should be Trade '91, not Trade '90)
□ 90 John Offerdahl .05 .02 .01
□ 91 Louis Oliver .05 .02 .01
□ 92 Reggie Roby .05 .02 .01
□ 93 Sammie Smith .05 .02 .01
□ 94 Hart Lee Dykes .05 .02 .01
□ 95 Irving Fryar .10 .05 .01
□ 96 Tommy Hodson .05 .02 .01
□ 97 Maurice Hurst .05 .02 .01
□ 98 John Stephens .05 .02 .01
□ 99 Andre Tippett .05 .02 .01
□ 100 Mark Boyer .05 .02 .01
□ 101 Kyle Clifton .05 .02 .01
□ 102 James Hasty .05 .02 .01
□ 103 Erik McMillan .05 .02 .01
□ 104 Rob Moore .25 .11 .03
□ 105 Joe Mott .05 .02 .01
□ 106 Ken O'Brien .05 .02 .01
□ 107 Ron Stallworth UER .05 .02 .01
(Acquired line should be Trade '91, not Draft 4-'89)
□ 108 Al Toon .10 .05 .01
□ 109 Gary Anderson K .05 .02 .01
□ 110 Bubby Brister .05 .02 .01
□ 111 Thomas Everett .05 .02 .01
□ 112 Merril Hoge .05 .02 .01
□ 113 Louis Lipps .05 .02 .01
□ 114 Greg Lloyd .25 .11 .03
□ 115 Hardy Nickerson .10 .05 .01
□ 116 Dwight Stone .05 .02 .01
□ 117 Rod Woodson .25 .11 .03
□ 118 Tim Worley .05 .02 .01
□ 119 Rod Bernstine .05 .02 .01
□ 120 Marion Butts .10 .05 .01
□ 121 Gill Byrd .05 .02 .01
□ 122 Arthur Cox .05 .02 .01
□ 123 Burt Grossman .05 .02 .01
□ 124 Ronnie Harmon .05 .02 .01
□ 125 Anthony Miller .10 .05 .01
□ 126 Leslie O'Neal .10 .05 .01
□ 127 Gary Plummer .05 .02 .01
□ 128 Sam Seale .05 .02 .01
□ 129 Junior Seau .40 .18 .05
□ 130 Broderick Thompson .05 .02 .01
□ 131 Billy Joe Tolliver .05 .02 .01
□ 132 Brian Blades .10 .05 .01
□ 133 Jeff Bryant .05 .02 .01
□ 134 Derrick Fenner .05 .02 .01
□ 135 Jacob Green .05 .02 .01
□ 136 Andy Heck .05 .02 .01
□ 137 Patrick Hunter UER .05 .02 .01
(Photos on back show 23 and 27)
□ 138 Norm Johnson .05 .02 .01
□ 139 Tommy Kane .05 .02 .01
□ 140 Dave Krieg .10 .05 .01
□ 141 John L. Williams .05 .02 .01
□ 142 Terry Wooden .05 .02 .01
□ 143 Steve Broussard .05 .02 .01
□ 144 Keith Jones .05 .02 .01
□ 145 Brian Jordan .10 .05 .01
□ 146 Chris Miller .10 .05 .01
□ 147 John Rade .05 .02 .01
□ 148 Andre Rison .10 .05 .01
□ 149 Mike Rozier .05 .02 .01
□ 150 Deion Sanders .60 .25 .07
□ 151 Neal Anderson .10 .05 .01
□ 152 Trace Armstrong .05 .02 .01

□ 153 Kevin Butler	.05	.02	.01
□ 154 Mark Carrier DB	.10	.05	.01
□ 155 Richard Dent	.10	.05	.01
□ 156 Dennis Gentry	.05	.02	.01
□ 157 Jim Harbaugh	.25	.11	.03
□ 158 Brad Muster	.05	.02	.01
□ 159 William Perry	.10	.05	.01
□ 160 Mike Singletary	.10	.05	.01
□ 161 Lemuel Stinson	.05	.02	.01
□ 162 Troy Aikman	1.00	.45	.12
□ 163 Michael Irvin	.25	.11	.03
□ 164 Mike Saxon	.05	.02	.01
□ 165 Emmitt Smith	2.00	.90	.25
□ 166 Jerry Ball	.05	.02	.01
□ 167 Michael Cofer	.05	.02	.01
□ 168 Rodney Peete	.10	.05	.01
□ 169 Barry Sanders	1.00	.45	.12
□ 170 Robert Brown	.05	.02	.01
□ 171 Anthony Dilweg	.05	.02	.01
□ 172 Tim Harris	.05	.02	.01
□ 173 Johnny Holland	.05	.02	.01
□ 174 Perry Kemp	.05	.02	.01
□ 175 Don Majkowski	.05	.02	.01
□ 176 Brian Noble	.05	.02	.01
□ 177 Jeff Query	.05	.02	.01
□ 178 Sterling Sharpe	.25	.11	.03
□ 179 Charles Wilson	.05	.02	.01
□ 180 Keith Woodside	.05	.02	.01
□ 181 Flipper Anderson UER (Back photo not him)	.05	.02	.01
□ 182 Bern Brostek	.05	.02	.01
□ 183 Pat Carter	.05	.02	.01
□ 184 Aaron Cox	.05	.02	.01
□ 185 Henry Ellard	.10	.05	.01
□ 186 Jim Everett	.10	.05	.01
□ 187 Cleveland Gary	.05	.02	.01
□ 188 Jerry Gray	.05	.02	.01
□ 189 Kevin Greene	.25	.11	.03
□ 190 Mike Wilcher	.05	.02	.01
□ 191 Alfred Anderson	.05	.02	.01
□ 192 Joey Browner	.05	.02	.01
□ 193 Anthony Carter	.10	.05	.01
□ 194 Chris Doleman	.05	.02	.01
□ 195 Rick Fenney	.05	.02	.01
□ 196 Darrell Fullington	.05	.02	.01
□ 197 Rich Gannon	.05	.02	.01
□ 198 Hassan Jones	.05	.02	.01
□ 199 Steve Jordan	.05	.02	.01
□ 200 Mike Merriweather	.05	.02	.01
□ 201 Al Noga	.05	.02	.01
□ 202 Herschel Walker	.10	.05	.01
□ 203 Wade Wilson	.10	.05	.01
□ 204 Morten Andersen	.05	.02	.01
□ 205 Gene Atkins	.05	.02	.01
□ 206 Toi Cook	.05	.02	.01
□ 207 Craig Heyward	.10	.05	.01
□ 208 Dalton Hilliard	.05	.02	.01
□ 209 Vaughan Johnson	.05	.02	.01
□ 210 Eric Martin	.05	.02	.01
□ 211 Brett Perriman	.25	.11	.03
□ 212 Pat Swilling	.10	.05	.01
□ 213 Steve Walsh	.05	.02	.01
□ 214 Ottis Anderson	.10	.05	.01
□ 215 Carl Banks	.05	.02	.01
□ 216 Maurice Carthon	.05	.02	.01
□ 217 Mark Collins	.05	.02	.01
□ 218 Rodney Hampton	.25	.11	.03
□ 219 Erik Howard	.05	.02	.01
□ 220 Mark Ingram	.10	.05	.01
□ 221 Pepper Johnson	.05	.02	.01
□ 222 Dave Meggett	.10	.05	.01
□ 223 Phil Simms	.10	.05	.01
□ 224 Lawrence Taylor	.25	.11	.03
□ 225 Lewis Tillman	.05	.02	.01
□ 226 Everson Walls	.05	.02	.01
□ 227 Fred Barnett	.25	.11	.03
□ 228 Jerome Brown	.05	.02	.01
□ 229 Keith Byars	.05	.02	.01
□ 230 Randall Cunningham	.10	.05	.01
□ 231 Byron Evans	.05	.02	.01
□ 232 Wes Hopkins	.05	.02	.01
□ 233 Keith Jackson	.10	.05	.01
□ 234 Heath Sherman	.05	.02	.01
□ 235 Anthony Toney	.05	.02	.01
□ 236 Reggie White	.25	.11	.03
□ 237 Rich Camarillo	.05	.02	.01
□ 238 Ken Harvey	.10	.05	.01
□ 239 Eric Hill	.05	.02	.01
□ 240 Johnny Johnson	.05	.02	.01
□ 241 Ernie Jones	.05	.02	.01
□ 242 Tim McDonald	.05	.02	.01
□ 243 Timm Rosenbach	.05	.02	.01
□ 244 Jay Taylor	.05	.02	.01
□ 245 Dexter Carter	.05	.02	.01
□ 246 Mike Cofer	.05	.02	.01
□ 247 Kevin Fagan	.05	.02	.01
□ 248 Don Griffin	.05	.02	.01
□ 249 Charles Haley	.10	.05	.01
□ 250 Brent Jones	.25	.11	.03
□ 251 Joe Montana UER (Born: Monongahela, not New Eagle)	1.00	.45	.12
□ 252 Darryl Pollard	.05	.02	.01
□ 253 Tom Rathman	.05	.02	.01
□ 254 Jerry Rice	1.00	.45	.12
□ 255 John Taylor	.10	.05	.01
□ 256 Steve Young	.75	.35	.09
□ 257 Gary Anderson RB	.05	.02	.01
□ 258 Mark Carrier WR	.25	.11	.03
□ 259 Chris Chandler	.10	.05	.01
□ 260 Reggie Cobb	.05	.02	.01
□ 261 Reuben Davis	.05	.02	.01
□ 262 Willie Drewrey	.05	.02	.01
□ 263 Ron Hall	.05	.02	.01
□ 264 Eugene Marve	.05	.02	.01
□ 265 Winston Moss UER (Acquired line should be Trade '91, not Draft 2-'87)	.05	.02	.01
□ 266 Vinny Testaverde	.10	.05	.01
□ 267 Broderick Thomas	.05	.02	.01
□ 268 Jeff Bostic	.05	.02	.01
□ 269 Earnest Byner	.05	.02	.01
□ 270 Gary Clark	.25	.11	.03
□ 271 Darrell Green	.05	.02	.01
□ 272 Jim Lachey	.05	.02	.01
□ 273 Wilber Marshall	.05	.02	.01
□ 274 Art Monk	.10	.05	.01
□ 275 Gerald Riggs	.05	.02	.01
□ 276 Mark Rypien	.10	.05	.01
□ 277 Ricky Sanders	.05	.02	.01
□ 278 Alvin Walton	.05	.02	.01
□ 279 Nick Bell	.05	.02	.01
□ 280 Eric Bieniemy	.05	.02	.01
□ 281 Jarrod Bunch	.05	.02	.01
□ 282 Mike Croel	.05	.02	.01
□ 283 Brett Favre	4.00	1.80	.50
□ 284 Moe Gardner	.05	.02	.01
□ 285 Pat Harlow	.05	.02	.01
□ 286 Randal Hill	.10	.05	.01
□ 287 Todd Marinovich	.05	.02	.01
□ 288 Russell Maryland	.25	.11	.03
□ 289 Dan McGwire	.05	.02	.01
□ 290 Ernie Mills UER (Patterns misspelled as patterson in first sentence)	.10	.05	.01
□ 291 Herman Moore	2.00	.90	.25
□ 292 Godfrey Myles	.05	.02	.01
□ 293 Browning Nagle	.05	.02	.01
□ 294 Mike Pritchard	.25	.11	.03
□ 295 Esera Tuaolo	.05	.02	.01
□ 296 Mark Vander Poel	.05	.02	.01
□ 297 Ricky Watters UER (Photo on back actually Ray Griggs)	1.50	.70	.19
□ 298 Chris Zorich	.25	.11	.03
□ 299 Checklist Card (Randall Cunningham and Emmitt Smith)	.10	.05	.01
□ 300 Checklist Card (Randall Cunningham and Emmitt Smith)	.10	.05	.01

1991 Ultra All-Stars

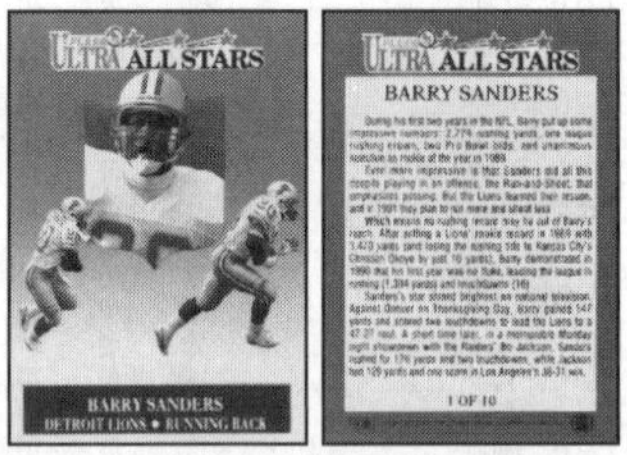

The 1991 Ultra All-Stars set consists of 10 standard-size cards. On the fronts, a color head shot of the player in a shield format is sandwiched between two smaller action shots of the player. The card face is gold, with player information provided in a green stripe at the bottom. Within a gold border on a white background, the backs present player profile. The cards were issued as inserts into the regular 1991 Ultra packs that were sold (primarily to the hobby) in black boxes.

	MINT	NRMT	EXC
COMPLETE SET (10)	12.00	5.50	1.50
COMMON CARD (1-10)	.50	.23	.06
□ 1 Barry Sanders	4.00	1.80	.50
□ 2 Keith Jackson	.50	.23	.06
□ 3 Bruce Smith	1.00	.45	.12
□ 4 Randall Cunningham	.50	.23	.06
□ 5 Dan Marino	6.00	2.70	.75
□ 6 Charles Haley	.50	.23	.06
□ 7 John L. Williams	.50	.23	.06
□ 8 Darrell Green	.50	.23	.06
□ 9 Stephone Paige	.50	.23	.06
□ 10 Kevin Greene	1.00	.45	.12

1991 Ultra Performances

This ten-card standard-size set was produced by Fleer to showcase outstanding NFL football players. The front features a color action player photo, banded above and below by silver stripes but bleeding to the edge of the card on the sides. To highlight the featured player, the background and other players in the picture are washed out.

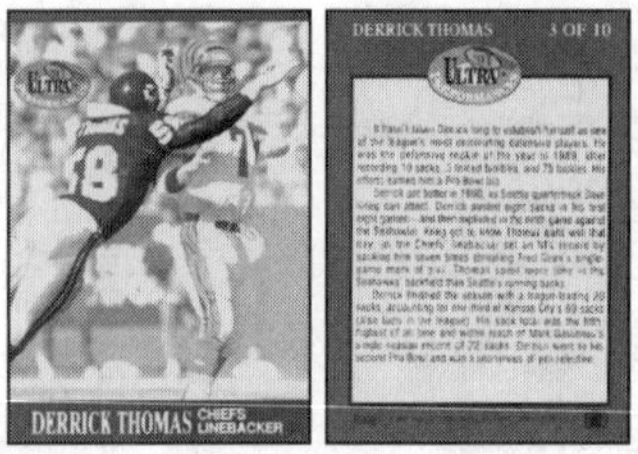

Inside black and silver borders, the back presents player profile. The cards were issued as inserts into the regular 1991 Ultra packs that were sold primarily to the retail industry in green boxes.

	MINT	NRMT	EXC
COMPLETE SET (10)	20.00	9.00	2.50
COMMON CARD (1-10)	.50	.23	.06
□ 1 Emmitt Smith	10.00	4.50	1.25
□ 2 Andre Rison	.50	.23	.06
□ 3 Derrick Thomas	1.00	.45	.12
□ 4 Joe Montana	5.00	2.20	.60
□ 5 Warren Moon	1.00	.45	.12
□ 6 Mike Singletary	.50	.23	.06
□ 7 Thurman Thomas	1.25	.55	.16
□ 8 Rod Woodson	1.00	.45	.12
□ 9 Jerry Rice	5.00	2.20	.60
□ 10 Reggie White	1.25	.55	.16

1991 Ultra Update

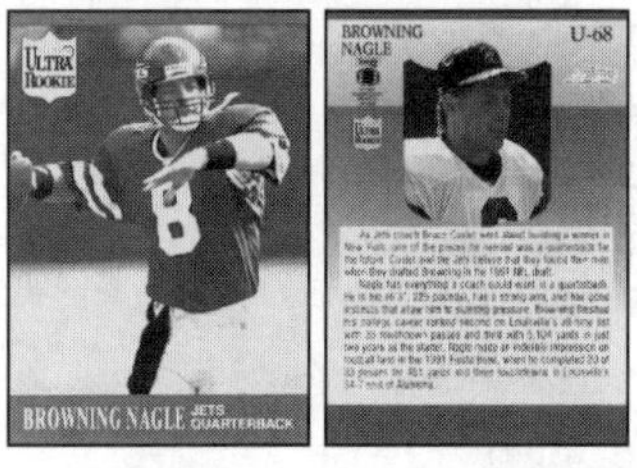

This 100-card standard-size set was produced by Fleer and featured some of the leading rookies and players who switched franchises during the 1991 season. The front design has a color action player photo, bleeding to the card sides but with silver borders above and beneath the picture. On most of the card backs, a color head shot of the player in a shield format is sandwiched between two smaller action shots of the player. The backs are accented in blue and green, with biography and statistics (1990 and career) at the bottom. The cards are numbered on the back and checklisted below alphabetically according to and within teams. Rookie Cards include Lawrence Dawsey, Ricky Ervins, Jeff Graham, Merton Hanks, Michael Jackson, Neil O'Donnell, Stanley Richard, Leonard Russell, Jon Vaughn and Harvey Williams. The cards are numbered with a "U" prefix.

	MINT	NRMT	EXC
COMPLETE FACT.SET (100)	25.00	11.00	3.10
COMMON CARD (U1-U100)	.08	.04	.01
□ U1 Brett Favre	20.00	9.00	2.50
□ U2 Moe Gardner	.08	.04	.01
□ U3 Tim McKyer	.08	.04	.01
□ U4 Bruce Pickens	.08	.04	.01
□ U5 Mike Pritchard	.30	.14	.04
□ U6 Cornelius Bennett	.15	.07	.02
□ U7 Phil Hansen	.08	.04	.01
□ U8 Henry Jones	.15	.07	.02
□ U9 Mark Kelso	.08	.04	.01
□ U10 James Lofton	.15	.07	.02
□ U11 Anthony Morgan	.08	.04	.01
□ U12 Stan Thomas	.08	.04	.01
□ U13 Chris Zorich	.15	.07	.02
□ U14 Reggie Rembert	.08	.04	.01
□ U15 Alfred Williams	.08	.04	.01
□ U16 Michael Jackson	.30	.14	.04
□ U17 Ed King	.08	.04	.01
□ U18 Joe Morris	.08	.04	.01
□ U19 Vince Newsome	.08	.04	.01
□ U20 Tony Casillas	.08	.04	.01
□ U21 Russell Maryland	.30	.14	.04
□ U22 Jay Novacek	.30	.14	.04
□ U23 Mike Croel	.08	.04	.01
□ U24 Gaston Green	.08	.04	.01
□ U25 Kenny Walker	.08	.04	.01
□ U26 Melvin Jenkins	.08	.04	.01
□ U27 Herman Moore	5.00	2.20	.60
□ U28 Kelvin Pritchett	.15	.07	.02
□ U29 Chris Spielman	.15	.07	.02
□ U30 Vinnie Clark	.08	.04	.01
□ U31 Allen Rice	.08	.04	.01
□ U32 Vai Sikahema	.08	.04	.01
□ U33 Esera Tuaolo	.08	.04	.01
□ U34 Mike Dumas	.08	.04	.01
□ U35 John Flannery	.08	.04	.01
□ U36 Allen Pinkett	.08	.04	.01
□ U37 Tim Barnett	.08	.04	.01
□ U38 Dan Saleaumua	.08	.04	.01
□ U39 Harvey Williams	.30	.14	.04
□ U40 Nick Bell	.08	.04	.01
□ U41 Roger Craig	.15	.07	.02
□ U42 Ronnie Lott	.15	.07	.02
□ U43 Todd Marinovich	.08	.04	.01
□ U44 Robert Delpino	.08	.04	.01
□ U45 Todd Lyght	.08	.04	.01
□ U46 Robert Young	.15	.07	.02
□ U47 Aaron Craver	.08	.04	.01
□ U48 Mark Higgs	.08	.04	.01
□ U49 Vestee Jackson	.08	.04	.01
□ U50 Carl Lee	.08	.04	.01
□ U51 Felix Wright	.08	.04	.01
□ U52 Darrell Fullington	.08	.04	.01
□ U53 Pat Harlow	.08	.04	.01
□ U54 Eugene Lockhart	.08	.04	.01
□ U55 Hugh Millen	.08	.04	.01
□ U56 Leonard Russell	.30	.14	.04
□ U57 Jon Vaughn	.08	.04	.01
□ U58 Quinn Early	.15	.07	.02
□ U59 Bobby Hebert	.08	.04	.01
□ U60 Rickey Jackson	.08	.04	.01
□ U61 Sam Mills	.15	.07	.02
□ U62 Jarrod Bunch	.08	.04	.01
□ U63 John Elliott	.08	.04	.01
□ U64 Jeff Hostetler	.15	.07	.02
□ U65 Ed McCaffrey	.15	.07	.02
□ U66 Kanavis McGhee	.08	.04	.01
□ U67 Mo Lewis	.15	.07	.02
□ U68 Browning Nagle	.08	.04	.01
□ U69 Blair Thomas	.08	.04	.01
□ U70 Antone Davis	.08	.04	.01
□ U71 Brad Goebel (See card U74)	.08	.04	.01
□ U72 Jim McMahon	.15	.07	.02
□ U73 Clyde Simmons	.08	.04	.01
□ U74 Randal Hill UER (Card number on back U71 instead of U74)	.15	.07	.02
□ U75 Eric Swann	.30	.14	.04
□ U76 Tom Tupa	.08	.04	.01
□ U77 Jeff Graham	.75	.35	.09
□ U78 Eric Green	.08	.04	.01
□ U79 Neil O'Donnell	1.50	.70	.19
□ U80 Huey Richardson	.08	.04	.01
□ U81 Eric Bieniemy	.08	.04	.01
□ U82 John Friesz	.30	.14	.04
□ U83 Eric Moten	.08	.04	.01
□ U84 Stanley Richard	.08	.04	.01
□ U85 Todd Bowles	.08	.04	.01
□ U86 Merton Hanks	.75	.35	.09
□ U87 Tim Harris	.08	.04	.01
□ U88 Pierce Holt	.08	.04	.01
□ U89 Ted Washington	.08	.04	.01
□ U90 John Kasay	.15	.07	.02
□ U91 Dan McGwire	.08	.04	.01
□ U92 Lawrence Dawsey	.15	.07	.02
□ U93 Charles McRae	.08	.04	.01
□ U94 Jesse Solomon	.08	.04	.01
□ U95 Robert Wilson	.08	.04	.01
□ U96 Ricky Ervins	.15	.07	.02
□ U97 Charles Mann	.08	.04	.01
□ U98 Bobby Wilson	.08	.04	.01
□ U99 Jerry Rice Pro-Visions	1.50	.70	.19
□ U100 Checklist 1-100 (Nick Bell and Jim McMahon)	.08	.04	.01

1992 Ultra

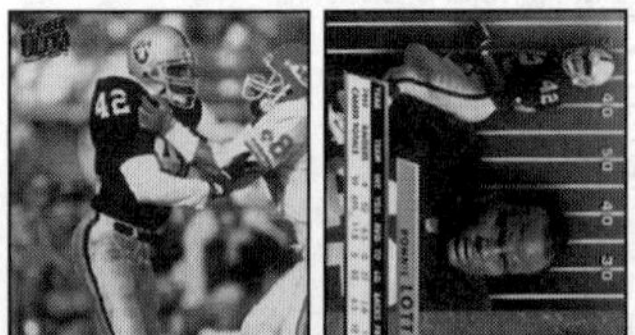

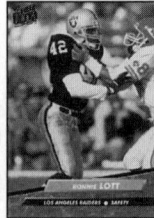

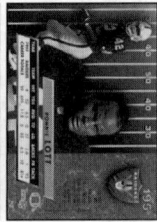

This 450-card standard-size set features color action player photos. Cards were issued in 14-card packs. The pictures are full-bleed except at the bottom where a diagonal gold foil stripe separates the photo from a green marbleized area. Within this area are bars in the team's colors that contain the player's name, team name, and position. The horizontal backs display both close-up and action cut-out player photos against a team-color coded football field design. Superimposed over the pictures are the player's name and statistics in bars matching the team colors. Rounding out the back is a green marbleized area on the right edge containing the team logo and a player biography. The cards are numbered on the back and checklisted below alphabetically according to teams. The set closes with Draft Picks (417-446). Rookie Cards include Edgar Bennett, Steve Bono, Terrell Buckley, Amp Lee, Kevin Turner and Tommy Vardell.

	MINT	NRMT	EXC
COMPLETE SET (450)	20.00	9.00	2.50
COMMON CARD (1-450)	.08	.04	.01
□ 1 Steve Broussard	.08	.04	.01
□ 2 Rick Bryan	.08	.04	.01
□ 3 Scott Case	.08	.04	.01

☐ 4 Darion Conner	.08	.04	.01
☐ 5 Bill Fralic	.08	.04	.01
☐ 6 Moe Gardner	.08	.04	.01
☐ 7 Tim Green	.08	.04	.01
☐ 8 Michael Haynes	.15	.07	.02
☐ 9 Chris Hinton	.08	.04	.01
☐ 10 Mike Kenn	.08	.04	.01
☐ 11 Tim McKyer	.08	.04	.01
☐ 12 Chris Miller	.15	.07	.02
☐ 13 Erric Pegram	.15	.07	.02
☐ 14 Mike Pritchard	.15	.07	.02
☐ 15 Andre Rison	.15	.07	.02
☐ 16 Jessie Tuggle	.08	.04	.01
☐ 17 Carlton Bailey	.15	.07	.02
☐ 18 Howard Ballard	.08	.04	.01
☐ 19 Cornelius Bennett	.15	.07	.02
☐ 20 Shane Conlan	.08	.04	.01
☐ 21 Kenneth Davis	.08	.04	.01
☐ 22 Kent Hull	.08	.04	.01
☐ 23 Mark Kelso	.08	.04	.01
☐ 24 James Lofton	.15	.07	.02
☐ 25 Keith McKeller	.08	.04	.01
☐ 26 Nate Odomes	.08	.04	.01
☐ 27 Jim Ritcher	.08	.04	.01
☐ 28 Leon Seals	.08	.04	.01
☐ 29 Darryl Talley	.08	.04	.01
☐ 30 Steve Tasker	.15	.07	.02
☐ 31 Thurman Thomas	.30	.14	.04
☐ 32 Will Wolford	.08	.04	.01
☐ 33 Jeff Wright	.08	.04	.01
☐ 34 Neal Anderson	.08	.04	.01
☐ 35 Trace Armstrong	.08	.04	.01
☐ 36 Mark Carrier DB	.08	.04	.01
☐ 37 Wendell Davis	.08	.04	.01
☐ 38 Richard Dent	.15	.07	.02
☐ 39 Shaun Gayle	.08	.04	.01
☐ 40 Jim Harbaugh	.30	.14	.04
☐ 41 Jay Hilgenberg	.08	.04	.01
☐ 42 Darren Lewis	.08	.04	.01
☐ 43 Steve McMichael	.15	.07	.02
☐ 44 Anthony Morgan	.08	.04	.01
☐ 45 Brad Muster	.08	.04	.01
☐ 46 William Perry	.15	.07	.02
☐ 47 John Roper	.08	.04	.01
☐ 48 Lemuel Stinson	.08	.04	.01
☐ 49 Tom Waddle	.08	.04	.01
☐ 50 Donnell Woolford	.08	.04	.01
☐ 51 Leo Barker	.08	.04	.01
☐ 52 Eddie Brown	.08	.04	.01
☐ 53 James Francis	.08	.04	.01
☐ 54 David Fulcher UER	.08	.04	.01
(Photo on back actually Eddie Brown)			
☐ 55 David Grant	.08	.04	.01
☐ 56 Harold Green	.08	.04	.01
☐ 57 Rodney Holman	.08	.04	.01
☐ 58 Lee Johnson	.08	.04	.01
☐ 59 Tim Krumrie	.08	.04	.01
☐ 60 Tim McGee	.08	.04	.01
☐ 61 Alonzo Mitz	.08	.04	.01
☐ 62 Anthony Munoz	.15	.07	.02
☐ 63 Alfred Williams	.08	.04	.01
☐ 64 Stephen Braggs	.08	.04	.01
☐ 65 Richard Brown	.08	.04	.01
☐ 66 Randy Hilliard	.08	.04	.01
☐ 67 Leroy Hoard	.15	.07	.02
☐ 68 Michael Jackson	.15	.07	.02
☐ 69 Mike Johnson	.08	.04	.01
☐ 70 James Jones	.08	.04	.01
☐ 71 Tony Jones	.08	.04	.01
☐ 72 Ed King	.08	.04	.01
☐ 73 Kevin Mack	.08	.04	.01
☐ 74 Clay Matthews	.15	.07	.02
☐ 75 Eric Metcalf	.15	.07	.02
☐ 76 Vince Newsome	.08	.04	.01
☐ 77 Steve Beuerlein	.08	.04	.01
☐ 78 Larry Brown DB	.08	.04	.01
☐ 79 Tony Casillas	.08	.04	.01
☐ 80 Alvin Harper	.15	.07	.02
☐ 81 Issiac Holt	.08	.04	.01
☐ 82 Ray Horton	.08	.04	.01
☐ 83 Michael Irvin	.30	.14	.04
☐ 84 Daryl Johnston	.30	.14	.04
☐ 85 Kelvin Martin	.08	.04	.01
☐ 86 Ken Norton	.30	.14	.04
☐ 87 Jay Novacek	.15	.07	.02
☐ 88 Emmitt Smith	5.00	2.20	.60
☐ 89 Vinson Smith	.08	.04	.01
☐ 90 Mark Stepnoski	.15	.07	.02
☐ 91 Tony Tolbert	.08	.04	.01
☐ 92 Alexander Wright	.08	.04	.01
☐ 93 Steve Atwater	.08	.04	.01
☐ 94 Tyrone Braxton	.08	.04	.01
☐ 95 Michael Brooks	.08	.04	.01
☐ 96 Mike Croel	.08	.04	.01
☐ 97 John Elway	1.50	.70	.19
☐ 98 Simon Fletcher	.08	.04	.01
☐ 99 Gaston Green	.08	.04	.01
☐ 100 Mark Jackson	.08	.04	.01
☐ 101 Keith Kartz	.08	.04	.01
☐ 102 Greg Kragen	.08	.04	.01
☐ 103 Greg Lewis	.08	.04	.01
☐ 104 Karl Mecklenburg	.08	.04	.01
☐ 105 Derek Russell	.08	.04	.01
☐ 106 Steve Sewell	.08	.04	.01
☐ 107 Dennis Smith	.08	.04	.01
☐ 108 David Treadwell	.08	.04	.01
☐ 109 Kenny Walker	.08	.04	.01
☐ 110 Michael Young	.08	.04	.01
☐ 111 Jerry Ball	.08	.04	.01
☐ 112 Bennie Blades	.08	.04	.01
☐ 113 Lomas Brown	.08	.04	.01
☐ 114 Scott Conover	.08	.04	.01
☐ 115 Ray Crockett	.08	.04	.01
☐ 116 Mel Gray	.15	.07	.02
☐ 117 Willie Green	.08	.04	.01
☐ 118 Erik Kramer	.15	.07	.02
☐ 119 Dan Owens	.08	.04	.01
☐ 120 Rodney Peete	.15	.07	.02
☐ 121 Brett Perriman	.30	.14	.04
☐ 122 Barry Sanders	2.50	1.10	.30
☐ 123 Chris Spielman	.15	.07	.02
☐ 124 Marc Spindler	.08	.04	.01
☐ 125 William White	.08	.04	.01
☐ 126 Tony Bennett	.08	.04	.01
☐ 127 Matt Brock	.08	.04	.01
☐ 128 LeRoy Butler	.08	.04	.01
☐ 129 Chuck Cecil	.08	.04	.01
☐ 130 Johnny Holland	.08	.04	.01
☐ 131 Perry Kemp	.08	.04	.01
☐ 132 Don Majkowski	.08	.04	.01
☐ 133 Tony Mandarich	.08	.04	.01
☐ 134 Brian Noble	.08	.04	.01
☐ 135 Bryce Paup	.30	.14	.04
☐ 136 Sterling Sharpe	.30	.14	.04
☐ 137 Darrell Thompson	.08	.04	.01
☐ 138 Mike Tomczak	.08	.04	.01
☐ 139 Vince Workman	.15	.07	.02
☐ 140 Ray Childress	.08	.04	.01
☐ 141 Cris Dishman	.08	.04	.01
☐ 142 Curtis Duncan	.08	.04	.01
☐ 143 William Fuller	.15	.07	.02
☐ 144 Ernest Givins	.15	.07	.02
☐ 145 Haywood Jeffires	.15	.07	.02
☐ 146 Sean Jones	.15	.07	.02
☐ 147 Lamar Lathon	.08	.04	.01
☐ 148 Bruce Matthews	.08	.04	.01
☐ 149 Bubba McDowell	.08	.04	.01
☐ 150 Johnny Meads	.08	.04	.01
☐ 151 Warren Moon	.30	.14	.04
☐ 152 Mike Munchak	.08	.04	.01
☐ 153 Bo Orlando	.08	.04	.01
☐ 154 Al Smith	.08	.04	.01
☐ 155 Doug Smith	.08	.04	.01
☐ 156 Lorenzo White	.08	.04	.01
☐ 157 Chip Banks	.08	.04	.01
☐ 158 Duane Bickett	.08	.04	.01
☐ 159 Bill Brooks	.08	.04	.01
☐ 160 Jon Hand	.08	.04	.01
☐ 161 Jeff Herrod	.08	.04	.01
☐ 162 Jessie Hester	.08	.04	.01
☐ 163 Scott Radecic	.08	.04	.01
☐ 164 Rohn Stark	.08	.04	.01
☐ 165 Clarence Verdin	.08	.04	.01
☐ 166 Eugene Daniel	.08	.04	.01
☐ 167 John Alt	.08	.04	.01
☐ 168 Tim Barnett	.08	.04	.01
☐ 169 Tim Grunhard	.08	.04	.01
☐ 170 Dino Hackett	.08	.04	.01
☐ 171 Jonathan Hayes	.08	.04	.01
☐ 172 Bill Maas	.08	.04	.01
☐ 173 Chris Martin	.08	.04	.01
☐ 174 Christian Okoye	.08	.04	.01
☐ 175 Stephone Paige	.08	.04	.01
☐ 176 Jayice Pearson	.08	.04	.01
☐ 177 Kevin Porter	.08	.04	.01
☐ 178 Kevin Ross	.08	.04	.01
☐ 179 Dan Saleaumua	.08	.04	.01
☐ 180 Tracy Simien	.08	.04	.01
☐ 181 Neil Smith	.30	.14	.04
☐ 182 Derrick Thomas	.30	.14	.04
☐ 183 Robb Thomas	.08	.04	.01
☐ 184 Barry Word	.08	.04	.01
☐ 185 Marcus Allen	.30	.14	.04
☐ 186 Eddie Anderson	.08	.04	.01
☐ 187 Nick Bell	.08	.04	.01
☐ 188 Tim Brown	.30	.14	.04
☐ 189 Mervyn Fernandez	.08	.04	.01
☐ 190 Willie Gault	.15	.07	.02
☐ 191 Jeff Gossett	.08	.04	.01
☐ 192 Ethan Horton	.08	.04	.01
☐ 193 Jeff Jaeger	.08	.04	.01
☐ 194 Howie Long	.15	.07	.02
☐ 195 Ronnie Lott	.15	.07	.02
☐ 196 Todd Marinovich	.08	.04	.01
☐ 197 Don Mosebar	.08	.04	.01
☐ 198 Jay Schroeder	.08	.04	.01
☐ 199 Anthony Smith	.08	.04	.01
☐ 200 Greg Townsend	.08	.04	.01
☐ 201 Lionel Washington	.08	.04	.01
☐ 202 Steve Wisniewski	.08	.04	.01
☐ 203 Flipper Anderson	.08	.04	.01
☐ 204 Robert Delpino	.08	.04	.01
☐ 205 Henry Ellard	.15	.07	.02
☐ 206 Jim Everett	.15	.07	.02
☐ 207 Kevin Greene	.30	.14	.04
☐ 208 Darryl Henley	.08	.04	.01
☐ 209 Damone Johnson	.08	.04	.01
☐ 210 Larry Kelm	.08	.04	.01
☐ 211 Todd Lyght	.08	.04	.01
☐ 212 Jackie Slater	.08	.04	.01
☐ 213 Michael Stewart	.08	.04	.01
☐ 214 Pat Terrell	.08	.04	.01
☐ 215 Robert Young	.08	.04	.01
☐ 216 Mark Clayton	.15	.07	.02
☐ 217 Bryan Cox	.15	.07	.02
☐ 218 Jeff Cross	.08	.04	.01
☐ 219 Mark Duper	.08	.04	.01
☐ 220 Harry Galbreath	.08	.04	.01
☐ 221 David Griggs	.08	.04	.01
☐ 222 Mark Higgs	.08	.04	.01
☐ 223 Vestee Jackson	.08	.04	.01
☐ 224 John Offerdahl	.08	.04	.01
☐ 225 Louis Oliver	.08	.04	.01
☐ 226 Tony Paige	.08	.04	.01
☐ 227 Reggie Roby	.08	.04	.01
☐ 228 Pete Stoyanovich	.08	.04	.01
☐ 229 Richmond Webb	.08	.04	.01
☐ 230 Terry Allen	.75	.35	.09
☐ 231 Ray Berry	.08	.04	.01
☐ 232 Anthony Carter	.15	.07	.02
☐ 233 Cris Carter	.30	.14	.04
☐ 234 Chris Doleman	.08	.04	.01
☐ 235 Rich Gannon	.08	.04	.01
☐ 236 Steve Jordan	.08	.04	.01
☐ 237 Carl Lee	.08	.04	.01
☐ 238 Randall McDaniel	.08	.04	.01
☐ 239 Mike Merriweather	.08	.04	.01
☐ 240 Harry Newsome	.08	.04	.01
☐ 241 John Randle	.15	.07	.02
☐ 242 Henry Thomas	.08	.04	.01
☐ 243 Bruce Armstrong	.08	.04	.01
☐ 244 Vincent Brown	.08	.04	.01
☐ 245 Marv Cook	.08	.04	.01
☐ 246 Irving Fryar	.15	.07	.02
☐ 247 Pat Harlow	.08	.04	.01
☐ 248 Maurice Hurst	.08	.04	.01
☐ 249 Eugene Lockhart	.08	.04	.01
☐ 250 Greg McMurtry	.08	.04	.01
☐ 251 Hugh Millen	.08	.04	.01
☐ 252 Leonard Russell	.15	.07	.02
☐ 253 Chris Singleton	.08	.04	.01
☐ 254 Andre Tippett	.08	.04	.01
☐ 255 Jon Vaughn	.08	.04	.01
☐ 256 Morten Andersen	.08	.04	.01
☐ 257 Gene Atkins	.08	.04	.01
☐ 258 Wesley Caroll	.08	.04	.01
☐ 259 Jim Dombrowski	.08	.04	.01
☐ 260 Quinn Early	.15	.07	.02
☐ 261 Bobby Hebert	.08	.04	.01
☐ 262 Joel Hilgenberg	.08	.04	.01
☐ 263 Rickey Jackson	.08	.04	.01
☐ 264 Vaughan Johnson	.08	.04	.01
☐ 265 Eric Martin	.08	.04	.01
☐ 266 Brett Maxie	.08	.04	.01
☐ 267 Fred McAfee	.08	.04	.01
☐ 268 Sam Mills	.08	.04	.01
☐ 269 Pat Swilling	.15	.07	.02
☐ 270 Floyd Turner	.08	.04	.01
☐ 271 Steve Walsh	.08	.04	.01
☐ 272 Stephen Baker	.08	.04	.01
☐ 273 Jarrod Bunch	.08	.04	.01
☐ 274 Mark Collins	.08	.04	.01
☐ 275 John Elliott	.08	.04	.01
☐ 276 Myron Guyton	.08	.04	.01
☐ 277 Rodney Hampton	.30	.14	.04
☐ 278 Jeff Hostetler	.15	.07	.02
☐ 279 Mark Ingram	.08	.04	.01
☐ 280 Pepper Johnson	.08	.04	.01
☐ 281 Sean Landeta	.08	.04	.01
☐ 282 Leonard Marshall	.08	.04	.01
☐ 283 Kanavis McGhee	.08	.04	.01
☐ 284 Dave Meggett	.15	.07	.02
☐ 285 Bart Oates	.08	.04	.01
☐ 286 Phil Simms	.15	.07	.02
☐ 287 Reyna Thompson	.08	.04	.01
☐ 288 Lewis Tillman	.08	.04	.01
☐ 289 Brad Baxter	.08	.04	.01
☐ 290 Mike Brim	.08	.04	.01
☐ 291 Chris Burkett	.08	.04	.01
☐ 292 Kyle Clifton	.08	.04	.01
☐ 293 James Hasty	.08	.04	.01
☐ 294 Joe Kelly	.08	.04	.01
☐ 295 Jeff Lageman	.08	.04	.01
☐ 296 Mo Lewis	.08	.04	.01
☐ 297 Erik McMillan	.08	.04	.01
☐ 298 Scott Mersereau	.08	.04	.01
☐ 299 Rob Moore	.15	.07	.02
☐ 300 Tony Stargell	.08	.04	.01
☐ 301 Jim Sweeney	.08	.04	.01
☐ 302 Marvin Washington	.08	.04	.01
☐ 303 Lonnie Young	.08	.04	.01
☐ 304 Eric Allen	.08	.04	.01
☐ 305 Fred Barnett	.30	.14	.04
☐ 306 Keith Byars	.08	.04	.01
☐ 307 Byron Evans	.08	.04	.01
☐ 308 Wes Hopkins	.08	.04	.01
☐ 309 Keith Jackson	.15	.07	.02
☐ 310 James Joseph	.08	.04	.01
☐ 311 Seth Joyner	.15	.07	.02
☐ 312 Roger Ruzek	.08	.04	.01
☐ 313 Clyde Simmons	.08	.04	.01
☐ 314 William Thomas	.08	.04	.01
☐ 315 Reggie White	.30	.14	.04
☐ 316 Calvin Williams	.15	.07	.02
☐ 317 Rich Camarillo	.08	.04	.01
☐ 318 Jeff Faulkner	.08	.04	.01
☐ 319 Ken Harvey	.08	.04	.01
☐ 320 Eric Hill	.08	.04	.01
☐ 321 Johnny Johnson	.08	.04	.01
☐ 322 Ernie Jones	.08	.04	.01
☐ 323 Tim McDonald	.08	.04	.01
☐ 324 Freddie Joe Nunn	.08	.04	.01
☐ 325 Luis Sharpe	.08	.04	.01
☐ 326 Eric Swann	.15	.07	.02
☐ 327 Aeneas Williams	.15	.07	.02
☐ 328 Michael Zordich	.08	.04	.01
☐ 329 Gary Anderson K	.08	.04	.01
☐ 330 Bubby Brister	.08	.04	.01
☐ 331 Barry Foster	.15	.07	.02
☐ 332 Eric Green	.08	.04	.01
☐ 333 Bryan Hinkle	.08	.04	.01
☐ 334 Tunch Ilkin	.08	.04	.01
☐ 335 Carnell Lake	.08	.04	.01
☐ 336 Louis Lipps	.08	.04	.01
☐ 337 David Little	.08	.04	.01
☐ 338 Greg Lloyd	.30	.14	.04
☐ 339 Neil O'Donnell	.30	.14	.04
☐ 340 Rod Woodson	.30	.14	.04
☐ 341 Rod Bernstine	.08	.04	.01
☐ 342 Marion Butts	.08	.04	.01
☐ 343 Gill Byrd	.08	.04	.01
☐ 344 John Friesz	.15	.07	.02
☐ 345 Burt Grossman	.08	.04	.01
☐ 346 Courtney Hall	.08	.04	.01
☐ 347 Ronnie Harmon	.08	.04	.01
☐ 348 Shawn Jefferson	.08	.04	.01
☐ 349 Nate Lewis	.08	.04	.01
☐ 350 Craig McEwen	.08	.04	.01
☐ 351 Eric Moten	.08	.04	.01
☐ 352 Gary Plummer	.08	.04	.01
☐ 353 Henry Rolling	.08	.04	.01
☐ 354 Broderick Thompson	.08	.04	.01
☐ 355 Derrick Walker	.08	.04	.01
☐ 356 Harris Barton	.08	.04	.01
☐ 357 Steve Bono	.40	.18	.05
☐ 358 Todd Bowles	.08	.04	.01
☐ 359 Dexter Carter	.08	.04	.01
☐ 360 Michael Carter	.08	.04	.01
☐ 361 Keith DeLong	.08	.04	.01
☐ 362 Charles Haley	.15	.07	.02
☐ 363 Merton Hanks	.15	.07	.02
☐ 364 Tim Harris	.08	.04	.01
☐ 365 Brent Jones	.15	.07	.02
☐ 366 Guy McIntyre	.08	.04	.01
☐ 367 Tom Rathman	.08	.04	.01
☐ 368 Bill Romanowski	.08	.04	.01
☐ 369 Jesse Sapolu	.08	.04	.01
☐ 370 John Taylor	.15	.07	.02
☐ 371 Steve Young	1.50	.70	.19
☐ 372 Robert Blackmon	.08	.04	.01
☐ 373 Brian Blades	.15	.07	.02
☐ 374 Jacob Green	.08	.04	.01
☐ 375 Dwayne Harper	.08	.04	.01
☐ 376 Andy Heck	.08	.04	.01
☐ 377 Tommy Kane	.08	.04	.01
☐ 378 John Kasay	.08	.04	.01
☐ 379 Cortez Kennedy	.15	.07	.02
☐ 380 Bryan Millard	.08	.04	.01
☐ 381 Rufus Porter	.08	.04	.01
☐ 382 Eugene Robinson	.08	.04	.01
☐ 383 John L. Williams	.08	.04	.01
☐ 384 Terry Wooden	.08	.04	.01
☐ 385 Gary Anderson RB	.08	.04	.01
☐ 386 Ian Beckles	.08	.04	.01
☐ 387 Mark Carrier WR	.15	.07	.02
☐ 388 Reggie Cobb	.08	.04	.01
☐ 389 Tony Covington	.08	.04	.01
☐ 390 Lawrence Dawsey	.15	.07	.02
☐ 391 Ron Hall	.08	.04	.01
☐ 392 Keith McCants	.08	.04	.01
☐ 393 Charles McRae	.08	.04	.01
☐ 394 Tim Newton	.08	.04	.01
☐ 395 Jesse Solomon	.08	.04	.01
☐ 396 Vinny Testaverde	.15	.07	.02
☐ 397 Broderick Thomas	.08	.04	.01
☐ 398 Robert Wilson	.08	.04	.01
☐ 399 Earnest Byner	.08	.04	.01
☐ 400 Gary Clark	.30	.14	.04
☐ 401 Andre Collins	.08	.04	.01
☐ 402 Brad Edwards	.08	.04	.01
☐ 403 Kurt Gouveia	.08	.04	.01
☐ 404 Darrell Green	.08	.04	.01
☐ 405 Joe Jacoby	.08	.04	.01
☐ 406 Jim Lachey	.08	.04	.01
☐ 407 Chip Lohmiller	.08	.04	.01
☐ 408 Charles Mann	.08	.04	.01
☐ 409 Wilber Marshall	.08	.04	.01
☐ 410 Brian Mitchell	.15	.07	.02
☐ 411 Art Monk	.15	.07	.02
☐ 412 Mark Rypien	.08	.04	.01
☐ 413 Ricky Sanders	.08	.04	.01
☐ 414 Mark Schlereth	.08	.04	.01
☐ 415 Fred Stokes	.08	.04	.01
☐ 416 Bobby Wilson	.08	.04	.01
☐ 417 Corey Barlow	.08	.04	.01
☐ 418 Edgar Bennett	1.25	.55	.16
☐ 419 Eddie Blake	.08	.04	.01
☐ 420 Terrell Buckley	.08	.04	.01
☐ 421 Willie Clay	.08	.04	.01

	MINT	NRMT	EXC
☐ 422 Rodney Culver	.08	.04	.01
☐ 423 Ed Cunningham	.08	.04	.01
☐ 424 Mark D'Onofrio	.08	.04	.01
☐ 425 Matt Darby	.08	.04	.01
☐ 426 Charles Davenport	.08	.04	.01
☐ 427 Will Furrer	.08	.04	.01
☐ 428 Keith Goganious	.08	.04	.01
☐ 429 Mario Bailey	.08	.04	.01
☐ 430 Chris Hakel	.08	.04	.01
☐ 431 Keith Hamilton	.08	.04	.01
☐ 432 Aaron Pierce	.08	.04	.01
☐ 433 Amp Lee	.08	.04	.01
☐ 434 Scott Lockwood	.08	.04	.01
☐ 435 Ricardo McDonald	.08	.04	.01
☐ 436 Dexter McNabb	.08	.04	.01
☐ 437 Chris Mims	.15	.07	.02
☐ 438 Mike Mooney	.08	.04	.01
☐ 439 Ray Roberts	.08	.04	.01
☐ 440 Patrick Rowe	.08	.04	.01
☐ 441 Leon Searcy	.15	.07	.02
☐ 442 Siran Stacy	.08	.04	.01
☐ 443 Kevin Turner	.08	.04	.01
☐ 444 Tommy Vardell	.15	.07	.02
☐ 445 Bob Whitfield	.08	.04	.01
☐ 446 Darryl Williams	.08	.04	.01
☐ 447 Checklist 1-110	.08	.04	.01
☐ 448 Checklist 111-224	.08	.04	.01
☐ 449 Checklist 230-340 UER (Missing 225-229)	.08	.04	.01
☐ 450 Checklist 341-450	.08	.04	.01

1992 Ultra Award Winners

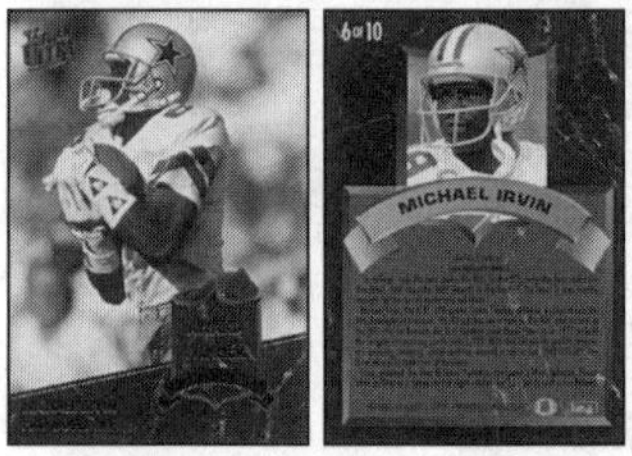

This ten-card standard-size set was randomly inserted in 1992 Ultra foil packs. Each player featured was a recipient of an award for his performance during the 1991 season. The player photos are full-bleed except at the bottom where a diagonal gold foil stripe separates the picture from a black marbleized area. The player's name and the award won are printed in gold foil in this marbleized area, and a black emblem with "Award Winner" and a banner in gold foil is superimposed toward the lower right corner.

	MINT	NRMT	EXC
COMPLETE SET (10)	16.00	7.25	2.00
COMMON CARD (1-10)	1.25	.55	.16
☐ 1 Mark Rypien	1.25	.55	.16
☐ 2 Cornelius Bennett UPI AFC Defensive POY	2.00	.90	.25
☐ 3 Anthony Munoz NFL Man of the Year	2.00	.90	.25
☐ 4 Lawrence Dawsey UPI NFC ROY	1.25	.55	.16
☐ 5 Thurman Thomas Pro Football Weekly NFL Offensive POY	3.00	1.35	.35
☐ 6 Michael Irvin Pro Bowl MVP	3.00	1.35	.35
☐ 7 Mike Croel UPI AFC ROY	1.25	.55	.16
☐ 8 Barry Sanders Maxwell Club POY	6.00	2.70	.75
☐ 9 Pat Swilling AP Defensive POY	1.25	.55	.16
☐ 10 Leonard Russell Pro Football Weekly NFL Offensive ROY	1.25	.55	.16

1992 Ultra Chris Miller

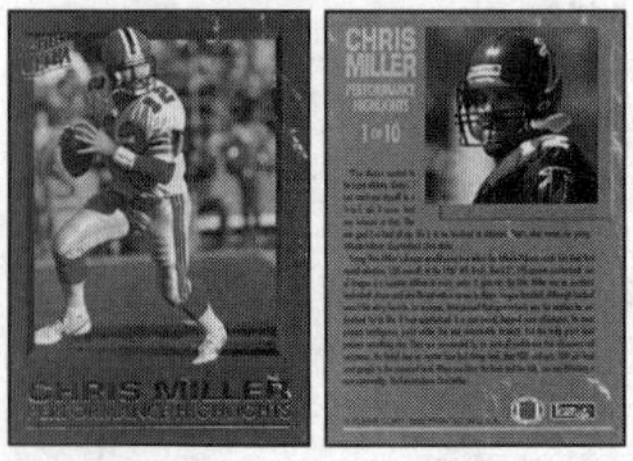

Randomly inserted in the foil packs, this ten-card standard-size set is part of Fleer's signature series. Miller signed over 2,000 of his subset cards. Card numbers 11-12 were available only by mail for ten '92 Ultra wrappers plus 2.00. The fronts display color action player photos with a grayish-black inner border and a maroon marbleized outer border. The player's name and the set title "Performance Highlights" appear in gold foil lettering in the bottom border. On a dusty rose marbleized background, the backs carry a color head shot and summary of Miller's football career.

	MINT	NRMT	EXC
COMPLETE SET (10)	10.00	4.50	1.25
COMMON C.MILLER (1-10)	1.25	.55	.16
COMMON SEND-OFF (11-12)	2.00	.90	.25
☐ 1 Chris Miller (Rolling out to pass white jersey)	1.25	.55	.16
☐ 2 Chris Miller (Ready to hand off ball, black jersey)	1.25	.55	.16
☐ 3 Chris Miller (Standing in pocket; prepared to pass)	1.25	.55	.16
☐ 4 Chris Miller (Ready to hand off)	1.25	.55	.16
☐ 5 Chris Miller (Poised to pass; ball held in one hand; black uniform)	1.25	.55	.16
☐ 6 Chris Miller (Poised to pass; both hands on ball)	1.25	.55	.16
☐ 7 Chris Miller (Running up field; black uniform)	1.25	.55	.16
☐ 8 Chris Miller (Rolling out and looking for receiver)	1.25	.55	.16
☐ 9 Chris Miller (Passing; arm cocked back)	1.25	.55	.16
☐ 10 Chris Miller (Running to right with ball at waist)	1.25	.55	.16
☐ 11 Chris Miller (Left side shot; ball cocked behind head)	2.00	.90	.25
☐ 12 Chris Miller (Front shot; just after ball released)	2.00	.90	.25
☐ AU Chris Miller AUTO (Certified autograph)	60.00	27.00	7.50

1992 Ultra Reggie White

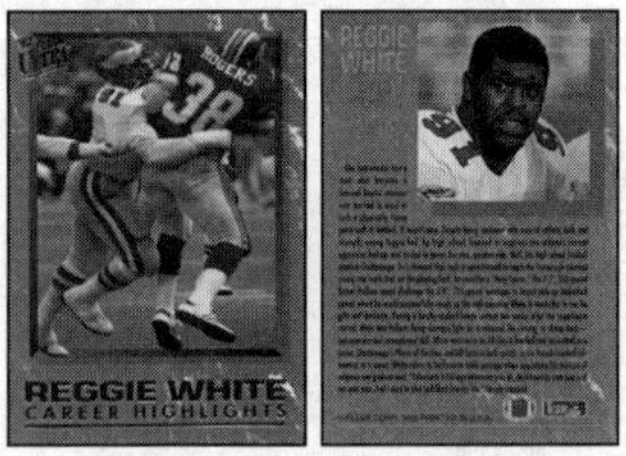

Randomly inserted in foil packs, this ten-card standard-size set is part of Ultra's signature series. White signed over 2,000 of his subset cards. Card numbers 11-12 were available only by mail for ten '92 Ultra wrappers plus 2.00. The fronts display color action player photos with a green inner border and a gray marbleized outer border. The player's name and the set title "Career Highlights" appear in gold foil lettering in the bottom border. On a gray marbleized background, the backs carry a color head shot and summary of White's football career. Card numbers 11-12 have rose-colored backs.

	MINT	NRMT	EXC
COMPLETE SET (10)	15.00	6.75	1.85
COMMON R.WHITE (1-10)	1.50	.70	.19
COMMON SEND-OFF (11-12)	2.50	1.10	.30
☐ 1 Reggie White (Rushing passer and being held by Cardinal)	1.50	.70	.19
☐ 2 Reggie White (Tackling George Rogers)	1.50	.70	.19
☐ 3 Reggie White (Rushing passer and beating Raider lineman)	1.50	.70	.19
☐ 4 Reggie White (Rushing passer with Redskin Don Warren in background)	1.50	.70	.19
☐ 5 Reggie White (Defensive posture in open field)	1.50	.70	.19
☐ 6 Reggie White (Rushing passer in dark green jersey)	1.50	.70	.19
☐ 7 Reggie White (Rushing passer with arms extended)	1.50	.70	.19
☐ 8 Reggie White (Fighting off block of Redskin Ed Simmons)	1.50	.70	.19
☐ 9 Reggie White (Watching from the sideline)	1.50	.70	.19
☐ 10 Reggie White (Fighting off block of Cardinal Walter Reeves)	1.50	.70	.19
☐ 11 Reggie White (Front shot; adjusting chin strap on helmet)	2.50	1.10	.30
☐ 12 Reggie White (Pass rushing to his left)	2.50	1.10	.30
☐ AU Reggie White AUTO (Certified autograph)	100.00	45.00	12.50

1993 Ultra

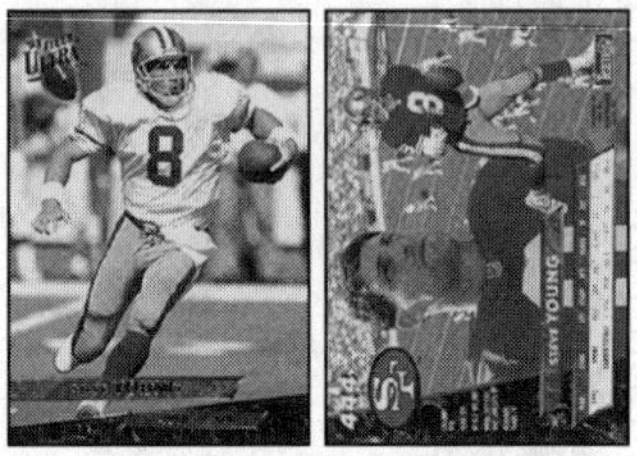

The 1993 Ultra set comprises 500 standard-size cards that were issued in 14 and 19-card packs. The front carries a color action player shot that is borderless, except at the bottom, where a black marbleized area set off by a gold-foil line carries the player's team name and position in gold foil. A team-colored marbleized bar immediately above carries the player's name. The horizontal back sports a close-up and action cut-out player photo against a football stadium graphic. The player's name, biography, and 1992 statistics all appear toward the lower left. The cards are numbered on the back and checklisted below alphabetically according to teams. Rookie Cards include Jerome Bettis, Drew Bledsoe, Vincent Brisby, Reggie Brooks, Curtis Conway, Troy Drayton, Garrison Hearst, Qadry Ismail, Terry Kirby, Leon Lett, O.J. McDuffie, Natrone Means, Glyn Milburn, Rick Mirer, Willie Roaf, Robert Smith and Dana Stubblefield.

	MINT	NRMT	EXC
COMPLETE SET (500)	50.00	22.00	6.25
COMMON CARD (1-500)	.15	.07	.02
☐ 1 Vinnie Clark	.15	.07	.02
☐ 2 Darion Conner	.15	.07	.02
☐ 3 Eric Dickerson	.30	.14	.04
☐ 4 Moe Gardner	.15	.07	.02
☐ 5 Tim Green	.15	.07	.02
☐ 6 Roger Harper	.15	.07	.02
☐ 7 Michael Haynes	.30	.14	.04
☐ 8 Bobby Hebert	.15	.07	.02
☐ 9 Chris Hinton	.15	.07	.02
☐ 10 Pierce Holt	.15	.07	.02
☐ 11 Mike Kenn	.15	.07	.02
☐ 12 Lincoln Kennedy	.15	.07	.02
☐ 13 Chris Miller	.30	.14	.04
☐ 14 Mike Pritchard	.30	.14	.04
☐ 15 Andre Rison	.30	.14	.04
☐ 16 Deion Sanders	2.00	.90	.25
☐ 17 Tony Smith	.15	.07	.02
☐ 18 Jessie Tuggle	.15	.07	.02
☐ 19 Howard Ballard	.15	.07	.02
☐ 20 Don Beebe	.15	.07	.02
☐ 21 Cornelius Bennett	.30	.14	.04
☐ 22 Bill Brooks	.15	.07	.02
☐ 23 Kenneth Davis	.15	.07	.02
☐ 24 Phil Hansen	.15	.07	.02
☐ 25 Henry Jones	.15	.07	.02
☐ 26 Jim Kelly	.50	.23	.06
☐ 27 Nate Odomes	.15	.07	.02
☐ 28 John Parrella	.15	.07	.02
☐ 29 Andre Reed	.30	.14	.04
☐ 30 Frank Reich	.30	.14	.04
☐ 31 Jim Ritcher	.15	.07	.02
☐ 32 Bruce Smith	.50	.23	.06
☐ 33 Thomas Smith	.30	.14	.04
☐ 34 Darryl Talley	.15	.07	.02
☐ 35 Steve Tasker	.30	.14	.04
☐ 36 Thurman Thomas	.50	.23	.06
☐ 37 Jeff Wright	.15	.07	.02
☐ 38 Neal Anderson	.15	.07	.02
☐ 39 Trace Armstrong	.15	.07	.02
☐ 40 Mark Carrier DB	.15	.07	.02
☐ 41 Curtis Conway	2.50	1.10	.30
☐ 42 Wendell Davis	.15	.07	.02
☐ 43 Richard Dent	.30	.14	.04
☐ 44 Shaun Gayle	.15	.07	.02
☐ 45 Jim Harbaugh	.50	.23	.06
☐ 46 Craig Heyward	.30	.14	.04
☐ 47 Darren Lewis	.15	.07	.02
☐ 48 Steve McMichael	.30	.14	.04
☐ 49 William Perry	.30	.14	.04
☐ 50 Carl Simpson	.15	.07	.02
☐ 51 Alonzo Spellman	.15	.07	.02
☐ 52 Keith Van Horne	.15	.07	.02
☐ 53 Tom Waddle	.15	.07	.02
☐ 54 Donnell Woolford	.15	.07	.02
☐ 55 John Copeland	.30	.14	.04
☐ 56 Derrick Fenner	.15	.07	.02
☐ 57 James Francis	.15	.07	.02
☐ 58 Harold Green	.15	.07	.02
☐ 59 David Klingler	.15	.07	.02
☐ 60 Tim Krumrie	.15	.07	.02
☐ 61 Ricardo McDonald	.15	.07	.02
☐ 62 Tony McGee	.30	.14	.04
☐ 63 Carl Pickens	2.00	.90	.25
☐ 64 Lamar Rogers	.15	.07	.02
☐ 65 Jay Schroeder	.15	.07	.02
☐ 66 Daniel Stubbs	.15	.07	.02
☐ 67 Steve Tovar	.15	.07	.02
☐ 68 Alfred Williams	.15	.07	.02
☐ 69 Darryl Williams	.15	.07	.02
☐ 70 Jerry Ball	.15	.07	.02
☐ 71 David Brandon	.15	.07	.02
☐ 72 Rob Burnett	.15	.07	.02
☐ 73 Mark Carrier WR	.30	.14	.04
☐ 74 Steve Everitt	.15	.07	.02
☐ 75 Dan Footman	.15	.07	.02
☐ 76 Leroy Hoard	.30	.14	.04
☐ 77 Michael Jackson	.30	.14	.04
☐ 78 Mike Johnson	.15	.07	.02
☐ 79 Bernie Kosar	.30	.14	.04
☐ 80 Clay Matthews	.30	.14	.04
☐ 81 Eric Metcalf	.30	.14	.04
☐ 82 Michael Dean Perry	.30	.14	.04
☐ 83 Vinny Testaverde	.30	.14	.04
☐ 84 Tommy Vardell	.15	.07	.02
☐ 85 Troy Aikman	3.00	1.35	.35
☐ 86 Larry Brown DB	.15	.07	.02
☐ 87 Tony Casillas	.15	.07	.02
☐ 88 Thomas Everett	.15	.07	.02
☐ 89 Charles Haley	.30	.14	.04
☐ 90 Alvin Harper	.30	.14	.04
☐ 91 Michael Irvin	.50	.23	.06
☐ 92 Jim Jeffcoat	.15	.07	.02
☐ 93 Daryl Johnston	.50	.23	.06
☐ 94 Robert Jones	.15	.07	.02
☐ 95 Leon Lett	.30	.14	.04
☐ 96 Russell Maryland	.15	.07	.02
☐ 97 Nate Newton	.30	.14	.04
☐ 98 Ken Norton	.30	.14	.04
☐ 99 Jay Novacek	.30	.14	.04
☐ 100 Darrin Smith	.30	.14	.04
☐ 101 Emmitt Smith	5.00	2.20	.60
☐ 102 Kevin Smith	.30	.14	.04
☐ 103 Mark Stepnoski	.15	.07	.02
☐ 104 Tony Tolbert	.15	.07	.02
☐ 105 Kevin Williams	.75	.35	.09
☐ 106 Steve Atwater	.15	.07	.02
☐ 107 Rod Bernstine	.15	.07	.02
☐ 108 Mike Croel	.15	.07	.02
☐ 109 Robert Delpino	.15	.07	.02
☐ 110 Shane Dronett	.15	.07	.02
☐ 111 John Elway	2.50	1.10	.30
☐ 112 Simon Fletcher	.15	.07	.02
☐ 113 Greg Kragen	.15	.07	.02
☐ 114 Tommy Maddox	.15	.07	.02
☐ 115 Arthur Marshall	.15	.07	.02
☐ 116 Karl Mecklenburg	.15	.07	.02
☐ 117 Glyn Milburn	.50	.23	.06
☐ 118 Reggie Rivers	.15	.07	.02
☐ 119 Shannon Sharpe	.50	.23	.06
☐ 120 Dennis Smith	.15	.07	.02
☐ 121 Kenny Walker	.15	.07	.02
☐ 122 Dan Williams	.15	.07	.02
☐ 123 Bennie Blades	.15	.07	.02
☐ 124 Lomas Brown	.15	.07	.02
☐ 125 Bill Fralic	.15	.07	.02
☐ 126 Mel Gray	.30	.14	.04
☐ 127 Willie Green	.15	.07	.02
☐ 128 Jason Hanson	.15	.07	.02
☐ 129 Antonio London	.15	.07	.02
☐ 130 Ryan McNeil	.15	.07	.02
☐ 131 Herman Moore	2.50	1.10	.30
☐ 132 Rodney Peete	.15	.07	.02
☐ 133 Brett Perriman	.50	.23	.06
☐ 134 Kelvin Pritchett	.15	.07	.02
☐ 135 Barry Sanders	3.00	1.35	.35
☐ 136 Tracy Scroggins	.15	.07	.02
☐ 137 Chris Spielman	.30	.14	.04
☐ 138 Pat Swilling	.15	.07	.02
☐ 139 Andre Ware	.15	.07	.02
☐ 140 Edgar Bennett	.50	.23	.06
☐ 141 Tony Bennett	.15	.07	.02
☐ 142 Matt Brock	.15	.07	.02
☐ 143 Terrell Buckley	.15	.07	.02
☐ 144 LeRoy Butler	.15	.07	.02
☐ 145 Mark Clayton	.15	.07	.02
☐ 146 Brett Favre	5.00	2.20	.60
☐ 147 Jackie Harris	.15	.07	.02
☐ 148 Johnny Holland	.15	.07	.02
☐ 149 Bill Maas	.15	.07	.02
☐ 150 Brian Noble	.15	.07	.02
☐ 151 Bryce Paup	.50	.23	.06
☐ 152 Ken Ruettgers	.15	.07	.02
☐ 153 Sterling Sharpe	.50	.23	.06
☐ 154 Wayne Simmons	.15	.07	.02
☐ 155 John Stephens	.15	.07	.02
☐ 156 George Teague	.30	.14	.04
☐ 157 Reggie White	.50	.23	.06
☐ 158 Micheal Barrow	.15	.07	.02
☐ 159 Cody Carlson	.15	.07	.02
☐ 160 Ray Childress	.15	.07	.02
☐ 161 Cris Dishman	.15	.07	.02
☐ 162 Curtis Duncan	.15	.07	.02
☐ 163 William Fuller	.15	.07	.02
☐ 164 Ernest Givins	.30	.14	.04
☐ 165 Brad Hopkins	.15	.07	.02
☐ 166 Haywood Jeffires	.30	.14	.04
☐ 167 Lamar Lathon	.15	.07	.02

☐ 168 Wilber Marshall	.15	.07	.02
☐ 169 Bruce Matthews	.15	.07	.02
☐ 170 Bubba McDowell	.15	.07	.02
☐ 171 Warren Moon	.50	.23	.06
☐ 172 Mike Munchak	.15	.07	.02
☐ 173 Eddie Robinson	.15	.07	.02
☐ 174 Al Smith	.15	.07	.02
☐ 175 Lorenzo White	.15	.07	.02
☐ 176 Lee Williams	.15	.07	.02
☐ 177 Chip Banks	.15	.07	.02
☐ 178 John Baylor	.15	.07	.02
☐ 179 Duane Bickett	.15	.07	.02
☐ 180 Kerry Cash	.15	.07	.02
☐ 181 Quentin Coryatt	.30	.14	.04
☐ 182 Rodney Culver	.15	.07	.02
☐ 183 Steve Emtman	.15	.07	.02
☐ 184 Jeff George	.50	.23	.06
☐ 185 Jeff Herrod	.15	.07	.02
☐ 186 Jessie Hester	.15	.07	.02
☐ 187 Anthony Johnson	.30	.14	.04
☐ 188 Reggie Langhorne	.15	.07	.02
☐ 189 Roosevelt Potts	.15	.07	.02
☐ 190 Rohn Stark	.15	.07	.02
☐ 191 Clarence Verdin	.15	.07	.02
☐ 192 Will Wolford	.15	.07	.02
☐ 193 Marcus Allen	.50	.23	.06
☐ 194 John Alt	.15	.07	.02
☐ 195 Tim Barnett	.15	.07	.02
☐ 196 J.J.Birden	.15	.07	.02
☐ 197 Dale Carter	.15	.07	.02
☐ 198 Willie Davis	.50	.23	.06
☐ 199 Jaime Fields	.15	.07	.02
☐ 200 Dave Krieg	.30	.14	.04
☐ 201 Nick Lowery	.15	.07	.02
☐ 202 Charles Mincy	.15	.07	.02
☐ 203 Joe Montana	3.00	1.35	.35
☐ 204 Christian Okoye	.15	.07	.02
☐ 205 Dan Saleaumua	.15	.07	.02
☐ 206 Will Shields	.15	.07	.02
☐ 207 Tracy Simien	.15	.07	.02
☐ 208 Neil Smith	.50	.23	.06
☐ 209 Derrick Thomas	.50	.23	.06
☐ 210 Harvey Williams	.30	.14	.04
☐ 211 Barry Word	.15	.07	.02
☐ 212 Eddie Anderson	.15	.07	.02
☐ 213 Patrick Bates	.15	.07	.02
☐ 214 Nick Bell	.15	.07	.02
☐ 215 Tim Brown	.50	.23	.06
☐ 216 Willie Gault	.15	.07	.02
☐ 217 Gaston Green	.15	.07	.02
☐ 218 Billy Joe Hobert	1.25	.55	.16
☐ 219 Ethan Horton	.15	.07	.02
☐ 220 Jeff Hostetler	.30	.14	.04
☐ 221 James Lofton	.30	.14	.04
☐ 222 Howie Long	.30	.14	.04
☐ 223 Todd Marinovich	.15	.07	.02
☐ 224 Terry McDaniel	.15	.07	.02
☐ 225 Winston Moss	.15	.07	.02
☐ 226 Anthony Smith	.15	.07	.02
☐ 227 Greg Townsend	.15	.07	.02
☐ 228 Aaron Wallace	.15	.07	.02
☐ 229 Lionel Washington	.15	.07	.02
☐ 230 Steve Wisniewski	.15	.07	.02
☐ 231 Flipper Anderson	.15	.07	.02
☐ 232 Jerome Bettis	4.00	1.80	.50
☐ 233 Marc Boutte	.15	.07	.02
☐ 234 Shane Conlan	.15	.07	.02
☐ 235 Troy Drayton	.30	.14	.04
☐ 236 Henry Ellard	.30	.14	.04
☐ 237 Jim Everett	.30	.14	.04
☐ 238 Cleveland Gary	.15	.07	.02
☐ 239 Sean Gilbert	.30	.14	.04
☐ 240 Darryl Henley	.15	.07	.02
☐ 241 David Lang	.15	.07	.02
☐ 242 Todd Lyght	.15	.07	.02
☐ 243 Anthony Newman	.15	.07	.02
☐ 244 Roman Phifer	.15	.07	.02
☐ 245 Gerald Robinson	.15	.07	.02
☐ 246 Henry Rolling	.15	.07	.02
☐ 247 Jackie Slater	.15	.07	.02
☐ 248 Keith Byars	.15	.07	.02
☐ 249 Marco Coleman	.15	.07	.02
☐ 250 Bryan Cox	.15	.07	.02
☐ 251 Jeff Cross	.15	.07	.02
☐ 252 Irving Fryar	.30	.14	.04
☐ 253 Mark Higgs	.15	.07	.02
☐ 254 Dwight Hollier	.15	.07	.02
☐ 255 Mark Ingram	.15	.07	.02
☐ 256 Keith Jackson	.30	.14	.04
☐ 257 Terry Kirby	.75	.35	.09
☐ 258 Dan Marino	5.00	2.20	.60
☐ 259 O.J.McDuffie	2.50	1.10	.30
☐ 260 John Offerdahl	.15	.07	.02
☐ 261 Louis Oliver	.15	.07	.02
☐ 262 Pete Stoyanovich	.15	.07	.02
☐ 263 Troy Vincent	.15	.07	.02
☐ 264 Richmond Webb	.15	.07	.02
☐ 265 Jarvis Williams	.15	.07	.02
☐ 266 Terry Allen	.50	.23	.06
☐ 267 Anthony Carter	.30	.14	.04
☐ 268 Cris Carter	.50	.23	.06
☐ 269 Roger Craig	.30	.14	.04
☐ 270 Jack Del Rio	.15	.07	.02
☐ 271 Chris Doleman	.15	.07	.02
☐ 272 Qadry Ismail	.50	.23	.06
☐ 273 Steve Jordan	.15	.07	.02
☐ 274 Randall McDaniel	.15	.07	.02
☐ 275 Audray McMillian	.15	.07	.02
☐ 276 John Randle	.15	.07	.02
☐ 277 Sean Salisbury	.15	.07	.02
☐ 278 Todd Scott	.15	.07	.02
☐ 279 Robert Smith	2.50	1.10	.30
☐ 280 Henry Thomas	.15	.07	.02
☐ 281 Ray Agnew	.15	.07	.02
☐ 282 Bruce Armstrong	.15	.07	.02
☐ 283 Drew Bledsoe	7.00	3.10	.85
☐ 284 Vincent Brisby	.50	.23	.06
☐ 285 Vincent Brown	.15	.07	.02
☐ 286 Eugene Chung	.15	.07	.02
☐ 287 Marv Cook	.15	.07	.02
☐ 288 Pat Harlow	.15	.07	.02
☐ 289 Jerome Henderson	.15	.07	.02
☐ 290 Greg McMurtry	.15	.07	.02
☐ 291 Leonard Russell	.30	.14	.04
☐ 292 Chris Singleton	.15	.07	.02
☐ 293 Chris Slade	.30	.14	.04
☐ 294 Andre Tippett	.15	.07	.02
☐ 295 Brent Williams	.15	.07	.02
☐ 296 Scott Zolak	.15	.07	.02
☐ 297 Morten Andersen	.15	.07	.02
☐ 298 Gene Atkins	.15	.07	.02
☐ 299 Mike Buck	.15	.07	.02
☐ 300 Toi Cook	.15	.07	.02
☐ 301 Jim Dombrowski	.15	.07	.02
☐ 302 Vaughn Dunbar	.15	.07	.02
☐ 303 Quinn Early	.30	.14	.04
☐ 304 Joel Hilgenberg	.15	.07	.02
☐ 305 Dalton Hilliard	.15	.07	.02
☐ 306 Rickey Jackson	.15	.07	.02
☐ 307 Vaughan Johnson	.15	.07	.02
☐ 308 Reginald Jones	.15	.07	.02
☐ 309 Eric Martin	.15	.07	.02
☐ 310 Wayne Martin	.15	.07	.02
☐ 311 Sam Mills	.15	.07	.02
☐ 312 Brad Muster	.15	.07	.02
☐ 313 Willie Roaf	.30	.14	.04
☐ 314 Irv Smith	.15	.07	.02
☐ 315 Wade Wilson	.15	.07	.02
☐ 316 Carlton Bailey	.15	.07	.02
☐ 317 Michael Brooks	.15	.07	.02
☐ 318 Derek Brown TE	.15	.07	.02
☐ 319 Marcus Buckley	.15	.07	.02
☐ 320 Jarrod Bunch	.15	.07	.02
☐ 321 Mark Collins	.15	.07	.02
☐ 322 Eric Dorsey	.15	.07	.02
☐ 323 Rodney Hampton	.50	.23	.06
☐ 324 Mark Jackson	.15	.07	.02
☐ 325 Pepper Johnson	.15	.07	.02
☐ 326 Ed McCaffrey	.15	.07	.02
☐ 327 Dave Meggett	.15	.07	.02
☐ 328 Bart Oates	.15	.07	.02
☐ 329 Mike Sherrard	.15	.07	.02
☐ 330 Phil Simms	.30	.14	.04
☐ 331 Michael Strahan	.15	.07	.02
☐ 332 Lawrence Taylor	.50	.23	.06
☐ 333 Brad Baxter	.15	.07	.02
☐ 334 Chris Burkett	.15	.07	.02
☐ 335 Kyle Clifton	.15	.07	.02
☐ 336 Boomer Esiason	.30	.14	.04
☐ 337 James Hasty	.15	.07	.02
☐ 338 Johnny Johnson	.15	.07	.02
☐ 339 Marvin Jones	.15	.07	.02
☐ 340 Jeff Lageman	.15	.07	.02
☐ 341 Mo Lewis	.15	.07	.02
☐ 342 Ronnie Lott	.30	.14	.04
☐ 343 Leonard Marshall	.15	.07	.02
☐ 344 Johnny Mitchell	.15	.07	.02
☐ 345 Rob Moore	.30	.14	.04
☐ 346 Browning Nagle	.15	.07	.02
☐ 347 Coleman Rudolph	.15	.07	.02
☐ 348 Blair Thomas	.15	.07	.02
☐ 349 Eric Thomas	.15	.07	.02
☐ 350 Brian Washington	.15	.07	.02
☐ 351 Marvin Washington	.15	.07	.02
☐ 352 Eric Allen	.15	.07	.02
☐ 353 Victor Bailey	.15	.07	.02
☐ 354 Fred Barnett	.30	.14	.04
☐ 355 Mark Bavaro	.15	.07	.02
☐ 356 Randall Cunningham	.30	.14	.04
☐ 357 Byron Evans	.15	.07	.02
☐ 358 Andy Harmon	.30	.14	.04
☐ 359 Tim Harris	.15	.07	.02
☐ 360 Lester Holmes	.15	.07	.02
☐ 361 Seth Joyner	.15	.07	.02
☐ 362 Keith Millard	.15	.07	.02
☐ 363 Leonard Renfro	.15	.07	.02
☐ 364 Heath Sherman	.15	.07	.02
☐ 365 Vai Sikahema	.15	.07	.02
☐ 366 Clyde Simmons	.15	.07	.02
☐ 367 William Thomas	.15	.07	.02
☐ 368 Herschel Walker	.30	.14	.04
☐ 369 Andre Waters	.15	.07	.02
☐ 370 Calvin Williams	.30	.14	.04
☐ 371 Johnny Bailey	.15	.07	.02
☐ 372 Steve Beuerlein	.15	.07	.02
☐ 373 Rich Camarillo	.15	.07	.02
☐ 374 Chuck Cecil	.15	.07	.02
☐ 375 Chris Chandler	.30	.14	.04
☐ 376 Gary Clark	.30	.14	.04
☐ 377 Ben Coleman	.15	.07	.02
☐ 378 Ernest Dye	.15	.07	.02
☐ 379 Ken Harvey	.15	.07	.02
☐ 380 Garrison Hearst	3.00	1.35	.35
☐ 381 Randal Hill	.15	.07	.02
☐ 382 Robert Massey	.15	.07	.02
☐ 383 Freddie Joe Nunn	.15	.07	.02
☐ 384 Ricky Proehl	.15	.07	.02
☐ 385 Luis Sharpe	.15	.07	.02
☐ 386 Tyronne Stowe	.15	.07	.02
☐ 387 Eric Swann	.30	.14	.04
☐ 388 Aeneas Williams	.15	.07	.02
☐ 389 Chad Brown	.30	.14	.04
☐ 390 Dermontti Dawson	.15	.07	.02
☐ 391 Donald Evans	.15	.07	.02
☐ 392 Deon Figures	.30	.14	.04
☐ 393 Barry Foster	.30	.14	.04
☐ 394 Jeff Graham	.30	.14	.04
☐ 395 Eric Green	.15	.07	.02
☐ 396 Kevin Greene	.50	.23	.06
☐ 397 Carlton Haselrig	.15	.07	.02
☐ 398 Andre Hastings	.50	.23	.06
☐ 399 D.J. Johnson	.15	.07	.02
☐ 400 Carnell Lake	.15	.07	.02
☐ 401 Greg Lloyd	.50	.23	.06
☐ 402 Neil O'Donnell	.50	.23	.06
☐ 403 Darren Perry	.15	.07	.02
☐ 404 Mike Tomczak	.15	.07	.02
☐ 405 Rod Woodson	.50	.23	.06
☐ 406 Eric Bieniemy	.15	.07	.02
☐ 407 Marion Butts	.15	.07	.02
☐ 408 Gill Byrd	.15	.07	.02
☐ 409 Darren Carrington	.15	.07	.02
☐ 410 Darrien Gordon	.15	.07	.02
☐ 411 Burt Grossman	.15	.07	.02
☐ 412 Courtney Hall	.15	.07	.02
☐ 413 Ronnie Harmon	.15	.07	.02
☐ 414 Stan Humphries	.50	.23	.06
☐ 415 Nate Lewis	.15	.07	.02
☐ 416 Natrone Means	3.00	1.35	.35
☐ 417 Anthony Miller	.30	.14	.04
☐ 418 Chris Mims	.15	.07	.02
☐ 419 Leslie O'Neal	.30	.14	.04
☐ 420 Gary Plummer	.15	.07	.02
☐ 421 Stanley Richard	.15	.07	.02
☐ 422 Junior Seau	.50	.23	.06
☐ 423 Harry Swayne	.15	.07	.02
☐ 424 Jerrol Williams	.15	.07	.02
☐ 425 Harris Barton	.15	.07	.02
☐ 426 Steve Bono	.50	.23	.06
☐ 427 Kevin Fagan	.15	.07	.02
☐ 428 Don Griffin	.15	.07	.02
☐ 429 Dana Hall	.15	.07	.02
☐ 430 Adrian Hardy	.15	.07	.02
☐ 431 Brent Jones	.30	.14	.04
☐ 432 Todd Kelly	.15	.07	.02
☐ 433 Amp Lee	.15	.07	.02
☐ 434 Tim McDonald	.15	.07	.02
☐ 435 Guy McIntyre	.15	.07	.02
☐ 436 Tom Rathman	.15	.07	.02
☐ 437 Jerry Rice	3.00	1.35	.35
☐ 438 Bill Romanowski	.15	.07	.02
☐ 439 Dana Stubblefield	.50	.23	.06
☐ 440 John Taylor	.30	.14	.04
☐ 441 Steve Wallace	.15	.07	.02
☐ 442 Michael Walter	.15	.07	.02
☐ 443 Ricky Watters	.50	.23	.06
☐ 444 Steve Young	2.50	1.10	.30
☐ 445 Robert Blackmon	.15	.07	.02
☐ 446 Brian Blades	.30	.14	.04
☐ 447 Jeff Bryant	.15	.07	.02
☐ 448 Ferrell Edmunds	.15	.07	.02
☐ 449 Carlton Gray	.15	.07	.02
☐ 450 Dwayne Harper	.15	.07	.02
☐ 451 Andy Heck	.15	.07	.02
☐ 452 Tommy Kane	.15	.07	.02
☐ 453 Cortez Kennedy	.30	.14	.04
☐ 454 Kelvin Martin	.15	.07	.02
☐ 455 Dan McGwire	.15	.07	.02
☐ 456 Rick Mirer	3.00	1.35	.35
☐ 457 Rufus Porter	.15	.07	.02
☐ 458 Ray Roberts	.15	.07	.02
☐ 459 Eugene Robinson	.15	.07	.02
☐ 460 Chris Warren	.30	.14	.04
☐ 461 John L. Williams	.15	.07	.02
☐ 462 Gary Anderson RB	.15	.07	.02
☐ 463 Tyji Armstrong	.15	.07	.02
☐ 464 Reggie Cobb	.15	.07	.02
☐ 465 Eric Curry	.15	.07	.02
☐ 466 Lawrence Dawsey	.15	.07	.02
☐ 467 Steve DeBerg	.15	.07	.02
☐ 468 Santana Dotson	.30	.14	.04
☐ 469 Demetrius DuBose	.15	.07	.02
☐ 470 Paul Gruber	.15	.07	.02
☐ 471 Ron Hall	.15	.07	.02
☐ 472 Courtney Hawkins	.15	.07	.02
☐ 473 Hardy Nickerson	.30	.14	.04
☐ 474 Ricky Reynolds	.15	.07	.02
☐ 475 Broderick Thomas	.15	.07	.02
☐ 476 Mark Wheeler	.15	.07	.02
☐ 477 Jimmy Williams	.15	.07	.02
☐ 478 Carl Banks	.15	.07	.02
☐ 479 Reggie Brooks	.30	.14	.04
☐ 480 Earnest Byner	.15	.07	.02
☐ 481 Tom Carter	.30	.14	.04
☐ 482 Andre Collins	.15	.07	.02
☐ 483 Brad Edwards	.15	.07	.02
☐ 484 Ricky Ervins	.15	.07	.02
☐ 485 Kurt Gouveia	.15	.07	.02
☐ 486 Darrell Green	.15	.07	.02
☐ 487 Desmond Howard	.30	.14	.04
☐ 488 Jim Lachey	.15	.07	.02
☐ 489 Chip Lohmiller	.15	.07	.02
☐ 490 Charles Mann	.15	.07	.02
☐ 491 Tim McGee	.15	.07	.02
☐ 492 Brian Mitchell	.30	.14	.04
☐ 493 Art Monk	.30	.14	.04
☐ 494 Mark Rypien	.15	.07	.02
☐ 495 Ricky Sanders	.15	.07	.02
☐ 496 Checklist 1-126 Chip Lohmiller	.15	.07	.02
☐ 497 Checklist 127-254 Ricky Proehl	.15	.07	.02
☐ 498 Checklist 255-382 Randall Cunningham	.15	.07	.02
☐ 499 Checklist 383-500 Dave Meggett	.15	.07	.02
☐ 500 Inserts Checklist William Perry	.15	.07	.02

1993 Ultra All-Rookies

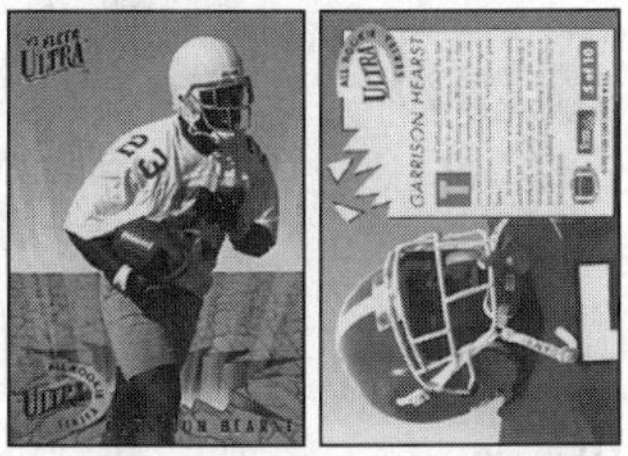

The 1993 Ultra All-Rookies set comprises 10 standard-size cards, randomly inserted in Ultra 14 and 19-card foil packs. The set spotlights first-year NFL players. The full-bleed fronts feature action player cut-outs on bright orange scorched-earth backgrounds. Stamped in gold-foil at the bottom of the picture is the set title and the player's name. The horizontal back displays a background of orange fading to yellow with a close-up player cut-out on the left side, and a white panel containing the player's name and highlights on the right. The cards are arranged in alphabetical order and are numbered on the back "X of 10."

	MINT	NRMT	EXC
COMPLETE SET (10)	75.00	34.00	9.50
COMMON CARD (1-10)	2.00	.90	.25
☐ 1 Patrick Bates	2.00	.90	.25
☐ 2 Jerome Bettis	15.00	6.75	1.85
☐ 3 Drew Bledsoe	25.00	11.00	3.10
☐ 4 Curtis Conway	8.00	3.60	1.00
☐ 5 Garrison Hearst	10.00	4.50	1.25
☐ 6 Qadry Ismail	4.00	1.80	.50
☐ 7 Marvin Jones	2.00	.90	.25
☐ 8 Glyn Milburn	4.00	1.80	.50
☐ 9 Rick Mirer	10.00	4.50	1.25
☐ 10 Kevin Williams	4.00	1.80	.50

1993 Ultra Award Winners

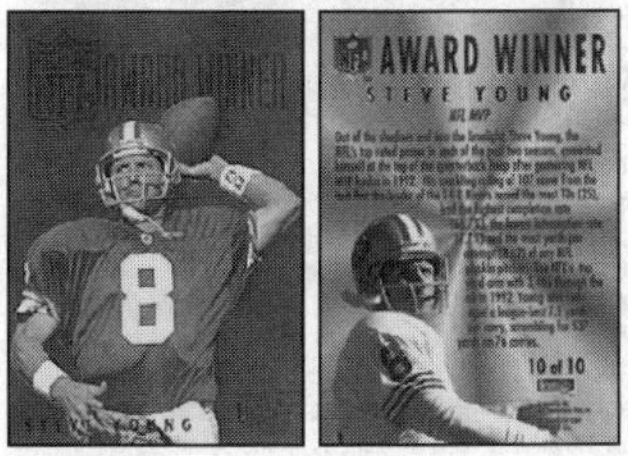

The 1993 Ultra Award Winners set comprises ten standard size cards, randomly inserted in Fleer Ultra 14- and 19-card foil packs. The set spotlights MVP's of the AFC and NFC, Rookies of the Year and other awards. The borderless fronts feature close-up posed or action player cut-outs on gold metallic backgrounds. The set title appears at the top, with the player's name printed across the bottom. The back sports a player cut-out on a gold metallic background with light gold rays radiating from the center. The set title and player's name are stamped in silver foil at the top followed by the player's 1992 award and career highlights. The cards are arranged in alphabetical order and numbered on the back "X of 10."

	MINT	NRMT	EXC
COMPLETE SET (10)	75.00	34.00	9.50
COMMON CARD (1-10)	4.00	1.80	.50
☐ 1 Troy Aikman	30.00	13.50	3.70
☐ 2 Dale Carter	4.00	1.80	.50
☐ 3 Chris Doleman	4.00	1.80	.50
☐ 4 Santana Dotson	4.00	1.80	.50
☐ 5 Barry Foster	6.00	2.70	.75
☐ 6 Jason Hanson	4.00	1.80	.50
☐ 7 Cortez Kennedy	6.00	2.70	.75
☐ 8 Carl Pickens	10.00	4.50	1.25
☐ 9 Steve Tasker	4.00	1.80	.50
☐ 10 Steve Young	20.00	9.00	2.50

1993 Ultra Michael Irvin

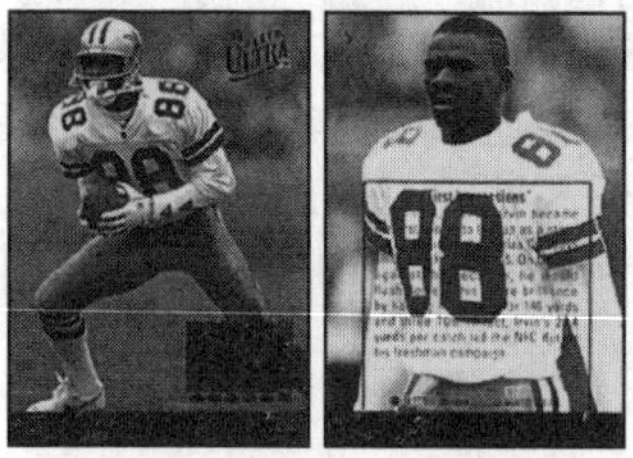

Subtitled Performance Highlights and randomly inserted in 1993 Fleer packs at a rate of one in 12, these ten standard-size cards feature on their fronts color action shots of Irvin that are borderless, except at the bottom, where the card is edged with a black marbleized stripe that carries the set's subtitle in silver-foil lettering. The set's logo appears in one corner. The back carries a color photo of Irvin, which is again bordered only on the bottom by a black marbleized stripe. Career highlights appear in silver-foil lettering within a blue-screened panel framed by a silver-foil line.

	MINT	NRMT	EXC
COMPLETE SET (10)	10.00	4.50	1.25
COMMON M.IRVIN (1-10)	1.25	.55	.16
COMMON SEND-OFF (11-12)	2.00	.90	.25
☐ 1 Michael Irvin The New Wave	1.25	.55	.16
☐ 2 Michael Irvin Eye of the Hurricane	1.25	.55	.16
☐ 3 Michael Irvin Dallas Delight	1.25	.55	.16
☐ 4 Michael Irvin Passing the Torch	1.25	.55	.16
☐ 5 Michael Irvin First Impressions	1.25	.55	.16
☐ 6 Michael Irvin Setback	1.25	.55	.16
☐ 7 Michael Irvin The Comeback Trail	1.25	.55	.16
☐ 8 Michael Irvin The Playmaker	1.25	.55	.16
☐ 9 Michael Irvin The Big Time	1.25	.55	.16
☐ 10 Michael Irvin All the Way	1.25	.55	.16
☐ 11 Michael Irvin	2.00	.90	.25
☐ 12 Michael Irvin	2.00	.90	.25
☐ AU Michael Irvin AUTO Certified Autograph	80.00	36.00	10.00

1993 Ultra League Leaders

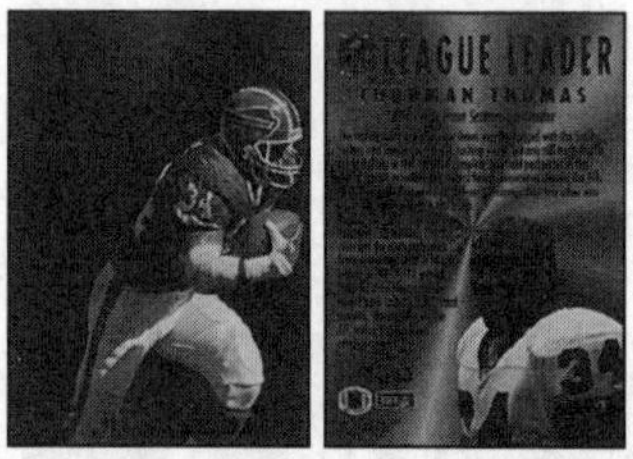

The 1993 Ultra League Leaders set comprises ten standard size cards, randomly inserted in Ultra 14 and 19-card foil packs. The set spotlights players who led their respective conferences in specific defensive or offensive categories. The borderless fronts feature close-up posed or action player cut-outs on silver metallic backgrounds. The set title appears at the top, with the player's name printed across the bottom. The back sports a player cut-out on a silver metallic background with light silver rays radiating from the center. The set title and player's name are stamped in silver foil at the top, followed by the category the player led in the 1992 season, and career highlights. The cards are arranged in alphabetical order and numbered on the back "X of 10."

	MINT	NRMT	EXC
COMPLETE SET (10)	100.00	45.00	12.50
COMMON CARD (1-10)	4.00	1.80	.50
☐ 1 Haywood Jeffires	6.00	2.70	.75
☐ 2 Henry Jones	4.00	1.80	.50
☐ 3 Audray McMillian	4.00	1.80	.50
☐ 4 Warren Moon	6.00	2.70	.75
☐ 5 Leslie O'Neal	4.00	1.80	.50
☐ 6 Deion Sanders	16.00	7.25	2.00
☐ 7 Sterling Sharpe	8.00	3.60	1.00
☐ 8 Clyde Simmons	4.00	1.80	.50
☐ 9 Emmitt Smith	50.00	22.00	6.25
☐ 10 Thurman Thomas	8.00	3.60	1.00

1993 Ultra Stars

The 1993 Ultra Stars set comprises ten standard-size cards, randomly inserted exclusively in Ultra 19-card jumbo packs. The set spotlights outstanding NFL players. The fronts feature close-up action player cut-outs superposed upon a ghosted U.S. flag and black-and-white background. Except for the gray marbleized stripe edging the bottom,

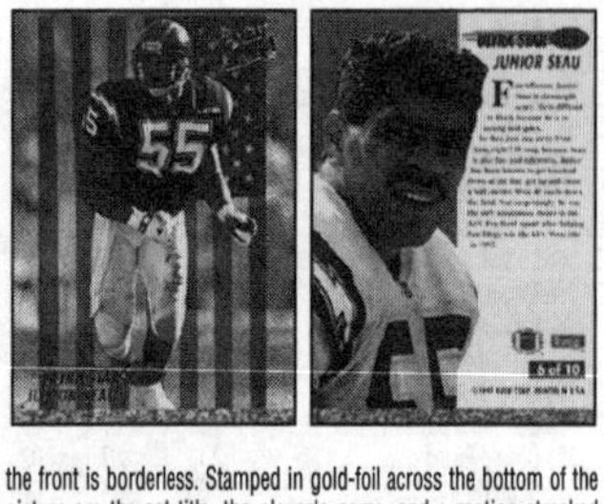

the front is borderless. Stamped in gold-foil across the bottom of the picture are the set title, the player's name, and a motion-streaked football icon. The back sports a close-up player cutout on one side, and career highlights on the other. The cards are arranged in alphabetical order.

	MINT	NRMT	EXC
COMPLETE SET (10)	120.00	55.00	15.00
COMMON CARD (1-10)	7.00	3.10	.85
☐ 1 Brett Favre	50.00	22.00	6.25
☐ 2 Barry Foster	7.00	3.10	.85
☐ 3 Michael Irvin	12.00	5.50	1.50
☐ 4 Cortez Kennedy	7.00	3.10	.85
☐ 5 Deion Sanders	20.00	9.00	2.50
☐ 6 Junior Seau	10.00	4.50	1.25
☐ 7 Derrick Thomas	10.00	4.50	1.25
☐ 8 Ricky Watters	10.00	4.50	1.25
☐ 9 Reggie White	12.00	5.50	1.50
☐ 10 Steve Young	25.00	11.00	3.10

1993 Ultra Touchdown Kings

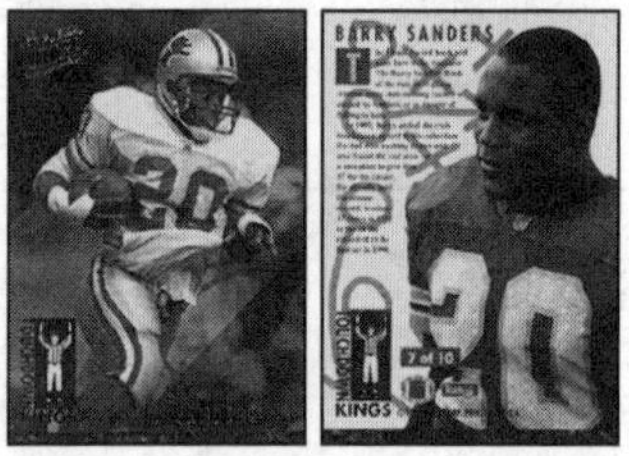

The 1993 Ultra Touchdown Kings set comprises ten standard-size cards, randomly inserted exclusively in Ultra 14 and 19-card packs. The set spotlights the NFL's best offensive players. The fronts feature a close-up action player cutout superposed upon a ghosted design of a football field and play diagrams. Stamped in gold foil across the bottom of the picture are the set title and the player's name. Except for a green marbleized lower edge, the front is borderless. The white back sports a close-up player cutout on a background of play diagrams, and includes the player's career highlights. The cards are arranged in alphabetical order.

	MINT	NRMT	EXC
COMPLETE SET (10)	80.00	36.00	10.00
COMMON CARD (1-10)	2.00	.90	.25
☐ 1 Rodney Hampton	4.00	1.80	.50
☐ 2 Dan Marino	20.00	9.00	2.50
☐ 3 Art Monk	2.00	.90	.25
☐ 4 Joe Montana	12.00	5.50	1.50
☐ 5 Jerry Rice	12.00	5.50	1.50
☐ 6 Andre Rison	2.00	.90	.25
☐ 7 Barry Sanders	12.00	5.50	1.50
☐ 8 Sterling Sharpe	4.00	1.80	.50
☐ 9 Emmitt Smith	20.00	9.00	2.50
☐ 10 Thurman Thomas	5.00	2.20	.60

1994 Ultra

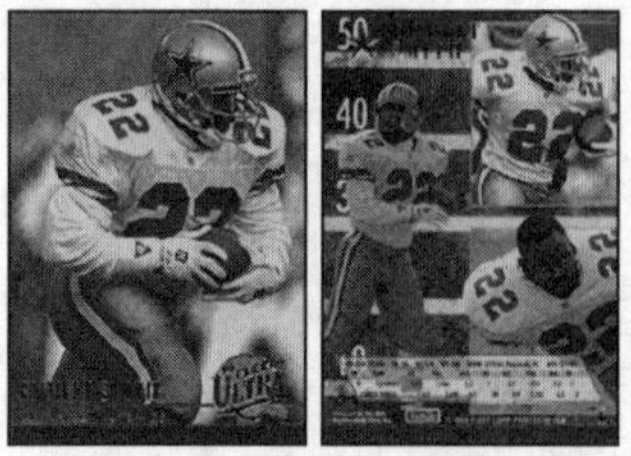

Cards from this 525-card standard size set were issued in two series of 325 and 200. Cards were issued in 14, 17, and 20-card packs. Card fronts have full-bleed photos with the player's name, team, position and a helmet in gold foil at the bottom. The backs have three photos and statistics. The cards are grouped alphabetically within teams, and checklisted below alphabetically according to teams. Rookie Cards include Derrick Alexander, Mario Bates, Isaac Bruce, Lake Dawson, Trent Dilfer, Bert Emanuel, Marshall Faulk, William Floyd, Greg Hill, Charles Johnson, Bam Morris, Errict Rhett, Darnay Scott and Heath Shuler.

	MINT	NRMT	EXC
COMPLETE SET (525)	50.00	22.00	6.25
COMPLETE SERIES 1 (325)	30.00	13.50	3.70
COMPLETE SERIES 2 (200)	20.00	9.00	2.50
COMMON CARD (1-525)	.10	.05	.01
☐ 1 Steve Beuerlein	.10	.05	.01
☐ 2 Gary Clark	.20	.09	.03
☐ 3 Randal Hill	.10	.05	.01
☐ 4 Seth Joyner	.10	.05	.01
☐ 5 Jamir Miller	.10	.05	.01
☐ 6 Ronald Moore	.10	.05	.01
☐ 7 Luis Sharpe	.10	.05	.01
☐ 8 Clyde Simmons	.10	.05	.01
☐ 9 Eric Swann	.20	.09	.03
☐ 10 Aeneas Williams	.10	.05	.01
☐ 11 Chris Doleman	.10	.05	.01
☐ 12 Bert Emanuel	1.50	.70	.19
☐ 13 Moe Gardner	.10	.05	.01
☐ 14 Jeff George	.30	.14	.04
☐ 15 Roger Harper	.10	.05	.01
☐ 16 Pierce Holt	.10	.05	.01
☐ 17 Lincoln Kennedy	.10	.05	.01
☐ 18 Erric Pegram	.10	.05	.01
☐ 19 Andre Rison	.20	.09	.03
☐ 20 Deion Sanders	1.00	.45	.12
☐ 21 Jessie Tuggle	.10	.05	.01
☐ 22 Cornelius Bennett	.20	.09	.03
☐ 23 Bill Brooks	.10	.05	.01
☐ 24 Jeff Burris	.20	.09	.03
☐ 25 Kent Hull	.10	.05	.01
☐ 26 Henry Jones	.10	.05	.01
☐ 27 Jim Kelly	.30	.14	.04
☐ 28 Marvcus Patton	.10	.05	.01
☐ 29 Andre Reed	.20	.09	.03
☐ 30 Bruce Smith	.30	.14	.04
☐ 31 Thomas Smith	.10	.05	.01
☐ 32 Thurman Thomas	.30	.14	.04
☐ 33 Jeff Wright	.10	.05	.01
☐ 34 Trace Armstrong	.10	.05	.01
☐ 35 Mark Carrier DB	.10	.05	.01
☐ 36 Dante Jones	.10	.05	.01
☐ 37 Erik Kramer	.20	.09	.03
☐ 38 Terry Obee	.10	.05	.01
☐ 39 Alonzo Spellman	.10	.05	.01
☐ 40 John Thierry	.10	.05	.01
☐ 41 Tom Waddle	.10	.05	.01
☐ 42 Donnell Woolford	.10	.05	.01
☐ 43 Tim Worley	.10	.05	.01
☐ 44 Chris Zorich	.10	.05	.01
☐ 45 John Copeland	.10	.05	.01
☐ 46 Harold Green	.10	.05	.01
☐ 47 David Klingler	.10	.05	.01
☐ 48 Ricardo McDonald	.10	.05	.01
☐ 49 Tony McGee	.10	.05	.01
☐ 50 Louis Oliver	.10	.05	.01
☐ 51 Carl Pickens	1.00	.45	.12
☐ 52 Darnay Scott	2.50	1.10	.30
☐ 53 Steve Tovar	.10	.05	.01
☐ 54 Dan Wilkinson	.20	.09	.03
☐ 55 Darryl Williams	.10	.05	.01
☐ 56 Derrick Alexander WR	.30	.14	.04
☐ 57 Michael Jackson	.20	.09	.03
☐ 58 Tony Jones	.10	.05	.01
☐ 59 Antonio Langham	.20	.09	.03
☐ 60 Eric Metcalf	.20	.09	.03
☐ 61 Stevon Moore	.10	.05	.01
☐ 62 Michael Dean Perry	.20	.09	.03
☐ 63 Anthony Pleasant	.10	.05	.01
☐ 64 Vinny Testaverde	.20	.09	.03
☐ 65 Eric Turner	.10	.05	.01
☐ 66 Tommy Vardell	.10	.05	.01
☐ 67 Troy Aikman	2.00	.90	.25
☐ 68 Larry Brown DB	.10	.05	.01
☐ 69 Shante Carver	.10	.05	.01
☐ 70 Charles Haley	.20	.09	.03
☐ 71 Michael Irvin	.30	.14	.04
☐ 72 Leon Lett	.10	.05	.01
☐ 73 Nate Newton	.10	.05	.01
☐ 74 Jay Novacek	.20	.09	.03
☐ 75 Darrin Smith	.10	.05	.01
☐ 76 Emmitt Smith	4.00	1.80	.50
☐ 77 Tony Tolbert	.10	.05	.01
☐ 78 Erik Williams	.10	.05	.01
☐ 79 Kevin Williams WR	.20	.09	.03
☐ 80 Steve Atwater	.10	.05	.01
☐ 81 Rod Bernstine	.10	.05	.01
☐ 82 Ray Crockett	.10	.05	.01
☐ 83 Mike Croel	.10	.05	.01
☐ 84 Shane Dronett	.10	.05	.01
☐ 85 Jason Elam	.10	.05	.01
☐ 86 John Elway	1.25	.55	.16
☐ 87 Simon Fletcher	.10	.05	.01
☐ 88 Glyn Milburn	.20	.09	.03
☐ 89 Anthony Miller	.20	.09	.03
☐ 90 Shannon Sharpe	.20	.09	.03
☐ 91 Gary Zimmerman	.10	.05	.01
☐ 92 Bennie Blades	.10	.05	.01
☐ 93 Lomas Brown	.10	.05	.01
☐ 94 Mel Gray	.10	.05	.01
☐ 95 Jason Hanson	.10	.05	.01
☐ 96 Ryan McNeil	.10	.05	.01
☐ 97 Scott Mitchell	.30	.14	.04
☐ 98 Herman Moore	.75	.35	.09
☐ 99 Johnnie Morton	.75	.35	.09
☐ 100 Robert Porcher	.10	.05	.01
☐ 101 Barry Sanders	2.00	.90	.25
☐ 102 Chris Spielman	.20	.09	.03
☐ 103 Pat Swilling	.10	.05	.01
☐ 104 Edgar Bennett	.30	.14	.04
☐ 105 Terrell Buckley	.10	.05	.01
☐ 106 Reggie Cobb	.10	.05	.01
☐ 107 Brett Favre	4.00	1.80	.50
☐ 108 Sean Jones	.10	.05	.01
☐ 109 Ken Ruettgers	.10	.05	.01
☐ 110 Sterling Sharpe	.20	.09	.03
☐ 111 Wayne Simmons	.10	.05	.01
☐ 112 Aaron Taylor	.10	.05	.01
☐ 113 George Teague	.10	.05	.01
☐ 114 Reggie White	.30	.14	.04
☐ 115 Micheal Barrow	.10	.05	.01
☐ 116 Gary Brown	.10	.05	.01
☐ 117 Cody Carlson	.10	.05	.01
☐ 118 Ray Childress	.10	.05	.01
☐ 119 Cris Dishman	.10	.05	.01
☐ 120 Henry Ford	.10	.05	.01
☐ 121 Haywood Jeffires	.20	.09	.03
☐ 122 Bruce Matthews	.10	.05	.01
☐ 123 Bubba McDowell	.10	.05	.01
☐ 124 Marcus Robertson	.10	.05	.01
☐ 125 Eddie Robinson	.10	.05	.01
☐ 126 Webster Slaughter	.10	.05	.01
☐ 127 Trev Alberts	.20	.09	.03
☐ 128 Tony Bennett	.10	.05	.01
☐ 129 Ray Buchanan	.10	.05	.01
☐ 130 Quentin Coryatt	.10	.05	.01
☐ 131 Eugene Daniel	.10	.05	.01
☐ 132 Steve Emtman	.10	.05	.01
☐ 133 Marshall Faulk	4.00	1.80	.50
☐ 134 Jim Harbaugh	.30	.14	.04
☐ 135 Roosevelt Potts	.10	.05	.01
☐ 136 Rohn Stark	.10	.05	.01
☐ 137 Marcus Allen	.30	.14	.04
☐ 138 Donnell Bennett	.10	.05	.01
☐ 139 Dale Carter	.10	.05	.01
☐ 140 Tony Casillas	.10	.05	.01
☐ 141 Mark Collins	.10	.05	.01
☐ 142 Willie Davis	.20	.09	.03
☐ 143 Tim Grunhard	.10	.05	.01
☐ 144 Greg Hill	1.00	.45	.12
☐ 145 Joe Montana	2.00	.90	.25
☐ 146 Tracy Simien	.10	.05	.01
☐ 147 Neil Smith	.30	.14	.04
☐ 148 Derrick Thomas	.30	.14	.04
☐ 149 Tim Brown	.30	.14	.04
☐ 150 James Folston	.10	.05	.01
☐ 151 Rob Fredrickson	.20	.09	.03
☐ 152 Jeff Hostetler	.20	.09	.03
☐ 153 Rocket Ismail	.20	.09	.03
☐ 154 James Jett	.10	.05	.01
☐ 155 Terry McDaniel	.10	.05	.01
☐ 156 Winston Moss	.10	.05	.01
☐ 157 Greg Robinson	.10	.05	.01
☐ 158 Anthony Smith	.10	.05	.01
☐ 159 Steve Wisniewski	.10	.05	.01
☐ 160 Flipper Anderson	.10	.05	.01
☐ 161 Jerome Bettis	1.00	.45	.12
☐ 162 Isaac Bruce	4.00	1.80	.50
☐ 163 Shane Conlan	.10	.05	.01
☐ 164 Wayne Gandy	.10	.05	.01
☐ 165 Sean Gilbert	.10	.05	.01
☐ 166 Todd Lyght	.10	.05	.01
☐ 167 Chris Miller	.10	.05	.01
☐ 168 Anthony Newman	.10	.05	.01
☐ 169 Roman Phifer	.10	.05	.01
☐ 170 Jackie Slater	.10	.05	.01
☐ 171 Gene Atkins	.10	.05	.01
☐ 172 Aubrey Beavers	.10	.05	.01
☐ 173 Tim Bowens	.20	.09	.03
☐ 174 J.B. Brown	.10	.05	.01
☐ 175 Marco Coleman	.10	.05	.01
☐ 176 Bryan Cox	.10	.05	.01
☐ 177 Irving Fryar	.20	.09	.03
☐ 178 Terry Kirby	.30	.14	.04
☐ 179 Dan Marino	4.00	1.80	.50
☐ 180 Troy Vincent	.10	.05	.01
☐ 181 Richmond Webb	.10	.05	.01
☐ 182 Terry Allen	.20	.09	.03
☐ 183 Cris Carter	.30	.14	.04
☐ 184 Jack Del Rio	.10	.05	.01
☐ 185 Vencie Glenn	.10	.05	.01
☐ 186 Randall McDaniel	.10	.05	.01
☐ 187 Warren Moon	.30	.14	.04
☐ 188 David Palmer	.20	.09	.03
☐ 189 John Randle	.10	.05	.01
☐ 190 Todd Scott	.10	.05	.01
☐ 191 Todd Steussie	.20	.09	.03
☐ 192 Henry Thomas	.10	.05	.01
☐ 193 Dewayne Washington	.20	.09	.03
☐ 194 Bruce Armstrong	.10	.05	.01
☐ 195 Harlon Barnett	.10	.05	.01
☐ 196 Drew Bledsoe	2.00	.90	.25
☐ 197 Vincent Brisby	.30	.14	.04
☐ 198 Vincent Brown	.10	.05	.01
☐ 199 Marion Butts	.10	.05	.01
☐ 200 Ben Coates	.30	.14	.04
☐ 201 Todd Collins	.10	.05	.01
☐ 202 Maurice Hurst	.10	.05	.01
☐ 203 Willie McGinest	.30	.14	.04
☐ 204 Ricky Reynolds	.10	.05	.01
☐ 205 Chris Slade	.10	.05	.01
☐ 206 Mario Bates	.75	.35	.09
☐ 207 Derek Brown RB	.10	.05	.01
☐ 208 Vince Buck	.10	.05	.01

☐ 209 Quinn Early	.20	.09	.03
☐ 210 Jim Everett	.20	.09	.03
☐ 211 Michael Haynes	.20	.09	.03
☐ 212 Tyrone Hughes	.20	.09	.03
☐ 213 Joe Johnson	.10	.05	.01
☐ 214 Vaughan Johnson	.10	.05	.01
☐ 215 Willie Roaf	.10	.05	.01
☐ 216 Renaldo Turnbull	.10	.05	.01
☐ 217 Michael Brooks	.10	.05	.01
☐ 218 Dave Brown	.20	.09	.03
☐ 219 Howard Cross	.10	.05	.01
☐ 220 Stacey Dillard	.10	.05	.01
☐ 221 Jumbo Elliott	.10	.05	.01
☐ 222 Keith Hamilton	.10	.05	.01
☐ 223 Rodney Hampton	.30	.14	.04
☐ 224 Thomas Lewis	.20	.09	.03
☐ 225 Dave Meggett	.10	.05	.01
☐ 226 Corey Miller	.10	.05	.01
☐ 227 Thomas Randolph	.10	.05	.01
☐ 228 Mike Sherrard	.10	.05	.01
☐ 229 Kyle Clifton	.10	.05	.01
☐ 230 Boomer Esiason	.20	.09	.03
☐ 231 Aaron Glenn	.20	.09	.03
☐ 232 James Hasty	.10	.05	.01
☐ 233 Bobby Houston	.10	.05	.01
☐ 234 Johnny Johnson	.10	.05	.01
☐ 235 Mo Lewis	.10	.05	.01
☐ 236 Ronnie Lott	.20	.09	.03
☐ 237 Rob Moore	.20	.09	.03
☐ 238 Marvin Washington	.10	.05	.01
☐ 239 Ryan Yarborough	.10	.05	.01
☐ 240 Eric Allen	.10	.05	.01
☐ 241 Victor Bailey	.10	.05	.01
☐ 242 Fred Barnett	.20	.09	.03
☐ 243 Mark Bavaro	.10	.05	.01
☐ 244 Randall Cunningham	.20	.09	.03
☐ 245 Byron Evans	.10	.05	.01
☐ 246 William Fuller	.10	.05	.01
☐ 247 Andy Harmon	.10	.05	.01
☐ 248 William Perry	.20	.09	.03
☐ 249 Herschel Walker	.20	.09	.03
☐ 250 Bernard Williams	.10	.05	.01
☐ 251 Dermontti Dawson	.10	.05	.01
☐ 252 Deon Figures	.10	.05	.01
☐ 253 Barry Foster	.10	.05	.01
☐ 254 Kevin Greene	.30	.14	.04
☐ 255 Charles Johnson	.75	.35	.09
☐ 256 Levon Kirkland	.10	.05	.01
☐ 257 Greg Lloyd	.30	.14	.04
☐ 258 Neil O'Donnell	.30	.14	.04
☐ 259 Darren Perry	.10	.05	.01
☐ 260 Dwight Stone	.10	.05	.01
☐ 261 Rod Woodson	.30	.14	.04
☐ 262 John Carney	.10	.05	.01
☐ 263 Issac Davis	.10	.05	.01
☐ 264 Courtney Hall	.10	.05	.01
☐ 265 Ronnie Harmon	.10	.05	.01
☐ 266 Stan Humphries	.30	.14	.04
☐ 267 Vance Johnson	.10	.05	.01
☐ 268 Natrone Means	.75	.35	.09
☐ 269 Chris Mims	.10	.05	.01
☐ 270 Leslie O'Neal	.10	.05	.01
☐ 271 Stanley Richard	.10	.05	.01
☐ 272 Junior Seau	.30	.14	.04
☐ 273 Harris Barton	.10	.05	.01
☐ 274 Dennis Brown	.10	.05	.01
☐ 275 Eric Davis	.10	.05	.01
☐ 276 William Floyd	1.50	.70	.19
☐ 277 John Johnson	.10	.05	.01
☐ 278 Tim McDonald	.10	.05	.01
☐ 279 Ken Norton Jr.	.20	.09	.03
☐ 280 Jerry Rice	2.00	.90	.25
☐ 281 Jesse Sapolu	.10	.05	.01
☐ 282 Dana Stubblefield	.30	.14	.04
☐ 283 Ricky Watters	.30	.14	.04
☐ 284 Bryant Young	.75	.35	.09
☐ 285 Steve Young	1.25	.55	.16
☐ 286 Sam Adams	.20	.09	.03
☐ 287 Brian Blades	.20	.09	.03
☐ 288 Ferrell Edmunds	.10	.05	.01
☐ 289 Patrick Hunter	.10	.05	.01
☐ 290 Cortez Kennedy	.20	.09	.03
☐ 291 Rick Mirer	.30	.14	.04
☐ 292 Nate Odomes	.10	.05	.01
☐ 293 Ray Roberts	.10	.05	.01
☐ 294 Eugene Robinson	.10	.05	.01
☐ 295 Rod Stephens	.10	.05	.01
☐ 296 Chris Warren	.20	.09	.03
☐ 297 Marty Carter	.10	.05	.01
☐ 298 Horace Copeland	.10	.05	.01
☐ 299 Eric Curry	.10	.05	.01
☐ 300 Santana Dotson	.20	.09	.03
☐ 301 Craig Erickson	.10	.05	.01
☐ 302 Paul Gruber	.10	.05	.01
☐ 303 Courtney Hawkins	.10	.05	.01
☐ 304 Martin Mayhew	.10	.05	.01
☐ 305 Hardy Nickerson	.20	.09	.03
☐ 306 Errict Rhett	2.00	.90	.25
☐ 307 Vince Workman	.10	.05	.01
☐ 308 Reggie Brooks	.20	.09	.03
☐ 309 Tom Carter	.10	.05	.01
☐ 310 Andre Collins	.10	.05	.01
☐ 311 Brad Edwards	.10	.05	.01
☐ 312 Kurt Gouveia	.10	.05	.01
☐ 313 Darrell Green	.10	.05	.01
☐ 314 Ethan Horton	.10	.05	.01
☐ 315 Desmond Howard	.20	.09	.03
☐ 316 Tre Johnson	.10	.05	.01
☐ 317 Sterling Palmer	.10	.05	.01
☐ 318 Heath Shuler	1.50	.70	.19
☐ 319 Tyronne Stowe	.10	.05	.01
☐ 320 NFL 75th Anniversary	.10	.05	.01
☐ 321 Checklist	.10	.05	.01
☐ 322 Checklist	.10	.05	.01
☐ 323 Checklist	.10	.05	.01
☐ 324 Checklist	.10	.05	.01
☐ 325 Checklist	.10	.05	.01
☐ 326 Garrison Hearst	.75	.35	.09
☐ 327 Eric Hill	.10	.05	.01
☐ 328 Seth Joyner	.10	.05	.01
☐ 329 Jim McMahon	.10	.05	.01
☐ 330 Jamir Miller	.10	.05	.01
☐ 331 Ricky Proehl	.10	.05	.01
☐ 332 Clyde Simmons	.10	.05	.01
☐ 333 Chris Doleman	.10	.05	.01
☐ 334 Bert Emanuel	.60	.25	.07
☐ 335 Jeff George	.30	.14	.04
☐ 336 D.J. Johnson	.10	.05	.01
☐ 337 Terance Mathis	.20	.09	.03
☐ 338 Clay Matthews	.10	.05	.01
☐ 339 Tony Smith	.10	.05	.01
☐ 340 Don Beebe	.10	.05	.01
☐ 341 Bucky Brooks	.10	.05	.01
☐ 342 Jeff Burris	.20	.09	.03
☐ 343 Kenneth Davis	.10	.05	.01
☐ 344 Phil Hansen	.10	.05	.01
☐ 345 Pete Metzelaars	.10	.05	.01
☐ 346 Darryl Talley	.10	.05	.01
☐ 347 Joe Cain	.10	.05	.01
☐ 348 Curtis Conway	.30	.14	.04
☐ 349 Shaun Gayle	.10	.05	.01
☐ 350 Chris Gedney	.10	.05	.01
☐ 351 Erik Kramer	.20	.09	.03
☐ 352 Vinson Smith	.10	.05	.01
☐ 353 John Thierry	.10	.05	.01
☐ 354 Lewis Tillman	.10	.05	.01
☐ 355 Mike Brim	.10	.05	.01
☐ 356 Derrick Fenner	.10	.05	.01
☐ 357 James Francis	.10	.05	.01
☐ 358 Louis Oliver	.10	.05	.01
☐ 359 Darnay Scott	1.00	.45	.12
☐ 360 Dan Wilkinson	.20	.09	.03
☐ 361 Alfred Williams	.10	.05	.01
☐ 362 Derrick Alexander WR	.30	.14	.04
☐ 363 Rob Burnett	.10	.05	.01
☐ 364 Mark Carrier WR	.20	.09	.03
☐ 365 Steve Everitt	.10	.05	.01
☐ 366 Leroy Hoard	.10	.05	.01
☐ 367 Pepper Johnson	.10	.05	.01
☐ 368 Antonio Langham	.20	.09	.03
☐ 369 Shante Carver	.10	.05	.01
☐ 370 Alvin Harper	.20	.09	.03
☐ 371 Daryl Johnston	.20	.09	.03
☐ 372 Russell Maryland	.10	.05	.01
☐ 373 Kevin Smith	.10	.05	.01
☐ 374 Mark Stepnoski	.10	.05	.01
☐ 375 Darren Woodson	.20	.09	.03
☐ 376 Allen Aldridge	.10	.05	.01
☐ 377 Ray Crockett	.10	.05	.01
☐ 378 Karl Mecklenburg	.10	.05	.01
☐ 379 Anthony Miller	.20	.09	.03
☐ 380 Mike Pritchard	.10	.05	.01
☐ 381 Leonard Russell	.10	.05	.01
☐ 382 Dennis Smith	.10	.05	.01
☐ 383 Anthony Carter	.20	.09	.03
☐ 384 Van Malone	.10	.05	.01
☐ 385 Robert Massey	.10	.05	.01
☐ 386 Scott Mitchell	.30	.14	.04
☐ 387 Johnnie Morton	.30	.14	.04
☐ 388 Brett Perriman	.20	.09	.03
☐ 389 Tracy Scroggins	.10	.05	.01
☐ 390 Robert Brooks	.60	.25	.07
☐ 391 LeRoy Butler	.10	.05	.01
☐ 392 Reggie Cobb	.10	.05	.01
☐ 393 Sean Jones	.10	.05	.01
☐ 394 George Koonce	.10	.05	.01
☐ 395 Steve McMichael	.20	.09	.03
☐ 396 Bryce Paup	.30	.14	.04
☐ 397 Aaron Taylor	.10	.05	.01
☐ 398 Henry Ford	.10	.05	.01
☐ 399 Ernest Givins	.20	.09	.03
☐ 400 Jeremy Nunley	.10	.05	.01
☐ 401 Bo Orlando	.10	.05	.01
☐ 402 Al Smith	.10	.05	.01
☐ 403 Barron Wortham	.10	.05	.01
☐ 404 Trev Alberts	.20	.09	.03
☐ 405 Tony Bennett	.10	.05	.01
☐ 406 Kerry Cash	.10	.05	.01
☐ 407 Sean Dawkins	.75	.35	.09
☐ 408 Marshall Faulk	1.50	.70	.19
☐ 409 Jim Harbaugh	.30	.14	.04
☐ 410 Jeff Herrod	.10	.05	.01
☐ 411 Kimble Anders	.20	.09	.03
☐ 412 Donnell Bennett	.10	.05	.01
☐ 413 J.J. Birden	.10	.05	.01
☐ 414 Mark Collins	.10	.05	.01
☐ 415 Lake Dawson	.75	.35	.09
☐ 416 Greg Hill	.30	.14	.04
☐ 417 Charles Mincy	.10	.05	.01
☐ 418 Greg Biekert	.10	.05	.01
☐ 419 Rob Fredrickson	.20	.09	.03
☐ 420 Nolan Harrison	.10	.05	.01
☐ 421 Jeff Jaeger	.10	.05	.01
☐ 422 Albert Lewis	.10	.05	.01
☐ 423 Chester McGlockton	.10	.05	.01
☐ 424 Tom Rathman	.10	.05	.01
☐ 425 Harvey Williams	.20	.09	.03
☐ 426 Isaac Bruce	2.00	.90	.25
☐ 427 Troy Drayton	.10	.05	.01
☐ 428 Wayne Gandy	.10	.05	.01
☐ 429 Fred Stokes	.10	.05	.01
☐ 430 Robert Young	.10	.05	.01
☐ 431 Gene Atkins	.10	.05	.01
☐ 432 Aubrey Beavers	.10	.05	.01
☐ 433 Tim Bowens	.20	.09	.03
☐ 434 Keith Byars	.10	.05	.01
☐ 435 Jeff Cross	.10	.05	.01
☐ 436 Mark Ingram	.10	.05	.01
☐ 437 Keith Jackson	.10	.05	.01
☐ 438 Michael Stewart	.10	.05	.01
☐ 439 Chris Hinton	.10	.05	.01
☐ 440 Qadry Ismail	.30	.14	.04
☐ 441 Carlos Jenkins	.10	.05	.01
☐ 442 Warren Moon	.30	.14	.04
☐ 443 David Palmer	.20	.09	.03
☐ 444 Jake Reed	.20	.09	.03
☐ 445 Robert Smith	.30	.14	.04
☐ 446 Todd Steussie	.20	.09	.03
☐ 447 Dewayne Washington	.20	.09	.03
☐ 448 Marion Butts	.10	.05	.01
☐ 449 Tim Goad	.10	.05	.01
☐ 450 Myron Guyton	.10	.05	.01
☐ 451 Kevin Lee	.10	.05	.01
☐ 452 Willie McGinest	.30	.14	.04
☐ 453 Ricky Reynolds	.10	.05	.01
☐ 454 Michael Timpson	.10	.05	.01
☐ 455 Morten Andersen	.10	.05	.01
☐ 456 Jim Everett	.20	.09	.03
☐ 457 Michael Haynes	.20	.09	.03
☐ 458 Joe Johnson	.10	.05	.01
☐ 459 Wayne Martin	.10	.05	.01
☐ 460 Sam Mills	.10	.05	.01
☐ 461 Irv Smith	.10	.05	.01
☐ 462 Carlton Bailey	.10	.05	.01
☐ 463 Chris Calloway	.10	.05	.01
☐ 464 Mark Jackson	.10	.05	.01
☐ 465 Thomas Lewis	.20	.09	.03
☐ 466 Thomas Randolph	.10	.05	.01
☐ 467 Stevie Anderson	.10	.05	.01
☐ 468 Brad Baxter	.10	.05	.01
☐ 469 Aaron Glenn	.20	.09	.03
☐ 470 Jeff Lageman	.10	.05	.01
☐ 471 Johnny Mitchell	.10	.05	.01
☐ 472 Art Monk	.20	.09	.03
☐ 473 William Fuller	.10	.05	.01
☐ 474 Charlie Garner	.20	.09	.03
☐ 475 Vaughn Hebron	.10	.05	.01
☐ 476 Bill Romanowski	.10	.05	.01
☐ 477 William Thomas	.10	.05	.01
☐ 478 Greg Townsend	.10	.05	.01
☐ 479 Bernard Williams	.10	.05	.01
☐ 480 Calvin Williams	.20	.09	.03
☐ 481 Eric Green	.10	.05	.01
☐ 482 Charles Johnson	.30	.14	.04
☐ 483 Carnell Lake	.10	.05	.01
☐ 484 Byron Bam Morris	.30	.14	.04
☐ 485 John L. Williams	.10	.05	.01
☐ 486 Darren Carrington	.10	.05	.01
☐ 487 Andre Coleman	.10	.05	.01
☐ 488 Isaac Davis	.10	.05	.01
☐ 489 Dwayne Harper	.10	.05	.01
☐ 490 Tony Martin	.30	.14	.04
☐ 491 Mark Seay	.30	.14	.04
☐ 492 Richard Dent	.20	.09	.03
☐ 493 William Floyd	.60	.25	.07
☐ 494 Rickey Jackson	.10	.05	.01
☐ 495 Brent Jones	.20	.09	.03
☐ 496 Ken Norton Jr.	.20	.09	.03
☐ 497 Gary Plummer	.10	.05	.01
☐ 498 Deion Sanders	1.00	.45	.12
☐ 499 John Taylor	.20	.09	.03
☐ 500 Lee Woodall	.10	.05	.01
☐ 501 Bryant Young	.30	.14	.04
☐ 502 Sam Adams	.20	.09	.03
☐ 503 Howard Ballard	.10	.05	.01
☐ 504 Michael Bates	.10	.05	.01
☐ 505 Robert Blackmon	.10	.05	.01
☐ 506 John Kasay	.10	.05	.01
☐ 507 Kelvin Martin	.10	.05	.01
☐ 508 Kevin Mawae	.10	.05	.01
☐ 509 Rufus Porter	.10	.05	.01
☐ 510 Lawrence Dawsey	.10	.05	.01
☐ 511 Trent Dilfer	1.25	.55	.16
☐ 512 Thomas Everett	.10	.05	.01
☐ 513 Jackie Harris	.10	.05	.01
☐ 514 Errict Rhett	.75	.35	.09
☐ 515 Henry Ellard	.20	.09	.03
☐ 516 John Friesz	.20	.09	.03
☐ 517 Ken Harvey	.10	.05	.01
☐ 518 Ethan Horton	.10	.05	.01
☐ 519 Tre Johnson	.10	.05	.01
☐ 520 Jim Lachey	.10	.05	.01
☐ 521 Heath Shuler	.60	.25	.07
☐ 522 Tony Woods	.10	.05	.01
☐ 523 Checklist	.10	.05	.01
☐ 524 Checklist	.10	.05	.01
☐ 525 Checklist	.10	.05	.01

1994 Ultra Achievement Awards

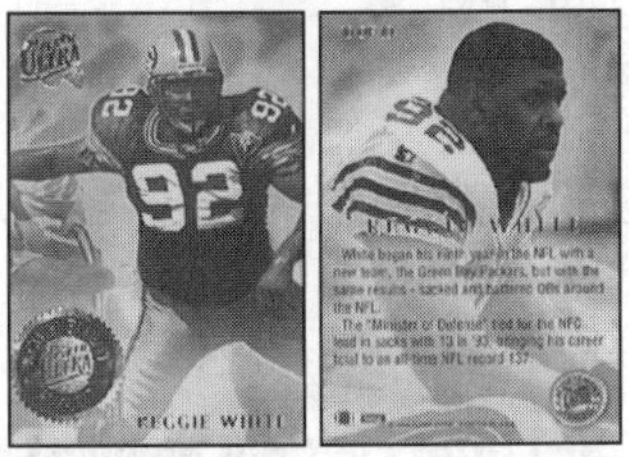

Randomly inserted in packs, this 10-card standard-size set features top players including those homing in on career milestones. Full-bleed fronts have a player photo superimposed over multi-color backgrounds. The player's name and set logo are in gold foil. The card backs have a photo with a similar background and highlights. The set is sequenced in alphabetical order. A jumbo version of this set was issued one set per hobby case. Those cards are valued as a multiple of the cards listed below.

	MINT	NRMT	EXC
COMPLETE SET (10)	12.00	5.50	1.50
COMMON CARD (1-10)	.50	.23	.06
COMPLETE JUMBO SET (10)	30.00	13.50	3.70
*JUMBO CARDS: 1.25X to 2.5X			

☐ 1 Marcus Allen	1.00	.45	.12
☐ 2 John Elway	1.50	.70	.19
☐ 3 Dan Marino	4.00	1.80	.50
☐ 4 Joe Montana	2.00	.90	.25
☐ 5 Jerry Rice	2.00	.90	.25
☐ 6 Barry Sanders	2.00	.90	.25
☐ 7 Sterling Sharpe	.50	.23	.06
☐ 8 Emmitt Smith	4.00	1.80	.50
☐ 9 Thurman Thomas	1.00	.45	.12
☐ 10 Reggie White	.75	.35	.09

1994 Ultra Award Winners

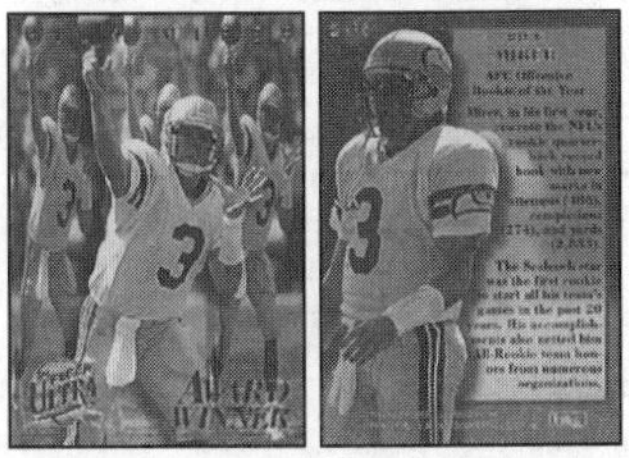

Randomly inserted in packs, this five-card standard-size set has a full-bleed design. A player photo is surpimposed over a background of three small versions of the same photo. The backs have a player photo and a write-up about the award. The set is sequenced in alphabetical order.

	MINT	NRMT	EXC
COMPLETE SET (5)	8.00	3.60	1.00
COMMON CARD (1-5)	.60	.25	.07

☐ 1 Jerome Bettis	1.25	.55	.16
☐ 2 Rick Mirer	1.00	.45	.12
☐ 3 Emmitt Smith	5.00	2.20	.60
☐ 4 Dana Stubblefield	.60	.25	.07
☐ 5 Rod Woodson	.60	.25	.07

1994 Ultra First Rounders

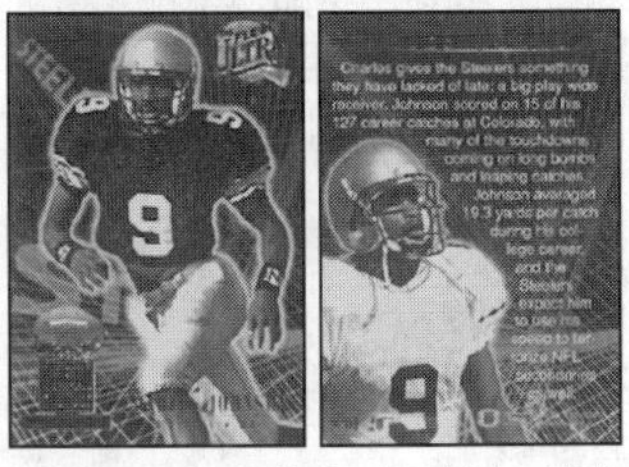

Randomly inserted in packs, this 20-card standard-size set depicts player selected in the first round of the 1994 NFL draft. Full-bleed fronts feature a player photo with a First Round logo at the bottom. The backs have a photo and information about the player's college career and why the team drafted him. The set is sequenced in alphabetical order.

	MINT	NRMT	EXC
COMPLETE SET (20)	15.00	6.75	1.85
COMMON CARD (1-20)	.40	.18	.05

☐ 1 Sam Adams	.40	.18	.05
☐ 2 Trev Alberts	.40	.18	.05

	MINT	NRMT	EXC
☐ 3 Shante Carver	.40	.18	.05
☐ 4 Marshall Faulk	3.00	1.35	.35
☐ 5 William Floyd	1.00	.45	.12
☐ 6 Rob Fredrickson	.40	.18	.05
☐ 7 Wayne Gandy	.40	.18	.05
☐ 8 Aaron Glenn	.40	.18	.05
☐ 9 Charles Johnson	.75	.35	.09
☐ 10 Joe Johnson	.40	.18	.05
☐ 11 Antonio Langham	.40	.18	.05
☐ 12 Willie McGinest	.40	.18	.05
☐ 13 Jamir Miller	.40	.18	.05
☐ 14 Johnnie Morton	.75	.35	.09
☐ 15 Heath Shuler	1.00	.45	.12
☐ 16 John Thierry	.40	.18	.05
☐ 17 Dewayne Washington	.40	.18	.05
☐ 18 Dan Wilkinson	.75	.35	.09
☐ 19 Bernard Williams	.40	.18	.05
☐ 20 Bryant Young	.75	.35	.09

1994 Ultra Flair Hot Numbers

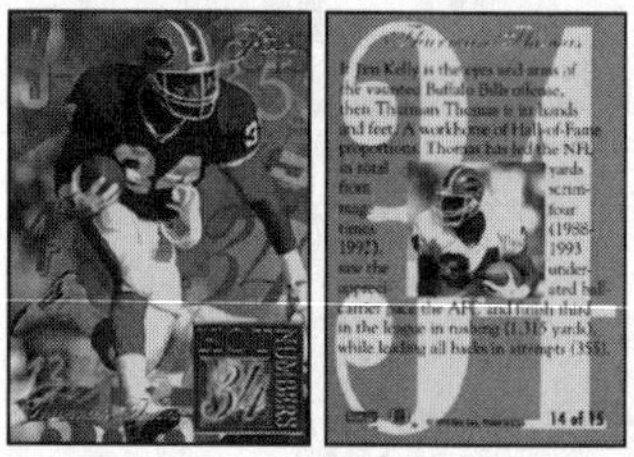

Randomly inserted in second series packs, this 15-card standard-size set is comprised of top offensive players. Card fronts have a player photo superimposed over a multi-color background. The Hot Number logo at bottom left or right includes the player's uniform number. The backs have a solid color background consistent with that player's team colors and the player uniform number. There is a small photo in the center and a write-up. The set is sequenced in alphabetical order.

	MINT	NRMT	EXC
COMPLETE SET (15)	20.00	9.00	2.50
COMMON CARD (1-15)	.50	.23	.06
☐ 1 Troy Aikman	2.50	1.10	.30
☐ 2 Jerome Bettis	1.25	.55	.16
☐ 3 Tim Brown	1.50	.70	.19
☐ 4 John Elway	2.00	.90	.25
☐ 5 Rodney Hampton	1.00	.45	.12
☐ 6 Michael Irvin	1.50	.70	.19
☐ 7 Dan Marino	5.00	2.20	.60
☐ 8 Joe Montana	2.50	1.10	.30
☐ 9 Jerry Rice	2.50	1.10	.30
☐ 10 Andre Rison	.50	.23	.06
☐ 11 Barry Sanders	2.50	1.10	.30
☐ 12 Sterling Sharpe	1.00	.45	.12
☐ 13 Emmitt Smith	5.00	2.20	.60
☐ 14 Thurman Thomas	1.50	.70	.19
☐ 15 Steve Young	2.00	.90	.25

1994 Ultra Flair Scoring Power

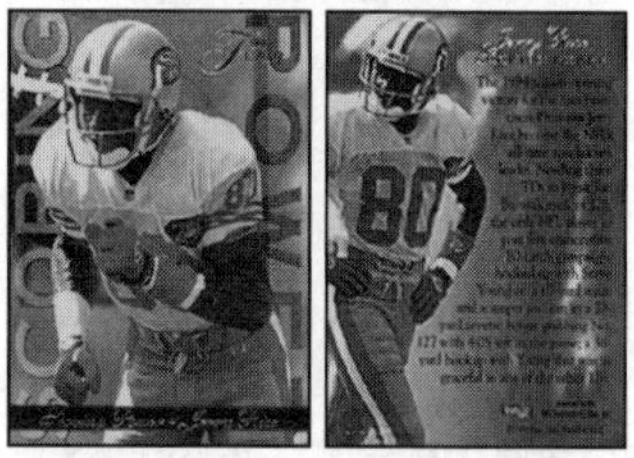

Randomly inserted in second series packs, this six-card standard-size set features touchdown leaders from the running back and wide receiver positions. The fronts contain a player photo superimposed over a multi-color background that includes the words "Scoring Power". The backs have a photo and highlights. The set is sequenced in alphabetical order.

	MINT	NRMT	EXC
COMPLETE SET (6)	16.00	7.25	2.00
COMMON CARD (1-6)	1.25	.55	.16
☐ 1 Marcus Allen	2.00	.90	.25
☐ 2 Natrone Means	3.00	1.35	.35
☐ 3 Jerry Rice	4.00	1.80	.50
☐ 4 Andre Rison	1.25	.55	.16
☐ 5 Emmitt Smith	8.00	3.60	1.00
☐ 6 Ricky Watters	1.25	.55	.16

1994 Ultra Flair Wave of the Future

Randomly inserted in second series, this six-card standard-size set focuses on top young players that could be household names for years to come. Card fronts feature a player photo superimposed over a solid color background that accentuates the uniform colors. The backs are similar and include highlights. The set is sequenced in alphabetical order.

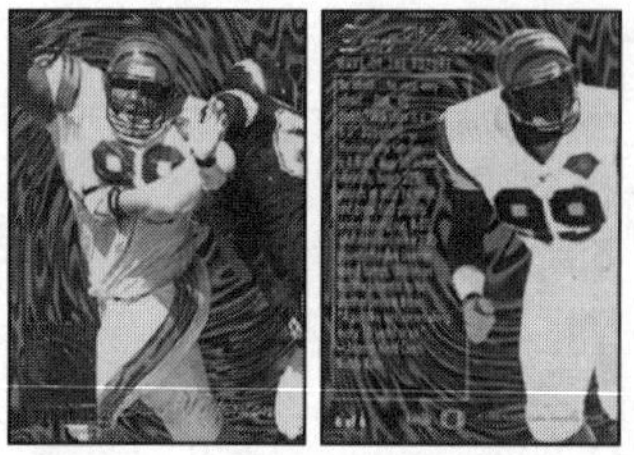

	MINT	NRMT	EXC
COMPLETE SET (6)	8.00	3.60	1.00
COMMON CARD (1-6)	.75	.35	.09
☐ 1 Trent Dilfer	1.00	.45	.12
☐ 2 Marshall Faulk	3.00	1.35	.35
☐ 3 Greg Hill	.75	.35	.09
☐ 4 Charles Johnson	.75	.35	.09
☐ 5 Heath Shuler	1.00	.45	.12
☐ 6 Dan Wilkinson	.75	.35	.09

1994 Ultra Rick Mirer

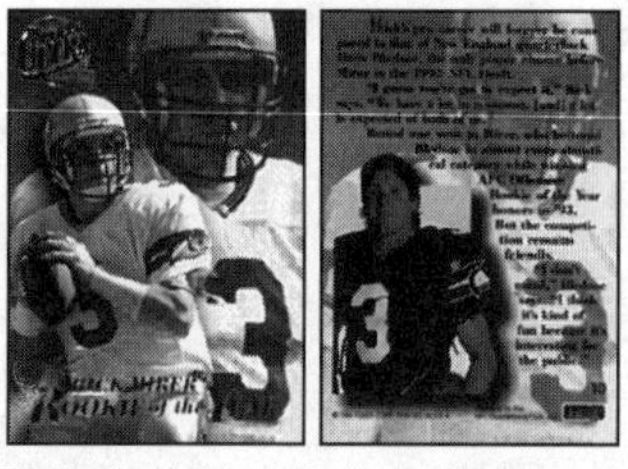

This 12-card standard-size set chronicles the collegiate career and rookie season of Seattle's Rick Mirer. The cards were randonly inserted in packs. The card fronts have two photos including an action shot that stands out from a larger faded photo used as background. The backs take a look at each stage of Mirer's career. Certified autographed cards of Mirer were randomly inserted as well. A two-card Promo sheet was produced and priced below.

	MINT	NRMT	EXC
COMPLETE SET (12)	5.00	2.20	.60
COMMON MIRER (1-10)	.50	.23	.06
COMMON SEND-OFF (11-12)	2.00	.90	.25
☐ 1 Rick Mirer (Rick's first start...)	.50	.23	.06
☐ 2 Rick Mirer ("Local Boy Makes Good"...)	.50	.23	.06
☐ 3 Rick Mirer (The comparisons to...)	.50	.23	.06
☐ 4 Rick Mirer (Entering the 1993 Draft...)	.50	.23	.06
☐ 5 Rick Mirer (The Seahawks knew...)	.50	.23	.06
☐ 6 Rick Mirer (The conventional wisdom...)	.50	.23	.06
☐ 7 Rick Mirer (When Rick arrived...)	.50	.23	.06
☐ 8 Rick Mirer (It took all of...)	.50	.23	.06
☐ 9 Rick Mirer (Rick's impressive rookie...)	.50	.23	.06
☐ 10 Rick Mirer (Rick's pro career...)	.50	.23	.06
☐ 11 Rick Mirer (Rick was a hero...)	2.00	.90	.25
☐ 12 Rick Mirer (Great quarterbacks...)	2.00	.90	.25
☐ AU1 Rick Mirer (Certified autograph)	125.00	55.00	15.50
☐ P1 Promo Sheet base brand card and insert	1.00	.45	.12

1994 Ultra Second Year Standouts

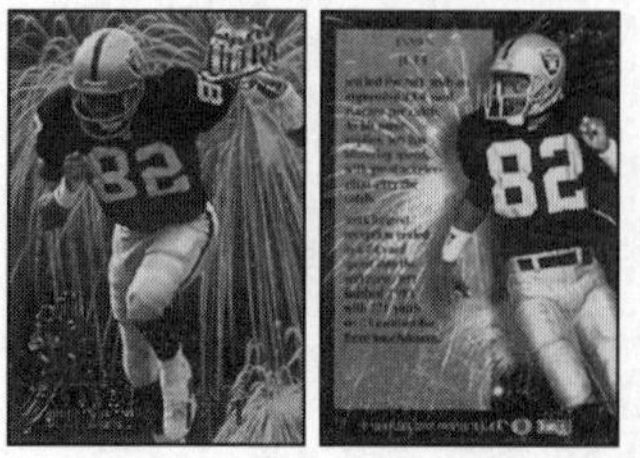

This 15-card standard-size set, honoring leading 1993 rookies, was randomly inserted into packs. The borderless fronts have a large photo of the player against a background of fireworks. The words "Second Year Standout" and the player's name are in gold foil lettering across the bottom. The backs feature another player photo with more fireworks in the background as well as highlights of his rookie season. The cards are arranged in alphabetical order.

	MINT	NRMT	EXC
COMPLETE SET (15)	15.00	6.75	1.85
COMMON CARD (1-15)	.50	.23	.06
☐ 1 Jerome Bettis	2.00	.90	.25
☐ 2 Drew Bledsoe	5.00	2.20	.60
☐ 3 Reggie Brooks	.50	.23	.06
☐ 4 Tom Carter	.50	.23	.06
☐ 5 Eric Curry	.50	.23	.06
☐ 6 Jason Elam	.50	.23	.06
☐ 7 Tyrone Hughes	1.00	.45	.12
☐ 8 James Jett	.50	.23	.06
☐ 9 Terry Kirby	1.25	.55	.16
☐ 10 Natrone Means	1.50	.70	.19
☐ 11 Rick Mirer	1.25	.55	.16
☐ 12 Ronald Moore	1.00	.45	.12
☐ 13 Willie Roaf	.50	.23	.06
☐ 14 Chris Slade	1.00	.45	.12
☐ 15 Dana Stubblefield	1.00	.45	.12

1994 Ultra Stars

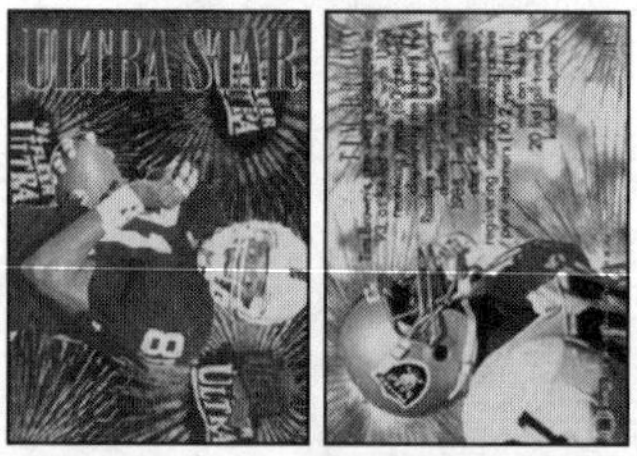

Randomly inserted in 17-card packs, this nine-card standard-size set showcases top offensive players. Horizontally designed, the card fronts have a player photo superimposed over a glossy background that differs in color according to the player's team. The backs have a player photo and highlights.The set is sequenced in alphabetical order.

	MINT	NRMT	EXC
COMPLETE SET (9)	120.00	55.00	15.00
COMMON CARD (1-9)	5.00	2.20	.60
☐ 1 Troy Aikman	20.00	9.00	2.50
☐ 2 Jerome Bettis	10.00	4.50	1.25
☐ 3 Tim Brown	8.00	3.60	1.00
☐ 4 Michael Irvin	8.00	3.60	1.00
☐ 5 Rick Mirer	8.00	3.60	1.00
☐ 6 Jerry Rice	20.00	9.00	2.50
☐ 7 Barry Sanders	20.00	9.00	2.50
☐ 8 Emmitt Smith	30.00	13.50	3.70
☐ 9 Rod Woodson	5.00	2.20	.60

1994 Ultra Touchdown Kings

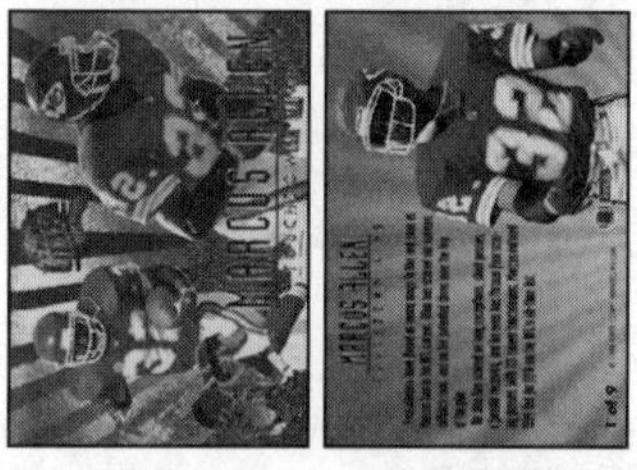

This nine-card standard-size set was randomly inserted in 14-card packs. Horizontally designed, the card fronts have two player photos over a glossy background that includes a football. The backs have a player photo with a write-up and a solid color background according to team. The set is sequenced in alphabetical order.

	MINT	NRMT	EXC
COMPLETE SET (9)	80.00	36.00	10.00
COMMON CARD (1-9)	3.00	1.35	.35
☐ 1 Marcus Allen	10.00	4.50	1.25
☐ 2 Dan Marino	20.00	9.00	2.50
☐ 3 Joe Montana	12.00	5.50	1.50
☐ 4 Jerry Rice	12.00	5.50	1.50
☐ 5 Andre Rison	3.00	1.35	.35
☐ 6 Sterling Sharpe	3.00	1.35	.35
☐ 7 Emmitt Smtih	20.00	9.00	2.50
☐ 8 Ricky Watters	5.00	2.20	.60
☐ 9 Steve Young	10.00	4.50	1.25

1995 Ultra

This standard-size set was printed in two series, which consisted of 550 standard-size cards. They were issued in 12 and 15 card packs with a suggested retail price of $2.29 and $2.99, respectively. Each pack comes with an insert card and a "Gold Medallion Edition" parallel set card. The series two set is also known as "Ultra Extra". The fronts have a full-color action photo with the player's name and team at the bottom in gold-foil. The backs have three photos, a color head shot, a color action and a black and white in the background, with career statistics at the bottom. Rookie cards include Ki-Jana Carter, Steve McNair, Michael Westbrook, Kerry Collins, Joey Galloway, J.J. Stokes, Tyrone Wheatley, Jeff Blake and Rashaan Salaam. The first series cards are numbered on the back grouped alphabetically within teams

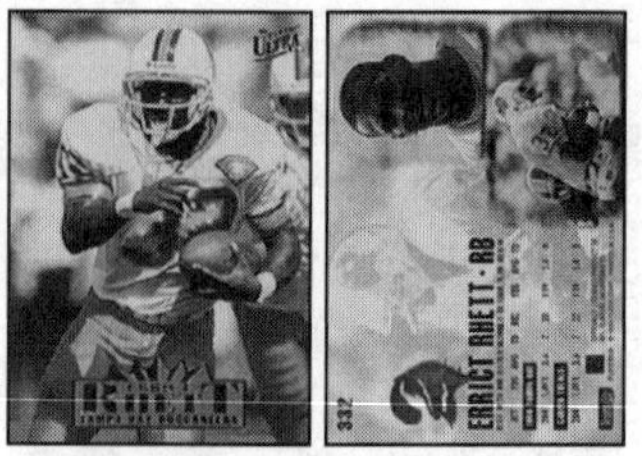

and checklisted below alphabetically according to teams. A Bam Morris prototype card was sent out as a promotion. It is very similar to the regular issue Morris, except that the prototype reads "1994 Steelers" instead of "1994 Pittsburgh" in the stat lines. A 4-card series two promo sheet was produced and priced below as an uncut sheet.

	MINT	NRMT	EXC
COMPLETE SET (550)	50.00	22.00	6.25
COMPLETE SERIES 1 (350)	30.00	13.50	3.70
COMPLETE SERIES 2 (200)	20.00	9.00	2.50
COMMON CARD (1-550)	.10	.05	.01
☐ 1 Michael Bankston	.10	.05	.01
☐ 2 Larry Centers	.20	.09	.03
☐ 3 Garrison Hearst	.30	.14	.04
☐ 4 Eric Hill	.10	.05	.01
☐ 5 Seth Joyner	.10	.05	.01
☐ 6 Lorenzo Lynch	.10	.05	.01
☐ 7 Jamir Miller	.10	.05	.01
☐ 8 Clyde Simmons	.10	.05	.01
☐ 9 Eric Swann	.20	.09	.03
☐ 10 Aeneas Williams	.10	.05	.01
☐ 11 Devin Bush	.10	.05	.01
☐ 12 Ron Davis	.10	.05	.01
☐ 13 Chris Doleman	.10	.05	.01
☐ 14 Bert Emanuel	.30	.14	.04
☐ 15 Jeff George	.20	.09	.03
☐ 16 Roger Harper	.10	.05	.01
☐ 17 Craig Heyward	.20	.09	.03
☐ 18 Pierce Holt	.10	.05	.01
☐ 19 D.J. Johnson	.10	.05	.01
☐ 20 Terance Mathis	.20	.09	.03
☐ 21 Chuck Smith	.10	.05	.01
☐ 22 Jessie Tuggle	.10	.05	.01
☐ 23 Cornelius Bennett	.20	.09	.03
☐ 24 Ruben Brown	.10	.05	.01
☐ 25 Jeff Burris	.10	.05	.01
☐ 26 Matt Darby	.10	.05	.01
☐ 27 Phil Hansen	.10	.05	.01
☐ 28 Henry Jones	.10	.05	.01
☐ 29 Jim Kelly	.30	.14	.04
☐ 30 Mark Maddox	.10	.05	.01
☐ 31 Andre Reed	.20	.09	.03
☐ 32 Bruce Smith	.30	.14	.04
☐ 33 Don Beebe	.10	.05	.01
☐ 34 Kerry Collins	4.00	1.80	.50
☐ 35 Darion Conner	.10	.05	.01
☐ 36 Pete Metzelaars	.10	.05	.01
☐ 37 Sam Mills	.20	.09	.03
☐ 38 Tyrone Poole	.20	.09	.03
☐ 39 Joe Cain	.10	.05	.01
☐ 40 Mark Carrier DB	.10	.05	.01
☐ 41 Curtis Conway	.30	.14	.04
☐ 42 Jeff Graham	.10	.05	.01
☐ 43 Raymont Harris	.10	.05	.01
☐ 44 Erik Kramer	.10	.05	.01
☐ 45 Rashaan Salaam	2.00	.90	.25
☐ 46 Lewis Tillman	.10	.05	.01
☐ 47 Donnell Woolford	.10	.05	.01
☐ 48 Chris Zorich	.10	.05	.01
☐ 49 Jeff Blake	2.00	.90	.25
☐ 50 Mike Brim	.10	.05	.01
☐ 51 Ki-Jana Carter	1.50	.70	.19
☐ 52 James Francis	.10	.05	.01
☐ 53 Carl Pickens	.30	.14	.04
☐ 54 Darnay Scott	.30	.14	.04
☐ 55 Steve Tovar	.10	.05	.01
☐ 56 Dan Wilkinson	.20	.09	.03
☐ 57 Alfred Williams	.10	.05	.01
☐ 58 Darryl Williams	.10	.05	.01
☐ 59 Derrick Alexander WR	.30	.14	.04
☐ 60 Rob Burnett	.10	.05	.01
☐ 61 Steve Everitt	.10	.05	.01
☐ 62 Leroy Hoard	.10	.05	.01
☐ 63 Michael Jackson	.20	.09	.03
☐ 64 Pepper Johnson	.10	.05	.01
☐ 65 Tony Jones	.10	.05	.01
☐ 66 Antonio Langham	.10	.05	.01
☐ 67 Anthony Pleasant	.10	.05	.01
☐ 68 Craig Powell	.10	.05	.01
☐ 69 Vinny Testaverde	.20	.09	.03
☐ 70 Eric Turner	.10	.05	.01
☐ 71 Troy Aikman	1.50	.70	.19
☐ 72 Charles Haley	.20	.09	.03
☐ 73 Michael Irvin	.30	.14	.04
☐ 74 Daryl Johnston	.20	.09	.03
☐ 75 Robert Jones	.10	.05	.01
☐ 76 Leon Lett	.10	.05	.01
☐ 77 Russell Maryland	.10	.05	.01
☐ 78 Jay Novacek	.20	.09	.03
☐ 79 Darrin Smith	.10	.05	.01
☐ 80 Emmitt Smith	3.00	1.35	.35

☐ 81 Kevin Smith	.10	.05	.01
☐ 82 Erik Williams	.10	.05	.01
☐ 83 Kevin Williams WR	.20	.09	.03
☐ 84 Sherman Williams	.10	.05	.01
☐ 85 Darren Woodson	.20	.09	.03
☐ 86 Elijah Alexander	.10	.05	.01
☐ 87 Steve Atwater	.10	.05	.01
☐ 88 Ray Crockett	.10	.05	.01
☐ 89 Shane Dronett	.10	.05	.01
☐ 90 Jason Elam	.10	.05	.01
☐ 91 John Elway	1.25	.55	.16
☐ 92 Simon Fletcher	.10	.05	.01
☐ 93 Glyn Milburn	.10	.05	.01
☐ 94 Anthony Miller	.20	.09	.03
☐ 95 Leonard Russell	.10	.05	.01
☐ 96 Shannon Sharpe	.20	.09	.03
☐ 97 Bennie Blades	.10	.05	.01
☐ 98 Lomas Brown	.10	.05	.01
☐ 99 Willie Clay	.10	.05	.01
☐ 100 Luther Elliss	.10	.05	.01
☐ 101 Mike Johnson	.10	.05	.01
☐ 102 Robert Massey	.10	.05	.01
☐ 103 Scott Mitchell	.20	.09	.03
☐ 104 Herman Moore	.75	.35	.09
☐ 105 Brett Perriman	.20	.09	.03
☐ 106 Robert Porcher	.10	.05	.01
☐ 107 Barry Sanders	1.50	.70	.19
☐ 108 Chris Spielman	.20	.09	.03
☐ 109 Edgar Bennett	.20	.09	.03
☐ 110 Robert Brooks	.30	.14	.04
☐ 111 LeRoy Butler	.10	.05	.01
☐ 112 Brett Favre	3.00	1.35	.35
☐ 113 Sean Jones	.10	.05	.01
☐ 114 John Jurkovic	.10	.05	.01
☐ 115 George Koonce	.10	.05	.01
☐ 116 Wayne Simmons	.10	.05	.01
☐ 117 George Teague	.10	.05	.01
☐ 118 Reggie White	.30	.14	.04
☐ 119 Micheal Barrow	.10	.05	.01
☐ 120 Gary Brown	.10	.05	.01
☐ 121 Cody Carlson	.10	.05	.01
☐ 122 Ray Childress	.10	.05	.01
☐ 123 Cris Dishman	.10	.05	.01
☐ 124 Bruce Matthews	.10	.05	.01
☐ 125 Steve McNair	3.50	1.55	.45
☐ 126 Marcus Robertson	.10	.05	.01
☐ 127 Webster Slaughter	.10	.05	.01
☐ 128 Al Smith	.10	.05	.01
☐ 129 Tony Bennett	.10	.05	.01
☐ 130 Ray Buchanan	.10	.05	.01
☐ 131 Quentin Coryatt	.20	.09	.03
☐ 132 Sean Dawkins	.20	.09	.03
☐ 133 Marshall Faulk	.75	.35	.09
☐ 134 Stephen Grant	.10	.05	.01
☐ 135 Jim Harbaugh	.20	.09	.03
☐ 136 Jeff Herrod	.10	.05	.01
☐ 137 Ellis Johnson	.10	.05	.01
☐ 138 Tony Siragusa	.10	.05	.01
☐ 139 Steve Beuerlein	.10	.05	.01
☐ 140 Tony Boselli	.20	.09	.03
☐ 141 Darren Carrington	.10	.05	.01
☐ 142 Reggie Cobb	.10	.05	.01
☐ 143 Kelvin Martin	.10	.05	.01
☐ 144 Kelvin Pritchett	.10	.05	.01
☐ 145 Joel Smeenge	.10	.05	.01
☐ 146 James O.Stewart	.20	.09	.03
☐ 147 Marcus Allen	.30	.14	.04
☐ 148 Kimble Anders	.20	.09	.03
☐ 149 Dale Carter	.20	.09	.03
☐ 150 Mark Collins	.10	.05	.01
☐ 151 Willie Davis	.20	.09	.03
☐ 152 Lake Dawson	.20	.09	.03
☐ 153 Greg Hill	.20	.09	.03
☐ 154 Trezelle Jenkins	.10	.05	.01
☐ 155 Darren Mickell	.10	.05	.01
☐ 156 Tracy Simien	.10	.05	.01
☐ 157 Neil Smith	.20	.09	.03
☐ 158 William White	.10	.05	.01
☐ 159 Joe Aska	.20	.09	.03
☐ 160 Greg Biekert	.10	.05	.01
☐ 161 Tim Brown	.30	.14	.04
☐ 162 Rob Fredrickson	.10	.05	.01
☐ 163 Andrew Glover	.10	.05	.01
☐ 164 Jeff Hostetler	.20	.09	.03
☐ 165 Rocket Ismail	.20	.09	.03
☐ 166 Napoleon Kaufman	1.50	.70	.19
☐ 167 Terry McDaniel	.10	.05	.01
☐ 168 Chester McGlockton	.20	.09	.03
☐ 169 Anthony Smith	.10	.05	.01
☐ 170 Harvey Williams	.10	.05	.01
☐ 171 Steve Wisniewski	.10	.05	.01
☐ 172 Gene Atkins	.10	.05	.01
☐ 173 Aubrey Beavers	.10	.05	.01
☐ 174 Tim Bowens	.10	.05	.01
☐ 175 Bryan Cox	.10	.05	.01
☐ 176 Jeff Cross	.10	.05	.01
☐ 177 Irving Fryar	.20	.09	.03
☐ 178 Dan Marino	3.00	1.35	.35
☐ 179 O.J. McDuffie	.30	.14	.04
☐ 180 Billy Milner	.10	.05	.01
☐ 181 Bernie Parmalee	.20	.09	.03
☐ 182 Troy Vincent	.10	.05	.01
☐ 183 Richmond Webb	.10	.05	.01
☐ 184 Derrick Alexander DE	.10	.05	.01
☐ 185 Cris Carter	.30	.14	.04
☐ 186 Jack Del Rio	.10	.05	.01
☐ 187 Qadry Ismail	.20	.09	.03
☐ 188 Ed McDaniel	.10	.05	.01
☐ 189 Randall McDaniel	.10	.05	.01
☐ 190 Warren Moon	.20	.09	.03
☐ 191 John Randle	.10	.05	.01
☐ 192 Jake Reed	.20	.09	.03
☐ 193 Fuad Reveiz	.10	.05	.01
☐ 194 Korey Stringer	.10	.05	.01
☐ 195 Dewayne Washington	.20	.09	.03
☐ 196 Bruce Armstrong	.10	.05	.01
☐ 197 Drew Bledsoe	1.50	.70	.19
☐ 198 Vincent Brisby	.10	.05	.01
☐ 199 Vincent Brown	.10	.05	.01
☐ 200 Marion Butts	.10	.05	.01
☐ 201 Ben Coates	.20	.09	.03
☐ 202 Myron Guyton	.10	.05	.01
☐ 203 Maurice Hurst	.10	.05	.01
☐ 204 Mike Jones	.10	.05	.01
☐ 205 Ty Law	.20	.09	.03
☐ 206 Willie McGinest	.20	.09	.03
☐ 207 Chris Slade	.20	.09	.03
☐ 208 Mario Bates	.30	.14	.04
☐ 209 Quinn Early	.20	.09	.03
☐ 210 Jim Everett	.10	.05	.01
☐ 211 Mark Fields	.10	.05	.01
☐ 212 Michael Haynes	.20	.09	.03
☐ 213 Tyrone Hughes	.20	.09	.03
☐ 214 Joe Johnson	.10	.05	.01
☐ 215 Wayne Martin	.10	.05	.01
☐ 216 Willie Roaf	.10	.05	.01
☐ 217 Irv Smith	.10	.05	.01
☐ 218 Jimmy Spencer	.10	.05	.01
☐ 219 Winfred Tubbs	.10	.05	.01
☐ 220 Renaldo Turnbull	.10	.05	.01
☐ 221 Michael Brooks	.10	.05	.01
☐ 222 Dave Brown	.20	.09	.03
☐ 223 Chris Calloway	.10	.05	.01
☐ 224 Howard Cross	.10	.05	.01
☐ 225 John Elliott	.10	.05	.01
☐ 226 Keith Hamilton	.10	.05	.01
☐ 227 Rodney Hampton	.20	.09	.03
☐ 228 Thomas Lewis	.20	.09	.03
☐ 229 Thomas Randolph	.10	.05	.01
☐ 230 Mike Sherrard	.10	.05	.01
☐ 231 Michael Strahan	.10	.05	.01
☐ 232 Tyrone Wheatley	.75	.35	.09
☐ 233 Brad Baxter	.10	.05	.01
☐ 234 Kyle Brady	.30	.14	.04
☐ 235 Kyle Clifton	.10	.05	.01
☐ 236 Hugh Douglas	.20	.09	.03
☐ 237 Boomer Esiason	.20	.09	.03
☐ 238 Aaron Glenn	.10	.05	.01
☐ 239 Bobby Houston	.10	.05	.01
☐ 240 Johnny Johnson	.10	.05	.01
☐ 241 Mo Lewis	.10	.05	.01
☐ 242 Johnny Mitchell	.10	.05	.01
☐ 243 Marvin Washington	.10	.05	.01
☐ 244 Fred Barnett	.20	.09	.03
☐ 245 Randall Cunningham	.20	.09	.03
☐ 246 William Fuller	.10	.05	.01
☐ 247 Charlie Garner	.20	.09	.03
☐ 248 Andy Harmon	.10	.05	.01
☐ 249 Greg Jackson	.10	.05	.01
☐ 250 Mike Mamula	.20	.09	.03
☐ 251 Bill Romanowski	.10	.05	.01
☐ 252 Bobby Taylor	.20	.09	.03
☐ 253 William Thomas	.10	.05	.01
☐ 254 Calvin Williams	.20	.09	.03
☐ 255 Michael Zordich	.10	.05	.01
☐ 256 Chad Brown	.20	.09	.03
☐ 257 Mark Bruener	.20	.09	.03
☐ 258 Dermontti Dawson	.20	.09	.03
☐ 259 Barry Foster	.20	.09	.03
☐ 260 Kevin Greene	.20	.09	.03
☐ 261 Charles Johnson	.20	.09	.03
☐ 262 Carnell Lake	.10	.05	.01
☐ 263 Greg Lloyd	.20	.09	.03
☐ 264 Byron Bam Morris	.20	.09	.03
☐ 265 Neil O'Donnell	.20	.09	.03
☐ 266 Darren Perry	.10	.05	.01
☐ 267 Ray Seals	.10	.05	.01
☐ 268 Kordell Stewart	4.00	1.80	.50
☐ 269 John L. Williams	.10	.05	.01
☐ 270 Rod Woodson	.20	.09	.03
☐ 271 Jerome Bettis	.50	.23	.06
☐ 272 Isaac Bruce	.75	.35	.09
☐ 273 Kevin Carter	.30	.14	.04
☐ 274 Shane Conlan	.10	.05	.01
☐ 275 Troy Drayton	.10	.05	.01
☐ 276 Sean Gilbert	.20	.09	.03
☐ 277 Todd Lyght	.10	.05	.01
☐ 278 Chris Miller	.10	.05	.01
☐ 279 Anthony Newman	.10	.05	.01
☐ 280 Roman Phifer	.10	.05	.01
☐ 281 Robert Young	.10	.05	.01
☐ 282 John Carney	.10	.05	.01
☐ 283 Andre Coleman	.10	.05	.01
☐ 284 Courtney Hall	.10	.05	.01
☐ 285 Ronnie Harmon	.10	.05	.01
☐ 286 Dwayne Harper	.10	.05	.01
☐ 287 Stan Humphries	.20	.09	.03
☐ 288 Shawn Jefferson	.10	.05	.01
☐ 289 Tony Martin	.20	.09	.03
☐ 290 Natrone Means	.30	.14	.04
☐ 291 Chris Mims	.10	.05	.01
☐ 292 Leslie O'Neal	.20	.09	.03
☐ 293 Junior Seau	.30	.14	.04
☐ 294 Mark Seay	.20	.09	.03
☐ 295 Eric Davis	.10	.05	.01
☐ 296 William Floyd	.30	.14	.04
☐ 297 Merton Hanks	.10	.05	.01
☐ 298 Brent Jones	.10	.05	.01
☐ 299 Ken Norton Jr.	.20	.09	.03
☐ 300 Gary Plummer	.10	.05	.01
☐ 301 Jerry Rice	1.50	.70	.19
☐ 302 Deion Sanders	1.00	.45	.12
☐ 303 Jesse Sapolu	.10	.05	.01
☐ 304 J.J. Stokes	1.50	.70	.19
☐ 305 Dana Stubblefield	.30	.14	.04
☐ 306 John Taylor	.10	.05	.01
☐ 307 Steve Wallace	.10	.05	.01
☐ 308 Lee Woodall	.10	.05	.01
☐ 309 Bryant Young	.20	.09	.03
☐ 310 Steve Young	1.25	.55	.16
☐ 311 Sam Adams	.10	.05	.01
☐ 312 Howard Ballard	.10	.05	.01
☐ 313 Robert Blackmon	.10	.05	.01
☐ 314 Brian Blades	.20	.09	.03
☐ 315 Joey Galloway	2.50	1.10	.30
☐ 316 Carlton Gray	.10	.05	.01
☐ 317 Cortez Kennedy	.20	.09	.03
☐ 318 Rick Mirer	.30	.14	.04
☐ 319 Eugene Robinson	.10	.05	.01
☐ 320 Chris Warren	.20	.09	.03
☐ 321 Terry Wooden	.10	.05	.01
☐ 322 Derrick Brooks	.10	.05	.01
☐ 323 Lawrence Dawsey	.10	.05	.01
☐ 324 Trent Dilfer	.30	.14	.04
☐ 325 Santana Dotson	.10	.05	.01
☐ 326 Thomas Everett	.10	.05	.01
☐ 327 Paul Gruber	.10	.05	.01
☐ 328 Jackie Harris	.10	.05	.01
☐ 329 Courtney Hawkins	.10	.05	.01
☐ 330 Martin Mayhew	.10	.05	.01
☐ 331 Hardy Nickerson	.10	.05	.01
☐ 332 Errict Rhett	.30	.14	.04
☐ 333 Warren Sapp	.20	.09	.03
☐ 334 Charles Wilson	.10	.05	.01
☐ 335 Reggie Brooks	.20	.09	.03
☐ 336 Tom Carter	.10	.05	.01
☐ 337 Henry Ellard	.20	.09	.03
☐ 338 Ricky Ervins	.10	.05	.01
☐ 339 Darrell Green	.10	.05	.01
☐ 340 Ken Harvey	.10	.05	.01
☐ 341 Brian Mitchell	.10	.05	.01
☐ 342 Cory Raymer	.10	.05	.01
☐ 343 Heath Shuler	.30	.14	.04
☐ 344 Michael Westbrook	2.00	.90	.25
☐ 345 Tony Woods	.10	.05	.01
☐ 346 Checklist	.10	.05	.01
☐ 347 Checklist	.10	.05	.01
☐ 348 Checklist	.10	.05	.01
☐ 349 Checklist	.10	.05	.01
☐ 350 Checklist	.10	.05	.01
☐ 351 Checklist	.10	.05	.01
☐ 352 Checklist	.10	.05	.01
☐ 353 Dave Krieg	.10	.05	.01
☐ 354 Rob Moore	.10	.05	.01
☐ 355 J.J. Birden	.10	.05	.01
☐ 356 Eric Metcalf	.20	.09	.03
☐ 357 Bryce Paup	.30	.14	.04
☐ 358 Willie Green	.20	.09	.03
☐ 359 Derrick Moore	.10	.05	.01
☐ 360 Michael Timpson	.10	.05	.01
☐ 361 Eric Bieniemy	.10	.05	.01
☐ 362 Keenan McCardell	.30	.14	.04
☐ 363 Andre Rison	.20	.09	.03
☐ 364 Lorenzo White	.10	.05	.01
☐ 365 Deion Sanders	1.00	.45	.12
☐ 366 Wade Wilson	.10	.05	.01
☐ 367 Aaron Craver	.10	.05	.01
☐ 368 Michael Dean Perry	.10	.05	.01
☐ 369 Rod Smith WR	.10	.05	.01
☐ 370 Henry Thomas	.10	.05	.01
☐ 371 Mark Ingram	.10	.05	.01
☐ 372 Chris Chandler	.20	.09	.03
☐ 373 Mel Gray	.10	.05	.01
☐ 374 Flipper Anderson	.10	.05	.01
☐ 375 Craig Erickson	.10	.05	.01
☐ 376 Mark Brunell	1.50	.70	.19
☐ 377 Ernest Givins	.10	.05	.01
☐ 378 Randy Jordan	.10	.05	.01
☐ 379 Webster Slaughter	.10	.05	.01
☐ 380 Tamarick Vanover	2.00	.90	.25
☐ 381 Gary Clark	.10	.05	.01
☐ 382 Steve Emtman	.10	.05	.01
☐ 383 Eric Green	.10	.05	.01
☐ 384 Louis Oliver	.10	.05	.01
☐ 385 Robert Smith	.30	.14	.04
☐ 386 Dave Meggett	.10	.05	.01
☐ 387 Eric Allen	.10	.05	.01
☐ 388 Wesley Walls	.20	.09	.03
☐ 389 Herschel Walker	.20	.09	.03
☐ 390 Ronald Moore	.10	.05	.01
☐ 391 Adrian Murrell	.20	.09	.03
☐ 392 Charles Wilson	.10	.05	.01
☐ 393 Derrick Fenner	.10	.05	.01
☐ 394 Pat Swilling	.10	.05	.01
☐ 395 Kelvin Martin	.10	.05	.01
☐ 396 Rodney Peete	.10	.05	.01
☐ 397 Ricky Watters	.30	.14	.04
☐ 398 Erric Pegram	.20	.09	.03
☐ 399 Leonard Russell	.10	.05	.01
☐ 400 Alexander Wright	.10	.05	.01
☐ 401 Darrien Gordon	.10	.05	.01
☐ 402 Alfred Pupunu	.10	.05	.01
☐ 403 Elvis Grbac	.30	.14	.04
☐ 404 Derek Loville	.10	.05	.01
☐ 405 Steve Broussard	.10	.05	.01
☐ 406 Ricky Proehl	.10	.05	.01
☐ 407 Bobby Joe Edmonds	.10	.05	.01
☐ 408 Alvin Harper	.10	.05	.01
☐ 409 Dave Moore	.10	.05	.01
☐ 410 Terry Allen	.20	.09	.03
☐ 411 Gus Frerotte	.75	.35	.09
☐ 412 Leslie Shepherd	.20	.09	.03
☐ 413 Stoney Case	.10	.05	.01
☐ 414 Frank Sanders	.30	.14	.04
☐ 415 Roell Preston	.10	.05	.01
☐ 416 Lorenzo Styles	.10	.05	.01
☐ 417 Justin Armour	.10	.05	.01
☐ 418 Todd Collins	.30	.14	.04
☐ 419 Darick Holmes	.75	.35	.09
☐ 420 Kerry Collins	2.00	.90	.25
☐ 421 Tyrone Poole	.20	.09	.03
☐ 422 Rashaan Salaam	1.00	.45	.12
☐ 423 Todd Sauerbrun	.10	.05	.01
☐ 424 Ki-Jana Carter	.30	.14	.04
☐ 425 David Dunn	.10	.05	.01
☐ 426 Ernest Hunter	.10	.05	.01
☐ 427 Eric Zeier	.30	.14	.04
☐ 428 Eric Bjornson	.20	.09	.03
☐ 429 Sherman Williams	.10	.05	.01
☐ 430 Terrell Davis	5.00	2.20	.60
☐ 431 Luther Elliss	.10	.05	.01
☐ 432 Kez McCorvey	.10	.05	.01
☐ 433 Antonio Freeman	3.00	1.35	.35
☐ 434 Craig Newsome	.10	.05	.01
☐ 435 Steve McNair	1.50	.70	.19
☐ 436 Chris Sanders	2.00	.90	.25
☐ 437 Zack Crockett	.10	.05	.01
☐ 438 Ellis Johnson	.10	.05	.01
☐ 439 Tony Boselli	.20	.09	.03
☐ 440 James O.Stewart	.20	.09	.03
☐ 441 Trezelle Jenkins	.10	.05	.01
☐ 442 Tamarick Vanover	1.00	.45	.12
☐ 443 Derrick Alexander DE	.10	.05	.01
☐ 444 Chad May	.10	.05	.01
☐ 445 James A.Stewart	.10	.05	.01
☐ 446 Ty Law	.20	.09	.03
☐ 447 Curtis Martin	5.00	2.20	.60
☐ 448 Will Moore	.10	.05	.01
☐ 449 Mark Fields	.10	.05	.01
☐ 450 Ray Zellars	.20	.09	.03
☐ 451 Charles Way	.10	.05	.01
☐ 452 Tyrone Wheatley	.30	.14	.04
☐ 453 Kyle Brady	.30	.14	.04
☐ 454 Wayne Chrebet	.30	.14	.04
☐ 455 Hugh Douglas	.20	.09	.03
☐ 456 Chris T.Jones	.30	.14	.04
☐ 457 Mike Mamula	.20	.09	.03
☐ 458 Fred McCrary	.10	.05	.01
☐ 459 Bobby Taylor	.20	.09	.03
☐ 460 Mark Bruener	.20	.09	.03
☐ 461 Kordell Stewart	2.00	.90	.25
☐ 462 Kevin Carter	.30	.14	.04
☐ 463 Lovell Pinkney	.10	.05	.01
☐ 464 Johnny Thomas	.10	.05	.01
☐ 465 Terrell Fletcher	.10	.05	.01
☐ 466 Jimmy Oliver	.10	.05	.01
☐ 467 J.J. Stokes	.75	.35	.09
☐ 468 Christian Fauria	.10	.05	.01
☐ 469 Joey Galloway	1.25	.55	.16
☐ 470 Derrick Brooks	.10	.05	.01
☐ 471 Warren Sapp	.20	.09	.03
☐ 472 Michael Westbrook	1.00	.45	.12
☐ 473 Garrison Hearst	.30	.14	.04
☐ 474 Jeff George	.20	.09	.03
☐ 475 Terance Mathis	.20	.09	.03
☐ 476 Andre Reed	.20	.09	.03
☐ 477 Bruce Smith	.30	.14	.04
☐ 478 Lamar Lathon	.10	.05	.01
☐ 479 Curtis Conway	.30	.14	.04
☐ 480 Jeff Blake	1.00	.45	.12
☐ 481 Carl Pickens	.30	.14	.04
☐ 482 Eric Turner	.10	.05	.01
☐ 483 Troy Aikman	.75	.35	.09
☐ 484 Michael Irvin	.30	.14	.04
☐ 485 Emmitt Smith	1.50	.70	.19
☐ 486 John Elway	.60	.25	.07
☐ 487 Shannon Sharpe	.20	.09	.03
☐ 488 Herman Moore	.30	.14	.04
☐ 489 Barry Sanders	.75	.35	.09
☐ 490 Brett Favre	1.50	.70	.19
☐ 491 Reggie White	.30	.14	.04
☐ 492 Haywood Jeffires	.10	.05	.01
☐ 493 Sean Dawkins	.10	.05	.01
☐ 494 Marshall Faulk	.30	.14	.04
☐ 495 Desmond Howard	.20	.09	.03
☐ 496 Steve Bono	.20	.09	.03
☐ 497 Derrick Thomas	.20	.09	.03
☐ 498 Irving Fryar	.20	.09	.03
☐ 499 Terry Kirby	.20	.09	.03
☐ 500 Dan Marino	1.50	.70	.19

		MINT	NRMT	EXC
☐ 501 O.J. McDuffie		.30	.14	.04
☐ 502 Cris Carter		.30	.14	.04
☐ 503 Warren Moon		.20	.09	.03
☐ 504 Jake Reed		.20	.09	.03
☐ 505 Drew Bledsoe		.75	.35	.09
☐ 506 Ben Coates		.20	.09	.03
☐ 507 Jim Everett		.10	.05	.01
☐ 508 Rodney Hampton		.20	.09	.03
☐ 509 Mo Lewis		.10	.05	.01
☐ 510 Tim Brown		.30	.14	.04
☐ 511 Jeff Hostetler		.20	.09	.03
☐ 512 Rocket Ismail		.20	.09	.03
☐ 513 Chester McGlockton		.20	.09	.03
☐ 514 Fred Barnett		.20	.09	.03
☐ 515 Greg Lloyd		.20	.09	.03
☐ 516 Byron Bam Morris		.20	.09	.03
☐ 517 Rod Woodson		.20	.09	.03
☐ 518 Jerome Bettis		.30	.14	.04
☐ 519 Isaac Bruce		.30	.14	.04
☐ 520 Stan Humphries		.20	.09	.03
☐ 521 Natrone Means		.30	.14	.04
☐ 522 Junior Seau		.30	.14	.04
☐ 523 William Floyd		.20	.09	.03
☐ 524 Jerry Rice		.75	.35	.09
☐ 525 Steve Young		.60	.25	.07
☐ 526 Cortez Kennedy		.20	.09	.03
☐ 527 Rick Mirer		.30	.14	.04
☐ 528 Chris Warren		.20	.09	.03
☐ 529 Trent Dilfer		.30	.14	.04
☐ 530 Errict Rhett		.30	.14	.04
☐ 531 Darrell Green		.10	.05	.01
☐ 532 Heath Shuler		.30	.14	.04
☐ 533 Stoney Case RO		.10	.05	.01
☐ 534 Eric Zeier RO		.30	.14	.04
☐ 535 Kerry Collins RO		1.50	.70	.19
☐ 536 Steve McNair RO		1.25	.55	.16
☐ 537 Kordell Stewart RO		1.50	.70	.19
☐ 538 Rob Johnson RO		.10	.05	.01
☐ 539 Eric Ball EE		.10	.05	.01
☐ 540 Darrick Brownlow EE		.10	.05	.01
☐ 541 Paul Butcher EE		.10	.05	.01
☐ 542 Carlester Crumpler EE		.10	.05	.01
☐ 543 Maurice Douglas EE		.10	.05	.01
☐ 544 Keith Elias EE		.10	.05	.01
☐ 545 Kenneth Gant EE		.10	.05	.01
☐ 546 Corey Harris EE		.10	.05	.01
☐ 547 Andre Hastings EE		.20	.09	.03
☐ 548 Thomas Homco EE		.10	.05	.01
☐ 549 Lenny McGill EE		.10	.05	.01
☐ 550 Mark Pike EE		.10	.05	.01
☐ P1 Promo Sheet		2.00	.90	.25

   Dave Meggett
   Justin Armour
   Brett Favre
   William Floyd

	MINT	NRMT	EXC
☐ P264 Byron Bam Morris	1.00	.45	.12

   Prototype Card
   back includes "1994 Steelers"
   in stat information

1995 Ultra Gold Medallion

This 550 card parallel set was randomly inserted into both series one and series two packs at a rate of one per pack. Card backs feature an all gold-foil background to differentiate it from the basic issue.

	MINT	NRMT	EXC
COMPLETE SET (550)	300.00	135.00	38.00
COMPLETE SERIES 1 (350)	180.00	80.00	22.00
COMPLETE SERIES 2 (200)	125.00	55.00	15.00
COMMON CARD (1-550)	.30	.14	.04
*STARS: 3X TO 6X BASIC CARDS			
*YOUNG STARS: 2X TO 4X BASIC CARDS			
*RCs: 1.5X TO 3X BASIC CARDS			

1995 Ultra Achievements

This 10-card set was randomly inserted into series one packs at a rate of one in seven packs and features outstanding achievements by individual players. Card fronts contain a colored background with different awards. The player's name and the card name "Ultra Achievement" are in gold foil along the bottom of the card. Card backs have a similar background with player commentary. This set also has a gold medallion parallel, which is identified by a gold seal on the front of the card.

	MINT	NRMT	EXC
COMPLETE SET (10)	10.00	4.50	1.25
COMMON CARD (1-10)	.50	.23	.06
COMPLETE GOLD MED.SET (10)	25.00	11.00	3.10
*GOLD MED.CARDS: 1X TO 2X			

	MINT	NRMT	EXC
☐ 1 Drew Bledsoe	2.50	1.10	.30
☐ 2 Cris Carter	.75	.35	.09
☐ 3 Ben Coates	.75	.35	.09
☐ 4 Mel Gray	.50	.23	.06
☐ 5 Jerry Rice	2.50	1.10	.30
☐ 6 Barry Sanders	2.50	1.10	.30
☐ 7 Deion Sanders	1.50	.70	.19
☐ 8 Herschel Walker	.50	.23	.06
☐ 9 Dewayne Washington	.50	.23	.06
☐ 10 Steve Young	2.00	.90	.25

1995 Ultra All-Rookie Team

 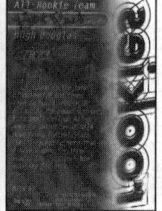

Randomly inserted at a rate of one in 55 series two packs, this 10 card set is printed on plastic stock and features top rookies from the 1995 season. Card fronts contain a full bleed photo on the right with the word "rookies" running along a clear background on the left. The player's name and the card title are located on the bottom right corner. Card backs feature a commentary on the rookie. A parallel of this set also exists - the All-Rookie Team Hot Pack. This set came only as a complete set inserted in packs at a rate of one in 360 packs. Cards have a "Hot Pack" designation on both the front and the back against a flame background. A cover card was included in the hot pack sets.

	MINT	NRMT	EXC
COMPLETE SET (10)	140.00	65.00	17.50
COMMON CARD (1-10)	10.00	4.50	1.25
COMP.HOT PACK SET (10)	70.00	32.00	8.75
*HOT PACK CARDS: HALF VALUE			

	MINT	NRMT	EXC
☐ 1 Michael Westbrook	15.00	6.75	1.85
☐ 2 Terrell Davis	35.00	16.00	4.40
☐ 3 Curtis Martin	35.00	16.00	4.40
☐ 4 Joey Galloway	25.00	11.00	3.10
☐ 5 Rashaan Salaam	18.00	8.00	2.20
☐ 6 J.J. Stokes	15.00	6.75	1.85
☐ 7 Napoleon Kaufman	10.00	4.50	1.25
☐ 8 Mike Mamula	10.00	4.50	1.25
☐ 9 Kyle Brady	10.00	4.50	1.25
☐ 10 Hugh Douglas	10.00	4.50	1.25

1995 Ultra Award Winners

This six card set was randomly inserted into series one packs at a rate of one in five and features award-winning players from the 1994 season. Card front backgrounds contain different "dummy" player shots with the player's name and card title in gold foil along the bottom of the card. Card backs contain a player shot with a commentary. A gold medallion parallel set also exists and is designated with a gold foil stamp on the front of the card.

	MINT	NRMT	EXC
COMPLETE SET (6)	8.00	3.60	1.00
COMMON CARD (1-6)	.50	.23	.06
COMP.GOLD MED.SET (6)	20.00	9.00	2.50
*GOLD MED.CARDS: 1X TO 2X			

	MINT	NRMT	EXC
☐ 1 Tim Bowens	.50	.23	.06
☐ 2 Marshall Faulk	.75	.35	.09
☐ 3 Dan Marino	3.00	1.35	.35
☐ 4 Barry Sanders	1.50	.70	.19
☐ 5 Deion Sanders	1.00	.45	.12
☐ 6 Steve Young	1.25	.55	.16

1995 Ultra First Rounders

This 20 card set was randomly inserted into series one packs at a rate of one in seven packs and features players who were chosen in the first round of the 1995 draft. Card fronts contain the team color in the background with helmets. The player's name and card title are located at the bottom. Card backs also contain a player shot with a commentary on the rookie. This set contains a gold medallion parallel which is designated on the front with a gold foil logo.

	MINT	NRMT	EXC
COMPLETE SET (20)	35.00	16.00	4.40
COMMON CARD (1-20)	.50	.23	.06
COMP.GOLD MED.SET (20)	80.00	36.00	10.00
*GOLD MED.CARDS: 1X TO 2X			

	MINT	NRMT	EXC
☐ 1 Derrick Alexander	.75	.35	.09
☐ 2 Tony Boselli	.75	.35	.09
☐ 3 Kyle Brady	.50	.23	.06
☐ 4 Mark Bruener	.50	.23	.06
☐ 5 Devin Bush	.50	.23	.06
☐ 6 Kevin Carter	.75	.35	.09
☐ 7 Ki-Jana Carter	2.00	.90	.25
☐ 8 Kerry Collins	7.00	3.10	.85
☐ 9 Mark Fields	.50	.23	.06
☐ 10 Joey Galloway	5.00	2.20	.60
☐ 11 Napoleon Kaufman	2.00	.90	.25
☐ 12 Ty Law	.75	.35	.09
☐ 13 Mike Mamula	.50	.23	.06
☐ 14 Steve McNair	6.00	2.70	.75
☐ 15 Rashaan Salaam	3.00	1.35	.35
☐ 16 Warren Sapp	.50	.23	.06
☐ 17 James O.Stewart	1.50	.70	.19
☐ 18 J.J.Stokes	2.00	.90	.25
☐ 19 Michael Westbrook	3.00	1.35	.35
☐ 20 Tyrone Wheatley	1.50	.70	.19

1995 Ultra Magna Force

This 20 card set was randomly inserted into series two hobby packs at a rate of one in 20 packs. Card fronts feature the title "Magna Force" in block letters on a silver foil background with the player's name at the bottom. Card backs feature a background action shot and a headshot in the upper right corner. A commentary on the player is also included.

	MINT	NRMT	EXC
COMPLETE SET (20)	125.00	55.00	15.50
COMMON CARD (1-20)	2.00	.90	.25

	MINT	NRMT	EXC
☐ 1 Emmitt Smith	25.00	11.00	3.10
☐ 2 Jerry Rice	10.00	4.50	1.25
☐ 3 Drew Bledsoe	10.00	4.50	1.25
☐ 4 Marshall Faulk	5.00	2.20	.60
☐ 5 Heath Shuler	3.00	1.35	.35
☐ 6 Carl Pickens	3.00	1.35	.35
☐ 7 Ben Coates	2.00	.90	.25
☐ 8 Terry Allen	2.00	.90	.25
☐ 9 Terance Mathis	2.00	.90	.25
☐ 10 Fred Barnett	2.00	.90	.25
☐ 11 O.J. McDuffie	3.00	1.35	.35
☐ 12 Garrison Hearst	3.00	1.35	.35
☐ 13 Deion Sanders	6.00	2.70	.75
☐ 14 Reggie White	3.00	1.35	.35
☐ 15 Herman Moore	5.00	2.20	.60
☐ 16 Brett Favre	25.00	11.00	3.10
☐ 17 William Floyd	2.00	.90	.25
☐ 18 Curtis Martin	20.00	9.00	2.50
☐ 19 Joey Galloway	10.00	4.50	1.25
☐ 20 Tyrone Wheatley	2.00	.90	.25

1995 Ultra Overdrive

This 20 card set was randomly inserted into series two retail packs at a rate of one in 20. Card fronts feature a colored swirl background with the card name running along the right and the player's name and position at the bottom. Card backs feature a background action shot with the player's head "boxed" and in color. A brief commentary on the player is under the headshot.

	MINT	NRMT	EXC
COMPLETE SET (20)	80.00	36.00	10.00
COMMON CARD (1-20)	2.00	.90	.25

	MINT	NRMT	EXC
☐ 1 Barry Sanders	10.00	4.50	1.25
☐ 2 Troy Aikman	10.00	4.50	1.25
☐ 3 Natrone Means	3.00	1.35	.35
☐ 4 Steve Young	8.00	3.60	1.00
☐ 5 Errict Rhett	3.00	1.35	.35
☐ 6 Terrell Davis	16.00	7.25	2.00
☐ 7 Michael Westbrook	5.00	2.20	.60
☐ 8 Michael Irvin	3.00	1.35	.35
☐ 9 Chris Warren	2.00	.90	.25
☐ 10 Tim Brown	3.00	1.35	.35
☐ 11 Jerome Bettis	3.00	1.35	.35

	MINT	NRMT	EXC
☐ 12 Ricky Watters	3.00	1.35	.35
☐ 13 Derrick Thomas	3.00	1.35	.35
☐ 14 Bruce Smith	3.00	1.35	.35
☐ 15 Rashaan Salaam	5.00	2.20	.60
☐ 16 Jeff Blake	5.00	2.20	.60
☐ 17 Alvin Harper	2.00	.90	.25
☐ 18 Shannon Sharpe	3.00	1.35	.35
☐ 19 Eric Swann	2.00	.90	.25
☐ 20 Andre Rison	2.00	.90	.25

1995 Ultra Rising Stars

This nine card set was randomly inserted into series one packs at a rate of one in 37 and features young players in an ultra-crystal design. Card fronts have a colorful space background on plastic stock with the player's name and card title "Rising Stars" in gold foil at the lower right. Card backs contain a commentary on the player. A gold medallion parallel of this set exists and is designated by a gold foil stamp on the front of the card.

	MINT	NRMT	EXC
COMPLETE SET (9)	50.00	22.00	6.25
COMMON CARD (1-9)	3.00	1.35	.35
COMP.GOLD MED.SET (9)	120.00	55.00	15.00
*GOLD MED.CARDS: 1X TO 2X			

	MINT	NRMT	EXC
☐ 1 Jerome Bettis	4.00	1.80	.50
☐ 2 Jeff Blake	6.00	2.70	.75
☐ 3 Drew Bledsoe	12.00	5.50	1.50
☐ 4 Ben Coates	3.00	1.35	.35
☐ 5 Marshall Faulk	6.00	2.70	.75
☐ 6 Brett Favre	25.00	11.00	3.10
☐ 7 Natrone Means	4.00	1.80	.50
☐ 8 Byron Bam Morris	3.00	1.35	.35
☐ 9 Eric Turner	3.00	1.35	.35

1995 Ultra Second Year Standouts

Randomly inserted into series one packs at a rate of one in five packs, this 15 card set focuses on 1994 rookies that made a big impact. Card fronts contain a colorful background with two player shots and the player's name and card title in gold foil along the bottom. Card backs contain another photo with a commentary. A gold medallion parallel of this set exists and is designated with a gold foil stamp on the front of the card.

	MINT	NRMT	EXC
COMPLETE SET (15)	12.00	5.50	1.50
COMMON CARD (1-15)	.50	.23	.06
COMP.GOLD MED.SET (15)	30.00	13.50	3.70
*GOLD MED.CARDS: 1X TO 2X			

	MINT	NRMT	EXC
☐ 1 Derrick Alexander WR	.75	.35	.09
☐ 2 Mario Bates	.50	.23	.06
☐ 3 Tim Bowens	.50	.23	.06
☐ 4 Bert Emanuel	.75	.35	.09
☐ 5 Marshall Faulk	2.00	.90	.25
☐ 6 William Floyd	.75	.35	.09
☐ 7 Rob Fredrickson	.50	.23	.06
☐ 8 Antonio Langham	.50	.23	.06
☐ 9 Byron Bam Morris	.75	.35	.09
☐ 10 Errict Rhett	.75	.35	.09
☐ 11 Darnay Scott	1.25	.55	.16
☐ 12 Heath Shuler	.75	.35	.09
☐ 13 Dewayne Washington	.50	.23	.06
☐ 14 Dan Wilkinson	.50	.23	.06
☐ 15 Bryant Young	.50	.23	.06

1995 Ultra Stars

Randomly inserted into series one jumbo 17 card packs only at a rate of one in seven packs, this 10 card set features some of the most popular NFL superstars. Card fronts contain a multi-photo background with the player's name and card title in silver foil. Card backs contain a photo and commentary. A gold medallion parallel of this set exists and is designated with a gold foil stamp on the front of the card.

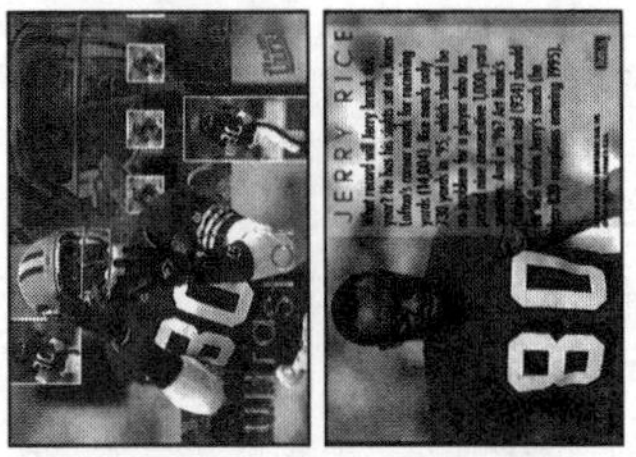

	MINT	NRMT	EXC
COMPLETE SET (10)	15.00	6.75	1.85
COMMON CARD (1-10)	.50	.23	.06
COMP.GOLD MED.SET (10)	35.00	16.00	4.40
*GOLD MED.CARDS: 1X TO 2X			

☐ 1 Tim Brown	.75	.35	.09
☐ 2 Marshall Faulk	1.00	.45	.12
☐ 3 Irving Fryar	.50	.23	.06
☐ 4 Dan Marino	4.00	1.80	.50
☐ 5 Natrone Means	.75	.35	.09
☐ 6 Jerry Rice	2.00	.90	.25
☐ 7 Barry Sanders	2.00	.90	.25
☐ 8 Deion Sanders	1.25	.55	.16
☐ 9 Emmitt Smith	4.00	1.80	.50
☐ 10 Rod Woodson	.50	.23	.06

1995 Ultra Touchdown Kings

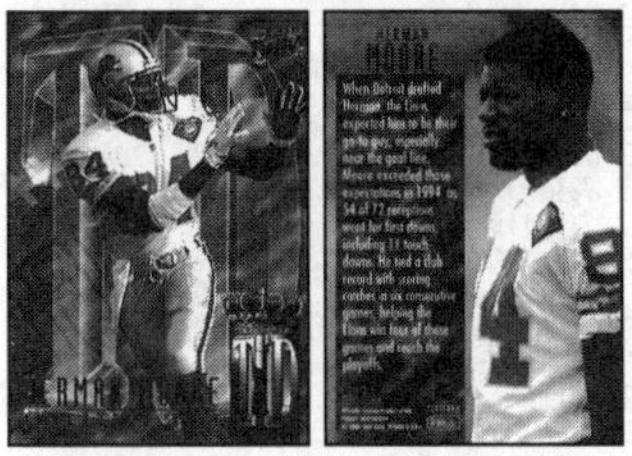

Randomly inserted into series one 12 card packs only at a rate of one in seven packs, this 10 card set features players with a knack for hitting pay dirt. Card fronts feature a colorful background with the letters "TD". The player's name and card title are located along the bottom in gold foil. Card backs feature a photo with commentary. A gold medallion parallel also exists and is designated by a gold foil stamp on the front of the card.

	MINT	NRMT	EXC
COMPLETE SET (10)	10.00	4.50	1.25
COMMON CARD (1-10)	.50	.23	.06
COMP. GOLD MED.SET (10)	20.00	9.00	2.50
*GOLD MED.CARDS: 1X TO 2X			

☐ 1 Marshall Faulk	1.00	.45	.12
☐ 2 Terance Mathis	.50	.23	.06
☐ 3 Natrone Means	.75	.35	.09
☐ 4 Herman Moore	.75	.35	.09
☐ 5 Carl Pickens	.75	.35	.09
☐ 6 Jerry Rice	2.00	.90	.25
☐ 7 Andre Rison	.50	.23	.06
☐ 8 Emmitt Smith	4.00	1.80	.50
☐ 9 Chris Warren	.50	.23	.06
☐ 10 Steve Young	1.50	.70	.19

1995 Ultra Ultrabilities

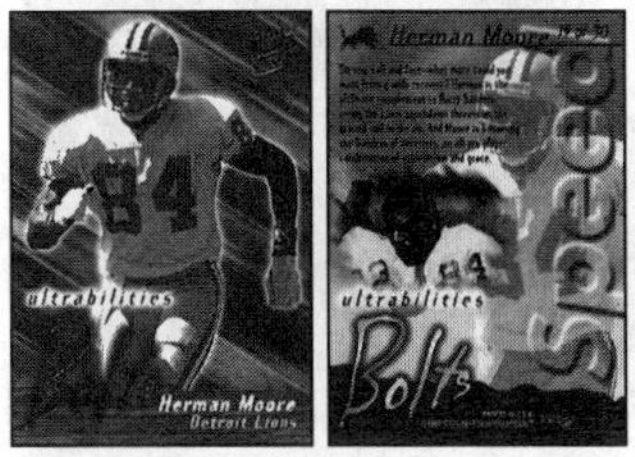

Randomly inserted into series two packs at a rate of one in five packs, this 30 card set is broken into three subsets: Blasts, Bolts and Guns. Blast card fronts contain an orange background with the title "Blasts" in gold foil and the player's name and team in white against an aqua background. Bolt card fronts contain an orange background with the title "Bolts" in gold foil and the player's name and team in white against a green background. Gun card fronts contain an orange swirl background with the title "Guns" in gold foil and the player's name and team in white against a red background. All card backs contain the player's name at the top followed by a brief commentary and a headshot.

	MINT	NRMT	EXC
COMPLETE SET (30)	50.00	22.00	6.25
COMMON CARD (1-30)	1.00	.45	.12

☐ 1 Dan Marino	8.00	3.60	1.00
☐ 2 Steve Young	3.00	1.35	.35
☐ 3 Drew Bledsoe	4.00	1.80	.50
☐ 4 Jeff Blake	2.00	.90	.25
☐ 5 Troy Aikman	4.00	1.80	.50
☐ 6 John Elway	3.00	1.35	.35
☐ 7 Trent Dilfer	1.50	.70	.19
☐ 8 Steve Bono	1.00	.45	.12
☐ 9 Brett Favre	8.00	3.60	1.00
☐ 10 Kerry Collins	6.00	2.70	.75
☐ 11 Barry Sanders	4.00	1.80	.50
☐ 12 Errict Rhett	2.00	.90	.25
☐ 13 Emmitt Smith	8.00	3.60	1.00
☐ 14 Chris Warren	1.00	.45	.12
☐ 15 Irving Fryar	1.00	.45	.12
☐ 16 Charlie Garner	1.00	.45	.12
☐ 17 Tim Brown	1.50	.70	.19
☐ 18 Eric Metcalf	1.00	.45	.12
☐ 19 Herman Moore	2.00	.90	.25
☐ 20 Robert Smith	1.50	.70	.19
☐ 21 Natrone Means	1.50	.70	.19
☐ 22 Derrick Thomas	1.50	.70	.19
☐ 23 Bruce Smith	1.50	.70	.19
☐ 24 Hugh Douglas	1.00	.45	.12
☐ 25 Mike Mamula	1.00	.45	.12
☐ 26 Jerome Bettis	2.00	.90	.25
☐ 27 Byron Bam Morris UER Rams helmet on back	1.50	.70	.19
☐ 28 Tim Bowens	1.00	.45	.12
☐ 29 William Floyd	1.50	.70	.19
☐ 30 Daryl Johnston	1.00	.45	.12

1996 Ultra

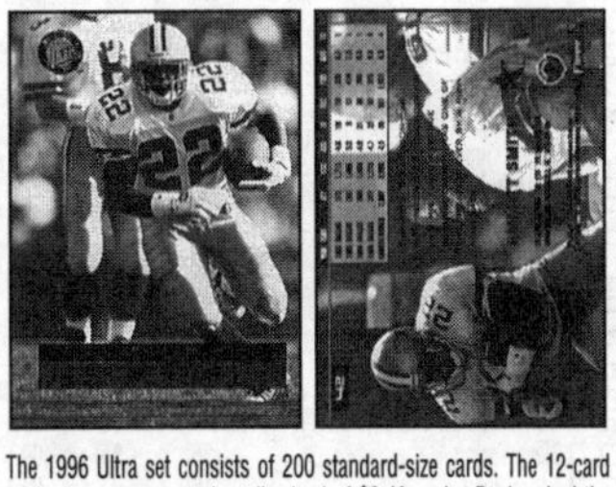

The 1996 Ultra set consists of 200 standard-size cards. The 12-card packs have a suggested retail priced of $2.49 each. Dealers had the option of purchasing either six, 12 or 30 box cases. Each case contained 24 packs per box with the 12 cards in the packs. The cards are grouped alphabetically within teams and checklisted below alphabetically according to teams. The following topical subsets are also part of the set: Rookies (164-178), First Impressions (179-188) and Secret Weapons (189-198). Rookie Cards include Tim Biakabutuka, Bobby Engram, Eddie George, Terry Glenn, Keyshawn Johnson, Leeland McElroy and Lawrence Phillips. A 3-card promo sheet was produced and priced below.

	MINT	NRMT	EXC
COMPLETE SET (200)	30.00	13.50	3.70
COMMON CARD (1-200)	.08	.04	.01

☐ 1 Larry Centers	.15	.07	.02
☐ 2 Garrison Hearst	.15	.07	.02
☐ 3 Rob Moore	.08	.04	.01
☐ 4 Eric Swann	.15	.07	.02
☐ 5 Aeneas Williams	.08	.04	.01
☐ 6 Bert Emanuel	.15	.07	.02
☐ 7 Jeff George	.15	.07	.02
☐ 8 Craig Heyward	.08	.04	.01
☐ 9 Terance Mathis	.08	.04	.01
☐ 10 Eric Metcalf	.15	.07	.02
☐ 11 Cornelius Bennett	.15	.07	.02
☐ 12 Darick Holmes	.15	.07	.02
☐ 13 Jim Kelly	.30	.14	.04
☐ 14 Bryce Paup	.15	.07	.02
☐ 15 Bruce Smith	.30	.14	.04
☐ 16 Mark Carrier WR	.15	.07	.02
☐ 17 Kerry Collins	1.50	.70	.19
☐ 18 Lamar Lathon	.08	.04	.01
☐ 19 Derrick Moore	.08	.04	.01
☐ 20 Tyrone Poole	.08	.04	.01
☐ 21 Curtis Conway	.30	.14	.04
☐ 22 Jeff Graham	.08	.04	.01
☐ 23 Raymont Harris	.08	.04	.01
☐ 24 Erik Kramer	.08	.04	.01
☐ 25 Rashaan Salaam	.30	.14	.04
☐ 26 Jeff Blake	.30	.14	.04
☐ 27 Ki-Jana Carter	.15	.07	.02
☐ 28 Carl Pickens	.30	.14	.04
☐ 29 Darnay Scott	.15	.07	.02
☐ 30 Dan Wilkinson	.08	.04	.01
☐ 31 Leroy Hoard	.08	.04	.01
☐ 32 Michael Jackson	.15	.07	.02
☐ 33 Andre Rison	.15	.07	.02
☐ 34 Vinny Testaverde	.15	.07	.02
☐ 35 Eric Turner	.08	.04	.01
☐ 36 Troy Aikman	1.25	.55	.16
☐ 37 Charles Haley	.15	.07	.02
☐ 38 Michael Irvin	.30	.14	.04
☐ 39 Daryl Johnston	.15	.07	.02
☐ 40 Jay Novacek	.15	.07	.02
☐ 41 Deion Sanders	.75	.35	.09
☐ 42 Emmitt Smith	2.50	1.10	.30
☐ 43 Steve Atwater	.08	.04	.01
☐ 44 Terrell Davis	2.00	.90	.25
☐ 45 John Elway	1.00	.45	.12
☐ 46 Anthony Miller	.15	.07	.02
☐ 47 Shannon Sharpe	.15	.07	.02
☐ 48 Scott Mitchell	.15	.07	.02
☐ 49 Herman Moore	.30	.14	.04
☐ 50 Johnnie Morton	.15	.07	.02
☐ 51 Brett Perriman	.15	.07	.02
☐ 52 Barry Sanders	1.25	.55	.16
☐ 53 Chris Spielman	.15	.07	.02
☐ 54 Edgar Bennett	.15	.07	.02
☐ 55 Robert Brooks	.30	.14	.04
☐ 56 Mark Chmura	.15	.07	.02
☐ 57 Brett Favre	2.50	1.10	.30
☐ 58 Reggie White	.30	.14	.04
☐ 59 Mel Gray	.08	.04	.01
☐ 60 Haywood Jeffires	.08	.04	.01
☐ 61 Steve McNair	1.25	.55	.16
☐ 62 Chris Sanders	.15	.07	.02
☐ 63 Rodney Thomas	.08	.04	.01
☐ 64 Quentin Coryatt	.08	.04	.01
☐ 65 Sean Dawkins	.08	.04	.01
☐ 66 Ken Dilger	.15	.07	.02
☐ 67 Marshall Faulk	.30	.14	.04
☐ 68 Jim Harbaugh	.15	.07	.02
☐ 69 Tony Boselli	.15	.07	.02
☐ 70 Mark Brunell	1.25	.55	.16
☐ 71 Desmond Howard	.15	.07	.02
☐ 72 Jimmy Smith	.15	.07	.02
☐ 73 James O. Stewart	.15	.07	.02
☐ 74 Marcus Allen	.30	.14	.04
☐ 75 Steve Bono	.15	.07	.02
☐ 76 Lake Dawson	.15	.07	.02
☐ 77 Neil Smith	.15	.07	.02
☐ 78 Derrick Thomas	.15	.07	.02
☐ 79 Tamarick Vanover	.30	.14	.04
☐ 80 Bryan Cox	.08	.04	.01
☐ 81 Irving Fryar	.15	.07	.02
☐ 82 Eric Green	.08	.04	.01
☐ 83 Dan Marino	2.50	1.10	.30
☐ 84 O.J. McDuffie	.15	.07	.02
☐ 85 Bernie Parmalee	.08	.04	.01
☐ 86 Cris Carter	.30	.14	.04
☐ 87 Qadry Ismail	.15	.07	.02
☐ 88 Warren Moon	.15	.07	.02
☐ 89 Jake Reed	.15	.07	.02
☐ 90 Robert Smith	.15	.07	.02
☐ 91 Drew Bledsoe	1.25	.55	.16
☐ 92 Vincent Brisby	.08	.04	.01
☐ 93 Ben Coates	.15	.07	.02
☐ 94 Curtis Martin	2.00	.90	.25
☐ 95 Willie McGinest	.08	.04	.01
☐ 96 Dave Meggett	.08	.04	.01
☐ 97 Mario Bates	.15	.07	.02
☐ 98 Quinn Early	.08	.04	.01
☐ 99 Jim Everett	.08	.04	.01
☐ 100 Michael Haynes	.15	.07	.02
☐ 101 Renaldo Turnbull	.08	.04	.01
☐ 102 Dave Brown	.15	.07	.02
☐ 103 Rodney Hampton	.15	.07	.02
☐ 104 Mike Sherrard	.08	.04	.01
☐ 105 Phillippi Sparks	.08	.04	.01
☐ 106 Tyrone Wheatley	.15	.07	.02
☐ 107 Hugh Douglas	.08	.04	.01
☐ 108 Boomer Esiason	.15	.07	.02
☐ 109 Aaron Glenn	.08	.04	.01
☐ 110 Mo Lewis	.08	.04	.01
☐ 111 Johnny Mitchell	.08	.04	.01
☐ 112 Tim Brown	.15	.07	.02
☐ 113 Jeff Hostetler	.15	.07	.02
☐ 114 Rocket Ismail	.15	.07	.02
☐ 115 Chester McGlockton	.08	.04	.01
☐ 116 Harvey Williams	.08	.04	.01
☐ 117 Fred Barnett	.15	.07	.02
☐ 118 William Fuller	.08	.04	.01
☐ 119 Charlie Garner	.08	.04	.01
☐ 120 Ricky Watters	.15	.07	.02
☐ 121 Calvin Williams	.30	.14	.04
☐ 122 Kevin Greene	.15	.07	.02
☐ 123 Greg Lloyd	.15	.07	.02
☐ 124 Byron Bam Morris	.15	.07	.02
☐ 125 Neil O'Donnell	.15	.07	.02
☐ 126 Erric Pegram	.15	.07	.02
☐ 127 Kordell Stewart	1.50	.70	.19
☐ 128 Yancey Thigpen	.15	.07	.02
☐ 129 Rod Woodson	.15	.07	.02
☐ 130 Jerome Bettis	.30	.14	.04
☐ 131 Isaac Bruce	.30	.14	.04
☐ 132 Troy Drayton	.08	.04	.01
☐ 133 Sean Gilbert	.08	.04	.01
☐ 134 Chris Miller	.08	.04	.01
☐ 135 Andre Coleman	.08	.04	.01
☐ 136 Ronnie Harmon	.08	.04	.01
☐ 137 Aaron Hayden	.15	.07	.02
☐ 138 Stan Humphries	.15	.07	.02
☐ 139 Natrone Means	.30	.14	.04
☐ 140 Junior Seau	.30	.14	.04
☐ 141 William Floyd	.15	.07	.02
☐ 142 Merton Hanks	.08	.04	.01
☐ 143 Brent Jones	.08	.04	.01
☐ 144 Derek Loville	.08	.04	.01
☐ 145 Jerry Rice	1.25	.55	.16
☐ 146 J.J. Stokes	.30	.14	.04
☐ 147 Steve Young	1.00	.45	.12
☐ 148 Brian Blades	.15	.07	.02
☐ 149 Joey Galloway	.60	.25	.07
☐ 150 Cortez Kennedy	.15	.07	.02
☐ 151 Rick Mirer	.15	.07	.02
☐ 152 Chris Warren	.15	.07	.02
☐ 153 Derrick Brooks	.08	.04	.01
☐ 154 Trent Dilfer	.15	.07	.02
☐ 155 Alvin Harper	.08	.04	.01
☐ 156 Jackie Harris	.08	.04	.01
☐ 157 Hardy Nickerson	.08	.04	.01
☐ 158 Errict Rhett	.15	.07	.02
☐ 159 Terry Allen	.15	.07	.02
☐ 160 Henry Ellard	.15	.07	.02
☐ 161 Brian Mitchell	.08	.04	.01
☐ 162 Heath Shuler	.30	.14	.04
☐ 163 Michael Westbrook	.30	.14	.04
☐ 164 Tim Biakabutuka	1.00	.45	.12
☐ 165 Tony Brackens	.15	.07	.02
☐ 166 Rickey Dudley	.30	.14	.04
☐ 167 Bobby Engram	1.00	.45	.12
☐ 168 Daryl Gardener	.15	.07	.02
☐ 169 Eddie George	4.00	1.80	.50
☐ 170 Terry Glenn	3.00	1.35	.35
☐ 171 Kevin Hardy	.15	.07	.02
☐ 172 Keyshawn Johnson	1.50	.70	.19
☐ 173 Cedric Jones	.15	.07	.02
☐ 174 Leeland McElroy	.30	.14	.04
☐ 175 Jonathan Ogden	.08	.04	.01
☐ 176 Lawrence Phillips	.50	.23	.06
☐ 177 Simeon Rice	.30	.14	.04
☐ 178 Regan Upshaw	.08	.04	.01
☐ 179 Justin Armour FI	.08	.04	.01
☐ 180 Kyle Brady FI	.15	.07	.02
☐ 181 Devin Bush FI	.08	.04	.01
☐ 182 Kevin Carter FI	.15	.07	.02
☐ 183 Wayne Chrebet FI	.15	.07	.02
☐ 184 Napoleon Kaufman FI	.15	.07	.02
☐ 185 Frank Sanders FI	.15	.07	.02
☐ 186 Warren Sapp FI	.08	.04	.01
☐ 187 Eric Zeier FI	.15	.07	.02
☐ 188 Ray Zellars FI	.08	.04	.01
☐ 189 Bill Brooks SW	.08	.04	.01
☐ 190 Chris Calloway SW	.08	.04	.01
☐ 191 Zack Crockett SW	.08	.04	.01
☐ 192 Antonio Freeman SW	.30	.14	.04
☐ 193 Tyrone Hughes SW	.08	.04	.01
☐ 194 Daryl Johnston SW	.15	.07	.02
☐ 195 Tony Martin SW	.08	.04	.01
☐ 196 Keenan McCardell SW	.30	.14	.04
☐ 197 Glyn Milburn SW	.08	.04	.01
☐ 198 David Palmer SW	.15	.07	.02
☐ 199 Checklist	.08	.04	.01
☐ 200 Checklist	.08	.04	.01
☐ P1 Promo Sheet Trent Dilfer Brett Favre Mr.Momentum Daryl Johnston Secret Weapon	2.00	.90	.25

1996 Ultra All-Rookie Die Cuts

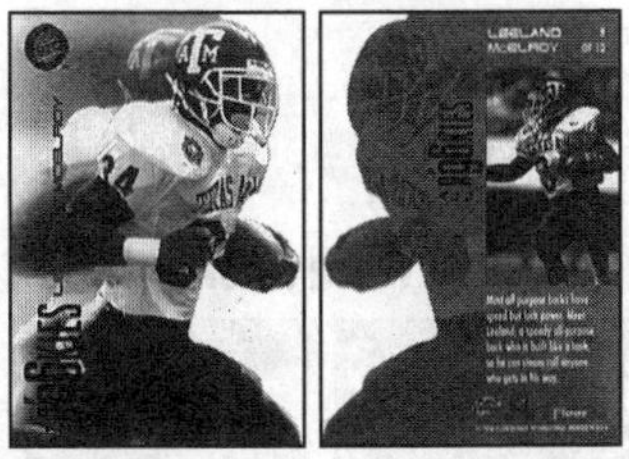

This 10 card die-cut set contains some of the better 1996 rookies. The cards were inserted at the rate of 1 in 180 Ultra packs and are numbered as "X" of 10.

	MINT	NRMT	EXC
COMPLETE SET (10)	200.00	90.00	25.00
COMMON CARD (1-10)	8.00	3.60	1.00

☐ 1 Bobby Engram	16.00	7.25	2.00
☐ 2 Daryl Gardener	8.00	3.60	1.00
☐ 3 Eddie George	50.00	22.00	6.25
☐ 4 Terry Glenn	40.00	18.00	5.00
☐ 5 Kevin Hardy	12.00	5.50	1.50
☐ 6 Keyshawn Johnson	25.00	11.00	3.10
☐ 7 Cedric Jones	8.00	3.60	1.00
☐ 8 Leeland McElroy	12.00	5.50	1.50
☐ 9 Jonathan Ogden	8.00	3.60	1.00
☐ 10 Simeon Rice	8.00	3.60	1.00

1996 Ultra Mr. Momentum

Randomly inserted in packs at a rate of one 10, this 20-card standard-size set features players who can dominate a game. The set is printed on special holographic-foil enhanced cards. The cards are sequenced in alphabetical order and numbered "X" of 20.

	MINT	NRMT	EXC
COMPLETE SET (20)	60.00	27.00	7.50
COMMON CARD (1-20)	2.00	.90	.25

☐ 1 Robert Brooks	3.50	1.55	.45
☐ 2 Isaac Bruce	5.00	2.20	.60
☐ 3 Terrell Davis	12.00	5.50	1.50
☐ 4 John Elway	6.00	2.70	.75
☐ 5 Marshall Faulk	5.00	2.20	.60

432 • 1996 Ultra Mr. Momentum

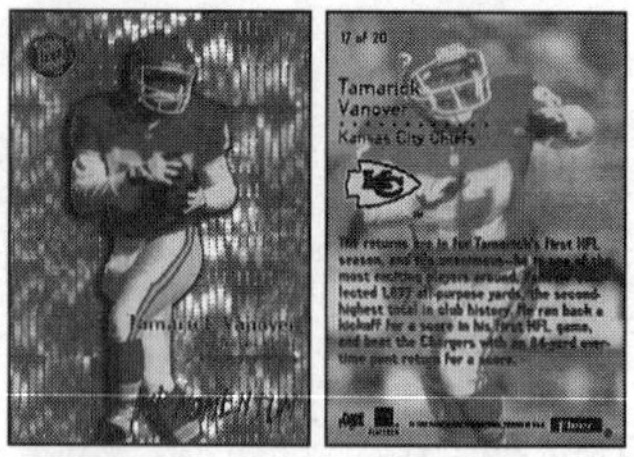

	MINT	NRMT	EXC
☐ 6 Brett Favre	15.00	6.75	1.85
☐ 7 Joey Galloway	5.00	2.20	.60
☐ 8 Dan Marino	15.00	6.75	1.85
☐ 9 Curtis Martin	12.00	5.50	1.50
☐ 10 Herman Moore	5.00	2.20	.60
☐ 11 Carl Pickens	3.50	1.55	.45
☐ 12 Jerry Rice	8.00	3.60	1.00
☐ 13 Barry Sanders	8.00	3.60	1.00
☐ 14 Chris Sanders	3.50	1.55	.45
☐ 15 Deion Sanders	5.00	2.20	.60
☐ 16 Kordell Stewart	10.00	4.50	1.25
☐ 17 Tamarick Vanover	5.00	2.20	.60
☐ 18 Chris Warren	2.00	.90	.25
☐ 19 Ricky Watters	2.00	.90	.25
☐ 20 Steve Young	6.00	2.70	.75

1996 Ultra Pulsating

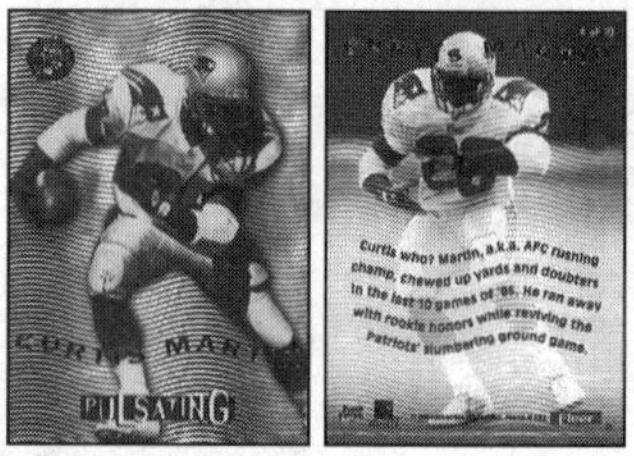

Randomly inserted in packs at a rate of one in 20, this 10-card standard-size set featured offensive skill position players. The set is printed on foil-enhanced cards. The cards are sequenced in alphabetical order and are numbered "X" of 10.

	MINT	NRMT	EXC
COMPLETE SET (10)	60.00	27.00	7.50
COMMON CARD (1-10)	2.00	.90	.25
☐ 1 Isaac Bruce	3.00	1.35	.35
☐ 2 Brett Favre	15.00	6.75	1.85
☐ 3 Joey Galloway	5.00	2.20	.60
☐ 4 Curtis Martin	12.00	5.50	1.50
☐ 5 Rashaan Salaam	4.00	1.80	.50
☐ 6 Barry Sanders	8.00	3.60	1.00
☐ 7 Deion Sanders	5.00	2.20	.60
☐ 8 Emmitt Smith	15.00	6.75	1.85
☐ 9 Kordell Stewart	10.00	4.50	1.25
☐ 10 Chris Warren	2.00	.90	.25

1996 Ultra Rookies

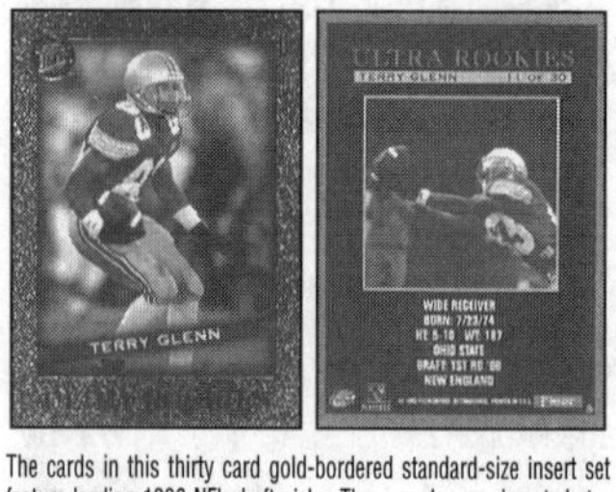

The cards in this thirty card gold-bordered standard-size insert set feature leading 1996 NFL draft picks. These cards were inserted at a ratio of 1 per 3 packs. The cards are sequenced in alphabetical order and were numbered as "X" of 30.

	MINT	NRMT	EXC
COMPLETE SET (30)	50.00	22.00	6.25
COMMON CARD (1-30)	1.00	.45	.12
☐ 1 Karim Abdul-Jabbar	6.00	2.70	.75
☐ 2 Mike Alstott	3.00	1.35	.35
☐ 3 Marco Battaglia	1.00	.45	.12
☐ 4 Tim Biakabutuka	2.00	.90	.25
☐ 5 Sean Boyd	1.00	.45	.12
☐ 6 Tony Brackens	2.00	.90	.25
☐ 7 Duane Clemons	1.00	.45	.12
☐ 8 Bobby Engram	3.00	1.35	.35
☐ 9 Daryl Gardener	2.00	.90	.25
☐ 10 Eddie George	10.00	4.50	1.25
☐ 11 Terry Glenn	8.00	3.60	1.00
☐ 12 Kevin Hardy	2.00	.90	.25
☐ 13 Marvin Harrison	4.00	1.80	.50
☐ 14 Dietrich Jells	1.00	.45	.12
☐ 15 Keyshawn Johnson	4.00	1.80	.50
☐ 16 Lance Johnstone	1.00	.45	.12
☐ 17 Cedric Jones	1.00	.45	.12
☐ 18 Marcus Jones	1.00	.45	.12
☐ 19 Danny Kanell	2.00	.90	.25
☐ 20 Markco Maddox	1.00	.45	.12
☐ 21 Derrick Mayes	2.00	.90	.25
☐ 22 Leeland McElroy	2.00	.90	.25
☐ 23 Dell McGee	1.00	.45	.12
☐ 24 Alex Molden	1.00	.45	.12
☐ 25 Eric Moulds	3.00	1.35	.35
☐ 26 Jonathan Ogden	1.00	.45	.12
☐ 27 Lawrence Phillips	3.00	1.35	.35
☐ 28 Simeon Rice	2.00	.90	.25
☐ 29 Regan Upshaw	1.00	.45	.12
☐ 30 Jerome Woods	1.00	.45	.12

1996 Ultra Sledgehammer

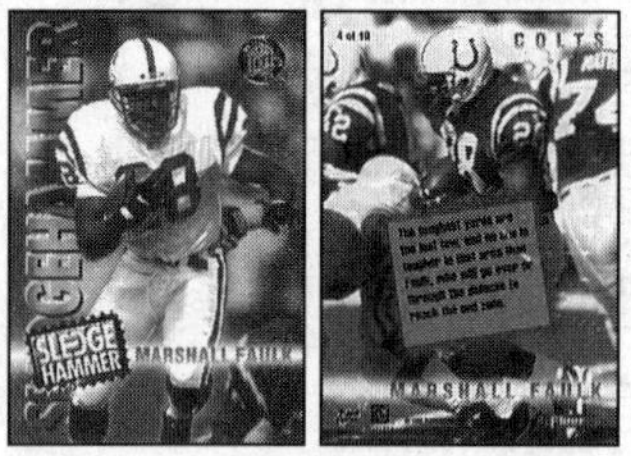

Randomly inserted in hobby packs only at a rate of one in 15, this 10-card embossed standard-size set highlights powerful offensive or defensive players. The cards are numbered as "X" of 10 and are sequenced in alphabetical order.

	MINT	NRMT	EXC
COMPLETE SET (10)	40.00	18.00	5.00
COMMON CARD (1-10)	3.00	1.35	.35
☐ 1 Jeff Blake	5.00	2.20	.60
☐ 2 Terrell Davis	8.00	3.60	1.00
☐ 3 Hugh Douglas	3.00	1.35	.35
☐ 4 Marshall Faulk	5.00	2.20	.60
☐ 5 Michael Irvin	5.00	2.20	.60
☐ 6 Steve McNair	6.00	2.70	.75
☐ 7 Natrone Means	4.00	1.80	.50
☐ 8 Errict Rhett	4.00	1.80	.50
☐ 9 Emmitt Smith	12.00	5.50	1.50
☐ 10 Rodney Thomas	3.00	1.35	.35

1997 Ultra

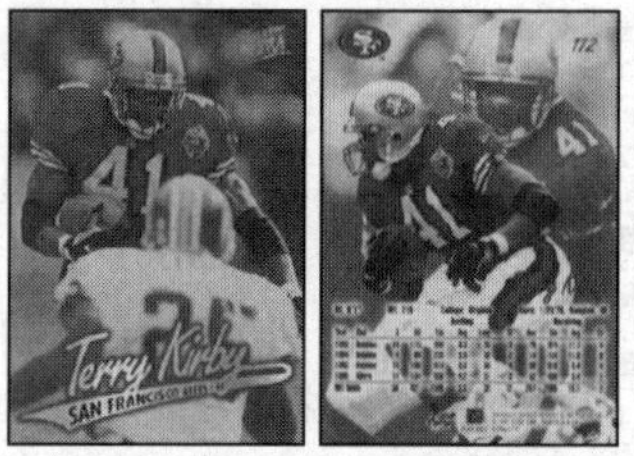

The 1997 Ultra set was released in one series totaling 200-cards with a large number of insert sets. Hobby packs also contained one Gold Medallion parallel card per pack with a Platinum Medallion parallel replacing the Gold version in 1:100 packs. The base cards feature the player's name and team name printed in silver holofoil on the card fronts. The cards were distributed in 24-pack hobby boxes with 10 cards per pack (2 inserts per pack).

	MINT	NRMT	EXC
COMPLETE SET (200)	30.00	13.50	3.70
COMMON CARD (1-200)	.10	.05	.01
☐ 1 Brett Favre	2.50	1.10	.30
☐ 2 Ricky Watters	.15	.07	.02
☐ 3 Dan Marino	2.50	1.10	.30
☐ 4 Bryan Still	.10	.05	.01
☐ 5 Chester McGlockton	.10	.05	.01
☐ 6 Tim Biakabutuka	.25	.11	.03
☐ 7 Dave Brown	.15	.07	.02
☐ 8 Mike Alstott	.25	.11	.03
☐ 9 O.J. McDuffie	.15	.07	.02
☐ 10 Mark Brunell	1.25	.55	.16
☐ 11 Michael Bates	.10	.05	.01
☐ 12 Tyrone Wheatley	.15	.07	.02
☐ 13 Eddie George	2.00	.90	.25
☐ 14 Kevin Greene	.15	.07	.02
☐ 15 Jerris McPhail	.10	.05	.01
☐ 16 Harvey Williams	.10	.05	.01
☐ 17 Eric Swann	.15	.07	.02
☐ 18 Carl Pickens	.25	.11	.03
☐ 19 Terrell Davis	1.25	.55	.16
☐ 20 Charles Way	.10	.05	.01
☐ 21 Jamie Asher	.15	.07	.02
☐ 22 Qadry Ismail	.15	.07	.02
☐ 23 Lawrence Phillips	.15	.07	.02
☐ 24 John Friesz	.10	.05	.01
☐ 25 Dorsey Levens	.15	.07	.02
☐ 26 Willie McGinest	.10	.05	.01
☐ 27 Chris T. Jones	.25	.11	.03
☐ 28 Cortez Kennedy	.15	.07	.02
☐ 29 Raymont Harris	.10	.05	.01
☐ 30 William Roaf	.10	.05	.01
☐ 31 Ted Johnson	.10	.05	.01
☐ 32 Tony Martin	.15	.07	.02
☐ 33 Jim Everett	.10	.05	.01
☐ 34 Ray Zellars	.10	.05	.01
☐ 35 Derrick Alexander WR	.15	.07	.02
☐ 36 Leonard Russell	.10	.05	.01
☐ 37 William Thomas	.10	.05	.01
☐ 38 Karim Abdul-Jabbar	1.00	.45	.12
☐ 39 Kevin Turner	.10	.05	.01
☐ 40 Robert Brooks	.25	.11	.03
☐ 41 Kent Graham	.15	.07	.02
☐ 42 Tony Brackens	.10	.05	.01
☐ 43 Rodney Hampton	.15	.07	.02
☐ 44 Drew Bledsoe	1.25	.55	.16
☐ 45 Barry Sanders	1.25	.55	.16
☐ 46 Tim Brown	.15	.07	.02
☐ 47 Reggie White	.25	.11	.03
☐ 48 Terry Allen	.15	.07	.02
☐ 49 Jim Harbaugh	.15	.07	.02
☐ 50 John Elway	1.00	.45	.12
☐ 51 William Floyd	.15	.07	.02
☐ 52 Michael Jackson	.15	.07	.02
☐ 53 Larry Centers	.15	.07	.02
☐ 54 Emmitt Smith	2.50	1.10	.30
☐ 55 Bruce Smith	.25	.11	.03
☐ 56 Terrell Owens	.75	.35	.09
☐ 57 Deion Sanders	.60	.25	.07
☐ 58 Neil O'Donnell	.15	.07	.02
☐ 59 Kordell Stewart	1.00	.45	.12
☐ 60 Bobby Engram	.15	.07	.02
☐ 61 Keenan McCardell	.15	.07	.02
☐ 62 Ben Coates	.15	.07	.02
☐ 63 Curtis Martin	1.25	.55	.16
☐ 64 Hugh Douglas	.10	.05	.01
☐ 65 Eric Moulds	.25	.11	.03
☐ 66 Derrick Thomas	.15	.07	.02
☐ 67 Byron Bam Morris	.15	.07	.02
☐ 68 Bryan Cox	.10	.05	.01
☐ 69 Rob Moore	.10	.05	.01
☐ 70 Michael Haynes	.15	.07	.02
☐ 71 Brian Mitchell	.10	.05	.01
☐ 72 Alex Molden	.10	.05	.01
☐ 73 Steve Young	.75	.35	.09
☐ 74 Andre Reed	.15	.07	.02
☐ 75 Michael Westbrook	.25	.11	.03
☐ 76 Eric Metcalf	.15	.07	.02
☐ 77 Tony Banks	.40	.18	.05
☐ 78 Ken Dilger	.15	.07	.02
☐ 79 John Henry Mills	.10	.05	.01
☐ 80 Ashley Ambrose	.10	.05	.01
☐ 81 Jason Dunn	.15	.07	.02
☐ 82 Trent Dilfer	.15	.07	.02
☐ 83 Wayne Chrebet	.10	.05	.01
☐ 84 Ty Detmer	.15	.07	.02
☐ 85 Aeneas Williams	.10	.05	.01
☐ 86 Frank Wycheck	.10	.05	.01
☐ 87 Jessie Tuggle	.10	.05	.01
☐ 88 Steve McNair	.75	.35	.09
☐ 89 Chris Slade	.10	.05	.01
☐ 90 Anthony Johnson	.15	.07	.02
☐ 91 Simeon Rice	.15	.07	.02
☐ 92 Mike Tomczak	.10	.05	.01
☐ 93 Sean Jones	.10	.05	.01
☐ 94 Wesley Walls	.10	.05	.01
☐ 95 Thurman Thomas	.25	.11	.03
☐ 96 Scott Mitchell	.15	.07	.02
☐ 97 Desmond Howard	.15	.07	.02
☐ 98 Chris Warren	.15	.07	.02
☐ 99 Glyn Milburn	.10	.05	.01
☐ 100 Vinny Testaverde	.15	.07	.02
☐ 101 James O.Stewart	.15	.07	.02
☐ 102 Iheanyi Uwaezuoke	.10	.05	.01
☐ 103 Stan Humphries	.15	.07	.02
☐ 104 Terance Mathis	.10	.05	.01
☐ 105 Thomas Lewis	.10	.05	.01
☐ 106 Eddie Kennison	.60	.25	.07
☐ 107 Rashaan Salaam	.25	.11	.03
☐ 108 Curtis Conway	.25	.11	.03
☐ 109 Chris Sanders	.15	.07	.02
☐ 110 Marcus Allen	.25	.11	.03
☐ 111 Gilbert Brown	.15	.07	.02
☐ 112 Jason Sehorn	.10	.05	.01
☐ 113 Zach Thomas	.40	.18	.05
☐ 114 Bobby Hebert	.10	.05	.01
☐ 115 Herman Moore	.25	.11	.03
☐ 116 Ray Lewis	.10	.05	.01
☐ 117 Darnay Scott	.15	.07	.02
☐ 118 Jamal Anderson	.15	.07	.02
☐ 119 Keyshawn Johnson	.60	.25	.07
☐ 120 Adrian Murrell	.15	.07	.02
☐ 121 Sam Mills	.15	.07	.02
☐ 122 Irving Fryar	.15	.07	.02
☐ 123 Ki-Jana Carter	.15	.07	.02
☐ 124 Gus Frerotte	.25	.11	.03
☐ 125 Terry Glenn	1.25	.55	.16
☐ 126 Quentin Coryatt	.10	.05	.01
☐ 127 Robert Smith	.15	.07	.02
☐ 128 Jeff Blake	.25	.11	.03
☐ 129 Natrone Means	.25	.11	.03
☐ 130 Isaac Bruce	.25	.11	.03
☐ 131 Lamar Lathon	.10	.05	.01
☐ 132 Johnnie Morton	.15	.07	.02
☐ 133 Jerry Rice	1.25	.55	.16
☐ 134 Errict Rhett	.15	.07	.02
☐ 135 Junior Seau	.25	.11	.03
☐ 136 Joey Galloway	.40	.18	.05
☐ 137 Napoleon Kaufman	.15	.07	.02
☐ 138 Troy Aikman	1.25	.55	.16
☐ 139 Kevin Hardy	.15	.07	.02
☐ 140 Jimmy Smith	.15	.07	.02
☐ 141 Edgar Bennett	.15	.07	.02
☐ 142 Hardy Nickerson	.10	.05	.01
☐ 143 Greg Lloyd	.15	.07	.02
☐ 144 Dale Carter	.10	.05	.01
☐ 145 Jake Reed	.15	.07	.02
☐ 146 Cris Carter	.25	.11	.03
☐ 147 Todd Collins	.15	.07	.02
☐ 148 Mel Gray	.10	.05	.01
☐ 149 Lawyer Milloy	.10	.05	.01
☐ 150 Kimble Anders	.10	.05	.01
☐ 151 Darick Holmes	.15	.07	.02
☐ 152 Bert Emanuel	.15	.07	.02
☐ 153 Marshall Faulk	.25	.11	.03
☐ 154 Frank Sanders	.15	.07	.02
☐ 155 Leeland McElroy	.15	.07	.02
☐ 156 Rickey Dudley	.15	.07	.02
☐ 157 Tamarick Vanover	.15	.07	.02
☐ 158 Kerry Collins	1.00	.45	.12
☐ 159 Jeff Graham	.10	.05	.01
☐ 160 Jerome Bettis	.25	.11	.03
☐ 161 Greg Hill	.15	.07	.02
☐ 162 John Mobley	.10	.05	.01
☐ 163 Michael Irvin	.25	.11	.03
☐ 164 Marvin Harrison	.60	.25	.07
☐ 165 Jim Schwantz	.10	.05	.01
☐ 166 Jermaine Lewis	.10	.05	.01
☐ 167 Levon Kirkland	.10	.05	.01
☐ 168 Nilo Silvan	.10	.05	.01
☐ 169 Ken Norton	.10	.05	.01
☐ 170 Yancey Thigpen	.15	.07	.02
☐ 171 Antonio Freeman	.40	.18	.05
☐ 172 Terry Kirby	.15	.07	.02
☐ 173 Brad Johnson	.15	.07	.02
☐ 174 Reidel Anthony	2.00	.90	.25
☐ 175 Tiki Barber	1.00	.45	.12
☐ 176 Pat Barnes	1.00	.45	.12
☐ 177 Michael Booker	.10	.05	.01
☐ 178 Peter Boulware	.10	.05	.01
☐ 179 Rae Carruth	1.25	.55	.16
☐ 180 Troy Davis	1.50	.70	.19
☐ 181 Corey Dillon	1.25	.55	.16
☐ 182 Jim Druckenmiller	2.50	1.10	.30
☐ 183 Warrick Dunn	3.00	1.35	.35
☐ 184 James Farrior	.10	.05	.01
☐ 185 Yatil Green	2.00	.90	.25
☐ 186 Walter Jones	.10	.05	.01
☐ 187 Tom Knight	.10	.05	.01
☐ 188 Sam Madison	.10	.05	.01
☐ 189 Tyrus McCloud	.10	.05	.01
☐ 190 Orlando Pace	.50	.23	.06
☐ 191 Jake Plummer	1.00	.45	.12
☐ 192 Dwayne Rudd	.10	.05	.01
☐ 193 Darrell Russell	.10	.05	.01
☐ 194 Sedrick Shaw	1.00	.45	.12
☐ 195 Shawn Springs	1.00	.45	.12
☐ 196 Bryant Westbrook	.25	.11	.03
☐ 197 Danny Wuerffel	2.50	1.10	.30
☐ 198 Reinard Wilson	.10	.05	.01
☐ 199 Checklist Rodney Hampton	.10	.05	.01
☐ 200 Checklist John Elway	.25	.11	.03
☐ S1 Terrell Davis Sample	3.00	1.35	.35

1997 Ultra Gold Medallion

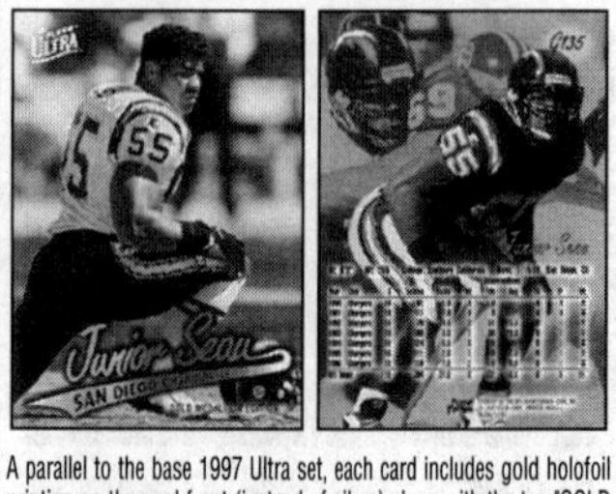

A parallel to the base 1997 Ultra set, each card includes gold holofoil printing on the card front (instead of silver) along with the tag "GOLD MEDALLION EDITION." The backs are numbered with a G prefix as well. Fleer used new photos on the card fronts for the parallel sets. The Gold Medallion cards were randomly inserted in hobby packs only at the rate of one per pack. The two checklist cards were not included in the parallel sets.

	MINT	NRMT	EXC
COMPLETE SET (198)	150.00	70.00	19.00
COMMON CARD (1-198)	.30	.14	.04

*STARS: 2X TO 4X BASIC CARDS
*YOUNG STARS: 1.5X TO 3X BASIC CARDS
*RCs: 1.5X TO 3X BASIC CARDS

1997 Ultra Platinum Medallion

A parallel to the base 1997 Ultra set, each card includes platinum holofoil printing on the card front (instead of silver). The backs are

numbered with a "P" prefix as well. Fleer used new photos on the card fronts for the parallel sets. The Platinum Medallion cards were randomly inserted in hobby packs only at the rate of 1:100 packs. Reportedly less than 150 of each card was produced.

	MINT	NRMT	EXC
COMMON CARD (1-198)	10.00	4.50	1.25
*STARS: 40X TO 80X BASIC CARDS			
*YOUNG STARS: 30X TO 60X BASIC CARDS			
*RCs: 20X TO 40X BASIC CARDS			

1997 Ultra Blitzkrieg

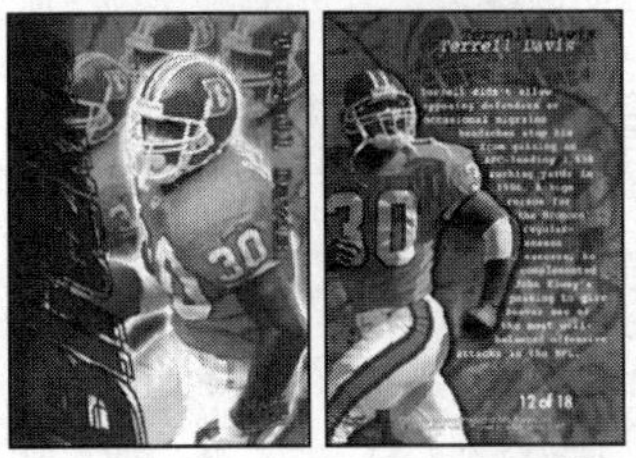

Randomly inserted in packs at a rate of one in 6, these cards feature top offensive players with a rainbow foil "blitzkrieg" logo running down the left side of the card front. A Die Cut parallel set was produced and randomly inserted at the rate of 1:36 packs.

	MINT	NRMT	EXC
COMPLETE SET (18)	80.00	36.00	10.00
COMMON CARD (1-18)	3.00	1.35	.35
*DIE CUTS: 1.5X TO 3X BASIC CARDS			
☐ 1 Eddie George	8.00	3.60	1.00
☐ 2 Terry Glenn	6.00	2.70	.75
☐ 3 Karim Abdul-Jabbar	5.00	2.20	.60
☐ 4 Emmitt Smith	12.00	5.50	1.50
☐ 5 Dan Marino	12.00	5.50	1.50
☐ 6 Brett Favre	12.00	5.50	1.50
☐ 7 Keyshawn Johnson	3.00	1.35	.35
☐ 8 Curtis Martin	6.00	2.70	.75
☐ 9 Marvin Harrison	4.00	1.80	.50
☐ 10 Barry Sanders	6.00	2.70	.75
☐ 11 Jerry Rice	6.00	2.70	.75
☐ 12 Terrell Davis	6.00	2.70	.75
☐ 13 Troy Aikman	6.00	2.70	.75
☐ 14 Drew Bledsoe	6.00	2.70	.75
☐ 15 John Elway	5.00	2.20	.60
☐ 16 Kordell Stewart	5.00	2.20	.60
☐ 17 Kerry Collins	5.00	2.20	.60
☐ 18 Steve Young	4.00	1.80	.50

1997 Ultra Play of the Game

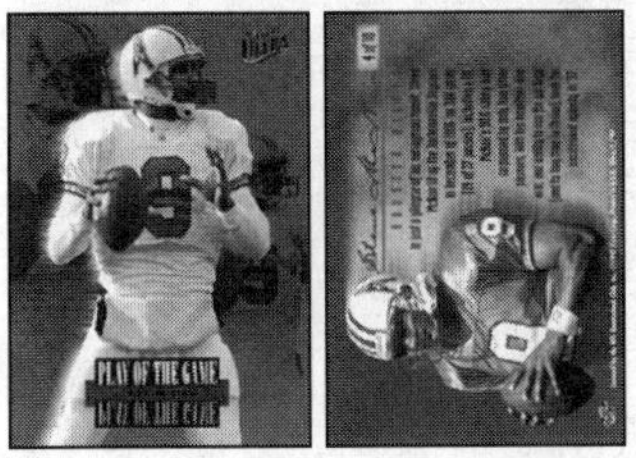

Cards from this set were randomly inserted in 1997 Ultra packs at the rate of 1:8. Each of these 10 cards feature a top offensive star with a short write-up about a great play or career game that player has had.

	MINT	NRMT	EXC
COMPLETE SET (10)	25.00	11.00	3.10
COMMON CARD (1-10)	1.50	.70	.19
☐ 1 Deion Sanders	3.00	1.35	.35
☐ 2 Jerry Rice	6.00	2.70	.75
☐ 3 Michael Westbrook	2.50	1.10	.30
☐ 4 Steve McNair	4.00	1.80	.50
☐ 5 Marshall Faulk	2.50	1.10	.30
☐ 6 Terrell Davis	6.00	2.70	.75
☐ 7 Mark Brunell	6.00	2.70	.75
☐ 8 Isaac Bruce	2.50	1.10	.30
☐ 9 Tony Banks	4.00	1.80	.50
☐ 10 Jamal Anderson	1.50	.70	.19

1997 Ultra Rookies

Rookies inserts were randomly seeded at a rate of one in 4. Each card was printed with the player's name and the Ultra logo in silver foil. A Gold Foil Embossed parallel version was also produced and randomly inserted at the rate of 1:18 packs.

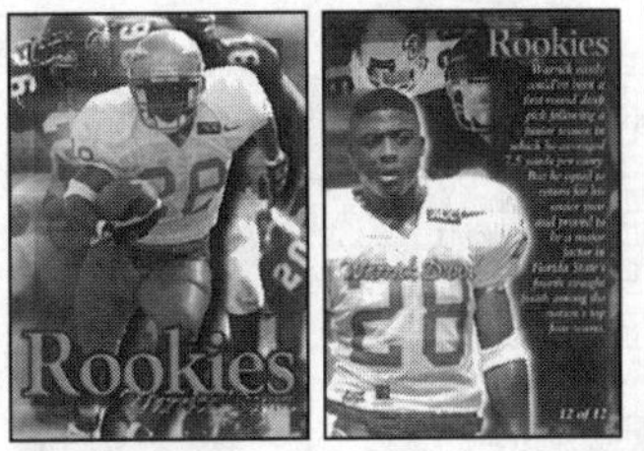

	MINT	NRMT	EXC
COMPLETE SET (12)	15.00	6.75	1.85
COMMON CARD (1-12)	.50	.23	.06
*GOLD EMBOSSED: 1.5X TO 3X			
☐ 1 Darnell Autry	1.50	.70	.19
☐ 2 Orlando Pace	1.00	.45	.12
☐ 3 Peter Boulware	.75	.35	.09
☐ 4 Shawn Springs	1.50	.70	.19
☐ 5 Bryant Westbrook	.50	.23	.06
☐ 6 Rae Carruth	2.00	.90	.25
☐ 7 Jim Druckenmiller	5.00	2.20	.60
☐ 8 Yatil Green	3.00	1.35	.35
☐ 9 James Farrior	.50	.23	.06
☐ 10 Dwayne Rudd	.50	.23	.06
☐ 11 Darrell Russell	.50	.23	.06
☐ 12 Warrick Dunn	6.00	2.70	.75

1997 Ultra Starring Role

This set was the toughest to pull of the non-parallel inserts in 1997 Ultra. Cards in this 10-card set were randomly inserted in packs at the rate of one in 288.

	MINT	NRMT	EXC
COMPLETE SET (10)	500.00	220.00	60.00
COMMON CARD (1-10)	30.00	13.50	3.70
☐ 1 Emmitt Smith	100.00	45.00	12.50
☐ 2 Barry Sanders	50.00	22.00	6.25
☐ 3 Curtis Martin	50.00	22.00	6.25
☐ 4 Dan Marino	100.00	45.00	12.50
☐ 5 Keyshawn Johnson	30.00	13.50	3.70
☐ 6 Marvin Harrison	30.00	13.50	3.70
☐ 7 Terry Glenn	50.00	22.00	6.25
☐ 8 Eddie George	70.00	32.00	8.75
☐ 9 Brett Favre	100.00	45.00	12.50
☐ 10 Karim Abdul-Jabbar	40.00	18.00	5.00

1997 Ultra Sunday School

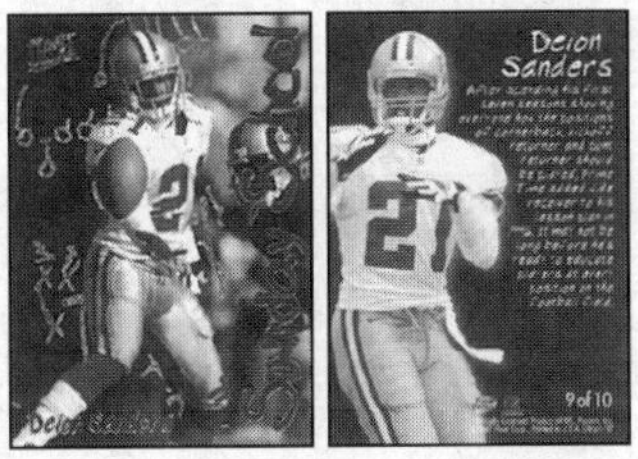

Randomly inserted in packs at a rate of one in 8, this 10-card set features an X's and O's type play diagram printed in silver foil on the card fronts.

	MINT	NRMT	EXC
COMPLETE SET (10)	30.00	13.50	3.70
COMMON CARD (1-10)	2.00	.90	.25
☐ 1 Marvin Harrison	4.00	1.80	.50
☐ 2 Barry Sanders	6.00	2.70	.75
☐ 3 Troy Aikman	6.00	2.70	.75
☐ 4 Drew Bledsoe	6.00	2.70	.75
☐ 5 John Elway	5.00	2.20	.60
☐ 6 Kordell Stewart	5.00	2.20	.60
☐ 7 Kerry Collins	5.00	2.20	.60
☐ 8 Steve Young	4.00	1.80	.50
☐ 9 Deion Sanders	3.00	1.35	.35
☐ 10 Joey Galloway	2.00	.90	.25

1997 Ultra Talent Show

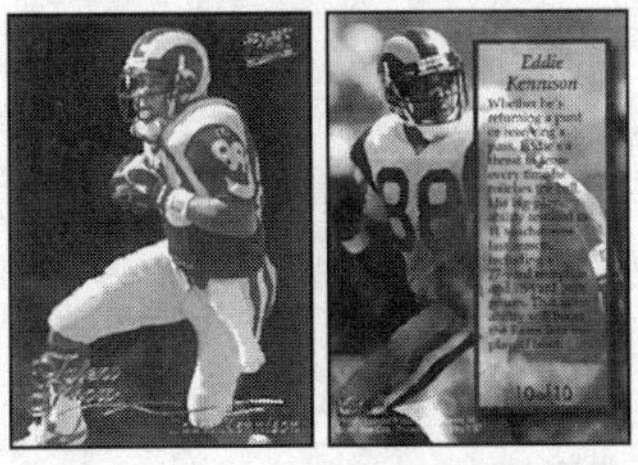

Randomly inserted in packs at a rate of one in 4, each card includes a player photo against a foil card stock background. The 10-card set focuses on up and coming NFL stars and includes gold foil lettering on the card fronts.

	MINT	NRMT	EXC
COMPLETE SET (10)	10.00	4.50	1.25
COMMON CARD (1-10)	.75	.35	.09
☐ 1 Joey Galloway	1.25	.55	.16
☐ 2 Steve McNair	2.00	.90	.25
☐ 3 Marshall Faulk	1.00	.45	.12
☐ 4 Isaac Bruce	1.00	.45	.12
☐ 5 Michael Westbrook	1.00	.45	.12
☐ 6 Zach Thomas	1.00	.45	.12
☐ 7 Jamal Anderson	.75	.35	.09
☐ 8 Mike Alstott	.75	.35	.09
☐ 9 Mark Brunell	3.00	1.35	.35
☐ 10 Eddie Kennison	2.00	.90	.25

1996 Ultra Sensations

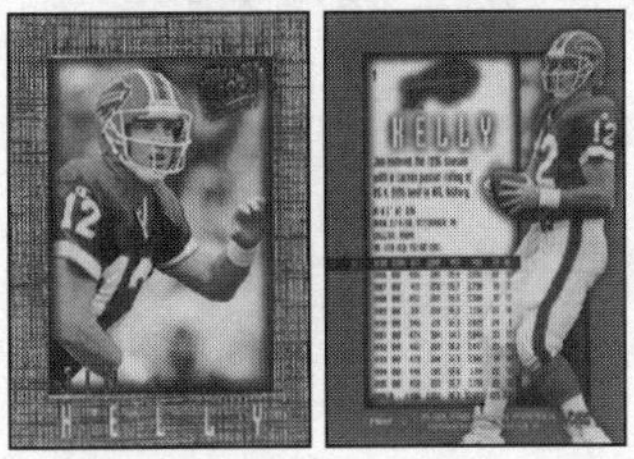

The 1996 Ultra Sensations set was issued in one series totalling 100 cards. The 12-card packs carried a suggested retail price of $2.49. Each card was produced in five different foil border colors with each inserted at various ratios. The Rainbow foil was the most difficult to pull (1% of total print run).

	MINT	NRMT	EXC
COMPLETE GOLD SET (100)	18.00	8.00	2.20
COMMON GOLD CARD (1-100)	.08	.04	.01
☐ 1 Leeland McElroy	.30	.14	.04
☐ 2 Frank Sanders	.15	.07	.02
☐ 3 Eric Swann	.15	.07	.02
☐ 4 Jeff George	.15	.07	.02
☐ 5 Terance Mathis	.08	.04	.01
☐ 6 Eric Metcalf	.15	.07	.02
☐ 7 Michael Jackson	.15	.07	.02
☐ 8 Eric Turner	.08	.04	.01
☐ 9 Jim Kelly	.30	.14	.04
☐ 10 Bryce Paup	.15	.07	.02
☐ 11 Bruce Smith	.30	.14	.04
☐ 12 Thurman Thomas	.30	.14	.04
☐ 13 Tim Biakabutuka	1.00	.45	.12
☐ 14 Kerry Collins	1.50	.70	.19
☐ 15 Muhsin Muhammad	1.25	.55	.16
☐ 16 Winslow Oliver	.08	.04	.01
☐ 17 Curtis Conway	.30	.14	.04
☐ 18 Bryan Cox	.08	.04	.01
☐ 19 Bobby Engram	1.00	.45	.12
☐ 20 Erik Kramer	.08	.04	.01
☐ 21 Rashaan Salaam	.30	.14	.04
☐ 22 Jeff Blake	.30	.14	.04
☐ 23 Ki-Jana Carter	.15	.07	.02
☐ 24 Carl Pickens	.30	.14	.04
☐ 25 Troy Aikman	1.25	.55	.16
☐ 26 Michael Irvin	.30	.14	.04
☐ 27 Daryl Johnston	.15	.07	.02
☐ 28 Deion Sanders	.75	.35	.09
☐ 29 Emmitt Smith	2.50	1.10	.30
☐ 30 Terrell Davis	2.00	.90	.25
☐ 31 John Elway	1.00	.45	.12
☐ 32 Anthony Miller	.15	.07	.02
☐ 33 John Mobley	.08	.04	.01
☐ 34 Scott Mitchell	.15	.07	.02
☐ 35 Herman Moore	.30	.14	.04
☐ 36 Barry Sanders	1.25	.55	.16
☐ 37 Edgar Bennett	.15	.07	.02
☐ 38 Robert Brooks	.30	.14	.04
☐ 39 Brett Favre	2.50	1.10	.30
☐ 40 Reggie White	.30	.14	.04
☐ 41 Eddie George	3.00	1.35	.35
☐ 42 Steve McNair	1.25	.55	.16
☐ 43 Chris Sanders	.15	.07	.02
☐ 44 Quentin Coryatt	.08	.04	.01
☐ 45 Marshall Faulk	.30	.14	.04
☐ 46 Jim Harbaugh	.15	.07	.02
☐ 47 Marvin Harrison	1.50	.70	.19
☐ 48 Mark Brunell	1.25	.55	.16
☐ 49 Natrone Means	.30	.14	.04
☐ 50 Andre Rison	.15	.07	.02
☐ 51 Marcus Allen	.30	.14	.04
☐ 52 Steve Bono	.15	.07	.02
☐ 53 Greg Hill	.15	.07	.02
☐ 54 Tamarick Vanover	.30	.14	.04
☐ 55 Karim Abdul-Jabbar	2.00	.90	.25
☐ 56 Dan Marino	2.50	1.10	.30
☐ 57 O.J. McDuffie	.15	.07	.02
☐ 58 Zach Thomas	1.25	.55	.16
☐ 59 Cris Carter	.30	.14	.04
☐ 60 Warren Moon	.15	.07	.02
☐ 61 Jake Reed	.15	.07	.02
☐ 62 Drew Bledsoe	1.25	.55	.16
☐ 63 Ben Coates	.15	.07	.02
☐ 64 Terry Glenn	2.50	1.10	.30
☐ 65 Curtis Martin	2.00	.90	.25
☐ 66 Mario Bates	.15	.07	.02
☐ 67 Michael Haynes	.15	.07	.02
☐ 68 Dave Brown	.15	.07	.02
☐ 69 Rodney Hampton	.15	.07	.02
☐ 70 Amani Toomer	.30	.14	.04
☐ 71 Tyrone Wheatley	.15	.07	.02
☐ 72 Keyshawn Johnson	1.50	.70	.19
☐ 73 Neil O'Donnell	.15	.07	.02
☐ 74 Tim Brown	.15	.07	.02
☐ 75 Rickey Dudley	.30	.14	.04
☐ 76 Napoleon Kaufman	.15	.07	.02
☐ 77 Chester McGlockton	.08	.04	.01
☐ 78 Charlie Garner	.08	.04	.01
☐ 79 Chris T. Jones	.30	.14	.04
☐ 80 Ricky Watters	.15	.07	.02
☐ 81 Jerome Bettis	.30	.14	.04
☐ 82 Kordell Stewart	1.50	.70	.19
☐ 83 Rod Woodson	.15	.07	.02
☐ 84 Aaron Hayden	.08	.04	.01
☐ 85 Stan Humphries	.15	.07	.02
☐ 86 Junior Seau	.30	.14	.04
☐ 87 Tony Banks	1.25	.55	.16
☐ 88 Isaac Bruce	.30	.14	.04
☐ 89 Lawrence Phillips	.50	.23	.06
☐ 90 Derek Loville	.08	.04	.01
☐ 91 Jerry Rice	1.25	.55	.16
☐ 92 J.J. Stokes	.30	.14	.04
☐ 93 Steve Young	1.00	.45	.12
☐ 94 Joey Galloway	.60	.25	.07
☐ 95 Rick Mirer	.15	.07	.02
☐ 96 Chris Warren	.15	.07	.02
☐ 97 Trent Dilfer	.15	.07	.02
☐ 98 Errict Rhett	.15	.07	.02
☐ 99 Terry Allen	.15	.07	.02
☐ 100 Michael Westbrook	.30	.14	.04
☐ NNO Brett Favre Checklist Card	2.50	1.10	.30
☐ NNO Promo Sheet Brett Favre Gold, Blue, and Marble Gold cards	3.50	1.55	.45

1996 Ultra Sensations Blue

A parallel to the base Gold set, each card features a blue foil colored border on front. Reportedly, the Blue cards were 30% of the total print run.

	MINT	NRMT	EXC
COMPLETE SET ()100)	25.00	11.00	3.10
COMMON CARD (1-100)	.10	.05	.01
*BLUE CARDS: .75X TO 1.5X			

1996 Ultra Sensations Rainbow

A parallel to the base Gold set, each card features a blue foil colored border on front. Reportedly, the Rainbow cards were 1% of the total print run.

	MINT	NRMT	EXC
COMPLETE SET ()100)	300.00	135.00	38.00
COMMON CARD (1-100)	1.25	.55	.16
*RAINBOW STARS: 7.5X TO 15X			
*RAINBOW YOUNG STARS: 6X TO 12X			
*RAINBOW RCs: 4X TO 8X			

1996 Ultra Sensations Marble Gold

A parallel to the base Gold set, each card features a blue foil colored border on front. Reportedly, the Marble Gold cards were 20% of the total print run.

	MINT	NRMT	EXC
COMPLETE SET (100)	30.00	13.50	3.70
COMMON CARD (1-100)	.15	.07	.02
*STARS: 1X TO 2X			
*YOUNG STARS/RCs: .75X TO 1.5X			

1996 Ultra Sensations Pewter

A parallel to the base Gold set, each card features a blue foil colored border on front. Reportedly, the Pewter cards were 9% of the total print run.

	MINT	NRMT	EXC
COMPLETE SET (100)	70.00	32.00	8.75
COMMON CARD (1-100)	.30	.14	.04
*PEWTER STARS: 2X TO 4X			
*PEWTER YOUNG STARS: 1.75X TO 3.5X			
*PEWTER RCs: 1.5X TO 3X			

1996 Ultra Sensations Creative Chaos

Randomly inserted in packs at a rate of one in 12, each card features two top NFL stars. Ten different players were paired together in all possible combinations to produce this 100-card set.

	MINT	NRMT	EXC
COMPLETE SET (100)	800.00	350.00	100.00
COMMON CARD (1-100)	4.00	1.80	.50
☐ 1A E.Smith/E.Smith	20.00	9.00	2.50
☐ 1B E.Smith/B.Favre	20.00	9.00	2.50
☐ 1C E.Smith/C.Martin	15.00	6.75	1.85
☐ 1D E.Smith/C.Warren	12.00	5.50	1.50

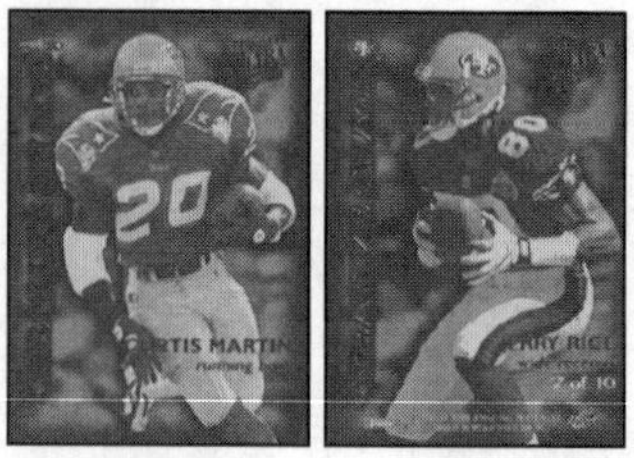

□ 1E E.Smith/D.Sanders	12.00	5.50	1.50
□ 1F E.Smith/S.Young	12.00	5.50	1.50
□ 1G E.Smith/J.Rice	15.00	6.75	1.85
□ 1H E.Smith/T.Davis	15.00	6.75	1.85
□ 1I E.Smith/C.Pickens	12.00	5.50	1.50
□ 1J E.Smith/M.Faulk	12.00	5.50	1.50
□ 2A B.Favre/E.Smith	20.00	9.00	2.50
□ 2B B.Favre/B.Favre	20.00	9.00	2.50
□ 2C B.Favre/C.Martin	15.00	6.75	1.85
□ 2D B.Favre/C.Warren	12.00	5.50	1.50
□ 2E B.Favre/D.Sanders	12.00	5.50	1.50
□ 2F B.Favre/S.Young	12.00	5.50	1.50
□ 2G B.Favre/J.Rice	15.00	6.75	1.85
□ 2H B.Favre/T.Davis	15.00	6.75	1.85
□ 2I B.Favre/C.Pickens	12.00	5.50	1.50
□ 2J B.Favre/M.Faulk	12.00	5.50	1.50
□ 3A C.Martin/E.Smith	15.00	6.75	1.85
□ 3B C.Martin/B.Favre	15.00	6.75	1.85
□ 3C C.Martin/C.Martin	12.00	5.50	1.50
□ 3D C.Martin/C.Warren	10.00	4.50	1.25
□ 3E C.Martin/D.Sanders	10.00	4.50	1.25
□ 3F C.Martin/S.Young	10.00	4.50	1.25
□ 3G C.Martin/J.Rice	10.00	4.50	1.25
□ 3H C.Martin/T.Davis	12.00	5.50	1.50
□ 3I C.Martin/C.Pickens	10.00	4.50	1.25
□ 3J C.Martin/M.Faulk	10.00	4.50	1.25
□ 4A C.Warren/E.Smith	12.00	5.50	1.50
□ 4B C.Warren/B.Favre	12.00	5.50	1.50
□ 4C C.Warren/C.Martin	10.00	4.50	1.25
□ 4D C.Warren/C.Warren	4.00	1.80	.50
□ 4E C.Warren/D.Sanders	6.00	2.70	.75
□ 4F C.Warren/S.Young	6.00	2.70	.75
□ 4G C.Warren/J.Rice	10.00	4.50	1.25
□ 4H C.Warren/T.Davis	10.00	4.50	1.25
□ 4I C.Warren/C.Pickens	4.00	1.80	.50
□ 4J C.Warren/M.Faulk	4.00	1.80	.50
□ 5A D.Sanders/E.Smith	12.00	5.50	1.50
□ 5B D.Sanders/B.Favre	12.00	5.50	1.50
□ 5C D.Sanders/C.Martin	10.00	4.50	1.25
□ 5D D.Sanders/C.Warren	6.00	2.70	.75
□ 5E D.Sanders/D.Sanders	6.00	2.70	.75
□ 5F D.Sanders/S.Young	6.00	2.70	.75
□ 5G D.Sanders/J.Rice	10.00	4.50	1.25
□ 5H D.Sanders/T.Davis	10.00	4.50	1.25
□ 5I D.Sanders/C.Pickens	6.00	2.70	.75
□ 5J D.Sanders/M.Faulk	6.00	2.70	.75
□ 6A S.Young/E.Smith	12.00	5.50	1.50
□ 6B S.Young/B.Favre	12.00	5.50	1.50
□ 6C S.Young/C.Martin	10.00	4.50	1.25
□ 6D S.Young/C.Warren	6.00	2.70	.75
□ 6E S.Young/D.Sanders	6.00	2.70	.75
□ 6F S.Young/S.Young	6.00	2.70	.75
□ 6G S.Young/J.Rice	10.00	4.50	1.25
□ 6H S.Young/T.Davis	10.00	4.50	1.25
□ 6I S.Young/C.Pickens	6.00	2.70	.75
□ 6J S.Young/M.Faulk	6.00	2.70	.75
□ 7A J.Rice/E.Smith	15.00	6.75	1.85
□ 7B J.Rice/B.Favre	15.00	6.75	1.85
□ 7C J.Rice/C.Martin	10.00	4.50	1.25
□ 7D J.Rice/C.Warren	10.00	4.50	1.25
□ 7E J.Rice/D.Sanders	10.00	4.50	1.25
□ 7F J.Rice/S.Young	10.00	4.50	1.25
□ 7G J.Rice/J.Rice	10.00	4.50	1.25
□ 7H J.Rice/T.Davis	10.00	4.50	1.25
□ 7I J.Rice/C.Pickens	10.00	4.50	1.25
□ 7J J.Rice/M.Faulk	10.00	4.50	1.25
□ 8A T.Davis/E.Smith	15.00	6.75	1.85
□ 8B T.Davis/B.Favre	15.00	6.75	1.85
□ 8C T.Davis/C.Martin	12.00	5.50	1.50
□ 8D T.Davis/C.Warren	10.00	4.50	1.25
□ 8E T.Davis/D.Sanders	10.00	4.50	1.25
□ 8F T.Davis/S.Young	10.00	4.50	1.25
□ 8G T.Davis/J.Rice	10.00	4.50	1.25
□ 8H T.Davis/T.Davis	12.00	5.50	1.50
□ 8I T.Davis/C.Pickens	10.00	4.50	1.25
□ 8J T.Davis/M.Faulk	10.00	4.50	1.25
□ 9A C.Pickens/E.Smith	12.00	5.50	1.50
□ 9B C.Pickens/B.Favre	12.00	5.50	1.50
□ 9C C.Pickens/C.Martin	10.00	4.50	1.25
□ 9D C.Pickens/C.Warren	4.00	1.80	.50
□ 9E C.Pickens/D.Sanders	6.00	2.70	.75
□ 9F C.Pickens/S.Young	6.00	2.70	.75
□ 9G C.Pickens/J.Rice	10.00	4.50	1.25
□ 9H C.Pickens/T.Davis	10.00	4.50	1.25
□ 9I C.Pickens/C.Pickens	4.00	1.80	.50
□ 9J C.Pickens/M.Faulk	4.00	1.80	.50
□ 10A M.Faulk/E.Smith	12.00	5.50	1.50
□ 10B M.Faulk/B.Favre	12.00	5.50	1.50
□ 10C M.Faulk/C.Martin	10.00	4.50	1.25
□ 10D M.Faulk/C.Warren	4.00	1.80	.50
□ 10E M.Faulk/D.Sanders	6.00	2.70	.75
□ 10F M.Faulk/S.Young	6.00	2.70	.75
□ 10G M.Faulk/J.Rice	10.00	4.50	1.25
□ 10H M.Faulk/T.Davis	10.00	4.50	1.25
□ 10I M.Faulk/C.Pickens	4.00	1.80	.50
□ 10J M.Faulk/M.Faulk	4.00	1.80	.50

1996 Ultra Sensations Random Rookies

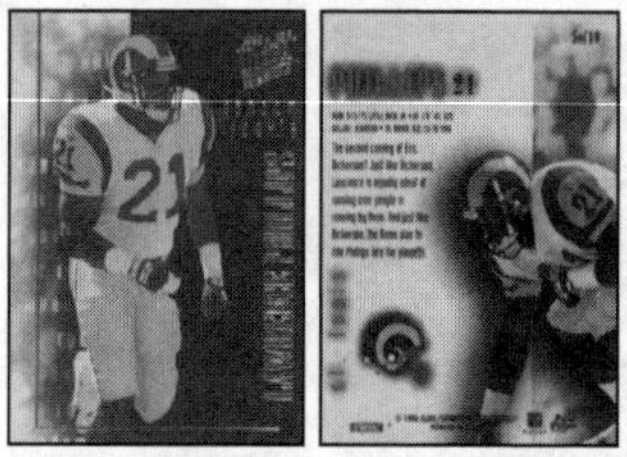

Randomly inserted in packs only at a rate of one in 48,each of these inserts features a top 1996 NFL rookie. Hobby packs contained cards #1-5), while #6-10 were inserted into retail packs. A Gold parallel version was also produced that comprised no more than 20% of the print run.

	MINT	NRMT	EXC
COMPLETE SET (10)	120.00	55.00	15.00
COMP.HOBBY SET (5)	60.00	27.00	7.50
COMP.RETAIL SET (5)	60.00	27.00	7.50
COMMON CARD (1-10)	8.00	3.60	1.00
COMP.GOLD SET (10)	250.00	110.00	31.00
COMMON GOLD CARD	20.00	9.00	2.50

*GOLD RANDOM ROOKIES: 1.25X TO 2.5X

□ 1 Keyshawn Johnson	12.00	5.50	1.50
□ 2 Eddie George	25.00	11.00	3.10
□ 3 Leeland McElroy	8.00	3.60	1.00
□ 4 Eric Moulds	8.00	3.60	1.00
□ 5 Lawrence Phillips	8.00	3.60	1.00
□ 6 Marvin Harrison	12.00	5.50	1.50
□ 7 Tim Biakabutuka	10.00	4.50	1.25
□ 8 Terry Glenn	20.00	9.00	2.50
□ 9 Rickey Dudley	8.00	3.60	1.00
□ 10 Tony Banks	10.00	4.50	1.25

1991 Upper Deck

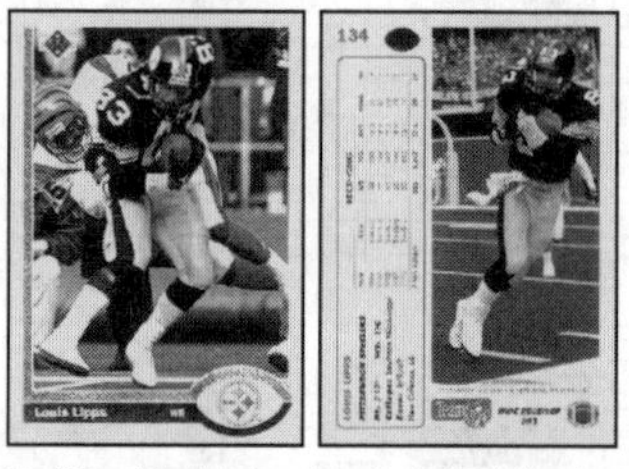

This 700-card standard size set was the first football card set produced by Upper Deck. The set was released in two series. The first series contains 500 cards and the high-number series contains 200 additional cards numbered in continuation of the low series. Factory sets were produced for each series. The cards have the typical Upper Deck look to them with attractive color photos on both sides of the card and statistics and a brief biography on the back. The front photos are accented by two color border stripes reflecting the team's colors, and the team's emblem appears in the lower right corner. Cards 72-99 feature team checklists with Vernon Wells drawings. Other subsets include Star Rookies (1-29), Aerial Threats (30-35), Season Leaders (401-406), Team MVP's (450-487), Rookie Force (AFC 601-626 and NFC 627-652) and an Arch Rivals subset with split-photo cards presenting one-on-one rivalries (653-658). Rookie Cards include Cody Carlson, Bryan Cox, Lawrence Dawsey, Ricky Ervins, Brett Favre, Jeff Graham, Alvin Harper, Randal Hill, Michael Jackson, Herman Moore, Bryce Paup, Erric Pegram, Mike Pritchard, Jake Reed, Leonard Russell, Ricky Watters and Harvey Williams. A Darrell Green insert (SP1) and an insert card commemorating Don Shula's historic 300th NFL victory (SP2) were randomly inserted in first and second series packs respectively. Two Promo cards were released to preview the set. We've listed them below, but they are not considered part of the complete set.

	MINT	NRMT	EXC
COMPLETE SET (700)	12.00	5.50	1.50
COMPLETE FACT.SET (700)	15.00	6.75	1.85
COMPLETE LO SERIES (500)	8.00	3.60	1.00
COMPLETE HI SERIES (200)	4.00	1.80	.50
COMPLETE FACT.HI SET (200)	4.00	1.80	.50
COMMON CARD (1-700)	.04	.02	.01

□ 1 Star Rookie Checklist Dan McGwire	.04	.02	.01
□ 2 Eric Bieniemy	.04	.02	.01
□ 3 Mike Dumas	.04	.02	.01
□ 4 Mike Croel	.04	.02	.01
□ 5 Russell Maryland	.25	.11	.03
□ 6 Charles McRae	.04	.02	.01
□ 7 Dan McGwire	.04	.02	.01
□ 8 Mike Pritchard	.25	.11	.03
□ 9 Ricky Watters	1.50	.70	.19
□ 10 Chris Zorich	.25	.11	.03
□ 11 Browning Nagle	.04	.02	.01
□ 12 Wesley Carroll	.04	.02	.01
□ 13 Brett Favre	4.00	1.80	.50
□ 14 Rob Carpenter	.04	.02	.01
□ 15 Eric Swann	.25	.11	.03
□ 16 Stanley Richard	.04	.02	.01
□ 17 Herman Moore	2.00	.90	.25
□ 18 Todd Marinovich	.04	.02	.01
□ 19 Aaron Craver	.04	.02	.01
□ 20 Chuck Webb	.04	.02	.01
□ 21 Todd Lyght	.04	.02	.01
□ 22 Greg Lewis	.04	.02	.01
□ 23 Eric Turner	.10	.05	.01
□ 24 Alvin Harper	.25	.11	.03
□ 25 Jarrod Bunch	.04	.02	.01
□ 26 Bruce Pickens	.04	.02	.01
□ 27 Harvey Williams	.25	.11	.03
□ 28 Randal Hill	.10	.05	.01
□ 29 Nick Bell	.04	.02	.01
□ 30 Jim Everett AT Henry Ellard	.10	.05	.01
□ 31 Randall Cunningham AT Keith Jackson	.04	.02	.01
□ 32 Steve DeBerg AT Stephone Paige	.04	.02	.01
□ 33 Warren Moon AT Drew Hill	.10	.05	.01
□ 34 Dan Marino AT Mark Clayton	.50	.23	.06
□ 35 Joe Montana AT Jerry Rice	.50	.23	.06
□ 36 Percy Snow	.04	.02	.01
□ 37 Kelvin Martin	.04	.02	.01
□ 38 Scott Case	.04	.02	.01
□ 39 John Gesek	.04	.02	.01
□ 40 Barry Word	.04	.02	.01
□ 41 Cornelius Bennett	.10	.05	.01
□ 42 Mike Kenn	.04	.02	.01
□ 43 Andre Reed	.10	.05	.01
□ 44 Bobby Hebert	.04	.02	.01
□ 45 William Perry	.10	.05	.01
□ 46 Dennis Byrd	.04	.02	.01
□ 47 Martin Mayhew	.04	.02	.01
□ 48 Issiac Holt	.04	.02	.01
□ 49 William White	.04	.02	.01
□ 50 JoJo Townsell	.04	.02	.01
□ 51 Jarvis Williams	.04	.02	.01
□ 52 Joey Browner	.04	.02	.01
□ 53 Pat Terrell	.04	.02	.01
□ 54 Joe Montana UER (Born Monongahela, not New Eagle)	1.00	.45	.12
□ 55 Jeff Herrod	.04	.02	.01
□ 56 Cris Carter	.25	.11	.03
□ 57 Jerry Rice	1.00	.45	.12
□ 58 Brett Perriman	.25	.11	.03
□ 59 Kevin Fagan	.04	.02	.01
□ 60 Wayne Haddix	.04	.02	.01
□ 61 Tommy Kane	.04	.02	.01
□ 62 Pat Beach	.04	.02	.01
□ 63 Jeff Lageman	.04	.02	.01
□ 64 Hassan Jones	.04	.02	.01
□ 65 Bennie Blades	.04	.02	.01
□ 66 Tim McGee	.04	.02	.01
□ 67 Robert Blackmon	.04	.02	.01
□ 68 Fred Stokes	.04	.02	.01
□ 69 Barney Bussey	.04	.02	.01
□ 70 Eric Metcalf	.10	.05	.01
□ 71 Mark Kelso	.04	.02	.01
□ 72 Neal Anderson TC	.04	.02	.01
□ 73 Boomer Esiason TC	.04	.02	.01
□ 74 Thurman Thomas TC	.25	.11	.03
□ 75 John Elway TC	.40	.18	.05
□ 76 Eric Metcalf TC	.10	.05	.01
□ 77 Vinny Testaverde TC	.10	.05	.01
□ 78 Johnny Johnson TC	.04	.02	.01
□ 79 Anthony Miller TC	.10	.05	.01
□ 80 Derrick Thomas TC	.10	.05	.01
□ 81 Jeff George TC	.10	.05	.01
□ 82 Troy Aikman TC	.50	.23	.06
□ 83 Dan Marino TC	.75	.35	.09
□ 84 Randall Cunningham TC	.10	.05	.01
□ 85 Deion Sanders TC	.04	.02	.01
□ 86 Jerry Rice TC	.50	.23	.06
□ 87 Lawrence Taylor TC	.10	.05	.01
□ 88 Al Toon TC	.04	.02	.01
□ 89 Barry Sanders TC	.50	.23	.06
□ 90 Warren Moon TC	.10	.05	.01
□ 91 Don Majkowski TC	.04	.02	.01
□ 92 Andre Tippett TC	.04	.02	.01
□ 93 Bo Jackson TC	.10	.05	.01
□ 94 Jim Everett TC	.10	.05	.01
□ 95 Art Monk TC	.10	.05	.01
□ 96 Morten Andersen TC	.04	.02	.01
□ 97 John L. Williams TC	.04	.02	.01
□ 98 Rod Woodson TC	.10	.05	.01
□ 99 Herschel Walker TC	.10	.05	.01
□ 100 Checklist 1-100	.04	.02	.01
□ 101 Steve Young	.75	.35	.09
□ 102 Jim Lachey	.04	.02	.01
□ 103 Tom Rathman	.04	.02	.01
□ 104 Earnest Byner	.04	.02	.01
□ 105 Karl Mecklenburg	.04	.02	.01
□ 106 Wes Hopkins	.04	.02	.01
□ 107 Michael Irvin	.25	.11	.03
□ 108 Burt Grossman	.04	.02	.01
□ 109 Jay Novacek UER (Wearing 82, but card says he wears 84)	.25	.11	.03
□ 110 Ben Smith	.04	.02	.01
□ 111 Rod Woodson	.25	.11	.03
□ 112 Ernie Jones	.04	.02	.01
□ 113 Bryan Hinkle	.04	.02	.01
□ 114 Vai Sikahema	.04	.02	.01
□ 115 Bubby Brister	.04	.02	.01
□ 116 Brian Blades	.10	.05	.01
□ 117 Don Majkowski	.04	.02	.01
□ 118 Rod Bernstine	.04	.02	.01
□ 119 Brian Noble	.04	.02	.01
□ 120 Eugene Robinson	.04	.02	.01
□ 121 John Taylor	.10	.05	.01
□ 122 Vance Johnson	.04	.02	.01
□ 123 Art Monk	.10	.05	.01
□ 124 John Elway	.75	.35	.09
□ 125 Dexter Carter	.04	.02	.01
□ 126 Anthony Miller	.10	.05	.01
□ 127 Keith Jackson	.10	.05	.01
□ 128 Albert Lewis	.04	.02	.01
□ 129 Billy Ray Smith	.04	.02	.01
□ 130 Clyde Simmons	.04	.02	.01
□ 131 Merril Hoge	.04	.02	.01
□ 132 Ricky Proehl	.04	.02	.01
□ 133 Tim McDonald	.04	.02	.01
□ 134 Louis Lipps	.04	.02	.01
□ 135 Ken Harvey	.10	.05	.01
□ 136 Sterling Sharpe	.10	.05	.01
□ 137 Gill Byrd	.04	.02	.01
□ 138 Tim Harris	.04	.02	.01
□ 139 Derrick Fenner	.04	.02	.01
□ 140 Johnny Holland	.04	.02	.01
□ 141 Ricky Sanders	.04	.02	.01
□ 142 Bobby Humphrey	.04	.02	.01
□ 143 Roger Craig	.10	.05	.01
□ 144 Steve Atwater	.04	.02	.01
□ 145 Ickey Woods	.04	.02	.01
□ 146 Randall Cunningham	.10	.05	.01
□ 147 Marion Butts	.10	.05	.01
□ 148 Reggie White	.25	.11	.03
□ 149 Ronnie Harmon	.04	.02	.01
□ 150 Mike Saxon	.04	.02	.01
□ 151 Greg Townsend	.04	.02	.01
□ 152 Troy Aikman	1.00	.45	.12
□ 153 Shane Conlan	.04	.02	.01
□ 154 Deion Sanders	.60	.25	.07
□ 155 Bo Jackson	.10	.05	.01
□ 156 Jeff Hostetler	.10	.05	.01
□ 157 Albert Bentley	.04	.02	.01
□ 158 James Williams	.04	.02	.01
□ 159 Bill Brooks	.04	.02	.01
□ 160 Nick Lowery	.04	.02	.01
□ 161 Ottis Anderson	.10	.05	.01
□ 162 Kevin Greene	.25	.11	.03
□ 163 Neil Smith	.25	.11	.03
□ 164 Jim Everett	.10	.05	.01
□ 165 Derrick Thomas	.25	.11	.03
□ 166 John L. Williams	.04	.02	.01
□ 167 Timm Rosenbach	.04	.02	.01
□ 168 Leslie O'Neal	.10	.05	.01
□ 169 Clarence Verdin	.04	.02	.01
□ 170 Dave Krieg	.10	.05	.01
□ 171 Steve Broussard	.04	.02	.01
□ 172 Emmitt Smith	2.00	.90	.25
□ 173 Andre Rison	.10	.05	.01
□ 174 Bruce Smith	.25	.11	.03
□ 175 Mark Clayton	.10	.05	.01
□ 176 Christian Okoye	.04	.02	.01
□ 177 Duane Bickett	.04	.02	.01
□ 178 Stephone Paige	.04	.02	.01
□ 179 Fredd Young	.04	.02	.01
□ 180 Mervyn Fernandez	.04	.02	.01
□ 181 Phil Simms	.10	.05	.01
□ 182 Pete Holohan	.04	.02	.01
□ 183 Pepper Johnson	.04	.02	.01
□ 184 Jackie Slater	.04	.02	.01
□ 185 Stephen Baker	.04	.02	.01
□ 186 Frank Cornish	.04	.02	.01
□ 187 Dave Waymer	.04	.02	.01
□ 188 Terance Mathis	.10	.05	.01
□ 189 Darryl Talley	.04	.02	.01
□ 190 James Hasty	.04	.02	.01
□ 191 Jay Schroeder	.04	.02	.01
□ 192 Kenneth Davis	.04	.02	.01
□ 193 Chris Miller	.10	.05	.01
□ 194 Scott Davis	.04	.02	.01
□ 195 Tim Green	.04	.02	.01
□ 196 Dan Saleaumua	.04	.02	.01
□ 197 Rohn Stark	.04	.02	.01
□ 198 John Alt	.04	.02	.01
□ 199 Steve Tasker	.10	.05	.01
□ 200 Checklist 101-200	.04	.02	.01
□ 201 Freddie Joe Nunn	.04	.02	.01
□ 202 Jim Breech	.04	.02	.01
□ 203 Roy Green	.04	.02	.01
□ 204 Gary Anderson RB	.04	.02	.01
□ 205 Rich Camarillo	.04	.02	.01
□ 206 Mark Bortz	.04	.02	.01
□ 207 Eddie Brown	.04	.02	.01
□ 208 Brad Muster	.04	.02	.01
□ 209 Anthony Munoz	.10	.05	.01

☐ 210 Dalton Hilliard	.04	.02	.01
☐ 211 Erik McMillan	.04	.02	.01
☐ 212 Perry Kemp	.04	.02	.01
☐ 213 Jim Thornton	.04	.02	.01
☐ 214 Anthony Dilweg	.04	.02	.01
☐ 215 Cleveland Gary	.04	.02	.01
☐ 216 Leo Goeas	.04	.02	.01
☐ 217 Mike Merriweather	.04	.02	.01
☐ 218 Courtney Hall	.04	.02	.01
☐ 219 Wade Wilson	.10	.05	.01
☐ 220 Billy Joe Tolliver	.04	.02	.01
☐ 221 Harold Green	.10	.05	.01
☐ 222 Al(Bubba) Baker	.10	.05	.01
☐ 223 Carl Zander	.04	.02	.01
☐ 224 Thane Gash	.04	.02	.01
☐ 225 Kevin Mack	.04	.02	.01
☐ 226 Morten Andersen	.04	.02	.01
☐ 227 Dennis Gentry	.04	.02	.01
☐ 228 Vince Buck	.04	.02	.01
☐ 229 Mike Singletary	.10	.05	.01
☐ 230 Rueben Mayes	.04	.02	.01
☐ 231 Mark Carrier WR	.25	.11	.03
☐ 232 Tony Mandarich	.04	.02	.01
☐ 233 Al Toon	.10	.05	.01
☐ 234 Renaldo Turnbull	.04	.02	.01
☐ 235 Broderick Thomas	.04	.02	.01
☐ 236 Anthony Carter	.10	.05	.01
☐ 237 Flipper Anderson	.04	.02	.01
☐ 238 Jerry Robinson	.04	.02	.01
☐ 239 Vince Newsome	.04	.02	.01
☐ 240 Keith Millard	.04	.02	.01
☐ 241 Reggie Langhorne	.04	.02	.01
☐ 242 James Francis	.04	.02	.01
☐ 243 Felix Wright	.04	.02	.01
☐ 244 Neal Anderson	.10	.05	.01
☐ 245 Boomer Esiason	.10	.05	.01
☐ 246 Pat Swilling	.10	.05	.01
☐ 247 Richard Dent	.10	.05	.01
☐ 248 Craig Heyward	.10	.05	.01
☐ 249 Ron Morris	.04	.02	.01
☐ 250 Eric Martin	.04	.02	.01
☐ 251 Jim C. Jensen	.04	.02	.01
☐ 252 Anthony Toney	.04	.02	.01
☐ 253 Sammie Smith	.04	.02	.01
☐ 254 Calvin Williams	.10	.05	.01
☐ 255 Dan Marino	1.50	.70	.19
☐ 256 Warren Moon	.25	.11	.03
☐ 257 Tommie Agee	.04	.02	.01
☐ 258 Haywood Jeffires	.10	.05	.01
☐ 259 Eugene Lockhart	.04	.02	.01
☐ 260 Drew Hill	.04	.02	.01
☐ 261 Vinny Testaverde	.10	.05	.01
☐ 262 Jim Arnold	.04	.02	.01
☐ 263 Steve Christie	.04	.02	.01
☐ 264 Chris Spielman	.10	.05	.01
☐ 265 Reggie Cobb	.04	.02	.01
☐ 266 John Stephens	.04	.02	.01
☐ 267 Jay Hilgenberg	.04	.02	.01
☐ 268 Brent Williams	.04	.02	.01
☐ 269 Rodney Hampton	.25	.11	.03
☐ 270 Irving Fryar	.10	.05	.01
☐ 271 Terry McDaniel	.04	.02	.01
☐ 272 Reggie Roby	.04	.02	.01
☐ 273 Allen Pinkett	.04	.02	.01
☐ 274 Tim McKyer	.04	.02	.01
☐ 275 Bob Golic	.04	.02	.01
☐ 276 Wilber Marshall	.04	.02	.01
☐ 277 Ray Childress	.04	.02	.01
☐ 278 Charles Mann	.04	.02	.01
☐ 279 Cris Dishman	.04	.02	.01
☐ 280 Mark Rypien	.10	.05	.01
☐ 281 Michael Cofer	.04	.02	.01
☐ 282 Keith Byars	.04	.02	.01
☐ 283 Mike Rozier	.04	.02	.01
☐ 284 Seth Joyner	.10	.05	.01
☐ 285 Jessie Tuggle	.04	.02	.01
☐ 286 Mark Bavaro	.04	.02	.01
☐ 287 Eddie Anderson	.04	.02	.01
☐ 288 Sean Landeta	.04	.02	.01
☐ 289 Howie Long	.10	.05	.01
(With George Brett)			
☐ 290 Reyna Thompson	.04	.02	.01
☐ 291 Ferrell Edmunds	.04	.02	.01
☐ 292 Willie Gault	.10	.05	.01
☐ 293 John Offerdahl	.04	.02	.01
☐ 294 Tim Brown	.25	.11	.03
☐ 295 Bruce Matthews	.10	.05	.01
☐ 296 Kevin Ross	.04	.02	.01
☐ 297 Lorenzo White	.04	.02	.01
☐ 298 Dino Hackett	.04	.02	.01
☐ 299 Curtis Duncan	.04	.02	.01
☐ 300 Checklist 201-300	.04	.02	.01
☐ 301 Andre Ware	.10	.05	.01
☐ 302 David Little	.04	.02	.01
☐ 303 Jerry Ball	.04	.02	.01
☐ 304 Dwight Stone UER	.04	.02	.01
(He's a WR, not RB)			
☐ 305 Rodney Peete	.10	.05	.01
☐ 306 Mike Baab	.04	.02	.01
☐ 307 Tim Worley	.04	.02	.01
☐ 308 Paul Farren	.04	.02	.01
☐ 309 Carnell Lake	.04	.02	.01
☐ 310 Clay Matthews	.10	.05	.01
☐ 311 Alton Montgomery	.04	.02	.01
☐ 312 Ernest Givins	.10	.05	.01
☐ 313 Mike Horan	.04	.02	.01
☐ 314 Sean Jones	.10	.05	.01
☐ 315 Leonard Smith	.04	.02	.01
☐ 316 Carl Banks	.04	.02	.01
☐ 317 Jerome Brown	.04	.02	.01
☐ 318 Everson Walls	.04	.02	.01
☐ 319 Ron Heller	.04	.02	.01
☐ 320 Mark Collins	.04	.02	.01
☐ 321 Eddie Murray	.04	.02	.01
☐ 322 Jim Harbaugh	.25	.11	.03
☐ 323 Mel Gray	.10	.05	.01
☐ 324 Keith Van Horne	.04	.02	.01
☐ 325 Lomas Brown	.04	.02	.01
☐ 326 Carl Lee	.04	.02	.01
☐ 327 Ken O'Brien	.04	.02	.01
☐ 328 Dermontti Dawson	.04	.02	.01
☐ 329 Brad Baxter	.04	.02	.01
☐ 330 Chris Doleman	.04	.02	.01
☐ 331 Louis Oliver	.04	.02	.01
☐ 332 Frank Stams	.04	.02	.01
☐ 333 Mike Munchak	.04	.02	.01
☐ 334 Fred Strickland	.04	.02	.01
☐ 335 Mark Duper	.10	.05	.01
☐ 336 Jacob Green	.04	.02	.01
☐ 337 Tony Paige	.04	.02	.01
☐ 338 Jeff Bryant	.04	.02	.01
☐ 339 Lemuel Stinson	.04	.02	.01
☐ 340 David Wyman	.04	.02	.01
☐ 341 Lee Williams	.04	.02	.01
☐ 342 Trace Armstrong	.04	.02	.01
☐ 343 Junior Seau	.40	.18	.05
☐ 344 John Roper	.04	.02	.01
☐ 345 Jeff George	.25	.11	.03
☐ 346 Herschel Walker	.10	.05	.01
☐ 347 Sam Clancy	.04	.02	.01
☐ 348 Steve Jordan	.04	.02	.01
☐ 349 Nate Odomes	.04	.02	.01
☐ 350 Martin Bayless	.04	.02	.01
☐ 351 Brent Jones	.25	.11	.03
☐ 352 Ray Agnew	.04	.02	.01
☐ 353 Charles Haley	.10	.05	.01
☐ 354 Andre Tippett	.04	.02	.01
☐ 355 Ronnie Lott	.10	.05	.01
☐ 356 Thurman Thomas	.25	.11	.03
☐ 357 Fred Barnett	.25	.11	.03
☐ 358 James Lofton	.10	.05	.01
☐ 359 William Frizzell	.04	.02	.01
☐ 360 Keith McKeller	.04	.02	.01
☐ 361 Rodney Holman	.04	.02	.01
☐ 362 Henry Ellard	.10	.05	.01
☐ 363 David Fulcher	.04	.02	.01
☐ 364 Jerry Gray	.04	.02	.01
☐ 365 James Brooks	.10	.05	.01
☐ 366 Tony Stargell	.04	.02	.01
☐ 367 Keith McCants	.04	.02	.01
☐ 368 Lewis Billups	.04	.02	.01
☐ 369 Ervin Randle	.04	.02	.01
☐ 370 Pat Leahy	.04	.02	.01
☐ 371 Bruce Armstrong	.04	.02	.01
☐ 372 Steve DeBerg	.04	.02	.01
☐ 373 Guy McIntyre	.04	.02	.01
☐ 374 Deron Cherry	.04	.02	.01
☐ 375 Fred Marion	.04	.02	.01
☐ 376 Michael Haddix	.04	.02	.01
☐ 377 Kent Hull	.04	.02	.01
☐ 378 Jerry Holmes	.04	.02	.01
☐ 379 Jim Richter	.04	.02	.01
☐ 380 Ed West	.04	.02	.01
☐ 381 Richmond Webb	.04	.02	.01
☐ 382 Mark Jackson	.04	.02	.01
☐ 383 Tom Newberry	.04	.02	.01
☐ 384 Ricky Nattiel	.04	.02	.01
☐ 385 Keith Sims	.04	.02	.01
☐ 386 Ron Hall	.04	.02	.01
☐ 387 Ken Norton	.25	.11	.03
☐ 388 Paul Gruber	.04	.02	.01
☐ 389 Daniel Stubbs	.04	.02	.01
☐ 390 Ian Beckles	.04	.02	.01
☐ 391 Hoby Brenner	.04	.02	.01
☐ 392 Tory Epps	.04	.02	.01
☐ 393 Sam Mills	.04	.02	.01
☐ 394 Chris Hinton	.04	.02	.01
☐ 395 Steve Walsh	.04	.02	.01
☐ 396 Simon Fletcher	.04	.02	.01
☐ 397 Tony Bennett	.10	.05	.01
☐ 398 Aundray Bruce	.04	.02	.01
☐ 399 Mark Murphy	.04	.02	.01
☐ 400 Checklist 301-400	.04	.02	.01
☐ 401 Barry Sanders LL	.50	.23	.06
☐ 402 Jerry Rice LL	.50	.23	.06
☐ 403 Warren Moon LL	.10	.05	.01
☐ 404 Derrick Thomas LL	.10	.05	.01
☐ 405 Nick Lowery LL	.10	.05	.01
☐ 406 Mark Carrier DB LL	.10	.05	.01
☐ 407 Michael Carter	.04	.02	.01
☐ 408 Chris Singleton	.04	.02	.01
☐ 409 Matt Millen	.10	.05	.01
☐ 410 Ronnie Lippett	.04	.02	.01
☐ 411 E.J. Junior	.04	.02	.01
☐ 412 Ray Donaldson	.04	.02	.01
☐ 413 Keith Willis	.04	.02	.01
☐ 414 Jessie Hester	.04	.02	.01
☐ 415 Jeff Cross	.04	.02	.01
☐ 416 Greg Jackson	.04	.02	.01
☐ 417 Alvin Walton	.04	.02	.01
☐ 418 Bart Oates	.04	.02	.01
☐ 419 Chip Lohmiller	.04	.02	.01
☐ 420 John Elliott	.04	.02	.01
☐ 421 Randall McDaniel	.04	.02	.01
☐ 422 Richard Johnson	.04	.02	.01
☐ 423 Al Noga	.04	.02	.01
☐ 424 Lamar Lathon	.04	.02	.01
☐ 425 Rick Fenney	.04	.02	.01
☐ 426 Jack Del Rio	.04	.02	.01
☐ 427 Don Mosebar	.04	.02	.01
☐ 428 Luis Sharpe	.04	.02	.01
☐ 429 Steve Wisniewski	.04	.02	.01
☐ 430 Jimmie Jones	.04	.02	.01
☐ 431 Freeman McNeil	.04	.02	.01
☐ 432 Ron Rivera	.04	.02	.01
☐ 433 Hart Lee Dykes	.04	.02	.01
☐ 434 Mark Carrier DB	.10	.05	.01
☐ 435 Rob Moore	.25	.11	.03
☐ 436 Gary Clark	.25	.11	.03
☐ 437 Heath Sherman	.04	.02	.01
☐ 438 Darrell Green	.04	.02	.01
☐ 439 Jessie Small	.04	.02	.01
☐ 440 Monte Coleman	.04	.02	.01
☐ 441 Leonard Marshall	.04	.02	.01
☐ 442 Richard Johnson	.04	.02	.01
☐ 443 Dave Meggett	.10	.05	.01
☐ 444 Barry Sanders	1.00	.45	.12
☐ 445 Lawrence Taylor	.25	.11	.03
☐ 446 Marcus Allen	.25	.11	.03
☐ 447 Johnny Johnson	.04	.02	.01
☐ 448 Aaron Wallace	.04	.02	.01
☐ 449 Anthony Thompson	.04	.02	.01
☐ 450 Steve DeBerg	.40	.18	.05
Dan Marino			
Team MVP CL 453-473			
☐ 451 Andre Rison MVP	.10	.05	.01
☐ 452 Thurman Thomas MVP	.10	.05	.01
☐ 453 Neal Anderson MVP	.04	.02	.01
☐ 454 Boomer Esiason MVP	.04	.02	.01
☐ 455 Eric Metcalf MVP	.10	.05	.01
☐ 456 Emmitt Smith MVP	1.00	.45	.12
☐ 457 Bobby Humphrey MVP	.04	.02	.01
☐ 458 Barry Sanders MVP	.50	.23	.06
☐ 459 Sterling Sharpe MVP	.10	.05	.01
☐ 460 Warren Moon MVP	.10	.05	.01
☐ 461 Albert Bentley MVP	.04	.02	.01
☐ 462 Steve DeBerg MVP	.04	.02	.01
☐ 463 Greg Townsend MVP	.04	.02	.01
☐ 464 Henry Ellard MVP	.10	.05	.01
☐ 465 Dan Marino MVP	.75	.35	.09
☐ 466 Anthony Carter MVP	.10	.05	.01
☐ 467 John Stephens MVP	.04	.02	.01
☐ 468 Pat Swilling MVP	.04	.02	.01
☐ 469 Ottis Anderson MVP	.10	.05	.01
☐ 470 Dennis Byrd MVP	.04	.02	.01
☐ 471 Randall Cunningham MVP	.10	.05	.01
☐ 472 Johnny Johnson MVP	.10	.05	.01
☐ 473 Rod Woodson MVP	.10	.05	.01
☐ 474 Anthony Miller MVP	.10	.05	.01
☐ 475 Jerry Rice MVP	.50	.23	.06
☐ 476 John L.Williams MVP	.04	.02	.01
☐ 477 Wayne Haddix MVP	.04	.02	.01
☐ 478 Earnest Byner MVP	.04	.02	.01
☐ 479 Doug Widell	.04	.02	.01
☐ 480 Tommy Hodson	.04	.02	.01
☐ 481 Shawn Collins	.04	.02	.01
☐ 482 Rickey Jackson	.04	.02	.01
☐ 483 Tony Casillas	.04	.02	.01
☐ 484 Vaughan Johnson	.04	.02	.01
☐ 485 Floyd Dixon	.04	.02	.01
☐ 486 Eric Green	.04	.02	.01
☐ 487 Harry Hamilton	.04	.02	.01
☐ 488 Gary Anderson K	.04	.02	.01
☐ 489 Bruce Hill	.04	.02	.01
☐ 490 Gerald Williams	.04	.02	.01
☐ 491 Cortez Kennedy	.25	.11	.03
☐ 492 Chet Brooks	.04	.02	.01
☐ 493 Dwayne Harper	.04	.02	.01
☐ 494 Don Griffin	.04	.02	.01
☐ 495 Andy Heck	.04	.02	.01
☐ 496 David Treadwell	.04	.02	.01
☐ 497 Irv Pankey	.04	.02	.01
☐ 498 Dennis Smith	.04	.02	.01
☐ 499 Marcus Dupree	.04	.02	.01
☐ 500 Checklist 401-500	.04	.02	.01
☐ 501 Wendell Davis	.04	.02	.01
☐ 502 Matt Bahr	.04	.02	.01
☐ 503 Rob Burnett	.04	.02	.01
☐ 504 Maurice Carthon	.04	.02	.01
☐ 505 Donnell Woolford	.04	.02	.01
☐ 506 Howard Ballard	.04	.02	.01
☐ 507 Mark Boyer	.04	.02	.01
☐ 508 Eugene Marve	.04	.02	.01
☐ 509 Joe Kelly	.04	.02	.01
☐ 510 Will Wolford	.04	.02	.01
☐ 511 Robert Clark	.04	.02	.01
☐ 512 Matt Brock	.04	.02	.01
☐ 513 Chris Warren	.40	.18	.05
☐ 514 Ken Willis	.04	.02	.01
☐ 515 George Jamison	.04	.02	.01
☐ 516 Rufus Porter	.04	.02	.01
☐ 517 Mark Higgs	.04	.02	.01
☐ 518 Thomas Everett	.04	.02	.01
☐ 519 Robert Brown	.04	.02	.01
☐ 520 Gene Atkins	.04	.02	.01
☐ 521 Hardy Nickerson	.10	.05	.01
☐ 522 Johnny Bailey	.04	.02	.01
☐ 523 William Frizzell	.04	.02	.01
☐ 524 Steve McMichael	.10	.05	.01
☐ 525 Kevin Porter	.04	.02	.01
☐ 526 Carwell Gardner	.04	.02	.01
☐ 527 Eugene Daniel	.04	.02	.01
☐ 528 Vestee Jackson	.04	.02	.01
☐ 529 Chris Goode	.04	.02	.01
☐ 530 Leon Seals	.04	.02	.01
☐ 531 Darion Conner	.04	.02	.01
☐ 532 Stan Brock	.04	.02	.01
☐ 533 Kirby Jackson	.04	.02	.01
☐ 534 Marv Cook	.04	.02	.01
☐ 535 Bill Fralic	.04	.02	.01
☐ 536 Keith Woodside	.04	.02	.01
☐ 537 Hugh Green	.04	.02	.01
☐ 538 Grant Feasel	.04	.02	.01
☐ 539 Bubba McDowell	.04	.02	.01
☐ 540 Vai Sikahema	.04	.02	.01
☐ 541 Aaron Cox	.04	.02	.01
☐ 542 Roger Craig	.10	.05	.01
☐ 543 Robb Thomas	.04	.02	.01
☐ 544 Ronnie Lott	.10	.05	.01
☐ 545 Robert Delpino	.04	.02	.01
☐ 546 Greg McMurtry	.04	.02	.01
☐ 547 Jim Morrissey	.04	.02	.01
☐ 548 Johnny Rembert	.04	.02	.01
☐ 549 Markus Paul	.04	.02	.01
☐ 550 Karl Wilson	.04	.02	.01
☐ 551 Gaston Green	.04	.02	.01
☐ 552 Willie Drewrey	.04	.02	.01
☐ 553 Michael Young	.04	.02	.01
☐ 554 Tom Tupa	.04	.02	.01
☐ 555 John Friesz	.25	.11	.03
☐ 556 Cody Carlson	.04	.02	.01
☐ 557 Eric Allen	.04	.02	.01
☐ 558 Thomas Benson	.04	.02	.01
☐ 559 Scott Mersereau	.04	.02	.01
☐ 560 Lionel Washington	.04	.02	.01
☐ 561 Brian Brennan	.04	.02	.01
☐ 562 Jim Jeffcoat	.04	.02	.01
☐ 563 Jeff Jaeger	.04	.02	.01
☐ 564 D.J. Johnson	.04	.02	.01
☐ 565 Danny Villa	.04	.02	.01
☐ 566 Don Beebe	.04	.02	.01
☐ 567 Michael Haynes	.25	.11	.03
☐ 568 Brett Faryniarz	.04	.02	.01
☐ 569 Mike Prior	.04	.02	.01
☐ 570 John Davis	.04	.02	.01
☐ 571 Vernon Turner	.04	.02	.01
☐ 572 Michael Brooks	.04	.02	.01
☐ 573 Mike Gann	.04	.02	.01
☐ 574 Ron Holmes	.04	.02	.01
☐ 575 Gary Plummer	.04	.02	.01
☐ 576 Bill Romanowski	.04	.02	.01
☐ 577 Chris Jacke	.04	.02	.01
☐ 578 Gary Reasons	.04	.02	.01
☐ 579 Tim Jorden	.04	.02	.01
☐ 580 Tim McKyer	.04	.02	.01
☐ 581 Johnnie Jackson	.04	.02	.01
☐ 582 Ethan Horton	.04	.02	.01
☐ 583 Pete Stoyanovich	.04	.02	.01
☐ 584 Jeff Query	.04	.02	.01
☐ 585 Frank Reich	.10	.05	.01
☐ 586 Riki Ellison	.04	.02	.01
☐ 587 Eric Hill	.04	.02	.01
☐ 588 Anthony Shelton	.04	.02	.01
☐ 589 Steve Smith	.04	.02	.01
☐ 590 Garth Jax	.04	.02	.01
☐ 591 Greg Davis	.04	.02	.01
☐ 592 Bill Maas	.04	.02	.01
☐ 593 Henry Rolling	.04	.02	.01
☐ 594 Keith Jones	.04	.02	.01
☐ 595 Tootie Robbins	.04	.02	.01
☐ 596 Brian Jordan	.10	.05	.01
☐ 597 Derrick Walker	.04	.02	.01
☐ 598 Jonathan Hayes	.04	.02	.01
☐ 599 Nate Lewis	.04	.02	.01
☐ 600 Checklist 501-600	.04	.02	.01
☐ 601 AFC Checklist RF	.04	.02	.01
Mike Croel			
Greg Lewis			
Keith Traylor			
Kenny Walker			
☐ 602 James Jones RF	.04	.02	.01
☐ 603 Tim Barnett RF	.04	.02	.01
☐ 604 Ed King RF	.04	.02	.01
☐ 605 Shane Curry RF	.04	.02	.01
☐ 606 Mike Croel RF	.04	.02	.01
☐ 607 Bryan Cox RF	.25	.11	.03
☐ 608 Shawn Jefferson RF	.10	.05	.01
☐ 609 Kenny Walker RF	.04	.02	.01
☐ 610 Michael Jackson RF	.25	.11	.03
☐ 611 Jon Vaughn RF	.04	.02	.01
☐ 612 Greg Lewis RF	.04	.02	.01
☐ 613 Joe Valerio RF	.04	.02	.01
☐ 614 Pat Harlow RF	.04	.02	.01
☐ 615 Henry Jones RF	.10	.05	.01
☐ 616 Jeff Graham RF	.25	.11	.03
☐ 617 Darryll Lewis RF	.10	.05	.01
☐ 618 Keith Traylor RF UER	.04	.02	.01
(Bronchos on back)			
☐ 619 Scott Miller RF	.04	.02	.01
☐ 620 Nick Bell RF	.04	.02	.01

	MINT	NRMT	EXC
☐ 621 John Flannery RF	.04	.02	.01
☐ 622 Leonard Russell RF	.10	.05	.01
☐ 623 Alfred Williams RF	.04	.02	.01
☐ 624 Browning Nagle RF	.04	.02	.01
☐ 625 Harvey Williams RF	.10	.05	.01
☐ 626 Dan McGwire RF	.04	.02	.01
☐ 627 NFC Checklist RF	.50	.23	.06
Brett Favre			
Moe Gardner			
Erric Pegram			
Bruce Pickens			
Mike Pritchard			
☐ 628 William Thomas RF	.04	.02	.01
☐ 629 Lawrence Dawsey RF	.10	.05	.01
☐ 630 Aeneas Williams RF	.10	.05	.01
☐ 631 Stan Thomas RF	.04	.02	.01
☐ 632 Randal Hill RF	.04	.02	.01
☐ 633 Moe Gardner RF	.04	.02	.01
☐ 634 Alvin Harper RF	.10	.05	.01
☐ 635 Esera Tuaolo RF	.04	.02	.01
☐ 636 Russell Maryland RF	.10	.05	.01
☐ 637 Anthony Morgan RF	.04	.02	.01
☐ 638 Erric Pegram RF	.25	.11	.03
☐ 639 Herman Moore RF	1.00	.45	.12
☐ 640 Ricky Ervins RF	.10	.05	.01
☐ 641 Kelvin Pritchett RF	.10	.05	.01
☐ 642 Roman Phifer RF	.04	.02	.01
☐ 643 Antone Davis RF	.04	.02	.01
☐ 644 Mike Pritchard RF	.10	.05	.01
☐ 645 Vinnie Clark RF	.04	.02	.01
☐ 646 Jake Reed RF	1.00	.45	.12
☐ 647 Brett Favre RF	2.00	.90	.25
☐ 648 Todd Lyght RF	.04	.02	.01
☐ 649 Bruce Pickens RF	.04	.02	.01
☐ 650 Darren Lewis RF	.04	.02	.01
☐ 651 Wesley Carroll RF	.04	.02	.01
☐ 652 James Joseph RF	.10	.05	.01
☐ 653 Robert Delpino AR	.04	.02	.01
Tim McDonald			
☐ 654 Vencie Glenn AR	.04	.02	.01
Deion Sanders			
☐ 655 Jerry Rice AR	.30	.14	.04
Terry McDaniel			
☐ 656 Barry Sanders AR	.40	.18	.05
Derrick Thomas			
☐ 657 Ken Tippins AR	.04	.02	.01
Lorenzo White			
☐ 658 Christian Okoye AR	.04	.02	.01
Jacob Green			
☐ 659 Rich Gannon	.04	.02	.01
☐ 660 Johnny Meads	.04	.02	.01
☐ 661 J.J. Birden	.10	.05	.01
☐ 662 Bruce Kozerski	.04	.02	.01
☐ 663 Felix Wright	.04	.02	.01
☐ 664 Al Smith	.04	.02	.01
☐ 665 Stan Humphries	.25	.11	.03
☐ 666 Alfred Anderson	.04	.02	.01
☐ 667 Nate Newton	.10	.05	.01
☐ 668 Vince Workman	.10	.05	.01
☐ 669 Ricky Reynolds	.04	.02	.01
☐ 670 Bryce Paup	.50	.23	.06
☐ 671 Gill Fenerty	.04	.02	.01
☐ 672 Darrell Thompson	.04	.02	.01
☐ 673 Anthony Smith	.04	.02	.01
☐ 674 Darryl Henley	.04	.02	.01
☐ 675 Brett Maxie	.04	.02	.01
☐ 676 Craig Taylor	.04	.02	.01
☐ 677 Steve Wallace	.10	.05	.01
☐ 678 Jeff Feagles	.04	.02	.01
☐ 679 James Washington	.04	.02	.01
☐ 680 Tim Harris	.04	.02	.01
☐ 681 Dennis Gibson	.04	.02	.01
☐ 682 Toi Cook	.04	.02	.01
☐ 683 Lorenzo Lynch	.04	.02	.01
☐ 684 Brad Edwards	.04	.02	.01
☐ 685 Ray Crockett	.04	.02	.01
☐ 686 Harris Barton	.04	.02	.01
☐ 687 Byron Evans	.04	.02	.01
☐ 688 Eric Thomas	.04	.02	.01
☐ 689 Jeff Criswell	.04	.02	.01
☐ 690 Eric Ball	.04	.02	.01
☐ 691 Brian Mitchell	.10	.05	.01
☐ 692 Quinn Early	.10	.05	.01
☐ 693 Aaron Jones	.04	.02	.01
☐ 694 Jim Dombrowski	.04	.02	.01
☐ 695 Jeff Bostic	.04	.02	.01
☐ 696 Tony Casillas	.04	.02	.01
☐ 697 Ken Lanier	.04	.02	.01
☐ 698 Henry Thomas	.04	.02	.01
☐ 699 Steve Beuerlein	.04	.02	.01
☐ 700 Checklist 601-700	.04	.02	.01
☐ P1 Joe Montana Promo	3.00	1.35	.35
Numbered 1			
☐ P2 Barry Sanders Promo	2.00	.90	.25
Numbered 500			
☐ SP1 Darrell Green	.50	.23	.06
NFL's Fastest Man			
☐ SP2 Don Shula CO	2.00	.90	.25
300th Victory			

1991 Upper Deck Game Breaker Holograms

This nine-card hologram standard-size set spotlights outstanding NFL running backs. Holograms 1-6 were randomly inserted in Upper Deck

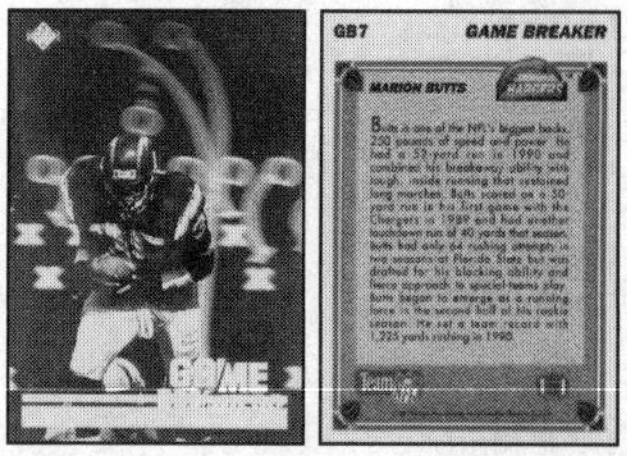

low series wax packs, and holograms 7-9 were inserted in the high series. The holograms feature a player action shot against the background of a football play diagram with X's and O's. The player's name appears in a stripe toward the bottom, with the words "Game Breaker" in the lower right corner. The backs have the team logo and career summary.

	MINT	NRMT	EXC
COMPLETE SET (9)	10.00	4.50	1.25
COMMON CARD (GB1-GB9)	.60	.25	.07
☐ GB1 Barry Sanders	3.00	1.35	.35
☐ GB2 Thurman Thomas	1.00	.45	.12
☐ GB3 Bobby Humphrey	.60	.25	.07
☐ GB4 Earnest Byner	.60	.25	.07
☐ GB5 Emmitt Smith	5.00	2.20	.60
☐ GB6 Neal Anderson	.60	.25	.07
☐ GB7 Marion Butts	.60	.25	.07
☐ GB8 James Brooks	.60	.25	.07
☐ GB9 Marcus Allen	1.00	.45	.12

1991 Upper Deck Joe Montana Heroes

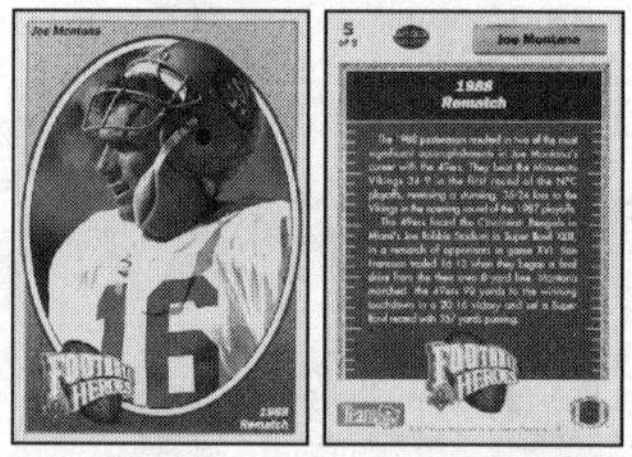

This ten-card Joe Montana standard-size set introduces Upper Deck's "Football Heroes" series, which were randomly inserted into 1991 Upper Deck first series foil packs. Montana personally autographed 2,500 of these cards, which feature a diamond hologram as a sign of authenticity. The front design has color player photos in an oval frame with white and blue borders, on a card face that shades from mustard to brown as one moves from top to bottom. The Upper Deck Football Heroes logo is superimposed at the lower left corner. The backs have a green football field design and summarize various high points in his career. Card number 9 features a portrait of Montana by noted sports artist Vernon Wells.

	MINT	NRMT	EXC
COMPLETE SET (10)	12.00	5.50	1.50
COMMON MONTANA (1-9)	.75	.35	.09
☐ 1 1974-78 College Years	.75	.35	.09
☐ 2 1981 A Star is Born	.75	.35	.09
☐ 3 1984 Super Bowl MVP	.75	.35	.09
☐ 4 1987 1st Passing Title	.75	.35	.09
☐ 5 1988 Rematch	.75	.35	.09
☐ 6 1989 NFL's MVP	.75	.35	.09
☐ 7 1989 Back-to-Back	.75	.35	.09
☐ 8 1990 Career Highs	.75	.35	.09
☐ 9 Checklist Heroes 1-9	.75	.35	.09
(Vernon Wells portrait			
of Joe Montana			
☐ AU Joe Montana AUTO	225.00	100.00	28.00
(Certified Autograph)			
☐ NNO Title/Header Card SP	8.00	3.60	1.00

1991 Upper Deck Heroes Montana Box Bottoms

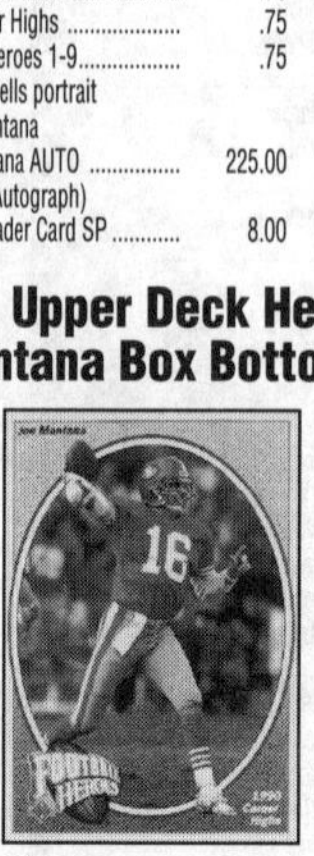

These eight oversized "cards" (approximately 5 1/4" by 7 1/4") were featured on the bottom of 1991 Upper Deck low series wax boxes. They are identical in design to the Montana Football Heroes insert cards, with the same color player photos in an oval frame. The backs are blank and the cards are unnumbered. We have checklisted them below according to their Heroes card numbering.

	MINT	NRMT	EXC
COMPLETE SET (8)	8.00	3.60	1.00
COMMON CARD (1-8)	1.25	.55	.16
☐ 1 1974-78 College Years	1.25	.55	.16
☐ 2 1981 A Star is Born	1.25	.55	.16
☐ 3 1984 Super Bowl MVP	1.25	.55	.16
☐ 4 1987 1st Passing Title	1.25	.55	.16
☐ 5 1988 Rematch	1.25	.55	.16
☐ 6 1989 NFL's MVP	1.25	.55	.16
☐ 7 1989 Back-to-Back	1.25	.55	.16
☐ 8 1990 Career Highs	1.25	.55	.16

1991 Upper Deck Joe Namath Heroes

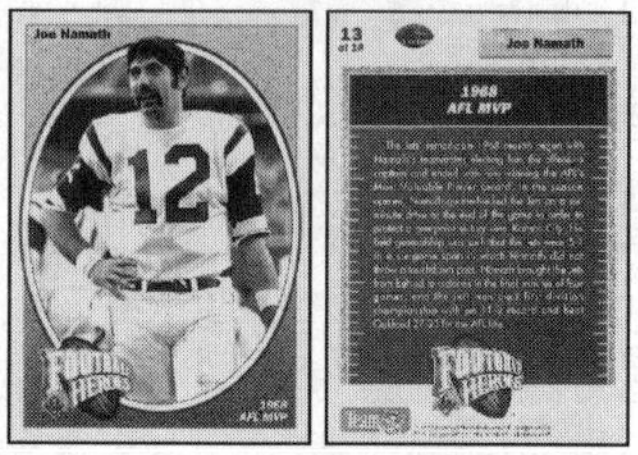

This ten-card Joe Namath standard-size set is the second part of Upper Deck's "Football Heroes" series, which were inserted in its High Number Series packs. Namath personally autographed 2,500 of these cards, and every 100th card was signed "Broadway Joe." The front design has color player photos in an oval frame with white and blue borders, on a card face that shades from mustard to brown as one moves from top to bottom. The Upper Deck Football Heroes logo is superimposed at the lower left corner. The backs have a green football field design and summarize various high points in his career. Card number 18 features a portrait of Namath by noted sports artist Vernon Wells. The cards are numbered (10-18) in continuation of the Joe Montana Heroes set.

	MINT	NRMT	EXC
COMPLETE SET (10)	12.00	5.50	1.50
COMMON NAMATH (10-18)	.75	.35	.09
☐ 10 1962-65 Crimson Tide	.75	.35	.09
☐ 11 1965 Broadway Joe	.75	.35	.09
☐ 12 1967 4,000 Yards	.75	.35	.09
Passing			
☐ 13 1968 AFL MVP	.75	.35	.09
☐ 14 1969 Super Bowl III	.75	.35	.09
☐ 15 1969 All-Pro	.75	.35	.09
☐ 16 1972 400 Yards	.75	.35	.09
☐ 17 1985 Hall of Fame	.75	.35	.09
☐ 18 Checklist Heroes 10-18	.75	.35	.09
(Vernon Wells portrait			
of Joe Namath)			
☐ AU Joe Montana AUTO	225.00	100.00	28.00
(Certified Autograph)			
☐ NNO Title/Header Card SP	8.00	3.60	1.00

1991 Upper Deck Heroes Namath Box Bottoms

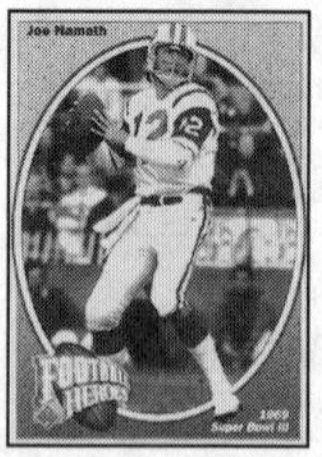

These eight oversized "cards" (approximately 5 1/4" by 7 1/4") were featured on the bottom of 1991 Upper Deck high series wax boxes. They are identical in design to the Namath Football Heroes insert cards, with the same color player photos in an oval frame. The backs are blank and the cards are unnumbered. We have checklisted them below according to the numbering of the Heroes cards.

	MINT	NRMT	EXC
COMPLETE SET (8)	8.00	3.60	1.00
COMMON CARD (10-17)	1.25	.55	.16
☐ 10 1962-65 Crimson Tide	1.25	.55	.16
☐ 11 1965 Broadway Joe	1.25	.55	.16
☐ 12 1967 4,000 Yards Passing	1.25	.55	.16
☐ 13 1968 AFL MVP	1.25	.55	.16
☐ 14 1969 Super Bowl III	1.25	.55	.16
☐ 15 1969 All-Pro	1.25	.55	.16
☐ 16 1972 400 Yards	1.25	.55	.16
☐ 17 1985 Hall of Fame	1.25	.55	.16

1991 Upper Deck Sheets

Upper Deck issued two football sheets in 1991. The 8 1/2" by 11" sheet to honor the Super Bowl XXV Champions features six Upper Deck Giants cards, which are listed as they appear counterclockwise beginning from the upper left corner. The background is a green

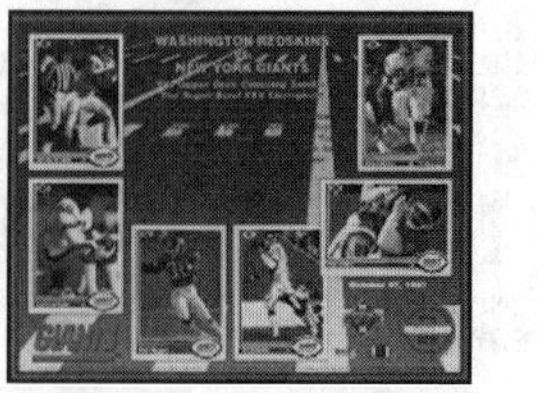

football field design. At the top are the words, "Washington Redskins vs. New York Giants" and "The Upper Deck Company Salutes The Super Bowl XXV Champions" in yellow lettering. In the center are game highlights in red lettering. The sheet is bordered by two blue and one red stripe. The issue date appears in the lower right corner as do the production run and issue number, which appear in the Upper Deck gold foil stamp. The Rams sheet commemorated the 40th anniversary of the 1951 Rams championship team. 60,000 numbered Ram sheets were distributed. The backs of both sheets are blank.

	MINT	NRMT	EXC
COMPLETE SET (2)	10.00	4.50	1.25
COMMON SHEET (1-2)	5.00	2.20	.60
☐ 1 Los Angeles Rams	5.00	2.20	.60
Commemorative Sheet			
October 1991 (60,000)			
☐ 2 New York Giants	5.00	2.20	.60
vs. Washington Redskins			
October 27, 1991			
(SB XXV Champions (72,000)			
Rodney Hampton			
Lawrence Taylor			
Dave Meggett			
Jeff Hostetler			
Mark Collins			
Ottis Anderson			

1992 Upper Deck

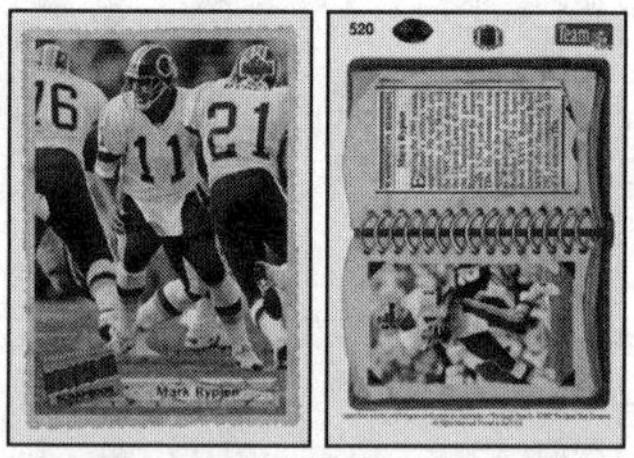

The 1992 Upper Deck football set was issued in two series and totaled 620 standard-size cards. No low series cards were included in this year's second series packs. First series packs featured the following random insert sets: a ten-card Walter Payton "Football Heroes"; a 15-card Pro Bowl; and five Game Breaker holograms (GB1, GB3, GB4, GB6, and GB8). Randomly inserted throughout series II foil packs were a ten-card Dan Marino "Football Heroes" subset, special cards of James Lofton (SP3) and Art Monk (SP4), and three Game Breaker holograms (GB2, GB5, and GB7). A 20-card "Coach's Report" insert set was featured only in hobby packs while ten "Fanimation" cards were included only in retail packs. Inside white borders, the fronts display color action player photos with shadow borders. The team logo appears on a granite slab at the lower left corner, and the player's name and position are printed on a granite bar extending to the right. A team color-coded bar accents the granite bar. The backs carry a second color player photo as well as biographical and statistical information on a granite slab. Topical subsets featured are Star Rookie (1-29), All-Rookie (30-55), Team Checklists (73-100), Season Leader (301-311), Team MVP (350-378), Rookie Force (401-426), and NFL Scrapbook (511-520). The cards are numbered on the back. Rookie Cards include Edgar Bennett, Steve Bono, Terrell Buckley, Amp Lee, Derrick Moore, Torrance Small, Tommy Vardell, Johnny Mitchell and Troy Vincent. Members of both NFL Properties and the NFL Players Association are included in the second series.

	MINT	NRMT	EXC
COMPLETE SET (620)	15.00	6.75	1.85
COMPLETE SERIES 1 (400)	10.00	4.50	1.25
COMPLETE SERIES 2 (220)	5.00	2.20	.60
COMMON CARD (1-620)	.05	.02	.01
☐ 1 Star Rookie Checklist	.10	.05	.01
Edgar Bennett			
Terrell Buckley			
Dexter McNabb			
☐ 2 Edgar Bennett	.75	.35	.09
☐ 3 Eddie Blake	.05	.02	.01
☐ 4 Brian Bollinger	.05	.02	.01
☐ 5 Joe Bowden	.05	.02	.01
☐ 6 Terrell Buckley	.05	.02	.01
☐ 7 Willie Clay	.05	.02	.01
☐ 8 Ed Cunningham	.05	.02	.01
☐ 9 Matt Darby	.05	.02	.01
☐ 10 Will Furrer	.05	.02	.01
☐ 11 Chris Hakel	.05	.02	.01
☐ 12 Carlos Huerta	.05	.02	.01
☐ 13 Amp Lee	.05	.02	.01
☐ 14 Ricardo McDonald	.05	.02	.01
☐ 15 Dexter McNabb	.05	.02	.01
☐ 16 Chris Mims	.10	.05	.01

☐ 17 Derrick Moore	.10	.05	.01
☐ 18 Mark D'Onofrio	.05	.02	.01
☐ 19 Patrick Rowe	.05	.02	.01
☐ 20 Leon Searcy	.10	.05	.01
☐ 21 Torrance Small	.25	.11	.03
☐ 22 Jimmy Smith	.25	.11	.03
☐ 23 Tony Smith	.05	.02	.01
☐ 24 Siran Stacy	.05	.02	.01
☐ 25 Kevin Turner	.05	.02	.01
☐ 26 Tommy Vardell	.10	.05	.01
☐ 27 Bob Whitfield	.05	.02	.01
☐ 28 Darryl Williams	.05	.02	.01
☐ 29 Jeff Sydner	.05	.02	.01
☐ 30 All-Rookie Checklist	.05	.02	.01
Mike Croel			
Leonard Russell			
☐ 31 Todd Marinovich AR	.05	.02	.01
☐ 32 Leonard Russell AR	.05	.02	.01
☐ 33 Nick Bell AR	.05	.02	.01
☐ 34 Alvin Harper AR	.05	.02	.01
☐ 35 Mike Pritchard AR	.05	.02	.01
☐ 36 Lawrence Dawsey AR	.05	.02	.01
☐ 37 Tim Barnett AR	.05	.02	.01
☐ 38 John Flannery AR	.05	.02	.01
☐ 39 Stan Thomas AR	.05	.02	.01
☐ 40 Ed King AR	.05	.02	.01
☐ 41 Charles McRae AR	.05	.02	.01
☐ 42 Eric Moten AR	.05	.02	.01
☐ 43 Moe Gardner AR	.05	.02	.01
☐ 44 Kenny Walker AR	.05	.02	.01
☐ 45 Esera Tuaolo AR	.05	.02	.01
☐ 46 Alfred Williams AR	.05	.02	.01
☐ 47 Bryan Cox AR	.05	.02	.01
☐ 48 Mo Lewis AR	.05	.02	.01
☐ 49 Mike Croel AR	.05	.02	.01
☐ 50 Stanley Richard AR	.05	.02	.01
☐ 51 Tony Covington AR	.05	.02	.01
☐ 52 Larry Brown DB AR	.05	.02	.01
☐ 53 Aeneas Williams AR	.05	.02	.01
☐ 54 John Kasay AR	.05	.02	.01
☐ 55 Jon Vaughn AR	.05	.02	.01
☐ 56 David Fulcher	.05	.02	.01
☐ 57 Barry Foster	.10	.05	.01
☐ 58 Terry Wooden	.05	.02	.01
☐ 59 Gary Anderson K	.05	.02	.01
☐ 60 Alfred Williams	.05	.02	.01
☐ 61 Robert Blackmon	.05	.02	.01
☐ 62 Brian Noble	.05	.02	.01
☐ 63 Terry Allen	.40	.18	.05
☐ 64 Darrell Green	.05	.02	.01
☐ 65 Darren Comeaux	.05	.02	.01
☐ 66 Rob Burnett	.05	.02	.01
☐ 67 Jarrod Bunch	.05	.02	.01
☐ 68 Michael Jackson	.10	.05	.01
☐ 69 Greg Lloyd	.25	.11	.03
☐ 70 Richard Brown	.05	.02	.01
☐ 71 Harold Green	.05	.02	.01
☐ 72 William Fuller	.10	.05	.01
☐ 73 Mark Carrier DB TC	.05	.02	.01
☐ 74 David Fulcher TC	.05	.02	.01
☐ 75 Cornelius Bennett TC	.05	.02	.01
☐ 76 Steve Atwater TC	.05	.02	.01
☐ 77 Kevin Mack TC	.05	.02	.01
☐ 78 Mark Carrier WR TC	.05	.02	.01
☐ 79 Tim McDonald TC	.05	.02	.01
☐ 80 Marion Butts TC	.05	.02	.01
☐ 81 Christian Okoye TC	.05	.02	.01
☐ 82 Jeff Herrod TC	.05	.02	.01
☐ 83 Emmitt Smith TC	1.00	.45	.12
☐ 84 Mark Duper TC	.05	.02	.01
☐ 85 Keith Jackson TC	.05	.02	.01
☐ 86 Andre Rison TC	.10	.05	.01
☐ 87 John Taylor TC	.05	.02	.01
☐ 88 Rodney Hampton TC	.10	.05	.01
☐ 89 Rob Moore TC	.05	.02	.01
☐ 90 Chris Spielman TC	.05	.02	.01
☐ 91 Haywood Jeffires TC	.05	.02	.01
☐ 92 Sterling Sharpe TC	.10	.05	.01
☐ 93 Irving Fryar TC	.10	.05	.01
☐ 94 Marcus Allen TC	.10	.05	.01
☐ 95 Henry Ellard TC	.05	.02	.01
☐ 96 Mark Rypien TC	.05	.02	.01
☐ 97 Pat Swilling TC	.05	.02	.01
☐ 98 Brian Blades TC	.05	.02	.01
☐ 99 Eric Green TC	.05	.02	.01
☐ 100 Anthony Carter TC	.05	.02	.01
☐ 101 Burt Grossman	.05	.02	.01
☐ 102 Gary Anderson RB	.05	.02	.01
☐ 103 Neil Smith	.25	.11	.03
☐ 104 Jeff Feagles	.05	.02	.01
☐ 105 Shane Conlan	.05	.02	.01
☐ 106 Jay Novacek	.10	.05	.01
☐ 107 Bill Brooks	.05	.02	.01
☐ 108 Mark Ingram	.05	.02	.01
☐ 109 Anthony Munoz	.10	.05	.01
☐ 110 Wendell Davis	.05	.02	.01
☐ 111 Jim Everett	.10	.05	.01
☐ 112 Bruce Matthews	.05	.02	.01
☐ 113 Mark Higgs	.05	.02	.01
☐ 114 Chris Warren	.25	.11	.03
☐ 115 Brad Baxter	.05	.02	.01
☐ 116 Greg Townsend	.05	.02	.01
☐ 117 Al Smith	.05	.02	.01
☐ 118 Jeff Cross	.05	.02	.01
☐ 119 Terry McDaniel	.05	.02	.01
☐ 120 Ernest Givins	.10	.05	.01
☐ 121 Fred Barnett	.25	.11	.03
☐ 122 Flipper Anderson	.05	.02	.01
☐ 123 Floyd Turner	.05	.02	.01
☐ 124 Stephen Baker	.05	.02	.01
☐ 125 Tim Johnson	.05	.02	.01
☐ 126 Brent Jones	.10	.05	.01
☐ 127 Leonard Marshall	.05	.02	.01
☐ 128 Jim Price	.05	.02	.01
☐ 129 Jessie Hester	.05	.02	.01
☐ 130 Mark Carrier WR	.10	.05	.01
☐ 131 Bubba McDowell	.05	.02	.01
☐ 132 Andre Tippett	.05	.02	.01
☐ 133 James Hasty	.05	.02	.01
☐ 134 Mel Gray	.10	.05	.01
☐ 135 Christian Okoye	.05	.02	.01
☐ 136 Earnest Byner	.05	.02	.01
☐ 137 Ferrell Edmunds	.05	.02	.01
☐ 138 Henry Ellard	.10	.05	.01
☐ 139 Rob Moore	.10	.05	.01
☐ 140 Brian Jordan	.10	.05	.01
☐ 141 Clarence Verdin	.05	.02	.01
☐ 142 Cornelius Bennett	.10	.05	.01
☐ 143 John Taylor	.10	.05	.01
☐ 144 Derrick Thomas	.25	.11	.03
☐ 145 Thurman Thomas	.25	.11	.03
☐ 146 Warren Moon	.25	.11	.03
☐ 147 Vinny Testaverde	.10	.05	.01
☐ 148 Steve Bono	.25	.11	.03
☐ 149 Robb Thomas	.05	.02	.01
☐ 150 John Friesz	.10	.05	.01
☐ 151 Richard Dent	.10	.05	.01
☐ 152 Eddie Anderson	.05	.02	.01
☐ 153 Kevin Greene	.25	.11	.03
☐ 154 Marion Butts	.05	.02	.01
☐ 155 Barry Sanders	1.00	.45	.12
☐ 156 Andre Rison	.10	.05	.01
☐ 157 Ronnie Lott	.10	.05	.01
☐ 158 Eric Allen	.05	.02	.01
☐ 159 Mark Clayton	.10	.05	.01
☐ 160 Terance Mathis	.10	.05	.01
☐ 161 Darryl Talley	.05	.02	.01
☐ 162 Eric Metcalf	.10	.05	.01
☐ 163 Reggie Cobb	.05	.02	.01
☐ 164 Ernie Jones	.05	.02	.01
☐ 165 David Griggs	.05	.02	.01
☐ 166 Tom Rathman	.05	.02	.01
☐ 167 Bubby Brister	.05	.02	.01
☐ 168 Broderick Thomas	.05	.02	.01
☐ 169 Chris Doleman	.05	.02	.01
☐ 170 Charles Haley	.10	.05	.01
☐ 171 Michael Haynes	.10	.05	.01
☐ 172 Rodney Hampton	.25	.11	.03
☐ 173 Nick Bell	.05	.02	.01
☐ 174 Gene Atkins	.05	.02	.01
☐ 175 Mike Merriweather	.05	.02	.01
☐ 176 Reggie Roby	.05	.02	.01
☐ 177 Bennie Blades	.05	.02	.01
☐ 178 John L. Williams	.05	.02	.01
☐ 179 Rodney Peete	.10	.05	.01
☐ 180 Greg Montgomery	.05	.02	.01
☐ 181 Vince Newsome	.05	.02	.01
☐ 182 Andre Collins	.05	.02	.01
☐ 183 Erik Kramer	.10	.05	.01
☐ 184 Bryan Hinkle	.05	.02	.01
☐ 185 Reggie White	.25	.11	.03
☐ 186 Bruce Armstrong	.05	.02	.01
☐ 187 Anthony Carter	.10	.05	.01
☐ 188 Pat Swilling	.10	.05	.01
☐ 189 Robert Delpino	.05	.02	.01
☐ 190 Brent Williams	.05	.02	.01
☐ 191 Johnny Johnson	.05	.02	.01
☐ 192 Aaron Craver	.05	.02	.01
☐ 193 Vincent Brown	.05	.02	.01
☐ 194 Herschel Walker	.10	.05	.01
☐ 195 Tim McDonald	.05	.02	.01
☐ 196 Gaston Green	.05	.02	.01
☐ 197 Brian Blades	.10	.05	.01
☐ 198 Rod Bernstine	.05	.02	.01
☐ 199 Brett Perriman	.25	.11	.03
☐ 200 John Elway	.60	.25	.07
☐ 201 Michael Carter	.05	.02	.01
☐ 202 Mark Carrier DB	.05	.02	.01
☐ 203 Cris Carter	.25	.11	.03
☐ 204 Kyle Clifton	.05	.02	.01
☐ 205 Alvin Wright	.05	.02	.01
☐ 206 Andre Ware	.05	.02	.01
☐ 207 Dave Waymer	.05	.02	.01
☐ 208 Darren Lewis	.05	.02	.01
☐ 209 Joey Browner	.05	.02	.01
☐ 210 Rich Miano	.05	.02	.01
☐ 211 Marcus Allen	.25	.11	.03
☐ 212 Steve Broussard	.05	.02	.01
☐ 213 Joel Hilgenberg	.05	.02	.01
☐ 214 Bo Orlando	.05	.02	.01
☐ 215 Clay Matthews	.10	.05	.01
☐ 216 Chris Hinton	.05	.02	.01
☐ 217 Al Edwards	.05	.02	.01
☐ 218 Tim Brown	.25	.11	.03
☐ 219 Sam Mills	.05	.02	.01
☐ 220 Don Majkowski	.05	.02	.01
☐ 221 James Francis	.05	.02	.01
☐ 222 Steve Hendrickson	.05	.02	.01
☐ 223 James Thornton	.05	.02	.01
☐ 224 Byron Evans	.05	.02	.01
☐ 225 Pepper Johnson	.05	.02	.01
☐ 226 Darryl Henley	.05	.02	.01
☐ 227 Simon Fletcher	.05	.02	.01
☐ 228 Hugh Millen	.05	.02	.01
☐ 229 Tim McGee	.05	.02	.01
☐ 230 Richmond Webb	.05	.02	.01
☐ 231 Tony Bennett	.05	.02	.01
☐ 232 Nate Odomes	.05	.02	.01
☐ 233 Scott Case	.05	.02	.01
☐ 234 Dalton Hilliard	.05	.02	.01
☐ 235 Paul Gruber	.05	.02	.01
☐ 236 Jeff Lageman	.05	.02	.01
☐ 237 Tony Mandarich	.05	.02	.01
☐ 238 Cris Dishman	.05	.02	.01
☐ 239 Steve Walsh	.05	.02	.01
☐ 240 Moe Gardner	.05	.02	.01
☐ 241 Bill Romanowski	.05	.02	.01
☐ 242 Chris Zorich	.10	.05	.01
☐ 243 Stephone Paige	.05	.02	.01
☐ 244 Mike Croel	.05	.02	.01
☐ 245 Leonard Russell	.10	.05	.01
☐ 246 Mark Rypien	.05	.02	.01
☐ 247 Aeneas Williams	.10	.05	.01
☐ 248 Steve Atwater	.05	.02	.01
☐ 249 Michael Stewart	.05	.02	.01
☐ 250 Pierce Holt	.05	.02	.01
☐ 251 Kevin Mack	.05	.02	.01
☐ 252 Sterling Sharpe	.25	.11	.03
☐ 253 Lawrence Dawsey	.10	.05	.01
☐ 254 Emmitt Smith	2.00	.90	.25
☐ 255 Todd Marinovich	.05	.02	.01
☐ 256 Neal Anderson	.05	.02	.01
☐ 257 Mo Lewis	.05	.02	.01
☐ 258 Vance Johnson	.05	.02	.01
☐ 259 Rickey Jackson	.05	.02	.01
☐ 260 Esera Tuaolo	.05	.02	.01
☐ 261 Wilber Marshall	.05	.02	.01
☐ 262 Keith Henderson	.05	.02	.01
☐ 263 William Thomas	.05	.02	.01
☐ 264 Rickey Dixon	.05	.02	.01
☐ 265 Dave Meggett	.10	.05	.01
☐ 266 Gerald Riggs	.05	.02	.01
☐ 267 Tim Harris	.05	.02	.01
☐ 268 Ken Harvey	.05	.02	.01
☐ 269 Clyde Simmons	.05	.02	.01
☐ 270 Irving Fryar	.10	.05	.01
☐ 271 Darion Conner	.05	.02	.01
☐ 272 Vince Workman	.10	.05	.01
☐ 273 Jim Harbaugh	.25	.11	.03
☐ 274 Lorenzo White	.05	.02	.01
☐ 275 Bobby Hebert	.05	.02	.01
☐ 276 Duane Bickett	.05	.02	.01
☐ 277 Jeff Bryant	.05	.02	.01
☐ 278 Scott Stephen	.05	.02	.01
☐ 279 Bob Golic	.05	.02	.01
☐ 280 Steve McMichael	.10	.05	.01
☐ 281 Jeff Graham	.25	.11	.03
☐ 282 Keith Jackson	.10	.05	.01
☐ 283 Howard Ballard	.05	.02	.01
☐ 284 Michael Brooks	.05	.02	.01
☐ 285 Freeman McNeil	.05	.02	.01
☐ 286 Rodney Holman	.05	.02	.01
☐ 287 Eric Bieniemy	.05	.02	.01
☐ 288 Seth Joyner	.10	.05	.01
☐ 289 Carwell Gardner	.05	.02	.01
☐ 290 Brian Mitchell	.10	.05	.01
☐ 291 Chris Miller	.10	.05	.01
☐ 292 Ray Berry	.05	.02	.01
☐ 293 Matt Brock	.05	.02	.01
☐ 294 Eric Thomas	.05	.02	.01
☐ 295 John Kasay	.05	.02	.01
☐ 296 Jay Hilgenberg	.05	.02	.01
☐ 297 Darrell Thompson	.05	.02	.01
☐ 298 Rich Gannon	.05	.02	.01
☐ 299 Steve Young	.60	.25	.07
☐ 300 Mike Kenn	.05	.02	.01
☐ 301 Emmitt Smith SL	1.00	.45	.12
☐ 302 Haywood Jeffires SL	.05	.02	.01
☐ 303 Michael Irvin SL	.25	.11	.03
☐ 304 Warren Moon SL	.10	.05	.01
☐ 305 Chip Lohmiller SL	.05	.02	.01
☐ 306 Barry Sanders SL	.50	.23	.06
☐ 307 Ronnie Lott SL	.10	.05	.01
☐ 308 Pat Swilling SL	.05	.02	.01
☐ 309 Thurman Thomas SL	.10	.05	.01
☐ 310 Reggie Roby SL	.05	.02	.01
☐ 311 Season Leader CL	.10	.05	.01
Warren Moon			
Michael Irvin			
Thurman Thomas			
☐ 312 Jacob Green	.05	.02	.01
☐ 313 Stephen Braggs	.05	.02	.01
☐ 314 Haywood Jeffires	.10	.05	.01
☐ 315 Freddie Joe Nunn	.05	.02	.01
☐ 316 Gary Clark	.25	.11	.03
☐ 317 Tim Barnett	.05	.02	.01
☐ 318 Mark Duper	.05	.02	.01
☐ 319 Eric Green	.05	.02	.01
☐ 320 Robert Wilson	.05	.02	.01
☐ 321 Michael Ball	.05	.02	.01
☐ 322 Eric Martin	.05	.02	.01
☐ 323 Alexander Wright	.05	.02	.01
☐ 324 Jessie Tuggle	.05	.02	.01
☐ 325 Ronnie Harmon	.05	.02	.01
☐ 326 Jeff Hostetler	.10	.05	.01
☐ 327 Eugene Daniel	.05	.02	.01
☐ 328 Ken Norton Jr.	.25	.11	.03
☐ 329 Reyna Thompson	.05	.02	.01
☐ 330 Jerry Ball	.05	.02	.01
☐ 331 Leroy Hoard	.10	.05	.01
☐ 332 Chris Martin	.05	.02	.01
☐ 333 Keith McKeller	.05	.02	.01
☐ 334 Brian Washington	.05	.02	.01
☐ 335 Eugene Robinson	.05	.02	.01
☐ 336 Maurice Hurst	.05	.02	.01
☐ 337 Dan Saleaumua	.05	.02	.01
☐ 338 Neil O'Donnell	.25	.11	.03
☐ 339 Dexter Davis	.05	.02	.01
☐ 340 Keith McCants	.05	.02	.01
☐ 341 Steve Beuerlein	.05	.02	.01
☐ 342 Roman Phifer	.05	.02	.01
☐ 343 Bryan Cox	.10	.05	.01
☐ 344 Art Monk	.10	.05	.01
☐ 345 Michael Irvin	.25	.11	.03
☐ 346 Vaughan Johnson	.05	.02	.01
☐ 347 Jeff Herrod	.05	.02	.01
☐ 348 Stanley Richard	.05	.02	.01
☐ 349 Michael Young	.05	.02	.01
☐ 350 Team MVP Checklist	.10	.05	.01
Rodney Hampton			
Reggie Cobb			
☐ 351 Jim Harbaugh MVP	.10	.05	.01
☐ 352 David Fulcher MVP	.05	.02	.01
☐ 353 Thurman Thomas MVP	.10	.05	.01
☐ 354 Gaston Green MVP	.05	.02	.01
☐ 355 Leroy Hoard MVP	.05	.02	.01
☐ 356 Reggie Cobb MVP	.05	.02	.01
☐ 357 Tim McDonald MVP	.05	.02	.01
☐ 358 Ronnie Harmon MVP UER	.05	.02	.01
(Bernstine misspelled			
as Bernstein)			
☐ 359 Derrick Thomas MVP	.10	.05	.01
☐ 360 Jeff Herrod MVP	.05	.02	.01
☐ 361 Michael Irvin MVP	.25	.11	.03
☐ 362 Mark Higgs MVP	.05	.02	.01
☐ 363 Reggie White MVP	.10	.05	.01
☐ 364 Chris Miller MVP	.05	.02	.01
☐ 365 Steve Young MVP	.30	.14	.04
☐ 366 Rodney Hampton MVP	.10	.05	.01
☐ 367 Jeff Lageman MVP	.05	.02	.01
☐ 368 Barry Sanders MVP	.50	.23	.06
☐ 369 Haywood Jeffires MVP	.05	.02	.01
☐ 370 Tony Bennett MVP	.05	.02	.01
☐ 371 Leonard Russell MVP	.05	.02	.01
☐ 372 Jeff Jaeger MVP	.05	.02	.01
☐ 373 Robert Delpino MVP	.05	.02	.01
☐ 374 Mark Rypien MVP	.05	.02	.01
☐ 375 Pat Swilling MVP	.05	.02	.01
☐ 376 Cortez Kennedy MVP	.10	.05	.01
☐ 377 Eric Green MVP	.05	.02	.01
☐ 378 Cris Carter MVP	.10	.05	.01
☐ 379 John Roper	.05	.02	.01
☐ 380 Barry Word	.05	.02	.01
☐ 381 Shawn Jefferson	.05	.02	.01
☐ 382 Tony Casillas	.05	.02	.01
☐ 383 John Baylor	.05	.02	.01
☐ 384 Al Noga	.05	.02	.01
☐ 385 Charles Mann	.05	.02	.01
☐ 386 Gill Byrd	.05	.02	.01
☐ 387 Chris Singleton	.05	.02	.01
☐ 388 James Joseph	.05	.02	.01
☐ 389 Larry Brown DB	.05	.02	.01
☐ 390 Chris Spielman	.10	.05	.01
☐ 391 Anthony Thompson	.05	.02	.01
☐ 392 Karl Mecklenburg	.05	.02	.01
☐ 393 Joe Kelly	.05	.02	.01
☐ 394 Kanavis McGhee	.05	.02	.01
☐ 395 Bill Maas	.05	.02	.01
☐ 396 Marv Cook	.05	.02	.01
☐ 397 Louis Lipps	.05	.02	.01
☐ 398 Marty Carter	.05	.02	.01
☐ 399 Louis Oliver	.05	.02	.01
☐ 400 Eric Swann	.10	.05	.01
☐ 401 Troy Auzenne	.05	.02	.01
☐ 402 Kurt Barber	.05	.02	.01
☐ 403 Marc Boutte	.05	.02	.01
☐ 404 Dale Carter	.10	.05	.01
☐ 405 Marco Coleman	.10	.05	.01
☐ 406 Quentin Coryatt	.25	.11	.03
☐ 407 Shane Dronett	.05	.02	.01
☐ 408 Vaughn Dunbar	.05	.02	.01
☐ 409 Steve Emtman	.05	.02	.01
☐ 410 Dana Hall	.10	.05	.01
☐ 411 Jason Hansen	.10	.05	.01
☐ 412 Courtney Hawkins	.10	.05	.01
☐ 413 Terrell Buckley	.05	.02	.01
☐ 414 Robert Jones	.05	.02	.01
☐ 415 David Klingler	.05	.02	.01
☐ 416 Tommy Maddox	.05	.02	.01
☐ 417 Johnny Mitchell	.05	.02	.01
☐ 418 Carl Pickens	1.00	.45	.12
☐ 419 Tracy Scroggins	.05	.02	.01
☐ 420 Tony Sacca	.05	.02	.01
☐ 421 Kevin Smith	.25	.11	.03
☐ 422 Alonzo Spellman	.10	.05	.01
☐ 423 Troy Vincent	.10	.05	.01
☐ 424 Sean Gilbert	.25	.11	.03
☐ 425 Larry Webster	.05	.02	.01
☐ 426 Rookie Force Checklist	.25	.11	.03
Carl Pickens			

David Klingler			
☐ 427 Bill Fralic	.05	.02	.01
☐ 428 Kevin Murphy	.05	.02	.01
☐ 429 Lemuel Stinson	.05	.02	.01
☐ 430 Harris Barton	.05	.02	.01
☐ 431 Dino Hackett	.05	.02	.01
☐ 432 John Stephens	.05	.02	.01
☐ 433 Keith Jennings	.05	.02	.01
☐ 434 Derrick Fenner	.05	.02	.01
☐ 435 Kenneth Gant	.05	.02	.01
☐ 436 Willie Gault	.10	.05	.01
☐ 437 Steve Jordan	.05	.02	.01
☐ 438 Charles Haley	.10	.05	.01
☐ 439 Keith Kartz	.05	.02	.01
☐ 440 Nate Lewis	.05	.02	.01
☐ 441 Doug Widell	.05	.02	.01
☐ 442 William White	.05	.02	.01
☐ 443 Eric Hill	.05	.02	.01
☐ 444 Melvin Jenkins	.05	.02	.01
☐ 445 David Wyman	.05	.02	.01
☐ 446 Ed West	.05	.02	.01
☐ 447 Brad Muster	.05	.02	.01
☐ 448 Ray Childress	.05	.02	.01
☐ 449 Kevin Ross	.05	.02	.01
☐ 450 Johnnie Jackson	.05	.02	.01
☐ 451 Tracy Simien	.05	.02	.01
☐ 452 Don Mosebar	.05	.02	.01
☐ 453 Jay Hilgenberg	.05	.02	.01
☐ 454 Wes Hopkins	.05	.02	.01
☐ 455 Jay Schroeder	.05	.02	.01
☐ 456 Jeff Bostic	.05	.02	.01
☐ 457 Bryce Paup	.25	.11	.03
☐ 458 Dave Waymer	.05	.02	.01
☐ 459 Toi Cook	.05	.02	.01
☐ 460 Anthony Smith	.05	.02	.01
☐ 461 Don Griffin	.05	.02	.01
☐ 462 Bill Hawkins	.05	.02	.01
☐ 463 Courtney Hall	.05	.02	.01
☐ 464 Jeff Uhlenhake	.05	.02	.01
☐ 465 Mike Sherrard	.05	.02	.01
☐ 466 James Jones	.05	.02	.01
☐ 467 Jerrol Williams	.05	.02	.01
☐ 468 Eric Ball	.05	.02	.01
☐ 469 Randall McDaniel	.05	.02	.01
☐ 470 Alvin Harper	.10	.05	.01
☐ 471 Tom Waddle	.05	.02	.01
☐ 472 Tony Woods	.05	.02	.01
☐ 473 Kelvin Martin	.05	.02	.01
☐ 474 Jon Vaughn	.05	.02	.01
☐ 475 Gill Fenerty	.05	.02	.01
☐ 476 Aundray Bruce	.05	.02	.01
☐ 477 Morten Andersen	.05	.02	.01
☐ 478 Lamar Lathon	.05	.02	.01
☐ 479 Steve DeOssie	.05	.02	.01
☐ 480 Marvin Washington	.05	.02	.01
☐ 481 Herschel Walker	.10	.05	.01
☐ 482 Howie Long	.10	.05	.01
☐ 483 Calvin Williams	.10	.05	.01
☐ 484 Brett Favre	2.50	1.10	.30
☐ 485 Johnny Bailey	.05	.02	.01
☐ 486 Jeff Gossett	.05	.02	.01
☐ 487 Carnell Lake	.05	.02	.01
☐ 488 Michael Zordich	.05	.02	.01
☐ 489 Henry Rolling	.05	.02	.01
☐ 490 Steve Smith	.05	.02	.01
☐ 491 Vestee Jackson	.05	.02	.01
☐ 492 Ray Crockett	.05	.02	.01
☐ 493 Dexter Carter	.05	.02	.01
☐ 494 Nick Lowery	.05	.02	.01
☐ 495 Cortez Kennedy	.10	.05	.01
☐ 496 Cleveland Gary	.05	.02	.01
☐ 497 Kelly Stouffer	.05	.02	.01
☐ 498 Carl Carter	.05	.02	.01
☐ 499 Shannon Sharpe	.25	.11	.03
☐ 500 Roger Craig	.10	.05	.01
☐ 501 Willie Drewrey	.05	.02	.01
☐ 502 Mark Schlereth	.05	.02	.01
☐ 503 Tony Martin	.25	.11	.03
☐ 504 Tom Newberry	.05	.02	.01
☐ 505 Ron Hall	.05	.02	.01
☐ 506 Scott Miller	.05	.02	.01
☐ 507 Donnell Woolford	.05	.02	.01
☐ 508 Dave Krieg	.10	.05	.01
☐ 509 Erric Pegram	.10	.05	.01
☐ 510 Checklist 401-510	.05	.02	.01
☐ 511 Barry Sanders SBK	.50	.23	.06
☐ 512 Thurman Thomas SBK	.10	.05	.01
☐ 513 Warren Moon SBK	.10	.05	.01
☐ 514 John Elway SBK	.30	.14	.04
☐ 515 Ronnie Lott SBK	.10	.05	.01
☐ 516 Emmitt Smith SBK	1.00	.45	.12
☐ 517 Andre Rison SBK	.10	.05	.01
☐ 518 Steve Atwater SBK	.05	.02	.01
☐ 519 Steve Young SBK	.30	.14	.04
☐ 520 Mark Rypien SBK	.05	.02	.01
☐ 521 Rich Camarillo	.05	.02	.01
☐ 522 Mark Bavaro	.05	.02	.01
☐ 523 Brad Edwards	.05	.02	.01
☐ 524 Chad Hennings	.10	.05	.01
☐ 525 Tony Paige	.05	.02	.01
☐ 526 Shawn Moore	.05	.02	.01
☐ 527 Sidney Johnson	.05	.02	.01
☐ 528 Sanjay Beach	.05	.02	.01
☐ 529 Kelvin Pritchett	.05	.02	.01
☐ 530 Jerry Holmes	.05	.02	.01
☐ 531 Al Del Greco	.05	.02	.01
☐ 532 Bob Gagliano	.05	.02	.01
☐ 533 Drew Hill	.05	.02	.01
☐ 534 Donald Frank	.05	.02	.01
☐ 535 Pio Sagapolutele	.05	.02	.01
☐ 536 Jackie Slater	.05	.02	.01
☐ 537 Vernon Turner	.05	.02	.01
☐ 538 Bobby Humphrey	.05	.02	.01
☐ 539 Audray McMillian	.05	.02	.01
☐ 540 Gary Brown	.05	.02	.01
☐ 541 Wesley Carroll	.05	.02	.01
☐ 542 Nate Newton	.10	.05	.01
☐ 543 Vai Sikahema	.05	.02	.01
☐ 544 Chris Chandler	.10	.05	.01
☐ 545 Nolan Harrison	.05	.02	.01
☐ 546 Mark Green	.05	.02	.01
☐ 547 Ricky Watters	.50	.23	.06
☐ 548 J.J. Birden	.05	.02	.01
☐ 549 Cody Carlson	.05	.02	.01
☐ 550 Tim Green	.05	.02	.01
☐ 551 Mark Jackson	.05	.02	.01
☐ 552 Vince Buck	.05	.02	.01
☐ 553 George Jamison	.05	.02	.01
☐ 554 Anthony Pleasant	.05	.02	.01
☐ 555 Reggie Johnson	.05	.02	.01
☐ 556 John Jackson	.05	.02	.01
☐ 557 Ian Beckles	.05	.02	.01
☐ 558 Buford McGee	.05	.02	.01
☐ 559 Fuad Reveiz UER (Born in Colombia, not Columbia)	.05	.02	.01
☐ 560 Joe Montana	1.00	.45	.12
☐ 561 Phil Simms	.10	.05	.01
☐ 562 Greg McMurtry	.05	.02	.01
☐ 563 Gerald Williams	.05	.02	.01
☐ 564 Dave Cadigan	.05	.02	.01
☐ 565 Rufus Porter	.05	.02	.01
☐ 566 Jim Kelly	.25	.11	.03
☐ 567 Deion Sanders	.50	.23	.06
☐ 568 Mike Singletary	.10	.05	.01
☐ 569 Boomer Esiason	.10	.05	.01
☐ 570 Andre Reed	.10	.05	.01
☐ 571 James Washington	.05	.02	.01
☐ 572 Jack Del Rio	.05	.02	.01
☐ 573 Gerald Perry	.05	.02	.01
☐ 574 Vinnie Clark	.05	.02	.01
☐ 575 Mike Piel	.05	.02	.01
☐ 576 Michael Dean Perry	.10	.05	.01
☐ 577 Ricky Proehl	.05	.02	.01
☐ 578 Leslie O'Neal	.10	.05	.01
☐ 579 Russell Maryland	.10	.05	.01
☐ 580 Eric Dickerson	.10	.05	.01
☐ 581 Fred Strickland	.05	.02	.01
☐ 582 Nick Lowery	.05	.02	.01
☐ 583 Joe Milinichik	.05	.02	.01
☐ 584 Mark Vlasic	.05	.02	.01
☐ 585 James Lofton	.10	.05	.01
☐ 586 Bruce Smith	.25	.11	.03
☐ 587 Harvey Williams	.25	.11	.03
☐ 588 Bernie Kosar	.10	.05	.01
☐ 589 Carl Banks	.05	.02	.01
☐ 590 Jeff George	.25	.11	.03
☐ 591 Fred Jones	.05	.02	.01
☐ 592 Todd Scott	.05	.02	.01
☐ 593 Keith Jones	.05	.02	.01
☐ 594A Tootie Robbins ERR (Card has him as a Denver Bronco)	.05	.02	.01
☐ 594B Tootie Robbins COR	.05	.02	.01
☐ 595 Todd Philcox	.05	.02	.01
☐ 596 Browning Nagle	.05	.02	.01
☐ 597 Troy Aikman	1.00	.45	.12
☐ 598 Dan Marino	1.50	.70	.19
☐ 599 Lawrence Taylor	.25	.11	.03
☐ 600 Webster Slaughter	.05	.02	.01
☐ 601 Aaron Cox	.05	.02	.01
☐ 602 Matt Stover	.05	.02	.01
☐ 603 Keith Sims	.05	.02	.01
☐ 604 Dennis Smith	.05	.02	.01
☐ 605 Kevin Porter	.05	.02	.01
☐ 606 Anthony Miller	.10	.05	.01
☐ 607 Ken O'Brien	.05	.02	.01
☐ 608 Randall Cunningham	.10	.05	.01
☐ 609 Timm Rosenbach	.05	.02	.01
☐ 610 Junior Seau	.25	.11	.03
☐ 611 Johnny Rembert	.05	.02	.01
☐ 612 Rick Tuten	.05	.02	.01
☐ 613 Willie Green	.05	.02	.01
☐ 614 Sean Salisbury UER (He is listed with Lions in 1990 and Chargers in 1991; he was with Vikings both years)	.05	.02	.01
☐ 615 Martin Bayless	.05	.02	.01
☐ 616 Jerry Rice	1.00	.45	.12
☐ 617 Randal Hill	.05	.02	.01
☐ 618 Dan McGwire	.05	.02	.01
☐ 619 Merril Hoge	.05	.02	.01
☐ 620 Checklist 571-620	.05	.02	.01
☐ SP3 James Lofton Yardage	1.00	.45	.12
☐ SP4 Art Monk Catches	.50	.23	.06

1992 Upper Deck Gold

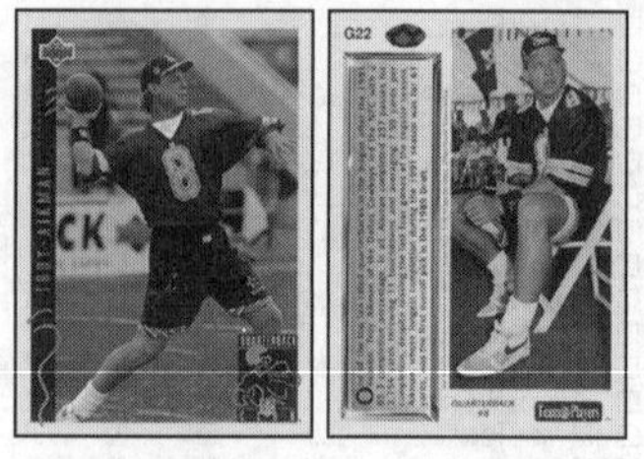

These 50 standard-size cards feature players licensed by NFL Properties. Each low series foil box contained one 15-card foil pack of these cards. Two Game Breaker holograms of Jerry Rice and Andre Reed were randomly inserted throughout these packs. The fronts of all cards display color action player photos bordered in white. On the Quarterback Club cards, the player's name is printed in a black stripe along the left edge, while the other cards have the player's name and position printed in different designs at the bottom. Though the backs of the Prospects cards feature a career summary, the backs of the remaining cards carry a color close-up photo as well as biography, statistics, or player profile. Two distinguishing features of the backs are a gold (instead of silver) Upper Deck hologram image and the NFL Properties logo. The cards are numbered on the back with a "G" prefix and subdivided into NFL Top Prospects (1-20), Quarterback Club (21-25), and veteran players (26-50). The key Rookie Cards in this set are Quentin Coryatt, Steve Emtman and Carl Pickens.

	MINT	NRMT	EXC
COMPLETE SET (50)	12.00	5.50	1.50
COMMON CARD (G1-G50)	.10	.05	.01
☐ G1 Steve Emtman	.10	.05	.01
☐ G2 Carl Pickens	2.00	.90	.25
☐ G3 Dale Carter	.30	.14	.04
☐ G4 Greg Skrepenak	.10	.05	.01
☐ G5 Kevin Smith	.30	.14	.04
☐ G6 Marco Coleman	.15	.07	.02
☐ G7 David Klingler	.15	.07	.02
☐ G8 Phillippi Sparks	.10	.05	.01
☐ G9 Tommy Maddox	.10	.05	.01
☐ G10 Quentin Coryatt	.15	.07	.02
☐ G11 Ty Detmer	.60	.25	.07
☐ G12 Vaughn Dunbar	.10	.05	.01
☐ G13 Ashley Ambrose	.15	.07	.02
☐ G14 Kurt Barber	.10	.05	.01
☐ G15 Chester McGlockton	.30	.14	.04
☐ G16 Todd Collins	.10	.05	.01
☐ G17 Steve Israel	.10	.05	.01
☐ G18 Marquez Pope	.10	.05	.01
☐ G19 Alonzo Spellman	.15	.07	.02
☐ G20 Tracy Scroggins	.10	.05	.01
☐ G21 Jim Kelly QC	.30	.14	.04
☐ G22 Troy Aikman QC	1.00	.45	.12
☐ G23 Randall Cunningham QC	.15	.07	.02
☐ G24 Bernie Kosar QC	.15	.07	.02
☐ G25 Dan Marino QC	1.50	.70	.19
☐ G26 Andre Reed	.15	.07	.02
☐ G27 Deion Sanders	.50	.23	.06
☐ G28 Randal Hill	.10	.05	.01
☐ G29 Eric Dickerson	.15	.07	.02
☐ G30 Jim Kelly	.30	.14	.04
☐ G31 Bernie Kosar	.15	.07	.02
☐ G32 Mike Singletary	.15	.07	.02
☐ G33 Anthony Miller	.15	.07	.02
☐ G34 Harvey Williams	.30	.14	.04
☐ G35 Randall Cunningham	.15	.07	.02
☐ G36 Joe Montana	1.00	.45	.12
☐ G37 Dan McGwire	.10	.05	.01
☐ G38 Al Toon	.15	.07	.02
☐ G39 Carl Banks	.10	.05	.01
☐ G40 Troy Aikman	1.00	.45	.12
☐ G41 Junior Seau	.30	.14	.04
☐ G42 Jeff George	.30	.14	.04
☐ G43 Michael Dean Perry	.15	.07	.02
☐ G44 Lawrence Taylor	.30	.14	.04
☐ G45 Dan Marino	1.50	.70	.19
☐ G46 Jerry Rice	1.00	.45	.12
☐ G47 Boomer Esiason	.15	.07	.02
☐ G48 Bruce Smith	.30	.14	.04
☐ G49 Leslie O'Neal	.15	.07	.02
☐ G50 Checklist Card	.10	.05	.01

1992 Upper Deck Coach's Report

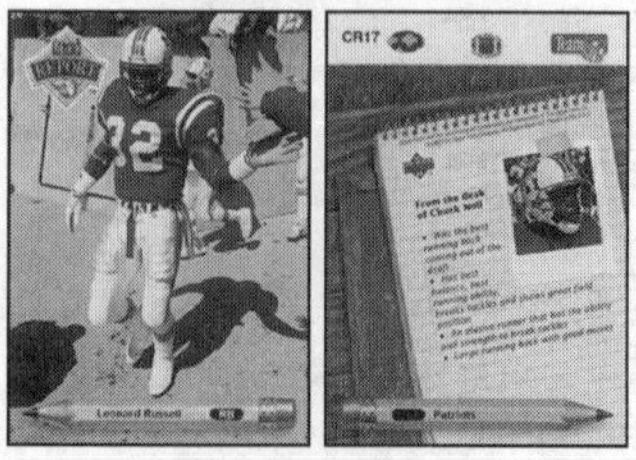

These 20 standard-size cards were randomly inserted throughout 1992 Upper Deck II hobby foil packs only. The set features Chuck Noll, former Steelers' head coach, analyzing 1992 rookies along with outstanding second-year players on their potential to achieve stardom in the NFL. The fronts feature full-bleed color action photos with the "Coach's Report" logo at one of the upper corners. The player's name and his position are printed on a short pencil toward the bottom of the card. The back has a yellow spiral-bound notepad resting on top of a chalkboard and wooden desk, with grass visible in the background. The top page has the words "From the desk of Chuck Noll" with his evaluation of the player's strengths as well as a color photograph taped to the page. The cards are numbered (with a "CR" prefix) on a white stripe that cuts across the top of the card.

	MINT	NRMT	EXC
COMPLETE SET (20)	16.00	7.25	2.00
COMMON CARD (CR1-CR20)	.40	.18	.05
☐ CR1 Mike Pritchard	.75	.35	.09
☐ CR2 Will Furrer	.40	.18	.05
☐ CR3 Alfred Williams	.40	.18	.05
☐ CR4 Tommy Vardell	.40	.18	.05
☐ CR5 Brett Favre	8.00	3.60	1.00
☐ CR6 Alvin Harper	.75	.35	.09
☐ CR7 Mike Croel	.40	.18	.05
☐ CR8 Herman Moore	3.50	1.55	.45
☐ CR9 Edgar Bennett	2.00	.90	.25
☐ CR10 Todd Marinovich	.40	.18	.05
☐ CR11 Aeneas Williams	.75	.35	.09
☐ CR12 Ricky Watters	2.00	.90	.25
☐ CR13 Amp Lee	.40	.18	.05
☐ CR14 Terrell Buckley	.40	.18	.05
☐ CR15 Tim Barnett	.40	.18	.05
☐ CR16 Nick Bell	.40	.18	.05
☐ CR17 Leonard Russell	.40	.18	.05
☐ CR18 Lawrence Dawsey	.75	.35	.09
☐ CR19 Robert Porcher	.40	.18	.05
☐ CR20 Checklist (Ricky Watters)	1.00	.45	.12

1992 Upper Deck Fanimation

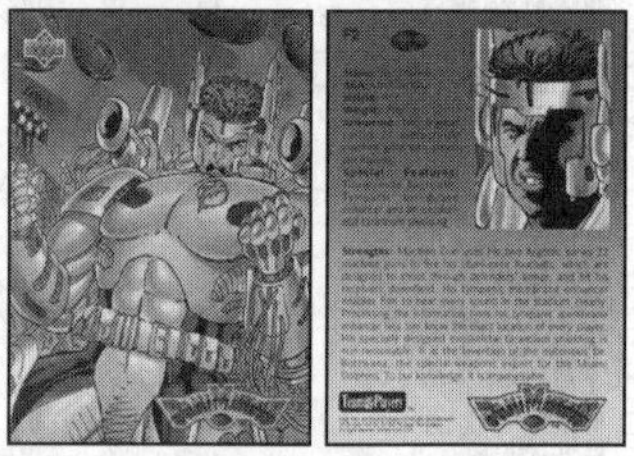

These ten standard-size cards were randomly inserted throughout 1992 Upper Deck second series retail foil packs only and were the work of artists Jim Lee and Rob Liefeld. The cards feature on the fronts full-bleed color cartoon illustrations that are based on NFL stars. The "Fanimation" logo appears in one of the lower corners. On a background that shades from red to orange to yellow, the backs have a head shot, biography (including topics such as "Armament" and "Special Features"), and a discussion of the character's strengths. The cards are numbered on the back in the upper left corner with an "F" prefix. The player's nickname is mentioned in the listing below.

	MINT	NRMT	EXC
COMPLETE SET (10)	25.00	11.00	3.10
COMMON CARD (F1-F10)	1.25	.55	.16
☐ F1 Jim Kelly (Shotgun Kelly)	2.00	.90	.25
☐ F2 Dan Marino (Machine Gun)	8.00	3.60	1.00
☐ F3 Lawrence Taylor (The Giant)	2.00	.90	.25
☐ F4 Deion Sanders (Neon Deion)	4.00	1.80	.50
☐ F5 Troy Aikman (The Marshall)	6.00	2.70	.75
☐ F6 Junior Seau (The Warrior)	2.00	.90	.25
☐ F7 Mike Singletary (Samurai)	1.25	.55	.16
☐ F8 Eric Dickerson (The Raider)	1.25	.55	.16
☐ F9 Jerry Rice (Goldfinger)	6.00	2.70	.75
☐ F10 Checklist Card Jim Kelly Dan Marino	4.00	1.80	.50

1992 Upper Deck Game Breaker Holograms

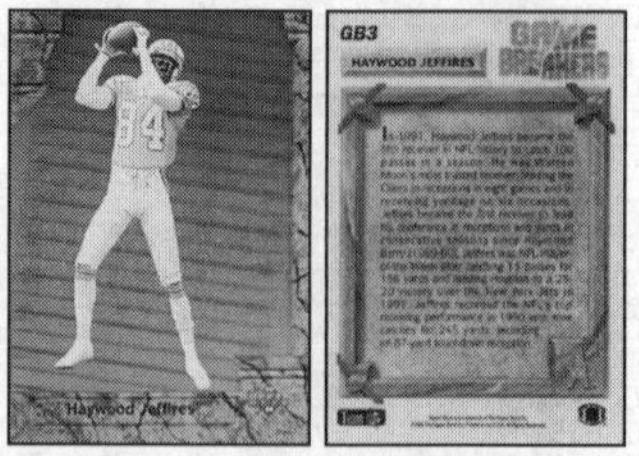

This nine-card hologram standard-size set showcases some of the NFL's standout wide receivers. Card numbers 1, 3, 4, 6, 8, and 9 were randomly inserted in 1992 Upper Deck first series packs while card numbers 2, 5, and 7 were found in the second series. The fronts

feature holographic action images of the players with a football field in the background and Roman architecture bordering the edges. The player's name appears at the bottom. The Upper Deck logo is at the lower left corner. On a white card face, the backs have contain a write-up on a beige marble-textured background. The words "Game Breakers" are at the top in verdigris marble-texture block letters. The player's name is printed in a beige bar to the left. The cards are numbered on the back with a "GB" prefix.

	MINT	NRMT	EXC
COMPLETE SET (9)	12.00	5.50	1.50
COMMON CARD (GB1-GB9)	1.25	.55	.16
☐ GB1 Art Monk	1.25	.55	.16
☐ GB2 Drew Hill	1.25	.55	.16
☐ GB3 Haywood Jeffires	1.25	.55	.16
☐ GB4 Andre Rison	2.00	.90	.25
☐ GB5 Mark Clayton	1.25	.55	.16
☐ GB6 Jerry Rice	4.00	1.80	.50
☐ GB7 Michael Haynes	1.25	.55	.16
☐ GB8 Andre Reed	2.00	.90	.25
☐ GB9 Michael Irvin	2.00	.90	.25

1992 Upper Deck Heroes Dan Marino

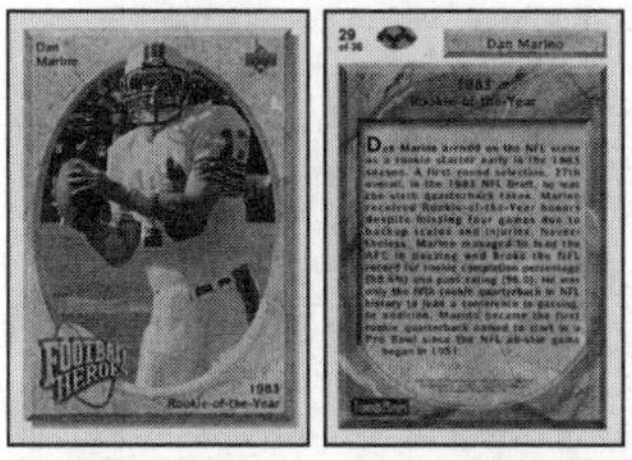

This ten-card standard-size set chronicles the collegiate and professional career of Dan Marino. The cards were randomly inserted in 1992 Upper Deck second series foil packs. The fronts feature color photos of Marino at various stages of his career within an oval picture frame on a marbleized slab. A shadow border makes the slab appear to hover over the white card face. The card subtitle appears in the lower right corner of the slab. The back design displays career highlights on a marbleized plaque framed by verdigris marbleized borders. The cards are numbered (28-36) in continuation of the Upper Deck Football Heroes set.

	MINT	NRMT	EXC
COMPLETE SET (10)	40.00	18.00	5.00
COMMON MARINO (28-36)	4.00	1.80	.50
☐ 28 1979-82 College Years	4.00	1.80	.50
☐ 29 1983 Rookie-of-the-Year	4.00	1.80	.50
☐ 30 1984 5,000 Yards Passing	4.00	1.80	.50
☐ 31 1985 Super Bowl XIX	4.00	1.80	.50
☐ 32 1986 4,000 Yards Passing	4.00	1.80	.50
☐ 33 1989 200th Touchdown Pass UER (Jurgensen misspelled as Jurgenson)	4.00	1.80	.50
☐ 34 1990 30,000 Yards	4.00	1.80	.50
☐ 35 1992 Still Counting...	4.00	1.80	.50
☐ 36 Checklist Heroes 28-36	4.00	1.80	.50
☐ AU Heroes AU Upper Deck Authenticated Numbered out of 2,800	100.00	45.00	12.50
☐ NNO Title/Header card	8.00	3.60	1.00

1992 Upper Deck Heroes Walter Payton

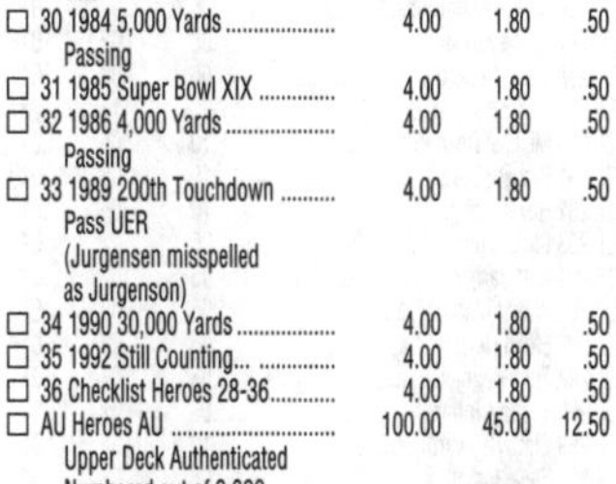

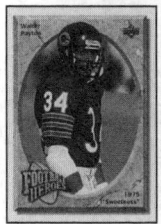

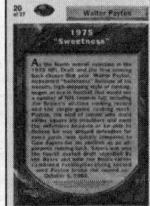

Randomly inserted in first series foil packs, this ten-card standard-size set depicts the former Chicago Bears running back Walter Payton during various stages of his career. The fronts feature color photos within an oval picture frame on a marbleized slab. A shadow border makes the slab appear to hover over the white card face. The card subtitle appears in the lower right corner of the slab. The back design displays capsule summaries on a marbleized plaque framed by dark gray marbleized borders. The cards are numbered (19-27) as a continuation of Upper Deck's "Football Heroes" series.

	MINT	NRMT	EXC
COMPLETE SET (10)	30.00	13.50	3.70
COMMON PAYTON (19-27)	3.00	1.35	.35
☐ 19 College Years 1971-74	3.00	1.35	.35
☐ 20 Sweetness 1975	3.00	1.35	.35
☐ 21 Career Year 1977	3.00	1.35	.35
☐ 22 NFL Rushing Rec. 1984	3.00	1.35	.35
☐ 23 2,000 Yard Seasons 1983-1985	3.00	1.35	.35
☐ 24 Super Bowl XX 1986	3.00	1.35	.35
☐ 25 Walter Payton Day 1987	3.00	1.35	.35
☐ 26 Hall of Fame Bound 1992	3.00	1.35	.35
☐ 27 Checklist Heroes 19-27	3.00	1.35	.35
☐ AU Autographed Card Numbered of 2,800 Upper Deck Authenticated	80.00	36.00	10.00
☐ NNO Title/Header Card	8.00	3.60	1.00

1992 Upper Deck Heroes Payton Box Bottoms

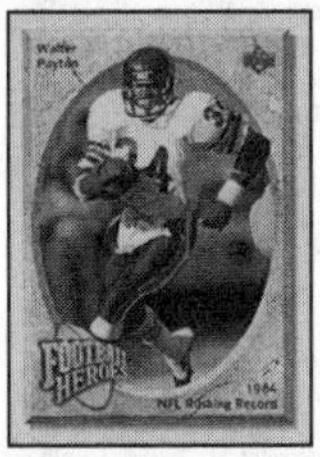

These eight oversized "cards" (approximately 5 1/4" by 7 1/4") were featured on the bottoms of 1992 Upper Deck first series waxboxes. They are identical in design to the Payton Football Heroes insert cards, with the same color player photos in an oval picture frame. The backs are blank and the cards are unnumbered. We have checklisted them below according to the numbering of the Heroes cards.

	MINT	NRMT	EXC
COMPLETE SET (8)	6.00	2.70	.75
COMMON CARD (19-26)	1.00	.45	.12
☐ 19 College Years 1971-74	1.00	.45	.12
☐ 20 Sweetness 1975	1.00	.45	.12
☐ 21 Career Year 1977	1.00	.45	.12
☐ 22 NFL Rushing Record 1984	1.00	.45	.12
☐ 23 2,000 Yard Seasons 1983-1985	1.00	.45	.12
☐ 24 Super Bowl XX 1986	1.00	.45	.12
☐ 25 Walter Payton Day 1987	1.00	.45	.12
☐ 26 Hall of Fame Bound 1992	1.00	.45	.12

1992 Upper Deck Pro Bowl

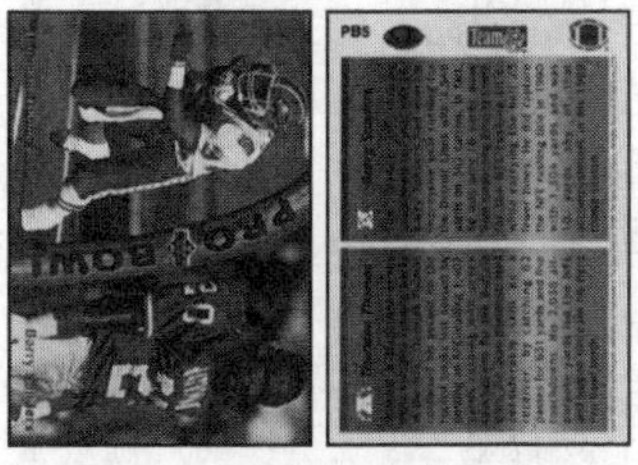

Randomly inserted in series I foil packs, this 16-card standard-size set featured players from the 1992 Pro Bowl in Hawaii. The horizontal fronts carry two full-bleed player photos; the left one features an AFC Pro Bowl player, while the right one has a NFC Pro Bowl player. The photos are separated by a rainbow consisting of six different color bands and overprinted with "Pro Bowl" in silver foil lettering. When rotated under a light, the bands reflect light in different directions. This unique look was produced by a process called prismatic lithography. The player's name in silver foil lettering at the bottom rounds out the front. On two rainbow-colored panels, the horizontal backs present a career summary for each player. The cards are numbered on the back with a "PB" prefix.

	MINT	NRMT	EXC
COMPLETE SET (16)	25.00	11.00	3.10
COMMON PAIR (PB1-PB16)	1.25	.55	.16
☐ PB1 Haywood Jeffires Michael Irvin	2.00	.90	.25
☐ PB2 Mark Clayton Gary Clark	1.25	.55	.16
☐ PB3 Anthony Munoz Jim Lachey	1.50	.70	.19
☐ PB4 Warren Moon Mark Rypien	1.50	.70	.19
☐ PB5 Thurman Thomas Barry Sanders	5.00	2.20	.60
☐ PB6 Marion Butts Emmitt Smith	8.00	3.60	1.00
☐ PB7 Greg Townsend Reggie White	2.00	.90	.25
☐ PB8 Cornelius Bennett Seth Joyner	1.25	.55	.16
☐ PB9 Derrick Thomas Pat Swilling	1.50	.70	.19
☐ PB10 Darryl Talley Chris Spielman	1.25	.55	.16
☐ PB11 Ronnie Lott Mark Carrier DB	1.50	.70	.19
☐ PB12 Steve Atwater Shaun Gayle	1.25	.55	.16
☐ PB13 Rod Woodson Darrell Green	1.50	.70	.19
☐ PB14 Jeff Gossett Chip Lohmiller	1.25	.55	.16
☐ PB15 Tim Brown Mel Gray	2.00	.90	.25
☐ PB16 Checklist Card	2.00	.90	.25

1992 Upper Deck NFL Sheets

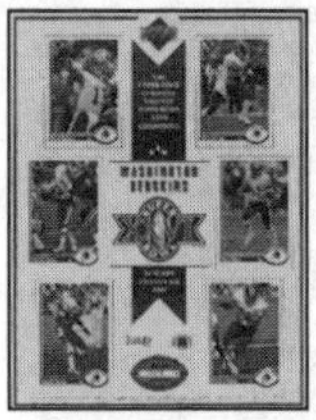

As an advertising promotion, Upper Deck released 8 1/2" by 11" commemorative sheets printed on card stock and picturing a series of Upper Deck cards. The fronts feature either captions indicating the event the sheet commemorates, or text advertising Upper Deck cards. The sheets have an Upper Deck stamp indicating the production run and serial number. The backs of the game sheets are blank. The backs of the advertising sheets are printed in black with the words "Upper Deck Limited Edition Commemorative Sheet." The AFC and NFC championship game commemorative sheets were distributed at Upper Deck's Super Bowl Card Show III and at the NFL Experience in Minneapolis. In the listing of sheets below, the players cards are listed beginning in the upper left corner of the sheet and moving toward the lower right corner. A sheet was also issued to promote Upper Deck's 1992 Comic Ball Comic Bowl IV cards. The front features a color photo of Lawrence Taylor, Jerry Rice, Thurman Thomas, Dan Marino, and various Looney Tunes characters set against a blue sky background. A green bottom border carries the issue number and production run in the Upper Deck gold foil stamp, the Looney Tunes logo, and product information. The Comic Ball logo overlaps the green border and the photo. The entire sheet is bordered by a thin black and wider white border.

	MINT	NRMT	EXC
COMPLETE SET (5	30.00	13.50	3.70
COMMON SHEET (1-5)	5.00	2.20	.60
☐ 1 AFC Championship vs. Buffalo Bills Jan. 12, 1992 (30,000) Thurman Thomas Cornelius Bennett Andre Reed John Elway Steve Atwater Gaston Green	5.00	2.20	.60
☐ 2 NFC Championship vs. Washington Redskins Jan. 12, 1992 (30,000) Mark Rypien Ricky Ervins Charles Mann Barry Sanders Chris Spielman Mel Gray	5.00	2.20	.60
☐ 3 Super Bowl XXVI Redskins Jan. 26, 1992 (15,000) Mark Rypien Ricky Ervins Charles Mann Gary Clark Darrell Green Earnest Byner	8.00	3.60	1.00
☐ 4 Super Bowl XXVI Bills Jan. 26, 1992 (15,000) Thurman Thomas Bruce Smith Abdre Reed Darryl Talley James Lofton Cornelius Bennett	5.00	2.20	.60
☐ 5 Comic Ball IV (15,000) Lawrence Taylor Jerry Rice Thurman Thomas Dan Marino Looney Tunes Characters	12.00	5.50	1.50

1992 Upper Deck SCD Sheets

Upper Deck produced eight different sheets for insertion into the Sept. 18, 1992, issue of Sports Collector's Digest. Reportedly 8,000 of each sheet were produced, and one was inserted into each SCD issue. Each 11" by 8 1/2" sheet features two rows of three cards each, on a speckled granite background. The backs are covered by the phrase "Upper Deck Limited Edition Commemorative Sheet." The sheets are numbered at the lower left corner "Version X of 8."

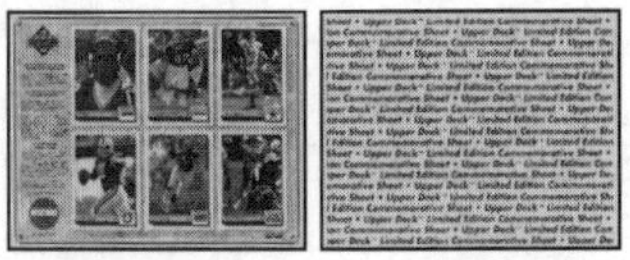

	MINT	NRMT	EXC
COMPLETE SET (8)	80.00	36.00	10.00
COMMON SHEET (1-8)	6.00	2.70	.75
☐ 1 Randall Cunningham David Klingler Dan Marino Troy Aikman Jim Kelly Bernie Kosar	16.00	7.25	2.00
☐ 2 Phillippi Sparks Dale Carter Steve Emtman Kevin Smith Marco Coleman Carl Pickens	6.00	2.70	.75
☐ 3 Quentin Coryatt Greg Skrepenak Chester McGlockton Kurt Barber Vaughn Dunbar Ashley Ambrose	6.00	2.70	.75
☐ 4 Ty Detmer Steve Israel Tracy Scroggins Todd Collins Alonzo Spellman Marquez Pope	6.00	2.70	.75
☐ 5 Eric Dickerson Randal Hill Jim Kelly Bernie Kosar Deion Sanders Andre Reed	8.00	3.60	1.00
☐ 6 Joe Montana Mike Singletary Randall Cunningham Anthony Miller Dan McGwire Harvey Williams	12.00	5.50	1.50
☐ 7 Al Toon Michael Dean Perry Troy Aikman Jeff George Carl Banks Junior Seau	10.00	4.50	1.25
☐ 8 Dan Marino Tommy Maddox Bruce Smith Leslie O'Neal Lawrence Taylor Jerry Rice	16.00	7.25	2.00

1992-93 Upper Deck NFL Experience

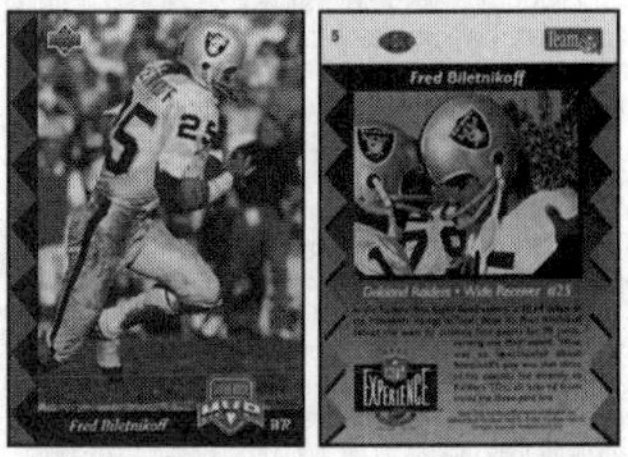

This 50-card standard-size set commemorates the stars of previous Super Bowls and potential stars of tomorrow. The set was produced in conjunction with the NFL Experience, a theme park held January 28-31, 1993, at the Rose Bowl (Pasadena, California), the site of Super Bowl XXVII. The set was available only through hobby dealers and was introduced at the Super Bowl Card Show at the NFL Experience. The fronts of card numbers 1-20 have full-bleed color player photos that are edged on two sides by various border stripes, while the fronts of cards numbers 21-50 feature color player photos tilted slightly to the left and bordered in the remaining area by a ghosted background. Some cards are accented with silver foil highlights, with at least one set in every case having gold-foil highlights. The gold set is valued at approximately five times the prices listed below. The backs present a color close-up photo, player profile, game performance summary, or player quote. The set is subdivided as follows: Super Bowl MVPs (1-5), Super Bowl Moments (6-10), Future Champions (11-20), and Super Bowl Dreams (21-50).

	MINT	NRMT	EXC
COMPLETE SET (50)	8.00	3.60	1.00
COMMON CARD (1-50)	.10	.05	.01
☐ 1 Joe Montana MVP	1.00	.45	.12
☐ 2 Roger Staubach MVP	.50	.23	.06
☐ 3 Bart Starr MVP	.25	.11	.03
☐ 4 Len Dawson MVP	.20	.09	.03
☐ 5 Fred Biletnikoff MVP	.20	.09	.03
☐ 6 Jim Plunkett	.20	.09	.03

☐ 7 Terry Bradshaw	.30	.14	.04
☐ 8 Jerry Rice	1.00	.45	.12
☐ 9 Doug Williams	.10	.05	.01
☐ 10 Dan Marino	2.00	.90	.25
☐ 11 David Klingler	.20	.09	.03
☐ 12 Steve Emtman	.10	.05	.01
☐ 13 Dale Carter	.10	.05	.01
☐ 14 Quentin Coryatt	.20	.09	.03
☐ 15 Tommy Maddox	.10	.05	.01
☐ 16 Vaughn Dunbar	.10	.05	.01
☐ 17 Marco Coleman	.10	.05	.01
☐ 18 Carl Pickens	.40	.18	.05
☐ 19 Sean Gilbert	.20	.09	.03
☐ 20 Tony Smith	.10	.05	.01
☐ 21 Jim Kelly	.40	.18	.05
☐ 22 Dan Marino	2.00	.90	.25
☐ 23 Boomer Esiason	.20	.09	.03
☐ 24 Bernie Kosar	.10	.05	.01
☐ 25 Ken O'Brien	.10	.05	.01
☐ 26 Deion Sanders	.75	.35	.09
☐ 27 Mike Singletary	.20	.09	.03
☐ 28 Andre Reed	.20	.09	.03
☐ 29 Michael Dean Perry	.10	.05	.01
☐ 30 Ricky Proehl	.10	.05	.01
☐ 31 Leslie O'Neal	.10	.05	.01
☐ 32 Jerry Rice	1.00	.45	.12
☐ 33 Eric Dickerson	.20	.09	.03
☐ 34 Troy Aikman	1.00	.45	.12
☐ 35 Bruce Smith	.20	.09	.03
☐ 36 Browning Nagle	.10	.05	.01
☐ 37 Carl Banks	.10	.05	.01
☐ 38 Harvey Williams	.20	.09	.03
☐ 39 Jeff George	.30	.14	.04
☐ 40 Lawrence Taylor	.25	.11	.03
☐ 41 Webster Slaughter	.10	.05	.01
☐ 42 Anthony Miller	.20	.09	.03
☐ 43 Randall Cunningham	.20	.09	.03
☐ 44 Timm Rosenbach	.10	.05	.01
☐ 45 Russell Maryland	.10	.05	.01
☐ 46 Randal Hill	.10	.05	.01
☐ 47 Dan McGwire	.10	.05	.01
☐ 48 Merril Hoge	.10	.05	.01
☐ 49 Kevin Fagan	.10	.05	.01
☐ 50 Junior Seau	.40	.18	.05

1993 Upper Deck

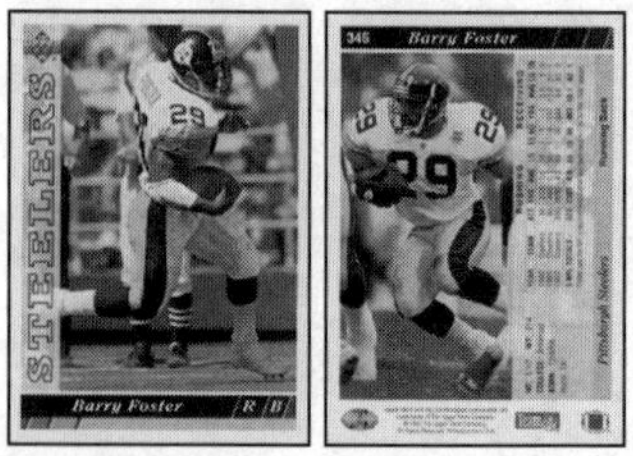

The 1993 Upper Deck football set was issued in a single series consisting of 530 standard-size cards. Cards were issued in 12-card hobby and retail packs and 22-card jumbo packs. The fronts feature color action player photos, with two stripes in the player's team colors at the bottom. The player's name and position are printed in the top stripe. On the left side of the card, the team name is printed in the teams' dominant color against a ghosted background. The backs carry a color close-up photo alongside biographical and statistical information that run the length of the card. The cards are numbered on the back. Topical subsets featured are Star Rookies (1-29), All-Rookie Team (30-55), Hitmen (56-62), Team Checklists (63-90), Season Leaders (421-431), and Berman's Best (432-442). Rookie Cards include Jerome Bettis, Drew Bledsoe, Reggie Brooks, Curtis Conway, Garrison Hearst, Terry Kirby, O.J. McDuffie, Natrone Means and Rick Mirer. An Eric Dickerson Promo card was produced to preview the set. It can easily be differentiated from the regular issue card by the team (Raiders for the promo card, Falcons for the regular issue).

	MINT	NRMT	EXC
COMPLETE SET (530)	30.00	13.50	3.70
COMMON CARD (1-530)	.05	.02	.01

☐ 1 Star Rookie Checklist Rick Mirer Garrison Hearst Curtis Conway Lincoln Kennedy	.40	.18	.05
☐ 2 Eric Curry SR	.05	.02	.01
☐ 3 Rick Mirer SR	1.25	.55	.16
☐ 4 Dan Williams SR	.05	.02	.01
☐ 5 Marvin Jones SR	.05	.02	.01
☐ 6 Willie Roaf SR	.05	.02	.01
☐ 7 Reggie Brooks SR	.10	.05	.01
☐ 8 Horace Copeland SR	.10	.05	.01
☐ 9 Lincoln Kennedy SR	.05	.02	.01
☐ 10 Curtis Conway SR	.75	.35	.09
☐ 11 Drew Bledsoe SR	3.00	1.35	.35
☐ 12 Patrick Bates SR	.05	.02	.01
☐ 13 Wayne Simmons SR	.05	.02	.01
☐ 14 Irv Smith SR	.05	.02	.01
☐ 15 Robert Smith SR	.75	.35	.09
☐ 16 O.J. McDuffie SR	.75	.35	.09
☐ 17 Darrien Gordon SR	.05	.02	.01
☐ 18 John Copeland SR	.10	.05	.01
☐ 19 Derek Brown RB SR	.05	.02	.01
☐ 20 Jerome Bettis SR	1.50	.70	.19
☐ 21 Deon Figures SR	.05	.02	.01
☐ 22 Glyn Milburn SR	.25	.11	.03
☐ 23 Garrison Hearst SR	1.25	.55	.16
☐ 24 Qadry Ismail SR	.25	.11	.03
☐ 25 Terry Kirby SR	.50	.23	.06
☐ 26 Lamar Thomas SR	.05	.02	.01
☐ 27 Tom Carter SR	.10	.05	.01
☐ 28 Andre Hastings SR	.25	.11	.03
☐ 29 George Teague SR	.10	.05	.01
☐ 30 All-Rookie Team CL Tommy Maddox	.25	.11	.03
☐ 31 David Klingler ART	.05	.02	.01
☐ 32 Tommy Maddox ART	.05	.02	.01
☐ 33 Vaughn Dunbar ART	.05	.02	.01
☐ 34 Rodney Culver ART	.05	.02	.01
☐ 35 Carl Pickens ART	.30	.14	.04
☐ 36 Courtney Hawkins ART	.05	.02	.01
☐ 37 Tyji Armstrong ART	.05	.02	.01
☐ 38 Ray Roberts ART	.05	.02	.01
☐ 39 Troy Auzenne ART	.05	.02	.01
☐ 40 Shane Dronett ART	.05	.02	.01
☐ 41 Chris Mims ART	.05	.02	.01
☐ 42 Sean Gilbert ART	.05	.02	.01
☐ 43 Steve Emtman ART	.05	.02	.01
☐ 44 Robert Jones ART	.05	.02	.01
☐ 45 Marco Coleman ART	.05	.02	.01
☐ 46 Ricardo McDonald ART	.05	.02	.01
☐ 47 Quentin Coryatt ART	.10	.05	.01
☐ 48 Dana Hall ART	.05	.02	.01
☐ 49 Darren Perry ART	.05	.02	.01
☐ 50 Darryl Williams ART	.05	.02	.01
☐ 51 Kevin Smith ART	.05	.02	.01
☐ 52 Terrell Buckley ART	.05	.02	.01
☐ 53 Troy Vincent ART	.05	.02	.01
☐ 54 Lin Elliott ART	.05	.02	.01
☐ 55 Dale Carter ART	.05	.02	.01
☐ 56 Steve Atwater HIT	.05	.02	.01
☐ 57 Junior Seau HIT	.10	.05	.01
☐ 58 Ronnie Lott HIT	.05	.02	.01
☐ 59 Louis Oliver HIT	.05	.02	.01
☐ 60 Cortez Kennedy HIT	.05	.02	.01
☐ 61 Pat Swilling HIT	.05	.02	.01
☐ 62 Hitmen Checklist	.05	.02	.01
☐ 63 Curtis Conway TC	.40	.18	.05
☐ 64 Alfred Williams TC	.05	.02	.01
☐ 65 Jim Kelly TC	.10	.05	.01
☐ 66 Simon Fletcher TC	.05	.02	.01
☐ 67 Eric Metcalf TC	.05	.02	.01
☐ 68 Lawrence Dawsey TC	.05	.02	.01
☐ 69 Garrison Hearst TC	.50	.23	.06
☐ 70 Anthony Miller TC	.05	.02	.01
☐ 71 Neil Smith TC	.05	.02	.01
☐ 72 Jeff George TC	.10	.05	.01
☐ 73 Emmitt Smith TC	1.00	.45	.12
☐ 74 Dan Marino TC	1.00	.45	.12
☐ 75 Clyde Simmons TC	.05	.02	.01
☐ 76 Deion Sanders TC	.30	.14	.04
☐ 77 Ricky Watters TC	.10	.05	.01
☐ 78 Rodney Hampton TC	.10	.05	.01
☐ 79 Brad Baxter TC	.05	.02	.01
☐ 80 Barry Sanders TC	.60	.25	.07
☐ 81 Warren Moon TC	.10	.05	.01
☐ 82 Brett Favre TC	1.00	.45	.12
☐ 83 Drew Bledsoe TC	1.25	.55	.16
☐ 84 Eric Dickerson TC	.10	.05	.01
☐ 85 Cleveland Gary TC	.05	.02	.01
☐ 86 Earnest Byner TC	.05	.02	.01
☐ 87 Wayne Martin TC	.05	.02	.01
☐ 88 Rick Mirer TC	.50	.23	.06
☐ 89 Barry Foster TC	.05	.02	.01
☐ 90 Terry Allen TC	.10	.05	.01
☐ 91 Vinnie Clark	.05	.02	.01
☐ 92 Howard Ballard	.05	.02	.01
☐ 93 Eric Ball	.05	.02	.01
☐ 94 Marc Boutte	.05	.02	.01
☐ 95 Larry Centers	.50	.23	.06
☐ 96 Gary Brown	.05	.02	.01
☐ 97 Hugh Millen	.05	.02	.01
☐ 98 Anthony Newman	.05	.02	.01
☐ 99 Darrell Thompson	.05	.02	.01
☐ 100 George Jamison	.05	.02	.01
☐ 101 James Francis	.05	.02	.01
☐ 102 Leonard Harris	.05	.02	.01
☐ 103 Lomas Brown	.05	.02	.01
☐ 104 James Lofton	.10	.05	.01
☐ 105 Jamie Dukes	.05	.02	.01
☐ 106 Quinn Early	.10	.05	.01
☐ 107 Ernie Jones	.05	.02	.01
☐ 108 Torrance Small	.05	.02	.01
☐ 109 Michael Carter	.05	.02	.01
☐ 110 Aeneas Williams	.05	.02	.01
☐ 111 Renaldo Turnbull	.05	.02	.01
☐ 112 Al Smith	.05	.02	.01
☐ 113 Troy Auzenne	.05	.02	.01
☐ 114 Stephen Baker	.05	.02	.01
☐ 115 Daniel Stubbs	.05	.02	.01
☐ 116 Dana Hall	.05	.02	.01
☐ 117 Lawrence Taylor	.25	.11	.03
☐ 118 Ron Hall	.05	.02	.01
☐ 119 Derrick Fenner	.05	.02	.01
☐ 120 Martin Mayhew	.05	.02	.01
☐ 121 Jay Schroeder	.05	.02	.01
☐ 122 Michael Zordich	.05	.02	.01
☐ 123 Ed McCaffrey	.05	.02	.01
☐ 124 John Stephens	.05	.02	.01
☐ 125 Brad Edwards	.05	.02	.01
☐ 126 Don Griffin	.05	.02	.01
☐ 127 Broderick Thomas	.05	.02	.01
☐ 128 Ted Washington	.05	.02	.01
☐ 129 Haywood Jeffires	.10	.05	.01
☐ 130 Gary Plummer	.05	.02	.01
☐ 131 Mark Wheeler	.05	.02	.01
☐ 132 Ty Detmer	.25	.11	.03
☐ 133 Derrick Walker	.05	.02	.01
☐ 134 Henry Ellard	.10	.05	.01
☐ 135 Neal Anderson	.05	.02	.01
☐ 136 Bruce Smith	.25	.11	.03
☐ 137 Cris Carter	.25	.11	.03
☐ 138 Vaughn Dunbar	.05	.02	.01
☐ 139 Dan Marino	2.00	.90	.25
☐ 140 Troy Aikman	1.00	.45	.12
☐ 141 Randall Cunningham	.10	.05	.01
☐ 142 Daryl Johnston	.25	.11	.03
☐ 143 Mark Clayton	.05	.02	.01
☐ 144 Rich Gannon	.05	.02	.01
☐ 145 Nate Newton	.10	.05	.01
☐ 146 Willie Gault	.05	.02	.01
☐ 147 Brian Washington	.05	.02	.01
☐ 148 Fred Barnett	.10	.05	.01
☐ 149 Gill Byrd	.05	.02	.01
☐ 150 Art Monk	.10	.05	.01
☐ 151 Stan Humphries	.25	.11	.03
☐ 152 Charles Mann	.05	.02	.01
☐ 153 Greg Lloyd	.25	.11	.03
☐ 154 Marvin Washington	.05	.02	.01
☐ 155 Bernie Kosar	.10	.05	.01
☐ 156 Pete Metzelaars	.05	.02	.01
☐ 157 Chris Hinton	.05	.02	.01
☐ 158 Jim Harbaugh	.25	.11	.03
☐ 159 Willie Davis	.25	.11	.03
☐ 160 Leroy Thompson	.05	.02	.01
☐ 161 Scott Miller	.05	.02	.01
☐ 162 Eugene Robinson	.05	.02	.01
☐ 163 David Little	.05	.02	.01
☐ 164 Pierce Holt	.05	.02	.01
☐ 165 James Hasty	.05	.02	.01
☐ 166 Dave Krieg	.10	.05	.01
☐ 167 Gerald Williams	.05	.02	.01
☐ 168 Kyle Clifton	.05	.02	.01
☐ 169 Bill Brooks	.05	.02	.01
☐ 170 Vance Johnson	.05	.02	.01
☐ 171 Greg Townsend	.05	.02	.01
☐ 172 Jason Belser	.05	.02	.01
☐ 173 Brett Perriman	.25	.11	.03
☐ 174 Steve Jordan	.05	.02	.01
☐ 175 Kelvin Martin	.05	.02	.01
☐ 176 Greg Kragen	.05	.02	.01
☐ 177 Kerry Cash	.05	.02	.01
☐ 178 Chester McGlockton	.10	.05	.01
☐ 179 Jim Kelly	.25	.11	.03
☐ 180 Todd McNair	.05	.02	.01
☐ 181 Leroy Hoard	.10	.05	.01
☐ 182 Seth Joyner	.05	.02	.01
☐ 183 Sam Gash	.05	.02	.01
☐ 184 Joe Nash	.05	.02	.01
☐ 185 Lin Elliott	.05	.02	.01
☐ 186 Robert Porcher	.05	.02	.01
☐ 187 Tommy Hodson	.05	.02	.01
☐ 188 Greg Lewis	.05	.02	.01
☐ 189 Dan Saleaumua	.05	.02	.01
☐ 190 Chris Goode	.05	.02	.01
☐ 191 Henry Thomas	.05	.02	.01
☐ 192 Bobby Hebert	.05	.02	.01
☐ 193 Clay Matthews	.10	.05	.01
☐ 194 Mark Carrier WR	.10	.05	.01
☐ 195 Anthony Pleasant	.05	.02	.01
☐ 196 Eric Dorsey	.05	.02	.01
☐ 197 Clarence Verdin	.05	.02	.01
☐ 198 Marc Spindler	.05	.02	.01
☐ 199 Tommy Maddox	.05	.02	.01
☐ 200 Wendell Davis	.05	.02	.01
☐ 201 John Fina	.05	.02	.01
☐ 202 Alonzo Spellman	.05	.02	.01
☐ 203 Darryl Williams	.05	.02	.01
☐ 204 Mike Croel	.05	.02	.01
☐ 205 Ken Norton Jr.	.10	.05	.01
☐ 206 Mel Gray	.10	.05	.01
☐ 207 Chuck Cecil	.05	.02	.01
☐ 208 John Flannery	.05	.02	.01
☐ 209 Chip Banks	.05	.02	.01
☐ 210 Chris Martin	.05	.02	.01
☐ 211 Dennis Brown	.05	.02	.01
☐ 212 Vinny Testaverde	.10	.05	.01
☐ 213 Nick Bell	.05	.02	.01
☐ 214 Robert Delpino	.05	.02	.01
☐ 215 Mark Higgs	.05	.02	.01
☐ 216 Al Noga	.05	.02	.01
☐ 217 Andre Tippett	.05	.02	.01
☐ 218 Pat Swilling	.05	.02	.01
☐ 219 Phil Simms	.10	.05	.01
☐ 220 Ricky Proehl	.05	.02	.01
☐ 221 William Thomas	.05	.02	.01
☐ 222 Jeff Graham	.10	.05	.01
☐ 223 Darion Conner	.05	.02	.01
☐ 224 Mark Carrier DB	.05	.02	.01
☐ 225 Willie Green	.05	.02	.01
☐ 226 Reggie Rivers	.05	.02	.01
☐ 227 Andre Reed	.10	.05	.01
☐ 228 Deion Sanders	.60	.25	.07
☐ 229 Chris Doleman	.05	.02	.01
☐ 230 Jerry Ball	.05	.02	.01
☐ 231 Eric Dickerson	.10	.05	.01
☐ 232 Carlos Jenkins	.05	.02	.01
☐ 233 Mike Johnson	.05	.02	.01
☐ 234 Marco Coleman	.05	.02	.01
☐ 235 Leslie O'Neal	.10	.05	.01
☐ 236 Browning Nagle	.05	.02	.01
☐ 237 Carl Pickens	.75	.35	.09
☐ 238 Steve Emtman	.05	.02	.01
☐ 239 Alvin Harper	.10	.05	.01
☐ 240 Keith Jackson	.10	.05	.01
☐ 241 Jerry Rice	1.00	.45	.12
☐ 242 Cortez Kennedy	.10	.05	.01
☐ 243 Tyji Armstrong	.05	.02	.01
☐ 244 Troy Vincent	.05	.02	.01
☐ 245 Randal Hill	.05	.02	.01
☐ 246 Robert Blackmon	.05	.02	.01
☐ 247 Junior Seau	.25	.11	.03
☐ 248 Sterling Sharpe	.25	.11	.03
☐ 249 Thurman Thomas	.25	.11	.03
☐ 250 David Klingler	.05	.02	.01
☐ 251 Jeff George	.25	.11	.03
☐ 252 Anthony Miller	.10	.05	.01
☐ 253 Earnest Byner	.05	.02	.01
☐ 254 Eric Swann	.10	.05	.01
☐ 255 Jeff Herrod	.05	.02	.01
☐ 256 Eddie Robinson	.05	.02	.01
☐ 257 Eric Allen	.05	.02	.01
☐ 258 John Taylor	.10	.05	.01
☐ 259 Sean Gilbert	.10	.05	.01
☐ 260 Ray Childress	.05	.02	.01
☐ 261 Michael Haynes	.10	.05	.01
☐ 262 Greg McMurtry	.05	.02	.01
☐ 263 Bill Romanowski	.05	.02	.01
☐ 264 Todd Lyght	.05	.02	.01
☐ 265 Clyde Simmons	.05	.02	.01
☐ 266 Webster Slaughter	.05	.02	.01
☐ 267 J.J. Birden	.05	.02	.01
☐ 268 Aaron Wallace	.05	.02	.01
☐ 269 Carl Banks	.05	.02	.01
☐ 270 Ricardo McDonald	.05	.02	.01
☐ 271 Michael Brooks	.05	.02	.01
☐ 272 Dale Carter	.05	.02	.01
☐ 273 Mike Pritchard	.10	.05	.01
☐ 274 Derek Brown TE	.05	.02	.01
☐ 275 Burt Grossman	.05	.02	.01
☐ 276 Mark Schlereth	.05	.02	.01
☐ 277 Karl Mecklenburg	.05	.02	.01
☐ 278 Rickey Jackson	.05	.02	.01
☐ 279 Ricky Ervins	.05	.02	.01
☐ 280 Jeff Bryant	.05	.02	.01
☐ 281 Eric Martin	.05	.02	.01
☐ 282 Carlton Haselrig	.05	.02	.01
☐ 283 Kevin Mack	.05	.02	.01
☐ 284 Brad Muster	.05	.02	.01
☐ 285 Kelvin Pritchett	.05	.02	.01
☐ 286 Courtney Hawkins	.05	.02	.01
☐ 287 Levon Kirkland	.05	.02	.01
☐ 288 Steve DeBerg	.05	.02	.01
☐ 289 Edgar Bennett	.25	.11	.03
☐ 290 Michael Dean Perry	.10	.05	.01
☐ 291 Richard Dent	.10	.05	.01
☐ 292 Howie Long	.10	.05	.01
☐ 293 Chris Mims	.05	.02	.01
☐ 294 Kurt Barber	.05	.02	.01
☐ 295 Wilber Marshall	.05	.02	.01
☐ 296 Ethan Horton	.05	.02	.01
☐ 297 Tony Bennett	.05	.02	.01
☐ 298 Johnny Johnson	.05	.02	.01
☐ 299 Craig Heyward	.10	.05	.01
☐ 300 Steve Israel	.05	.02	.01
☐ 301 Kenneth Gant	.05	.02	.01
☐ 302 Eugene Chung	.05	.02	.01
☐ 303 Harvey Williams	.10	.05	.01
☐ 304 Jarrod Bunch	.05	.02	.01
☐ 305 Darren Perry	.05	.02	.01
☐ 306 Steve Christie	.05	.02	.01
☐ 307 John Randle	.05	.02	.01
☐ 308 Warren Moon	.25	.11	.03
☐ 309 Charles Haley	.10	.05	.01
☐ 310 Tony Smith	.05	.02	.01
☐ 311 Steve Broussard	.05	.02	.01
☐ 312 Alfred Williams	.05	.02	.01
☐ 313 Terrell Buckley	.05	.02	.01
☐ 314 Trace Armstrong	.05	.02	.01
☐ 315 Brian Mitchell	.10	.05	.01
☐ 316 Steve Atwater	.05	.02	.01
☐ 317 Nate Lewis	.05	.02	.01
☐ 318 Richard Brown	.05	.02	.01
☐ 319 Rufus Porter	.05	.02	.01
☐ 320 Pat Harlow	.05	.02	.01
☐ 321 Anthony Smith	.05	.02	.01
☐ 322 Jack Del Rio	.05	.02	.01
☐ 323 Darryl Talley	.05	.02	.01
☐ 324 Sam Mills	.05	.02	.01
☐ 325 Chris Miller	.10	.05	.01
☐ 326 Ken Harvey	.05	.02	.01
☐ 327 Rod Woodson	.25	.11	.03
☐ 328 Tony Tolbert	.05	.02	.01
☐ 329 Todd Kinchen	.05	.02	.01
☐ 330 Brian Noble	.05	.02	.01
☐ 331 Dave Meggett	.05	.02	.01
☐ 332 Chris Spielman	.10	.05	.01

	MINT	NRMT	EXC
☐ 333 Barry Word	.05	.02	.01
☐ 334 Jessie Hester	.05	.02	.01
☐ 335 Michael Jackson	.10	.05	.01
☐ 336 Mitchell Price	.05	.02	.01
☐ 337 Michael Irvin	.25	.11	.03
☐ 338 Simon Fletcher	.05	.02	.01
☐ 339 Keith Jennings	.05	.02	.01
☐ 340 Vai Sikahema	.05	.02	.01
☐ 341 Roger Craig	.10	.05	.01
☐ 342 Ricky Watters	.25	.11	.03
☐ 343 Reggie Cobb	.05	.02	.01
☐ 344 Kanavis McGhee	.05	.02	.01
☐ 345 Barry Foster	.10	.05	.01
☐ 346 Marion Butts	.05	.02	.01
☐ 347 Bryan Cox	.05	.02	.01
☐ 348 Wayne Martin	.05	.02	.01
☐ 349 Jim Everett	.10	.05	.01
☐ 350 Nate Odomes	.05	.02	.01
☐ 351 Anthony Johnson	.10	.05	.01
☐ 352 Rodney Hampton	.25	.11	.03
☐ 353 Terry Allen	.25	.11	.03
☐ 354 Derrick Thomas	.25	.11	.03
☐ 355 Calvin Williams	.10	.05	.01
☐ 356 Pepper Johnson	.05	.02	.01
☐ 357 John Elway	.75	.35	.09
☐ 358 Steve Young	.75	.35	.09
☐ 359 Emmitt Smith	2.00	.90	.25
☐ 360 Brett Favre	2.00	.90	.25
☐ 361 Cody Carlson	.05	.02	.01
☐ 362 Vincent Brown	.05	.02	.01
☐ 363 Gary Anderson RB	.05	.02	.01
☐ 364 Jon Vaughn	.05	.02	.01
☐ 365 Todd Marinovich	.05	.02	.01
☐ 366 Carnell Lake	.05	.02	.01
☐ 367 Kurt Gouveia	.05	.02	.01
☐ 368 Lawrence Dawsey	.05	.02	.01
☐ 369 Neil O'Donnell	.25	.11	.03
☐ 370 Duane Bickett	.05	.02	.01
☐ 371 Ronnie Harmon	.05	.02	.01
☐ 372 Rodney Peete	.05	.02	.01
☐ 373 Cornelius Bennett	.10	.05	.01
☐ 374 Brad Baxter	.05	.02	.01
☐ 375 Ernest Givins	.10	.05	.01
☐ 376 Keith Byars	.05	.02	.01
☐ 377 Eric Bieniemy	.05	.02	.01
☐ 378 Mike Brim	.05	.02	.01
☐ 379 Darren Lewis	.05	.02	.01
☐ 380 Heath Sherman	.05	.02	.01
☐ 381 Leonard Russell	.10	.05	.01
☐ 382 Brent Jones	.10	.05	.01
☐ 383 David Whitmore	.05	.02	.01
☐ 384 Ray Roberts	.05	.02	.01
☐ 385 John Offerdahl	.05	.02	.01
☐ 386 Keith McCants	.05	.02	.01
☐ 387 John Baylor	.05	.02	.01
☐ 388 Amp Lee	.05	.02	.01
☐ 389 Chris Warren	.10	.05	.01
☐ 390 Herman Moore	.75	.35	.09
☐ 391 Johnny Bailey	.05	.02	.01
☐ 392 Tim Johnson	.05	.02	.01
☐ 393 Eric Metcalf	.10	.05	.01
☐ 394 Chris Chandler	.10	.05	.01
☐ 395 Mark Rypien	.05	.02	.01
☐ 396 Christian Okoye	.05	.02	.01
☐ 397 Shannon Sharpe	.25	.11	.03
☐ 398 Eric Hill	.05	.02	.01
☐ 399 David Lang	.05	.02	.01
☐ 400 Bruce Matthews	.05	.02	.01
☐ 401 Harold Green	.05	.02	.01
☐ 402 Mo Lewis	.05	.02	.01
☐ 403 Terry McDaniel	.05	.02	.01
☐ 404 Wesley Carroll	.05	.02	.01
☐ 405 Richmond Webb	.05	.02	.01
☐ 406 Andre Rison	.10	.05	.01
☐ 407 Lonnie Young	.05	.02	.01
☐ 408 Tommy Vardell	.05	.02	.01
☐ 409 Gene Atkins	.05	.02	.01
☐ 410 Sean Salisbury	.05	.02	.01
☐ 411 Kenneth Davis	.05	.02	.01
☐ 412 John L. Williams	.05	.02	.01
☐ 413 Roman Phifer	.05	.02	.01
☐ 414 Bennie Blades	.05	.02	.01
☐ 415 Tim Brown	.25	.11	.03
☐ 416 Lorenzo White	.05	.02	.01
☐ 417 Tony Casillas	.05	.02	.01
☐ 418 Tom Waddle	.05	.02	.01
☐ 419 David Fulcher	.05	.02	.01
☐ 420 Jessie Tuggle	.05	.02	.01
☐ 421 Emmitt Smith SL	1.00	.45	.12
☐ 422 Clyde Simmons SL	.05	.02	.01
☐ 423 Sterling Sharpe SL	.10	.05	.01
☐ 424 Sterling Sharpe SL	.10	.05	.01
☐ 425 Emmitt Smith SL	1.00	.45	.12
☐ 426 Dan Marino SL	1.00	.45	.12
☐ 427 Henry Jones SL Audray McMillian	.05	.02	.01
☐ 428 Thurman Thomas SL	.10	.05	.01
☐ 429 Greg Montgomery SL	.05	.02	.01
☐ 430 Pete Stoyanovich SL	.05	.02	.01
☐ 431 Season Leaders CL Emmitt Smith	.50	.23	.06
☐ 432 Steve Young BB	.40	.18	.05
☐ 433 Jerry Rice BB	.60	.25	.07
☐ 434 Ricky Watters BB	.10	.05	.01
☐ 435 Barry Foster BB	.05	.02	.01
☐ 436 Cortez Kennedy BB	.05	.02	.01
☐ 437 Warren Moon BB	.10	.05	.01
☐ 438 Thurman Thomas BB	.10	.05	.01
☐ 439 Brett Favre BB	1.00	.45	.12
☐ 440 Andre Rison BB	.10	.05	.01
☐ 441 Barry Sanders BB	.60	.25	.07
☐ 442 Berman's Best CL Chris Berman	.05	.02	.01
☐ 443 Moe Gardner	.05	.02	.01
☐ 444 Robert Jones	.05	.02	.01
☐ 445 Reggie Langhorne	.05	.02	.01
☐ 446 Flipper Anderson	.05	.02	.01
☐ 447 James Washington	.05	.02	.01
☐ 448 Aaron Craver	.05	.02	.01
☐ 449 Jack Trudeau	.05	.02	.01
☐ 450 Neil Smith	.25	.11	.03
☐ 451 Chris Burkett	.05	.02	.01
☐ 452 Russell Maryland	.05	.02	.01
☐ 453 Drew Hill	.05	.02	.01
☐ 454 Barry Sanders	1.00	.45	.12
☐ 455 Jeff Cross	.05	.02	.01
☐ 456 Bennie Thompson	.05	.02	.01
☐ 457 Marcus Allen	.25	.11	.03
☐ 458 Tracy Scroggins	.05	.02	.01
☐ 459 LeRoy Butler	.05	.02	.01
☐ 460 Joe Montana	1.00	.45	.12
☐ 461 Eddie Anderson	.05	.02	.01
☐ 462 Tim McDonald	.05	.02	.01
☐ 463 Ronnie Lott	.10	.05	.01
☐ 464 Gaston Green	.05	.02	.01
☐ 465 Shane Conlan	.05	.02	.01
☐ 466 Leonard Marshall	.05	.02	.01
☐ 467 Melvin Jenkins	.05	.02	.01
☐ 468 Don Beebe	.05	.02	.01
☐ 469 Johnny Mitchell	.05	.02	.01
☐ 470 Darryl Henley	.05	.02	.01
☐ 471 Boomer Esiason	.10	.05	.01
☐ 472 Mark Kelso	.05	.02	.01
☐ 473 John Booty	.05	.02	.01
☐ 474 Pete Stoyanovich	.05	.02	.01
☐ 475 Thomas Smith	.10	.05	.01
☐ 476 Carlton Gray	.05	.02	.01
☐ 477 Dana Stubblefield	.25	.11	.03
☐ 478 Ryan McNeil	.05	.02	.01
☐ 479 Natrone Means	1.25	.55	.16
☐ 480 Carl Simpson	.05	.02	.01
☐ 481 Robert O'Neal	.05	.02	.01
☐ 482 Demetrius DuBose	.05	.02	.01
☐ 483 Darrin Smith	.10	.05	.01
☐ 484 Micheal Barrow	.05	.02	.01
☐ 485 Chris Slade	.10	.05	.01
☐ 486 Steve Tovar	.05	.02	.01
☐ 487 Ron George	.05	.02	.01
☐ 488 Steve Tasker	.10	.05	.01
☐ 489 Will Furrer	.05	.02	.01
☐ 490 Reggie White	.25	.11	.03
☐ 491 Sean Jones	.05	.02	.01
☐ 492 Gary Clark	.10	.05	.01
☐ 493 Donnell Woolford	.05	.02	.01
☐ 494 Steve Beuerlein	.05	.02	.01
☐ 495 Anthony Carter	.10	.05	.01
☐ 496 Louis Oliver	.05	.02	.01
☐ 497 Chris Zorich	.05	.02	.01
☐ 498 David Brandon	.05	.02	.01
☐ 499 Bubba McDowell	.05	.02	.01
☐ 500 Adrian Cooper	.05	.02	.01
☐ 501 Bill Johnson	.05	.02	.01
☐ 502 Shawn Jefferson	.05	.02	.01
☐ 503 Siran Stacy	.05	.02	.01
☐ 504 James Jones	.05	.02	.01
☐ 505 Tom Rathman	.05	.02	.01
☐ 506 Vince Buck	.05	.02	.01
☐ 507 Kent Graham	.25	.11	.03
☐ 508 Darren Carrington	.05	.02	.01
☐ 509 Rickey Dixon	.05	.02	.01
☐ 510 Toi Cook	.05	.02	.01
☐ 511 Steve Smith	.05	.02	.01
☐ 512 Ostell Miles	.05	.02	.01
☐ 513 Phillippi Sparks	.05	.02	.01
☐ 514 Lee Williams	.05	.02	.01
☐ 515 Gary Reasons	.05	.02	.01
☐ 516 Shane Dronett	.05	.02	.01
☐ 517 Jay Novacek	.05	.02	.01
☐ 518 Kevin Greene	.25	.11	.03
☐ 519 Derek Russell	.05	.02	.01
☐ 520 Quentin Coryatt	.10	.05	.01
☐ 521 Santana Dotson	.10	.05	.01
☐ 522 Donald Frank	.05	.02	.01
☐ 523 Mike Prior	.05	.02	.01
☐ 524 Dwight Hollier	.05	.02	.01
☐ 525 Eric Davis	.05	.02	.01
☐ 526 Dalton Hilliard	.05	.02	.01
☐ 527 Rodney Culver	.05	.02	.01
☐ 528 Jeff Hostetler	.10	.05	.01
☐ 529 Ernie Mills	.05	.02	.01
☐ 530 Craig Erickson	.10	.05	.01
☐ P1 Eric Dickerson Promo Numbered 231	2.00	.90	.25

1993 Upper Deck America's Team

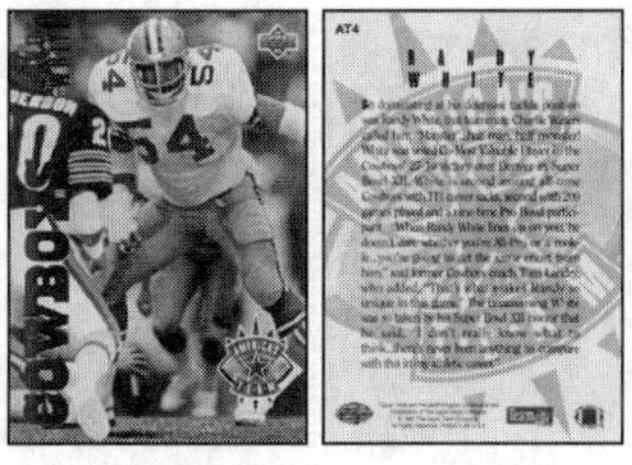

Randomly inserted in hobby foil packs at a rate of one in 25, this 15-card standard-size set showcases past and present Super Bowl champions from the Dallas Cowboys. Card numbers 1-6 feature Cowboys who participated in Super Bowl XII while card numbers 7-13 highlight Cowboys from Super Bowl XXVII. The fronts display full-bleed color action player photos; the team name and the player's name are silver foil-stamped and run up the edge of the card. A special "America's Team" emblem adorns the bottom corner. With a faded and enlarged version of this special emblem as a background, the backs presents a career summary, highlighting the player's performance in the Super Bowl. The cards are numbered on the back with an "AT" prefix. There is also a jumbo version of this set.

	MINT	NRMT	EXC
COMPLETE SET (15)	120.00	55.00	15.00
COMMON CARD (AT1-AT14)	4.00	1.80	.50
*JUMBO CARDS: .15X TO .3X BASIC CARDS			
☐ AT1 Roger Staubach	12.00	5.50	1.50
☐ AT2 Chuck Howley	4.00	1.80	.50
☐ AT3 Harvey Martin	4.00	1.80	.50
☐ AT4 Randy White	6.00	2.70	.75
☐ AT5 Bob Lilly	6.00	2.70	.75
☐ AT6 Drew Pearson	6.00	2.70	.75
☐ AT7 Emmitt Smith	40.00	18.00	5.00
☐ AT8 Troy Aikman	20.00	9.00	2.50
☐ AT9 Ken Norton Jr.	6.00	2.70	.75
☐ AT10 Robert Jones	4.00	1.80	.50
☐ AT11 Russell Maryland	4.00	1.80	.50
☐ AT12 Jay Novacek	6.00	2.70	.75
☐ AT13 Michael Irvin	8.00	3.60	1.00
☐ AT14 Checklist Card Troy Aikman	10.00	4.50	1.25
☐ NNO Header Card Emmitt Smith	16.00	7.25	2.00

1993 Upper Deck Future Heroes

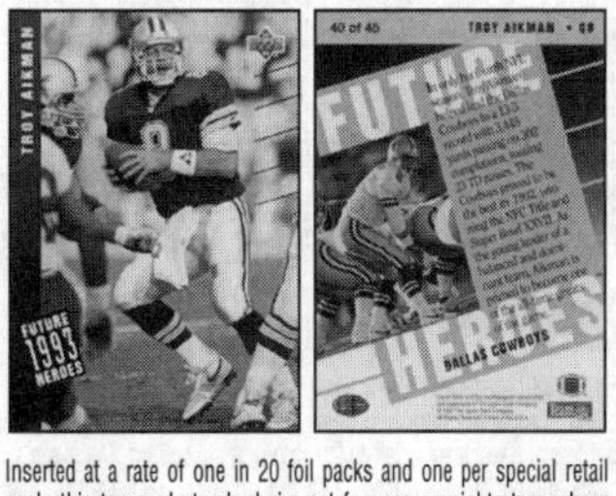

Inserted at a rate of one in 20 foil packs and one per special retail pack, this ten-card standard-size set focuses on eight stars whose current performance may one day land them in the Pro Football Hall of Fame. The color action player photos are full-bleed on three sides but edged on the left by a team color-coded stripe carrying the player's name. Short diagonal stripes and a "1993 Future Heroes" logo are done in gold foil and accent the card front. The backs have a team color-coded panel tilted to the left and carrying player profile and a small color player photo that bleeds off the left edge. Player identification as well as card number appear in a stripe at the top. The cards are numbered 37-45 in continuation of previous years "Football Heroes" series.

	MINT	NRMT	EXC
COMPLETE SET (10)	20.00	9.00	2.50
COMMON CARD (37-45)	.75	.35	.09
☐ 37 Barry Foster	.75	.35	.09
☐ 38 Junior Seau	1.25	.55	.16
☐ 39 Emmitt Smith	6.00	2.70	.75
☐ 40 Troy Aikman	4.00	1.80	.50
☐ 41 David Klingler	.75	.35	.09
☐ 42 Ricky Watters	1.25	.55	.16
☐ 43 Barry Sanders	4.00	1.80	.50
☐ 44 Brett Favre	6.00	2.70	.75
☐ 45 Emmitt Smith Checklist	2.50	1.10	.30
☐ NNO Ricky Watters Header	.75	.35	.09

1993 Upper Deck Pro Bowl

Randomly inserted in retail foil packs at a rate of one in 25, this 15-card standard-size set highlights the top NFC and AFC participants in last year's Pro Bowl. Produced with Upper Deck's new "Electric" printing technology, the horizontal fronts display glossy color player photos that are full-bleed on the top and right and bordered on the left and bottom by holographic stripes. A second color player photo is inset on the right portion of the card, while the 1993 Pro Bowl logo appears at the lower left corner. On a panel that shades from blue to white, the horizontal backs present career summary. The cards are numbered on the back with a "PB" prefix.

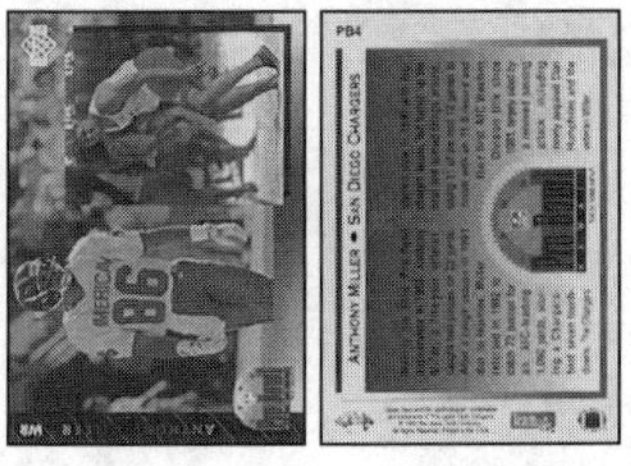

	MINT	NRMT	EXC
COMPLETE SET (20)	175.00	80.00	22.00
COMMON CARD (PB1-PB20)	4.00	1.80	.50
☐ PB1 Andre Reed	8.00	3.60	1.00
☐ PB2 Dan Marino	35.00	16.00	4.40
☐ PB3 Warren Moon	6.00	2.70	.75
☐ PB4 Anthony Miller	6.00	2.70	.75
☐ PB5 Barry Foster	4.00	1.80	.50
☐ PB6 Steve Atwater	4.00	1.80	.50
☐ PB7 Cortez Kennedy	6.00	2.70	.75
☐ PB8 Junior Seau	8.00	3.60	1.00
☐ PB9 Jerry Rice	25.00	11.00	3.10
☐ PB10 Michael Irvin	8.00	3.60	1.00
☐ PB11 Sterling Sharpe	8.00	3.60	1.00
☐ PB12 Steve Young	20.00	9.00	2.50
☐ PB13 Troy Aikman	25.00	11.00	3.10
☐ PB14 Brett Favre	35.00	16.00	4.40
☐ PB15 Emmitt Smith	35.00	16.00	4.40
☐ PB16 Rodney Hampton	8.00	3.60	1.00
☐ PB17 Barry Sanders	25.00	11.00	3.10
☐ PB18 Ricky Watters	8.00	3.60	1.00
☐ PB19 Pat Swilling	4.00	1.80	.50
☐ PB20 Checklist Card	5.00	2.20	.60

1993 Upper Deck Rookie Exchange

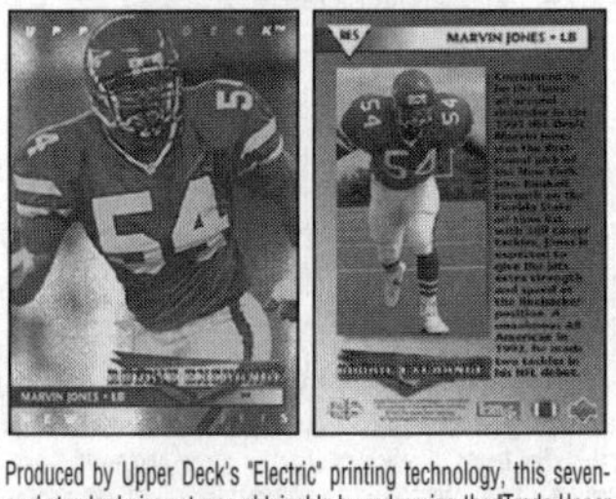

Produced by Upper Deck's "Electric" printing technology, this seven-card standard-size set was obtainable by redeeming the "Trade Upper Deck" card. One of these special trade cards was reportedly inserted in every 72 packs. The fronts feature borderless color player action shots that have the metallic quality of the "Electric" printing process. The player's name and position appear within a team color-coded bar near the bottom, and his team's name appears in silver lettering below. The back carries another color player photo on the left side, with his 1993 season highlights shown on the right, all overlaid upon a team color-coded background that lightens toward the bottom left. The player's name and position are again shown within a team color-coded bar, this time near the top. The cards are numbered on the back with an "RE" prefix.

	MINT	NRMT	EXC
COMPLETE SET (6)	16.00	7.25	2.00
COMMON CARD (RE2-RE7)	1.00	.45	.12
☐ RE1 Trade Upper Deck Card Expired	.50	.23	.06
☐ RE1X Trade Upper Deck Card Punched	.50	.23	.06
☐ RE2 Drew Bledsoe	6.00	2.70	.75
☐ RE3 Rick Mirer	3.00	1.35	.35
☐ RE4 Garrison Hearst	3.00	1.35	.35
☐ RE5 Marvin Jones	1.00	.45	.12
☐ RE6 Curtis Conway	2.00	.90	.25
☐ RE7 Jerome Bettis	3.50	1.55	.45

1993 Upper Deck Team MVPs

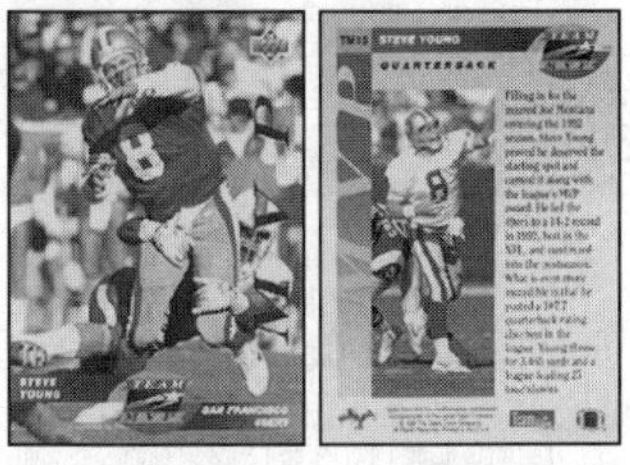

Issued one per jumbo pack, this 29-card standard-size set spotlights the Most Valuable Player on each of the NFL's 28 teams. The fronts carry full-bleed color action player photos. The player's name and team name appear respectively on two team color-coded stripes that intersect a Team MVP logo at the bottom center. Inside team color-coded stripes that edge the left and top, the gray-fading-to white

backs have different color player photos alongside career highlights. The cards are numbered on the back with a "TM" prefix.

	MINT	NRMT	EXC
COMPLETE SET (29)	25.00	11.00	3.10
COMMON CARD (TM1-TM29)	.50	.23	.06
☐ TM1 Neal Anderson	.50	.23	.06
☐ TM2 Harold Green	.50	.23	.06
☐ TM3 Thurman Thomas	1.25	.55	.16
☐ TM4 John Elway	2.50	1.10	.30
☐ TM5 Eric Metcalf	.75	.35	.09
☐ TM6 Reggie Cobb	.50	.23	.06
☐ TM7 Johnny Bailey	.50	.23	.06
☐ TM8 Junior Seau	1.25	.55	.16
☐ TM9 Derrick Thomas	.75	.35	.09
☐ TM10 Steve Emtman	.50	.23	.06
☐ TM11 Troy Aikman	4.00	1.80	.50
☐ TM12 Dan Marino	7.00	3.10	.85
☐ TM13 Clyde Simmons	.50	.23	.06
☐ TM14 Andre Rison	1.25	.55	.16
☐ TM15 Steve Young	2.50	1.10	.30
☐ TM16 Rodney Hampton	1.25	.55	.16
☐ TM17 Rob Moore	.75	.35	.09
☐ TM18 Barry Sanders	4.00	1.80	.50
☐ TM19 Warren Moon	.75	.35	.09
☐ TM20 Sterling Sharpe	1.25	.55	.16
☐ TM21 Jon Vaughn	.50	.23	.06
☐ TM22 Tim Brown	1.25	.55	.16
☐ TM23 Jim Everett	.75	.35	.09
☐ TM24 Gary Clark	.75	.35	.09
☐ TM25 Wayne Martin	.50	.23	.06
☐ TM26 Cortez Kennedy	.75	.35	.09
☐ TM27 Barry Foster	.50	.23	.06
☐ TM28 Terry Allen	1.25	.55	.16
☐ TM29 Checklist Card	.50	.23	.06

1993 Upper Deck Team Chiefs

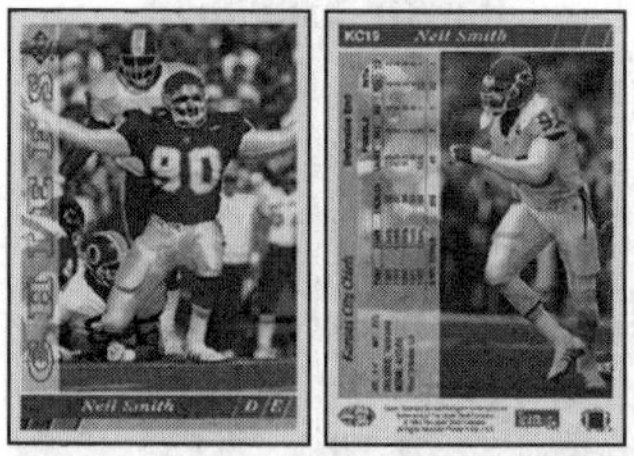

The 1993 Upper Deck Chiefs Team Set consists of 25 standard-size cards. The fronts display a color action player photo with white borders and two team color-coded stripes at the bottom. The player's name and position are printed in the top stripe. On the left side of the card, the team name is printed in a team color against a ghosted background. The backs carry a second photo alongside biographical and statistical information. The cards are numbered on the back with a "KC" prefix.

	MINT	NRMT	EXC
COMPLETE SET (25)	5.00	2.20	.60
COMMON CARD (KC1-KC25)	.20	.09	.03
☐ KC1 Nick Lowery	.20	.09	.03
☐ KC2 Lonnie Marts	.20	.09	.03
☐ KC3 Marcus Allen	.75	.35	.09
☐ KC4 Bennie Thompson	.20	.09	.03
☐ KC5 Bryan Barker	.20	.09	.03
☐ KC6 Christian Okoye	.30	.14	.04
☐ KC7 Dale Carter	.30	.14	.04
☐ KC8 Dan Saleaumua	.20	.09	.03
☐ KC9 Dave Krieg	.30	.14	.04
☐ KC10 Derrick Thomas	.50	.23	.06
☐ KC11 Doug Terry	.20	.09	.03
☐ KC12 Fred Jones	.20	.09	.03
☐ KC13 Harvey Williams	.30	.14	.04
☐ KC14 J.J. Birden	.20	.09	.03
☐ KC15 Joe Montana	2.00	.90	.25
☐ KC16 John Alt	.20	.09	.03
☐ KC17 Leonard Griffin	.20	.09	.03
☐ KC18 Matt Blundin	.20	.09	.03
☐ KC19 Neil Smith	.30	.14	.04
☐ KC20 Tim Barnett	.20	.09	.03
☐ KC21 Tim Grunhard	.20	.09	.03
☐ KC22 Todd McNair	.20	.09	.03
☐ KC23 Tracy Simien	.20	.09	.03
☐ KC24 Willie Davis	.30	.14	.04
☐ KC25 Joe Montana (Checklist back)	1.00	.45	.12

1993 Upper Deck Team Cowboys

The 1993 Upper Deck Cowboys Team Set consists of 25 standard-size cards. The fronts display a color action player photo with white borders and two team color-coded stripes at the bottom. The player's name and position are printed in the top stripe. On the left side of the card, the team name is printed in a team color against a ghosted background. The backs carry a second photo alongside biographical and statistical information. The cards are numbered on the back with a "D" prefix.

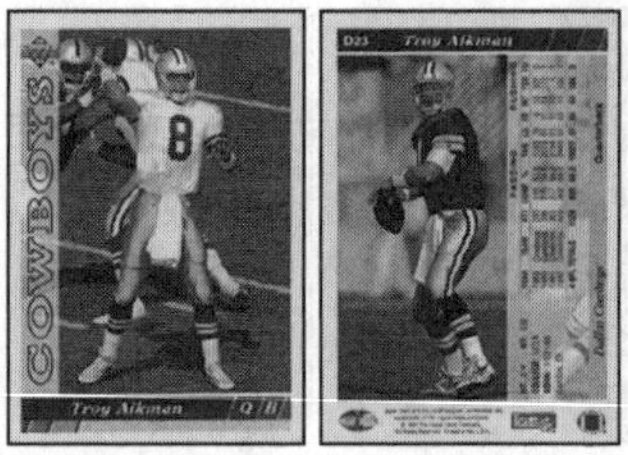

	MINT	NRMT	EXC
COMPLETE SET (25)	8.00	3.60	1.00
COMMON CARD (D1-D25)	.20	.09	.03
☐ D1 Alvin Harper	.30	.14	.04
☐ D2 Charles Haley	.30	.14	.04
☐ D3 Jimmy Smith	.20	.09	.03
☐ D4 Darrin Smith	.20	.09	.03
☐ D5 Jim Jeffcoat	.20	.09	.03
☐ D6 Daryl Johnston	.40	.18	.05
☐ D7 Dixon Edwards	.20	.09	.03
☐ D8 Emmitt Smith	3.00	1.35	.35
☐ D9 James Washington	.20	.09	.03
☐ D10 Jay Novacek	.30	.14	.04
☐ D11 Ken Norton Jr.	.30	.14	.04
☐ D12 Kenneth Gant	.20	.09	.03
☐ D13 Larry Brown DB	.30	.14	.04
☐ D14 Leon Lett	.30	.14	.04
☐ D15 Lin Elliott	.20	.09	.03
☐ D16 Mark Tuinei	.20	.09	.03
☐ D17 Michael Irvin	.60	.25	.07
☐ D18 Nate Newton	.20	.09	.03
☐ D19 Robert Jones	.20	.09	.03
☐ D20 Thomas Everett UER (Photo actually Brock Marion)	.20	.09	.03
☐ D21 Tony Casillas	.20	.09	.03
☐ D22 Tony Tolbert	.20	.09	.03
☐ D23 Troy Aikman	2.00	.90	.25
☐ D24 Russell Maryland	.20	.09	.03
☐ D25 Troy Aikman (Checklist back)	1.00	.45	.12

1993 Upper Deck Team 49ers

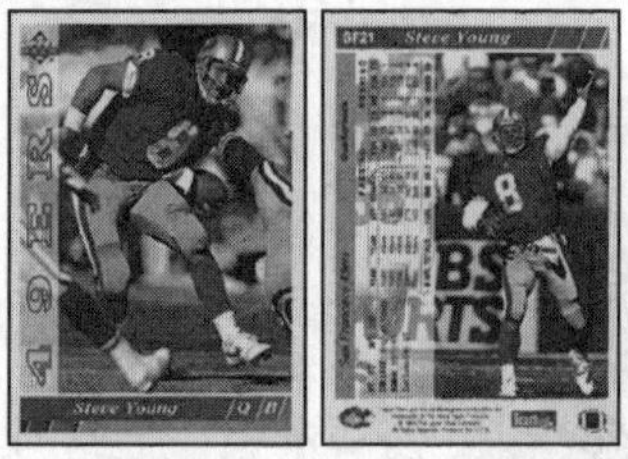

The 1993 Upper Deck 49ers Team Set consists of 25 standard-size cards. The fronts display a color action player photo with white borders and two team color-coded stripes at the bottom. The player's name and position are printed in the top stripe. On the left side of the card, the team name is printed in a team color against a ghosted background. The backs carry a second photo alongside biographical and statistical information. The cards are numbered on the back with an "SF" prefix.

	MINT	NRMT	EXC
COMPLETE SET (25)	7.50	3.40	.95
COMMON CARD (SF1-SF25)	.20	.09	.03
☐ SF1 Amp Lee	.20	.09	.03
☐ SF2 Bill Romanowski	.20	.09	.03
☐ SF3 Brent Jones	.30	.14	.04
☐ SF4 Dana Hall	.20	.09	.03
☐ SF5 Dana Stubblefield	.60	.25	.07
☐ SF6 Dennis Brown	.20	.09	.03
☐ SF7 Dexter Carter	.20	.09	.03
☐ SF8 Don Griffin	.20	.09	.03
☐ SF9 Eric Davis	.30	.14	.04
☐ SF10 Guy McIntyre	.20	.09	.03
☐ SF11 Jamie Williams	.20	.09	.03
☐ SF12 Jerry Rice	2.00	.90	.25
☐ SF13 John Taylor	.30	.14	.04
☐ SF14 Keith DeLong	.20	.09	.03
☐ SF15 Marc Logan	.20	.09	.03
☐ SF16 Michael Walter	.20	.09	.03
☐ SF17 Mike Cofer	.20	.09	.03
☐ SF18 Odessa Turner	.20	.09	.03
☐ SF19 Ricky Watters	.60	.25	.07
☐ SF20 Steve Bono	.50	.23	.06
☐ SF21 Steve Young	1.50	.70	.19
☐ SF22 Ted Washington	.20	.09	.03
☐ SF23 Tom Rathman	.30	.14	.04
☐ SF24 Jesse Sapolu	.20	.09	.03
☐ SF25 Steve Young (Checklist back)	.75	.35	.09

1993 Upper Deck 24K Gold

This 8-card set was issued by Upper Deck only through their hobby channels. The black and gold fronts are horizontal and have the player's facsimile signature on the left with an etched portrait on the right. Although the cards are numbered on the back out of 2500, reportedly only 1500 of each card was produced. Six quarterbacks and two running backs are featured in this set.

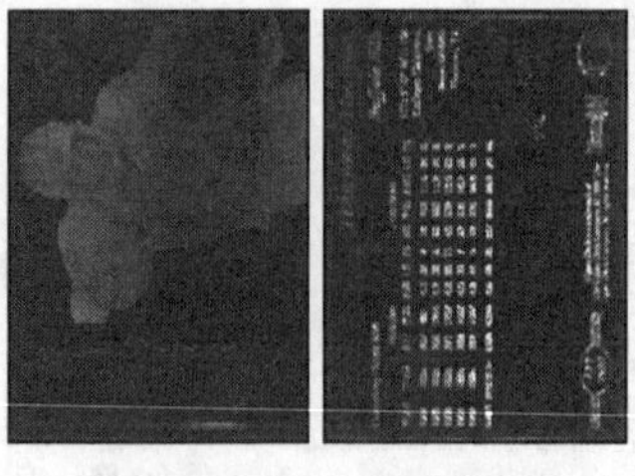

	MINT	NRMT	EXC
COMPLETE SET (8)	700.00	325.00	90.00
COMMON CARD (1-8)	50.00	22.00	6.25
☐ 1 Joe Montana	100.00	45.00	12.50
☐ 2 Emmitt Smith	150.00	70.00	19.00
☐ 3 Drew Bledsoe	90.00	40.00	11.00
☐ 4 Troy Aikman	90.00	40.00	11.00
☐ 5 Rick Mirer	50.00	22.00	6.25
☐ 6 Dan Marino	150.00	70.00	19.00
☐ 7 Steve Young	75.00	34.00	9.50
☐ 8 Thurman Thomas	50.00	22.00	6.25

1993 Upper Deck Authenticated Classic Confronations

This 3 1/2" by 5" card feature the opposing quarterbacks from Super Bowl 19. Dan Marino and Joe Montana are pictured on the card along with the score of the game. The words "Classic Confrontations XIX" are printed on the right. The card is sequentially numbered out of 20,000. The back describes 1984 seasonal and Super Bowl highlights for each player.

	MINT	NRMT	EXC
COMPLETE SET (1)	18.00	8.00	2.20
COMMON CARD	18.00	8.00	2.20
☐ 1 Joe Montana Dan Marino Classic Confrontation	18.00	8.00	2.20

1993-94 Upper Deck Miller Lite SB

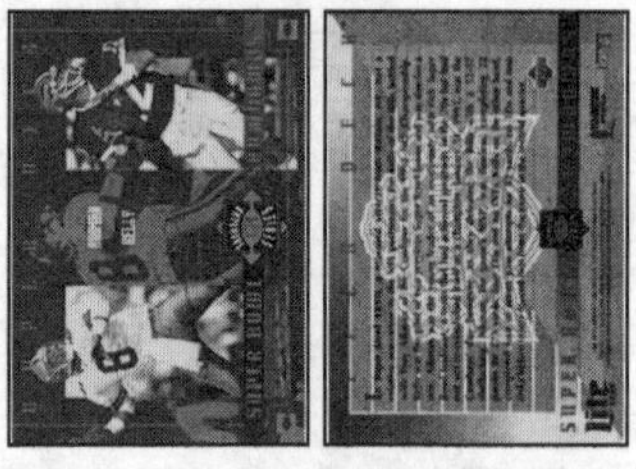

Sponsored by Miller Lite Beer and Tombstone Pizza, the 1993 Upper Deck Super Bowl Showdown Series consists of five cards measuring approximately 5" by 3 1/2". One card was included in specially-marked half-cases of Miller Lite beer. Furthermore, the set could be obtained by mailing in the official certificate (included in each specially-marked case), along with three UPC symbols from three 24-packs (or case equivalents) of 12-ounce Miller Lite cans and the dated cash register receipt. All certificates must be received by March 18, 1994. All entries were entered in a random drawing for 1,000 sweepstakes prizes of a Joe Montana personally autographed collector sheet. The horizontal card fronts feature the starting quarterbacks from competing Super Bowl teams. On each side of the front is a color action player cut-out photo superimposed over a ghosted game photo. The quarterbacks' last names appear in the center of the card in white print above the Super Bowl depicted on the card, the final score, and the date all printed in gold foil lettering. A blue stripe intersects the lower portion of the left photo containing the words "Super Bowl," and "Showdowns" appears on a red stripe intersecting the right photo. A ghosted Super Bowl logo for the play-off depicted on the front, serves as a background for highlights of the quarterbacks' accomplishments during the game. The backs are bordered in team color-coded borders that fade to a metallic silver. Sponsor logos are printed on the lower edge. The cards are numbered on the front.

	MINT	NRMT	EXC
COMPLETE SET (5)	12.00	5.50	1.50
COMMON CARD (1-5)	2.50	1.10	.30
☐ 1 Troy Aikman Jim Kelly Super Bowl XXVII	3.50	1.55	.45
☐ 2 Jim Kelly Mark Rypien Super Bowl XXVI	2.00	.90	.25
☐ 3 John Elway Joe Montana Super Bowl XXIV	3.50	1.55	.45
☐ 4 John Elway Phil Simms Super Bowl XXI	3.00	1.35	.35
☐ 5 Joe Montana Dan Marino Super Bowl XIX	5.00	2.20	.60

1994 Upper Deck Pro Bowl Samples

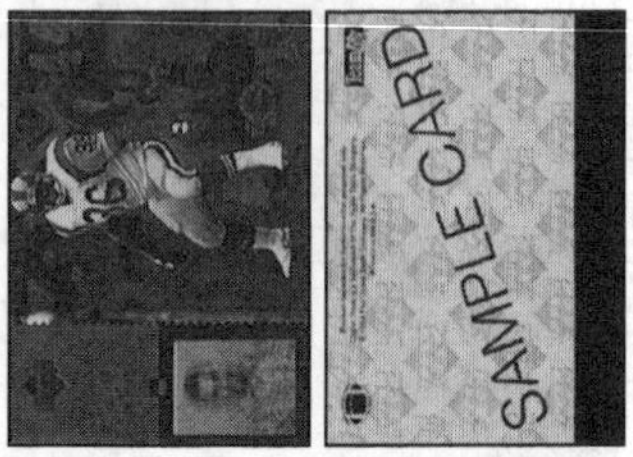

Measuring the standard-size, this six-card sample set spotlights players who participated in the Pro Bowl. The cards were originally passed out at the National Convention in Houston. On the left edge, the horizontal fronts have a purple stripe carrying the player's name, team name, and a holographic headshot framed by a black border. The rest of the front displays a full-bleed color action player photo with a metallic sheen. On a white screened background of a gray Upper Deck logos, the backs have the disclaimer "SAMPLE CARD" printed diagonally. The cards are unnumbered and checklisted below in alphabetical order.

	MINT	NRMT	EXC
COMPLETE SET (6)	35.00	16.00	4.40
COMMON CARD (1-6)	3.50	1.55	.45
☐ 1 Jerome Bettis	3.50	1.55	.45
☐ 2 Brett Favre	15.00	6.75	1.85
☐ 3 John Elway	6.00	2.70	.75
☐ 4 Thurman Thomas	3.50	1.55	.45
☐ 5 Jerry Rice	7.50	3.40	.95
☐ 6 Steve Young	6.00	2.70	.75

1994 Upper Deck

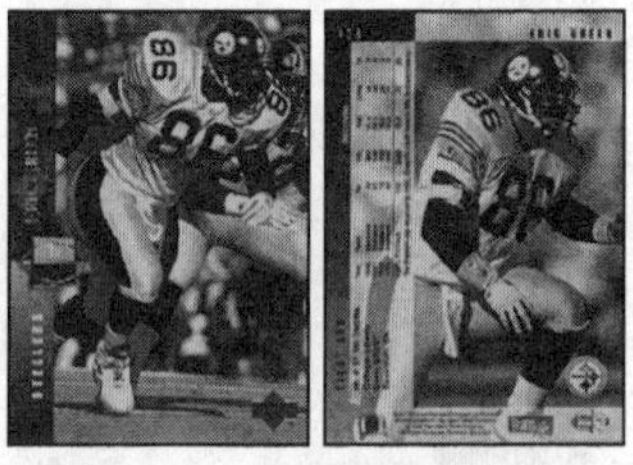

This 330-card standard-size set was released in one series. They were issued in 12-card packs with a suggested retail price of $1.99. The following subsets include Rookies (1-30) and Heavy Weights (31-40). The fronts are dominated by a full-color photo of the player extending to the borderless right side. The left side features the player's name in gold foil, his position and team identification. The backs have biographical information, recent seasonal and career statistics as well as a photo on the right. The cards are numbered in the upper-left corner. Rookie Cards include Isaac Bruce, Trent Dilfer, Marshall Faulk, William Floyd, Errict Rhett, and Heath Shuler. A Joe Montana Promo card was produced and priced below.

	MINT	NRMT	EXC
COMPLETE SET (330)	35.00	16.00	4.40
COMMON CARD (1-330)	.10	.05	.01
☐ 1 Dan Wilkinson	.20	.09	.03
☐ 2 Antonio Langham	.20	.09	.03
☐ 3 Derrick Alexander WR	.30	.14	.04
☐ 4 Charles Johnson	.60	.25	.07
☐ 5 Bucky Brooks	.10	.05	.01
☐ 6 Trev Alberts	.20	.09	.03
☐ 7 Marshall Faulk	3.50	1.55	.45
☐ 8 Willie McGinest	.30	.14	.04
☐ 9 Aaron Glenn	.20	.09	.03
☐ 10 Ryan Yarborough	.10	.05	.01
☐ 11 Greg Hill	.75	.35	.09
☐ 12 Sam Adams	.20	.09	.03
☐ 13 John Thierry	.10	.05	.01
☐ 14 Johnnie Morton	.60	.25	.07
☐ 15 LeShon Johnson	.20	.09	.03
☐ 16 David Palmer	.20	.09	.03
☐ 17 Trent Dilfer	1.00	.45	.12
☐ 18 Jamir Miller	.10	.05	.01
☐ 19 Thomas Lewis	.20	.09	.03
☐ 20 Heath Shuler	1.25	.55	.16
☐ 21 Wayne Gandy	.10	.05	.01
☐ 22 Isaac Bruce	3.50	1.55	.45
☐ 23 Joe Johnson	.10	.05	.01
☐ 24 Mario Bates	.60	.25	.07
☐ 25 Bryant Young	.60	.25	.07
☐ 26 William Floyd	1.25	.55	.16
☐ 27 Errict Rhett	1.50	.70	.19
☐ 28 Chuck Levy	.10	.05	.01

29 Darnay Scott	2.00	.90	.25
30 Rob Fredrickson	.20	.09	.03
31 Jamir Miller HW	.10	.05	.01
32 Thomas Lewis HW	.10	.05	.01
33 John Thierry HW	.10	.05	.01
34 Sam Adams HW	.10	.05	.01
35 Joe Johnson HW	.10	.05	.01
36 Bryant Young HW	.20	.09	.03
37 Wayne Gandy HW	.10	.05	.01
38 LeShon Johnson HW	.10	.05	.01
39 Mario Bates HW	.20	.09	.03
40 Greg Hill HW	.20	.09	.03
41 Andy Heck	.10	.05	.01
42 Warren Moon	.30	.14	.04
43 Jim Everett	.20	.09	.03
44 Bill Romanowski	.10	.05	.01
45 Michael Haynes	.20	.09	.03
46 Chris Doleman	.10	.05	.01
47 Merril Hoge	.10	.05	.01
48 Chris Miller	.10	.05	.01
49 Clyde Simmons	.10	.05	.01
50 Jeff George	.30	.14	.04
51 Jeff Burris	.20	.09	.03
52 Ethan Horton	.10	.05	.01
53 Scott Mitchell	.30	.14	.04
54 Howard Ballard	.10	.05	.01
55 Lewis Tillman	.10	.05	.01
56 Marion Butts	.10	.05	.01
57 Erik Kramer	.20	.09	.03
58 Ken Norton Jr.	.20	.09	.03
59 Anthony Miller	.20	.09	.03
60 Chris Hinton	.10	.05	.01
61 Ricky Proehl	.10	.05	.01
62 Craig Heyward	.20	.09	.03
63 Darryl Talley	.10	.05	.01
64 Tim Worley	.10	.05	.01
65 Derrick Fenner	.10	.05	.01
66 Jerry Ball	.10	.05	.01
67 Darrin Smith	.10	.05	.01
68 Mike Croel	.10	.05	.01
69 Ray Crockett	.10	.05	.01
70 Tony Bennett	.10	.05	.01
71 Webster Slaughter	.10	.05	.01
72 Anthony Johnson	.20	.09	.03
73 Charles Mincy	.10	.05	.01
74 Calvin Jones	.10	.05	.01
75 Henry Ellard	.20	.09	.03
76 Troy Vincent	.10	.05	.01
77 Sean Salisbury	.10	.05	.01
78 Pat Harlow	.10	.05	.01
79 James Williams	.10	.05	.01
80 Dave Brown	.20	.09	.03
81 Kent Graham	.20	.09	.03
82 Seth Joyner	.10	.05	.01
83 Deon Figures	.10	.05	.01
84 Stanley Richard	.10	.05	.01
85 Tom Rathman	.10	.05	.01
86 Rod Stephens	.10	.05	.01
87 Ray Seals	.10	.05	.01
88 Andre Collins	.10	.05	.01
89 Cornelius Bennett	.20	.09	.03
90 Richard Dent	.20	.09	.03
91 Louis Oliver	.10	.05	.01
92 Rodney Peete	.10	.05	.01
93 Jackie Harris	.10	.05	.01
94 Tracy Simien	.10	.05	.01
95 Greg Townsend	.10	.05	.01
96 Michael Stewart	.10	.05	.01
97 Irving Fryar	.20	.09	.03
98 Todd Collins	.10	.05	.01
99 Irv Smith	.10	.05	.01
100 Chris Calloway	.10	.05	.01
101 Kevin Greene	.30	.14	.04
102 John Friesz	.20	.09	.03
103 Steve Bono	.20	.09	.03
104 Brian Blades	.20	.09	.03
105 Reggie Cobb	.10	.05	.01
106 Eric Swann	.20	.09	.03
107 Mike Pritchard	.10	.05	.01
108 Bill Brooks	.10	.05	.01
109 Jim Harbaugh	.30	.14	.04
110 David Whitmore	.10	.05	.01
111 Eddie Anderson	.10	.05	.01
112 Ray Crittenden	.10	.05	.01
113 Mark Collins	.10	.05	.01
114 Brian Washington	.10	.05	.01
115 Barry Foster	.10	.05	.01
116 Gary Plummer	.10	.05	.01
117 Marc Logan	.10	.05	.01
118 John L. Williams	.10	.05	.01
119 Marty Carter	.10	.05	.01
120 Kurt Gouveia	.10	.05	.01
121 Ronald Moore	.10	.05	.01
122 Pierce Holt	.10	.05	.01
123 Henry Jones	.10	.05	.01
124 Donnell Woolford	.10	.05	.01
125 Steve Tovar	.10	.05	.01
126 Anthony Pleasant	.10	.05	.01
127 Jay Novacek	.20	.09	.03
128 Dan Williams	.10	.05	.01
129 Barry Sanders	1.50	.70	.19
130 Robert Brooks	.60	.25	.07
131 Lorenzo White	.10	.05	.01
132 Kerry Cash	.10	.05	.01
133 Joe Montana	1.50	.70	.19
134 Jeff Hostetler	.20	.09	.03
135 Jerome Bettis	.75	.35	.09
136 Dan Marino	3.00	1.35	.35
137 Vencie Glenn	.10	.05	.01
138 Vincent Brown	.10	.05	.01
139 Rickey Jackson	.10	.05	.01
140 Carlton Bailey	.10	.05	.01
141 Jeff Lageman	.10	.05	.01
142 William Thomas	.10	.05	.01
143 Neil O'Donnell	.30	.14	.04
144 Shawn Jefferson	.10	.05	.01
145 Steve Young	1.00	.45	.12
146 Chris Warren	.20	.09	.03
147 Courtney Hawkins	.10	.05	.01
148 Brad Edwards	.10	.05	.01
149 O.J. McDuffie	.30	.14	.04
150 David Lang	.10	.05	.01
151 Chuck Cecil	.10	.05	.01
152 Norm Johnson	.10	.05	.01
153 Pete Metzelaars	.10	.05	.01
154 Shaun Gayle	.10	.05	.01
155 Alfred Williams	.10	.05	.01
156 Eric Turner	.10	.05	.01
157A Emmitt Smith ERR incorrect stat totals	3.00	1.35	.35
157B Emmitt Smith COR corrected stats	3.00	1.35	.35
158 Steve Atwater	.10	.05	.01
159 Robert Porcher	.10	.05	.01
160 Edgar Bennett	.30	.14	.04
161 Bubba McDowell	.10	.05	.01
162 Jeff Herrod	.10	.05	.01
163 Keith Cash	.10	.05	.01
164 Patrick Bates	.10	.05	.01
165 Todd Lyght	.10	.05	.01
166 Mark Higgs	.10	.05	.01
167 Carlos Jenkins	.10	.05	.01
168 Drew Bledsoe	1.50	.70	.19
169 Wayne Martin	.10	.05	.01
170 Mike Sherrard	.10	.05	.01
171 Ronnie Lott	.20	.09	.03
172 Fred Barnett	.20	.09	.03
173 Eric Green	.10	.05	.01
174 Leslie O'Neal	.10	.05	.01
175 Brent Jones	.20	.09	.03
176 Jon Vaughn	.10	.05	.01
177 Vince Workman	.10	.05	.01
178 Ron Middleton	.10	.05	.01
179 Terry McDaniel	.10	.05	.01
180 Willie Davis	.20	.09	.03
181 Gary Clark	.20	.09	.03
182 Bobby Hebert	.10	.05	.01
183 Russell Copeland	.10	.05	.01
184 Chris Gedney	.10	.05	.01
185 Tony McGee	.10	.05	.01
186 Rob Burnett	.10	.05	.01
187 Charles Haley	.20	.09	.03
188 Shannon Sharpe	.20	.09	.03
189 Mel Gray	.10	.05	.01
190 George Teague	.10	.05	.01
191 Ernest Givins	.20	.09	.03
192 Ray Buchanan	.10	.05	.01
193 J.J. Birden	.10	.05	.01
194 Tim Brown	.30	.14	.04
195 Tim Lester	.10	.05	.01
196 Marco Coleman	.10	.05	.01
197 Randall McDaniel	.10	.05	.01
198 Bruce Armstrong	.10	.05	.01
199 Willie Roaf	.10	.05	.01
200 Greg Jackson	.10	.05	.01
201 Johnny Mitchell	.10	.05	.01
202 Calvin Williams	.20	.09	.03
203 Jeff Graham	.10	.05	.01
204 Darren Carrington	.10	.05	.01
205 Jerry Rice	1.50	.70	.19
206 Cortez Kennedy	.20	.09	.03
207 Charles Wilson	.10	.05	.01
208 James Jenkins	.10	.05	.01
209 Ray Childress	.10	.05	.01
210 LeRoy Butler	.10	.05	.01
211 Randal Hill	.10	.05	.01
212 Lincoln Kennedy	.10	.05	.01
213 Kenneth Davis	.10	.05	.01
214 Terry Obee	.10	.05	.01
215 Ricardo McDonald	.10	.05	.01
216 Pepper Johnson	.10	.05	.01
217 Alvin Harper	.20	.09	.03
218 John Elway	1.00	.45	.12
219 Derrick Moore	.10	.05	.01
220 Terrell Buckley	.10	.05	.01
221 Haywood Jeffires	.20	.09	.03
222 Jessie Hester	.10	.05	.01
223 Kimble Anders	.20	.09	.03
224 Rocket Ismail	.20	.09	.03
225 Roman Phifer	.10	.05	.01
226 Bryan Cox	.10	.05	.01
227 Cris Carter	.30	.14	.04
228 Sam Gash	.10	.05	.01
229 Renaldo Turnbull	.10	.05	.01
230 Rodney Hampton	.30	.14	.04
231 Johnny Johnson	.10	.05	.01
232 Tim Harris	.10	.05	.01
233 Leroy Thompson	.10	.05	.01
234 Junior Seau	.30	.14	.04
235 Tim McDonald	.10	.05	.01
236 Eugene Robinson	.10	.05	.01
237 Lawrence Dawsey	.10	.05	.01
238 Tim Johnson	.10	.05	.01
239 Jason Elam	.10	.05	.01
240 Willie Green	.10	.05	.01
241 Larry Centers	.30	.14	.04
242 Erric Pegram	.10	.05	.01
243 Bruce Smith	.30	.14	.04
244 Alonzo Spellman	.10	.05	.01
245 Carl Pickens	.75	.35	.09
246 Michael Jackson	.20	.09	.03
247 Kevin Williams	.20	.09	.03
248 Glyn Milburn	.20	.09	.03
249 Herman Moore	.75	.35	.09
250 Brett Favre	3.00	1.35	.35
251 Al Smith	.10	.05	.01
252 Roosevelt Potts	.10	.05	.01
253 Marcus Allen	.30	.14	.04
254 Anthony Smith	.10	.05	.01
255 Sean Gilbert	.10	.05	.01
256 Keith Byars	.10	.05	.01
257 Scottie Graham	.20	.09	.03
258 Leonard Russell	.10	.05	.01
259 Eric Martin	.10	.05	.01
260 Jarrod Bunch	.10	.05	.01
261 Rob Moore	.20	.09	.03
262 Herschel Walker	.20	.09	.03
263 Levon Kirkland	.10	.05	.01
264 Chris Mims	.10	.05	.01
265 Ricky Watters	.30	.14	.04
266 Rick Mirer	.30	.14	.04
267 Santana Dotson	.20	.09	.03
268 Reggie Brooks	.20	.09	.03
269 Garrison Hearst	.75	.35	.09
270 Thurman Thomas	.30	.14	.04
271 Johnny Bailey	.10	.05	.01
272 Andre Rison	.20	.09	.03
273 Jim Kelly	.30	.14	.04
274 Mark Carrier DB	.10	.05	.01
275 David Klingler	.10	.05	.01
276 Eric Metcalf	.20	.09	.03
277 Troy Aikman	1.50	.70	.19
278 Simon Fletcher	.10	.05	.01
279 Pat Swilling	.10	.05	.01
280 Sterling Sharpe	.20	.09	.03
281 Cody Carlson	.10	.05	.01
282 Steve Emtman	.10	.05	.01
283 Neil Smith	.30	.14	.04
284 James Jett	.10	.05	.01
285 Shane Conlan	.10	.05	.01
286 Keith Jackson	.10	.05	.01
287 Qadry Ismail	.30	.14	.04
288 Chris Slade	.10	.05	.01
289 Derek Brown RB	.10	.05	.01
290 Phil Simms	.20	.09	.03
291 Boomer Esiason	.20	.09	.03
292 Eric Allen	.10	.05	.01
293 Rod Woodson	.30	.14	.04
294 Ronnie Harmon	.10	.05	.01
295 John Taylor	.20	.09	.03
296 Ferrell Edmunds	.10	.05	.01
297 Craig Erickson	.10	.05	.01
298 Brian Mitchell	.10	.05	.01
299 Dante Jones	.10	.05	.01
300 John Copeland	.10	.05	.01
301 Steve Beuerlein	.10	.05	.01
302 Deion Sanders	.75	.35	.09
303 Andre Reed	.20	.09	.03
304 Curtis Conway	.30	.14	.04
305 Harold Green	.10	.05	.01
306 Vinny Testaverde	.20	.09	.03
307 Michael Irvin	.30	.14	.04
308 Rod Bernstine	.10	.05	.01
309 Chris Spielman	.20	.09	.03
310 Reggie White	.30	.14	.04
311 Gary Brown	.10	.05	.01
312 Quentin Coryatt	.10	.05	.01
313 Derrick Thomas	.30	.14	.04
314 Greg Robinson	.10	.05	.01
315 Troy Drayton	.10	.05	.01
316 Terry Kirby	.30	.14	.04
317 John Randle	.10	.05	.01
318 Ben Coates	.30	.14	.04
319 Tyrone Hughes	.20	.09	.03
320 Corey Miller	.10	.05	.01
321 Brad Baxter	.10	.05	.01
322 Randall Cunningham	.20	.09	.03
323 Greg Lloyd	.30	.14	.04
324 Stan Humphries	.30	.14	.04
325 Dana Stubblefield	.30	.14	.04
326 Kelvin Martin	.10	.05	.01
327 Hardy Nickerson	.20	.09	.03
328 Desmond Howard	.20	.09	.03
329 Mark Carrier WR	.20	.09	.03
330 Daryl Johnston	.20	.09	.03
P19 Joe Montana Promo	2.00	.90	.25

1994 Upper Deck Electric Gold

Inserted one per hobby box and randomly inserted in special retail packs, this 330-card standard-size set is a parallel to the basic Upper Deck issue. They can be distinguished by the gold electric logo at the bottom. They differ from the silver version in that the Electric Gold logo was produced with prismatic foil.

	MINT	NRMT	EXC
COMPLETE SET (330)	1600.00	700.00	200.00
COMMON CARD (1-330)	2.50	1.10	.30
*STARS: 17.5X TO 35X BASIC CARDS			
*RCs: 10X TO 18X BASIC CARDS			

1994 Upper Deck Electric Silver

Inserted one per hobby pack and two per special retail pack, this 330 card standard-size set is a parallel to the basic Upper Deck pack. The cards can be distinguished by the silver Electric logo at the bottom. They differ from the gold versions in that the logo was produced with a flat foil finish instead of prismatic.

	MINT	NRMT	EXC
COMPLETE SET (330)	120.00	55.00	15.00
COMMON CARD (1-330)	.25	.11	.03
*STARS: 2X TO 4X BASIC CARDS			
*RCs: 1.25X TO 2.5X BASIC CARDS			

1994 Upper Deck Predictor Award Winners

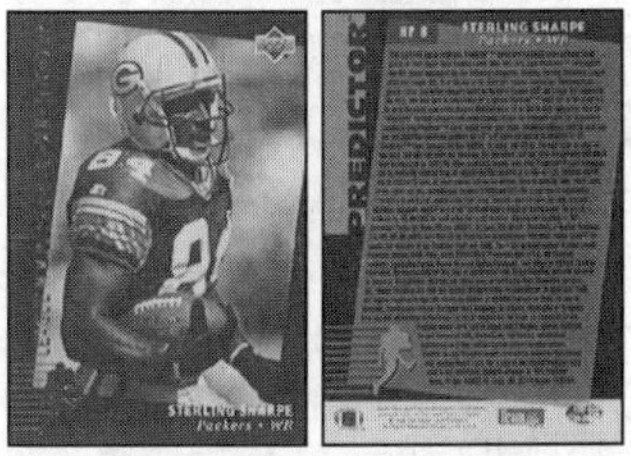

Randomly inserted in Hobby packs at a rate of one in 20, this set was designed to include a potential league MVP and Rookie of the Year. The card of the player that won an award could have been redeemed for a special foil enhanced 20-card Predictor set including the league MVP (Longshot, Steve Young) and Rookie of the Year (Marshall Faulk) game cards. The card of a second place finisher (Barry Sanders MVP, several tied for Longshot ROY) could have been redeemed for a foil enhanced 10-card Predictor set for the category with which the player placed second. The offer expired March 31, 1995. The cards feature a color photo on front with the Predictor category on the left border that is broken into two solid colors. The player's name, team and position are at bottom right. The backs contain game rules. The cards are numbered with an "HP" prefix.

	MINT	NRMT	EXC
COMPLETE SET (20)	90.00	40.00	11.00
COMMON CARD (HP1-HP20)	1.25	.55	.16
H PREFIX PRIZE SET (20)	50.00	22.00	6.25
*H PREFIX PRIZES: .2X TO .4X BASIC CARDS			

HP1 Emmitt Smith	10.00	4.50	1.25
HP2 Barry Sanders W2	8.00	3.60	1.00
HP3 Jerome Bettis	3.00	1.35	.35
HP4 Joe Montana	6.00	2.70	.75
HP5 Dan Marino	10.00	4.50	1.25
HP6 Marshall Faulk	5.00	2.20	.60
HP7 Dan Wilkinson	1.25	.55	.16
HP8 Sterling Sharpe	1.25	.55	.16
HP9 Thurman Thomas	2.00	.90	.25
HP10 The Longshot W1	3.00	1.35	.35
HP11 Marshall Faulk W1	6.00	2.70	.75
HP12 Trent Dilfer	2.00	.90	.25
HP13 Heath Shuler	2.00	.90	.25
HP14 David Palmer	1.25	.55	.16
HP15 Charles Johnson	1.25	.55	.16
HP16 Greg Hill	1.25	.55	.16
HP17 Johnnie Morton	1.25	.55	.16
HP18 Errict Rhett	2.50	1.10	.30
HP19 Darnay Scott	2.00	.90	.25
HP20 The Longshot W2	3.00	1.35	.35

1994 Upper Deck Predictor League Leaders

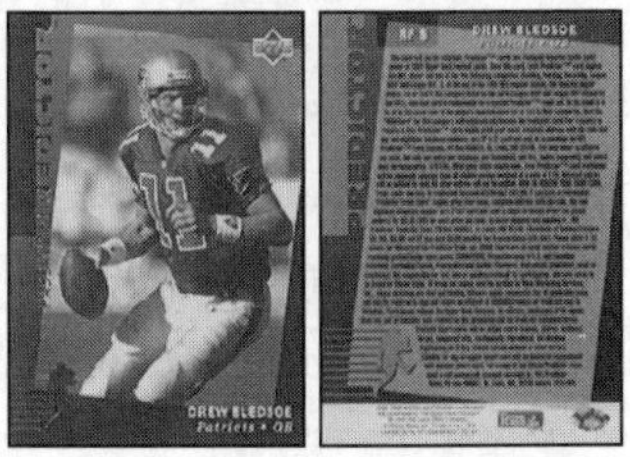

Randomly inserted in Retail packs at a rate of one in 20, this 30-card standard-size set was designed to include potential top passers (1-9), rushers (11-19) and receivers (21-29). There are also three Longshot cards. If the players within a certain category did not finish first or second, the Longshot card could be redeemed. If one of the players included in either of the three categories finished first, that card could be redeemed for a special foil enhanced 30-card Predictor set which includes the Rushing, Passing and Receiving category game cards. Cards of second place finishers could be exchanged for a 10-card foil

enhanced Predictor set for that category. Winning cards are noted below. The cardbacks contain the game rules and each card is numbered with an "RP" prefix.

	MINT	NRMT	EXC
COMPLETE SET (30)	120.00	55.00	15.00
COMMON CARD (RP1-RP30)	1.25	.55	.16
R PREFIX PRIZE SET (30)	60.00	27.00	7.50

*R PREFIX PRIZES: .2X to .4X BASIC CARDS

☐ RP1 Troy Aikman	5.00	2.20	.60
☐ RP2 Steve Young	4.00	1.80	.50
☐ RP3 John Elway	4.00	1.80	.50
☐ RP4 Joe Montana	6.00	2.70	.75
☐ RP5 Brett Favre	10.00	4.50	1.25
☐ RP6 Heath Shuler	2.50	1.10	.30
☐ RP7 Dan Marino W2	12.00	5.50	1.50
☐ RP8 Rick Mirer	2.50	1.10	.30
☐ RP9 Drew Bledsoe W1	8.00	3.60	1.00
☐ RP10 The Longshot	1.25	.55	.16
☐ RP11 Emmitt Smith	10.00	4.50	1.25
☐ RP12 Barry Sanders W1	8.00	3.60	1.00
☐ RP13 Jerome Bettis	3.00	1.35	.35
☐ RP14 Rodney Hampton	2.50	1.10	.30
☐ RP15 Thurman Thomas	2.50	1.10	.30
☐ RP16 Marshall Faulk	5.00	2.20	.60
☐ RP17 Barry Foster	1.25	.55	.16
☐ RP18 Reggie Brooks	1.25	.55	.16
☐ RP19 Ricky Watters	2.50	1.10	.30
☐ RP20 The Longshot W2	2.50	1.10	.30
☐ RP21 Jerry Rice	8.00	3.60	1.00
☐ RP22 Sterling Sharpe	2.50	1.10	.30
☐ RP23 Andre Rison	2.50	1.10	.30
☐ RP24 Michael Irvin	2.50	1.10	.30
☐ RP25 Tim Brown	2.50	1.10	.30
☐ RP26 Shannon Sharpe	1.25	.55	.16
☐ RP27 Andre Reed	2.50	1.10	.30
☐ RP28 Irving Fryar	1.25	.55	.16
☐ RP29 Charles Johnson	2.50	1.10	.30
☐ RP30 The Longshot W2	2.50	1.10	.30

1994 Upper Deck Pro Bowl

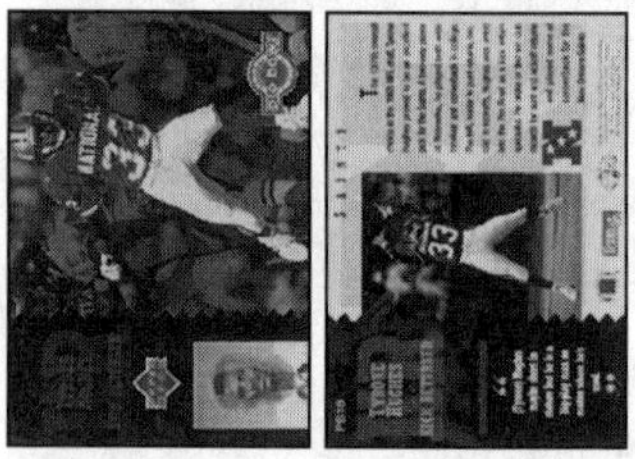

Randomly inserted in both Hobby and Retail packs, this 20-card standard-size set reflects on performers in the 1994 Pro Bowl. Horizontally designed cards feature the debut of Upper Deck's Holoview process. An action photo from the Pro Bowl covers most of the card front. The left side has a small hologram and the player's name and position. The back contains a photo, 1993 season highlights and a player quote. The backs are numbered with a "PB" prefix.

	MINT	NRMT	EXC
COMPLETE SET (20)	100.00	45.00	12.50
COMMON CARD (PB1-PB20)	2.00	.90	.25
☐ PB1 Jerome Bettis	5.00	2.20	.60
☐ PB2 Jay Novacek	3.00	1.35	.35
☐ PB3 Shannon Sharpe	2.00	.90	.25
☐ PB4 Brent Jones	2.00	.90	.25
☐ PB5 Andre Rison	3.00	1.35	.35
☐ PB6 Tim Brown	4.00	1.80	.50
☐ PB7 Anthony Miller	2.00	.90	.25
☐ PB8 Jerry Rice	15.00	6.75	1.85
☐ PB9 Brett Favre	30.00	13.50	3.70
☐ PB10 Emmitt Smith	30.00	13.50	3.70
☐ PB11 Steve Young	12.00	5.50	1.50
☐ PB12 John Elway	12.00	5.50	1.50
☐ PB13 Warren Moon	3.00	1.35	.35
☐ PB14 Thurman Thomas	4.00	1.80	.50
☐ PB15 Ricky Watters	3.00	1.35	.35
☐ PB16 Rod Woodson	3.00	1.35	.35
☐ PB17 Reggie White	4.00	1.80	.50
☐ PB18 Tyrone Hughes	2.00	.90	.25
☐ PB19 Derrick Thomas	3.00	1.35	.35
☐ PB20 Checklist	2.00	.90	.25

1994-95 Upper Deck Sheets

These 11" by 8.5" sheets were issued by Upper Deck. The autograph sheet was given out during the 1995 Super Bowl Card Show VI for collectors to have signed by players appearing at the show. The Dan Marino was issued in 1995 to commemorate Marino's record breaking season.

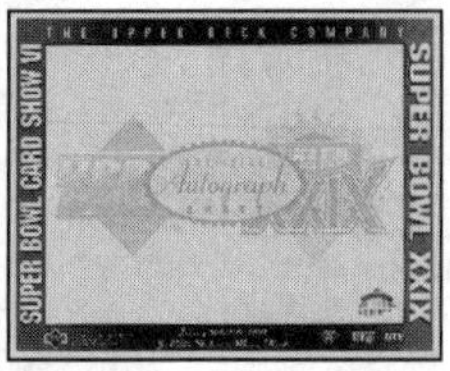

	MINT	NRMT	EXC
COMPLETE SET (4)	30.00	13.50	3.70
COMMON SHEET	4.00	1.80	.50
☐ NNO Super Bowl XXIX Autograph Sheet Jan. 26-29, 1995	4.00	1.80	.50
☐ NNO Rookie Class 1994 Dan Wilkinson Heath Shuler Trev Alberts Greg Hill Marshall Faulk Johnnie Morton	8.00	3.60	1.00
☐ NNO Upper Deck Salutes St. Louis Rams Undated numbered of 30,000 Sean Gilbert Kevin Carter Isaac Bruce Jerome Bettis Chris Miller Shane Conlan	8.00	3.60	1.00
☐ NNO Dan Marino 1995 Record Breaker Numbered of 30,000	12.00	5.50	1.50

1995 Upper Deck

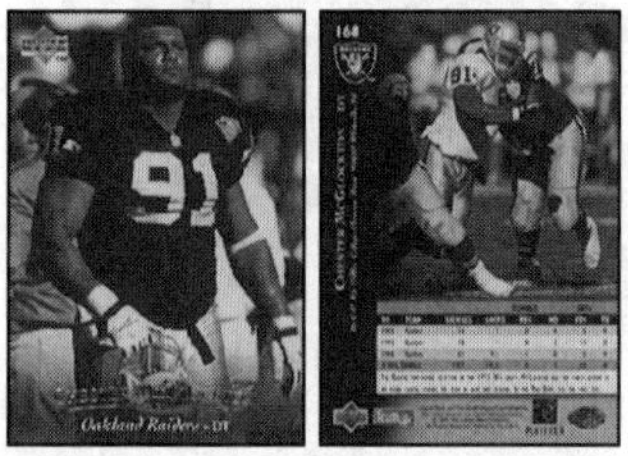

This 300-card standard-size set was released in one series. They were issued in 12-card packs with a suggested retail price of $1.99. There is one subset, Rookies (1-30). The fronts have a full-color photo of the player with his name in gold-foil at the bottom while the team name is in white underneath that. The backs have a color-action photo in the top portion with statistics at the bottom. Rookie Cards include Jeff Blake, Ki-Jana Carter, Kerry Collins, Joey Galloway, Curtis Martin, Steve McNair, Rashaan Salaam, J.J. Stokes, Michael Westbrook and Tyrone Wheatley. Two parallels exist which were randomly inserted into retail packs only: Electric and Electric Gold. The Electric insert set feature a silver foil logo on the front and is inserted one per pack. The Electric Gold insert set features a gold foil logo on the front and is inserted at a rate of one in 35 packs. Joe Montana (#19) and Marshall Faulk (PB95) Promo cards were produced and listed below.

	MINT	NRMT	EXC
COMPLETE SET (300)	30.00	13.50	3.70
COMMON CARD (1-300)	.10	.05	.01
☐ 1 Ki-Jana Carter	1.50	.70	.19
☐ 2 Tony Boselli	.15	.07	.02
☐ 3 Steve McNair	4.00	1.80	.50
☐ 4 Michael Westbrook	2.00	.90	.25
☐ 5 Kerry Collins	5.00	2.20	.60
☐ 6 Kevin Carter	.30	.14	.04
☐ 7 James A.Stewart	.10	.05	.01
☐ 8 Joey Galloway	3.00	1.35	.35
☐ 9 Kyle Brady	.30	.14	.04
☐ 10 J.J. Stokes	1.50	.70	.19
☐ 11 Derrick Alexander DE	.10	.05	.01
☐ 12 Warren Sapp	.15	.07	.02
☐ 13 Mark Fields UER Linebacker on front, running back on back	.10	.05	.01
☐ 14 Tyrone Wheatley	.75	.35	.09
☐ 15 Napoleon Kaufman	1.50	.70	.19
☐ 16 James O. Stewart	.15	.07	.02
☐ 17 Luther Elliss	.10	.05	.01
☐ 18 Rashaan Salaam	2.00	.90	.25
☐ 19 Jimmy Oliver	.10	.05	.01
☐ 20 Mark Bruener	.15	.07	.02
☐ 21 Derrick Brooks	.10	.05	.01
☐ 22 Christian Fauria	.10	.05	.01
☐ 23 Ray Zellars	.15	.07	.02
☐ 24 Todd Collins	.30	.14	.04
☐ 25 Sherman Williams	.10	.05	.01
☐ 26 Frank Sanders	.30	.14	.04
☐ 27 Rodney Thomas	.30	.14	.04
☐ 28 Rob Johnson	.10	.05	.01
☐ 29 Steve Stenstrom	.10	.05	.01
☐ 30 Curtis Martin	6.00	2.70	.75
☐ 31 Gary Clark	.10	.05	.01
☐ 32 Troy Aikman	1.50	.70	.19
☐ 33 Mike Sherrard	.10	.05	.01
☐ 34 Fred Barnett	.15	.07	.02
☐ 35 Henry Ellard	.15	.07	.02
☐ 36 Terry Allen	.15	.07	.02
☐ 37 Jeff Graham	.10	.05	.01
☐ 38 Herman Moore	.75	.35	.09
☐ 39 Brett Favre	3.00	1.35	.35
☐ 40 Trent Dilfer	.30	.14	.04
☐ 41 Derek Brown RB	.10	.05	.01
☐ 42 Andre Rison	.15	.07	.02
☐ 43 Flipper Anderson	.10	.05	.01
☐ 44 Jerry Rice	1.50	.70	.19
☐ 45 Andre Reed	.15	.07	.02
☐ 46 Sean Dawkins	.15	.07	.02
☐ 47 Irving Fryar	.15	.07	.02
☐ 48 Vincent Brisby	.10	.05	.01
☐ 49 Rob Moore	.10	.05	.01
☐ 50 Carl Pickens	.30	.14	.04
☐ 51 Vinny Testaverde	.15	.07	.02
☐ 52 Ray Childress	.10	.05	.01
☐ 53 Eric Green	.10	.05	.01
☐ 54 Anthony Miller	.15	.07	.02
☐ 55 Lake Dawson	.15	.07	.02
☐ 56 Tim Brown	.30	.14	.04
☐ 57 Stan Humphries	.15	.07	.02
☐ 58 Rick Mirer	.30	.14	.04
☐ 59 Randal Hill	.10	.05	.01
☐ 60 Charles Haley	.15	.07	.02
☐ 61 Chris Calloway	.10	.05	.01
☐ 62 Calvin Williams	.15	.07	.02
☐ 63 Ethan Horton	.10	.05	.01
☐ 64 Cris Carter	.30	.14	.04
☐ 65 Curtis Conway	.30	.14	.04
☐ 66 Scott Mitchell	.15	.07	.02
☐ 67 Edgar Bennett	.15	.07	.02
☐ 68 Craig Erickson	.10	.05	.01
☐ 69 Jim Everett	.10	.05	.01
☐ 70 Terance Mathis	.15	.07	.02
☐ 71 Robert Young	.10	.05	.01
☐ 72 Brent Jones	.10	.05	.01
☐ 73 Thurman Thomas	.30	.14	.04
☐ 74 Marshall Faulk	.75	.35	.09
☐ 75 O.J. McDuffie	.30	.14	.04
☐ 76 Ben Coates	.15	.07	.02
☐ 77 Johnny Mitchell	.10	.05	.01
☐ 78 Darnay Scott	.30	.14	.04
☐ 79 Derrick Alexander WR	.30	.14	.04
☐ 80 Lorenzo White	.10	.05	.01
☐ 81 Charles Johnson	.15	.07	.02
☐ 82 John Elway	1.25	.55	.16
☐ 83 Willie Davis	.15	.07	.02
☐ 84 James Jett	.15	.07	.02
☐ 85 Mark Seay	.15	.07	.02
☐ 86 Brian Blades	.15	.07	.02
☐ 87 Ronald Moore	.10	.05	.01
☐ 88 Alvin Harper	.10	.05	.01
☐ 89 Dave Brown	.15	.07	.02
☐ 90 Randall Cunningham	.15	.07	.02
☐ 91 Heath Shuler	.30	.14	.04
☐ 92 Jake Reed	.15	.07	.02
☐ 93 Donnell Woolford	.10	.05	.01
☐ 94 Barry Sanders	1.50	.70	.19
☐ 95 Reggie White	.30	.14	.04
☐ 96 Lawrence Dawsey	.10	.05	.01
☐ 97 Michael Haynes	.15	.07	.02
☐ 98 Bert Emanuel	.30	.14	.04
☐ 99 Troy Drayton	.10	.05	.01
☐ 100 Steve Young	1.25	.55	.16
☐ 101 Bruce Smith	.30	.14	.04
☐ 102 Roosevelt Potts	.10	.05	.01
☐ 103 Dan Marino	3.00	1.35	.35
☐ 104 Michael Timpson	.10	.05	.01
☐ 105 Boomer Esiason	.15	.07	.02
☐ 106 David Klingler	.15	.07	.02
☐ 107 Eric Metcalf	.15	.07	.02
☐ 108 Gary Brown	.10	.05	.01
☐ 109 Neil O'Donnell	.15	.07	.02
☐ 110 Shannon Sharpe	.15	.07	.02
☐ 111 Joe Montana	1.50	.70	.19
☐ 112 Jeff Hostetler	.15	.07	.02
☐ 113 Ronnie Harmon	.10	.05	.01
☐ 114 Chris Warren	.15	.07	.02
☐ 115 Larry Centers	.15	.07	.02
☐ 116 Michael Irvin	.30	.14	.04
☐ 117 Rodney Hampton	.15	.07	.02
☐ 118 Herschel Walker	.15	.07	.02
☐ 119 Reggie Brooks	.15	.07	.02
☐ 120 Qadry Ismail	.15	.07	.02
☐ 121 Chris Zorich	.10	.05	.01
☐ 122 Chris Spielman	.15	.07	.02
☐ 123 Sean Jones	.10	.05	.01
☐ 124 Errict Rhett	.30	.14	.04
☐ 125 Tyrone Hughes	.15	.07	.02
☐ 126 Jeff George	.15	.07	.02
☐ 127 Chris Miller	.10	.05	.01
☐ 128 Ricky Watters	.30	.14	.04
☐ 129 Jim Kelly	.30	.14	.04
☐ 130 Tony Bennett	.10	.05	.01
☐ 131 Terry Kirby	.15	.07	.02
☐ 132 Drew Bledsoe	1.50	.70	.19
☐ 133 Johnny Johnson	.10	.05	.01
☐ 134 Dan Wilkinson	.15	.07	.02
☐ 135 Leroy Hoard	.10	.05	.01
☐ 136 Darryll Lewis	.10	.05	.01
☐ 137 Barry Foster	.15	.07	.02
☐ 138 Shane Dronett	.10	.05	.01
☐ 139 Marcus Allen	.30	.14	.04
☐ 140 Harvey Williams	.10	.05	.01
☐ 141 Tony Martin	.15	.07	.02
☐ 142 Rod Stephens	.10	.05	.01
☐ 143 Eric Swann	.15	.07	.02
☐ 144 Daryl Johnston	.15	.07	.02
☐ 145 Dave Meggett	.10	.05	.01
☐ 146 Charlie Garner	.15	.07	.02
☐ 147 Ken Harvey	.10	.05	.01
☐ 148 Warren Moon	.15	.07	.02
☐ 149 Steve Walsh	.10	.05	.01
☐ 150 Pat Swilling	.10	.05	.01
☐ 151 Terrell Buckley	.10	.05	.01
☐ 152 Courtney Hawkins	.10	.05	.01
☐ 153 Willie Roaf	.10	.05	.01
☐ 154 Chris Doleman	.10	.05	.01
☐ 155 Jerome Bettis	.50	.23	.06
☐ 156 Dana Stubblefield	.30	.14	.04
☐ 157 Cornelius Bennett	.15	.07	.02
☐ 158 Quentin Coryatt	.15	.07	.02
☐ 159 Bryan Cox	.10	.05	.01
☐ 160 Marion Butts	.10	.05	.01
☐ 161 Aaron Glenn	.10	.05	.01
☐ 162 Louis Oliver	.10	.05	.01
☐ 163 Eric Turner	.10	.05	.01
☐ 164 Cris Dishman	.10	.05	.01
☐ 165 John L. Williams	.10	.05	.01
☐ 166 Simon Fletcher	.10	.05	.01
☐ 167 Neil Smith	.15	.07	.02
☐ 168 Chester McGlockton	.15	.07	.02
☐ 169 Natrone Means	.30	.14	.04
☐ 170 Sam Adams	.10	.05	.01
☐ 171 Clyde Simmons	.10	.05	.01
☐ 172 Jay Novacek	.15	.07	.02
☐ 173 Keith Hamilton	.10	.05	.01
☐ 174 William Fuller	.10	.05	.01
☐ 175 Tom Carter	.10	.05	.01
☐ 176 John Randle	.10	.05	.01
☐ 177 Lewis Tillman	.10	.05	.01
☐ 178 Mel Gray	.10	.05	.01
☐ 179 George Teague	.10	.05	.01
☐ 180 Hardy Nickerson	.10	.05	.01
☐ 181 Mario Bates	.30	.14	.04
☐ 182 D.J. Johnson	.10	.05	.01
☐ 183 Sean Gilbert	.15	.07	.02
☐ 184 Bryant Young	.15	.07	.02
☐ 185 Jeff Burris	.10	.05	.01
☐ 186 Floyd Turner	.10	.05	.01
☐ 187 Troy Vincent	.10	.05	.01
☐ 188 Willie McGinest	.15	.07	.02
☐ 189 James Hasty	.10	.05	.01
☐ 190 Jeff Blake	2.00	.90	.25
☐ 191 Stevon Moore	.10	.05	.01
☐ 192 Ernest Givins	.10	.05	.01
☐ 193 Byron Bam Morris	.15	.07	.02
☐ 194 Ray Crockett	.10	.05	.01
☐ 195 Dale Carter	.15	.07	.02
☐ 196 Terry McDaniel	.10	.05	.01
☐ 197 Leslie O'Neal	.15	.07	.02
☐ 198 Cortez Kennedy	.15	.07	.02
☐ 199 Seth Joyner	.10	.05	.01
☐ 200 Emmitt Smith	3.00	1.35	.35
☐ 201 Thomas Lewis	.15	.07	.02
☐ 202 Andy Harmon	.10	.05	.01
☐ 203 Ricky Ervins	.10	.05	.01
☐ 204 Fuad Reveiz	.10	.05	.01
☐ 205 John Thierry	.10	.05	.01
☐ 206 Bennie Blades	.10	.05	.01
☐ 207 LeShon Johnson	.15	.07	.02
☐ 208 Charles Wilson	.10	.05	.01
☐ 209 Joe Johnson	.10	.05	.01
☐ 210 Chuck Smith	.10	.05	.01
☐ 211 Roman Phifer	.10	.05	.01
☐ 212 Ken Norton Jr.	.15	.07	.02
☐ 213 Bucky Brooks	.10	.05	.01
☐ 214 Ray Buchanan	.10	.05	.01
☐ 215 Tim Bowens	.10	.05	.01
☐ 216 Vincent Brown	.10	.05	.01
☐ 217 Marcus Turner	.10	.05	.01
☐ 218 Derrick Fenner	.10	.05	.01
☐ 219 Antonio Langham	.10	.05	.01
☐ 220 Cody Carlson	.10	.05	.01
☐ 221 Greg Lloyd	.15	.07	.02
☐ 222 Steve Atwater	.10	.05	.01
☐ 223 Donnell Bennett	.10	.05	.01
☐ 224 Rocket Ismail	.15	.07	.02
☐ 225 John Carney	.10	.05	.01
☐ 226 Eugene Robinson	.10	.05	.01
☐ 227 Aeneas Williams	.10	.05	.01
☐ 228 Darrin Smith	.10	.05	.01
☐ 229 Phillippi Sparks	.10	.05	.01
☐ 230 Eric Allen	.10	.05	.01
☐ 231 Brian Mitchell	.10	.05	.01
☐ 232 David Palmer	.15	.07	.02
☐ 233 Mark Carrier DB	.10	.05	.01
☐ 234 Dave Krieg	.10	.05	.01
☐ 235 Robert Brooks	.30	.14	.04
☐ 236 Eric Curry	.10	.05	.01
☐ 237 Wayne Martin	.10	.05	.01
☐ 238 Craig Heyward	.15	.07	.02
☐ 239 Isaac Bruce	.75	.35	.09
☐ 240 Deion Sanders	1.00	.45	.12
☐ 241 Steve Tasker	.15	.07	.02
☐ 242 Jim Harbaugh	.15	.07	.02
☐ 243 Aubrey Beavers	.10	.05	.01
☐ 244 Chris Slade	.15	.07	.02
☐ 245 Mo Lewis	.10	.05	.01
☐ 246 Alfred Williams	.10	.05	.01
☐ 247 Michael Dean Perry	.10	.05	.01
☐ 248 Marcus Robertson	.10	.05	.01
☐ 249 Kevin Greene	.15	.07	.02

☐ 250 Leonard Russell	.10	.05	.01
☐ 251 Greg Hill	.15	.07	.02
☐ 252 Rob Fredrickson	.10	.05	.01
☐ 253 Junior Seau	.30	.14	.04
☐ 254 Rick Tuten	.10	.05	.01
☐ 255 Garrison Hearst	.30	.14	.04
☐ 256 Russell Maryland	.10	.05	.01
☐ 257 Michael Brooks	.10	.05	.01
☐ 258 Bernard Williams	.10	.05	.01
☐ 259 Reggie Roby	.10	.05	.01
☐ 260 Dewayne Washington	.15	.07	.02
☐ 261 Raymont Harris	.10	.05	.01
☐ 262 Brett Perriman	.15	.07	.02
☐ 263 LeRoy Butler	.10	.05	.01
☐ 264 Santana Dotson	.10	.05	.01
☐ 265 Irv Smith	.10	.05	.01
☐ 266 Ron George	.10	.05	.01
☐ 267 Marquez Pope	.10	.05	.01
☐ 268 William Floyd	.30	.14	.04
☐ 269 Matt Darby	.10	.05	.01
☐ 270 Jeff Herrod	.10	.05	.01
☐ 271 Bernie Parmalee	.15	.07	.02
☐ 272 Leroy Thompson	.10	.05	.01
☐ 273 Ronnie Lott	.15	.07	.02
☐ 274 Steve Tovar	.10	.05	.01
☐ 275 Michael Jackson	.15	.07	.02
☐ 276 Al Smith	.10	.05	.01
☐ 277 Rod Woodson	.15	.07	.02
☐ 278 Glyn Milburn	.10	.05	.01
☐ 279 Kimble Anders	.15	.07	.02
☐ 280 Anthony Smith	.10	.05	.01
☐ 281 Andre Coleman	.10	.05	.01
☐ 282 Terry Wooden	.10	.05	.01
☐ 283 Mickey Washington	.10	.05	.01
☐ 284 Steve Beuerlein	.10	.05	.01
☐ 285 Mark Brunell	1.50	.70	.19
☐ 286 Keith Goganious	.10	.05	.01
☐ 287 Desmond Howard	.15	.07	.02
☐ 288 Darren Carrington	.10	.05	.01
☐ 289 Derek Brown TE	.10	.05	.01
☐ 290 Reggie Cobb	.10	.05	.01
☐ 291 Jeff Lageman	.10	.05	.01
☐ 292 Lamar Lathon	.10	.05	.01
☐ 293 Sam Mills	.15	.07	.02
☐ 294 Carlton Bailey	.10	.05	.01
☐ 295 Mark Carrier WR	.15	.07	.02
☐ 296 Willie Green	.15	.07	.02
☐ 297 Frank Reich	.10	.05	.01
☐ 298 Don Beebe	.10	.05	.01
☐ 299 Tim McKyer	.10	.05	.01
☐ 300 Pete Metzelaars	.10	.05	.01
☐ P1 Joe Montana Promo base brand card Numbered 19	2.00	.90	.25
☐ P2 Joe Montana Promo Predictor card Numbered 19	2.50	1.10	.30
☐ P3 Marshall Faulk Promo Pro Bowl hologram card Numbered PB95	2.00	.90	.25

1995 Upper Deck Electric Gold

This 300 card parallel set was randomly inserted into packs at a rate of one per 35 hobby or retail packs. The cards are differentiated by having a gold foil "Electric" logo on the card front.

	MINT	NRMT	EXC
COMPLETE SET (300)	800.00	350.00	100.00
COMMON CARD (1-300)	1.50	.70	.19
*GOLD STARS: 15X TO 30X BASIC CARDS			
*YOUNG STARS: 10X TO 20X BASIC CARDS			
*RCs: 8X TO 16X BASIC CARDS			

1995 Upper Deck Electric Silver

This 300 card parallel set was inserted into 1995 Upper Deck hobby and retail packs at a rate of one per pack. A special retail pack was also produced with two silvers per pack. The cards are differentiated by having a silver foil "Electric" logo on the card front.

	MINT	NRMT	EXC
COMPLETE SET (300)	125.00	55.00	15.50
COMMON CARD (1-300)	.20	.09	.03
*STARS: 2X TO 4X BASIC CARDS			
*YOUNG STARS: 1.5X TO 3X BASIC CARDS			
*RCs: 1.25X TO 2.5X BASIC CARDS			

1995 Upper Deck Joe Montana Trilogy

This 23 card standard size set was issued in three parts: part one (MT1-MT8) was in 1995 Collector's Choice, part two (MT9-MT16) was in 1995 Upper Deck and part three (MT17-MT21) was in 1995 SP. The cards come one in 12 packs in Collector's Choice and Upper Deck and one in 29 SP packs. The fronts have a full-color photo with a small head shot in the left corner. The bottoms have information on a major point in his career and a title on a gold-foil background. The backs have a small-color photo with more information about him on the bottom.

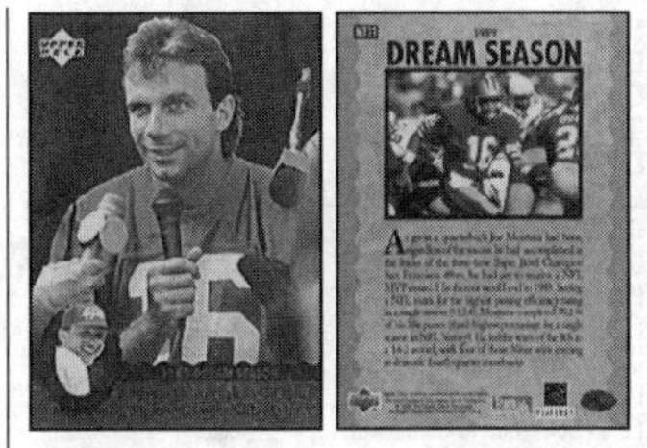

	MINT	NRMT	EXC
COMPLETE SET (23)	70.00	32.00	8.75
COMPLETE CC SERIES 1 (9)	20.00	9.00	2.50
COMPLETE UD SERIES 2 (9)	30.00	13.50	3.70
COMPLETE SP SERIES 3 (5)	20.00	9.00	2.50
COMMON CC CARD (MT1-MT8)	3.00	1.35	.35
COMMON UD CARD (MT9-MT16)	4.00	1.80	.50
COMMON SP CARD (MT17-MT20)	5.00	2.20	.60
☐ MT1 Joe Montana 1977-NCAA Champs	3.00	1.35	.35
☐ MT2 Joe Montana 1978-Cotton Bowl	3.00	1.35	.35
☐ MT3 Joe Montana The 1978 NFL Draft	3.00	1.35	.35
☐ MT4 Joe Montana The Catch	3.00	1.35	.35
☐ MT5 Joe Montana Super Bowl XVI	3.00	1.35	.35
☐ MT6 Joe Montana Super Bowl XVI MVP	3.00	1.35	.35
☐ MT7 Joe Montana Super Bowl XIX	3.00	1.35	.35
☐ MT8 Joe Montana Super Bowl XIX MVP	3.00	1.35	.35
☐ MT9 Joe Montana The Drive	4.00	1.80	.50
☐ MT10 Joe Montana Super Bowl XXIII	4.00	1.80	.50
☐ MT11 Joe Montana 1989-Dream Season	4.00	1.80	.50
☐ MT12 Joe Montana NFL MVP Back-To-Back	4.00	1.80	.50
☐ MT13 Joe Montana Super Bowl XXIV	4.00	1.80	.50
☐ MT14 Joe Montana Super Bowl XXIV MVP	4.00	1.80	.50
☐ MT15 Joe Montana Back-To-Back Super Bowls	4.00	1.80	.50
☐ MT16 Joe Montana The Comeback	4.00	1.80	.50
☐ MT17 Joe Montana	5.00	2.20	.60
☐ MT18 Joe Montana	5.00	2.20	.60
☐ MT19 Joe Montana	5.00	2.20	.60
☐ MT20 Joe Montana	5.00	2.20	.60
☐ CCH Collector's Choice Header	3.00	1.35	.35
☐ SPH SP Header	4.00	1.80	.50
☐ UDH Upper Deck Header	5.00	2.20	.60

1995 Upper Deck Predictor Award Winners

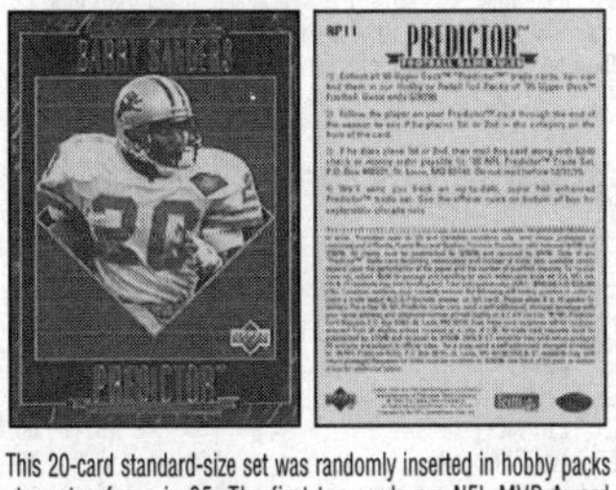

This 20-card standard-size set was randomly inserted in hobby packs at a rate of one in 35. The first ten cards are NFL MVP Award predictors and the second ten are Rookie-of-the-Year Award predictors. The cardfronts have a color action photo with the player's name above and the set title and award category below the picture in copper foil. The backs contain the contest rules. If the player featured won, in the category included on the card, the collector could exchange his card (plus $3 postage) for a special foil enhanced parallel redemption prize set. Each card is numbered with an "HP" for hobby predictor. The exchange cards expired 3/30/96.

	MINT	NRMT	EXC
COMPLETE SET (20)	70.00	32.00	8.75
COMMON CARD (HP1-HP20)	2.00	.90	.25
☐ HP1 Dan Marino	10.00	4.50	1.25
☐ HP2 Steve Young	5.00	2.20	.60
☐ HP3 Drew Bledsoe	6.00	2.70	.75
☐ HP4 Troy Aikman	6.00	2.70	.75
☐ HP5 Barry Sanders	6.00	2.70	.75
☐ HP6 Emmitt Smith	10.00	4.50	1.25
☐ HP7 Jerry Rice W2	10.00	4.50	1.25
☐ HP8 Steve McNair	4.00	1.80	.50
☐ HP9 Natrone Means	3.00	1.35	.35
☐ HP10 The Longshot W1	2.00	.90	.25
☐ HP11 Ki-Jana Carter	3.00	1.35	.35
☐ HP12 Steve McNair	8.00	3.60	1.00
☐ HP13 Michael Westbrook	3.00	1.35	.35
☐ HP14 Kerry Collins	8.00	3.60	1.00
☐ HP15 Joey Galloway	5.00	2.20	.60
☐ HP16 Kyle Brady	2.00	.90	.25
☐ HP17 Napoleon Kaufman	2.00	.90	.25
☐ HP18 Tyrone Wheatley	2.00	.90	.25
☐ HP19 Rashaan Salaam	4.00	1.80	.50
☐ HP20 The Longshot W1	2.00	.90	.25

1995 Upper Deck Predictor League Leaders

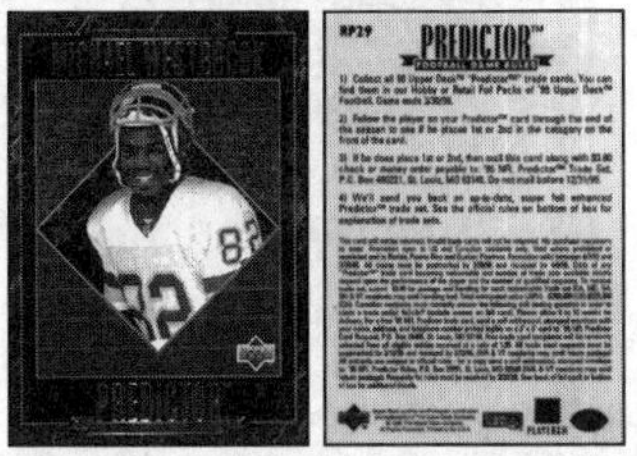

This 30-card standard-size set was randomly inserted in retail packs at a rate of one in 30. The first ten cards are passing efficiency predictors, the second ten rushing yardage and the final ten receiving yardage predictors. The fronts contain a color action photo with the player's name above and the set title and category below the photo. Cardbacks contained the game rules. If the featured player finished first or second in the category included on the card, the collector could exchange his card (plus $3 postage) for a foil enhanced parallel prize set. The exchange cards expired 3/30/96.

	MINT	NRMT	EXC
COMPLETE SET (30)	100.00	45.00	12.50
COMMON CARD (RP1-RP30)	2.00	.90	.25
☐ RP1 Dan Marino	10.00	4.50	1.25
☐ RP2 Steve Young	5.00	2.20	.60
☐ RP3 Drew Bledsoe	6.00	2.70	.75
☐ RP4 Troy Aikman	6.00	2.70	.75
☐ RP5 John Elway	5.00	2.20	.60
☐ RP6 Brett Favre W2	15.00	6.75	1.85
☐ RP7 Stan Humphries	2.00	.90	.25
☐ RP8 Jeff George	3.00	1.35	.35
☐ RP9 Kerry Collins	6.00	2.70	.75
☐ RP10 The Longshot W1	2.00	.90	.25
☐ RP11 Barry Sanders W2	10.00	4.50	1.25
☐ RP12 Chris Warren	2.00	.90	.25
☐ RP13 Emmitt Smith W1	15.00	6.75	1.85
☐ RP14 Natrone Means	3.00	1.35	.35
☐ RP15 Rodney Hampton	2.00	.90	.25
☐ RP16 Marshall Faulk	4.00	1.80	.50
☐ RP17 Errict Rhett	3.00	1.35	.35
☐ RP18 Napoleon Kaufman	2.00	.90	.25
☐ RP19 Ki-Jana Carter	4.00	1.80	.50
☐ RP20 The Longshot	2.00	.90	.25
☐ RP21 Jerry Rice W1	10.00	4.50	1.25
☐ RP22 Ben Coates	2.00	.90	.25
☐ RP23 Cris Carter	3.00	1.35	.35
☐ RP24 Andre Reed	2.00	.90	.25
☐ RP25 Andre Rison	2.00	.90	.25
☐ RP26 Tim Brown	3.00	1.35	.35
☐ RP27 Michael Irvin	4.00	1.80	.50
☐ RP28 Irving Fryar	2.00	.90	.25
☐ RP29 Michael Westbrook	4.00	1.80	.50
☐ RP30 The Longshot W2	2.00	.90	.25

1995 Upper Deck Pro Bowl

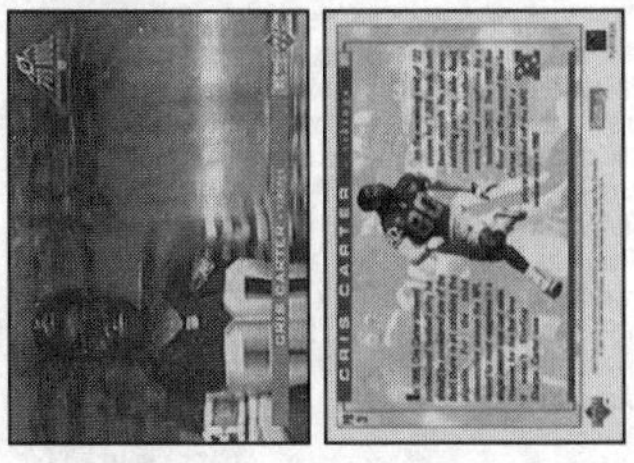

This 25 card standard-size set was randomly inserted in packs at a rate of one in 25. The set commemorates the players who went to the 1995 Pro Bowl. The fronts are laid out horizontally with a 3-D holoview image of the player and palm trees behind him. The backs have a color-action player photo in his Pro Bowl uniform with information on his 1994 season that got him to Hawaii. Card backs contain a "PB" prefix.

	MINT	NRMT	EXC
COMPLETE SET (25)	150.00	70.00	19.00
COMMON CARD (PB1-PB25)	3.00	1.35	.35
☐ PB1 Barry Sanders	15.00	6.75	1.85
☐ PB2 Brent Jones	3.00	1.35	.35
☐ PB3 Cris Carter	5.00	2.20	.60
☐ PB4 Emmitt Smith	30.00	13.50	3.70
☐ PB5 Jay Novacek	3.00	1.35	.35
☐ PB6 Jerome Bettis			
☐ PB7 Jerry Rice	15.00	6.75	1.85
☐ PB8 Michael Irvin			
☐ PB9 Ricky Watters	5.00	2.20	.60
☐ PB10 Steve Young	12.00	5.50	1.50
☐ PB11 Troy Aikman	15.00	6.75	1.85
☐ PB12 Warren Moon	5.00	2.20	.60
☐ PB13 Terance Mathis	3.00	1.35	.35
☐ PB14 Ben Coates	3.00	1.35	.35
☐ PB15 Chris Warren	5.00	2.20	.60
☐ PB16 Dan Marino	30.00	13.50	3.70
☐ PB17 Drew Bledsoe	15.00	6.75	1.85
☐ PB18 Irving Fryar	3.00	1.35	.35
☐ PB19 Jeff Hostetler	3.00	1.35	.35
☐ PB20 John Elway	12.00	5.50	1.50
☐ PB21 Leroy Hoard	3.00	1.35	.35
☐ PB22 Marshall Faulk	8.00	3.60	1.00
☐ PB23 Natrone Means	5.00	2.20	.60
☐ PB24 Tim Brown	5.00	2.20	.60
☐ PB25 Checklist	5.00	2.20	.60

1995 Upper Deck Special Edition

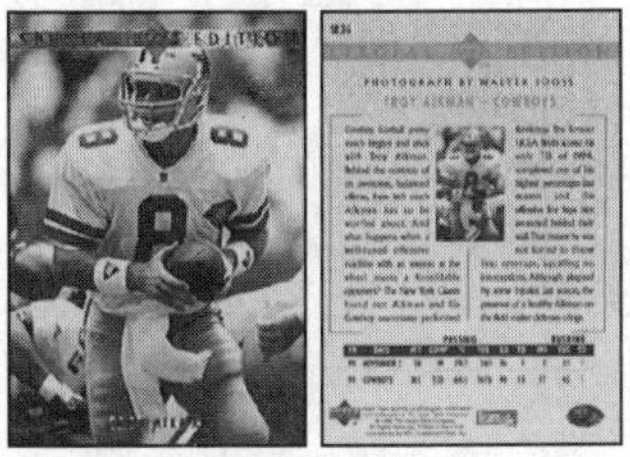

This 90-card standard-size set was inserted in each hobby pack. The fronts have a full-bleed color photo. The words "Special Edition" with Upper Deck between them are in at the top of the card with the player's name at the bottom, all of which are in silver-foil. The backs have a small version of the picture from the front with the player's name above it and "Special Edition" above that in silver. Information and statistics are on the bottom of the card. A gold version of the set also exists and was inserted into packs at a rate of one in 35.

	MINT	NRMT	EXC
COMPLETE SET (90)	40.00	18.00	5.00
COMMON CARD (SE1-SE90)	.25	.11	.03
COMPLETE GOLD SE (90)	600.00	275.00	75.00
COMMON GOLD SPEC.EDIT.	1.50	.70	.19
*GOLD SE STARS: 3X to 6X			
*GOLD SE YOUNG STARS: 2.5X to 5X			
☐ SE1 Terry Kirby	.25	.11	.03
☐ SE2 Marcus Allen	1.00	.45	.12
☐ SE3 Bernie Parmalee	.25	.11	.03
☐ SE4 Vernon Turner	.25	.11	.03
☐ SE5 Dolphins Defense	.25	.11	.03
☐ SE6 Kevin Turner	.25	.11	.03
☐ SE7 Henry Thomas	.25	.11	.03
☐ SE8 Barry Sanders	2.50	1.10	.30
☐ SE9 Marshall Faulk	1.25	.55	.16
☐ SE10 Bill Bates	.25	.11	.03
☐ SE11 Stan Humphries	.50	.23	.06
☐ SE12 Barry Foster	.25	.11	.03
☐ SE13 Shannon Sharpe	.50	.23	.06
☐ SE14 Joe Montana	2.50	1.10	.30
☐ SE15 Bryan Cox	.25	.11	.03
☐ SE16 Dale Carter	.25	.11	.03
☐ SE17 Drew Bledsoe	2.50	1.10	.30
☐ SE18 Dan Marino	5.00	2.20	.60
☐ SE19 Ricky Watters	1.00	.45	.12
☐ SE20 Alvin Harper	.25	.11	.03
☐ SE21 Harris Barton	.25	.11	.03
☐ SE22 Dan Marino	5.00	2.20	.60
☐ SE23 Ronnie Harmon	.25	.11	.03
☐ SE24 Michael Irvin	1.00	.45	.12
☐ SE25 Emmitt Smith	5.00	2.20	.60
☐ SE26 Jeff Christy	.25	.11	.03
☐ SE27 Terry Allen	.50	.23	.06
☐ SE28 Randall Cunningham	.50	.23	.06
☐ SE29 Todd Steussie	.25	.11	.03
☐ SE30 Warren Moon	.50	.23	.06
☐ SE31 Robert Griffith	.25	.11	.03
☐ SE32 Tony Tolbert	.25	.11	.03
☐ SE33 William Fuller	.25	.11	.03
☐ SE34 Bernard Williams	.25	.11	.03
☐ SE35 Charlie Garner	.25	.11	.03
☐ SE36 Troy Aikman	2.50	1.10	.30
☐ SE37 Alvin Harper	.25	.11	.03
☐ SE38 Kenneth Gant	.25	.11	.03
☐ SE39 Daryl Johnston	.25	.11	.03
☐ SE40 Ben Coates	.50	.23	.06
☐ SE41 Rickey Jackson	.25	.11	.03
☐ SE42 O.J. McDuffie	.50	.23	.06
☐ SE43 Marion Butts	.25	.11	.03
☐ SE44 The Snap	.25	.11	.03
☐ SE45 Kimble Anders	.25	.11	.03
☐ SE46 Chiefs Defense	.25	.11	.03
☐ SE47 Richmond Webb	.25	.11	.03
☐ SE48 Carlos Jenkins	.25	.11	.03

☐ SE49 James Harris DE	.25	.11	.03
☐ SE50 Dexter Carter	.25	.11	.03
☐ SE51 Qadry Ismail	.50	.23	.06
☐ SE52 Jeff Herrod	.25	.11	.03
☐ SE53 Sean Jones	.25	.11	.03
☐ SE54 Keith Sims	.25	.11	.03
☐ SE55 William Floyd	.50	.23	.06
☐ SE56 Don Majkowski	.25	.11	.03
☐ SE57 Chargers Defense	.25	.11	.03
☐ SE58 Byron Evans	.25	.11	.03
☐ SE59 Chad Hennings	.25	.11	.03
☐ SE60 Eric Allen	.25	.11	.03
☐ SE61 Curtis Martin	5.00	2.20	.60
☐ SE62 Napoleon Kaufman	.50	.23	.06
☐ SE63 Kevin Carter	.50	.23	.06
☐ SE64 Luther Elliss	.25	.11	.03
☐ SE65 Frank Sanders	.50	.23	.06
☐ SE66 Rob Johnson	.25	.11	.03
☐ SE67 Christian Fauria	.25	.11	.03
☐ SE68 Kyle Brady	.25	.11	.03
☐ SE69 Ray Zellars	.25	.11	.03
☐ SE70 James A.Stewart	.25	.11	.03
☐ SE71 Ty Law	.25	.11	.03
☐ SE72 Rodney Thomas	.50	.23	.06
☐ SE73 Jimmy Oliver	.25	.11	.03
☐ SE74 James O.Stewart	.50	.23	.06
☐ SE75 Dave Barr	.25	.11	.03
☐ SE76 Kordell Stewart	4.00	1.80	.50
☐ SE77 Michael Westbrook	2.00	.90	.25
☐ SE78 Bobby Taylor	.25	.11	.03
☐ SE79 Mark Fields	.25	.11	.03
☐ SE80 Kerry Collins	4.00	1.80	.50
☐ SE81 Natrone Means	.50	.23	.06
☐ SE82 Mark Seay	.25	.11	.03
☐ SE83 Deion Sanders	1.50	.70	.19
☐ SE84 Dana Stubblefield	.25	.11	.03
☐ SE85 49ers Defense	.25	.11	.03
☐ SE86 Alfred Pupunu	.25	.11	.03
☐ SE87 Tim Harris	.25	.11	.03
☐ SE88 Jerry Rice	2.50	1.10	.30
☐ SE89 Steve Young	2.00	.90	.25
☐ SE90 Steve Young Jerry Rice	2.00	.90	.25

1995 Upper Deck Authenticated Marino

These oversized (3 1/2" by 5") cards were issued only through Upper Deck Authenticated. UDA, through their contract with Dan Marino, were able to issue a group of special cards to honor his record breaking season in 1995.

	MINT	NRMT	EXC
COMPLETE SET (3)	60.00	27.00	7.50
COMMON CARD (1-3)	15.00	6.75	1.85
☐ 1 Dan Marino 343 Gold Foil 5,000 Cards Printed Honors Career Touchdown Record	30.00	13.50	3.70
☐ 2 Dan Marino Most 3,000 Yard Seasons 10,000 Cards Printed	15.00	6.75	1.85
☐ 3 Dan Marino Total Passing Yards Numbered out of 5,000	15.00	6.75	1.85

1995 Upper Deck/GTE Phone Cards AFC

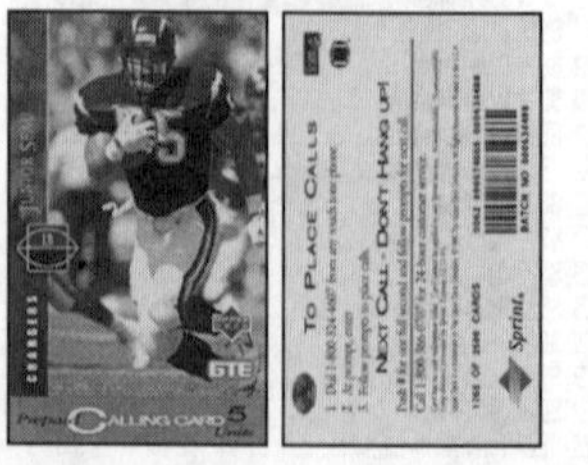

Upper Deck and GTE joined together to produce these 15 prepaid phone cards. Measuring approximately 3 3/8" by 2 1/8", the cards have rounded corners and carry 5 units of U.S. long distance calling. The fronts feature color action player photos of AFC football players, with the player's name, position and team in a team color-coded bar alongside the left. A red bar below the photo carries the words "Prepaid Calling Card, 5 Units". The backs have instructions on how to use the calling cards. The cards are unnumbered and checklisted below in alphabetical order. Just 2,500 of each card were produced, and they are individually numbered on the back. A special card with more detailed instructions was included with each set.

	MINT	NRMT	EXC
COMPLETE SET (15)	75.00	34.00	9.50
COMMON CARD (1-15)	3.00	1.35	.35
☐ 1 Marcus Allen	4.00	1.80	.50
☐ 2 Drew Bledsoe	8.00	3.60	1.00
☐ 3 Gary Brown	3.00	1.35	.35
☐ 4 Tim Brown	4.00	1.80	.50
☐ 5 John Elway	7.00	3.10	.85
☐ 6 Marshall Faulk	10.00	4.50	1.25
☐ 7 Barry Foster	3.00	1.35	.35
☐ 8 Jim Kelly	4.00	1.80	.50
☐ 9 Ronnie Lott	3.00	1.35	.35
☐ 10 Dan Marino	15.00	6.75	1.85
☐ 11 Rick Mirer	4.00	1.80	.50
☐ 12 Carl Pickens	4.00	1.80	.50
☐ 13 Junior Seau	4.00	1.80	.50
☐ 14 Vinny Testaverde	3.00	1.35	.35
☐ 15 Title Card	3.00	1.35	.35

1995 Upper Deck/GTE Phone Cards NFC

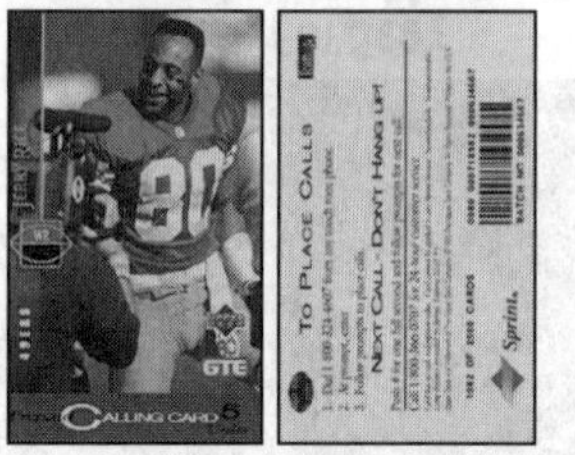

Upper Deck and GTE joined together to produce these 15 prepaid phone cards. Measuring approximately 3 3/8" by 2 1/8", the cards have rounded corners and carry five units of U.S. long distance calling. The fronts feature color action player photos of NFC football players, with the player's name, position and team in a team color-coded bar alongside the left. A blue bar below the photo carries the words "Prepaid Calling Card, 5 Units". The backs have instructions on how to use the calling cards. They are unnumbered and checklisted below in alphabetical order. Only 2,500 of each card were produced, and they are individually numbered on the back. A special card with more detailed instructions was included with each set.

	MINT	NRMT	EXC
COMPLETE SET (15)	60.00	27.00	7.50
COMMON CARD (1-15)	3.00	1.35	.35
☐ 1 Jerome Bettis	4.00	1.80	.50
☐ 2 Gary Clark	3.00	1.35	.35
☐ 3 Curtis Conway	4.00	1.80	.50
☐ 4 Randall Cunningham	3.00	1.35	.35
☐ 5 Rodney Hampton	3.00	1.35	.35
☐ 6 Michael Haynes	3.00	1.35	.35
☐ 7 Michael Irvin	4.00	1.80	.50
☐ 8 Warren Moon	3.00	1.35	.35
☐ 9 Hardy Nickerson	3.00	1.35	.35
☐ 10 Jerry Rice	8.00	3.60	1.00
☐ 11 Andre Rison	3.00	1.35	.35
☐ 12 Barry Sanders	8.00	3.60	1.00
☐ 13 Sterling Sharpe	4.00	1.80	.50
☐ 14 Heath Shuler	4.00	1.80	.50
☐ 15 Title Card	4.00	1.80	.50

1995 Upper Deck Joe Montana Box Set

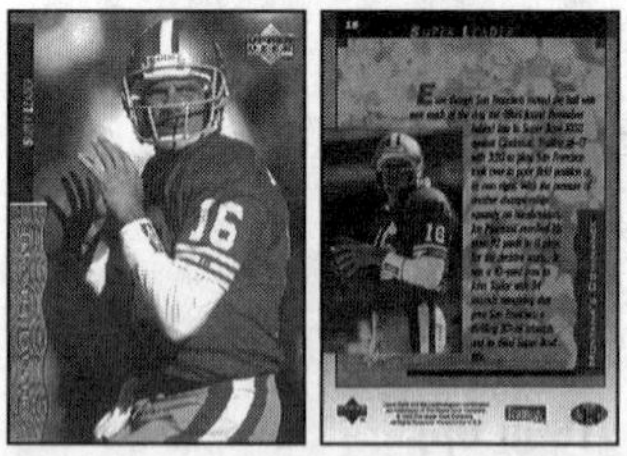

This 45-card, boxed set summarizes the career of Joe Montana from the Pennsylvania Pee-Wee Leagues through his NFL career. On the fronts, the full-bleed photos are edged by a gold foil design and a black-and-red bar. The backs feature a second color photo and commentary summarizing various facets of his career. The set is subdivided as follows: The Early Years (1-5), Montana's Dominance (6-25), The New Chief (26-30), Joe's Numbers (31-40), and Teammates (41-45). The set includes an oversized (8 1/8" by 3 3/8") card commemorating the quarterback duel between Montana and Dan Marino in Super Bowl XIX on January 20, 1985. Though not numbered as part of the set, this oversized card carries a serial number out of 38,000.

	MINT	NRMT	EXC
COMPLETE SET (45)	20.00	9.00	2.50
COMMON CARD (1-45)	.60	.25	.07
☐ 1 A Star Is Born	.60	.25	.07
☐ 2 Quarterback State	.60	.25	.07
☐ 3 Making Of A Hero	.60	.25	.07
☐ 4 National Champion	.60	.25	.07
☐ 5 Never-Say-Die	.60	.25	.07
☐ 6 The Protege	.60	.25	.07
☐ 7 New Orleans-The First Victim	.60	.25	.07
☐ 8 The Catch	.60	.25	.07
☐ 9 Super Bowl Fever	.60	.25	.07
☐ 10 Super Bowl XVI	.60	.25	.07
☐ 11 Emergence Of A Record-Breaker	.60	.25	.07
☐ 12 Career-Year	.60	.25	.07
☐ 13 Heroic Comeback	.60	.25	.07
☐ 14 Super Bowl XIX	.60	.25	.07
☐ 15 Repeat Performance	.60	.25	.07
☐ 16 First Passing Crown	.60	.25	.07
☐ 17 Super Bowl XXIII	.60	.25	.07
☐ 18 Super Leader	.60	.25	.07
☐ 19 Best Of The Best	.60	.25	.07
☐ 20 Super Bowl XXIV	.60	.25	.07
☐ 21 Four-Time Champs	.60	.25	.07
☐ 22 Team Of The 80's	.60	.25	.07
☐ 23 Back-To-Back MVP's	.60	.25	.07
☐ 24 Down, But Far From Out	.60	.25	.07
☐ 25 Farewell Performance	.60	.25	.07
☐ 26 The Trade	.60	.25	.07
☐ 27 First K.C. Comeback	.60	.25	.07
☐ 28 Playoff Magic	.60	.25	.07
☐ 29 Dueling Quarterbacks	.60	.25	.07
☐ 30 Another Milestone Falls	.60	.25	.07
☐ 31 39 300-Yard Games	.60	.25	.07
☐ 32 273 Touchdowns	.60	.25	.07
☐ 33 112.4 Pass Efficiency Rating	.60	.25	.07
☐ 34 92.3 Pass Efficiency Rating	.60	.25	.07
☐ 35 117 Wins	.60	.25	.07
☐ 36 31 Comeback Victories	.60	.25	.07
☐ 37 5,391 Attempts	.60	.25	.07
☐ 38 3 Super Bowl MVP's	.60	.25	.07
☐ 39 3,409 Completions	.60	.25	.07
☐ 40 40,551 Yards	.60	.25	.07
☐ 41 Bill Walsh	.60	.25	.07
☐ 42 Russ Francis	.60	.25	.07
☐ 43 Roger Craig	.60	.25	.07
☐ 44 Jerry Rice	.60	.25	.07
☐ 45 Dwight Clark	.60	.25	.07
☐ NNO Super Bowl XIX Quarterback Duel numbered of 38,000 Joe Montana Dan Marino	5.00	2.20	.60
☐ JM16 Joe Montana Promo	2.00	.90	.25

1996 Upper Deck

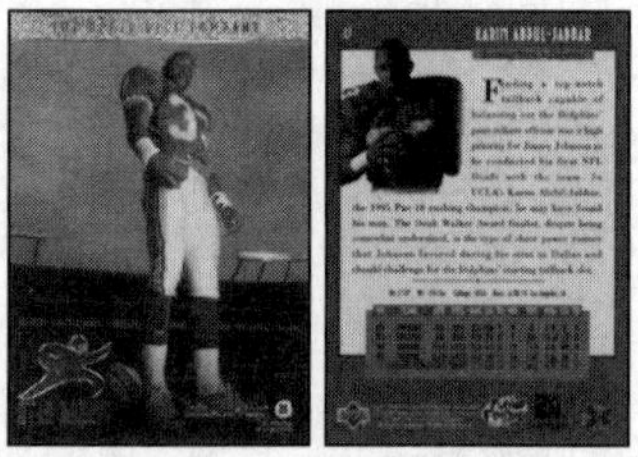

The 1996 Upper Deck set was issued in one series totalling 300-cards. The 12-card packs originally retailed for $2.99 each. The set contains a 33-card Star Rookies subset and numerous insert sets. Also included as an insert, in both Collector's Choice and Upper Deck packs (1:4 packs), was a game piece for the Meet the Stars promotion. Each game piece featured multiple choice trivia questions about football. A collector could scratch of the box next to the answer that they felt best matched the question to determine if they won. Instant win game pieces were also inserted one in 72 packs. Winning game pieces could be sent to Upper Deck for prize drawings. The Grand Prize was a chance to meet Dan Marino. Prizes for 2nd through 4th were for Upper Deck Authenticated shopping sprees. The 5th prize was two special Dan Marino Meet the Stars cards. The blankbacked die cut cards measure roughly 5" X 7"and are entitled Dynamic Debut and Magic Memories. These two cards are priced at the bottom of the base set below.

	MINT	NRMT	EXC
COMPLETE SET (300)	40.00	18.00	5.00
COMMON CARD (1-300)	.08	.04	.01
☐ 1 Keyshawn Johnson	1.50	.70	.19
☐ 2 Kevin Hardy	.15	.07	.02
☐ 3 Simeon Rice	.30	.14	.04
☐ 4 Jonathan Ogden	.08	.04	.01
☐ 5 Cedric Jones	.15	.07	.02
☐ 6 Lawrence Phillips	.50	.23	.06
☐ 7 Tim Biakabutuka	1.00	.45	.12
☐ 8 Terry Glenn	3.00	1.35	.35
☐ 9 Rickey Dudley	.30	.14	.04
☐ 10 Willie Anderson	.08	.04	.01
☐ 11 Alex Molden	.08	.04	.01
☐ 12 Regan Upshaw	.08	.04	.01
☐ 13 Walt Harris	.08	.04	.01
☐ 14 Eddie George	4.00	1.80	.50
☐ 15 John Mobley	.08	.04	.01
☐ 16 Duane Clemons	.08	.04	.01
☐ 17 Eddie Kennison	1.50	.70	.19
☐ 18 Marvin Harrison	1.50	.70	.19
☐ 19 Daryl Gardener	.15	.07	.02
☐ 20 Leeland McElroy	.30	.14	.04
☐ 21 Eric Moulds	1.00	.45	.12
☐ 22 Alex Van Dyke	.15	.07	.02
☐ 23 Mike Alstott	.50	.23	.06
☐ 24 Jeff Lewis	.15	.07	.02
☐ 25 Bobby Engram	1.00	.45	.12
☐ 26 Derrick Mayes	1.00	.45	.12
☐ 27 Karim Abdul-Jabbar	2.50	1.10	.30
☐ 28 Bobby Hoying	.30	.14	.04
☐ 29 Stepfret Williams	.08	.04	.01
☐ 30 Chris Darkins	.15	.07	.02
☐ 31 Stephen Davis	.30	.14	.04
☐ 32 Danny Kanell	.30	.14	.04
☐ 33 Tony Brackens	.15	.07	.02
☐ 34 Leslie O'Neal	.08	.04	.01
☐ 35 Chris Doleman	.08	.04	.01
☐ 36 Larry Brown	.08	.04	.01
☐ 37 Ronnie Harmon	.08	.04	.01
☐ 38 Chris Spielman	.15	.07	.02
☐ 39 John Jurkovic	.08	.04	.01
☐ 40 Shawn Jefferson	.08	.04	.01
☐ 41 William Floyd	.15	.07	.02
☐ 42 Eric Davis	.08	.04	.01
☐ 43 Willie Clay	.08	.04	.01
☐ 44 Marco Coleman	.08	.04	.01
☐ 45 Lorenzo White	.08	.04	.01
☐ 46 Neil O'Donnell	.15	.07	.02
☐ 47 Natrone Means	.30	.14	.04
☐ 48 Cornelius Bennett	.15	.07	.02
☐ 49 Steve Walsh	.08	.04	.01
☐ 50 Jerome Bettis	.30	.14	.04
☐ 51 Boomer Esiason	.15	.07	.02
☐ 52 Glyn Milburn	.08	.04	.01
☐ 53 Kevin Greene	.15	.07	.02
☐ 54 Seth Joyner	.08	.04	.01
☐ 55 Jeff Graham	.08	.04	.01
☐ 56 Darren Woodson	.15	.07	.02
☐ 57 Dale Carter	.08	.04	.01
☐ 58 Lorenzo Lynch	.08	.04	.01
☐ 59 Tim Brown	.15	.07	.02
☐ 60 Jerry Rice	1.25	.55	.16
☐ 61 Garrison Hearst	.15	.07	.02
☐ 62 Eric Metcalf	.15	.07	.02
☐ 63 Leroy Hoard	.08	.04	.01
☐ 64 Thurman Thomas	.30	.14	.04
☐ 65 Sam Mills	.15	.07	.02
☐ 66 Curtis Conway	.30	.14	.04
☐ 67 Carl Pickens	.30	.14	.04
☐ 68 Deion Sanders	.75	.35	.09
☐ 69 Shannon Sharpe	.15	.07	.02
☐ 70 Herman Moore	.30	.14	.04
☐ 71 Robert Brooks	.30	.14	.04
☐ 72 Rodney Thomas	.08	.04	.01
☐ 73 Ken Dilger	.15	.07	.02
☐ 74 Mark Brunell	1.25	.55	.16
☐ 75 Marcus Allen	.30	.14	.04
☐ 76 Dan Marino	2.50	1.10	.30
☐ 77 Robert Smith	.15	.07	.02
☐ 78 Drew Bledsoe	1.25	.55	.16
☐ 79 Jim Everett	.08	.04	.01
☐ 80 Rodney Hampton	.15	.07	.02
☐ 81 Adrian Murrell	.15	.07	.02
☐ 82 Daryl Hobbs	.08	.04	.01
☐ 83 Ricky Watters	.15	.07	.02
☐ 84 Yancey Thigpen	.15	.07	.02
☐ 85 Roman Phifer	.08	.04	.01
☐ 86 Tony Martin	.15	.07	.02
☐ 87 Dana Stubblefield	.15	.07	.02
☐ 88 Joey Galloway	.60	.25	.07
☐ 89 Errict Rhett	.15	.07	.02
☐ 90 Terry Allen	.15	.07	.02
☐ 91 Aeneas Williams	.08	.04	.01
☐ 92 Craig Heyward	.08	.04	.01
☐ 93 Vinny Testaverde	.15	.07	.02
☐ 94 Bryce Paup	.15	.07	.02
☐ 95 Kerry Collins	1.50	.70	.19
☐ 96 Rashaan Salaam	.30	.14	.04
☐ 97 Dan Wilkinson	.08	.04	.01
☐ 98 Jay Novacek	.15	.07	.02
☐ 99 John Elway	1.00	.45	.12
☐ 100 Bennie Blades	.08	.04	.01
☐ 101 Edgar Bennett	.15	.07	.02
☐ 102 Darryll Lewis	.08	.04	.01
☐ 103 Marshall Faulk	.30	.14	.04
☐ 104 Bryan Schwartz	.08	.04	.01
☐ 105 Tamarick Vanover	.30	.14	.04
☐ 106 Terry Kirby	.15	.07	.02
☐ 107 John Randle	.08	.04	.01
☐ 108 Ted Johnson	.08	.04	.01
☐ 109 Mario Bates	.15	.07	.02
☐ 110 Philippi Sparks	.08	.04	.01
☐ 111 Marvin Washington	.08	.04	.01
☐ 112 Terry McDaniel	.08	.04	.01
☐ 113 Bobby Taylor	.15	.07	.02
☐ 114 Carnell Lake	.08	.04	.01
☐ 115 Troy Drayton	.08	.04	.01
☐ 116 Darren Bennett	.08	.04	.01
☐ 117 J.J. Stokes	.30	.14	.04
☐ 118 Rick Mirer	.15	.07	.02
☐ 119 Jackie Harris	.08	.04	.01
☐ 120 Ken Harvey	.08	.04	.01
☐ 121 Rob Moore	.08	.04	.01
☐ 122 Jeff George	.15	.07	.02
☐ 123 Andre Rison	.15	.07	.02
☐ 124 Darick Holmes	.15	.07	.02
☐ 125 Tim McKyer	.08	.04	.01
☐ 126 Alonzo Spellman	.08	.04	.01
☐ 127 Jeff Blake	.30	.14	.04
☐ 128 Kevin Williams	.08	.04	.01
☐ 129 Anthony Miller	.15	.07	.02
☐ 130 Barry Sanders	1.25	.55	.16
☐ 131 Brett Favre	2.50	1.10	.30
☐ 132 Steve McNair	1.25	.55	.16
☐ 133 Jim Harbaugh	.15	.07	.02
☐ 134 Desmond Howard	.15	.07	.02

□ 135 Steve Bono	.15	.07	.02
□ 136 Bernie Parmalee	.08	.04	.01
□ 137 Warren Moon	.15	.07	.02
□ 138 Curtis Martin	2.00	.90	.25
□ 139 Irv Smith	.08	.04	.01
□ 140 Thomas Lewis	.08	.04	.01
□ 141 Kyle Brady	.15	.07	.02
□ 142 Napoleon Kaufman	.15	.07	.02
□ 143 Mike Mamula	.08	.04	.01
□ 144 Erric Pegram	.15	.07	.02
□ 145 Isaac Bruce	.30	.14	.04
□ 146 Andre Coleman	.08	.04	.01
□ 147 Merton Hanks	.08	.04	.01
□ 148 Brian Blades	.15	.07	.02
□ 149 Hardy Nickerson	.08	.04	.01
□ 150 Michael Westbrook	.30	.14	.04
□ 151 Larry Centers	.15	.07	.02
□ 152 Morten Andersen	.08	.04	.01
□ 153 Michael Jackson	.15	.07	.02
□ 154 Bruce Smith	.30	.14	.04
□ 155 Derrick Moore	.08	.04	.01
□ 156 Mark Carrier	.08	.04	.01
□ 157 John Copeland	.08	.04	.01
□ 158 Emmitt Smith	2.50	1.10	.30
□ 159 Jason Elam	.08	.04	.01
□ 160 Scott Mitchell	.15	.07	.02
□ 161 Mark Chmura	.15	.07	.02
□ 162 Blaine Bishop	.08	.04	.01
□ 163 Tony Bennett	.08	.04	.01
□ 164 Pete Mitchell	.08	.04	.01
□ 165 Dan Saleaumua	.08	.04	.01
□ 166 Pete Stoyanovich	.08	.04	.01
□ 167 Cris Carter	.30	.14	.04
□ 168 Vince Brisby	.08	.04	.01
□ 169 Wayne Martin	.08	.04	.01
□ 170 Tyrone Wheatley	.15	.07	.02
□ 171 Mo Lewis	.08	.04	.01
□ 172 Harvey Williams	.08	.04	.01
□ 173 Calvin Williams	.08	.04	.01
□ 174 Norm Johnson	.08	.04	.01
□ 175 Mark Rypien	.08	.04	.01
□ 176 Stan Humphries	.15	.07	.02
□ 177 Derek Loville	.08	.04	.01
□ 178 Christian Fauria	.08	.04	.01
□ 179 Warren Sapp	.08	.04	.01
□ 180 Henry Ellard	.15	.07	.02
□ 181 Jamir Miller	.08	.04	.01
□ 182 Jessie Tuggle	.08	.04	.01
□ 183 Stevon Moore	.08	.04	.01
□ 184 Jim Kelly	.30	.14	.04
□ 185 Mark Carrier	.08	.04	.01
□ 186 Chris Zorich	.08	.04	.01
□ 187 Harold Green	.08	.04	.01
□ 188 Chris Boniol	.08	.04	.01
□ 189 Allen Aldridge	.08	.04	.01
□ 190 Brett Perriman	.15	.07	.02
□ 191 Chris Jacke	.08	.04	.01
□ 192 Todd McNair	.08	.04	.01
□ 193 Floyd Turner	.08	.04	.01
□ 194 Jeff Lageman	.08	.04	.01
□ 195 Derrick Thomas	.15	.07	.02
□ 196 Eric Green	.08	.04	.01
□ 197 Orlando Thomas	.08	.04	.01
□ 198 Ben Coates	.15	.07	.02
□ 199 Tyrone Hughes	.08	.04	.01
□ 200 Dave Brown	.15	.07	.02
□ 201 Brad Baxter	.08	.04	.01
□ 202 Chester McGlockton	.08	.04	.01
□ 203 Rodney Peete	.08	.04	.01
□ 204 Willie Williams	.08	.04	.01
□ 205 Kevin Carter	.15	.07	.02
□ 206 Aaron Hayden	.08	.04	.01
□ 207 Steve Young	1.00	.45	.12
□ 208 Chris Warren	.15	.07	.02
□ 209 Eric Curry	.08	.04	.01
□ 210 Brian Mitchell	.08	.04	.01
□ 211 Frank Sanders	.15	.07	.02
□ 212 Terance Mathis UER name misspelled Terence	.08	.04	.01
□ 213 Eric Turner	.08	.04	.01
□ 214 Bill Brooks	.08	.04	.01
□ 215 John Kasay	.08	.04	.01
□ 216 Erik Kramer	.08	.04	.01
□ 217 Darnay Scott	.15	.07	.02
□ 218 Charles Haley	.15	.07	.02
□ 219 Steve Atwater	.08	.04	.01
□ 220 Jason Hanson	.08	.04	.01
□ 221 LeRoy Butler	.08	.04	.01
□ 222 Cris Dishman	.08	.04	.01
□ 223 Sean Dawkins	.08	.04	.01
□ 224 James O. Stewart	.15	.07	.02
□ 225 Greg Hill	.15	.07	.02
□ 226 Jeff Cross	.08	.04	.01
□ 227 Qadry Ismail	.15	.07	.02
□ 228 Dave Meggett	.08	.04	.01
□ 229 Eric Allen	.08	.04	.01
□ 230 Chris Calloway	.08	.04	.01
□ 231 Wayne Chrebet	.15	.07	.02
□ 232 Jeff Hostetler	.15	.07	.02
□ 233 Andy Harmon	.08	.04	.01
□ 234 Greg Lloyd	.15	.07	.02
□ 235 Toby Wright	.08	.04	.01
□ 236 Junior Seau	.30	.14	.04
□ 237 Bryant Young	.15	.07	.02
□ 238 Robert Blackmon	.08	.04	.01
□ 239 Trent Dilfer	.15	.07	.02
□ 240 Leslie Shepherd	.08	.04	.01
□ 241 Eric Swann	.15	.07	.02
□ 242 Bert Emanuel	.15	.07	.02
□ 243 Antonio Langham	.08	.04	.01
□ 244 Steve Christie	.08	.04	.01
□ 245 Tyrone Poole	.08	.04	.01
□ 246 Jim Flanigan	.08	.04	.01
□ 247 Tony McGee	.08	.04	.01
□ 248 Michael Irvin	.30	.14	.04
□ 249 Byron Bam Morris	.15	.07	.02
□ 250 Terrell Davis	2.00	.90	.25
□ 251 Johnnie Morton	.15	.07	.02
□ 252 Sean Jones	.08	.04	.01
□ 253 Chris Sanders	.15	.07	.02
□ 254 Quentin Coryatt	.08	.04	.01
□ 255 Willie Jackson	.15	.07	.02
□ 256 Mark Collins	.08	.04	.01
□ 257 Randal Hill	.08	.04	.01
□ 258 David Palmer	.15	.07	.02
□ 259 Will Moore	.08	.04	.01
□ 260 Michael Haynes	.15	.07	.02
□ 261 Mike Sherrard	.08	.04	.01
□ 262 William Thomas	.08	.04	.01
□ 263 Kordell Stewart	1.50	.70	.19
□ 264 D'Marco Farr	.08	.04	.01
□ 265 Terrell Fletcher	.08	.04	.01
□ 266 Lee Woodall	.08	.04	.01
□ 267 Eugene Robinson	.08	.04	.01
□ 268 Alvin Harper	.08	.04	.01
□ 269 Gus Frerotte	.30	.14	.04
□ 270 Antonio Freeman	.60	.25	.07
□ 271 Clyde Simmons	.08	.04	.01
□ 272 Chuck Smith	.08	.04	.01
□ 273 Steve Tasker	.08	.04	.01
□ 274 Kevin Butler	.08	.04	.01
□ 275 Steve Tovar	.08	.04	.01
□ 276 Troy Aikman	1.25	.55	.16
□ 277 Aaron Craver	.08	.04	.01
□ 278 Henry Thomas	.08	.04	.01
□ 279 Craig Newsome	.08	.04	.01
□ 280 Brent Jones	.08	.04	.01
□ 281 Micheal Barrow	.08	.04	.01
□ 282 Ray Buchanan	.08	.04	.01
□ 283 Jimmy Smith	.15	.07	.02
□ 284 Neil Smith	.15	.07	.02
□ 285 O.J. McDuffie	.15	.07	.02
□ 286 Jake Reed	.15	.07	.02
□ 287 Ty Law	.08	.04	.01
□ 288 Torrance Small	.08	.04	.01
□ 289 Hugh Douglas	.08	.04	.01
□ 290 Pat Swilling	.08	.04	.01
□ 291 Charlie Garner	.08	.04	.01
□ 292 Ernie Mills	.08	.04	.01
□ 293 John Carney	.08	.04	.01
□ 294 Ken Norton	.15	.07	.02
□ 295 Cortez Kennedy	.15	.07	.02
□ 296 Derrick Brooks	.08	.04	.01
□ 297 Heath Shuler	.30	.14	.04
□ 298 Reggie White	.30	.14	.04
□ 299 Kimble Anders	.08	.04	.01
□ 300 Willie McGinest	.08	.04	.01
□ MS1 Dan Marino Dynamic Debut Meet the Stars Prize	5.00	2.20	.60
□ MS2 Dan Marino Magic Memories Meet the Stars Prize	5.00	2.20	.60

1996 Upper Deck Game Face

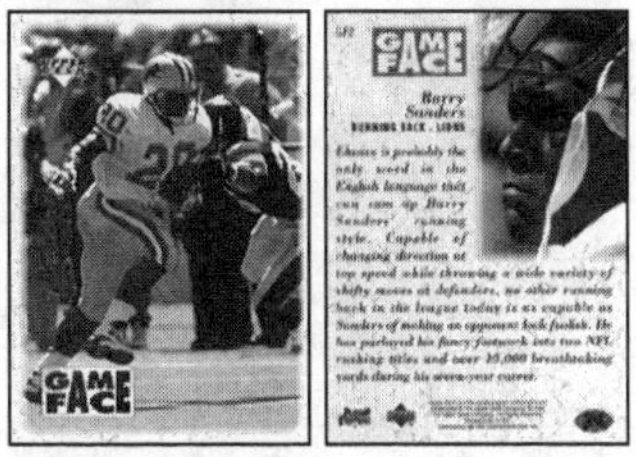

This 10 card standard-sized set was inserted one per pack in 1996 Upper Deck special retail packs.The front of the card has a photo of the player, his name, team, and positon, and a Game Face logo in the lower left hand corner of the card. The back of the card has a color photo in the upper right hand side of the card, with a short analysis of that player's skills.

	MINT	NRMT	EXC
COMPLETE SET (10)	12.00	5.50	1.50
COMMON CARD (GF1-GF10)	.75	.35	.09
□ GF1 Dan Marino	4.00	1.80	.50
□ GF2 Barry Sanders	2.00	.90	.25
□ GF3 Jerry Rice	2.00	.90	.25
□ GF4 Stan Humphries	.75	.35	.09
□ GF5 Drew Bledsoe	2.00	.90	.25
□ GF6 Greg Lloyd	.75	.35	.09
□ GF7 Jim Harbaugh	.75	.35	.09
□ GF8 Rashaan Salaam	1.00	.45	.12
□ GF9 Jeff Blake	1.00	.45	.12
□ GF10 Reggie White	1.00	.45	.12

1996 Upper Deck Game Jersey

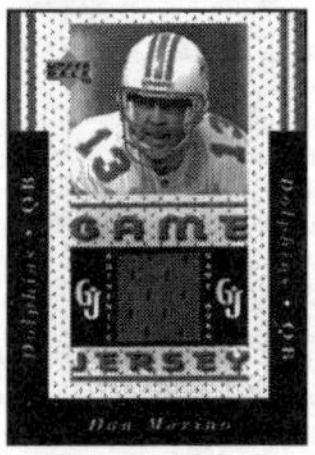

Randomly inserted in packs at a rate of one in 2500, this 10-card standard-sized insert set features an actual piece of a game-used jersey from the particular player featured on the card. The front of the card features a color picture of the player, the player's name, team, and the piece of jersey, with the insert name "Game Jersey" surrounding it.

	MINT	NRMT	EXC
COMPLETE SET (10)	3200.00	1450.00	400.00
COMMON CARD (GJ1-GJ10)	150.00	70.00	19.00
□ GJ1 Dan Marino	600.00	275.00	75.00
□ GJ2 Jerry Rice	350.00	160.00	45.00
□ GJ3 Joe Montana	500.00	220.00	60.00
□ GJ4 Jerry Rice	350.00	160.00	45.00
□ GJ5 Rashaan Salaam	150.00	70.00	19.00
□ GJ6 Marshall Faulk	200.00	90.00	25.00
□ GJ7 Dan Marino	600.00	275.00	75.00
□ GJ8 Steve Young	300.00	135.00	38.00
□ GJ9 Barry Sanders	350.00	160.00	45.00
□ GJ10 Mark Brunell	300.00	135.00	38.00

1996 Upper Deck Hot Properties

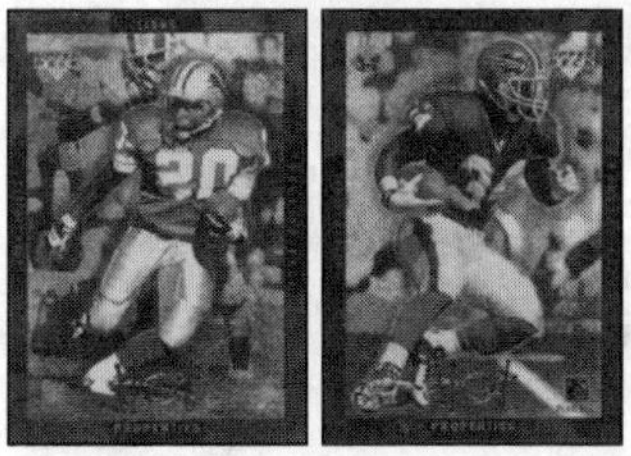

Randomly inserted in packs at a rate of one in 11, this 20-card standard-sized set featured two players on opposite sides of the card who were considered to be "hot" players within the NFL. The cards have a outlined player photo on both sides of the card, as well as name and position, with a "Hot Properties" logo in the bottom center of the card. The cards are numbered with a "HT" prefix. There is also a gold parallel version of this set that was inserted at a rate of 1:71 packs.

	MINT	NRMT	EXC
COMPLETE SET (20)	150.00	70.00	19.00
COMMON CARD (HT1-HT20)	2.50	1.10	.30
COMP.GOLD SET (20)	400.00	180.00	50.00
COMMON GOLD (HT1-HT20)	8.00	3.60	1.00
*GOLD CARDS: 1X TO 2X REDS			
□ HT1 Dan Marino Drew Bledsoe	20.00	9.00	2.50
□ HT2 Jerry Rice J.J. Stokes	8.00	3.60	1.00
□ HT3 Kordell Stewart Deion Sanders	8.00	3.60	1.00
□ HT4 Brett Favre Rick Mirer	20.00	9.00	2.50
□ HT5 Jeff Blake Steve McNair	6.00	2.70	.75
□ HT6 Emmitt Smith Errict Rhett	20.00	9.00	2.50
□ HT7 John Elway Warren Moon	6.00	2.70	.75
□ HT8 Steve Young Mark Brunell	8.00	3.60	1.00
□ HT9 Troy Aikman Kerry Collins	12.00	5.50	1.50
□ HT10 Joey Galloway Chris Sanders	5.00	2.20	.60
□ HT11 Herman Moore Cris Carter	4.00	1.80	.50
□ HT12 Rodney Hampton Terrell Davis	12.00	5.50	1.50
□ HT13 Carl Pickens Isaac Bruce	4.00	1.80	.50
□ HT14 Rashaan Salaam Michael Westbrook	4.00	1.80	.50
□ HT15 Marshall Faulk Curtis Martin	12.00	5.50	1.50
□ HT16 Tamarick Vanover Eric Metcalf	4.00	1.80	.50
□ HT17 Keyshawn Johnson Terry Glenn	15.00	6.75	1.85
□ HT18 Lawrence Phillips Tim Biakabutuka	6.00	2.70	.75
□ HT19 Kevin Hardy Simeon Rice	2.50	1.10	.30
□ HT20 Barry Sanders Thurman Thomas	8.00	3.60	1.00

1996 Upper Deck Predictors

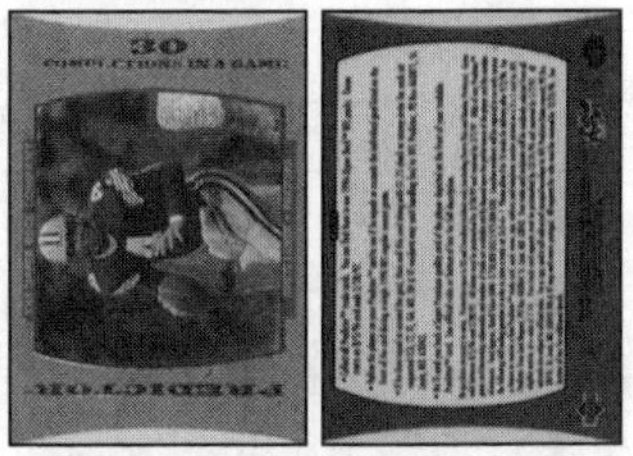

The 1996 Upper Deck Predictors were randomly inserted in both hobby and retail packs at a rate of one in 23, with stated odds of 1:14 in some special retail packs. These otherwise standard-sized insert cards had a small concave die-cut into the ends of the card, which had a gold border surrounding a picture of the player. This interactive insert listed an accomplishment (i.e., 14 receptions in a game, 450 yards passing in a game, etc.) that the player pictured had to reach during the 1996 NFL season for the card to be redeemable for a "TV-Cel" upgrade of the particular card. The results listed after the player below by a W (winner) or L (loser) reflects their success in meeting those goals. The predictors inserted in hobby packs have a "PH" prefix, while the retail predictors have a "PR" prefix.

	MINT	NRMT	EXC
COMP.HOBBY SET (20)	60.00	27.00	7.50
COMP.RETAIL SET (20)	60.00	27.00	7.50
COMMON CARD	.75	.35	.09
□ PH1 Dan Marino 450 Yards Passing L	8.00	3.60	1.00
□ PH2 Steve Young 35 Completions L	3.00	1.35	.35
□ PH3 Brett Favre 375 Yards Passing W	8.00	3.60	1.00
□ PH4 Drew Bledsoe 35 Completions W	4.00	1.80	.50
□ PH5 Jeff George 380 Yards Passing L	.75	.35	.09
□ PH6 John Elway 30 Completions W	3.00	1.35	.35
□ PH7 Barry Sanders 190 Total Yards W	4.00	1.80	.50
□ PH8 Curtis Martin 58 Yard Play L	5.00	2.20	.60
□ PH9 Marshall Faulk 195 Total Yards L	2.00	.90	.25
□ PH10 Emmitt Smith 75 Yard Play L	8.00	3.60	1.00
□ PH11 Terrell Davis 150 Yards Rushing W	5.00	2.20	.60
□ PH12 Errict Rhett 50 Yard Play L	1.50	.70	.19
□ PH13 Lawrence Phillips 55 Yard Play L	1.50	.70	.19
□ PH14 Jerry Rice 14 Receptions L	4.00	1.80	.50
□ PH15 Michael Irvin 130 Yards Receiving W	2.00	.90	.25
□ PH16 Joey Galloway 10 Receptions L	2.00	.90	.25
□ PH17 Herman Moore 190 Yards Receiving L	2.00	.90	.25
□ PH18 Isaac Bruce 12 Receptions L	2.00	.90	.25
□ PH19 Carl Pickens 150 Yards Receiving W	.75	.35	.09
□ PH20 Keyshawn Johnson 11 Receptions L	2.50	1.10	.30
□ PR1 Dan Marino 35 Completions L	8.00	3.60	1.00
□ PR2 Steve Young 435 Total Yards W	3.00	1.35	.35
□ PR3 Brett Favre 30 Completions L	8.00	3.60	1.00
□ PR4 Drew Bledsoe 350 Yards Passing W	4.00	1.80	.50
□ PR5 Jeff George 35 Completions L	.75	.35	.09
□ PR6 John Elway 350 Yards Passing W	3.00	1.35	.35
□ PR7 Barry Sanders 70 Yard Play L	4.00	1.80	.50
□ PR8 Curtis Martin 160 Yards Rushing W	5.00	2.20	.60
□ PR9 Marshall Faulk 75 Yard Play L	2.00	.90	.25
□ PR10 Emmitt Smith 195 Total Yards L	8.00	3.60	1.00
□ PR11 Terrell Davis 59 Yard Play W	5.00	2.20	.60
□ PR12 Errict Rhett 150 Yards Rushing L	1.50	.70	.19
□ PR13 Lawrence Phillips	1.50	.70	.19

	MINT	NRMT	EXC
130 Yards Rushing L			
☐ PR14 Jerry Rice	4.00	1.80	.50
200 Yards Receiving L			
☐ PR15 Michael Irvin	2.00	.90	.25
12 Receptions W			
☐ PR16 Joey Galloway	2.00	.90	.25
250 Total Yards L			
☐ PR17 Herman Moore	2.00	.90	.25
12 Receptions W			
☐ PR18 Isaac Bruce	2.00	.90	.25
200 Yards Receiving W			
☐ PR19 Carl Pickens	.75	.35	.09
10 Receptions W			
☐ PR20 Keyshawn Johnson	2.50	1.10	.30
140 Yards Receiving L			

1996 Upper Deck Pro Bowl

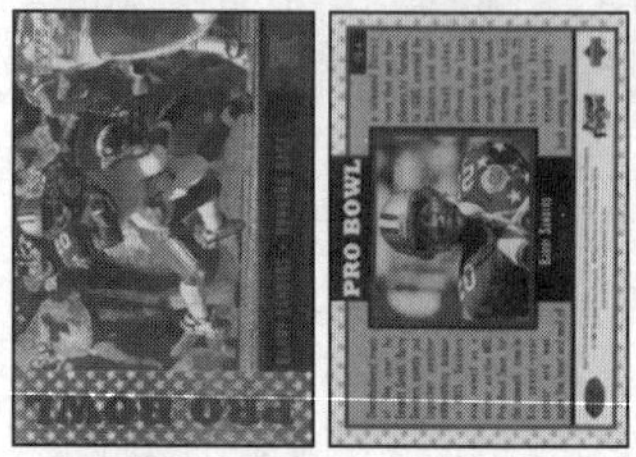

This standard-sized set of 20 cards was inserted at a rate of 1:33 packs in 1996 Upper Deck hobby and retail issues. The front of the card features the player in Pro Bowl action with the words "Pro Bowl" prominently displayed on the left side of the card, and the player, position, and conference symbol listed at the bottom of the card. The card backs have a photo of the player in the center of the card, as well as a short biography on the player.

	MINT	NRMT	EXC
COMPLETE SET (20)	135.00	60.00	17.00
COMMON CARD (PB1-PB20)	3.00	1.35	.35
☐ PB1 Warren Moon	3.00	1.35	.35
☐ PB2 Brett Favre	25.00	11.00	3.10
☐ PB3 Steve Young	10.00	4.50	1.25
☐ PB4 Barry Sanders	12.00	5.50	1.50
☐ PB5 Emmitt Smith	25.00	11.00	3.10
☐ PB6 Jerry Rice	12.00	5.50	1.50
☐ PB7 Herman Moore	5.00	2.20	.60
☐ PB8 Michael Irvin	5.00	2.20	.60
☐ PB9 Mark Chmura	3.00	1.35	.35
☐ PB10 Reggie White	5.00	2.20	.60
☐ PB11 Jim Harbaugh	3.00	1.35	.35
☐ PB12 Jeff Blake	5.00	2.20	.60
☐ PB13 Curtis Martin	15.00	6.75	1.85
☐ PB14 Marshall Faulk	5.00	2.20	.60
☐ PB15 Chris Warren	3.00	1.35	.35
☐ PB16 Bryan Cox	3.00	1.35	.35
☐ PB17 Junior Seau	3.00	1.35	.35
☐ PB18 Carl Pickens	3.00	1.35	.35
☐ PB19 Yancey Thigpen	3.00	1.35	.35
☐ PB20 Ben Coates	3.00	1.35	.35

1996 Upper Deck Proview

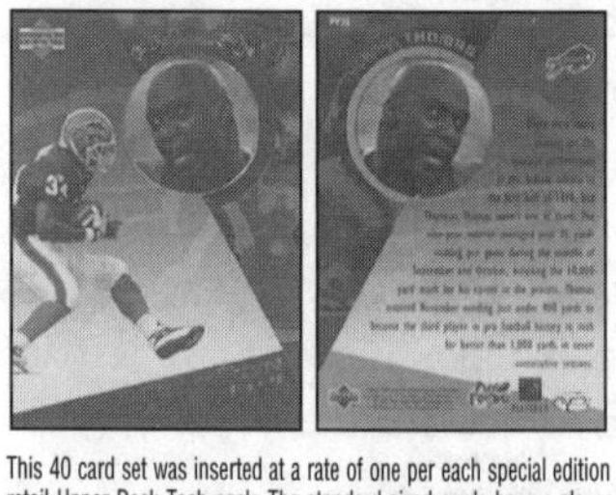

This 40 card set was inserted at a rate of one per each special edition retail Upper Deck Tech pack. The standard-sized cards have a player photo on the front, with a half-dollar sized player photo cel inserted on the upper right side of the card, with the player's name and position listed on the lower right-hand side of the card. The back of the card identifies the player and gives a short biography, and the cards are numbered with a "PV" prefix. These cards were also inserted in parallel silver (1:35 UD Tech packs) and gold (1:143 UD Tech packs).

	MINT	NRMT	EXC
COMPLETE SET (40)	125.00	55.00	15.50
COMMON CARD (PV1-PV40)	1.25	.55	.16
*SILVER CARDS: 2.5X TO 5X BASIC CARDS			
*GOLD CARDS: 7.5X TO 15X BASIC CARDS			
☐ PV1 Warren Moon	1.25	.55	.16
☐ PV2 Jerry Rice	8.00	3.60	1.00
☐ PV3 Brett Favre	15.00	6.75	1.85
☐ PV4 Jim Harbaugh	2.00	.90	.25
☐ PV5 Junior Seau	2.00	.90	.25
☐ PV6 Jeff Blake	3.00	1.35	.35
☐ PV7 John Elway	6.00	2.70	.75
☐ PV8 Troy Aikman	8.00	3.60	1.00
☐ PV9 Steve Young	6.00	2.70	.75
☐ PV10 Kordell Stewart	8.00	3.60	1.00
☐ PV11 Drew Bledsoe	8.00	3.60	1.00
☐ PV12 Jim Kelly	3.00	1.35	.35
☐ PV13 Dan Marino	15.00	6.75	1.85
☐ PV14 Kerry Collins	8.00	3.60	1.00
☐ PV15 Jeff Hostetler	1.25	.55	.16
☐ PV16 Terry Allen	2.00	.90	.25
☐ PV17 Carl Pickens	2.00	.90	.25
☐ PV18 Mark Brunell	8.00	3.60	1.00
☐ PV19 Keyshawn Johnson	4.00	1.80	.50
☐ PV20 Barry Sanders	8.00	3.60	1.00
☐ PV21 Deion Sanders	4.00	1.80	.50
☐ PV22 Emmitt Smith	15.00	6.75	1.85
☐ PV23 Curtis Conway	1.25	.55	.16
☐ PV24 Herman Moore	3.00	1.35	.35
☐ PV25 Joey Galloway	3.00	1.35	.35
☐ PV26 Robert Smith	1.25	.55	.16
☐ PV27 Eddie George	12.00	5.50	1.50
☐ PV28 Curtis Martin	10.00	4.50	1.25
☐ PV29 Marshall Faulk	3.00	1.35	.35
☐ PV30 Terrell Davis	10.00	4.50	1.25
☐ PV31 Rashaan Salaam	3.00	1.35	.35
☐ PV32 Jamal Anderson	1.25	.55	.16
☐ PV33 Karim Abdul-Jabbar	8.00	3.60	1.00
☐ PV34 Edgar Bennett	1.25	.55	.16
☐ PV35 Thurman Thomas	3.00	1.35	.35
☐ PV36 Jerome Bettis	3.00	1.35	.35
☐ PV37 Tim Brown	2.00	.90	.25
☐ PV38 Chris Sanders	1.25	.55	.16
☐ PV39 Eddie Kennison	4.00	1.80	.50
☐ PV40 Shannon Sharpe	1.25	.55	.16

1996 Upper Deck Team Trio

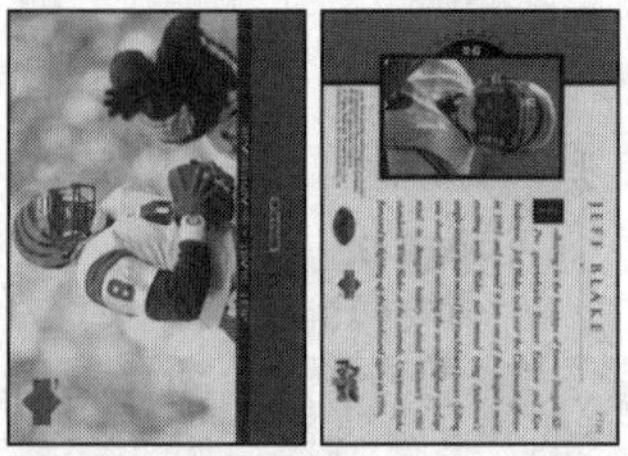

Randomly inserted in packs at a rate of one in 4, this 90-card set features die-cutting on 60 of the 90 cards as well as 30 standard-sized cards within the set. Each of the 30 NFL teams has 3 cards within the set, which when placed together forms the "Team Trio". The cards that would be on the left and right hand sides of the "Team Trio" have a rounded die-cut edge. The front of each card gives the player's name, position, and the insert name, while the backs give a snapshot photo and biography.

	MINT	NRMT	EXC
COMPLETE SET (90)	100.00	45.00	12.50
COMMON CARD (TT1-TT90)	.50	.23	.06
☐ TT1 Curtis Conway	1.00	.45	.12
☐ TT2 Darnay Scott	1.00	.45	.12
☐ TT3 Bryce Paup	.50	.23	.06
☐ TT4 Terrell Davis	5.00	2.20	.60
☐ TT5 Hardy Nickerson	.50	.23	.06
☐ TT6 Frank Sanders	1.00	.45	.12
☐ TT7 Stan Humphries	1.00	.45	.12
☐ TT8 Tamarick Vanover	1.50	.70	.19
☐ TT9 Sean Dawkins	.50	.23	.06
☐ TT10 Deion Sanders	2.00	.90	.25
☐ TT11 Dan Marino	5.00	2.20	.60
☐ TT12 Charlie Garner	.50	.23	.06
☐ TT13 Eric Metcalf	1.00	.45	.12
☐ TT14 J.J. Stokes	1.50	.70	.19
☐ TT15 Chris Calloway	.50	.23	.06
☐ TT16 Pete Mitchell	.50	.23	.06
☐ TT17 Wayne Chrebet	1.00	.45	.12
☐ TT18 Herman Moore	1.50	.70	.19
☐ TT19 Steve McNair	3.00	1.35	.35
☐ TT20 Edgar Bennett	1.00	.45	.12
☐ TT21 Kerry Collins	4.00	1.80	.50
☐ TT22 Vincent Brisby	.50	.23	.06
☐ TT23 Jeff Hostetler	.50	.23	.06
☐ TT24 Kevin Carter	.50	.23	.06
☐ TT25 Michael Jackson	.50	.23	.06
☐ TT26 Michael Westbrook	1.50	.70	.19
☐ TT27 Tyrone Hughes	.50	.23	.06
☐ TT28 Joey Galloway	2.00	.90	.25
☐ TT29 Byron Bam Morris	1.00	.45	.12
☐ TT30 Warren Moon	1.00	.45	.12
☐ TT31 Rashaan Salaam	1.50	.70	.19
☐ TT32 Jeff Blake	1.50	.70	.19
☐ TT33 Thurman Thomas	1.50	.70	.19
☐ TT34 John Elway	2.50	1.10	.30
☐ TT35 Errict Rhett	1.00	.45	.12
☐ TT36 Garrison Hearst	1.00	.45	.12
☐ TT37 Andre Coleman	.50	.23	.06
☐ TT38 Steve Bono	.50	.23	.06
☐ TT39 Marshall Faulk	1.50	.70	.19
☐ TT40 Troy Aikman	3.00	1.35	.35
☐ TT41 Terry Kirby	1.00	.45	.12
☐ TT42 Rodney Peete	.50	.23	.06
☐ TT43 Craig Heyward	.50	.23	.06
☐ TT44 Steve Young	2.50	1.10	.30
☐ TT45 Rodney Hampton	.50	.23	.06
☐ TT46 Mark Brunell	3.00	1.35	.35
☐ TT47 Kyle Brady	.50	.23	.06
☐ TT48 Scott Mitchell	.50	.23	.06
☐ TT49 Chris Sanders	1.00	.45	.12
☐ TT50 Brett Favre	5.00	2.20	.60
☐ TT51 Mark Carrier WR	1.00	.45	.12
☐ TT52 Drew Bledsoe	3.00	1.35	.35
☐ TT53 Napoleon Kaufman	.50	.23	.06
☐ TT54 Mark Rypien	.50	.23	.06
☐ TT55 Andre Rison	1.00	.45	.12
☐ TT56 Terry Allen	1.00	.45	.12
☐ TT57 Jim Everett	.50	.23	.06
☐ TT58 Chris Warren	1.00	.45	.12
☐ TT59 Kordell Stewart	4.00	1.80	.50
☐ TT60 Jake Reed	.50	.23	.06
☐ TT61 Erik Kramer	.50	.23	.06
☐ TT62 Carl Pickens	1.00	.45	.12
☐ TT63 Jim Kelly	1.50	.70	.19
☐ TT64 Anthony Miller	.50	.23	.06
☐ TT65 Trent Dilfer	1.00	.45	.12
☐ TT66 Larry Centers	.50	.23	.06
☐ TT67 Junior Seau	1.00	.45	.12
☐ TT68 Marcus Allen	1.50	.70	.19
☐ TT69 Jim Harbaugh	1.00	.45	.12
☐ TT70 Emmitt Smith	5.00	2.20	.60
☐ TT71 O.J.McDuffie	1.00	.45	.12
☐ TT72 Ricky Watters	1.00	.45	.12
☐ TT73 Jeff George	1.00	.45	.12
☐ TT74 Jerry Rice	3.00	1.35	.35
☐ TT75 Dave Brown	1.00	.45	.12
☐ TT76 James O. Stewart	1.00	.45	.12
☐ TT77 Adrian Murrell	1.00	.45	.12
☐ TT78 Barry Sanders	3.00	1.35	.35
☐ TT79 Rodney Thomas	1.00	.45	.12
☐ TT80 Robert Brooks	1.50	.70	.19
☐ TT81 Derrick Moore	.50	.23	.06
☐ TT82 Curtis Martin	5.00	2.20	.60
☐ TT83 Tim Brown	1.00	.45	.12
☐ TT84 Isaac Bruce	1.50	.70	.19
☐ TT85 Vinny Testaverde	.50	.23	.06
☐ TT86 Henry Ellard	.50	.23	.06
☐ TT87 Mario Bates	.50	.23	.06
☐ TT88 Rick Mirer	1.00	.45	.12
☐ TT89 Yancey Thigpen	1.00	.45	.12
☐ TT90 Cris Carter	1.00	.45	.12

1996 Upper Deck TV-Cels

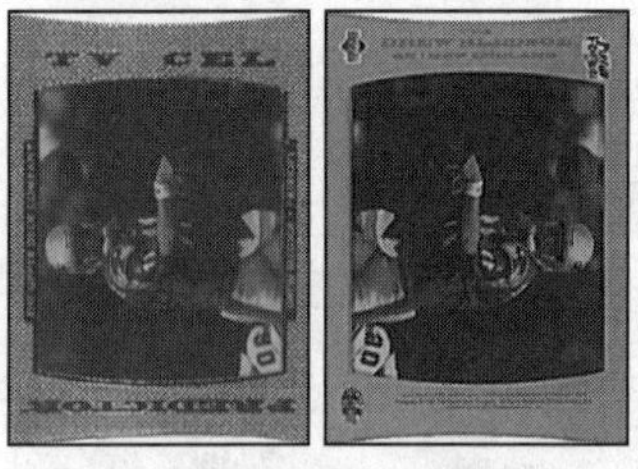

This 20 card insert set contains a "TV-Cel" in the middle of the card surrounded by gold border that identifies the player, and also, the fact that the card is a "TV-Cel" and has slightly concave die-cuts on the end of the card. If measured by the outside edges of the card, it is a standard-sized card. The distribution of these cards were as follows: A maximum of 500 TV-Cels of each player were inserted in 1996 Upper Deck packs, while in addition, these cards were also available as the redemption prizes for a particular players winning Predictor card. The amount of times that a player's predictor card won is listed after their name on the list below.

	MINT	NRMT	EXC
COMPLETE SET (20)	1000.00	450.00	125.00
COMMON CARD (1-20)	20.00	9.00	2.50
COMMON WIN (15/17-19)	20.00	9.00	2.50
☐ 1 Dan Marino	160.00	70.00	20.00
☐ 2 Steve Young 1W	40.00	18.00	5.00
☐ 3 Brett Favre 1W	100.00	45.00	12.50
☐ 4 Drew Bledsoe 2W	60.00	27.00	7.50
☐ 5 Jeff George 2W	20.00	9.00	2.50
☐ 6 John Elway 2W	50.00	22.00	6.25
☐ 7 Barry Sanders 1W	60.00	27.00	7.50
☐ 8 Curtis Martin 1W	50.00	22.00	6.25
☐ 9 Marshall Faulk	30.00	13.50	3.70
☐ 10 Emmitt Smith	160.00	70.00	20.00
☐ 11 Terrell Davis 1W	40.00	18.00	5.00
☐ 12 Errict Rhett	30.00	13.50	3.70
☐ 13 Lawrence Phillips	30.00	13.50	3.70
☐ 14 Jerry Rice	75.00	34.00	9.50
☐ 15 Michael Irvin	30.00	13.50	3.70
☐ 16 Joey Galloway	50.00	22.00	6.25
☐ 17 Herman Moore	30.00	13.50	3.70
☐ 18 Isaac Bruce	30.00	13.50	3.70
☐ 19 Carl Pickens	20.00	9.00	2.50
☐ 20 Keyshawn Johnson	50.00	22.00	6.25

1997 Upper Deck Crash the Game Super Bowl XXXI

This special Crash the Game set for Super Bowl XXXI in New Orleans was produced by Upper Deck and distributed primarily through the hobby publication SCD. Each of the eight cards carries the Super Bowl date (Jan. 26) on the cardfront in gold foil along with a player photo

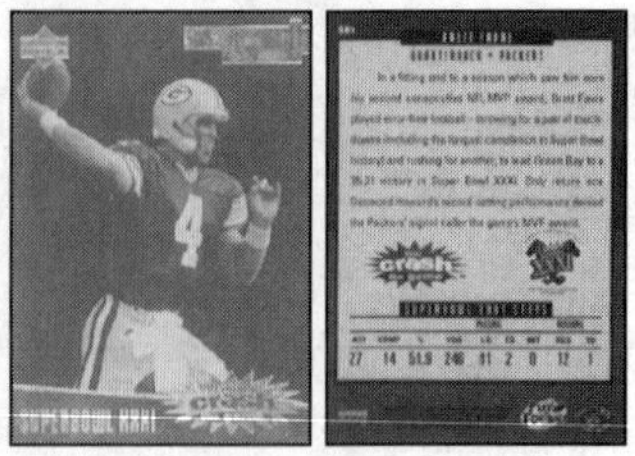

set against a purple colored background. The featured player must have scored a touchdown or passed for a touchdown in the game for the card to be exchangeable. Winning cards have been noted below. Collectors could exchange those winners, along with $2 for postage, for a parallel complete set printed on foil stock. A header card was also included with the prize set. The contest cards expired on February 29, 1997.

	MINT	NRMT	EXC
COMPLETE SET (8)	15.00	6.75	1.85
COMMON CARD (A1-N4)	.75	.35	.09
COMP.FOIL PRIZE SET (9)	10.00	4.50	1.25
COMMON FOIL PRIZE (SB1-SB9)	.75	.35	.09
☐ A1 Drew Bledsoe	1.50	.70	.19
☐ A2 Curtis Martin	1.50	.70	.19
☐ A3 Ben Coates	.75	.35	.09
☐ A4 Terry Glenn	1.50	.70	.19
☐ N1 Brett Favre	3.00	1.35	.35
☐ N2 Edgar Bennett	.75	.35	.09
☐ N3 Don Beebe	.75	.35	.09
☐ N4 Antonio Freeman	1.00	.45	.12

1997 Upper Deck Black Diamond

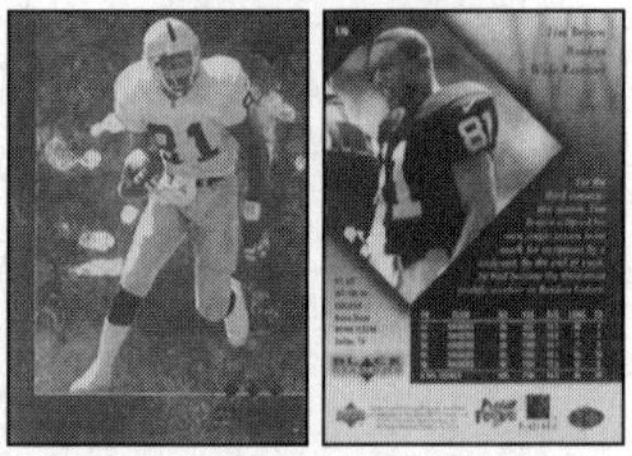

The 1997 Upper Deck Black Diamond set totals 180-cards and was distributed in six card packs with a suggested retail of $3.49. The set was produced essentially in three series together: Black Diamond (1-90), Double Black Diamond (91-150) inserted one in every four packs, and Triple Black Diamond (151-180) inserted one in every 30 packs. The fronts feature color action player photos reproduced on Light F/X card stock with one, two, or three Black Diamonds on the front designating its rarity. The backs carry player information and statistics.

	MINT	NRMT	EXC
COMPLETE SET (180)	525.00	240.00	65.00
COMP.SERIES 1 (90)	25.00	11.00	3.10
COMMON CARD (1-90)	.20	.09	.03
COMP.SERIES 2 (60)	100.00	45.00	12.50
COMMON DOUBLE (91-150)	1.50	.70	.19
COMP.SERIES 3 (30)	400.00	180.00	50.00
COMMON TRIPLE (151-180)	8.00	3.60	1.00
☐ 1 Alfred Williams	.20	.09	.03
☐ 2 Alvin Harper	.20	.09	.03
☐ 3 Andre Hastings	.30	.14	.04
☐ 4 Andre Reed	.30	.14	.04
☐ 5 Anthony Johnson	.30	.14	.04
☐ 6 Anthony Miller	.30	.14	.04
☐ 7 Byron Bam Morris	.30	.14	.04
☐ 8 Bobby Hebert	.20	.09	.03
☐ 9 Bobby Taylor	.30	.14	.04
☐ 10 Boomer Esiason	.30	.14	.04
☐ 11 Brett Perriman	.30	.14	.04
☐ 12 Brian Blades	.30	.14	.04
☐ 13 Bryan Cox	.20	.09	.03
☐ 14 Bryant Young	.30	.14	.04
☐ 15 Bryce Paup	.20	.09	.03
☐ 16 Carnell Lake	.20	.09	.03
☐ 17 Cedric Jones	.20	.09	.03
☐ 18 Chad Brown	.30	.14	.04
☐ 19 Charlie Garner	.20	.09	.03
☐ 20 Chris Chandler	.30	.14	.04
☐ 21 Cornelius Bennett	.30	.14	.04
☐ 22 Cortez Kennedy	.30	.14	.04
☐ 23 Cris Carter	.50	.23	.06
☐ 24 Dale Carter	.20	.09	.03
☐ 25 Daryl Gardener	.30	.14	.04
☐ 26 Derrick Alexander WR	.30	.14	.04
☐ 27 Derrick Mayes	.30	.14	.04
☐ 28 Don Beebe	.20	.09	.03
☐ 29 Eric Allen	.20	.09	.03
☐ 30 Eric Moulds	.50	.23	.06
☐ 31 Errict Rhett	.30	.14	.04
☐ 32 Frank Sanders	.30	.14	.04
☐ 33 Glyn Milburn	.20	.09	.03

	MINT	NRMT	EXC
☐ 34 Henry Ellard	.30	.14	.04
☐ 35 Jamal Anderson	.30	.14	.04
☐ 36 James O. Stewart	.30	.14	.04
☐ 37 Jason Dunn	.30	.14	.04
☐ 38 Jerry Rice	3.00	1.35	.35
☐ 39 Jim Everett	.20	.09	.03
☐ 40 Jim Kelly	.50	.23	.06
☐ 41 Joey Galloway	.75	.35	.09
☐ 42 John Carney	.20	.09	.03
☐ 43 John Elway	2.00	.90	.25
☐ 44 John Randle	.20	.09	.03
☐ 45 Karim Abdul-Jabbar	2.50	1.10	.30
☐ 46 Keenan McCardell	.30	.14	.04
☐ 47 Ken Dilger	.30	.14	.04
☐ 48 Ken Norton	.20	.09	.03
☐ 49 Ki-Jana Carter	.30	.14	.04
☐ 50 Kordell Stewart	2.00	.90	.25
☐ 51 Lawrence Phillips	.30	.14	.04
☐ 52 Leslie O'Neal	.20	.09	.03
☐ 53 Mark Chmura	.30	.14	.04
☐ 54 Marshall Faulk	.50	.23	.06
☐ 55 Michael Haynes	.30	.14	.04
☐ 56 Michael Irvin	.50	.23	.06
☐ 57 Michael Jackson	.30	.14	.04
☐ 58 Michael Westbrook	.50	.23	.06
☐ 59 Mike Tomczak	.20	.09	.03
☐ 60 Napoleon Kaufman	.30	.14	.04
☐ 61 Neil O'Donnell	.30	.14	.04
☐ 62 Neil Smith	.30	.14	.04
☐ 63 O.J. McDuffie	.30	.14	.04
☐ 64 Orlando Thomas	.20	.09	.03
☐ 65 Rashaan Salaam	.50	.23	.06
☐ 66 Regan Upshaw	.20	.09	.03
☐ 67 Rick Mirer	.30	.14	.04
☐ 68 Rob Moore	.20	.09	.03
☐ 69 Ronnie Harmon	.20	.09	.03
☐ 70 Sam Mills	.30	.14	.04
☐ 71 Sean Dawkins	.20	.09	.03
☐ 72 Shawn Jefferson	.20	.09	.03
☐ 73 Stan Humphries	.30	.14	.04
☐ 74 Stepfret Williams	.20	.09	.03
☐ 75 Stephen Davis	.30	.14	.04
☐ 76 Steve Atwater	.20	.09	.03
☐ 77 Terance Mathis	.20	.09	.03
☐ 78 Terrell Fletcher	.20	.09	.03
☐ 79 Terry Glenn	3.00	1.35	.35
☐ 80 Terry McDaniel	.20	.09	.03
☐ 81 Tony McGee	.20	.09	.03
☐ 82 Trent Dilfer	.30	.14	.04
☐ 83 Troy Drayton	.20	.09	.03
☐ 84 Ty Detmer	.30	.14	.04
☐ 85 Tyrone Hughes	.20	.09	.03
☐ 86 Walt Harris	.20	.09	.03
☐ 87 Wayne Chrebet	.20	.09	.03
☐ 88 Wesley Walls	.20	.09	.03
☐ 89 Willie Davis	.30	.14	.04
☐ 90 Willie McGinest	.20	.09	.03
☐ 91 Adrian Murrell	2.00	.90	.25
☐ 92 Alex Molden	1.50	.70	.19
☐ 93 Alex Van Dyke	2.00	.90	.25
☐ 94 Andre Coleman	1.50	.70	.19
☐ 95 Ben Coates	2.00	.90	.25
☐ 96 Bobby Engram	2.00	.90	.25
☐ 97 Bruce Smith	3.00	1.35	.35
☐ 98 Charles Johnson	2.00	.90	.25
☐ 99 Chris Sanders	2.00	.90	.25
☐ 100 Chris T. Jones	3.00	1.35	.35
☐ 101 Chris Warren	2.00	.90	.25
☐ 102 Darnay Scott	2.00	.90	.25
☐ 103 Dave Brown	2.00	.90	.25
☐ 104 Derrick Thomas	2.00	.90	.25
☐ 105 Drew Bledsoe	10.00	4.50	1.25
☐ 106 Edgar Bennett	2.00	.90	.25
☐ 107 Emmitt Smith	20.00	9.00	2.50
☐ 108 Eric Bjornson	1.50	.70	.19
☐ 109 Eric Metcalf	2.00	.90	.25
☐ 110 Garrison Hearst	2.00	.90	.25
☐ 111 Gus Frerotte	3.00	1.35	.35
☐ 112 Hardy Nickerson	1.50	.70	.19
☐ 113 Herman Moore	3.00	1.35	.35
☐ 114 Hugh Douglas	1.50	.70	.19
☐ 115 Irving Fryar	2.00	.90	.25
☐ 116 J.J. Stokes	2.00	.90	.25
☐ 117 Jake Reed	2.00	.90	.25
☐ 118 Jeff Hostetler	2.00	.90	.25
☐ 119 Jeff Lewis	2.00	.90	.25
☐ 120 Jim Harbaugh	2.00	.90	.25
☐ 121 Johnnie Morton	2.00	.90	.25
☐ 122 Jonathan Ogden	1.50	.70	.19
☐ 123 Kevin Carter	1.50	.70	.19
☐ 124 Kevin Greene	2.00	.90	.25
☐ 125 Kevin Hardy	2.00	.90	.25
☐ 126 Leeland McElroy	2.00	.90	.25
☐ 127 Mike Alstott	3.00	1.35	.35
☐ 128 Muhsin Muhammad	6.00	2.70	.75
☐ 129 Natrone Means	3.00	1.35	.35
☐ 130 Quentin Coryatt	1.50	.70	.19
☐ 131 Ray Lewis	1.50	.70	.19
☐ 132 Ray Zellars	1.50	.70	.19
☐ 133 Rickey Dudley	2.00	.90	.25
☐ 134 Ricky Watters	2.00	.90	.25
☐ 135 Robert Smith	2.00	.90	.25
☐ 136 Scott Mitchell	2.00	.90	.25
☐ 137 Sean Gilbert	1.50	.70	.19
☐ 138 Shannon Sharpe	2.00	.90	.25
☐ 139 Simeon Rice	2.00	.90	.25
☐ 140 Stanley Pritchett	1.50	.70	.19
☐ 141 Steve McNair	6.00	2.70	.75
☐ 142 Steve Young	8.00	3.60	1.00
☐ 143 Tamarick Vanover	2.00	.90	.25
☐ 144 Terry Allen	2.00	.90	.25
☐ 145 Thurman Thomas	3.00	1.35	.35
☐ 146 Tony Banks	6.00	2.70	.75
☐ 147 Tony Martin	2.00	.90	.25
☐ 148 Tyrone Wheatley	2.00	.90	.25
☐ 149 Vinny Testaverde	2.00	.90	.25
☐ 150 Zach Thomas	6.00	2.70	.75
☐ 151 Amani Toomer	8.00	3.60	1.00
☐ 152 Barry Sanders	35.00	16.00	4.40
☐ 153 Bobby Hoying	8.00	3.60	1.00
☐ 154 Brett Favre	70.00	32.00	8.75
☐ 155 Carl Pickens	12.00	5.50	1.50
☐ 156 Curtis Conway	12.00	5.50	1.50
☐ 157 Curtis Martin	35.00	16.00	4.40
☐ 158 Dan Marino	70.00	32.00	8.75
☐ 159 Deion Sanders	15.00	6.75	1.85
☐ 160 Eddie George	50.00	22.00	6.25
☐ 161 Eddie Kennison	15.00	6.75	1.85
☐ 162 Elvis Grbac	8.00	3.60	1.00
☐ 163 Isaac Bruce	12.00	5.50	1.50
☐ 164 Jeff Blake	12.00	5.50	1.50
☐ 165 Jerome Bettis	12.00	5.50	1.50
☐ 166 Junior Seau	12.00	5.50	1.50
☐ 167 Kerry Collins	30.00	13.50	3.70
☐ 168 Keyshawn Johnson	15.00	6.75	1.85
☐ 169 Larry Centers	8.00	3.60	1.00
☐ 170 Marcus Allen	12.00	5.50	1.50
☐ 171 Mark Brunell	35.00	16.00	4.40
☐ 172 Marvin Harrison	15.00	6.75	1.85
☐ 173 Reggie White	12.00	5.50	1.50
☐ 174 Rodney Hampton	8.00	3.60	1.00
☐ 175 Terrell Davis	35.00	16.00	4.40
☐ 176 Tim Brown	8.00	3.60	1.00
☐ 177 Todd Collins	8.00	3.60	1.00
☐ 178 Troy Aikman	35.00	16.00	4.40
☐ 179 Tim Biakabutuka	12.00	5.50	1.50
☐ 180 Warren Moon	8.00	3.60	1.00
☐ BD1 Troy Aikman Promo	2.00	.90	.25

1997 Upper Deck Black Diamond Gold

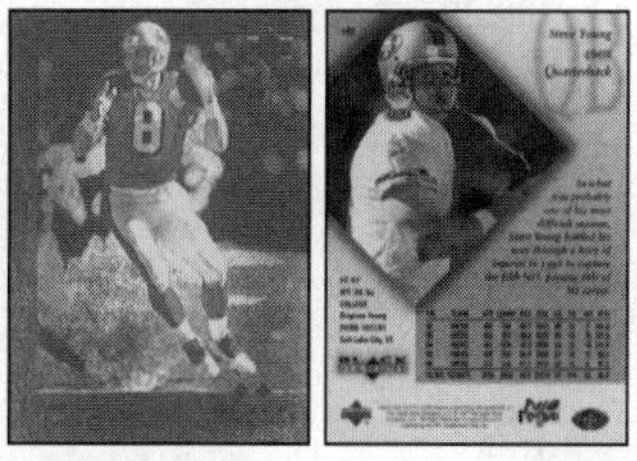

These cards were randomly inserted in packs at a rate of one in 15 for single Black Diamond Gold (1-90), one in 46 for Double Black Diamond Gold (91-150) and a total print run of 50 for each Triple Black Diamond Gold (151-180). This Black Diamond Gold set is parallel to the regular set and was reproduced with a gold light F/X foil.

	MINT	NRMT	EXC
COMPLETE SET (180)	3500.00	1600.00	450.00
COMP.SERIES 1 (90)	200.00	90.00	25.00
COMMON CARD (1-90)	2.50	1.10	.30
*SER.1 STARS: 3X TO 7X BASIC CARDS			
*SER.1 YOUNG STARS: 3X TO 6X BASIC CARDS			
COMP.SERIES 2 (60)	300.00	135.00	38.00
COMMON DOUBLE (91-150)	4.00	1.80	.50
*SER.2 STARS: 2X TO 4X BASIC CARDS			
*SER.2 YOUNG STARS: 1.5X TO 3X BASIC CARDS			
COMP.SERIES 3 (30)	3000.00	1350.00	375.00
COMMON TRIPLE (151-180)	20.00	9.00	2.50
*SER.3 STARS: 3X TO 7X BASIC CARDS			
*SER.3 YOUNG STARS: 2.5X TO 6X BASIC CARDS			

☐ 38 Jerry Rice	20.00	9.00	2.50
☐ 43 John Elway	15.00	6.75	1.85
☐ 45 Karim Abdul-Jabbar	15.00	6.75	1.85
☐ 50 Kordell Stewart	15.00	6.75	1.85
☐ 79 Terry Glenn	20.00	9.00	2.50
☐ 105 Drew Bledsoe	40.00	18.00	5.00
☐ 107 Emmitt Smith	80.00	36.00	10.00
☐ 141 Steve McNair	25.00	11.00	3.10
☐ 142 Steve Young	30.00	13.50	3.70
☐ 152 Barry Sanders	300.00	135.00	38.00
☐ 154 Brett Favre	500.00	220.00	60.00
☐ 157 Curtis Martin	200.00	90.00	25.00
☐ 158 Dan Marino	500.00	220.00	60.00
☐ 159 Deion Sanders	120.00	55.00	15.00
☐ 160 Eddie George	250.00	110.00	31.00
☐ 161 Eddie Kennison	100.00	45.00	12.50
☐ 167 Kerry Collins	200.00	90.00	25.00
☐ 168 Keyshawn Johnson	100.00	45.00	12.50
☐ 171 Mark Brunell	250.00	110.00	31.00
☐ 172 Marvin Harrison	100.00	45.00	12.50
☐ 175 Terrell Davis	200.00	90.00	25.00
☐ 178 Troy Aikman	300.00	135.00	38.00

1997 Upper Deck Black Diamond Title Quest

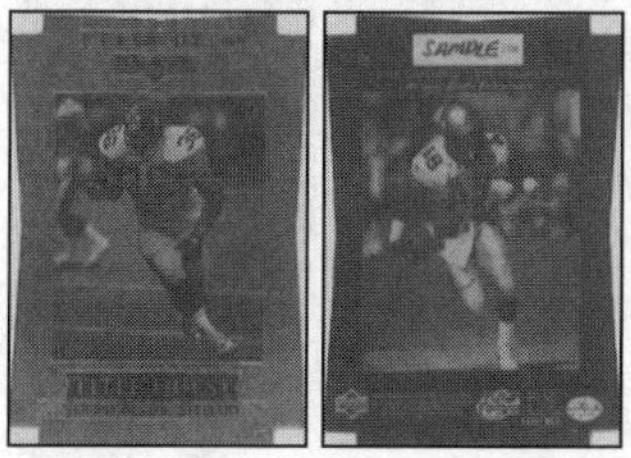

This 20-card insert set features color action player photos of NFL superstars reproduced on a die-cut card utilizing cell technology and gold etching. Only 100 of each card were produced, and they are sequentially numbered.

	MINT	NRMT	EXC
COMPLETE SET (20)	3500.00	1600.00	450.00
COMMON CARD (1-20)	50.00	22.00	6.25

☐ 1 Dan Marino	400.00	180.00	50.00
☐ 2 Jerry Rice	250.00	110.00	31.00
☐ 3 Drew Bledsoe	250.00	110.00	31.00
☐ 4 Emmitt Smith	400.00	180.00	50.00
☐ 5 Troy Aikman	250.00	110.00	31.00
☐ 6 Steve Young	175.00	80.00	22.00
☐ 7 Brett Favre	400.00	180.00	50.00
☐ 8 John Elway	200.00	90.00	25.00
☐ 9 Barry Sanders	250.00	110.00	31.00
☐ 10 Jerome Bettis	100.00	45.00	12.50
☐ 11 Deion Sanders	125.00	55.00	15.50
☐ 12 Karim Abdul-Jabbar	150.00	70.00	19.00
☐ 13 Terrell Davis	200.00	90.00	25.00
☐ 14 Marshall Faulk	50.00	22.00	6.25
☐ 15 Curtis Martin	200.00	90.00	25.00
☐ 16 Eddie George	300.00	135.00	38.00
☐ 17 Steve McNair	150.00	70.00	19.00
☐ 18 Terry Glenn	200.00	90.00	25.00
☐ 19 Joey Galloway	100.00	45.00	12.50
☐ 20 Keyshawn Johnson	50.00	22.00	6.25

1996 Upper Deck Silver

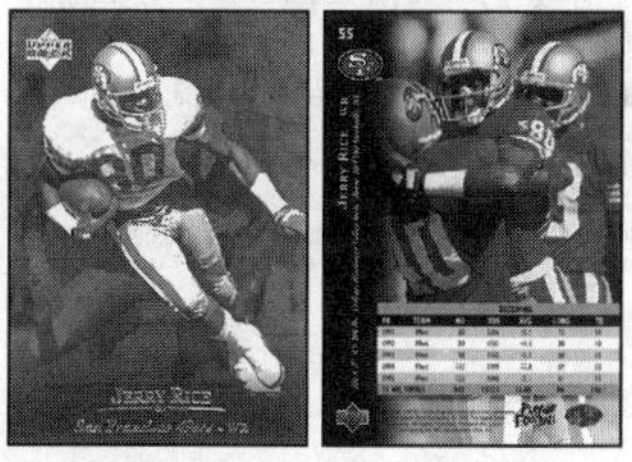

The 1996 Upper Deck Silver set was issued only through Upper Deck's hobby channels. The set was issued in one series totalling 225 standard-size cards. The 10-card packs had a suggested retail price of $2.49 each. 28 packs were in a box and 20 boxes made up a case. The set contains the topical subset Season Leaders (211-225).

	MINT	NRMT	EXC
COMPLETE SET (225)	25.00	11.00	3.10
COMMON CARD (1-225)	.05	.02	.01

☐ 1 Larry Centers	.10	.05	.01
☐ 2 Terance Mathis	.05	.02	.01
☐ 3 Justin Armour	.05	.02	.01
☐ 4 Kerry Collins	1.25	.55	.16
☐ 5 Jim Flanigan UER Mike on front	.05	.02	.01
☐ 6 Dan Wilkinson	.05	.02	.01
☐ 7 Eric Zeier	.10	.05	.01
☐ 8 Deion Sanders	.50	.23	.06
☐ 9 Steve Atwater	.05	.02	.01
☐ 10 Johnnie Morton	.10	.05	.01
☐ 11 Craig Newsome	.05	.02	.01
☐ 12 Broncos Offensive Line	.05	.02	.01
☐ 13 Ken Dilger	.10	.05	.01
☐ 14 Mark Brunell	1.00	.45	.12
☐ 15 Tamarick Vanover	.20	.09	.03
☐ 16 Bernie Parmalee	.05	.02	.01
☐ 17 Orlando Thomas	.05	.02	.01
☐ 18 Will Moore	.05	.02	.01
☐ 19 Mark Fields	.05	.02	.01
☐ 20 Tyrone Wheatley	.10	.05	.01
☐ 21 Kyle Brady	.10	.05	.01
☐ 22 Napoleon Kaufman	.10	.05	.01
☐ 23 Mike Mamula	.05	.02	.01
☐ 24 Erric Pegram	.10	.05	.01
☐ 25 Brent Jones	.05	.02	.01
☐ 26 Aaron Hayden	.10	.05	.01
☐ 27 Christian Fauria	.05	.02	.01
☐ 28 Cowboys Offensive Line with Troy Aikman	.05	.02	.01
☐ 29 Derrick Brooks	.05	.02	.01
☐ 30 Brian Mitchell	.05	.02	.01
☐ 31 Garrison Hearst	.10	.05	.01
☐ 32 Devin Bush	.05	.02	.01
☐ 33 Andre Reed	.10	.05	.01
☐ 34 Derrick Moore	.05	.02	.01
☐ 35 Erik Kramer	.05	.02	.01
☐ 36 Jeff Blake	.20	.09	.03
☐ 37 Andre Rison	.10	.05	.01
☐ 38 Troy Aikman	1.00	.45	.12
☐ 39 Anthony Miller	.10	.05	.01
☐ 40 Scott Mitchell	.10	.05	.01
☐ 41 Reggie White	.20	.09	.03
☐ 42 Chris Sanders	.10	.05	.01
☐ 43 Ellis Johnson	.05	.02	.01
☐ 44 Willie Jackson	.10	.05	.01
☐ 45 Steve Bono	.10	.05	.01
☐ 46 Terry Kirby	.10	.05	.01
☐ 47 Jake Reed	.10	.05	.01
☐ 48 Vincent Brisby	.05	.02	.01
☐ 49 Quinn Early	.05	.02	.01
☐ 50 Thomas Lewis	.05	.02	.01
☐ 51 Wayne Chrebet	.10	.05	.01
☐ 52 Pat Swilling	.05	.02	.01
☐ 53 Bobby Taylor	.10	.05	.01
☐ 54 Mark Bruener	.05	.02	.01
☐ 55 Jerry Rice	1.00	.45	.12
☐ 56 Natrone Means	.20	.09	.03
☐ 57 Rick Mirer	.10	.05	.01
☐ 58 Kevin Carter	.10	.05	.01
☐ 59 Hardy Nickerson	.05	.02	.01
☐ 60 Lions Offensive Line with Scott Mitchell	.05	.02	.01
☐ 61 Eric Swann	.10	.05	.01
☐ 62 Eric Metcalf	.10	.05	.01
☐ 63 Russell Copeland	.05	.02	.01
☐ 64 Pete Metzelaars	.05	.02	.01
☐ 65 Curtis Conway	.20	.09	.03
☐ 66 Darnay Scott	.10	.05	.01
☐ 67 Leroy Hoard	.05	.02	.01
☐ 68 Darren Woodson	.10	.05	.01
☐ 69 John Elway	.60	.25	.07
☐ 70 Brett Perriman	.10	.05	.01
☐ 71 Mark Chmura	.10	.05	.01
☐ 72 Chris Chandler	.10	.05	.01
☐ 73 Marshall Faulk	.20	.09	.03
☐ 74 Pete Mitchell	.05	.02	.01
☐ 75 Willie Davis	.10	.05	.01
☐ 76 Irving Fryar	.10	.05	.01
☐ 77 Robert Smith	.10	.05	.01
☐ 78 Drew Bledsoe	1.00	.45	.12
☐ 79 Mario Bates	.10	.05	.01
☐ 80 Chris Calloway	.05	.02	.01
☐ 81 Boomer Esiason	.10	.05	.01
☐ 82 Harvey Williams	.05	.02	.01
☐ 83 Fred Barnett	.10	.05	.01
☐ 84 Neil O'Donnell	.10	.05	.01
☐ 85 Lee Woodall	.05	.02	.01
☐ 86 Junior Seau	.20	.09	.03
☐ 87 Brian Blades	.10	.05	.01
☐ 88 Chris Miller	.05	.02	.01
☐ 89 Warren Sapp	.05	.02	.01
☐ 90 Terry Allen	.10	.05	.01
☐ 91 Dave Krieg	.05	.02	.01
☐ 92 Bert Emanuel	.10	.05	.01
☐ 93 Jim Kelly	.20	.09	.03
☐ 94 Mark Carrier	.05	.02	.01
☐ 95 Jeff Graham	.05	.02	.01
☐ 96 Tony McGee	.05	.02	.01
☐ 97 Vinny Testaverde	.10	.05	.01
☐ 98 Michael Irvin	.20	.09	.03
☐ 99 Shannon Sharpe	.10	.05	.01
☐ 100 Chris Spielman	.10	.05	.01
☐ 101 Edgar Bennett	.10	.05	.01
☐ 102 Haywood Jeffires	.05	.02	.01
☐ 103 Quentin Coryatt	.05	.02	.01
☐ 104 Jeff Lageman	.05	.02	.01
☐ 105 Neil Smith	.10	.05	.01
☐ 106 O.J. McDuffie	.10	.05	.01
☐ 107 Warren Moon	.10	.05	.01
☐ 108 Ben Coates	.10	.05	.01
☐ 109 Michael Haynes	.10	.05	.01
☐ 110 Mike Sherrard	.05	.02	.01
☐ 111 Adrian Murrell	.10	.05	.01
☐ 112 Jeff Hostetler	.10	.05	.01
☐ 113 Charlie Garner	.05	.02	.01
☐ 114 Yancey Thigpen	.10	.05	.01
☐ 115 Steve Young	.60	.25	.07
☐ 116 Tony Martin	.10	.05	.01
☐ 117 49ers Offensive Line	.05	.02	.01
☐ 118 Jerome Bettis	.20	.09	.03
☐ 119 Alvin Harper	.05	.02	.01
☐ 120 Heath Shuler	.20	.09	.03
☐ 121 Rob Moore	.05	.02	.01
☐ 122 Chris Doleman	.05	.02	.01
☐ 123 Bruce Smith	.20	.09	.03
☐ 124 Sam Mills	.10	.05	.01
☐ 125 Donnell Woolford	.05	.02	.01
☐ 126 Harold Green	.05	.02	.01
☐ 127 Antonio Langham	.05	.02	.01
☐ 128 Charles Haley	.10	.05	.01
☐ 129 Aaron Craver	.05	.02	.01
☐ 130 Barry Sanders	1.00	.45	.12
☐ 131 Sean Jones	.05	.02	.01
☐ 132 Steve McNair	.75	.35	.09
☐ 133 Tony Bennett	.05	.02	.01
☐ 134 Dolphins Offensive Line with Dan Marino	.05	.02	.01

☐ 135 Greg Hill	.10	.05	.01
☐ 136 Eric Green	.05	.02	.01
☐ 137 John Randle	.05	.02	.01
☐ 138 Dave Meggett	.05	.02	.01
☐ 139 Irv Smith	.05	.02	.01
☐ 140 Dave Brown	.10	.05	.01
☐ 141 Raiders Offensive Line	.05	.02	.01
☐ 142 Rocket Ismail	.10	.05	.01
☐ 143 Rodney Peete	.05	.02	.01
☐ 144 Kevin Greene	.10	.05	.01
☐ 145 Derek Loville	.05	.02	.01
☐ 146 Leslie O'Neal	.05	.02	.01
☐ 147 Cortez Kennedy	.10	.05	.01
☐ 148 Sean Gilbert	.05	.02	.01
☐ 149 Jackie Harris	.05	.02	.01
☐ 150 Henry Ellard	.10	.05	.01
☐ 151 Frank Sanders	.10	.05	.01
☐ 152 Jeff George	.10	.05	.01
☐ 153 Darick Holmes	.10	.05	.01
☐ 154 Tyrone Poole	.05	.02	.01
☐ 155 Rashaan Salaam	.20	.09	.03
☐ 156 Carl Pickens	.20	.09	.03
☐ 157 Eric Turner	.05	.02	.01
☐ 158 Jay Novacek	.10	.05	.01
☐ 159 Terrell Davis	1.50	.70	.19
☐ 160 Herman Moore	.20	.09	.03
☐ 161 Robert Brooks	.20	.09	.03
☐ 162 Rodney Thomas	.05	.02	.01
☐ 163 Sean Dawkins	.05	.02	.01
☐ 164 James O. Stewart	.10	.05	.01
☐ 165 Marcus Allen	.20	.09	.03
☐ 166 Dan Marino	2.00	.90	.25
☐ 167 Cris Carter	.20	.09	.03
☐ 168 Curtis Martin	1.50	.70	.19
☐ 169 Tyrone Hughes	.05	.02	.01
☐ 170 Rodney Hampton	.10	.05	.01
☐ 171 Hugh Douglas	.05	.02	.01
☐ 172 Tim Brown	.10	.05	.01
☐ 173 Ricky Watters	.10	.05	.01
☐ 174 Kordell Stewart	1.25	.55	.16
☐ 175 Stan Humphries	.10	.05	.01
☐ 176 J.J. Stokes	.20	.09	.03
☐ 177 Joey Galloway	.40	.18	.05
☐ 178 Isaac Bruce	.20	.09	.03
☐ 179 Errict Rhett	.10	.05	.01
☐ 180 Michael Westbrook	.20	.09	.03
☐ 181 Steelers Offensive Line	.05	.02	.01
☐ 182 Craig Heyward	.05	.02	.01
☐ 183 Bryce Paup	.10	.05	.01
☐ 184 Brett Maxie	.05	.02	.01
☐ 185 Kevin Butler	.05	.02	.01
☐ 186 John Copeland	.05	.02	.01
☐ 187 Keenan McCardell	.20	.09	.03
☐ 188 Emmitt Smith	2.00	.90	.25
☐ 189 Glyn Milburn	.05	.02	.01
☐ 190 Jason Hanson	.05	.02	.01
☐ 191 Brett Favre	2.00	.90	.25
☐ 192 Darryll Lewis UER name spelled Darryl on front	.05	.02	.01
☐ 193 Jim Harbaugh	.10	.05	.01
☐ 194 Desmond Howard	.10	.05	.01
☐ 195 Derrick Thomas	.10	.05	.01
☐ 196 Bryan Cox	.05	.02	.01
☐ 197 Amp Lee	.05	.02	.01
☐ 198 Ty Law	.05	.02	.01
☐ 199 Jim Everett	.05	.02	.01
☐ 200 Vencie Glenn	.05	.02	.01
☐ 201 Charles Wilson	.05	.02	.01
☐ 202 Terry McDaniel	.05	.02	.01
☐ 203 Calvin Williams	.20	.09	.03
☐ 204 Greg Lloyd	.10	.05	.01
☐ 205 Merton Hanks	.05	.02	.01
☐ 206 Andre Coleman	.05	.02	.01
☐ 207 Chris Warren	.10	.05	.01
☐ 208 D'Marco Farr	.05	.02	.01
☐ 209 Trent Dilfer	.10	.05	.01
☐ 210 Ken Harvey	.05	.02	.01
☐ 211 Jim Harbaugh SL	.10	.05	.01
☐ 212 Brett Favre SL	1.00	.45	.12
☐ 213 Curtis Martin SL	1.00	.45	.12
☐ 214 Carl Pickens SL	.20	.09	.03
☐ 215 Norm Johnson SL	.05	.02	.01
☐ 216 Bryce Paup SL	.10	.05	.01
☐ 217 Herman Moore SL	.20	.09	.03
☐ 218 Jerry Rice SL	.50	.23	.06
☐ 219 Orlando Thomas SL	.05	.02	.01
☐ 220 Emmitt Smith SL	1.00	.45	.12
☐ 221 Tyrone Hughes SL	.05	.02	.01
☐ 222 Tamarick Vanover SL	.20	.09	.03
☐ 223 Rick Tuten SL	.05	.02	.01
☐ 224 49ers Defense SL	.05	.02	.01
☐ 225 Lions Offensive Line SL	.05	.02	.01

1996 Upper Deck Silver All-NFL

Randomly inserted in packs at a rate of one in 5, this 20-card set highlights some of the top players selected to the Upper Deck All-NFL Team. The cards feature Light F/X Technology and a die-cut design with a football type texture. The cards are numbered with an "AN" prefix.

	MINT	NRMT	EXC
COMPLETE SET (20)	50.00	22.00	6.25
COMMON CARD (AN1-AN20)	1.00	.45	.12

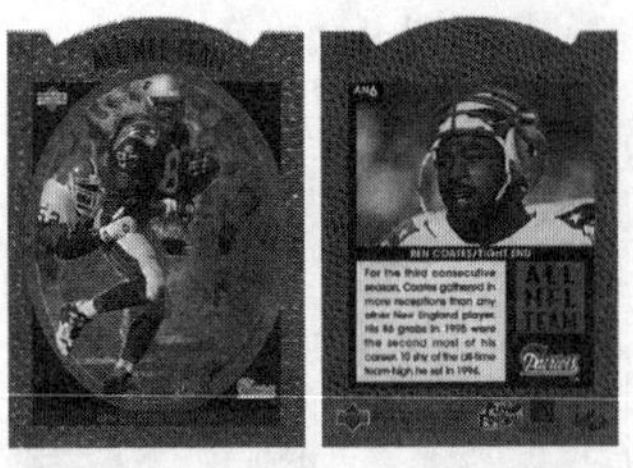

☐ AN1 Herman Moore	3.00	1.35	.35
☐ AN2 Isaac Bruce	3.00	1.35	.35
☐ AN3 Jerry Rice	5.00	2.20	.60
☐ AN4 Michael Irvin	3.00	1.35	.35
☐ AN5 Eric Metcalf	1.00	.45	.12
☐ AN6 Ben Coates	2.00	.90	.25
☐ AN7 Brett Favre	10.00	4.50	1.25
☐ AN8 Jim Harbaugh	2.00	.90	.25
☐ AN9 Emmitt Smith	10.00	4.50	1.25
☐ AN10 Barry Sanders	5.00	2.20	.60
☐ AN11 Chris Warren	2.00	.90	.25
☐ AN12 Curtis Martin	10.00	4.50	1.25
☐ AN13 Hugh Douglas	1.00	.45	.12
☐ AN14 Neil Smith	1.00	.45	.12
☐ AN15 Reggie White	3.00	1.35	.35
☐ AN16 Bryce Paup	1.00	.45	.12
☐ AN17 Greg Lloyd	2.00	.90	.25
☐ AN18 Carnell Lake	1.00	.45	.12
☐ AN19 Merton Hanks	1.00	.45	.12
☐ AN20 Tamarick Vanover	3.00	1.35	.35

1996 Upper Deck Silver All-Rookie Team

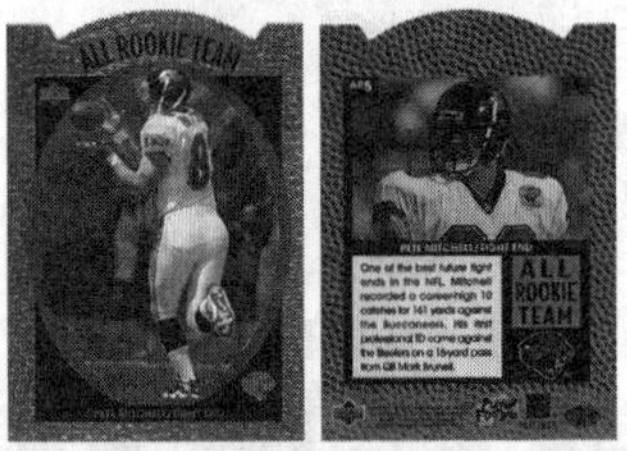

Randomly inserted in packs at a rate of one in 18, this 20-card set features some of the top rookies selected to the Upper Deck All-Rookie Team. These cards also showcase Light F/X Technology and a die-cut design with a unique football texture. The cards differentiate from the All-NFL cards in that these cards have a golden color to them. The cards are numbered with an "AR" prefix.

	MINT	NRMT	EXC
COMPLETE SET (20)	100.00	45.00	12.50
COMMON CARD (AR1-AR20)	2.50	1.10	.30

☐ AR1 Joey Galloway	8.00	3.60	1.00
☐ AR2 Chris Sanders	4.00	1.80	.50
☐ AR3 J.J. Stokes	5.00	2.20	.60
☐ AR4 Ken Dilger	4.00	1.80	.50
☐ AR5 Pete Mitchell	2.50	1.10	.30
☐ AR6 Kordell Stewart	16.00	7.25	2.00
☐ AR7 Kerry Collins	16.00	7.25	2.00
☐ AR8 Tony Boselli	4.00	1.80	.50
☐ AR9 Terrell Davis	20.00	9.00	2.50
☐ AR10 Rodney Thomas	4.00	1.80	.50
☐ AR11 Rashaan Salaam	5.00	2.20	.60
☐ AR12 Curtis Martin	20.00	9.00	2.50
☐ AR13 Napoleon Kaufman	4.00	1.80	.50
☐ AR14 Hugh Douglas	2.50	1.10	.30
☐ AR15 Ellis Johnson	2.50	1.10	.30
☐ AR16 Kevin Carter	2.50	1.10	.30
☐ AR17 Derrick Brooks	2.50	1.10	.30
☐ AR18 Craig Newsome	2.50	1.10	.30
☐ AR19 Orlanda Thomas	2.50	1.10	.30
☐ AR20 Tamarick Vanover	5.00	2.20	.60

1996 Upper Deck Silver Helmet Cards

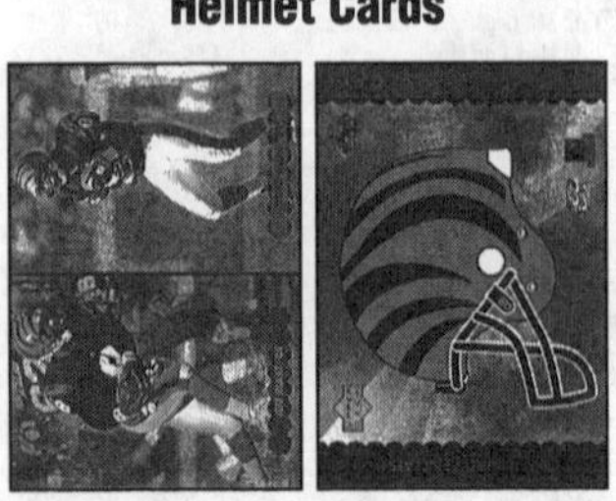

Randomly inserted in packs at a rate of one in 18, this 30-card standard-size set features double front Light F/X technology with each of the 30 NFL teams helmets on one side and two top stars on the other. We have sequenced this set below in alphabetical order within division order.

	MINT	NRMT	EXC
COMPLETE SET (30)	250.00	110.00	31.00
COMMON CARD	3.00	1.35	.35

☐ AC1 Jeff Blake David Dunn	6.00	2.70	.75
☐ AC2 Vinny Testaverde Eric Zeier	3.00	1.35	.35
☐ AC3 Rodney Thomas Chris Sanders	4.00	1.80	.50
☐ AC4 Mark Brunell James O.Stewart	10.00	4.50	1.25
☐ AC5 Greg Lloyd Kordell Stewart	16.00	7.25	2.00
☐ AE1 Marshall Faulk Ken Dilger	6.00	2.70	.75
☐ AE2 Wayne Chrebet Hugh Douglas	3.00	1.35	.35
☐ AE3 Dan Marino Billy Milner	35.00	16.00	4.40
☐ AE4 Jim Kelly Darick Holmes	6.00	2.70	.75
☐ AE5 Drew Bledsoe Curtis Martin	25.00	11.00	3.10
☐ AW1 Steve Bono Tamarick Vanover UER name spelled Tamerick on front	6.00	2.70	.75
☐ AW2 Chris Warren Joey Galloway	8.00	3.60	1.00
☐ AW3 Natrone Means Aaron Hayden	4.00	1.80	.50
☐ AW4 Tim Brown Napoleon Kaufman	4.00	1.80	.50
☐ AW5 John Elway Terrell Davis	20.00	9.00	2.50
☐ NC1 Erik Kramer Rashaan Salaam	6.00	2.70	.75
☐ NC2 Herman Moore Luther Elliss	6.00	2.70	.75
☐ NC3 Cris Carter Orlanda Thomas	4.00	1.80	.50
☐ NC4 Errict Rhett Derrick Brooks	10.00	4.50	1.25
☐ NC5 Robert Brooks Craig Newsome	6.00	2.70	.75
☐ NE1 Garrison Hearst Frank Sanders	4.00	1.80	.50
☐ NE2 Rodney Hampton Tyrone Wheatley	4.00	1.80	.50
☐ NE3 Ricky Watters Mike Mamula	4.00	1.80	.50
☐ NE4 Terry Allen Michael Westbrook	6.00	2.70	.75
☐ NE5 Emmitt Smith Sherman Williams	35.00	16.00	4.40
☐ NW1 Jeff George Devin Bush	4.00	1.80	.50
☐ NW2 Sam Mills Kerry Collins	16.00	7.25	2.00
☐ NW3 Mario Bates Mark Fields	3.00	1.35	.35
☐ NW4 Isaac Bruce Kevin Carter	6.00	2.70	.75
☐ NW5 Jerry Rice J.J.Stokes	20.00	9.00	2.50

1996 Upper Deck Silver Dan Marino

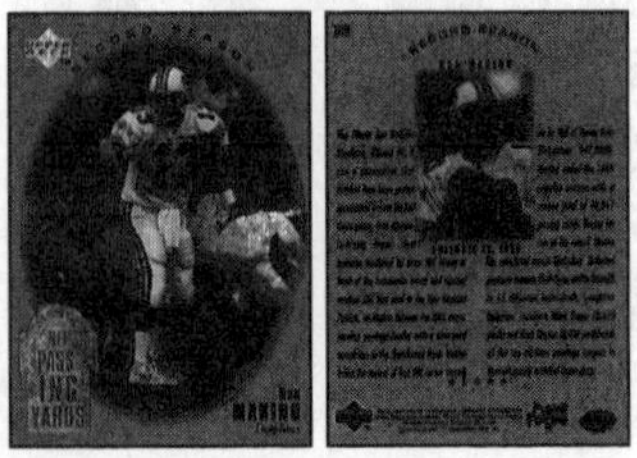

Randomly inserted in packs at a rate of one in 81, this 4-card standard-size set commemorates Dan's record breaking performances from the previous NFL season. The cards are numbered with an "RS" prefix.

	MINT	NRMT	EXC
COMPLETE SET (4)	60.00	27.00	7.50
COMMON CARD (RS1-RS4)	15.00	6.75	1.85

☐ RS1 All-Time Completions	15.00	6.75	1.85
☐ RS2 All-Time Passing Yards	15.00	6.75	1.85
☐ RS3 All-Time TD Passes	15.00	6.75	1.85
☐ RS4 300-Yard Games	15.00	6.75	1.85

1996 Upper Deck Silver Prime Choice Rookies

This standard sized redemption set was available by returning a trade card randomly inserted in 1996 Upper Deck Silver. The cards contain an inset photo of the player and a full length foil accented shot of the player with "Prime Choice Rookie" placed in the upper left hand corner

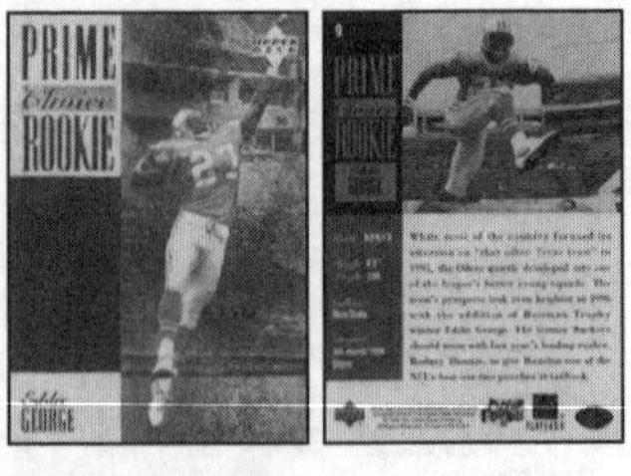

of the card with the player's name in the lower left hand corner. The backs contain a short biography with a color picture of the player. The redemption expired 8/30/96.

	MINT	NRMT	EXC
COMPLETE SET (20)	30.00	13.50	3.70
COMMON CARD (1-20)	.50	.23	.06

☐ 1 Keyshawn Johnson	2.00	.90	.25
☐ 2 Kevin Hardy	.75	.35	.09
☐ 3 Simeon Rice	.50	.23	.06
☐ 4 Tim Biakabutuka	1.25	.55	.16
☐ 5 Terry Glenn	6.00	2.70	.75
☐ 6 Rickey Dudley	.75	.35	.09
☐ 7 Alex Molden	.50	.23	.06
☐ 8 Regan Upshaw	.50	.23	.06
☐ 9 Eddie George	8.00	3.60	1.00
☐ 10 John Mobley	.50	.23	.06
☐ 11 Eddie Kennison	2.00	.90	.25
☐ 12 Marvin Harrison	2.00	.90	.25
☐ 13 Leeland McElroy	.75	.35	.09
☐ 14 Eric Moulds	1.25	.55	.16
☐ 15 Mike Alstott	1.00	.45	.12
☐ 16 Bobby Engram	1.25	.55	.16
☐ 17 Derrick Mayes	.75	.35	.09
☐ 18 Karim Abdul-Jabbar	4.00	1.80	.50
☐ 19 Stepfret Williams	.50	.23	.06
☐ 20 Jeff Lewis	.50	.23	.06
☐ NNO Redemption Card Expired	1.00	.45	.12

1995 Upper Deck Authenticated Joe Montana Jumbos

Upper Deck released this 4-card set through it's Authenticated cataloge. The cards of the 49ers' great quarterback measure approximately 5" by 3 1/2" and feature color action photos of Joe Montana playing in four Super Bowls. Each card came packaged in its own snap together plastic holder. The backs carry regular and post season statistics as well as the card's number.

	MINT	NRMT	EXC
COMPLETE SET (4)	40.00	18.00	5.00
COMMON CARD (1-4)	10.00	4.50	1.25

☐ 1 Joe Montana Super Bowl XVI	10.00	4.50	1.25
☐ 2 Joe Montana Super Bowl XIX	10.00	4.50	1.25
☐ 3 Joe Montana Super Bowl XXIII	10.00	4.50	1.25
☐ 4 Joe Montana Super Bowl XXIV	10.00	4.50	1.25

1993 U.S. Playing Cards Ditka's Picks

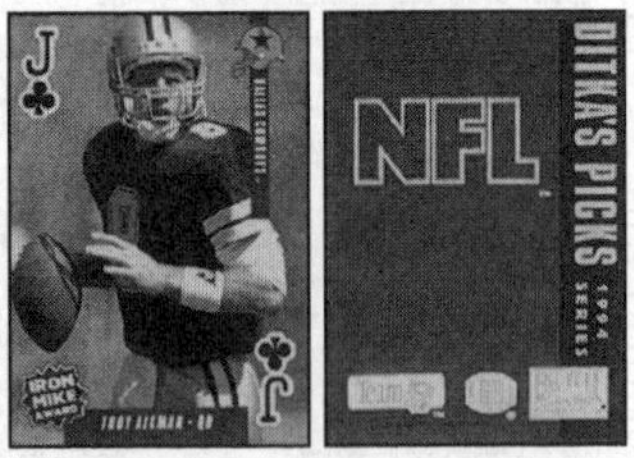

Part of the Bicycle Sports Collection, these 56 playing cards, featuring Mike Ditka's NFL player picks, measure the standard-size and have rounded corners. The fronts feature borderless color player action shots with slightly ghosted backgrounds. The player's name appears in white lettering within a green rectangle at the bottom. His team name and helmet appear at the upper right. The backs are black, gold, and green and, besides carrying the set's title, also display the logos for the Bicycle Sports Collection, NFL, and NFLPA. The set is checklisted below in playing card order by suits and assigned numbers to Aces (1), Jacks (11), Queens (12), and Kings (13).

	MINT	NRMT	EXC
COMPLETE SET (56)	5.00	2.20	.60
COMMON CARD	.05	.02	.01

☐ 1C Steve Young	.50	.23	.06
☐ 1D Joe Montana	.75	.35	.09
☐ 1H Dan Marino	.05	.02	.01
☐ 1S Troy Aikman	.75	.35	.09
☐ 2C Jim Lachey	.05	.02	.01

☐ 2D Richmond Webb	.05	.02	.01
☐ 2H Wilber Marshall	.05	.02	.01
☐ 2S Ronnie Lott	.10	.05	.01
☐ 3C Sean Gilbert	.05	.02	.01
☐ 3D Clay Matthews	.10	.05	.01
☐ 3H Jeff Lageman	.05	.02	.01
☐ 3S Audray McMillian	.05	.02	.01
☐ 4C Morten Andersen	.05	.02	.01
☐ 4D Pete Stoyanovich	.05	.02	.01
☐ 4H Rohn Stark	.05	.02	.01
☐ 4S Sean Landeta	.05	.02	.01
☐ 5C Broderick Thomas	.05	.02	.01
☐ 5D James Francis	.05	.02	.01
☐ 5H Derrick Thomas	.20	.09	.03
☐ 5S Tony Bennett	.05	.02	.01
☐ 6C Seth Joyner	.05	.02	.01
☐ 6D Percy Snow	.05	.02	.01
☐ 6H Junior Seau	.20	.09	.03
☐ 6S Chris Spielman	.05	.02	.01
☐ 7C Pierce Holt	.05	.02	.01
☐ 7D Rod Woodson	.20	.09	.03
☐ 7H Ray Childress	.05	.02	.01
☐ 7S Deion Sanders	.40	.18	.05
☐ 8C Jay Novacek	.10	.05	.01
☐ 8D Eric Green	.05	.02	.01
☐ 8H Marv Cook	.05	.02	.01
☐ 8S Brent Jones	.05	.02	.01
☐ 9C Randall McDaniel	.05	.02	.01
☐ 9D Mike Munchak	.05	.02	.01
☐ 9H Bruce Matthews	.05	.02	.01
☐ 9S Mark Stepnoski	.05	.02	.01
☐ 10C Harris Barton	.05	.02	.01
☐ 10D Steve Atwater	.05	.02	.01
☐ 10H Henry Jones	.05	.02	.01
☐ 10S Chuck Cecil	.05	.02	.01
☐ 11C Sterling Sharpe	.20	.09	.03
☐ 11D Anthony Miller	.10	.05	.01
☐ 11H Haywood Jeffires	.10	.05	.01
☐ 11S Jerry Rice	.75	.35	.09
☐ 12C Reggie White	.20	.09	.03
☐ 12D Howie Long	.10	.05	.01
☐ 12H Cortez Kennedy	.10	.05	.01
☐ 12S Chris Doleman	.05	.02	.01
☐ 13C Emmitt Smith	.05	.02	.01
☐ 13D Thurman Thomas	.20	.09	.03
☐ 13H Barry Foster	.05	.02	.01
☐ 13S Barry Sanders	.75	.35	.09
☐ WILD Tom Waddle	.05	.02	.01
☐ WILD Steve Wisniewski	.05	.02	.01
☐ NNO Ditka's AFC Picks	.10	.05	.01
☐ NNO Ditka's NFC Picks	.10	.05	.01

1994 U.S. Playing Cards Ditka's Picks

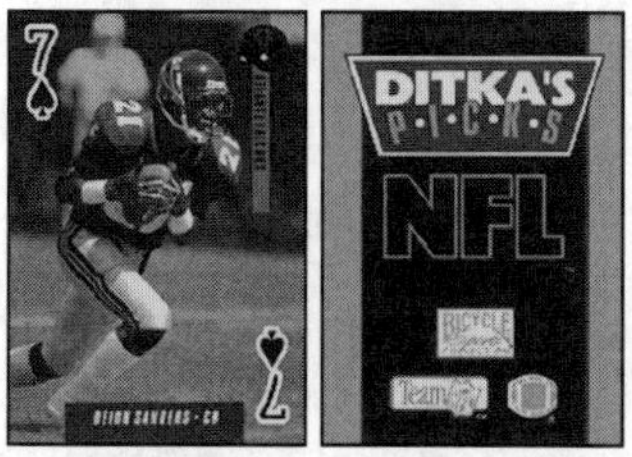

Part of the Bicycle Sports Collection, these 56 playing cards, featuring Mike Ditka's NFL player picks, measure the standard size and have rounded corners. The fronts feature boderless color player action shots with black-and-white backgrounds. The player's name appears in white lettering within a blue bar at the bottom. His team name and helmet appear at the upper right. The backs are black, silver, and blue and, besides carrying the set's title, display the logos for the Bicycle Sports Collection, NFL, and NFLPA. The set is checklisted below in playing card order by suits, with numbers assigned to Aces (1), Jacks (11), Queens (12), and Kings (13).

	MINT	NRMT	EXC
COMPLETE SET (56)	5.00	2.20	.60
COMMON CARD	.05	.02	.01
☐ 1C Sterling Sharpe	.10	.05	.01
☐ 1D Rickey Jackson	.05	.02	.01
☐ 1H Emmitt Smith	1.50	.70	.19
☐ 1S Rod Woodson	.10	.05	.01
☐ 2C Marcus Robertson	.05	.02	.01
☐ 2D Rohn Stark	.05	.02	.01
☐ 2H Dave Cadigan	.05	.02	.01
☐ 2S Kevin Williams	.10	.05	.01
☐ 3C John Kasay	.05	.02	.01
☐ 3D Carlton Haselrig	.05	.02	.01
☐ 3H Donnell Woolford	.05	.02	.01
☐ 3S Dan Wilkinson	.10	.05	.01
☐ 4C Marshall Faulk	.75	.35	.09
☐ 4D Greg Montgomery	.05	.02	.01
☐ 4H Leslie O'Neal	.05	.02	.01
☐ 4S Eric Curry	.05	.02	.01
☐ 5C Eric Turner	.05	.02	.01
☐ 5D Rick Mirer	.20	.09	.03
☐ 5H Kevin Smith	.05	.02	.01
☐ 5S Troy Vincent	.05	.02	.01
☐ 6C Cornelius Bennett	.10	.05	.01
☐ 6D Seth Joyner	.10	.05	.01
☐ 6H Gary Zimmerman	.05	.02	.01
☐ 6S LeRoy Butler	.05	.02	.01
☐ 7C Tommy Vardell	.05	.02	.01
☐ 7D Richmond Webb	.05	.02	.01
☐ 7H Ben Coates	.20	.09	.03
☐ 7S Steve Everitt	.05	.02	.01
☐ 8C Tom Rathman	.05	.02	.01
☐ 8D Ray Childress	.05	.02	.01
☐ 8H Tim Brown	.20	.09	.03
☐ 8S Mark Bavaro	.05	.02	.01
☐ 9C Bennie Blades	.05	.02	.01
☐ 9D John(Jumbo) Elliott	.05	.02	.01
☐ 9H Jim Lachey	.05	.02	.01
☐ 9S Neil Smith	.10	.05	.01
☐ 10C Sean Gilbert	.05	.02	.01
☐ 10D Steve Tasker	.05	.02	.01
☐ 10H Chris Zorich	.05	.02	.01
☐ 10S Haywood Jeffires	.10	.05	.01
☐ 11C Troy Aikman	.75	.35	.09
☐ 11D Jeff Hostetler	.10	.05	.01
☐ 11H Junior Seau	.20	.09	.03
☐ 11S Mark Stepnoski	.05	.02	.01
☐ 12C Chris Spielman	.05	.02	.01
☐ 12D Marcus Allen	.20	.09	.03
☐ 12H Reggie White	.20	.09	.03
☐ 12S Harris Barton	.05	.02	.01
☐ 13C Andre Rison	.10	.05	.01
☐ 13D Randall McDaniel	.05	.02	.01
☐ 13H Cortez Kennedy	.05	.02	.01
☐ 13S Norm Johnson	.05	.02	.01
☐ WILD Heath Shuler	.40	.18	.05
☐ WILD Shannon Sharpe	.10	.05	.01
☐ NNO Ditka's AFC Picks	.10	.05	.01
☐ NNO Ditka's NFC Picks	.10	.05	.01

1995 U.S. Playing Cards Ditka's Picks

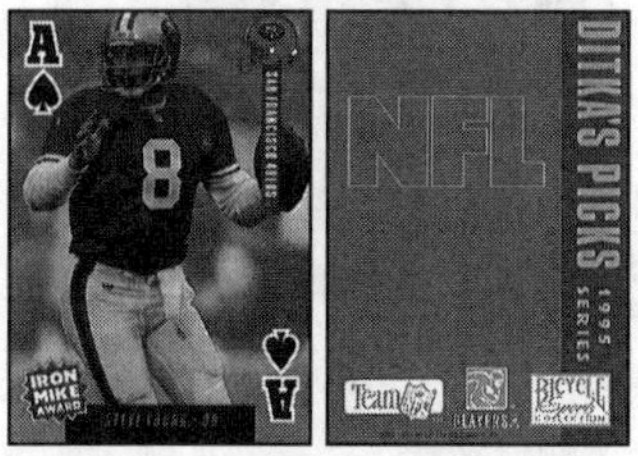

Part of the Bicycle Sports Collection, these 56 playing cards, featuring Mike Ditka's NFL player picks, measure the standard size and have rounded corners. The fronts feature borderless color action player images with black-and-white backgrounds. The player's name and position appear in gold lettering within a black bar at the bottom. His team name and helmet appear at the upper right. The backs are burgundy, gold, and black and, besides carrying the set's title, also display the logos for the Bicycle Sports Collection, NFL, and NFLPA. The set is checklisted below in playing card order by suits with numbers assigned to Aces (1), Jacks (11), Queens (12), and Kings (13).

	MINT	NRMT	EXC
COMPLETE SET (56)	5.00	2.20	.60
COMMON CARD	.05	.02	.01
☐ 1C Randall McDaniel	.05	.02	.01
☐ 1D Dan Marino	1.50	.70	.19
☐ 1H Drew Bledsoe	.75	.35	.09
☐ 1S Steve Young	.50	.23	.06
☐ 2C Renaldo Turnbull	.05	.02	.01
☐ 2D Tony Boselli	.10	.05	.01
☐ 2H Ki-Jana Carter	.20	.09	.03
☐ 2S Todd Sauerbrun	.05	.02	.01
☐ 3C Aeneas Williams	.05	.02	.01
☐ 3D Bruce Smith	.20	.09	.03
☐ 3H Shawn Jefferson	.05	.02	.01
☐ 3S Andy Harmon	.05	.02	.01
☐ 4C Donnell Woolford	.05	.02	.01
☐ 4D Ronnie Lott	.10	.05	.01
☐ 4H Tim Brown	.20	.09	.03
☐ 4S Charles Haley	.05	.02	.01
☐ 5C Merton Hanks	.05	.02	.01
☐ 5D Eric Turner	.05	.02	.01
☐ 5H Ben Coates	.20	.09	.03
☐ 5S Brian Williams	.05	.02	.01
☐ 6C Eric Metcalf	.10	.05	.01
☐ 6D Dave Meggett	.05	.02	.01
☐ 6H Neil Smith	.10	.05	.01
☐ 6S Ian Beckles	.05	.02	.01
☐ 7C Herman Moore	.20	.09	.03
☐ 7D Mel Gray	.05	.02	.01
☐ 7H Ray Childress	.05	.02	.01
☐ 7S Jim Lachey	.05	.02	.01
☐ 8C Bennie Blades	.05	.02	.01
☐ 8D Kevin Greene	.10	.05	.01
☐ 8H Gary Zimmerman	.05	.02	.01
☐ 8S William Roaf	.05	.02	.01
☐ 9C Bryant Young	.10	.05	.01
☐ 9D Bruce Matthews	.05	.02	.01
☐ 9H Richmond Webb	.05	.02	.01
☐ 9S Howard Cross	.05	.02	.01
☐ 10C Seth Joyner	.05	.02	.01
☐ 10D Marshall Faulk	.40	.18	.05
☐ 10H Jeff Dellenbach	.05	.02	.01
☐ 10S Cris Carter	.20	.09	.03
☐ 11C Sean Gilbert	.05	.02	.01
☐ 11D John Carney	.05	.02	.01
☐ 11H Rohn Stark	.05	.02	.01
☐ 11S Jerry Rice	.75	.35	.09
☐ 12C Reggie White	.20	.09	.03
☐ 12D Terry McDaniel	.05	.02	.01
☐ 12H Rod Woodson	.20	.09	.03
☐ 12S Daryl Johnston	.10	.05	.01
☐ 13C Norm Johnson	.05	.02	.01
☐ 13D Cortez Kennedy	.05	.02	.01
☐ 13H Cornelius Bennett	.10	.05	.01
☐ 13S Barry Sanders	.75	.35	.09
☐ WILD Junior Seau	.20	.09	.03
☐ WILD Chris Spielman	.05	.02	.01
☐ NNO Ditka's AFC Picks	.10	.05	.01
☐ NNO Ditka's NFC Picks	.10	.05	.01

1963-64 Vikings Team Issue

This 20-card set of the Minnesota Vikings measures approximately 5" by 7" and features black-and-white borderless player portraits with the players position, name and team in a bar at the card bottom. The photos were likely issued over a number of years. Either a Vikings or Minnesota name can be found on the cardfronts.The backs are blank. The cards are unnumbered and checklisted below in alphabetical order.

	NRMT	VG-E	GOOD
COMPLETE SET (20)	100.00	45.00	12.50
COMMON CARD (1-20)	5.00	2.20	.60
☐ 1 Jim Battle	5.00	2.20	.60
☐ 2 Larry Bowie	5.00	2.20	.60
☐ 3 Bill Butler	5.00	2.20	.60
☐ 4 Lee Calland	5.00	2.20	.60
☐ 5 John Campbell	5.00	2.20	.60
☐ 6 Leon Clarke	5.00	2.20	.60
☐ 7 Paul Dickson	5.00	2.20	.60
☐ 8 Terry Dillon	5.00	2.20	.60
☐ 9 Paul Flatley	7.50	3.40	.95
☐ 10 Tom Frankhauser	5.00	2.20	.60
☐ 11 Rip Hawkins	6.00	2.70	.75
☐ 12 Don Hultz	6.00	2.70	.75
☐ 13 Errol Linden	5.00	2.20	.60
☐ 14 Mike Mercer	6.00	2.70	.75
☐ 15 Ray Poage	5.00	2.20	.60
☐ 16 Jim Prestel	5.00	2.20	.60
☐ 17 Jerry Reichow	6.00	2.70	.75
☐ 18 Ed Sharockman	6.00	2.70	.75
☐ 19 Gordon Smith	5.00	2.20	.60
☐ 20 Tom Wilson	6.00	2.70	.75

1965 Vikings Team Issue

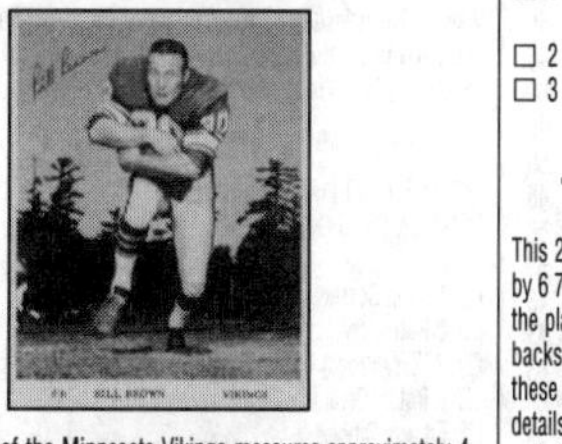

This 10-card set of the Minnesota Vikings measures approximately 4 1/4" by 5 1/2" and features black-and-white player portraits with the players position (appreviated), name and team in a bar at the card bottom. The photos were likely issued over a number of years and vary slightly in text style and size. The cardbacks are blank; each is unnumbered and checklisted below in alphabetical order.

	NRMT	VG-E	GOOD
COMPLETE SET (10)	50.00	22.00	6.25
COMMON CARD (1-10)	5.00	2.20	.60
☐ 1 Larry Bowie	5.00	2.20	.60
☐ 2 Bill Brown	6.00	2.70	.75
☐ 3 Fred Cox	5.00	2.20	.60
☐ 4 Paul Dickson	5.00	2.20	.60
☐ 5 Carl Eller	8.00	3.60	1.00
☐ 6 Rip Hawkins	5.00	2.20	.60
☐ 7 Karl Kassulke	5.00	2.20	.60
☐ 8 Mick Tingelhoff	6.00	2.70	.75
☐ 9 Norm Van Brocklin CO	8.00	3.60	1.00
☐ 10 Ron Vanderkelen	5.00	2.20	.60

1966 Vikings Team Issue

These large photo cards are approximately 8" by 10" and feature black-and-white player photos. Each has a white border and was printed on thick glossy stock. The cards are unnumbered and checklisted below in alphabetical order. They are very similar to the 1967 and 1968 issues, but can be differentiated by the player's position, name, and then team name spread out across the border below the photo. Any additions to the checklist below are appreciated.

	NRMT	VG-E	GOOD
COMPLETE SET (3)	15.00	6.75	1.85
COMMON CARD (1-3)	5.00	2.20	.60
☐ 1 Larry Bowie	5.00	2.20	.60
☐ 2 Dave Tobey	5.00	2.20	.60
☐ 3 Ron Vanderkelen	5.00	2.20	.60

1967 Vikings Team Issue

These large photo cards are approximately 8" by 10" and feature black-and-white player photos. Each has a white border and was printed on thick glossy stock. The cards are unnumbered and checklisted below in alphabetical order. They are very similar to the 1966 and 1968 issues, but can be differentiated by the player's name, postion, and team name tightly arranged in the border below the photo.

	NRMT	VG-E	GOOD
COMPLETE SET (23)	110.00	50.00	14.00
COMMON CARD (1-23)	5.00	2.20	.60
☐ 1 Grady Alderman (Offensive lineman)	7.50	3.40	.95
☐ 2 John Beasley	5.00	2.20	.60
☐ 3 Bob Berry	5.00	2.20	.60
☐ 4 Doug Davis	5.00	2.20	.60
☐ 5 Paul Dickinson	5.00	2.20	.60
☐ 6 Paul Flatley	6.00	2.70	.75
☐ 7 Bob Grim	6.00	2.70	.75
☐ 8 Dale Hackbart	5.00	2.20	.60
☐ 9 Don Hansen	5.00	2.20	.60
☐ 10 Jim Hargrove	5.00	2.20	.60
☐ 11 Clint Jones	6.00	2.70	.75
☐ 12 Jeff Jordan	5.00	2.20	.60
☐ 13 Joe Kapp	7.50	3.40	.95
☐ 14 John Kirby	5.00	2.20	.60
☐ 15 Gary Larsen	6.00	2.70	.75
☐ 16 Earsell Mackbee	5.00	2.20	.60
☐ 17 Marlin McKeever	5.00	2.20	.60
☐ 18 Milt Sunde	5.00	2.20	.60
☐ 19 Jim Vellone	5.00	2.20	.60
☐ 20 Bobby Walden	5.00	2.20	.60
☐ 21 Lonnie Warwick	5.00	2.20	.60
☐ 22 Gene Washington (End)	6.00	2.70	.75
☐ 23 Roy Winston	5.00	2.20	.60

1968 Vikings Team Issue

These large photo cards are approximately 8" by 10" and feature black-and-white player photos. Each has a white border and was printed on thick glossy stock. The cards are unnumbered and checklisted below in alphabetical order. They are very similar to the 1966 and 1967 issues, but can be differentiated by the player's name, postion (initial), and team name loosely arranged in the border below the photo.

	NRMT-MT	EXC	G-VG
COMPLETE SET (3)	12.00	5.50	1.50
COMMON CARD (1-3)	4.00	1.80	.50
☐ 1 Grady Alderman Tackle	4.00	1.80	.50
☐ 2 Gary Cuozzo	4.00	1.80	.50
☐ 3 Gene Washington Wide receiver	4.00	1.80	.50

1969 Vikings Team Issue

This 27-card set of the Minnesota Vikings measures approximately 5" by 6 7/8" and features black-and-white borderless player portraits with the players name, position and team in a wide bar at the bottom. The backs are blank. Although similar to earlier Vikings' team issues, these photos can be differentiated by the order in which the player details are listed at the bottom of the card. The cards are unnumbered and checklisted below in alphabetical order.

	NRMT-MT	EXC	G-VG
COMPLETE SET (27)	100.00	45.00	12.50
COMMON CARD (1-27)	4.00	1.80	.50
☐ 1 Bookie Bolin	4.00	1.80	.50
☐ 2 Bobby Bryant	6.00	2.70	.75
☐ 3 John Beasley	4.00	1.80	.50
☐ 4 Gary Cuozzo	6.00	2.70	.75
☐ 5 Doug Davis	4.00	1.80	.50
☐ 6 Paul Dickson	4.00	1.80	.50
☐ 7 Bob Grim	5.00	2.20	.60
☐ 8 Dale Hackbart	4.00	1.80	.50
☐ 9 Jim Hargrove	4.00	1.80	.50
☐ 10 John Henderson	4.00	1.80	.50
☐ 11 Wally Hilgenberg	5.00	2.20	.60
☐ 12 Clinton Jones	5.00	2.20	.60
☐ 13 Karl Kassulke	4.00	1.80	.50
☐ 14 Kent Kramer	4.00	1.80	.50
☐ 15 Gary Larsen	5.00	2.20	.60
☐ 16 Bob Lee	5.00	2.20	.60
☐ 17 Jim Lindsey	4.00	1.80	.50
☐ 18 Earsell Mackbee	4.00	1.80	.50
☐ 19 Mike McGill	4.00	1.80	.50
☐ 20 Oscar Reed	4.00	1.80	.50
☐ 21 Ed Sharockman	4.00	1.80	.50
☐ 22 Steve Smith	4.00	1.80	.50
☐ 23 Milt Sunde	4.00	1.80	.50
☐ 24 Jim Vellone	4.00	1.80	.50
☐ 25 Lonnie Warwick	4.00	1.80	.50
☐ 26 Gene Washington	6.00	2.70	.75
☐ 27 Charlie West	4.00	1.80	.50

1970-71 Vikings Team Issue

This 17-card set of the Minnesota Vikings measures approximately 5" by 7" and features black-and-white borderless player portraits with the players name and team name only in a wide bar at the bottom. The

backs are blank. The photos were likely issued over a number of years due to the different type styles used on the photo's text. The cards are unnumbered and checklisted below in alphabetical order. Any additions to this checklist would be greatly appreciated.

	NRMT-MT	EXC	G-VG
COMPLETE SET (17)	60.00	27.00	7.50
COMMON CARD (1-17)	4.00	1.80	.50
☐ 1 John Beasley	4.00	1.80	.50
☐ 2 Doug Davis	4.00	1.80	.50
☐ 3 Paul Dickson	4.00	1.80	.50
☐ 4 Bob Grim	5.00	2.20	.60
☐ 5 Jim Hargrove	4.00	1.80	.50
☐ 6 John Henderson	4.00	1.80	.50
☐ 7 Clint Jones	4.00	1.80	.50
☐ 8 Bob Lee	5.00	2.20	.60
☐ 9 Jim Lindsey	4.00	1.80	.50
☐ 10 Oscar Reed	4.00	1.80	.50
☐ 11 Ed Sharockman	4.00	1.80	.50
☐ 12 Steve Smith	4.00	1.80	.50
☐ 13 Milt Sunde	4.00	1.80	.50
☐ 14 Dave Tobey	4.00	1.80	.50
☐ 15 Jim Vellone	4.00	1.80	.50
☐ 16 John Ward	4.00	1.80	.50
☐ 17 Charlie West	5.00	2.20	.60

1971 Vikings Photos

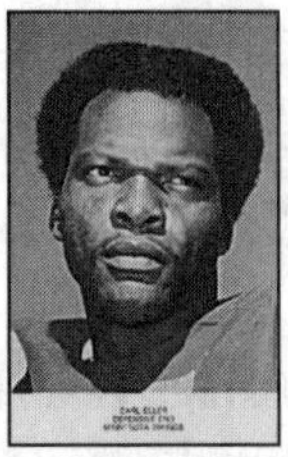

Issued in the late summer of 1971 (preseason), this team-issued set consists of 49 four-color close-up photos printed on thin paper stock. Each photo measures approximately 5" by 7 7/16". The player's name, position, and team name appear in a white bottom border. The backs are blank. The cards are unnumbered and checklisted below in alphabetical order.

	NRMT-MT	EXC	G-VG
COMPLETE SET (52)	200.00	90.00	25.00
COMMON CARD	3.50	1.55	.45
☐ 1 Grady Alderman	5.00	2.20	.60
☐ 2 Neill Armstrong CO	3.50	1.55	.45
☐ 3 John Beasley	3.50	1.55	.45
☐ 4 Bill Brown	5.00	2.20	.60
☐ 5 Bob Brown	3.50	1.55	.45
☐ 6 Bobby Bryant	4.00	1.80	.50
☐ 7 Jerry Burns CO	3.50	1.55	.45
☐ 8 Fred Cox	4.00	1.80	.50
☐ 9 Gary Cuozzo	4.00	1.80	.50
☐ 10 Doug Davis	3.50	1.55	.45
☐ 11 Al Denson	3.50	1.55	.45
☐ 12 Paul Dickson	3.50	1.55	.45
☐ 13 Carl Eller	8.00	3.60	1.00
☐ 14 Bud Grant CO	10.00	4.50	1.25
☐ 15 Bob Grim	4.00	1.80	.50
☐ 16 Leo Hayden	3.50	1.55	.45
☐ 17 John Henderson	3.50	1.55	.45
☐ 18 Wally Hilgenberg	4.00	1.80	.50
☐ 19 Noel Jenke	3.50	1.55	.45
☐ 20 Clint Jones	4.00	1.80	.50
☐ 21 Karl Kassulke	3.50	1.55	.45
☐ 22 Paul Krause	6.00	2.70	.75
☐ 23 Gary Larsen	4.00	1.80	.50
☐ 24 Bob Lee	4.00	1.80	.50
☐ 25 Jim Lindsey	3.50	1.55	.45
☐ 26 Jim Marshall	8.00	3.60	1.00
☐ 27 Bus Mertes CO	3.50	1.55	.45
☐ 28 John Michels CO	3.50	1.55	.45
☐ 29 Jocko Nelson CO	3.50	1.55	.45
☐ 30 Dave Osborn	5.00	2.20	.60
☐ 31 Alan Page	12.00	5.50	1.50
☐ 32 Jack Patera CO	3.50	1.55	.45
☐ 33 Jerry Patton	3.50	1.55	.45
☐ 34 Pete Perreault	3.50	1.55	.45
☐ 35 Oscar Reed	3.50	1.55	.45
☐ 36 Ed Sharockman	3.50	1.55	.45
☐ 37 Norm Snead	5.00	2.20	.60
☐ 38 Milt Sunde	3.50	1.55	.45
☐ 39 Doug Sutherland	3.50	1.55	.45
☐ 40 Mick Tingelhoff	5.00	2.20	.60
☐ 41 Stu Voigt	4.00	1.80	.50
☐ 42 John Ward	3.50	1.55	.45
☐ 43 Lonnie Warwick	3.50	1.55	.45
☐ 44 Gene Washington	5.00	2.20	.60
☐ 45 Charlie West	3.50	1.55	.45
☐ 46 Ed White	5.00	2.20	.60
☐ 47 Carl Winfrey	3.50	1.55	.45
☐ 48 Roy Winston	4.00	1.80	.50
☐ 49 Jeff Wright	3.50	1.55	.45
☐ 50 Nate Wright	4.00	1.80	.50
☐ 51 Ron Yary	5.00	2.20	.60
☐ 52 Godfrey Zaunbrecher	3.50	1.55	.45

1971 Vikings Postcards

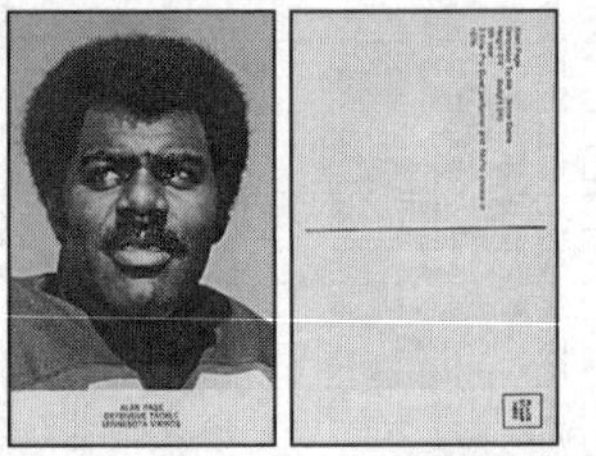

This 19-card set measures roughly 5" by 7 1/2" and features posed color close-up photos on the fronts. These cards were issued after the season had begun and may have been sold at the stadium. The player's name, position, and team name appear in a white bottom border. As with a postcard, the horizontal backs are divided into two sections by a thin black stripe. Brief biographical information is given at the upper left corner, while a box for the stamp is printed at the upper right corner. The cards are unnumbered and checklisted below in alphabetical order.

	NRMT-MT	EXC	G-VG
COMPLETE SET (19)	70.00	32.00	8.75
COMMON CARD (1-19)	3.00	1.35	.35
☐ 1 Grady Alderman	4.00	1.80	.50
☐ 2 Neill Armstrong CO	3.00	1.35	.35
☐ 3 John Beasley	3.00	1.35	.35
☐ 4 Paul Dickson	3.00	1.35	.35
☐ 5 Bud Grant CO	10.00	4.50	1.25
☐ 6 Wally Hilgenberg	4.00	1.80	.50
☐ 7 Noel Jenke	3.00	1.35	.35
☐ 8 Paul Krause	5.00	2.20	.60
☐ 9 Gary Larsen	4.00	1.80	.50
☐ 10 Dave Osborn	4.00	1.80	.50
☐ 11 Alan Page	12.00	5.50	1.50
☐ 12 Jerry Patton	3.00	1.35	.35
☐ 13 Doug Sutherland	3.00	1.35	.35
☐ 14 Mick Tingelhoff	4.00	1.80	.50
☐ 15 Lonnie Warwick	3.00	1.35	.35
☐ 16 Charlie West	3.00	1.35	.35
☐ 17 Jeff Wright	3.00	1.35	.35
☐ 18 Nate Wright	4.00	1.80	.50
☐ 19 Godfrey Zaunbrecher	3.00	1.35	.35

1973 Vikings Team Issue

This 17-card set of the Minnesota Vikings measures roughly 5" by 7". The fronts feature white bordered black-and-white player portraits with the player's name and team in the bottom wide margin. The backs are blank. The photos can be differentiated from previous Vikings Team Issues by the distinctive white borders and scripted team name on the card fronts. The cards are unnumbered and checklisted below in alphabetical order.

	NRMT-MT	EXC	G-VG
COMPLETE SET (17)	45.00	20.00	5.50
COMMON CARD (1-17)	3.00	1.35	.35
☐ 1 John Beasley	3.00	1.35	.35
☐ 2 Bob Berry	4.00	1.80	.50
☐ 3 Terry Brown	3.00	1.35	.35
☐ 4 Bobby Bryant	4.00	1.80	.50
☐ 5 Larry Dibbles	3.00	1.35	.35
☐ 6 Mike Eischeid	3.00	1.35	.35
☐ 7 Charles Goodrum	3.00	1.35	.35
☐ 8 Neil Graff	3.00	1.35	.35
☐ 9 Wally Hilgenberg	4.00	1.80	.50
☐ 10 Amos Martin	3.00	1.35	.35
☐ 11 Brent McClanahan	4.00	1.80	.50
☐ 12 John Michels	3.00	1.35	.35
☐ 13 Oscar Reed	3.00	1.35	.35
☐ 14 John Ward	3.00	1.35	.35
☐ 15 Charlie West	3.00	1.35	.35
☐ 16 Jeff Wright	3.00	1.35	.35
☐ 17 Nate Wright	4.00	1.80	.50

1978 Vikings Country Kitchen

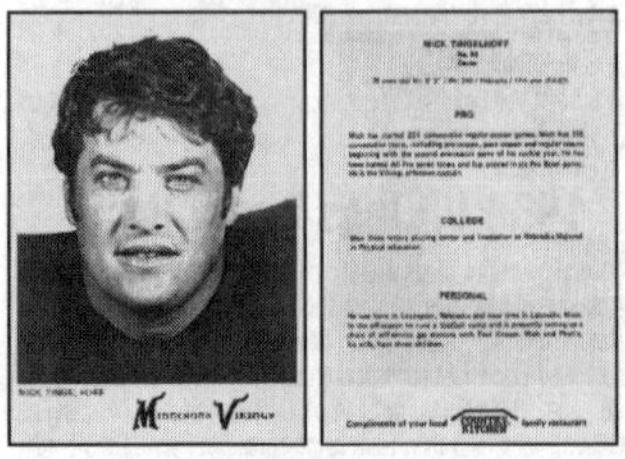

This seven-card set was sponsored by Country Kitchen Restaurants and measures approximately 5" by 7". The front features a black and white head shot of the player. The card backs have biographical and statistical information. The cards are unnumbered and hence are listed alphabetically below.

	NRMT-MT	EXC	G-VG
COMPLETE SET (7)	45.00	20.00	5.50
COMMON CARD (1-7)	5.00	2.20	.60
☐ 1 Bobby Bryant	5.00	2.20	.60
☐ 2 Tommy Kramer	6.00	2.70	.75
☐ 3 Paul Krause	7.50	3.40	.95
☐ 4 Ahmad Rashad	10.00	4.50	1.25
☐ 5 Jeff Siemon	5.00	2.20	.60
☐ 6 Mick Tingelhoff	6.00	2.70	.75
☐ 7 Sammie White	7.50	3.40	.95

1979 Vikings SuperAmerica

The 1979 SuperAmerica Vikings set was distributed through the SuperAmerica convenience stores with a fill-up of gasoline. These 10" by 12" unnumbered sepia posters display watercolor art of the player in action, with a write-up about his career in the top third of the poster. The bottom third of the poster shows a watercolor close-up of the particular player along with a descriptive cutline for the poster. The posters are cataloged in alphabetical order below. There are seven known posters.

	NRMT-MT	EXC	G-VG
COMPLETE SET (7)	40.00	18.00	5.00
COMMON CARD (1-7)	4.00	1.80	.50
☐ 1 Bill Brown	5.00	2.20	.60
☐ 2 Karl Kassulke	4.00	1.80	.50
☐ 3 Jim Marshall	6.00	2.70	.75
☐ 4 Hugh McElhenny	7.50	3.40	.95
☐ 5 Dave Osborn	4.00	1.80	.50
☐ 6 Fran Tarkenton	12.00	5.50	1.50
☐ 7 Gene Washington	5.00	2.20	.60

1983 Vikings Police

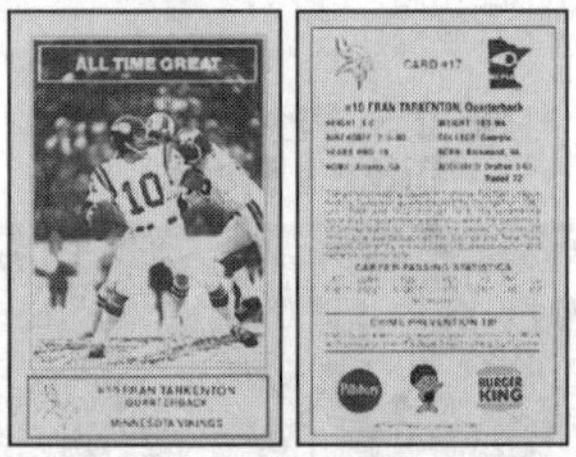

The 1983 Minnesota Vikings set contains 17 numbered cards. The cards measure approximately 2 5/8" by 4 1/8". This first Viking police set is sponsored by Pillsbury, Minnesota Crime Prevention Officers Association, Green Giant, and Burger King. In addition to the Vikings' logo, logos of all five organizations appear on the backs. The fronts contain a Vikings logo.

	MINT	NRMT	EXC
COMPLETE SET (17)	10.00	4.50	1.25
COMMON CARD (1-17)	.50	.23	.06
☐ 1 Checklist Card	.75	.35	.09
☐ 2 Tommy Kramer	1.00	.45	.12
☐ 3 Ted Brown	.50	.23	.06
☐ 4 Joe Senser	.50	.23	.06
☐ 5 Sammie White	1.00	.45	.12
☐ 6 Doug Martin	.50	.23	.06
☐ 7 Matt Blair	.75	.35	.09
☐ 8 Bud Grant CO	2.00	.90	.25
☐ 9 Scott Studwell	.75	.35	.09
☐ 10 Greg Coleman	.50	.23	.06
☐ 11 John Turner	.50	.23	.06
☐ 12 Jim Hough	.50	.23	.06
☐ 13 Joey Browner	1.00	.45	.12
☐ 14 Dennis Swilley	.50	.23	.06
☐ 15 Darrin Nelson	.75	.35	.09
☐ 16 Mark Mullaney	.50	.23	.06
☐ 17 Fran Tarkenton (All-Time Great)	3.50	1.55	.45

1984 Vikings Police

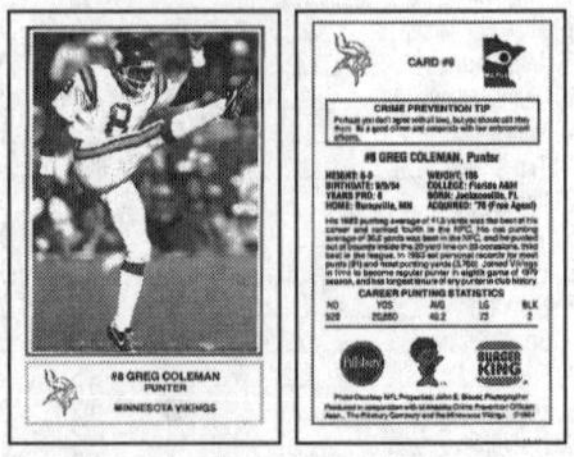

This numbered 18-card set features the Minnesota Vikings. Cards measure approximately 2 5/8" by 4 1/8" and are dated in the lower right corner of the reverse. The set was printed on thick card stock. Logos on the card backs are printed in color. The set was sponsored by Pillsbury, Burger King, and the Minnesota Crime Prevention Officers Association.

	MINT	NRMT	EXC
COMPLETE SET (18)	8.00	3.60	1.00
COMMON CARD (1-18)	.40	.18	.05
☐ 1 Checklist Card	.60	.25	.07
☐ 2 Keith Nord	.40	.18	.05
☐ 3 Joe Senser	.40	.18	.05
☐ 4 Tommy Kramer	.75	.35	.09
☐ 5 Darrin Nelson	.60	.25	.07
☐ 6 Tim Irwin	.40	.18	.05
☐ 7 Mark Mullaney	.40	.18	.05
☐ 8 Les Steckel CO	.40	.18	.05
☐ 9 Greg Coleman	.40	.18	.05
☐ 10 Tommy Hannon	.40	.18	.05
☐ 11 Curtis Rouse	.40	.18	.05
☐ 12 Scott Studwell	.60	.25	.07
☐ 13 Steve Jordan	.75	.35	.09
☐ 14 Willie Teal	.40	.18	.05
☐ 15 Ted Brown	.60	.25	.07
☐ 16 Sammie White	.75	.35	.09
☐ 17 Matt Blair	.60	.25	.07
☐ 18 Jim Marshall (All Time Great)	2.00	.90	.25

1985 Vikings Police

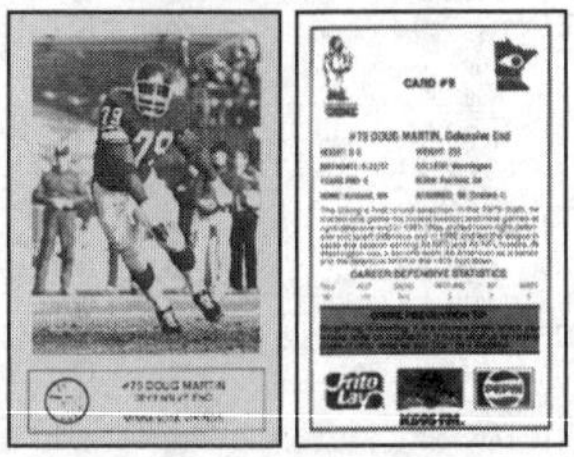

This 16-card set of Minnesota Vikings is numbered on the back. Cards measure approximately 2 5/8" by 4 1/8" and the backs contain a "Crime Prevention Tip". The set was sponsored by Frito-Lay, Pepsi-Cola, KS95-FM, and local area law enforcement agencies. Card backs are written in red and blue on white card stock. The set commemorates the 25th (Silver) Anniversary Season for the Vikings. The checklist card tells which week each card was available.

	MINT	NRMT	EXC
COMPLETE SET (16)	7.00	3.10	.85
COMMON CARD (1-16)	.40	.18	.05
☐ 1 Checklist Card	.60	.25	.07
☐ 2 Bud Grant CO	1.25	.55	.16
☐ 3 Matt Blair	.60	.25	.07
☐ 4 Alfred Anderson	.40	.18	.05
☐ 5 Fred McNeill	.40	.18	.05
☐ 6 Tommy Kramer	.75	.35	.09
☐ 7 Jan Stenerud	1.00	.45	.12
☐ 8 Sammie White	.75	.35	.09
☐ 9 Doug Martin	.40	.18	.05
☐ 10 Greg Coleman	.40	.18	.05
☐ 11 Steve Riley	.40	.18	.05
☐ 12 Walker Lee Ashley	.40	.18	.05
☐ 13 Tim Irwin	.40	.18	.05
☐ 14 Scott Studwell	.40	.18	.05
☐ 15 Darrin Nelson	.60	.25	.07
☐ 16 Mick Tingelhoff (All-Time Great)	.75	.35	.09

1986 Vikings Police

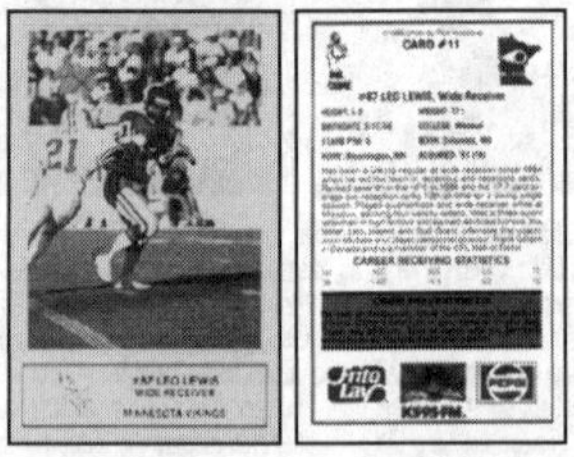

This 14-card set of Minnesota Vikings is numbered on the back. Cards measure approximately 2 5/8" by 4 1/8" and the backs contain a "Crime Prevention Tip". The checklist for the set is on the back of the head coach card.

	MINT	NRMT	EXC
COMPLETE SET (14)	8.00	3.60	1.00
COMMON CARD (1-14)	.40	.18	.05
☐ 1 Jerry Burns CO (Checklist back)	.40	.18	.05
☐ 2 Darrin Nelson	.60	.25	.07
☐ 3 Tommy Kramer	.75	.35	.09
☐ 4 Anthony Carter	1.50	.70	.19
☐ 5 Scott Studwell	.40	.18	.05
☐ 6 Chris Doleman	1.50	.70	.19
☐ 7 Joey Browner	.75	.35	.09
☐ 8 Steve Jordan	.75	.35	.09
☐ 9 David Howard	.40	.18	.05
☐ 10 Tim Newton	.40	.18	.05
☐ 11 Leo Lewis	.40	.18	.05
☐ 12 Keith Millard	.75	.35	.09
☐ 13 Doug Martin	.40	.18	.05
☐ 14 Bill Brown (All-Time Great)	.60	.25	.07

1987 Vikings Police

This 14-card set of Minnesota Vikings is numbered on the back. Cards measure approximately 2 5/8" by 4 1/8" and are in full color on the

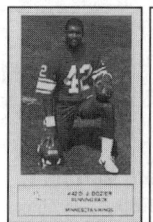 

front. The backs contain a "Crime Prevention Tip". The checklist for the set is on the back of the first card. Purple Power '87 is actually an action montage by artist Cliff Spohn. Reportedly 2.1 million cards were distributed during the 14-week promotion. The set was sponsored by the Vikings, Frito-Lay, Campbell's Soup, and KSTP-FM in cooperation with the Minnesota Crime Prevention Officers Association.

	MINT	NRMT	EXC
COMPLETE SET (14)	8.00	3.60	1.00
COMMON CARD (1-14)	.40	.18	.05
☐ 1 Vikings Theme Art	.60	.25	.07
(checklist back)			
☐ 2 Jerry Burns CO	.60	.25	.07
☐ 3 Scott Studwell	.40	.18	.05
☐ 4 Tommy Kramer	.75	.35	.09
☐ 5 Gerald Robinson	.40	.18	.05
☐ 6 Wade Wilson	1.00	.45	.12
☐ 7 Anthony Carter	1.50	.70	.19
☐ 8 Terry Tausch	.40	.18	.05
☐ 9 Leo Lewis	.40	.18	.05
☐ 10 Keith Millard	.75	.35	.09
☐ 11 Carl Lee	.40	.18	.05
☐ 12 Steve Jordan	.60	.25	.07
☐ 13 D.J. Dozier	.60	.25	.07
☐ 14 Alan Page ATG	1.50	.70	.19

1988 Vikings Police

The 1988 Police Minnesota Vikings set contains 12 numbered cards measuring approximately 2 5/8" by 4 1/8". There are nine cards of current players, plus one checklist card, one "Vikings Defense" card, and one of "All-Time Great" Paul Krause.

	MINT	NRMT	EXC
COMPLETE SET (12)	6.00	2.70	.75
COMMON CARD (1-12)	.40	.18	.05
☐ 1 Vikings Offense	.60	.25	.07
(Checklist on back)			
☐ 2 Jesse Solomon	.40	.18	.05
☐ 3 Kirk Lowdermilk	.40	.18	.05
☐ 4 Darrin Nelson	.60	.25	.07
☐ 5 Chris Doleman	.75	.35	.09
☐ 6 D.J. Dozier	.60	.25	.07
☐ 7 Gary Zimmerman	.60	.25	.07
☐ 8 Allen Rice	.40	.18	.05
☐ 9 Joey Browner	.60	.25	.07
☐ 10 Anthony Carter	1.00	.45	.12
☐ 11 Vikings Defense	.60	.25	.07
☐ 12 Paul Krause	1.00	.45	.12
(All-Time Great)			

1989 Vikings Police

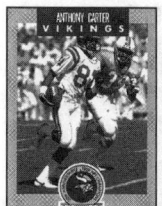 

The 1989 Police Minnesota Vikings set contains ten standard-size cards. The fronts have gray borders and color action photos; the horizontally oriented backs have safety tips, bios, and career highlights. It has been reported that 175,000 cards of each player were given away by the police officers in the state of Minnesota.

	MINT	NRMT	EXC
COMPLETE SET (10)	6.00	2.70	.75
COMMON CARD (1-10)	.40	.18	.05

☐ 1 Team Card	.60	.25	.07
(schedule on back)			
☐ 2 Henry Thomas	1.00	.45	.12
☐ 3 Rick Fenney	.40	.18	.05
☐ 4 Chuck Nelson	.40	.18	.05
☐ 5 Jim Gustafson	.40	.18	.05
☐ 6 Wade Wilson	.75	.35	.09
☐ 7 Randall McDaniel	1.00	.45	.12
☐ 8 Jesse Solomon	.40	.18	.05
☐ 9 Anthony Carter	1.00	.45	.12
☐ 10 Joe Kapp	.75	.35	.09
(All-Time Great)			

1989 Vikings Taystee Discs

 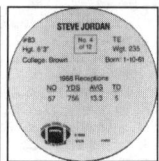

The 1989 Taystee Minnesota Vikings set contains 12 white-bordered, approximately 2 3/4" diameter discs. The fronts have helmetless color mug shots; the backs are white and have sparse bio and stats. One disc was included in each specially-marked Taystee product, distributed only in the Minnesota area.

	MINT	NRMT	EXC
COMPLETE SET (12)	6.00	2.70	.75
COMMON CARD (1-12)	.40	.18	.05
☐ 1 Anthony Carter	1.00	.45	.12
☐ 2 Chris Doleman	1.00	.45	.12
☐ 3 Joey Browner	.60	.25	.07
☐ 4 Steve Jordan	.60	.25	.07
☐ 5 Scott Studwell	.40	.18	.05
☐ 6 Wade Wilson	.60	.25	.07
☐ 7 Kirk Lowdermilk	.40	.18	.05
☐ 8 Tommy Kramer	.60	.25	.07
☐ 9 Keith Millard	.60	.25	.07
☐ 10 Rick Fenney	.40	.18	.05
☐ 11 Gary Zimmerman	.40	.18	.05
☐ 12 Darrin Nelson	.60	.25	.07

1990 Vikings Police

This ten-card standard-size set was issued to promote safety in the Minneapolis area by using members of the 1990 Minnesota Vikings. The card photos have posed action shots on the front along with an advertisement for Gatorade on the front and a crime prevention tip on the back. We have checklisted the cards in this set in alphabetical order.

	MINT	NRMT	EXC
COMPLETE SET (10)	5.00	2.20	.60
COMMON CARD (1-10)	.35	.16	.04
☐ 1 Ray Berry	.35	.16	.04
☐ 2 Anthony Carter	1.00	.45	.12
☐ 3 Chris Doleman	.75	.35	.09
☐ 4 Rick Fenney	.35	.16	.04
☐ 5 Hassan Jones	.50	.23	.06
☐ 6 Carl Lee	.35	.16	.04
☐ 7 Mike Merriweather	.50	.23	.06
☐ 8 Scott Studwell	.35	.16	.04
☐ 9 Herschel Walker	1.25	.55	.16
☐ 10 Wade Wilson	.75	.35	.09

1991 Vikings Police

This ten-card standard-size set was sponsored by Gatorade. The cards were distributed by participating Minnesota police departments, one per week, beginning on Aug. 23 with Rick Fenney, and concluding on Oct. 27 with Chris Doleman. Card fronts display an action player photo enclosed in a purple border, while player's name is printed at

---

the top in a gray rectangle. Gatorade's logo appears at the bottom of the picture. The first card's back lists the Vikings' game schedule. The horizontally oriented backs of the remaining cards feature a black and white close-up of the player and a biographical sketch on the left portion. Player's name, position, and jersey number appear in a black box at the top right, while the Vikadontis Rex mascot appears below. A crime prevention tip appears under the card number, while sponsor logos of Super Bowl XXVI, KFAN Sports Radio, and K102 Radio round out the back design.

	MINT	NRMT	EXC
COMPLETE SET (10)	5.00	2.20	.60
COMMON CARD (1-10)	.35	.16	.04
☐ 1 Rick Fenney	.35	.16	.04
☐ 2 Wade Wilson	.75	.35	.09
☐ 3 Mike Merriweather	.50	.23	.06
☐ 4 Hassan Jones	.35	.16	.04
☐ 5 Rich Gannon	.75	.35	.09
☐ 6 Mark Dusbabek	.35	.16	.04
☐ 7 Sean Salisbury	.50	.23	.06
☐ 8 Reggie Rutland	.50	.23	.06
☐ 9 Tim Irwin	.35	.16	.04
☐ 10 Chris Doleman	.75	.35	.09

1992 Vikings Police

This ten-card standard size set was primarily sponsored by Gatorade. The card fronts display an action color player photo framed by a purple border, while the player's name and team name appear in a gray rectangle at the top. The Gatorade logo appears at the bottom of the picture. The horizontally oriented backs carry a black-and-white close-up of the player and biographical information within a black outline box on the left side of the card. The player's name and position appear in a black bar at the top. Below are Vikadontis Rex (the team mascot), a crime prevention tip, and other sponsor logos (KFAN Sports Radio AM 1130 and K102).

	MINT	NRMT	EXC
COMPLETE SET (10)	6.00	2.70	.75
COMMON CARD (1-10)	.35	.16	.04
☐ 1 Dennis Green CO	.50	.23	.06
(Schedule on back)			
☐ 2 John Randle	.50	.23	.06
☐ 3 Todd Scott	.35	.16	.04
☐ 4 Anthony Carter	.75	.35	.09
☐ 5 Steve Jordan	.50	.23	.06
☐ 6 Terry Allen	2.00	.90	.25
☐ 7 Brian Habib	.35	.16	.04
☐ 8 Fuad Reveiz	.35	.16	.04
☐ 9 Roger Craig	.50	.23	.06
☐ 10 Cris Carter	1.50	.70	.19

1993 Vikings Police

This ten-card standard-size set was primarily sponsored by Gatorade, and the cards feature on their fronts purple-bordered color player photos. The player's name and team name appear within a gray rectangle at the top, and the Gatorade logo is displayed at the bottom. The white and horizontal back carries a black-and-white player headshot in the upper left, with his biography shown below. His name, position, and uniform number appear in the black stripe at the top. Below are Vikadontis Rex (the team mascot), a crime prevention tip, and other sponsor logos (KFAN Sports Radio and K102).

	MINT	NRMT	EXC
COMPLETE SET (10)	5.00	2.20	.60
COMMON CARD (1-10)	.30	.14	.04
☐ 1 Dennis Green CO	.50	.23	.06
(CL/schedule on back)			
☐ 2 Henry Thomas	.50	.23	.06
☐ 3 Todd Scott	.30	.14	.04
☐ 4 Jack Del Rio	.50	.23	.06
☐ 5 Vencie Glenn	.30	.14	.04
☐ 6 Fuad Reveiz	.50	.23	.06
☐ 7 Cris Carter	1.25	.55	.16
☐ 8 Terry Allen	1.25	.55	.16

☐ 9 Roger Craig	.75	.35	.09
☐ 10 Carlos Jenkins	.30	.14	.04

1995 Vikings Police

This ten-card set was primarily sponsored by Gatorade, and these standard sized cars feature on the front purple-bordered player photos. The player's and team name appear within a gray rectangle at the top of the card, and the Gatorade logo, as well as an 35th team anniversary logo are positioned at the bottom corners of the card. The white and horizontal back features a black and white headshot with the players biography below the photo. The players name, position, and number are in a black stripe on the top of the back of the card. Below are Vikadontis Rex (the team mascot), a crime prevention tip, and other sponsor logos (KFAN Sports Radio and K102) The cards are numbered on the back directly over the crime prevention tip.

	MINT	NRMT	EXC
COMPLETE SET (10)	5.00	2.20	.60
COMMON CARD	.40	.18	.05
☐ 1 Warren Moon	1.00	.45	.12
(CL/Schedule on the back)			
☐ 2 Randall McDaniel	.40	.18	.05
☐ 3 Jake Reed	1.00	.45	.12
☐ 4 Jack Del Rio	.50	.23	.06
☐ 5 Cris Carter	1.00	.45	.12
☐ 6 Fuad Reveiz	.40	.18	.05
☐ 7 Amp Lee	.40	.18	.05
☐ 8 John Randle	.50	.23	.06
☐ 9 Andrew Jordan	.40	.18	.05
☐ 10 DeWayne Washington	.75	.35	.09

1928 W560 Playing Cards

Cards in this set are the known football players in the W560 multisport set. The cards were issued in strips and follow a standard playing card design. We've numbered the cards below according to the playing card number and suit. All are college players of the 1928 era.

	EX	VG	GOOD
COMPLETE SET (6)	35.00	16.00	4.40
COMMON CARD	6.00	2.70	.75
☐ 1D Dutch Loud	6.00	2.70	.75
☐ 2D Chris Cagle	6.00	2.70	.75
☐ 6H B.T. Dumont	6.00	2.70	.75
☐ 9H Al Lassman	6.00	2.70	.75
☐ 10D D.A. Lowry UER	6.00	2.70	.75
misspelled Lowery			
☐ 12H M.E. Sprague	6.00	2.70	.75

1986 Waddingtons Game

This boxed set of 40 oversized (3 1/2" by 5 11/16") playing cards was produced in England and comes complete with a plastic tray and game rules. The object of the game is to play all of one's cards onto a central pattern based on typical movements in an American Football Game. The fronts feature colorful illustrations of five of the most famous teams in the NFL. Each team is portrayed on seven cards; moreover, there are five interception cards, which show merely the NFL logo. The backs of all the cards are printed in two colors of blue and have an oversized NFL logo. The cards have been checklisted below alphabetically according to teams, with the interception cards listed at the end. We've included the names of recognizable but unidentified players on the card fronts. Most of the art was apparently produced in the early 1980s based on the players featured.

	MINT	NRMT	EXC
COMPLETE SET (40)	50.00	22.00	6.25
COMMON CARD (1-40)	.50	.23	.06
☐ 1 Bears 10	3.00	1.35	.35
Walter Payton			
☐ 2 Bears 20	3.00	1.35	.35
Walter Payton			
☐ 3 Bears 40	3.00	1.35	.35
Walter Payton			

□ 4 Bears 50	3.00	1.35	.35
Walter Payton			
□ 5 Bears First Down	3.00	1.35	.35
Walter Payton			
□ 6 Bears Punt	3.00	1.35	.35
Walter Payton			
□ 7 Bears Touchdown	3.00	1.35	.35
Walter Payton			
□ 8 Cowboys 10	1.00	.45	.12
Danny White			
Tony Dorsett			
□ 9 Cowboys 20	1.00	.45	.12
Danny White			
Tony Dorsett			
□ 10 Cowboys 40	1.00	.45	.12
Danny White			
Tony Dorsett			
□ 11 Cowboys 50	1.00	.45	.12
Danny White			
Tony Dorsett			
□ 12 Cowboys First Down	1.00	.45	.12
Danny White			
Tony Dorsett			
□ 13 Cowboys Punt	1.00	.45	.12
Danny White			
Tony Dorsett			
□ 14 Cowboys Touchdown	1.00	.45	.12
Danny White			
Tony Dorsett			
□ 15 Dolphins 10	.50	.23	.06
Lorenzo Hampton			
Eric Laakso			
□ 16 Dolphins 20	.50	.23	.06
Lorenzo Hampton			
Eric Laakso			
□ 17 Dolphins 40	.50	.23	.06
Lorenzo Hampton			
Eric Laakso			
□ 18 Dolphins 50	.50	.23	.06
Lorenzo Hampton			
Eric Laakso			
□ 19 Dolphins First Down	.50	.23	.06
Lorenzo Hampton			
Eric Laakso			
□ 20 Dolphins Punt	.50	.23	.06
Lorenzo Hampton			
Eric Laakso			
□ 21 Dolphins Touchdown	.50	.23	.06
Lorenzo Hampton			
Eric Laakso			
□ 22 Redskins 10	1.00	.45	.12
John Riggins			
Joe Theismann			
□ 23 Redskins 20	1.00	.45	.12
John Riggins			
Joe Theismann			
□ 24 Redskins 40	1.00	.45	.12
John Riggins			
Joe Theismann			
□ 25 Redskins 50	1.00	.45	.12
John Riggins			
Joe Theismann			
□ 26 Redskins First Down	1.00	.45	.12
John Riggins			
Joe Theismann			
□ 27 Redskins Punt	1.00	.45	.12
John Riggins			
Joe Theismann			
□ 28 Redskins Touchdown	1.00	.45	.12
John Riggins			
Joe Theismann			
□ 29 Steelers 10	2.00	.90	.25
Terry Bradshaw			
Lynn Swann			
□ 30 Steelers 20	2.00	.90	.25
Terry Bradshaw			
Lynn Swann			
□ 31 Steelers 40	2.00	.90	.25
Terry Bradshaw			
Lynn Swann			
□ 32 Steelers 50	2.00	.90	.25
Terry Bradshaw			
Lynn Swann			
□ 33 Steelers First Down	2.00	.90	.25
Terry Bradshaw			
Lynn Swann			
□ 34 Steelers Punt	2.00	.90	.25
Terry Bradshaw			
Lynn Swann			
□ 35 Steelers Touchdown	2.00	.90	.25
Terry Bradshaw			
Lynn Swann			
□ 36 Interception Card	.50	.23	.06
□ 37 Interception Card	.50	.23	.06
□ 38 Interception Card	.50	.23	.06
□ 39 Interception Card	.50	.23	.06
□ 40 Interception Card	.50	.23	.06

1988 Wagon Wheel

This attractive set of eight large cards was issued in the United Kingdom by Burtons as an insert in a box of Chocolate Biscuits (cookies). Players in the set are recognizable but not explicitly identified on the card. The theme of the set is the explanation of American football to the British. The cards measure approximately 6

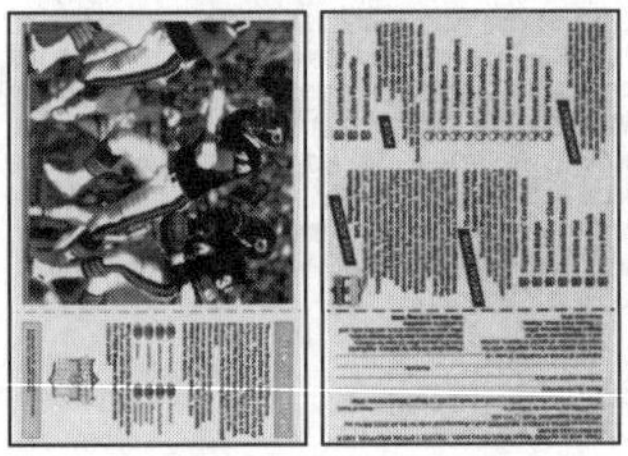

5/16" by 4 5/16" and are unnumbered. The card backs provide information on related mail order products available until May 31, 1988.

	MINT	NRMT	EXC
COMPLETE SET (8)	75.00	34.00	9.50
COMMON CARD (1-8)	6.00	2.70	.75
□ 1 Defensive Back	6.00	2.70	.75
(Todd Bowles cover-ing Mark Bavaro)			
□ 2 Defensive Lineman	8.00	3.60	1.00
(Ed Too Tall Jones and Neil Lomax)			
□ 3 Kicker	6.00	2.70	.75
(Kevin Butler)			
□ 4 Linebacker	6.00	2.70	.75
(Bob Brudzinski)			
□ 5 Offensive Lineman	18.00	8.00	2.20
(Keith Van Horne leading Walter Payton)			
□ 6 Quarterback	30.00	13.50	3.70
(John Elway)			
□ 7 Receiver	12.00	5.50	1.50
(Steve Largent between Vann McElroy and Mike Haynes)			
□ 8 Running Back	6.00	2.70	.75
(Rodney Carter of the Steelers)			

1964 Wheaties Stamps

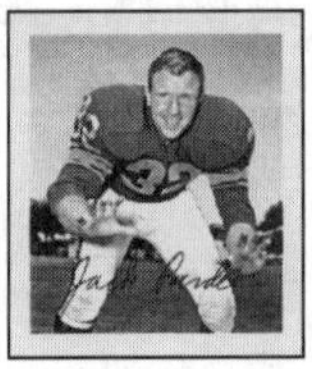

This set of 74 stamps was issued perforated within a 48-page album. There were 70 players and four team logo stamps bound into the album as six pages of 12 stamps each plus two stamps attached to the inside front cover. In fact, they are typically found this way, still bound into the album. The stamps measure approximately 2 1/2" by 2 3/4" and are unnumbered. The album itself measures approximately 8 1/8" by 11" and is entitled "Pro Bowl Football Player Stamp Album". The stamp list below has been alphabetized for convenience. Each player stamp has a facsimile autograph on the front. Note that there are no spaces in the album for Joe Schmidt, Y.A.Tittle, or the four team emblem stamps.

	NRMT	VG-E	GOOD
COMPLETE SET (74)	250.00	110.00	31.00
COMMON CARD (1-74)	2.50	1.10	.30
□ 1 Herb Adderley	6.00	2.70	.75
□ 2 Grady Alderman	2.50	1.10	.30
□ 3 Doug Atkins	6.00	2.70	.75
□ 4 Sam Baker	2.50	1.10	.30
(In Cowboys' uniform)			
□ 5 Erich Barnes	2.50	1.10	.30
(In Bears' jersey)			
□ 6 Terry Barr	2.50	1.10	.30
□ 7 Dick Bass	3.50	1.55	.45
□ 8 Maxie Baughan	2.50	1.10	.30
□ 9 Raymond Berry	8.00	3.60	1.00
□ 10 Charley Bradshaw	2.50	1.10	.30
(In Rams' jersey)			
□ 11 Jim Brown	35.00	16.00	4.40
□ 12 Roger Brown	2.50	1.10	.30
□ 13 Timmy Brown	3.50	1.55	.45
□ 14 Gail Cogdill	2.50	1.10	.30
□ 15 Tommy Davis	2.50	1.10	.30
□ 16 Willie Davis	6.00	2.70	.75
□ 17 Bob DeMarco	2.50	1.10	.30
□ 18 Darrell Dess	2.50	1.10	.30
□ 19 Buddy Dial	2.50	1.10	.30
(In Steelers' jersey)			
□ 20 Mike Ditka	20.00	9.00	2.50
□ 21 Galen Fiss	2.50	1.10	.30
□ 22 Lee Folkins	2.50	1.10	.30
□ 23 Joe Fortunato	2.50	1.10	.30
□ 24 Bill Glass	3.50	1.55	.45
□ 25 John Gordy	2.50	1.10	.30
□ 26 Ken Gray	2.50	1.10	.30
□ 27 Forrest Gregg	5.00	2.20	.60
□ 28 Rip Hawkins	2.50	1.10	.30
□ 29 Charlie Johnson	3.50	1.55	.45
□ 30 John Henry Johnson	6.00	2.70	.75
□ 31 Hank Jordan	5.00	2.20	.60
□ 32 Jim Katcavage	2.50	1.10	.30
□ 33 Jerry Kramer	5.00	2.20	.60
□ 34 Joe Krupa	2.50	1.10	.30
□ 35 John LoVetere	2.50	1.10	.30
(In Rams' jersey)			
□ 36 Dick Lynch	2.50	1.10	.30
□ 37 Gino Marchetti	6.00	2.70	.75
□ 38 Joe Marconi	2.50	1.10	.30
□ 39 Tommy Mason	3.50	1.55	.45
□ 40 Dale Meinert	2.50	1.10	.30
□ 41 Lou Michaels	2.50	1.10	.30
□ 42 Minnesota Vikings	3.50	1.55	.45
Emblem			
□ 43 Bobby Mitchell	6.00	2.70	.75
□ 44 John Morrow	2.50	1.10	.30
□ 45 New York Giants	3.50	1.55	.45
Emblem			
□ 46 Merlin Olsen	10.00	4.50	1.25
□ 47 Jack Pardee	5.00	2.20	.60
□ 48 Jim Parker	5.00	2.20	.60
□ 49 Bernie Parrish	2.50	1.10	.30
□ 50 Don Perkins	3.50	1.55	.45
□ 51 Richie Petitbon	3.50	1.55	.45
□ 52 Vince Promuto	2.50	1.10	.30
□ 53 Myron Pottios	2.50	1.10	.30
□ 54 Mike Pyle	2.50	1.10	.30
□ 55 Pete Retzlaff	3.50	1.55	.45
□ 56 Jim Ringo	5.00	2.20	.60
(In Packers' jersey)			
□ 57 Joe Rutgens	2.50	1.10	.30
□ 58 St. Louis Cardinals	3.50	1.55	.45
Emblem			
□ 59 San Francisco 49ers	3.50	1.55	.45
Emblem			
□ 60 Dick Schafrath	2.50	1.10	.30
□ 61 Joe Schmidt	6.00	2.70	.75
□ 62 Del Shofner	3.50	1.55	.45
□ 63 Norm Snead	3.50	1.55	.45
□ 64 Bart Starr	15.00	6.75	1.85
□ 65 Jim Taylor	10.00	4.50	1.25
□ 66 Roosevelt Taylor	3.50	1.55	.45
□ 67 Clendon Thomas	2.50	1.10	.30
(In Rams' jersey)			
□ 68 Y.A. Tittle	12.00	5.50	1.50
(In 49ers' jersey)			
□ 69 Johnny Unitas	20.00	9.00	2.50
□ 70 Bill Wade	3.50	1.55	.45
□ 71 Wayne Walker	3.50	1.55	.45
□ 72 Jesse Whittenton	2.50	1.10	.30
□ 73 Larry Wilson	5.00	2.20	.60
□ 74 Abe Woodson	2.50	1.10	.30
□ NNO Stamp Album	20.00	9.00	2.50

1987 Wheaties

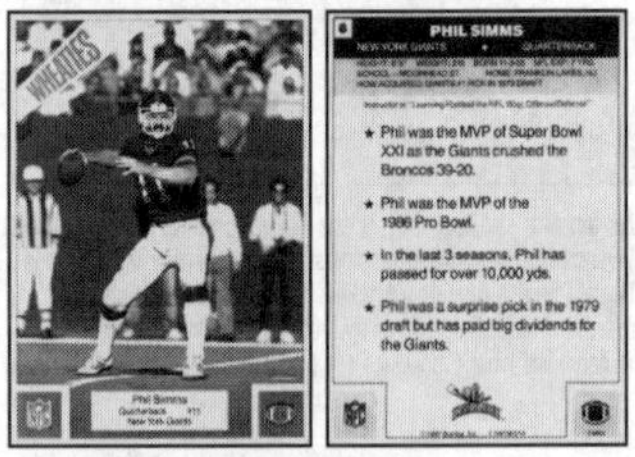

This 26-card set was distributed one per box in the specially marked packages of Wheaties cereal. Each "card" (actually they are more like mini-posters) came folded and inside a thin cellophane wrap. These 5" by 7" color photos are attractive. Individual player information and statistics are printed in black and white on the card backs. The cards are numbered on the back in the upper left corner. This project was organized by Mike Schechter Associates and produced by Starline Inc. in conjunction with the NFL Players Association. Bernie Kosar is very difficult to find and is not even listed as being in the set on the checklists Wheaties provides on the cereal box. Kosar may have been pulled from the set since, Ohio Edison held Bernie's advertising rights with some exclusivity.

	MINT	NRMT	EXC
COMPLETE SET (26)	175.00	80.00	22.00
COMMON CARD (1-26)	2.00	.90	.25
□ 1 Tony Dorsett	5.00	2.20	.60
□ 2 Herschel Walker	3.00	1.35	.35
□ 3 Marcus Allen	8.00	3.60	1.00
□ 4 Eric Dickerson	4.00	1.80	.50
□ 5 Walter Payton	12.00	5.50	1.50
□ 6 Phil Simms	4.00	1.80	.50
□ 7 Tommy Kramer	2.00	.90	.25
□ 8 Joe Morris	2.00	.90	.25
□ 9 Roger Craig	4.00	1.80	.50
□ 10 Curt Warner	3.00	1.35	.35
□ 11 Andre Tippett	2.00	.90	.25
□ 12 Joe Montana	30.00	13.50	3.70
□ 13 Jim McMahon	3.00	1.35	.35
□ 14 Bernie Kosar SP	20.00	9.00	2.50
□ 15 Jay Schroeder	2.00	.90	.25
□ 16 Al Toon	2.00	.90	.25
□ 17 Mark Gastineau	2.00	.90	.25
□ 18 Kenny Easley	2.00	.90	.25
□ 19 Howie Long	4.00	1.80	.50
□ 20 Dan Marino	40.00	18.00	5.00
□ 21 Karl Mecklenburg	2.00	.90	.25
□ 22 John Elway	20.00	9.00	2.50
□ 23 Boomer Esiason	4.00	1.80	.50
□ 24 Dan Fouts	4.00	1.80	.50
□ 25 Jim Kelly	10.00	4.50	1.25
□ 26 Louis Lipps	2.00	.90	.25

1991 Wild Card National Promos

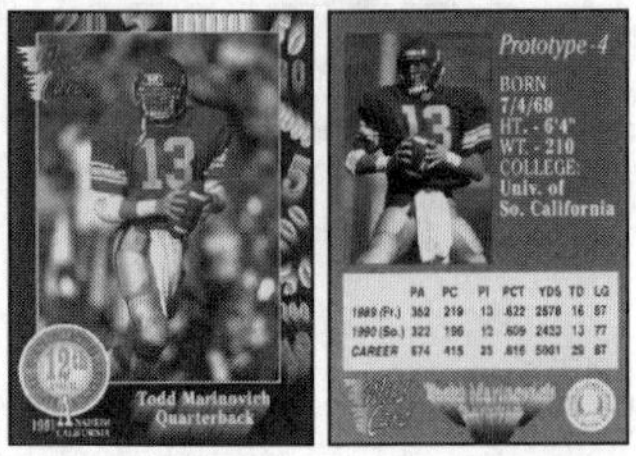

These cards were given away at the 1991 12th Annual Sports Collectors Convention in Anaheim, California. The fronts of these standard-size cards have high gloss color player photos on a black card face with different colored numbers above and to the right of the picture. On a background that changes from fuchsia to purple as one moves down the card, the backs have a color player photo, biography, and statistics. Striped versions of these cards with a football-shaped hologram in the upper left corner were also issued. The cards are numbered in the upper right corner as "Prototype-2" and following.

	MINT	NRMT	EXC
COMPLETE SET (3)	3.00	1.35	.35
COMMON CARD (P2-P4)	1.00	.45	.12
□ P2 Dan McGwire	1.00	.45	.12
San Diego State			
□ P3 Randal Hill	1.25	.55	.16
Miami			
□ P4 Todd Marinovich	1.00	.45	.12
USC			

1991 Wild Card NFL Prototypes

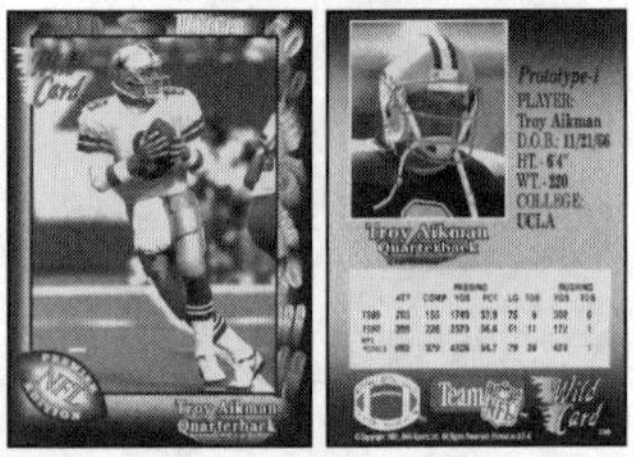

This six-card Wild Card Prototype set measures the standard-size. The front design features glossy color action player photos, on a black card face with yellow highlighting around the picture and different color numbers appearing in the top and right borders. A football icon with the words "NFL Premier Edition" overlays the lower left corner of the picture. The backs shade from black to yellow and have a color headshot, biography, and statistics for the last three years. The cards are numbered in the upper right corner.

	MINT	NRMT	EXC
COMPLETE SET (6)	8.00	3.60	1.00
COMMON CARD (1-6)	.75	.35	.09
□ 1 Troy Aikman	1.50	.70	.19
□ 2 Barry Sanders	1.50	.70	.19
□ 3 Thurman Thomas	.75	.35	.09
□ 4 Emmitt Smith	3.00	1.35	.35
□ 5 Jerry Rice	1.50	.70	.19
□ 6 Lawrence Taylor	.75	.35	.09

1991 Wild Card

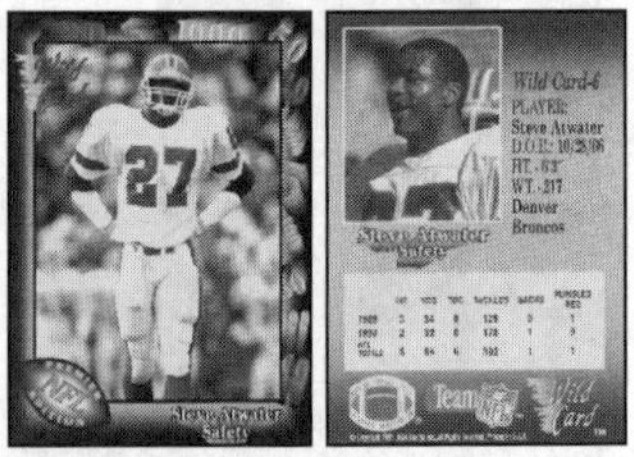

The Wild Card NFL contains 160 standard-size cards. Reportedly, production quantities were limited to 30,000 numbered ten-box cases. The series included three bonus cards (Wild Card Case Card, Wild Card Box Card, and Wild Card Hot Card) that were redeemable for the item pictured. Surprise wild card number 126 could be exchanged for a ten-card NFL Experience set, featuring five players each from the Washington Redskins and the Buffalo Bills. This set resembles that

given away at the Super Bowl Show, except that the cards bear no date. The front design features glossy color action player photos, highlighted in mustard on a black card face. Different color numbers appear in the top and right borders. The words "NFL Premier Edition" in a football icon overlay the lower left corner of the picture. The backs shade from black to mustard and carry a color headshot, biography, statistics, and card number. The secondary market value of the striped cards did not prove to be as strong as Wild Card anticipated. There have been numerous examples available at card shows and stores of higher stripe cards being offered heavily discounted off their theoretical value based on multiplying the stripe number times the single card value. Rookie Cards in this set include Ricky Ervins, Alvin Harper, Randal Hill, Michael Jackson, Herman Moore, Neil O'Donnell, Mike Pritchard, and Leonard Russell.

	MINT	NRMT	EXC
COMPLETE SET (160)	6.00	2.70	.75
COMMON CARD (1-160)	.04	.02	.01

*5 STRIPES: 1X TO 2X BASIC CARDS
10 STRIPES: 1.5X TO 3X BASIC CARDS
*20 STRIPES: 2.5X TO 5X BASIC CARDS
*50 STRIPES: 4X TO 8X BASIC CARDS
*100 STRIPES: 7X TO 15X BASIC CARDS
*1000 STRIPES: 40X TO 100X BASIC CARDS

	MINT	NRMT	EXC
☐ 1 Jeff George	.20	.09	.03
☐ 2 Sean Jones	.20	.09	.03
☐ 3 Duane Bickett	.04	.02	.01
☐ 4 John Elway	.60	.25	.07
☐ 5 Christian Okoye	.20	.09	.03
☐ 6 Steve Atwater	.04	.02	.01
☐ 7 Anthony Munoz	.20	.09	.03
☐ 8 Dave Krieg	.20	.09	.03
☐ 9 Nick Lowery	.04	.02	.01
☐ 10 Albert Bentley	.04	.02	.01
☐ 11 Mark Jackson	.04	.02	.01
☐ 12 Jeff Bryant	.04	.02	.01
☐ 13 Johnny Hector	.04	.02	.01
☐ 14 John L. Williams	.04	.02	.01
☐ 15 Jim Everett	.20	.09	.03
☐ 16 Mark Duper	.20	.09	.03
☐ 17 Drew Hill UER (Reversed negative on card front)	.20	.09	.03
☐ 18 Randal Hill	.20	.09	.03
☐ 19 Ernest Givins	.20	.09	.03
☐ 20 Ken O'Brien	.04	.02	.01
☐ 21 Blair Thomas UER (Says he caught 204 passes in 1990)	.20	.09	.03
☐ 22 Derrick Thomas	.20	.09	.03
☐ 23 Harvey Williams	.10	.05	.01
☐ 24 Simon Fletcher	.04	.02	.01
☐ 25 Stephone Paige	.04	.02	.01
☐ 26 Barry Word	.04	.02	.01
☐ 27 Warren Moon	.20	.09	.03
☐ 28 Derrick Fenner	.04	.02	.01
☐ 29 Shane Conlan	.04	.02	.01
☐ 30 Karl Mecklenburg	.04	.02	.01
☐ 31 Gary Anderson RB	.04	.02	.01
☐ 32 Sammie Smith	.04	.02	.01
☐ 33 Steve DeBerg	.20	.09	.03
☐ 34 Dan McGwire UER (TD stats say 29, should be 27)	.04	.02	.01
☐ 35 Roger Craig	.20	.09	.03
☐ 36 Tom Tupa	.04	.02	.01
☐ 37 Rod Woodson	.20	.09	.03
☐ 38 Junior Seau	.10	.05	.01
☐ 39 Bruce Pickens	.04	.02	.01
☐ 40 Greg Townsend	.04	.02	.01
☐ 41 Gary Clark	.20	.09	.03
☐ 42 Broderick Thomas	.04	.02	.01
☐ 43 Charles Mann	.20	.09	.03
☐ 44 Browning Nagle	.20	.09	.03
☐ 45 James Joseph	.20	.09	.03
☐ 46 Emmitt Smith UER (Scoring 1 TD, should be 11)	1.50	.70	.19
☐ 47 Cornelius Bennett	.20	.09	.03
☐ 48 Maurice Hurst	.04	.02	.01
☐ 49 Art Monk	.20	.09	.03
☐ 50 Louis Lipps	.20	.09	.03
☐ 51 Mark Rypien	.20	.09	.03
☐ 52 Bubby Brister	.20	.09	.03
☐ 53 John Stephens	.04	.02	.01
☐ 54 Merril Hoge	.04	.02	.01
☐ 55 Kevin Mack	.04	.02	.01
☐ 56 Al Toon	.20	.09	.03
☐ 57 Ronnie Lott	.20	.09	.03
☐ 58 Eric Metcalf	.20	.09	.03
☐ 59 Vinny Testaverde	.20	.09	.03
☐ 60 Darrell Green	.04	.02	.01
☐ 61 Randall Cunningham	.20	.09	.03
☐ 62 Charles Haley	.20	.09	.03
☐ 63 Mark Carrier	.20	.09	.03
☐ 64 Jim Harbaugh	.20	.09	.03
☐ 65 Richard Dent	.20	.09	.03
☐ 66 Stan Thomas	.04	.02	.01
☐ 67 Neal Anderson	.20	.09	.03
☐ 68 Troy Aikman	.75	.35	.09
☐ 69 Mike Pritchard	.20	.09	.03
☐ 70 Deion Sanders	.40	.18	.05
☐ 71 Andre Rison	.20	.09	.03
☐ 72 Keith Millard	.04	.02	.01
☐ 73 Jerry Rice	.75	.35	.09
☐ 74 Johnny Johnson	.04	.02	.01
☐ 75 Tim McDonald	.04	.02	.01
☐ 76 Leonard Russell	.20	.09	.03
☐ 77 Keith Jackson	.20	.09	.03
☐ 78 Keith Byars	.20	.09	.03
☐ 79 Ricky Proehl	.04	.02	.01
☐ 80 Dexter Carter	.04	.02	.01
☐ 81 Alvin Harper	.20	.09	.03
☐ 82 Irving Fryar	.20	.09	.03
☐ 83 Marion Butts	.20	.09	.03
☐ 84 Alfred Williams	.04	.02	.01
☐ 85 Timm Rosenbach	.04	.02	.01
☐ 86 Steve Young	.60	.25	.07
☐ 87 Albert Lewis	.04	.02	.01
☐ 88 Rodney Peete	.20	.09	.03
☐ 89 Barry Sanders	.75	.35	.09
☐ 90 Bennie Blades	.04	.02	.01
☐ 91 Chris Spielman	.20	.09	.03
☐ 92 John Friesz	.20	.09	.03
☐ 93 Jerome Brown	.20	.09	.03
☐ 94 Reggie White	.10	.05	.01
☐ 95 Michael Irvin	.10	.05	.01
☐ 96 Keith McCants	.04	.02	.01
☐ 97 Vinnie Clark	.20	.09	.03
☐ 98 Louis Oliver	.04	.02	.01
☐ 99 Mark Clayton	.20	.09	.03
☐ 100 John Offerdahl	.04	.02	.01
☐ 101 Michael Carter	.04	.02	.01
☐ 102 John Taylor	.20	.09	.03
☐ 103 William Perry	.20	.09	.03
☐ 104 Gill Byrd	.04	.02	.01
☐ 105 Burt Grossman	.04	.02	.01
☐ 106 Herman Moore	1.50	.70	.19
☐ 107 Howie Long	.20	.09	.03
☐ 108 Bo Jackson	.10	.05	.01
☐ 109 Kelvin Pritchett	.04	.02	.01
☐ 110 Jacob Green	.04	.02	.01
☐ 111 Chris Doleman	.20	.09	.03
☐ 112 Herschel Walker	.20	.09	.03
☐ 113 Russell Maryland	.20	.09	.03
☐ 114 Anthony Carter	.20	.09	.03
☐ 115 Joey Browner	.04	.02	.01
☐ 116 Tony Mandarich	.04	.02	.01
☐ 117 Don Majkowski	.04	.02	.01
☐ 118 Ricky Ervins	.20	.09	.03
☐ 119 Sterling Sharpe	.10	.05	.01
☐ 120 Tim Harris	.04	.02	.01
☐ 121 Hugh Millen	.04	.02	.01
☐ 122 Mike Rozier	.04	.02	.01
☐ 123 Chris Miller	.20	.09	.03
☐ 124 Morten Andersen	.04	.02	.01
☐ 125 Neil O'Donnell	.10	.05	.01
☐ 126 Surprise Wild Card (Exchangeable for ten-card NFL Experience set)	.20	.09	.03
☐ 127 Eddie Brown	.04	.02	.01
☐ 128 James Francis	.04	.02	.01
☐ 129 James Brooks	.20	.09	.03
☐ 130 David Fulcher	.04	.02	.01
☐ 131 Michael Jackson	.10	.05	.01
☐ 132 Clay Matthews	.20	.09	.03
☐ 133 Scott Norwood	.04	.02	.01
☐ 134 Wesley Carroll	.20	.09	.03
☐ 135 Thurman Thomas	.10	.05	.01
☐ 136 Mark Ingram	.20	.09	.03
☐ 137 Bobby Hebert	.20	.09	.03
☐ 138 Bobby Wilson	.04	.02	.01
☐ 139 Craig Heyward	.20	.09	.03
☐ 140 Dalton Hilliard	.04	.02	.01
☐ 141 Jeff Hostetler	.20	.09	.03
☐ 142 Dave Meggett	.20	.09	.03
☐ 143 Cris Dishman	.20	.09	.03
☐ 144 Lawrence Taylor	.20	.09	.03
☐ 145 Leonard Marshall	.04	.02	.01
☐ 146 Pepper Johnson	.04	.02	.01
☐ 147 Todd Marinovich	.04	.02	.01
☐ 148 Mike Croel	.04	.02	.01
☐ 149 Erik McMillan	.04	.02	.01
☐ 150 Flipper Anderson	.04	.02	.01
☐ 151 Cleveland Gary	.04	.02	.01
☐ 152 Henry Ellard	.20	.09	.03
☐ 153 Kevin Greene	.20	.09	.03
☐ 154 Michael Cofer	.04	.02	.01
☐ 155 Todd Lyght	.20	.09	.03
☐ 156 Bruce Smith	.10	.05	.01
☐ 157 Checklist 1	.04	.02	.01
☐ 158 Checklist 2	.04	.02	.01
☐ 159 Checklist 3	.04	.02	.01
☐ 160 Checklist 4	.04	.02	.01

1991 Wild Card NFL Redemption Cards

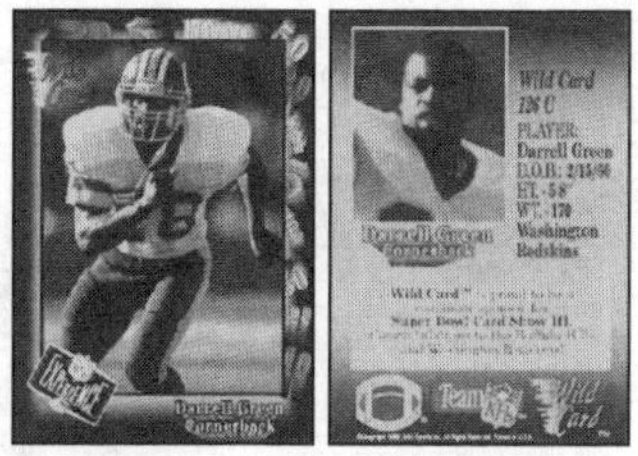

This ten-card standard-size set commemorates Super Bowl XXVI and features five players from each team. These cards were exchanged for Wild Card surprise card number 126, and thus they are numbered 126A-J. Cards 126A-126E feature Washington Redskins, whereas cards 126F-126J feature Buffalo Bills. In design, these redemption cards are identical to the 1991 Wild Card NFL Super Bowl Promos/NFL Experience set. The only detectible difference is that the Super Bowl promos have the date and location of the Super Bowl Card Show III on the back, while these redemption cards do not carry that information and are numbered differently.

	MINT	NRMT	EXC
COMPLETE SET (10)	3.00	1.35	.35
COMMON CARD (126A-126J)	.15	.07	.02
☐ 126A Mark Rypien	.15	.07	.02
☐ 126B Ricky Ervins	.15	.07	.02
☐ 126C Darrell Green	.15	.07	.02
☐ 126D Charles Mann	.15	.07	.02
☐ 126E Art Monk	.25	.11	.03
☐ 126F Thurman Thomas	.60	.25	.07
☐ 126G Bruce Smith	.25	.11	.03
☐ 126H Cornelius Bennett	.25	.11	.03
☐ 126I Scott Norwood	.15	.07	.02
☐ 126J Shane Conlan	.15	.07	.02

1991 Wild Card NFL Super Bowl Promos

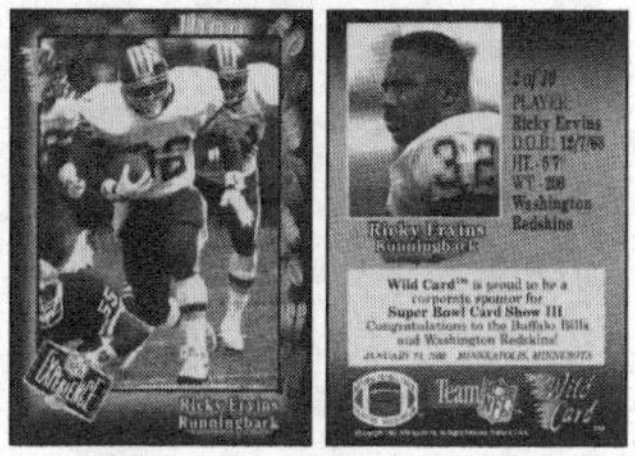

This ten-card standard-size set commemorates Super Bowl XXVI and features five players from each team. The cards were given away during the SuperBowl Card Show III by Wild Card, a corporate sponsor of the show. Prominently displayed on the card front is the "NFL Experience" logo. The fronts have high gloss color player photos, on a black and yellow card face that has different colored numbers above and to the right of the picture. On a background that shades from black to yellow and to black again, the backs have a color head shot, biography, and a sponsor's advertisement. The cards are numbered in the upper right corner. Cards 1-5 feature Washington Redskins, whereas cards 6-10 feature Buffalo Bills.

	MINT	NRMT	EXC
COMPLETE SET (10)	3.50	1.55	.45
COMMON CARD (1-10)	.25	.11	.03
☐ 1 Mark Rypien	.25	.11	.03
☐ 2 Ricky Ervins	.25	.11	.03
☐ 3 Darrell Green	.25	.11	.03
☐ 4 Charles Mann	.25	.11	.03
☐ 5 Art Monk	.40	.18	.05
☐ 6 Thurman Thomas	1.25	.55	.16
☐ 7 Bruce Smith	.40	.18	.05
☐ 8 Cornelius Bennett	.40	.18	.05
☐ 9 Scott Norwood	.25	.11	.03
☐ 10 Shane Conlan	.25	.11	.03

1991-92 Wild Card Redemption Prototypes

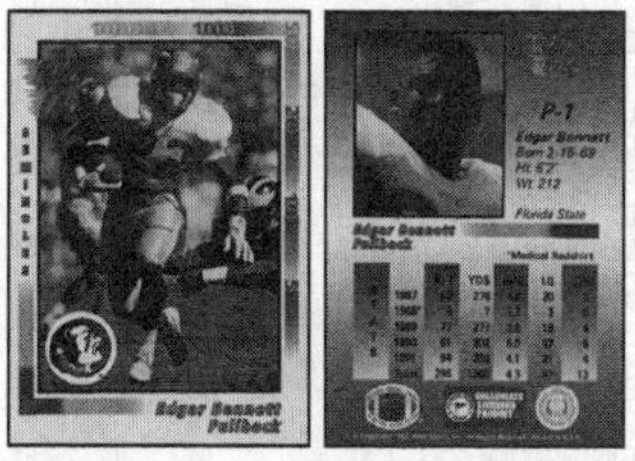

Collectors who redeemed their three Collegiate Football Surprise wild cards before April 30, 1992 received as a bonus this six-card set of 1992 Collegiate Football Redemption Prototype cards. The standard-size cards feature glossy color player photos bordered in white. Different color numbers (1000, 100, 50, 20, 10 and 5) edge the top and right side of the photo in the white border, and the team name and team colors frame the picture on the left side and bottom. The player's name and position appear in the bottom white border. The backs shade from purple to white and back to purple and carry a color head shot, biography, and statistics. The cards are numbered on the back with a "P" prefix.

	MINT	NRMT	EXC
COMPLETE SET (6)	1.50	.70	.19
COMMON CARD (P1-P6)	.20	.09	.03
☐ P1 Edgar Bennett Florida State	.75	.35	.09
☐ P2 Jimmy Smith Jackson State	.30	.14	.04
☐ P3 Will Furrer Virginia Tech	.20	.09	.03
☐ P4 Terrell Buckley Florida State	.20	.09	.03
☐ P5 Tommy Vardell Stanford	.30	.14	.04
☐ P6 Amp Lee Florida State	.20	.09	.03

1992 Wild Card NFL Prototypes

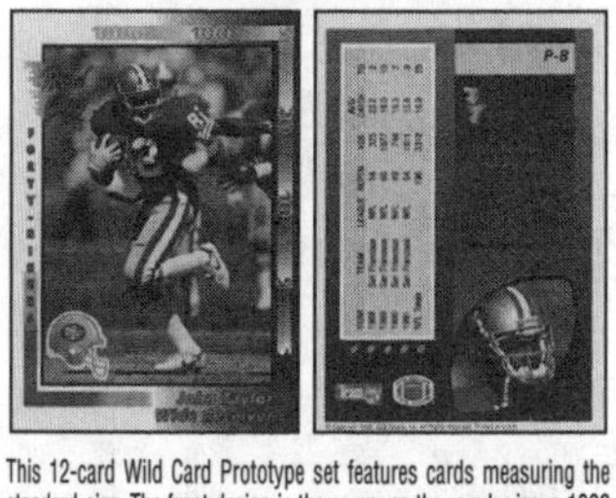

This 12-card Wild Card Prototype set features cards measuring the standard-size. The front design is the samer as the regular issue 1992 Wild Card NFL cards. The cards are numbered in the upper right corner of the reverse with a "P" prefix. The set numbering starts where the 1991 Wild Card Prototypes set left off.

	MINT	NRMT	EXC
COMPLETE SET (12)	10.00	4.50	1.25
COMMON CARD (P7-P18)	.50	.23	.06
☐ P7 Barry Sanders	2.00	.90	.25
☐ P8 John Taylor	.50	.23	.06
☐ P9 John Elway	1.50	.70	.19
☐ P10 Erik Kramer	.50	.23	.06
☐ P11 Christian Okoye	.50	.23	.06
☐ P12 Leonard Russell	.50	.23	.06
☐ P13 Barry Sanders	2.00	.90	.25
☐ P14 Earnest Byner	.50	.23	.06
☐ P15 Warren Moon	.75	.35	.09
☐ P16 Ronnie Lott	.75	.35	.09
☐ P17 Michael Irvin	1.00	.45	.12
☐ P18 Haywood Jeffires	.50	.23	.06

1992 Wild Card

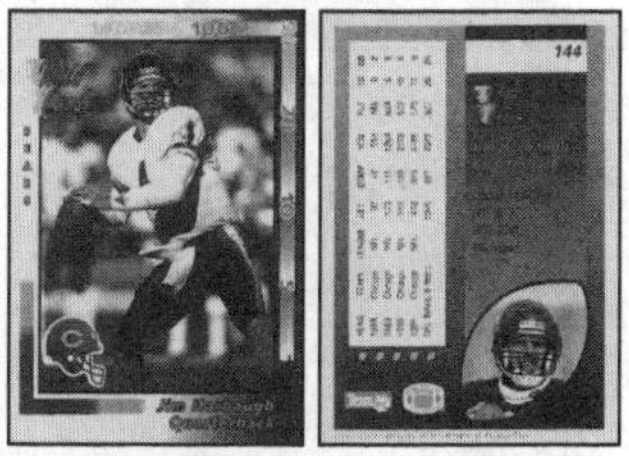

The 1992 Wild Card NFL set contains 460 standard-size cards issued in two series of 250 and 210 cards, respectively. It is reported that the first series production run was limited to 30,000 ten-box numbered foil cases. One hundred "case cards" and one thousand box cards were randomly inserted into the foil packs. Also cards from the Red Hot Rookie set were inserted in the packs. The left half of the card face is white while the right half shades from gray to black. The fronts display glossy color action photos, with the player's name and position beneath the picture. In the lower left corner, the pictures are accented by a two-color stripe (reflecting the team's colors); a numbered stripe with the denominations 5, 10, 20, 50, 100, and 1,000 accents the upper right corner. The backs exhibit different shades of jade and present biographical and statistical information. At the bottom, a color head shot appears inside a football. The first series is checklisted by teams. Subsets include Draft Picks (223-239) and League Leaders (240-245). Through a mail-in offer, the surprise card could be exchanged for a four-card cello pack featuring a P1 Barry Sanders (with first series Surprise Card 1) or P2 Emmitt Smith (with second series Surprise Card 251) Stat Smasher foil card, a Red Hot Rookie card, a Field Force card, and either a silver or gold Field Force card. Every jumbo pack included ten Series I cards, ten Series II cards, one Stat Smasher, one gold or silver foil Red Hot Rookie, and one gold or silver foil Running Wild. Rookie Cards include Edgar Bennett, Steve Bono, Terrell Buckley, Marco Coleman, Amp Lee, Johnny Mitchell and Tommy Vardell. A Barry Sanders promo card was produced and distributed at the 1992 National Sports Collectors Convention. The card contains The National logo and was issued in striped values of 5, 10, 20, 50 and 100.

	MINT	NRMT	EXC
COMPLETE SET (460)	10.00	4.50	1.25
COMPLETE SERIES 1 (250)	5.00	2.20	.60
COMPLETE SERIES 2 (210)	5.00	2.20	.60
COMMON CARD (1-460)	.04	.02	.01

*5 STRIPES: 1X TO 2X BASIC CARDS
*10 STRIPES: 1.5X TO 3X BASIC CARDS
*20 STRIPES: 2.5X TO 5X BASIC CARDS
*50 STRIPES: 4X TO 8X BASIC CARDS
*100 STRIPES: 7X TO 15X BASIC CARDS
*1000 STRIPES: 40X TO 100X BASIC CARDS

☐ 1 Surprise Card	.04	.02	.01
☐ 2 Marcus Dupree	.04	.02	.01
☐ 3 Jackie Slater	.04	.02	.01
☐ 4 Robert Delpino	.04	.02	.01
☐ 5 Jerry Gray	.04	.02	.01
☐ 6 Jim Everett	.10	.05	.01
☐ 7 Roman Phifer	.04	.02	.01
☐ 8 Alvin Wright	.04	.02	.01
☐ 9 Todd Lyght	.04	.02	.01
☐ 10 Reggie White	.20	.09	.03
☐ 11 Randal Hill	.04	.02	.01
☐ 12 Keith Byars	.04	.02	.01
☐ 13 Clyde Simmons	.10	.05	.01
☐ 14 Keith Jackson	.10	.05	.01
☐ 15 Seth Joyner	.10	.05	.01
☐ 16 James Joseph	.04	.02	.01
☐ 17 Eric Allen	.04	.02	.01
☐ 18 Sammie Smith	.04	.02	.01
☐ 19 Mark Clayton	.10	.05	.01
☐ 20 Aaron Craver	.04	.02	.01
☐ 21 Hugh Green	.04	.02	.01
☐ 22 John Offerdahl	.04	.02	.01
☐ 23 Jeff Cross	.04	.02	.01
☐ 24 Ferrell Edmunds	.04	.02	.01
☐ 25 Mark Duper	.10	.05	.01
☐ 26 Ronnie Harmon	.04	.02	.01
☐ 27 Derrick Walker	.04	.02	.01
☐ 28 Gary Plummer	.04	.02	.01
☐ 29 Rod Bernstine	.04	.02	.01
☐ 30 Burt Grossman	.04	.02	.01
☐ 31 Donnie Elder	.04	.02	.01
☐ 32 John Friesz	.10	.05	.01
☐ 33 Billy Ray Smith	.04	.02	.01
☐ 34 Luis Sharpe	.04	.02	.01
☐ 35 Aeneas Williams	.10	.05	.01
☐ 36 Ken Harvey	.10	.05	.01
☐ 37 Johnny Johnson UER	.04	.02	.01
(1990 rushing stats are wrong)			
☐ 38 Eric Swann	.10	.05	.01
☐ 39 Tom Tupa	.04	.02	.01
☐ 40 Anthony Thompson	.04	.02	.01
☐ 41 Broderick Thomas	.04	.02	.01
☐ 42 Vinny Testaverde	.10	.05	.01
☐ 43 Mark Carrier WR	.10	.05	.01
☐ 44 Gary Anderson RB	.04	.02	.01
☐ 45 Keith McCants	.04	.02	.01
☐ 46 Reggie Cobb	.04	.02	.01
☐ 47 Lawrence Dawsey	.10	.05	.01
☐ 48 Kevin Murphy	.04	.02	.01
☐ 49 Keith Woodside	.04	.02	.01
☐ 50 Darrell Thompson	.04	.02	.01
☐ 51 Vinnie Clark	.04	.02	.01
☐ 52 Sterling Sharpe	.10	.05	.01
☐ 53 Mike Tomczak	.04	.02	.01
☐ 54A Don Majkowski ERR	.10	.05	.01
(Listed as Dan)			
☐ 54B Don Majikowski COR	.10	.05	.01
☐ 55 Tony Mandarich	.04	.02	.01
☐ 56 Mark Murphy	.04	.02	.01
☐ 57 Dexter McNabb	.04	.02	.01
☐ 58 Rick Fenney	.04	.02	.01
☐ 59 Cris Carter	.20	.09	.03
☐ 60 Wade Wilson	.04	.02	.01
☐ 61 Mike Merriweather	.04	.02	.01
☐ 62 Rich Gannon	.04	.02	.01
☐ 63 Herschel Walker	.10	.05	.01
☐ 64 Chris Doleman	.10	.05	.01
☐ 65 Al Noga UER	.04	.02	.01
(On front, he's a DE; on back, he's a DT)			
☐ 66 Chris Mims	.04	.02	.01
☐ 67 Ed Cunningham	.04	.02	.01
☐ 68 Marcus Allen	.20	.09	.03
☐ 69 Kevin Turner	.10	.05	.01
☐ 70 Howie Long	.10	.05	.01
☐ 71 Tim Brown	.10	.05	.01
☐ 72 Nick Bell	.04	.02	.01
☐ 73 Todd Marinovich	.04	.02	.01
☐ 74 Jay Schroeder	.04	.02	.01
☐ 75 Mervyn Fernandez	.04	.02	.01
☐ 76 Tony Smith	.04	.02	.01
☐ 77 John Alt	.04	.02	.01
☐ 78 Christian Okoye	.04	.02	.01
☐ 79 Nick Lowery	.04	.02	.01
☐ 80 Derrick Thomas	.20	.09	.03
☐ 81 Bill Maas	.04	.02	.01
☐ 82 Dino Hackett	.04	.02	.01
☐ 83 Deron Cherry	.04	.02	.01
☐ 84 Barry Word	.04	.02	.01
☐ 85 Mike Mooney	.04	.02	.01
☐ 86 Cris Dishman	.04	.02	.01
☐ 87 Bruce Matthews	.04	.02	.01
☐ 88 Tony Jones	.04	.02	.01
☐ 89 William Fuller	.04	.02	.01
☐ 90 Ray Childress	.04	.02	.01
☐ 91 Warren Moon	.10	.05	.01
☐ 92 Lorenzo White	.04	.02	.01
☐ 93 Joe Bowden	.04	.02	.01
☐ 94 Tom Rathman	.04	.02	.01
☐ 95 Keith Henderson	.04	.02	.01
☐ 96 Jesse Sapolu	.04	.02	.01
☐ 97 Charles Haley	.10	.05	.01
☐ 98 Steve Young	.50	.23	.06
☐ 99 John Taylor	.10	.05	.01
☐ 100 Tim Harris	.04	.02	.01
☐ 101 Scott Davis	.04	.02	.01
☐ 102 Steve Bono	.30	.14	.04
☐ 103 Mike Kenn	.04	.02	.01
☐ 104 Mike Farr	.04	.02	.01
☐ 105 Rodney Peete	.10	.05	.01
☐ 106 Jerry Ball	.04	.02	.01
☐ 107 Chris Spielman	.10	.05	.01
☐ 108 Barry Sanders	.75	.35	.09
☐ 109 Bennie Blades	.04	.02	.01
☐ 110 Herman Moore	.60	.25	.07
☐ 111 Erik Kramer	.10	.05	.01
☐ 112 Vance Johnson	.04	.02	.01
☐ 113 Mike Croel	.04	.02	.01
☐ 114 Mark Jackson	.04	.02	.01
☐ 115 Steve Atwater	.04	.02	.01
☐ 116 Gaston Green	.04	.02	.01
☐ 117 John Elway	.50	.23	.06
☐ 118 Simon Fletcher	.04	.02	.01
☐ 119 Karl Mecklenburg	.04	.02	.01
☐ 120 Hart Lee Dykes	.04	.02	.01
☐ 121 Jerome Henderson	.04	.02	.01
☐ 122 Chris Singleton	.04	.02	.01
☐ 123 Marv Cook	.04	.02	.01
☐ 124 Leonard Russell	.04	.02	.01
☐ 125 Hugh Millen	.04	.02	.01
☐ 126 Pat Harlow	.04	.02	.01
☐ 127 Andre Tippett	.04	.02	.01
☐ 128 Bruce Armstrong	.04	.02	.01
☐ 129 Gary Clark	.10	.05	.01
☐ 130 Art Monk	.10	.05	.01
☐ 131 Darrell Green	.04	.02	.01
☐ 132 Wilber Marshall	.04	.02	.01
☐ 133 Jim Lachey	.04	.02	.01
☐ 134 Earnest Byner	.04	.02	.01
☐ 135 Chip Lohmiller	.04	.02	.01
☐ 136 Mark Rypien	.04	.02	.01
☐ 137 Ricky Sanders	.04	.02	.01
☐ 138 Stan Thomas	.04	.02	.01
☐ 139 Neal Anderson	.10	.05	.01
☐ 140 Trace Armstrong	.04	.02	.01
☐ 141 Kevin Butler	.04	.02	.01
☐ 142 Mark Carrier DB	.04	.02	.01
☐ 143 Dennis Gentry	.04	.02	.01
☐ 144 Jim Harbaugh	.10	.05	.01
☐ 145 Richard Dent	.10	.05	.01
☐ 146 Andre Rison	.20	.09	.03
☐ 147 Bruce Pickens	.04	.02	.01
☐ 148 Chris Hinton UER	.04	.02	.01
(Dealt to Falcons in 1990, not 1989)			
☐ 149 Brian Jordan	.10	.05	.01
☐ 150 Chris Miller	.04	.02	.01
☐ 151 Moe Gardner	.04	.02	.01
☐ 152 Bill Fralic	.04	.02	.01
☐ 153 Michael Haynes	.10	.05	.01
☐ 154 Mike Pritchard	.10	.05	.01
☐ 155 Dean Biasucci	.04	.02	.01
☐ 156 Clarence Verdin	.04	.02	.01
☐ 157 Donnell Thompson	.04	.02	.01
☐ 158 Duane Bickett	.04	.02	.01
☐ 159 Jon Hand	.04	.02	.01
☐ 160 Sam Graddy	.04	.02	.01
☐ 161 Emmitt Smith	1.50	.70	.19
☐ 162 Michael Irvin	.20	.09	.03
☐ 163 Danny Noonan	.04	.02	.01
☐ 164 Jack Del Rio	.04	.02	.01
☐ 165 Jim Jeffcoat	.04	.02	.01
☐ 166 Alexander Wright	.04	.02	.01
☐ 167 Frank Minnifield	.04	.02	.01
☐ 168 Ed King	.04	.02	.01
☐ 169 Reggie Langhorne	.04	.02	.01
☐ 170 Mike Baab	.04	.02	.01
☐ 171 Eric Metcalf	.10	.05	.01
☐ 172 Clay Matthews	.04	.02	.01
☐ 173 Kevin Mack	.04	.02	.01
☐ 174 Mike Johnson	.04	.02	.01
☐ 175 Jeff Lageman	.04	.02	.01
☐ 176 Freeman McNeil	.10	.05	.01
☐ 177 Erik McMillan	.04	.02	.01
☐ 178 James Hasty	.04	.02	.01
☐ 179 Kyle Clifton	.04	.02	.01
☐ 180 Joe Kelly	.04	.02	.01
☐ 181 Phil Simms	.10	.05	.01
☐ 182 Everson Walls	.04	.02	.01
☐ 183 Jeff Hostetler	.10	.05	.01
☐ 184 Dave Meggett	.10	.05	.01
☐ 185 Matt Bahr	.04	.02	.01
☐ 186 Mark Ingram	.04	.02	.01
☐ 187 Rodney Hampton	.10	.05	.01
☐ 188 Kanavis McGhee	.04	.02	.01
☐ 189 Tim McGee	.04	.02	.01
☐ 190 Eddie Brown	.04	.02	.01
☐ 191 Rodney Holman	.04	.02	.01
☐ 192 Harold Green	.10	.05	.01
☐ 193 James Francis	.04	.02	.01
☐ 194 Anthony Munoz	.10	.05	.01
☐ 195 David Fulcher	.04	.02	.01
☐ 196 Tim Krumrie	.04	.02	.01
☐ 197 Bubby Brister	.10	.05	.01
☐ 198 Rod Woodson	.10	.05	.01
☐ 199 Louis Lipps	.04	.02	.01
☐ 200 Carnell Lake	.04	.02	.01
☐ 201 Don Beebe	.04	.02	.01
☐ 202 Thurman Thomas	.20	.09	.03
☐ 203 Cornelius Bennett	.10	.05	.01
☐ 204 Mark Kelso	.04	.02	.01
☐ 205 James Lofton	.10	.05	.01
☐ 206 Darryl Talley	.04	.02	.01
☐ 207 Morten Andersen	.04	.02	.01
☐ 208 Vince Buck	.04	.02	.01
☐ 209 Wesley Carroll	.04	.02	.01
☐ 210 Bobby Hebert	.04	.02	.01
☐ 211 Craig Heyward	.10	.05	.01
☐ 212 Dalton Hilliard	.04	.02	.01
☐ 213 Rickey Jackson	.04	.02	.01
☐ 214 Eric Martin	.04	.02	.01
☐ 215 Pat Swilling	.10	.05	.01
☐ 216 Steve Walsh	.04	.02	.01
☐ 217 Torrance Small	.04	.02	.01
☐ 218 Jacob Green	.04	.02	.01
☐ 219 Cortez Kennedy	.10	.05	.01
☐ 220 John L. Williams	.04	.02	.01
☐ 221 Terry Wooden	.04	.02	.01
☐ 222 Grant Feasel	.04	.02	.01
☐ 223 Siran Stacy	.04	.02	.01
☐ 224 Chris Hakel	.04	.02	.01
☐ 225 Todd Harrison	.04	.02	.01
☐ 226 Bob Whitfield	.04	.02	.01
☐ 227 Eddie Blake	.04	.02	.01
☐ 228 Keith Hamilton	.04	.02	.01
☐ 229 Darryl Williams	.04	.02	.01
☐ 230 Ricardo McDonald	.04	.02	.01
☐ 231 Alan Haller	.04	.02	.01
☐ 232 Leon Searcy	.10	.05	.01
☐ 233 Patrick Rowe	.04	.02	.01
☐ 234 Edgar Bennett	.60	.25	.07
☐ 235 Terrell Buckley	.10	.05	.01
☐ 236 Will Furrer	.10	.05	.01
☐ 237 Amp Lee UER	.04	.02	.01
(Front photo actually Edgar Bennett)			
☐ 238 Jimmy Smith	.10	.05	.01
☐ 239 Tommy Vardell	.10	.05	.01
☐ 240 Leonard Russell	.04	.02	.01
'91 Offensive ROY			
☐ 241 Mike Croel	.04	.02	.01
'91 Defensive ROY			
☐ 242 Warren Moon	.10	.05	.01
'91 AFC Passing Leader			
☐ 243 Mark Rypien	.04	.02	.01
'91 NFC Passing Leader			
☐ 244 Thurman Thomas	.20	.09	.03
'91 AFC Rushing Leader			
☐ 245 Emmitt Smith	.75	.35	.09
'91 NFC Rushing Leader			
☐ 246 Checklist 1-50	.04	.02	.01
☐ 247 Checklist 51-100	.04	.02	.01
☐ 248 Checklist 101-150	.04	.02	.01
☐ 249 Checklist 151-200	.04	.02	.01
☐ 250 Checklist 201-250	.04	.02	.01
☐ 251 Surprise Card	.04	.02	.01
☐ 252 Erric Pegram	.10	.05	.01
☐ 253 Anthony Carter	.10	.05	.01
☐ 254 Roger Craig	.10	.05	.01
☐ 255 Hassan Jones	.04	.02	.01
☐ 256 Steve Jordan	.04	.02	.01
☐ 257 Randall McDaniel	.04	.02	.01
☐ 258 Henry Thomas	.04	.02	.01
☐ 259 Carl Lee	.04	.02	.01
☐ 260 Ray Agnew	.04	.02	.01
☐ 261 Irving Fryar	.10	.05	.01
☐ 262 Tom Waddle	.04	.02	.01
☐ 263 Greg McMurtry	.04	.02	.01
☐ 264 Stephen Baker	.04	.02	.01
☐ 265 Mark Collins	.04	.02	.01
☐ 266 Howard Cross	.04	.02	.01
☐ 267 Pepper Johnson	.04	.02	.01
☐ 268 Fred Barnett	.10	.05	.01
☐ 269 Heath Sherman	.04	.02	.01
☐ 270 William Thomas	.04	.02	.01
☐ 271 Bill Bates	.10	.05	.01
☐ 272 Issiac Holt	.04	.02	.01
☐ 273 Emmitt Smith	1.50	.70	.19
☐ 274 Eric Bieniemy	.04	.02	.01
☐ 275 Marion Butts	.04	.02	.01
☐ 276 Gill Byrd	.04	.02	.01
☐ 277 Robert Blackmon	.04	.02	.01
☐ 278 Brian Blades	.10	.05	.01
☐ 279 Joe Nash	.04	.02	.01
☐ 280 Bill Brooks	.04	.02	.01
☐ 281 Mel Gray	.04	.02	.01
☐ 282 Andre Ware	.10	.05	.01
☐ 283 Steve McMichael	.04	.02	.01
☐ 284 Brad Muster	.04	.02	.01
☐ 285 Ron Rivera	.04	.02	.01
☐ 286 Chris Zorich	.10	.05	.01
☐ 287 Chris Burkett	.04	.02	.01
☐ 288 Irv Eatman	.04	.02	.01
☐ 289 Rob Moore	.10	.05	.01
☐ 290 Joe Mott	.04	.02	.01
☐ 291 Brian Washington	.04	.02	.01
☐ 292 Michael Carter	.04	.02	.01
☐ 293 Dexter Carter	.04	.02	.01
☐ 294 Don Griffin	.04	.02	.01
☐ 295 John Taylor	.10	.05	.01
☐ 296 Ted Washington	.04	.02	.01
☐ 297 Monte Coleman	.04	.02	.01
☐ 298 Andre Collins	.04	.02	.01
☐ 299 Charles Mann	.04	.02	.01
☐ 300 Shane Conlan	.04	.02	.01
☐ 301 Keith McKeller	.04	.02	.01
☐ 302 Nate Odomes	.04	.02	.01
☐ 303 Riki Ellison	.04	.02	.01
☐ 304 Willie Gault	.04	.02	.01
☐ 305 Bob Golic	.04	.02	.01
☐ 306 Ethan Horton	.04	.02	.01
☐ 307 Ronnie Lott	.10	.05	.01
☐ 308 Don Mosebar	.04	.02	.01
☐ 309 Aaron Wallace	.04	.02	.01
☐ 310 Wymon Henderson	.04	.02	.01
☐ 311 Vance Johnson	.04	.02	.01
☐ 312 Ken Lanier	.04	.02	.01
☐ 313 Steve Sewell	.04	.02	.01
☐ 314 Dennis Smith	.04	.02	.01
☐ 315 Kenny Walker	.04	.02	.01
☐ 316 Chris Martin	.04	.02	.01
☐ 317 Albert Lewis	.04	.02	.01
☐ 318 Todd McNair	.04	.02	.01
☐ 319 Tracy Simien	.04	.02	.01
☐ 320 Percy Snow	.04	.02	.01
☐ 321 Mark Rypien	.04	.02	.01
☐ 322 Bryan Hinkle	.04	.02	.01
☐ 323 David Little	.04	.02	.01
☐ 324 Dwight Stone	.04	.02	.01
☐ 325 Van Waiters	.04	.02	.01
☐ 326 Pio Sagapolutele	.04	.02	.01
☐ 327 Michael Jackson	.10	.05	.01
☐ 328 Vestee Jackson	.04	.02	.01
☐ 329 Tony Paige	.04	.02	.01
☐ 330 Reggie Roby	.04	.02	.01
☐ 331 Haywood Jeffires	.10	.05	.01
☐ 332 Lamar Lathon	.04	.02	.01
☐ 333 Bubba McDowell	.04	.02	.01
☐ 334 Doug Smith	.04	.02	.01
☐ 335 Dean Steinkuhler	.04	.02	.01
☐ 336 Jessie Tuggle	.04	.02	.01
☐ 337 Freddie Joe Nunn	.04	.02	.01
☐ 338 Pat Terrell	.04	.02	.01
☐ 339 Tom McHale	.04	.02	.01
☐ 340 Sam Mills	.10	.05	.01
☐ 341 John Tice	.04	.02	.01
☐ 342 Brent Jones	.10	.05	.01
☐ 343 Robert Porcher	.04	.02	.01
☐ 344 Mark D'Onofrio	.04	.02	.01
☐ 345 David Tate	.04	.02	.01
☐ 346 Courtney Hawkins	.10	.05	.01
☐ 347 Ricky Watters	.10	.05	.01
☐ 348 Amp Lee	.04	.02	.01
☐ 349 Steve Young	.50	.23	.06
☐ 350 Natu Tuatagaloa	.04	.02	.01
☐ 351 Alfred Williams	.04	.02	.01
☐ 352 Derek Brown TE	.04	.02	.01
☐ 353 Marco Coleman UER	.10	.05	.01
(Back photo actually a Denver Bronco)			
☐ 354 Tommy Maddox	.04	.02	.01
☐ 355 Siran Stacy	.04	.02	.01
☐ 356 Greg Lewis	.04	.02	.01
☐ 357 Paul Gruber	.04	.02	.01
☐ 358 Troy Vincent	.10	.05	.01
☐ 359 Robert Wilson	.04	.02	.01
☐ 360 Jessie Hester	.04	.02	.01
☐ 361 Shaun Gayle	.04	.02	.01
☐ 362 Deron Cherry	.04	.02	.01
☐ 363 Wendell Davis	.04	.02	.01
☐ 364 David Klingler UER	.10	.05	.01
(Bio misspells his name as Klinger)			
☐ 365 Jason Hanson	.10	.05	.01
☐ 366 Marquez Pope	.04	.02	.01
☐ 367 Robert Williams	.04	.02	.01
☐ 368 Kelvin Pritchett	.04	.02	.01
☐ 369 Dana Hall	.10	.05	.01
☐ 370 David Brandon	.04	.02	.01
☐ 371 Tim McKyer	.04	.02	.01
☐ 372 Darion Conner	.04	.02	.01
☐ 373 Derrick Fenner	.04	.02	.01
☐ 374 Hugh Millen	.04	.02	.01
☐ 375 Bill Jones	.04	.02	.01
☐ 376 J.J. Birden	.04	.02	.01
☐ 377 Ty Detmer	.20	.09	.03
☐ 378 Alonzo Spellman	.10	.05	.01
☐ 379 Sammie Smith	.04	.02	.01
☐ 380 Al Smith	.04	.02	.01
☐ 381 Louis Clark	.04	.02	.01
☐ 382 Vernice Smith	.04	.02	.01
☐ 383 Tony Martin	.20	.09	.03
☐ 384 Willie Green	.04	.02	.01
☐ 385 Sean Gilbert	.10	.05	.01
☐ 386 Eugene Chung	.04	.02	.01
☐ 387 Toi Cook	.04	.02	.01
☐ 388 Brett Maxie	.04	.02	.01
☐ 389 Steve Israel	.04	.02	.01
☐ 390 Mike Mularkey	.04	.02	.01
☐ 391 Barry Foster	.10	.05	.01
☐ 392 Hardy Nickerson	.10	.05	.01
☐ 393 Johnny Mitchell	.04	.02	.01
☐ 394 Thurman Thomas	.20	.09	.03
☐ 395 Tony Smith	.04	.02	.01
☐ 396 Keith Goganious	.04	.02	.01
☐ 397 Matt Darby	.04	.02	.01
☐ 398 Nate Turner	.04	.02	.01
☐ 399 Keith Jennings	.04	.02	.01
☐ 400 Mitchell Benson	.04	.02	.01

☐ 401 Kurt Barber	.04	.02	.01
☐ 402 Tony Sacca	.04	.02	.01
☐ 403 Steve Hendrickson	.04	.02	.01
☐ 404 Johnny Johnson	.04	.02	.01
☐ 405 Lorenzo Lynch	.04	.02	.01
☐ 406 Luis Sharpe	.04	.02	.01
☐ 407 Jim Everett	.10	.05	.01
☐ 408 Neal Anderson	.10	.05	.01
☐ 409 Ashley Ambrose	.04	.02	.01
☐ 410 George Williams	.04	.02	.01
☐ 411 Clarence Kay	.04	.02	.01
☐ 412 Dave Krieg	.10	.05	.01
☐ 413 Terrell Buckley	.10	.05	.01
☐ 414 Ricardo McDonald	.04	.02	.01
☐ 415 Kelly Stouffer	.04	.02	.01
☐ 416 Barney Bussey	.04	.02	.01
☐ 417 Ray Roberts	.04	.02	.01
☐ 418 Fred McAfee	.04	.02	.01
☐ 419 Fred Banks	.04	.02	.01
☐ 420 Tim McDonald	.04	.02	.01
☐ 421 Darryl Williams	.04	.02	.01
☐ 422 Bobby Abrams	.04	.02	.01
☐ 423 Tommy Vardell	.10	.05	.01
☐ 424 William White	.04	.02	.01
☐ 425 Billy Ray Smith	.04	.02	.01
☐ 426 Lemuel Stinson	.04	.02	.01
☐ 427 Brad Johnson	.04	.02	.01
☐ 428 Herschel Walker	.10	.05	.01
☐ 429 Eric Thomas	.04	.02	.01
☐ 430 Anthony Thompson	.04	.02	.01
☐ 431 Ed West	.04	.02	.01
☐ 432 Edgar Bennett	.10	.05	.01
☐ 433 Warren Powers	.04	.02	.01
☐ 434 Byron Evans	.04	.02	.01
☐ 435 Rodney Culver	.04	.02	.01
☐ 436 Ray Horton	.04	.02	.01
☐ 437 Richmond Webb	.04	.02	.01
☐ 438 Mark McMillian	.04	.02	.01
☐ 439 Subset Checklist	.04	.02	.01
☐ 440 Lawrence Pete	.04	.02	.01
☐ 441 Rod Smith DB	.04	.02	.01
☐ 442 Mark Rodenhauser	.04	.02	.01
☐ 443 Scott Lockwood	.04	.02	.01
☐ 444 Charles Davenport	.04	.02	.01
☐ 445 Terry McDaniel	.04	.02	.01
☐ 446 Darren Perry	.04	.02	.01
☐ 447 Darrick Owens	.04	.02	.01
☐ 448 Alvin Wright	.04	.02	.01
☐ 449 Frank Stams	.04	.02	.01
☐ 450 Santana Dotson	.10	.05	.01
☐ 451 Mark Carrier DB	.04	.02	.01
☐ 452 Kevin Murphy	.04	.02	.01
☐ 453 Jeff Bryant	.04	.02	.01
☐ 454 Eric Allen	.04	.02	.01
☐ 455 Brian Bollinger	.04	.02	.01
☐ 456 Elston Ridgle	.04	.02	.01
☐ 457 Jim Riggs	.04	.02	.01
☐ 458 Checklist 251-320	.04	.02	.01
☐ 459 Checklist 321-391	.04	.02	.01
☐ 460 Checklist 392-460	.04	.02	.01
☐ P1 Barry Sanders National Promo	1.00	.45	.12
☐ P2 Barry Sanders (5-card National Promo sheet)	2.00	.90	.25

1992 Wild Card Class Back Attack

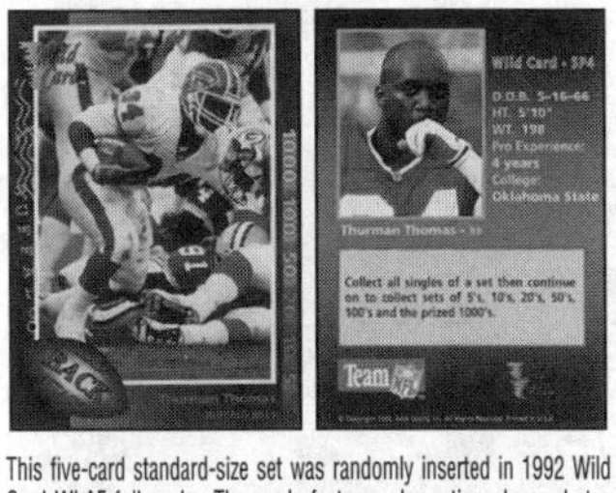

This five-card standard-size set was randomly inserted in 1992 Wild Card WLAF foil packs. The cards feature color action player photos with white borders. The picture is set against a black and green card face with multi-colored numbers on the right edge and a mustard graphic design on the left. A football icon at the lower left is printed with the words "Class Back Attack" (1-4) or "Red Hot Rookie" (5). The player's name and position appear in the lower right corner. The backs are green and sport a close-up shot and biographical information. A pale green box with a red border contains an explanation of the odds of getting a wild card in packs or boxes. David Klingler was redeemable for a Surprise Card.

	MINT	NRMT	EXC
COMPLETE SET (5)	7.00	3.10	.85
COMMON CARD (SP1-SP5)	.50	.23	.06

☐ SP1 Vaughn Dunbar	.50	.23	.06
☐ SP2 Barry Sanders	2.00	.90	.25
☐ SP3 Emmitt Smith	4.00	1.80	.50
☐ SP4 Thurman Thomas	1.00	.45	.12
☐ SP5 David Klingler (Red Hot Rookie; Surprise Card Redemption)	.50	.23	.06

1992 Wild Card Field Force

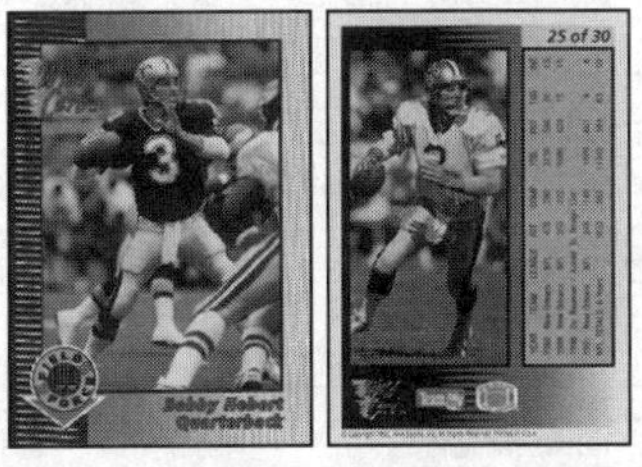

This 30-card standard-size set was randomly inserted in 1992 Wild Card NFL II foil packs. Gold and silver foil versions of each card were also produced and randomly inserted in packs. The Golds were the toughest version to pull. The front design features glossy color player photos. Against a dark plum background, a silver or gold foil pattern similar to the teeth on a comb runs the length of the card on the left. The remaining border is purple and turns into wavy purple lines on white as one moves toward the right card edge. The backs carry a second color player photo and player profile or statistics are presented on a pastel green panel.

	MINT	NRMT	EXC
COMPLETE SET (30)	15.00	6.75	1.85
COMMON CARD (1-30)	.20	.09	.03

*5 STRIPES: 1X to 2X BASIC CARDS
*10 STRIPES: 1.5X to 3X BASIC CARDS
*20 STRIPES: 2X to 4X BASIC CARDS
*50 STRIPES: 3X to 7X BASIC CARDS
*100 STRIPES: 7X to 15X BASIC CARDS
*1000 STRIPES: 40X to 80X BASIC CARDS
*SILVER CARDS: 1X to 2X BASIC CARDS
*GOLD CARDS: 1.5X to 3X BASIC CARDS

☐ 1 Joe Montana	1.25	.55	.16
☐ 2 Quentin Coryatt	.20	.09	.03
☐ 3 Tommy Vardell	.20	.09	.03
☐ 4 Jim Kelly	.50	.23	.06
☐ 5 John Elway	1.00	.45	.12
☐ 6 Ricky Watters	.30	.14	.04
☐ 7 Vinny Testaverde	.20	.09	.03
☐ 8 Randal Hill	.20	.09	.03
☐ 9 Amp Lee	.20	.09	.03
☐ 10 Vaughn Dunbar	.20	.09	.03
☐ 11 Troy Aikman	1.25	.55	.16
☐ 12 Deion Sanders	.75	.35	.09
☐ 13 Rodney Hampton	.30	.14	.04
☐ 14 Brett Favre	2.50	1.10	.30
☐ 15 Warren Moon	.30	.14	.04
☐ 16 Browning Nagle	.20	.09	.03
☐ 17 Terrell Buckley	.20	.09	.03
☐ 18 Barry Sanders	1.25	.55	.16
☐ 19 Dan Marino	2.50	1.10	.30
☐ 20 Carl Pickens	.50	.23	.06
☐ 21 Herschel Walker	.30	.14	.04
☐ 22 Ronnie Lott	.30	.14	.04
☐ 23 Steve Emtman	.20	.09	.03
☐ 24 Mark Rypien	.20	.09	.03
☐ 25 Bobby Hebert	.20	.09	.03
☐ 26 Dan McGwire	.20	.09	.03
☐ 27 Neil O'Donnell	.50	.23	.06
☐ 28 Cris Carter	.50	.23	.06
☐ 29 Randall Cunningham	.30	.14	.04
☐ 30 Jerry Rice	1.25	.55	.16

1992 Wild Card Pro Picks

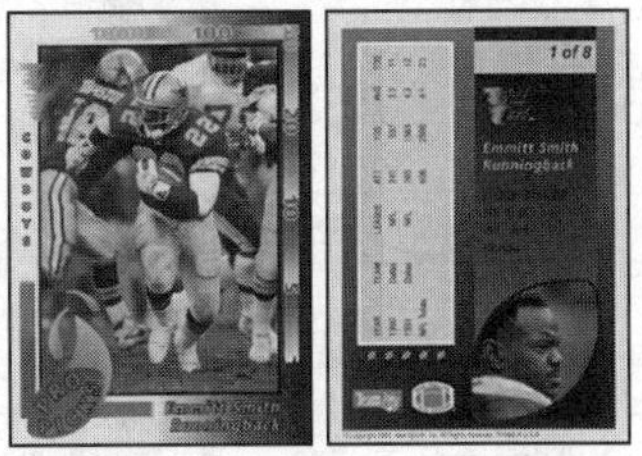

This eight-card standard-size set was randomly inserted one per card in retail jumbo packs. The cards feature color action player photos with thin black borders. The picture is set against a black and white card face with multi-colored numbers on the top and right edge. A football icon at the lower left is printed with the words "Pro Picks". The player's name and position appear in the lower right corner. The backs are magenta shading to burgundy and sport a close-up, football-shaped shot, biographical information and statistics.

	MINT	NRMT	EXC
COMPLETE SET (8)	7.00	3.10	.85
COMMON CARD (1-8)	.20	.09	.03

☐ 1 Emmitt Smith	3.00	1.35	.35
☐ 2 Mark Rypien	.20	.09	.03
☐ 3 Warren Moon	.40	.18	.05
☐ 4 Leonard Russell	.20	.09	.03
☐ 5 Thurman Thomas	.60	.25	.07
☐ 6 John Elway	1.00	.45	.12
☐ 7 Barry Sanders	1.50	.70	.19
☐ 8 Steve Young	1.00	.45	.12

1992 Wild Card Red Hot Rookies

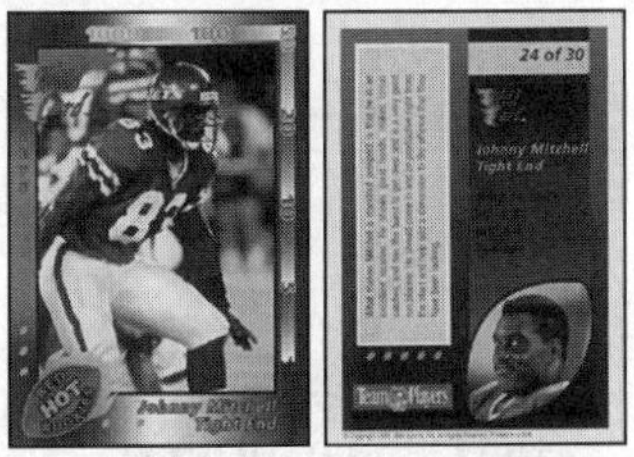

This 30-card standard-size set was randomly inserted in 1992 Wild Card NFL second series foil packs. The fronts feature glossy color player photos inside black inner borders. The outer borders shade from red to white and then to black as one moves from left to right across the card face, and the customary series of colored numbers (1000, 100, 50, 20, 10, and 5) form a right angle at the upper right corner of the photo. A flaming football with the words "Red Hot Rookies" appears at the lower left corner. The backs are streaked with different shades of red and bordered in white. A player profile appears on a pastel green panel. A color head shot inside a football-shaped icon rounds out the back. Gold and Silver parallel versions were also available one per jumbo pack.

	MINT	NRMT	EXC
COMPLETE SET (30)	12.00	5.50	1.50
COMPLETE SERIES 1 (10)	4.00	1.80	.50
COMPLETE SERIES 2 (20)	8.00	3.60	1.00
COMMON CARD (1-30)	.30	.14	.04

*5 STRIPES: 1X to 2X BASIC CARDS
*10 STRIPES: 1.5X to 3X BASIC CARDS
*20 STRIPES: 2X to 4X BASIC CARDS
*50 STRIPES: 3X to 7X BASIC CARDS
*100 STRIPES: 7X to 15X BASIC CARDS
*1000 STRIPES: 40X to 80X BASIC CARDS
*GOLD CARDS: .5X to 1X BASIC CARDS
*SILVER CARDS: .35X to .75X BASIC CARDS

☐ 1 Darryl Williams	.30	.14	.04
☐ 2 Amp Lee	.30	.14	.04
☐ 3 Will Furrer	.30	.14	.04
☐ 4 Edgar Bennett	1.25	.55	.16
☐ 5 Terrell Buckley	.50	.23	.06
☐ 6 Bob Whitfield	.30	.14	.04
☐ 7 Siran Stacy	.30	.14	.04
☐ 8 Jimmy Smith	.75	.35	.09
☐ 9 Kevin Turner	.50	.23	.06
☐ 10 Tommy Vardell	.50	.23	.06
☐ 11 Surprise Card	.30	.14	.04
☐ 12 Derek Brown TE	.30	.14	.04
☐ 13 Marco Coleman	.50	.23	.06
☐ 14 Quentin Coryatt	.50	.23	.06
☐ 15 Rodney Culver	.30	.14	.04
☐ 16 Ty Detmer	.75	.35	.09
☐ 17 Vaughn Dunbar	.30	.14	.04
☐ 18 Steve Emtman	.50	.23	.06
☐ 19 Sean Gilbert	.50	.23	.06
☐ 20 Courtney Hawkins	.50	.23	.06
☐ 21 David Klingler	.50	.23	.06
☐ 22 Amp Lee	.30	.14	.04
☐ 23 Tommy Maddox	.30	.14	.04
☐ 24 Johnny Mitchell	.30	.14	.04
☐ 25 Darren Perry	.30	.14	.04
☐ 26 Carl Pickens	1.00	.45	.12
☐ 27 Robert Porcher	.30	.14	.04
☐ 28 Tony Smith	.30	.14	.04
☐ 29 Alonzo Spellman	.50	.23	.06
☐ 30 Troy Vincent	.50	.23	.06

1992 Wild Card Running Wild

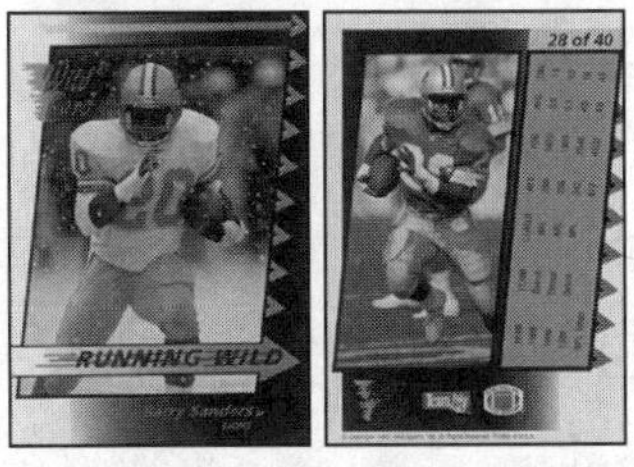

This 40-card standard-size set was inserted one card per pack in 1992 Wild Card NFL series 2 jumbo packs. The cards feature action color player photos set in a parallelogram shape against a background that shades from white to black. Near the bottom of the picture, a gradated green arrow icon runs from left to right stamped in gold foil with the words "Running Wild". Smaller versions of the arrow icon appear at the right edge of the photo as though they are running behind it. The player's name and team appear at the bottom right in red. A parallel Gold foil version was also randomly inserted in packs. It's slightly tougher to find.

	MINT	NRMT	EXC
COMPLETE SET (40)	15.00	6.75	1.85
COMMON CARD (1-40)	.25	.11	.03

*5 STRIPES: 1X TO 2X BASIC CARDS
*10 STRIPES: 1.5X TO 3X BASIC CARDS
*20 STRIPES: 2X TO 4X BASIC CARDS
*50 STRIPES: 3X TO 7X BASIC CARDS
*100 STRIPES: 7X TO 15X BASIC CARDS
*1000 STRIPES: 40X TO 80X BASIC CARDS
*GOLD CARDS: .75X to 1.5X SILVERS

☐ 1 Terry Allen	.40	.18	.05
☐ 2 Neal Anderson	.40	.18	.05
☐ 3 Eric Ball	.25	.11	.03
☐ 4 Nick Bell	.25	.11	.03
☐ 5 Edgar Bennett	.75	.35	.09
☐ 6 Rod Bernstine	.25	.11	.03
☐ 7 Marion Butts	.25	.11	.03
☐ 8 Keith Byars	.25	.11	.03
☐ 9 Earnest Byner	.25	.11	.03
☐ 10 Reggie Cobb	.25	.11	.03
☐ 11 Roger Craig	.40	.18	.05
☐ 12 Rodney Culver	.25	.11	.03
☐ 13 Barry Foster	.40	.18	.05
☐ 14 Cleveland Gary	.25	.11	.03
☐ 15 Harold Green	.25	.11	.03
☐ 16 Gaston Green	.25	.11	.03
☐ 17 Rodney Hampton	.40	.18	.05
☐ 18 Mark Higgs	.25	.11	.03
☐ 19 Dalton Hilliard	.25	.11	.03
☐ 20 Bobby Humphrey UER (Misspelled Humphries)	.25	.11	.03
☐ 21 Amp Lee	.25	.11	.03
☐ 22 Kevin Mack	.25	.11	.03
☐ 23 Eric Metcalf	.40	.18	.05
☐ 24 Brad Muster	.25	.11	.03
☐ 25 Christian Okoye	.25	.11	.03
☐ 26 Tom Rathman	.25	.11	.03
☐ 27 Leonard Russell	.25	.11	.03
☐ 28 Barry Sanders	2.00	.90	.25
☐ 29 Heath Sherman	.25	.11	.03
☐ 30 Emmitt Smith	3.50	1.55	.45
☐ 31 Blair Thomas	.25	.11	.03
☐ 32 Thurman Thomas	.75	.35	.09
☐ 33 Tommy Vardell	.40	.18	.05
☐ 34 Herschel Walker	.40	.18	.05
☐ 35 Chris Warren	.40	.18	.05
☐ 36 Ricky Watters	.75	.35	.09
☐ 37 Lorenzo White	.25	.11	.03
☐ 38 John L. Williams	.25	.11	.03
☐ 39 Barry Word	.25	.11	.03
☐ 40 Vince Workman	.25	.11	.03

1992 Wild Card Stat Smashers

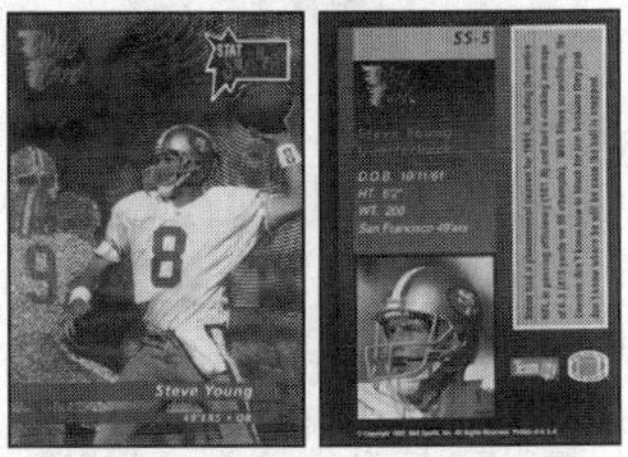

This 52-card insert standard-size set was randomly inserted in 1992 Wild Card NFL packs. Card numbers 1-16 were randomly inserted in 1992 Wild Card NFL II foil packs, while card numbers 17-52 were inserted one per pack in second series jumbo packs. The collector could also obtain a Barry Sanders Stat Smasher card through a mail-in offer in exchange for the surprise card in series one. The second series surprise card coulld be exchanged for an Emmitt Smith SS promo (P2). The fronts feature color player cut-outs superimposed on a full-bleed metallic foil background texturized in various patterns. The player's name, team name, and his position appear in lilac and purple stripes that cut across the bottom of the card face. Each stripe becomes jagged at the right edge of the card. The Stat Smashers icon in the upper right completes the front. The backs have black borders and display a panel that shades from violet to a deep, brownish-purple from top to bottom. Featured on the panel are a color head shot, biography, and a 1991 season summary of the player's achievements. The cards are numbered on the back with an "SS" prefix.

	MINT	NRMT	EXC
COMPLETE SET (52)	40.00	18.00	5.00
COMPLETE SERIES 1 (16)	20.00	9.00	2.50
COMPLETE SERIES 2 (36)	20.00	9.00	2.50
COMMON CARD (SS1-SS16)	.75	.35	.09
COMMON CARD (SS17-SS52)	.40	.18	.05

*5 STRIPES: 1X to 2X BASIC CARDS
*10 STRIPES: 1.5X to 3X BASIC CARDS
*20 STRIPES: 2X to 4X BASIC CARDS
*50 STRIPES: 3X to 7X BASIC CARDS
*100 STRIPES: 7X to 15X BASIC CARDS
*1000 STRIPES: 40X to 100X BASIC CARDS

☐ SS1 Barry Sanders	3.00	1.35	.35
☐ SS2 Leonard Russell	.75	.35	.09
☐ SS3 Thurman Thomas	2.00	.90	.25
☐ SS4 John Elway	2.50	1.10	.30
☐ SS5 Steve Young	2.50	1.10	.30
☐ SS6 Warren Moon	1.25	.55	.16
☐ SS7 Terrell Buckley	.75	.35	.09
☐ SS8 Randall Cunningham	1.25	.55	.16
☐ SS9 Steve Emtman	.75	.35	.09
☐ SS10 Dan Marino	6.00	2.70	.75

	MINT	NRMT	EXC
☐ SS11 Joe Montana	4.00	1.80	.50
☐ SS12 Carl Pickens	2.00	.90	.25
☐ SS13 Jerry Rice	3.00	1.35	.35
☐ SS14 Deion Sanders	1.50	.70	.19
☐ SS15 Tommy Vardell	.75	.35	.09
☐ SS16 Ricky Watters	1.25	.55	.16
☐ SS17 Troy Aikman	2.00	.90	.25
☐ SS18 Dale Carter	.40	.18	.05
☐ SS19 Quentin Coryatt	.60	.25	.07
☐ SS20 Vaughn Dunbar	.40	.18	.05
☐ SS21 Mark Duper	.40	.18	.05
☐ SS22 Eric Metcalf	.60	.25	.07
☐ SS23 Brett Favre	4.00	1.80	.50
☐ SS24 Barry Foster	.60	.25	.07
☐ SS25 Jeff George	.60	.25	.07
☐ SS26 Sean Gilbert UER ("Stan" on front)	.40	.18	.05
☐ SS27 Jim Harbaugh	1.00	.45	.12
☐ SS28 Courtney Hawkins	.40	.18	.05
☐ SS29 Charles Haley	.40	.18	.05
☐ SS30 Bobby Hebert	.40	.18	.05
☐ SS31 Stan Humphries	.60	.25	.07
☐ SS32 Michael Irvin	1.00	.45	.12
☐ SS33 Jim Kelly	1.00	.45	.12
☐ SS34 David Klingler	.40	.18	.05
☐ SS35 Ronnie Lott	.60	.25	.07
☐ SS36 Tommy Maddox	.40	.18	.05
☐ SS37 Todd Marinovich	.40	.18	.05
☐ SS38 Hugh Millen	.40	.18	.05
☐ SS39 Art Monk	.60	.25	.07
☐ SS40 Browning Nagle	.40	.18	.05
☐ SS41 Neil O'Donnell	.60	.25	.07
☐ SS42 Tom Rathman	.40	.18	.05
☐ SS43 Andre Rison	.60	.25	.07
☐ SS44 Mike Singletary	.60	.25	.07
☐ SS45 Tony Smith	.40	.18	.05
☐ SS46 Emmitt Smith	4.00	1.80	.50
☐ SS47 Pete Stoyanovich	.40	.18	.05
☐ SS48 John Taylor	.40	.18	.05
☐ SS49 Troy Vincent	.40	.18	.05
☐ SS50 Herschel Walker	.60	.25	.07
☐ SS51 Lorenzo White	.40	.18	.05
☐ SS52 Rodney Culver	.40	.18	.05
☐ P1 Barry Sanders Promo	2.00	.90	.25
☐ P2 Emmitt Smith Promo	4.00	1.80	.50

1992 Wild Card NASDAM/SCAI Miami

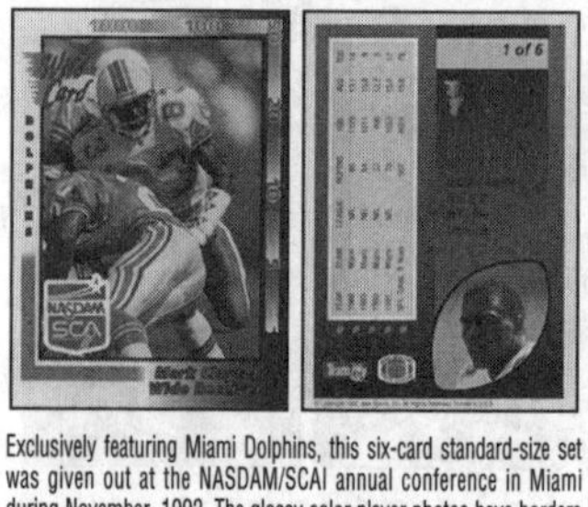

Exclusively featuring Miami Dolphins, this six-card standard-size set was given out at the NASDAM/SCAI annual conference in Miami during November, 1992. The glossy color player photos have borders shading from white to black as one moves across the card face. The team color-coded stripes form a right angle at the lower left corner, while the customary series of colored numbers (1000, 100, 50, 20, 10, and 5) form a right angle at the upper right corner of the photo. On the back statistics appear on a pastel green panel. A color head shot inside a football-shaped icon and biographical information rounds out the back.

	MINT	NRMT	EXC
COMPLETE SET (6)	3.00	1.35	.35
COMMON CARD (1-6)	.50	.23	.06
☐ 1 Mark Clayton	.75	.35	.09
☐ 2 Aaron Craver	.50	.23	.06
☐ 3 Tony Paige	.50	.23	.06
☐ 4 Mark Duper	.75	.35	.09
☐ 5 Tony Martin	1.00	.45	.12
☐ 6 Reggie Roby	.50	.23	.06

1992 Wild Card Sacramento CardFest

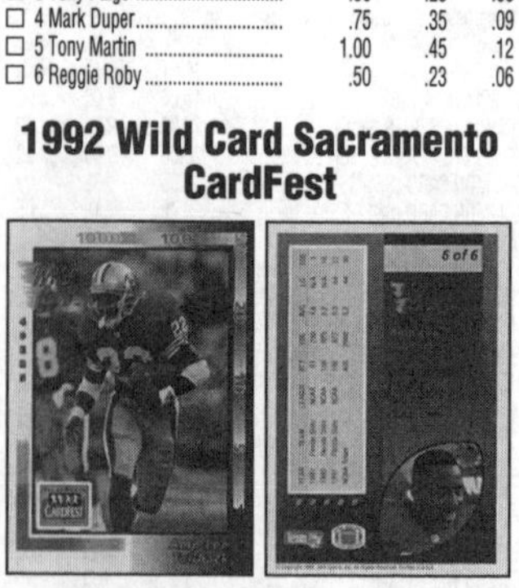

This six-card standard-size set (of San Francisco 49ers) features color action player photos with thin black borders. The picture is set against a black and white card face with multi-colored numbers on the top and right edge. A Sacramento CardFest icon is superimposed on the photo at the lower left. The player's name and position appear in the lower right corner. The backs are blue-green shading to black and sport a close-up, football-shaped picture, biographical information, and statistics.

	MINT	NRMT	EXC
COMPLETE SET (6)	3.00	1.35	.35
COMMON CARD (1-6)	.40	.18	.05
☐ 1 Tom Rathman	.40	.18	.05
☐ 2 Steve Young	1.00	.45	.12
☐ 3 Steve Bono	.60	.25	.07
☐ 4 Brent Jones	.40	.18	.05
☐ 5 Ricky Watters	.60	.25	.07
☐ 6 Amp Lee	.40	.18	.05

1992 Wild Card WLAF

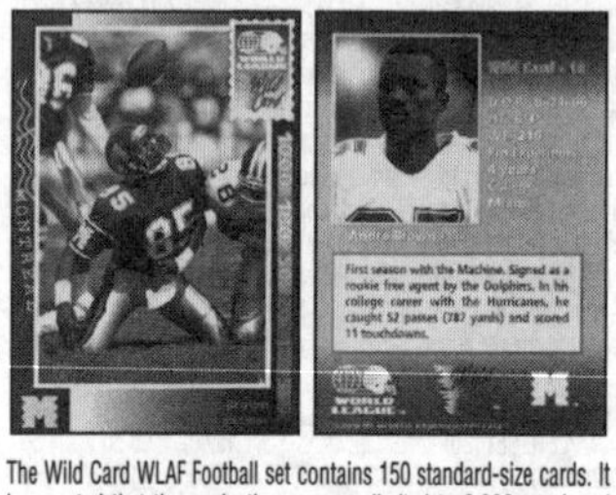

The Wild Card WLAF Football set contains 150 standard-size cards. It is reported that the production run was limited to 6,000 numbered ten-box cases, and that no factory sets were produced. The fronts display glossy color action player photos, on a black and gray card face with a white frame around the picture and different color numbers in the right border. The Wild Card World League logo resembles a postage stamp in the upper right corner. On a background with different shades of blue, the backs have a head shot, biography, and career highlights. The cards are numbered on the back and checklisted below according to teams.

	MINT	NRMT	EXC
COMPLETE SET (150)	6.00	2.70	.75
COMMON CARD (1-150)	.05	.02	.01
☐ 1 World Bowl Champs	.05	.02	.01
☐ 2 Pete Mandley	.10	.05	.01
☐ 3 Steve Williams	.05	.02	.01
☐ 4 Dee Thomas	.05	.02	.01
☐ 5 Emanuel King	.05	.02	.01
☐ 6 Anthony Dilweg	.10	.05	.01
☐ 7 Ben Brown	.05	.02	.01
☐ 8 Darryl Harris	.05	.02	.01
☐ 9 Aaron Emanuel	.05	.02	.01
☐ 10 Andre Brown	.05	.02	.01
☐ 11 Reggie McKenzie	.10	.05	.01
☐ 12 Darryl Holmes	.05	.02	.01
☐ 13 Michael Proctor	.05	.02	.01
☐ 14 Ricky Johnson	.05	.02	.01
☐ 15 Ray Savage	.05	.02	.01
☐ 16 George Searcy	.05	.02	.01
☐ 17 Titus Dixon	.05	.02	.01
☐ 18 Willie Fears	.05	.02	.01
☐ 19 Terrence Cooks	.05	.02	.01
☐ 20 Ivory Lee Brown	.05	.02	.01
☐ 21 Mike Johnson	.10	.05	.01
☐ 22 Doug Williams	.05	.02	.01
☐ 23 Brad Goebel	.10	.05	.01
☐ 24 Tony Boles	.05	.02	.01
☐ 25 Cisco Richard	.05	.02	.01
☐ 26 Robb White	.05	.02	.01
☐ 27 Darrell Colbert	.05	.02	.01
☐ 28 Wayne Walker	.05	.02	.01
☐ 29 Ronnie Williams	.05	.02	.01
☐ 30 Erik Norgard	.05	.02	.01
☐ 31 Darren Willis	.05	.02	.01
☐ 32 Kent Wells	.05	.02	.01
☐ 33 Phil Logan	.05	.02	.01
☐ 34 Pat O'Hara	.05	.02	.01
☐ 35 Melvin Patterson	.05	.02	.01
☐ 36 Amir Rasul	.05	.02	.01
☐ 37 Tom Rouen	.05	.02	.01
☐ 38 Chris Cochrane	.05	.02	.01
☐ 39 Randy Bethel	.05	.02	.01
☐ 40 Eric Harmon	.05	.02	.01
☐ 41 Archie Herring	.05	.02	.01
☐ 42 Tim James	.05	.02	.01
☐ 43 Babe Laufenberg	.10	.05	.01
☐ 44 Herb Welch	.05	.02	.01
☐ 45 Stefon Adams	.05	.02	.01
☐ 46 Tony Burse	.05	.02	.01
☐ 47 Carl Parker	.05	.02	.01
☐ 48 Mike Prugle	.05	.02	.01
☐ 49 Mike Jones	.10	.05	.01
☐ 50 David Archer	.50	.23	.06
☐ 51 Corian Freeman	.05	.02	.01
☐ 52 Eddie Brown	.05	.02	.01
☐ 53 Paul Green	.05	.02	.01
☐ 54 Basil Proctor	.05	.02	.01
☐ 55 Mike Sinclair	.05	.02	.01
☐ 56 Louis Riddick	.05	.02	.01
☐ 57 Roman Matuez	.05	.02	.01
☐ 58 Darryl Clack	.05	.02	.01
☐ 59 Willie Davis	.50	.23	.06
☐ 60 Glen Rodgers	.05	.02	.01
☐ 61 Grantis Bell	.05	.02	.01
☐ 62 Joe Howard-Johnson	.05	.02	.01
☐ 63 Rocen Keeton	.05	.02	.01
☐ 64 Dean Witkowski	.05	.02	.01
☐ 65 Stacey Simmons	.05	.02	.01
☐ 66 Roger Vick	.05	.02	.01
☐ 67 Scott Mitchell	1.00	.45	.12
☐ 68 Todd Krumm	.05	.02	.01
☐ 69 Kerwin Bell	.10	.05	.01
☐ 70 Richard Carey	.05	.02	.01
☐ 71 Kip Lewis	.05	.02	.01
☐ 72 Andre Alexander	.05	.02	.01
☐ 73 Reggie Slack	.05	.02	.01
☐ 74 Falanda Newton	.05	.02	.01
☐ 75 Tony Woods	.20	.09	.03
☐ 76 Chris McLemore	.05	.02	.01
☐ 77 Eric Wilkerson	.05	.02	.01
☐ 78 Cornell Burbage	.05	.02	.01
☐ 79 Doug Pederson	.20	.09	.03
☐ 80 Brent Pease	.05	.02	.01
☐ 81 Monty Gilbreath	.05	.02	.01
☐ 82 Wes Pritchett	.05	.02	.01
☐ 83 Byron Williams	.05	.02	.01
☐ 84 Ron Sancho	.05	.02	.01
☐ 85 Tony Jones	.20	.09	.03
☐ 86 Anthony Wallace	.05	.02	.01
☐ 87 Mike Perez	.10	.05	.01
☐ 88 Steve Bartalo	.05	.02	.01
☐ 89 Teddy Garcia	.05	.02	.01
☐ 90 Joe Greenwood	.05	.02	.01
☐ 91 Tony Baker	.20	.09	.03
☐ 92 Glenn Cobb	.05	.02	.01
☐ 93 Mark Tucker	.05	.02	.01
☐ 94 Lyneil Mayo	.05	.02	.01
☐ 95 Alex Espinoza	.05	.02	.01
☐ 96 Mike Norseth	.05	.02	.01
☐ 97 Steven Avery	.05	.02	.01
☐ 98 John Brantley	.05	.02	.01
☐ 99 Eddie Britton	.05	.02	.01
☐ 100 Philip Doyle	.05	.02	.01
☐ 101 Elroy Harris	.05	.02	.01
☐ 102 John R. Holland	.05	.02	.01
☐ 103 Mark Hopkins	.05	.02	.01
☐ 104 Arthur Hunter	.05	.02	.01
☐ 105 Paul McGowan	.05	.02	.01
☐ 106 John Miller	.05	.02	.01
☐ 107 Shawn Moore	.10	.05	.01
☐ 108 Phil Ross	.05	.02	.01
☐ 109 Eugene Rowell	.05	.02	.01
☐ 110 Joe Valerio	.05	.02	.01
☐ 111 Harvey Wilson	.05	.02	.01
☐ 112 Irvin Smith	.05	.02	.01
☐ 113 Tony Sargent	.05	.02	.01
☐ 114 Ricky Shaw	.05	.02	.01
☐ 115 Curtis Moore	.05	.02	.01
☐ 116 Fred McNair	.05	.02	.01
☐ 117 Danny Lockett	.05	.02	.01
☐ 118 William Kirksey	.05	.02	.01
☐ 119 Stan Gelbaugh	.20	.09	.03
☐ 120 Judd Garrett	.10	.05	.01
☐ 121 Dedrick Dodge	.05	.02	.01
☐ 122 Dan Crossman	.05	.02	.01
☐ 123 Jeff Alexander	.05	.02	.01
☐ 124 Lew Barnes	.05	.02	.01
☐ 125 Willie Don Wright	.05	.02	.01
☐ 126 Johnny Thomas	.05	.02	.01
☐ 127 Richard Buchanan	.05	.02	.01
☐ 128 Chad Fortune	.05	.02	.01
☐ 129 Eric Lindstrom	.05	.02	.01
☐ 130 Ron Goetz	.05	.02	.01
☐ 131 Bruce Clark	.05	.02	.01
☐ 132 Anthony Greene	.05	.02	.01
☐ 133 Demetrius Davis	.10	.05	.01
☐ 134 Mike Roth	.05	.02	.01
☐ 135 Tony Moss	.05	.02	.01
☐ 136 Scott Erney	.05	.02	.01
☐ 137 Brad Henke	.05	.02	.01
☐ 138 Malcolm Frank	.05	.02	.01
☐ 139 Sean Foster	.05	.02	.01
☐ 140 Michael Titley	.05	.02	.01
☐ 141 Rickey Williams	.05	.02	.01
☐ 142 Karl Dunbar	.05	.02	.01
☐ 143 Carl Bax	.05	.02	.01
☐ 144 Willie Bouyer	.05	.02	.01
☐ 145 Howard Feggins	.05	.02	.01
☐ 146 David Smith	.05	.02	.01
☐ 147 Bernard Ford	.05	.02	.01
☐ 148 Checklist 1	.05	.02	.01
☐ 149 Checklist 2	.05	.02	.01
☐ 150 Checklist 3	.05	.02	.01
☐ NNO Box Card (Redeemable for box of WLAF; inserted in various Wild Card products)	.05	.02	.01

1992-93 Wild Card San Francisco

Exclusively featuring San Francisco 49ers, this six-card, standard-size set was originally given out at the Sports Collectors Card Expo held in San Francisco in September, 1992 and then reissued (with a slightly different show logo, different individual card numbers, and two replacement players) at the Spring National Sports Collectors Convention in San Francisco in March 1993. The two sets are

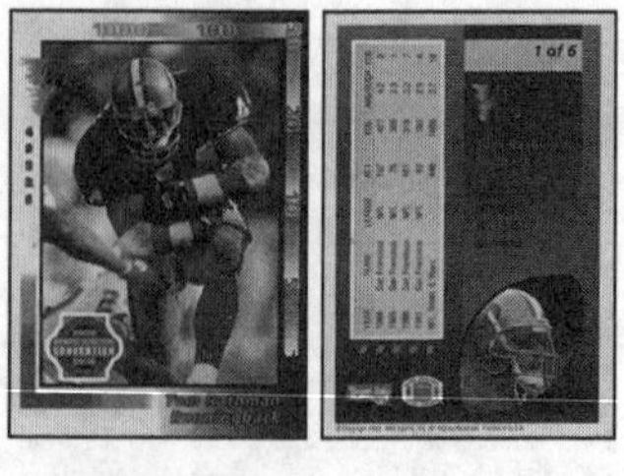

indistinguishable except for the different show logo in the lower left corner of each obverse and the card numbering. The two sets currently are valued equally. The glossy color player photos have borders shading from white to black as one moves across the card face. The team color-coded stripes form a right angle at the lower left corner, while the customary series of colored numbers (1000, 100, 50, 20, 10, and 5) form a right angle at the upper right corner of the photo. On the back statistics appear on a pastel green panel. A color head shot inside a football-shaped icon and biographical information rounds out the back. The cards are numbered on the back; cards designated below as A are from the original 1992 set, whereas the B versions are from the 1993 reissue set. The complete set below applies to either set.

	MINT	NRMT	EXC
COMPLETE SET (6)	4.00	1.80	.50
COMMON CARD (1-6)	.30	.14	.04
☐ 1A John Taylor	.30	.14	.04
☐ 1B Tom Rathman	.30	.14	.04
☐ 2A Amp Lee	.30	.14	.04
☐ 2B Steve Young	.75	.35	.09
☐ 3A Steve Bono	.50	.23	.06
☐ 3B Steve Bono	.50	.23	.06
☐ 4A Steve Young	.75	.35	.09
☐ 4B Brent Jones	.30	.14	.04
☐ 5A Tom Rathman	.30	.14	.04
☐ 5B Ricky Watters	.50	.23	.06
☐ 6A Don Griffin	.30	.14	.04
☐ 6B Amp Lee	.30	.14	.04

1993 Wild Card Prototypes

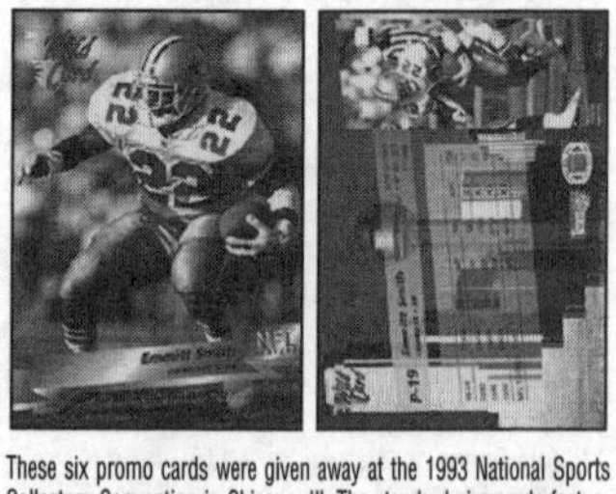

These six promo cards were given away at the 1993 National Sports Collectors Convention in Chicago, Ill. The standard-size cards feature full-bleed color action player photos. The player's name and team name appear in a gold lightning stripe that cuts across the bottom of the card. Against a background of the home team's city skyline, the horizontal backs carry a second, smaller color action photo, biography, and career summary. The cards are numbered on the back with a "P" prefix. The set numbering starts where the 1992 Wild Card Prototypes left off. A Superchrome version was also produced of each card. These were actually re-numbered (#SCP1-SCP6) but have been priced below using a multiplier.

	MINT	NRMT	EXC
COMPLETE SET (6)	5.00	2.20	.60
COMMON CARD (P19-P24)	.40	.18	.05
*SUPERCHROME CARDS: .75X TO 1.5X			
☐ P19 Emmitt Smith	2.00	.90	.25
☐ P20 Ricky Watters	.75	.35	.09
☐ P21 Drew Bledsoe	1.50	.70	.19
☐ P22 Garrison Hearst	.75	.35	.09
☐ P23 Barry Foster	.40	.18	.05
☐ P24 Rick Mirer	.75	.35	.09

1993 Wild Card

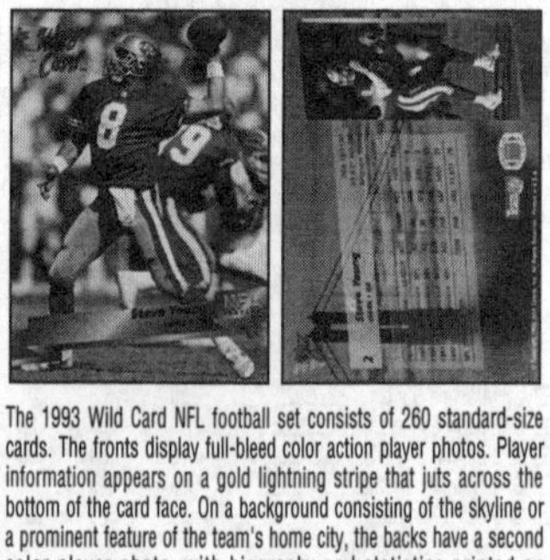

The 1993 Wild Card NFL football set consists of 260 standard-size cards. The fronts display full-bleed color action player photos. Player information appears on a gold lightning stripe that juts across the bottom of the card face. On a background consisting of the skyline or a prominent feature of the team's home city, the backs have a second color player photo, with biography and statistics printed on

transparent panels. The first series cards are numbered on the back and checklisted below according to teams. Randomly inserted in early 1993 Wild Card packs were cards from the 1993 Stat Smashers, Field Force, and Red Hot Rookies sets. A different packaging scheme begun early in 1994 featured six Superchrome counterparts to the regular cards inserted in special Superchrome 15-card low-series and 13-card high-series hobby packs, and are valued at four to nine times the value of the regular issue cards. One of ten Superchrome Back-to-Back inserts, featuring a Field Force player on the front and a Red Hot Rookie on the back, was inserted in each 18-pack box. Also, special striped cards were randomly inserted into regular Wild Card packs. These cards came in varying "denominations" of stripes, ranging from five to 1,000, and the corresponding values for them are noted in the header below. Rookie Cards include Jerome Bettis, Drew Bledsoe, Reggie Brooks, Derek Brown, Garrison Hearst, O.J. McDuffie and Rick Mirer.

	MINT	NRMT	EXC
COMPLETE SET (260)	10.00	4.50	1.25
COMPLETE SERIES 1 (200)	5.00	2.20	.60
COMPLETE SERIES 2 (60)	5.00	2.20	.60
COMMON CARD (1-260)	.04	.02	.01

*5 STRIPES: 1X TO 2X BASIC CARDS
*10 STRIPES: 1.5X TO 3X BASIC CARDS
*20 STRIPES: 2.5X TO 5X BASIC CARDS
*50 STRIPES: 4X TO 8X BASIC CARDS
*100 STRIPES: 7X TO 15X BASIC CARDS
*1000 STRIPES: 40X TO 100X BASIC CARDS

☐ 1 Surprise Card	.04	.02	.01
☐ 2 Steve Young	.50	.23	.06
☐ 3 John Taylor	.10	.05	.01
☐ 4 Jerry Rice	.75	.35	.09
☐ 5 Brent Jones	.10	.05	.01
☐ 6 Ricky Watters	.10	.05	.01
☐ 7 Elvis Grbac	.10	.05	.01
☐ 8 Amp Lee	.04	.02	.01
☐ 9 Steve Bono	.10	.05	.01
☐ 10 Wendell Davis	.04	.02	.01
☐ 11 Mark Carrier DB	.04	.02	.01
☐ 12 Jim Harbaugh	.10	.05	.01
☐ 13 Curtis Conway	.60	.25	.07
☐ 14 Neal Anderson	.04	.02	.01
☐ 15 Tom Waddle	.04	.02	.01
☐ 16 Jeff Query	.04	.02	.01
☐ 17 David Klingler	.04	.02	.01
☐ 18 Eric Ball	.04	.02	.01
☐ 19 Derrick Fenner	.04	.02	.01
☐ 20 Steve Tovar	.04	.02	.01
☐ 21 Carl Pickens	.10	.05	.01
☐ 22 Ricardo McDonald	.04	.02	.01
☐ 23 Harold Green	.04	.02	.01
☐ 24 Keith McKeller	.04	.02	.01
☐ 25 Steve Christie	.04	.02	.01
☐ 26 Andre Reed	.10	.05	.01
☐ 27 Kenneth Davis	.04	.02	.01
☐ 28 Frank Reich	.04	.02	.01
☐ 29 Jim Kelly	.20	.09	.03
☐ 30 Bruce Smith	.20	.09	.03
☐ 31 Thurman Thomas	.20	.09	.03
☐ 32 Glyn Milburn	.10	.05	.01
☐ 33 John Elway	.50	.23	.06
☐ 34 Vance Johnson	.04	.02	.01
☐ 35 Greg Lewis	.04	.02	.01
☐ 36 Steve Atwater	.04	.02	.01
☐ 37 Shannon Sharpe	.10	.05	.01
☐ 38 Mike Croel	.04	.02	.01
☐ 39 Kevin Mack	.04	.02	.01
☐ 40 Lawyer Tillman	.04	.02	.01
☐ 41 Tommy Vardell	.04	.02	.01
☐ 42 Bernie Kosar	.10	.05	.01
☐ 43 Eric Metcalf	.10	.05	.01
☐ 44 Clay Matthews	.04	.02	.01
☐ 45 Keith McCants	.04	.02	.01
☐ 46 Broderick Thomas	.04	.02	.01
☐ 47 Lawrence Dawsey	.04	.02	.01
☐ 48 Reggie Cobb	.04	.02	.01
☐ 49 Lamar Thomas	.04	.02	.01
☐ 50 Courtney Hawkins	.10	.05	.01
☐ 51 Ivory Lee Brown	.04	.02	.01
☐ 52 Ernie Jones	.04	.02	.01
☐ 53 Freddie Joe Nunn	.04	.02	.01
☐ 54 Chris Chandler	.10	.05	.01
☐ 55 Randal Hill	.04	.02	.01
☐ 56 Lorenzo Lynch	.04	.02	.01
☐ 57 Garrison Hearst	1.00	.45	.12
☐ 58 Marion Butts	.04	.02	.01
☐ 59 Anthony Miller	.10	.05	.01
☐ 60 Eric Bieniemy	.04	.02	.01
☐ 61 Ronnie Harmon	.04	.02	.01
☐ 62 Junior Seau	.10	.05	.01
☐ 63 Gill Byrd	.04	.02	.01
☐ 64 Stan Humphries	.10	.05	.01
☐ 65 John Friesz	.04	.02	.01
☐ 66 J.J. Birden	.10	.05	.01
☐ 67 Joe Montana	.75	.35	.09
☐ 68 Christian Okoye	.10	.05	.01
☐ 69 Dale Carter	.04	.02	.01
☐ 70 Barry Word	.04	.02	.01
☐ 71 Derrick Thomas	.10	.05	.01
☐ 72 Todd McNair	.04	.02	.01
☐ 73 Harvey Williams	.04	.02	.01
☐ 74 Jack Trudeau	.04	.02	.01
☐ 75 Rodney Culver	.04	.02	.01
☐ 76 Anthony Johnson	.04	.02	.01
☐ 77 Steve Emtman	.04	.02	.01
☐ 78 Quentin Coryatt	.10	.05	.01
☐ 79 Kerry Cash	.04	.02	.01
☐ 80 Jeff George	.10	.05	.01
☐ 81 Darrin Smith	.04	.02	.01
☐ 82 Jay Novacek	.10	.05	.01
☐ 83 Michael Irvin	.20	.09	.03
☐ 84 Alvin Harper	.10	.05	.01
☐ 85 Kevin Williams	1.00	.45	.12
☐ 86 Troy Aikman	.75	.35	.09
☐ 87 Emmitt Smith	1.50	.70	.19
☐ 88 O.J. McDuffie	.35	.16	.04
☐ 89 Mike Williams	.04	.02	.01
☐ 90 Dan Marino	1.50	.70	.19
☐ 91 Aaron Craver	.04	.02	.01
☐ 92 Troy Vincent	.04	.02	.01
☐ 93 Keith Jackson	.10	.05	.01
☐ 94 Marco Coleman	.04	.02	.01
☐ 95 Mark Higgs	.04	.02	.01
☐ 96 Fred Barnett	.10	.05	.01
☐ 97 Wes Hopkins	.04	.02	.01
☐ 98 Randall Cunningham	.10	.05	.01
☐ 99 Heath Sherman	.04	.02	.01
☐ 100 Vai Sikahema	.04	.02	.01
☐ 101 Tony Smith	.04	.02	.01
☐ 102 Andre Rison	.10	.05	.01
☐ 103 Chris Miller	.04	.02	.01
☐ 104 Deion Sanders	.35	.16	.04
☐ 105 Mike Pritchard	.10	.05	.01
☐ 106 Steve Broussard	.04	.02	.01
☐ 107 Stephen Baker	.04	.02	.01
☐ 108 Carl Banks	.04	.02	.01
☐ 109 Jarrod Bunch	.04	.02	.01
☐ 110 Phil Simms	.10	.05	.01
☐ 111 Rodney Hampton	.10	.05	.01
☐ 112 Dave Meggett	.04	.02	.01
☐ 113 Pepper Johnson	.04	.02	.01
☐ 114 Coleman Rudolph	.04	.02	.01
☐ 115 Boomer Esiason	.10	.05	.01
☐ 116 Browning Nagle	.04	.02	.01
☐ 117 Rob Moore	.10	.05	.01
☐ 118 Marvin Jones	.04	.02	.01
☐ 119 Herman Moore	.35	.16	.04
☐ 120 Bennie Blades	.04	.02	.01
☐ 121 Erik Kramer	.04	.02	.01
☐ 122 Mel Gray	.04	.02	.01
☐ 123 Rodney Peete	.04	.02	.01
☐ 124 Barry Sanders	.75	.35	.09
☐ 125 Chris Spielman	.04	.02	.01
☐ 126 Lamar Lathon	.04	.02	.01
☐ 127 Ernest Givins	.10	.05	.01
☐ 128 Lorenzo White	.10	.05	.01
☐ 129 Micheal Barrow	.04	.02	.01
☐ 130 Warren Moon	.10	.05	.01
☐ 131 Cody Carlson	.04	.02	.01
☐ 132 Reggie White	.20	.09	.03
☐ 133 Terrell Buckley	.04	.02	.01
☐ 134 Ed West	.04	.02	.01
☐ 135 Mark Brunell	2.00	.90	.25
☐ 136 Brett Favre	2.00	.90	.25
☐ 137 Edgar Bennett	.10	.05	.01
☐ 138 Sterling Sharpe	.10	.05	.01
☐ 139 George Teague	.04	.02	.01
☐ 140 Leonard Russell	.10	.05	.01
☐ 141 Drew Bledsoe	2.00	.90	.25
☐ 142 Eugene Chung	.04	.02	.01
☐ 143 Walter Stanley	.04	.02	.01
☐ 144 Scott Zolak	.04	.02	.01
☐ 145 Jon Vaughn	.04	.02	.01
☐ 146 Andre Tippett	.04	.02	.01
☐ 147 Alexander Wright	.04	.02	.01
☐ 148 Billy Joe Hobert	.20	.09	.03
☐ 149 Terry McDaniel	.04	.02	.01
☐ 150 Tim Brown	.10	.05	.01
☐ 151 Willie Gault	.04	.02	.01
☐ 152 Howie Long	.10	.05	.01
☐ 153 Todd Marinovich	.04	.02	.01
☐ 154 Jim Everett	.10	.05	.01
☐ 155 David Lang	.04	.02	.01
☐ 156 Henry Ellard	.10	.05	.01
☐ 157 Cleveland Gary	.04	.02	.01
☐ 158 Steve Israel	.04	.02	.01
☐ 159 Jerome Bettis	1.25	.55	.16
☐ 160 Jackie Slater	.04	.02	.01
☐ 161 Art Monk	.10	.05	.01
☐ 162 Ricky Sanders	.04	.02	.01
☐ 163 Brian Mitchell	.04	.02	.01
☐ 164 Reggie Brooks	.04	.02	.01
☐ 165 Mark Rypien	.04	.02	.01
☐ 166 Earnest Byner	.04	.02	.01
☐ 167 Andre Collins	.04	.02	.01
☐ 168 Quinn Early	.10	.05	.01
☐ 169 Fred McAfee	.04	.02	.01
☐ 170 Wesley Carroll	.04	.02	.01
☐ 171 Gene Atkins	.04	.02	.01
☐ 172 Derek Brown RB UER (Name spelled Derrek on front)	.20	.09	.03
☐ 173 Vaughn Dunbar	.04	.02	.01
☐ 174 Rickey Jackson UER (Name spelled Ricky on front)	.04	.02	.01
☐ 175 John L. Williams	.04	.02	.01
☐ 176 Carlton Gray	.04	.02	.01
☐ 177 Cortez Kennedy	.10	.05	.01
☐ 178 Kelly Stouffer	.04	.02	.01
☐ 179 Rick Mirer	.75	.35	.09
☐ 180 Dan McGwire	.04	.02	.01
☐ 181 Chris Warren	.10	.05	.01
☐ 182 Barry Foster	.10	.05	.01
☐ 183 Merril Hoge	.04	.02	.01
☐ 184 Darren Perry	.04	.02	.01
☐ 185 Deon Figures	.10	.05	.01
☐ 186A Jeff Graham ERR (Name misspelled Grahm on front)	.20	.09	.03
☐ 186B Jeff Graham COR (Name spelled correctly)	.20	.09	.03
☐ 187 Dwight Stone	.04	.02	.01
☐ 188 Neil O'Donnell	.10	.05	.01
☐ 189 Rod Woodson	.10	.05	.01
☐ 190 Alex Van Pelt	.04	.02	.01
☐ 191 Steve Jordan	.04	.02	.01
☐ 192 Roger Craig	.10	.05	.01
☐ 193 Qadry Ismail UER (Misspelled Quadry on card front)	.10	.05	.01
☐ 194 Robert Smith	.20	.09	.03
☐ 195 Gino Torretta	.10	.05	.01
☐ 196 Anthony Carter	.10	.05	.01
☐ 197 Terry Allen	.10	.05	.01
☐ 198 Rich Gannon	.10	.05	.01
☐ 199 Checklist 1-100	.04	.02	.01
☐ 200 Checklist 101-200	.04	.02	.01
☐ 201 Victor Bailey	.04	.02	.01
☐ 202 Micheal Barrow	.04	.02	.01
☐ 203 Patrick Bates	.04	.02	.01
☐ 204 Jerome Bettis	1.00	.45	.12
☐ 205 Drew Bledsoe	1.00	.45	.12
☐ 206 Vincent Brisby	.10	.05	.01
☐ 207 Reggie Brooks	.10	.05	.01
☐ 208 Derek Brown RB	.10	.05	.01
☐ 209 Keith Byars	.04	.02	.01
☐ 210 Tom Carter	.04	.02	.01
☐ 211 Curtis Conway	.20	.09	.03
☐ 212 Russell Copeland	.10	.05	.01
☐ 213 John Copeland	.10	.05	.01
☐ 214 Eric Curry	.10	.05	.01
☐ 215 Troy Drayton	.10	.05	.01
☐ 216 Jason Elam	.04	.02	.01
☐ 217 Steve Everitt	.04	.02	.01
☐ 218 Deon Figures	.10	.05	.01
☐ 219 Irving Fryar	.10	.05	.01
☐ 220 Darrien Gordon	.04	.02	.01
☐ 221 Carlton Gray	.04	.02	.01
☐ 222 Kevin Greene	.10	.05	.01
☐ 223 Andre Hastings	.10	.05	.01
☐ 224 Michael Haynes	.10	.05	.01
☐ 225 Garrison Hearst	.20	.09	.03
☐ 226 Bobby Hebert	.04	.02	.01
☐ 227 Lester Holmes	.04	.02	.01
☐ 228 Jeff Hostetler	.10	.05	.01
☐ 229 Desmond Howard	.10	.05	.01
☐ 230 Tyrone Hughes	.10	.05	.01
☐ 231 Qadry Ismail	.10	.05	.01
☐ 232 Rocket Ismail	.10	.05	.01
☐ 233 James Jett	.10	.05	.01
☐ 234 Marvin Jones	.04	.02	.01
☐ 235 Todd Kelly	.04	.02	.01
☐ 236 Lincoln Kennedy	.04	.02	.01
☐ 237 Terry Kirby	.10	.05	.01
☐ 238 Bernie Kosar	.10	.05	.01
☐ 239 Derrick Lassic	.04	.02	.01
☐ 240 Wilber Marshall	.04	.02	.01
☐ 241 O.J. McDuffie	.35	.16	.04
☐ 242 Ryan McNeil	.04	.02	.01
☐ 243 Natrone Means	.75	.35	.09
☐ 244 Glyn Milburn	.10	.05	.01
☐ 245 Rick Mirer	.35	.16	.04
☐ 246 Scott Mitchell	.20	.09	.03
☐ 247 Ronald Moore	.10	.05	.01
☐ 248 Lorenzo Neal	.04	.02	.01
☐ 249 Erric Pegram	.10	.05	.01
☐ 250 Roosevelt Potts	.04	.02	.01
☐ 251 Leonard Renfro	.04	.02	.01
☐ 252 Greg Robinson	.04	.02	.01
☐ 253 Wayne Simmons	.04	.02	.01
☐ 254 Chris Slade	.10	.05	.01
☐ 255 Irv Smith	.10	.05	.01
☐ 256 Robert Smith	.35	.16	.04
☐ 257 Dana Stubblefield	.20	.09	.03
☐ 258 George Teague	.04	.02	.01
☐ 259 Kevin Williams WR	.10	.05	.01
☐ 260 Checklist 201-260	.04	.02	.01

1993 Wild Card Superchrome

The Superchrome set was distributed in its own packaging, but is essentially a parallel to the base 1993 Wild Card set. The cards feature a metallized foil look and included many of the same inserts as the base product.

	MINT	NRMT	EXC
COMPLETE SET (260)	15.00	6.75	1.85
COMPLETE SERIES 1 (200)	7.50	3.40	.95
COMPLETE SERIES 2 (60)	7.50	3.40	.95
COMMON CARD (1-260)	.10	.05	.01

*SUPERCHROMES: .75X to 1.5X BASIC CARDS

1993 Wild Card Bomb Squad

One of these 30 standard-size cards was inserted in each 1993 Wild Card high-number (201-260) pack. Reportedly, 10,000 Bomb Squad sets were produced. The cards feature on their metallic fronts

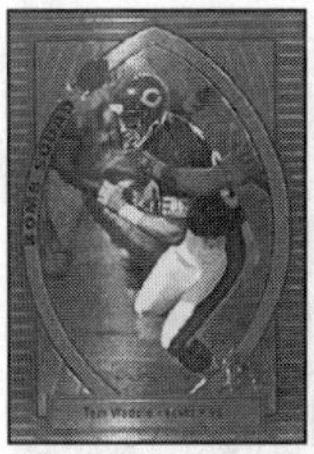

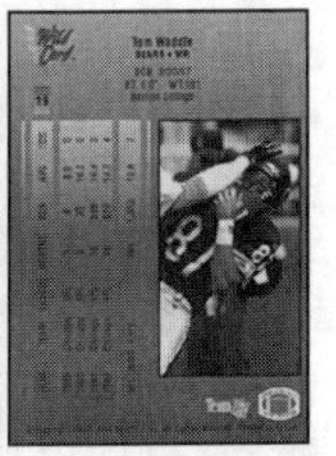

embossed color action photos of the NFL's top receivers within lined silver and bronze borders. The player's name, team, and position appear at the bottom. The orangeish back carries the player's name, team, and position at the top, followed below by biography, a horizontal stat table, and player action shot.

	MINT	NRMT	EXC
COMPLETE SET (30)	12.00	5.50	1.50
COMMON CARD (1-30)	.30	.14	.04

☐ 1 Jerry Rice	2.00	.90	.25
☐ 2 John Taylor	.30	.14	.04
☐ 3 J.J. Birden	.30	.14	.04
☐ 4 Stephen Baker	.30	.14	.04
☐ 5 Victor Bailey	.30	.14	.04
☐ 6 O.J. McDuffie	.75	.35	.09
☐ 7 Haywood Jeffires	.50	.23	.06
☐ 8 Eric Green	.30	.14	.04
☐ 9 Johnny Mitchell	.30	.14	.04
☐ 10 Art Monk	.50	.23	.06
☐ 11 Quinn Early	.50	.23	.06
☐ 12 Troy Drayton	.30	.14	.04
☐ 13 Vincent Brisby	.50	.23	.06
☐ 14 Courtney Hawkins	.30	.14	.04
☐ 15 Tom Waddle	.30	.14	.04
☐ 16 Curtis Conway	.75	.35	.09
☐ 17 Andre Reed	.50	.23	.06
☐ 18 Carl Pickens	.75	.35	.09
☐ 19 Sterling Sharpe	.50	.23	.06
☐ 20 Shannon Sharpe	.75	.35	.09
☐ 21 Qadry Ismail	.50	.23	.06
☐ 22 Rocket Ismail	.50	.23	.06
☐ 23 Andre Rison	.50	.23	.06
☐ 24 Michael Haynes	.50	.23	.06
☐ 25 Alvin Harper	.50	.23	.06
☐ 26 Michael Irvin	.75	.35	.09
☐ 27 Michael Jackson	.50	.23	.06
☐ 28 Herman Moore	1.00	.45	.12
☐ 29 Anthony Miller	.50	.23	.06
☐ 30 Gary Clark	.50	.23	.06

1993 Wild Card Bomb Squad B/B

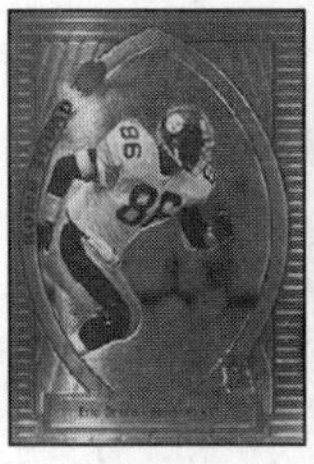

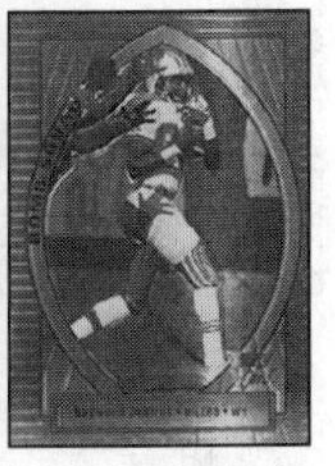

These 15 standard-size cards are double-front (two-player) versions of the 30-card Bomb Squad set. One was randomly inserted in each 20-pack box of 1993 Wild Card high-number jumbo packs. Reportedly, 1,000 of these double-sided sets were made. The cards' designs are identical to the fronts of the regular Bomb Squad cards. The cards are numbered on one side.

	MINT	NRMT	EXC
COMPLETE SET (15)	20.00	9.00	2.50
COMMON PAIR (1-15)	1.00	.45	.12

☐ 1 Jerry Rice John Taylor	4.00	1.80	.50
☐ 2 Tom Waddle Curtis Conway	1.50	.70	.19
☐ 3 Andre Reed Carl Pickens	1.50	.70	.19
☐ 4 Sterling Sharpe Shannon Sharpe	2.50	1.10	.30
☐ 5 Qadry Ismail Rocket Ismail	1.50	.70	.19
☐ 6 Andre Rison Michael Haynes	1.50	.70	.19
☐ 7 Alvin Harper Michael Irvin	2.50	1.10	.30
☐ 8 Michael Jackson Herman Moore	2.50	1.10	.30
☐ 9 Anthony Miller Gary Clark	1.00	.45	.12
☐ 10 J.J. Birden Stephen Baker	1.00	.45	.12
☐ 11 Victor Bailey O.J. McDuffie	1.50	.70	.19
☐ 12 Haywood Jeffires	1.00	.45	.12

Eric Green			
☐ 13 Johnny Mitchell	1.00	.45	.12
Art Monk			
☐ 14 Quinn Early	1.00	.45	.12
Troy Drayton			
☐ 15 Vincent Brisby	1.50	.70	.19
Courtney Hawkins			

1993 Wild Card Field Force

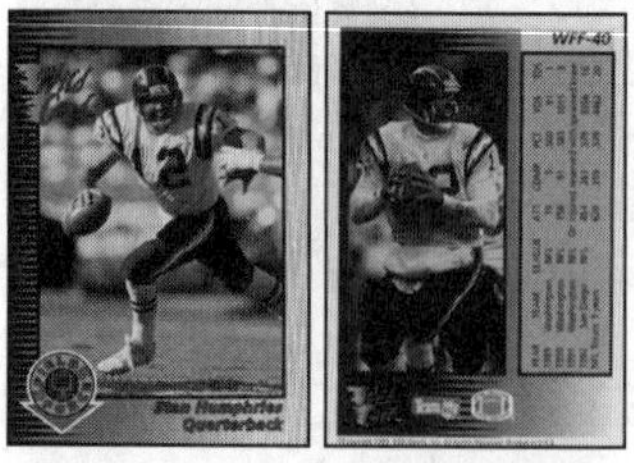

Randomly inserted in foil packs, this 90-card standard-size set was issued in three 30-card series based on Division alignments. Gold and Silver parallel cards were also randomly inserted in packs. The composite border has black and blue straight lines on the left side, blending into blue and white wavy lines on the right. The player's name and position appear in red on the right side of the bottom border, and the team name, also in red, appears vertically on the left. The Field Force logo appears at the lower left corner. Cards 31-60 are numbered on the back with a "WFF" prefix. Cards 61-90 are numbered with an "EFF" prefix and cards 91-120 with a "CFF" prefix. Early in 1994, Superchrome counterparts to 10 Field Force cards were randomly inserted in Wild Card Superchrome foil packs.

	MINT	NRMT	EXC
COMPLETE SET (90)	30.00	13.50	3.70
COMPLETE WEST SERIES (30)	10.00	4.50	1.25
COMPLETE EAST SERIES (30)	10.00	4.50	1.25
COMPLETE CENT.SERIES (30)	10.00	4.50	1.25
COMMON CARD (31-120)	.25	.11	.03
*SILVER CARDS: .6X to 1.25X BASIC CARDS			
*GOLD CARDS: .75X to 1.5X BASIC CARDS			

☐ 31 Jerry Rice	1.00	.45	.12
☐ 32 Ricky Watters	.35	.16	.04
☐ 33 Steve Bono	.25	.11	.03
☐ 34 Amp Lee	.25	.11	.03
☐ 35 Steve Young	1.00	.45	.12
☐ 36 Tommy Maddox	.25	.11	.03
☐ 37 Cleveland Gary	.25	.11	.03
☐ 38 John Elway	.75	.35	.09
☐ 39 Glyn Milburn	.35	.16	.04
☐ 40 Stan Humphries	.35	.16	.04
☐ 41 Junior Seau	.35	.16	.04
☐ 42 Natrone Means	.75	.35	.09
☐ 43 Dale Carter	.25	.11	.03
☐ 44 Joe Montana	1.00	.45	.12
☐ 45 Christian Okoye	.25	.11	.03
☐ 46 Deion Sanders	.60	.25	.07
☐ 47 Roger Harper	.25	.11	.03
☐ 48 Steve Broussard	.25	.11	.03
☐ 49 Todd Marinovich	.25	.11	.03
☐ 50 Billy Joe Hobert	.50	.23	.06
☐ 51 Patrick Bates	.25	.11	.03
☐ 52 Jerome Bettis	1.00	.45	.12
☐ 53 Flipper Anderson	.25	.11	.03
☐ 54 Irv Smith	.25	.11	.03
☐ 55 Quinn Early	.25	.11	.03
☐ 56 Vaughn Dunbar	.25	.11	.03
☐ 57 Rick Mirer	.75	.35	.09
☐ 58 Carlton Gray	.25	.11	.03
☐ 59 Chris Warren	.35	.16	.04
☐ 60 Dan McGwire	.25	.11	.03
☐ 61 Pete Metzelaars	.25	.11	.03
☐ 62 Kenneth Davis	.25	.11	.03
☐ 63 Thurman Thomas	.50	.23	.06
☐ 64 Chris Chandler	.25	.11	.03
☐ 65 Garrison Hearst	.75	.35	.09
☐ 66 Ricky Proehl	.25	.11	.03
☐ 67 Steve Emtman	.25	.11	.03
☐ 68 Jeff George	.35	.16	.04
☐ 69 Clarence Verdin	.25	.11	.03
☐ 70 Troy Aikman	1.00	.45	.12
☐ 71 Emmitt Smith	2.00	.90	.25
☐ 72 Alvin Harper	.25	.11	.03
☐ 73 Michael Irvin	.50	.23	.06
☐ 74 O.J. McDuffie	.50	.23	.06
☐ 75 Troy Vincent	.25	.11	.03
☐ 76 Keith Jackson	.25	.11	.03
☐ 77 Dan Marino	2.00	.90	.25
☐ 78 Leonard Renfro	.25	.11	.03
☐ 79 Heath Sherman	.25	.11	.03
☐ 80 Derek Brown TE	.25	.11	.03
☐ 81 Rodney Hampton	.35	.16	.04
☐ 82 James Hasty	.25	.11	.03
☐ 83 Johnny Mitchell	.25	.11	.03
☐ 84 Brad Baxter	.25	.11	.03
☐ 85 Leonard Russell	.25	.11	.03
☐ 86 Marv Cook	.25	.11	.03
☐ 87 Drew Bledsoe	2.00	.90	.25
☐ 88 Ricky Ervins	.25	.11	.03
☐ 89 Art Monk	.35	.16	.04
☐ 90 Earnest Byner	.25	.11	.03
☐ 91 Tom Waddle	.25	.11	.03
☐ 92 Neal Anderson	.25	.11	.03
☐ 93 Curtis Conway	.50	.23	.06
☐ 94 Harold Green	.25	.11	.03
☐ 95 Jeff Query	.25	.11	.03
☐ 96 Carl Pickens	.35	.16	.04
☐ 97 David Klingler	.25	.11	.03
☐ 98 Michael Jackson	.35	.16	.04
☐ 99 Eric Metcalf	.35	.16	.04
☐ 100 Courtney Hawkins	.25	.11	.03
☐ 101 Eric Curry	.25	.11	.03
☐ 102 Reggie Cobb	.25	.11	.03
☐ 103 Mel Gray	.25	.11	.03
☐ 104 Barry Sanders	1.00	.45	.12
☐ 105 Rodney Peete	.25	.11	.03
☐ 106 Haywood Jeffires	.25	.11	.03
☐ 107 Cody Carlson	.25	.11	.03
☐ 108 Curtis Duncan	.25	.11	.03
☐ 109 Edgar Bennett	.35	.16	.04
☐ 110 George Teague	.25	.11	.03
☐ 111 Terrell Buckley	.25	.11	.03
☐ 112 Brett Favre	2.00	.90	.25
☐ 113 Deon Figures	.25	.11	.03
☐ 114 Rod Woodson	.35	.16	.04
☐ 115 Neil O'Donnell	.35	.16	.04
☐ 116 Barry Foster	.25	.11	.03
☐ 117 Cris Carter	.35	.16	.04
☐ 118 Gino Torretta	.25	.11	.03
☐ 119 Terry Allen	.35	.16	.04
☐ 120 Qadry Ismail	.35	.16	.04

1993 Wild Card Field Force Superchrome

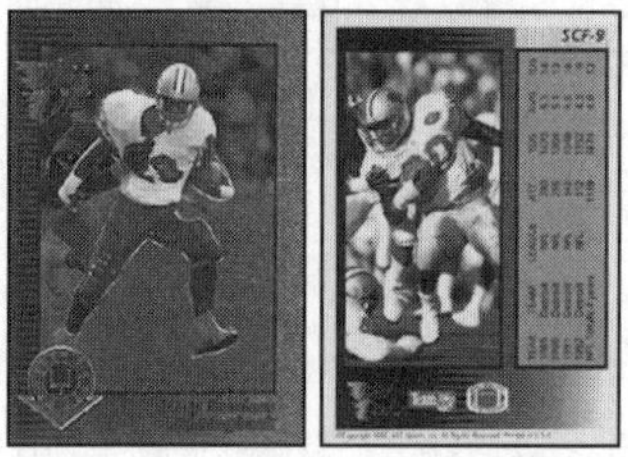

These 10 standard-size cards are Superchrome counterparts to selected cards from the 1993 Wild Card Field Force set. They were randomly inserted in 1993 Wild Card Superchrome foil packs. They feature on their metallic fronts embossed color player action shots within black, white, and blue borders highlighted by wavy and straight lines. The player's name and position appear in red lettering at the lower right. The white-bordered back carries another color player action shot on the left, and a horizontal stat table on the right. Aside from their special foil finish and the "SCF" prefix on their numbered (1-10) backs, they are otherwise identical to the regular Field Force cards. Twenty high-number Superchrome Field Force cards could be obtained by sending 29.95 to Wild Card. According to information on Superchrome foil packs, production of the high-number set was limited to 10,000 sets.

	MINT	NRMT	EXC
COMPLETE SET (10)	12.00	5.50	1.50
COMMON CARD (1-10)	.30	.14	.04

☐ 1 Jerry Rice	1.25	.55	.16
☐ 2 Glyn Milburn	.30	.14	.04
☐ 3 Joe Montana	1.25	.55	.16
☐ 4 Rick Mirer	1.00	.45	.12
☐ 5 Troy Aikman	1.25	.55	.16
☐ 6 Emmitt Smith	2.50	1.10	.30
☐ 7 Dan Marino	2.50	1.10	.30
☐ 8 Drew Bledsoe	2.00	.90	.25
☐ 9 Barry Sanders	1.25	.55	.16
☐ 10 Brett Favre	2.50	1.10	.30

1993 Wild Card Red Hot Rookies

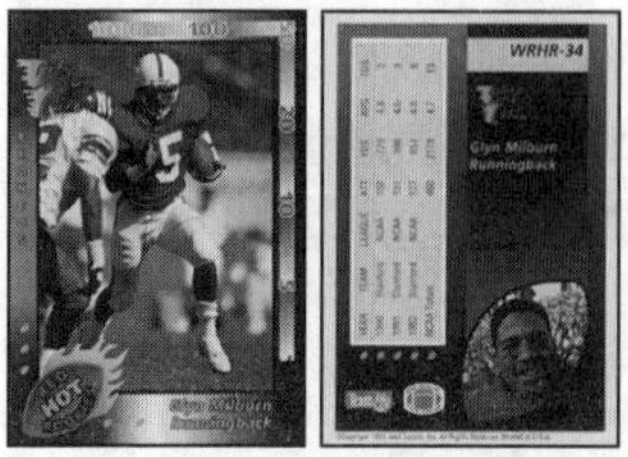

Randomly inserted in foil packs, this 30-card standard-size set is divided into three 10-card subsets based on divisional alignment. The fronts feature bordered glossy color player action photos. Different color numbers and stripes appear in the top and right borders. A football icon with the words "Red Hot Rookies" straddles the lower left corner of the photo and border. The player's name and position appear in the lower right of the border, and the team name appears vertically on the left, both in mustard yellow. The white-bordered back has a posed color player close-up within a football icon in the lower right and stats displayed horizontally in a green rectangle down the left side, all on a reddish brown background. Cards 31-40 are numbered on the back with a "WRHR" prefix. Cards 41-50 are numbered with an "ERHR" prefix and cards 51-60 with a "CRHR" prefix. Early in 1994, Superchrome counterparts to 10 Red Hot Rookies cards were randomly inserted in Wild Card Superchrome foil packs.

	MINT	NRMT	EXC
COMPLETE SET (30)	15.00	6.75	1.85
COMPLETE WEST SERIES (10)	6.00	2.70	.75
COMPLETE EAST SERIES (10)	6.00	2.70	.75
COMPLETE CENT.SERIES (10)	4.00	1.80	.50
COMMON CARD (31-60)	.25	.11	.03

☐ 31 Dana Stubblefield	.60	.25	.07
☐ 32 Todd Kelly	.25	.11	.03
☐ 33 Dan Williams	.25	.11	.03
☐ 34 Glyn Milburn	.40	.18	.05
☐ 35 Natrone Means	1.25	.55	.16
☐ 36 Lincoln Kennedy	.25	.11	.03
☐ 37 Patrick Bates	.25	.11	.03
☐ 38 Jerome Bettis	1.50	.70	.19
☐ 39 Irv Smith	.25	.11	.03
☐ 40 Rick Mirer	1.25	.55	.16
☐ 41 Garrison Hearst	1.25	.55	.16
☐ 42 Kevin Williams	.50	.23	.06
☐ 43 Terry Kirby	.60	.25	.07
☐ 44 O.J. McDuffie	1.00	.45	.12
☐ 45 Leonard Renfro	.25	.11	.03
☐ 46 Victor Bailey	.25	.11	.03
☐ 47 Marvin Jones	.25	.11	.03
☐ 48 Drew Bledsoe	3.00	1.35	.35
☐ 49 Reggie Brooks UER (Missing career college stats)	.40	.18	.05
☐ 50 Tom Carter	.25	.11	.03
☐ 51 Curtis Conway	1.00	.45	.12
☐ 52 Dan Footman	.25	.11	.03
☐ 53 Lamar Thomas	.25	.11	.03
☐ 54 Eric Curry	.40	.18	.05
☐ 55 Ryan McNeil	.25	.11	.03
☐ 56 Micheal Barrow	.25	.11	.03
☐ 57 Wayne Simmons	.25	.11	.03
☐ 58 George Teague	.40	.18	.05
☐ 59 Robert Smith	1.00	.45	.12
☐ 60 Qadry Ismail	.60	.25	.07

1993 Wild Card Red Hot Rookies Superchrome

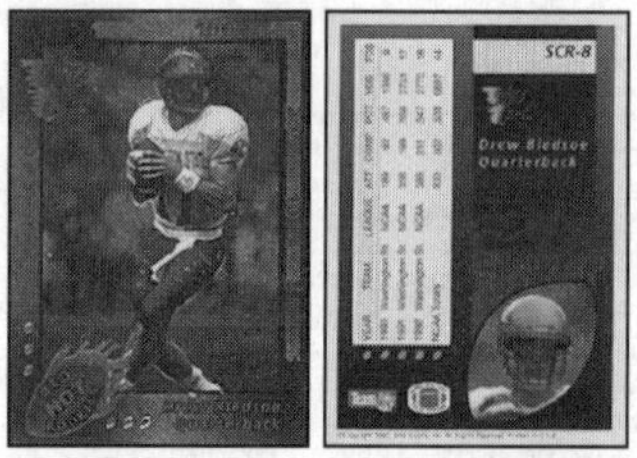

These 10 standard-size cards are Superchrome counterparts to selected cards from the 1993 Wild Card Red Hot Rookies set. They were randomly inserted in 1993 Wild Card Superchrome foil packs. They feature on their metallic fronts embossed color action shots of NFL rookies in their college uniforms within colorful borders highlighted by numbers. The player's name and position appear in gold-colored lettering at the lower right. His team name appears vertically in the left margin. The white-bordered back carries a horizontal stat table on the left, with the player's name, position, biography, and headshot on the right. Aside from their special foil finish and the "SCR" prefix on their numbered (1-10) backs, they are otherwise identical to the regular Red Hot Rookies cards.

	MINT	NRMT	EXC
COMPLETE SET (10)	15.00	6.75	1.85
COMMON CARD (1-10)	.75	.35	.09

☐ 1 Dana Stubblefield	1.00	.45	.12
☐ 2 Glyn Milburn	.75	.35	.09
☐ 3 Jerome Bettis	2.50	1.10	.30
☐ 4 Rick Mirer	2.00	.90	.25
☐ 5 Garrison Hearst	2.00	.90	.25
☐ 6 Terry Kirby	1.00	.45	.12
☐ 7 Victor Bailey	.75	.35	.09
☐ 8 Drew Bledsoe	5.00	2.20	.60
☐ 9 Reggie Brooks	.75	.35	.09
☐ 10 Qadry Ismail	1.00	.45	.12

1993 Wild Card Stat Smashers

Randomly inserted in foil packs, this 60-card standard-size set was issued in three subsets of 20 cards based on divisional alignment. The action player photos on the fronts stand out against action scenes that have a silver metallic sheen to them. The player's name as well as team name and position appear on colored stripes that jut across the bottom of the picture. The black-bordered backs carry biographical information and a close-up player photo (in the lower left corner), with career summary appearing horizontally in a box on the right portion.

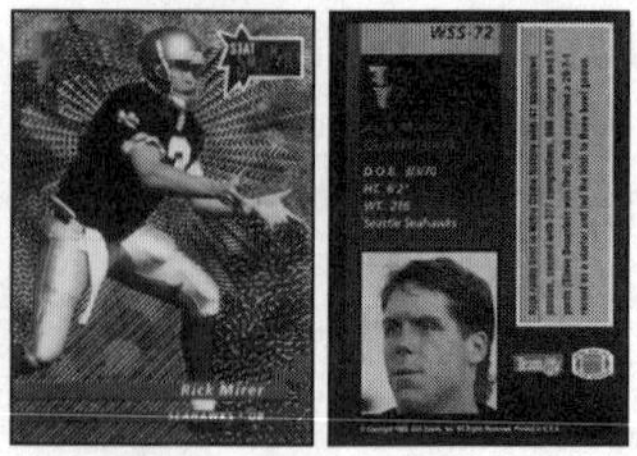

	MINT	NRMT	EXC
COMPLETE SET (60)	50.00	22.00	6.25
COMPLETE WEST SERIES (20)	18.00	8.00	2.20
COMPLETE EAST SERIES (20)	18.00	8.00	2.20
COMPLETE CENT.SERIES (20)	18.00	8.00	2.20
COMMON CARD (53-112)	.50	.23	.06
*GOLD CARDS: SAME PRICE			

☐ 53 Ricky Watters	.75	.35	.09
☐ 54 Jerry Rice	2.00	.90	.25
☐ 55 Steve Young	1.50	.70	.19
☐ 56 Shannon Sharpe	.75	.35	.09
☐ 57 John Elway	1.50	.70	.19
☐ 58 Glyn Milburn	.75	.35	.09
☐ 59 Marion Butts	.50	.23	.06
☐ 60 Junior Seau	.75	.35	.09
☐ 61 Natrone Means	1.50	.70	.19
☐ 62 Joe Montana	2.50	1.10	.30
☐ 63 J.J. Birden	.50	.23	.06
☐ 64 Michael Haynes	.75	.35	.09
☐ 65 Deion Sanders	1.25	.55	.16
☐ 66 Billy Joe Hobert	1.00	.45	.12
☐ 67 Nick Bell	.50	.23	.06
☐ 68 Jerome Bettis	2.00	.90	.25
☐ 69 Vaughn Dunbar	.50	.23	.06
☐ 70 Quinn Early	.75	.35	.09
☐ 71 Dan McGwire	.50	.23	.06
☐ 72 Rick Mirer	1.50	.70	.19
☐ 73 Kenneth Davis	.50	.23	.06
☐ 74 Thurman Thomas	1.00	.45	.12
☐ 75 Garrison Hearst	1.50	.70	.19
☐ 76 Ricky Proehl	.50	.23	.06
☐ 77 Jeff George	.75	.35	.09
☐ 78 Rodney Culver	.50	.23	.06
☐ 79 Troy Aikman	2.00	.90	.25
☐ 80 Emmitt Smith	4.00	1.80	.50
☐ 81 Michael Irvin	1.00	.45	.12
☐ 82 O.J. McDuffie	1.25	.55	.16
☐ 83 Keith Jackson	.50	.23	.06
☐ 84 Dan Marino	4.00	1.80	.50
☐ 85 Heath Sherman	.50	.23	.06
☐ 86 Fred Barnett	.50	.23	.06
☐ 87 Rodney Hampton	.75	.35	.09
☐ 88 Marvin Jones	.50	.23	.06
☐ 89 Brad Baxter	.50	.23	.06
☐ 90 Drew Bledsoe	4.00	1.80	.50
☐ 91 Ricky Ervins	.50	.23	.06
☐ 92 Art Monk	.75	.35	.09
☐ 93 Neal Anderson	.50	.23	.06
☐ 94 Curtis Conway	1.50	.70	.19
☐ 95 John Copeland	.50	.23	.06
☐ 96 Carl Pickens	.75	.35	.09
☐ 97 David Klingler	.50	.23	.06
☐ 98 Michael Jackson	.75	.35	.09
☐ 99 Kevin Mack	.50	.23	.06
☐ 100 Eric Curry	.50	.23	.06
☐ 101 Reggie Cobb	.50	.23	.06
☐ 102 Willie Green	.50	.23	.06
☐ 103 Barry Sanders	2.00	.90	.25
☐ 104 Haywood Jeffires	.75	.35	.09
☐ 105 Lorenzo White	.50	.23	.06
☐ 106 Sterling Sharpe	.75	.35	.09
☐ 107 Brett Favre	4.00	1.80	.50
☐ 108 Neil O'Donnell	.75	.35	.09
☐ 109 Barry Foster	.75	.35	.09
☐ 110 Rich Gannon	.50	.23	.06
☐ 111 Robert Smith	1.25	.55	.16
☐ 112 Qadry Ismail	.75	.35	.09

1993 Wild Card Stat Smashers Rookies

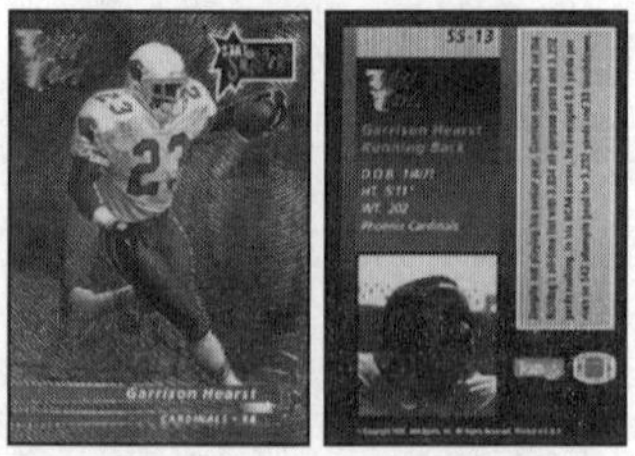

This 52-card standard-size set was issued in gold or silver form. These cards (either type) were inserted one per jumbo pack.This set features an assortment of 1993 NFL rookies.

	MINT	NRMT	EXC
COMPLETE SET (52)	15.00	6.75	1.85

COMMON CARD (1-52)	.20	.09	.03
COMPLETE GOLD SET (52)	25.00	11.00	3.10

*GOLD CARDS: .75X to 1.5X BASIC CARDS

☐ 1 Todd Kelly	.20	.09	.03
☐ 2 Dana Stubblefield	.30	.14	.04
☐ 3 Curtis Conway	.75	.35	.09
☐ 4 John Copeland	.20	.09	.03
☐ 5 Russell Copeland	.20	.09	.03
☐ 6 Thomas Smith	.30	.14	.04
☐ 7 Glyn Milburn	.30	.14	.04
☐ 8 Jason Elam	.30	.14	.04
☐ 9 Steve Everitt	.30	.14	.04
☐ 10 Eric Curry	.20	.09	.03
☐ 11 Horace Copeland	.30	.14	.04
☐ 12 Ronald Moore	.30	.14	.04
☐ 13 Garrison Hearst	1.00	.45	.12
☐ 14 Natrone Means	1.00	.45	.12
☐ 15 Darrien Gordon	.30	.14	.04
☐ 16 Roosevelt Potts	.20	.09	.03
☐ 17 Kevin Williams	.50	.23	.06
☐ 18 Derrick Lassic	.20	.09	.03
☐ 19 O.J. McDuffie	.75	.35	.09
☐ 20 Terry Kirby	.50	.23	.06
☐ 21 Scott Mitchell	.50	.23	.06
☐ 22 Victor Bailey	.20	.09	.03
☐ 23 Vaughn Hebron	.20	.09	.03
☐ 24 Lincoln Kennedy	.20	.09	.03
☐ 25 Michael Strahan	.20	.09	.03
☐ 26 Marvin Jones	.20	.09	.03
☐ 27 Tony McGee	.30	.14	.04
☐ 28 Ryan McNeil	.20	.09	.03
☐ 29 Micheal Barrow	.20	.09	.03
☐ 30 Wayne Simmons	.20	.09	.03
☐ 31 George Teague	.20	.09	.03
☐ 32 Vincent Brisby	.50	.23	.06
☐ 33 Drew Bledsoe	2.50	1.10	.30
☐ 34 Rocket Ismail	.30	.14	.04
☐ 35 Patrick Bates	.20	.09	.03
☐ 36 James Jett	.20	.09	.03
☐ 37 Jerome Bettis	1.25	.55	.16
☐ 38 Troy Drayton	.30	.14	.04
☐ 39 Tom Carter	.20	.09	.03
☐ 40 Reggie Brooks	.30	.14	.04
☐ 41 Lorenzo Neal	.20	.09	.03
☐ 42 Derek Brown RB	.20	.09	.03
☐ 43 Tyrone Hughes	.30	.14	.04
☐ 44 Rick Mirer	1.00	.45	.12
☐ 45 Carlton Gray	.20	.09	.03
☐ 46 Andre Hastings	.30	.14	.04
☐ 47 Deon Figures	.20	.09	.03
☐ 48 Qadry Ismail	.30	.14	.04
☐ 49 Robert Smith	.75	.35	.09
☐ 50 Irv Smith	.30	.14	.04
☐ 51 Chris Slade	.30	.14	.04
☐ 52 Willie Roaf	.30	.14	.04

1993 Wild Card Superchrome FF/RHR B/B

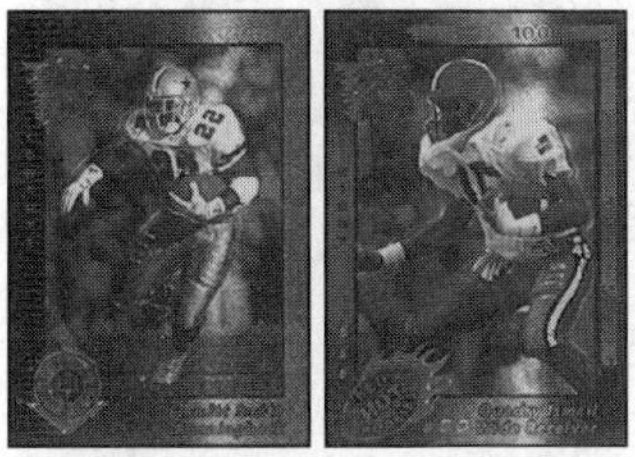

This set is frequently called "Red Hot Rookies and Field Force -- Back to Back." Measuring the standard-size, these cards were randomly inserted in Superchrome series two packs. The cards are double-sided, with a Red Hot Rookies on one side and a Field Force on the other. The cards are unnumbered and checklisted below alphabetically by the Field Force player.

	MINT	NRMT	EXC
COMPLETE SET (10)	20.00	9.00	2.50
COMMON PAIR (1-10)	1.00	.45	.12
☐ 1 Troy Aikman Dana Stubblefield	2.00	.90	.25
☐ 2 Drew Bledsoe Drew Bledsoe	3.00	1.35	.35
☐ 3 Brett Favre Terry Kirby	4.00	1.80	.50
☐ 4 Dan Marino Reggie Brooks	4.00	1.80	.50
☐ 5 Glyn Milburn Rick Mirer	1.00	.45	.12
☐ 6 Rick Mirer Glyn Milburn	1.00	.45	.12
☐ 7 Joe Montana Jerome Bettis	2.50	1.10	.30
☐ 8 Jerry Rice Garrison Hearst	2.00	.90	.25
☐ 9 Barry Sanders Victor Bailey	2.00	.90	.25
☐ 10 Emmitt Smith Qadry Ismail UER (Misspelled Quadry)	4.00	1.80	.50

1993 Wild Card Superchrome Rookies Promos

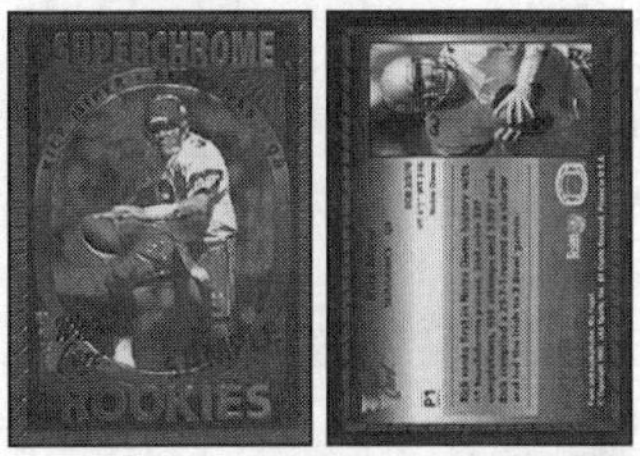

These five standard-size promo cards feature on their fronts metallic purple-bordered color player action shots set within gold elliptical inner borders. The player's name, team, and position appear within the gold inner border. The "Sample" disclaimer appears near the bottom of the photo. The black- and purple-bordered horizontal back carries the player's name, team, and position at the top, followed below by biography, statistics, and, on the right, another color player action shot. The cards are numbered on the back with a "P" prefix.

	MINT	NRMT	EXC
COMPLETE SET (5)	6.00	2.70	.75
COMMON CARD (P1-P5)	.75	.35	.09
☐ P1 Rick Mirer	1.25	.55	.16
☐ P2 Reggie Brooks	.75	.35	.09
☐ P3 Glyn Milburn	.75	.35	.09
☐ P4 Drew Bledsoe	2.50	1.10	.30
☐ P5 Jerome Bettis	1.50	.70	.19

1993 Wild Card Superchrome Rookies

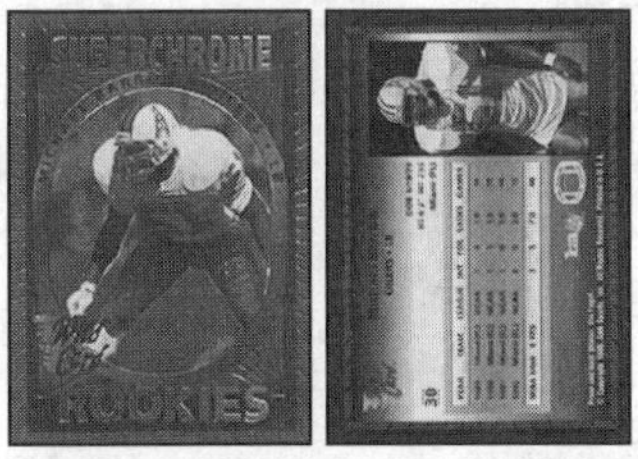

These 50 standard-size cards issued early in 1994 were inserted, six per pack, in each special Superchrome Rookies 15-card foil pack. (The remaining cards in the pack were regular 1993 Wild Cards.) They feature on their foil fronts color player action shots with multicolored borders. The player's name, team and position appear within the oval gold-colored inner border. The black- and purple-bordered horizontal back carries the player's name, team and position at the top, followed below by biography and statistics. A small color player action shot appears on the right. The set is sequenced in team order. Scott Mitchell is the only non-rookie in this set.

	MINT	NRMT	EXC
COMPLETE SET (50)	20.00	9.00	2.50
COMMON CARD (1-50)	.20	.09	.03
☐ 1 Dana Stubblefield	.50	.23	.06
☐ 2 Todd Kelly	.20	.09	.03
☐ 3 Curtis Conway	.75	.35	.09
☐ 4 John Copeland	.30	.14	.04
☐ 5 Tony McGee	.30	.14	.04
☐ 6 Russell Copeland	.20	.09	.03
☐ 7 Thomas Smith	.20	.09	.03
☐ 8 Jason Elam	.30	.14	.04
☐ 9 Glyn Milburn	.30	.14	.04
☐ 10 Steve Everitt	.20	.09	.03
☐ 11 Demetrius DuBose	.20	.09	.03
☐ 12 Eric Curry	.30	.14	.04
☐ 13 Garrison Hearst	1.25	.55	.16
☐ 14 Ronald Moore	.30	.14	.04
☐ 15 Darrien Gordon	.20	.09	.03
☐ 16 Natrone Means	1.25	.55	.16
☐ 17 Roosevelt Potts	.20	.09	.03
☐ 18 Derrick Lassic	.20	.09	.03
☐ 19 Kevin Williams	.50	.23	.06
☐ 20 Scott Mitchell UER (Text indicates drafted in '91; should be '90)	.50	.23	.06
☐ 21 O.J. McDuffie	.75	.35	.09
☐ 22 Terry Kirby	.50	.23	.06
☐ 23 Vaughn Hebron	.20	.09	.03
☐ 24 Victor Bailey	.20	.09	.03
☐ 25 Lincoln Kennedy	.20	.09	.03
☐ 26 Michael Strahan	.20	.09	.03
☐ 27 Marvin Jones	.20	.09	.03
☐ 28 Will Shields	.20	.09	.03
☐ 29 Ryan McNeil	.20	.09	.03
☐ 30 Micheal Barrow	.20	.09	.03
☐ 31 George Teague	.20	.09	.03
☐ 32 Wayne Simmons	.20	.09	.03
☐ 33 Vincent Brisby	.30	.14	.04
☐ 34 Drew Bledsoe	3.00	1.35	.35
☐ 35 Patrick Bates	.20	.09	.03
☐ 36 James Jett	.20	.09	.03
☐ 37 Rocket Ismail	.30	.14	.04
☐ 38 Troy Drayton	.30	.14	.04
☐ 39 Jerome Bettis	1.50	.70	.19
☐ 40 Tom Carter	.20	.09	.03
☐ 41 Reggie Brooks	.30	.14	.04
☐ 42 Tyrone Hughes	.30	.14	.04
☐ 43 Derek Brown RB	.30	.14	.04
☐ 44 Willie Roaf	.30	.14	.04
☐ 45 Carlton Gray	.20	.09	.03
☐ 46 Rick Mirer	1.25	.55	.16
☐ 47 Andre Hastings	.30	.14	.04
☐ 48 Deon Figures	.30	.14	.04
☐ 49 Qadry Ismail	.30	.14	.04
☐ 50 Robert Smith	.75	.35	.09

1993 Wild Card Superchrome Rookies B/B

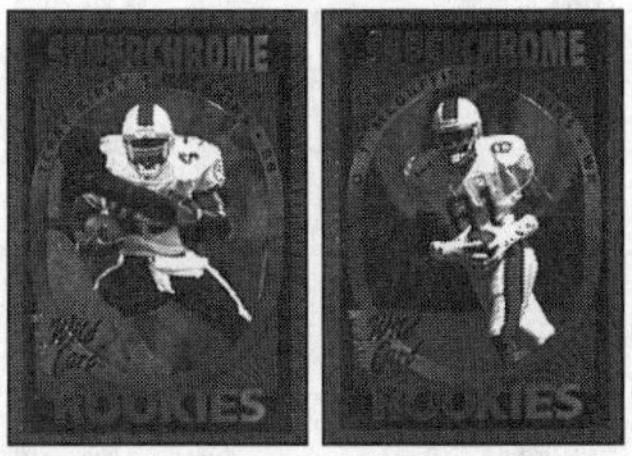

Randomly inserted in 1993 Wild Card Superchrome Rookies foil packs, these 25 standard-size cards feature on both metallic sides embossed color action shots of NFL rookies in their NFL uniforms within purple, black, blue, and gold borders. The player's name, team, and position appear above the photo within the oval gold inner border. The cards are unnumbered and checklisted below in alphabetical order.

	MINT	NRMT	EXC
COMPLETE SET (25)	30.00	13.50	3.70
COMMON PAIR (1-25)	.75	.35	.09
☐ 1 Victor Bailey Vaughn Hebron	.75	.35	.09
☐ 2 Micheal Barrow Ryan McNeil	.75	.35	.09
☐ 3 Patrick Bates Vincent Brisby	.75	.35	.09
☐ 4 Jerome Bettis Natrone Means	2.50	1.10	.30
☐ 5 Drew Bledsoe Rick Mirer	5.00	2.20	.60
☐ 6 Reggie Brooks Glyn Milburn	1.25	.55	.16
☐ 7 Derek Brown RB Tyrone Hughes	.75	.35	.09
☐ 8 Tom Carter Jason Elam	.75	.35	.09
☐ 9 Curtis Conway Steve Everitt	2.00	.90	.25
☐ 10 John Copeland Tony McGee	.75	.35	.09
☐ 11 Russell Copeland Thomas Smith	.75	.35	.09
☐ 12 Eric Curry Demetrius DuBose	.75	.35	.09
☐ 13 Troy Drayton Darrien Gordon	.75	.35	.09
☐ 14 Deon Figures Andre Hastings	.75	.35	.09
☐ 15 Carlton Gray Willie Roaf	.75	.35	.09
☐ 16 Garrison Hearst Ronald Moore	2.00	.90	.25
☐ 17 Qadry Ismail Rocket Ismail	1.25	.55	.16
☐ 18 James Jett Robert Smith	1.50	.70	.19
☐ 19 Marvin Jones Will Shields	.75	.35	.09
☐ 20 Todd Kelly Dana Stubblefield	1.25	.55	.16
☐ 21 Lincoln Kennedy Michael Strahan	.75	.35	.09
☐ 22 Terry Kirby O.J. McDuffie	2.00	.90	.25
☐ 23 Derrick Lassic Kevin Williams	1.25	.55	.16
☐ 24 Scott Mitchell Roosevelt Potts	1.25	.55	.16
☐ 25 Wayne Simmons George Teague	.75	.35	.09

1967 Williams Portraits

This set consists of 512 charcoal portraits of NFL players. Each portrait measures approximately 8" by 10", and they were sold in sets of eight for 1.00 and the end flap from Velveeta, or a front label from Kraft Deluxe Slices or Singles, Cracker Barrel Cheddar or Kraft Sliced Natural Cheese. There were four eight-portrait groups for each of the 16 NFL teams. Moreover, an official NFL portrait album which would hold 32 portraits was offered for 2.00. The player's name and position were printed beneath the charcoal portrait. The backs are blank. The portraits are unnumbered and have been checklisted below

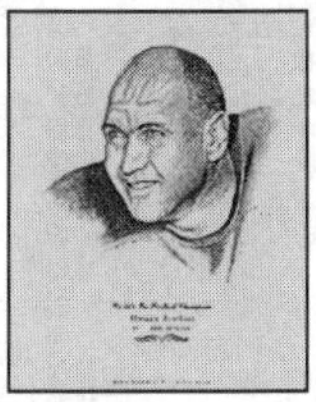

alphabetically according to team. A checklist sheet (8" by 10") was produced, but is not considered a card. The Redskins and Packers sets appear to be the easiest to find. Popular players issued in their Rookie Card year include Leroy Kelly, Tommy Nobis, Dan Reeves and Jackie Smith. Players issued before their Rookie Card year include Lem Barney, Brian Piccolo, Bubba Smith and Steve Spurrier.

	NRMT	VG-E	GOOD
COMPLETE SET (512)	6500.00	2900.00	800.00
COMMON CARD (1-512)	8.00	3.60	1.00
☐ 1 Taz Anderson	15.00	6.75	1.85
☐ 2 Gary Barnes	15.00	6.75	1.85
☐ 3 Lee Calland	15.00	6.75	1.85
☐ 4 Junior Coffey	15.00	6.75	1.85
☐ 5 Ed Cook	15.00	6.75	1.85
☐ 6 Perry Lee Dunn	15.00	6.75	1.85
☐ 7 Dan Grimm	15.00	6.75	1.85
☐ 8 Alex Hawkins	12.00	5.50	1.50
☐ 9 Randy Johnson	15.00	6.75	1.85
☐ 10 Lou Kirouac	15.00	6.75	1.85
☐ 11 Errol Linden	15.00	6.75	1.85
☐ 12 Billy Lothridge	15.00	6.75	1.85
☐ 13 Frank Marchlewski	15.00	6.75	1.85
☐ 14 Rich Marshall	15.00	6.75	1.85
☐ 15 Billy Martin	15.00	6.75	1.85
☐ 16 Tom Moore	12.00	5.50	1.50
☐ 17 Tommy Nobis	20.00	9.00	2.50
☐ 18 Jim Norton	15.00	6.75	1.85
☐ 19 Nick Rassas	15.00	6.75	1.85
☐ 20 Ken Reaves	15.00	6.75	1.85
☐ 21 Bobby Richards	15.00	6.75	1.85
☐ 22 Jerry Richardson	15.00	6.75	1.85
☐ 23 Bob Riggle	15.00	6.75	1.85
☐ 24 Karl Rubke	15.00	6.75	1.85
☐ 25 Marion Rushing	15.00	6.75	1.85
☐ 26 Chuck Sieminski	15.00	6.75	1.85
☐ 27 Steve Sloan	15.00	6.75	1.85
☐ 28 Ron Smith	15.00	6.75	1.85
☐ 29 Don Talbert	15.00	6.75	1.85
☐ 30 Ernie Wheelwright	15.00	6.75	1.85
☐ 31 Sam Williams	15.00	6.75	1.85
☐ 32 Jim Wilson	15.00	6.75	1.85
☐ 33 Sam Ball	15.00	6.75	1.85
☐ 34 Raymond Berry	30.00	13.50	3.70
☐ 35 Bob Boyd	15.00	6.75	1.85
☐ 36 Ordell Braase	15.00	6.75	1.85
☐ 37 Barry Brown	15.00	6.75	1.85
☐ 38 Bill Curry	15.00	6.75	1.85
☐ 39 Mike Curtis	12.00	5.50	1.50
☐ 40 Alvin Haymond	15.00	6.75	1.85
☐ 41 Jerry Hill	15.00	6.75	1.85
☐ 42 David Lee	15.00	6.75	1.85
☐ 43 Jerry Logan	15.00	6.75	1.85
☐ 44 Tony Lorick	15.00	6.75	1.85
☐ 45 Lenny Lyles	15.00	6.75	1.85
☐ 46 John Mackey	18.00	8.00	2.20
☐ 47 Tom Matte	12.00	5.50	1.50
☐ 48 Lou Michaels	12.00	5.50	1.50
☐ 49 Fred Miller	15.00	6.75	1.85
☐ 50 Lenny Moore	30.00	13.50	3.70
☐ 51 Jimmy Orr	15.00	6.75	1.85
☐ 52 Jim Parker	18.00	8.00	2.20
☐ 53 Glenn Ressler	15.00	6.75	1.85
☐ 54 Willie Richardson	15.00	6.75	1.85
☐ 55 Don Shinnick	15.00	6.75	1.85
☐ 56 Billy Ray Smith	15.00	6.75	1.85
☐ 57 Bubba Smith	20.00	9.00	2.50
☐ 58 Dan Sullivan	15.00	6.75	1.85
☐ 59 Dick Szymanski	15.00	6.75	1.85
☐ 60 Johnny Unitas	60.00	27.00	7.50
☐ 61 Bob Vogel	15.00	6.75	1.85
☐ 62 Rick Volk	15.00	6.75	1.85
☐ 63 Jim Welch	15.00	6.75	1.85
☐ 64 Butch Wilson	15.00	6.75	1.85
☐ 65 Charlie Bivins	15.00	6.75	1.85
☐ 66 Charlie Brown	15.00	6.75	1.85
☐ 67 Doug Buffone	15.00	6.75	1.85
☐ 68 Rudy Bukich	15.00	6.75	1.85
☐ 69 Ron Bull	15.00	6.75	1.85
☐ 70 Dick Butkus	50.00	22.00	6.25
☐ 71 Jim Cadile	15.00	6.75	1.85
☐ 72 Jack Concannon	15.00	6.75	1.85
☐ 73 Frank Cornish	15.00	6.75	1.85
☐ 74 Don Croftcheck	15.00	6.75	1.85
☐ 75 Dick Evey	15.00	6.75	1.85
☐ 76 Joe Fortunato	15.00	6.75	1.85
☐ 77 Curtis Gentry	15.00	6.75	1.85
☐ 78 Bobby Joe Green	15.00	6.75	1.85
☐ 79 John Henry Johnson	18.00	8.00	2.20
☐ 80 Bob Jones	15.00	6.75	1.85
☐ 81 Jimmy Jones	15.00	6.75	1.85
☐ 82 Ralph Kurek	15.00	6.75	1.85

☐ 83 Roger LeClerc	15.00	6.75	1.85
☐ 84 Andy Livingston	15.00	6.75	1.85
☐ 85 Bennie McRae	15.00	6.75	1.85
☐ 86 Johnny Morris	15.00	6.75	1.85
☐ 87 Richie Petitbon	15.00	6.75	1.85
☐ 88 Loyd Phillips	15.00	6.75	1.85
☐ 89 Brian Piccolo	50.00	22.00	6.25
☐ 90 Jim Purnell	15.00	6.75	1.85
☐ 91 Mike Pyle	15.00	6.75	1.85
☐ 92 Mike Reilly	15.00	6.75	1.85
☐ 93 Gale Sayers	50.00	22.00	6.25
☐ 94 George Seals	15.00	6.75	1.85
☐ 95 Roosevelt Taylor	12.00	5.50	1.50
☐ 96 Bob Wetoska	15.00	6.75	1.85
☐ 97 Erich Barnes	15.00	6.75	1.85
☐ 98 Johnny Brewer	15.00	6.75	1.85
☐ 99 Monte Clark	15.00	6.75	1.85
☐ 100 Gary Collins	12.00	5.50	1.50
☐ 101 Larry Conjar	15.00	6.75	1.85
☐ 102 Vince Costello	15.00	6.75	1.85
☐ 103 Ross Fichtner	15.00	6.75	1.85
☐ 104 Bill Glass	15.00	6.75	1.85
☐ 105 Ernie Green	15.00	6.75	1.85
☐ 106 Jack Gregory	15.00	6.75	1.85
☐ 107 Charlie Harraway	15.00	6.75	1.85
☐ 108 Gene Hickerson	15.00	6.75	1.85
☐ 109 Fred Hoaglin	15.00	6.75	1.85
☐ 110 Jim Houston	15.00	6.75	1.85
☐ 111 Mike Howell	15.00	6.75	1.85
☐ 112 Joe Bob Isbell	15.00	6.75	1.85
☐ 113 Walter Johnson	15.00	6.75	1.85
☐ 114 Jim Kanicki	15.00	6.75	1.85
☐ 115 Ernie Kellerman	15.00	6.75	1.85
☐ 116 Leroy Kelly	20.00	9.00	2.50
☐ 117 Dale Lindsey	15.00	6.75	1.85
☐ 118 Clifton McNeil	15.00	6.75	1.85
☐ 119 Milt Morin	15.00	6.75	1.85
☐ 120 Nick Pietrosante	15.00	6.75	1.85
☐ 121 Frank Ryan	12.00	5.50	1.50
☐ 122 Dick Schafrath	15.00	6.75	1.85
☐ 123 Randy Schultz	15.00	6.75	1.85
☐ 124 Ralph Smith	15.00	6.75	1.85
☐ 125 Carl Ward	15.00	6.75	1.85
☐ 126 Paul Warfield	20.00	9.00	2.50
☐ 127 Paul Wiggin	15.00	6.75	1.85
☐ 128 John Wooten	15.00	6.75	1.85
☐ 129 George Andrie	15.00	6.75	1.85
☐ 130 Jim Boeke	15.00	6.75	1.85
☐ 131 Frank Clarke	12.00	5.50	1.50
☐ 132 Mike Connelly	15.00	6.75	1.85
☐ 133 Buddy Dial	15.00	6.75	1.85
☐ 134 Leon Donohue	15.00	6.75	1.85
☐ 135 Dave Edwards	15.00	6.75	1.85
☐ 136 Mike Gaechter	15.00	6.75	1.85
☐ 137 Walt Garrison	18.00	8.00	2.20
☐ 138 Pete Gent	15.00	6.75	1.85
☐ 139 Cornell Green	12.00	5.50	1.50
☐ 140 Bob Hayes	20.00	9.00	2.50
☐ 141 Chuck Howley	18.00	8.00	2.20
☐ 142 Lee Roy Jordan	18.00	8.00	2.20
☐ 143 Bob Lilly	30.00	13.50	3.70
☐ 144 Tony Liscio	15.00	6.75	1.85
☐ 145 Warren Livingston	15.00	6.75	1.85
☐ 146 Dave Manders	15.00	6.75	1.85
☐ 147 Don Meredith	35.00	16.00	4.40
☐ 148 Ralph Neely	15.00	6.75	1.85
☐ 149 John Niland	15.00	6.75	1.85
☐ 150 Pettis Norman	15.00	6.75	1.85
☐ 151 Don Perkins	12.00	5.50	1.50
☐ 152 Jethro Pugh	12.00	5.50	1.50
☐ 153 Dan Reeves	25.00	11.00	3.10
☐ 154 Mel Renfro	18.00	8.00	2.20
☐ 155 Jerry Rhome	12.00	5.50	1.50
☐ 156 Les Shy	15.00	6.75	1.85
☐ 157 J.D. Smith	15.00	6.75	1.85
☐ 158 Willie Townes	15.00	6.75	1.85
☐ 159 Danny Villanueva	15.00	6.75	1.85
☐ 160 John Wilbur	15.00	6.75	1.85
☐ 161 Mike Alford	15.00	6.75	1.85
☐ 162 Lem Barney	18.00	8.00	2.20
☐ 163 Charley Bradshaw	15.00	6.75	1.85
☐ 164 Roger Brown	12.00	5.50	1.50
☐ 165 Ernie Clark	15.00	6.75	1.85
☐ 166 Gail Cogdill	15.00	6.75	1.85
☐ 167 Nick Eddy	15.00	6.75	1.85
☐ 168 Mel Farr	15.00	6.75	1.85
☐ 169 Bobby Felts	15.00	6.75	1.85
☐ 170 Ed Flanagan	15.00	6.75	1.85
☐ 171 Jim Gibbons	12.00	5.50	1.50
☐ 172 John Gordy	15.00	6.75	1.85
☐ 173 Larry Hand	15.00	6.75	1.85
☐ 174 Wally Hilgenberg	15.00	6.75	1.85
☐ 175 Alex Karras	20.00	9.00	2.50
☐ 176 Bob Kowalkowski	15.00	6.75	1.85
☐ 177 Ron Kramer	15.00	6.75	1.85
☐ 178 Mike Lucci	15.00	6.75	1.85
☐ 179 Bruce Maher	15.00	6.75	1.85
☐ 180 Amos Marsh	15.00	6.75	1.85
☐ 181 Darris McCord	15.00	6.75	1.85
☐ 182 Tom Nowatzke	15.00	6.75	1.85
☐ 183 Milt Plum	12.00	5.50	1.50
☐ 184 Wayne Rasmussen	15.00	6.75	1.85
☐ 185 Roger Shoals	15.00	6.75	1.85
☐ 186 Pat Studstill	12.00	5.50	1.50
☐ 187 Karl Sweetan	15.00	6.75	1.85
☐ 188 Bobby Thompson DB	15.00	6.75	1.85
☐ 189 Doug Van Horn	15.00	6.75	1.85
☐ 190 Wayne Walker	15.00	6.75	1.85
☐ 191 Tommy Watkins	15.00	6.75	1.85
☐ 192 Garo Yepremian	12.00	5.50	1.50
☐ 193 Herb Adderley	15.00	6.75	1.85
☐ 194 Lionel Aldridge	8.00	3.60	1.00
☐ 195 Donny Anderson	10.00	4.50	1.25
☐ 196 Ken Bowman	8.00	3.60	1.00
☐ 197 Zeke Bratkowski	10.00	4.50	1.25
☐ 198 Bob Brown DT	8.00	3.60	1.00
☐ 199 Tom Brown	8.00	3.60	1.00
☐ 200 Lee Roy Caffey	8.00	3.60	1.00
☐ 201 Don Chandler	10.00	4.50	1.25
☐ 202 Tommy Crutcher	8.00	3.60	1.00
☐ 203 Carroll Dale	10.00	4.50	1.25
☐ 204 Willie Davis	15.00	6.75	1.85
☐ 205 Boyd Dowler	10.00	4.50	1.25
☐ 206 Marv Fleming	10.00	4.50	1.25
☐ 207 Gale Gillingham	8.00	3.60	1.00
☐ 208 Jim Grabowski	8.00	3.60	1.00
☐ 209 Forrest Gregg	15.00	6.75	1.85
☐ 210 Doug Hart	8.00	3.60	1.00
☐ 211 Bob Jeter	8.00	3.60	1.00
☐ 212 Hank Jordan	12.00	5.50	1.50
☐ 213 Ron Kostelnik	8.00	3.60	1.00
☐ 214 Jerry Kramer	12.00	5.50	1.50
☐ 215 Bob Long	8.00	3.60	1.00
☐ 216 Max McGee	10.00	4.50	1.25
☐ 217 Ray Nitschke	20.00	9.00	2.50
☐ 218 Elijah Pitts	10.00	4.50	1.25
☐ 219 Dave Robinson	8.00	3.60	1.00
☐ 220 Bob Skoronski	8.00	3.60	1.00
☐ 221 Bart Starr	25.00	11.00	3.10
☐ 222 Fred Thurston	10.00	4.50	1.25
☐ 223 Willie Wood	15.00	6.75	1.85
☐ 224 Steve Wright	8.00	3.60	1.00
☐ 225 Dick Bass	12.00	5.50	1.50
☐ 226 Maxie Baughan	15.00	6.75	1.85
☐ 227 Joe Carollo	15.00	6.75	1.85
☐ 228 Bernie Casey	15.00	6.75	1.85
☐ 229 Don Chuy	15.00	6.75	1.85
☐ 230 Charlie Cowan	15.00	6.75	1.85
☐ 231 Irv Cross	15.00	6.75	1.85
☐ 232 Willie Ellison	15.00	6.75	1.85
☐ 233 Roman Gabriel	18.00	8.00	2.20
☐ 234 Bruce Gossett	15.00	6.75	1.85
☐ 235 Roosevelt Grier	18.00	8.00	2.20
☐ 236 Tony Guillory	15.00	6.75	1.85
☐ 237 Ken Iman	15.00	6.75	1.85
☐ 238 Deacon Jones	20.00	9.00	2.50
☐ 239 Les Josephson	15.00	6.75	1.85
☐ 240 Jon Kilgore	15.00	6.75	1.85
☐ 241 Chuck Lamson	15.00	6.75	1.85
☐ 242 Lamar Lundy	12.00	5.50	1.50
☐ 243 Tom Mack	18.00	8.00	2.20
☐ 244 Tommy Mason	12.00	5.50	1.50
☐ 245 Tommy McDonald	12.00	5.50	1.50
☐ 246 Ed Meador	15.00	6.75	1.85
☐ 247 Bill Munson	12.00	5.50	1.50
☐ 248 Bob Nichols	15.00	6.75	1.85
☐ 249 Merlin Olsen	25.00	11.00	3.10
☐ 250 Jack Pardee	12.00	5.50	1.50
☐ 251 Bucky Pope	15.00	6.75	1.85
☐ 252 Joe Scibelli	15.00	6.75	1.85
☐ 253 Jack Snow	12.00	5.50	1.50
☐ 254 Billy Truax	15.00	6.75	1.85
☐ 255 Clancy Williams	15.00	6.75	1.85
☐ 256 Doug Woodlief	10.00	4.50	1.25
☐ 257 Grady Alderman	12.00	5.50	1.50
☐ 258 John Beasley	15.00	6.75	1.85
☐ 259 Bob Berry	15.00	6.75	1.85
☐ 260 Larry Bowie	15.00	6.75	1.85
☐ 261 Bill Brown	12.00	5.50	1.50
☐ 262 Fred Cox	12.00	5.50	1.50
☐ 263 Doug Davis	15.00	6.75	1.85
☐ 264 Paul Dickson	15.00	6.75	1.85
☐ 265 Carl Eller	18.00	8.00	2.20
☐ 266 Paul Flatley	15.00	6.75	1.85
☐ 267 Dale Hackbart	15.00	6.75	1.85
☐ 268 Don Hansen	15.00	6.75	1.85
☐ 269 Clint Jones	15.00	6.75	1.85
☐ 270 Jeff Jordan	15.00	6.75	1.85
☐ 271 Karl Kassulke	15.00	6.75	1.85
☐ 272 John Kirby	15.00	6.75	1.85
☐ 273 Gary Larsen	15.00	6.75	1.85
☐ 274 Jim Lindsey	15.00	6.75	1.85
☐ 275 Earsell Mackbee	15.00	6.75	1.85
☐ 276 Jim Marshall	18.00	8.00	2.20
☐ 277 Marlin McKeever	15.00	6.75	1.85
☐ 278 Dave Osborn	15.00	6.75	1.85
☐ 279 Jim Phillips	15.00	6.75	1.85
☐ 280 Ed Sharockman	15.00	6.75	1.85
☐ 281 Jerry Shay	15.00	6.75	1.85
☐ 282 Milt Sunde	15.00	6.75	1.85
☐ 283 Archie Sutton	15.00	6.75	1.85
☐ 284 Mick Tingelhoff	12.00	5.50	1.50
☐ 285 Ron VanderKelen	15.00	6.75	1.85
☐ 286 Jim Vellone	15.00	6.75	1.85
☐ 287 Lonnie Warwick	15.00	6.75	1.85
☐ 288 Roy Winston	15.00	6.75	1.85
☐ 289 Doug Atkins	20.00	9.00	2.50
☐ 290 Vern Burke	15.00	6.75	1.85
☐ 291 Bruce Cortez	15.00	6.75	1.85
☐ 292 Gary Cuozzo	12.00	5.50	1.50
☐ 293 Ted Davis	15.00	6.75	1.85
☐ 294 John Douglas	15.00	6.75	1.85
☐ 295 Jim Garcia	15.00	6.75	1.85
☐ 296 Tom Hall	15.00	6.75	1.85
☐ 297 Jim Heidel	15.00	6.75	1.85
☐ 298 Leslie Kelley	15.00	6.75	1.85
☐ 299 Billy Kilmer	18.00	8.00	2.20
☐ 300 Kent Kramer	15.00	6.75	1.85
☐ 301 Jake Kupp	15.00	6.75	1.85
☐ 302 Earl Leggett	15.00	6.75	1.85
☐ 303 Obert Logan	15.00	6.75	1.85
☐ 304 Tom McNeill	15.00	6.75	1.85
☐ 305 John Morrow	15.00	6.75	1.85
☐ 306 Ray Ogden	15.00	6.75	1.85
☐ 307 Ray Rissmiller	15.00	6.75	1.85
☐ 308 George Rose	15.00	6.75	1.85
☐ 309 Dave Rowe	15.00	6.75	1.85
☐ 310 Brian Schweda	15.00	6.75	1.85
☐ 311 Dave Simmons	15.00	6.75	1.85
☐ 312 Jerry Simmons	15.00	6.75	1.85
☐ 313 Steve Stonebreaker	15.00	6.75	1.85
☐ 314 Jim Taylor	20.00	9.00	2.50
☐ 315 Mike Tilleman	10.00	4.50	1.25
☐ 316 Phil Vandersea	10.00	4.50	1.25
☐ 317 Joe Wendryhoski	10.00	4.50	1.25
☐ 318 Dave Whitsell	12.00	5.50	1.50
☐ 319 Fred Whittingham	10.00	4.50	1.25
☐ 320 Gary Wood	10.00	4.50	1.25
☐ 321 Ken Avery	10.00	4.50	1.25
☐ 322 Bookie Bolin	15.00	6.75	1.85
☐ 323 Henry Carr	12.00	5.50	1.50
☐ 324 Pete Case	15.00	6.75	1.85
☐ 325 Clarence Childs	15.00	6.75	1.85
☐ 326 Mike Ciccolella	15.00	6.75	1.85
☐ 327 Glen Condren	15.00	6.75	1.85
☐ 328 Bob Crespino	15.00	6.75	1.85
☐ 329 Don Davis	15.00	6.75	1.85
☐ 330 Tucker Frederickson	12.00	5.50	1.50
☐ 331 Charlie Harper	15.00	6.75	1.85
☐ 332 Phil Harris	15.00	6.75	1.85
☐ 333 Allen Jacobs	15.00	6.75	1.85
☐ 334 Homer Jones	15.00	6.75	1.85
☐ 335 Jim Katcavage	15.00	6.75	1.85
☐ 336 Tom Kennedy	15.00	6.75	1.85
☐ 337 Ernie Koy	15.00	6.75	1.85
☐ 338 Greg Larson	15.00	6.75	1.85
☐ 339 Spider Lockhart	15.00	6.75	1.85
☐ 340 Chuck Mercein	15.00	6.75	1.85
☐ 341 Jim Moran	15.00	6.75	1.85
☐ 342 Earl Morrall	12.00	5.50	1.50
☐ 343 Joe Morrison	15.00	6.75	1.85
☐ 344 Francis Peay	15.00	6.75	1.85
☐ 345 Del Shofner	12.00	5.50	1.50
☐ 346 Jeff Smith	15.00	6.75	1.85
☐ 347 Fran Tarkenton	40.00	18.00	5.00
☐ 348 Aaron Thomas	15.00	6.75	1.85
☐ 349 Larry Vargo	15.00	6.75	1.85
☐ 350 Freeman White	15.00	6.75	1.85
☐ 351 Sidney Williams	15.00	6.75	1.85
☐ 352 Willie Young	15.00	6.75	1.85
☐ 353 Sam Baker	15.00	6.75	1.85
☐ 354 Gary Ballman	15.00	6.75	1.85
☐ 355 Randy Beisler	15.00	6.75	1.85
☐ 356 Bob Brown OT	12.00	5.50	1.50
☐ 357 Timmy Brown	20.00	9.00	2.50
☐ 358 Mike Ditka	50.00	22.00	6.25
☐ 359 Dave Graham	15.00	6.75	1.85
☐ 360 Ben Hawkins	15.00	6.75	1.85
☐ 361 Fred Hill	15.00	6.75	1.85
☐ 362 King Hill	15.00	6.75	1.85
☐ 363 Lynn Hoyem	15.00	6.75	1.85
☐ 364 Don Hultz	15.00	6.75	1.85
☐ 365 Dwight Kelley	15.00	6.75	1.85
☐ 366 Israel Lang	15.00	6.75	1.85
☐ 367 Dave Lloyd	15.00	6.75	1.85
☐ 368 Aaron Martin	15.00	6.75	1.85
☐ 369 Ron Medved	15.00	6.75	1.85
☐ 370 John Meyers	15.00	6.75	1.85
☐ 371 Mike Morgan	15.00	6.75	1.85
☐ 372 Al Nelson	15.00	6.75	1.85
☐ 373 Jim Nettles	15.00	6.75	1.85
☐ 374 Floyd Peters	15.00	6.75	1.85
☐ 375 Gary Pettigrew	15.00	6.75	1.85
☐ 376 Ray Poage	15.00	6.75	1.85
☐ 377 Nate Ramsey	15.00	6.75	1.85
☐ 378 Dave Recher	15.00	6.75	1.85
☐ 379 Jim Ringo	15.00	6.75	1.85
☐ 380 Joe Scarpati	15.00	6.75	1.85
☐ 381 Jim Skaggs	15.00	6.75	1.85
☐ 382 Norm Snead	18.00	8.00	2.20
☐ 383 Harold Wells	15.00	6.75	1.85
☐ 384 Tom Woodeshick	15.00	6.75	1.85
☐ 385 Bill Asbury	15.00	6.75	1.85
☐ 386 John Baker	15.00	6.75	1.85
☐ 387 Jim Bradshaw	15.00	6.75	1.85
☐ 388 Rod Breedlove	15.00	6.75	1.85
☐ 389 John Brown	15.00	6.75	1.85
☐ 390 Amos Bullocks	15.00	6.75	1.85
☐ 391 Jim Butler	15.00	6.75	1.85
☐ 392 John Campbell	15.00	6.75	1.85
☐ 393 Mike Clark	15.00	6.75	1.85
☐ 394 Larry Gagner	15.00	6.75	1.85
☐ 395 Earl Gros	15.00	6.75	1.85
☐ 396 John Hilton	15.00	6.75	1.85
☐ 397 Dick Hoak	15.00	6.75	1.85
☐ 398 Roy Jefferson	12.00	5.50	1.50
☐ 399 Tony Jeter	15.00	6.75	1.85
☐ 400 Brady Keys	15.00	6.75	1.85
☐ 401 Ken Kortas	15.00	6.75	1.85
☐ 402 Ray Mansfield	15.00	6.75	1.85
☐ 403 Paul Martha	15.00	6.75	1.85
☐ 404 Ben McGee	15.00	6.75	1.85
☐ 405 Bill Nelsen	12.00	5.50	1.50
☐ 406 Kent Nix	15.00	6.75	1.85
☐ 407 Fran O'Brien	15.00	6.75	1.85
☐ 408 Andy Russell	20.00	9.00	2.50
☐ 409 Bill Saul	15.00	6.75	1.85
☐ 410 Don Shy	15.00	6.75	1.85
☐ 411 Clendon Thomas	15.00	6.75	1.85
☐ 412 Bruce Van Dyke	15.00	6.75	1.85
☐ 413 Lloyd Voss	15.00	6.75	1.85
☐ 414 Ralph Wenzel	15.00	6.75	1.85
☐ 415 J.R. Wilburn	15.00	6.75	1.85
☐ 416 Marv Woodson	15.00	6.75	1.85
☐ 417 Jim Bakken	12.00	5.50	1.50
☐ 418 Don Brumm	15.00	6.75	1.85
☐ 419 Vidal Carlin	15.00	6.75	1.85
☐ 420 Bobby Joe Conrad	12.00	5.50	1.50
☐ 421 Willis Crenshaw	15.00	6.75	1.85
☐ 422 Bob DeMarco	15.00	6.75	1.85
☐ 423 Pat Fischer	12.00	5.50	1.50
☐ 424 Billy Gambrell	15.00	6.75	1.85
☐ 425 Prentice Gautt	15.00	6.75	1.85
☐ 426 Ken Gray	15.00	6.75	1.85
☐ 427 Jerry Hillebrand	15.00	6.75	1.85
☐ 428 Charlie Johnson	12.00	5.50	1.50
☐ 429 Bill Koman	15.00	6.75	1.85
☐ 430 Dave Long	15.00	6.75	1.85
☐ 431 Ernie McMillan	15.00	6.75	1.85
☐ 432 Dave Meggysey	15.00	6.75	1.85
☐ 433 Dale Meinert	15.00	6.75	1.85
☐ 434 Mike Melinkovich	15.00	6.75	1.85
☐ 435 Dave O'Brien	15.00	6.75	1.85
☐ 436 Sonny Randle	15.00	6.75	1.85
☐ 437 Bob Reynolds	15.00	6.75	1.85
☐ 438 Joe Robb	15.00	6.75	1.85
☐ 439 Johnny Roland	15.00	6.75	1.85
☐ 440 Roy Shivers	15.00	6.75	1.85
☐ 441 Sam Silas	15.00	6.75	1.85
☐ 442 Jackie Smith	18.00	8.00	2.20
☐ 443 Rick Sortun	15.00	6.75	1.85
☐ 444 Jerry Stovall	15.00	6.75	1.85
☐ 445 Chuck Walker	15.00	6.75	1.85
☐ 446 Bobby Williams	15.00	6.75	1.85
☐ 447 Dave Williams	15.00	6.75	1.85
☐ 448 Larry Wilson	18.00	8.00	2.20
☐ 449 Kermit Alexander	15.00	6.75	1.85
☐ 450 Cas Banaszek	15.00	6.75	1.85
☐ 451 Bruce Bosley	15.00	6.75	1.85
☐ 452 John Brodie	20.00	9.00	2.50
☐ 453 Joe Cerne	15.00	6.75	1.85
☐ 454 John David Crow	20.00	9.00	2.50
☐ 455 Tommy Davis	15.00	6.75	1.85
☐ 456 Bob Harrison	15.00	6.75	1.85
☐ 457 Matt Hazeltine	15.00	6.75	1.85
☐ 458 Stan Hindman	15.00	6.75	1.85
☐ 459 Charlie Johnson	12.00	5.50	1.50
☐ 460 Jim Johnson	18.00	8.00	2.20
☐ 461 Dave Kopay	12.00	5.50	1.50
☐ 462 Charlie Krueger	15.00	6.75	1.85
☐ 463 Roland Lakes	15.00	6.75	1.85
☐ 464 Gary Lewis	15.00	6.75	1.85
☐ 465 Dave McCormick	15.00	6.75	1.85
☐ 466 Kay McFarland	15.00	6.75	1.85
☐ 467 Clark Miller	15.00	6.75	1.85
☐ 468 George Mira	15.00	6.75	1.85
☐ 469 Howard Mudd	15.00	6.75	1.85
☐ 470 Frank Nunley	15.00	6.75	1.85
☐ 471 Dave Parks	15.00	6.75	1.85
☐ 472 Walter Rock	15.00	6.75	1.85
☐ 473 Len Rohde	15.00	6.75	1.85
☐ 474 Steve Spurrier	40.00	18.00	5.00
☐ 475 Monty Stickles	15.00	6.75	1.85
☐ 476 John Thomas	15.00	6.75	1.85
☐ 477 Bill Tucker	15.00	6.75	1.85
☐ 478 Dave Wilcox	12.00	5.50	1.50
☐ 479 Ken Willard	15.00	6.75	1.85
☐ 480 Dick Witcher	10.00	4.50	1.25
☐ 481 Willie Adams	8.00	3.60	1.00
☐ 482 Walt Barnes	8.00	3.60	1.00
☐ 483 Jim Carroll	8.00	3.60	1.00
☐ 484 Dave Crossan	8.00	3.60	1.00
☐ 485 Charlie Gogolak	8.00	3.60	1.00
☐ 486 Tom Goosby	8.00	3.60	1.00
☐ 487 Chris Hanburger	10.00	4.50	1.25
☐ 488 Rickie Harris	8.00	3.60	1.00
☐ 489 Len Hauss	8.00	3.60	1.00
☐ 490 Sam Huff	20.00	9.00	2.50
☐ 491 Steve Jackson	8.00	3.60	1.00
☐ 492 Mitch Johnson	8.00	3.60	1.00
☐ 493 Sonny Jurgensen	18.00	8.00	2.20
☐ 494 Carl Kammerer	8.00	3.60	1.00
☐ 495 Paul Krause	12.00	5.50	1.50
☐ 496 Joe Don Looney	10.00	4.50	1.25
☐ 497 Ray McDonald	8.00	3.60	1.00
☐ 498 Bobby Mitchell	12.00	5.50	1.50
☐ 499 Jim Ninowski	8.00	3.60	1.00
☐ 500 Brig Owens	8.00	3.60	1.00
☐ 501 Vince Promuto	8.00	3.60	1.00
☐ 502 Pat Richter	8.00	3.60	1.00

	MINT	NRMT	EXC
☐ 503 Joe Rutgens	8.00	3.60	1.00
☐ 504 Lonnie Sanders	8.00	3.60	1.00
☐ 505 Ray Schoenke	8.00	3.60	1.00
☐ 506 Jim Shorter	8.00	3.60	1.00
☐ 507 Jerry Smith	8.00	3.60	1.00
☐ 508 Ron Snidow	8.00	3.60	1.00
☐ 509 Jim Snowden	8.00	3.60	1.00
☐ 510 Charley Taylor	18.00	8.00	2.20
☐ 511 Steve Thurlow	8.00	3.60	1.00
☐ 512 A.D. Whitfield	8.00	3.60	1.00

1994 Ted Williams

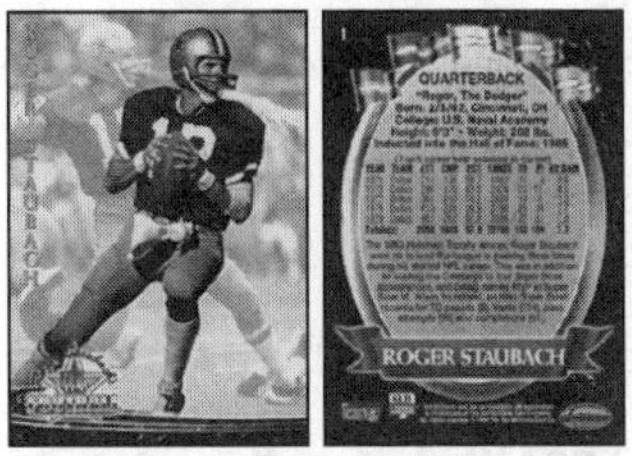

The 1994 Ted Williams Roger Staubach's NFL Football Preview Edition consists of 90 standard-size cards. Only 5,000 twelve box cases were produced. The fronts feature borderless color player action shots superimposed on a ghosted action player photo. The player's name appears in vertical silver lettering near the left edge. The set's embossed logo appears in the lower left corner. The navy blue backs carry the player's position, biography, stats, and career highlights within a silver-colored, oval plaque highlighted by flags. The cards are numbered on the back and checklisted below according to teams. The series closes with three topical subsets: Chalkboard Legends (64-72), Golden Arms (73-81), and Dawning of a Legacy (82-90). Randomly inserted in foil packs were three special chase cards: Charles Barkley, Fred Dryer, and Ted Williams. Two promo cards were produced and are listed below. They carry different photos than the regular issue cards.

	MINT	NRMT	EXC
COMPLETE SET (90)	8.00	3.60	1.00
COMMON CARD (1-90)	.05	.02	.01
☐ 1 Roger Staubach	1.00	.45	.12
☐ 2 Tony Dorsett	.50	.23	.06
☐ 3 Bob Lilly	.20	.09	.03
☐ 4 Art Donovan	.20	.09	.03
☐ 5 Bert Jones UER (Text states he was 1985 HOF inductee. Jones is not in HOF)	.05	.02	.01
☐ 6 Johnny Unitas	.75	.35	.09
☐ 7 Jack Kemp	1.00	.45	.12
☐ 8 O.J. Simpson	.75	.35	.09
☐ 9 Dick Butkus	.75	.35	.09
☐ 10 Gale Sayers	.75	.35	.09
☐ 11 Mike Singletary	.10	.05	.01
☐ 12 Bronko Nagurski	.20	.09	.03
☐ 13 Ken Anderson	.10	.05	.01
☐ 14 Otto Graham	.40	.18	.05
☐ 15 Lou Groza	.20	.09	.03
☐ 16 Marion Motley	.10	.05	.01
☐ 17 Floyd Little	.05	.02	.01
☐ 18 Haven Moses	.05	.02	.01
☐ 19 Lem Barney	.10	.05	.01
☐ 20 Dick(Night Train) Lane	.10	.05	.01
☐ 21 Bobby Layne	.40	.18	.05
☐ 22 Ray Nitschke	.20	.09	.03
☐ 23 Willie Wood	.10	.05	.01
☐ 24 Billy(White Shoes) Johnson	.05	.02	.01
☐ 25 Mike Bell	.05	.02	.01
☐ 26 Buck Buchanan	.10	.05	.01
☐ 27 Len Dawson	.20	.09	.03
☐ 28 Roman Gabriel	.05	.02	.01
☐ 29 LeRoy Irvin	.05	.02	.01
☐ 30 Deacon Jones	.10	.05	.01
☐ 31 Bob Waterfield	.20	.09	.03
☐ 32 Bob Griese	.40	.18	.05
☐ 33 Carl Eller	.10	.05	.01
☐ 34 Fran Tarkenton	.40	.18	.05
☐ 35 John Hannah	.10	.05	.01
☐ 36 Jim Plunkett	.10	.05	.01
☐ 37 Tom Dempsey	.05	.02	.01
☐ 38 Archie Manning	.10	.05	.01
☐ 39 Sam Huff	.20	.09	.03
☐ 40 Andy Robustelli	.10	.05	.01
☐ 41 Charley Conerly	.10	.05	.01
☐ 42 Don Maynard	.20	.09	.03
☐ 43 Matt Snell	.05	.02	.01
☐ 44 Wesley Walker	.05	.02	.01
☐ 45 George Blanda	.20	.09	.03
☐ 46 Ben Davidson	.05	.02	.01
☐ 47 Jim Otto	.10	.05	.01
☐ 48 Norm Van Brocklin	.20	.09	.03
☐ 49 Harold Carmichael	.10	.05	.01
☐ 50 Joe Greene	.20	.09	.03
☐ 51 L.C. Greenwood	.10	.05	.01
☐ 52 Jack Lambert	.20	.09	.03
☐ 53 Lance Alworth	.20	.09	.03
☐ 54 Dan Fouts	.20	.09	.03
☐ 55 John Brodie	.20	.09	.03
☐ 56 Steve Largent	.40	.18	.05
☐ 57 Jim Zorn	.05	.02	.01
☐ 58 Jim Hart	.05	.02	.01
☐ 59 Mel Gray	.05	.02	.01
☐ 60 Lee Roy Selmon	.05	.02	.01
☐ 61 Sonny Jurgensen	.20	.09	.03
☐ 62 Sammy Baugh	.60	.25	.07
☐ 63 Checklist UER (Players on card nos. 61 and 62 reversed)	.05	.02	.01
☐ 64 George Allen CO	.10	.05	.01
☐ 65 George Halas CO	.40	.18	.05
☐ 66 Tom Landry CO	.40	.18	.05
☐ 67 Vince Lombardi CO	.50	.23	.06
☐ 68 John Madden CO	.50	.23	.06
☐ 69 Chuck Noll CO	.20	.09	.03
☐ 70 Don Shula CO	.20	.09	.03
☐ 71 Hank Stram CO	.10	.05	.01
☐ 72 Checklist	.05	.02	.01
☐ 73 Terry Bradshaw	.75	.35	.09
☐ 74 Len Dawson	.20	.09	.03
☐ 75 Dan Fouts	.20	.09	.03
☐ 76 Bart Starr	.40	.18	.05
☐ 77 Roger Staubach	1.00	.45	.12
☐ 78 Fran Tarkenton	.40	.18	.05
☐ 79 Y.A. Tittle	.40	.18	.05
☐ 80 Johnny Unitas	.75	.35	.09
☐ 81 Checklist	.05	.02	.01
☐ 82 Brett Favre Pack-ing Up	1.25	.55	.16
☐ 83 Brett Favre A Memorable Week	1.25	.55	.16
☐ 84 Brett Favre What A Year	1.25	.55	.16
☐ 85 Brett Favre Ready for 1993	1.25	.55	.16
☐ 86 Neil O'Donnell 1991	.10	.05	.01
☐ 87 Neil O'Donnell College	.10	.05	.01
☐ 88 Neil O'Donnell High Notes	.10	.05	.01
☐ 89 Neil O'Donnell 1992	.10	.05	.01
☐ 90 Checklist Card	.05	.02	.01
☐ P1 Roger Staubach Promo	2.00	.90	.25
☐ P73 Terry Bradshaw Promo	2.00	.90	.25
☐ CB1 Charles Barkley	2.00	.90	.25
☐ CB1AU Charles Barkley AU (Certified autograph) AU/34	400.00	180.00	50.00
☐ HM1 Fred Dryer Hollywood Makeovers	2.00	.90	.25
☐ TW1 Ted Williams Teddy Football	5.00	2.20	.60
☐ TW1AU Ted Williams AU/54 (Certified autograph)	400.00	180.00	50.00

1994 Ted Williams Auckland Collection

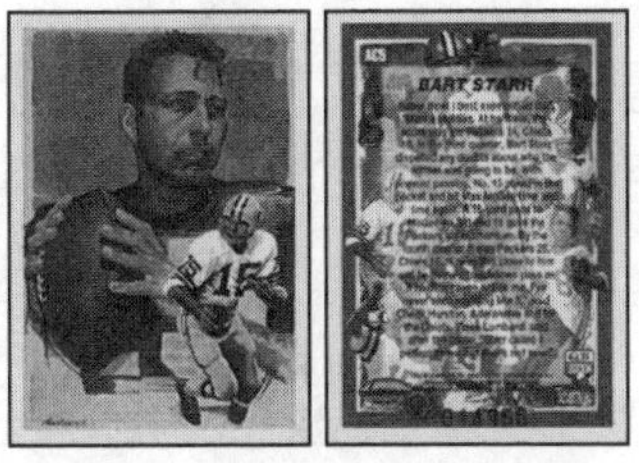

Randomly inserted in hobby packs only, the nine-card standard-size set consists of an illustrated series by one of the country's foremost sports artists, Jim Auckland. The cards are printed on a special matte finish paper stock. The white bordered fronts have illustrations from noted sports artist, Jim Auckland. The red and white bordered backs have a ghosted multi-player illustration with a player summary. The cards are numbered on the back with an "AC" prefix.

	MINT	NRMT	EXC
COMPLETE SET (9)	25.00	11.00	3.10
COMMON CARD (AC1-AC9)	1.00	.45	.12
☐ AC1 Brett Favre	10.00	4.50	1.25
☐ AC2 Vince Lombardi	3.00	1.35	.35
☐ AC3 Walter Payton	4.00	1.80	.50
☐ AC4 Phil Simms	2.00	.90	.25
☐ AC5 Bart Starr	3.00	1.35	.35
☐ AC6 Roger Staubach	4.00	1.80	.50
☐ AC7 Jim Thorpe	3.00	1.35	.35
☐ AC8 Johnny Unitas	3.00	1.35	.35
☐ AC9 Checklist	1.00	.45	.12

1994 Ted Williams Etched In Stone Unitas

Randomly inserted in packs, this nine-card 1994 Ted Williams Etched in Stone standard-size set highlights the career of football legend Johnny Unitas. The full-bleed color and sepia photos have a gold edged upper left and lower right corner. Unitas' name is printed within the lower right gold corner and the set title appears in the lower left corner. The backs are brick red with a puzzle design. When all nine

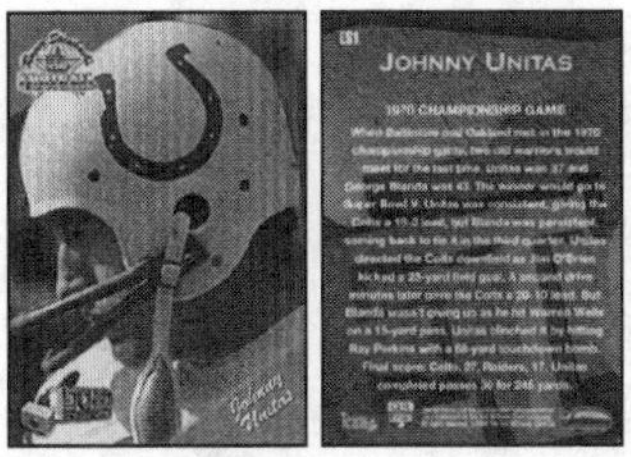

cards are placed in a protective card sheet, the words "Etched in Stone," a gold star, and a stone mallet become visible. The narrative format on the back chronicals Unitas' career beginning with college football. The cards are numbered on the back with an "ES" prefix.

	MINT	NRMT	EXC
COMPLETE SET (9)	10.00	4.50	1.25
COMMON CARD (ES1-ES9)	1.25	.55	.16
☐ ES1 Johnny Unitas 1970 Championship Game	1.25	.55	.16
☐ ES2 Johnny Unitas Super Bowl V	1.25	.55	.16
☐ ES3 Johnny Unitas Memories	1.25	.55	.16
☐ ES4 Johnny Unitas Injuries	1.25	.55	.16
☐ ES5 Johnny Unitas 1959 Rematch	1.25	.55	.16
☐ ES6 Johnny Unitas College Days	1.25	.55	.16
☐ ES7 Johnny Unitas 1972	1.25	.55	.16
☐ ES8 Johnny Unitas Greatest Game Ever	1.25	.55	.16
☐ ES9 Checklist Card	1.25	.55	.16

1994 Ted Williams Instant Replays

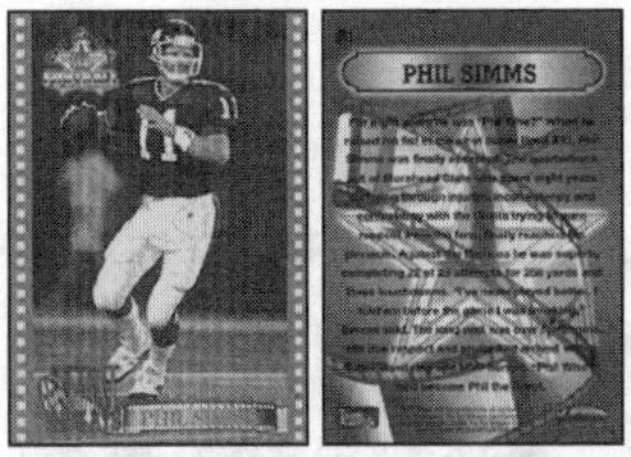

Randomly inserted in hobby packs only, this 17-card standard-size set highlights four of the greatest dynasties in NFL history. The four teams were distributed by region. The card front features a color or sepia-toned action player photo with gold film strip designed borders to the left and right side of the photo. The photo has a striped finish effect somewhat similar to a Sportflic card, but with only a single player photo. The set name is printed in the lower left corner and the player's name appears on a film strip styled stripe across the bottom. The orange backs have a ghosted star wrapped with gray film strip and carry player summary and highlights. The player's name is printed on a gold bar across the top. The set is organized according to teams as follows: New York Giants (1-4), Green Bay Packers (5-8), Pittsburgh Steelers (9-12), and Oakland/L.A. Raiders (13-16). The cards are numbered on the back with an "IR" prefix.

	MINT	NRMT	EXC
COMPLETE SET (17)	15.00	6.75	1.85
COMMON CARD (IR1-IR17)	.50	.23	.06
☐ IR1 Phil Simms	.75	.35	.09
☐ IR2 Y.A. Tittle	1.00	.45	.12
☐ IR3 Sam Huff	1.00	.45	.12
☐ IR4 Brad Van Pelt	.50	.23	.06
☐ IR5 Brett Favre	5.00	2.20	.60
☐ IR6 Bart Starr	1.50	.70	.19
☐ IR7 Paul Hornung	1.50	.70	.19
☐ IR8 Ray Nitschke	1.00	.45	.12
☐ IR9 Neil O'Donnell	.75	.35	.09
☐ IR10 Terry Bradshaw	2.00	.90	.25
☐ IR11 Joe Greene	1.00	.45	.12
☐ IR12 Jack Lambert	1.00	.45	.12
☐ IR13 Jeff Hostetler	.50	.23	.06
☐ IR14 Lyle Alzado	.50	.23	.06
☐ IR15 Dave Casper	.50	.23	.06
☐ IR16 Ken Stabler	1.50	.70	.19
☐ IR17 Checklist Card	.50	.23	.06

1994 Ted Williams Path to Greatness

Randomly inserted into packs, this nine-card standard-size set features collegiate players who went on to successful NFL careers. The cards feature great collegiate players and coaches who went on to successful NFL careers. The fronts carry sepia-toned or color action player photos. A narrow gold border is located along the upper and left side. The photo has a striped finish effect somewhat similar to a Sportflic card, but with only a single player photo. In gold foil, the player's name is stamped on a white banner across the bottom of the

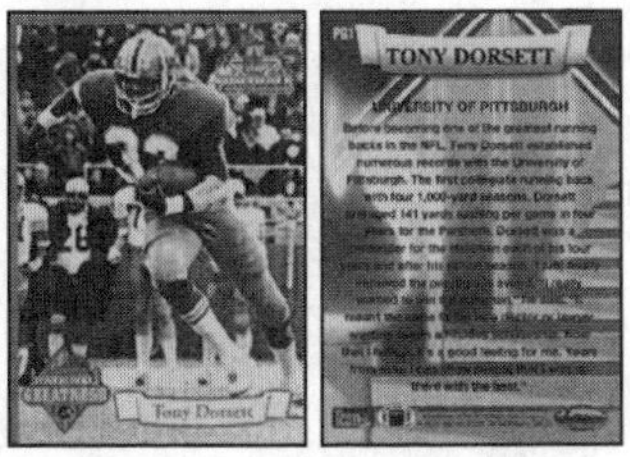

picture. The set title appears in the lower left corner. The colorful backs are borderless with gray stairs leading from a torch in the lower left corner. The player's name is printed on a white banner across the top. The player's collegiate football highlights are listed in narrative format. The cards are numbered on the back with a "PG" prefix.

	MINT	NRMT	EXC
COMPLETE SET (9)	12.00	5.50	1.50
COMMON CARD (PG1-PG9)	.50	.23	.06
☐ PG1 Tony Dorsett	2.00	.90	.25
☐ PG2 Red Grange	2.00	.90	.25
☐ PG3 Bob Griese	1.25	.55	.16
☐ PG4 Jeff Hostetler	.50	.23	.06
☐ PG5 Neil O'Donnell	.50	.23	.06
☐ PG6 Jim Plunkett	.75	.35	.09
☐ PG7 O.J. Simpson	2.00	.90	.25
☐ PG8 Roger Staubach	3.00	1.35	.35
☐ PG9 Checklist Card	.50	.23	.06

1994 Ted Williams Walter Payton

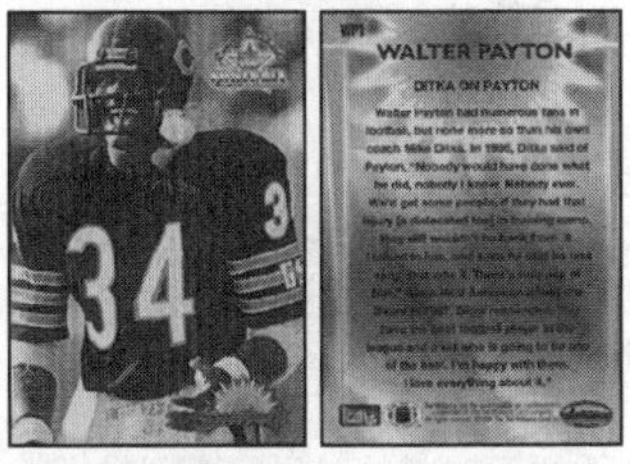

Available only in jumbo packs sold in mass market retail outlets, this nine-card set spotlights the career of one of football's greatest running backs, Walter Payton. The standard size cards feature full-bleed color action shots. The photo has a striped finish effect somewhat similar to a Sportflic card, but with only a single photo exposure. The set title appears in the lower right corner. The borderless blue backs have a sun design at the top, with the title of the card appearing below Payton's name. Each card chronicles a specific time of Payton's career beginning with college, and including a card listing career statistics. The cards are numbered on the back with a "WP" prefix.

	MINT	NRMT	EXC
COMPLETE SET (9)	12.00	5.50	1.50
COMMON CARD (WP1-WP9)	1.50	.70	.19
☐ WP1 Walter Payton Ditka On Payton	1.50	.70	.19
☐ WP2 Walter Payton Winning It All	1.50	.70	.19
☐ WP3 Walter Payton Rookie	1.50	.70	.19
☐ WP4 Walter Payton 1977	1.50	.70	.19
☐ WP5 Walter Payton College	1.50	.70	.19
☐ WP6 Walter Payton Payton vs. O.J.	1.50	.70	.19
☐ WP7 Walter Payton Sweetness	1.50	.70	.19
☐ WP8 Walter Payton The Records	1.50	.70	.19
☐ WP9 Checklist Card	1.50	.70	.19

1994 Ted Williams POG Cards

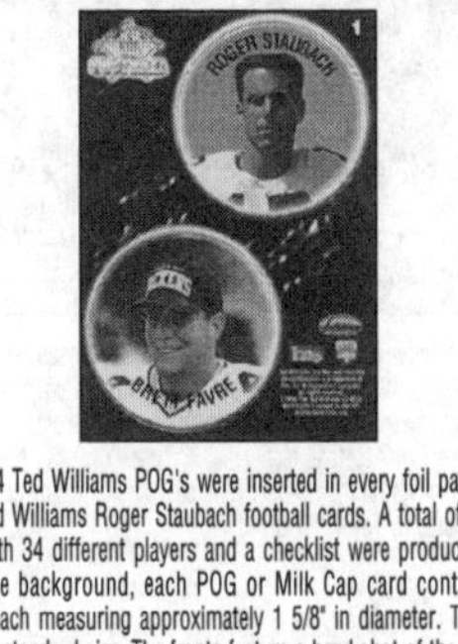

The 1994 Ted Williams POG's were inserted in every foil pack of the 1994 Ted Williams Roger Staubach football cards. A total of 18 POG cards with 34 different players and a checklist were produced. On a dark blue background, each POG or Milk Cap card contains two POG's, each measuring approximately 1 5/8" in diameter. The cards measure standard size. The fronts feature a head shot of the player in

color or black and white with the player's name printed above or below the photo. The white backs are blank. The cards are numbered on the front.

	MINT	NRMT	EXC
COMPLETE SET (18)	3.00	1.35	.35
COMMON CARD (1-18)	.20	.09	.03

☐ 1 Roger Staubach	1.00	.45	.12
Brett Favre			
☐ 2 Roman Gabriel	.20	.09	.03
Lee Roy Jordan			
☐ 3 Dan Fouts	.25	.11	.03
John Brodie			
☐ 4 Terry Bradshaw	.40	.18	.05
Bart Starr			
☐ 5 O.J. Simpson	.40	.18	.05
Floyd Little			
☐ 6 Pete Pihos	.25	.11	.03
Larry Csonka			
☐ 7 Dick(Night Train) Lane	.20	.09	.03
Carl Eller			
☐ 8 Sam Huff	.20	.09	.03
Ben Davidson			
☐ 9 Jack Lambert	.20	.09	.03
Jethro Pugh			
☐ 10 Mike Singletary	.20	.09	.03
Harold Carmichael			
☐ 11 Chuck Noll CO	.20	.09	.03
Bud Grant CO			
☐ 12 John Madden CO	.30	.14	.04
Lyle Alzado			
☐ 13 Walter Payton	.50	.23	.06
Gale Sayers			
☐ 14 Fred Dryer	.20	.09	.03
Ron Mix			
☐ 15 Bob Griese	.25	.11	.03
Doug Williams			
☐ 16 Tony Dorsett	.30	.14	.04
Red Grange			
☐ 17 Sonny Jurgensen	.20	.09	.03
Jeff Hostetler			
☐ 18 Checklist Card	.20	.09	.03

1994 Ted Williams Trade for Staubach

A special "Trade for Roger" card was randomly inserted in foil packs, at a rate of one per case in all 5,000 cases. Collectors received one of 5,000 nine-card sets by sending in the redemption card with 3.00 for postage and handling. The deadline for the redemption was April 15, 1994, and the redemption card itself was also returned to the collector with a validation stamp on it. The fronts feature a mix of full-bleed color or sepia-toned photos, with the player's name in silver foil along the left edge. The backs carry the card subtitle and summarize various highlights during his career.

	MINT	NRMT	EXC
COMPLETE SET (10)	25.00	11.00	3.10
COMMON CARD (TR1-TR9)	3.00	1.35	.35

☐ TR1 Roger Staubach	3.00	1.35	.35
The Dodger			
☐ TR2 Roger Staubach	3.00	1.35	.35
College Years			
☐ TR3 Roger Staubach	3.00	1.35	.35
The Heisman Trophy			
☐ TR4 Roger Staubach	3.00	1.35	.35
The Draft			
☐ TR5 Roger Staubach	3.00	1.35	.35
Coach's Decision			
☐ TR6 Roger Staubach	3.00	1.35	.35
A Leader			
☐ TR7 Roger Staubach	3.00	1.35	.35
MVP Year			
☐ TR8 Roger Staubach	3.00	1.35	.35
Hall of Fame			
☐ TR9 Checklist	3.00	1.35	.35
☐ NNO Trade for Roger	3.00	1.35	.35
Redemption Card			

1974 Wonder Bread

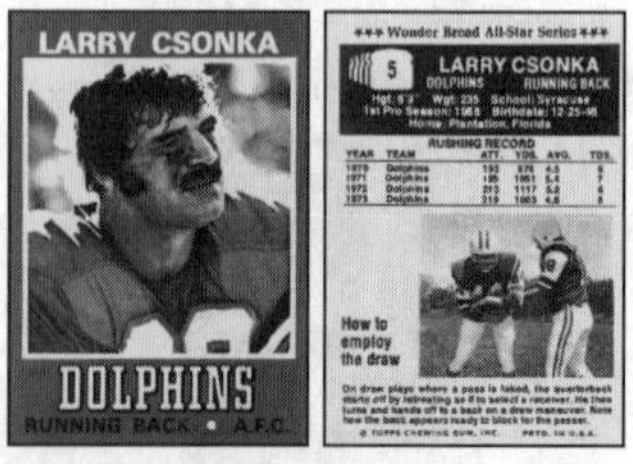

The 1974 Wonder Bread Football set features 30 standard-size cards with colored borders and color photographs of the players on the front. Season by season records are given on the back of the cards as well as a particular football technique. A "Topps Chewing Gum, Inc." copyright appears on the reverse. A parallel version of the cards was also distributed by Town Talk Bread.

	NRMT-MT	EXC	G-VG
COMPLETE SET (30)	30.00	13.50	3.70
COMMON CARD (1-30)	.60	.25	.07

☐ 1 Jim Bakken	.60	.25	.07
☐ 2 Forrest Blue	.60	.25	.07
☐ 3 Bill Bradley	.60	.25	.07
☐ 4 Willie Brown	1.25	.55	.16
☐ 5 Larry Csonka	6.00	2.70	.75
☐ 6 Ken Ellis	.60	.25	.07
☐ 7 Bruce Gossett	.60	.25	.07
☐ 8 Bob Griese	6.00	2.70	.75
☐ 9 Chris Hanburger	.60	.25	.07
☐ 10 Winston Hill	.60	.25	.07
☐ 11 Jim Johnson	1.25	.55	.16
☐ 12 Paul Krause	1.00	.45	.12
☐ 13 Ted Kwalick	.60	.25	.07
☐ 14 Willie Lanier	1.25	.55	.16
☐ 15 Tom Mack	1.00	.45	.12
☐ 16 Jim Otto	1.25	.55	.16
☐ 17 Alan Page	1.50	.70	.19
☐ 18 Frank Pitts	.60	.25	.07
☐ 19 Jim Plunkett	1.25	.55	.16
☐ 20 Mike Reid	1.25	.55	.16
☐ 21 Paul Smith	.60	.25	.07
☐ 22 Bob Tucker	.60	.25	.07
☐ 23 Jim Tyrer	.60	.25	.07
☐ 24 Gene Upshaw	1.25	.55	.16
☐ 25 Phil Villapiano	.60	.25	.07
☐ 26 Paul Warfield	4.00	1.80	.50
☐ 27 Dwight White	1.00	.45	.12
☐ 28 Steve Owens	1.00	.45	.12
☐ 29 Jerrel Wilson	.60	.25	.07
☐ 30 Ron Yary	.60	.25	.07

1974 Wonder Bread/Town Talk

The 1974 Town Talk Bread set features 30 standard-size cards with colored borders and color photographs of the players on the front. The cards are essentially a parallel version of the 1974 Wonder Bread release, but were distributed through Town Talk Bread products. A "Topps Chewing Gum, Inc." copyright appears on the reverse. These Town Talk cards are more difficult to find and are priced using the multiplier line given below. They are distinguished from the Wonder Bread issue by the absence of a credit line at the top of the cardback.

	NRMT-MT	EXC	G-VG
COMPLETE SET (30)	200.00	90.00	25.00
COMMON CARD (1-30)	4.00	1.80	.50

*TOWN TALKS: 3X TO 5X BASIC CARDS

1975 Wonder Bread

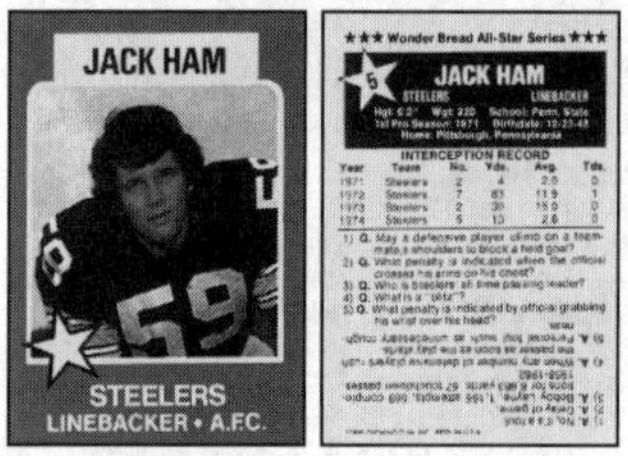

The 1975 Wonder Bread Football card set contains 24 standard-size cards with either blue (7-18) or red (1-6 and 19-24) borders. The backs feature several questions (about the player and the game of football) whose answers could be determined by turning the card upside down and reading the answers to the corresponding questions. The words "Topps Chewing Gum, Inc." appears at the bottom of the reverse of the card. Wonder Bread also produced a saver sheet and album for this set. A parallel version of the cards was also produced by Town Talk Bread.

	NRMT-MT	EXC	G-VG
COMPLETE SET (24)	18.00	8.00	2.20
COMMON CARD (1-24)	.50	.23	.06

☐ 1 Alan Page	1.00	.45	.12
☐ 2 Emmitt Thomas	.50	.23	.06
☐ 3 John Mendenhall	.50	.23	.06
☐ 4 Ken Houston	.75	.35	.09
☐ 5 Jack Ham	1.50	.70	.19
☐ 6 L.C. Greenwood	.75	.35	.09
☐ 7 Tom Mack	.50	.23	.06
☐ 8 Winston Hill	.50	.23	.06
☐ 9 Isaac Curtis	.50	.23	.06
☐ 10 Terry Owens	.50	.23	.06
☐ 11 Drew Pearson	1.50	.70	.19
☐ 12 Don Cockroft	.50	.23	.06
☐ 13 Bob Griese	3.00	1.35	.35
☐ 14 Riley Odoms	.50	.23	.06
☐ 15 Chuck Foreman	.75	.35	.09
☐ 16 Forrest Blue	.50	.23	.06
☐ 17 Franco Harris	3.00	1.35	.35
☐ 18 Larry Little	.75	.35	.09
☐ 19 Bill Bergey	.50	.23	.06
☐ 20 Ray Guy	.75	.35	.09
☐ 21 Ted Hendricks	1.00	.45	.12
☐ 22 Levi Johnson	.50	.23	.06
☐ 23 Jack Mildren	.50	.23	.06
☐ 24 Mel Tom	.50	.23	.06

1975 Wonder Bread/Town Talk

The 1975 Town Talk Bread card set contains 24 standard-size cards with either blue (7-18) or red (1-6 and 19-24) borders. The cards are essentially a parallel to the Wonder Bread issue. The words "Topps Chewing Gum, Inc." appears at the bottom of the cardback. These Town Talk cards are more difficult to find and are priced using the multiplier line given below. They are distinguished by the different "Town Talk" credit line at the top of the cardback.

	NRMT-MT	EXC	G-VG
COMPLETE SET (24)	150.00	70.00	19.00
COMMON CARD (1-24)	4.00	1.80	.50

*TOWN TALKS: 4X TO 8X BASIC CARDS

1976 Wonder Bread

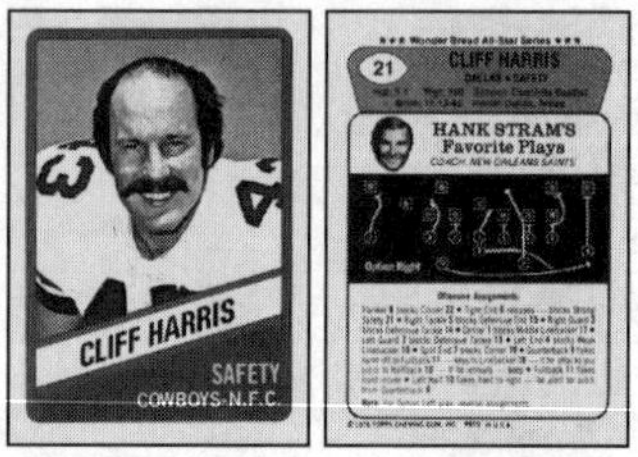

The 1976 Wonder Bread Football Card set features 24 colored standard-size cards with red or blue frame lines and white borders. The first 12 cards (1-12) in the set feature offensive players with a blue frame and the last 12 cards (13-24) feature defensive players with a red frame. The backs feature one of coach Hank Stram's favorite plays, with a football diagram and a text listing each offensive player's assignments of the particular play. The "Topps Chewing Gum, Inc." copyright appears at the bottom on the cardback. A parallel version of the cards was also produced by Town Talk Bread.

	NRMT-MT	EXC	G-VG
COMPLETE SET (24)	5.00	2.20	.60
COMMON CARD (1-24)	.20	.09	.03

☐ 1 Craig Morton	.50	.23	.06
☐ 2 Chuck Foreman	.35	.16	.04
☐ 3 Franco Harris	1.25	.55	.16
☐ 4 Mel Gray	.35	.16	.04
☐ 5 Charley Taylor	.75	.35	.09
☐ 6 Richard Caster	.20	.09	.03
☐ 7 George Kunz	.20	.09	.03
☐ 8 Rayfield Wright	.20	.09	.03
☐ 9 Gene Upshaw	.50	.23	.06
☐ 10 Tom Mack	.20	.09	.03
☐ 11 Len Hauss	.20	.09	.03
☐ 12 Garo Yepremian	.20	.09	.03
☐ 13 Cedrick Hardman	.20	.09	.03
☐ 14 Jack Youngblood	.50	.23	.06
☐ 15 Wally Chambers	.20	.09	.03
☐ 16 Jerry Sherk	.20	.09	.03
☐ 17 Bill Bergey	.20	.09	.03
☐ 18 Jack Ham	.75	.35	.09
☐ 19 Fred Carr	.20	.09	.03
☐ 20 Jack Tatum	.35	.16	.04
☐ 21 Cliff Harris	.50	.23	.06
☐ 22 Emmitt Thomas	.20	.09	.03
☐ 23 Ken Riley	.20	.09	.03
☐ 24 Ray Guy	.50	.23	.06

1976 Wonder Bread/Town Talk

The 1976 Town Talk Bread football card set features 24 colored standard-size cards with red or blue frame lines and white borders. The cards are essentially a parallel version to the Wonder Bread release. The "Topps Chewing Gum, Inc." copyright appears at the bottom on the cardback. These Town Talk cards are more difficult to find than the Wonder Bread issue and are priced using the multiplier line given below. They are distinguished by the different credit line at the top of the cardback.

	NRMT-MT	EXC	G-VG
COMPLETE SET (24)	75.00	34.00	9.50
COMMON CARD (1-24)	3.00	1.35	.35

*TOWN TALKS: 6X TO 12X BASIC CARDS

1984 Wranglers Carl's Jr. USFL

This ten-card USFL set was sponsored by Carl's Jr. Restaurants and distributed by the local police department in Tempe, Arizona. The cards measure approximately 2 1/2" by 3 5/8". On the front, the company logo and name appears in the lower right hand corner, and the USFL logo in the lower left hand corner. These emblems and the team name "Arizona Wranglers" on the top are in red print. The black and white posed photo in the middle has the player's name and position below in black ink. The back includes biographical information and an advertisement for Carl's Jr. Restaurants. The cards are listed below alphabetically, with the jersey number after the player's name.

	MINT	NRMT	EXC
COMPLETE SET (10)	30.00	13.50	3.70
COMMON CARD (1-10)	2.50	1.10	.30

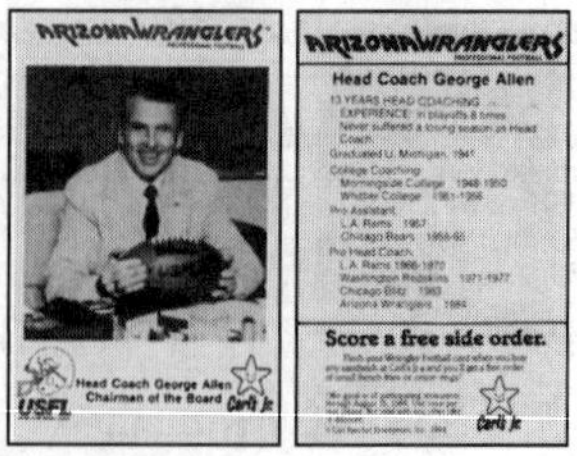

☐ 1 George Allen CO	8.00	3.60	1.00
☐ 2 Luther Bradley 27	2.50	1.10	.30
☐ 3 Trumaine Johnson 2	2.50	1.10	.30
☐ 4 Greg Landry 11	6.00	2.70	.75
☐ 5 Kit Lathrop 70	2.50	1.10	.30
☐ 6 John Lee 64	2.50	1.10	.30
☐ 7 Keith Long 33	2.50	1.10	.30
☐ 8 Alan Risher 7	2.50	1.10	.30
☐ 9 Tim Spencer 46	3.50	1.55	.45
☐ 10 Lenny Willis 89	2.50	1.10	.30

1984 Wranglers Team Issue USFL

These eight (approximately) 8" by 10" glossy, horizontally oriented sheets feature the 1984 Arizona Wranglers of the USFL. Each sheet features two rows of four black-and-white photos each, with player identification printed immediately beneath the picture. The team and USFL logos fill out the bottom corners. The backs are blank. Each sheet is numbered at the bottom in the middle "X of 8."

	MINT	NRMT	EXC
COMPLETE SET (8)	40.00	18.00	5.00
COMMON PANEL (1-8)	5.00	2.20	.60

☐ 1 Edward Diethrich PRES	8.00	3.60	1.00
Bill Harris VP			
George Allen CO			
G. Bruce Allen GM			
Robert Barnes			
Dennis Bishop			
Mack Boatner			
Luther Bradley			
☐ 2 Clay Brown	5.00	2.20	.60
Eddie Brown			
Wamon Buggs			
Bob Clasby			
Frank Corral			
Doug Cozen			
Doug Dennison			
Robert Dillon			
☐ 3 Larry Douglas	5.00	2.20	.60
Joe Ehrmann			
Nick Eyre			
Jim Fahnhorst			
Doak Field			
Bruce Gheesling			
Frank Giddens			
Alfondia Hill			
☐ 4 Dave Huffman	7.00	3.10	.85
Hubert Hurst			
Donnie Johnson			
Randy Johnson			
Trumaine Johnson			
Jeff Kiewel			
Bruce Laird			
Greg Landry			
☐ 5 Kit Lathrop	5.00	2.20	.60
John Lee			
Alva Liles			
Dan Lloyd			
Kevin Long			
Karl Lorch			
Andy Melontree			
Frank Minnifield			
☐ 6 Tom Piette	5.00	2.20	.60
Tom Porras			
Paul Ricker			
Alan Risher			
Don Schwartz			
Bobby Scott			
Lance Shields			
Ed Smith			
☐ 7 Robert Smith	5.00	2.20	.60
Tim Spencer			
John Stadnik			
Mark Stevenson			
Dave Steif			
Gerry Sullivan			
Ted Sutton			
Motrandy Taylor			
☐ 8 Rob Taylor T	5.00	2.20	.60
Tom Thayer			
Todd Thomas			
Ted Walton			
Stan White			
Lenny Willis			
Tim Wrightman			
Wilbur Young			

1995 Zenith Promos

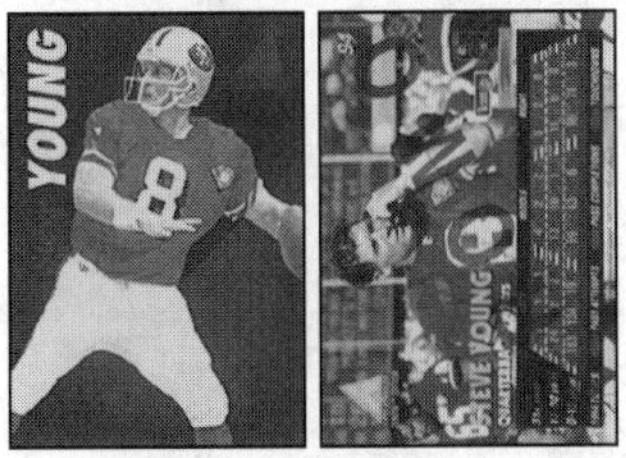

Commemorating the 1994 achievements of three Future Hall of Famers, this 4-card promo set was issued to herald the release of the 1995 Pinnacle Zenith series. Measuring the standard size, the cards are printed on 24-point card stock utilizing Pinnacle's all-foil metalized printing technology. The fronts display color action cutouts on a brown geometric design and bronze metallized brick design. The horizontal backs carry a color closeup photo and 1994 statistics presented on a football field graphic. The disclaimer "PROMO" is printed diagonally across the backs.

	MINT	NRMT	EXC
COMPLETE SET (4)	25.00	11.00	3.10
COMMON CARD	1.00	.45	.12
☐ 1 Emmitt Smith	10.00	4.50	1.25
☐ 94 Steve Young	5.00	2.20	.60
☐ 97 Dan Marino	10.00	4.50	1.25
☐ NNO Title Card	1.00	.45	.12

1995 Zenith

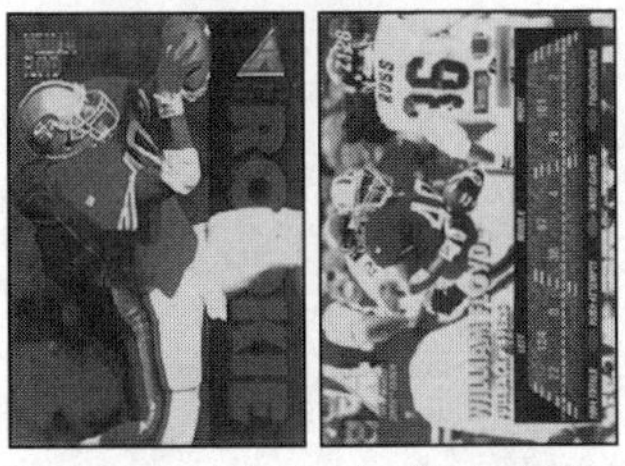

This 150-card standard-size set was issued by Pinnacle to honor some of the top NFL players. The cards are printed on 24-point card stock utilizing Pinnacle's all-foil metalized printing technology. The fronts display color action photos superimposed over a brown geometric design and bronze metalized printing technology. The horizontal backs carry a color close-up and 1994 statistics presented on a football field graphic. The only key Rookie Card is Jeff Blake.

	MINT	NRMT	EXC
COMPLETE SET (150)	60.00	27.00	7.50
COMMON CARD (Z1-Z150)	.40	.18	.05
☐ Z1 Emmitt Smith	10.00	4.50	1.25
☐ Z2 Chris Spielman	.75	.35	.09
☐ Z3 Johnny Mitchell	.40	.18	.05
☐ Z4 Boomer Esiason	.75	.35	.09
☐ Z5 Jackie Harris	.40	.18	.05
☐ Z6 Warren Moon	.75	.35	.09
☐ Z7 Harvey Williams	.40	.18	.05
☐ Z8 Steve Walsh	.40	.18	.05
☐ Z9 Cris Carter	1.25	.55	.16
☐ Z10 Natrone Means	1.25	.55	.16
☐ Z11 Art Monk	.75	.35	.09
☐ Z12 Leslie O'Neal	.75	.35	.09
☐ Z13 Adrian Murrell	.75	.35	.09
☐ Z14 John Elway	5.00	2.20	.60
☐ Z15 Larry Centers	.75	.35	.09
☐ Z16 Ricky Ervins	.40	.18	.05
☐ Z17 Jeff Graham	.40	.18	.05
☐ Z18 Ricky Watters	1.25	.55	.16
☐ Z19 Eric Green	.40	.18	.05
☐ Z20 Curtis Conway	1.25	.55	.16
☐ Z21 Jake Reed	.75	.35	.09
☐ Z22 Michael Timpson	.40	.18	.05
☐ Z23 Marcus Allen	1.25	.55	.16
☐ Z24 Andre Rison	.75	.35	.09
☐ Z25 Terry Kirby	.75	.35	.09
☐ Z26 Reggie White	1.25	.55	.16
☐ Z27 Randall Cunningham	.75	.35	.09
☐ Z28 Jim Kelly	1.25	.55	.16
☐ Z29 Robert Brooks	1.25	.55	.16
☐ Z30 Terance Mathis	.75	.35	.09
☐ Z31 Anthony Miller	.75	.35	.09
☐ Z32 Neil O'Donnell	.75	.35	.09
☐ Z33 Jeff Hostetler	.75	.35	.09
☐ Z34 Drew Bledsoe	6.00	2.70	.75
☐ Z35 Irving Spikes	.75	.35	.09
☐ Z36 Keith Byars	.40	.18	.05
☐ Z37 Rod Woodson	.75	.35	.09
☐ Z38 Rob Moore	.40	.18	.05
☐ Z39 Scott Mitchell	.75	.35	.09
☐ Z40 Cody Carlson	.40	.18	.05
☐ Z41 Alvin Harper	.40	.18	.05
☐ Z42 Chris Warren	.75	.35	.09
☐ Z43 Ben Coates	.75	.35	.09
☐ Z44 Jim Everett	.40	.18	.05
☐ Z45 Vinny Testaverde	.75	.35	.09
☐ Z46 Glyn Milburn	.40	.18	.05
☐ Z47 Calvin Williams	.75	.35	.09
☐ Z48 Fred Barnett	.75	.35	.09
☐ Z49 Tim Brown	1.25	.55	.16
☐ Z50 Lorenzo White	.40	.18	.05
☐ Z51 Brent Jones	.40	.18	.05
☐ Z52 Henry Ellard	.75	.35	.09
☐ Z53 Rick Mirer	1.25	.55	.16
☐ Z54 Junior Seau	1.25	.55	.16
☐ Z55 Jeff Blake	4.00	1.80	.50
☐ Z56 Desmond Howard	.75	.35	.09
☐ Z57 Jerry Rice	6.00	2.70	.75
☐ Z58 Lewis Tillman	.40	.18	.05
☐ Z59 Roosevelt Potts	.40	.18	.05
☐ Z60 Rocket Ismail	.75	.35	.09
☐ Z61 Eric Hill	.40	.18	.05
☐ Z62 Brett Favre	10.00	4.50	1.25
☐ Z63 Haywood Jeffires	.40	.18	.05
☐ Z64 Barry Foster	.75	.35	.09
☐ Z65 Flipper Anderson	.40	.18	.05
☐ Z66 Troy Aikman	6.00	2.70	.75
☐ Z67 Herschel Walker	.75	.35	.09
☐ Z68 Sean Dawkins	.75	.35	.09
☐ Z69 Erric Pegram	.75	.35	.09
☐ Z70 Irving Fryar	.75	.35	.09
☐ Z71 Thurman Thomas	1.25	.55	.16
☐ Z72 Eric Metcalf	.75	.35	.09
☐ Z73 John Taylor	.40	.18	.05
☐ Z74 Jeff George	.75	.35	.09
☐ Z75 Courtney Hawkins	.40	.18	.05
☐ Z76 Carl Pickens	1.25	.55	.16
☐ Z77 Mike Sherrard	.40	.18	.05
☐ Z78 Rodney Hampton	.75	.35	.09
☐ Z79 Joe Montana	6.00	2.70	.75
☐ Z80 Willie Davis	.75	.35	.09
☐ Z81 Chris Penn	.40	.18	.05
☐ Z82 Dave Brown	.75	.35	.09
☐ Z83 Gary Brown	.40	.18	.05
☐ Z84 Andre Reed	.75	.35	.09
☐ Z85 Michael Irvin	1.25	.55	.16
☐ Z86 Vincent Brisby	.40	.18	.05
☐ Z87 Barry Sanders	6.00	2.70	.75
☐ Z88 Qadry Ismail	.75	.35	.09
☐ Z89 Reggie Brooks	.75	.35	.09
☐ Z90 Bruce Smith	1.25	.55	.16
☐ Z91 David Klingler	.75	.35	.09
☐ Z92 Michael Haynes	.75	.35	.09
☐ Z93 Derek Russell	.40	.18	.05
☐ Z94 Steve Young	5.00	2.20	.60
☐ Z95 Terry Allen	.75	.35	.09
☐ Z96 Mark Seay	.75	.35	.09
☐ Z97 Dan Marino	10.00	4.50	1.25
☐ Z98 Jerry Rice 1994 Record Wrecker	6.00	2.70	.75
☐ Z99 Cris Carter 1994 Record Wrecker	1.25	.55	.16
☐ Z100 Art Monk Record Wrecker	.75	.35	.09
☐ Z102 Stan Humphries	.75	.35	.09
☐ Z103 Herman Moore	3.00	1.35	.35
☐ Z104 Ronald Moore	.40	.18	.05
☐ Z105 Greg Lloyd	.75	.35	.09
☐ Z106 Jerome Bettis	2.00	.90	.25
☐ Z107 Craig Erickson	.40	.18	.05
☐ Z108 Keith Jackson	.40	.18	.05
☐ Z109 Sterling Sharpe	.75	.35	.09
☐ Z110 Ronnie Harmon	.40	.18	.05
☐ Z111 Deion Sanders	4.00	1.80	.50
☐ Z112 Charles Haley	.75	.35	.09
☐ Z113 Bernie Parmalee	.75	.35	.09
☐ Z114 Leroy Hoard	.40	.18	.05
☐ Z115 O.J. McDuffie	1.25	.55	.16
☐ Z116 Garrison Hearst	1.25	.55	.16
☐ Z117 Kevin Greene	.75	.35	.09
☐ Z118 Derek Brown	.40	.18	.05
☐ Z119 Mark Brunell	6.00	2.70	.75
☐ Z120 Kevin Williams	.75	.35	.09
☐ Z121 Dan Wilkinson	.75	.35	.09
☐ Z122 Chuck Levy	.40	.18	.05
☐ Z123 Derrick Alexander	1.25	.55	.16
☐ Z124 Aaron Bailey	.40	.18	.05
☐ Z125 Thomas Lewis	.75	.35	.09
☐ Z126 Antonio Langham	.40	.18	.05
☐ Z127 Bryan Reeves	.40	.18	.05
☐ Z128 William Floyd	1.25	.55	.16
☐ Z129 Lake Dawson	.75	.35	.09
☐ Z130 Bert Emanuel	1.25	.55	.16
☐ Z131 Marshall Faulk	3.00	1.35	.35
☐ Z132 Heath Shuler	1.25	.55	.16
☐ Z133 David Palmer	.75	.35	.09
☐ Z134 Willie McGinest	.75	.35	.09
☐ Z135 Mario Bates	1.25	.55	.16
☐ Z136 Byron Bam Morris	.75	.35	.09
☐ Z137 Tim Bowens	.40	.18	.05
☐ Z138 Errict Rhett	1.25	.55	.16
☐ Z139 Charlie Garner	.75	.35	.09
☐ Z140 Darnay Scott	2.50	1.10	.30
☐ Z141 Greg Hill	.75	.35	.09
☐ Z142 LeShon Johnson	.75	.35	.09
☐ Z143 Charles Johnson	.75	.35	.09
☐ Z144 Trent Dilfer	1.25	.55	.16
☐ Z145 Gus Frerotte	3.00	1.35	.35
☐ Z146 Johnnie Morton	.75	.35	.09
☐ Z147 Glenn Foley	.40	.18	.05
☐ Z148 Perry Klein	.40	.18	.05
☐ Z149 Ryan Yarborough	.75	.35	.09
☐ Z150 Tydus Winans	.40	.18	.05

1995 Zenith Rookie Roll Call

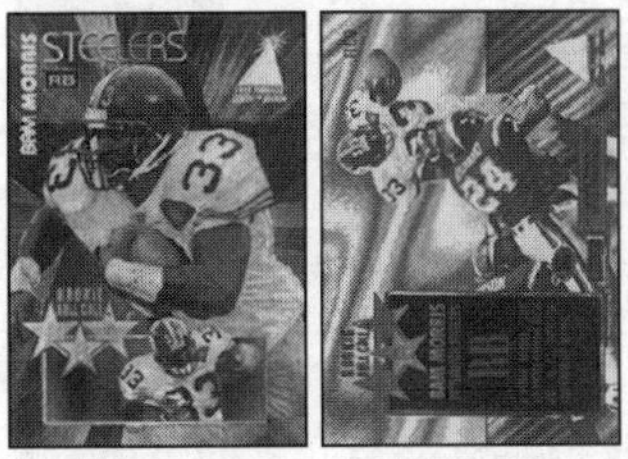

This 18 card standard-size set was randomly inserted into packs at a rate of one in 72. These cards, limited to not more than 1,200 of each, feature leading 1994 rookies. The fronts feature player metalized images framed against a large star in the middle. The player is identified in gold foil in the upper left corner while the team name is placed across the top. A smaller player shot is located near the bottom. Horizontal backs contain a brief player information blurb, as well as another metalized photo. The cards are numbered with a "RC" prefix.

	MINT	NRMT	EXC
COMPLETE SET (18)	300.00	135.00	38.00
COMMON CARD (RC1-RC18)	15.00	6.75	1.85
☐ RC1 Marshall Faulk	60.00	27.00	7.50
☐ RC2 Charlie Garner	15.00	6.75	1.85
☐ RC3 Derrick Alexander WR	25.00	11.00	3.10
☐ RC4 Heath Shuler	35.00	16.00	4.40
☐ RC5 Glenn Foley	15.00	6.75	1.85
☐ RC6 Trent Dilfer	35.00	16.00	4.40
☐ RC7 David Palmer	15.00	6.75	1.85
☐ RC8 Gus Frerotte	40.00	18.00	5.00
☐ RC9 Byron Bam Morris	25.00	11.00	3.10
☐ RC10 Mario Bates	25.00	11.00	3.10
☐ RC11 Greg Hill	25.00	11.00	3.10
☐ RC12 Errict Rhett	35.00	16.00	4.40
☐ RC13 Darnay Scott	40.00	18.00	5.00
☐ RC14 Lake Dawson	25.00	11.00	3.10
☐ RC15 Bert Emanuel	25.00	11.00	3.10
☐ RC16 LeShon Johnson	15.00	6.75	1.85
☐ RC17 William Floyd	25.00	11.00	3.10
☐ RC18 Charles Johnson	15.00	6.75	1.85

1995 Zenith Second Season

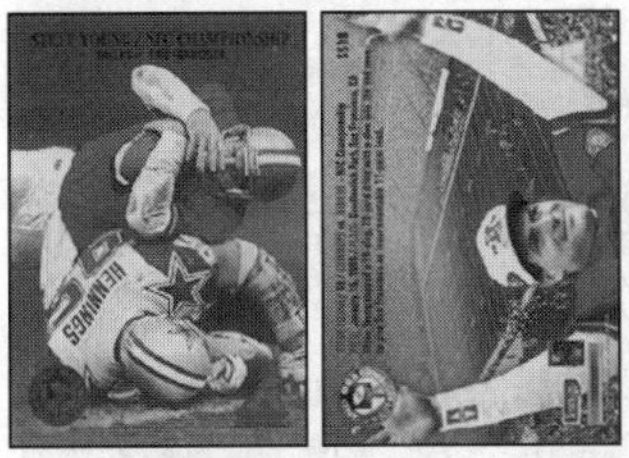

This 25 card standard-size set was randomly inserted into packs at a rate of one in six. The fronts feature photography from the game with which card was produced for. The particular game is identified in black lettering across the top. The words "Second Season" are located in the bottom left corner. The horizontal backs have information about the game and a large head shot of the player(s). All cards are numbered with a "SS" prefix in the upper right corner. Each card is set against the same generic game action background. The set is sequenced in playoff game order.

	MINT	NRMT	EXC
COMPLETE SET (25)	140.00	65.00	17.50
COMMON CARD (SS1-SS25)	3.00	1.35	.35
☐ SS1 Brett Favre	16.00	7.25	2.00
☐ SS2 Dan Marino	16.00	7.25	2.00
☐ SS3 Marcus Allen	5.00	2.20	.60
☐ SS4 Joe Montana	10.00	4.50	1.25
☐ SS5 Vinny Testaverde	3.00	1.35	.35
☐ SS6 Emmitt Smith	16.00	7.25	2.00
☐ SS7 Troy Aikman	10.00	4.50	1.25
☐ SS8 Steve Young	8.00	3.60	1.00
☐ SS9 William Floyd	3.00	1.35	.35
☐ SS10 Yancey Thigpen	5.00	2.20	.60
☐ SS11 Barry Foster	3.00	1.35	.35
☐ SS12 Natrone Means	5.00	2.20	.60
☐ SS13 Mark Seay	3.00	1.35	.35
☐ SS14 Stan Humphries	3.00	1.35	.35
☐ SS15 Tony Martin	3.00	1.35	.35
☐ SS16 Jerry Rice	10.00	4.50	1.25
☐ SS17 Deion Sanders	6.00	2.70	.75
☐ SS18 Steve Young	8.00	3.60	1.00
☐ SS19 Steve Young	8.00	3.60	1.00
☐ SS20 Emmitt Smith	16.00	7.25	2.00
☐ SS21 Troy Aikman	10.00	4.50	1.25
☐ SS22 Jerry Rice	10.00	4.50	1.25
☐ SS23 Ricky Watters	3.00	1.35	.35
☐ SS24 Steve Young	8.00	3.60	1.00
☐ SS25 Jerry Rice Steve Young	10.00	4.50	1.25

1995 Zenith Z-Team

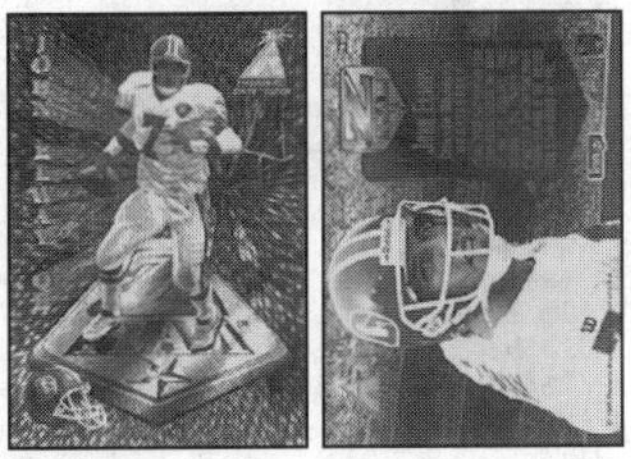

This 18 card standard-size set was randomly inserted into packs at a rate of one in 24 and features star offensive players. The fronts have the player's name and position down the left side. The player's photo is located on a Z-team pedestal with a prismatic and metallic background that contains various colors. The back includes brief player information as well as a color player photo. Cards are numbered with a "ZT" prefix.

	MINT	NRMT	EXC
COMPLETE SET (18)	500.00	220.00	60.00
COMMON CARD (ZT1-ZT18)	15.00	6.75	1.85
☐ ZT1 Dan Marino	80.00	36.00	10.00
☐ ZT2 Troy Aikman	40.00	18.00	5.00
☐ ZT3 Emmitt Smith	80.00	36.00	10.00
☐ ZT4 Barry Sanders	40.00	18.00	5.00
☐ ZT5 Joe Montana	40.00	18.00	5.00
☐ ZT6 Jerry Rice	40.00	18.00	5.00
☐ ZT7 John Elway	30.00	13.50	3.70
☐ ZT8 Marshall Faulk	20.00	9.00	2.50
☐ ZT9 Brett Favre	80.00	36.00	10.00
☐ ZT10 Steve Young	25.00	11.00	3.10
☐ ZT11 Sterling Sharpe	15.00	6.75	1.85
☐ ZT12 Drew Bledsoe	40.00	18.00	5.00
☐ ZT13 Ricky Watters	15.00	6.75	1.85
☐ ZT14 Cris Carter	15.00	6.75	1.85
☐ ZT15 Warren Moon	15.00	6.75	1.85
☐ ZT16 Natrone Means	15.00	6.75	1.85
☐ ZT17 Michael Irvin	20.00	9.00	2.50
☐ ZT18 Chris Warren	15.00	6.75	1.85

1996 Zenith Promos

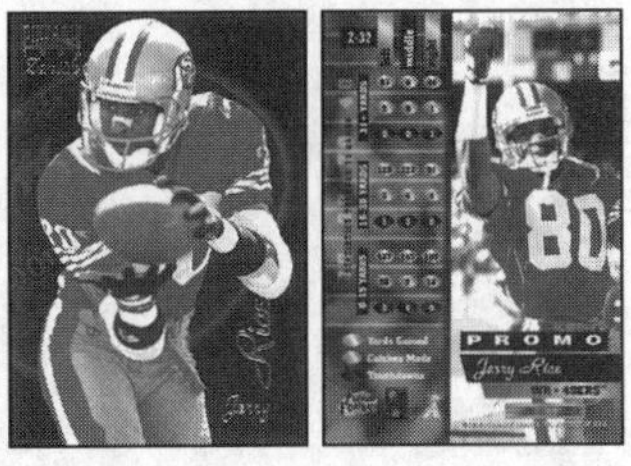

This four-card set was issued by Pinnacle to preview its 1996 Zenith release. The cards are identical to their regular issue and Z-Team issue counterparts, except for the word "Promo" printed on the back of the card.

	MINT	NRMT	EXC
COMPLETE SET (4)	35.00	16.00	4.40
COMMON CARD	.50	.23	.06
☐ 4 Emmitt Smith Z-Team	20.00	9.00	2.50
☐ 32 Jerry Rice	10.00	4.50	1.25
☐ 36 John Elway	8.00	3.60	1.00
☐ NNO Title Card	.50	.23	.06

1996 Zenith

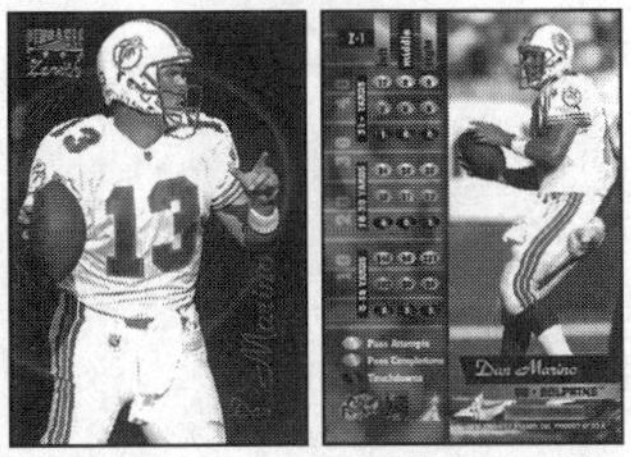

The 1996 Zenith set was issued in one series totaling 150 standard-size cards. This was the second year Pinnacle Brands used the Zenith line to produce a high end football set during the off-season. The 6-card packs had a suggested retail price of $2.59 each. They were issued in 16 box cases with 24 packs in each box. Topical subsets in the set include 1995 Rookies (97-131), Proof Positive (132-146) and Checklist Cards (148-150). The Dallas Cowboy Triplets: Troy Aikman, Michael Irvin and Emmitt Smith are featured on card #147. There are no key Rookie Cards in this set.

	MINT	NRMT	EXC
COMPLETE SET (150)	50.00	22.00	6.25
COMMON CARD (1-150)	.15	.07	.02

	MINT	NRMT	EXC
☐ 1 Dan Marino	5.00	2.20	.60
☐ 2 Yancey Thigpen	.30	.14	.04
☐ 3 Marcus Allen	.60	.25	.07
☐ 4 Curtis Conway	.60	.25	.07
☐ 5 Troy Aikman	3.00	1.35	.35
☐ 6 William Floyd	.30	.14	.04
☐ 7 Ricky Watters	.30	.14	.04
☐ 8 Herman Moore	.60	.25	.07
☐ 9 Jim Harbaugh	.30	.14	.04
☐ 10 Isaac Bruce	.60	.25	.07
☐ 11 Drew Bledsoe	3.00	1.35	.35
☐ 12 Jeff Blake	.60	.25	.07
☐ 13 Tim Brown	.30	.14	.04
☐ 14 Deion Sanders	2.00	.90	.25
☐ 15 Greg Hill	.30	.14	.04
☐ 16 Ben Coates	.30	.14	.04
☐ 17 Errict Rhett	.30	.14	.04
☐ 18 Barry Sanders	3.00	1.35	.35
☐ 19 Erik Kramer	.15	.07	.02
☐ 20 Emmitt Smith	5.00	2.20	.60
☐ 21 Brett Favre	5.00	2.20	.60
☐ 22 Jerome Bettis	.60	.25	.07
☐ 23 Garrison Hearst	.30	.14	.04
☐ 24 Michael Irvin	.60	.25	.07
☐ 25 Chris Warren	.30	.14	.04
☐ 26 Steve Young	2.50	1.10	.30
☐ 27 Cris Carter	.60	.25	.07
☐ 28 Carl Pickens	.60	.25	.07
☐ 29 Lake Dawson	.30	.14	.04
☐ 30 Marshall Faulk	.60	.25	.07
☐ 31 Vincent Brisby	.15	.07	.02
☐ 32 Jerry Rice	3.00	1.35	.35
☐ 33 Eric Metcalf	.30	.14	.04
☐ 34 Natrone Means	.60	.25	.07
☐ 35 Steve Bono	.30	.14	.04
☐ 36 John Elway	2.50	1.10	.30
☐ 37 Jeff Hostetler	.30	.14	.04
☐ 38 Scott Mitchell	.30	.14	.04
☐ 39 Andre Rison	.30	.14	.04
☐ 40 Daryl Johnston	.30	.14	.04
☐ 41 Mark Brunell	3.00	1.35	.35
☐ 42 Jeff George	.30	.14	.04
☐ 43 Mario Bates	.30	.14	.04
☐ 44 Erric Pegram	.30	.14	.04
☐ 45 Brent Jones	.15	.07	.02
☐ 46 Trent Dilfer	.30	.14	.04
☐ 47 Larry Centers	.30	.14	.04
☐ 48 Anthony Miller	.30	.14	.04
☐ 49 Reggie White	.60	.25	.07
☐ 50 Bill Brooks	.15	.07	.02
☐ 51 Chris Zorich	.15	.07	.02
☐ 52 Jim Kelly	.60	.25	.07
☐ 53 Junior Seau	.60	.25	.07
☐ 54 Chris Miller	.15	.07	.02
☐ 55 Gus Frerotte	.60	.25	.07
☐ 56 Andre Reed	.30	.14	.04
☐ 57 Darnay Scott	.30	.14	.04
☐ 58 Brett Perriman	.30	.14	.04
☐ 59 Edgar Bennett	.30	.14	.04
☐ 60 Warren Moon	.30	.14	.04
☐ 61 Neil O'Donnell	.30	.14	.04
☐ 62 Jay Novacek	.30	.14	.04
☐ 63 Byron Bam Morris	.30	.14	.04
☐ 64 Jim Everett	.15	.07	.02
☐ 65 Ken Norton, Jr.	.30	.14	.04
☐ 66 Tony Martin	.30	.14	.04
☐ 67 Steve Atwater	.15	.07	.02
☐ 68 Henry Ellard	.30	.14	.04
☐ 69 Rodney Hampton	.30	.14	.04
☐ 70 Derrick Thomas	.30	.14	.04
☐ 71 Stan Humphries	.30	.14	.04
☐ 72 Harvey Williams	.15	.07	.02
☐ 73 Greg Lloyd	.30	.14	.04
☐ 74 Jake Reed	.30	.14	.04
☐ 75 Charles Haley	.30	.14	.04
☐ 76 Quinn Early	.15	.07	.02
☐ 77 Rodney Peete	.15	.07	.02
☐ 78 Brian Blades	.30	.14	.04
☐ 79 Robert Brooks	.60	.25	.07
☐ 80 Terry Allen	.30	.14	.04
☐ 81 Dave Brown	.30	.14	.04
☐ 82 Derrick Alexander	.30	.14	.04
☐ 83 Terance Mathis	.15	.07	.02
☐ 84 Rick Mirer	.30	.14	.04
☐ 85 Herschel Walker	.30	.14	.04
☐ 86 Charlie Garner	.15	.07	.02
☐ 87 Jeff Graham	.15	.07	.02
☐ 88 Bruce Smith	.60	.25	.07
☐ 89 Terry Kirby	.30	.14	.04
☐ 90 Craig Heyward	.15	.07	.02
☐ 91 Bernie Parmalee	.15	.07	.02
☐ 92 Adrian Murrell	.30	.14	.04
☐ 93 Derek Loville	.15	.07	.02
☐ 94 Heath Shuler	.60	.25	.07
☐ 95 Shannon Sharpe	.30	.14	.04
☐ 96 Bert Emanuel	.30	.14	.04
☐ 97 Hugh Douglas	.15	.07	.02
☐ 98 Lovell Pinkney	.15	.07	.02
☐ 99 Sherman Williams	.15	.07	.02
☐ 100 Tony Boselli	.30	.14	.04
☐ 101 Wayne Chrebet	.30	.14	.04
☐ 102 Orlando Thomas	.15	.07	.02
☐ 103 Darick Holmes	.30	.14	.04
☐ 104 Tyrone Wheatley	.30	.14	.04
☐ 105 Christian Fauria	.15	.07	.02
☐ 106 Frank Sanders	.30	.14	.04
☐ 107 Chad May	.15	.07	.02
☐ 108 James O. Stewart	.30	.14	.04
☐ 109 Ken Dilger	.30	.14	.04
☐ 110 Kyle Brady	.30	.14	.04
☐ 111 Todd Collins	.30	.14	.04
☐ 112 Terrell Fletcher	.15	.07	.02
☐ 113 Eric Bjornson	.15	.07	.02
☐ 114 Justin Armour	.15	.07	.02
☐ 115 Rob Johnson	.15	.07	.02
☐ 116 Terrell Davis	4.00	1.80	.50
☐ 117 J.J. Stokes	.60	.25	.07
☐ 118 Rashaan Salaam	.60	.25	.07
☐ 119 Chris Sanders	.30	.14	.04
☐ 120 Kerry Collins	3.00	1.35	.35
☐ 121 Michael Westbrook	.60	.25	.07
☐ 122 Eric Zeier	.30	.14	.04
☐ 123 Curtis Martin	4.00	1.80	.50
☐ 124 Rodney Thomas	.15	.07	.02
☐ 125 Kordell Stewart	3.00	1.35	.35
☐ 126 Joey Galloway	1.50	.70	.19
☐ 127 Steve McNair	2.50	1.10	.30
☐ 128 Napoleon Kaufman	.30	.14	.04
☐ 129 Tamarick Vanover	.60	.25	.07
☐ 130 Stoney Case	.15	.07	.02
☐ 131 James A. Stewart	.15	.07	.02
☐ 132 Carl Pickens PP	.60	.25	.07
☐ 133 Jim Harbaugh PP	.30	.14	.04
☐ 134 Yancey Thigpen PP	.30	.14	.04
☐ 135 Ricky Watters PP	.30	.14	.04
☐ 136 Isaac Bruce PP	.60	.25	.07
☐ 137 Kordell Stewart PP	1.50	.70	.19
☐ 138 Jeff Blake PP	.30	.14	.04
☐ 139 Terrell Davis PP	2.00	.90	.25
☐ 140 Scott Mitchell PP	.15	.07	.02
☐ 141 Rodney Thomas PP	.15	.07	.02
☐ 142 Robert Brooks PP	.60	.25	.07
☐ 143 Joey Galloway PP	.75	.35	.09
☐ 144 Brett Favre PP	2.50	1.10	.30
☐ 145 Kerry Collins PP	1.50	.70	.19
☐ 146 Herman Moore PP	.60	.25	.07
☐ 147 Michael Irvin Emmitt Smith Troy Aikman	3.50	1.55	.45
☐ 148 Dan Marino Checklist	1.00	.45	.12
☐ 149 Jerry Rice Checklist	.75	.35	.09
☐ 150 Emmitt Smith Checklist	1.00	.45	.12

1996 Zenith Artist's Proofs

This 150 card standard-size set is a parallel to the regular Zenith issue. Inserted approximately one every 23 packs, the cards have an "Artist Proof" logo in the lower left.

	MINT	NRMT	EXC
COMP.AP SET (150)	1800.00	800.00	220.00
COMMON CARD (1-150)	5.00	2.20	.60

*AP STARS: 12.5X TO 25X BASIC CARDS
*AP YOUNG STARS: 10X TO 20X BASIC CARDS

1996 Zenith Noteworthy '95

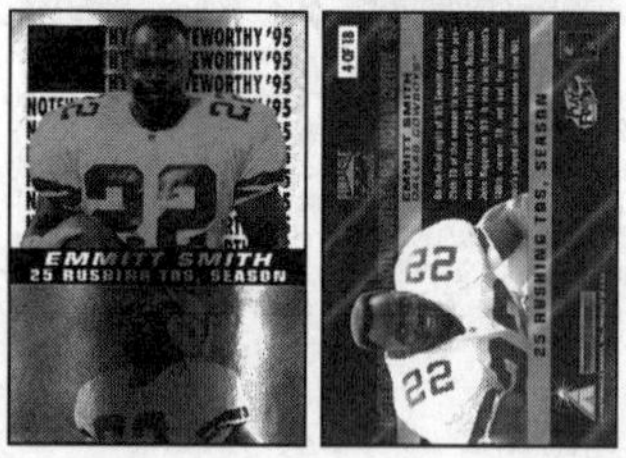

Randomly inserted in packs at a rate of one in 12, this 18-card set focuses on noteworthy accomplishments of players during the 1995 season. The fronts have two player photos on a foil background as well as the identification of the feat. The cards are numbered "X" of 18.

	MINT	NRMT	EXC
COMPLETE SET (18)	80.00	36.00	10.00
COMMON CARD (1-18)	1.50	.70	.19
☐ 1 Dan Marino	12.00	5.50	1.50
☐ 2 Jerry Rice	6.00	2.70	.75
☐ 3 Michael Irvin	3.00	1.35	.35
☐ 4 Emmitt Smith	12.00	5.50	1.50
☐ 5 Michael Irvin Emmitt Smith	10.00	4.50	1.25
☐ 6 Herman Moore	3.00	1.35	.35
☐ 7 Brett Favre	12.00	5.50	1.50
☐ 8 Barry Sanders	6.00	2.70	.75
☐ 9 Marcus Allen	3.00	1.35	.35
☐ 10 Steve Young	4.00	1.80	.50
☐ 11 John Elway	4.00	1.80	.50
☐ 12 Warren Moon	2.50	1.10	.30
☐ 13 Jim Kelly	3.00	1.35	.35
☐ 14 Jim Everett	1.50	.70	.19
☐ 15 Charles Haley	1.50	.70	.19
☐ 16 Emmitt Smith	12.00	5.50	1.50
☐ 17 Troy Aikman	6.00	2.70	.75
☐ 18 Larry Brown	1.50	.70	.19

1996 Zenith Rookie Rising

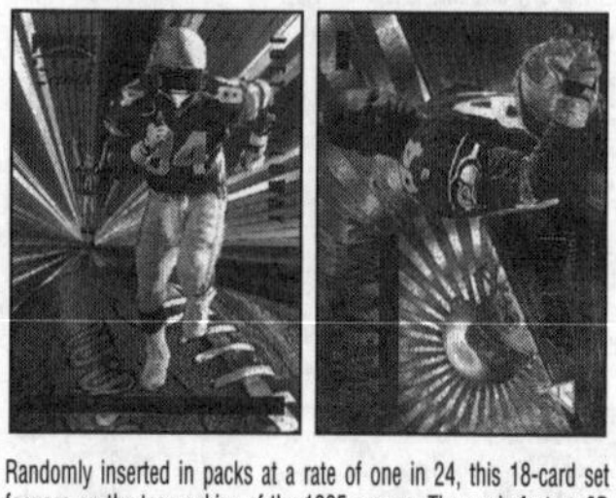

Randomly inserted in packs at a rate of one in 24, this 18-card set focuses on the top rookies of the 1995 season. The cards feature 3D printing with each side utilizing the dufex technology. The horizontal backs are numbered as "X" of 18.

	MINT	NRMT	EXC
COMPLETE SET (18)	300.00	135.00	38.00
COMMON CARD (1-18)	8.00	3.60	1.00
☐ 1 Sherman Williams	8.00	3.60	1.00
☐ 2 Curtis Martin	35.00	16.00	4.40
☐ 3 Michael Westbrook	15.00	6.75	1.85
☐ 4 Darick Holmes	8.00	3.60	1.00
☐ 5 James O.Stewart	10.00	4.50	1.25
☐ 6 Eric Zeier	8.00	3.60	1.00
☐ 7 Tamarick Vanover	15.00	6.75	1.85
☐ 8 J.J. Stokes	15.00	6.75	1.85
☐ 9 Kordell Stewart	30.00	13.50	3.70
☐ 10 Rodney Thomas	8.00	3.60	1.00
☐ 11 Kerry Collins	35.00	16.00	4.40
☐ 12 Terrell Davis	35.00	16.00	4.40
☐ 13 Steve McNair	30.00	13.50	3.70
☐ 14 Rashaan Salaam	15.00	6.75	1.85
☐ 15 Joey Galloway	18.00	8.00	2.20
☐ 16 Wayne Chrebet	8.00	3.60	1.00
☐ 17 Chris Sanders	10.00	4.50	1.25
☐ 18 Frank Sanders	10.00	4.50	1.25

1996 Zenith Z-Team

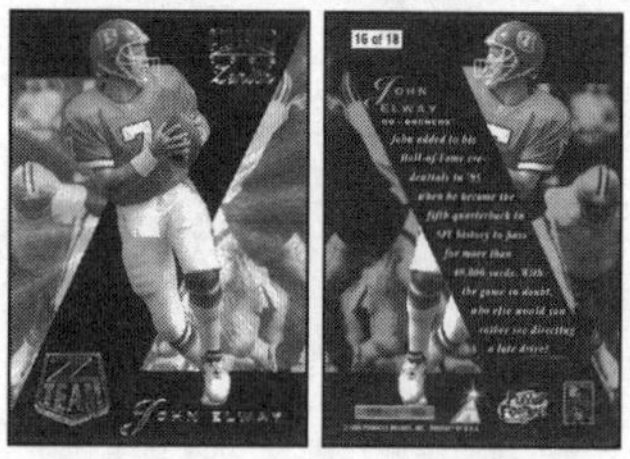

Randomly inserted in packs at a rate of one in 72, this 18-card set consists of the best players in the NFL during the 1995 season. The printing technology used for these sets was gold-foil stamped SpectroView printing. The cards are numbered as "X" of 18.

	MINT	NRMT	EXC
COMPLETE SET (18)	600.00	275.00	75.00
COMMON CARD (1-18)	15.00	6.75	1.85
☐ 1 Troy Aikman	50.00	22.00	6.25
☐ 2 Drew Bledsoe	50.00	22.00	6.25
☐ 3 Errict Rhett	20.00	9.00	2.50
☐ 4 Emmitt Smith	90.00	40.00	11.00
☐ 5 Jerry Rice	50.00	22.00	6.25
☐ 6 Cris Carter	15.00	6.75	1.85
☐ 7 Curtis Martin	50.00	22.00	6.25
☐ 8 Deion Sanders	25.00	11.00	3.10
☐ 9 Brett Favre	90.00	40.00	11.00
☐ 10 Michael Irvin	25.00	11.00	3.10
☐ 11 Chris Warren	15.00	6.75	1.85
☐ 12 Dan Marino	90.00	40.00	11.00
☐ 13 Steve Young	30.00	13.50	3.70
☐ 14 Marshall Faulk	25.00	11.00	3.10
☐ 15 Barry Sanders	50.00	22.00	6.25
☐ 16 John Elway	35.00	16.00	4.40
☐ 17 Isaac Bruce	25.00	11.00	3.10
☐ 18 Carl Pickens	20.00	9.00	2.50

1997 Zenith

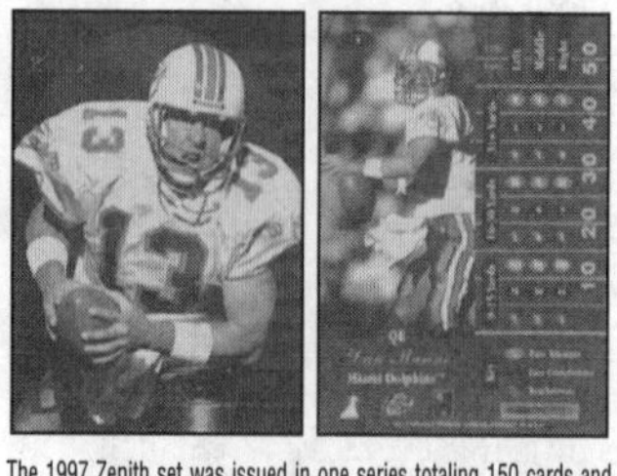

The 1997 Zenith set was issued in one series totaling 150 cards and was distributed in six-card packs with a suggested retail of $3.99. The fronts feature color player photos printed on 24 point card stock. The backs carry player information.

	MINT	NRMT	EXC
COMPLETE SET (150)	50.00	22.00	6.25
COMMON CARD (1-150)	.15	.07	.02
☐ 1 Brett Favre	5.00	2.20	.60
☐ 2 Jerry Rice	2.50	1.10	.30
☐ 3 Shannon Sharpe	.30	.14	.04
☐ 4 Dan Marino	5.00	2.20	.60
☐ 5 James O.Stewart	.30	.14	.04
☐ 6 Warren Moon	.30	.14	.04
☐ 7 Emmitt Smith	5.00	2.20	.60
☐ 8 Kordell Stewart	2.00	.90	.25
☐ 9 Kerry Collins	2.00	.90	.25
☐ 10 Ricky Watters	.30	.14	.04
☐ 11 Gus Frerotte	.60	.25	.07
☐ 12 Barry Sanders	2.50	1.10	.30
☐ 13 Joey Galloway	.75	.35	.09
☐ 14 Marshall Faulk	.60	.25	.07
☐ 15 Todd Collins	.30	.14	.04
☐ 16 Steve McNair	1.50	.70	.19
☐ 17 Tyrone Wheatley	.30	.14	.04
☐ 18 Isaac Bruce	.60	.25	.07
☐ 19 Troy Aikman	2.50	1.10	.30
☐ 20 Larry Centers	.30	.14	.04
☐ 21 Alvin Harper	.15	.07	.02
☐ 22 Rashaan Salaam	.60	.25	.07
☐ 23 Eric Metcalf	.30	.14	.04
☐ 24 Jim Everett	.15	.07	.02
☐ 25 Ken Dilger	.30	.14	.04
☐ 26 Curtis Martin	2.50	1.10	.30
☐ 27 Neil O'Donnell	.30	.14	.04
☐ 28 Thurman Thomas	.60	.25	.07
☐ 29 Andre Rison	.30	.14	.04
☐ 30 Steve Bono	.15	.07	.02
☐ 31 Garrison Hearst	.30	.14	.04
☐ 32 Junior Seau	.60	.25	.07
☐ 33 Napoleon Kaufman	.30	.14	.04
☐ 34 Jerome Bettis	.60	.25	.07
☐ 35 Frank Wycheck	.15	.07	.02
☐ 36 Lamar Smith	.15	.07	.02
☐ 37 Derrick Alexander WR	.30	.14	.04
☐ 38 Steve Young	1.50	.70	.19
☐ 39 Cris Carter	.60	.25	.07
☐ 40 O.J. McDuffie	.30	.14	.04
☐ 41 Deion Sanders	1.25	.55	.16
☐ 42 Robert Brooks	.60	.25	.07
☐ 43 Jeff Blake	.60	.25	.07
☐ 44 Marcus Allen	.60	.25	.07
☐ 45 Herman Moore	.60	.25	.07
☐ 46 Ray Zellars	.15	.07	.02
☐ 47 Tim Brown	.30	.14	.04
☐ 48 John Elway	2.00	.90	.25
☐ 49 Charles Johnson	.30	.14	.04
☐ 50 Rodney Peete	.15	.07	.02
☐ 51 Curtis Conway	.60	.25	.07
☐ 52 Kevin Greene	.30	.14	.04
☐ 53 Andre Reed	.30	.14	.04
☐ 54 Mark Brunell	2.50	1.10	.30
☐ 55 Tony Martin	.30	.14	.04
☐ 56 Elvis Grbac	.30	.14	.04
☐ 57 Wayne Chrebet	.15	.07	.02
☐ 58 Vinny Testaverde	.30	.14	.04
☐ 59 Terry Allen	.30	.14	.04
☐ 60 Dave Brown	.30	.14	.04
☐ 61 LeShon Johnson	.15	.07	.02
☐ 62 Trent Dilfer	.30	.14	.04
☐ 63 Chris Warren	.30	.14	.04
☐ 64 Chris Sanders	.30	.14	.04
☐ 65 Kevin Carter	.15	.07	.02
☐ 66 Jim Harbaugh	.30	.14	.04
☐ 67 Terance Mathis	.15	.07	.02
☐ 68 Ben Coates	.30	.14	.04
☐ 69 Robert Smith	.30	.14	.04
☐ 70 Drew Bledsoe	2.50	1.10	.30
☐ 71 Henry Ellard	.30	.14	.04
☐ 72 Scott Mitchell	.30	.14	.04
☐ 73 Andre Hastings	.30	.14	.04
☐ 74 Rodney Hampton	.30	.14	.04
☐ 75 Michael Jackson	.30	.14	.04
☐ 76 Jeff Hostetler	.30	.14	.04
☐ 77 Reggie White	.60	.25	.07
☐ 78 Desmond Howard	.30	.14	.04
☐ 79 Adrian Murrell	.30	.14	.04
☐ 80 Carl Pickens	.60	.25	.07
☐ 81 Erik Kramer	.15	.07	.02
☐ 82 Terrell Davis	2.50	1.10	.30
☐ 83 Sean Dawkins	.15	.07	.02
☐ 84 Jamal Anderson	.30	.14	.04
☐ 85 Stan Humphries	.30	.14	.04
☐ 86 Chris T. Jones	.60	.25	.07
☐ 87 Hardy Nickerson	.15	.07	.02
☐ 88 Anthony Johnson	.30	.14	.04
☐ 89 Michael Haynes	.30	.14	.04
☐ 90 Irving Spikes	.15	.07	.02
☐ 91 Bruce Smith	.60	.25	.07
☐ 92 Keenan McCardell	.30	.14	.04
☐ 93 Chris Chandler	.30	.14	.04
☐ 94 Tamarick Vanover	.30	.14	.04
☐ 95 Dorsey Levens	.30	.14	.04
☐ 96 Roman Phifer	.15	.07	.02
☐ 97 Michael Irvin	.60	.25	.07
☐ 98 Tim Biakabutuka	.60	.25	.07
☐ 99 Stepfret Williams	.15	.07	.02
☐ 100 Eddie George	4.00	1.80	.50
☐ 101 Karim Abdul-Jabbar	2.50	1.10	.30
☐ 102 Amani Toomer	.30	.14	.04

☐ 103 Tony Banks	1.00	.45	.12
☐ 104 Regan Upshaw	.15	.07	.02
☐ 105 Leeland McElroy	.30	.14	.04
☐ 106 Jason Dunn	.30	.14	.04
☐ 107 Keyshawn Johnson	1.50	.70	.19
☐ 108 Winslow Oliver	.15	.07	.02
☐ 109 Walt Harris	.15	.07	.02
☐ 110 Stanley Pritchett	.15	.07	.02
☐ 111 Eddie Kennison	1.50	.70	.19
☐ 112 Terrell Owens	2.00	.90	.25
☐ 113 Duane Clemons	.15	.07	.02
☐ 114 John Mobley	.15	.07	.02
☐ 115 Simeon Rice	.30	.14	.04
☐ 116 Tony Brackens	.15	.07	.02
☐ 117 Eric Moulds	.60	.25	.07
☐ 118 Marvin Harrison	1.50	.70	.19
☐ 119 Rickey Dudley	.30	.14	.04
☐ 120 Mike Alstott	.60	.25	.07
☐ 121 Terry Glenn	3.00	1.35	.35
☐ 122 Brian Dawkins	.15	.07	.02
☐ 123 Kevin Hardy	.30	.14	.04
☐ 124 Bobby Engram	.30	.14	.04
☐ 125 Alex Van Dyke	.30	.14	.04
☐ 126 Zach Thomas	1.00	.45	.12
☐ 127 Bryan Still	.15	.07	.02
☐ 128 Detron Smith	.15	.07	.02
☐ 129 Jerome Woods	.15	.07	.02
☐ 130 Muhsin Muhammad	1.00	.45	.12
☐ 131 Lawrence Phillips	.30	.14	.04
☐ 132 Alex Molden	.15	.07	.02
☐ 133 Steve Young SH	1.00	.45	.12
☐ 134 Troy Aikman SH	1.25	.55	.16
☐ 135 Junior Seau SH	.30	.14	.04
☐ 136 John Elway SH	1.00	.45	.12
☐ 137 Dan Marino SH	2.50	1.10	.30
☐ 138 Desmond Howard SH	.30	.14	.04
☐ 139 Brett Favre SH	2.50	1.10	.30
☐ 140 Jerry Rice SH	1.25	.55	.16
☐ 141 Kerry Collins SH	1.00	.45	.12
☐ 142 Barry Sanders SH	1.25	.55	.16
☐ 143 Mark Brunell SH	1.25	.55	.16
☐ 144 Drew Bledsoe SH	1.25	.55	.16
☐ 145 Eddie Kennison SH	.60	.25	.07
☐ 146 Marvin Harrison SH	.60	.25	.07
☐ 147 Emmitt Smith SH	2.50	1.10	.30
☐ 148 Eddie George Terry Glenn Rickey Dudley Bobby Hoying Awesome Foursome	2.00	.90	.25
☐ 149 Emmitt Smith Checklist back	1.25	.55	.16
☐ 150 Dan Marino Checklist back	1.25	.55	.16

1997 Zenith Artist's Proofs

Randomly inserted in packs at the rate of one in 47, this 150-card set is a parallel version of the regular set and is similar in design. The distinction is seen in the gold, rainbow holographic foil stamp on each card.

	MINT	NRMT	EXC
COMPLETE SET (150)	1800.00	800.00	220.00
COMMON CARD (1-150)	6.00	2.70	.75

*AP STARS: 15X TO 25X BASIC CARDS
*AP YOUNG STARS: 10X TO 20X BASIC CARDS

☐ 1 Brett Favre	135.00	60.00	17.00
☐ 2 Jerry Rice	60.00	27.00	7.50
☐ 4 Dan Marino	135.00	60.00	17.00
☐ 7 Emmitt Smith	135.00	60.00	17.00
☐ 8 Kordell Stewart	50.00	22.00	6.25
☐ 9 Kerry Collins	60.00	27.00	7.50
☐ 12 Barry Sanders	60.00	27.00	7.50
☐ 16 Steve McNair	40.00	18.00	5.00
☐ 19 Troy Aikman	60.00	27.00	7.50
☐ 26 Curtis Martin	60.00	27.00	7.50
☐ 38 Steve Young	40.00	18.00	5.00
☐ 41 Deion Sanders	40.00	18.00	5.00
☐ 48 John Elway	50.00	22.00	6.25
☐ 54 Mark Brunell	60.00	27.00	7.50
☐ 70 Drew Bledsoe	60.00	27.00	7.50
☐ 82 Terrell Davis	60.00	27.00	7.50
☐ 100 Eddie George	80.00	36.00	10.00
☐ 101 Karim Abdul-Jabbar	50.00	22.00	6.25
☐ 112 Terrell Owens	40.00	18.00	5.00
☐ 121 Terry Glenn	60.00	27.00	7.50
☐ 134 Troy Aikman SH	30.00	13.50	3.70
☐ 137 Dan Marino SH	60.00	27.00	7.50
☐ 139 Brett Favre SH	60.00	27.00	7.50
☐ 140 Jerry Rice SH	30.00	13.50	3.70
☐ 142 Barry Sanders SH	30.00	13.50	3.70
☐ 143 Mark Brunell SH	30.00	13.50	3.70
☐ 144 Drew Bledsoe SH	30.00	13.50	3.70
☐ 147 Emmitt Smith SH	60.00	27.00	7.50
☐ 148 Eddie George Terry Glenn Rickey Dudley Bobby Hoying Awesome Foursome	40.00	18.00	5.00

1997 Zenith Rookie Rising

Randomly inserted in packs at a rate of one in 11, this 24-card set features color player photos of potential future young stars with all-foil Dufex printing.

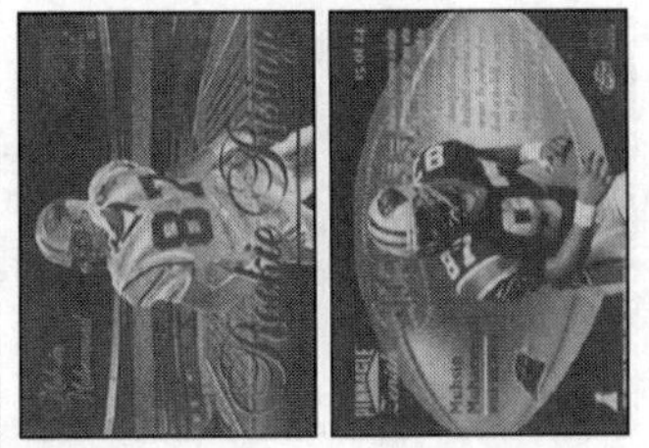

	MINT	NRMT	EXC
COMPLETE SET (24)	175.00	80.00	22.00
COMMON CARD (1-24)	4.00	1.80	.50

☐ 1 Eddie Kennison	10.00	4.50	1.25
☐ 2 Marvin Harrison	10.00	4.50	1.25
☐ 3 Keyshawn Johnson	10.00	4.50	1.25
☐ 4 Leeland McElroy	6.00	2.70	.75
☐ 5 Terrell Owens	15.00	6.75	1.85
☐ 6 Terry Glenn	25.00	11.00	3.10
☐ 7 Bobby Engram	6.00	2.70	.75
☐ 8 Karim Abdul-Jabbar	20.00	9.00	2.50
☐ 9 Lawrence Phillips	8.00	3.60	1.00
☐ 10 Amani Toomer	6.00	2.70	.75
☐ 11 Eric Moulds	8.00	3.60	1.00
☐ 12 Jason Dunn	4.00	1.80	.50
☐ 13 Stanley Pritchett	4.00	1.80	.50
☐ 14 Eddie George	30.00	13.50	3.70
☐ 15 Muhsin Muhammad	12.00	5.50	1.50
☐ 16 Rickey Dudley	6.00	2.70	.75
☐ 17 Tony Banks	12.00	5.50	1.50
☐ 18 Bryan Still	4.00	1.80	.50
☐ 19 Tim Biakabutuka	8.00	3.60	1.00
☐ 20 Simeon Rice	4.00	1.80	.50
☐ 21 Zach Thomas	12.00	5.50	1.50
☐ 22 Kevin Hardy	6.00	2.70	.75
☐ 23 Jerris McPhail	4.00	1.80	.50
☐ 24 Mike Alstott	6.00	2.70	.75

1997 Zenith V2

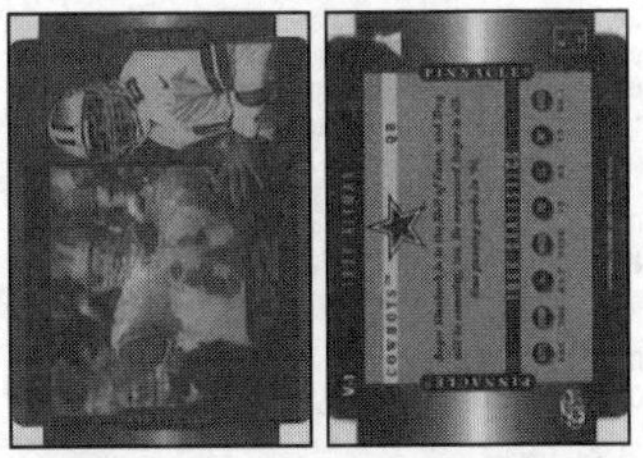

Randomly inserted in packs at a rate of one in 23, this multi-phase animated set captures the achievements of 18 modern day legends in full motion lenticular technology with strip foil stamping. Each card delivers up to two seconds of actual game film footage.

	MINT	NRMT	EXC
COMPLETE SET (18)	350.00	160.00	45.00
COMMON CARD (V1-V18)	5.00	2.20	.60

☐ V1 Troy Aikman	25.00	11.00	3.10
☐ V2 John Elway	20.00	9.00	2.50
☐ V3 Jim Harbaugh	5.00	2.20	.60
☐ V4 Barry Sanders	25.00	11.00	3.10
☐ V5 Deion Sanders	10.00	4.50	1.25
☐ V6 Drew Bledsoe	25.00	11.00	3.10
☐ V7 Dan Marino	50.00	22.00	6.25
☐ V8 Terrell Davis	20.00	9.00	2.50
☐ V9 Isaac Bruce	8.00	3.60	1.00
☐ V10 Jerome Bettis	8.00	3.60	1.00
☐ V11 Emmitt Smith	50.00	22.00	6.25
☐ V12 Brett Favre	50.00	22.00	6.25
☐ V13 Steve Young	15.00	6.75	1.85
☐ V14 Mark Brunell	25.00	11.00	3.10
☐ V15 Joey Galloway	8.00	3.60	1.00
☐ V16 Kordell Stewart	15.00	6.75	1.85
☐ V17 Jerry Rice	25.00	11.00	3.10
☐ V18 Curtis Martin	20.00	9.00	2.50

1997 Zenith Z-Team

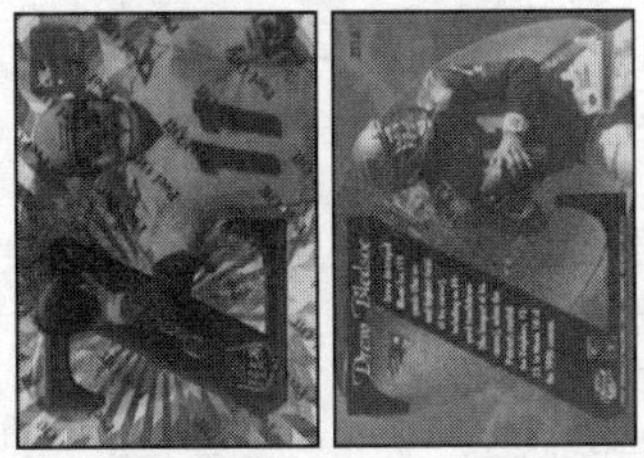

Randomly inserted in packs at a rate of one in 71, this 18-card set features color player photos of some of the NFL's top stars printed with mirror mylar micro-etched technology.

	MINT	NRMT	EXC
COMPLETE SET (18)	600.00	275.00	75.00
COMMON CARD (ZT1-ZT18)	20.00	9.00	2.50

*MIRROR GOLDS: 1.25X TO 2.5X BASIC CARDS

☐ ZT1 Emmitt Smith	80.00	36.00	10.00
☐ ZT2 Dan Marino	80.00	36.00	10.00
☐ ZT3 Jerry Rice	40.00	18.00	5.00
☐ ZT4 John Elway	35.00	16.00	4.40
☐ ZT5 Curtis Martin	40.00	18.00	5.00
☐ ZT6 Deion Sanders	25.00	11.00	3.10
☐ ZT7 Tony Banks	25.00	11.00	3.10
☐ ZT8 Jim Harbaugh	20.00	9.00	2.50
☐ ZT9 Joey Galloway	25.00	11.00	3.10
☐ ZT10 Troy Aikman	40.00	18.00	5.00
☐ ZT11 Brett Favre	80.00	36.00	10.00
☐ ZT12 Keyshawn Johnson	25.00	11.00	3.10
☐ ZT13 Eddie George	40.00	18.00	5.00
☐ ZT14 Barry Sanders	40.00	18.00	5.00
☐ ZT15 Kordell Stewart	30.00	13.50	3.70
☐ ZT16 Steve Young	30.00	13.50	3.70
☐ ZT17 Terrell Davis	40.00	18.00	5.00
☐ ZT18 Drew Bledsoe	40.00	18.00	5.00

1991 Classic Promos

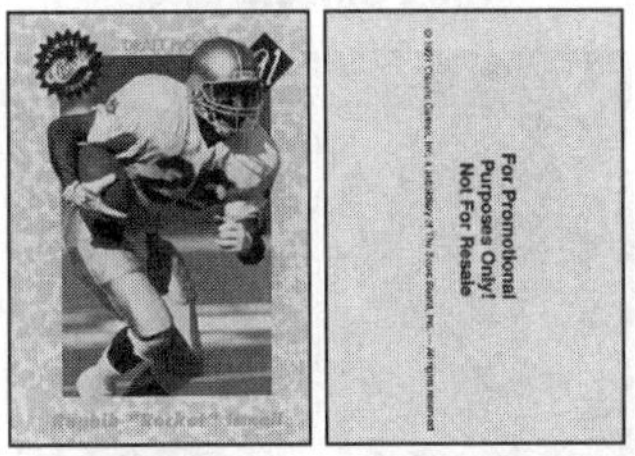

These 1991 Classic Football Draft Pick promos measure the standard size. The front features an action color photo on a two-toned spotted gray background of the player with his name below in aqua or black print. The borders are a white and gray spotty pattern, with "Premiere Classic Edition" in the upper left hand corner and "'91" in the upper right hand corner. The back states that these cards are for promotional purposes only. These five player cards (minus the "B" variations) were also issued as an unperforated promo sheet that measures approximately 7 1/2" by 7 1/8". The sheets were given away during the 1991 12th National Sports Collectors Convention in Anaheim (July 2nd-7th). The promo sheets bear a unique serial number("X of 10,000"). The backs have the warning "For Promotional Use Only" plastered over the Premier Classic Edition logo.

	MINT	NRMT	EXC
COMPLETE SET (7)	7.50	3.40	.95
COMMON CARD (1-5)	.75	.35	.09

☐ 1 Antone Davis Black print on front	.75	.35	.09
☐ 2A Raghib Rocket Ismail Black print on front	2.00	.90	.25
☐ 2B Raghib Rocket Ismail Blue print on front	2.00	.90	.25
☐ 3A Todd Lyght Black print on front	.75	.35	.09
☐ 3B Todd Lyght Blue print on front	.75	.35	.09
☐ 4 Russell Maryland Black print on front	1.00	.45	.12
☐ 5 Eric Turner Black print on front	1.00	.45	.12

1991 Classic

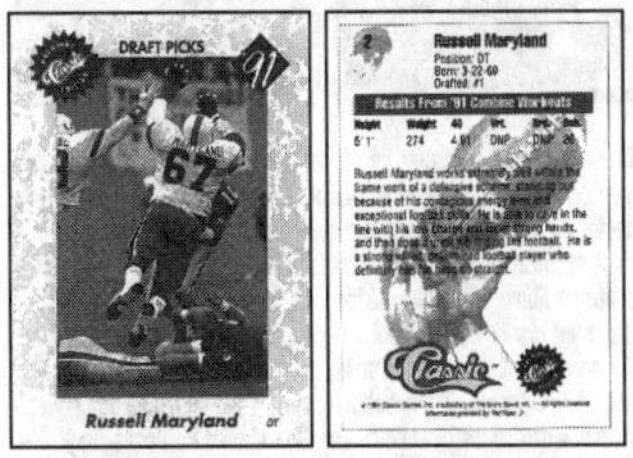

This 50-card set was distributed by Classic Games in factory set form. Top players from the 1991 NFL Draft are featured, including early cards of Brett Favre and Ricky Watters. Neither NFL team nor college team names are mentioned on the cards.

	MINT	NRMT	EXC
COMPLETE SET (50)	4.00	1.80	.50
COMMON CARD (1-50)	.04	.02	.01

☐ 1 Raghib "Rocket" Ismail	.50	.23	.06
☐ 2 Russell Maryland	.25	.11	.03
☐ 3 Eric Turner	.25	.11	.03
☐ 4 Bruce Pickens	.04	.02	.01
☐ 5 Mike Croel	.04	.02	.01
☐ 6 Todd Lyght	.04	.02	.01
☐ 7 Eric Swann	.25	.11	.03
☐ 8 Antone Davis	.04	.02	.01
☐ 9 Stanley Richard	.04	.02	.01
☐ 10 Pat Harlow	.04	.02	.01
☐ 11 Alvin Harper	.25	.11	.03
☐ 12 Mike Pritchard	.25	.11	.03
☐ 13 Leonard Russell	.25	.11	.03
☐ 14 Dan McGwire	.04	.02	.01
☐ 15 Bobby Wilson	.04	.02	.01
☐ 16 Alfred Williams	.04	.02	.01
☐ 17 Vinnie Clark	.04	.02	.01
☐ 18 Kelvin Pritchett	.04	.02	.01
☐ 19 Harvey Williams	.50	.23	.06
☐ 20 Stan Thomas	.04	.02	.01
☐ 21 Randal Hill	.25	.11	.03
☐ 22 Todd Marinovich	.04	.02	.01
☐ 23 Henry Jones	.04	.02	.01
☐ 24 Jarrod Bunch	.04	.02	.01
☐ 25 Mike Dumas	.04	.02	.01
☐ 26 Ed King	.04	.02	.01
☐ 27 Reggie Johnson	.04	.02	.01
☐ 28 Roman Phifer	.04	.02	.01
☐ 29 Mike Jones	.04	.02	.01
☐ 30 Brett Favre	2.00	.90	.25
☐ 31 Browning Nagle	.04	.02	.01
☐ 32 Esera Tuaolo	.04	.02	.01
☐ 33 George Thornton	.04	.02	.01
☐ 34 Dixon Edwards	.04	.02	.01
☐ 35 Darryl Lewis	.25	.11	.03
☐ 36 Eric Bieniemy	.04	.02	.01
☐ 37 Shane Curry	.04	.02	.01
☐ 38 Jerome Henderson	.04	.02	.01
☐ 39 Wesley Carroll	.25	.11	.03
☐ 40 Nick Bell	.04	.02	.01
☐ 41 John Flannery	.04	.02	.01
☐ 42 Ricky Watters	1.25	.55	.16
☐ 43 Jeff Graham	.50	.23	.06
☐ 44 Eric Moten	.04	.02	.01
☐ 45 Jesse Campbell	.04	.02	.01
☐ 46 Chris Zorich	.04	.02	.01
☐ 47 Doug Thomas	.04	.02	.01
☐ 48 Phil Hansen	.04	.02	.01
☐ 49 Kanavis McGhee	.04	.02	.01
☐ 50 Reggie Barrett	.04	.02	.01

1992 Classic Promos

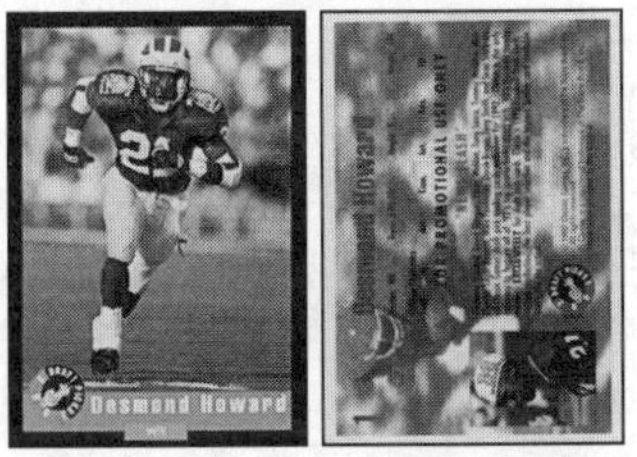

This six-card standard-size set was issued by Classic to preview the forthcoming draft pick issue. As with the regular issue foil and blister pack cards, the fronts have glossy color player photos enclosed by thin black borders. However, the color player photos on these promo cards differ from those used in the regular issue set. The Classic logo in the lower left corner is superimposed over a blue bottom stripe that includes player information. For background, the backs display the same unfocused image of a ball carrier breaking through the line in the deep, rich purple and maroon of the blister-pack cards. The backs present biography, but only the headings of the college stat categories appear. Further, the color close-up photos are also different, and the career summary has been replaced by a "News Flash" in the form of an advertisement for the draft pick set. Finally, the disclaimer "For Promotional Purposes Only" is stamped where the statistics would have been listed.

	MINT	NRMT	EXC
COMPLETE SET (6)	7.00	3.10	.85
COMMON CARD (1-6)	.75	.35	.09

☐ 1 Desmond Howard	1.00	.45	.12
☐ 2 David Klingler	1.00	.45	.12
☐ 3 Quentin Coryatt	1.00	.45	.12
☐ 4 Carl Pickens	2.50	1.10	.30
☐ 5 Derek Brown	.75	.35	.09
☐ 6 Casey Weldon	.75	.35	.09

1992 Classic

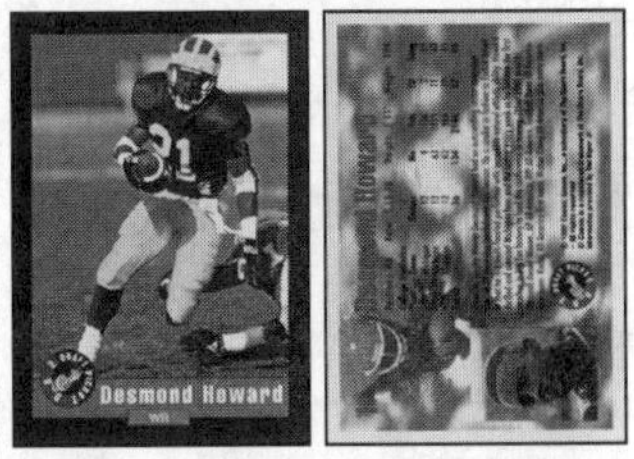

The 1992 Classic Draft Picks Foil set contains 100 standard-size cards featuring the highest rated football players eligible for the 1992 NFL draft. The production run of the foil was limited to 14,000, ten-box cases, and to 40,000 of each bonus card. The fronts have glossy color player photos enclosed by thin black borders. A Classic logo in the lower left corner is superimposed over a blue bottom stripe that

includes player information. Against the background of an unfocused image of a ball carrier breaking through the line, the backs have biography, college statistics, and career summary, with a color head shot in the lower left corner. This 100-card set needs to be distinguished from the 60-card set sold in blister packs only. Though both sets are identical in design, the photos displayed on the fronts are different, as are the head shots on the backs. On some of the cards, the career summary also differs. However, the most distinctive feature is that background on the backs of the foil-pack cards are ghosted, whereas the same background on the blister-pack cards exhibits a deep, rich purple and maroon. Key cards include Edgar Bennett, Marco Coleman, Quentin Coryatt, Sean Gilbert, Desmond Howard, David Klingler, Johnny Mitchell and Carl Pickens.

	MINT	EXC	G-VG
COMPLETE BLISTER SET (60)	7.00	3.10	.85
COMPLETE FOIL SET (100)	10.00	4.50	1.25
COMMON CARD (1-100)	.05	.02	.01
☐ 1 Desmond Howard	.50	.23	.06
☐ 2 David Klingler	.25	.11	.03
☐ 3 Quentin Coryatt	.25	.11	.03
☐ 4 Bill Johnson	.05	.02	.01
☐ 5 Eugene Chung	.05	.02	.01
☐ 6 Derek Brown TE	.25	.11	.03
☐ 7 Carl Pickens	1.50	.70	.19
☐ 8 Chris Mims	.25	.11	.03
☐ 9 Charles Davenport	.05	.02	.01
☐ 10 Ray Roberts	.05	.02	.01
☐ 11 Chuck Smith	.05	.02	.01
☐ 12 Joe Bowden	.05	.02	.01
☐ 13 Mirko Jurkovic	.05	.02	.01
☐ 14 Tony Smith	.05	.02	.01
☐ 15 Ken Swilling	.05	.02	.01
☐ 16 Greg Skrepenak	.05	.02	.01
☐ 17 Phillippi Sparks	.25	.11	.03
☐ 18 Alonzo Spellman	.25	.11	.03
☐ 19 Bernard Dafney	.05	.02	.01
☐ 20 Edgar Bennett	1.25	.55	.16
☐ 21 Shane Dronett	.05	.02	.01
☐ 22 Jeremy Lincoln	.05	.02	.01
☐ 23 Dion Lambert	.05	.02	.01
☐ 24 Siran Stacy	.25	.11	.03
☐ 25 Tony Sacca	.25	.11	.03
☐ 26 Sean Lumpkin	.05	.02	.01
☐ 27 Tommy Vardell	.25	.11	.03
☐ 28 Keith Hamilton	.25	.11	.03
☐ 29 Ashley Ambrose	.25	.11	.03
☐ 30B John Rays	.50	.23	.06
☐ 30F Sean Gilbert	.50	.23	.06
☐ 31 Casey Weldon	.25	.11	.03
☐ 32 Marc Boutte	.05	.02	.01
☐ 33 Santana Dotson	.25	.11	.03
☐ 34 Ronnie West	.05	.02	.01
☐ 35 Michael Bankston	.05	.02	.01
☐ 36 Mike Pawlawski	.05	.02	.01
☐ 37 Dale Carter	.50	.23	.06
☐ 38 Carlos Snow	.05	.02	.01
☐ 39 Corey Barlow	.05	.02	.01
☐ 40 Mark D'Onofrio	.05	.02	.01
☐ 41 Matt Blundin	.05	.02	.01
☐ 42 George Rooks	.05	.02	.01
☐ 43 Patrick Rowe	.05	.02	.01
☐ 44 Dwight Hollier	.05	.02	.01
☐ 45 Joel Steed	.05	.02	.01
☐ 46 Erick Anderson	.05	.02	.01
☐ 47 Rodney Culver	.25	.11	.03
☐ 48 Chris Hakel	.05	.02	.01
☐ 49 Luke Fisher	.05	.02	.01
☐ 50 Kevin Smith	.25	.11	.03
☐ 51 Robert Brooks	1.00	.45	.12
☐ 52 Bucky Richardson	.05	.02	.01
☐ 53 Steve Israel	.25	.11	.03
☐ 54B Tyrone Ashley	.50	.23	.06
☐ 54F Marco Coleman	.50	.23	.06
☐ 55 Johnny Mitchell	.25	.11	.03
☐ 56 Scottie Graham	.25	.11	.03
☐ 57 Keith Goganious	.25	.11	.03
☐ 58 Tommy Maddox	.05	.02	.01
☐ 59 Terrell Buckley	.25	.11	.03
☐ 60 Dana Hall	.25	.11	.03
☐ 61 Ty Detmer	.50	.23	.06
☐ 62 Darryl Williams	.25	.11	.03
☐ 63 Jason Hanson	.25	.11	.03
☐ 64 Leon Searcy	.25	.11	.03
☐ 65 Gene McGuire	.05	.02	.01
☐ 66 Will Furrer	.05	.02	.01
☐ 67 Darren Woodson	.25	.11	.03
☐ 68 Tracy Scroggins	.25	.11	.03
☐ 69 Corey Widmer	.05	.02	.01
☐ 70 Robert Harris	.25	.11	.03
☐ 71 Larry Tharpe	.05	.02	.01
☐ 72 Lance Olberding	.05	.02	.01
☐ 73 Stacey Dillard	.05	.02	.01
☐ 74 Troy Auzenne	.05	.02	.01
☐ 75 Tommy Jeter	.05	.02	.01
☐ 76 Mike Evans	.05	.02	.01
☐ 77 Shane Collins	.05	.02	.01
☐ 78 Mark Thomas	.05	.02	.01
☐ 79 Chester McGlockton	.25	.11	.03
☐ 80 Robert Porcher	.25	.11	.03
☐ 81 Marquez Pope	.25	.11	.03
☐ 82 Rico Smith	.05	.02	.01
☐ 83 Tyrone Williams	.25	.11	.03
☐ 84 Rod Smith	.25	.11	.03
☐ 85 Tyrone Legette	.05	.02	.01
☐ 86 Wayne Hawkins	.05	.02	.01
☐ 87 Derrick Moore	.25	.11	.03
☐ 88 Tim Lester	.05	.02	.01
☐ 89 Calvin Holmes	.05	.02	.01
☐ 90 Reggie Dwight	.05	.02	.01
☐ 91 Eddie Robinson	.05	.02	.01
☐ 92 Robert Jones	.25	.11	.03
☐ 93 Ricardo McDonald	.05	.02	.01
☐ 94 Howard Dinkins	.05	.02	.01
☐ 95 Todd Collins	.05	.02	.01
☐ 96 Eddie Blake	.05	.02	.01
☐ 97 Classic Quarterbacks Matt Blundin David Klingler Tommy Maddox Mike Pawlawski Tony Sacca Casey Weldon	.50	.23	.06
☐ 98 Back to Back Ty Detmer Desmond Howard	.50	.23	.06
☐ NNO Checklist 2	.05	.02	.01
☐ NNO Checklist 1	.05	.02	.01

1992 Classic LPs

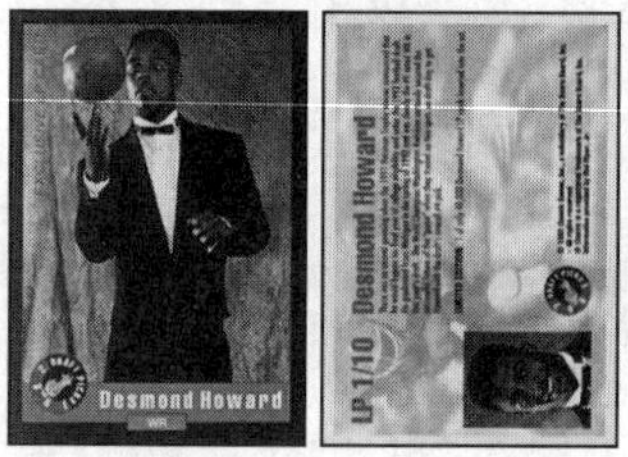

The 1992 Classic Draft Picks Gold LP Insert set contains ten standard-size cards featuring the highest rated football players eligible for the 1992 NFL draft. These ten gold foil stamped bonus cards were randomly inserted in foil packs. The production run of the foil was limited to 14,000, ten-box cases, and to 40,000 of each bonus card.

	MINT	EXC	G-VG
COMPLETE SET (10)	4.00	1.80	.50
COMMON CARD (LP1-LP10)	.75	.35	.09
☐ LP1 Desmond Howard	1.00	.45	.12
☐ LP2 David Klingler	.75	.35	.09
☐ LP3 Siran Stacy	.75	.35	.09
☐ LP4 Casey Weldon	.75	.35	.09
☐ LP5 Sean Gilbert	.75	.35	.09
☐ LP6 Matt Blundin	.75	.35	.09
☐ LP7 Tommy Maddox	.75	.35	.09
☐ LP8 Derek Brown TE	.75	.35	.09
☐ LP9 Tony Smith RB	.75	.35	.09
☐ LP10 Tony Sacca	.75	.35	.09

1993 Classic Gold Promos

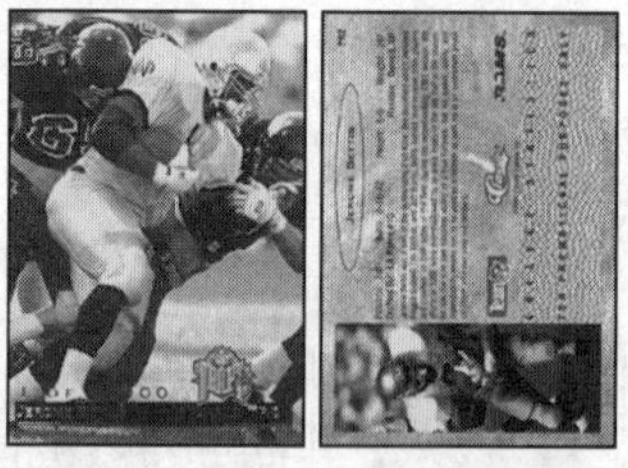

These standard-size promo cards were sent to Classic Collectors Club members. The fronts feature color action player photos. The player's name, the word "Gold," and his position are gold foil stamped in a black stripe at the bottom. The production run "1 of 5,000" is gold foil stamped above this black stripe. The gold foil Classic logo at the upper left rounds out the front. On a blue-gray variegated background, the horizontal back has a narrowly cropped action photo, biography, and player profile. A tan pebble-grain panel designed for college statistics carries the disclaimer "For Promotional Purposes Only." The card is numbered on the back with a "PR" prefix.

	MINT	NRMT	EXC
COMPLETE SET (2)	6.00	2.70	.75
COMMON CARD (1-2)	2.00	.90	.25
☐ PR1 Terry Kirby	2.00	.90	.25
☐ PR2 Jerome Bettis	4.00	1.80	.50

1993 Classic Preview

This standard-size card was issued to preview the design of the 1993 Classic Football Draft Picks series. The front features a color action player photo with bluish-gray variegated borders. The player's name, position, and the Classic 1993 Draft emblem appear in the mustard stripe that edges the bottom of the picture. The horizontal back carries a second color action photo, biography, player profile, and complete collegiate statistics.

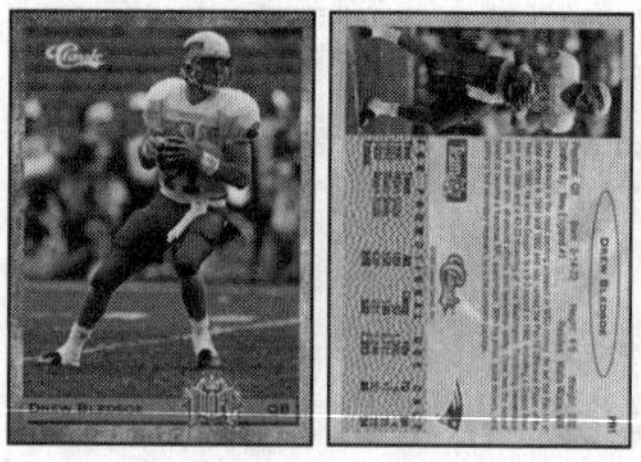

	MINT	NRMT	EXC
COMPLETE SET (1)	5.00	2.20	.60
COMMON CARD	5.00	2.20	.60
☐ PR1 Drew Bledsoe	5.00	2.20	.60

1993 Classic

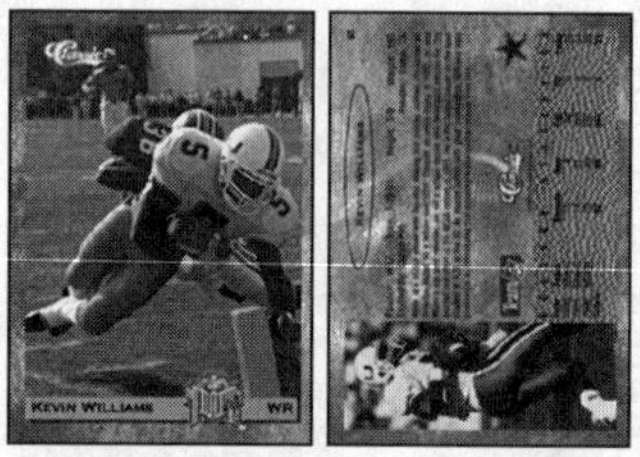

The 1993 Classic Football Draft Picks set consists of 100 standard-size cards. Randomly inserted throughout the foil packs were ten limited-print foil stamped cards, 1993 Classic Basketball Draft Pick Preview cards, 1993 Classic NFL Pro Line Preview cards, and 1,000 autographed cards by Super Bowl MVP Troy Aikman. Cards of number one pick Drew Bledsoe and number two pick Rick Mirer were exclusive to Classic until these players signed their NFL contracts. The production figures were 15,000 ten-box sequentially numbered cases, with 36 ten-card packs per box. The fronts feature color action player photos with blue stone-textured borders. The player's name and position is printed in a mustard bar at the bottom of the picture. The Classic Draft Picks logo overlaps the bar and the photo slightly to the right of center. The horizontal backs carry a small action photo, biographical information, statistics, and a player profile. Key cards include Jerome Bettis, Drew Bledsoe, Terry Kirby and Rick Mirer. Classic also issued 5,000 Gold Factory sets which include autographed cards of Drew Bledsoe and Rick Mirer.

	MINT	EXC	G-VG
COMPLETE SET (100)	7.00	3.10	.85
COMMON CARD (1-100)	.05	.02	.01
☐ 1 Drew Bledsoe	1.50	.70	.19
☐ 2 Rick Mirer	.50	.23	.06
☐ 3 Garrison Hearst	.50	.23	.06
☐ 4 Marvin Jones	.25	.11	.03
☐ 5 John Copeland	.25	.11	.03
☐ 6 Eric Curry	.25	.11	.03
☐ 7 Curtis Conway	.75	.35	.09
☐ 8 Willie Roaf	.25	.11	.03
☐ 9 Lincoln Kennedy	.25	.11	.03
☐ 10 Jerome Bettis	1.00	.45	.12
☐ 11 Mike Compton	.05	.02	.01
☐ 12 John Gerak	.05	.02	.01
☐ 13 Will Shields	.25	.11	.03
☐ 14 Ben Coleman	.05	.02	.01
☐ 15 Ernest Dye	.25	.11	.03
☐ 16 Lester Holmes	.05	.02	.01
☐ 17 Brad Hopkins	.25	.11	.03
☐ 18 Everett Lindsay	.05	.02	.01
☐ 19 Todd Rucci	.05	.02	.01
☐ 20 Lance Gunn	.05	.02	.01
☐ 21 Elvis Grbac	.50	.23	.06
☐ 22 Shane Matthews	.05	.02	.01
☐ 23 Rudy Harris	.05	.02	.01
☐ 24 Richie Anderson	.05	.02	.01
☐ 25 Derek Brown RB	.25	.11	.03
☐ 26 Roger Harper	.05	.02	.01
☐ 27 Terry Kirby	.50	.23	.06
☐ 28 Natrone Means	.75	.35	.09
☐ 29 Glyn Milburn	.25	.11	.03
☐ 30 Adrian Murrell	.50	.23	.06
☐ 31 Lorenzo Neal	.25	.11	.03
☐ 32 Roosevelt Potts	.25	.11	.03
☐ 33 Kevin Williams RB	.05	.02	.01
☐ 34 Russell Copeland	.25	.11	.03
☐ 35 Fred Baxter	.05	.02	.01
☐ 36 Troy Drayton	.25	.11	.03
☐ 37 Chris Gedney	.25	.11	.03
☐ 38 Irv Smith	.25	.11	.03
☐ 39 Olanda Truitt	.25	.11	.03
☐ 40 Victor Bailey	.25	.11	.03
☐ 41 Horace Copeland	.25	.11	.03
☐ 42 Ron Dickerson Jr.	.05	.02	.01
☐ 43 Willie Harris	.05	.02	.01
☐ 44 Tyrone Hughes	.25	.11	.03
☐ 45 Qadry Ismail	.50	.23	.06
☐ 46 Reggie Brooks	.25	.11	.03
☐ 47 Sean LaChapelle	.05	.02	.01
☐ 48 O.J.McDuffie UER	.50	.23	.06
☐ 49 Larry Ryans	.05	.02	.01
☐ 50 Kenny Shedd	.05	.02	.01
☐ 51 Brian Stablein	.05	.02	.01
☐ 52 Lamar Thomas	.25	.11	.03
☐ 53 Kevin Williams WR	.50	.23	.06
☐ 54 Othello Henderson	.05	.02	.01
☐ 55 Kevin Henry	.05	.02	.01
☐ 56 Todd Kelly	.25	.11	.03
☐ 57 Devon McDonald	.25	.11	.03
☐ 58 Michael Strahan	.25	.11	.03
☐ 59 Dan Williams	.25	.11	.03
☐ 60 Golbert Brown	.05	.02	.01
☐ 61 Mark Caesar	.05	.02	.01
☐ 62 Ronnie Dixon	.05	.02	.01
☐ 63 John Parrella	.05	.02	.01
☐ 64 Leonard Renfro	.05	.02	.01
☐ 65 Coleman Rudolph	.05	.02	.01
☐ 66 Ronnie Bradford	.05	.02	.01
☐ 67 Tom Carter	.25	.11	.03
☐ 68 Deon Figures	.25	.11	.03
☐ 69 Derrick Frazier	.25	.11	.03
☐ 70 Darrien Gordon	.25	.11	.03
☐ 71 Carlton Gray	.05	.02	.01
☐ 72 Adrian Hardy	.05	.02	.01
☐ 73 Mike Reid	.05	.02	.01
☐ 74 Thomas Smith	.25	.11	.03
☐ 75 Robert O'Neal	.05	.02	.01
☐ 76 Chad Brown	.25	.11	.03
☐ 77 Demetrius DuBose	.25	.11	.03
☐ 78 Reggie Givens	.05	.02	.01
☐ 79 Travis Hill	.05	.02	.01
☐ 80 Rich McKenzie	.05	.02	.01
☐ 81 Barry Minter	.05	.02	.01
☐ 82 Darrin Smith	.25	.11	.03
☐ 83 Steve Tovar	.05	.02	.01
☐ 84 Patrick Bates	.25	.11	.03
☐ 85 Dan Footman	.25	.11	.03
☐ 86 Ryan McNeil	.25	.11	.03
☐ 87 Danan Hughes	.25	.11	.03
☐ 88 Mark Brunell	1.50	.70	.19
☐ 89 Ron Moore	.25	.11	.03
☐ 90 Antonio London	.25	.11	.03
☐ 91 Steve Everitt	.25	.11	.03
☐ 92 Wayne Simmons	.25	.11	.03
☐ 93 Robert Smith	.50	.23	.06
☐ 94 Dana Stubblefield	.50	.23	.06
☐ 95 George Teague	.25	.11	.03
☐ 96 Carl Simpson	.05	.02	.01
☐ 97 Billy Joe Hobert	.50	.23	.06
☐ 98 Gino Torretta	.25	.11	.03
☐ 99 Checklist 1	.05	.02	.01
☐ 100 Checklist 2	.05	.02	.01
☐ AU1 Troy Aikman AU/1000 Certified autograph	175.00	80.00	22.00
☐ AU2 Drew Bledsoe AU/5000	80.00	36.00	10.00
☐ AU3 Rick Mirer AU/5000	30.00	13.50	3.70

1993 Classic Draft Stars

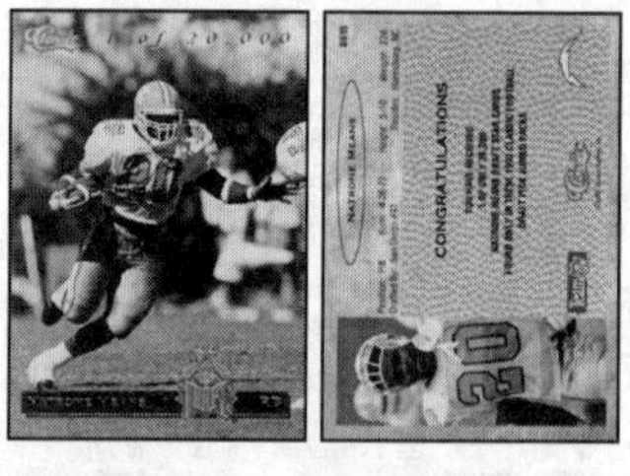

These standard-size cards were issued one per 1993 Classic Football Draft Pick jumbo pack. This 20-card set features "Draft Stars". The cards have a "DS" prefix on the card numbers. There was reportedly approximately one Bledsoe/Mirer "Jumbo card" in every other box.

	MINT	EXC	G-VG
COMPLETE SET (20)	25.00	11.00	3.10
COMMON CARD (DS1-DS20)	.50	.23	.06
☐ DS1 Drew Bledsoe	4.00	1.80	.50
☐ DS2 Rick Mirer	1.00	.45	.12
☐ DS3 Garrison Hearst	1.00	.45	.12
☐ DS4 Marvin Jones	.50	.23	.06
☐ DS5 John Copeland	.50	.23	.06
☐ DS6 Eric Curry	.50	.23	.06
☐ DS7 Curtis Conway	1.00	.45	.12
☐ DS8 Jerome Bettis	2.50	1.10	.30
☐ DS9 Patrick Bates	.50	.23	.06
☐ DS10 Tom Carter	.50	.23	.06
☐ DS11 Irv Smith	.50	.23	.06
☐ DS12 Robert Smith	1.00	.45	.12
☐ DS13 O.J.McDuffie	1.00	.45	.12
☐ DS14 Roosevelt Potts	.50	.23	.06
☐ DS15 Natrone Means	1.00	.45	.12
☐ DS16 Glyn Milburn	.50	.23	.06
☐ DS17 Reggie Brooks	.50	.23	.06
☐ DS18 Kevin Williams WR	1.00	.45	.12
☐ DS19 Qadry Ismail	1.00	.45	.12
☐ DS20 Billy Joe Hobert	1.00	.45	.12
☐ NNO Drew Bledsoe Rick Mirer Jumbo Card	15.00	6.75	1.85

1993 Classic LPs

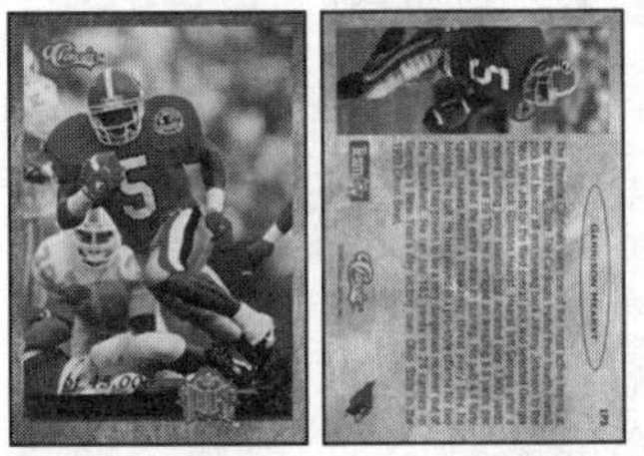

These limited print, foil-stamped cards were randomly inserted in 1993 Classic Football Draft Pick foil packs. The cards measure the standard size, and 45,000 of each card were produced. The fronts feature color action player photos with bluish-gray variegated borders. The player's name, position, and the Classic 1993 Draft emblem appear in the golden foil stripe that edges the bottom of the picture. In addition, "1 of 45,000" and "LP" are gold foil stamped just above the stripe. On a bluish-gray background, the horizontal back carries a second color action photo and player profile.

	MINT	EXC	G-VG
COMPLETE SET (10)	30.00	13.50	3.70
COMMON CARD (LP1-LP10)	1.50	.70	.19
☐ LP1 Drew Bledsoe	10.00	4.50	1.25
☐ LP2 Rick Mirer	2.50	1.10	.30
☐ LP3 Garrison Hearst	2.50	1.10	.30
☐ LP4 Marvin Jones	1.50	.70	.19
☐ LP5 John Copeland	1.50	.70	.19
☐ LP6 Eric Curry	1.50	.70	.19
☐ LP7 Curtis Conway	2.50	1.10	.30
☐ LP8 Jerome Bettis	6.00	2.70	.75
☐ LP9 Reggie Brooks	1.50	.70	.19
☐ LP10 Qadry Ismail	1.50	.70	.19

1993 Classic Superhero Comics

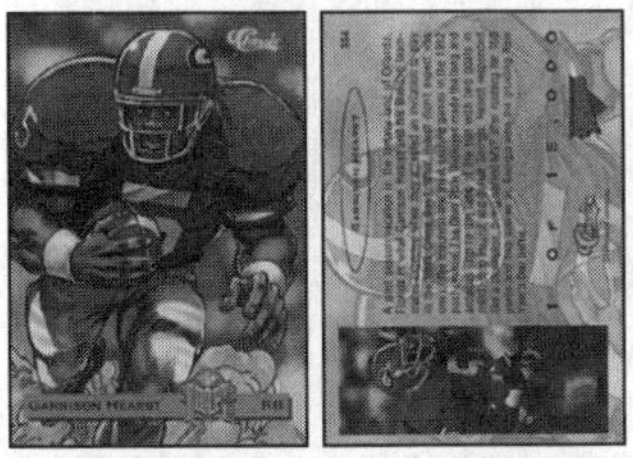

Illustrated by Neal Adams of Deathwatch 2,000 fame, these four standard-size cards were randomly inserted in 1993 Classic Football Draft Pick foil packs. 15,000 of each card were produced. The fronts feature full-bleed color comic-style action poses of the player. The player's name and position appear in a mustard stripe toward the bottom of the picture. Over a ghosted version of the front photo, the horizontal backs carry a small color action photo and a summary of the player's performance. The cards are numbered on the back with an "SH" prefix.

	MINT	EXC	G-VG
COMPLETE SET (4)	40.00	18.00	5.00
COMMON CARD (SH1-SH4)	8.00	3.60	1.00
☐ SH1 Troy Aikman	20.00	9.00	2.50
☐ SH2 Drew Bledsoe	15.00	6.75	1.85
☐ SH3 Rick Mirer	8.00	3.60	1.00
☐ SH4 Garrison Hearst	8.00	3.60	1.00

1994 Classic Previews

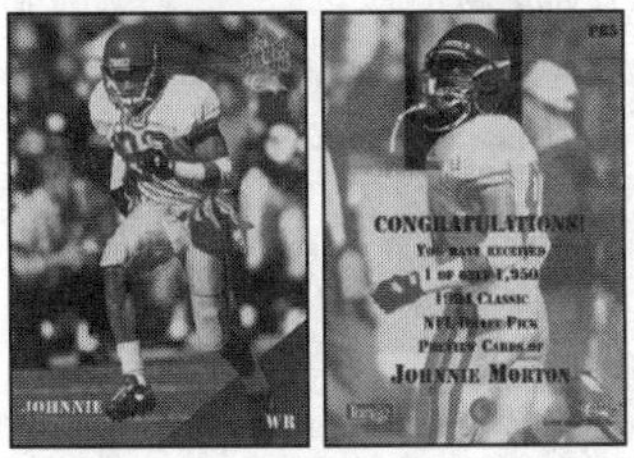

Randomly inserted in Images packs, this five-card standard-size set features color player action shots on the fronts. These photos are borderless, except for the blue triangle in a lower corner that carries the player's position in white lettering. The player's name appears in the other lower corner. The back carries a borderless color player action shot, which is ghosted, except for the area around the player's head. A congratulatory message at the bottom gives the number of sets produced: 1,950. The cards are numbered on the back with a "PR" prefix.

	MINT	EXC	G-VG
COMPLETE SET (5)	8.00	3.60	1.00
COMMON CARD (PR1-PR5)	1.00	.45	.12
☐ PR1 Heath Shuler	4.00	1.80	.50
☐ PR2 Trent Dilfer	2.00	.90	.25
☐ PR3 Dan Wilkinson	1.00	.45	.12
☐ PR4 David Palmer	1.00	.45	.12
☐ PR5 Johnnie Morton	1.00	.45	.12

1994 Classic Promos

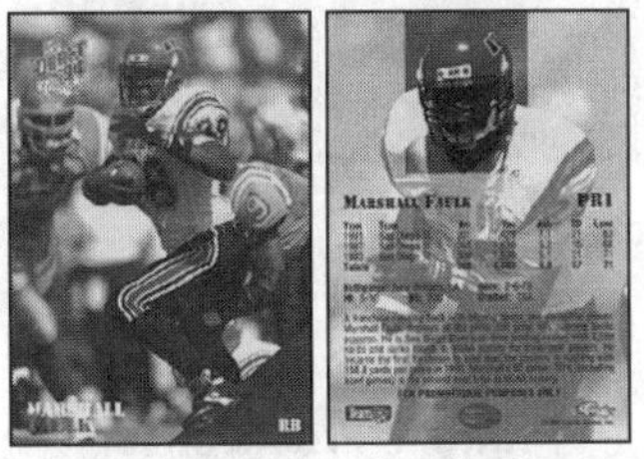

These standard-size cards were issued to preview the design of the 1994 Classic Football Draft Picks series. The fronts feature color action shots of the players in their college uniforms. The photos are borderless, except for a royal blue lower corner that carries the player's position. The player's name is printed in the other lower corner. The borderless back carries a player action shot that is ghosted, with the exception of the area around the player's head. Player biography, statistics, and career highlights round out the back. Along the bottom are the words, "For promotional purposes only." The cards are numbered on the back with a "PR" prefix.

	MINT	NRMT	EXC
COMPLETE SET(3)	14.00	6.25	1.75
COMMON CARD (PR1-PR3)	5.00	2.20	.60
☐ PR1 Marshall Faulk	6.00	2.70	.75
☐ PR2 Heath Shuler	5.00	2.20	.60
☐ PR3 Heath Shuler	5.00	2.20	.60

1994 Classic

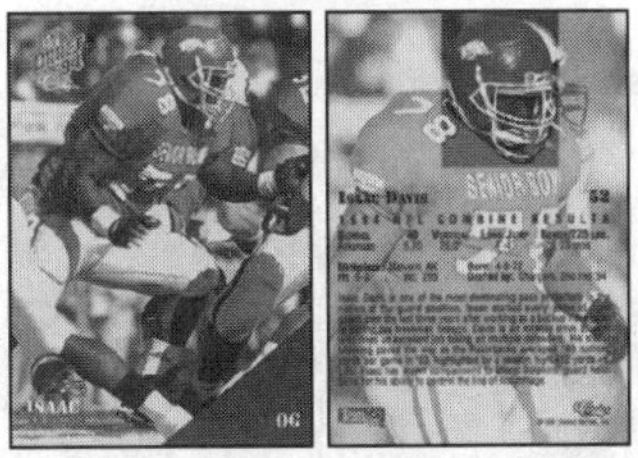

This 105-card standard-size set features color player action shots on the fronts. These photos are borderless, except for the blue triangle in a lower corner that carries the player's position in white lettering. The draftee's name and his new NFL team helmet logo appear in the other corner. The back carries a borderless color player action shot, which is ghosted, except for the area around the player's head. The player's statistics, brief biography, and career highlights round out the back. A parallel gold set was issued one per pack. The cards are valued as a multiple of the regular cards. Key players in this set include Isaac Bruce, Marshall Faulk and Errict Rhett. Two special inserts (one signed) featuring Jerry Rice were randomly inserted into packs, both in honor of Rice becoming the all-time TD reception leader.

	MINT	EXC	G-VG
COMPLETE SET (105)	7.00	3.10	.85
COMMON CARD (1-105)	.05	.02	.01
☐ 1 Heath Shuler	.50	.23	.06
☐ 2 Trent Dilfer	.50	.23	.06
☐ 3 Marshall Faulk	1.25	.55	.16
☐ 4 Errict Rhett	.50	.23	.06
☐ 5 Charlie Garner	.25	.11	.03
☐ 6 Sam Adams	.25	.11	.03
☐ 7 Shante Carver	.25	.11	.03
☐ 8 Dwayne Chandler	.05	.02	.01
☐ 9 Andre Coleman	.25	.11	.03
☐ 10 Carlester Crumpler	.05	.02	.01
☐ 11 Charles Johnson	.25	.11	.03
☐ 12 David Palmer	.25	.11	.03
☐ 13 Dan Wilkinson	.25	.11	.03
☐ 14 LeShon Johnson	.25	.11	.03
☐ 15 Mario Bates	.25	.11	.03
☐ 16 Glenn Foley	.25	.11	.03
☐ 17 William Gaines	.25	.11	.03
☐ 18 Wayne Gandy	.25	.11	.03
☐ 19 Jason Gildon	.05	.02	.01
☐ 20 Eric Gant	.05	.02	.01
☐ 21 Tre Johnson	.25	.11	.03
☐ 22 Calvin Jones	.25	.11	.03
☐ 23 Jake Kelchner	.05	.02	.01
☐ 24 Perry Klein	.25	.11	.03
☐ 25 Chuck Levy	.25	.11	.03
☐ 26 Corey Louchiey	.05	.02	.01
☐ 27 Chris Maumalanga	.05	.02	.01
☐ 28 Jamir Miller	.25	.11	.03
☐ 29 Jim Miller	.25	.11	.03
☐ 30 Johnnie Morton	.25	.11	.03
☐ 31 Doug Nussmeier	.25	.11	.03
☐ 32 Vaughn Parker	.25	.11	.03
☐ 33 Darnay Scott	.50	.23	.06
☐ 34 Fernando Smith	.25	.11	.03
☐ 35 Lamar Smith	.25	.11	.03
☐ 36 Marcus Spears	.05	.02	.01
☐ 37 Irving Spikes	.25	.11	.03
☐ 38 Todd Steussie	.25	.11	.03
☐ 39 Aaron Taylor	.25	.11	.03
☐ 40 John Thierry	.25	.11	.03
☐ 41 Dewayne Washington	.25	.11	.03
☐ 42 Jason Winrow	.05	.02	.01
☐ 43 Ronnie Woolford	.25	.11	.03
☐ 44 Bryant Young	.25	.11	.03
☐ 45 Arthur Bussie	.05	.02	.01
☐ 46 Derrick Alexander WR	.50	.23	.06
☐ 47 Larry Allen	.25	.11	.03
☐ 48 Aubrey Beavers	.05	.02	.01
☐ 49 James Bostic	.25	.11	.03
☐ 50 Jeff Burris	.25	.11	.03
☐ 51 Lindsey Chapman	.05	.02	.01
☐ 52 Isaac Davis	.25	.11	.03
☐ 53 Lake Dawson	.50	.23	.06
☐ 54 Tyronne Drakeford	.25	.11	.03
☐ 55 William Floyd	.25	.11	.03
☐ 56 Henry Ford	.25	.11	.03
☐ 57 Rob Fredrickson	.25	.11	.03
☐ 58 Aaron Glenn	.25	.11	.03
☐ 59 Shelby Hill	.05	.02	.01
☐ 60 Willie Jackson	.25	.11	.03
☐ 61 Joe Johnson	.25	.11	.03
☐ 62 Aaron Laing	.25	.11	.03
☐ 63 Kevin Lee	.25	.11	.03
☐ 64 Eric Mahlum	.25	.11	.03
☐ 65 Steve Matthews	.25	.11	.03
☐ 66 Willie McGinest	.25	.11	.03
☐ 67 Kevin Mitchell	.25	.11	.03
☐ 68 Byron Bam Morris	.50	.23	.06
☐ 69 Thomas Randolph	.25	.11	.03
☐ 70 Tony Richardson	.25	.11	.03
☐ 71 Corey Sawyer	.25	.11	.03
☐ 72 Jason Sehorn	.25	.11	.03
☐ 73 Rob Waldrop	.05	.02	.01
☐ 74 Jay Walker	.25	.11	.03
☐ 75 Bernard Williams	.05	.02	.01
☐ 76 Marvin Goodwin	.05	.02	.01
☐ 77 Romeo Bandison	.05	.02	.01
☐ 78 Bucky Brooks	.25	.11	.03
☐ 79 James Folston	.05	.02	.01
☐ 80 Donnell Bennett	.25	.11	.03
☐ 81 Charlie Ward	.50	.23	.06
☐ 82 Antonio Langham	.25	.11	.03
☐ 83 Greg Hill	.50	.23	.06
☐ 84 Anthony Phillips	.05	.02	.01
☐ 85 Winfred Tubbs	.25	.11	.03
☐ 86 Trev Alberts	.25	.11	.03
☐ 87 Tim Bowens	.25	.11	.03
☐ 88 Thomas Lewis	.25	.11	.03
☐ 89 Allen Aldridge	.05	.02	.01
☐ 90 Bert Emanuel	.50	.23	.06
☐ 91 Ryan Yarborough	.25	.11	.03
☐ 92 Lonnie Johnson	.05	.02	.01
☐ 93 Isaac Bruce	1.25	.55	.16
☐ 94 Checklist 1	.05	.02	.01
☐ 95 Checklist 2	.05	.02	.01
☐ 96 Troy Aikman FLB	.50	.23	.06
☐ 97 Steve Young FLB	.50	.23	.06
☐ 98 Rick Mirer FLB	.50	.23	.06
☐ 99 Drew Bledsoe FLB	.50	.23	.06
☐ 100 Jerry Rice FLB	.50	.23	.06
☐ 101 Heath Shuler COMIC SP	.50	.23	.06
☐ 102 Marshall Faulk COMIC SP	.75	.35	.09
☐ 103 Trent Dilfer COMIC SP	.25	.11	.03
☐ 104 Dan Wilkinson COMIC SP	.25	.11	.03
☐ 105 David Palmer COMIC SP	.25	.11	.03
☐ JR1 Jerry Rice Special	15.00	6.75	1.85
☐ NNO Jerry Rice AU/1994	130.00	57.50	16.00

1994 Classic Draft Stars

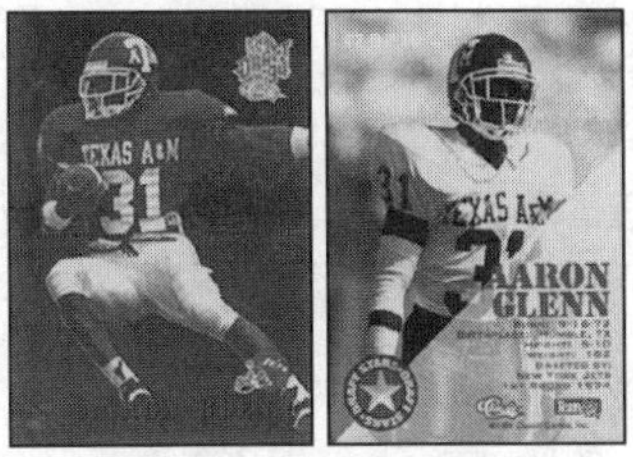

Inserted one per periodical pack, this 20-card standard-size set features some of the NFL's top draft picks. The full-bleed color action photos on the fronts have a metallic sheen to them. The player's name, position, and the helmet of the team which drafted him are printed toward the bottom. A second color photo appears on the back. A diagonal line divides the photo into two, and on the lower ghosted portion appears biographical information. The cards are numbered on the back "X of 20." The Rick Mirer card was a special insert randomly placed in periodical packs.

	MINT	EXC	G-VG
COMPLETE SET (20)	15.00	6.75	1.85
COMMON CARD (1-20)	.25	.11	.03
☐ 1 Trev Alberts	.50	.23	.06
☐ 2 Jeff Burris	.50	.23	.06
☐ 3 Shante Carver	.25	.11	.03
☐ 4 Trent Dilfer	1.00	.45	.12
☐ 5 Marshall Faulk	4.00	1.80	.50
☐ 6 William Floyd	.50	.23	.06
☐ 7 Aaron Glenn	.50	.23	.06
☐ 8 Greg Hill	1.00	.45	.12
☐ 9 Charles Johnson	.50	.23	.06
☐ 10 Calvin Jones	.25	.11	.03
☐ 11 Antonio Langham	.50	.23	.06
☐ 12 Thomas Lewis	.50	.23	.06
☐ 13 Willie McGinest	.50	.23	.06
☐ 14 Jamir Miller	.25	.11	.03
☐ 15 Johnnie Morton	.50	.23	.06
☐ 16 David Palmer	.50	.23	.06
☐ 17 Darnay Scott	1.00	.45	.12
☐ 18 Heath Shuler	1.00	.45	.12
☐ 19 Dan Wilkinson	.50	.23	.06
☐ 20 Bryant Young	.50	.23	.06
☐ NNO Rick Mirer Special	4.00	1.80	.50

1994 Classic Picks

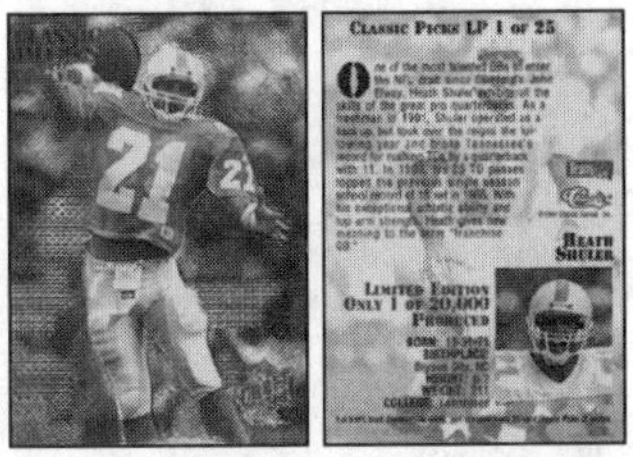

Randomly inserted in packs, these five standard-size cards have borderless fronts featuring color action player cutouts set on textured metallic backgrounds. The player's name appears in an upper corner in colored metallic lettering. The back carries a borderless ghosted color player action shot. A color headshot appears in a lower corner. Career highlights appear near the top and a brief player biography appears near the bottom. A message in blue lettering states that production was limited to 20,000 of each card. The cards are numbered on the back with an "LP" prefix.

	MINT	EXC	G-VG
COMPLETE SET (5)	20.00	9.00	2.50
COMMON CARD (1-5)	2.50	1.10	.30
☐ 1 Heath Shuler	3.00	1.35	.35
☐ 2 Trent Dilfer	3.00	1.35	.35
☐ 3 Johnnie Morton	2.50	1.10	.30
☐ 4 David Palmer	2.50	1.10	.30
☐ 5 Marshall Faulk	15.00	6.75	1.85

1994 Classic ROY Sweepstakes

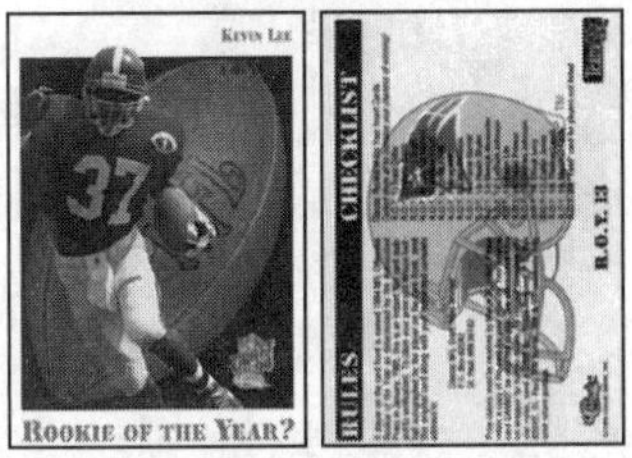

Randomly inserted in packs, these 20 standard-size cards feature candidates for the '94 NFL offensive Rookie of the Year. The card of the player who won the award was redeemable for a football signed by the player. The white-bordered fronts feature color action player cutouts set on an image of a football. The player's name appears in red lettering within the margin above the photo. The question, "Rookie of the Year" appears in the margin below the picture. The production run of 2,500 appears in gold foil within an upper corner of the photo. The white horizontal back carries sweepstake rules and set checklist. The player's ghosted NFL team helmet also appears. The cards are numbered on the back with a "ROY" prefix. The prizes were redeemable until March 31, 1995.

	MINT	EXC	G-VG
COMPLETE SET (20)	60.00	27.00	7.50
COMMON CARD (ROY1-ROY20)	1.50	.70	.19
☐ ROY1 Trent Dilfer	4.00	1.80	.50
☐ ROY2 Mario Bates	2.50	1.10	.30
☐ ROY3 Darnay Scott	4.00	1.80	.50
☐ ROY4 Johnnie Morton	2.50	1.10	.30
☐ ROY5 William Floyd	2.50	1.10	.30
☐ ROY6 Errict Rhett	8.00	3.60	1.00
☐ ROY7 Greg Hill	2.50	1.10	.30
☐ ROY8 Lake Dawson	2.50	1.10	.30
☐ ROY9 Charlie Garner	2.50	1.10	.30
☐ ROY10 Heath Shuler	4.00	1.80	.50
☐ ROY11 Derrick Alexander WR	2.50	1.10	.30
☐ ROY12 LeShon Johnson	2.50	1.10	.30
☐ ROY13 Kevin Lee	1.50	.70	.19
☐ ROY14 David Palmer	2.50	1.10	.30

☐ ROY15 Charles Johnson	2.50	1.10	.30
☐ ROY16 Chuck Levy	1.50	.70	.19
☐ ROY17 Calvin Jones	1.50	.70	.19
☐ ROY18 Thomas Lewis	2.50	1.10	.30
☐ ROY19 Marshall Faulk Expired	20.00	9.00	2.50
☐ ROY20 Field Card	1.50	.70	.19

1994 Classic Game Cards

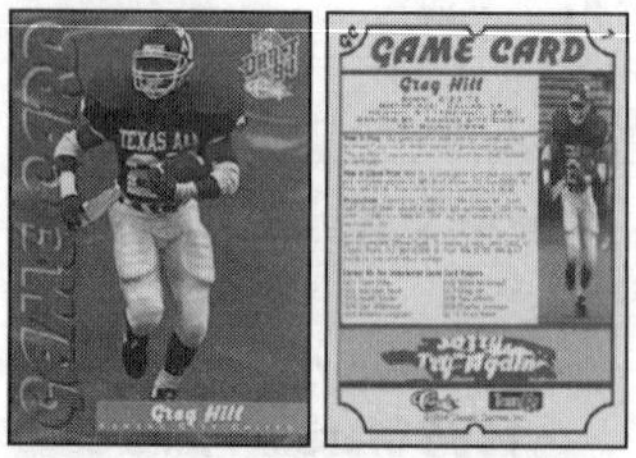

Inserted one per jumbo pack, this ten-card set measures the standard size. The fronts feature borderless color action player photos on a computer-generated background resembling water. The player's name and the team name appear on the bottom, while the words "Game Card" are printed alongside the left. The backs carry a small sepia-toned player photo, along with biography, rules on how to play the game and a checklist. Unnumbered Drew Bledsoe cards were randomly inserted in jumbo packs. Winning cards were redeemable for a 1994 Classic NFL Draft Gold Uncut Sheet, or a 1994 NFL Draft Day Set. The cards were redeemable until February 28, 1995.

	MINT	EXC	G-VG
COMPLETE SET (10)	10.00	4.50	1.25
COMMON CARD (GC1-GC10)	.25	.11	.03
*PRIZE BOX SCRATCHED:HALF VALUE			

☐ DB1 Drew Bledsoe Special	15.00	6.75	1.85
☐ GC1 Trent Dilfer	.75	.35	.09
☐ GC2 Marshall Faulk	3.00	1.35	.35
☐ GC3 Heath Shuler	.75	.35	.09
☐ GC4 Dan Wilkinson	.25	.11	.03
☐ GC5 Antonio Langham	.25	.11	.03
☐ GC6 Willie McGinest	.40	.18	.05
☐ GC7 Greg Hill	.40	.18	.05
☐ GC8 Trev Alberts	.25	.11	.03
☐ GC9 Charles Johnson	.40	.18	.05
☐ GC10 Errict Rhett	1.25	.55	.16

1995 Classic NFL Rookies

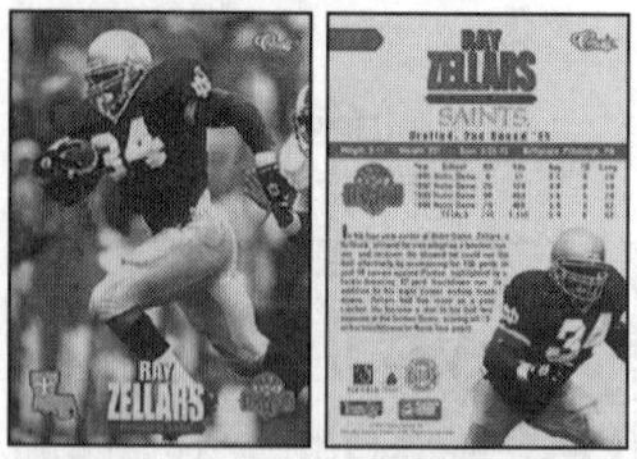

This 110-card standard-size set features first-year NFL players. The cards were issued in 10-card packs, with 36 packs in a box and 12 boxes per case. For the card hobby, 2,950 sequentially numbered cases were produced. This set includes all 32 first round draft choices as well as many prominent later round picks. The set closes with an "Award Winner" subset at cards (101-105) as well as a flashback set of leading NFL players (106-110). Printed in 18-point stock, the full-bleed fronts feature color action photos. The player is identified in white lettering near the bottom. His position is in red lettering directly underneath his name. The backs contain biographical information, collegiate states and a player profile. The bottom right is dedicated to another player photo. All of this information is set against a white background. Key players in this set include Kerry Collins, Terrell Davis, Joey Galloway, Curtis Martin, Rashaan Salaam, Kordell Stewart, J.J. Stokes and Michael Westbrook.

	MINT	EXC	G-VG
COMPLETE SET (110)	15.00	6.75	1.85
COMMON CARD (1-110)	.05	.02	.01

☐ 1 Ki-Jana Carter	.50	.23	.06
☐ 2 Tony Boselli	.25	.11	.03
☐ 3 Steve McNair	1.00	.45	.12
☐ 4 Michael Westbrook	.50	.23	.06
☐ 5 Kerry Collins	1.50	.70	.19
☐ 6 Kevin Carter	.25	.11	.03
☐ 7 Mike Mamula	.25	.11	.03
☐ 8 Joey Galloway	.75	.35	.09
☐ 9 Kyle Brady	.25	.11	.03
☐ 10 J.J. Stokes	.50	.23	.06
☐ 11 Derrick Alexander	.25	.11	.03
☐ 12 Warren Sapp	.25	.11	.03
☐ 13 Mark Fields	.05	.02	.01
☐ 14 Ruben Brown	.05	.02	.01
☐ 15 Ellis Johnson	.05	.02	.01
☐ 16 Hugh Douglas	.25	.11	.03
☐ 17 Tyrone Wheatley	.25	.11	.03
☐ 18 Napoleon Kaufman	.50	.23	.06
☐ 19 James O. Stewart	.50	.23	.06
☐ 20 Luther Ellis	.05	.02	.01
☐ 21 Rashaan Salaam	.50	.23	.06
☐ 22 Tyrone Poole	.25	.11	.03
☐ 23 Ty Law	.25	.11	.03
☐ 24 Korey Stringer	.05	.02	.01
☐ 25 Billy Milner	.05	.02	.01
☐ 26 Devin Bush	.05	.02	.01
☐ 27 Mark Bruener	.25	.11	.03
☐ 28 Derrick Brooks	.05	.02	.01
☐ 29 Blake Brockermeyer	.05	.02	.01
☐ 30 Craig Powell	.05	.02	.01
☐ 31 Trezelle Jenkins	.05	.02	.01
☐ 32 Craig Newsome	.05	.02	.01
☐ 33 Thomas Bailey	.05	.02	.01
☐ 34 Chad May	.05	.02	.01
☐ 35 J.J. Smith	.05	.02	.01
☐ 36 Lorenzo Styles	.05	.02	.01
☐ 37 Brian Williams	.05	.02	.01
☐ 38 Damien Covington	.05	.02	.01
☐ 39 Steve Stenstrom	.05	.02	.01
☐ 40 Darius Holland	.05	.02	.01
☐ 41 Pete Mitchell	.05	.02	.01
☐ 42 Todd Collins	.50	.23	.06
☐ 43 Kordell Stewart	1.50	.70	.19
☐ 44 Eric Zeier	.75	.35	.09
☐ 45 Frank Sanders	.75	.35	.09
☐ 46 Ben Talley	.05	.02	.01
☐ 47 Billy Williams	.05	.02	.01
☐ 48 Chris T. Jones	.50	.23	.06
☐ 49 Tamarick Vanover	.50	.23	.06
☐ 50 Jimmy Hitchcock	.05	.02	.01
☐ 51 Chris Hudson	.05	.02	.01
☐ 52 Terrell Fletcher	.50	.23	.06
☐ 53 Brent Moss	.05	.02	.01
☐ 54 Terrell Davis	2.00	.90	.25
☐ 55 Rodney Thomas	.50	.23	.06
☐ 56 Larry Jones	.05	.02	.01
☐ 57 Ray Zellars	.25	.11	.03
☐ 58 David Sloan	.25	.11	.03
☐ 59 Brandon Bennett	.05	.02	.01
☐ 60 Brian DeMarco	.05	.02	.01
☐ 61 Bryan Schwartz	.05	.02	.01
☐ 62 Jack Jackson	.05	.02	.01
☐ 63 Bobby Taylor	.25	.11	.03
☐ 64 Kevin Hickman	.05	.02	.01
☐ 65 Matt O'Dwyer	.05	.02	.01
☐ 66 Patrick Riley	.05	.02	.01
☐ 67 Ki-Jana Carter	.50	.23	.06
☐ 68 Kerry Collins	1.50	.70	.19
☐ 69 Steve McNair	1.00	.45	.12
☐ 70 Tyrone Wheatley	.50	.23	.06
☐ 71 Antonio Freeman	1.25	.55	.16
☐ 72 Clifton Abraham	.05	.02	.01
☐ 73 Kez McCorvey	.05	.02	.01
☐ 74 Lovell Pinkney	.05	.02	.01
☐ 75 Lee DeRamus	.05	.02	.01
☐ 76 John Walsh	.05	.02	.01
☐ 77 Cory Raymer	.05	.02	.01
☐ 78 Corey Fuller	.05	.02	.01
☐ 79 Tyrone Davis	.05	.02	.01
☐ 80 David Dunn	.25	.11	.03
☐ 81 Dana Howard	.05	.02	.01
☐ 82 Melvin Johnson	.05	.02	.01
☐ 83 Robert Baldwin	.05	.02	.01
☐ 84 Curtis Martin	2.00	.90	.25
☐ 85 Zack Crockett	.05	.02	.01
☐ 86 Jay Barker	.05	.02	.01
☐ 87 Christian Fauria	.25	.11	.03
☐ 88 Zach Wiegert	.05	.02	.01
☐ 89 Barrett Brooks	.05	.02	.01
☐ 90 Ken Dilger	.25	.11	.03
☐ 91 James A. Stewart	.05	.02	.01
☐ 92 Ed Hervey	.05	.02	.01
☐ 93 Torey Hunter	.05	.02	.01
☐ 94 Sherman Williams	.25	.11	.03
☐ 95 Shawn King	.05	.02	.01
☐ 96 Dave Barr	.05	.02	.01
☐ 97 Rob Johnson	.05	.02	.01
☐ 98 Stoney Case	.05	.02	.01
☐ 99 Ki-Jana Carter CL	.30	.14	.04
☐ 100 Steve McNair CL	.30	.14	.04
☐ 101 Rashaan Salaam AW	.75	.35	.09
☐ 102 Kerry Collins AW	.50	.23	.06
☐ 103 Rashaan Salaam AW	.75	.35	.09
☐ 104 Kerry Collins AW	.50	.23	.06
☐ 105 Jay Barker	.05	.02	.01
☐ 106 Drew Bledsoe	.75	.35	.09
☐ 107 Marshall Faulk	.50	.23	.06
☐ 108 Steve Young	.50	.23	.06
☐ 109 Troy Aikman	.50	.23	.06
☐ 110 Emmitt Smith	.75	.35	.09
☐ MF1 Marshall Faulk	15.00	6.75	1.85

1995 Classic NFL Rookies Printer's Proofs

Inserted at a rate of two per box in hobby cases only, 595 of each regular card were issued as Printer's proof cards. Printed in 18-point stock, the fronts feature full-bleed color action photos. The player's name is printed across the bottom between the team logo and the 1995 Draft logo. The backs carry complete collegiate statistics, updated information on all players, and a second action photo. The set closes with Award Winners (101-105) and Draft Retro (106-110).

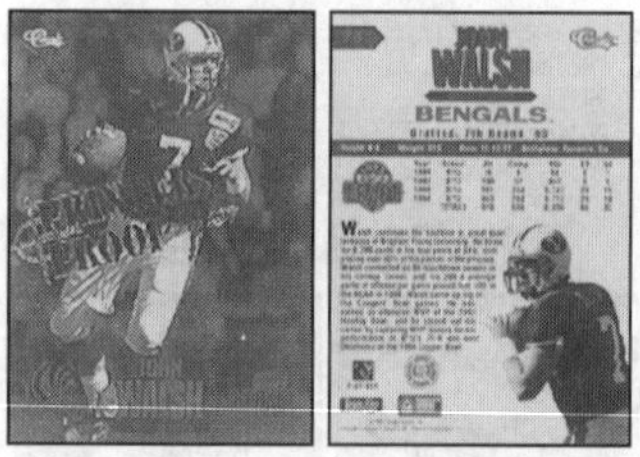

	MINT	NRMT	EXC
COMPLETE SET (110)	300.00	135.00	38.00
COMMON CARD (1-110)	1.00	.45	.12
*STARS:12X TO 20X BASIC CARDS			

1995 Classic NFL Rookies Printer's Proofs Silver

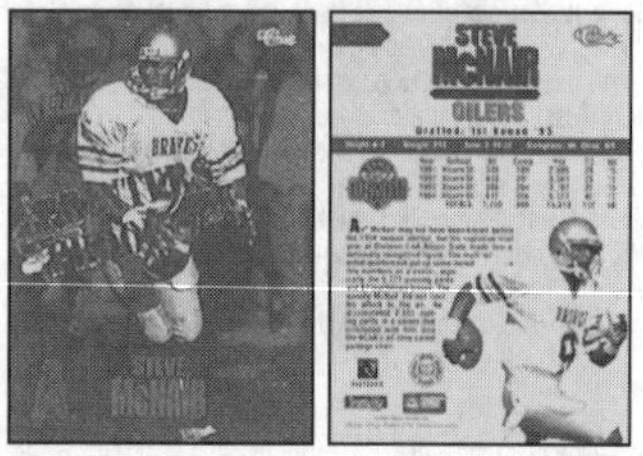

Inserted at a rate of one per box in hobby cases only, 297 of each silver series card were issued as Printer's Proof cards. The fronts feature full-bleed color action photos. The player's name is printed across the bottom between the team logo and the 1995 Draft logo. The backs carry complete collegiate statistics, updated information on all players, and a second action photo. The set closes with Award Winners (101-105) and Draft Retro (106-110).

	MINT	NRMT	EXC
COMPLETE SET (110)	450.00	200.00	55.00
COMMON CARD (1-110)	1.50	.70	.19
*STARS:18X TO 30X BASIC CARDS			

1995 Classic NFL Rookies Silver

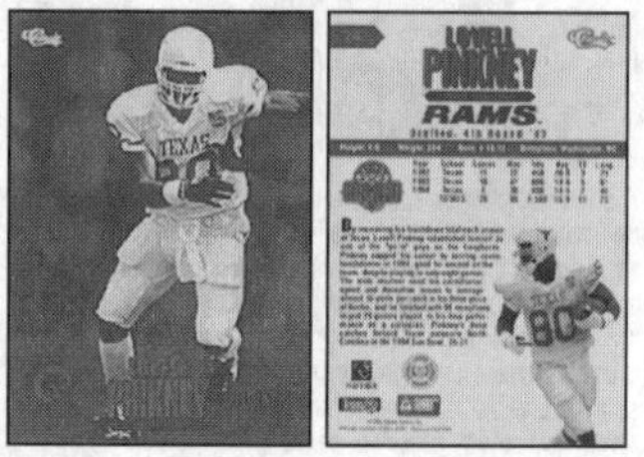

This 110-card parallel standard-size set was inserted one per foil pack and printed on silver foil board. The fronts feature full-bleed color action photos. The player's name is printed across the bottom between the team logo and the 1995 Draft logo. The backs carry complete collegiate statistics, updated information on all players, and a second action photo. The set closes with Award Winners (101-105) and Draft Retro (106-110).

	MINT	NRMT	EXC
COMPLETE SET (110)	45.00	20.00	5.50
COMMON CARD (1-110)	.10	.05	.01
*STARS: 2X TO 3X BASIC CARDS			

1995 Classic NFL Rookies Die Cuts

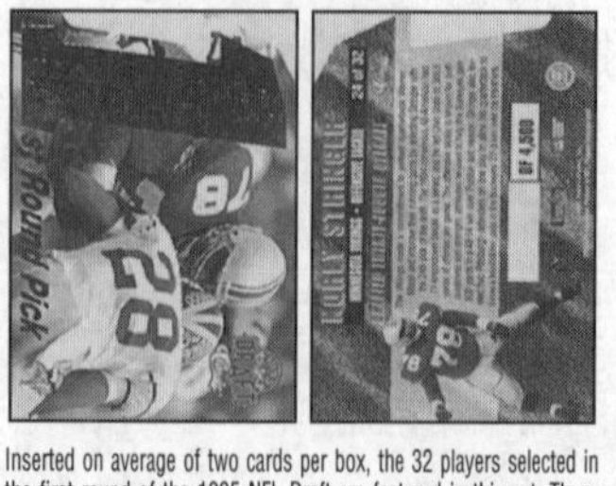

Inserted on average of two cards per box, the 32 players selected in the first round of the 1995 NFL Draft are featured in this set. These retail-only cards display an action photo die-cut in the shape of the number 1. They are sequentially numbered to 4,500.

	MINT	EXC	G-VG
COMPLETE SET (32)	100.00	45.00	12.50
COMMON CARD (1-32)	.75	.35	.09
COMP. PRINT PROOF (32)	1200.00	550.00	150.00
COMMON PRINTER'S PROOF	10.00	4.50	1.25
*STARS: 9X TO 15X BASIC CARDS			
COMP. SILVER SIG. (32)	250.00	110.00	31.00
COMMON SILVER SIGNATURE	2.00	.90	.25
*STARS:1.5X TO 3X BASIC CARDS			

☐ 1 Ki-Jana Carter	4.00	1.80	.50
☐ 2 Tony Boselli	2.00	.90	.25
☐ 3 Steve McNair	8.00	3.60	1.00
☐ 4 Michael Westbrook	4.00	1.80	.50
☐ 5 Kerry Collins	12.00	5.50	1.50
☐ 6 Kevin Carter	2.00	.90	.25
☐ 7 Mike Mamula	2.00	.90	.25
☐ 8 Joey Galloway	6.00	2.70	.75
☐ 9 Kyle Brady	2.00	.90	.25
☐ 10 J.J. Stokes	4.00	1.80	.50
☐ 11 Derrick Alexander	2.00	.90	.25
☐ 12 Warren Sapp	2.00	.90	.25
☐ 13 Mark Fields	.75	.35	.09
☐ 14 Ruben Brown	.75	.35	.09
☐ 15 Ellis Johnson	.75	.35	.09
☐ 16 Hugh Douglas	2.00	.90	.25
☐ 17 Tyrone Wheatley	2.00	.90	.25
☐ 18 Napoleon Kaufman	4.00	1.80	.50
☐ 19 James O. Stewart	4.00	1.80	.50
☐ 20 Luther Ellis	.75	.35	.09
☐ 21 Rashaan Salaam	4.00	1.80	.50
☐ 22 Tyrone Poole	2.00	.90	.25
☐ 23 Ty Law	2.00	.90	.25
☐ 24 Korey Stringer	.75	.35	.09
☐ 25 Billy Milner	.75	.35	.09
☐ 26 Devin Bush	.75	.35	.09
☐ 27 Mark Bruener	2.00	.90	.25
☐ 28 Derrick Brooks	.75	.35	.09
☐ 29 Blake Brockermeyer	2.00	.90	.25
☐ 30 Craig Powell	.75	.35	.09
☐ 31 Trezelle Jenkins	.75	.35	.09
☐ 32 Craig Newsome	.75	.35	.09

1995 Classic NFL Rookies Draft Review

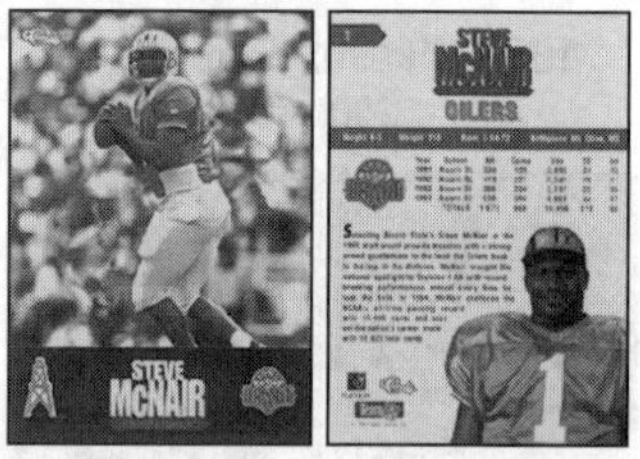

The first fourteen cards of this standard-size set was originally handed out to the media on NFL Draft Day (April 22) but were later reissued at a rate of one per three Classic NFL Rookies Retail rack packs. The original checklist card number 14 was replaced with a card featuring Emmitt Smith and additional eight cards that updated team selections where issued to complete the 22-card set. The original 14-card set also came with a certificate numbered out of 19,995 sets. The fronts feature full-bleed color action photos except at the bottom, where a red foil stripe edges the picture and displays the team logo, player's name and position, and a 1995 NFL Draft emblem. Since a player could be drafted by several different teams, the players are pictured in different pro uniforms. The backs carry biography, complete collegiate statistics, player profile, and a color player cutout.

	MINT	EXC	G-VG
COMPLETE SET (23)	25.00	11.00	3.10
COMMON CARD (1-22)	.25	.11	.03

☐ 1 Steve McNair-Oilers	2.50	1.10	.30
☐ 2 Steve McNair-Vikings	1.00	.45	.12
☐ 3 Steve McNair-Jaguars	1.00	.45	.12
☐ 4 Ki-Jana Carter-Panthers	1.00	.45	.12
☐ 5 Ki-Jana Carter-Jaguars	1.00	.45	.12
☐ 6 Kerry Collins-Bills	1.50	.70	.19
☐ 7 Kerry Collins-Colts	1.50	.70	.19
☐ 8 Kerry Collins-Cardinals	1.50	.70	.19
☐ 9 John Walsh-Panthers	.25	.11	.03
☐ 10 John Walsh-Vikings	.25	.11	.03
☐ 11 John Walsh-Dolphins	.25	.11	.03
☐ 12 J.J. Stokes-Seahawks	.50	.23	.06
☐ 13 J.J. Stokes-Rams	.50	.23	.06
☐ 14 Emmitt Smith	3.00	1.35	.35
☐ 14A Checklist John Walsh Steve McNair Kerry Collins	1.00	.45	.12
☐ 15 Steve Young	1.50	.70	.19
☐ 16 Marshall Faulk	2.00	.90	.25
☐ 17 Troy Aikman	1.50	.70	.19
☐ 18 Ki-Jana Carter-Bengals	1.25	.55	.16
☐ 19 Kerry Collins-Panthers	4.00	1.80	.50
☐ 20 J.J. Stokes-49ers	1.00	.45	.12
☐ 21 Michael Westbrook-Redskins	1.25	.55	.16
☐ 22 Kyle Brady-Jets	.25	.11	.03

1995 Classic NFL Rookies Instant Energy

This 20-card standard-size set was inserted one per rack pack. On a background streaked with lightning, the fronts feature a full-bleed color player photo with a metallic sheen. The player's name and team

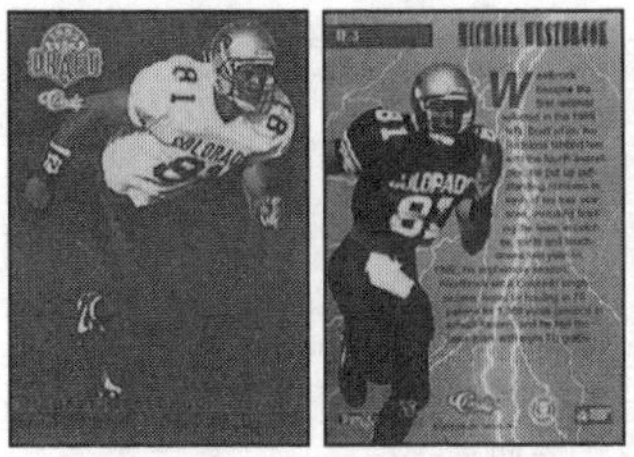

name appear in a silver and black stripe across the bottom. The back carries a color player cutout and a player profile, again on a lightning-streaked background.

	MINT	EXC	G-VG
COMPLETE SET (20)	20.00	9.00	2.50
COMMON CARD (IE1-IE20)	.25	.11	.03
☐ IE1 Ki-Jana Carter	.50	.23	.06
☐ IE2 Steve McNair	2.00	.90	.25
☐ IE3 Michael Westbrook	1.00	.45	.12
☐ IE4 Joey Galloway	1.50	.70	.19
☐ IE5 Tyrone Wheatley	.50	.23	.06
☐ IE6 Napoleon Kaufman	.50	.23	.06
☐ IE7 Warren Sapp	.25	.11	.03
☐ IE8 Kevin Carter	.25	.11	.03
☐ IE9 Todd Collins	.50	.23	.06
☐ IE10 Rob Johnson	.25	.11	.03
☐ IE11 Chad May	.25	.11	.03
☐ IE12 Mike Mamula	.25	.11	.03
☐ IE13 Sherman Williams	.25	.11	.03
☐ IE14 Tony Boselli	.25	.11	.03
☐ IE15 Kerry Collins	3.00	1.35	.35
☐ IE16 J.J. Stokes	.50	.23	.06
☐ IE17 Rashaan Salaam	1.00	.45	.12
☐ IE18 Kordell Stewart	3.00	1.35	.35
☐ IE19 Derrick Brooks	.25	.11	.03
☐ IE20 Frank Sanders	.50	.23	.06

1995 Classic NFL Rookies ROY Redemption

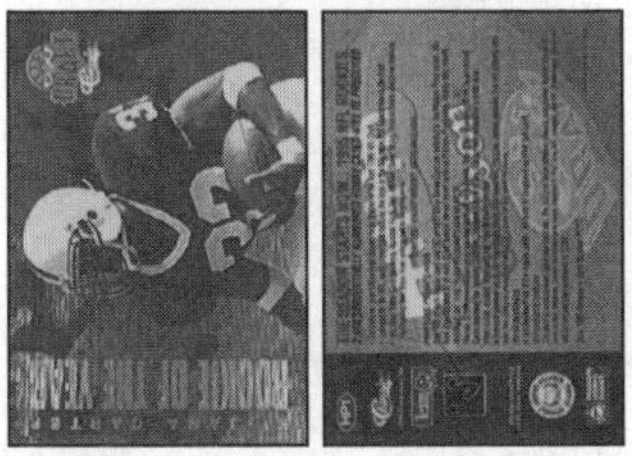

Inserted on average of one card every three boxes, these 20 interactive, holographic cards feature 19 players and one field card. Cards featuring the 1995 Associated Press NFL Offensive Rookie of the Year were redeemable for a 50.00 phone card of the player. The fronts feature a large holographic area and an action photo. Each card is numbered one of 2,500.

	MINT	EXC	G-VG
COMPLETE SET (20)	200.00	90.00	25.00
COMMON CARD (1-20)	2.00	.90	.25
☐ 1 Ki-Jana Carter	6.00	2.70	.75
☐ 2 Tony Boselli	2.00	.90	.25
☐ 3 Steve McNair	12.00	5.50	1.50
☐ 4 Michael Westbrook	6.00	2.70	.75
☐ 5 Kerry Collins	20.00	9.00	2.50
☐ 6 Joey Galloway	10.00	4.50	1.25
☐ 7 Kyle Brady	2.00	.90	.25
☐ 8 J.J. Stokes	15.00	6.75	1.85
☐ 9 Tyrone Wheatley	2.00	.90	.25
☐ 10 Napoleon Kaufman	3.00	1.35	.35
☐ 11 Rashaan Salaam	6.00	2.70	.75
☐ 12 Kordell Stewart	20.00	9.00	2.50
☐ 13 James O. Stewart	5.00	2.20	.60
☐ 14 Frank Sanders	10.00	4.50	1.25
☐ 15 Ray Zellars	2.00	.90	.25
☐ 16 Zack Crockett	2.00	.90	.25
☐ 17 Tamarick Vanover	3.00	1.35	.35
☐ 18 Chad May	2.00	.90	.25
☐ 19 Eric Zeier	2.00	.90	.25
☐ 20 Field Card-C.Martin	2.00	.90	.25
☐ ROY1 Curtis Martin $50 PC	80.00	36.00	10.00

1995 Classic NFL Rookies Rookie Spotlight

This 30-card standard-size set was inserted one per rack pack. The fronts feature a full-bleed color player photo with a metallic sheen. The player's name and position appear in silver foil lettering at the lower right corner. On a background consisting of a blue-tinted action photo, the back carries a player profile, "Spotlight" feature, and a color headshot.

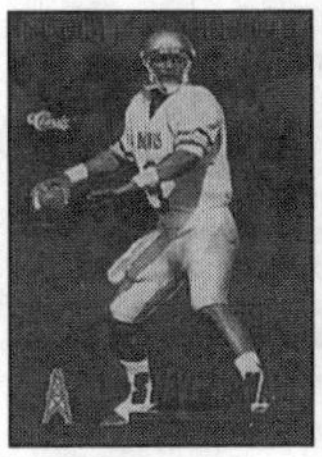

	MINT	EXC	G-VG
COMPLETE SET (30)	20.00	9.00	2.50
COMMON CARD (RS1-RS30)	.25	.11	.03
HOLOGRAPHIC CARDS:5X BASIC CARDS			
☐ RS1 Ki-Jana Carter	1.00	.45	.12
☐ RS2 Steve McNair	2.00	.90	.25
☐ RS3 Michael Westbrook	1.00	.45	.12
☐ RS4 Joey Galloway	1.50	.70	.19
☐ RS5 Tyrone Wheatley	.50	.23	.06
☐ RS6 Napoleon Kaufman	.50	.23	.06
☐ RS7 Kordell Stewart	2.50	1.10	.30
☐ RS8 Frank Sanders	.50	.23	.06
☐ RS9 Zack Crockett	.25	.11	.03
☐ RS10 Tamarick Vanover	.50	.23	.06
☐ RS11 Chad May	.25	.11	.03
☐ RS12 Eric Zeier	.50	.23	.06
☐ RS13 Mike Mamula	.25	.11	.03
☐ RS14 Warren Sapp	.25	.11	.03
☐ RS15 Kevin Carter	.25	.11	.03
☐ RS16 Derrick Brooks	.25	.11	.03
☐ RS17 Todd Collins	.50	.23	.06
☐ RS18 Rob Johnson	.25	.11	.03
☐ RS19 Chris T. Jones	1.00	.45	.12
☐ RS20 Terrell Fletcher	.50	.23	.06
☐ RS21 Sherman Williams	.25	.11	.03
☐ RS22 Tony Boselli	.25	.11	.03
☐ RS23 Kerry Collins	3.00	1.35	.35
☐ RS24 J.J. Stokes	.50	.23	.06
☐ RS25 Rashaan Salaam	1.00	.45	.12
☐ RS26 James O. Stewart	.50	.23	.06
☐ RS27 Rodney Thomas	.50	.23	.06
☐ RS28 Jack Jackson	.25	.11	.03
☐ RS29 Lovell Pinkney	.25	.11	.03
☐ RS30 Ruben Brown	.25	.11	.03

1996 Classic NFL Draft Day

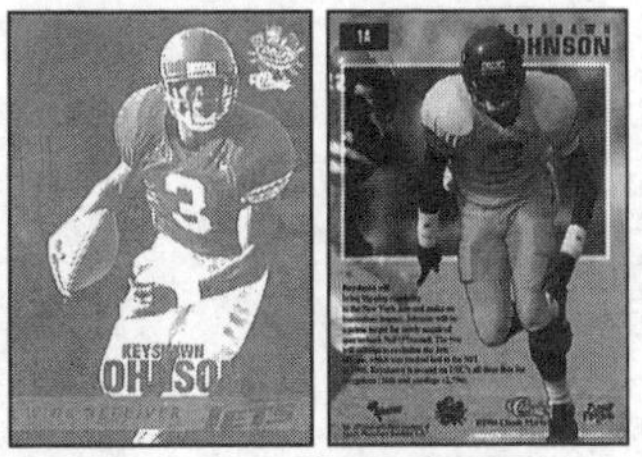

This 15-card set was distributed at the 1996 NFL Draft in New York. It was designed to match the top picks with the team that selected them; therefore three players appear with three different team options. NFL veterans and the previous Heisman Award winner are also included. Each set came with a certificate of authenticity numbered of 9,996.

	MINT	NRMT	EXC
COMPLETE SET (15)	30.00	13.50	3.70
COMMON CARD (1-9)	1.00	.45	.12
☐ 1A Keyshawn Johnson Jets	1.50	.70	.19
☐ 1B Keyshawn Johnson Jaguars	1.50	.70	.19
☐ 1C Keyshawn Johnson Redskins	1.50	.70	.19
☐ 2A Kevin Hardy Jaguars	1.00	.45	.12
☐ 2B Kevin Hardy Redskins	1.00	.45	.12
☐ 2C Kevin Hardy Cardinals	1.00	.45	.12
☐ 3A Terry Glenn Patriots	3.00	1.35	.35
☐ 3B Terry Glenn Giants	3.00	1.35	.35
☐ 3C Terry Glenn Jets	3.00	1.35	.35
☐ 4 Eddie George	4.00	1.80	.50
☐ 5 Emmitt Smith	4.00	1.80	.50
☐ 6 Troy Aikman	2.50	1.10	.30
☐ 7 Drew Bledsoe	2.50	1.10	.30
☐ 8 Kerry Collins	2.50	1.10	.30
☐ 9 Title Card Checklist Back	1.00	.45	.12

1996 Classic NFL Rookies

The 1996 Classic NFL Rookies set was issued in one series totaling 100 standard-size cards. The set was issued in 10-card packs with 36 packs in a box and 12 boxes in a case. Among the topical subsets are: All-Americans (65-74), NFL Greats (75-79) and Checklists (99-100). There is also a gold parallel set that was issued one per special retail jumbo pack. The key players in this set are Terry Glenn, Keyshawn Johnson and Lawrence Phillips.

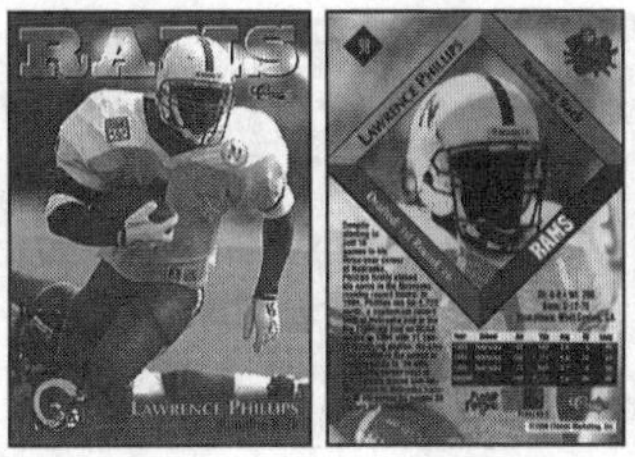

	MINT	NRMT	EXC
COMPLETE SET (100)	10.00	4.50	1.25
COMMON CARD (1-100)	.05	.02	.01
☐ 1 Keyshawn Johnson	1.00	.45	.12
☐ 2 Jonathan Ogden	.05	.02	.01
☐ 3 Kevin Hardy	.25	.11	.03
☐ 4 Leeland McElroy	.50	.23	.06
☐ 5 Terry Glenn	2.50	1.10	.30
☐ 6 Tim Biakabutuka	.50	.23	.06
☐ 7 Tony Brackens	.25	.11	.03
☐ 8 Duane Clemons	.20	.09	.03
☐ 9 Willie Anderson	.05	.02	.01
☐ 10 Karim Abdul-Jabbar	1.50	.70	.19
☐ 11 Daryl Gardener	.20	.09	.03
☐ 12 Simeon Rice	.20	.09	.03
☐ 13 Eddie George	2.50	1.10	.30
☐ 14 Andre Johnson	.05	.02	.01
☐ 15 Jon Runyan	.05	.02	.01
☐ 16 Jevon Langford	.05	.02	.01
☐ 17 Derrick Mayes	.60	.25	.07
☐ 18 Stephen Davis	.50	.23	.06
☐ 19 Ray Farmer	.05	.02	.01
☐ 20 Chris Doering	.05	.02	.01
☐ 21 Jimmy Herndon	.05	.02	.01
☐ 22 Jerome Woods	.05	.02	.01
☐ 23 Scott Greene	.05	.02	.01
☐ 24 Jamain Stephens	.05	.02	.01
☐ 25 Tommie Frazier	.75	.35	.09
☐ 26 Dusty Zeigler	.05	.02	.01
☐ 27 Alex Molden	.05	.02	.01
☐ 28 Dietrich Jells	.05	.02	.01
☐ 29 Brian Roche	.05	.02	.01
☐ 30 Danny Kanell	.25	.11	.03
☐ 31 Roman Oben	.05	.02	.01
☐ 32 Chris Darkins	.05	.02	.01
☐ 33 Christian Peter	.05	.02	.01
☐ 34 Jeff Hartings	.05	.02	.01
☐ 35 Bobby Hoying	.05	.02	.01
☐ 36 Steve Taneyhill	.05	.02	.01
☐ 37 Lance Johnstone	.05	.02	.01
☐ 38 Zach Thomas	.50	.23	.06
☐ 39 Donnie Edwards	.05	.02	.01
☐ 40 Eric Moulds	.25	.11	.03
☐ 41 Amani Toomer	.25	.11	.03
☐ 42 Scott Slutzker	.05	.02	.01
☐ 43 Matt Stevens	.05	.02	.01
☐ 44 Randall Godfrey	.05	.02	.01
☐ 45 Orpheus Roye	.05	.02	.01
☐ 46 Jason Odom	.05	.02	.01
☐ 47 Je'Rod Cherry	.05	.02	.01
☐ 48 Jeff Lewis	.05	.02	.01
☐ 49 Mike Alstott	.25	.11	.03
☐ 50 Tony Banks	1.25	.55	.16
☐ 51 Stepfret Williams	.05	.02	.01
☐ 52 Michael Cheever	.05	.02	.01
☐ 53 Bryant Mix	.05	.02	.01
☐ 54 James Ritchey	.05	.02	.01
☐ 55 Marcus Coleman	.25	.11	.03
☐ 56 Sedric Clark	.05	.02	.01
☐ 57 Kyle Wachholtz	.05	.02	.01
☐ 58 Johnny McWilliams	.05	.02	.01
☐ 59 Lawyer Milloy	.05	.02	.01
☐ 60 Alex Van Dyke	.25	.11	.03
☐ 61 Stanley Pritchett	.25	.11	.03
☐ 62 Ray Mickens	.05	.02	.01
☐ 63 Toraino Singleton	.05	.02	.01
☐ 64 Richard Huntley	.05	.02	.01
☐ 65 Eddie George AA	1.25	.55	.16
☐ 66 Terry Glenn AA	1.25	.55	.16
☐ 67 Keyshawn Johnson AA	.50	.23	.06
☐ 68 Jonathan Ogden AA	.05	.02	.01
☐ 69 Tommie Frazier AA	.50	.23	.06
☐ 70 Kevin Hardy AA	.25	.11	.03
☐ 71 Zach Thomas AA	.25	.11	.03
☐ 72 Tony Brackens AA	.05	.02	.01
☐ 73 Lawyer Milloy AA	.05	.02	.01
☐ 74 Leeland McElroy AA	.25	.11	.03
☐ 75 Emmitt Smith	.75	.35	.09
☐ 76 Steve McNair	.50	.23	.06
☐ 77 Kerry Collins	.50	.23	.06
☐ 78 Drew Bledsoe	.50	.23	.06
☐ 79 Marshall Faulk	.50	.23	.06
☐ 80 Pete Kendall	.05	.02	.01
☐ 81 Regan Upshaw	.20	.09	.03
☐ 82 Mercury Hayes	.05	.02	.01
☐ 83 Dou Innocent	.05	.02	.01
☐ 84 DeRon Jenkins	.05	.02	.01
☐ 85 Marco Battaglia	.05	.02	.01
☐ 86 John Mobley	.05	.02	.01
☐ 87 Cedric Jones	.05	.02	.01
☐ 88 Marvin Harrison	1.00	.45	.12
☐ 89 Israel Ifeanyl	.05	.02	.01
☐ 90 Reggie Brown	.05	.02	.01
☐ 91 Jermane Mayberry	.05	.02	.01
☐ 92 Brian Dawkins	.05	.02	.01
☐ 93 Tady Bruschi	.05	.02	.01
☐ 94 Terrell Owens	1.00	.45	.12
☐ 95 Jermaine Lewis	.05	.02	.01
☐ 96 Sean Boyd	.05	.02	.01
☐ 97 Phillip Daniels	.05	.02	.01
☐ 98 Lawrence Phillips	.50	.23	.06
☐ 99 Keyshawn Johnson CL	.25	.11	.03
☐ 100 Terry Glenn CL	1.00	.45	.12
☐ P1 Keyshawn Johnson Promo	3.00	1.35	.35

1996 Classic NFL Rookie Die Cuts

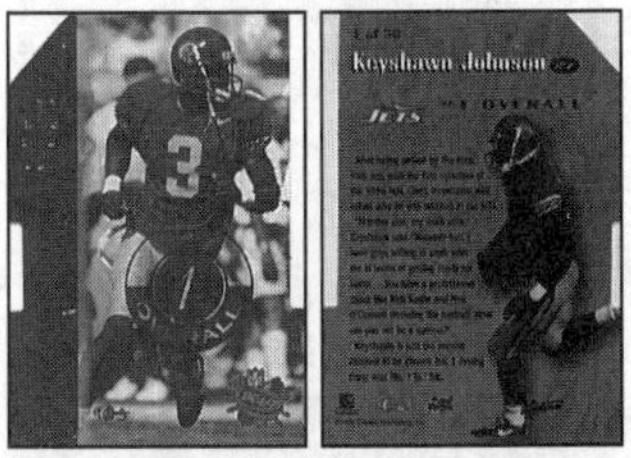

Randomly inserted in retail packs, these cards feature the players drafted in the first round of the 1996 NFL draft. The set is sequenced in draft order and the cards are numbered as "X" of 30.

	MINT	NRMT	EXC
COMPLETE SET (30)	350.00	160.00	45.00
COMMON CARD (1-30)	6.00	2.70	.75
☐ 1 Keyshawn Johnson	30.00	13.50	3.70
☐ 2 Kevin Hardy	10.00	4.50	1.25
☐ 3 Simeon Rice	10.00	4.50	1.25
☐ 4 Jonathan Ogden	10.00	4.50	1.25
☐ 5 Cedric Jones	6.00	2.70	.75
☐ 6 Lawrence Phillips	20.00	9.00	2.50
☐ 7 Terry Glenn	70.00	32.00	8.75
☐ 8 Tim Biakabutuka	20.00	9.00	2.50
☐ 9 Emmitt Smith	50.00	22.00	6.25
☐ 10 Willie Anderson	10.00	4.50	1.25
☐ 11 Alex Molden	6.00	2.70	.75
☐ 12 Regan Upshaw	6.00	2.70	.75
☐ 13 Kerry Collins	20.00	9.00	2.50
☐ 14 Eddie George	70.00	32.00	8.75
☐ 15 John Mobley	6.00	2.70	.75
☐ 16 Duane Clemons	6.00	2.70	.75
☐ 17 Reggie Brown	6.00	2.70	.75
☐ 18 Marshall Faulk	20.00	9.00	2.50
☐ 19 Marvin Harrison	30.00	13.50	3.70
☐ 20 Daryl Gardener	10.00	4.50	1.25
☐ 21 Pete Kendall	6.00	2.70	.75
☐ 22 Joey Galloway	20.00	9.00	2.50
☐ 23 Jeff Hartings	6.00	2.70	.75
☐ 24 Eric Moulds	10.00	4.50	1.25
☐ 25 Jermaine Mayberry	6.00	2.70	.75
☐ 26 Steve McNair	20.00	9.00	2.50
☐ 27 Kyle Brady	6.00	2.70	.75
☐ 28 Jerome Woods	6.00	2.70	.75
☐ 29 Jamain Stephens	6.00	2.70	.75
☐ 30 Andre Johnson	6.00	2.70	.75

1996 Classic NFL Rookies NFL Home/Road Jerseys

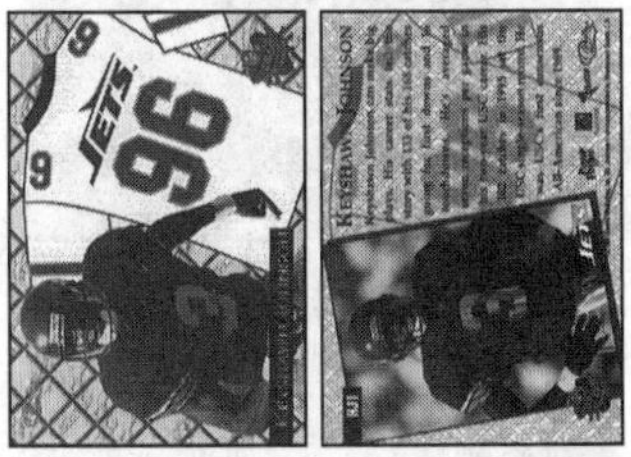

Randomly inserted in packs at a rate of one in 15, this 30-card horizontal insert set features some leading 1996 NFL Rookies as well as using a "mesh" type emboss to give the feel and look of the drafted player's offical jersey. The Road Jerseys are exclusive to hobby packs and Home Jerseys are exclusive to retail packs.

	MINT	NRMT	EXC
COMPLETE SET (30)	80.00	36.00	10.00
COMMON CARD (1-30)	1.25	.55	.16
☐ 1 Keyshawn Johnson	10.00	4.50	1.25
☐ 2 Kevin Hardy	2.00	.90	.25
☐ 3 Jonathan Ogden	1.25	.55	.16
☐ 4 Terry Glenn	20.00	9.00	2.50
☐ 5 Tim Biakabutuka	12.00	5.50	1.50
☐ 6 Karim Abdul-Jabbar	12.00	5.50	1.50
☐ 7 Simeon Rice	4.00	1.80	.50
☐ 8 Eric Moulds	6.00	2.70	.75

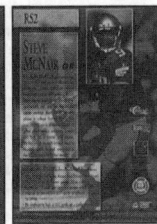

□ 9 Mike Alstott	6.00	2.70	.75
□ 10 Leeland McElroy	6.00	2.70	.75
□ 11 Daryl Gardener	4.00	1.80	.50
□ 12 Eddie George	20.00	9.00	2.50
□ 13 Amani Toomer	4.00	1.80	.50
□ 14H Johnny McWilliams	6.00	2.70	.75
□ 14R Marvin Harrison	10.00	4.50	1.25
□ 15 Derrick Mayes	4.00	1.80	.50
□ 16H Duane Clemons	1.25	.55	.16
□ 16R Dietrich Jells	1.25	.55	.16
□ 17 Chris Darkins	4.00	1.80	.50
□ 18 Ray Farmer	1.25	.55	.16
□ 19 Danny Kanell	4.00	1.80	.50
□ 20 Bobby Hoying	4.00	1.80	.50
□ 21 Zach Thomas	4.00	1.80	.50
□ 22H Tony Banks	10.00	4.50	1.25
□ 22R Kyle Wachholtz	1.25	.55	.16
□ 23 Alex Van Dyke	4.00	1.80	.50
□ 24 Stepfret Williams	1.25	.55	.16
□ 25 Chris Doering	1.25	.55	.16
□ 26 Lance Johnstone	1.25	.55	.16
□ 27 Stephen Davis	4.00	1.80	.50
□ 28 Scott Greene	1.25	.55	.16
□ 29 Tony Brackens	4.00	1.80	.50
□ 30 Jevon Langford	1.25	.55	.16

1996 Classic NFL Rookies Rookie Lasers

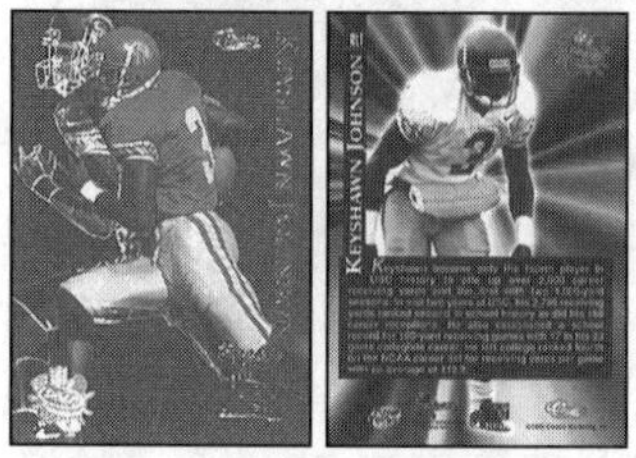

Randomly inserted in hobby packs only at a rate of one in 100, this 10-card insert standard-size set features the most explosive first-year players. The cards feature a dual player image, the words "Rookie Lasers" in the lower right and the player's name on the right. The cards are numbered with an "RL" prefix.

	MINT	NRMT	EXC
COMPLETE SET (10)	325.00	145.00	40.00
COMMON CARD (RL1-RL10)	8.00	3.60	1.00
STATED ODDS 1:100 HOBBY			
□ RL1 Keyshawn Johnson	40.00	18.00	5.00
□ RL2 Jonathan Ogden	8.00	3.60	1.00
□ RL3 Eddie George	80.00	36.00	10.00
□ RL4 Terry Glenn	80.00	36.00	10.00
□ RL5 Tommy Frazier	30.00	13.50	3.70
□ RL6 Karim Abdul-Jabbar	60.00	27.00	7.50
□ RL7 Duane Clemons	8.00	3.60	1.00
□ RL8 Leeland McElroy	40.00	18.00	5.00
□ RL9 Tim Biakabutuka	60.00	27.00	7.50
□ RL10 Kevin Hardy	12.00	5.50	1.50

1996 Classic NFL Rookies ROY Contenders

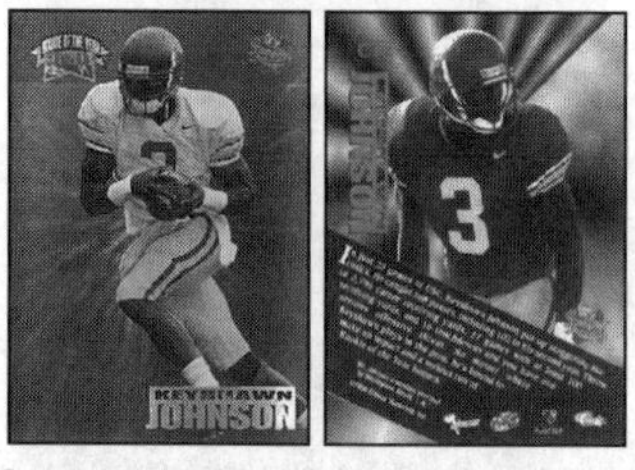
KEYSHAWN JOHNSON

Randomly inserted in retail packs, these cards feature 10 players expected to be strong candidates for NFL Offensive Rookie of the Year honors. The cards are numbered with a "C" prefix.

	MINT	NRMT	EXC
COMPLETE SET (10)	70.00	32.00	8.75
COMMON CARD (C1-C10)	1.50	.70	.19
□ C1 Keyshawn Johnson	10.00	4.50	1.25
□ C2 Jonathan Ogden	1.50	.70	.19
□ C3 Eddie George	20.00	9.00	2.50
□ C4 Terry Glenn	20.00	9.00	2.50
□ C5 Eric Moulds	6.00	2.70	.75
□ C6 Karim Abdul-Jabbar	12.00	5.50	1.50
□ C7 Leeland McElroy	10.00	4.50	1.25
□ C8 Tim Biakabutuka	5.00	2.20	.60
□ C9 Bobby Hoying	6.00	2.70	.75
□ C10 Stephen Davis	5.00	2.20	.60

1996 Classic NFL Rookies ROY Interactive

Randomly inserted in packs at a rate of one in 35, this 20-card insert standard-size set features the top candidates eligible to win the AP

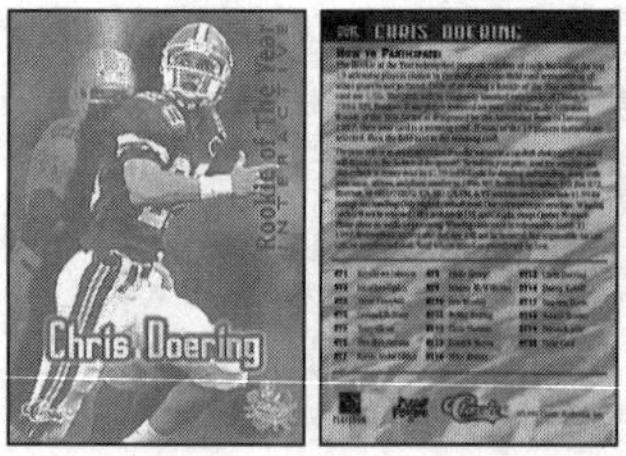
Chris Doering

NFL Offensive Rookie of the Year award. If the player on your card wins the award, you win too. Winning cards can be redeemed for an autographed collectible. The winning cards were to be redeemed by March 31, 1997 and the winning cards were not returned after being redeemed. The cards are numbered with an "RY" prefix.

	MINT	NRMT	EXC
COMPLETE SET (20)	100.00	45.00	12.50
COMMON CARD (RY1-RY20)	2.50	1.10	.30
□ RY1 Keyshawn Johnson	10.00	4.50	1.25
□ RY2 Jonathan Ogden	2.50	1.10	.30
□ RY3 Steve Taneyhill	2.50	1.10	.30
□ RY4 Leeland McElroy	6.00	2.70	.75
□ RY5 Terry Glenn	20.00	9.00	2.50
□ RY6 Tim Biakabutuka	6.00	2.70	.75
□ RY7 Karim Abdul-Jabbar	12.00	5.50	1.50
□ RY8 Eddie George	25.00	11.00	3.10
□ RY9 Johnny McWilliams	2.50	1.10	.30
□ RY10 Eric Moulds	8.00	3.60	1.00
□ RY11 Bobby Hoying	8.00	3.60	1.00
□ RY12 Chris Darkins	6.00	2.70	.75
□ RY13 Derrick Mayes	8.00	3.60	1.00
□ RY14 Mike Alstott	6.00	2.70	.75
□ RY15 Chris Doering	2.50	1.10	.30
□ RY16 Danny Kanell	8.00	3.60	1.00
□ RY17 Stephen Davis	6.00	2.70	.75
□ RY18 Amani Toomer	8.00	3.60	1.00
□ RY19 Dietrich Jells	2.50	1.10	.30
□ RY20 Field Card	12.00	5.50	1.50

1992 Courtside Promos

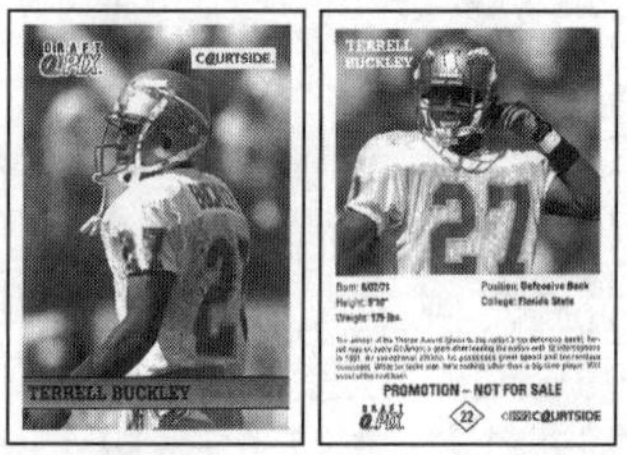
TERRELL BUCKLEY
PROMOTION – NOT FOR SALE

The 1992 Courtside Draft Pix Promo set contains eight player cards. These promos are sometimes found with red overprint stamps on the back commemorating the show where they were available as give-aways. The style of these promo cards is very similar to that of the 1992 Courtside regular issue cards. All these promo cards are marked on the back clearly with "Promotion Not For Sale". Two number 20's were issued. The cards are standard-size and feature glossy color action photos bordered in white.

	MINT	NRMT	EXC
COMPLETE SET (8)	5.00	2.20	.60
COMMON CARD	.25	.11	.03
□ 20A Tony Brooks	.25	.11	.03
□ 20B Amp Lee	.25	.11	.03
□ 22 Terrell Buckley	.50	.23	.06
□ 30 Tommy Vardell	.50	.23	.06
□ 40 Carl Pickens	2.50	1.10	.30
□ 44 Quentin Coryatt	.50	.23	.06
□ 50 Mike Gaddis	.25	.11	.03
□ 60 Steve Emtman (No statistics or bio on card back)	.50	.23	.06

1992 Courtside

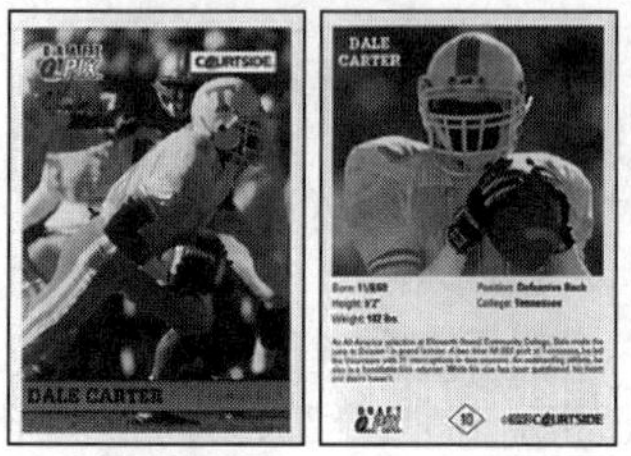
DALE CARTER

The 1992 Courtside Draft Pix football set contains 140 player cards. Ten short printed insert cards (five Award Winner and five All-America) were randomly inserted in the foil packs. This set also includes a foilgram card featuring Steve Emtman. Fifty thousand foilgram cards were printed, and collectors could receive one by sending in ten foil pack wrappers. Moreover, one set of foilgram cards and 20 free promo cards were offered to dealers for each case order. It has been reported that the production run was limited to 7,500 numbered cases, and that no factory sets were issued. Gold, silver, and bronze foil versions of the regular cards were randomly inserted within the foil cases in quantities of 1,000, 2,000, and 3,000 respectively. Reportedly more than 70,000 autographed cards were also inserted. The standard-size cards feature on the fronts glossy color action photos bordered in white (some of the cards are oriented horizontally). The player's name and position appear in a gold stripe cutting across the bottom. On the backs, the upper half has a color close-up photo, with biography and collegiate statistics below. Key cards include Quentin Coryatt, Amp Lee, Johnny Mitchell, Carl Pickens and Tommy Vardell.

	MINT	EXC	G-VG
COMPLETE SET (140)	6.00	2.70	.75
COMMON CARD (1-140)	.05	.02	.01
STAR AUTOGRAPHS 15X TO 30X BASIC CARDS			
□ 1 Steve Emtman	.25	.11	.03
□ 2 Quentin Coryatt	.25	.11	.03
□ 3 Ken Swilling	.05	.02	.01
□ 4 Jay Leeuwenburg	.05	.02	.01
□ 5 Mazio Royster	.05	.02	.01
□ 6 Matt Veatch	.05	.02	.01
□ 7A Scott Lockwood ERR (No career totals)	.05	.02	.01
□ 7B Scott Lockwood COR	.05	.02	.01
□ 8 Todd Collins	.25	.11	.03
□ 9 Gene McGuire	.05	.02	.01
□ 10 Dale Carter	.25	.11	.03
□ 11 Michael Bankston	.25	.11	.03
□ 12 Jeremy Lincoln	.05	.02	.01
□ 13A Troy Auzenne ERR (Misspelled Auzene)	.05	.02	.01
□ 13B Troy Auzenne COR	.05	.02	.01
□ 14 Rod Smith	.25	.11	.03
□ 15 Andy Kelly	.05	.02	.01
□ 16 Chris Holder	.05	.02	.01
□ 17 Rico Smith	.05	.02	.01
□ 18 Chris Pedersen	.05	.02	.01
□ 19 Brian Treggs	.05	.02	.01
□ 20 Eugene Chung	.05	.02	.01
□ 21 Joel Steed	.05	.02	.01
□ 22 Ricardo McDonald	.05	.02	.01
□ 23 Nate Turner	.05	.02	.01
□ 24 Sean Lumpkin	.05	.02	.01
□ 25 Ty Detmer	.50	.23	.06
□ 26 Matt Darby	.05	.02	.01
□ 27 Michael Warfield	.05	.02	.01
□ 28 Tracy Scroggins	.05	.02	.01
□ 29 Carl Pickens	1.50	.70	.19
□ 30 Chris Mims	.25	.11	.03
□ 31 Mark D'Onofrio	.05	.02	.01
□ 32 Dwight Hollier	.05	.02	.01
□ 33 Siupeli Malamala	.05	.02	.01
□ 34A Mark Barsotti ERR (Back stats jumbled with no career totals)	.05	.02	.01
□ 34B Mark Barsotti COR	.05	.02	.01
□ 35 Charles Davenport	.05	.02	.01
□ 36 Brian Bollinger	.05	.02	.01
□ 37 Willie McClendon	.05	.02	.01
□ 38 Calvin Holmes	.05	.02	.01
□ 39 Phillippi Sparks	.25	.11	.03
□ 40 Darryl Williams	.05	.02	.01
□ 41 Greg Skrepenak	.25	.11	.03
□ 42 Larry Webster	.05	.02	.01
□ 43 Dion Lambert	.05	.02	.01
□ 44 Sam Gash	.25	.11	.03
□ 45 Patrick Rowe	.05	.02	.01
□ 46 Scottie Graham	.25	.11	.03
□ 47 Darian Hagan	.05	.02	.01
□ 48 Arthur Marshall	.25	.11	.03
□ 49 Amp Lee	.05	.02	.01
□ 50 Tommy Vardell	.25	.11	.03
□ 51 Robert Porcher	.25	.11	.03
□ 52 Reggie Dwight	.05	.02	.01
□ 53 Torrance Small	.25	.11	.03
□ 54 Ronnie West	.05	.02	.01
□ 55 Tony Brooks	.05	.02	.01
□ 56 Anthony McDowell	.05	.02	.01
□ 57 Chris Hakel	.05	.02	.01
□ 58 Ed Cunningham	.05	.02	.01
□ 59 Ashley Ambrose	.25	.11	.03
□ 60 Alonzo Spellman	.25	.11	.03
□ 61 Harold Heath	.05	.02	.01
□ 62 Ron Lopez	.05	.02	.01
□ 63 Bill Johnson	.05	.02	.01
□ 64 Kent Graham	.25	.11	.03
□ 65 Aaron Pierce	.05	.02	.01
□ 66 Bucky Richardson	.25	.11	.03
□ 67A Todd Kinchen ERR (Long reception for '91 is on a different line)	.05	.02	.01
□ 67B Todd Kinchen COR	.05	.02	.01
□ 68 Ken Ealy	.05	.02	.01
□ 69 Carlos Snow	.05	.02	.01
□ 70 Dana Hall	.25	.11	.03
□ 71 Matt Rodgers	.05	.02	.01
□ 72 Howard Dinkins	.05	.02	.01
□ 73 Tim Lester	.05	.02	.01
□ 74 Mark Chmura	.50	.23	.06
□ 75 Johnny Mitchell	.25	.11	.03
□ 76 Mirko Jurkovic	.05	.02	.01
□ 77 Anthony Lynn	.05	.02	.01
□ 78 Roosevelt Potts	.25	.11	.03
□ 79 Tony Sands	.05	.02	.01
□ 80 Kevin Smith	.25	.11	.03
□ 81 Tony Brown	.05	.02	.01
□ 82 Bobby Fuller	.05	.02	.01
□ 83 Darryl Ashmore	.05	.02	.01
□ 84 Tyrone Legette	.05	.02	.01
□ 85 Mike Gaddis	.05	.02	.01
□ 86A Cal Dixon ERR (Should be number 101)	.05	.02	.01
□ 86B Gerald Dixon COR	.05	.02	.01
□ 87 T.J. Rubley	.25	.11	.03
□ 88 Mark Thomas	.05	.02	.01
□ 89 Corey Widmer	.25	.11	.03
□ 90 Robert Jones	.25	.11	.03
□ 91 Eddie Robinson	.25	.11	.03
□ 92 Rob Tomlinson	.05	.02	.01
□ 93 Russ Campbell	.05	.02	.01
□ 94 Keith Goganious	.25	.11	.03
□ 95 Rod Moore	.05	.02	.01
□ 96 Jerry Ostroski	.05	.02	.01
□ 97 Tyji Armstrong	.05	.02	.01
□ 98 Ronald Humphrey	.05	.02	.01
□ 99 Corey Harris	.05	.02	.01
□ 100 Terrell Buckley	.25	.11	.03
□ 101 Cal Dixon (See card number 86A)	.05	.02	.01
□ 102 Tyrone Williams	.05	.02	.01
□ 103 Joe Bowden	.05	.02	.01
□ 104 Santana Dotson	.25	.11	.03
□ 105 Jeff Blake	1.50	.70	.19
□ 106 Erick Anderson	.05	.02	.01
□ 107 Steve Israel	.05	.02	.01
□ 108 Chad Roghair	.05	.02	.01
□ 109 Todd Harrison	.05	.02	.01
□ 110 Chester McGlockton	.25	.11	.03
□ 111 Marquez Pope	.25	.11	.03
□ 112 George Rooks	.05	.02	.01
□ 113 Dion Johnson	.05	.02	.01
□ 114 Tim Simpson	.05	.02	.01
□ 115 Chris Walsh	.05	.02	.01
□ 116 Marc Boutte	.05	.02	.01
□ 117 Jamie Gill	.05	.02	.01
□ 118 Willie Clay	.25	.11	.03
□ 119 Tim Paulk	.05	.02	.01
□ 120 Ray Roberts	.05	.02	.01
□ 121 Jeff Thomason	.05	.02	.01
□ 122 Leodis Flowers	.05	.02	.01
□ 123 Robert Brooks	1.00	.45	.12
□ 124 Jeff Ellis	.05	.02	.01
□ 125 John Fina	.05	.02	.01
□ 126A Michael Smith ERR (Back stats jumbled with no career totals)	.05	.02	.01
□ 126B Michael Smith COR	.05	.02	.01
□ 127 Mike Saunders	.50	.23	.06
□ 128 John Brown III	.05	.02	.01
□ 129 Reggie Yarbrough	.05	.02	.01
□ 130 Leon Searcy	.25	.11	.03
□ 131 Marcus Woods	.05	.02	.01
□ 132 Shane Collins	.25	.11	.03
□ 133 Chuck Smith	.05	.02	.01
□ 134 Keith Hamilton	.25	.11	.03
□ 135 Rodney Blackshear	.05	.02	.01
□ 136 Corey Barlow	.05	.02	.01
□ 137 Robert Harris	.05	.02	.01
□ 138 Tony Smith	.25	.11	.03
□ 139 Checklist 1 (Some have 139 Auzenne spelled Auzene)	.05	.02	.01
□ 140 Checklist 2	.05	.02	.01

1992 Courtside Foilgrams

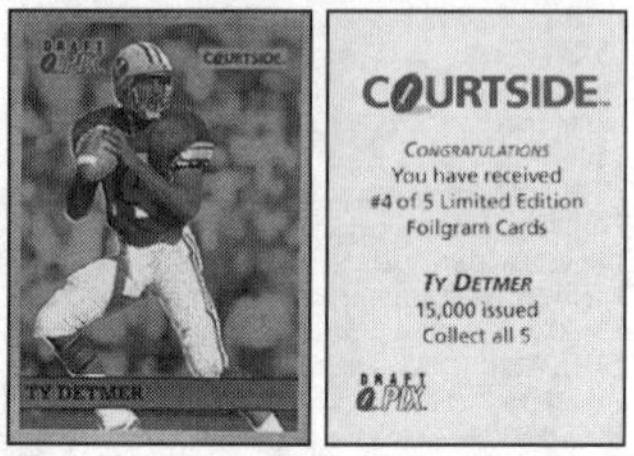
TY DETMER
COURTSIDE
Congratulations
You have received
#4 of 5 Limited Edition
Foilgram Cards
Ty Detmer
15,000 issued
Collect all 5

These five special foilgram standard-size cards were redeemable by mail via a wrapper offer. They feature some leading prospects of the 1992 draft.

	MINT	NRMT	EXC
COMPLETE SET (5)	4.00	1.80	.50
COMMON CARD (1-5)	.75	.35	.09
□ 1 Steve Emtman	.75	.35	.09
□ 2 Tommy Vardell	.75	.35	.09
□ 3 Terrell Buckley	.75	.35	.09
□ 4 Ty Detmer	1.50	.70	.19
□ 5 Amp Lee	.75	.35	.09

1992 Courtside Inserts

These ten special insert cards were included as random inserts within foil cases of 1992 Courtside Draft Pix football. They consist of five Award Winners and five All-America cards. The fronts of these standard-size cards have glossy color action photos enclosed by

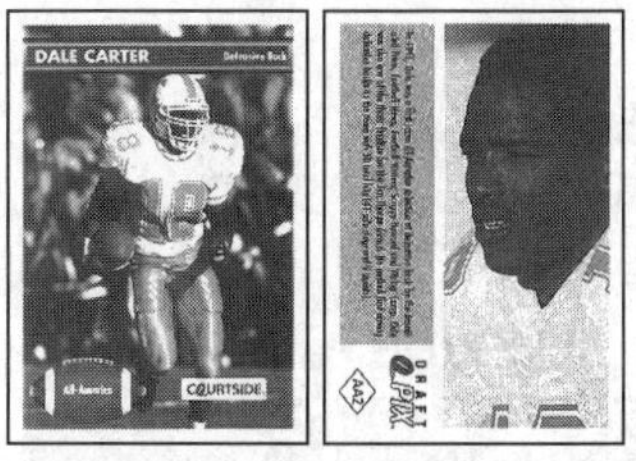

white borders. The player's name and position appear in a stripe that cuts across the top of the picture; a football icon with the words "All-America" or the award won appears in the lower left corner. The backs have a close-up player photo, with player profile printed on a color box alongside the picture.

	MINT	EXC	G-VG
COMPLETE SET (10)	10.00	4.50	1.25
COMMON CARD	.50	.23	.06
☐ AA1 Carl Pickens	3.00	1.35	.35
☐ AA2 Dale Carter	.75	.35	.09
☐ AA3 Tommy Vardell	.75	.35	.09
☐ AA4 Amp Lee	.50	.23	.06
☐ AA5 Leon Searcy	.50	.23	.06
☐ AW1 Steve Emtman	.50	.23	.06
☐ AW2 Ty Detmer/Heisman	1.50	.70	.19
☐ AW3 Steve Emtman	.50	.23	.06
☐ AW4 Terrell Buckley	.50	.23	.06
☐ AW5 Erick Anderson	.50	.23	.06

1993 Courtside Sean Dawkins

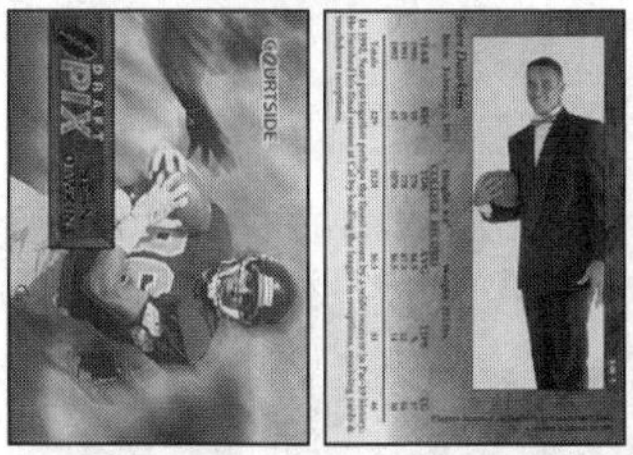

Sean Dawkins, who was drafted in the first round by the Indianapolis Colts, is showcased in this five-card, standard-size set. Only 20,000 sets of each player were produced, and Dawkins personally autographed 5,000 cards for random insertion within the sets. The fronts display full-bleed glossy action photos, with the backgrounds blurred to highlight the player. Each card has a color bar carrying a gold foil football icon, the words "Draft Pix," and the player's name in gold foil lettering. On a background reflecting the same color as the front bar, the backs have a second color action photo and either biography, statistics, player profile, or highlights. The complete set price below is a sealed price since it is not known if there is an autograph sealed inside. Card number 3 was also issued as a promo which was identical to the regular issue, except that the disclaimer "Promotional Not for Sale" is stamped on the front in a circular format, and the words "Authentic Signature" are printed in silver lettering toward the bottom of the front.

	MINT	NRMT	EXC
COMPLETE SET (5)	5.00	2.20	.60
COMMON CARD (1-5)	1.00	.45	.12
☐ 1 Sean Dawkins (Ball cradled in right arm; running up field)	1.00	.45	.12
☐ 2 Sean Dawkins (Hands outstretched to catch ball)	1.00	.45	.12
☐ 3 Sean Dawkins (Being handchecked by cornerback)	1.00	.45	.12
☐ 4 Sean Dawkins (Kneeling pose)	1.00	.45	.12
☐ 5 Sean Dawkins (Dressed in tuxedo)	1.00	.45	.12
☐ AU1 Sean Dawkins AU/5000 (Certified autograph)	12.00	5.50	1.50

1993 Courtside Russell White

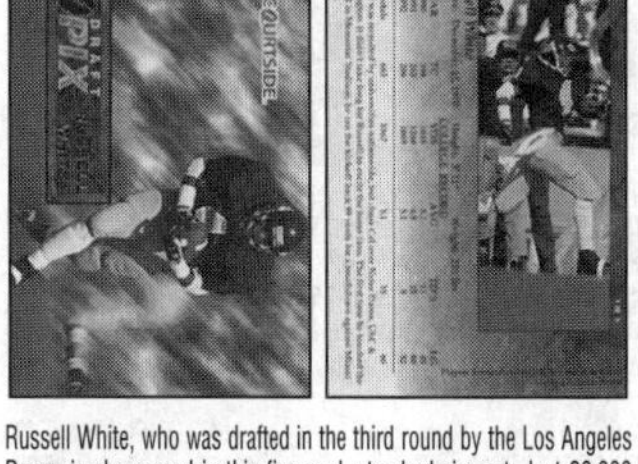

Russell White, who was drafted in the third round by the Los Angeles Rams, is showcased in this five-card, standard-size set. Just 20,000 sets of each player were produced, and White personally autographed 5,000 cards for random insertion within the sets. The fronts display full-bleed glossy action photos, with the backgrounds blurred to highlight the player. Each card has a color bar carrying a gold foil football icon, the words "Draft Pix," and the player's name in gold foil lettering. On a background reflecting the same color as the front bar, the backs have a second color action photo and either biography, statistics, player profile, or highlights. The complete set price below is a sealed price since it is not known if there is an autograph sealed inside. Card numbers 3-5 were also issued as promos. They are identical to their regular issues, except that the disclaimer "Promotional Not for Sale" is stamped on their fronts in a circular format, and the words "Authentic Signature" are printed in silver lettering toward the bottom of the front.

	MINT	NRMT	EXC
COMPLETE SET (5)	2.50	1.10	.30
COMMON CARD (1-5)	.50	.23	.06
☐ 1 Russell White (Running almost straight ahead)	.50	.23	.06
☐ 2 Russell White (Running toward the right)	.50	.23	.06
☐ 3 Russell White (Running toward defensive player number 78)	.50	.23	.06
☐ 4 Russell White (Running upfield; side view)	.50	.23	.06
☐ 5 Russell White (Dressed in tuxedo)	.50	.23	.06
☐ AU1 Russell White AU/5000 (Certified autograph)	5.00	2.20	.60

1996 Press Pass

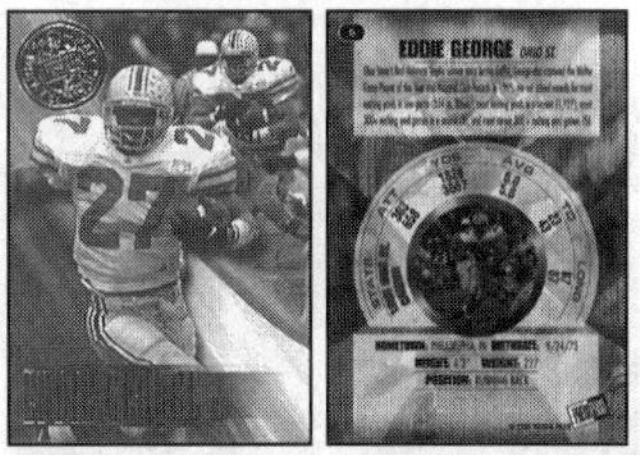

The Press Pass set was issued in one series totalling 55 standard-size cards. The set was issued in three card packs. The fronts have two photos as well as the player's name and position on the bottom. The '96 Press Pass Draft Pick' logo is in the upper left. The backs include vital statistics, statistical information and some career information.

	MINT	NRMT	EXC
COMPLETE SET (55)	15.00	6.75	1.85
COMMON CARD (1-55)	.10	.05	.01
☐ 1 Keyshawn Johnson	2.00	.90	.25
☐ 2 Jonathan Ogden	.10	.05	.01
☐ 3 Duane Clemons	.40	.18	.05
☐ 4 Kevin Hardy	.50	.23	.06
☐ 5 Eddie George	4.00	1.80	.50
☐ 6 Karim Abdul-Jabbar	2.50	1.10	.30
☐ 7 Terry Glenn	4.00	1.80	.50
☐ 8 Leeland McElroy	.75	.35	.09
☐ 9 Simeon Rice	.40	.18	.05
☐ 10 Roman Oben	.10	.05	.01
☐ 11 Daryl Gardener	.40	.18	.05
☐ 12 Marcus Coleman	.10	.05	.01
☐ 13 Christian Peter	.10	.05	.01
☐ 14 Tim Biakabutuka	.75	.35	.09
☐ 15 Eric Moulds	.75	.35	.09
☐ 16 Chris Darkins	1.00	.45	.12
☐ 17 Andre Johnson	.10	.05	.01
☐ 18 Lawyer Milloy	.10	.05	.01
☐ 19 Jon Runyan	.10	.05	.01
☐ 20 Mike Alstott	.75	.35	.09
☐ 21 Jeff Hartings	.10	.05	.01
☐ 22 Amani Toomer	.75	.35	.09
☐ 23 Danny Kanell	.75	.35	.09
☐ 24 Marco Battaglia	.60	.25	.07
☐ 25 Stephen Davis	1.00	.45	.12
☐ 26 Johnny McWilliams	.40	.18	.05
☐ 27 Israel Ifeanyi	.10	.05	.01
☐ 28 Scott Slutzker	.10	.05	.01
☐ 29 Bryant Mix	.10	.05	.01
☐ 30 Brian Roche	.10	.05	.01
☐ 31 Stanley Pritchett	.40	.18	.05
☐ 32 Jerome Woods	.10	.05	.01
☐ 33 Tommie Frazier	1.25	.55	.16
☐ 34 Stepfret Williams	.75	.35	.09
☐ 35 Ray Mickens	.10	.05	.01
☐ 36 Alex Van Dyke	1.00	.45	.12
☐ 37 Bobby Hoying	.75	.35	.09
☐ 38 Tony Brackens	.40	.18	.05
☐ 39 Dietrich Jells	.10	.05	.01
☐ 40 Jason Odom	.10	.05	.01
☐ 41 Randall Godfrey	.10	.05	.01
☐ 42 Willie Anderson	.10	.05	.01
☐ 43 Tony Banks	2.00	.90	.25
☐ 44 Michael Cheever	.10	.05	.01
☐ 45 Je'Rod Cherry	.10	.05	.01
☐ 46 Chris Doering	.30	.14	.04
☐ 47 Steve Taneyhill	.40	.18	.05
☐ 48 Kyle Wachholtz	.10	.05	.01
☐ 49 Dusty Zeigler	.10	.05	.01
☐ 50 Derrick Mayes	.75	.35	.09
☐ 51 Orpheus Roye	.10	.05	.01
☐ 52 Sedric Clark	.10	.05	.01
☐ 53 Richard Huntley	.10	.05	.01
☐ 54 Donnie Edwards	.10	.05	.01
☐ 55 Zach Thomas CL	.40	.18	.05
☐ P1 Tim Biakabutuka Promo	3.00	1.35	.35
☐ RED Lawrence Phillips	15.00	6.75	1.85

1996 Press Pass Holofoil

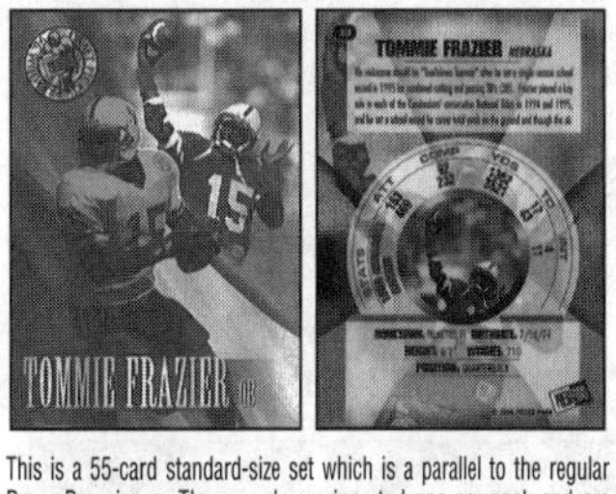

This is a 55-card standard-size set which is a parallel to the regular Press Pass issue. These cards are inserted one per pack and are printed on holofoil paper stock.

	MINT	NRMT	EXC
COMPLETE SET (55)	45.00	20.00	5.50
COMMON CARD (1-55)	.30	.14	.04
*STARS:2X TO 3X BASIC CARDS			

1996 Press Pass Holofoil Emerald Proofs

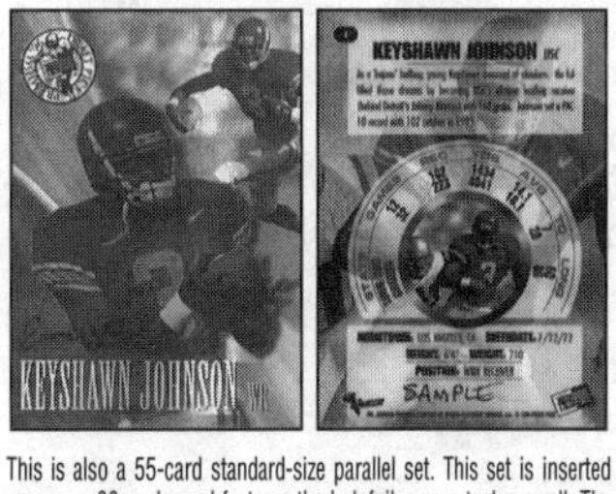

This is also a 55-card standard-size parallel set. This set is inserted one every 36 packs and features the holofoil paper stock as well. The words "Emerald Proof" are printed on the front. Each card is numbered as being one of 280.

	MINT	NRMT	EXC
COMPLETE SET (55)	300.00	135.00	38.00
COMMON CARD (1-55)	1.00	.45	.12
*STARS:12X TO 20X BASIC CARDS			

1996 Press Pass Autographs

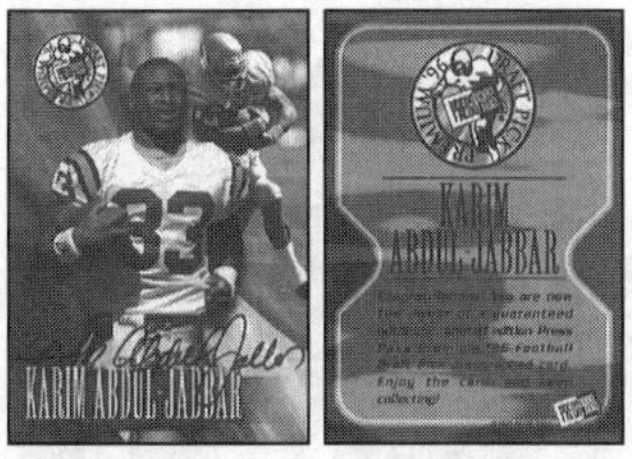

These cards were inserted approximately one every 72 packs. The cards have a player autograph on the front. The backs of the card state that the collector has received an authentic, limited edition Press Pass autograph card. The cards are unnumbered and we have sequenced them in alphabetical order.

	MINT	NRMT	EXC
COMPLETE SET (12)	225.00	100.00	28.00
COMMON CARD (1-12)	10.00	4.50	1.25
☐ 1 Karim Abdul-Jabbar	60.00	27.00	7.50
☐ 2 Tony Banks	50.00	22.00	6.25
☐ 3 Tim Biakabutuka	25.00	11.00	3.10
☐ 4 Duane Clemons	10.00	4.50	1.25
☐ 5 Stephen Davis	15.00	6.75	1.85
☐ 6 Chris Doering	10.00	4.50	1.25
☐ 7 Bobby Hoying	15.00	6.75	1.85
☐ 8 Keyshawn Johnson	40.00	18.00	5.00
☐ 9 Danny Kanell	15.00	6.75	1.85
☐ 10 Leeland McElroy	15.00	6.75	1.85
☐ 11 Jonathan Ogden	10.00	4.50	1.25
☐ 12 Steve Taneyhill	10.00	4.50	1.25

1996 Press Pass Crystal Ball

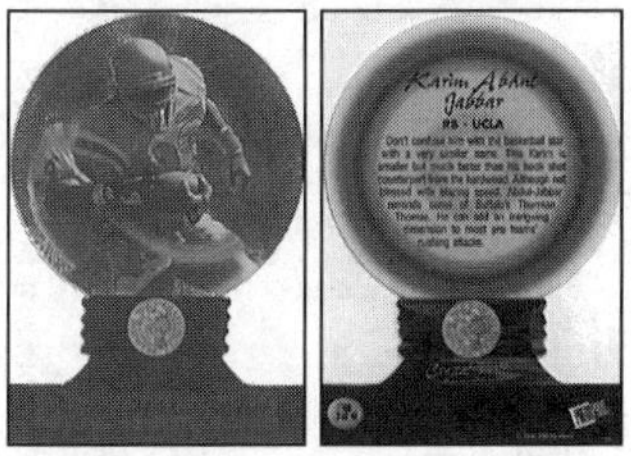

These cards were inserted one every 18 packs. The die cut cards feature a player's photo within a multi-colored crystal ball. The words "Crystal Ball" as well as the player's name are on the bottom. The cards are numbered with a "CB" prefix and are also numbered as "X" of 12.

	MINT	NRMT	EXC
COMPLETE SET (12)	70.00	32.00	8.75
COMMON CARD (CB1-CB12)	2.50	1.10	.30
☐ CB1 Lawyer Milloy	2.50	1.10	.30
☐ CB2 Terry Glenn	20.00	9.00	2.50
☐ CB3 Duane Clemons	2.50	1.10	.30
☐ CB4 Kevin Hardy	4.00	1.80	.50
☐ CB5 Eddie George	20.00	9.00	2.50
☐ CB6 Jonathan Ogden	2.50	1.10	.30
☐ CB7 Karim Abdul-Jabbar	12.00	5.50	1.50
☐ CB8 Tim Biakabutuka	15.00	6.75	1.85
☐ CB9 Eric Moulds	6.00	2.70	.75
☐ CB10 Danny Kanell	6.00	2.70	.75
☐ CB11 Leeland McElroy	10.00	4.50	1.25
☐ CB12 Keyshawn Johnson	10.00	4.50	1.25

1996 Press Pass Phone Cards $5/$10/$20

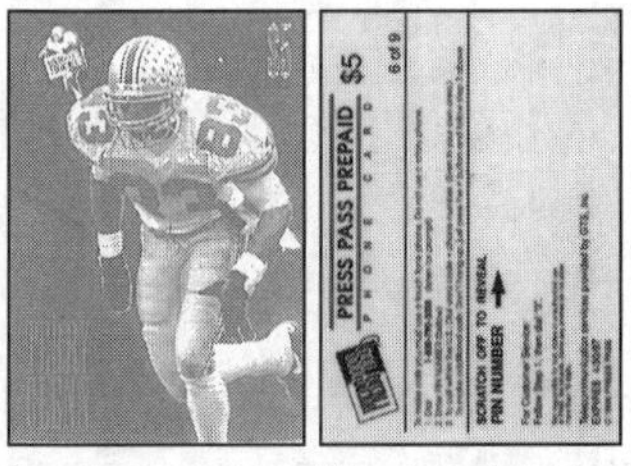

These cards were randomly inserted into packs. The checklists for all three sets are the same; however, they were inserted in different ratios. The $5 cards were inserted one every 36 packs, while the $10 were included one every 216 packs and the $20 phone cards were included one every 864 packs. There are also $1996 phone cards and those cards were inserted one every forty-four thousand packs. These $1996 cards are not valued at the present. The standard-size cards feature a player photo. The dollar amount of the card is located in the upper right with the player's name in the lower left. The back has user information, with the cards usable until April 30, 1997. The cards are numbered as 'X' of nine.

	MINT	NRMT	EXC
COMPLETE SET (9)	90.00	40.00	11.00
COMMON CARD (PT1-PT9)	5.00	2.20	.60
TEN DOLLAR CARDS:2X BASIC CARDS			
TWENTY DOLLAR CARDS: 5X BASIC CARDS			
☐ PT1 Keyshawn Johnson	10.00	4.50	1.25
☐ PT2 Jonathan Ogden	5.00	2.20	.60
☐ PT3 Tommie Frazier	8.00	3.60	1.00
☐ PT4 Eddie George	20.00	9.00	2.50
☐ PT5 Karim Abdul-Jabbar	12.00	5.50	1.50
☐ PT6 Terry Glenn	20.00	9.00	2.50
☐ PT7 Leeland McElroy	15.00	6.75	1.85
☐ PT8 Tim Biakabutuka	8.00	3.60	1.00
☐ PT9 Kevin Hardy	10.00	4.50	1.25

1996 Press Pass Paydirt

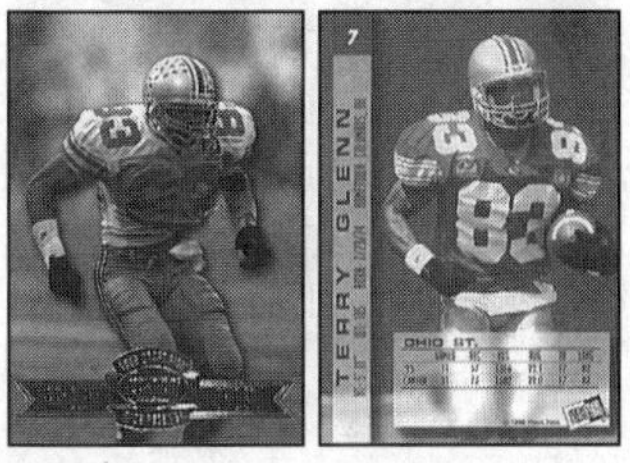

These 75 standard-size cards were issued in five-card packs. This set is the retail version of Press Pass and also features various insert cards. This set features players projected to be among the leading rookies of the 1996 NFL season. The RED Lawrence Phillips card was the prize for an expired mail order pack redemption.

	MINT	NRMT	EXC
COMPLETE SET (75)	25.00	11.00	3.10
COMMON CARD (1-75)	.10	.05	.01
☐ 1 Keyshawn Johnson	2.00	.90	.25
☐ 2 Jonathan Ogden	.10	.05	.01
☐ 3 Duane Clemons	.10	.05	.01
☐ 4 Kevin Hardy	.40	.18	.05
☐ 5 Eddie George	4.00	1.80	.50
☐ 6 Karim Abdul-Jabbar	2.50	1.10	.30
☐ 7 Terry Glenn	4.00	1.80	.50
☐ 8 Leeland McElroy	.40	.18	.05
☐ 9 Simeon Rice	.40	.18	.05
☐ 10 Roman Oben	.10	.05	.01
☐ 11 Daryl Gardener	.40	.18	.05
☐ 12 Marcus Coleman	.10	.05	.01
☐ 13 Christian Peter	.10	.05	.01
☐ 14 Tim Biakabutuka	.75	.35	.09
☐ 15 Eric Moulds	.75	.35	.09
☐ 16 Chris Darkins	.10	.05	.01
☐ 17 Andre Johnson	.10	.05	.01
☐ 18 Lawyer Milloy	.10	.05	.01
☐ 19 Jon Runyan	.10	.05	.01
☐ 20 Mike Alstott	.40	.18	.05
☐ 21 Jeff Hartings	.10	.05	.01
☐ 22 Amani Toomer	.75	.35	.09
☐ 23 Danny Kanell	.40	.18	.05
☐ 24 Marco Battaglia	.10	.05	.01
☐ 25 Stephen Davis	.40	.18	.05
☐ 26 Johnny McWilliams	.10	.05	.01
☐ 27 Israel Ifeanyi	.10	.05	.01
☐ 28 Scott Slutzker	.10	.05	.01
☐ 29 Bryant Mix	.10	.05	.01
☐ 30 Brian Roche	.10	.05	.01
☐ 31 Stanley Pritchett	.40	.18	.05
☐ 32 Jerome Woods	.10	.05	.01
☐ 33 Tommie Frazier	1.25	.55	.16
☐ 34 Stepfret Williams	.10	.05	.01
☐ 35 Ray Mickens	.10	.05	.01
☐ 36 Alex Van Dyke	.40	.18	.05
☐ 37 Bobby Hoying	.40	.18	.05
☐ 38 Tony Brackens	.40	.18	.05
☐ 39 Dietrich Jells	.10	.05	.01
☐ 40 Jason Odom	.10	.05	.01
☐ 41 Randall Godfrey	.10	.05	.01
☐ 42 Willie Anderson	.10	.05	.01
☐ 43 Tony Banks	2.00	.90	.25
☐ 44 Michael Cheever	.10	.05	.01
☐ 45 Je'Rod Cherry	.10	.05	.01
☐ 46 Chris Doering	.10	.05	.01
☐ 47 Steve Taneyhill	.10	.05	.01
☐ 48 Kyle Wachholtz	.10	.05	.01
☐ 49 Dusty Zeigler	.10	.05	.01
☐ 50 Derrick Mayes	.40	.18	.05
☐ 51 Orpheus Roye	.10	.05	.01
☐ 52 Sedric Clark	.10	.05	.01
☐ 53 Richard Huntley	.10	.05	.01
☐ 54 Donnie Edwards	.10	.05	.01
☐ 55 Zach Thomas	.75	.35	.09
☐ 56 Alex Molden	.10	.05	.01
☐ 57 Jimmy Herndon	.10	.05	.01
☐ 58 Mike Alstott	.75	.35	.09
☐ 59 Scott Greene	.10	.05	.01
☐ 60 Danny Kanell	.40	.18	.05
☐ 61 Jonathan Ogden	.10	.05	.01
☐ 62 Simeon Rice	.40	.18	.05
☐ 63 Kevin Hardy	.40	.18	.05
☐ 64 Jon Runyan	.10	.05	.01
☐ 65 Stephen Davis	.40	.18	.05
☐ 66 Tim Biakabutuka	.75	.35	.09
☐ 67 Terry Glenn	4.00	1.80	.50
☐ 68 Leeland McElroy	.40	.18	.05
☐ 69 Eric Moulds	.75	.35	.09
☐ 70 Karim Abdul-Jabbar	2.50	1.10	.30
☐ 71 Lawyer Milloy	.10	.05	.01
☐ 72 Derrick Mayes	.75	.35	.09
☐ 73 Tommie Frazier	1.25	.55	.16
☐ 74 Bobby Hoying	.40	.18	.05
☐ 75 Kyle Wachholtz CL	.10	.05	.01
☐ RED Lawrence Phillips	15.00	6.75	1.85

1996 Press Pass Paydirt Holofoil

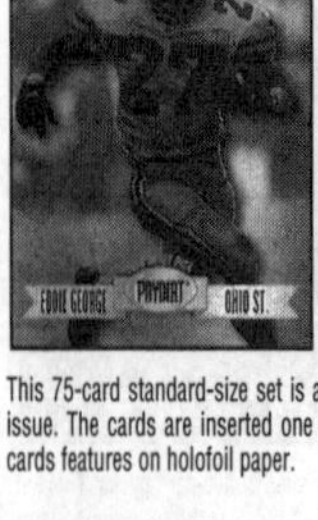

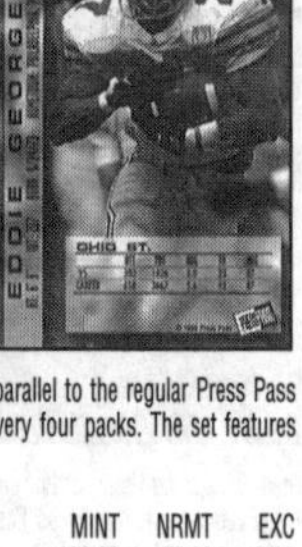

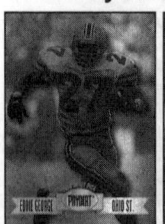

This 75-card standard-size set is a parallel to the regular Press Pass issue. The cards are inserted one every four packs. The set features cards features on holofoil paper.

	MINT	NRMT	EXC
COMPLETE SET (75)	120.00	55.00	15.00
COMMON CARD (1-75)	.40	.18	.05
*STARS:2X TO 4X BASIC CARDS			

1996 Press Pass Paydirt Red Foil

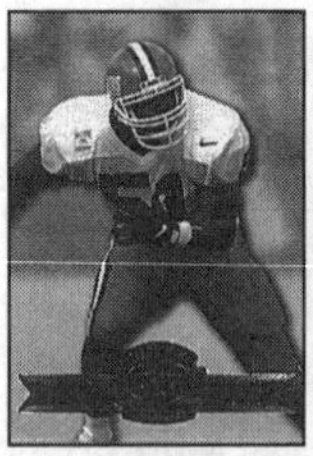

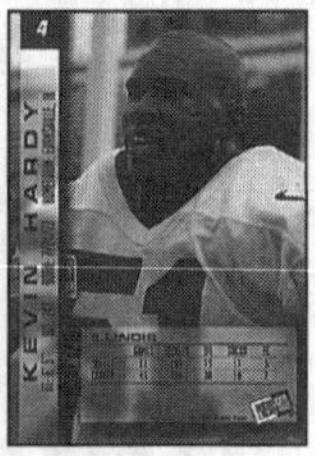

These cards, which are also called "Torquers" were inserted one per pack. This 75 card standard-size parallel set actually features "Red Foil" not the blue foil as described on the wrapper.

	MINT	NRMT	EXC
COMPLETE SET (75)	60.00	27.00	7.50
COMMON CARD (1-75)	.20	.09	.03
*STARS:1X TO 2X BASIC CARDS			

1996 Press Pass Paydirt Autographs

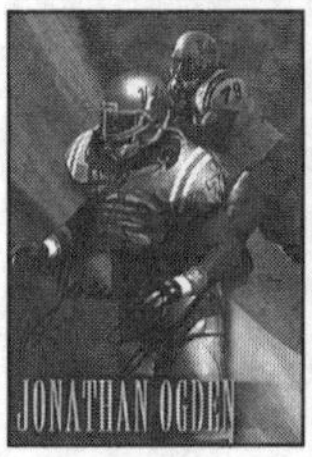

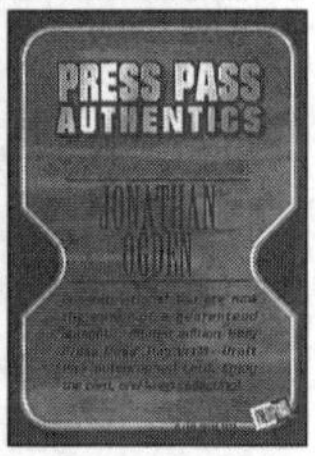

These cards are insetrted one every 72 packs. The cards are autographed on the front and have the words "You have received an authentic limited-edition Press Pass Paydirt card on the back. These cards are unnumbered and we have sequenced them in alphabetical order.

	MINT	NRMT	EXC
COMPLETE SET (16)	250.00	110.00	31.00
COMMON CARD (1-16)	10.00	4.50	1.25
☐ 1 Karim Abdul-Jabbar	60.00	27.00	7.50
☐ 2 Tony Banks	50.00	22.00	6.25
☐ 3 Tim Biakabutuka	25.00	11.00	3.10
☐ 4 Duane Clemons	10.00	4.50	1.25
☐ 5 Stephen Davis	15.00	6.75	1.85
☐ 6 Chris Doering	10.00	4.50	1.25
☐ 7 Bobby Hoying	15.00	6.75	1.85
☐ 8 Keyshawn Johnson	40.00	18.00	5.00
☐ 9 Danny Kanell	15.00	6.75	1.85
☐ 10 Derrick Mayes	15.00	6.75	1.85
☐ 11 Leeland McElroy	15.00	6.75	1.85
☐ 12 Lawyer Milloy	10.00	4.50	1.25
☐ 13 Eric Moulds	15.00	6.75	1.85
☐ 14 Jonathan Ogden	10.00	4.50	1.25
☐ 15 Steve Tanneyhill	10.00	4.50	1.25
☐ 16 Alex Van Dyke	15.00	6.75	1.85

1996 Press Pass Paydirt Eddie George

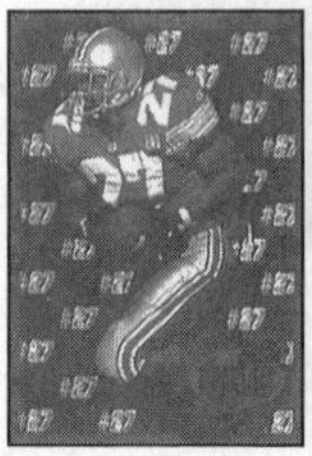

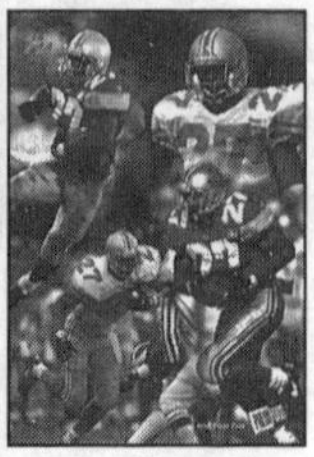

1995 Heisman Trophy winner Eddie George is featured in this four-card standard-size set. The cards were inserted into packs at a staggered rate: Card #1 was one in 36, Card #2 was one in 72, Card #3 was one in 216, and Card #4 was one in 864 packs. The fronts feature a photo of George against a silver background of his name repeating while the backs contain four different action shots. The cards are numbered with an "EG" prefix.

	MINT	NRMT	EXC
COMPLETE SET (4)	125.00	55.00	15.50
COMMON CARD(EG1-EG4)	6.00	2.70	.75
☐ EG1 Eddie George	6.00	2.70	.75
☐ EG2 Eddie George	10.00	4.50	1.25
☐ EG3 Eddie George	30.00	13.50	3.70
☐ EG4 Eddie George	90.00	40.00	11.00

1996 Press Pass Paydirt Game Breakers

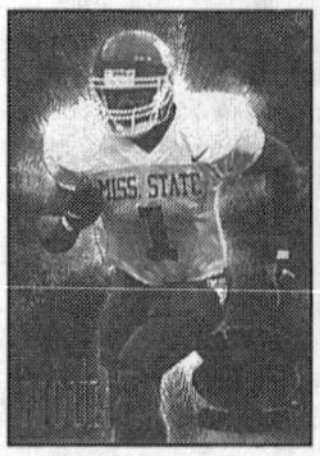

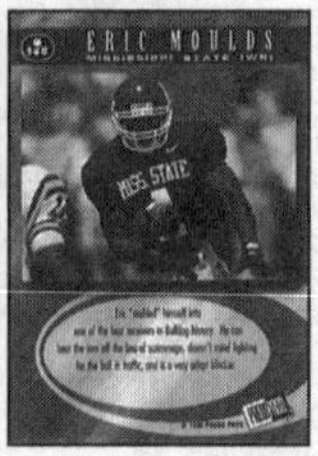

This 12-card standard-size set features players who dominated games in college. The cards were inserted one every 18 packs. The set is numbered with a "GB" prefix.

	MINT	NRMT	EXC
COMPLETE SET (12)	70.00	32.00	8.75
COMMON CARD (GB1-GB12)	2.50	1.10	.30
☐ GB1 Lawyer Milloy	2.50	1.10	.30
☐ GB2 Terry Glenn	20.00	9.00	2.50
☐ GB3 Duane Clemons	2.50	1.10	.30
☐ GB4 Kevin Hardy	4.00	1.80	.50
☐ GB5 Eddie George	20.00	9.00	2.50
☐ GB6 Jonathan Ogden	2.50	1.10	.30
☐ GB7 Karim Abdul-Jabbar	12.00	5.50	1.50
☐ GB8 Tim Biakabutuka	6.00	2.70	.75
☐ GB9 Eric Moulds	4.00	1.80	.50
☐ GB10 Danny Kanell	4.00	1.80	.50
☐ GB11 Leeland McElroy	4.00	1.80	.50
☐ GB12 Keyshawn Johnson	10.00	4.50	1.25

1997 Press Pass

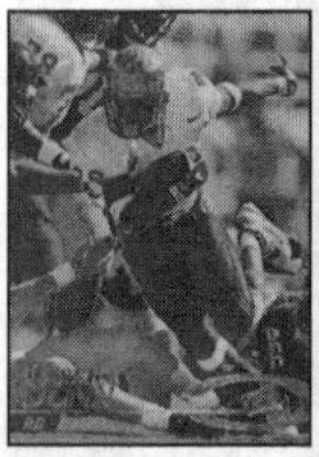

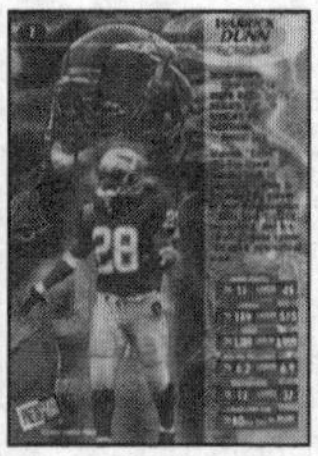

This 50 card set features some leading NFL prospects entering the 1997 season. The borderless full color shots feature an action photo on the front with the players name and position on the bottom. The backs feature biographical information, a brief blurb as well as collegiate stats for these players.

	MINT	NRMT	EXC
COMPLETE SET (49)	15.00	6.75	1.85
COMMON CARD (1-50)	.10	.05	.01
☐ 1 Orlando Pace	.20	.09	.03
☐ 2 Warrick Dunn	2.00	.90	.25
☐ 3 Danny Wuerffel	1.50	.70	.19
☐ 4 Darnell Autry	.60	.25	.07
☐ 5 Troy Davis	1.00	.45	.12
☐ 6 Jake Plummer	.60	.25	.07
☐ 7 Corey Dillon	.75	.35	.09
☐ 8 Reidel Anthony	1.25	.55	.16
☐ 9 Byron Hanspard	.75	.35	.09
☐ 10 Tiki Barber	.60	.25	.07
☐ 11 Ike Hilliard	1.25	.55	.16
☐ 12 Rae Carruth	.75	.35	.09
☐ 13 Yatil Green	1.25	.55	.16
☐ 14 Peter Boulware	.20	.09	.03
☐ 15 Jim Druckenmiller	1.50	.70	.19
☐ 16 Pat Barnes	.10	.05	.01
☐ 17 Trevor Pryce	.10	.05	.01
☐ 18 Kevin Lockett	.10	.05	.01
☐ 19 Koy Detmer	.20	.09	.03
☐ 20 Bryant Westbrook	.10	.05	.01
☐ 21 Darrell Russell	.20	.09	.03
☐ 22 Tony Gonzalez	.40	.18	.05
☐ 23 Shawn Springs	.60	.25	.07
☐ 24 Chris Canty	.20	.09	.03
☐ 25 David LaFleur	.60	.25	.07
☐ 26 Dwayne Rudd	.10	.05	.01
☐ 27 Bob Sapp	.10	.05	.01
☐ 28 Mike Vrabel	.10	.05	.01
☐ 29 Antowain Smith	.60	.25	.07
☐ 30 Keith Poole	.10	.05	.01
☐ 31 Sedrick Shaw	.10	.05	.01
☐ 32 Tremain Mack	.10	.05	.01
☐ 33 Matt Russell	.10	.05	.01
☐ 34 Reinard Wilson	.20	.09	.03
☐ 35 Marc Edwards	.10	.05	.01
☐ 36 Greg Jones	.10	.05	.01
☐ 37 Michael Booker	.20	.09	.03
☐ 38 James Farrior	.10	.05	.01
☐ 39 Danny Wuerffel HL	.75	.35	.09
☐ 40 Troy Davis HL	.50	.23	.06
☐ 41 Corey Dillon HL	.20	.09	.03
☐ 42 Jake Plummer HL	.10	.05	.01
☐ 43 Peter Boulware HL (sacking Danny Wuerffel)	.40	.18	.05
☐ 44 Eddie Robinson CO	.20	.09	.03
☐ 45 Bobby Bowden CO	.75	.35	.09
☐ 46 Steve Spurrier CO	1.25	.55	.16
☐ 47 Gary Barnett CO	.10	.05	.01
☐ 49 Tom Osborne CO	.75	.35	.09
☐ 50 Jarrett Irons CL	.20	.09	.03

1997 Press Pass Combine

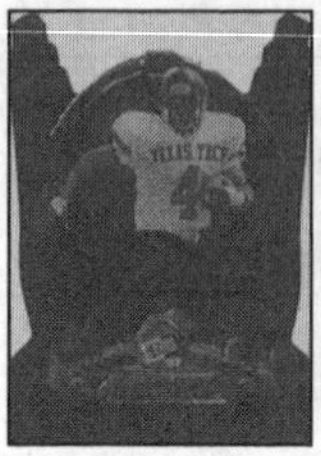

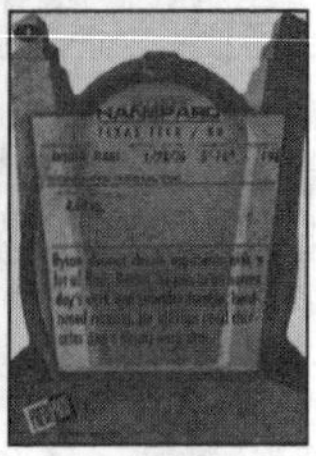

This 45 card set is a mini parallel to the regular Press Pass issue. The cards in this set feature the players only, not any of the coaches in the Press Pass set.

	MINT	NRMT	EXC
COMPLETE SET (45)	30.00	13.50	3.70
COMMON CARD (1-45)	.25	.11	.03
*STARS: 2X BASIC CARDS			

1997 Press Pass Red Zone

This set is another parallel to the regular Press Pass set. This time, all the cards are pictured in the parallel issue.

	MINT	NRMT	EXC
COMPLETE SET (49)	30.00	13.50	3.70
COMMON CARD (1-50)	.25	.11	.03
*STARS: 2X BASIC CARDS			

1997 Press Pass Big 12

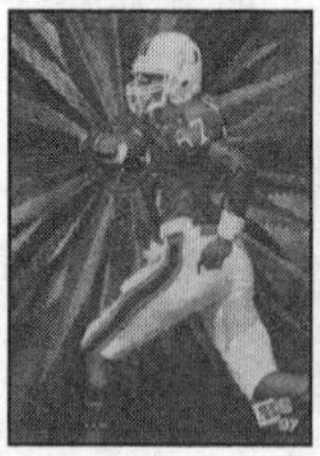

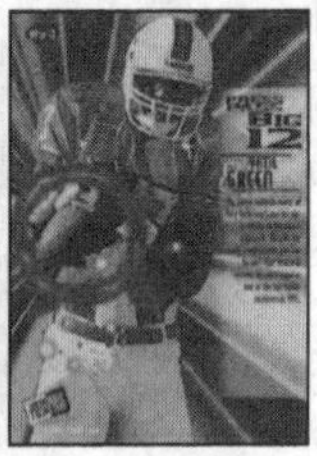

This set features not players only from the collegiate conference but features 12 players who look like they will have sucsessfull pro careers. These cards are inserted one every 12 packs and are numbered with a "B" prefix on the card.

	MINT	NRMT	EXC
COMPLETE SET (12)	40.00	18.00	5.00
COMMON CARD (B1-B12)	3.00	1.35	.35
☐ B1 Orlando Pace	4.00	1.80	.50
☐ B2 Peter Boulware	3.00	1.35	.35
☐ B3 Shawn Springs	4.00	1.80	.50
☐ B4 Warrick Dunn	10.00	4.50	1.25
☐ B5 Dwayne Rudd	3.00	1.35	.35
☐ B6 Rae Carruth	4.00	1.80	.50
☐ B7 Bryant Westbrook	3.00	1.35	.35
☐ B8 Darrell Russell	3.00	1.35	.35
☐ B9 Yatil Green	5.00	2.20	.60
☐ B10 David LaFleur	4.00	1.80	.50
☐ B11 Jim Druckenmiller	8.00	3.60	1.00
☐ B12 Reidel Anthony	5.00	2.20	.60

1997 Press Pass Can't Miss

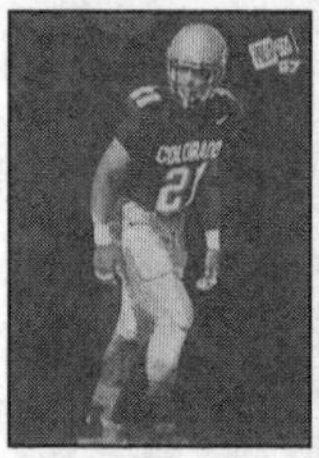

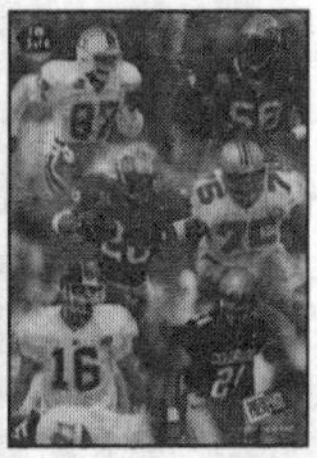

This six card set features the players Press Pass believed would be the best players in their draft class. The cards are printed in ascending difficulty with card #1 being inserted one every 720 packs, card #2 one every 360, card #3 is one of 180; card #4 are one every 90; card #5 is one every 45 and card #6 is one every 36. The cards are numbered with a "CM" prefix on the back.

	MINT	NRMT	EXC
COMPLETE SET (6)	200.00	90.00	25.00
COMMON CARD (CM1-CM6)	8.00	3.60	1.00

☐ CM1 Warrick Dunn	80.00	36.00	10.00
☐ CM2 Jim Druckenmiller	50.00	22.00	6.25
☐ CM3 Yatil Green	40.00	18.00	5.00
☐ CM4 Orlando Pace	20.00	9.00	2.50
☐ CM5 Rae Carruth	20.00	9.00	2.50
☐ CM6 Peter Boulware	8.00	3.60	1.00

1997 Press Pass Head Butt

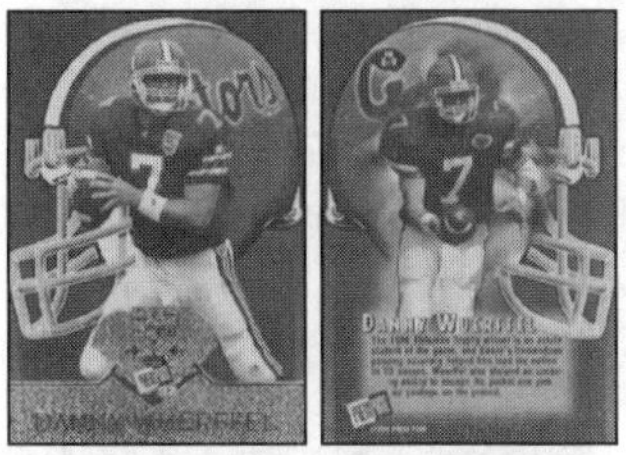

These cards feature leading NFL prospects as of the beginning of the 1997 season. The cards are numbered with a "HB" parallel on the back and there is also a die-cut parallel version.

	MINT	NRMT	EXC
COMPLETE SET (9)	50.00	22.00	6.25
COMMON CARD (HB1-HB9)	4.00	1.80	.50
DIE CUTS: 2X VALUE			
☐ HB1 Warrick Dunn	15.00	6.75	1.85
☐ HB2 Orlando Pace	4.00	1.80	.50
☐ HB3 Troy Davis	6.00	2.70	.75
☐ HB4 Reidel Anthony	10.00	4.50	1.25
☐ HB5 Rae Carruth	6.00	2.70	.75
☐ HB6 Yatil Green	10.00	4.50	1.25
☐ HB7 Corey Dillon	6.00	2.70	.75
☐ HB8 Danny Wuerffel	10.00	4.50	1.25
☐ HB9 Darnell Autry	6.00	2.70	.75

1997 Press Pass Marquee Matchups

This nine card insert set was issued one every 18 packs. Each cards pictures two players who are both looking to make an NFL impact at the same position.

	MINT	NRMT	EXC
COMPLETE SET (9)	30.00	13.50	3.70
COMMON CARD (MM1-MM9)	2.00	.90	.25
☐ MM1 Jim Druckenmiller Danny Wuerffel	10.00	4.50	1.25
☐ MM2 Warrick Dunn Corey Dillon	8.00	3.60	1.00
☐ MM3 Darnell Autry Troy Davis	6.00	2.70	.75
☐ MM4 Byron Hanspard Tiki Barber	6.00	2.70	.75
☐ MM5 Reidel Anthony Bryant Westbrook	2.50	1.10	.30
☐ MM6 Peter Boulware Orlando Pace	2.00	.90	.25
☐ MM7 Rae Carruth Ike Hilliard	4.00	1.80	.50
☐ MM8 Yatil Green Shawn Springs	3.00	1.35	.35
☐ MM9 David LaFleur Tony Gonzalez	2.50	1.10	.30

1997 Score Board NFL Rookies

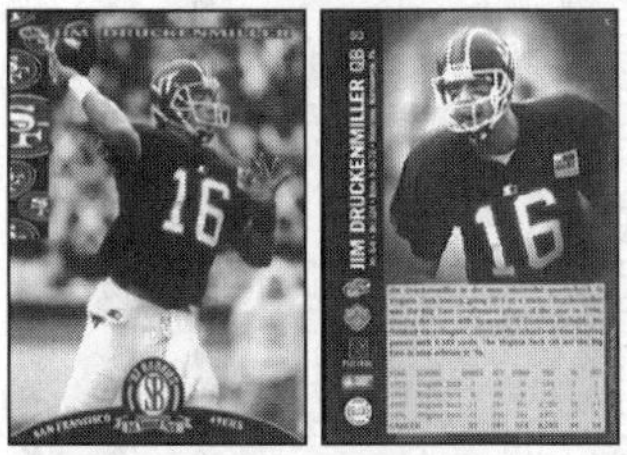

The 1997 Score Board NFL Rookies set was issued in one series totaling 100 standard-size cards. The set was issued in 8-card packs with 36 packs in a box and 12 boxes in a case. Among the topical subsets are: All-Americans (94-98) and Checklists (99-100). The key players in this set are Warrick Dunn and Jim Druckenmiller.

	MINT	NRMT	EXC
COMPLETE SET (100)	10.00	4.50	1.25
COMMON CARD (1-100)	.05	.02	.01
☐ 1 Jake Plummer	.40	.18	.05
☐ 2 Tony Gonzalez	.25	.11	.03
☐ 3 Trevor Pryce	.05	.02	.01
☐ 4 Greg Jones	.05	.02	.01
☐ 5 Koy Detmer	.10	.05	.01
☐ 6 Rae Carruth	.50	.23	.06
☐ 7 Peter Boulware	.10	.05	.01
☐ 8 Warrick Dunn	1.25	.55	.16
☐ 9 Antowain Smith	.40	.18	.05
☐ 10 Troy Davis	.60	.25	.07
☐ 11 David LaFleur	.40	.18	.05
☐ 12 Yatil Green	.75	.35	.09
☐ 13 Michael Booker	.10	.05	.01
☐ 14 Shawn Springs	.40	.18	.05
☐ 15 Bryant Westbrook	.05	.02	.01
☐ 16 Byron Hanspard	.50	.23	.06
☐ 17 Darrell Russell	.10	.05	.01
☐ 18 Corey Dillon	.50	.23	.06
☐ 19 Tyrus McCloud	.05	.02	.01
☐ 20 Reinard Wilson	.10	.05	.01
☐ 21 Adam Meadows	.05	.02	.01
☐ 22 Tremain Mack	.05	.02	.01
☐ 23 Ricky Parker	.05	.02	.01
☐ 24 George Jones	.05	.02	.01
☐ 25 Terry Battle	.05	.02	.01
☐ 26 Will Blackwell	.05	.02	.01
☐ 27 Jerald Sowell	.05	.02	.01
☐ 28 Isaac Byrd	.05	.02	.01
☐ 29 Chris Naeole	.05	.02	.01
☐ 30 Kevin Lockett	.05	.02	.01
☐ 31 Freddie Jones	.10	.05	.01
☐ 32 Pat Barnes	.05	.02	.01
☐ 33 Torrian Gray	.05	.02	.01
☐ 34 Brian Manning	.05	.02	.01
☐ 35 Dedric Ward	.05	.02	.01
☐ 36 Pete Monty	.05	.02	.01
☐ 37 Sam Madison	.05	.02	.01
☐ 38 Sedrick Shaw	.40	.18	.05
☐ 39 Mike Logan	.05	.02	.01
☐ 40 Albert Connell	.05	.02	.01
☐ 41 Canute Curtis	.05	.02	.01
☐ 42 Ronde Barber	.05	.02	.01
☐ 43 Orlando Pace	.10	.05	.01
☐ 44 Edward Perry	.05	.02	.01
☐ 45 Tiki Barber	.40	.18	.05
☐ 46 Kevin Jackson	.05	.02	.01
☐ 47 Jerry Wunsch	.05	.02	.01
☐ 48 Michael Hamilton	.05	.02	.01
☐ 49 Darnell Autry	.40	.18	.05
☐ 50 Jim Druckenmiller	1.00	.45	.12
☐ 51 James Farrior	.05	.02	.01
☐ 52 Derrick Mason	.05	.02	.01
☐ 53 Ty Howard	.05	.02	.01
☐ 54 Jason Taylor	.05	.02	.01
☐ 55 Reidel Anthony	.75	.35	.09
☐ 56 Bert Berry	.05	.02	.01
☐ 57 Marc Edwards	.05	.02	.01
☐ 58 James Hamilton	.05	.02	.01
☐ 59 Ike Hilliard	.75	.35	.09
☐ 60 Tommy Knight	.05	.02	.01
☐ 61 Walter Jones	.05	.02	.01
☐ 62 Chad Levitt	.05	.02	.01
☐ 63 Pratt Lyons	.05	.02	.01
☐ 64 Greg Clark	.05	.02	.01
☐ 65 Ryan Phillips	.05	.02	.01
☐ 66 Jason Martin	.05	.02	.01
☐ 67 Scott Sanderson	.05	.02	.01
☐ 68 Alshermond Singleton	.05	.02	.01
☐ 69 Duce Staley	.05	.02	.01
☐ 70 Jared Tomich	.05	.02	.01
☐ 71 Ross Verba	.05	.02	.01
☐ 72 Derrick Rodgers	.05	.02	.01
☐ 73 Mike Vrabel	.05	.02	.01
☐ 74 John Allred	.05	.02	.01
☐ 75 Bob Sapp	.05	.02	.01
☐ 76 Brad Otton	.05	.02	.01
☐ 77 Tarik Glenn	.05	.02	.01
☐ 78 Chad Scott	.05	.02	.01
☐ 79 Nathan Davis	.05	.02	.01
☐ 80 Henri Crockett	.05	.02	.01
☐ 81 Tarik Saleh	.05	.02	.01
☐ 82 Seth Payne	.05	.02	.01
☐ 83 Pete Chryplewicz	.05	.02	.01
☐ 84 Reidel Anthony AA	.25	.11	.03
☐ 85 Reinard Wilson AA	.05	.02	.01
☐ 86 Byron Hanspard AA	.25	.11	.03
☐ 87 Shawn Springs AA	.10	.05	.01
☐ 88 David LaFleur AA	.10	.05	.01
☐ 89 Troy Davis AA	.25	.11	.03
☐ 90 Warrick Dunn AA	.60	.25	.07
☐ 91 Peter Boulware AA	.10	.05	.01
☐ 92 Rae Carruth AA	.10	.05	.01
☐ 93 Tony Gonzalez AA	.10	.05	.01
☐ 94 Jake Plummer AA	.10	.05	.01
☐ 95 Orlando Pace AA	.10	.05	.01
☐ 96 Ike Hilliard AA	.05	.02	.01
☐ 97 Kevin Jackson AA	.10	.05	.01
☐ 98 Jim Druckenmiller AA	.50	.23	.06
☐ 99 Shawn Springs CL	.10	.05	.01
☐ 100 Warrick Dunn CL	.50	.23	.06

1997 Score Board NFL Rookies Dean's List

This 100-card standard-size set is a parallel to the regular Score Board issue. The cards are inserted one every five packs. The set features cards with gold foil.

	MINT	NRMT	EXC
COMPLETE SET (100)	40.00	18.00	5.00
COMMON CARD (1-100)	.25	.11	.03
*STARS : 4X BASIC CARDS			

1997 Score Board NFL Rookies Varsity Club

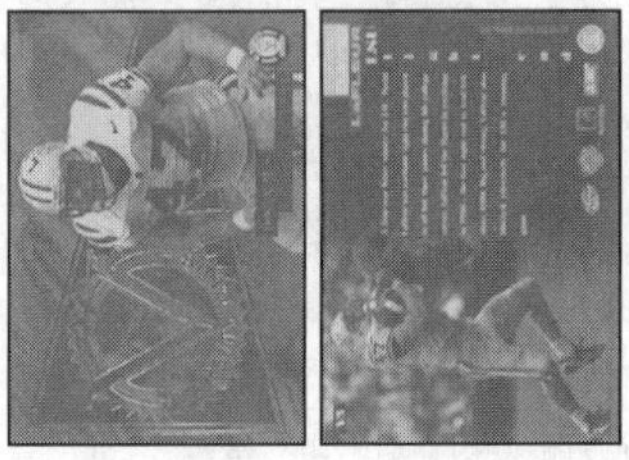

This 30-card horizontal insert set features some of the leading 1997 NFL Rookies with their school pennant. The cards are numbered with an "V" prefix and are randomly inserted in packs at a rate of one in 36.

	MINT	NRMT	EXC
COMPLETE SET (30)	100.00	45.00	12.50
COMMON CARD (V1-V30)	2.00	.90	.25
☐ V1 Tiki Barber	5.00	2.20	.60
☐ V2 Sedrick Shaw	5.00	2.20	.60
☐ V3 Kevin Lockett	2.00	.90	.25
☐ V4 Byron Hanspard	6.00	2.70	.75
☐ V5 David LaFleur	5.00	2.20	.60
☐ V6 Warrick Dunn	12.00	5.50	1.50
☐ V7 Yatil Green	8.00	3.60	1.00
☐ V8 Corey Dillon	6.00	2.70	.75
☐ V9 Orlando Pace	3.00	1.35	.35
☐ V10 Tony Gonzalez	4.00	1.80	.50
☐ V11 Darrell Russell	3.00	1.35	.35
☐ V12 Jake Plummer	5.00	2.20	.60
☐ V13 Peter Boulware	3.00	1.35	.35
☐ V14 Shawn Springs	5.00	2.20	.60
☐ V15 Bryant Westbrook	2.00	.90	.25
☐ V16 Rae Carruth	6.00	2.70	.75
☐ V17 Antowain Smith	5.00	2.20	.60
☐ V18 Reidel Anthony	8.00	3.60	1.00
☐ V19 Michael Booker	3.00	1.35	.35
☐ V20 Freddie Jones	2.00	.90	.25
☐ V21 Pat Barnes	2.00	.90	.25
☐ V22 Troy Davis	7.00	3.10	.85
☐ V23 Walter Jones	2.00	.90	.25
☐ V24 Reinard Wilson	3.00	1.35	.35
☐ V25 George Jones	2.00	.90	.25
☐ V26 Terry Battle	2.00	.90	.25
☐ V27 Tommy Knight	2.00	.90	.25
☐ V28 Termain Mack	2.00	.90	.25
☐ V29 Jim Druckenmiller	10.00	4.50	1.25
☐ V30 Ike Hilliard	8.00	3.60	1.00

1997 Score Board NFL Rookies War Room

This 20-card insert set features some of the leading 1997 NFL Rookies. The cards are numbered with an "W" prefix and are randomly inserted in packs at a rate of one in 100.

	MINT	NRMT	EXC
COMPLETE SET (20)	150.00	70.00	19.00
COMMON CARD (W1-W20)	5.00	2.20	.60
☐ W1 Yatil Green	15.00	6.75	1.85
☐ W2 Antowain Smith	8.00	3.60	1.00
☐ W3 Tony Gonzalez	6.00	2.70	.75
☐ W4 Corey Dillon	10.00	4.50	1.25
☐ W5 Jake Plummer	8.00	3.60	1.00
☐ W6 Peter Boulware	6.00	2.70	.75
☐ W7 Orlando Pace	6.00	2.70	.75
☐ W8 Darrell Russell	6.00	2.70	.75
☐ W9 Reinard Wilson	6.00	2.70	.75
☐ W10 Shawn Springs	8.00	3.60	1.00
☐ W11 Bryant Westbrook	5.00	2.20	.60
☐ W12 Rae Carruth	10.00	4.50	1.25
☐ W13 Warrick Dunn	25.00	11.00	3.10
☐ W14 David LaFleur	8.00	3.60	1.00
☐ W15 Byron Hanspard	10.00	4.50	1.25
☐ W16 Michael Booker	5.00	2.20	.60
☐ W17 Reidel Anthony	15.00	6.75	1.85
☐ W18 Troy Davis	12.00	5.50	1.50
☐ W19 Chris Naeole	5.00	2.20	.60
☐ W20 Jim Druckenmiller	20.00	9.00	2.50

1994 Signature Rookies

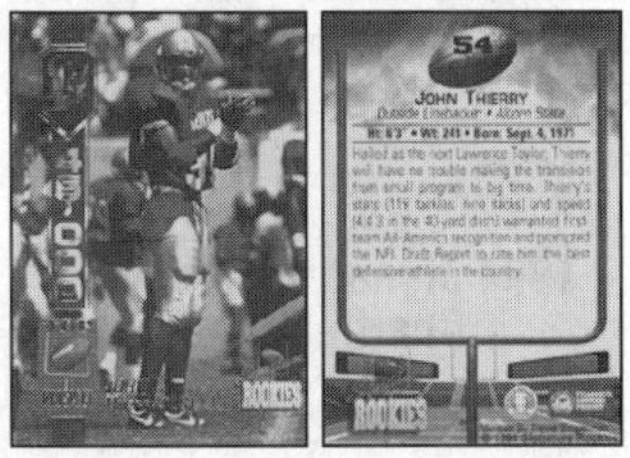

These 60 standard-size cards feature borderless color action shots of top NFL prospects in their college uniforms. A wide gold-foil stripe adorns the left side and carries the words "1 of 45,000" or, for the autographed card included in every six-card pack, "Authentic Signature." The player's name and position appear at the bottom. Production was limited to 12,500 numbered boxes. Special subsets include the five-card Charlie Ward set, 2,500 cards of which were hand signed by the Heisman Trophy winner; the five-card "Hottest Prospect" set, 2,000 of which were hand signed by each of the five players; and also sets of Gale Sayers and Tony Dorsett, of which 2,000 and 1,000 cards, respectively, were autographed.

	MINT	EXC	G-VG
COMPLETE SET (60)	7.00	3.10	.85
COMMON CARD (1-60)	.05	.02	.01
☐ 1 Sam Adams	.25	.11	.03
☐ 2 Trev Alberts	.25	.11	.03
☐ 3 Derrick Alexander WR	.50	.23	.06
☐ 4 Larry Allen	.25	.11	.03
☐ 5 Aubrey Beavers	.05	.02	.01
☐ 6 Lou Benfatti	.05	.02	.01
☐ 7 James Bostic	.05	.02	.01
☐ 8 Tim Bowens	.25	.11	.03
☐ 9 Rich Braham	.05	.02	.01
☐ 10 Isaac Bruce	1.25	.55	.16
☐ 11 Vaughn Bryant	.05	.02	.01
☐ 12 Brentson Buckner	.25	.11	.03
☐ 13 Jeff Burris	.25	.11	.03
☐ 14 Carlester Crumpler	.05	.02	.01
☐ 15 Lake Dawson	.30	.14	.04
☐ 16 Tyronne Drakeford	.25	.11	.03
☐ 17 Dan Eichloff	.05	.02	.01
☐ 18 Rob Fredrickson	.25	.11	.03
☐ 19 Gus Frerotte	.75	.35	.09
☐ 20 William Gaines	.05	.02	.01
☐ 21 Wayne Gandy	.05	.02	.01
☐ 22 Jason Gildon	.05	.02	.01
☐ 23 Lemanski Hall	.05	.02	.01
☐ 24 Shelby Hill	.05	.02	.01
☐ 25 Willie Jackson	.25	.11	.03
☐ 26 LeShon Johnson	.25	.11	.03
☐ 27 Tre Johnson	.05	.02	.01
☐ 28 Alan Kline	.05	.02	.01
☐ 29 Darren Krein	.05	.02	.01
☐ 30 Antonio Langham	.25	.11	.03
☐ 31 Corey Louchiey	.05	.02	.01
☐ 32 Keith Lyle	.05	.02	.01
☐ 33 Eric Mahlum	.05	.02	.01
☐ 34 Van Malone	.05	.02	.01
☐ 35 Chris Maumalanga	.05	.02	.01
☐ 36 Jamir Miller	.25	.11	.03
☐ 37 Jim Miller	.25	.11	.03
☐ 38 Byron Bam Morris	.50	.23	.06
☐ 39 Aaron Mundy	.05	.02	.01
☐ 40 Jeremy Nunley	.05	.02	.01
☐ 41 Turhonn O'Bannon	.05	.02	.01
☐ 42 Brad Ottis	.05	.02	.01
☐ 43 David Palmer	.25	.11	.03
☐ 44 Joe Panos	.05	.02	.01
☐ 45 Jim Pyne	.05	.02	.01
☐ 46 John Reece	.05	.02	.01
☐ 47 Errict Rhett	1.50	.70	.19
☐ 48 Tony Richardson	.05	.02	.01
☐ 49 Sam Rogers	.05	.02	.01
☐ 50 Tim Ruddy	.05	.02	.01
☐ 51 Corey Sawyer	.05	.02	.01
☐ 52 Malcolm Seabron	.05	.02	.01
☐ 53 Jason Sehorn	.05	.02	.01
☐ 54 John Thierry	.25	.11	.03
☐ 55 Jason Winrow	.05	.02	.01
☐ 56 Ronnie Woolford	.05	.02	.01
☐ 57 Toby Wright	.05	.02	.01
☐ 58 Ryan Yarborough	.05	.02	.01
☐ 59 Eric Zomalt	.05	.02	.01
☐ 60 Checklist	.05	.02	.01

1994 SR Signatures

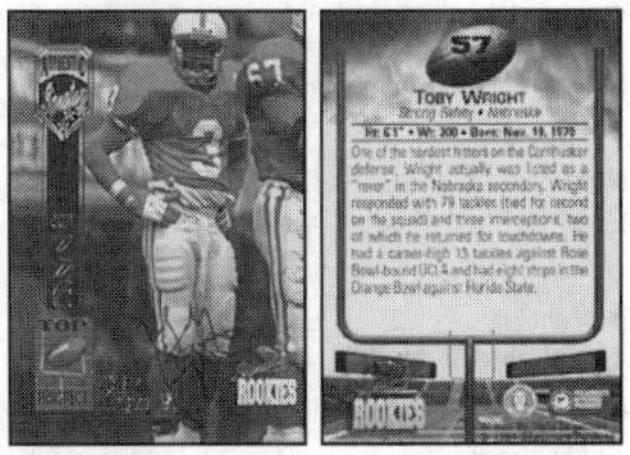

These 59 standard-size cards were available in autographed form; an autographed card was promised in every six-card pack of Signature Rookies. Production was limited to 12,500 numbered boxes. Each signed card was numbered out of 7750. Seven hundred Errict Rhett signatures are not authentic. If these cards were sent in, Signature Rookies then did a verification check.

	MINT	EXC	G-VG
COMPLETE SET (59)	250.00	110.00	31.00
COMMON SIGNATURE (1-59)	4.00	1.80	.50
☐ 1 Sam Adams	6.00	2.70	.75
☐ 2 Trev Alberts	6.00	2.70	.75
☐ 3 Derrick Alexander WR	6.00	2.70	.75
☐ 4 Larry Allen	6.00	2.70	.75
☐ 5 Aubrey Beavers	4.00	1.80	.50

☐ 6 Lou Benfatti	4.00	1.80	.50
☐ 7 James Bostic	4.00	1.80	.50
☐ 8 Tim Bowens	6.00	2.70	.75
☐ 9 Rich Braham	4.00	1.80	.50
☐ 10 Isaac Bruce	20.00	9.00	2.50
☐ 11 Vaughn Bryant	4.00	1.80	.50
☐ 12 Brentson Buckner	4.00	1.80	.50
☐ 13 Jeff Burris	6.00	2.70	.75
☐ 14 Carlester Crumpler	4.00	1.80	.50
☐ 15 Lake Dawson	7.00	3.10	.85
☐ 16 Tyronne Drakeford	6.00	2.70	.75
☐ 17 Dan Eichloff	4.00	1.80	.50
☐ 18 Rob Fredrickson	6.00	2.70	.75
☐ 19 Gus Frerotte	15.00	6.75	1.85
☐ 20 William Gaines	4.00	1.80	.50
☐ 21 Wayne Gandy	4.00	1.80	.50
☐ 22 Jason Gildon	4.00	1.80	.50
☐ 23 Lemanski Hall	4.00	1.80	.50
☐ 24 Shelby Hill	4.00	1.80	.50
☐ 25 Willie Jackson	6.00	2.70	.75
☐ 26 LeShon Johnson	6.00	2.70	.75
☐ 27 Tre Johnson	6.00	2.70	.75
☐ 28 Alan Kline	4.00	1.80	.50
☐ 29 Darren Krein	4.00	1.80	.50
☐ 30 Antonio Langham	6.00	2.70	.75
☐ 31 Corey Louchiey	4.00	1.80	.50
☐ 32 Keith Lyle	4.00	1.80	.50
☐ 33 Eric Mahlum	4.00	1.80	.50
☐ 34 Van Malone	4.00	1.80	.50
☐ 35 Chris Maumalanga	4.00	1.80	.50
☐ 36 Jamir Miller	6.00	2.70	.75
☐ 37 Jim Miller	10.00	4.50	1.25
☐ 38 Byron Bam Morris	10.00	4.50	1.25
☐ 39 Aaron Mundy	4.00	1.80	.50
☐ 40 Jeremy Nunley	4.00	1.80	.50
☐ 41 Turhonn O'Bannon	4.00	1.80	.50
☐ 42 Brad Ottis	4.00	1.80	.50
☐ 43 David Palmer	6.00	2.70	.75
☐ 44 Joe Panos	4.00	1.80	.50
☐ 45 Jim Pyne	4.00	1.80	.50
☐ 46 John Reece	4.00	1.80	.50
☐ 47 Errict Rhett	12.00	5.50	1.50
☐ 48 Tony Richardson	4.00	1.80	.50
☐ 49 Sam Rogers	4.00	1.80	.50
☐ 50 Tim Ruddy	4.00	1.80	.50
☐ 51 Corey Sawyer	4.00	1.80	.50
☐ 52 Malcom Seabron	4.00	1.80	.50
☐ 53 Jason Sehorn	4.00	1.80	.50
☐ 54 John Thierry	6.00	2.70	.75
☐ 55 Jason Winrow	4.00	1.80	.50
☐ 56 Ronnie Woolford	4.00	1.80	.50
☐ 57 Toby Wright	4.00	1.80	.50
☐ 58 Ryan Yarborough	6.00	2.70	.75
☐ 59 Eric Zomalt	4.00	1.80	.50

1994 Signature Rookies Bonus Signatures

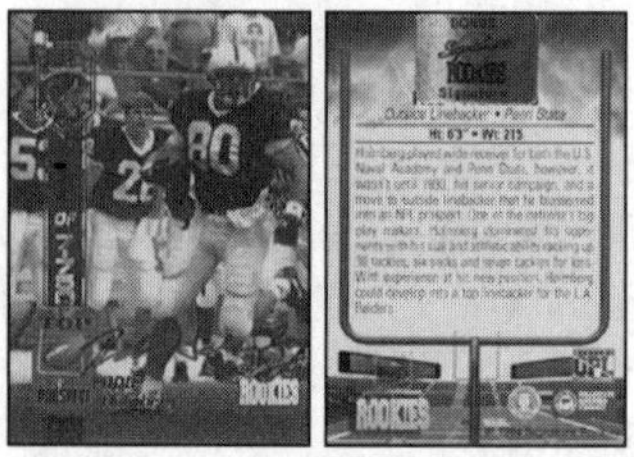

Randomly inserted in 1994 Tetrad packs, each card in this 15-card standard-size set was hand-numbered out of 7,750. The fronts display color action player photos, with a gold foil stripe accenting the left side. The player's signature appears across the bottom. The back carries biography, player profile, and a Signature Rookies Bonus Signature gold foil seal. The cards are unnumbered and checklisted below in alphabetical order.

	MINT	EXC	G-VG
COMPLETE SET (15)	30.00	13.50	3.70
COMMON SIGNATURE (1-15)	3.00	1.35	.35
☐ 1 Jamal Anderson	3.00	1.35	.35
☐ 2 Myron Bell	3.00	1.35	.35
☐ 3 Mitch Berger	3.00	1.35	.35
☐ 4 Jocelyn Borgella	3.00	1.35	.35
☐ 5 Chris Brantley	3.00	1.35	.35
☐ 6 Ron Edwards	3.00	1.35	.35
☐ 7 Rob Holmberg	3.00	1.35	.35
☐ 8 Fred Lester	3.00	1.35	.35
☐ 9 Joseph Patton	3.00	1.35	.35
☐ 10 Eric Ravotti	3.00	1.35	.35
☐ 11 Jim Reid	3.00	1.35	.35
☐ 12 Jerry Reynolds	3.00	1.35	.35
☐ 13 Bracey Walker	3.00	1.35	.35
☐ 14 Gabe Wilkins	3.00	1.35	.35
☐ 15 Brant Boyer	3.00	1.35	.35

1994 Signature Rookies Tony Dorsett

Randomly inserted in packs, these two standard-size cards feature borderless color action shots. A wide gold-foil stripe adorns the left

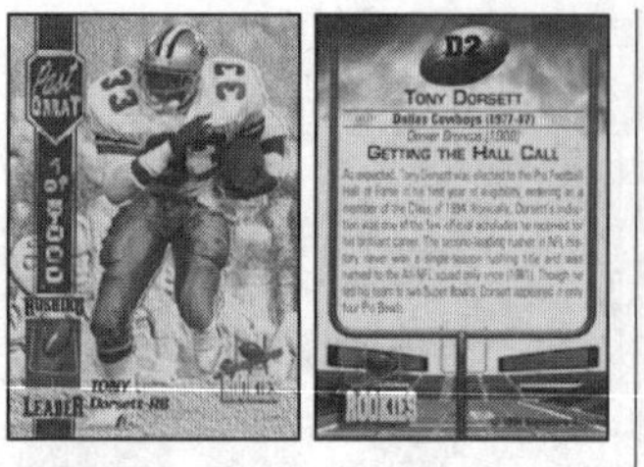

side and carries the words "1 of 5,000". The player's name and position appear at the bottom. The backs carry player biography and profile. Dorsett autographed 1,000 of his cards.

	MINT	EXC	G-VG
COMPLETE SET (2)	6.00	2.70	.75
COMMON DORSETT (D1-D2)	3.00	1.35	.35
COMP.SIGNATURE SET (2)	80.00	36.00	10.00
TONY DORSETT AU/1000	40.00	18.00	5.00
☐ D1 Tony Dorsett Holding ball in left hand	3.00	1.35	.35
☐ D2 Tony Dorsett Holding ball in both hands	3.00	1.35	.35

1994 SR Hottest Prospects

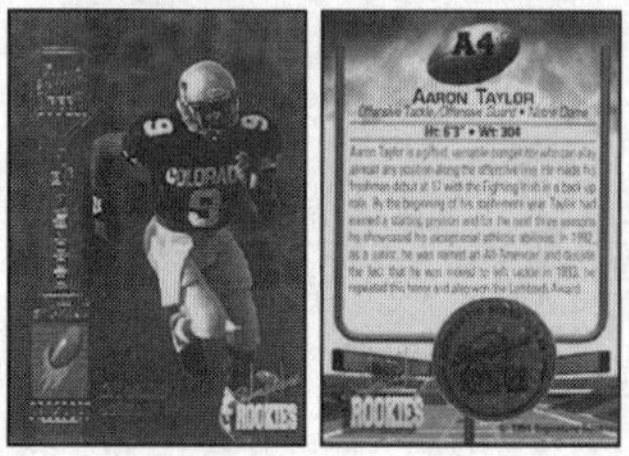

Randomly inserted in packs, these five standard-size cards feature borderless color action shots of top NFL prospects in their college uniforms. A gold-foil stripe adorns the left side and carries the words "1 of 15,000." The player's name and position are gold-foil stamped across the bottom. The backs carry player biography and profile.

	MINT	EXC	G-VG
COMPLETE SET (5)	8.00	3.60	1.00
COMMON CARD (A1-A5)	1.50	.70	.19
*SIGNATURES:4X VALUE			
☐ A1 Willie McGinest	3.00	1.35	.35
☐ A2 Bryant Young	4.00	1.80	.50
☐ A3 Dewayne Washington	1.50	.70	.19
☐ A4 Aaron Taylor	1.50	.70	.19
☐ A5 Charles Johnson	2.50	1.10	.30

1994 Signature Rookies Gale Sayers

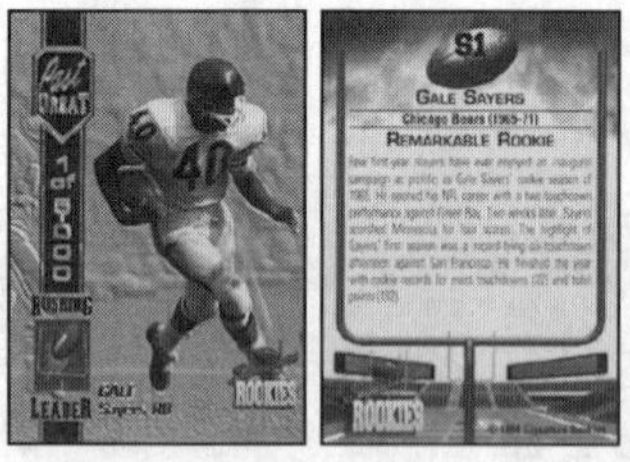

Randomly inserted in packs, these two standard-size cards feature borderless color action shots. A wide gold-foil stripe adorns the left side and carries the words "1 of 5,000". The player's name and position appear at the bottom. The backs carry player biography and profile. Sayers autographed 1,000 of his cards.

	MINT	EXC	G-VG
COMPLETE SET (2)	8.00	3.60	1.00
COMMON SAYERS (S1-S2)	4.00	1.80	.50
COMP. SIGNATURE SET (2)	80.00	36.00	10.00
GALE SAYERS AU/1000	40.00	18.00	5.00
☐ S1 Gale Sayers Holding ball in right hand	4.00	1.80	.50
☐ S2 Gale Sayers Holding ball in both hands	4.00	1.80	.50

1994 Signature Rookies Charlie Ward

Randomly inserted in packs, this 5-card standard-size set spotlights Charlie Ward, the 1993 Heisman Trophy Winner. On the front, the left side features in gold the words Future Great, the 5,000 of each card production number and the identification of Ward as a 2 sport star. The remainder of the card is used for a full-color photo which bleeds

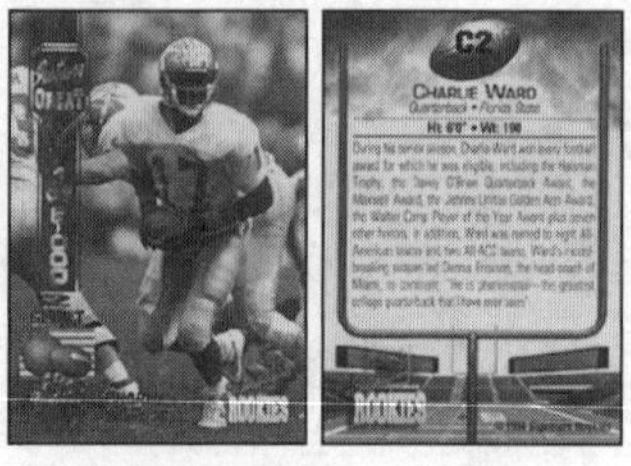

to the corner. The backs are numbered on the top of the card. Underneath the top, information about Ward is placed between two goal posts. Each card includes information pertaining to Ward's career at Florida State. Ward autographed 525 of his cards.

	MINT	EXC	G-VG
COMPLETE SET (5)	4.00	1.80	.50
COMMON WARD (C1-C5)	1.00	.45	.12
COMP. SIGNED SET (5)	100.00	45.00	12.50
CHARLIE WARD AU/525	20.00	9.00	2.50
☐ C1 Charlie Ward In throwing motion	1.00	.45	.12
☐ C2 Charlie Ward Ready to hand-off	1.00	.45	.12
☐ C3 Charlie Ward Posed Football shot	1.00	.45	.12
☐ C4 Charlie Ward Holding Basketball at waist	1.00	.45	.12
☐ C5 Charlie Ward Holding Basketball overhead	1.00	.45	.12

1995 SR Auto-Phonex

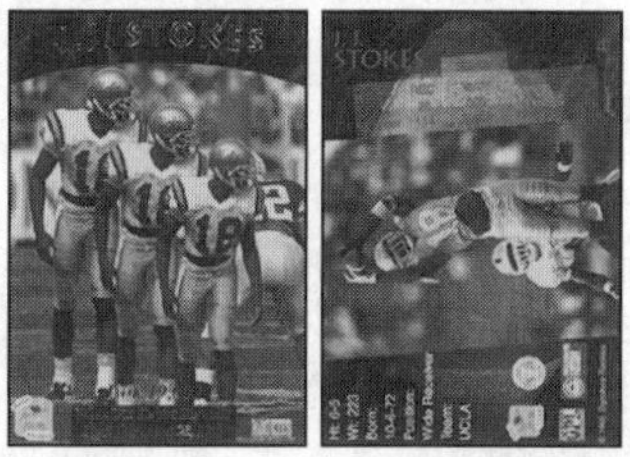

These 40 standard-size cards feature 1995 NFL Draft picks. The fronts feature triple-exposure-like color action player photos. The player's name in gold-foil letters appears on a marbleized background above the photo, while "1 of 19,000" is printed on the bottom. The horizontal backs carry another color action player photo with biography and stats. Four hundred and ninety-nine 16-box cases were produced. Every case of Auto-Phonex contained randomly inserted Hot Packs, which included an MCI autographed phone card and five additional autographed cards. Each pack contained five regular cards and one calling card worth $2.00, $5.00, or $25.00 in phone time. Five dollar calling cards feature J.J. Stokes; the odds of finding one of these 500 cards is 1:287. Twenty-five dollar calling cards feature Kevin Carter; the odds of finding one of these 100 cards is 1:1,437. Ten cash cards worth 100.00 featuring Warren Sapp were randomly inserted; odds of finding one are 1:14,371. Also eight $1,000.00 cash cards featuring either Ki-Jana Carter or Rashaan Salaam were randomly inserted; odds of finding one of these are 1:35,928.

	MINT	EXC	G-VG
COMPLETE SET (40)	6.00	2.70	.75
COMMON CARD (1-40)	.10	.05	.01
☐ 1 Warren Sapp	.25	.11	.03
☐ 2 Kevin Carter	.25	.11	.03
☐ 3 Ki-Jana Carter	.50	.23	.06
☐ 4 J.J.Stokes	.50	.23	.06
☐ 5 Derrick Alexander	.25	.11	.03
☐ 6 Rashaan Salaam	.50	.23	.06
☐ 7 Jamal Willis	.10	.05	.01
☐ 8 Frank Sanders	.50	.23	.06
☐ 9 Rob Johnson	.25	.11	.03
☐ 10 Derrick Brooks	.10	.05	.01
☐ 11 Sherman Williams	.25	.11	.03
☐ 12 Dave Barr	.10	.05	.01
☐ 13 Christian Fauria	.10	.05	.01
☐ 14 Stoney Case	.10	.05	.01
☐ 15 Rodney Thomas	.60	.25	.07
☐ 16 James A. Stewart	.10	.05	.01
☐ 17 Ray Zellars	.25	.11	.03
☐ 18 Jack Jackson	.10	.05	.01
☐ 19 Terrell Davis	1.50	.70	.19
☐ 20 Kyle Brady	.25	.11	.03
☐ 21 Ruben Brown	.10	.05	.01
☐ 22 Brent Moss	.10	.05	.01
☐ 23 John Sacca	.10	.05	.01
☐ 24 David Dunn	.10	.05	.01
☐ 25 Eddie Goines	.10	.05	.01
☐ 26 Curtis Martin	1.50	.70	.19
☐ 27 Billy Williams	.10	.05	.01
☐ 28 Steve Stenstrom	.10	.05	.01
☐ 29 Mark Bruener	.25	.11	.03
☐ 30 Kelvin Anderson	.10	.05	.01
☐ 31 Ellis Johnson	.10	.05	.01
☐ 32 Steve Ingram	.10	.05	.01
☐ 33 Larry Jones	.10	.05	.01
☐ 34 Bobby Taylor	.25	.11	.03
☐ 35 Joe Aska	.10	.05	.01
☐ 36 Jerrott Williard	.10	.05	.01
☐ 37 Chris T. Jones	.50	.23	.06
☐ 38 Mark Birchmeier	.10	.05	.01
☐ 39 Jimmy Hitchcock	.10	.05	.01
☐ 40 Tyrone Davis	.10	.05	.01
☐ NNO Ki-Jana Carter CL	.30	.14	.04

1995 SR Auto-Phonex Phone Card Signatures

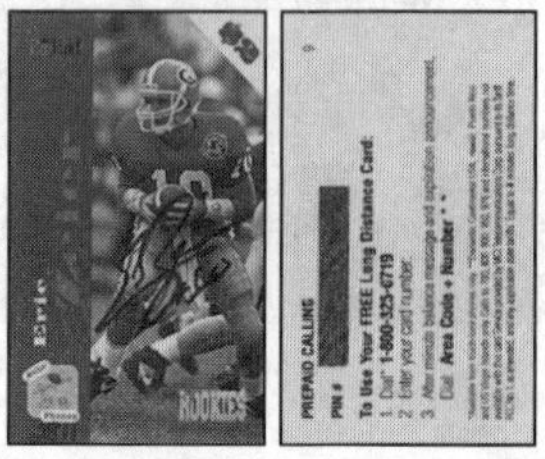

Inserted one per pack, these 40 phone cards feature the 1995 NFL Draft picks. They measure 2 3/8" by 3 1/8", have rounded corners and carry $2.00 worth of U.S. long distance calling. The fronts feature color action player photos, with the player's name in a bar alongside the left. The backs have instructions on how to use the card. The $2.00 phone cards are numbered out of 3,750. Four hundred and ninety-nine 16-box cases were produced. Every case of Auto-Phonex contained randomly-inserted Hot Packs, which included an MCI autographed phone card and five additional autographed cards. Each pack contained five regular cards and one calling card worth $2.00, $5.00, or $25.00 in phone time. Five dollar phone cards feature J.J. Stokes; the odds of finding one of these 500 cards is 1:287. Twenty-five dollar phone cards feature Kevin Carter; the odds of finding one of these 100 cards is 1:1,437. Ten cash cards worth $100.00 featuring Warren Sapp were randomly inserted; odds of finding one are 1:14,371. Also eight $1,000.00 cash cards featuring either Ki-Jana Carter or Rashaan Salaam were randomly inserted; odds of finding one of these are 1:35,928.

	MINT	EXC	G-VG
COMPLETE SET (40)	225.00	100.00	28.00
COMMON SIGN. (1-40)	3.00	1.35	.35
☐ 1 Warren Sapp	5.00	2.20	.60
☐ 2 Kevin Carter	5.00	2.20	.60
☐ 3 Ki-Jana Carter	8.00	3.60	1.00
☐ 4 J.J.Stokes	8.00	3.60	1.00
☐ 5 Derrick Alexander	3.00	1.35	.35
☐ 6 Rashaan Salaam	8.00	3.60	1.00
☐ 7 Jamal Willis	3.00	1.35	.35
☐ 8 Frank Sanders	8.00	3.60	1.00
☐ 9 Eric Zeier	5.00	2.20	.60
☐ 10 Derrick Brooks	3.00	1.35	.35
☐ 11 Sherman Williams	5.00	2.20	.60
☐ 12 Dave Barr	3.00	1.35	.35
☐ 13 Christian Fauria	3.00	1.35	.35
☐ 14 Stoney Case	3.00	1.35	.35
☐ 15 Rodney Thomas	5.00	2.20	.60
☐ 16 James A. Stewart	3.00	1.35	.35
☐ 17 Ray Zellars	5.00	2.20	.60
☐ 18 Jack Jackson	3.00	1.35	.35
☐ 19 Terrell Davis	30.00	13.50	3.70
☐ 20 Kyle Brady	5.00	2.20	.60
☐ 21 Ruben Brown	3.00	1.35	.35
☐ 22 Brent Moss	3.00	1.35	.35
☐ 23 John Sacca	3.00	1.35	.35
☐ 24 David Dunn	3.00	1.35	.35
☐ 25 Eddie Goines	3.00	1.35	.35
☐ 26 Curtis Martin	30.00	13.50	3.70
☐ 27 Billy Williams	3.00	1.35	.35
☐ 28 Steve Stenstrom	3.00	1.35	.35
☐ 29 Mark Bruener	5.00	2.20	.60
☐ 30 Kelvin Anderson	3.00	1.35	.35
☐ 31 Ellis Johnson	3.00	1.35	.35
☐ 32 Steve Ingram	3.00	1.35	.35
☐ 33 Larry Jones	3.00	1.35	.35
☐ 34 Bobby Taylor	5.00	2.20	.60
☐ 35 Joe Aska	3.00	1.35	.35
☐ 36 Jerrott Williard	3.00	1.35	.35
☐ 37 Chris T. Jones	8.00	3.60	1.00
☐ 38 Mark Birchmeier	3.00	1.35	.35
☐ 39 Jimmy Hitchcock	3.00	1.35	.35
☐ 40 Tyrone Davis	3.00	1.35	.35
☐ NNO J.J. Stokes $5 Card	20.00	9.00	2.50
☐ NNO Kevin Carter $25 Card	40.00	18.00	5.00

1995 SR Auto-Phonex Signatures

Every case of Auto-Phonex contained randomly inserted Hot Packs, which included an MCI autographed phone card and five additional autographed cards. By sending in a redemption insert, the collector received one of two 5-card hot packs. The cards are identical in design to their regular issue counterparts except for the signatures. Also each card is numbered out of 300.

	MINT	EXC	G-VG
COMPLETE SET (10)	300.00	135.00	38.00
COMMON SIGN. (1-10)	15.00	6.75	1.85

	MINT	EXC	G-VG
3A Ki-Jana Carter	70.00	32.00	8.75
6A Rashaan Salaam	70.00	32.00	8.75
8A Frank Sanders	70.00	32.00	8.75
11A Sherman Williams	15.00	6.75	1.85
12A Dave Barr	15.00	6.75	1.85
14A Stoney Case	15.00	6.75	1.85
16A James A.Stewart	15.00	6.75	1.85
17A Ray Zellars	30.00	13.50	3.70
20A Kyle Brady	30.00	13.50	3.70
23A John Sacca	15.00	6.75	1.85

1995 SR Draft Preview

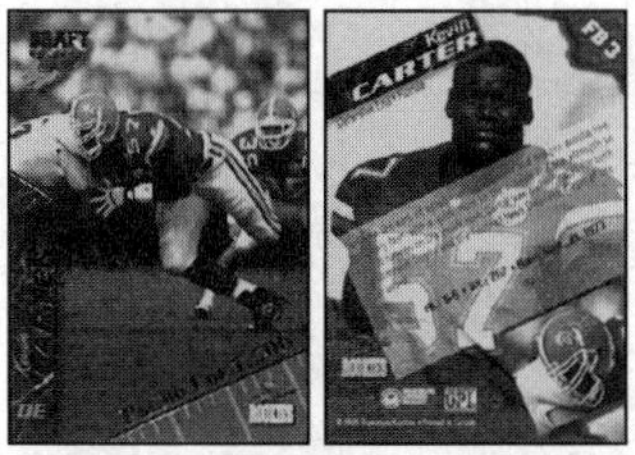

These standard-size six-card packs retailed for 5.00 and included an autographed card. Each player autographed 7,750 of his own cards, and 39,000 of each card were produced. The fronts display a color action player photo. At the lower left corner, a black marblized stripe outlined in gold foil carries the player's name. The lower right corner has a triangular-shaped green football field design. Edged at the upper right and lower left corners with green grass, the backs show a closeup photo, with a ghosted panel carrying bio and player profile. The cards are numbered in the top right corner. An international version of this set was also issued; in which; players signed 2,750 of their own cards, and 13,500 of each card produced. These cards are similiar to the original set except they are stamped in silver foil with the words international appearing on the card fronts.

	MINT	EXC	G-VG
COMPLETE SET (80)	10.00	4.50	1.25
COMMON CARD (1-80)	.10	.05	.01
1 Derrick Alexander	.10	.05	.01
2 Kelvin Anderson	.10	.05	.01
3 Antonio Armstrong	.10	.05	.01
4 Jamie Asher	.10	.05	.01
5 Joe Aska	.10	.05	.01
6 Dave Barr	.10	.05	.01
7 Brandon Bennett	.10	.05	.01
8 Tony Berti	.10	.05	.01
9 Mark Birchmeier	.10	.05	.01
10 Tony Boselli	.25	.11	.03
11 Derrick Brooks	.10	.05	.01
12 Anthony Brown	.10	.05	.01
13 Ruben Brown	.10	.05	.01
14 Mark Bruener	.30	.14	.04
15 Ontiwaun Carter	.10	.05	.01
16 Stoney Case	.10	.05	.01
17 Byron Chamberlain	.10	.05	.01
18 Shannon Clavelle	.10	.05	.01
19 Jamal Cox	.10	.05	.01
20 Zack Crockett	.25	.11	.03
21 Terrell Davis	2.00	.90	.25
22 Tyrone Davis	.10	.05	.01
23 Lee DeRamus	.10	.05	.01
24 Ken Dilger	.40	.18	.05
25 Hugh Douglas	.50	.23	.06
26 David Dunn	.10	.05	.01
27 Chad Eaton	.10	.05	.01
28 Hicham El-Mashtoub	.10	.05	.01
29 Christian Fauria	.10	.05	.01
30 Terrell Fletcher	.30	.14	.04
31 Antonio Freeman	1.25	.55	.16
32 Eddie Goines	.10	.05	.01
33 Roger Graham	.10	.05	.01
34 Carl Greenwood	.10	.05	.01
35 Ed Hervey	.10	.05	.01
36 Jimmy Hitchcock	.10	.05	.01
37 Darius Holland	.10	.05	.01
38 Torey Hunter	.10	.05	.01
39 Steve Ingram	.10	.05	.01
40 Jack Jackson	.10	.05	.01
41 Trezelle Jenkins	.10	.05	.01
42 Ellis Johnson	.10	.05	.01
43 Eric Johnson	.10	.05	.01
44 Rob Johnson	.25	.11	.03
45 Chris T. Jones	.50	.23	.06
46 Larry Jones	.10	.05	.01
47 Shawn King	.10	.05	.01
48 Scotty Lewis	.10	.05	.01
49 Curtis Martin	2.00	.90	.25
50 Oscar McBride	.10	.05	.01
51 Kez McCorvey	.10	.05	.01
52 Bronzell Miller	.10	.05	.01
53 Pete Mitchell	.10	.05	.01
54 Brent Moss	.10	.05	.01
55 Craig Newsome	.10	.05	.01
56 Herman O'Berry	.10	.05	.01
57 Matt O'Dwyer	.10	.05	.01
58 Tyrone Poole	.25	.11	.03
59 Brian Pruitt	.10	.05	.01
60 Cory Raymer	.10	.05	.01
61 John Sacca	.10	.05	.01
62 Frank Sanders	.50	.23	.06
63 J.J. Smith	.10	.05	.01
64 Brendan Stai	.10	.05	.01
65 Steve Stenstrom	.10	.05	.01
66 James O. Stewart	.50	.23	.06
67 Kordell Stewart	1.50	.70	.19
68 Ben Talley	.10	.05	.01
69 Bobby Taylor	.25	.11	.03
70 Johnny Thomas	.10	.05	.01
71 Orlando Thomas	.25	.11	.03
72 Rodney Thomas	.25	.11	.03
73 Zach Wiegert	.10	.05	.01
74 Jerrott Willard	.10	.05	.01
75 Billy Williams	.10	.05	.01
76 Sherman Williams	.10	.05	.01
77 Jamal Willis	.10	.05	.01
78 Dave Wohlabaugh	.10	.05	.01
79 Eric Zeier	.25	.11	.03
80 Checklist	.10	.05	.01

1995 SR Draft Preview Signatures

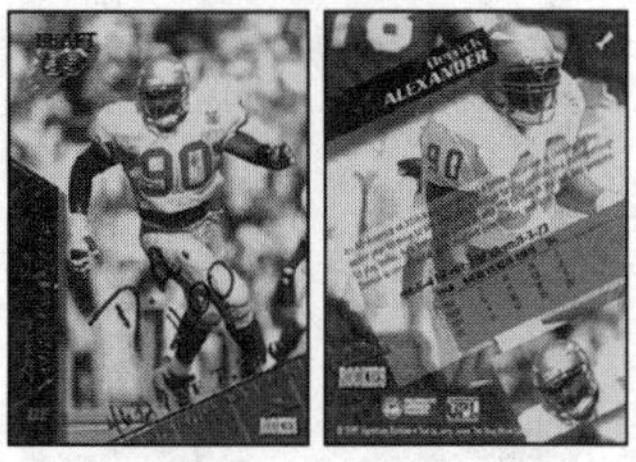

These 79 standard-size cards were also available in autographed form; an autograph card was included in each six-card pack. Each player autographed 7,750 of his own cards, and 39,000 of each regular card were produced. The design is identical to that of the regular issue, except for the autograph inscribed across the front. An international version of this set was included in each six-card pack; in which; players signed 2,750 of their own cards, and 13,500 of each card produced. These cards are similiar to the original set except they are stamped in silver foil with the words international appearing on the card fronts.

	MINT	EXC	G-VG
COMPLETE SET (79)	250.00	110.00	31.00
COMMON SIGN. (1-79)	2.50	1.10	.30
INTERNATIONAL: 2X BASIC CARDS ..			
1 Derrick Alexander	2.50	1.10	.30
2 Kelvin Anderson	2.50	1.10	.30
3 Antonio Armstrong	2.50	1.10	.30
4 Jamie Asher	2.50	1.10	.30
5 Joe Aska	2.50	1.10	.30
6 Dave Barr	2.50	1.10	.30
7 Brandon Bennett	2.50	1.10	.30
8 Tony Berti	2.50	1.10	.30
9 Mark Birchmeier	2.50	1.10	.30
10 Tony Boselli	4.00	1.80	.50
11 Derrick Brooks	2.50	1.10	.30
12 Anthony Brown	2.50	1.10	.30
13 Ruben Brown	2.50	1.10	.30
14 Mark Bruener	4.00	1.80	.50
15 Ontiwaun Carter	2.50	1.10	.30
16 Stoney Case	2.50	1.10	.30
17 Byron Chamberlain	2.50	1.10	.30
18 Shannon Clavelle	2.50	1.10	.30
19 Jamal Cox	2.50	1.10	.30
20 Zack Crockett	4.00	1.80	.50
21 Terrell Davis	20.00	9.00	2.50
22 Tyrone Davis	2.50	1.10	.30
23 Lee DeRamus	2.50	1.10	.30
24 Ken Dilger	5.00	2.20	.60
25 Hugh Douglas	5.00	2.20	.60
26 David Dunn	2.50	1.10	.30
27 Chad Eaton	2.50	1.10	.30
28 Hicham El-Mashtoub	2.50	1.10	.30
29 Christian Fauria	2.50	1.10	.30
30 Terrell Fletcher	4.00	1.80	.50
31 Antonio Freeman	12.00	5.50	1.50
32 Eddie Goines	2.50	1.10	.30
33 Roger Graham	2.50	1.10	.30
34 Carl Greenwood	2.50	1.10	.30
35 Ed Hervey	2.50	1.10	.30
36 Jimmy Hitchcock	2.50	1.10	.30
37 Darius Holland	2.50	1.10	.30
38 Torey Hunter	2.50	1.10	.30
39 Steve Ingram	2.50	1.10	.30
40 Jack Jackson	2.50	1.10	.30
41 Trezelle Jenkins	2.50	1.10	.30
42 Ellis Johnson	2.50	1.10	.30
43 Eric Johnson	2.50	1.10	.30
44 Rob Johnson	4.00	1.80	.50
45 Chris T. Jones	8.00	3.60	1.00
46 Larry Jones	2.50	1.10	.30
47 Shawn King	2.50	1.10	.30
48 Scotty Lewis	2.50	1.10	.30
49 Curtis Martin	20.00	9.00	2.50
50 Oscar McBride	2.50	1.10	.30
51 Kez McCorvey	2.50	1.10	.30
52 Bronzell Miller	2.50	1.10	.30
53 Pete Mitchell	2.50	1.10	.30
54 Brent Moss	2.50	1.10	.30
55 Craig Newsome	2.50	1.10	.30
56 Herman O'Berry	2.50	1.10	.30
57 Matt O'Dwyer	2.50	1.10	.30
58 Tyrone Poole	4.00	1.80	.50
59 Brian Pruitt	2.50	1.10	.30
60 Cory Raymer	2.50	1.10	.30
61 John Sacca	2.50	1.10	.30
62 Frank Sanders	8.00	3.60	1.00
63 J.J. Smith	2.50	1.10	.30
64 Brendan Stai	2.50	1.10	.30
65 Steve Stenstrom	2.50	1.10	.30
66 James O. Stewart	5.00	2.20	.60
67 Kordell Stewart	15.00	6.75	1.85
68 Ben Talley	2.50	1.10	.30
69 Bobby Taylor	4.00	1.80	.50
70 Johnny Thomas	2.50	1.10	.30
71 Orlando Thomas	4.00	1.80	.50
72 Rodney Thomas	8.00	3.60	1.00
73 Zach Wiegert	2.50	1.10	.30
74 Jerrott Willard	2.50	1.10	.30
75 Billy Williams	2.50	1.10	.30
76 Sherman Williams	4.00	1.80	.50
77 Jamal Willis	2.50	1.10	.30
78 Dave Wohlabaugh	2.50	1.10	.30
79 Eric Zeier	8.00	3.60	1.00

1995 SR Draft Preview Franchise Rookies

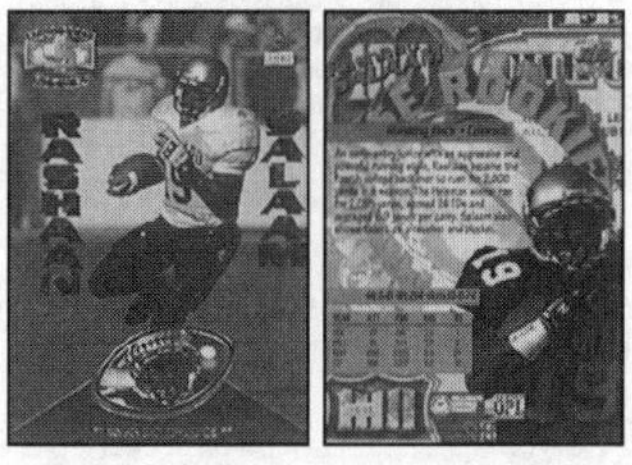

Randomly inserted at a ratio of one per every eight packs, this 10-card standard-size set captures some top draft picks. Each player autographed 2,500 of his own cards, and just 10,000 sets were produced. The fronts feature a player action photo with a small head shot at the bottom in a gold football frame on top a gold triangle. The player's first name runs along the left side with the last name on the right. The backs carry the player's name, position, school, college statistics, biographical information and career highlights on a background of a hundred dollar bill. An international version of this set was also issued. These cards are similiar to the original set except they are stamped in silver foil with the words international appearing on the card fronts.

	MINT	EXC	G-VG
COMPLETE SET (R1-10)	12.00	5.50	1.50
COMMON CARD (R1-R10)	.50	.23	.06
INTERNATIONAL: 2X BASIC CARDS ..			
R1 Kyle Brady	.75	.35	.09
R2 Kevin Carter	.50	.23	.06
R3 Ki-Jana Carter	4.00	1.80	.50
R4 Luther Ellis	.50	.23	.06
R5 Rashaan Salaam	5.00	2.20	.60
R6 Warren Sapp	.75	.35	.09
R7 James A. Stewart	.50	.23	.06
R8 J.J. Stokes	4.00	1.80	.50
R9 Michael Westbrook	3.50	1.55	.45
R10 Ray Zellars	.75	.35	.09

1995 SR Draft Preview Franchise Rookies Signatures

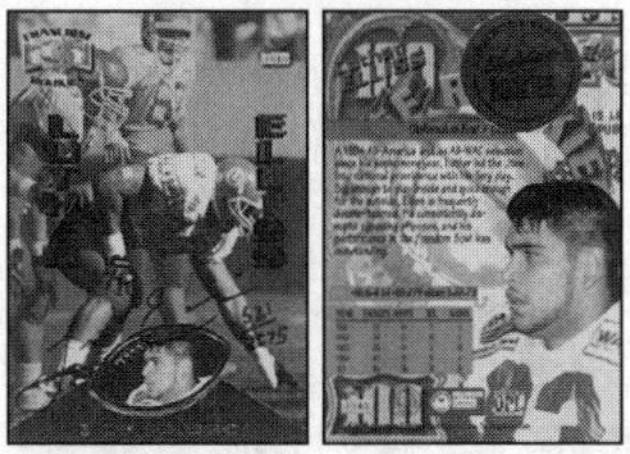

Randomly inserted at a ratio of one per every eight packs, this 10-card standard-size set was also available in autographed form. Each player autographed 2,575 of his own cards, and just 10,000 sets were produced. The design is identical to that of the regular issue, except for the autograph inscribed across the front.

	MINT	EXC	G-VG
COMPLETE SET (R1-10)	125.00	55.00	15.50
COMMON SIGN. (R1-R10)	4.00	1.80	.50
R1 Kyle Brady	5.00	2.20	.60
R2 Kevin Carter	4.00	1.80	.50
R3 Ki-Jana Carter	18.00	8.00	2.20
R4 Luther Ellis	4.00	1.80	.50
R5 Rashaan Salaam	30.00	13.50	3.70
R6 Warren Sapp/1125	10.00	4.50	1.25
R7 James A. Stewart	4.00	1.80	.50
R8 J.J. Stokes	25.00	11.00	3.10
R9 Michael Westbrook	20.00	9.00	2.50
R10 Ray Zellars	5.00	2.20	.60

1995 SR Draft Preview International Franchise Duo

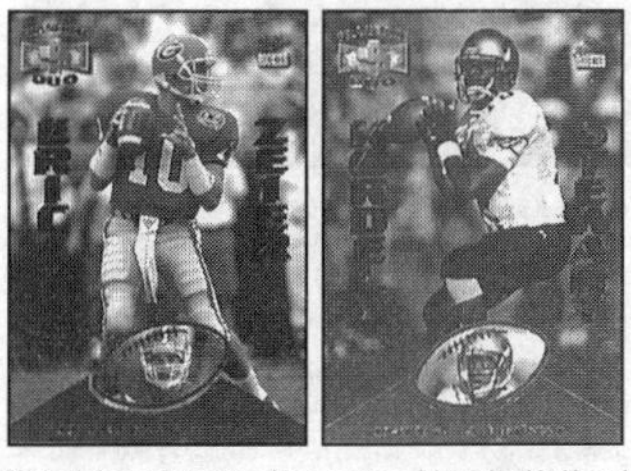

Randomly inserted at a ratio of one per every eight packs, this 10-card standard-size set captures one top draft pick on each side of the card. Each player autographed a number of his own cards, The fronts feature a player action photo with a small head shot at the bottom in a silver football frame on top a silver triangle. The word international appears in the silver triangle. The player's first name runs along the left side with the last name on the right.

	MINT	EXC	G-VG
COMPLETE SET (10)	20.00	9.00	2.50
COMMON CARD (1-10)	1.50	.70	.19
1 Ki-Jana Carter Kevin Carter	3.00	1.35	.35
2 Warren Sapp Derrick Alexander	1.50	.70	.19
3 James A. Stewart James O. Stewart	3.00	1.35	.35
4 Michael Westbrook J.J. Stokes	4.00	1.80	.50
5 Kyle Brady Kerry Collins	3.00	1.35	.35
6 Steve McNair Kerry Collins	5.00	2.20	.60
7 Eric Zeier Kordell Stewart	5.00	2.20	.60
8 Rob Johnson Stoney Case	1.50	.70	.19
9 Rashaan Salaam Ki-Jana Carter	5.00	2.20	.60
10 Ray Zellars Sherman Williams	2.00	.90	.25

1995 SR Draft Preview International Franchise Duo Signatures

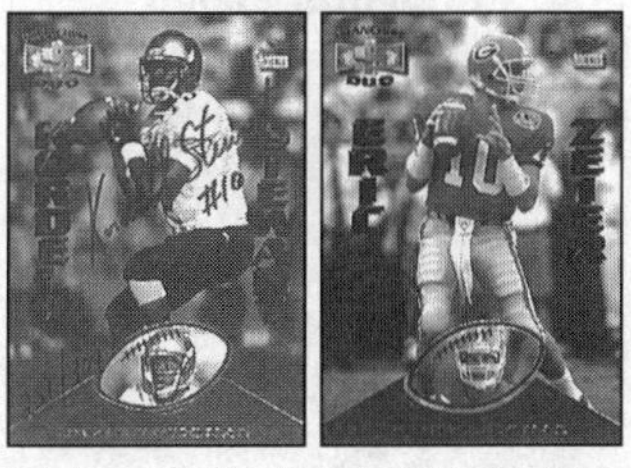

Randomly inserted into international packs, this 16-card standard-size set captures one top draft pick on each side of the card. Each player autographed a number of his own cards. The number of cards each player autographed appears below. James A. Stewart and Warren Sapp were the only players featured in this set that did not autograph any of their own cards. The design is identical to that of the regular issue, except for the autograph inscribed across the front and the authentic signature sticker that appears on the opposite side.

	MINT	EXC	G-VG
COMPLETE SET (16)	700.00	325.00	90.00
COMMON CARD (1-16)	15.00	6.75	1.85
1 Derrick Alexander AU/200	15.00	6.75	1.85
2 Kyle Brady AU/242	20.00	9.00	2.50
3 Kevin Carter AU/315	15.00	6.75	1.85
4 Ki-Jana Carter AU/400	60.00	27.00	7.50
5 Stoney Case AU/200	15.00	6.75	1.85
6 Kerry Collins AU/600	70.00	32.00	8.75
7 Rob Johnson AU/309	20.00	9.00	2.50
8 Steve McNair AU/600	60.00	27.00	7.50
9 Rashaan Salaam AU/299	70.00	32.00	8.75
10 Kordell Stewart AU/309	125.00	55.00	15.50
11 James O. Stewart AU/200	70.00	32.00	8.75
13 J.J. Stokes AU/284	60.00	27.00	7.50
14 Michael Westbrook AU/282	70.00	32.00	8.75
15 Sherman Williams AU/312	20.00	9.00	2.50
16 Eric Zeier AU/314	20.00	9.00	2.50
17 Ray Zellars AU/310	20.00	9.00	2.50

1995 SR Draft Preview Masters Of The Mic

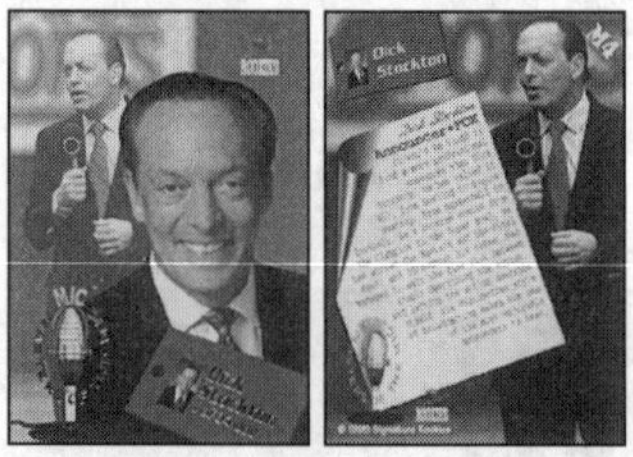

Randomly inserted at a ratio of one card per every four packs, this 5-card standard-size set profiles some top sports announcers. Each announcer autographed 1,000 of his own cards, and just 30,000 sets were produced. The fronts feature a picture of the announcer on a photo background with a small head shot on a blue press pass in the right lower corner. The backs carry the same large photo with a short profile on a white background over the picture. The cards are numbered in the top right corner. An international version of this set was also issued. These cards are similiar to the original set except they are stamped in silver foil with the words international appearing on the card fronts.

	MINT	EXC	G-VG
COMPLETE SET (5)	10.00	4.50	1.25
COMMON CARD (M1-M5)	2.00	.90	.25
INTERNATIONAL: 2X BASIC CARDS			
☐ M1 Todd Christensen	2.00	.90	.25
☐ M2 Jerry Glanville	2.00	.90	.25
☐ M3 Howie Long	2.00	.90	.25
☐ M4 Dick Stockton	2.00	.90	.25
☐ M5 Joe Theismann UER	2.00	.90	.25

1995 SR Draft Preview Masters Of The Mic Signatures

Randomly inserted at a ratio of one card per every four packs, this 5-card standard-size set was available in autographed form. Each announcer autographed 1,030 of his own cards, and just 30,000 sets were produced. The design is identical to that of the regular issue, except for the autograph inscribed across the front.

	MINT	EXC	G-VG
COMPLETE SET (5)	65.00	29.00	8.00
COMMON SIGN. (M1-M5)	14.00	6.25	1.75
☐ M1 Todd Christensen	14.00	6.25	1.75
☐ M2 Jerry Glanville	14.00	6.25	1.75
☐ M3 Howie Long	14.00	6.25	1.75
☐ M4 Dick Stockton	14.00	6.25	1.75
☐ M5 Joe Theismann UER	14.00	6.25	1.75

1995 SR Draft Preview Peripheral Vision

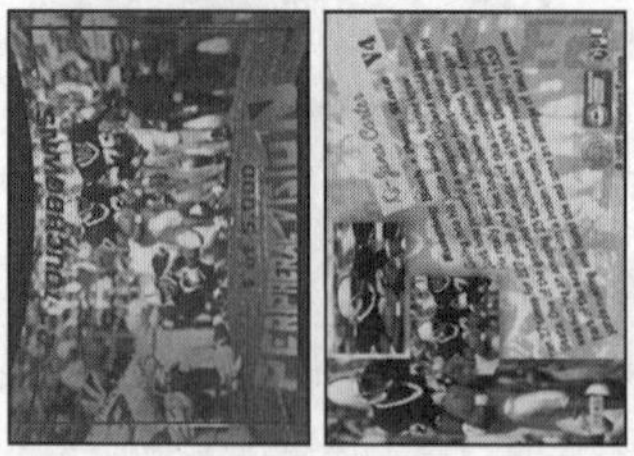

Randomly inserted at a ratio of one per every 24 packs, this 5-card standard-size set spotlights two outstanding running backs. Each player signed 100 of his own cards. The set consists of two Salaam cards, two Carter cards, and a Head-to-Head card featuring both players. One hundred Head-to-Head cards bear signatures by both players. An international version of this set was also issued. These cards are similiar to the original set except they are stamped in silver foil with the words international appearing on the card fronts.

	MINT	EXC	G-VG
COMPLETE SET (5)	8.00	3.60	1.00
COMMON CARD (V1-V5)	2.00	.90	.25
INTERNATIONAL: 2X BASIC CARDS			
☐ 1/2 Rashaan Salaam	2.00	.90	.25
☐ 3/4 Ki-Jana Carter	2.00	.90	.25
☐ 5 Ki-Jana Carter Rashaan Salaam	2.50	1.10	.30
☐ V2 Rashaan Salaam	2.00	.90	.25
☐ V4 Ki-Jana Carter	2.00	.90	.25

1995 SR Draft Preview Peripheral Vision Signatures

Randomly inserted at a ratio of one per every 24 packs, this 5-card standard-size set was available in autographed form. The design is identical to that of the regular issue, except for the autograph inscribed across the front. Approximately 105 of each autograph exist.

	MINT	EXC	G-VG
COMPLETE SET (5)	550.00	250.00	70.00
COMMON SIGN. (V1-V5)	80.00	36.00	10.00
☐ 1/2 Rashaan Salaam	80.00	36.00	10.00
☐ 3/4 Ki-Jana Carter	80.00	36.00	10.00
☐ 5 Ki-Jana Carter Rashaan Salaam	250.00	110.00	31.00
☐ V2 Rashaan Salaam	150.00	70.00	19.00
☐ V4 Ki-Jana Carter	90.00	40.00	11.00

1995 SR Draft Preview Old Judge Previews

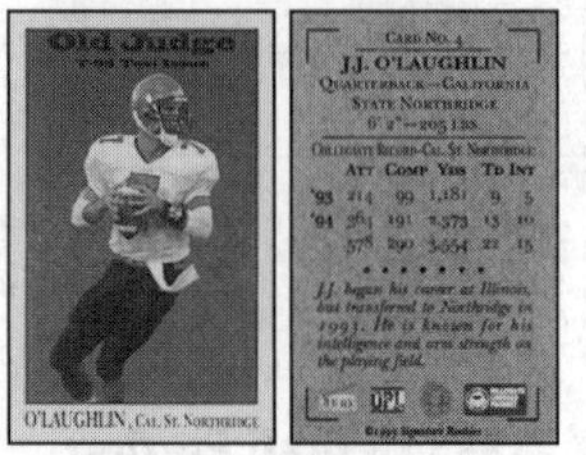

Randomly inserted at a ratio of one per every 24 packs, this 5-card set spotlights some collegiate stars. Just 5,000 sets were produced, with 515 autographs of each player. The cards measure 2" by 3". Inside white borders, the fronts display a color action cutout on a solid color background. The series name "Old Judge, T-95 Test Issue" is printed across the top, while the player's last name and school appear in the bottom white border. The backs carry biographical and statistical information.

	MINT	EXC	G-VG
COMPLETE SET (5)	20.00	9.00	2.50
COMMON CARD (1-5)	1.50	.70	.19
*SIGNATURES:10X VALUE			
☐ 1 Blake Brockermeyer	1.50	.70	.19
☐ 2 Kerry Collins	10.00	4.50	1.25
☐ 3 Steve McNair	6.00	2.70	.75
☐ 4 J.J. O'Laughlin	1.50	.70	.19
☐ 5 John Walsh	1.50	.70	.19

1995 SR Draft Preview Old Judge Previews Signatures

Randomly inserted at a ratio of one per 24 packs, this 5-card standard-size set was also available in autographed form. Each player autographed 515 of his cards. The cards are identical to their regular issue counterparts, except for the autograph inscribed across the front.

	MINT	EXC	G-VG
COMPLETE SET (5)	200.00	90.00	25.00
COMMON SIGN. (1-5)	15.00	6.75	1.85
☐ 1 Blake Brockermeyer	15.00	6.75	1.85
☐ 2 Kerry Collins	100.00	45.00	12.50
☐ 3 Steve McNair	60.00	27.00	7.50
☐ 4 J.J. O'Laughlin	15.00	6.75	1.85
☐ 5 John Walsh	15.00	6.75	1.85

1995 SR Signature Prime Previews

Randomly inserted in Basketball Autobilia packs, this five-card standard-size set features color player action shots on the fronts. These photos are borderless and carries the player's name in gold lettering in a red stripe that appears on the left side of the card. The red stripe starts with the Signature Prime logo and ends with the Signature Rookies logo. The back carries an additional photo the player; his position and college stats.

	MINT	EXC	G-VG
COMPLETE SET (5)	12.00	5.50	1.50
COMMON CARD (1-5)	1.00	.45	.12
☐ 1 Ki-Jana Carter	2.00	.90	.25
☐ 2 Kyle Brady	1.00	.45	.12
☐ 3 J.J. Stokes	2.50	1.10	.30
☐ 4 Rashaan Salaam	3.00	1.35	.35
☐ 5 Steve McNair	5.00	2.20	.60

1995 SR Signature Prime

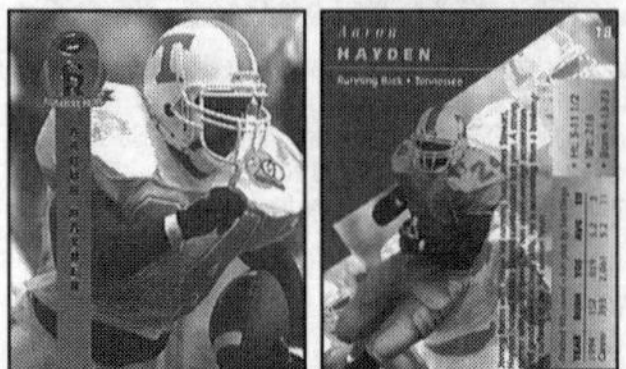

This 50-card standard-size set features color player action shots on the fronts. Each player autographed 3,000 of his own cards. These photos are borderless and carries the player's name in gold lettering in a red stripe that appears on the left side of the card. The red stripe starts with the Signature Prime logo and ends with the Signature Rookies logo. The back carries an additional photo the player; his position and college stats.

	MINT	EXC	G-VG
COMPLETE SET (50)	20.00	9.00	2.50
COMMON CARD (1-50)	.15	.07	.02
CHECKLIST (NNO)	.10	.05	.01
☐ 1 Justin Armour	.15	.07	.02
☐ 2 Joe Aska	.15	.07	.02
☐ 3 Henry Bailey	.15	.07	.02
☐ 4 Jay Barker	.15	.07	.02
☐ 5 Dave Barr	.15	.07	.02
☐ 6 Kevin Bouie	.15	.07	.02
☐ 7 Mark Bruener	.40	.18	.05
☐ 8 Stoney Case	.15	.07	.02
☐ 9 Curtis Ceaser	.15	.07	.02
☐ 10 Todd Collins	.75	.35	.09
☐ 11 Jerry Colquitt	.15	.07	.02
☐ 12 Terrell Davis	4.00	1.80	.50
☐ 13 David Dunn	.40	.18	.05
☐ 14 O'Mar Ellison	.15	.07	.02
☐ 15 Christian Fauria	.40	.18	.05
☐ 16 Antonio Freeman	2.50	1.10	.30
☐ 17 Eddie Goines	.15	.07	.02
☐ 18 Aaron Hayden	.40	.18	.05
☐ 19 William Henderson	.15	.07	.02
☐ 20 Kevin Hickman	.15	.07	.02
☐ 21 Jack Jackson	.15	.07	.02
☐ 22 Travis Jervey	.15	.07	.02
☐ 23 Rob Johnson	.40	.18	.05
☐ 24 Chris T. Jones	.75	.35	.09
☐ 25 Larry Jones	.15	.07	.02
☐ 26 Curtis Marsh	.15	.07	.02
☐ 27 Curtis Martin	4.00	1.80	.50
☐ 28 Fred McCrary	.15	.07	.02
☐ 29 Mike Miller	.15	.07	.02
☐ 30 Shannon Myers	.15	.07	.02
☐ 31 Jimmy Oliver	.15	.07	.02
☐ 32 Dino Philyaw	.15	.07	.02
☐ 33 Lovell Pinkney	.15	.07	.02
☐ 34 Michael Roan	.15	.07	.02
☐ 35 Chris Sanders	.75	.35	.09
☐ 36 Frank Sanders	.75	.35	.09
☐ 37 Cory Schlesinger	.40	.18	.05
☐ 38 Charlie Simmons	.15	.07	.02
☐ 39 David Sloan	.40	.18	.05
☐ 40 Steve Stenstrom	.15	.07	.02
☐ 41 James A. Stewart	.15	.07	.02
☐ 42 Rodney Thomas	.40	.18	.05
☐ 43 A.C. Tellison	.15	.07	.02
☐ 44 Tamarick Vanover	.75	.35	.09
☐ 45 John Walsh	.15	.07	.02
☐ 46 Kendell Watkins	.15	.07	.02
☐ 47 Charles Way	.40	.18	.05
☐ 48 Craig Whelihan	.15	.07	.02
☐ 49 Eric Zeier	.40	.18	.05
☐ 50 Ray Zellars	.40	.18	.05

1995 SR Signature Prime Signatures

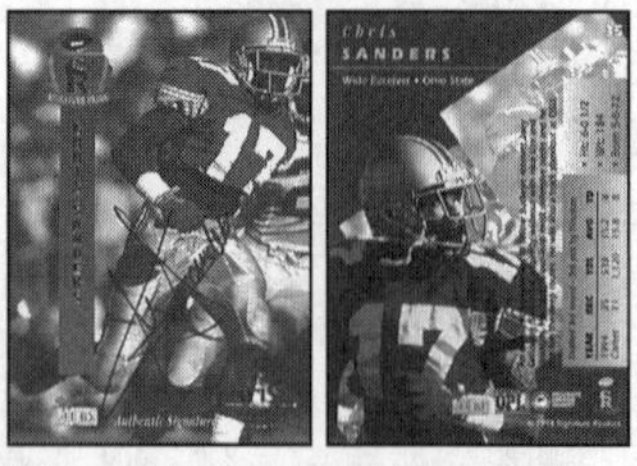

This 50-card standard-size set features color player action shots on the fronts. Each player autographed 3,000 of his own cards. These autographed cards were inserted at a rate of one per pack and were sealed in a protective holder. The design is identical to that of the regular issue, except for the autograph, the words authentic signature and the numbering appearing in an outlined gold foil football in the bottom right hand corner on the front of the card.

	MINT	EXC	G-VG
COMPLETE SET (50)	275.00	125.00	34.00
COMMON CARD (1-50)	4.00	1.80	.50
☐ 1 Justin Armour	4.00	1.80	.50
☐ 2 Joe Aska	4.00	1.80	.50
☐ 3 Henry Bailey	4.00	1.80	.50
☐ 4 Jay Barker	4.00	1.80	.50
☐ 5 Dave Barr	4.00	1.80	.50
☐ 6 Kevin Bouie	4.00	1.80	.50
☐ 7 Mark Bruener	8.00	3.60	1.00
☐ 8 Stoney Case	4.00	1.80	.50
☐ 9 Curtis Ceaser	4.00	1.80	.50
☐ 10 Todd Collins	8.00	3.60	1.00
☐ 11 Jerry Colquitt	4.00	1.80	.50
☐ 12 Terrell Davis	30.00	13.50	3.70
☐ 13 David Dunn	8.00	3.60	1.00
☐ 14 O'Mar Ellison	4.00	1.80	.50
☐ 15 Christian Fauria	8.00	3.60	1.00
☐ 16 Antonio Freeman	20.00	9.00	2.50
☐ 17 Eddie Goines	4.00	1.80	.50
☐ 18 Aaron Hayden	8.00	3.60	1.00
☐ 19 William Henderson	4.00	1.80	.50
☐ 20 Kevin Hickman	4.00	1.80	.50
☐ 21 Jack Jackson	4.00	1.80	.50
☐ 22 Travis Jervey	4.00	1.80	.50
☐ 23 Rob Johnson	4.00	1.80	.50
☐ 24 Chris T. Jones	12.00	5.50	1.50
☐ 25 Larry Jones	4.00	1.80	.50
☐ 26 Curtis Marsh	4.00	1.80	.50
☐ 27 Curtis Martin	30.00	13.50	3.70
☐ 28 Fred McCrary	4.00	1.80	.50
☐ 29 Mike Miller	4.00	1.80	.50
☐ 30 Shannon Myers	4.00	1.80	.50
☐ 31 Jimmy Oliver	4.00	1.80	.50
☐ 32 Dino Philyaw	4.00	1.80	.50
☐ 33 Lovell Pinkney	4.00	1.80	.50
☐ 34 Michael Roan	4.00	1.80	.50
☐ 35 Chris Sanders	12.00	5.50	1.50
☐ 36 Frank Sanders	12.00	5.50	1.50
☐ 37 Cory Schlesinger	8.00	3.60	1.00
☐ 38 Charlie Simmons	4.00	1.80	.50
☐ 39 David Sloan	8.00	3.60	1.00
☐ 40 Steve Stenstrom	4.00	1.80	.50
☐ 41 James A. Stewart	4.00	1.80	.50
☐ 42 Rodney Thomas	8.00	3.60	1.00
☐ 43 A.C. Tellison	4.00	1.80	.50
☐ 44 Tamarick Vanover	12.00	5.50	1.50
☐ 45 John Walsh	4.00	1.80	.50
☐ 46 Kendell Watkins	4.00	1.80	.50
☐ 47 Charles Way	8.00	3.60	1.00
☐ 48 Craig Whelihan	4.00	1.80	.50
☐ 49 Eric Zeier	8.00	3.60	1.00
☐ 50 Ray Zellars	8.00	3.60	1.00

1995 SR Signature Prime TD Club

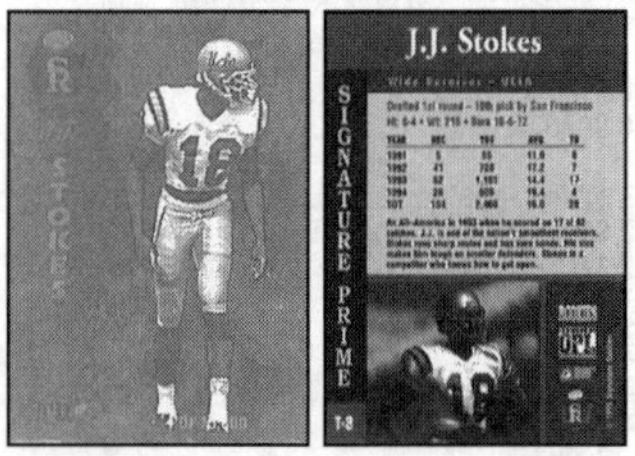

This 10-card set was inserted at a rate of one per pack. Each player autographed 1,000 of his own cards of the 15,000 cards produced. A photo of the player appears on the right side of the card front with a silver foil background. The player's name appears on the left side of the card with a green/blue background with the Signature Prime and TD Club logos.

	MINT	EXC	G-VG
COMPLETE SET (10)	12.00	5.50	1.50
COMMON CARD (T1-T10)	.50	.23	.06
☐ T1 Kyle Brady	.50	.23	.06
☐ T2 Ki-Jana Carter	2.00	.90	.25
☐ T3 Kerry Collins	3.00	1.35	.35
☐ T4 Joey Galloway	1.50	.70	.19
☐ T5 Steve McNair	2.00	.90	.25
☐ T6 Rashaan Salaam	3.00	1.35	.35
☐ T7 James O. Stewart	.75	.35	.09
☐ T8 J.J. Stokes	2.50	1.10	.30
☐ T9 Michael Westbrook	2.00	.90	.25
☐ T10 Sherman Williams	.50	.23	.06

1995 SR Signature Prime TD Club Signatures

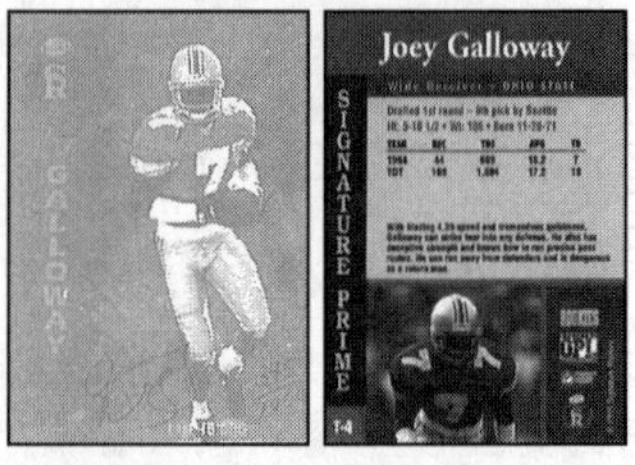

This 10-card signature set was randomly inserted in packs. Each player autographed 1,000 of his own cards of the 15,000 cards produced. Each autograph came sealed in a protective holder. The design is identical to that of the regular issue, except for the autograph and numbering on the front.

	MINT	EXC	G-VG
COMPLETE SET (10)	300.00	135.00	38.00
COMMON CARD (1-10)	15.00	6.75	1.85
☐ T1 Kyle Brady	15.00	6.75	1.85
☐ T2 Ki-Jana Carter	25.00	11.00	3.10
☐ T3 Kerry Collins	70.00	32.00	8.75
☐ T4 Joey Galloway	40.00	18.00	5.00

☐ T5 Steve McNair	50.00	22.00	6.25
☐ T6 Rashaan Salaam	30.00	13.50	3.70
☐ T7 James O. Stewart	25.00	11.00	3.10
☐ T8 J.J. Stokes	25.00	11.00	3.10
☐ T9 Michael Westbrook	30.00	13.50	3.70
☐ T10 Sherman Williams	15.00	6.75	1.85

1996 SR Autobilia

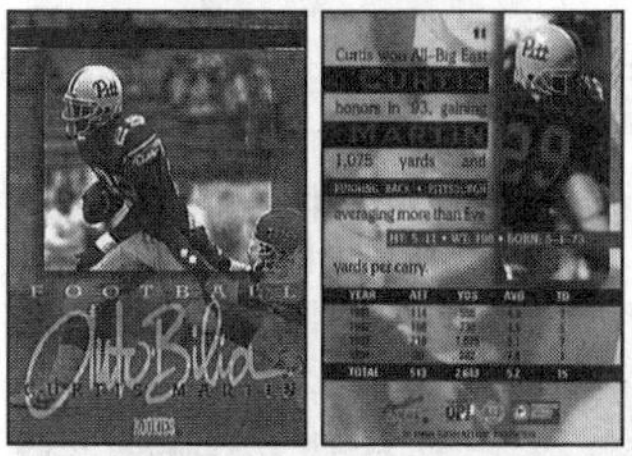

This 55 card standard-size set was issued by Signature Rookies The fronts feature a player photo as well as the words "Autobilia" on the front. The back has vital statistics, seasonal and career information as well as another player photo. Rookies from the 1995 season as well as those for the upcoming 1996 season are featured in this set.

	MINT	NRMT	EXC
COMPLETE SET (55)	15.00	6.75	1.85
COMMON CARD (1-55)	.10	.05	.01
☐ 1 Ruben Brown	.10	.05	.01
☐ 2 Kevin Carter	.10	.05	.01
☐ 3 Ki-Jana Carter	.25	.11	.03
☐ 4 Stoney Case	.10	.05	.01
☐ 5 Kerry Collins	.75	.35	.09
☐ 6 Terrell Davis	1.00	.45	.12
☐ 7 Antonio Freeman	.50	.23	.06
☐ 8 Joey Galloway	.75	.35	.09
☐ 9 Darick Holmes	.25	.11	.03
☐ 10 Jack Jackson	.10	.05	.01
☐ 11 Curtis Martin	1.00	.45	.12
☐ 12 O.J. McDuffie	.25	.11	.03
☐ 13 Steve McNair	.30	.14	.04
☐ 14 Byron "Bam" Morris	.50	.23	.06
☐ 15 Craig Newsome	.10	.05	.01
☐ 16 Errict Rhett	.50	.23	.06
☐ 17 Rashaan Salaam	.75	.35	.09
☐ 18 Frank Sanders	.25	.11	.03
☐ 19 James O. Stewart	.25	.11	.03
☐ 20 Kordell Stewart	.75	.35	.09
☐ 21 J.J. Stokes	.50	.23	.06
☐ 22 Rodney Thomas	.25	.11	.03
☐ 23 Tamarick Vanover	.50	.23	.06
☐ 24 Michael Westbrook	.50	.23	.06
☐ 25 Sherman Williams	.10	.05	.01
☐ 26 Eric Zeier	.40	.18	.05
☐ 27 Karim Abdul-Jabbar	1.50	.70	.19
☐ 28 Mike Alstott	1.00	.45	.12
☐ 29 Willie Anderson	.10	.05	.01
☐ 30 Tony Banks	1.25	.55	.16
☐ 31 Marco Battaglia	.40	.18	.05
☐ 32 Tim Biakabutuka	2.00	.90	.25
☐ 33 Stephen Davis	.60	.25	.07
☐ 34 Chris Doering	.10	.05	.01
☐ 35 Daryl Gardener	.10	.05	.01
☐ 36 Eddie George	2.50	1.10	.30
☐ 37 Terry Glenn	2.50	1.10	.30
☐ 38 Randall Godfrey	.10	.05	.01
☐ 39 Marvin Harrison	1.00	.45	.12
☐ 40 Aaron Hayden	.25	.11	.03
☐ 41 Mercury Hayes	.40	.18	.05
☐ 42 Dietrich Jells	.10	.05	.01
☐ 43 Cedric Jones	.10	.05	.01
☐ 44 Jeff Lewis	.30	.14	.04
☐ 45 Derrick Mayes	.75	.35	.09
☐ 46 Leland McElroy	1.25	.55	.16
☐ 47 Jerald Moore	.40	.18	.05
☐ 48 Eric Moulds	.75	.35	.09
☐ 49 Kendrick Nord	.10	.05	.01
☐ 50 Stanley Pritchett	.25	.11	.03
☐ 51 Jon Stark	.10	.05	.01
☐ 52 Steve Taneyhill	.10	.05	.01
☐ 53 Amani Toomer	.75	.35	.09
☐ 54 Stepfret Williams	.50	.23	.06
☐ 55 Checklist	.10	.05	.01

1991 Star Pics Promos

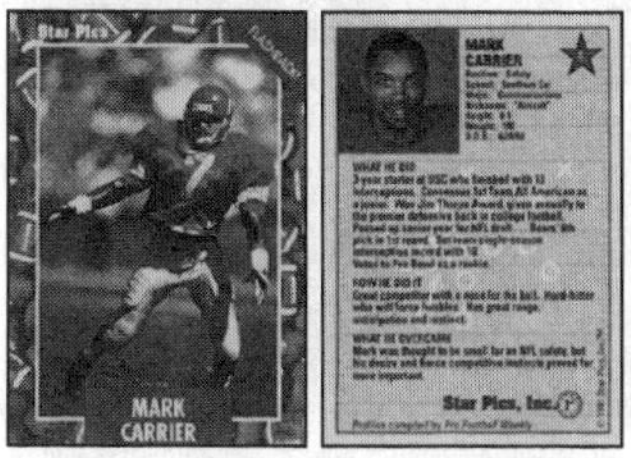

These promo cards measure the standard size and preview the style of the 1991 Star Pics football set. The cards were distributed in two-card panels with Aaron Craver paired with Mark Carrier and Dan McGwire paired with Eric Turner. These promos were quite plentiful because they were also bound into the Pro Football Weekly annual football preview publication. The fronts feature action color player photos. The photo is framed in white and bordered by footballs. The player's name appears in a maroon box at the bottom. The backs have a mint-green football field background with plays drawn in. Printed on the field is a close-up color photo, biography, career highlights, and player profile.

	MINT	NRMT	EXC
COMPLETE SET (4)	4.00	1.80	.50
COMMON CARD (1-4)	1.00	.45	.12
☐ 1 Mark Carrier DB	1.00	.45	.12
☐ 2 Aaron Craver	1.00	.45	.12
☐ 3 Dan McGwire	1.00	.45	.12
☐ 4 Eric Turner	1.25	.55	.16

1991 Star Pics

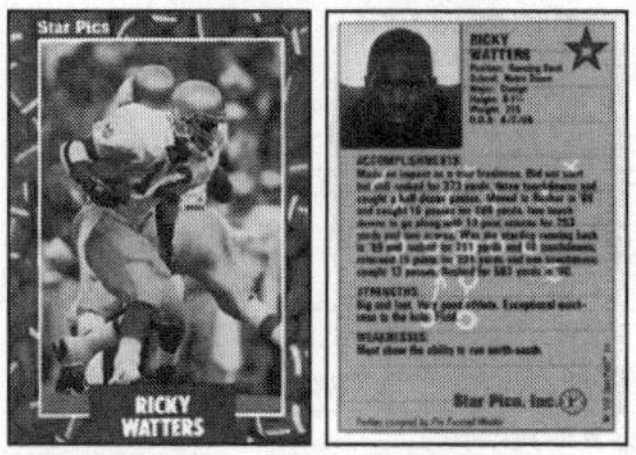

This 112-card standard-size set features on the front an action color photo enclosed by a thin white border against a background of footballs. The player's name appears in white print on a maroon-colored box below the picture. The back has a full-color posed photo in the upper left hand corner and the card number (enclosed in a red star) in the upper right hand corner. The biographical information, including accomplishments, strengths, and weaknesses, is printed on a pale green diagram of a football field with a diagrammed play. The set also includes player agents and flashback cards of top young players. Autographed cards were inserted in some of the sets on a random basis. The key players in this set are Brett Favre, Alvin Harper, Randal Hill, Herman Moore, Mike Pritchard, and Ricky Watters.

	MINT	EXC	G-VG
COMPLETE FACTORY SET (113)	6.00	2.70	.75
COMMON CARD (1-112)	.04	.02	.01
COMMON AUTOGRAPH	7.00	3.10	.85
COMMON FLB AUTOGRAPH	20.00	9.00	2.50
FLB AUTOGRAPHS 250X TO 400X BASIC CARDS			
STAR AUTOGRAPHS 20X TO 40X BASIC CARDS			
☐ 1 1991 NFL Draft Overview	.04	.02	.01
☐ 2 Barry Sanders FLB	.50	.23	.06
☐ 3 Nick Bell	.25	.11	.03
☐ 4 Kelvin Pritchett	.04	.02	.01
☐ 5 Huey Richardson	.04	.02	.01
☐ 6 Mike Croel	.25	.11	.03
☐ 7 Paul Justin	.04	.02	.01
☐ 8 Ivory Lee Brown	.04	.02	.01
☐ 9 Herman Moore	1.50	.70	.19
☐ 10 Derrick Thomas FLB	.25	.11	.03
☐ 11 Keith Traylor	.04	.02	.01
☐ 12 Joe Johnson	.04	.02	.01
☐ 13 Dan McGwire	.04	.02	.01
☐ 14 Harvey Williams	.50	.23	.06
☐ 15 Eric Moten	.04	.02	.01
☐ 16 Steve Zucker	.04	.02	.01
☐ 17 Randal Hill	.25	.11	.03
☐ 18 Browning Nagle	.25	.11	.03
☐ 19 Stan Thomas	.04	.02	.01
☐ 20 Emmitt Smith FLB	.50	.23	.06
☐ 21 Ted Washington	.04	.02	.01
☐ 22 Lamar Rogers	.04	.02	.01
☐ 23 Kenny Walker	.04	.02	.01
☐ 24 Howard Griffith	.04	.02	.01
☐ 25 Reggie Johnson	.04	.02	.01
☐ 26 Lawrence Dawsey	.25	.11	.03
☐ 27 Joe Garten	.04	.02	.01
☐ 28 Moe Gardner	.25	.11	.03
☐ 29 Michael Stonebreaker	.04	.02	.01
☐ 30 Jeff George FLB	.25	.11	.03
☐ 31 Leigh Steinberg	.04	.02	.01
☐ 32 John Flannery	.04	.02	.01
☐ 33 Pat Harlow	.04	.02	.01
☐ 34 Kanavis McGhee	.04	.02	.01
☐ 35 Mike Dumas	.04	.02	.01
☐ 36 Godfrey Myles	.04	.02	.01
☐ 37 Shawn Moore	.04	.02	.01
☐ 38 Jeff Graham	.50	.23	.06
☐ 39 Ricky Watters	1.25	.55	.16
☐ 40 Andre Ware	.25	.11	.03
☐ 41 Henry Jones	.25	.11	.03
☐ 42 Eric Turner	.25	.11	.03
☐ 43 Bob Woolf	.04	.02	.01
☐ 44 Randy Baldwin	.04	.02	.01
☐ 45 Mo Lewis	.25	.11	.03
☐ 46 Jerry Evans	.04	.02	.01
☐ 47 Derek Russell	.04	.02	.01
☐ 48 Merton Hanks	.25	.11	.03
☐ 49 Kevin Donnalley	.04	.02	.01
☐ 50 Troy Aikman FLB	.50	.23	.06
☐ 51 William Thomas	.25	.11	.03
☐ 52 Chris Thome	.04	.02	.01
☐ 53 Ricky Ervins	.25	.11	.03
☐ 54 Jake Reed	.75	.35	.09
☐ 55 Jerome Henderson	.04	.02	.01
☐ 56 Mark Vander Poel	.04	.02	.01
☐ 57 Bernard Ellison	.04	.02	.01
☐ 58 Jack Mills	.04	.02	.01
☐ 59 Jarrod Bunch	.04	.02	.01
☐ 60 Mark Carrier DB	.25	.11	.03
☐ 61 Rocen Keeton	.04	.02	.01
☐ 62 Louis Riddick	.04	.02	.01
☐ 63 Bobby Wilson	.04	.02	.01
☐ 64 Steve Jackson	.25	.11	.03
☐ 65 Brett Favre	2.00	.90	.25
☐ 66 Ernie Mills	.25	.11	.03
☐ 67 Joe Valerio	.04	.02	.01
☐ 68 Chris Smith	.04	.02	.01
☐ 69 Ralph Cindrich	.04	.02	.01
☐ 70 Christian Okoye	.04	.02	.01
☐ 71 Charles McRae	.04	.02	.01
☐ 72 Jon Vaughn	.04	.02	.01
☐ 73 Eric Swann	.25	.11	.03
☐ 74 Bill Musgrave	.04	.02	.01
☐ 75 Eric Bieniemy	.25	.11	.03
☐ 76 Pat Tyrance	.04	.02	.01
☐ 77 Vinnie Clark	.04	.02	.01
☐ 78 Eugene Williams	.04	.02	.01
☐ 79 Rob Carpenter	.04	.02	.01
☐ 80 Deion Sanders FLB	.50	.23	.06
☐ 81 Roman Phifer	.25	.11	.03
☐ 82 Greg Lewis	.04	.02	.01
☐ 83 John Johnson	.04	.02	.01
☐ 84 Richard Howell	.04	.02	.01
☐ 85 Jesse Campbell	.04	.02	.01
☐ 86 Stanley Richard	.25	.11	.03
☐ 87 Alfred Williams	.25	.11	.03
☐ 88 Mike Pritchard	.25	.11	.03
☐ 89 Mel Agee	.04	.02	.01
☐ 90 Aaron Craver	.04	.02	.01
☐ 91 Tim Barnett	.04	.02	.01
☐ 92 Wesley Carroll	.25	.11	.03
☐ 93 Kevin Scott	.04	.02	.01
☐ 94 Darren Lewis	.04	.02	.01
☐ 95 Tim Bruton	.04	.02	.01
☐ 96 Tim James	.04	.02	.01
☐ 97 Darryll Lewis	.25	.11	.03
☐ 98 Shawn Jefferson	.25	.11	.03
☐ 99 Mitch Donahue	.04	.02	.01
☐ 100 Marvin Demoff	.04	.02	.01
☐ 101 Adrian Cooper	.04	.02	.01
☐ 102 Bruce Pickens	.04	.02	.01
☐ 103 Scott Zolak	.04	.02	.01
☐ 104 Phil Hansen	.25	.11	.03
☐ 105 Ed King	.04	.02	.01
☐ 106 Mike Jones	.04	.02	.01
☐ 107 Alvin Harper	.25	.11	.03
☐ 108 Robert Young	.25	.11	.03
☐ 109 Offensive Prospects Nick Bell Brett Favre Alvin Harper Charles McRae	.50	.23	.06
☐ 110 Defensive Prospects Mike Croel Eric Swann Eric Turner	.25	.11	.03
☐ 111 Checklist 1	.04	.02	.01
☐ 112 Checklist 2	.04	.02	.01
☐ NNO Salute/Advertisement American Flag background	.04	.02	.01

1992 Star Pics

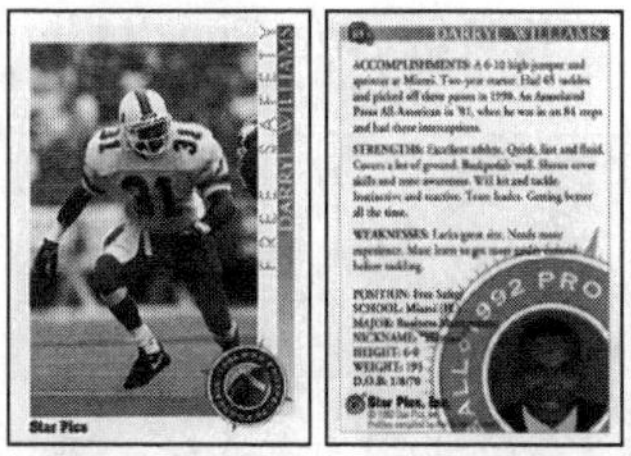

This 100-card standard-size set highlights more than 80 of the top college prospects in the country. The set was available in ten-card foil StarPaks and factory sets, with randomly inserted autograph cards in both. It was reported that the production run did not exceed 195,000 factory sets and 12,000 ten-box foil cases. The fronts feature glossy color action photos bordered in white. A color stripe runs the length of the card on the right side, and the player's position and name are printed vertically. The Star Pics logo is superimposed at the lower right corner. The backs present an in-depth scouting report (accomplishments, strengths, and weaknesses), biographical information, and a color head shot in a circular format at the lower right corner. The five-card Flashback subset (10, 20, 30, 50, 70) displays illustrations by sports artist Scott Medlock. The StarStat subset, ten cards in all, compares the top pro prospects' stats to the collegiate stats of NFL greats; two of these were included in each set and eight others were randomly inserted in the foil packs. Autographed cards were inserted in sets and wax on a random basis. The key players in this set are Robert Brooks, Quentin Coryatt, Johnny Mitchell, Carl Pickens, and Tommy Vardell.

	MINT	EXC	G-VG
COMPLETE SET (100)	6.00	2.70	.75
COMMON CARD (1-100)	.05	.02	.01
STAR AUTOGRAPHS 20X TO 40X BASIC CARDS			
☐ 1 Steve Emtman SS	.25	.11	.03
☐ 2 Chris Hakel	.05	.02	.01
☐ 3 Phillippi Sparks	.05	.02	.01
☐ 4 Howard Dinkins	.05	.02	.01
☐ 5 Robert Brooks	1.00	.45	.12
☐ 6 Chris Pederson	.05	.02	.01
☐ 7 Bucky Richardson	.25	.11	.03
☐ 8 Keith Goganious	.05	.02	.01
☐ 9 Robert Porcher	.25	.11	.03
☐ 10 Andre Rison FLB	.50	.23	.06
☐ 11 Jason Hanson	.25	.11	.03
☐ 12 Tommy Vardell	.25	.11	.03
☐ 13 Kurt Barber	.05	.02	.01
☐ 14 Bernard Dafney	.05	.02	.01
☐ 15 Levon Kirkland	.05	.02	.01
☐ 16 Corey Widmer	.05	.02	.01
☐ 17 Santana Dotson	.25	.11	.03
☐ 18 Chris Holder	.05	.02	.01
☐ 19 Elbert Turner	.05	.02	.01
☐ 20 Mike Croel	.05	.02	.01
☐ 21 Darren Perry	.05	.02	.01
☐ 22 Troy Vincent	.25	.11	.03
☐ 23 Quentin Coryatt	.25	.11	.03
☐ 24 John Brown III	.05	.02	.01
☐ 25 John Ray	.05	.02	.01
☐ 26 Vaughn Dunbar	.05	.02	.01
☐ 27 Stacey Dillard	.05	.02	.01
☐ 28 Alonzo Spellman	.25	.11	.03
☐ 29 Darren Woodson	.25	.11	.03
☐ 30 Pat Swilling	.25	.11	.03
☐ 31 Eddie Robinson	.05	.02	.01
☐ 32 Tyji Armstrong	.05	.02	.01
☐ 33 Bill Johnson	.05	.02	.01
☐ 34 Eugene Chung	.05	.02	.01
☐ 35 Ricardo McDonald	.05	.02	.01
☐ 36 Sean Lumpkin	.05	.02	.01
☐ 37 Greg Skrepenak	.05	.02	.01
☐ 38 Ashley Ambrose	.25	.11	.03
☐ 39 Kevin Smith	.25	.11	.03
☐ 40 Todd Collins	.05	.02	.01
☐ 41 Shane Dronett	.25	.11	.03
☐ 42 Ronnie West	.05	.02	.01
☐ 43 Darryl Williams	.25	.11	.03
☐ 44 Rodney Blackshear	.05	.02	.01
☐ 45 Dion Lambert	.05	.02	.01
☐ 46 Mike Saunders	.50	.23	.06
☐ 47 Keo Coleman	.05	.02	.01
☐ 48 Dana Hall	.25	.11	.03
☐ 49 Arthur Marshall	.05	.02	.01
☐ 50 Leonard Russell	.25	.11	.03
☐ 51 Matt Rodgers	.05	.02	.01
☐ 52 Shane Collins	.05	.02	.01
☐ 53 Courtney Hawkins	.25	.11	.03
☐ 54 Chuck Smith	.05	.02	.01
☐ 55 Joe Bowden	.05	.02	.01
☐ 56 Gene McGuire	.05	.02	.01
☐ 57 Tracy Scroggins	.05	.02	.01
☐ 58 Mark D'Onofrio	.05	.02	.01
☐ 59 Jimmy Smith	.25	.11	.03
☐ 60 Carl Pickens	1.50	.70	.19
☐ 61 Robert Harris	.05	.02	.01
☐ 62 Erick Anderson	.05	.02	.01
☐ 63 Doug Rigby	.05	.02	.01
☐ 64 Keith Hamilton	.25	.11	.03
☐ 65 Vaughn Dunbar	.05	.02	.01
☐ 66 Willie Clay	.05	.02	.01
☐ 67 Robert Jones	.25	.11	.03
☐ 68 Leon Searcy	.25	.11	.03
☐ 69 Elliot Pilton	.05	.02	.01
☐ 70 Thurman Thomas FLB	.50	.23	.06
☐ 71 Mark Wheeler	.05	.02	.01
☐ 72 Jeremy Lincoln	.05	.02	.01
☐ 73 Tony McCoy	.05	.02	.01
☐ 74 Charles Davenport	.05	.02	.01
☐ 75 Patrick Rowe	.05	.02	.01
☐ 76 Tommy Jeter	.05	.02	.01
☐ 77 Rod Smith	.25	.11	.03
☐ 78 Johnny Mitchell	.25	.11	.03
☐ 79 Corey Barlow	.05	.02	.01
☐ 80 Scottie Graham	.25	.11	.03
☐ 81 Mark Bounds	.05	.02	.01
☐ 82 Chester McGlockton	.25	.11	.03
☐ 83 Ray Roberts	.05	.02	.01
☐ 84 Dale Carter	.25	.11	.03
☐ 85 James Patton	.05	.02	.01
☐ 86 Tyrone Legette	.05	.02	.01
☐ 87 Leodis Flowers	.05	.02	.01
☐ 88 Rico Smith	.05	.02	.01
☐ 89 Kevin Turner	.25	.11	.03
☐ 90 Steve Emtman	.25	.11	.03
☐ 91 Rodney Culver	.05	.02	.01
☐ 92 Chris Mims	.25	.11	.03
☐ 93 Carlos Snow	.05	.02	.01
☐ 94 Corey Harris	.05	.02	.01
☐ 95 Nate Williams	.05	.02	.01
☐ 96 Timothy Roberts	.05	.02	.01
☐ 97 Steve Israel	.05	.02	.01

□ 98 Tony Smith (WR)	.05	.02	.01
□ 99 Dwayne Sabb	.05	.02	.01
□ 100 Checklist	.05	.02	.01

1992 Star Pics StarStat Bonus

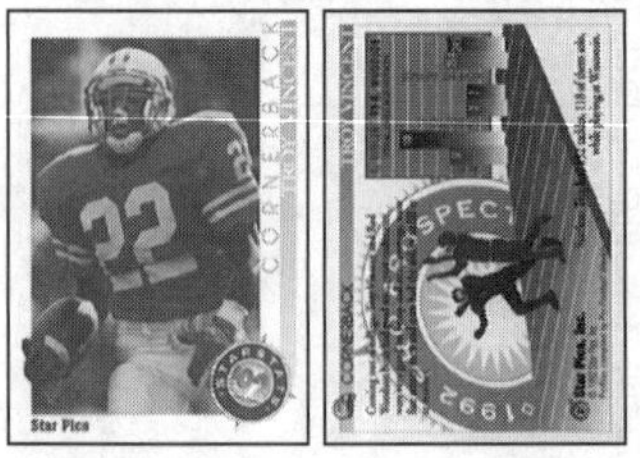

This eight-card standard-size set highlights top college prospects. The cards were available as an insert in ten-card foil StarPaks. The StarStat concept compares top pro prospects' stats to the collegiate stats of NFL greats.

	MINT	EXC	G-VG
COMPLETE SET (8)	8.00	3.60	1.00
COMMON CARD (SS1-SS8)	.50	.23	.06
□ SS1 Dale Carter	.75	.35	.09
□ SS2 Carl Pickens	4.00	1.80	.50
□ SS3 Alonzo Spellman	.50	.23	.06
□ SS4 Jimmy Smith	.50	.23	.06
□ SS5 Quentin Coryatt	.75	.35	.09
□ SS6 Troy Vincent	.50	.23	.06
□ SS7 Darryl Williams	.50	.23	.06
□ SS8 Courtney Hawkins	.50	.23	.06

1994 Superior Rookies Promos

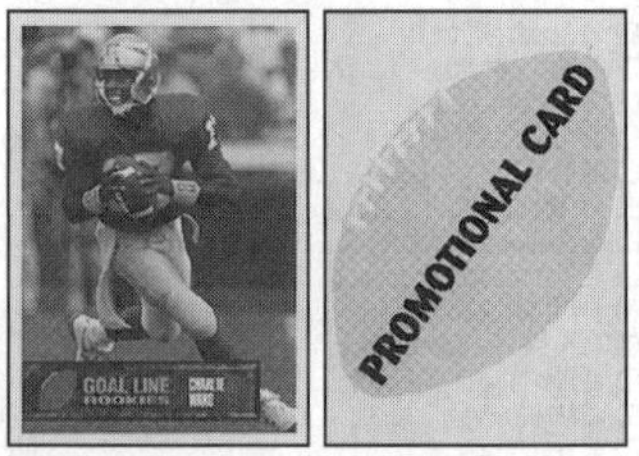

These two promo cards measure the standard size and feature white-bordered color action shots of the players in their college uniforms. The player's name, the set's title, and a football icon appear within a brownish marbleized bar near the bottom. Aside from the "Promotional Card" disclaimer printed diagonally within a ghosted gray football, the backs are blank. The cards are unnumbered and checklisted below in alphabetical order. The company was previously named Goal Line and Side Line.

	MINT	NRMT	EXC
COMPLETE SET (2)	3.00	1.35	.35
COMMON CARD (1-2)	1.00	.45	.12
□ 1 Rick Mirer	2.00	.90	.25
□ 2 Charlie Ward	1.00	.45	.12

1994 Superior Rookies

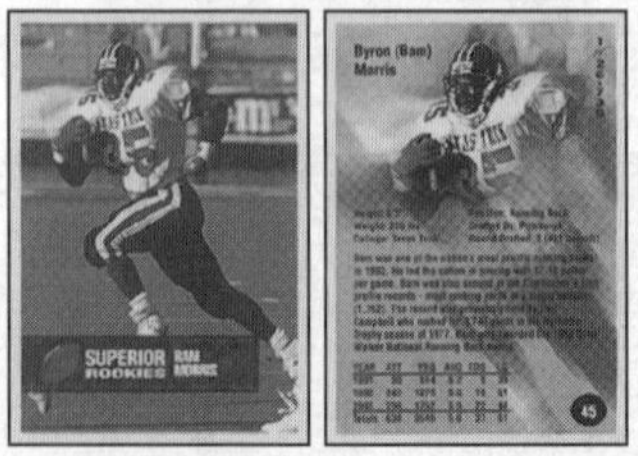

These 80 standard-size cards were issued by Superior Rookies. The white-bordered fronts carry color action shots of NFL rookies in their college uniforms. The player's name, set name, and a football icon appear in a color marbleized bar near the bottom. Over a ghosted player photo, the white-bordered back carries the player's name, biography, career highlights, and statistics. The production figures are given as "1 of 26,730". Just 9,900 boxes were produced. Each case included 144 autographed cards and 144 gold foil-stamped cards. The first 300 two-case orders received an individually numbered autographed Jerome Bettis card.

	MINT	EXC	G-VG
COMPLETE SET (80)	8.00	3.60	1.00
COMMON CARD (1-80)	.05	.02	.01
□ 1 Rick Mirer FLB	.50	.23	.06
□ 2 Jerome Bettis	.50	.23	.06
□ 3 Reggie Brooks	.25	.11	.03
□ 4 Trent Pollard	.05	.02	.01
□ 5 Willie Clark	.05	.02	.01
□ 6 Tim Ruddy	.05	.02	.01
□ 7 Lindsey Chapman	.05	.02	.01
□ 8 Van Malone	.05	.02	.01
□ 9 Jeff Burris	.25	.11	.03
□ 10 Charles Johnson	.25	.11	.03
□ 11 Brice Adams	.05	.02	.01
□ 12 Steve Shine	.05	.02	.01
□ 13 Brentson Buckner	.25	.11	.03
□ 14 Marty Moore	.05	.02	.01
□ 15 Ryan Yarborough	.25	.11	.03
□ 16 Aaron Taylor	.25	.11	.03
□ 17 Charlie Ward	.25	.11	.03
□ 18 Aubrey Beavers	.05	.02	.01
□ 19 Zane Beehn	.05	.02	.01
□ 20 Johnnie Morton	.25	.11	.03
□ 21 Jeremy Nunley	.05	.02	.01
□ 22 Bucky Brooks	.25	.11	.03
□ 23 Dewayne Washington	.25	.11	.03
□ 24 Mario Bates	.25	.11	.03
□ 25 David Palmer	.25	.11	.03
□ 26 Kevin Mawae	.05	.02	.01
□ 27 Chris Brantley	.05	.02	.01
□ 28 Bruce Walker	.05	.02	.01
□ 29 Jamir Miller	.05	.02	.01
□ 30 Thomas Lewis	.25	.11	.03
□ 31 Chad Bratzke	.05	.02	.01
□ 32 Anthony Phillips	.05	.02	.01
□ 33 Errict Rhett	.50	.23	.06
□ 34 Tre Johnson	.05	.02	.01
□ 35 Perry Klein	.05	.02	.01
□ 36 Tyronne Drakeford	.05	.02	.01
□ 37 Bernard Williams	.05	.02	.01
□ 38 Carlester Crumpler	.05	.02	.01
□ 39 Myron Bell	.05	.02	.01
□ 40 Greg Hill	.25	.11	.03
□ 41 James Burton	.05	.02	.01
□ 42 Lloyd Hill	.05	.02	.01
□ 43 Antonio Langham	.25	.11	.03
□ 44 Jim Flanigan	.05	.02	.01
□ 45 Byron Bam Morris	.25	.11	.03
□ 46 Brad Ottis	.05	.02	.01
□ 47 Wayne Gandy	.05	.02	.01
□ 48 Rob Holmberg	.05	.02	.01
□ 49 Bryant Young	.25	.11	.03
□ 50 William Floyd	.50	.23	.06
□ 51 Kevin Mitchell	.05	.02	.01
□ 52 Ervin Collier	.05	.02	.01
□ 53 Winfred Tubbs	.05	.02	.01
□ 54 Mark Montgomery	.05	.02	.01
□ 55 Willie McGinest	.25	.11	.03
□ 56 Jim Miller	.25	.11	.03
□ 57 Doug Nussmeier	.05	.02	.01
□ 58 Joe Panos	.05	.02	.01
□ 59 Sam Adams	.05	.02	.01
□ 60 Derrick Alexander WR	.50	.23	.06
□ 61 Pete Bercich	.05	.02	.01
□ 62 Eric Ravotti	.05	.02	.01
□ 63 Eric Mahlum	.05	.02	.01
□ 64 Corey Louchiey	.05	.02	.01
□ 65 Lake Dawson	.50	.23	.06
□ 66 Rob Fredrickson	.05	.02	.01
□ 67 Sam Rogers	.05	.02	.01
□ 68 John Covington	.05	.02	.01
□ 69 Larry Allen	.05	.02	.01
□ 70 LeShon Johnson	.25	.11	.03
□ 71 Jerry Reynolds	.05	.02	.01
□ 72 Eric Zomalt	.05	.02	.01
□ 73 Gus Frerotte	.75	.35	.09
□ 74 Jason Winrow	.05	.02	.01
□ 75 Corey Sawyer	.05	.02	.01
□ 76 Malcolm Seabron	.05	.02	.01
□ 77 Cory Fleming	.05	.02	.01
□ 78 Chris Maumalanga	.05	.02	.01
□ 79 Chris Penn	.05	.02	.01
□ 80 Checklist	.05	.02	.01

1994 Superior Rookies Autographs

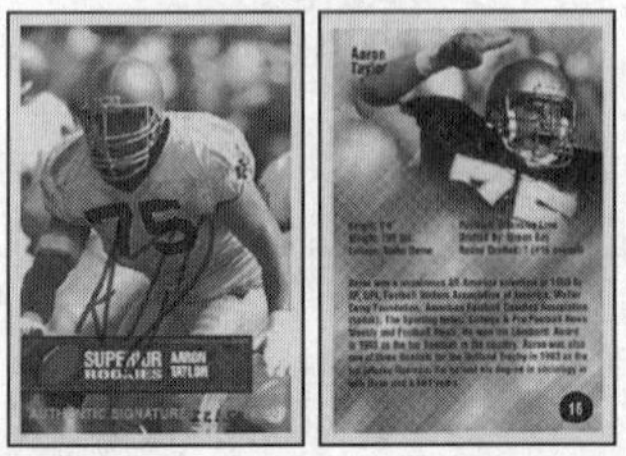

These 79 standard-size autograph cards were issued one per pack by Superior Rookies. The white-bordered fronts carry color action shots of NFL rookies in their college uniforms. The player's autograph appears on the front. His name, the set name, and a football icon appear in a brown marbleized bar near the bottom. Over a ghosted player photo, the white-bordered back carries the player's name, biography, career highlights, and statistics. The cards are numbered on the back and listed below with the number of cards each player autographed.

	MINT	EXC	G-VG
COMPLETE SET (79)	250.00	110.00	31.00
COMMON AUTOGRAPH	2.00	.90	.25
□ 1 Rick Mirer FLB/1000	25.00	11.00	3.10
□ 2 Jerome Bettis FLB/1000	40.00	18.00	5.00
□ 3 Reggie Brooks FLB/1000	3.00	1.35	.35
□ 4 Trent Pollard/6000	2.00	.90	.25
□ 5 Willie Clark/5000	2.00	.90	.25
□ 6 Tim Ruddy/5000	2.00	.90	.25
□ 7 Lindsey Chapman/6000	2.00	.90	.25
□ 8 Van Malone/5000	2.00	.90	.25
□ 9 Jeff Burris/4000	3.00	1.35	.35
□ 10 Charles Johnson/5000	3.00	1.35	.35
□ 11 Brice Adams/6000	2.00	.90	.25
□ 12 Steve Shine/6000	2.00	.90	.25
□ 13 Brentson Buckner/4000	3.00	1.35	.35
□ 14 Marty Moore/6000	2.00	.90	.25
□ 15 Ryan Yarborough/5000	3.00	1.35	.35
□ 16 Aaron Taylor/4000	2.00	.90	.25
□ 17 Charlie Ward/4000	3.00	1.35	.35
□ 18 Aubrey Beavers/5000	2.00	.90	.25
□ 19 Zane Beehn/6000	2.00	.90	.25
□ 20 Johnnie Morton/4000	3.00	1.35	.35
□ 21 Jeremy Nunley/5000	2.00	.90	.25
□ 22 Bucky Brooks/5000	3.00	1.35	.35
□ 23 Dewayne Washington/4000	3.00	1.35	.35
□ 24 Mario Bates/5000	6.00	2.70	.75
□ 25 David Palmer/4000	3.00	1.35	.35
□ 26 Kevin Mawae/5000	2.00	.90	.25
□ 27 Chris Brantley/5000	2.00	.90	.25
□ 28 Bruce Walker/5000	2.00	.90	.25
□ 29 Jamir Miller/4000	2.00	.90	.25
□ 30 Thomas Lewis/5000	3.00	1.35	.35
□ 31 Chad Bratzke/6000	2.00	.90	.25
□ 32 Anthony Phillips/5000	2.00	.90	.25
□ 33 Errict Rhett/5000	12.00	5.50	1.50
□ 34 Tre Johnson/4000	2.00	.90	.25
□ 35 Perry Klein/5000	2.00	.90	.25
□ 36 Tyronne Drakeford/5000	2.00	.90	.25
□ 37 Bernard Williams/4000	2.00	.90	.25
□ 38 Carlester Crumpler/6000	2.00	.90	.25
□ 39 Myron Bell/6000	2.00	.90	.25
□ 40 Greg Hill/5000	3.00	1.35	.35
□ 41 James Burton/6000	2.00	.90	.25
□ 42 Lloyd Hill/5000	2.00	.90	.25
□ 43 Antonio Langham/4000	3.00	1.35	.35
□ 44 Jim Flanigan/5000	2.00	.90	.25
□ 45 Byron Bam Morris/5000	3.00	1.35	.35
□ 46 Brad Ottis/5000	2.00	.90	.25
□ 47 Wayne Gandy/4000	2.00	.90	.25
□ 48 Rob Holmberg/6000	2.00	.90	.25
□ 49 Bryant Young/4000	3.00	1.35	.35
□ 50 William Floyd/5000	5.00	2.20	.60
□ 51 Kevin Mitchell/5000	2.00	.90	.25
□ 52 Ervin Collier/5000	2.00	.90	.25
□ 53 Winfred Tubbs/5000	2.00	.90	.25
□ 54 Mark Montgomery/6000	2.00	.90	.25
□ 55 Willie McGinest/4000	3.00	1.35	.35
□ 56 Jim Miller/5000	3.00	1.35	.35
□ 57 Doug Nussmeier/6000	2.00	.90	.25
□ 58 Joe Panos/6000	2.00	.90	.25
□ 59 Sam Adams/5000	2.00	.90	.25
□ 60 Derrick Alexander/5000	5.00	2.20	.60
□ 61 Pete Bercich/6000	2.00	.90	.25
□ 62 Eric Ravotti/6000	2.00	.90	.25
□ 63 Eric Mahlum/4000	2.00	.90	.25
□ 64 Corey Louchiey/5000	2.00	.90	.25
□ 65 Lake Dawson/5000	4.00	1.80	.50
□ 66 Rob Fredrickson/4000	2.00	.90	.25
□ 67 Sam Rogers/5000	2.00	.90	.25
□ 68 John Covington/6000	2.00	.90	.25
□ 69 Larry Allen/5000	2.00	.90	.25
□ 70 LeShon Johnson/5000	3.00	1.35	.35
□ 71 Jerry Reynolds/6000	2.00	.90	.25
□ 72 Eric Zomalt/5000	2.00	.90	.25
□ 73 Gus Frerotte/5000	15.00	6.75	1.85
□ 74 Jason Winrow/6000	2.00	.90	.25
□ 75 Corey Sawyer/6000	2.00	.90	.25
□ 76 Malcolm Seabron/5000	2.00	.90	.25
□ 77 Cory Fleming/5000	2.00	.90	.25
□ 78 Chris Maumalanga/5000	2.00	.90	.25
□ 79 Chris Penn/6000	2.00	.90	.25

1994 Superior Rookies Deep Threat

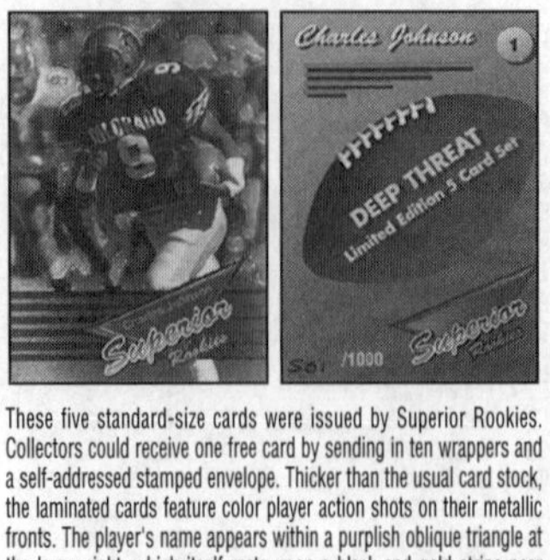

These five standard-size cards were issued by Superior Rookies. Collectors could receive one free card by sending in ten wrappers and a self-addressed stamped envelope. Thicker than the usual card stock, the laminated cards feature color player action shots on their metallic fronts. The player's name appears within a purplish oblique triangle at the lower right, which itself rests upon a black and gold stripe near the bottom. The borderless back carries the player's name in yellow cursive lettering at the upper left. A large football icon in the middle carries the set's name. The cards are individually numbered out of 1,000.

	MINT	EXC	G-VG
COMPLETE SET (5)	10.00	4.50	1.25
COMMON CARD (1-5)	2.50	1.10	.30
□ 1 Charles Johnson	3.00	1.35	.35
□ 2 Johnnie Morton	4.00	1.80	.50
□ 3 Derrick Alexander	3.00	1.35	.35
□ 4 David Palmer	2.50	1.10	.30
□ 5 Thomas Lewis	2.50	1.10	.30

1994 Superior Rookies Instant Impact

Randomly inserted in packs, these 10 standard-size cards were issued by Superior Rookies. Thicker than the usual card stock, the laminated cards feature color player action shots on their metallic fronts. The player's name appears within a purplish oblique triangle at the lower right, which itself rests upon a black and gold stripe near the bottom. The borderless back carries the player's name in yellow cursive lettering at the upper left. A large football icon in the middle carries the set's name. The cards are individually numbered out of 2,970.

	MINT	EXC	G-VG
COMPLETE SET (10)	15.00	6.75	1.85
COMMON CARD (1-10)	1.00	.45	.12
□ 1 Rick Mirer	2.00	.90	.25
□ 2 Jerome Bettis	5.00	2.20	.60
□ 3 Reggie Brooks	1.00	.45	.12
□ 4 Charlie Ward	1.00	.45	.12
□ 5 Willie McGinest	1.00	.45	.12
□ 6 Greg Hill	2.00	.90	.25
□ 7 William Floyd	2.00	.90	.25
□ 8 Bryant Young	1.00	.45	.12
□ 9 Errict Rhett	5.00	2.20	.60
□ 10 Sam Adams	1.00	.45	.12

1995 Superior Pix Promos

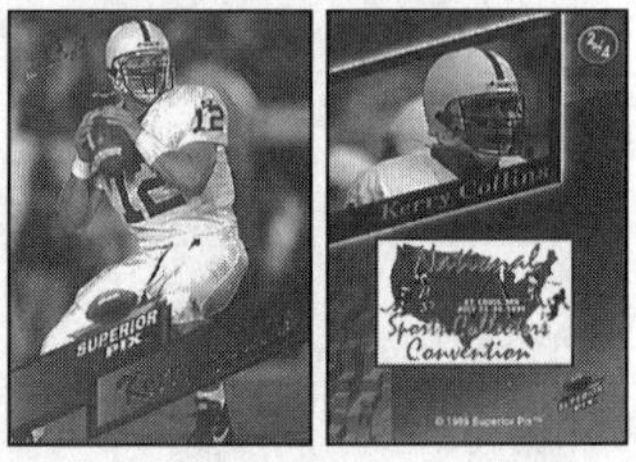

This 4-card set was issued to preview the 1995 Superior Pix Draft series. The set was mailed out as well as distributed at the National Sports Collectors Convention in St. Louis (July 24-30, 1995). The fronts display full-bleed color action photos, with the player's name in a red variegated diagonal bar across the bottom. A second diagonal bar carries the manufacturer's name. The backs carry a head shot and the National Convention logo.

	MINT	NRMT	EXC
COMPLETE SET (4)	8.00	3.60	1.00
COMMON CARD (1-4)	1.00	.45	.12
□ 1 Steve McNair	2.00	.90	.25
□ 2 Kerry Collins	3.00	1.35	.35
□ 3 Tyrone Wheatley	1.00	.45	.12
□ 4 Joey Galloway	2.00	.90	.25

1995 Superior Pix

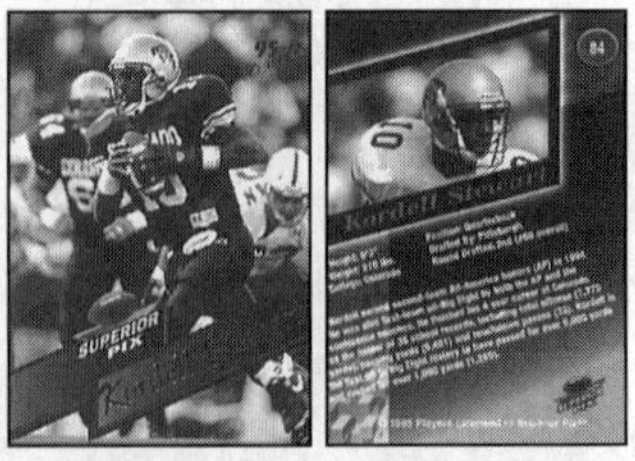

These standard-size cards came in eight-card packs with an autographed card in each pack. Each player autographed a number of his own cards. The fronts display a color action player photo with the

words '95 Draft in gold foil in either at the top right of left hand corner of the card. The players name and the Superior Pix logo appear on two stripes that appear at an angle across the bottom of the card. The backs includes a box with a head shot photo of the player at the top left hand corner followed by some facts and history on the player.

	MINT	EXC	G-VG
COMPLETE SET (110)	10.00	4.50	1.25
COMMON CARD (1-110)	.05	.02	.01
☐ 1 Ki-Jana Carter	.25	.11	.03
☐ 2 Tony Boselli	.25	.11	.03
☐ 3 Steve McNair	1.00	.45	.12
☐ 4 Michael Westbrook	.50	.23	.06
☐ 5 Kerry Collins	1.50	.70	.19
☐ 6 Terrell Davis	2.00	.90	.25
☐ 7 Kevin Bouie	.05	.02	.01
☐ 8 Brian Williams	.05	.02	.01
☐ 9 Kez McCorvey	.05	.02	.01
☐ 10 Kyle Brady	.25	.11	.03
☐ 11 Rob Johnson	.25	.11	.03
☐ 12 Carl Greenwood	.05	.02	.01
☐ 13 Mark Fields	.05	.02	.01
☐ 14 Andrew Greene	.05	.02	.01
☐ 15 Orlando Thomas	.05	.02	.01
☐ 16 Don Sasa	.05	.02	.01
☐ 17 Brent Moss	.05	.02	.01
☐ 18 Jamal Willis	.05	.02	.01
☐ 19 Michael Hendricks	.05	.02	.01
☐ 20 Rashaan Salaam	.50	.23	.06
☐ 21 John Sacca	.05	.02	.01
☐ 22 Cory Raymer	.05	.02	.01
☐ 23 Kirby Dar Dar	.05	.02	.01
☐ 24 Lee DeRamus	.05	.02	.01
☐ 25 Joey Galloway	.75	.35	.09
☐ 26 Mike Frederick	.05	.02	.01
☐ 27 Todd Collins	.50	.23	.06
☐ 28 Stoney Case	.05	.02	.01
☐ 29 Devin Bush	.05	.02	.01
☐ 30 Chad May	.05	.02	.01
☐ 31 Darrick Holmes	.25	.11	.03
☐ 32 Johnny Thomas	.05	.02	.01
☐ 33 Luther Ellis	.05	.02	.01
☐ 34 Tyrone Wheatley	.25	.11	.03
☐ 35 Terry Connealy	.05	.02	.01
☐ 36 Ruben Brown	.05	.02	.01
☐ 37 Kelvin Anderson	.05	.02	.01
☐ 38 Tony Berti	.05	.02	.01
☐ 39 Steve Ingram	.05	.02	.01
☐ 40 Kevin Carter	.25	.11	.03
☐ 41 Dave Wohlabaugh	.05	.02	.01
☐ 42 Mike Morton	.05	.02	.01
☐ 43 Steve Stenstrom	.05	.02	.01
☐ 44 Zach Wiegert	.05	.02	.01
☐ 45 Rodney Thomas	.25	.11	.03
☐ 46 Eddie Goines	.05	.02	.01
☐ 47 Kenny Gales	.05	.02	.01
☐ 48 Jamal Ellis	.05	.02	.01
☐ 49 Demetrius Edwards	.05	.02	.01
☐ 50 Justin Armour	.05	.02	.01
☐ 51 Billy Williams	.05	.02	.01
☐ 52 Ed Hervey	.05	.02	.01
☐ 53 Antonio Armstrong	.05	.02	.01
☐ 54 Oliver Gibson	.05	.02	.01
☐ 55 David Dunn	.25	.11	.03
☐ 56 Tyrone Davis	.05	.02	.01
☐ 57 Craig Newsome	.05	.02	.01
☐ 58 William Strong	.05	.02	.01
☐ 59 Sherman Williams	.05	.02	.01
☐ 60 James O. Stewart	.25	.11	.03
☐ 61 Bryan Schwartz	.05	.02	.01
☐ 62 Frank Sanders	.25	.11	.03
☐ 63 Barret Robbins	.05	.02	.01
☐ 64 Bronzell Miller	.05	.02	.01
☐ 65 Curtis Martin	2.00	.90	.25
☐ 66 Chris T. Jones	.50	.23	.06
☐ 67 Dave Barr	.05	.02	.01
☐ 68 Anthony Brown	.05	.02	.01
☐ 69 Ken Dilger	.25	.11	.03
☐ 70 Warren Sapp	.25	.11	.03
☐ 71 James A. Stewart	.05	.02	.01
☐ 72 Corey Fuller	.05	.02	.01
☐ 73 Christian Fauria	.25	.11	.03
☐ 74 Brian DeMarco	.05	.02	.01
☐ 75 J.J. Stokes	.50	.23	.06
☐ 76 Hicham El-Mashtoub	.05	.02	.01
☐ 77 Anthony Cook	.05	.02	.01
☐ 78 Mark Bruener	.25	.11	.03
☐ 79 Blake Brockermeyer	.05	.02	.01
☐ 80 Derrick Brooks	.05	.02	.01
☐ 81 Joe Aska	.05	.02	.01
☐ 82 Lance Brown	.05	.02	.01
☐ 83 Pete Mitchell	.05	.02	.01
☐ 84 Kordell Stewart	1.50	.70	.19
☐ 85 Bobby Taylor	.25	.11	.03
☐ 86 Jimmy Hitchcock	.05	.02	.01
☐ 87 Jack Jackson	.05	.02	.01
☐ 88 Ray Zellars	.05	.02	.01
☐ 89 Darius Holland	.05	.02	.01
☐ 90 Derrick Alexander	.25	.11	.03
☐ 91 Torey Hunter	.05	.02	.01
☐ 92 Scotty Lewis	.05	.02	.01
☐ 93 Carl Reeves	.05	.02	.01
☐ 94 Terrell Fletcher	.05	.02	.01
☐ 95 Ontiwaun Carter	.05	.02	.01
☐ 96 Trezelle Jenkins	.05	.02	.01
☐ 97 Mark Birchmeier	.05	.02	.01
☐ 98 Len Raney	.05	.02	.01
☐ 99 Ronald Cherry	.05	.02	.01
☐ 100 Tyrone Wheatley	.25	.11	.03
☐ 101 John Jones	.05	.02	.01
☐ 102 Zack Crockett	.05	.02	.01
☐ 103 Larry Jones	.05	.02	.01
☐ 104 Michael McCoy	.05	.02	.01
☐ 105 Ellis Johnson	.05	.02	.01
☐ 106 Jerrott Willard	.05	.02	.01
☐ 107 Jason James	.05	.02	.01
☐ 108 J.J. Smith	.05	.02	.01
☐ 109 Mike Mamula	.05	.02	.01
☐ 110 Checklist	.05	.02	.01

1995 Superior Pix Autographs

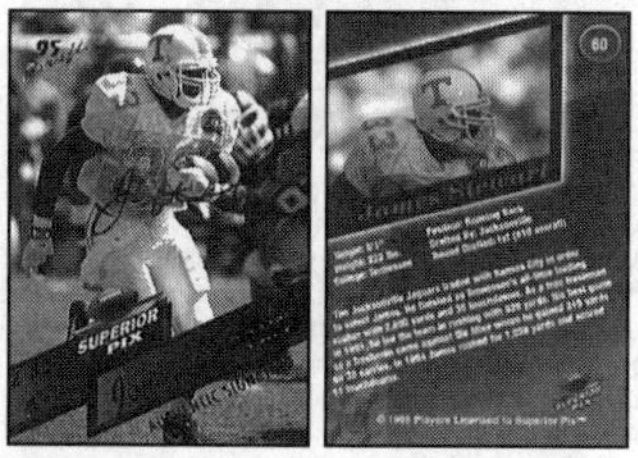

These standard-size cards came in eight-card packs with an autographed card in each pack. Each player autographed a different number of his own cards. The number of cards each player autographed appears below. The design is identical to that of the regular issue, except for the autograph, the words authentic signature and numbering on the front.

	MINT	EXC	G-VG
COMPLETE SET (109)	300.00	135.00	38.00
COMMON CARD (1-109)	2.00	.90	.25
☐ 1 Ki-Jana Carter/1000	20.00	9.00	2.50
☐ 2 Tony Boselli/4000	3.00	1.35	.35
☐ 3 Steve McNair/3000	12.00	5.50	1.50
☐ 4 Michael Westbrook/4000	7.00	3.10	.85
☐ 5 Kerry Collins/3000	15.00	6.75	1.85
☐ 6 Terrell Davis/5000	18.00	8.00	2.20
☐ 7 Kevin Bouie	2.00	.90	.25
☐ 8 Brian Williams	2.00	.90	.25
☐ 9 Kez McCorvey/6500	2.00	.90	.25
☐ 10 Kyle Brady/3500	3.00	1.35	.35
☐ 11 Rob Johnson/3000	2.00	.90	.25
☐ 12 Carl Greenwood	2.00	.90	.25
☐ 13 Mark Fields/5000	2.00	.90	.25
☐ 14 Andrew Greene/5000	2.00	.90	.25
☐ 15 Orlando Thomas/6000	2.00	.90	.25
☐ 16 Don Sasa/6500	2.00	.90	.25
☐ 17 Brent Moss	2.00	.90	.25
☐ 18 Jamal Willis	2.00	.90	.25
☐ 19 Michael Hendricks	2.00	.90	.25
☐ 20 Rashaan Salaam/3500	7.00	3.10	.85
☐ 21 John Sacca	2.00	.90	.25
☐ 22 Cory Raymer/6000	2.00	.90	.25
☐ 23 Kirby Dar Dar	2.00	.90	.25
☐ 24 Lee DeRamus/6500	2.00	.90	.25
☐ 25 Joey Galloway/4000	10.00	4.50	1.25
☐ 26 Mike Frederick/6000	2.00	.90	.25
☐ 27 Todd Collins/5000	3.00	1.35	.35
☐ 28 Stoney Case/4000	2.00	.90	.25
☐ 29 Devin Bush/5000	2.00	.90	.25
☐ 30 Chad May/4000	2.00	.90	.25
☐ 31 Darrick Holmes/6500	8.00	3.60	1.00
☐ 32 Johnny Thomas/6500	2.00	.90	.25
☐ 33 Luther Ellis/5000	2.00	.90	.25
☐ 34 Tyrone Wheatley/5000	3.00	1.35	.35
☐ 35 Terry Connealy/6500	2.00	.90	.25
☐ 36 Ruben Brown/3500	2.00	.90	.25
☐ 37 Kelvin Anderson	2.00	.90	.25
☐ 38 Tony Berti	2.00	.90	.25
☐ 39 Steve Ingram	2.00	.90	.25
☐ 40 Kevin Carter/4000	3.00	1.35	.35
☐ 41 Dave Wohlabaugh/6500	2.00	.90	.25
☐ 42 Mike Morton/4000	2.00	.90	.25
☐ 43 Steve Stenstrom/5000	2.00	.90	.25
☐ 44 Zach Wiegert/5000	2.00	.90	.25
☐ 45 Rodney Thomas/5000	3.00	1.35	.35
☐ 46 Eddie Goines	2.00	.90	.25
☐ 47 Kenny Gales/6500	2.00	.90	.25
☐ 48 Jamal Ellis/6500	2.00	.90	.25
☐ 49 Demetrius Edwards/6500	2.00	.90	.25
☐ 50 Justin Armour/5000	2.00	.90	.25
☐ 51 Billy Williams	2.00	.90	.25
☐ 52 Ed Hervey	2.00	.90	.25
☐ 53 Antonio Armstrong	2.00	.90	.25
☐ 54 Oliver Gibson	2.00	.90	.25
☐ 55 David Dunn/5000	3.00	1.35	.35
☐ 56 Tyrone Davis	2.00	.90	.25
☐ 57 Craig Newsome/4000	2.00	.90	.25
☐ 58 William Strong	2.00	.90	.25
☐ 59 Sherman Williams/3500	2.00	.90	.25
☐ 60 James O. Stewart/4000	3.00	1.35	.35
☐ 61 Bryan Schwartz/6000	2.00	.90	.25
☐ 62 Frank Sanders/5000	7.00	3.10	.85
☐ 63 Barret Robbins/6000	2.00	.90	.25
☐ 64 Bronzell Miller	2.00	.90	.25
☐ 65 Curtis Martin/4000	18.00	8.00	2.20
☐ 66 Chris T. Jones/4000	7.00	3.10	.85
☐ 67 Dave Barr/5000	2.00	.90	.25
☐ 68 Anthony Brown/6500	2.00	.90	.25
☐ 69 Ken Dilger/6000	3.00	1.35	.35
☐ 70 Warren Sapp/4000	3.00	1.35	.35
☐ 71 James A. Stewart	2.00	.90	.25
☐ 72 Corey Fuller/5000	2.00	.90	.25
☐ 73 Christian Fauria/5000	3.00	1.35	.35
☐ 74 Brian DeMarco/6000	2.00	.90	.25
☐ 75 J.J. Stokes/1000	16.00	7.25	2.00
☐ 76 Hicham El-Mashtoub	2.00	.90	.25
☐ 77 Anthony Cook/6000	2.00	.90	.25
☐ 78 Mark Bruener/4000	3.00	1.35	.35
☐ 79 Blake Brockermeyer/4000	2.00	.90	.25
☐ 80 Derrick Brooks/4000	2.00	.90	.25
☐ 81 Joe Aska/4000	2.00	.90	.25
☐ 82 Lance Brown/6500	2.00	.90	.25
☐ 83 Pete Mitchell/6500	2.00	.90	.25
☐ 84 Kordell Stewart/6500	12.00	5.50	1.50
☐ 85 Bobby Taylor/4000	3.00	1.35	.35
☐ 86 Jimmy Hitchcock	2.00	.90	.25
☐ 87 Jack Jackson/5000	2.00	.90	.25
☐ 88 Ray Zellars/4000	3.00	1.35	.35
☐ 89 Darius Holland	2.00	.90	.25
☐ 90 Derrick Alexander/4000	3.00	1.35	.35
☐ 91 Torey Hunter/6000	2.00	.90	.25
☐ 92 Scotty Lewis/6500	2.00	.90	.25
☐ 93 Carl Reeves	2.00	.90	.25
☐ 94 Terrell Fletcher/6000	3.00	1.35	.35
☐ 95 Ontiwaun Carter/6500	2.00	.90	.25
☐ 96 Trezelle Jenkins/5000	2.00	.90	.25
☐ 97 Mark Birchmeier	2.00	.90	.25
☐ 98 Len Raney	2.00	.90	.25
☐ 99 Ronald Cherry/6500	2.00	.90	.25
☐ 100 Tyrone Wheatley/6500	3.00	1.35	.35
☐ 101 John Jones	2.00	.90	.25
☐ 102 Zack Crockett/6000	2.00	.90	.25
☐ 103 Larry Jones/4000	2.00	.90	.25
☐ 104 Michael McCoy	2.00	.90	.25
☐ 105 Ellis Johnson/3500	2.00	.90	.25
☐ 106 Jerrott Willard/5000	2.00	.90	.25
☐ 107 Jason James	2.00	.90	.25
☐ 108 J.J. Smith	2.00	.90	.25
☐ 109 Mike Mamula/4000	2.00	.90	.25

1995 Superior Pix Deep Threat

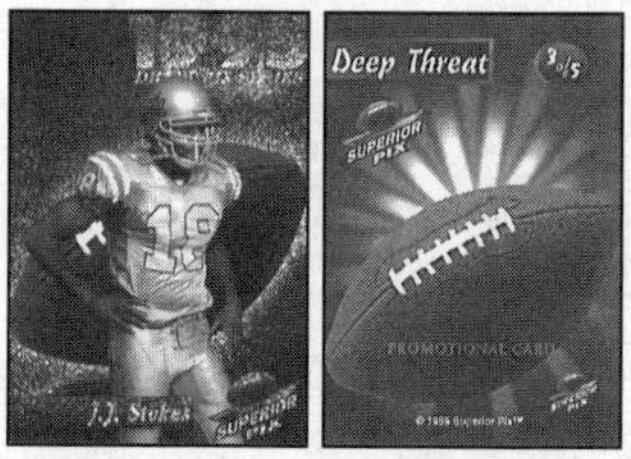

Randomly inserted at a rate of one in nine packs, these 5 standard-size cards display a color player photo in front of a football with a prism background of sorted colors with the players name appearing in silver in a stripe across the bottom of the card. The words 1995 Draft Pix Series appears at the top of the card with the Superior Pix logo appearing in the bottom right hand corner. This set features the top wide receiver prospect from the draft.

	MINT	EXC	G-VG
COMPLETE SET (5)	8.00	3.60	1.00
COMMON CARD (1-5)	1.25	.55	.16
☐ 1 Michael Westbrook	2.00	.90	.25
☐ 2 Joey Galloway	2.50	1.10	.30
☐ 3 J.J. Stokes	2.00	.90	.25
☐ 4 Kyle Brady	1.25	.55	.16
☐ 5 Frank Sanders	2.00	.90	.25

1995 Superior Pix Instant Impact

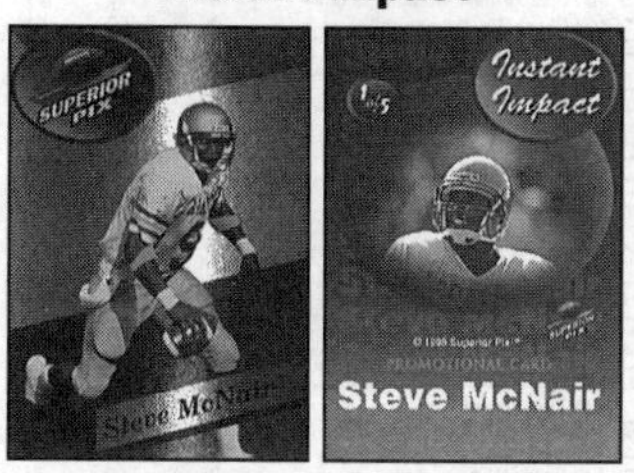

Randomly inserted at a rate of one in 18 packs, these 5 standard-size cards display a color action player photo with a split blue/silver/green foil background. The player's name appears within a gold/purple strip across the lower right hand corner of the card. The Superior Pix logo appears across the upper left hand corner of the card. This set features those players expected to have the most immediate impact in the league.

	MINT	EXC	G-VG
COMPLETE SET (5)	8.00	3.60	1.00
COMMON CARD (1-5)	.75	.35	.09
☐ 1 Steve McNair	2.00	.90	.25
☐ 2 Kerry Collins	3.00	1.35	.35
☐ 3 Tyrone Wheatley	.75	.35	.09
☐ 4 Joey Galloway	1.50	.70	.19
☐ 5 Tony Boselli	.75	.35	.09

1995 Superior Pix Open Field

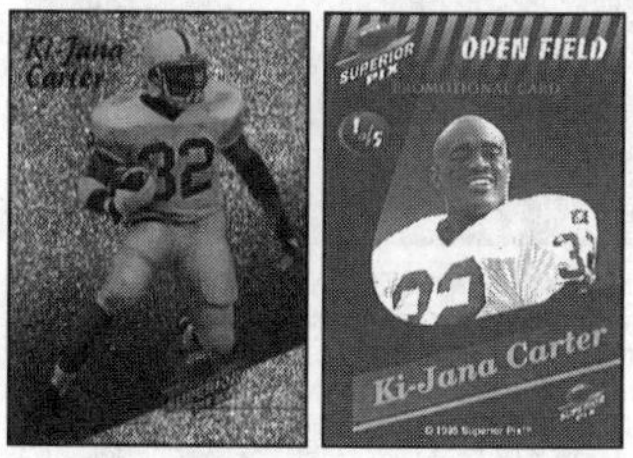

Randomly inserted at a rate of one in 18 packs, these 5 standard-size cards display a color action player photo with a split silver/purple prism like background. The player's name appears in black in the top left or right of the card with the Superior Pix logo appearing in the bottom left or right section of the card. This set features the top running back prospects from the draft.

	MINT	EXC	G-VG
COMPLETE SET (5)	6.00	2.70	.75
COMMON CARD (1-5)	.75	.35	.09
☐ 1 Ki-Jana Carter	1.25	.55	.16
☐ 2 Tyrone Wheatley	.75	.35	.09
☐ 3 James O. Stewart	1.25	.55	.16
☐ 4 Rashaan Salaam	2.00	.90	.25
☐ 5 Ray Zellars	.75	.35	.09

1995 Superior Pix Top Defender

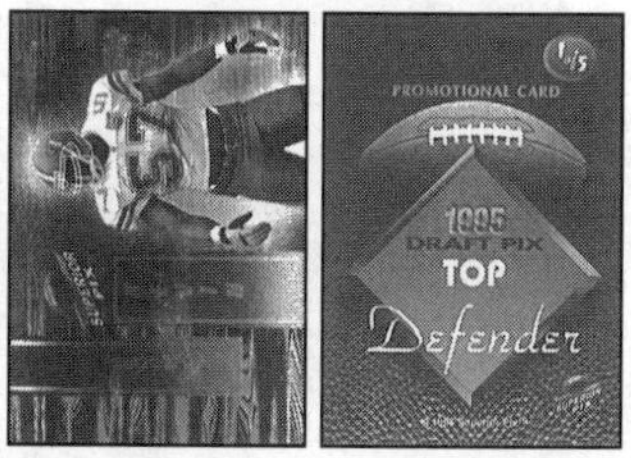

Randomly inserted at a rate of one in nine packs, these five standard-size cards display a color player photo in front of a split blue/gold wood grain background. The player's first and last name appear in two separate stripes to the immediate left of the player. This set features the top defensive lineman prospects from the draft.

	MINT	EXC	G-VG
COMPLETE SET (5)	4.00	1.80	.50
COMMON CARD (1-5)	1.00	.45	.12
☐ 1 Kevin Carter	1.00	.45	.12
☐ 2 Derrick Alexander	1.00	.45	.12
☐ 3 Warren Sapp	1.00	.45	.12
☐ 4 Derrick Brooks	1.00	.45	.12
☐ 5 Mike Mamula	1.00	.45	.12

1991 Wild Card National Promos

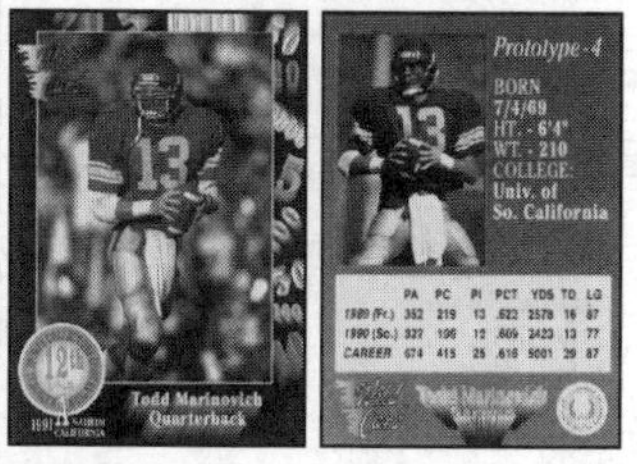

These cards were given away at the 1991 12th Annual Sports Collectors Convention in Anaheim, California. The fronts of these standard-size cards have high gloss color player photos on a black card face with different colored numbers above and to the right of the picture. Striped versions of these cards with a football-shaped hologram in the upper left corner were also issued. The cards are numbered in the upper right corner of the cardback and begin with Prototype-2.

	MINT	NRMT	EXC
COMPLETE SET (3)	2.00	.90	.25
COMMON CARD (P2-P4)	.75	.35	.09

☐ P2 Dan McGwire	.75	.35	.09
☐ P3 Randal Hill	1.00	.45	.12
☐ P4 Todd Marinovich	.75	.35	.09

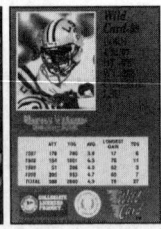

1991 Wild Card

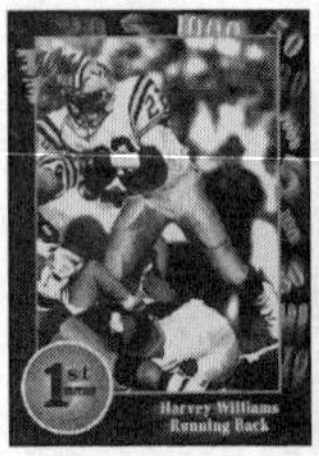

The Wild Card College Football Draft Picks set contains 160 cards measuring the standard size. Reportedly, production quantities were limited to 20,000 numbered cases (or 630,000 sets). The front design features glossy color action player photos on a black card face with an orange frame around the picture and different color numbers appearing in the top and right borders. The words "1st edition" in a circular emblem overlay the lower left corner of the picture. One of out every 100 cards is "wild," with a numbered stripe to indicate how many cards it can be redeemed for. There are 5, 10, 20, 50, 100, and 1000 denominations, with the highest numbers the scarcest. Whatever the "wild" number, the card could be redeemed for that number of regular cards of the same player (plus a redemption fee of $4.95). The set included three surprise wild cards (#1, #15, and #22). If these cards were redeemed before April 30, 1992, the collector received three cards to complete the set (listed below as B versions) and a bonus set of six 1992 collegiate football prototype cards. Collectors who redeemed their cards after April 30 did not receive the prototype cards. Also, Kenny Anderson and Larry Johnson promo cards, numbers P2 and P1 respectively, were randomly inserted, and they could be redeemed after January 2, 1992 for then-unknown player cards. Key cards in this set include Bryan Cox, Craig Erickson, Brett Favre, Alvin Harper, Randal Hill, Rocket Ismail (issued as a surprise card), Herman Moore, Mike Pritchard, Leonard Russell and Ricky Watters.

	MINT	NRMT	EXC
COMPLETE SET (160)	6.00	2.70	.75
COMMON CARD (1-160)	.05	.02	.01

5 STRIPES: 1X TO 2X
10 STRIPES: 1.5X TO 3X
20 STRIPES: 2.5X TO 5X
50 STRIPES: 4X TO 8X
100 STRIPES: 7X TO 15X
1000 STRIPES: 40X TO 100X

☐ 1A Wild Card 1	.05	.02	.01
☐ 1B Todd Lyght	.10	.05	.01
☐ 2 Kelvin Pritchett	.10	.05	.01
☐ 3 Robert Young	.10	.05	.01
☐ 4 Reggie Johnson	.05	.02	.01
☐ 5 Eric Turner	.10	.05	.01
☐ 6 Pat Tyrance	.05	.02	.01
☐ 7 Curvin Richards	.05	.02	.01
☐ 8 Calvin Stephens	.05	.02	.01
☐ 9 Corey Miller	.05	.02	.01
☐ 10 Michael Jackson	.20	.09	.03
☐ 11 Simmie Carter	.05	.02	.01
☐ 12 Roland Smith	.05	.02	.01
☐ 13 Pat O'Hara	.05	.02	.01
☐ 14 Scott Conover	.05	.02	.01
☐ 15A Wild Card 2	.05	.02	.01
☐ 15B Russell Maryland	.10	.05	.01
☐ 16 Greg Amsler	.05	.02	.01
☐ 17 Moe Gardner	.05	.02	.01
☐ 18 Howard Griffith	.05	.02	.01
☐ 19 David Daniels	.05	.02	.01
☐ 20 Henry Jones	.10	.05	.01
☐ 21 Don Davey	.05	.02	.01
☐ 22A Wild Card 3	.05	.02	.01
☐ 22B Raghib Ismail	.20	.09	.03
☐ 23 Richie Andrews	.05	.02	.01
☐ 24 Shawn Moore	.05	.02	.01
☐ 25 Anthony Moss	.05	.02	.01
☐ 26 Vince Moore	.05	.02	.01
☐ 27 Leroy Thompson	.05	.02	.01
☐ 28 Darrick Brown	.05	.02	.01
☐ 29 Mel Agee	.05	.02	.01
☐ 30 Darryll Lewis	.05	.02	.01
☐ 31 Hyland Hickson	.05	.02	.01
☐ 32 Leonard Russell	.10	.05	.01
☐ 33 Floyd Fields	.05	.02	.01
☐ 34 Esera Tuaolo	.05	.02	.01
☐ 35 Todd Marinovich	.05	.02	.01
☐ 36 Gary Wellman	.05	.02	.01
☐ 37 Ricky Ervins	.10	.05	.01
☐ 38 Pat Harlow	.05	.02	.01
☐ 39 Mo Lewis	.05	.02	.01
☐ 40 John Kasay	.05	.02	.01
☐ 41 Phil Hansen	.05	.02	.01
☐ 42 Kevin Donnalley	.05	.02	.01
☐ 43 Dexter Davis	.05	.02	.01
☐ 44 Vance Hammond	.05	.02	.01
☐ 45 Chris Gardocki	.05	.02	.01
☐ 46 Bruce Pickens	.05	.02	.01
☐ 47 Godfrey Myles	.05	.02	.01
☐ 48 Ernie Mills	.10	.05	.01
☐ 49 Derek Russell	.05	.02	.01
☐ 50 Chris Zorich	.05	.02	.01
☐ 51 Alfred Williams	.05	.02	.01
☐ 52 Jon Vaughn	.05	.02	.01
☐ 53 Adrian Cooper	.05	.02	.01
☐ 54 Eric Bieniemy	.10	.05	.01
☐ 55 Robert Bailey	.05	.02	.01
☐ 56 Ricky Watters	.75	.35	.09
☐ 57 Mark Vander Poel	.05	.02	.01
☐ 58 James Joseph	.05	.02	.01
☐ 59 Darren Lewis	.05	.02	.01
☐ 60 Wesley Carroll	.10	.05	.01
☐ 61 Dave Key	.05	.02	.01
☐ 62 Mike Pritchard	.10	.05	.01
☐ 63 Craig Erickson	.10	.05	.01
☐ 64 Browning Nagle	.05	.02	.01
☐ 65 Mike Dumas	.05	.02	.01
☐ 66 Andre Jones	.05	.02	.01
☐ 67 Herman Moore	1.00	.45	.12
☐ 68 Greg Lewis	.05	.02	.01
☐ 69 James Good	.05	.02	.01
☐ 70 Stan Thomas	.05	.02	.01
☐ 71 Jerome Henderson	.05	.02	.01
☐ 72 Doug Thomas	.05	.02	.01
☐ 73 Tony Covington	.05	.02	.01
☐ 74 Charles Mincy	.05	.02	.01
☐ 75 Kanavis McGhee	.05	.02	.01
☐ 76 Tom Backes	.05	.02	.01
☐ 77 Fernandus Vinson	.05	.02	.01
☐ 78 Marcus Robertson	.05	.02	.01
☐ 79 Eric Harmon	.05	.02	.01
☐ 80 Rob Selby	.05	.02	.01
☐ 81 Ed King	.05	.02	.01
☐ 82 William Thomas	.05	.02	.01
☐ 83 Mike Jones	.05	.02	.01
☐ 84 Paul Justin	.05	.02	.01
☐ 85 Robert Wilson	.05	.02	.01
☐ 86 Jesse Campbell	.05	.02	.01
☐ 87 Hayward Haynes	.05	.02	.01
☐ 88 Mike Croel	.05	.02	.01
☐ 89 Jeff Graham	.30	.14	.04
☐ 90 Vinnie Clark	.05	.02	.01
☐ 91 Keith Cash	.05	.02	.01
☐ 92 Tim Ryan	.05	.02	.01
☐ 93 Jarrod Bunch	.05	.02	.01
☐ 94 Stanley Richard	.05	.02	.01
☐ 95 Alvin Harper	.20	.09	.03
☐ 96 Bob Dahl	.05	.02	.01
☐ 97 Mark Gunn	.05	.02	.01
☐ 98 Frank Blevins	.05	.02	.01
☐ 99 Harvey Williams	.30	.14	.04
☐ 100 Dixon Edwards	.05	.02	.01
☐ 101 Blake Miller	.05	.02	.01
☐ 102 Bobby Wilson	.05	.02	.01
☐ 103 Chuck Webb	.05	.02	.01
☐ 104 Randal Hill	.20	.09	.03
☐ 105 Shane Curry	.05	.02	.01
☐ 106 Barry Sanders	1.00	.45	.12
☐ 107 Richard Fain	.05	.02	.01
☐ 108 Joe Garten	.05	.02	.01
☐ 109 Dean Dingman	.05	.02	.01
☐ 110 Mark Tucker	.05	.02	.01
☐ 111 Dan McGwire	.05	.02	.01
☐ 112 Paul Glonek	.05	.02	.01
☐ 113 Tom Dohring	.05	.02	.01
☐ 114 Joe Sims	.05	.02	.01
☐ 115 Bryan Cox	.10	.05	.01
☐ 116 Bobby Olive	.05	.02	.01
☐ 117 Blaise Bryant	.05	.02	.01
☐ 118 Charles Johnson	.05	.02	.01
☐ 119 Brett Favre	2.00	.90	.25
☐ 120 Luis Cristobal	.05	.02	.01
☐ 121 Don Gibson	.05	.02	.01
☐ 122 Scott Ross	.05	.02	.01
☐ 123 Huey Richardson	.05	.02	.01
☐ 124 Chris Smith	.05	.02	.01
☐ 125 Duane Young	.05	.02	.01
☐ 126 Eric Swann	.20	.09	.03
☐ 127 Jeff Fite	.05	.02	.01
☐ 128 Eugene Williams	.05	.02	.01
☐ 129 Harlan Davis	.05	.02	.01
☐ 130 James Bradley	.05	.02	.01
☐ 131 Rob Carpenter	.05	.02	.01
☐ 132 Dennis Ransom	.05	.02	.01
☐ 133 Mike Arthur	.05	.02	.01
☐ 134 Chuck Weatherspoon	.05	.02	.01
☐ 135 Darrell Malone	.05	.02	.01
☐ 136 George Thornton	.05	.02	.01
☐ 137 Lamar McGriggs	.05	.02	.01
☐ 138 Alex Johnson	.05	.02	.01
☐ 139 Eric Moten	.05	.02	.01
☐ 140 Joe Valerio	.05	.02	.01
☐ 141 Jake Reed	.30	.14	.04
☐ 142 Ernie Thompson	.05	.02	.01
☐ 143 Roland Poles	.05	.02	.01
☐ 144 Randy Bethel	.05	.02	.01
☐ 145 Terry Bagsby	.05	.02	.01
☐ 146 Tim James	.05	.02	.01
☐ 147 Kenny Walker	.05	.02	.01
☐ 148 Nolan Harrison	.05	.02	.01
☐ 149 Keith Traylor	.05	.02	.01
☐ 150 Nick Subis	.05	.02	.01
☐ 151 Scott Zolak	.05	.02	.01
☐ 152 Pio Sagapolutele	.05	.02	.01
☐ 153 James Jones	.05	.02	.01
☐ 154 Mike Sullivan	.05	.02	.01
☐ 155 Joe Johnson	.05	.02	.01
☐ 156 Todd Scott	.05	.02	.01
☐ 157 Checklist 1	.05	.02	.01
☐ 158 Checklist 2	.05	.02	.01
☐ 159 Checklist 3	.05	.02	.01
☐ 160 Checklist 4	.05	.02	.01

1992 Wild Card NASDAM

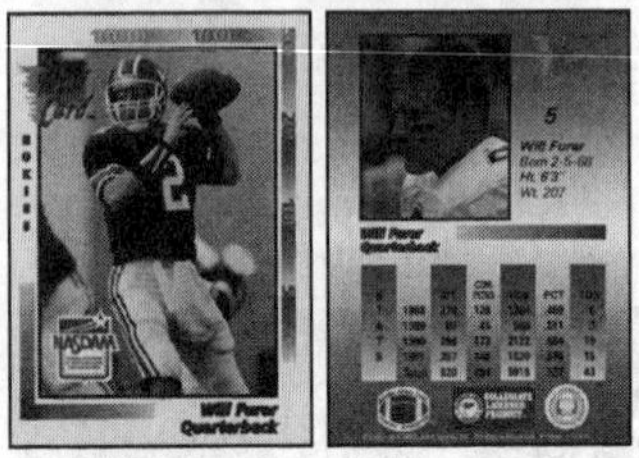

These five promo standard-size cards were given away at the NASDAM trade show in Orlando in the spring of 1992. The cards features color action player photos with white borders. Team color-coded stripes form a right angle at the lower left corner, while the customary series of colored numbers (1000, 100, 50, 20, 10, and 5) form a right angle at the upper right corner of the photo. On a blue and white background, the backs carry a color headshot, biography, and statistics.

	MINT	NRMT	EXC
COMPLETE SET (5)	2.00	.90	.25
COMMON CARD (1-5)	.30	.14	.04
☐ 1 Edgar Bennett	1.00	.45	.12
☐ 2 Amp Lee	.30	.14	.04
☐ 3 Terrell Buckley	.50	.23	.06
☐ 4 Tony Smith	.30	.14	.04
☐ 5 Will Furrer UER (Misspelled Furer)	.30	.14	.04

1993 Air Force Smokey

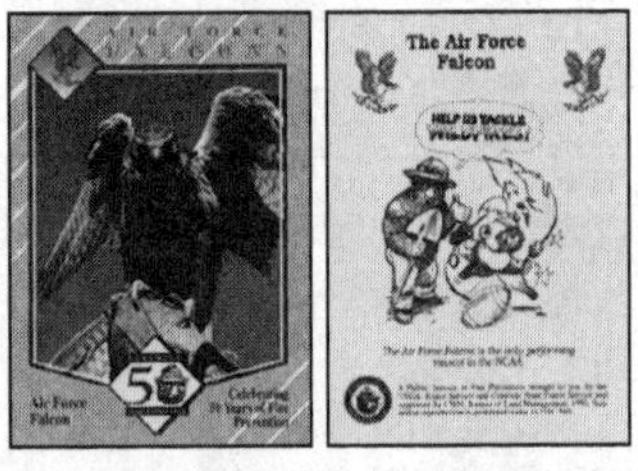

These 16 standard-size cards feature on their fronts color player action shots set within gray borders with white diagonal stripes. The player's name and position appear on the left side underneath the photo. The team name and logo appear above the photo. The plain white back carries the player's name and position at the top, followed by a Smokey safety tip, and the player's career highlights. The cards are unnumbered and checklisted below in alphabetical order.

	MINT	NRMT	EXC
COMPLETE SET (16)	15.00	6.75	1.85
COMMON CARD (1-16)	.75	.35	.09
☐ 1 Fisher DeBerry CO	1.00	.45	.12
☐ 2 Dee Dowis	2.50	1.10	.30
☐ 3 Chad Hennings	5.00	2.20	.60
☐ 4 Carlton MacDonald	1.00	.45	.12
☐ 5 Terry Maki	1.00	.45	.12
☐ 6 Reggie Minton CO	1.00	.45	.12
☐ 7 Air Force Falcon	.75	.35	.09
☐ 8 Air Force Thunderbirds	.75	.35	.09
☐ 9 Cadet Field House	.75	.35	.09
☐ 10 Chapel	.75	.35	.09
☐ 11 Color Guard	.75	.35	.09
☐ 12 Commander-in-Chief's Trophy	.75	.35	.09
☐ 13 Drum and Bugle Corp	.75	.35	.09
☐ 14 Falcon Stadium	.75	.35	.09
☐ 15 Parachute Team	.75	.35	.09
☐ 16 Talon T-38	.75	.35	.09

1971 Alabama Team Sheets

These six sheets measure approximately 8" by 9". The fronts feature twelve black-and-white player portraits arranged in three rows of four portraits per row. The player's name is printed under the photo. The backs are blank. The sheets are unnumbered and checklisted below in alphabetical order.

	NRMT-MT	EXC	G-VG
COMPLETE SET (6)	50.00	22.00	6.25
COMMON PANEL (1-6)	7.00	3.10	.85
☐ 1 Mike Raines Pat Raines Terry Rowell Gary Rutledge Bubba Sawyer Bill Sexton Wayne Wheeler Jack White Steve Williams Dexter Wood	10.00	4.50	1.25
☐ 2 Johnny Musso Lanny Norris Robin Parkhouse Jim Patterson Steve Root Jimmy Rosser Jeff Rouzie Robby Rowan Chuck Strickland Tom Surlas Steve Wade David Watkins	12.00	5.50	1.50
☐ 3 Fred Marshall Noah Miller John Mitchell Randy Moore Gary Reynolds Benny Rippetoe Ronny Robertson John Rogers Jim Simmons Paul Spivey Steve Sprayberry Rod Steakley	7.00	3.10	.85
☐ 4 Richard Bryan Chip Burke Jerry Cash Don Cokely Greg Gantt Jim Grammer Wayne Hall John Hannah Rand Lambert Tom Lusk Bobby McKinney David McMakin	10.00	4.50	1.25
☐ 5 Ellis Beck Steve Bisceglia Jeff Blitz Buddy Brown Steve Dean Mike Denson Joe Doughty Mike Eckenrod Pat Keever David Knapp Jim Krapf Joe LaBue	7.00	3.10	.85
☐ 6 Wayne Adkinson David Bailey Marvin Barron Jeff Beard Andy Cross John Croyle Bill Davis Terry Davis Steve Higginbotham Ed Hines Jimmy Horton Wilbur Jackson	7.00	3.10	.85

1972 Alabama

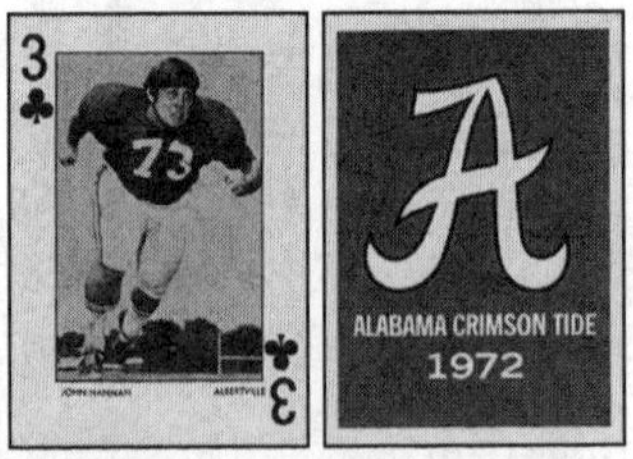

This 54-card standard-size set was issued in a box as a playing card deck through the Alabama University bookstore. The cards have rounded corners and the typical playing card finish. The fronts feature black-and-white posed action photos of helmetless players in their uniforms. A white border surrounds each picture and contains the card number and suit designation in the upper left corner and again, but inverted, in the lower right. The player's name and hometown appear just beneath the photo. The white-bordered crimson backs all have the Alabama "A" logo in white and the year of issue, 1972. The name Alabama Crimson Tide also appears on the backs. Since the set is similar to a playing card set, the set is arranged just like a card deck and checklisted below accordingly. In the checklist below S means Spades, D means Diamonds, C means Clubs, H means Hearts, and JK means Joker. The cards are checklisted below in playing card order by suits and numbers are assigned to Aces (1), Jacks (11), Queens (12), and Kings (13). The jokers are unnumbered and listed at the end. Key cards in the set are early cards of coaching legend Paul "Bear" Bryant and lineman John Hannah.

	NRMT-MT	EXC	G-VG
COMPLETE SET (54)	110.00	50.00	14.00
COMMON CARD	1.50	.70	.19
☐ 1C Skip Kubelius	1.50	.70	.19
☐ 1D Terry Davis	2.50	1.10	.30

☐ 1H Robert Fraley	1.50	.70	.19
☐ 1S Paul(Bear) Bryant CO	35.00	16.00	4.40
☐ 2C David Watkins	1.50	.70	.19
☐ 2D Bobby McKinney	1.50	.70	.19
☐ 2H Dexter Wood	1.50	.70	.19
☐ 2S Chuck Strickland	1.50	.70	.19
☐ 3C John Hannah	18.00	8.00	2.20
☐ 3D Tom Lusk	1.50	.70	.19
☐ 3H Jim Krapf	1.50	.70	.19
☐ 3S Warren Dyar	1.50	.70	.19
☐ 4C Greg Gantt	2.50	1.10	.30
☐ 4D Johnny Sharpless	1.50	.70	.19
☐ 4H Steve Wade	1.50	.70	.19
☐ 4S John Rogers	1.50	.70	.19
☐ 5C Doug Faust	1.50	.70	.19
☐ 5D Jeff Rouzie	1.50	.70	.19
☐ 5H Buddy Brown	1.50	.70	.19
☐ 5S Randy Moore	1.50	.70	.19
☐ 6C David Knapp	2.50	1.10	.30
☐ 6D Lanny Norris	1.50	.70	.19
☐ 6H Paul Spivey	1.50	.70	.19
☐ 6S Pat Raines	1.50	.70	.19
☐ 7C Pete Pappas	1.50	.70	.19
☐ 7D Ed Hines	1.50	.70	.19
☐ 7H Mike Washington	1.50	.70	.19
☐ 7S David McMakin	2.50	1.10	.30
☐ 8C Steve Dean	1.50	.70	.19
☐ 8D Joe LaBue	1.50	.70	.19
☐ 8H John Croyle	1.50	.70	.19
☐ 8S Noah Miller	1.50	.70	.19
☐ 9C Bobby Stanford	1.50	.70	.19
☐ 9D Sylvester Croom	2.50	1.10	.30
☐ 9H Wilbur Jackson	8.00	3.60	1.00
☐ 9S Ellis Beck	1.50	.70	.19
☐ 10C Steve Bisceglia	1.50	.70	.19
☐ 10D Andy Cross	1.50	.70	.19
☐ 10H John Mitchell	2.50	1.10	.30
☐ 10S Bill Davis	1.50	.70	.19
☐ 11C Gary Rutledge	2.50	1.10	.30
☐ 11D Randy Billingsley	1.50	.70	.19
☐ 11H Randy Hall	1.50	.70	.19
☐ 11S Ralph Stokes	1.50	.70	.19
☐ 12C Jeff Blitz	1.50	.70	.19
☐ 12D Robby Rowan	1.50	.70	.19
☐ 12H Mike Raines	1.50	.70	.19
☐ 12S Wayne Wheeler	1.50	.70	.19
☐ 13C Steve Sprayberry	1.50	.70	.19
☐ 13D Wayne Hall	2.50	1.10	.30
☐ 13H Morris Hunt	1.50	.70	.19
☐ 13S Butch Norman	1.50	.70	.19
☐ JK1 Denny Stadium	1.50	.70	.19
☐ JK2 Memorial Coliseum	1.50	.70	.19

1973 Alabama

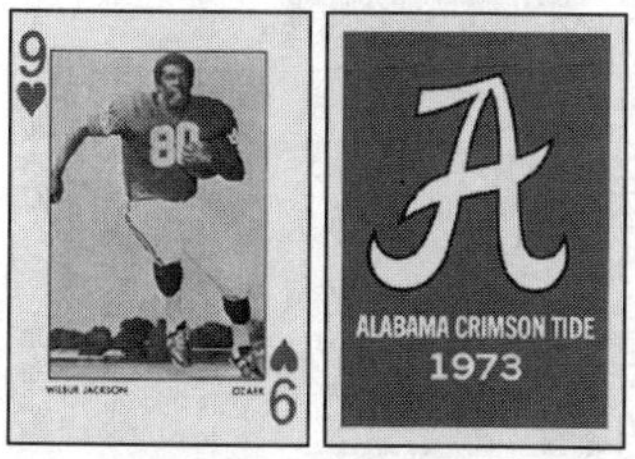

These 54 standard-size playing cards have rounded corners and the typical playing card finish The cards were sold through the Alabama University bookstore. The fronts feature black-and-white posed action photos of helmetless players in their uniforms. A white border surrounds each picture and contains the card number and suit designation in the upper left corner and again, but inverted, in the lower right. The player's name and hometown appear just beneath the photo. The white-bordered crimson backs all have the Alabama "A" logo in white and the year of issue, 1973. The name Alabama Crimson Tide also appears on the backs. Since this is a set of playing cards, the set is checklisted below accordingly. In the checklist below S means Spades, D means Diamonds, C means Clubs, H means Hearts, and JK means Joker. The cards are in playing card order by suits and numbers are assigned to Aces (1), Jacks (11), Queens (12), and Kings (13). The jokers are unnumbered and listed at the end.

	NRMT-MT	EXC	G-VG
COMPLETE SET (54)	90.00	40.00	11.00
COMMON CARD	1.50	.70	.19
☐ 1C Skip Kubelius	1.50	.70	.19
☐ 1D Mark Prudhomme	1.50	.70	.19
☐ 1H Robert Fraley	1.50	.70	.19
☐ 1S Paul(Bear) Bryant CO	25.00	11.00	3.10
☐ 2C David Watkins	1.50	.70	.19
☐ 2D Richard Todd	12.00	5.50	1.50
☐ 2H Buddy Pope	1.50	.70	.19
☐ 2S Chuck Strickland	1.50	.70	.19
☐ 3C Bob Bryan	1.50	.70	.19
☐ 3D Gary Hanrahan	1.50	.70	.19
☐ 3H Greg Montgomery	1.50	.70	.19
☐ 3S Warren Dyar	1.50	.70	.19
☐ 4C Greg Gantt	2.50	1.10	.30
☐ 4D Johnny Sharpless	1.50	.70	.19
☐ 4H Rick Watson	1.50	.70	.19
☐ 4S John Rogers	1.50	.70	.19
☐ 5C George Pugh	2.50	1.10	.30
☐ 5D Jeff Rouzie	1.50	.70	.19
☐ 5H Buddy Brown	1.50	.70	.19
☐ 5S Randy Moore	1.50	.70	.19
☐ 6C Ray Maxwell	1.50	.70	.19
☐ 6D Alan Pizzitola	1.50	.70	.19
☐ 6H Paul Spivey	1.50	.70	.19
☐ 6S Ron Robertson	1.50	.70	.19
☐ 7C Pete Pappas	1.50	.70	.19
☐ 7D Steve Kulback	1.50	.70	.19
☐ 7H Mike Washington	1.50	.70	.19
☐ 7S David McMakin	2.50	1.10	.30
☐ 8C Steve Dean	1.50	.70	.19
☐ 8D Jerry Brown	1.50	.70	.19
☐ 8H John Croyle	1.50	.70	.19
☐ 8S Noah Miller	1.50	.70	.19
☐ 9C Leroy Cook	1.50	.70	.19
☐ 9D Sylvester Croom	2.50	1.10	.30
☐ 9H Wilbur Jackson	6.00	2.70	.75
☐ 9S Ellis Beck	1.50	.70	.19
☐ 10C Tyrone King	1.50	.70	.19
☐ 10D Mike Stock	1.50	.70	.19
☐ 10H Mike Dubose	1.50	.70	.19
☐ 10S Bill Davis	1.50	.70	.19
☐ 11C Gary Rutledge	2.50	1.10	.30
☐ 11D Randy Billingsley	1.50	.70	.19
☐ 11H Randy Hall	1.50	.70	.19
☐ 11S Ralph Stokes	1.50	.70	.19
☐ 12C Woodrow Lowe	6.00	2.70	.75
☐ 12D Marvin Barron	1.50	.70	.19
☐ 12H Mike Raines	1.50	.70	.19
☐ 12S Wayne Wheeler	1.50	.70	.19
☐ 13C Steve Sprayberry	1.50	.70	.19
☐ 13D Wayne Hall	2.50	1.10	.30
☐ 13H Morris Hunt	1.50	.70	.19
☐ 13S Butch Norman	1.50	.70	.19
☐ JK1 Denny Stadium	1.50	.70	.19
☐ JK2 Memorial Coliseum	1.50	.70	.19

1988 Alabama Winners

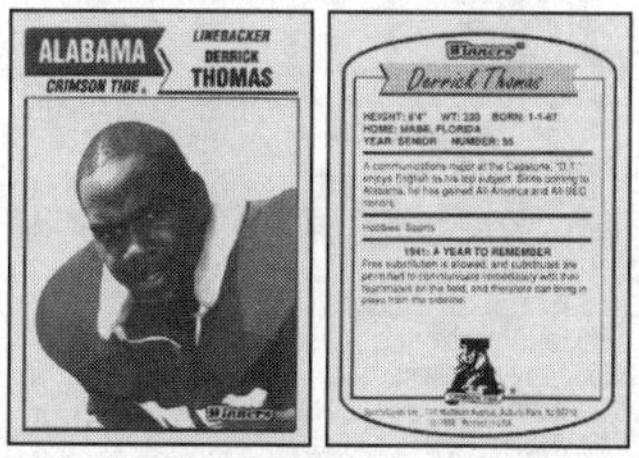

The 1988 Alabama Winners set contains 73 standard-size cards. The fronts have color portrait photos with "Alabama" and name banners in school colors; the vertically oriented backs have brief profiles and Crimson Tide highlights from specific seasons. The card numbering is essentially in order alphabetically by subject's name. The set features an early card of Derrick Thomas.

	MINT	NRMT	EXC
COMPLETE SET (73)	12.00	5.50	1.50
COMMON CARD (1-73)	.15	.07	.02
☐ 1 Title Card (Schedule on back)	.25	.11	.03
☐ 2 Charlie Abrams	.15	.07	.02
☐ 3 Sam Atkins	.15	.07	.02
☐ 4 Marco Battle	.15	.07	.02
☐ 5 George Bethune	.15	.07	.02
☐ 6 Scott Bolt	.15	.07	.02
☐ 7 Tommy Bowden	.25	.11	.03
☐ 8 Danny Cash	.15	.07	.02
☐ 9 John Cassimus	.15	.07	.02
☐ 10 David Casteal	.15	.07	.02
☐ 11 Terrill Chatman	.15	.07	.02
☐ 12 Andy Christoff	.15	.07	.02
☐ 13 Tommy Cole	.15	.07	.02
☐ 14 Tony Cox	.15	.07	.02
☐ 15 Howard Cross	.75	.35	.09
☐ 16 Bill Curry CO	.25	.11	.03
☐ 17 Johnny Davis	.25	.11	.03
☐ 18 Vantreise Davis	.15	.07	.02
☐ 19 Joe Demos	.15	.07	.02
☐ 20 Philip Doyle	.25	.11	.03
☐ 21 Jeff Dunn	.15	.07	.02
☐ 22 John Fruhmorgen	.15	.07	.02
☐ 23 Jim Fuller	.15	.07	.02
☐ 24 Greg Gilbert	.15	.07	.02
☐ 25 Pierre Goode	.25	.11	.03
☐ 26 John Guy	.15	.07	.02
☐ 27 Spencer Hammond	.15	.07	.02
☐ 28 Stacy Harrison	.15	.07	.02
☐ 29 Murry Hill	.15	.07	.02
☐ 30 Byron Holdbrooks	.15	.07	.02
☐ 31 Ben Holt	.15	.07	.02
☐ 32 Bobby Humphrey	.75	.35	.09
☐ 33 Gene Jelks	.50	.23	.06
☐ 34 Kermit Kendrick	.15	.07	.02
☐ 35 William Kent	.15	.07	.02
☐ 36 David Lenoir	.15	.07	.02
☐ 37 Butch Lewis	.15	.07	.02
☐ 38 Don Lindsey	.15	.07	.02
☐ 39 John Mangum	.50	.23	.06
☐ 40 Tim Matheny	.15	.07	.02
☐ 41 Mac McWhorter	.25	.11	.03
☐ 42 Chris Mohr	.25	.11	.03
☐ 43 Larry New	.15	.07	.02
☐ 44 Gene Newberry	.15	.07	.02
☐ 45 Lee Ozmint	.15	.07	.02
☐ 46 Trent Patterson	.15	.07	.02
☐ 47 Greg Payne	.15	.07	.02
☐ 48 Thomas Rayam	.15	.07	.02
☐ 49 Chris Robinette	.15	.07	.02
☐ 50 Larry Rose	.15	.07	.02
☐ 51 Derrick Rushton	.15	.07	.02
☐ 52 Lamonde Russell	.15	.07	.02
☐ 53 Craig Sanderson	.15	.07	.02
☐ 54 Wayne Shaw	.15	.07	.02
☐ 55 Willie Shepherd	.15	.07	.02
☐ 56 Roger Shultz	.15	.07	.02
☐ 57 David Smith	.15	.07	.02
☐ 58 Homer Smith	.15	.07	.02
☐ 59 Mike Smith	.15	.07	.02
☐ 60 Byron Sneed	.15	.07	.02
☐ 61 Robert Stewart	.15	.07	.02
☐ 62 Vince Strickland	.15	.07	.02
☐ 63 Brian Stutson	.15	.07	.02
☐ 64 Vince Sutton	.15	.07	.02
☐ 65 Derrick Thomas	5.00	2.20	.60
☐ 66 Steve Turner	.15	.07	.02
☐ 67 Alan Ward	.15	.07	.02
☐ 68 Lorenzo Ward	.15	.07	.02
☐ 69 Steve Webb	.15	.07	.02
☐ 70 Woody Wilson	.15	.07	.02
☐ 71 Chip Wisdom	.15	.07	.02
☐ 72 Willie Wyatt	.15	.07	.02
☐ 73 Mike Zuga	.15	.07	.02

1989 Alabama Coke 20

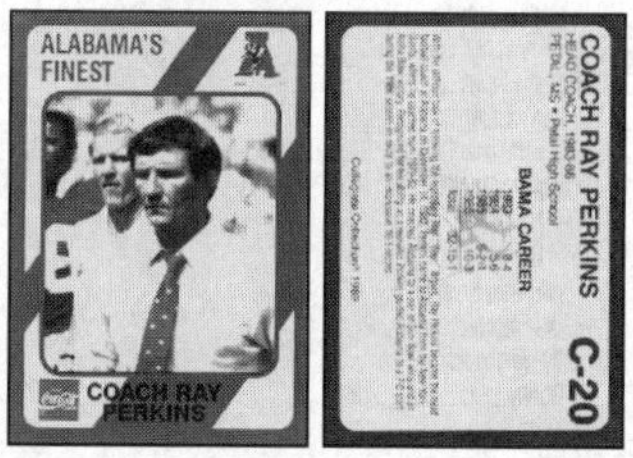

The 1989 Coke University of Alabama football set contains 20 standard-size cards, depicting former Crimson Tide greats. The fronts have vintage photos; the horizontally oriented backs feature player profiles. Both sides have crimson borders. These cards were printed on very thin stock.

	MINT	NRMT	EXC
COMPLETE SET (20)	12.00	5.50	1.50
COMMON CARD (C1-C20)	.35	.16	.04
☐ C1 Paul(Bear) Bryant CO	2.00	.90	.25
☐ C2 John Hannah	.75	.35	.09
☐ C3 Fred Sington	.35	.16	.04
☐ C4 Derrick Thomas	1.50	.70	.19
☐ C5 Dwight Stephenson	.75	.35	.09
☐ C6 Cornelius Bennett	1.00	.45	.12
☐ C7 Ozzie Newsome	1.00	.45	.12
☐ C8 Joe Namath (Art)	2.50	1.10	.30
☐ C9 Steve Sloan	.60	.25	.07
☐ C10 Bill Curry CO	.35	.16	.04
☐ C11 Paul(Bear) Bryant CO	2.00	.90	.25
☐ C12 Big Al (Mascot)	.35	.16	.04
☐ C13 Scott Hunter	.50	.23	.06
☐ C14 Lee Roy Jordan	.75	.35	.09
☐ C15 Walter Lewis	.35	.16	.04
☐ C16 Bobby Humphrey	.35	.16	.04
☐ C17 John Mitchell	.35	.16	.04
☐ C18 Johnny Musso	.75	.35	.09
☐ C19 Pat Trammell	.35	.16	.04
☐ C20 Ray Perkins CO	.60	.25	.07

1989 Alabama Coke 580

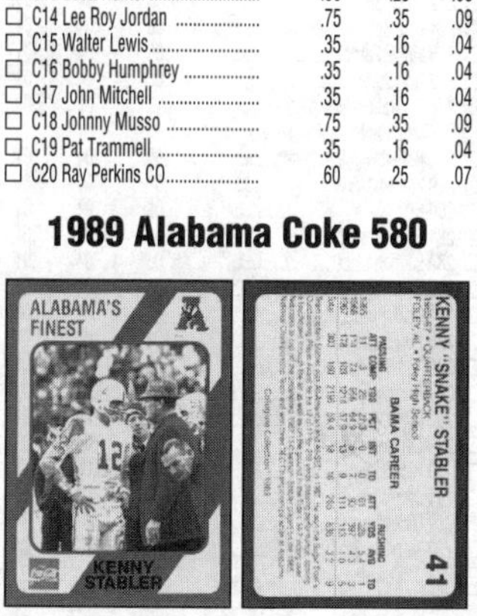

The 1989 Coke University of Alabama football set contains 580 standard-size cards, depicting former Crimson Tide greats. The fronts contain vintage photos; the horizontally oriented backs feature player profiles. Both sides have crimson borders. The cards were distributed in sets and in poly packs. These cards were printed on very thin stock.

	MINT	NRMT	EXC
COMPLETE SET (580)	35.00	16.00	4.40
COMMON CARD (1-580)	.08	.04	.01
☐ 1 Paul(Bear) Bryant CO	.75	.35	.09
☐ 2 W.T. Van De Graff	.08	.04	.01
☐ 3 A.T.S. Hubert	.08	.04	.01
☐ 4 Bill Buckler	.08	.04	.01
☐ 5 Hoyt(Wu) Winslett	.08	.04	.01
☐ 6 Tony Holm	.08	.04	.01
☐ 7 Fred Sington Sr.	.15	.07	.02
☐ 8 John Suther	.08	.04	.01
☐ 9 Johnny Cain	.08	.04	.01
☐ 10 Tom Hupke	.15	.07	.02
☐ 11 Millard Howell	.25	.11	.03
☐ 12 Steve Wright	.08	.04	.01
☐ 13 Bill Searcey	.08	.04	.01
☐ 14 Riley Smith	.08	.04	.01
☐ 15 Arthur Tarzan White	.08	.04	.01
☐ 16 Joe Kilgrow	.08	.04	.01
☐ 17 Leroy Monsky	.08	.04	.01
☐ 18 James Ryba	.08	.04	.01
☐ 19 Carey Cox	.08	.04	.01
☐ 20 Holt Rast	.08	.04	.01
☐ 21 Joe Domnanovich	.08	.04	.01
☐ 22 Don Whitmire	.15	.07	.02
☐ 23 Harry Gilmer	.25	.11	.03
☐ 24 Vaughn Mancha	.08	.04	.01
☐ 25 Ed Salem	.08	.04	.01
☐ 26 Bobby Marlow	.30	.14	.04
☐ 27 George Mason	.08	.04	.01
☐ 28 Billy Neighbors	.25	.11	.03
☐ 29 Lee Roy Jordan	.50	.23	.06
☐ 30 Wayne Freeman	.08	.04	.01
☐ 31 Dan Kearley	.08	.04	.01
☐ 32 Joe Namath	1.00	.45	.12
☐ 33 David Ray	.15	.07	.02
☐ 34 Paul Crane	.08	.04	.01
☐ 35 Steve Sloan	.25	.11	.03
☐ 36 Richard Cole	.08	.04	.01
☐ 37 Cecil Dowdy	.15	.07	.02
☐ 38 Bobby Johns	.08	.04	.01
☐ 39 Ray Perkins	.30	.14	.04
☐ 40 Dennis Homan	.25	.11	.03
☐ 41 Ken Stabler	.75	.35	.09
☐ 42 Robert W. Boylston	.08	.04	.01
☐ 43 Mike Hall	.08	.04	.01
☐ 44 Alvin Samples	.08	.04	.01
☐ 45 Johnny Musso with Bear Bryant	.25	.11	.03
☐ 46 Bryant-Denney Stadium	.08	.04	.01
☐ 47 Tom Surlas	.08	.04	.01
☐ 48 John Hannah	.30	.14	.04
☐ 49 Jim Krapf	.08	.04	.01
☐ 50 John Mitchell	.15	.07	.02
☐ 51 Buddy Brown	.08	.04	.01
☐ 52 Woodrow Lowe	.15	.07	.02
☐ 53 Wayne Wheeler	.08	.04	.01
☐ 54 Leroy Cook	.08	.04	.01
☐ 55 Sylvester Croom	.15	.07	.02
☐ 56 Mike Washington	.08	.04	.01
☐ 57 Ozzie Newsome	.50	.23	.06
☐ 58 Barry Krauss	.15	.07	.02
☐ 59 Marty Lyons	.25	.11	.03
☐ 60 Jim Bunch	.08	.04	.01
☐ 61 Don McNeal	.15	.07	.02
☐ 62 Dwight Stephenson	.30	.14	.04
☐ 63 Bill Davis	.08	.04	.01
☐ 64 E.J. Junior	.15	.07	.02
☐ 65 Tommy Wilcox	.15	.07	.02
☐ 66 Jeremiah Castille	.15	.07	.02
☐ 67 Bobby Swafford	.08	.04	.01
☐ 68 Cornelius Bennett	.50	.23	.06
☐ 69 David Knapp	.15	.07	.02
☐ 70 Bobby Humphrey	.30	.14	.04
☐ 71 Van Tiffin	.08	.04	.01
☐ 72 Sid Smith	.08	.04	.01
☐ 73 Pat Trammell	.25	.11	.03
☐ 74 Mickey Andrews	.08	.04	.01
☐ 75 Steve Bowman	.08	.04	.01
☐ 76 Bob Baumhower	.25	.11	.03
☐ 77 Bob Cryder	.08	.04	.01
☐ 78 Byron Braggs	.15	.07	.02
☐ 79 Warren Lyles	.08	.04	.01
☐ 80 Steve Mott	.08	.04	.01
☐ 81 Walter Lewis	.15	.07	.02
☐ 82 Ricky Moore	.08	.04	.01
☐ 83 Wes Neighbors	.08	.04	.01
☐ 84 Derrick Thomas	.60	.25	.07
☐ 85 Kermit Kendrick	.08	.04	.01
☐ 86 Larry Rose	.08	.04	.01
☐ 87 Charlie Marr	.08	.04	.01
☐ 88 James Whatley	.08	.04	.01
☐ 89 Erin Warren	.08	.04	.01
☐ 90 Charlie Holm	.08	.04	.01
☐ 91 Fred Davis	.08	.04	.01
☐ 92 John Wyhonic	.08	.04	.01
☐ 93 Jimmy Nelson	.08	.04	.01
☐ 94 Roy Steiner	.15	.07	.02
☐ 95 Tom Whitley	.08	.04	.01
☐ 96 John Wozniak	.08	.04	.01
☐ 97 Ed Holdnak	.08	.04	.01
☐ 98 Al Lary	.08	.04	.01
☐ 99 Mike Mizerany	.08	.04	.01
☐ 100 Pat O'Sullivan	.08	.04	.01
☐ 101 Jerry Watford	.08	.04	.01
☐ 102 Cecil Ingram	.15	.07	.02
☐ 103 Mike Fracchia	.08	.04	.01
☐ 104 Benny Nelson	.08	.04	.01

☐ 105 Tommy Tolleson .08 .04 .01
☐ 106 Creed Gilmer .08 .04 .01
☐ 107 John Calvert .08 .04 .01
☐ 108 Derrick Slaughter .08 .04 .01
☐ 109 Mike Ford .08 .04 .01
☐ 110 Bruce Stephens .08 .04 .01
☐ 111 Danny Ford .25 .11 .03
☐ 112 Jimmy Grammer .08 .04 .01
☐ 113 Steve Higginbotham .08 .04 .01
☐ 114 David Bailey .08 .04 .01
☐ 115 Greg Gantt .25 .11 .03
☐ 116 Terry Davis .15 .07 .02
☐ 117 Chuck Strickland .08 .04 .01
☐ 118 Bobby McKinney .08 .04 .01
☐ 119 Wilbur Jackson .25 .11 .03
☐ 120 Mike Raines .08 .04 .01
☐ 121 Steve Sprayberry .08 .04 .01
☐ 122 David McMakin .15 .07 .02
☐ 123 Ben Smith .08 .04 .01
☐ 124 Steadman Shealy .25 .11 .03
☐ 125 John Rogers .08 .04 .01
☐ 126 Ricky Davis .15 .07 .02
☐ 127 Conley Duncan .08 .04 .01
☐ 128 Wayne Rhodes .08 .04 .01
☐ 129 Buddy Seay .08 .04 .01
☐ 130 Alan Pizzitola .08 .04 .01
☐ 131 Richard Todd .25 .11 .03
☐ 132 Charlie Ferguson .08 .04 .01
☐ 133 Charley Hannah .15 .07 .02
☐ 134 Wiley Barnes .08 .04 .01
☐ 135 Mike Brock .08 .04 .01
☐ 136 Murray Legg .08 .04 .01
☐ 137 Wayne Hamilton .08 .04 .01
☐ 138 David Hannah .08 .04 .01
☐ 139 Jim Bob Harris .08 .04 .01
☐ 140 Bart Krout .08 .04 .01
☐ 141 Bob Cayavec .08 .04 .01
☐ 142 Joe Beazley .08 .04 .01
☐ 143 Mike Adcock .08 .04 .01
☐ 144 Albert Bell .08 .04 .01
☐ 145 Mike Shula .40 .18 .05
☐ 146 Curt Jarvis .08 .04 .01
☐ 147 Freddie Robinson .08 .04 .01
☐ 148 Bill Condon .08 .04 .01
☐ 149 Howard Cross .30 .14 .04
☐ 150 Joe Demyanovich .08 .04 .01
☐ 151 Major Ogilvie .25 .11 .03
☐ 152 Perron Shoemaker .08 .04 .01
☐ 153 Mike Jones .08 .04 .01
☐ 154 Vic Bradford .08 .04 .01
☐ 155 Ed Hickerson .08 .04 .01
☐ 156 Mitchell Olenski .08 .04 .01
☐ 157 George Hecht .08 .04 .01
☐ 158 Russ Craft .08 .04 .01
☐ 159 Joey Jones .25 .11 .03
☐ 160 Jack Green .08 .04 .01
☐ 161 Lowell Tew .15 .07 .02
☐ 162 Lamar Moye .08 .04 .01
☐ 163 Jesse Richardson .15 .07 .02
☐ 164 Harold Lutz .08 .04 .01
☐ 165 Travis Hunt .08 .04 .01
☐ 166 Ed Culpepper .08 .04 .01
☐ 167 Nick Germanos .08 .04 .01
☐ 168 Billy Rains .08 .04 .01
☐ 169 Don Cochran .08 .04 .01
☐ 170 Cotton Clark .08 .04 .01
☐ 171 Gaylon McCollogh .08 .04 .01
☐ 172 Tim Bates .08 .04 .01
☐ 173 Wayne Cook .08 .04 .01
☐ 174 Jerry Duncan .08 .04 .01
☐ 175 Steve Davis .08 .04 .01
☐ 176 Donnie Sutton .08 .04 .01
☐ 177 Randy Barron .08 .04 .01
☐ 178 Frank Mann .08 .04 .01
☐ 179 Jeff Rouzie .08 .04 .01
☐ 180 John Croyle .08 .04 .01
☐ 181 Skip Kubelius .08 .04 .01
☐ 182 Steve Bisceglia .08 .04 .01
☐ 183 Gary Rutledge .15 .07 .02
☐ 184 Mike Dubose .08 .04 .01
☐ 185 Johnny Davis .25 .11 .03
☐ 186 K.J. Lazenby .08 .04 .01
☐ 187 Jeff Rutledge .25 .11 .03
☐ 188 Mike Tucker .08 .04 .01
☐ 189 Tony Nathan .25 .11 .03
☐ 190 Buddy Aydelette .08 .04 .01
☐ 191 Steve Whitman .08 .04 .01
☐ 192 Ricky Tucker .08 .04 .01
☐ 193 Randy Scott .08 .04 .01
☐ 194 Warren Averitte .08 .04 .01
☐ 195 Doug Vickers .08 .04 .01
☐ 196 Jackie Cline .08 .04 .01
☐ 197 Wayne Davis .08 .04 .01
☐ 198 Hardy Walker .08 .04 .01
☐ 199 Paul Ott Carruth .15 .07 .02
☐ 200 Paul(Bear) Bryant CO .75 .35 .09
☐ 201 Randy Rockwell .08 .04 .01
☐ 202 Chris Mohr .15 .07 .02
☐ 203 Walter Merrill .08 .04 .01
☐ 204 Johnny Sullivan .08 .04 .01
☐ 205 Harold Newman .08 .04 .01
☐ 206 Erskine Walker .08 .04 .01
☐ 207 Ted Cook .08 .04 .01
☐ 208 Charles Compton .08 .04 .01
☐ 209 Bill Cadenhead .08 .04 .01
☐ 210 Butch Avinger .08 .04 .01
☐ 211 Bobby Wilson .08 .04 .01
☐ 212 Sid Youngelman .25 .11 .03
☐ 213 Leon Fuller .08 .04 .01
☐ 214 Tommy Brooker .15 .07 .02
☐ 215 Richard Williamson .25 .11 .03
☐ 216 Riggs Stephenson .25 .11 .03
☐ 217 Al Clemens .08 .04 .01
☐ 218 Grant Gillis .08 .04 .01
☐ 219 Johnny Mack Brown .50 .23 .06
☐ 220 Major Ogilvie .25 .11 .03
with Bear Bryant
☐ 221 Fred Pickhard .08 .04 .01
☐ 222 Herschel Caldwell .08 .04 .01
☐ 223 Emile Barnes .08 .04 .01
☐ 224 Mike McQueen .08 .04 .01
☐ 225 Ray Abruzzese .15 .07 .02
☐ 226 Jesse Bendross .25 .11 .03
☐ 227 Lew Bostick .08 .04 .01
☐ 228 Jimmy Bowdoin .08 .04 .01
☐ 229 Dave Brown .08 .04 .01
☐ 230 Tom Calvin .08 .04 .01
☐ 231 Ken Emerson .08 .04 .01
☐ 232 Calvin Frey .08 .04 .01
☐ 233 Thornton Chandler .15 .07 .02
☐ 234 George Weeks .08 .04 .01
☐ 235 Randy Edwards .08 .04 .01
☐ 236 Phillip Brown .08 .04 .01
☐ 237 Clay Whitehurst .08 .04 .01
☐ 238 Chris Goode .08 .04 .01
☐ 239 Preston Gothard .08 .04 .01
☐ 240 Herb Hannah .08 .04 .01
☐ 241 John M. Snoderly .08 .04 .01
☐ 242 Scott Hunter .25 .11 .03
☐ 243 Bobby Jackson .08 .04 .01
☐ 244 Bruce Jones .08 .04 .01
☐ 245 Robbie Jones .08 .04 .01
☐ 246 Terry Jones .08 .04 .01
☐ 247 Leslie Kelley .08 .04 .01
☐ 248 Larry Lauer .08 .04 .01
☐ 249 '61 National Champs .25 .11 .03
(Tommy Brooker,
Pat Trammell,
Lee Roy Jordan,
Paul(Bear) Bryant,
Mike Fracchia, and
Billy Neighbors)
☐ 250 Bobby Luna .08 .04 .01
☐ 251 Keith Pugh .08 .04 .01
☐ 252 Alan McElroy .08 .04 .01
☐ 253 '25 National Champs .15 .07 .02
(Team Photo)
☐ 254 Curtis McGriff .25 .11 .03
☐ 255 Norman Mosley .08 .04 .01
☐ 256 Herky Mosley .08 .04 .01
☐ 257 Ray Ogden .15 .07 .02
☐ 258 Pete Jilleba .08 .04 .01
☐ 259 Benny Perrin .08 .04 .01
☐ 260 Claude Perry .08 .04 .01
☐ 261 Tommy Cole .08 .04 .01
☐ 262 Ed Versprille .08 .04 .01
☐ 263 '30 National Champs .15 .07 .02
(Team Photo)
☐ 264 Don Jacobs .08 .04 .01
☐ 265 Robert Skelton .08 .04 .01
☐ 266 Joe Curtis .08 .04 .01
☐ 267 Bart Starr .75 .35 .09
☐ 268 Young Boozer .08 .04 .01
☐ 269 Tommy Lewis .15 .07 .02
☐ 270 Woody Umphrey .08 .04 .01
☐ 271 Carney Laslie .08 .04 .01
☐ 272 Russ Wood .08 .04 .01
☐ 273 David Smith .08 .04 .01
☐ 274 Paul Spivey .08 .04 .01
☐ 275 Linnie Patrick .08 .04 .01
☐ 276 Ron Durby .08 .04 .01
☐ 277 '26 National Champs .15 .07 .02
(Team Photo)
☐ 278 Robert Higginbotham .08 .04 .01
☐ 279 William Oliver .08 .04 .01
☐ 280 Stan Moss .08 .04 .01
☐ 281 Eddie Propst .08 .04 .01
☐ 282 Laurien Stapp .08 .04 .01
☐ 283 Clem Gryska .08 .04 .01
☐ 284 Clark Pearce .08 .04 .01
☐ 285 Pete Cavan .08 .04 .01
☐ 286 Tom Newton .08 .04 .01
☐ 287 Rich Wingo .15 .07 .02
☐ 288 Rickey Gilliland .08 .04 .01
☐ 289 Conrad Fowler .08 .04 .01
☐ 290 Rick Neal .08 .04 .01
☐ 291 James Blevins .08 .04 .01
☐ 292 Dick Flowers .08 .04 .01
☐ 293 Marshall Brown .08 .04 .01
☐ 294 Jeff Beard .08 .04 .01
☐ 295 Pete Moore .08 .04 .01
☐ 296 Vince Boothe .08 .04 .01
☐ 297 Charley Boswell .08 .04 .01
☐ 298 Van Marcus .08 .04 .01
☐ 299 Randy Billingsley .15 .07 .02
☐ 300 Paul(Bear) Bryant CO .75 .35 .09
☐ 301 Gene Blackwell .08 .04 .01
☐ 302 Johnny Mosley .08 .04 .01
☐ 303 Ray Perkins CO .25 .11 .03
☐ 304 Harold Drew CO .08 .04 .01
☐ 305 Frank Thomas CO .25 .11 .03
(Not the Frank Thomas
that went to Auburn)
☐ 306 Wallace Wade CO .15 .07 .02
☐ 307 Newton Godfree .08 .04 .01
☐ 308 Steve Williams .08 .04 .01
☐ 309 Al Lewis .08 .04 .01
☐ 310 Fred Grant .08 .04 .01
☐ 311 Jerry Brown .08 .04 .01
☐ 312 Mal Moore CO .15 .07 .02
with Bear Bryant
☐ 313 Tilden Campbell .08 .04 .01
☐ 314 Jack Smalley .08 .04 .01
☐ 315 Paul(Bear) Bryant CO .75 .35 .09
☐ 316 C.B. Clements .08 .04 .01
☐ 317 Billy Piper .08 .04 .01
☐ 318 Robert Lee Hamner .08 .04 .01
☐ 319 Donnie Faust .08 .04 .01
☐ 320 Gary Bramblett .08 .04 .01
☐ 321 Peter Kim .08 .04 .01
☐ 322 Fred Berrey .08 .04 .01
☐ 323 Paul(Bear) Bryant CO .75 .35 .09
☐ 324 John Fruhmorgen .08 .04 .01
☐ 325 Jim Fuller .08 .04 .01
with Bear Bryant
☐ 326 Doug Allen .08 .04 .01
☐ 327 Russ Mosley .08 .04 .01
☐ 328 Ricky Thomas .08 .04 .01
☐ 329 Vince Sutton .08 .04 .01
☐ 330 Larry Roberts .15 .07 .02
☐ 331 Rick McLain .08 .04 .01
☐ 332 Charles Eckerly .08 .04 .01
☐ 333 '34 National Champs .15 .07 .02
(Team Photo)
☐ 334 Eddie McCombs .08 .04 .01
☐ 335 Scott Allison .08 .04 .01
☐ 336 Vince Cowell .08 .04 .01
☐ 337 David Watkins .08 .04 .01
☐ 338 Jim Duke .08 .04 .01
☐ 339 Don Harris .08 .04 .01
☐ 340 Lanny Norris .08 .04 .01
☐ 341 Thad Flanagan .08 .04 .01
☐ 342 Albert Elmore Jr. .08 .04 .01
☐ 343 Alan Gray .08 .04 .01
☐ 344 David Gilmer .08 .04 .01
☐ 345 Hal Self .08 .04 .01
☐ 346 Ben McLeod .08 .04 .01
☐ 347 Clell(Butch) Hobson .50 .23 .06
☐ 348 Jimmy Carroll .08 .04 .01
☐ 349 Frank Canterbury .08 .04 .01
☐ 350 John Byrd Williams .08 .04 .01
☐ 351 Marvin Barron .08 .04 .01
☐ 352 William J. Stone .08 .04 .01
☐ 353 Barry Smith .15 .07 .02
☐ 354 Jerrill Sprinkle .08 .04 .01
☐ 355 Hank Crisp CO .08 .04 .01
☐ 356 Bobby Smith .08 .04 .01
☐ 357 Charles Gray .08 .04 .01
☐ 358 Marlin Dyess .08 .04 .01
☐ 359 '41 National Champs .15 .07 .02
(Team Photo)
☐ 360 Robert Moore .08 .04 .01
☐ 361 1961 National Champs .15 .07 .02
Billy Neighbors
Pat Trammell
Darwin Holt
☐ 362 Tommy White .08 .04 .01
☐ 363 Earl Wesley .08 .04 .01
☐ 364 John O'Linger .08 .04 .01
☐ 365 Bill Battle .08 .04 .01
☐ 366 Butch Wilson .08 .04 .01
☐ 367 Tim Davis .08 .04 .01
☐ 368 Larry Wall .08 .04 .01
☐ 369 Hudson Harris .08 .04 .01
☐ 370 Mike Hopper .08 .04 .01
☐ 371 Jackie Sherrill .40 .18 .05
☐ 372 Tom Somerville .08 .04 .01
☐ 373 David Chatwood .08 .04 .01
☐ 374 George Ranager .08 .04 .01
☐ 375 Tommy Wade .25 .11 .03
☐ 376 '64 National Champs .60 .25 .07
(Joe Namath)
☐ 377 Reid Drinkard .08 .04 .01
☐ 378 Mike Hand .08 .04 .01
☐ 379 Ed White .25 .11 .03
☐ 380 Angelo Stafford .08 .04 .01
☐ 381 Ellis Beck .08 .04 .01
☐ 382 Wayne Hall .15 .07 .02
☐ 383 Randy Hall .08 .04 .01
☐ 384 Jack O'Rear .08 .04 .01
☐ 385 Colenzo Hubbard .08 .04 .01
☐ 386 Gus White .08 .04 .01
☐ 387 Rick Watson .08 .04 .01
☐ 388 Steve Allen .08 .04 .01
☐ 389 John David Crow Jr. .15 .07 .02
☐ 390 Britton Cooper .08 .04 .01
☐ 391 Mike Rodriguez .08 .04 .01
☐ 392 Steve Wade .08 .04 .01
☐ 393 William J. Rice .08 .04 .01
☐ 394 Greg Richardson .08 .04 .01
☐ 395 Joe Jones .15 .07 .02
☐ 396 Todd Richardson .08 .04 .01
☐ 397 Anthony Smiley .08 .04 .01
☐ 398 Duff Morrison .08 .04 .01
☐ 399 Jay Grogan .08 .04 .01
☐ 400 Steve Booker .08 .04 .01
☐ 401 Larry Abney .08 .04 .01
☐ 402 Bill Abston .08 .04 .01
☐ 403 Wayne Adkinson .08 .04 .01
☐ 404 Charles Allen .08 .04 .01
☐ 405 Phil Allman .08 .04 .01
☐ 406 1965 National Champs .25 .11 .03
(1965 Seniors)
Steve Sloan
Paul Crane
David Ray
Tommy Tolleson
Ben McLeod
Jackie Sherrill
Tim Bates
Creed Gilmer
Steve Bowman
☐ 407 James Angelich .08 .04 .01
☐ 408 Troy Barker .08 .04 .01
☐ 409 George Bethune .08 .04 .01
☐ 410 Bill Blair .08 .04 .01
☐ 411 Clark Boler .08 .04 .01
☐ 412 Duffy Boles .08 .04 .01
☐ 413 Ray Bolden .08 .04 .01
☐ 414 Bruce Bolton .08 .04 .01
☐ 415 Alvin Davis .08 .04 .01
☐ 416 Baxter Booth .08 .04 .01
☐ 417 Paul Boschung .08 .04 .01
☐ 418 1979 National Champs .25 .11 .03
(Team Photo)
☐ 419 Richard Brewer .08 .04 .01
☐ 420 Jack Brown .08 .04 .01
☐ 421 Larry Brown TE .08 .04 .01
☐ 422 David Brungard .08 .04 .01
☐ 423 Jim Burkett .08 .04 .01
☐ 424 Auxford Burks .08 .04 .01
☐ 425 Jim Cain .08 .04 .01
☐ 426 Dick Turpin .08 .04 .01
☐ 427 Neil Callaway .08 .04 .01
☐ 428 David Casteal .08 .04 .01
☐ 429 Phil Chaffin .08 .04 .01
☐ 430 Howard Chappell .08 .04 .01
☐ 431 Bob Childs .08 .04 .01
☐ 432 Knute Rockne Christian .08 .04 .01
☐ 433 Richard Ciemny .08 .04 .01
☐ 434 J.B. Whitworth .08 .04 .01
☐ 435 Mike Clements .08 .04 .01
☐ 436 1973 National Champs .25 .11 .03
(Coaching Staff)
☐ 437 Rocky Colburn .08 .04 .01
☐ 438 Danny Collins .08 .04 .01
☐ 439 James Taylor .08 .04 .01
☐ 440 Joe Compton .08 .04 .01
☐ 441 Bob Conway .08 .04 .01
☐ 442 Charlie Stephens .08 .04 .01
☐ 443 Kerry Goode .15 .07 .02
☐ 444 Joe LaBue .08 .04 .01
☐ 445 Allen Crumbley .08 .04 .01
☐ 446 Bill Curry CO .15 .07 .02
☐ 447 David Bedwell .08 .04 .01
☐ 448 Jim Davis .08 .04 .01
☐ 449 Mike Dean .08 .04 .01
☐ 450 Steve Dean .08 .04 .01
☐ 451 Vince DeLaurentis .08 .04 .01
☐ 452 Gary Deniro .08 .04 .01
☐ 453 Jim Dildy .08 .04 .01
☐ 454 Joe Dildy .08 .04 .01
☐ 455 Jimmy Dill .08 .04 .01
☐ 456 Joe Dismuke .08 .04 .01
☐ 457 Junior Davis .08 .04 .01
☐ 458 Warren Dyar .08 .04 .01
☐ 459 Hugh Morrow .08 .04 .01
☐ 460 Grady Elmore .08 .04 .01
☐ 461 1978 National Champs .25 .11 .03
(Jeff Rutledge,
Tony Nathan,
Barry Krauss,
Marty Lyons,
and Rich Wingo)
☐ 462 Ed Hines .08 .04 .01
☐ 463 D.Joe Gambrell .08 .04 .01
☐ 464 Kavanaugh(Kay) Francis .08 .04 .01
☐ 465 Robert Fraley .08 .04 .01
☐ 466 Milton Frank .08 .04 .01
☐ 467 Jim Franko .08 .04 .01
☐ 468 Buddy French .08 .04 .01
☐ 469 Wayne Rhoads .08 .04 .01
☐ 470 Ralph Gandy .08 .04 .01
☐ 471 Danny Gilbert .08 .04 .01
☐ 472 Greg Gilbert .08 .04 .01
☐ 473 Joe Godwin .08 .04 .01
☐ 474 Richard Grammer .08 .04 .01
☐ 475 Louis Green .08 .04 .01
☐ 476 Gary Martin .08 .04 .01
☐ 477 Bill Hannah .08 .04 .01
☐ 478 Allen Harpole .08 .04 .01
☐ 479 Neb Hayden .08 .04 .01
☐ 480 Butch Henry .08 .04 .01
☐ 481 Norwood Hodges .08 .04 .01
☐ 482 Earl Smith .08 .04 .01
☐ 483 Darwin Holt .08 .04 .01
☐ 484 Scott Homan .08 .04 .01
☐ 485 Nathan Rustin .08 .04 .01
☐ 486 Gene Raburn .08 .04 .01
☐ 487 Ellis Houston .08 .04 .01

☐ 488 Frank Howard	.08	.04	.01
☐ 489 Larry Hughes	.08	.04	.01
☐ 490 Joe Kelley	.08	.04	.01
☐ 491 Charlie Harris	.08	.04	.01
☐ 492 Legion Field	.08	.04	.01
☐ 493 Tim Hurst	.08	.04	.01
☐ 494 Hunter Husband	.08	.04	.01
☐ 495 Lou Ikner	.08	.04	.01
☐ 496 Craig Epps	.08	.04	.01
☐ 497 Jug Jenkins	.08	.04	.01
☐ 498 Billy Johnson	.08	.04	.01
☐ 499 David Johnson	.08	.04	.01
☐ 500 Jon Hand	.25	.11	.03
☐ 501 Max Kelley	.08	.04	.01
☐ 502 Terry Killgore	.08	.04	.01
☐ 503 Eddie Lowe	.08	.04	.01
☐ 504 Noah Langdale	.08	.04	.01
☐ 505 Ed Lary	.08	.04	.01
☐ 506 Foy Leach	.08	.04	.01
☐ 507 Harry Lee	.08	.04	.01
☐ 508 Jim Loftin	.08	.04	.01
☐ 509 Curtis Lynch	.08	.04	.01
☐ 510 John Mauro	.08	.04	.01
☐ 511 Ray Maxwell	.08	.04	.01
☐ 512 Frank McClendon	.08	.04	.01
☐ 513 Tom McCrary	.08	.04	.01
☐ 514 Sonny McGahey	.08	.04	.01
☐ 515 John McIntosh	.08	.04	.01
☐ 516 David McIntyre	.08	.04	.01
☐ 517 Wes Thompson	.08	.04	.01
☐ 518 James Melton	.08	.04	.01
☐ 519 John Miller	.08	.04	.01
☐ 520 Fred Mims	.08	.04	.01
☐ 521 Dewey Mitchell	.08	.04	.01
☐ 522 Lydell Mitchell (Linebacker)	.08	.04	.01
☐ 523 Greg Montgomery	.15	.07	.02
☐ 524 Jimmie Moore	.08	.04	.01
☐ 525 Randy Moore	.08	.04	.01
☐ 526 Ed Morgan	.08	.04	.01
☐ 527 Norris Hamer	.08	.04	.01
☐ 528 Frank Mosely	.08	.04	.01
☐ 529 Sidney Neighbors	.08	.04	.01
☐ 530 Rod Nelson	.08	.04	.01
☐ 531 James Nisbet	.08	.04	.01
☐ 532 Mark Nix	.08	.04	.01
☐ 533 L.W. Noonan	.08	.04	.01
☐ 534 Louis Thompson	.08	.04	.01
☐ 535 William Oliver	.08	.04	.01
☐ 536 Gary Otten	.08	.04	.01
☐ 537 Wayne Owen	.08	.04	.01
☐ 538 Steve Patterson	.08	.04	.01
☐ 539 Charley Pell	.25	.11	.03
☐ 540 Bob Pettee	.08	.04	.01
☐ 541 Gordon Pettus	.08	.04	.01
☐ 542 Gary Phillips	.08	.04	.01
☐ 543 Clay Walls	.08	.04	.01
☐ 544 Douglas Potts	.08	.04	.01
☐ 545 Mike Stock	.08	.04	.01
☐ 546 John Mark Prudhomme	.08	.04	.01
☐ 547 George Pugh	.15	.07	.02
☐ 548 Pat Raines	.08	.04	.01
☐ 549 Joe Riley	.08	.04	.01
☐ 550 Wayne Trimble	.08	.04	.01
☐ 551 Darryl White	.08	.04	.01
☐ 552 Bill Richardson	.08	.04	.01
☐ 553 Ray Richeson	.08	.04	.01
☐ 554 Danny Ridgeway	.08	.04	.01
☐ 555 Terry Sanders	.08	.04	.01
☐ 556 Kenneth Roberts	.08	.04	.01
☐ 557 Jimmy Watts	.08	.04	.01
☐ 558 Ron Robertson	.08	.04	.01
☐ 559 Norbie Ronsonet	.08	.04	.01
☐ 560 Jimmy Lynn Rosser	.08	.04	.01
☐ 561 Terry Rowell	.08	.04	.01
☐ 562 Larry Joe Ruffin	.08	.04	.01
☐ 563 Jack Rutledge	.08	.04	.01
☐ 564 Al Sabo	.08	.04	.01
☐ 565 David Sadler	.08	.04	.01
☐ 566 Donald Sanford	.08	.04	.01
☐ 567 Hayward Sanford	.08	.04	.01
☐ 568 Paul Tripoli	.08	.04	.01
☐ 569 Lou Scales	.08	.04	.01
☐ 570 Kurt Schmissrauter	.08	.04	.01
☐ 571 Willard Scissum	.08	.04	.01
☐ 572 Joe Sewell	.15	.07	.02
☐ 573 Jimmy Sharpe	.08	.04	.01
☐ 574 Willie Shepherd	.08	.04	.01
☐ 575 Jack Smalley Jr.	.08	.04	.01
☐ 576 Jim Simmons (Tight End)	.08	.04	.01
☐ 577 Jim Simmons (Tackle)	.08	.04	.01
☐ 578 Malcolm Simmons	.08	.04	.01
☐ 579 Dave Sington	.08	.04	.01
☐ 580 Fred Sington Jr.	.15	.07	.02

1992 Alabama Greats Hoby

This 42-card standard-size set was issued to commemorate a special Centennial Festival weekend. It features 42 Team of the Century candidates as selected by the fans. The fronts display a mix of glossy black and white or color player photos with rounded corners on a crimson card face. The "Century of Champions" logo is superimposed

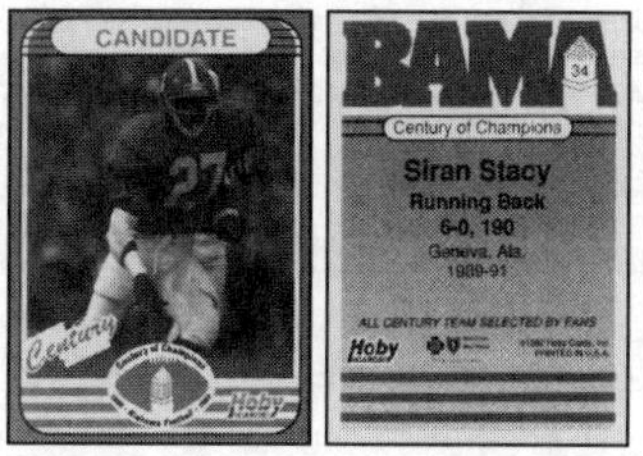

at the bottom of the picture over a white and crimson stripe pattern. On the crimson-colored backs, "Bama" appears in large block lettering at the top, with the player's name and brief biographical information presented below.

	MINT	NRMT	EXC
COMPLETE SET (42)	14.00	6.25	1.75
COMMON CARD (1-42)	.25	.11	.03
☐ 1 Bob Baumhower	.50	.23	.06
☐ 2 Cornelius Bennett	.75	.35	.09
☐ 3 Buddy Brown	.25	.11	.03
☐ 4 Paul(Bear) Bryant CO	1.50	.70	.19
☐ 5 Johnny Cain	.25	.11	.03
☐ 6 Jeremiah Castille	.35	.16	.04
☐ 7 Leroy Cook	.25	.11	.03
☐ 8 Paul Crane	.35	.16	.04
☐ 9 Philip Doyle	.25	.11	.03
☐ 10 Harry Gilmer	.35	.16	.04
☐ 11 Jon Hand	.50	.23	.06
☐ 12 Herb Hannah	.25	.11	.03
☐ 13 John Hannah	.75	.35	.09
☐ 14 Dennis Homan	.35	.16	.04
☐ 15 Dixie Howell	.35	.16	.04
☐ 16 Bobby Humphrey	.35	.16	.04
☐ 17 Don Hutson	1.00	.45	.12
☐ 18 Curt Jarvis	.35	.16	.04
☐ 19 Lee Roy Jordan	.75	.35	.09
☐ 20 Barry Krauss	.35	.16	.04
☐ 21 Woodrow Lowe	.35	.16	.04
☐ 22 Marty Lyons	.35	.16	.04
☐ 23 Vaughn Mancha	.25	.11	.03
☐ 24 John Mangum	.35	.16	.04
☐ 25 Bobby Marlow	.35	.16	.04
☐ 26 Don McNeal	.35	.16	.04
☐ 27 Chris Mohr	.35	.16	.04
☐ 28 Johnny Musso	.50	.23	.06
☐ 29 Billy Neighbors	.35	.16	.04
☐ 30 Ozzie Newsome	.75	.35	.09
☐ 31 Ray Perkins	.50	.23	.06
☐ 32 Fred Sington	.25	.11	.03
☐ 33 Ken Stabler	1.25	.55	.16
☐ 34 Siran Stacy	.35	.16	.04
☐ 35 Dwight Stephenson	.50	.23	.06
☐ 36 Robert Stewart	.25	.11	.03
☐ 37 Derrick Thomas	1.00	.45	.12
☐ 38 Van Tiffin	.25	.11	.03
☐ 39 Mike Washington	.25	.11	.03
☐ 40 Arthur Tarzan White	.25	.11	.03
☐ 41 Tommy Wilcox	.35	.16	.04
☐ 42 Willie Wyatt	.25	.11	.03

1980 Arizona Police

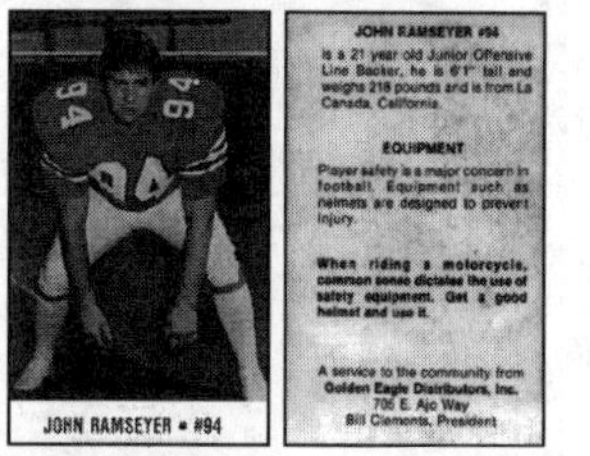

The 1980 University of Arizona Police set contains 24 cards measuring approximately 2 7/16" by 3 3/4". The fronts have borderless color player photos, with the player's name and jersey number in a white stripe beneath the picture. The backs have brief biographical information and safety tips. The cards are unnumbered and checklisted below in alphabetical order. Reportedly the Reggie Ware card is very difficult to find.

	MINT	NRMT	EXC
COMPLETE SET (24)	100.00	45.00	12.50
COMMON CARD (1-24)	3.00	1.35	.35
☐ 1 Brian Clifford	3.00	1.35	.35
☐ 2 Mark Fulcher	3.00	1.35	.35
☐ 3 Bob Gareeb	3.00	1.35	.35
☐ 4 Marcellus Green	4.00	1.80	.50
☐ 5 Drew Hardville	3.00	1.35	.35
☐ 6 Neal Harris	3.00	1.35	.35
☐ 7 Richard Hersey	3.00	1.35	.35
☐ 8 Alfondia Hill	3.00	1.35	.35
☐ 9 Tim Holmes	3.00	1.35	.35
☐ 10 Jack Housley	3.00	1.35	.35
☐ 11 Glenn Hutchinson	3.00	1.35	.35
☐ 12 Bill Jensen	3.00	1.35	.35
☐ 13 Frank Kalil	3.00	1.35	.35
☐ 14 Dave Liggins	3.00	1.35	.35
☐ 15 Tom Manno	3.00	1.35	.35
☐ 16 Bill Nettling	3.00	1.35	.35
☐ 17 Hubie Oliver	6.00	2.70	.75
☐ 18 Glenn Perkins	3.00	1.35	.35
☐ 19 John Ramseyer	3.00	1.35	.35
☐ 20 Mike Robinson	3.00	1.35	.35
☐ 21 Chris Schultz	4.00	1.80	.50
☐ 22 Larry Smith CO	4.00	1.80	.50
☐ 23 Reggie Ware SP	30.00	13.50	3.70
☐ 24 Bill Zivic	3.00	1.35	.35

1981 Arizona Police

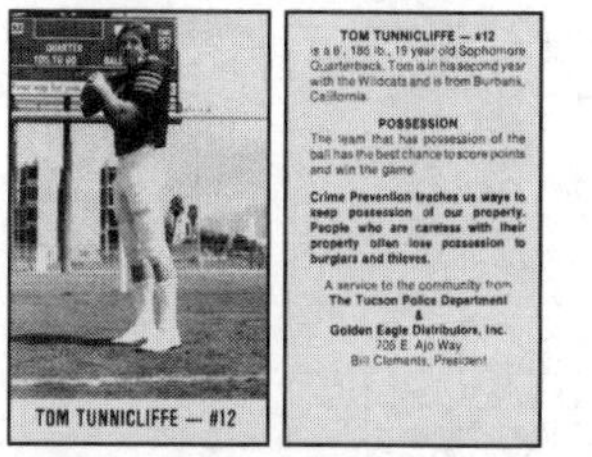

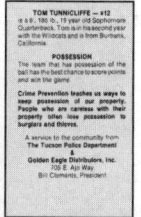

The 1981 University of Arizona Police set contains 27 cards measuring approximately 2 3/8" by 3 1/2". The fronts have borderless color player photos, with the player's name and jersey number in a white stripe beneath the picture. The backs have brief biographical information and safety tips. The cards are unnumbered and checklisted below in alphabetical order.

	MINT	NRMT	EXC
COMPLETE SET (27)	40.00	18.00	5.00
COMMON CARD (1-27)	2.00	.90	.25
☐ 1 Moe Ankney ACO	3.00	1.35	.35
☐ 2 Van Brandon	2.00	.90	.25
☐ 3 Bob Carter	2.00	.90	.25
☐ 4 Brian Christiansen	2.00	.90	.25
☐ 5 Mark Fulcher	2.00	.90	.25
☐ 6 Bob Gareeb	2.00	.90	.25
☐ 7 Gary Gibson	2.00	.90	.25
☐ 8 Mark Gobel	2.00	.90	.25
☐ 9 Al Gross	2.00	.90	.25
☐ 10 Kevin Hardcastle	2.00	.90	.25
☐ 11 Neal Harris	2.00	.90	.25
☐ 12 Brian Holland	2.00	.90	.25
☐ 13 Ricky Hunley	4.00	1.80	.50
☐ 14 Frank Kalil	2.00	.90	.25
☐ 15 Jeff Kiewel	2.00	.90	.25
☐ 16 Chris Knudsen	2.00	.90	.25
☐ 17 Ivan Lesnik	2.00	.90	.25
☐ 18 Tony Neely	2.00	.90	.25
☐ 19 Glenn Perkins	2.00	.90	.25
☐ 20 Randy Robbins	2.00	.90	.25
☐ 21 Gerald Roper	2.00	.90	.25
☐ 22 Chris Schultz	3.00	1.35	.35
☐ 23 Gary Shaw	2.00	.90	.25
☐ 24 Larry Smith CO	3.00	1.35	.35
☐ 25 Tom Tunnicliffe	3.00	1.35	.35
☐ 26 Sergio Vega	2.00	.90	.25
☐ 27 Brett Weber	3.00	1.35	.35

1982 Arizona Police

The 1982 University of Arizona Police set contains 26 cards. The fronts have borderless color player photos, with the player's name and jersey number in a white stripe beneath the picture. The backs have brief biographical information and safety tips. The cards are unnumbered and checklisted below in alphabetical order.

	MINT	NRMT	EXC
COMPLETE SET (26)	35.00	16.00	4.40
COMMON CARD (1-26)	1.50	.70	.19
☐ 1 Brad Anderson	1.50	.70	.19
☐ 2 Steve Boadway	1.50	.70	.19
☐ 3 Bruce Bush	1.50	.70	.19
☐ 4 Mike Freeman	1.50	.70	.19
☐ 5 Marsharne Graves	1.50	.70	.19
☐ 6 Courtney Griffin	1.50	.70	.19
☐ 7 Al Gross	2.00	.90	.25
☐ 8 Julius Holt	1.50	.70	.19
☐ 9 Lamonte Hunley	2.00	.90	.25
☐ 10 Ricky Hunley	2.50	1.10	.30
☐ 11 Vance Johnson	5.00	2.20	.60
☐ 12 Chris Kaesman	1.50	.70	.19
☐ 13 John Kaiser	1.50	.70	.19
☐ 14 Mark Keel	1.50	.70	.19
☐ 15 Jeff Kiewel	1.50	.70	.19
☐ 16 Ivan Lesnik	1.50	.70	.19
☐ 17 Glenn McCormick	1.50	.70	.19
☐ 18 Ray Moret	1.50	.70	.19
☐ 19 Tony Neely	1.50	.70	.19
☐ 20 Byron Nelson	2.00	.90	.25
☐ 21 Glenn Perkins	1.50	.70	.19
☐ 22 Randy Robbins	1.50	.70	.19
☐ 23 Larry Smith CO	2.00	.90	.25
☐ 24 Tom Tunnicliffe	2.00	.90	.25
☐ 25 Kevin Ward	1.50	.70	.19
☐ 26 David Wood	1.50	.70	.19

1983 Arizona Police

The 1983 University of Arizona Police set contains 24 cards. The fronts have borderless color player photos, with the player's name and jersey number in a white stripe beneath the picture. The backs have brief biographical information and safety tips. The cards are unnumbered and checklisted below in alphabetical order.

	MINT	NRMT	EXC
COMPLETE SET (24)	35.00	16.00	4.40
COMMON CARD (1-24)	1.50	.70	.19
☐ 1 John Barthalt	1.50	.70	.19
☐ 2 Steve Boadway	1.50	.70	.19
☐ 3 Chris Brewer	1.50	.70	.19
☐ 4 Lynnden Brown	1.50	.70	.19
☐ 5 Charlie Dickey	1.50	.70	.19
☐ 6 Jay Dobins	1.50	.70	.19
☐ 7 Joe Drake	1.50	.70	.19
☐ 8 Allen Durden	2.00	.90	.25
☐ 9 Byron Evans	5.00	2.20	.60
☐ 10 Nils Fox	1.50	.70	.19
☐ 11 Mike Freeman	1.50	.70	.19
☐ 12 Marsharne Graves	1.50	.70	.19
☐ 13 Lamonte Hunley	2.00	.90	.25
☐ 14 Vance Johnson	4.00	1.80	.50
☐ 15 John Kaiser	1.50	.70	.19
☐ 16 Ivan Lesnik	1.50	.70	.19
☐ 17 Byron Nelson	2.00	.90	.25
☐ 18 Randy Robbins	1.50	.70	.19
☐ 19 Craig Schiller	1.50	.70	.19
☐ 20 Larry Smith CO	2.00	.90	.25
☐ 21 Tom Tunnicliffe	2.00	.90	.25
☐ 22 Mark Walczak	1.50	.70	.19
☐ 23 David Wood	1.50	.70	.19
☐ 24 Max Zendejas	2.00	.90	.25

1984 Arizona Police

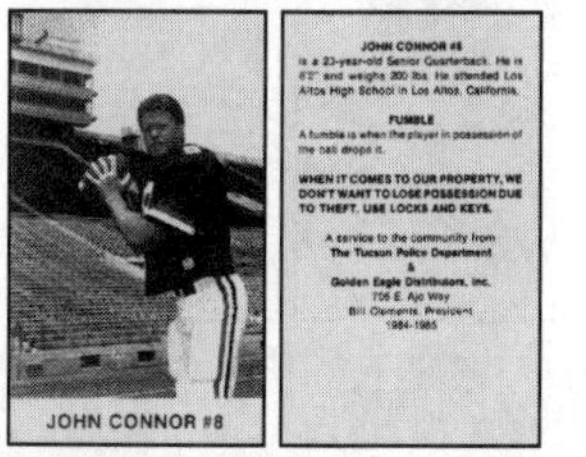

The 1984 University of Arizona Police set contains 25 cards measuring approximately 2 1/4" by 3 5/8". The fronts have borderless color photos; the vertically oriented backs have brief bios and safety tips. The cards are unnumbered, so are listed by jersey numbers. These cards are printed on very thin stock. The set is described on the back of each card as 1984-85.

	MINT	NRMT	EXC
COMPLETE SET (25)	15.00	6.75	1.85
COMMON CARD (1-25)	.75	.35	.09
☐ 1 Alfred Jenkins	2.00	.90	.25
☐ 8 John Connor	1.00	.45	.12
☐ 13 Max Zendejas	1.00	.45	.12
☐ 15 Gordon Bunch	.75	.35	.09
☐ 19 Allen Durden	1.00	.45	.12
☐ 23 Lynnden Brown	.75	.35	.09
☐ 25 Vance Johnson	2.00	.90	.25
☐ 28 Tom Bayse	.75	.35	.09
☐ 35 Brent Wood	.75	.35	.09
☐ 40 Greg Turner	.75	.35	.09
☐ 47 Steve Boadway	.75	.35	.09
☐ 52 Nils Fox	.75	.35	.09
☐ 54 Craig Vesling	.75	.35	.09
☐ 62 David Connor	.75	.35	.09
☐ 67 Charlie Dickey	.75	.35	.09
☐ 71 Brian Denton	.75	.35	.09
☐ 78 John DuBose	.75	.35	.09
☐ 79 Joe Drake	.75	.35	.09
☐ 82 Joy Dobyns	.75	.35	.09
☐ 85 Mark Walczak	.75	.35	.09
☐ 86 Jon Horton	.75	.35	.09
☐ 92 David Wood	.75	.35	.09
☐ 98 Lamonte Hunley	1.00	.45	.12
☐ 99 John Barthalt	.75	.35	.09
☐ NNO Larry Smith CO	1.00	.45	.12

1985 Arizona Police

The 1985 University of Arizona Police set contains 23 cards measuring 2 1/4" by 3 5/8". The fronts have borderless color photos; the vertically oriented backs have brief bios and safety tips. The cards are unnumbered, so are listed by jersey numbers. These cards are printed on very thin stock. The set is described on the back of each card as 1985-86.

	MINT	NRMT	EXC
COMPLETE SET (23)	15.00	6.75	1.85
COMMON CARD (1-23)	.75	.35	.09
☐ 1 Alfred Jenkins	1.50	.70	.19
☐ 2 David Adams	.75	.35	.09
☐ 6 Chuck Cecil	2.00	.90	.25
☐ 13 Max Zendejas	1.00	.45	.12

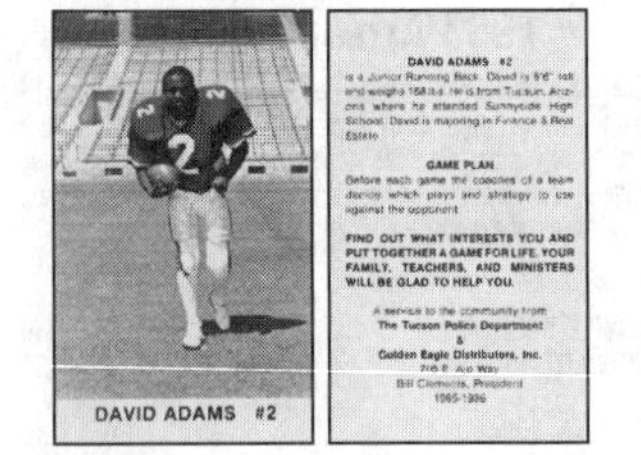

DAVID ADAMS #2
is a Junior Running Back. David is 6'6", tall and weighs 198 lbs. He is from Tucson, Arizona where he attended Sunnyside High School. David is majoring in Finance & Real Estate.

GAME PLAN
Before each game the coaches of a team decide which plays and strategy to use against the opponent.

FIND OUT WHAT INTERESTS YOU AND PUT TOGETHER A GAME FOR LIFE. YOUR FAMILY, TEACHERS, AND MINISTERS WILL BE GLAD TO HELP YOU.

A service to the community from
The Tucson Police Department
&
Golden Eagle Distributors, Inc.
Bill Clements, President
1985-1986

DAVID ADAMS #2

	MINT	NRMT	EXC
☐ 15 Gordon Bunch	.75	.35	.09
☐ 18 Jeff Fairholm	1.00	.45	.12
☐ 19 Allen Durden	1.00	.45	.12
☐ 29 Don Be'ans	.75	.35	.09
☐ 32 Joe Prior	.75	.35	.09
☐ 42 Blake Custer	.75	.35	.09
☐ 44 Boomer Gibson	.75	.35	.09
☐ 48 Byron Evans	3.00	1.35	.35
☐ 50 Val Bichekas	.75	.35	.09
☐ 52 Joe Tofflemire	1.00	.45	.12
☐ 54 Craig Vesling	.75	.35	.09
☐ 59 Jim Birmingham	.75	.35	.09
☐ 72 Curt DiGiacomo	.75	.35	.09
☐ 73 Lee Brunelli	.75	.35	.09
☐ 78 John DuBose	.75	.35	.09
☐ 83 Gary Parrish	.75	.35	.09
☐ 95 Cliff Thorpe	.75	.35	.09
☐ 96 Glenn Howell	.75	.35	.09
☐ NNO Larry Smith CO	1.00	.45	.12

1986 Arizona Police

DEREK HILL #82
is a 19 year old Sophomore Flanker. He is 6' 3" tall and weighs 178 lbs. Derek is from Carson, CA where he attended Carson High. Derek is a Public recreation major.

SAFETY
This occurs when a player with the ball is tackled behind his own goal line. The other team earns two points for a safety.

REMEMBER WHEN CROSSING THE STREET TO CROSS AT THE CORNER OR IN A CROSSWALK. YIELD TO ALL ONCOMING TRAFFIC AND MAINTAIN YOUR OWN SAFETY.

A service to the community from
The Tucson Police Department
&
Golden Eagle Distributors, Inc.
706 E. Ajo Way
Bill Clements, President
1986-1987

DEREK HILL #82

This 24-card set was cosponsored by the Tucson Police Department and Golden Eagle Distributors. The cards measure approximately 2 1/4" by 3 5/8". The fronts feature borderless posed color player photos, with the player's name and uniform number in the white stripe beneath the picture. The backs present player profile, a discussion or definition of some aspect of football, and a safety message. The cards are unnumbered and checklisted below in alphabetical order. The set is described on the back of each card as 1986-87.

	MINT	NRMT	EXC
COMPLETE SET (24)	15.00	6.75	1.85
COMMON CARD (1-24)	.75	.35	.09
☐ 1 David Adams	.75	.35	.09
☐ 2 Frank Arriola	.75	.35	.09
☐ 3 Val Biehekas	.75	.35	.09
☐ 4 Jim Birmingham	.75	.35	.09
☐ 5 Chuck Cecil	1.50	.70	.19
☐ 6 James Debow	.75	.35	.09
☐ 7 Brian Denton	.75	.35	.09
☐ 8 Byron Evans	2.00	.90	.25
☐ 9 Jeff Fairholm	1.00	.45	.12
☐ 10 Boomer Gibson	.75	.35	.09
☐ 11 Eugene Hardy	.75	.35	.09
☐ 12 Derek Hill	1.50	.70	.19
☐ 13 Jon Horton	.75	.35	.09
☐ 14 Alfred Jenkins	1.25	.55	.16
☐ 15 Danny Lockett	1.00	.45	.12
☐ 16 Stan Mataele	.75	.35	.09
☐ 17 Chris McLemore	.75	.35	.09
☐ 18 Jeff Rinehart	.75	.35	.09
☐ 19 Ruben Rodriguez	1.00	.45	.12
☐ 20 Martin Rudolph	.75	.35	.09
☐ 21 Larry Smith CO	1.00	.45	.12
☐ 22 Joe Tofflemire	1.00	.45	.12
☐ 23 Dana Wells	.75	.35	.09
☐ 24 Brent Wood	.75	.35	.09

1987 Arizona Police

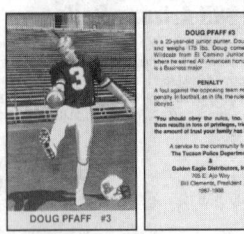

DOUG PFAFF #3
is a 20-year-old junior punter. Doug is 6-10 and weighs 175 lbs. Doug comes to the Wildcats from El Camino Junior College where he earned All American honors. Doug is a Business major.

PENALTY
A foul against the opposing team results in a penalty in football, as in life, the rules must be obeyed.

"You should obey the rules, too. Breaking them results in loss of privileges, friends, and the amount of trust your family has in you."

A service to the community from
The Tucson Police Department
&
Golden Eagle Distributors, Inc.
706 E. Ajo Way
Bill Clements, President
1987-1988

DOUG PFAFF #3

The 1987 University of Arizona Police set contains 23 cards measuring approximately 2 1/4" by 3 5/8". The fronts have borderless color photos; the vertically oriented backs have brief bios and safety

---

tips. The cards are unnumbered, so they are listed by jersey numbers. These cards are printed on very thin stock. The set is described on the back of each card as 1987-88.

	MINT	NRMT	EXC
COMPLETE SET (23)	15.00	6.75	1.85
COMMON CARD (1-23)	.75	.35	.09
☐ 2 Bobby Watters	1.00	.45	.12
☐ 3 Doug Pfaff	.75	.35	.09
☐ 6 Chuck Cecil	1.50	.70	.19
☐ 11 Gary Coston	.75	.35	.09
☐ 18 Jeff Fairholm	1.00	.45	.12
☐ 22 Eugene Hardy	.75	.35	.09
☐ 26 Troy Cephers	.75	.35	.09
☐ 34 Charles Webb	.75	.35	.09
☐ 38 James Debow	.75	.35	.09
☐ 40 Art Greathouse	.75	.35	.09
☐ 43 Jerry Beasley	.75	.35	.09
☐ 44 Boomer Gibson	.75	.35	.09
☐ 47 Gallen Allen	.75	.35	.09
☐ 52 Joe Tofflemire	1.00	.45	.12
☐ 60 Jeff Rinehart	.75	.35	.09
☐ 64 Kevin McKinney	.75	.35	.09
☐ 68 Tom Lynch	.75	.35	.09
☐ 82 Derek Hill	1.25	.55	.16
☐ 84 Kevin Singleton	1.00	.45	.12
☐ 87 Chris Singleton	2.00	.90	.25
☐ 97 George Hinkle	.75	.35	.09
☐ 99 Dana Wells	.75	.35	.09
☐ NNO Dick Tomey CO	1.25	.55	.16

1988 Arizona Police

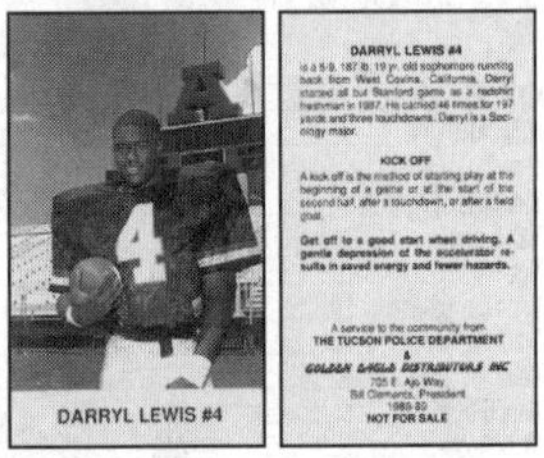

DARRYL LEWIS #4
is 6-6, 187 lb, 19 yr. old sophomore running back from West Covina, California. Darryl stored all but Stanford gains as a marked freshman in 1987. He carried all nines for 147 yards and three touchdowns. Darryl is a Sociology major.

KICK OFF
A kick off is the method of starting play at the beginning of a game or at the start of the second half after a touchdown, or after a field goal.

Get off to a good start when driving. A gentle depression of the accelerator results in saved energy and fewer hazards.

A service to the community from
THE TUCSON POLICE DEPARTMENT
&
GOLDEN EAGLE DISTRIBUTORS INC
706 E. Ajo Way
Bill Clements, President
1988-89
NOT FOR SALE

DARRYL LEWIS #4

The 1988 University of Arizona Police set contains 25 cards measuring approximately 2 5/16" by 3 3/4". The fronts have borderless color photos; the vertically oriented backs have brief bios and safety tips. The cards are unnumbered, so they are listed by jersey numbers. These cards are printed on very thin stock. The set is described on the back of each card as 1988-89.

	MINT	NRMT	EXC
COMPLETE SET (25)	15.00	6.75	1.85
COMMON CARD (1-25)	.75	.35	.09
☐ 2 Bobby Watters	1.00	.45	.12
☐ 4 Darryll Lewis UER	2.00	.90	.25
name misspelled Darryl			
☐ 5 Durrell Jones	.75	.35	.09
☐ 8 Reggie McGill	.75	.35	.09
☐ 10 Ronald Veal	1.00	.45	.12
☐ 15 Jeff Hammerschmidt	.75	.35	.09
☐ 22 Scott Geyer	.75	.35	.09
☐ 24 R. Groppenbacher	.75	.35	.09
☐ 25 David Eldridge	.75	.35	.09
☐ 35 Mario Hampton	.75	.35	.09
☐ 38 James Debow	.75	.35	.09
☐ 40 Art Greathouse	.75	.35	.09
☐ 50 Darren Case	.75	.35	.09
☐ 51 Doug Penner	.75	.35	.09
☐ 52 Joe Tofflemire	1.00	.45	.12
☐ 63 John Brandom	.75	.35	.09
☐ 65 Ken Hakes	.75	.35	.09
☐ 74 Glenn Parker	1.25	.55	.16
☐ 78 Rob Woods	.75	.35	.09
☐ 82 Derek Hill	1.25	.55	.16
☐ 84 Kevin Singleton	1.00	.45	.12
☐ 87 Chris Singleton	1.50	.70	.19
☐ 96 Brad Henke	.75	.35	.09
☐ 99 Dana Wells	.75	.35	.09
☐ NNO Dick Tomey CO	1.00	.45	.12

1989 Arizona Police

CHRIS SINGLETON #87
is 6-3, 246 lb 22 yr. old senior outside linebacker from Pomona, California. Chris was named the outside linebacker of the defensive team of the year for 1988. He notched 89 tackles, and was credited five times for bringing the quarterback down for a loss. Chris had 116 tackles including nine tackles for losses in 1988. Also received a fumble and broke up four passes. Chris is a General Studies major.

PRIDE
We take pride in our football team. They exercise and discipline themselves daily to present many and do their best.

Take pride in your body! Keep it in through exercise. Don't poison yourself with narcotics or alcohol. You are playing for keeps.

A service to the community from
THE TUCSON POLICE DEPARTMENT
&
GOLDEN EAGLE DISTRIBUTORS INC
706 E. Ajo Way
Bill Clements, President
1989-90
NOT FOR SALE

CHRIS SINGLETON #87

This 26-card set was co-sponsored by the Tucson Police Department and Golden Eagle Distributors. The cards measure approximately 2 1/4" by 3 3/4". The fronts feature borderless posed color player photos, with the player's name and uniform number in the white stripe beneath the picture. The backs present player profile, a

---

discussion or definition of some aspect of football, and a safety message. The cards are unnumbered and checklisted below in alphabetical order. The set is described on the back of each card as 1989-90.

	MINT	NRMT	EXC
COMPLETE SET (26)	12.00	5.50	1.50
COMMON CARD (1-26)	.60	.25	.07
☐ 1 Zeno Alexander	.60	.25	.07
☐ 2 John Brandom	.60	.25	.07
☐ 3 Todd Burden	.60	.25	.07
☐ 4 Darren Case	.60	.25	.07
☐ 5 David Eldridge	.60	.25	.07
☐ 6 Nick Fineanganofo	.60	.25	.07
☐ 7 Scott Geyer	.60	.25	.07
☐ 8 Art Greathouse	.60	.25	.07
☐ 9 Richard Griffith	.60	.25	.07
☐ 10 Ken Hakes	.60	.25	.07
☐ 11 Jeff Hammerschmidt	.60	.25	.07
☐ 12 Mario Hampton	.60	.25	.07
☐ 13 Darryll Lewis	1.50	.70	.19
☐ 14 Kip Lewis	.60	.25	.07
☐ 15 George Malauulu	.75	.35	.09
☐ 16 Reggie McGill	.60	.25	.07
☐ 17 John Nies	.60	.25	.07
☐ 18 Glenn Parker	1.00	.45	.12
☐ 19 Mike Parker	.60	.25	.07
☐ 20 Doug Pfaff	.60	.25	.07
☐ 21 David Roney	.60	.25	.07
☐ 22 Pete Russell	.60	.25	.07
☐ 23 Chris Singleton	1.25	.55	.16
☐ 24 Paul Tofflemire	.60	.25	.07
☐ 25 Dick Tomey CO	.75	.35	.09
☐ 26 Ronald Veal	.75	.35	.09

1992 Arizona Police

 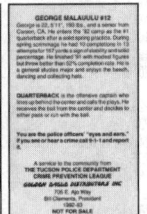

GEORGE MALAUULU #12
George is 22, 5'11", 180 lbs. and a senior from Carson, CA. He enters his 6G camp as the #1 quarterback after a wild spring practice. During the spring, he completed 52% of his attempts for 167 yards a page of stability and added spring. George will be expected to lead and hold but throw better than 62% completion rate. He is a general studies major and enjoys the beach, dancing and collecting hats.

QUARTERBACK is the offensive captain who lines up behind the center and calls the plays. He receives the ball from the center and decides to either pass or run with the ball.

You are the police officers' "eyes and ears." If you see or hear a crime call 9-1-1 and report it.

A service to the community from
THE TUCSON POLICE DEPARTMENT
CRIME PREVENTION LEAGUE
&
GOLDEN EAGLE DISTRIBUTORS INC
706 E. Ajo Way
Bill Clements, President
1992-93
NOT FOR SALE

GEORGE MALAUULU #12

This 21-card set was sponsored by the Tucson Police Department and Golden Eagle Distributors. The cards measure approximately 2" by 3 3/4". The fronts feature borderless color photos of the players posed at the football stadium, with bleaches and scoreboard in the background. The player's name and jersey number are printed in the white stripe at the bottom. The backs are white and carry player information, an explanation of some aspect of football, and a safety message. The cards are unnumbered and checklisted below in alphabetical order.

	MINT	NRMT	EXC
COMPLETE SET (21)	10.00	4.50	1.25
COMMON CARD (1-21)	.50	.23	.06
☐ 1 Tony Bouie	1.00	.45	.12
☐ 2 Heath Bray	.50	.23	.06
☐ 3 Charlie Camp	.50	.23	.06
☐ 4 Ontiwaun Carter	.60	.25	.07
☐ 5 Richard Griffith	.50	.23	.06
☐ 6 Sean Harris	.75	.35	.09
☐ 7 Mike Heemsbergen	.50	.23	.06
☐ 8 Jimmy Hopkins	.50	.23	.06
☐ 9 Billy Johnson	.50	.23	.06
☐ 10 Keshon Johnson	.50	.23	.06
☐ 11 Chuck Levy	1.25	.55	.16
☐ 12 Richard Maddox	.50	.23	.06
☐ 13 George Malauulu	.60	.25	.07
☐ 14 Darryl Morrison	.75	.35	.09
☐ 15 Mani Ott	.50	.23	.06
☐ 16 Ty Parten	.75	.35	.09
☐ 17 Mike Scurlock	.75	.35	.09
☐ 18 Warner Smith	.50	.23	.06
☐ 19 Dick Tomey CO	.50	.23	.06
☐ 20 Terry Vaughn	.75	.35	.09
☐ 21 Rob Waldrop	.75	.35	.09

1991 Army Smokey

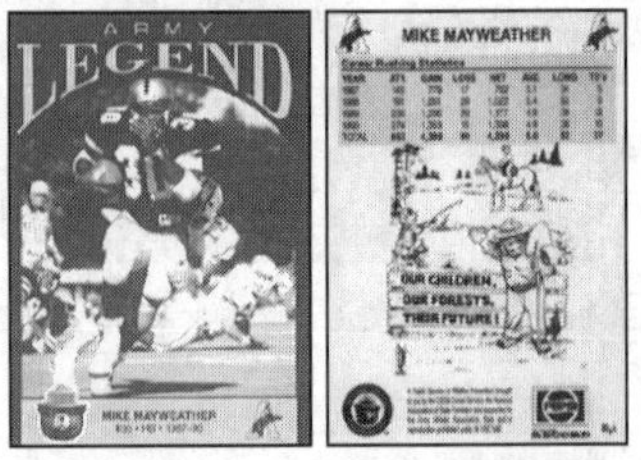

MIKE MAYWEATHER

MIKE MAYWEATHER
RB • HB • 1987-90

Printed on thin card stock, this set was sponsored by the Forest Service and Pepsi. The fronts feature color player action shots framed by a black border with gold-colored lettering. The white backs carry

---

player profile and a fire prevention cartoon starring Smokey. The cards are unnumbered and checklisted below in alphabetical order. The checklist below is thought to be incomplete. Any additions to this list are appreciated.

	MINT	NRMT	EXC
COMPLETE SET (13)	10.00	4.50	1.25
COMMON CARD (1-13)	.75	.35	.09
☐ 1 Steve Chaloult	.75	.35	.09
☐ 2 Lance Chambers	.75	.35	.09
☐ 3 Pete Dawkins	1.50	.70	.19
☐ 4 Trey Gilmore	.75	.35	.09
☐ 5 Mike Mayweather	.75	.35	.09
☐ 6 Willie McMillian	.75	.35	.09
☐ 7 Dan Menendez	.75	.35	.09
☐ 8 Edrian Oliver	.75	.35	.09
☐ 9 Arlen Smith	.75	.35	.09
☐ 10 Bob Sutton CO	1.00	.45	.12
☐ 11 Callian Thomas	.75	.35	.09
☐ 12 Myreon Williams	.75	.35	.09
☐ 13 Michie Stadium	.75	.35	.09

1993 Army Smokey

Printed on thin card stock, this 15-card standard-size set was sponsored by the USDA, the Forest Service, other state and federal agencies, Pepsi, Freihofer's, and The Times Herald Record. Smokey sets issued in 1993 have a special 50th year anniversary logo on the front. The fronts feature color player action shots framed by thin white and black lines and with gold-colored borders highlighted by oblique white stripes. The team's name appears within the upper margin, and the player's name and position, along with the Smokey 50-year celebration logo, rest in the lower margin. The white backs carry player profile and a fire prevention cartoon starring Smokey. The cards are unnumbered and checklisted below in alphabetical order.

	MINT	NRMT	EXC
COMPLETE SET (15)	12.00	5.50	1.50
COMMON CARD (1-15)	.75	.35	.09
☐ 1 Paul Andrzejewski	.75	.35	.09
☐ 2 Kevin Czarnecki	.75	.35	.09
☐ 3 Chad Davis	.75	.35	.09
☐ 4 Glenn Davis	3.00	1.35	.35
☐ 5 Mark Escobedo	.75	.35	.09
☐ 6 Gary Graves	.75	.35	.09
☐ 7 Leamon Hall	1.00	.45	.12
☐ 8 Jason Miller	1.00	.45	.12
☐ 9 Mike Plaia	.75	.35	.09
☐ 10 Rick Roper	1.00	.45	.12
☐ 11 Jim Slomka	.75	.35	.09
☐ 12 Bob Sutton CO	.75	.35	.09
☐ 13 Jason Sutton	.75	.35	.09
☐ 14 Pat Zelley	.75	.35	.09
☐ 15 Army Mule (Mascot)	.75	.35	.09

1972 Auburn Tigers

This 54-card standard-size set was issued in a playing card deck box. The cards have rounded corners and the typical playing card finish. The fronts feature black-and-white posed photos of helmetless players in their uniforms. A white border surrounds each picture and contains the card number and suit designation in the upper left corner and again, but inverted, in the lower right. The player's name and hometown appear just beneath the photo. The white-bordered orange backs all have the Auburn "AU" logo in navy blue and orange and white outlines. The the year of issue, 1972, and the name "Auburn Tigers" also appears on the backs. Since the set is similar to a playing card set, it is arranged just like a card deck and checklisted below accordingly. In the checklist below C means Clubs, D means Diamonds, H means Hearts, S means Spades and JK means Joker. Numbers are assigned to Aces (1), Jacks (11), Queens (12), and Kings (13). The jokers are unnumbered and listed at the end.

	NRMT-MT	EXC	G-VG
COMPLETE SET (54)	75.00	34.00	9.50
COMMON CARD	1.50	.70	.19

☐ 1C Ken Calleja	1.50	.70	.19
☐ 1D James Owens	1.50	.70	.19
☐ 1H Mac Lorendo	1.50	.70	.19
☐ 1S Ralph(Shug) Jordan CO	6.00	2.70	.75
☐ 2C Rick Neel	1.50	.70	.19
☐ 2D Ted Smith	1.50	.70	.19
☐ 2H Eddie Welch	1.50	.70	.19
☐ 2S Mike Neel	1.50	.70	.19
☐ 3C Larry Taylor	1.50	.70	.19
☐ 3D Rett Davis	1.50	.70	.19
☐ 3H Rusty Fuller	1.50	.70	.19
☐ 3S Lee Gross	1.50	.70	.19
☐ 4C Bruce Evans	1.50	.70	.19
☐ 4D Rusty Deen	1.50	.70	.19
☐ 4H Johnny Simmons	1.50	.70	.19
☐ 4S Bill Newton	1.50	.70	.19
☐ 5C Dave Beverly	2.50	1.10	.30
☐ 5D Dave Lyon	1.50	.70	.19
☐ 5H Mike Fuller	4.00	1.80	.50
☐ 5S Bill Luka	1.50	.70	.19
☐ 6C Ken Bernich	1.50	.70	.19
☐ 6D Andy Steele	1.50	.70	.19
☐ 6H Wade Whatley	1.50	.70	.19
☐ 6S Bob Newton	2.50	1.10	.30
☐ 7C Benny Sivley	2.00	.90	.25
☐ 7D Gardner Jett	2.00	.90	.25
☐ 7H Rob Spivey	2.00	.90	.25
☐ 7S Jay Casey	1.50	.70	.19
☐ 8C David Langner	1.50	.70	.19
☐ 8D Terry Henley	1.50	.70	.19
☐ 8H Thomas Gossom	1.50	.70	.19
☐ 8S Joe Tanory	1.50	.70	.19
☐ 9C Chris Linderman	1.50	.70	.19
☐ 9D Harry Unger	1.50	.70	.19
☐ 9H Kenny Burks	1.50	.70	.19
☐ 9S Sandy Cannon	1.50	.70	.19
☐ 10C Roger Mitchell	1.50	.70	.19
☐ 10D Jim McKinney	1.50	.70	.19
☐ 10H Gaines Lanier	1.50	.70	.19
☐ 10S Dave Beck	1.50	.70	.19
☐ 11C Bob Farrior	1.50	.70	.19
☐ 11D Miles Jones	1.50	.70	.19
☐ 11H Tres Rogers	1.50	.70	.19
☐ 11S David Hughes	1.50	.70	.19
☐ 12C Sherman Moon	1.50	.70	.19
☐ 12D Danny Sanspree	1.50	.70	.19
☐ 12H Steve Taylor	1.50	.70	.19
☐ 12S Randy Walls	1.50	.70	.19
☐ 13C Steve Wilson	1.50	.70	.19
☐ 13D Bobby Davis	1.50	.70	.19
☐ 13H Hamlin Caldwell	1.50	.70	.19
☐ 13S Dan Nugent	1.50	.70	.19
☐ JK1 Joker Auburn Memorial Coliseum	1.50	.70	.19
☐ JK2 Joker Cliff Hare Stadium	1.50	.70	.19

1973 Auburn Tigers

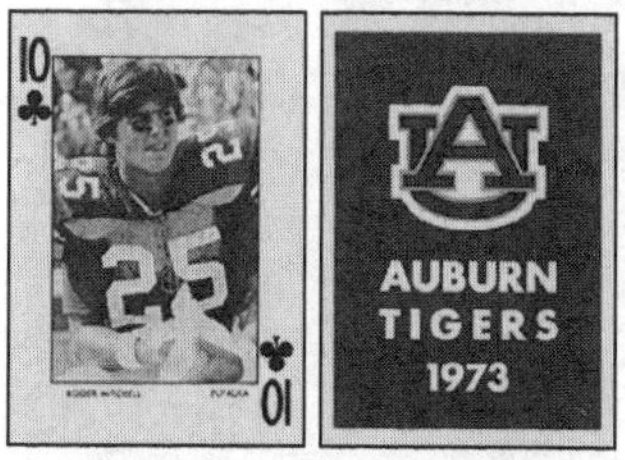

This 54-card standard-size set was issued in a playing card deck box. The cards have rounded corners and the typical playing card finish. The fronts feature black-and-white posed photos of helmetless players in their uniforms. A white border surrounds each picture and contains the card number and suit designation in the upper left corner and again, but inverted, in the lower right. The player's name and hometown appear just beneath the photo. The white-bordered navy blue backs all have the Auburn "AU" logo in navy blue and orange and white outlines. The the year of issue, 1973, and the name "Auburn Tigers" also appears on the backs. Since the set is similar to a playing card set, it is arranged just like a card deck and checklisted below accordingly. In the checklist below C means Clubs, D means Diamonds, H means Hearts, S means Spades and JK means Joker. Numbers are assigned to Aces (1), Jacks (11), Queens (12), and Kings (13). The jokers are unnumbered and listed at the end.

	NRMT-MT	EXC	G-VG
COMPLETE SET (54)	65.00	29.00	8.00
COMMON CARD	1.50	.70	.19
☐ 1C Ken Calleja	1.50	.70	.19
☐ 1D Chris Wilson	1.50	.70	.19
☐ 1H Lee Hayley	1.50	.70	.19
☐ 1S Ralph(Shug) Jordan CO	5.00	2.20	.60
☐ 2C Rick Neel	1.50	.70	.19
☐ 2D Johnny Sumner	1.50	.70	.19
☐ 2H Mitzi Jackson	1.50	.70	.19
☐ 2S Jim Pitts	1.50	.70	.19
☐ 3C Steve Stanaland	1.50	.70	.19
☐ 3D Rett Davis	1.50	.70	.19
☐ 3H Rusty Fuller	1.50	.70	.19
☐ 3S Lee Gross	1.50	.70	.19
☐ 4C Bruce Evans	1.50	.70	.19
☐ 4D Rusty Deen	1.50	.70	.19
☐ 4H Liston Eddins	1.50	.70	.19
☐ 4S Bill Newton	1.50	.70	.19
☐ 5C Jimmy Sirmans	1.50	.70	.19
☐ 5D Harry Ward	1.50	.70	.19
☐ 5H Mike Fuller	2.50	1.10	.30
☐ 5S Bill Luka	1.50	.70	.19
☐ 6C Ken Bernich	1.50	.70	.19
☐ 6D Andy Steele	1.50	.70	.19
☐ 6H Wade Whatley	1.50	.70	.19
☐ 6S Bob Newton	2.00	.90	.25
☐ 7C Benny Sivley	2.00	.90	.25
☐ 7D Rick Telhiard	2.00	.90	.25
☐ 7H Rob Spivey	2.00	.90	.25
☐ 7S David Williams	1.50	.70	.19
☐ 8C David Langner	1.50	.70	.19
☐ 8D Chuck Fletcher	1.50	.70	.19
☐ 8H Thomas Gossom	1.50	.70	.19
☐ 8S Holley Caldwell	1.50	.70	.19
☐ 9C Chris Linderman	1.50	.70	.19
☐ 9D Ed Butler	1.50	.70	.19
☐ 9H Kenny Burks	1.50	.70	.19
☐ 9S Mike Flynn	1.50	.70	.19
☐ 10C Roger Mitchell	1.50	.70	.19
☐ 10D Jim McKinney	1.50	.70	.19
☐ 10H Gaines Lanier	1.50	.70	.19
☐ 10S Carl Hubbard	1.50	.70	.19
☐ 11C Bob Farrior	1.50	.70	.19
☐ 11D Ronnie Jones	1.50	.70	.19
☐ 11H Billy Woods	1.50	.70	.19
☐ 11S David Hughes	1.50	.70	.19
☐ 12C Sherman Moon	1.50	.70	.19
☐ 12D Mike Gates	1.50	.70	.19
☐ 12H Steve Taylor	1.50	.70	.19
☐ 12S Randy Walls	1.50	.70	.19
☐ 13C Roger Pruett	1.50	.70	.19
☐ 13D Bobby Davis	1.50	.70	.19
☐ 13H Hamlin Caldwell	1.50	.70	.19
☐ 13S Dan Nugent	1.50	.70	.19
☐ JK1 Joker Auburn Memorial Coliseum	1.50	.70	.19
☐ JK2 Joker Cliff Hare Stadium	1.50	.70	.19

1989 Auburn Coke 20

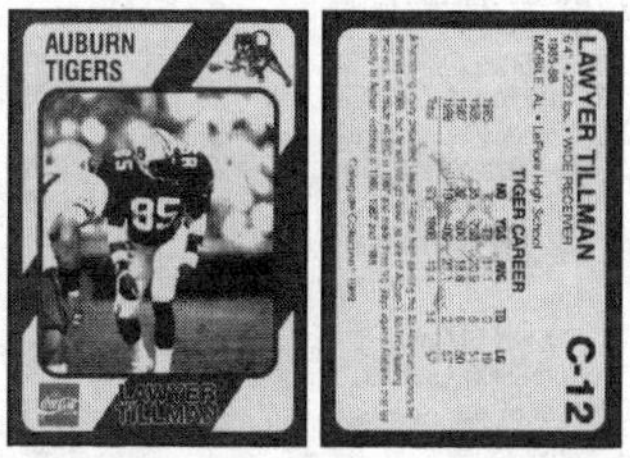

The 1989 Coke Auburn University football set contains 20 standard-size cards, depicting former Auburn greats. The fronts contain vintage photos; the horizontally oriented backs feature player profiles. Both sides have navy borders. These cards were printed on very thin stock.

	MINT	NRMT	EXC
COMPLETE SET (20)	10.00	4.50	1.25
COMMON CARD (C1-C20)	.35	.16	.04
☐ C1 Pat Dye CO	.60	.25	.07
☐ C2 Zeke Smith	.35	.16	.04
☐ C3 War Eagle (Mascot)	.50	.23	.06
☐ C4 Tucker Frederickson	.50	.23	.06
☐ C5 John Heisman	.50	.23	.06
☐ C6 Ralph(Shug) Jordan CO	.35	.16	.04
☐ C7 Pat Sullivan	.50	.23	.06
☐ C8 Terry Beasley	.35	.16	.04
☐ C9 Punt Bama Punt Ralph(Shug) Jordan and Paul(Bear) Bryant	.50	.23	.06
☐ C10 Retired Jerseys (Pat Sullivan and Terry Beasley)	.50	.23	.06
☐ C11 Bo Jackson	2.00	.90	.25
☐ C12 Lawyer Tillman	.50	.23	.06
☐ C13 Gregg Carr	.35	.16	.04
☐ C14 Lionel James	.60	.25	.07
☐ C15 Joe Cribbs	.75	.35	.09
☐ C16 Heisman Winners (Pat Sullivan, Bo Jackson, and Pat Dye CO)	1.00	.45	.12
☐ C17 Aundray Bruce	.50	.23	.06
☐ C18 Aubie (Mascot)	.35	.16	.04
☐ C19 Tracy Rocker	.35	.16	.04
☐ C20 James Brooks	1.00	.45	.12

1989 Auburn Coke 580

The 1989 Coke Auburn University football set contains 580 standard-size cards, depicting former Auburn greats. The fronts contain vintage photos; the horizontally oriented backs feature player profiles. Both sides have navy borders. The cards were distributed in sets and in poly packs. These cards were printed on very thin stock. This set is notable for its inclusion of several Bo Jackson cards.

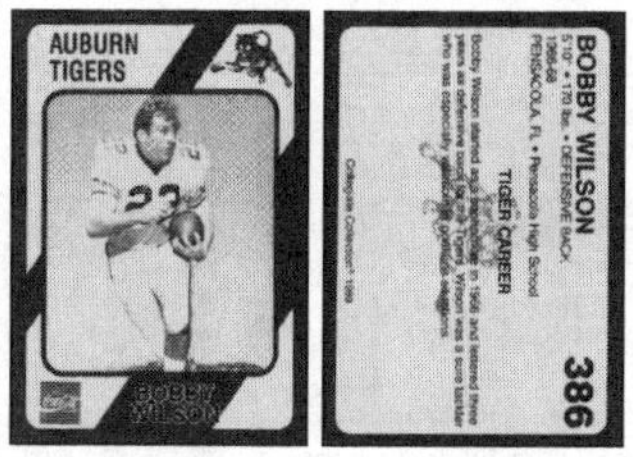

	MINT	NRMT	EXC
COMPLETE SET (580)	30.00	13.50	3.70
COMMON CARD (1-580)	.07	.03	.01
☐ 1 Pat Dye CO (His First Game)	.25	.11	.03
☐ 2 Auburn's First Team (1892 Team Photo)	.15	.07	.02
☐ 3 Pat Sullivan	.25	.11	.03
☐ 4 Bo (Jackson) Over The Top	.75	.35	.09
☐ 5 Jimmy Hitchcock	.07	.03	.01
☐ 6 Walter Gilbert	.07	.03	.01
☐ 7 Monk Gafford	.07	.03	.01
☐ 8 Frank D'Agostino	.07	.03	.01
☐ 9 Joe Childress	.15	.07	.02
☐ 10 Jim Pyburn	.15	.07	.02
☐ 11 Tex Warrington	.07	.03	.01
☐ 12 Travis Tidwell	.15	.07	.02
☐ 13 Fob James	.07	.03	.01
☐ 14 Jim Phillips	.15	.07	.02
☐ 15 Zeke Smith	.07	.03	.01
☐ 16 Mike Fuller	.15	.07	.02
☐ 17 Ed Dyas	.07	.03	.01
☐ 18 Jack Thornton	.07	.03	.01
☐ 19 Ken Rice	.07	.03	.01
☐ 20 Freddie Hyatt	.07	.03	.01
☐ 21 Jackie Burkett	.15	.07	.02
☐ 22 Jimmy Sidle	.15	.07	.02
☐ 23 Buddy McClinton	.07	.03	.01
☐ 24 Larry Willingham	.15	.07	.02
☐ 25 Bob Harris	.07	.03	.01
☐ 26 Bill Cody	.07	.03	.01
☐ 27 Lewis Colbert	.07	.03	.01
☐ 28 Brent Fullwood	.25	.11	.03
☐ 29 Tracy Rocker	.15	.07	.02
☐ 30 Kurt Grain	.07	.03	.01
☐ 31 Walter Reeves	.15	.07	.02
☐ 32 Jordan-Hare Stadium	.07	.03	.01
☐ 33 Ben Tamburello	.07	.03	.01
☐ 34 Benji Roland	.07	.03	.01
☐ 35 Chris Knapp	.07	.03	.01
☐ 36 Dowe Aughtman	.07	.03	.01
☐ 37 Auburn Tigers Logo	.07	.03	.01
☐ 38 Tommie Agee	.15	.07	.02
☐ 39 Bo Jackson	.75	.35	.09
☐ 40 Freddy Weygand	.15	.07	.02
☐ 41 Rodney Garner	.07	.03	.01
☐ 42 Brian Shulman	.07	.03	.01
☐ 43 Jim Thompson	.07	.03	.01
☐ 44 Shan Morris	.07	.03	.01
☐ 45 Ralph(Shug) Jordan CO	.15	.07	.02
☐ 46 Stacy Searels	.07	.03	.01
☐ 47 1957 Champs (Team Photo)	.15	.07	.02
☐ 48 Mike Kolen	.15	.07	.02
☐ 49 A Challenge Met (Pat Dye)	.15	.07	.02
☐ 50 Mark Dorminey	.07	.03	.01
☐ 51 Greg Staples	.07	.03	.01
☐ 52 Randy Campbell	.07	.03	.01
☐ 53 Duke Donaldson	.07	.03	.01
☐ 54 Yann Cowart	.07	.03	.01
☐ 55 Second Blocked Punt (Vs. Alabama 1972) Bill Newton David Langner	.15	.07	.02
☐ 56 Keith Uecker	.15	.07	.02
☐ 57 David Jordan	.07	.03	.01
☐ 58 Tim Drinkard	.07	.03	.01
☐ 59 Connie Frederick	.07	.03	.01
☐ 60 Pat Arrington	.07	.03	.01
☐ 61 Willie Howell	.07	.03	.01
☐ 62 Terry Page	.07	.03	.01
☐ 63 Ben Thomas	.07	.03	.01
☐ 64 Ron Stallworth	.15	.07	.02
☐ 65 Charlie Trotman	.07	.03	.01
☐ 66 Ed West	.15	.07	.02
☐ 67 James Brooks	.50	.23	.06
☐ 68 Changing of the Guard Doug Barfield and Ralph(Shug) Jordan	.15	.07	.02
☐ 69 Ken Bernich	.07	.03	.01
☐ 70 Chris Woods	.07	.03	.01
☐ 71 Ralph(Shug) Jordan CO	.15	.07	.02
☐ 72 Steve Dennis CO	.07	.03	.01
☐ 73 Reggie Herring CO	.07	.03	.01
☐ 74 Al Del Greco	.15	.07	.02
☐ 75 Wayne Hall CO	.07	.03	.01
☐ 76 Langdon Hall	.07	.03	.01
☐ 77 Donnie Humphrey	.07	.03	.01
☐ 78 Jeff Burger	.15	.07	.02
☐ 79 Vernon Blackard	.07	.03	.01
☐ 80 Larry Blakeney CO	.07	.03	.01
☐ 81 Doug Smith	.07	.03	.01
☐ 82 Two Eras Meet Ralph(Shug) Jordan and Vince Dooley	.15	.07	.02
☐ 83 Kyle Collins	.07	.03	.01
☐ 84 Bobby Freeman	.07	.03	.01
☐ 85 Pat Sullivan CO	.25	.11	.03
☐ 86 Neil Callaway CO	.07	.03	.01
☐ 87 William Andrews	.25	.11	.03
☐ 88 Curtis Kuykendall	.07	.03	.01
☐ 89 David Campbell	.07	.03	.01
☐ 90 Seniors of '83	.25	.11	.03
☐ 91 Bud Casey CO	.07	.03	.01
☐ 92 Jay Jacobs CO	.07	.03	.01
☐ 93 Al Del Greco	.15	.07	.02
☐ 94 Pate Mote	.07	.03	.01
☐ 95 Rob Shuler	.07	.03	.01
☐ 96 Jerry Beasley	.07	.03	.01
☐ 97 Pat Washington	.07	.03	.01
☐ 98 Ed Graham	.07	.03	.01
☐ 99 Leon Myers	.07	.03	.01
☐ 100 Paul Davis CO	.07	.03	.01
☐ 101 Tom Banks Jr.	.15	.07	.02
☐ 102 Mike Simmons	.07	.03	.01
☐ 103 Alex Bowden	.07	.03	.01
☐ 104 Jim Bone	.07	.03	.01
☐ 105 Wincent Harris	.07	.03	.01
☐ 106 James Daniel CO	.07	.03	.01
☐ 107 Jimmy Carter	.07	.03	.01
☐ 108 Leading Passers (Pat Sullivan)	.25	.11	.03
☐ 109 Alvin Mitchell	.07	.03	.01
☐ 110 Mark Clement	.07	.03	.01
☐ 111 Bob Brown	.07	.03	.01
☐ 112 Shot Senn	.07	.03	.01
☐ 113 Loran Carter	.07	.03	.01
☐ 114 Pat Dye's First Team (Team Photo)	.15	.07	.02
☐ 115 Bob Hix	.07	.03	.01
☐ 116 Bo Russell	.07	.03	.01
☐ 117 Mike Mann	.07	.03	.01
☐ 118 Mike Shirey	.07	.03	.01
☐ 119 Pat Dye CO	.15	.07	.02
☐ 120 Kevin Greene	.25	.11	.03
☐ 121 Auburn Creed	.07	.03	.01
☐ 122 Jordan's All-Americans (Ralph(Shug) Jordan, Tucker Frederickson, and Jimmy Sidle)	.15	.07	.02
☐ 123 Dave Blanks	.07	.03	.01
☐ 124 Scott Bolton	.07	.03	.01
☐ 125 Vince Dooley	.25	.11	.03
☐ 126 Tim Jessie	.07	.03	.01
☐ 127 Joe Davis	.07	.03	.01
☐ 128 Clayton Beauford	.07	.03	.01
☐ 129 Wilbur Hutsell AD	.07	.03	.01
☐ 130 Joe Whit CO	.07	.03	.01
☐ 131 Gary Kelley	.07	.03	.01
☐ 132 Bo Jackson	.75	.35	.09
☐ 133 Aundray Bruce	.25	.11	.03
☐ 134 Ronny Bellew	.07	.03	.01
☐ 135 Hindman Wall	.07	.03	.01
☐ 136 Frank Warren	.07	.03	.01
☐ 137 Abb Chrietzberg	.07	.03	.01
☐ 138 Collis Campbell	.07	.03	.01
☐ 139 Randy Stokes	.07	.03	.01
☐ 140 Teedy Faulk	.07	.03	.01
☐ 141 Reese McCall	.15	.07	.02
☐ 142 Jeff Jackson	.07	.03	.01
☐ 143 Bill Burgess	.07	.03	.01
☐ 144 Willie Huntley	.07	.03	.01
☐ 145 Doug Huntley	.07	.03	.01
☐ 146 Bacardi Bowl (Walter Gilbert)	.07	.03	.01
☐ 147 Russ Carreker	.07	.03	.01
☐ 148 Joe Moon	.07	.03	.01
☐ 149 A Look Ahead (Pat Dye CO)	.15	.07	.02
☐ 150 Joe Sullivan	.07	.03	.01
☐ 151 Scott Riley	.07	.03	.01
☐ 152 Larry Ellis	.07	.03	.01
☐ 153 Jeff Parks	.07	.03	.01
☐ 154 Gerald Williams	.07	.03	.01
☐ 155 Lee Griffith	.07	.03	.01
☐ 156 First Blocked Punt (Vs. Alabama 1972) Bill Newton	.15	.07	.02
☐ 157 Bill Beckwith ADMIN	.07	.03	.01
☐ 158 Celebration (1957 Action Photo)	.15	.07	.02
☐ 159 Tommy Carroll	.15	.07	.02
☐ 160 John Dailey	.07	.03	.01
☐ 161 George Stephenson	.07	.03	.01
☐ 162 Danny Arnold	.07	.03	.01
☐ 163 Mike Edwards	.07	.03	.01
☐ 164 1894 Auburn-Alabama Trophy	.15	.07	.02
☐ 165 Don Anderson	.07	.03	.01
☐ 166 Alvin Briggs	.07	.03	.01
☐ 167 Herb Waldrop CO	.07	.03	.01
☐ 168 Jim Skuthan	.07	.03	.01
☐ 169 Alan Hardin	.07	.03	.01
☐ 170 Coaching Generations	.25	.11	.03

(Pat Sullivan and Bobby Freeman)			
171 Georgia Celebration (1971 Locker Room)	.07	.03	.01
172 Auburn 17, Alabama 16 (1972 Scoreboard)	.15	.07	.02
173 Nat Ceasar	.07	.03	.01
174 Billy Hitchcock	.15	.07	.02
175 SEC Championship Trophy	.15	.07	.02
176 Dr. James E. Martin PRES	.07	.03	.01
177 Ricky Westbrook	.15	.07	.02
178 Fob James	.15	.07	.02
179 Stacy Dunn	.07	.03	.01
180 Tracy Turner	.07	.03	.01
181 Pat Dye CO	.15	.07	.02
182 Terry Beasley in the Record Book	.07	.03	.01
183 Ed(Foots) Bauer	.07	.03	.01
184 1984 Sugar Bowl Scoreboard	.07	.03	.01
185 Mark Robbins	.07	.03	.01
186 Paul White CO	.07	.03	.01
187 Hindman Wall AD	.07	.03	.01
188 Dave Beverly	.15	.07	.02
189 Sugar Bowl Trophy	.07	.03	.01
190 Edmund Nelson	.07	.03	.01
191 Edmund Nelson	.07	.03	.01
192 Cliff Hare	.07	.03	.01
193 Byron Franklin	.15	.07	.02
194 Richard Manry	.07	.03	.01
195 Malcolm McCary	.07	.03	.01
196 Patrick Waters ADMIN	.07	.03	.01
197 Chester Willis	.07	.03	.01
198 Alex Dudchock	.07	.03	.01
199 Pat Sullivan in the Record Book	.25	.11	.03
200 Victory Ride (Pat Dye CO)	.15	.07	.02
201 Dr. George Petrie CO	.07	.03	.01
202 D.M. Balliet CO	.07	.03	.01
203 G.H. Harvey CO	.07	.03	.01
204 F.M. Hall CO	.07	.03	.01
205 John Heisman CO	.25	.11	.03
206 Billy Watkins CO	.07	.03	.01
207 J.R. Kent CO	.07	.03	.01
208 Mike Harvey CO	.07	.03	.01
209 Billy Bates CO	.07	.03	.01
210 Mike Donahue CO	.07	.03	.01
211 W.S. Kienholz CO	.07	.03	.01
212 Mike Donahue CO	.07	.03	.01
213 Boozer Pitts CO	.07	.03	.01
214 Dave Morey CO	.07	.03	.01
215 George Bohler CO	.07	.03	.01
216 John Floyd CO	.07	.03	.01
217 Chet Wynne CO	.07	.03	.01
218 Jack Meagher CO	.07	.03	.01
219 Carl Voyles CO	.07	.03	.01
220 Earl Brown CO	.07	.03	.01
221 Ralph(Shug) Jordan CO	.15	.07	.02
222 Doug Barfield CO	.15	.07	.02
223 Most Career Points (Bo Jackson)	.35	.16	.04
224 Sonny Ferguson	.07	.03	.01
225 Ronnie Ross	.07	.03	.01
226 Gardner Jett	.15	.07	.02
227 Jerry Wilson	.07	.03	.01
228 Dick Schmalz	.07	.03	.01
229 Morris Savage	.07	.03	.01
230 James Owens	.07	.03	.01
231 Eddie Welch	.07	.03	.01
232 Lee Hayley	.07	.03	.01
233 Dick Hayley	.07	.03	.01
234 Jeff McCollum	.07	.03	.01
235 Rick Freeman	.07	.03	.01
236 Bobby Freeman CO	.07	.03	.01
237 Auburn 32, Alabama 22 (Trophy)	.15	.07	.02
238 Chip Powell	.07	.03	.01
239 Nick Ardillo	.07	.03	.01
240 Don Bristow	.07	.03	.01
241 Bucky Waid	.07	.03	.01
242 Greg Robert	.07	.03	.01
243 Ray Rollins	.07	.03	.01
244 Tommy Hicks	.07	.03	.01
245 Steve Wallace	.15	.07	.02
246 David Hughes	.07	.03	.01
247 Chuck Hurston	.07	.03	.01
248 Jimmy Long	.07	.03	.01
249 John Cochran AD	.07	.03	.01
250 Bobby Davis	.07	.03	.01
251 G.W. Clapp	.07	.03	.01
252 Jere Colley	.07	.03	.01
253 Tim James	.07	.03	.01
254 Joe Dolan	.07	.03	.01
255 Jerry Gordon	.07	.03	.01
256 Billy Edge	.07	.03	.01
257 Lawyer Tillman	.25	.11	.03
258 John McAfee	.07	.03	.01
259 Scotty Long	.07	.03	.01
260 Billy Austin	.07	.03	.01
261 Tracy Rocker	.15	.07	.02
262 Mickey Sutton	.07	.03	.01
263 Tommy Traylor	.07	.03	.01
264 Bill Van Dyke	.07	.03	.01
265 Sam McClurkin	.07	.03	.01
266 Mike Flynn	.07	.03	.01
267 Jimmy Sirmans	.07	.03	.01
268 Reggie Ware	.15	.07	.02
269 Bill Luka	.07	.03	.01
270 Don Machen	.07	.03	.01
271 Bill Grisham	.07	.03	.01
272 Bruce Evans	.07	.03	.01
273 Hank Hall	.07	.03	.01
274 Tommy Lunceford	.07	.03	.01
275 Pat Thomas	.07	.03	.01
276 Marvin Trott	.07	.03	.01
277 Brad Everett	.07	.03	.01
278 Frank Reeves	.07	.03	.01
279 Bishop Reeves	.07	.03	.01
280 Carver Reeves	.07	.03	.01
281 Billy Haas	.07	.03	.01
282 Dye's First AU Bowl (Pat Dye CO)	.15	.07	.02
283 Nate Hill	.07	.03	.01
284 Bucky Howard	.07	.03	.01
285 Tim Christian	.07	.03	.01
286 Tim Christian CO	.07	.03	.01
287 Tom Nettleman	.07	.03	.01
288 Carl Hubbard	.07	.03	.01
289 Auburn's Biggest Wins (Chart)	.07	.03	.01
290 Jay Jacobs	.07	.03	.01
291 Jimmy Pettus	.07	.03	.01
292 Cliff Hare Stadium	.07	.03	.01
293 Richard Wood	.15	.07	.02
294 Sandy Cannon	.07	.03	.01
295 Bill Braswell	.07	.03	.01
296 Foy Thompson	.07	.03	.01
297 Robert Margeson	.07	.03	.01
298 Pipeline to the Pros (Seven Pro Players) Gerald Williams Ed West Gregg Carr Donnie Humphrey Al Del Greco Ben Thomas Edmund Nelson	.25	.11	.03
299 Bill Evans	.07	.03	.01
300 Marvin Tucker	.07	.03	.01
301 Jack Locklear	.07	.03	.01
302 Mike Locklear	.07	.03	.01
303 Harry Unger	.07	.03	.01
304 Lee Marke Sellers	.07	.03	.01
305 Ted Foret	.07	.03	.01
306 Bobby Foret	.07	.03	.01
307 Mike Neel	.07	.03	.01
308 Rick Neel	.07	.03	.01
309 Mike Alford	.07	.03	.01
310 Mac Crawford	.07	.03	.01
311 Bill Cunningham	.07	.03	.01
312 Legends (Pat Sullivan and Jeff Burger)	.25	.11	.03
313 Frank LaRussa	.07	.03	.01
314 Chris Vacarella	.07	.03	.01
315 Gerald Robinson	.15	.07	.02
316 Ronnie Baynes	.07	.03	.01
317 Dave Edwards	.07	.03	.01
318 Steve Taylor	.07	.03	.01
319 Phillip Gilchrist	.07	.03	.01
320 Ben McCurdy	.07	.03	.01
321 Dave Hill	.07	.03	.01
322 Jim Reynolds	.07	.03	.01
323 Chuck Fletcher	.07	.03	.01
324 Bogue Miller	.07	.03	.01
325 Dave Beck	.07	.03	.01
326 Johnny Simmons	.07	.03	.01
327 Howard Simpson	.07	.03	.01
328 Benny Sivley	.15	.07	.02
329 1987 SEC Champions (Team Photo)	.15	.07	.02
330 Frank Cox	.07	.03	.01
331 Phil Gargis	.07	.03	.01
332 Don Webb	.07	.03	.01
333 Dan Presley	.07	.03	.01
334 Al Giffin	.07	.03	.01
335 Don Lewis	.07	.03	.01
336 Eric Floyd	.15	.07	.02
337 Jordan and Stadium (Ralph(Shug) Jordan)	.15	.07	.02
338 Terry Hendy	.07	.03	.01
339 Bill Atkins	.07	.03	.01
340 Tony Long	.07	.03	.01
341 Jimmy Clemmer	.07	.03	.01
342 John Valentine	.07	.03	.01
343 Bruce Bylsma	.07	.03	.01
344 Merrill Shirley	.07	.03	.01
345 Kenny Howard CO	.07	.03	.01
346 Hal Hamrick	.07	.03	.01
347 Greg Zipp	.07	.03	.01
348 Mac Champion	.07	.03	.01
349 Most Tackles in One Game (Kurt Crain)	.07	.03	.01
350 Leading Career Rushers (Bo Jackson)	.35	.16	.04
351 Homer Williams	.07	.03	.01
352 Mike Gates	.07	.03	.01
353 Rusty Fuller	.07	.03	.01
354 Rusty Deen	.07	.03	.01
355 Stalwart Defenders (Bob Harris and Mark Dorminey)	.07	.03	.01
356 Heroes of '56 (Ralph(Shug) Jordan, Jerry Elliott, and Frank Reeves)	.15	.07	.02
357 Road to the Top (Cartoon)	.15	.07	.02
358 Cleve Wester	.07	.03	.01
359 Line Stars (Jackie Burkett and Zeke Smith)	.15	.07	.02
360 Bob Scarbrough	.07	.03	.01
361 Jimmy Speigner	.07	.03	.01
362 Danny Speigner	.07	.03	.01
363 Alvin Bresler	.07	.03	.01
364 Wade Whatley	.07	.03	.01
365 Lance Hill	.07	.03	.01
366 Andy Steele	.07	.03	.01
367 John Whatley	.07	.03	.01
368 Alton Shell	.07	.03	.01
369 Larry Blakeney	.07	.03	.01
370 Mickey Zofko	.07	.03	.01
371 Gene Lorendo CO	.07	.03	.01
372 Mac Lorendo	.07	.03	.01
373 Buddy Davidson AD	.07	.03	.01
374 Dave Woodward	.07	.03	.01
375 Richard Guthrie	.07	.03	.01
376 George Rose	.07	.03	.01
377 Alan Bollinger	.07	.03	.01
378 Danny Sanspree	.07	.03	.01
379 Winky Giddens	.07	.03	.01
380 Franklin Fuller	.07	.03	.01
381 Charlie Collins	.07	.03	.01
382 Auburn, 23-22 (Scoreboard)	.07	.03	.01
383 Jeff Weekley	.07	.03	.01
384 Larry Haynie	.07	.03	.01
385 Miles Jones	.07	.03	.01
386 Bobby Wilson	.15	.07	.02
387 Bobby Lauder	.07	.03	.01
388 Charlie Glenn	.07	.03	.01
389 Claude Saia	.07	.03	.01
390 Tom Bryan	.07	.03	.01
391 Lee Gross	.07	.03	.01
392 Jerry Popwell	.07	.03	.01
393 Tommy Groat	.07	.03	.01
394 Neal Dettmering	.07	.03	.01
395 Dr. W.S. Bailey ADMIN	.07	.03	.01
396 Jim Pitts	.07	.03	.01
397 College Football History (Cliff Hare Stadium)	.07	.03	.01
398 Doc Griffith	.07	.03	.01
399 Liston Eddins	.07	.03	.01
400 Woody Woodall	.07	.03	.01
401 Auburn Helmet	.07	.03	.01
402 Skip Johnston	.07	.03	.01
403 Trey Gainous	.07	.03	.01
404 Randy Walls	.07	.03	.01
405 Jimmy Partin	.07	.03	.01
406 Dick Ingwerson	.07	.03	.01
407 David Shelby	.07	.03	.01
408 Harry Ward	.07	.03	.01
409 Thomas Gossom	.07	.03	.01
410 Samford T. Gower	.07	.03	.01
411 Architects of the Future (Jeff Beard and Ralph(Shug) Jordan)	.15	.07	.02
412 Ed Butler	.07	.03	.01
413 Bob Butler	.07	.03	.01
414 Ben Strickland	.07	.03	.01
415 Jeff Lott	.07	.03	.01
416 Harris Rabren	.07	.03	.01
417 Mike McQuaig	.07	.03	.01
418 Steve Wilson	.07	.03	.01
419 Jorge Portela	.07	.03	.01
420 Dave Middleton	.15	.07	.02
421 Tommy Yearout	.07	.03	.01
422 Gusty Yearout	.07	.03	.01
423 The Auburn Stadium	.07	.03	.01
424 Cliff Hare Stadium	.07	.03	.01
425 Oscar Burford	.07	.03	.01
426 Cliff Hare Stadium	.07	.03	.01
427 Cliff Hare Stadium	.07	.03	.01
428 Jordan-Hare Stadium	.07	.03	.01
429 Jack Meagher CO	.07	.03	.01
430 Jeff Beard AD	.07	.03	.01
431 Frank Young ADMIN	.07	.03	.01
432 Frank Riley	.07	.03	.01
433 Ernie Warren	.07	.03	.01
434 Brian Atkins	.07	.03	.01
435 George Atkins	.07	.03	.01
436 Ricky Sanders	.35	.16	.04
437 George Kenmore	.07	.03	.01
438 Don Heller	.07	.03	.01
439 Pat Meagher	.07	.03	.01
440 Tim Davis	.07	.03	.01
441 Tiger Meat (Cooks)	.07	.03	.01
442 Joe Connally CO	.07	.03	.01
443 Bob Newton	.15	.07	.02
444 Bill Newton	.07	.03	.01
445 David Langner	.07	.03	.01
446 Charlie Langner	.07	.03	.01
447 Brownie Flournoy ADMIN	.07	.03	.01
448 Mike Hicks	.07	.03	.01
449 Larry Hill	.07	.03	.01
450 Tim Baker	.07	.03	.01
451 Danny Bentley	.07	.03	.01
452 Tommy Lowry	.07	.03	.01
453 Jim Price	.07	.03	.01
454 Lloyd Nix	.07	.03	.01
455 Kenny Burks	.07	.03	.01
456 Rusty and Sallie Deen ADMIN	.07	.03	.01
457 Johnny Sumner	.07	.03	.01
458 Scott Blackmon	.07	.03	.01
459 Chuck Maxime	.07	.03	.01
460 Big SEC Wins (Chart)	.07	.03	.01
461 Bo Davis	.07	.03	.01
462 George Rose	.07	.03	.01
463 Bob Bradley	.07	.03	.01
464 Steve Osburne	.07	.03	.01
465 George Gross	.07	.03	.01
466 Andy Gross	.07	.03	.01
467 M.L. Brackett	.07	.03	.01
468 Herman Wilkes	.07	.03	.01
469 Roger Mitchell	.07	.03	.01
470 Bobby Beaird	.07	.03	.01
471 Sammy Oates	.07	.03	.01
472 Jimmy Ricketts	.07	.03	.01
473 Bucky Ayters	.07	.03	.01
474 Bill James	.07	.03	.01
475 Johnny Wallis	.07	.03	.01
476 Chris Jornson	.07	.03	.01
477 Joe Overton	.07	.03	.01
478 Tommy Lorino	.07	.03	.01
479 James Warren	.07	.03	.01
480 Lynn Johnson	.07	.03	.01
481 Sam Mitchell	.07	.03	.01
482 Sedrick McIntyre	.07	.03	.01
483 Mike Holtzclaw	.07	.03	.01
484 Dave Ostrowski	.07	.03	.01
485 Jim Walsh	.07	.03	.01
486 Mike Henley	.07	.03	.01
487 Roy Tatum	.07	.03	.01
488 Al Parks	.07	.03	.01
489 Billy Wilson	.15	.07	.02
490 Ken Luke	.07	.03	.01
491 Phillip Hall	.07	.03	.01
492 Bruce Yates	.07	.03	.01
493 Dan Hataway	.07	.03	.01
494 Joe Leichtnam	.07	.03	.01
495 Danny Fulford	.07	.03	.01
496 Ken Hardy	.07	.03	.01
497 Rob Spivey	.07	.03	.01
498 Rick Telhiard	.07	.03	.01
499 Ron Yarbrough	.07	.03	.01
500 Leo Sexton	.07	.03	.01
501 Dick McGowen CO	.07	.03	.01
502 Lee Kidd	.07	.03	.01
503 Rex McKissick	.07	.03	.01
504 Fagen Canzoneri and Zach Jenkins	.07	.03	.01
505 Jim Bouchillon	.07	.03	.01
506 Forrest Blue	.25	.11	.03
507 Mike Helms	.07	.03	.01
508 Bobby Hunt	.15	.07	.02
509 John Liptak	.07	.03	.01
510 Jim McKinney	.07	.03	.01
511 Ed Baker	.07	.03	.01
512 Heisman Trophies	.25	.11	.03
513 Eddy Jackson	.07	.03	.01
514 Jimmy Powell	.07	.03	.01
515 Jerry Elliott	.07	.03	.01
516 Jimmy Jones	.07	.03	.01
517 Jimmy Laster	.07	.03	.01
518 Larry Laster	.07	.03	.01
519 Jerry Sansom	.07	.03	.01
520 Don Downs	.07	.03	.01
521 Danny Skutack	.07	.03	.01
522 Keith Green	.07	.03	.01
523 Spence McCracken	.07	.03	.01
524 Lloyd Cheattom	.07	.03	.01
525 Mike Shows	.07	.03	.01
526 Spec Kelley	.07	.03	.01
527 Dick McGowen	.07	.03	.01
528 Jon Kilgore	.07	.03	.01
529 Frank Gatski	.25	.11	.03
530 Joel Eaves	.07	.03	.01
531 John Adcock	.07	.03	.01
532 Jimmy Fenton	.07	.03	.01
533 Mike McCartney	.07	.03	.01
534 Harrison McCraw	.07	.03	.01
535 Mailon Kent	.07	.03	.01
536 Dickie Flournoy	.07	.03	.01
537 Coker Barton	.07	.03	.01
538 Scotty Elam	.07	.03	.01
539 Tim Wood	.07	.03	.01
540 Terry Fuller	.07	.03	.01
541 Johnny Kern	.07	.03	.01
542 Mike Currier	.07	.03	.01
543 Richard Cheek	.07	.03	.01
544 Dan Dickerson	.07	.03	.01
545 Arnold Fagen	.07	.03	.01
546 John"Rat" Riley	.07	.03	.01

		MINT	NRMT	EXC
☐ 547	Jim Burson	.15	.07	.02
☐ 548	Bob Fleming	.07	.03	.01
☐ 549	Mike Fitzhugh	.07	.03	.01
☐ 550	Jim Patton	.25	.11	.03
☐ 551	Bryant Harvard	.07	.03	.01
☐ 552	Leon Cochran	.07	.03	.01
☐ 553	Wayne Frazier	.07	.03	.01
☐ 554	Phillip Dembowski	.07	.03	.01
☐ 555	Alex Spurlin and Ed Spurlin	.07	.03	.01
☐ 556	Bill Kilpatrick	.07	.03	.01
☐ 557	Gaines Lanier	.07	.03	.01
☐ 558	Johnny McDonald	.07	.03	.01
☐ 559	Ray Powell	.07	.03	.01
☐ 560	Jimmy Putman	.07	.03	.01
☐ 561	Bobby Wasden	.07	.03	.01
☐ 562	Roger Pruett	.07	.03	.01
☐ 563	Don Braswell	.07	.03	.01
☐ 564	John Jeffery	.07	.03	.01
☐ 565	Auburn-A TV Favorite (Pat Dye CO)	.15	.07	.02
☐ 566	Lamar Rawson	.07	.03	.01
☐ 567	Larry Rawson	.07	.03	.01
☐ 568	David Rawson	.07	.03	.01
☐ 569	Hal Herring CO	.07	.03	.01
☐ 570	Pat Sullivan	.25	.11	.03
☐ 571	John Cochran	.07	.03	.01
☐ 572	Jerry Gulledge	.07	.03	.01
☐ 573	Steve Stanaland	.15	.07	.02
☐ 574	Greg Zipp	.07	.03	.01
☐ 575	John Trotman	.07	.03	.01
☐ 576	Clyde Baumgartner	.07	.03	.01
☐ 577	Jay Casey	.07	.03	.01
☐ 578	Ralph O'Gwynne	.07	.03	.01
☐ 579	Sid Scarborough	.07	.03	.01
☐ 580	Tom Banks Sr.	.15	.07	.02

1991 Auburn Hoby

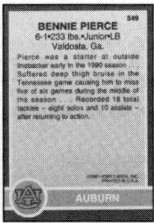

This 42-card standard-size set was produced by Hoby and features the 1991 Auburn football team. Five hundred uncut press sheets were also produced, and they were signed and numbered by Pat Dye. The cards feature on the fronts a mix of posed and action color photos, with thin white borders on a royal blue card face. The school logo occurs in the lower left corner in an orange circle, with the player's name in a gold stripe extending to the right. On a light orange background, the backs carry biography, player profile, or statistics.

		MINT	NRMT	EXC
COMPLETE SET (42)		10.00	4.50	1.25
COMMON CARD (523-564)		.25	.11	.03
☐ 523	Thomas Bailey	.25	.11	.03
☐ 524	Corey Barlow	.35	.16	.04
☐ 525	Reggie Barlow	.35	.16	.04
☐ 526	Fred Baxter	.35	.16	.04
☐ 527	Eddie Blake	.35	.16	.04
☐ 528	Herbert Casey	.25	.11	.03
☐ 529	Pedro Cherry	.25	.11	.03
☐ 530	Darrel Crawford	.35	.16	.04
☐ 531	Tim Cromartie	.35	.16	.04
☐ 532	Juan Crum	.25	.11	.03
☐ 533	Karekin Cunningham	.25	.11	.03
☐ 534	Alonzo Etheridge	.25	.11	.03
☐ 535	Joe Frazier	.25	.11	.03
☐ 536	Pat Dye AD/CO	.50	.23	.06
☐ 537	Thery George	.25	.11	.03
☐ 538	Chris Gray	.35	.16	.04
☐ 539	Victor Hall	.25	.11	.03
☐ 540	Randy Hart	.25	.11	.03
☐ 541	Chris Holland	.25	.11	.03
☐ 542	Chuckie Johnson	.25	.11	.03
☐ 543	Anthony Judge	.25	.11	.03
☐ 544	Corey Lewis	.25	.11	.03
☐ 545	Reid McMilion	.25	.11	.03
☐ 546	Bob Meeks	.25	.11	.03
☐ 547	Dale Overton	.25	.11	.03
☐ 548	Mike Pelton	.50	.23	.06
☐ 549	Bennie Pierce	.25	.11	.03
☐ 550	Mike Pina	.25	.11	.03
☐ 551	Anthony Redmon	.25	.11	.03
☐ 552	Tony Richardson	.50	.23	.06
☐ 553	Richard Shea	.25	.11	.03
☐ 554	Fred Smith	.35	.16	.04
☐ 555	Otis Mounds	.25	.11	.03
☐ 556	Ricky Sutton	.25	.11	.03
☐ 557	Alex Thomas	.25	.11	.03
☐ 558	Greg Thompson	.25	.11	.03
☐ 559	Tim Tillman	.25	.11	.03
☐ 560	Jim Von Wyl	.25	.11	.03
☐ 561	Stan White	.50	.23	.06
☐ 562	Darrell Williams	.25	.11	.03
☐ 563	James Willis	.25	.11	.03
☐ 564	Jon Wilson	.25	.11	.03

1993 Baylor

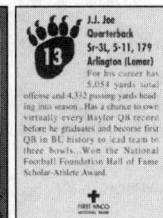

Sponsored by First Waco National Bank, the 21 cards comprising this set were issued as perforated game program insert sheets. The three perforated sheets measure approximately 7 5/8" by 11". Each sheet consists of seven player cards and a sponsor card, which is the size of two player cards. Each perforated player card measures approximately 2 7/16" by 3 5/16" and features green-bordered posed color head shots of helmetless players. The player's name and position appear within an orange banner at the bottom. The team name, Baylor Bears, appears in white lettering within a black bar at the upper right. The player's uniform number is shown in white within a black circle at the upper left. The white back carries the player's name, position, and biography in bold black lettering at the upper right. Previous season highlights follow below. The player's uniform number appears in white within a black icon of a bear's paw at the upper left, but otherwise the cards are unnumbered and so checklisted below in alphabetical order.

		MINT	NRMT	EXC
COMPLETE SET (21)		16.00	7.25	2.00
COMMON CARD (1-21)		.75	.35	.09
☐ 1	Lamone Alexander	.75	.35	.09
☐ 2	Joseph Asbell	.75	.35	.09
☐ 3	Marvin Callies	.75	.35	.09
☐ 4	Todd Crawford	.75	.35	.09
☐ 5	Earnest Crownover	.75	.35	.09
☐ 6	Will Davidson	1.00	.45	.12
☐ 7	Chris Dull	.75	.35	.09
☐ 8	Raynor Finley	.75	.35	.09
☐ 9	J.J. Joe	2.00	.90	.25
☐ 10	Phillip Kent	.75	.35	.09
☐ 11	David Leaks	.75	.35	.09
☐ 12	Scotty Lewis	1.00	.45	.12
☐ 13	Fred Miller	1.00	.45	.12
☐ 14	Bruce Nowak	.75	.35	.09
☐ 15	Mike Oatis	.75	.35	.09
☐ 16	Chuck Pope	.75	.35	.09
☐ 17	Adrian Robinson	2.00	.90	.25
☐ 18	Tyrone Smith	.75	.35	.09
☐ 19	Andrew Swasey	.75	.35	.09
☐ 20	Byron Thompson	.75	.35	.09
☐ 21	Tony Tubbs	.75	.35	.09

1984 BYU All-Time Greats

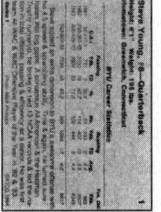

This 15-card standard-size set features BYU's all-time great football players since 1958. The sets were sold in a plastic bag, and the back of the attached paper tab indicated that additional sets could be purchased for 2.00 plus 75 cents for postage and handling. On a white card face, the fronts display both close-up and action player photos that have a purple tint. The top reads "All-Time Cougar Greats B.Y.U.," with the words "Cougar Greats" in a purple banner. The player's name is printed in purple in the bottom white border. The horizontal backs are gray and carry biography, BYU career statistics, and a career summary. Steve Young is featured in one of his earliest card appearances.

		MINT	NRMT	EXC
COMPLETE SET (15)		20.00	9.00	2.50
COMMON CARD (1-15)		.50	.23	.06
☐ 1	Steve Young	15.00	6.75	1.85
☐ 2	Eldon Fortie	.50	.23	.06
☐ 3	Bart Oates	2.00	.90	.25
☐ 4	Pete Van Valkenburg	.60	.25	.07
☐ 5	Mike Mees	.50	.23	.06
☐ 6	Wayne Baker	.50	.23	.06
☐ 7	Gordon Gravelle	.60	.25	.07
☐ 8	Gordon Hudson	.60	.25	.07
☐ 9	Kurt Gunther	.50	.23	.06
☐ 10	Todd Shell	.60	.25	.07
☐ 11	Chris Farasopoulos	1.00	.45	.12
☐ 12	Paul Howard	.50	.23	.06
☐ 13	Dave Atkinson	.50	.23	.06

		MINT	NRMT	EXC
☐ 14	Paul Linford	.50	.23	.06
☐ 15	Phil Odle	.60	.25	.07

1984-85 BYU National Champions

This 15-card standard-size set features the 1984 BYU National Championship team. The bordered front features a player action shot. The back features a banner carrying the phrase "BYU - 1984 National Champions", and a helmet immediately underneath. A player profile completes the back. The cards are unnumbered and checklisted below in alphabetical order.

		MINT	NRMT	EXC
COMPLETE SET (15)		25.00	11.00	3.10
COMMON CARD (1-15)		1.50	.70	.19
☐ 1	Mark Allen	1.50	.70	.19
☐ 2	Adam Hysbert	1.50	.70	.19
☐ 3	Larry Hamilton	1.50	.70	.19
☐ 4	Jim Herrmann	1.50	.70	.19
☐ 5	Kyle Morrell	2.00	.90	.25
☐ 6	Lee Johnson	2.00	.90	.25
☐ 7	David Mills	1.50	.70	.19
☐ 8	Dave Wright Craig Garrick Trevor Matich Robert Anae Louis Wong	3.00	1.35	.35
☐ 9	Jim Herrmann Larry Hamilton Smith	2.00	.90	.25
☐ 10	Louis Wong	1.50	.70	.19
☐ 11	Bosco in Holiday Bowl (Robbie Bosco)	5.00	2.20	.60
☐ 12	BYU Cougar Stadium	1.50	.70	.19
☐ 13	UPI Final Top 20	1.50	.70	.19
☐ 14	BYU National Championship Roster	1.50	.70	.19
☐ 15	Schedule and Scores For 1984	1.50	.70	.19

1990 BYU Safety

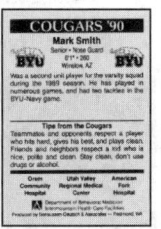

This 12-card standard-size set was issued in Utah in conjunction with three area hospitals to promote safety. The fronts of the cards feature the hospitals' names on the top while underneath them are full-color action shots framed in the blue and white colors of the Cougars. The word "Cougars" is on top of the photo with the year "1990" on the right side and the player's name and position on the bottom of the card. The backs have biographical information as well as various safety tips. The set was issued in three strips of four cards. Since the cards are unnumbered, we are listing them in alphabetical order. This set features an early card of 1990 Heisman trophy winner Ty Detmer.

		MINT	NRMT	EXC
COMPLETE SET (12)		16.00	7.25	2.00
COMMON CARD (1-12)		1.00	.45	.12
☐ 1	Rocky Beigel	1.00	.45	.12
☐ 2	Matt Bellini	1.50	.70	.19
☐ 3	Tony Crutchfield	1.00	.45	.12
☐ 4	Ty Detmer	8.00	3.60	1.00
☐ 5	Norm Dixon	1.00	.45	.12
☐ 6	Earl Kauffman	1.00	.45	.12
☐ 7	Rich Kaufusi	1.50	.70	.19
☐ 8	Bryan May	1.00	.45	.12
☐ 9	Brent Nyberg	1.00	.45	.12
☐ 10	Chris Smith	1.50	.70	.19
☐ 11	Mark Smith	1.00	.45	.12
☐ 12	Robert Stephens	1.00	.45	.12

1991 BYU Safety

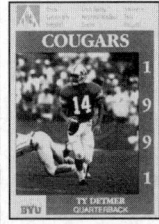
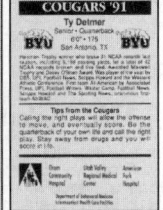

This 16-card standard-size set was sponsored by Orem Community Hospital, Utah Valley Regional Medical Center, and American Fork Hospital. The cards were issued in four-card perforated strips at four different home games. The fronts feature a full-color action shot enclosed in a three-sided blue drop border and a small white border

---

at the left. The name "Cougars" is in white reversed-out letters in the top blue border, while 1991 runs down the right side, and the player's name and position are in the bottom border. Sponsor logos appear in aqua lettering at the top, while the school logo is in blue in the lower left corner. Card backs feature player profile, "Tips from the Cougars" (anti-drug or alcohol messages), and sponsor names. The cards are unnumbered and checklisted below in alphabetical order.

		MINT	NRMT	EXC
COMPLETE SET (16)		12.00	5.50	1.50
COMMON CARD (1-16)		.75	.35	.09
☐ 1	Josh Arnold	.75	.35	.09
☐ 2	Rocky Beigel	.75	.35	.09
☐ 3	Scott Charlton	.75	.35	.09
☐ 4	Tony Crutchfield	.75	.35	.09
☐ 5	Ty Detmer	5.00	2.20	.60
☐ 6	LaVell Edwards CO	1.50	.70	.19
☐ 7	Scott Giles	.75	.35	.09
☐ 8	Derwin Gray	1.00	.45	.12
☐ 9	Shad Hansen	.75	.35	.09
☐ 10	Brad Hunter	.75	.35	.09
☐ 11	Earl Kauffman	.75	.35	.09
☐ 12	Jared Leavitt	.75	.35	.09
☐ 13	Micah Matsuzaki	.75	.35	.09
☐ 14	Bryan May	.75	.35	.09
☐ 15	Peter Tuipulotu	.75	.35	.09
☐ 16	Matt Zundel	.75	.35	.09

1992 BYU Safety

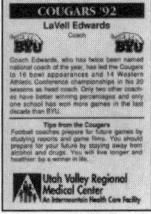

This 16-card standard-size set was sponsored by Fillmore Medical Center, an Intermountain Health Care facility. The cards were issued in four-card perforated strips. The fronts feature a glossy full-color action shot enclosed by a three-sided blue border and a small white border at the left. The name "Cougars" is in white lettering in the top blue border, "1992" runs down the right side, and the player's name and position are in the bottom border. The sponsor logo appears in blue lettering at the top, while the school logo is in blue at the lower left corner. The card backs feature a player profile, "Tips from the Cougars" (anti-drug or alcohol messages), and sponsor names. The cards are unnumbered and checklisted below in alphabetical order.

		MINT	NRMT	EXC
COMPLETE SET (16)		10.00	4.50	1.25
COMMON CARD (1-16)		.60	.25	.07
☐ 1	Tyler Anderson	.60	.25	.07
☐ 2	Randy Brock	.60	.25	.07
☐ 3	Brad Clark	.60	.25	.07
☐ 4	Eric Drage	1.00	.45	.12
☐ 5	LaVell Edwards CO	1.00	.45	.12
☐ 6	Mike Empey	.60	.25	.07
☐ 7	Lenny Gomes	.60	.25	.07
☐ 8	Derwin Gray	1.00	.45	.12
☐ 9	Shad Hansen	.60	.25	.07
☐ 10	Eli Herring	1.00	.45	.12
☐ 11	Micah Matsuzaki	.60	.25	.07
☐ 12	Patrick Mitchell	.75	.35	.09
☐ 13	Garry Pay	.60	.25	.07
☐ 14	Greg Pitts	.60	.25	.07
☐ 15	Byron Rex	.75	.35	.09
☐ 16	Jamal Willis	1.00	.45	.12

1993 BYU

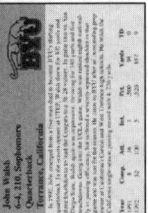

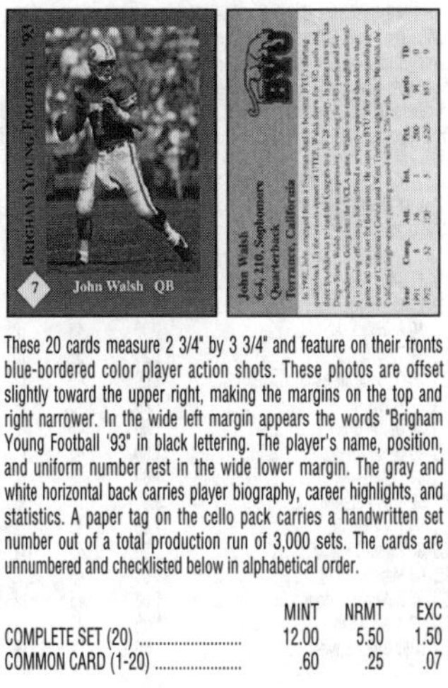

These 20 cards measure 2 3/4" by 3 3/4" and feature on their fronts blue-bordered color player action shots. These photos are offset slightly toward the upper right, making the margins on the top and right narrower. In the wide left margin appears the words "Brigham Young Football '93" in black lettering. The player's name, position, and uniform number rest in the wide lower margin. The gray and white horizontal back carries player biography, career highlights, and statistics. A paper tag on the cello pack carries a handwritten set number out of a total production run of 3,000 sets. The cards are unnumbered and checklisted below in alphabetical order.

		MINT	NRMT	EXC
COMPLETE SET (20)		12.00	5.50	1.50
COMMON CARD (1-20)		.60	.25	.07

☐ 1 Tyler Anderson	.60	.25	.07
☐ 2 Randy Brock	.75	.35	.09
☐ 3 Frank Christianson	.60	.25	.07
☐ 4 Eric Drage	1.00	.45	.12
☐ 5 LaVell Edwards CO	.75	.35	.09
☐ 6 Mike Empey	.60	.25	.07
☐ 7 Lenny Gomes	.75	.35	.09
☐ 8 Kalin Hall	.60	.25	.07
☐ 9 Nathan Hall	.60	.25	.07
☐ 10 Hema Heimuli	1.00	.45	.12
☐ 11 Todd Herget	.60	.25	.07
☐ 12 Eli Herring	.75	.35	.09
☐ 13 Micah Matsuzaki	.60	.25	.07
☐ 14 Casey Mazzota	.60	.25	.07
☐ 15 Patrick Mitchell	.60	.25	.07
☐ 16 Evan Pilgrim	1.00	.45	.12
☐ 17 Greg Pitts	.60	.25	.07
☐ 18 Vic Tarleton	.60	.25	.07
☐ 19 John Walsh	2.50	1.10	.30
☐ 20 Jamal Willis	1.00	.45	.12

1988 California Smokey

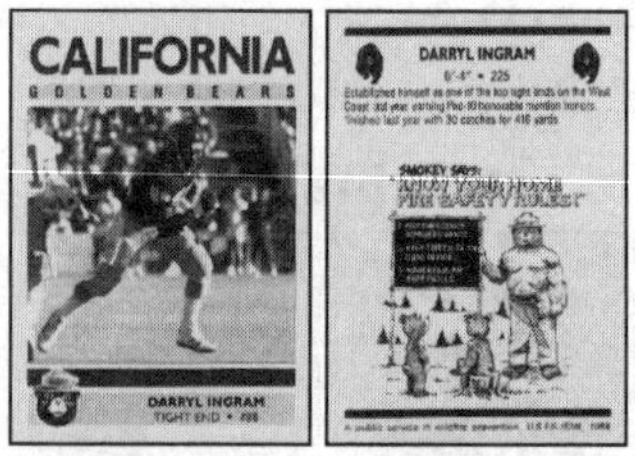

The 1988 California Bears Smokey set contains 12 standard-size cards. The fronts feature color action photos with name, position, and jersey number. The vertically oriented backs have brief career highlights. The cards are unnumbered, so they are listed in alphabetical order by subject's name. The card fronts contain a yellow stripe on the top and bottom that includes the team and player names.

	MINT	NRMT	EXC
COMPLETE SET (12)	15.00	6.75	1.85
COMMON CARD (1-12)	1.25	.55	.16
☐ 1 Rob Bimson	1.25	.55	.16
☐ 2 Joel Dickson	1.25	.55	.16
☐ 3 Robert DosRemedios	1.25	.55	.16
☐ 4 Mike Ford	1.25	.55	.16
☐ 5 Darryl Ingram	1.25	.55	.16
☐ 6 David Ortega	1.25	.55	.16
☐ 7 Chris Richards	1.25	.55	.16
☐ 8 Bruce Snyder CO	2.00	.90	.25
☐ 9 Troy Taylor	2.00	.90	.25
☐ 10 Natu Tuatagaloa	2.00	.90	.25
☐ 11 Majett Whiteside	1.25	.55	.16
☐ 12 Dave Zawatson	1.25	.55	.16

1989 California Smokey

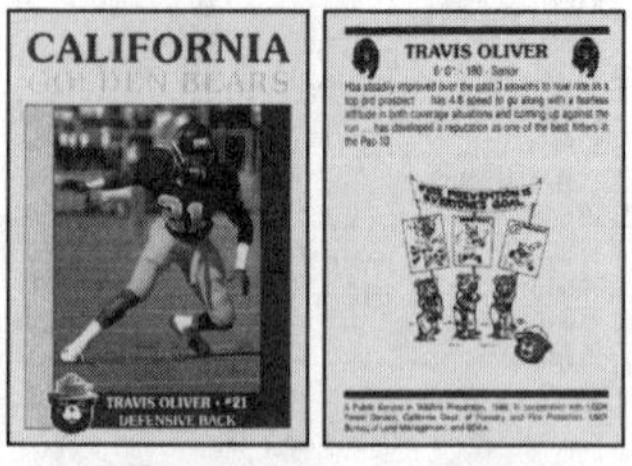

The 1989 California Bears Smokey set contains 16 standard-size cards. The fronts feature color action photos with name, position, and jersey number. The vertically oriented backs have brief career highlights. The cards are unnumbered, so they are listed by jersey numbers. The card fronts contain a player photo bordered on the left by a yellow stripe and a blue stripe on the right and below the photo.

	MINT	NRMT	EXC
COMPLETE SET (16)	15.00	6.75	1.85
COMMON CARD (1-16)	1.00	.45	.12
☐ 1 John Hardy	1.00	.45	.12
☐ 2 Mike Ford	1.00	.45	.12
☐ 10 Robbie Keen	1.00	.45	.12
☐ 11 Troy Taylor	1.25	.55	.16
☐ 20 Dwayne Jones	1.00	.45	.12
☐ 21 Travis Oliver	1.00	.45	.12
☐ 34 Darrin Greer	1.00	.45	.12
☐ 40 David Ortega	1.00	.45	.12
☐ 41 Dan Slevin	1.00	.45	.12
☐ 52 Troy Auzenne	3.00	1.35	.35
☐ 69 Tony Smith	1.00	.45	.12
☐ 80 Junior Tagaloa	1.00	.45	.12
☐ 83 Michael Smith	1.00	.45	.12
☐ 95 DeWayne Odom	1.00	.45	.12
☐ 99 Joel Dickson	1.00	.45	.12
☐ NNO Bruce Snyder CO	1.50	.70	.19

1990 California Smokey

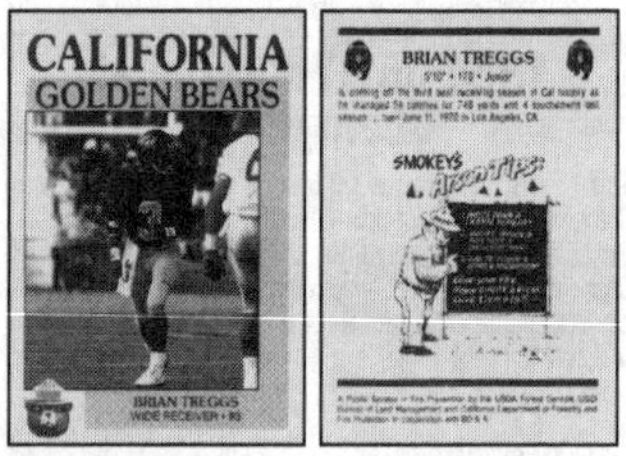

The 1990 California Bears Smokey set contains 16 standard-size cards. The fronts feature a color action photo bordered in yellow on three sides, with the player's name, position, and jersey number below the picture. The backs have brief career highlights and a fire prevention cartoon starring Smokey the Bear. These unnumbered cards are listed in alphabetical order below for convenience. The card fronts contain a player photo bordered on three sides by a yellow stripe.

	MINT	NRMT	EXC
COMPLETE SET (16)	12.00	5.50	1.50
COMMON CARD (1-16)	.75	.35	.09
☐ 1 Troy Auzenne 52	2.00	.90	.25
☐ 2 John Belli 61	.75	.35	.09
☐ 3 Joel Dickson 99	.75	.35	.09
☐ 4 Ron English 42	.75	.35	.09
☐ 5 Rhett Hall 57	2.50	1.10	.30
☐ 6 John Hardy 1	.75	.35	.09
☐ 7 Robbie Keen 10	.75	.35	.09
☐ 8 DeWayne Odom 95	1.00	.45	.12
☐ 9 Mike Pawlawski 9	1.50	.70	.19
☐ 10 Castle Redmond 37	.75	.35	.09
☐ 11 James Richards 64	.75	.35	.09
☐ 12 Ernie Rogers 68	.75	.35	.09
☐ 13 Bruce Snyder CO	1.25	.55	.16
☐ 14 Brian Treggs 3	1.00	.45	.12
☐ 15 Anthony Wallace 6	.75	.35	.09
☐ 16 Greg Zomalt 28	.75	.35	.09

1991 California Smokey

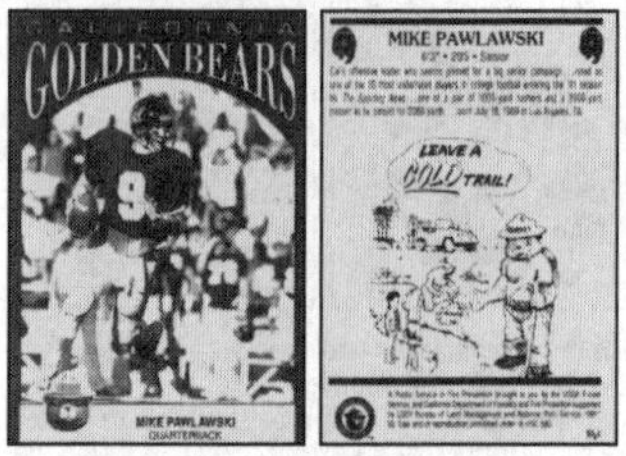

This 16-card standard size set was sponsored by the USDA Forest Service and other agencies. The cards were printed on thin cardboard stock. The card fronts are accented in the team's colors (dark blue and yellow) and have glossy color action player photos. The top of the pictures is curved to resemble an archway, and the team name follows the curve of the arch. The player's name and position appear in a stripe below the picture. The backs present player profile and a fire prevention cartoon starring Smokey. The cards are unnumbered and checklisted below in alphabetical order. An early card of Sean Dawkins is featured in this set.

	MINT	NRMT	EXC
COMPLETE SET (16)	15.00	6.75	1.85
COMMON CARD (1-16)	.75	.35	.09
☐ 1 Troy Auzenne	1.50	.70	.19
☐ 2 Chris Cannon	.75	.35	.09
☐ 3 Cornell Collier	.75	.35	.09
☐ 4 Sean Dawkins	3.00	1.35	.35
☐ 5 Steve Gordon	.75	.35	.09
☐ 6 Mike Pawlawski	1.25	.55	.16
☐ 7 Bruce Snyder CO	1.25	.55	.16
☐ 8 Todd Steussie	2.00	.90	.25
☐ 9 Mack Travis	.75	.35	.09
☐ 10 Brian Treggs	1.00	.45	.12
☐ 11 Russell White	2.00	.90	.25
☐ 12 Jason Wilborn	.75	.35	.09
☐ 13 David Wilson	.75	.35	.09
☐ 14 Brent Woodall	.75	.35	.09
☐ 15 Eric Zomalt	1.25	.55	.16
☐ 16 Greg Zomalt	.75	.35	.09

1992 California Smokey

This 16-card standard-size set was sponsored by the USDA Forest Service and other state and federal agencies. The cards are printed on thin card stock. The fronts carry a color action player photo on a navy blue card face. The team name and year appear above the photo in yellow print on a navy blue bar that partially rests on a yellow bar with notched ends. Below the photo, the player's name and sponsor logos appear in a yellow border stripe. The backs carry player profile and a fire prevention cartoon starring Smokey. The cards are unnumbered and checklisted below in alphabetical order.

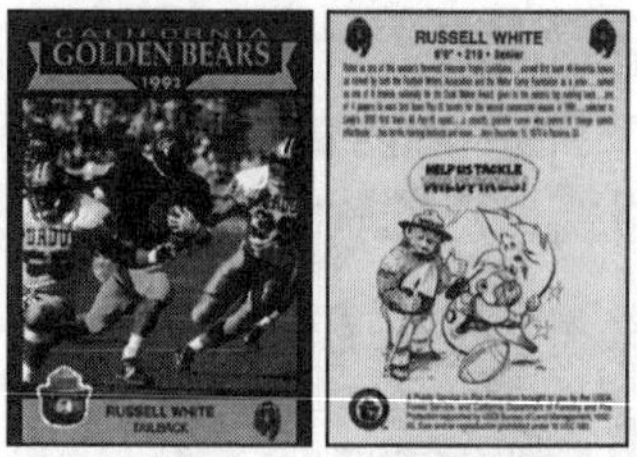

	MINT	NRMT	EXC
COMPLETE SET (16)	12.00	5.50	1.50
COMMON CARD (1-16)	.60	.25	.07
☐ 1 Chidi Ahanotu	1.00	.45	.12
☐ 2 Wolf Barber	.60	.25	.07
☐ 3 Mick Barsala	.60	.25	.07
☐ 4 Doug Brien	1.50	.70	.19
☐ 5 Al Casner	.60	.25	.07
☐ 6 Lindsey Chapman	.60	.25	.07
☐ 7 Sean Dawkins	2.50	1.10	.30
☐ 8 Keith Gilbertson CO	.75	.35	.09
☐ 9 Eric Mahlum	.75	.35	.09
☐ 10 Chris Noonan	.60	.25	.07
☐ 11 Todd Steussie	1.50	.70	.19
☐ 12 Mack Travis	.60	.25	.07
☐ 13 Russell White	1.50	.70	.19
☐ 14 Jerrott Willard	.75	.35	.09
☐ 15 Eric Zomalt	1.00	.45	.12
☐ 16 Greg Zomalt	.60	.25	.07

1993 California Smokey

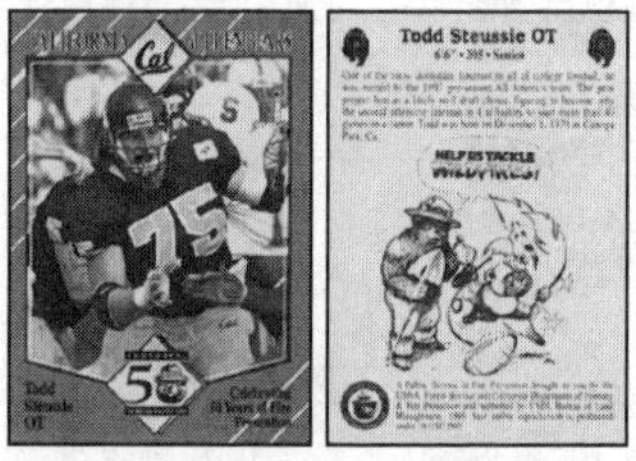

Printed on thin card stock, this 16-card standard-size set was sponsored by the USDA, the Forest Service, and other state and federal agencies. The fronts feature color player action shots framed by thin white and black lines and with gold-colored borders highlighted by oblique white stripes. The team's name appears within the upper margin, and the player's name and position, along with the Smokey 50-year celebration logo, rest in the lower margin. The white backs carry player profile and a fire prevention cartoon starring Smokey. The cards are unnumbered and checklisted below in alphabetical order.

	MINT	NRMT	EXC
COMPLETE SET (16)	10.00	4.50	1.25
COMMON CARD (1-16)	.60	.25	.07
☐ 1 Dave Barr	2.00	.90	.25
☐ 2 Doug Brien	1.25	.55	.16
☐ 3 Mike Caldwell	.75	.35	.09
☐ 4 Lindsey Chapman	.60	.25	.07
☐ 5 Je'Rod Cherry	1.00	.45	.12
☐ 6 Michael Davis	.60	.25	.07
☐ 7 Tyrone Edwards	.60	.25	.07
☐ 8 Keith Gilbertson CO	.60	.25	.07
☐ 9 Jody Graham	.60	.25	.07
☐ 10 Marty Holly	.60	.25	.07
☐ 11 Paul Joiner	.60	.25	.07
☐ 12 Eric Mahlum	.60	.25	.07
☐ 13 Damien Semien	.60	.25	.07
☐ 14 Todd Steussie	1.25	.55	.16
☐ 15 Jerrott Willard	.60	.25	.07
☐ 16 Eric Zomalt	.75	.35	.09

1995 California Smokey

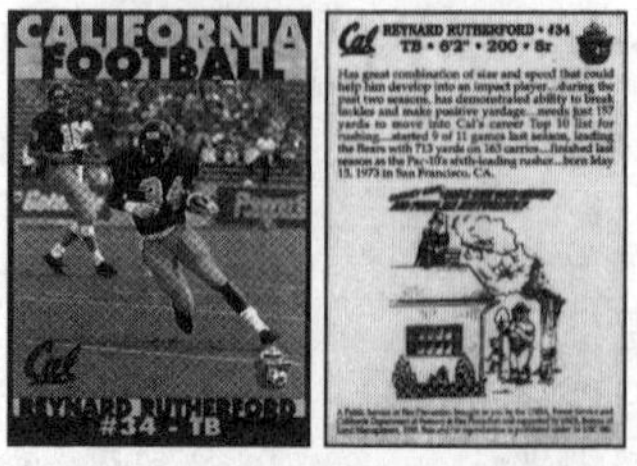

This 16-card set was sponsored by the USDA Forest Service and other agencies. The cards are printed on thin card stock. The fronts feature color action photos; the phrase "California Football" and player identification are printed in block lettering and reversed out on team color-coded borders. In black print on a white background, the backs present biography, player profile, and a fire prevention cartoon starring Smokey. The cards are unnumbered and checklisted below in alphabetical order.

	MINT	NRMT	EXC
COMPLETE SET (16)	12.00	5.50	1.50
COMMON CARD (1-16)	.50	.23	.06
☐ 1 Pat Barnes	2.50	1.10	.30
☐ 2 Na'il Benjamin	.60	.25	.07
☐ 3 Sean Bullard	.50	.23	.06
☐ 4 Je'Rod Cherry	.60	.25	.07
☐ 5 Duane Clemons	1.50	.70	.19
☐ 6 Dante Depaola	.50	.23	.06
☐ 7 Kevin Devine	.50	.23	.06
☐ 8 Keith Gilbertson CO	.50	.23	.06
☐ 9 Andy Jacobs	.50	.23	.06
☐ 10 Ryan Longwell	.50	.23	.06
☐ 11 Ben Lynch	.50	.23	.06
☐ 12 Reynard Rutherford	.50	.23	.06
☐ 13 James Stallworth	.50	.23	.06
☐ 14 Regan Upshaw	2.00	.90	.25
☐ 15 Iheanyi Uwaezuoke	2.00	.90	.25
☐ 16 Brandon Whiting	.50	.23	.06

1989 Clemson

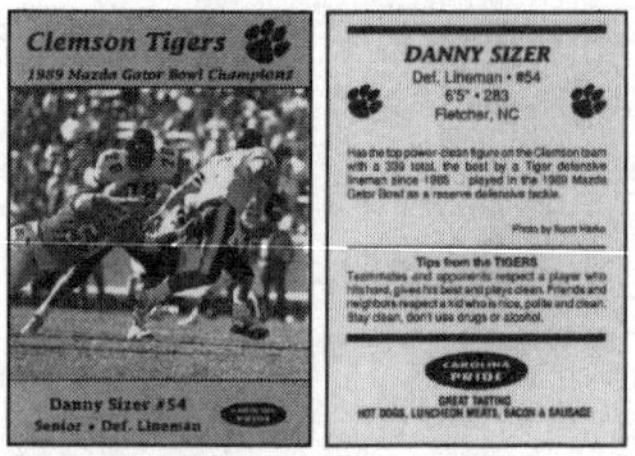

This 32-card standard-size set commemorates the Clemson Tigers as the 1989 Mazda Gator Bowl Champions. It was sponsored by Carolina Pride. The front presents either a posed or action color photo. Two orange bands with black lettering on the top and bottom have the school, player's name, number, classification, and position. The Carolina Pride logo appears in the lower left hand corner and the Tiger pawprint appears in the upper left hand corner. The back has biographical information and a tip from the Tigers in the form of an anti-drug or alcohol message. The cards are unnumbered and are listed below in alphabetical order by subject.

	MINT	NRMT	EXC
COMPLETE SET (32)	20.00	9.00	2.50
COMMON CARD (1-32)	.75	.35	.09
☐ 1 Wally Ake CO	.75	.35	.09
☐ 2 Larry Beckman CO	.75	.35	.09
☐ 3 Mitch Belton 32	.75	.35	.09
☐ 4 Scott Beville 61	.75	.35	.09
☐ 5 Doug Brewster 92	.75	.35	.09
☐ 6 Larry Brinson CO	1.00	.45	.12
☐ 7 Reggie Demps 30	.75	.35	.09
☐ 8 Robin Eaves 44	.75	.35	.09
☐ 9 Barney Farrar CO	.75	.35	.09
☐ 10 Stacy Fields 46	.75	.35	.09
☐ 11 Vance Hammond 90	.75	.35	.09
☐ 12 Eric Harmon 76	.75	.35	.09
☐ 13 Ken Hatfield CO	1.50	.70	.19
☐ 14 Jerome Henderson 36	1.50	.70	.19
☐ 15 Les Herrin CO	.75	.35	.09
☐ 16 Roger Hinshaw CO	.75	.35	.09
☐ 17 John Johnson 12	1.50	.70	.19
☐ 18 Reggie Lawrence 34	.75	.35	.09
☐ 19 Stacy Long 67	.75	.35	.09
☐ 20 Eric Mader 82	.75	.35	.09
☐ 21 Arlington Nunn 39	.75	.35	.09
☐ 22 David Puckett 68	.75	.35	.09
☐ 23 Danny Sizer 54	.75	.35	.09
☐ 24 Robbie Spector 2	.75	.35	.09
☐ 25 Rick Stockstill CO	1.00	.45	.12
☐ 26 Bruce Taylor 6	.75	.35	.09
☐ 27 Doug Thomas 41	.75	.35	.09
☐ 28 The Tiger (Mascot)	.75	.35	.09
☐ 29 Tiger Paw Title Card	.75	.35	.09
☐ 30 Bob Trott CO	.75	.35	.09
☐ 31 Larry Van Der Heyden CO	.75	.35	.09
☐ 32 Richard Wilson CO	.75	.35	.09

1950 C.O.P. Betsy Ross

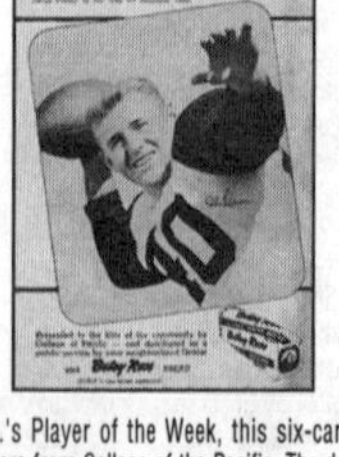

Subtitled C.O.P.'s Player of the Week, this six-card set features outstanding players from College of the Pacific. The date of the set is fixed by the Eddie LeBaron card, which listed him as a senior. The oversized cards measure approximately 5" by 7" and are printed on thin paper stock. The fronts feature black-and-white posed action shots that are tilted slightly to the left and have rounded corners. The

top stripe carries brief biographical information and career highlights. The bottom stripe notes that these cards were distributed "as a public service by your neighborhood Grocer and Betsy Ross Bread." The bread company's logo at the lower right corner rounds out the back. Other cards may belong to this set. The backs are blank and the unnumbered cards are listed below in alphabetical order.

	NRMT	VG-E	GOOD
COMPLETE SET (6)	90.00	40.00	11.00
COMMON CARD (1-6)	10.00	4.50	1.25
☐ 1 Don Campora	10.00	4.50	1.25
☐ 2 Don Hardey	10.00	4.50	1.25
☐ 3 Robert Klein	10.00	4.50	1.25
☐ 4 Eddie LeBaron	40.00	18.00	5.00
☐ 5 Eddie Macon	20.00	9.00	2.50
☐ 6 John Rohde	10.00	4.50	1.25

1990 Colorado Smokey

This 16-card standard-size set was issued to honor the eventual co-National Champion Colorado Buffaloes as well as to promote fire safety. This set was distributed at the final Colorado home game of the 1990 season at Folsom Field. Featured are some of the leading players on the Buffaloes including Eric Bieniemy, Darian Hagan, Charles Johnson, and Butkus Award winner Alfred Williams. The set was issued in a sheet of 16 cards which, when perforated, measure the standard size. The cards feature full-color action photos of the players on the front and a brief biography along with a safety tip featuring the popular safety figure, Smokey the Bear. This unnumbered set has been checklisted below in alphabetical order.

	MINT	NRMT	EXC
COMPLETE SET (16)	18.00	8.00	2.20
COMMON CARD (1-16)	.60	.25	.07
☐ 1 Eric Bieniemy	2.00	.90	.25
☐ 2 Joe Garten	1.00	.45	.12
☐ 3 Darian Hagan	2.00	.90	.25
☐ 4 George Hemingway	.60	.25	.07
☐ 5 Garry Howe	.60	.25	.07
☐ 6 Tim James	.60	.25	.07
☐ 7 Charles Johnson	3.00	1.35	.35
☐ 8 Bill McCartney CO	2.00	.90	.25
☐ 9 Dave McCloughan	1.00	.45	.12
☐ 10 Kanavis McGhee	1.00	.45	.12
☐ 11 Mike Pritchard	5.00	2.20	.60
☐ 12 Tom Rouen	1.00	.45	.12
☐ 13 Michael Simmons	.60	.25	.07
☐ 14 Mark Vander Poel	1.00	.45	.12
☐ 15 Alfred Williams	2.00	.90	.25
☐ 16 Ralphie (Mascot)	.60	.25	.07

1992 Colorado Pepsi

Originally issued in perforated sheets, these 12 standard-size cards feature on their fronts color player posed and action shots set within black borders and framed by a yellowish line. The player's name and position, along with the Pepsi logo, appear underneath the photo. The team name and logo appear above the photo. The plain white back carries the player's name and jersey number at the top, followed below by position, height, weight, class, hometown, major, and career highlights. The cards are unnumbered and checklisted below in alphabetical order.

	MINT	NRMT	EXC
COMPLETE SET (12)	15.00	6.75	1.85
COMMON CARD (1-12)	.75	.35	.09
☐ 1 Greg Biekert	2.00	.90	.25
☐ 3 Ronnie Bradford	1.00	.45	.12
☐ 4 Chad Brown	3.00	1.35	.35
☐ 5 Marcellus Elder	1.00	.45	.12
☐ 6 Deon Figures	2.50	1.10	.30
☐ 7 Jim Hansen	.75	.35	.09
☐ 8 Jack Keys	.75	.35	.09
☐ 9 Bill McCartney CO	2.00	.90	.25
☐ 10 Clint Moles	.75	.35	.09
☐ 11 Jason Perkins	.75	.35	.09
☐ 12 Scott Starr	.75	.35	.09

1993 Colorado Smokey

Originally issued in perforated sheets, these 12 standard-size cards feature on their fronts color player posed and action shots set within black borders and framed by a yellowish line. The player's name and position, along with the Pepsi logo, appear underneath the photo. The team name and logo appear above the photo. The plain white back carries the player's name and jersey number at the top, followed below by position, height, weight, class, hometown, major, and career highlights. The cards are unnumbered and checklisted below in alphabetical order.

	MINT	NRMT	EXC
COMPLETE SET (16)	15.00	6.75	1.85
COMMON CARD (1-16)	1.00	.45	.12
☐ 1 Craig Anderson	1.00	.45	.12
☐ 2 Mitch Berger	1.50	.70	.19
☐ 3 Jeff Brunner	1.00	.45	.12
☐ 4 Dennis Collier	1.00	.45	.12
☐ 5 Dwayne Davis	1.00	.45	.12
☐ 6 Brian Dyet	1.00	.45	.12
☐ 7 Sean Embree	1.00	.45	.12
☐ 8 Garrett Ford	1.00	.45	.12
☐ 9 James Hill	1.00	.45	.12
☐ 10 Charles Johnson	3.00	1.35	.35
☐ 11 Greg Lindsey	1.00	.45	.12
☐ 12 Sam Rogers	1.00	.45	.12
☐ 13 Mark Smith	1.00	.45	.12
☐ 14 Duke Tobin	1.00	.45	.12
☐ 15 Ronnie Woolfork	1.50	.70	.19
☐ 16 Derek Agnew	1.00	.45	.12

1994 Colorado Smokey

Measuring 10 1/4" by 14 1/4", this perforated sheet consists of sixteen standard-size cards arranged in four 4-card rows. On a yellow card face, the fronts feature color action photos inside black-and-white inner borders. Short white diagonal stripes accent the front on the left and right sides. Player information and the slogan "Partners in Fire Prevention" appear at the bottom. The backs present biographical information and a fire prevention cartoon starring Smokey. The cards are unnumbered and checklisted below in alphabetical order.

	MINT	NRMT	EXC
COMPLETE SET (16)	25.00	11.00	3.10
COMMON CARD (1-16)	.75	.35	.09
☐ 1 Blake Anderson	.75	.35	.09
☐ 2 Norm Barnett	.75	.35	.09
☐ 3 Tony Berti	1.25	.55	.16
☐ 4 Ken Browne	.75	.35	.09
☐ 5 Christian Fauria	2.00	.90	.25
☐ 6 Darius Holland	1.25	.55	.16
☐ 7 Chris Hudson	1.25	.55	.16
☐ 8 Ted Johnson	1.50	.70	.19
☐ 9 Vance Joseph	.75	.35	.09
☐ 10 Jon Knutson	.75	.35	.09
☐ 11 Bill McCartney CO	1.50	.70	.19
☐ 12 Erik Mitchell	.75	.35	.09
☐ 13 Kordell Stewart	10.00	4.50	1.25
☐ 14 Derek West	.75	.35	.09
☐ 15 Michael Westbrook	5.00	2.20	.60
☐ 16 Team logo	.75	.35	.09

1973 Colorado State

The 1973 Colorado State football set consists of eight cards, measuring approximately 2 1/2" by 3 3/4". The set was sponsored by Poudre Valley Dairy Foods. The fronts display green-tinted posed action shots with rounded corners and green borders. The words "1973 CSU Football" appear in the top border while the player's name and position are printed in the bottom border. The horizontal backs present the 1973 football schedule. Reportedly, the Stuebbe and Simpson cards are more difficult to obtain because they were given out to the public before hobbyists began to collect the set. Best known among the players is Willie Miller, who played for the Los Angeles Rams. The cards are unnumbered and checklisted below in alphabetical order.

	NRMT-MT	EXC	G-VG
COMPLETE SET (8)	80.00	36.00	10.00
COMMON CARD (1-8)	8.00	3.60	1.00
☐ 1 Wes Cerveny	8.00	3.60	1.00
☐ 2 Mark Driscoll	8.00	3.60	1.00
☐ 3 Jim Kennedy	8.00	3.60	1.00
☐ 4 Greg Kuhn	8.00	3.60	1.00
☐ 5 Willie Miller	20.00	9.00	2.50
☐ 6 Al Simpson SP	12.00	5.50	1.50
☐ 7 Jan Stuebbe SP	12.00	5.50	1.50
☐ 8 Tom Wallace	8.00	3.60	1.00

1987 Duke Police

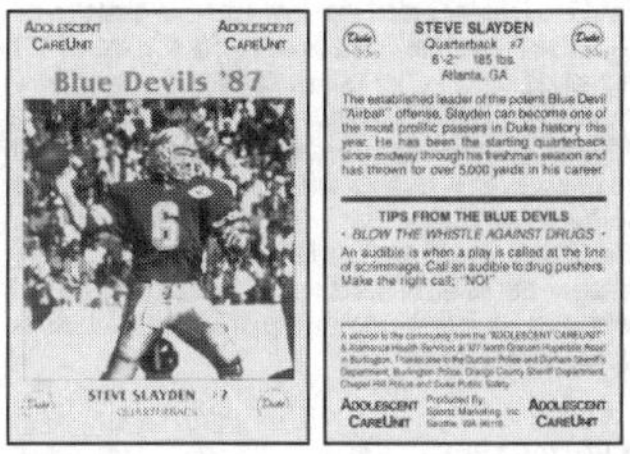

This 16-card, standard-size set features players on Duke University's 1987 Blue Devils football team. The set was distributed to elementary school children in North Carolina by local law enforcement representatives as part of a drug education program. The front has a color action player photo, with Adolescent CareUnit logos in the upper corners and the player's name, uniform number, and position centered beneath the picture. The back has two Duke helmet logos in the upper corners, biographical information, and an anti-drug tip. The cards are unnumbered and checklisted below in alphabetical order.

	MINT	NRMT	EXC
COMPLETE SET (16)	30.00	13.50	3.70
COMMON CARD (1-16)	1.50	.70	.19
☐ 1 Andy Andreasik 60	1.50	.70	.19
☐ 2 Brian Bernard 93	1.50	.70	.19
☐ 3 Bob Calamari 31	1.50	.70	.19
☐ 4 Jason Cooper 22	1.50	.70	.19
☐ 5 Dave Demore 92	1.50	.70	.19
☐ 6 Mike Diminick 21	1.50	.70	.19
☐ 7 Jim Godfrey 56	1.50	.70	.19
☐ 8 Doug Green 5	1.50	.70	.19
☐ 9 Stanley Monk 24	1.50	.70	.19
☐ 10 Chris Port 73	2.00	.90	.25
☐ 11 Steve Ryan 63	1.50	.70	.19
☐ 12 Steve Slayden 7	2.00	.90	.25
☐ 13 Steve Spurrier CO	12.00	5.50	1.50
☐ 14 Dewayne Terry 27	1.50	.70	.19
☐ 15 Fonda Williams 19	1.50	.70	.19
☐ 16 Blue Devil (Mascot)	2.00	.90	.25

1995 FlickBall College Teams

Flickball released a set of 60 college mascot "paper footballs" in 1995. These flickballs were distributed in 6 count blister packs.

	MINT	NRMT	EXC
COMPLETE SET (60)	20.00	9.00	2.50
COMMON CARD (1-60)	.25	.11	.03
☐ 1 Alabama	.50	.23	.06
☐ 2 Auburn	.50	.23	.06
☐ 3 Boston Universary	.25	.11	.03
☐ 4 Boston College	.40	.18	.05
☐ 5 BYU	.40	.18	.05
☐ 6 Citadel	.25	.11	.03
☐ 7 Columbia	.25	.11	.03
☐ 8 Florida	.50	.23	.06
☐ 9 Georgia	.50	.23	.06
☐ 10 Houston	.25	.11	.03
☐ 11 Illinois	.40	.18	.05
☐ 12 Kansas State	.40	.18	.05
☐ 13 Kentucky	.40	.18	.05
☐ 14 Maine	.25	.11	.03
☐ 15 Marquette	.25	.11	.03
☐ 16 Memphis	.25	.11	.03
☐ 17 Michigan	.50	.23	.06
☐ 18 Mississippi	.40	.18	.05
☐ 19 Carolina Greensboro	.25	.11	.03
☐ 20 North Carolina State	.40	.18	.05
☐ 21 Nebraska	.50	.23	.06
☐ 22 New Mexico	.25	.11	.03
☐ 23 North Carolina	.50	.23	.06
☐ 24 Oklahoma State	.40	.18	.05
☐ 25 Pittsburgh	.40	.18	.05
☐ 26 Purdue	.40	.18	.05
☐ 27 Rhode Island	.25	.11	.03
☐ 28 Seton Hall	.25	.11	.03
☐ 29 South Carolina	.40	.18	.05
☐ 30 South Connecticut	.25	.11	.03
☐ 31 St. Johns	.25	.11	.03
☐ 32 Stony Brook	.25	.11	.03
☐ 33 Temple	.25	.11	.03
☐ 34 Tennessee	.50	.23	.06
☐ 35 Tulane	.25	.11	.03
☐ 36 Army	.40	.18	.05
☐ 37 Vanderbilt	.40	.18	.05
☐ 38 Virginia	.40	.18	.05
☐ 39 Wisconsin	.40	.18	.05
☐ 40 Wyoming	.25	.11	.03
☐ 41 Duke	.40	.18	.05
☐ 42 North Carolina Central	.25	.11	.03
☐ 43 Georgia Tech	.40	.18	.05
☐ 44 New York U.	.25	.11	.03
☐ 45 San Francisco State	.25	.11	.03
☐ 46 San Diego State	.25	.11	.03
☐ 47 Wake Forest	.40	.18	.05
☐ 48 Minnesota	.40	.18	.05
☐ 49 Penn State	.50	.23	.06
☐ 50 Villanova	.25	.11	.03
☐ 51 Clemson	.40	.18	.05
☐ 52 Fresno State	.25	.11	.03
☐ 53 Colorado State	.25	.11	.03
☐ 54 LSU	.50	.23	.06
☐ 55 Georgetown	.40	.18	.05
☐ 56 UNC Charlotte	.25	.11	.03
☐ 57 University of San Francisco	.25	.11	.03
☐ 58 Arizona	.50	.23	.06
☐ 59 Florida State	.50	.23	.06
☐ 60 Yale	.25	.11	.03

1973 Florida Gators

This set was issued in a playing card deck box. The cards have rounded corners and the typical playing card format. The fronts feature black-and-white posed photos of helmetless players in their uniforms. A white border surrounds each picture and contains the card number and suit designation in the upper left corner and again, but inverted, in the lower right. The player's name and position initials appear just beneath the photo. The orange backs all feature the "Fighting Gators" logo. The the year of issue, 1973, is included on the schedule card. Since the set is similar to a playing card set, it is arranged just like a card deck and checklisted below accordingly. In the checklist below C means Clubs, D means Diamonds, H means Hearts, S means Spades and JK means Joker. Numbers are assigned to Aces (1), Jacks (11), Queens (12), and Kings (13). The jokers are unnumbered and listed at the end.

	NRMT-MT	EXC	G-VG
COMPLETE SET (54)	100.00	45.00	12.50
COMMON CARD	2.00	.90	.25
☐ 1C Kris Anderson	2.00	.90	.25
☐ 1D David Bowden	2.00	.90	.25
☐ 1H Nat Moore	10.00	4.50	1.25
☐ 1S Doug Dickey CO	3.00	1.35	.35
☐ 2C Gary Padgett	2.00	.90	.25
☐ 2D Tom Dolfi	2.00	.90	.25
☐ 2H Sammy Green	2.00	.90	.25
☐ 2S Scott Nugent	2.00	.90	.25
☐ 3C Joel Parker	2.00	.90	.25
☐ 3D Don Gaffney	2.00	.90	.25
☐ 3H Andy Summers	2.00	.90	.25
☐ 3S Joe Wunderly	2.00	.90	.25
☐ 4C George Nicholas	2.00	.90	.25
☐ 4D Hank Foldberg	5.00	2.20	.60
☐ 4H Jimmy DuBose	2.00	.90	.25
☐ 4S David Starkey	2.00	.90	.25
☐ 5C Buster Morrison	2.00	.90	.25
☐ 5D Mike Williams	2.00	.90	.25
☐ 5H David Hitchcock	2.00	.90	.25
☐ 5S Glenn Cameron	2.00	.90	.25
☐ 6C Mike Moore	2.00	.90	.25
☐ 6D Chan Gailey	2.00	.90	.25
☐ 6H John Williams	2.00	.90	.25
☐ 6S Eddie Sirmons	2.00	.90	.25
☐ 7C Roy Mallory	2.00	.90	.25
☐ 7D Mike Smith	2.00	.90	.25
☐ 7H Glenn Sever	2.00	.90	.25
☐ 7S Ward Eastman	2.00	.90	.25
☐ 8C Lee McGriff	2.00	.90	.25
☐ 8D Carey Geiger	2.00	.90	.25
☐ 8H Andy Wade	2.00	.90	.25
☐ 8S Robbie Davis	2.00	.90	.25
☐ 9C Chris McCoun	2.00	.90	.25

☐ 9D Preston Kendrick	2.00	.90	.25
☐ 9H Jim Revels	2.00	.90	.25
☐ 9S Robby Ball	2.00	.90	.25
☐ 10C Burton Lawless	3.00	1.35	.35
☐ 10D Clint Griffith	2.00	.90	.25
☐ 10H Alvin Butler	5.00	2.20	.60
☐ 10S Thom Clifford	2.00	.90	.25
☐ 11C Jimbo Kynes	2.00	.90	.25
☐ 11D Al Darby	2.00	.90	.25
☐ 11H Hollis Boardman	2.00	.90	.25
☐ 11S Ricky Browne	2.00	.90	.25
☐ 12C Randy Talbot	2.00	.90	.25
☐ 12D Mike Stanfield	2.00	.90	.25
☐ 12H Paul Parker	2.00	.90	.25
☐ 12S John Lacer	2.00	.90	.25
☐ 13C Tyson Sever	2.00	.90	.25
☐ 13D Wayne Fields	2.00	.90	.25
☐ 13H Vince Kendrick	2.00	.90	.25
☐ 13S Ralph Ortega	2.00	.90	.25
☐ J1 Schedule Card	2.00	.90	.25
☐ J2 Joker	2.00	.90	.25

1988 Florida Burger King

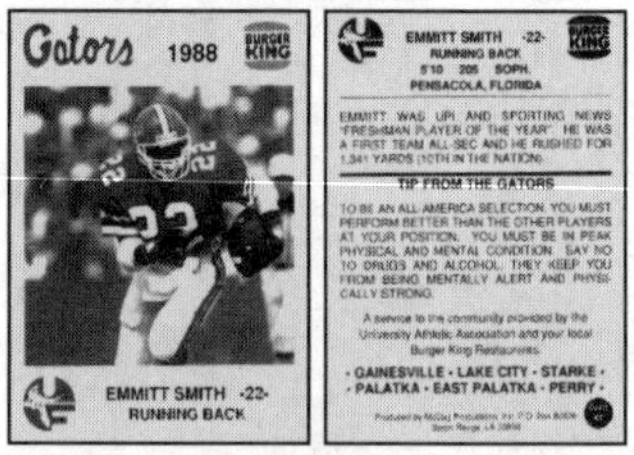

This 16-card standard-size set features then-current football players at the University of Florida. The cards are numbered on the back in the lower right corner. The set was produced by McDag Productions and sponsored by Burger King. The set is also considered to be a police/safety set due to the "Tip from the Gators" on each card back. The Emmitt Smith card from this set has been illegally reprinted; all known reprints (counterfeits) are missing the Burger King logo on the card front. Collectors are urged to be especially cautious when purchasing single Emmitt Smith cards without the rest of the set.

	MINT	NRMT	EXC
COMPLETE SET (16)	70.00	32.00	8.75
COMMON CARD (1-16)	.75	.35	.09
☐ 1 Florida Gators Team	5.00	2.20	.60
☐ 2 Emmitt Smith 22	55.00	25.00	7.00
☐ 3 David Williams 73	1.50	.70	.19
☐ 4 Jeff Roth 96	.75	.35	.09
☐ 5 Rhondy Weston 68	1.00	.45	.12
☐ 6 Stacey Simmons 25	1.00	.45	.12
☐ 7 Huey Richardson 90	1.50	.70	.19
☐ 8 Wayne Williams 23	1.00	.45	.12
☐ 9 Charlie Wright 79	.75	.35	.09
☐ 10 Tracy Daniels 63	.75	.35	.09
☐ 11 Ernie Mills 14	3.00	1.35	.35
☐ 12 Willie McGrady 38	.75	.35	.09
☐ 13 Chris Bromley 52	.75	.35	.09
☐ 14 Louis Oliver 18	2.50	1.10	.30
☐ 15 Galen Hall CO	1.50	.70	.19
☐ 16 Albert the Alligator (Mascot)	.75	.35	.09

1989 Florida

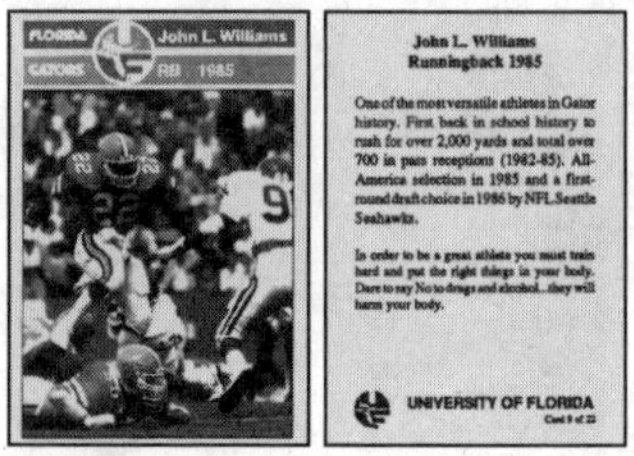

The 1989 Florida Gators football set contains 22 standard-size cards of past players, i.e., all-time Gators. The fronts have vintage or color action photos with white borders; the vertically oriented backs have player profiles. These cards were distributed as a complete set. A safety message is included near the bottom of each reverse along with a card number.

	MINT	NRMT	EXC
COMPLETE SET (22)	18.00	8.00	2.20
COMMON CARD (1-22)	.50	.23	.06
☐ 1 Dale Van Sickle	.50	.23	.06
☐ 2 Cris Collinsworth	1.25	.55	.16
☐ 3 Wilber Marshall	1.50	.70	.19
☐ 4 Jack Youngblood	1.25	.55	.16
☐ 5 Steve Spurrier	6.00	2.70	.75
☐ 6 David Little	.75	.35	.09
☐ 7 Bruce Bennett	.50	.23	.06
☐ 8 Charlie LaPradd	.50	.23	.06
☐ 9 John L. Williams	1.50	.70	.19
☐ 10 Steve Tannen	.75	.35	.09
☐ 11 Neal Anderson	1.50	.70	.19
☐ 12 Larry Dupree	.50	.23	.06
☐ 13 Guy Dennis	.50	.23	.06
☐ 14 Jarvis Williams	.75	.35	.09
☐ 15 Bill Carr	.50	.23	.06
☐ 16 Clifford Charlton	.50	.23	.06
☐ 17 Wes Chandler	1.25	.55	.16
☐ 18 David Galloway	.50	.23	.06
☐ 19 Carlos Alvarez	.50	.23	.06
☐ 20 Lomas Brown	1.25	.55	.16
☐ 21 Larry Smith	.50	.23	.06
☐ 22 Ricky Nattiel	.75	.35	.09

1989 Florida Smokey

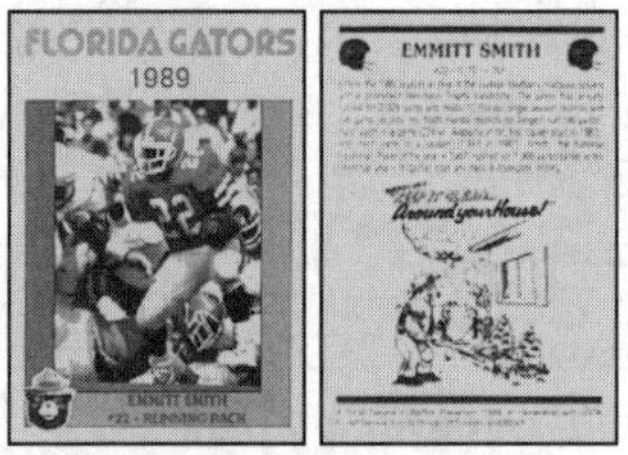

This 16-card standard size set was issued with the cooperation of the USDA Forest Service, the Florida Division of Forestry, and the BDA and features members of the 1989 Florida Gators. The cards feature the words "Florida Gators 1989" on top of an action photo and a biography of the player and a fire prevention cartoon on the back. We have checklisted this set in alphabetical order and put the uniform number next to the player's name. Sets are sometimes found with only 15 cards, missing the Galen Hall card, which was apparently withdrawn after his termination as coach of the Gators. The key card in this set is Emmitt Smith, who would go on to professional success with the Dallas Cowboys.

	MINT	NRMT	EXC
COMPLETE SET (16)	50.00	22.00	6.25
COMMON CARD (1-16)	1.00	.45	.12
☐ 1 Chris Bromley 52	1.00	.45	.12
☐ 2 Richard Fain 28	1.50	.70	.19
☐ 3 John David Francis 7	1.00	.45	.12
☐ 4 Galen Hall CO SP	10.00	4.50	1.25
☐ 5 Tony Lomack 20	1.00	.45	.12
☐ 6 Willie McClendon 5	1.00	.45	.12
☐ 7 Pat Moorer 45	1.00	.45	.12
☐ 8 Kyle Morris 1	1.00	.45	.12
☐ 9 Huey Richardson 90	1.50	.70	.19
☐ 10 Stacey Simmons 25	1.00	.45	.12
☐ 11 Emmitt Smith 22	40.00	18.00	5.00
☐ 12 Richard Starowesky 75	1.00	.45	.12
☐ 13 Kerry Watkins 4	1.00	.45	.12
☐ 14 Albert (Mascot)	1.00	.45	.12
☐ 15 Cheerleaders	1.50	.70	.19
☐ 16 Gator Helmet	1.00	.45	.12

1990 Florida Smokey

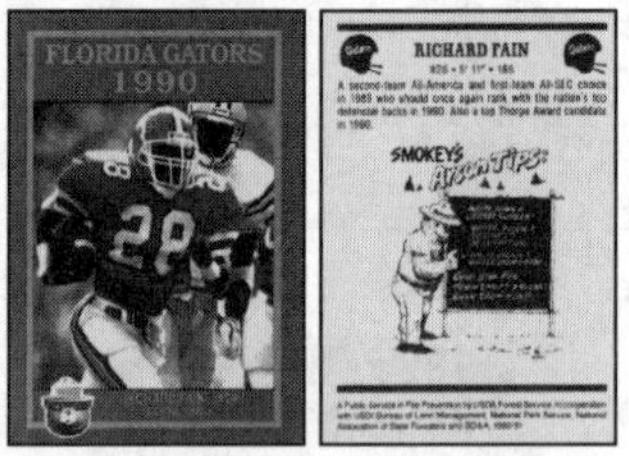

This 12-card standard-size set was sponsored by the USDA Forest Service in conjunction with several other federal agencies. The cards have color action shots, with orange lettering and borders on a purple card face. The back has two Florida helmet icons at the top and features a player profile and a fire prevention cartoon starring Smokey. The cards are unnumbered and checklisted below in alphabetical order, with the uniform number after the name.

	MINT	NRMT	EXC
COMPLETE SET (12)	15.00	6.75	1.85
COMMON CARD (1-12)	1.00	.45	.12
☐ 1 Terence Barber 3	1.00	.45	.12
☐ 2 Chris Bromley 52	1.00	.45	.12
☐ 3 Richard Fain 28	1.25	.55	.16
☐ 4 Willie McClendon 5	1.25	.55	.16
☐ 5 Dexter McNabb 21	1.25	.55	.16
☐ 6 Ernie Mills 14	2.50	1.10	.30
☐ 7 Mark Murray 54	1.00	.45	.12
☐ 8 Jerry Odom 57	1.00	.45	.12
☐ 9 Huey Richardson 90	1.25	.55	.16
☐ 10 Steve Spurrier CO	5.00	2.20	.60
☐ 11 Albert and Alberta (Mascots)	1.00	.45	.12
☐ 12 Mr. Two-Bits (Fan)	1.00	.45	.12

1991 Florida Smokey

This 12-card standard-size set was sponsored by the USDA Forest Service and other agencies. The cards are printed on thin cardboard

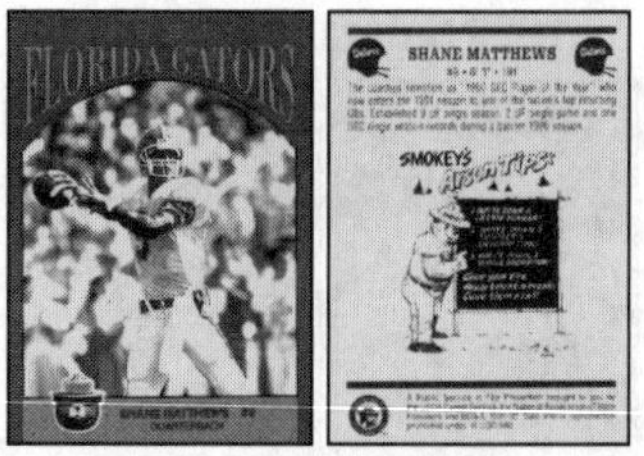

stock. The card fronts are accented in the team's colors (blue and red-orange) and have glossy color action player photos. The top of the pictures is curved to resemble an archway, and the team name follows the curve of the arch. The player's name and position appear in a stripe below the picture. The backs present a player profile and a fire prevention cartoon starring Smokey the Bear. The cards are unnumbered and checklisted below in alphabetical order.

	MINT	NRMT	EXC
COMPLETE SET (12)	15.00	6.75	1.85
COMMON CARD (1-12)	1.00	.45	.12
☐ 1 Ephesians Bartley	1.25	.55	.16
☐ 2 Michael Brandon	1.00	.45	.12
☐ 3 Brad Culpepper	1.50	.70	.19
☐ 4 Arden Czyzewski	1.00	.45	.12
☐ 5 Cal Dixon	1.25	.55	.16
☐ 6 Tre Everett	1.00	.45	.12
☐ 7 Hesham Ismail	1.00	.45	.12
☐ 8 Shane Matthews	2.50	1.10	.30
☐ 9 Steve Spurrier CO	5.00	2.20	.60
☐ 10 Mark White	1.00	.45	.12
☐ 11 Will White	1.00	.45	.12
☐ 12 Albert and Alberta (Mascots)	1.00	.45	.12

1993 Florida State

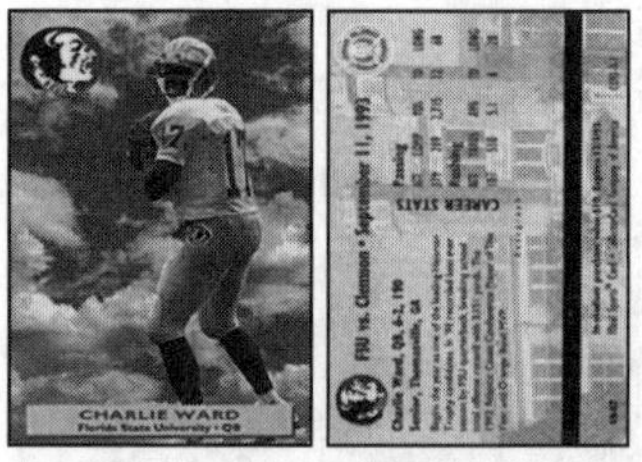

These six football "credit" cards each contained 10.00 of food and merchandise value at FSU concession stands specially equipped with scanners to read the value in the cards. The cards were sold for 15.00 each exclusively through the Florida State Athletic Department and could be purchased individually or as a six-card set. Charlie Ward was the first card issued (for the Seminoles' home opener against Clemson) with an additional card issued at each successive home game. Reportedly only 12,000 sets were produced. The cards were manufactured by CollectorCard of America in Minneapolis. The cards have rounded corners and measure 2 1/8" by 3 3/8". The fronts feature borderless color player cutouts superposed upon a background of sky and clouds. The player's name and position appear within a light blue rectangle at the bottom. The horizontal back has a borderless ghosted color photo of an FSU campus building as the background. At the top are shown the FSU opponent and date for the game at which the card was first available. The player's name, position, height, weight, class, hometown, and 1992 season highlights appear on the left side; his career statistics appear on the right. The black scanning stripe appears across the back near the bottom. The cards are unnumbered and checklisted below in alphabetical order.

	MINT	NRMT	EXC
COMPLETE SET (6)	85.00	38.00	10.50
COMMON CARD (1-6)	6.00	2.70	.75
☐ 1 Bobby Bowden CO	15.00	6.75	1.85
☐ 2 Derrick Brooks	15.00	6.75	1.85
☐ 3 Corey Sawyer	10.00	4.50	1.25
☐ 4 Tamarick Vanover	30.00	13.50	3.70
☐ 5 Charlie Ward	25.00	11.00	3.10
☐ 6 Chief Osceola (Mascot)	6.00	2.70	.75

1996 Florida State

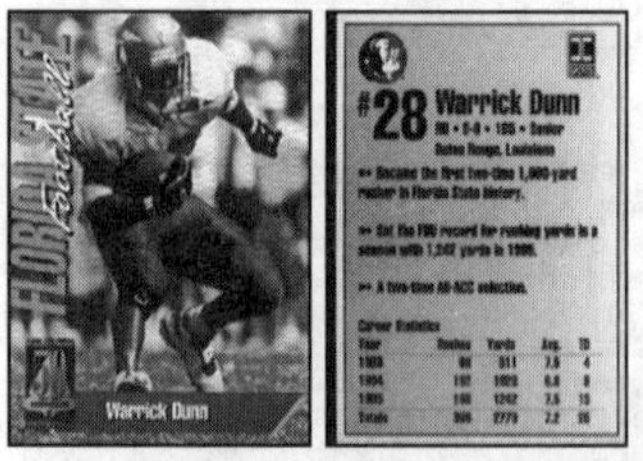

The 1996 Florida State set was produced by Host Communications and handed out in conjunction with program sales made at the various Florida State home games during the 1996 football season. The cards were issued as a complete sheet of 12 cards, which was attached to a cover entitled the "1996 Florida State Football Photo Album". The inside of the "album" had action and practice photos of the Florida State team, while the cover had a defensive action shot with an inset photo of Bobby Bowden. The perforated color front cards measure approximately 3 1/8" by 2 1/2", with the sheet measuring approximately 12 1/2" by 7 1/2". The cards have the players name across the bottom of the card in a red border, while the left side of the card has Florida State in a orange hue with "football" scripted in white over the school name. The backs of the cards are white with black printing and contain the Host Communications logo in the upper right hand corner.The 12 card set is comprised of seniors from the Florida State team, including notable players such as Andre Cooper, Warrick Dunn, Wayne Messam, Connell Spain and Reynard Wilson. The only dual player card in this set features offensive linemen Chad Bates and Todd Fordham. Since the cards are only numbered by jersey number on the back, they are checklisted in alphabetical order below.

	MINT	NRMT	EXC
COMPLETE SET (12)	12.00	5.50	1.50
COMMON CARD (1-12)	.50	.23	.06
☐ 1 Chad Bates Todd Fordham	.50	.23	.06
☐ 2 Scott Bentley	1.00	.45	.12
☐ 3 Byron Capers	.75	.35	.09
☐ 4 James Colzie	.75	.35	.09
☐ 5 Andre Cooper	1.50	.70	.19
☐ 6 Henri Crockett	1.00	.45	.12
☐ 7 Warrick Dunn	4.00	1.80	.50
☐ 8 Sean Hamlet	.75	.35	.09
☐ 9 Sean Liss	.75	.35	.09
☐ 10 Wayne Messam	1.50	.70	.19
☐ 11 Connell Spain	1.00	.45	.12
☐ 12 Reinard Wilson	2.00	.90	.25

1986 Fort Hayes State

This set features 27 standard-size cards. The card fronts feature a player head shot with the team name arcing above. The player's name and position appear below the picture. The back features the player's name, position, and biography at the top with the player's statistics and profile below. The cards are unnumbered and checklisted below in alphabetical order.

	MINT	NRMT	EXC
COMPLETE SET (27)	30.00	13.50	3.70
COMMON CARD (1-27)	1.25	.55	.16
☐ 1 Kelly Barnard	1.25	.55	.16
☐ 2 James Bess	1.25	.55	.16
☐ 3 Eric Busenbark	1.25	.55	.16
☐ 4 Sylvester Butler	1.25	.55	.16
☐ 5 Channing Day	1.25	.55	.16
☐ 6 Edward Faagai	1.25	.55	.16
☐ 7 Randy Fayette	1.25	.55	.16
☐ 8 Gerald Hall	1.25	.55	.16
☐ 9 Mike Hipp	1.25	.55	.16
☐ 10 Sam Holloway	1.25	.55	.16
☐ 11 Howard Hood	1.25	.55	.16
☐ 12 James Jermon	1.25	.55	.16
☐ 13 Randy Jordan	1.25	.55	.16
☐ 14 John Kelsh	1.25	.55	.16
☐ 15 Randy Knox	1.25	.55	.16
☐ 16 Robert Long	1.25	.55	.16
☐ 17 Les Miller	1.25	.55	.16
☐ 18 Frankie Neal	1.25	.55	.16
☐ 19 Paul Nelson	1.25	.55	.16
☐ 20 Darryl Pittman	1.25	.55	.16
☐ 21 Mike Shoff	1.25	.55	.16
☐ 22 Kip Stewart	1.25	.55	.16
☐ 23 Rod Timmons	1.25	.55	.16
☐ 24 Rob Ukleya	1.25	.55	.16
☐ 25 John Vincent CO	1.25	.55	.16
☐ 26 Rick Wheeler	1.25	.55	.16
☐ 27 Mike Worth	1.25	.55	.16

1987 Fresno State Burger King

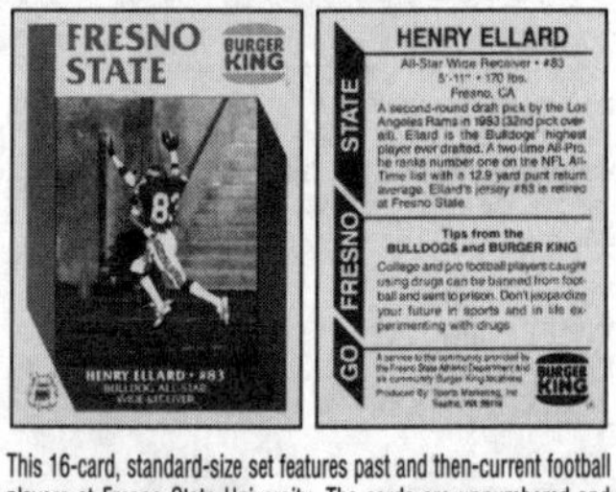

This 16-card, standard-size set features past and then-current football players at Fresno State University. The cards are unnumbered and hence are listed below in uniform number order. The set was produced by Sports Marketing Inc. and sponsored by Burger King. The set is also considered to be a police/safety set due to the "Tip from the Bulldogs" on each card back.

	MINT	NRMT	EXC
COMPLETE SET (16)	25.00	11.00	3.10
COMMON CARD (1-16)	1.50	.70	.19

☐ 1 Gene Taylor	1.50	.70	.19
☐ 5 Michael Stewart	2.00	.90	.25
☐ 9 Kevin Sweeney	2.00	.90	.25
☐ 12 Eric Buechele	1.50	.70	.19
☐ 19 Rod Webster	1.50	.70	.19
☐ 26 Kelly Skipper	1.50	.70	.19
☐ 27 Barry Belli	1.50	.70	.19
☐ 32 Kelly Brooks	1.50	.70	.19
☐ 45 David Grayson	2.00	.90	.25
☐ 67 Jethro Franklin	1.50	.70	.19
☐ 71 Jeff Truschel	1.50	.70	.19
☐ 80 John O'Leary	1.50	.70	.19
☐ 81 Stephen Baker	3.00	1.35	.35
☐ 83 Henry Ellard	6.00	2.70	.75
☐ 86 Stephone Paige	4.00	1.80	.50
☐ NNO Jim Sweeney CO	3.00	1.35	.35

1989 Fresno State Smokey

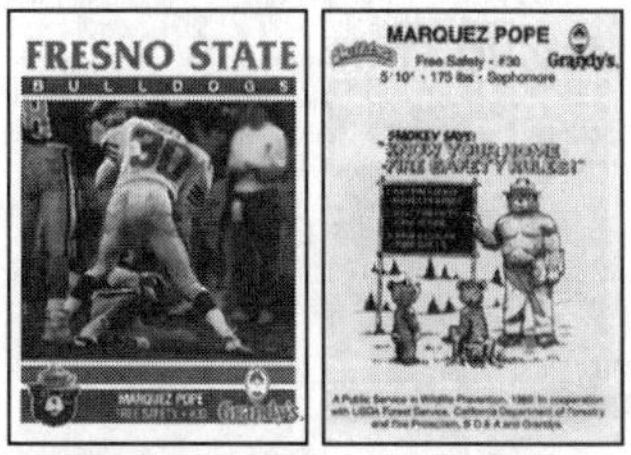

This unnumbered 16-card set measures the standard size. The set was sponsored by the USDA Forest Service and issued with the cooperation of Grandy's restaurants. The fronts feature a color player photo bounded on top and bottom by red and blue-colored strips. At the bottom the player's name, position, and jersey number are sandwiched between the Smokey the Bear picture and Grandy's logo. The back has biographical information and a public service announcement (with cartoon) concerning fire prevention along with the year of issued -- 1989.

	MINT	NRMT	EXC
COMPLETE SET (16)	15.00	6.75	1.85
COMMON CARD (1-16)	1.00	.45	.12
☐ 1 Mark Barsotti	1.50	.70	.19
☐ 2 Rich Bartlewski	1.00	.45	.12
☐ 3 Ron Cox	2.50	1.10	.30
☐ 4 Myron Jones	1.00	.45	.12
☐ 5 Steve Loop	1.00	.45	.12
☐ 6 Fil Lujan	1.00	.45	.12
☐ 7 Darrel Martin	1.00	.45	.12
☐ 8 Lance Oberparleiter	1.00	.45	.12
☐ 9 Dwight Pickens	1.00	.45	.12
☐ 10 Marquez Pope	3.00	1.35	.35
☐ 11 Nick Ruggeroli	1.00	.45	.12
☐ 12 Jim Sweeney CO	1.50	.70	.19
☐ 13 Jeff Thiesen	1.00	.45	.12
☐ 14 Paul Vial	1.00	.45	.12
☐ 15 James Williams	1.50	.70	.19
☐ 16 Bulldog Stadium	1.00	.45	.12

1990 Fresno State Smokey

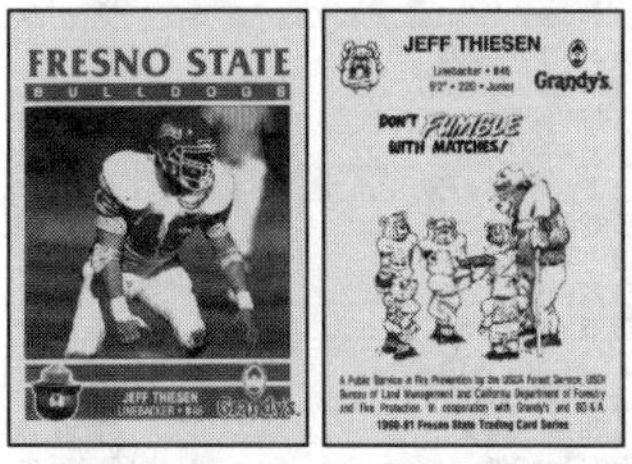

This unnumbered, 16-card set measures the standard size. The set was sponsored by the USDA Forest Service and issued with the cooperation of Grandy's and the BDA. The front features an action color photo, bounded on top and bottom by red and purple strips. At the bottom the player's name, position, and jersey number are sandwiched between the Smokey the Bear picture and Grandy's logo. The back has biographical information and a public service announcement (with cartoon) concerning fire prevention. Future NFL players included in this set are Ron Cox, Aaron Craver, Marquez Pope, and James Williams.

	MINT	NRMT	EXC
COMPLETE SET (16)	15.00	6.75	1.85
COMMON CARD (1-16)	1.00	.45	.12
☐ 1 Mark Barsotti	1.25	.55	.16
☐ 2 Ron Cox	2.00	.90	.25
☐ 3 Aaron Craver	2.00	.90	.25
☐ 4 DeVonne Edwards	1.00	.45	.12
☐ 5 Courtney Griffin	1.00	.45	.12
☐ 6 Jesse Hardwick	1.00	.45	.12
☐ 7 Melvin Johnson	1.00	.45	.12
☐ 8 Brian Lasho	1.00	.45	.12
☐ 9 Kelvin Means	1.00	.45	.12
☐ 10 Marquez Pope	2.50	1.10	.30
☐ 11 Zack Rix	1.00	.45	.12
☐ 12 Nick Ruggeroli	1.00	.45	.12
☐ 13 Jim Sweeney CO	1.50	.70	.19
☐ 14 Erick Tanuvasa	1.00	.45	.12
☐ 15 Jeff Thiesen	1.00	.45	.12
☐ 16 James Williams	1.25	.55	.16

1988 Georgia McDag

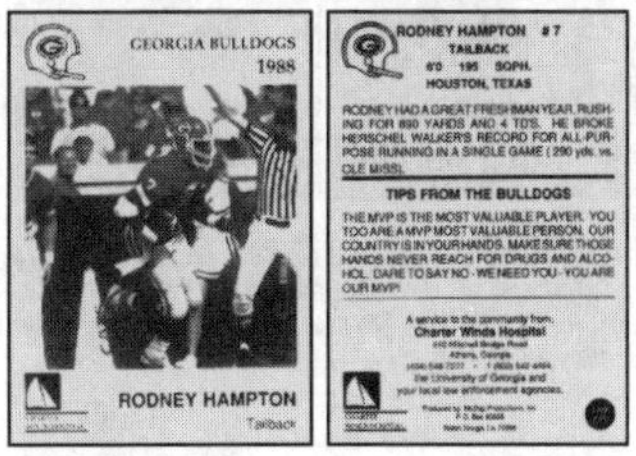

This 16-card set features then-current football players at the University of Georgia. The cards measure approximately 2 1/2" by 3 1/2". The set was produced by McDag Productions. The set is also considered to be a police/safety set due to the "Tip from the Bulldogs" on each card back. The key card in the set is Rodney Hampton.

	MINT	NRMT	EXC
COMPLETE SET (16)	20.00	9.00	2.50
COMMON CARD (1-16)	1.00	.45	.12
☐ 1 UGA IV (Mascot)	1.00	.45	.12
☐ 2 Vince Dooley AD/CO	3.00	1.35	.35
☐ 3 Steve Crumley	1.00	.45	.12
☐ 4 Aaron Chubb	1.00	.45	.12
☐ 5 Keith Henderson	2.00	.90	.25
☐ 6 Steve Harmon	1.00	.45	.12
☐ 7 Terrie Webster	1.00	.45	.12
☐ 8 John Kasay	3.00	1.35	.35
☐ 9 Wayne Johnson	1.00	.45	.12
☐ 10 Tim Worley	2.00	.90	.25
☐ 11 Wycliffe Lovelace	1.00	.45	.12
☐ 12 Brent Collins	1.00	.45	.12
☐ 13 Vince Guthrie	1.00	.45	.12
☐ 14 Todd Wheeler	1.00	.45	.12
☐ 15 Bill Goldberg	1.00	.45	.12
☐ 16 Rodney Hampton	8.00	3.60	1.00

1989 Georgia 200

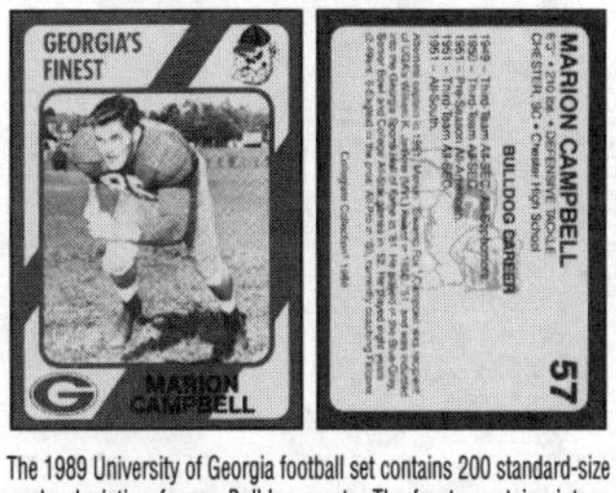

The 1989 University of Georgia football set contains 200 standard-size cards, depicting former Bulldog greats. The fronts contain vintage photos; the horizontally oriented backs feature player profiles. Both sides have red borders. The cards were distributed in sets and in poly packs. These cards were printed on very thin stock. This set is notable for its inclusion of several Herschel Walker cards.

	MINT	NRMT	EXC
COMPLETE SET (200)	18.00	8.00	2.20
COMMON CARD (1-200)	.10	.05	.01
☐ 1 Vince Dooley AD	.20	.09	.03
☐ 2 Ivy M. Shiver	.10	.05	.01
☐ 3 Vince Dooley CO	.20	.09	.03
☐ 4 Vince Dooley CO	.20	.09	.03
☐ 5 Ray Goff CO	.20	.09	.03
☐ 6 Ray Goff CO	.20	.09	.03
☐ 7 Wally Butts CO	.20	.09	.03
☐ 8 Wally Butts CO	.20	.09	.03
☐ 9 Herschel Walker	.75	.35	.09
☐ 10 Frank Sinkwich	.40	.18	.05
☐ 11 Bob McWhorter	.10	.05	.01
☐ 12 Joe Bennett	.10	.05	.01
☐ 13 Dan Edwards	.10	.05	.01
☐ 14 Tom A. Nash	.10	.05	.01
☐ 15 Herb Maffett	.10	.05	.01
☐ 16 Ralph Maddox	.10	.05	.01
☐ 17 Vernon Smith	.10	.05	.01
☐ 18 Bill Hartman Jr.	.10	.05	.01
☐ 19 Frank Sinkwich	.20	.09	.03
☐ 20 Joe O'Malley	.10	.05	.01
☐ 21 Mike Castronis	.10	.05	.01
☐ 22 Aschel M. Day	.10	.05	.01
☐ 23 Herb St. John	.10	.05	.01
☐ 24 Craig Hertwig	.10	.05	.01
☐ 25 John Rauch	.20	.09	.03
☐ 26 Harry Babcock	.10	.05	.01
☐ 27 Bruce Kemp	.10	.05	.01
☐ 28 Pat Dye	.20	.09	.03
☐ 29 Fran Tarkenton	1.00	.45	.12
☐ 30 Larry Kohn	.10	.05	.01
☐ 31 Ray Rissmiller	.10	.05	.01
☐ 32 George Patton	.20	.09	.03
☐ 33 Mixon Robinson	.10	.05	.01
☐ 34 Lynn Hughes	.10	.05	.01
☐ 35 Bill Stanfill	.20	.09	.03
☐ 36 Robert Dicks	.10	.05	.01
☐ 37 Lynn Hunnicutt	.10	.05	.01
☐ 38 Tommy Lyons	.10	.05	.01
☐ 39 Royce Smith	.10	.05	.01
☐ 40 Steve Greer	.10	.05	.01
☐ 41 Randy Johnson	.40	.18	.05
☐ 42 Mike Wilson	.10	.05	.01
☐ 43 Joel Parrish	.10	.05	.01
☐ 44 Ben Zambiasi	.20	.09	.03
☐ 45 Allan Leavitt	.10	.05	.01
☐ 46 George Collins	.10	.05	.01
☐ 47 Rex Robinson	.10	.05	.01
☐ 48 Scott Woerner	.10	.05	.01
☐ 49 Herschel Walker	.75	.35	.09
☐ 50 Bob Burns	.10	.05	.01
☐ 51 Jimmy Payne	.10	.05	.01
☐ 52 Fred Brown	.10	.05	.01
☐ 53 Kevin Butler	.20	.09	.03
☐ 54 Don Porterfield	.10	.05	.01
☐ 55 Mac McWhorter	.10	.05	.01
☐ 56 John Little	.10	.05	.01
☐ 57 Marion Campbell	.40	.18	.05
☐ 58 Zeke Bratkowski	.40	.18	.05
☐ 59 Buck Belue	.20	.09	.03
☐ 60 Duward Pennington	.10	.05	.01
☐ 61 Lamar Davis	.10	.05	.01
☐ 62 Steve Wilson	.10	.05	.01
☐ 63 Leman L. Rosenberg	.10	.05	.01
☐ 64 Dennis Hughes	.10	.05	.01
☐ 65 Wayne Radloff	.10	.05	.01
☐ 66 Lindsay Scott	.20	.09	.03
☐ 67 Wayne Swinford	.10	.05	.01
☐ 68 Kim Stephens	.10	.05	.01
☐ 69 Willie McClendon	.20	.09	.03
☐ 70 Ron Jenkins	.10	.05	.01
☐ 71 Jeff Lewis	.10	.05	.01
☐ 72 Larry Rakestraw	.10	.05	.01
☐ 73 Spike Jones	.20	.09	.03
☐ 74 Tom Nash Jr.	.10	.05	.01
☐ 75 Vassa Cate	.10	.05	.01
☐ 76 Theron Sapp	.20	.09	.03
☐ 77 Claude Hipps	.20	.09	.03
☐ 78 Charley Trippi	.40	.18	.05
☐ 79 Mike Weaver	.10	.05	.01
☐ 80 Anderson Johnson	.10	.05	.01
☐ 81 Matt Robinson	.20	.09	.03
☐ 82 Bill Krug	.10	.05	.01
☐ 83 Todd Wheeler	.10	.05	.01
☐ 84 Mack Guest	.10	.05	.01
☐ 85 Frank Ros	.10	.05	.01
☐ 86 Jeff Hipp	.10	.05	.01
☐ 87 Milton Leathers	.10	.05	.01
☐ 88 George Morton	.10	.05	.01
☐ 89 Jim Broadway	.10	.05	.01
☐ 90 Tim Morrison	.10	.05	.01
☐ 91 Homer Key	.10	.05	.01
☐ 92 Richard Tardits	.20	.09	.03
☐ 93 Tommy Thurson	.10	.05	.01
☐ 94 Bob Kelley	.10	.05	.01
☐ 95 Bob McWhorter	.10	.05	.01
☐ 96 Vernon Smith	.10	.05	.01
☐ 97 Eddie Weaver	.10	.05	.01
☐ 98 Bill Stanfill	.20	.09	.03
☐ 99 Scott Williams	.10	.05	.01
☐ 100 Checklist Card	.10	.05	.01
☐ 101 Len Hauss	.20	.09	.03
☐ 102 Jim Griffith	.10	.05	.01
☐ 103 Nat Dye	.10	.05	.01
☐ 104 Quinton Lumpkin	.10	.05	.01
☐ 105 Mike Garrett	.10	.05	.01
☐ 106 Glynn Harrison	.10	.05	.01
☐ 107 Aaron Chubb	.10	.05	.01
☐ 108 John Brantley	.10	.05	.01
☐ 109 Pat Hodgson	.10	.05	.01
☐ 110 Guy McIntyre	.40	.18	.05
☐ 111 Keith Harris	.10	.05	.01
☐ 112 Mike Cavan	.10	.05	.01
☐ 113 Kevin Jackson	.10	.05	.01
☐ 114 Jim Cagle	.10	.05	.01
☐ 115 Charles Whittemore	.10	.05	.01
☐ 116 Graham Batchelor	.10	.05	.01
☐ 117 Art DeCarlo	.20	.09	.03
☐ 118 Kendall Keith	.10	.05	.01
☐ 119 Jeff Pyburn	.20	.09	.03
☐ 120 James Ray	.10	.05	.01
☐ 121 Mack Burroughs	.10	.05	.01
☐ 122 Jimmy Vickers	.10	.05	.01
☐ 123 Charley Britt	.10	.05	.01
☐ 124 Matt Braswell	.10	.05	.01
☐ 125 Jake Richardson	.10	.05	.01
☐ 126 Ronnie Stewart	.10	.05	.01
☐ 127 Tim Crowe	.10	.05	.01
☐ 128 Troy Sadowski	.10	.05	.01
☐ 129 Robert Honeycutt	.10	.05	.01
☐ 130 Warren Gray	.10	.05	.01
☐ 131 David Guthrie	.10	.05	.01
☐ 132 John Lastinger	.20	.09	.03
☐ 133 Chip Wisdom	.10	.05	.01
☐ 134 Butch Box	.10	.05	.01
☐ 135 Tony Cushenberry	.10	.05	.01
☐ 136 Vince Guthrie	.10	.05	.01
☐ 137 Floyd Reid Jr.	.20	.09	.03
☐ 138 Mark Hodge	.10	.05	.01
☐ 139 Joe Happe	.10	.05	.01
☐ 140 Al Bodine	.10	.05	.01
☐ 141 Gene Chandler	.10	.05	.01
☐ 142 Tommy Lawhorne	.10	.05	.01
☐ 143 Bobby Walden	.20	.09	.03
☐ 144 Douglas McFalls	.10	.05	.01
☐ 145 Jim Milo	.10	.05	.01
☐ 146 Billy Payne	.75	.35	.09
☐ 147 Paul Holmes	.10	.05	.01
☐ 148 Bob Clemens	.10	.05	.01
☐ 149 Kenny Sims	.10	.05	.01
☐ 150 Reid Moseley Jr.	.10	.05	.01
☐ 151 Tim Callaway	.10	.05	.01
☐ 152 Rusty Russell	.10	.05	.01
☐ 153 Jim McCollough	.10	.05	.01
☐ 154 Wally Williamson	.10	.05	.01
☐ 155 John Bond	.10	.05	.01
☐ 156 Charley Trippi	.40	.18	.05
☐ 157 The Play (Lindsay Scott)	.20	.09	.03
☐ 158 Joe Boland	.10	.05	.01
☐ 159 Michael Babb	.10	.05	.01
☐ 160 Jimmy Poulos	.10	.05	.01
☐ 161 Chris McCarthy	.10	.05	.01
☐ 162 Billy Mixon	.10	.05	.01
☐ 163 Dicky Clark	.10	.05	.01
☐ 164 David Rholetter	.10	.05	.01
☐ 165 Chuck Heard	.10	.05	.01
☐ 166 Pat Field	.10	.05	.01
☐ 167 Preston Ridlehuber	.10	.05	.01
☐ 168 Heyward Allen	.10	.05	.01
☐ 169 Kirby Moore	.10	.05	.01
☐ 170 Chris Welton	.10	.05	.01
☐ 171 Bill McKenny	.10	.05	.01
☐ 172 Steve Boswell	.10	.05	.01
☐ 173 Bob Towns	.10	.05	.01
☐ 174 Anthony Towns	.10	.05	.01
☐ 175 Porter Payne	.10	.05	.01
☐ 176 Bobby Garrard	.10	.05	.01
☐ 177 Jack Griffith	.10	.05	.01
☐ 178 Herschel Walker	.75	.35	.09
☐ 179 Andy Perhach	.10	.05	.01
☐ 180 Dr. Charles Herty CO	.10	.05	.01
☐ 181 Kent Lawrence	.20	.09	.03
☐ 182 David McKnight	.10	.05	.01
☐ 183 Joe Tereshinski Jr.	.10	.05	.01
☐ 184 Cicero Lucas	.10	.05	.01
☐ 185 Glenn(Pop) Warner CO	.20	.09	.03
☐ 186 Tony Flack	.10	.05	.01
☐ 187 Kevin Butler	.20	.09	.03
☐ 188 Bill Mitchell	.10	.05	.01
☐ 189 Poulos vs. Tech (Jimmy Poulos)	.10	.05	.01
☐ 190 Pete Case	.20	.09	.03
☐ 191 Pete Tinsley	.10	.05	.01
☐ 192 Joe Tereshinski	.20	.09	.03
☐ 193 Jimmy Harper	.10	.05	.01
☐ 194 Don Leebern	.10	.05	.01
☐ 195 Harry Mehre CO	.10	.05	.01
☐ 196 Retired Jerseys (Herschel Walker, Theron Sapp, Charley Trippi, and Frank Sinkwich)	.40	.18	.05
☐ 197 Terrie Webster	.10	.05	.01
☐ 198 George Woodruff CO	.10	.05	.01
☐ 199 First Georgia Team (1892 Team Photo)	.10	.05	.01
☐ 200 Checklist Card	.10	.05	.01

1989 Georgia Police

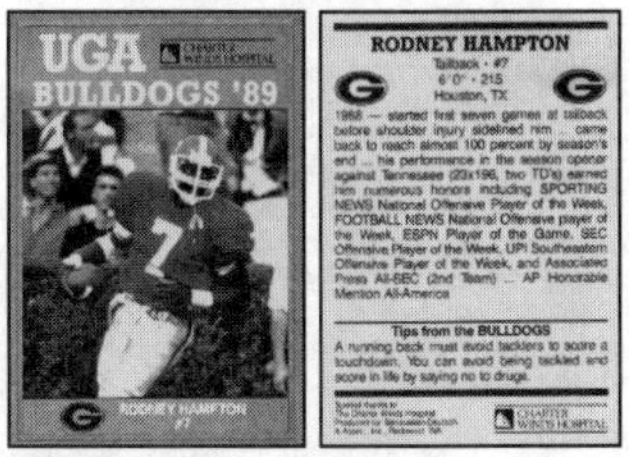

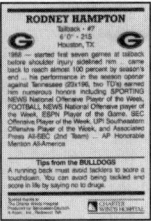

This 16-card set was sponsored by Charter Winds Hospital. The cards were issued on an uncut sheet with four rows of four cards each; if cut, the cards would measure the standard size. The color action photos on the fronts are bordered in gray, and card face itself is red. The words "UGA Bulldogs '89" appear in white lettering above the picture. The backs have biography, career summary, and "Tips from the Bulldogs" in the form of anti-drug or alcohol messages. The cards are unnumbered and checklisted below in alphabetical order, with the uniform number after the name. Again, Rodney Hampton is the key card in this set.

	MINT	NRMT	EXC
COMPLETE SET (16)	15.00	6.75	1.85
COMMON CARD (1-16)	.75	.35	.09
☐ 1 Hiawatha Berry 58	.75	.35	.09
☐ 2 Brian Cleveland 37	.75	.35	.09
☐ 3 Demetrius Douglas 53	.75	.35	.09
☐ 4 Alphonso Ellis 33	.75	.35	.09

☐ 5 Ray Goff CO	1.00	.45	.12
☐ 6 Bill Goldberg 95	.75	.35	.09
☐ 7 Rodney Hampton 7	6.00	2.70	.75
☐ 8 David Hargett 25	.75	.35	.09
☐ 9 Joey Hester 1	.75	.35	.09
☐ 10 John Kasay 3	2.00	.90	.25
☐ 11 Mo Lewis 57	3.00	1.35	.35
☐ 12 Arthur Marshall 12	1.50	.70	.19
☐ 13 Curt Mull 50	.75	.35	.09
☐ 14 Ben Smith 26	1.50	.70	.19
☐ 15 Greg Talley 11	.75	.35	.09
☐ 16 Kirk Warner 83	.75	.35	.09

1990 Georgia Police

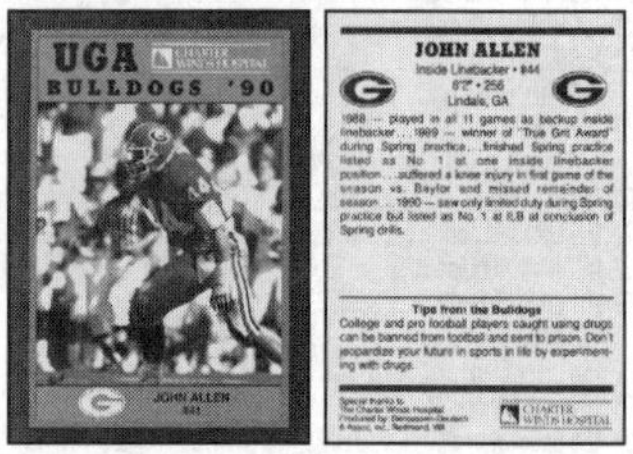

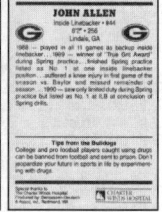

This 14-card standard size set was sponsored by Charter Winds Hospital and features the University of Georgia Bulldogs. The front design has red stripes above and below the color action player photo, with gray borders on a black card face. The back has biographical information, player profile, and "Tips from the Bulldogs" in the form of anti-drug and alcohol messages. The cards are unnumbered and checklisted below in alphabetical order, with the uniform number after the name.

	MINT	NRMT	EXC
COMPLETE SET (14)	10.00	4.50	1.25
COMMON CARD (1-14)	.75	.35	.09
☐ 1 John Allen 44	.75	.35	.09
☐ 2 Brian Cleveland 37	.75	.35	.09
☐ 3 Norman Cowins 59	.75	.35	.09
☐ 4 Alphonso Ellis 33	.75	.35	.09
☐ 5 Ray Goff CO	1.00	.45	.12
☐ 6 David Hargett 25	.75	.35	.09
☐ 7 Sean Hunnings 6	.75	.35	.09
☐ 8 Preston Jones 14	1.00	.45	.12
☐ 9 John Kasay 3	1.50	.70	.19
☐ 10 Arthur Marshall 12	1.25	.55	.16
☐ 11 Jack Swan 76	.75	.35	.09
☐ 12 Greg Talley 11	.75	.35	.09
☐ 13 Lemonte Tellis 77	.75	.35	.09
☐ 14 Chris Wilson 16	.75	.35	.09

1991 Georgia Police

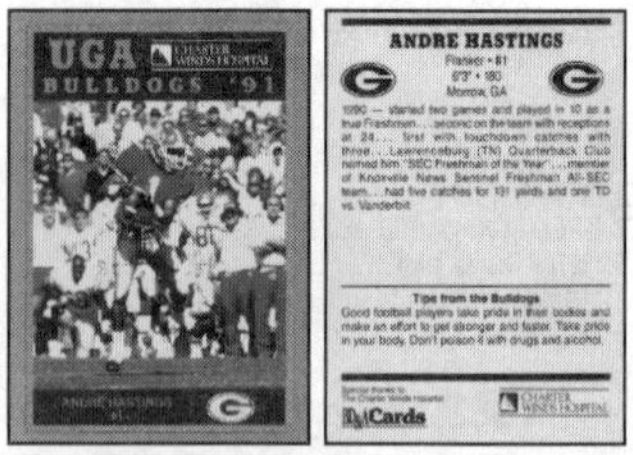

The 1991 Georgia Bulldog set was sponsored by Charter Winds Hospital, and its company logo appears on both sides of the cards. The cards measure the standard size and were issued on an unperforated sheet. Fronts feature a mix of glossy color action or posed player photos, with a gray border stripe on a red card face. The words "UGA Bulldogs '91" appear in a black stripe above the picture, while player identification is given in a black stripe below the picture. The backs have biography, career summary, and "Tips from the Bulldogs" in the form of anti-drug or alcohol messages. The cards are unnumbered and checklisted below in alphabetical order. The key card in the set is Garrison Hearst.

	MINT	NRMT	EXC
COMPLETE SET (16)	15.00	6.75	1.85
COMMON CARD (1-16)	.75	.35	.09
☐ 1 John Allen	.75	.35	.09
☐ 2 Chuck Carswell	.75	.35	.09
☐ 3 Russell DeFoor	.75	.35	.09
☐ 4 Ray Goff CO	1.00	.45	.12
☐ 5 David Hargett	.75	.35	.09
☐ 6 Andre Hastings	2.50	1.10	.30
☐ 7 Garrison Hearst	6.00	2.70	.75
☐ 8 Arthur Marshall	1.00	.45	.12
☐ 9 Kevin Maxwell	.75	.35	.09
☐ 10 DeWayne Simmons	.75	.35	.09
☐ 11 Jack Swan	.75	.35	.09
☐ 12 Greg Talley	.75	.35	.09
☐ 13 Lemonte Tellis	.75	.35	.09
☐ 14 Chris Wilson	.75	.35	.09
☐ 15 George Wynn	.75	.35	.09
☐ 16 UGA V (Mascot)	.75	.35	.09

1992 Georgia Police

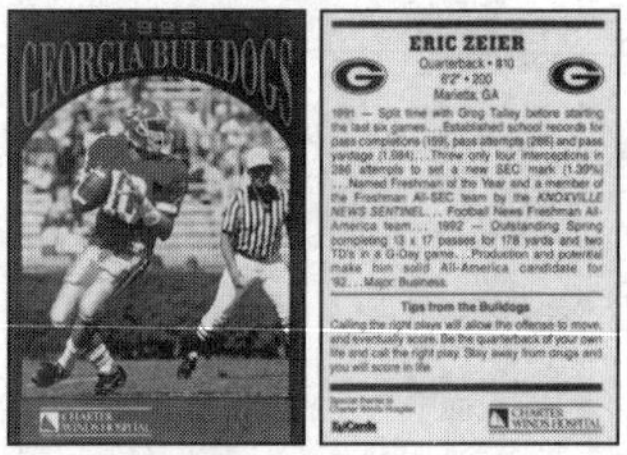

This 15-card standard-size set was sponsored by Charter Winds Hospital and produced by BD and A cards. The fronts feature color action player photos against a black card face. The top of the picture is arched, and the year and words "Georgia Bulldogs" are printed in red above the arch. The player's name is printed in a gray stripe at the bottom. The backs are white with black print and contain career highlights and "Tips from the Bulldogs." Sponsor logos appear at the bottom. The set features Eric Zeier and Garrison Hearst on early college cards.

	MINT	NRMT	EXC
COMPLETE SET (15)	12.00	5.50	1.50
COMMON CARD (1-15)	.50	.23	.06
☐ 1 Mitch Davis	.60	.25	.07
☐ 2 Damon Evans	.50	.23	.06
☐ 3 Torrey Evans	.50	.23	.06
☐ 4 Ray Goff CO	.60	.25	.07
☐ 5 Andre Hastings	2.00	.90	.25
☐ 6 Garrison Hearst	4.00	1.80	.50
☐ 7 Donnie Maib	.50	.23	.06
☐ 8 Alec Millen	.50	.23	.06
☐ 9 Shannon Mitchell	.60	.25	.07
☐ 10 Mack Strong	1.00	.45	.12
☐ 11 Jack Swan	.50	.23	.06
☐ 12 UGA (Mascot)	.50	.23	.06
☐ 13 Bernard Williams	.60	.25	.07
☐ 14 Chris Wilson	.50	.23	.06
☐ 15 Eric Zeier	5.00	2.20	.60

1993 Georgia Police

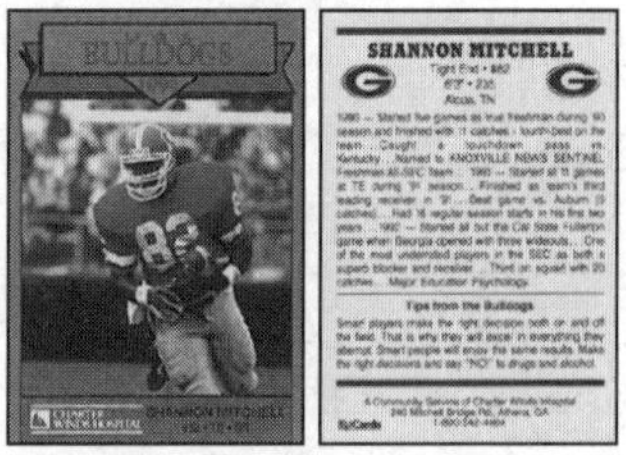

Originally issued in perforated sheets, this 16-card set was sponsored by Charter Winds Hospital and produced by BD and A cards. The cards measure the standard size. The fronts feature color action and posed player photos against a red card face. The year and words "Georgia Bulldogs" are printed in gray lettering above the photo. The player's name, jersey number, position, and class are printed in a gray stripe at the bottom. The plain white backs carry the player's name, position, jersey number, height, weight, and hometown at the top, followed below by career highlights and "Tips from the Bulldogs." The cards are unnumbered and checklisted below in alphabetical order. The set features an early card of Terrell Davis.

	MINT	NRMT	EXC
COMPLETE SET (16)	18.00	8.00	2.20
COMMON CARD (1-16)	.50	.23	.06
☐ 1 Scot Armstrong	.50	.23	.06
☐ 2 Brian Bohannon	.50	.23	.06
☐ 3 Carlo Butler	.50	.23	.06
☐ 4 Charlie Clemons	.50	.23	.06
☐ 5 Mitch Davis	.60	.25	.07
☐ 6 Terrell Davis	10.00	4.50	1.25
☐ 7 Randall Godfrey	1.00	.45	.12
☐ 8 Ray Goff CO	.60	.25	.07
☐ 9 Frank Harvey	.50	.23	.06
☐ 10 Travis Jones	.50	.23	.06
☐ 11 Shannon Mitchell	.50	.23	.06
☐ 12 Greg Tremble	.50	.23	.06
☐ 13 Bernard Williams	.60	.25	.07
☐ 14 Chad Wilson	.50	.23	.06
☐ 15 Eric Zeier	4.00	1.80	.50
☐ 16 UGA (Mascot)	.50	.23	.06

1991 Georgia Southern

Produced by TJR Marketing, this 45-card set features All-American players and school record holders from Georgia Southern University. Twenty-five hundred numbered sets were printed and sold to the public; each set was accompanied by a certificate of limited edition. One hundred numbered and uncut sheets were also offered. An additional 275 proof sets and another 100 unnumbered uncut sheets with different backs were produced. The 275 proof sets differ from the 2500 limited sets in that the former have a light blue (rather than a dark blue) back border and the word "proof" on the card backs. The fronts feature a full-color photo within a small yellow border enclosed

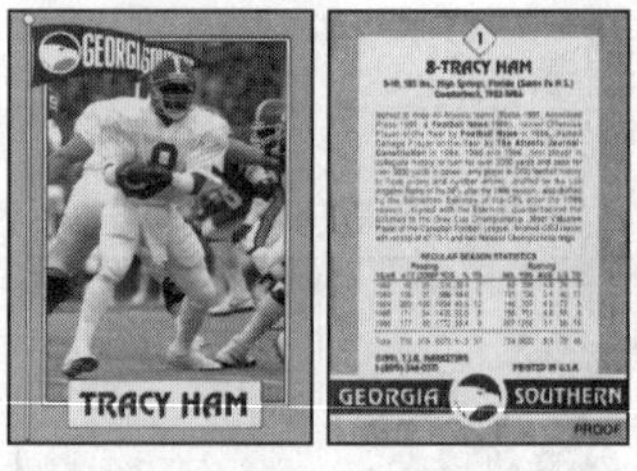

in a turquoise border. A yellow flag pole with a Georgia Southern flag highlights the left side of the card while the player's name is in a white box beneath the photo. The back contains biography, career summary, and statistics.

	MINT	NRMT	EXC
COMPLETE SET (45)	30.00	13.50	3.70
COMMON CARD (1-45)	.60	.25	.07
☐ 1 Tracey Ham	4.00	1.80	.50
☐ 2 Tim Foley	1.50	.70	.19
☐ 3 Vance Pike	.60	.25	.07
☐ 4 Dennis Franklin	.60	.25	.07
☐ 5 Ernie Thompson	.60	.25	.07
☐ 6 Giff Smith	.60	.25	.07
☐ 7 Flint Matthews	.60	.25	.07
☐ 8 Joe Ross	.60	.25	.07
☐ 9 Gerald Harris	.60	.25	.07
☐ 10 Monty Sharpe	.60	.25	.07
☐ 11 The Beginning Erskine(Erk) Russell CO	1.00	.45	.12
☐ 12 Mike West	.60	.25	.07
☐ 13 Jessie Jenkins	.60	.25	.07
☐ 14 '85 Championship (Ring)	.60	.25	.07
☐ 15 Erskine(Erk) Russell CO	1.00	.45	.12
☐ 16 Tim Brown	.75	.35	.09
☐ 17 Taz Dixon	.60	.25	.07
☐ 18 '86 Championship	.60	.25	.07
☐ 19 Sean Gainey	.60	.25	.07
☐ 20 James(Peanut) Carter	.75	.35	.09
☐ 21 Ricky Harris	.75	.35	.09
☐ 22 Fred Stokes	2.00	.90	.25
☐ 23 Randell Boone	.60	.25	.07
☐ 24 Ronald Warnock	.60	.25	.07
☐ 25 Raymond Gross	.60	.25	.07
☐ 26 Robert Underwood	.60	.25	.07
☐ 27 Frank Johnson	.60	.25	.07
☐ 28 Darren Alford	.60	.25	.07
☐ 29 Darrell Hendrix	.60	.25	.07
☐ 30 Raymond Gross	.60	.25	.07
☐ 31 Hugo Rossignol	.60	.25	.07
☐ 32 Charles Carper	.60	.25	.07
☐ 33 Melvin Bell	.60	.25	.07
☐ 34 The Catch (Tracey Ham to Frank Johnson)	1.50	.70	.19
☐ 35 Karl Miller	.60	.25	.07
☐ 36 Our House Allen E. Paulson Stadium	.60	.25	.07
☐ 37 Danny Durham	.60	.25	.07
☐ 38 '89 Championship	.60	.25	.07
☐ 39 Tony Belser	.60	.25	.07
☐ 40 Nay Young	.60	.25	.07
☐ 41 Steve Bussoletti	.60	.25	.07
☐ 42 Tim Stowers CO	.60	.25	.07
☐ 43 Rodney Oglesby	.60	.25	.07
☐ 44 '90 Championship	.60	.25	.07
☐ 45 Tracey Ham	4.00	1.80	.50

1992 Gridiron Promos

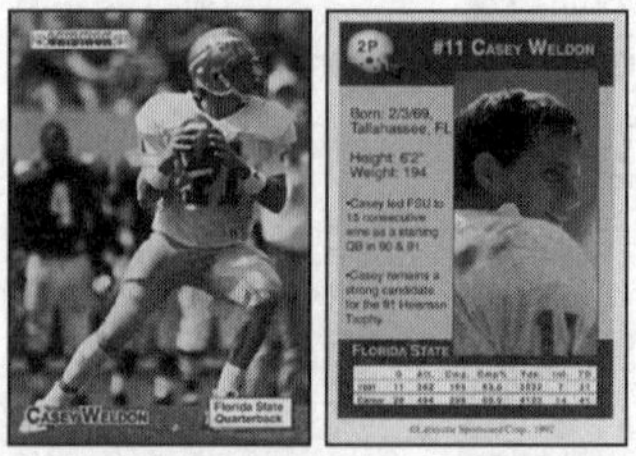

Produced by Lafayette Sportscard Corporation, this four-card promo set was issued to show the design of the 1992 Gridiron set. The standard-size cards feature full-bleed action color player photos. The picture on card number 1P is horizontal. The player's name appears at the lower left in team color-coded lettering; his school and position are at the lower right. On a background of team color-coded panels, the backs display a vertical close-up photo, biography, player profile information, and college statistics.

	MINT	NRMT	EXC
COMPLETE SET (4)	6.00	2.70	.75
COMMON CARD (1P-4P)	.50	.23	.06
☐ 1P Siran Stacy	.50	.23	.06
☐ 2P Casey Weldon	.75	.35	.09
☐ 3P Mike Saunders	.50	.23	.06
☐ 4P Jeff Blake	5.00	2.20	.60

1992 Gridiron

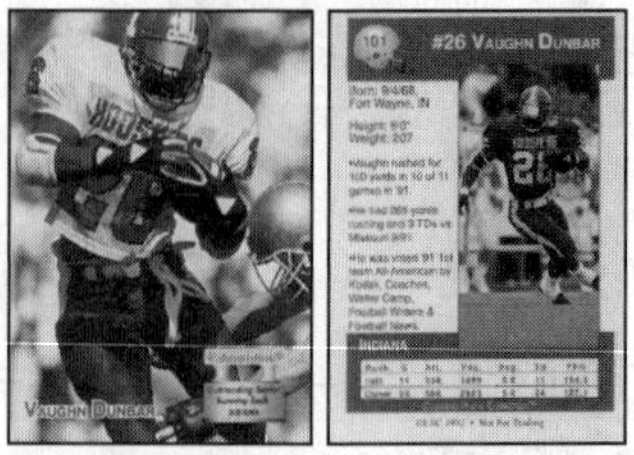

The 1992 Gridiron football set was produced by Lafayette Sportscard Corporation. The 110 standard-size cards pay tribute to graduating seniors and coaches from the top 25 college teams of 1991. Three players and one coach represent each team. Reportedly the production run was limited to 50,000 sets or 2,500 numbered cases. The full-bleed glossy color photos dominate the card fronts; the producer's logo, player's name, team name, and position are placed in the corners. In addition to a second color player photo, the back carries biography, career highlights, and statistics (1991 and career), on panels reflecting the team colors. Only the four Desmond Howard cards (13B, 33B, 105B, and 107B) have a letter suffix after the card number.

	MINT	NRMT	EXC
COMPLETE SET (110)	30.00	13.50	3.70
COMMON CARD (1-107)	.10	.05	.01
☐ 1 Rob Perez	.20	.09	.03
☐ 2 Jason Jones	.10	.05	.01
☐ 3 Jason Christ	.10	.05	.01
☐ 4 Fisher DeBerry CO	.20	.09	.03
☐ 5 Danny Woodson	.10	.05	.01
☐ 6 Siran Stacy	.20	.09	.03
☐ 7 Robert Stewart	.10	.05	.01
☐ 8 Gene Stallings CO	1.00	.45	.12
☐ 9 Santana Dotson	.75	.35	.09
☐ 10 Curtis Hafford	.10	.05	.01
☐ 11 John Turnpaugh	.10	.05	.01
☐ 12 Grant Teaff CO	.35	.16	.04
☐ 13B Desmond Howard	.75	.35	.09
☐ 14 Brian Treggs	.10	.05	.01
☐ 15 Troy Auzenne	.20	.09	.03
☐ 16 Bruce Snyder CO	.35	.16	.04
☐ 17 DeChane Cameron	.10	.05	.01
☐ 18 Levon Kirkland	.35	.16	.04
☐ 19 Ed McDaniel	.20	.09	.03
☐ 20 Ken Hatfield CO	.25	.11	.03
☐ 21 Darian Hagan	.20	.09	.03
☐ 22 Rico Smith	.20	.09	.03
☐ 23 Joel Steed	.20	.09	.03
☐ 24 Bill McCartney CO	1.00	.45	.12
☐ 25 Jeff Blake	4.00	1.80	.50
☐ 26 David Daniels	.10	.05	.01
☐ 27 Robert Jones	.20	.09	.03
☐ 28 Bill Lewis CO	.20	.09	.03
☐ 29 Tim Paulk	.10	.05	.01
☐ 30 Arden Czyzewski	.10	.05	.01
☐ 31 Cal Dixon	.10	.05	.01
☐ 32 Steve Spurrier CO	3.00	1.35	.35
☐ 33B Desmond Howard	.75	.35	.09
☐ 34 Casey Weldon	.35	.16	.04
☐ 35 Kirk Carruthers	.10	.05	.01
☐ 36 Bobby Bowden CO	2.50	1.10	.30
☐ 37 Mark Barsotti	.10	.05	.01
☐ 38 Kelvin Means	.10	.05	.01
☐ 39 Marquez Pope	.20	.09	.03
☐ 40 Jim Sweeney CO	.35	.16	.04
☐ 41 Kameno Bell	.10	.05	.01
☐ 42 Elbert Turner	.10	.05	.01
☐ 43 Marlin Primous	.10	.05	.01
☐ 44 John Mackovic CO	.50	.23	.06
☐ 45 Matt Rodgers	.20	.09	.03
☐ 46 Mike Saunders	.20	.09	.03
☐ 47 John Derby	.10	.05	.01
☐ 48 Hayden Fry CO	1.00	.45	.12
☐ 49 Carlos Huerta	.20	.09	.03
☐ 50 Leon Searcy	.20	.09	.03
☐ 51 Claude Jones	.10	.05	.01
☐ 52 Dennis Erickson CO	1.00	.45	.12
☐ 53 Erick Anderson	.20	.09	.03
☐ 54 J.D. Carlson	.10	.05	.01
☐ 55 Greg Skrepenak	.35	.16	.04
☐ 56 Gary Moeller CO	.20	.09	.03
☐ 57 Keithen McCant	.20	.09	.03
☐ 58 Nate Turner	.10	.05	.01
☐ 59 Pat Englebert	.10	.05	.01
☐ 60 Tom Osborne CO	2.50	1.10	.30
☐ 61 Charles Davenport	.10	.05	.01
☐ 62 Mark Thomas	.10	.05	.01
☐ 63 Clyde Hawley	.10	.05	.01
☐ 64 Dick Sheridan CO	.20	.09	.03
☐ 65 Derek Brown TE	.20	.09	.03
☐ 66 Rodney Culver	.20	.09	.03
☐ 67 Tony Smith	.20	.09	.03
☐ 68 Lou Holtz CO	2.50	1.10	.30
☐ 69 Kent Graham	.35	.16	.04
☐ 70 Scottie Graham	1.00	.45	.12
☐ 71 John Kacherski	.10	.05	.01
☐ 72 John Cooper CO	.50	.23	.06
☐ 73 Mike Gaddis	.20	.09	.03

☐ 74 Joe Bowden	.20	.09	.03
☐ 75 Mike McKinley	.10	.05	.01
☐ 76 Gary Gibbs CO	.10	.05	.01
☐ 77 Sam Gash	.20	.09	.03
☐ 78 Keith Goganious	.20	.09	.03
☐ 79 Darren Perry	.35	.16	.04
☐ 80 Joe Paterno CO	3.00	1.35	.35
☐ 81 Steve Israel	.20	.09	.03
☐ 82 Eric Seaman	.10	.05	.01
☐ 83 Glen Deveaux	.10	.05	.01
☐ 84 Paul Hackett CO	.35	.16	.04
☐ 85 Tommy Vardell	.35	.16	.04
☐ 86 Chris Walsh	.10	.05	.01
☐ 87 Jason Palumbis	.10	.05	.01
☐ 88 Dennis Green CO	.75	.35	.09
☐ 89 Andy Kelly	.10	.05	.01
☐ 90 Dale Carter	.75	.35	.09
☐ 91 Shon Walker	.10	.05	.01
☐ 92 Johnny Majors CO	.50	.23	.06
☐ 93 Bucky Richardson	.20	.09	.03
☐ 94 Quentin Coryatt	1.25	.55	.16
☐ 95 Kevin Smith	.75	.35	.09
☐ 96 R.C. Slocum CO	.75	.35	.09
☐ 97 Ed Cunningham	.20	.09	.03
☐ 98 Mario Bailey	.20	.09	.03
☐ 99 Donald Jones	.10	.05	.01
☐ 100 Don James CO	1.00	.45	.12
☐ 101 Vaughn Dunbar	.35	.16	.04
☐ 102 Reggie Yarbrough	.10	.05	.01
☐ 103 Matt Blundin	.35	.16	.04
☐ 104 Tony Sands	.10	.05	.01
☐ 105B Desmond Howard	.75	.35	.09
☐ 106 Ty Detmer	1.50	.70	.19
☐ 107B Desmond Howard	.75	.35	.09
☐ NNO Mario Bailey CL Jeff Blake	1.00	.45	.12
☐ NNO Mike Gaddis CL Tommy Vardell	.20	.09	.03
☐ NNO Title Card	.10	.05	.01

1905 Harvard Postcards

This set was produced by the University Post Card Company in 1905. Each includes the standard postcard style back with the fronts featuring a player photo to the left and an action scene to the right. The player's name and school seal are included at the top of the card. Any additional information on this set would be appreciated.

	EX	VG	GOOD
COMPLETE SET (1)	60.00	27.00	7.50
COMMON CARD (1)	60.00	27.00	7.50
☐ 1 Daniel Hurley	60.00	27.00	7.50

1989 Hawaii

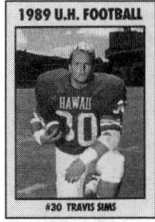
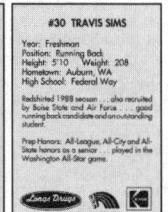

This 25-card set features current football players at the University of Hawaii. The cards are unnumbered, so they are listed below according to uniform number, which is prominently displayed on both sides of the card. The cards measure approximately 2 1/2" by 3 1/2". The set was sponsored by Longs Drugs and Kodak.

	MINT	NRMT	EXC
COMPLETE SET (25)	12.00	5.50	1.50
COMMON CARD (1-25)	.50	.23	.06
☐ 3 Michael Coulson	.50	.23	.06
☐ 4 Walter Briggs	.50	.23	.06
☐ 5 Gavin Robertson	.50	.23	.06
☐ 7 Jason Elam	3.00	1.35	.35
☐ 16 Clayton Mahuka	.50	.23	.06
☐ 18 Garrett Gabriel	.75	.35	.09
☐ 19 Kim McCloud	.50	.23	.06
☐ 27 Kyle Ah Loo	.50	.23	.06
☐ 28 Dane McArthur	.50	.23	.06
☐ 30 Travis Sims	.50	.23	.06
☐ 31 David Maeva	.50	.23	.06
☐ 37 Mike Tresler	.50	.23	.06
☐ 43 Jamal Farmer	.60	.25	.07
☐ 56 Mark Odom	.50	.23	.06
☐ 61 Allen Smith	.50	.23	.06
☐ 66 Manly Williams	.50	.23	.06
☐ 67 Larry Jones	.50	.23	.06
☐ 71 Sean Robinson	.50	.23	.06
☐ 72 Shawn Alivado	.50	.23	.06
☐ 79 Leo Goeas	1.00	.45	.12
☐ 86 Larry Khan-Smith	.50	.23	.06
☐ 89 Chris Roscoe	.50	.23	.06
☐ 91 Augie Apelu	.50	.23	.06
☐ 97 Dana Directo	.50	.23	.06
☐ NNO Bob Wagner CO	.60	.25	.07

1990 Hawaii 7-Eleven

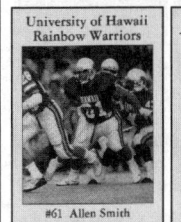

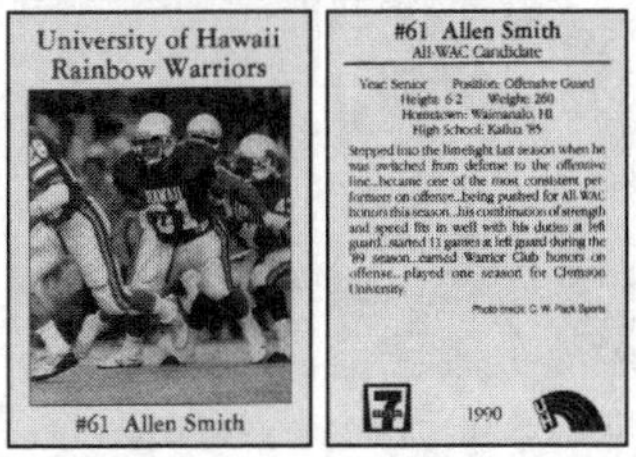

This 50-card standard size set features members of the 1990 Hawaii Rainbow Warriors Football team. The cards have white borders framing a full-color photo on the front and biographical information on the back of the card. We have checklisted this set in alphabetical order and placed the uniform number of the player next to the name of the player.

	MINT	NRMT	EXC
COMPLETE SET (50)	16.00	7.25	2.00
COMMON CARD (1-50)	.35	.16	.04
☐ 1 Sean Abreu 40	.35	.16	.04
☐ 2 Joaquin Barnett 53	.35	.16	.04
☐ 3 Darrick Branch 87	.35	.16	.04
☐ 4 David Brantley 9	.35	.16	.04
☐ 5 Akili Calhoun 98	.35	.16	.04
☐ 6 Michael Carter 3	.35	.16	.04
☐ 7 Shawn Ching 72	.35	.16	.04
☐ 8 Jason Elam 7	2.00	.90	.25
☐ 9 Jamal Farmer 43	.50	.23	.06
☐ 10 Garrett Gabriel 18	.50	.23	.06
☐ 11 Brian Gordon 15	.35	.16	.04
☐ 12 Kenny Harper 6	.35	.16	.04
☐ 13 Mitchell Kaaialii 57	.35	.16	.04
☐ 14 Larry Khan-Smith 86	.35	.16	.04
☐ 15 Haku Kahoano 95	.35	.16	.04
☐ 16 Nuuanu Kaulia 94	.35	.16	.04
☐ 17 Eddie Kealoha 38	.35	.16	.04
☐ 18 Zerin Khan 14	.35	.16	.04
☐ 19 David Maeva 31	.35	.16	.04
☐ 20 Dane McArthur 28	.35	.16	.04
☐ 21 Kim McCloud 19	.35	.16	.04
☐ 22 Jeff Newman 1	.35	.16	.04
☐ 23 Mark Odom 56	.35	.16	.04
☐ 24 Louis Randall 51	.35	.16	.04
☐ 25 Gavin Robertson 5	.35	.16	.04
☐ 26 Sean Robinson 71	.35	.16	.04
☐ 27 Tavita Sagapolu 77	.35	.16	.04
☐ 28 Lyno Samana 45	.35	.16	.04
☐ 29 Walter Santiago 12	.35	.16	.04
☐ 30 Joe Sardo 21	.35	.16	.04
☐ 31 Travis Sims 30	.35	.16	.04
☐ 32 Allen Smith 61	.35	.16	.04
☐ 33 Jeff Sydner 26	1.00	.45	.12
☐ 34 Richard Stevenson 33	.35	.16	.04
☐ 35 David Tanuvasa 44	.35	.16	.04
☐ 36 Mike Tresler 37	.35	.16	.04
☐ 37 Lemoe Tua 60	.35	.16	.04
☐ 38 Peter Viliamu 69	.35	.16	.04
☐ 39 Bob Wagner CO	.50	.23	.06
☐ 40 Terry Whitaker 2	.35	.16	.04
☐ 41 Manly Williams 66	.35	.16	.04
☐ 42 Jerry Winfrey 90	.35	.16	.04
☐ 43 Aloha Stadium	.35	.16	.04
☐ 44 Assistant Coaches	.35	.16	.04
☐ 45 Defense (Nuuanu Kaulia)	.35	.16	.04
☐ 46 Offense (Jamal Farmer)	.50	.23	.06
☐ 47 Special Teams (Jason Elam)	.75	.35	.09
☐ 48 BYU Victory (Jamal Farmer)	.50	.23	.06
☐ 49 UH Logo	.35	.16	.04
☐ 50 WAC Logo	.35	.16	.04

1991 Hoby SEC Stars

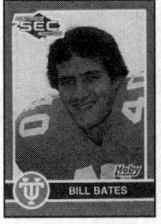

The premier edition of Hoby's Stars of the Southeastern Conference football card set contains 396 standard-size cards. Each institution is represented by 36 prominent past players. The front design features a mix of color or black and white, posed or action player photos, with thin white borders on a gold card face. The school logo appears in the lower left corner of the picture, with the player's name in a blue stripe extending to the right. The color of the backs reflects the team's primary color; the backs present biography, statistics, or career highlights. The cards are checklisted alphabetically according to

teams, with athletic director, coach, and checklist cards listed at the end. The set closes with an SEC Rivalries subset (390-395) and a Commissioner card (396). The numbering below reflects the actual numbering on the cards and checklists. A mistake occurred when Tennessee's players began with 299 rather than 289; thus no cards are numbered 289-298, and both Tennessee and Vanderbilt cards share the numbers 325-334.

	MINT	NRMT	EXC
COMPLETE SET (396)	65.00	29.00	8.00
COMMON CARD (1-396)	.20	.09	.03
☐ 1 Paul(Bear) Bryant CO	2.00	.90	.25
☐ 2 Johnny Musso	.50	.23	.06
☐ 3 Keith McCants	.30	.14	.04
☐ 4 Cecil Dowdy	.20	.09	.03
☐ 5 Thomas Rayam	.20	.09	.03
☐ 6 Van Tiffin	.20	.09	.03
☐ 7 Efrum Thomas	.20	.09	.03
☐ 8 Jon Hand	.30	.14	.04
☐ 9 David Smith	.20	.09	.03
☐ 10 Larry Rose	.20	.09	.03
☐ 11 Lamonde Russell	.30	.14	.04
☐ 12 Mike Washington	.20	.09	.03
☐ 13 Tommy Cole	.20	.09	.03
☐ 14 Roger Shultz	.20	.09	.03
☐ 15 Spencer Hammond	.20	.09	.03
☐ 16 John Fruhmorgen	.20	.09	.03
☐ 17 Gene Jelks	.30	.14	.04
☐ 18 John Mangum	.30	.14	.04
☐ 19 George Thornton	.20	.09	.03
☐ 20 Billy Neighbors	.30	.14	.04
☐ 21 Howard Cross	.40	.18	.05
☐ 22 Jeremiah Castille	.30	.14	.04
☐ 23 Derrick Thomas	1.00	.45	.12
☐ 24 Terrill Chatman	.20	.09	.03
☐ 25 Ken Stabler	1.50	.70	.19
☐ 26 Lee Ozmint	.20	.09	.03
☐ 27 Philip Doyle	.20	.09	.03
☐ 28 Kermit Kendrick	.20	.09	.03
☐ 29 Chris Mohr	.20	.09	.03
☐ 30 Tommy Wilcox	.20	.09	.03
☐ 31 Gary Hollingsworth	.20	.09	.03
☐ 32 Sylvester Croom	.30	.14	.04
☐ 33 Willie Wyatt	.20	.09	.03
☐ 34 Pooley Hubert	.20	.09	.03
☐ 35 Bobby Humphrey	.30	.14	.04
☐ 36 Vaughn Mancha	.20	.09	.03
☐ 37 Reggie Slack	.40	.18	.05
☐ 38 Vince Dooley CO	.40	.18	.05
☐ 39 Ed King	.30	.14	.04
☐ 40 Connie Frederick	.20	.09	.03
☐ 41 Jeff Burger	.30	.14	.04
☐ 42 Monk Gafford	.20	.09	.03
☐ 43 David Rocker	.20	.09	.03
☐ 44 Jim Pyburn	.20	.09	.03
☐ 45 Bob Harris	.20	.09	.03
☐ 46 Travis Tidwell	.20	.09	.03
☐ 47 Shug Jordan CO	.40	.18	.05
☐ 48 Zeke Smith	.30	.14	.04
☐ 49 Terry Beasley	.30	.14	.04
☐ 50 Pat Sullivan	.50	.23	.06
☐ 51 Stacy Danley	.30	.14	.04
☐ 52 Jimmy Hitchcock	.20	.09	.03
☐ 53 John Wiley	.20	.09	.03
☐ 54 Greg Taylor	.20	.09	.03
☐ 55 Lamar Rogers	.30	.14	.04
☐ 56 Rob Selby	.20	.09	.03
☐ 57 James Joseph	.30	.14	.04
☐ 58 Mike Kolen	.30	.14	.04
☐ 59 Kevin Greene	.75	.35	.09
☐ 60 Ben Thomas	.20	.09	.03
☐ 61 Shayne Wasden	.20	.09	.03
☐ 62 Tex Warrington	.20	.09	.03
☐ 63 Tommie Agee	.30	.14	.04
☐ 64 Jim Phillips	.20	.09	.03
☐ 65 Lawyer Tillman	.30	.14	.04
☐ 66 Mark Dorminey	.20	.09	.03
☐ 67 Steve Wallace	.30	.14	.04
☐ 68 Ed Dyas	.20	.09	.03
☐ 69 Alexander Wright	.30	.14	.04
☐ 70 Lionel James	.30	.14	.04
☐ 71 Aundray Bruce	.30	.14	.04
☐ 72 Edmund Nelson	.20	.09	.03
☐ 73 Jack Youngblood	.75	.35	.09
☐ 74 Carlos Alvarez	.30	.14	.04
☐ 75 Ricky Nattiel	.30	.14	.04
☐ 76 Bill Carr	.20	.09	.03
☐ 77 Guy Dennis	.20	.09	.03
☐ 78 Charles Casey	.20	.09	.03
☐ 79 Louis Oliver	.40	.18	.05
☐ 80 John Reaves	.30	.14	.04
☐ 81 Wayne Peace	.30	.14	.04
☐ 82 Charlie LaPradd	.20	.09	.03
☐ 83 Wes Chandler	.40	.18	.05
☐ 84 Richard Trapp	.20	.09	.03
☐ 85 Ralph Ortega	.20	.09	.03
☐ 86 Tommy Durrance	.20	.09	.03
☐ 87 Burton Lawless	.30	.14	.04
☐ 88 Bruce Bennett	.20	.09	.03
☐ 89 Huey Richardson	.20	.09	.03
☐ 90 Larry Smith	.20	.09	.03
☐ 91 Trace Armstrong	.40	.18	.05
☐ 92 Nat Moore	.40	.18	.05
☐ 93 James Jones	.40	.18	.05
☐ 94 Kay Stephenson	.30	.14	.04

☐ 95 Scot Brantley	.20	.09	.03
☐ 96 Ray Criswell	.20	.09	.03
☐ 97 Steve Tannen	.30	.14	.04
☐ 98 Ernie Mills	.40	.18	.05
☐ 99 Bruce Vaughn	.20	.09	.03
☐ 100 Steve Spurrier	3.00	1.35	.35
☐ 101 Crawford Ker	.30	.14	.04
☐ 102 David Galloway	.30	.14	.04
☐ 103 David Williams	.30	.14	.04
☐ 104 Lomas Brown	.40	.18	.05
☐ 105 Fernando Jackson	.20	.09	.03
☐ 106 Jeff Roth	.20	.09	.03
☐ 107 Mark Murray	.20	.09	.03
☐ 108 Kirk Kirkpatrick	.20	.09	.03
☐ 109 Ray Goff CO	.30	.14	.04
☐ 110 Quinton Lumpkin	.20	.09	.03
☐ 111 Royce Smith	.20	.09	.03
☐ 112 Larry Rakestraw	.30	.14	.04
☐ 113 Kevin Butler	.30	.14	.04
☐ 114 Aschel M. Day	.20	.09	.03
☐ 115 Scott Woerner	.30	.14	.04
☐ 116 Herb St. John	.20	.09	.03
☐ 117 Ray Rissmiller	.20	.09	.03
☐ 118 Buck Belue	.30	.14	.04
☐ 119 George Collins	.20	.09	.03
☐ 120 Joel Parrish	.20	.09	.03
☐ 121 Terry Hoage	.30	.14	.04
☐ 122 Frank Sinkwich	.50	.23	.06
☐ 123 Billy Payne	.50	.23	.06
☐ 124 Zeke Bratkowski	.40	.18	.05
☐ 125 Herschel Walker	1.00	.45	.12
☐ 126 Pat Dye CO	.40	.18	.05
☐ 127 Vernon Smith	.20	.09	.03
☐ 128 Rex Robinson	.20	.09	.03
☐ 129 Mike Castronis	.20	.09	.03
☐ 130 Pop Warner CO	.40	.18	.05
☐ 131 George Patton	.30	.14	.04
☐ 132 Harry Babcock	.20	.09	.03
☐ 133 Lindsay Scott	.30	.14	.04
☐ 134 Bill Stanfill	.30	.14	.04
☐ 135 Bill Hartman Jr.	.20	.09	.03
☐ 136 Eddie Weaver	.20	.09	.03
☐ 137 Tim Worley	.40	.18	.05
☐ 138 Ben Zambiasi	.40	.18	.05
☐ 139 Bob McWhorter	.20	.09	.03
☐ 140 Rodney Hampton	1.00	.45	.12
☐ 141 Len Hauss	.30	.14	.04
☐ 142 Wally Butts CO	.30	.14	.04
☐ 143 Andy Johnson	.30	.14	.04
☐ 144 M. Shiver Jr.	.20	.09	.03
☐ 145 Clyde Johnson	.20	.09	.03
☐ 146 Steve Meilinger	.20	.09	.03
☐ 147 Howard Schnellenberger CO	.50	.23	.06
☐ 148 Irv Goode	.30	.14	.04
☐ 149 Sam Ball	.20	.09	.03
☐ 150 Babe Parilli	.40	.18	.05
☐ 151 Rick Norton	.30	.14	.04
☐ 152 Warren Bryant	.20	.09	.03
☐ 153 Mike Pfeifer	.20	.09	.03
☐ 154 Sonny Collins	.30	.14	.04
☐ 155 Mark Higgs	.40	.18	.05
☐ 156 Randy Holleran	.20	.09	.03
☐ 157 Bill Ransdell	.20	.09	.03
☐ 158 Joey Worley	.20	.09	.03
☐ 159 Jim Kovach	.30	.14	.04
☐ 160 Joe Federspiel	.30	.14	.04
☐ 161 Larry Seiple	.30	.14	.04
☐ 162 Darryl Bishop	.20	.09	.03
☐ 163 George Blanda	1.00	.45	.12
☐ 164 Oliver Barnett	.30	.14	.04
☐ 165 Paul Calhoun	.20	.09	.03
☐ 166 Dick Lyons	.20	.09	.03
☐ 167 Tom Hutchinson	.30	.14	.04
☐ 168 George Adams	.30	.14	.04
☐ 169 Derrick Ramsey	.30	.14	.04
☐ 170 Rick Kestner	.20	.09	.03
☐ 171 Art Still	.40	.18	.05
☐ 172 Rick Nuzum	.20	.09	.03
☐ 173 Richard Jaffe	.20	.09	.03
☐ 174 Rodger Bird	.20	.09	.03
☐ 175 Jeff Van Note	.40	.18	.05
☐ 176 Herschel Turner	.20	.09	.03
☐ 177 Lou Michaels	.30	.14	.04
☐ 178 Ray Correll	.20	.09	.03
☐ 179 Doug Moseley	.20	.09	.03
☐ 180 Bob Gain	.40	.18	.05
☐ 181 Tommy Casanova	.40	.18	.05
☐ 182 Mike Anderson	.20	.09	.03
☐ 183 Craig Burns	.20	.09	.03
☐ 184 A.J. Duhe	.30	.14	.04
☐ 185 Lyman White	.20	.09	.03
☐ 186 Paul Dietzel CO	.40	.18	.05
☐ 187 Paul Lyons	.20	.09	.03
☐ 188 Eddie Ray	.30	.14	.04
☐ 189 Roy Winston	.30	.14	.04
☐ 190 Brad Davis	.20	.09	.03
☐ 191 Mike Williams	.30	.14	.04
☐ 192 Karl Wilson	.20	.09	.03
☐ 193 Ron Estay	.20	.09	.03
☐ 194 Malcolm Scott	.20	.09	.03
☐ 195 Greg Jackson	.30	.14	.04
☐ 196 Willie Teal	.20	.09	.03
☐ 197 Eddie Fuller	.20	.09	.03
☐ 198 Ralph Norwood	.20	.09	.03
☐ 199 Bert Jones	.50	.23	.06

☐ 200 Y.A. Tittle	.75	.35	.09
☐ 201 Jerry Stovall	.40	.18	.05
☐ 202 Henry Thomas	.40	.18	.05
☐ 203 Lance Smith	.20	.09	.03
☐ 204 Doug Moreau	.30	.14	.04
☐ 205 Tyler LaFauci	.20	.09	.03
☐ 206 George Bevan	.20	.09	.03
☐ 207 Robert Dugas	.20	.09	.03
☐ 208 Carlos Carson	.30	.14	.04
☐ 209 Andy Hamilton	.30	.14	.04
☐ 210 James Britt	.20	.09	.03
☐ 211 Wendell Davis	.40	.18	.05
☐ 212 Ron Sancho	.30	.14	.04
☐ 213 Johnny Robinson	.40	.18	.05
☐ 214 Eric Martin	.40	.18	.05
☐ 215 Michael Brooks	.30	.14	.04
☐ 216 Toby Caston	.30	.14	.04
☐ 217 Jesse Anderson	.20	.09	.03
☐ 218 Jimmy Webb	.20	.09	.03
☐ 219 Mardye McDole	.20	.09	.03
☐ 220 David Smith	.20	.09	.03
☐ 221 Dana Moore	.20	.09	.03
☐ 222 Cedric Corse	.20	.09	.03
☐ 223 Louis Clark	.20	.09	.03
☐ 224 Walter Packer	.20	.09	.03
☐ 225 George Wonsley	.30	.14	.04
☐ 226 Billy Jackson	.30	.14	.04
☐ 227 Bruce Plummer	.20	.09	.03
☐ 228 Aaron Pearson	.20	.09	.03
☐ 229 Glen Collins	.20	.09	.03
☐ 230 Paul Davis CO	.20	.09	.03
☐ 231 Wayne Jones	.20	.09	.03
☐ 232 John Bond	.20	.09	.03
☐ 233 Johnie Cooks	.30	.14	.04
☐ 234 Robert Young	.20	.09	.03
☐ 235 Don Smith	.20	.09	.03
☐ 236 Kent Hull	.40	.18	.05
☐ 237 Tony Shell	.20	.09	.03
☐ 238 Steve Freeman	.30	.14	.04
☐ 239 James Williams	.20	.09	.03
☐ 240 Tom Goode	.30	.14	.04
☐ 241 Stan Black	.20	.09	.03
☐ 242 Bo Russell	.20	.09	.03
☐ 243 Richard Byrd	.20	.09	.03
☐ 244 Frank Dowsing	.20	.09	.03
☐ 245 Wayne Harris	.40	.18	.05
☐ 246 Richard Keys	.20	.09	.03
☐ 247 Artie Cosby	.20	.09	.03
☐ 248 Dave Marler	.20	.09	.03
☐ 249 Michael Haddix	.30	.14	.04
☐ 250 Jerry Clower	.40	.18	.05
☐ 251 Bill Bell	.30	.14	.04
☐ 252 Jerry Bouldin	.20	.09	.03
☐ 253 Parker Hall	.20	.09	.03
☐ 254 Allen Brown	.20	.09	.03
☐ 255 Bill Smith	.20	.09	.03
☐ 256 Freddie Joe Nunn	.40	.18	.05
☐ 257 John Vaught CO	.30	.14	.04
☐ 258 Buford McGee	.30	.14	.04
☐ 259 Kenny Dill	.20	.09	.03
☐ 260 Jim Miller	.20	.09	.03
☐ 261 Doug Jacobs	.20	.09	.03
☐ 262 John Dottley	.30	.14	.04
☐ 263 Willie Green	.40	.18	.05
☐ 264 Tony Bennett	.40	.18	.05
☐ 265 Stan Hindman	.20	.09	.03
☐ 266 Charles Childers	.20	.09	.03
☐ 267 Harry Harrison	.20	.09	.03
☐ 268 Todd Sandroni	.20	.09	.03
☐ 269 Glynn Griffing	.20	.09	.03
☐ 270 Chris Mitchell	.20	.09	.03
☐ 271 Shawn Cobb	.20	.09	.03
☐ 272 Doug Elmore	.20	.09	.03
☐ 273 Dawson Pruett	.20	.09	.03
☐ 274 Warner Alford	.20	.09	.03
☐ 275 Archie Manning	1.50	.70	.19
☐ 276 Kelvin Pritchett	.30	.14	.04
☐ 277 Pat Coleman	.20	.09	.03
☐ 278 Stevon Moore	.30	.14	.04
☐ 279 John Darnell	.20	.09	.03
☐ 280 Wesley Walls	.40	.18	.05
☐ 281 Billy Brewer	.30	.14	.04
☐ 282 Mark Young	.20	.09	.03
☐ 283 Andre Townsend	.30	.14	.04
☐ 284 Billy Ray Adams	.20	.09	.03
☐ 285 Jim Dunaway	.30	.14	.04
☐ 286 Paige Cothren	.30	.14	.04
☐ 287 Jake Gibbs	.40	.18	.05
☐ 288 Jim Urbanek	.20	.09	.03
☐ 299 Tony Thompson	.20	.09	.03
☐ 300 Johnny Majors CO	.40	.18	.05
☐ 301 Roland Poles	.20	.09	.03
☐ 302 Alvin Harper	.50	.23	.06
☐ 303 Doug Baird	.20	.09	.03
☐ 304 Greg Burke	.20	.09	.03
☐ 305 Sterling Henton	.20	.09	.03
☐ 306 Preston Warren	.20	.09	.03
☐ 307 Stanley Morgan	.50	.23	.06
☐ 308 Bobby Scott	.30	.14	.04
☐ 309 Doug Atkins	.50	.23	.06
☐ 310 Bill Young	.20	.09	.03
☐ 311 Bob Garmon	.20	.09	.03
☐ 312 Herman Weaver	.30	.14	.04
☐ 313 Dewey Warren	.20	.09	.03
☐ 314 John Boynton	.30	.14	.04
☐ 315 Bob Davis	.20	.09	.03
☐ 316 Pat Ryan	.20	.09	.03
☐ 317 Keith DeLong	.30	.14	.04
☐ 318 Bobby Dodd CO	.40	.18	.05
☐ 319 Ricky Townsend	.20	.09	.03
☐ 320 Eddie Brown	.30	.14	.04
☐ 321 Herman Hickman CO	.30	.14	.04
☐ 322 Nathan Dougherty	.20	.09	.03
☐ 323 Mickey Marvin	.20	.09	.03
☐ 324 Reggie Cobb	.40	.18	.05
☐ 325A Condredge Holloway	.50	.23	.06
☐ 325B Josh Cody	.20	.09	.03
☐ 326A Anthony Hancock	.40	.18	.05
☐ 326B Jack Jenkins	.20	.09	.03
☐ 327A Steve Kiner	.20	.09	.03
☐ 327B Bob Goodridge	.20	.09	.03
☐ 328A Mike Mauck	.20	.09	.03
☐ 328B Chris Gaines	.20	.09	.03
☐ 329A Bill Bates	.50	.23	.06
☐ 329B Willie Geny	.20	.09	.03
☐ 330A Austin Denney	.30	.14	.04
☐ 330B Bob Laws	.20	.09	.03
☐ 331A Robert Neyland CO	.50	.23	.06
☐ 331B Rob Monaco	.20	.09	.03
☐ 332A Bob Suffridge	.20	.09	.03
☐ 332B Chuck Scott	.20	.09	.03
☐ 333A Abe Shires	.20	.09	.03
☐ 333B Hek Wakefield	.20	.09	.03
☐ 334A Robert Shaw	.40	.18	.05
☐ 334B Ken Stone	.20	.09	.03
☐ 335 Mark Adams	.20	.09	.03
☐ 336 Ed Smith	.20	.09	.03
☐ 337 Dan McGugin CO	.20	.09	.03
☐ 338 Doug Mathews	.20	.09	.03
☐ 339 Whit Taylor	.40	.18	.05
☐ 340 Gene Moshier	.20	.09	.03
☐ 341 Christie Hauck	.20	.09	.03
☐ 342 Lee Nalley	.20	.09	.03
☐ 343 Wamon Buggs	.20	.09	.03
☐ 344 Jim Arnold	.30	.14	.04
☐ 345 Buford Ray	.30	.14	.04
☐ 346 Will Wolford	.30	.14	.04
☐ 347 Steve Bearden	.20	.09	.03
☐ 348 Frank Mordica	.20	.09	.03
☐ 349 Barry Burton	.20	.09	.03
☐ 350 Bill Wade	.40	.18	.05
☐ 351 Tommy Woodroof	.20	.09	.03
☐ 352 Steve Wade	.20	.09	.03
☐ 353 Preston Brown	.20	.09	.03
☐ 354 Ben Roderick	.20	.09	.03
☐ 355 Charles Horton	.20	.09	.03
☐ 356 DeMond Winston	.20	.09	.03
☐ 357 John North	.20	.09	.03
☐ 358 Don Orr	.20	.09	.03
☐ 359 Art Demmas	.20	.09	.03
☐ 360 Mark Johnson	.20	.09	.03
☐ 361 Hootie Ingram AD	.30	.14	.04
☐ 362 Gene Stallings CO	.50	.23	.06
☐ 363 Alabama Checklist	.20	.09	.03
☐ 364 Pat Dye CO	.40	.18	.05
☐ 365 Auburn Checklist	.20	.09	.03
☐ 366 Vince Dooley AD	.30	.14	.04
☐ 367 Ray Goff CO	.30	.14	.04
☐ 368 Georgia Checklist	.20	.09	.03
☐ 369 C.M. Newton AD	.30	.14	.04
☐ 370 Bill Curry CO	.30	.14	.04
☐ 371 Kentucky Checklist	.20	.09	.03
☐ 372 Joe Dean AD	.30	.14	.04
☐ 373 Curley Hallman CO	.30	.14	.04
☐ 374 LSU Checklist	.20	.09	.03
☐ 375 Warner Alford AD	.20	.09	.03
☐ 376 Billy Brewer CO	.30	.14	.04
☐ 377 Ole Miss Checklist	.20	.09	.03
☐ 378 Larry Templeton AD	.20	.09	.03
☐ 379 Jackie Sherrill CO	.40	.18	.05
☐ 380 Miss. State Checklist	.20	.09	.03
☐ 381 Bill Arnsparger AD	.30	.14	.04
☐ 382 Steve Spurrier CO	2.00	.90	.25
☐ 383 Florida Checklist	.20	.09	.03
☐ 384 Doug Dickey AD	.20	.09	.03
☐ 385 Johnny Majors CO	.40	.18	.05
☐ 386 Tennessee Checklist	.20	.09	.03
☐ 387 Paul Hoolahan AD	.20	.09	.03
☐ 388 Gerry DiNardo CO	.40	.18	.05
☐ 389 Vanderbilt Checklist	.20	.09	.03
☐ 390 The Iron Bowl Alabama vs. Auburn	.40	.18	.05
☐ 391 Largest Outdoor Cocktail Party Florida vs. Georgia	.20	.09	.03
☐ 392 The Egg Bowl Mississippi State vs. Ole Miss	.20	.09	.03
☐ 393 The Beer Barrel Kentucky vs. Tennessee	.20	.09	.03
☐ 394 Drama on Halloween LSU vs. Ole Miss	.20	.09	.03
☐ 395 Tennessee Hoedown Tennessee vs. Vanderbilt	.20	.09	.03
☐ 396 Roy Kramer COMM	.20	.09	.03

1991 Hoby SEC Stars Signature

These ten specially designed signature series cards feature a prominent player from each SEC institution. They were randomly

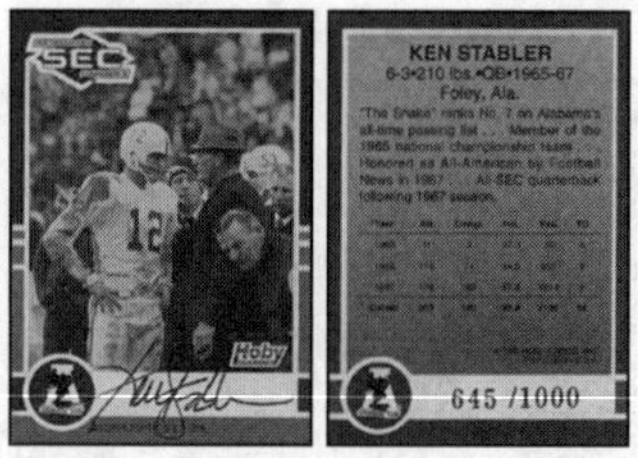

inserted in the 1991 SEC Stars Hoby gold-foil packs. Each player selected autographed 1,000 cards, and each card bears a unique serial number. The cards are identical in size and design with the corresponding player cards in the regular series, with four exceptions: 1) the stripe at the bottom of the card face is left blank for the player's autograph; 2) the numbering of the complete set has been removed; 3) the pattern of gold and blue borders on the front differs slightly from the regular issue; and 4) the Manning card displays a different photo on the front than its counterpart in the regular set. Since the cards are unnumbered, they are checklisted below in alphabetical order.

	MINT	NRMT	EXC
COMPLETE SET (10)	400.00	180.00	50.00
COMMON CARD (1-10)	20.00	9.00	2.50
☐ 1 Carlos Alvarez	20.00	9.00	2.50
☐ 2 Zeke Bratkowski	30.00	13.50	3.70
☐ 3 Jerry Clower	20.00	9.00	2.50
☐ 4 Condredge Holloway	25.00	11.00	3.10
☐ 5 Bert Jones	50.00	22.00	6.25
☐ 6 Archie Manning	75.00	34.00	9.50
☐ 7 Ken Stabler	100.00	45.00	12.50
☐ 8 Pat Sullivan	50.00	22.00	6.25
☐ 9 Jeff Van Note	25.00	11.00	3.10
☐ 10 Bill Wade	30.00	13.50	3.70

1992 Houston Motion Sports

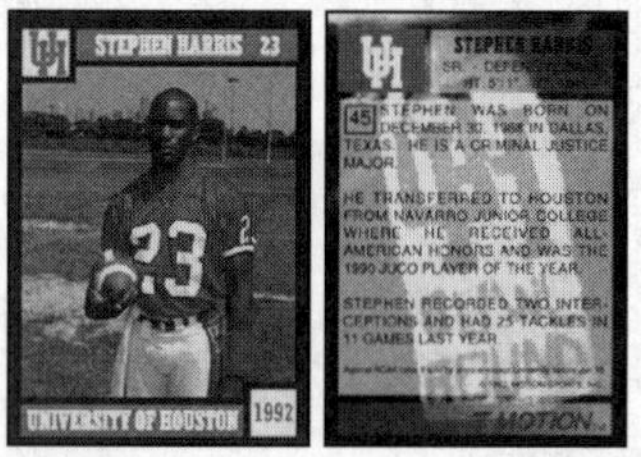

Produced by Motion Sports Inc., these 66 standard-size cards feature on their fronts black-bordered color player photos, mostly posed, with the player's name and uniform number appearing in white lettering within a red stripe at the top. The back carries a borderless action photo, upon which are ghosted panels that contain the player's biography and Houston highlights.

	MINT	NRMT	EXC
COMPLETE SET (66)	30.00	13.50	3.70
COMMON CARD (1-62)	.50	.23	.06
☐ 1 Freddie Gilbert	.60	.25	.07
☐ 2 Lorenzo Dickson	.50	.23	.06
☐ 3 Sherman Smith	1.00	.45	.12
☐ 4 Brad Whigham	.50	.23	.06
☐ 5 Allen Aldridge	1.00	.45	.12
☐ 6 Truett Akin	.50	.23	.06
☐ 7 Nahala Johnson	.60	.25	.07
☐ 8 1980 Garden State Bowl Terald Clark	.50	.23	.06
☐ 9 1977 Cotton Bowl	.60	.25	.07
☐ 10 Tyrone Davis	.50	.23	.06
☐ 11 Kevin Bleier	.50	.23	.06
☐ 12 Nigel Ventress	.50	.23	.06
☐ 13 Darren Woods	.50	.23	.06
☐ 14 Linton Weatherspoon	.50	.23	.06
☐ 15 John R. Morris	.50	.23	.06
☐ 16 Kevin Batiste	.60	.25	.07
☐ 17 Kelvin McKnight	.50	.23	.06
☐ 18 Stewart Carpenter	.50	.23	.06
☐ 19 Ron Peters	.50	.23	.06
☐ 20 Stephen Dixon	.60	.25	.07
☐ 21 Chandler Evans	.50	.23	.06
☐ 22 Tyler Mucho	.50	.23	.06
☐ 23 Kevin Labay	.50	.23	.06
☐ 24 Steve Clarke	.50	.23	.06
☐ 25 Keith Jack	.50	.23	.06
☐ 26 Steve Matejka	.50	.23	.06
☐ 27 The Astrodome	.50	.23	.06
☐ 28 Roman Anderson	.50	.23	.06
☐ 29 Quarterback U. Andre Ware David Klingler	1.50	.70	.19
☐ 30 Cougar Pride Andre Ware David Klingler	1.50	.70	.19
☐ 31 Bayou Bucket (Annual Houston vs. Rice game)	.50	.23	.06
☐ 32 Jeff Tait	.50	.23	.06
☐ 33 Donald Douglas	.50	.23	.06
☐ 34 Victor Mamich	.50	.23	.06
☐ 35 John W.Brown	.50	.23	.06
☐ 36 Zach Chatman	.50	.23	.06
☐ 37 Jason Youngblood	.50	.23	.06
☐ 38 David Klingler	2.00	.90	.25
☐ 39 John H.Brown	.50	.23	.06
☐ 40 Tommy Guy	.50	.23	.06
☐ 41 1980 Cotton Bowl (Game action)	.60	.25	.07
☐ 42 1973 Bluebonnet Bowl (Marshall Johnson)	.60	.25	.07
☐ 43 Chris Pezman	.50	.23	.06
☐ 44 Tracy Good	.50	.23	.06
☐ 45 Stephen Harris	.50	.23	.06
☐ 46 Ryan McCoy	.60	.25	.07
☐ 47 Michael Newhouse	.50	.23	.06
☐ 48 Jimmy Klingler	1.50	.70	.19
☐ 49 Joe Wheeler	.50	.23	.06
☐ 50 Eric Harrison	.50	.23	.06
☐ 51 Craig Hall	.50	.23	.06
☐ 52 Shasta (Mascot)	.50	.23	.06
☐ 53 NCAA Records (Passing and Receiving)	.60	.25	.07
☐ 54 Darrell Clapp	.60	.25	.07
☐ 55 Eric Blount	.50	.23	.06
☐ 56 Tiandre Sanders	.50	.23	.06
☐ 57 Kyle Allen	.50	.23	.06
☐ 58 Brisket Howard	.50	.23	.06
☐ 59 Greg Thornburgh	.50	.23	.06
☐ 60 Wilson Whitley	1.00	.45	.12
☐ 61 Andre Ware	2.00	.90	.25
☐ 62 John Jenkins CO	.60	.25	.07
☐ NNO Ad Card Motion Sports	.50	.23	.06
☐ NNO Front Card	.50	.23	.06
☐ NNO Back Card	.50	.23	.06
☐ NNO Checklist	.50	.23	.06

1988 Humboldt State Smokey

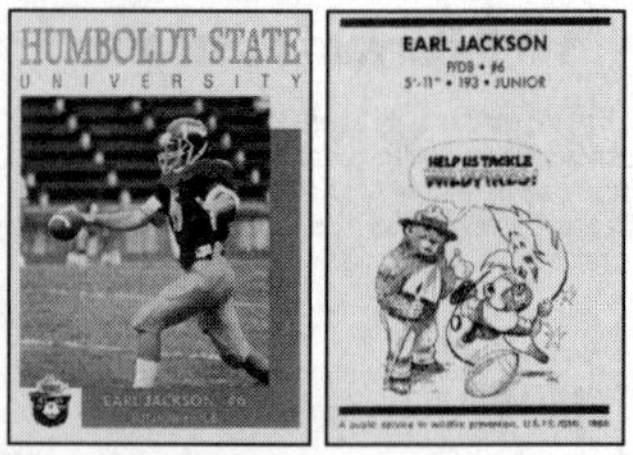

This unnumbered, 11-card standard-size set was issued by the Humboldt State University football team and sponsored by the U. S. Forest Service. The cards feature posed color photos on the front. The cards are bordered right and below in green, with player information below the photo in gold lettering. The Smokey Bear logo is in the lower left corner. The backs have biographical information on the player and a cartoon concerning fire prevention.

	MINT	NRMT	EXC
COMPLETE SET (11)	12.00	5.50	1.50
COMMON CARD (1-11)	1.25	.55	.16
☐ 1 Richard Ashe 1	1.25	.55	.16
☐ 2 Darin Bradbury 64	1.25	.55	.16
☐ 3 Rodney Dorsett 7	1.25	.55	.16
☐ 4 Dave Harper 55	1.25	.55	.16
☐ 5 Earl Jackson 6	1.25	.55	.16
☐ 6 Derek Mallard 82	1.25	.55	.16
☐ 7 Scott Reagan 60	1.25	.55	.16
☐ 8 Wesley White 1	1.25	.55	.16
☐ 9 Paul Wienecke 40	1.25	.55	.16
☐ 10 William Williams 14	1.25	.55	.16
☐ 11 Kelvin Windham 30	1.25	.55	.16

1989 Idaho

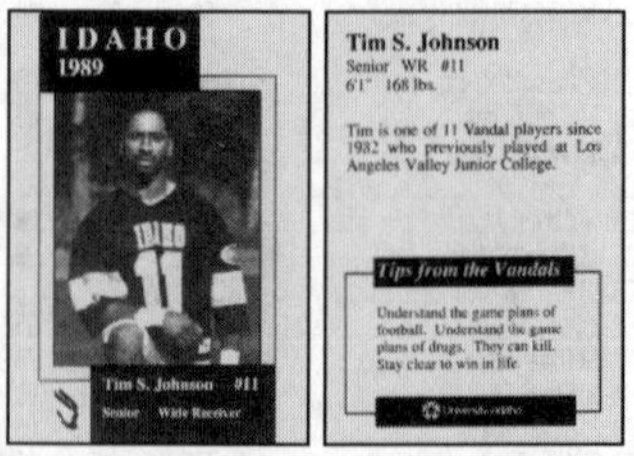

This 12-card set features then-current football players at the University of Idaho. The cards are unnumbered, so they are listed below according to uniform number, which is displayed on both sides of the card. The photos are in black and white. The cards in the set contain "Tips from the Vandals" on the reverses and measure approximately 2 1/2" by 3 1/2".

	MINT	NRMT	EXC
COMPLETE SET (12)	12.00	5.50	1.50
COMMON CARD	.75	.35	.09
☐ 3 Brian Smith	.75	.35	.09
☐ 11 Tim S. Johnson	.75	.35	.09

☐ 16 Lee Allen	.75	.35	.09
☐ 17 John Friesz	6.00	2.70	.75
☐ 20 Todd Hoiness	.75	.35	.09
☐ 25 David Jackson	.75	.35	.09
☐ 53 Steve Unger	.75	.35	.09
☐ 58 John Rust	.75	.35	.09
☐ 63 Troy Wright	.75	.35	.09
☐ 67 Todd Neu	.75	.35	.09
☐ 83 Michael Davis	.75	.35	.09
☐ 93 Mike Zeller	.75	.35	.09

1990 Illinois Centennial

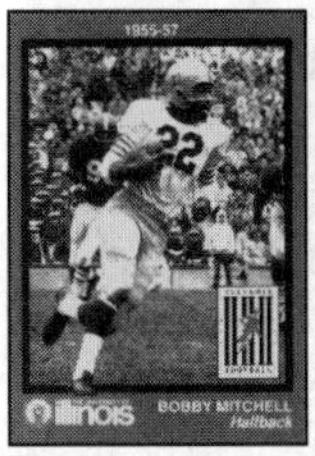

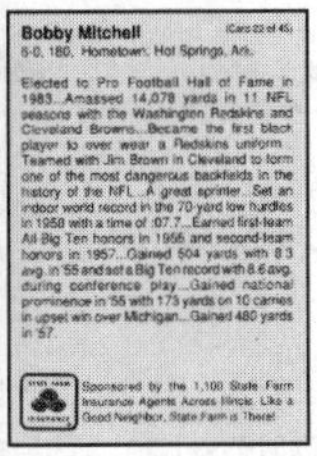

This 45-card set measures the standard size and was issued to celebrate 100 years of football at the University of Illinois. The set was produced by College Classics and the State Farm Insurance agents in Illinois. The front features either a color or black and white photo of the player with a dark blue border on an orange background. The back has biographical information as well as the card number.

	MINT	NRMT	EXC
COMPLETE SET (45)	30.00	13.50	3.70
COMMON CARD (1-45)	.40	.18	.05
☐ 1 Red Grange	4.00	1.80	.50
☐ 2 Dick Butkus	3.00	1.35	.35
☐ 3 Ray Nitschke	2.00	.90	.25
☐ 4 Jim Grabowski	.50	.23	.06
☐ 5 Alex Agase	.50	.23	.06
☐ 6 Claude Young	.50	.23	.06
☐ 7 Scott Studwell	.50	.23	.06
☐ 8 Tony Eason	.50	.23	.06
☐ 9 John Mackovic	.75	.35	.09
☐ 10 Jack Trudeau	.75	.35	.09
☐ 11 Jeff George	2.00	.90	.25
☐ 12 Rose Bowl Coaches	.40	.18	.05
Ray Eliot			
Pete Elliott			
Mike White			
☐ 13 George Huff	.40	.18	.05
☐ 14 David Williams	.40	.18	.05
☐ 15 Bob Zuppke	.75	.35	.09
☐ 16 George Halas	2.00	.90	.25
☐ 17 Dike Eddleman	.40	.18	.05
☐ 18 Dave Wilson	.40	.18	.05
☐ 19 Tab Bennett	.40	.18	.05
☐ 20 Jim Juriga	.40	.18	.05
☐ 21 John Karras	.40	.18	.05
☐ 22 Bobby Mitchell	1.00	.45	.12
☐ 23 Dan Beaver	.40	.18	.05
☐ 24 Joe Rutgens	.50	.23	.06
☐ 25 Bill Burrell	.40	.18	.05
☐ 26 J.C. Caroline	.50	.23	.06
☐ 27 Al Brosky	.40	.18	.05
☐ 28 Don Thorp	.40	.18	.05
☐ 29 First Football Team	.40	.18	.05
☐ 30 Red Grange Retired	2.00	.90	.25
☐ 31 Memorial Stadium	.40	.18	.05
☐ 32 Chris White	.40	.18	.05
☐ 33 Early Stars	.40	.18	.05
Ralph Chapman			
Perry Graves			
Bart Macomber			
☐ 34 Early Stars	.40	.18	.05
John Depler			
Charles Carney			
Jim McMillen			
☐ 35 Early Stars	.40	.18	.05
Burt Ingwerson			
Butch Nowack			
Bernie Shively			
☐ 36 Great Quarterbacks	.40	.18	.05
Fred Custardo			
Mike Wells			
Tom O'Connell			
☐ 37 Great Running Backs	.50	.23	.06
Thomas Rooks			
Abe Woodson			
Keith Jones			
☐ 38 Great Receivers	.50	.23	.06
Mike Bellamy			
Doug Dieken			
John Wright			
☐ 39 Great Offensive	.40	.18	.05
Forrest Van Hook			
Larry McCarren			
Chris Babyar			
☐ 40 Great Defensive Backs	.40	.18	.05
Craig Swope			
George Donnelly			
Mike Gower			
☐ 41 Great Linebackers	.40	.18	.05
Charles Boerio			
Don Hansen			
John Sullivan			
☐ 42 Defensive Linemen	.40	.18	.05
Archie Sutton			
Chuck Studley			
Scott Davis			
☐ 43 Great Kickers	.40	.18	.05
Mike Bass K			
Bill Brown			
Frosty Peters			
☐ 44 Retired Numbers	1.50	.70	.19
Dick Butkus			
☐ 45 Football Centennial	.40	.18	.05
Logo			

1992 Illinois

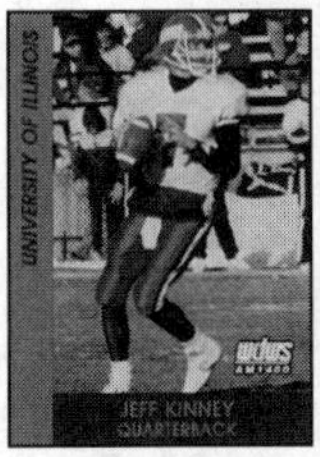

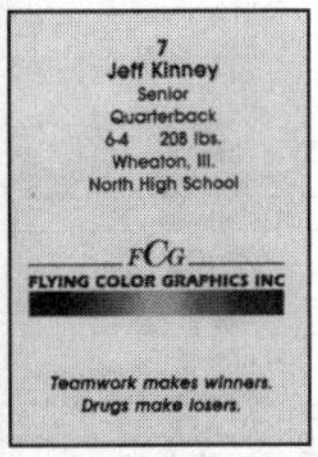

Produced by Flying Color Graphics Inc. and sponsored by WDWS radio station (AM 1400), this 48-card standard-size set features the University of Illinois football team. The cards are printed on thin card stock. The fronts feature a mix of posed or action color player photos. The pictures are bordered on the left by an orange stripe and at the bottom by a purple stripe. The player's name and position are printed in the purple stripe. The backs carry biographical information, the producer's logo, and a brief public service announcement. The cards are unnumbered and checklisted below in alphabetical order.

	MINT	NRMT	EXC
COMPLETE SET (48)	20.00	9.00	2.50
COMMON CARD (1-48)	.35	.16	.04
☐ 1 Derek Allen	.35	.16	.04
☐ 2 Jeff Arneson	.35	.16	.04
☐ 3 Randy Bierman	.35	.16	.04
☐ 4 Darren Boyer	.35	.16	.04
☐ 5 Rod Boykin	.35	.16	.04
☐ 6 Mike Cole	.35	.16	.04
☐ 7 Chad Copher	.35	.16	.04
☐ 8 Fred Cox	.50	.23	.06
☐ 9 Robert Crumpton	.50	.23	.06
☐ 10 Ken Dilger	2.50	1.10	.30
☐ 11 Jason Edwards	.35	.16	.04
☐ 12 Greg Engel	.35	.16	.04
☐ 13 Steve Feagin	.35	.16	.04
☐ 14 Erik Foggey	.35	.16	.04
☐ 15 Kevin Hardy	4.00	1.80	.50
☐ 16 Jeff Hasenstab	.35	.16	.04
☐ 17 John Holecek	.50	.23	.06
☐ 18 Brad Hopkins	1.00	.45	.12
☐ 19 John Horn	.35	.16	.04
☐ 20 Dana Howard	1.00	.45	.12
☐ 21 Filmel Johnson	.35	.16	.04
☐ 22 Jon Kerr	.35	.16	.04
☐ 23 Jeff Kinney	.50	.23	.06
☐ 24 Jim Klein	.35	.16	.04
☐ 25 Todd Leach	.35	.16	.04
☐ 26 Wagner Lester	.35	.16	.04
☐ 27 Lashon Ludington	.35	.16	.04
☐ 28 Clinton Lynch	.35	.16	.04
☐ 29 Tim McCloud	.35	.16	.04
☐ 30 David Olson	.35	.16	.04
☐ 31 Antwoine Patton	.50	.23	.06
☐ 32 Jim Pesek	.35	.16	.04
☐ 33 Alfred Pierce	.35	.16	.04
☐ 34 Mark Qualls	.35	.16	.04
☐ 35 Phil Rathke	.35	.16	.04
☐ 36 Chris Richardson	.50	.23	.06
☐ 37 Derrick Rucker	.35	.16	.04
☐ 38 Aaron Shelby	.35	.16	.04
☐ 39 John Sidari	.35	.16	.04
☐ 40 J.J. Strong	.35	.16	.04
☐ 41 Mike Suarez	.35	.16	.04
☐ 42 Lou Tepper CO	.50	.23	.06
☐ 43 Scott Turner	.35	.16	.04
☐ 44 Jason Verduzco	1.00	.45	.12
☐ 45 Tyrone Washington	.35	.16	.04
☐ 46 Forry Wells	.35	.16	.04
☐ 47 Pat Wendt	.35	.16	.04
☐ 48 John Wright	.35	.16	.04

1982 Indiana State Police

This 64-card police set was sponsored by First National Bank (Terre Haute), 7-Up, and WTHI/TV (Channel 10). The cards measure approximately 2 5/8" by 4 1/8". A white diagonal cutting across the bottom of the card face has a drawing of the school mascot (an Indian with tomahawk in hand) and the words "Sycamore Rampage." The backs have brief biographical information, a trivia feature about the player, an anti-drug or alcohol message, and sponsor logos. The cards are unnumbered and checklisted below in alphabetical order by subject.

	MINT	NRMT	EXC
COMPLETE SET (64)	150.00	70.00	19.00
COMMON CARD (1-64)	3.00	1.35	.35
☐ 1 David Allen	3.00	1.35	.35
☐ 2 Doug Arnold	3.00	1.35	.35
☐ 3 James Banks	3.00	1.35	.35
☐ 4 Scott Bartel	3.00	1.35	.35
☐ 5 Kurt Bell	3.00	1.35	.35
☐ 6 Terry Bell	3.00	1.35	.35
☐ 7 Steve Bidwell	3.00	1.35	.35
☐ 8 Keith Bonney	3.00	1.35	.35
☐ 9 Mark Boster	3.00	1.35	.35
☐ 10 Bobby Boyce	3.00	1.35	.35
☐ 11 Steve Brickey CO	3.00	1.35	.35
☐ 12 Mark Bryson	3.00	1.35	.35
☐ 13 Steve Buxton	3.00	1.35	.35
☐ 14 Ed Campbell	3.00	1.35	.35
☐ 15 Jeff Campbell	4.00	1.80	.50
☐ 16 Tom Chapman	3.00	1.35	.35
☐ 17 Cheerleaders	3.00	1.35	.35
(Ruth Ann Medworth DIR)			
☐ 18 Darrold Clardy	3.00	1.35	.35
☐ 19 Wayne Davis	3.00	1.35	.35
☐ 20 Herbert Dawson	3.00	1.35	.35
☐ 21 Richard Dawson	3.00	1.35	.35
☐ 22 Chris Delaplaine	3.00	1.35	.35
☐ 23 Max Dillon	3.00	1.35	.35
☐ 24 Rick Dwenger	3.00	1.35	.35
☐ 25 Ed Foggs	3.00	1.35	.35
☐ 26 Allen Hartwig	3.00	1.35	.35
☐ 27 Pat Henderson CO	3.00	1.35	.35
☐ 28 Don Hitz	3.00	1.35	.35
☐ 29 Pete Hoener CO	3.00	1.35	.35
☐ 30 Bob Hopkins	3.00	1.35	.35
☐ 31 Kris Huber	3.00	1.35	.35
Baton Twirler			
☐ 32 Leroy Irvin	4.00	1.80	.50
☐ 33 Mike Johannes	3.00	1.35	.35
☐ 34 Anthony Kimball	3.00	1.35	.35
☐ 35 Gregg Kimbrough	3.00	1.35	.35
☐ 36 Bob Koehne	3.00	1.35	.35
☐ 37 Jerry Lasko CO	3.00	1.35	.35
☐ 38 Kevin Lynch	3.00	1.35	.35
☐ 39 Dan Maher	3.00	1.35	.35
☐ 40 Ed Martin	3.00	1.35	.35
☐ 41 Regis Mason	3.00	1.35	.35
☐ 42 Rob McIntyre	3.00	1.35	.35
☐ 43 Quintin Mikell	3.00	1.35	.35
☐ 44 Jeff Miller	3.00	1.35	.35
☐ 45 Mark Miller	3.00	1.35	.35
☐ 46 Mike Osborne	3.00	1.35	.35
☐ 47 Max Payne CO	3.00	1.35	.35
☐ 48 Scott Piercy	3.00	1.35	.35
☐ 49 Dennis Raetz CO	3.00	1.35	.35
☐ 50 Kevin Ramsey	3.00	1.35	.35
☐ 51 Dean Reader	3.00	1.35	.35
☐ 52 Eric Robinson	3.00	1.35	.35
☐ 53 Walter Seaphus	3.00	1.35	.35
☐ 54 Sparkettes	3.00	1.35	.35
(Marthann Markler DIR)			
☐ 55 John Spradley	3.00	1.35	.35
☐ 56 Manual Studway	3.00	1.35	.35
☐ 57 Sam Suggs	3.00	1.35	.35
☐ 58 Larry Swart	3.00	1.35	.35
☐ 59 Bob Tyree	3.00	1.35	.35
☐ 60 Bob Turner CO	3.00	1.35	.35
☐ 61 Brad Verdun	3.00	1.35	.35
☐ 62 Keith Ward	3.00	1.35	.35
☐ 63 Sean Whiten	3.00	1.35	.35
☐ 64 Perry Willett	3.00	1.35	.35

1971 Iowa Team Photos

This 32-player University of Iowa photo set was issued as four sheets measuring approximately 8" by 10" featuring eight black and white player portraits. The backs are blank. We have arranged the photos in order alphabetically by the player in the upper left hand corner.

	NRMT-MT	EXC	G-VG
COMPLETE SET (4)	30.00	13.50	3.70
COMMON SHEET	7.00	3.10	.85
☐ 1 Geoff Mickelson	10.00	4.50	1.25
Craig Clemons			
Frank Holmes			
Levi Mitchell			
Charles Podolak			
Lorin Lynch			
Steve Penney			
Larry Horton			
☐ 2 Alan Schaefer	7.00	3.10	.85
Dave Triplett			
John Muller			
Jim Kaiser			
Wendell Bell			
Clark Malmer			
Rich Solomon			
Kelly Disser			
☐ 3 Bill Schoonover	7.00	3.10	.85
Frank Sunderman			
Craig Darling			
Tom Cabalka			
Dave Simms			
Bill Rose			
Buster Hoinkes			
Charles Cross			
☐ 4 Kyle Skogman	7.00	3.10	.85
Kerry Reardon			
Dave Harris			
Rob Fick			
Mike Dillner			
Ike White			
Mark Nelson			
Harry Kokolus			

1984 Iowa

The 1984 Iowa Hawkeyes set contains 60 standard-size cards. The fronts feature color portrait photos bordered in black. The backs provide brief profiles. The cards are unnumbered and so they are listed in alphabetical order.

	MINT	NRMT	EXC
COMPLETE SET (60)	50.00	22.00	6.25
COMMON CARD (1-60)	.75	.35	.09
☐ 1 Kevin Angel	.75	.35	.09
☐ 2 Kerry Burt	.75	.35	.09
☐ 3 Fred Bush	.75	.35	.09
☐ 4 Craig Clark	.75	.35	.09
☐ 5 Zane Corbin	.75	.35	.09
☐ 6 Nate Creer	.75	.35	.09
☐ 7 Dave Croston	.75	.35	.09
☐ 8 George Davis	.75	.35	.09
☐ 9 Jeff Drost	.75	.35	.09
☐ 10 Quinn Early	5.00	2.20	.60
☐ 11 Mike Flagg	.75	.35	.09
☐ 12 Hayden Fry CO	2.50	1.10	.30
☐ 13 Bruce Gear	.75	.35	.09
☐ 14 Owen Gill	2.00	.90	.25
☐ 15 Bill Glass	1.00	.45	.12
☐ 16 Mike Haight	1.50	.70	.19
☐ 17 Bill Happel	.75	.35	.09
☐ 18 Kevin Harmon	1.00	.45	.12
☐ 19 Ronnie Harmon	5.00	2.20	.60
☐ 20 Craig Hartman	.75	.35	.09
☐ 21 Jonathan Hayes	2.00	.90	.25
☐ 22 Erric Hedgeman	.75	.35	.09
☐ 23 Scott Helverson	.75	.35	.09
☐ 24 Mike Hooks	.75	.35	.09
☐ 25 Paul Hufford	.75	.35	.09
☐ 26 Keith Hunter	.75	.35	.09
☐ 27 George Little	.75	.35	.09
☐ 28 Chuck Long	2.00	.90	.25
☐ 29 J.C. Love-Jordan	.75	.35	.09
☐ 30 George Millett	.75	.35	.09
☐ 31 Devon Mitchell	1.00	.45	.12
☐ 32 Tom Nichol	.75	.35	.09
☐ 33 Kelly O'Brien	.75	.35	.09
☐ 34 Hap Peterson	.75	.35	.09
☐ 35 Joe Schuster	1.00	.45	.12
☐ 36 Tim Sennott	.75	.35	.09
☐ 37 Ken Sims	.75	.35	.09
☐ 38 Mark Sindlinger	.75	.35	.09
☐ 39 Robert Smith	.75	.35	.09
☐ 40 Kevin Spitzig	.75	.35	.09
☐ 41 Larry Station	.75	.35	.09
☐ 42 Mike Stoops	.75	.35	.09
☐ 43 Dave Strobel	.75	.35	.09
☐ 44 Mark Vlasic	2.00	.90	.25
☐ 45 Jon Vrieze	.75	.35	.09
☐ 46 Tony Wancket	.75	.35	.09
☐ 47 Herb Webster	.75	.35	.09
☐ 48 Coaching Staff	1.00	.45	.12
☐ 49 Captains	1.50	.70	.19
☐ 50 Bowl Players	1.00	.45	.12
☐ 51 Kevin Harmon	1.50	.70	.19
Ronnie Harmon			
Harmon Brothers			
☐ 52 Cheerleaders	.75	.35	.09
☐ 53 Pompons	1.00	.45	.12
☐ 54 Kinnick Stadium	.75	.35	.09
☐ 55 Herky the Hawk	.75	.35	.09
(Mascot)			
☐ 56 Rose Bowl Ring	.75	.35	.09
☐ 57 Peach Bowl Trophy	.75	.35	.09
☐ 58 Gator Bowl Stadium	.75	.35	.09
☐ 59 Floyd of Rosedale	.75	.35	.09
(Trophy)			
☐ 60 Checklist Card	.75	.35	.09

1987 Iowa

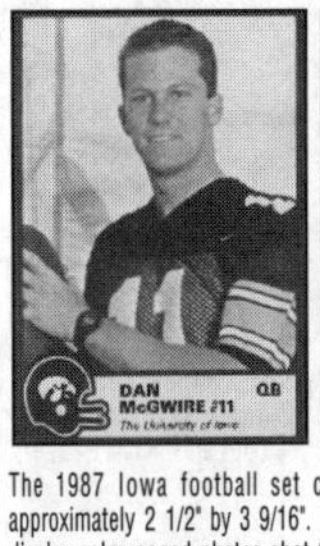

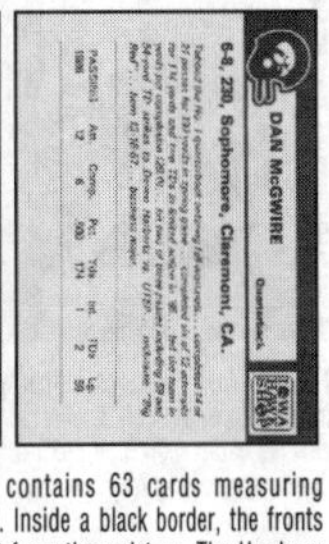

The 1987 Iowa football set contains 63 cards measuring approximately 2 1/2" by 3 9/16". Inside a black border, the fronts display color posed photos shot from the waist up. The Hawkeye helmet appears in the lower left corner, with player information in a yellow stripe extending to the right. The horizontally oriented backs

have biographical information, player profile, and bowl game emblems. The cards are unnumbered and checklisted below in alphabetical order, with non-player cards listed at the end.

	MINT	NRMT	EXC
COMPLETE SET (63)	40.00	18.00	5.00
COMMON CARD (1-63)	.60	.25	.07
☐ 1 Mark Adams	.60	.25	.07
☐ 2 Dave Alexander	1.00	.45	.12
☐ 3 Bill Anderson	.60	.25	.07
☐ 4 Tim Anderson	.60	.25	.07
☐ 5 Rick Bayless	.60	.25	.07
☐ 6 Jeff Beard	.60	.25	.07
☐ 7 Mike Burke	.60	.25	.07
☐ 8 Kerry Burt	.60	.25	.07
☐ 9 Malcolm Christie	.60	.25	.07
☐ 10 Craig Clark	.60	.25	.07
☐ 11 Marv Cook	2.00	.90	.25
☐ 12 Jeff Croston	.60	.25	.07
☐ 13 Greg Divis	.60	.25	.07
☐ 14 Quinn Early	3.00	1.35	.35
☐ 15 Greg Fedders	.60	.25	.07
☐ 16 Mike Flagg	.60	.25	.07
☐ 17 Melvin Foster	.60	.25	.07
☐ 18 Hayden Fry CO	2.00	.90	.25
☐ 19 Grant Goodman	.60	.25	.07
☐ 20 Dave Haight	1.00	.45	.12
☐ 21 Merton Hanks	3.00	1.35	.35
☐ 22 Deven Harberts	.60	.25	.07
☐ 23 Kevin Harmon	.75	.35	.09
☐ 24 Chuck Hartlieb	1.25	.55	.16
☐ 25 Tork Hook	.60	.25	.07
☐ 26 Rob Houghtlin	.60	.25	.07
☐ 27 David Hudson	.60	.25	.07
☐ 28 Myron Keppy	.60	.25	.07
☐ 29 Jeff Koeppel	.60	.25	.07
☐ 30 Bob Kratch	1.50	.70	.19
☐ 31 Peter Marciano	.60	.25	.07
☐ 32 Jim Mauro	.60	.25	.07
☐ 33 Marc Mazzeri	.60	.25	.07
☐ 34 Dan McGwire	2.00	.90	.25
☐ 35 Mike Miller	.60	.25	.07
☐ 36 Joe Mott	1.00	.45	.12
☐ 37 James Pipkins	.60	.25	.07
☐ 38 Tom Poholsky	.75	.35	.09
☐ 39 Jim Poynton	.60	.25	.07
☐ 40 J.J. Puk	.60	.25	.07
☐ 41 Brad Quast	.60	.25	.07
☐ 42 Jim Reilly	.60	.25	.07
☐ 43 Matt Ruhland	.60	.25	.07
☐ 44 Bob Schmitt	.60	.25	.07
☐ 45 Joe Schuster	.60	.25	.07
☐ 46 Dwight Sistrunk	.75	.35	.09
☐ 47 Mark Stoops	.60	.25	.07
☐ 48 Steve Thomas	.60	.25	.07
☐ 49 Kent Thompson	.60	.25	.07
☐ 50 Travis Watkins	.60	.25	.07
☐ 51 Herb Wester	.60	.25	.07
☐ 52 Anthony Wright	.60	.25	.07
☐ 53 Big 10 Championship Ring and Rose Bowl Ring	.60	.25	.07
☐ 54 Cheerleaders	.60	.25	.07
☐ 55 Floyd of Rosedale (Trophy)	.60	.25	.07
☐ 56 Freedom Bowl (Game Action Photo)	.75	.35	.09
☐ 57 Herky the Hawk (Mascot)	.60	.25	.07
☐ 58 Holiday Bowl (Game Action Photo)	.75	.35	.09
☐ 59 Indoor Practice Facility	.60	.25	.07
☐ 60 Iowa Team Captains (Quinn Early and five others)	1.50	.70	.19
☐ 61 Kinnick Stadium	.60	.25	.07
☐ 62 Peach Bowl (Game Action Photo)	.60	.25	.07
☐ 63 Pom Pons (Cheerleaders)	.60	.25	.07

1988 Iowa

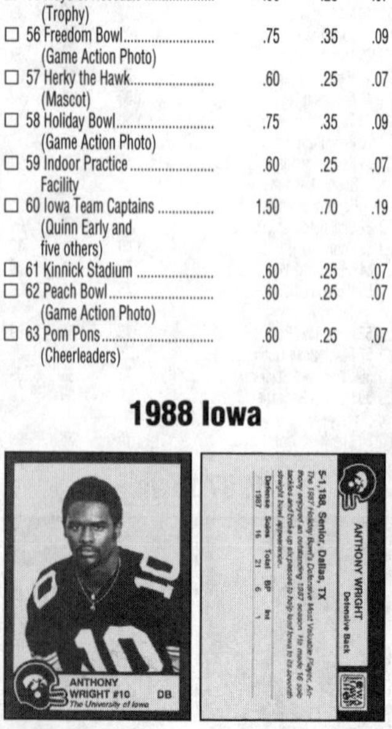

The 1988 Iowa Hawkeyes set contains 64 standard-size cards. The fronts feature color portrait photos bordered in black. The horizontally oriented backs show brief profiles. The cards are unnumbered and, therefore, listed by jersey numbers.

	MINT	NRMT	EXC
COMPLETE SET (64)	30.00	13.50	3.70
COMMON CARD	.50	.23	.06
☐ 2 Travis Watkins	.60	.25	.07
☐ 4 James Pipkins	.50	.23	.06
☐ 5 Mike Burke	.50	.23	.06
☐ 8 Chuck Hartlieb	1.00	.45	.12
☐ 10 Anthony Wright	.50	.23	.06
☐ 14 Tom Poholsky	.60	.25	.07
☐ 16 Deven Harberts	.50	.23	.06
☐ 18 Leroy Smith	.50	.23	.06
☐ 20 David Hudson	.50	.23	.06
☐ 21 Tony Stewart	.50	.23	.06
☐ 22 Sean Smith	.50	.23	.06
☐ 23 Richard Bass	.50	.23	.06
☐ 26 Peter Marciano	.50	.23	.06
☐ 29 Greg Brown	.50	.23	.06
☐ 30 Grant Goodman	.50	.23	.06
☐ 31 John Derby	.50	.23	.06
☐ 32 Mike Saunders	1.00	.45	.12
☐ 35 Brad Quast	.50	.23	.06
☐ 38 Chet Davis	.50	.23	.06
☐ 40 Marc Mazzeri	.50	.23	.06
☐ 41 Mark Stoops	.50	.23	.06
☐ 42 Tork Hook	.50	.23	.06
☐ 44 Keaton Smiley	.50	.23	.06
☐ 45 Merton Hanks	2.50	1.10	.30
☐ 48 Tyrone Berrie	.50	.23	.06
☐ 50 Bill Anderson	.50	.23	.06
☐ 51 Jeff Koeppel	.50	.23	.06
☐ 53 Greg Fedders	.50	.23	.06
☐ 57 Matt Ruhland	.50	.23	.06
☐ 58 Greg Davis	.50	.23	.06
☐ 60 Bob Schmitt	.50	.23	.06
☐ 61 Dave Turner	.50	.23	.06
☐ 64 Dave Haight	.75	.35	.09
☐ 66 Melvin Foster	.50	.23	.06
☐ 67 Jim Poynton	.50	.23	.06
☐ 68 Tim Anderson	.50	.23	.06
☐ 70 Bob Kratch	1.00	.45	.12
☐ 71 Jim Johnson	.50	.23	.06
☐ 74 George Hawthorne	.50	.23	.06
☐ 75 Greg Aegerter	.50	.23	.06
☐ 77 Paul Glonek	.50	.23	.06
☐ 80 Steve Green	.50	.23	.06
☐ 81 Brian Wise	.50	.23	.06
☐ 82 Jon Filloon	.50	.23	.06
☐ 84 Marv Cook	2.00	.90	.25
☐ 85 John Palmer	.60	.25	.07
☐ 87 Jeff Skillett	.50	.23	.06
☐ 88 Tom Ward	.50	.23	.06
☐ 95 Jim Reilly	.50	.23	.06
☐ 96 Ron Geater	.50	.23	.06
☐ 97 Joe Mott	.75	.35	.09
☐ 99 Moses Santos	.50	.23	.06
☐ NNO Team Captains (Marv Cook and four others)	1.00	.45	.12
☐ NNO Hayden Fry CO	1.50	.70	.19
☐ NNO Holiday Bowl 1987 Hayden Fry CO)	.75	.35	.09
☐ NNO Peach Bowl (Game Action Photo)	.60	.25	.07
☐ NNO Holiday Bowl 1986 (Game Action Photo)	.60	.25	.07
☐ NNO Herky the Hawk(Mascot)	.50	.23	.06
☐ NNO Cheerleaders	.50	.23	.06
☐ NNO Kinnick Stadium	.50	.23	.06
☐ NNO Pom Pons (Cheerleaders)	.50	.23	.06
☐ NNO Championship Rings	.50	.23	.06
☐ NNO Indoor Practice Facility	.50	.23	.06
☐ NNO Symbolic Tiger Hawk (Helmet)	.50	.23	.06

1989 Iowa

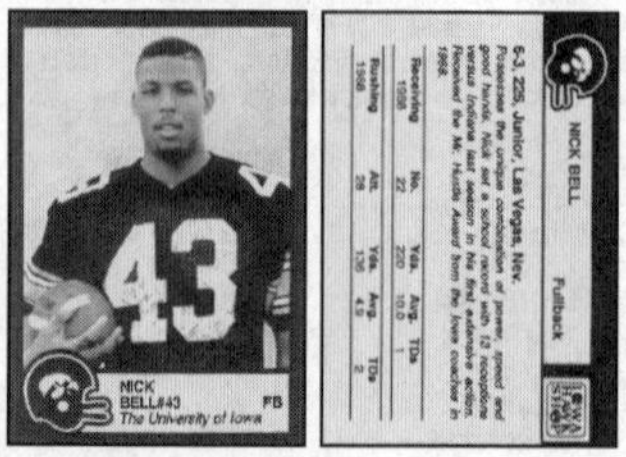

The 1989 Iowa football set contains 90 cards measuring approximately 2 1/2" by 3 9/16". Inside a black border, the fronts display color posed photos shot from the waist up. The team helmet appears in the lower left corner, with player information in a yellow stripe extending to the right. The horizontally oriented backs have biographical information, player profile, and bowl game emblems. The cards are unnumbered and checklisted below in alphabetical order, with non-player cards listed at the end.

	MINT	NRMT	EXC
COMPLETE SET (90)	30.00	13.50	3.70
COMMON CARD (1-90)	.40	.18	.05
☐ 1 Greg Aegerter	.40	.18	.05
☐ 2 Kevin Allendorf	.40	.18	.05
☐ 3 Bill Anderson	.40	.18	.05
☐ 4 Richard Bass	.40	.18	.05
☐ 5 Rob Baxley	.40	.18	.05
☐ 6 Nick Bell	1.50	.70	.19
☐ 7 Phil Bradley	.40	.18	.05
☐ 8 Greg Brown	.40	.18	.05
☐ 9 Doug Buch	.40	.18	.05
☐ 10 Gary Clark	.40	.18	.05
☐ 11 Roderick Davis	.40	.18	.05
☐ 12 Scott Davis	1.00	.45	.12
☐ 13 John Derby	.50	.23	.06
☐ 14 Mike Devlin	.40	.18	.05
☐ 15 Jason Dumont	.40	.18	.05
☐ 16 Mike Ertz	.40	.18	.05
☐ 17 Ted Faley	.40	.18	.05
☐ 18 Greg Fedders	.40	.18	.05
☐ 19 Mike Ferroni	.50	.23	.06
☐ 20 Jon Filloon	.40	.18	.05
☐ 21 Melvin Foster	.50	.23	.06
☐ 22 Hayden Fry CO	1.00	.45	.12
☐ 23 Ron Geater	.40	.18	.05
☐ 24 Ed Gochenour	.40	.18	.05
☐ 25 Merton Hanks	2.00	.90	.25
☐ 26 Jim Hartlieb	.50	.23	.06
☐ 27 George Hawthorne	.40	.18	.05
☐ 28 Tork Hook	.40	.18	.05
☐ 29 Danan Hughes	1.50	.70	.19
☐ 30 Jim Johnson	.40	.18	.05
☐ 31 Jeff Koeppel	.40	.18	.05
☐ 32 Marvin Lampkin	.40	.18	.05
☐ 33 Peter Marciano	.40	.18	.05
☐ 34 Ed Marshall	.40	.18	.05
☐ 35 Kirk McGowan	.40	.18	.05
☐ 36 Mike Miller	.40	.18	.05
☐ 37 Lew Montgomery	.40	.18	.05
☐ 38 George Murphy	.40	.18	.05
☐ 39 John Palmer	.50	.23	.06
☐ 40 James Pipkins	.40	.18	.05
☐ 41 Tom Poholsky	.50	.23	.06
☐ 42 Eddie Polly	.40	.18	.05
☐ 43 Jim Poynton	.40	.18	.05
☐ 44 Brad Quast	.40	.18	.05
☐ 45 Matt Rodgers	.75	.35	.09
☐ 46 Matt Ruhland	.40	.18	.05
☐ 47 Ron Ryan	.40	.18	.05
☐ 48 Moses Santos	.40	.18	.05
☐ 49 Mike Saunders	.75	.35	.09
☐ 50 Doug Scott	.40	.18	.05
☐ 51 Jeff Skillett	.40	.18	.05
☐ 52 Leroy Smith	.40	.18	.05
☐ 53 Sean Smith	.40	.18	.05
☐ 54 Sean Snyder	.40	.18	.05
☐ 55 Tony Stewart	.40	.18	.05
☐ 56 Mark Stoops	.40	.18	.05
☐ 57 Dave Turner	.40	.18	.05
☐ 58 Darin Vande Zande	.40	.18	.05
☐ 59 Ted Velicer	.40	.18	.05
☐ 60 Travis Watkins	.40	.18	.05
☐ 61 Dusty Weiland	.40	.18	.05
☐ 62 Ladd Wessels	.40	.18	.05
☐ 63 Matt Whitaker	.40	.18	.05
☐ 64 Brian Wise	.40	.18	.05
☐ 65 Anthony Wright	.40	.18	.05
☐ 66 100 Years of Iowa Football (Logo)	.40	.18	.05
☐ 67 The Tigerhawk (School Logo)	.40	.18	.05
☐ 68 Herky The Hawk (Mascot)	.40	.18	.05
☐ 69 Kinnick Stadium	.40	.18	.05
☐ 70 Hawkeye Fans	.40	.18	.05
☐ 71 NFL Tradition (Logo)	.40	.18	.05
☐ 72 1982 Peach Bowl (Logo)	.40	.18	.05
☐ 73 1982 Rose Bowl (Logo)	.40	.18	.05
☐ 74 1983 Gator Bowl (Logo)	.40	.18	.05
☐ 75 1984 Freedom Bowl (Logo)	.40	.18	.05
☐ 76 1986 Holiday Bowl (Logo)	.40	.18	.05
☐ 77 1986 Rose Bowl (Logo)	.40	.18	.05
☐ 78 1987 Holiday Bowl (Logo)	.40	.18	.05
☐ 79 1988 Peach Bowl (Logo)	.40	.18	.05
☐ 80 Big Ten Conference (Logo)	.40	.18	.05
☐ 81 Iowa Marching Band	.40	.18	.05
☐ 82 Indoor Practice Facility	.40	.18	.05
☐ 83 Iowa Locker Rooms	.40	.18	.05
☐ 84 Iowa Weight Room	.40	.18	.05
☐ 85 Iowa Class Rooms	.40	.18	.05
☐ 86 Players' Lounge	.40	.18	.05
☐ 87 Floyd of Rosedale (Trophy)	.40	.18	.05
☐ 88 Medical Facilities	.40	.18	.05
☐ 89 Media Coverage	.40	.18	.05
☐ 90 Television Coverage (Camera)	.40	.18	.05

1993 Iowa

The 1993 Iowa set consists of 64 standard-size cards. The fronts feature black-bordered color player photos, mostly posed, with the player's name and uniform number appearing in gold-colored lettering within the top margin. The team name and the player's postion are shown in gold-colored lettering within the bottom margin. The yellow horizontal back carries the player's name, position, and biography in white lettering within the black stripe across the top. Below are the

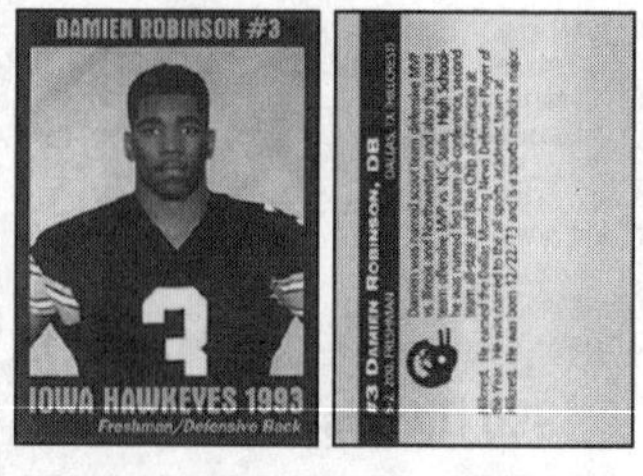

player's high school and college football highlights. The cards are unnumbered and checklisted below in alphabetical order, with nonplayer cards listed at the end.

	MINT	NRMT	EXC
COMPLETE SET (64)	30.00	13.50	3.70
COMMON CARD (1-64)	.40	.18	.05
☐ 1 Ryan Abraham	.75	.35	.09
☐ 2 Greg Allen	.40	.18	.05
☐ 3 Jeff Andrews	.40	.18	.05
☐ 4 Jeff Anttila	.40	.18	.05
☐ 5 Jefferson Bates	.40	.18	.05
☐ 6 George Bennett	.40	.18	.05
☐ 7 Lloyd Bickham	.40	.18	.05
☐ 8 Larry Blue	.40	.18	.05
☐ 9 Pat Boone	.40	.18	.05
☐ 10 Tyrone Boudreaux	.40	.18	.05
☐ 11 Paul Burmeister	.75	.35	.09
☐ 12 Tyler Casey	.40	.18	.05
☐ 13 Billy Coats	.40	.18	.05
☐ 14 Maurea Crain	.40	.18	.05
☐ 15 Ernest Crank	.50	.23	.06
☐ 16 Mike Dailey	.40	.18	.05
☐ 17 Anthony Dean	.50	.23	.06
☐ 18 Bobby Diaco	.40	.18	.05
☐ 19 Mike Duprey	.40	.18	.05
☐ 20 Billy Ennis-Inge	.75	.35	.09
☐ 21 Matt Eyde	.40	.18	.05
☐ 22 Fritz Fequiere	.75	.35	.09
☐ 23 Hayden Fry CO	1.00	.45	.12
☐ 24 Willie Guy	.40	.18	.05
☐ 25 John Hartlieb	.50	.23	.06
☐ 26 Jason Henlon	.40	.18	.05
☐ 27 Matt Hilliard	.40	.18	.05
☐ 28 Mike Hornaday	.40	.18	.05
☐ 29 Rob Huber	.40	.18	.05
☐ 30 Chris Jackson	.40	.18	.05
☐ 31 Harold Jasper	.75	.35	.09
☐ 32 Jamar Jones	.40	.18	.05
☐ 33 Kent Kahl	.40	.18	.05
☐ 34 Cliff King	.40	.18	.05
☐ 35 John Kline	.40	.18	.05
☐ 36 Tom Knight	2.00	.90	.25
☐ 37 Aaron Kooiker	.40	.18	.05
☐ 38 Andy Kreider	.40	.18	.05
☐ 39 Bill Lange	.40	.18	.05
☐ 40 Doug Laufenberg	.40	.18	.05
☐ 41 Hal Mady	.50	.23	.06
☐ 42 Brian McCullouch	.40	.18	.05
☐ 43 Jason Olejniczak	.40	.18	.05
☐ 44 Chris Palmer	.40	.18	.05
☐ 45 Scott Plate	.50	.23	.06
☐ 46 Marquis Porter	.50	.23	.06
☐ 47 Matt Purdy	.40	.18	.05
☐ 48 Matt Quest	.40	.18	.05
☐ 49 Damien Robinson	.50	.23	.06
☐ 50 Todd Romano	.40	.18	.05
☐ 51 Mark Roussell	.40	.18	.05
☐ 52 Ted Serama	.40	.18	.05
☐ 53 Scott Sether	.40	.18	.05
☐ 54 Sedrick Shaw	4.00	1.80	.50
☐ 55 Scott Slutzker	.50	.23	.06
☐ 56 Ryan Terry	.50	.23	.06
☐ 57 Mike Wells	.40	.18	.05
☐ 58 Casey Wiegmann	.40	.18	.05
☐ 59 Parker Wildeman	.40	.18	.05
☐ 60 Big Ten Conference (Logo card)	.40	.18	.05
☐ 61 Hawkeyes Schedule	.40	.18	.05
☐ 62 Herky (Mascot)	.40	.18	.05
☐ 63 Indoor Practice Facility	.40	.18	.05
☐ 64 Kinnick Stadium	.40	.18	.05

1997 Iowa

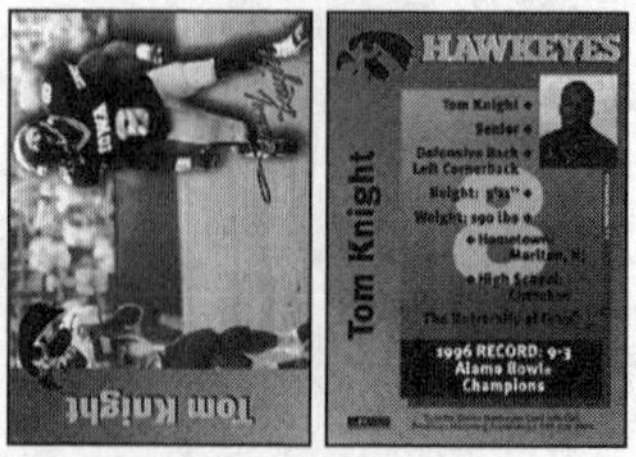

This 19 card standard-sized set was issued in 1997 by American Marketing Associates to commemorate the 1996 Alamo Bowl

champions. The cards are done in a horizontal fashion, with a full bleed photo and facsimile signature on the front with the player's name on the left side of the card. Reportedly 2,000 sets were produced. The set is listed below in alphabetical order.

	MINT	NRMT	EXC
COMPLETE SET (19)	30.00	13.50	3.70
COMMON CARD (1-19)	1.50	.70	.19

☐ 1 Brett Chambers	1.50	.70	.19
☐ 2 Billy Coats	1.50	.70	.19
☐ 3 Ryan Driscoll	2.00	.90	.25
☐ 4 Bill Ennis-Inge	2.50	1.10	.30
☐ 5 Rodney Filer	1.50	.70	.19
☐ 6 Hayden Fry	2.50	1.10	.30
☐ 7 Nick Gallery	1.50	.70	.19
☐ 8 Aaron Granquist	1.50	.70	.19
☐ 9 Brion Hurley	1.50	.70	.19
☐ 10 Tom Knight	3.00	1.35	.35
☐ 11 Mark Mitchell	1.50	.70	.19
☐ 12 Demo Odems	1.50	.70	.19
☐ 13 Jon Ortlieb	1.50	.70	.19
☐ 14 Bill Reardon	1.50	.70	.19
☐ 15 Damien Robinson	2.50	1.10	.30
☐ 16 Ted Serama	1.50	.70	.19
☐ 17 Ross Verba	2.50	1.10	.30
☐ 18 Hawk Watch 1996 Seniors Iowa Hawkeyes Football	2.00	.90	.25
☐ 19 Hawkeyes Logo	1.50	.70	.19

1907 Ivy League Postcards

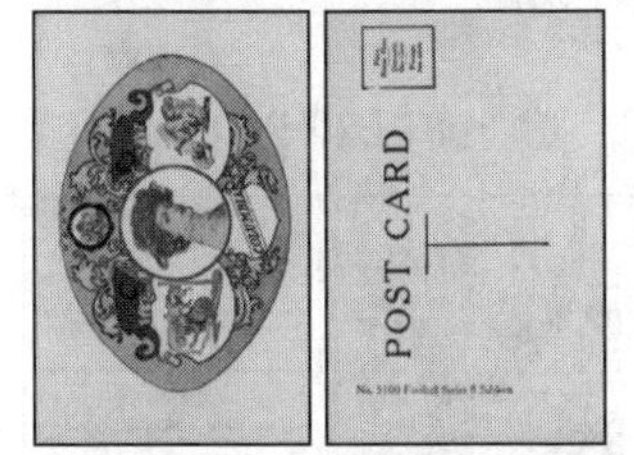

This postcard series features schools of the Ivy League. Each card (3 5/8" by 5 1/2") includes an artist's rendering of a woman's face surrounded by two football action scenes within the outline of a football. The copyright line reads "1907 P.Gordon" and the back features a standard postcard design. The title "No. 5100 Football Series 8 Subjects" is included on the cardback as well.

	EX	VG	GOOD
COMPLETE SET (8)	200.00	90.00	25.00
COMMON CARD	25.00	11.00	3.10

☐ 1 Brown	25.00	11.00	3.10
☐ 2 Columbia	25.00	11.00	3.10
☐ 3 Cornell	25.00	11.00	3.10
☐ 4 Dartmouth	25.00	11.00	3.10
☐ 5 Harvard	30.00	13.50	3.70
☐ 6 Pennsylvania	25.00	11.00	3.10
☐ 7 Princeton	30.00	13.50	3.70
☐ 8 Yale	30.00	13.50	3.70

1989 Kansas

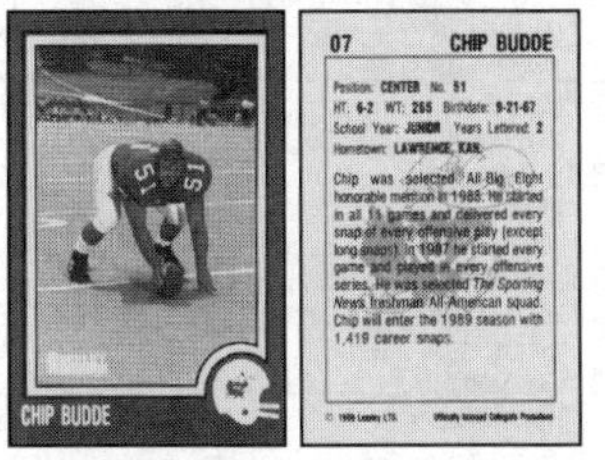

The 1989 University of Kansas set contains 40 standard-size cards. The fronts feature color photos bordered in blue. The vertically oriented backs show brief profiles. The cards are numbered on the back in the upper left corner. The set was produced by Leesley, Ltd. for the University of Kansas. The set was originally available from the KU Bookstore for 6.00 plus 1.50 for postage.

	MINT	NRMT	EXC
COMPLETE SET (40)	15.00	6.75	1.85
COMMON CARD (1-40)	.35	.16	.04

☐ 1 Kelly Donohoe	.75	.35	.09
☐ 2 Roger Robben	.35	.16	.04
☐ 3 Tony Sands	.35	.16	.04
☐ 4 Paul Zaffaroni	.35	.16	.04
☐ 5 Lance Flachsbarth	.35	.16	.04
☐ 6 Brad Fleeman	.35	.16	.04
☐ 7 Chip Budde	.50	.23	.06
☐ 8 Bill Hundelt	.35	.16	.04
☐ 9 Dan Newbrough	.35	.16	.04
☐ 10 Gary Oatis	.35	.16	.04
☐ 11 B.J. Lohsen	.50	.23	.06
☐ 12 John Fritch	.35	.16	.04
☐ 13 Russ Bowen	.35	.16	.04
☐ 14 Smith Holland	.35	.16	.04
☐ 15 Jason Priest	.50	.23	.06
☐ 16 Scott McCabe	.35	.16	.04
☐ 17 Jason Tyrer	.35	.16	.04
☐ 18 Mongo Allen	.35	.16	.04
☐ 19 Glen Mason CO	1.00	.45	.12
☐ 20 Deral Boykin	.50	.23	.06
☐ 21 Quintin Smith	.35	.16	.04
☐ 22 Mark Koncz	.50	.23	.06
☐ 23 John Baker	.50	.23	.06
☐ 24 Football Staff (schedule on back)	.50	.23	.06
☐ 25 Maurice Hooks	.35	.16	.04
☐ 26 Frank Hatchett	.35	.16	.04
☐ 27 Paul Friday	.35	.16	.04
☐ 28 Doug Terry	.35	.16	.04
☐ 29 Kenny Drayton	.35	.16	.04
☐ 30 Jim New	.35	.16	.04
☐ 31 Christopher Perez	.35	.16	.04
☐ 32 Maurice Douglas	1.00	.45	.12
☐ 33 Curtis Moore	.35	.16	.04
☐ 34 David Gordon	.35	.16	.04
☐ 35 Matt Nolen	.35	.16	.04
☐ 36 Dave Walton	.35	.16	.04
☐ 37 King Dixon	.50	.23	.06
☐ 38 Memorial Stadium	.35	.16	.04
☐ 39 Jayhawks in Action (Kelly Donohue)	.50	.23	.06
☐ 40 Jayhawks in Action (John Baker OL)	.50	.23	.06
☐ NNO Title Card	.75	.35	.09

1992 Kansas

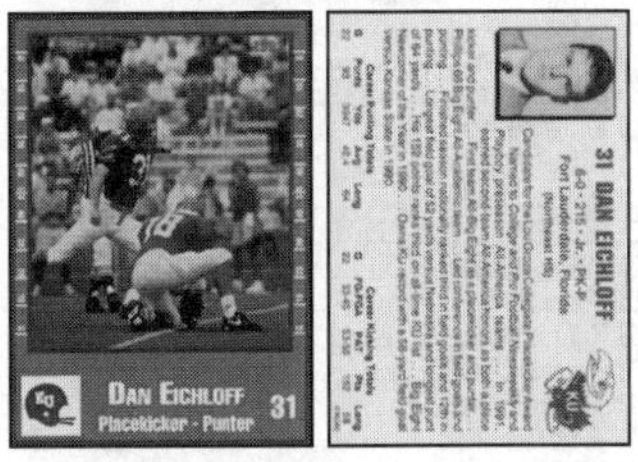

This 52-card standard-size set features the 1992 Kansas Jayhawks football team. The fronts display either posed or action color player photos inside green and blue borders. The green border has white yard markers as found on a football field. The team helmet, player's name, position, and uniform number are presented in a red bar beneath the picture. The horizontal backs carry a black-and-white head shot, biographical information, player profile, or statistics. The cards are unnumbered and checklisted below in alphabetical order.

	MINT	NRMT	EXC
COMPLETE SET (52)	20.00	9.00	2.50
COMMON CARD (1-50)	.40	.18	.05

☐ 1 Mark Allison	.40	.18	.05
☐ 2 Hassan Bailey	.50	.23	.06
☐ 3 Greg Ballard	.40	.18	.05
☐ 4 Marlin Blakeney	.40	.18	.05
☐ 5 Khristopher Booth	.40	.18	.05
☐ 6 Charley Bowen	.40	.18	.05
☐ 7 Gilbert Brown	3.00	1.35	.35
☐ 8 Dwayne Chandler	.40	.18	.05
☐ 9 Brian Christian	.40	.18	.05
☐ 10 David Converse	.40	.18	.05
☐ 11 Monte Cozzens	.40	.18	.05
☐ 12 Don Davis	.40	.18	.05
☐ 13 Maurice Douglas	1.00	.45	.12
☐ 14 Dan Eichloff	.50	.23	.06
☐ 15 Chad Fette	.40	.18	.05
☐ 16 Matt Gay	.40	.18	.05
☐ 17 Harold Harris	.40	.18	.05
☐ 18 Rodney Harris	.50	.23	.06
☐ 19 Steve Harvey	.40	.18	.05
☐ 20 Hessley Hempstead	.40	.18	.05
☐ 21 Chip Hilleary	1.00	.45	.12
☐ 22 Dick Holt	.40	.18	.05
☐ 23 Guy Howard	.40	.18	.05
☐ 24 Chaka Johnson	.40	.18	.05
☐ 25 John Jones	.40	.18	.05
☐ 26 Rod Jones	.40	.18	.05
☐ 27 Kwamie Lassiter	.50	.23	.06
☐ 28 Rob Licursi	.40	.18	.05
☐ 29 Trace Liggett	.40	.18	.05
☐ 30 Keith Loneker	.40	.18	.05
☐ 31 Dave Marcum	.40	.18	.05
☐ 32 Glen Mason CO	1.00	.45	.12
☐ 33 Chris Maumalanga	1.00	.45	.12
☐ 34 Gerald McBurrows	.40	.18	.05
☐ 35 Robert Mitchell	.40	.18	.05
☐ 36 Ty Moeder	.40	.18	.05
☐ 37 Kyle Moore	.40	.18	.05
☐ 38 Ron Page	.40	.18	.05
☐ 39 Chris Powell	.40	.18	.05
☐ 40 Dan Schmidt	.40	.18	.05
☐ 41 Ashaundai Smith	.40	.18	.05
☐ 42 Mike Steele	.40	.18	.05
☐ 43 Dana Stubblefield	3.00	1.35	.35
☐ 44 Wes Swinford	.40	.18	.05
☐ 45 Larry Thiel	.40	.18	.05
☐ 46 Fredrick Thomas	.50	.23	.06
☐ 47 Pete Vang	.40	.18	.05
☐ 48 Robert Vaughn	.40	.18	.05
☐ 49 George White	.50	.23	.06
☐ 50 Sylvester Wright	.40	.18	.05
☐ NNO Schedule Card	.40	.18	.05
☐ NNO Coaching Staff	.40	.18	.05

1982 Kentucky Schedules

This 19-card set measures approximately 2 1/4" by 3 3/4". The borderless front features a player head shot with the player's name below. The horizontal back features the 1982 season schedule. The cards are unnumbered and checklisted below in alphabetical order.

	MINT	NRMT	EXC
COMPLETE SET (19)	45.00	20.00	5.50
COMMON CARD (1-19)	3.00	1.35	.35

☐ 1 Richard Abraham	3.00	1.35	.35
☐ 2 Glenn Amerson	3.00	1.35	.35
☐ 3 Effley Brooks	3.00	1.35	.35
☐ 4 Shawn Donigan	3.00	1.35	.35
☐ 5 Rod Francis	3.00	1.35	.35
☐ 6 Terry Henry	3.00	1.35	.35
☐ 7 Ben Johnson	3.00	1.35	.35
☐ 8 Dave Lyons	3.00	1.35	.35
☐ 9 John Maddox	3.00	1.35	.35
☐ 10 Rob Mangas	3.00	1.35	.35
☐ 11 David(Buzz) Meers	3.00	1.35	.35
☐ 12 Andy Molls	3.00	1.35	.35
☐ 13 Tom Petty	3.00	1.35	.35
☐ 14 Don Roe	3.00	1.35	.35
☐ 15 Todd Shadowen	3.00	1.35	.35
☐ 16 Gerald Smyth	3.00	1.35	.35
☐ 17 Pete Venable	3.00	1.35	.35
☐ 18 Allan Watson	3.00	1.35	.35
☐ 19 Steve Williams	3.00	1.35	.35

1986 Kentucky Schedules

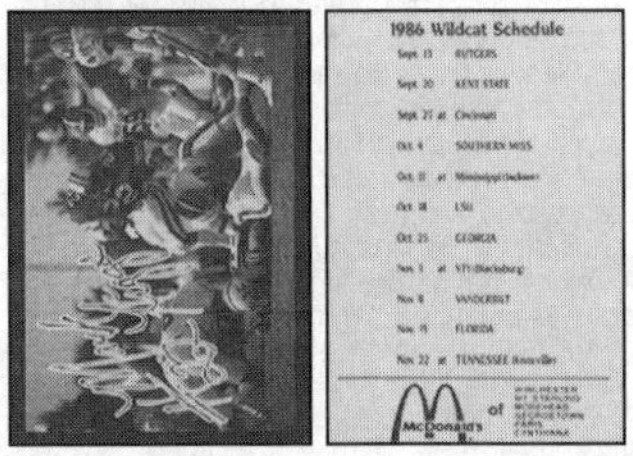

Sponsored by several McDonald's restaurants, this four-card schedule set measures approximately 2 1/4" by 3 1/2" and is printed on cardboard stock. Inside black borders, the horizontal fronts feature color photos, with the player's (or coach's) signature inscribed across the picture. The players also wrote their jersey numbers. The backs present the 1986 Wildcat schedule; a sponsor logo at the bottom completes the back. The cards are unnumbered and checklisted below in alphabetical order.

	MINT	NRMT	EXC
COMPLETE SET (4)	15.00	6.75	1.85
COMMON CARD (1-4)	4.00	1.80	.50

☐ 1 Jerry Claiborne CO	4.00	1.80	.50
☐ 2 Mark Higgs	6.00	2.70	.75
☐ 3 Marc Logan	6.00	2.70	.75
☐ 4 Bill Ransdell	4.00	1.80	.50

1981 Louisville Police

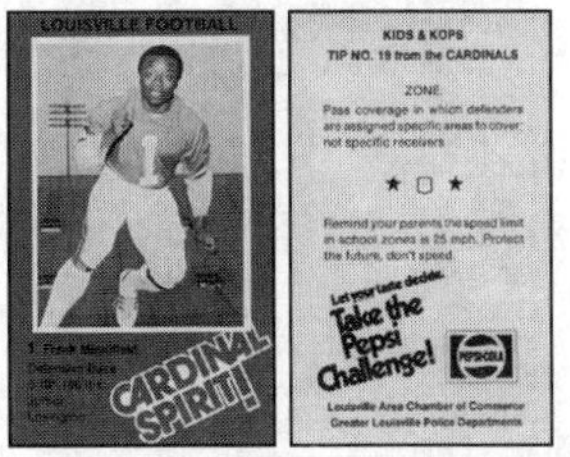

This 64-card set, which measures approximately 2 5/8" by 4 1/8", was sponsored by Pepsi-Cola (Take the Pepsi Challenge), The Louisville Area Chamber of Commerce, and the Greater Louisville Police Departments. The card front features red borders surrounding a black-and-white photo of the player. The backs feature definitions of football terms and a brief safety tip. This set features future professional star Mark Clayton in one of his earliest card appearances. Reportedly the Title/Logo card is very difficult to find. The cards are numbered on the back by safety tips.

	MINT	NRMT	EXC
COMPLETE SET (64)	125.00	55.00	15.50
COMMON CARD (1-64)	1.00	.45	.12

☐ 1 Title Card SP (Catch That Cardinal Spirit)	50.00	22.00	6.25
☐ 2 Bob Weber CO	1.00	.45	.12
☐ 3 Assistant Coaches	1.00	.45	.12
☐ 4 Jay Trautwein	1.00	.45	.12
☐ 5 Darrell Wimberly	1.00	.45	.12
☐ 6 Jeff Van Camp	1.00	.45	.12
☐ 7 Joe Welch	1.00	.45	.12
☐ 8 Fred Blackmon	1.00	.45	.12
☐ 9 Lamar(Toot) Evans	1.00	.45	.12
☐ 10 Tom Blair	1.00	.45	.12
☐ 11 Joe Kader	1.00	.45	.12
☐ 12 Mike Trainor	1.00	.45	.12
☐ 13 Richard Tharpe	1.00	.45	.12
☐ 14 Gene Hagan	1.00	.45	.12
☐ 15 Greg Jones	1.00	.45	.12
☐ 16 Leon Williams	1.00	.45	.12
☐ 17 Ellsworth Larkins	1.00	.45	.12
☐ 18 Sebastian Curry	1.00	.45	.12
☐ 19 Frank Minnifield	7.50	3.40	.95
☐ 20 Roger Clay	1.00	.45	.12
☐ 21 Mark Blasinsky	1.00	.45	.12
☐ 22 Mike Cruz	1.00	.45	.12
☐ 23 David Arthur	1.00	.45	.12
☐ 24 Johnny Unitas (In front background, list of Cardinals who played pro ball)	20.00	9.00	2.50
☐ 25 John DeMarco	1.00	.45	.12
☐ 26 Eric Rollins	1.00	.45	.12
☐ 27 Jack Pok	1.00	.45	.12
☐ 28 Pete McCartney	1.00	.45	.12
☐ 29 Mark Clayton	15.00	6.75	1.85
☐ 30 Jeff Hortert	1.00	.45	.12
☐ 31 Pete Bowen	1.00	.45	.12
☐ 32 Robert Niece	1.00	.45	.12
☐ 33 Todd McMahan	1.00	.45	.12
☐ 34 John Wall	1.00	.45	.12
☐ 35 Kelly Stickrod	1.00	.45	.12
☐ 36 Jim Miller	1.00	.45	.12
☐ 37 Tom Moore	1.00	.45	.12
☐ 38 Kurt Knop	1.00	.45	.12
☐ 39 Mark Musgrave	1.00	.45	.12
☐ 40 Tony Campbell	1.00	.45	.12
☐ 41 Mark Wilson	1.00	.45	.12
☐ 42 Robert Mitchell	1.00	.45	.12
☐ 43 Courtney Jeter	1.00	.45	.12
☐ 44 Wayne Taylor	1.00	.45	.12
☐ 45 Jeff Speedy	1.50	.70	.19
☐ 46 Donnie Craft	1.00	.45	.12
☐ 47 Glenn Hunter	1.00	.45	.12
☐ 48 1981 Louisville Schedule	1.00	.45	.12
☐ 49 Greg Hickman	1.00	.45	.12
☐ 50 Nate Dozier	1.00	.45	.12
☐ 51 Pat Patterson	1.00	.45	.12
☐ 52 Scott Gannon	1.00	.45	.12
☐ 53 Dean May	1.00	.45	.12
☐ 54 David Hatfield	1.00	.45	.12
☐ 55 Mike Nuzzolese	1.00	.45	.12
☐ 56 John Ayers	1.00	.45	.12
☐ 57 Lamar Cummins	1.00	.45	.12
☐ 58 Bill Olsen AD	1.00	.45	.12
☐ 59 Tailgating	1.00	.45	.12
☐ 60 Football Complex	1.00	.45	.12
☐ 61 Marching Band	1.00	.45	.12
☐ 62 Cheerleaders	1.00	.45	.12
☐ 63 Administration Bldg.	1.00	.45	.12
☐ 64 Cardinal Bird	1.00	.45	.12

1990 Louisville Smokey

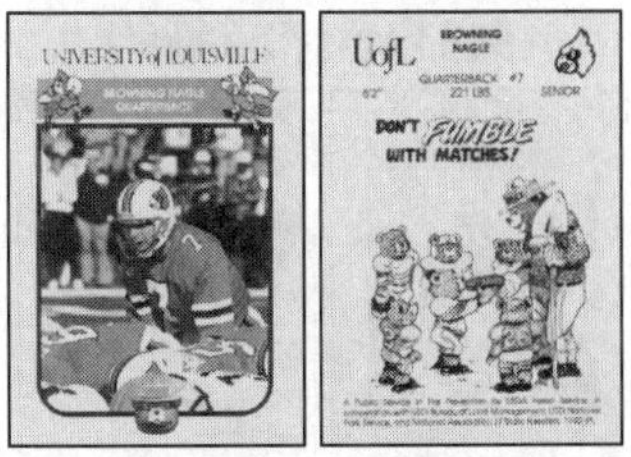

This 16-card standard-size set was sponsored by the USDA Forest Service in cooperation with several other federal agencies. On white card stock, the fronts display color action player photos with rounded bottom corners. The player's name and position appear between two Cardinal logos in a red stripe above the picture. The cards have brief biographical information and a safety cartoon featuring Smokey the Bear. The cards are unnumbered and checklisted below in alphabetical order.

	MINT	NRMT	EXC
COMPLETE SET (16)	25.00	11.00	3.10
COMMON CARD (1-16)	1.25	.55	.16

☐ 1 Greg Brohm	1.25	.55	.16
☐ 2 Jeff Brohm	1.50	.70	.19
☐ 3 Pete Burkey	1.25	.55	.16
☐ 4 Mike Flores	1.25	.55	.16
☐ 5 Dan Gangwer	1.25	.55	.16
☐ 6 Reggie Johnson	1.50	.70	.19
☐ 7 Scott McAllister	1.25	.55	.16
☐ 8 Ken McKay	1.25	.55	.16
☐ 9 Browning Nagle	4.00	1.80	.50
☐ 10 Ed Reynolds	1.25	.55	.16
☐ 11 Mark Sander	1.25	.55	.16

		MINT	NRMT	EXC
☐ 12	Howard Schnellenberger CO	5.00	2.20	.60
☐ 13	Ted Washington	2.50	1.10	.30
☐ 14	Klaus Wilmsmeyer	2.00	.90	.25
☐ 15	Cardinal Bird Mascot	1.25	.55	.16
☐ 16	Cardinal Stadium	1.25	.55	.16

1992 Louisville Kraft

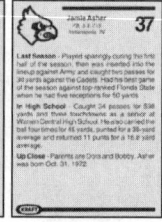

Originally issued in perforated sheets, this 30-card set was sponsored by Kraft. After being cut, the cards measure the standard size. The fronts feature color posed player photos against a white card face. The team's name appears in red above the photo. Below the photo are team helmet, two horizonal red stripes, and the player's name, jersey number, position, and class. The plain white backs carry the player's name, position, jersey number, height, weight, and hometown at the top, followed below by career highlights. The cards are unnumbered and checklisted below in alphabetical order.

		MINT	NRMT	EXC
	COMPLETE SET (30)	18.00	8.00	2.20
	COMMON CARD (1-30)	.60	.25	.07
☐ 1	Jamie Asher	2.00	.90	.25
☐ 2	Xzavia Atkins	.60	.25	.07
☐ 3	Kevin Blumeier	.60	.25	.07
☐ 4	Greg Brohm	.75	.35	.09
☐ 5	Jeff Brohm	1.50	.70	.19
☐ 6	Brandon Brookfield	.60	.25	.07
☐ 7	Ray Buchanan	2.50	1.10	.30
☐ 8	Rawle Bynoe	.60	.25	.07
☐ 9	Tom Cavallo	.60	.25	.07
☐ 10	Kevin Cook	.60	.25	.07
☐ 11	Andy Culley	.60	.25	.07
☐ 12	Ralph Dawkins	.75	.35	.09
☐ 13	Dave Debold	.60	.25	.07
☐ 14	Chris Fitzpatrick	.60	.25	.07
☐ 15	Kevin Gaines	.60	.25	.07
☐ 16	Jose Gonzalez	.60	.25	.07
☐ 17	Jim Hanna	.60	.25	.07
☐ 18	Ken Harnden	.60	.25	.07
☐ 19	Ivey Henderson	.60	.25	.07
☐ 20	Joe Johnson	1.00	.45	.12
☐ 21	Robert Knuutila	.60	.25	.07
☐ 22	Marty Lowe	1.00	.45	.12
☐ 23	Roman Oben	1.25	.55	.16
☐ 24	Garin Patrick	.60	.25	.07
☐ 25	Leonard Ray	.60	.25	.07
☐ 26	Shawn Rodriguez	.60	.25	.07
☐ 27	Anthony Shelman	1.00	.45	.12
☐ 28	Brevin Smith	.60	.25	.07
☐ 29	Jason Stinson	.75	.35	.09
☐ 30	Ben Sumpter	.75	.35	.09

1993 Louisville Kraft

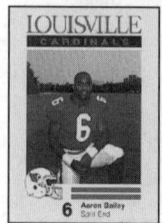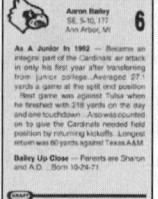

Originally issued in perforated sheets, this 30-card set was sponsored by Kraft. The cards measure the standard size. The fronts feature color posed player photos against a white card face. The team's name appears in red above the photo. Below the photo are team helmet, two horizonal red stripes, and the player's name, jersey number, position, and class. The plain white backs carry the player's name, position, jersey number, height, weight, and hometown at the top, followed below by career highlights. The cards are unnumbered and checklisted below in alphabetical order.

		MINT	NRMT	EXC
	COMPLETE SET (30)	18.00	8.00	2.20
	COMMON CARD (1-30)	.60	.25	.07
☐ 1	Jamie Asher	1.50	.70	.19
☐ 2	Aaron Bailey	1.50	.70	.19
☐ 3	Zoe Barney	.60	.25	.07
☐ 4	Anthony Bridges	.60	.25	.07
☐ 5	Jeff Brohm	1.00	.45	.12
☐ 6	Brandon Brookfield	.60	.25	.07
☐ 7	Kendall Brown	.60	.25	.07
☐ 8	Tom Carrol	.60	.25	.07

		MINT	NRMT	EXC
☐ 9	Tom Cavallo	.60	.25	.07
☐ 10	Kevin Cook	.60	.25	.07
☐ 11	Ralph Dawkins	.75	.35	.09
☐ 12	Dave Debold	.60	.25	.07
☐ 13	Reggie Ferguson	.60	.25	.07
☐ 14	Chris Fitzpatrick	.60	.25	.07
☐ 15	Johnny Frost	.60	.25	.07
☐ 16	Jim Hanna	.60	.25	.07
☐ 17	Ivey Henderson	.60	.25	.07
☐ 18	Marcus Hill	.60	.25	.07
☐ 19	Shawn Jackson	.60	.25	.07
☐ 20	Joe Johnson	.75	.35	.09
☐ 21	Marty Lowe	.75	.35	.09
☐ 22	Vertis McKinney	.60	.25	.07
☐ 23	Greg Minnis	.60	.25	.07
☐ 24	Roman Oben	1.00	.45	.12
☐ 25	Garin Patrick	.60	.25	.07
☐ 26	Terry Quinn	.75	.35	.09
☐ 27	Leonard Ray	.60	.25	.07
☐ 28	Anthony Shelman	.75	.35	.09
☐ 29	Jason Stinson	.60	.25	.07
☐ 30	Ben Sumpter	.60	.25	.07

1983 LSU Sunbeam

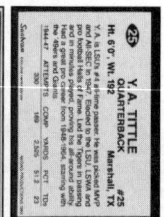

This set features 100 standard-size cards remembering ex-football players from Louisiana State University (LSU). The posed pictures on the front are black and white, bordered on the top and sides by a goal post in the school's colors, purple and gold. The horizontally oriented backs feature purple printing with biographical information and the card number in the upper left hand corner. Some of the former and current NFL stars included in this set are Billy Cannon, Carlos Carson, Tommy Casanova, Tommy Davis, Sid Fournet, Bo Harris, Bert Jones, Leonard Marshall, Jim Taylor, Y.A. Tittle, Steve Van Buren, Roy Winston, and David Woodley. The set was sponsored by Sunbeam Bread in conjunction with McDAG Productions.

		MINT	NRMT	EXC
	COMPLETE SET (100)	12.00	5.50	1.50
	COMMON CARD (1-100)	.10	.05	.01
☐ 1	1958 LSU National Championship Team	.30	.14	.04
☐ 2	Abe Mickal	.10	.05	.01
☐ 3	Carlos Carson	.20	.09	.03
☐ 4	Charles Alexander	.30	.14	.04
☐ 5	Steve Ensminger	.10	.05	.01
☐ 6	Ken Kavanaugh Sr.	.20	.09	.03
☐ 7	Bert Jones	.50	.23	.06
☐ 8	David Woodley	.20	.09	.03
☐ 9	Jerry Marchand	.10	.05	.01
☐ 10	Clyde Lindsey	.10	.05	.01
☐ 11	James Britt	.10	.05	.01
☐ 12	Warren Rabb	.20	.09	.03
☐ 13	Mike Hillman	.10	.05	.01
☐ 14	Nelson Stokley	.10	.05	.01
☐ 15	Abner Wimberly	.10	.05	.01
☐ 16	Terry Robiskie	.20	.09	.03
☐ 17	Steve Van Buren	.50	.23	.06
☐ 18	Doug Moreau	.20	.09	.03
☐ 19	George Tarasovic	.20	.09	.03
☐ 20	Billy Cannon	.50	.23	.06
☐ 21	Jerry Stovall	.20	.09	.03
☐ 22	Joe Labruzzo	.10	.05	.01
☐ 23	Mickey Mangham	.10	.05	.01
☐ 24	Craig Burns	.10	.05	.01
☐ 25	Y.A. Tittle	1.00	.45	.12
☐ 26	Wendell Harris	.20	.09	.03
☐ 27	Leroy Labat	.10	.05	.01
☐ 28	Hokie Gajan	.20	.09	.03
☐ 29	Mike Williams	.10	.05	.01
☐ 30	Sammy Grezaffi	.20	.09	.03
☐ 31	Clinton Burrell	.10	.05	.01
☐ 32	Orlando McDaniel	.10	.05	.01
☐ 33	George Bevan	.10	.05	.01
☐ 34	Johnny Robinson	.30	.14	.04
☐ 35	Billy Masters	.10	.05	.01
☐ 36	J.W. Brodnax	.10	.05	.01
☐ 37	Tommy Casanova	.30	.14	.04
☐ 38	Fred Miller	.10	.05	.01
☐ 39	George Rice	.10	.05	.01
☐ 40	Earl Gros	.20	.09	.03
☐ 41	Lynn LeBlanc	.10	.05	.01
☐ 42	Jim Taylor	.50	.23	.06
☐ 43	Joe Tumenello	.10	.05	.01
☐ 44	Tommy Davis	.20	.09	.03
☐ 45	Alvin Dark	.30	.14	.04
☐ 46	Richard Picou	.10	.05	.01
☐ 47	Chaille Percy	.10	.05	.01
☐ 48	John Garlington	.20	.09	.03
☐ 49	Mike Morgan	.10	.05	.01
☐ 50	Charles(Bo) Strange	.10	.05	.01

		MINT	NRMT	EXC
☐ 51	Max Fugler	.30	.14	.04
☐ 52	Don Schwab	.10	.05	.01
☐ 53	Dennis Gaubatz	.20	.09	.03
☐ 54	Jimmy Field	.10	.05	.01
☐ 55	Warren Capone	.10	.05	.01
☐ 56	Albert Richardson	.10	.05	.01
☐ 57	Charley Cusiman	.10	.05	.01
☐ 58	Brad Davis	.10	.05	.01
☐ 59	Gaynell(Gus) Kinchen	.10	.05	.01
☐ 60	Roy(Moonie) Winston	.20	.09	.03
☐ 61	Mike Anderson	.10	.05	.01
☐ 62	Jesse Fatherree	.10	.05	.01
☐ 63	Gene"Red" Knight	.10	.05	.01
☐ 64	Tyler LaFauci	.10	.05	.01
☐ 65	Emile Fournet	.10	.05	.01
☐ 66	Gaynell"Gus" Tinsley	.20	.09	.03
☐ 67	Remi Prudhomme	.10	.05	.01
☐ 68	Marvin"Moose"Stewart	.10	.05	.01
☐ 69	Jerry Guillot	.10	.05	.01
☐ 70	Steve Cassidy	.10	.05	.01
☐ 71	Bo Harris	.20	.09	.03
☐ 72	Robert Dugas	.10	.05	.01
☐ 73	Malcolm Scott	.10	.05	.01
☐ 74	Charles(Pinky) Rohm	.10	.05	.01
☐ 75	Gerald Keigley	.10	.05	.01
☐ 76	Don Alexander	.10	.05	.01
☐ 77	A.J. Duhe	.20	.09	.03
☐ 78	Ron Estay	.10	.05	.01
☐ 79	John Wood	.10	.05	.01
☐ 80	Andy Hamilton	.10	.05	.01
☐ 81	Jay Michaelson	.10	.05	.01
☐ 82	Kenny Konz	.20	.09	.03
☐ 83	Tracy Porter	.10	.05	.01
☐ 84	Billy Truax	.10	.05	.01
☐ 85	Alan Risher	.10	.05	.01
☐ 86	John Adams	.10	.05	.01
☐ 87	Tommy Neck	.10	.05	.01
☐ 88	Brad Boyd	.10	.05	.01
☐ 89	Greg LaFleur	.10	.05	.01
☐ 90	Bill Elko	.10	.05	.01
☐ 91	Binks Miciotto	.10	.05	.01
☐ 92	Lew Sibley	.10	.05	.01
☐ 93	Willie Teal	.10	.05	.01
☐ 94	Lyman White	.10	.05	.01
☐ 95	Chris Williams	.10	.05	.01
☐ 96	Sid Fournet	.10	.05	.01
☐ 97	Leonard Marshall	.20	.09	.03
☐ 98	Ramsey Dardar	.10	.05	.01
☐ 99	Ken Bordelon	.10	.05	.01
☐ 100	Fred(Skinny) Hall	.10	.05	.01

1985 LSU Police

The 1985 LSU Police set contains 16 standard-size cards. The fronts have color action photos bordered in white; the vertically oriented backs have brief career highlights and safety tips. The cards are unnumbered, so they are listed below alphabetically by subject's name. These cards are printed on very thin stock. The set was produced by McDag Productions. Card backs contain "Tips from the Tigers," while card fronts contain a blue Louisiana Savings logo.

		MINT	NRMT	EXC
	COMPLETE SET (16)	8.00	3.60	1.00
	COMMON CARD (1-16)	.60	.25	.07
☐ 1	Mitch Andrews	.60	.25	.07
☐ 2	Bill Arnsparger CO	1.00	.45	.12
☐ 3	Roland Barbay	.60	.25	.07
☐ 4	Michael Brooks	1.00	.45	.12
☐ 5	Shawn Burks	.60	.25	.07
☐ 6	Tommy Clapp	.60	.25	.07
☐ 7	Matt DeFrank	.60	.25	.07
☐ 8	Kevin Guidry	.60	.25	.07
☐ 9	Dalton Hilliard	1.50	.70	.19
☐ 10	Garry James	1.00	.45	.12
☐ 11	Norman Jefferson	.60	.25	.07
☐ 12	Rogie Magee	.60	.25	.07
☐ 13	Mike the Tiger(Mascot)	.60	.25	.07
☐ 14	Craig Rathjen	.60	.25	.07
☐ 15	Jeff Wickersham	.75	.35	.09
☐ 16	Karl Wilson	.75	.35	.09

1986 LSU Police

The 1986 LSU Police set contains 16 standard-size cards. The fronts have color action photos bordered in white; the vertically oriented backs have brief career highlights and safety tips. The cards are unnumbered, so they are listed below alphabetically by subject's name. These cards are printed on very thin stock. The set was produced by McDag Productions. Card backs contain "Tips from the Tigers," while card fronts contain logos for The General and the Chemical Dependency Unit of Baton Rouge.

1990 Louisville Smokey / Tigers

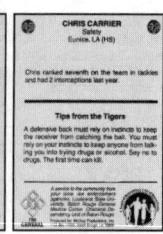

CHRIS CARRIER — Safety
Eunice, LA (HS)

Chris ranked seventh on the team in tackles and had 2 interceptions last year.

Tips from the Tigers

A defensive back must rely on instinct to keep the receiver from catching the ball. You must rely on your instincts to keep anyone from talking you into trying drugs or alcohol. Say no to drugs. The first time can kill.

		MINT	NRMT	EXC
	COMPLETE SET (16)	8.00	3.60	1.00
	COMMON CARD (1-16)	.50	.23	.06
☐ 1	Nacho Albergamo	.50	.23	.06
☐ 2	Eric Andolsek	1.00	.45	.12
☐ 3	Bill Arnsparger CO	.75	.35	.09
☐ 4	Roland Barbay	.50	.23	.06
☐ 5	Michael Brooks	1.00	.45	.12
☐ 6	Chris Carrier	.50	.23	.06
☐ 7	Toby Caston	1.00	.45	.12
☐ 8	Wendell Davis	1.50	.70	.19
☐ 9	Kevin Guidry	.50	.23	.06
☐ 10	John Hazard	.50	.23	.06
☐ 11	Oliver Lawrence	.50	.23	.06
☐ 12	Rogie Magee	.50	.23	.06
☐ 13	Sammy Martin	.75	.35	.09
☐ 14	Darrell Phillips	.50	.23	.06
☐ 15	Steve Rehage	.50	.23	.06
☐ 16	Ron Sancho	.75	.35	.09

1987 LSU Police

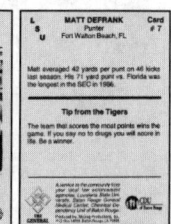

MATT DEFRANK — Punter
Fort Walton Beach, FL

Matt averaged 42 yards per punt on 46 kicks last season. His 71 yard punt vs. Florida was the longest in the SEC in 1986.

Tip from the Tigers

The team that scores the most points wins the game. If you say no to drugs you will score in life. Be a winner.

The 1987 LSU Police set contains 16 standard-size cards. The fronts have color action photos bordered in white; the vertically oriented backs have brief career highlights and safety tips. These cards are printed on very thin stock. This set was distributed at the Oct. 17, 1987 game vs. Kentucky. The set was produced by McDag Productions. Card backs contain "Tips from the Tigers." The cards are unnumbered, so they are listed below alphabetically by subject's name. The key card in the set is Harvey Williams' first card.

		MINT	NRMT	EXC
	COMPLETE SET (16)	10.00	4.50	1.25
	COMMON CARD (1-16)	.50	.23	.06
☐ 1	Nacho Albergamo	.50	.23	.06
☐ 2	Eric Andolsek	.75	.35	.09
☐ 3	Mike Archer CO	.75	.35	.09
☐ 4	David Browndyke	.50	.23	.06
☐ 5	Chris Carrier	.50	.23	.06
☐ 6	Wendell Davis	1.00	.45	.12
☐ 7	Matt DeFrank	.50	.23	.06
☐ 8	Nicky Hazard	.50	.23	.06
☐ 9	Eric Hill	1.00	.45	.12
☐ 10	Tommy Hodson	1.50	.70	.19
☐ 11	Greg Jackson	1.00	.45	.12
☐ 12	Brian Kinchen	1.00	.45	.12
☐ 13	Darren Malbrough	.50	.23	.06
☐ 14	Sammy Martin	.50	.23	.06
☐ 15	Ron Sancho	.50	.23	.06
☐ 16	Harvey Williams	3.50	1.55	.45

1988 LSU Police

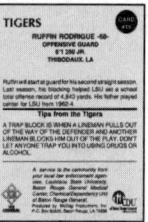

RUFFIN RODRIGUE — Offensive Guard
#1286 JR.
Thibodaux, LA

Ruffin will start at guard for his second straight season. Last season, his blocking helped LSU set a school total offense record of 4,843 yards. His father played center for LSU from 1962-4.

Tips from the Tigers

A TRAP BLOCK IS WHEN A LINEMAN PULLS OUT OF THE WAY OF THE DEFENDER AND ANOTHER LINEMAN BLOCKS HIM OUT OF THE PLAY. DON'T LET ANYONE TRAP YOU INTO USING DRUGS OR ALCOHOL.

The 1988 LSU football set contains 16 standard-size cards. The fronts have color action photos with white borders and black lettering; the vertically oriented backs have career highlights. These cards were distributed as a set, which was produced by McDag Productions. Card backs contain "Tips from the Tigers".

		MINT	NRMT	EXC
	COMPLETE SET (16)	8.00	3.60	1.00
	COMMON CARD (1-16)	.50	.23	.06

☐ 1 Mike The Tiger(Mascot)	.50	.23	.06
☐ 2 Mike Archer CO	.75	.35	.09
☐ 3 Tommy Hodson	1.50	.70	.19
☐ 4 Harvey Williams	2.50	1.10	.30
☐ 5 David Browndyke	.50	.23	.06
☐ 6 Karl Dunbar	.50	.23	.06
☐ 7 Eddie Fuller	.50	.23	.06
☐ 8 Mickey Guidry	.50	.23	.06
☐ 9 Greg Jackson	.75	.35	.09
☐ 10 Clint James	.50	.23	.06
☐ 11 Victor Jones	.50	.23	.06
☐ 12 Tony Moss	.50	.23	.06
☐ 13 Ralph Norwood	.50	.23	.06
☐ 14 Darrell Phillips	.50	.23	.06
☐ 15 Ruffin Rodrigue	.50	.23	.06
☐ 16 Ron Sancho	.50	.23	.06

1989 LSU Police

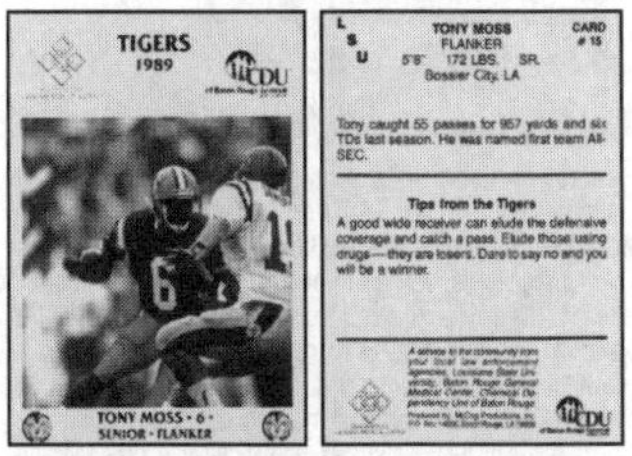

The 1989 LSU football set contains 16 standard-size cards. The fronts have color action photos with white borders and black lettering; the vertically oriented backs have career highlights. These cards were distributed as a set, which was produced by McDag Productions. Card backs contain "Tips from the Tigers".

	MINT	NRMT	EXC
COMPLETE SET (16)	8.00	3.60	1.00
COMMON CARD (1-16)	.50	.23	.06
☐ 1 Mike the Tiger(Mascot)	.50	.23	.06
☐ 2 David Browndyke 4	.50	.23	.06
☐ 3 Mike Archer CO	.75	.35	.09
☐ 4 Ruffin Rodrigue 68	.50	.23	.06
☐ 5 Marc Boutte 95	1.00	.45	.12
☐ 6 Clint James 70	.50	.23	.06
☐ 7 Jimmy Young 5	.50	.23	.06
☐ 8 Alvin Lee 26	.50	.23	.06
☐ 9 Eddie Fuller 33	.50	.23	.06
☐ 10 Tiger Stadium	.50	.23	.06
☐ 11 Harvey Williams 22	2.00	.90	.25
☐ 12 Verge Ausberry 98	.50	.23	.06
☐ 13 Karl Dunbar 63	.50	.23	.06
☐ 14 Tommy Hodson 13	1.25	.55	.16
☐ 15 Tony Moss 6	.50	.23	.06
☐ 16 The Golden Girls (Cheerleaders)	.50	.23	.06

1992 LSU McDag

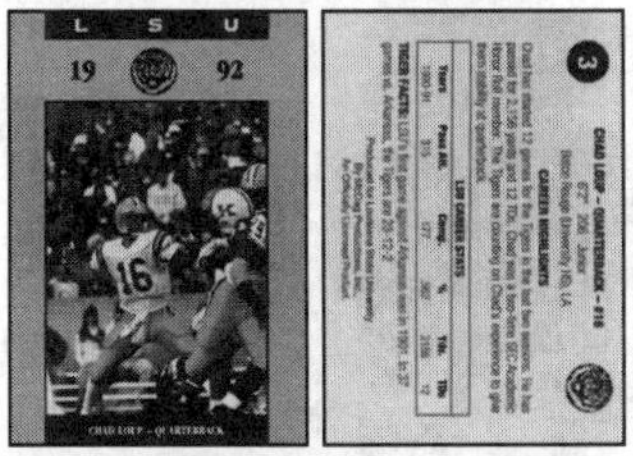

This 16-card standard-size set was produced for Louisiana State University by McDag Productions Inc. The cards are printed on thin stock and feature on the fronts action color player shots framed in purple on a mustard background. A purple bar at the top contains "LSU" in white lettering with the year and team logo (a tiger's head) immediately below on the mustard top border. The white backs are printed in purple and feature biography, career highlights, statistics, and "Tiger Facts".

	MINT	NRMT	EXC
COMPLETE SET (16)	6.00	2.70	.75
COMMON CARD (1-16)	.50	.23	.06
☐ 1 Curley Hallman CO	.75	.35	.09
☐ 2 Ray Adams	.50	.23	.06
☐ 3 Chad Loup	.75	.35	.09
☐ 4 Odell Beckham	.50	.23	.06
☐ 5 Wesley Jacob	.50	.23	.06
☐ 6 Kevin Mawae	1.00	.45	.12
☐ 7 Clayton Mouton	.50	.23	.06
☐ 8 Roovelroe Swan	.50	.23	.06
☐ 9 Ricardo Washington	.50	.23	.06
☐ 10 David Walkup	.50	.23	.06
☐ 11 Jessie Daigle	.50	.23	.06
☐ 12 Carlton Buckles	.50	.23	.06
☐ 13 Anthony Williams	.50	.23	.06
☐ 14 Darron Landry	.50	.23	.06
☐ 15 Frank Godfrey	.50	.23	.06
☐ 16 Pedro Suarez	.50	.23	.06

1969 Maryland Team Sheets

These six sheets measure approximately 8" by 10". The fronts feature two rows of four black-and-white player portraits each. The player's name is printed under the photo. The backs are blank. The sheets are unnumbered and checklisted below in alphabetical order according to the first player (or coach) listed.

	NRMT-MT	EXC	G-VG
COMPLETE SET (6)	30.00	13.50	3.70
COMMON PANEL (1-6)	6.00	2.70	.75
☐ 1 Bill Backus Lou Bracken Sonny Demczuk Roland Merritt Rich Slaninka Ralph Sonntag Mike Stubljar Jim Stull	6.00	2.70	.75
☐ 2 Bill Bell CO George Boutselis CO Albert Ferguson CO James Kehoe AD Roy Lester CO Dim Montero CO Lee Royer CO	6.00	2.70	.75
☐ 3 Pat Burke John Dyer Craig Gienger Tony Greene Bob MacBride Bill Meister Russ Nolan Ray Soporowski	6.00	2.70	.75
☐ 4 Steve Ciambor Kenny Dutton Dan Kecman Bob Mahnic Len Santacroce David Seifert Len Spicer Rick Stoll	6.00	2.70	.75
☐ 5 Bob Colbert John Dill Henry Gareis Bill Grant Glenn Kubany Bill Reilly Wally Stalnaker Gary Vansickler	6.00	2.70	.75
☐ 6 Paul Fitzpatrick Larry Marshall Tom Miller Will Morris Dennis O'Hara Scott Shank Jeff Shugars Al Thomas	6.00	2.70	.75

1991 Maryland High School Big 33

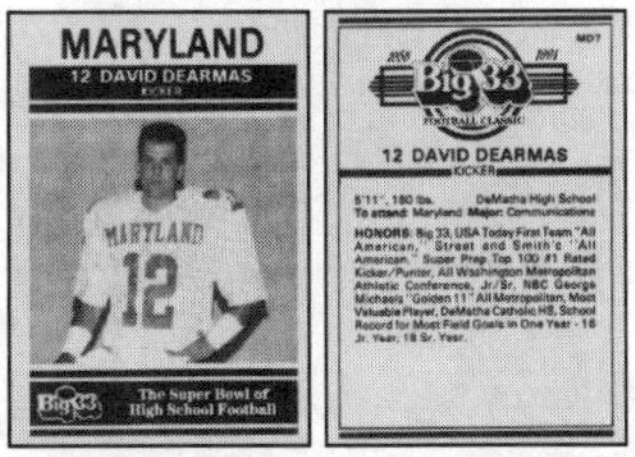

This 34-card standard-size high school football set was issued to commemorate the Big 33 Football Classic. The fronts feature a posed black and white player photo enclosed in a white border. State name appears at top. Player number and position appear as white reversed-out lettering within a black bar. The Big 33 logo and The Super Bowl of High School Football appear at the bottom. The backs feature biographical information and honors received within a thin black border.

	MINT	NRMT	EXC
COMPLETE SET (34)	20.00	9.00	2.50
COMMON CARD (MD1-MD34)	.75	.35	.09
☐ MD1 Asim Penny	1.00	.45	.12
☐ MD2 Louis Jason	1.00	.45	.12
☐ MD3 Mark McCain	1.00	.45	.12
☐ MD4 Matthew Byrne	.75	.35	.09
☐ MD5 Mike Gillespie	.75	.35	.09
☐ MD6 Ricky Rowe	.75	.35	.09
☐ MD7 David DeArmas	1.00	.45	.12
☐ MD8 Duane Ashman	.75	.35	.09
☐ MD9 James Cunningham	.75	.35	.09
☐ MD10 Keith Kormanik	.75	.35	.09
☐ MD11 Leonard Green	.75	.35	.09
☐ MD12 Larry Washington	.75	.35	.09
☐ MD13 Raphael Wall	.75	.35	.09
☐ MD14 Kai Hebron	.75	.35	.09
☐ MD15 Coy Gibbs	1.00	.45	.12
☐ MD16 Lenard Marcus	.75	.35	.09
☐ MD17 John Taliaferro	1.00	.45	.12
☐ MD18 J.C. Price	.75	.35	.09
☐ MD19 Jamal Cox	1.00	.45	.12
☐ MD20 Rick Budd	.75	.35	.09
☐ MD21 Shaun Marshall	.75	.35	.09
☐ MD22 Allan Jenkins	.75	.35	.09
☐ MD23 Bryon Turner	.75	.35	.09
☐ MD24 Ryan Foran	.75	.35	.09
☐ MD25 John Summerday	.75	.35	.09
☐ MD26 Joshua Austin	.75	.35	.09
☐ MD27 Emile Palmer	.75	.35	.09
☐ MD28 John Teter	.75	.35	.09
☐ MD29 John Kennedy	.75	.35	.09
☐ MD30 Clarence Collins	.75	.35	.09
☐ MD31 Daryl Smith	.75	.35	.09
☐ MD32 David Wilkins	.75	.35	.09
☐ MD33 David Thomas	.75	.35	.09
☐ MD34 Russell Thomas	1.00	.45	.12

1992 Maryland High School Big 33

This standard-size high school football set was issued to commemorate the Big 33 Football Classic. The fronts feature posed player photos enclosed by a white border. The state name appears at the top of the card along with the player's name, number, and position. The Big 33 logo appears below the photo. The backs feature the player's biographical information along with a notation to which college he plans to attend. The unnumbered cards are listed below alphabetically.

	MINT	NRMT	EXC
COMPLETE SET (35)	20.00	9.00	2.50
COMMON CARD (1-35)	.75	.35	.09
☐ 1 George Addison	.75	.35	.09
☐ 2 Calvin Arrington	.75	.35	.09
☐ 3 Damon Atwater	.75	.35	.09
☐ 4 Bruce Ballard	.75	.35	.09
☐ 5 Mike Bertoni	.75	.35	.09
☐ 6 Demont Blackmon	.75	.35	.09
☐ 7 Jason Buckhanan	.75	.35	.09
☐ 8 Jay Cammon	.75	.35	.09
☐ 9 James Easterly	.75	.35	.09
☐ 10 Marlon Evans	.75	.35	.09
☐ 11 Effrem Gordon	.75	.35	.09
☐ 12 Ray Gray	.75	.35	.09
☐ 13 Brent Guyton	.75	.35	.09
☐ 14 Michael Kelly	.75	.35	.09
☐ 15 Eric Knight	.75	.35	.09
☐ 16 Bill Krumpe	.75	.35	.09
☐ 17 Ted Kwalick Honorary Chairman	1.00	.45	.12
☐ 18 Brandon Lallis	.75	.35	.09
☐ 19 David Lee	.75	.35	.09
☐ 20 Jermaine Lewis	1.25	.55	.16
☐ 21 Matt Lilly	.75	.35	.09
☐ 22 Andre Martin	.75	.35	.09
☐ 23 Rhad Miles	.75	.35	.09
☐ 24 Julian Norment	.75	.35	.09
☐ 25 Steve Oliver	.75	.35	.09
☐ 26 Jeremy Raley	.75	.35	.09
☐ 27 Richard Snowden	.75	.35	.09
☐ 28 Robert St. Pierre	.75	.35	.09
☐ 29 Jack Sykes	.75	.35	.09
☐ 30 Allen Syring	.75	.35	.09
☐ 31 Troy Turner	.75	.35	.09
☐ 32 David Vernier	.75	.35	.09
☐ 33 Anthony Walker	.75	.35	.09
☐ 34 Phillip White	.75	.35	.09
☐ 35 Joe Wright	.75	.35	.09

1988 McNeese State McDag/Police

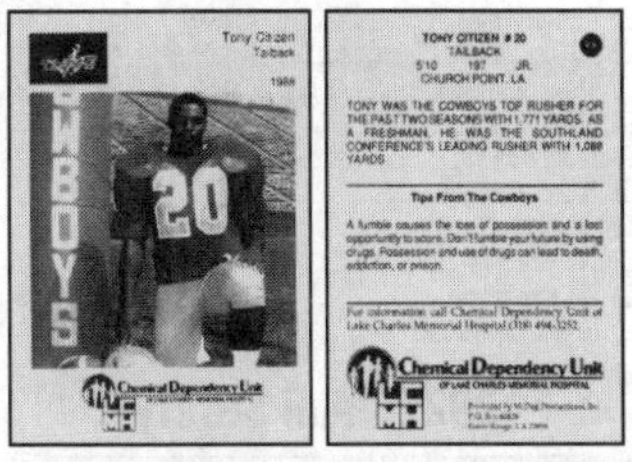

This 16-card standard-size set is printed on thin card stock. It is sponsored by the Behavioral Health and Chemical Dependency Units of Lake Charles Memorial Hospital. Card front has a posed picture enclosed in a white border. Team logo appears in upper left while player's name, position, and the year appear in upper right corner. The sponsor logos appear at the bottom. Horizontally oriented backs present biography, player profile, "Tips From the Cowboys" in the form of anti-drug messages, and sponsor logos at the bottom.

	MINT	NRMT	EXC
COMPLETE SET (16)	6.00	2.70	.75
COMMON CARD (1-16)	.50	.23	.06
☐ 1 Sonny Jackson CO	.50	.23	.06
☐ 2 Lance Wiley	.50	.23	.06
☐ 3 Brian McZeal	.50	.23	.06
☐ 4 Berwick Davenport	.50	.23	.06
☐ 5 Gary Irvin	.50	.23	.06
☐ 6 Glenn Koch	.50	.23	.06
☐ 7 Chad Habetz	.50	.23	.06
☐ 8 Pete Sinclair	.50	.23	.06
☐ 9 Tony Citizen	.50	.23	.06
☐ 10 Scott Dieterich	.50	.23	.06
☐ 11 Hud Jackson	.50	.23	.06
☐ 12 Darrin Andrus	.50	.23	.06
☐ 13 Jeff Mathews	.50	.23	.06
☐ 14 Devin Babineaux	.50	.23	.06
☐ 15 Jeff Delhomme	.50	.23	.06
☐ 16 Eric LeBlanc Mike Pierce	.50	.23	.06

1989 McNeese State McDag/Police

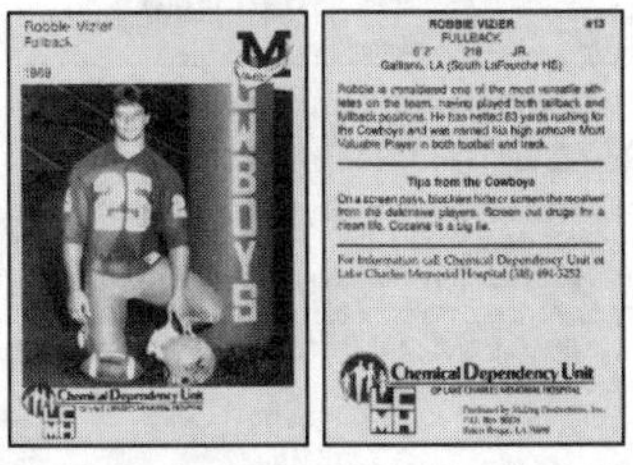

This 16-card standard-size set is printed on thin card stock. It is sponsored by the Behavioral Health and Chemical Dependency Units of Lake Charles Memorial Hospital. The fronts feature color posed photos enclosed by light blue borders. The player's name, position, year, and school logo are in the top border while the sponsor logo appears beneath the picture. The backs carry biography, player profile, and "Tips From The Cowboys" in the form of anti-drug or mental health messages. The cards are numbered on the back in the upper right corner.

	MINT	NRMT	EXC
COMPLETE SET (16)	6.00	2.70	.75
COMMON CARD (1-16)	.50	.23	.06
☐ 1 Marc Stampley	.50	.23	.06
☐ 2 Mark LeBlanc	.50	.23	.06
☐ 3 Kip Texada	.60	.25	.07
☐ 4 Brian Champagne	.50	.23	.06
☐ 5 Ronald Scott	.50	.23	.06
☐ 6 Jimmy Poirier	.50	.23	.06
☐ 7 Cliff Buckner	.50	.23	.06
☐ 8 Jericho Loupe	.50	.23	.06
☐ 9 Vaughn Calbert	.50	.23	.06
☐ 10 Rodney Burks	.50	.23	.06
☐ 11 Troy Jones	.50	.23	.06
☐ 12 Chris Andrus	.50	.23	.06
☐ 13 Robbie Vizier	.50	.23	.06
☐ 14 Kenneth Pierce	.50	.23	.06
☐ 15 Bobby Smith	.50	.23	.06
☐ 16 Trent Lee	.50	.23	.06

1990 McNeese State McDag/Police

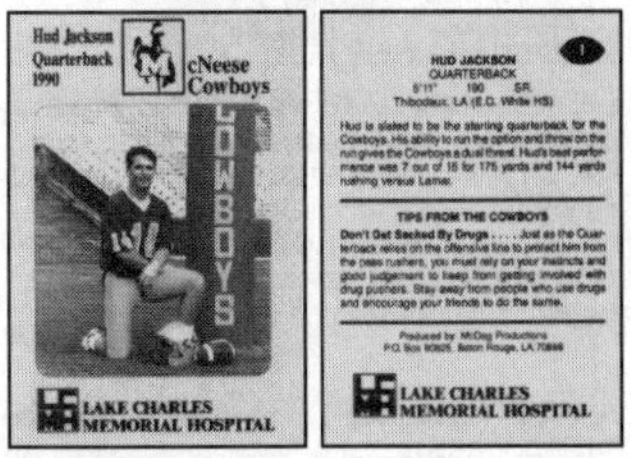

The 1990 McNeese State Cowboys football set contains 16 standard-size cards and is basically the same design as previous years. The card front features a posed player photo, with rounded corners and enclosed by a light blue border. The player's name, position, year, and school logo are in the top border while the sponsor's name and logo (Lake Charles Memorial Hospital) are beneath the picture. Backs feature biography, player profile, and "Tips From The Cowboys" in the form of anti-drug or mental health messages.

	MINT	NRMT	EXC
COMPLETE SET (16)	6.00	2.70	.75
COMMON CARD (1-16)	.50	.23	.06
☐ 1 Hud Jackson	.50	.23	.06
☐ 2 Wes Watts	.50	.23	.06
☐ 3 Mark LeBlanc	.50	.23	.06
☐ 4 Jeff Delhomme	.50	.23	.06
☐ 5 Mike Reed	.50	.23	.06
☐ 6 Chuck Esponge	.50	.23	.06
☐ 7 Ronald Scott	.50	.23	.06
☐ 8 Ken Naquin	.50	.23	.06
☐ 9 Steve Aultman	.50	.23	.06
☐ 10 Sean Judge	.50	.23	.06
☐ 11 Greg Rayson	.50	.23	.06
☐ 12 Kip Texada	.60	.25	.07
☐ 13 Mike Pierce	.50	.23	.06

	MINT	NRMT	EXC
☐ 14 Jimmy Poirier	.50	.23	.06
☐ 15 Ronald Solomon	.50	.23	.06
☐ 16 Eric Foster	.50	.23	.06

1991 McNeese State McDag/Police

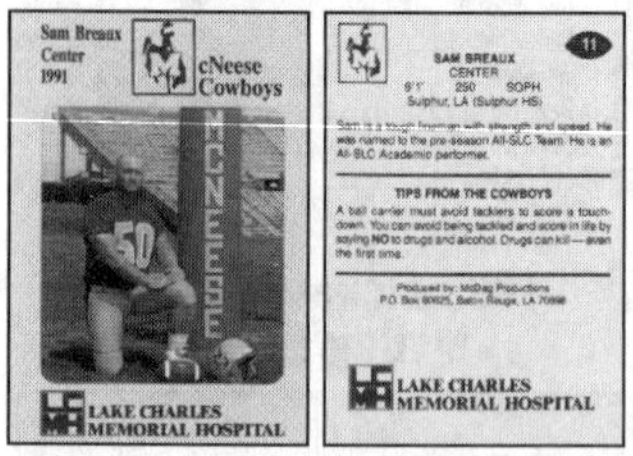

This 16-card standard-size set was produced by McDag Productions and sponsored by Lake Charles Memorial Hospital. The print run was reportedly limited to 3,500 sets. Each of the cards features a posed color photo of the player kneeling beside the goalpost, with the stadium in the background. The pictures have rounded corners and light blue borders. Player information appears above the picture, while the sponsor's logo adorns the bottom of the card. The backs have biography, player profile, and "Tips from the Cowboys" in the form of anti-drug and alcohol messages.

	MINT	NRMT	EXC
COMPLETE SET (16)	6.00	2.70	.75
COMMON CARD (1-16)	.50	.23	.06
☐ 1 Eric Roberts	.50	.23	.06
☐ 2 Erwin Brown	.50	.23	.06
☐ 3 Marcus Bowie	.50	.23	.06
☐ 4 Wes Watts	.50	.23	.06
☐ 5 Brian Brumfield	.50	.23	.06
☐ 6 Marc Stampley	.50	.23	.06
☐ 7 Sean Judge	.50	.23	.06
☐ 8 Joey Bernard	.50	.23	.06
☐ 9 Ken Naquin	.50	.23	.06
☐ 10 Bobby Smith	.50	.23	.06
☐ 11 Sam Breaux	.50	.23	.06
☐ 12 Ronald Scott	.50	.23	.06
☐ 13 Edward Dyer	.50	.23	.06
☐ 14 Greg Rayson	.50	.23	.06
☐ 15 Eric Kidd	.50	.23	.06
☐ 16 Bobby Keasler CO	.50	.23	.06

1992 McNeese State McDag/Police

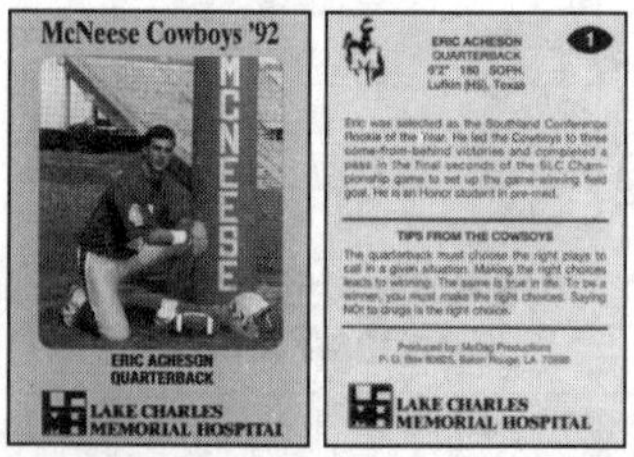

This 16-card standard-size set was produced by McDag Productions and sponsored by Lake Charles Memorial Hospital. The set is printed on thin card stock. The fronts feature rounded-corner posed color player photos on a mustard card face. The player's name and position appear below the picture. The backs have a white background and carry biographical information, player profile, and anti-drug or alcohol messages under the heading "Tips from the Cowboys."

	MINT	NRMT	EXC
COMPLETE SET (16)	6.00	2.70	.75
COMMON CARD (1-16)	.50	.23	.06
☐ 1 Eric Acheson	.50	.23	.06
☐ 2 Pat Neck	.50	.23	.06
☐ 3 Marcus Bowie	.50	.23	.06
☐ 4 Marty Posey	.50	.23	.06
☐ 5 Brian Brumfield	.50	.23	.06
☐ 6 Terry Irving	.75	.35	.09
☐ 7 Eric Fleming	.50	.23	.06
☐ 8 Lance Guidry	.50	.23	.06
☐ 9 Ken Naquin	.50	.23	.06
☐ 10 Chris Fontenette	.50	.23	.06
☐ 11 Sam Breaux	.50	.23	.06
☐ 12 Dana Scott	.50	.23	.06
☐ 13 Edward Dyer	.50	.23	.06
☐ 14 Blayne Rush	.50	.23	.06
☐ 15 Ronald Solomon	.50	.23	.06
☐ 16 Steve Aultman	.50	.23	.06

1990 Miami Smokey

The 1990 Miami Hurricanes Smokey set was issued in a sheet of 16 cards which, when perforated, measure the standard size. The fronts feature color action photos bordered in orange on green background, with the player's name, position, and jersey number below the picture. The backs have biographical information (in English and Spanish) and a fire prevention cartoon starring Smokey. The cards are unnumbered, so they are listed below alphabetically by subject's name. Key players in this set include Craig Erickson, Randal Hill and Russell Maryland.

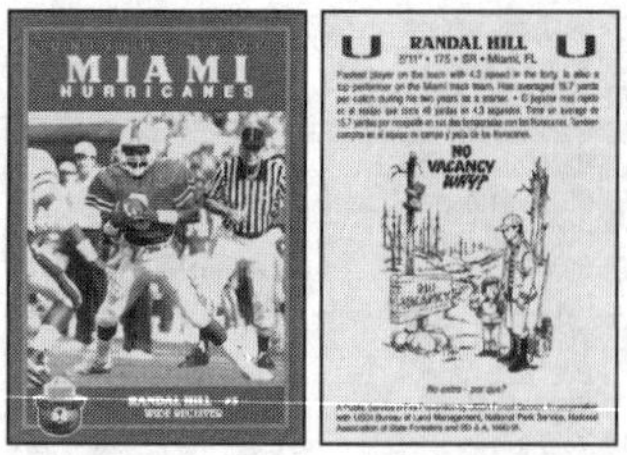

	MINT	NRMT	EXC
COMPLETE SET (16)	18.00	8.00	2.20
COMMON CARD (1-16)	.75	.35	.09
☐ 1 Randy Bethel 93	.75	.35	.09
☐ 2 Wesley Carroll 81	2.00	.90	.25
☐ 3 Rob Chudzinski 84	.75	.35	.09
☐ 4 Leonard Conley 28	1.00	.45	.12
☐ 5 Luis Cristobal 59	.75	.35	.09
☐ 6 Maurice Crum 49	.75	.35	.09
☐ 7 Shane Curry 44	1.00	.45	.12
☐ 8 Craig Erickson 7	3.00	1.35	.35
☐ 9 Dennis Erickson CO	2.00	.90	.25
☐ 10 Darren Handy 66	.75	.35	.09
☐ 11 Randal Hill 3	3.00	1.35	.35
☐ 12 Carlos Huerta 27	1.00	.45	.12
☐ 13 Russell Maryland 67	3.00	1.35	.35
☐ 14 Stephen McGuire 30	1.00	.45	.12
☐ 15 Roland Smith 16	.75	.35	.09
☐ 16 Mike Sullivan 79	.75	.35	.09

1991 Miami Police

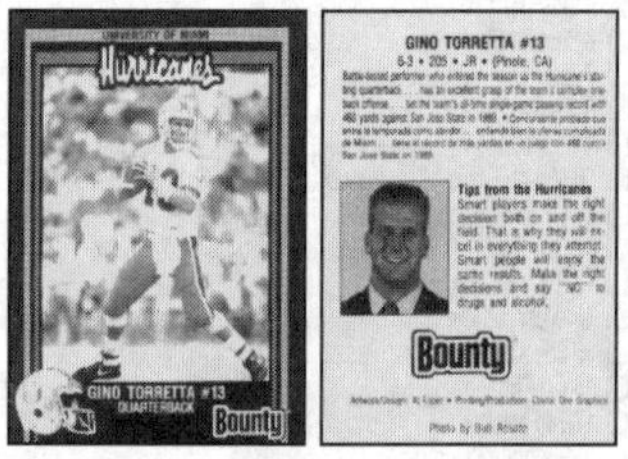

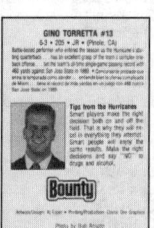

This 16-card standard-size set was sponsored by Bounty. Approximately 5,000 sets were issued, and they were given away at the Nov. 9 game against West Virginia at the Orange Bowl. The player action photos on the fronts are enclosed in black, orange, and green borders. College and team name are printed inside top borders while player information appears between the team helmet and Bounty logo at the bottom of the card face. Horizontally oriented backs provide player profile (in English and Spanish), biographical information, a head shot, and "Tips from the Hurricanes" in form of public service announcements. Sponsor logo and photo credits also appear on the back. The cards are unnumbered and checklisted below in alphabetical order.

	MINT	NRMT	EXC
COMPLETE SET (16)	15.00	6.75	1.85
COMMON CARD (1-16)	1.00	.45	.12
☐ 1 Jessie Armstead	1.50	.70	.19
☐ 2 Micheal Barrow	2.00	.90	.25
☐ 3 Hurlie Brown	1.00	.45	.12
☐ 4 Dennis Erickson CO	2.00	.90	.25
☐ 5 Anthony Hamlet	1.00	.45	.12
☐ 6 Carlos Huerta	1.50	.70	.19
☐ 7 Herbert James	1.00	.45	.12
☐ 8 Claude Jones	1.00	.45	.12
☐ 9 Stephen McGuire	1.50	.70	.19
☐ 10 Eric Miller	1.00	.45	.12
☐ 11 Joe Moore	1.00	.45	.12
☐ 12 Charles Pharms	1.00	.45	.12
☐ 13 Leon Searcy	2.00	.90	.25
☐ 14 Darrin Smith	2.00	.90	.25
☐ 15 Lamar Thomas	1.50	.70	.19
☐ 16 Gino Torretta	2.50	1.10	.30

1992 Miami Safety

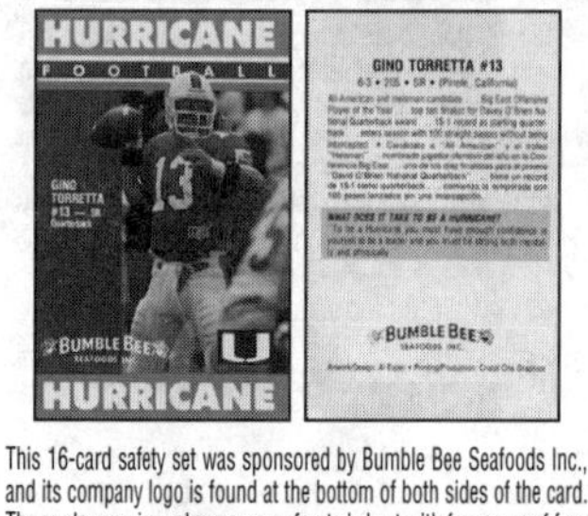

This 16-card safety set was sponsored by Bumble Bee Seafoods Inc., and its company logo is found at the bottom of both sides of the card. The cards were issued as an unperforated sheet with four rows of four cards each. If the cards were cut, they would measure the standard size. The color player photos on the fronts bleed off the bottom and right side but are edged by a thick green stripe on the left. The words "Hurricane Football" are printed in orange and green stripes that cut across the top of the front. The backs present biography, career summary, and "What Does It Take to Be a Hurricane" feature, which consists of a quote stressing a positive mental attitude. The cards are unnumbered and checklisted below in alphabetical order. The set features the second collegiate card of 1992 Heismann Trophy winner Gino Torretta as well as a card of wide receiver Kevin Williams.

	MINT	NRMT	EXC
COMPLETE SET (16)	15.00	6.75	1.85
COMMON CARD (1-16)	.75	.35	.09
☐ 1 Jessie Armstead	1.00	.45	.12
☐ 2 Micheal Barrow	1.50	.70	.19
☐ 3 Coleman Bell	.75	.35	.09
☐ 4 Mark Caesar	.75	.35	.09
☐ 5 Horace Copeland UER (Name misspelled Horrace on front)	2.50	1.10	.30
☐ 6 Mario Cristobal	.75	.35	.09
☐ 7 Dennis Erickson CO	1.50	.70	.19
☐ 8 Casey Greer	.75	.35	.09
☐ 9 Stephen McGuire	1.00	.45	.12
☐ 10 Ryan McNeil	2.00	.90	.25
☐ 11 Rusty Medearis	.75	.35	.09
☐ 12 Darrin Smith	1.50	.70	.19
☐ 13 Darryl Spencer	.75	.35	.09
☐ 14 Lamar Thomas	2.00	.90	.25
☐ 15 Gino Torretta	2.00	.90	.25
☐ 16 Kevin Williams WR	2.50	1.10	.30

1993 Miami Bumble Bee

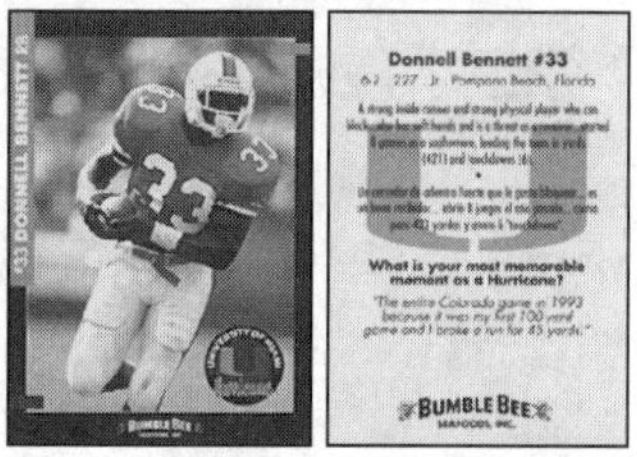

Sponsored by Bumble Bee, the 16 cards comprising this set were issued in one 16-card perforated sheet. The sheet measures approximately 10" by 14" and consists of four rows of four cards each. Each card measures the standard size and carries on its front a black-bordered color player action shot. The player's name, uniform number, and position appear vertically in white lettering within the orange stripe at the upper left. The Hurricanes' logo is displayed within a lower corner of the player photo. The Bumble Bee logo in white lettering rests in the lower black margin. The white back carries the player's name, uniform number, biography, highlights in both English and Spanish, and the player's "Most memorable moment as a Hurricane." The Bumble Bee logo at the bottom rounds out the card. The cards are unnumbered and checklisted below in alphabetical order.

	MINT	NRMT	EXC
COMPLETE SET (16)	12.00	5.50	1.50
COMMON CARD (1-16)	.60	.25	.07
☐ 1 Rudy Barber	.60	.25	.07
☐ 2 Robert Bass	.60	.25	.07
☐ 3 Donnell Bennett	2.00	.90	.25
☐ 4 Jason Budroni	.60	.25	.07
☐ 5 Marcus Carey	.60	.25	.07
☐ 6 Ryan Collins	1.00	.45	.12
☐ 7 Frank Costa	1.00	.45	.12
☐ 8 Dennis Erickson CO	1.25	.55	.16
☐ 9 Terris Harris	.60	.25	.07
☐ 10 Chris T. Jones	3.00	1.35	.35
☐ 11 Larry Jones	1.50	.70	.19
☐ 12 Darren Krein	1.00	.45	.12
☐ 13 Kenny Lopez	.60	.25	.07
☐ 14 Kevin Patrick	.60	.25	.07
☐ 15 Dexter Seigler	.60	.25	.07
☐ 16 Paul White	.60	.25	.07

1907 Michigan Dietsche Postcards

This set features members of the University of Michigan football team on postcard back cards. The catalog designation for this set is PC765-3. Each card features a black and white player photo on front and a postcard back complete with a short player write-up. The A.C. Dietsche copyright line also appears on the back.

	EXC	VG	G
COMPLETE SET (15)	750.00	350.00	95.00
COMMON CARD (1-15)	40.00	18.00	5.00
☐ 1 Dave Allerdice	50.00	22.00	6.25
☐ 2 William Casey	40.00	18.00	5.00
☐ 3 William Embs	40.00	18.00	5.00
☐ 4 Keene Fitzpatrick TR	40.00	18.00	5.00
☐ 5 Flanagan	40.00	18.00	5.00
☐ 6 Walter Graham	40.00	18.00	5.00
☐ 7 H.S. Hammond	40.00	18.00	5.00
☐ 8 John Loell	40.00	18.00	5.00
☐ 9 Paul Magoffin	50.00	22.00	6.25
☐ 10 James Miller	40.00	18.00	5.00
☐ 11 Walter Rheinschild	40.00	18.00	5.00
☐ 12 Mason Rumney	40.00	18.00	5.00
☐ 13 Adolph(Germany) Schultz	125.00	55.00	15.50
☐ 14 William Wasmund	40.00	18.00	5.00
☐ 15 Fielding Yost CO	125.00	55.00	15.50

1977 Michigan

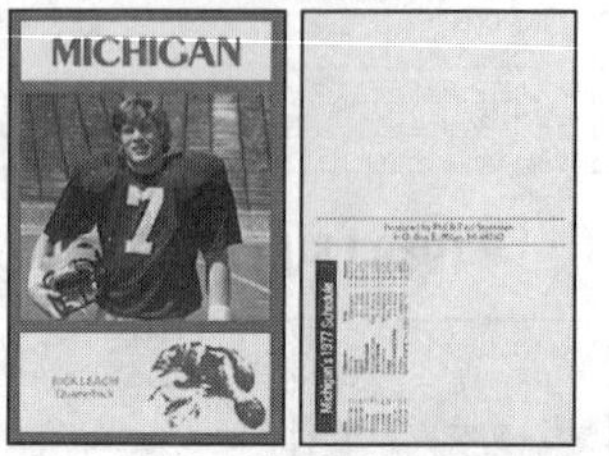

Produced by Stommen Enterprises, this 21-card postcard size (approximately 3 1/2" by 5 1/2") set features the 1977 Michigan Wolverines. Bordered in blue, the fronts divide into three registers. The top register is pale yellow and carries "Michigan" in block lettering. The middle register displays a color posed photo of the player in uniform holding his helmet. The bottom register is pale yellow and has the player's name, position, and a drawing of the mascot, all in blue. The horizontal backs are divided down the middle by two thin bluish-purple stripes, and Michigan's 1977 schedule appears in the same color ink on the upper left. Three cards, those of Giesler, Stephenson, and Szara, have an additional feature on their backs, an order blank printed on the right side. The order blank speaks of the "entire set of 18" and goes on to state "also available at the gates before and after the games." It appears that these three cards may have been produced or distributed later than the other eighteen.

	NRMT-MT	EXC	G-VG
COMPLETE SET (21)	20.00	9.00	2.50
COMMON CARD (1-21)	.75	.35	.09
☐ 1 John Anderson	1.25	.55	.16
☐ 2 Russell Davis	1.25	.55	.16
☐ 3 Mark Donahue	.75	.35	.09
☐ 4 Walt Downing	.75	.35	.09
☐ 5 Bill Dufek	1.25	.55	.16
☐ 6 Jon Giesler SP	2.00	.90	.25
☐ 7 Steve Graves	.75	.35	.09
☐ 8 Curtis Greer	2.00	.90	.25
☐ 9 Dwight Hicks	2.50	1.10	.30
☐ 10 Derek Howard	.75	.35	.09
☐ 11 Harlan Huckleby	2.50	1.10	.30
☐ 12 Gene Johnson	.75	.35	.09
☐ 13 Dale Keitz	.75	.35	.09
☐ 14 Mike Kenn	2.50	1.10	.30
☐ 15 Rick Leach	3.00	1.35	.35
☐ 16 Mark Schmerge	.75	.35	.09
☐ 17 Ron Simpkins	1.25	.55	.16
☐ 18 Curt Stephenson SP	2.00	.90	.25
☐ 19 Gerry Szara SP	2.00	.90	.25
☐ 20 Rick White	.75	.35	.09
☐ 21 Gregg Willner	.75	.35	.09

1989 Michigan

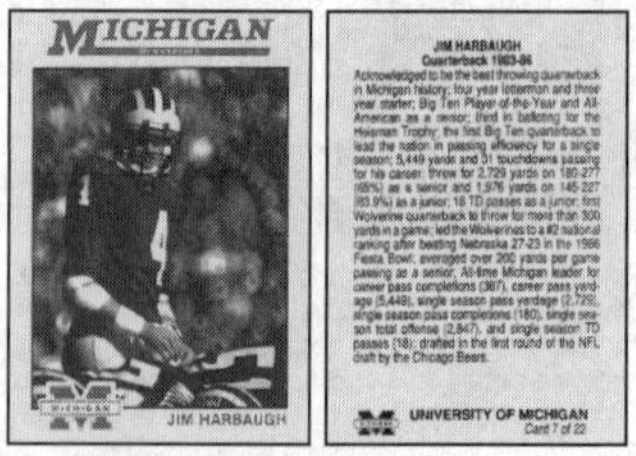

The 1989 Michigan football set contains 22 standard-size cards. The fronts have vintage or color action photos with white borders; the vertically oriented backs have detailed profiles. These cards were distributed as a set.

	MINT	NRMT	EXC
COMPLETE SET (22)	15.00	6.75	1.85
COMMON CARD (1-22)	.50	.23	.06
☐ 1 H.O.(Fritz) Crisler CO	.75	.35	.09
☐ 2 Anthony Carter	1.50	.70	.19
☐ 3 Willie Heston	.50	.23	.06
☐ 4 Reggie McKenzie	.50	.23	.06
☐ 5 Bo Schembechler CO	2.00	.90	.25
☐ 6 Dan Dierdorf	2.00	.90	.25
☐ 7 Jim Harbaugh	2.00	.90	.25
☐ 8 Bennie Oosterbaan	.50	.23	.06
☐ 9 Jamie Morris	.60	.25	.07
☐ 10 Gerald R. Ford	2.00	.90	.25
☐ 11 Curtis Greer	.60	.25	.07
☐ 12 Ron Kramer	.60	.25	.07
☐ 13 Calvin O'Neal	.50	.23	.06
☐ 14 Bob Chappuis	.50	.23	.06

☐ 15 Fielding H. Yost CO	1.00	.45	.12
☐ 16 Dennis Franklin	.50	.23	.06
☐ 17 Benny Friedman	.60	.25	.07
☐ 18 Jim Mandich	.60	.25	.07
☐ 19 Rob Lytle	.60	.25	.07
☐ 20 Bump Elliott	.60	.25	.07
☐ 21 Harry Kipke	.50	.23	.06
☐ 22 Dave Brown	.60	.25	.07

1988 Mississippi McDag

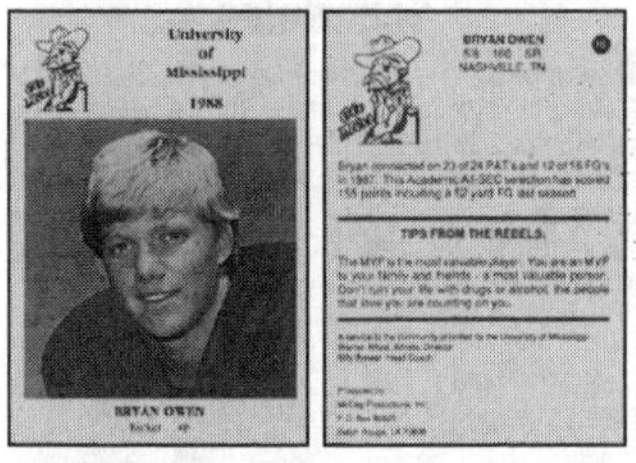

Apparently, McDag Productions only issued two standard-size cards in this set. Each front displays a color posed head and shoulders shot enclosed by white borders. The school logo, name, and year appear in the top white border while player information is printed beneath the picture. The back has biographical information, a summary of the player's performance in 1987, and "Tips from the Rebels" that consist of anti-drug and alcohol messages.

	MINT	NRMT	EXC
COMPLETE SET (2)	4.00	1.80	.50
COMMON CARD (15-16)	2.00	.90	.25
☐ 15 Mark Young	2.00	.90	.25
☐ 16 Bryan Owen	2.00	.90	.25

1991 Mississippi Hoby

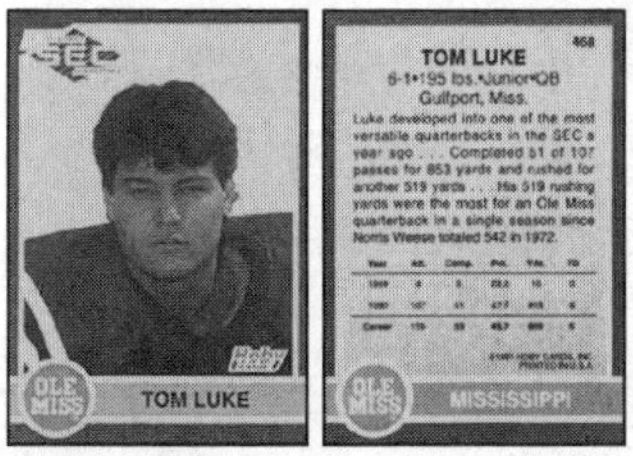

This 42-card standard-size set was produced by Hoby and features the 1991 Ole Miss football team. Five hundred uncut press sheets were also produced, and they were signed and numbered by Billy Brewer. The cards feature on the fronts color head and shoulders shots, with thin white borders on a royal blue card face. The school logo occurs in the lower left corner in a red circle, with the player's name in a gold stripe extending to the right. On a light red background, the backs carry biography, player profile, and statistics. The cards are numbered on the back and are ordered alphabetically by player's name.

	MINT	NRMT	EXC
COMPLETE SET (42)	9.00	4.00	1.10
COMMON CARD (439-480)	.25	.11	.03
☐ 439 Gary Abide	.25	.11	.03
☐ 440 Dwayne Amos	.25	.11	.03
☐ 441 Tyji Armstrong	1.00	.45	.12
☐ 442 Tyrone Ashley	.25	.11	.03
☐ 443 Darron Billings	.25	.11	.03
☐ 444 Danny Boyd	.25	.11	.03
☐ 445 Billy Brewer CO	.35	.16	.04
☐ 446 Chad Brown	.25	.11	.03
☐ 447 Tony Brown	.25	.11	.03
☐ 448 Vincent Brownlee	.35	.16	.04
☐ 449 Jeff Carter	.35	.16	.04
☐ 450 Richard Chisolm	.25	.11	.03
☐ 451 Clint Conlee	.25	.11	.03
☐ 452 Marvin Courtney	.25	.11	.03
☐ 453 Cliff Dew	.25	.11	.03
☐ 454 Johnny Dixon	.25	.11	.03
☐ 455 Artis Ford	.25	.11	.03
☐ 456 Chauncey Godwin	.25	.11	.03
☐ 457 Brian Harper	.25	.11	.03
☐ 458 David Harris	.25	.11	.03
☐ 459 Pete Harris	.25	.11	.03
☐ 460 David Herring	.25	.11	.03
☐ 461 James Holcombe	.25	.11	.03
☐ 462 Kevin Ingram	.25	.11	.03
☐ 463 Phillip Kent	.35	.16	.04
☐ 464 Derrick King	.25	.11	.03
☐ 465 Brian Lee	.25	.11	.03
☐ 466 Jim Lentz	.25	.11	.03
☐ 467 Everett Lindsay	.25	.11	.03
☐ 468 Tom Luke	.25	.11	.03
☐ 469 Thomas McLeish	.25	.11	.03
☐ 470 Wesley Melton	.25	.11	.03
☐ 471 Tyrone Montgomery	.75	.35	.09
☐ 472 Deano Orr	.25	.11	.03
☐ 473 Darrick Owens	.35	.16	.04
☐ 474 Lynn Ross	.25	.11	.03
☐ 475 Russ Shows	.25	.11	.03
☐ 476 Eddie Small	.35	.16	.04
☐ 477 Trea Southerland	.25	.11	.03
☐ 478 Gerald Vaughn	.25	.11	.03
☐ 479 Abner White	.25	.11	.03
☐ 480 Sebastian Williams	.25	.11	.03

1991 Mississippi State Hoby

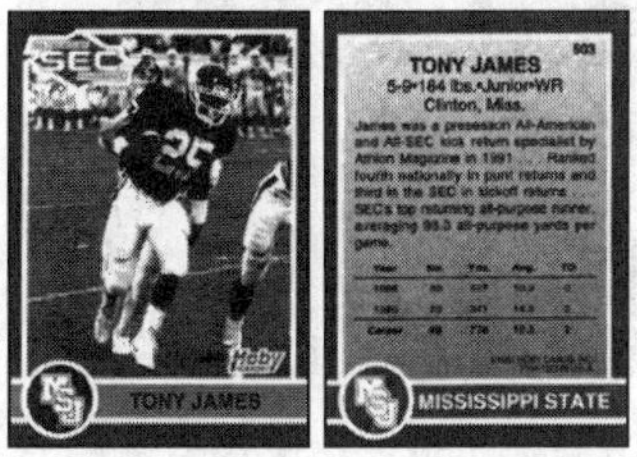

This 42-card standard-size set was produced by Hoby and features the 1991 Mississippi State football team. The cards feature on the fronts color head shots, with thin white borders on a royal blue card face. The school logo occurs in the lower left corner in a maroon circle, with the player's name in a gold stripe extending to the right. On a light maroon background, the backs carry biography, player profile, and statistics. The cards are numbered on the back and are ordered alphabetically by player's name.

	MINT	NRMT	EXC
COMPLETE SET (42)	9.00	4.00	1.10
COMMON CARD (481-522)	.25	.11	.03
☐ 481 Lance Aldridge	.25	.11	.03
☐ 482 Treddis Anderson	.25	.11	.03
☐ 483 Shea Bell	.25	.11	.03
☐ 484 Chris Bosarge	.25	.11	.03
☐ 485 Daniel Boyd	.25	.11	.03
☐ 486 Jerome Brown	.25	.11	.03
☐ 487 Torrance Brown	.25	.11	.03
☐ 488 Keith Carr	.25	.11	.03
☐ 489 Herman Carroll	.25	.11	.03
☐ 490 Keo Coleman	.35	.16	.04
☐ 491 Michael Davis	.25	.11	.03
☐ 492 Trenell Edwards	.25	.11	.03
☐ 493 Chris Firle	.25	.11	.03
☐ 494 Lee Ford	.25	.11	.03
☐ 495 Tay Galloway	.25	.11	.03
☐ 496 Chris Gardner	.25	.11	.03
☐ 497 Arleye Gibson	.25	.11	.03
☐ 498 Tony Harris	.25	.11	.03
☐ 499 Willie Harris	.25	.11	.03
☐ 500 Kevin Henry	.35	.16	.04
☐ 501 Jackie Sherrill CO	.50	.23	.06
☐ 502 John James	.25	.11	.03
☐ 503 Tony James	.25	.11	.03
☐ 504 Todd Jordan	.25	.11	.03
☐ 505 Keith Joseph	.25	.11	.03
☐ 506 Kelvin Knight	.25	.11	.03
☐ 507 Lee Lipscomb	.25	.11	.03
☐ 508 Juan Long	.25	.11	.03
☐ 509 Kyle McCoy	.25	.11	.03
☐ 510 Tommy Morrell	.25	.11	.03
☐ 511 Kelly Ray	.25	.11	.03
☐ 512 Mike Riley	.25	.11	.03
☐ 513 Kenny Roberts	.25	.11	.03
☐ 514 William Robinson	.25	.11	.03
☐ 515 Bill Sartin	.25	.11	.03
☐ 516 Kenny Stewart	.25	.11	.03
☐ 517 Rodney Stowers	.50	.23	.06
☐ 518 Anthony Thames	.25	.11	.03
☐ 519 Edward Williams	.25	.11	.03
☐ 520 Nate Williams	.25	.11	.03
☐ 521 Karl Williamson	.25	.11	.03
☐ 522 Marc Woodard	.25	.11	.03

1907 Missouri Postcards

These Missouri Postcards were issued in 1907. Any additions or information on the checklist below would be appreciated.

	EXC	VG	G
COMPLETE SET (3)	90.00	40.00	11.00
COMMON CARD (1-3)	30.00	13.50	3.70
☐ 1 W.N.Deatherage	30.00	13.50	3.70
☐ 2 W.L.Driver	30.00	13.50	3.70
☐ 3 E.L.Miller	30.00	13.50	3.70

1992 Mobil Cotton Bowl

This 24-card set captures "Classic Moments" from the Mobil Cotton Bowl. The fronts feature sepia-toned player photos, edged on the left and below by dark blue borders, and on right and below by pink shadow borders. A red triangle superposed on the picture carries the player's name, school, and the year that he played in the Cotton Bowl game. On a white card face with a ghosted version of the Cotton Bowl logo, the horizontal backs summarize the player's outstanding performance. The cards are numbered on the back "X/24."

	MINT	NRMT	EXC
COMPLETE SET (24)	40.00	18.00	5.00
COMMON CARD (1-24)	1.00	.45	.12
☐ 1 The Cotton Bowl	1.00	.45	.12
☐ 2 Sammy Baugh	3.00	1.35	.35
☐ 3 Doak Walker	2.00	.90	.25
☐ 4 Dick Moegle	1.00	.45	.12
☐ 5 Bobby Layne	3.00	1.35	.35
☐ 6 Curtis Sanford Founder	1.00	.45	.12
☐ 7 John Kimbrough	1.00	.45	.12
☐ 8 Ernie Davis	5.00	2.20	.60
☐ 9 Lance Alworth	2.00	.90	.25
☐ 10 James Street Darrell Royal CO	1.50	.70	.19
☐ 11 Mike Singletary	1.50	.70	.19
☐ 12 Roger Staubach	5.00	2.20	.60
☐ 13 Earl Campbell	4.00	1.80	.50
☐ 14 Wilson Whitley	1.00	.45	.12
☐ 15 Jim Swink	1.00	.45	.12
☐ 16 Martin Ruby	1.00	.45	.12
☐ 17 Davey O'Brien	1.50	.70	.19
☐ 18 Gene Stallings CO Paul(Bear) Bryant CO	3.00	1.35	.35
☐ 19 Bo Jackson	2.00	.90	.25
☐ 20 Joe Theismann	1.50	.70	.19
☐ 21 Field Scovell Mr. Cotton Bowl	1.00	.45	.12
☐ 22 Ken Hatfield	1.00	.45	.12
☐ 23 Joe Montana	6.00	2.70	.75
☐ 24 Mobil Cotton Bowl Classic CL	1.00	.45	.12

1974 Nebraska

This is a 54-card set of playing cards each measuring approximately 2 1/4" by 3 1/2". The front features the words "Go Big Red" and "Nebraska" in the shape of a football helmet. The back features a player head shot with the player's name below. The cards are numbered as a deck of cards. This set features an early card of coaching great Tom Osborne.

	NRMT-MT	EXC	G-VG
COMPLETE SET (54)	100.00	45.00	12.50
COMMON CARD (1-54)	1.50	.70	.19
☐ 1 Tom Osborne CO	25.00	11.00	3.10
☐ 2 Terry Rogers	1.50	.70	.19
☐ 3 Tom Ruud	2.00	.90	.25
☐ 4 Jeff Schneider	1.50	.70	.19
☐ 5 Mark Heydorff	1.50	.70	.19
☐ 6 Dean Gissler	1.50	.70	.19
☐ 7 Jim Burrow	1.50	.70	.19
☐ 8 Al Eveland	1.50	.70	.19
☐ 9 Chuck Jones	1.50	.70	.19
☐ 10 Brad Jenkins	1.50	.70	.19
☐ 11 Dave Butterfield	1.50	.70	.19
☐ 12 Rich Duda	2.00	.90	.25
☐ 13 Steve Hoins	1.50	.70	.19
☐ 14 Ron Pruitt	1.50	.70	.19
☐ 15 Tony Davis	2.00	.90	.25
☐ 16 Mike Fultz	1.50	.70	.19
☐ 17 Chad Leonardi	1.50	.70	.19
☐ 18 John Starkebaum	1.50	.70	.19
☐ 19 Marvin Crenshaw	2.00	.90	.25
☐ 20 Larry Mushinskie	1.50	.70	.19
☐ 21 Tom Pate	1.50	.70	.19
☐ 22 Dave Humm	5.00	2.20	.60
☐ 23 Willie Thornton	2.00	.90	.25
☐ 24 Dave Redding	1.50	.70	.19
☐ 25 Dave Shamblin	1.50	.70	.19
☐ 26 Earl Everett	1.50	.70	.19
☐ 27 Rik Bonness	2.00	.90	.25
☐ 28 Mark Doak	1.50	.70	.19
☐ 29 John Lee	1.50	.70	.19
☐ 30 Mike Coyle	1.50	.70	.19
☐ 31 George Kyros	1.50	.70	.19
☐ 32 Gary Higgs	1.50	.70	.19
☐ 33 Dennis Pavelka	1.50	.70	.19
☐ 34 Jeff Moran	1.50	.70	.19
☐ 35 John O'Leary	1.50	.70	.19
☐ 36 Percy Eichelberger	1.50	.70	.19
☐ 37 Greg Jorgensen	1.50	.70	.19
☐ 38 George Mills	1.50	.70	.19
☐ 39 Terry Luck	1.50	.70	.19
☐ 40 Don Westbrook	1.50	.70	.19
☐ 41 Mike Offner	1.50	.70	.19
☐ 42 Stan Waldemore	1.50	.70	.19
☐ 43 Stan Hegener	1.50	.70	.19
☐ 44 Bobby Thomas	1.50	.70	.19
☐ 45 Bob Martin	1.50	.70	.19
☐ 46 Ritch Bahe	1.50	.70	.19
☐ 47 Tom Heiser	1.50	.70	.19
☐ 48 Steve Wieser	1.50	.70	.19
☐ 49 Ardell Johnson	1.50	.70	.19
☐ 50 Chuck Malito	1.50	.70	.19
☐ 51 Bob Lingenfelter	1.50	.70	.19
☐ 52 Wonder Monds	2.00	.90	.25
☐ 53 Bob Nelson	2.00	.90	.25
☐ 54 Memorial Stadium	2.00	.90	.25

1977 Nebraska

This 54-card set of playing cards measures 2 1/4" by 3 1/2". The front features the words "Go Big Red" and "Nebraska" in the shape of a football helmet. The back features a player head shot with the player's name below. The cards are numbered as a deck of cards.

	NRMT-MT	EXC	G-VG
COMPLETE SET (54)	75.00	34.00	9.50
COMMON CARD (1-54)	1.25	.55	.16
SEMISTARS	1.50	.70	.19
☐ 1 Tom Osborne CO	20.00	9.00	2.50
☐ 2 Tom Alward	1.25	.55	.16
☐ 3 Dan Anderson	1.25	.55	.16
☐ 4 Frosty Anderson	1.25	.55	.16
☐ 5 Al Austin	1.25	.55	.16
☐ 6 Ritch Bahe	1.25	.55	.16
☐ 7 John Bell	1.25	.55	.16
☐ 8 Rik Bonness	1.50	.70	.19
☐ 9 Randy Borg	1.25	.55	.16
☐ 10 Rich Costanzo	1.25	.55	.16
☐ 11 Maury Damkroger	1.50	.70	.19
☐ 12 Tony Davis	1.50	.70	.19
☐ 13 Mark Doak	1.25	.55	.16
☐ 14 Richard Duda	1.50	.70	.19
☐ 15 John Dutton	4.00	1.80	.50
☐ 16 Pat Fischer	4.00	1.80	.50
☐ 17 Marvin Crenshaw	1.50	.70	.19
☐ 18 Dean Gissler	1.25	.55	.16
☐ 19 Dave Goeller	1.25	.55	.16
☐ 20 Percy Eichelberger	1.25	.55	.16
☐ 21 Stan Hegener	1.25	.55	.16
☐ 22 Dave Humm	3.00	1.35	.35
☐ 23 Ardell Johnson	1.25	.55	.16
☐ 24 Doug Johnson	1.25	.55	.16
☐ 25 Chuck Jones	1.25	.55	.16
☐ 26 Wonder Monds	1.50	.70	.19
☐ 27 Terry Rogers	1.25	.55	.16
☐ 28 Bob Revelle	1.25	.55	.16
☐ 29 Tom Pate	1.25	.55	.16
☐ 30 Mike O'Holleran	1.25	.55	.16
☐ 31 Ron Pruitt	1.25	.55	.16
☐ 32 Bob Nelson	1.50	.70	.19
☐ 33 Larry Mushinskie	1.25	.55	.16
☐ 34 Jeff Moran	1.25	.55	.16
☐ 35 Bob Martin	1.25	.55	.16
☐ 36 Ralph Powell	1.25	.55	.16
☐ 37 Steve Manstedt	1.25	.55	.16
☐ 38 Brent Longwell	1.25	.55	.16
☐ 39 George Kyros	1.25	.55	.16
☐ 40 Zaven Yaralian	1.25	.55	.16
☐ 41 Bob Wolfe	1.25	.55	.16
☐ 42 Steve Wieser	1.25	.55	.16
☐ 43 Daryl White	1.25	.55	.16
☐ 44 Bob Thornton	1.25	.55	.16
☐ 45 John Starkebaum	1.25	.55	.16
☐ 46 Dave Shamblin	1.25	.55	.16
☐ 48 Bob Schmit	1.50	.70	.19
☐ 49 Rich Sanger	1.25	.55	.16
☐ 50 Willie Thornton	1.50	.70	.19
☐ 51 Tom Ruud	1.50	.70	.19
☐ 52 Steve Runty	1.25	.55	.16
☐ JK Stadium (Red)	1.50	.70	.19
☐ JK Stadium (Black)	1.50	.70	.19

1989 Nebraska 100

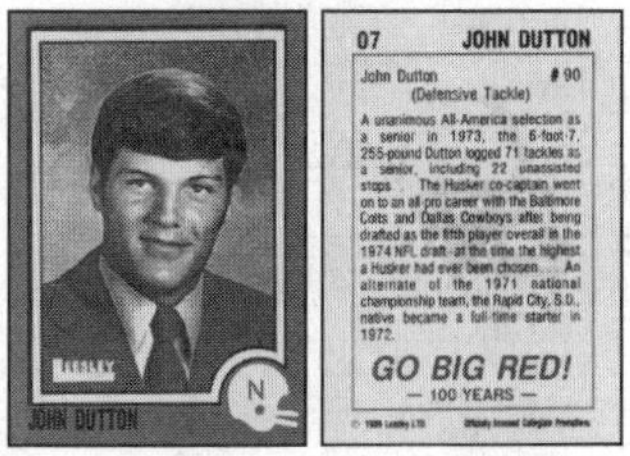

This 100-card standard-size set was sponsored and produced by Leesley Ltd. The set is sometimes subtitled as "100 Years of Nebraska Football" as it features past University of Nebraska football players. Many of the pictures are actually color portrait drawings rather than photos. The cards have thick red borders. The vertically oriented backs have detailed profiles. These cards were distributed as a complete set and as eight-card cello packs. The cards are numbered on the back in the upper left corner.

	MINT	NRMT	EXC
COMPLETE SET (100)	40.00	18.00	5.00
COMMON CARD (1-100)	.35	.16	.04
☐ 1 Tony Davis	.50	.23	.06
☐ 2 Keith Jones	.35	.16	.04
☐ 3 Turner Gill	1.25	.55	.16
☐ 4 Dave Butterfield	.35	.16	.04
☐ 5 Wonder Monds	.50	.23	.06
☐ 6 Dave Rimington	.75	.35	.09
☐ 7 John Dutton	.75	.35	.09
☐ 8 Irving Fryar	3.00	1.35	.35
☐ 9 Dean Steinkuhler	.75	.35	.09
☐ 10 Mike Rozier	1.25	.55	.16
☐ 11 Jarvis Redwine	.75	.35	.09
☐ 12 Randy Schleusener	.35	.16	.04
☐ 13 Junior Miller	.50	.23	.06
☐ 14 Broderick Thomas	1.25	.55	.16
☐ 15 Steve Taylor	.50	.23	.06
☐ 16 Neil Smith	2.00	.90	.25
☐ 17 John McCormick	.35	.16	.04
☐ 18 Danny Noonan	.50	.23	.06
☐ 19 Mike Fultz	.35	.16	.04
☐ 20 Vince Ferragamo	1.00	.45	.12

☐ 21 Jerry Tagge	.75	.35	.09
☐ 22 Jeff Kinney	.50	.23	.06
☐ 23 Rich Glover	.50	.23	.06
☐ 24 Johnny Rodgers	1.25	.55	.16
☐ 25 Rik Bonness	.50	.23	.06
☐ 26 Dave Humm	.50	.23	.06
☐ 27 Mark Traynowicz	.50	.23	.06
☐ 28 Harry Grimminger	.35	.16	.04
☐ 29 Bill Lewis	.50	.23	.06
☐ 30 Jim Skow	.50	.23	.06
☐ 31 Larry Kramer	.35	.16	.04
☐ 32 Tony Jeter	.50	.23	.06
☐ 33 Robert Brown	.35	.16	.04
☐ 34 Larry Wachholtz	.35	.16	.04
☐ 35 Wayne Meylan	.50	.23	.06
☐ 36 Bob Newton	.35	.16	.04
☐ 37 Willie Harper	.50	.23	.06
☐ 38 Bob Martin	.50	.23	.06
☐ 39 Jerry Murtaugh	.50	.23	.06
☐ 40 Daryl White	.35	.16	.04
☐ 41 Larry Jacobson	.35	.16	.04
☐ 42 Joe Armstrong	.35	.16	.04
☐ 43 Laverne Allers	.35	.16	.04
☐ 44 Freeman White	.50	.23	.06
☐ 45 Marvin Crenshaw	.50	.23	.06
☐ 46 Forrest Behm	.35	.16	.04
☐ 47 Jerry Minnick	.35	.16	.04
☐ 48 Tom Davis	.35	.16	.04
☐ 49 Kelvin Clark	.50	.23	.06
☐ 50 Tom Rathman	1.25	.55	.16
☐ 51 Sam Francis	.35	.16	.04
☐ 52 Joe Orduna	.50	.23	.06
☐ 53 Ed Weir	.35	.16	.04
☐ 54 Bill Thornton	.35	.16	.04
☐ 55 Bob Devaney CO	.75	.35	.09
☐ 56 Bret Clark	.35	.16	.04
☐ 57 Frank Solich	.35	.16	.04
☐ 58 Tim Smith	.35	.16	.04
☐ 59 George Andrews	.50	.23	.06
☐ 60 Rick Berns	.50	.23	.06
☐ 61 Monte Johnson	.50	.23	.06
☐ 62 Walt Barnes	.35	.16	.04
☐ 63 Jim McFarland	.35	.16	.04
☐ 64 Jimmy Williams	.35	.16	.04
☐ 65 Vic Halligan	.35	.16	.04
☐ 66 Guy Chamberlin	.35	.16	.04
☐ 67 Hugh Rhea	.35	.16	.04
☐ 68 George Sauer	.50	.23	.06
☐ 69 E.O. Stiehm CO	.35	.16	.04
☐ 70 Walter G. Booth CO	.35	.16	.04
☐ 71 First Night Game	.35	.16	.04
(Memorial Stadium)			
☐ 72 Memorial Stadium	.35	.16	.04
☐ 73 M-Stadium Expansions	.35	.16	.04
☐ 74 Andra Franklin	.75	.35	.09
☐ 75 Ron McDole	.50	.23	.06
☐ 76 Pat Fischer	.50	.23	.06
☐ 77 Dan McMullen	.35	.16	.04
☐ 78 Charles Brock	.35	.16	.04
☐ 79 Verne Lewellen	.35	.16	.04
☐ 80 Bob Nelson	.50	.23	.06
☐ 81 Roger Craig	3.00	1.35	.35
☐ 82 Fred Shirey	.35	.16	.04
☐ 83 Tom Novak	.35	.16	.04
☐ 84 Ray Richards	.35	.16	.04
☐ 85 Warren Alfson	.35	.16	.04
☐ 86 Lawrence Ely	.35	.16	.04
☐ 87 Mike Rozier	1.25	.55	.16
☐ 88 Dean Steinkuhler	.75	.35	.09
☐ 89 John Dutton	.75	.35	.09
☐ 90 Dave Rimington	.75	.35	.09
☐ 91 Johnny Rodgers	1.25	.55	.16
☐ 92 Herbie Husker (Mascot)	.35	.16	.04
☐ 93 Tom Osborne CO	1.50	.70	.19
☐ 94 Broderick Thomas	1.25	.55	.16
☐ 95 Bob Reynolds	.35	.16	.04
☐ 96 Mick Tingelhoff UER	.75	.35	.09
(Name misspelled Tinglehoff)			
☐ 97 Lloyd Cardwell	.35	.16	.04
☐ 98 Johnny Rodgers	1.25	.55	.16
☐ 99 '70 National Champs	.50	.23	.06
(Team Photo)			
☐ 100 '71 National Champs	.50	.23	.06
(Team Photo)			
☐ NNO Title Card	.50	.23	.06
(Contest on back)			

1993 Nebraska *

This 25-card set of the Nebraska Huskers features color action player photos in a white border. Athlete's from various sports categories are represented with extra descriptions following the non-football

---

athletes. The player's name, position, and hometown are printed in the wide bottom margin. The backs carry a Husker tip and a crime prevention tip. The cards are unnumbered and checklisted below in alphabetical order.

	MINT	NRMT	EXC
COMPLETE SET (25)	15.00	6.75	1.85
COMMON CARD (1-25)	.50	.23	.06
☐ 1 Trev Alberts	2.00	.90	.25
☐ 2 Mike Anderson	.75	.35	.09
☐ 3 Ernie Beler	.75	.35	.09
☐ 4 Byron Bennett	.75	.35	.09
☐ 5 Troy Bromawn	.50	.23	.06
(Men's baseball)			
☐ 6 NaFeesah Brown	.50	.23	.06
(Women's basketball)			
☐ 7 Jed Dalton	.50	.23	.06
(Men's baseball)			
☐ 8 Sumner Darling	.50	.23	.06
(Men's gymnastics)			
☐ 9 Corey Dixon	.75	.35	.09
☐ 10 Troy Dumas	.75	.35	.09
☐ 11 Nicole Duval	.50	.23	.06
(Women's gymnastics)			
☐ 12 Mike Eierman	.50	.23	.06
(Wrestling)			
☐ 13 Amy Erlenbusch	.50	.23	.06
(Women's softball)			
☐ 14 Dennis Harrison	.50	.23	.06
(Men's gymnastics)			
☐ 15 Jamar Johnson	1.00	.45	.12
(Men's basketball)			
☐ 16 Calvin Jones	1.50	.70	.19
☐ 17 Laura Luther	.50	.23	.06
(Women's volleyball)			
☐ 18 Denise McMillen	.50	.23	.06
(Women's softball)			
☐ 19 Bruce Moore	.75	.35	.09
☐ 20 David Noonan	1.00	.45	.12
☐ 21 Lori Phillips	.50	.23	.06
(Women's gymnastics)			
☐ 22 Eric Piatkowski	2.00	.90	.25
(Men's basketball)			
☐ 23 Nikki Stricker	.50	.23	.06
(Women's volleyball)			
☐ 24 Frank Velazquez	.50	.23	.06
(Wrestling)			
☐ 25 Meggan Yedsena	.50	.23	.06
(Women's basketball)			

1994 Nebraska *

This 21-card set of the Nebraska Huskers features color action player photos from several sports surrounded by a black border. The player's name, college year, position, and hometown are printed in the wide bottom margin. The backs carry a crime prevention tip. The cards are unnumbered and checklisted below in alphabetical order.

	MINT	NRMT	EXC
COMPLETE SET (21)	15.00	6.75	1.85
COMMON CARD (1-21)	.50	.23	.06
☐ 1 Kelly Aspergren	.50	.23	.06
(Women's volleyball)			
☐ 2 Jaron Boone	1.00	.45	.12
(Men's basketball)			
☐ 3 Terry Connealy	.75	.35	.09
☐ 4 Jed Dalton	.50	.23	.06
(Men's baseball)			
☐ 5 Troy Dumas	.75	.35	.09
☐ 6 Cody Dusenberry	.50	.23	.06
(Women's softball)			
☐ 7 Nicole Duval	.50	.23	.06
(Women's gymnastics)			
☐ 8 Richard Grace	.50	.23	.06
(Men's gymnastics)			
☐ 9 Donta Jones	1.50	.70	.19
☐ 10 Rick Kleffer	.50	.23	.06
(Men's gymnastics)			
☐ 11 Barron Miles	1.00	.45	.12
☐ 12 Darin Petersen	.50	.23	.06
(Men's gymnastics)			
☐ 13 Cory Schlesinger	2.00	.90	.25
☐ 14 Ed Stewart	.75	.35	.09
☐ 15 Erick Strickland	2.00	.90	.25
(Men's basketball)			
☐ 16 Joy Taylor	.50	.23	.06
(Women's gymnastics)			
☐ 17 Emily Thompson	.50	.23	.06
(Women's basketball)			
☐ 18 Tanya Upthegrove	.50	.23	.06
(Women's basketball)			

☐ 19 Zach Wiegert	1.50	.70	.19
☐ 20 Billie Winsett	.50	.23	.06
(Women's volleyball)			
☐ 21 Rob Zatechka	1.50	.70	.19

1996 Nebraska

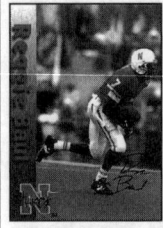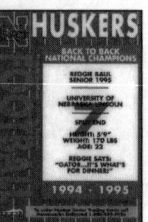

The 22 card Nebraska standard-size set was produced by Homeworks Unlimited and was sold in set form. The 21 seniors from the 1995-6 Nebraska National Championship team are included within the set, as well as a checklist card. Key players within this set include Clinton Childs, Tommie Frazier, Aaron Graham, and Jeff Makovicka. In addition, there is a Brook Berringer tribute card, which details his tragic death from a plane crash. While the players' uniform number is listed on each of these cards, they are arranged in alphabetical order below. Each plastic card has a facsimile autograph on the front.

	MINT	NRMT	EXC
COMPLETE SET (22)	35.00	16.00	4.40
COMMON CARD (1-22)	1.50	.70	.19
☐ 1 Jacques Allen	1.50	.70	.19
☐ 2 Reggie Baul	1.75	.80	.22
☐ 3 Brook Berringer	4.00	1.80	.50
☐ 4 Clinton Childs	2.00	.90	.25
☐ 5 Doug Colman	1.50	.70	.19
☐ 6 Phil Ellis	1.50	.70	.19
☐ 7 Tommie Frazier	5.00	2.20	.60
☐ 8 Mark Gilman	1.50	.70	.19
☐ 9 Aaron Graham	2.00	.90	.25
☐ 10 Luther Hardin	1.50	.70	.19
☐ 11 Jason Jenkins	1.50	.70	.19
☐ 12 Clester Johnson	1.50	.70	.19
☐ 13 Jeff Makovicka	1.75	.80	.22
☐ 14 Brian Nunns	1.50	.70	.19
☐ 15 Steve Ott	1.50	.70	.19
☐ 16 Aaron Penland	1.50	.70	.19
☐ 17 Christian Peter	2.00	.90	.25
☐ 18 Darren Schmadeke	2.00	.90	.25
☐ 19 Tony Veland	1.50	.70	.19
☐ 20 Steve Volin	1.50	.70	.19
☐ 21 Tyrone Williams	2.00	.90	.25
☐ 22 Checklist Card	1.50	.70	.19
Team Logo			

1979 North Carolina Schedules

This four-card set was apparently issued by the Department of Athletics at North Carolina (Chapel Hill) and partially sponsored by Hardee's. The cards measure approximately 2 3/8" by 3 3/8". The card front features a full-bleed head shot of the player, with the player's name and jersey number burned into the bottom portion of the picture. The backs carry the 1979 varsity football schedule. The cards are unnumbered and checklisted below in alphabetical order.

	NRMT-MT	EXC	G-VG
COMPLETE SET (4)	12.00	5.50	1.50
COMMON CARD (1-4)	3.00	1.35	.35
☐ 1 Ricky Barden	3.00	1.35	.35
☐ 2 Steve Junkman	3.00	1.35	.35
☐ 3 Matt Kupec	4.00	1.80	.50
☐ 4 Doug Paschal	3.00	1.35	.35

1982 North Carolina Schedules

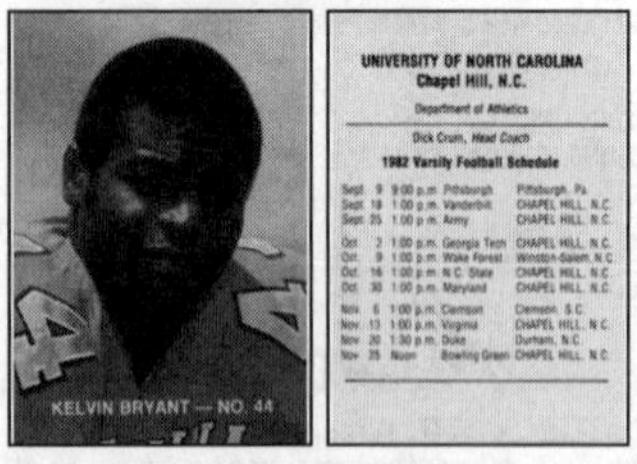

This eight-card set was apparently issued by the Department of Athletics at North Carolina (Chapel Hill). The cards measure approximately 2 3/8" by 3 3/8". The card front features a full-bleed head shot of the player, with the player's name and jersey number burned into the bottom portion of the picture. The backs carry the 1982 varsity football schedule. The cards are unnumbered and checklisted below in alphabetical order.

	MINT	NRMT	EXC
COMPLETE SET (8)	25.00	11.00	3.10
COMMON CARD (1-8)	3.00	1.35	.35

☐ 1 Kelvin Bryant	7.50	3.40	.95
☐ 2 Alan Burrus	3.00	1.35	.35
☐ 3 David Drechsler	3.00	1.35	.35
☐ 4 Rod Elkins	4.00	1.80	.50
☐ 5 Jack Parry	3.00	1.35	.35
☐ 6 Greg Poole	3.00	1.35	.35
☐ 7 Ron Spruill	3.00	1.35	.35
☐ 8 Mike Wilcher	4.00	1.80	.50

1986 North Carolina Schedules

This four-card set was apparently issued by the Department of Athletics at North Carolina (Chapel Hill). The cards measure approximately 2 3/8" by 3 3/8". The card front features a full-bleed head shot of the player, with the player's name and jersey number burned into the bottom portion of the picture. The backs carry the 1986 varsity football schedule. The cards are unnumbered and checklisted below in alphabetical order.

	MINT	NRMT	EXC
COMPLETE SET (4)	15.00	6.75	1.85
COMMON CARD (1-4)	3.00	1.35	.35
☐ 1 Walter Bailey	3.00	1.35	.35
☐ 2 Harris Barton	6.00	2.70	.75
☐ 3 C.A. Brooks	3.00	1.35	.35
☐ 4 Eric Streater	4.00	1.80	.50

1988 North Carolina

This 16-card set was produced by Sports Marketing and features color player portraits with sponsor logos in the top margin and player's name, jersey number, academic year, and position listed in the bottom border. The backs carry the player's name, position, jersey number, biographical and career information with team tips and sponsors listed below. The cards are unnumbered and checklisted below in alphabetical order.

	MINT	NRMT	EXC
COMPLETE SET (16)	15.00	6.75	1.85
COMMON CARD (1-16)	1.00	.45	.12
☐ 1 Mack Brown CO	1.50	.70	.19
☐ 2 Pat Crowley	1.00	.45	.12
☐ 3 Torin Dorn	2.00	.90	.25
☐ 4 Jeff Garnica	1.00	.45	.12
☐ 5 Antonio Goss	1.00	.45	.12
☐ 6 Jonathan Hall	1.50	.70	.19
☐ 7 Darrell Hamilton	1.00	.45	.12
☐ 8 Creighton Incorminias	1.00	.45	.12
☐ 9 John Keller	1.00	.45	.12
☐ 10 Randy Marriott	1.00	.45	.12
☐ 11 Deems May	1.00	.45	.12
☐ 12 John Reed	1.00	.45	.12
☐ 13 James Thompson	1.50	.70	.19
☐ 14 Steve Steinbacher	1.00	.45	.12
☐ 15 Dan Vooletich	1.00	.45	.12
☐ 16 Mitch Wike	1.00	.45	.12

1991 North Carolina Schedules

This three-card set was apparently issued by the Department of Athletics at North Carolina (Chapel Hill) and partially sponsored by Hardee's. The cards measure approximately 2 3/8" by 3 3/8". The card front features a full-bleed head shot of the player, with the player's name and jersey number burned into the bottom portion of the picture. The backs carry the 1991 varsity football schedule. The cards are unnumbered and checklisted below in alphabetical order.

	MINT	NRMT	EXC
COMPLETE SET (3)	7.00	3.10	.85
COMMON CARD (1-3)	2.00	.90	.25
☐ 1 Eric Gash	2.00	.90	.25
☐ 2 Dwight Hollier	4.00	1.80	.50
☐ 3 Tommy Thigpen	2.00	.90	.25

1993 North Carolina State

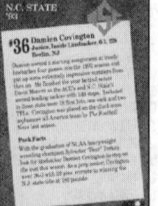

These 56 standard-size cards were produced by Action Graphics. They feature on their fronts color tilted player action and posed shots set within red borders. The team's name appears reversed out of a black bar above the photo. The player's name appears in white lettering within a black bar near the bottom of the photo. The gray-bordered back carries the team name and year at the top. The player's name, position, number, biography, and career highlights follow within a white area below. The cards are unnumbered and checklisted below in alphabetical order.

	MINT	NRMT	EXC
COMPLETE SET (56)	25.00	11.00	3.10
COMMON CARD (1-56)	.50	.23	.06
☐ 1 John Akins	.75	.35	.09
☐ 2 Darryl Beard	.50	.23	.06
☐ 3 Ricky Bell	.50	.23	.06
☐ 4 Geoff Bender	.50	.23	.06
☐ 5 Chuck Browning	.50	.23	.06
☐ 6 Chuck Cole	.50	.23	.06
☐ 7 Chris Cotton	.50	.23	.06
☐ 8 Eric Counts	.50	.23	.06
☐ 9 Damien Covington	1.50	.70	.19
☐ 10 Dallas Dickerson	.50	.23	.06
☐ 11 Gary Downs	.50	.23	.06
☐ 12 Brian Fitzgerald	.50	.23	.06
☐ 13 Ed Gallon	.50	.23	.06
☐ 14 Ledel George	.50	.23	.06
☐ 15 Walt Gerard	.50	.23	.06
☐ 16 Gregg Giannamore	.50	.23	.06
☐ 17 Eddie Goines	1.00	.45	.12
☐ 18 Ray Griffis	.50	.23	.06
☐ 19 Mike Harrison	.50	.23	.06
☐ 20 Terry Harvey	.50	.23	.06
☐ 21 George Hegamin	1.00	.45	.12
☐ 22 Chris Hennie-Roed	.50	.23	.06
☐ 23 Adrian Hill	.50	.23	.06
☐ 24 Robert Hinton	.50	.23	.06
☐ 25 David Inman	.50	.23	.06
☐ 26 Dave Janik	.50	.23	.06
☐ 27 Shawn Johnson	.50	.23	.06
☐ 28 Tyler Lawrence	.50	.23	.06
☐ 29 Miller Lawson	.50	.23	.06
☐ 30 Sean Maguire	.50	.23	.06
☐ 31 Drea Major	.50	.23	.06
☐ 32 Mike Moore	.50	.23	.06
☐ 33 James Newsome	.50	.23	.06
☐ 34 Mike O'Cain CO	.75	.35	.09
☐ 35 Loren Pinkney	.50	.23	.06
☐ 36 Carlos Pruitt	.50	.23	.06
☐ 37 Carl Reeves	1.00	.45	.12
☐ 38 Jon Rissler	.50	.23	.06
☐ 39 Chad Robinson	.50	.23	.06
☐ 40 Ryan Schultz	.75	.35	.09
☐ 41 William Strong	1.00	.45	.12
☐ 42 Jimmy Sziksai	.50	.23	.06
☐ 43 Eric Taylor	.50	.23	.06
☐ 44 Pat Threatt	.50	.23	.06
☐ 45 Steve Videtich	.75	.35	.09
☐ 46 James Walker	.75	.35	.09
☐ 47 Todd Ward	.75	.35	.09
☐ 48 Dewayne Washington	2.00	.90	.25
☐ 49 Heath Woods	.50	.23	.06
☐ 50 Scott Woods	.50	.23	.06
☐ 51 Defensive Coaches	.50	.23	.06
Buddy Green			
Kent Briggs			
Ken Pettus			
Jeff Snipes			
Henry Trevathan			
☐ 52 Offensive Coaches	.50	.23	.06
Ted Cain			
Robbie Caldwell			
Jimmy Kiser			
Brette Simmons			
Dick Portee			
☐ 53 Tri-Captains	.75	.35	.09
John Akins			
Todd Ward			
Dewayne Washington			
☐ 54 Carter-Finley Stadium	.50	.23	.06
☐ 55 Checklist	.50	.23	.06
☐ 56 Title Card	.75	.35	.09

1989 North Texas McDag

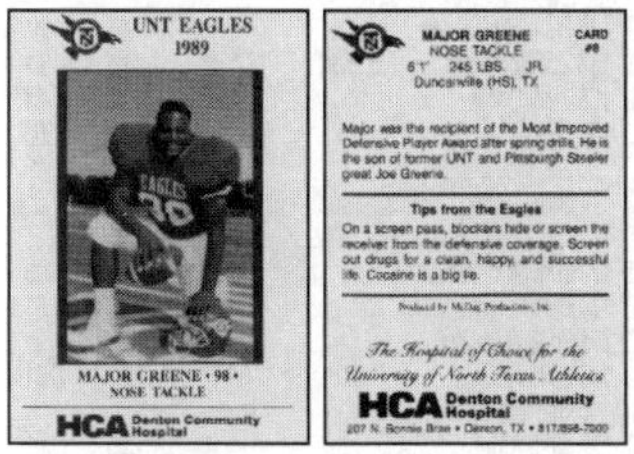

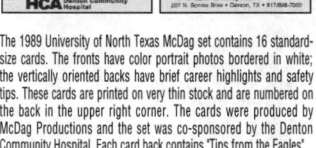

The 1989 University of North Texas McDag set contains 16 standard-size cards. The fronts have color portrait photos bordered in white; the vertically oriented backs have brief career highlights and safety tips. These cards are printed on very thin stock and are numbered on the back in the upper right corner. The cards were produced by McDag Productions and the set was co-sponsored by the Denton Community Hospital. Each card back contains "Tips from the Eagles".

	MINT	NRMT	EXC
COMPLETE SET (16)	7.00	3.10	.85
COMMON CARD (1-16)	.50	.23	.06
☐ 1 Clay Bode	.50	.23	.06
☐ 2 Scott Bowles	.50	.23	.06
☐ 3 Keith Chapman	.50	.23	.06
☐ 4 Darrin Collins	.50	.23	.06
☐ 5 Tony Cook	.50	.23	.06
☐ 6 Scott Davis	1.00	.45	.12
☐ 7 Byron Gross	.50	.23	.06
☐ 8 Larry Green	.50	.23	.06
☐ 9 Major Greene	1.00	.45	.12
☐ 10 Carl Brewer	.50	.23	.06
☐ 11 J.D. Martinez	.50	.23	.06
☐ 12 Charles Monroe	.50	.23	.06
☐ 13 Kregg Sanders	.50	.23	.06
☐ 14 Lou Smith	.50	.23	.06
☐ 15 Jeff Tutson	.50	.23	.06
☐ 16 Trent Touchstone	.50	.23	.06

1990 North Texas McDag

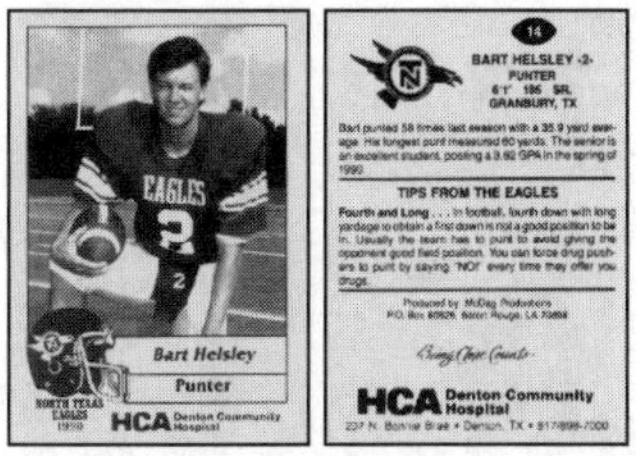

This 16-card standard-size set was sponsored by the HCA Denton Community Hospital, whose company name appears at the bottom on both sides of the card. The front features a color posed photo, with the player in a kneeling posture and the football in his hand. The picture is framed by a thin dark green border on a white card face, with the player's name and position below the picture. In the lower left corner a North Texas Eagles' helmet appears in the school's colors, green and white. The back has biographical information and a tip from the Eagles in the form of an anti-drug or alcohol message. The set features an early card of running back Erric Pegram.

	MINT	NRMT	EXC
COMPLETE SET (16)	10.00	4.50	1.25
COMMON CARD (1-16)	.50	.23	.06
☐ 1 Scott Davis	.75	.35	.09
☐ 2 Byron Gross	.50	.23	.06
☐ 3 Tony Cook	.50	.23	.06
☐ 4 Walter Casey	.50	.23	.06
☐ 5 Erric Pegram	4.00	1.80	.50
☐ 6 Clay Bode	.50	.23	.06
☐ 7 Scott Bowles	.50	.23	.06
☐ 8 Shawn Wash	.50	.23	.06
☐ 9 Isaac Barnett	.50	.23	.06
☐ 10 Paul Gallamore	.50	.23	.06
☐ 11 J.D. Martinez	.50	.23	.06
☐ 12 Velton Morgan	.50	.23	.06
☐ 13 Major Greene	.75	.35	.09
☐ 14 Bart Helsley	.50	.23	.06
☐ 15 Jeff Tutson	.50	.23	.06
☐ 16 Tony Walker	.50	.23	.06

1992 Northwestern Louisiana State

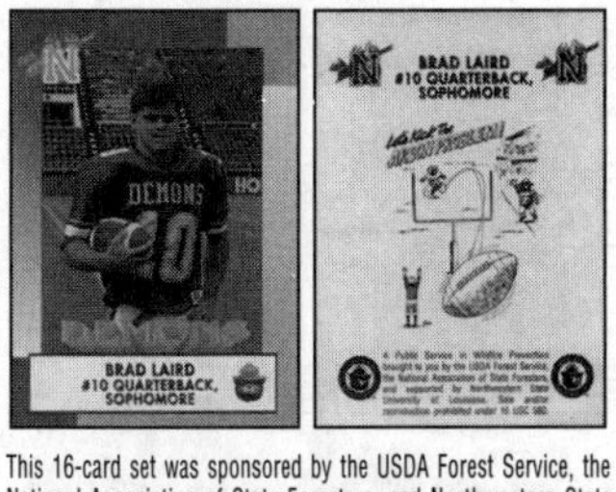

This 16-card set was sponsored by the USDA Forest Service, the National Association of State Foresters, and Northwestern State University of Louisiana. The cards measure approximately 2 5/8" by 3 5/8" and are printed on thin card stock. The fronts feature posed color player photos (from the waist up) that are bordered in the team's colors (purple and orange). Player information and the Smokey logo appear in a white box superimposed toward the bottom. In black on white, the backs present basic player information and a fire prevention cartoon starring Smokey. The cards are unnumbered and checklisted below in alphabetical order.

	MINT	NRMT	EXC
COMPLETE SET (16)	8.00	3.60	1.00
COMMON CARD (1-16)	.50	.23	.06
☐ 1 Darius Adams	.50	.23	.06
☐ 2 Paul Arevalo	.50	.23	.06
☐ 3 Brad Brown	.50	.23	.06
☐ 4 Steve Brown	.60	.25	.07
☐ 5 J.J. Eldridge	.50	.23	.06
☐ 6 Sam Goodwin CO	.60	.25	.07
☐ 7 Adrian Hardy	.60	.25	.07
☐ 8 Guy Hedrick	.50	.23	.06
☐ 9 Brad Laird	.60	.25	.07
☐ 10 Lawann Latson	.50	.23	.06
☐ 11 Deon Ridgell	.50	.23	.06
☐ 12 Bryan Roussell	.50	.23	.06
☐ 13 Brannon Rowlett	.50	.23	.06
☐ 14 Marcus Spears	1.00	.45	.12
☐ 15 Carlos Treadway	.60	.25	.07
☐ 16 Vic (Team Mascot)	.50	.23	.06

1930 Notre Dame Postcards

Notre Dame issued this postcard set with the intention of fans to have each card autographed and game score recorded as a momento of the game featured. Each of the postcards covers a specific 1930 Notre Dame game with the date and opponent included on the cardfront. 1930 would prove to be Knute Rockne's last season as coach of the Fighting Irish as he would perish in a plane crash early in 1931. The cards are unnumbered and listed below alphabetically.

	EX-MT	VG-EX	G
COMPLETE SET (25)	900.00	400.00	110.00
COMMON CARD	35.00	16.00	4.40
☐ 1 Marty Brill	40.00	18.00	5.00
☐ 2 Frank Carideo	35.00	16.00	4.40
☐ 3 Tom Conley	35.00	16.00	4.40
☐ 4 Al Culver	35.00	16.00	4.40
October 25			
☐ 5 Dick Donaghue	35.00	16.00	4.40
October 18			
☐ 6 Nordy Hoffman	35.00	16.00	4.40
☐ 7 Al Howard	35.00	16.00	4.40
November 15			
☐ 8 Chuck Jaskwich	35.00	16.00	4.40
November 22			
☐ 9 Clarence Kaplan	35.00	16.00	4.40
October 18			
☐ 10 Tom Kassis	35.00	16.00	4.40
☐ 11 Ed Koska	35.00	16.00	4.40
November 22			
☐ 12 Joe Kurth	40.00	18.00	5.00
☐ 13 Bernie Leahy	50.00	22.00	6.25
☐ 14 Frank Leahy	125.00	55.00	15.50
☐ 15 Dick Mahoney	35.00	16.00	4.40
November 8			
☐ 16 Art McManmon	35.00	16.00	4.40
November 1			
☐ 17 Bert Metzger	35.00	16.00	4.40
☐ 18 Larry Moon Mullins	50.00	22.00	6.25
☐ 19 John O'Brien	35.00	16.00	4.40
☐ 20 Bucky O'Connor	35.00	16.00	4.40
☐ 21 Joe Savoldi	40.00	18.00	5.00
☐ 22 Marchmont Schwartz	40.00	18.00	5.00
☐ 23 Robert Terlaak	35.00	16.00	4.40
November 8			
☐ 24 George Vlk	35.00	16.00	4.40
October 25			
☐ 25 Tom Yarr	40.00	18.00	5.00

1988 Notre Dame

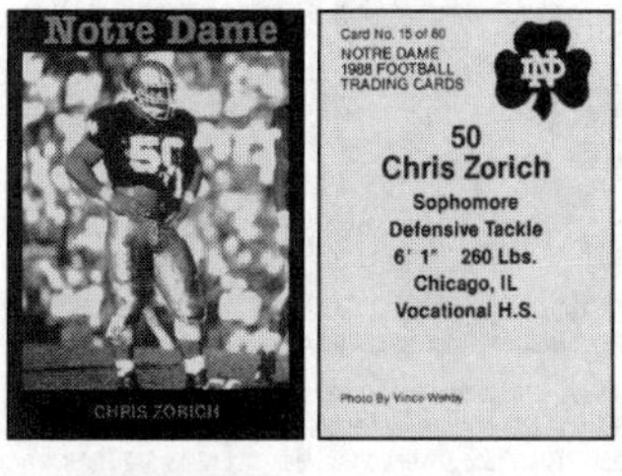

The 1988 Notre Dame football set contains 60 standard-size cards depicting the 1988 National Champions. The fronts have sharp color action photos with dark blue borders and gold lettering; the vertically oriented backs have biographical information. These cards were distributed as a complete set. There are 58 cards of players from the National Championship team, plus one coach card and one for the Golden Dome. The key cards in the set are Raghib Ismail and Ricky Watters.

	MINT	NRMT	EXC
COMPLETE SET (60)	25.00	11.00	3.10
COMMON CARD (1-60)	.25	.11	.03
☐ 1 Golden Dome	.50	.23	.06
☐ 2 Lou Holtz CO	2.00	.90	.25
☐ 3 Mark Green	.50	.23	.06
☐ 4 Andy Heck	1.00	.45	.12
☐ 5 Ned Bolcar	.50	.23	.06
☐ 6 Anthony Johnson	2.00	.90	.25
☐ 7 Flash Gordon	.25	.11	.03
☐ 8 Pat Eilers	.50	.23	.06
☐ 9 Raghib(Rocket) Ismail	4.00	1.80	.50
☐ 10 Ted FitzGerald	.25	.11	.03
☐ 11 Ted Healy	.25	.11	.03
☐ 12 Braxston Banks	.50	.23	.06
☐ 13 Steve Belles	.25	.11	.03
☐ 14 Steve Alaniz	.25	.11	.03
☐ 15 Chris Zorich	2.00	.90	.25
☐ 16 Kent Graham	2.00	.90	.25
☐ 17 Mike Brennan	.25	.11	.03
☐ 18 Marty Lippincott	.25	.11	.03
☐ 19 Rod West	.25	.11	.03
☐ 20 Dean Brown	.25	.11	.03
☐ 21 Tom Gorman	.25	.11	.03
☐ 22 Tony Rice	1.50	.70	.19
☐ 23 Steve Roddy	.25	.11	.03
☐ 24 Reggie Ho	.50	.23	.06
☐ 25 Pat Terrell	1.00	.45	.12
☐ 26 Joe Jarosz	.25	.11	.03
☐ 27 Mike Stonebreaker	1.00	.45	.12
☐ 28 David Jandric	.25	.11	.03
☐ 29 Jeff Alm	.75	.35	.09
☐ 30 Pete Graham	.25	.11	.03
☐ 31 Corny Southall	.25	.11	.03
☐ 32 Joe Allen	.25	.11	.03
☐ 33 Jim Sexton	.25	.11	.03
☐ 34 Michael Crounse	.25	.11	.03
☐ 35 Kurt Zackrison	.25	.11	.03
☐ 36 Stan Smagala	.50	.23	.06
☐ 37 Mike Heldt	.25	.11	.03
☐ 38 Frank Stams	1.00	.45	.12
☐ 39 D'Juan Francisco	.50	.23	.06
☐ 40 Tim Ryan	.50	.23	.06
☐ 41 Arnold Ale	.25	.11	.03
☐ 42 Andre Jones	.25	.11	.03
☐ 43 Wes Pritchett	.25	.11	.03
☐ 44 Tim Grunhard	1.00	.45	.12
☐ 45 Chuck Killian	.25	.11	.03
☐ 46 Scott Kowalkowski	.50	.23	.06
☐ 47 George Streeter	.25	.11	.03
☐ 48 Donn Grimm	.25	.11	.03
☐ 49 Ricky Watters	7.00	3.10	.85
☐ 50 Ryan Mihalko	.25	.11	.03
☐ 51 Tony Brooks	.75	.35	.09
☐ 52 Todd Lyght	1.00	.45	.12
☐ 53 Winston Sandri	.25	.11	.03
☐ 54 Aaron Robb	.25	.11	.03
☐ 55 Derek Brown TE	1.00	.45	.12
☐ 56 Bryan Flannery	.25	.11	.03
☐ 57 Kevin McShane	.25	.11	.03
☐ 58 Billy Hackett	.25	.11	.03
☐ 59 George Williams	.50	.23	.06
☐ 60 Frank Jacobs	.25	.11	.03

1988 Notre Dame Smokey *

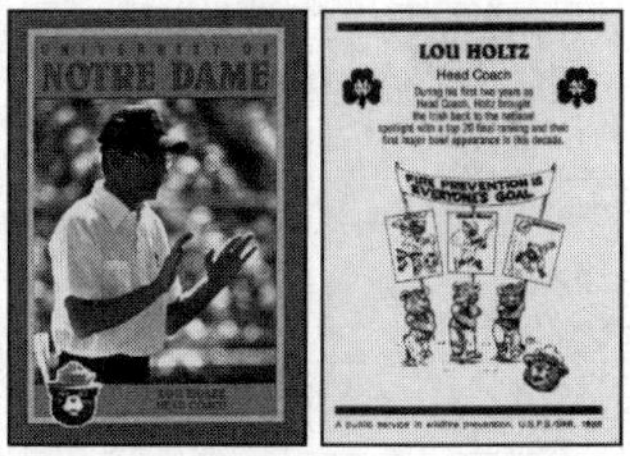

This 14-card standard size set was sponsored by the U. S. Forestry Service. The front features a color action photo, with orange and green borders on a purple background. The back has biographical information (or a schedule) and a fire prevention cartoon starring Smokey the Bear. These unnumbered cards are ordered alphabetically within type for convenience. Ricky Watters is featured in this set.

	MINT	NRMT	EXC
COMPLETE SET (14)	35.00	16.00	4.40
COMMON CARD (1-10)	2.00	.90	.25
COMMON SPORT (11-14)	1.50	.70	.19
☐ 1 Braxston Banks 39	3.00	1.35	.35
☐ 2 Ned Bolcar 47	3.00	1.35	.35
☐ 3 Tom Gorman 87	2.00	.90	.25
☐ 4 Mark Green 24	3.00	1.35	.35
☐ 5 Andy Heck 66	3.00	1.35	.35
☐ 6 Lou Holtz CO	4.00	1.80	.50
☐ 7 Anthony Johnson 22	4.00	1.80	.50
☐ 8 Wes Pritchett 34	2.00	.90	.25
☐ 9 George Streeter 27	2.00	.90	.25
☐ 10 Ricky Watters 12	10.00	4.50	1.25
☐ 11 Men's Soccer	1.50	.70	.19
☐ 12 Volleyball	1.50	.70	.19
☐ 13 Women's Basketball	1.50	.70	.19
☐ 14 Women's Tennis	1.50	.70	.19

1989 Notre Dame 1903-32

The 1989 Notre Dame Football I set contains 22 standard-size cards depicting the Irish stars from 1903-32. The fronts have vintage photos with white borders and gold lettering; the vertically oriented backs have detailed profiles. These cards were distributed as a set.

	MINT	NRMT	EXC
COMPLETE SET (22)	7.00	3.10	.85
COMMON CARD (1-22)	.35	.16	.04
☐ 1 Hunk Anderson	.50	.23	.06
☐ 2 Bert Metzger	.35	.16	.04

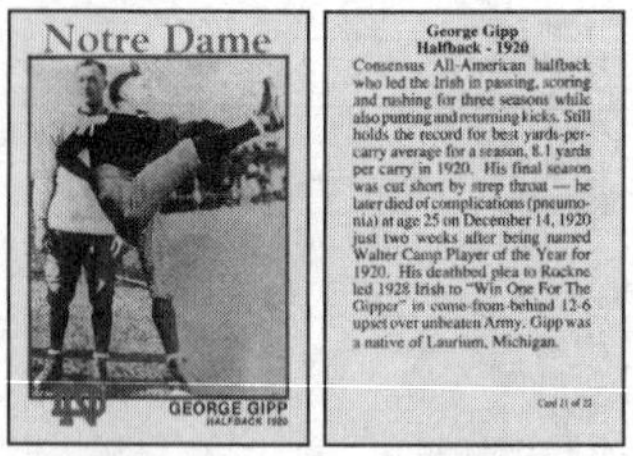

Notre Dame

George Gipp
Halfback - 1920
Consensus All-American halfback who led the Irish in passing, scoring and rushing for three seasons while also punting and running kicks. Still holds the record for best yards-per-carry average for a season, 8.1 yards per carry in 1920. His final season was cut short by strep throat — he later died of complications (pneumonia) at age 25 on December 14, 1920 just two weeks after being named Walter Camp Player of the Year for 1920. His deathbed plea to Knute led 1928 Irish to "Win One For The Gipper" in come-from-behind 12-6 upset over unbeaten Army. Gipp was a native of Laurium, Michigan.

GEORGE GIPP
HALFBACK 1920
Card 21 of 22

☐ 3 Roger Kiley	.35	.16	.04
☐ 4 Nordy Hoffman	.35	.16	.04
☐ 5 Knute Rockne CO	10.00	4.50	1.25
☐ 6 Elmer Layden	.75	.35	.09
☐ 7 Gus Dorais	.50	.23	.06
☐ 8 Ray Eichenlaub	.35	.16	.04
☐ 9 Don Miller	.75	.35	.09
☐ 10 Moose Krause	.75	.35	.09
☐ 11 Jesse Harper	.35	.16	.04
☐ 12 Jack Cannon	.35	.16	.04
☐ 13 Eddie Anderson	.35	.16	.04
☐ 14 Louis Salmon	.35	.16	.04
☐ 15 John Smith	.35	.16	.04
☐ 16 Harry Stuhldreher	.75	.35	.09
☐ 17 Joe Kurth	.35	.16	.04
☐ 18 Frank Carideo	.35	.16	.04
☐ 19 Marchy Schwartz	.35	.16	.04
☐ 20 Adam Walsh	.35	.16	.04
☐ 21 George Gipp	2.00	.90	.25
☐ 22 Jim Crowley	.75	.35	.09

1989 Notre Dame 1935-59

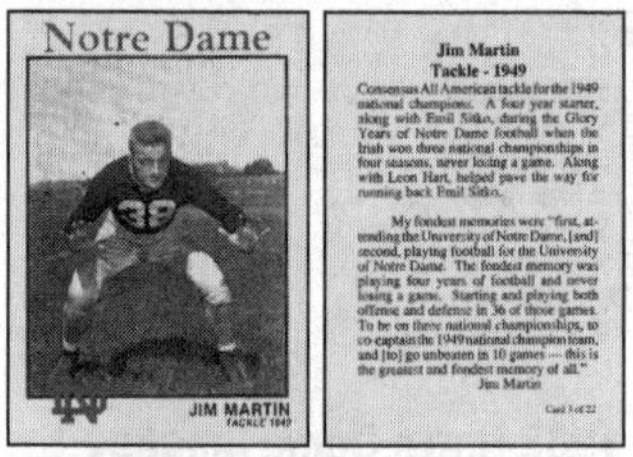

Notre Dame

Jim Martin
Tackle - 1949
Consensus All American tackle for the 1949 national champions. A four year starter, along with Emil Sitko, during the Glory Years of Notre Dame football when the Irish won three national championships in four seasons, never losing a game. Along with Leon Hart, helped pave the way for winning back Emil Sitko.

My fondest memories were "first, attending the University of Notre Dame, [and] second, playing football for the University of Notre Dame. The fondest memory was playing four years of football and never losing a game. Starting and playing both offense and defense in 36 of those games. To be on three national championships, to co-captain the 1949 national champion team, and [to] go undefeated in 10 games — this is the greatest and fondest memory of all." Jim Martin

JIM MARTIN
TACKLE 1949
Card 3 of 22

The 1989 Notre Dame Football II set contains 22 standard-size cards depicting the Irish stars from 1935-59. The fronts have vintage photos with white borders and gold lettering; the vertically oriented backs have detailed profiles. These cards were distributed as a set.

	MINT	NRMT	EXC
COMPLETE SET (22)	10.00	4.50	1.25
COMMON CARD (1-22)	.35	.16	.04

☐ 1 Frank Leahy CO	1.00	.45	.12
☐ 2 John Lattner	1.00	.45	.12
☐ 3 Jim Martin	.50	.23	.06
☐ 4 Joe Heap	.35	.16	.04
☐ 5 Paul Hornung	2.00	.90	.25
☐ 6 Bill Shakespeare	.75	.35	.09
☐ 7 Bob Dove	.35	.16	.04
☐ 8 Bob Williams	.35	.16	.04
☐ 9 Al Ecuyer	.35	.16	.04
☐ 10 George Connor	.75	.35	.09
☐ 11 Leon Hart	1.00	.45	.12
☐ 12 Joe Beinor	.35	.16	.04
☐ 13 Bill Fischer	.35	.16	.04
☐ 14 Angelo Bertelli	1.00	.45	.12
☐ 15 Ralph Guglielmi	.50	.23	.06
☐ 16 Pat Filley	.35	.16	.04
☐ 17 Emil Sitko	.50	.23	.06
☐ 18 Don Schaefer	.35	.16	.04
☐ 19 Monty Stickles	.50	.23	.06
☐ 20 Creighton Miller	.35	.16	.04
☐ 21 Chuck Sweeney	.35	.16	.04
☐ 22 Johnny Lujack	1.50	.70	.19

1989 Notre Dame 1964-87

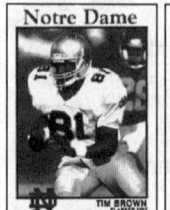

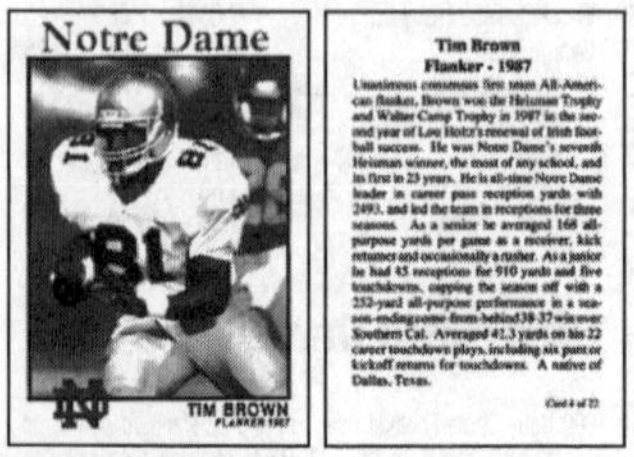

Notre Dame

Tim Brown
Flanker - 1987
Unanimous consensus first team All-American flanker. Brown won the Heisman Trophy and Walter Camp Trophy in 1987 in the second year of Lou Holtz's renewal of Irish football success. He was Notre Dame's seventh Heisman winner, the most of any school, and its first in 20 years. He is all-time Notre Dame leader in career pass reception yards with 2493, and led the team in receptions for three seasons. As a senior he averaged 168 all-purpose yards per game as a receiver, kick returner and occasionally a rusher. As a junior he had 45 receptions for 910 yards and five touchdowns, topping the season off with a 253-yard all-purpose performance in a season-ending game from behind 38-37 win over Southern Cal. Averaged 41.3 yards on his 22 career touchdown plays, including six punt or kickoff returns for touchdowns. A native of Dallas, Texas.

TIM BROWN
FLANKER 1987
Card 4 of 22

The 1989 Notre Dame Football III set contains 22 standard-size cards depicting the Irish stars from 1964-87. The fronts have vintage and color photos with white borders and gold lettering; the vertically oriented backs have detailed profiles. These cards were distributed as a set.

	MINT	NRMT	EXC
COMPLETE SET (22)	10.00	4.50	1.25
COMMON CARD (1-22)	.35	.16	.04

☐ 1 Dan Devine CO	.50	.23	.06
☐ 2 Joe Theismann	1.50	.70	.19
☐ 3 Tom Gatewood	.50	.23	.06
☐ 4 Tim Brown	1.50	.70	.19
☐ 5 Ara Parseghian CO	1.50	.70	.19
☐ 6 Jim Lynch	.50	.23	.06
☐ 7 Luther Bradley	.35	.16	.04
☐ 8 Ross Browner	.50	.23	.06
☐ 9 John Huarte	1.00	.45	.12
☐ 10 Bob Crable	.50	.23	.06
☐ 11 Ken MacAfee	.50	.23	.06
☐ 12 Alan Page	1.00	.45	.12
☐ 13 Vagas Ferguson	.50	.23	.06
☐ 14 Dick Arrington	.35	.16	.04
☐ 15 Bob Golic	.50	.23	.06
☐ 16 Mike Townsend	.35	.16	.04
☐ 17 Walt Patulski	.50	.23	.06
☐ 18 Allen Pinkett	.50	.23	.06
☐ 19 Terry Hanratty	.75	.35	.09
☐ 20 Dave Casper	.75	.35	.09
☐ 21 Jack Snow	.75	.35	.09
☐ 22 Nick Eddy	.50	.23	.06

1990 Notre Dame Promos

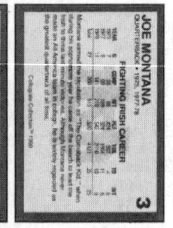

This ten-card standard-size set was issued by Collegiate Collection to honor some of the leading figures in Fighting Irish history. This set has a mix of the most famous Notre Dame coaches and some of the offensive stars of Notre Dame's long history. The featured subjects active after 1960 are shown in color photos.

	MINT	NRMT	EXC
COMPLETE SET (10)	10.00	4.50	1.25
COMMON CARD (1-10)	.50	.23	.06

☐ 1 Knute Rockne CO	2.00	.90	.25
☐ 2 Joe Theismann	1.00	.45	.12
☐ 3 Joe Montana	4.00	1.80	.50
☐ 4 George Gipp	2.00	.90	.25
☐ 5 Notre Dame Stadium	.50	.23	.06
☐ 6 Ara Parseghian CO	.75	.35	.09
☐ 7 Frank Leahy CO	.75	.35	.09
☐ 8 Lou Holtz CO	.75	.35	.09
☐ 9 Tony Rice	.50	.23	.06
☐ 10 Rocky Bleier	.75	.35	.09

1990 Notre Dame 200

This 200-card standard size set was issued by Collegiate Collection in 1990 and features many of the great players and figures of Notre Dame history. The set was available in wax packs and features a mixture of black and white or color photos, posed and action, with a yellow border against a blue background. The horizontally oriented backs are numbered in the upper right hand corner and provide career highlights. There were 2000 special George Gipp cards randomly inserted in wax packs as a bonus. These Gipp's are rarely seen in the secondary market and no value has been attached to them.

	MINT	NRMT	EXC
COMPLETE SET (200)	20.00	9.00	2.50
COMMON CARD (1-200)	.10	.05	.01

☐ 1 Joe Montana	1.25	.55	.16
☐ 2 Tim Brown	.50	.23	.06
☐ 3 Reggie Barnett	.25	.11	.03
☐ 4 Joe Theismann	.50	.23	.06
☐ 5 Bob Clasby	.10	.05	.01
☐ 6 Dave Casper	.25	.11	.03
☐ 7 George Kunz	.25	.11	.03
☐ 8 Vince Phelan	.10	.05	.01
☐ 9 Tom Gibbons	.10	.05	.01
☐ 10 Tom Thayer	.10	.05	.01
☐ 11 Notre Dame Helmet	.10	.05	.01
☐ 12 John Scully	.10	.05	.01
☐ 13 Lou Holtz CO	.40	.18	.05
☐ 14 Larry Dinardo	.25	.11	.03
☐ 15 Greg Marx	.10	.05	.01
☐ 16 Greg Dingens	.10	.05	.01

☐ 17 Jim Seymour	.25	.11	.03
☐ 18 1979 Cotton Bowl (Program)	.25	.11	.03
☐ 19 Mike Kadish	.25	.11	.03
☐ 20 Bob Crable	.25	.11	.03
☐ 21 Tony Rice (pneumo	.25	.11	.03
☐ 22 Phil Carter	.10	.05	.01
☐ 23 Ken MacAfee	.25	.11	.03
☐ 24 Nick Eddy	.25	.11	.03
☐ 25 1988 National Champs (Trophies)	.25	.11	.03
☐ 26 Clarence Ellis	.25	.11	.03
☐ 27 Joe Restic	.10	.05	.01
☐ 28 Dan Devine CO	.25	.11	.03
☐ 29 John K. Carney	.10	.05	.01
☐ 30 Stacey Toran	.25	.11	.03
☐ 31 47th Sugar Bowl (Program)	.10	.05	.01
☐ 32 J. Heavens	.10	.05	.01
☐ 33 Mike Fanning	.10	.05	.01
☐ 34 Dave Vinson	.10	.05	.01
☐ 35 Ralph Guglielmi	.10	.05	.01
☐ 36 Reggie Ho	.10	.05	.01
☐ 37 Allen Pinkett	.25	.11	.03
☐ 38 Jim Browner	.25	.11	.03
☐ 39 Blair Kiel	.25	.11	.03
☐ 40 Joe Montana	1.25	.55	.16
☐ 41 Rocky Bleier	.40	.18	.05
☐ 42 Terry Hanratty	.40	.18	.05
☐ 43 Tom Regner	.25	.11	.03
☐ 44 Pete Holohan	.10	.05	.01
☐ 45 Greg Bell	.25	.11	.03
☐ 46 Dave Duerson	.25	.11	.03
☐ 47 Frank Varrichione	.25	.11	.03
☐ 48 1988 Championship (Team Photo)	.25	.11	.03
☐ 49 Ted Burgmeier	.10	.05	.01
☐ 50 Ara Parseghian CO	.40	.18	.05
☐ 51 Mike Townsend	.10	.05	.01
☐ 52 Liberty Bowl 1983 (Program)	.10	.05	.01
☐ 53 Tony Furjanic	.10	.05	.01
☐ 54 Luther Bradley	.25	.11	.03
☐ 55 Steve Niehaus	.25	.11	.03
☐ 56 56th Orange Bowl (Program)	.10	.05	.01
☐ 57 32nd Gator Bowl (Program)	.10	.05	.01
☐ 58 40th Sugar Bowl (Program)	.10	.05	.01
☐ 59 52nd Cotton Bowl (Program)	.10	.05	.01
☐ 60 1975 Orange Bowl (Program)	.10	.05	.01
☐ 61 Wayne Bullock	.10	.05	.01
☐ 62 Larry Moriarty	.10	.05	.01
☐ 63 Jim Lynch	.25	.11	.03
☐ 64 Mike McCoy	.25	.11	.03
☐ 65 Tony Hunter	.25	.11	.03
☐ 66 1984 Aloha Bowl (Program)	.10	.05	.01
☐ 67 Dave Huffman	.10	.05	.01
☐ 68 John Lattner	.40	.18	.05
☐ 69 Tom Gatewood	.25	.11	.03
☐ 70 Knute Rockne CO	.75	.35	.09
☐ 71 Phil Pozderac	.10	.05	.01
☐ 72 Ross Browner	.25	.11	.03
☐ 73 Pete Demmerle	.10	.05	.01
☐ 74 Sunkist Fiesta Bowl (Program)	.10	.05	.01
☐ 75 Walt Patulski	.25	.11	.03
☐ 76 George Gipp	.75	.35	.09
☐ 77 LeRoy Leopold	.10	.05	.01
☐ 78 John Huarte	.40	.18	.05
☐ 79 Tony Yelovich CO	.10	.05	.01
☐ 80 Johnny Lujack	.40	.18	.05
☐ 81 Cotton Bowl Classic (Program)	.10	.05	.01
☐ 82 Tim Huffman	.10	.05	.01
☐ 83 Bob Golic	.25	.11	.03
☐ 84 Tom Clements	.25	.11	.03
☐ 85 39th Orange Bowl (Program)	.10	.05	.01
☐ 86 James J. White ADMIN	.10	.05	.01
☐ 87 Frank Carideo	.10	.05	.01
☐ 88 Vinny Cerrato	.10	.05	.01
☐ 89 Louis Salmon	.10	.05	.01
☐ 90 Bob Burger	.10	.05	.01
☐ 91 Gerry Dinardo	.25	.11	.03
☐ 92 Mike Creaney	.10	.05	.01
☐ 93 John Krimm	.10	.05	.01
☐ 94 Vagas Ferguson	.25	.11	.03
☐ 95 Kris Haines	.10	.05	.01
☐ 96 Gus Dorais	.25	.11	.03
☐ 97 Tom Schoen	.10	.05	.01
☐ 98 Jack Robinson	.10	.05	.01
☐ 99 Joe Heap	.10	.05	.01
☐ 100 Checklist 1-99	.10	.05	.01
☐ 101 Gary Darnell CO	.10	.05	.01
☐ 102 Peter Vaas CO	.10	.05	.01
☐ 103 1924 National Champs (Team Photo)	.40	.18	.05
☐ 104 Wayne Millner	.25	.11	.03
☐ 105 Moose Krause	.25	.11	.03
☐ 106 Jack Cannon	.10	.05	.01

☐ 107 Christy Flanagan	.10	.05	.01
☐ 108 Bob Lehmann	.10	.05	.01
☐ 109 1947 Champions (Team Photo)	.25	.11	.03
☐ 110 Joe Kurth	.10	.05	.01
☐ 111 Tommy Yarr	.10	.05	.01
☐ 112 Nick Buoniconti	.40	.18	.05
☐ 113 Jim Smithberger	.10	.05	.01
☐ 114 Joe Beinor	.10	.05	.01
☐ 115 Pete Cordelli CO	.10	.05	.01
☐ 116 Daryle Lamonica	.40	.18	.05
☐ 117 Kevin Hardy	.10	.05	.01
☐ 118 Creighton Miller	.25	.11	.03
☐ 119 Bob Gladieux	.25	.11	.03
☐ 120 Fred Miller (Later Miller Brewing)	.25	.11	.03
☐ 121 Gary Potempa	.10	.05	.01
☐ 122 Bob Kuechenberg	.25	.11	.03
☐ 123 Jesse Harper	.10	.05	.01
☐ 124 1929 National Champs (Team Photo)	.25	.11	.03
☐ 125 Alan Page	.40	.18	.05
☐ 126 Don Miller	.40	.18	.05
☐ 127 1943 National Champs (Team Photo)	.25	.11	.03
☐ 128 Bob Wetoska	.10	.05	.01
☐ 129 Skip Holtz CO	.10	.05	.01
☐ 130 Hunk Anderson CO	.25	.11	.03
☐ 131 Bob Williams	.10	.05	.01
☐ 132 1966 National Champs (Team Photo)	.10	.05	.01
☐ 133 Jim Reilly	.10	.05	.01
☐ 134 Earl(Curly) Lambeau	.40	.18	.05
☐ 135 Ernie Hughes	.10	.05	.01
☐ 136 Dick Bumpas CO	.10	.05	.01
☐ 137 Jay Haynes CO	.10	.05	.01
☐ 138 Harry Stuhldreher	.40	.18	.05
☐ 139 1971 Cotton Bowl (Game Photo)	.25	.11	.03
☐ 140 1930 National Champs (Team Photo)	.25	.11	.03
☐ 141 Larry Conjar	.25	.11	.03
☐ 142 1977 National Champs (Team Photo)	.25	.11	.03
☐ 143 Pete Duranko	.25	.11	.03
☐ 144 Heisman Winners	.40	.18	.05
Tim Brown			
Johnny Lujack			
Angelo Bertelli			
Leon Hart			
Paul Hornung			
John Huarte			
John Lattner			
☐ 145 Bill Fischer	.10	.05	.01
☐ 146 Marchy Schwartz	.10	.05	.01
☐ 147 Chuck Heater CO	.10	.05	.01
☐ 148 Bert Metzger	.10	.05	.01
☐ 149 Bill Shakespeare	.25	.11	.03
☐ 150 Adam Walsh	.10	.05	.01
☐ 151 Nordy Hoffman	.10	.05	.01
☐ 152 Ted Gradel	.10	.05	.01
☐ 153 Monty Stickles	.25	.11	.03
☐ 154 Neil Worden	.10	.05	.01
☐ 155 Pat Filley	.10	.05	.01
☐ 156 Angelo Bertelli	.25	.11	.03
☐ 157 Nick Pietrosante	.25	.11	.03
☐ 158 Art Hunter	.10	.05	.01
☐ 159 Ziggy Czarobski	.10	.05	.01
☐ 160 1925 Rose Bowl (Program)	.10	.05	.01
☐ 161 Al Ecuyer	.10	.05	.01
☐ 162 1949 Notre Dame Champs (Team Photo)	.10	.05	.01
☐ 163 Elmer Layden	.40	.18	.05
☐ 164 Joe Moore CO	.10	.05	.01
☐ 165 1946 National Champs (Team Photo)	.10	.05	.01
☐ 166 Frank Rydzewski	.10	.05	.01
☐ 167 Bud Boeringer	.10	.05	.01
☐ 168 Jerry Groom	.10	.05	.01
☐ 169 Jack Snow	.25	.11	.03
☐ 170 Joe Montana	1.25	.55	.16
☐ 171 John Smith	.10	.05	.01
☐ 172 Frank Leahy CO	.40	.18	.05
☐ 173 Emil Sitko	.25	.11	.03
☐ 174 Dick Arrington	.10	.05	.01
☐ 175 Eddie Anderson	.10	.05	.01
☐ 176 1928 Army (Logo and score)	.10	.05	.01
☐ 177 1913 Army (Logo and score)	.10	.05	.01
☐ 178 1935 Ohio State (Logo and game score)	.10	.05	.01
☐ 179 1946 Army (Logo and game score)	.10	.05	.01
☐ 180 1953 Georgia Tech (Logo and game score)	.10	.05	.01
☐ 181 Don Schaefer	.10	.05	.01
☐ 182 1973 Football Team (Team Photo)	.25	.11	.03
☐ 183 Bob Dove	.10	.05	.01
☐ 184 Dick Szymanski	.10	.05	.01
☐ 185 Jim Martin	.25	.11	.03
☐ 186 1957 Oklahoma (Logo and game score)	.10	.05	.01

☐ 187 1966 Michigan State (Logo and game score)	.10	.05	.01
☐ 188 1973 USC (Logo and game score)	.10	.05	.01
☐ 189 1980 Michigan (Logo and game score)	.10	.05	.01
☐ 190 1982 Michigan (Logo and game score)	.10	.05	.01
☐ 191 Chuck Sweeney	.10	.05	.01
☐ 192 Notre Dame Stadium	.10	.05	.01
☐ 193 Roger Kiley	.10	.05	.01
☐ 194 Ray Eichenlaub	.10	.05	.01
☐ 195 George Connor	.25	.11	.03
☐ 196 1982 Pittsburgh (Logo and game score)	.10	.05	.01
☐ 197 1986 USC (Logo and game score)	.10	.05	.01
☐ 198 1988 Miami (Logo and game score)	.10	.05	.01
☐ 199 1988 USC (Logo and game score)	.10	.05	.01
☐ 200 Checklist 101-199	.10	.05	.01

1990 Notre Dame 60

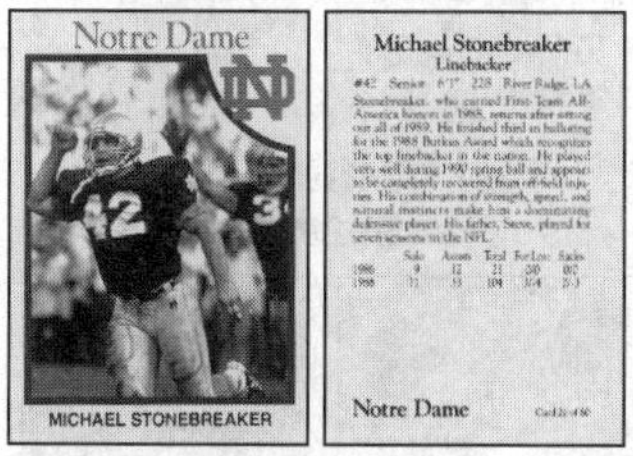
Notre Dame
Michael Stonebreaker
Linebacker
MICHAEL STONEBREAKER
Notre Dame

This 60-card set measures approximately 2 1/2" by 3 1/2" and was issued to celebrate the 1990 Notre Dame football team. The key cards in this set feature Reggie Brooks, Raghib "Rocket" Ismail, Rick Mirer, and Ricky Watters. There is a full color photo on the front, with the Notre Dame logo in the lower right-hand corner of the card. The back has biographical information about the player. The set was produced by College Classics; reportedly 10,000 sets were produced and distributed.

	MINT	NRMT	EXC
COMPLETE SET (60)	25.00	11.00	3.10
COMMON CARD (1-60)	.35	.16	.04
☐ 1 Joe Allen	.35	.16	.04
☐ 2 William Pollard	.35	.16	.04
☐ 3 Tony Smith	.35	.16	.04
☐ 4 Tony Brooks	.75	.35	.09
☐ 5 Kenny Spears	.35	.16	.04
☐ 6 Mike Heldt	.35	.16	.04
☐ 7 Derek Brown TE	.75	.35	.09
☐ 8 Rodney Culver	.75	.35	.09
☐ 9 Ricky Watters	5.00	2.20	.60
☐ 10 Raghib(Rocket) Ismail	2.50	1.10	.30
☐ 11 Lou Holtz CO	1.00	.45	.12
☐ 12 Chris Zorich	1.50	.70	.19
☐ 13 Erik Simien	.35	.16	.04
☐ 14 Shawn Davis	.35	.16	.04
☐ 15 Greg Davis	.35	.16	.04
☐ 16 Walter Boyd	.35	.16	.04
☐ 17 Tim Ryan	.50	.23	.06
☐ 18 Lindsay Knapp	.35	.16	.04
☐ 19 Junior Bryant	.35	.16	.04
☐ 20 Mike Stonebreaker	.50	.23	.06
☐ 21 Randy Scianna	.35	.16	.04
☐ 22 Rick Mirer	6.00	2.70	.75
☐ 23 Ryan Mihalko	.35	.16	.04
☐ 24 Todd Lyght	.75	.35	.09
☐ 25 Andre Jones	.75	.35	.09
☐ 26 Rod Smith DB	.50	.23	.06
☐ 27 Winston Sandri	.35	.16	.04
☐ 28 Bob Dahl	.50	.23	.06
☐ 29 Stuart Tyner	.35	.16	.04
☐ 30 Brian Shannon	.35	.16	.04
☐ 31 Shawn Smith	.35	.16	.04
☐ 32 Jim Sexton	.35	.16	.04
☐ 33 Dorsey Levens	4.00	1.80	.50
☐ 34 Lance Johnson	.35	.16	.04
☐ 35 George Poorman	.35	.16	.04
☐ 36 Irv Smith	1.00	.45	.12
☐ 37 George Williams	.35	.16	.04
☐ 38 George Marshall	.50	.23	.06
☐ 39 Reggie Brooks	2.00	.90	.25
☐ 40 Scott Kowalkowski	.50	.23	.06
☐ 41 Jerry Bodine	.35	.16	.04
☐ 42 Karmeeleyah McGill	.35	.16	.04
☐ 43 Donn Grimm	.35	.16	.04
☐ 44 Billy Hackett	.35	.16	.04
☐ 45 Jordan Halter	.35	.16	.04
☐ 46 Mirko Jurkovic	.75	.35	.09
☐ 47 Mike Callan	.35	.16	.04
☐ 48 Justin Hall	.35	.16	.04
☐ 49 Nick Smith	.35	.16	.04
☐ 50 Brian Ratigan	.35	.16	.04
☐ 51 Eric Jones	.35	.16	.04
☐ 52 Todd Norman	.35	.16	.04
☐ 53 Devon McDonald	.50	.23	.06
☐ 54 Marc deManigold	.35	.16	.04
☐ 55 Bret Hankins	.35	.16	.04
☐ 56 Adrian Jarrell	.50	.23	.06
☐ 57 Craig Hentrich	.50	.23	.06
☐ 58 Demetrius DuBose	.75	.35	.09
☐ 59 Gene McGuire	.75	.35	.09
☐ 60 Ray Griggs	.35	.16	.04

1990 Notre Dame Greats

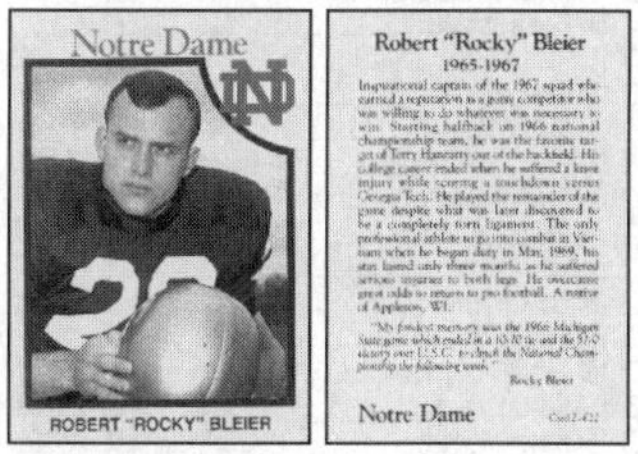
Notre Dame
Robert "Rocky" Bleier
1965-1967
ROBERT "ROCKY" BLEIER
Notre Dame

This 22-card standard-size set celebrates 22 of the All-Americans and past greats who attended Notre Dame. The cards have a mix of color and black and white photos on the front of the card and the back of the card has a biography of the player which describes his career at Notre Dame.

	MINT	NRMT	EXC
COMPLETE SET (22)	10.00	4.50	1.25
COMMON CARD (1-22)	.35	.16	.04
☐ 1 Clarence Ellis	.50	.23	.06
☐ 2 Rocky Bleier	.75	.35	.09
☐ 3 Tom Regner	.50	.23	.06
☐ 4 Jim Seymour	.35	.16	.04
☐ 5 Joe Montana	3.00	1.35	.35
☐ 6 Art Hunter	.50	.23	.06
☐ 7 Mike McCoy	.50	.23	.06
☐ 8 Bud Boeringer	.35	.16	.04
☐ 9 Greg Marx	.35	.16	.04
☐ 10 Nick Buoniconti	.75	.35	.09
☐ 11 Pete Demmerle	.35	.16	.04
☐ 12 Fred Miller	.35	.16	.04
☐ 13 Tommy Yarr	.35	.16	.04
☐ 14 Frank Rydzewski	.35	.16	.04
☐ 15 Dave Duerson	.50	.23	.06
☐ 16 Ziggy Czarobski	.35	.16	.04
☐ 17 Jim White	.50	.23	.06
☐ 18 Larry DiNardo	.50	.23	.06
☐ 19 George Kunz	.50	.23	.06
☐ 20 Jack Robinson	.35	.16	.04
☐ 21 Steve Niehaus	.50	.23	.06
☐ 22 John Scully	.50	.23	.06

1992 Notre Dame

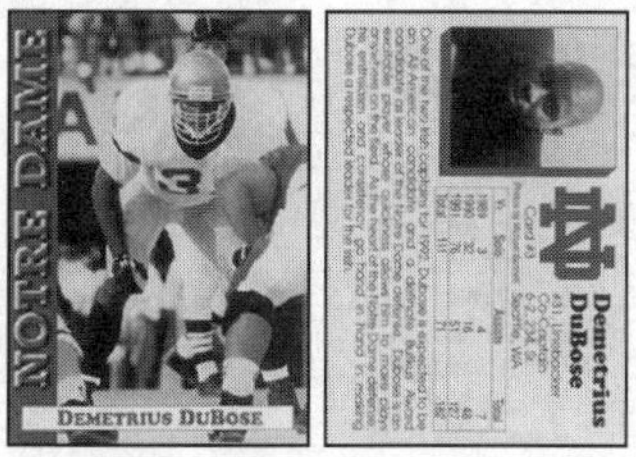
NOTRE DAME
DEMETRIUS DUBOSE
Demetrius DuBose

This 59-card standard-size set features color action player photos bordered on the left or right edge by a gray stripe containing the team name. The player's name appears in gold lettering on a white stripe at the bottom. The horizontal backs feature close-up player pictures with shadow box borders. The white background is printed with a profile of the player. The school logo and biographical information appear at the top. The cards are numbered on the back and are arranged alphabetically (with a few exceptions) after leading off with Coach Lou Holtz, Rick Mirer, and Demetrius DuBose. Other noteworthy cards in the set are Jerome Bettis, Reggie Brooks, Lake Dawson and Ray Zellars.

	MINT	NRMT	EXC
COMPLETE SET (59)	25.00	11.00	3.10
COMMON CARD (1-59)	.35	.16	.04
☐ 1 Lou Holtz CO	1.00	.45	.12
☐ 2 Rick Mirer	4.00	1.80	.50
☐ 3 Demetrius DuBose	.75	.35	.09
☐ 4 Lee Becton	1.25	.55	.16
☐ 5 Pete Bercich	.50	.23	.06
☐ 6 Jerome Bettis	4.00	1.80	.50
☐ 7 Reggie Brooks	1.50	.70	.19
☐ 8 Junior Bryant	.35	.16	.04
☐ 9 Jeff Burris	1.25	.55	.16
☐ 10 Tom Carter	1.00	.45	.12
☐ 11 Willie Clark	.35	.16	.04
☐ 12 John Covington	.50	.23	.06
☐ 13 Travis Davis	.35	.16	.04
☐ 14 Lake Dawson	1.50	.70	.19
☐ 15 Mark Zataveski	.35	.16	.04
☐ 16 Paul Failla	.75	.35	.09
☐ 17 Jim Flanigan	.75	.35	.09
☐ 18 Oliver Gibson	.35	.16	.04
☐ 19 Justin Goheen	.50	.23	.06
☐ 20 Tracy Graham	.35	.16	.04
☐ 21 Ray Griggs	.35	.16	.04
☐ 22 Justin Hall	.35	.16	.04
☐ 23 Jordan Halter	.35	.16	.04
☐ 24 Brian Hamilton	.50	.23	.06
☐ 25 Craig Hentrich	.50	.23	.06
☐ 26 Germaine Holden	.35	.16	.04
☐ 27 Adrian Jarrell	.50	.23	.06
☐ 28 Clint Johnson	.50	.23	.06
☐ 29 Lance Johnson	.35	.16	.04
☐ 30 Lindsay Knapp	.50	.23	.06
☐ 31 Ryan Leahy (Not alphabetical order)	.50	.23	.06
☐ 32 Greg Lane	.50	.23	.06
☐ 33 Dean Lytle	.35	.16	.04
☐ 34 Bernard Mannelly	.35	.16	.04
☐ 35 Oscar McBride	.50	.23	.06
☐ 36 Devon McDonald	.75	.35	.09
☐ 37 Kevin McDougal	1.00	.45	.12
☐ 38 Karl McGill	.35	.16	.04
☐ 39 Mike McGlinn	.35	.16	.04
☐ 40 Mike Miller	.75	.35	.09
☐ 41 Jeremy Nau	.35	.16	.04
☐ 42 Todd Norman	.50	.23	.06
☐ 43 Tim Ruddy (Not alphabetical order)	.50	.23	.06
☐ 44 William Pollard	.35	.16	.04
☐ 45 Brian Ratigan	.35	.16	.04
☐ 46 Leshane Saddler	.35	.16	.04
☐ 47 Jeremy Sample	.35	.16	.04
☐ 48 Irv Smith	1.00	.45	.12
☐ 49 Laron Moore (Not alphabetical order)	.35	.16	.04
☐ 50 Anthony Peterson (Not alphabetical order)	.50	.23	.06
☐ 51 Charles Stafford	.35	.16	.04
☐ 52 Nick Smith	.35	.16	.04
☐ 53 Greg Stec	.35	.16	.04
☐ 54 John Taliaferro	.35	.16	.04
☐ 55 Aaron Taylor	1.00	.45	.12
☐ 56 Stuart Tyner	.35	.16	.04
☐ 57 Ray Zellars (Not alphabetical order)	1.50	.70	.19
☐ 58 Tyler Young (Not alphabetical order)	.35	.16	.04
☐ 59 Bryant Young	2.00	.90	.25

1993 Notre Dame

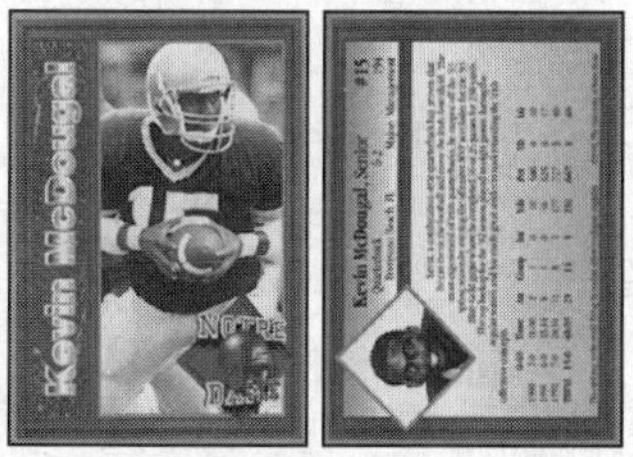
Kevin McDougal

These 72 standard-size cards feature on their fronts color player action shots. These photos are bordered in either blue, gold, green, or white, and each variety has its own checklist. All the cards have gold-colored outer borders. The player's name appears vertically in multicolored lettering within a photo of a football stadium near the left side. The horizontal back is bordered in the same color as its front, and carries a color player head shot within a diamond at the upper left, which is framed by a gold-colored line. The player's name, class, position, uniform number, and biography appear within a grayish rectangle at the top. His Notre Dame highlights and stats follow within the greenish panel below. The cards are unnumbered and checklisted below in alphabetical order.

	MINT	NRMT	EXC
COMPLETE SET (72)	20.00	9.00	2.50
COMMON CARD (1-72)	.25	.11	.03
☐ 1 Jeremy Akers	.35	.16	.04
☐ 2 Joe Babey	.25	.11	.03
☐ 3 Huntley Bakich	.25	.11	.03
☐ 4 Jason Beckwith	.25	.11	.03
☐ 5 Lee Becton	.75	.35	.09
☐ 6 Pete Bercich	.35	.16	.04
☐ 7 Jeff Burris	1.25	.55	.16
☐ 8 Pete Chryplewicz	.25	.11	.03
☐ 9 Willie Clark	.25	.11	.03
☐ 10 John Covington	.35	.16	.04
☐ 11 Travis Davis	.25	.11	.03
☐ 12 Lake Dawson	1.25	.55	.16
☐ 13 Paul Failla	.50	.23	.06
☐ 14 Jim Flanigan	.50	.23	.06
☐ 15 Reggie Fleurima	.25	.11	.03
☐ 16 Ben Foos	.25	.11	.03
☐ 17 Herbert Gibson	.25	.11	.03
☐ 18 Oliver Gibson	.50	.23	.06
☐ 19 Justin Goheen	.35	.16	.04
☐ 20 Tracy Graham	.25	.11	.03
☐ 21 Paul Grasmanis	.35	.16	.04
☐ 22 Jordan Halter	.25	.11	.03
☐ 23 Brian Hamilton	.35	.16	.04
☐ 24 Germaine Holden	.25	.11	.03
☐ 25 Lou Holtz CO	1.00	.45	.12
☐ 26 Robert Hughes	.25	.11	.03
☐ 27 Adrian Jarrell	.35	.16	.04
☐ 28 Clint Johnson	.35	.16	.04
☐ 29 Lance Johnson	.25	.11	.03
☐ 30 Thomas Knight	.35	.16	.04
☐ 31 Jim Kordas	.25	.11	.03
☐ 32 Greg Lane	.35	.16	.04
☐ 33 Ryan Leahy	.35	.16	.04
☐ 34 Will Lyell	.35	.16	.04
☐ 35 Dean Lytle	.25	.11	.03
☐ 36 Brian Magee	.25	.11	.03
☐ 37 Alton Maiden	.25	.11	.03
☐ 38 Derrick Mayes	1.50	.70	.19
☐ 39 Oscar McBride	.35	.16	.04
☐ 40 Mike McCullough	.50	.23	.06
☐ 41 Kevin McDougal	.50	.23	.06
☐ 42 Mike McGlinn	.25	.11	.03
☐ 43 Brian Meter	.25	.11	.03
☐ 44 Mike Miller	.50	.23	.06
☐ 45 Steve Misetic	.25	.11	.03
☐ 46 Jeremy Nau	.25	.11	.03
☐ 47 Todd Norman	.35	.16	.04
☐ 48 Kevin Pendergast	.35	.16	.04
☐ 49 Anthony Peterson	.25	.11	.03
☐ 50 David Quist	.25	.11	.03
☐ 51 Jeff Riney	.25	.11	.03
☐ 52 Tim Ruddy	.35	.16	.04
☐ 53 LeShane Saddler	.25	.11	.03
☐ 54 Jeremy Sample	.25	.11	.03
☐ 55 Charles Stafford	.25	.11	.03
☐ 56 Greg Stec	.25	.11	.03
☐ 57 Cliff Stroud	.25	.11	.03
☐ 58 John Taliaferro	.25	.11	.03
☐ 59 Aaron Taylor	1.25	.55	.16
☐ 60 Bobby Taylor	1.25	.55	.16
☐ 61 Bill Wagasy	.25	.11	.03
☐ 62 Leon Wallace	.25	.11	.03
☐ 63 Shawn Wooden	.35	.16	.04
☐ 64 Renaldo Wynn	.35	.16	.04
☐ 65 Bryant Young	1.50	.70	.19
☐ 66 Mark Zataveski	.35	.16	.04
☐ 67 Dusty Zeigler	.35	.16	.04
☐ 68 Ray Zellars	1.25	.55	.16
☐ 69 Blue Roster Checklist	.25	.11	.03
☐ 70 Gold Roster Checklist	.25	.11	.03
☐ 71 Green Roster Checklist	.25	.11	.03
☐ 72 White Roster Checklist	.25	.11	.03

1961 Nu-Card

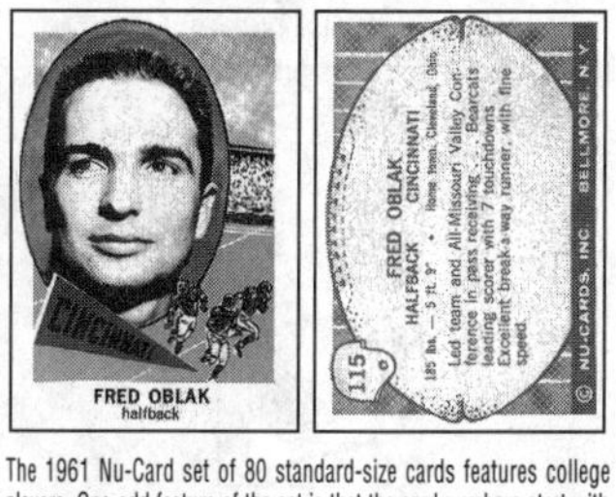
FRED OBLAK
halfback
FRED OBLAK
CINCINNATI
HALFBACK
115

The 1961 Nu-Card set of 80 standard-size cards features college players. One odd feature of the set is that the card numbers start with the number 101. The set features the first nationally distributed cards of Ernie Davis, Roman Gabriel, and John Hadl.

	NRMT	VG-E	GOOD
COMPLETE SET (80)	200.00	90.00	25.00
COMMON CARD (101-180)	2.50	1.10	.30
☐ 101 Bob Ferguson	6.00	2.70	.75
☐ 102 Ron Snidow	3.00	1.35	.35
☐ 103 Steve Barnett	2.50	1.10	.30
☐ 104 Greg Mather	2.50	1.10	.30
☐ 105 Vern Von Sydow	2.50	1.10	.30
☐ 106 John Hewitt	2.50	1.10	.30
☐ 107 Eddie Johns	2.50	1.10	.30
☐ 108 Walt Rappold	2.50	1.10	.30
☐ 109 Roy Winston	4.00	1.80	.50
☐ 110 Bob Boyda	2.50	1.10	.30
☐ 111 Billy Neighbors	4.00	1.80	.50
☐ 112 Don Purcell	2.50	1.10	.30
☐ 113 Ken Byers	2.50	1.10	.30
☐ 114 Ed Pine	2.50	1.10	.30
☐ 115 Fred Oblak	2.50	1.10	.30
☐ 116 Bobby Iles	2.50	1.10	.30
☐ 117 John Hadl	15.00	6.75	1.85
☐ 118 Charlie Mitchell	2.50	1.10	.30
☐ 119 Bill Swinford	2.50	1.10	.30
☐ 120 Bill King	2.50	1.10	.30
☐ 121 Mike Lucci	5.00	2.20	.60
☐ 122 Dave Sarette	2.50	1.10	.30
☐ 123 Alex Kroll	3.00	1.35	.35
☐ 124 Steve Bauwer	2.50	1.10	.30
☐ 125 Jimmy Saxton	3.00	1.35	.35
☐ 126 Steve Simms	2.50	1.10	.30
☐ 127 Andy Timura	2.50	1.10	.30
☐ 128 Gary Collins	7.00	3.10	.85
☐ 129 Ron Taylor	2.50	1.10	.30
☐ 130 Bobby Dodd	7.00	3.10	.85
☐ 131 Curtis McClinton	7.00	3.10	.85
☐ 132 Ray Poage	3.00	1.35	.35
☐ 133 Gus Gonzales	2.50	1.10	.30
☐ 134 Dick Locke	2.50	1.10	.30

☐ 135 Larry Libertore	2.50	1.10	.30
☐ 136 Stan Sczurek	2.50	1.10	.30
☐ 137 Pete Case	3.00	1.35	.35
☐ 138 Jesse Bradford	2.50	1.10	.30
☐ 139 Coolidge Hunt	2.50	1.10	.30
☐ 140 Walter Doleschal	2.50	1.10	.30
☐ 141 Bill Williamson	2.50	1.10	.30
☐ 142 Pat Trammell	6.00	2.70	.75
☐ 143 Ernie Davis	60.00	27.00	7.50
☐ 144 Chuck Lamson	2.50	1.10	.30
☐ 145 Bobby Plummer	3.00	1.35	.35
☐ 146 Sonny Gibbs	3.00	1.35	.35
☐ 147 Joe Eilers	2.50	1.10	.30
☐ 148 Roger Kochman	2.50	1.10	.30
☐ 149 Norman Beal	2.50	1.10	.30
☐ 150 Sherwyn Torson	2.50	1.10	.30
☐ 151 Russ Hepner	2.50	1.10	.30
☐ 152 Joe Romig	2.50	1.10	.30
☐ 153 Larry Thompson T	2.50	1.10	.30
☐ 154 Tom Perdue	2.50	1.10	.30
☐ 155 Ken Bolin	2.50	1.10	.30
☐ 156 Art Perkins	2.50	1.10	.30
☐ 157 Jim Sanderson	2.50	1.10	.30
☐ 158 Bob Asack	2.50	1.10	.30
☐ 159 Dan Celoni	2.50	1.10	.30
☐ 160 Bill McGuirt	2.50	1.10	.30
☐ 161 Dave Hoppmann	2.50	1.10	.30
☐ 162 Gary Barnes	2.50	1.10	.30
☐ 163 Don Lisbon	3.00	1.35	.35
☐ 164 Jerry Cross	2.50	1.10	.30
☐ 165 George Pierovich	2.50	1.10	.30
☐ 166 Roman Gabriel	20.00	9.00	2.50
☐ 167 Billy White	2.50	1.10	.30
☐ 168 Gale Weidner	2.50	1.10	.30
☐ 169 Charles Rieves	2.50	1.10	.30
☐ 170 Jim Furlong	2.50	1.10	.30
☐ 171 Tom Hutchinson	3.00	1.35	.35
☐ 172 Galen Hall	6.00	2.70	.75
☐ 173 Wilburn Hollis	2.50	1.10	.30
☐ 174 Don Kasso	2.50	1.10	.30
☐ 175 Bill Miller	3.00	1.35	.35
☐ 176 Ron Miller	2.50	1.10	.30
☐ 177 Joe Williams	2.50	1.10	.30
☐ 178 Mel Mellin	2.50	1.10	.30
☐ 179 Tom Vassell	2.50	1.10	.30
☐ 180 Mike Cotton	3.00	1.35	.35

1961 Nu-Card Pennant Inserts

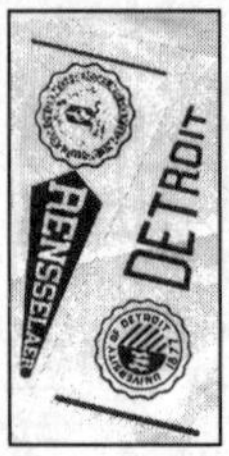

This set of pennant sticker pairs was inserted with the 1961 Nu-Card regular issue college football set. These inserts are actually 1 1/2" by 3 7/16" and one pair was to be inserted in each wax pack. The pennant pairs were printed with several different ink colors (orange, light blue, navy blue, purple, green, black, and red) on several different paper stock colors (white, red, gray, orange, and yellow). The pennant pairs are unnumbered and are ordered below alphabetically according to the lowest alphabetical member of the pair. Many of the teams are available paired with several different other colleges. Any additions to this list below would be welcome.

	NRMT	VG-E	GOOD
COMPLETE SET (265)	750.00	350.00	95.00
COMMON STICKER	3.00	1.35	.35
☐ 1 Air Force/Georgetown	3.00	1.35	.35
☐ 2 Air Force/Queens	3.00	1.35	.35
☐ 3 Air Force/Upsala	3.00	1.35	.35
☐ 4 Alabama/Boston U.	4.00	1.80	.50
☐ 5 Alabama/Cornell	4.00	1.80	.50
☐ 6 Alabama/Detroit	4.00	1.80	.50
☐ 7 Alabama/Harvard	4.00	1.80	.50
☐ 8 Alabama/Wisconsin	4.00	1.80	.50
☐ 9 Allegheny/Colorado St.	3.00	1.35	.35
☐ 10 Allegheny/Oregon	3.00	1.35	.35
☐ 11 Allegheny/Piedmont	3.00	1.35	.35
☐ 12 Allegheny/Wm.and Mary	3.00	1.35	.35
☐ 13 Arizona/Kansas	3.00	1.35	.35
☐ 14 Arizona/Mississippi	3.00	1.35	.35
☐ 15 Arizona/Pennsylvania	3.00	1.35	.35
☐ 16 Arizona/S.M.U.	3.00	1.35	.35
☐ 17 Army/Ga.Tech	3.00	1.35	.35
☐ 18 Army/Iowa	3.00	1.35	.35
☐ 19 Army/Johns Hopkins	3.00	1.35	.35
☐ 20 Army/Maryland	3.00	1.35	.35
☐ 21 Army/Missouri	3.00	1.35	.35
☐ 22 Army/Pratt	3.00	1.35	.35
☐ 23 Army/Purdue	3.00	1.35	.35
☐ 24 Auburn/Florida	4.00	1.80	.50
☐ 25 Auburn/Gettysburg	3.00	1.35	.35
☐ 26 Auburn/Illinois	4.00	1.80	.50
☐ 27 Auburn/Syracuse	4.00	1.80	.50
☐ 28 Auburn/Virginia	4.00	1.80	.50
☐ 29 Barnard/Columbia	3.00	1.35	.35
☐ 30 Barnard/Maine	3.00	1.35	.35
☐ 31 Barnard/N.Carolina	3.00	1.35	.35
☐ 32 Baylor/Colorado St.	3.00	1.35	.35
☐ 33 Baylor/Drew	3.00	1.35	.35
☐ 34 Baylor/Oregon	3.00	1.35	.35
☐ 35 Baylor/Piedmont	3.00	1.35	.35
☐ 36 Boston Coll./Minnesota	3.00	1.35	.35
☐ 37 Boston Coll./Norwich	3.00	1.35	.35
☐ 38 Boston Coll./Winthrop	3.00	1.35	.35
☐ 39 Boston U./Cornell	3.00	1.35	.35
☐ 40 Boston U./Rensselaer	3.00	1.35	.35
☐ 41 Boston U./Stanford	3.00	1.35	.35
☐ 42 Boston U./Temple	3.00	1.35	.35
☐ 43 Boston U./Utah State	3.00	1.35	.35
☐ 44 Bridgeport/Holy Cross	3.00	1.35	.35
☐ 45 Bridgeport/N.Y.U.	3.00	1.35	.35
☐ 46 Bridgeport/Northwestrn	3.00	1.35	.35
☐ 47 Bucknell/Illinois	3.00	1.35	.35
☐ 48 Bucknell/Syracuse	3.00	1.35	.35
☐ 49 Bucknell/Virginia	3.00	1.35	.35
☐ 50 California/Delaware	3.00	1.35	.35
☐ 51 California/Hofstra	3.00	1.35	.35
☐ 52 California/Kentucky	3.00	1.35	.35
☐ 53 California/Marquette	3.00	1.35	.35
☐ 54 California/Michigan	4.00	1.80	.50
☐ 55 California/Notre Dame	7.50	3.40	.95
☐ 56 California/Wingate	3.00	1.35	.35
☐ 57 Charleston/Dickinson	3.00	1.35	.35
☐ 58 Charleston/Lafayette	3.00	1.35	.35
☐ 59 Charleston/U.of Mass.	3.00	1.35	.35
☐ 60 Cincinnati/Maine	3.00	1.35	.35
☐ 61 Cincinnati/Ohio Wesl.	3.00	1.35	.35
☐ 62 Citadel/Columbia	3.00	1.35	.35
☐ 63 Citadel/Maine	3.00	1.35	.35
☐ 64 Citadel/N.Carolina	3.00	1.35	.35
☐ 65 Coast Guard/Drake	3.00	1.35	.35
☐ 66 Coast Guard/Penn St.	3.00	1.35	.35
☐ 67 Coast Guard/Yale	3.00	1.35	.35
☐ 68 Coker/UCLA	3.00	1.35	.35
☐ 69 Coker/Wingate	3.00	1.35	.35
☐ 70 Colby/Kings Point	3.00	1.35	.35
☐ 71 Colby/Queens	3.00	1.35	.35
☐ 72 Colby/Rice	3.00	1.35	.35
☐ 73 Colby/Upsala	3.00	1.35	.35
☐ 74 Colgate/Dickinson	3.00	1.35	.35
☐ 75 Colgate/Lafayette	3.00	1.35	.35
☐ 76 Colgate/U.of Mass.	3.00	1.35	.35
☐ 77 Colgate/Springfield	3.00	1.35	.35
☐ 78 Colgate/Texas AM	3.00	1.35	.35
☐ 79 C.O.P./Princeton	3.00	1.35	.35
☐ 80 C.O.P./Oklahoma St.	3.00	1.35	.35
☐ 81 C.O.P./Oregon St.	3.00	1.35	.35
☐ 82 Colo.St./Drew	3.00	1.35	.35
☐ 83 Colo.St./Oregon	3.00	1.35	.35
☐ 84 Colo.St./Piedmont	3.00	1.35	.35
☐ 85 Colo.St./Wm.and Mary	3.00	1.35	.35
☐ 86 Columbia/Dominican	3.00	1.35	.35
☐ 87 Columbia/Maine	3.00	1.35	.35
☐ 88 Columbia/N.Carolina	3.00	1.35	.35
☐ 89 Cornell/Harvard	3.00	1.35	.35
☐ 90 Cornell/Rensselaer	3.00	1.35	.35
☐ 91 Cornell/Stanford	3.00	1.35	.35
☐ 92 Cornell/Wisconsin	3.00	1.35	.35
☐ 93 Dartmouth/Mich.St.	3.00	1.35	.35
☐ 94 Dartmouth/Ohio U.	3.00	1.35	.35
☐ 95 Dartmouth/Wagner	3.00	1.35	.35
☐ 96 Davidson/Ohio Wesl.	3.00	1.35	.35
☐ 97 Davidson/S.Carolina	3.00	1.35	.35
☐ 98 Davidson/Texas Tech	3.00	1.35	.35
☐ 99 Delaware/Marquette	3.00	1.35	.35
☐ 100 Delaware/Michigan	3.00	1.35	.35
☐ 101 Delaware/Notre Dame	5.00	2.20	.60
☐ 102 Delaware/UCLA	3.00	1.35	.35
☐ 103 Denver/Florida State	4.00	1.80	.50
☐ 104 Denver/Indiana	3.00	1.35	.35
☐ 105 Denver/Iowa State	3.00	1.35	.35
☐ 106 Denver/USC	3.00	1.35	.35
☐ 107 Denver/VMI	3.00	1.35	.35
☐ 108 Detroit/Harvard	3.00	1.35	.35
☐ 109 Detroit/Rensselaer	3.00	1.35	.35
☐ 110 Detroit/Stanford	3.00	1.35	.35
☐ 111 Detroit/Utah State	3.00	1.35	.35
☐ 112 Dickinson/U.of Mass.	3.00	1.35	.35
☐ 113 Dickinson/Regis	3.00	1.35	.35
☐ 114 Dickinson/Springfield	3.00	1.35	.35
☐ 115 Dickinson/Texas AM	3.00	1.35	.35
☐ 116 Dominican/North Car.	3.00	1.35	.35
☐ 117 Drake/Duke	3.00	1.35	.35
☐ 118 Drake/Kentucky	3.00	1.35	.35
☐ 119 Drake/Middlebury	3.00	1.35	.35
☐ 120 Drake/Penn St.	3.00	1.35	.35
☐ 121 Drake/St. Peters	3.00	1.35	.35
☐ 122 Drake/Yale	3.00	1.35	.35
☐ 123 Drew/Middlebury	3.00	1.35	.35
☐ 124 Drew/Oregon	3.00	1.35	.35
☐ 125 Drew/Piedmont	3.00	1.35	.35
☐ 126 Drew/Wm. and Mary	3.00	1.35	.35
☐ 127 Duke/Middlebury	3.00	1.35	.35
☐ 128 Duke/Rhode Island	3.00	1.35	.35
☐ 129 Duke/Seton Hall	3.00	1.35	.35
☐ 130 Duke/Yale	3.00	1.35	.35
☐ 131 Finch/Long Island AT	3.00	1.35	.35
☐ 132 Finch/Michigan St.	3.00	1.35	.35
☐ 133 Finch/Ohio U.	3.00	1.35	.35
☐ 134 Finch/Wagner	3.00	1.35	.35
☐ 135 Florida/Gettysburg	3.00	1.35	.35
☐ 136 Florida/Illinois	4.00	1.80	.50
☐ 137 Florida/Syracuse	4.00	1.80	.50
☐ 138 Florida/Virginia	4.00	1.80	.50
☐ 139 Florida St./Indiana	4.00	1.80	.50
☐ 140 Florida St./Iowa St.	4.00	1.80	.50
☐ 141 Florida St./So.Cal.	4.00	1.80	.50
☐ 142 Florida St./VMI	4.00	1.80	.50
☐ 143 Georgetown/Kings Point	3.00	1.35	.35
☐ 144 Georgetown/Rice	3.00	1.35	.35
☐ 145 Georgia/Missouri	4.00	1.80	.50
☐ 146 Georgia/Ohio Wesleyan	3.00	1.35	.35
☐ 147 Georgia/Rutgers	3.00	1.35	.35
☐ 148 Georgia/So.Carolina	4.00	1.80	.50
☐ 149 Ga.Tech/Johns Hopkins	3.00	1.35	.35
☐ 150 Ga.Tech/Maryland	3.00	1.35	.35
☐ 151 Ga.Tech/Missouri	3.00	1.35	.35
☐ 152 Gettysburg/Syracuse	3.00	1.35	.35
☐ 153 Harvard/Miami	4.00	1.80	.50
☐ 154 Harvard/NC State	3.00	1.35	.35
☐ 155 Harvard/Stanford	3.00	1.35	.35
☐ 156 Harvard/Utah State	3.00	1.35	.35
☐ 157 Harvard/Wisconsin	3.00	1.35	.35
☐ 158 Hofstra/Marquette	3.00	1.35	.35
☐ 159 Hofstra/Michigan	4.00	1.80	.50
☐ 160 Hofstra/Navy	3.00	1.35	.35
☐ 161 Hofstra/UCLA	3.00	1.35	.35
☐ 162 Holy Cross/Navy	3.00	1.35	.35
☐ 163 Holy Cross/New York	3.00	1.35	.35
☐ 164 Holy Cross/N'western	3.00	1.35	.35
☐ 165 Holy Cross/Nyack	3.00	1.35	.35
☐ 166 Howard/Kentucky	3.00	1.35	.35
☐ 167 Howard/Villanova	3.00	1.35	.35
☐ 168 Illinois/Syracuse	3.00	1.35	.35
☐ 169 Indiana/Iowa State	3.00	1.35	.35
☐ 170 Indiana/V.M.I.	3.00	1.35	.35
☐ 171 Iowa/Maryland	3.00	1.35	.35
☐ 172 Iowa/Missouri	3.00	1.35	.35
☐ 173 Iowa/Pratt	3.00	1.35	.35
☐ 174 Iowa State/So.Cal.	4.00	1.80	.50
☐ 175 Johns Hopkins/Pratt	3.00	1.35	.35
☐ 176 Johns Hopkins/Purdue	3.00	1.35	.35
☐ 177 Kansas/St.Francis	3.00	1.35	.35
☐ 178 Kansas/S.M.U.	3.00	1.35	.35
☐ 179 Kansas State/N.Y.U.	3.00	1.35	.35
☐ 180 Kansas State/T.C.U.	3.00	1.35	.35
☐ 181 Kentucky/Maryland	3.00	1.35	.35
☐ 182 Kentucky/Middlebury	3.00	1.35	.35
☐ 183 Kentucky/New Hampsh.	3.00	1.35	.35
☐ 184 Kentucky/Penn State	5.00	2.20	.60
☐ 185 Kentucky/Rhode Island	3.00	1.35	.35
☐ 186 Kentucky/St.Peter's	3.00	1.35	.35
☐ 187 Kentucky/Seton Hall	3.00	1.35	.35
☐ 188 Kentucky/Villanova	3.00	1.35	.35
☐ 189 Kings Point/Queens	3.00	1.35	.35
☐ 190 Kings Point/Rice	3.00	1.35	.35
☐ 191 Kings Point/Upsala	3.00	1.35	.35
☐ 192 Lafayette/U.of Mass.	3.00	1.35	.35
☐ 193 Lafayette/Regis	3.00	1.35	.35
☐ 194 Long Isl. AT/Mich.St.	3.00	1.35	.35
☐ 195 Long Isl. AT/Ohio U.	3.00	1.35	.35
☐ 196 Long Isl. AT/Wagner	3.00	1.35	.35
☐ 197 Loyola/Minnesota	3.00	1.35	.35
☐ 198 Loyola/Norwich	3.00	1.35	.35
☐ 199 Loyola/Winthrop	3.00	1.35	.35
☐ 200 Marquette/Michigan	4.00	1.80	.50
☐ 201 Marquette/Navy	3.00	1.35	.35
☐ 202 Marquette/New Platz	3.00	1.35	.35
☐ 203 Marquette/Notre Dame	5.00	2.20	.60
☐ 204 Marquette/UCLA	3.00	1.35	.35
☐ 205 Maryland/Missouri	3.00	1.35	.35
☐ 206 Mass./Regis	3.00	1.35	.35
☐ 207 Mass./Springfield	3.00	1.35	.35
☐ 208 Mass./Texas AM	3.00	1.35	.35
☐ 209 Michigan/Navy	4.00	1.80	.50
☐ 210 Michigan/New Platz	3.00	1.35	.35
☐ 211 Michigan/UCLA	4.00	1.80	.50
☐ 212 Michigan St./Ohio U.	3.00	1.35	.35
☐ 213 Michigan St./Wagner	3.00	1.35	.35
☐ 214 Middlebury/Penn St.	3.00	1.35	.35
☐ 215 Middlebury/Yale	3.00	1.35	.35
☐ 216 Minnesota/Norwich	3.00	1.35	.35
☐ 217 Minnesota/Winthrop	3.00	1.35	.35
☐ 218 Mississippi/Penn	3.00	1.35	.35
☐ 219 Mississippi/St.Francis	3.00	1.35	.35
☐ 220 Missouri/Purdue	3.00	1.35	.35
☐ 221 Navy/Notre Dame	7.50	3.40	.95
☐ 222 Navy/UCLA	4.00	1.80	.50
☐ 223 Navy/Wingate	3.00	1.35	.35
☐ 224 New Hamp./Villanova	3.00	1.35	.35
☐ 225 N.Y.U./Northwestern	3.00	1.35	.35
☐ 226 NCE/Temple	3.00	1.35	.35
☐ 227 NCE/Wisconsin	3.00	1.35	.35
☐ 228 NC State/Temple	3.00	1.35	.35
☐ 229 Northwestern/TCU	3.00	1.35	.35
☐ 230 Norwich/Winthrop	3.00	1.35	.35
☐ 231 Notre Dame/UCLA	7.50	3.40	.95
☐ 232 Notre Dame/Wingate	5.00	2.20	.60
☐ 233 Ohio U./Wagner	3.00	1.35	.35
☐ 234 Ohio Wesl./Roberts	3.00	1.35	.35
☐ 235 Ohio Wesl./S.Carolina	3.00	1.35	.35
☐ 236 Okla.St./Oregon St.	3.00	1.35	.35
☐ 237 Okla.St./Princeton	3.00	1.35	.35
☐ 238 Oregon/Piedmont	3.00	1.35	.35
☐ 239 Oregon/Wm.and Mary	3.00	1.35	.35
☐ 240 Oregon St./Princeton	3.00	1.35	.35
☐ 241 Penn State/St.Peter's	3.00	1.35	.35
☐ 242 Penn State/Seton Hall	3.00	1.35	.35
☐ 243 Penn State/Yale	3.00	1.35	.35
☐ 244 Penn/S.M.U.	3.00	1.35	.35
☐ 245 Penn/St.Francis	3.00	1.35	.35
☐ 246 Queens/Rice	3.00	1.35	.35
☐ 247 Queens/Upsala	3.00	1.35	.35
☐ 248 Rensselaer/Stanford	3.00	1.35	.35
☐ 249 Rensselaer/Temple	3.00	1.35	.35
☐ 250 Rensselaer/Utah State	3.00	1.35	.35
☐ 251 Rhode Island/Yale	3.00	1.35	.35
☐ 252 Rice/Upsala	3.00	1.35	.35
☐ 253 Roberts/So.Carolina	3.00	1.35	.35
☐ 254 Roberts/Texas Tech	3.00	1.35	.35
☐ 255 Rutgers/So.Carolina	3.00	1.35	.35
☐ 256 St.Francis/S.M.U.	3.00	1.35	.35
☐ 257 St.Peter's/Villanova	3.00	1.35	.35
☐ 258 St.Peter's/Yale	3.00	1.35	.35
☐ 259 So.California/VMI	4.00	1.80	.50
☐ 260 So.Carolina/Texas Tech	3.00	1.35	.35
☐ 261 Syracuse/Virginia	3.00	1.35	.35
☐ 262 Temple/Wisconsin	3.00	1.35	.35
☐ 263 UCLA/Wingate	4.00	1.80	.50
☐ 264 Utah State/Wisconsin	3.00	1.35	.35
☐ 265 Villanova/Yale	3.00	1.35	.35

1991 Oberlin College Heisman Club

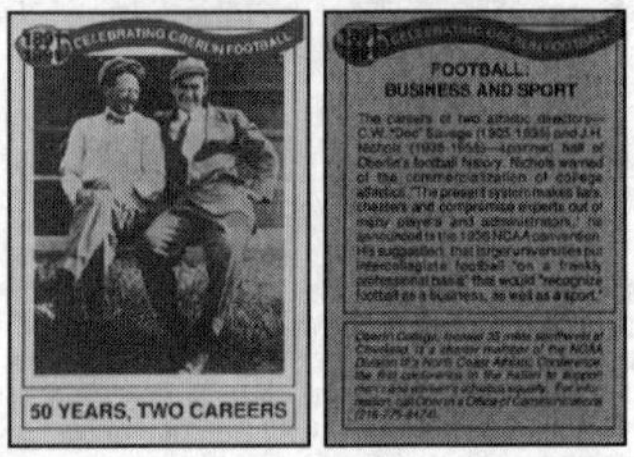

This five-card standard-size set was issued to commemorate 100 years of Oberlin football. The cards feature black-and-white posed and action photos of coaches and players significant to Oberlin's history. The front picture rests on a white card face, and a thin maroon line frames the photo and forms a box around the player's name at the bottom. A football icon in the upper left corner contains the years 1891-1991, and a maroon banner emanating from the football is printed with the words "Celebrating Oberlin Football". The backs are plain cardboard. A thin maroon line forms a box containing information about the front photos. In a smaller box is information about Oberlin College, including the Oberlin Office of Communications' phone number. The cards are unnumbered and checklisted below in alphabetical order.

	MINT	NRMT	EXC
COMPLETE SET (5)	5.00	2.20	.60
COMMON CARD (1-5)	1.00	.45	.12
☐ 1 50 Years, Two Careers C.W.(Doc) Savage J.H. Nichols (Athletic Directors)	1.00	.45	.12
☐ 2 John W. Heisman CO	2.00	.90	.25
☐ 3 Oberlin's 1892 Team	1.00	.45	.12
☐ 4 Oberlin's Fauver Twins Doc Edgar Fauver Doc Edwin Fauver	1.00	.45	.12
☐ 5 Oberlin's Four Horsemen Carl Semple Carl Williams H.K. Regal C.W.(Doc) Savage	1.00	.45	.12

1994 Ohio High School Big 33

This standard-size high school football set was issued to commemorate the 37th annual Big 33 Ohio Football Classic. The cardfronts feature posed player photos enclosed by a white border. The state name appears at the top of the card along with the player's name, number, and position. The backs feature player's biographical information and future college plans if known. The cards are unnumbered and listed below alphabetically.

	MINT	NRMT	EXC
COMPLETE SET (35)	25.00	11.00	3.10
COMMON CARD (1-35)	.60	.25	.07
☐ 1 Ryan Beougher	.60	.25	.07
☐ 2 Jeremy Beutler	.60	.25	.07
☐ 3 Chioke Bradley	.60	.25	.07
☐ 4 Calvin Brown	.60	.25	.07
☐ 5 Che Bryant	.60	.25	.07
☐ 6 Brooks Burris	.60	.25	.07
☐ 7 Todd Bush	.60	.25	.07
☐ 8 Mike Buzin	.60	.25	.07
☐ 9 John Cappelletti Honorary Chairman	1.00	.45	.12
☐ 10 Eric deGroh	.60	.25	.07
☐ 11 Keith Dimmy	.60	.25	.07
☐ 12 Chad Duff	.60	.25	.07

	MINT	NRMT	EXC
☐ 13 Curtis Enis	3.00	1.35	.35
☐ 14 Dennis Fitzgerald	.60	.25	.07
☐ 15 Eric Gohlstin	1.00	.45	.12
☐ 16 Eric Haddad	.60	.25	.07
☐ 17 Jason Hughes	.60	.25	.07
☐ 18 Dontey Hunter	.60	.25	.07
☐ 19 Kevin Huntley	.75	.35	.09
☐ 20 Jermon Jackson	.60	.25	.07
☐ 21 Kevin Jones	.60	.25	.07
☐ 22 Todd Kollar	.75	.35	.09
☐ 23 John Lumpkin	.60	.25	.07
☐ 24 Marvin Major	.60	.25	.07
☐ 25 Andy McCullough	.60	.25	.07
☐ 26 Dee Miller	.75	.35	.09
☐ 27 Damon Moore	.60	.25	.07
☐ 28 Scott Mutryn	.60	.25	.07
☐ 29 Orlando Pace	4.00	1.80	.50
☐ 30 BJ Payne	.60	.25	.07
☐ 31 Pepe Pearson	2.00	.90	.25
☐ 32 Marcus Ray	.60	.25	.07
☐ 33 Chad Smithberger	.60	.25	.07
☐ 34 Rasche Sumpter	.60	.25	.07
☐ 35 Sean Williams	.60	.25	.07

1995 Ohio High School Big 33

This standard-size high school football set was issued to commemorate the Big 33 Ohio Football Classic. The cardfronts feature posed player photos enclosed by a white border. The state name and year appear at the top of the card along with the player's name, number, and position. The backs feature player's biographical information and future college plans if known. The cards are unnumbered and listed below alphabetically.

	MINT	NRMT	EXC
COMPLETE SET (35)	18.00	8.00	2.20
COMMON CARD (1-35)	.60	.25	.07
☐ 1 Juan Armour	.60	.25	.07
☐ 2 Matt Borgmann	1.00	.45	.12
☐ 3 Jason Caswell	.60	.25	.07
☐ 4 Brian Coleman	.75	.35	.09
☐ 5 Tony Eisenhard	.60	.25	.07
☐ 6 Mike Furrey	.60	.25	.07
☐ 7 Michael Gantous	.60	.25	.07
☐ 8 Michael Glassmeyer	.60	.25	.07
☐ 9 Andy Habing	.60	.25	.07
☐ 10 Brent Hanni	.60	.25	.07
☐ 11 Murad Holliday	.60	.25	.07
☐ 12 Chris Huelsman	.60	.25	.07
☐ 13 Nathaniel Johnson	.60	.25	.07
☐ 14 Craig Kantz	.60	.25	.07
☐ 15 Percy King	.60	.25	.07
☐ 16 Chris Kirk	.75	.35	.09
☐ 17 Patrick Kratus	.60	.25	.07
☐ 18 Matthew Lavrar	.60	.25	.07
☐ 19 Courtney Ledyard	.60	.25	.07
☐ 20 Tim Lewis Honorary Chairman	.60	.25	.07
☐ 21 Jason Lucas	.60	.25	.07
☐ 22 Rob Majoy	.60	.25	.07
☐ 23 Josh McDaniels	.60	.25	.07
☐ 24 Tobey McKee	.60	.25	.07
☐ 25 Rob Murphy	.60	.25	.07
☐ 26 Ahmed Plummer	.60	.25	.07
☐ 27 Vanness Provitt	.60	.25	.07
☐ 28 Nathan Shaffer	.60	.25	.07
☐ 29 Eric Smith	.60	.25	.07
☐ 30 Willie Spencer	.60	.25	.07
☐ 31 Charles Tincher	.60	.25	.07
☐ 32 T.J. Upshaw	.75	.35	.09
☐ 33 Torrence Wilson	.60	.25	.07
☐ 34 Antoine Winfield	.60	.25	.07
☐ 35 Steven Wisniewski	.60	.25	.07

1996 Ohio High School Big 33

This standard-size high school football set was issued to commemorate the Big 33 Ohio Football Classic. The cardfronts feature posed player photos enclosed by a white border. The state initials and year appear at the top of the card along with the player's name, number, and position. The backs feature player's biographical information and future college plans if known. The cards are unnumbered and listed below alphabetically.

	MINT	NRMT	EXC
COMPLETE SET (35)	18.00	8.00	2.20
COMMON CARD (1-35)	.60	.25	.07
☐ 1 Mike Austin	.60	.25	.07
☐ 2 Mike Bath	.60	.25	.07
☐ 3 Gary Berry	.60	.25	.07
☐ 4 Kevin Coffey	.60	.25	.07
☐ 5 Jim Covert Honorary Chairman	1.00	.45	.12
☐ 6 Chris Della Vella	.60	.25	.07
☐ 7 Corey Estell	.60	.25	.07
☐ 8 Matt Feschak	.60	.25	.07
☐ 9 Aaron Focht	.60	.25	.07
☐ 10 Derek Fox	.60	.25	.07
☐ 11 Ben Gilbert	.60	.25	.07
☐ 12 Nick Goings	.75	.35	.09
☐ 13 Kevin Houser	.60	.25	.07
☐ 14 Christopher Hovan	.60	.25	.07
☐ 15 Robert Johnson	.60	.25	.07
☐ 16 Andy Katzemoyer	1.50	.70	.19
☐ 17 Jefferson Kelley	.60	.25	.07
☐ 18 Marc Kielmeyer	.60	.25	.07
☐ 19 Jeremy Manns	.60	.25	.07
☐ 20 Shaun Mason	.60	.25	.07
☐ 21 Chris Modelski	.60	.25	.07
☐ 22 Mike Montgomery	.60	.25	.07
☐ 23 Kurt Murphy	.60	.25	.07
☐ 24 Daniel Norris	.60	.25	.07
☐ 25 Danny O'Leary	.60	.25	.07
☐ 26 Renauld Ray	.60	.25	.07
☐ 27 Jermaine Sheffield	.60	.25	.07
☐ 28 Rolland Steele	.60	.25	.07
☐ 29 Brian Stephan	.60	.25	.07
☐ 30 Dan Stultz	.60	.25	.07
☐ 31 Jeremiah Taylor	.60	.25	.07
☐ 32 Jason Turner	.60	.25	.07
☐ 33 Tyson Walter	.60	.25	.07
☐ 34 Shawn Wright	.60	.25	.07
☐ 35 Eric Zbinovec	.60	.25	.07

1979 Ohio State Greats

This 53-card set contains all the Ohio State football players and coaches who obtained All-American or National Football Hall of Fame status through 1978. The cards were issued in the playing card format, and each card measures approximately 2 1/2" by 3 1/4". The fronts feature a close-up photograph of the player in an octagon frame. Those cards with two stars in the octagon frame indicate those players voted into the National Football Hall of Fame. The backs feature a collage of Ohio State players within an octagon border with "All-Americans, National Football Hall of Famers" at the bottom. Because this set is similar to a playing card set, the set is arranged just like a card deck and checklisted below as follows: C means Clubs, D means Diamonds, H means Hearts, S means Spades, and JK means Joker. The cards are checklisted below in playing card order by suits and numbers are assigned to Aces (1), Jacks (11), Queens (12), and Kings (13). The joker is listed at the end.

	NRMT-MT	EXC	G-VG
COMPLETE SET (53)	40.00	18.00	5.00
COMMON CARD	.75	.35	.09
☐ 1C Chris Ward	.75	.35	.09
☐ 1D Jan White	1.00	.45	.12
☐ 1H Ernest R. Godfrey ACO	.75	.35	.09
☐ 1S Ray Pryor	.75	.35	.09
☐ 2C Ray Griffin	1.00	.45	.12
☐ 2D Tom Deleone	1.00	.45	.12
☐ 2H Francis A. Schmidt CO	.75	.35	.09
☐ 2S Dave Foley	1.00	.45	.12
☐ 3C Tom Cousineau	1.25	.55	.16
☐ 3D Randy Gradishar	2.00	.90	.25
☐ 3H Jim Parker	2.00	.90	.25
☐ 3S Rufus Mayes	1.00	.45	.12
☐ 4C Aaron Brown	1.00	.45	.12
☐ 4D John Hicks	1.25	.55	.16
☐ 4H Vic Janowicz	2.00	.90	.25
☐ 4S Rex Kern	1.50	.70	.19
☐ 5C Chris Ward	.75	.35	.09
☐ 5D Van Decree	.75	.35	.09
☐ 5H Les Horvath	1.50	.70	.19
☐ 5S Jim Otis	1.50	.70	.19
☐ 6C Tom Skladany	1.00	.45	.12
☐ 6D Randy Gradishar	2.00	.90	.25
☐ 6H Bill Willis	1.25	.55	.16
☐ 6S Ted Provost	.75	.35	.09
☐ 7C Bob Brudzinski	1.00	.45	.12
☐ 7D Archie Griffin	2.50	1.10	.30
☐ 7H James Daniell	.75	.35	.09
☐ 7S Jim Stillwagon	1.25	.55	.16
☐ 8C Ted Smith	.75	.35	.09
☐ 8D John Hicks	1.25	.55	.16
☐ 8H Gust Zarnas	.75	.35	.09
☐ 8S Jack Tatum	1.50	.70	.19
☐ 9C Tom Skladany	1.25	.55	.16
☐ 9D Neal Colzie	1.00	.45	.12
☐ 9H Gomer Jones	.75	.35	.09
☐ 9S Tim Anderson	.75	.35	.09
☐ 10C Archie Griffin	2.50	1.10	.30
☐ 10D Pete Cusick	.75	.35	.09
☐ 10H Wes Fesler	1.00	.45	.12
☐ 10S John Brockington	1.50	.70	.19
☐ 11C Tim Fox	1.00	.45	.12
☐ 11D Van Decree	.75	.35	.09
☐ 11H Gaylord Stinchcomb	.75	.35	.09
☐ 11S Mike Sensibaugh	1.00	.45	.12
☐ 12C Tom Skladany	1.00	.45	.12
☐ 12D Archie Griffin	2.50	1.10	.30
☐ 12H Chic Harley	.75	.35	.09
☐ 12S Jim Stillwagon	1.25	.55	.16
☐ 13C Kurt Schumacher	1.00	.45	.12
☐ 13D Steve Meyers	1.00	.45	.12
☐ 13H Tom Cousineau	1.25	.55	.16
☐ 13S Jack Tatum	1.50	.70	.19
☐ JK Howard Jones CO	1.00	.45	.12

1988 Ohio State

The 1988 Ohio State University football set contains 22 standard-size cards. The fronts have vintage or color action photos with white borders; the vertically oriented backs have detailed profiles. These cards were distributed as a set. The set is unnumbered, so the cards are listed alphabetically.

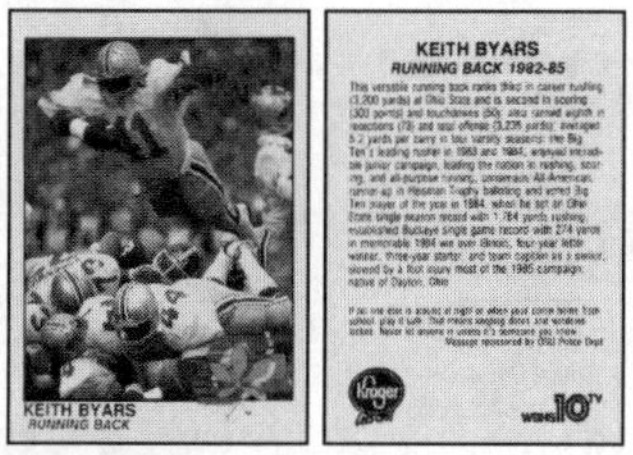
KEITH BYARS
RUNNING BACK 1982-85
KEITH BYARS
RUNNING BACK

	MINT	NRMT	EXC
COMPLETE SET (22)	15.00	6.75	1.85
COMMON CARD (1-22)	.40	.18	.05
☐ 1 Bob Brudzinski	.50	.23	.06
☐ 2 Keith Byars	1.00	.45	.12
☐ 3 Hopalong Cassady	1.00	.45	.12
☐ 4 Arnold Chonko	.50	.23	.06
☐ 5 Wes Fesler	.40	.18	.05
☐ 6 Randy Gradishar	1.00	.45	.12
☐ 7 Archie Griffin	1.50	.70	.19
☐ 8 Chic Harley	.40	.18	.05
☐ 9 Woody Hayes CO	1.25	.55	.16
☐ 10 John Hicks	.50	.23	.06
☐ 11 Les Horvath	1.00	.45	.12
☐ 12 Jim Houston	.75	.35	.09
☐ 13 Vic Janowicz	1.25	.55	.16
☐ 14 Pepper Johnson	.75	.35	.09
☐ 15 Ike Kelley	.40	.18	.05
☐ 16 Rex Kern	.75	.35	.09
☐ 17 Jim Lachey	.75	.35	.09
☐ 18 Jim Parker	1.00	.45	.12
☐ 19 Tom Skladany	.50	.23	.06
☐ 20 Chris Spielman	1.00	.45	.12
☐ 21 Jim Stillwagon	.75	.35	.09
☐ 22 Jack Tatum	1.00	.45	.12

1989 Ohio State

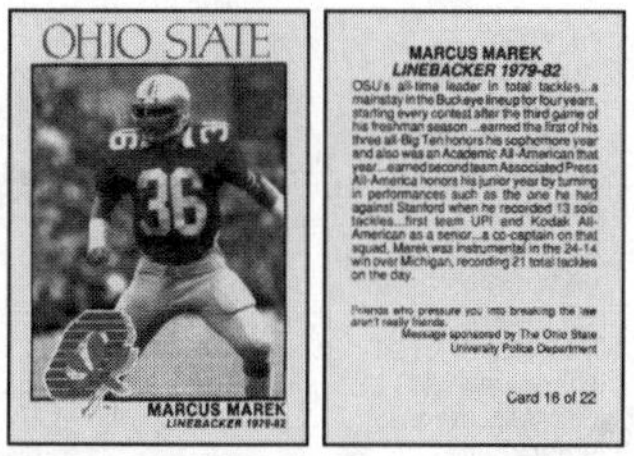
OHIO STATE
MARCUS MAREK
LINEBACKER 1979-82
MARCUS MAREK
Card 16 of 22

The 1989 Ohio State University football set contains 22 standard-size cards. The fronts have vintage or color action photos with white borders; the vertically oriented backs have detailed profiles. These cards were distributed as a set and are numbered on the backs.

	MINT	NRMT	EXC
COMPLETE SET (22)	10.00	4.50	1.25
COMMON CARD (1-22)	.40	.18	.05
☐ 1 Mike Tomczak	1.00	.45	.12
☐ 2 Paul Warfield	1.50	.70	.19
☐ 3 Kirk Lowdermilk	.50	.23	.06
☐ 4 Bob Ferguson	.50	.23	.06
☐ 5 Jack Graf	.40	.18	.05
☐ 6 Tim Fox	.50	.23	.06
☐ 7 Eric Kumerow	.50	.23	.06
☐ 8 Neal Colzie	.50	.23	.06
☐ 9 Jim Otis	.75	.35	.09
☐ 10 John Brockington	1.00	.45	.12
☐ 11 Cornelius Greene	.40	.18	.05
☐ 12 Jim Marshall	1.00	.45	.12
☐ 13 Tim Spencer	.50	.23	.06
☐ 14 Don Scott	.40	.18	.05
☐ 15 Chris Ward	.50	.23	.06
☐ 16 Marcus Marek	.50	.23	.06
☐ 17 Dave Foley	.50	.23	.06
☐ 18 Bill Willis	.75	.35	.09
☐ 19 John Frank	.75	.35	.09
☐ 20 Rufus Mayes	.50	.23	.06
☐ 21 Tom Tupa	.75	.35	.09
☐ 22 Jan White	.50	.23	.06

1990 Ohio State

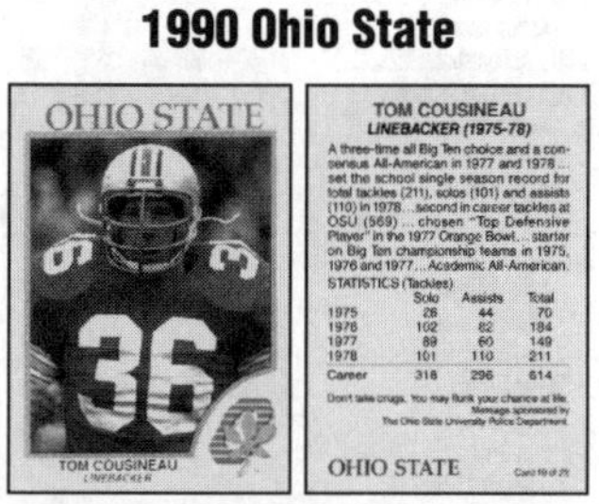
OHIO STATE
TOM COUSINEAU
LINEBACKER (1975-78)
TOM COUSINEAU
OHIO STATE

This 22-card set measures the standard size. There is a full color photograph on the front, and the Ohio State logo on the lower right-hand corner. The back has biographical information about the player. The set was produced by College Classics and features past and current players.

	MINT	NRMT	EXC
COMPLETE SET (22)	8.00	3.60	1.00
COMMON CARD (1-22)	.35	.16	.04
☐ 1 Jeff Uhlenhake	.50	.23	.06
☐ 2 Ray Ellis	.35	.16	.04
☐ 3 Todd Bell	.50	.23	.06
☐ 4 Jeff Logan	.35	.16	.04
☐ 5 Pete Johnson	.75	.35	.09
☐ 6 Van DeCree	.35	.16	.04
☐ 7 Ted Provost	.35	.16	.04
☐ 8 Mike Lanese	.35	.16	.04
☐ 9 Aaron Brown	.50	.23	.06
☐ 10 Pete Cusick	.35	.16	.04
☐ 11 Vlade Janakievski	.35	.16	.04
☐ 12 Steve Myers	.35	.16	.04
☐ 13 Ted Smith	.35	.16	.04
☐ 14 Doug Donley	.50	.23	.06
☐ 15 Ron Springs	.50	.23	.06
☐ 16 Ken Fritz	.35	.16	.04
☐ 17 Jeff Davidson	.35	.16	.04
☐ 18 Art Schlichter	.75	.35	.09
☐ 19 Tom Cousineau	.75	.35	.09
☐ 20 Call Murray	.35	.16	.04
☐ 21 Brian Baschnagel	.50	.23	.06
☐ 22 Joe Staysniak	.35	.16	.04

1992 Ohio State

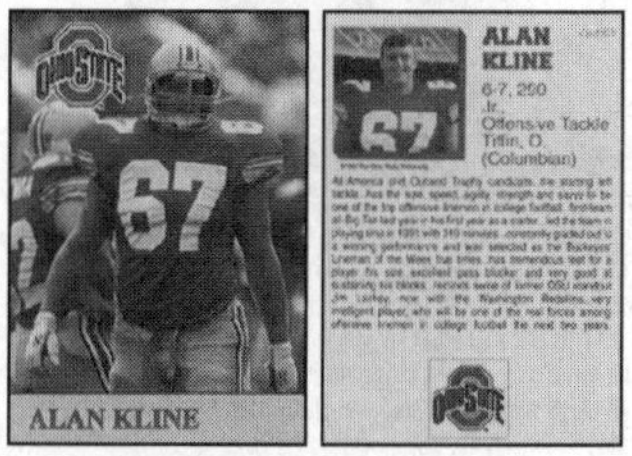
ALAN KLINE
6-7, 250
Offensive Tackle
Tiffin, O.
ALAN KLINE

This 1992 Ohio State University football set contains 59 standard-size cards. Packaged in a cardboard sleeve, the cards were available only through the Ohio State Department of Athletics, the Arena Shop and its affiliated University bookstores. They originally sold this card set for 14.00, but the set was later closed out at a lower price. The fronts feature full-bleed action and posed color photos. The player's name is printed in red lettering inside a gray bar at the bottom, and the school logo also appears in different corners on the fronts. On a white background, the backs carry a small color close-up shot, short player biography, a detailed profile, career stats, and the school logo. Robert Smith and Greg Smith were not featured in this 59-card set because they reportedly refused to sign the NCAA waiver that must accompany their appearance in a profit-making endeavor on behalf of their school. Joey Galloway and Eddie George are the key cards in this set, but there are several other NFL draftees and players in this set.

	MINT	NRMT	EXC
COMPLETE SET (59)	25.00	11.00	3.10
COMMON CARD (1-58)	.25	.11	.03
☐ 1 John Cooper CO	.75	.35	.09
☐ 2 Kirk Herbstreit	.50	.23	.06
☐ 3 Steve Tovar	1.00	.45	.12
☐ 4 Chico Nelson	.25	.11	.03
☐ 5 Tim Patillo	.25	.11	.03
☐ 6 Tito Paul	.50	.23	.06
☐ 7 Jim Borchers	.25	.11	.03
☐ 8 Craig Powell	.75	.35	.09
☐ 9 Deron Brown	.25	.11	.03
☐ 10 Alex Rodriguez	.25	.11	.03
☐ 11 Chris Sanders	3.00	1.35	.35
☐ 12 Cedric Saunders	.25	.11	.03
☐ 13 Walter Taylor	.40	.18	.05
☐ 14 Jack Thrush	.25	.11	.03
☐ 15 Brian Stablein	.50	.23	.06
☐ 16 Tim Walton	.25	.11	.03
☐ 17 Rod Smith	.50	.23	.06
☐ 18 Brad Pope	.25	.11	.03
☐ 19 William Houston	.25	.11	.03
☐ 20 Dan Wilkinson	1.50	.70	.19
☐ 21 Jason Winrow	.40	.18	.05
☐ 22 Mark Williams	.25	.11	.03
☐ 23 Jason Simmons	.50	.23	.06
☐ 24 Luke Fickell	.50	.23	.06
☐ 25 Tim Williams	.25	.11	.03
☐ 26 Raymont Harris	2.00	.90	.25
☐ 27 Preston Harrison	.25	.11	.03
☐ 28 Len Hartman	.25	.11	.03
☐ 29 Eddie George	8.00	3.60	1.00
☐ 30 Jayson Gwinn	.50	.23	.06
☐ 31 Korey Stringer	1.00	.45	.12
☐ 32 Tom Lease	.25	.11	.03
☐ 33 Randall Brown	.25	.11	.03
☐ 34 DeWayne Carter	.25	.11	.03
☐ 35 Bryan Cook	.25	.11	.03
☐ 36 Allen DeGraffenreid	.50	.23	.06
☐ 37 Brian Stoughton	.25	.11	.03
☐ 38 Derrick Foster	.25	.11	.03
☐ 39 Butler By'not'e	.75	.35	.09
☐ 40 Jeff Cothran	.75	.35	.09
☐ 41 Robert Davis	.25	.11	.03
☐ 42 Joey Galloway	5.00	2.20	.60
☐ 43 Roger Harper	.75	.35	.09

	MINT	NRMT	EXC
☐ 44 Bobby Hoying	2.50	1.10	.30
☐ 45 C.J. Kelly	.40	.18	.05
☐ 46 Brent Johnson	.25	.11	.03
☐ 47 Paul Long	.25	.11	.03
☐ 48 Joe Metzger	.25	.11	.03
☐ 49 Jason Louis	.25	.11	.03
☐ 50 Dave Monnot	.25	.11	.03
☐ 51 Greg Beatty	.25	.11	.03
☐ 52 Pete Beckman	.25	.11	.03
☐ 53 Matt Bonhaus	.25	.11	.03
☐ 54 Marlon Kerner	.50	.23	.06
☐ 55 Alan Kline	.25	.11	.03
☐ 56 Greg Kuszmaul	.25	.11	.03
☐ 57 Jim Otis	.40	.18	.05
Buckeye Flashback			
October 12, 1968			
☐ 58 Buckeye Flashback	.40	.18	.05
September 30, 1972			
☐ NNO Title Card CL	.40	.18	.05

1997 Ohio State

This fully laminated, limited edition set of the 1997 Ohio State Rose Bowl Champion Buckeyes is distributed by American Marketing Associates. The fronts feature full color player action shots with the team logo and a facsimile autograph printed in red across the bottom. The backs carry player information and the team 1996 season record. The cards are unnumbered and checklisted below in alphabetical order. Reportedly 4000 sets were produced.

	MINT	NRMT	EXC
COMPLETE SET (24)	30.00	13.50	3.70
COMMON CARD (1-24)	1.25	.55	.16
☐ 1 Greg Bellisari	1.50	.70	.19
☐ 2 Matt Calhoun	1.25	.55	.16
☐ 3 Shane Clark	1.25	.55	.16
☐ 4 Dan Colson	1.25	.55	.16
☐ 5 John Cooper CO	1.50	.70	.19
☐ 6 LeShun Daniels	1.25	.55	.16
☐ 7 Luke Fickell	1.25	.55	.16
☐ 8 Matt Finkes	2.00	.90	.25
☐ 9 Anthony Gwinn	1.50	.70	.19
☐ 10 Bob Houser	1.50	.70	.19
☐ 11 Ty Howard	1.50	.70	.19
☐ 12 Josh Jackson	1.25	.55	.16
☐ 13 D.J. Jones	1.25	.55	.16
☐ 14 Rob Kelly	1.50	.70	.19
☐ 15 Heath Knisely	1.25	.55	.16
☐ 16 Ryan Miller	1.25	.55	.16
☐ 17 Juan Porter	1.25	.55	.16
☐ 18 Chad Pulliam	1.25	.55	.16
☐ 19 Dimitrious Stanley	1.50	.70	.19
☐ 20 Buster Tillman	1.50	.70	.19
☐ 21 Mike Vrabel	2.00	.90	.25
☐ 22 American Marketing Associates	1.25	.55	.16
☐ 23 1997 Senior Rose Bowl Champions	1.50	.70	.19
☐ 24 Team Logo	1.25	.55	.16
☐ 25 Sponsor card	1.25	.55	.16

1982 Oklahoma Playing Cards

Manufactured for OU by TransMedia, these 56 playing cards measure approximately 2 3/8" by 3 3/8" and have rounded corners and the typical playing card finish. Some of the fronts feature color action shots, some carry black-and-white head shots, and still others have no photos at all, just text. The red backs carry the white OU logo. The set is checklisted below in playing card order by suits, with numbers assigned to Aces (1), Jacks (11), Queens (12), and Kings (13).

	MINT	NRMT	EXC
COMPLETE SET (56)	40.00	18.00	5.00
COMMON CARD	.50	.23	.06
☐ C1 Joe Washington	1.00	.45	.12
Action shot			
☐ C2 Coaches 1895-1934	.50	.23	.06

	MINT	NRMT	EXC
☐ C3 Buddy Burris	1.00	.45	.12
All-Americans 1946-48			
☐ C4 Buck McPhail	1.00	.45	.12
J.D.Roberts			
Max Boydston			
Kurt Burris			
All-Americans 1953-54			
☐ C5 Ralph Neely	1.00	.45	.12
Carl McAdams			
Bob Kalsu			
Steve Owens			
All-Americans 1963-69			
☐ C6 Kyle Davis	1.00	.45	.12
Tinker Owens			
Dewey Selmon			
Lee Roy Selmon			
All-Americans 1974-75			
☐ C7 Jim Weatherall 1951	1.00	.45	.12
☐ C8 Billy Vessels 1952	1.00	.45	.12
☐ C9 NCAA Champions 1955	1.00	.45	.12
☐ C10 Uwe Von Schamann	.50	.23	.06
Action shot			
☐ C11 Tony DiRienzo	.50	.23	.06
Action shot			
☐ C12 Joe Washington	1.00	.45	.12
Action shot			
☐ C13 Tinker Owens	1.00	.45	.12
Action shot			
☐ D1 Joe Washington	1.00	.45	.12
Action shot			
☐ D2 Coaches 1935-1982	.50	.23	.06
☐ D3 Jimmy Owens	1.00	.45	.12
Darrell Royal			
All-Americans 1949			
☐ D4 Bo Bolinger	1.00	.45	.12
Ed Gray			
Jerry Tubbs			
Terry McDonald			
All-Americans 1955-56			
☐ D5 Granville Liggins	1.00	.45	.12
Steve Zabel			
Ken Mendenhall			
Jack Mildren			
All-Americans 1966-71			
☐ D6 Terry Webb	1.00	.45	.12
Billy Brooks			
Jimbo Elrod			
Mike Vaughan			
All-Americans 1975-76			
☐ D7 J.D. Roberts 1953	1.00	.45	.12
☐ D8 Steve Owens 1969	1.50	.70	.19
☐ D9 NCAA Champions 1956	1.00	.45	.12
☐ D10 Barry Switzer CO	.50	.23	.06
☐ D11 Lucius Selmon	.50	.23	.06
Action shot			
☐ D12 Elvis Peacock	.50	.23	.06
Action shot			
☐ D13 Billy Sims	1.00	.45	.12
Action shot			
☐ H1 Jimbo Elrod	.50	.23	.06
Action shot			
☐ H2 All-Americans 1913-37	1.00	.45	.12
☐ H3 Jim Weatherall	1.00	.45	.12
All-Americans 1949-51			
☐ H4 Bill Krisher	1.00	.45	.12
Clendon Thomas			
Bob Harrison			
Jerry Thompson			
All-Americans 1957-59			
☐ H5 Greg Pruitt	1.00	.45	.12
Tom Brahaney			
Derland Moore			
Rod Shoate			
All-Americans 1971-74			
☐ H6 Zac Henderson	1.00	.45	.12
Greg Roberts			
Daryl Hunt			
George Cumby			
All-Americans 1976-78			
☐ H7 Lee Roy Selmon 1975	1.50	.70	.19
☐ H8 Billy Sims 1978	1.50	.70	.19
☐ H9 NCAA Champions 1974	1.00	.45	.12
☐ H10 Lee Roy Selmon	1.00	.45	.12
Action shot			
☐ H11 Tinker Owens	.50	.23	.06
Action shot			
☐ H12 Action shot	.50	.23	.06
☐ H13 Lee Roy Selmon	1.00	.45	.12
Action shot			
☐ S1 Horace Ivory	.50	.23	.06
Action shot			
☐ S2 All-Americans 1938-46	1.00	.45	.12
☐ S3 Tom Catlin	1.00	.45	.12
Billy Vessels			
Eddie Crowder			
All-Americans 1951-52			
☐ S4 Leon Cross	1.00	.45	.12
Wayne Lee			
Jim Grisham			
Joe Don Looney			
All-Americans 1962-63			
☐ S5 Lucius Selmon	1.00	.45	.12
Eddie Foster			
John Roush			
Joe Washington			

	MINT	NRMT	EXC
All-Americans 1973-75			
☐ S6 Reggie Kinlaw	1.00	.45	.12
Billy Sims			
Louis Oubre			
Terry Crouch			
All-Americans 1978-81			
☐ S7 Greg Roberts 1978	1.00	.45	.12
☐ S8 NCAA Champions 1950	1.00	.45	.12
☐ S9 NCAA Champions 1975	1.00	.45	.12
☐ S10 Bobby Proctor CO	.50	.23	.06
Action shot			
☐ S11 Steve Davis	.50	.23	.06
Action shot			
☐ S12 Greg Pruitt	1.00	.45	.12
Action shot			
☐ S13 Elvis Peacock	.50	.23	.06
Action shot			
☐ JK1 Sooner Schooner	.50	.23	.06
☐ JK2 Sooner Schooner	.50	.23	.06
☐ NNO Mail order card	.50	.23	.06
☐ NNO Mail order card	.50	.23	.06

1986 Oklahoma

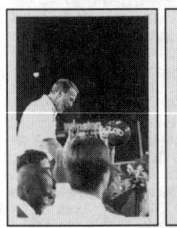

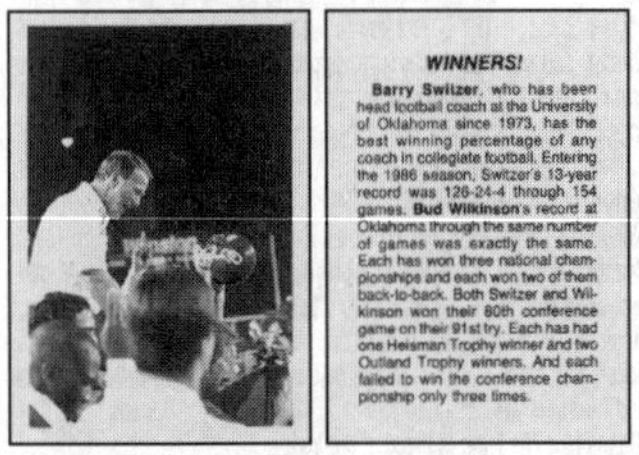

WINNERS!
Barry Switzer, who has been head football coach at the University of Oklahoma since 1973, has the best winning percentage of any coach in collegiate football. Entering the 1986 season, Switzer's 13-year record was 126-24-4 through 154 games. Bud Wilkinson's record at Oklahoma through the same number of games was exactly the same. Each has won three national championships and each won two of them back-to-back. Both Switzer and Wilkinson won their 80th straight conference game on their 91st try. Each has had one Heisman Trophy winner and two Outland Trophy winners. And each failed to win the conference championship only three times.

The 1986 Oklahoma National Championship set contains 16 unnumbered, standard-size cards. The fronts are 'pure' with color photos, thin white borders and no printing; the backs describe the front photos. These cards were printed on very thin stock. This set sports several unusual and/or attractive pictures.

	MINT	NRMT	EXC
COMPLETE SET (16)	8.00	3.60	1.00
COMMON CARD (1-16)	.35	.16	.04
☐ 1 Championship Ring	.50	.23	.06
1985 National Champs			
☐ 2 Orange Bowl	.35	.16	.04
(In Bowl Play)			
☐ 3 On the Road to Record	.35	.16	.04
☐ 4 Graduation Record	.35	.16	.04
☐ 5 Lawrence G. Rawl	.35	.16	.04
President of Exxon			
☐ 6 Barry Switzer	1.50	.70	.19
(Winners)			
☐ 7 Win Streaks Hold	.35	.16	.04
Records			
☐ 8 Brian Bosworth	1.00	.45	.12
☐ 9 Heisman Trophy	.75	.35	.09
Billy Vessels 1952			
Steve Owens 1969			
Billy Sims 1978			
☐ 10 All-America Sooners	.75	.35	.09
(Tony Casillas)			
☐ 11 Jamelle Holieway	.50	.23	.06
☐ 12 Sooner Strength	.35	.16	.04
☐ 13 Sooner Support	.35	.16	.04
☐ 14 Go Sooners	.35	.16	.04
(Crimson and Cream)			
☐ 15 Border Battle	.50	.23	.06
(Oklahoma vs. Texas)			
☐ 16 Barry Switzer CO SP	2.50	1.10	.30
(Caricature; "I Want			
You ...; '86 OU foot-			
ball schedule on back)			

1986 Oklahoma McDag

The 1986 Oklahoma McDag set contains 16 standard-size cards printed on very thin stock. The fronts have color action photos bordered in white; the vertically oriented backs have brief career highlights and safety tips. The cards are unnumbered, so they are listed alphabetically by player's name. The key card in the set features tight end Keith Jackson.

	MINT	NRMT	EXC
COMPLETE SET (16)	20.00	9.00	2.50
COMMON CARD (1-16)	1.00	.45	.12
☐ 1 Brian Bosworth	3.00	1.35	.35
☐ 2 Sonny Brown	1.00	.45	.12

	MINT	NRMT	EXC
☐ 3 Steve Bryan	1.00	.45	.12
☐ 4 Lydell Carr	1.50	.70	.19
☐ 5 Patrick Collins	1.50	.70	.19
☐ 6 Jamelle Holieway	2.00	.90	.25
☐ 7 Mark Hutson	1.00	.45	.12
☐ 8 Keith Jackson	6.00	2.70	.75
☐ 9 Troy Johnson	1.00	.45	.12
☐ 10 Dante Jones	3.00	1.35	.35
☐ 11 Tim Lashar	1.00	.45	.12
☐ 12 Paul Migliazzo	1.00	.45	.12
☐ 13 Anthony Phillips	1.00	.45	.12
☐ 14 Darrell Reed	1.00	.45	.12
☐ 15 Derrick Shepard	1.50	.70	.19
☐ 16 Spencer Tillman	1.50	.70	.19

1987 Oklahoma Police

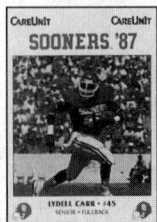
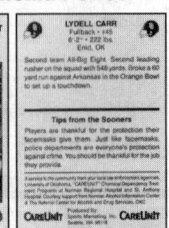

The 1987 Oklahoma Police set consists of 16 standard-size cards printed on thin card stock. The fronts feature color action player photos on a white card face. CareUnit logos and the words 'Sooners '87' are printed in the top margin, while player information between two helmets fill the bottom margin. The backs carry player biography, career highlights, and "Tips from the Sooners" in the form of anti-crime messages. The cards are unnumbered and checklisted below according to uniform number.

	MINT	NRMT	EXC
COMPLETE SET (16)	18.00	8.00	2.20
COMMON CARD	.75	.35	.09
☐ 1 Eric Mitchel	1.25	.55	.16
☐ 4 Jamelle Holieway	2.00	.90	.25
☐ 10 David Vickers	.75	.35	.09
☐ 25 Anthony Stafford	1.25	.55	.16
☐ 29 Rickey Dixon	2.00	.90	.25
☐ 33 Patrick Collins	1.25	.55	.16
☐ 40 Darrell Reed	.75	.35	.09
☐ 45 Lydell Carr	1.25	.55	.16
☐ 50 Dante Jones	2.00	.90	.25
☐ 66 Jon Phillips and	.75	.35	.09
68 Anthony Phillips			
☐ 75 Greg Johnson	.75	.35	.09
☐ 79 Mark Hutson	.75	.35	.09
☐ 80 Troy Johnson	.75	.35	.09
☐ 88 Keith Jackson	6.00	2.70	.75
☐ 98 Dante Williams	.75	.35	.09
☐ NNO Barry Switzer CO	3.00	1.35	.35

1988 Oklahoma Greats

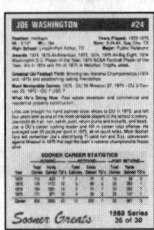

The 1988 Oklahoma Greats set features 30 standard-size cards. The fronts have color photos bordered in white and red. The vertically oriented backs feature detailed biographical information, statistics, and highlights.

	MINT	NRMT	EXC
COMPLETE SET (30)	8.00	3.60	1.00
COMMON CARD (1-30)	.25	.11	.03
☐ 1 Jerry Anderson	.25	.11	.03
☐ 2 Dee Andros	.40	.18	.05
☐ 3 Dean Blevins	.25	.11	.03
☐ 4 Rick Bryan	.50	.23	.06
☐ 5 Paul(Buddy) Burris	.25	.11	.03
☐ 6 Eddie Crowder	.40	.18	.05
☐ 7 Jack Ging	.25	.11	.03
☐ 8 Jim Grisham	.40	.18	.05
☐ 9 Jimmy Harris	.40	.18	.05
☐ 10 Scott Hill	.25	.11	.03
☐ 11 Eddie Hinton	.40	.18	.05
☐ 12 Earl Johnson	.25	.11	.03
☐ 13 Don Key	.25	.11	.03
☐ 14 Tim Lashar	.25	.11	.03
☐ 15 Granville Liggins	.50	.23	.06
☐ 16 Thomas Lott	.40	.18	.05
☐ 17 Carl McAdams	.40	.18	.05
☐ 18 Jack Mitchell	.40	.18	.05
☐ 19 Billy Pricer	.25	.11	.03
☐ 20 John Roush	.25	.11	.03

☐ 21 Darrell Royal	.50	.23	.06
☐ 22 Lucious Selmon	.40	.18	.05
☐ 23 Ron Shotts	.25	.11	.03
☐ 24 Jerry Tubbs	.40	.18	.05
☐ 25 Bob Warmack	.25	.11	.03
☐ 26 Joe Washington	.50	.23	.06
☐ 27 Jim Weatherall	.40	.18	.05
☐ 28 '86 Sooner Great Game	.25	.11	.03
☐ 29 '75 Sooners	.25	.11	.03
☐ 30 Checklist Card	.40	.18	.05

1988 Oklahoma Police

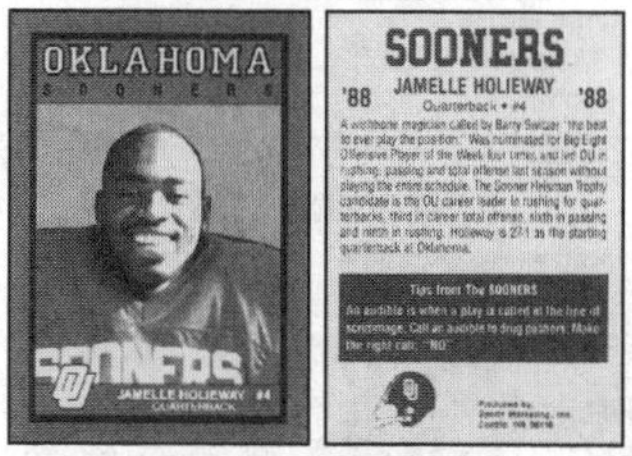

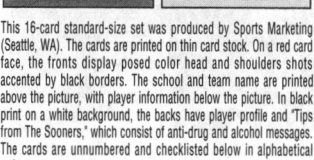

This 16-card standard-size set was produced by Sports Marketing (Seattle, WA). The cards are printed on thin card stock. On a red card face, the fronts display posed color head and shoulders shots accented by black borders. The school and team name are printed above the picture, with player information below the picture. In black print on a white background, the backs have player profile and "Tips from The Sooners," which consist of anti-drug and alcohol messages. The cards are unnumbered and checklisted below in alphabetical order.

	MINT	NRMT	EXC
COMPLETE SET (16)	18.00	8.00	2.20
COMMON CARD (1-16)	1.00	.45	.12
☐ 1 Rotnei Anderson	1.50	.70	.19
☐ 2 Eric Bross	1.00	.45	.12
☐ 3 Mike Gaddis	2.00	.90	.25
☐ 4 Scott Garl	1.00	.45	.12
☐ 5 James Goode	1.00	.45	.12
☐ 6 Jamelle Holieway	2.00	.90	.25
☐ 7 Bob Latham	1.00	.45	.12
☐ 8 Ken McMichel	1.00	.45	.12
☐ 9 Eric Mitchel	1.50	.70	.19
☐ 10 Leon Perry	1.50	.70	.19
☐ 11 Anthony Phillips	1.00	.45	.12
☐ 12 Anthony Stafford	1.50	.70	.19
☐ 13 Barry Switzer CO	4.00	1.80	.50
☐ 14 Mark Vankeirsbilck	1.00	.45	.12
☐ 15 Curtice Williams	1.00	.45	.12
☐ 16 Dante Williams	1.00	.45	.12

1989 Oklahoma Police

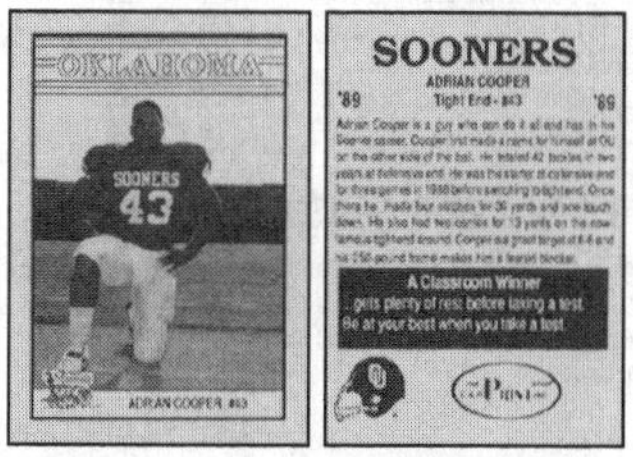

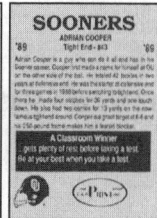

This 16-card standard-size set was produced by The C and R Print Shop Inc. and features members of the Oklahoma Sooners football team. The fronts feature posed color player photos inside a black picture frame with white outer borders. The players are pictured in uniform with one knee on the ground. The school name appears above the picture in red print and accented by black horizontal lines; the player's name, number, and the team's logo (a covered wagon) are printed below the picture. The backs present a player profile and, in a black box, a tip for becoming "A Classroom Winner." The team helmet and the producer's logo round out the back. The cards are unnumbered and checklisted below in alphabetical order.

	MINT	NRMT	EXC
COMPLETE SET (16)	15.00	6.75	1.85
COMMON CARD (1-16)	1.00	.45	.12
☐ 1 Tom Backes	1.00	.45	.12
☐ 2 Frank Blevins	1.00	.45	.12
☐ 3 Eric Bross	1.00	.45	.12
☐ 4 Adrian Cooper	3.00	1.35	.35
☐ 5 Scott Evans	1.00	.45	.12
☐ 6 Mike Gaddis	2.00	.90	.25
☐ 7 Gary Gibbs CO	1.50	.70	.19
☐ 8 James Goode	1.00	.45	.12
☐ 9 Ken McMichel	1.00	.45	.12
☐ 10 Leon Perry	1.50	.70	.19
☐ 11 Mike Sawatzky	1.00	.45	.12
☐ 12 Don Smitherman	1.00	.45	.12
☐ 13 Kevin Thompson	1.00	.45	.12
☐ 14 Mark VanKeirsbilck	1.00	.45	.12
☐ 15 Mike Wise	1.00	.45	.12
☐ 16 Dante Williams	1.00	.45	.12

1990 Oklahoma Police

This (16??)-card Police set was sponsored by the Bank of Oklahoma and given away during the season. The standard sized cards feature color player photos with many of the players posed with one knee on the ground. The border trim and school name at top were printed in red. The player's name is printed in capital lettering beneath the picture. The cardbacks list career highlights and a player quote in the form of safety messages. The cards are unnumbered and arranged below alphabetically. Any additional information on this set would be greatly appreciated.

	MINT	NRMT	EXC
COMPLETE SET (7)	8.00	3.60	1.00
COMMON CARD (1-7)	1.00	.45	.12
☐ 1 Joe Bowden	2.00	.90	.25
☐ 2 Scott Evans	1.00	.45	.12
☐ 3 Mike Gaddis	1.50	.70	.19
☐ 4 James Goode	1.00	.45	.12
☐ 5 Arthur Guess	1.00	.45	.12
☐ 6 Mike McKinley	1.00	.45	.12
☐ 7 Randy Wallace	1.00	.45	.12

1991 Oklahoma Police

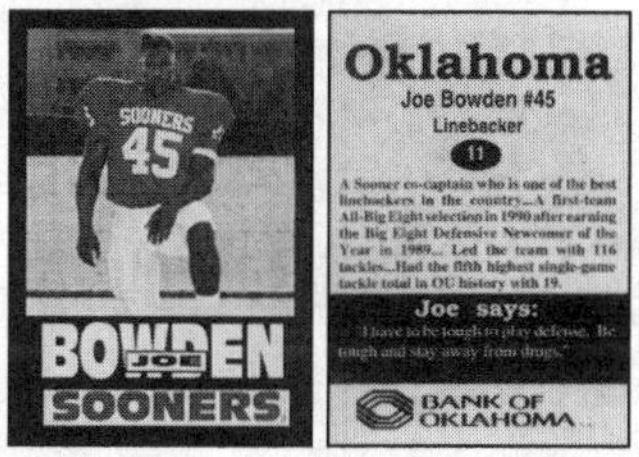

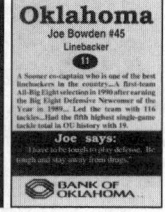

This 16-card Police set was sponsored by the Bank of Oklahoma and given away during the season. The cards were issued on an uncut sheet measuring approximately 10 1/2" by 17". If the cards were cut, each would measure approximately 2 1/2" by 4 1/4". The fronts feature color player photos with the players posed with one knee on the ground. The borders are black. The player's name and team name are printed in large block lettering beneath the picture. The backs list career highlights and a player quote in the form of anti-drug messages. The cards are numbered on the back in a black oval.

	MINT	NRMT	EXC
COMPLETE SET (16)	15.00	6.75	1.85
COMMON CARD (1-16)	1.00	.45	.12
☐ 1 Gary Gibbs CO	1.50	.70	.19
☐ 2 Cale Gundy	2.00	.90	.25
☐ 3 Charles Franks	1.00	.45	.12
☐ 4 Mike Gaddis	1.50	.70	.19
☐ 5 Brad Reddell	1.00	.45	.12
☐ 6 Brandon Houston	1.00	.45	.12
☐ 7 Chris Wilson	1.00	.45	.12
☐ 8 Darnell Walker	1.00	.45	.12
☐ 9 Mike McKinley	1.00	.45	.12
☐ 10 Kenyon Rasheed	2.00	.90	.25
☐ 11 Joe Bowden	2.00	.90	.25
☐ 12 Jason Belser	2.00	.90	.25
☐ 13 Steve Collins	1.00	.45	.12
☐ 14 Reggie Barnes	1.00	.45	.12
☐ 15 Randy Wallace	1.00	.45	.12
☐ 16 Proctor Land	1.00	.45	.12

1953 Oregon

This 20-card set measures the standard size. The fronts feature a posed action photo, with player information appearing in handwritten script in a white box toward the bottom of the picture. Below the motto "Football is Fun," the backs have a list of locations where adult tickets can be purchased and a Knothole Gang membership offer. The cards are unnumbered and checklisted below in alphabetical order.

	NRMT	VG-E	GOOD
COMPLETE SET (20)	400.00	180.00	50.00
COMMON CARD (1-20)	20.00	9.00	2.50
☐ 1 Farrell Albright	25.00	11.00	3.10
☐ 2 Ted Anderson	20.00	9.00	2.50
☐ 3 Len Berrie	20.00	9.00	2.50
☐ 4 Tom Elliott	20.00	9.00	2.50
☐ 5 Tim Flaherty	20.00	9.00	2.50
☐ 6 Cecil Hodges	20.00	9.00	2.50
☐ 7 Barney Holland	20.00	9.00	2.50
☐ 8 Dick James	30.00	13.50	3.70
☐ 9 Harry Johnson	20.00	9.00	2.50
☐ 10 Dave Lowe	20.00	9.00	2.50
☐ 11 Jack Patera	40.00	18.00	5.00
☐ 12 Ron Pheister	25.00	11.00	3.10
☐ 13 John Reed	20.00	9.00	2.50
☐ 14 Hal Reeve	25.00	11.00	3.10
☐ 15 Larry Rose	20.00	9.00	2.50
☐ 16 George Shaw	30.00	13.50	3.70
☐ 17 Lon Stiner Jr.	20.00	9.00	2.50
☐ 18 Ken Sweitzer	20.00	9.00	2.50
☐ 19 Keith Tucker	20.00	9.00	2.50
☐ 20 Dean Van Leuven	20.00	9.00	2.50

1956 Oregon

This 19-card set measures the standard size. The fronts feature a posed action photo, with player information appearing in a white box toward the bottom of the picture. Below the motto "Follow the Ducks," the backs have schedule information and a list of locations where adult tickets can be purchased. The cards are unnumbered and checklisted below in alphabetical order.

	NRMT	VG-E	GOOD
COMPLETE SET (19)	325.00	145.00	40.00
COMMON CARD (1-19)	20.00	9.00	2.50
☐ 1 Bruce Brenn	20.00	9.00	2.50
☐ 2 Jack Brown	20.00	9.00	2.50
☐ 3 Reanous Cochran	20.00	9.00	2.50
☐ 4 Jack Crabtree	25.00	11.00	3.10
☐ 5 Tom Crabtree	20.00	9.00	2.50
☐ 6 Tom Hale	20.00	9.00	2.50
☐ 7 Spike Hillstrom	20.00	9.00	2.50
☐ 8 Jim Linden	20.00	9.00	2.50
☐ 9 Hank Loumena	20.00	9.00	2.50
☐ 10 Nick Markulis	20.00	9.00	2.50
☐ 11 Phil McHugh	20.00	9.00	2.50
☐ 13 Harry Mondale	20.00	9.00	2.50
☐ 14 Leroy Phelps	20.00	9.00	2.50
☐ 15 Jack Pocock	20.00	9.00	2.50
☐ 16 John Roventos	20.00	9.00	2.50
☐ 17 Jim Shanley	20.00	9.00	2.50
☐ 18 Ron Stover	25.00	11.00	3.10
☐ 19 J.C. Wheeler	20.00	9.00	2.50

1958 Oregon

This 20-card set measures approximately 2 1/4" by 3 9/16". The fronts feature a posed action player photo with player information in the white border beneath the picture. The cards are unnumbered and checklisted below in alphabetical order.

	NRMT	VG-E	GOOD
COMPLETE SET (20)	350.00	160.00	45.00
COMMON CARD (1-20)	20.00	9.00	2.50
☐ 1 Greg Altenhofen	20.00	9.00	2.50
☐ 2 Darrel Aschbacher	25.00	11.00	3.10
☐ 3 Dave Fish	20.00	9.00	2.50
☐ 4 Sandy Fraser	20.00	9.00	2.50
☐ 5 Dave Grosz	25.00	11.00	3.10
☐ 6 Bob Grottkau	25.00	11.00	3.10
☐ 7 Marlan Holland	20.00	9.00	2.50
☐ 8 Tom Keele	20.00	9.00	2.50
☐ 9 Alden Kimbrough	20.00	9.00	2.50
☐ 10 Don Laudenslager	20.00	9.00	2.50
☐ 11 Riley Mattson	30.00	13.50	3.70
☐ 12 Bob Peterson	20.00	9.00	2.50
☐ 13 Dave Powell	20.00	9.00	2.50
☐ 14 Len Read	20.00	9.00	2.50
☐ 15 Will Reeve	20.00	9.00	2.50
☐ 16 Joe Schaffeld	20.00	9.00	2.50
☐ 17 Charlie Tourville	20.00	9.00	2.50
☐ 18 Dave Urell	20.00	9.00	2.50
☐ 19 Pete Welch	20.00	9.00	2.50
☐ 20 Willie West	30.00	13.50	3.70

1991 Oregon Smokey

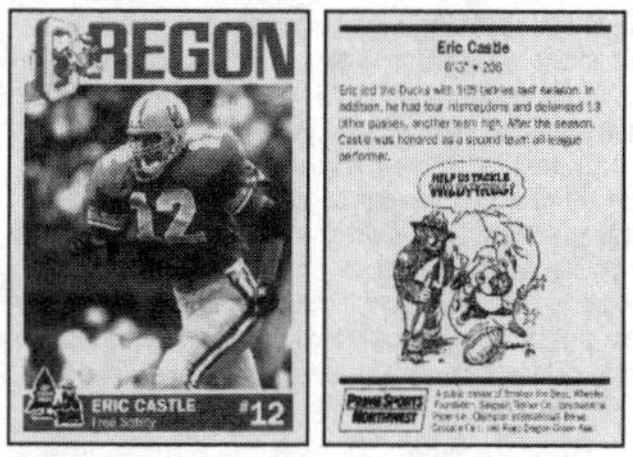

This 12-card (approximately 3" by 4") set was issued as a perforated sheet. Distinctive green and gold fronts feature player action photos printed on white card stock. Oregon appears at the top of each picture while the Smokey logo, player name, position, and number are reversed-out white letters in the green bar at the bottom. The backs have biographical information and a fire prevention cartoon starring Smokey the Bear. The cards are unnumbered and checklisted below in alphabetical order.

	MINT	NRMT	EXC
COMPLETE SET (12)	12.00	5.50	1.50
COMMON CARD (1-12)	1.00	.45	.12
☐ 1 Bud Bowie	1.00	.45	.12
☐ 2 Rich Brooks CO	3.00	1.35	.35
☐ 3 Sean Burwell	1.00	.45	.12
☐ 4 Eric Castle	1.50	.70	.19
☐ 5 Andy Conner	1.00	.45	.12
☐ 6 Joe Farwell	1.00	.45	.12
☐ 7 Matt LaBounty	1.50	.70	.19
☐ 8 Gregg McCallum	1.00	.45	.12
☐ 9 Daryle Smith	1.00	.45	.12
☐ 10 Jeff Thomason	1.50	.70	.19
☐ 11 Tommy Thompson	1.00	.45	.12
☐ 12 Marcus Woods	1.25	.55	.16

1988 Oregon State Smokey

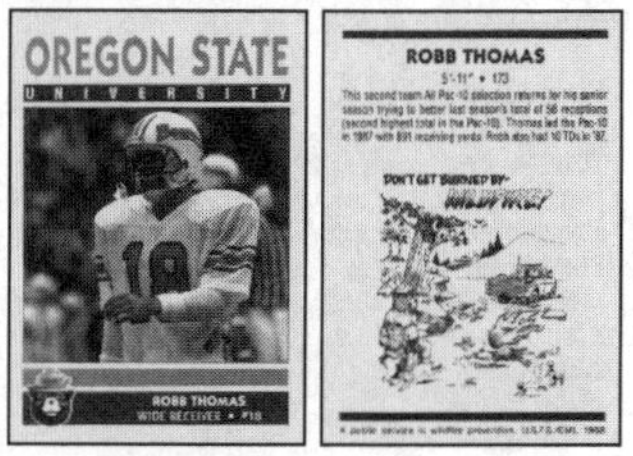

The 1988 Oregon State Smokey set contains 12 standard-size cards. The fronts feature color action photos with name, position, and jersey number. The vertically oriented backs have brief career highlights as well as a brief message from Smokey. The cards are unnumbered, but listed alphabetically below.

	MINT	NRMT	EXC
COMPLETE SET (12)	12.00	5.50	1.50
COMMON CARD (1-12)	1.25	.55	.16
☐ 1 Troy Bussanich	1.25	.55	.16
☐ 2 Andre Harris	1.25	.55	.16
☐ 3 Teddy Johnson	1.25	.55	.16
☐ 4 Jason Kent	1.25	.55	.16
☐ 5 Dave Kragthorpe CO	1.25	.55	.16
☐ 6 Mike Matthews	1.25	.55	.16
☐ 7 Phil Ross	1.25	.55	.16
☐ 8 Brian Taylor	1.25	.55	.16
☐ 9 Robb Thomas	2.50	1.10	.30
☐ 10 Esera Tuaolo	2.00	.90	.25
☐ 11 Erik Wilhelm	2.50	1.10	.30
☐ 12 Dowell Williams	1.25	.55	.16

1990 Oregon State Smokey

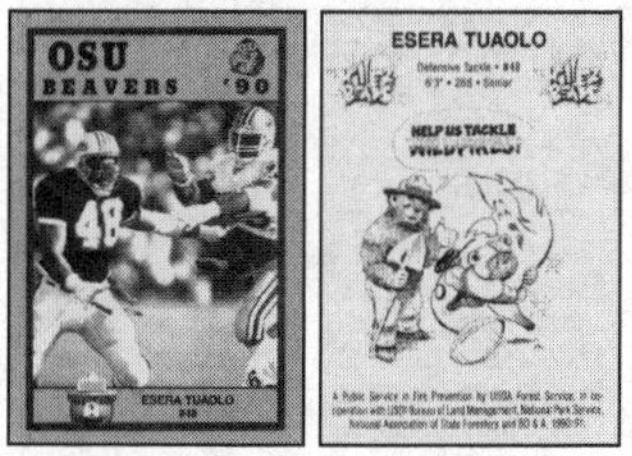

This 16-card set was sponsored by the USDA Forest Service in cooperation with other federal and state agencies. The cards were issued on a sheet with four rows of four cards each; after perforation, they measure the standard size. The fronts feature a mix of color action or posed shots of the players, with black lettering and borders on an orange card face. The backs have player information and a fire prevention cartoon starring Smokey. The cards are unnumbered and checklisted below in alphabetical order.

	MINT	NRMT	EXC
COMPLETE SET (16)	12.00	5.50	1.50
COMMON CARD (1-16)	1.00	.45	.12
☐ 1 Brian Beck	1.00	.45	.12
☐ 2 Martin Billings	1.00	.45	.12
☐ 3 Matt Booher	1.00	.45	.12
☐ 4 George Breland	1.00	.45	.12
☐ 5 Brad D'Ancona	1.00	.45	.12
☐ 6 Dennis Edwards	1.00	.45	.12
☐ 7 Brent Huff	1.00	.45	.12
☐ 8 James Jones	1.00	.45	.12
☐ 9 Dave Kragthorpe CO	1.00	.45	.12
☐ 10 Todd McKinney	1.00	.45	.12
☐ 11 Torey Overstreet	1.00	.45	.12
☐ 12 Reggie Pitchford	1.00	.45	.12
☐ 13 Todd Sahlfeld	1.00	.45	.12
☐ 14 Scott Thompson	1.00	.45	.12
☐ 15 Esera Tuaolo	1.50	.70	.19
☐ 16 Maurice Wilson	1.00	.45	.12

1991 Oregon State Smokey

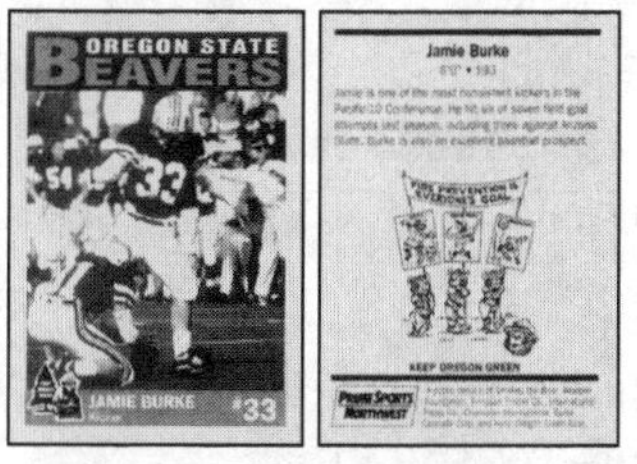

This 12-card set was sponsored by Prime Sports Northwest and other companies to promote fire safety in Oregon. The oversized cards were issued as a perforated sheet and measure approximately 3" by 4". The fronts feature action player photos banded by a black stripe above and an orange stripe below. A Smokey logo and player information are given in the bottom orange stripe. Horizontally oriented backs present career summary and a fire prevention cartoon starring Smokey. The cards are unnumbered and checklisted below in alphabetical order.

	MINT	NRMT	EXC
COMPLETE SET (12)	10.00	4.50	1.25
COMMON CARD (1-12)	1.00	.45	.12
☐ 1 Adam Albaugh	1.00	.45	.12
☐ 2 Jamie Burke	1.00	.45	.12
☐ 3 Chad de Sully	1.00	.45	.12
☐ 4 Dennis Edwards	1.00	.45	.12
☐ 5 James Jones	1.00	.45	.12
☐ 6 Fletcher Keister	1.00	.45	.12
☐ 7 Tom Nordquist	1.00	.45	.12
☐ 8 Tony O'Billovich	1.25	.55	.16
☐ 9 Jerry Pettibone CO	1.25	.55	.16
☐ 10 Mark Price	1.00	.45	.12
☐ 11 Todd Sahlfeld	1.00	.45	.12
☐ 12 Earl Zackery	1.00	.45	.12

1992 Oregon State Smokey

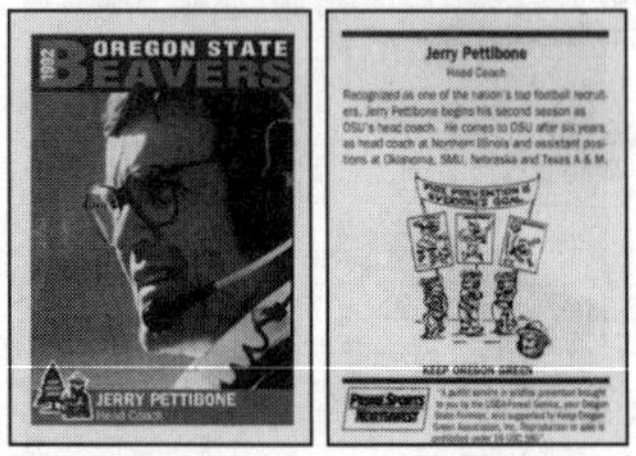

Sponsored by Prime Sports Northwest, this 12-card set was issued on thin card stock as a perforated sheet; after perforation, each card would measure approximately 3" by 4". The fronts show color player photos bordered in white. The school and team name appear in a black bar above the picture, while the player's name, jersey number, and position are printed on a orange bar beneath the picture. In black print on a white background, the backs feature a player profile and a fire prevention cartoon starring Smokey. The cards are unnumbered and checklisted below in alphabetical order.

	MINT	NRMT	EXC
COMPLETE SET (12)	9.00	4.00	1.10
COMMON CARD (1-12)	.75	.35	.09
☐ 1 Zechariah Davis	.75	.35	.09
☐ 2 Chad De Sully	.75	.35	.09
☐ 3 Michael Hale	.75	.35	.09
☐ 4 Fletcher Keister	.75	.35	.09
☐ 5 Chad Paulson	.75	.35	.09
☐ 6 Rico Petrini	.75	.35	.09
☐ 7 Jerry Pettibone CO	1.00	.45	.12
☐ 8 Sailusi Poulivaati	.75	.35	.09
☐ 9 Tony O'Billovich	1.00	.45	.12
☐ 10 Dwayne Owens	.75	.35	.09
☐ 11 J.J. Young	1.50	.70	.19
☐ 12 Maurice Wilson	.75	.35	.09

1994 Oregon State Smokey

Sponsored by Prime Sports Northwest, this 12-card set was issued on thin card stock as a perforated sheet; after perforation, each card would measure approximately 3" by 4". The fronts show color player photos bordered in white. The school, team name and year appear in a black bar above the picture, while the player's name and position are printed on a orange bar beneath the picture. In black print on a white background, the backs feature a player profile and a fire prevention cartoon starring Smokey. The cards are unnumbered and checklisted below in alphabetical order.

	MINT	NRMT	EXC
COMPLETE SET (12)	9.00	4.00	1.10
COMMON CARD (1-12)	.75	.35	.09
☐ 1 William Ephraim	.75	.35	.09
☐ 2 Johnny Feinga	.75	.35	.09
☐ 3 John Garrett	.75	.35	.09
☐ 4 Michael Hale	.75	.35	.09
☐ 5 Tom Holmes	.75	.35	.09
☐ 6 Cory Huot	.75	.35	.09
☐ 7 Rico Petrini	.75	.35	.09
☐ 8 Cameron Reynolds	.75	.35	.09
☐ 9 Kane Rogers	.75	.35	.09
☐ 10 Don Shanklin	1.00	.45	.12
☐ 11 Reggie Tongue	1.25	.55	.16
☐ 12 J.J.Young	1.00	.45	.12

1988 Penn State

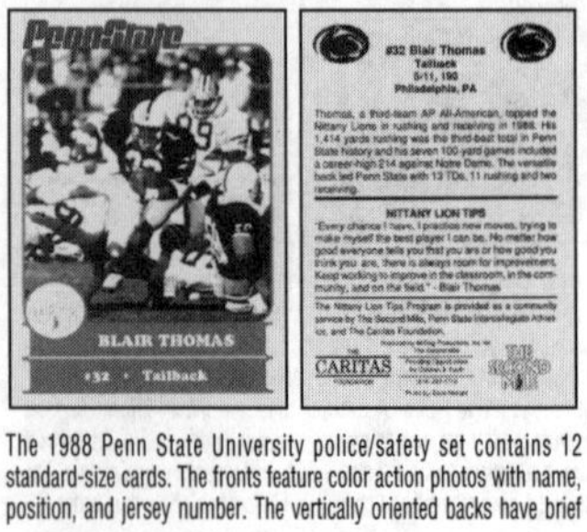

The 1988 Penn State University police/safety set contains 12 standard-size cards. The fronts feature color action photos with name, position, and jersey number. The vertically oriented backs have brief career highlights and "Nittany Lion Tips". The set was produced by McDag Productions. The set is subtitled "The Second Mile" on the front and back of each card. The set is unnumbered and hence are numbered by uniform number which is given on both sides of each player's card.

	MINT	NRMT	EXC
COMPLETE SET (12)	25.00	11.00	3.10
COMMON CARD	1.25	.55	.16
☐ 5 Michael Timpson	4.00	1.80	.50
☐ 20 John Greene	1.25	.55	.16
☐ 28 Brian Chizmar	1.25	.55	.16
☐ 31 Andre Collins	4.00	1.80	.50
☐ 32 Blair Thomas	4.00	1.80	.50
☐ 39 Eddie Johnson	1.25	.55	.16
☐ 66 Steve Wisniewski	4.00	1.80	.50
☐ 75 Rich Schonewolf	1.25	.55	.16
☐ 78 Roger Duffy	1.50	.70	.19
☐ 84 Keith Karpinski	1.50	.70	.19
☐ NNO Joe Paterno CO	6.00	2.70	.75
☐ NNO Penn State Mascot The Nittany Lion	1.50	.70	.19

1989 Penn State

This 15-card standard-size set was sponsored by "The Second Mile" (a non-profit organization) in conjunction with IBM. The fronts feature a mix of action and posed player photos, with the player's name and position listed below the picture. The backs carry career highlights and "Nittany Lion Tips." The cards are unnumbered and checklisted below in alphabetical order.

	MINT	NRMT	EXC
COMPLETE SET (15)	20.00	9.00	2.50
COMMON CARD (1-15)	1.00	.45	.12
☐ 1 Brian Chizmar	1.00	.45	.12
☐ 2 Andre Collins	2.50	1.10	.30
☐ 3 David Daniels	2.50	1.10	.30
☐ 4 Roger Duffy	1.25	.55	.16
☐ 5 Tim Freeman	1.00	.45	.12
☐ 6 Scott Gob	1.00	.45	.12
☐ 7 David Jakob	1.00	.45	.12
☐ 8 Geoff Japchen	1.00	.45	.12
☐ 9 Joe Paterno CO	5.00	2.20	.60
☐ 10 Sherrod Rainge	1.00	.45	.12
☐ 11 Rich Schonewolf	1.00	.45	.12
☐ 12 David Szott	2.50	1.10	.30
☐ 13 Blair Thomas	2.50	1.10	.30
☐ 14 Leroy Thompson	2.50	1.10	.30
☐ 15 Nittany Lion (Mascot)	1.00	.45	.12

1990 Penn State

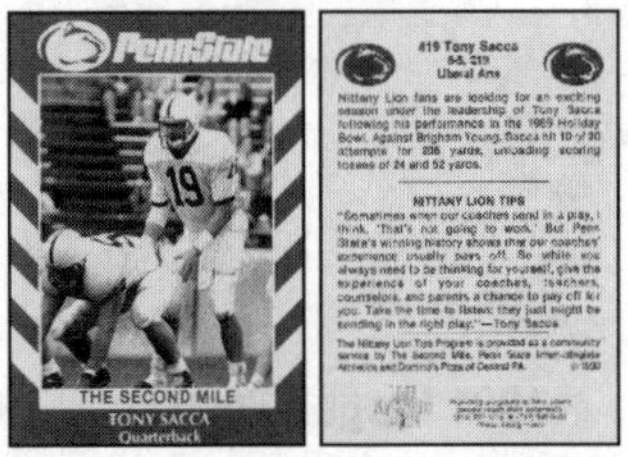

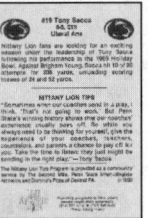

The 16-card police/safety standard-size set was sponsored by "The Second Mile," a nonprofit organization that helps needy children. The set was underwritten in part by the Mellon Family Foundation. The cards are printed on thin card stock. The fronts display a mix of posed or action color photos, with solid blue borders above and below, and blue and white striped borders on the sides. The school logo and name are printed in the top blue border while the sponsor's name and player information appear beneath the picture. The backs have brief biographical information, player profile, and "Nittany Lion Tips" in the form of player quotes. A sponsor advertisement at the bottom rounds out the card back. The cards are unnumbered and checklisted below in alphabetical order.

	MINT	NRMT	EXC
COMPLETE SET (16)	18.00	8.00	2.20
COMMON CARD (1-16)	.75	.35	.09
☐ 1 Gerry Collins	.75	.35	.09
☐ 2 David Daniels	1.25	.55	.16
☐ 3 Jim Deter	.75	.35	.09
☐ 4 Mark D'Onofrio	1.25	.55	.16
☐ 5 Sam Gash	2.00	.90	.25
☐ 6 Frank Giannetti	.75	.35	.09
☐ 7 Keith Goganious	1.25	.55	.16
☐ 8 Doug Helkowski	.75	.35	.09
☐ 9 Hernon Henderson	.75	.35	.09
☐ 10 Matt McCartin	.75	.35	.09
☐ 11 Joe Paterno CO	4.00	1.80	.50
☐ 12 Darren Perry	2.00	.90	.25
☐ 13 Tony Sacca	2.00	.90	.25
☐ 14 Terry Smith	.75	.35	.09
☐ 15 Willie Thomas	.75	.35	.09
☐ 16 Leroy Thompson	2.00	.90	.25

1991 Penn State Book Store

The Penn State Book Store offered this 9-card set printed on one perforated sheet. Each unnumbered card includes a Penn State football highlight with the featured player mentioned only on the cardback.

	MINT	NRMT	EXC
COMPLETE SET (9)	12.00	5.50	1.50
COMMON CARD (1-9)	1.50	.70	.19
☐ 1 Anything But the Pits Kenny Jackson	1.50	.70	.19
☐ 2 A Defensive Fiesta Don Graham sacking Vinny Testaverde	1.50	.70	.19
☐ 3 Miracle of Mount Nittany Kirk Bowman	1.50	.70	.19
☐ 4 Nittany Lions Turn the Tide Tim Johnson Shane Conlan	2.00	.90	.25
☐ 5 Orangemen Get Run Over John Shaffer	1.50	.70	.19
☐ 6 Quieting the Echoes Curt Warner	2.00	.90	.25
☐ 7 Run For No. 1 D.J. Dozier	2.00	.90	.25
☐ 8 A Sweet Sugar Bowl Catch Gregg Garrity	1.50	.70	.19
☐ 9 Title Card 1991 Schedule on back	1.50	.70	.19

1991-92 Penn State Legends

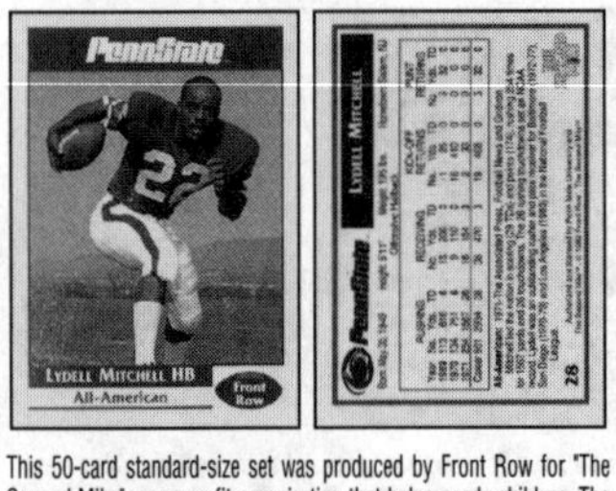

This 50-card standard-size set was produced by Front Row for "The Second Mile," a non-profit organization that helps needy children. The set spotlights All-Americans who played at Penn State from 1923 to 1991. The production run was limited to 20,000 sets. The fronts feature a mix of color and black and white, as well as posed and action, player photos with white borders. Card top carries Penn State in white on a blue border while the bottom has the player's name in a blue border and All-American in red. Front Row's logo appears at the bottom right. Horizontally printed backs have statistics and biography within a red border. An unnumbered insert has a checklist on one side and acknowledgments on the other. The cards are numbered on the back, with the player cards arranged in alphabetical order. Front Row also produced three promo cards prior to the general release of the set; they are distinguished by the fact that "Promo" is stamped diagonally across the back.

	MINT	NRMT	EXC
COMPLETE SET (51)	20.00	9.00	2.50
COMMON CARD (1-50)	.35	.16	.04
☐ 1 Joe Paterno CO	2.00	.90	.25
☐ 2 Kurt Allerman	.35	.16	.04
☐ 3 Chris Bahr	.50	.23	.06
☐ 4 Matt Bahr	.50	.23	.06
☐ 5 Bruce Bannon	.35	.16	.04
☐ 6 Greg Buttle	.50	.23	.06
☐ 7 John Cappelletti	.75	.35	.09
☐ 8 Bruce Clark	.35	.16	.04
☐ 9 Andre Collins	.75	.35	.09
☐ 10 Shane Conlan	.75	.35	.09
☐ 11 Chris Conlin	.35	.16	.04
☐ 12 Randy Crowder	.50	.23	.06
☐ 13 Keith Dorney	.50	.23	.06
☐ 14 D.J. Dozier	.75	.35	.09
☐ 15 Bill Dugan	.35	.16	.04
☐ 16 Chuck Fusina	.50	.23	.06
☐ 17 Leon Gajecki	.35	.16	.04
☐ 18 Jack Ham	1.50	.70	.19
☐ 19 Bob Higgins	.35	.16	.04
☐ 20 John Hufnagel	.75	.35	.09
☐ 21 Kenny Jackson	.50	.23	.06
☐ 22 Tim Johnson	.35	.16	.04
☐ 23 Dave Joyner	.35	.16	.04
☐ 24 Roger Kochman	.35	.16	.04
☐ 25 Ted Kwalick	.50	.23	.06
☐ 26 Richie Lucas	.75	.35	.09
☐ 27 Matt Millen	.75	.35	.09
☐ 28 Lydell Mitchell	.75	.35	.09
☐ 29 Bob Mitinger	.35	.16	.04
☐ 30 John Nessel	.35	.16	.04
☐ 31 Ed O'Neil	.50	.23	.06
☐ 32 Dennis Onkotz	.35	.16	.04
☐ 33 Darren Perry	.50	.23	.06
☐ 34 Charlie Pittman	.50	.23	.06
☐ 35A Tom Rafferty ERR (Photo actually T. Quinn)	5.00	2.20	.60
☐ 35B Tom Rafferty COR	1.25	.55	.16
☐ 36 Mike Reid UER (Reversed negative)	1.25	.55	.16
☐ 37 Glenn Ressler	.50	.23	.06
☐ 38 Dave Robinson	.50	.23	.06
☐ 39 Mark Robinson	.35	.16	.04
☐ 40 Randy Sidler	.35	.16	.04
☐ 41 John Skorupan	.50	.23	.06
☐ 42 Neal Smith	.35	.16	.04
☐ 43 Steve Suhey	.50	.23	.06
☐ 44 Sam Tamburo	.35	.16	.04
☐ 45 Blair Thomas	1.25	.55	.16
☐ 46 Curt Warner	1.50	.70	.19
☐ 47 Steve Wisniewski	.75	.35	.09
☐ 48 Charlie Zapiec	.35	.16	.04
☐ 49 Michael Zordich	.50	.23	.06
☐ 50 Harry Wilson and Joe Bedenk	.35	.16	.04
☐ P1 Joe Paterno CO (Promo)	4.00	1.80	.50
☐ P10 Shane Conlan (Promo)	2.00	.90	.25
☐ P18 Jack Ham (Promo)	2.50	1.10	.30
☐ NNO Checklist Card	.35	.16	.04

1992 Penn State

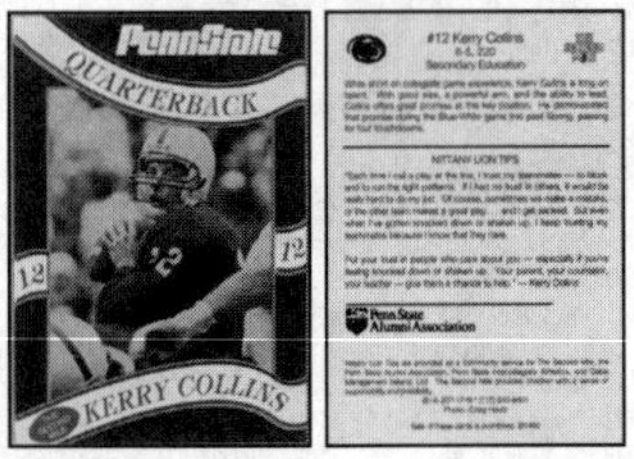

Sponsored by The Second Mile, this 16-card standard-size set features posed and action color player photos against a royal blue background that is also edged in light blue. White banners, outlined with red and light blue, run across the top and bottom, and behind the middle of the picture. The banners contain the player's position, jersey number, and name. The backs have biographical information, a player profile, and "Nittany Lion Tips" in the form of player quotes. A sponsor message at the bottom rounds out the card back. The cards are unnumbered and checklisted below in alphabetical order. The key cards in the set feature Kyle Brady, Kerry Collins, and O.J. McDuffie.

	MINT	NRMT	EXC
COMPLETE SET (16)	25.00	11.00	3.10
COMMON CARD (1-16)	.60	.25	.07
☐ 1 Richie Anderson	2.00	.90	.25
☐ 2 Lou Benfatti	1.00	.45	.12
☐ 3 Derek Bochna	.60	.25	.07
☐ 4 Kyle Brady	3.00	1.35	.35
☐ 5 Kerry Collins	12.00	5.50	1.50
☐ 6 Troy Drayton	2.00	.90	.25
☐ 7 John Gerak	1.00	.45	.12
☐ 8 Reggie Givens	1.00	.45	.12
☐ 9 Shelly Hammonds	1.00	.45	.12
☐ 10 Greg Huntington	.60	.25	.07
☐ 11 Tyoka Jackson	1.00	.45	.12
☐ 12 O.J. McDuffie	5.00	2.20	.60
☐ 13 Lee Rubin	.60	.25	.07
☐ 14 E.J. Sandusky	.60	.25	.07
☐ 15 Tisen Thomas	.60	.25	.07
☐ 16 Brett Wright	.60	.25	.07

1992 Penn State Book Store

The Penn State Book Store offered this 9-card set printed on one perforated sheet. Each unnumbered card includes an all-time great Penn State football player light with career highlights mentioned on the cardback.

	MINT	NRMT	EXC
COMPLETE SET (9)	8.00	3.60	1.00
COMMON CARD (1-9)	1.00	.45	.12
☐ 1 Kurt Allerman	1.00	.45	.12
☐ 2 Bruce Bannon	1.00	.45	.12
☐ 3 Todd Blackledge	1.50	.70	.19
☐ 4 John Bruno	1.00	.45	.12
☐ 5 Greg Garrity	1.50	.70	.19
☐ 6 Dave Joyner	1.00	.45	.12
☐ 7 Massimo Manca	1.00	.45	.12
☐ 8 Dennis Onkotz	1.00	.45	.12
☐ 9 Title Card	1.00	.45	.12

1993 Penn State

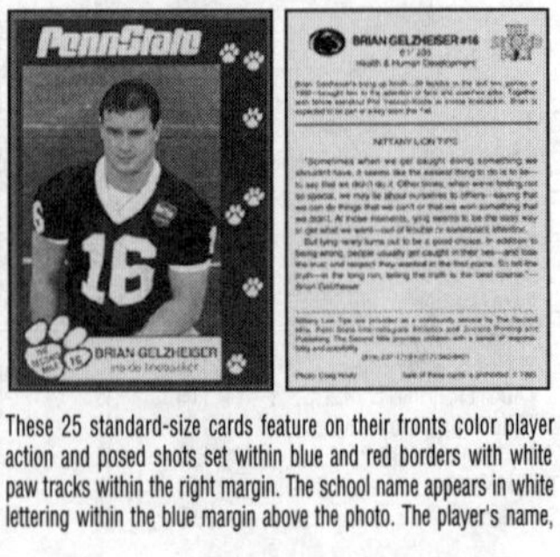

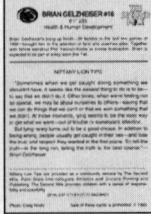

These 25 standard-size cards feature on their fronts color player action and posed shots set within blue and red borders with white paw tracks within the right margin. The school name appears in white lettering within the blue margin above the photo. The player's name,

number, and position appear in blue lettering in a white rectangle below the photo. The white back carries the player's name, number, and profile at the top. Below is a Nittany Lions tip given by each player. The cards are unnumbered and checklisted below in alphabetical order.

	MINT	NRMT	EXC
COMPLETE SET (25)	25.00	11.00	3.10
COMMON CARD (1-25)	.50	.23	.06
☐ 1 Mike Archie Ki-Jana Carter Stephen Pitts	5.00	2.20	.60
☐ 2 Lou Benfatti	.75	.35	.09
☐ 3 Derek Bochna	.50	.23	.06
☐ 4 Kyle Brady	2.00	.90	.25
☐ 5 Kerry Collins	8.00	3.60	1.00
☐ 6 Criag Fayak	.50	.23	.06
☐ 7 Marlon Forbes	.50	.23	.06
☐ 8 Brian Gelzheiser	1.00	.45	.12
☐ 9 Bucky Greeley	.50	.23	.06
☐ 10 Ryan Grube	.75	.35	.09
☐ 11 Shelly Hammonds	.75	.35	.09
☐ 12 Jeff Hartings	.75	.35	.09
☐ 13 Rob Holmberg	1.00	.45	.12
☐ 14 Tyoka Jackson	.75	.35	.09
☐ 15 Mike Malinoski	.75	.35	.09
☐ 16 Brian Monaghan	.50	.23	.06
☐ 17 Brian O'Neal	.75	.35	.09
☐ 18 Jeff Perry	.50	.23	.06
☐ 19 Derick Pickett	.50	.23	.06
☐ 20 Tony Pittman	.50	.23	.06
☐ 21 Eric Ravotti	.75	.35	.09
☐ 22 Lee Rubin	.50	.23	.06
☐ 23 Vin Stewart	.50	.23	.06
☐ 24 Tisen Thomas	.50	.23	.06
☐ 25 Phil Yeboah-Kodie	.75	.35	.09

1994 Penn State

These 25 standard-size cards feature on their fronts color player action and posed shots with a white paw track in the lower right hand corner. The school name appears above the photo. The cards are unnumbered and checklisted below in alphabetical order.

	MINT	NRMT	EXC
COMPLETE SET (25)	20.00	9.00	2.50
COMMON CARD (1-25)	.50	.23	.06
☐ 1 Mike Archie	2.00	.90	.25
☐ 2 Todd Atkins	.50	.23	.06
☐ 3 Kyle Brady	2.00	.90	.25
☐ 4 Ki-Jana Carter	4.00	1.80	.50
☐ 5 Eric Clair	.50	.23	.06
☐ 6 Kerry Collins	7.00	3.10	.85
☐ 7 Cliff Dingle	.50	.23	.06
☐ 8 Bobby Engram	3.00	1.35	.35
☐ 9 Brian Gelzheiser	.75	.35	.09
☐ 10 Andre Johnson	.75	.35	.09
☐ 11 Josh Kroell	.50	.23	.06
☐ 12 Brian Milne	1.00	.45	.12
☐ 13 Jeff Perry	.50	.23	.06
☐ 14 Tony Pittman	.50	.23	.06
☐ 15 Stephen Pitts	.50	.23	.06
☐ 16 Wally Richardson	1.50	.70	.19
☐ 17 Marco Rivera	.50	.23	.06
☐ 18 Vin Stewart	.50	.23	.06
☐ 19 Jon Witman	1.50	.70	.19

1995 Penn State

These 25 standard-size cards feature on their fronts color player action and posed shots with the now common white Lion paw print at the above the photo with the school name below the photo. The cards are unnumbered and checklisted below in alphabetical order.

	MINT	NRMT	EXC
COMPLETE SET (25)	15.00	6.75	1.85
COMMON CARD (1-25)	.50	.23	.06
☐ 1 Todd Atkins	.50	.23	.06
☐ 2 Mike Archie	1.50	.70	.19
☐ 3 Eric Clair	.50	.23	.06
☐ 4 Jason Collins	.75	.35	.09
☐ 5 Keith Conlin	.50	.23	.06
☐ 6 Brett Conway	.75	.35	.09
☐ 7 Jeff Davis	.50	.23	.06
☐ 8 Bobby Engram	2.00	.90	.25
☐ 9 Eric Gallman	.50	.23	.06
☐ 10 Carl Gray	.50	.23	.06
☐ 11 Jeff Hartings	1.50	.70	.19
☐ 12 Kim Herring	.50	.23	.06
☐ 13 Clint Holes	.50	.23	.06
☐ 14 Andre Johnson	1.00	.45	.12
☐ 15 Terry Killens	.75	.35	.09
☐ 16 Brian King	.50	.23	.06
☐ 17 Brian Miller	.50	.23	.06
☐ 18 Brian Milne	.75	.35	.09
☐ 19 Brandon Noble	.50	.23	.06
☐ 20 Stephen Pitts	.75	.35	.09
☐ 21 Wally Richardson	1.25	.55	.16
☐ 22 Marco Rivera	.50	.23	.06
☐ 23 Freddie Scott	1.50	.70	.19
☐ 24 Mark Tate	.50	.23	.06
☐ 25 Jon Witman	1.00	.45	.12

1996 Penn State

These 25 standard-size cards feature on their fronts color player action and posed shots with a white paw print in the lower right hand corner. The school name appears above the photo. The cards are unnumbered and checklisted below in alphabetical order.

	MINT	NRMT	EXC
COMPLETE SET (25)	12.00	5.50	1.50
COMMON CARD (1-25)	.50	.23	.06
☐ 1 Aaron Collins	.50	.23	.06
☐ 2 Brett Conway	.50	.23	.06
☐ 3 Chris Eberly	.50	.23	.06
☐ 4 Curtis Enis	2.00	.90	.25
☐ 5 Gerald Filardi	.50	.23	.06
☐ 6 Matt Fornadel	.50	.23	.06
☐ 7 Mike Gonzalez	.50	.23	.06
☐ 8 Jason Henderson	.50	.23	.06
☐ 9 Kim Herring	.50	.23	.06
☐ 10 Joe Jurevicius	1.00	.45	.12
☐ 11 Brad Jones	.50	.23	.06
☐ 12 Darrell Kania	.50	.23	.06
☐ 13 Shawn Lee	.75	.35	.09
☐ 14 Brian Miller	.50	.23	.06
☐ 15 Joe Nastasi	.50	.23	.06
☐ 16 Jim Nelson	.50	.23	.06
☐ 17 Brandon Norle	.50	.23	.06
☐ 18 Keith Olsommer	.75	.35	.09
☐ 19 Phil Ostrowski	.50	.23	.06
☐ 20 Chuck Penzenik	.50	.23	.06
☐ 21 Wally Richardson	1.00	.45	.12
☐ 22 Jason Sload	.50	.23	.06
☐ 23 Chris Snyder	.50	.23	.06
☐ 24 Mark Tate	.50	.23	.06
☐ 25 Barry Tielsch	.50	.23	.06

1991 Pennsylvania High School Big 33

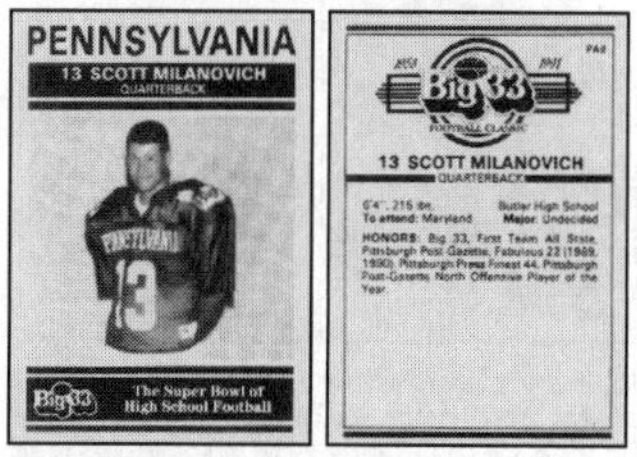

This 36-card standard-size high school football set was issued to commemorate the Big 33 Football Classic, an annual high school football game begun in 1958 and featuring Pennsylvania versus Maryland for the past seven games. The fronts feature posed black and white player photos enclosed by a white border. State name appears at top of card while player name, number, and position appear in white reversed-out lettering in black. The Big 33 logo and The Super Bowl of High School Football appear in same reverse-out fashion at bottom. The backs feature player's biographical information enclosed within a thin black border. The key cards in this set feature Mike Archie, Marvin Harrison, Curtis Martin and Ray Zellars.

	MINT	NRMT	EXC
COMPLETE SET (36)	40.00	18.00	5.00
COMMON CARD (PA1-PA36)	.50	.23	.06
☐ PA1 Dietrich Jells	2.00	.90	.25
☐ PA2 Mike Archie	3.00	1.35	.35
☐ PA3 Tony Miller	.50	.23	.06
☐ PA4 Edmund Robinson	.50	.23	.06
☐ PA5 Brian Miller	.75	.35	.09
☐ PA6 Marvin Harrison	6.00	2.70	.75
☐ PA7 Mike Cawley	.50	.23	.06
☐ PA8 Thomas Marchese	.50	.23	.06
☐ PA9 Scott Milanovich	2.00	.90	.25
☐ PA10 Shawn Wooden	1.50	.70	.19
☐ PA11 Curtis Martin	15.00	6.75	1.85
☐ PA12 William Khayat	.50	.23	.06
☐ PA13 Jermell Fleming	.50	.23	.06
☐ PA14 Ray Zellars	5.00	2.20	.60
☐ PA15 Jon Witman	1.50	.70	.19
☐ PA16 Chris McCartney	.50	.23	.06
☐ PA17 David Rebar	.50	.23	.06
☐ PA18 Mark Zataveski	.75	.35	.09
☐ PA19 Todd Atkins	.75	.35	.09
☐ PA20 Shannon Stevens	.50	.23	.06
☐ PA21 Keith Conlin	.75	.35	.09
☐ PA22 John Bowman	.50	.23	.06
☐ PA23 Maurice Lawrence	.50	.23	.06
☐ PA24 Mike Halapin	.50	.23	.06
☐ PA25 Steve Keim	.50	.23	.06
☐ PA26 Dennis Martin	.50	.23	.06
☐ PA27 Keith Morris	.50	.23	.06
☐ PA28 Chris Villarrial	1.00	.45	.12
☐ PA29 Thomas Tumulty	.50	.23	.06
☐ PA30 Jason Augustino	.50	.23	.06
☐ PA31 Gregory Delong	.50	.23	.06
☐ PA32 James Moore	.50	.23	.06
☐ PA33 Eric Clair	.75	.35	.09
☐ PA34 Tyler Young	.50	.23	.06
☐ PA35 Jeffrey Sauve	.50	.23	.06
☐ PA36 Terry Hammons	.50	.23	.06

1992 Pennsylvania High School Big 33

This standard-size high school football set was issued to commemorate the Pennsylvania Big 33 Football Classic. The fronts feature posed player photos enclosed by a white border. The state name appears at the top of the card along with the player's name, number, and position. The Big 33 logo appears below the photo. The backs feature the player's biographical information along with a notation to which college he plans to attend. The unnumbered cards are listed below alphabetically.

	MINT	NRMT	EXC
COMPLETE SET (35)	16.00	7.25	2.00
COMMON CARD (1-35)	.50	.23	.06
☐ 1 Bill Anderson	.50	.23	.06
☐ 2 Larry Austin	.50	.23	.06
☐ 3 Brandon Bailey	.50	.23	.06
☐ 4 Richard Brooks Jr.	.50	.23	.06
☐ 5 Ken Buczynski	.50	.23	.06
☐ 6 Jason Chavis	.50	.23	.06
☐ 7 Matt Cope	.50	.23	.06
☐ 8 Jeff Craig	.50	.23	.06
☐ 9 Jamaal Crawford	.50	.23	.06
☐ 10 Todd Durish	.50	.23	.06
☐ 11 Jon Dylewski	.50	.23	.06
☐ 12 Scott Florence	.50	.23	.06
☐ 13 David Gathman	.50	.23	.06
☐ 14 Darrell Harding	.50	.23	.06
☐ 15 Anthony Hardy	.50	.23	.06
☐ 16 Clinton Holes	.50	.23	.06
☐ 17 Michael Horn	.50	.23	.06
☐ 18 Matt Hosilyk	.50	.23	.06
☐ 19 Jay Jones	.50	.23	.06
☐ 20 Jason Killian	.50	.23	.06
☐ 21 Ted Kwalick Honorary Chairman	1.00	.45	.12
☐ 22 Tajuan Law	.50	.23	.06
☐ 23 Mark Libiano	.50	.23	.06
☐ 24 Mike Logan	.50	.23	.06
☐ 25 Michael Mohring	.50	.23	.06
☐ 26 Justin Morabito	.50	.23	.06
☐ 27 Mark Nori	.50	.23	.06
☐ 28 Keith Olsommer	1.50	.70	.19
☐ 29 Harvey Penneypacker	.50	.23	.06
☐ 30 Cliff Stroud	.50	.23	.06
☐ 31 Lorenzo Styles	1.00	.45	.12
☐ 32 Mark Tate	.50	.23	.06
☐ 33 Gerald Thompson	.50	.23	.06
☐ 34 Barry Tielsch	.50	.23	.06
☐ 35 Scott Weaver	.50	.23	.06

1994 Pennsylvania High School Big 33

This standard-size high school football set was issued to commemorate the 37th annual Pennsylvania Big 33 Football Classic. The fronts feature posed player photos enclosed by a white border. The state name appears at the top of the card along with the player's name, number, and position. The Big 33 logo appears below the photo. The backs feature the player's biographical information along with a notation to which college he plans to attend. The unnumbered cards are listed below alphabetically.

	MINT	NRMT	EXC
COMPLETE SET (35)	16.00	7.25	2.00
COMMON CARD (1-35)	.50	.23	.06
☐ 1 Lamar Campbell	.50	.23	.06
☐ 2 John Cappelletti Honorary Chairman	1.00	.45	.12
☐ 3 Timothy Cramsey	.50	.23	.06
☐ 4 Cliff Crosby	.50	.23	.06
☐ 5 Jon Curry	.50	.23	.06
☐ 6 Darryl Daniel	.50	.23	.06
☐ 7 Ted Daniels	.50	.23	.06
☐ 8 Dan Drogan	.50	.23	.06
☐ 9 Jamaal Edwards	.75	.35	.09
☐ 10 Ryan Fagan	.50	.23	.06
☐ 11 Charles Fisher	.50	.23	.06
☐ 12 Matt Gubba	.50	.23	.06
☐ 13 Artrell Hawkins	.50	.23	.06
☐ 14 Tom Indio	.50	.23	.06
☐ 15 Isaac Jones	.50	.23	.06
☐ 16 Eric Kasperowicz	.50	.23	.06
☐ 17 Brad Keller	.50	.23	.06
☐ 18 Brian Kuklick	.50	.23	.06
☐ 19 Shawn Lee	.50	.23	.06
☐ 20 Frank Lockett	.50	.23	.06
☐ 21 Troy Logan	.50	.23	.06
☐ 22 Seamus Murphy	.50	.23	.06
☐ 23 Joseph Nastasi	.50	.23	.06
☐ 24 Chris Nocco	.50	.23	.06
☐ 25 Doug Ostrosky	.50	.23	.06
☐ 26 Darren Oswald	.50	.23	.06
☐ 27 James Pizano	.50	.23	.06
☐ 28 Matt Rader	.50	.23	.06
☐ 29 Jason Richards	.50	.23	.06
☐ 30 Chris Schneider	.50	.23	.06
☐ 31 Brad Scioli	.50	.23	.06
☐ 32 Clint Seace	.50	.23	.06
☐ 33 Shawn Summerville	.75	.35	.09
☐ 34 John Thorton	.50	.23	.06
☐ 35 Tim Zeglin	.50	.23	.06

1995 Pennsylvania High School Big 33

This standard-size high school football set was issued to commemorate the 38th annual Pennsylvania Big 33 Football Classic. The fronts feature posed player photos enclosed by a white border. The state name and year appear at the top of the card along with the player's name, number, and position. The Big 33 logo appears below the photo. The backs feature the player's biographical information along with a notation to which college he plans to attend. The unnumbered cards are listed below alphabetically.

	MINT	NRMT	EXC
COMPLETE SET (35)	15.00	6.75	1.85
COMMON CARD (1-35)	.50	.23	.06
☐ 1 Askari Adams	.50	.23	.06
☐ 2 Bryan Arndt	.50	.23	.06
☐ 3 Michael Bennett	.50	.23	.06
☐ 4 Bryan Boggs	.50	.23	.06
☐ 5 Aaron Brady	.50	.23	.06
☐ 6 Stephen Brominski	.50	.23	.06
☐ 7 Marc Bulger	.50	.23	.06
☐ 8 Rich Butcofski	.50	.23	.06
☐ 9 Anthony Cleary	.50	.23	.06
☐ 10 Melvin Cobbs	.50	.23	.06
☐ 11 Eric Cole	.50	.23	.06
☐ 12 William B. Craver	.50	.23	.06
☐ 13 Jermaine Cromerdie	.50	.23	.06
☐ 14 Troy Davidson	.50	.23	.06
☐ 15 Darnell Dinkins	.50	.23	.06
☐ 16 Rashonn Drayton	.75	.35	.09
☐ 17 Chafie Fields	.50	.23	.06
☐ 18 Joshua George	.50	.23	.06
☐ 19 Mike Gimbol	.50	.23	.06
☐ 20 Julian Graham	.50	.23	.06
☐ 21 Aaron Harris	.50	.23	.06
☐ 22 Randy Homa	.50	.23	.06
☐ 23 Corey Jones	.50	.23	.06
☐ 24 Chad Knoell	.50	.23	.06
☐ 25 Dan Kreider	.50	.23	.06
☐ 26 Noel Lamontagne	.50	.23	.06
☐ 27 Marc Lapadula	.50	.23	.06
☐ 28 Tim Lewis Honorary Chairman	.50	.23	.06
☐ 29 Matt Mapes	.50	.23	.06
☐ 30 Vince Pellis	.50	.23	.06
☐ 31 Henry Poteat	.50	.23	.06
☐ 32 Brandon Short	.50	.23	.06
☐ 33 Rich Stankewicz	.50	.23	.06
☐ 34 Brandon Streeter	.50	.23	.06
☐ 35 Ethan Weidle	.50	.23	.06

1996 Pennsylvania High School Big 33

This standard-size high school football set was issued to commemorate the 39th annual Pennsylvania Big 33 Football Classic. The fronts feature posed player photos enclosed by a white border. The state name and year appear at the top of the card along with the player's name, number, and position. The Big 33 logo appears below the photo. The backs feature the player's biographical information along with a notation to which college he plans to attend. The unnumbered cards are listed below alphabetically.

	MINT	NRMT	EXC
COMPLETE SET (35)	15.00	6.75	1.85
COMMON CARD (1-35)	.50	.23	.06
☐ 1 Randy Ament	.50	.23	.06
☐ 2 Imani Bell	.50	.23	.06
☐ 3 John Blick	.50	.23	.06
☐ 4 Rick Bolinsky	.50	.23	.06
☐ 5 Chance Bright	.50	.23	.06
☐ 6 Mike Cerimele	.50	.23	.06
☐ 7 Bilal Cook	.50	.23	.06
☐ 8 David Costa	.75	.35	.09
☐ 9 Jim Covert Honorary Chairman	1.00	.45	.12
☐ 10 Paul Fath	.50	.23	.06
☐ 11 Aaron Gatten	.50	.23	.06
☐ 12 Demond Gibson	.50	.23	.06
☐ 13 Rick Gilliam	.50	.23	.06
☐ 14 Cullen Hawkins	.50	.23	.06
☐ 15 Lee Holmes	.50	.23	.06
☐ 16 Seth Hornacek	.50	.23	.06
☐ 17 Brad Jones	.50	.23	.06
☐ 18 Ben Kopp	.50	.23	.06
☐ 19 Justin Kurpeikis	.50	.23	.06
☐ 20 Tim Long	.50	.23	.06
☐ 21 Brian Minehart	.50	.23	.06
☐ 22 Andy Molinaro	.50	.23	.06
☐ 23 Robert Mowl	.50	.23	.06
☐ 24 Jonathan Murphy	.50	.23	.06
☐ 25 Raki Nelson	.50	.23	.06
☐ 26 Brian Remley	.50	.23	.06
☐ 27 David Robbins III	.50	.23	.06
☐ 28 Sean Ruffing	.50	.23	.06
☐ 29 Jordan Scott	.50	.23	.06
☐ 30 Ben Thomas	.50	.23	.06
☐ 31 Jason Wallace	.50	.23	.06
☐ 32 Garrett Watkins	.50	.23	.06
☐ 33 Kenny Watson	.50	.23	.06
☐ 34 Michael White	.50	.23	.06
☐ 35 Tony Zimmerman	.50	.23	.06

1989 Pittsburgh

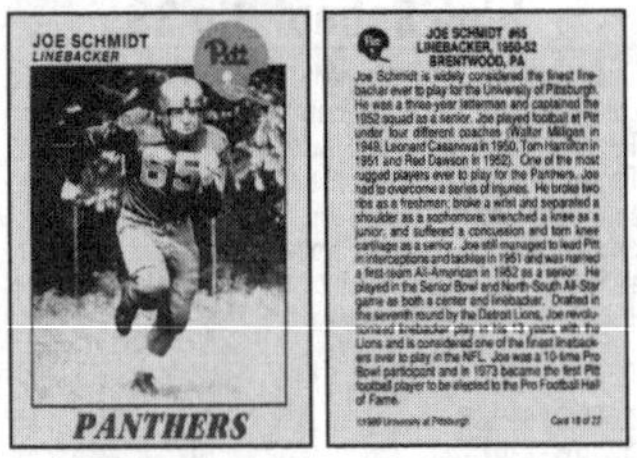

The 1989 Pitt football set contains 22 standard-size cards. The fronts have vintage or color action photos with white borders; the vertically oriented backs have detailed profiles. These cards were distributed as a set.

	MINT	NRMT	EXC
COMPLETE SET (22)	12.00	5.50	1.50
COMMON CARD (1-22)	.30	.14	.04
☐ 1 Tony Dorsett	2.50	1.10	.30
☐ 2 Pop Warner CO	.40	.18	.05
☐ 3 Hugh Green	.60	.25	.07
☐ 4 Matt Cavanaugh	.50	.23	.06
☐ 5 Mike Gottfried	.40	.18	.05
☐ 6 Jim Covert	.50	.23	.06
☐ 7 Bob Peck	.30	.14	.04
☐ 8 Gibby Welch	.30	.14	.04
☐ 9 Bill Daddio	.40	.18	.05
☐ 10 Jock Sutherland CO	.40	.18	.05
☐ 11 Joe Walton	.40	.18	.05
☐ 12 Dan Marino	5.00	2.20	.60
☐ 13 Russ Grimm	.40	.18	.05
☐ 14 Mike Ditka	2.50	1.10	.30
☐ 15 Marshall Goldberg	.50	.23	.06
☐ 16 Bill Fralic	.40	.18	.05
☐ 17 Paul Martha	.40	.18	.05
☐ 18 Joe Schmidt	.75	.35	.09
☐ 19 Rickey Jackson	.60	.25	.07
☐ 20 Ave Daniell	.30	.14	.04
☐ 21 Bill Maas	.40	.18	.05
☐ 22 Mark May	.40	.18	.05

1990 Pitt Foodland

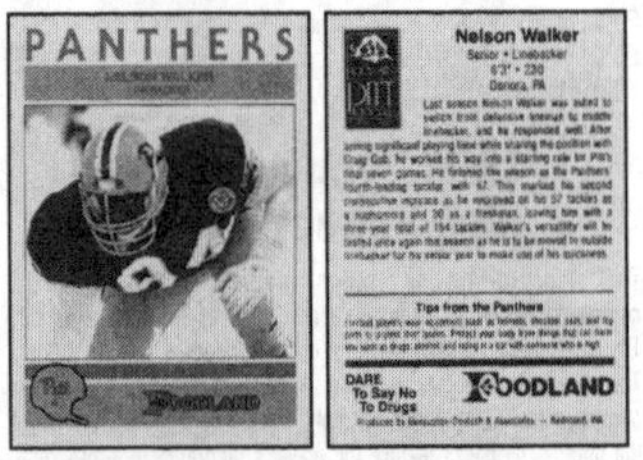

This 12-card standard-size set was sponsored by Foodland to promote anti-drug involvement in the Pittsburgh area. This set features members of the 1990 Pittsburgh Panthers football team. The front features a color action photo, with the team name, player's name, and position at the top. The Pitt helmet appears at the bottom left hand corner and the Foodland logo below the picture. The back contains biographical information and a tip from the Panthers in the form of an anti-drug message. The set was produced by Bensussen-Deutsch and Association from Redmond, Washington. For convenient reference, these unnumbered cards are checklisted below in alphabetical order.

	MINT	NRMT	EXC
COMPLETE SET (12)	8.00	3.60	1.00
COMMON CARD (1-12)	.50	.23	.06
☐ 1 Curtis Bray	.50	.23	.06
☐ 2 Craig Gob	.50	.23	.06
☐ 3 Paul Hackett CO	.50	.23	.06
☐ 4 Keith Hamilton	1.50	.70	.19
☐ 5 Ricardo McDonald	1.50	.70	.19
☐ 6 Ronald Redmon	.50	.23	.06
☐ 7 Curvin Richards	.75	.35	.09
☐ 8 Louis Riddick	1.50	.70	.19
☐ 9 Chris Sestili	.50	.23	.06
☐ 10 Olanda Truitt	1.50	.70	.19
☐ 11 Alex Van Pelt	1.50	.70	.19
☐ 12 Nelson Walker	.50	.23	.06

1991 Pitt Foodland

This 12-card standard-size set was sponsored by Foodland and features the 1991 Pittsburgh Panthers. The cards are printed on thin cardboard stock. The set was issued as individual cards or as an unperforated sheet. The card fronts are accented in the team's colors (blue and yellow) and have glossy color action player photos. The top of the pictures is curved to resemble an archway, and the team name follows the curve of the arch. The player's name and position appear in a yellow stripe below the picture. In black print on white, the backs have the team logo, biography, player profile, and "Tips from the Panthers" in the form of anti-drug messages. The cards are unnumbered and checklisted below in alphabetical order.

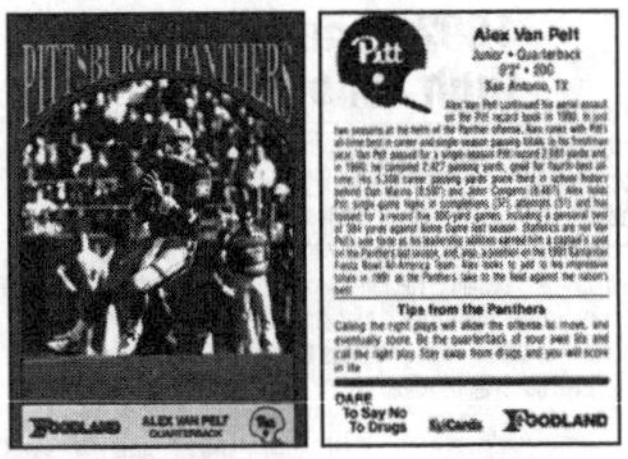

	MINT	NRMT	EXC
COMPLETE SET (12)	8.00	3.60	1.00
COMMON CARD (1-12)	.75	.35	.09
☐ 1 Richard Allen	.75	.35	.09
☐ 2 Curtis Bray	.75	.35	.09
☐ 3 Jeff Christy	1.00	.45	.12
☐ 4 Steve Israel	1.00	.45	.12
☐ 5 Scott Kaplan	.75	.35	.09
☐ 6 Ricardo McDonald	1.00	.45	.12
☐ 7 Dave Moore	.75	.35	.09
☐ 8 Eric Seaman	.75	.35	.09
☐ 9 Chris Sestili	.75	.35	.09
☐ 10 Alex Van Pelt	1.50	.70	.19
☐ 11 Nelson Walker	.75	.35	.09
☐ 12 Kevin Williams HB	.75	.35	.09

1991 Pitt State

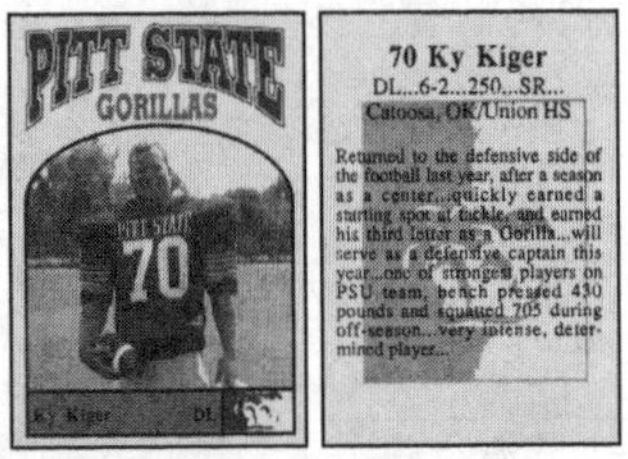

The 1991 Pitt State Gorillas set consists of 18 standard-size cards. Printed on thin white card stock, fronts show player in either a posed or an action photo placed within an arch design. College and team name appears at top of each card while player's name is in a gold bar at bottom next to a picture of the mascot. The backs present biography and player profile superimposed over a drawing of the mascot. A checklist is included with the set on a paper insert. The key player in this set is NFL running back Ron Moore. Also appearing in the set is Ronnie West, who was the Gorillas' Harlon Hill Award candidate. The cards are unnumbered and listed alphabetically below.

	MINT	NRMT	EXC
COMPLETE SET (18)	12.00	5.50	1.50
COMMON CARD (1-18)	.60	.25	.07
☐ 1 Chuck Broyles CO	.60	.25	.07
☐ 2 Darren Dawson	.60	.25	.07
☐ 3 Kendall Gammon	.60	.25	.07
☐ 4 Jamie Goodson	.60	.25	.07
☐ 5 Brian Hoover	.60	.25	.07
☐ 6 James Jenkins	.60	.25	.07
☐ 7 Ky Kiger	.60	.25	.07
☐ 8 Phil McCoy	.60	.25	.07
☐ 9 Kline Minniefield	.60	.25	.07
☐ 10 Ronald Moore	4.00	1.80	.50
☐ 11 Jeff Mundhenke	.60	.25	.07
☐ 12 Brian Pinamonti	.60	.25	.07
☐ 13 Michael Rose	.60	.25	.07
☐ 14 Shane Tafoya	.60	.25	.07
☐ 15 Ronnie West	1.00	.45	.12
☐ 16 Michael Wilber	.60	.25	.07
☐ 17 Troy Wilson	1.50	.70	.19
☐ 18 Team Photo	1.25	.55	.16

1992 Pitt State

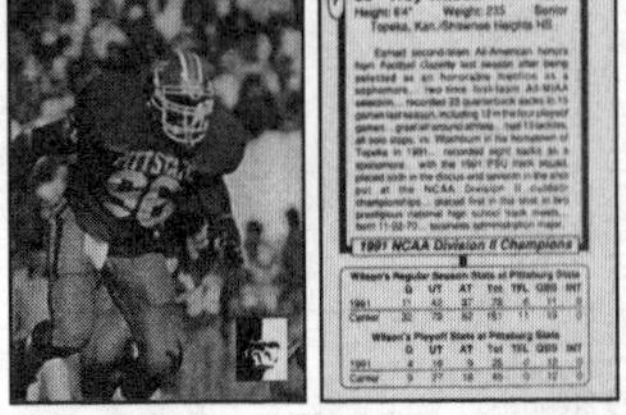

Initiated by Students in Free Enterprise (SIFE), this 18-card set was produced to raise funds for the Pitt State athletic department. The cards could be purchased at football games, the University Post Office, or Kelce room 220. The production run figures were 3,000 numbered packaged sets and 750 uncut sheets. One thousand of the packaged sets contained a Ronnie West bonus card. In addition to the 18 standard-size cards, the set included one paper insert providing card history, a checklist, and set serial number, and another paper insert with cartoons about four different "Isms" (socialism, communism, nazism, and capitalism) and a list of examples of "Big Government" waste in spending. The set features full-bleed color action player photos. The backs are plain white card stock printed with black and contain biographies and player photos. Some cards also carry Pitt State trivia, while others have statistics. The key card in the set features running back Ron Moore.

	MINT	NRMT	EXC
COMPLETE SET (18)	10.00	4.50	1.25
COMMON CARD (1-18)	.60	.25	.07
☐ 1 Ronald Moore	2.00	.90	.25
☐ 2 Craig Jordan	.60	.25	.07
☐ 3 Joel Thornton	.60	.25	.07
☐ 4 Don Tolar	.60	.25	.07
☐ 5 Andy Kesinger	.60	.25	.07
☐ 6 Mike Brockel	.60	.25	.07
☐ 7 Troy Wilson	1.25	.55	.16
☐ 8 Brian Hutchins	.60	.25	.07
☐ 9 Chris Hanna	.60	.25	.07
☐ 10 Coaching Staff	.60	.25	.07
☐ 11 Gus Gorilla (Mascot)	.60	.25	.07
☐ 12 Lance Gosch	.60	.25	.07
☐ 13 Jerry Boone / Chad Watskey	.60	.25	.07
☐ 14 Jeff Moreland / Scott Lutz	.60	.25	.07
☐ 15 Ronnie Fuller / Mickey Beagle	.60	.25	.07
☐ 16 Todd Hafner / Kevin Duncan	.60	.25	.07
☐ 17 Duke Palmer / Eric Perks	.60	.25	.07
☐ 18 Kris Mengarelli	.60	.25	.07

1989 Purdue Legends Smokey

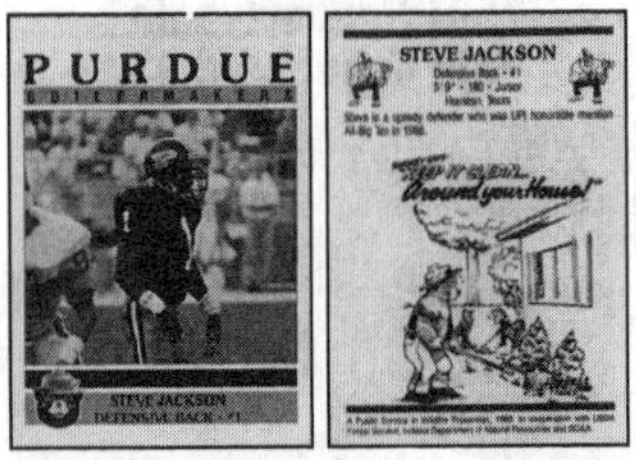

This 16-card set features members of the 1989 Purdue Boilermakers as well as some stars of the past. These sets were distributed at the Purdue/Iowa game in 1989 and have a full-color action photo on the front underneath the Purdue Boilermaker name on top and the player's name, uniform number, and position underneath his photo. The card backs have biographical information as well as a fire safety tip. This set was sponsored by the USDA Forest Service, Indiana Department of Natural Resources, and BDA. We have checklisted this set in alphabetical order and put the initials LEG next to the alumni.

	MINT	NRMT	EXC
COMPLETE SET (16)	30.00	13.50	3.70
COMMON CARD (1-16)	1.25	.55	.16
☐ 1 Fred Akers CO	1.50	.70	.19
☐ 2 Jim Everett LEG	3.00	1.35	.35
☐ 3 Bob Griese LEG	6.00	2.70	.75
☐ 4 Mark Herrmann LEG	2.00	.90	.25
☐ 5 Bill Hitchcock	1.25	.55	.16
☐ 6 Steve Jackson	1.50	.70	.19
☐ 7 Derrick Kelson	1.25	.55	.16
☐ 8 Leroy Keyes LEG	2.00	.90	.25
☐ 9 Shawn McCarthy	1.25	.55	.16
☐ 10 Dwayne O'Connor	1.25	.55	.16
☐ 11 Mike Phipps LEG	2.00	.90	.25
☐ 12 Darren Trieb	1.25	.55	.16
☐ 13 Tony Vinson	1.25	.55	.16
☐ 14 Calvin Williams	2.50	1.10	.30
☐ 15 Rod Woodson LEG	5.00	2.20	.60
☐ 16 Dave Young LEG	1.25	.55	.16

1990 Rice Aetna

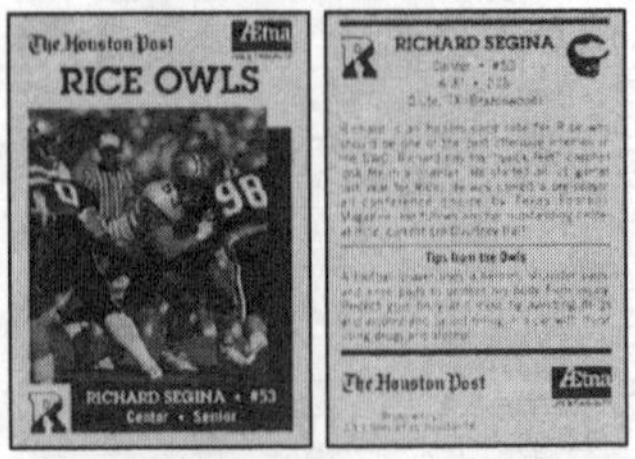

This 12-card standard-size set was sponsored by The Houston Post and Aetna Life and Casualty. The cards feature color action player photos with a navy-blue shadow border on a white card face. The player's name, uniform number, position, and classification appear in the shadow border at the bottom. The team name and sponsor logos are at the top. The backs feature navy-blue print on a white background and include biographical information, player profile, and anti-drug or alcohol messages under the heading "Tips from the Owls". The cards are unnumbered and checklisted below in alphabetical order. The sole distribution of the cards was as giveaways to fans at the Owls' home game against Texas; reportedly 25,000 sets were given away.

	MINT	NRMT	EXC
COMPLETE SET (12)	12.00	5.50	1.50
COMMON CARD (1-12)	1.00	.45	.12
☐ 1 O.J. Brigance	1.50	.70	.19
☐ 2 Trevor Cobb	2.00	.90	.25
☐ 3 Tim Fitzpatrick	1.00	.45	.12
☐ 4 Fred Goldsmith CO	2.00	.90	.25
☐ 5 David Griffin	1.00	.45	.12
☐ 6 Eric Henley	1.50	.70	.19
☐ 7 Donald Hollas	2.00	.90	.25
☐ 8 Richard Segina	1.00	.45	.12
☐ 9 Matt Sign	1.00	.45	.12
☐ 10 Bill Stone	1.00	.45	.12
☐ 11 Trey Teichelman UER (Misspelled Tichelman on front and back)	1.00	.45	.12
☐ 12 Alonzo Williams	1.00	.45	.12

1991 Rice Aetna

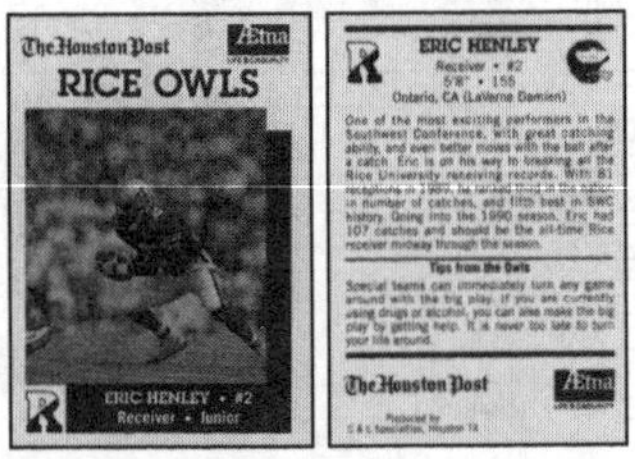

Sponsored by the Houston Post and Aetna Life and Casualty, these 12 standard-size cards feature color action player photos with gray inner borders and white outer borders. The player's name, uniform number, position, and class appear within a navy blue stripe below the photo. The words "Rice Owls '91" appear within a navy blue stripe above the picture. The backs feature navy-colored lettering on a white background and include biographical information, player profile, and anti-drug and alcohol messages under the heading "Tips from the Owls." At the lower right the cards are labeled "series 2." The cards are unnumbered and checklisted below in alphabetical order. The sole distribution of the cards was as giveaways to fans at the Owls' home game against Texas A and M; reportedly 25,000 sets were given away.

	MINT	NRMT	EXC
COMPLETE SET (12)	12.00	5.50	1.50
COMMON CARD (1-12)	1.00	.45	.12
☐ 1 Mike Appelbaum	1.00	.45	.12
☐ 2 Louis Balady	1.00	.45	.12
☐ 3 Nathan Bennett	1.00	.45	.12
☐ 4 Trevor Cobb	1.50	.70	.19
☐ 5 Herschel Crowe	1.00	.45	.12
☐ 6 David Griffin	1.00	.45	.12
☐ 7 Eric Henley	1.50	.70	.19
☐ 8 Matt Sign	1.00	.45	.12
☐ 9 Larry Stuppy	1.00	.45	.12
☐ 10 Trey Teichelman	1.00	.45	.12
☐ 11 Alonzo Williams	1.00	.45	.12
☐ 12 Greg Willig	1.00	.45	.12

1992 Rice Taco Cabana

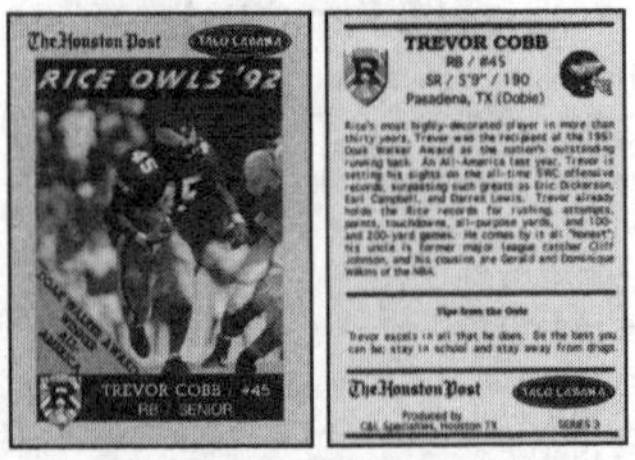

This 12-card set was sponsored by The Houston Post and Taco Cabana, and their company logos appear in the top white border. The fronts feature color action player photos bordered in white. A navy blue bar above the picture carries the words "Rice Owls '92", while a navy blue bar below the picture has the school logo and player information. The backs feature navy-blue print on a white background and include biographical information, player profile, and anti-drug or alcohol messages under the heading "Tips from the Owls". The cards are unnumbered and checklisted below in alphabetical order. The sole distribution of the cards was as giveaways to fans at the Owls' home game against Texas; reportedly 25,000 sets were given away.

	MINT	NRMT	EXC
COMPLETE SET (12)	12.00	5.50	1.50
COMMON CARD (1-12)	1.00	.45	.12
☐ 1 Shawn Alberding	1.00	.45	.12
☐ 2 Mike Appelbaum	1.00	.45	.12
☐ 3 Louis Balady	1.00	.45	.12
☐ 4 Nathan Bennett	1.00	.45	.12
☐ 5 Trevor Cobb	1.50	.70	.19
☐ 6 Josh LaRocca	1.00	.45	.12

	MINT	NRMT	EXC
☐ 7 Jimmy Lee	1.25	.55	.16
☐ 8 Corey Seymour	1.00	.45	.12
☐ 9 Matt Sign	1.00	.45	.12
☐ 10 Emmett Waldron	1.25	.55	.16
☐ 11 Alonzo Williams	1.00	.45	.12
☐ 12 Taco Cabana (Advertisement)	1.00	.45	.12

1993 Rice Taco Cabana

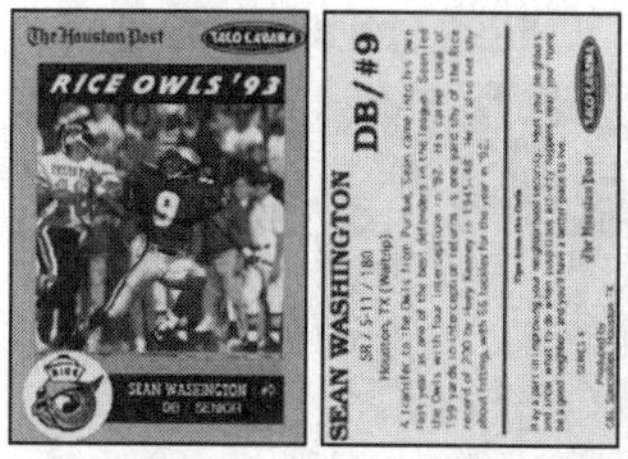

This 12-card standard size set was sponsored by The Houston Post and Taco Cabana. The fronts feature color action player photos against a gray card face. The year and team name are shown in white lettering within a blue bar above the photo. The player's name, jersey number, position, and class are printed in white lettering within a blue bar at the bottom. The horizontal white backs carry the player's name, position, jersey number, height, weight, and hometown at the top, followed below by career highlights and "Tips from the Owls." The cards are unnumbered and checklisted below in alphabetical order. Bert Emanuel is the key player in this set.

	MINT	NRMT	EXC
COMPLETE SET (12)	12.00	5.50	1.50
COMMON CARD (1-12)	1.00	.45	.12
☐ 1 Nathan Bennett	1.00	.45	.12
☐ 2 Cris Cooley	1.25	.55	.16
☐ 3 Bert Emanuel	5.00	2.20	.60
☐ 4 Jimmy Golden	1.00	.45	.12
☐ 5 Tom Hetherington	1.00	.45	.12
☐ 6 Ed Howard	1.00	.45	.12
☐ 7 Jimmy Lee	1.25	.55	.16
☐ 8 Corey Seymour	1.00	.45	.12
☐ 9 Clemente Torres	1.00	.45	.12
☐ 10 Emmett Waldron	1.25	.55	.16
☐ 11 Sean Washington	1.00	.45	.12
☐ 12 Taco Cabana Ad Card	1.00	.45	.12

1995 Roox HS

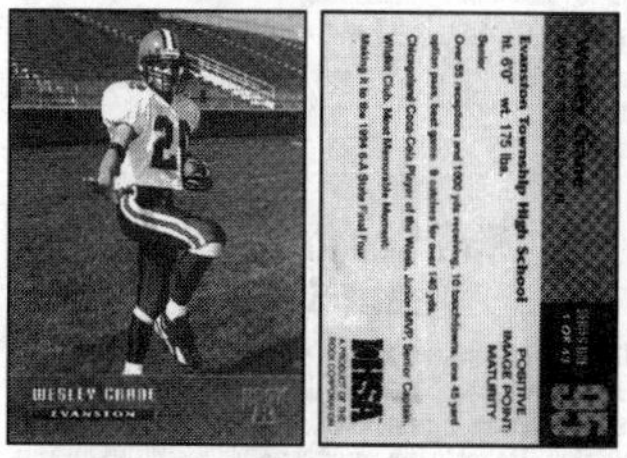

This 39-card set features football players of various Illinois high schools. Cards 35-39 were not issued. The fronts display color player photos with the player's name and school in a brown marblized stripe at the bottom. The backs carry the player's name, position, biographical information, and a "Positive Image Point."

	MINT	NRMT	EXC
COMPLETE SET (39)	20.00	9.00	2.50
COMMON CARD (1-43)	.60	.25	.07
☐ 1 Wesley Crane	.60	.25	.07
☐ 2 Nii Hammond	.60	.25	.07
☐ 3 Daniel Anglin	.60	.25	.07
☐ 4 Ronnie Williams	.60	.25	.07
☐ 5 Harold Blackmon	.60	.25	.07
☐ 6 Tim Lavery	.60	.25	.07
☐ 7 Babatunde Ridley	.60	.25	.07
☐ 8 Fred Wakefield	.60	.25	.07
☐ 9 Bobie Singleton	.60	.25	.07
☐ 10 Chris Janek	.60	.25	.07
☐ 11 Steffan Nicholson	.60	.25	.07
☐ 12 Scott Mullen	.60	.25	.07
☐ 13 Jason Scherer	.60	.25	.07
☐ 14 Kevin Beard, Jr.	.60	.25	.07
☐ 15 Michael Sergeant	.60	.25	.07
☐ 16 Marcus Smith	.60	.25	.07
☐ 17 Eric Garrett	.60	.25	.07
☐ 18 Chris Pickett	.60	.25	.07
☐ 19 Michael Burden	.60	.25	.07
☐ 20 Nick Abruzzo	.60	.25	.07
☐ 21 Stanley Williams	.60	.25	.07
☐ 22 Joey Goodspeed	.60	.25	.07
☐ 23 Stephen Olien	.60	.25	.07
☐ 24 R.J. Luke	.60	.25	.07
☐ 25 Matt Kelly	.60	.25	.07
☐ 26 Ricardo King	.60	.25	.07
☐ 27 Tamaine Hills	.60	.25	.07
☐ 28 Michael Yarborough	.60	.25	.07
☐ 29 Brian Schmitz	.60	.25	.07
☐ 30 Joe Carroll	.60	.25	.07
☐ 31 Roy Sessions	.60	.25	.07
☐ 32 Marcus Hood	.60	.25	.07
☐ 33 Lorenzo Smith	.60	.25	.07
☐ 34 Karlton Thomas	.60	.25	.07
☐ 40 Carlos Polk	.60	.25	.07
☐ 41 Montinez Williams	.60	.25	.07
☐ 42 Neil Carroll	.60	.25	.07
☐ 43 Shaka Jones	.60	.25	.07
☐ NNO Cover Card blankbacked	.10	.05	.01

1996 Roox Shrine Bowl HS

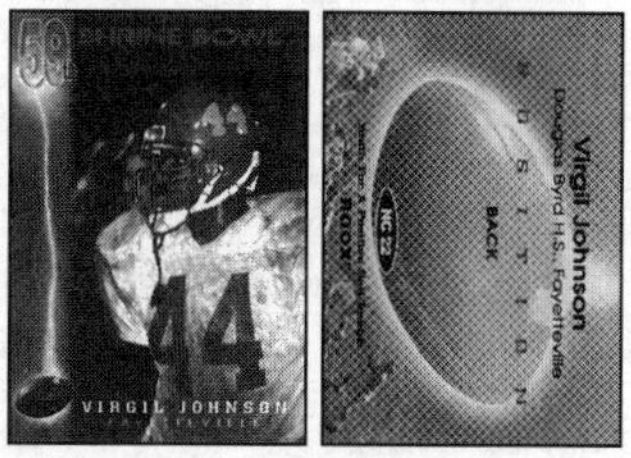

Roox Corp. released this 74-card set commemorating the 59th Shrine Bowl between North Carolina and South Carolina High Schools. The cards feature color player photos of members of both teams. Although the cards are not numbered as one set, they are commonly sold as a set of 74.

	MINT	NRMT	EXC
COMPLETE SET (74)	40.00	18.00	5.00
COMMON CARD (NC1-NC36)	.60	.25	.07
COMMON CARD (SC1-SC36)	.60	.25	.07
☐ NC1 Rocky Hunt	.60	.25	.07
☐ NC2 Cam Holland	.60	.25	.07
☐ NC3 Derrick Chambers	.60	.25	.07
☐ NC4 Ramondo North	.60	.25	.07
☐ NC5 Bo Manis	.60	.25	.07
☐ NC6 Antonio Graham	.60	.25	.07
☐ NC7 Clayton White	.60	.25	.07
☐ NC8 Billy Young	.60	.25	.07
☐ NC9 Joshua Tucker	.60	.25	.07
☐ NC10 Rod Emery	.60	.25	.07
☐ NC11 Matt Burdick	.60	.25	.07
☐ NC12 Chad Gathings	.60	.25	.07
☐ NC13 Brian Ray	.60	.25	.07
☐ NC14 Brandon Spoon	.60	.25	.07
☐ NC15 Dauntae Finger	.60	.25	.07
☐ NC16 Raymond Massey	.60	.25	.07
☐ NC17 Damien Bennett	.60	.25	.07
☐ NC18 Bennie Griffin	.60	.25	.07
☐ NC19 Randolph Galloway	.60	.25	.07
☐ NC20 Titus Pettigrew	.60	.25	.07
☐ NC21 Chris McCoy	.60	.25	.07
☐ NC22 Virgil Johnson	.60	.25	.07
☐ NC23 Marcus Reaves	.60	.25	.07
☐ NC24 Scottie Stepp	.60	.25	.07
☐ NC25 Julius Bell	.60	.25	.07
☐ NC26 Robert Williams	.60	.25	.07
☐ NC27 Rashad Burke	.60	.25	.07
☐ NC28 Michael Cox	.60	.25	.07
☐ NC29 Kwabena Greene	.60	.25	.07
☐ NC30 Tim Burgess	.60	.25	.07
☐ NC31 Scott Smith	.60	.25	.07
☐ NC32 Steven Lindsey	.60	.25	.07
☐ NC33 Charles Berry	.60	.25	.07
☐ NC34 Chris Satterfield	.60	.25	.07
☐ NC35 Eric Leak	.60	.25	.07
☐ NC36 Nick Means MG	.60	.25	.07
☐ SC1 Ikie Curry	.60	.25	.07
☐ SC2 Shaun Ellis	.60	.25	.07
☐ SC3 Zabeion McRoy	.60	.25	.07
☐ SC4 Will McLaurin	.60	.25	.07
☐ SC5 Jarvis Davis	.60	.25	.07
☐ SC6 Justin Hill	.60	.25	.07
☐ SC7 Antwon Black	.60	.25	.07
☐ SC8 Justin Watts	.60	.25	.07
☐ SC9 Ray Mazyck	.60	.25	.07
☐ SC10 Chris McGee	.60	.25	.07
☐ SC11 Stan Manning	.60	.25	.07
☐ SC12 Micale Chandler	.60	.25	.07
☐ SC13 Deveron Harper	.60	.25	.07
☐ SC14 Brian Wofford	.60	.25	.07
☐ SC15 Tim Winfield	.60	.25	.07
☐ SC16 Donovan Norman	.60	.25	.07
☐ SC17 Chip Brogden	.60	.25	.07
☐ SC18 Seth Stoddard	.60	.25	.07
☐ SC19 Nakia Adderson	.60	.25	.07
☐ SC20 Adam Varnadore	.60	.25	.07
☐ SC21 Lance Legree	.60	.25	.07
☐ SC22 Scott Greer	.60	.25	.07
☐ SC23 B.J. Little	.60	.25	.07
☐ SC24 Kinte Wilson	.60	.25	.07
☐ SC25 Rod Joseph	.60	.25	.07
☐ SC26 Benji Wallace	.60	.25	.07
☐ SC27 Don Moore	.60	.25	.07
☐ SC28 Cecil Caldwell	.60	.25	.07
☐ SC29 Thomas Washington	.60	.25	.07
☐ SC30 Rory Gallman	.60	.25	.07
☐ SC31 Courtney Brown	.60	.25	.07
☐ SC32 Jermale Kelly	.60	.25	.07
☐ SC33 Walsh Dingle	.60	.25	.07
☐ SC34 Mal Lawyer	.60	.25	.07
☐ SC35 Will Gainey	.60	.25	.07
☐ SC36 Bird Bourne MG	.60	.25	.07
☐ NNO South Carolina Title Card	.10	.05	.01
☐ NNO North Carolina Title Card	.10	.05	.01

1996 Roox Prep Star AT/EA/SE

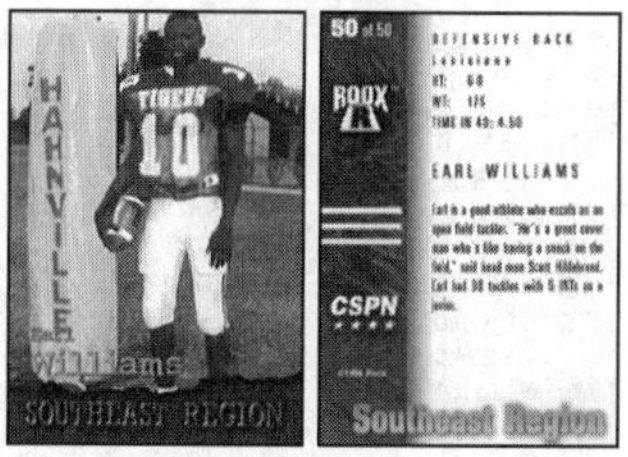

This 142 card standard size boxed set was produced by Roox featuring high school players that played in 1996, and includes standouts from the following states: Alabama, Arkansas, Canada, Connecticut, Delaware, the District of Columbia, Florida, Georgia, Kentucky, Louisiana, Maryland, Massachusetts, Mississippi, New Jersey, New York, North Carolina, Pennsylvania, South Carolina, Virginia, and West Virginia. Reportedly, 1000 sets were produced.

	MINT	NRMT	EXC
COMPLETE SET (142)	80.00	36.00	10.00
COMMON CARD	.60	.25	.07
☐ AT1 David Garrard	.60	.25	.07
☐ AT2 Erik Lipton	.60	.25	.07
☐ AT3 Tim Olmstead	.60	.25	.07
☐ AT4 Craig Powers	.60	.25	.07
☐ AT5 Jason Thompson	.60	.25	.07
☐ AT6 William Combs	.60	.25	.07
☐ AT7 Gil Harris	.60	.25	.07
☐ AT8 Golden Myers	.60	.25	.07
☐ AT9 Chris Willetts	.60	.25	.07
☐ AT10 Chris Ramseur	.60	.25	.07
☐ AT11 Anthony Sanders	.60	.25	.07
☐ AT12 Ali Culpepper	.60	.25	.07
☐ AT13 Dominique Stevenson	.60	.25	.07
☐ AT14 Rondell White	.60	.25	.07
☐ AT15 David Foster	.60	.25	.07
☐ AT16 Luis Moreno	.60	.25	.07
☐ AT17 Sherman Scott	.60	.25	.07
☐ AT18 Doug Bost	.60	.25	.07
☐ AT19 Terry Denoon	.60	.25	.07
☐ AT20 Dave Johnson	.60	.25	.07
☐ AT21 Dain Lewis	.60	.25	.07
☐ AT22 Chris McDaniel	.60	.25	.07
☐ AT23 Chadwick Scott	.60	.25	.07
☐ AT24 Brian Scott	.60	.25	.07
☐ AT25 Bobby Graham	.60	.25	.07
☐ AT26 Steve Shipp	.60	.25	.07
☐ AT27 Jimmy Caldwell	.60	.25	.07
☐ AT28 Rico Gladden	.60	.25	.07
☐ AT29 Evan Kay	.60	.25	.07
☐ AT30 Rashad Slade	.60	.25	.07
☐ AT31 Nate Krill	.60	.25	.07
☐ AT32 Chris Luzar	.60	.25	.07
☐ AT33 Graham Manley	.60	.25	.07
☐ AT34 Neely Page	.60	.25	.07
☐ AT35 David Pugh	.60	.25	.07
☐ AT36 Jason Cox	.60	.25	.07
☐ AT37 Jason McFeasters	.60	.25	.07
☐ AT38 John Miller	.60	.25	.07
☐ AT39 Bobby Dameron	.60	.25	.07
☐ AT40 Keith Esteppe	.60	.25	.07
☐ AT41 Tim Falls	.60	.25	.07
☐ AT42 Jeman Jacobs	.60	.25	.07
☐ AT43 Scott McLain	.60	.25	.07
☐ AT44 Ty Hunt	.60	.25	.07
☐ AT45 Jeff Chambers	.60	.25	.07
☐ AT46 Nick Gilliland	.60	.25	.07
☐ AT47 Buddy Young	.60	.25	.07
☐ AT48 DeAngelo Lloyd	.60	.25	.07
☐ AT49 Ben Bacot	.60	.25	.07
☐ AT50 Corey Nelson	.60	.25	.07
☐ AT51 Jimi Massey	.60	.25	.07
☐ AT52 Sam Scott	.60	.25	.07
☐ AT53 Mike Winfield	.60	.25	.07
☐ AT54 Jayvon McKinney	.60	.25	.07
☐ EA1 Luke Richmond	.60	.25	.07
☐ EA2 Mike Gaydosz	.60	.25	.07
☐ EA3 Eddie Campbell	.60	.25	.07
☐ EA4 Dan Ellis	.60	.25	.07
☐ EA5 Darin Miller	.60	.25	.07
☐ EA6 Ravon Anderson	.60	.25	.07
☐ EA7 Jason Murray	.60	.25	.07
☐ EA8 Brett Aurilla	.60	.25	.07
☐ EA9 Tremayne Bendross	.60	.25	.07
☐ EA10 Sean Fisher	.60	.25	.07
☐ EA11 J.R. Johnson	.60	.25	.07
☐ EA12 Victor Strader	.60	.25	.07
☐ EA13 Dennis Thomas	.60	.25	.07
☐ EA14 Quentin Harris	.60	.25	.07
☐ EA15 Reggie Garrett	.60	.25	.07
☐ EA16 Patrick O'Brien	.60	.25	.07
☐ EA17 Guenter Kryszon	.60	.25	.07
☐ EA18 Kareem McKenzie	.60	.25	.07
☐ EA19 Martin Bibla	.60	.25	.07
☐ EA20 Joe Collins	.60	.25	.07
☐ EA21 John Kuchmek	.60	.25	.07
☐ EA22 Greg Ransom	.60	.25	.07
☐ EA23 Tim Sample	.60	.25	.07
☐ EA24 Marty Wensel	.60	.25	.07
☐ EA25 Jack Bloom	.60	.25	.07
☐ EA26 Nate Ritzenhaler	.60	.25	.07
☐ EA27 Charley Powell	.60	.25	.07
☐ EA28 Ron Graham	.60	.25	.07
☐ EA29 Joe McKinney	.60	.25	.07
☐ EA30 Jeremiah Clarke	.60	.25	.07
☐ EA31 Frank Fodera	.60	.25	.07
☐ EA32 John Yura	.60	.25	.07
☐ EA33 Jonathon Harris	.60	.25	.07
☐ EA34 Ben Martin	.60	.25	.07
☐ EA35 Cory Wire	.60	.25	.07
☐ EA36 Sean Bell	.60	.25	.07
☐ EA37 Brad Eissler	.60	.25	.07
☐ EA38 LaVrar Arrington	.60	.25	.07
☐ SE1 Kenny Kelly	.60	.25	.07
☐ SE2 Daniel Cobb	.60	.25	.07
☐ SE3 Phillip Deas	.60	.25	.07
☐ SE4 Adam Cox	.60	.25	.07
☐ SE5 Ron Johnson	.60	.25	.07
☐ SE6 Tommy Banks	.60	.25	.07
☐ SE7 Sherrod Dickson	.60	.25	.07
☐ SE8 Davey Ford Jr.	.60	.25	.07
☐ SE9 Travis Henry	.60	.25	.07
☐ SE10 William McCray	.60	.25	.07
☐ SE11 Dan Morgan	.60	.25	.07
☐ SE12 Adrian Peterson	.60	.25	.07
☐ SE13 Darrell Jackson	.60	.25	.07
☐ SE14 Orlando Iglesias	.60	.25	.07
☐ SE15 Eddie Williams	.60	.25	.07
☐ SE16 Matt Wright	.60	.25	.07
☐ SE17 Fred Weary	.60	.25	.07
☐ SE18 Braxton Anderson	.60	.25	.07
☐ SE19 Romaro Miller	.60	.25	.07
☐ SE20 Ronald Boldin	.60	.25	.07
☐ SE21 Otis Duhart	.60	.25	.07
☐ SE22 Jabari Ellison	.60	.25	.07
☐ SE23 Tom Hillard	.60	.25	.07
☐ SE24 Ryan Smith	.60	.25	.07
☐ SE25 Erik Strange	.60	.25	.07
☐ SE26 Sam Matthews	.60	.25	.07
☐ SE27 Thomas Pittman	.60	.25	.07
☐ SE28 Andrew Zow	.60	.25	.07
☐ SE29 Gerard Warren	.60	.25	.07
☐ SE30 Adrian Wilson	.60	.25	.07
☐ SE31 Char-Ron Dorsey	.60	.25	.07
☐ SE32 Kennard Ellis	.60	.25	.07
☐ SE33 Jabari Holloway	.60	.25	.07
☐ SE34 Melvin Richey	.60	.25	.07
☐ SE35 Willie Sams	.60	.25	.07
☐ SE36 Josh Weldon	.60	.25	.07
☐ SE37 Travis Carroll	.60	.25	.07
☐ SE38 Cortez Allen	.60	.25	.07
☐ SE39 Andra Davis	.60	.25	.07
☐ SE40 Matt Miller	.60	.25	.07
☐ SE41 Whit Smith	.60	.25	.07
☐ SE42 Stanford Simmons	.60	.25	.07
☐ SE43 Tony Dixon	.60	.25	.07
☐ SE44 Clifton Robinson	.60	.25	.07
☐ SE45 Hugh Holmes	.60	.25	.07
☐ SE46 Abdul Howard	.60	.25	.07
☐ SE47 Rob Pate	.60	.25	.07
☐ SE48 Matt Howard	.60	.25	.07
☐ SE49 Terrence Trammell	.60	.25	.07
☐ SE50 Earl Williams	.60	.25	.07
☐ NNO Jesse Palmer	.60	.25	.07

1996 Roox Prep Star C/W

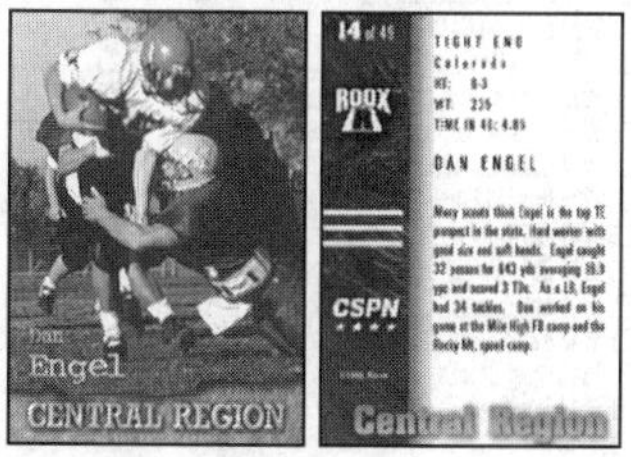

This 142 card standard size boxed set was produced by Roox featuring high school players that played in 1996, and includes standouts from the following states: Arizona, California, Colorado, Hawaii, Idaho, Kansas, Missouri, Nebraska, Nevada, New Mexico, Oklahoma, Oregon, Utah, Washington, and Wyoming. Reportedly, 1000 sets were produced.

	MINT	NRMT	EXC
COMPLETE SET(145)	80.00	36.00	10.00
COMMON CARD (C1-C49/W1-W95)	.60	.25	.07
☐ C1 B.J. Tiger	.60	.25	.07
☐ C2 Ryan Lown	.60	.25	.07
☐ C3 Sherard Poteete	.60	.25	.07
☐ C4 Eric Gooden	.60	.25	.07

□ C5 Ken Alsop	.60	.25	.07
□ C6 Levi Mehl	.60	.25	.07
□ C7 Justin Gallimore	.60	.25	.07
□ C8 Dallas Davis	.60	.25	.07
□ C9 Ahmed Kabba	.60	.25	.07
□ C10 Aaron Lockett	.60	.25	.07
□ C11 Kevin Wendling	.60	.25	.07
□ C12 Ryan Humphrey	.60	.25	.07
□ C13 Brandon Stephens	.60	.25	.07
□ C14 Dan Engel	.60	.25	.07
□ C15 Jared Holland	.60	.25	.07
□ C16 Tango McCauley	.60	.25	.07
□ C17 Kyle Jenson	.60	.25	.07
□ C18 Kody Hergert	.60	.25	.07
□ C19 Jon Rutherford	.60	.25	.07
□ C20 John Teasdale	.60	.25	.07
□ C21 Steve Wiedower	.60	.25	.07
□ C22 Joshua Graham	.60	.25	.07
□ C23 John Robertson	.60	.25	.07
□ C24 Austin Lee	.60	.25	.07
□ C25 Brandon Washington	.60	.25	.07
□ C26 Andy Wisne	.60	.25	.07
□ C27 Bary Holleyman	.60	.25	.07
□ C28 Darren Palladino	.60	.25	.07
□ C29 Mike Burke	.60	.25	.07
□ C30 Thomas Fortune	.60	.25	.07
□ C31 Pete Battisti	.60	.25	.07
□ C32 Monty Beisel	.60	.25	.07
□ C33 John Paul Keserich	.60	.25	.07
□ C34 Garrett Masters	.60	.25	.07
□ C35 Bubba Babb	.60	.25	.07
□ C36 Marlon Guess	.60	.25	.07
□ C37 Stanley Peters	.60	.25	.07
□ C38 Harold Burgess	.60	.25	.07
□ C39 Courtney Hysaw	.60	.25	.07
□ C40 Darcey Levy	.60	.25	.07
□ C41 Zach Magalei	.60	.25	.07
□ C42 Drew Smith	.60	.25	.07
□ C43 Jeff Ferguson	.60	.25	.07
□ C44 Eric Rosel	.60	.25	.07
□ C45 Jeremy Toles	.60	.25	.07
□ C46 Jason Krause	.60	.25	.07
□ C47 Jeff Gloy	.60	.25	.07
□ C48 Brandan Kramer	.60	.25	.07
□ C49 Marques Spivey	.60	.25	.07
□ W1 Randy Fasani	.60	.25	.07
□ W2 Todd Mortensen	.60	.25	.07
□ W3 Spencer Brinton	.60	.25	.07
□ W4 Greg Cicero	.60	.25	.07
□ W5 Scott McEwan	.60	.25	.07
□ W6 Drew Miller	.60	.25	.07
□ W7 Austin Moherman	.60	.25	.07
□ W8 David Priestley	.60	.25	.07
□ W9 David Carr	.60	.25	.07
□ W10 Chris Czernek	.60	.25	.07
□ W11 Jared Flint	.60	.25	.07
□ W12 Josh Rogers	.60	.25	.07
□ W13 Damion Barton	.60	.25	.07
□ W14 Eddie Gayles	.60	.25	.07
□ W15 Mike Rhodes	.60	.25	.07
□ W16 Donovan Calhoun	.60	.25	.07
□ W17 Dante Clay	.60	.25	.07
□ W18 James Creason	.60	.25	.07
□ W19 Tony Elam	.60	.25	.07
□ W20 Brian Palmer	.60	.25	.07
□ W21 Roderick Walker	.60	.25	.07
□ W22 Terrynce White	.60	.25	.07
□ W23 Michael Yancy	.60	.25	.07
□ W24 Ken-Yon Rambo	.60	.25	.07
□ W25 Eddie Gorton	.60	.25	.07
□ W26 Ja'Warren Hooker	.60	.25	.07
□ W27 Jeff Johnson	.60	.25	.07
□ W28 Cody Joyce	.60	.25	.07
□ W29 Rossi Martin	.60	.25	.07
□ W30 Rashawn Owens	.60	.25	.07
□ W31 Joey Getherall	.60	.25	.07
□ W32 Jamien McCullum	.60	.25	.07
□ W33 Brandon Nash	.60	.25	.07
□ W34 Tafiti Uso	.60	.25	.07
□ W35 Lonnie Ford	.60	.25	.07
□ W36 Antoine Harris	.60	.25	.07
□ W37 Corey Lee Smith	.60	.25	.07
□ W38 Donnell Burch	.60	.25	.07
□ W39 Lee Turner	.60	.25	.07
□ W40 Brian Polak	.60	.25	.07
□ W41 Mike Souza	.60	.25	.07
□ W42 Kurt Vollers	.60	.25	.07
□ W43 Craig Brooks	.60	.25	.07
□ W44 Ron Price	.60	.25	.07
□ W45 Mike Wambolt	.60	.25	.07
□ W46 Ralph Zarate	.60	.25	.07
□ W47 Jim Adams	.60	.25	.07
□ W48 Ed Anderson	.60	.25	.07
□ W49 Justin David	.60	.25	.07
□ W50 Brian Hart	.60	.25	.07
□ W51 Nic Hawkins	.60	.25	.07
□ W52 Brandon Hoopes	.60	.25	.07
□ W53 Kris Keene	.60	.25	.07
□ W54 Travis Pfeifer	.60	.25	.07
□ W55 Langston Walker	.60	.25	.07
□ W56 Andre Carter	.60	.25	.07
□ W57 John Jackson	.60	.25	.07
□ W58 Welton Kage	.60	.25	.07
□ W59 Anthony Thomas	.60	.25	.07
□ W60 Justin Bannan	.60	.25	.07
□ W61 Ryan Nielsen	.60	.25	.07
□ W62 Brandon Manumaleuna	.60	.25	.07
□ W63 Kyle Roselle	.60	.25	.07
□ W64 Darrell Daniels	.60	.25	.07
□ W65 Bobby Demars	.60	.25	.07
□ W66 Tracy Hunt	.60	.25	.07
□ W67 Zeke Moreno	.60	.25	.07
□ W68 Tim Shear	.60	.25	.07
□ W69 Kori Dickerson	.60	.25	.07
□ W70 Ty Gregorak	.60	.25	.07
□ W71 Malachi Keddington	.60	.25	.07
□ W72 Don Meyers	.60	.25	.07
□ W73 Tony Thompson	.60	.25	.07
□ W74 Ife Ohalete	.60	.25	.07
□ W75 Antuan Simmons	.60	.25	.07
□ W76 Albus Brooks	.60	.25	.07
□ W77 Dewey Hale	.60	.25	.07
□ W78 Kameron Jones	.60	.25	.07
□ W79 Lamont Thompson	.60	.25	.07
□ W80 Fred Washington	.60	.25	.07
□ W81 Shanga Wilson	.60	.25	.07
□ W82 Marques Anderson	.60	.25	.07
□ W83 DeMario Franklin	.60	.25	.07
□ W84 Melvin Justice	.60	.25	.07
□ W85 Kris Richard	.60	.25	.07
□ W86 Julius Thompson	.60	.25	.07
□ W87 Wes Tufaga	.60	.25	.07
□ W88 Zak Haselmo	.60	.25	.07
□ W89 Jeremy Kelly	.60	.25	.07
□ W90 John Gonzalez	.60	.25	.07
□ W91 Robert Jackson	.60	.25	.07
□ W92 Rod Perry Jr.	.60	.25	.07
□ W93 Charles Tharp	.60	.25	.07
□ W94 Marcus Brady	.60	.25	.07
□ W95 Merle Sango	.60	.25	.07

1996 Roox Prep Star MW/SW

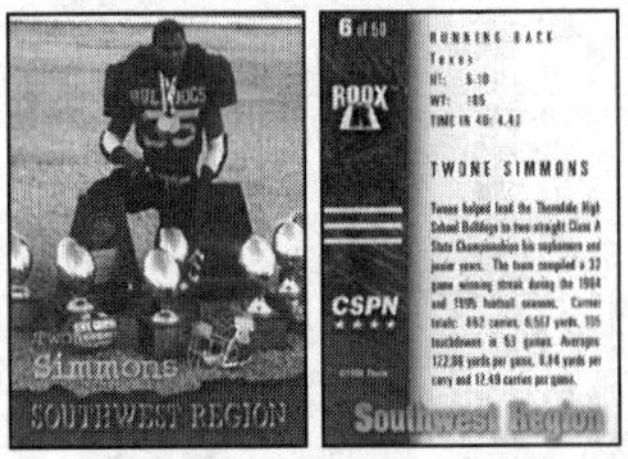

This 142 card standard size boxed set was produced by Roox featuring high school players that played in 1996, and includes standouts from the following states: Illinois, Indiana, Iowa, Michigan, Minnesota, Ohio, Texas, and Wisconsin. Reportedly, 1000 sets were produced.

	MINT	NRMT	EXC
COMPLETE SET(115)	80.00	36.00	10.00
COMMON CARD	.75	.35	.09

□ MW1 Zack Kustock	.75	.35	.09
□ MW2 Tyler Evans	.75	.35	.09
□ MW3 Rob Johnson	.75	.35	.09
□ MW4 Chris Ludban	.75	.35	.09
□ MW5 Ken Stopka	.75	.35	.09
□ MW6 Kyle Van Sluys	.75	.35	.09
□ MW7 Sean Penny	.75	.35	.09
□ MW8 Bill Andrews	.75	.35	.09
□ MW9 James Harrison	.75	.35	.09
□ MW10 De'Wayne Hogan	.75	.35	.09
□ MW11 Carlos Honare'	.75	.35	.09
□ MW12 Ray Jackson	.75	.35	.09
□ MW13 Greg Simpson	.75	.35	.09
□ MW14 Israel Thompson	.75	.35	.09
□ MW15 Ernest Brown	.75	.35	.09
□ MW16 Sam Crenshaw	.75	.35	.09
□ MW17 Adrian Duncan	.75	.35	.09
□ MW18 Kahlil Hill	.75	.35	.09
□ MW19 Teddy Johnson	.75	.35	.09
□ MW20 Omari Jordan	.75	.35	.09
□ MW21 Jason Kemble	.75	.35	.09
□ MW22 Jace Sayler	.75	.35	.09
□ MW23 Tim Stratton	.75	.35	.09
□ MW24 Adam Fay	.75	.35	.09
□ MW25 Josh Jakubowski	.75	.35	.09
□ MW26 Ben Mast	.75	.35	.09
□ MW27 Mike Collins	.75	.35	.09
□ MW28 Oliver King	.75	.35	.09
□ MW29 Rocky Nease	.75	.35	.09
□ MW30 Josh Parrish	.75	.35	.09
□ MW31 Clifton Reta	.75	.35	.09
□ MW32 Brian Wise	.75	.35	.09
□ MW33 Maurice Williams	.75	.35	.09
□ MW34 Kevin Bell	.75	.35	.09
□ MW35 Derek Burns	.75	.35	.09
□ MW36 Anwar Cooper	.75	.35	.09
□ MW37 Jeremy Dox	.75	.35	.09
□ MW38 Raesche Hill	.75	.35	.09
□ MW39 Jason Ptak	.75	.35	.09
□ MW40 Ben Pulfer	.75	.35	.09
□ MW41 Heath Queen	.75	.35	.09
□ MW42 Bill Seymour	.75	.35	.09
□ MW43 Demetrius Smith	.75	.35	.09
□ MW44 Ben Sobieski	.75	.35	.09
□ MW45 Hubert Thompson	.75	.35	.09
□ MW46 Jake Frysinger	.75	.35	.09
□ MW47 Jason Ott	.75	.35	.09
□ MW48 Kyle Vanden Bosch	.75	.35	.09
□ MW49 Kurt Anderson	.75	.35	.09
□ MW50 Napoleon Harris	.75	.35	.09
□ MW51 Jason Manson	.75	.35	.09
□ MW52 Joel Mesman	.75	.35	.09
□ MW53 Jeff Skibitsky	.75	.35	.09
□ MW54 T.J. Turner	.75	.35	.09
□ MW55 Mike Clinkscale	.75	.35	.09
□ MW56 Jamie Grant	.75	.35	.09
□ MW57 Kyle Moffatt	.75	.35	.09
□ MW58 Abdullah Muhammad	.75	.35	.09
□ MW59 Eric Parker	.75	.35	.09
□ MW60 Mike Young	.75	.35	.09
□ MW61 Pat Gibson	.75	.35	.09
□ MW62 Brendan Rauh	.75	.35	.09
□ MW63 Antwan Randle El	.75	.35	.09
□ MW64 Levron Williams	.75	.35	.09
□ SW1 Edmond Stansbury	.75	.35	.09
□ SW2 Grant Elam	.75	.35	.09
□ SW3 Regan George	.75	.35	.09
□ SW4 Matt Schobel	.75	.35	.09
□ SW5 Hodges Mitchell	.75	.35	.09
□ SW6 Twone Simmons	.75	.35	.09
□ SW7 Donald Williams	.75	.35	.09
□ SW8 Jason Coffey	.75	.35	.09
□ SW9 Corey Harris	.75	.35	.09
□ SW10 Shon Jones	.75	.35	.09
□ SW11 Burnest Rhodes	.75	.35	.09
□ SW12 Adrian Thomas	.75	.35	.09
□ SW13 Robert Williams	.75	.35	.09
□ SW14 Daniel Belcha	.75	.35	.09
□ SW15 Damon Daniels	.75	.35	.09
□ SW16 Raymond Turner	.75	.35	.09
□ SW17 Chad Irwin	.75	.35	.09
□ SW18 Ed Kelly	.75	.35	.09
□ SW19 Miles Koon	.75	.35	.09
□ SW20 Luke Nichols	.75	.35	.09
□ SW21 Dennis Jones	.75	.35	.09
□ SW22 Rodney Endsley	.75	.35	.09
□ SW23 Norman McKinney	.75	.35	.09
□ SW24 Terry Williams	.75	.35	.09
□ SW25 David Warren	.75	.35	.09
□ SW26 Lonnie Madison	.75	.35	.09
□ SW27 Shaun Rogers	.75	.35	.09
□ SW28 Mike Minott	.75	.35	.09
□ SW29 Evan Perroni	.75	.35	.09
□ SW30 Grant Irons	.75	.35	.09
□ SW31 Josh Spoerl	.75	.35	.09
□ SW32 Tommy Tull	.75	.35	.09
□ SW33 Chad Chester	.75	.35	.09
□ SW34 Devon Lemons	.75	.35	.09
□ SW35 Antowan Alexander	.75	.35	.09
□ SW36 Jay Brooks	.75	.35	.09
□ SW37 Quenton Jammer	.75	.35	.09
□ SW38 Derrick Yates	.75	.35	.09
□ SW39 Gary Baxter	.75	.35	.09
□ SW40 Danny Black	.75	.35	.09
□ SW41 Brandon Couts	.75	.35	.09
□ SW42 Derek Dorris	.75	.35	.09
□ SW43 Michael Jameson	.75	.35	.09
□ SW44 Mickey Jones	.75	.35	.09
□ SW45 Kevon Morton	.75	.35	.09
□ SW46 Rod Sheppard	.75	.35	.09
□ SW47 J.R. Pouncey	.75	.35	.09
□ SW48 Sterlin Gilbert	.75	.35	.09
□ SW49 Terry Burrell	.75	.35	.09
□ SW50 Jason Stevenson	.75	.35	.09

1990 San Jose State Smokey

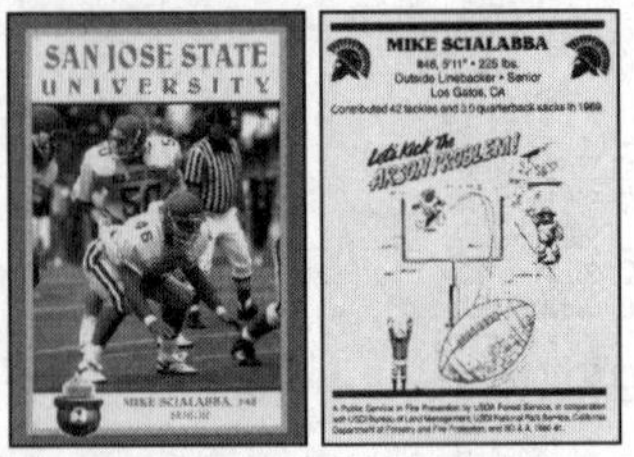

This 15-card standard-size set features members of the 1990 San Jose State football team. The front has a color action photo, with the school name above the picture and the player's name, uniform number, and school year below. The picture is enframed by an orange border on a blue background. The back provides information on the player and features a fire prevention cartoon starring Smokey the Bear. For convenient reference, these unnumbered cards are checklisted below in alphabetical order.

	MINT	NRMT	EXC
COMPLETE SET (15)	10.00	4.50	1.25
COMMON CARD (1-15)	.75	.35	.09

□ 1 Bob Bleisch 90	.75	.35	.09
□ 2 Sheldon Canley 20	.75	.35	.09
□ 3 Paul Franklin 37	.75	.35	.09
□ 4 Anthony Gallegos 72	.75	.35	.09
□ 5 Steve Hieber 48	.75	.35	.09
□ 6 Everett Lampkins 43	.75	.35	.09
□ 7 Kelly Liebengood 21	.75	.35	.09
□ 8 Ralph Martini 9	.75	.35	.09
□ 9 Lyneil Mayo 62	.75	.35	.09
□ 10 Mike Powers 57	.75	.35	.09
□ 11 Mike Scialabba 46	.75	.35	.09
□ 12 Terry Shea CO	.75	.35	.09
□ 13 Freddie Smith 4	.75	.35	.09
□ 14 Eddie Thomas 26	.75	.35	.09
□ 15 Brian Woods 64	.75	.35	.09

1992 San Jose State

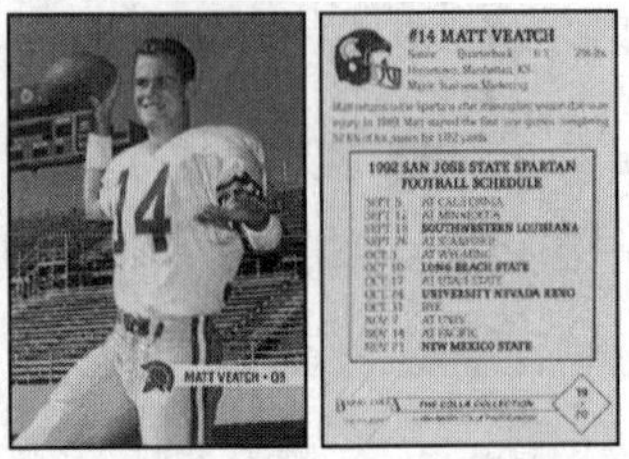

These 20 standard-size cards of the 1992 San Jose State Spartans feature posed color "action" shots by Barry Colla on their borderless fronts. The player's name and position appear within a yellow strip in one corner. The white back carries a Spartan helmet logo at the upper left. The player's jersey number, name, and biography appear alongside the right. The 1992 Spartan game schedule at the bottom rounds out each card. The cards are numbered on the back in alphabetical order as "X of 20".

	MINT	NRMT	EXC
COMPLETE SET (20)	10.00	4.50	1.25
COMMON CARD (1-20)	.60	.25	.07

□ 1 Maceo Barbosa	.60	.25	.07
□ 2 Bobby Blackmon	.60	.25	.07
□ 3 David Blakes	.60	.25	.07
□ 4 Walter Brooks Jr.	.60	.25	.07
□ 5 Greg Bruggeman	.60	.25	.07
□ 6 Bryce Burnett	.60	.25	.07
□ 7 Doug Calcagno	.60	.25	.07
□ 8 Gary Charlton	.60	.25	.07
□ 9 Chris Clarke	.60	.25	.07
□ 10 Hesh Colar	.60	.25	.07
□ 11 Jeff Greeney	.60	.25	.07
□ 12 Leon Hawthorne	.60	.25	.07
□ 13 Peni Iosefa	.60	.25	.07
□ 14 Byron Jackson	.60	.25	.07
□ 15 Robbie Miller	.60	.25	.07
□ 16 Freddie Smith	.60	.25	.07
□ 17 Spencer Smith	.60	.25	.07
□ 18 Simon Vaoifi	.60	.25	.07
□ 19 Matt Veatch	1.00	.45	.12
□ 20 Blair Zerr	.60	.25	.07

1969 South Carolina Team Sheets

These six sheets measure approximately 8" by 10". The fronts feature two rows of five black-and-white player portraits each. The player's name, position and home town are printed under the photo. The backs are blank. The sheets are unnumbered and checklisted below in alphabetical order according to the first player listed.

	NRMT-MT	EXC	G-VG
COMPLETE SET (6)	45.00	20.00	5.50
COMMON PANEL (1-6)	7.00	3.10	.85

□ 1 Tim Bice Candler Boyd Don Buckner Ronald Bunch Bob Cole Carl Cowart Don Dunning Mike Fair Tony Fusaro Benny Galloway	7.00	3.10	.85
□ 2 Allen Brown Don Somma Billy Tharp Scott Townsend Pat Watson Bob Wehmeyer Bob White Curtis Williams Tom Wingard Fred Zeigler	7.00	3.10	.85
□ 3 Andy Chavous Wally Orrel Ronnie Palmer Hyrum Pierce Jimmy Poole Roy Don Reeves Larry Royal Gene Schwarting Fletcher Spigner Frank Tetterton	7.00	3.10	.85
□ 4 Paul Dietzel CO Larry Jones CO Johnny Menger CO	15.00	6.75	1.85

Pride Ratterree CO Bill Rowe CO Bill Shalosky CO Lou Holtz CO Don Purvis CO Jack Powers CO Dick Weldon CO			
□ 5 Ben Garnto Gordon Gibson Johnny Glass Jimmy Gobble Dave Grant Johnny Gregory Bob Harris Rudy Holloman Earl Hunter Jack James	7.00	3.10	.85
□ 6 Jimmy Killen Joe Komoroski Dave Lucas Bob Mauro George McCarthy Toy McCord Wally Medlin Bob Morris Warren Muir Jim Mulvihill	7.00	3.10	.85

1974 Southern Cal Discs

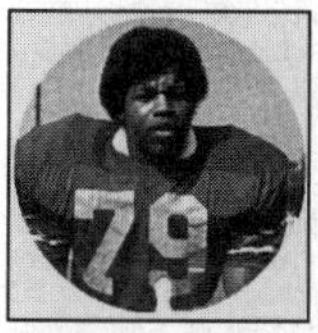
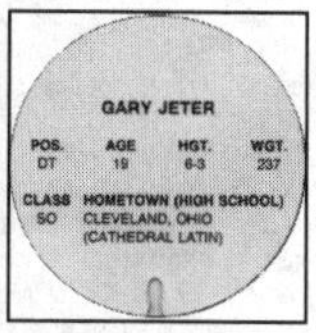

This 30-disc set was issued inside a miniature plastic football display holder, sitting on a red stand that reads "Trojans 1974". The discs measure approximately 2 5/16" in diameter and feature borderless color glossy player photos, shot from the waist up. The backs have biographical information, including the high school attended in the player's hometown. The discs are unnumbered and are listed alphabetically below. The set was reportedly produced and sold by Photo Sports (under the name Foto Ball) during Southern Cal's homecoming week the Fall of 1974.

	NRMT-MT	EXC	G-VG
COMPLETE SET (30)	80.00	36.00	10.00
COMMON DISC (1-30)	2.00	.90	.25
□ 1 Bill Bain	2.50	1.10	.30
□ 2 Otha Bradley	2.50	1.10	.30
□ 3 Kevin Bruce	2.00	.90	.25
□ 4 Mario Celotto	2.00	.90	.25
□ 5 Marvin Cobb	4.00	1.80	.50
□ 6 Anthony Davis	8.00	3.60	1.00
□ 7 Joe Davis	2.00	.90	.25
□ 8 Shelton Diggs	2.50	1.10	.30
□ 9 Dave Farmer	2.50	1.10	.30
□ 10 Pat Haden	10.00	4.50	1.25
□ 11 Donnie Hickman	2.00	.90	.25
□ 12 Doug Hogan	2.00	.90	.25
□ 13 Mike Howell	2.00	.90	.25
□ 14 Gary Jeter	4.00	1.80	.50
□ 15 Steve Knutson	2.00	.90	.25
□ 16 Chris Limahelu	2.50	1.10	.30
□ 17 Bob McCaffrey	2.00	.90	.25
□ 18 J.K. McKay	4.00	1.80	.50
□ 19 John McKay CO	5.00	2.20	.60
□ 20 Jim O'Bradovich	4.00	1.80	.50
□ 21 Charles Phillips	2.50	1.10	.30
□ 22 Ed Powell	2.00	.90	.25
□ 23 Marvin Powell	4.00	1.80	.50
□ 24 Danny Reece	2.50	1.10	.30
□ 25 Art Riley	2.00	.90	.25
□ 26 Traveller II and Richard Sako	2.50	1.10	.30
□ 27 Tommy Trojan Trojan Statue	2.50	1.10	.30
□ 28 USC Song Girls	2.00	.90	.25
□ 29 USC Song Girls	2.00	.90	.25
□ 30 Richard Wood	4.00	1.80	.50

1988 Southern Cal Smokey

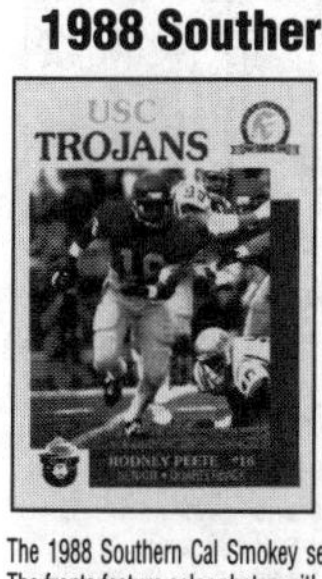

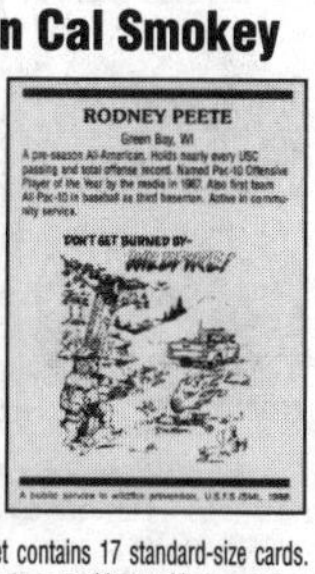

The 1988 Southern Cal Smokey set contains 17 standard-size cards. The fronts feature color photos with name, position, and jersey number. The vertically oriented backs have brief career highlights. The cards are unnumbered, so they are listed alphabetically by subject's name.

	MINT	NRMT	EXC
COMPLETE SET (17)	12.00	5.50	1.50
COMMON CARD (1-17)	.75	.35	.09
□ 1 Erik Affholter	1.25	.55	.16
□ 2 Gene Arrington	.75	.35	.09
□ 3 Scott Brennan	.75	.35	.09
□ 4 Jeff Brown	.75	.35	.09
□ 5 Tracy Butts	.75	.35	.09
□ 6 Martin Chesley	.75	.35	.09
□ 7 Paul Green	.75	.35	.09
□ 8 John Guerrero	.75	.35	.09
□ 9 Chris Hale	.75	.35	.09
□ 10 Rodney Peete	4.00	1.80	.50
□ 11 Dave Powroznik	.75	.35	.09
□ 12 Mark Sager	.75	.35	.09
□ 13 Mike Serpa	.75	.35	.09
□ 14 Larry Smith CO	1.25	.55	.16
□ 15 Chris Sperle	.75	.35	.09
□ 16 Joe Walshe	.75	.35	.09
□ 17 Steven Webster	.75	.35	.09

1988 Southern Cal Winners

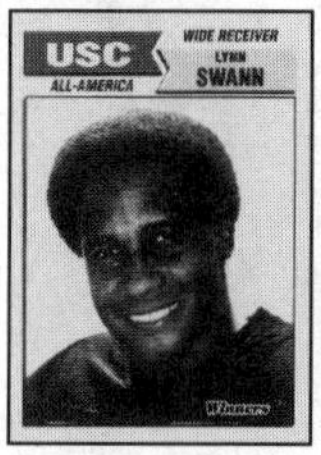

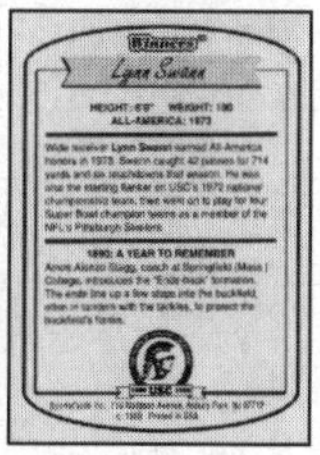

The 1988 Southern Cal Winners set contains 73 standard-size cards. The fronts have black and white mugshots with USC and name banners in school colors; the vertically oriented backs have brief profiles and Trojan highlights from specific seasons. The set was sold by the USC bookstore. The cards are unnumbered, so they are listed alphabetically by type.

	MINT	NRMT	EXC
COMPLETE SET (73)	15.00	6.75	1.85
COMMON CARD (1-73)	.20	.09	.03
□ 1 Title Card (schedule on back)	.30	.14	.04
□ 2 George Achica	.30	.14	.04
□ 3 Marcus Allen	2.50	1.10	.30
□ 4 Jon Arnett	.40	.18	.05
□ 5 Johnny Baker	.20	.09	.03
□ 6 Damon Bame	.20	.09	.03
□ 7 Chip Banks	.40	.18	.05
□ 8 Mike Battle	.30	.14	.04
□ 9 Hal Bedsole	.30	.14	.04
□ 10 Ricky Bell	.40	.18	.05
□ 11 Jeff Bregel	.20	.09	.03
□ 12 Tay Brown	.20	.09	.03
□ 13 Brad Budde	.30	.14	.04
□ 14 Dave Cadigan	.30	.14	.04
□ 15 Pat Cannamela	.20	.09	.03
□ 16 Paul Cleary	.20	.09	.03
□ 17 Sam Cunningham	.40	.18	.05
□ 18 Anthony Davis	.75	.35	.09
□ 19 Clarence Davis	.30	.14	.04
□ 20 Morley Drury	.20	.09	.03
□ 21 John Ferraro	.20	.09	.03
□ 22 Bill Fisk	.20	.09	.03
□ 23 Roy Foster	.30	.14	.04
□ 24 Mike Garrett	.40	.18	.05
□ 25 Frank Gifford	1.50	.70	.19
□ 26 Ralph Heywood	.20	.09	.03
□ 27 Pat Howell	.20	.09	.03
□ 28 Gary Jeter	.30	.14	.04
□ 29 Dennis Johnson	.20	.09	.03
□ 30 Mort Kaer	.20	.09	.03
□ 31 Grenny Lansdell	.20	.09	.03
□ 32 Ronnie Lott	1.50	.70	.19
□ 33 Paul McDonald	.30	.14	.04
□ 34 Tim McDonald	.40	.18	.05
□ 35 Ron Mix	.40	.18	.05
□ 36 Don Mosebar	.40	.18	.05
□ 37 Artimus Parker	.30	.14	.04
□ 38 Charles Phillips	.20	.09	.03
□ 39 Erny Pinckert	.20	.09	.03
□ 40 Marvin Powell	.30	.14	.04
□ 41 Aaron Rosenberg	.20	.09	.03
□ 42 Tim Rossovich	.30	.14	.04
□ 43 Jim Sears	.20	.09	.03
□ 44 Gus Shaver	.20	.09	.03
□ 45 Nate Shaw	.20	.09	.03
□ 46 O.J. Simpson	4.00	1.80	.50
□ 47 Ernie Smith	.20	.09	.03
□ 48 Harry Smith	.20	.09	.03
□ 49 Larry Stevens	.20	.09	.03
□ 50 Lynn Swann	1.50	.70	.19
□ 51 Brice Taylor	.20	.09	.03
□ 52 Dennis Thurman	.30	.14	.04
□ 53 Keith Van Horne	.30	.14	.04
□ 54 Cotton Warburton	.20	.09	.03
□ 55 Charles White	.75	.35	.09
□ 56 Elmer Willhoite	.20	.09	.03
□ 57 Richard Wood	.30	.14	.04
□ 58 Ron Yary	.40	.18	.05
□ 59 Adrian Young	.20	.09	.03
□ 60 Charles Young UER (listed as Adrian Young on card front)	.30	.14	.04
□ 61 Pete Adams and John Grant	.20	.09	.03
□ 62 Bill Bain and Jim O'Bradovich	.30	.14	.04
□ 63 Nate Barrager and Francis Tappan	.20	.09	.03
□ 64 Booker Brown and Steve Riley	.20	.09	.03
□ 65 Al Cowlings, Jimmy Gunn, and Charles Weaver	.50	.23	.06
□ 66 Jack Del Rio and Duane Bickett	.50	.23	.06
□ 67 Clay Matthews and Bruce Matthews	.75	.35	.09
□ 68 Marlin McKeever and Mike McKeever	.40	.18	.05
□ 69 Orv Mohler and Garrett Arbelbide	.20	.09	.03
□ 70 Sid Smith and Marv Montgomery	.20	.09	.03
□ 71 John Vella and Willie Hall	.30	.14	.04
□ 72 Don Williams and Jesse Hibbs	.20	.09	.03
□ 73 Stan Williamson and Tony Slaton	.20	.09	.03

1989 Southern Cal Smokey

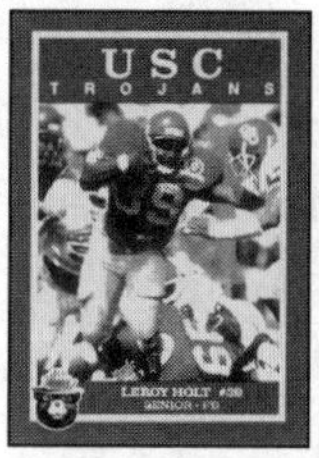

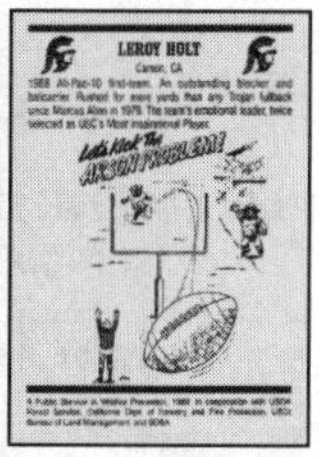

The 1989 Smokey USC football set contains 23 standard-size cards. The fronts have color action photos with maroon borders; the vertically oriented backs have fire prevention tips. These cards were distributed as a set. The cards are unnumbered, so the cards are listed below alphabetically by subject.

	MINT	NRMT	EXC
COMPLETE SET (23)	12.00	5.50	1.50
COMMON CARD (1-23)	.60	.25	.07
□ 1 Dan Barnes	.60	.25	.07
□ 2 Dwight Carner	.60	.25	.07
□ 3 Delmar Chesley	.60	.25	.07
□ 4 Cleveland Colter	.60	.25	.07
□ 5 Aaron Emanuel	1.25	.55	.16
□ 6 Scott Galbraith	1.25	.55	.16
□ 7 Leroy Holt	.75	.35	.09
□ 8 Randy Hord	.60	.25	.07
□ 9 John Jackson	1.25	.55	.16
□ 10 Brad Leggett	.60	.25	.07
□ 11 Marching Band	.60	.25	.07
□ 12 Dan Owens	1.50	.70	.19
□ 13 Brent Parkinson	.60	.25	.07
□ 14 Tim Ryan	1.50	.70	.19
□ 15 Bill Schultz	.60	.25	.07
□ 16 Larry Smith CO	.75	.35	.09
□ 17 Ernest Spears	.75	.35	.09
□ 18 J.P. Sullivan	.60	.25	.07
□ 19 Cordell Sweeney	.60	.25	.07
□ 20 Traveler (Horse Mascot)	.60	.25	.07
□ 21 Marlon Washington	.60	.25	.07
□ 22 Michael Williams	.60	.25	.07
□ 23 Yell Leaders and Song Girls	.60	.25	.07

1991 Southern Cal College Classics *

Produced by College Classics Inc., this 100-card standard-size set honors former Trojan athletes. The white-bordered fronts feature color and black-and-white player photos, mostly action shots, which are framed by red lines. The player's name appears in red lettering within a yellow rectangle at the bottom. The white back carries the player's name, position (or sport if not football), and the years he or she played for USC, all in red lettering within the yellow rectangle at the top. Career highlights follow below. The cards are numbered on the back. The complete set comes with a blank-backed white card that carries the set's production number out of a total of 20,000 produced. In addition, 1,400 cards autographed by John Naber, Ron Fairly, Tom Seaver, Charles White, Dave Stockton, Mike Garrett, Anthony Davis, and Fred Lynn were randomly inserted throughout 1,000 of these sets.

	MINT	NRMT	EXC
COMPLETE SET (100)	30.00	13.50	3.70
COMMON CARD (1-100)	.25	.11	.03
□ 1 Charles White	.75	.35	.09
□ 2 Anthony Davis	.75	.35	.09
□ 3 Clay Matthews	.75	.35	.09
□ 4 Hoby Brenner	.35	.16	.04
□ 5 Mike Garrett	.50	.23	.06
□ 6 Bill Sharman (Basketball)	1.25	.55	.16
□ 7 Bob Seagren (Track)	.35	.16	.04
□ 8 Mike McKeever	.35	.16	.04
□ 9 Celso Kalache (Volleyball)	.25	.11	.03
□ 10 John Williams CO (Water polo)	.25	.11	.03
□ 11 John Naber (Swimming)	.50	.23	.06
□ 12 Brad Budde	.35	.16	.04
□ 13 Tim Ryan	.35	.16	.04
□ 14 Mark Tucker	.25	.11	.03
□ 15 Rodney Peete	1.00	.45	.12
□ 16 Art Mazmanian (Baseball)	.25	.11	.03
□ 17 Red Badgro (Baseball)	.35	.16	.04
□ 18 Sue Habernigg (Women's swimming)	.25	.11	.03
□ 19 Craig Fertig	.25	.11	.03
□ 20 John Block (Basketball)	.50	.23	.06
□ 21 Jen-Kai Liu (Volleyball)	.25	.11	.03
□ 22 Kim Ruddins (Women's volleyball)	.25	.11	.03
□ 23 Al Cowlings	.50	.23	.06
□ 24 Ronnie Lott	1.25	.55	.16
□ 25 Adam Johnson (Volleyball)	1.50	.70	.19
□ 26 Fred Lynn (Baseball)	.50	.23	.06
□ 27 Rick Leach (Tennis)	.25	.11	.03
□ 28 Tim Rossovich	.35	.16	.04
□ 29 Marvin Powell	.35	.16	.04
□ 30 Ron Yary	.50	.23	.06
□ 31 Ken Ruettgers	.50	.23	.06
□ 32 Bob Yoder CO (Men's volleyball)	.25	.11	.03
□ 33 Megan McCallister (Women's volleyball)	.25	.11	.03
□ 34 Dave Cadigan	.35	.16	.04
□ 35 Jeff Bregel	.25	.11	.03
□ 36 Michael Wayman (Tennis)	.25	.11	.03
□ 37 Sippy Woodhead-Kantzer (Women's swimming)	.35	.16	.04
□ 38 Tim Hovland (Volleyball)	1.00	.45	.12
□ 39 Steve Busby (Baseball)	.50	.23	.06
□ 40 Tom Seaver (Baseball)	2.00	.90	.25
□ 41 Anthony Colorito	.25	.11	.03
□ 42 Wayne Carlander (Basketball)	.35	.16	.04
□ 43 Erik Affholter	.35	.16	.04
□ 44 Jim Obradovich	.35	.16	.04
□ 45 Duane Bickett	.50	.23	.06
□ 46 Leslie Daland (Women's swimming)	.25	.11	.03
□ 47 Ole Oleson (Track)	.25	.11	.03
□ 48 Ed Putnam (Baseball)	.25	.11	.03
□ 49 Stan Smith (Tennis)	.75	.35	.09
□ 50 Jeff Hart (Golf)	.25	.11	.03
□ 51 Jack Del Rio	.50	.23	.06
□ 52 Bob Boyd CO (Basketball)	.35	.16	.04
□ 53 Pat Haden	1.00	.45	.12
□ 54 John Lambert (Basketball)	.35	.16	.04
□ 55 Pete Beathard	.75	.35	.09
□ 56 Anna-Maria Fernandez (Women's tennis)	.35	.16	.04
□ 57 Marta Figueras-Dotti (Women's golf)	.35	.16	.04
□ 58 Don Mosebar	.35	.16	.04
□ 59 Don Doll	.35	.16	.04
□ 60 Dave Stockton (Golf)	.75	.35	.09
□ 61 Trisha Laux (Women's tennis)	.25	.11	.03
□ 62 Roy Foster	.35	.16	.04
□ 63 Bruce Matthews	.50	.23	.06
□ 64 Steve Sogge	.35	.16	.04
□ 65 Tracy Nakamura (Women's golf)	.35	.16	.04
□ 66 Marv Montgomery	.25	.11	.03
□ 67 Jack Tingley (Swimming)	.25	.11	.03
□ 68 Larry Stevens	.25	.11	.03
□ 69 Harry Smith	.25	.11	.03
□ 70 Bill Bain	.25	.11	.03

	MINT	NRMT	EXC
☐ 71 Mark McGwire (Baseball)	3.00	1.35	.35
☐ 72 Brad Brink (Baseball)	.25	.11	.03
☐ 73 Richard Wood	.35	.16	.04
☐ 74 Rod Dedeaux CO (Baseball)	.50	.23	.06
☐ 75 Paul Westphal (Basketball)	1.25	.55	.16
☐ 76 Al Krueger	.25	.11	.03
☐ 77 James McConica (Swimming)	.25	.11	.03
☐ 78 Rod Martin	.35	.16	.04
☐ 79 Bill Yardley (Volleyball)	.25	.11	.03
☐ 80 Bill Stetson (Volleyball)	.25	.11	.03
☐ 81 Ray Looze (Swimming)	.25	.11	.03
☐ 82 Dan Jorgensen (Swimming)	.25	.11	.03
☐ 83 Anna-Lucia Fernandez (Women's tennis)	.35	.16	.04
☐ 84 Terri O'Loughlin (Women's swimming)	.25	.11	.03
☐ 85 John Grant	.25	.11	.03
☐ 86 Chris Lewis (Tennis)	.25	.11	.03
☐ 87 Steve Timmons (Volleyball)	2.00	.90	.25
☐ 88 Dr. Dallas Long (Track)	.35	.16	.04
☐ 89 John McKay CO	.50	.23	.06
☐ 90 Joe Bottom (Swimming)	.25	.11	.03
☐ 91 John Jackson	.35	.16	.04
☐ 92 Paul McDonald	.35	.16	.04
☐ 93 Jimmy Gunn	.25	.11	.03
☐ 94 Rod Sherman	.35	.16	.04
☐ 95 Cecilia Fernandez (Women's tennis)	.25	.11	.03
☐ 96 Doug Adler (Tennis)	.25	.11	.03
☐ 97 Ron Orr (Swimming)	.25	.11	.03
☐ 98 Debbie Landreth Brown (Women's volleyball)	.25	.11	.03
☐ 99 Debbie Green (Women's volleyball)	.25	.11	.03
☐ 100 Pat Harrison (Baseball)	.25	.11	.03

1991 Southern Cal Smokey

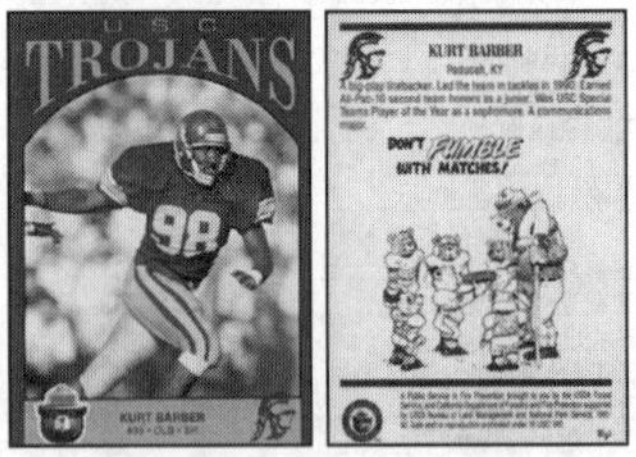

This 16-card standard-size set was sponsored by the USDA Forest Service as well as other federal and state agencies. The front features color action player photos bordered in maroon. The top of the pictures is curved to resemble an archway, and the team name follows the curve of the arch. Player information and logos appear in a mustard stripe beneath the picture. In black on white, the backs carry player profile and a fire prevention cartoon starring Smokey. The cards are unnumbered and checklisted below in alphabetical order.

	MINT	NRMT	EXC
COMPLETE SET (16)	8.00	3.60	1.00
COMMON CARD (1-16)	.60	.25	.07
☐ 1 Kurt Barber	1.25	.55	.16
☐ 2 Ron Dale	.60	.25	.07
☐ 3 Derrick Deese	1.00	.45	.12
☐ 4 Michael Gaytan	.60	.25	.07
☐ 5 Matt Gee	.60	.25	.07
☐ 6 Calvin Holmes	1.00	.45	.12
☐ 7 Scott Lockwood	1.00	.45	.12
☐ 8 Michael Moody	.60	.25	.07
☐ 9 Marvin Pollard	.60	.25	.07
☐ 10 Mark Raab	.60	.25	.07
☐ 11 Larry Smith CO	.75	.35	.09
☐ 12 Raoul Spears	.60	.25	.07
☐ 13 Matt Willig	.60	.25	.07
☐ 14 Alan Wilson	.60	.25	.07
☐ 15 James Wilson	.60	.25	.07
☐ 16 Traveler (The Trojan Horse)	.60	.25	.07

1992 Southern Cal Smokey

This 16-card standard-size set was sponsored by the USDA Forest Service and other state and federal agencies. The cards are printed on thin card stock. The fronts carry a color action player photo on a brick-red card face. The team name and year appear above the photo in gold print on a brick-red bar that partially rests on a gold bar with

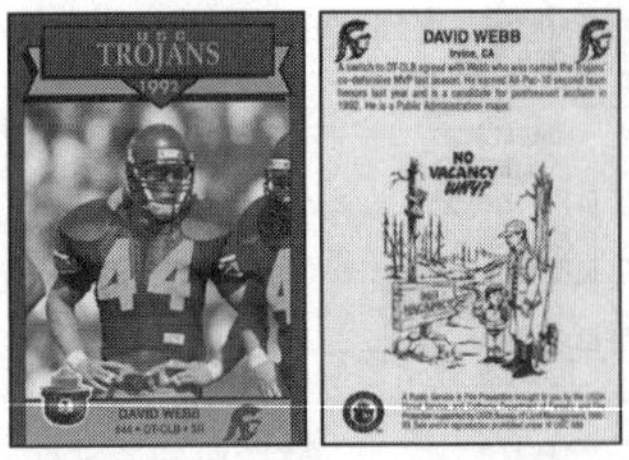

notched ends. Below the photo, the player's name and sponsor logos appear in a gold border stripe. The backs carry player profile and a fire prevention cartoon starring Smokey. The cards are unnumbered and checklisted below in alphabetical order.

	MINT	NRMT	EXC
COMPLETE SET (16)	8.00	3.60	1.00
COMMON CARD (1-16)	.60	.25	.07
☐ 1 Wes Bender	.60	.25	.07
☐ 2 Estrus Crayton	.60	.25	.07
☐ 3 Eric Dixon	.60	.25	.07
☐ 4 Travis Hannah	1.50	.70	.19
☐ 5 Zuri Hector	.60	.25	.07
☐ 6 Lamont Hollinquest	.60	.25	.07
☐ 7 Yonnie Jackson	.60	.25	.07
☐ 8 Bruce Luizzi	.60	.25	.07
☐ 9 Mike Mooney	.75	.35	.09
☐ 10 Stephon Pace	.60	.25	.07
☐ 11 Joel Scott	.60	.25	.07
☐ 12 DeNail Sparks	.60	.25	.07
☐ 13 Titus Tuiasosopo	.60	.25	.07
☐ 14 Larry Wallace	.60	.25	.07
☐ 15 David Webb	.60	.25	.07
☐ 16 Title Card ART	.60	.25	.07

1988 Southwestern Louisiana McDag *

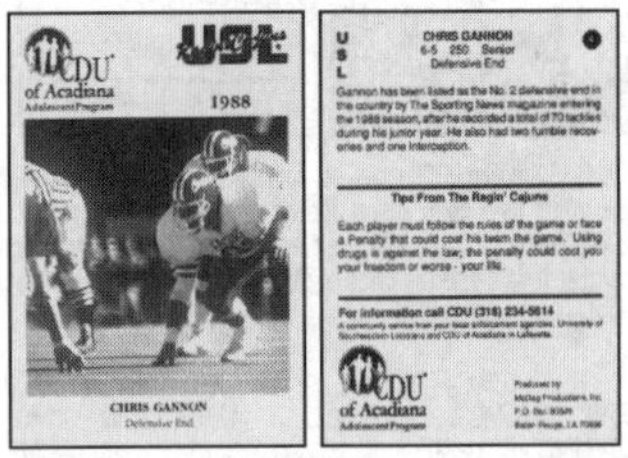

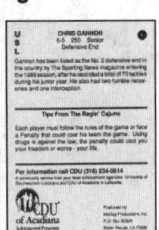

Produced by McDag, this standard-size card set features USL action player photos printed on white card stock. Card numbers 1-10 are player cards; cards 11 and 12 feature dance team members. The CDU of Acadiana Adolescent Program logo appears at the top of each card as well as USL Ragin' Cajuns and year. Player's name appears at bottom in white border. The backs carry biographical information, "Tips from the Ragin' Cajuns" in the form of anti-drug messages, and sponsor advertisement.

	MINT	NRMT	EXC
COMPLETE SET (12)	6.00	2.70	.75
COMMON CARD (1-12)	.50	.23	.06
☐ 1 Brian Mitchell (QB rolling out)	2.00	.90	.25
☐ 2 Brian Mitchell (QB over center)	2.00	.90	.25
☐ 3 Chris Gannon (DE signalling sideline)	.50	.23	.06
☐ 4 Chris Gannon (DE awaiting snap)	.50	.23	.06
☐ 5 Willie Culpepper	.75	.35	.09
☐ 6 Greg Eagles	.50	.23	.06
☐ 7 Steve McKinney	.50	.23	.06
☐ 8 Pat Decuir	.50	.23	.06
☐ 9 Leslie Luquette	.50	.23	.06
☐ 10 Robert Johnson	.50	.23	.06
☐ 11 Lisa McCoy (Cheerleader)	.50	.23	.06
☐ 12 Michelle Aubert (Cheerleader)	.50	.23	.06

1991 Stanford All-Century

This 100-card standard-size set is an All-Century commemorative set issued to honor outstanding players at Stanford during the past 100 years. The set was issued in perforated strips of six cards each. The first card of each strip, redeemable at Togo's for a free Pepsi with any purchase, lists the 1991 home schedule on back. Reportedly only 5,000 sets were produced. Card fronts are pale yellow and feature a close-up black and white player photo in a circle surrounded by palm branches. A gold banner with the words "1891 Stanford Football 1991" appears at bottom of picture while "All-Century Team" rounds out the top of picture. The player's name appears in a red stripe at the bottom of the card face. In mauve print on white, card backs have biographical information and sponsor logos at the bottom. The cards are unnumbered and checklisted below in alphabetical order.

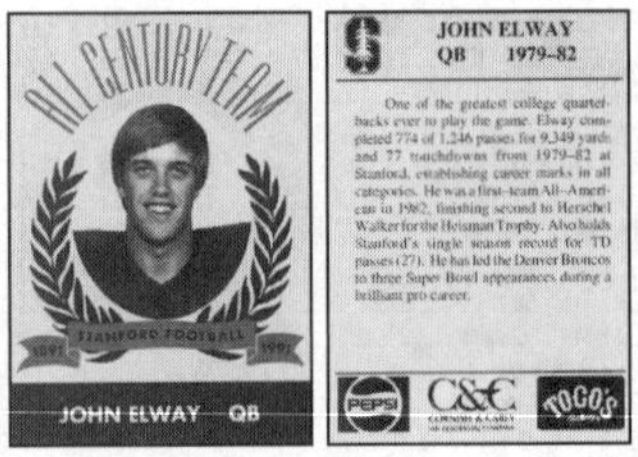

	MINT	NRMT	EXC
COMPLETE SET (100)	110.00	50.00	14.00
COMMON CARD (1-100)	.75	.35	.09
☐ 1 Frankie Albert	1.25	.55	.16
☐ 2 Lester Archambeau	1.00	.45	.12
☐ 3 Bruno Banducci	.75	.35	.09
☐ 4 Benny Barnes	1.00	.45	.12
☐ 5 Guy Benjamin	2.00	.90	.25
☐ 6 Mike Boryla	1.25	.55	.16
☐ 7 Marty Brill	.75	.35	.09
☐ 8 John Brodie	6.00	2.70	.75
☐ 9 Jackie Brown	.75	.35	.09
☐ 10 George Buehler	1.00	.45	.12
☐ 11 Don Bunce	1.25	.55	.16
☐ 12 Chris Burford	1.25	.55	.16
☐ 13 Walter Camp CO	2.50	1.10	.30
☐ 14 Gordy Ceresino	.75	.35	.09
☐ 15 Jack Chapple	.75	.35	.09
☐ 16 Toi Cook	2.00	.90	.25
☐ 17 Bill Corbus	.75	.35	.09
☐ 18 Steve Dils	2.50	1.10	.30
☐ 19 Pat Donovan	1.25	.55	.16
☐ 20 John Elway	25.00	11.00	3.10
☐ 21 Chuck Evans	.75	.35	.09
☐ 22 Skip Face	.75	.35	.09
☐ 23 Hugh Gallarneau	.75	.35	.09
☐ 24 Rod Garcia	.75	.35	.09
☐ 25 Bob Garrett	.75	.35	.09
☐ 26 Rick Gervais	.75	.35	.09
☐ 27 John Gillory	.75	.35	.09
☐ 28 Bobby Grayson	1.00	.45	.12
☐ 29 Bones Hamilton	1.00	.45	.12
☐ 30 Ray Handley	2.00	.90	.25
☐ 31 Mark Harmon	.75	.35	.09
☐ 32 Marv Harris	.75	.35	.09
☐ 33 Emile Harry	1.25	.55	.16
☐ 34 Tony Hill	2.50	1.10	.30
☐ 35 Brian Holloway	1.25	.55	.16
☐ 36 John Hopkins	.75	.35	.09
☐ 37 Dick Horn	.75	.35	.09
☐ 38 Jeff James	1.00	.45	.12
☐ 39 Gary Kerkorian	.75	.35	.09
☐ 40 Gordon King	1.00	.45	.12
☐ 41 Younger Klippert	.75	.35	.09
☐ 42 Pete Kmetovic	.75	.35	.09
☐ 43 Jim Lawson	.75	.35	.09
☐ 44 Pete Lazetich	.75	.35	.09
☐ 45 Dave Lewis	1.00	.45	.12
☐ 46 Vic Lindskog	.75	.35	.09
☐ 47 James Lofton	6.00	2.70	.75
☐ 48 Ken Margerum	1.25	.55	.16
☐ 49 Ed McCaffrey	2.00	.90	.25
☐ 50 Charles McCloud	.75	.35	.09
☐ 51 Bill McColl	1.00	.45	.12
☐ 52 Duncan McColl	.75	.35	.09
☐ 53 Milt McColl	.75	.35	.09
☐ 54 Jim Merlo	1.00	.45	.12
☐ 55 Phil Moffatt	.75	.35	.09
☐ 56 Bob Moore	1.00	.45	.12
☐ 57 Sam Morley	.75	.35	.09
☐ 58 Monk Moscrip	.75	.35	.09
☐ 59 Brad Muster	2.50	1.10	.30
☐ 60 Ken Naber	.75	.35	.09
☐ 61 Darrin Nelson	2.00	.90	.25
☐ 62 Ernie Nevers	4.00	1.80	.50
☐ 63 Dick Norman	.75	.35	.09
☐ 64 Blaine Nye	1.25	.55	.16
☐ 65 Don Parish	.75	.35	.09
☐ 66 John Paye	2.00	.90	.25
☐ 67 Gary Pettigrew	1.00	.45	.12
☐ 68 Jim Plunkett	6.00	2.70	.75
☐ 69 Randy Poltl	.75	.35	.09
☐ 70 Seraphim Post	.75	.35	.09
☐ 71 John Ralston CO	1.25	.55	.16
☐ 72 Bob Reynolds	.75	.35	.09
☐ 73 Don Robesky	.75	.35	.09
☐ 74 Doug Robison	.75	.35	.09
☐ 75 Greg Sampson	.75	.35	.09
☐ 76 John Sande	.75	.35	.09
☐ 77 Turk Schonert	2.00	.90	.25
☐ 78 Jack Schultz	.75	.35	.09
☐ 79 Clark Shaughnessy CO	1.25	.55	.16
☐ 80 Ted Shipkey	.75	.35	.09
☐ 81 Jeff Siemon	2.00	.90	.25
☐ 82 Andy Sinclair	.75	.35	.09
☐ 83 Malcolm Snider	1.00	.45	.12
☐ 84 Norm Standlee	1.00	.45	.12
☐ 85 Roger Stillwell	.75	.35	.09
☐ 86 Chuck Taylor CO	.75	.35	.09
☐ 87 Dink Templeton	.75	.35	.09
☐ 88 Tiny Thornhill CO	.75	.35	.09
☐ 89 Dave Tipton	.75	.35	.09
☐ 90 Keith Topping	.75	.35	.09
☐ 91 Randy Vataha	1.00	.45	.12
☐ 92 Garin Veris	1.25	.55	.16
☐ 93 Jon Volpe	2.50	1.10	.30
☐ 94 Bill Walsh CO	5.00	2.20	.60
☐ 95 Pop Warner CO	2.00	.90	.25
☐ 96 Gene Washington	2.00	.90	.25
☐ 97 Vincent White	.75	.35	.09
☐ 98 Paul Wiggin	1.25	.55	.16
☐ 99 John Wilbur	1.00	.45	.12
☐ 100 David Wyman	1.25	.55	.16

1992 Stanford

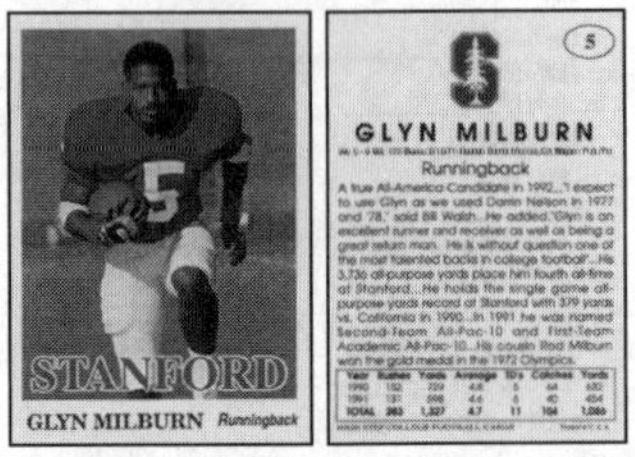

This 35-card standard-size set was manufactured by High Step College Football Cards (Turlock, California). The cards were given away individually at home games. Complete sets could be purchased for 10.00 at the Stanford Stadium, the Track House, or by mail order. Production was reportedly limited to 10,000 sets with only 7,500 being sold as complete sets. The cards were also available in five-card packs; the packs were .75 each and could only be purchased in lots of 20 for 15.00. The cards feature posed action color player photos with white borders. The player's name and position appear in the bottom border. The word "Stanford" is printed in brick-red with a white outline either at the top or bottom of the picture. The backs are white and carry biographical and statistical information and career highlights. The player's uniform number appears in a football icon at the upper right corner. The cards are unnumbered and checklisted below in alphabetical order. The key card in the set is Glyn Milburn.

	MINT	NRMT	EXC
COMPLETE SET (35)	18.00	8.00	2.20
COMMON CARD (1-35)	.35	.16	.04
☐ 1 Seyon Albert	.35	.16	.04
☐ 2 Estevan Avila	.50	.23	.06
☐ 3 Tyler Batson	.35	.16	.04
☐ 4 Guy Benjamin ACO	.60	.25	.07
☐ 5 David Calomese	.35	.16	.04
☐ 6 Mike Cook	.50	.23	.06
☐ 7 Chris Dalman	.75	.35	.09
☐ 8 Dave Garnett	.35	.16	.04
☐ 9 Ron George	1.00	.45	.12
☐ 10 Darrien Gordon	2.00	.90	.25
☐ 11 Tom Holmoe ACO	.60	.25	.07
☐ 12 Derron Klafter	.35	.16	.04
☐ 13 J.J. Lasley	.50	.23	.06
☐ 14 John Lynch	.60	.25	.07
☐ 15 Glyn Milburn	3.00	1.35	.35
☐ 16 Fernando Montes ACO	.50	.23	.06
☐ 17 Vince Otoupal	.35	.16	.04
☐ 18 Rick Pallow	.35	.16	.04
☐ 19 Ron Redell	.35	.16	.04
☐ 20 Aaron Rembisz	.35	.16	.04
☐ 21 Bill Ring ACO	.50	.23	.06
☐ 22 Ellery Roberts	.60	.25	.07
☐ 23 Scott Schuhmann ACO	.35	.16	.04
☐ 24 Terry Shea ACO	.35	.16	.04
☐ 25 Bill Singler ACO	.35	.16	.04
☐ 26 Paul Stonehouse	.35	.16	.04
☐ 27 Dave Tipton ACO	.35	.16	.04
☐ 28 Keena Turner ACO	.75	.35	.09
☐ 29 Fred von Appen ACO	.35	.16	.04
☐ 30 Bill Walsh CO	3.00	1.35	.35
☐ 31 Ryan Wetnight	2.00	.90	.25
☐ 32 Tom Williams	.35	.16	.04
☐ 33 Mike Wilson ACO	.50	.23	.06
☐ 34 Billy Wittman	.35	.16	.04
☐ 35 Checklist Card (J.J. Lasley)	.50	.23	.06

1993 Stanford

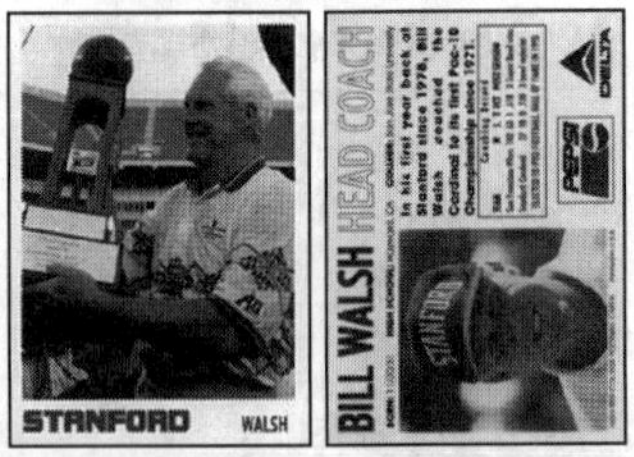

These 18 standard-size cards feature on their fronts color player action shots set within white borders. The player's name appears underneath the photo. The white horizonal back carries the player's name, position, number, and biography at the top. On the left is a player head shot, and on the right, the player's career highlights. The cards are unnumbered and checklisted below in alphabetical order.

	MINT	NRMT	EXC
COMPLETE SET (18)	10.00	4.50	1.25
COMMON CARD (1-18)	.50	.23	.06
☐ 1 Jeff Bailey	.50	.23	.06
☐ 2 Parker Bailey	.50	.23	.06
☐ 3 Roger Boden	.50	.23	.06
☐ 4 Hartwell Brown	.50	.23	.06
☐ 5 Vaughn Bryant	.60	.25	.07
☐ 6 Brian Cassidy	.50	.23	.06
☐ 7 Glen Cavanaugh	.50	.23	.06
☐ 8 Kevin Garnett	.50	.23	.06
☐ 9 Mark Hatzenbuhler	.50	.23	.06
☐ 10 Steve Hoyem	.60	.25	.07
☐ 11 Mike Jerich	.50	.23	.06
☐ 12 Paul Nickel	.50	.23	.06
☐ 13 Toby Norwood	.60	.25	.07
☐ 14 Tyrone Parker	.60	.25	.07
☐ 15 Ellery Roberts	.60	.25	.07
☐ 16 David Shaw	.50	.23	.06
☐ 17 Bill Walsh CO	2.50	1.10	.30
☐ 18 Josh Wright	.50	.23	.06

1976 Sunbeam SEC Die Cuts

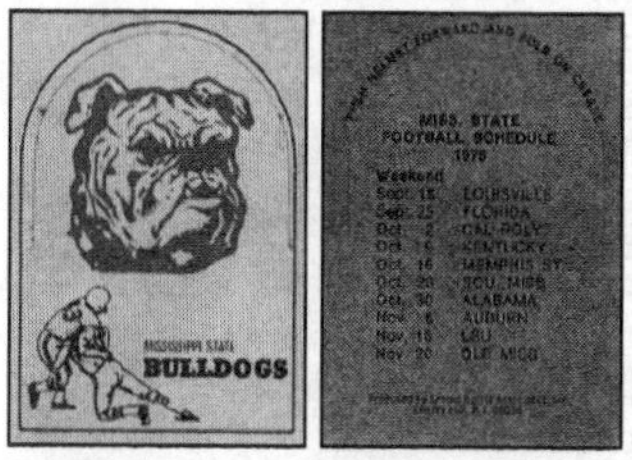

Produced by Arnold Harris Associates Inc. (Cherry Hill, New Jersey), each one of these twenty standard-size cards was inserted in specially-marked loaves of Sunbeam bread. Sunbeam also issued a 4" by 9" "Stand-up Trading Card Saver Book" to hold the cards. This book features pictures of all the fronts with instructions to put the corners of the cards in the slots indicated by the arrows. The team profile cards display the team helmet, an ink drawing of a football action scene, and the team name. The white backs profile the coach and team. The schedule cards show the mascot, another ink drawing of a football action scene, and the team name. The gray backs carry the 1976 football schedule. Both cards are perforated in an arc. The cards are unnumbered; they are checklisted below alphabetically as presented in the saver book.

	NRMT-MT	EXC	G-VG
COMPLETE SET (20)	125.00	55.00	15.50
COMMON CARD (1-20)	5.00	2.20	.60
☐ 1 Alabama Crimson Tide Team Profile	12.00	5.50	1.50
☐ 2 Alabama Crimson Tide Schedule	12.00	5.50	1.50
☐ 3 Auburn War Eagle Team Profile	6.00	2.70	.75
☐ 4 Auburn War Eagle Schedule	6.00	2.70	.75
☐ 5 Florida Gators Team Profile	10.00	4.50	1.25
☐ 6 Florida Gators Schedule	10.00	4.50	1.25
☐ 7 Georgia Bulldogs Team Profile	6.00	2.70	.75
☐ 8 Georgia Bulldogs Schedule	6.00	2.70	.75
☐ 9 Kentucky Wildcats Team Profile	6.00	2.70	.75
☐ 10 Kentucky Wildcats Schedule	6.00	2.70	.75
☐ 11 Louisiana St. Tigers Team Profile	6.00	2.70	.75
☐ 12 Louisiana St. Tigers Schedule	6.00	2.70	.75
☐ 13 Miss. St. Bulldogs Team Profile	5.00	2.20	.60
☐ 14 Miss. St. Bulldogs Schedule	5.00	2.20	.60
☐ 15 Ole Miss Rebels Team Profile	5.00	2.20	.60
☐ 16 Ole Miss Rebels Schedule	5.00	2.20	.60
☐ 17 Tennessee Volunteers Team Profile	8.00	3.60	1.00
☐ 18 Tennessee Volunteers Schedule	8.00	3.60	1.00
☐ 19 Vanderbilt Commodores Team Profile	5.00	2.20	.60
☐ 20 Vanderbilt Commodores Schedule	5.00	2.20	.60

1989 Syracuse Burger King

This 15-card set, featuring cards measuring approximately 2 1/2" by 3 1/2", was produced to honor members of the 1989 Syracuse football team. The fronts of the card have an action photo of the player along with the identification "Syracuse University 1989" and the players

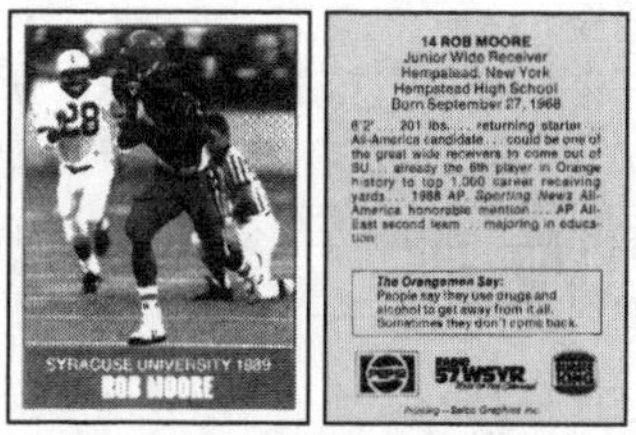

name while the back has biography and a safety tip. This set was sponsored by WYSR radio, Burger King, and Pepsi. Since the set is unnumbered, we have checklisted it in alphabetical order. The key card in the set is wide receiver Rob Moore.

	MINT	NRMT	EXC
COMPLETE SET (15)	18.00	8.00	2.20
COMMON CARD (1-15)	1.00	.45	.12
☐ 1 David Bavaro	1.50	.70	.19
☐ 2 Blake Bednars	1.00	.45	.12
☐ 3 Alban Brown	1.00	.45	.12
☐ 4 Dan Burey	1.00	.45	.12
☐ 5 Rob Burnett	2.50	1.10	.30
☐ 6 Fred DeRiggi	1.00	.45	.12
☐ 7 John Flannery	2.00	.90	.25
☐ 8 Duane Kinnon	1.00	.45	.12
☐ 9 Dick MacPherson CO	2.00	.90	.25
☐ 10 Rob Moore	5.00	2.20	.60
☐ 11 Michael Owens	1.50	.70	.19
☐ 12 Bill Scharr	1.00	.45	.12
☐ 13 Turnell Sims	1.00	.45	.12
☐ 14 Sean Whiteman	1.00	.45	.12
☐ 15 Terry Wooden	2.50	1.10	.30

1991 Syracuse Program Cards

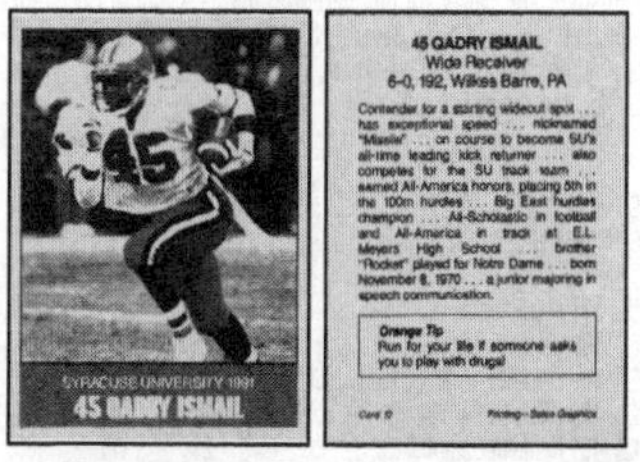

The 1991 Syracuse football set was sponsored by Drumlins Travel and available as inserts in Syracuse University football game programs. Each perforated insert measures approximately 8" by 11" and displays three rows of three cards each. The top two rows consist of six approximately 2 5/8" by 3 1/2" player cards, while the third row has three cards with a sponsor advertisement, a 1991-92 basketball schedule, and the university's logo respectively. The player cards feature glossy color action photos bordered in white, with text reversed-out in white in a burnt orange stripe beneath the picture. The backs have biography, career summary, and an "Orange Tip" in the form of an anti-drug message. Qadry Ismail is the key player in this set.

	MINT	NRMT	EXC
COMPLETE SET (36)	30.00	13.50	3.70
COMMON CARD (1-36)	.75	.35	.09
☐ 1 George Rooks	.75	.35	.09
☐ 2 Marvin Graves	4.00	1.80	.50
☐ 3 Andrew Dees	.75	.35	.09
☐ 4 Glen Young	1.00	.45	.12
☐ 5 Chris Gedney	2.00	.90	.25
☐ 6 Paul Pasqualoni CO	1.00	.45	.12
☐ 7 Terrence Wisdom	.75	.35	.09
☐ 8 John Biskup	.75	.35	.09
☐ 9 Mark McDonald	.75	.35	.09
☐ 10 Dan Conley	1.00	.45	.12
☐ 11 Kevin Mitchell	.75	.35	.09
☐ 12 Qadry Ismail	6.00	2.70	.75
☐ 13 John Lusardi	.75	.35	.09
☐ 14 David Walker	.75	.35	.09
☐ 15 John Capachione	.75	.35	.09
☐ 16 Shelby Hill	1.25	.55	.16
☐ 17 Dwayne Joseph	.75	.35	.09
☐ 18 Greg Walker	.75	.35	.09
☐ 19 Jerry Sharp	.75	.35	.09
☐ 20 Tim Sandquist	.75	.35	.09
☐ 21 Chuck Bull	.75	.35	.09
☐ 22 Jo Jo Wooden	.75	.35	.09
☐ 23 Terry Richardson	.75	.35	.09
☐ 24 Doug Womack	.75	.35	.09
☐ 25 Reggie Terry	.75	.35	.09
☐ 26 Garland Hawkins	.75	.35	.09
☐ 27 Tony Montemorra	.75	.35	.09
☐ 28 Chip Todd	.75	.35	.09
☐ 29 Pat O'Neill	1.00	.45	.12
☐ 30 Kevin Barker	.75	.35	.09
☐ 31 John Reagan	.75	.35	.09
☐ 32 Pat O'Rourke	.75	.35	.09
☐ 33 Jim Wentworth	.75	.35	.09
☐ 34 Ernie Brown	.75	.35	.09
☐ 35 John Nilsen	.75	.35	.09
☐ 36 Al Wooten	.75	.35	.09

1980 Tennessee Police

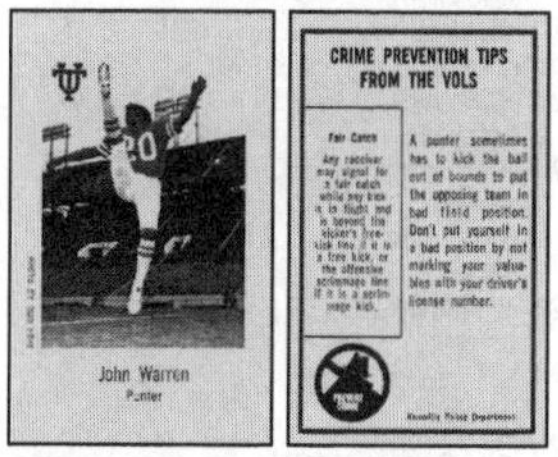

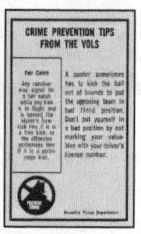

The 1980 Tennessee Police Set features 19 cards measuring approximately 2 5/8" by 4 3/16". The fronts have color photos bordered in white; the vertically oriented backs feature football terminology and safety tips. The cards are unnumbered, so they are listed alphabetically by subject's name. The key player in this set is longtime Cowboy special team star Bill Bates.

	MINT	NRMT	EXC
COMPLETE SET (19)	50.00	22.00	6.25
COMMON CARD (1-19)	2.00	.90	.25
☐ 1 Bill Bates	12.00	5.50	1.50
☐ 2 James Berry	2.00	.90	.25
☐ 3 Chris Bolton	2.00	.90	.25
☐ 4 Mike L. Cofer	6.00	2.70	.75
☐ 5 Glenn Ford	2.00	.90	.25
☐ 6 Anthony Hancock	6.00	2.70	.75
☐ 7 Brian Ingram	2.00	.90	.25
☐ 8 Tim Irwin	4.00	1.80	.50
☐ 9 Kenny Jones	2.00	.90	.25
☐ 10 Wilbert Jones	2.00	.90	.25
☐ 11 Johnny Majors CO	6.00	2.70	.75
☐ 12 Bill Marren	2.00	.90	.25
☐ 13 Danny Martin	2.00	.90	.25
☐ 14 Jim Noonan	2.00	.90	.25
☐ 15 Lee North	2.00	.90	.25
☐ 16 Hubert Simpson	3.00	1.35	.35
☐ 17 Danny Spradlin	3.00	1.35	.35
☐ 18 John Warren	3.00	1.35	.35
☐ 19 Brad White	2.00	.90	.25

1990 Tennessee Centennial

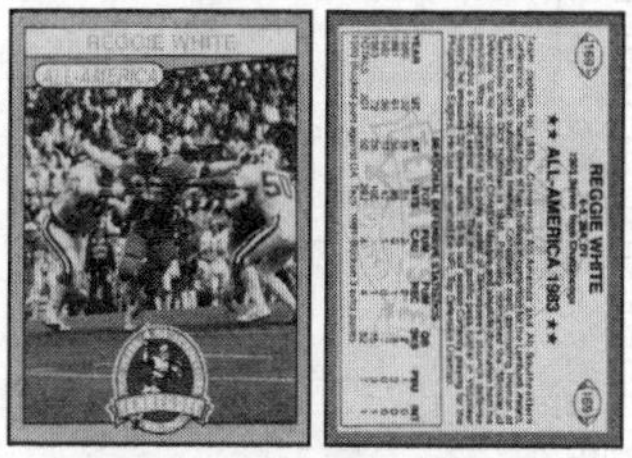

The 1990 Tennessee Volunteers set contains 294 standard-size cards. The fronts feature a mix of color or black and white player photos, enframed by orange borders. The player's name appears in a white stripe above the picture, and a Tennessee insignia with the words "100 Years of Volunteers" is superimposed at the bottom of the picture. In a horizontal format, the backs have player profiles in black lettering overlaying an indistinct version of the same insignia as on the card fronts. The cards are numbered on the backs in both upper corners.

	MINT	NRMT	EXC
COMPLETE SET (294)	35.00	16.00	4.40
COMMON CARD (1-294)	.10	.05	.01
☐ 1 Vince Moore	.20	.09	.03
☐ 2 Steve Matthews	.10	.05	.01
☐ 3 Joey Chapman	.10	.05	.01
☐ 4 Terence Cleveland	.10	.05	.01
☐ 5 Thomas Wood	.10	.05	.01
☐ 6 J.J. McCleskey	.10	.05	.01
☐ 7 Jason Julian	.10	.05	.01
☐ 8 Andy Kelly	.20	.09	.03
☐ 9 Derrick Folsom	.10	.05	.01
☐ 10 Chip McCallum	.10	.05	.01
☐ 11 Lloyd Kerr	.10	.05	.01
☐ 12 Cory Fleming	.30	.14	.04
☐ 13 Kevin Zurcher	.10	.05	.01
☐ 14 Lee England	.10	.05	.01
☐ 15 Carl Pickens	2.00	.90	.25
☐ 16 Sterling Henton	.10	.05	.01
☐ 17 Lee Wood	.10	.05	.01
☐ 18 Kent Elmore	.10	.05	.01
☐ 19 Craig Faulkner	.10	.05	.01
☐ 20 Keith Denson	.10	.05	.01
☐ 21 Preston Warren	.10	.05	.01
☐ 22 Floyd Miley	.10	.05	.01
☐ 23 Earnest Fields	.10	.05	.01
☐ 24 Tony Thompson	.10	.05	.01
☐ 25 Jeremy Lincoln	.30	.14	.04
☐ 26 David Bennett	.10	.05	.01
☐ 27 Greg Burke	.10	.05	.01
☐ 28 Tavio Henson	.10	.05	.01
☐ 29 Kevin Wendelboe	.10	.05	.01
☐ 30 Cedric Kline	.10	.05	.01
☐ 31 Keith Jeter	.10	.05	.01
☐ 32 Chris Russ	.10	.05	.01
☐ 33 DeWayne Dotson	.10	.05	.01
☐ 34 Mike Rapien	.10	.05	.01
☐ 35 Clemons McCroskey	.10	.05	.01
☐ 36 Mark Fletcher	.10	.05	.01
☐ 37 Chuck Smith	.20	.09	.03
☐ 38 Jeff Tullis	.10	.05	.01
☐ 39 Kelly Days	.10	.05	.01
☐ 40 Shazzon Bradley	.10	.05	.01
☐ 41 Reggie Ingram	.10	.05	.01
☐ 42 Roland Poles	.10	.05	.01
☐ 43 Tracy Smith	.10	.05	.01
☐ 44 Chuck Webb	.30	.14	.04
☐ 45 Shon Walker	.20	.09	.03
☐ 46 Eric Riffer	.10	.05	.01
☐ 47 Greg Amsler	.10	.05	.01
☐ 48 J.J. Surlas	.10	.05	.01
☐ 49 Brian Bradley	.10	.05	.01
☐ 50 Tom Myslinski	.20	.09	.03
☐ 51 John Fisher	.10	.05	.01
☐ 52 Craig Martin	.10	.05	.01
☐ 53 Carey Bailey	.10	.05	.01
☐ 54 Houston Thomas	.10	.05	.01
☐ 55 Ryan Patterson	.10	.05	.01
☐ 56 Chad Goodin	.10	.05	.01
☐ 57 Brian Spivey	.10	.05	.01
☐ 58 Todd Kelly	.10	.05	.01
☐ 59 Mike Stowell	.10	.05	.01
☐ 60 Jim Fenwick	.10	.05	.01
☐ 61 Marc Jones	.10	.05	.01
☐ 62 Chris Ragan	.10	.05	.01
☐ 63 Rodney Gordon	.10	.05	.01
☐ 64 Mark Needham	.10	.05	.01
☐ 65 Patrick Lenoir	.10	.05	.01
☐ 66 Martin Williams	.10	.05	.01
☐ 67 Brad Seiber	.10	.05	.01
☐ 68 Larry Smith	.10	.05	.01
☐ 69 Jerry Teel	.10	.05	.01
☐ 70 Charles McRae	.30	.14	.04
☐ 71 Rex Hargrove	.10	.05	.01
☐ 72 James Wilson	.10	.05	.01
☐ 73 Doug Baird	.10	.05	.01
☐ 74 Mark Moore	.10	.05	.01
☐ 75 Lance Nelson	.10	.05	.01
☐ 76 Robert Todd	.10	.05	.01
☐ 77 Greg Gerardi	.10	.05	.01
☐ 78 Antone Davis	.30	.14	.04
☐ 79 Eric Still	.10	.05	.01
☐ 80 Anthony Morgan	.75	.35	.09
☐ 81 Alvin Harper	1.00	.45	.12
☐ 82 Charles Longmire	.10	.05	.01
☐ 83 Mark Adams	.10	.05	.01
☐ 84 Chris Benson	.10	.05	.01
☐ 85 Horace Morris	.10	.05	.01
☐ 86 Harlan Davis	.10	.05	.01
☐ 87 Darryl Hardy	.10	.05	.01
☐ 88 Tracy Hayworth	.20	.09	.03
☐ 89 Von Reeves	.10	.05	.01
☐ 90 Marion Hobby	.10	.05	.01
☐ 91 John Ward ANN	.10	.05	.01
☐ 92 Roderick Lewis	.10	.05	.01
☐ 93 Orion McCants	.10	.05	.01
☐ 94 James Warren	.10	.05	.01
☐ 95 Mario Brunson	.10	.05	.01
☐ 96 Joe Davis	.10	.05	.01
☐ 97 Shawn Truss	.10	.05	.01
☐ 98 Keith Steed	.10	.05	.01
☐ 99 Kacy Rodgers	.10	.05	.01
☐ 100 Johnny Majors CO	.30	.14	.04
☐ 101 Phillip Fulmer CO	.30	.14	.04
☐ 102 Larry Lacewell CO	.20	.09	.03
☐ 103 Charlie Coe CO	.10	.05	.01
☐ 104 Tommy West CO	.10	.05	.01
☐ 105 David Cutcliffe CO	.10	.05	.01
☐ 106 Jack Sells CO	.10	.05	.01
☐ 107 Rex Norris CO	.10	.05	.01
☐ 108 John Chavis CO	.10	.05	.01
☐ 109 Tim Keane CO	.10	.05	.01
☐ 110 Tim Mingey Recruiter	.10	.05	.01
☐ 111 Bill Higdon Sr. Admin. Asst.	.10	.05	.01
☐ 112 Tim Kerin TR	.10	.05	.01
☐ 113 Bruno Pauletto CO	.10	.05	.01
☐ 114 Vols 17, Co.State 14 (Chuck Webb)	.20	.09	.03
☐ 115 Vols 24, UCLA 6 (Chuck Webb)	.20	.09	.03
☐ 116 Vols 28, Duke 6 (Game action photo)	.10	.05	.01
☐ 117 Vols 21, Auburn 14 (Game action photo)	.10	.05	.01
☐ 118 Vols 17, Georgia 14 (Jason Julian)	.10	.05	.01
☐ 119 Vols 30, Alabama 47 (Roland Poles)	.10	.05	.01
☐ 120 Vols 45, LSU 39 (Charles McRae)	.20	.09	.03
☐ 121 Vols 52, Akron 9 (Brian Spivey)	.10	.05	.01
☐ 122 Vols 33, Ole Miss 21 (Alvin Harper)	.30	.14	.04
☐ 123 Vols 31, Kentucky 10 (Kelly Days)	.10	.05	.01
☐ 124 Vols 17, Vanderbilt 10	.10	.05	.01

(Game action photo)			
☐ 125 '90 Mobil Cotton	.10	.05	.01
Bowl 1 (Jason Julian)			
☐ 126 '90 Mobil Cotton	.10	.05	.01
Bowl 2 (Andy Kelly)			
☐ 127 '90 Mobil Cotton	.20	.09	.03
Bowl 3 (Chuck Webb)			
☐ 128 '90 Mobil Cotton	.10	.05	.01
Bowl 4 (Scoreboard)			
☐ 129 Eric Still	.10	.05	.01
☐ 130 Chris Benson	.10	.05	.01
☐ 131 Preston Warren	.10	.05	.01
☐ 132 Lee England	.10	.05	.01
☐ 133 Kent Elmore	.10	.05	.01
☐ 134 Eric Still	.10	.05	.01
☐ 135 Chuck Webb	.30	.14	.04
☐ 136 Marion Hobby	.10	.05	.01
☐ 137 Kent Elmore	.10	.05	.01
☐ 138 Antone Davis	.30	.14	.04
☐ 139 Thomas Woods	.10	.05	.01
☐ 140 Charles McRae	.30	.14	.04
☐ 141 Preston Warren	.10	.05	.01
☐ 142 Darryl Hardy	.10	.05	.01
☐ 143 Offense or Defense	1.00	.45	.12
(Carl Pickens)			
☐ 144 Carl Pickens	2.00	.90	.25
☐ 145 Chuck Webb	.30	.14	.04
☐ 146 Thomas Woods	.10	.05	.01
☐ 147 Total Offense Game	.10	.05	.01
(Andy Kelly)			
☐ 148 The TVA	.10	.05	.01
(Offensive Line)			
Antone Davis			
Eric Still			
Tom Myslinski			
John Fisher			
☐ 149 Smokey (Mascot)	.10	.05	.01
☐ 150 Doug Dickey	.10	.05	.01
Director of Athletics			
☐ 151 Neyland Stadium	.10	.05	.01
☐ 152 Neyland-Thompson Ctr	.10	.05	.01
☐ 153 Gibbs Hall	.10	.05	.01
(Dormitory)			
☐ 154 Academics and	.10	.05	.01
Athletics			
(Carmen Tegano Asst.AD)			
☐ 155 Gene McEver HOF	.10	.05	.01
☐ 156 Beattie Feathers HOF	.30	.14	.04
☐ 157 Robert Neyland HOF CO	.75	.35	.09
☐ 158 Herman Hickman HOF	.20	.09	.03
☐ 159 Bowden Wyatt HOF	.20	.09	.03
☐ 160 Hank Lauricella HOF	.10	.05	.01
☐ 161 Doug Atkins HOF	.30	.14	.04
☐ 162 Johnny Majors HOF	.30	.14	.04
☐ 163 Bobby Dodd HOF	.30	.14	.04
☐ 164 Bob Suffridge HOF	.10	.05	.01
☐ 165 Nathan Dougherty HOF	.10	.05	.01
☐ 166 George Cafego HOF	.10	.05	.01
☐ 167 Bob Johnson HOF	.20	.09	.03
☐ 168 Ed Molinski HOF	.10	.05	.01
☐ 169 Reggie White	2.50	1.10	.30
☐ 170 Willie Gault	.60	.25	.07
☐ 171 Doug Atkins	.30	.14	.04
☐ 172 Keith DeLong	.30	.14	.04
☐ 173 Ron Widby	.20	.09	.03
☐ 174 Bill Johnson	.20	.09	.03
☐ 175 Jack Reynolds	.30	.14	.04
☐ 176 Tim McGee	.50	.23	.06
☐ 177 Harry Galbreath	.20	.09	.03
☐ 178 Roland James	.20	.09	.03
☐ 179 Abe Shires	.10	.05	.01
☐ 180 Ted Daffer	.10	.05	.01
☐ 181 Bob Foxx	.10	.05	.01
☐ 182 Richmond Flowers	.30	.14	.04
☐ 183 Beattie Feathers	.30	.14	.04
☐ 184 Condredge Holloway	.50	.23	.06
☐ 185 Larry Sievers	.20	.09	.03
☐ 186 Johnnie Jones	.10	.05	.01
☐ 187 Carl Zander	.20	.09	.03
☐ 188 Dale Jones	.10	.05	.01
☐ 189 Bruce Wilkerson	.20	.09	.03
☐ 190 Terry McDaniel	.30	.14	.04
☐ 191 Craig Colquitt	.20	.09	.03
☐ 192 Stanley Morgan	.75	.35	.09
☐ 193 Curt Watson	.10	.05	.01
☐ 194 Bobby Majors	.10	.05	.01
☐ 195 Steve Kiner	.20	.09	.03
☐ 196 Paul Naumoff	.20	.09	.03
☐ 197 Bud Sherrod	.10	.05	.01
☐ 198 Murray Warmath	.20	.09	.03
☐ 199 Steve DeLong	.20	.09	.03
☐ 200 Bill Pearman	.10	.05	.01
☐ 201 Bobby Gordon	.10	.05	.01
☐ 202 John Michels	.10	.05	.01
☐ 203 Bill Mayo	.10	.05	.01
☐ 204 Andy Kozar	.10	.05	.01
☐ 205 1892 Volunteers	.10	.05	.01
(Team photo)			
☐ 206 1900 Volunteers	.10	.05	.01
(Team photo)			
☐ 207 1905 Volunteers	.10	.05	.01
(Team photo)			
☐ 208 1907 Volunteers	.10	.05	.01
(Individual player photos)			
☐ 209 1916 Volunteers	.10	.05	.01
(Team photo)			
☐ 210 1914 Volunteers	.10	.05	.01
(Team photo)			
☐ 211 1896 Volunteers	.10	.05	.01
(Team photo)			
☐ 212 1908 Volunteers	.10	.05	.01
(Team photo)			
☐ 213 1926 Volunteers	.10	.05	.01
(Team photo)			
☐ 214 1930 Volunteers	.10	.05	.01
(Team photo)			
☐ 215 1934 Volunteers	.10	.05	.01
(Team photo)			
☐ 216 1938 Volunteers	.10	.05	.01
(Team photo)			
☐ 217 1940 Volunteers	.10	.05	.01
(Team photo)			
☐ 218 1944 Volunteers	.10	.05	.01
(Team photo)			
☐ 219 1945 Volunteers	.10	.05	.01
(Team photo)			
☐ 220 1954 Volunteers	.10	.05	.01
(Team photo)			
☐ 221 1969 Volunteers	.10	.05	.01
(Team photo)			
☐ 222 1962 Volunteers	.10	.05	.01
(Team photo)			
☐ 223 1976 Volunteers	.10	.05	.01
(Team photo)			
☐ 224 1985 Volunteers	.10	.05	.01
(Team photo)			
☐ 225 1978 Volunteers	.10	.05	.01
(Team photo)			
☐ 226 1980 Volunteeers	.10	.05	.01
(Team photo)			
☐ 227 1984 Volunteers	.10	.05	.01
(Team photo)			
☐ 228 1988 Volunteers	.10	.05	.01
(Team photo)			
☐ 229 James Baird	.10	.05	.01
☐ 230 Condredge Holloway	.50	.23	.06
☐ 231 J.G. Lowe	.10	.05	.01
☐ 232 E.A. McLean	.10	.05	.01
☐ 233 Lemont Holt Jeffers	.10	.05	.01
☐ 234 Howard Johnson	.10	.05	.01
☐ 235 Malcolm Aiken	.10	.05	.01
☐ 236 Toby Palmer	.10	.05	.01
☐ 237 Sam Bartholomew	.10	.05	.01
☐ 238 Ray Graves	.10	.05	.01
☐ 239 Billy Bevis	.10	.05	.01
☐ 240 Bert Rechichar	.20	.09	.03
☐ 241 Jim Beutel	.10	.05	.01
☐ 242 Mike Lucci	.30	.14	.04
☐ 243 Hal Wantland	.10	.05	.01
☐ 244 Jackie Walker	.10	.05	.01
☐ 245 Ron McCartney	.10	.05	.01
☐ 246 Robert Shaw	.30	.14	.04
☐ 247 Lee North	.10	.05	.01
☐ 248 James Berry	.10	.05	.01
☐ 249 Carl Zander	.20	.09	.03
☐ 250 Chris White	.10	.05	.01
☐ 251 Tommy Sims	.10	.05	.01
☐ 252 Tim McGee	.50	.23	.06
☐ 253 Keith DeLong	.30	.14	.04
☐ 254 1931 NY Charity Game	.10	.05	.01
(Program)			
☐ 255 1941 Sugar Bowl	.10	.05	.01
(Program)			
☐ 256 1945 Rose Bowl	.10	.05	.01
(Program)			
☐ 257 1957 Gator Bowl	.10	.05	.01
(Program)			
☐ 258 1968 Orange Bowl	.10	.05	.01
(Program)			
☐ 259 1972 Bluebonnet Bowl	.10	.05	.01
(Program)			
☐ 260 1981 Garden State	.10	.05	.01
Bowl (Program)			
☐ 261 1968 Sugar Bowl	.10	.05	.01
(Program)			
☐ 262 Checklist 1-76	.10	.05	.01
☐ 263 Checklist 77-152	.10	.05	.01
☐ 264 Checklist 153-228	.10	.05	.01
☐ 265 Checklist 229-294	.10	.05	.01
☐ 266 Chris White	.10	.05	.01
☐ 267 Kelsey Finch	.10	.05	.01
☐ 268 Johnnie Jones	.10	.05	.01
☐ 269 Johnnie Jones	.10	.05	.01
☐ 270 Curt Watson	.10	.05	.01
☐ 271 William Howard	.10	.05	.01
☐ 272 Bubba Wyche	.75	.35	.09
☐ 273 Tony Robinson	.30	.14	.04
☐ 274 Daryl Dickey	.30	.14	.04
☐ 275 Alan Cockrell To	.30	.14	.04
Willie Gault			
☐ 276 Alan Cockrell	.30	.14	.04
☐ 277 Bobby Scott	.30	.14	.04
☐ 278 Tony Robinson	.30	.14	.04
☐ 279 Jeff Francis	.20	.09	.03
☐ 280 Alvin Harper	1.00	.45	.12
☐ 281 Johnny Mills	.10	.05	.01
☐ 282 Thomas Woods	.10	.05	.01
☐ 283 Bob Lund	.10	.05	.01
☐ 284 Gene McEver	.10	.05	.01
☐ 285 Stanley Morgan	.75	.35	.09
☐ 286 Fuad Reveiz	.30	.14	.04
☐ 287 Kent Elmore	.10	.05	.01
☐ 288 Jimmy Colquitt	.10	.05	.01
☐ 289 Willie Gault	.60	.25	.07
☐ 290 100 Years	.75	.35	.09
Celebration			
(Reggie White)			
☐ 291 The 100 Years Kickoff	.10	.05	.01
(Group photo)			
☐ 292 Like Father, Like Son	.30	.14	.04
Keith DeLong			
Steve DeLong			
☐ 293 Offense and Defense	.20	.09	.03
Raleigh McKenzie			
Reggie McKenzie			
☐ 294 It's Football Time	.20	.09	.03
(1990 schedule on back)			

1991 Tennessee Hoby

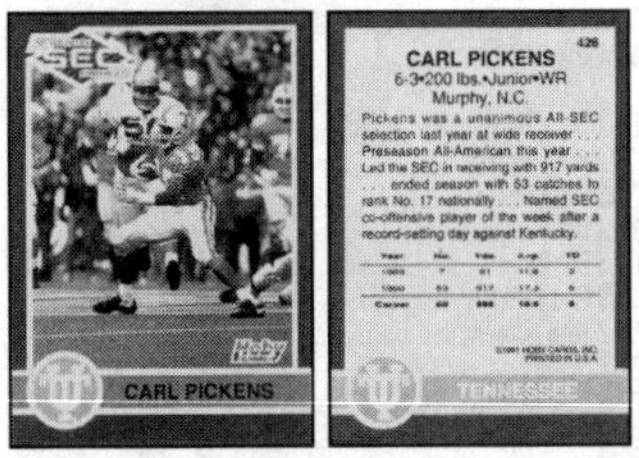

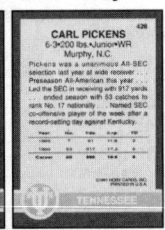

This 42-card standard-size set was produced by Hoby and features the 1991 Tennessee football team. Five hundred uncut press sheets were also produced, and they were signed and numbered by Johnny Majors. The cards feature on the fronts a mix of posed and action color photos, with thin white borders on a royal blue card face. The school logo appears in the lower left corner in an orange circle, with the player's name in a gold stripe extending to the right. On a light orange background, the backs carry biography, player profile, or statistics. The cards are numbered on the back and are ordered alphabetically by player. Several NFL players make their first card appearance in this set: Dale Carter, Chris Mims, Carl Pickens, Heath Shuler, and James Stewart.

	MINT	NRMT	EXC
COMPLETE SET (42)	25.00	11.00	3.10
COMMON CARD (397-438)	.25	.11	.03
☐ 397 Mark Adams	.25	.11	.03
☐ 398 Carey Bailey	.25	.11	.03
☐ 399 David Bennett	.25	.11	.03
☐ 400 Shazzon Bradley	.25	.11	.03
☐ 401 Kenneth Campbell	.25	.11	.03
☐ 402 Dale Carter	2.00	.90	.25
☐ 403 Joey Chapman	.25	.11	.03
☐ 404 Jerry Colquitt	.50	.23	.06
☐ 405 Bernard Dafney	.50	.23	.06
☐ 406 Craig Faulkner	.25	.11	.03
☐ 407 Earnest Fields	.25	.11	.03
☐ 408 John Fisher	.25	.11	.03
☐ 409 Cory Fleming	.75	.35	.09
☐ 410 Mark Fletcher	.25	.11	.03
☐ 411 Tom Fuhler	.25	.11	.03
☐ 412 Johnny Majors CO	.50	.23	.06
☐ 413 Darryl Hardy	.25	.11	.03
☐ 414 Aaron Hayden	2.50	1.10	.30
☐ 415 Tavio Henson	.25	.11	.03
☐ 416 Reggie Ingram	.25	.11	.03
☐ 417 Andy Kelly	.50	.23	.06
☐ 418 Todd Kelly	.75	.35	.09
☐ 419 Patrick Lenoir	.25	.11	.03
☐ 420 Roderick Lewis	.25	.11	.03
☐ 421 Jeremy Lincoln	1.50	.70	.19
☐ 422 J.J. McCleskey	.35	.16	.04
☐ 423 Floyd Miley	.25	.11	.03
☐ 424 Chris Mims	1.50	.70	.19
☐ 425 Tom Myslinski	.35	.16	.04
☐ 426 Carl Pickens	5.00	2.20	.60
☐ 427 Roc Powe	.25	.11	.03
☐ 428 Von Reeves	.25	.11	.03
☐ 429 Eric Riffer	.25	.11	.03
☐ 430 Kacy Rodgers	.25	.11	.03
☐ 431 Steve Session	.25	.11	.03
☐ 432 Heath Shuler	6.00	2.70	.75
☐ 433 Chuck Smith	.35	.16	.04
☐ 434 James O.Stewart	3.00	1.35	.35
☐ 435 Mike Stowell	.25	.11	.03
☐ 436 J.J. Surlas	.25	.11	.03
☐ 437 Shon Walker	.35	.16	.04
☐ 438 James Wilson	.25	.11	.03

1991 Texas HS Legends

This 25-card standard-size set was sponsored by Pepsi and issued by the Texas High School Football Hall of Fame. Apparently the set was sold in five five-card packs; each pack featured four player cards and a numbered cover card. On a black card face, the fronts feature sepia-toned player photos. The words "Texas High School Football Legend" and logos adorn the top of the front, while the player's name, high school, and years attended are presented below the picture. In red and blue print on a white panel, the backs carry biographical information, career summary under four subheadings (performance chart; college/pro honors; unforgettable moment; expert opinion), and the player's signature. The cards are unnumbered and checklisted below in alphabetical order, with the cover cards listed at the end.

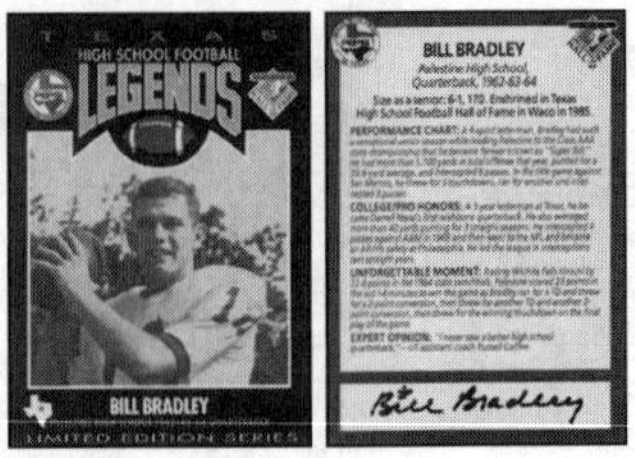

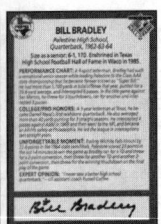

	MINT	NRMT	EXC
COMPLETE SET (25)	18.00	8.00	2.20
COMMON CARD (1-25)	.60	.25	.07
☐ 1 Marty Akins	.60	.25	.07
☐ 2 Gil Bartosh	.60	.25	.07
☐ 3 Bill Bradley	1.00	.45	.12
☐ 4 Chris Gilbert	1.25	.55	.16
☐ 5 Glynn Gregory	.75	.35	.09
☐ 6 Charlie Haas	.60	.25	.07
☐ 7 Craig James	2.00	.90	.25
☐ 8 Boody Johnson	.60	.25	.07
☐ 9 Ernie Koy Jr.	.75	.35	.09
☐ 10 Glenn Lippman	.60	.25	.07
☐ 11 Jack Pardee	1.00	.45	.12
☐ 12 Billy Patterson	.60	.25	.07
☐ 13 Billy Sims	3.00	1.35	.35
☐ 14 Byron Townsend	.60	.25	.07
☐ 15 Doyle Traylor	.60	.25	.07
☐ 16 Joe Washington Jr.	1.00	.45	.12
☐ 17 Allie White	.60	.25	.07
☐ 18 Wilson Whitley	.75	.35	.09
☐ 19 Gordon Wood	.75	.35	.09
☐ 20 Willie Zapalac	.60	.25	.07
☐ 21 Cover Card 1	.60	.25	.07
☐ 22 Cover Card 2	.60	.25	.07
☐ 23 Cover Card 3	.60	.25	.07
☐ 24 Cover Card 4	.60	.25	.07
☐ 25 Cover Card 5	.60	.25	.07

1993 Texas Taco Bell

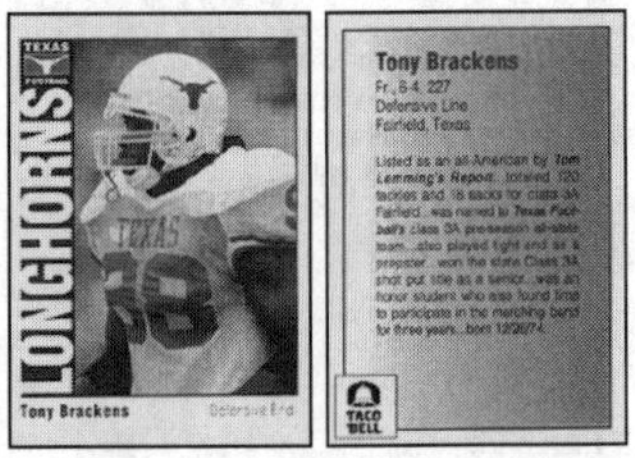

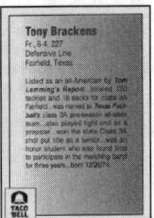

Sponsored by Taco Bell, the 50 cards comprising this set were issued in perforated game program insert sheets. The sheets measure approximately 8" by 10 7/8". Each card measures approximately 2 3/8" by 3 3/8" and carries on its front a white-bordered color player action shot. The player's name and position appear in black lettering within the white border at the bottom. The words "Texas Longhorns" in white lettering, along with the team logo, appear within the vertical black bar along the photo's left side. Each back carries the player's name in orange lettering at the upper left, followed below by his class, position, hometown, and highlights. The Taco Bell logo at the lower left rounds out the card. The cards are unnumbered and checklisted below in alphabetical order.

	MINT	NRMT	EXC
COMPLETE SET (50)	30.00	13.50	3.70
COMMON CARD (1-50)	.50	.23	.06
☐ 1 Mike Adams	2.00	.90	.25
☐ 2 Thomas Baskin	.50	.23	.06
☐ 3 Tony Brackens	2.00	.90	.25
☐ 4 Steve Bradley	.50	.23	.06
☐ 5 Blake Brockermeyer	1.50	.70	.19
(Wearing home jersey)			
☐ 6 Blake Brockermeyer	1.50	.70	.19
(Wearing away jersey)			
☐ 7 Phil Brown	.50	.23	.06
☐ 8 Chris Carter	.50	.23	.06
☐ 9 Stonie Clark	.75	.35	.09
☐ 10 Gerald Crawford	.50	.23	.06
☐ 12 Trent Elliot	.50	.23	.06
☐ 13 Joey Ellis	.75	.35	.09
☐ 14 John Elmore	.75	.35	.09
☐ 15 Jon Feick	.50	.23	.06
☐ 16 Victor Frazier	.50	.23	.06
☐ 17 Jimmy Hakes	.50	.23	.06
☐ 18 Anthony Holmes	.50	.23	.06
☐ 19 Brian Howard	.50	.23	.06
☐ 20 Jon Hunter	.50	.23	.06
☐ 21 Curtis Jackson	.75	.35	.09
☐ 22 Eric Jackson	.50	.23	.06
☐ 23 Bryan Johnson	.75	.35	.09
☐ 24 James Lane	.50	.23	.06
☐ 25 Doug Livingston	.50	.23	.06
☐ 26 Chad Lucas	.50	.23	.06
☐ 27 John Mackovic CO	1.00	.45	.12
☐ 28 Van Malone	1.25	.55	.16
☐ 29 Justin McLemore	.75	.35	.09

	MINT	NRMT	EXC
☐ 30 Shea Morenz	2.50	1.10	.30
☐ 31 Dan Neil	1.00	.45	.12
☐ 32 Cosmo Palmieri	.50	.23	.06
☐ 33 Joe Phillips	.50	.23	.06
☐ 34 Lovell Pinkney	2.50	1.10	.30
☐ 35 Chris Rapp	.50	.23	.06
☐ 36 Robert Reed	.50	.23	.06
☐ 37 Jason Reeves	.50	.23	.06
☐ 38 Troy Riemer	.50	.23	.06
☐ 39 Scott Szeredy	.50	.23	.06
☐ 40 Tre Thomas	.75	.35	.09
☐ 41 Winfred Tubbs	1.50	.70	.19
☐ 42 Duane Vacek	.75	.35	.09
☐ 43 Brian Vasek	.75	.35	.09
☐ 44 Rodrick Walker	1.00	.45	.12
☐ 45 Norman Watkins	.50	.23	.06
☐ 46 Kevin Watler	.50	.23	.06
☐ 47 Pascal Watty	.50	.23	.06
☐ 48 Bryant Westbrook	3.00	1.35	.35
☐ 49 Longhorns Band	.50	.23	.06
☐ 50 Taco Bell logo card 1993 Texas schedule	.50	.23	.06

1992 Texas A and M

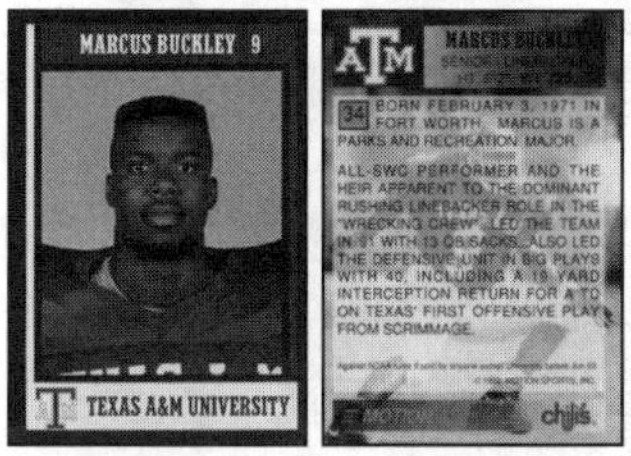

Produced by Motions Sports Inc., this 64-card standard-size set was sponsored by Pepsi Cola and Chili's restaurants. The cards were to be sold only at the campus bookstore of Texas A and M University. The fronts feature posed color player photos on a black card face. The photo is framed in black and has a white border at the right and bottom and a maroon border at the top and left. The player's name and number appear in the top maroon border and "Texas A and M University" appear in the bottom white border. On a ghosted player photo, the backs present a player profile in a transparent white box. Key cards in this set are Greg Hill and Rodney Thomas.

	MINT	NRMT	EXC
COMPLETE SET (65)	30.00	13.50	3.70
COMMON CARD (1-62)	.35	.16	.04
☐ 1 Matt Miller	.50	.23	.06
☐ 2 Steve Emerson	.35	.16	.04
☐ 3 Brad Cooper	.35	.16	.04
☐ 4 Mike Hendricks	.50	.23	.06
☐ 5 Dexter Wesley	.35	.16	.04
☐ 6 Darrell Red	.35	.16	.04
☐ 7 Antonio Shorter	.75	.35	.09
☐ 8 Larry Wallace	.35	.16	.04
☐ 9 Kefa Chatham	.35	.16	.04
☐ 10 Billy Mitchell	.35	.16	.04
☐ 11 Patrick Bates	2.00	.90	.25
☐ 12 Greg Hill	4.00	1.80	.50
☐ 13 Tommy Preston	.35	.16	.04
☐ 14 Ryan Mathews	.35	.16	.04
☐ 15 Steve Kenney	.35	.16	.04
☐ 16 John Richard	.35	.16	.04
☐ 17 John Ellisor	.35	.16	.04
☐ 18 Ryan Kern	.35	.16	.04
☐ 19 Jeff Jones	.35	.16	.04
☐ 20 Chris Sanders	.35	.16	.04
☐ 21 Reggie Graham	.35	.16	.04
☐ 22 David Davis	.35	.16	.04
☐ 23 Tony Harrison	.50	.23	.06
☐ 24 Jason Mathews	.50	.23	.06
☐ 25 Otis Nealy	.35	.16	.04
☐ 26 Kent Petty	.35	.16	.04
☐ 27 Rodney Thomas	4.00	1.80	.50
☐ 28 Sam Adams	2.00	.90	.25
☐ 29 Clif Groce	.35	.16	.04
☐ 30 Tyler Harrison	.35	.16	.04
☐ 31 Eric England	.35	.16	.04
☐ 32 Jason Atkinson	.50	.23	.06
☐ 33 Lance Teichelman	.35	.16	.04
☐ 34 Marcus Buckley	2.00	.90	.25
☐ 35 Steve Solari	.50	.23	.06
☐ 36 Aggie Coaches	.50	.23	.06
☐ 37 Derrick Frazier	.50	.23	.06
☐ 38 James McKeehan	.50	.23	.06
☐ 39 Doug Carter	.35	.16	.04
☐ 40 Larry Jackson	.35	.16	.04
☐ 41 Brian Mitchell	.50	.23	.06
☐ 42 Greg Schorp	.50	.23	.06
☐ 43 Greg Cook	.35	.16	.04
☐ 44 Kyle Maxfield	.35	.16	.04
☐ 45 Todd Mathison	.35	.16	.04
☐ 46 Chris Dausin	.35	.16	.04
☐ 47 Junior White	.35	.16	.04
☐ 48 Wilbert Biggens	.35	.16	.04
☐ 49 Terry Venetoulias	.35	.16	.04
☐ 50 Jessie Cox	.35	.16	.04
☐ 51 R.C. Slocum CO	1.00	.45	.12
☐ 52 Defensive Coaches Bob Davie Kirk Doll Bill Johnson Trent Walters	.50	.23	.06
☐ 53 Offensive Coaches Mike Sherman Shawn Slocum Bob Toledo Gary Kubiak David Culley	.50	.23	.06
☐ 54 Tim Cassidy Recruiting Coordinator	.35	.16	.04
☐ 55 Yell Leaders Steve Scanlon Adin Pfeuffer Tim Isgitt Ronnie McDonald Mark Rollins	.35	.16	.04
☐ 56 A and M Band	.35	.16	.04
☐ 57 Reveille V Mascot	.35	.16	.04
☐ 58 Twelfth Man Statue	.50	.23	.06
☐ 59 Bonfire	.35	.16	.04
☐ 60 Training Facility	.35	.16	.04
☐ 61 Kyle Field	.35	.16	.04
☐ 62 Texas A and M Campus	.35	.16	.04
☐ NNO Front Card (Texas A and M logo)	.35	.16	.04
☐ NNO Back Card	.35	.16	.04
☐ NNO Checklist Card	.35	.16	.04

1995 Tony's Pizza College Mascots

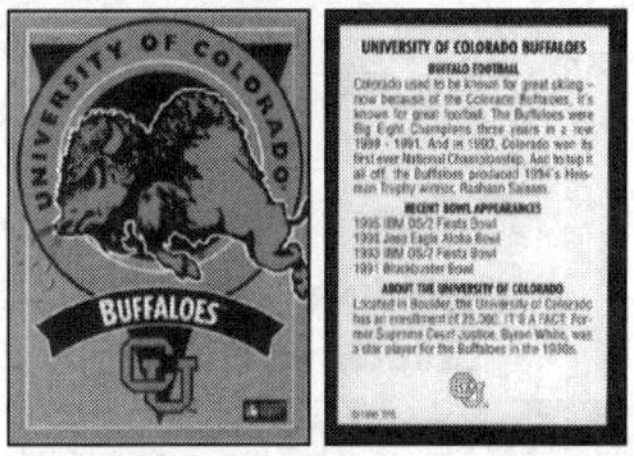

These 20 standard-size cards were issued on the back panels of specially-marked Tony's Italian Pastry and Tony's Pizza D'Primo packages. The cards were not perforated but could be removed from the back panel by cutting along the dotted line. Two cards were featured on each panel as well as an offer for a college sweatshirt. The fronts feature team color-coded drawings of football team mascots, while the backs carry interesting facts and highlights about the college and its football program. The cards are unnumbered and checklisted below in alphabetical order.

	MINT	NRMT	EXC
COMPLETE SET (20)	7.00	3.10	.85
COMMON CARD	.25	.11	.03
☐ 1 Alabama Crimson Tide	.50	.23	.06
☐ 2 Auburn Tigers	.40	.18	.05
☐ 3 Arizona Wildcats	.25	.11	.03
☐ 4 Boston College Eagles	.25	.11	.03
☐ 5 Colorado Buffaloes	.40	.18	.05
☐ 6 Florida State Seminoles	.50	.23	.06
☐ 7 Florida Gators	.50	.23	.06
☐ 8 Kansas State Wildcats	.25	.11	.03
☐ 9 Miami Hurricanes	.50	.23	.06
☐ 10 Michigan Wolverines	.50	.23	.06
☐ 11 Nebraska Cornhuskers	.50	.23	.06
☐ 12 Notre Dame Fightin' Irish	.50	.23	.06
☐ 13 Penn State Nittany Lions	.50	.23	.06
☐ 14 Tennessee Volunteers	.50	.23	.06
☐ 15 Texas Longhorns	.40	.18	.05
☐ 16 Texas A,M Aggies	.40	.18	.05
☐ 17 UCLA Bruins	.50	.23	.06
☐ 18 USC Trojans	.50	.23	.06
☐ 19 Washington Huskies	.40	.18	.05
☐ 20 Wisconsin Badgers	.25	.11	.03

1991 UNLV

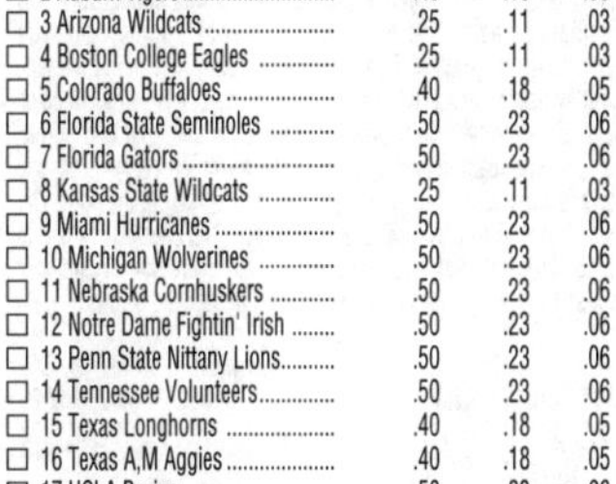

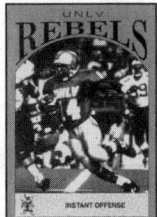

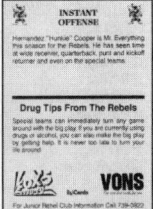

This 12-card standard size set was sponsored by KVVU TV (Fox 5), BDA, and Vons. The cards were printed on thin card stock and issued on a perforated sheet measuring approximately 10" by 10 1/2". The fronts feature color action photos bordered in red. The top of the pictures is curved to resemble an archway, and the team name follows the curve of the arch. The player's name and position appear in a gray stripe below the picture. The backs carry comments, "Drug Tips From The Rebels," sponsor logos, and a phone number for Junior Rebel Club Information. The cards are unnumbered and checklisted below in alphabetical order.

	MINT	NRMT	EXC
COMPLETE SET (12)	8.00	3.60	1.00
COMMON CARD (1-12)	.75	.35	.09
☐ 1 Cheerleaders and Songleaders	.75	.35	.09
☐ 2 Gang Tackle	.75	.35	.09
☐ 3 Instant Offense Hernandez Cooper	.75	.35	.09
☐ 4 No Escape	.75	.35	.09
☐ 5 On the Move	.75	.35	.09
☐ 6 Punching It In	.75	.35	.09
☐ 7 Ready to Fire Derek Stott	.75	.35	.09
☐ 8 Rebel Fever	.75	.35	.09
☐ 9 Rebel Sack	.75	.35	.09
☐ 10 Sam Boyd Silver Bowl	.75	.35	.09
☐ 11 Jim Strong CO	.75	.35	.09
☐ 12 Team Photo	1.00	.45	.12

1991 Utah State Schedules

These Utah State schedules were distributed during the 1991 season. They are listed below in alphabetical order. If there are any additions to the players checklisted below, that information would be appreciated.

	MINT	NRMT	EXC
COMPLETE SET (7)	10.00	4.50	1.25
COMMON CARD	1.50	.70	.19
☐ 1 Warren Bowers	1.50	.70	.19
☐ 2 Floyd Foreman	1.50	.70	.19
☐ 3 Ron Lopez	1.50	.70	.19
☐ 4 Del Lyles	1.50	.70	.19
☐ 5 Charlie Smith	1.50	.70	.19
☐ 6 Toby Tyler	1.50	.70	.19
☐ 7 Rob Van De Pol	1.50	.70	.19

1990 Versailles HS

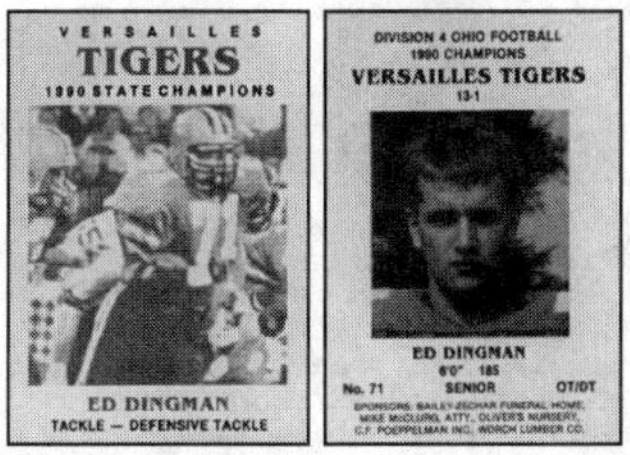

This 20-card set features the Versailles Tigers, the 1990 State Champions of Division 4 Ohio Football. The set was issued as a perforated sheet consisting of five rows of four cards each; after perforation, each individual card measures the standard size (2 1/2" by 3 1/2"). On a white card face, the fronts feature black and white action game shots. The player's name team name above the photo and the player's name below it are printed in orange lettering; other information on the fronts is in black lettering. The backs are dominated by a black and white head shot with biography and a list of sponsors immediately below the pictures. The cards are unnumbered and checklisted below alphabetically.

	MINT	NRMT	EXC
COMPLETE SET (20)	8.00	3.60	1.00
COMMON CARD (1-20)	.50	.23	.06
☐ 1 Kevin Bergman	.50	.23	.06
☐ 2 A.J. Bey	.50	.23	.06
☐ 3 Brad Bey	.50	.23	.06
☐ 4 Ed Dingman	.75	.35	.09
☐ 5 Brian Griesdorn	.50	.23	.06
☐ 6 Al Hetrick CO	.75	.35	.09
☐ 7 Garth Hoellrich	.50	.23	.06
☐ 8 Trent Huff	.50	.23	.06
☐ 9 Brian Keiser	.50	.23	.06
☐ 10 Lane Knore	.50	.23	.06
☐ 11 Brian Kunk	.50	.23	.06
☐ 12 Keenan Leichty	.50	.23	.06
☐ 13 Marc Litten	.50	.23	.06
☐ 14 Craig Oliver	.50	.23	.06
☐ 15 Jon Pothast	.50	.23	.06
☐ 16 Joe Rush	.50	.23	.06
☐ 17 Shane Schultz	.50	.23	.06
☐ 18 Mark Siekman	.50	.23	.06
☐ 19 Matt Stall	.50	.23	.06
☐ 20 Nathan Subler	.50	.23	.06

1990 Virginia

This 16-card standard size set was issued to celebrate the 1990 Virginia Cavalier team, which contended for the National Title. This set features a good mix of action photography and portrait shots on the front with biographical information on the back. The set was issued as a perforated sheet with four rows of four cards each. This set was sponsored by the Charter Hospital of Charlottesville and was given out to those fans in attendance at the Sept. 29, 1990 game against William and Mary. The cards are unnumbered and listed below in alphabetical order. The key card in this set is wide receiver Herman Moore.

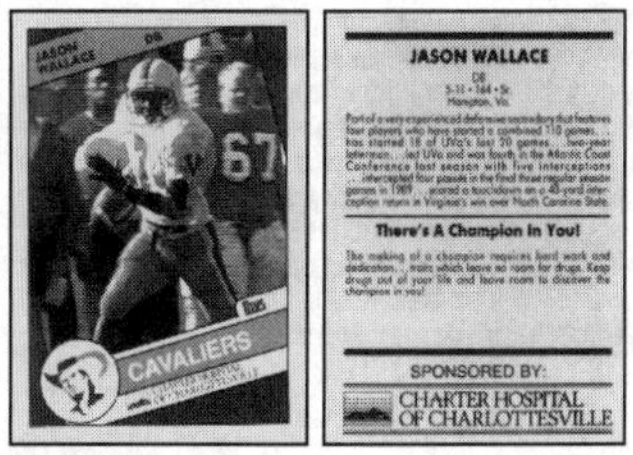

	MINT	NRMT	EXC
COMPLETE SET (16)	25.00	11.00	3.10
COMMON CARD (1-16)	1.25	.55	.16
☐ 1 Chris Borsari	1.25	.55	.16
☐ 2 Ron Carey	1.25	.55	.16
☐ 3 Paul Collins	1.25	.55	.16
☐ 4 Tony Covington	2.00	.90	.25
☐ 5 Derek Dooley	1.25	.55	.16
☐ 6 Joe Hall	1.25	.55	.16
☐ 7 Myron Martin	1.25	.55	.16
☐ 8 Bruce McGonnigal	1.50	.70	.19
☐ 9 Jake McInerney	1.25	.55	.16
☐ 10 Keith McMeans	1.25	.55	.16
☐ 11 Herman Moore	12.00	5.50	1.50
☐ 12 Shawn Moore	3.00	1.35	.35
☐ 13 Trevor Ryals	1.25	.55	.16
☐ 14 Chris Stearns	1.25	.55	.16
☐ 15 Jason Wallace	1.25	.55	.16
☐ 16 George Welsh CO	1.50	.70	.19

1992 Virginia Coca-Cola

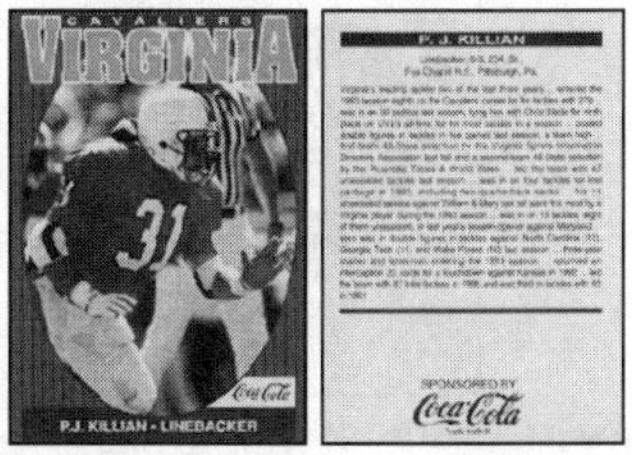

Sponsored by Coca-Cola, the 16 cards comprising this set were issued in one 16-card insert sheet. The perforated sheet measures approximately 10" by 14" and consists of four rows of four cards each. Each card measures the standard size and carries on its front a blue-bordered color player action shot. The player's name and position appear in white lettering within a dark blue bar set off by white lines at the bottom of the player photo. "Virginia" appears in orange lettering within the blue border above the photo. The Cavaliers logo is shown in one corner of the photo, and the word "Cavs" appears in orange lettering within a white rectangle at the lower left corner of the player photo. The Coca-Cola logo rests within the blue border at the bottom. The white back carries the player's name, position, biography, and highlights. The Coca-Cola logo at the bottom rounds out the card. The cards are unnumbered and checklisted below in alphabetical order. The key card in this set is running back Terry Kirby.

	MINT	NRMT	EXC
COMPLETE SET (16)	15.00	6.75	1.85
COMMON CARD (1-16)	1.00	.45	.12
☐ 1 Bobby Goodman	1.25	.55	.16
☐ 2 Michael Husted	2.00	.90	.25
☐ 3 Greg Jeffries	1.50	.70	.19
☐ 4 Charles Keiningham	1.00	.45	.12
☐ 5 Terry Kirby	5.00	2.20	.60
☐ 6 Kenneth Miles	1.00	.45	.12
☐ 7 Tim Samec	1.00	.45	.12
☐ 8 Chris Slade	3.50	1.55	.45
☐ 9 Alvin Snead	1.00	.45	.12
☐ 10 Gary Steele	1.00	.45	.12
☐ 11 Jeff Tomlin	1.00	.45	.12
☐ 12 Terrence Tomlin	1.00	.45	.12
☐ 13 David Ware	1.00	.45	.12
☐ 14 George Welsh CO	1.25	.55	.16
☐ 15 Virginia 20, Clemson 7; Sept. 8, 1990	1.00	.45	.12
☐ 16 Virginia 20, N.Carolina 17; Nov. 14, 1987	1.00	.45	.12

1993 Virginia Coca-Cola

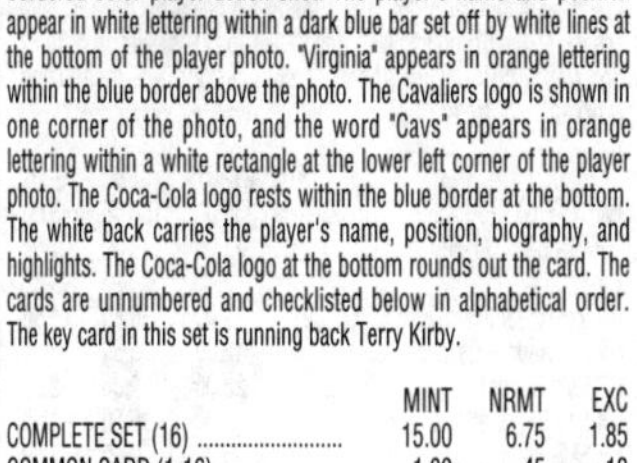

Sponsored by Coca-Cola, the 16 cards comprising this set were issued in one 16-card game program insert sheet. The perforated

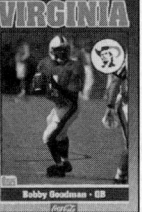

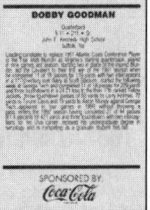

sheet measures approximately 10" by 14" and consists of four rows of four cards each. Each card measures the standard size and carries on its front an elliptical color player action shot bordered in blue with black vertical stirpes. The player's name and position appear in white lettering within a dark blue stripe at the bottom. The team name appears in orange and white lettering above the photo. The Coca-Cola logo appears at the lower right. The white back carries the player's name, position, biography, and highlights. The Coca-Cola logo at the bottom rounds out the card. The cards are unnumbered and checklisted below in alphabetical order.

	MINT	NRMT	EXC
COMPLETE SET (16)	15.00	6.75	1.85
COMMON CARD (1-16)	1.00	.45	.12
☐ 1 Tom Burns	1.00	.45	.12
☐ 2 Peter Collins	1.00	.45	.12
☐ 3 Bill Curry	1.00	.45	.12
☐ 4 Mark Dixon	1.00	.45	.12
☐ 5 Bill Edwards	1.00	.45	.12
☐ 6 P.J. Killian	1.00	.45	.12
☐ 7 Keith Lyle	1.00	.45	.12
☐ 8 Greg McClellan	1.00	.45	.12
☐ 9 Matt Mikeska	1.00	.45	.12
☐ 10 Aaron Mundy	1.00	.45	.12
☐ 11 Jim Reid	1.00	.45	.12
☐ 12 Josh Schrader	1.00	.45	.12
☐ 13 Jerrod Washington	1.00	.45	.12
☐ 14 George Welsh CO	1.25	.55	.16
☐ 15 Cavalier Spirit (Cheerleaders)	1.00	.45	.12
☐ 16 Cavalier Mascot	1.00	.45	.12

1973 Washington KFC

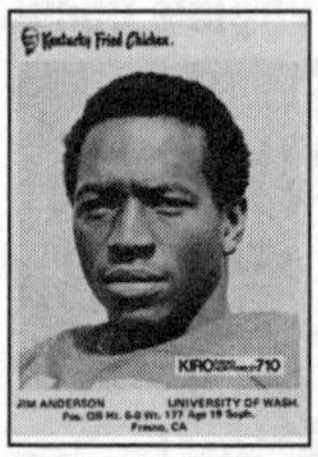

Sponsored by Kentucky Fried Chicken and KIRO (Radio Northwest 710), these 30 cards measure approximately 3" by 4" and are printed on thick card stock. The fronts feature posed black-and-white head shots with white borders. The Kentucky Fried Chicken logo is in the top border, while player information is printed in the bottom border. The backs are blank. The cards are unnumbered and checklisted below in alphabetical order. The cards were given out by KFC with purchase of their product. Also distributed to purchasers of 5.00 or more was a color team photo or coaches picture measuring approximately 8" by 10".

	NRMT-MT	EXC	G-VG
COMPLETE SET (30)	350.00	160.00	45.00
COMMON CARD (1-30)	12.00	5.50	1.50
☐ 1 Jim Anderson	12.00	5.50	1.50
☐ 2 Jim Andrilenas	12.00	5.50	1.50
☐ 3 Glen Bonner	20.00	9.00	2.50
☐ 4 Bob Boustead	12.00	5.50	1.50
☐ 5 Skip Boyd	20.00	9.00	2.50
☐ 6 Gordie Bronson	12.00	5.50	1.50
☐ 7 Reggie Brown	12.00	5.50	1.50
☐ 8 Dan Celoni CO	12.00	5.50	1.50
☐ 9 Brian Daheny	12.00	5.50	1.50
☐ 10 Fred Dean	12.00	5.50	1.50
☐ 11 Pete Elswick	12.00	5.50	1.50
☐ 12 Dennis Fitzpatrick	12.00	5.50	1.50
☐ 13 Bob Graves	12.00	5.50	1.50
☐ 14 Pedro Hawkins	12.00	5.50	1.50
☐ 15 Rick Hayes	12.00	5.50	1.50
☐ 16 Barry Houlihan	12.00	5.50	1.50
☐ 17 Roberto Jourdan	12.00	5.50	1.50
☐ 18 Washington Keenan	12.00	5.50	1.50
☐ 19 Eddie King	12.00	5.50	1.50
☐ 20 Jim Kristoff	12.00	5.50	1.50
☐ 21 Murphy McFarland	12.00	5.50	1.50
☐ 22 Walter Oldes	12.00	5.50	1.50
☐ 23 Louis Quinn	12.00	5.50	1.50
☐ 24 Frank Reed	20.00	9.00	2.50
☐ 25 Dain Rodwell	12.00	5.50	1.50
☐ 26 Ron Stanley	12.00	5.50	1.50
☐ 27 Joe Tabor	12.00	5.50	1.50
☐ 28 Pete Taggares	12.00	5.50	1.50
☐ 29 John Whitacre	12.00	5.50	1.50
☐ 30 Hans Woldseth	12.00	5.50	1.50
☐ NNO Color Team Photo (Large 8x10)	20.00	9.00	2.50
☐ NNO Coaches Photo (Large 8x10)	25.00	11.00	3.10

1988 Washington Smokey

The 1988 University of Washington Smokey set contains 16 standard-size cards. The fronts feature color photos bordered in deep purple, with name, position, and jersey number. The vertically oriented backs have fire prevention cartoons. The cards are unnumbered and are listed below in alphabetical order.

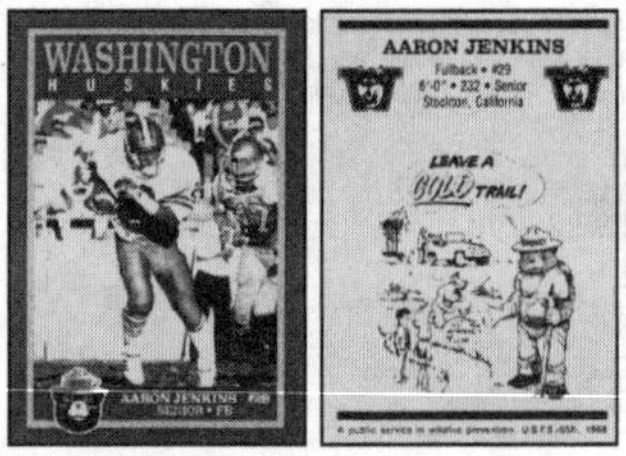

	MINT	NRMT	EXC
COMPLETE SET (16)	15.00	6.75	1.85
COMMON CARD (1-16)	1.00	.45	.12
☐ 1 Ricky Andrews	1.00	.45	.12
☐ 2 Bern Brostek	2.00	.90	.25
☐ 3 Dennis Brown	2.00	.90	.25
☐ 4 Cary Conklin	2.00	.90	.25
☐ 5 Tony Covington	1.00	.45	.12
☐ 6 Darryl Hall	1.00	.45	.12
☐ 7 Martin Harrison	2.00	.90	.25
☐ 8 Don James CO	2.00	.90	.25
☐ 9 Aaron Jenkins	1.00	.45	.12
☐ 10 Le-Lo Lang	2.00	.90	.25
☐ 11 Art Malone	1.00	.45	.12
☐ 12 Andre Riley	1.00	.45	.12
☐ 13 Brian Slater	1.00	.45	.12
☐ 14 Vince Weathersby	1.00	.45	.12
☐ 15 Brett Wiese	1.00	.45	.12
☐ 16 Mike Zandofsky	1.50	.70	.19

1990 Washington Smokey *

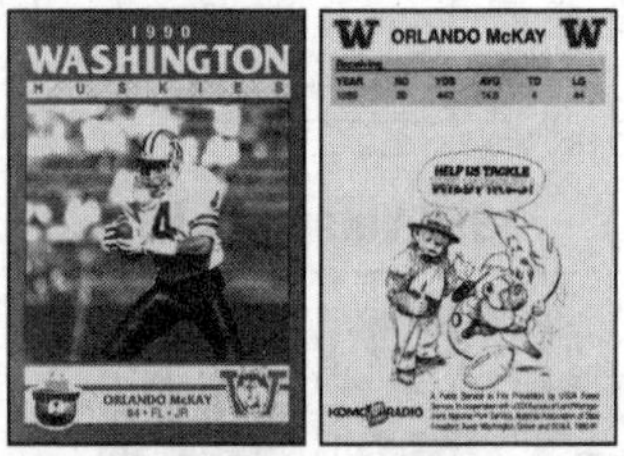

This 16-card standard size set was issued to promote fire safety. The fronts of the cards are purple bordered with "1990 Washington Huskies" on the top of the card. A full-color action photo is in the middle of the card and the player's name, uniform number, and position are underneath. On the lower left hand corner is the Smokey symbol and in the lower right-hand corner is the Washington Huskies logo. On the back is biographical information about the player and a fire safety tip. The set was issued with cooperation from the USDI Bureau of Land Management, the National Park Service, the National Association of State Foresters, Keep Washington Green, BDA, and KOMO Radio. We have checklisted this set alphabetically within player type and put the uniform number, where applicable, next to the player's name. The set was also issued in an unperforated sheet with four rows of four cards each. The last row of cards features women volleyball players. The key card in this set is quarterback Mark Brunell.

	MINT	NRMT	EXC
COMPLETE SET (16)	30.00	13.50	3.70
COMMON CARD (1-16)	.75	.35	.09
☐ 1 Eric Briscoe 28	.75	.35	.09
☐ 2 Mark Brunell 11	20.00	9.00	2.50
☐ 3 James Clifford 53	.75	.35	.09
☐ 4 John Cook 93	.75	.35	.09
☐ 5 Ed Cunningham 79	2.00	.90	.25
☐ 6 Dana Hall 5	2.50	1.10	.30
☐ 7 Don James CO	1.50	.70	.19
☐ 8 Donald Jones 48	.75	.35	.09
☐ 9 Dean Kirkland 51	.75	.35	.09
☐ 10 Greg Lewis 20	2.00	.90	.25
☐ 11 Orlando McKay 4	.75	.35	.09
☐ 12 Travis Richardson 58	.75	.35	.09
☐ 13 Kelley Larsen (Women's volleyball)	.75	.35	.09
☐ 14 Michelle Reid (Women's volleyball)	.75	.35	.09
☐ 15 Ashleigh Robertson (Women's volleyball)	.75	.35	.09
☐ 16 Gail Thorpe (Women's volleyball)	.75	.35	.09

1991 Washington Smokey *

This 16-card standard size set was sponsored by the USDA Forest Service and other federal agencies. The cards are printed on thin cardboard stock. The set was issued in two different forms. Ten thousand 12-card sets were distributed at the Huskies' home game against the University of Toledo. This set was also issued as a 16-card unperforated sheet, with the final row featuring four women volleyball players. The card fronts are accented in the team's colors (purple and gold) and have glossy color action player photos. The top of the pictures is curved to resemble an archway, and the team name follows the curve of the arch. The player's name and position appear in a stripe below the picture. The backs present statistics and a fire

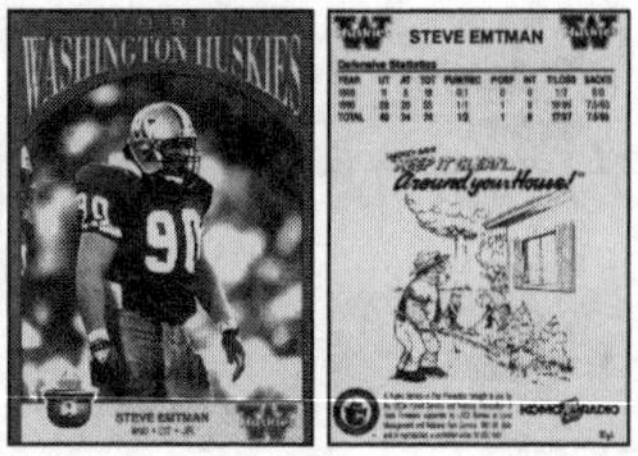

prevention cartoon starring Smokey. The cards are unnumbered and checklisted below in alphabetical order, with the women volleyball players listed at the end. The key card in this set is quarterback Billy Joe Hobert.

	MINT	NRMT	EXC
COMPLETE SET (16)	15.00	6.75	1.85
COMMON CARD (1-16)	.75	.35	.09
☐ 1 Mario Bailey	1.50	.70	.19
☐ 2 Beno Bryant	1.50	.70	.19
☐ 3 Brett Collins	.75	.35	.09
☐ 4 Ed Cunningham	1.50	.70	.19
☐ 5 Steve Emtman	2.00	.90	.25
☐ 6 Dana Hall	2.00	.90	.25
☐ 7 Billy Joe Hobert	5.00	2.20	.60
☐ 8 Dave Hoffmann	.75	.35	.09
☐ 9 Don James CO	1.25	.55	.16
☐ 10 Donald Jones	.75	.35	.09
☐ 11 Siupeli Malamala	1.50	.70	.19
☐ 12 Orlando McKay	.75	.35	.09
☐ 13 Diane Flick (Women's volleyball)	.75	.35	.09
☐ 14 Kelley Larsen (Women's volleyball)	.75	.35	.09
☐ 15 Ashleigh Robertson (Women's volleyball)	.75	.35	.09
☐ 16 Dana Thompson (Women's volleyball)	.75	.35	.09

1992 Washington Greats/Pacific

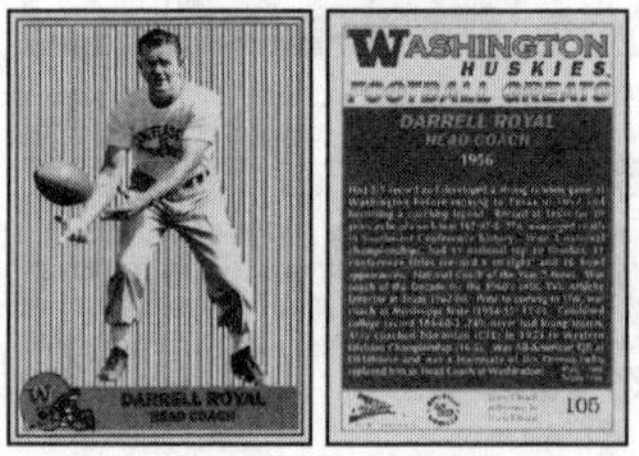

This 110-card standard-size set highlights 100 years of Huskies football. The cards were produced by Pacific Trading Cards, who donated a portion of the proceeds from their sale to the University of Washington and the Don James Endowment Fund for athletic scholarships. Reportedly the production run was limited to 2,500 numbered cases; moreover, 1,000 serial numbered cards autographed by Hugh McElhenny were randomly inserted in the ten-card foil packs. On a white card face, the fronts display a mix of color or black and white player photos enclosed by thin gold and purple borders. The team helmet appears in the lower left corner, with the player's name and position in a gold stripe extending to the right. The backs carry biography and career summary. The checklist card was randomly inserted at a reported rate of one every one or two wax boxes; it is not included in the complete set price listed below.

	MINT	NRMT	EXC
COMPLETE SET (110)	18.00	8.00	2.20
COMMON CARD (1-110)	.15	.07	.02
☐ 1 Don James CO	.50	.23	.06
☐ 2 Cary Conklin	.50	.23	.06
☐ 3 Tom Cowan	.15	.07	.02
☐ 4 Thane Cleland	.15	.07	.02
☐ 5 Steve Pelluer	.50	.23	.06
☐ 6 Sonny Sixkiller	.50	.23	.06
☐ 7 Koll Hagen	.15	.07	.02
☐ 8 Danny Greene	.15	.07	.02
☐ 9 George Black	.15	.07	.02
☐ 10 Mike Baldassin	.15	.07	.02
☐ 11 Bill Douglas	.15	.07	.02
☐ 12 Tom Flick	.25	.11	.03
☐ 13 Brian Slater	.15	.07	.02
☐ 14 Dick Sprague	.15	.07	.02
☐ 15 Bob Schloredt	.35	.16	.04
☐ 16 Bill Smith	.15	.07	.02
☐ 17 Marv Bergmann	.15	.07	.02
☐ 18 Sam Mitchell	.25	.11	.03
☐ 19 Bill Earley	.15	.07	.02
☐ 20 Clarence Dirks	.15	.07	.02
☐ 21 Jimmie Cain	.15	.07	.02
☐ 22 Don Heinrich	.35	.16	.04
☐ 23 Paul(Socko) Sulkosky	.15	.07	.02
☐ 24 By Haines	.15	.07	.02
☐ 25 Joe Steele	.15	.07	.02
☐ 26 Bob Monroe	.15	.07	.02
☐ 27 Roy McKasson	.15	.07	.02
☐ 28 Charlie Mitchell	.25	.11	.03
☐ 29 Ernie Steele	.15	.07	.02
☐ 30 Kyle Heinrich	.25	.11	.03
☐ 31 Travis Richardson	.15	.07	.02
☐ 32 Hugh McElhenny	1.00	.45	.12
☐ 33 George Wildcat Wilson	.15	.07	.02
☐ 34 Merle Hufford	.15	.07	.02
☐ 35 Steve Thompson	.15	.07	.02
☐ 36 Jim Krieg	.15	.07	.02
☐ 37 Chuck Olson	.15	.07	.02
☐ 38 Charley Russell	.15	.07	.02
☐ 39 Duane Wardlow	.15	.07	.02
☐ 40 Jay MacDowell	.15	.07	.02
☐ 41 Alf Hemstad	.15	.07	.02
☐ 42 Max Starcevich	.15	.07	.02
☐ 43 Ray Mansfield	.25	.11	.03
☐ 44 Brooks Biddle	.15	.07	.02
☐ 45 Toussaint Tyler	.35	.16	.04
☐ 46 Randy Van Diver	.15	.07	.02
☐ 47 John Cook	.15	.07	.02
☐ 48 Paul Skansi	.25	.11	.03
☐ 49 Tim Meamber	.15	.07	.02
☐ 50 Milt Bohart	.15	.07	.02
☐ 51 Curt Marsh	.25	.11	.03
☐ 52 Antowaine Richardson	.15	.07	.02
☐ 53 Jim Rodgers	.15	.07	.02
☐ 54 Mike Rohrbach	.15	.07	.02
☐ 55 Dan Agen	.15	.07	.02
☐ 56 Tom Turnure	.15	.07	.02
☐ 57 Ron Medved	.25	.11	.03
☐ 58 Vic Markov	.15	.07	.02
☐ 59 Carl(Bud) Ericksen	.15	.07	.02
☐ 60 Bill Kinnune	.15	.07	.02
☐ 61 Karsten(Corky) Lewis	.15	.07	.02
☐ 62 Sam Robinson	.25	.11	.03
☐ 63 Dave Nisbet	.15	.07	.02
☐ 64 Barry Bullard	.15	.07	.02
☐ 65 Norm Dicks	.15	.07	.02
☐ 66 Rick Redman	.25	.11	.03
☐ 67 Mark Jerue	.25	.11	.03
☐ 68 Jeff Toews	.15	.07	.02
☐ 69 Fletcher Jenkins	.15	.07	.02
☐ 70 Ray Horton	.25	.11	.03
☐ 71 Tom Erlandson	.15	.07	.02
☐ 72 Steve Alvord	.15	.07	.02
☐ 73 Dean Browning	.15	.07	.02
☐ 74 Scott Greenwood	.15	.07	.02
☐ 75 Bo Yates	.15	.07	.02
☐ 76 Jake Kupp	.25	.11	.03
☐ 77 Jim Owens CO	.15	.07	.02
☐ 78 Don McKeta	.15	.07	.02
☐ 79 Ben Davidson	.50	.23	.06
☐ 80 Tim Bullard	.15	.07	.02
☐ 81 Bill Albrecht	.15	.07	.02
☐ 82 Jim Cope	.15	.07	.02
☐ 83 Earl Monlux	.15	.07	.02
☐ 84 Paul Schwegler	.15	.07	.02
☐ 85 Steve Bramwell	.15	.07	.02
☐ 86 Ted Holzknecht	.15	.07	.02
☐ 87 Larry Hatch	.15	.07	.02
☐ 88 John Brady	.15	.07	.02
☐ 89 Bob Hivner	.15	.07	.02
☐ 90 Chuck Nelson	.25	.11	.03
☐ 91 Jeff Jaeger	.25	.11	.03
☐ 92 Rich Camarillo	.25	.11	.03
☐ 93 Jim Houston	.25	.11	.03
☐ 94 Jim Skaggs	.25	.11	.03
☐ 95 John Cherberg CO	.15	.07	.02
☐ 96 Bo Cornell	.25	.11	.03
☐ 97 Bill Cahill	.15	.07	.02
☐ 98 Dean McAdams	.15	.07	.02
☐ 99 Gil Dobie CO	.25	.11	.03
☐ 100 Walter Shiel	.15	.07	.02
☐ 101 Enoch Bagshaw CO	.15	.07	.02
☐ 102 Ray Eckmann	.15	.07	.02
☐ 103 Luther Carr	.15	.07	.02
☐ 104 Jimmy Bryan	.15	.07	.02
☐ 105 Darrell Royal	.35	.16	.04
☐ 106 Ray Frankowski	.15	.07	.02
☐ 107 Ray Pinney	.25	.11	.03
☐ 108 Skip Boyd	.15	.07	.02
☐ 109 Al Burleson	.15	.07	.02
☐ 110 Dennis Fitzpatrick	.25	.11	.03
☐ NNO Checklist Card	3.00	1.35	.35
☐ AU32 Hugh McElhenny (Certified Autograph, serially numbered of 1000)	50.00	22.00	6.25

1992 Washington Pay Less

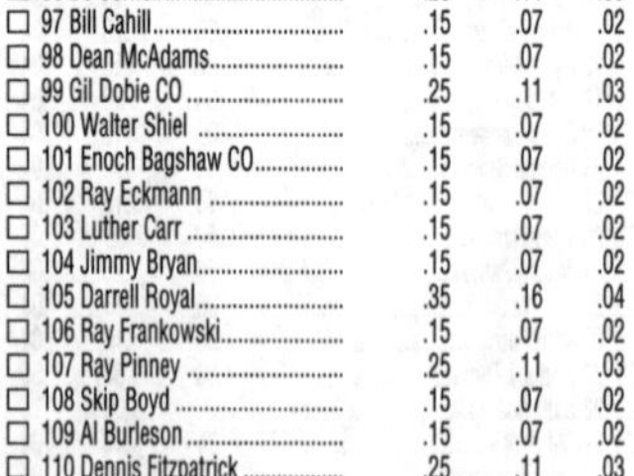

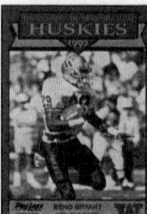

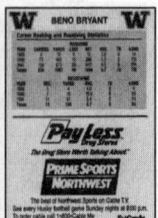

This 16-card standard-size set was sponsored by Pay Less Drug Stores and Prime Sports Northwest. The cards are printed on thin card stock. The fronts carry a color action player photo on a purple

card face. The team name and year appear above the photo in gold print on a purple bar that partially rests on a gold bar with notched ends. Below the photo, the player's name and sponsor logos appear in a gold border stripe. The backs carry statistics and sponsor advertisements. The cards are unnumbered and checklisted below in alphabetical order. The Billy Joe Hobart card was reportedly pulled from circulation after his suspension from the team.

	MINT	NRMT	EXC
COMPLETE SET (16)	25.00	11.00	3.10
COMMON CARD (1-16)	.75	.35	.09
☐ 1 Walter Bailey	.75	.35	.09
☐ 2 Jay Barry	.75	.35	.09
☐ 3 Mark Brunell	12.00	5.50	1.50
☐ 4 Beno Bryant	1.00	.45	.12
☐ 5 James Clifford	.75	.35	.09
☐ 6 Jaime Fields	.75	.35	.09
☐ 7 Travis Hanson	.75	.35	.09
☐ 8 Billy Joe Hobert SP	5.00	2.20	.60
☐ 9 Dave Hoffmann	.75	.35	.09
☐ 10 Matt Jones	.75	.35	.09
☐ 11 Lincoln Kennedy	2.00	.90	.25
☐ 12 Andy Mason	.75	.35	.09
☐ 13 Shane Pahukoa	.75	.35	.09
☐ 14 Tommie Smith	.75	.35	.09
☐ 15 Darius Turner	.75	.35	.09
☐ 16 Team Photo (Schedule)	.75	.35	.09

1993 Washington Safeway

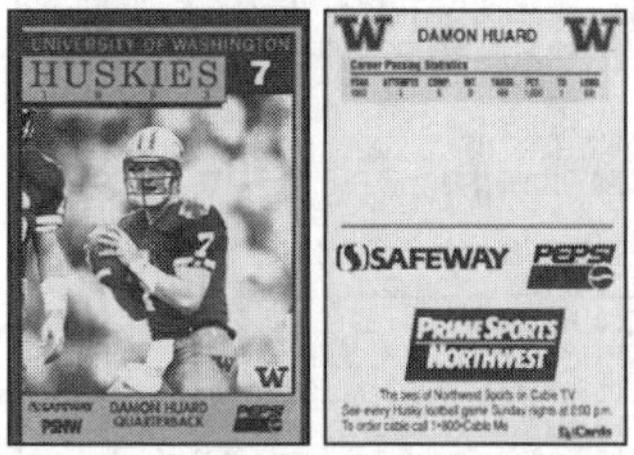

The 16 standard-size cards comprising this Huskies set sponsored by Safeway food stores, Pepsi, and Prime Sports Northwest, were printed on thin card stock and feature on their fronts purple- and gold-bordered color player action shots. The player's name and position, along with the sponsors' logos, appear within the gold margin at the bottom. The words "Huskies 1993" appear in purple lettering within a gold bar at the upper left. The player's uniform number appears in white lettering at the upper right. The white back carries the player's name at the top, followed below by a stat table or player highlights. The sponsors' logos at the bottom round out the card. The cards are unnumbered and checklisted below in alphabetical order. The key card in this set is Napoleon Kaufman.

	MINT	NRMT	EXC
COMPLETE SET (16)	12.00	5.50	1.50
COMMON CARD (1-16)	.75	.35	.09
☐ 1 Beno Bryant	1.00	.45	.12
☐ 2 Hillary Butler	.75	.35	.09
☐ 3 D'Marco Farr	1.50	.70	.19
☐ 4 Jamal Fountaine	.75	.35	.09
☐ 5 Tom Gallagher	.75	.35	.09
☐ 6 Travis Hanson	.75	.35	.09
☐ 7 Damon Huard	1.50	.70	.19
☐ 8 Matt Jones	.75	.35	.09
☐ 9 Pete Kaligis	.75	.35	.09
☐ 10 Napoleon Kaufman	4.00	1.80	.50
☐ 11 Joe Kralik	.75	.35	.09
☐ 12 Andy Mason	.75	.35	.09
☐ 13 Jim Nevelle	.75	.35	.09
☐ 14 Pete Pierson	.75	.35	.09
☐ 15 Steve Springstead	.75	.35	.09
☐ 16 John Werdel	.75	.35	.09

1994 Washington

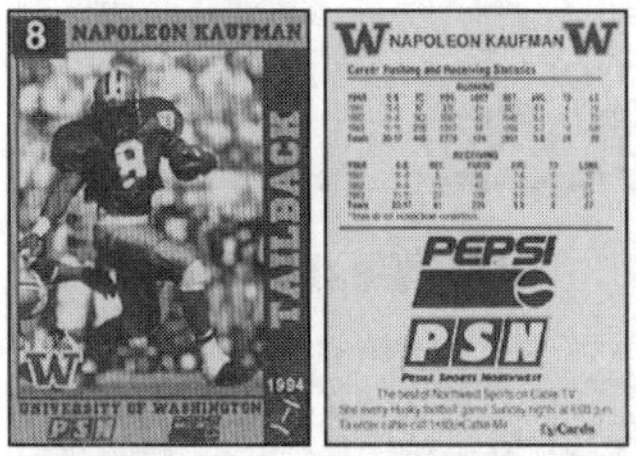

Produced by BD and A Cards, this 12-card standard-size set was jointly sponsored by Pepsi and PSN (Prime Sports Northwest) Cable T.V. Printed on thin card stock, the fronts display color player photos that are framed by purple and gold borders. The player's name is printed in the top border, his position in the right border, and sponsor logos in the bottom border. In black print on a white background, the backs present career statistics. The cards are unnumbered and checklisted below in alphabetical order. The set was also issued as a 10 3/8" by 10 3/4" uncut sheet.

	MINT	NRMT	EXC
COMPLETE SET (12)	12.00	5.50	1.50
COMMON CARD (1-12)	.60	.25	.07
☐ 1 Eric Bjornson	3.00	1.35	.35
☐ 2 Mark Bruener	3.00	1.35	.35
☐ 3 Richie Chambers	1.00	.45	.12
☐ 4 Frank Garcia	1.00	.45	.12
☐ 5 Russell Hairston	.60	.25	.07
☐ 6 Damon Huard	1.25	.55	.16
☐ 7 Napoleon Kaufman	3.00	1.35	.35
☐ 8 David Killpatrick	.60	.25	.07
☐ 9 Lamar Lyons	.60	.25	.07
☐ 10 Andrew Peterson	1.00	.45	.12
☐ 11 Donovan Schmidt	.60	.25	.07
☐ 12 Richard Thomas	.60	.25	.07

1995 Washington

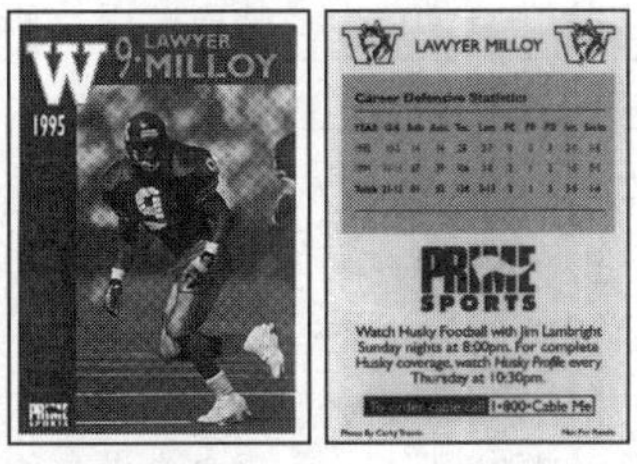

This 16-card set released by the University of Washington Huskies features color action player photos with a team-color partial border containing the player's name and position. The backs carry player career highlights. The cards are unnumbered and checklisted below in alphabetical order.

	MINT	NRMT	EXC
COMPLETE SET (16)	10.00	4.50	1.25
COMMON CARD (1-16)	.50	.23	.06
☐ 1 Ink Aleaga	1.00	.45	.12
☐ 2 Eric Battle	.75	.35	.09
☐ 3 Ernie Conwell	.50	.23	.06
☐ 4 Deke Devers	.50	.23	.06
☐ 5 Mike Ewaliko	.50	.23	.06
☐ 6 Scott Greenlaw	.50	.23	.06
☐ 7 Trevor Highfield	.50	.23	.06
☐ 8 Stephen Hoffmann	.50	.23	.06
☐ 9 Damon Huard	.75	.35	.09
☐ 10 Dave Janoski	.50	.23	.06
☐ 11 Patrick Kesi	.50	.23	.06
☐ 12 Jim Lambright CO	1.00	.45	.12
☐ 13 Lawyer Milloy	2.50	1.10	.30
☐ 14 Leon Neal	.50	.23	.06
☐ 15 Reggie Reser	.50	.23	.06
☐ 16 Richard Thomas	.50	.23	.06

1988 Washington State Smokey

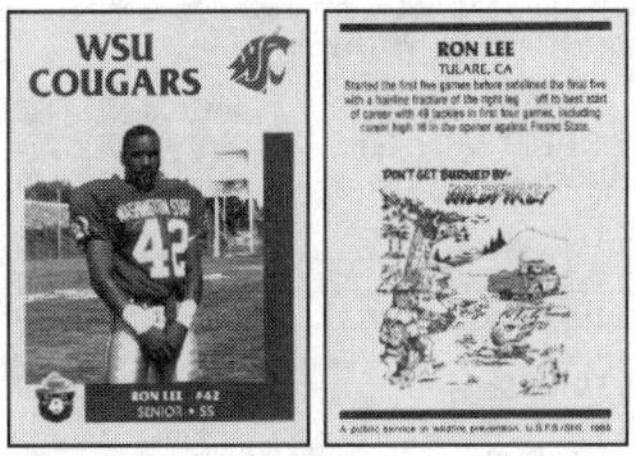

The 1988 Washington State University Smokey set contains 12 standard-size cards. The fronts feature color photos bordered in white and maroon, with name, position, and jersey number. The vertically oriented backs have fire prevention cartoons. The cards are unnumbered, so are listed by jersey numbers. The set is also noteworthy in that it contains one of the few cards of Mike Utley, the courageous Detroit Lions' lineman, who was paralyzed as a result of an on-field injury during a game in 1991.

	MINT	NRMT	EXC
COMPLETE SET (12)	12.00	5.50	1.50
COMMON CARD	1.00	.45	.12
☐ 3 Timm Rosenbach	2.00	.90	.25
☐ 18 Shawn Landrum	1.00	.45	.12
☐ 19 Artie Holmes	1.00	.45	.12
☐ 31 Steve Broussard	2.00	.90	.25
☐ 42 Ron Lee	1.00	.45	.12
☐ 55 Tuineau Alipate	1.00	.45	.12
☐ 60 Mike Utley	4.00	1.80	.50
☐ 68 Chris Dyko	1.00	.45	.12
☐ 74 Jim Michalczik	1.00	.45	.12
☐ 75 Tony Savage	1.00	.45	.12
☐ 76 Ivan Cook	1.00	.45	.12
☐ 82 Doug Wellsandt	1.00	.45	.12

1990 Washington State Smokey *

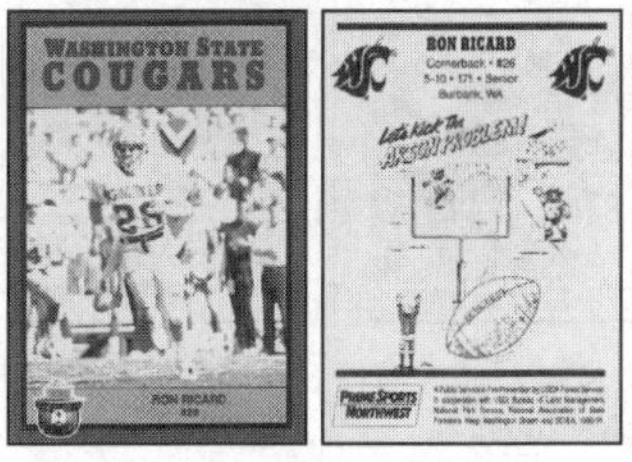

This 16-card standard-size set was sponsored by the USDA Forest Service in cooperation with several other federal agencies. Apart from four female volleyball players (2, 11, 13, and 14), the set features football players. The front presents an action color photo with text and borders in the school's colors maroon and silver. The Smokey the Bear picture appears in the lower left hand corner. The back includes biographical information and a public service announcement (with cartoon) concerning fire prevention. The cards are unnumbered, so they are listed alphabetically by subject's name.

	MINT	NRMT	EXC
COMPLETE SET (16)	10.00	4.50	1.25
COMMON CARD (1-16)	.75	.35	.09
☐ 1 Lewis Bush 48	.75	.35	.09
☐ 2 Carrie Couturier (Women's volleyball)	.75	.35	.09
☐ 3 Steve Cromer 70	.75	.35	.09
☐ 4 C.J. Davis 1	.75	.35	.09
☐ 5 John Diggs 22	.75	.35	.09
☐ 6 Alvin Dunn 27	.75	.35	.09
☐ 7 Aaron Garcia 9	.75	.35	.09
☐ 8 Bob Garman 74	.75	.35	.09
☐ 9 Brad Gossen 12	1.00	.45	.12
☐ 10 Calvin Griggs 5	.75	.35	.09
☐ 11 Kelly Hankins (Women's volleyball)	.75	.35	.09
☐ 12 Jason Hanson 4	2.50	1.10	.30
☐ 13 Kristen Hovde (Women's volleyball)	.75	.35	.09
☐ 14 Keri Killebrew (Women's volleyball)	.75	.35	.09
☐ 15 Chris Moton 6	.75	.35	.09
☐ 16 Ron Ricard 26	.75	.35	.09

1991 Washington State Smokey *

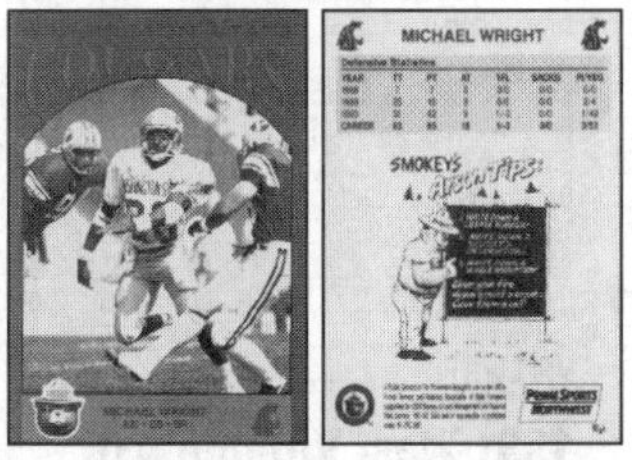

This 16-card standard-size set was sponsored by the USDA Forest Service and other federal agencies. The cards are printed on thin cardboard stock. The set was issued as a perforated sheet and as an uncut sheet without perforations. The final row of the sheet features four women volleyball players. The card fronts are accented in the team's colors (dark red and gray) and have either glossy color action or posed player photos. The top of the pictures is curved to resemble an archway, and the team name follows the curve of the arch. The player's name and position appear in a stripe below the picture. The backs present statistics and a fire prevention cartoon starring Smokey. The cards are unnumbered and checklisted below in alphabetical order, with the women volleyball players

	MINT	NRMT	EXC
COMPLETE SET (16)	10.00	4.50	1.25
COMMON CARD (1-16)	.75	.35	.09
☐ 1 Lewis Bush	1.25	.55	.16
☐ 2 Chad Cushing	.75	.35	.09
☐ 3 C.J. Davis	.75	.35	.09
☐ 4 Bob Garman	.75	.35	.09
☐ 5 Jason Hanson	2.00	.90	.25
☐ 6 Gabriel Oladipo	.75	.35	.09
☐ 7 Anthony Prior	1.25	.55	.16
☐ 8 Jay Reyna	.75	.35	.09
☐ 9 Lee Tilleman	.75	.35	.09
☐ 10 Kirk Westerfield	.75	.35	.09
☐ 11 Butch Williams	.75	.35	.09
☐ 12 Michael Wright	.75	.35	.09
☐ 13 Carrie Couturier (Women's volleyball)	.75	.35	.09
☐ 14 Kelly Hankins (Women's volleyball)	.75	.35	.09
☐ 15 Kristen Hovde (Women's volleyball)	.75	.35	.09
☐ 16 Keri Killebrew (Women's volleyball)	.75	.35	.09

1992 Washington State Smokey *

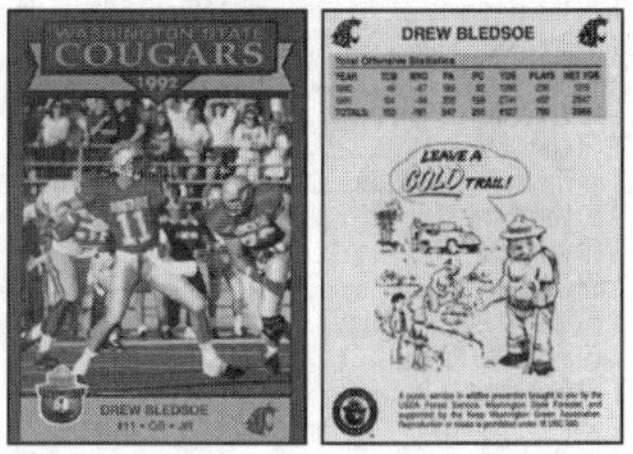

This 20-card standard size set was sponsored by the USDA Forest Service and other federal agencies. The cards are printed on thin cardboard stock. The set was issued as a perforated sheet. The last two rows of the sheet feature women volleyball players. The card fronts are accented in the team's colors (brick-red and gray) and have color action player photos. The team name and year appear above the photo in gray print on a brick-red bar that partially rests on a gray bar with notched ends. Below the photo, the player's name and sponsor logos appear in a gray border stripe. The cards are unnumbered and checklisted below in alphabetical order with the volleyball players listed at the end. The key card is Drew Bledsoe, featured in his first card appearence.

	MINT	NRMT	EXC
COMPLETE SET (20)	30.00	13.50	3.70
COMMON CARD (1-20)	.60	.25	.07
☐ 1 Drew Bledsoe	20.00	9.00	2.50
☐ 2 Phillip Bobo	1.00	.45	.12
☐ 3 Lewis Bush	.60	.25	.07
☐ 4 C.J. Davis	.60	.25	.07
☐ 5 Shaumbe Wright-Fair	1.00	.45	.12
☐ 6 Bob Garman	.60	.25	.07
☐ 7 Ray Hall	.60	.25	.07
☐ 8 Torey Hunter	1.00	.45	.12
☐ 9 Kurt Loertscher	.60	.25	.07
☐ 10 Anthony McClanahan	.60	.25	.07
☐ 11 John Rushing	.60	.25	.07
☐ 12 Clarence Williams	1.00	.45	.12
☐ 13 Betty Bartram (Women's volleyball)	.60	.25	.07
☐ 14 Krista Beightol (Women's volleyball)	.60	.25	.07
☐ 15 Carrie Gilley (Women's volleyball)	.60	.25	.07
☐ 16 Shannan Griffin (Women's volleyball)	.60	.25	.07
☐ 17 Becky Howlett (Women's volleyball)	.60	.25	.07
☐ 18 Kristen Hovde (Women's volleyball)	.60	.25	.07
☐ 19 Keri Killebrew (Women's volleyball)	.60	.25	.07
☐ 20 Cindy Fredrick CO M. Farokhmanesh ACO Gweyn Leabo ACO (Women's volleyball)	.60	.25	.07

1974 West Virginia

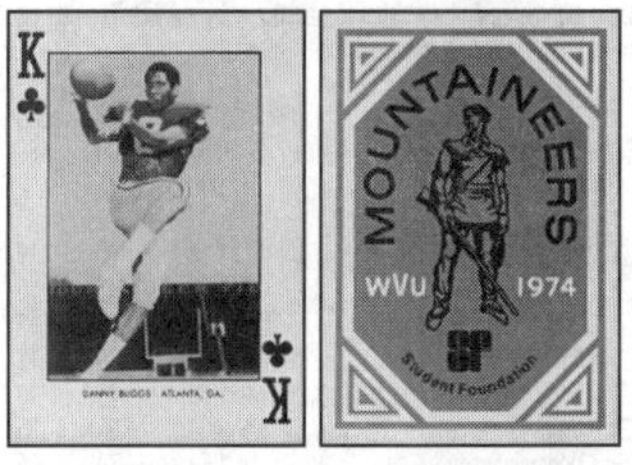

This 53-card set was sponsored by the Student Foundation, a non-profit campus development group. The cards were issued in the playing card format, and each card measures approximately 2 1/8" by 3 1/8". The fronts feature either close-ups or posed action shots of the players. Card backs feature a line drawing of a West Virginia Mountaineer, with the four corners cut off to create triangles. There are two different card backs, same design, but either blue or gold. Because this set is similar to a playing card set, the set is arranged just like a card deck and checklisted below as follows: C means Clubs, D means Diamonds, H means Hearts, S means Spades, and JK means Joker. The cards are checklisted below in playing card order by suits and numbers are assigned to Aces (1), Jacks (11), Queens (12), and Kings (13). The joker is listed at the end. The key card in the set is coach Bobby Bowden.

	NRMT-MT	EXC	G-VG
COMPLETE SET (53)	90.00	40.00	11.00
COMMON CARD	1.50	.70	.19
☐ 1C Stu Wolpert	1.50	.70	.19
☐ 1D Mountaineer Coaches	5.00	2.20	.60
☐ 1H Leland Byrd AD	1.50	.70	.19
☐ 1S Bobby Bowden CO	25.00	11.00	3.10
☐ 2C Jay Sheehan	1.50	.70	.19
☐ 2D Tom Brandner	1.50	.70	.19
☐ 2H Tom Bowden	1.50	.70	.19

	MINT	NRMT	EXC
☐ 2S Chuck Smith	1.50	.70	.19
☐ 3C Ray Marshall	1.50	.70	.19
☐ 3D Randy Swinson	1.50	.70	.19
☐ 3H Tom Loadman	1.50	.70	.19
☐ 3S Bob Kaminski	1.50	.70	.19
☐ 4C Ron Lee	3.00	1.35	.35
☐ 4D Kirk Lewis	1.50	.70	.19
☐ 4H Greg Dorn	1.50	.70	.19
☐ 4S Emil Ros	1.50	.70	.19
☐ 5C Mark Burke	1.50	.70	.19
☐ 5D Rory Fields	1.50	.70	.19
☐ 5H Gary Lombard	1.50	.70	.19
☐ 5S Brian Gates	1.50	.70	.19
☐ 6C John Schell	1.50	.70	.19
☐ 6D Paul Jordan	1.50	.70	.19
☐ 6H Mike Hubbard	1.50	.70	.19
☐ 6S Chuck Kelly	1.50	.70	.19
☐ 7C Rick Pennypacker	2.00	.90	.25
☐ 7D Heywood Smith	1.50	.70	.19
☐ 7H Jack Eastwood	1.50	.70	.19
☐ 7S Andy Peters	1.50	.70	.19
☐ 8C Steve Dunlap	1.50	.70	.19
☐ 8D Dave Wilcher	2.00	.90	.25
☐ 8H Greg Anderson	1.50	.70	.19
☐ 8S Ken Culbertson	1.50	.70	.19
☐ 9C David Van Halanger	1.50	.70	.19
☐ 9D Rick Shaffer	1.50	.70	.19
☐ 9H Rich Lukowski	1.50	.70	.19
☐ 9S Al Gluchoski	1.50	.70	.19
☐ 10C Dwayne Woods	1.50	.70	.19
☐ 10D Ben Williams	2.00	.90	.25
☐ 10H John Adams	1.50	.70	.19
☐ 10S Tom Florence	1.50	.70	.19
☐ 11C Marcus Mauney	1.50	.70	.19
☐ 11D John Spraggins	1.50	.70	.19
☐ 11H Bruce Huffman	1.50	.70	.19
☐ 11S Bernie Kirchner	1.50	.70	.19
☐ 12C Artie Owens	2.00	.90	.25
☐ 12D Charlie Miller	1.50	.70	.19
☐ 12H 1974 Cheerleaders	1.50	.70	.19
☐ 12S Eddie Russell	1.50	.70	.19
☐ 13C Danny Buggs	5.00	2.20	.60
☐ 13D Marshall Mills	1.50	.70	.19
☐ 13H John Everly	1.50	.70	.19
☐ 13S Jeff Merrow	4.00	1.80	.50
☐ JK Student Foundation	1.50	.70	.19

1988 West Virginia

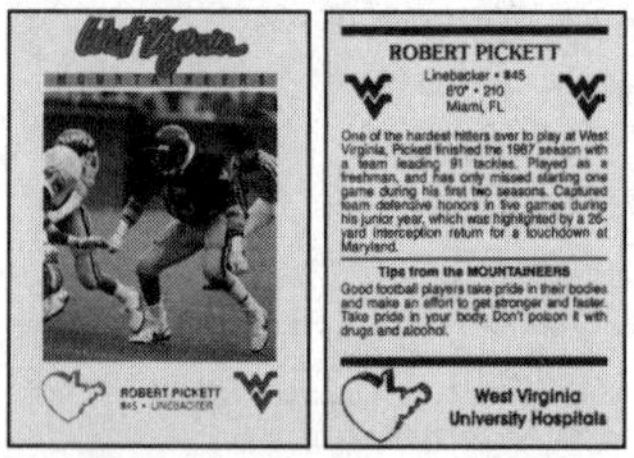

The 1988 West Virginia University set contains 16 standard-size cards. The fronts feature color photos bordered in white, with name, position, and jersey number. The vertically oriented backs have brief biographical information and "Tips from the Mountaineers." The cards are unnumbered and are listed alphabetically by subject. The set was sponsored by West Virginia University Hospitals.

	MINT	NRMT	EXC
COMPLETE SET (16)	20.00	9.00	2.50
COMMON CARD (1-16)	1.00	.45	.12
☐ 1 Charlie Baumann	1.50	.70	.19
☐ 2 Anthony Brown	1.00	.45	.12
☐ 3 Willie Edwards	1.00	.45	.12
☐ 4 Theron Ellis	1.50	.70	.19
☐ 5 Chris Haering	1.50	.70	.19
☐ 6 Major Harris	3.00	1.35	.35
☐ 7 Undra Johnson	1.50	.70	.19
☐ 8 Kevin Koken	1.00	.45	.12
☐ 9 Pat Marlatt	1.00	.45	.12
☐ 10 Eugene Napoleon	1.00	.45	.12
☐ 11 Don Nehlen CO	2.00	.90	.25
☐ 12 Bo Orlando	3.00	1.35	.35
☐ 13 Chris Parker	1.00	.45	.12
☐ 14 Robert Pickett	1.00	.45	.12
☐ 15 Brian Smider	1.00	.45	.12
☐ 16 John Stroia	1.00	.45	.12

1990 West Virginia Program Cards

Sponsored by Gatorade Thirst Quencher, the 1990 West Virginia Mountaineers football set consists of 49 standard-size cards printed on thin card stock. The set was available as a complete set or in seven-card perforated sheets featured in issues of Mountaineer Illustrated Magazine. The fronts feature posed color action shots bordered in white. The words "West Virginia Mountaineers" is shown in the team's colors above the picture. Below the picture are the team helmet, a green broken stripe, and player information. The back has biographical information, player profile, and "Mountaineer Tips" that consist of encouragements to stay in school. The cards are unnumbered and checklisted below in alphabetical order. Key cards in the set include James Jett and baseball's Darrell Whitmore.

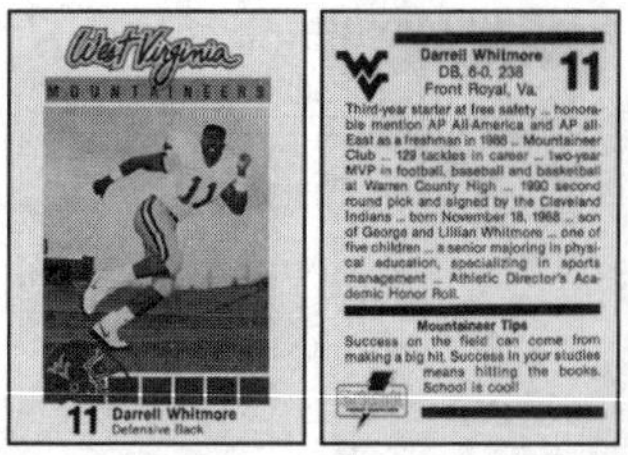

	MINT	NRMT	EXC
COMPLETE SET (49)	35.00	16.00	4.40
COMMON CARD (1-49)	.75	.35	.09
☐ 1 Tarris Alexander	.75	.35	.09
☐ 2 Leroy Axem	.75	.35	.09
☐ 3 Michael Beasley	.75	.35	.09
☐ 4 Calvin Bell	.75	.35	.09
☐ 5 Matt Bland	.75	.35	.09
☐ 6 John Brown	1.25	.55	.16
☐ 7 Brad Carroll	.75	.35	.09
☐ 8 Mike Collins	.75	.35	.09
☐ 9 Mike Compton	1.25	.55	.16
☐ 10 Cecil Doggette	.75	.35	.09
☐ 11 Rick Dolly	.75	.35	.09
☐ 12 Theron Ellis	1.25	.55	.16
☐ 13 Charlie Fedorco	.75	.35	.09
☐ 14 Garrett Ford	.75	.35	.09
☐ 15 Scott Gaskins	.75	.35	.09
☐ 16 Boris Graham	.75	.35	.09
☐ 17 Keith Graley	.75	.35	.09
☐ 18 Chris Gray	.75	.35	.09
☐ 19 Greg Hertzog	.75	.35	.09
☐ 20 Ed Hill	.75	.35	.09
☐ 21 Verne Howard	.75	.35	.09
☐ 22 James Jett	3.00	1.35	.35
☐ 23 Greg Jones	.75	.35	.09
☐ 24 Jon Jones	.75	.35	.09
☐ 25 Ted Kester	.75	.35	.09
☐ 26 Darroll Mitchell	.75	.35	.09
☐ 27 John Murphy	.75	.35	.09
☐ 28 Don Nehlen CO	2.50	1.10	.30
☐ 29 Tim Newsom	.75	.35	.09
☐ 30 Joe Pabian	.75	.35	.09
☐ 31 John Ray	.75	.35	.09
☐ 32 Steve Redd	.75	.35	.09
☐ 33 Joe Ruth	.75	.35	.09
☐ 34 Alex Shook	.75	.35	.09
☐ 35 Jeff Sniffen	.75	.35	.09
☐ 36 Ray Staton	.75	.35	.09
☐ 37 Rick Stead	.75	.35	.09
☐ 38 Darren Studstill	2.00	.90	.25
☐ 39 Lorenzo Styles	2.00	.90	.25
☐ 40 Gary Tillis	.75	.35	.09
☐ 41 Rico Tyler	.75	.35	.09
☐ 42 Darrell Whitmore	2.00	.90	.25
☐ 43 E.J. Wheeler	.75	.35	.09
☐ 44 Darrick Wiley	.75	.35	.09
☐ 45 Tim Williams	.75	.35	.09
☐ 46 Sam Wilson	.75	.35	.09
☐ 47 Dale Wolfley	.75	.35	.09
☐ 48 Rob Yachini	.75	.35	.09
☐ 49 Mountaineer Field	.75	.35	.09

1991 West Virginia ATG

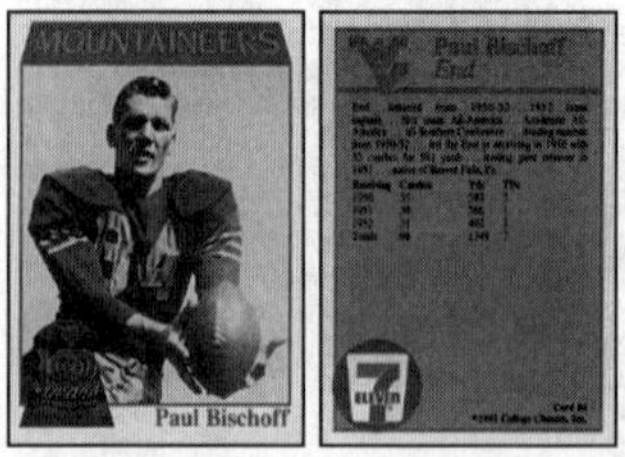

The 1991 West Virginia All-Time Greats football set was produced by College Classics to celebrate the university's 100th year anniversary. It was sponsored and sold by 7-Eleven Stores. The 50 standard-size cards display action photos, with the team name above and the player's name in the white border beneath the picture. A "100 Years" emblem is superimposed at the lower right corner. The backs have biographical information, career statistics, and "Mountaineer Tips" in the form of "stay in school" messages.

	MINT	NRMT	EXC
COMPLETE SET (50)	20.00	9.00	2.50
COMMON CARD (1-50)	.35	.16	.04
☐ 1 Jeff Hostetler	2.50	1.10	.30
☐ 2 Tom Allman	.35	.16	.04
☐ 3 Russ Bailey	.35	.16	.04
☐ 4 Paul Bischoff	.35	.16	.04
☐ 5 Bruce Bosley	.50	.23	.06
☐ 6 Jim Braxton	.50	.23	.06
☐ 7 Danny Buggs	.50	.23	.06
☐ 8 Harry Clarke	.35	.16	.04
☐ 9 Ken Culbertson	.35	.16	.04
☐ 10 Willie Drewrey	.50	.23	.06
☐ 11 Steve Dunlap	.35	.16	.04
☐ 12 Garrett Ford	.35	.16	.04
☐ 13 Dennis Fowlkes	.35	.16	.04
☐ 14 Bob Gresham	.50	.23	.06
☐ 15 Chris Haering	.50	.23	.06
☐ 16 Major Harris	1.00	.45	.12
☐ 17 Steve Hathaway	.35	.16	.04
☐ 18 Rick Hollins	.35	.16	.04
☐ 19 Chuck Howley	1.00	.45	.12
☐ 20 Sam Huff	2.00	.90	.25
☐ 21 Brian Jozwiak	.50	.23	.06
☐ 22 Gene Lamone	.35	.16	.04
☐ 23 Oliver Luck	.75	.35	.09
☐ 24 Kerry Marbury	.35	.16	.04
☐ 25 Joe Marconi	.50	.23	.06
☐ 26 Jeff Merrow	.50	.23	.06
☐ 27 Steve Newberry	.35	.16	.04
☐ 28 Bob Orders	.35	.16	.04
☐ 29 Artie Owens	.50	.23	.06
☐ 30 Tom Pridemore	.50	.23	.06
☐ 31 Mark Raugh	.35	.16	.04
☐ 32 Reggie Rembert	.50	.23	.06
☐ 33 Ira Rodgers	.35	.16	.04
☐ 34 Mike Sherwood	.35	.16	.04
☐ 35 Joe Stydahar	.50	.23	.06
☐ 36 Renaldo Turnbull	1.25	.55	.16
☐ 37 Paul Woodside	.35	.16	.04
☐ 38 Fred Wyant	.35	.16	.04
☐ 39 Carl Leatherwood	.35	.16	.04
☐ 40 Darryl Talley	1.00	.45	.12
☐ 41 David Grant	.50	.23	.06
☐ 42 Bobby Bowden CO	2.00	.90	.25
☐ 43 Jim Carlen CO	.35	.16	.04
☐ 44 Frank Cignetti CO	.35	.16	.04
☐ 45 Gene Corum CO	.35	.16	.04
☐ 46 Art Lewis CO	.35	.16	.04
☐ 47 Don Nehlen CO	.50	.23	.06
☐ 48 New Mountaineer Field	.35	.16	.04
☐ 49 Old Mountaineer Field	.35	.16	.04
☐ 50 Lambert Trophy	.50	.23	.06

1991 West Virginia Program Cards

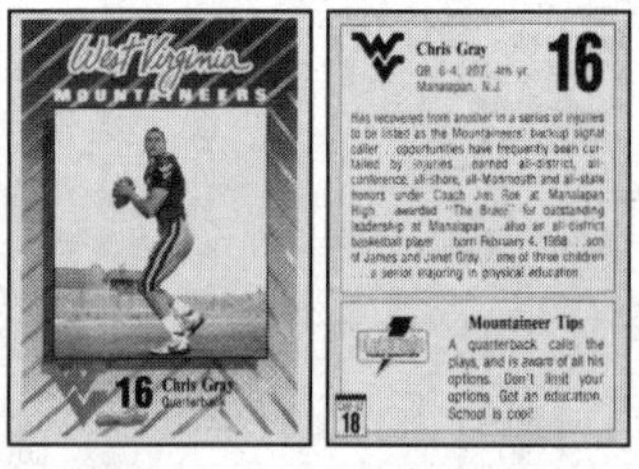

This 42-card standard-size set was printed on thin card stock with white borders; the card fronts carry a posed action player photo against a screened blue background with blue and gold diagonal lines. West Virginia Mountaineers is imprinted over blue background at top while jersey number, name, and position appear at bottom. The backs have biography, "Mountaineer Tips" consisting of school advice, and the Gatorade Thirst Quencher logo. The cards are numbered on the back; the numbering is essentially alphabetical by player's name. Seven different cards were featured in each of the team's six home game Mountaineer Illustrated programs.

	MINT	NRMT	EXC
COMPLETE SET (42)	30.00	13.50	3.70
COMMON CARD (1-42)	.75	.35	.09
☐ 1 Tarris Alexander	.75	.35	.09
☐ 2 Johnathan Allen	.75	.35	.09
☐ 3 Leroy Axem	.75	.35	.09
☐ 4 Joe Ayuso	.75	.35	.09
☐ 5 Michael Beasley	.75	.35	.09
☐ 6 Rich Braham	1.00	.45	.12
☐ 7 Tom Briggs	.75	.35	.09
☐ 8 John Cappa	.75	.35	.09
☐ 9 Mike Collins	1.00	.45	.12
☐ 10 Mike Compton	1.00	.45	.12
☐ 11 Doug Cooley	.75	.35	.09
☐ 12 Cecil Doggette	.75	.35	.09
☐ 13 Rick Dolly	.75	.35	.09
☐ 14 Garrett Ford	.75	.35	.09
☐ 15 Scott Gaskins	1.00	.45	.12
☐ 16 Boris Graham	.75	.35	.09
☐ 17 Keith Graley	.75	.35	.09
☐ 18 Chris Gray	.75	.35	.09
☐ 19 Barry Hawkins	.75	.35	.09
☐ 20 Ed Hill	1.00	.45	.12
☐ 21 James Jett	3.00	1.35	.35
☐ 22 Jon Jones	.75	.35	.09
☐ 23 Jim LeBlanc	1.00	.45	.12
☐ 24 David Mayfield	1.00	.45	.12
☐ 25 Adrian Murrell	5.00	2.20	.60
☐ 26 Sam Mustipher	.75	.35	.09
☐ 27 Tim Newsom	.75	.35	.09
☐ 28 Tommy Orr	.75	.35	.09
☐ 29 Joe Pabian	.75	.35	.09
☐ 30 John Ray	.75	.35	.09
☐ 31 Wes Richardson	1.00	.45	.12
☐ 32 Nate Rine	.75	.35	.09
☐ 33 Joe Ruth	.75	.35	.09
☐ 34 Alex Shook	.75	.35	.09
☐ 35 Kwame Smith	.75	.35	.09
☐ 36 Darren Studstill	2.00	.90	.25
☐ 37 Lorenzo Styles	1.50	.70	.19
☐ 38 Gary Tillis	.75	.35	.09
☐ 39 Ron Weaver	.75	.35	.09
☐ 40 Darrell Whitmore	2.50	1.10	.30
☐ 41 Darrick Wiley	.75	.35	.09
☐ 42 Rodney Woodard	.75	.35	.09

1992 West Virginia Program Cards

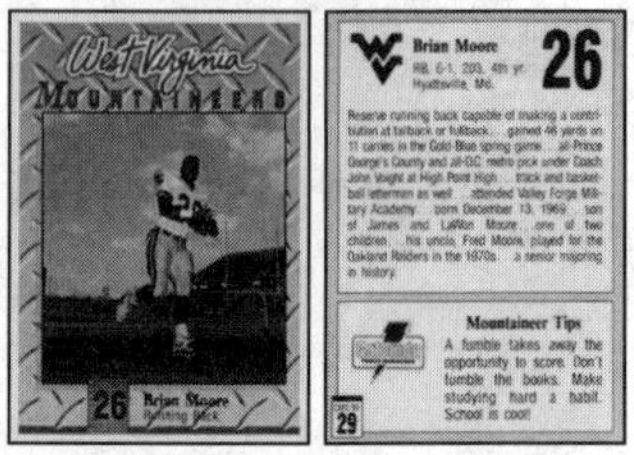

This 49-card standard-size set was available in the team's home game Mountaineer Illustrated Programs. The cards were printed on thin stock. The white-bordered fronts carry a posed action player photo on an orange-yellow background with short diagonal maroon and gray lines. West Virginia Mountaineers is imprinted at the top above the player's photo. The jersey number, name and position appear at the bottom. The backs have biography, "Mountaineer Tips," consisting of school advice, and the Gatorade logo.

	MINT	NRMT	EXC
COMPLETE SET (49)	30.00	13.50	3.70
COMMON CARD (1-49)	.75	.35	.09
☐ 1 Tarris Alexander	.75	.35	.09
☐ 2 Joe Avila	.75	.35	.09
☐ 3 Leroy Axem	.75	.35	.09
☐ 4 Mike Baker	.75	.35	.09
☐ 5 Sean Biser	.75	.35	.09
☐ 6 Mike Booth	.75	.35	.09
☐ 7 Rich Braham	1.00	.45	.12
☐ 8 Tom Briggs	.75	.35	.09
☐ 9 Tim Brown	.75	.35	.09
☐ 10 Darius Burwell	.75	.35	.09
☐ 11 John Cappa	.75	.35	.09
☐ 12 Matt Ceglie	.75	.35	.09
☐ 13 Mike Collins	.75	.35	.09
☐ 14 Mike Compton	1.00	.45	.12
☐ 15 Rick Dolly	.75	.35	.09
☐ 16 Garrett Ford	.75	.35	.09
☐ 17 Scott Gaskins	1.00	.45	.12
☐ 18 Boris Graham	.75	.35	.09
☐ 19 Dan Harless	.75	.35	.09
☐ 20 Barry Hawkins	.75	.35	.09
☐ 21 Ed Hill	1.00	.45	.12
☐ 22 James Jett	2.50	1.10	.30
☐ 23 Mark Johnson	.75	.35	.09
☐ 24 Jon Jones	.75	.35	.09
☐ 25 Jake Kelchner	2.50	1.10	.30
☐ 26 Harold Kidd	.75	.35	.09
☐ 27 Jim LeBlanc	1.00	.45	.12
☐ 28 David Mayfield	1.00	.45	.12
☐ 29 Brian Moore	.75	.35	.09
☐ 30 Adrian Murrell	4.00	1.80	.50
☐ 31 Robert Nelson	.75	.35	.09
☐ 32 Tommy Orr	.75	.35	.09
☐ 33 Joe Pabian	.75	.35	.09
☐ 34 Brett Parise	.75	.35	.09
☐ 35 Steve Perkins	.75	.35	.09
☐ 36 Steve Redd	.75	.35	.09
☐ 37 Wes Richardson	1.00	.45	.12
☐ 38 Nate Rine	.75	.35	.09
☐ 39 Tom Robsock	.75	.35	.09
☐ 40 Kwame Smith	.75	.35	.09
☐ 41 Darren Studstill	1.50	.70	.19
☐ 42 Lorenzo Styles	1.50	.70	.19
☐ 43 Matt Taffoni	.75	.35	.09
☐ 44 Mark Ulmer	.75	.35	.09
☐ 45 Mike Vanderjagt	1.00	.45	.12
☐ 46 Darrick Wiley	.75	.35	.09
☐ 47 Dale Williams	.75	.35	.09
☐ 48 Rodney Woodard	.75	.35	.09
☐ 49 James Wright	.75	.35	.09

1993 West Virginia

These 49 standard-size cards feature on their fronts posed color player photos set within blue marbleized borders. The player's name and position appear in a yellowish rectangle underneath the photo. The gray bordered back carries the player's name, position, uniform number and biography at the top, followed by the player's career highlights. Two different sets were issued. The fronts are identical in both sets but the backs differ slightly. The first set was the program set sponsored by Gatorade; the second set was the Big East Champions set. The WVU Sports Information office originally sold the program set for 5.00 and the Big East Champions sets for 7.00. Also there was a variation in these sets. In the program set, card number 13 is Daymeian Gallimore; in the Big East set, he is replaced by the Big East Trophy.

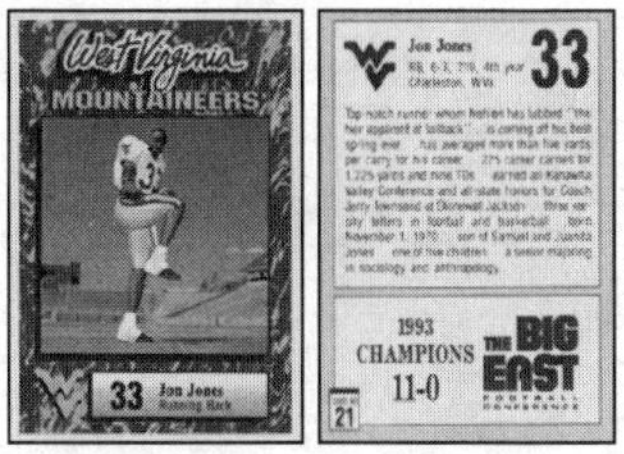

	MINT	NRMT	EXC
COMPLETE SET (49)	25.00	11.00	3.10
COMMON CARD (1-49)	.50	.23	.06

	MINT	NRMT	EXC
☐ 1 Zach Abraham	.50	.23	.06
☐ 2 Tarris Alexander	.50	.23	.06
☐ 3 Mike Baker	.50	.23	.06
☐ 4 Aaron Beasley	.50	.23	.06
☐ 5 Derrick Bell	.50	.23	.06
☐ 6 Mike Booth	.50	.23	.06
☐ 7 Rich Braham	.75	.35	.09
☐ 8 Tim Brown	.50	.23	.06
☐ 9 Mike Collins	.75	.35	.09
☐ 10 Doug Costin	.50	.23	.06
☐ 11 Calvin Edwards	.50	.23	.06
☐ 12 Jim Freeman	.50	.23	.06
☐ 13A Big East Trophy	1.50	.70	.19
☐ 13B Daymeian Gallimore	1.50	.70	.19
☐ 14 Jimmy Gary	.50	.23	.06
☐ 15 Scott Gaskins	.75	.35	.09
☐ 16 Buddy Hager	.50	.23	.06
☐ 17 Dan Harless	.50	.23	.06
☐ 18 John Harper	.50	.23	.06
☐ 19 Barry Hawkins	.75	.35	.09
☐ 20 Ed Hill	.75	.35	.09
☐ 21 Jon Jones	.50	.23	.06
☐ 22 Jay Kearney	.50	.23	.06
☐ 23 Jake Kelchner	2.00	.90	.25
☐ 24 Harold Kidd	.50	.23	.06
☐ 25 Chris Klick	.50	.23	.06
☐ 26 Jim LeBlanc	.75	.35	.09
☐ 27 Chris Ling	.50	.23	.06
☐ 28 David Mayfield	.75	.35	.09
☐ 29 Keith Morris	.50	.23	.06
☐ 30 Tommy Orr	.50	.23	.06
☐ 31 Joe Pabian	.50	.23	.06
☐ 32 Ken Painter	.50	.23	.06
☐ 33 Steve Perkins	.50	.23	.06
☐ 34 Maurice Richards	.50	.23	.06
☐ 35 Wes Richardson	.75	.35	.09
☐ 36 Nate Rine	.50	.23	.06
☐ 37 Tom Robsock	.50	.23	.06
☐ 38 Todd Sauerbrun	2.00	.90	.25
☐ 39 Darren Studstill	1.50	.70	.19
☐ 40 Matt Taffoni	.50	.23	.06
☐ 41 Keith Taparausky	.50	.23	.06
☐ 42 Mark Ulmer	.50	.23	.06
☐ 43 Robert Walker	1.25	.55	.16
☐ 44 Charles Washington	.50	.23	.06
☐ 45 Darrick Wiley	.50	.23	.06
☐ 46 Dale Williams	.50	.23	.06
☐ 47 James(Puppy) Wright	.50	.23	.06
☐ 48 Don Nehlen CO	1.00	.45	.12
☐ 49 Mountaineer Field	.50	.23	.06

1992 Wisconsin Program Cards

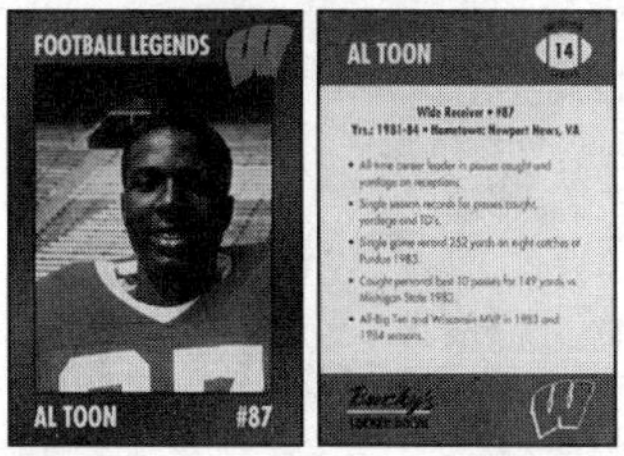

This 27-card standard-size set was issued in three Badger game programs in October 1992, each containing one nine-card sheet. The fronts feature former Badger football legends pictured in various poses, some in color, others in black-and-white, on a red-bordered card that has the red Wisconsin "W" logo in the top right. The player's name and uniform number appear in white in the bottom margin. The back has the player's name in white on a red stripe at the top. Another red stripe at the bottom contains the "W" logo and the logo of the sponsor, Bucky's Locker Room. Between the red stripes, a brief player biography appears in the white middle portion.

	MINT	NRMT	EXC
COMPLETE SET (27)	25.00	11.00	3.10
COMMON CARD (1-27)	.75	.35	.09

	MINT	NRMT	EXC
☐ 1 Troy Vincent	2.50	1.10	.30
☐ 2 Tim Krumrie	1.25	.55	.16
☐ 3 Barry Alvarez CO	1.50	.70	.19
☐ 4 Pat Richter	1.25	.55	.16
☐ 5 Nate Odomes	1.25	.55	.16
☐ 6 Ron Vander Kelen	1.50	.70	.19
☐ 7 Don Davey	1.25	.55	.16
☐ 8 Alan Ameche	2.00	.90	.25
☐ 9 Randy Wright	1.25	.55	.16
☐ 10 Ken Bowman	1.00	.45	.12
☐ 11 Chuck Belin	.75	.35	.09
☐ 12 Elroy Hirsch	2.00	.90	.25
☐ 13 Paul Gruber	1.25	.55	.16
☐ 14 Al Toon	1.50	.70	.19
☐ 15 Richard Johnson	1.00	.45	.12
☐ 16 Pat Harder	1.00	.45	.12
☐ 17 Gary Casper	.75	.35	.09
☐ 18 Rufus Ferguson	.75	.35	.09
☐ 19 Pat O'Donahue	.75	.35	.09
☐ 20 Dennis Lick	.75	.35	.09
☐ 21 Jeff Dellenbach	1.00	.45	.12
☐ 22 Jim Bakken	1.00	.45	.12
☐ 23 Milt Bruhn CO	.75	.35	.09
☐ 24 Mike Webster	1.50	.70	.19
☐ 25 Dave McClain CO	.75	.35	.09
☐ 26 Bill Marek	.75	.35	.09
☐ 27 Rick Graf	.75	.35	.09

1990 Wyoming Smokey

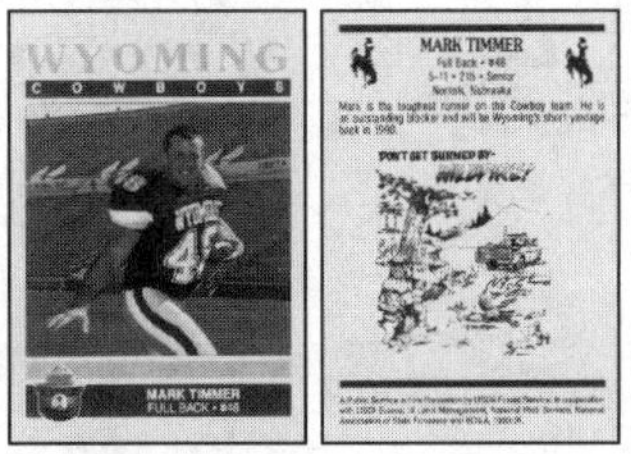

The 1990 Wyoming Cowboys Smokey set was issued in a sheet of 16 cards which, when perforated, measure the standard size (2 1/2" by 3 1/2"). The fronts feature color photos with the player's name, position, and jersey number below the picture. The backs have biographical information and a fire prevention cartoon starring Smokey. The cards are unnumbered, so they are listed below in alphabetical order by subject.

	MINT	NRMT	EXC
COMPLETE SET (16)	20.00	9.00	2.50
COMMON CARD (1-16)	1.50	.70	.19

	MINT	NRMT	EXC
☐ 1 Tom Corontzos 18	1.50	.70	.19
☐ 2 Jay Daffer 34	1.50	.70	.19
☐ 3 Mitch Donahue 49	2.00	.90	.25
☐ 4 Sean Fleming 42	1.50	.70	.19
☐ 5 Pete Gosar 53	1.50	.70	.19
☐ 6 Robert Midgett 57	1.50	.70	.19
☐ 7 Bryan Mooney 9	1.50	.70	.19
☐ 8 Doug Rigby 77	1.50	.70	.19
☐ 9 Paul Roach CO	2.00	.90	.25
☐ 10 Mark Timmer 48	1.50	.70	.19
☐ 11 Paul Wallace 29	1.50	.70	.19
☐ 12 Shawn Wiggins 15	1.50	.70	.19
☐ 13 Gordy Wood 95	1.50	.70	.19
☐ 14 Willie Wright 96	1.50	.70	.19
☐ 15 Cowboy Joe Mascot	1.50	.70	.19
☐ 16 Title Card Cowboy logo	1.50	.70	.19

1993 Wyoming Smokey

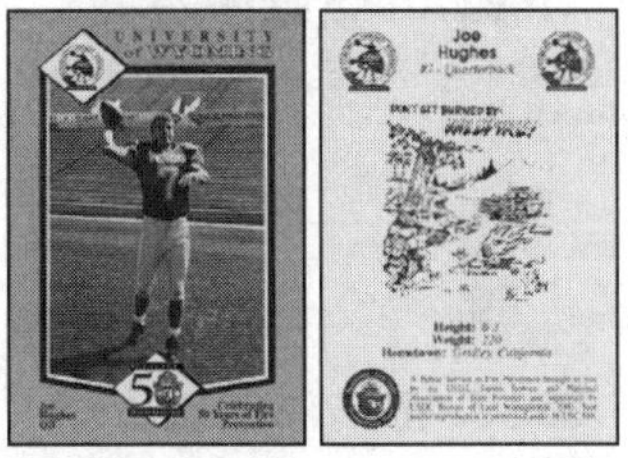

These 16 standard-size cards feature on their fronts color player action shots set within yellow borders. The player's name and position appear on the left side beneath the photo; the team name and logo appear above the photo. The plain white back carries the player's name and position at the top, followed by a Smokey safety tip, and the player's career highlights. The cards are unnumbered and checklisted below in alphabetical order.

	MINT	NRMT	EXC
COMPLETE SET (16)	12.00	5.50	1.50
COMMON CARD (1-16)	.75	.35	.09

	MINT	NRMT	EXC
☐ 1 John Burrough	.75	.35	.09
☐ 2 Wade Constance	.75	.35	.09
☐ 3 Mike Fitzgerald	.75	.35	.09
☐ 4 Jarrod Heidmann	.75	.35	.09
☐ 5 Joe Hughes	.75	.35	.09
☐ 6 Kenny Johnson	1.00	.45	.12
☐ 7 Mike Jones	1.00	.45	.12
☐ 8 Cody Kelly	.75	.35	.09
☐ 9 Rob Levin	.75	.35	.09
☐ 10 Prentice Rhone	.75	.35	.09
☐ 11 Greg Scanlan	1.00	.45	.12
☐ 12 Cory Talich	.75	.35	.09
☐ 13 Kurt Whitehead	.75	.35	.09
☐ 14 Thomas Williams	.75	.35	.09
☐ 15 Tyrone Williams	.75	.35	.09
☐ 16 Ryan Yarborough	3.00	1.35	.35

1992 Youngstown State

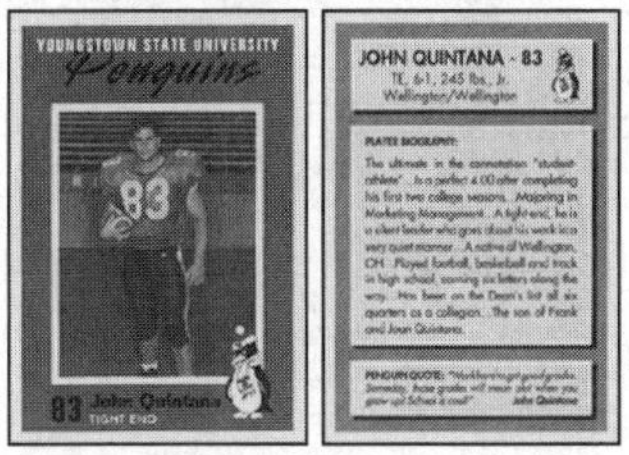

These 54 standard-size cards feature on their fronts posed black-and-white player photos set within red borders. The player's name, position, and jersey number appear beneath the photo. The gray-bordered back carries the player's name, position, uniform number and biography at the top, followed by the player's career highlights. The cards are unnumbered and checklisted below in alphabetical order.

	MINT	NRMT	EXC
COMPLETE SET (54)	20.00	9.00	2.50
COMMON CARD (1-54)	.40	.18	.05

	MINT	NRMT	EXC
☐ 1 Ramon Amill	.40	.18	.05
☐ 2 Dan Black	.40	.18	.05
☐ 3 Trent Boykin	.40	.18	.05
☐ 4 Reginald Brown	.40	.18	.05
☐ 5 Mark Brungard	1.00	.45	.12
☐ 6 Larry Bucciarelli	.40	.18	.05
☐ 7 David Burch	.40	.18	.05
☐ 8 Nick Cochran	.40	.18	.05
☐ 9 Brian Coman	.40	.18	.05
☐ 10 Ken Conatser ACO	.40	.18	.05
☐ 11 Darnell Clark	1.00	.45	.12
☐ 12 Dave DelBoccio	.40	.18	.05
☐ 13 Tom Dillingham	.40	.18	.05
☐ 14 John Englehardt	.40	.18	.05
☐ 15 Marcus Evans	.40	.18	.05
☐ 16 Malcolm Everette	.40	.18	.05
☐ 17 Drew Gerber	.40	.18	.05
☐ 18 Michael Ghent	.40	.18	.05
☐ 19 Aaron Green	.40	.18	.05
☐ 20 Jon Heacock ACO	.40	.18	.05
☐ 21 Alfred Hill	.40	.18	.05
☐ 22 Terica Jones	.40	.18	.05
☐ 23 Craig Kertesz	.40	.18	.05
☐ 24 Paul Kokos Jr.	.40	.18	.05
☐ 25 Reginald Lee	.50	.23	.06
☐ 26 Raymond Miller	.50	.23	.06
☐ 27 Brian Moore ACO	.40	.18	.05
☐ 28 Mike Nezbeth	.40	.18	.05
☐ 29 William Norris	.40	.18	.05
☐ 30 James Panozzo	.40	.18	.05
☐ 31 Derek Pixley	.40	.18	.05
☐ 32 Jeff Powers	.40	.18	.05
☐ 33 David Quick	.40	.18	.05
☐ 34 John Quintana	.40	.18	.05
☐ 35 Mike Rekstis	.40	.18	.05
☐ 36 Demario Ridgeway	.40	.18	.05
☐ 37 Dave Roberts	.40	.18	.05
☐ 38 Chris Sammarone	.50	.23	.06
☐ 39 Randy Smith	.40	.18	.05
☐ 40 Tamron Smith	.50	.23	.06
☐ 41 John Steele	.40	.18	.05
☐ 42 Jim Tressel CO	1.00	.45	.12
☐ 43 Chris Vecchione	.40	.18	.05
☐ 44 Lester Weaver	.50	.23	.06
☐ 45 Jeff Wilkins	.50	.23	.06
☐ 46 Herb Williams	.40	.18	.05
☐ 47 Ryan Wood	.40	.18	.05
☐ 48 Don Zwisler	.40	.18	.05
☐ 49 Penguin Pros Card 1	.50	.23	.06
☐ 50 Penguin Pros Card 2	.50	.23	.06
☐ 51 First-Team All-American	.50	.23	.06
☐ 52 Did You Know 1	.40	.18	.05
☐ 53 Did You Know 2	.40	.18	.05
☐ 54 Did You Know 3	.40	.18	.05

1991 All World CFL

The premier edition of the 1991 All World Canadian Football set contains of 110 standard-size cards. The cards were produced in both set and foil cases, and in both English and French versions. This set includes legends of the CFL (designated below by LEG) and an eight-card "Rocket" subset. In addition, 2,000 personally signed Rocket Ismail cards were randomly inserted in the packs: 1600 in the English foil cases and 400 in the French foil cases. The cards are numbered from 1-1600 in the English and 1-400 in the French. The front design has high gloss color action photos trimmed in red, on a royal blue background with diagonal white pinstripes. The player's name appears in red lettering in the lower left corner, and the CFL helmet logo is in the lower right corner. The backs are horizontally oriented and have royal blue borders. While the veteran player cards have head and shoulders color shots and player information on the backs, the

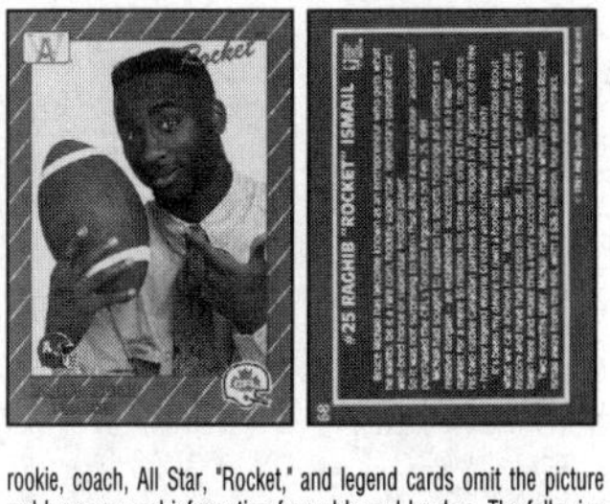

rookie, coach, All Star, "Rocket," and legend cards omit the picture and have personal information framed by red borders. The following cards are designated as "Rookie" on the card front: 4, 16, 28, 33, 53, 63, 66, 68, 78, 84, 92, 101, and 110. The premium for the French version is very slight, just ten percent above the prices listed below. A Rocket Ismail promo card was released and is priced below.

	MINT	NRMT	EXC
COMPLETE SET (110)	3.00	1.35	.35
COMMON CARD (1-110)	.04	.02	.01

	MINT	NRMT	EXC
☐ 1 Raghib(Rocket) Ismail	.25	.11	.03
☐ 2 Bruce McNall Owner	.04	.02	.01
☐ 3 Ray Alexander	.08	.04	.01
☐ 4 Matt Clark	.08	.04	.01
☐ 5 Bobby Jurasin	.08	.04	.01
☐ 6 Dieter Brock LEG	.08	.04	.01
☐ 7 Doug Flutie	.50	.23	.06
☐ 8 Stewart Hill	.08	.04	.01
☐ 9 James Mills	.08	.04	.01
☐ 10 Raghib(Rocket) Ismail (With Bruce McNall)	.25	.11	.03
☐ 11 Tom Clements LEG	.15	.07	.02
☐ 12 Lui Passaglia	.15	.07	.02
☐ 13 Ian Sinclair	.08	.04	.01
☐ 14 Chris Skinner	.08	.04	.01
☐ 15 Joe Theismann LEG	.15	.07	.02
☐ 16 Jon Volpe	.25	.11	.03
☐ 17 Deatrich Wise	.04	.02	.01
☐ 18 Danny Barrett	.15	.07	.02
☐ 19 Warren Moon LEG	.25	.11	.03
☐ 20 Leo Blanchard	.04	.02	.01
☐ 21 Derrick Crawford	.08	.04	.01
☐ 22 Lloyd Fairbanks	.04	.02	.01
☐ 23 David Beckman CO	.04	.02	.01
☐ 24 Matt Finlay	.04	.02	.01
☐ 25 Darryl Hall	.08	.04	.01
☐ 26 Ron Hopkins	.08	.04	.01
☐ 27 Wally Buono CO	.04	.02	.01
☐ 28 Kenton Leonard	.08	.04	.01
☐ 29 Brent Matich	.04	.02	.01
☐ 30 Greg Peterson	.04	.02	.01
☐ 31 Steve Goldman CO	.04	.02	.01
☐ 32 Allen Pitts	.15	.07	.02
☐ 33 Raghib(Rocket) Ismail	.25	.11	.03
☐ 34 Danny Bass	.08	.04	.01
☐ 35 John Gregory CO	.08	.04	.01
☐ 36 Rod Connop	.04	.02	.01
☐ 37 Craig Ellis	.08	.04	.01
☐ 38 Raghib(Rocket) Ismail Rookie	.25	.11	.03
☐ 39 Ron Lancaster CO	.08	.04	.01
☐ 40 Tracey Ham	.35	.16	.04
☐ 41 Ray Macoritti	.08	.04	.01
☐ 42 Willie Pless	.15	.07	.02
☐ 43 Bob O'Billovich CO	.04	.02	.01
☐ 44 Michael Soles	.08	.04	.01
☐ 45 Reggie Taylor	.15	.07	.02
☐ 46 Henry Williams	.20	.09	.03
☐ 47 Adam Rita CO	.04	.02	.01
☐ 48 Larry Wruck	.08	.04	.01
☐ 49 Grover Covington	.15	.07	.02
☐ 50 Rocky DiPietro	.08	.04	.01
☐ 51 Darryl Rogers CO	.04	.02	.01
☐ 52 Peter Giftopoulus	.08	.04	.01
☐ 53 Herman Heard	.08	.04	.01
☐ 54 Mike Kerrigan	.20	.09	.03
☐ 55 Reggie Barnes AS	.08	.04	.01
☐ 56 Derrick McAdoo	.08	.04	.01
☐ 57 Paul Osbaldiston	.08	.04	.01
☐ 58 Earl Winfield	.15	.07	.02
☐ 59 Greg Battle AS	.15	.07	.02
☐ 60 Damon Allen	.25	.11	.03
☐ 61 Reggie Barnes	.15	.07	.02
☐ 62 Bob Molle	.04	.02	.01
☐ 63 Raghib(Rocket) Ismail	.25	.11	.03
☐ 64 Irv Daymond	.04	.02	.01
☐ 65 Andre Francis	.08	.04	.01
☐ 66 Bart Hull	.15	.07	.02
☐ 67 Stephen Jones	.15	.07	.02
☐ 68 Raghib(Rocket) Ismail	.25	.11	.03
☐ 69 Glenn Kulka	.08	.04	.01
☐ 70 Loyd Lewis	.04	.02	.01
☐ 71 Rob Smith	.08	.04	.01
☐ 72 Roger Aldag	.08	.04	.01
☐ 73 Kent Austin	.15	.07	.02
☐ 74 Ray Elgaard	.15	.07	.02
☐ 75 Mike Clemons AS	.25	.11	.03
☐ 76 Jeff Fairholm	.08	.04	.01
☐ 77 Richie Hall	.08	.04	.01
☐ 78 Willis Jacox	.08	.04	.01
☐ 79 Eddie Lowe	.08	.04	.01

☐ 80 Ray Elgaard AS	.08	.04	.01
☐ 81 Donald Narcisse	.15	.07	.02
☐ 82 James Mills AS	.08	.04	.01
☐ 83 Dave Ridgway	.15	.07	.02
☐ 84 Ted Wahl	.08	.04	.01
☐ 85 Carl Brazley	.08	.04	.01
☐ 86 Mike Clemons	.50	.23	.06
☐ 87 Matt Dunigan	.35	.16	.04
☐ 88 Grey Cup Checklist 1	.04	.02	.01
☐ 89 Harold Hallman	.08	.04	.01
☐ 90 Rodney Harding	.08	.04	.01
☐ 91 Don Moen	.08	.04	.01
☐ 92 Raghib(Rocket) Ismail	.25	.11	.03
☐ 93 Reggie Pleasant	.15	.07	.02
☐ 94 Darrell Smith UER (One L on front, two on back)	.15	.07	.02
☐ 95 Group Shot Checklist 2	.04	.02	.01
☐ 96 Chris Schultz	.08	.04	.01
☐ 97 Don Wilson	.04	.02	.01
☐ 98 Greg Battle	.15	.07	.02
☐ 99 Lyle Bauer	.04	.02	.01
☐ 100 Less Browne	.08	.04	.01
☐ 101 Raghib(Rocket) Ismail	.25	.11	.03
☐ 102 Tom Burgess	.15	.07	.02
☐ 103 Mike Gray	.04	.02	.01
☐ 104 Rod Hill	.08	.04	.01
☐ 105 Warren Hudson	.08	.04	.01
☐ 106 Tyrone Jones	.15	.07	.02
☐ 107 Stan Mikawos	.04	.02	.01
☐ 108 Robert Mimbs	.50	.23	.06
☐ 109 James West	.15	.07	.02
☐ 110 Raghib(Rocket) Ismail	.25	.11	.03
☐ NNO Rocket Ismail (Autographed card/1600)	50.00	22.00	6.25
☐ P1 Rocket Ismail Promo (numbered P)	1.00	.45	.12

1992 All World CFL

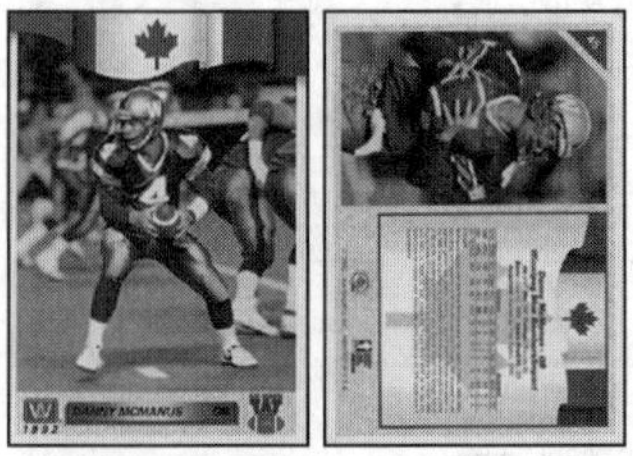

The 1992 All World CFL set consists of 180 standard-size cards. The production run was 4,000 individually numbered foil cases and 8,000 numbered factory sets. Foil embossed maple leaf cards and 1,000 autographed Doug Flutie cards were randomly inserted into foil packs. Special insert sets focus on Rookies (eight cards), Trophy Winners (12 cards), Road to the Cup (four cards), and Memorable Grey Cups (four cards). The color action player photos on the fronts are accented above by a Canadian flag that bleeds off the card top. The backs present statistics, another player photo, biography, and an import designation to indicate a player is non-Canadian. Two Promo cards were produced and are priced below.

	MINT	NRMT	EXC
COMPLETE SET (180)	8.00	3.60	1.00
COMMON CARD (1-180)	.05	.02	.01

☐ 1 Checklist 1-90	.05	.02	.01
☐ 2 Draft Picks Checklist	.05	.02	.01
☐ 3 Western Final	.05	.02	.01
☐ 4 Eastern Final	.05	.02	.01
☐ 5 79th Grey Cup	.05	.02	.01
☐ 6 Grey Cup Most Outstanding Player Rocket Ismail	.20	.09	.03
☐ 7 Memorable Grey Cups 1909	.05	.02	.01
☐ 8 Memorable Grey Cups 1969	.05	.02	.01
☐ 9 Memorable Grey Cups 1982	.05	.02	.01
☐ 10 Memorable Grey Cups 1989	.05	.02	.01
☐ 11 Jeff Braswell	.10	.05	.01
☐ 12 Glenn Kulka	.10	.05	.01
☐ 13 Will Johnson	.20	.09	.03
☐ 14 Lance Chomyc	.10	.05	.01
☐ 15 Stan Mikawos	.05	.02	.01
☐ 16 Bobby Jurasin	.20	.09	.03
☐ 17 Terry Baker	.10	.05	.01
☐ 18 Tracey Ham	.60	.25	.07
☐ 19 Todd Wiseman	.05	.02	.01
☐ 20 Rob Crifo	.05	.02	.01
☐ 21 Chris Morris	.20	.09	.03
☐ 22 Jon Volpe	.50	.23	.06
☐ 23 Donald Narcisse	.20	.09	.03
☐ 24 David Williams	.20	.09	.03
☐ 25 Paul Clatney	.05	.02	.01
☐ 26 Willie Pless	.20	.09	.03
☐ 27 Rickey Foggie	.20	.09	.03
☐ 28 Denny Chronopoulos	.05	.02	.01
☐ 29 Darryl Sampson	.05	.02	.01
☐ 30 Patrick Wayne	.05	.02	.01
☐ 31 Terrence Jones	.20	.09	.03
☐ 32 Larry Wruck	.10	.05	.01
☐ 33 Angelo Snipes	.30	.14	.04
☐ 34 Tony Champion	.20	.09	.03
☐ 35 Steve Taylor	.20	.09	.03
☐ 36 Lorne King	.05	.02	.01
☐ 37 Roger Aldag	.10	.05	.01
☐ 38 Damon Allen	.40	.18	.05
☐ 39 Chris Walby	.20	.09	.03
☐ 40 Doug Davies	.05	.02	.01
☐ 41 Dan Rashovich	.05	.02	.01
☐ 42 Mark Scott	.05	.02	.01
☐ 43 Reggie Pleasant	.20	.09	.03
☐ 44 Bob Cameron	.20	.09	.03
☐ 45 Danny McManus	.20	.09	.03
☐ 46 Matt Clark	.10	.05	.01
☐ 47 Bart Hull	.10	.05	.01
☐ 48 Hank Ilesic	.20	.09	.03
☐ 49 Pee Wee Smith	.30	.14	.04
☐ 50 Irv Daymond	.05	.02	.01
☐ 51 Greg Battle J.P. McCaffrey Trophy	.20	.09	.03
☐ 52 Will Johnson Norm Fieldgate Trophy	.20	.09	.03
☐ 53 Lance Chomyc Lew Hayman Trophy	.10	.05	.01
☐ 54 Jim Mills DeMarco-Becket Memorial Trophy	.10	.05	.01
☐ 55 Jon Volpe Jackie Parker Trophy	.20	.09	.03
☐ 56 Raghib(Rocket) Ismail Frank M. Gibson Trophy	.30	.14	.04
☐ 57 Dave Ridgway David Dryburgh Memorial Trophy	.20	.09	.03
☐ 58 Chris Walby Leo Dandurand Trophy	.20	.09	.03
☐ 59 Doug Flutie Jeff Nicklin Memorial Trophy	.50	.23	.06
☐ 60 Robert Mimbs Jeff Russell Memorial Trophy	.35	.16	.04
☐ 61 Jon Volpe Eddie James Memorial Trophy	.20	.09	.03
☐ 62 Blake Marshall Dr. Beattie Martin Trophy	.10	.05	.01
☐ 63 Eric Streater	.20	.09	.03
☐ 64 Carl Brazley	.10	.05	.01
☐ 65 Kent Warnock	.10	.05	.01
☐ 66 Brian Bonner	.05	.02	.01
☐ 67 Tom Burgess	.20	.09	.03
☐ 68 Bob Gordon	.05	.02	.01
☐ 69 Milson Jones	.10	.05	.01
☐ 70 Todd Dillon	.10	.05	.01
☐ 71 Keyvan Jenkins	.20	.09	.03
☐ 72 Ken Evraire	.20	.09	.03
☐ 73 Willis Jacox	.20	.09	.03
☐ 74 Carl Bland	.05	.02	.01
☐ 75 Daniel Hunter	.05	.02	.01
☐ 76 Chris Schultz	.10	.05	.01
☐ 77 Earl Winfield	.20	.09	.03
☐ 78 Henry Williams	.30	.14	.04
☐ 79 Matt Dunigan	.60	.25	.07
☐ 80 Mark McLoughlin	.05	.02	.01
☐ 81 Craig Ellis	.10	.05	.01
☐ 82 Rodney Harding	.20	.09	.03
☐ 83 Scott Douglas	.05	.02	.01
☐ 84 Ray Elgaard	.20	.09	.03
☐ 85 Doug Flutie	1.00	.45	.12
☐ 86 Gary Lewis	.05	.02	.01
☐ 87 Rod Hill	.05	.02	.01
☐ 88 Gregg Stumon	.10	.05	.01
☐ 89 Ray Alexander	.10	.05	.01
☐ 90 Blake Dermott	.10	.05	.01
☐ 91 Checklist 91-180	.05	.02	.01
☐ 92 Trophy Winners CL	.10	.05	.01
☐ 93 British Columbia CL	.05	.02	.01
☐ 94 Calgary CL	.05	.02	.01
☐ 95 Edmonton CL	.05	.02	.01
☐ 96 Saskatchewan CL	.05	.02	.01
☐ 97 Hamilton CL	.05	.02	.01
☐ 98 Ottawa CL	.05	.02	.01
☐ 99 Toronto CL	.05	.02	.01
☐ 100 Winnipeg CL	.05	.02	.01
☐ 101 James West	.20	.09	.03
☐ 102 Jeff Fairholm	.10	.05	.01
☐ 103 Mike Campbell	.10	.05	.01
☐ 104 Darren Flutie	.60	.25	.07
☐ 105 Blake Marshall	.20	.09	.03
☐ 106 Loyd Lewis	.05	.02	.01
☐ 107 Enis Jackson	.05	.02	.01
☐ 108 John Motton	.20	.09	.03
☐ 109 Ken Walcott	.05	.02	.01
☐ 110 Richie Hall	.10	.05	.01
☐ 111 Greg Peterson	.05	.02	.01
☐ 112 Wally Zatylny	.05	.02	.01
☐ 113 Lui Passaglia	.20	.09	.03
☐ 114 Darryl Hall	.10	.05	.01
☐ 115 Michael Soles	.10	.05	.01
☐ 116 Doug Brewster	.05	.02	.01
☐ 117 Mike Gray	.05	.02	.01
☐ 118 Mike Trevathan	.20	.09	.03
☐ 119 Don Moen	.10	.05	.01
☐ 120 Chris Armstrong	.40	.18	.05
☐ 121 Lucius Floyd	.05	.02	.01
☐ 122 Ken Pettway	.05	.02	.01
☐ 123 Anthony Drawhorn	.10	.05	.01
☐ 124 Brian Walling	.20	.09	.03
☐ 125 Troy Westwood	.20	.09	.03
☐ 126 Reggie Barnes	.20	.09	.03
☐ 127 Raghib(Rocket) Ismail	.50	.23	.06
☐ 128 Rod Connop	.05	.02	.01
☐ 129 Chris Major	.20	.09	.03
☐ 130 Dave Bovell	.05	.02	.01
☐ 131 Quency Williams	.05	.02	.01
☐ 132 Michel Bourgeau	.10	.05	.01
☐ 133 Harold Hallman	.10	.05	.01
☐ 134 Junior Thurman	.20	.09	.03
☐ 135 Stewart Hill	.10	.05	.01
☐ 136 Brent Matich	.05	.02	.01
☐ 137 Leroy Blugh	.10	.05	.01
☐ 138 Nick Mazzoli	.05	.02	.01
☐ 139 Dave Ridgway	.20	.09	.03
☐ 140 Matt Finlay	.05	.02	.01
☐ 141 Mike Clemons	1.00	.45	.12
☐ 142 Jason Riley	.05	.02	.01
☐ 143 Stacey Hairston	.05	.02	.01
☐ 144 Jim Mills	.10	.05	.01
☐ 145 Paul Randolph	.05	.02	.01
☐ 146 David Sapunjis	.20	.09	.03
☐ 147 Charles Gordon	.05	.02	.01
☐ 148 Chris Tsangaris	.05	.02	.01
☐ 149 Darrell K. Smith	.20	.09	.03
☐ 150 Leo Groenewegen	.05	.02	.01
☐ 151 Greg Battle	.20	.09	.03
☐ 152 Bruce Covernton	.20	.09	.03
☐ 153 Paul Osbaldiston	.10	.05	.01
☐ 154 Don Wilson	.05	.02	.01
☐ 155 Kent Austin	.30	.14	.04
☐ 156 Jamie Morris	.20	.09	.03
☐ 157 Andre Francis	.10	.05	.01
☐ 158 O.J. Brigance	.30	.14	.04
☐ 159 Less Browne	.10	.05	.01
☐ 160 Alondra Johnson	.10	.05	.01
☐ 161 Dexter Manley	.10	.05	.01
☐ 162 Bob Poley	.05	.02	.01
☐ 163 Ed Berry	.05	.02	.01
☐ 164 Peter Giftopoulos	.10	.05	.01
☐ 165 Glen Suitor	.10	.05	.01
☐ 166 Eddie Thomas	.05	.02	.01
☐ 167 Danny Barrett	.20	.09	.03
☐ 168 Robert Mimbs	.35	.16	.04
☐ 169 Jim Sandusky	.20	.09	.03
☐ 170 Maurice Smith	.05	.02	.01
☐ 171 David Conrad	.05	.02	.01
☐ 172 Larry Willis	.10	.05	.01
☐ 173 Ian Sinclair	.10	.05	.01
☐ 174 Allen Pitts	.30	.14	.04
☐ 175 Don McPherson	.20	.09	.03
☐ 176 Ray Bernard	.05	.02	.01
☐ 177 Dale Sanderson	.05	.02	.01
☐ 178 Dan Ferrone	.10	.05	.01
☐ 179 Vic Stevenson	.05	.02	.01
☐ 180 Rob Smith	.10	.05	.01
☐ P1 Doug Flutie Promo (Numbered P)	1.50	.70	.19
☐ P2 Rocket Ismail Promo (Numbered P)	1.00	.45	.12

1992 Arena Holograms

Arena Trading Cards produced this Grey Cup Trophy hologram card. It was released at the 1992 Toronto Sky Dome card show.

	MINT	NRMT	EXC
COMPLETE SET (1)	5.00	2.20	.60
COMMON CARD	5.00	2.20	.60

☐ 1 Grey Cup Trophy	5.00	2.20	.60

1982 Bantam/FBI CFL Discs

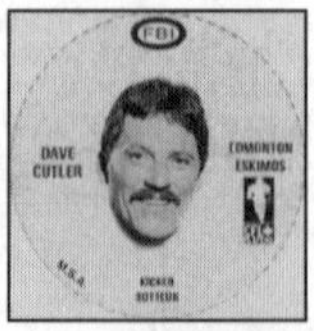

The disks in this set measure approximately 2 7/8" in diameter and two were available on the bottoms of specially marked Bantam Orange Drink and FBI Juice product boxes. The disks were perforated for removal. Each disk carries a black-and-white photo of the player's face against a white background. The player's name and team are printed on either side of the photo, while the player's position is printed below. The card backs are blank. The cards are unnumbered and checklisted below in alphabetical order.

	MINT	NRMT	EXC
COMPLETE SET (31)	175.00	80.00	22.00
COMMON CARD (1-31)	4.00	1.80	.50

☐ 1 Junior Ah You	6.00	2.70	.75
☐ 2 Zenon Andrusyshyn	6.00	2.70	.75
☐ 3 Leon Bright	6.00	2.70	.75
☐ 4 Bob Cameron	6.00	2.70	.75
☐ 5 Tom Clements	15.00	6.75	1.85
☐ 6 Jim Corrigall	6.00	2.70	.75
☐ 7 Tom Cousineau	8.00	3.60	1.00
☐ 8 Carl Crennell	6.00	2.70	.75
☐ 9 Dave Cutler	6.00	2.70	.75
☐ 10 Peter Dalla Riva	8.00	3.60	1.00
☐ 11 Dave Fennell	6.00	2.70	.75
☐ 12 Vince Ferragamo	10.00	4.50	1.25
☐ 13 Tom Forzani	4.00	1.80	.50
☐ 14 Tony Gabriel	10.00	4.50	1.25
☐ 15 Gabriel Gregoire	4.00	1.80	.50
☐ 16 Billy Hardee	4.00	1.80	.50
☐ 17 Larry Highbaugh	6.00	2.70	.75
☐ 18 Condredge Holloway	10.00	4.50	1.25
☐ 19 Mark Jackson QB	4.00	1.80	.50
☐ 20 Billy Johnson (White Shoes)	10.00	4.50	1.25
☐ 21 Larry Key	4.00	1.80	.50
☐ 22 Marc Lacelle	4.00	1.80	.50
☐ 23 Ian Mofford	6.00	2.70	.75
☐ 24 Gerry Organ	4.00	1.80	.50
☐ 25 Tony Petruccio	4.00	1.80	.50
☐ 26 Tony Proudfoot	6.00	2.70	.75
☐ 27 Randy Rhino	8.00	3.60	1.00
☐ 28 Ian Santer	4.00	1.80	.50
☐ 29 Jerry Tagge	8.00	3.60	1.00
☐ 30 Jim Washington	6.00	2.70	.75
☐ 31 Tom Wilkinson	8.00	3.60	1.00

1954 Blue Ribbon Tea CFL

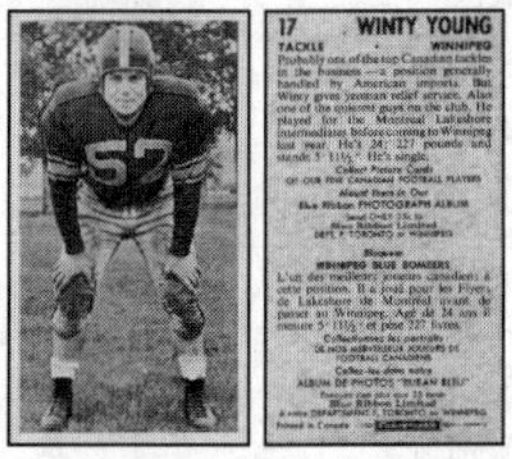

The 1954 Blue Ribbon Tea set contains 80 color cards of CFL players. The cards measure 2 1/4" by 4". The pictures on the front are obviously posed rather than actual action shots. The backs of the cards contain biographical data in both English and French. An album for this set exists as an offer for this album is listed on the back. The set is printed in Canada, presumably by a firm called Colorgraphic, as this firm's logo appears at the bottom on the back of the card. Cards are numbered in team order, i.e., Winnipeg Blue Bombers (1-19), Ottawa Rough Riders (20-29), Hamilton Tiger-Cats (30-39), Edmonton Eskimos (40-50), Calgary Stampeders (51-60), and Montreal Alouettes (61-80).

	NRMT	VG-E	GOOD
COMPLETE SET (80)	12000.00	5400.00	1500.00
COMMON CARD (1-80)	110.00	50.00	14.00

☐ 1 Jack Jacobs	200.00	90.00	25.00
☐ 2 Neill Armstrong	125.00	55.00	15.50
☐ 3 Lorne Benson	110.00	50.00	14.00
☐ 4 Tom Casey	125.00	55.00	15.50
☐ 5 Vinnie Drake	110.00	50.00	14.00
☐ 6 Tommy Ford	110.00	50.00	14.00
☐ 7 Bud Grant	600.00	275.00	75.00
☐ 8 Dick Huffman	125.00	55.00	15.50
☐ 9 Gerry James	150.00	70.00	19.00
☐ 10 Bud Korchak	110.00	50.00	14.00
☐ 11 Thomas Lumsden	110.00	50.00	14.00
☐ 12 Steve Patrick	110.00	50.00	14.00
☐ 13 Keith Pearce	110.00	50.00	14.00
☐ 14 Jesse Thomas	110.00	50.00	14.00
☐ 15 Buddy Tinsley	125.00	55.00	15.50
☐ 16 Alan Scott Wiley	110.00	50.00	14.00
☐ 17 Winty Young	110.00	50.00	14.00
☐ 18 Joseph Zaleski	110.00	50.00	14.00
☐ 19 Ron Vaccher	110.00	50.00	14.00
☐ 20 John Gramling	110.00	50.00	14.00
☐ 21 Bob Simpson	150.00	70.00	19.00
☐ 22 Bruno Bitkowski	125.00	55.00	15.50
☐ 23 Kaye Vaughan	125.00	55.00	15.50
☐ 24 Don Carter	110.00	50.00	14.00
☐ 25 Gene Roberts	110.00	50.00	14.00
☐ 26 Howie Turner	110.00	50.00	14.00
☐ 27 Avatus Stone	110.00	50.00	14.00
☐ 28 Tom McHugh	110.00	50.00	14.00
☐ 29 Clyde Bennett	110.00	50.00	14.00
☐ 30 Bill Berezowski	110.00	50.00	14.00
☐ 31 Eddie Bevan	110.00	50.00	14.00
☐ 32 Dick Brown	110.00	50.00	14.00
☐ 33 Bernie Custis	125.00	55.00	15.50
☐ 34 Merle Hapes	125.00	55.00	15.50
☐ 35 Tip Logan	110.00	50.00	14.00
☐ 36 Vince Mazza	125.00	55.00	15.50
☐ 37 Pete Neumann	125.00	55.00	15.50
☐ 38 Vince Scott	125.00	55.00	15.50
☐ 39 Ralph Toohy	110.00	50.00	14.00
☐ 40 Frank Anderson	110.00	50.00	14.00
☐ 41 Bob Dean	110.00	50.00	14.00

☐ 42 Leon Manley	110.00	50.00	14.00
☐ 43 Bill Zock	125.00	55.00	15.50
☐ 44 Frank Morris	150.00	70.00	19.00
☐ 45 Jim Quondamatteo	110.00	50.00	14.00
☐ 46 Eagle Keys	150.00	70.00	19.00
☐ 47 Bernie Faloney	350.00	160.00	45.00
☐ 48 Jackie Parker	500.00	220.00	60.00
☐ 49 Ray Willsey	110.00	50.00	14.00
☐ 50 Mike King	110.00	50.00	14.00
☐ 51 Johnny Bright	350.00	160.00	45.00
☐ 52 Gene Brito	125.00	55.00	15.50
☐ 53 Stan Heath	125.00	55.00	15.50
☐ 54 Roy Jenson	110.00	50.00	14.00
☐ 55 Don Loney	110.00	50.00	14.00
☐ 56 Eddie Macon	110.00	50.00	14.00
☐ 57 Peter Maxwell-Muir	110.00	50.00	14.00
☐ 58 Tom Miner	110.00	50.00	14.00
☐ 59 Jim Prewett	110.00	50.00	14.00
☐ 60 Lowell Wagner	110.00	50.00	14.00
☐ 61 Red O'Quinn	125.00	55.00	15.50
☐ 62 Ray Poole	125.00	55.00	15.50
☐ 63 Jim Staton	110.00	50.00	14.00
☐ 64 Alex Webster	200.00	90.00	25.00
☐ 65 Al Dekdebruin	110.00	50.00	14.00
☐ 66 Ed Bradley	110.00	50.00	14.00
☐ 67 Tex Coulter	150.00	70.00	19.00
☐ 68 Sam Etcheverry	500.00	220.00	60.00
☐ 69 Larry Grigg	110.00	50.00	14.00
☐ 70 Tom Hugo	110.00	50.00	14.00
☐ 71 Chuck Hunsinger	110.00	50.00	14.00
☐ 72 Herb Trawick	125.00	55.00	15.50
☐ 73 Virgil Wagner	125.00	55.00	15.50
☐ 74 Phil Adrian	110.00	50.00	14.00
☐ 75 Bruce Coulter	110.00	50.00	14.00
☐ 76 Jim Miller	110.00	50.00	14.00
☐ 77 Jim Mitchener	110.00	50.00	14.00
☐ 78 Tom Moran	110.00	50.00	14.00
☐ 79 Doug McNichol	110.00	50.00	14.00
☐ 80 Joey Pal	110.00	50.00	14.00
☐ NNO Saver Album	500.00	220.00	60.00

1988 Bootlegger B.C. Lions

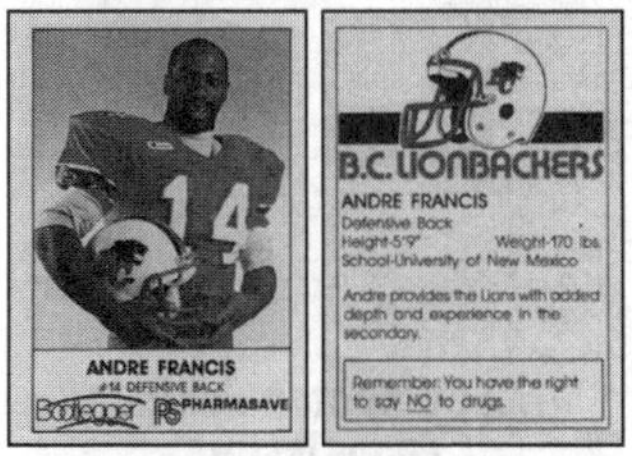

This 13-card standard-size safety set features members of the British Columbia Lions and was co-sponsored by Bootlegger and PS Pharmasave, whose company logos adorn the bottom of the card face. These cards display posed color player photos, shot from the waist up against a sky blue background. The photos are framed by white borders, with player information immediately below the pictures. The backs have an icon of the team helmet, biography, and an anti-drug message. A different "Just Say No To Drugs" message is included on each card. The sponsor title card lists a total of 36 different companies who financed the drug awareness program. The cards are unnumbered and checklisted below in alphabetical order.

	MINT	NRMT	EXC
COMPLETE SET (13)	20.00	9.00	2.50
COMMON CARD (1-12)	1.25	.55	.16
☐ 1 Jamie Buis	1.25	.55	.16
☐ 2 Jan Carinci	1.25	.55	.16
☐ 3 Dwayne Derban	1.25	.55	.16
☐ 4 Roy Dewalt	3.00	1.35	.35
☐ 5 Andre Francis	1.50	.70	.19
☐ 6 Rick Klassen	2.00	.90	.25
☐ 7 Kevin Konar	1.50	.70	.19
☐ 8 Scott Lecky	1.25	.55	.16
☐ 9 James Parker	3.00	1.35	.35
☐ 10 John Ulmer	1.25	.55	.16
☐ 11 Peter VandenBos	1.25	.55	.16
☐ 12 Todd Wiseman	1.25	.55	.16
☐ NNO Title Card Corporate Sponsors	1.50	.70	.19

1971 Chevron B.C. Lions

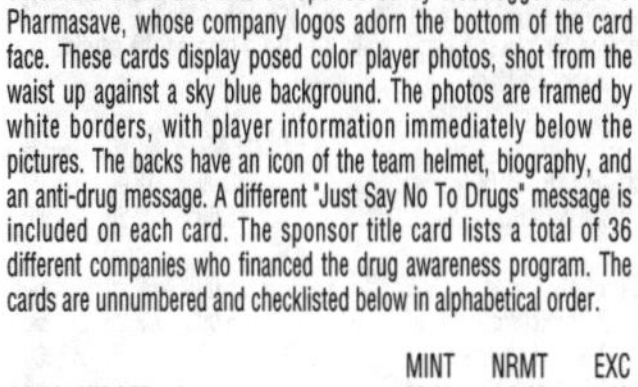

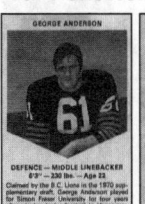

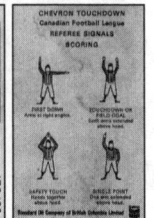

This 23-card set of the British Columbia Lions measures approximately 3" by 4 1/2" and was distributed by Standard Oil Company. The unnumbered cards were apparently originally attached in complete sheet form as perforations can by found on the cards' edges. The fronts feature color player portraits and player information on a white background. The backs carry information about the Canadian Football League. A plastic folded "wallet" was produced to house the set with the words "Chevron Touchdown Cards" on the cover. Cards 3,7,11,22, 27,28,33,44 and 46 were bonus cards added later and therefore considered tougher to find.

	NRMT-MT	EXC	G-VG
COMPLETE SET (50)	225.00	100.00	28.00
COMMON CARD (1-50)	3.00	1.35	.35
COMMON SP	12.00	5.50	1.50
☐ 1 George Anderson	3.00	1.35	.35
☐ 2 Josh Ashton	4.00	1.80	.50
☐ 3 Ross Boice SP	12.00	5.50	1.50
☐ 4 Paul Brothers	3.00	1.35	.35
☐ 5 Tom Cassese	3.00	1.35	.35
☐ 6 Roy Cavallin	3.00	1.35	.35
☐ 7 Rusty Clark SP	12.00	5.50	1.50
☐ 8 Owen Dejanovich CO	3.00	1.35	.35
☐ 9 Dave Denny	3.00	1.35	.35
☐ 10 Brian Donnelly	3.00	1.35	.35
☐ 11 Steve Duich SP	12.00	5.50	1.50
☐ 12 Jim Duke	3.00	1.35	.35
☐ 13 Dave Easley	3.00	1.35	.35
☐ 14 Trevor Ekdahl	4.00	1.80	.50
☐ 15 Jim Evenson	4.00	1.80	.50
☐ 16 Greg Findlay	3.00	1.35	.35
☐ 17 Ted Gerela	3.00	1.35	.35
☐ 18 Dave Golinsky	3.00	1.35	.35
☐ 19 Lefty Hendrickson	3.00	1.35	.35
☐ 20 Lach Heron	4.00	1.80	.50
☐ 21 Gerry Herron	3.00	1.35	.35
☐ 22 Larry Highbaugh SP	12.00	5.50	1.50
☐ 23 Wayne Holm	3.00	1.35	.35
☐ 24 Bob Howes	3.00	1.35	.35
☐ 25 Max Huber	3.00	1.35	.35
☐ 26 Garrett Hunsperger	3.00	1.35	.35
☐ 27 Lawrence James SP	12.00	5.50	1.50
☐ 28 Brian Kelsey SP	12.00	5.50	1.50
☐ 29 Eagle Keys CO	4.00	1.80	.50
☐ 30 Mike Leveille	3.00	1.35	.35
☐ 31 John Love	3.00	1.35	.35
☐ 32 Ray Lychak	3.00	1.35	.35
☐ 33 Dick Lyons SP	12.00	5.50	1.50
☐ 34 Wayne Matherne	3.00	1.35	.35
☐ 35 Ken McCullough CO	3.00	1.35	.35
☐ 36 Don Moorhead	3.00	1.35	.35
☐ 37 Pete Palmer	3.00	1.35	.35
☐ 38 Jackie Parker GM	12.00	5.50	1.50
☐ 39 Ken Phillips	3.00	1.35	.35
☐ 40 Cliff Powell	3.00	1.35	.35
☐ 41 Gary Robinson	3.00	1.35	.35
☐ 42 Ken Sugarman	4.00	1.80	.50
☐ 43 Bruce Taupier	3.00	1.35	.35
☐ 44 Jim Tomlin SP	12.00	5.50	1.50
☐ 45 Bud Tynes CO	3.00	1.35	.35
☐ 46 Carl Weathers SP	12.00	5.50	1.50
☐ 47 Jim White	3.00	1.35	.35
☐ 48 Mike Wilson	3.00	1.35	.35
☐ 49 Jim Young	8.00	3.60	1.00
☐ 50 Contest Card For Chevron	3.00	1.35	.35

1971 Chiquita CFL All-Stars

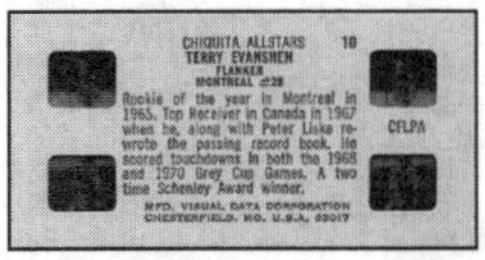

This set of CFL All-Stars actually consists of 13 slides which were intended to be viewed by a specially yellow Chiquita viewer. Each slide measures approximately 1 3/4" by 3 5/8" and contains four small color slides showing two views of two players. Each side has a player summary on its middle portion, with two small color action slides at each end stacked one above the other. When the slide is placed in the viewer, the two bottom slides, which are identical, reveal the first player. Flipping the slide over reveals the other player biography and enables one to view the other two slides, which show the second player. Each side of the slides is numbered as listed below. The set is considered complete without the yellow viewer.

	NRMT-MT	EXC	G-VG
COMPLETE SET (13)	235.00	105.00	29.00
COMMON PAIR	15.00	6.75	1.85
☐ 1 Bill Baker 2 Ken Sugarman	20.00	9.00	2.50
☐ 3 Wayne Giardino 4 Peter Dalla Riva	20.00	9.00	2.50
☐ 5 Leon McQuay 6 Jim Thorpe	25.00	11.00	3.10
☐ 7 George Reed 8 Jerry Campbell	20.00	9.00	2.50
☐ 9 Tommy Joe Coffey 10 Terry Evanshen	25.00	11.00	3.10
☐ 11 Jim Young 12 Mark Kosmos	20.00	9.00	2.50
☐ 13 Ron Forwick 14 Jack Abendschan	15.00	6.75	1.85
☐ 15 Don Jonas 16 Al Marcellin	20.00	9.00	2.50
☐ 17 Joe Theismann 18 Jim Corrigall	50.00	22.00	6.25
☐ 19 Ed George 20 Dick Dupuis	15.00	6.75	1.85
☐ 21 Ted Dushinski 22 Bob Swift	15.00	6.75	1.85
☐ 23 John Lagrone 24 Bill Danychuk	15.00	6.75	1.85
☐ 25 Garney Henley 26 John Williams	20.00	9.00	2.50
☐ NNO Yellow Viewer	45.00	20.00	5.50

1961 CKNW B.C. Lions

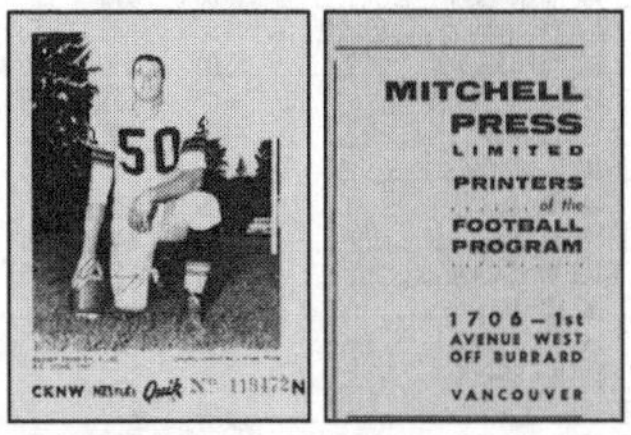

Each of these photos measure approximately 3 7/8" by 5 1/2". Inside white borders, the fronts feature black-and-white posed action photos. The player's facsimile autograph is written across the picture; on most of the cards it is in red ink. Immediately below the picture in small print are player information and "Graphic Industries Limited Photo." The wider white bottom border also carries sponsor information and a five- or six-digit serial number. Apparently the photos were primarily sponsored by CKNW (a radio station), which appears on every photo, and various other co-sponsors that may vary from card to card. The photos show signs of perforation as they were originally issued in game programs. The backs display various advertisements. The photos are unnumbered and checklisted below in alphabetical order. The co-sponsors (listed on the card front) are also listed below. The set can be distinguished from the set of the following year by the presence of the set's date in the lower left corner of the cardfront.

	NRMT	VG-E	GOOD
COMPLETE SET (30)	200.00	90.00	25.00
COMMON CARD (1-30)	6.00	2.70	.75
☐ 1 By Bailey	15.00	6.75	1.85
☐ 2 Nub Beamer	6.00	2.70	.75
☐ 3 Bob Belak Kings Drive-In	6.00	2.70	.75
☐ 4 Neil Beaumont	6.00	2.70	.75
☐ 5 Bill Britton Nestle's Quik	6.00	2.70	.75
☐ 6 Tom Brown Kings Drive-In	8.00	3.60	1.00
☐ 7 Mike Cacic	6.00	2.70	.75
☐ 8 Jim Carphin	6.00	2.70	.75
☐ 9 Bruce Claridge	6.00	2.70	.75
☐ 10 Pat Claridge	6.00	2.70	.75
☐ 11 Steve Cotter	6.00	2.70	.75
☐ 12 Lonnie Dennis Nestle's Quik	6.00	2.70	.75
☐ 13 Norm Fieldgate	8.00	3.60	1.00
☐ 14 Willie Fleming	18.00	8.00	2.20
☐ 15 George Grant	6.00	2.70	.75
☐ 16 Sonny Homer Nestle's Quik	8.00	3.60	1.00
☐ 17 Bob Jeter	10.00	4.50	1.25
☐ 18 Dick Johnson	6.00	2.70	.75
☐ 19 Earl Keeley	6.00	2.70	.75
☐ 20 Vic Kristopaitis	6.00	2.70	.75
☐ 21 Gordie Mitchell	6.00	2.70	.75
☐ 22 Rae Ross Nestle's Quik	6.00	2.70	.75
☐ 23 Bob Schloredt	8.00	3.60	1.00
☐ 24 Gary Schwertfeger	6.00	2.70	.75
☐ 25 Mel Semenko Kings Drive-In	6.00	2.70	.75
☐ 26 Ed Sullivan	8.00	3.60	1.00
☐ 27 Barney Therrien Nestle's Quik	6.00	2.70	.75
☐ 28 Ed Vereb	6.00	2.70	.75
☐ 29 Don Vicic	6.00	2.70	.75
☐ 30 Ron Watton	6.00	2.70	.75

1962 CKNW B.C. Lions

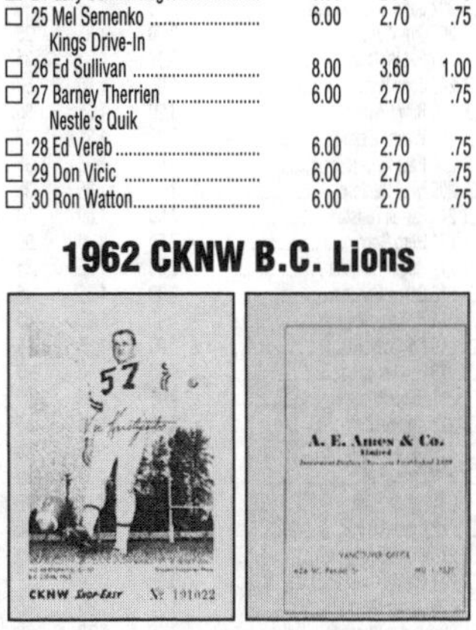

Each of these photos measure approximately 3 7/8" by 5 1/2". Inside white borders, the fronts feature black-and-white posed action photos. The player's facsimile autograph is written across the picture; on most of the cards it is in red ink. Immediately below the picture in small print are player information and "Graphic Industries Limited Photo." The wider white bottom border also carries sponsor information and a five- or six-digit serial number. Apparently the photos were primarily sponsored by CKNW (a radio station), which appears on every photo, and various other co-sponsors that may vary from card to card. The photos show signs of perforation as they were originally issued in game programs. The backs display various advertisements. The photos are unnumbered and checklisted below in alphabetical order. The co-sponsors are also listed below. The set can be distinguished from the set of the previous year by the presence of the set's date in the lower left corner of the cardfront.

	NRMT	VG-E	GOOD
COMPLETE SET (32)	200.00	90.00	25.00
COMMON CARD (1-32)	6.00	2.70	.75
☐ 1 By Bailey	15.00	6.75	1.85
☐ 2 Nub Beamer	6.00	2.70	.75
☐ 3 Neil Beaumont	8.00	3.60	1.00
☐ 4 Bob Belak	6.00	2.70	.75
☐ 5 Walt Bilicki	6.00	2.70	.75
☐ 6 Tom Brown Shop-Easy	8.00	3.60	1.00
☐ 7 Mack Burton Shop-Easy	8.00	3.60	1.00
☐ 8 Mike Cacic	6.00	2.70	.75
☐ 9 Jim Carphin	6.00	2.70	.75
☐ 10 Pat Claridge	6.00	2.70	.75
☐ 11 Steve Cotter	6.00	2.70	.75
☐ 12 Lonnie Dennis	6.00	2.70	.75
☐ 13 Norm Fieldgate	8.00	3.60	1.00
☐ 14 Willie Fleming Shop-Easy	18.00	8.00	2.20
☐ 15 Dick Fouts	8.00	3.60	1.00
☐ 16 George Grant	6.00	2.70	.75
☐ 17 Ian Hagemoen	6.00	2.70	.75
☐ 18 Tommy Hinton	8.00	3.60	1.00
☐ 19 Sonny Homer	8.00	3.60	1.00
☐ 20 Joe Kapp	25.00	11.00	3.10
☐ 21 Earl Keeley	6.00	2.70	.75
☐ 22 Vic Kristopaitis Shop-Easy	6.00	2.70	.75
☐ 23 Tom Larscheid	6.00	2.70	.75
☐ 24 Mike Martin	6.00	2.70	.75
☐ 25 Gordie Mitchell	6.00	2.70	.75
☐ 26 Baz Nagle	6.00	2.70	.75
☐ 27 Bob Schloredt	8.00	3.60	1.00
☐ 28 Gary Schwertfeger	6.00	2.70	.75
☐ 29 Willie Taylor	8.00	3.60	1.00
☐ 30 Barney Therrien	6.00	2.70	.75
☐ 31 Don Vicic	6.00	2.70	.75
☐ 32 Tom Walker	6.00	2.70	.75

1965 Coke Caps CFL

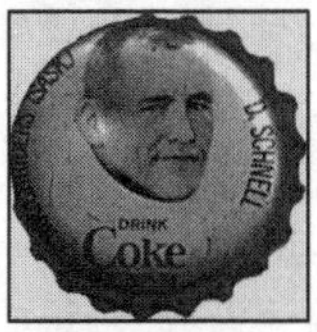

This set of 230 Coke caps was issued on bottled soft drinks and featured CFL players. The caps measure approximately one inch in diameter. The outside of the cap exhibits a black-and-white photo of the player's face, with a Coke (or Sprite) advertisement below the picture. Sprite caps are harder to find and are valued using the multiplier line below. The player's team name is written vertically on the left side, following the curve of the bottle cap, and likewise for the player's name on the right side. The players are listed in alphabetical order within their teams, and the teams are arranged alphabetically. Three players appear twice with two different teams, Don Fuell, Hal Ledyard, and L. Tomlinson. A plastic holder measuring approximately 14" by 16" was also available. The caps were available in French and English, the difference being "Drink Coke" or "Bovez Coke" under the player photo.

	NRMT	VG-E	GOOD
COMPLETE SET (230)	700.00	325.00	90.00
COMMON CAP (1-230)	3.00	1.35	.35
*SPRITE CAPS: 1.5X TO 2.5X			
*FRENCH CAPS: 1.25X TO 2X			
☐ 1 Neil Beaumont	4.00	1.80	.50
☐ 2 Tom Brown	6.00	2.70	.75
☐ 3 Mack Burton	3.00	1.35	.35
☐ 4 Mike Cacic	3.00	1.35	.35
☐ 5 Pat Claridge	3.00	1.35	.35
☐ 6 Steve Cotter	3.00	1.35	.35
☐ 7 Norm Fieldgate	6.00	2.70	.75
☐ 8 Greg Findlay	3.00	1.35	.35
☐ 9 Willie Fleming	7.50	3.40	.95
☐ 10 Dick Fouts	3.00	1.35	.35
☐ 11 Tom Hinton	6.00	2.70	.75
☐ 12 Sonny Homer	4.00	1.80	.50
☐ 13 Joe Kapp	15.00	6.75	1.85
☐ 14 G. Kasapis	3.00	1.35	.35
☐ 15 Peter Kempf	3.00	1.35	.35
☐ 16 Bill Lasseter	3.00	1.35	.35
☐ 17 Mike Martin	3.00	1.35	.35
☐ 18 Ron Morris	3.00	1.35	.35

☐ 19 Bill Munsey	3.00	1.35	.35
☐ 20 Paul Seale	3.00	1.35	.35
☐ 21 Steve Shafer	3.00	1.35	.35
☐ 22 Ken Sugarman	4.00	1.80	.50
☐ 23 Bob Swift	3.00	1.35	.35
☐ 24 J. Williams	3.00	1.35	.35
☐ 25 Ron Albright UER (misspelled Allbright)	3.00	1.35	.35
☐ 26 Lu Bain	3.00	1.35	.35
☐ 27 Frank Budd	3.00	1.35	.35
☐ 28 Lovell Coleman	4.00	1.80	.50
☐ 29 Eagle Day	6.00	2.70	.75
☐ 30 Paul Dudley	3.00	1.35	.35
☐ 31 Jim Furlong	3.00	1.35	.35
☐ 32 George Hansen	3.00	1.35	.35
☐ 33 Wayne Harris	10.00	4.50	1.25
☐ 34 Herman Harrison	6.00	2.70	.75
☐ 35 Pat Holmes	3.00	1.35	.35
☐ 36 Art Johnson	3.00	1.35	.35
☐ 37 Jerry Keeling	6.00	2.70	.75
☐ 38 Roger Kramer	4.00	1.80	.50
☐ 39 Hal Krebs	3.00	1.35	.35
☐ 40 Don Luzzi	6.00	2.70	.75
☐ 41 Pete Manning	3.00	1.35	.35
☐ 42 Dale Parsons	3.00	1.35	.35
☐ 43 Ron Payne	3.00	1.35	.35
☐ 44 Larry Robinson	4.00	1.80	.50
☐ 45 Gerry Shaw	3.00	1.35	.35
☐ 46 Don Stephenson	3.00	1.35	.35
☐ 47 Bob Taylor	4.00	1.80	.50
☐ 48 Ted Woods	3.00	1.35	.35
☐ 49 Jon Anabo	3.00	1.35	.35
☐ 50 R. Ash	3.00	1.35	.35
☐ 51 Jim Battle	3.00	1.35	.35
☐ 52 Charlie Brown	3.00	1.35	.35
☐ 53 Tommy Joe Coffey	10.00	4.50	1.25
☐ 54 Marcel Deleeuw	3.00	1.35	.35
☐ 55 Al Ecuyer	3.00	1.35	.35
☐ 56 Ron Forwick	3.00	1.35	.35
☐ 57 Jim Higgins	3.00	1.35	.35
☐ 58 H. Huth	3.00	1.35	.35
☐ 59 Randy Kerbow	3.00	1.35	.35
☐ 60 Oscar Kruger	3.00	1.35	.35
☐ 61 Tom Machan	3.00	1.35	.35
☐ 62 G. McKee	3.00	1.35	.35
☐ 63 Bill Mitchell	3.00	1.35	.35
☐ 64 Barry Mitchelson	3.00	1.35	.35
☐ 65 Roger Nelson	6.00	2.70	.75
☐ 66 Bill Redell	3.00	1.35	.35
☐ 67 M. Rohliser	3.00	1.35	.35
☐ 68 Howie Schumm	3.00	1.35	.35
☐ 69 E.A. Sims	3.00	1.35	.35
☐ 70 John Sklopan	3.00	1.35	.35
☐ 71 Jim Stinnette	3.00	1.35	.35
☐ 72 Barney Therrien	3.00	1.35	.35
☐ 73 Jim Thomas	3.00	1.35	.35
☐ 74 Neil Thomas	3.00	1.35	.35
☐ 75 Bill Tobin	3.00	1.35	.35
☐ 76 Terry Wilson	3.00	1.35	.35
☐ 77 Art Baker	3.00	1.35	.35
☐ 78 John Barrow	6.00	2.70	.75
☐ 79 Gene Ceppetelli	3.00	1.35	.35
☐ 80 John Cimba	3.00	1.35	.35
☐ 81 Dick Cohee	3.00	1.35	.35
☐ 82 Frank Cosentino	4.00	1.80	.50
☐ 83 Johnny Counts	3.00	1.35	.35
☐ 84 Stan Crisson	3.00	1.35	.35
☐ 85 Tommy Grant	7.50	3.40	.95
☐ 86 Garney Henley	7.50	3.40	.95
☐ 87 E. Hoerster	3.00	1.35	.35
☐ 88 Zeno Karcz	4.00	1.80	.50
☐ 89 Ellison Kelly	7.50	3.40	.95
☐ 90 Bob Krouse	3.00	1.35	.35
☐ 91 Billy Ray Locklin	3.00	1.35	.35
☐ 92 Chet Miksza	3.00	1.35	.35
☐ 93 Angelo Mosca	15.00	6.75	1.85
☐ 94 Bronko Nagurski	7.50	3.40	.95
☐ 95 Ted Page	3.00	1.35	.35
☐ 96 Don Sutherin	6.00	2.70	.75
☐ 97 Dave Viti	3.00	1.35	.35
☐ 98 Dick Walton	3.00	1.35	.35
☐ 99 Billy Wayte	3.00	1.35	.35
☐ 100 Joe Zuger	3.00	1.35	.35
☐ 101 Jim Andreotti	4.00	1.80	.50
☐ 102 John Baker	4.00	1.80	.50
☐ 103 Gino Beretta	3.00	1.35	.35
☐ 104 Bill Bewley	4.00	1.80	.50
☐ 105 Garland Boyette	4.00	1.80	.50
☐ 106 Doug Daigneault	3.00	1.35	.35
☐ 107 George Dixon	7.50	3.40	.95
☐ 108 D. Dolatri	3.00	1.35	.35
☐ 109 Ted Elsby	3.00	1.35	.35
☐ 110 Don Estes	3.00	1.35	.35
☐ 111 Terry Evenshen	10.00	4.50	1.25
☐ 112 Clare Exelby	3.00	1.35	.35
☐ 113 Larry Fairholm	4.00	1.80	.50
☐ 114 Bernie Faloney	15.00	6.75	1.85
☐ 115 Don Fuell	3.00	1.35	.35
☐ 116 Mike Gibbons	3.00	1.35	.35
☐ 117 Ralph Goldston	4.00	1.80	.50
☐ 118 Al Irwin	3.00	1.35	.35
☐ 119 John Kennerson	3.00	1.35	.35
☐ 120 Ed Learn	3.00	1.35	.35
☐ 121 Moe Levesque	3.00	1.35	.35
☐ 122 Bob Minihane	3.00	1.35	.35
☐ 123 Jim Reynolds	3.00	1.35	.35
☐ 124 Billy Roy	3.00	1.35	.35
☐ 125 Larry Tomlinson	3.00	1.35	.35
☐ 126 Ernie White	3.00	1.35	.35
☐ 127 Rick Black	3.00	1.35	.35
☐ 128 Mike Blum	3.00	1.35	.35
☐ 129 Billy Joe Booth	3.00	1.35	.35
☐ 130 Jim Cain	3.00	1.35	.35
☐ 131 Bill Cline	3.00	1.35	.35
☐ 132 Merv Collins	3.00	1.35	.35
☐ 133 Jim Conroy	4.00	1.80	.50
☐ 134 Larry DeGraw	3.00	1.35	.35
☐ 135 Jim Dillard	3.00	1.35	.35
☐ 136 Gene Gaines	6.00	2.70	.75
☐ 137 Don Gilbert	3.00	1.35	.35
☐ 138 Russ Jackson	15.00	6.75	1.85
☐ 139 Ken Lehmann	4.00	1.80	.50
☐ 140 Bob O'Billovich	3.00	1.35	.35
☐ 141 John Pentecost	3.00	1.35	.35
☐ 142 Joe Poirier	4.00	1.80	.50
☐ 143 Moe Racine	3.00	1.35	.35
☐ 144 Sam Scoccia	3.00	1.35	.35
☐ 145 Bo Scott	7.50	3.40	.95
☐ 146 Jerry Selinger	3.00	1.35	.35
☐ 147 Marshall Shirk	3.00	1.35	.35
☐ 148 Bill Siekierski	3.00	1.35	.35
☐ 149 Ron Stewart	7.50	3.40	.95
☐ 150 Whit Tucker	6.00	2.70	.75
☐ 151 Ron Atchison	6.00	2.70	.75
☐ 152 Al Benecick	3.00	1.35	.35
☐ 153 Clyde Brock	3.00	1.35	.35
☐ 154 Ed Buchanan	3.00	1.35	.35
☐ 155 R. Cameron	3.00	1.35	.35
☐ 156 Hugh Campbell	7.50	3.40	.95
☐ 157 Henry Dorsch	3.00	1.35	.35
☐ 158 Larry Dumelie	3.00	1.35	.35
☐ 159 Garner Ekstran	4.00	1.80	.50
☐ 160 Martin Fabi	3.00	1.35	.35
☐ 161 Bob Good	3.00	1.35	.35
☐ 162 Bob Kosid	3.00	1.35	.35
☐ 163 Ron Lancaster	10.00	4.50	1.25
☐ 164 Hal Ledyard	3.00	1.35	.35
☐ 165 Len Legault	3.00	1.35	.35
☐ 166 Ron Meadmore	3.00	1.35	.35
☐ 167 Bob Ptacek	3.00	1.35	.35
☐ 168 George Reed	10.00	4.50	1.25
☐ 169 Dick Schnell	3.00	1.35	.35
☐ 170 Wayne Shaw	3.00	1.35	.35
☐ 171 Ted Urness	6.00	2.70	.75
☐ 172 Dale West	4.00	1.80	.50
☐ 173 Reg Whitehouse	3.00	1.35	.35
☐ 174 Gene Wlasiuk	3.00	1.35	.35
☐ 175 Jim Worden	3.00	1.35	.35
☐ 176 Dick Aldridge	3.00	1.35	.35
☐ 177 Walt Balasiuk	3.00	1.35	.35
☐ 178 Ron Brewer	3.00	1.35	.35
☐ 179 W. Dickey	3.00	1.35	.35
☐ 180 Bob Dugan	3.00	1.35	.35
☐ 181 Larry Ferguson	3.00	1.35	.35
☐ 182 Don Fuell	3.00	1.35	.35
☐ 183 Ed Harrington	4.00	1.80	.50
☐ 184 Ron Howell	3.00	1.35	.35
☐ 185 F. Laroue	3.00	1.35	.35
☐ 186 Sherman Lewis	7.50	3.40	.95
☐ 187 Marv Luster	6.00	2.70	.75
☐ 188 Dave Mann	4.00	1.80	.50
☐ 189 Pete Martin	3.00	1.35	.35
☐ 190 Marty Martinello	3.00	1.35	.35
☐ 191 Lamar McHan	6.00	2.70	.75
☐ 192 Danny Nykoluk	3.00	1.35	.35
☐ 193 Jackie Parker	20.00	9.00	2.50
☐ 194 Dave Pivec	3.00	1.35	.35
☐ 195 Jim Rountree	3.00	1.35	.35
☐ 196 Dick Shatto	7.50	3.40	.95
☐ 197 Billy Shipp	3.00	1.35	.35
☐ 198 Len Sparks	3.00	1.35	.35
☐ 199 Dave Still	3.00	1.35	.35
☐ 200 Norm Stoneburgh	3.00	1.35	.35
☐ 201 Dave Thelen	6.00	2.70	.75
☐ 202 John Vilanus	3.00	1.35	.35
☐ 203 Jim Walter	3.00	1.35	.35
☐ 204 Pat Watson	3.00	1.35	.35
☐ 205 John Wydareny	4.00	1.80	.50
☐ 206 Billy Cooper	3.00	1.35	.35
☐ 207 Wayne Dennis	3.00	1.35	.35
☐ 208 Paul Desjardins	3.00	1.35	.35
☐ 209 Noel Dunford	3.00	1.35	.35
☐ 210 Farrell Funston	4.00	1.80	.50
☐ 211 Herb Gray	7.50	3.40	.95
☐ 212 Roger Hamelin	3.00	1.35	.35
☐ 213 Barrie Hansen	3.00	1.35	.35
☐ 214 Henry Janzen	4.00	1.80	.50
☐ 215 Hal Ledyard	3.00	1.35	.35
☐ 216 Leo Lewis	7.50	3.40	.95
☐ 217 Brian Palmer	3.00	1.35	.35
☐ 218 Art Perkins	3.00	1.35	.35
☐ 219 Cornel Piper	3.00	1.35	.35
☐ 220 Ernie Pitts	3.00	1.35	.35
☐ 221 Kenny Ploen	7.50	3.40	.95
☐ 222 Dave Raimey	4.00	1.80	.50
☐ 223 Norm Rauhaus	4.00	1.80	.50
☐ 224 Frank Rigney	6.00	2.70	.75
☐ 225 Roger Savoie	3.00	1.35	.35
☐ 226 Jackie Simpson	6.00	2.70	.75
☐ 227 Dick Thornton	4.00	1.80	.50
☐ 228 Sherwyn Thorson	3.00	1.35	.35
☐ 229 Ed Ulmer	3.00	1.35	.35
☐ 230 Bill Whisler	3.00	1.35	.35

1952 Crown Brand

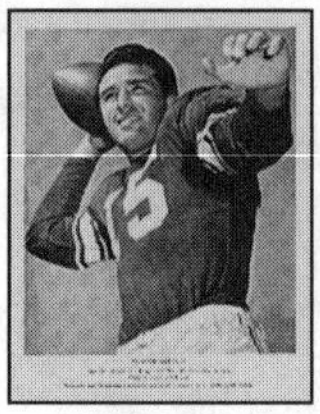
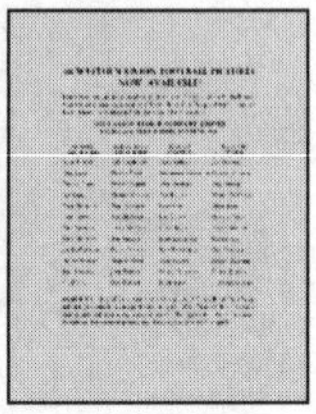

This set of 48 pictures was distributed by Crown Brand Corn Syrup. The collection of the complete set of pictures involved a mail-in offer: one label or cone top from a tin of Crown Brand Corn Syrup and 10 cents for two pictures; or two labels and 25 cents for seven pictures. The photos measure approximately 7" by 8 1/4" and feature a posed photo of the player, with player information below. The back has a checklist of all 48 players included in the set. Hall of Famers included in this set are Tom Casey, Dick Huffman, Jack Jacobs, Martin Ruby, Buddy Tinsley, and Frank Morris. The photos are listed below in alphabetical order according to their teams.

	NRMT	VG-E	GOOD
COMPLETE SET (48)	2000.00	900.00	250.00
COMMON CARD (1-48)	50.00	22.00	6.25
☐ 1 John Brown	50.00	22.00	6.25
☐ 2 Tom Casey	75.00	34.00	9.50
☐ 3 Tommy Ford	50.00	22.00	6.25
☐ 4 Ian Gibb	50.00	22.00	6.25
☐ 5 Dick Huffman	75.00	34.00	9.50
☐ 6 Jack Jacobs	100.00	45.00	12.50
☐ 7 Thomas Lumsden	50.00	22.00	6.25
☐ 8 George McPhail	50.00	22.00	6.25
☐ 9 Jim McPherson	50.00	22.00	6.25
☐ 10 Buddy Tinsley	75.00	34.00	9.50
☐ 11 Ron Vaccher	50.00	22.00	6.25
☐ 12 Al Wiley	50.00	22.00	6.25
☐ 13 Ken Charlton	75.00	34.00	9.50
☐ 14 Glenn Dobbs	75.00	34.00	9.50
☐ 15 Sully Glasser	50.00	22.00	6.25
☐ 16 Nelson Greene	50.00	22.00	6.25
☐ 17 Bert Iannone	50.00	22.00	6.25
☐ 18 Art McEwan	50.00	22.00	6.25
☐ 19 Jimmy McFaul	50.00	22.00	6.25
☐ 20 Bob Pelling	50.00	22.00	6.25
☐ 21 Chuck Radley	50.00	22.00	6.25
☐ 22 Martin Ruby	75.00	34.00	9.50
☐ 23 Jack Russell	50.00	22.00	6.25
☐ 24 Roy Wright	50.00	22.00	6.25
☐ 25 Paul Alford	50.00	22.00	6.25
☐ 26 Sugarfoot Anderson	50.00	22.00	6.25
☐ 27 Dick Bradley	50.00	22.00	6.25
☐ 28 Bob Bryant	50.00	22.00	6.25
☐ 29 Cliff Cyr	50.00	22.00	6.25
☐ 30 Cal Green	50.00	22.00	6.25
☐ 31 Stan Heath	75.00	34.00	9.50
☐ 32 Stan Kaluznick	50.00	22.00	6.25
☐ 33 Guss Knickerhm	50.00	22.00	6.25
☐ 34 Paul Salata	50.00	22.00	6.25
☐ 35 Murry Sullivan	50.00	22.00	6.25
☐ 36 Dave West	50.00	22.00	6.25
☐ 37 Joe Aguirre	50.00	22.00	6.25
☐ 38 Claude Arnold	50.00	22.00	6.25
☐ 39 Bill Briggs	50.00	22.00	6.25
☐ 40 Mario DeMarco	50.00	22.00	6.25
☐ 41 Mike King	50.00	22.00	6.25
☐ 42 Donald Lord	50.00	22.00	6.25
☐ 43 Frank Morris	75.00	34.00	9.50
☐ 44 Gayle Pace	50.00	22.00	6.25
☐ 45 Rod Pantages	50.00	22.00	6.25
☐ 46 Rollin Prather	50.00	22.00	6.25
☐ 47 Chuck Quilter	50.00	22.00	6.25
☐ 48 Jim Quondamatteo	50.00	22.00	6.25

1993 Dairy Lids Saskatchewan Roughride

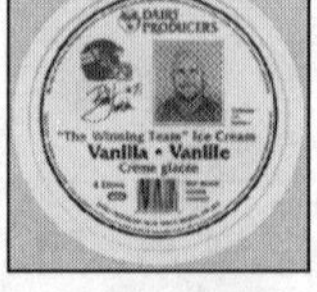

Issued in Saskatchewan and featuring 1993 Roughriders players, these six 1993 Dairy Producers Ice Cream collector lids were issued on four-litre ice cream cartons. Each white plastic lid measures approximately 8 1/4" in diameter. Inside a black border, the circular lids display a head shot, team helmet, and facsimile autograph on the upper portion, with information about the ice cream on the lower portion. The lids are unnumbered and checklisted below in alphabetical order.

	MINT	NRMT	EXC
COMPLETE SET (6)	20.00	9.00	2.50
COMMON LID (1-6)	2.50	1.10	.30
☐ 1 Kent Austin	6.00	2.70	.75
☐ 2 Ray Elgaard	5.00	2.20	.60
☐ 3 Jeff Fairholm	5.00	2.20	.60
☐ 4 Bobby Jurasin	3.50	1.55	.45
☐ 5 Dave Ridgway UER (Misspelled Ridgeway)	3.50	1.55	.45
☐ 6 Glen Suitor	2.50	1.10	.30

1993 Dream Cards Winnipeg Blue Bombers

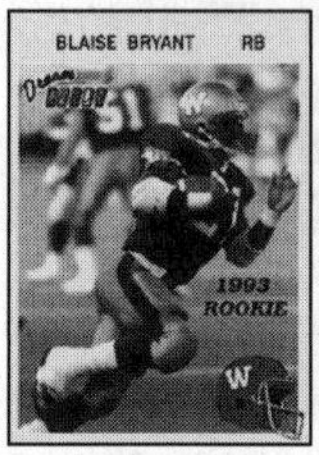

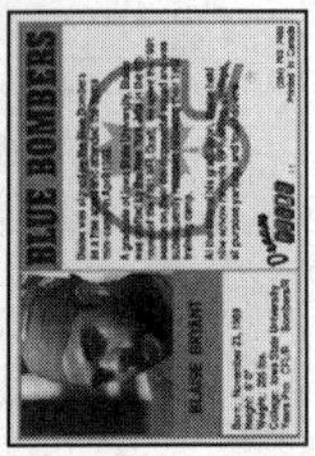

Printed on thin card stock, these 12 standard-size cards feature on their fronts white-bordered color player action shots. The player's name and position appear in black lettering within the wide upper margin. The white-bordered horizontal back is framed by a blue line and carries a color player head shot at the upper left. The player's name and biography appear below, and his career highlights are shown to the right.

	MINT	NRMT	EXC
COMPLETE SET (12)	4.00	1.80	.50
COMMON CARD (1-12)	.30	.14	.04
☐ 1 Matt Dunigan	1.50	.70	.19
☐ 2 Greg Battle	.75	.35	.09
☐ 3 Nathaniel Bolton	.30	.14	.04
☐ 4 Stan Mikawos	.30	.14	.04
☐ 5 Miles Gorrell	.30	.14	.04
☐ 6 Troy Westwood	.75	.35	.09
☐ 7 Michael Richardson	.75	.35	.09
☐ 8 David Black	.30	.14	.04
☐ 9 Chris Walby	.50	.23	.06
☐ 10 David Williams	.50	.23	.06
☐ 11 Blaise Bryant	.50	.23	.06
☐ 12 Bob Cameron	.50	.23	.06

1972 Edmonton Eskimos Team Issue

The Eskimos issued this set of player photos. Each includes a black-and-white player photo on thin card stock. The roughly 7" by 9" cards include the player's name, stats, and team logo on the cardfronts. Cardbacks are blank.

	NRMT-MT	EXC	G-VG
COMPLETE SET (9)	40.00	18.00	5.00
COMMON CARD (1-9)	5.00	2.20	.60
☐ 1 Gene Foster	5.00	2.20	.60
☐ 2 Jim Henshall	5.00	2.20	.60
☐ 3 Garry Lefebvre	5.00	2.20	.60
☐ 4 Ed Molstad	5.00	2.20	.60
☐ 5 Bayne Norrie	5.00	2.20	.60
☐ 6 Dave Syme	5.00	2.20	.60
☐ 7 Peter Travis	5.00	2.20	.60
☐ 8 Charlie Turner	5.00	2.20	.60
☐ 9 Tom Wilkinson	10.00	4.50	1.25

1981 Red Rooster Edmonton Eskimos Cups

Red Rooster Food Stores sponsored a series of 10-cups featuring the 1981 Edmonton Eskimos. Each cup included four black and white photos of Edmonton players, except for the coaches cup that included five coaches. Warren Moon is the key player in the set.

	MINT	NRMT	EXC
COMPLETE SET (10)	50.00	22.00	6.25
COMMON CUP (1-10)	3.00	1.35	.35
☐ 1 Neil Lumsden Warren Moon Hector Pothier Dale Potter	20.00	9.00	2.50
☐ 2 Eric Upton Don Warrington Tom Wilkinson Mike Wilson	8.00	3.60	1.00
☐ 3 Coaches Dan Daniel Joe Faragalli Don Matthews Hugh Campbell Cal Murphy	3.00	1.35	.35
☐ 4 Stu Lang Pete Lavorato Ted Milian	3.00	1.35	.35

Dave Fennell
		MINT	NRMT	EXC
☐ 5	Ed Jones	5.00	2.20	.60

Brian Kelly
Dan Kepley
John Konihowski
| ☐ 6 | Dan Kearns | 5.00 | 2.20 | .60 |

James Parker
Angelo San Tucci
Tom Scott
| ☐ 7 | Waddell Smith | 3.00 | 1.35 | .35 |

Bill Stevenson
Tom Towns
Hank Ilesic
| ☐ 8 | David Boone | 5.00 | 2.20 | .60 |

Gregg Butler
Dave Cutler
Ron Estay
| ☐ 9 | Emilio Fraietta | 3.00 | 1.35 | .35 |

Brian Fryer
Jim Germany
York Hentschel
| ☐ 10 | Larry Highbaugh UER(Laray) | 3.00 | 1.35 | .35 |

Joe Hollimon
Bob Howes
Leo Blanchard

1981 Edmonton Journal Eskimos

This 16-card set measures approximately 3" by 5" and was sponsored by the Edmonton Journal. The set features black-and-white posed player photos with white borders. The player's name and position is printed at the bottom. The Edmonton helmet icon is printed at the bottom. The backs are blank. The cards are unnumbered and checklisted below in alphabetical order. Warren Moon is featured in one of his earliest card appearances.

		MINT	NRMT	EXC
	COMPLETE SET (16)	175.00	80.00	22.00
	COMMON CARD (1-16)	5.00	2.20	.60
☐ 1	Dave Fennell	7.50	3.40	.95
☐ 2	Brian Fryer	5.00	2.20	.60
☐ 3	Jim Germany	6.00	2.70	.75
☐ 4	Gary Hayes	5.00	2.20	.60
☐ 5	Larry Highbaugh	10.00	4.50	1.25
☐ 6	Joe Hollimon	5.00	2.20	.60
☐ 7	Ed Jones	5.00	2.20	.60
☐ 8	Dan Kearns	5.00	2.20	.60
☐ 9	Brian Kelly	15.00	6.75	1.85
☐ 10	Dan Kepley	10.00	4.50	1.25
☐ 11	Neil Lumsden	6.00	2.70	.75
☐ 12	Warren Moon	75.00	34.00	9.50
☐ 13	James Parker	15.00	6.75	1.85
☐ 14	Tom Scott	10.00	4.50	1.25
☐ 15	Waddell Smith	5.00	2.20	.60
☐ 16	Bill Stevenson	6.00	2.70	.75

1984 Edmonton Journal Eskimos

This 13-card set measures approximately 3" by 5" and was sponsored by the Edmonton Journal. The set features black-and-white posed player photos with white borders. The player's name and position is printed at the bottom. The sponsor's logo and a Edmonton helmet icon are printed at the top. The backs are blank. The cards are unnumbered and checklisted below in alphabetical order.

		MINT	NRMT	EXC
	COMPLETE SET (13)	40.00	18.00	5.00
	COMMON CARD (1-13)	3.50	1.55	.45
☐ 1	Leo Blanchard	3.50	1.55	.45
☐ 2	Marco Cyncar	5.00	2.20	.60
☐ 3	Blake Dermott	5.00	2.20	.60
☐ 4	Brian Fryer	3.50	1.55	.45
☐ 5	Joe Hollimon	3.50	1.55	.45
☐ 6	James Hunter	3.50	1.55	.45

		MINT	NRMT	EXC
☐ 7	Greg Marshall	5.00	2.20	.60
☐ 8	Mike Nelson CO	3.50	1.55	.45
☐ 9	Hector Pothier	3.50	1.55	.45
☐ 10	Paul G. Rudzinski ACO	3.50	1.55	.45
☐ 11	Bill Stevenson	5.00	2.20	.60
☐ 12	Tom Towns	3.50	1.55	.45
☐ 13	Eric Upton	3.50	1.55	.45

1981 JOGO CFL B/W

This Canadian Football League set consists of 50 numbered black and white cards with blue printing on the backs of the cards. Cards were printed in Canada and measure 3 1/2" by 5". J.C. Watts (card number 4) was added to the set after he was the MVP of the Grey Cup in 1981 replacing Greg Marshall. According to the producer, there were three press runs (500 sets, 500 sets, and 300 sets) for this set; only the third contained the J.C. Watts card. The set price below includes both number 4's. The key card in the set is Warren Moon, representing his first card of any kind.

		MINT	NRMT	EXC
	COMPLETE SET (51)	200.00	90.00	25.00
	COMMON CARD (1-50)	1.00	.45	.12
☐ 1	Richard Crump	2.00	.90	.25
☐ 2	Tony Gabriel	7.50	3.40	.95
☐ 3	Gerry Organ	1.00	.45	.12
☐ 4A	Greg Marshall	2.00	.90	.25
☐ 4B	J.C. Watts SP	60.00	27.00	7.50
☐ 5	Mike Raines	1.00	.45	.12
☐ 6	Larry Brune	1.00	.45	.12
☐ 7	Randy Rhino	2.50	1.10	.30
☐ 8	Bruce Clark	3.00	1.35	.35
☐ 9	Condredge Holloway	7.50	3.40	.95
☐ 10	Dave Newman	1.00	.45	.12
☐ 11	Cedric Minter	1.00	.45	.12
☐ 12	Peter Muller	1.00	.45	.12
☐ 13	Vince Ferragamo	7.50	3.40	.95
☐ 14	James Scott	2.00	.90	.25
☐ 15	Billy Johnson (White Shoes)	6.00	2.70	.75
☐ 16	David Overstreet	6.00	2.70	.75
☐ 17	Keith Gary	1.00	.45	.12
☐ 18	Tom Clements	15.00	6.75	1.85
☐ 19	Keith Baker	1.00	.45	.12
☐ 20	David Shaw	1.00	.45	.12
☐ 21	Ben Zambiasi	3.00	1.35	.35
☐ 22	John Priestner	2.00	.90	.25
☐ 23	Warren Moon	90.00	40.00	11.00
☐ 24	Tom Wilkinson	3.00	1.35	.35
☐ 25	Brian Kelly	6.00	2.70	.75
☐ 26	Dan Kepley	2.00	.90	.25
☐ 27	Larry Highbaugh	2.00	.90	.25
☐ 28	David Boone	1.00	.45	.12
☐ 29	John Henry White	1.00	.45	.12
☐ 30	Joe Paopao	3.00	1.35	.35
☐ 31	Larry Key	1.00	.45	.12
☐ 32	Glen Jackson	1.00	.45	.12
☐ 33	Joe Hollimon	1.00	.45	.12
☐ 34	Dieter Brock	6.00	2.70	.75
☐ 35	Mike Holmes	1.00	.45	.12
☐ 36	William Miller	1.00	.45	.12
☐ 37	John Helton	3.00	1.35	.35
☐ 38	Joe Poplawski	2.00	.90	.25
☐ 39	Joe Barnes	5.00	2.20	.60
☐ 40	John Hufnagel	6.00	2.70	.75
☐ 41	Bobby Thompson T	1.00	.45	.12
☐ 42	Steve Stapler	2.00	.90	.25
☐ 43	Tom Cousineau	6.00	2.70	.75
☐ 44	Bruce Threadgill	1.00	.45	.12
☐ 45	Ed McAleney	1.00	.45	.12
☐ 46	Leif Petterson	1.00	.45	.12
☐ 47	Paul Bennett	1.00	.45	.12
☐ 48	James Reed	1.00	.45	.12
☐ 49	Gerry Dattilio	1.00	.45	.12
☐ 50	Checklist Card	2.00	.90	.25

1982 JOGO Ottawa

These 24 large (approximately 3 1/2" by 5") cards featuring the Ottawa Rough Riders of the CFL have full color fronts while the backs are printed in red and black on white stock. Cards are numbered inside a leaf in the middle of the back of the card; player's uniform number is also given on the back of the card. A sample card of Rick Sowieta (with blank back) is also available with overstruck "Collector's Series" in red ink diagonally across the front of the card. These cards were endorsed by the CFL Players Association and produced by JOGO and were available for sale in some confectionary stores.

		MINT	NRMT	EXC
	COMPLETE SET (24)	7.50	3.40	.95
	COMMON CARD (1-24)	.35	.16	.04

		MINT	NRMT	EXC
☐ 1	Jordan Case	.35	.16	.04
☐ 2	Larry Brune	.35	.16	.04
☐ 3	Val Belcher	.35	.16	.04
☐ 4	Greg Marshall	.50	.23	.06
☐ 5	Mike Raines	.35	.16	.04
☐ 6	Rick Sowieta	.35	.16	.04
☐ 7	John Glassford	.35	.16	.04
☐ 8	Bruce Walker	.35	.16	.04
☐ 9	Jim Reid	.50	.23	.06
☐ 10	Kevin Powell	.35	.16	.04
☐ 11	Jim Piaskoski	.35	.16	.04
☐ 12	Kelvin Kirk	.35	.16	.04
☐ 13	Gerry Organ	.35	.16	.04
☐ 14	Carl Brazley	.50	.23	.06
☐ 15	William Mitchell	.35	.16	.04
☐ 16	Billy Hardee	.35	.16	.04
☐ 17	Jonathan Sutton	.35	.16	.04
☐ 18	Doug Seymour	.35	.16	.04
☐ 19	Pat Staub	.35	.16	.04
☐ 20	Larry Tittley	.35	.16	.04
☐ 21	Pat Stoqua	.35	.16	.04
☐ 22	Sam Platt	.35	.16	.04
☐ 23	Gary Dulin	.35	.16	.04
☐ 24	John Holland	.35	.16	.04

1982 JOGO Ottawa Past

This set consists of 16 black and white numbered cards measuring approximately 3 1/2" by 5". They feature ex-Ottawa players with the front of the card giving the position and years that the player played for the Rough Riders. The cards are numbered on the front in the lower right corner and the backs are blank except for the words "Printed in Canada by The Runge Press Limited." The first series (1-12) was issued as an insert to the 1982 color set of Rough Riders; the next series of four (13-16) were added later. In the first series, six of the cards were double printed; these are designated with a DP in the checklist below. The cards were also re-issued in 1984 as inserts in the Ottawa Rough Rider game programs. These 1984 cards are part of the Ottawa Yesterday's Heroes set and contain a different cardback complete with sponsor logos and a player write-up.

		MINT	NRMT	EXC
	COMPLETE SET (16)	30.00	13.50	3.70
	COMMON CARD (1-12)	1.25	.55	.16
	COMMON CARD (13-16)	2.00	.90	.25
	COMMON DP	.75	.35	.09
☐ 1	Tony Gabriel	3.00	1.35	.35
☐ 2	Whit Tucker DP	1.50	.70	.19
☐ 3	Dave Thelen	2.50	1.10	.30
☐ 4	Ron Stewart DP	2.00	.90	.25
☐ 5	Russ Jackson DP	3.50	1.55	.45
☐ 6	Kaye Vaughan	2.00	.90	.25
☐ 7	Bob Simpson	2.00	.90	.25
☐ 8	Ken Lehmann	1.50	.70	.19
☐ 9	Lou Bruce	1.25	.55	.16
☐ 10	Wayne Giardino DP	1.25	.55	.16
☐ 11	Moe Racine	1.25	.55	.16
☐ 12	Gary Schreider	1.25	.55	.16
☐ 13	Don Sutherin	4.00	1.80	.50
☐ 14	Mark Kosmos DP	1.25	.55	.16
☐ 15	Jim Foley DP	2.00	.90	.25
☐ 16	Jim Conroy	.75	.35	.09

1983 JOGO CFL Limited

This unnumbered set of 110 color cards was printed in very limited quantities (only 600 sets of which 500 were numbered according to the producer) and features players in the Canadian Football League. The backs of the cards appear to be on off-white card stock. The checklist below is organized in alphabetical order within each team, although the player's uniform number is given on the back of the cards. The cards are listed by team order. Cards of Warren Moon and Dieter Brock are especially difficult to find since both of these players purchased quantities of their own card directly from the producer for distribution to their fans. Each of the registered sets is numbered on the Darrell Moir (Calgary number 110) card.

		MINT	NRMT	EXC
	COMPLETE SET (110)	900.00	400.00	110.00
	COMMON CARD (1-110)	5.00	2.20	.60
☐ 1	Steve Ackroyd	5.00	2.20	.60
☐ 2	Joe Barnes	12.00	5.50	1.50
☐ 3	Bob Bronk	5.00	2.20	.60
☐ 4	Jan Carinci	5.00	2.20	.60
☐ 5	Gordon Elser	5.00	2.20	.60
☐ 6	Dan Ferrone	6.00	2.70	.75
☐ 7	Terry Greer	12.00	5.50	1.50
☐ 8	Mike Hameluck	5.00	2.20	.60
☐ 9	Condredge Holloway	15.00	6.75	1.85
☐ 10	Greg Holmes	5.00	2.20	.60
☐ 11	Hank Ilesic	10.00	4.50	1.25
☐ 12	John Malinosky	5.00	2.20	.60
☐ 13	Cedric Minter	5.00	2.20	.60
☐ 14	Don Moen	6.00	2.70	.75
☐ 15	Rick Mohr	5.00	2.20	.60
☐ 16	Darrell Nicholson	6.00	2.70	.75
☐ 17	Paul Pearson	6.00	2.70	.75
☐ 18	Matthew Teague	5.00	2.20	.60
☐ 19	Geoff Townsend	5.00	2.20	.60
☐ 20	Tom Trifaux	5.00	2.20	.60
☐ 21	Darrell Wilson	5.00	2.20	.60
☐ 22	Earl Wilson	5.00	2.20	.60
☐ 23	Ricky Barden	5.00	2.20	.60
☐ 24	Roger Cattelan	5.00	2.20	.60
☐ 25	Michael Collymore	5.00	2.20	.60
☐ 26	Charles Cornelius	5.00	2.20	.60
☐ 27	Mariet Ford	5.00	2.20	.60
☐ 28	Tyron Gray	6.00	2.70	.75
☐ 29	Steve Harrison	5.00	2.20	.60
☐ 30	Tim Hook	5.00	2.20	.60
☐ 31	Greg Marshall	6.00	2.70	.75
☐ 32	Ken Miller	5.00	2.20	.60
☐ 33	Dave Newman	5.00	2.20	.60
☐ 34	Rudy Phillips	6.00	2.70	.75
☐ 35	Jim Reid	5.00	2.20	.60
☐ 36	Junior Robinson	5.00	2.20	.60
☐ 37	Mark Seale	5.00	2.20	.60
☐ 38	Rick Sowieta	5.00	2.20	.60
☐ 39	Pat Stoqua	5.00	2.20	.60
☐ 40	Skip Walker	10.00	4.50	1.25
☐ 41	Al Washington	5.00	2.20	.60
☐ 42	J.C. Watts	60.00	27.00	7.50
☐ 43	Keith Baker	5.00	2.20	.60
☐ 44	Dieter Brock	35.00	16.00	4.40
☐ 45	Rocky DiPietro	20.00	9.00	2.50
☐ 46	Howard Fields	5.00	2.20	.60
☐ 47	Ron Johnson	6.00	2.70	.75
☐ 48	John Priestner	5.00	2.20	.60
☐ 49	Johnny Shepherd	5.00	2.20	.60
☐ 50	Mike Walker	6.00	2.70	.75
☐ 51	Ben Zambiasi	12.00	5.50	1.50
☐ 52	Nick Arakgi	6.00	2.70	.75
☐ 53	Brian DeRoo	5.00	2.20	.60
☐ 54	Denny Ferdinand	5.00	2.20	.60
☐ 55	Willie Hampton	5.00	2.20	.60
☐ 56	Kevin Starkey	5.00	2.20	.60
☐ 57	Glen Weir	5.00	2.20	.60
☐ 58	Larry Crawford	6.00	2.70	.75
☐ 59	Tyrone Crews	5.00	2.20	.60
☐ 60	James Curry	10.00	4.50	1.25
☐ 61	Roy DeWalt	12.00	5.50	1.50
☐ 62	Mervyn Fernandez	40.00	18.00	5.00
☐ 63	Sammy Greene	5.00	2.20	.60
☐ 64	Glen Jackson	5.00	2.20	.60
☐ 65	Glenn Leonhard	5.00	2.20	.60
☐ 66	Nelson Martin	5.00	2.20	.60
☐ 67	Joe Paopao	7.50	3.40	.95
☐ 68	Lui Passaglia	10.00	4.50	1.25
☐ 69	Al Wilson	5.00	2.20	.60
☐ 70	Nick Bastaja	5.00	2.20	.60
☐ 71	Paul Bennett	5.00	2.20	.60
☐ 72	John Bonk	5.00	2.20	.60
☐ 73	Aaron Brown	5.00	2.20	.60
☐ 74	Bob Cameron	10.00	4.50	1.25
☐ 75	Tom Clements	60.00	27.00	7.50
☐ 76	Rick House	6.00	2.70	.75
☐ 77	John Hufnagel	15.00	6.75	1.85
☐ 78	Sean Kehoe	5.00	2.20	.60
☐ 79	James Murphy	12.00	5.50	1.50
☐ 80	Tony Norman	5.00	2.20	.60
☐ 81	Joe Poplawski	5.00	2.20	.60
☐ 82	Willard Reaves	15.00	6.75	1.85
☐ 83	Bobby Thompson T	5.00	2.20	.60
☐ 84	Wylie Turner	5.00	2.20	.60
☐ 85	Dave Fennell	7.50	3.40	.95
☐ 86	Jim Germany	6.00	2.70	.75
☐ 87	Larry Highbaugh	7.50	3.40	.95
☐ 88	Joe Hollimon	5.00	2.20	.60

 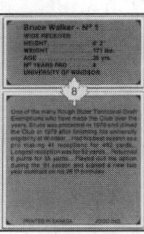 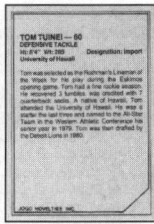

☐ 89 Dan Kepley	10.00	4.50	1.25
☐ 90 Neil Lumsden	5.00	2.20	.60
☐ 91 Warren Moon	400.00	180.00	50.00
☐ 92 James Parker	12.00	5.50	1.50
☐ 93 Dale Potter	5.00	2.20	.60
☐ 94 Angelo Santucci	5.00	2.20	.60
☐ 95 Tom Towns	5.00	2.20	.60
☐ 96 Tom Tuinei	6.00	2.70	.75
☐ 97 Danny Bass	12.00	5.50	1.50
☐ 98 Ray Crouse	5.00	2.20	.60
☐ 99 Gerry Dattilio	7.50	3.40	.95
☐ 100 Tom Forzani	5.00	2.20	.60
☐ 101 Mike Levenseller	5.00	2.20	.60
☐ 102 Mike McTague	6.00	2.70	.75
☐ 103 Bernie Morrison	5.00	2.20	.60
☐ 104 Darrell Toussaint	5.00	2.20	.60
☐ 105 Chris DeFrance	5.00	2.20	.60
☐ 106 Dwight Edwards	6.00	2.70	.75
☐ 107 Vince Goldsmith	10.00	4.50	1.25
☐ 108 Homer Jordan	5.00	2.20	.60
☐ 109 Mike Washington	5.00	2.20	.60
☐ 110A Darrell Moir (Set number on back)	12.00	5.50	1.50
☐ 110B Darrell Moir (Without set number)	50.00	22.00	6.25

1983 JOGO Hall of Fame A

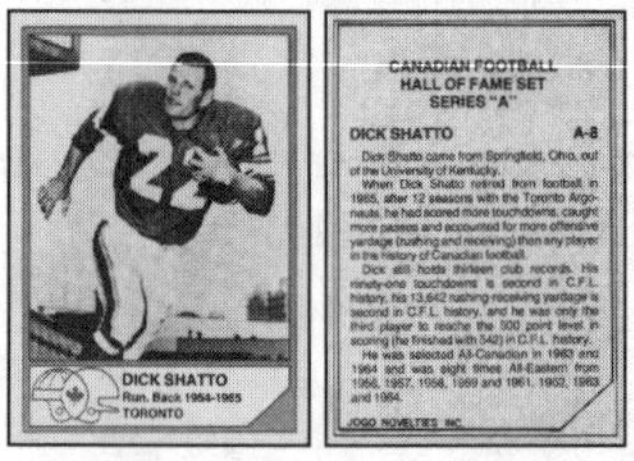

This 25-card standard-size set features members of the Canadian Football Hall of Fame. Cards were produced by JOGO Novelties. These black and white standard sized cards have a red border. On the back they are numbered (with the prefix A) and contain biographical information.

	MINT	NRMT	EXC
COMPLETE SET (25)	35.00	16.00	4.40
COMMON CARD (A1-A25)	.75	.35	.09
☐ A1 Russ Jackson	5.00	2.20	.60
☐ A2 Harvey Wylie	.75	.35	.09
☐ A3 Kenny Ploen	2.00	.90	.25
☐ A4 Garney Henley	2.00	.90	.25
☐ A5 Hal Patterson	2.50	1.10	.30
☐ A6 Carl Cronin	.75	.35	.09
☐ A7 Bob Simpson	.75	.35	.09
☐ A8 Dick Shatto	1.25	.55	.16
☐ A9 John Red O'Quinn	.75	.35	.09
☐ A10 Johnny Bright	2.00	.90	.25
☐ A11 Ernest Cox	.75	.35	.09
☐ A12 Rollie Miles	.75	.35	.09
☐ A13 Leo Lewis	2.00	.90	.25
☐ A14 Bud Grant	12.00	5.50	1.50
☐ A15 Herb Trawick	.75	.35	.09
☐ A16 Wayne Harris	1.25	.55	.16
☐ A17 Earl Lunsford	.75	.35	.09
☐ A18 Tony Golab	.75	.35	.09
☐ A19 George Reed	2.00	.90	.25
☐ A20 By Bailey	.75	.35	.09
☐ A21 Harry Batstone	.75	.35	.09
☐ A22 Ron Atchison	1.25	.55	.16
☐ A23 Willie Fleming	1.25	.55	.16
☐ A24 Frank Leadlay	.75	.35	.09
☐ A25 Lionel Conacher	3.00	1.35	.35

1983 JOGO Hall of Fame B

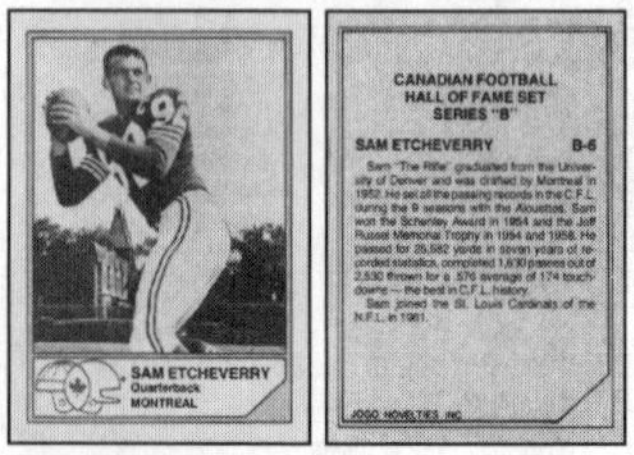

This 25-card standard-size set features members of the Canadian Football Hall of Fame. Cards were produced by JOGO Novelties. These black and white standard-sized cards have a red border. On the back they are numbered (with the prefix B) and contain biographical information. The title card is not required (or considered below) as part of the complete set as priced below; however the title card is indeed somewhat harder to find separately as there were reportedly only half as many title cards printed as there were cards for each player.

	MINT	NRMT	EXC
COMPLETE SET (25)	35.00	16.00	4.40
COMMON CARD (B1-B25)	.75	.35	.09
☐ B1 Bernie Faloney	4.00	1.80	.50
☐ B2 George Dixon	2.00	.90	.25
☐ B3 John Barrow	2.00	.90	.25
☐ B4 Jackie Parker	6.00	2.70	.75
☐ B5 Jack Jacobs	.75	.35	.09
☐ B6 Sam Etcheverry	4.00	1.80	.50
☐ B7 Norm Fieldgate	1.25	.55	.16
☐ B8 John Ferrard	.75	.35	.09
☐ B9 Tommy Joe Coffey	2.00	.90	.25
☐ B10 Martin Ruby	.75	.35	.09
☐ B11 Ted Reeve	.75	.35	.09
☐ B12 Kaye Vaughan	.75	.35	.09
☐ B13 Ron Lancaster	3.00	1.35	.35
☐ B14 Smirle Lawson	.75	.35	.09
☐ B15 Fritz Hanson	.75	.35	.09
☐ B16 Vince Scott	.75	.35	.09
☐ B17 Frank Morris	.75	.35	.09
☐ B18 Normie Kwong	2.00	.90	.25
☐ B19 Dr. Tom Casey	1.25	.55	.16
☐ B20 Herb Gray	2.00	.90	.25
☐ B21 Gerry James	1.25	.55	.16
☐ B22 Pete Neumann	.75	.35	.09
☐ B23 Joe Krol	.75	.35	.09
☐ B24 Ron Stewart	1.25	.55	.16
☐ B25 Buddy Tinsley	.75	.35	.09
☐ NNO Title Card SP (Map to HOF on back)	6.00	2.70	.75

1983 JOGO Quarterbacks

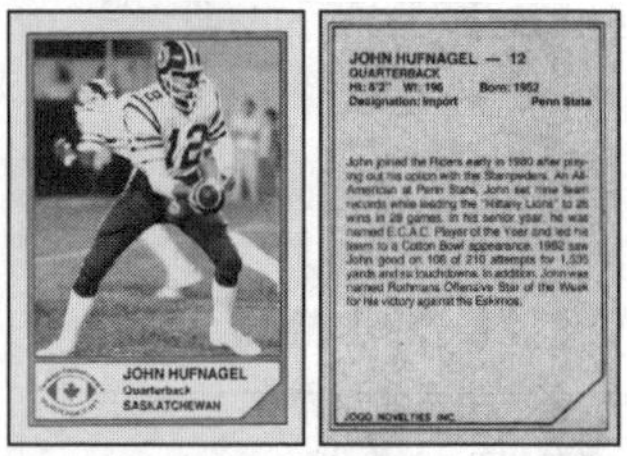

This nine-card black and white (with red border) standard-size set contains several well-known quarterbacks performing in the CFL. The cards are unnumbered although each player's uniform number is given on the back of his card. The cards are numbered in alphabetical order in the checklist below for convenience.

	MINT	NRMT	EXC
COMPLETE SET (9)	80.00	36.00	10.00
COMMON CARD (1-9)	1.50	.70	.19
☐ 1 Dieter Brock	4.00	1.80	.50
☐ 2 Tom Clements	7.50	3.40	.95
☐ 3 Gerry Dattilio	1.50	.70	.19
☐ 4 Roy DeWalt	3.00	1.35	.35
☐ 5 Johnny Evans	1.50	.70	.19
☐ 6 Condredge Holloway	4.00	1.80	.50
☐ 7 John Hufnagel	4.00	1.80	.50
☐ 8 Warren Moon	40.00	18.00	5.00
☐ 9 J.C. Watts	30.00	13.50	3.70

1984 JOGO CFL

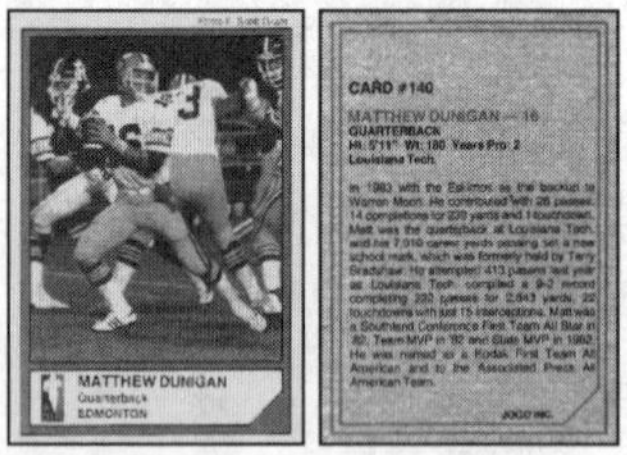

This full-color set of 160 standard-size cards produced by JOGO consists of two series: the first series is 1-110 and the second series runs from 111-160. According to the producer, there were 400 more sets of the first series printed than were printed of the second series; hence the second series is slightly more valuable per card. The cards are numbered on the back; the backs contain printing in red and black ink. The second series was printed on a gray cardboard stock whereas the first series is on a cream-colored stock. Photos were taken by F. Scott Grant, who is credited on the fronts of the cards. The cards feature players in the Canadian Football League. Some players are featured in both series.

	MINT	NRMT	EXC
COMPLETE SET (160)	200.00	90.00	25.00
COMPLETE SERIES 1 (110)	125.00	55.00	15.50
COMPLETE SERIES 2 (50)	90.00	40.00	11.00
COMMON CARD (1-110)	.75	.35	.09
COMMON CARD (111-160)	2.00	.90	.25
☐ 1 Mike Hameluck	1.25	.55	.16
☐ 2 Bob Bronk	.75	.35	.09
☐ 3 Paul Pearson	.75	.35	.09
☐ 4 Dan Ferrone	1.25	.55	.16
☐ 5 Paul Bennett	.75	.35	.09
☐ 6 Joe Barnes	4.00	1.80	.50
☐ 7 Condredge Holloway	6.00	2.70	.75
☐ 8 Terry Greer	5.00	2.20	.60
☐ 9 Vince Goldsmith	3.00	1.35	.35
☐ 10 Darrell Wilson	.75	.35	.09
☐ 11 Tom Trifaux	.75	.35	.09
☐ 12 Kelvin Pruenster	.75	.35	.09
☐ 13 Earl Wilson	.75	.35	.09
☐ 14 Hank Ilesic	2.50	1.10	.30
☐ 15 Stephen Del Col	.75	.35	.09
☐ 16 Lamont Meacham	.75	.35	.09
☐ 17 Lester Brown	.75	.35	.09
☐ 18 Rob Forbes	.75	.35	.09
☐ 19 Darrell Nicholson	.75	.35	.09
☐ 20 James Curry	2.50	1.10	.30
☐ 21 Skip Walker	2.50	1.10	.30
☐ 22 J.C. Watts	30.00	13.50	3.70
☐ 23 Kevin Powell	.75	.35	.09
☐ 24 Dean Dorsey	2.00	.90	.25
☐ 25 Tyron Gray	2.00	.90	.25
☐ 26 Mike Hudson	1.25	.55	.16
☐ 27 Dan Rashovich	.75	.35	.09
☐ 28 Rudy Phillips	1.25	.55	.16
☐ 29 Larry Tittley	.75	.35	.09
☐ 30 Ricky Barden UER (Number missing)	.75	.35	.09
☐ 31 Mark Seale	.75	.35	.09
☐ 32 Prince McJunkins	1.25	.55	.16
☐ 33 Kevin Dalliday	.75	.35	.09
☐ 34 Rick Sowieta	.75	.35	.09
☐ 35 Roger Cattelan	.75	.35	.09
☐ 36 Damir Dupin	.75	.35	.09
☐ 37 Jack Williams	.75	.35	.09
☐ 38 Dave Newman	.75	.35	.09
☐ 39 Maurice Doyle	.75	.35	.09
☐ 40 Tim Hook	.75	.35	.09
☐ 41 Dieter Brock	10.00	4.50	1.25
☐ 42 Rufus Crawford	5.00	2.20	.60
☐ 43 Steve Kearns	.75	.35	.09
☐ 44 Ross Francis	.75	.35	.09
☐ 45 Henry Waszczuk	.75	.35	.09
☐ 46 Mark Streeter	.75	.35	.09
☐ 47 Mike McIntyre	.75	.35	.09
☐ 48 John Priestner	.75	.35	.09
☐ 49 Paul Palma	.75	.35	.09
☐ 50 Mike Walker	1.25	.55	.16
☐ 51 Mike Barker	.75	.35	.09
☐ 52 Todd Brown	.75	.35	.09
☐ 53 Andre Francis	2.00	.90	.25
☐ 54 Glenn Keeble	.75	.35	.09
☐ 55 Turner Gill	10.00	4.50	1.25
☐ 56 Eugene Belliveau	.75	.35	.09
☐ 57 Willie Hampton	.75	.35	.09
☐ 58 Ken Ciancone	.75	.35	.09
☐ 59 Preston Young	.75	.35	.09
☐ 60 Stanley Washington	.75	.35	.09
☐ 61 Denny Ferdinand	.75	.35	.09
☐ 62 Steve Smith	.75	.35	.09
☐ 63 Rick Klassen	1.25	.55	.16
☐ 64 Larry Crawford	1.25	.55	.16
☐ 65 John Henry White	.75	.35	.09
☐ 66 Bernie Glier	.75	.35	.09
☐ 67 Don Taylor	.75	.35	.09
☐ 68 Roy DeWalt	3.00	1.35	.35
☐ 69 Mervyn Fernandez	20.00	9.00	2.50
☐ 70 John Blain	.75	.35	.09
☐ 71 James Parker	4.00	1.80	.50
☐ 72 Henry Vereen	.75	.35	.09
☐ 73 Gerald Roper	.75	.35	.09
☐ 74 Jim Sandusky	10.00	4.50	1.25
☐ 75 John Pankratz	.75	.35	.09
☐ 76 Tom Clements	10.00	4.50	1.25
☐ 77 Vernon Pahl	.75	.35	.09
☐ 78 Trevor Kennerd	2.50	1.10	.30
☐ 79 Stan Mikawos	.75	.35	.09
☐ 80 Ken Hailey	.75	.35	.09
☐ 81 James Murphy	4.00	1.80	.50
☐ 82 Jeff Boyd	2.00	.90	.25
☐ 83 Bob Cameron	3.00	1.35	.35
☐ 84 Jerome Erdman	2.00	.90	.25
☐ 85 Tyrone Jones	2.50	1.10	.30
☐ 86 John Bonk	.75	.35	.09
☐ 87 John Sturdivant	2.00	.90	.25
☐ 88 Dan Huclack	.75	.35	.09
☐ 89 Tony Norman	.75	.35	.09
☐ 90 Kevin Neiles	.75	.35	.09
☐ 91 Dave Kirzinger	.75	.35	.09
☐ 92 Kevin Molle	.75	.35	.09
☐ 93 Jerry Debrouolny	.75	.35	.09
☐ 94 Larry Hogue	.75	.35	.09
☐ 95 Ken Moore	.75	.35	.09
☐ 96 Jerry Friesen	.75	.35	.09
☐ 97 Mike McTague	1.25	.55	.16
☐ 98 Jason Riley	.75	.35	.09
☐ 99 Roger Aldag	2.00	.90	.25
☐ 100 Dave Ridgway	4.00	1.80	.50
☐ 101 Eric Upton	.75	.35	.09
☐ 102 Laurent DesLauriers	.75	.35	.09
☐ 103 Brian Fryer	.75	.35	.09
☐ 104 Brian DeRoo	.75	.35	.09
☐ 105 Neil Lumsden	.75	.35	.09
☐ 106 Hector Pothier	.75	.35	.09
☐ 107 Brian Kelly	12.00	5.50	1.50
☐ 108 Dan Kepley	3.00	1.35	.35
☐ 109 Danny Bass	5.00	2.20	.60
☐ 110 Nick Arakgi	1.25	.55	.16
☐ 111 Lyle Bauer	2.00	.90	.25
☐ 112 Al Washington	2.00	.90	.25
☐ 113 Michel Bourgeau	2.50	1.10	.30
☐ 114 Keith Gooch	2.00	.90	.25
☐ 115 Sean Kehoe	.75	.35	.09
☐ 116 Ken Clark	2.50	1.10	.30
☐ 117 Orlando Flanagan	2.00	.90	.25
☐ 118 Greg Vavra	2.00	.90	.25
☐ 119 Mark Bragagnolo	2.00	.90	.25
☐ 120 Dave Cutler	7.50	3.40	.95
☐ 121 Nick Hebeler	2.00	.90	.25
☐ 122 Harry Skipper	5.00	2.20	.60
☐ 123 Frank Robinson	2.50	1.10	.30
☐ 124 DeWayne Jett	2.50	1.10	.30
☐ 125 Mark Young	2.00	.90	.25
☐ 126 Felix Wright	20.00	9.00	2.50
☐ 127 Bob Poley	2.00	.90	.25
☐ 128 Leo Ezerins	2.00	.90	.25
☐ 129 Johnny Shepherd	2.50	1.10	.30
☐ 130 Jeff Inglis	2.00	.90	.25
☐ 131 Dwaine Wilson	2.00	.90	.25
☐ 132 Aaron Hill	2.00	.90	.25
☐ 133 Brian Dudley	2.00	.90	.25
☐ 134 Ned Armour	2.00	.90	.25
☐ 135 Darryl Hall	2.00	.90	.25
☐ 136 Vince Phason	2.00	.90	.25
☐ 137 Terry Lymon	2.00	.90	.25
☐ 138 Jerry Dobrovolny	2.00	.90	.25
☐ 139 Richard Nemeth	2.00	.90	.25
☐ 140 Matt Dunigan	50.00	22.00	6.25
☐ 141 Rick Mohr	2.00	.90	.25
☐ 142 Lawrie Skolrood	2.00	.90	.25
☐ 143 Craig Ellis	6.00	2.70	.75
☐ 144 Steve Johnson	2.00	.90	.25
☐ 145 Glen Suitor	2.50	1.10	.30
☐ 146 Jeff Roberts	2.00	.90	.25
☐ 147 Greg Fieger	2.00	.90	.25
☐ 148 Sterling Hinds	2.00	.90	.25
☐ 149 Willard Reaves	8.00	3.60	1.00
☐ 150 John Pitts	2.00	.90	.25
☐ 151 Delbert Fowler	2.50	1.10	.30
☐ 152 Mark Hopkins	2.00	.90	.25
☐ 153 Pat Cantner	2.00	.90	.25
☐ 154 Scott Flagel	2.50	1.10	.30
☐ 155 Donovan Rose	2.00	.90	.25
☐ 156 David Shaw	2.00	.90	.25
☐ 157 Mark Moors	2.00	.90	.25
☐ 158 Chris Walby	5.00	2.20	.60
☐ 159 Eugene Belliveau	2.00	.90	.25
☐ 160 Trevor Kennerd	10.00	4.50	1.25

1984 JOGO Ottawa Yesterday's Heroes

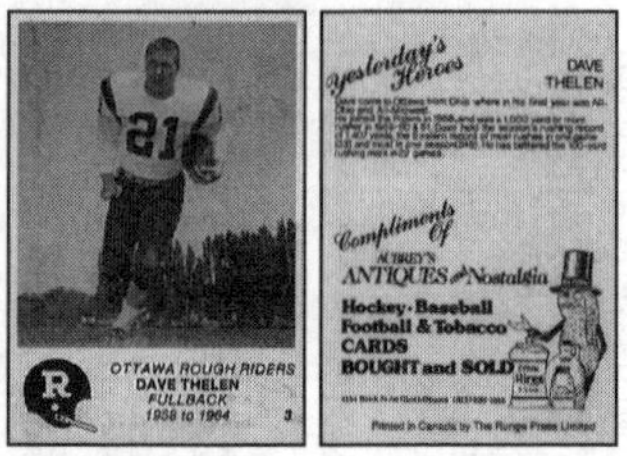

JOGO released this 22-card set as inserts into 1984 Ottawa Rough Rider game programs. The first 16-cards of this set were re-issued from the 1982 Jogo Ottawa Past set, with the primary difference being the complete player write-up on the cardbacks. The title "Yesterday's Heroes" as well as sponsor logos also are included on the cardbacks.

	MINT	NRMT	EXC
COMPLETE SET (22)	100.00	45.00	12.50
COMMON CARD (1-22)	4.00	1.80	.50
☐ 1 Tony Gabriel	6.00	2.70	.75
☐ 2 Whit Tucker	4.00	1.80	.50
☐ 3 Dave Thelen	4.00	1.80	.50
☐ 4 Ron Stewart	4.00	1.80	.50
☐ 5 Russ Jackson	15.00	6.75	1.85
☐ 6 Kaye Vaughan	4.00	1.80	.50
☐ 7 Bob Simpson	4.00	1.80	.50
☐ 8 Ken Lehmann	4.00	1.80	.50
☐ 9 Lou Bruce	4.00	1.80	.50
☐ 10 Wayne Giardino	4.00	1.80	.50
☐ 11 Moe Racine	4.00	1.80	.50
☐ 12 Gary Schreider	4.00	1.80	.50
☐ 13 Don Sutherin	6.00	2.70	.75
☐ 14 Mark Kosmos	4.00	1.80	.50
☐ 15 Jim Foley	4.00	1.80	.50
☐ 16 Jim Conroy	4.00	1.80	.50
☐ 17 George Brancato	5.00	2.20	.60
☐ 18 Art Green	5.00	2.20	.60
☐ 19 Rudy Sims	5.00	2.20	.60
☐ 20 Jim Coode	5.00	2.20	.60
☐ 21 Jerry Campbell	5.00	2.20	.60
☐ 22 Jim Piaskoski	5.00	2.20	.60

1985 JOGO CFL

The 1985 JOGO CFL set is standard size and was distributed as a single series of 110 cards, numbered 1-110. With some exceptions, the number ordering of the set is by teams.

	MINT	NRMT	EXC
COMPLETE SET (110)	125.00	55.00	15.50
COMMON CARD (1-110)	.75	.35	.09
☐ 1 Mike Hameluck	1.25	.55	.16
☐ 2 Michel Bourgeau	1.25	.55	.16
☐ 3 Waymon Alridge	.75	.35	.09
☐ 4 Daric Zeno	.75	.35	.09
☐ 5 J.C. Watts	20.00	9.00	2.50
☐ 6 Kevin Gray	.75	.35	.09
☐ 7 Steve Harrison	.75	.35	.09
☐ 8 Ralph Dixon	.75	.35	.09
☐ 9 Jo Jo Heath	.75	.35	.09
☐ 10 Rick Sowieta	.75	.35	.09
☐ 11 Brad Fawcett	.75	.35	.09
☐ 12 Lamont Meacham	.75	.35	.09
☐ 13 Dean Dorsey	2.00	.90	.25
☐ 14 Bernard Quarles	.75	.35	.09
☐ 15 Mike Caterbone	.75	.35	.09
☐ 16 Bob Stephen	.75	.35	.09
☐ 17 Nick Benjamin	1.25	.55	.16
☐ 18 Tim McCray	1.25	.55	.16
☐ 19 Chris Sigler	.75	.35	.09
☐ 20 Tony Johns	.75	.35	.09
☐ 21 Jason Riley	.75	.35	.09
☐ 22 Ralph Scholz	.75	.35	.09
☐ 23 Ken Hobart	2.50	1.10	.30
☐ 24 Paul Bennett	.75	.35	.09
☐ 25 Dan Ferrone	1.25	.55	.16
☐ 26 Jim Kalafat	.75	.35	.09
☐ 27 William Mitchell	.75	.35	.09
☐ 28 Denny Ferdinand	.75	.35	.09
☐ 29 James Curry	2.50	1.10	.30
☐ 30 Jeff Inglis	.75	.35	.09
☐ 31 Bob Bronk	.75	.35	.09
☐ 32 Dan Petschenig	.75	.35	.09
☐ 33 Terry Greer	4.00	1.80	.50
☐ 34 Condredge Holloway	5.00	2.20	.60
☐ 35 Ian Beckstead	.75	.35	.09
☐ 36 James Parker	3.00	1.35	.35
☐ 37 Tim Cowan	1.25	.55	.16
☐ 38 Roy DeWalt	2.50	1.10	.30
☐ 39 Mervyn Fernandez	10.00	4.50	1.25
☐ 40 Bernie Glier	.75	.35	.09
☐ 41 Keyvan Jenkins	3.00	1.35	.35
☐ 42 Melvin Byrd	2.00	.90	.25
☐ 43 Ron Robinson	2.00	.90	.25
☐ 44 Andre Jones	.75	.35	.09
☐ 45 Jim Sandusky	5.00	2.20	.60
☐ 46 Darnell Clash	2.50	1.10	.30
☐ 47 Rick Klassen	1.25	.55	.16
☐ 48 Brian Kelly	6.00	2.70	.75
☐ 49 Rick House	1.25	.55	.16
☐ 50 Stewart Hill	3.00	1.35	.35
☐ 51 Chris Woods	3.00	1.35	.35
☐ 52 Darryl Hall	1.25	.55	.16
☐ 53 Laurent DesLauriers	.75	.35	.09
☐ 54 Larry Cowan	.75	.35	.09
☐ 55 Matt Dunigan	12.00	5.50	1.50
☐ 56 Andre Francis	1.25	.55	.16
☐ 57 Roy Kurtz	.75	.35	.09
☐ 58 Steve Raquet	.75	.35	.09
☐ 59 Turner Gill	4.00	1.80	.50
☐ 60 Sandy Armstrong	.75	.35	.09
☐ 61 Nick Arakgi	1.25	.55	.16
☐ 62 Mike McTague	1.25	.55	.16
☐ 63 Aaron Hill	1.25	.55	.16
☐ 64 Brett Williams	2.00	.90	.25
☐ 65 Trevor Bowles	1.25	.55	.16
☐ 66 Mark Hopkins	.75	.35	.09
☐ 67 Frank Kosec	.75	.35	.09
☐ 68 Ken Ciancone	.75	.35	.09
☐ 69 Dwaine Wilson	.75	.35	.09
☐ 70 Mark Stevens	.75	.35	.09
☐ 71 George Voelk	.75	.35	.09
☐ 72 Doug Scott	.75	.35	.09
☐ 73 Rob Smith	2.00	.90	.25
☐ 74 Alan Reid	.75	.35	.09
☐ 75 Rick Mohr	.75	.35	.09
☐ 76 Dave Ridgway	3.00	1.35	.35
☐ 77 Homer Jordan	.75	.35	.09
☐ 78 Terry Leschuk	.75	.35	.09
☐ 79 Rick Goltz	.75	.35	.09
☐ 80 Neil Quilter	.75	.35	.09
☐ 81 Joe Paopao	2.50	1.10	.30
☐ 82 Stephen Jones	2.50	1.10	.30
☐ 83 Scott Redl	.75	.35	.09
☐ 84 Tony Dennis	.75	.35	.09
☐ 85 Glen Suitor	1.25	.55	.16
☐ 86 Mike Anderson	.75	.35	.09
☐ 87 Stewart Fraser	.75	.35	.09
☐ 88 Fran McDermott	.75	.35	.09
☐ 89 Craig Ellis	3.00	1.35	.35
☐ 90 Eddie Ray Walker	2.00	.90	.25
☐ 91 Trevor Kennerd	4.00	1.80	.50
☐ 92 Pat Cantner	.75	.35	.09
☐ 93 Tom Clements	10.00	4.50	1.25
☐ 94 Glen Steele	.75	.35	.09
☐ 95 Willard Reaves	4.00	1.80	.50
☐ 96 Tony Norman	.75	.35	.09
☐ 97 Tyrone Jones	2.50	1.10	.30
☐ 98 Jerome Erdman	.75	.35	.09
☐ 99 Sean Kehoe	.75	.35	.09
☐ 100 Kevin Neiles	.75	.35	.09
☐ 101 Ken Hailey	.75	.35	.09
☐ 102 Scott Flagel	1.25	.55	.16
☐ 103 Mark Moors	.75	.35	.09
☐ 104 Gerry McGrath	.75	.35	.09
☐ 105 James Hood	.75	.35	.09
☐ 106 Randy Ambrosie	1.25	.55	.16
☐ 107 Terry Irvin	.75	.35	.09
☐ 108 Joe Barnes	3.00	1.35	.35
☐ 109 Richard Nemeth	.75	.35	.09
☐ 110 Darrell Patterson	.75	.35	.09

1985 JOGO Ottawa Program Inserts

These inserts were featured in Ottawa home game programs. The cards are black-and-white with a white border and measure approximately 3 3/8" by 5 1/8". They are numbered in the lower right hand corner.

	MINT	NRMT	EXC
COMPLETE SET (9)	35.00	16.00	4.40
COMMON CARD (1-9)	4.00	1.80	.50
☐ 1 1960 Grey Cup Team	4.00	1.80	.50
☐ 2 Russ Jackson	10.00	4.50	1.25
☐ 3 Angelo Mosca	8.00	3.60	1.00
☐ 4 Joe Poirier	4.00	1.80	.50
☐ 5 Sam Scoccia	4.00	1.80	.50
☐ 6 Gilles Archambeault	4.00	1.80	.50
☐ 7 Ron Lancaster	6.00	2.70	.75
☐ 8 Tom Jones	4.00	1.80	.50
☐ 9 Gerry Nesbitt	4.00	1.80	.50

1986 JOGO CFL

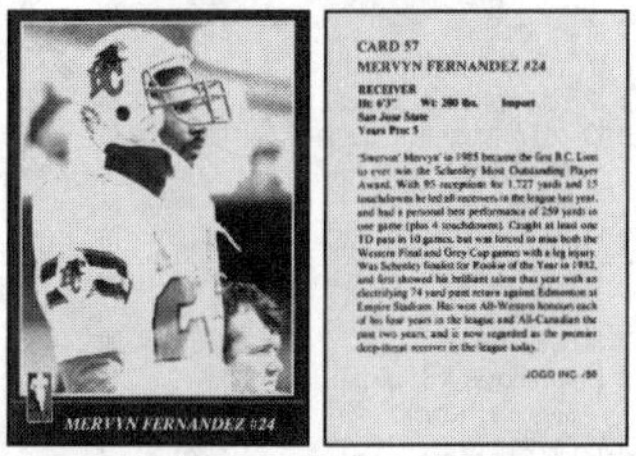

The 1986 JOGO CFL set is standard size. These numbered cards were issued in two different series, 1-110 and 111-169. A few players appear in both series. This year's set from JOGO has a distinctive black border on the front of the card. Card backs are printed in red and black on white card stock. The player's name and uniform number are given on the front of the card. The player's team is not explicitly listed anywhere on the card. An interesting card in this is set is #83 Brian Pillman, who later went on to fame as wrestler "Flyin Brian".

	MINT	NRMT	EXC
COMPLETE SET (169)	100.00	45.00	12.50
COMPLETE SERIES 1 (110)	60.00	27.00	7.50
COMPLETE SERIES 2 (59)	40.00	18.00	5.00
COMMON CARD (1-110)	.60	.25	.07
COMMON CARD (111-169)	.60	.25	.07
☐ 1 Ken Hobart	2.00	.90	.25
☐ 2 Tom Porras	1.00	.45	.12
☐ 3 Jason Riley	.60	.25	.07
☐ 4 Ron Ingram	.60	.25	.07
☐ 5 Steve Stapler	1.00	.45	.12
☐ 6 Mike Derks	.60	.25	.07
☐ 7 Grover Covington	4.00	1.80	.50
☐ 8 Lance Shields	1.00	.45	.12
☐ 9 Mike Robinson	.60	.25	.07
☐ 10 Mark Napiorkowski	.60	.25	.07
☐ 11 Romel Andrews	.60	.25	.07
☐ 12 Ed Gataveckas	.60	.25	.07
☐ 13 Tony Champion	4.00	1.80	.50
☐ 14 Dale Sanderson	.60	.25	.07
☐ 15 Mark Barousse	.60	.25	.07
☐ 16 Nick Benjamin	1.00	.45	.12
☐ 17 Reginal Butts	.60	.25	.07
☐ 18 Tom Burgess	5.00	2.20	.60
☐ 19 Todd Dillon	3.00	1.35	.35
☐ 20 Jim Reid	1.00	.45	.12
☐ 21 Robert Reid	.60	.25	.07
☐ 22 Roger Cattelan	.60	.25	.07
☐ 23 Kevin Powell	.60	.25	.07
☐ 24 Randy Fabi	.60	.25	.07
☐ 25 Gerry Hornett	.60	.25	.07
☐ 26 Rick Sowieta	.60	.25	.07
☐ 27 Warren Hudson	1.00	.45	.12
☐ 28 Steven Cox	.60	.25	.07
☐ 29 Dean Dorsey	1.00	.45	.12
☐ 30 Michel Bourgeau	1.00	.45	.12
☐ 31 Ken Joiner	.60	.25	.07
☐ 32 Mark Seale	.60	.25	.07
☐ 33 Condredge Holloway	4.00	1.80	.50
☐ 34 Bob Bronk	.60	.25	.07
☐ 35 Jeff Inglis	.60	.25	.07
☐ 36 Lance Chomyc	1.50	.70	.19
☐ 37 Craig Ellis	2.00	.90	.25
☐ 38 Marcellus Greene	.60	.25	.07
☐ 39 David Marshall	.60	.25	.07
☐ 40 Kerry Parker	.60	.25	.07
☐ 41 Darrell Wilson	.60	.25	.07
☐ 42 Walter Lewis	3.00	1.35	.35
☐ 43 Sandy Armstrong	.60	.25	.07
☐ 44 Ken Ciancone	.60	.25	.07
☐ 45 Steve Raquet	.60	.25	.07
☐ 46 Lemont Jeffers	.60	.25	.07
☐ 47 Paul Gray	.60	.25	.07
☐ 48 Jacques Chapdelaine	.60	.25	.07
☐ 49 Rick Ryan	.60	.25	.07
☐ 50 Mark Hopkins	.60	.25	.07
☐ 51 Glenn Keeble	.60	.25	.07
☐ 52 Roy Kurtz	.60	.25	.07
☐ 53 Brian Dudley	.60	.25	.07
☐ 54 Mike Gray	.60	.25	.07
☐ 55 Tyrone Crews	.60	.25	.07
☐ 56 Roy DeWalt	2.50	1.10	.30
☐ 57 Mervyn Fernandez	5.00	2.20	.60
☐ 58 Bernie Glier	.60	.25	.07
☐ 59 James Parker	3.00	1.35	.35
☐ 60 Bruce Barnett	.60	.25	.07
☐ 61 Keyvan Jenkins	1.50	.70	.19
☐ 62 Al Wilson	.60	.25	.07
☐ 63 Delbert Fowler	1.00	.45	.12
☐ 64 James Jefferson	5.00	2.20	.60
☐ 65 James West	6.00	2.70	.75
☐ 66 Laurent DesLauriers	.60	.25	.07
☐ 67 Damon Allen	15.00	6.75	1.85
☐ 68 Roy Bennett	3.00	1.35	.35
☐ 69 Hasson Arbubakrr	.60	.25	.07
☐ 70 Tom Clements	7.50	3.40	.95
☐ 71 Trevor Kennerd	1.50	.70	.19
☐ 72 Perry Tuttle	3.00	1.35	.35
☐ 73 Pat Cantner	.60	.25	.07
☐ 74 Mike Hameluck	.60	.25	.07
☐ 75 Rob Prodanovic	.60	.25	.07
☐ 76 James Bell	1.00	.45	.12
☐ 77 Hector Pothier	.60	.25	.07
☐ 78 Milson Jones	2.00	.90	.25
☐ 79 Craig Shaffer	.60	.25	.07
☐ 80 Chris Skinner	1.00	.45	.12
☐ 81 Matt Dunigan	7.50	3.40	.95
☐ 82 Tom Dixon	.60	.25	.07
☐ 83 Brian Pillman	.60	.25	.07
☐ 84 Randy Ambrosie	.60	.25	.07
☐ 85 Rick Johnson	3.00	1.35	.35
☐ 86 Larry Hogue	.60	.25	.07
☐ 87 Garrett Doll	.60	.25	.07
☐ 88 Stu Laird	1.00	.45	.12
☐ 89 Greg Fieger	.60	.25	.07
☐ 90 Sean McKeown	.60	.25	.07
☐ 91 Rob Bresciani	.60	.25	.07
☐ 92 Harold Hallman	2.50	1.10	.30
☐ 93 Jamie Harris	.60	.25	.07
☐ 94 Dan Rashovich	.60	.25	.07
☐ 95 David Conrad	.60	.25	.07
☐ 96 Glen Suitor	1.00	.45	.12
☐ 97 Mike Siroishka	.60	.25	.07
☐ 98 Mike McGruder	3.00	1.35	.35
☐ 99 Brad Calip	.60	.25	.07
☐ 100 Mike Anderson	.60	.25	.07
☐ 101 Trent Bryant	.60	.25	.07
☐ 102 Gary Lewis	.60	.25	.07
☐ 103 Tony Dennis	.60	.25	.07
☐ 104 Paul Tripoli	.60	.25	.07
☐ 105 Daric Zeno	.60	.25	.07
☐ 106 Michael Elarms	.60	.25	.07
☐ 107 Donohue Grant	.60	.25	.07
☐ 108 Ray Elgaard	12.00	5.50	1.50
☐ 109 Joe Paopao	2.00	.90	.25
☐ 110 Dave Ridgway	2.50	1.10	.30
☐ 111 Rudy Phillips	1.00	.45	.12
☐ 112 Carl Brazley	1.00	.45	.12
☐ 113 Andre Francis	.60	.25	.07
☐ 114 Mitchell Price	1.00	.45	.12
☐ 115 Wayne Lee	.60	.25	.07
☐ 116 Tim McCray	1.50	.70	.19
☐ 117 Scott Virkus	.60	.25	.07
☐ 118 Nick Hebeler	.60	.25	.07
☐ 119 Eddie Ray Walker	1.00	.45	.12
☐ 120 Bobby Johnson	.60	.25	.07
☐ 121 Mike McTague	.60	.25	.07
☐ 122 Jeff Inglis	.60	.25	.07
☐ 123 Joe Fuller	.60	.25	.07
☐ 124 Steve Crane	.60	.25	.07
☐ 125 Bill Henry	.60	.25	.07
☐ 126 Ron Brown	.60	.25	.07
☐ 127 Henry Taylor	.60	.25	.07
☐ 128 Greg Holmes	.60	.25	.07
☐ 129 Steve Harrison	.60	.25	.07
☐ 130 Paul Osbaldiston	3.00	1.35	.35
☐ 131 Craig Walls	.60	.25	.07
☐ 132 Clorindo Grilli	.60	.25	.07
☐ 133 Marty Palazeti	.60	.25	.07
☐ 134 Darryl Hall	.60	.25	.07
☐ 135 David Black	.60	.25	.07
☐ 136 Bennie Thompson	2.50	1.10	.30
☐ 137 Darryl Sampson	.60	.25	.07
☐ 138 James Murphy	2.50	1.10	.30
☐ 139 Scott Flagel	.60	.25	.07
☐ 140 Trevor Kennerd	2.00	.90	.25
☐ 141 Bob Molle	.60	.25	.07
☐ 142 Darrell Patterson	.60	.25	.07
☐ 143 Stan Mikawos	.60	.25	.07
☐ 144 John Sturdivant	.60	.25	.07
☐ 145 Tyrone Jones	2.00	.90	.25
☐ 146 Jim Zorn	12.00	5.50	1.50
☐ 147 Steve Howlett	.60	.25	.07
☐ 148 Jeff Volpe	.60	.25	.07
☐ 149 Jerome Erdman	.60	.25	.07
☐ 150 Ned Armour	.60	.25	.07
☐ 151 Rick Klassen	1.00	.45	.12
☐ 152 Brett Williams	2.00	.90	.25
☐ 153 Richie Hall	.60	.25	.07
☐ 154 Ray Alexander	2.50	1.10	.30
☐ 155 Willie Pless	6.00	2.70	.75
☐ 156 Marlon Jones	.60	.25	.07
☐ 157 Danny Bass	3.00	1.35	.35
☐ 158 Frank Balkovec	.60	.25	.07
☐ 159 Less Browne	4.00	1.80	.50
☐ 160 Paul Osbaldiston	1.50	.70	.19
☐ 161 Trevor Bowles	.60	.25	.07
☐ 162 David Daniels	.60	.25	.07
☐ 163 Kevin Konar	1.50	.70	.19
☐ 164 Gary Allen	2.00	.90	.25
☐ 165 Karlton Watson	.60	.25	.07
☐ 166 Ron Hopkins	1.00	.45	.12
☐ 167 Rob Smith	.60	.25	.07
☐ 168 Garrett Doll	.60	.25	.07
☐ 169 Rod Skillman	2.00	.90	.25

1987 JOGO CFL

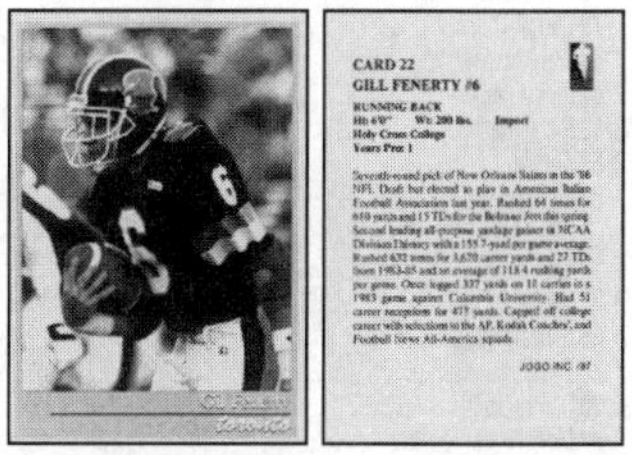

The 1987 JOGO CFL set is standard size. These numbered cards were issued essentially in team order. A color photo is framed by a blue border. Card backs are printed in black on white card stock except for the CFLPA (Canadian Football League Players' Association) logo in the upper right corner which is red and black.

	MINT	NRMT	EXC
COMPLETE SET (110)	80.00	36.00	10.00
COMMON CARD (1-110)	.50	.23	.06
☐ 1 Jim Reid	1.00	.45	.12
☐ 2 Nick Benjamin	.75	.35	.09
☐ 3 Dean Dorsey	1.00	.45	.12
☐ 4 Hasson Arbubakrr	.50	.23	.06
☐ 5 Gerald Alphin	6.00	2.70	.75
☐ 6 Larry Willis	3.00	1.35	.35
☐ 7 Rick Wolkensperg	.50	.23	.06
☐ 8 Roy DeWalt	1.50	.70	.19
☐ 9 Michel Bourgeau	.75	.35	.09
☐ 10 Anthony Woodson	.50	.23	.06
☐ 11 Marv Allemang	.50	.23	.06
☐ 12 Jerry Dobrovolny	.50	.23	.06
☐ 13 Larry Mohr	.50	.23	.06
☐ 14 Kyle Hall	.50	.23	.06
☐ 15 Irv Daymond	.50	.23	.06
☐ 16 Ken Ford	.50	.23	.06
☐ 17 Leo Groenewegen	.50	.23	.06
☐ 18 Michael Cline	.50	.23	.06
☐ 19 Gilbert Renfroe	3.00	1.35	.35
☐ 20 Danny Barrett	6.00	2.70	.75
☐ 21 Dan Petschenig	.50	.23	.06
☐ 22 Gill Fenerty UER (Misspelled Gil on card front)	10.00	4.50	1.25
☐ 23 Lance Chomyc	.75	.35	.09
☐ 24 Jake Vaughan	.50	.23	.06
☐ 25 John Congemi	1.50	.70	.19
☐ 26 Kelvin Pruenster	.50	.23	.06
☐ 27 Mike Siroishka	.50	.23	.06
☐ 28 Dwight Edwards	.75	.35	.09
☐ 29 Darnell Clash	1.00	.45	.12
☐ 30 Glenn Kulka	1.00	.45	.12
☐ 31 Jim Kardash	.50	.23	.06
☐ 32 Selwyn Drain	.50	.23	.06
☐ 33 Ian Sinclair	1.00	.45	.12
☐ 34 Pat Cantner	.50	.23	.06
☐ 35 Trevor Kennerd	2.50	1.10	.30
☐ 36 Bob Cameron	1.00	.45	.12
☐ 37 Willard Reaves	3.00	1.35	.35
☐ 38 Jeff Treftlin	.50	.23	.06
☐ 39 David Black	.50	.23	.06
☐ 40 Chris Walby	2.00	.90	.25
☐ 41 Tom Clements	4.00	1.80	.50
☐ 42 Mike Gray	.50	.23	.06
☐ 43 Bennie Thompson	1.00	.45	.12
☐ 44 Tyrone Jones	1.50	.70	.19
☐ 45 Ken Winey	.50	.23	.06
☐ 46 Nick Arakgi	.75	.35	.09
☐ 47 James West	2.50	1.10	.30
☐ 48 Ken Pettway	.50	.23	.06
☐ 49 James Murphy	2.50	1.10	.30
☐ 50 Carl Fodor	.50	.23	.06
☐ 51 Tom Muecke	1.50	.70	.19
☐ 52 Alvis Satele	.50	.23	.06
☐ 53 Grover Covington	2.00	.90	.25
☐ 54 Tom Porras	.75	.35	.09
☐ 55 Jason Riley	.50	.23	.06

	MINT	NRMT	EXC
☐ 56 Jed Tommy	.50	.23	.06
☐ 57 Bernie Ruoff	.75	.35	.09
☐ 58 Ed Gataveckas	.50	.23	.06
☐ 59 Wayne Lee	.50	.23	.06
☐ 60 Ken Hobart	1.00	.45	.12
☐ 61 Frank Robinson	.75	.35	.09
☐ 62 Mike Robinson	.50	.23	.06
☐ 63 Ben Zambiasi UER (No team listed on front of card)	1.50	.70	.19
☐ 64 Byron Williams	.50	.23	.06
☐ 65 Lance Shields	.75	.35	.09
☐ 66 Ralph Scholz	.50	.23	.06
☐ 67 Earl Winfield	5.00	2.20	.60
☐ 68 Terry Lehne	.50	.23	.06
☐ 69 Alvin Bailey	.50	.23	.06
☐ 70 David Sauve	.50	.23	.06
☐ 71 Bernie Glier	.50	.23	.06
☐ 72 Nelson Martin	.50	.23	.06
☐ 73 Kevin Konar	1.00	.45	.12
☐ 74 Greg Peterson	.50	.23	.06
☐ 75 Harold Hallman	1.00	.45	.12
☐ 76 Sandy Armstrong	.50	.23	.06
☐ 77 Glenn Harper	.50	.23	.06
☐ 78 Rick Worman	1.00	.45	.12
☐ 79 Darrell Toussaint	.50	.23	.06
☐ 80 Larry Hogue	.50	.23	.06
☐ 81 Rick Johnson	2.50	1.10	.30
☐ 82 Richie Hall	.75	.35	.09
☐ 83 Stu Laird	.75	.35	.09
☐ 84 Mike Emery	.50	.23	.06
☐ 85 Cliff Toney	.50	.23	.06
☐ 86 Matt Dunigan	6.00	2.70	.75
☐ 87 Hector Pothier	.50	.23	.06
☐ 88 Stewart Hill	1.00	.45	.12
☐ 89 Stephen Jones	1.00	.45	.12
☐ 90 Dan Huclack	.50	.23	.06
☐ 91 Mark Napiorkowski	.50	.23	.06
☐ 92 Mike Derks	.50	.23	.06
☐ 93 Mike Walker	1.00	.45	.12
☐ 94 Mike McGruder	1.50	.70	.19
☐ 95 Terry Baker	3.00	1.35	.35
☐ 96 Bobby Jurasin	4.00	1.80	.50
☐ 97 James Curry	2.50	1.10	.30
☐ 98 Tracey Mack	.50	.23	.06
☐ 99 Tom Burgess	3.50	1.55	.45
☐ 100 Steve Crane	.50	.23	.06
☐ 101 Glen Suitor	.75	.35	.09
☐ 102 Walter Bender	.50	.23	.06
☐ 103 Jeff Bentrim	2.00	.90	.25
☐ 104 Eric Florence	.50	.23	.06
☐ 105 Terry Cochrane	.50	.23	.06
☐ 106 Tony Dennis	.50	.23	.06
☐ 107 David Albright	.50	.23	.06
☐ 108 David Sidoo	.50	.23	.06
☐ 109 Harry Skipper	.75	.35	.09
☐ 110 Dave Ridgway	2.00	.90	.25

1988 JOGO CFL

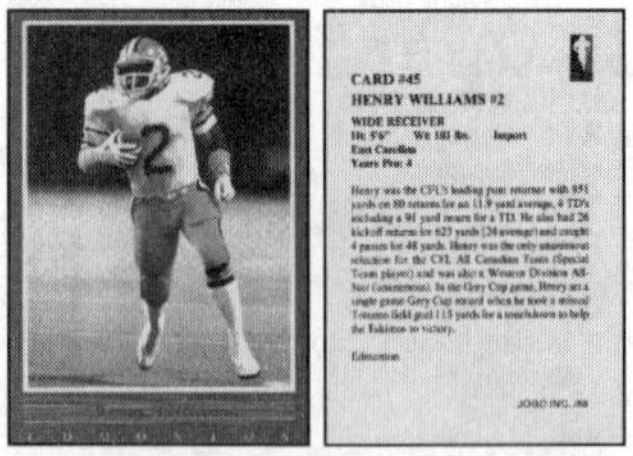

The 1988 JOGO CFL set is standard size. These numbered cards were issued essentially in team order. A color photo is framed by a blue border with a white inner outline. Card backs are printed in black on white card stock, except for the CFLPA (Canadian Football League Players' Association) logo in the upper right corner which is red and black. The cards are arranged according to teams.

	MINT	NRMT	EXC
COMPLETE SET (110)	90.00	40.00	11.00
COMMON CARD (1-110)	.50	.23	.06
☐ 1 Roy DeWalt	2.00	.90	.25
☐ 2 Jim Reid	1.00	.45	.12
☐ 3 Patrick Wayne	.50	.23	.06
☐ 4 Jerome Erdman	.50	.23	.06
☐ 5 Tom Dixon	.50	.23	.06
☐ 6 Brad Fawcett	.50	.23	.06
☐ 7 Tom Muecke	1.25	.55	.16
☐ 8 Mike Hudson	.50	.23	.06
☐ 9 Orville Lee	1.00	.45	.12
☐ 10 Michel Bourgeau	.75	.35	.09
☐ 11 Dan Sellers	.50	.23	.06
☐ 12 Rob Pavan	.50	.23	.06
☐ 13 Rae Robirtis	.50	.23	.06
☐ 14 Rod Brown	.50	.23	.06
☐ 15 Ken Evraire	.75	.35	.09
☐ 16 Irv Daymond	.50	.23	.06
☐ 17 Tim Jessie	1.00	.45	.12
☐ 18 Jim Sandusky	4.00	1.80	.50
☐ 19 Blake Dermott	1.00	.45	.12
☐ 20 Brian Warren	.50	.23	.06
☐ 21 Mike Walker	3.00	1.35	.35
☐ 22 Tom Porras	.75	.35	.09
☐ 23 Less Browne	1.00	.45	.12
☐ 24 Paul Osbaldiston	1.00	.45	.12
☐ 25 Vernell Quinn	.50	.23	.06
☐ 26 Mike Derks	.50	.23	.06
☐ 27 Arnold Grevious	.50	.23	.06
☐ 28 Tim Lorenz	.50	.23	.06
☐ 29 Mike Robinson	.50	.23	.06
☐ 30 Doug Davies	.50	.23	.06
☐ 31 Earl Winfield	3.00	1.35	.35
☐ 32 Wally Zatylny	2.00	.90	.25
☐ 33 Martin Sartin	.50	.23	.06
☐ 34 Lee Knight	.50	.23	.06
☐ 35 Jason Riley	.50	.23	.06
☐ 36 Darrell Corbin	.50	.23	.06
☐ 37 Tony Champion	2.50	1.10	.30
☐ 38 Steve Stapler	.75	.35	.09
☐ 39 Scott Flagel	.75	.35	.09
☐ 40 Grover Covington	1.50	.70	.19
☐ 41 Mark Napiorkowski	.50	.23	.06
☐ 42 Jacques Chapdelaine	.50	.23	.06
☐ 43 Lance Shields	.75	.35	.09
☐ 44 Donohue Grant	.50	.23	.06
☐ 45 Henry Williams	25.00	11.00	3.10
☐ 46 Trevor Bowles	.75	.35	.09
☐ 47 Don Wilson	.50	.23	.06
☐ 48 Tracey Ham	15.00	6.75	1.85
☐ 49 Richie Hall	.75	.35	.09
☐ 50 Rob Bresciani	.50	.23	.06
☐ 51 James Curry	1.00	.45	.12
☐ 52 Kent Austin	12.00	5.50	1.50
☐ 53 Jeff Bentrim	.75	.35	.09
☐ 54 Dave Ridgway	1.25	.55	.16
☐ 55 Terry Baker	.75	.35	.09
☐ 56 Lance Chomyc	.75	.35	.09
☐ 57 Paul Sandor	.50	.23	.06
☐ 58 Kevin Cummings	.50	.23	.06
☐ 59 John Congemi	1.00	.45	.12
☐ 60 Gilbert Renfroe	1.50	.70	.19
☐ 61 Jake Vaughan	.50	.23	.06
☐ 62 Doran Major	.50	.23	.06
☐ 63 Dwight Edwards	.75	.35	.09
☐ 64 Bruce Elliott	.50	.23	.06
☐ 65 Lorenzo Graham	.75	.35	.09
☐ 66 Jim Kardash	.50	.23	.06
☐ 67 Reggie Pleasant	2.50	1.10	.30
☐ 68 Carl Brazley	.75	.35	.09
☐ 69 Gill Fenerty	6.00	2.70	.75
☐ 70 Selwyn Drain	.50	.23	.06
☐ 71 Warren Hudson	.75	.35	.09
☐ 72 Willie Fears	1.00	.45	.12
☐ 73 Randy Ambrosie	.50	.23	.06
☐ 74 George Ganas	.50	.23	.06
☐ 75 Glenn Kulka	.75	.35	.09
☐ 76 Kelvin Pruenster	.50	.23	.06
☐ 77 Darrell Smith	1.50	.70	.19
☐ 78 Jearld Baylis	1.50	.70	.19
☐ 79 Blaine Schmidt	.50	.23	.06
☐ 80 Tony Visco	1.00	.45	.12
☐ 81 Carl Fodor	.50	.23	.06
☐ 82 Rudy Phillips	.75	.35	.09
☐ 83 Craig Watson	.75	.35	.09
☐ 84 Kent Warnock	.75	.35	.09
☐ 85 Ken Ford	.50	.23	.06
☐ 86 Blake Marshall	2.00	.90	.25
☐ 87 Terry Cochrane	.50	.23	.06
☐ 88 Shawn Faulkner	.50	.23	.06
☐ 89 Marshall Toner	.50	.23	.06
☐ 90 Darren Yewshyn	.50	.23	.06
☐ 91 Eugene Belliveau	.50	.23	.06
☐ 92 Jay Christensen	1.00	.45	.12
☐ 93 Anthony Parker	1.25	.55	.16
☐ 94 Walter Ballard	.50	.23	.06
☐ 95 Matt Dunigan	6.00	2.70	.75
☐ 96 Andre Francis	.75	.35	.09
☐ 97 Rickey Foggie	5.00	2.20	.60
☐ 98 Delbert Fowler	.75	.35	.09
☐ 99 Michael Allen	1.00	.45	.12
☐ 100 Greg Battle	5.00	2.20	.60
☐ 101 Mike Gray	.50	.23	.06
☐ 102 Dan Wicklum	.50	.23	.06
☐ 103 Paul Shorten	.50	.23	.06
☐ 104 Paul Clatney	.50	.23	.06
☐ 105 Rod Hill	1.50	.70	.19
☐ 106 Steve Rodehutskors	1.00	.45	.12
☐ 107 Sean Salisbury	3.00	1.35	.35
☐ 108 Vernon Pahl	.50	.23	.06
☐ 109 Trevor Kennerd	.75	.35	.09
☐ 110 David Williams	2.50	1.10	.30

1988 JOGO CFL League

This 106-card set was produced and distributed before the CFL season started. The set was produced expressly for the league. There were to be 13 players for each of the eight teams with, reportedly, 3000 complete sets printed. Since the cards were intended for promotional purposes, each team was responsible for distributing their own cards making complete sets rather difficult. After the cards were printed, roster changes caused some of the cards to be withdrawn. All the cards were distributed by the players and teams except for three cards: Tom Clements number 105 (retired), Nick Arakgi number 54 (retired), and the checklist number 106, which were only available from hobby distributors of JOGO products. In addition, players who were victims of early trades or injuries, are also more difficult to find, e.g., Kevin Powell (traded to Edmonton), Greg Marshall (injured and retired), Willard Reaves (signed with

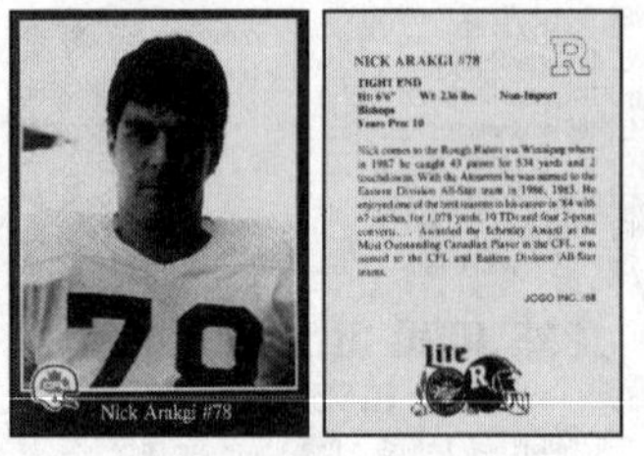

Washington Redskins), Milson Jones (traded to Saskatchewan), Scott Flagel (traded to Hamilton), and Jim Sandusky (traded to Edmonton). Cards are unnumbered except for uniform number which is prominently displayed on both sides of the card. The cards are ordered below alphabetically within team.

	MINT	NRMT	EXC
COMPLETE SET (106)	200.00	90.00	25.00
COMMON CARD (1-106)	1.00	.45	.12
☐ 1 Walter Ballard	1.00	.45	.12
☐ 2 Jan Carinci	1.00	.45	.12
☐ 3 Larry Crawford	2.00	.90	.25
☐ 4 Tyrone Crews	1.00	.45	.12
☐ 5 Andre Francis	1.50	.70	.19
☐ 6 Bernie Glier	1.00	.45	.12
☐ 7 Keith Gooch	1.00	.45	.12
☐ 8 Kevin Konar	1.50	.70	.19
☐ 9 Scott Lecky	1.00	.45	.12
☐ 10 James Parker	3.00	1.35	.35
☐ 11 Jim Sandusky (Traded)	8.00	3.60	1.00
☐ 12 Gregg Stumon	2.00	.90	.25
☐ 13 Todd Wiseman (Not listed on checklist card)	1.00	.45	.12
☐ 14 Gary Allen	1.50	.70	.19
☐ 15 Scott Flagel (Traded)	2.00	.90	.25
☐ 16 Harold Hallman	2.00	.90	.25
☐ 17 Larry Hogue UER (Misspelled Hoque)	1.00	.45	.12
☐ 18 Ron Hopkins	1.00	.45	.12
☐ 19 Stu Laird	1.50	.70	.19
☐ 20 Andy McVey	1.00	.45	.12
☐ 21 Bernie Morrison	1.00	.45	.12
☐ 22 Tim Petros	2.00	.90	.25
☐ 23 Bob Poley	1.00	.45	.12
☐ 24 Tom Spoletini	1.00	.45	.12
☐ 25 Emanuel Tolbert	3.00	1.35	.35
☐ 26 Larry Willis	1.50	.70	.19
☐ 27 Damon Allen	10.00	4.50	1.25
☐ 28 Danny Bass	3.00	1.35	.35
☐ 29 Stanley Blair	1.00	.45	.12
☐ 30 Marco Cyncar	1.50	.70	.19
☐ 31 Tracey Ham	25.00	11.00	3.10
☐ 32 Milson Jones (Traded)	3.00	1.35	.35
☐ 33 Stephen Jones	2.00	.90	.25
☐ 34 Jerry Kauric	2.00	.90	.25
☐ 35 Hector Pothier	1.00	.45	.12
☐ 36 Tom Richards	3.00	1.35	.35
☐ 37 Chris Skinner	1.50	.70	.19
☐ 38 Henry Williams	35.00	16.00	4.40
☐ 39 Larry Wruck	1.50	.70	.19
☐ 40 Pat Brady	1.00	.45	.12
☐ 41 Grover Covington	3.00	1.35	.35
☐ 42 Rocky DiPietro	3.00	1.35	.35
☐ 43 Howard Fields	1.00	.45	.12
☐ 44 Miles Gorrell	1.00	.45	.12
☐ 45 Johnnie Jones	1.00	.45	.12
☐ 46 Tom Porras	1.50	.70	.19
☐ 47 Jason Riley	1.00	.45	.12
☐ 48 Dale Sanderson	1.00	.45	.12
☐ 49 Ralph Scholz	1.00	.45	.12
☐ 50 Lance Shields	1.50	.70	.19
☐ 51 Steve Stapler	1.50	.70	.19
☐ 52 Mike Walker	3.00	1.35	.35
☐ 53 Gerald Alphin	4.00	1.80	.50
☐ 54 Nick Arakgi SP (Retired before season)	20.00	9.00	2.50
☐ 55 Nick Benjamin	1.50	.70	.19
☐ 56 Tom Dixon	1.00	.45	.12
☐ 57 Leo Groenewegen	1.00	.45	.12
☐ 58 Will Lewis	1.50	.70	.19
☐ 59 Greg Marshall (Injured and retired)	4.00	1.80	.50
☐ 60 Larry Mohr	1.00	.45	.12
☐ 61 Kevin Powell (Traded)	2.00	.90	.25
☐ 62 Jim Reid	2.00	.90	.25
☐ 63 Art Schlichter	5.00	2.20	.60
☐ 64 Rick Wolkensperg	1.00	.45	.12
☐ 65 Anthony Woodson	1.00	.45	.12
☐ 66 David Albright	1.00	.45	.12
☐ 67 Roger Aldag	1.50	.70	.19
☐ 68 Mike Anderson	1.00	.45	.12
☐ 69 Kent Austin	15.00	6.75	1.85
☐ 70 Tom Burgess	5.00	2.20	.60
☐ 71 James Curry	2.00	.90	.25
☐ 72 Ray Elgaard	5.00	2.20	.60
☐ 73 Denny Ferdinand	1.00	.45	.12
☐ 74 Bobby Jurasin	5.00	2.20	.60
☐ 75 Gary Lewis	1.00	.45	.12
☐ 76 Dave Ridgway	3.00	1.35	.35
☐ 77 Harry Skipper	1.50	.70	.19
☐ 78 Glen Suitor	1.50	.70	.19
☐ 79 Ian Beckstead	1.00	.45	.12
☐ 80 Lance Chomyc	1.50	.70	.19
☐ 81 John Congemi	2.00	.90	.25
☐ 82 Gill Fenerty	8.00	3.60	1.00
☐ 83 Dan Ferrone	1.50	.70	.19
☐ 84 Warren Hudson	1.50	.70	.19
☐ 85 Hank Ilesic	3.00	1.35	.35
☐ 86 Jim Kardash	1.00	.45	.12
☐ 87 Glenn Kulka	1.50	.70	.19
☐ 88 Don Moen	1.50	.70	.19
☐ 89 Gilbert Renfroe	2.00	.90	.25
☐ 90 Chris Schultz	1.50	.70	.19
☐ 91 Darrell Smith	2.00	.90	.25
☐ 92 Lyle Bauer	1.00	.45	.12
☐ 93 Nick Bastaja	1.00	.45	.12
☐ 94 David Black	1.00	.45	.12
☐ 95 Bob Cameron	2.00	.90	.25
☐ 96 Randy Fabi	1.00	.45	.12
☐ 97 James Jefferson	5.00	2.20	.60
☐ 98 Stan Mikawos	1.00	.45	.12
☐ 99 James Murphy	2.00	.90	.25
☐ 100 Ken Pettway	1.00	.45	.12
☐ 101 Willard Reaves (Signed with Redskins)	10.00	4.50	1.25
☐ 102 Darryl Sampson	1.00	.45	.12
☐ 103 Chris Walby	4.00	1.80	.50
☐ 104 James West	4.00	1.80	.50
☐ 105 Tom Clements SP (Retired before season)	20.00	9.00	2.50
☐ 106 Checklist Card SP	6.00	2.70	.75

1989 JOGO CFL

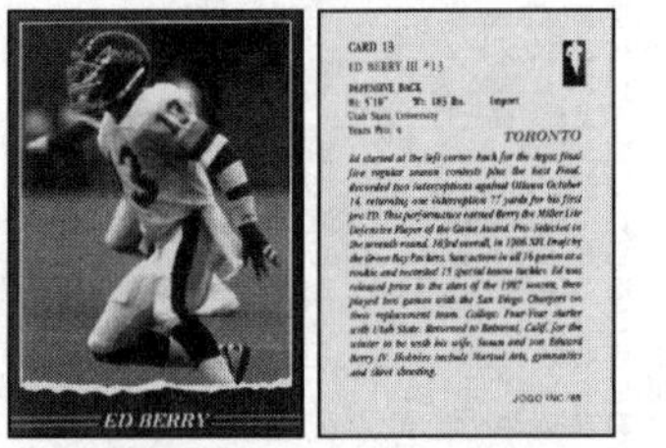

The 1989 JOGO CFL set contains 160 standard-size cards. The cards were issued in two series, 1-110 and 111-160. Except for the card numbering, the two series are indistinguishable. The fronts have color action photos with dark blue borders and yellow lettering; the vertically oriented backs have biographical information and career highlights. The first 200 sets of the first series cards came out with purple borders; these rather scarce color variations are valued at approximately triple the values listed below. The cards are numbered on the back and checklisted below according to teams.

	MINT	NRMT	EXC
COMPLETE SET (160)	60.00	27.00	7.50
COMPLETE SERIES 1 (110)	35.00	16.00	4.40
COMPLETE SERIES 2 (50)	25.00	11.00	3.10
COMMON CARD (1-160)	.50	.23	.06
☐ 1 Mike Kerrigan	2.00	.90	.25
☐ 2 Ian Beckstead	.50	.23	.06
☐ 3 Lance Chomyc	.75	.35	.09
☐ 4 Gill Fenerty	3.00	1.35	.35
☐ 5 Lee Morris	.50	.23	.06
☐ 6 Todd Wiseman	.50	.23	.06
☐ 7 John Congemi	.75	.35	.09
☐ 8 Harold Hallman	.75	.35	.09
☐ 9 Jim Kardash	.50	.23	.06
☐ 10 Kelvin Pruenster	.50	.23	.06
☐ 11 Blaine Schmidt	.50	.23	.06
☐ 12 Bruce Holmes	.50	.23	.06
☐ 13 Ed Berry	.50	.23	.06
☐ 14 Bobby McAllister	2.00	.90	.25
☐ 15 Frank Robinson	.75	.35	.09
☐ 16 Darrell Corbin	.50	.23	.06
☐ 17 Jason Riley	.50	.23	.06
☐ 18 Darrell Patterson	.50	.23	.06
☐ 19 Darrell Harle	.50	.23	.06
☐ 20 Mark Napiorkowski	.50	.23	.06
☐ 21 Derrick McAdoo	1.50	.70	.19
☐ 22 Sam Loucks	.50	.23	.06
☐ 23 Ronnie Glanton	.50	.23	.06
☐ 24 Lance Shields	.50	.23	.06
☐ 25 Tony Champion	1.50	.70	.19
☐ 26 Floyd Salazar	.50	.23	.06
☐ 27 Tony Visco	.75	.35	.09
☐ 28 Glenn Kulka	.75	.35	.09
☐ 29 Reggie Pleasant	1.00	.45	.12
☐ 30 Rod Skillman	.50	.23	.06
☐ 31 Grover Covington	1.00	.45	.12
☐ 32 Gerald Alphin	2.00	.90	.25
☐ 33 Gerald Wilcox	.75	.35	.09
☐ 34 Daniel Hunter	.50	.23	.06
☐ 35 Tony Kimbrough	.75	.35	.09
☐ 36 Willie Fears	.75	.35	.09
☐ 37 Tyrone Thurman	3.00	1.35	.35
☐ 38 Dean Dorsey	.75	.35	.09

Card	MINT	NRMT	EXC
☐ 39 Tom Schimmer	.50	.23	.06
☐ 40 Ken Evraire	.75	.35	.09
☐ 41 Steve Wiggins	.50	.23	.06
☐ 42 Donovan Wright	.50	.23	.06
☐ 43 Tuineau Alipate	.75	.35	.09
☐ 44 Richie Hall	.50	.23	.06
☐ 45 Rob Bresciani	.50	.23	.06
☐ 46 Tom Burgess	1.00	.45	.12
☐ 47 Jeff Fairholm	3.00	1.35	.35
☐ 48 John Hoffman	.50	.23	.06
☐ 49 Dave Ridgway	1.25	.55	.16
☐ 50 Terry Baker	.75	.35	.09
☐ 51 Mike Hildebrand	.50	.23	.06
☐ 52 Danny Bass	2.00	.90	.25
☐ 53 Jeff Braswell	.75	.35	.09
☐ 54 Michel Bourgeau	.75	.35	.09
☐ 55 Ken Ford	.50	.23	.06
☐ 56 Enis Jackson	.50	.23	.06
☐ 57 Tony Hunter	1.00	.45	.12
☐ 58 Andre Francis	.75	.35	.09
☐ 59 Larry Wruck	.75	.35	.09
☐ 60 Pierre Vercheval	1.00	.45	.12
☐ 61 Keith Wright	.50	.23	.06
☐ 62 Andrew McConnell	.50	.23	.06
☐ 63 Gregg Stumon	.75	.35	.09
☐ 64 Steve Taylor	2.50	1.10	.30
☐ 65 Brett Williams	.75	.35	.09
☐ 66 Tracey Ham	5.00	2.20	.60
☐ 67 Stewart Hill	.75	.35	.09
☐ 68 Eugene Belliveau	.50	.23	.06
☐ 69 Tom Porras	.75	.35	.09
☐ 70 Jay Christensen	.50	.23	.06
☐ 71 Michael Soles	1.00	.45	.12
☐ 72 John Mandarich	1.00	.45	.12
☐ 73 Dan Wicklum	.50	.23	.06
☐ 74 Shawn Daniels	.50	.23	.06
☐ 75 Marshall Toner	.50	.23	.06
☐ 76 Kent Warnock	.75	.35	.09
☐ 77 Terrence Jones	3.00	1.35	.35
☐ 78 Damon Allen	4.00	1.80	.50
☐ 79 Kevin Konar	.75	.35	.09
☐ 80 Phillip Smith	.50	.23	.06
☐ 81 Marcus Thomas	.50	.23	.06
☐ 82 Jamie Taras	.50	.23	.06
☐ 83 Rob Moretto	.50	.23	.06
☐ 84 Eugene Mingo	.50	.23	.06
☐ 85 Matt Dunigan	4.00	1.80	.50
☐ 86 Jan Carinci	.50	.23	.06
☐ 87 Anthony Parker	2.00	.90	.25
☐ 88 Keith Gooch	.50	.23	.06
☐ 89 Ron Howard	.50	.23	.06
☐ 90 David Williams	1.50	.70	.19
☐ 91 Less Browne	.75	.35	.09
☐ 92 Quency Williams	.50	.23	.06
☐ 93 Tim McCray	.75	.35	.09
☐ 94 Jeff Croonen	.50	.23	.06
☐ 95 Greg Battle	2.00	.90	.25
☐ 96 Moustafa Ali	.50	.23	.06
☐ 97 Michael Allen	.50	.23	.06
☐ 98 David Black	.50	.23	.06
☐ 99 Paul Randolph	.50	.23	.06
☐ 100 Trevor Kennerd	.75	.35	.09
☐ 101 Ken Pettway	.50	.23	.06
☐ 102 Sean Salisbury	2.00	.90	.25
☐ 103 Bob Cameron	.75	.35	.09
☐ 104 Tim Jessie	.75	.35	.09
☐ 105 Leon Hatziioannou	.50	.23	.06
☐ 106 Matt Pearce	.50	.23	.06
☐ 107 Paul Clatney	.50	.23	.06
☐ 108 Randy Fabi	.50	.23	.06
☐ 109 Mike Gray	.50	.23	.06
☐ 110 James Murphy	1.50	.70	.19
☐ 111 Danny Barrett	1.50	.70	.19
☐ 112 Wally Zatylny	.75	.35	.09
☐ 113 Tony Truelove	.50	.23	.06
☐ 114 Leroy Blugh	.75	.35	.09
☐ 115 Reggie Taylor	1.00	.45	.12
☐ 116 Mark Zeno	2.00	.90	.25
☐ 117 Paul Wetmore	.50	.23	.06
☐ 118 Mark McLoughlin	.50	.23	.06
☐ 119 Randy Ambrosie	.50	.23	.06
☐ 120 Will Johnson	.75	.35	.09
☐ 121 Brock Smith	.50	.23	.06
☐ 122 Willie Gillus	.50	.23	.06
☐ 123 Andy McVey	.50	.23	.06
☐ 124 Wes Cooper	.50	.23	.06
☐ 125 Tyrone Pope	.50	.23	.06
☐ 126 Craig Ellis	1.00	.45	.12
☐ 127 Darrel Hopper	.50	.23	.06
☐ 128 Brad Fawcett	.50	.23	.06
☐ 129 Pat Miller	.50	.23	.06
☐ 130 Irv Daymond	.50	.23	.06
☐ 131 Bob Molle	.50	.23	.06
☐ 132 James Mills	2.50	1.10	.30
☐ 133 Darrell Wallace	.75	.35	.09
☐ 134 Jerry Beasley	.50	.23	.06
☐ 135 Loyd Lewis	.50	.23	.06
☐ 136 Bernie Glier	.50	.23	.06
☐ 137 Eric Streater	2.00	.90	.25
☐ 138 Gerald Roper	.50	.23	.06
☐ 139 Brad Tierney	.50	.23	.06
☐ 140 Patrick Wayne	.50	.23	.06
☐ 141 Craig Watson	.50	.23	.06
☐ 142 Doug(Tank) Landry	2.50	1.10	.30
☐ 143 Orville Lee	1.00	.45	.12
☐ 144 Rocco Romano	.50	.23	.06
☐ 145 Todd Dillon	1.00	.45	.12
☐ 146 Michel Lamy	.50	.23	.06
☐ 147 Tony Cherry	2.50	1.10	.30
☐ 148 Flint Fleming	.50	.23	.06
☐ 149 Kennard Martin	.50	.23	.06
☐ 150 Lorenzo Graham	.50	.23	.06
☐ 151 Junior Thurman	1.00	.45	.12
☐ 152 Darnell Graham	.50	.23	.06
☐ 153 Dan Ferrone	.75	.35	.09
☐ 154 Matt Finlay	.50	.23	.06
☐ 155 Brent Matich	.50	.23	.06
☐ 156 Kent Austin	4.00	1.80	.50
☐ 157 Will Lewis	.50	.23	.06
☐ 158 Mike Walker	1.00	.45	.12
☐ 159 Tim Petros	.75	.35	.09
☐ 160 Stu Laird	1.50	.70	.19

1990 JOGO CFL

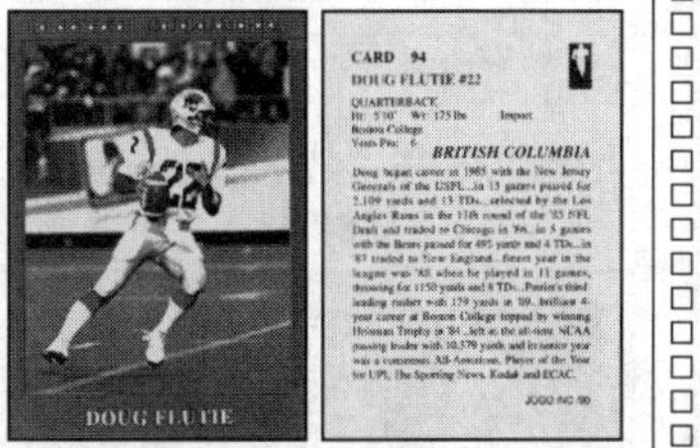

This 220-card standard-size set of JOGO Canadian Football League cards was issued in two series of 110 cards. The first series card fronts feature an action shot of the player, enframed by a thin red border on blue background, with team name above the photo and player's name below. The second series card fronts feature solid blue borders surrounding an action shot of the player with the team's name on the top of the card and the player's name underneath. The card number and player information are found on the back. Three British Columbia players featured in the set that are of interest to American collectors are Doug Flutie, Mark Gastineau, and Major Harris. The complete set price below includes only one of the variations of card 84. First series cards are arranged according to teams.

	MINT	NRMT	EXC
COMPLETE SET (220)	50.00	22.00	6.25
COMPLETE SERIES 1 (110)	25.00	11.00	3.10
COMPLETE SERIES 2 (110)	25.00	11.00	3.10
COMMON CARD (1-220)	.20	.09	.03

Card	MINT	NRMT	EXC
☐ 1A Grey Cup Champs ERR (Roughriders because...)	.75	.35	.09
☐ 1B Grey Cup Champs COR (Roughriders became...)	4.00	1.80	.50
☐ 2 Kent Austin	1.50	.70	.19
☐ 3 James Ellingson	.35	.16	.04
☐ 4 Vince Goldsmith	.35	.16	.04
☐ 5 Gary Lewis	.20	.09	.03
☐ 6 Bobby Jurasin	.75	.35	.09
☐ 7 Tim McCray	.35	.16	.04
☐ 8 Chuck Klingbeil	.75	.35	.09
☐ 9 Albert Brown	.20	.09	.03
☐ 10 Dave Ridgway	.50	.23	.06
☐ 11 Tony Rice	2.00	.90	.25
☐ 12 Richie Hall	.20	.09	.03
☐ 13 Jeff Fairholm	.75	.35	.09
☐ 14 Ray Elgaard	1.25	.55	.16
☐ 15 Sonny Gordon	.20	.09	.03
☐ 16 Peter Giftopoulos	.50	.23	.06
☐ 17 Mike Kerrigan	.75	.35	.09
☐ 18 Jason Riley	.20	.09	.03
☐ 19 Wally Zatylny	.35	.16	.04
☐ 20 Derrick McAdoo	.35	.16	.04
☐ 21 Dale Sanderson	.20	.09	.03
☐ 22 Paul Osbaldiston	.35	.16	.04
☐ 23 Todd Dillon	.35	.16	.04
☐ 24 Miles Gorrell	.20	.09	.03
☐ 25 Earl Winfield	.50	.23	.06
☐ 26 Bill Henry	.20	.09	.03
☐ 27 Darrell Harle	.20	.09	.03
☐ 28 Ernie Schramayr	.20	.09	.03
☐ 29 Greg Peterson	.20	.09	.03
☐ 30 Marshall Toner	.20	.09	.03
☐ 31 Danny Barrett	1.00	.45	.12
☐ 32 Mike Palumbo	.20	.09	.03
☐ 33 Ken Ford	.20	.09	.03
☐ 34 Brock Smith	.20	.09	.03
☐ 35 Tom Spoletini	.20	.09	.03
☐ 36 Will Johnson	.35	.16	.04
☐ 37 Terrence Jones	1.00	.45	.12
☐ 38 Darcy Kopp	.20	.09	.03
☐ 39 Tim Petros	.35	.16	.04
☐ 40 Mitchell Price	.20	.09	.03
☐ 41 Junior Thurman	.75	.35	.09
☐ 42 Kent Warnock	.35	.16	.04
☐ 43 Darrell Smith	.75	.35	.09
☐ 44 Chris Schultz UER (No team on back)	.35	.16	.04
☐ 45 Kelvin Pruenster	.20	.09	.03
☐ 46 Matt Dunigan	2.00	.90	.25
☐ 47 Lance Chomyc	.20	.09	.03
☐ 48 John Congemi	.50	.23	.06
☐ 49 Mike Clemons	8.00	3.60	1.00
☐ 50 Glenn Harper	.20	.09	.03
☐ 51 Branko Vincic	.20	.09	.03
☐ 52 Tom Porras	.35	.16	.04
☐ 53 Reggie Pleasant	.35	.16	.04
☐ 54 Randy Marriott	.20	.09	.03
☐ 55 James Parker	.50	.23	.06
☐ 56 Don Moen	.35	.16	.04
☐ 57 James West	.75	.35	.09
☐ 58 Trevor Kennerd	.50	.23	.06
☐ 59 Warren Hudson	.35	.16	.04
☐ 60 Tom Burgess	1.00	.45	.12
☐ 61 David Black	.20	.09	.03
☐ 62 Matt Pearce	.20	.09	.03
☐ 63 Steve Rodehutskors	.20	.09	.03
☐ 64 Rod Hill	.35	.16	.04
☐ 65 Nick Benjamin	.35	.16	.04
☐ 66 Bob Cameron	.35	.16	.04
☐ 67 Leon Hatziioannou	.20	.09	.03
☐ 68 Robert Mimbs	2.50	1.10	.30
☐ 69 Mike Gray	.20	.09	.03
☐ 70 Ken Winey	.20	.09	.03
☐ 71 Mike Hildebrand	.20	.09	.03
☐ 72 Brett Williams	.35	.16	.04
☐ 73 Tracey Ham	2.50	1.10	.30
☐ 74 Danny Bass	.50	.23	.06
☐ 75 Mark Norman	.20	.09	.03
☐ 76 Andre Francis	.35	.16	.04
☐ 77 Todd Storme	.20	.09	.03
☐ 78 Henry Williams	4.00	1.80	.50
☐ 79 Kevin Clark	.50	.23	.06
☐ 80 Enis Jackson	.20	.09	.03
☐ 81 Leroy Blugh	.20	.09	.03
☐ 82 Jeff Braswell	.20	.09	.03
☐ 83 Larry Wruck	.35	.16	.04
☐ 84A Mike McLean ERR (Photo actually 24 Mike Hildebrand)	2.00	.90	.25
☐ 84B Mike McLean COR (Two players shown)	4.00	1.80	.50
☐ 85 Leo Groenewegen UER (Misspelled Groenewegan on card back)	.20	.09	.03
☐ 86 Mark Gastineau	1.00	.45	.12
☐ 87 Rocco Romano	.20	.09	.03
☐ 88 Major Harris	1.50	.70	.19
☐ 89 Ray Alexander	.35	.16	.04
☐ 90 Joe Paopao	.35	.16	.04
☐ 91 Ian Sinclair	.35	.16	.04
☐ 92 Tony Visco UER (British Columbia on front, correctly has team as Toronto on front)	.20	.09	.03
☐ 93 Lui Passaglia	.50	.23	.06
☐ 94 Doug Flutie	12.00	5.50	1.50
☐ 95 Glenn Kulka	.35	.16	.04
☐ 96 Bruce Holmes	.20	.09	.03
☐ 97 Stacey Dawsey	.20	.09	.03
☐ 98 Damon Allen	.50	.23	.06
☐ 99 Ken Evraire	.35	.16	.04
☐ 100 David Williams	.50	.23	.06
☐ 101 Gregg Stumon	.35	.16	.04
☐ 102 Scott Flagel	.35	.16	.04
☐ 103 Gerald Roper	.20	.09	.03
☐ 104 Tony Cherry	.75	.35	.09
☐ 105 Jim Mills	.35	.16	.04
☐ 106 Dean Dorsey	.20	.09	.03
☐ 107 Patrick Wayne	.20	.09	.03
☐ 108 Reggie Barnes	1.50	.70	.19
☐ 109 Kari Yli-Renko	.20	.09	.03
☐ 110 Ken Hobart	.50	.23	.06
☐ 111 Doug Flutie	10.00	4.50	1.25
☐ 112 Grover Covington	.50	.23	.06
☐ 113 Michael Allen	.20	.09	.03
☐ 114 Mike Walker	.50	.23	.06
☐ 115 Danny McManus	3.00	1.35	.35
☐ 116 Greg Battle	1.00	.45	.12
☐ 117 Quency Williams	.20	.09	.03
☐ 118 Jeff Croonen	.20	.09	.03
☐ 119 Paul Randolph	.20	.09	.03
☐ 120 Rick House	.35	.16	.04
☐ 121 Rob Smith	.35	.16	.04
☐ 122 Mark Napiorkowski	.20	.09	.03
☐ 123 Ed Berry	.20	.09	.03
☐ 124 Rob Crifo	.20	.09	.03
☐ 125 Gord Weber	.20	.09	.03
☐ 126 Jeff Boyd	.35	.16	.04
☐ 127 Paul McGowan	.35	.16	.04
☐ 128 Reggie Taylor	.50	.23	.06
☐ 129 Warren Jones	.20	.09	.03
☐ 130 Blake Marshall	.35	.16	.04
☐ 131 Darrell Corbin	.20	.09	.03
☐ 132 Jim Rockford	.35	.16	.04
☐ 133 Richard Nurse	.20	.09	.03
☐ 134 Bryan Illerbrun	.20	.09	.03
☐ 135 Mark Waterman	.20	.09	.03
☐ 136 Doug(Tank) Landry	1.00	.45	.12
☐ 137 Ronnie Glanton	.20	.09	.03
☐ 138 Mark Guy	.35	.16	.04
☐ 139 Mike Anderson	.20	.09	.03
☐ 140 Remi Trudel	.20	.09	.03
☐ 141 Stephen Jones	.75	.35	.09
☐ 142 Mike Derks	.20	.09	.03
☐ 143 Michel Bourgeau Edmonton Oilers	.35	.16	.04
☐ 144 Jeff Bentrim	.35	.16	.04
☐ 145 Roger Aldag	.35	.16	.04
☐ 146 Donald Narcisse	2.00	.90	.25
☐ 147 Troy Wilson	.20	.09	.03
☐ 148 Glen Suitor	.35	.16	.04
☐ 149 Stewart Hill	.75	.35	.09
☐ 150 Chris Johnstone	.20	.09	.03
☐ 151 Mark Mathis	.20	.09	.03
☐ 152 Blaine Schmidt	.20	.09	.03
☐ 153 Craig Ellis	.50	.23	.06
☐ 154 John Mandarich	.35	.16	.04
☐ 155 Steve Zatylny	.20	.09	.03
☐ 156 Michel Lamy	.20	.09	.03
☐ 157 Irv Daymond	.20	.09	.03
☐ 158 Tom Porras	.35	.16	.04
☐ 159 Rick Worman	.35	.16	.04
☐ 160 Major Harris	1.00	.45	.12
☐ 161 Darryl Hall	.35	.16	.04
☐ 162 Terry Andrysiak	.35	.16	.04
☐ 163 Harold Hallman	.35	.16	.04
☐ 164 Carl Brazley	.20	.09	.03
☐ 165 Kevin Smellie	.20	.09	.03
☐ 166 Mark Campbell	.35	.16	.04
☐ 167 Andy McVey	.20	.09	.03
☐ 168 Derrick Crawford	.35	.16	.04
☐ 169 Howard Dell	.20	.09	.03
☐ 170 Dave Van Belleghem	.20	.09	.03
☐ 171 Don Wilson	.20	.09	.03
☐ 172 Robert Smith	.35	.16	.04
☐ 173 Keith Browner	.35	.16	.04
☐ 174 Chris Munford	.20	.09	.03
☐ 175 Gary Wilkerson	.20	.09	.03
☐ 176 Rickey Foggie UER (Misspelled Foogie on card front)	1.00	.45	.12
☐ 177 Robin Belanger	.20	.09	.03
☐ 178 Andrew Murray	.20	.09	.03
☐ 179 Paul Masotti	.35	.16	.04
☐ 180 Chris Gaines	.20	.09	.03
☐ 181 Joe Clausi	.20	.09	.03
☐ 182 Greg Harris	.20	.09	.03
☐ 183 Dave Bovell	.20	.09	.03
☐ 184 Eric Streater	.35	.16	.04
☐ 185 Larry Hogue	.20	.09	.03
☐ 186 Jan Carinci	.20	.09	.03
☐ 187 Floyd Salazar	.20	.09	.03
☐ 188 Alondra Johnson	.35	.16	.04
☐ 189 Jay Christensen UER (Misspelled Christenson on card front)	.35	.16	.04
☐ 190 Rick Ryan	.20	.09	.03
☐ 191 Willie Pless	1.50	.70	.19
☐ 192 Walter Ballard	.20	.09	.03
☐ 193 Lee Knight	.20	.09	.03
☐ 194 Ray Macoritti	.35	.16	.04
☐ 195 Dan Payne	.20	.09	.03
☐ 196 Dan Sellers	.20	.09	.03
☐ 197 Rae Robirtis	.20	.09	.03
☐ 198 Dave Mossman	.20	.09	.03
☐ 199 Sam Loucks	.20	.09	.03
☐ 200 Derek MacCready	.20	.09	.03
☐ 201 Tony Cherry	.50	.23	.06
☐ 202 Moustafa Ali	.35	.16	.04
☐ 203 Terry Baker	.35	.16	.04
☐ 204 Matt Finlay	.20	.09	.03
☐ 205 Daniel Hunter	.20	.09	.03
☐ 206 Chris Major	1.50	.70	.19
☐ 207 Henry Smith	.20	.09	.03
☐ 208 David Sapunjis	3.00	1.35	.35
☐ 209 Darrell Wallace	.35	.16	.04
☐ 210 Mark Singer	.20	.09	.03
☐ 211 Tuineau Alipate	.20	.09	.03
☐ 212 Tony Champion	1.00	.45	.12
☐ 213 Mike Lazecki	.20	.09	.03
☐ 214 Larry Clarkson	.20	.09	.03
☐ 215 Lorenzo Graham	.20	.09	.03
☐ 216 Tony Martino	.20	.09	.03
☐ 217 Ken Watson	.20	.09	.03
☐ 218 Paul Clatney	.20	.09	.03
☐ 219 Ken Pettway	.20	.09	.03
☐ 220 Tyrone Jones	.75	.35	.09

1991 JOGO CFL

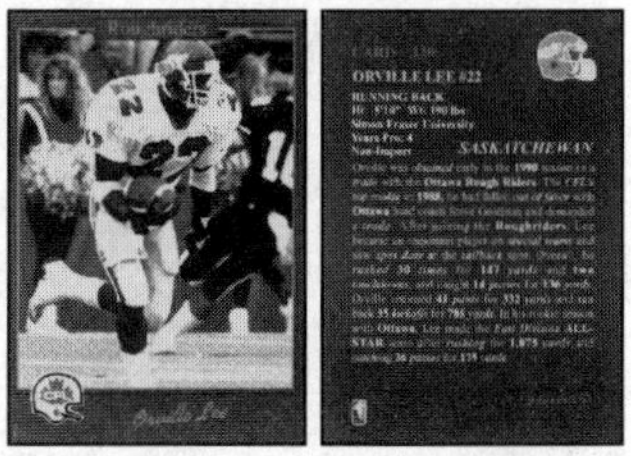

The 1991 JOGO CFL football set contains 220 standard-size cards. The set was released in two series, 1-110 and 111-220. The set was distributed in factory sets and in foil packs (10 cards per pack). The front design has glossy color action shots, with thin gray and red borders against a royal blue card face. The team name appears above the picture, while the CFL helmet logo and the player's name appear at the bottom of the card face. The backs have red, green, and yellow lettering on a black background. They feature biography and career

summary. The team logo and card number round out the back. The cards are numbered on the back and checklisted below according to teams. It is estimated that 30,000 sets were produced. Rocket Ismail was originally planned for inclusion in the set, but was removed based on litigation. Ismail had signed an exclusive with All World, which apparently took precedence over JOGO's attempt to include him in the set based on his membership in the CFL Players' Association.

	MINT	NRMT	EXC
COMPLETE SET (220)	6.00	2.70	.75
COMPLETE SERIES 1 (110)	3.00	1.35	.35
COMPLETE SERIES 2 (110)	3.00	1.35	.35
COMMON CARD (1-220)	.04	.02	.01
□ 1 Tracey Ham	.35	.16	.04
□ 2 Larry Wruck	.08	.04	.01
□ 3 Pierre Vercheval	.04	.02	.01
□ 4 Rod Connop	.04	.02	.01
□ 5 Michel Bourgeau	.04	.02	.01
□ 6 Leroy Blugh	.04	.02	.01
□ 7 Mike Walker	.04	.02	.01
□ 8 Ray Macoritti	.04	.02	.01
□ 9 Michael Soles	.04	.02	.01
□ 10 Brett Williams	.08	.04	.01
□ 11 Blake Marshall	.08	.04	.01
□ 12 David Williams	.08	.04	.01
□ 13 Enis Jackson	.04	.02	.01
□ 14 Craig Ellis	.08	.04	.01
□ 15 Reggie Taylor	.08	.04	.01
□ 16 Mike McLean	.04	.02	.01
□ 17 Blake Dermott	.04	.02	.01
□ 18 Henry Williams	.50	.23	.06
□ 19 Jordan Gaertner	.04	.02	.01
□ 20 Willie Pless	.15	.07	.02
□ 21 Danny Bass	.15	.07	.02
□ 22 Trevor Bowles	.04	.02	.01
□ 23 Rob Davidson	.04	.02	.01
□ 24 Mark Norman	.04	.02	.01
□ 25 Ron Lancaster CO	.10	.05	.01
□ 26 Chris Johnstone	.04	.02	.01
□ 27 Randy Ambrosie	.04	.02	.01
□ 28 Glenn Kulka	.04	.02	.01
□ 29 Gerald Wilcox	.04	.02	.01
□ 30 Kari Yli-Renko	.04	.02	.01
□ 31 Daniel Hunter	.04	.02	.01
□ 32 Bryan Illerbrun	.04	.02	.01
□ 33 Terry Baker	.04	.02	.01
□ 34 Jeff Braswell	.04	.02	.01
□ 35 Andre Francis	.04	.02	.01
□ 36 Irv Daymond	.04	.02	.01
□ 37 Sean Foudy	.04	.02	.01
□ 38 Brad Tierney	.04	.02	.01
□ 39 Gregg Stumon	.04	.02	.01
□ 40 Scott Flagel	.04	.02	.01
□ 41 Gerald Roper	.04	.02	.01
□ 42 Charles Wright	.04	.02	.01
□ 43 Rob Smith	.04	.02	.01
□ 44 James Ellingson	.04	.02	.01
□ 45 Damon Allen	.30	.14	.04
□ 46 John Congemi	.04	.02	.01
□ 47 Reggie Barnes	.20	.09	.03
□ 48 Stephen Jones	.15	.07	.02
□ 49 Rob Prodanovic	.04	.02	.01
□ 50 Steve Goldman	.04	.02	.01
□ 51 Patrick Wayne	.04	.02	.01
□ 52 David Conrad	.04	.02	.01
□ 53 John Krupke	.04	.02	.01
□ 54 Loyd Lewis	.04	.02	.01
□ 55 Tony Cherry	.20	.09	.03
□ 56 Terrence Jones	.25	.11	.03
□ 57 Dan Wicklum	.04	.02	.01
□ 58 Allen Pitts	.40	.18	.05
□ 59 Junior Thurman	.04	.02	.01
□ 60 Ron Hopkins	.04	.02	.01
□ 61 Andy McVey	.04	.02	.01
□ 62 Leo Blanchard	.04	.02	.01
□ 63 Mark Singer	.04	.02	.01
□ 64 Darryl Hall	.04	.02	.01
□ 65 David McCrary	.04	.02	.01
□ 66 Mark Guy	.04	.02	.01
□ 67 Marshall Toner	.04	.02	.01
□ 68 Derrick Crawford	.04	.02	.01
□ 69 Danny Barrett	.20	.09	.03
□ 70 Kent Warnock	.08	.04	.01
□ 71 Brent Matich	.04	.02	.01
□ 72 Mark McLoughlin	.04	.02	.01
□ 73 Joe Clausi	.04	.02	.01
□ 74 Wally Buono CO	.04	.02	.01
□ 75 Will Johnson	.08	.04	.01
□ 76 Walter Ballard	.04	.02	.01
□ 77 Matt Finlay	.04	.02	.01
□ 78 David Sapunjis	.35	.16	.04
□ 79 Greg Peterson	.04	.02	.01
□ 80 Paul Clatney	.04	.02	.01
□ 81 Lloyd Fairbanks	.04	.02	.01
□ 82 Herman Heard	.15	.07	.02
□ 83 Richard Nurse	.04	.02	.01
□ 84 Dave Richardson	.04	.02	.01
□ 85 Ernie Schramayr	.04	.02	.01
□ 86 Todd Dillon	.04	.02	.01
□ 87 Tuineau Alipate	.04	.02	.01
□ 88 Peter Giftopoulos	.04	.02	.01
□ 89 Miles Gorrell	.04	.02	.01
□ 90 Earl Winfield	.20	.09	.03
□ 91 Paul Osbaldiston	.04	.02	.01
□ 92 Dale Sanderson	.04	.02	.01
□ 93 Jason Riley	.04	.02	.01
□ 94 Ken Evraire	.04	.02	.01
□ 95 Lee Knight	.04	.02	.01
□ 96 Tim Lorenz	.04	.02	.01
□ 97 Derrick McAdoo	.08	.04	.01
□ 98 Bobby Dawson	.04	.02	.01
□ 99 Rickey Royal	.04	.02	.01
□ 100 Ronald Veal	.20	.09	.03
□ 101 Grover Covington	.08	.04	.01
□ 102 Mike Kerrigan	.20	.09	.03
□ 103 Rocky DiPietro	.20	.09	.03
□ 104 Mark Dennis	.04	.02	.01
□ 105 Tony Champion	.20	.09	.03
□ 106 Tony Visco	.04	.02	.01
□ 107 Darrell Harle	.04	.02	.01
□ 108 Wally Zatylny	.04	.02	.01
□ 109 David Beckman CO	.04	.02	.01
□ 110 Checklist 1-110	.04	.02	.01
□ 111 Jeff Fairholm	.04	.02	.01
□ 112 Roger Aldag	.04	.02	.01
□ 113 David Albright	.04	.02	.01
□ 114 Gary Lewis	.04	.02	.01
□ 115 Dan Rashovich	.04	.02	.01
□ 116 Lucius Floyd	.04	.02	.01
□ 117 Bob Poley	.04	.02	.01
□ 118 Donald Narcisse	.20	.09	.03
□ 119 Bobby Jurasin	.15	.07	.02
□ 120 Orville Lee	.08	.04	.01
□ 121 Stacey Hairston	.04	.02	.01
□ 122 Richie Hall	.04	.02	.01
□ 123 John Gregory CO	.04	.02	.01
□ 124 Rick Worman	.04	.02	.01
□ 125 Dave Ridgway	.15	.07	.02
□ 126 Wayne Drinkwalter	.04	.02	.01
□ 127 Eddie Lowe	.04	.02	.01
□ 128 Mike Hogue	.04	.02	.01
□ 129 Larry Hogue	.04	.02	.01
□ 130 Milson Jones	.04	.02	.01
□ 131 Ray Elgaard	.20	.09	.03
□ 132 Dave Pitcher	.04	.02	.01
□ 133 Vic Stevenson	.04	.02	.01
□ 134 Albert Brown	.04	.02	.01
□ 135 Mike Anderson	.04	.02	.01
□ 136 Glen Suitor	.04	.02	.01
□ 137 Kent Austin	.30	.14	.04
□ 138 Mike Gray	.04	.02	.01
□ 139 Steve Rodehutskors	.04	.02	.01
□ 140 Eric Streater	.08	.04	.01
□ 141 David Black	.04	.02	.01
□ 142 James West	.15	.07	.02
□ 143 Danny McManus	.30	.14	.04
□ 144 Darryl Sampson	.04	.02	.01
□ 145 Bob Cameron	.08	.04	.01
□ 146 Tom Burgess	.35	.16	.04
□ 147 Rick House	.04	.02	.01
□ 148 Chris Walby	.15	.07	.02
□ 149 Michael Allen	.04	.02	.01
□ 150 Warren Hudson	.04	.02	.01
□ 151 Dave Bovell	.04	.02	.01
□ 152 Rob Crifo	.04	.02	.01
□ 153 Lyle Bauer	.04	.02	.01
□ 154 Trevor Kennerd	.20	.09	.03
□ 155 Troy Johnson	.04	.02	.01
□ 156 Less Browne	.04	.02	.01
□ 157 Nick Benjamin	.04	.02	.01
□ 158 Matt Pearce	.04	.02	.01
□ 159 Tyrone Jones	.04	.02	.01
□ 160 Rod Hill	.04	.02	.01
□ 161 Bob Molle	.04	.02	.01
□ 162 Lee Hull	.04	.02	.01
□ 163 Greg Battle	.20	.09	.03
□ 164 Robert Mimbs	.50	.23	.06
□ 165 Giulio Caravatta	.04	.02	.01
□ 166 James Mills	.15	.07	.02
□ 167 Ian Sinclair	.04	.02	.01
□ 168 Robin Belanger	.04	.02	.01
□ 169 Deatrich Wise	.04	.02	.01
□ 170 Chris Skinner	.04	.02	.01
□ 171 Norman Jefferson	.04	.02	.01
□ 172 Larry Clarkson	.04	.02	.01
□ 173 Chris Major	.35	.16	.04
□ 174 Stewart Hill	.04	.02	.01
□ 175 Tony Hunter	.04	.02	.01
□ 176 Stacey Dawsey	.04	.02	.01
□ 177 Doug Flutie	1.00	.45	.12
□ 178 Mike Trevathan	.08	.04	.01
□ 179 Jearld Baylis	.08	.04	.01
□ 180 Matt Clark	.25	.11	.03
□ 181 Ken Pettway	.04	.02	.01
□ 182 Lloyd Joseph	.04	.02	.01
□ 183 Jon Volpe	1.00	.45	.12
□ 184 Leo Groenewegen	.04	.02	.01
□ 185 Carl Coulter	.04	.02	.01
□ 186 O.J. Brigance	1.00	.45	.12
□ 187 Ryan Hanson	.04	.02	.01
□ 188 Rocco Romano	.04	.02	.01
□ 189 Ray Alexander	.04	.02	.01
□ 190 Bob O'Billovich CO	.04	.02	.01
□ 191 Paul Wetmore	.04	.02	.01
□ 192 Harold Hallman	.04	.02	.01
□ 193 Ed Berry	.04	.02	.01
□ 194 Brian Warren	.04	.02	.01
□ 195 Matt Dunigan	.40	.18	.05
□ 196 Kelvin Pruenster	.04	.02	.01
□ 197 Ian Beckstead	.04	.02	.01
□ 198 Carl Brazley	.04	.02	.01
□ 199 Trevor Kennerd	.15	.07	.02
□ 200 Reggie Pleasant	.08	.04	.01
□ 201 Kevin Smellie	.04	.02	.01
□ 202 Don Moen	.04	.02	.01
□ 203 Blaine Schmidt	.04	.02	.01
□ 204 Chris Schultz	.04	.02	.01
□ 205 Lance Chomyc	.04	.02	.01
□ 206 Darrell Smith	.20	.09	.03
□ 207 Dan Ferrone	.04	.02	.01
□ 208 Chris Gaines	.04	.02	.01
□ 209 Keith Castello	.04	.02	.01
□ 210 Chris Munford	.04	.02	.01
□ 211 Rodney Harding	.04	.02	.01
□ 212 Darryl Ford	.04	.02	.01
□ 213 Rickey Foggie	.20	.09	.03
□ 214 Don Wilson	.04	.02	.01
□ 215 Andrew Murray	.04	.02	.01
□ 216 Jim Kardash	.04	.02	.01
□ 217 Mike Clemons	1.25	.55	.16
□ 218 Bruce Elliott	.04	.02	.01
□ 219 Mike McCarthy	.04	.02	.01
□ 220 Checklist Card	.04	.02	.01

1991 JOGO CFL Stamp Card Inserts

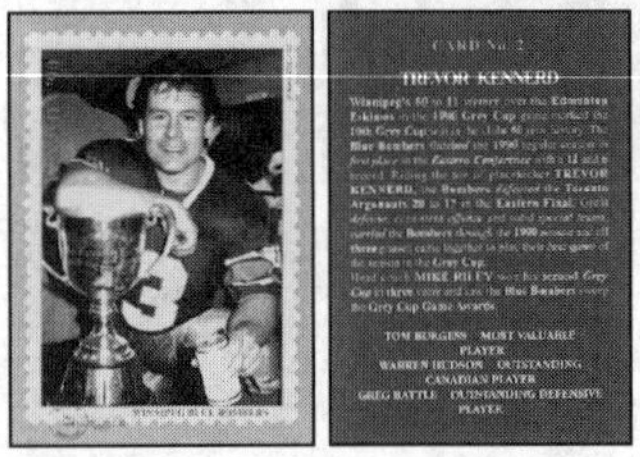

These three standard-size insert cards have photos on their fronts within a white postage stamp border. In red, green, and yellow print on a black background, the backs present commentary to the front pictures. The first two cards are numbered on the back, while the card picturing the Grey Cup Trophy is unnumbered.

	MINT	NRMT	EXC
COMPLETE SET (3)	25.00	11.00	3.10
COMMON CARD	8.00	3.60	1.00
□ 1 Albert Henry George Grey	8.00	3.60	1.00
□ 2 Trevor Kennerd	10.00	4.50	1.25
□ NNO Grey Cup Trophy (Grey Cup Winners listed on card back)	8.00	3.60	1.00

1992 JOGO CFL Promos

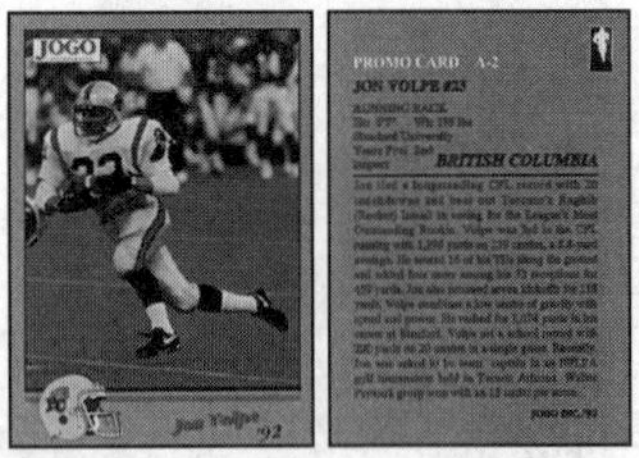

JOGO produced the first two of the five Promo cards with a color action player photo on a silver cardfront. The team helmet and player's name appear in the bottom silver border. The third card features Rocket Rat, the JOGO Card Company "mascot." The back presents his biography and closes with an educational message ("Education Equals More Freedom"). Reportedly only 6,000 of each card were released. Two other cards (P1-P2) were inserted into the second edition of the Charlton CFL Football Card Price Guide as an uncut sheet of two. Reportedly, 5500 of the two card sheets were produced. The two Ken Danby Collector's Classic Library cards were produced to promote the Libraries series as well as a Ken Danby Grey Cup lithograph.

	MINT	NRMT	EXC
COMPLETE SET (7)	12.00	5.50	1.50
COMMON CARD	.75	.35	.09
□ A1 Mike(Pinball) Clemons	2.00	.90	.25
□ A2 Jon Volpe	2.00	.90	.25
□ A3 Rocket Rat (Cartoon character)	.75	.35	.09
□ P1 Mike(Pinball) Clemons	3.00	1.35	.35
□ P2 Jon Volpe	3.00	1.35	.35
□ CC1 Ken Danby Art Collector's Classic Library	.75	.35	.09
□ CC2 Ken Danby Art Collector's Classic Library	.75	.35	.09

1992 JOGO CFL

The 1992 JOGO CFL set contains 220 standard-size cards. Reportedly there were less than 1200 cases produced. The cards feature color action player photos on a silver card face. The team helmet and

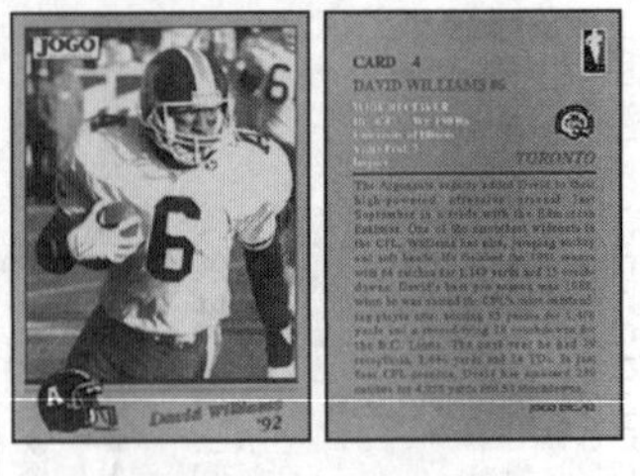

player's name appear in the bottom silver border. In yellow, red, and green print on a silver background, the back has biography and player profile. The cards are numbered on the back and checklisted below according to teams.

	MINT	NRMT	EXC
COMPLETE SET (220)	18.00	8.00	2.20
COMMON CARD (1-220)	.05	.02	.01
□ 1 Dave Bovell	.05	.02	.01
□ 2 Don Moen	.10	.05	.01
□ 3 Ian Beckstead	.05	.02	.01
□ 4 David Williams	.10	.05	.01
□ 5 Hank Ilesic	.20	.09	.03
□ 6 Brian Warren	.05	.02	.01
□ 7 Paul Masotti	.10	.05	.01
□ 8 Kelvin Pruenster	.05	.02	.01
□ 9 Mike Clemons	1.25	.55	.16
□ 10 Chris Schultz	.10	.05	.01
□ 11 Andrew Murray	.05	.02	.01
□ 12 Lance Chomyc	.10	.05	.01
□ 13 Ed Berry	.05	.02	.01
□ 14 Harold Hallman	.10	.05	.01
□ 15 Dave Van Belleghem	.05	.02	.01
□ 16 Rodney Harding	.10	.05	.01
□ 17 Rickey Foggie	.20	.09	.03
□ 18 Darrell Smith	.20	.09	.03
□ 19 Bob Skemp	.05	.02	.01
□ 20 Carl Brazley	.10	.05	.01
□ 21 J.P. Izquierdo	.05	.02	.01
□ 22 Mike Campbell	.10	.05	.01
□ 23 Reggie Pleasant	.20	.09	.03
□ 24 Dan Ferrone	.10	.05	.01
□ 25 Kevin Smellie	.05	.02	.01
□ 26 Don Wilson	.05	.02	.01
□ 27 Adam Rita CO	.05	.02	.01
□ 28 Greg Peterson	.05	.02	.01
□ 29 David Sapunjis	.50	.23	.06
□ 30 Srecko Zizakovic	.10	.05	.01
□ 31 Carl Bland	.05	.02	.01
□ 32 Errol Tucker	.05	.02	.01
□ 33 Allen Pitts	.25	.11	.03
□ 34 Pee Wee Smith	.30	.14	.04
□ 35 Will Johnson	.20	.09	.03
□ 36 Kent Warnock	.10	.05	.01
□ 37 Brent Matich	.05	.02	.01
□ 38 Stu Laird	.10	.05	.01
□ 39 Shawn Beals	.05	.02	.01
□ 40 Darcy Kopp	.05	.02	.01
□ 41 Ken Moore	.05	.02	.01
□ 42 Alondra Johnson	.10	.05	.01
□ 43 Matt Finlay	.05	.02	.01
□ 44 Andy McVey	.05	.02	.01
□ 45 Paul Clatney	.05	.02	.01
□ 46 Karl Anthony	.05	.02	.01
□ 47 Bruce Covernton	.35	.16	.04
□ 48 Mark McLoughlin UER (Name misspelled several times on the card back)	.05	.02	.01
□ 49 Pat Hinds	.05	.02	.01
□ 50 Eric Mitchel UER (Misspelled Mitchell on both sides)	.20	.09	.03
□ 51 Dan Wicklum	.05	.02	.01
□ 52 Tim Cofield	.50	.23	.06
□ 53 Steve Taylor	.35	.16	.04
□ 54 Darryl Hall	.10	.05	.01
□ 55 Angelo Snipes	.60	.25	.07
□ 56 Shawn Daniels	.05	.02	.01
□ 57 Terrence Jones	.25	.11	.03
□ 58 Brian Bonner	.05	.02	.01
□ 59 Kari Yli-Renko	.05	.02	.01
□ 60 Denny Chronopoulos	.05	.02	.01
□ 61 Damon Allen	.30	.14	.04
□ 62 Reggie Barnes	.20	.09	.03
□ 63 Andre Francis UER (Misspelled Frances on card front)	.10	.05	.01
□ 64 Rob Smith	.10	.05	.01
□ 65 Anthony Drawhorn	.10	.05	.01
□ 66 David Conrad UER (Back text says team is Green Riders)	.05	.02	.01
□ 67 Irv Daymond	.05	.02	.01
□ 68 Terry Baker	.10	.05	.01
□ 69 Daniel Hunter	.05	.02	.01
□ 70 Gord Weber	.05	.02	.01
□ 71 Tom Burgess	.30	.14	.04
□ 72 Charles Gordon	.05	.02	.01
□ 73 Bobby Gordon	.05	.02	.01
□ 74 Jock Climie	.25	.11	.03
□ 75 Patrick Wayne	.05	.02	.01

□ 76 Sean Foudy	.05	.02	.01
□ 77 James Ellingson	.10	.05	.01
□ 78 Gregg Stumon	.10	.05	.01
□ 79 John Kropke	.10	.05	.01
□ 80 Stephen Jones	.25	.11	.03
□ 81 Ron Smeltzer	.05	.02	.01
□ 82 Scott Campbell	.50	.23	.06
□ 83 Henry Williams	1.25	.55	.16
□ 84 Willie Pless	.60	.25	.07
□ 85 Dan Murphy	.05	.02	.01
□ 86 Chris Armstrong	.20	.09	.03
□ 87 Tracey Ham	.50	.23	.06
□ 88 Larry Wruck	.10	.05	.01
□ 89 Rod Connop	.05	.02	.01
□ 90 Jim Sandusky	.25	.11	.03
□ 91 Randy Ambrosie	.05	.02	.01
□ 92 Michel Bourgeau	.10	.05	.01
□ 93 Bennie Goods UER (Misspelled Benny)	.25	.11	.03
□ 94 Rob Davidson	.05	.02	.01
□ 95 Leroy Blugh	.10	.05	.01
□ 96 Brian Walling	.20	.09	.03
□ 97 Michael Soles	.10	.05	.01
□ 98 Craig Ellis	.10	.05	.01
□ 99 Pierre Vercheval	.10	.05	.01
□ 100 Matt Dunigan	.50	.23	.06
□ 101 Enis Jackson	.05	.02	.01
□ 102 Tom Muecke	.20	.09	.03
□ 103 Jed Roberts	.05	.02	.01
□ 104 Steve Krupey	.05	.02	.01
□ 105 Blake Marshall	.35	.16	.04
□ 106 Trevor Bowles	.10	.05	.01
□ 107 Eddie Thomas	.05	.02	.01
□ 108 Rocket Rat (JOGO Mascot)	.10	.05	.01
□ 109 Checklist 1-110 UER (50 Eric Mitchell 93 Benny Goods)	.10	.05	.01
□ 110 Tom Burgess	.35	.16	.04
□ 111 Bob Cameron	.20	.09	.03
□ 112 James West	.20	.09	.03
□ 113 Chris Walby	.15	.07	.02
□ 114 David Black	.05	.02	.01
□ 115 Nick Benjamin	.10	.05	.01
□ 116 Matt Pearce	.05	.02	.01
□ 117 Bob Molle	.05	.02	.01
□ 118 Rod Hill	.05	.02	.01
□ 119 Kyle Hall	.05	.02	.01
□ 120 Danny McManus	.35	.16	.04
□ 121 Cal Murphy	.15	.07	.02
□ 122 Stan Mikawos	.05	.02	.01
□ 123 Bobby Evans	.05	.02	.01
□ 124 Larry Willis	.10	.05	.01
□ 125 Eric Streater	.20	.09	.03
□ 126 Perry Tuttle	.20	.09	.03
□ 127 Leon Hatziioannou	.05	.02	.01
□ 128 Sammy Garza	.05	.02	.01
□ 129 Greg Battle	.25	.11	.03
□ 130 Elfrid Payton	.25	.11	.03
□ 131 Troy Westwood	.20	.09	.03
□ 132 Mike Gray	.05	.02	.01
□ 133 Dave Vankoughnett	.05	.02	.01
□ 134 Paul Randolph	.05	.02	.01
□ 135 Darryl Sampson	.05	.02	.01
□ 136 Less Browne	.10	.05	.01
□ 137 Quency Williams	.05	.02	.01
□ 138 Robert Mimbs	.50	.23	.06
□ 139 Matt Dunigan	1.25	.55	.16
□ 140 Dan Rashovich	.05	.02	.01
□ 141 Dan Farthing	.05	.02	.01
□ 142 Bruce Boyko	.05	.02	.01
□ 143 Kim McCloud	.05	.02	.01
□ 144 Richie Hall	.10	.05	.01
□ 145 Paul Vajda	.05	.02	.01
□ 146 Willis Jacox	.25	.11	.03
□ 147 Glen Scrivener	.05	.02	.01
□ 148 Dave Ridgway	.20	.09	.03
□ 149 Lucius Floyd	.10	.05	.01
□ 150 James King	.05	.02	.01
□ 151 Kent Austin	.50	.23	.06
□ 152 Jeff Fairholm	.10	.05	.01
□ 153 Roger Aldag	.10	.05	.01
□ 154 Albert Brown	.05	.02	.01
□ 155 Chris Gioskos	.05	.02	.01
□ 156 Stacey Hairston	.05	.02	.01
□ 157 Glen Suitor	.10	.05	.01
□ 158 Milson Jones	.10	.05	.01
□ 159 Vic Stevenson	.05	.02	.01
□ 160 Bob Poley	.05	.02	.01
□ 161 Bobby Jurasin	.20	.09	.03
□ 162 Gary Lewis	.05	.02	.01
□ 163 Donald Narcisse	.20	.09	.03
□ 164 Mike Anderson	.05	.02	.01
□ 165 Nick Mazzoli	.05	.02	.01
□ 166 Lance Trumble	.05	.02	.01
□ 167 Dale Sanderson	.05	.02	.01
□ 168 Todd Wiseman	.05	.02	.01
□ 169 Mark Dennis	.10	.05	.01
□ 170 Peter Giftopoulos	.10	.05	.01
□ 171 Ken Evraire	.10	.05	.01
□ 172 Darrell Harle	.05	.02	.01
□ 173 Terry Wright	.05	.02	.01
□ 174 Jamie Morris	.20	.09	.03
□ 175 Corris Ervin	.05	.02	.01
□ 176 Don McPherson	.20	.09	.03
□ 177 Jason Riley	.05	.02	.01
□ 178 Tim Jackson	.05	.02	.01
□ 179 Todd Dillon	.10	.05	.01
□ 180 Lee Knight	.05	.02	.01
□ 181 Scott Douglas	.05	.02	.01
□ 182 Dave Richardson	.05	.02	.01
□ 183 Wally Zatylny	.10	.05	.01
□ 184 Rickey Martin	.05	.02	.01
□ 185 John Motton	.30	.14	.04
□ 186 Mark Waterman	.05	.02	.01
□ 187 Ernie Schramayr	.05	.02	.01
□ 188 Miles Gorrell	.05	.02	.01
□ 189 Tony Champion	.20	.09	.03
□ 190 Earl Winfield	.25	.11	.03
□ 191 John Zajdel	.05	.02	.01
□ 192 Danny Barrett	.30	.14	.04
□ 193 Ian Sinclair	.10	.05	.01
□ 194 Norman Jefferson	.05	.02	.01
□ 195 Ryan Hanson	.05	.02	.01
□ 196 Matt Clark	.15	.07	.02
□ 197 Leo Groenewegen	.05	.02	.01
□ 198 Ray Alexander	.10	.05	.01
□ 199 James Mills	.20	.09	.03
□ 200 Jon Volpe	.60	.25	.07
□ 201 Doug Hocking	.05	.02	.01
□ 202 Tony Kimbrough	.10	.05	.01
□ 203 Lui Passaglia	.20	.09	.03
□ 204 Bruce Holmes	.05	.02	.01
□ 205 Jamie Taras	.05	.02	.01
□ 206 Derek MacCready	.05	.02	.01
□ 207 Jay Christensen	.10	.05	.01
□ 208 O.J. Brigance	.50	.23	.06
□ 209 Robin Belanger	.05	.02	.01
□ 210 Stewart Hill	.10	.05	.01
□ 211 Mike Marasco	.05	.02	.01
□ 212 Mike Trevathan	.20	.09	.03
□ 213 Chris Major	.20	.09	.03
□ 214 Steve Rodehutskors	.10	.05	.01
□ 215 Paul Wetmore	.05	.02	.01
□ 216 Ken Pettway	.05	.02	.01
□ 217 Darren Flutie	2.00	.90	.25
□ 218 Giulio Caravatta	.05	.02	.01
□ 219 Murray Pezim	.10	.05	.01
□ 220 Checklist 111-220	.10	.05	.01

1992 JOGO CFL Missing Years

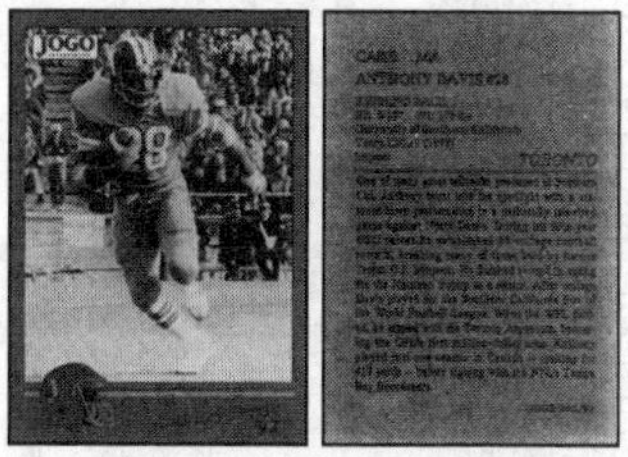

Since no CFL cards were produced from 1972 to 1981, JOGO created this set of "Missing Years" players to provide CFL fans with memories of their favorite players of the 70's. This 22-card standard-size set was randomly inserted in the packs. The fronts carry action black-and-white player photos on a gold metallic face. A red, blue, and orange stripe borders the bottom of the picture. A blue helmet with the JOGO "J" is in the lower left corner and the player's name appears in red in the bottom border. The backs are metallic gold with red and green print. They carry biographical information and a player profile. The cards are numbered on the back with an "A" suffix.

	MINT	NRMT	EXC
COMPLETE SET (22)	20.00	9.00	2.50
COMMON CARD (1-22)	1.00	.45	.12
□ 1 Larry Smith	1.50	.70	.19
□ 2 Mike Nelms	1.50	.70	.19
□ 3 John Sciarra	2.00	.90	.25
□ 4 Ed Chalupka	1.00	.45	.12
□ 5 Mike Rae	1.50	.70	.19
□ 6 Terry Metcalf UER (His CFL years were 78-80, not 78-90)	2.50	1.10	.30
□ 7 Chuck Ealey	5.00	2.20	.60
□ 8 Junior Ah-You	1.50	.70	.19
□ 9 Mike Samples	1.00	.45	.12
□ 10 Ray Nettles	1.00	.45	.12
□ 11 Dickie Harris	1.00	.45	.12
□ 12 Willie Burden	3.00	1.35	.35
□ 13 Johnny Rodgers	5.00	2.20	.60
□ 14 Anthony Davis	3.00	1.35	.35
□ 15 Joe Pisarcik UER (His CFL years were 74-76, not 74-75)	1.50	.70	.19
□ 16 Jim Washington	1.00	.45	.12
□ 17 Tom Scott UER (11 years in CFL, not 10)	1.50	.70	.19
□ 18 Butch Norman	1.00	.45	.12
□ 19 Steve Molnar	1.00	.45	.12
□ 20 Jerry Tagge	2.50	1.10	.30
□ 21 Leon Bright UER (His CFL years were 77-80, not 77-79)	2.50	1.10	.30
□ 22 Waddell Smith	2.00	.90	.25

1992 JOGO CFL Stamp Cards

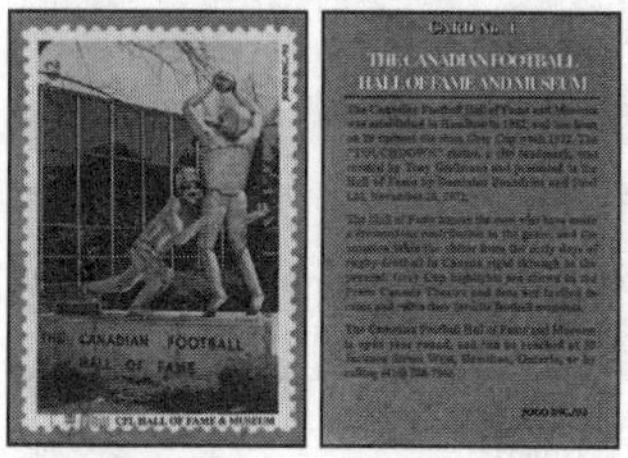

This five-card standard-size set was randomly inserted in foil packs. There were only two sets per foil case and only 1,200 cases of foil made according to JOGO. The fronts feature color photos with white postage stamp borders. In green, yellow, and red print on a silver metallic background, the backs provide information about the pictures on the front.

	MINT	NRMT	EXC
COMPLETE SET (5)	25.00	11.00	3.10
COMMON CARD (1-5)	6.00	2.70	.75
□ 1 CFL Hall of Fame Museum and Statue	6.00	2.70	.75
□ 2 Toronto Argonauts 1991 Grey Cup Champs	6.00	2.70	.75
□ 3 Tom Pate Memorial Trophy	6.00	2.70	.75
□ 4 Russ Jackson MVP	6.00	2.70	.75
□ 5 Oldest Trophy in The Hall of Fame (Montreal Football Challenge Cup)	6.00	2.70	.75

1993 JOGO CFL

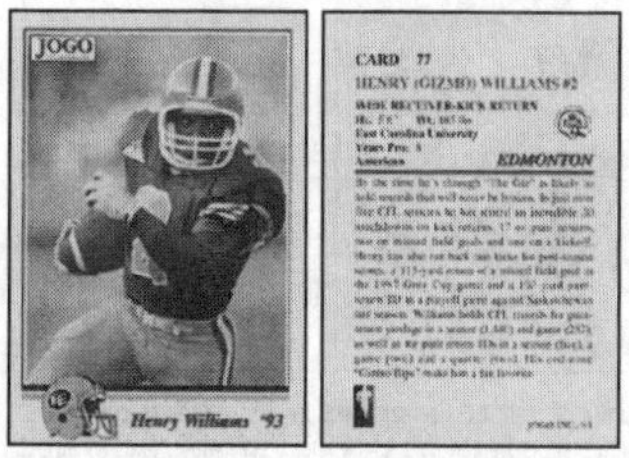

The 1993 JOGO CFL set consists of 220 standard-size cards. Just 1,300 numbered sets and 440 sets for the players were produced. The fronts feature color action player photos on a light gray card face with ghosted JOGO CFL lettering. A team-color coded stripe highlights the bottom edge of the picture. The team helmet and player's name appear in the bottom border. The white backs contain biography and player profiles which are printed in red and black. The cards are numbered on the back according to teams.

	MINT	NRMT	EXC
COMPLETE SET (220)	40.00	18.00	5.00
COMPLETE SERIES 1 (110)	25.00	11.00	3.10
COMPLETE SERIES 2 (110)	18.00	8.00	2.20
COMMON CARD (1-220)	.15	.07	.02
□ 1 Stephen Jones	.50	.23	.06
□ 2 Chris Gioskos	.15	.07	.02
□ 3 Treamelle Taylor	.15	.07	.02
□ 4 Irv Daymond	.15	.07	.02
□ 5 Gord Weber	.15	.07	.02
□ 6 James Ellingson	.25	.11	.03
□ 7 Lybrant Robinson	.15	.07	.02
□ 8 Michael Allen	.25	.11	.03
□ 9 Gregg Stumon	.25	.11	.03
□ 10 Darren Joseph	.40	.18	.05
□ 11 Terry Baker	.25	.11	.03
□ 12 Denny Chronopoulos	.15	.07	.02
□ 13 Tom Burgess	1.00	.45	.12
□ 14 Wayne Walker	.50	.23	.06
□ 15 Brendan Rogers	.15	.07	.02
□ 16 Matt Pearce	.15	.07	.02
□ 17 Chris Tsangaris	.15	.07	.02
□ 18 Leon Hatziioannou	.15	.07	.02
□ 19 Bob Cameron	.40	.18	.05
□ 20 Donald Smith	.15	.07	.02
□ 21 Michael Richardson	1.00	.45	.12
□ 22 Jayson Dzikowicz	.15	.07	.02
□ 23 Matt Dunigan	1.50	.70	.19
□ 24 Steve Grant	.15	.07	.02
□ 25 Rob Crifo	.15	.07	.02
□ 26 Dave Vankoughnett	.15	.07	.02
□ 27 Paul Masotti	.25	.11	.03
□ 28 Blaine Schmidt	.15	.07	.02
□ 29 Dave Van Belleghem	.15	.07	.02
□ 30 Brian Warren	.15	.07	.02
□ 31 Reggie Pleasant	.40	.18	.05
□ 32 Tracey Ham	.75	.35	.09
□ 33 Mike Clemons	1.50	.70	.19
□ 34 Lance Chomyc	.25	.11	.03
□ 35 Ken Benson	.15	.07	.02
□ 36 Chris Green	.15	.07	.02
□ 37 Mike Campbell	.15	.07	.02
□ 38 Chris Schultz	.25	.11	.03
□ 39 Reggie Rogers	.25	.11	.03
□ 40 John Hood	.25	.11	.03
□ 41 Dave Richardson	.15	.07	.02
□ 42 Mike Jovanovich	.25	.11	.03
□ 43 Joey Jauch	.25	.11	.03
□ 44 Lubo Zizakovic	.15	.07	.02
□ 45 Don McPherson	.25	.11	.03
□ 46 Brett Williams	.40	.18	.05
□ 47 Todd Wiseman	.15	.07	.02
□ 48 Jim Jauch	.15	.07	.02
□ 49 Eros Sanchez	.25	.11	.03
□ 50 Scott Walker	.15	.07	.02
□ 51 Roger Hennig	.15	.07	.02
□ 52 Glen Suitor	.25	.11	.03
□ 53 Bobby Jurasin	.25	.11	.03
□ 54 Scott Hendrickson	.15	.07	.02
□ 55 Ventson Donelson	.15	.07	.02
□ 56 Dan Rashovich	.15	.07	.02
□ 57 Kent Austin	.75	.35	.09
□ 58 Ray Elgaard	.40	.18	.05
□ 59 Dave Ridgway	.40	.18	.05
□ 60 Byron K. Williams	.15	.07	.02
□ 61 Larry Ryckman PRES	.15	.07	.02
□ 62 Karl Anthony	.15	.07	.02
□ 63 Greg Knox	.15	.07	.02
□ 64 Ken Moore	.15	.07	.02
□ 65 Allen Pitts	.40	.18	.05
□ 66 Matt Finlay	.25	.11	.03
□ 67 Tony Martino	.15	.07	.02
□ 68 Harald Hasselbach	1.50	.70	.19
□ 69 David Sapunjis	1.50	.70	.19
□ 70 Andy McVey	.15	.07	.02
□ 71 Stu Laird	.25	.11	.03
□ 72 Derrick Crawford	.25	.11	.03
□ 73 Mark McLoughlin	.15	.07	.02
□ 74A Will Johnson ERR (Eskimo logo)	2.00	.90	.25
□ 74B Will Johnson COR (Stampeder logo)	.75	.35	.09
□ 75 Don Wilson	.15	.07	.02
□ 76 J.P. Izquierdo	.15	.07	.02
□ 77 Henry Williams	1.25	.55	.16
□ 78 Larry Wruck	.25	.11	.03
□ 79 David Shelton	.25	.11	.03
□ 80 Damion Lyons	.15	.07	.02
□ 81 Jed Roberts	.15	.07	.02
□ 82 Trent Brown	.15	.07	.02
□ 83 Michel Bourgeau	.25	.11	.03
□ 84 Blake Dermott	.25	.11	.03
□ 85 Willie Pless	.50	.23	.06
□ 86 Leroy Blugh	.25	.11	.03
□ 87 Steve Krupey	.15	.07	.02
□ 88 Jim Sandusky	.25	.11	.03
□ 89 Danny Barrett	.50	.23	.06
□ 90 James West	.40	.18	.05
□ 91 Glen Scrivener	.15	.07	.02
□ 92 Tyrone Jones	.25	.11	.03
□ 93A Jon Volpe ERR (Photo has poor color)	.50	.23	.06
□ 93B Jon Volpe COR	2.00	.90	.25
□ 94 Less Browne	.25	.11	.03
□ 95 Matt Clark	.25	.11	.03
□ 96 Andre Francis	.25	.11	.03
□ 97 Darren Flutie	2.00	.90	.25
□ 98 Ray Alexander	.25	.11	.03
□ 99 Rob Smith	.25	.11	.03
□ 100 Fred Anderson Managing General Partner	.25	.11	.03
□ 101 Robb White UER Rob on front and back	.15	.07	.02
□ 102 Bobby Humphery	.25	.11	.03
□ 103 Willie Bouyer	.15	.07	.02
□ 104 Titus Dixon	.25	.11	.03
□ 105 John Wiley	.15	.07	.02
□ 106 Kerwin Bell	1.00	.45	.12
□ 107 Carl Parker	.15	.07	.02
□ 108 Mike Oliphant	.75	.35	.09
□ 109 David Archer	2.50	1.10	.30
□ 110 Freeman Baysinger	.25	.11	.03
□ 111 Gerald Alphin	.25	.11	.03
□ 112 Gerald Wilcox	.25	.11	.03
□ 113 Reggie Barnes	.40	.18	.05
□ 114 Michel Raby	.15	.07	.02
□ 115 Charles Wright	.15	.07	.02
□ 116 Brett Young	.25	.11	.03
□ 117 Charles Gordon	.15	.07	.02
□ 118 Anthony Drawhorn	.25	.11	.03
□ 119 Daved Benefield	.25	.11	.03
□ 120 Patrick Burke	.15	.07	.02
□ 121 Joe Sardo	.15	.07	.02
□ 122 Dexter Manley	.25	.11	.03
□ 123 Bruce Beaton	.15	.07	.02
□ 124 Joe Fuller	.15	.07	.02
□ 125 Michel Lamy	.15	.07	.02
□ 126 Terrence Jones	.50	.23	.06
□ 127 Jeff Croonen	.15	.07	.02
□ 128 Leonard Johnson	.15	.07	.02
□ 129 Dan Payne	.15	.07	.02
□ 130 Carlton Lance	.15	.07	.02
□ 131 Errol Brown	.15	.07	.02
□ 132 Wayne Drinkwalter	.15	.07	.02
□ 133 Malvin Hunter	.15	.07	.02
□ 134 Maurice Crum	.15	.07	.02
□ 135 Brooks Findlay	.15	.07	.02

☐ 136 Ray Bernard	.15	.07	.02
☐ 137 Paul Osbaldiston	.25	.11	.03
☐ 138 Mark Dennis	.25	.11	.03
☐ 139 Glenn Kulka	.25	.11	.03
☐ 140 Lee Knight	.15	.07	.02
☐ 141 Mike O'Shea	1.25	.55	.16
☐ 142 Paul Bushey	.15	.07	.02
☐ 143 Nick Mazzoli	.15	.07	.02
☐ 144 Earl Winfield	.50	.23	.06
☐ 145 Gary Wilkerson	.15	.07	.02
☐ 146 Jason Riley	.15	.07	.02
☐ 147 Bob MacDonald	.15	.07	.02
☐ 148 Dale Sanderson	.15	.07	.02
☐ 149 Bobby Dawson	.15	.07	.02
☐ 150 Rod Connop	.15	.07	.02
☐ 151 Tony Woods	.25	.11	.03
☐ 152 Dan Murphy	.15	.07	.02
☐ 153 Mike DuMaresq	.15	.07	.02
☐ 154 Allan Boyko	.15	.07	.02
☐ 155 Vaughn Booker	.75	.35	.09
☐ 156 Elfrid Payton	.25	.11	.03
☐ 157 Mike Kerrigan	.50	.23	.06
☐ 158 Charles Anthony	.15	.07	.02
☐ 159 Brent Matich	.15	.07	.02
☐ 160 Craig Hendrickson	.15	.07	.02
☐ 161 Dave Pitcher	.15	.07	.02
☐ 162 Stewart Hill	.25	.11	.03
☐ 163 Terryl Ulmer	.15	.07	.02
☐ 164 Paul Cranmer	.15	.07	.02
☐ 165 Mike Saunders	1.25	.55	.16
☐ 166 Doug Flutie	2.00	.90	.25
☐ 167 Keilan Matthews	.15	.07	.02
☐ 168 Kip Texada	.15	.07	.02
☐ 169 Jonathan Wilson	.15	.07	.02
☐ 170 Bruce Dickson	.15	.07	.02
☐ 171 Mike Trevathan	.40	.18	.05
☐ 172 Vic Stevenson	.15	.07	.02
☐ 173 Keith Powe	.15	.07	.02
☐ 174 Eddie Taylor	.15	.07	.02
☐ 175 Tim Lorenz	.15	.07	.02
☐ 176 Sean Millington	.25	.11	.03
☐ 177 Ryan Hanson	.15	.07	.02
☐ 178 Ed Berry	.15	.07	.02
☐ 179 Kent Warnock	.25	.11	.03
☐ 180 Spencer McLennan	.15	.07	.02
☐ 181 Brian Walling	.25	.11	.03
☐ 182 Danny McManus	.75	.35	.09
☐ 183 Donovan Wright	.15	.07	.02
☐ 184 Giulio Caravatta	.15	.07	.02
☐ 185 Derek MacCready	.15	.07	.02
☐ 186 Greg Eaglin	.15	.07	.02
☐ 187 Jim Mills	.15	.07	.02
☐ 188 Tom Europe	.15	.07	.02
☐ 189 Zock Allen	.15	.07	.02
☐ 190 Ian Sinclair	.25	.11	.03
☐ 191 O.J. Brigance	1.50	.70	.19
☐ 192 Steve Rodehutskors	.25	.11	.03
☐ 193 Lou Cafazzo	.15	.07	.02
☐ 194 Mark Dube	.15	.07	.02
☐ 195 Srecko Zizakovic	.15	.07	.02
☐ 196 Alondra Johnson	.25	.11	.03
☐ 197 Rocco Romano	.15	.07	.02
☐ 198 Raymond Biggs	.15	.07	.02
☐ 199 Frank Marof	.15	.07	.02
☐ 200 Brian Wiggins	.25	.11	.03
☐ 201 Marvin Pope	.15	.07	.02
☐ 202 Gerald Vaughn	.15	.07	.02
☐ 203 Todd Storme	.15	.07	.02
☐ 204 Blair Zerr	.15	.07	.02
☐ 205 Eric Johnson	.25	.11	.03
☐ 206 Mark Pearce	.15	.07	.02
☐ 207 Will Moore	1.00	.45	.12
☐ 208 Bruce Plummer	.15	.07	.02
☐ 209 Kari Yli-Renko	.15	.07	.02
☐ 210 Doug Parrish	.15	.07	.02
☐ 211 Warren Hudson	.25	.11	.03
☐ 212 Kevin Whitley	.15	.07	.02
☐ 213 Enis Jackson	.15	.07	.02
☐ 214 Wally Zatylny	.25	.11	.03
☐ 215 Bruce Elliott	.15	.07	.02
☐ 216 Harold Hallman	.25	.11	.03
☐ 217 Glenn Rogers	.15	.07	.02
☐ 218 Manny Hazard	.50	.23	.06
☐ 219 Robert Clark	.25	.11	.03
☐ 220 Doug Flutie UER (Three misspelled Tree on back)	2.00	.90	.25

1993 JOGO CFL Missing Years

For the second year, JOGO created a "Missing Years" set to provide CFL fans with memories of their favorite players of the '70s, since no CFL cards were produced from 1972 to 1981. These cards were randomly inserted in packs. The 22 standard-size cards feature on their fronts black-and-white player photos with metallic gold borders. Blue, white, and orange stripes border the bottom of the picture. A blue helmet with the JOGO "J" is in the lower left corner, and the player's name appears in red lettering within the lower gold margin. The white back has black and red lettering and carries the player's name, uniform number, position, biography, team name, and career highlights. The cards are numbered on the back with a "B" suffix.

	MINT	NRMT	EXC
COMPLETE SET (22)	15.00	6.75	1.85
COMMON CARD (1B-22B)	.60	.25	.07

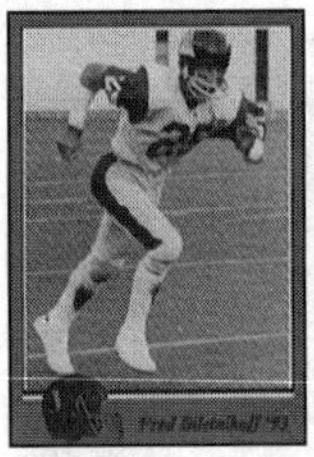

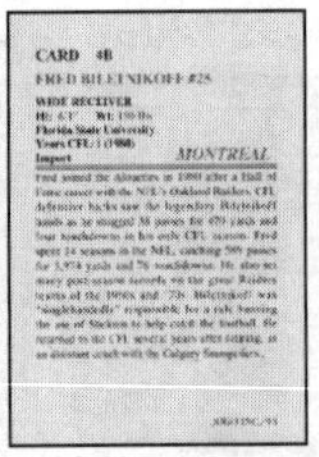

☐ 1B Jimmy Edwards	1.00	.45	.12
☐ 2B Lou Harris	.60	.25	.07
☐ 3B George Mira	1.25	.55	.16
☐ 4B Fred Biletnikoff	3.50	1.55	.45
☐ 5B Randy Halsall	.60	.25	.07
☐ 6B Don Sweet	.60	.25	.07
☐ 7B Jim Coode	.60	.25	.07
☐ 8B Steve Mazurak	.75	.35	.09
☐ 9B Wayne Allison	.60	.25	.07
☐ 10B Paul Williams	.60	.25	.07
☐ 11B Eric Allen	1.25	.55	.16
☐ 12B M.L. Harris	.75	.35	.09
☐ 13B James Sykes	1.50	.70	.19
☐ 14B Chuck Zapiec	.75	.35	.09
☐ 15B George McGowan	.60	.25	.07
☐ 16B Bob Macoritti	.75	.35	.09
☐ 17B Chuck Walton	.60	.25	.07
☐ 18B Willie Armstead	.75	.35	.09
☐ 19B Rocky Long	.60	.25	.07
☐ 20B Gene Mack	.60	.25	.07
☐ 21B David Green	1.25	.55	.16
☐ 22B Don Warrington	.75	.35	.09

1994 JOGO CFL Caravan

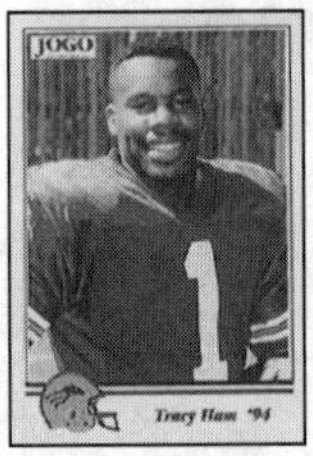

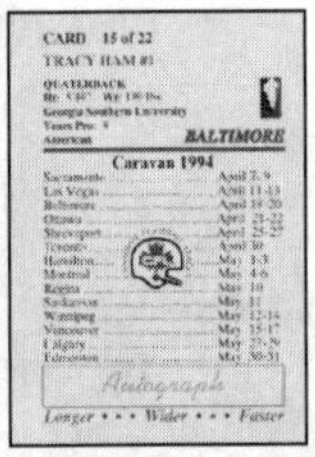

These 22 standard-size cards feature white-bordered color player action shots framed by a black line. Black, white, and red stripes border the bottom of the picture. The player's name appears in red lettering within the bottom white margin; his team helmet rests at the lower left. The white back has black and red lettering and carries the player's name, uniform number, position, biography, nationality, and team name. Below is the show schedule that lists the North American cities and dates for "Caravan 1994." The cards are numbered on the back as "X of 22." The cards are organized by team.

	MINT	NRMT	EXC
COMPLETE SET (22)	40.00	18.00	5.00
COMMON CARD (1-22)	1.00	.45	.12
☐ 1 Glenn Kulka	1.50	.70	.19
☐ 2 Jock Climie	2.00	.90	.25
☐ 3 Danny Barrett	3.00	1.35	.35
☐ 4 Stephen Jones	2.00	.90	.25
☐ 5 Mike Clemons	4.00	1.80	.50
☐ 6 Pierre Vercheval	1.50	.70	.19
☐ 7 Ken Evraire	1.50	.70	.19
☐ 8 Brett Williams UER (Misspelled Willians on card front)	1.50	.70	.19
☐ 9 Wally Zatylny	1.50	.70	.19
☐ 10 Mike O'Shea	2.50	1.10	.30
☐ 11 Earl Winfield	2.00	.90	.25
☐ 12 Mike Oliphant	2.00	.90	.25
☐ 13 Matt Dunigan	3.00	1.35	.35
☐ 14 Chris Walby	2.00	.90	.25
☐ 15 Tracey Ham	3.00	1.35	.35
☐ 16 Darrell K. Smith	2.00	.90	.25
☐ 17 Glen Suitor	1.50	.70	.19
☐ 18 Mark McLoughlin	1.00	.45	.12
☐ 19 Bruce Covernton	1.50	.70	.19
☐ 20 Willie Pless	2.00	.90	.25
☐ 21 Henry Williams	4.00	1.80	.50
☐ 22 Lui Passaglia	2.00	.90	.25

1994 JOGO CFL

The 1994 JOGO set consists of 310 standard-size cards released in three series. Reportedly 2,000 numbered sets were produced. The fronts feature color action player photos on a white card face, with a team color-coded jagged stripe on the bottom. The team helmet, player's name and position appear under the picture. The white backs contain biography and player profiles which are printed in red and black. The cards are numbered on the back according to teams.

	MINT	NRMT	EXC
COMPLETE SET (310)	75.00	34.00	9.50
COMPLETE SERIES 1 (110)	20.00	9.00	2.50
COMPLETE SERIES 2 (110)	20.00	9.00	2.50
COMPLETE SERIES 3 (90)	35.00	16.00	4.40

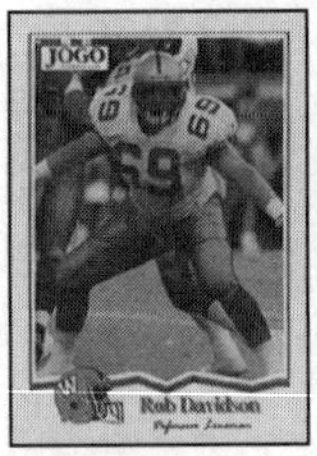

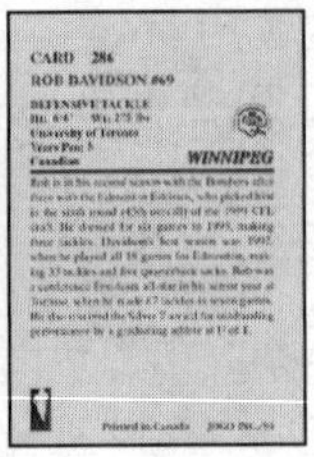

COMMON CARD (1-110)	.15	.07	.02
COMMON CARD (111-220)	.15	.07	.02
COMMON CARD (221-310)	.30	.14	.04
☐ 1 Danny Barrett	.50	.23	.06
☐ 2 Remi Trudel	.15	.07	.02
☐ 3 Terry Baker	.25	.11	.03
☐ 4 Paul Clatney	.15	.07	.02
☐ 5 Michael Richardson	.75	.35	.09
☐ 6 John Kropke	.25	.11	.03
☐ 7 Glenn Kulka	.25	.11	.03
☐ 8 Daved Benefield	.25	.11	.03
☐ 9 Derek MacCready	.15	.07	.02
☐ 10 Jessie Small	.25	.11	.03
☐ 11 Chris Gioskos	.15	.07	.02
☐ 12 Gregg Stumon	.25	.11	.03
☐ 13 Lee Johnson	.25	.11	.03
☐ 14 Michael Jefferson Jr.	.15	.07	.02
☐ 15 Mario Perry	.15	.07	.02
☐ 16 Joe Mero	.15	.07	.02
☐ 17 Reggie Barnes	.25	.11	.03
☐ 18 Mike Stowell	.15	.07	.02
☐ 19 Tony Moss	.15	.07	.02
☐ 20 Antoine Worthman	.15	.07	.02
☐ 21 Joe Fuller	.15	.07	.02
☐ 22 Daniel Hunter	.15	.07	.02
☐ 23 Doug Flutie	2.50	1.10	.30
☐ 24 Douglas Craft	.50	.23	.06
☐ 25 Lubo Zizakovic	.15	.07	.02
☐ 26 Srecko Zizakovic	.15	.07	.02
☐ 27 Stu Laird	.25	.11	.03
☐ 28 Brian Wiggins	.25	.11	.03
☐ 29 Will Johnson	.60	.25	.07
☐ 30 David Sapunjis	1.00	.45	.12
☐ 31 Rocco Romano	.15	.07	.02
☐ 32 Raymond Biggs	.15	.07	.02
☐ 33 Ken Moore	.15	.07	.02
☐ 34 Matt Finlay	.25	.11	.03
☐ 35 Ian Sinclair	.25	.11	.03
☐ 36 Glen Scrivener	.15	.07	.02
☐ 37 Less Browne	.25	.11	.03
☐ 38 Darren Flutie	1.50	.70	.19
☐ 39 Freeman Baysinger	.15	.07	.02
☐ 40 Kent Austin	.50	.23	.06
☐ 41 Donovan Wright	.15	.07	.02
☐ 42 Cory Philpot	1.50	.70	.19
☐ 43 Tom Europe	.15	.07	.02
☐ 44 Giulio Caravatta	.15	.07	.02
☐ 45 Mike Clemons	1.50	.70	.19
☐ 46 Leon Hatziioannou	.15	.07	.02
☐ 47 Blaine Schmidt	.15	.07	.02
☐ 48 Reggie Pleasant	.60	.25	.07
☐ 49 Paul Masotti	.25	.11	.03
☐ 50 Pierre Vercheval	.25	.11	.03
☐ 51 Duane Forde	.15	.07	.02
☐ 52 Jeff Fairholm	.25	.11	.03
☐ 53 Carl Coulter	.15	.07	.02
☐ 54 Bobby Gordon	.15	.07	.02
☐ 55 Mike Jovanovich	.15	.07	.02
☐ 56 Chris Johnstone	.15	.07	.02
☐ 57 Matt Pearce	.15	.07	.02
☐ 58 Bob Cameron	.60	.25	.07
☐ 59 Brett MacNeil	.15	.07	.02
☐ 60 Blaise Bryant	.40	.18	.05
☐ 61 Chris Tsangaris	.15	.07	.02
☐ 62 Dave Vankoughnett	.15	.07	.02
☐ 63 Gerald Alphin	.25	.11	.03
☐ 64 Alfred Jackson	2.00	.90	.25
☐ 65 Jayson Dzikowicz	.15	.07	.02
☐ 66 Bobby Evans	.15	.07	.02
☐ 67 Dave Ridgway	.60	.25	.07
☐ 68 Bobby Jurasin	.25	.11	.03
☐ 69 Dan Payne	.15	.07	.02
☐ 70 Ray Elgaard	.60	.25	.07
☐ 71 Dan Farthing	.15	.07	.02
☐ 72 Glen Suitor	.25	.11	.03
☐ 73 Mike Saunders	1.00	.45	.12
☐ 74 Brent Matich	.15	.07	.02
☐ 75 Scott Hendrickson	.15	.07	.02
☐ 76 Dan Rashovich	.15	.07	.02
☐ 77 Wayne Drinkwalter	.15	.07	.02
☐ 78 Larry Wruck	.25	.11	.03
☐ 79 J.P. Izquierdo	.15	.07	.02
☐ 80 Jed Roberts	.15	.07	.02
☐ 81 Michel Bourgeau	.25	.11	.03
☐ 82 Malvin Hunter	.15	.07	.02
☐ 83 Bruce Dickson	.15	.07	.02
☐ 84 Jim Sandusky	.25	.11	.03
☐ 85 Mike DuMaresq	.15	.07	.02
☐ 86 Tracy Gravely	.25	.11	.03
☐ 87 Tracey Ham	1.00	.45	.12
☐ 88 John Congemi	.25	.11	.03
☐ 89 Darrell Corbin	.15	.07	.02
☐ 90 Maurice Kelly	.25	.11	.03
☐ 91 Doug Flutie MVP	2.50	1.10	.30
☐ 92 Alfred Jordan	.25	.11	.03
☐ 93 Curtis Mayfield	.40	.18	.05
☐ 94 David Hollis	.15	.07	.02
☐ 95 James Blake	.15	.07	.02
☐ 96 Anthony Blue	.25	.11	.03
☐ 97 Jeffrey Sawyer	.15	.07	.02
☐ 98 Al Whiting	.15	.07	.02
☐ 99 Brad LaCombe	.15	.07	.02
☐ 100 Wally Zatylny	.25	.11	.03
☐ 101 Bob Torrance	.15	.07	.02
☐ 102 Jeffery Fields	.15	.07	.02
☐ 103 John G. Motton Jr.	.25	.11	.03
☐ 104 Todd Wiseman	.15	.07	.02
☐ 105 Mike O'Shea	1.00	.45	.12
☐ 106 Scott Douglas	.15	.07	.02
☐ 107 Dale Sanderson	.15	.07	.02
☐ 108 David Diaz-Infante	.25	.11	.03
☐ 109 Michael Kiselak	.15	.07	.02
☐ 110 Chris Thieneman	.15	.07	.02
☐ 111 Horace Brooks	.25	.11	.03
☐ 112 Andre Francis	.25	.11	.03
☐ 113 Nick Mazzoli	.15	.07	.02
☐ 114 Irv Daymond	.15	.07	.02
☐ 115 Alfred Smith	.15	.07	.02
☐ 116 Stephen Jones	.40	.18	.05
☐ 117 Bruce Beaton	.15	.07	.02
☐ 118 Corey Dowden	.15	.07	.02
☐ 119 Gerald Collins	.25	.11	.03
☐ 120 Joe Washington	.25	.11	.03
☐ 121 Irvin Smith	.15	.07	.02
☐ 122 Harold Nash Jr.	.25	.11	.03
☐ 123 Ray Savage Jr.	.15	.07	.02
☐ 124 Billy Scott	.15	.07	.02
☐ 125 Aaron Kanner	.15	.07	.02
☐ 126 Ben Williams	.40	.18	.05
☐ 127 Keith Browner	.25	.11	.03
☐ 128 Eros Sanchez	.25	.11	.03
☐ 129 Don Caparotti	.15	.07	.02
☐ 130 Earnest Fields	.15	.07	.02
☐ 131 O.J. Brigance	1.00	.45	.12
☐ 132 Walter Wilson	.25	.11	.03
☐ 133 Allen Pitts	.40	.18	.05
☐ 134 Tony Stewart	.25	.11	.03
☐ 135 Marvin Pope	.15	.07	.02
☐ 136 Tony Martino	.15	.07	.02
☐ 137 Vince Danielsen	.15	.07	.02
☐ 138 Pee Wee Smith	.50	.23	.06
☐ 139 Bruce Covernton	.60	.25	.07
☐ 140 Greg Knox	.15	.07	.02
☐ 141 Gerald Vaughn	.15	.07	.02
☐ 142 Jay McNeil	.15	.07	.02
☐ 143 Larry Ryckman OWN	.15	.07	.02
☐ 144 Blair Zerr	.15	.07	.02
☐ 145 Danny McManus	.75	.35	.09
☐ 146 Jamie Taras	.15	.07	.02
☐ 147 Kelly Sims	.25	.11	.03
☐ 148 Denny Chronopoulos	.15	.07	.02
☐ 149 Enis Jackson	.15	.07	.02
☐ 150 Virgil Robertson	.15	.07	.02
☐ 151 Tyrone Chatman	.15	.07	.02
☐ 152 Brian Forde	.15	.07	.02
☐ 153 Andrew Stewart	.15	.07	.02
☐ 154 Ryan Hanson	.15	.07	.02
☐ 155 Francois Belanger	.15	.07	.02
☐ 156 Tony O'Billovich	.15	.07	.02
☐ 157 Erik White	.25	.11	.03
☐ 158 Kevin Whitley	.15	.07	.02
☐ 159 Chris Schultz	.25	.11	.03
☐ 160 Mike Campbell	.15	.07	.02
☐ 161 Wayne Lammle	.15	.07	.02
☐ 162 Keith Ballard	.15	.07	.02
☐ 163 Neil Fort	.15	.07	.02
☐ 164 Charles Anthony	.15	.07	.02
☐ 165 John Buddenberg	.15	.07	.02
☐ 166 Allan Boyko	.15	.07	.02
☐ 167 Paul Randolph	.15	.07	.02
☐ 168 Gerald Wilcox	.25	.11	.03
☐ 169 Brendan Rogers	.15	.07	.02
☐ 170 Kim Phillips	.15	.07	.02
☐ 171 David Williams	.25	.11	.03
☐ 172 James Pruitt	.25	.11	.03
☐ 173 Kevin O'Brien	.25	.11	.03
☐ 174 Tre Everett	.25	.11	.03
☐ 175 Hurlie Brown	.15	.07	.02
☐ 176 Malcolm Frank	.15	.07	.02
☐ 177 Sean Brantley	.15	.07	.02
☐ 178 Aaron Ruffin	.15	.07	.02
☐ 179 Anthony Drawhorn	.25	.11	.03
☐ 180 Larry Thompson	.75	.35	.09
☐ 181 Brooks Findlay	.15	.07	.02
☐ 182 Dallas Rysavy	.15	.07	.02
☐ 183 Ray Bernard	.15	.07	.02
☐ 184 Donald Narcisse	.60	.25	.07
☐ 185 Warren Jones	.25	.11	.03
☐ 186 Tom Gerhart	.15	.07	.02
☐ 187 David Robinson Jr.	.50	.23	.06
☐ 188 Damon Allen	.60	.25	.07
☐ 189 Henry Williams	1.00	.45	.12
☐ 190 Jay Christensen	.25	.11	.03
☐ 191 Trent Brown	.15	.07	.02
☐ 192 Rod Connop	.15	.07	.02
☐ 193 Michael Soles	.25	.11	.03

☐ 194 Vance Hammond	.15	.07	.02
☐ 195 Maurice Miller	.15	.07	.02
☐ 196 Shar Pourdanesh	2.00	.90	.25
☐ 197 Elfrid Payton	.25	.11	.03
☐ 198 Ken Benson	.15	.07	.02
☐ 199 David Maeva	.15	.07	.02
☐ 200 Carlos Huerta	.25	.11	.03
☐ 201 Prince Wimbley III	.25	.11	.03
☐ 202 Anthony Calvillo	2.00	.90	.25
☐ 203 Kenny Wilhite	.60	.25	.07
☐ 204 Peter Shorts	.15	.07	.02
☐ 205 Willie Fears	.25	.11	.03
☐ 206 Rod Harris	.75	.35	.09
☐ 207 Terry Wright	.15	.07	.02
☐ 208 Stephen Bates	.25	.11	.03
☐ 209 John Hood	.25	.11	.03
☐ 210 Steven McKee	.15	.07	.02
☐ 211 Richard Nurse	.15	.07	.02
☐ 212 Lee Knight	.15	.07	.02
☐ 213 Joey Jauch	.25	.11	.03
☐ 214 Dave Richardson	.15	.07	.02
☐ 215 Paul Bushey	.15	.07	.02
☐ 216 Lou Cafazzo	.15	.07	.02
☐ 217 Don Odegard	.15	.07	.02
☐ 218 Mark Ledbetter	.15	.07	.02
☐ 219 Curtis Moore	.15	.07	.02
☐ 220 CFL Team Helmets (Set number card)	.25	.11	.03
☐ 221 Patrick Burke	.30	.14	.04
☐ 222 Dean Noel	.60	.25	.07
☐ 223 Leonard Johnson	.30	.14	.04
☐ 224 Darren Joseph	.25	.11	.03
☐ 225 Adam Rita CO	.30	.14	.04
☐ 226 Fred Ward	.60	.25	.07
☐ 227 Tony Bailey	.30	.14	.04
☐ 228 Frank Marof	.30	.14	.04
☐ 229 Andrew Thomas	.60	.25	.07
☐ 230 Peter Tuipulotu	.60	.25	.07
☐ 231 Shawn Beals	.30	.14	.04
☐ 232 Ken Watson	.30	.14	.04
☐ 233 Robert Holland	.30	.14	.04
☐ 234 John Terry	.30	.14	.04
☐ 235 Michael Philbrick	.30	.14	.04
☐ 236 Reggie Slack	1.25	.55	.16
☐ 237 Gary Wilkerson UER (First name misspelled Garry on back)	.30	.14	.04
☐ 238 Brett Young	.30	.14	.04
☐ 239 Eric Carter	.60	.25	.07
☐ 240 Sheldon Canley	.60	.25	.07
☐ 241 Lester Smith	.30	.14	.04
☐ 242 Donald Igwebuike	.60	.25	.07
☐ 243 Keith Ballard	.30	.14	.04
☐ 244 Roger Reinson	.30	.14	.04
☐ 245 Duane Dmytryshyn	.30	.14	.04
☐ 246 Marvin Coleman	.30	.14	.04
☐ 247 Ken Burress	.30	.14	.04
☐ 248 Jearld Baylis	.60	.25	.07
☐ 249 Rickey Foggie	.75	.35	.09
☐ 250 Dave Dinnall	.60	.25	.07
☐ 251 Darrell Harle	.30	.14	.04
☐ 252 P.J. Martin	.60	.25	.07
☐ 253 Val St. Germain	.30	.14	.04
☐ 254 Tim Cofield	.75	.35	.09
☐ 255 Charles Gordon	.30	.14	.04
☐ 256 Keilly Rush	.30	.14	.04
☐ 257 James Pruitt	.60	.25	.07
☐ 258 Brian McCurdy	.60	.25	.07
☐ 259 Joe Johnson UER (Front says last name is Jackson)	.60	.25	.07
☐ 260 Joe Burgos	.30	.14	.04
☐ 261 Tim Jackson	.30	.14	.04
☐ 262 George Nimako	.60	.25	.07
☐ 263 Hency Charles	.30	.14	.04
☐ 264 Eric Drage	.60	.25	.07
☐ 265 Joe Sardo	.30	.14	.04
☐ 266 Norm Casola	.30	.14	.04
☐ 267 Dave Irwin	.60	.25	.07
☐ 268 Tommy Henry	.30	.14	.04
☐ 269 Taly Williams	.30	.14	.04
☐ 270 Swift Burch III	.30	.14	.04
☐ 271 Keita Crespina	.30	.14	.04
☐ 272 Michael Brooks	.60	.25	.07
☐ 273 Chris Armstrong	.60	.25	.07
☐ 274 Karl Anthony	.30	.14	.04
☐ 275 David Archer	3.00	1.35	.35
☐ 276 Kevin Robson	.30	.14	.04
☐ 277 Jamie Holland	.60	.25	.07
☐ 278 Don Smith	.30	.14	.04
☐ 279 Norris Thomas	.60	.25	.07
☐ 280 Matt Dunigan	1.25	.55	.16
☐ 281 Greg Clarke	.30	.14	.04
☐ 282 Del Lyles	.30	.14	.04
☐ 283 Alan Wetmore	.30	.14	.04
☐ 284 Errol Brown	.30	.14	.04
☐ 285 Ryan Carey	.30	.14	.04
☐ 286 Rob Davidson	.30	.14	.04
☐ 287 Ed Kucy SP	1.50	.70	.19
☐ 288 Tom Burgess	1.00	.45	.12
☐ 289 Peter Miller	.30	.14	.04
☐ 290 Dale Joseph	.30	.14	.04
☐ 291 Chris Burns	.30	.14	.04
☐ 292 Nathaniel Bolton	.60	.25	.07
☐ 293 Byron Williams	.15	.07	.02
☐ 294 David Harper	.30	.14	.04
☐ 295 Jason K. Wallace	.30	.14	.04
☐ 296 Greg Joelson	.30	.14	.04
☐ 297 Doug Parrish	.30	.14	.04
☐ 298 Sean Fleming	.30	.14	.04
☐ 299 Mike Lee	.60	.25	.07
☐ 300 Chris Morris	.60	.25	.07
☐ 301 Eddie Brown	1.00	.45	.12
☐ 302 Blake Dermott	.30	.14	.04
☐ 303 Brian Walling	.25	.11	.03
☐ 304 Charles Miles	.60	.25	.07
☐ 305 Robin Crifo	.60	.25	.07
☐ 306 Nick Benjamin	.25	.11	.03
☐ 307 Jim Speros PR/OWN	.60	.25	.07
☐ 308 Robert Presbury	.30	.14	.04
☐ 309 Mike Pringle	2.50	1.10	.30
☐ 310 Jon Volpe	1.00	.45	.12

1994 JOGO CFL Hall of Fame C

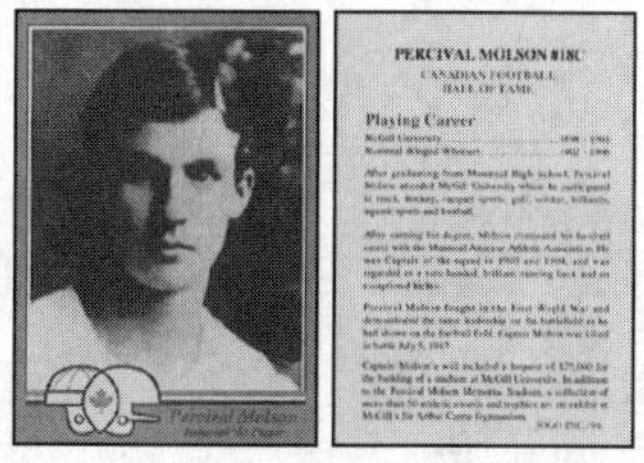

These 25 cards measure the standard size. The fronts feature black-and-white player photos with metallic gold borders. Red, white, and blue stripes edge the bottom of the picture. The player's name appears in red lettering within the lower gold margin. On a white background, the backs carry the player's career years along with awards and honors he received.

	MINT	NRMT	EXC
COMPLETE SET (25)	18.00	8.00	2.20
COMMON CARD (C1-C25)	.75	.35	.09
☐ C1 Leo Lewis	2.00	.90	.25
☐ C2 Tom Brown	.75	.35	.09
☐ C3 Samuel Berger	.75	.35	.09
☐ C4 Dave Fennell	1.25	.55	.16
☐ C5 Arthur Chipman	.75	.35	.09
☐ C6 Tony Gabriel	1.25	.55	.16
☐ C7 Frank Clair	.75	.35	.09
☐ C8 Dean Griffing	.75	.35	.09
☐ C9 Hec Crighton	.75	.35	.09
☐ C10 Eddie James	.75	.35	.09
☐ C11 Andrew Currie	.75	.35	.09
☐ C12 Ab Box	.75	.35	.09
☐ C13 Gord Perry	.75	.35	.09
☐ C14 Terry Evanshen	2.00	.90	.25
☐ C15 Syd Halter	.75	.35	.09
☐ C16 Don Luzzi	1.25	.55	.16
☐ C17 Norm Kimball	.75	.35	.09
☐ C18 Percival Molson	.75	.35	.09
☐ C19 Bob Kramer	.75	.35	.09
☐ C20 Angelo Mosca	2.50	1.10	.30
☐ C21 Ralph Cooper	.75	.35	.09
☐ C22 Ken Charlton	.75	.35	.09
☐ C23 Jim Young	1.25	.55	.16
☐ C24 Joe Tubman	.75	.35	.09
☐ C25 Virgil Wagner	1.25	.55	.16

1994 JOGO CFL Hall of Fame D

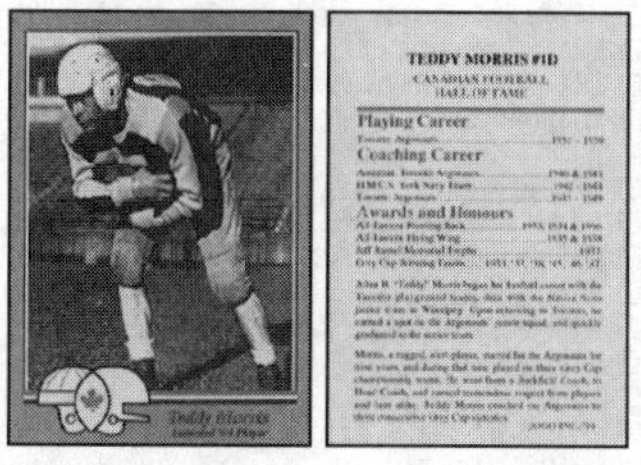

These 25 cards measure the standard size. The fronts feature black-and-white player photos with metallic gold borders. Red, white, and blue stripes edge the bottom of the picture. The player's name appears in red lettering within the lower gold margin. On a white background, the backs carry the player's career years along with awards and honors he received.

	MINT	NRMT	EXC
COMPLETE SET (25)	18.00	8.00	2.20
COMMON CARD (D1-D25)	.75	.35	.09
☐ D1 Teddy Morris	.75	.35	.09
☐ D2 John Ferraro	.75	.35	.09
☐ D3 Len Back	.75	.35	.09
☐ D4 Harold Ballard	1.25	.55	.16
☐ D5 Seppi DuMoulin	.75	.35	.09
☐ D6 Herm Harrison	1.25	.55	.16
☐ D7 William Foulds	.75	.35	.09
☐ D8 Peter Dalla Riva	1.25	.55	.16
☐ D9 John Metras	.75	.35	.09
☐ D10 Don Sutherin	1.25	.55	.16
☐ D11 Ken Preston	.75	.35	.09
☐ D12 Ellison Kelly	1.25	.55	.16
☐ D13 Annis Stukus	.75	.35	.09
☐ D14 Brian Timmis	.75	.35	.09
☐ D15 Ralph Sazio	.75	.35	.09
☐ D16 Hugh Stirling	.75	.35	.09
☐ D17 Jimmie Simpson	.75	.35	.09
☐ D18 Russ Rebholz	.75	.35	.09
☐ D19 Seymour Wilson	.75	.35	.09
☐ D20 Paul Rowe	.75	.35	.09
☐ D21 Jeff Russel	.75	.35	.09
☐ D22 Art Stevenson	.75	.35	.09
☐ D23 Whit Tucker	1.25	.55	.16
☐ D24 Dave Thelen	1.25	.55	.16
☐ D25 Tom Wilkinson	2.00	.90	.25

1994 JOGO CFL Hall of Fame Inductees

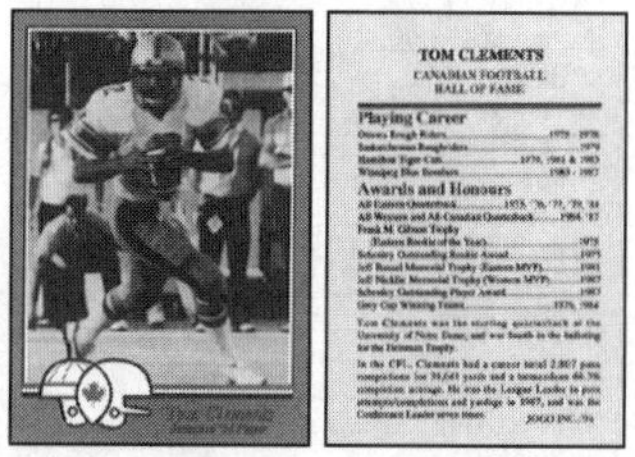

This five-card standard-size set honors the 1994 inductees of the Canadian Football Hall of Fame. The fronts feature black-and-white player photos with metallic gold borders. Red, white, and black stripes edge the bottom of the picture. The player's name appears in red lettering within the lower gold margin. On a white background, the backs carry the player's career years along with awards and honors he received.

	MINT	NRMT	EXC
COMPLETE SET (5)	5.00	2.20	.60
COMMON CARD (1-5)	.75	.35	.09
☐ 1 Bill Baker	1.00	.45	.12
☐ 2 Tom Clements	2.50	1.10	.30
☐ 3 Gene Gaines	1.00	.45	.12
☐ 4 Don McNaughton	.75	.35	.09
☐ 5 Title Card	.75	.35	.09

1994 JOGO CFL Missing Years

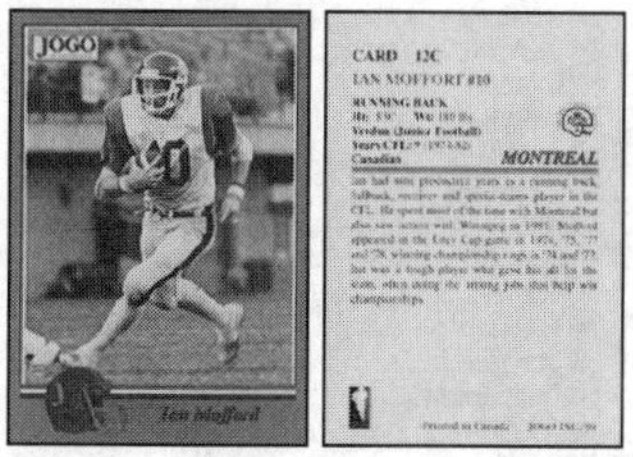

For the third year, JOGO created a "Missing Link" set to provide CFL fans with memories of their favorite players of the 1970s, since no CFL cards were produced from 1972-1981. JOGO produced 1,700 sets, of which 500 were broken to provide individual players with cards. Of the 1,200 complete sets, 200 were used for press and promotional give-aways. The 20-card set measures the standard size. The fronts feature black-and-white player photos with metallic gold borders. Red, white, and blue stripes edge the bottom of the picture. A blue helmet with the JOGO "J" is in the lower left corner, and the player's name appears in red lettering within the lower gold margin. On a white background, the backs carry player biography and career highlights.

	MINT	NRMT	EXC
COMPLETE SET (20)	12.00	5.50	1.50
COMMON CARD (C1-C20)	.50	.23	.06
☐ C1 Steve Ferrughelli UER (Photo actually John O'Leary)	1.50	.70	.19
☐ C2 Rhome Nixon	.75	.35	.09
☐ C3 Don Moorhead	.50	.23	.06
☐ C4 Mike Widger	.75	.35	.09
☐ C5 Pete Catan	.75	.35	.09
☐ C6 Ron Meeks	.50	.23	.06
☐ C7 Ezzret Anderson	1.25	.55	.16
☐ C8 Bill Hatanaka	.50	.23	.06
☐ C9 Joe Jackson	.75	.35	.09
☐ C10 Tom Campana	.75	.35	.09
☐ C11 Vernon Perry	1.00	.45	.12
☐ C12 Ian Mofford	.75	.35	.09
☐ C13 Wally Highsmith	.75	.35	.09
☐ C14 Jake Dunlop	.75	.35	.09
☐ C15 Bill Stevenson	.50	.23	.06
☐ C16 Pete Lavorato	.50	.23	.06
☐ C17 Cyril McFall	.50	.23	.06
☐ C18 Maurice Butler	.50	.23	.06
☐ C19 Tom Pate	1.25	.55	.16
☐ C20 Eugene Clark	1.25	.55	.16

1995 JOGO CFL

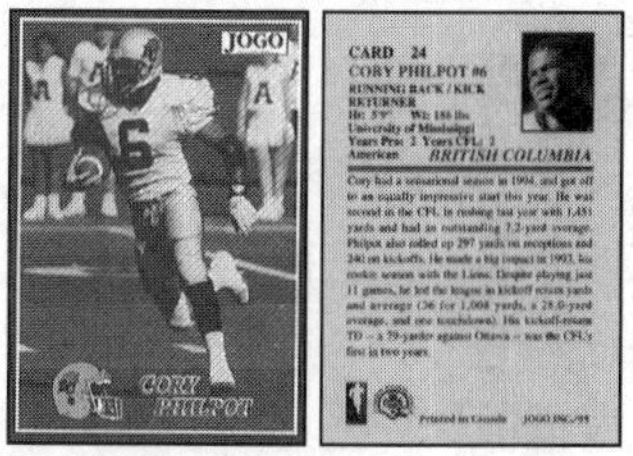

This 399-card standard-size set of CFL players was released by Jogo in three series and one Update series. The cards feature color player photos inside a thin white and blue outside border. The player's name and team helmet are printed below. The backs carry biographical and career information. Jogo reports there were 1000 numbered sets of series 1-3 produced for sale to the hobby and 200 additional sets distributed to the players. The Update set was limited to 850 sets produced. The Doug Flutie M.V.P. card (#330) carries the set number.

	MINT	NRMT	EXC
COMPLETE SET (399)	145.00	65.00	18.00
COMPLETE SERIES 1 (110)	40.00	18.00	5.00
COMPLETE SERIES 2 (110)	40.00	18.00	5.00
COMPLETE SERIES 3 (110)	40.00	18.00	5.00
COMPLETE UPDATE SET (69)	25.00	11.00	3.10
COMMON CARD (1-399)	.20	.09	.03
☐ 1 Doug Flutie	3.00	1.35	.35
☐ 2 Lubo Zizakovic	.20	.09	.03
☐ 3 Srecko Zizakovic	.20	.09	.03
☐ 4 Greg Knox	.20	.09	.03
☐ 5 Kenny Walker	.35	.16	.04
☐ 6 Raymond Biggs	.20	.09	.03
☐ 7 Stu Laird	.35	.16	.04
☐ 8 Jeff Garcia	1.00	.45	.12
☐ 9 Alfred Jordan	.35	.16	.04
☐ 10 Tracy Gravely	.35	.16	.04
☐ 11 Tracy Ham	1.00	.45	.12
☐ 12 O.J. Brigance	1.25	.55	.16
☐ 13 Mike Pringle	1.50	.70	.19
☐ 14 Nick Subis	.20	.09	.03
☐ 15 Irvin Smith	.20	.09	.03
☐ 16 Shar Pourdanesh	1.25	.55	.16
☐ 17 Lester Smith	.20	.09	.03
☐ 18 Josh Miller	.20	.09	.03
☐ 19 Jamie Taras	.20	.09	.03
☐ 20 Darren Flutie	1.50	.70	.19
☐ 21 Danny McManus	.75	.35	.09
☐ 22 Spencer McLennan	.20	.09	.03
☐ 23 Tony Collier	.20	.09	.03
☐ 24 Cory Philpot	1.00	.45	.12
☐ 25 Ian Sinclair	.35	.16	.04
☐ 26 Dave Chaytors	.20	.09	.03
☐ 27 Dave Ritchie UER Richie on front	.20	.09	.03
☐ 28 Rob Wallow	.20	.09	.03
☐ 29 Brad Breedlove	.50	.23	.06
☐ 30 Adrion Smith	.20	.09	.03
☐ 31 Stephen Bates	.20	.09	.03
☐ 32 Don Odegard	.20	.09	.03
☐ 33 Eric Nelson	.20	.09	.03
☐ 34 Danton Barto	.20	.09	.03
☐ 35 Donald Smith	.20	.09	.03
☐ 36 Gary Morris	.20	.09	.03
☐ 37 Michael Jovanovich	.20	.09	.03
☐ 38 Danny Barrett	.50	.23	.06
☐ 39 Ray Alexander	.35	.16	.04
☐ 40 John Kropke	.35	.16	.04
☐ 41 Remi Trudel	.20	.09	.03
☐ 42 Ray Bernard	.20	.09	.03
☐ 43 Pat Mahon	.20	.09	.03
☐ 44 Dan Murphy	.20	.09	.03
☐ 45 Stefen Reid	.20	.09	.03
☐ 46 Marcus Gates	.20	.09	.03
☐ 47 Tom Gerhart	.20	.09	.03
☐ 48 Mike Kiselak	.20	.09	.03
☐ 49 David Archer	2.00	.90	.25
☐ 50 Tommie Smith	.20	.09	.03
☐ 51 Roman Anderson	.20	.09	.03
☐ 52 Tony Burse	.20	.09	.03
☐ 53 Todd Jordan	.20	.09	.03
☐ 54 Peter Shorts	.20	.09	.03
☐ 55 Jimmy Klingler	.75	.35	.09
☐ 56 Mark Ledbetter	.20	.09	.03
☐ 57 Thomas Rayam	.20	.09	.03
☐ 58 Andre Strode	.20	.09	.03
☐ 59 Eddie Davis	.20	.09	.03
☐ 60 Jimmie Reed	.20	.09	.03
☐ 61 Fernando Thomas	.20	.09	.03
☐ 62 Craig Gibson	.20	.09	.03
☐ 63 Akaba Delaney	.20	.09	.03
☐ 64 Mike Clemons	1.25	.55	.16
☐ 65 Kent Austin	.50	.23	.06
☐ 66 Joe Burgos	.20	.09	.03

□ 67 John Terry .20 .09 .03
□ 68 Don Wilson .20 .09 .03
□ 69 Eric Blount DE .20 .09 .03
□ 70 Reggie Barnes .35 .16 .04
□ 71 Darrick Branch .20 .09 .03
□ 72 P.J. Gleason .20 .09 .03
□ 73 Rod Connop .20 .09 .03
□ 74 J.P. Izquierdo .20 .09 .03
□ 75 Jed Roberts .20 .09 .03
□ 76 Jim Sandusky .35 .16 .04
□ 77 Chris Vargas .20 .09 .03
□ 78 Henry Williams .75 .35 .09
□ 79 Michael Soles .35 .16 .04
□ 80 Robert Holland .20 .09 .03
□ 81 Larry Wruck .35 .16 .04
□ 82 Dale Sanderson .20 .09 .03
□ 83 Anthony Calvillo .75 .35 .09
□ 84 Kalin Hall .20 .09 .03
□ 85 Sam Rogers .20 .09 .03
□ 86 Lee Knight .20 .09 .03
□ 87 Wally Zatylny .35 .16 .04
□ 88 Earl Winfield .50 .23 .06
□ 89 Dave Richardson .20 .09 .03
□ 90 Mike O'Shea .75 .35 .09
□ 91 Bruce Boyko .20 .09 .03
□ 92 Dave Ridgway .50 .23 .06
□ 93 Dave Van Belleghem .20 .09 .03
□ 94 Mike Anderson .20 .09 .03
□ 95 Ray Elgaard .50 .23 .06
□ 96 Dan Rashovich .20 .09 .03
□ 97 Wayne Drinkwalter .20 .09 .03
□ 98 Brent Matich .20 .09 .03
□ 99 Joe Fuller .20 .09 .03
□ 100 Freeman Baysinger Jr. .20 .09 .03
□ 101 Billy Joe Tolliver .50 .23 .06
□ 102 Martin Patton .20 .09 .03
□ 103 Wayne Walker .35 .16 .04
□ 104 Bjorn Nittmo .75 .35 .09
□ 105 Alan Wetmore .20 .09 .03
□ 106 K.D. Williams .20 .09 .03
□ 107 Bob Cameron .50 .23 .06
□ 108 Ken Burress .20 .09 .03
□ 109 Chris Johnstone .20 .09 .03
□ 110 Allan Boyko .20 .09 .03
□ 111 David Sapunjis 1.00 .45 .12
□ 112 Matt Finlay .35 .16 .04
□ 113 Jamie Crysdale .20 .09 .03
□ 114 Marvin Pope .20 .09 .03
□ 115 Craig Brenner .20 .09 .03
□ 116 Vince Danielsen .20 .09 .03
□ 117 Will Johnson .50 .23 .06
□ 118 Tony Stewart .20 .09 .03
□ 119 Chris Wright .50 .23 .06
□ 120 Grant Carter .20 .09 .03
□ 121 Karl Anthony .20 .09 .03
□ 122 Elfrid Payton .35 .16 .04
□ 123 Ken Watson .20 .09 .03
□ 124 Cory Mantyka .20 .09 .03
□ 125 Todd Furdyk .20 .09 .03
□ 126 Keithen McCant .20 .09 .03
□ 127 Ryan Hanson .20 .09 .03
□ 128 Glen Scrivener .20 .09 .03
□ 129 Mike Trevathan .50 .23 .06
□ 130 Tom Europe .20 .09 .03
□ 131 Giulio Caravatta .20 .09 .03
□ 132 Eddie Lee Thomas .20 .09 .03
□ 133 Shelton Quarles .20 .09 .03
□ 134 Robert E. Davis II .20 .09 .03
□ 135 Damon Allen .60 .25 .07
□ 136 Derek Brown .20 .09 .03
□ 137 Joe Horn .50 .23 .06
□ 138 John Tweet Martin .20 .09 .03
□ 139 Greg Battle .50 .23 .06
□ 140 Ed Berry .20 .09 .03
□ 141 Irv Daymond .20 .09 .03
□ 142 Jay Christensen .35 .16 .04
□ 143 Michael Richardson .50 .23 .06
□ 144 James Ellingson .35 .16 .04
□ 145 Brett Young .35 .16 .04
□ 146 Kai Bjorn .20 .09 .03
□ 147 James Monroe .20 .09 .03
□ 148 Eric Geter .20 .09 .03
□ 149 Emanuel Martin .20 .09 .03
□ 150 DeWayne Knight .20 .09 .03
□ 151 Mike Saunders 1.00 .45 .12
□ 152 David Harper .20 .09 .03
□ 153 Bobby Humphery .35 .16 .04
□ 154 Charles Franks .20 .09 .03
□ 155 Jeff Sawyer .20 .09 .03
□ 156 John Buddenberg .20 .09 .03
□ 157 Willie Fears .35 .16 .04
□ 158 Jason Wallace .20 .09 .03
□ 159 Robert Gordon .20 .09 .03
□ 160 Scott Player .35 .16 .04
□ 161 York Kurinsky .20 .09 .03
□ 162 Stephen Anderson .20 .09 .03
□ 163 Shonte Peoples .20 .09 .03
□ 164 Angelo Snipes .50 .23 .06
□ 165 Ted Long .20 .09 .03
□ 166 Anthony Drawhorn .35 .16 .04
□ 167 Marvin Graves .20 .09 .03
□ 168 Joe Sardo .20 .09 .03
□ 169 Duane Forde .20 .09 .03
□ 170 P.J. Martin .20 .09 .03
□ 171 Jock Climie .20 .09 .03
□ 172 Jeff Fairholm .35 .16 .04
□ 173 Tommy Henry .20 .09 .03
□ 174 Paul Masotti .35 .16 .04
□ 175 Chris Green .20 .09 .03
□ 176 Bruce Dickson .20 .09 .03
□ 177 Darian Hagan .20 .09 .03
□ 178 Malvin Hunter .20 .09 .03
□ 179 Steve Krupey .20 .09 .03
□ 180 Sean Fleming .20 .09 .03
□ 181 Blake Dermott .35 .16 .04
□ 182 Leroy Blugh .35 .16 .04
□ 183 Steve Taylor .50 .23 .06
□ 184 Eric Carter .35 .16 .04
□ 185 Jessie Small .35 .16 .04
□ 186 Blaine Schmidt .20 .09 .03
□ 187 Lou Cafazzo .20 .09 .03
□ 188 Doug Davies .20 .09 .03
□ 189 Kelvin Means .20 .09 .03
□ 190 Derek R. Grier .20 .09 .03
□ 191 Darren Joseph .35 .16 .04
□ 192 Aaron Ruffin .20 .09 .03
□ 193 Dan Farthing .20 .09 .03
□ 194 Dan Payne .20 .09 .03
□ 195 Brooks Findlay .20 .09 .03
□ 196 Paul Vajda .20 .09 .03
□ 197 Ron Goetz .20 .09 .03
□ 198 Tim Broady .20 .09 .03
□ 199 Terryl Ulmer .20 .09 .03
□ 200 Harold Nash Jr. .20 .09 .03
□ 201 Mike Stowell .20 .09 .03
□ 202 Ben Williams .35 .16 .04
□ 203 Curtis Mayfield .35 .16 .04
□ 204 Reggie Rogers .35 .16 .04
□ 205 Donnell Johnson .20 .09 .03
□ 206 Jon Heidenreich .20 .09 .03
□ 207 Ronald Perry .20 .09 .03
□ 208 Robbie Keen .20 .09 .03
□ 209 Alex Mash Jr. .20 .09 .03
□ 210 Jason Mallett .20 .09 .03
□ 211 Miles Gorrell .20 .09 .03
□ 212 Juran Bolden .75 .35 .09
□ 213 Greg Clark .20 .09 .03
□ 214 Ryan Carey .20 .09 .03
□ 215 Del Lyles .20 .09 .03
□ 216 Brendan Rogers .20 .09 .03
□ 217 Kevin Robson .20 .09 .03
□ 218 Paul Randolph .20 .09 .03
□ 219 Shannon Garrett .20 .09 .03
□ 220 Charlie Clemons .20 .09 .03
□ 221 Matt Dunigan 1.25 .55 .16
□ 222 Jay McNeil .20 .09 .03
□ 223 Denny Chronopoulos .20 .09 .03
□ 224 Bobby Pandelidis .20 .09 .03
□ 225 Bruce Beaton .20 .09 .03
□ 226 Mark Pearce .20 .09 .03
□ 227 Rocco Romano .20 .09 .03
□ 228 Alondra Johnson .35 .16 .04
□ 229 Tony Martino .20 .09 .03
□ 230 John James .20 .09 .03
□ 231 Courtney Griffin .20 .09 .03
□ 232 Robert Davis .20 .09 .03
□ 233 Manny Hazard .35 .16 .04
□ 234 Joe Mero .20 .09 .03
□ 235 Maurice Kelly .35 .16 .04
□ 236 Michael Morreale .20 .09 .03
□ 237 Reggie Slack .50 .23 .06
□ 238 Greg Eaglin .20 .09 .03
□ 239 Noah Cantor .20 .09 .03
□ 240 Shawn Daniels .20 .09 .03
□ 241 Charles Gordon .20 .09 .03
□ 242 Enis Jackson .20 .09 .03
□ 243 Matt Clark .35 .16 .04
□ 244 David Lucas .20 .09 .03
□ 245 Roger Hennig .20 .09 .03
□ 246 Leonard Nelson .20 .09 .03
□ 247 George Bethune .20 .09 .03
□ 248 Maurice Miller .20 .09 .03
□ 249 Kenny Walker .35 .16 .04
□ 250 Andre Ware 1.50 .70 .19
□ 251 Jay Macias .20 .09 .03
□ 252 Mark Ricks .20 .09 .03
□ 253 Chris Tsangaris .20 .09 .03
□ 254 Wayne Lammle .20 .09 .03
□ 255 Derek MacCready .20 .09 .03
□ 256 Paul Yatkowski .20 .09 .03
□ 257 Horace Brooks .35 .16 .04
□ 258 Kerry Brown .20 .09 .03
□ 259 Jude St. John .20 .09 .03
□ 260 Mike Schad 1.50 .70 .19
□ 261 Malcolm Frank .20 .09 .03
□ 262 Kenny Wilhite .35 .16 .04
□ 263 Billy Hess .20 .09 .03
□ 264 Grady Cavness .35 .16 .04
□ 265 Roosevelt Collins Jr. .20 .09 .03
□ 266 Darren Muilenberg .20 .09 .03
□ 267 Kitrick Taylor .75 .35 .09
□ 268 Chuck Esty .20 .09 .03
□ 269 Myron M. Wise .20 .09 .03
□ 270 James King .20 .09 .03
□ 271 Jim Kemp .75 .35 .09
□ 272 Oscar Giles .50 .23 .06
□ 273 Dave Ritchie CO .20 .09 .03
□ 274 Joe Kralik .20 .09 .03
□ 275 Troy Mills .20 .09 .03
□ 276 Mark Stock .20 .09 .03
□ 277 Pierre Vercheval .35 .16 .04
□ 278 Terry Baker .35 .16 .04
□ 279 Scott Douglas .20 .09 .03
□ 280 Leon Hatziioannou .20 .09 .03
□ 281 Jeff Cummins .50 .23 .06
□ 282 Allen Pitts .50 .23 .06
□ 283 Ken Walcott .20 .09 .03
□ 284 Swift Burch III .20 .09 .03
□ 285 Charles Davis .20 .09 .03
□ 286 Leo Groenewegen .20 .09 .03
□ 287 Bennie Goods .35 .16 .04
□ 288 Craig Hendrickson .20 .09 .03
□ 289 John Kalin .20 .09 .03
□ 290 Trent Brown .20 .09 .03
□ 291 Marc Tobert .20 .09 .03
□ 292 Nick Mazzoli .20 .09 .03
□ 293 Singor Mobley .20 .09 .03
□ 294 Dondre Owens .20 .09 .03
□ 295 Kerwin Bell .75 .35 .09
□ 296 Mike Kerrigan .50 .23 .06
□ 297 Hassan Bailey .20 .09 .03
□ 298 Frank Marof .20 .09 .03
□ 299 Derrick McAdoo .35 .16 .04
□ 300 Brian McCurdy .35 .16 .04
□ 301 Larry Thompson .50 .23 .06
□ 302 Errol Brown .20 .09 .03
□ 303 Troy Alexander .20 .09 .03
□ 304 Dave Pitcher .20 .09 .03
□ 305 Joey Jauch .35 .16 .04
□ 306 Gene Makowsky .20 .09 .03
□ 307 Ventson Donelson .20 .09 .03
□ 308 Gary Rogers .20 .09 .03
□ 309 Carl Coulter .20 .09 .03
□ 310 Chris Gioskos .20 .09 .03
□ 311 Michael DuMaresq .20 .09 .03
□ 312 Rob Crifo .20 .09 .03
□ 313 Terry Smith .20 .09 .03
□ 314 Don Robinson .20 .09 .03
□ 315 Uzooma Okeke .20 .09 .03
□ 316 Eldonta Osborne .20 .09 .03
□ 317 Rob Hitchcock .20 .09 .03
□ 318 Ray Savage Jr. .20 .09 .03
□ 319 Terry Beauford .20 .09 .03
□ 320 Cliff Baskerville .20 .09 .03
□ 321 David Gamble .20 .09 .03
□ 322 Darrius Watson .20 .09 .03
□ 323 Tim Daniel .20 .09 .03
□ 324 Len Johnson .20 .09 .03
□ 325 Blaise Bryant .35 .16 .04
□ 326 Doug Hocking .20 .09 .03
□ 327 Sean Graham .20 .09 .03
□ 328 Jamie Holland .35 .16 .04
□ 329 Matt Pearce .20 .09 .03
□ 330 Doug Flutie C.F.L. MVP 2.00 .90 .25
□ 331 Donald Narcisse .50 .23 .06
□ 332 Chuck Reed .20 .09 .03
□ 333 Sheldon Benoit .20 .09 .03
□ 334 John Motton .35 .16 .04
□ 335 Franco Grilla .20 .09 .03
□ 336 Brett MacNeil .20 .09 .03
□ 337 Wade Miller .20 .09 .03
□ 338 Steven McKee .20 .09 .03
□ 339 Brad Elberg .20 .09 .03
□ 340 Greg Patrick .20 .09 .03
□ 341 Andrew Grigg .20 .09 .03
□ 342 Kevin McDougal .20 .09 .03
□ 343 Prince Wimbley III .35 .16 .04
□ 344 Sam Hairston .20 .09 .03
□ 345 Curtis Gordon .35 .16 .04
□ 346 Chris Keneally .20 .09 .03
□ 347 Michael Philbrick .20 .09 .03
□ 348 Keith Embray .20 .09 .03
□ 349 Steve Grant .20 .09 .03
□ 350 Taly Williams .20 .09 .03
□ 351 Garry Sawatzky .20 .09 .03
□ 352 Dean Noel .35 .16 .04
□ 353 Mike Armstrong .20 .09 .03
□ 354 David Pool .20 .09 .03
□ 355 Tyrone Edwards .20 .09 .03
□ 356 Tim Cofield 1.25 .55 .16
□ 357 Gerald Vaughn .20 .09 .03
□ 358 Mark McLoughlin .20 .09 .03
□ 359 Robert Dougherty .20 .09 .03
□ 360 Norm Casola .20 .09 .03
□ 361 Shawn Knight .20 .09 .03
□ 362 Kelvin Means .20 .09 .03
□ 363 Reggie Pleasant .50 .23 .06
□ 364 Jim Smyrl .20 .09 .03
□ 365 Fred Montgomery .20 .09 .03
□ 366 Ron Perry .20 .09 .03
□ 367 Jami Anderson .20 .09 .03
□ 368 Jeff Reinebold .20 .09 .03
□ 369 Steve Brannon .20 .09 .03
□ 370 Jimmy Cunningham 1.00 .45 .12
□ 371 Damion Lyons .20 .09 .03
□ 372 John Tweet Martin .20 .09 .03
□ 373 Mike Campbell .20 .09 .03
□ 374 Jonathan Wilson .20 .09 .03
□ 375 Sandy Annunziata .20 .09 .03
□ 376 Brian Walling .35 .16 .04
□ 377 Eric Blount RB .50 .23 .06
□ 378 Tom Gerhart .20 .09 .03
□ 379 Milt Stegall .20 .09 .03
□ 380 Bob Kronenberg .20 .09 .03
□ 381 Barry Rose .20 .09 .03
□ 382 Tim Walton .20 .09 .03
□ 383 Kelvin Harris .20 .09 .03
□ 384 Dwayne Provo .20 .09 .03
□ 385 Jayson Dzikowicz .20 .09 .03
□ 386 Melendez Byrd .20 .09 .03
□ 387 Val St. Germain .20 .09 .03
□ 388 Dave Vankoughnett .20 .09 .03
□ 389 Aaron Kanner .20 .09 .03
□ 390 Nick Richards .20 .09 .03
□ 391 Rohan Marley .50 .23 .06
□ 392 Chris Burns .20 .09 .03
□ 393 Joe Fuller .20 .09 .03
□ 394 Donovan Gans .20 .09 .03
□ 395 Jermaine Chaney .20 .09 .03
□ 396 Jackie Kellogg .20 .09 .03
□ 397 Ray Savage Jr. .20 .09 .03
□ 398 Oscar Giles .50 .23 .06
□ 399 Jeff Neal .20 .09 .03

1995 JOGO CFL Athletes in Action

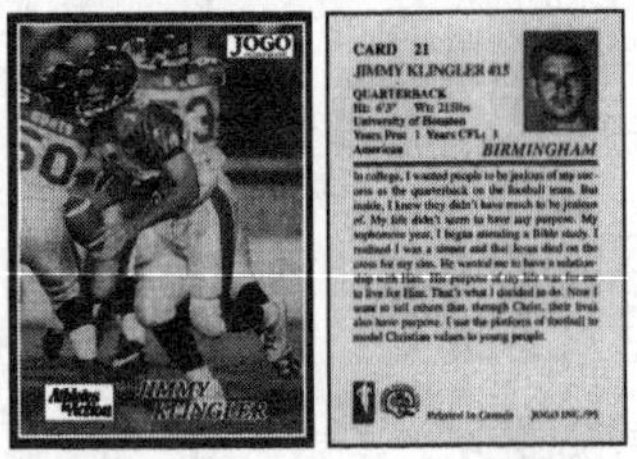

This 21-card standard-size set of players in the Canadian Football League features front color action player photos with the AIA logo. The backs carry a small black-and-white head photo of the player with biographical information and the importance of religion in that player's life in his own words.

	MINT	NRMT	EXC
COMPLETE SET (21)	8.00	3.60	1.00
COMMON CARD (1-21)	.40	.18	.05

□ 1 Kelly Sims .75 .35 .09
□ 2 Craig Hendrickson .40 .18 .05
□ 3 Kerwin Bell 1.25 .55 .16
□ 4 Glenn Harper .40 .18 .05
□ 5 Jim Sandusky .75 .35 .09
□ 6 Eldonta Osborne .40 .18 .05
□ 7 Guy Earle .40 .18 .05
□ 8 Charles Anthony .40 .18 .05
□ 9 O.J. Brigance 2.00 .90 .25
□ 10 Junior Thurman .75 .35 .09
□ 11 Erik White .75 .35 .09
□ 12 Henry Newby .40 .18 .05
□ 13 Darryl Sampson .40 .18 .05
□ 14 Tony Woods .75 .35 .09
□ 15 Sean Brantley .40 .18 .05
□ 16 Shalon Baker .40 .18 .05
□ 17 Greg Frers .40 .18 .05
□ 18 Danny Barrett .75 .35 .09
□ 19 John Earle .40 .18 .05
□ 20 Tracy Ham 2.00 .90 .25
□ 21 Jimmy Klingler .75 .35 .09

1995 JOGO CFL Missing Years

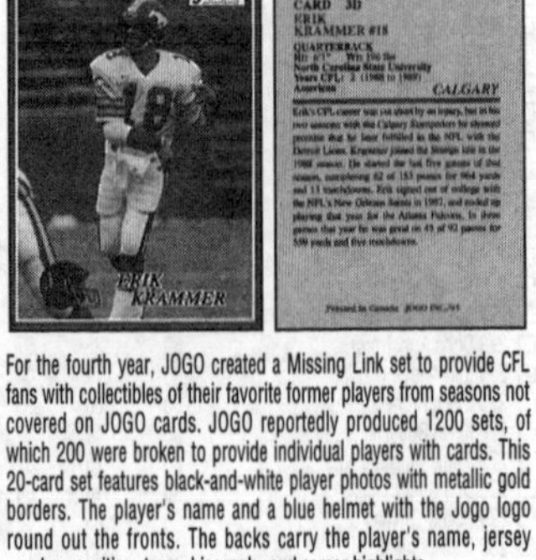

For the fourth year, JOGO created a Missing Link set to provide CFL fans with collectibles of their favorite former players from seasons not covered on JOGO cards. JOGO reportedly produced 1200 sets, of which 200 were broken to provide individual players with cards. This 20-card set features black-and-white player photos with metallic gold borders. The player's name and a blue helmet with the Jogo logo round out the fronts. The backs carry the player's name, jersey number, position, team, biography and career highlights.

	MINT	NRMT	EXC
COMPLETE SET (20)	10.00	4.50	1.25
COMMON CARD (1D-20D)	.50	.23	.06

□ 1D Jimmy Jones .75 .35 .09
□ 2D Charlie Brandon .50 .23 .06
□ 3D Erik Kramer UER 3.00 1.35 .35
name spelled Krammer
□ 4D Jeff Avery .50 .23 .06
□ 5D Wally Buono .50 .23 .06
□ 6D Mike Strickland .75 .35 .09
□ 7D Bob Toogood .75 .35 .09

	MINT	NRMT	EXC
☐ 8D Joe Hernandez	.50	.23	.06
☐ 9D Doug Battershill	.50	.23	.06
☐ 10D Al Brenner	.50	.23	.06
☐ 11D Tim Anderson	.50	.23	.06
☐ 12D Ted Provost	.50	.23	.06
☐ 13D Eugene Goodlow	.75	.35	.09
☐ 14D Rudy Florio	.50	.23	.06
☐ 15D Joey Walters	.75	.35	.09
☐ 16D Bob Viccars	.50	.23	.06
☐ 17D Tyrone Walls	.75	.35	.09
☐ 18D John Harvey	.75	.35	.09
☐ 19D Dick Aldridge	.50	.23	.06
☐ 20D Grady Cavness	.75	.35	.09

1996 JOGO CFL

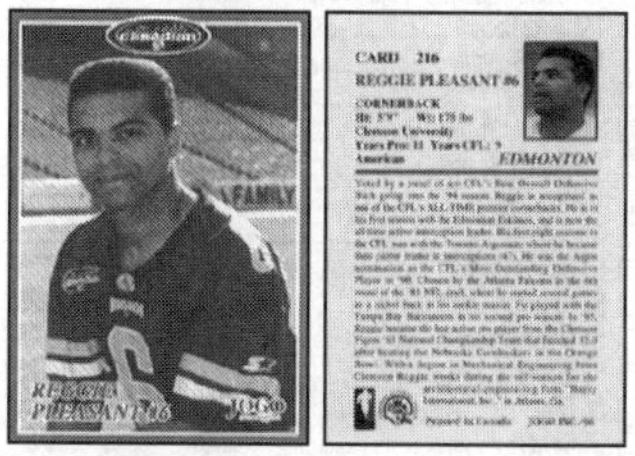

The 1996 JOGO set was released in one series. Several top players are featured on their first cards in the set.

	MINT	NRMT	EXC
COMPLETE SET (220)	50.00	22.00	6.25
COMMON CARD (1-220)	.20	.09	.03
☐ 1 Jeff Garcia	.50	.23	.06
☐ 2 Jeff Cummins	.50	.23	.06
☐ 3 Terry Baker	.35	.16	.04
☐ 4 James Taras	.20	.09	.03
☐ 5 Eric Blount RB	.50	.23	.06
☐ 6 Dan Rashovich	.20	.09	.03
☐ 7 Dale Sanderson	.20	.09	.03
☐ 8 Paul Masotti	.35	.16	.04
☐ 9 Giulio Caravatta	.20	.09	.03
☐ 10 Stefen Reid	.20	.09	.03
☐ 11 Lee Knight	.20	.09	.03
☐ 12 Dave Vankoughnett	.20	.09	.03
☐ 13 Stu Laird	.35	.16	.04
☐ 14 Todd Storme	.20	.09	.03
☐ 15 Glenn Rogers Jr.	.20	.09	.03
☐ 16 Miles Gorrell	.20	.09	.03
☐ 17 Mike Kiselak	.20	.09	.03
☐ 18 Mike Trevathan	.50	.23	.06
☐ 19 Troy Westwood	.50	.23	.06
☐ 20 Michael Jovanovich	.20	.09	.03
☐ 21 Alan Wetmore	.20	.09	.03
☐ 22 Bruce Covernton	.35	.16	.04
☐ 23 Ryan Carey	.20	.09	.03
☐ 24 Larry Wruck	.35	.16	.04
☐ 25 Lou Cafazzo	.20	.09	.03
☐ 26 Mac Cody	1.00	.45	.12
☐ 27 Todd Furdyk	.20	.09	.03
☐ 28 Shannon Garrett	.20	.09	.03
☐ 29 Kenny Wilhite	.35	.16	.04
☐ 30 Bruce Beaton	.20	.09	.03
☐ 31 Tony Martino	.20	.09	.03
☐ 32 Brooks Findlay	.20	.09	.03
☐ 33 Matt Dunigan	1.00	.45	.12
☐ 34 Ed Kucy	.20	.09	.03
☐ 35 Mike Clemons	1.00	.45	.12
☐ 36 Cory Philpot	1.00	.45	.12
☐ 37 Steve Taylor	.50	.23	.06
☐ 38 Jackie Kellogg	.20	.09	.03
☐ 39 Spencer McLennan	.20	.09	.03
☐ 40 Jason Mallett	.20	.09	.03
☐ 41 Robert Mimbs	.75	.35	.09
☐ 42 Doug Davies	.20	.09	.03
☐ 43 Malvin Hunter	.20	.09	.03
☐ 44 Wayne Lammle	.20	.09	.03
☐ 45 David Maeva	.20	.09	.03
☐ 46 Jay McNeil	.20	.09	.03
☐ 47 Ed Berry	.20	.09	.03
☐ 48 Irvin Smith	.20	.09	.03
☐ 49 Wade Miller	.20	.09	.03
☐ 50 Dan Farthing	.20	.09	.03
☐ 51 Tom Gerhart	.20	.09	.03
☐ 52 Ray Bernard	.20	.09	.03
☐ 53 Jude St. John	.20	.09	.03
☐ 54 Terry Vaughn	.20	.09	.03
☐ 55 Shelton Quarles	.20	.09	.03
☐ 56 Kelvin Anderson	1.50	.70	.19
☐ 57 Mike Withycombe	.20	.09	.03
☐ 58 Sean Graham	.20	.09	.03
☐ 59 Errol Brown	.20	.09	.03
☐ 60 Swift Burch III	.20	.09	.03
☐ 61 Jed Roberts	.20	.09	.03
☐ 62 Ted Long	.20	.09	.03
☐ 63 Mike Morreale	.20	.09	.03
☐ 64 Tyrone Chatman	.20	.09	.03
☐ 65 Anthony McClanahan	.20	.09	.03
☐ 66 David Pitcher	.20	.09	.03
☐ 67 Shannon Baker	.20	.09	.03
☐ 68 Fred Childress	.20	.09	.03
☐ 69 John Terry	.20	.09	.03
☐ 70 Chris Morris	.50	.23	.06
☐ 71 Andrew Grigg	.20	.09	.03
☐ 72 Reggie Givens	.50	.23	.06
☐ 73 Cory Mantyka	.20	.09	.03
☐ 74 Alfred Jordan	.35	.16	.04
☐ 75 Harold Nash Jr.	.20	.09	.03
☐ 76 Brett MacNeil	.20	.09	.03
☐ 77 Brent Matich	.20	.09	.03
☐ 78 Gerry Collins	.20	.09	.03
☐ 79 Johnson Joseph	.20	.09	.03
☐ 80 Jimmy Cunningham	.50	.23	.06
☐ 81 Eddie Davis	.20	.09	.03
☐ 82 Tom Europe	.20	.09	.03
☐ 83 Darryl Hall	.35	.16	.04
☐ 84 Tracy Gravely	.20	.09	.03
☐ 85 Bob Cameron	.50	.23	.06
☐ 86 Paul McCallum	.20	.09	.03
☐ 87 Tyrone Williams	.20	.09	.03
☐ 88 Maurice Kelly	.35	.16	.04
☐ 89 Sammie Brennan	.20	.09	.03
☐ 90 Ken Benson	.20	.09	.03
☐ 91 Sean Millington	.20	.09	.03
☐ 92 Greg Knox	.20	.09	.03
☐ 93 Kevin Robson	.20	.09	.03
☐ 94 Rod Harris	.50	.23	.06
☐ 95 Charles Gordon	.20	.09	.03
☐ 96 Donald Smith	.20	.09	.03
☐ 97 Joe Mero	.20	.09	.03
☐ 98 Reggie Slack	.50	.23	.06
☐ 99 Garry Sawatzky	.20	.09	.03
☐ 100 Adrion Smith	.20	.09	.03
☐ 101 Allan Boyko	.20	.09	.03
☐ 102 Scott Hendrickson	.20	.09	.03
☐ 103 Eddie Britton	.20	.09	.03
☐ 104 Will Johnson	.50	.23	.06
☐ 105 John Raposo	.20	.09	.03
☐ 106 Chris Tsangaris	.20	.09	.03
☐ 107 Cooper Harris	.20	.09	.03
☐ 108 Quinn Magnuson	.20	.09	.03
☐ 109 Blaine Schmidt	.20	.09	.03
☐ 110 David Archer	2.00	.90	.25
☐ 111 David Sapunjis	.75	.35	.09
☐ 112 Stephen Anderson	.20	.09	.03
☐ 113 Raymond Biggs	.20	.09	.03
☐ 114 Jean-Agnes Charles	.20	.09	.03
☐ 115 Vince Danielsen	.20	.09	.03
☐ 116 Wayne Drinkwalter	.35	.16	.04
☐ 117 Farell Duclair	.20	.09	.03
☐ 118 Duane Forde	.20	.09	.03
☐ 119 Rohn Meyer	.20	.09	.03
☐ 120 Travis Moore	.20	.09	.03
☐ 121 Kevin Reid	.20	.09	.03
☐ 122 Roger Reinson	.20	.09	.03
☐ 123 Gonzalo Floyd	.20	.09	.03
☐ 124 Dwayne Provo	.20	.09	.03
☐ 125 Peter Tuipulotu	.20	.09	.03
☐ 126 Curtis Mayfield	.35	.16	.04
☐ 127 Ray Elgaard	.50	.23	.06
☐ 128 John James	.20	.09	.03
☐ 129 Dave Van Belleghem	.20	.09	.03
☐ 130 J.P. Izquierdo	.20	.09	.03
☐ 131 Darren Joseph	.35	.16	.04
☐ 132 Frank Jagas	.20	.09	.03
☐ 133 Heath Rylance	.20	.09	.03
☐ 134 Rick Walters	.20	.09	.03
☐ 135 Michael Philbrick	.20	.09	.03
☐ 136 Val St. Germain	.20	.09	.03
☐ 137 Justin Ring	.20	.09	.03
☐ 138 Mike Campbell	.20	.09	.03
☐ 139 Burt Thornton	.20	.09	.03
☐ 140 Jason Kaiser	.20	.09	.03
☐ 141 Tim Brown	.20	.09	.03
☐ 142 Ken Watson	.20	.09	.03
☐ 143 Tommie Frasier	2.50	1.10	.30
☐ 144 Tyrone Rodgers	.20	.09	.03
☐ 145 Craig Hendrickson	.20	.09	.03
☐ 146 Johnny R. Scott	.20	.09	.03
☐ 147 Mark Pimiskern	.20	.09	.03
☐ 148 Frank Pimiskern	.20	.09	.03
☐ 149 Carl Coulter	.20	.09	.03
☐ 150 Reggie Carthon	.20	.09	.03
☐ 151 Ronald Williams	.20	.09	.03
☐ 152 Ted Alford	.20	.09	.03
☐ 153 Dave Chaytors	.20	.09	.03
☐ 154 Robert Gordon	.20	.09	.03
☐ 155 Jayson Dzikowicz	.20	.09	.03
☐ 156 Lubo Zizakovic	.20	.09	.03
☐ 157 Mike Hendricks	.20	.09	.03
☐ 158 Obie Spanic	.20	.09	.03
☐ 159 Andre Bolduc	.20	.09	.03
☐ 160 Robert Drummond	.50	.23	.06
☐ 161 Chuck Esty	.20	.09	.03
☐ 162 Tommy Henry	.20	.09	.03
☐ 163 Nick Richards	.20	.09	.03
☐ 164 Profail Grier	.20	.09	.03
☐ 165 Melvin Aldridge	.20	.09	.03
☐ 166 Uzooma Okeke	.20	.09	.03
☐ 167 Courtney Griffin	.20	.09	.03
☐ 168 Leonard Humphries	.20	.09	.03
☐ 169 Jason Wallace	.20	.09	.03
☐ 170 Derek MacCready	.20	.09	.03
☐ 171 Franky West	.20	.09	.03
☐ 172 Kelvin Means	.20	.09	.03
☐ 173 David Harper	.20	.09	.03
☐ 174 Rob Stevenson	.20	.09	.03
☐ 175 John Kalin	.20	.09	.03
☐ 176 Nigel Williams	.20	.09	.03
☐ 177 Chris Armstrong	.50	.23	.06
☐ 178 Douglas Craft	.50	.23	.06
☐ 179 Michael Soles	.35	.16	.04
☐ 180 Mike Saunders	1.00	.45	.12
☐ 181 Michel Lamy	.20	.09	.03
☐ 182 Jock Climie	.50	.23	.06
☐ 183 Grant Carter	.20	.09	.03
☐ 184 Hency Charles	.20	.09	.03
☐ 185 Jason Bryant	.20	.09	.03
☐ 186 Dexter Dawson	.20	.09	.03
☐ 187 Glen Scrivener	.20	.09	.03
☐ 188 K.D. Williams	.20	.09	.03
☐ 189 Dean Lytle	.20	.09	.03
☐ 190 Donovan Wright	.20	.09	.03
☐ 191 Andrew Henry	.20	.09	.03
☐ 192 Doug Flutie	3.00	1.35	.35
☐ 193 Brendan Rogers	.20	.09	.03
☐ 194 Darian Hagan	.20	.09	.03
☐ 195 Jeff Fairholm	.35	.16	.04
☐ 196 Marcello Simmons	.20	.09	.03
☐ 197 Oscar Giles	.35	.16	.04
☐ 198 Chris Gioskos	.20	.09	.03
☐ 199 Dan Murphy	.20	.09	.03
☐ 200 Norm Casola	.20	.09	.03
☐ 201 Vic Stevenson	.20	.09	.03
☐ 202 Duane Dmytryshyn	.20	.09	.03
☐ 203 Christopher Perez	.20	.09	.03
☐ 204 Noah Cantor	.20	.09	.03
☐ 205 Mike Vanderjagt	.20	.09	.03
☐ 206 George Nimako	.35	.16	.04
☐ 207 Andrew Stewart	.20	.09	.03
☐ 208 Pierre Vercheval	.35	.16	.04
☐ 209 Chris Green	.20	.09	.03
☐ 210 Maurice Miller	.20	.09	.03
☐ 211 Leroy Blugh	.35	.16	.04
☐ 212 Jim Sandusky	.35	.16	.04
☐ 213 Thomas Rayam	.20	.09	.03
☐ 214 Cody Ledbetter	.20	.09	.03
☐ 215 Michael Sellers	.20	.09	.03
☐ 216 Reggie Pleasant	.50	.23	.06
☐ 217 Errol Martin	.20	.09	.03
☐ 218 Trent Brown	.20	.09	.03
☐ 219 Bruce Dickson	.20	.09	.03
☐ 220 Dan Payne	.20	.09	.03

1989 KFC Calgary

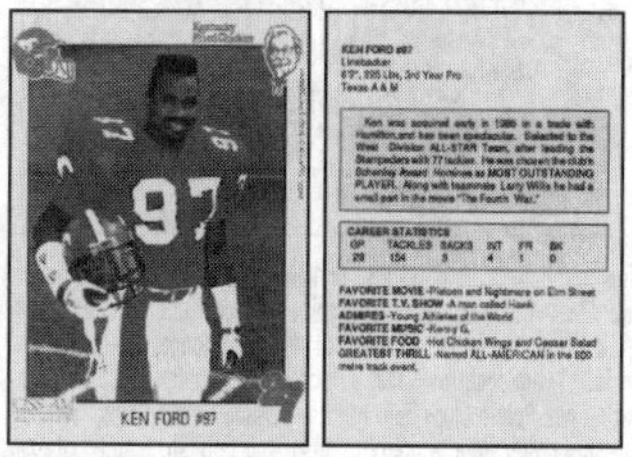

The 1989 KFC Calgary Stampeders set contains 24 cards measuring approximately 2 7/16" by 3 5/16". The fronts have color portrait photos bordered in white; the vertically oriented backs have detailed profiles and statistics. The cards come as perforated strips of four player cards and one discount card for 2.00 off any 1989 Stampeder home game ticket purchase. The cards are ordered on the strips by uniform number such that by looking at the reverse of each strip, the cards are in almost perfect numerical order. The only exception is that card 9 comes before 8.

	MINT	NRMT	EXC
COMPLETE SET (24)	10.00	4.50	1.25
COMMON CARD (1-24)	.40	.18	.05
☐ 3 David McCrary	.40	.18	.05
☐ 4 Brent Matich	.60	.25	.07
☐ 8 Danny Barrett	1.50	.70	.19
☐ 9 Terrence Jones	1.25	.55	.16
☐ 12 Tim Petros	.60	.25	.07
☐ 13 Mark McLoughlin	.40	.18	.05
☐ 15 Ron Hopkins	.60	.25	.07
☐ 20 Chris Major	1.25	.55	.16
☐ 24 Greg Peterson	.40	.18	.05
☐ 25 Shawn Faulkner	.40	.18	.05
☐ 32 Darcy Kopp	.40	.18	.05
☐ 34 Andy McVey	.40	.18	.05
☐ 39 Doug(Tank) Landry	1.00	.45	.12
☐ 59 Leo Blanchard	.40	.18	.05
☐ 61 Tom Spoletini	.40	.18	.05
☐ 65 Mike Palumbo	.40	.18	.05
☐ 66 Dan Ferrone	.60	.25	.07
☐ 74 Mitchell Price	.60	.25	.07
☐ 76 Marshall Toner	.40	.18	.05
☐ 84 Eugene Belliveau	.60	.25	.07
☐ 85 Brock Smith	.40	.18	.05
☐ 89 Larry Willis	.75	.35	.09
☐ 93 Kent Warnock	.75	.35	.09
☐ 97 Ken Ford	.40	.18	.05

1990 KFC Calgary

The 1990 KFC Calgary Stampeders set contains 24 cards measuring approximately 2 7/16" by 3 5/16". The fronts have color portrait photos bordered in white. The cards come as perforated strips of four player cards and one discount card for 2.00 off any 1990 Stampeder home game ticket purchase. The cards are ordered alphabetically in the list below.

	MINT	NRMT	EXC
COMPLETE SET (24)	10.00	4.50	1.25
COMMON CARD (1-24)	.50	.23	.06
☐ 1 Walter Ballard	.50	.23	.06
☐ 2 Danny Barrett	1.50	.70	.19
☐ 3 Eddie Brown	1.25	.55	.16
☐ 4 Joe Clausi	.50	.23	.06
☐ 5 Lloyd Fairbanks	.75	.35	.09
☐ 6 Matt Finlay	.75	.35	.09
☐ 7 Ken Ford	.50	.23	.06
☐ 8 Ron Hopkins	.75	.35	.09
☐ 9 Keyvan Jenkins	1.25	.55	.16
☐ 10 Will Johnson	.75	.35	.09
☐ 11 Terrence Jones	1.25	.55	.16
☐ 12 David McCrary	.50	.23	.06
☐ 13 Mark McLoughlin	.50	.23	.06
☐ 14 Andy McVey	.50	.23	.06
☐ 15 Brent Matich	.50	.23	.06
☐ 16 Mike Palumbo	.50	.23	.06
☐ 17 Greg Peterson	.50	.23	.06
☐ 18 Tim Petros	.75	.35	.09
☐ 19 Mitchell Price	.75	.35	.09
☐ 20 Brock Smith	.50	.23	.06
☐ 21 Tom Spoletini	.50	.23	.06
☐ 22 Junior Thurman	1.25	.55	.16
☐ 23 Marshall Toner	.50	.23	.06
☐ 24 Kent Warnock	.75	.35	.09

1984 McDonald's Ottawa

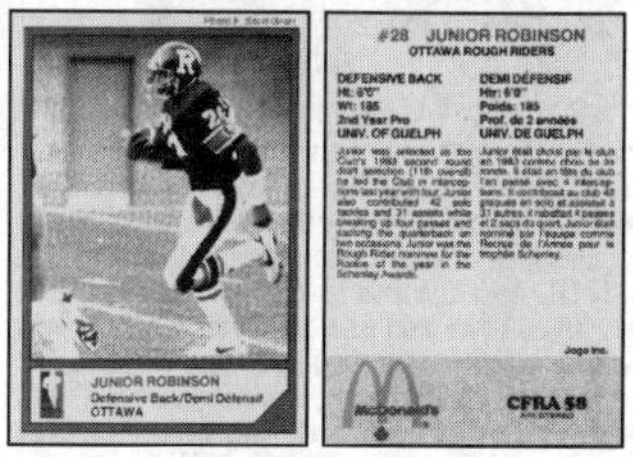

This 4 panel (12 card) full-color set was issued in panels of three over a four-week period as a promotion of McDonald's and radio station CFRA 58 AM. It was reported that 210,000 panels were given away at McDonald's. Cards were produced in conjunction with JOGO Novelties. The cards can be separated as they are perforated. The cards are unnumbered although the player's uniform number is given on the back of the card. The numbering below refers to the week (of the promotion) during which the panel was distributed. Photos were taken by F. Scott Grant, who is credited on the fronts of the cards. The cards measure approximately 2 1/2" by 3 1/2".

	MINT	NRMT	EXC
COMPLETE SET (4)	12.00	5.50	1.50
COMMON PANEL (1-4)	2.00	.90	.25
☐ 1 Ken Miller Rudy Phillips Jim Reid	2.00	.90	.25
☐ 2 Gary Dulin Greg Marshall Junior Robinson	2.00	.90	.25
☐ 3 Kevin Powell Tyron Gray Skip Walker	2.00	.90	.25
☐ 4 Rick Sowieta Bruce Walker J.C. Watts	7.50	3.40	.95

1983 Mohawk B.C. Lions

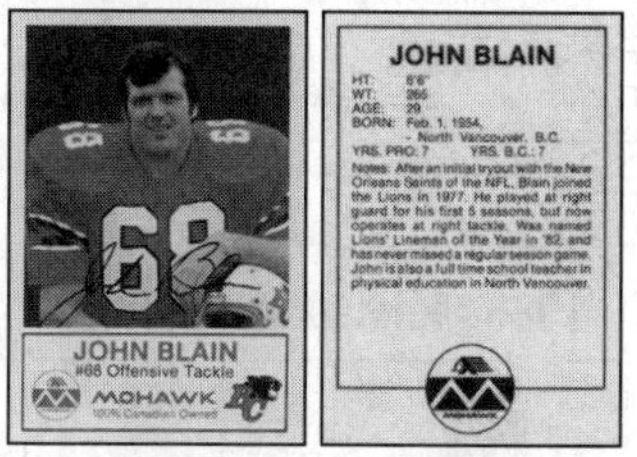

This 24-card set of the CFL's British Columbia Lions was only issued in British Columbia by Mohawk Oil as a premium at its gas stations. Posed color player's photos appear on a white card face. The cards measure approximately 2 1/2" by 3 5/8". A thin black line forms a box at the bottom that contains the player's name, jersey number, position, team logo, and sponsor logo. Each card has a facsimile autograph of the player on the front. The backs have biographical information and career notes printed in blue. The cards are unnumbered and checklisted below in alphabetical order.

	MINT	NRMT	EXC
COMPLETE SET (24)	20.00	9.00	2.50
COMMON CARD (1-24)	.75	.35	.09

☐ 1 John Blain	.75	.35	.09
☐ 2 Tim Cowan	1.00	.45	.12
☐ 3 Larry Crawford	1.00	.45	.12
☐ 4 Tyrone Crews	.75	.35	.09
☐ 5 James Curry	1.00	.45	.12
☐ 6 Roy Dewalt	1.50	.70	.19
☐ 7 Mervyn Fernandez	2.50	1.10	.30
☐ 8 Sammy Greene	.75	.35	.09
☐ 9 Jo Jo Heath	.75	.35	.09
☐ 10 Nick Hebeler	1.00	.45	.12
☐ 11 Glen Jackson	.75	.35	.09
☐ 12 Tim Kearse	.75	.35	.09
☐ 13 Rick Klassen	1.00	.45	.12
☐ 14 Kevin Konar	1.00	.45	.12
☐ 15 Glenn Leonhard	.75	.35	.09
☐ 16 Nelson Martin	.75	.35	.09
☐ 17 Mack Moore	.75	.35	.09
☐ 18 John Pankratz	.75	.35	.09
☐ 19 Joe Paopao	1.25	.55	.16
☐ 20 Lui Passaglia	2.50	1.10	.30
☐ 21 Don Taylor	.75	.35	.09
☐ 22 Mike Washburn	.75	.35	.09
☐ 23 John Henry White	.75	.35	.09
☐ 24 Al Wilson	.75	.35	.09

1984 Mohawk B.C. Lions

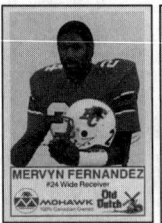

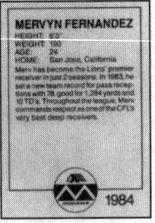

This 32-card set was co-sponsored by Mohawk and Old Dutch, and only issued in British Columbia by Mohawk Oil as a premium at its gas stations. The set features members of the British Columbia Lions of the CFL. The cards measure approximately 2 1/2" by 3 5/8". The front features a posed color player photo, with white borders and a facsimile autograph across the picture. Player information and sponsors' logos appear in a rectangle below the picture. In blue print on white, the back has biography and player profile. The cards are unnumbered and checklisted below in alphabetical order.

	MINT	NRMT	EXC
COMPLETE SET (32)	20.00	9.00	2.50
COMMON CARD (1-32)	.60	.25	.07
☐ 1 Ned Armour	1.00	.45	.12
☐ 2 John Blain	.60	.25	.07
☐ 3 Melvin Byrd	1.00	.45	.12
☐ 4 Darnell Clash	1.00	.45	.12
☐ 5 Tim Cowan	1.00	.45	.12
☐ 6 Larry Crawford	1.00	.45	.12
☐ 7 Tyrone Crews	.60	.25	.07
☐ 8 Roy DeWalt	1.50	.70	.19
☐ 9 Mervyn Fernandez	2.50	1.10	.30
☐ 10 Bernie Glier	.60	.25	.07
☐ 11 Dennis Guevin	.60	.25	.07
☐ 12 Nick Hebeler	.60	.25	.07
☐ 13 Bryan Illerbrun	.60	.25	.07
☐ 14 Glen Jackson	.60	.25	.07
☐ 15 Andre Jones	.60	.25	.07
☐ 16 Rick Klassen	1.00	.45	.12
☐ 17 Kevin Konar	1.00	.45	.12
☐ 18 Glenn Leonhard	.60	.25	.07
☐ 19 Nelson Martin	.60	.25	.07
☐ 20 Billy McBride	.60	.25	.07
☐ 21 Mack Moore	.60	.25	.07
☐ 22 John Pankratz	.60	.25	.07
☐ 23 James Parker	1.50	.70	.19
☐ 24 Lui Passaglia	2.50	1.10	.30
☐ 25 Ryan Potter	.60	.25	.07
☐ 26 Gerald Roper	.60	.25	.07
☐ 27 Jim Sandusky	2.00	.90	.25
☐ 28 Don Taylor	.60	.25	.07
☐ 29 John Henry White	.60	.25	.07
☐ 30 Al Wilson	.60	.25	.07
☐ 31 Team Card	1.00	.45	.12
☐ 32 Checklist	1.00	.45	.12

1985 Mohawk B.C. Lions

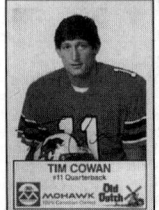

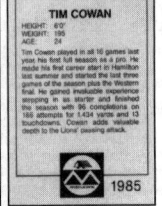

This 32-card set was co-sponsored by Mohawk and Old Dutch, and only issued in British Columbia by Mohawk Oil as a premium at its gas stations. Measuring approximately 2 1/2" by 3 5/8", the card fronts feature posed, color player photos with white borders. A facsimile autograph is inscribed across the picture. At the bottom, a white box that is outlined by a thin black line carries the player's name, jersey number, position, and sponsor logos. In blue print, the backs carry biographical information and a player profile. The cards are unnumbered and checklisted below in alphabetical order.

	MINT	NRMT	EXC
COMPLETE SET (32)	20.00	9.00	2.50
COMMON CARD (1-32)	.50	.23	.06
☐ 1 John Blain	.50	.23	.06
☐ 2 Jamie Buis	.50	.23	.06
☐ 3 Melvin Byrd	.75	.35	.09
☐ 4 Darnell Clash	1.00	.45	.12
☐ 5 Tim Cowan	.75	.35	.09
☐ 6 Tyrone Crews	.50	.23	.06
☐ 7 Mark DeBrueys	.50	.23	.06
☐ 8 Roy Dewalt	1.50	.70	.19
☐ 9 Mervyn Fernandez	2.50	1.10	.30
☐ 10 Bernie Glier	.50	.23	.06
☐ 11 Keith Gooch	.50	.23	.06
☐ 12 Dennis Guevin	.50	.23	.06
☐ 13 Nick Hebeler	.50	.23	.06
☐ 14 Bryan Illerbrun	.50	.23	.06
☐ 15 Glen Jackson	.50	.23	.06
☐ 16 Keyvan Jenkins	1.00	.45	.12
☐ 17 Andre Jones	.50	.23	.06
☐ 18 Rick Klassen	.75	.35	.09
☐ 19 Kevin Konar	.75	.35	.09
☐ 20 Glenn Leonhard	.50	.23	.06
☐ 21 Nelson Martin	.50	.23	.06
☐ 22 John Pankratz	.50	.23	.06
☐ 23 James Parker	1.25	.55	.16
☐ 24 Lui Passaglia	2.50	1.10	.30
☐ 25 Ryan Potter	.50	.23	.06
☐ 26 Ron Robinson	.75	.35	.09
☐ 27 Gerald Roper	.50	.23	.06
☐ 28 Jim Sandusky	2.00	.90	.25
☐ 29 John Henry White	.50	.23	.06
☐ 30 Al Wilson	.50	.23	.06
☐ 31 Team Photo	.75	.35	.09
☐ 32 Checklist	.75	.35	.09

1963 Nalley's Coins

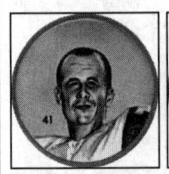

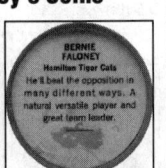

This 160-coin set is difficult to complete due to the fact that within every team grouping, the last ten coins are much tougher to find. The back of the coin is hard plastic, but also see-through. The coins can be found with sponsors Nalley's Potato Chips, Hunter's Potato Chips, Krun-Chee Potato Chips, and Humpty Dumpty Potato Chips. Humpty Dumpty coins were printed in French and English, instead of just English. The coins can also be found without sponsor names. Eight of the nine CFL teams are represented. The coins measure approximately 1 3/8" in diameter. Shields to hold the coins were also issued; these shields are also very collectible and are listed at the end of the list below, with the prefix S. The shields are not included in the complete set price.

	NRMT	VG-E	GOOD
COMPLETE SET (160)	3000.00	1350.00	375.00
COMMON COIN (1-160)	5.00	2.20	.60
☐ 1 Jackie Parker	20.00	9.00	2.50
☐ 2 Dick Shatto	8.00	3.60	1.00
☐ 3 Dave Mann	6.00	2.70	.75
☐ 4 Danny Nykoluk	5.00	2.20	.60
☐ 5 Billy Shipp	5.00	2.20	.60
☐ 6 Doug McNichol	5.00	2.20	.60
☐ 7 Jim Rountree	5.00	2.20	.60
☐ 8 Art Johnson	5.00	2.20	.60
☐ 9 Walt Radzick	5.00	2.20	.60
☐ 10 Jim Andreotti	6.00	2.70	.75
☐ 11 Gerry Philip	20.00	9.00	2.50
☐ 12 Lynn Bottoms	20.00	9.00	2.50
☐ 13 Ron Morris SP	110.00	50.00	14.00
☐ 14 Nobby Wirkowski CO	20.00	9.00	2.50
☐ 15 John Wydareny	20.00	9.00	2.50
☐ 16 Gerry Wilson	20.00	9.00	2.50
☐ 17 Gerry Patrick SP	50.00	22.00	6.25
☐ 18 Aubrey Linne	20.00	9.00	2.50
☐ 19 Norm Stoneburgh	20.00	9.00	2.50
☐ 20 Ken Beck	20.00	9.00	2.50
☐ 21 Russ Jackson	15.00	6.75	1.85
☐ 22 Kaye Vaughan	8.00	3.60	1.00
☐ 23 Dave Thelen	8.00	3.60	1.00
☐ 24 Ron Stewart	8.00	3.60	1.00
☐ 25 Moe Racine	5.00	2.20	.60
☐ 26 Jim Conroy	6.00	2.70	.75
☐ 27 Joe Poirier	6.00	2.70	.75
☐ 28 Mel Seminko	5.00	2.20	.60
☐ 29 Whit Tucker	8.00	3.60	1.00
☐ 30 Ernie White	5.00	2.20	.60
☐ 31 Frank Clair CO	20.00	9.00	2.50
☐ 32 Marv Bevan	20.00	9.00	2.50
☐ 33 Jerry Selinger	20.00	9.00	2.50
☐ 34 Jim Cain	20.00	9.00	2.50
☐ 35 Mike Snodgrass	20.00	9.00	2.50
☐ 36 Ted Smale	20.00	9.00	2.50
☐ 37 Billy Joe Booth	20.00	9.00	2.50
☐ 38 Len Chandler	20.00	9.00	2.50
☐ 39 Rick Black	20.00	9.00	2.50
☐ 40 Allen Schau	20.00	9.00	2.50
☐ 41 Bernie Faloney	15.00	6.75	1.85
☐ 42 Bobby Kuntz	6.00	2.70	.75
☐ 43 Joe Zuger	6.00	2.70	.75
☐ 44 Hal Patterson	12.00	5.50	1.50
☐ 45 Bronko Nagurski	10.00	4.50	1.25
☐ 46 Zeno Karcz	6.00	2.70	.75
☐ 47 Hardiman Cureton	5.00	2.20	.60
☐ 48 John Barrow	8.00	3.60	1.00
☐ 49 Tommy Grant	8.00	3.60	1.00
☐ 50 Garney Henley	8.00	3.60	1.00
☐ 51 Dick Easterly	20.00	9.00	2.50
☐ 52 Frank Cosentino	20.00	9.00	2.50
☐ 53 Geno DeNobile	20.00	9.00	2.50
☐ 54 Ralph Goldston	20.00	9.00	2.50
☐ 55 Chet Miksza	20.00	9.00	2.50
☐ 56 Bob Minihane	20.00	9.00	2.50
☐ 57 Don Sutherin	40.00	18.00	5.00
☐ 58 Ralph Sazio CO	20.00	9.00	2.50
☐ 59 Dave Viti SP	35.00	16.00	4.40
☐ 60 Angelo Mosca SP	125.00	55.00	15.50
☐ 61 Sandy Stephens	8.00	3.60	1.00
☐ 62 George Dixon	8.00	3.60	1.00
☐ 63 Don Clark	6.00	2.70	.75
☐ 64 Don Paquette	5.00	2.20	.60
☐ 65 Billy Wayte	5.00	2.20	.60
☐ 66 Ed Nickla	5.00	2.20	.60
☐ 67 Marv Luster	8.00	3.60	1.00
☐ 68 Joe Stracini	5.00	2.20	.60
☐ 69 Bobby Jack Oliver	6.00	2.70	.75
☐ 70 Ted Elsby	5.00	2.20	.60
☐ 71 Jim Trimble CO	20.00	9.00	2.50
☐ 72 Bob Leblanc	20.00	9.00	2.50
☐ 73 Dick Schnell	20.00	9.00	2.50
☐ 74 Milt Crain	20.00	9.00	2.50
☐ 75 Dick Dalatri	20.00	9.00	2.50
☐ 76 Billy Roy	20.00	9.00	2.50
☐ 77 Dave Hoppmann	20.00	9.00	2.50
☐ 78 Billy Ray Locklin	20.00	9.00	2.50
☐ 79 Ed Learn SP	125.00	55.00	15.50
☐ 80 Meco Poliziani SP	40.00	18.00	5.00
☐ 81 Leo Lewis	8.00	3.60	1.00
☐ 82 Kenny Ploen	8.00	3.60	1.00
☐ 83 Steve Patrick	5.00	2.20	.60
☐ 84 Farrell Funston	6.00	2.70	.75
☐ 85 Charlie Shepard	6.00	2.70	.75
☐ 86 Ronnie Latourelle	5.00	2.20	.60
☐ 87 Gord Rowland	6.00	2.70	.75
☐ 88 Frank Rigney	6.00	2.70	.75
☐ 89 Cornel Piper	5.00	2.20	.60
☐ 90 Ernie Pitts	5.00	2.20	.60
☐ 91 Roger Hagberg	30.00	13.50	3.70
☐ 92 Herb Gray	50.00	22.00	6.25
☐ 93 Jack Delveaux	20.00	9.00	2.50
☐ 94 Roger Savoie	20.00	9.00	2.50
☐ 95 Nick Miller	20.00	9.00	2.50
☐ 96 Norm Rauhaus	20.00	9.00	2.50
☐ 97 Cec Luining	20.00	9.00	2.50
☐ 98 Hal Ledyard	20.00	9.00	2.50
☐ 99 Neil Thomas	20.00	9.00	2.50
☐ 100 Bud Grant CO	90.00	40.00	11.00
☐ 101 Eagle Keys CO	8.00	3.60	1.00
☐ 102 Mike Wicklum	5.00	2.20	.60
☐ 103 Bill Mitchell	5.00	2.20	.60
☐ 104 Mike Lashuk	5.00	2.20	.60
☐ 105 Tommy Joe Coffey	8.00	3.60	1.00
☐ 106 Zeke Smith	5.00	2.20	.60
☐ 107 Joe Hernandez	5.00	2.20	.60
☐ 108 Johnny Bright	8.00	3.60	1.00
☐ 109 Don Getty	8.00	3.60	1.00
☐ 110 Nat Dye	5.00	2.20	.60
☐ 111 James Earl Wright	20.00	9.00	2.50
☐ 112 Mike Volcan SP	35.00	16.00	4.40
☐ 113 Jon Rechner	20.00	9.00	2.50
☐ 114 Len Vella	20.00	9.00	2.50
☐ 115 Ted Frechette	20.00	9.00	2.50
☐ 116 Larry Fleisher	20.00	9.00	2.50
☐ 117 Oscar Kruger	20.00	9.00	2.50
☐ 118 Ken Peterson	20.00	9.00	2.50
☐ 119 Bobby Walden	6.00	2.70	.75
☐ 120 Mickey Ording	20.00	9.00	2.50
☐ 121 Pete Manning	5.00	2.20	.60
☐ 122 Harvey Wylie	6.00	2.70	.75
☐ 123 Tony Pajaczkowski	8.00	3.60	1.00
☐ 124 Wayne Harris	10.00	4.50	1.25
☐ 125 Earl Lunsford	8.00	3.60	1.00
☐ 126 Don Luzzi	6.00	2.70	.75
☐ 127 Ed Buckanan	5.00	2.20	.60
☐ 128 Lovell Coleman	6.00	2.70	.75
☐ 129 Hal Krebs	5.00	2.20	.60
☐ 130 Eagle Day	8.00	3.60	1.00
☐ 131 Bobby Dobbs CO	20.00	9.00	2.50
☐ 132 George Hansen	20.00	9.00	2.50
☐ 133 Roy Jokanovich SP	90.00	40.00	11.00
☐ 134 Jerry Keeling	30.00	13.50	3.70
☐ 135 Larry Anderson	20.00	9.00	2.50
☐ 136 Bill Crawford	20.00	9.00	2.50
☐ 137 Ron Albright	20.00	9.00	2.50
☐ 138 Bill Britton	20.00	9.00	2.50
☐ 139 Jim Dillard	20.00	9.00	2.50
☐ 140 Jim Furlong	20.00	9.00	2.50
☐ 141 Dave Skrien CO	5.00	2.20	.60
☐ 142 Willie Fleming	10.00	4.50	1.25
☐ 143 Nub Beamer	5.00	2.20	.60
☐ 144 Norm Fieldgate	8.00	3.60	1.00
☐ 145 Joe Kapp	35.00	16.00	4.40
☐ 146 Tom Hinton	8.00	3.60	1.00
☐ 147 Pat Claridge	5.00	2.20	.60
☐ 148 Bill Munsey	5.00	2.20	.60
☐ 149 Mike Martin	5.00	2.20	.60
☐ 150 Tom Brown	8.00	3.60	1.00
☐ 151 Ian Hagemoen	20.00	9.00	2.50
☐ 152 Jim Carphin	20.00	9.00	2.50
☐ 153 By Bailey	40.00	18.00	5.00
☐ 154 Steve Cotter	20.00	9.00	2.50
☐ 155 Mike Cacic	20.00	9.00	2.50
☐ 156 Neil Beaumont	20.00	9.00	2.50
☐ 157 Lonnie Dennis	20.00	9.00	2.50
☐ 158 Barney Therrien	20.00	9.00	2.50
☐ 159 Sonny Homer	20.00	9.00	2.50
☐ 160 Walt Bilicki	20.00	9.00	2.50
☐ S1 Toronto Shield	50.00	22.00	6.25
☐ S2 Ottawa Shield	50.00	22.00	6.25
☐ S3 Hamilton Shield	50.00	22.00	6.25
☐ S4 Montreal Shield	50.00	22.00	6.25
☐ S5 Winnipeg Shield	50.00	22.00	6.25
☐ S6 Edmonton Shield	50.00	22.00	6.25
☐ S7 Calgary Shield	50.00	22.00	6.25
☐ S8 British Columbia Shield	50.00	22.00	6.25

1964 Nalley's Coins

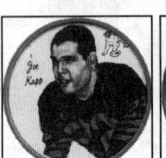

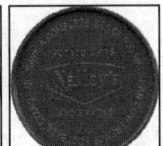

This 100-coin set is very similar to the set from the previous year except that there are no real distribution scarcities. The backs of the coins are plastic, but not see-through. No specific information about the player, as in the previous year, is included. The coins were sponsored by Nalley's Potato Chips and packaged one per box of chips. The set numbering is in team order. The coins measure approximately 1 3/8" in diameter. Shields to hold the coins were also issued; these shields are also very collectible and are listed at the end of the list below with the prefix "S". The shields are not included in the complete set price. Only teams from the Western Conference of the CFL were included.

	NRMT	VG-E	GOOD
COMPLETE SET (100)	750.00	350.00	95.00
COMMON COIN (1-100)	5.00	2.20	.60
☐ 1 Joe Kapp	30.00	13.50	3.70
☐ 2 Willie Fleming	10.00	4.50	1.25
☐ 3 Norm Fieldgate	8.00	3.60	1.00
☐ 4 Bill Murray	5.00	2.20	.60
☐ 5 Tom Brown	10.00	4.50	1.25
☐ 6 Neil Beaumont	6.00	2.70	.75
☐ 7 Sonny Homer	6.00	2.70	.75
☐ 8 Lonnie Dennis	5.00	2.20	.60
☐ 9 Dave Skrien	5.00	2.20	.60
☐ 10 Dick Fouts CO	5.00	2.20	.60
☐ 11 Paul Seale	5.00	2.20	.60
☐ 12 Peter Kempf	5.00	2.20	.60
☐ 13 Steve Shafer	5.00	2.20	.60
☐ 14 Tom Hinton	8.00	3.60	1.00
☐ 15 Pat Claridge	5.00	2.20	.60
☐ 16 By Bailey	8.00	3.60	1.00
☐ 17 Nub Beamer	6.00	2.70	.75
☐ 18 Steve Cotter	5.00	2.20	.60
☐ 19 Mike Cacic	5.00	2.20	.60
☐ 20 Mike Martin	5.00	2.20	.60
☐ 21 Eagle Day	15.00	6.75	1.85
☐ 22 Jim Dillard	5.00	2.20	.60
☐ 23 Pete Murray	5.00	2.20	.60
☐ 24 Tony Pajaczkowski	8.00	3.60	1.00
☐ 25 Don Luzzi	6.00	2.70	.75
☐ 26 Wayne Harris	10.00	4.50	1.25
☐ 27 Harvey Wylie	6.00	2.70	.75
☐ 28 Bill Crawford	5.00	2.20	.60
☐ 29 Jim Furlong	5.00	2.20	.60
☐ 30 Lovell Coleman	6.00	2.70	.75
☐ 31 Pat Haines	5.00	2.20	.60
☐ 32 Bob Taylor	6.00	2.70	.75
☐ 33 Ernie Danjean	5.00	2.20	.60
☐ 34 Jerry Keeling	8.00	3.60	1.00
☐ 35 Larry Robinson	6.00	2.70	.75
☐ 36 George Hansen	5.00	2.20	.60
☐ 37 Ron Albright	5.00	2.20	.60
☐ 38 Larry Anderson	5.00	2.20	.60
☐ 39 Bill Miller	5.00	2.20	.60
☐ 40 Bill Britton	5.00	2.20	.60
☐ 41 Lynn Amadee	8.00	3.60	1.00
☐ 42 Mike Lashuk	5.00	2.20	.60
☐ 43 Tommy Joe Coffey	8.00	3.60	1.00
☐ 44 Junior Hawthorne	5.00	2.20	.60
☐ 45 Nat Dye	5.00	2.20	.60
☐ 46 Al Ecuyer	5.00	2.20	.60
☐ 47 Howie Schumm	5.00	2.20	.60

☐ 48 Zeke Smith	5.00	2.20	.60
☐ 49 Mike Wicklum	5.00	2.20	.60
☐ 50 Mike Volcan	5.00	2.20	.60
☐ 51 E.A. Sims	5.00	2.20	.60
☐ 52 Bill Mitchell	5.00	2.20	.60
☐ 53 Ken Reed	5.00	2.20	.60
☐ 54 Len Vella	5.00	2.20	.60
☐ 55 Johnny Bright	8.00	3.60	1.00
☐ 56 Don Getty	8.00	3.60	1.00
☐ 57 Oscar Kruger	5.00	2.20	.60
☐ 58 Ted Frechette	5.00	2.20	.60
☐ 59 James Earl Wright	5.00	2.20	.60
☐ 60 Roger Nelson	5.00	2.20	.60
☐ 61 Ron Lancaster	12.00	5.50	1.50
☐ 62 Bill Clarke	5.00	2.20	.60
☐ 63 Bob Shaw	5.00	2.20	.60
☐ 64 Ray Purdin	5.00	2.20	.60
☐ 65 Ron Atchison	8.00	3.60	1.00
☐ 66 Ted Urness	8.00	3.60	1.00
☐ 67 Bob Ptacek	5.00	2.20	.60
☐ 68 Neil Habig	5.00	2.20	.60
☐ 69 Garner Ekstran	6.00	2.70	.75
☐ 70 Gene Wlasiuk	5.00	2.20	.60
☐ 71 Jack Gotta	6.00	2.70	.75
☐ 72 Dick Cohee	5.00	2.20	.60
☐ 73 Ron Meadmore	5.00	2.20	.60
☐ 74 Martin Fabi	5.00	2.20	.60
☐ 75 Bob Good	5.00	2.20	.60
☐ 76 Len Legault	5.00	2.20	.60
☐ 77 Al Benecick	5.00	2.20	.60
☐ 78 Dale West	6.00	2.70	.75
☐ 79 Reg Whitehouse	5.00	2.20	.60
☐ 80 George Reed	10.00	4.50	1.25
☐ 81 Kenny Ploen	8.00	3.60	1.00
☐ 82 Leo Lewis	12.00	5.50	1.50
☐ 83 Dick Thornton	6.00	2.70	.75
☐ 84 Steve Patrick	5.00	2.20	.60
☐ 85 Frank Rigney	6.00	2.70	.75
☐ 86 Cornel Piper	5.00	2.20	.60
☐ 87 Sherwyn Thorson	5.00	2.20	.60
☐ 88 Ernie Pitts	5.00	2.20	.60
☐ 89 Roger Hagberg	6.00	2.70	.75
☐ 90 Bud Grant CO	50.00	22.00	6.25
☐ 91 Jack Delveaux	5.00	2.20	.60
☐ 92 Farrell Funston	6.00	2.70	.75
☐ 93 Ronnie Latourelle	5.00	2.20	.60
☐ 94 Roger Hamelin	5.00	2.20	.60
☐ 95 Gord Rowland	6.00	2.70	.75
☐ 96 Herb Gray	10.00	4.50	1.25
☐ 97 Nick Miller	5.00	2.20	.60
☐ 98 Norm Rauhaus	6.00	2.70	.75
☐ 99 Bill Whisler	5.00	2.20	.60
☐ 100 Hal Ledyard	5.00	2.20	.60
☐ S1 British Columbia Shield	45.00	20.00	5.50
☐ S2 Calgary Shield	45.00	20.00	5.50
☐ S3 Edmonton Shield	45.00	20.00	5.50
☐ S4 Saskatchewan Shield	45.00	20.00	5.50
☐ S5 Winnipeg Shield	45.00	20.00	5.50

1976 Nalley's Chips CFL

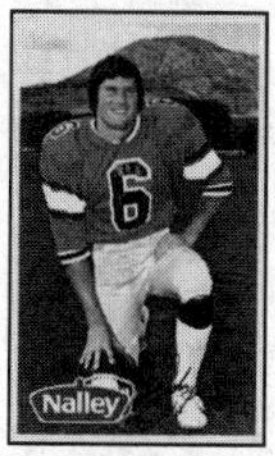

This 30-card set was distributed in Western Canada in boxes of Nalley's potato chips. The cards measure approximately 3 3/8" by 5 1/2" and feature posed color photos of the player, with the Nalley company name and player's signature below the picture. These blank-backed, unnumbered cards are listed below in alphabetical order according to their teams: British Columbia Lions (1-10), Edmonton Eskimos (11-20), and Calgary Stampeders (21-30).

	NRMT-MT	EXC	G-VG
COMPLETE SET (30)	350.00	160.00	45.00
COMMON CARD (1-30)	8.00	3.60	1.00
☐ 1 Bill Baker	20.00	9.00	2.50
☐ 2 Eric Guthrie	8.00	3.60	1.00
☐ 3 Lou Harris	10.00	4.50	1.25
☐ 4 Layne McDowell	8.00	3.60	1.00
☐ 5 Ray Nettles	8.00	3.60	1.00
☐ 6 Lui Passaglia	30.00	13.50	3.70
☐ 7 John Sciarra	15.00	6.75	1.85
☐ 8 Wayne Smith	8.00	3.60	1.00
☐ 9 Michael Strickland	8.00	3.60	1.00
☐ 10 Jim Young	20.00	9.00	2.50
☐ 11 Dave Cutler	15.00	6.75	1.85
☐ 12 Larry Highbaugh	12.00	5.50	1.50
☐ 13 John Konihowski	8.00	3.60	1.00
☐ 14 Bruce Lemmerman	10.00	4.50	1.25
☐ 15 George McGowan	12.00	5.50	1.50
☐ 16 Dale Potter	8.00	3.60	1.00
☐ 17 Charlie Turner	8.00	3.60	1.00
☐ 18 Tyrone Walls	10.00	4.50	1.25
☐ 19 Don Warrington	8.00	3.60	1.00
☐ 20 Tom Wilkinson	25.00	11.00	3.10
☐ 21 Willie Burden	35.00	16.00	4.40
☐ 22 Larry Cates	8.00	3.60	1.00
☐ 23 Lloyd Fairbanks	12.00	5.50	1.50
☐ 24 Joe Forzani	10.00	4.50	1.25
☐ 25 Tom Forzani	8.00	3.60	1.00
☐ 26 Rick Galbos	8.00	3.60	1.00
☐ 27 John Helton	15.00	6.75	1.85
☐ 28 Harold Holton	8.00	3.60	1.00
☐ 29 Rudy Linterman	12.00	5.50	1.50
☐ 30 Joe Pisarcik	15.00	6.75	1.85

1968 O-Pee-Chee CFL

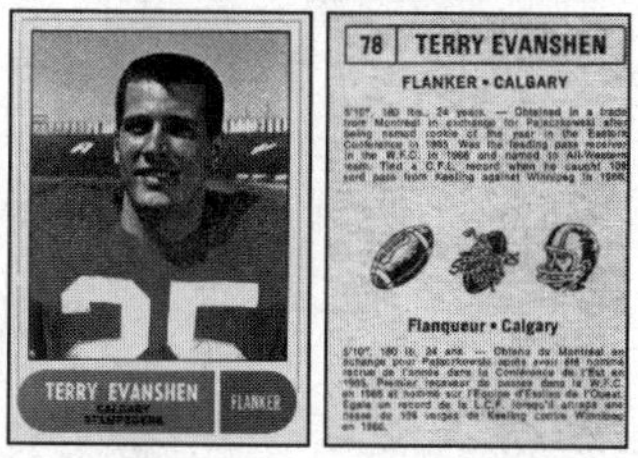

The 1968 O-Pee-Chee CFL set of 132 standard-size cards received limited distribution and is considered by some to be a test set. The card backs are written in English and French in green ink on yellowish card stock. The cards are ordered by teams. A complete checklist is given on card number 132. The card front design is similar to the design of the 1968 Topps NFL set.

	NRMT-MT	EXC	G-VG
COMPLETE SET (132)	1200.00	550.00	150.00
COMMON CARD (1-132)	7.50	3.40	.95
☐ 1 Roger Murphy	15.00	3.70	1.50
☐ 2 Charlie Parker	7.50	3.40	.95
☐ 3 Mike Webster	7.50	3.40	.95
☐ 4 Carroll Williams	7.50	3.40	.95
☐ 5 Phil Brady	7.50	3.40	.95
☐ 6 Dave Lewis	7.50	3.40	.95
☐ 7 John Baker	7.50	3.40	.95
☐ 8 Basil Bark	7.50	3.40	.95
☐ 9 Donnie Davis	7.50	3.40	.95
☐ 10 Pierre Desjardins	7.50	3.40	.95
☐ 11 Larry Fairholm	7.50	3.40	.95
☐ 12 Peter Paquette	7.50	3.40	.95
☐ 13 Ray Lychak	7.50	3.40	.95
☐ 14 Ted Collins	7.50	3.40	.95
☐ 15 Margene Adkins	12.00	5.50	1.50
☐ 16 Ron Stewart	20.00	9.00	2.50
☐ 17 Russ Jackson	40.00	18.00	5.00
☐ 18 Bo Scott	15.00	6.75	1.85
☐ 19 Joe Poirier	10.00	4.50	1.25
☐ 20 Wayne Giardino	7.50	3.40	.95
☐ 21 Gene Gaines	15.00	6.75	1.85
☐ 22 Billy Joe Booth	7.50	3.40	.95
☐ 23 Whit Tucker	15.00	6.75	1.85
☐ 24 Rick Black	7.50	3.40	.95
☐ 25 Ken Lehmann	12.00	5.50	1.50
☐ 26 Bob Brown	7.50	3.40	.95
☐ 27 Moe Racine	7.50	3.40	.95
☐ 28 Dick Thornton	10.00	4.50	1.25
☐ 29 Bob Taylor	10.00	4.50	1.25
☐ 30 Mel Profit	12.00	5.50	1.50
☐ 31 Dave Mann	10.00	4.50	1.25
☐ 32 Marv Luster	12.00	5.50	1.50
☐ 33 Ed Buchanan	7.50	3.40	.95
☐ 34 Ed Harrington	10.00	4.50	1.25
☐ 35 Jim Dillard	7.50	3.40	.95
☐ 36 Bob Taylor	10.00	4.50	1.25
☐ 37 Ron Arends	7.50	3.40	.95
☐ 38 Mike Wadsworth	7.50	3.40	.95
☐ 39 Wally Gabler	12.00	5.50	1.50
☐ 40 Pete Martin	7.50	3.40	.95
☐ 41 Danny Nykoluk	7.50	3.40	.95
☐ 42 Bill Frank	7.50	3.40	.95
☐ 43 Gordon Christian	7.50	3.40	.95
☐ 44 Tommy Joe Coffey	20.00	9.00	2.50
☐ 45 Ellison Kelly	20.00	9.00	2.50
☐ 46 Angelo Mosca	35.00	16.00	4.40
☐ 47 John Barrow	20.00	9.00	2.50
☐ 48 Bill Danychuk	12.00	5.50	1.50
☐ 49 Jon Hohman	7.50	3.40	.95
☐ 50 Bill Redell	7.50	3.40	.95
☐ 51 Joe Zuger	10.00	4.50	1.25
☐ 52 Willie Bethea	12.00	5.50	1.50
☐ 53 Dick Cohee	7.50	3.40	.95
☐ 54 Tommy Grant	15.00	6.75	1.85
☐ 55 Garney Henley	20.00	9.00	2.50
☐ 56 Ted Page	7.50	3.40	.95
☐ 57 Bob Krouse	7.50	3.40	.95
☐ 58 Phil Minnick	7.50	3.40	.95
☐ 59 Butch Pressley	7.50	3.40	.95
☐ 60 Dave Raimey	10.00	4.50	1.25
☐ 61 Sherwyn Thorson	7.50	3.40	.95
☐ 62 Bill Whisler	7.50	3.40	.95
☐ 63 Roger Hamelin	7.50	3.40	.95
☐ 64 Chuck Harrison	7.50	3.40	.95
☐ 65 Ken Nielsen	12.00	5.50	1.50
☐ 66 Ernie Pitts	7.50	3.40	.95
☐ 67 Mitch Zainasky	7.50	3.40	.95
☐ 68 John Schneider	7.50	3.40	.95
☐ 69 Ron Kirkland	7.50	3.40	.95
☐ 70 Paul Desjardins	7.50	3.40	.95
☐ 71 Luther Selbo	7.50	3.40	.95
☐ 72 Don Gilbert	7.50	3.40	.95
☐ 73 Bob Lueck	7.50	3.40	.95
☐ 74 Gerry Shaw	7.50	3.40	.95
☐ 75 Chuck Zickefoose	7.50	3.40	.95
☐ 76 Frank Andruski	7.50	3.40	.95
☐ 77 Lanny Boleski	7.50	3.40	.95
☐ 78 Terry Evanshen	20.00	9.00	2.50
☐ 79 Jim Furlong	7.50	3.40	.95
☐ 80 Wayne Harris	20.00	9.00	2.50
☐ 81 Jerry Keeling	15.00	6.75	1.85
☐ 82 Roger Kramer	10.00	4.50	1.25
☐ 83 Pete Liske	20.00	9.00	2.50
☐ 84 Dick Suderman	12.00	5.50	1.50
☐ 85 Granville Liggins	20.00	9.00	2.50
☐ 86 George Reed	30.00	13.50	3.70
☐ 87 Ron Lancaster	30.00	13.50	3.70
☐ 88 Alan Ford	7.50	3.40	.95
☐ 89 Gordon Barwell	7.50	3.40	.95
☐ 90 Wayne Shaw	7.50	3.40	.95
☐ 91 Bruce Bennett	15.00	6.75	1.85
☐ 92 Henry Dorsch	7.50	3.40	.95
☐ 93 Ken Reed	7.50	3.40	.95
☐ 94 Ron Atchison	15.00	6.75	1.85
☐ 95 Clyde Brock	7.50	3.40	.95
☐ 96 Al Benecick	7.50	3.40	.95
☐ 97 Ted Urness	12.00	5.50	1.50
☐ 98 Wally Dempsey	7.50	3.40	.95
☐ 99 Don Gerhardt	7.50	3.40	.95
☐ 100 Ted Dushinski	7.50	3.40	.95
☐ 101 Ed McQuarters	12.00	5.50	1.50
☐ 102 Bob Kosid	7.50	3.40	.95
☐ 103 Gary Brandt	7.50	3.40	.95
☐ 104 John Wydareny	10.00	4.50	1.25
☐ 105 Jim Thomas	7.50	3.40	.95
☐ 106 Art Perkins	7.50	3.40	.95
☐ 107 Frank Cosentino	12.00	5.50	1.50
☐ 108 Earl Edwards	10.00	4.50	1.25
☐ 109 Garry Lefebvre	7.50	3.40	.95
☐ 110 Greg Pipes	10.00	4.50	1.25
☐ 111 Ian MacLeod	7.50	3.40	.95
☐ 112 Dick Dupuis	7.50	3.40	.95
☐ 113 Ron Forwick	7.50	3.40	.95
☐ 114 Jerry Griffin	7.50	3.40	.95
☐ 115 John LaGrone	12.00	5.50	1.50
☐ 116 E.A. Sims	7.50	3.40	.95
☐ 117 Greenard Poles	7.50	3.40	.95
☐ 118 Leroy Sledge	7.50	3.40	.95
☐ 119 Ken Sugarman	10.00	4.50	1.25
☐ 120 Jim Young	30.00	13.50	3.70
☐ 121 Garner Ekstran	10.00	4.50	1.25
☐ 122 Jim Evenson	12.00	5.50	1.50
☐ 123 Greg Findlay	7.50	3.40	.95
☐ 124 Ted Gerela	10.00	4.50	1.25
☐ 125 Lach Heron	10.00	4.50	1.25
☐ 126 Mike Martin	7.50	3.40	.95
☐ 127 Craig Murray	7.50	3.40	.95
☐ 128 Pete Ohler	7.50	3.40	.95
☐ 129 Sonny Homer	10.00	4.50	1.25
☐ 130 Bill Lasseter	7.50	3.40	.95
☐ 131 John McDowell	7.50	3.40	.95
☐ 132 Checklist Card	70.00	17.50	7.00

1968 O-Pee-Chee CFL Poster Inserts

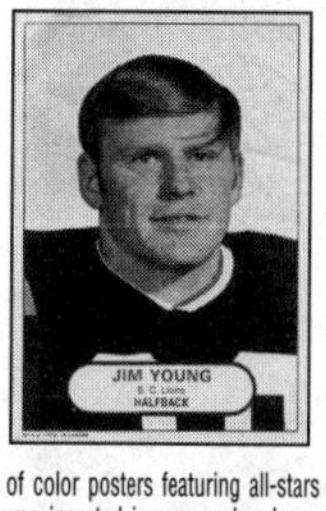

This 16-card set of color posters featuring all-stars of the Canadian Football League was inserted in wax packs along with the regular issue of 1968 O-Pee-Chee CFL cards. These (approximately) 5" by 7" posters were folded twice in order to fit in the wax packs. They are unnumbered and are blank on the back. They were printed on very thin paper. These posters are similar in appearance to the 1967 Topps baseball and 1968 Topps football poster inserts.

	NRMT-MT	EXC	G-VG
COMPLETE SET (16)	325.00	145.00	40.00
COMMON CARD (1-16)	15.00	6.75	1.85
☐ 1 Margene Adkins	18.00	8.00	2.20
☐ 2 Tommy Joe Coffey	25.00	11.00	3.10
☐ 3 Frank Cosentino	18.00	8.00	2.20
☐ 4 Terry Evanshen	25.00	11.00	3.10
☐ 5 Larry Fairholm	15.00	6.75	1.85
☐ 6 Wally Gabler	15.00	6.75	1.85
☐ 7 Russ Jackson	35.00	16.00	4.40
☐ 8 Ron Lancaster	30.00	13.50	3.70
☐ 9 Pete Liske	25.00	11.00	3.10
☐ 10 Dave Mann	18.00	8.00	2.20
☐ 11 Ken Nielsen	18.00	8.00	2.20
☐ 12 Dave Raimey	18.00	8.00	2.20
☐ 13 George Reed	30.00	13.50	3.70
☐ 14 Carroll Williams	15.00	6.75	1.85
☐ 15 Jim Young	30.00	13.50	3.70
☐ 16 Joe Zuger	15.00	6.75	1.85

1970 O-Pee-Chee CFL

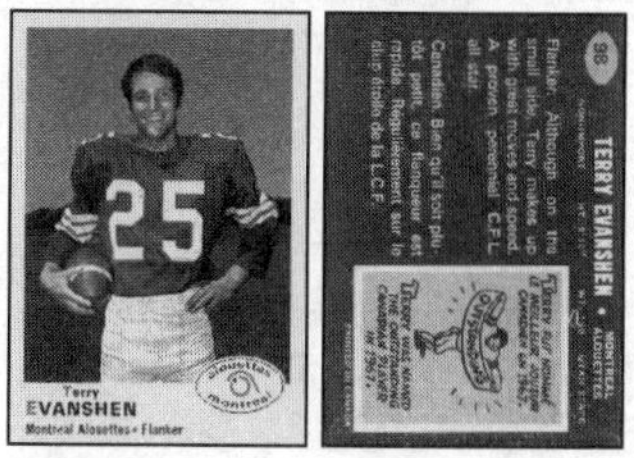

The 1970 O-Pee-Chee CFL set features 115 standard-size cards ordered by teams. The design of these cards is very similar to the 1969 Topps NFL football issue. The card backs are written in French and English; the card back is predominantly black with white lettering and green accent. Six miscellaneous special feature cards comprise cards numbered 110-115.

	NRMT-MT	EXC	G-VG
COMPLETE SET (115)	325.00	145.00	40.00
COMMON CARD (1-115)	2.00	.90	.25
☐ 1 Ed Harrington	3.00	.75	.30
☐ 2 Danny Nykoluk	2.00	.90	.25
☐ 3 Marv Luster	4.00	1.80	.50
☐ 4 Dave Raimey	3.00	1.35	.35
☐ 5 Bill Symons	3.00	1.35	.35
☐ 6 Tom Wilkinson	20.00	9.00	2.50
☐ 7 Mike Wadsworth	2.00	.90	.25
☐ 8 Dick Thornton	3.00	1.35	.35
☐ 9 Jim Tomlin	2.00	.90	.25
☐ 10 Mel Profit	3.00	1.35	.35
☐ 11 Bob Taylor	3.00	1.35	.35
☐ 12 Dave Mann	3.00	1.35	.35
☐ 13 Tommy Joe Coffey	5.00	2.20	.60
☐ 14 Angelo Mosca	18.00	8.00	2.20
☐ 15 Joe Zuger	3.00	1.35	.35
☐ 16 Garney Henley	10.00	4.50	1.25
☐ 17 Mike Strofolino	2.00	.90	.25
☐ 18 Billy Ray Locklin	2.00	.90	.25
☐ 19 Ted Page	2.00	.90	.25
☐ 20 Bill Danychuk	3.00	1.35	.35
☐ 21 Bob Krouse	2.00	.90	.25
☐ 22 John Reid	2.00	.90	.25
☐ 23 Dick Wesolowski	2.00	.90	.25
☐ 24 Willie Bethea	3.00	1.35	.35
☐ 25 Ken Sugarman	3.00	1.35	.35
☐ 26 Rich Robinson	2.00	.90	.25
☐ 27 Dave Tobey	2.00	.90	.25
☐ 28 Paul Brothers	2.00	.90	.25
☐ 29 Charlie Brown RB	2.00	.90	.25
☐ 30 Jerry Bradley	2.00	.90	.25
☐ 31 Ted Gerela	3.00	1.35	.35
☐ 32 Jim Young	8.00	3.60	1.00
☐ 33 Gary Robinson	2.00	.90	.25
☐ 34 Bob Howes	2.00	.90	.25
☐ 35 Greg Findlay	2.00	.90	.25
☐ 36 Trevor Ekdahl	3.00	1.35	.35
☐ 37 Ron Stewart	6.00	2.70	.75
☐ 38 Joe Poirier	3.00	1.35	.35
☐ 39 Wayne Giardino	2.00	.90	.25
☐ 40 Tom Schuette	2.00	.90	.25
☐ 41 Roger Perdrix	2.00	.90	.25
☐ 42 Jim Mankins	2.00	.90	.25
☐ 43 Jay Roberts	2.00	.90	.25
☐ 44 Ken Lehmann	3.00	1.35	.35
☐ 45 Jerry Campbell	3.00	1.35	.35
☐ 46 Billy Joe Booth	3.00	1.35	.35
☐ 47 Whit Tucker	5.00	2.20	.60
☐ 48 Moe Racine	2.00	.90	.25
☐ 49 Corey Colehour	3.00	1.35	.35
☐ 50 Dave Gasser	2.00	.90	.25
☐ 51 Jerry Griffin	2.00	.90	.25
☐ 52 Greg Pipes	3.00	1.35	.35
☐ 53 Roy Shatzko	2.00	.90	.25
☐ 54 Ron Forwick	2.00	.90	.25
☐ 55 Ed Molstad	2.00	.90	.25
☐ 56 Ken Ferguson	2.00	.90	.25
☐ 57 Terry Swarn	5.00	2.20	.60
☐ 58 Tom Nettles	2.00	.90	.25
☐ 59 John Wydareny	3.00	1.35	.35
☐ 60 Bayne Norrie	2.00	.90	.25
☐ 61 Wally Gabler	3.00	1.35	.35
☐ 62 Paul Desjardins	2.00	.90	.25
☐ 63 Peter Francis	2.00	.90	.25
☐ 64 Bill Frank	2.00	.90	.25
☐ 65 Chuck Harrison	2.00	.90	.25
☐ 66 Gene Lakusiak	2.00	.90	.25
☐ 67 Phil Minnick	2.00	.90	.25
☐ 68 Doug Strong	2.00	.90	.25
☐ 69 Glen Schapansky	2.00	.90	.25
☐ 70 Ed Ulmer	2.00	.90	.25
☐ 71 Bill Whisler	2.00	.90	.25
☐ 72 Ted Collins	2.00	.90	.25

□ 73 Larry DeGraw	2.00	.90	.25
□ 74 Henry Dorsch	2.00	.90	.25
□ 75 Alan Ford	2.00	.90	.25
□ 76 Ron Lancaster	20.00	9.00	2.50
□ 77 Bob Kosid	2.00	.90	.25
□ 78 Bobby Thompson	2.00	.90	.25
□ 79 Ted Dushinski	2.00	.90	.25
□ 80 Bruce Bennett	4.00	1.80	.50
□ 81 George Reed	15.00	6.75	1.85
□ 82 Wayne Shaw	2.00	.90	.25
□ 83 Cliff Shaw	2.00	.90	.25
□ 84 Jack Abendschan	3.00	1.35	.35
□ 85 Ed McQuarters	5.00	2.20	.60
□ 86 Jerry Keeling	5.00	2.20	.60
□ 87 Gerry Shaw	2.00	.90	.25
□ 88 Basil Bark UER (Misspelled Back)	2.00	.90	.25
□ 89 Wayne Harris	6.00	2.70	.75
□ 90 Jim Furlong	2.00	.90	.25
□ 91 Larry Robinson	3.00	1.35	.35
□ 92 John Helton	10.00	4.50	1.25
□ 93 Dave Cranmer	2.00	.90	.25
□ 94 Lanny Boleski UER (Misspelled Larry)	2.00	.90	.25
□ 95 Herman Harrison	5.00	2.20	.60
□ 96 Granville Liggins	5.00	2.20	.60
□ 97 Joe Forzani	3.00	1.35	.35
□ 98 Terry Evanshen	8.00	3.60	1.00
□ 99 Sonny Wade	6.00	2.70	.75
□ 100 Dennis Duncan	2.00	.90	.25
□ 101 Al Phaneuf	3.00	1.35	.35
□ 102 Larry Fairholm	2.00	.90	.25
□ 103 Moses Denson	4.00	1.80	.50
□ 104 Gino Baretta	2.00	.90	.25
□ 105 Gene Ceppetelli	2.00	.90	.25
□ 106 Dick Smith	2.00	.90	.25
□ 107 Gordon Judges	2.00	.90	.25
□ 108 Harry Olszewski	2.00	.90	.25
□ 109 Mike Webster	2.00	.90	.25
□ 110 Checklist 1-115	30.00	7.50	3.00
□ 111 Outstanding Player (list from 1953-1969)	8.00	3.60	1.00
□ 112 Player of the Year (list from 1954-1969)	8.00	3.60	1.00
□ 113 Lineman of the Year (list from 1955-1969)	6.00	2.70	.75
□ 114 CFL Coaches (listed on card front)	6.00	2.70	.75
□ 115 Identifying Player (explanation of uniform numbering system)	15.00	6.75	1.85

1970 O-Pee-Chee CFL Push-Out Inserts

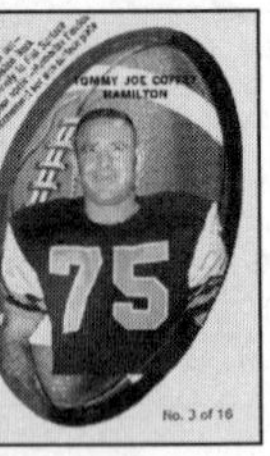
No. 3 of 16

This attractive set of 16 push-out inserts features players in the Canadian Football League. The cards are standard size, but are actually stickers, if the backs are moistened. The cards are numbered at the bottom and the backs are blank. Instructions on the front (upper left corner) are written in both English and French. Each player's team is identified on his card under his name. The player is shown superimposed over a football; the push-out area is essentially the football.

	NRMT-MT	EXC	G-VG
COMPLETE SET (16)	250.00	110.00	31.00
COMMON CARD (1-16)	12.00	5.50	1.50
□ 1 Ed Harrington	12.00	5.50	1.50
□ 2 Danny Nykoluk	12.00	5.50	1.50
□ 3 Tommy Joe Coffey	25.00	11.00	3.10
□ 4 Angelo Mosca	35.00	16.00	4.40
□ 5 Ken Sugarman	15.00	6.75	1.85
□ 6 Jay Roberts	12.00	5.50	1.50
□ 7 Joe Poirier	15.00	6.75	1.85
□ 8 Corey Colehour	12.00	5.50	1.50
□ 9 Dave Gasser	12.00	5.50	1.50
□ 10 Wally Gabler	15.00	6.75	1.85
□ 11 Paul Desjardins	12.00	5.50	1.50
□ 12 Larry DeGraw	12.00	5.50	1.50
□ 13 Jerry Keeling	20.00	9.00	2.50
□ 14 Gerry Shaw	12.00	5.50	1.50
□ 15 Terry Evanshen	25.00	11.00	3.10
□ 16 Sonny Wade	15.00	6.75	1.85

1971 O-Pee-Chee CFL

The 1971 O-Pee-Chee CFL set features 132 standard-size cards ordered by teams. The card fronts feature a bright red border. The card backs are written in French and English. A complete checklist is given on card number 132. The key card in the set is Joe Theismann, which is his first professional card and predates his entry into the NFL.

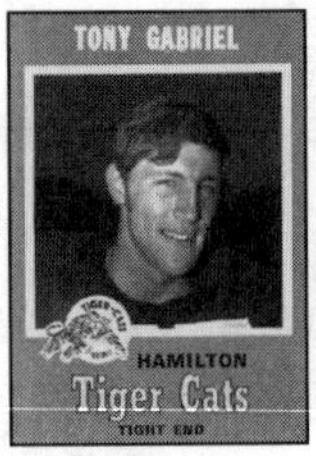
TONY GABRIEL
HAMILTON
Tiger Cats
TIGHT END

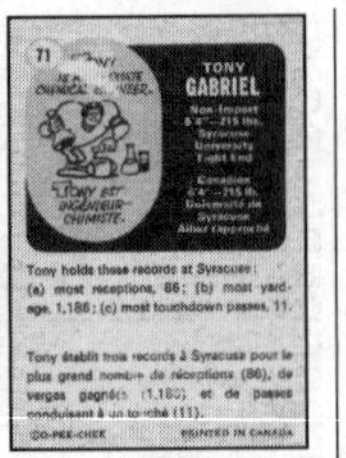
TONY GABRIEL

	NRMT-MT	EXC	G-VG
COMPLETE SET (132)	250.00	110.00	31.00
COMMON CARD (1-132)	1.00	.45	.12
□ 1 Bill Symons	1.50	.35	.15
□ 2 Mel Profit	1.50	.70	.19
□ 3 Jim Tomlin	1.00	.45	.12
□ 4 Ed Harrington	1.50	.70	.19
□ 5 Jim Corrigall	4.00	1.80	.50
□ 6 Chip Barrett	1.00	.45	.12
□ 7 Marv Luster	3.00	1.35	.35
□ 8 Ellison Kelly	4.00	1.80	.50
□ 9 Charlie Bray	1.00	.45	.12
□ 10 Pete Martin	1.00	.45	.12
□ 11 Tony Moro	1.00	.45	.12
□ 12 Dave Raimey	1.50	.70	.19
□ 13 Joe Theismann	100.00	45.00	12.50
□ 14 Greg Barton	6.00	2.70	.75
□ 15 Leon McQuay	6.00	2.70	.75
□ 16 Don Jonas	6.00	2.70	.75
□ 17 Doug Strong	1.00	.45	.12
□ 18 Paul Brule	1.00	.45	.12
□ 19 Bill Frank	1.00	.45	.12
□ 20 Joe Critchlow	1.00	.45	.12
□ 21 Chuck Liebrock	1.00	.45	.12
□ 22 Rob McLaren	1.00	.45	.12
□ 23 Bob Swift	1.00	.45	.12
□ 24 Rick Shaw	1.00	.45	.12
□ 25 Ross Richardson	1.00	.45	.12
□ 26 Benji Dial	1.00	.45	.12
□ 27 Jim Heighton	1.00	.45	.12
□ 28 Ed Ulmer	1.00	.45	.12
□ 29 Glen Schapansky	1.00	.45	.12
□ 30 Larry Slagle	1.00	.45	.12
□ 31 Tom Cassese	1.00	.45	.12
□ 32 Ted Gerela	1.00	.45	.12
□ 33 Bob Howes	1.00	.45	.12
□ 34 Ken Sugarman	1.50	.70	.19
□ 35 A.D. Whitfield	1.50	.70	.19
□ 36 Jim Young	6.00	2.70	.75
□ 37 Tom Wilkinson	10.00	4.50	1.25
□ 38 Lefty Hendrickson	1.00	.45	.12
□ 39 Dave Golinsky	1.00	.45	.12
□ 40 Gerry Herron	1.00	.45	.12
□ 41 Jim Evenson	1.50	.70	.19
□ 42 Greg Findlay	1.00	.45	.12
□ 43 Garrett Hunsperger	1.00	.45	.12
□ 44 Jerry Bradley	1.00	.45	.12
□ 45 Trevor Ekdahl	1.50	.70	.19
□ 46 Bayne Norrie	1.00	.45	.12
□ 47 Henry King	1.00	.45	.12
□ 48 Terry Swarn	1.50	.70	.19
□ 49 Jim Thomas	1.50	.70	.19
□ 50 Bob Houmard	1.00	.45	.12
□ 51 Don Trull	3.00	1.35	.35
□ 52 Dave Cutler	8.00	3.60	1.00
□ 53 Mike Law	1.00	.45	.12
□ 54 Dick Dupuis	1.50	.70	.19
□ 55 Dave Gasser	1.00	.45	.12
□ 56 Ron Forwick	1.00	.45	.12
□ 57 John LaGrone	1.50	.70	.19
□ 58 Greg Pipes	1.50	.70	.19
□ 59 Ted Page	1.00	.45	.12
□ 60 John Wydareny	1.50	.70	.19
□ 61 Joe Zuger	1.50	.70	.19
□ 62 Tommy Joe Coffey	6.00	2.70	.75
□ 63 Rensi Perdoni	1.00	.45	.12
□ 64 Bob Taylor	1.50	.70	.19
□ 65 Garney Henley	6.00	2.70	.75
□ 66 Dick Wesolowski	1.00	.45	.12
□ 67 Dave Fleming	1.00	.45	.12
□ 68 Bill Danychuk	1.50	.70	.19
□ 69 Angelo Mosca	18.00	8.00	2.20
□ 70 Bob Krouse	1.00	.45	.12
□ 71 Tony Gabriel	18.00	8.00	2.20
□ 72 Wally Gabler	1.50	.70	.19
□ 73 Bob Steiner	1.00	.45	.12
□ 74 John Reid	1.00	.45	.12
□ 75 Jon Hohman	1.00	.45	.12
□ 76 Barry Ardern	1.00	.45	.12
□ 77 Jerry Campbell	1.50	.70	.19
□ 78 Billy Cooper	1.00	.45	.12
□ 79 Dave Braggins	1.00	.45	.12
□ 80 Tom Schuette	1.00	.45	.12
□ 81 Dennis Duncan	1.00	.45	.12
□ 82 Moe Racine	1.00	.45	.12
□ 83 Rod Woodward	1.00	.45	.12
□ 84 Al Marcelin	1.50	.70	.19
□ 85 Garry Wood	5.00	2.20	.60
□ 86 Wayne Giardino	1.00	.45	.12
□ 87 Roger Perdrix	1.00	.45	.12
□ 88 Hugh Oldham	1.00	.45	.12
□ 89 Rick Cassatta	2.50	1.10	.30
□ 90 Jack Abendschan	1.50	.70	.19
□ 91 Don Bahnuik	1.00	.45	.12
□ 92 Bill Baker	10.00	4.50	1.25
□ 93 Gordon Barwell	1.00	.45	.12
□ 94 Gary Brandt	1.00	.45	.12
□ 95 Henry Dorsch	1.00	.45	.12
□ 96 Ted Dushinski	1.00	.45	.12
□ 97 Alan Ford	1.00	.45	.12
□ 98 Ken Frith	1.00	.45	.12
□ 99 Ralph Galloway	1.00	.45	.12
□ 100 Bob Kosid	1.00	.45	.12
□ 101 Ron Lancaster	15.00	6.75	1.85
□ 102 Silas McKinnie	1.00	.45	.12
□ 103 George Reed	8.00	3.60	1.00
□ 104 Gene Ceppetelli	1.00	.45	.12
□ 105 Merl Code	1.00	.45	.12
□ 106 Peter Dalla Riva	8.00	3.60	1.00
□ 107 Moses Denson	2.50	1.10	.30
□ 108 Pierre Desjardins	1.00	.45	.12
□ 109 Terry Evanshen	6.00	2.70	.75
□ 110 Larry Fairholm	1.50	.70	.19
□ 111 Gene Gaines	5.00	2.20	.60
□ 112 Ed George	1.50	.70	.19
□ 113 Gordon Judges	1.00	.45	.12
□ 114 Garry Lefebvre	1.00	.45	.12
□ 115 Al Phaneuf	1.50	.70	.19
□ 116 Steve Smear	5.00	2.20	.60
□ 117 Sonny Wade	3.00	1.35	.35
□ 118 Frank Andruski	1.00	.45	.12
□ 119 Basil Bark	1.00	.45	.12
□ 120 Lanny Boleski	1.00	.45	.12
□ 121 Joe Forzani	1.50	.70	.19
□ 122 Jim Furlong	1.00	.45	.12
□ 123 Wayne Harris	6.00	2.70	.75
□ 124 Herman Harrison	4.00	1.80	.50
□ 125 John Helton	4.00	1.80	.50
□ 126 Wayne Holm	1.00	.45	.12
□ 127 Fred James	1.00	.45	.12
□ 128 Jerry Keeling	4.00	1.80	.50
□ 129 Rudy Linterman	1.50	.70	.19
□ 130 Larry Robinson	1.50	.70	.19
□ 131 Gerry Shaw	1.00	.45	.12
□ 132 Checklist Card	25.00	6.25	2.50

1971 O-Pee-Chee CFL Poster Inserts

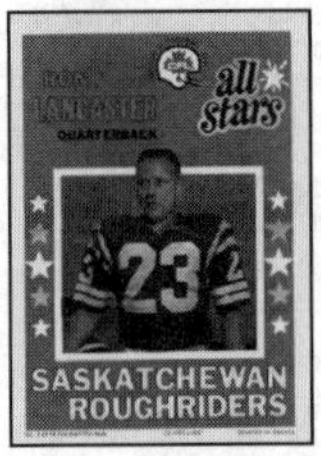
all stars
QUARTERBACK
SASKATCHEWAN
ROUGHRIDERS

This 16-card set of posters featuring all-stars of the Canadian Football League was inserted in wax packs along with the regular issue of O-Pee-Chee cards. These 5" by 7" posters were folded twice in order to fit in the wax packs. They are numbered at the bottom and are blank on the back. These posters are somewhat similar in appearance to the Topps football poster inserts of 1971.

	NRMT-MT	EXC	G-VG
COMPLETE SET (16)	175.00	80.00	22.00
COMMON CARD (1-16)	8.00	3.60	1.00
□ 1 Tommy Joe Coffey	15.00	6.75	1.85
□ 2 Herman Harrison	15.00	6.75	1.85
□ 3 Bill Frank	8.00	3.60	1.00
□ 4 Ellison Kelly	10.00	4.50	1.25
□ 5 Charlie Bray	8.00	3.60	1.00
□ 6 Bill Danychuk	10.00	4.50	1.25
□ 7 Ron Lancaster	20.00	9.00	2.50
□ 8 Bill Symons	10.00	4.50	1.25
□ 9 Steve Smear	10.00	4.50	1.25
□ 10 Angelo Mosca	20.00	9.00	2.50
□ 11 Wayne Harris	15.00	6.75	1.85
□ 12 Greg Findlay	8.00	3.60	1.00
□ 13 John Wydareny	10.00	4.50	1.25
□ 14 Garney Henley	15.00	6.75	1.85
□ 15 Al Phaneuf	10.00	4.50	1.25
□ 16 Ed Harrington	10.00	4.50	1.25

1972 O-Pee-Chee CFL

The 1972 O-Pee-Chee CFL set of 132 standard-size cards is the last O-Pee-Chee CFL issue to date. Cards are ordered by teams. The card backs are written in French and English; card back is blue and green print on white card stock. Fourteen Pro-Action cards (118-131) and a checklist card (132) complete the set. The key card in the set is Joe Theismann. The cards were originally sold in ten-cent wax packs with eight cards and a piece of bubble gum.

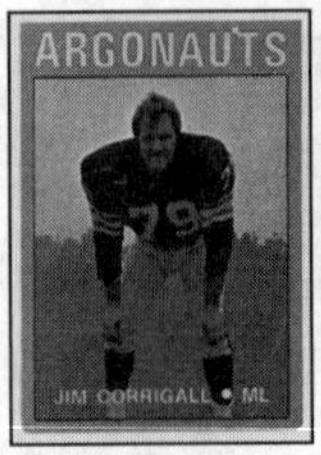
ARGONAUTS
JIM CORRIGALL • ML

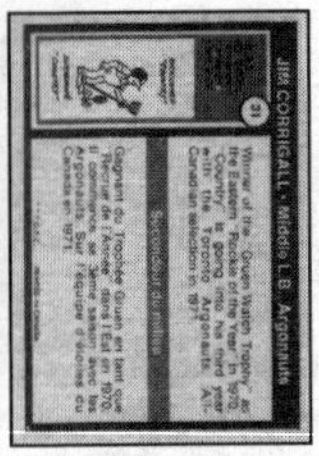

	NRMT-MT	EXC	G-VG
COMPLETE SET (132)	200.00	90.00	25.00
COMMON CARD (1-132)	1.00	.45	.12
□ 1 Bob Krouse	1.00	.25	.10
□ 2 John Williams	1.00	.45	.12
□ 3 Garney Henley	6.00	2.70	.75
□ 4 Dick Wesolowski	1.00	.45	.12
□ 5 Paul McKay	1.00	.45	.12
□ 6 Bill Danychuk	1.50	.70	.19
□ 7 Angelo Mosca	12.00	5.50	1.50
□ 8 Tommy Joe Coffey	5.00	2.20	.60
□ 9 Tony Gabriel	10.00	4.50	1.25
□ 10 Mike Blum	1.00	.45	.12
□ 11 Doug Mitchell	1.00	.45	.12
□ 12 Emery Hicks	1.00	.45	.12
□ 13 Max Anderson	1.00	.45	.12
□ 14 Ed George	1.50	.70	.19
□ 15 Mark Kosmos	1.50	.70	.19
□ 16 Ted Collins	1.00	.45	.12
□ 17 Peter Dalla Riva	5.00	2.20	.60
□ 18 Pierre Desjardins	1.00	.45	.12
□ 19 Terry Evanshen	6.00	2.70	.75
□ 20 Larry Fairholm	1.50	.70	.19
□ 21 Jim Foley	1.50	.70	.19
□ 22 Gordon Judges	1.00	.45	.12
□ 23 Barry Randall	1.00	.45	.12
□ 24 Brad Upshaw	1.00	.45	.12
□ 25 Jorma Kuisma	1.00	.45	.12
□ 26 Mike Widger	1.00	.45	.12
□ 27 Joe Theismann	50.00	22.00	6.25
□ 28 Greg Barton	4.00	1.80	.50
□ 29 Bill Symons	1.50	.70	.19
□ 30 Leon McQuay	4.00	1.80	.50
□ 31 Jim Corrigall	4.00	1.80	.50
□ 32 Jim Stillwagon	4.00	1.80	.50
□ 33 Dick Thornton	1.50	.70	.19
□ 34 Marv Luster	4.00	1.80	.50
□ 35 Paul Desjardins	1.00	.45	.12
□ 36 Mike Eben	1.00	.45	.12
□ 37 Eric Allen	5.00	2.20	.60
□ 38 Chip Barrett	1.00	.45	.12
□ 39 Noah Jackson	3.00	1.35	.35
□ 40 Jim Young	6.00	2.70	.75
□ 41 Trevor Ekdahl	1.50	.70	.19
□ 42 Garrett Hunsperger	1.00	.45	.12
□ 43 Willie Postler	1.00	.45	.12
□ 44 George Anderson	1.00	.45	.12
□ 45 Ron Estay	1.00	.45	.12
□ 46 Johnny Musso	15.00	6.75	1.85
□ 47 Eric Guthrie	1.00	.45	.12
□ 48 Monroe Eley	1.00	.45	.12
□ 49 Don Bunce	5.00	2.20	.60
□ 50 Jim Evenson	1.50	.70	.19
□ 51 Ken Sugarman	1.50	.70	.19
□ 52 Dave Golinsky	1.00	.45	.12
□ 53 Wayne Harris	5.00	2.20	.60
□ 54 Jerry Keeling	4.00	1.80	.50
□ 55 Herman Harrison	4.00	1.80	.50
□ 56 Larry Robinson	1.50	.70	.19
□ 57 John Helton	4.00	1.80	.50
□ 58 Gerry Shaw	1.00	.45	.12
□ 59 Frank Andruski	1.00	.45	.12
□ 60 Basil Bark	1.00	.45	.12
□ 61 Joe Forzani	1.50	.70	.19
□ 62 Jim Furlong	1.00	.45	.12
□ 63 Rudy Linterman	1.50	.70	.19
□ 64 Granville Liggins	4.00	1.80	.50
□ 65 Lanny Boleski	1.00	.45	.12
□ 66 Hugh Oldham	1.00	.45	.12
□ 67 Dave Braggins	1.00	.45	.12
□ 68 Jerry Campbell	1.50	.70	.19
□ 69 Al Marcelin	1.50	.70	.19
□ 70 Tom Pullen	1.00	.45	.12
□ 71 Rudy Sims	1.00	.45	.12
□ 72 Marshall Shirk	1.00	.45	.12
□ 73 Tom Laputka	1.00	.45	.12
□ 74 Barry Ardern	1.00	.45	.12
□ 75 Billy Cooper	1.00	.45	.12
□ 76 Dan Deever	1.00	.45	.12
□ 77 Wayne Giardino	1.00	.45	.12
□ 78 Terry Wellesley	1.00	.45	.12
□ 79 Ron Lancaster	12.00	5.50	1.50
□ 80 George Reed	10.00	4.50	1.25
□ 81 Bobby Thompson	1.00	.45	.12
□ 82 Jack Abendschan	1.50	.70	.19
□ 83 Ed McQuarters	3.00	1.35	.35
□ 84 Bruce Bennett	3.00	1.35	.35
□ 85 Bill Baker	5.00	2.20	.60
□ 86 Don Bahnuik	1.00	.45	.12
□ 87 Gary Brandt	1.00	.45	.12
□ 88 Henry Dorach	1.00	.45	.12
□ 89 Ted Dushinski	1.00	.45	.12
□ 90 Alan Ford	1.00	.45	.12
□ 91 Bob Kosid	1.00	.45	.12
□ 92 Greg Pipes	1.50	.70	.19
□ 93 John LaGrone	1.50	.70	.19
□ 94 Dave Gasser	1.00	.45	.12

☐ 95 Bob Taylor	1.50	.70	.19
☐ 96 Dave Cutler	5.00	2.20	.60
☐ 97 Dick Dupuis	1.00	.45	.12
☐ 98 Ron Forwick	1.00	.45	.12
☐ 99 Bayne Norrie	1.00	.45	.12
☐ 100 Jim Henshall	1.00	.45	.12
☐ 101 Charlie Turner	1.00	.45	.12
☐ 102 Fred Dunn	1.00	.45	.12
☐ 103 Sam Scarber	1.00	.45	.12
☐ 104 Bruce Lemmerman	5.00	2.20	.60
☐ 105 Don Jonas	6.00	2.70	.75
☐ 106 Doug Strong	1.00	.45	.12
☐ 107 Ed Williams	1.00	.45	.12
☐ 108 Paul Markle	1.00	.45	.12
☐ 109 Gene Lakusiak	1.00	.45	.12
☐ 110 Bob LaRose	1.00	.45	.12
☐ 111 Rob McLaren	1.00	.45	.12
☐ 112 Pete Ribbins	1.00	.45	.12
☐ 113 Bill Frank	1.00	.45	.12
☐ 114 Bob Swift	1.00	.45	.12
☐ 115 Chuck Liebrock	1.00	.45	.12
☐ 116 Joe Critchlow	1.00	.45	.12
☐ 117 Paul Williams	1.00	.45	.12
☐ 118 Pro Action	1.00	.45	.12
Max Anderson			
☐ 119 Pro Action	1.00	.45	.12
Max Anderson			
☐ 120 Pro Action	1.00	.45	.12
☐ 121 Pro Action	1.00	.45	.12
☐ 122 Pro Action	1.00	.45	.12
Emery Hicks			
Frank Andruski			
☐ 123 Pro Action	1.00	.45	.12
Greg Barton			
☐ 124 Pro Action	1.00	.45	.12
☐ 125 Pro Action	1.00	.45	.12
Paul Markle			
☐ 126 Pro Action	1.00	.45	.12
☐ 127 Pro Action	2.00	.90	.25
Don Jonas			
☐ 128 Pro Action	2.00	.90	.25
Don Jonas			
☐ 129 Pro Action	1.00	.45	.12
☐ 130 Pro Action	10.00	4.50	1.25
Joe Theismann			
☐ 131 Pro Action	1.00	.45	.12
Paul McKay			
☐ 132 Checklist Card	35.00	8.75	3.50

1972 O-Pee-Chee CFL Trio Sticker Inserts

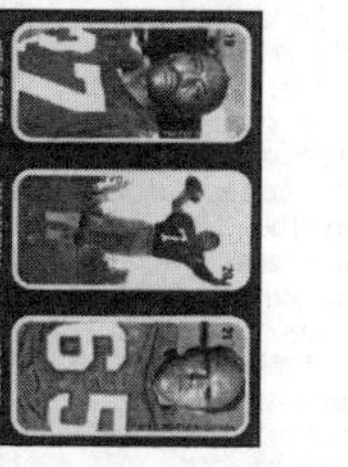

Issued with the 1972 CFL regular cards was this 24-card set of trio peel-off sticker inserts. These blank-backed panels of three small stickers are 2 1/2" by 3 1/2" and have a distinctive black border around an inner white border. Each individual player is numbered in the upper corner of his card; the player's name and team are given below the player's picture in the black border. The copyright notation (O.P.C. Printed in Canada) is overprinted in the picture area of the card.

	NRMT-MT	EXC	G-VG
COMPLETE SET (24)	300.00	135.00	38.00
COMMON PANEL	10.00	4.50	1.25
☐ 1 Johnny Musso	40.00	18.00	5.00
2 Ron Lancaster			
3 Don Jonas			
☐ 4 Jerry Campbell	10.00	4.50	1.25
5 Bill Symons			
6 Ted Collins			
☐ 7 Dave Cutler	12.00	5.50	1.50
8 Paul McKay			
9 Rudy Sims			
☐ 10 Wayne Harris	25.00	11.00	3.10
11 Greg Pipes			
12 Chuck Ealey			
☐ 13 Ron Estay	10.00	4.50	1.25
14 Jack Abendschan			
15 Paul Markle			
☐ 16 Jim Stillwagon	12.00	5.50	1.50
17 Terry Evanshen			
18 Willie Postler			
☐ 19 Hugh Oldham	40.00	18.00	5.00
20 Joe Theismann			
21 Ed George			
☐ 22 Larry Robinson	12.00	5.50	1.50
23 Bruce Lemmerman			
24 Garney Henley			
☐ 25 Bill Baker	12.00	5.50	1.50
26 Bob LaRose			
27 Frank Andruski			
☐ 28 Don Bunce	15.00	6.75	1.85
29 George Reed			
30 Doug Strong			
☐ 31 Al Marcelin	12.00	5.50	1.50
32 Leon McQuay			
33 Peter Dalla Riva			
☐ 34 Dick Dupuis	10.00	4.50	1.25
35 Bill Danychuk			
36 Marshall Shirk			
☐ 37 Jerry Keeling	12.00	5.50	1.50
38 John LaGrone			
39 Bob Krouse			
☐ 40 Jim Young	12.00	5.50	1.50
41 Ed McQuarters			
42 Gene Lakusiak			
☐ 43 Dick Thornton	10.00	4.50	1.25
44 Larry Fairholm			
45 Garrett Hunsperger			
☐ 46 Dave Braggins	12.00	5.50	1.50
47 Greg Barton			
48 Mark Kosmos			
☐ 49 John Helton	12.00	5.50	1.50
50 Bobby Taylor			
51 Dick Wesolowski			
☐ 52 Don Bahnuik	10.00	4.50	1.25
53 Rob McLaren			
54 Granville Liggins			
☐ 55 Monroe Eley	10.00	4.50	1.25
56 Bob Thompson			
57 Ed Williams			
☐ 58 Tom Pullen	10.00	4.50	1.25
59 Jim Corrigall			
60 Pierre Desjardins			
☐ 61 Ron Forwick	18.00	8.00	2.20
62 Angelo Mosca			
63 Tom Laputka			
☐ 64 Herman Harrison	10.00	4.50	1.25
65 Dave Gasser			
66 John Williams			
☐ 67 Trevor Ekdahl	10.00	4.50	1.25
68 Bruce Bennett			
69 Gerry Shaw			
☐ 70 Jim Foley	10.00	4.50	1.25
71 Pete Ribbins			
72 Marv Luster			

1952 Parkhurst CFL

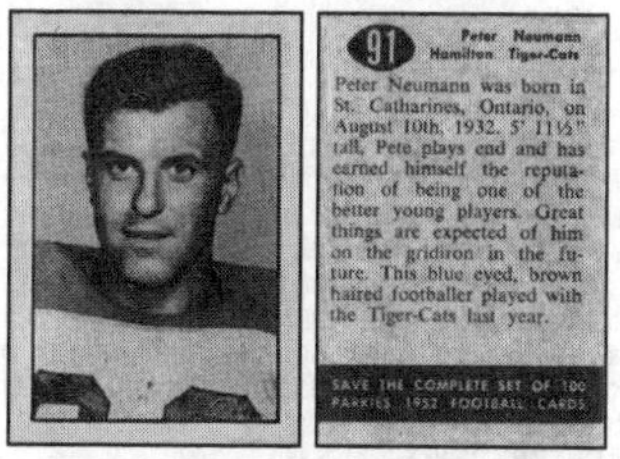

The 1952 Parkhurst CFL set of 100 cards is the earliest known CFL issue. Features include the four Eastern teams: Toronto Argonauts (20-40), Montreal Alouettes (41-61), Ottawa Rough Riders (63-78, 100), and Hamilton Tiger-Cats (79-99), as well as 19 instructional artwork cards (1-19). These small cards measure approximately 1 7/8" by 2 3/4". There are two different number 58's and card number 62 does not exist.

	NRMT	VG-E	GOOD
COMPLETE SET (100)	3000.00	1350.00	375.00
COMMON CARD (1-19)	20.00	9.00	2.50
COMMON CARD (20-100)	30.00	13.50	3.70
☐ 1 Watch the games	50.00	12.50	5.00
☐ 2 Teamwork	20.00	9.00	2.50
☐ 3 Football Equipment	20.00	9.00	2.50
☐ 4 Hang onto the ball	20.00	9.00	2.50
☐ 5 The head on tackle	20.00	9.00	2.50
☐ 6 The football field	20.00	9.00	2.50
☐ 7 The Lineman's Stance	20.00	9.00	2.50
☐ 8 Centre's spiral pass	20.00	9.00	2.50
☐ 9 The lineman	20.00	9.00	2.50
☐ 10 The place kick	20.00	9.00	2.50
☐ 11 The cross-body block	20.00	9.00	2.50
☐ 12 T formation	20.00	9.00	2.50
☐ 13 Falling on the ball	20.00	9.00	2.50
☐ 14 The throw	20.00	9.00	2.50
☐ 15 Breaking from tackle	20.00	9.00	2.50
☐ 16 How to catch a pass	20.00	9.00	2.50
☐ 17 The punt	20.00	9.00	2.50
☐ 18 Shifting the ball	20.00	9.00	2.50
☐ 19 Penalty signals	20.00	9.00	2.50
☐ 20 Leslie Ascott	30.00	13.50	3.70
☐ 21 Robert Marshall	30.00	13.50	3.70
☐ 22 Tom Harpley	30.00	13.50	3.70
☐ 23 Robert McClelland	30.00	13.50	3.70
☐ 24 Rod Smylie	30.00	13.50	3.70
☐ 25 Bill Bass	30.00	13.50	3.70
☐ 26 Fred Black	30.00	13.50	3.70
☐ 27 Jack Carpenter	30.00	13.50	3.70
☐ 28 Bob Hack	30.00	13.50	3.70
☐ 29 Ulysses Curtis	30.00	13.50	3.70
☐ 30 Nobby Wirkowski	50.00	22.00	6.25
☐ 31 George Arnett	30.00	13.50	3.70
☐ 32 Lorne Parkin	30.00	13.50	3.70
☐ 33 Alex Toogood	30.00	13.50	3.70
☐ 34 Marshall Haymes	30.00	13.50	3.70
☐ 35 Shanty McKenzie	30.00	13.50	3.70
☐ 36 Byron Karrys	30.00	13.50	3.70
☐ 37 George Rooks	30.00	13.50	3.70
☐ 38 Red Ettinger	30.00	13.50	3.70
☐ 39 Al Bruno	40.00	18.00	5.00
☐ 40 Stephen Karrys	30.00	13.50	3.70
☐ 41 Herb Trawick	50.00	22.00	6.25
☐ 42 Sam Etcheverry	350.00	160.00	45.00
☐ 43 Marv Melrowitz	30.00	13.50	3.70
☐ 44 John Red O'Quinn	50.00	22.00	6.25
☐ 45 Jim Ostendarp	30.00	13.50	3.70
☐ 46 Tom Tofaute	30.00	13.50	3.70
☐ 47 Joey Pal	30.00	13.50	3.70
☐ 48 Ray Cicia	30.00	13.50	3.70
☐ 49 Bruce Coulter	35.00	16.00	4.40
☐ 50 Jim Mitchener	30.00	13.50	3.70
☐ 51 Lally Lalonde	30.00	13.50	3.70
☐ 52 Jim Staton	30.00	13.50	3.70
☐ 53 Glenn Douglas	30.00	13.50	3.70
☐ 54 Dave Tomlinson	30.00	13.50	3.70
☐ 55 Ed Salem	30.00	13.50	3.70
☐ 56 Virgil Wagner	50.00	22.00	6.25
☐ 57 Dawson Tilley	30.00	13.50	3.70
☐ 58A Cec Findlay	40.00	18.00	5.00
☐ 58B Tommy Manastersky	40.00	18.00	5.00
☐ 59 Frank Nable	30.00	13.50	3.70
☐ 60 Chuck Anderson	30.00	13.50	3.70
☐ 61 Charlie Hubbard	30.00	13.50	3.70
☐ 63 Benny MacDonnell	30.00	13.50	3.70
☐ 64 Peter Karpuk	30.00	13.50	3.70
☐ 65 Tom O'Malley	30.00	13.50	3.70
☐ 66 Bill Stanton	30.00	13.50	3.70
☐ 67 Matt Anthony	30.00	13.50	3.70
☐ 68 John Morneau	30.00	13.50	3.70
☐ 69 Howie Turner	30.00	13.50	3.70
☐ 70 Alton Baldwin	30.00	13.50	3.70
☐ 71 John Bovey	30.00	13.50	3.70
☐ 72 Bruno Bitkowski	35.00	16.00	4.40
☐ 73 Gene Roberts	30.00	13.50	3.70
☐ 74 John Wagoner	30.00	13.50	3.70
☐ 75 Ted MacLarty	30.00	13.50	3.70
☐ 76 Jerry Lefebvre	30.00	13.50	3.70
☐ 77 Buck Rogers	30.00	13.50	3.70
☐ 78 Bruce Cummings	30.00	13.50	3.70
☐ 79 Hal Wagner	40.00	18.00	5.00
☐ 80 Joe Shinn	30.00	13.50	3.70
☐ 81 Eddie Bevan	30.00	13.50	3.70
☐ 82 Ralph Sazio	50.00	22.00	6.25
☐ 83 Bob McDonald	30.00	13.50	3.70
☐ 84 Vince Scott	40.00	18.00	5.00
☐ 85 Jack Stewart	30.00	13.50	3.70
☐ 86 Ralph Bartolini	30.00	13.50	3.70
☐ 87 Blake Taylor	30.00	13.50	3.70
☐ 88 Richard Brown	30.00	13.50	3.70
☐ 89 Douglas Gray	30.00	13.50	3.70
☐ 90 Alex Muzyka	30.00	13.50	3.70
☐ 91 Pete Neumann	50.00	22.00	6.25
☐ 92 Jack Rogers	30.00	13.50	3.70
☐ 93 Bernie Custis	40.00	18.00	5.00
☐ 94 Cam Fraser	30.00	13.50	3.70
☐ 95 Vince Mazza	40.00	18.00	5.00
☐ 96 Peter Wooley	30.00	13.50	3.70
☐ 97 Earl Valiquette	30.00	13.50	3.70
☐ 98 Floyd Cooper	30.00	13.50	3.70
☐ 99 Louis DiFrancisco	30.00	13.50	3.70
☐ 100 Robert Simpson	135.00	34.00	13.50

1956 Parkhurst CFL

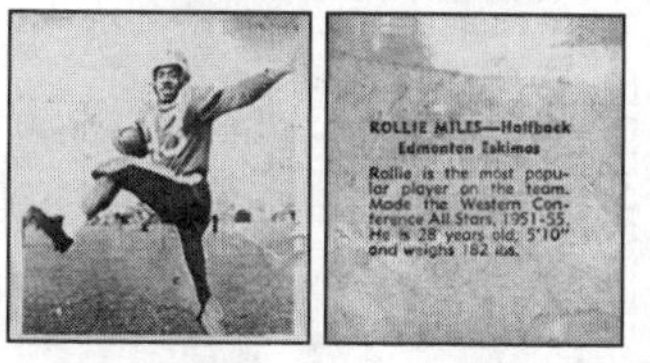

The 1956 Parkhurst CFL set of 50 cards features ten players from each of five teams: Edmonton Eskimos (1-10), Saskatchewan Roughriders (11-20), Calgary Stampeders (21-30), Winnipeg Blue Bombers (31-40), and Montreal Alouettes (41-50). Cards are numbered on the front. The cards measure approximately 1 3/4" by 1 7/8". The cards were sold in wax boxes of 48 five-cent wax packs each containing cards and gum. The set features an early card of Bud Grant, who later coached the Minnesota Vikings.

	NRMT	VG-E	GOOD
COMPLETE SET (50)	3500.00	1600.00	450.00
COMMON CARD (1-50)	40.00	18.00	5.00
☐ 1 Art Walker	80.00	20.00	8.00
☐ 2 Frank Anderson	40.00	18.00	5.00
☐ 3 Normie Kwong	150.00	70.00	19.00
☐ 4 Johnny Bright	150.00	70.00	19.00
☐ 5 Jackie Parker	400.00	180.00	50.00
☐ 6 Bob Dean	40.00	18.00	5.00
☐ 7 Don Getty	125.00	55.00	15.50
☐ 8 Rollie Miles	100.00	45.00	12.50
☐ 9 Ted Tully	40.00	18.00	5.00
☐ 10 Frank Morris	90.00	40.00	11.00
☐ 11 Martin Ruby	60.00	27.00	7.50
☐ 12 Mel Becket	80.00	36.00	10.00
☐ 13 Bill Clarke	40.00	18.00	5.00
☐ 14 John Wozniak	40.00	18.00	5.00
☐ 15 Larry Isbell	40.00	18.00	5.00
☐ 16 Ken Carpenter	80.00	36.00	10.00
☐ 17 Sully Glasser	40.00	18.00	5.00
☐ 18 Bobby Marlow	90.00	40.00	11.00
☐ 19 Paul Anderson	60.00	27.00	7.50
☐ 20 Gord Sturtridge	80.00	36.00	10.00
☐ 21 Alex Macklin	40.00	18.00	5.00
☐ 22 Duke Cook	40.00	18.00	5.00
☐ 23 Bill Stevenson	40.00	18.00	5.00
☐ 24 Lynn Bottoms	80.00	36.00	10.00
☐ 25 Aramis Dandoy	40.00	18.00	5.00
☐ 26 Peter Muir	60.00	27.00	7.50
☐ 27 Harvey Wylie	80.00	36.00	10.00
☐ 28 Joe Yamauchi	40.00	18.00	5.00
☐ 29 John Alderton	40.00	18.00	5.00
☐ 30 Bill McKenna	40.00	18.00	5.00
☐ 31 Edward Kotowich	40.00	18.00	5.00
☐ 32 Herb Gray	100.00	45.00	12.50
☐ 33 Calvin Jones	150.00	70.00	19.00
☐ 34 Herman Day	40.00	18.00	5.00
☐ 35 Buddy Leake	40.00	18.00	5.00
☐ 36 Robert McNamara	40.00	18.00	5.00
☐ 37 Bud Grant	350.00	160.00	45.00
☐ 38 Gord Rowland	60.00	27.00	7.50
☐ 39 Glen McWhinney	40.00	18.00	5.00
☐ 40 Lorne Benson	40.00	18.00	5.00
☐ 41 Sam Etcheverry	300.00	135.00	38.00
☐ 42 Joey Pal	40.00	18.00	5.00
☐ 43 Tom Hugo	40.00	18.00	5.00
☐ 44 Tex Coulter	60.00	27.00	7.50
☐ 45 Doug McNichol	40.00	18.00	5.00
☐ 46 Tom Moran	40.00	18.00	5.00
☐ 47 Red O'Quinn	80.00	36.00	10.00
☐ 48 Hal Patterson	200.00	90.00	25.00
☐ 49 Jacques Belec	40.00	18.00	5.00
☐ 50 Pat Abruzzi	100.00	25.00	10.00

1981 Police Saskatchewan

The 1981 Police Saskatchewan set is very similar to other Rough Riders police issues. The cards measure approximately 2 5/8" by 4 1/8" and were printed on thin white stock. The unnumbered cards are listed below alphabetically with the player's jersey number also included.

	MINT	NRMT	EXC
COMPLETE SET (10)	18.00	8.00	2.20
COMMON CARD	1.50	.70	.19
☐ 1 Roger Aldag 44	2.00	.90	.25
☐ 2 Joe Barnes 7	2.00	.90	.25
☐ 3 Lester Brown 22	1.50	.70	.19
☐ 4 Dwight Edwards 33	2.00	.90	.25
☐ 5 Vince Goldsmith 78	2.00	.90	.25
☐ 6 John Hufnagel 12	5.00	2.20	.60
☐ 7 Ken McEachern 20	1.50	.70	.19
☐ 8 Mike Samples 66	1.50	.70	.19
☐ 9 Joey Walters 17	1.50	.70	.19
☐ 10 Lyall Woznesensky 76	1.50	.70	.19

1982 Police Hamilton

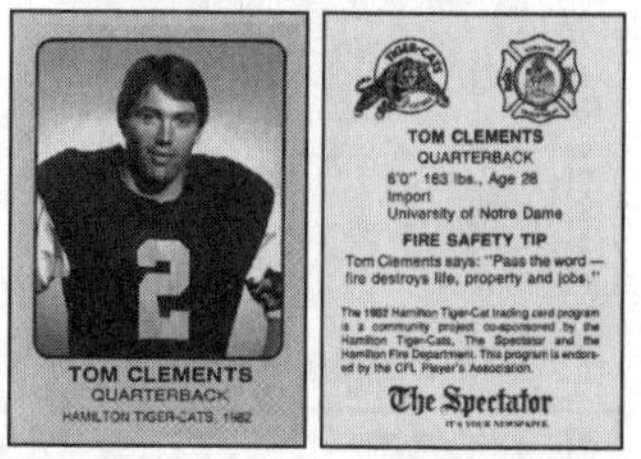

This 35-card safety standard-size set was co-sponsored by the Hamilton Tiger-Cats, The Spectator (newspaper), and the Hamilton Fire Department. These cards were printed on thin cardboard stock and feature posed color player photos, shot from the waist up against a light blue background. The surrounding card face is gold, with player information in black below the picture. The backs have biography, a fire safety tip in the form of a player quote, as well as team and sponsor logos. The cards are unnumbered and checklisted below in alphabetical order. Four additional cards were produced but not released as part of the set (since the players were released from the team at mid-season) and hence are not included below. These four cards (Mike Horton, Joe Kuklo, Peter Martel, and Mathews) are quite scarce as they were only issued to press members and a few distinguished guests at a Hamilton Tiger-Cat game.

	MINT	NRMT	EXC
COMPLETE SET (35)	20.00	9.00	2.50
COMMON CARD (1-35)	.50	.23	.06
☐ 1 Marv Allemang	.50	.23	.06
☐ 2 Jeff Arp	.50	.23	.06
☐ 3 Keith Baker	.50	.23	.06
☐ 4 Gerald Bess	.75	.35	.09
☐ 5 Mark Bragagnolo	.50	.23	.06
☐ 6 Carmelo Carteri	.50	.23	.06
☐ 7 Tom Clements	7.50	3.40	.95
☐ 8 Grover Covington	3.00	1.35	.35

☐ 9 Rocky DiPietro	4.00	1.80	.50
☐ 10 Howard Fields	.50	.23	.06
☐ 11 Ross Francis	.50	.23	.06
☐ 12 Ed Fulton	.50	.23	.06
☐ 13 Peter Gales	.50	.23	.06
☐ 14 Ed Gataveckas	.50	.23	.06
☐ 15 Dave Graffi	.50	.23	.06
☐ 16 Obie Graves	.50	.23	.06
☐ 17 Hazen Henderson	.50	.23	.06
☐ 18 Ron Johnson	1.25	.55	.16
☐ 19 Dave Marler	.75	.35	.09
☐ 20 Jim Muller	.50	.23	.06
☐ 21 Leroy Paul	.50	.23	.06
☐ 22 John Priestner	.75	.35	.09
☐ 23 Dave Purves	.50	.23	.06
☐ 24 James Ramey	.50	.23	.06
☐ 25 Doug Redl	.50	.23	.06
☐ 26 Bernie Ruoff	.75	.35	.09
☐ 27 David Sauve	.50	.23	.06
☐ 28 David Shaw	.50	.23	.06
☐ 29 Kerry Smith	.50	.23	.06
☐ 30 Steve Stapler	.75	.35	.09
☐ 31 Kyle Stevens	.50	.23	.06
☐ 32 Mike Walker	2.00	.90	.25
☐ 33 Henry Waszczuk	.50	.23	.06
☐ 34 Harold Woods	.50	.23	.06
☐ 35 Ben Zambiasi	2.50	1.10	.30

1982 Police Saskatchewan

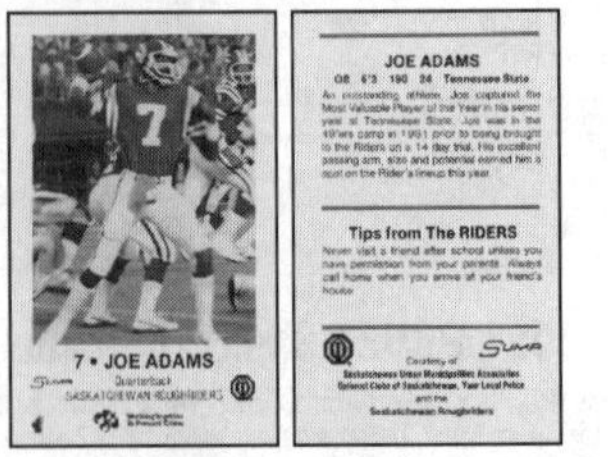

The 1982 Police SUMA (Saskatchewan Urban Municipalities Association) Saskatchewan Roughriders set contains 16 cards measuring approximately 2 5/8" by 4 1/8". The fronts have color action photos bordered in white; the vertically oriented backs have career highlights and safety tips. The card backs have black printing with green accent on white card stock. The cards are printed on thin stock. The cards are unnumbered, so they are listed below by uniform number.

	MINT	NRMT	EXC
COMPLETE SET (16)	12.00	5.50	1.50
COMMON CARD	.75	.35	.09
☐ 2 Greg Fieger	1.00	.45	.12
☐ 7 Joe Adams	.75	.35	.09
☐ 12 John Hufnagel	4.00	1.80	.50
☐ 17 Joey Walters	.75	.35	.09
☐ 20 Ken McEachern	.75	.35	.09
☐ 21 Marcellus Greene	.75	.35	.09
☐ 25 Steve Dennis	.75	.35	.09
☐ 29 Fran McDermott	.75	.35	.09
☐ 37 Frank Robinson	1.00	.45	.12
☐ 44 Roger Aldag	1.25	.55	.16
☐ 57 Bob Poley	1.00	.45	.12
☐ 66 Mike Samples	.75	.35	.09
☐ 69 Don Swafford	.75	.35	.09
☐ 74 Chris DeFrance	.75	.35	.09
☐ 76 Lyall Woznesensky	.75	.35	.09
☐ 78 Vince Goldsmith	1.50	.70	.19

1982 Police Winnipeg

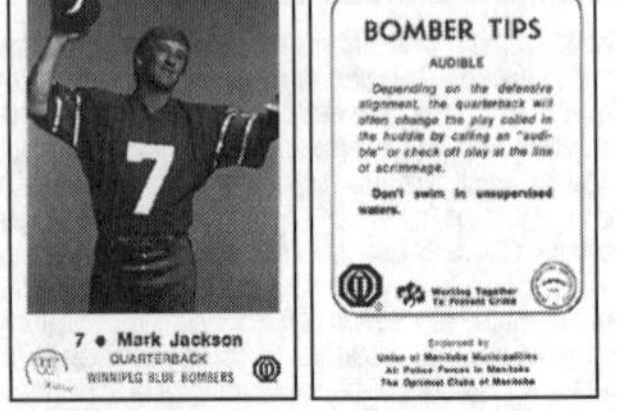

This 24-card Police set was sponsored by the Union of Manitoba Municipalities, all Police Forces in Manitoba, and The Optimist Clubs of Manitoba. The cards measure approximately 2 5/8" by 3 7/8" and were issued in two-card perforated panels one per week over a 12-week period. The panel pairs were Kennerd/Phason, Jackson/Walby, Pierson/House, Miller/Mikawos, Goodlow/Bennett, Bonk/Helton, Catan/Ezerins, Norman/Jones, Smith/Williams, Thompson/Poplawski, Bastaja/Reed, and Jauch/Brock. The fronts have posed color player photos, bordered in white with player information below the picture. The backs have "Bomber Tips" that consist of public safety announcements. These thin-stock cards are unnumbered and checklisted below in alphabetical order.

	MINT	NRMT	EXC
COMPLETE SET (24)	12.00	5.50	1.50
COMMON CARD (1-24)	.40	.18	.05
☐ 1 Nick Bastaja	.40	.18	.05
☐ 2 Paul Bennett	.40	.18	.05
☐ 3 John Bonk	.40	.18	.05
☐ 4 Dieter Brock	2.50	1.10	.30
☐ 5 Pete Catan	.40	.18	.05
☐ 6 Leo Ezerins	.40	.18	.05
☐ 7 Eugene Goodlow	.60	.25	.07
☐ 8 John Helton	1.50	.70	.19
☐ 9 Rick House	.60	.25	.07
☐ 10 Mark Jackson	.60	.25	.07
☐ 11 Ray Jauch CO	.40	.18	.05
☐ 12 Milson Jones	1.00	.45	.12
☐ 13 Trevor Kennerd	1.50	.70	.19
☐ 14 Stan Mikawos	.40	.18	.05
☐ 15 William Miller	.60	.25	.07
☐ 16 Tony Norman	.40	.18	.05
☐ 17 Vince Phason	.40	.18	.05
☐ 18 Reggie Pierson	.40	.18	.05
☐ 19 Joe Poplawski	.60	.25	.07
☐ 20 James Reed	.40	.18	.05
☐ 21 Franky Smith	.40	.18	.05
☐ 22 Bobby Thompson T	.40	.18	.05
☐ 23 Chris Walby	1.00	.45	.12
☐ 24 Charles Williams	.40	.18	.05

1983 Police Hamilton

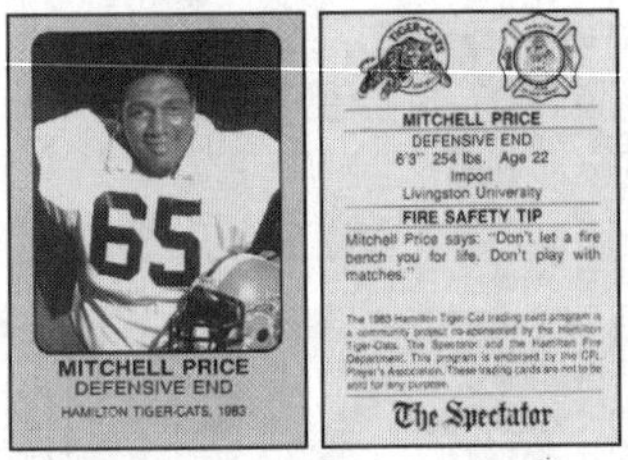

This 37-card police standard-size set was jointly sponsored by the Hamilton Tiger-Cats, The Spectator (a newspaper), and the Hamilton Fire Department. The cards are printed on thin card stock and feature posed color player photos, shot from the waist up against a black background. The surrounding card face is gold, with player information in black print below the picture. The backs have biographical information, a fire safety tip in the form of a player quote, as well as team and sponsor logos. The cards are unnumbered and checklisted below in alphabetical order.

	MINT	NRMT	EXC
COMPLETE SET (37)	20.00	9.00	2.50
COMMON CARD (1-37)	.50	.23	.06
☐ 1 Marv Allemang	.50	.23	.06
☐ 2 Jeff Arp	.50	.23	.06
☐ 3 Keith Baker	.50	.23	.06
☐ 4 Harold E. Ballard PRES	2.00	.90	.25
☐ 5 Mike Barker	.50	.23	.06
☐ 6 Gerald Bess	.75	.35	.09
☐ 7 Pat Brady	.50	.23	.06
☐ 8 Mark Bragagnolo	.50	.23	.06
☐ 9 Tom Clements	7.50	3.40	.95
☐ 10 Grover Covington	3.00	1.35	.35
☐ 11 Rufus Crawford	2.00	.90	.25
☐ 12 Rocky DiPietro	4.00	1.80	.50
☐ 13 Leo Ezerins	.50	.23	.06
☐ 14 Howard Fields	.50	.23	.06
☐ 15 Ross Francis	.50	.23	.06
☐ 16 Peter Gales	.50	.23	.06
☐ 17 Ed Gataveckas	.50	.23	.06
☐ 18 Paul Gohier	.50	.23	.06
☐ 19 Dave Graffi	.50	.23	.06
☐ 20 Ron Johnson	1.25	.55	.16
☐ 21 Steve Kearns	.50	.23	.06
☐ 22 Wayne Lee	.50	.23	.06
☐ 23 Mike McIntyre	.50	.23	.06
☐ 24 Paul Palma	.50	.23	.06
☐ 25 George Piva	.50	.23	.06
☐ 26 Mitchell Price	.75	.35	.09
☐ 27 John Priestner	.75	.35	.09
☐ 28 Bernie Ruoff	.75	.35	.09
☐ 29 David Sauve	.50	.23	.06
☐ 30 Johnny Shepherd	.50	.23	.06
☐ 31 Steve Stapler	1.00	.45	.12
☐ 32 Mark Streeter	.50	.23	.06
☐ 33 Jeff Tedford	.50	.23	.06
☐ 34 Mike Walker	2.00	.90	.25
☐ 35 Henry Waszczuk	.50	.23	.06
☐ 36 Felix Wright	2.50	1.10	.30
☐ 37 Ben Zambiasi	2.50	1.10	.30

1983 Police Saskatchewan

The 1983 Police SUMA (Saskatchewan Urban Municipalities Association) Saskatchewan Roughriders set contains 16 cards measuring approximately 2 5/8" by 4 1/8". The fronts have color action photos bordered in white; the vertically oriented backs have career highlights and safety tips. The card backs have black printing with green accent on white card stock. The cards are printed on thin stock. The cards are unnumbered, so they are listed below by uniform number. The 1983 set is distinguished from the similar 1982 SUMA set by the presence of facsimile autographs on the 1983 version.

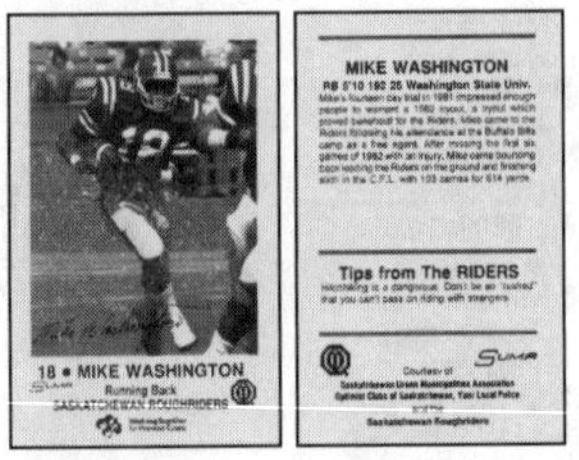

	MINT	NRMT	EXC
COMPLETE SET (16)	12.00	5.50	1.50
COMMON CARD	.75	.35	.09
☐ 9 Ron Robinson	1.00	.45	.12
☐ 12 John Hufnagel	3.00	1.35	.35
☐ 13 Ken Clark	1.00	.45	.12
☐ 18 Mike Washington	1.00	.45	.12
☐ 24 Marshall Hamilton	.75	.35	.09
☐ 25 Mike Emery	.75	.35	.09
☐ 30 Duane Galloway	.75	.35	.09
☐ 33 Dwight Edwards	1.00	.45	.12
☐ 36 Dave Ridgway	2.00	.90	.25
☐ 42 Eddie Lowe	1.00	.45	.12
☐ 58 J.C. Pelusi	.75	.35	.09
☐ 60 Karl Morgan	.75	.35	.09
☐ 61 Bryan Illerbrun	.75	.35	.09
☐ 65 Neil Quilter	.75	.35	.09
☐ 72 Ray Elgaard	3.00	1.35	.35
☐ 74 Chris DeFrance	.75	.35	.09

1984 Police Ottawa

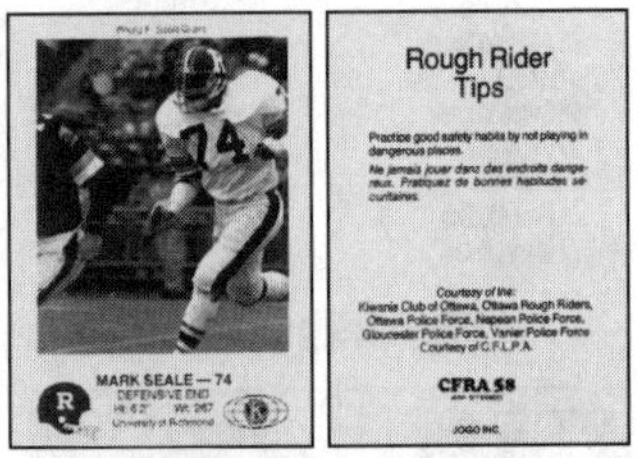

This ten-card full-color set was given away over a ten-week period. The sponsors were Kiwanis, several Police Forces, and radio station CFRA 58 AM. Cards were produced in conjunction with JOGO Inc. The cards are unnumbered although the player's uniform number is given on the front of the card. The numbering below is in alphabetical order for convenience. The cards measure approximately 2 1/2" by 3 1/2". Photos were taken by F. Scott Grant, who is credited on the fronts of the cards. Mark Seale was the card for the tenth and final week; he was printed in a much smaller quantity than the other cards. It was reported that 6,000 of each of the first nine players were given away, whereas only 500 Mark Seale cards were given out.

	MINT	NRMT	EXC
COMPLETE SET (10)	35.00	16.00	4.40
COMMON CARD (1-10)	.75	.35	.09
☐ 1 Greg Marshall	1.25	.55	.16
☐ 2 Dave Newman	.75	.35	.09
☐ 3 Rudy Phillips	1.25	.55	.16
☐ 4 Jim Reid	1.25	.55	.16
☐ 5 Mark Seale SP	20.00	9.00	2.50
☐ 6 Rick Sowieta	1.25	.55	.16
☐ 7 Pat Stoqua	1.25	.55	.16
☐ 8 Skip Walker	2.50	1.10	.30
☐ 9 Al Washington	.75	.35	.09
☐ 10 J.C. Watts	10.00	4.50	1.25

1985 Police Ottawa

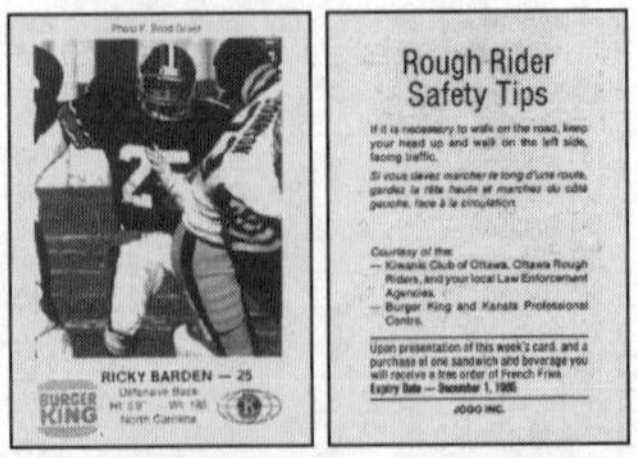

This ten-card set was also sponsored by Burger King as indicated on the front of each card and JOGO Inc. as indicated on the back. The cards measure approximately 2 1/2" by 3 1/2". Card photos (by photographer F. Scott Grant) all show Ottawa Rough Riders in game action. The numbering below is in alphabetical order for convenience.

	MINT	NRMT	EXC
COMPLETE SET (10)	6.00	2.70	.75
COMMON CARD (1-10)	.40	.18	.05
☐ 1 Ricky Barden	.40	.18	.05
☐ 2 Michel Bourgeau	.60	.25	.07
☐ 3 Roger Cattelan	.40	.18	.05
☐ 4 Ken Clark	.60	.25	.07
☐ 5 Dean Dorsey	.60	.25	.07
☐ 6 Greg Marshall	.60	.25	.07
☐ 7 Kevin Powell	.40	.18	.05
☐ 8 Jim Reid	.60	.25	.07
☐ 9 Rick Sowieta	.60	.25	.07
☐ 10 J.C. Watts	3.50	1.55	.45

1962 Post Cereal CFL

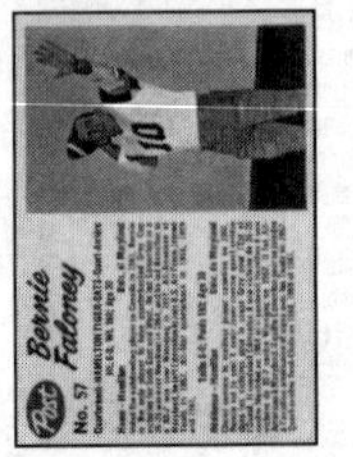

The 1962 Post Cereal CFL set is the first of two Post Cereal Canadian Football issues. The cards measure the standard size. The cards were issued on the backs of boxes of Post Cereals distributed in Canada. Cards were not available directly from the company via a send-in offer as with other Post Cereal issues. Cards which are marked as SP are considered somewhat shorter printed and more limited in supply. Many of these short-printed cards have backs that are not the typical brown color but rather white. The cards are arranged according to teams. An album for the cards was also produced for this set and is relatively hard to find.

	NRMT	VG-E	GOOD
COMPLETE SET (137)	1600.00	700.00	200.00
COMMON CARD (1-137)	7.50	3.40	.95
☐ 1A Don Clark (Brown back)	20.00	9.00	2.50
☐ 1B Don Clark SP (White back)	60.00	27.00	7.50
☐ 2 Ed Meadows	7.50	3.40	.95
☐ 3 Meco Poliziani	7.50	3.40	.95
☐ 4 George Dixon	20.00	9.00	2.50
☐ 5 Bobby Jack Oliver	10.00	4.50	1.25
☐ 6 Ross Buckle	7.50	3.40	.95
☐ 7 Jack Espenship	7.50	3.40	.95
☐ 8 Howard Cissell	7.50	3.40	.95
☐ 9 Ed Nickla	7.50	3.40	.95
☐ 10 Ed Learn	7.50	3.40	.95
☐ 11 Billy Ray Locklin	7.50	3.40	.95
☐ 12 Don Paquette	7.50	3.40	.95
☐ 13 Milt Crain	10.00	4.50	1.25
☐ 14 Dick Schnell	7.50	3.40	.95
☐ 15 Dick Cohee	10.00	4.50	1.25
☐ 16 Joe Francis	10.00	4.50	1.25
☐ 17 Gilles Archambeault	7.50	3.40	.95
☐ 18 Angelo Mosca	30.00	13.50	3.70
☐ 19 Ernie White	7.50	3.40	.95
☐ 20 George Brancato	10.00	4.50	1.25
☐ 21 Ron Lancaster	30.00	13.50	3.70
☐ 22 Jim Cain	7.50	3.40	.95
☐ 23 Gerry Nesbitt	7.50	3.40	.95
☐ 24 Russ Jackson	30.00	13.50	3.70
☐ 25 Bob Simpson	18.00	8.00	2.20
☐ 26 Sam Scoccia	7.50	3.40	.95
☐ 27 Tom Jones	7.50	3.40	.95
☐ 28 Kaye Vaughan	15.00	6.75	1.85
☐ 29 Chuck Stanley	7.50	3.40	.95
☐ 30 Dave Thelen	15.00	6.75	1.85
☐ 31 Gary Schreider	7.50	3.40	.95
☐ 32 Jim Reynolds	7.50	3.40	.95
☐ 33 Doug Daigneault	7.50	3.40	.95
☐ 34 Joe Poirier	10.00	4.50	1.25
☐ 35 Clare Exelby	7.50	3.40	.95
☐ 36 Art Johnson	7.50	3.40	.95
☐ 37 Menan Schriewer	7.50	3.40	.95
☐ 38 Art Darch	7.50	3.40	.95
☐ 39 Cookie Gilchrist	25.00	11.00	3.10
☐ 40 Brian Aston	7.50	3.40	.95
☐ 41 Bobby Kuntz SP	50.00	22.00	6.25
☐ 42 Gerry Patrick	7.50	3.40	.95
☐ 43 Norm Stoneburgh	7.50	3.40	.95
☐ 44 Billy Shipp	7.50	3.40	.95
☐ 45 Jim Andreotti	15.00	6.75	1.85
☐ 46 Tobin Rote	20.00	9.00	2.50
☐ 47 Dick Shatto	15.00	6.75	1.85
☐ 48 Dave Mann	10.00	4.50	1.25
☐ 49 Ron Morris	7.50	3.40	.95
☐ 50 Lynn Bottoms	10.00	4.50	1.25
☐ 51 Jim Rountree	10.00	4.50	1.25
☐ 52 Bill Mitchell	7.50	3.40	.95
☐ 53 Wes Gideon SP	50.00	22.00	6.25
☐ 54 Boyd Carter	7.50	3.40	.95
☐ 55 Ron Howell	10.00	4.50	1.25
☐ 56 John Barrow	15.00	6.75	1.85
☐ 57 Bernie Faloney	30.00	13.50	3.70
☐ 58 Ron Ray	7.50	3.40	.95
☐ 59 Don Sutherin	15.00	6.75	1.85
☐ 60 Frank Cosentino	10.00	4.50	1.25
☐ 61 Hardiman Cureton	7.50	3.40	.95
☐ 62 Hal Patterson	20.00	9.00	2.50
☐ 63 Ralph Goldston	10.00	4.50	1.25
☐ 64 Tommy Grant	15.00	6.75	1.85
☐ 65 Larry Hickman	10.00	4.50	1.25

☐ 66 Zeno Karcz	10.00	4.50	1.25
☐ 67 Garney Henley	20.00	9.00	2.50
☐ 68 Gerry McDougall	10.00	4.50	1.25
☐ 69 Vince Scott	12.00	5.50	1.50
☐ 70 Gerry James	15.00	6.75	1.85
☐ 71 Roger Hagberg	10.00	4.50	1.25
☐ 72 Gord Rowland	10.00	4.50	1.25
☐ 73 Ernie Pitts	7.50	3.40	.95
☐ 74 Frank Rigney	12.00	5.50	1.50
☐ 75 Norm Rauhaus	12.00	5.50	1.50
☐ 76 Leo Lewis	20.00	9.00	2.50
☐ 77 Mike Wright	7.50	3.40	.95
☐ 78 Jack Delveaux	7.50	3.40	.95
☐ 79 Steve Patrick	7.50	3.40	.95
☐ 80 Dave Burkholder	7.50	3.40	.95
☐ 81 Charlie Shepard	10.00	4.50	1.25
☐ 82 Kenny Ploen	20.00	9.00	2.50
☐ 83 Ronnie Latourelle	7.50	3.40	.95
☐ 84 Herb Gray	15.00	6.75	1.85
☐ 85 Hal Ledyard	7.50	3.40	.95
☐ 86 Cornel Piper SP	50.00	22.00	6.25
☐ 87 Farrell Funston	10.00	4.50	1.25
☐ 88 Ray Smith	7.50	3.40	.95
☐ 89 Clair Branch	7.50	3.40	.95
☐ 90 Fred Burket	7.50	3.40	.95
☐ 91 Dave Grosz	7.50	3.40	.95
☐ 92 Bob Golic	10.00	4.50	1.25
☐ 93 Billy Gray	7.50	3.40	.95
☐ 94 Neil Habig	7.50	3.40	.95
☐ 95 Reg Whitehouse	7.50	3.40	.95
☐ 96 Jack Gotta	10.00	4.50	1.25
☐ 97 Bob Ptacek	10.00	4.50	1.25
☐ 98 Jerry Keeling	15.00	6.75	1.85
☐ 99 Ernie Danjean	7.50	3.40	.95
☐ 100 Don Luzzi	12.00	5.50	1.50
☐ 101 Wayne Harris	20.00	9.00	2.50
☐ 102 Tony Pajaczkowski	15.00	6.75	1.85
☐ 103 Earl Lunsford	15.00	6.75	1.85
☐ 104 Ernie Warlick	12.00	5.50	1.50
☐ 105 Gene Filipski	12.00	5.50	1.50
☐ 106 Eagle Day	15.00	6.75	1.85
☐ 107 Bill Crawford	7.50	3.40	.95
☐ 108 Oscar Kruger	7.50	3.40	.95
☐ 109 Gino Fracas	10.00	4.50	1.25
☐ 110 Don Stephenson	7.50	3.40	.95
☐ 111 Jim Letcavits	7.50	3.40	.95
☐ 112 Howie Schumm	7.50	3.40	.95
☐ 113 Jackie Parker	40.00	18.00	5.00
☐ 114 Rollie Miles	15.00	6.75	1.85
☐ 115 Johnny Bright	20.00	9.00	2.50
☐ 116 Don Getty	15.00	6.75	1.85
☐ 117 Bobby Walden	10.00	4.50	1.25
☐ 118 Roger Nelson	15.00	6.75	1.85
☐ 119 Al Ecuyer	7.50	3.40	.95
☐ 120 Ed Gray	7.50	3.40	.95
☐ 121 Vic Chapman SP	50.00	22.00	6.25
☐ 122 Earl Keeley	7.50	3.40	.95
☐ 123 Sonny Homer	7.50	3.40	.95
☐ 124 Bob Jeter	20.00	9.00	2.50
☐ 125 Jim Carphin	7.50	3.40	.95
☐ 126 By Bailey	15.00	6.75	1.85
☐ 127 Norm Fieldgate	15.00	6.75	1.85
☐ 128 Vic Kristopaitis	7.50	3.40	.95
☐ 129 Willie Fleming	20.00	9.00	2.50
☐ 130 Don Vicic	7.50	3.40	.95
☐ 131 Tom Brown SP	50.00	22.00	6.25
☐ 132 Tom Hinton SP	50.00	22.00	6.25
☐ 133 Pat Claridge	7.50	3.40	.95
☐ 134 Bill Britton	7.50	3.40	.95
☐ 135 Neil Beaumont	10.00	4.50	1.25
☐ 136 Nub Beamer SP	50.00	22.00	6.25
☐ 137 Joe Kapp	60.00	27.00	7.50
☐ NNO Post Album	75.00	34.00	9.50

1963 Post Cereal CFL

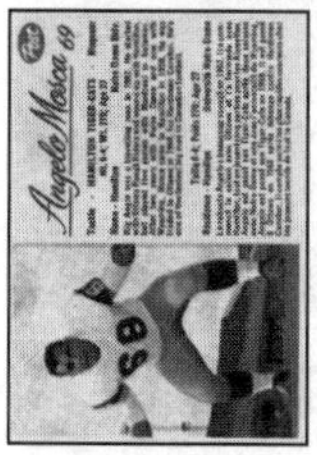

The 1963 Post Cereal CFL set was issued on backs of boxes of Post Cereals in Canada. The cards measure 2 1/2" by 3 1/2". Cards could also be obtained from an order-by-number offer during 1963 from Post's Canadian affiliate. Cards are numbered and ordered within the set according to team. An album for the cards was also produced for this set and is relatively hard to find.

	NRMT	VG-E	GOOD
COMPLETE SET (160)	900.00	400.00	110.00
COMMON CARD (1-160)	5.00	2.20	.60
☐ 1 Larry Hickman	7.50	3.40	.95
☐ 2 Dick Schnell	5.00	2.20	.60
☐ 3 Don Clark	7.50	3.40	.95
☐ 4 Ted Page	5.00	2.20	.60
☐ 5 Milt Crain	7.50	3.40	.95
☐ 6 George Dixon	10.00	4.50	1.25
☐ 7 Ed Nickla	5.00	2.20	.60
☐ 8 Barrie Hansen	5.00	2.20	.60
☐ 9 Ed Learn	5.00	2.20	.60
☐ 10 Billy Ray Locklin	5.00	2.20	.60
☐ 11 Bobby Jack Oliver	7.50	3.40	.95
☐ 12 Don Paquette	5.00	2.20	.60
☐ 13 Sandy Stephens	12.00	5.50	1.50
☐ 14 Billy Wayte	5.00	2.20	.60
☐ 15 Jim Reynolds	5.00	2.20	.60
☐ 16 Ross Buckle	5.00	2.20	.60
☐ 17 Bob Geary	5.00	2.20	.60
☐ 18 Bobby Lee Thompson	5.00	2.20	.60
☐ 19 Mike Snodgrass	5.00	2.20	.60
☐ 20 Billy Joe Booth	7.50	3.40	.95
☐ 21 Jim Cain	5.00	2.20	.60
☐ 22 Kaye Vaughan	10.00	4.50	1.25
☐ 23 Doug Daigneault	5.00	2.20	.60
☐ 24 Millard Flemming	5.00	2.20	.60
☐ 25 Russ Jackson	25.00	11.00	3.10
☐ 26 Joe Poirier	7.50	3.40	.95
☐ 27 Moe Racine	5.00	2.20	.60
☐ 28 Norb Roy	5.00	2.20	.60
☐ 29 Ted Smale	5.00	2.20	.60
☐ 30 Ernie White	5.00	2.20	.60
☐ 31 Whit Tucker	10.00	4.50	1.25
☐ 32 Dave Thelen	10.00	4.50	1.25
☐ 33 Len Chandler	5.00	2.20	.60
☐ 34 Jim Conroy	7.50	3.40	.95
☐ 35 Jerry Selinger	5.00	2.20	.60
☐ 36 Ron Stewart	12.00	5.50	1.50
☐ 37 Jim Andreotti	7.50	3.40	.95
☐ 38 Jackie Parker	25.00	11.00	3.10
☐ 39 Lynn Bottoms	7.50	3.40	.95
☐ 40 Gerry Patrick	5.00	2.20	.60
☐ 41 Gerry Philip	5.00	2.20	.60
☐ 42 Art Johnson	5.00	2.20	.60
☐ 43 Aubrey Linne	5.00	2.20	.60
☐ 44 Dave Mann	7.50	3.40	.95
☐ 45 Marty Martinello	5.00	2.20	.60
☐ 46 Doug McNichol	5.00	2.20	.60
☐ 47 Ron Morris	5.00	2.20	.60
☐ 48 Walt Radzick	5.00	2.20	.60
☐ 49 Jim Rountree	5.00	2.20	.60
☐ 50 Dick Shatto	10.00	4.50	1.25
☐ 51 Billy Shipp	5.00	2.20	.60
☐ 52 Norm Stoneburgh	5.00	2.20	.60
☐ 53 Gerry Wilson	5.00	2.20	.60
☐ 54 Danny Nykoluk	5.00	2.20	.60
☐ 55 John Barrow	10.00	4.50	1.25
☐ 56 Frank Cosentino	7.50	3.40	.95
☐ 57 Hardiman Cureton	5.00	2.20	.60
☐ 58 Bobby Kuntz	7.50	3.40	.95
☐ 59 Bernie Faloney	20.00	9.00	2.50
☐ 60 Garney Henley	12.00	5.50	1.50
☐ 61 Zeno Karcz	7.50	3.40	.95
☐ 62 Dick Easterly	5.00	2.20	.60
☐ 63 Bronko Nagurski	12.00	5.50	1.50
☐ 64 Hal Patterson	15.00	6.75	1.85
☐ 65 Ron Ray	5.00	2.20	.60
☐ 66 Don Sutherin	7.50	3.40	.95
☐ 67 Dave Viti	5.00	2.20	.60
☐ 68 Joe Zuger	7.50	3.40	.95
☐ 69 Angelo Mosca	20.00	9.00	2.50
☐ 70 Ralph Goldston	7.50	3.40	.95
☐ 71 Tommy Grant	10.00	4.50	1.25
☐ 72 Geno DeNobile	5.00	2.20	.60
☐ 73 Dave Burkholder	5.00	2.20	.60
☐ 74 Jack Delveaux	5.00	2.20	.60
☐ 75 Farrell Funston	7.50	3.40	.95
☐ 76 Herb Gray	10.00	4.50	1.25
☐ 77 Roger Hagberg	7.50	3.40	.95
☐ 78 Henry Janzen	7.50	3.40	.95
☐ 79 Ronnie Latourelle	5.00	2.20	.60
☐ 80 Leo Lewis	10.00	4.50	1.25
☐ 81 Cornel Piper	5.00	2.20	.60
☐ 82 Ernie Pitts	5.00	2.20	.60
☐ 83 Kenny Ploen	10.00	4.50	1.25
☐ 84 Norm Rauhaus	7.50	3.40	.95
☐ 85 Charlie Shepard	7.50	3.40	.95
☐ 86 Gar Warren	5.00	2.20	.60
☐ 87 Dick Thornton	7.50	3.40	.95
☐ 88 Hal Ledyard	5.00	2.20	.60
☐ 89 Frank Rigney	7.50	3.40	.95
☐ 90 Gord Rowland	7.50	3.40	.95
☐ 91 Don Walsh	5.00	2.20	.60
☐ 92 Bill Burrell	5.00	2.20	.60
☐ 93 Ron Atchison	9.00	4.00	1.10
☐ 94 Billy Gray	5.00	2.20	.60
☐ 95 Neil Habig	5.00	2.20	.60
☐ 96 Bob Ptacek	5.00	2.20	.60
☐ 97 Ray Purdin	5.00	2.20	.60
☐ 98 Ted Urness	7.50	3.40	.95
☐ 99 Dale West	7.50	3.40	.95
☐ 100 Reg Whitehouse	5.00	2.20	.60
☐ 101 Clair Branch	5.00	2.20	.60
☐ 102 Bill Clarke	5.00	2.20	.60
☐ 103 Garner Ekstran	7.50	3.40	.95
☐ 104 Jack Gotta	7.50	3.40	.95
☐ 105 Len Legault	5.00	2.20	.60
☐ 106 Larry Dumelie	5.00	2.20	.60
☐ 107 Bill Britton	5.00	2.20	.60
☐ 108 Ed Buchanan	5.00	2.20	.60
☐ 109 Lovell Coleman	7.50	3.40	.95
☐ 110 Bill Crawford	5.00	2.20	.60
☐ 111 Ernie Danjean	5.00	2.20	.60
☐ 112 Eagle Day	9.00	4.00	1.10
☐ 113 Jim Furlong	5.00	2.20	.60
☐ 114 Wayne Harris	15.00	6.75	1.85
☐ 115 Roy Jakanovich	5.00	2.20	.60
☐ 116 Phil Lohmann	5.00	2.20	.60
☐ 117 Earl Lunsford	7.50	3.40	.95
☐ 118 Don Luzzi	7.50	3.40	.95
☐ 119 Tony Pajaczkowski	7.50	3.40	.95
☐ 120 Pete Manning	7.50	3.40	.95
☐ 121 Harvey Wylie	7.50	3.40	.95
☐ 122 George Hansen	5.00	2.20	.60
☐ 123 Pat Holmes	5.00	2.20	.60
☐ 124 Larry Robinson	7.50	3.40	.95
☐ 125 Johnny Bright	15.00	6.75	1.85
☐ 126 Jon Rechner	5.00	2.20	.60
☐ 127 Al Ecuyer	5.00	2.20	.60
☐ 128 Don Getty	12.00	5.50	1.50
☐ 129 Ed Gray	5.00	2.20	.60
☐ 130 Oscar Kruger	5.00	2.20	.60
☐ 131 Jim Letcavits	5.00	2.20	.60
☐ 132 Mike Lashuk	5.00	2.20	.60
☐ 133 Don Duncalfe	5.00	2.20	.60
☐ 134 Bobby Walden	7.50	3.40	.95
☐ 135 Tommy Joe Coffey	12.00	5.50	1.50
☐ 136 Nat Dye	5.00	2.20	.60
☐ 137 Roy Stevenson	5.00	2.20	.60
☐ 138 Howie Schumm	5.00	2.20	.60
☐ 139 Roger Nelson	7.50	3.40	.95
☐ 140 Larry Fleisher	7.50	3.40	.95
☐ 141 Dunc Harvey	5.00	2.20	.60
☐ 142 James Earl Wright	7.50	3.40	.95
☐ 143 By Bailey	8.00	3.60	1.00
☐ 144 Nub Beamer	5.00	2.20	.60
☐ 145 Neil Beaumont	7.50	3.40	.95
☐ 146 Tom Brown	7.50	3.40	.95
☐ 147 Pat Claridge	5.00	2.20	.60
☐ 148 Lonnie Dennis	7.50	3.40	.95
☐ 149 Norm Fieldgate	7.50	3.40	.95
☐ 150 Willie Fleming	12.00	5.50	1.50
☐ 151 Dick Fouts	7.50	3.40	.95
☐ 152 Tom Hinton	7.50	3.40	.95
☐ 153 Sonny Homer	7.50	3.40	.95
☐ 154 Joe Kapp	30.00	13.50	3.70
☐ 155 Tom Larscheid	5.00	2.20	.60
☐ 156 Mike Martin	5.00	2.20	.60
☐ 157 Mel Mein	5.00	2.20	.60
☐ 158 Mike Cacic	5.00	2.20	.60
☐ 159 Walt Bilicki	5.00	2.20	.60
☐ 160 Earl Keeley	5.00	2.20	.60
☐ NNO Post Album	75.00	34.00	9.50

1958 Puritan Meats B.C. Lions

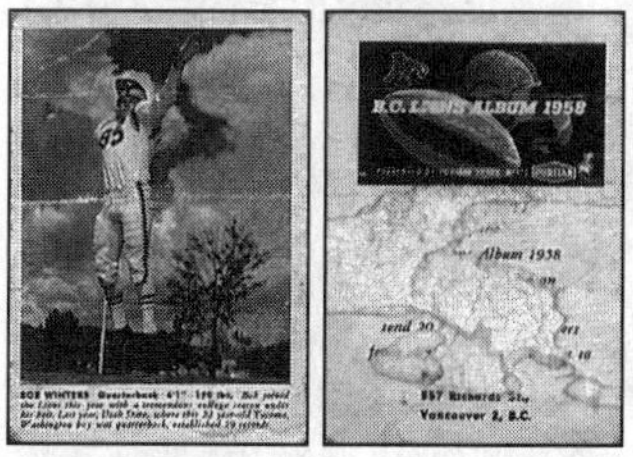

Measuring 2 1/4 by 3 3/8", these cards were distributed with Puritan canned meat products. The fronts feature black-and-white posed action photos inside white borders. In bold black lettering, the player's name, position, height, and weight are given. Immediately after in italic print is a player profile. In addition to a team logo, the back carries an offer for a 1958 B.C. Lions album for three Puritan product wrappers and 20 cents. The cards are unnumbered and checklisted below in alphabetical order. Any additions to this list would be appreciated.

	NRMT	VG-E	GOOD
COMPLETE SET (3)	50.00	22.00	6.25
COMMON CARD (1-3)	15.00	6.75	1.85
☐ 1 Ted Hunt	15.00	6.75	1.85
☐ 2 Howard Schnellenberger	25.00	11.00	3.10
☐ 3 Bob Winters	15.00	6.75	1.85

1991 Queen's University

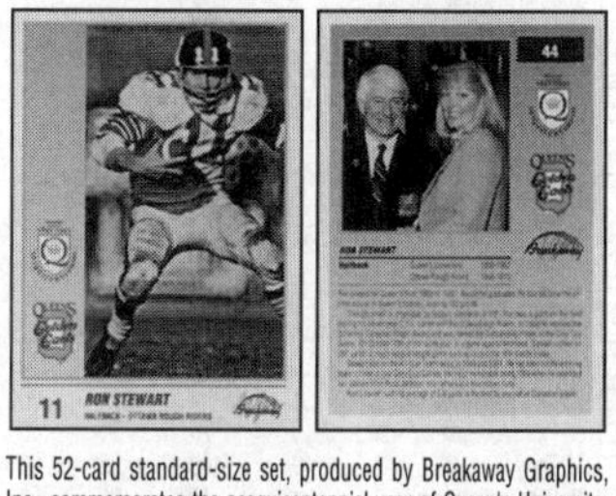

This 52-card standard-size set, produced by Breakaway Graphics, Inc., commemorates the sesquicentennial year of Queen's University. This Golden Gaels football set is the first ever to be issued by a Canadian college football organization. Reportedly only 5,725 sets and 275 uncut sheets were printed. The card fronts feature color player photos inside a gold border, with a pale green strip running down the left side of the picture. On a pale green background, the backs have a color head shot, biography, player profile, and statistics. Five special promotional cards were also included with this commemorative set. Five hundred autographed promo cards were randomly inserted in the production run, including 100 by Mike Schad and Jock Climie and 300 by Ron Stewart.

	MINT	NRMT	EXC
COMPLETE SET (52)	12.00	5.50	1.50
COMMON CARD (1-51)	.30	.14	.04
COMMON CARD (P1-P5)	3.00	1.35	.35
☐ 1 First Rugby Team Team photo	.75	.35	.09
☐ 2 Grey Cup Years Harry Batstone Frank R. Leadlay	.75	.35	.09
☐ 3 1978 Vanier Cup Champs	.30	.14	.04
☐ 4 1978 Vanier Cup Champs	.30	.14	.04
☐ 5 Tim Pendergast	.30	.14	.04
☐ 6 Brad Elberg	.30	.14	.04
☐ 7 Ken Kirkwood	.30	.14	.04
☐ 8 Kyle Wanzel	.30	.14	.04
☐ 9 Brian Alford	.30	.14	.04
☐ 10 Paul Kozan	.30	.14	.04
☐ 11 Paul Beresford	.30	.14	.04
☐ 12 Ron Herman	.30	.14	.04
☐ 13 Mike Ross	.30	.14	.04
☐ 14 Tom Black	.30	.14	.04
☐ 15 Steve Yovetich	.30	.14	.04
☐ 16 Mark Robinson	.30	.14	.04
☐ 17 Don Rorwick	.30	.14	.04
☐ 18 Ed Kidd	.30	.14	.04
☐ 19 Jamie Galloway	.30	.14	.04
☐ 20 Dan Wright	.30	.14	.04
☐ 21 Scott Gray	.30	.14	.04
☐ 22 Dan McCullough	.30	.14	.04
☐ 23 Steve Othen	.30	.14	.04
☐ 24 Doug Hargreaves CO	.30	.14	.04
☐ 25 Sue Bolton CO	.30	.14	.04
☐ 26 Coaching Staff	.50	.23	.06
☐ 27 Joel Dagnone	.30	.14	.04
☐ 28 Mark Morrison	.30	.14	.04
☐ 29 Rob Krog	.30	.14	.04
☐ 30 Dan Pawliw	.30	.14	.04
☐ 31 Greg Bryk	.30	.14	.04
☐ 32 Eric Dell	.30	.14	.04
☐ 33 Mike Boone	.30	.14	.04
☐ 34 James Paterson	.30	.14	.04
☐ 35 Jeff Yach	.30	.14	.04
☐ 36 Peter Pain	.30	.14	.04
☐ 37 Aron Campbell	.30	.14	.04
☐ 38 Chris McCormick	.30	.14	.04
☐ 39 Jason Moller	.30	.14	.04
☐ 40 Terry Huhtala	.30	.14	.04
☐ 41 Matt Zarowny	.30	.14	.04
☐ 42 David St. Amour	.30	.14	.04
☐ 43 Frank Tindall	.30	.14	.04
☐ 44 Ron Stewart	1.00	.45	.12
☐ 45 Jim Young	1.00	.45	.12
☐ 46 Bob Howes	.30	.14	.04
☐ 47 Stu Lang	.30	.14	.04
☐ 48 Mike Schad (In college uniform)	.75	.35	.09
☐ 49 Mike Schad (In Philadelphia Eagles uniform)	.75	.35	.09
☐ 50 Jock Climie	1.00	.45	.12
☐ 51 Checklist	.30	.14	.04
☐ P1 Jock Climie	3.00	1.35	.35
☐ P1AU Jock Climie AU/100	30.00	13.50	3.70
☐ P2 Ron Stewart	4.00	1.80	.50
☐ P2AU Ron Stewart AU/300	30.00	13.50	3.70
☐ P3 Jim Young	4.00	1.80	.50
☐ P4 Stu Lang	3.00	1.35	.35
☐ P5 Mike Schad	3.00	1.35	.35
☐ P5AU Mike Schad AU/100	30.00	13.50	3.70
☐ NNO Title Card	.75	.35	.09

1978 Redpath Sugar Montreal Alouettes

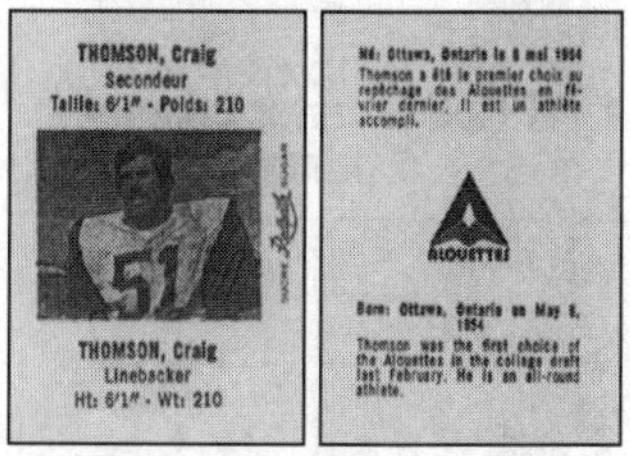

Redpath Sugar produced small (roughly 1 5/8" by 2 1/2") sugar packets featuring Alouette players for distribution in the Montreal area. Each is unnumbered and includes a small color photo of the player on the front along with his name, position, and vital information in both French and English. The back of the sugar packet includes an Alouettes logo and a short player bio. Any additions to this checklist are appreciated.

	NRMT-MT	EXC	G-VG
COMPLETE SET (3)	15.00	6.75	1.85
COMMON PACKET (1-3)	5.00	2.20	.60
□ 1 Dan Diebert Trainer	5.00	2.20	.60
□ 2 Mark Jackson	5.00	2.20	.60
□ 3 Craig Thomson	5.00	2.20	.60

1981 Red Rooster Calgary Stampeders

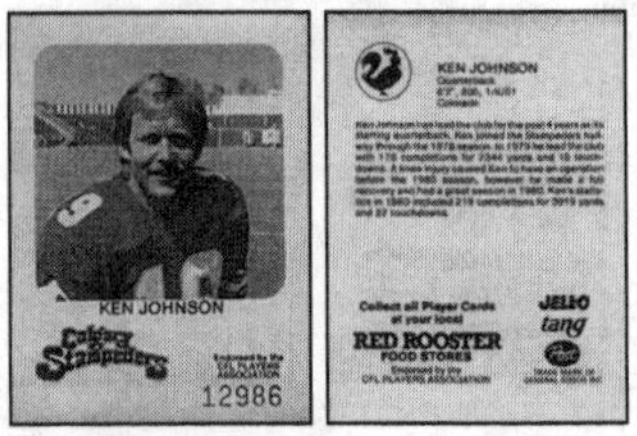

This 40-card set, distributed by Red Rooster Food Stores, measures approximately 2 3/4" by 3 5/8" and features posed, color player photos with rounded corners on a white card face. Since the card edges are perforated, the cards were apparently issued as a sheet. The player's name is printed below the photo, as is the team name and a CFL Players Association endorsement. (Some of the cards have a serial number below the endorsement). The backs carry biographical information and a player profile. Sponsor logos and names are printed at the bottom. The cards are unnumbered and checklisted below in alphabetical order.

	MINT	NRMT	EXC
COMPLETE SET (40)	30.00	13.50	3.70
COMMON CARD (1-40)	.60	.25	.07
□ 1 Willie Armstead	.60	.25	.07
□ 2 Doug Battershill	.60	.25	.07
□ 3 Willie Burden (From waist up)	3.00	1.35	.35
□ 4 Willie Burden (Head and shoulders)	3.00	1.35	.35
□ 5 Scott Burk UER (Misspelled Burke 4th line of bio)	.60	.25	.07
□ 6 Al Burleson	.60	.25	.07
□ 7 Ken Dombrowski	.60	.25	.07
□ 8 Lloyd Fairbanks	1.25	.55	.16
□ 9 Rob Forbes	.60	.25	.07
□ 10 Tom Forzani	1.00	.45	.12
□ 11 Miles Gorrell	.60	.25	.07
□ 12 J.T. Hay	.60	.25	.07
□ 13 John Holland	1.00	.45	.12
□ 14 Norm Hopely	.60	.25	.07
□ 15 Jeff Inglis	1.00	.45	.12
□ 16 Lepoleon Ingram	.60	.25	.07
□ 17 Terry Irvin	.60	.25	.07
□ 18 Ken Johnson	1.00	.45	.12
□ 19 Franklin King	.60	.25	.07
□ 20 Dave Kirzinger	.60	.25	.07
□ 21 Frank Kosec	.60	.25	.07
□ 22 Tom Krebs	.60	.25	.07
□ 23 Reggie Lewis	.60	.25	.07
□ 24 Robert Lubig	.60	.25	.07
□ 25 Scott MacArthur	.60	.25	.07
□ 26 Ed McAleney	.60	.25	.07
□ 27 Mike McTague	1.00	.45	.12
□ 28 Mark Moors	1.00	.45	.12
□ 29 Bernie Morrison	.60	.25	.07
□ 30 Mark Nelson	.60	.25	.07
□ 31 Ray Odums	.60	.25	.07
□ 32 Ronnie Paggett	.60	.25	.07
□ 33 John Palazeti	.60	.25	.07
□ 34 John Prassas	.60	.25	.07
□ 35 Tom Reimer	.60	.25	.07
□ 36 James Sykes (Close-up)	3.00	1.35	.35
□ 37 James Sykes (From waist up)	3.00	1.35	.35
□ 38 Bruce Threadgill	.60	.25	.07
□ 39 Bob Viccars	.60	.25	.07
□ 40 Merv Walker	.60	.25	.07

1981 Red Rooster Edmonton Eskimos

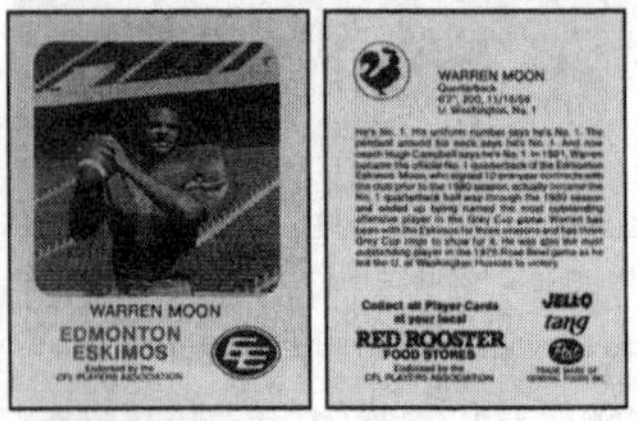

This 40-card set, distributed by Red Rooster Food Stores, measures approximately 2 3/4" by 3 1/2" and features posed, color player photos with rounded corners on a white card face. Since the card edges are perforated, the cards were apparently issued as a sheet. The player's name is printed below the photo, as is the team name and a CFL Players Association endorsement. The backs carry biographical information and a player profile. Sponsor logos and names are printed at the bottom. The cards are unnumbered and checklisted below in alphabetical order.

	MINT	NRMT	EXC
COMPLETE SET (40)	55.00	25.00	7.00
COMMON CARD (1-40)	.60	.25	.07
□ 1 Leo Blanchard	.60	.25	.07
□ 2 David Boone	.60	.25	.07
□ 3 Brian Broomell	.60	.25	.07
□ 4 Hugh Campbell CO	1.25	.55	.16
□ 5 Dave Cutler	3.00	1.35	.35
□ 6 Marco Cyncar	1.00	.45	.12
□ 7 Ron Estay	.60	.25	.07
□ 8 Dave Fennell	1.00	.45	.12
□ 9 Emilio Fraietta	.60	.25	.07
□ 10 Brian Fryer	.60	.25	.07
□ 11 Jim Germany	1.00	.45	.12
□ 12 Gary Hayes	.60	.25	.07
□ 13 Larry Highbaugh	1.25	.55	.16
□ 14 Joe Hollimon	.60	.25	.07
□ 15 Hank Ilesic	1.25	.55	.16
□ 16 Ed Jones	.60	.25	.07
□ 17 Dan Kearns	.60	.25	.07
□ 18 Sean Kehoe	.60	.25	.07
□ 19 Brian Kelly	2.50	1.10	.30
□ 20 Dan Kepley	1.25	.55	.16
□ 21 Stu Lang	.60	.25	.07
□ 22 Pete Lavorato	.60	.25	.07
□ 23 Neil Lumsden	1.00	.45	.12
□ 24 Bill Manchuk	.60	.25	.07
□ 25 Mike McLeod	.60	.25	.07
□ 26 Ted Milian	.60	.25	.07
□ 27 Warren Moon	25.00	11.00	3.10
□ 28 James Parker	2.50	1.10	.30
□ 29 John Pointer	.60	.25	.07
□ 30 Hector Pothier	.60	.25	.07
□ 31 Dale Potter	.60	.25	.07
□ 32 Angelo Santucci	.60	.25	.07
□ 33 Tom Scott	1.00	.45	.12
□ 34 Waddell Smith	1.00	.45	.12
□ 35 Bill Stevenson	1.00	.45	.12
□ 36 Tom Towns	.60	.25	.07
□ 37 Eric Upton	.60	.25	.07
□ 38 Mark Wald	.60	.25	.07
□ 39 Ken Walter	.60	.25	.07
□ 40 Tom Wilkinson	4.00	1.80	.50

1995 R.E.L. CFL

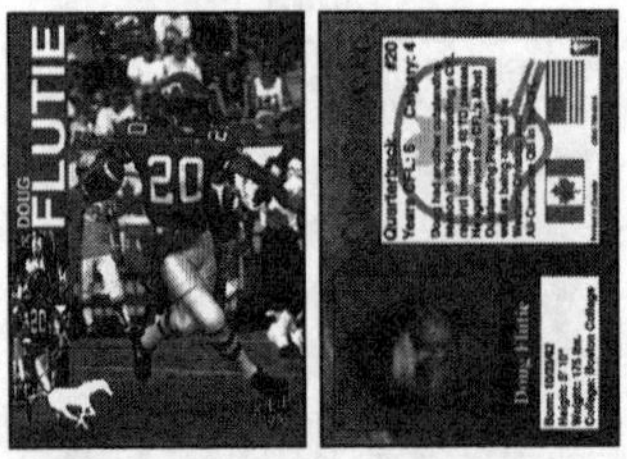

This 250-card set of the CFL was produced by Hammer Slammer Canada and Robindale Enterprises LTD. The cards feature color action player photos with the player's name in the left team-colored border above a small black-and-white player action photo. The team and card logos at the bottom round out the front. The backs carry a black-and-white player portrait with the team name, position, jersey number, and biographical and career information on a background of blended team colors. Reportedly, 3999 individually numbered sets were produced and distributed in 10-set cases. Each case also included an individually numbered (of 399) Doug Flutie card. The 14 logo cards near the end of the set listing are actually unnumbered, but have been assigned numbers below according to the checklist card. A Doug Flutie Promo card was issued as well to promote the new set.

	MINT	NRMT	EXC
COMPLETE SET (250)	30.00	13.50	3.70
COMMON CARD (1-250)	.10	.05	.01
□ 1 Doug Flutie	1.25	.55	.16
□ 2 Bruce Covernton	.20	.09	.03
□ 3 Jamie Crysdale	.10	.05	.01
□ 4 Matt Finlay	.20	.09	.03
□ 5 Alondra Johnson	.20	.09	.03
□ 6 Will Johnson	.25	.11	.03
□ 7 Greg Knox	.10	.05	.01
□ 8 Stu Laird	.20	.09	.03
□ 9 Kenton Leonard	.10	.05	.01
□ 10 Tony Martino	.10	.05	.01
□ 11 Mark McLoughlin	.10	.05	.01
□ 12 Allen Pitts	.25	.11	.03
□ 13 Marvin Pope	.10	.05	.01
□ 14 Rocco Romano	.10	.05	.01
□ 15 David Sapunjis	.50	.23	.06
□ 16 Pee Wee Smith	.25	.11	.03
□ 17 Tony Stewart	.10	.05	.01
□ 18 Srecko Zizakovic	.10	.05	.01
□ 19 Kerwin Bell	.35	.16	.04
□ 20 Leroy Blugh	.20	.09	.03
□ 21 Rod Connop	.10	.05	.01
□ 22 Blake Dermott	.20	.09	.03
□ 23 Lucius Floyd	.10	.05	.01
□ 24 Bennie Goods	.20	.09	.03
□ 25 Glenn Harper	.10	.05	.01
□ 26 Craig Hendrickson	.10	.05	.01
□ 27 Robert Holland	.10	.05	.01
□ 28 Malvin Hunter	.10	.05	.01
□ 29 John Kalin	.10	.05	.01
□ 30 Nick Mazzoli	.10	.05	.01
□ 31 Willie Pless	.40	.18	.05
□ 32 Jim Sandusky	.20	.09	.03
□ 33 Michael Soles	.20	.09	.03
□ 34 Marc Tobert	.10	.05	.01
□ 35 Henry Williams	.40	.18	.05
□ 36 Larry Wruck	.20	.09	.03
□ 37 Lee Knight	.10	.05	.01
□ 38 Shawn Prendergast	.10	.05	.01
□ 39 Richard Nurse	.10	.05	.01
□ 40 Eric Carter	.20	.09	.03
□ 41 Frank Marof	.10	.05	.01
□ 42 Roger Hennig	.10	.05	.01
□ 43 Derek Grier	.10	.05	.01
□ 44 Kelvin Means	.10	.05	.01
□ 45 Michael Philbrick	.10	.05	.01
□ 46 Jessie Small	.20	.09	.03
□ 47 Mike O'Shea	.35	.16	.04
□ 48 Marcus Cotton	.10	.05	.01
□ 49 Hassan Bailey	.10	.05	.01
□ 50 Anthony Calvillo	.50	.23	.06
□ 51 Mike Kerrigan	.25	.11	.03
□ 52 Hank Ilesic	.25	.11	.03
□ 53 Paul Osbaldiston	.20	.09	.03
□ 54 Earl Winfield	.25	.11	.03
□ 55 Danton Barto	.10	.05	.01
□ 56 Tim Cofield	.25	.11	.03
□ 57 Bruce Perkins	.10	.05	.01
□ 58 Damion Lyons	.10	.05	.01
□ 59 Joe Horn	.25	.11	.03
□ 60 Rickey Foggie	.25	.11	.03
□ 61 Bobby Dawson	.10	.05	.01
□ 62 Eddie Brown	.25	.11	.03
□ 63 Vance Hammond	.10	.05	.01
□ 64 Ed Berry	.10	.05	.01
□ 65 Stephen Bates	.10	.05	.01
□ 66 Greg Battle	.25	.11	.03
□ 67 Gary Anderson	.10	.05	.01
□ 68 Donald Smith	.10	.05	.01
□ 69 Adrion Smith	.10	.05	.01
□ 70 Rodney Harding	.20	.09	.03
□ 71 Damon Allen	.40	.18	.05
□ 72 Junior Robinson	.10	.05	.01
□ 73 Ken Watson	.10	.05	.01
□ 74 Nick Subis	.10	.05	.01
□ 75 Mike Pringle	1.00	.45	.12
□ 76 Shar Pourdanesh	.40	.18	.05
□ 77 Elfrid Payton	.20	.09	.03
□ 78 Josh Miller	.10	.05	.01
□ 79 Carlos Huerta	.20	.09	.03
□ 80 Tracy Ham	.50	.23	.06
□ 81 Tracey Gravely	.10	.05	.01
□ 82 Matt Goodwin	.10	.05	.01
□ 83 Neil Fort	.10	.05	.01
□ 84 O.J. Brigance	.75	.35	.09
□ 85 Jearld Baylis	.25	.11	.03
□ 86 Mike Alexander	.10	.05	.01
□ 87 Shannon Culver	.10	.05	.01
□ 88 Robert Clark	.20	.09	.03
□ 89 Courtney Griffin	.10	.05	.01
□ 90 Demetrious Maxie	.10	.05	.01
□ 91 Dave Ridgway	.25	.11	.03
□ 92 Terryl Ulmer	.10	.05	.01
□ 93 Lybrant Robinson	.10	.05	.01
□ 94 Troy Alexander	.10	.05	.01
□ 95 Darren Joseph	.20	.09	.03
□ 96 Warren Jones	.20	.09	.03
□ 97 Dan Rashovich	.10	.05	.01
□ 98 Glenn Kulka	.20	.09	.03
□ 99 Dale Joseph	.10	.05	.01
□ 100 Scott Hendrickson	.10	.05	.01
□ 101 Ron Goetz	.10	.05	.01
□ 102 Ventson Donelson	.10	.05	.01
□ 103 Mike Anderson	.10	.05	.01
□ 104 Brent Matich	.10	.05	.01
□ 105 Donald Narcisse	.25	.11	.03
□ 106 Tom Burgess	.35	.16	.04
□ 107 Bobby Jurasin	.20	.09	.03
□ 108 Ray Elgaard	.25	.11	.03
□ 109 Brian Bonner	.10	.05	.01
□ 110 Robbie Keen	.10	.05	.01
□ 111 Bjorn Nittmo	.35	.16	.04
□ 112 Martin Patton	.10	.05	.01
□ 113 Rod Harris	.25	.11	.03
□ 114 Mike Johnson	.10	.05	.01
□ 115 Billy Joe Tolliver	.25	.11	.03
□ 116 Curtis Mayfield	.20	.09	.03
□ 117 Ben Jefferson	.10	.05	.01
□ 118 Jon Heidenreich	.10	.05	.01
□ 119 Mike Stowell	.10	.05	.01
□ 120 Alex Mash	.10	.05	.01
□ 121 Ray Savage	.10	.05	.01
□ 122 Mario Perry	.10	.05	.01
□ 123 Ron Perry	.10	.05	.01
□ 124 Joe Fuller	.10	.05	.01
□ 125 Jonathan Wilson	.10	.05	.01
□ 126 Anthony Shelton	.10	.05	.01
□ 127 Emanuel Martin	.10	.05	.01
□ 128 Ray Alexander	.20	.09	.03
□ 129 Michael Richardson	.25	.11	.03
□ 130 Irv Daymond	.10	.05	.01
□ 131 Terry Baker	.20	.09	.03
□ 132 Danny Barrett	.25	.11	.03
□ 133 James Ellingson	.20	.09	.03
□ 134 John Kropke	.20	.09	.03
□ 135 Garry Lewis	.10	.05	.01
□ 136 James Monroe	.10	.05	.01
□ 137 Brett Young	.20	.09	.03
□ 138 Remi Trudel	.10	.05	.01
□ 139 Jed Tommy	.10	.05	.01
□ 140 Odessa Turner	.20	.09	.03
□ 141 David Black	.10	.05	.01
□ 142 Eric Geter	.10	.05	.01
□ 143 Sammy Garza	.10	.05	.01
□ 144 Loyd Lewis	.10	.05	.01
□ 145 Enis Jackson	.10	.05	.01
□ 146 Danny McManus	.35	.16	.04
□ 148 Cory Philpot	.75	.35	.09
□ 149 Glen Scrivener	.10	.05	.01
□ 150 Ian Sinclair	.20	.09	.03
□ 151 Vic Stevenson	.10	.05	.01
□ 152 Andrew Stewart	.10	.05	.01
□ 153 Jamie Taras	.10	.05	.01
□ 154 Robert Gordon	.10	.05	.01
□ 155 Tom Europe	.10	.05	.01
□ 156 Spencer McLennan	.10	.05	.01
□ 157 Mike Trevathan	.25	.11	.03
□ 158 Matt Clark	.20	.09	.03
□ 159 Daved Benefield	.20	.09	.03
□ 160 Darren Flutie	.75	.35	.09
□ 161 Charles Gordon	.10	.05	.01
□ 162 Ryan Hanson	.10	.05	.01
□ 163 Kent Austin	.25	.11	.03
□ 164 Reggie Barnes	.20	.09	.03
□ 165 Mike Clemons	.75	.35	.09
□ 166 Jock Climie	.10	.05	.01
□ 167 Duane Forde	.10	.05	.01
□ 168 Leon Hatziioannou	.10	.05	.01
□ 169 Wayne Lammle	.10	.05	.01
□ 170 Paul Masotti	.20	.09	.03
□ 171 George Nimako	.20	.09	.03
□ 172 Calvin Tiggle	.10	.05	.01
□ 173 Don Wilson	.10	.05	.01
□ 174 Chris Tsangaris	.10	.05	.01
□ 174 Lui Passaglia	.30	.14	.04
□ 175 Darrick Branch	.10	.05	.01
□ 176 Carl Coulter	.10	.05	.01
□ 177 P.J. Martin	.10	.05	.01
□ 178 Eric Blount DE	.10	.05	.01
□ 179 Norm Casola	.10	.05	.01
□ 180 Joe Burgos	.10	.05	.01
□ 181 John Buddenberg	.10	.05	.01
□ 182 George Bethune	.10	.05	.01
□ 183 Oscar Giles	.25	.11	.03
□ 184 Myron Wise	.10	.05	.01
□ 185 Roman Anderson	.10	.05	.01
□ 186 Dave Harper	.10	.05	.01
□ 187 Mike Saunders	.50	.23	.06
□ 188 Roosevelt Collins	.10	.05	.01
□ 189 Peter Shorts	.10	.05	.01
□ 190 Willie Fears	.20	.09	.03
□ 191 Mike Kiselak	.10	.05	.01
□ 192 Malcolm Frank	.10	.05	.01
□ 193 Joe Kralik	.10	.05	.01
□ 194 David Archer	1.25	.55	.16
□ 195 Billy Hess	.10	.05	.01
□ 196 Mark Stock	.10	.05	.01
□ 197 James King	.10	.05	.01
□ 198 Tony Burse	.10	.05	.01
□ 199 Donovan Gans	.10	.05	.01
□ 200 Keith Woodside	.10	.05	.01
□ 201 Anthony Drawhorn	.20	.09	.03
□ 202 Jimmy Klingler	.35	.16	.04
□ 203 Matt Dunigan	.60	.25	.07
□ 204 John Motton	.20	.09	.03
□ 205 Scott Player	.20	.09	.03
□ 206 Franco Grilla	.10	.05	.01
□ 207 Shonte Peoples	.10	.05	.01
□ 208 Derrick Crawford	.20	.09	.03
□ 209 Fernando Thomas	.10	.05	.01
□ 210 Delius Morris	.10	.05	.01
□ 211 Roosevelt Patterson	.10	.05	.01
□ 212 Willie McClendon	.10	.05	.01
□ 213 Jason Phillips	.10	.05	.01
□ 214 Mike James	.10	.05	.01
□ 215 Andre Strode	.10	.05	.01
□ 216 Chris Dyko	.10	.05	.01
□ 217 Chris Walby	.25	.11	.03
□ 218 Miles Gorrell	.10	.05	.01
□ 219 Dave Vankoughnett	.10	.05	.01
□ 220 Del Lyles	.10	.05	.01
□ 221 Bob Cameron	.25	.11	.03
□ 222 Troy Westwood	.25	.11	.03
□ 223 Reggie Slack	.25	.11	.03
□ 224 Blaise Bryant	.20	.09	.03
□ 225 Gerald Wilcox	.20	.09	.03
□ 226 David Williams	.20	.09	.03
□ 227 Kelly Rush	.10	.05	.01
□ 228 Stan Mikawos	.10	.05	.01
□ 229 Paul Randolph	.10	.05	.01

230 Greg Clark	.10	.05	.01
231 Jason Mallett	.10	.05	.01
232 Juran Bolden	.35	.16	.04
233 Brett MacNeil	.10	.05	.01
234 Chris Johnstone	.10	.05	.01
235 Toronto Argonauts Logo	.10	.05	.01
236 Ottawa Rough Riders Logo	.10	.05	.01
237 Hamilton Tiger-Cats Logo	.10	.05	.01
238 Winnipeg Blue Bombers Logo	.10	.05	.01
239 Saskatchewan Roughriders Logo	.10	.05	.01
240 Calgary Stampeders Logo	.10	.05	.01
241 Edmonton Eskimos Logo	.10	.05	.01
242 B.C. Lions Logo	.10	.05	.01
243 Memphis Mad Dogs Logo	.10	.05	.01
244 Birmingham Barracudas Logo	.10	.05	.01
245 San Antonio Texans Logo	.10	.05	.01
246 Shreveport Pirates Logo	.10	.05	.01
247 Baltimore Stallions Logo	.10	.05	.01
248 Grey Cup Logo	.10	.05	.01
249 Checklist #1	.20	.09	.03
250 Checklist #2	.20	.09	.03
P1 Doug Flutie Promo numbered one of 2500	2.00	.90	.25
AU1 Doug Flutie AUTO signed card	50.00	22.00	6.25

1971 Royal Bank B.C. Lions

This 16-photo set of the CFL's British Columbia Lions was sponsored by Royal Bank. Each black-and-white, blank-backed picture measures approximately 5" by 7" and features a white-bordered posed action photo and a facsimile autograph inscribed across it. The sponsor logo appears in black in each corner of the bottom margin. The photos are unnumbered and checklisted below in alphabetical order.

	NRMT-MT	EXC	G-VG
COMPLETE SET (16)	50.00	22.00	6.25
COMMON CARD (1-16)	2.50	1.10	.30
1 George Anderson	2.50	1.10	.30
2 Paul Brothers	2.50	1.10	.30
3 Brian Donnelly	2.50	1.10	.30
4 Dave Easley	2.50	1.10	.30
5 Trevor Ekdahl	3.50	1.55	.45
6 Jim Evenson	3.50	1.55	.45
7 Greg Findlay	2.50	1.10	.30
8 Lefty Hendrickson	2.50	1.10	.30
9 Bob Howes	2.50	1.10	.30
10 Garrett Hunsperger	2.50	1.10	.30
11 Wayne Matherne	2.50	1.10	.30
12 Don Moorhead	2.50	1.10	.30
13 Ken Phillips	2.50	1.10	.30
14 Ken Sugarman	3.50	1.55	.45
15 Tom Wilkinson	10.00	4.50	1.25
16 Jim Young	8.00	3.60	1.00

1972 Royal Bank B.C. Lions

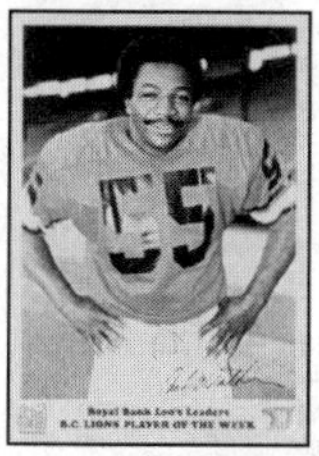

This set of 16 photos was sponsored by Royal Bank. They measure approximately 5" by 7" and are printed on thin glossy paper. The color posed player photos are bordered in white. A facsimile autograph is inscribed across the picture. At the bottom of the front, the words "Royal Leaders, B.C. Lions Player of the Week" are printed between the sponsor's logo and the Lions' logo. The backs are blank. The photos are unnumbered and checklisted below in alphabetical order. One noteworthy card in the set is Carl Weathers, who went on to acting fame as Apollo Creed in Sylvester Stallone's popular "Rocky" movies.

	NRMT-MT	EXC	G-VG
COMPLETE SET (16)	50.00	22.00	6.25
COMMON CARD (1-16)	2.50	1.10	.30
1 George Anderson	2.50	1.10	.30
2 Brian Donnelly	2.50	1.10	.30
3 Dave Easley	2.50	1.10	.30
4 Trevor Ekdahl	3.50	1.55	.45
5 Ron Estay	2.50	1.10	.30
6 Jim Evenson	3.50	1.55	.45
7 Dave Golinsky	2.50	1.10	.30
8 Larry Highbaugh	3.50	1.55	.45
9 Garrett Hunsperger	2.50	1.10	.30
10 Don Moorhead	2.50	1.10	.30
11 Johnny Musso	7.50	3.40	.95
12 Ray Nettles	2.50	1.10	.30
13 Willie Postler	2.50	1.10	.30
14 Carl Weathers	15.00	6.75	1.85
15 Jim Young	7.50	3.40	.95
16 Coaching Staff Bud Tynes Ken McCullough Owen Dejanovich Eagle Keys	3.50	1.55	.45

1973 Royal Bank B.C. Lions

This set of 16 photos was sponsored by Royal Bank. They measure approximately 5" by 7" and are printed on thin glossy paper. The color posed action shots are bordered in white. A facsimile autograph is inscribed across the picture. At the bottom of the front, the words "Royal Leaders, B.C. Lions Player of the Week" are printed between the sponsor's logo and the Lions' logo. The set includes two Moorhead cards, and only these have borders around the picture. Moreover, one has a black border, while the other has a silver border. Only the Matherne photo has a black stripe at the bottom. This black stripe appears to be covering up a wrong signature, that of Don Moorhead. The backs are blank. The photos are unnumbered and checklisted below in alphabetical order.

	NRMT-MT	EXC	G-VG
COMPLETE SET (16)	50.00	22.00	6.25
COMMON CARD (1-15)	2.50	1.10	.30
1 Barry Ardern	2.50	1.10	.30
2 Monroe Eley	3.50	1.55	.45
3 Bob Friend	2.50	1.10	.30
4 Eric Guthrie	2.50	1.10	.30
5 Garrett Hunsperger	2.50	1.10	.30
6 Wayne Matherne	2.50	1.10	.30
7A Don Moorhead (Black border)	2.50	1.10	.30
7B Don Moorhead (Silver border)	2.50	1.10	.30
8 Johnny Musso	7.50	3.40	.95
9 Ray Nettles	2.50	1.10	.30
10 Pete Palmer	2.50	1.10	.30
11 Gary Robinson SP	20.00	9.00	2.50
12 Al Wilson	2.50	1.10	.30
13 Mike Wilson	2.50	1.10	.30
14 Jim Young	7.50	3.40	.95
15 Coaches Bud Tynes Ken McCullough Owen Dejanovich Eagle Keys	3.50	1.55	.45

1974 Royal Bank B.C. Lions

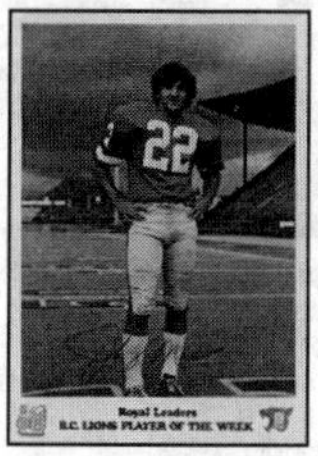

This blank-backed 14-photo color set was sponsored by Royal Bank. Each posed and bordered CFL Lions player's photo measures approximately 5" by 7" and carries a facsimile autograph across it. The sponsor logo appears in the lower left corner while the team logo is in the lower right corner. The photos are unnumbered and checklisted below in alphabetical order.

	NRMT-MT	EXC	G-VG
COMPLETE SET (14)	40.00	18.00	5.00
COMMON CARD (1-14)	2.50	1.10	.30
1 Bill Baker	6.00	2.70	.75
2 Karl Douglas	2.50	1.10	.30
3 Layne McDowell	2.50	1.10	.30
4 Ivan MacMillan	2.50	1.10	.30
5 Bud Magrum	2.50	1.10	.30
6 Don Moorhead	2.50	1.10	.30
7 Johnny Musso	7.50	3.40	.95
8 Ray Nettles	2.50	1.10	.30
9 Brian Sopatyk	2.50	1.10	.30
10 Curtis Wester	3.50	1.55	.45
11 Slade Willis	2.50	1.10	.30
12 Al Wilson	2.50	1.10	.30
13 Jim Young	7.50	3.40	.95
14 Coaching Staff	3.50	1.55	.45

1975 Royal Bank B.C. Lions

Royal Bank sponsored this 14-photo set. Each photo measures approximately 5 1/4" by 6". The photos are unnumbered and checklisted below in alphabetical order.

	NRMT-MT	EXC	G-VG
COMPLETE SET (14)	40.00	18.00	5.00
COMMON CARD (1-14)	2.50	1.10	.30
1 Brock Ansley	2.50	1.10	.30
2 Terry Bailey	2.50	1.10	.30
3 Bill Baker	6.00	2.70	.75
4 Elton Brown	2.50	1.10	.30
5 Grady Cavness	3.50	1.55	.45
6 Ross Clarkson	2.50	1.10	.30
7 Joe Fourqurean	2.50	1.10	.30
8 Lou Harris	3.50	1.55	.45
9 Layne McDowell	2.50	1.10	.30
10 Don Moorhead	2.50	1.10	.30
11 Tony Moro	2.50	1.10	.30
12 Ray Nettles	2.50	1.10	.30
13 Curtis Wester	3.50	1.55	.45
14 Jim Young	7.50	3.40	.95

1976 Royal Bank B.C. Lions

This set of 15 photos was sponsored by Royal Bank. They measure approximately 5 1/4" by 6" and are printed on thin glossy paper. The color posed player shots (from the waist up) are bordered in white. A facsimile autograph is inscribed across the picture. At the bottom of the front, the words "1976 Royal Leaders, B.C. Lions Player of the Week" are printed between the sponsor's logo and the Lions' logo. The backs are blank. The photos are unnumbered and checklisted below in alphabetical order.

	NRMT-MT	EXC	G-VG
COMPLETE SET (15)	40.00	18.00	5.00
COMMON CARD (1-15)	2.50	1.10	.30
1 Terry Bailey	2.50	1.10	.30
2 Bill Baker	6.00	2.70	.75
3 Ted Dushinski	2.50	1.10	.30
4 Eric Guthrie	2.50	1.10	.30
5 Lou Harris	3.50	1.55	.45
6 Glen Jackson	2.50	1.10	.30
7 Rocky Long	2.50	1.10	.30
8 Layne McDowell	2.50	1.10	.30
9 Ray Nettles	2.50	1.10	.30
10 Gary Robinson	2.50	1.10	.30
11 John Sciarra	6.00	2.70	.75
12 Wayne Smith	2.50	1.10	.30
13 Michael Strickland	2.50	1.10	.30
14 Al Wilson	2.50	1.10	.30
15 Jim Young	7.50	3.40	.95

1977 Royal Bank B.C. Lions

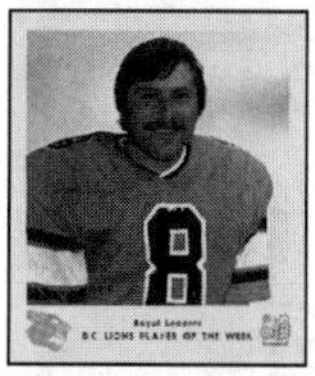

This set of 12 photos was sponsored by Royal Bank. They measure approximately 4 3/4" by 5 3/8" and are printed on thin glossy paper. The color head and shoulders shots are bordered in white. A facsimile autograph is inscribed across the picture. At the bottom of the front, the words "Royal Leaders, B.C. Lions Player of the Week" are printed between the Lions' logo and the sponsor's logo. The backs are blank. The photos are unnumbered and checklisted below in alphabetical order.

	NRMT-MT	EXC	G-VG
COMPLETE SET (12)	40.00	18.00	5.00
COMMON CARD (1-12)	2.50	1.10	.30
1 Doug Carlson	2.50	1.10	.30
2 Sam Cvijanovich	2.50	1.10	.30
3 Ted Dushinski	2.50	1.10	.30
4 Paul Giroday	2.50	1.10	.30
5 Glen Jackson	2.50	1.10	.30
6 Frank Landy	2.50	1.10	.30
7 Lui Passaglia	7.50	3.40	.95
8 John Sciarra	6.00	2.70	.75
9 Michael Strickland	2.50	1.10	.30
10 Jerry Tagge	7.50	3.40	.95
11 Al Wilson	2.50	1.10	.30
12 Jim Young	7.50	3.40	.95

1978 Royal Bank B.C. Lions

Royal Bank sponsored this 12-photo set. Each photo measures approximately 4 1/4" by 5 1/2". The photos are unnumbered and checklisted below in alphabetical order.

	NRMT-MT	EXC	G-VG
COMPLETE SET (12)	40.00	18.00	5.00
COMMON CARD (1-12)	2.50	1.10	.30
1 Terry Bailey	2.50	1.10	.30
2 Leon Bright	5.00	2.20	.60
3 Doug Carlson	2.50	1.10	.30
4 Grady Cavness	3.50	1.55	.45
5 Al Charuk	2.50	1.10	.30
6 Paul Giroday	2.50	1.10	.30
7 Larry Key	2.50	1.10	.30
8 Frank Landy	2.50	1.10	.30
9 Lui Passaglia	7.50	3.40	.95
10 Jerry Tagge	7.50	3.40	.95
11 Al Wilson	2.50	1.10	.30
12 Jim Young	7.50	3.40	.95

1987 Royal Studios Regina Rams

Standard size; Front: color photo, white and green stripe border, player name and number. Back: black on white card stock, position, resume.

	MINT	NRMT	EXC
COMPLETE SET (20)	35.00	16.00	4.40
COMMON CARD	2.00	.90	.25
1 Jami Anderson	2.00	.90	.25
2 Tim Burnie	2.00	.90	.25
3 Doug Dorsch	2.00	.90	.25
4 Brian Eltom	2.00	.90	.25
5 Dave Gebert	2.00	.90	.25
6 Ryan Hall	2.00	.90	.25
7 Dan Johnston	2.00	.90	.25
8 Sam Khuber	2.00	.90	.25
9 Lance Lascue	2.00	.90	.25
10 Mike Lazecki	2.00	.90	.25
11 Dean Mihalicz	2.00	.90	.25
12 Ken Neiszner	2.00	.90	.25
13 Dean Picton	2.00	.90	.25
14 Tim Relke	2.00	.90	.25
15 Cliff Rusconi	2.00	.90	.25
16 Rob Sillinger	2.00	.90	.25
17 Richard Sutcliffe	2.00	.90	.25
18 Wendell Toth	2.00	.90	.25
19 Steve Tunison	2.00	.90	.25
20 Jim Warnecke	2.00	.90	.25

1987 Royal Studios Saskatchewan Roughriders

This 40-card standard-size set features members of the Saskatchewan Roughriders. The card fronts are in color, with white and green striped border, with the player's name and uniform number at the bottom. The card backs are black on white card stock, with the player's name, number, position, team, and resume at the top. The cards are unnumbered and are listed below in alphabetical order by subject.

	MINT	NRMT	EXC
COMPLETE SET (40)	35.00	16.00	4.40
COMMON CARD (1-40)	.75	.35	.09
1 Dave Albright	.75	.35	.09
2 Roger Aldag	1.00	.45	.12
3 Mike Anderson	.75	.35	.09
4 Tron Armstrong	.75	.35	.09
5 Terry Baker	1.00	.45	.12
6 Walter Bender	1.25	.55	.16
7 Jeff Bentrim	1.25	.55	.16
8 Todd Brown	.75	.35	.09
9 Tom Burgess	3.00	1.35	.35
10 Coaching Staff John Hufnagel Dick Adams John Gregory Ted Heath Gary Hoffman M. Samples	1.00	.45	.12
11 Terry Cochrane	.75	.35	.09
12 David Conrad	.75	.35	.09
13 Steve Crane	.75	.35	.09
14 James Curry	2.00	.90	.25
15 Tony Dennis	.75	.35	.09
16 Ray Elgaard	3.00	1.35	.35
17 Denny Ferdinand	.75	.35	.09
18 Roderick Fisher	.75	.35	.09
19 Joe Fuller	.75	.35	.09
20 Gainer The Gopher (Team Mascot)	.75	.35	.09
21 Norris Gibbs	.75	.35	.09
22 Nick Hebeler	.75	.35	.09
23 Bryan Illerbrun	1.00	.45	.12
24 Alan Johns	.75	.35	.09
25 Bobby Jurasin	3.00	1.35	.35
26 Eddie Lowe	1.00	.45	.12
27 Tracey Mack	.75	.35	.09
28 Tim McCray	1.50	.70	.19
29 Mike McGruder	1.00	.45	.12
30 Ken Moore	.75	.35	.09
31 Dan Rashovich	.75	.35	.09
32 Scott Redl	.75	.35	.09
33 Dave Ridgway	1.25	.55	.16
34 Dave Sidoo	.75	.35	.09
35 Harry Skipper	1.00	.45	.12
36 Lawrie Skolrood	1.00	.45	.12
37 Vic Stevenson	.75	.35	.09
38 Glen Suitor	1.00	.45	.12
39 Brendan Taman Asst.EQ MG Ivan Gutfriend Athletic Therapist Norm Fong EQ MG	.75	.35	.09
40 Mark Urness	.75	.35	.09

1988 Royal Studios Saskatchewan Roughriders

This 54-card standard-size set features members of the Saskatchewan Roughriders. The card fronts are in color, with white and green striped border, with the player's name and number at the bottom. The card backs are black on white card stock, with the player's name, number, position, team, and resume at the top. The cards are unnumbered and listed below in alphabetical order by subject. The cards were printed on three different 20-card sheets, necessitating six double-printed cards as noted below.

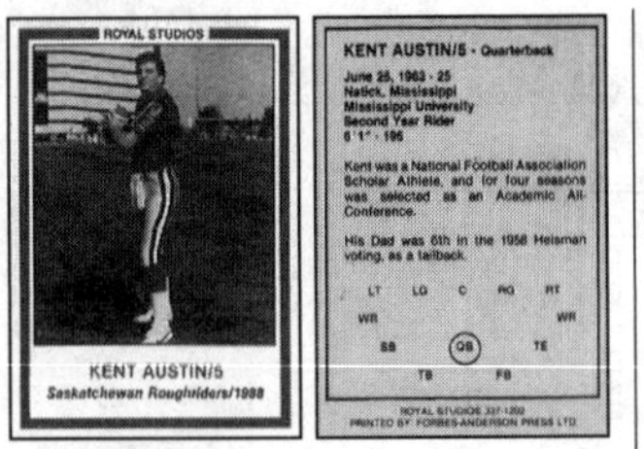

	MINT	NRMT	EXC
COMPLETE SET (54)	40.00	18.00	5.00
COMMON CARD (1-54)	.50	.23	.06
☐ 1 Dave Albright	.50	.23	.06
☐ 2 Roger Aldag DP	.75	.35	.09
☐ 3 Mike Anderson	.50	.23	.06
☐ 4 Kent Austin DP	3.00	1.35	.35
☐ 5 Terry Baker	.75	.35	.09
☐ 6 Jeff Bentrim	.75	.35	.09
☐ 7 Rob Bresciani	.50	.23	.06
☐ 8 Albert Brown	.75	.35	.09
☐ 9 Tom Burgess DP	2.50	1.10	.30
☐ 10 Coaching Staff Gary Hoffman Dick Adams Dan Daniel Ted Heath John Gregory Steve Goldman	.75	.35	.09
☐ 11 Dick Cohee and The Store	.50	.23	.06
☐ 12 David Conrad	.50	.23	.06
☐ 13 Steve Crane	.50	.23	.06
☐ 14 James Curry DP	1.25	.55	.16
☐ 15 Dream Team (Cheerleaders)	1.25	.55	.16
☐ 16 Ray Elgaard	2.50	1.10	.30
☐ 17 James Ellingson	.75	.35	.09
☐ 18 Jeff Fairholm	1.25	.55	.16
☐ 19 Denny Ferdinand	.50	.23	.06
☐ 20 The Flame (Team Mascot)	.50	.23	.06
☐ 21 Norm Fong and Ivan Gutfriend (Equipment/Trainer)	.50	.23	.06
☐ 22 Joe Fuller	.50	.23	.06
☐ 23 Gainer The Gopher (Team Mascot)	.50	.23	.06
☐ 24 Vince Goldsmith	1.00	.45	.12
☐ 25 John Gregory CO	.75	.35	.09
☐ 26 Richie Hall	.50	.23	.06
☐ 27 Bill Henry	.50	.23	.06
☐ 28 James Hood	.50	.23	.06
☐ 29 Bryan Illerbrun UER (Name misspelled Brian on front and back)	.75	.35	.09
☐ 30 Milson Jones	1.25	.55	.16
☐ 31 Bobby Jurasin DP	2.50	1.10	.30
☐ 32 Tim Kearse	.50	.23	.06
☐ 33 Rick Klassen	.75	.35	.09
☐ 34 Gary Lewis	.50	.23	.06
☐ 35 Eddie Lowe	.75	.35	.09
☐ 36 Greg McCormack	.50	.23	.06
☐ 37 Tim McCray	1.00	.45	.12
☐ 38 Ray McDonald	.75	.35	.09
☐ 39 Mike McGruder	.75	.35	.09
☐ 40 Ken Moore	.50	.23	.06
☐ 41 Donald Narcisse	2.00	.90	.25
☐ 42 Dan Rambo and Brendan Taman (Rider Scouting)	.50	.23	.06
☐ 43 Dan Rashovich	.50	.23	.06
☐ 44 Dameon Reilly	.75	.35	.09
☐ 45 Dave Ridgway DP	1.00	.45	.12
☐ 46 Rocco Romano	.50	.23	.06
☐ 47 Harry Skipper	.75	.35	.09
☐ 48 Vic Stevenson	.50	.23	.06
☐ 49 Glen Suitor	.75	.35	.09
☐ 50 Jeff Treftlin	.50	.23	.06
☐ 51 Mark Urness	.50	.23	.06
☐ 52 Eddie Ray Walker	.75	.35	.09
☐ 53 John Walker	.75	.35	.09
☐ 54 Jeff Watson	.50	.23	.06

1989 Royal Studios Saskatchewan Roughriders

This 54-card standard-size set features members of the Saskatchewan Roughriders. The card fronts are in color, with white and green striped border, with the player's name and uniform number at the bottom. The card backs are black on white card stock, with the player's name, number, position, team, and resume at the top. The cards are unnumbered and are listed below in alphabetical order by subject. The cards were printed on three different 20-card sheets, necessitating six double-printed cards as noted below.

	MINT	NRMT	EXC
COMPLETE SET (54)	35.00	16.00	4.40
COMMON CARD (1-54)	.50	.23	.06
☐ 1 Dave Albright	.50	.23	.06
☐ 2 Roger Aldag DP	.75	.35	.09
☐ 3 Tuineau Alipate	.75	.35	.09
☐ 4 Mike Anderson	.50	.23	.06
☐ 5 Kent Austin	3.00	1.35	.35
☐ 6 Terry Baker	.75	.35	.09
☐ 7 Jeff Bentrim	.75	.35	.09
☐ 8 Rob Bresciani	.50	.23	.06
☐ 9 Albert Brown	.75	.35	.09
☐ 10 Tom Burgess DP	2.50	1.10	.30
☐ 11 Coaching Staff	.75	.35	.09
☐ 12 Steve Crane	.50	.23	.06
☐ 13 James Curry	1.25	.55	.16
☐ 14 Kevin Dixon	.50	.23	.06
☐ 15 Dream Team (Cheerleaders sponsored by CKRM)	1.00	.45	.12
☐ 16 Wayne Drinkwalter	.75	.35	.09
☐ 17 Ray Elgaard	2.00	.90	.25
☐ 18 James Ellingson	.75	.35	.09
☐ 19 Jeff Fairholm	.75	.35	.09
☐ 20 The Flame	.50	.23	.06
☐ 21 Norm Fong and Ivan Gutfriend (Equipment/Trainer)	.50	.23	.06
☐ 22 Gainer The Gopher DP (Team Mascot)	.50	.23	.06
☐ 23 John Gregory CO	.75	.35	.09
☐ 24 Vince Goldsmith	.75	.35	.09
☐ 25 Mark Guy	.75	.35	.09
☐ 26 Richie Hall DP	.50	.23	.06
☐ 27 John Hoffman	.50	.23	.06
☐ 28 Bryan Illerbrun UER (Name misspelled Brian on front and back)	.75	.35	.09
☐ 29 Milson Jones	.75	.35	.09
☐ 30 Bobby Jurasin DP	2.00	.90	.25
☐ 31 Chuck Klingbeil	.75	.35	.09
☐ 32 Gary Lewis	.75	.35	.09
☐ 33 Eddie Lowe	.75	.35	.09
☐ 34 Greg McCormack	.50	.23	.06
☐ 35 Tim McCray	1.00	.45	.12
☐ 36 Ray McDonald	.50	.23	.06
☐ 37 Ken Moore	.50	.23	.06
☐ 38 Cedric Moses	.50	.23	.06
☐ 39 Donald Narcisse	1.50	.70	.19
☐ 40 Dan Payne	.50	.23	.06
☐ 41 Bob Poley	.50	.23	.06
☐ 42 Dan Rashovich	.50	.23	.06
☐ 43 Dave Ridgway DP	1.00	.45	.12
☐ 44 Junior Robinson	.75	.35	.09
☐ 45 Harry Skipper	.75	.35	.09
☐ 46 Vic Stevenson	.50	.23	.06
☐ 47 Glen Suitor	1.00	.45	.12
☐ 48 Jeff Treftlin	.50	.23	.06
☐ 49 Kelly Trithart	.75	.35	.09
☐ 50 Mark Urness	.50	.23	.06
☐ 51 Lionel Vital	.50	.23	.06
☐ 52 Eddie Ray Walker	.75	.35	.09
☐ 53 Steve Wiggins	.50	.23	.06
☐ 54 Donovan Wright	.50	.23	.06

1990 Royal Studios Saskatchewan Roughriders

This 60-card standard size set features members of the Saskatchewan Roughriders. The card fronts are in color, with white and green striped border, with the player's name and uniform number at the bottom. The card backs are black on white card stock, with the player's name, number, position, team, and resume at the top. The cards are unnumbered and are listed below in alphabetical order by subject.

	MINT	NRMT	EXC
COMPLETE SET (60)	35.00	16.00	4.40
COMMON CARD (1-60)	.50	.23	.06
☐ 1 Dick Adams CO	.50	.23	.06
☐ 2 Dave Albright	.50	.23	.06
☐ 3 Roger Aldag	.75	.35	.09
☐ 4 Tuineau Alipate	.75	.35	.09
☐ 5 Mike Anderson	.50	.23	.06
☐ 6 Kent Austin	2.50	1.10	.30
☐ 7 Tony Belser	.50	.23	.06
☐ 8 Jeff Bentrim	.75	.35	.09
☐ 9 Bruce Boyko	.75	.35	.09
☐ 10 Albert Brown	.75	.35	.09
☐ 11 Paul Bushey	.50	.23	.06
☐ 12 Larry Donovan CO	.50	.23	.06
☐ 13 Dream Team (Cheerleaders sponsored by CKRM)	.75	.35	.09
☐ 14 Wayne Drinkwalter	.75	.35	.09
☐ 15 Sean Dykes	.50	.23	.06
☐ 16 Ray Elgaard	2.50	1.10	.30
☐ 17 Jeff Fairholm	1.00	.45	.12
☐ 18 Norman Fong MG Ivan Gutfriend MG	.50	.23	.06
☐ 19 Alan Ford GM	.50	.23	.06
☐ 20 Lucius Floyd	.75	.35	.09
☐ 21 Gainer The Gopher (Team Mascot)	.50	.23	.06
☐ 22 Chris Gioskos	.50	.23	.06
☐ 23 Vince Goldsmith	1.00	.45	.12
☐ 24 John Gregory CO	.75	.35	.09
☐ 25 Mark Guy	.75	.35	.09
☐ 26 Stacey Hairston	.75	.35	.09
☐ 27 Richie Hall	.75	.35	.09
☐ 28 Greg Harris	.50	.23	.06
☐ 29 Ted Heath CO	.50	.23	.06
☐ 30 Gary Hoffman CO	.50	.23	.06
☐ 31 John Hoffman	.50	.23	.06
☐ 32 Larry Hogue	.75	.35	.09
☐ 33 Bobby Jurasin	2.00	.90	.25
☐ 34 Milson Jones	1.00	.45	.12
☐ 35 James King	.50	.23	.06
☐ 36 Chuck Klingbeil	1.00	.45	.12
☐ 37 Mike Lazecki	.50	.23	.06
☐ 38 Orville Lee	1.50	.70	.19
☐ 39 Gary Lewis	.75	.35	.09
☐ 40 Eddie Lowe	.75	.35	.09
☐ 41 Greg McCormack	.50	.23	.06
☐ 42 Tim McCray	1.00	.45	.12
☐ 43 Ken Moore	.50	.23	.06
☐ 44 Donald Narcisse	1.50	.70	.19
☐ 45 Dave Pitcher	.50	.23	.06
☐ 46 Bob Poley	.50	.23	.06
☐ 47 Brent Pollack	.50	.23	.06
☐ 48 Dan Rashovich	.50	.23	.06
☐ 49 Tony Rice	1.50	.70	.19
☐ 50 Dave Ridgway	1.00	.45	.12
☐ 51 Pal Sartori	.50	.23	.06
☐ 52 Saskatchewan Roughriders	1.00	.45	.12
☐ 53 Glen Scrivener	.50	.23	.06
☐ 54 Tony Simmons	.50	.23	.06
☐ 55 Vic Stevenson	.50	.23	.06
☐ 56 Glen Suitor	1.00	.45	.12
☐ 57 Jeff Treftlin	.50	.23	.06
☐ 58 Kelly Trithart UER (Name misspelled Trihart on front and back)	.75	.35	.09
☐ 59 Lionel Vital	.50	.23	.06
☐ 60 Slater Zaleski	.50	.23	.06

1991 Royal Studios Saskatchewan Roughriders

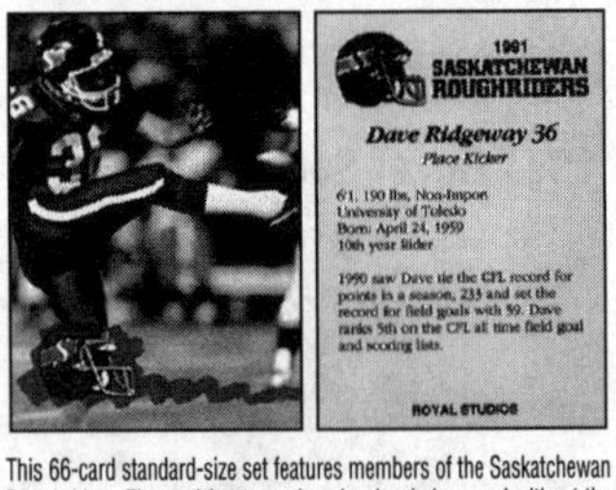

This 66-card standard-size set features members of the Saskatchewan Roughriders. The card fronts are in color, borderless, and without the player identification except through the photo. The card backs are black on white card stock, with the player's name, number, position, team, and resume at the top. The cards are unnumbered and are listed below in alphabetical order by subject.

	MINT	NRMT	EXC
COMPLETE SET (66)	35.00	16.00	4.40
COMMON CARD (1-66)	.40	.18	.05
☐ 1 Dick Adams CO	.40	.18	.05
☐ 2 Dave Albright	.40	.18	.05
☐ 3 Roger Aldag	.60	.25	.07
☐ 4 Mike Anderson	.40	.18	.05
☐ 5 Kent Austin	3.00	1.35	.35
☐ 6 John Bankhead	.60	.25	.07
☐ 7 Kerry Beutler 1990 Miss Grey Cup	.60	.25	.07
☐ 8 Allan Boyko	.60	.25	.07
☐ 9 Bruce Boyko	.60	.25	.07
☐ 10 Doug Brewster	.40	.18	.05
☐ 11 Albert Brown	.60	.25	.07
☐ 12 Paul Bushey	.40	.18	.05
☐ 13 Coaching Staff	.40	.18	.05
☐ 14 Larry Donovan CO	.40	.18	.05
☐ 15 Wayne Drinkwalter	.60	.25	.07
☐ 16 Sean Dykes	.40	.18	.05
☐ 17 Ray Elgaard	2.00	.90	.25
☐ 18 Jeff Fairholm	1.00	.45	.12
☐ 19 Dan Farthing	.40	.18	.05
☐ 20 Lucius Floyd	.60	.25	.07
☐ 21 Gainer The Gopher Team Mascot	.40	.18	.05
☐ 22 Chris Gioskos UER (Name misspelled Gioskas on front)	.40	.18	.05
☐ 23 Sonny Gordon	.40	.18	.05
☐ 24 John Gregory CO	.60	.25	.07
☐ 25 Stacey Hairston	.60	.25	.07
☐ 26 Richie Hall	.60	.25	.07
☐ 27 Greg Harris	.40	.18	.05
☐ 28 Major Harris	1.50	.70	.19
☐ 29 Ted Heath CO	.40	.18	.05
☐ 30 Gary Hoffman CO	.40	.18	.05
☐ 31 John Hoffman	.40	.18	.05
☐ 32 Larry Hogue	.60	.25	.07
☐ 33 Willis Jacox	1.50	.70	.19
☐ 34 Ray Jauch CO	.60	.25	.07
☐ 35 Gene Jelks	1.50	.70	.19
☐ 36 Milson Jones	1.00	.45	.12
☐ 37 Bobby Jurasin	2.00	.90	.25
☐ 38 James King	.40	.18	.05
☐ 39 Mike Lazecki	.40	.18	.05
☐ 40 Orville Lee	1.50	.70	.19
☐ 41 Gary Lewis	.60	.25	.07
☐ 42 Eddie Lowe	.60	.25	.07
☐ 43 Paul Maines	.40	.18	.05
☐ 44 Don Matthews CO	.40	.18	.05
☐ 45 Dane McArthur	.40	.18	.05
☐ 46 David McCrary	.40	.18	.05
☐ 47 Donald Narcisse	1.50	.70	.19
☐ 48 Offensive Line	.40	.18	.05
☐ 49 Dave Pitcher	.40	.18	.05
☐ 50 Bob Poley	.40	.18	.05
☐ 51 Brent Pollack	.40	.18	.05
☐ 52 Basil Proctor	.40	.18	.05
☐ 53 Dan Rashovich	.40	.18	.05
☐ 54 Dave Ridgway UER (Name misspelled Ridgeway on back)	1.00	.45	.12
☐ 55 Roughriders vs. The Rocket	1.00	.45	.12
☐ 56 Roughriders Team	.60	.25	.07
☐ 57 Glen Scrivener	.40	.18	.05
☐ 58 Keith Stephens	.40	.18	.05
☐ 59 Vic Stevenson	.40	.18	.05
☐ 60 Glen Suitor	1.00	.45	.12
☐ 61 Chris Thieneman	.40	.18	.05
☐ 62 Jeff Treftlin	.40	.18	.05
☐ 63 Kelly Trithart	.60	.25	.07
☐ 64 Paul Vajda	.40	.18	.05
☐ 65 Ted Wahl	.40	.18	.05
☐ 66 Rick Worman	1.00	.45	.12

1991 Royal Studios Roughriders Grey Cup 1966-91

Standard size. Front: black-and-white, silver border, name. Back: black on white card stock, player's name, number, position, resume.

	MINT	NRMT	EXC
COMPLETE SET (40)	35.00	16.00	4.40
COMMON CARD (1-40)	.60	.25	.07
☐ 1 Jack Abendschan	1.00	.45	.12
☐ 2 Sandy Archer TR	.60	.25	.07
☐ 3 Ron Atchison	3.00	1.35	.35
☐ 4 Gord Barwell	.60	.25	.07
☐ 5 Al Benecick	.60	.25	.07
☐ 6 Bruce Bennett	1.00	.45	.12
☐ 7 Tom Beynon	.60	.25	.07
☐ 8 Clyde Brock	.60	.25	.07
☐ 9 Ed Buchanan	.60	.25	.07
☐ 10 Hugh Campbell	1.00	.45	.12
☐ 11 Wally Dempsey	.60	.25	.07
☐ 12 Henry Dorsch	.60	.25	.07
☐ 13 Paul Dudley	.60	.25	.07
☐ 14 Larry Dumelie	.60	.25	.07
☐ 15 Ted Dushinski	.60	.25	.07
☐ 16 Garner Ekstran	1.00	.45	.12
☐ 17 Alan Ford	.60	.25	.07
☐ 18 Alan Ford The Catch	.60	.25	.07
☐ 19 Don Gerhardt	.60	.25	.07
☐ 20 Eagle Keys CO	1.50	.70	.19
☐ 21 Bob Kosid	.60	.25	.07
☐ 22 Ron Lancaster	3.00	1.35	.35
☐ 23 Ron Lancaster Hugh Campbell	2.50	1.10	.30
☐ 24 Moe Levesque	.60	.25	.07
☐ 25 Ed McQuarters	.60	.25	.07
☐ 26 Gil Petmanis	.60	.25	.07
☐ 27 Ken Preston GM	1.50	.70	.19
☐ 28 George Reed	1.50	.70	.19
☐ 29 Ken Reed	.60	.25	.07
☐ 30 Cliff Shaw	.60	.25	.07
☐ 31 Wayne Shaw	.60	.25	.07
☐ 32 Ted Urness	1.00	.45	.12
☐ 33 Galen Wahlmeier	.60	.25	.07
☐ 34 Dale West	1.00	.45	.12
☐ 35 Reg Whitehouse	.60	.25	.07
☐ 36 Gene Wlasiuk	.60	.25	.07
☐ 37 Jim Worden	.60	.25	.07
☐ 38 Saskatchewan Roughriders 1966 Grey Cup Lineup	.60	.25	.07
☐ 39 The Ticket 40th Annual Grey Cup	.60	.25	.07
☐ 40 The Grey Cup 40th Annual Grey Cup	.60	.25	.07

1971 Sargent Promotions Stamps

This photo album, measuring approximately 10 3/4" by 13", features 225 players from nine Canadian Football League teams. The set was sponsored by Eddie Sargent Promotions and is completely bi-lingual. The collector completed the set by purchasing a different picture packet from a participating food store each week. There were 16 different picture packets, with 14 color stickers per packet. After a general introduction, the album is divided into team sections, with two pages devoted to each team. A brief history of each team is presented,

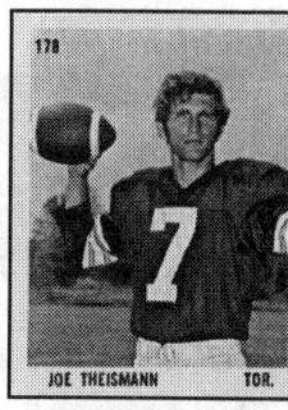

followed by 25 numbered sticker slots. Each sticker measures approximately 2" by 2 1/2" and has a posed color player photo with white borders. The player's name and team affiliation are indicated in the bottom white border. Biographical information and career summary appear below each sticker slot on the page itself. The stickers are numbered on the front and checklisted below alphabetically according to teams.

	NRMT-MT	EXC	G-VG
COMPLETE SET (225)	225.00	100.00	28.00
COMMON CARD (1-225)	.75	.35	.09
☐ 1 Jim Young	7.50	3.40	.95
☐ 2 Trevor Ekdahl	1.25	.55	.16
☐ 3 Ted Gerela	1.25	.55	.16
☐ 4 Jim Evenson	1.25	.55	.16
☐ 5 Ray Lychak	.75	.35	.09
☐ 6 Dave Golinsky	.75	.35	.09
☐ 7 Ted Warkentin	.75	.35	.09
☐ 8 A.D. Whitfield	1.25	.55	.16
☐ 9 Lach Heron	1.25	.55	.16
☐ 10 Ken Phillips	.75	.35	.09
☐ 11 Lefty Hendrickson	.75	.35	.09
☐ 12 Paul Brothers	.75	.35	.09
☐ 13 Eagle Keys CO	1.50	.70	.19
☐ 14 Garrett Hunsperger	.75	.35	.09
☐ 15 Greg Findlay	.75	.35	.09
☐ 16 Dave Easley	.75	.35	.09
☐ 17 Barrie Hansen	.75	.35	.09
☐ 18 Wayne Dennis	.75	.35	.09
☐ 19 Jerry Bradley	.75	.35	.09
☐ 20 Gerry Herron	.75	.35	.09
☐ 21 Gary Robinson	.75	.35	.09
☐ 22 Bill Whisler	.75	.35	.09
☐ 23 Bob Howes	.75	.35	.09
☐ 24 Tom Wilkinson	6.00	2.70	.75
☐ 25 Tom Cassese	.75	.35	.09
☐ 26 Dick Suderman	1.25	.55	.16
☐ 27 Jerry Keeling	4.00	1.80	.50
☐ 28 John Helton	4.00	1.80	.50
☐ 29 Jim Furlong	.75	.35	.09
☐ 30 Fred James	.75	.35	.09
☐ 31 Howard Starks	.75	.35	.09
☐ 32 Craig Koinzan	.75	.35	.09
☐ 33 Frank Andruski	.75	.35	.09
☐ 34 Joe Forzani	1.25	.55	.16
☐ 35 Herb Schumn	.75	.35	.09
☐ 36 Gerry Shaw	.75	.35	.09
☐ 37 Lanny Boleski	.75	.35	.09
☐ 38 Jim Duncan CO	.75	.35	.09
☐ 39 Hugh McKinnis	.75	.35	.09
☐ 40 Basil Bark	.75	.35	.09
☐ 41 Herman Harrison	4.00	1.80	.50
☐ 42 Larry Robinson	1.25	.55	.16
☐ 43 Larry Lawrence	.75	.35	.09
☐ 44 Granville Liggins	2.00	.90	.25
☐ 45 Wayne Harris	4.00	1.80	.50
☐ 46 John Atamian	.75	.35	.09
☐ 47 Wayne Holm	.75	.35	.09
☐ 48 Rudy Linterman	1.25	.55	.16
☐ 49 Jim Sillye	.75	.35	.09
☐ 50 Terry Wilson	.75	.35	.09
☐ 51 Don Trull	2.00	.90	.25
☐ 52 Rusty Clark	.75	.35	.09
☐ 53 Ted Page	.75	.35	.09
☐ 54 Ken Ferguson	.75	.35	.09
☐ 55 Alan Pitcaithley	.75	.35	.09
☐ 56 Bayne Norrie	.75	.35	.09
☐ 57 Dave Gasser	.75	.35	.09
☐ 58 Jim Thomas	.75	.35	.09
☐ 59 Terry Swarn	1.25	.55	.16
☐ 60 Ron Forwick	.75	.35	.09
☐ 61 Henry King	.75	.35	.09
☐ 62 John Wydareny	1.25	.55	.16
☐ 63 Ray Jauch CO	1.25	.55	.16
☐ 64 Jim Henshall	.75	.35	.09
☐ 65 Dave Cutler	4.00	1.80	.50
☐ 66 Fred Dunn	.75	.35	.09
☐ 67 Dick Dupuis	1.25	.55	.16
☐ 68 Fritz Greenlee	.75	.35	.09
☐ 69 Jerry Griffin	1.25	.55	.16
☐ 70 Allen Ische	.75	.35	.09
☐ 71 John LaGrone	1.25	.55	.16
☐ 72 Mike Law	.75	.35	.09
☐ 73 Ed Molstad	.75	.35	.09
☐ 74 Greg Pipes	1.25	.55	.16
☐ 75 Roy Shatzko	.75	.35	.09
☐ 76 Joe Zuger	1.25	.55	.16
☐ 77 Wally Gabler	1.25	.55	.16
☐ 78 Tony Gabriel	6.00	2.70	.75
☐ 79 John Reid	.75	.35	.09
☐ 80 Dave Fleming	.75	.35	.09
☐ 81 Jon Hohman	.75	.35	.09
☐ 82 Tommy Joe Coffey	5.00	2.20	.60
☐ 83 Dick Wesolowski	.75	.35	.09
☐ 84 Gordon Christian	.75	.35	.09
☐ 85 Steve Worster	6.00	2.70	.75
☐ 86 Bob Taylor	1.25	.55	.16
☐ 87 Doug Mitchell	.75	.35	.09
☐ 88 Al Dorow CO	1.25	.55	.16
☐ 89 Angelo Mosca	7.50	3.40	.95
☐ 90 Bill Danychuk	1.25	.55	.16
☐ 91 Mike Blum	.75	.35	.09
☐ 92 Garney Henley	6.00	2.70	.75
☐ 93 Bob Steiner	.75	.35	.09
☐ 94 John Manel	.75	.35	.09
☐ 95 Bob Krouse	.75	.35	.09
☐ 96 John Williams	.75	.35	.09
☐ 97 Scott Henderson	.75	.35	.09
☐ 98 Ed Chalupka	.75	.35	.09
☐ 99 Paul McKay	.75	.35	.09
☐ 100 Rensi Perdoni	.75	.35	.09
☐ 101 Ed George	1.25	.55	.16
☐ 102 Al Phaneuf	1.25	.55	.16
☐ 103 Sonny Wade	2.00	.90	.25
☐ 104 Moses Denson	2.00	.90	.25
☐ 105 Terry Evanshen	6.00	2.70	.75
☐ 106 Pierre Desjardins	.75	.35	.09
☐ 107 Larry Fairholm	.75	.35	.09
☐ 108 Gene Gaines	4.00	1.80	.50
☐ 109 Bobby Lee Thompson	.75	.35	.09
☐ 110 Mike Widger	.75	.35	.09
☐ 111 Gene Ceppetelli	.75	.35	.09
☐ 112 Barry Randall	.75	.35	.09
☐ 113 Sam Etcheverry CO	2.50	1.10	.30
☐ 114 Mark Kosmos	1.25	.55	.16
☐ 115 Peter Dalla Riva	4.00	1.80	.50
☐ 116 Ted Collins	.75	.35	.09
☐ 117 John Couture	.75	.35	.09
☐ 118 Tony Passander	.75	.35	.09
☐ 119 Garry Lefebvre	.75	.35	.09
☐ 120 George Springate	.75	.35	.09
☐ 121 Gordon Judges	.75	.35	.09
☐ 122 Steve Smear	2.50	1.10	.30
☐ 123 Tom Pullen	.75	.35	.09
☐ 124 Merl Code	.75	.35	.09
☐ 125 Steve Booras	.75	.35	.09
☐ 126 Hugh Oldham	.75	.35	.09
☐ 127 Moe Racine	.75	.35	.09
☐ 128 John Kruspe	.75	.35	.09
☐ 129 Ken Lehmann	1.25	.55	.16
☐ 130 Billy Cooper	.75	.35	.09
☐ 131 Marshall Shirk	.75	.35	.09
☐ 132 Tom Schuette	.75	.35	.09
☐ 133 Doug Specht	.75	.35	.09
☐ 134 Dennis Duncan	.75	.35	.09
☐ 135 Jerry Campbell	1.25	.55	.16
☐ 136 Wayne Giardino	.75	.35	.09
☐ 137 Roger Perdrix	.75	.35	.09
☐ 138 Jack Gotta CO	1.25	.55	.16
☐ 139 Terry Wellesley	.75	.35	.09
☐ 140 Dave Braggins	.75	.35	.09
☐ 141 Dave Pivec	.75	.35	.09
☐ 142 Rod Woodward	.75	.35	.09
☐ 143 Garry Wood	2.00	.90	.25
☐ 144 Al Marcelin	1.25	.55	.16
☐ 145 Dan Dever	.75	.35	.09
☐ 146 Ivan MacMillan	.75	.35	.09
☐ 147 Wayne Smith	.75	.35	.09
☐ 148 Barry Ardern	.75	.35	.09
☐ 149 Rick Cassatta	1.25	.55	.16
☐ 150 Bill Van Burkleo	.75	.35	.09
☐ 151 Ron Lancaster	6.00	2.70	.75
☐ 152 Wayne Shaw	.75	.35	.09
☐ 153 Bob Kosid	.75	.35	.09
☐ 154 George Reed	7.50	3.40	.95
☐ 155 Don Bahnuik	.75	.35	.09
☐ 156 Gordon Barwell	.75	.35	.09
☐ 157 Clyde Brock	.75	.35	.09
☐ 158 Alan Ford	.75	.35	.09
☐ 159 Jack Abendschan	1.25	.55	.16
☐ 160 Steve Molnar	.75	.35	.09
☐ 161 Al Rankin	.75	.35	.09
☐ 162 Bobby Thompson	.75	.35	.09
☐ 163 Dave Skrien CO	.75	.35	.09
☐ 164 Nolan Bailey	.75	.35	.09
☐ 165 Bill Baker	5.00	2.20	.60
☐ 166 Bruce Bennett	1.50	.70	.19
☐ 167 Gary Brandt	.75	.35	.09
☐ 168 Charlie Collins	.75	.35	.09
☐ 169 Henry Dorsch	.75	.35	.09
☐ 170 Ted Dushinski	.75	.35	.09
☐ 171 Bruce Gainer	.75	.35	.09
☐ 172 Ralph Galloway	.75	.35	.09
☐ 173 Ken Frith	.75	.35	.09
☐ 174 Cliff Shaw	.75	.35	.09
☐ 175 Silas McKinnie	.75	.35	.09
☐ 176 Mike Eben	.75	.35	.09
☐ 177 Greg Barton	2.00	.90	.25
☐ 178 Joe Theismann	25.00	11.00	3.10
☐ 179 Charlie Bray	.75	.35	.09
☐ 180 Roger Scales	.75	.35	.09
☐ 181 Bob Hudspeth	.75	.35	.09
☐ 182 Bill Symons	1.25	.55	.16
☐ 183 Dave Raimey	1.25	.55	.16
☐ 184 Dave Cranmer	1.25	.55	.16
☐ 185 Mel Profit	1.25	.55	.16
☐ 186 Paul Desjardins	.75	.35	.09
☐ 187 Tony Moro	.75	.35	.09
☐ 188 Leo Cahill CO	.75	.35	.09
☐ 189 Chip Barrett	.75	.35	.09
☐ 190 Pete Martin	.75	.35	.09
☐ 191 Walt Balasiuk	.75	.35	.09
☐ 192 Jim Corrigall	1.25	.55	.16
☐ 193 Ellison Kelly	5.00	2.20	.60
☐ 194 Jim Tomlin	.75	.35	.09
☐ 195 Marv Luster	2.00	.90	.25
☐ 196 Jim Thorpe	2.00	.90	.25
☐ 197 Jim Stillwagon	4.00	1.80	.50
☐ 198 Ed Harrington	.75	.35	.09
☐ 199 Jim Dye	.75	.35	.09
☐ 200 Leon McQuay	2.50	1.10	.30
☐ 201 Rob McLaren	.75	.35	.09
☐ 202 Benji Dial	.75	.35	.09
☐ 203 Chuck Liebrock	.75	.35	.09
☐ 204 Glen Schapansky	.75	.35	.09
☐ 205 Ed Ulmer	.75	.35	.09
☐ 206 Ross Richardson	.75	.35	.09
☐ 207 Lou Andrus	.75	.35	.09
☐ 208 Paul Robson	.75	.35	.09
☐ 209 Paul Brule	.75	.35	.09
☐ 210 Doug Strong	.75	.35	.09
☐ 211 Dick Smith	.75	.35	.09
☐ 212 Bill Frank	.75	.35	.09
☐ 213 Jim Spavital CO	.75	.35	.09
☐ 214 Rick Shaw	.75	.35	.09
☐ 215 Joe Critchlow	.75	.35	.09
☐ 216 Don Jonas	3.00	1.35	.35
☐ 217 Bob Swift	.75	.35	.09
☐ 218 Larry Kerychuk	.75	.35	.09
☐ 219 Bob McCarthy	.75	.35	.09
☐ 220 Gene Lakusiak	.75	.35	.09
☐ 221 Jim Heighton	.75	.35	.09
☐ 222 Chuck Harrison	.75	.35	.09
☐ 223 Lance Fletcher	.75	.35	.09
☐ 224 Larry Slagle	.75	.35	.09
☐ 225 Wayne Giesbrecht	.75	.35	.09

1956 Shredded Wheat CFL

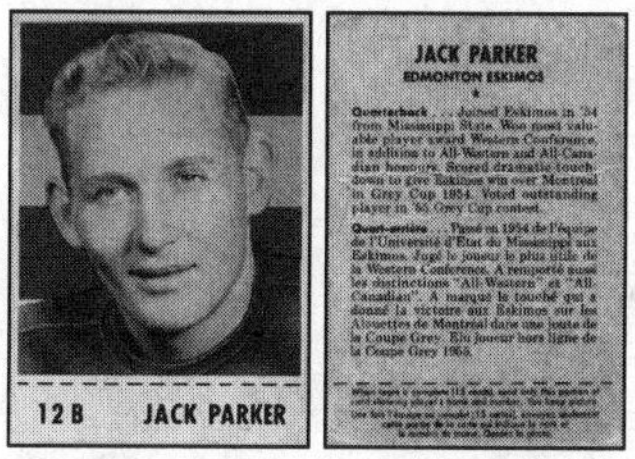

The 1956 Shredded Wheat CFL football card set contains 105 cards portraying CFL players. The cards measure 2 1/2" by 3 1/2". The fronts of the cards contain a black and white portrait photo of the player on a one-color striped background. The lower 1/2" of the front contains the card number and the player's name below a dashed line. This lower portion of the card was presumably connected with a premium offer, as the back indicates such an offer, in both English and French, on the bottom. The backs contain brief biographical data in both English and French. Each letter prefix corresponds to a team, e.g., A: Calgary Stampeders, B: Edmonton Eskimos, C: Winnipeg Blue Bombers, D: Hamilton Tiger-Cats, E: Toronto Argonauts, F: Saskatchewan Roughriders, and G: Ottawa Rough Riders.

	NRMT	VG-E	GOOD
COMPLETE SET (105)	9000.00	4000.00	1100.00
COMMON CARD (1-105)	80.00	36.00	10.00
☐ A1 Peter Muir	90.00	40.00	11.00
☐ A2 Harry Langford	80.00	36.00	10.00
☐ A3 Tony Pajaczkowski	150.00	70.00	19.00
☐ A4 Bob Morgan	80.00	36.00	10.00
☐ A5 Baz Nagle	80.00	36.00	10.00
☐ A6 Alex Macklin	80.00	36.00	10.00
☐ A7 Bob Geary	80.00	36.00	10.00
☐ A8 Don Klosterman	125.00	55.00	15.50
☐ A9 Bill McKenna	80.00	36.00	10.00
☐ A10 Bill Stevenson	80.00	36.00	10.00
☐ A11 Charles Baillie	80.00	36.00	10.00
☐ A12 Berdett Hess	80.00	36.00	10.00
☐ A13 Lynn Bottoms	90.00	40.00	11.00
☐ A14 Doug Brown	80.00	36.00	10.00
☐ A15 Jack Hennemier	80.00	36.00	10.00
☐ B1 Frank Anderson	80.00	36.00	10.00
☐ B2 Don Barry	80.00	36.00	10.00
☐ B3 Johnny Bright	200.00	90.00	25.00
☐ B4 Kurt Burris	80.00	36.00	10.00
☐ B5 Bob Dean	80.00	36.00	10.00
☐ B6 Don Getty	150.00	70.00	19.00
☐ B7 Normie Kwong	200.00	90.00	25.00
☐ B8 Earl Lindley	80.00	36.00	10.00
☐ B9 Art Walker	100.00	45.00	12.50
☐ B10 Rollie Miles	125.00	55.00	15.50
☐ B11 Frank Morris	125.00	55.00	15.50
☐ B12 Jackie Parker	300.00	135.00	38.00
☐ B13 Ted Tully	80.00	36.00	10.00
☐ B14 Frank Ivy	90.00	40.00	11.00
☐ B15 Bill Rowekamp	80.00	36.00	10.00
☐ C1 Al Sherman	80.00	36.00	10.00
☐ C2 Larry Cabrelli	80.00	36.00	10.00
☐ C3 Ron Kelly	80.00	36.00	10.00
☐ C4 Edward Kotowich	80.00	36.00	10.00
☐ C5 Buddy Leake	100.00	45.00	12.50
☐ C6 Thomas Lumsden	80.00	36.00	10.00
☐ C7 Bill Smitiuk	80.00	36.00	10.00
☐ C8 Buddy Tinsley	125.00	55.00	15.50
☐ C9 Ron Vaccher	80.00	36.00	10.00
☐ C10 Eagle Day	125.00	55.00	15.50
☐ C11 Buddy Allison	80.00	36.00	10.00
☐ C12 Bob Haas	90.00	40.00	11.00
☐ C13 Steve Patrick	80.00	36.00	10.00
☐ C14 Keith Pearce UER (Misspelled Pierce on front)	80.00	36.00	10.00
☐ C15 Lorne Benson	80.00	36.00	10.00
☐ D1 George Arnett	80.00	36.00	10.00
☐ D2 Eddie Bevan	80.00	36.00	10.00
☐ D3 Art Darch	80.00	36.00	10.00
☐ D4 John Fedosoff	80.00	36.00	10.00
☐ D5 Cam Fraser	80.00	36.00	10.00
☐ D6 Ron Howell	90.00	40.00	11.00
☐ D7 Alex Muzyka	90.00	40.00	11.00
☐ D8 Chet Miksza	80.00	36.00	10.00
☐ D9 Walt Nikorak	80.00	36.00	10.00
☐ D10 Pete Neumann	125.00	55.00	15.50
☐ D11 Steve Oneschuk	80.00	36.00	10.00
☐ D12 Vince Scott	125.00	55.00	15.50
☐ D13 Ralph Toohy	80.00	36.00	10.00
☐ D14 Ray Truant	80.00	36.00	10.00
☐ D15 Nobby Wirkowski	100.00	45.00	12.50
☐ E1 Pete Bennett	80.00	36.00	10.00
☐ E2 Fred Black	80.00	36.00	10.00
☐ E3 Jim Copeland	80.00	36.00	10.00
☐ E4 Al Pfeifer	90.00	40.00	11.00
☐ E5 Ron Albright	80.00	36.00	10.00
☐ E6 Tom Dublinski	80.00	36.00	10.00
☐ E7 Billy Shipp	80.00	36.00	10.00
☐ E8 Baz Mackie	80.00	36.00	10.00
☐ E9 Bill McFarlane	80.00	36.00	10.00
☐ E10 John Sopinka	100.00	45.00	12.50
☐ E11 Dick Brown	80.00	36.00	10.00
☐ E12 Gerry Doucette	80.00	36.00	10.00
☐ E13 Dan Shaw	80.00	36.00	10.00
☐ E14 Dick Shatto	175.00	80.00	22.00
☐ E15 Bill Swiacki	100.00	45.00	12.50
☐ F1 Ray Syrnyk	80.00	36.00	10.00
☐ F2 Martin Ruby	125.00	55.00	15.50
☐ F3 Bobby Marlow	125.00	55.00	15.50
☐ F4 Doug Kiloh	80.00	36.00	10.00
☐ F5 Gord Sturtridge	90.00	40.00	11.00
☐ F6 Stan Williams	80.00	36.00	10.00
☐ F7 Larry Isbell	80.00	36.00	10.00
☐ F8 Ken Casner	80.00	36.00	10.00
☐ F9 Mel Becket	100.00	45.00	12.50
☐ F10 Reg Whitehouse	80.00	36.00	10.00
☐ F11 Harry Lampman	80.00	36.00	10.00
☐ F12 Mario DeMarco	90.00	40.00	11.00
☐ F13 Ken Carpenter	100.00	45.00	12.50
☐ F14 Frank Filchock	100.00	45.00	12.50
☐ F15 Frank Tripucka	125.00	55.00	15.50
☐ G1 Tom Tracy	150.00	70.00	19.00
☐ G2 Pete Ladygo	80.00	36.00	10.00
☐ G3 Sam Scoccia	80.00	36.00	10.00
☐ G4 Joe Upton	80.00	36.00	10.00
☐ G5 Bob Simpson	150.00	70.00	19.00
☐ G6 Bruno Bitkowski	90.00	40.00	11.00
☐ G7 Joe Stracini UER (Misspelled Straccini on card front)	80.00	36.00	10.00
☐ G8 Hal Ledyard	80.00	36.00	10.00
☐ G9 Milt Graham	80.00	36.00	10.00
☐ G10 Bill Sowalski	80.00	36.00	10.00
☐ G11 Avatus Stone	80.00	36.00	10.00
☐ G12 John Boich	100.00	45.00	12.50
☐ G13 Don Pinhey UER (Misspelled Bob Pinkney on card front)	80.00	36.00	10.00
☐ G14 Peter Karpuk	80.00	36.00	10.00
☐ G15 Frank Clair	125.00	55.00	15.50

1994 Smokey Sacramento

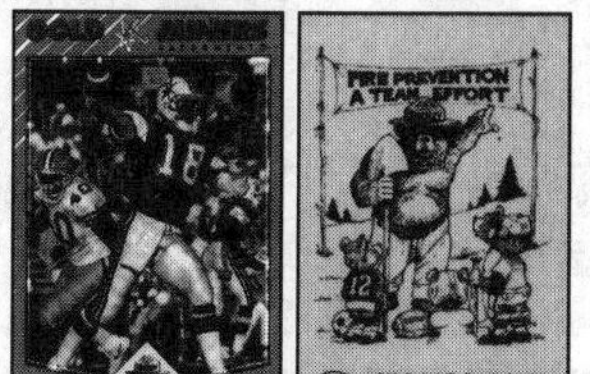

This Smokey sponsored set features members of the Sacramento Gold Miners and measures approximately 2 1/4" by 3 1/2." The cardfronts include a color player photo with the team name above the photo and the player's name, position and vital statistics below. Cardbacks contain a fire prevention message from Smokey.

	MINT	NRMT	EXC
COMPLETE SET (18)	30.00	13.50	3.70
COMMON CARD	1.25	.55	.16

☐ 1 Fred Anderson CEO	1.50	.70	.19
☐ 2 David Archer	6.00	2.70	.75
☐ 3 George Bethune	1.25	.55	.16
☐ 4 David Diaz-Infante	1.50	.70	.19
☐ 5 Willie Fears	1.50	.70	.19
☐ 6 Corian Freeman	1.25	.55	.16
☐ 7 Pete Gardere	1.50	.70	.19
☐ 8 Tom Gerhart	1.25	.55	.16
☐ 9 Rod Harris	1.25	.55	.16
☐ 10 Bobby Humphery	2.00	.90	.25
☐ 11 Mike Kiselak	1.25	.55	.16
☐ 12 Mark Ledbetter	1.25	.55	.16
☐ 13 Maurice Miller	1.25	.55	.16
☐ 14 Troy Mills	1.25	.55	.16
☐ 15 Mike Oliphant	3.00	1.35	.35
☐ 16 James Pruitt	1.50	.70	.19
☐ 17 Junior Robinson	1.25	.55	.16
☐ 18 Kay Stephenson CO	1.25	.55	.16

1993 Sport Chek Calgary Stampeders

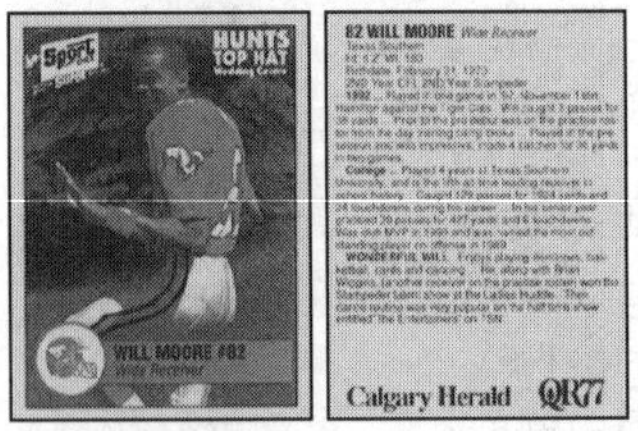

Measuring approximately 12 1/2" by 19 1/2", this perforated sheet displays twenty-four player cards and six coupons. After perforation, the individual cards measure approximately 2 1/2" by 3 1/4". The fronts show posed color shots inside white borders. Some of these photos are overexposed. The upper corners hold sponsor logos, while at the bottom the team logo and player identification are provided. In black print on a white background, the backs carry biography, season summary, and personal information. The sheets were given away to fans at two Stampeder home games during the season. Also four-card mini-sheets, depicting Flutie, Thurman, Zizakovic, and Sapunjis, were included in each 1993 Grey Cup Fan Fest welcome package. The cards are unnumbered and checklisted below in alphabetical order.

	MINT	NRMT	EXC
COMPLETE SET (24)	18.00	8.00	2.20
COMMON CARD (1-24)	.60	.25	.07
☐ 1 Karl Anthony	.60	.25	.07
☐ 2 Raymond Biggs	.60	.25	.07
☐ 3 Douglas Craft	.60	.25	.07
☐ 4 Doug Davies	.60	.25	.07
☐ 5 Mark Dube	.60	.25	.07
☐ 6 Matt Finlay	.60	.25	.07
☐ 7 Doug Flutie	5.00	2.20	.60
☐ 8 Fred Gatlin	.60	.25	.07
☐ 9 Keyvan Jenkins	1.00	.45	.12
☐ 10 Alondra Johnson	.60	.25	.07
☐ 11 Pat Mahon	.60	.25	.07
☐ 12 Tony Martino	.60	.25	.07
☐ 13 Mark McLoughlin	.60	.25	.07
☐ 14 Andy McVey	.60	.25	.07
☐ 15 Will Moore	2.00	.90	.25
☐ 16 Mark Pearce	.60	.25	.07
☐ 17 Allen Pitts	1.25	.55	.16
☐ 18 David Sapunjis	1.50	.70	.19
☐ 19 Junior Thurman	1.25	.55	.16
☐ 20 Gerald Vaughn	.60	.25	.07
☐ 21 Ken Watson	.60	.25	.07
☐ 22 Brian Wiggins	1.00	.45	.12
☐ 23 Blair Zerr	.60	.25	.07
☐ 24 Srecko Zizakovic	.60	.25	.07

1958 Topps CFL

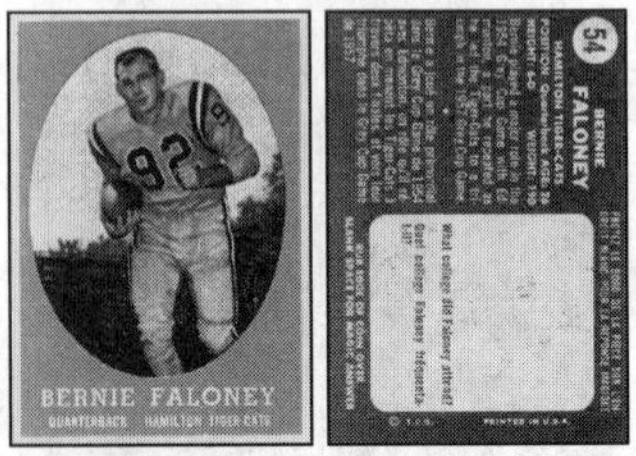

The 1958 Topps CFL set features eight of the nine Canadian Football League teams, excluding Montreal. The cards measure the standard size. This first Topps Canadian issue is very similar in format to the 1958 Topps NFL issue. The cards were sold in wax boxes containing 36 five-cent wax packs. The card backs feature a "Rub-a-coin" quiz along with the typical biographical and statistical information. The set features the first card of Cookie Gilchrist, who later led the AFL in rushing twice.

	NRMT	VG-E	GOOD
COMPLETE SET (88)	500.00	220.00	60.00
COMMON CARD (1-88)	5.00	2.20	.60
☐ 1 Paul Anderson	6.00	1.50	.60
☐ 2 Leigh McMillan	5.00	2.20	.60
☐ 3 Vic Chapman	5.00	2.20	.60
☐ 4 Bobby Marlow	12.00	5.50	1.50
☐ 5 Mike Cacic	5.00	2.20	.60
☐ 6 Ron Pawlowski	5.00	2.20	.60
☐ 7 Frank Morris	9.00	4.00	1.10
☐ 8 Earl Keeley	6.00	2.70	.75
☐ 9 Don Walsh	5.00	2.20	.60
☐ 10 Bryan Engram	5.00	2.20	.60
☐ 11 Bobby Kuntz	6.00	2.70	.75
☐ 12 Jerry Janes	5.00	2.20	.60
☐ 13 Don Bingham	5.00	2.20	.60
☐ 14 Paul Fedor	5.00	2.20	.60
☐ 15 Tommy Grant	12.00	5.50	1.50
☐ 16 Don Getty	20.00	9.00	2.50
☐ 17 George Brancato	6.00	2.70	.75
☐ 18 Jackie Parker	40.00	18.00	5.00
☐ 19 Alan Valdes	5.00	2.20	.60
☐ 20 Paul Dekker	5.00	2.20	.60
☐ 21 Frank Tripucka	12.00	5.50	1.50
☐ 22 Gerry McDougall	9.00	4.00	1.10
☐ 23 Willard Dewveall	6.00	2.70	.75
☐ 24 Ted Smale	5.00	2.20	.60
☐ 25 Tony Pajaczkowski	12.00	5.50	1.50
☐ 26 Don Pinhey	5.00	2.20	.60
☐ 27 Buddy Tinsley	12.00	5.50	1.50
☐ 28 Cookie Gilchrist	40.00	18.00	5.00
☐ 29 Larry Isbell	5.00	2.20	.60
☐ 30 Bob Kelley	5.00	2.20	.60
☐ 31 Thomas(Corky) Tharp	6.00	2.70	.75
☐ 32 Steve Patrick	5.00	2.20	.60
☐ 33 Hardiman Cureton	5.00	2.20	.60
☐ 34 Joe Mobra	5.00	2.20	.60
☐ 35 Harry Lunn	5.00	2.20	.60
☐ 36 Gord Rowland	6.00	2.70	.75
☐ 37 Herb Gray	15.00	6.75	1.85
☐ 38 Bob Simpson	15.00	6.75	1.85
☐ 39 Cam Fraser	5.00	2.20	.60
☐ 40 Kenny Ploen	18.00	8.00	2.20
☐ 41 Lynn Bottoms	6.00	2.70	.75
☐ 42 Bill Stevenson	5.00	2.20	.60
☐ 43 Jerry Selinger	5.00	2.20	.60
☐ 44 Oscar Kruger	9.00	4.00	1.10
☐ 45 Gerry James	15.00	6.75	1.85
☐ 46 Dave Mann	12.00	5.50	1.50
☐ 47 Tom Dimitroff	5.00	2.20	.60
☐ 48 Vince Scott	12.00	5.50	1.50
☐ 49 Fran Rogel	6.00	2.70	.75
☐ 50 Henry Hair	5.00	2.20	.60
☐ 51 Bob Brady	5.00	2.20	.60
☐ 52 Gerry Doucette	5.00	2.20	.60
☐ 53 Ken Carpenter	6.00	2.70	.75
☐ 54 Bernie Faloney	25.00	11.00	3.10
☐ 55 John Barrow	20.00	9.00	2.50
☐ 56 George Druxman	5.00	2.20	.60
☐ 57 Rollie Miles	12.00	5.50	1.50
☐ 58 Jerry Cornelison	5.00	2.20	.60
☐ 59 Harry Langford	5.00	2.20	.60
☐ 60 Johnny Bright	20.00	9.00	2.50
☐ 61 Ron Clinkscale	5.00	2.20	.60
☐ 62 Jack Hill	5.00	2.20	.60
☐ 63 Ron Quillian	5.00	2.20	.60
☐ 64 Ted Tully	5.00	2.20	.60
☐ 65 Pete Neft	5.00	2.20	.60
☐ 66 Arvyd Buntins	5.00	2.20	.60
☐ 67 Normie Kwong	20.00	9.00	2.50
☐ 68 Matt Phillips	5.00	2.20	.60
☐ 69 Pete Bennett	5.00	2.20	.60
☐ 70 Vern Lofstrom	5.00	2.20	.60
☐ 71 Norm Stoneburgh	5.00	2.20	.60
☐ 72 Danny Nykoluk	5.00	2.20	.60
☐ 73 Chuck Dubuque	5.00	2.20	.60
☐ 74 John Varone	5.00	2.20	.60
☐ 75 Bob Kimoff	5.00	2.20	.60
☐ 76 John Pyeatt	5.00	2.20	.60
☐ 77 Pete Neumann	12.00	5.50	1.50
☐ 78 Ernie Pitts	9.00	4.00	1.10
☐ 79 Steve Oneschuk	5.00	2.20	.60
☐ 80 Kaye Vaughan	12.00	5.50	1.50
☐ 81 Joe Yamauchi	5.00	2.20	.60
☐ 82 Harvey Wylie	9.00	4.00	1.10
☐ 83 Berdett Hess	5.00	2.20	.60
☐ 84 Dick Shatto	20.00	9.00	2.50
☐ 85 Floyd Harrawood	5.00	2.20	.60
☐ 86 Ron Atchison	12.00	5.50	1.50
☐ 87 Bobby Judd	5.00	2.20	.60
☐ 88 Keith Pearce	9.00	2.20	.90

1959 Topps CFL

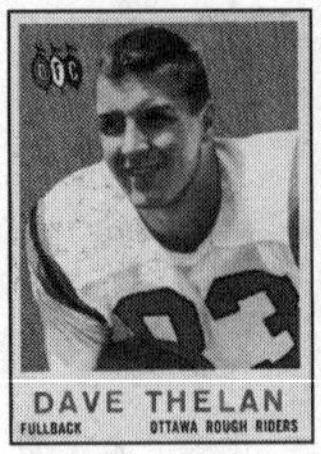

The 1959 Topps CFL set features cards grouped by teams. The cards measure the standard size. Checklists are given on the backs of card number 15 (1-44) and card number 44 (45-88). The issue is very similar to the Topps 1959 NFL issue. The cards were originally sold in five-cent wax packs with gum.

	NRMT	VG-E	GOOD
COMPLETE SET (88)	400.00	180.00	50.00
COMMON CARD (1-88)	4.00	1.80	.50
☐ 1 Norm Rauhaus	10.00	2.50	1.00
☐ 2 Cornel Piper UER (Misspelled Cornell on both sides)	4.00	1.80	.50
☐ 3 Leo Lewis	20.00	9.00	2.50
☐ 4 Roger Savoie	4.00	1.80	.50
☐ 5 Jim Van Pelt	10.00	4.50	1.25
☐ 6 Herb Gray	10.00	4.50	1.25
☐ 7 Gerry James	10.00	4.50	1.25
☐ 8 By Bailey	12.00	5.50	1.50
☐ 9 Tom Hinton	8.00	3.60	1.00
☐ 10 Chuck Quilter	4.00	1.80	.50
☐ 11 Mel Gillett	4.00	1.80	.50
☐ 12 Ted Hunt	4.00	1.80	.50
☐ 13 Sonny Homer	5.00	2.20	.60
☐ 14 Bill Jessup	4.00	1.80	.50
☐ 15 Al Dorow (Checklist 1-44 back)	20.00	6.00	2.00
☐ 16 Norm Fieldgate	12.00	5.50	1.50
☐ 17 Urban Henry	5.00	2.20	.60
☐ 18 Paul Cameron	4.00	1.80	.50
☐ 19 Bruce Claridge	4.00	1.80	.50
☐ 20 Jim Bakhtiar	4.00	1.80	.50
☐ 21 Earl Lunsford	12.00	5.50	1.50
☐ 22 Walt Radzick	4.00	1.80	.50
☐ 23 Ron Albright	4.00	1.80	.50
☐ 24 Art Scullion	4.00	1.80	.50
☐ 25 Ernie Warlick	6.00	2.70	.75
☐ 26 Nobby Wirkowski	5.00	2.20	.60
☐ 27 Harvey Wylie	9.00	4.00	1.10
☐ 28 Gordon Brown	4.00	1.80	.50
☐ 29 Don Luzzi	10.00	4.50	1.25
☐ 30 Hal Patterson	20.00	9.00	2.50
☐ 31 Jackie Simpson	15.00	6.75	1.85
☐ 32 Doug McNichol	4.00	1.80	.50
☐ 33 Bob MacLellan	4.00	1.80	.50
☐ 34 Ted Elsby	4.00	1.80	.50
☐ 35 Mike Kovac	4.00	1.80	.50
☐ 36 Bob Leary	4.00	1.80	.50
☐ 37 Hal Krebs	4.00	1.80	.50
☐ 38 Steve Jennings	4.00	1.80	.50
☐ 39 Don Getty	12.00	5.50	1.50
☐ 40 Normie Kwong	12.00	5.50	1.50
☐ 41 Johnny Bright	15.00	6.75	1.85
☐ 42 Art Walker	5.00	2.20	.60
☐ 43 Jackie Parker UER (Incorrectly listed as Tackle on card front)	35.00	16.00	4.40
☐ 44 Don Barry (Checklist 45-88 back)	20.00	6.00	2.00
☐ 45 Tommy Joe Coffey	25.00	11.00	3.10
☐ 46 Mike Volcan	4.00	1.80	.50
☐ 47 Stan Renning	4.00	1.80	.50
☐ 48 Gino Fracas	9.00	4.00	1.10
☐ 49 Ted Smale	4.00	1.80	.50
☐ 50 Mack Yoho	5.00	2.20	.60
☐ 51 Bobby Gravens	4.00	1.80	.50
☐ 52 Milt Graham	4.00	1.80	.50
☐ 53 Lou Bruce	4.00	1.80	.50
☐ 54 Bob Simpson	12.00	5.50	1.50
☐ 55 Bill Sowalski	4.00	1.80	.50
☐ 56 Russ Jackson	40.00	18.00	5.00
☐ 57 Don Clark	10.00	4.50	1.25
☐ 58 Dave Thelen	10.00	4.50	1.25
☐ 59 Larry Cowart	4.00	1.80	.50
☐ 60 Dave Mann	5.00	2.20	.60
☐ 61 Norm Stoneburgh UER (Misspelled Stoneburg)	4.00	1.80	.50
☐ 62 Ronnie Knox	9.00	4.00	1.10
☐ 63 Dick Shatto	12.00	5.50	1.50
☐ 64 Bobby Kuntz	5.00	2.20	.60
☐ 65 Phil Muntz	4.00	1.80	.50
☐ 66 Gerry Doucette	4.00	1.80	.50
☐ 67 Sam DeLuca	5.00	2.20	.60
☐ 68 Boyd Carter	4.00	1.80	.50
☐ 69 Vic Kristopaitis	9.00	4.00	1.10
☐ 70 Gerry McDougall UER (Misspelled Jerry)	5.00	2.20	.60
☐ 71 Vince Scott	10.00	4.50	1.25
☐ 72 Angelo Mosca	35.00	16.00	4.40
☐ 73 Chet Miksza	4.00	1.80	.50
☐ 74 Eddie Macon	4.00	1.80	.50
☐ 75 Harry Lampman	4.00	1.80	.50
☐ 76 Bill Graham	4.00	1.80	.50
☐ 77 Ralph Goldston	5.00	2.20	.60
☐ 78 Cam Fraser	4.00	1.80	.50
☐ 79 Ron Dundas	4.00	1.80	.50
☐ 80 Bill Clarke	4.00	1.80	.50
☐ 81 Len Legault	4.00	1.80	.50
☐ 82 Reg Whitehouse	4.00	1.80	.50
☐ 83 Dale Parsons	4.00	1.80	.50
☐ 84 Doug Kiloh	4.00	1.80	.50
☐ 85 Tom Whitehouse	4.00	1.80	.50
☐ 86 Mike Hagler	4.00	1.80	.50
☐ 87 Paul Anderson	4.00	1.80	.50
☐ 88 Danny Banda	5.00	1.25	.50

1960 Topps CFL

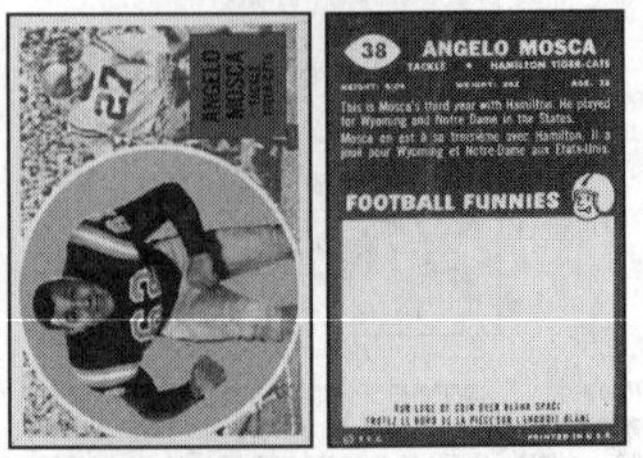

The 1960 Topps CFL set features cards grouped by teams. The cards measure the standard size. Checklists are given on the backs of card number 14 (1-44) and card number 45 (45-88). The issue is very similar in format to the Topps NFL issue of 1960. The set features a card of Gerry James, who also played in the National Hockey League.

	NRMT	VG-E	GOOD
COMPLETE SET (88)	500.00	220.00	60.00
COMMON CARD (1-88)	4.00	1.80	.50
☐ 1 By Bailey	12.00	3.00	1.20
☐ 2 Paul Cameron	4.00	1.80	.50
☐ 3 Bruce Claridge	4.00	1.80	.50
☐ 4 Chuck Dubuque	4.00	1.80	.50
☐ 5 Randy Duncan	12.00	5.50	1.50
☐ 6 Norm Fieldgate	10.00	4.50	1.25
☐ 7 Urban Henry	5.00	2.20	.60
☐ 8 Ted Hunt	4.00	1.80	.50
☐ 9 Bill Jessup	4.00	1.80	.50
☐ 10 Ted Tully	4.00	1.80	.50
☐ 11 Vic Chapman	4.00	1.80	.50
☐ 12 Gino Fracas	5.00	2.20	.60
☐ 13 Don Getty	10.00	4.50	1.25
☐ 14 Ed Gray	4.00	1.80	.50
☐ 15 Oscar Kruger (Checklist 1-44 back)	20.00	5.00	2.00
☐ 16 Rollie Miles	10.00	4.50	1.25
☐ 17 Jackie Parker	30.00	13.50	3.70
☐ 18 Joe-Bob Smith UER (Misspelled Bob-Joe on both sides)	4.00	1.80	.50
☐ 19 Mike Volcan	4.00	1.80	.50
☐ 20 Art Walker	5.00	2.20	.60
☐ 21 Ron Albright	4.00	1.80	.50
☐ 22 Jim Bakhtiar	4.00	1.80	.50
☐ 23 Lynn Bottoms	5.00	2.20	.60
☐ 24 Jack Gotta	8.00	3.60	1.00
☐ 25 Joe Kapp	50.00	22.00	6.25
☐ 26 Earl Lunsford	9.00	4.00	1.10
☐ 27 Don Luzzi	9.00	4.00	1.10
☐ 28 Art Scullion	4.00	1.80	.50
☐ 29 Hugh Simpson	4.00	1.80	.50
☐ 30 Ernie Warlick	8.00	3.60	1.00
☐ 31 John Barrow	12.00	5.50	1.50
☐ 32 Paul Dekker	4.00	1.80	.50
☐ 33 Bernie Faloney	20.00	9.00	2.50
☐ 34 Cam Fraser	4.00	1.80	.50
☐ 35 Ralph Goldston	5.00	2.20	.60
☐ 36 Ron Howell	5.00	2.20	.60
☐ 37 Gerry McDougall UER (Misspelled Jerry)	5.00	2.20	.60
☐ 38 Angelo Mosca	20.00	9.00	2.50
☐ 39 Pete Neumann	8.00	3.60	1.00
☐ 40 Vince Scott	8.00	3.60	1.00
☐ 41 Ted Elsby	4.00	1.80	.50
☐ 42 Sam Etcheverry	25.00	11.00	3.10
☐ 43 Mike Kovac	4.00	1.80	.50
☐ 44 Ed Learn	4.00	1.80	.50
☐ 45 Ivan Livingstone (Checklist 45-88 back)	20.00	5.00	2.00
☐ 46 Hal Patterson	18.00	8.00	2.20
☐ 47 Jackie Simpson	12.00	5.50	1.50
☐ 48 Veryl Switzer	4.00	1.80	.50
☐ 49 Bill Bewley	9.00	4.00	1.10
☐ 50 Joel Wells	4.00	1.80	.50
☐ 51 Ron Atchison	9.00	4.00	1.10
☐ 52 Ken Carpenter	5.00	2.20	.60
☐ 53 Bill Clarke	4.00	1.80	.50
☐ 54 Ron Dundas	4.00	1.80	.50
☐ 55 Mike Hagler	4.00	1.80	.50
☐ 56 Jack Hill	4.00	1.80	.50
☐ 57 Doug Kiloh	4.00	1.80	.50
☐ 58 Bobby Marlow	10.00	4.50	1.25
☐ 59 Bob Mulgado	4.00	1.80	.50
☐ 60 George Brancato	5.00	2.20	.60
☐ 61 Lou Bruce	4.00	1.80	.50
☐ 62 Hardiman Cureton	4.00	1.80	.50
☐ 63 Russ Jackson	25.00	11.00	3.10
☐ 64 Gerry Nesbitt	4.00	1.80	.50
☐ 65 Bob Simpson	10.00	4.50	1.25
☐ 66 Ted Smale	4.00	1.80	.50
☐ 67 Dave Thelen	9.00	4.00	1.10
☐ 68 Kaye Vaughan	8.00	3.60	1.00
☐ 69 Pete Bennett	4.00	1.80	.50
☐ 70 Boyd Carter	4.00	1.80	.50
☐ 71 Gerry Doucette	4.00	1.80	.50
☐ 72 Bobby Kuntz	5.00	2.20	.60
☐ 73 Alex Panton	4.00	1.80	.50
☐ 74 Tobin Rote	18.00	8.00	2.20
☐ 75 Jim Rountree	5.00	2.20	.60

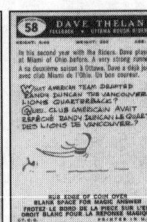

☐ 76 Dick Shatto	10.00	4.50	1.25
☐ 77 Norm Stoneburgh	4.00	1.80	.50
☐ 78 Thomas(Corky) Tharp	5.00	2.20	.60
☐ 79 George Druxman	4.00	1.80	.50
☐ 80 Herb Gray	10.00	4.50	1.25
☐ 81 Gerry James	10.00	4.50	1.25
☐ 82 Leo Lewis	10.00	4.50	1.25
☐ 83 Ernie Pitts	5.00	2.20	.60
☐ 84 Kenny Ploen	15.00	6.75	1.85
☐ 85 Norm Rauhaus	5.00	2.20	.60
☐ 86 Gord Rowland	5.00	2.20	.60
☐ 87 Charlie Shepard	5.00	2.20	.60
☐ 88 Don Clark	8.00	3.60	1.00

1961 Topps CFL

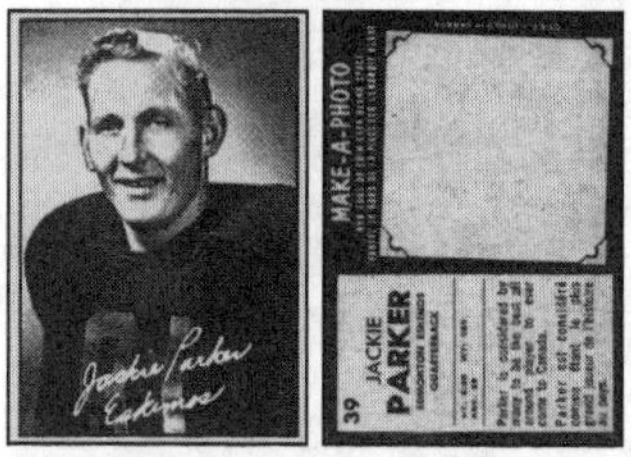

The 1961 Topps CFL set features cards grouped by teams with the team picture last in the sequence. The cards measure the standard size. Card number 102 gives the full set checklist. Although the T.C.G. trademark appears on these cards, they were printed in Canada by O-Pee-Chee.

	NRMT	VG-E	GOOD
COMPLETE SET (132)	900.00	400.00	110.00
COMMON CARD (1-132)	6.00	2.70	.75
☐ 1 By Bailey	15.00	6.75	1.85
☐ 2 Bruce Claridge	6.00	2.70	.75
☐ 3 Norm Fieldgate	12.00	5.50	1.50
☐ 4 Willie Fleming	20.00	9.00	2.50
☐ 5 Urban Henry	7.50	3.40	.95
☐ 6 Bill Herron	6.00	2.70	.75
☐ 7 Tom Hinton	10.00	4.50	1.25
☐ 8 Sonny Homer	7.50	3.40	.95
☐ 9 Bob Jeter	15.00	6.75	1.85
☐ 10 Vic Kristopaitis	6.00	2.70	.75
☐ 11 Baz Nagle	6.00	2.70	.75
☐ 12 Ron Watton	6.00	2.70	.75
☐ 13 Joe Yamauchi	6.00	2.70	.75
☐ 14 Bob Schloredt	15.00	6.75	1.85
☐ 15 B.C. Lions Team	12.00	5.50	1.50
☐ 16 Ron Albright	6.00	2.70	.75
☐ 17 Gordon Brown	6.00	2.70	.75
☐ 18 Gerry Doucette	6.00	2.70	.75
☐ 19 Gene Filipski	12.00	5.50	1.50
☐ 20 Joe Kapp	30.00	13.50	3.70
☐ 21 Earl Lunsford	12.00	5.50	1.50
☐ 22 Don Luzzi	12.00	5.50	1.50
☐ 23 Bill McKenna	6.00	2.70	.75
☐ 24 Ron Morris	6.00	2.70	.75
☐ 25 Tony Pajaczkowski	12.00	5.50	1.50
☐ 26 Lorne Reid	6.00	2.70	.75
☐ 27 Art Scullion	6.00	2.70	.75
☐ 28 Ernie Warlick	10.00	4.50	1.25
☐ 29 Stampeders Team	12.00	5.50	1.50
☐ 30 Johnny Bright	15.00	6.75	1.85
☐ 31 Vic Chapman	6.00	2.70	.75
☐ 32 Gino Fracas	7.50	3.40	.95
☐ 33 Tommy Joe Coffey	18.00	8.00	2.20
☐ 34 Don Getty	15.00	6.75	1.85
☐ 35 Ed Gray	6.00	2.70	.75
☐ 36 Oscar Kruger	7.50	3.40	.95
☐ 37 Rollie Miles	12.00	5.50	1.50
☐ 38 Roger Nelson	12.00	5.50	1.50
☐ 39 Jackie Parker	35.00	16.00	4.40
☐ 40 Howie Schumm	6.00	2.70	.75
☐ 41 Joe-Bob Smith UER (Misspelled Bob-Joe on both sides)	6.00	2.70	.75
☐ 42 Art Walker	7.50	3.40	.95
☐ 43 Eskimos Team	12.00	5.50	1.50
☐ 44 John Barrow	15.00	6.75	1.85
☐ 45 Paul Dekker	6.00	2.70	.75
☐ 46 Tom Dublinski	6.00	2.70	.75
☐ 47 Bernie Faloney	25.00	11.00	3.10
☐ 48 Cam Fraser	6.00	2.70	.75
☐ 49 Ralph Goldston	7.50	3.40	.95
☐ 50 Ron Howell	7.50	3.40	.95
☐ 51 Gerry McDougall	7.50	3.40	.95
☐ 52 Pete Neumann	12.00	5.50	1.50
☐ 53 Bronko Nagurski	15.00	6.75	1.85
☐ 54 Vince Scott	10.00	4.50	1.25
☐ 55 Steve Oneschuk	7.50	3.40	.95
☐ 56 Hal Patterson	20.00	9.00	2.50
☐ 57 Jim Taylor	7.50	3.40	.95
☐ 58 Hamilton Tiger-Cats Team	12.00	5.50	1.50
☐ 59 Ted Elsby	6.00	2.70	.75
☐ 60 Don Clark	7.50	3.40	.95
☐ 61 Dick Cohee	10.00	4.50	1.25
☐ 62 George Dixon	20.00	9.00	2.50
☐ 63 Wes Gideon	6.00	2.70	.75
☐ 64 Harry Lampman	6.00	2.70	.75
☐ 65 Meco Poliziani	6.00	2.70	.75
☐ 66 Charles Baillie	6.00	2.70	.75
☐ 67 Howard Cissell	6.00	2.70	.75
☐ 68 Ed Learn	6.00	2.70	.75
☐ 69 Tom Moran	6.00	2.70	.75
☐ 70 Jack Simpson	12.00	5.50	1.50
☐ 71 Bill Bewley	7.50	3.40	.95
☐ 72 Tom Hugo	6.00	2.70	.75
☐ 73 Alouettes Team	15.00	6.75	1.85
☐ 74 Gilles Archambeault	6.00	2.70	.75
☐ 75 Lou Bruce	6.00	2.70	.75
☐ 76 Russ Jackson	30.00	13.50	3.70
☐ 77 Tom Jones	6.00	2.70	.75
☐ 78 Gerry Nesbitt	6.00	2.70	.75
☐ 79 Ron Lancaster	40.00	18.00	5.00
☐ 80 Joe Kelly	6.00	2.70	.75
☐ 81 Joe Poirier	7.50	3.40	.95
☐ 82 Doug Daigneault	6.00	2.70	.75
☐ 83 Kaye Vaughan	10.00	4.50	1.25
☐ 84 Dave Thelen	15.00	6.75	1.85
☐ 85 Ron Stewart	25.00	11.00	3.10
☐ 86 Ted Smale	6.00	2.70	.75
☐ 87 Bob Simpson	15.00	6.75	1.85
☐ 88 Ottawa Rough Riders Team	12.00	5.50	1.50
☐ 89 Don Allard	6.00	2.70	.75
☐ 90 Ron Atchison	12.00	5.50	1.50
☐ 91 Bill Clarke	6.00	2.70	.75
☐ 92 Ron Dundas	6.00	2.70	.75
☐ 93 Jack Gotta	10.00	4.50	1.25
☐ 94 Bob Golic	7.50	3.40	.95
☐ 95 Jack Hill	6.00	2.70	.75
☐ 96 Doug Kiloh	6.00	2.70	.75
☐ 97 Len Legault	6.00	2.70	.75
☐ 98 Doug McKenzie	6.00	2.70	.75
☐ 99 Bob Ptacek	7.50	3.40	.95
☐ 100 Roy Smith	6.00	2.70	.75
☐ 101 Saskatchewan Roughriders Team	12.00	5.50	1.50
☐ 102 Checklist 1-132	90.00	22.00	9.00
☐ 103 Jim Andreotti	7.50	3.40	.95
☐ 104 Boyd Carter	6.00	2.70	.75
☐ 105 Dick Fouts	7.50	3.40	.95
☐ 106 Cookie Gilchrist	25.00	11.00	3.10
☐ 107 Bobby Kuntz	7.50	3.40	.95
☐ 108 Jim Rountree	7.50	3.40	.95
☐ 109 Dick Shatto	15.00	6.75	1.85
☐ 110 Norm Stoneburgh	6.00	2.70	.75
☐ 111 Dave Mann	7.50	3.40	.95
☐ 112 Ed Ochiena	6.00	2.70	.75
☐ 113 Bill Stribling	6.00	2.70	.75
☐ 114 Tobin Rote	20.00	9.00	2.50
☐ 115 Stan Wallace	6.00	2.70	.75
☐ 116 Billy Shipp	6.00	2.70	.75
☐ 117 Argonauts Team	15.00	6.75	1.85
☐ 118 Dave Burkholder	6.00	2.70	.75
☐ 119 Jack Delveaux	6.00	2.70	.75
☐ 120 George Druxman	6.00	2.70	.75
☐ 121 Farrell Funston	7.50	3.40	.95
☐ 122 Herb Gray	12.00	5.50	1.50
☐ 123 Gerry James	12.00	5.50	1.50
☐ 124 Ronnie Latourelle	6.00	2.70	.75
☐ 125 Leo Lewis	15.00	6.75	1.85
☐ 126 Steve Patrick	6.00	2.70	.75
☐ 127 Ernie Pitts	7.50	3.40	.95
☐ 128 Kenny Ploen	15.00	6.75	1.85
☐ 129 Norm Rauhaus	7.50	3.40	.95
☐ 130 Gord Rowland	7.50	3.40	.95
☐ 131 Charlie Shepard	7.50	3.40	.95
☐ 132 Winnipeg Blue Bombers Team Card	20.00	5.00	2.00

1961 Topps CFL Transfers

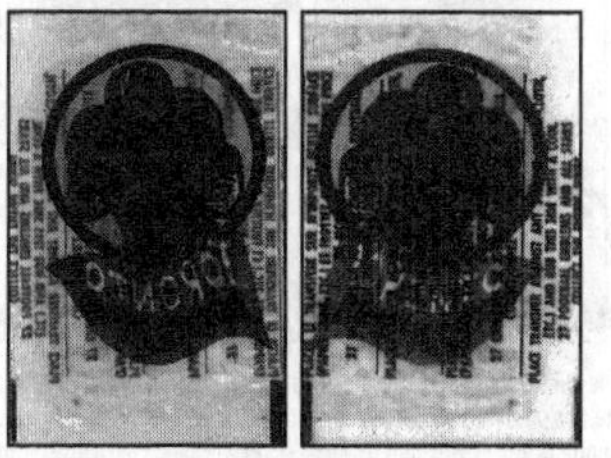

There were 27 transfers inserted in Topps CFL wax packs issued in 1961. The transfers measure approximately 2" by 3" and feature players, logos, and pennants of the CFL teams. After placing the transfer against any surface, the collector could apply the transfer by rubbing the top side with a coin. The top side carried instructions for applying the transfers. The pictures on the transfers are done in five basic colors: reddish orange, yellow, blue, black, and green. The transfers are unnumbered and are checklisted below alphabetically according to players (1-15) and teams (19-27). The set price below is only for the 24 players and team cards that we currently list. Any additional information on the other players that were contained in this set would be appreciated.

	NRMT	VG-E	GOOD
COMPLETE SET (24)	750.00	350.00	95.00
COMMON CARD (1-15)	30.00	13.50	3.70
COMMON TEAM (19-27)	20.00	9.00	2.50
☐ 1 Don Clark	35.00	16.00	4.40
☐ 2 Gene Filipski	35.00	16.00	4.40
☐ 3 Willie Fleming	40.00	18.00	5.00
☐ 4 Cookie Gilchrist	40.00	18.00	5.00
☐ 5 Jack Hill	30.00	13.50	3.70
☐ 6 Bob Jeter	35.00	16.00	4.40
☐ 7 Joe Kapp	60.00	27.00	7.50
☐ 8 Leo Lewis	40.00	18.00	5.00
☐ 9 Gerry McDougall	20.00	9.00	2.50
☐ 10 Jackie Parker	50.00	22.00	6.25
☐ 11 Hal Patterson	40.00	18.00	5.00
☐ 12 Kenny Ploen	40.00	18.00	5.00
☐ 13 Bob Ptacek	20.00	9.00	2.50
☐ 14 Ron Stewart	40.00	18.00	5.00
☐ 15 Dave Thelen	40.00	18.00	5.00
☐ 19 British Columbia Lions Logo/Pennant	20.00	9.00	2.50
☐ 20 Calgary Stampeders Logo/Pennant	20.00	9.00	2.50
☐ 21 Edmonton Eskimos Logo/Pennant	20.00	9.00	2.50
☐ 22 Hamilton Tiger-Cats Logo/Pennant	20.00	9.00	2.50
☐ 23 Montreal Alouettes Logo/Pennant	20.00	9.00	2.50
☐ 24 Ottawa Rough Riders Logo/Pennant	20.00	9.00	2.50
☐ 25 Saskatchewan Roughriders Logo/Pennant	20.00	9.00	2.50
☐ 26 Toronto Argonauts Logo/Pennant	20.00	9.00	2.50
☐ 27 Winnipeg Blue Bombers Logo/Pennant	20.00	9.00	2.50

1962 Topps CFL

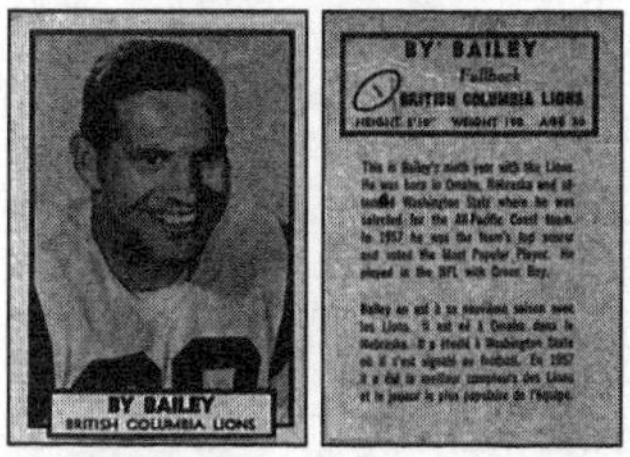

This 1962 Topps CFL set features 169 different numbered cards in perforated pairs. The cards measure 1 1/4" by 2 1/2" individually and 2 1/2" by 3 1/2" as a pair. The team cards contain a team checklist on the reverse side. The players preceding the team cards belong to the respective teams. Teams are in alphabetical order and players within teams are also in alphabetical order. The cards are ordered by team. Although the T.C.G. trademark appears on the cards, they were printed in Canada by O-Pee-Chee.

	NRMT	VG-E	GOOD
COMPLETE SET (169)	500.00	220.00	60.00
COMMON CARD (1-169)	2.00	.90	.25
☐ 1 By Bailey	6.00	1.50	.60
☐ 2 Nub Beamer	2.00	.90	.25
☐ 3 Tom Brown	8.00	3.60	1.00
☐ 4 Mack Burton	2.00	.90	.25
☐ 5 Mike Cacic	2.00	.90	.25
☐ 6 Pat Claridge	2.00	.90	.25
☐ 7 Steve Cotter	2.00	.90	.25
☐ 8 Lonnie Dennis	2.00	.90	.25
☐ 9 Norm Fieldgate	5.00	2.20	.60
☐ 10 Willie Fleming	10.00	4.50	1.25
☐ 11 Tom Hinton	4.00	1.80	.50
☐ 12 Sonny Homer	3.00	1.35	.35
☐ 13 Joe Kapp	15.00	6.75	1.85
☐ 14 Tom Larscheid	2.00	.90	.25
☐ 15 Gordie Mitchell	2.00	.90	.25
☐ 16 Baz Nagle	2.00	.90	.25
☐ 17 Norris Stevenson	2.00	.90	.25
☐ 18 Barney Therrien UER (Misspelled Therien on card front)	2.00	.90	.25
☐ 19 Don Vicic	2.00	.90	.25
☐ 20 B.C. Lions Team	8.00	3.60	1.00
☐ 21 Ed Buchanan	2.00	.90	.25
☐ 22 Joe Carruthers	2.00	.90	.25
☐ 23 Lovell Coleman	3.00	1.35	.35
☐ 24 Barrie Cyr	2.00	.90	.25
☐ 25 Ernie Danjean	2.00	.90	.25
☐ 26 Gene Filipski	4.00	1.80	.50
☐ 27 George Hansen	2.00	.90	.25
☐ 28 Earl Lunsford	5.00	2.20	.60
☐ 29 Don Luzzi	3.00	1.35	.35
☐ 30 Bill McKenna	2.00	.90	.25
☐ 31 Tony Pajaczkowski	4.00	1.80	.50
☐ 32 Chuck Quilter	2.00	.90	.25
☐ 33 Lorne Reid	2.00	.90	.25
☐ 34 Art Scullion	2.00	.90	.25
☐ 35 Jim Walden	2.00	.90	.25
☐ 36 Harvey Wylie	4.00	1.80	.50
☐ 37 Calgary Stampeders Team Card	8.00	3.60	1.00
☐ 38 Johnny Bright	10.00	4.50	1.25
☐ 39 Vic Chapman	2.00	.90	.25
☐ 40 Marion Drew Deese	2.00	.90	.25
☐ 41 Al Ecuyer	2.00	.90	.25
☐ 42 Gino Fracas	3.00	1.35	.35
☐ 43 Don Getty	6.00	2.70	.75
☐ 44 Ed Gray	2.00	.90	.25
☐ 45 Urban Henry	3.00	1.35	.35
☐ 46 Bill Hill	2.00	.90	.25
☐ 47 Mike Kmeche	2.00	.90	.25
☐ 48 Oscar Kruger	3.00	1.35	.35
☐ 49 Mike Lashuk	2.00	.90	.25
☐ 50 Jim Letcavits	2.00	.90	.25
☐ 51 Roger Nelson	4.00	1.80	.50
☐ 52 Jackie Parker	15.00	6.75	1.85
☐ 53 Howie Schumm	2.00	.90	.25
☐ 54 Jim Shipka	2.00	.90	.25
☐ 55 Bill Smith	2.00	.90	.25
☐ 56 Joe-Bob Smith	2.00	.90	.25
☐ 57 Art Walker	3.00	1.35	.35
☐ 58 Edmonton Eskimos Team card	8.00	3.60	1.00
☐ 59 John Barrow	8.00	3.60	1.00
☐ 60 Hardiman Cureton	2.00	.90	.25
☐ 61 Geno DeNobile	2.00	.90	.25
☐ 62 Tom Dublinski	2.00	.90	.25
☐ 63 Bernie Faloney	12.00	5.50	1.50
☐ 64 Cam Fraser	2.00	.90	.25
☐ 65 Ralph Goldston	3.00	1.35	.35
☐ 66 Tommy Grant	7.00	3.10	.85
☐ 67 Garney Henley	15.00	6.75	1.85
☐ 68 Ron Howell	3.00	1.35	.35
☐ 69 Zeno Karcz	3.00	1.35	.35
☐ 70 Gerry McDougall UER (Misspelled Jerry)	3.00	1.35	.35
☐ 71 Chet Miksza	2.00	.90	.25
☐ 72 Bronko Nagurski	6.00	2.70	.75
☐ 73 Hal Patterson	10.00	4.50	1.25
☐ 74 George Scott	2.00	.90	.25
☐ 75 Vince Scott	4.00	1.80	.50
☐ 76 Hamilton Tiger-Cats Team card	8.00	3.60	1.00
☐ 77 Ron Brewer	3.00	1.35	.35
☐ 78 Ron Brooks	2.00	.90	.25
☐ 79 Howard Cissell	2.00	.90	.25
☐ 80 Don Clark	3.00	1.35	.35
☐ 81 Dick Cohee	3.00	1.35	.35
☐ 82 John Conroy	2.00	.90	.25
☐ 83 Milt Crain	3.00	1.35	.35
☐ 84 Ted Elsby	2.00	.90	.25
☐ 85 Joe Francis	3.00	1.35	.35
☐ 86 Gene Gaines	8.00	3.60	1.00
☐ 87 Barrie Hansen	2.00	.90	.25
☐ 88 Mike Kovac	2.00	.90	.25
☐ 89 Ed Learn	2.00	.90	.25
☐ 90 Billy Ray Locklin	2.00	.90	.25
☐ 91 Marv Luster	6.00	2.70	.75
☐ 92 Bobby Jack Oliver	3.00	1.35	.35
☐ 93 Sandy Stephens	8.00	3.60	1.00
☐ 94 Montreal Alouettes Team Card	10.00	4.50	1.25
☐ 95 Gilles Archambeault	2.00	.90	.25
☐ 96 Bruno Bitkowski	3.00	1.35	.35
☐ 97 Jim Conroy	3.00	1.35	.35
☐ 98 Doug Daigneault	2.00	.90	.25
☐ 99 Dick Desmarais	2.00	.90	.25
☐ 100 Russ Jackson	15.00	6.75	1.85
☐ 101 Tom Jones	2.00	.90	.25
☐ 102 Ron Lancaster	20.00	9.00	2.50
☐ 103 Angelo Mosca	15.00	6.75	1.85
☐ 104 Gerry Nesbitt	2.00	.90	.25
☐ 105 Joe Poirier	3.00	1.35	.35
☐ 106 Moe Racine	2.00	.90	.25
☐ 107 Gary Schreider	2.00	.90	.25
☐ 108 Bob Simpson	6.00	2.70	.75
☐ 109 Ted Smale	2.00	.90	.25
☐ 110 Ron Stewart	7.00	3.10	.85
☐ 111 Dave Thelen	6.00	2.70	.75
☐ 112 Kaye Vaughan	4.00	1.80	.50
☐ 113 Ottawa Rough Riders Team card	8.00	3.60	1.00
☐ 114 Ron Atchison UER (Misspelled Atcheson on card front)	4.00	1.80	.50
☐ 115 Danny Banda	2.00	.90	.25
☐ 116 Al Benecick	2.00	.90	.25
☐ 117 Clair Branch	2.00	.90	.25
☐ 118 Fred Burket	2.00	.90	.25
☐ 119 Bill Clarke	2.00	.90	.25
☐ 120 Jim Copeland	2.00	.90	.25
☐ 121 Ron Dundas	2.00	.90	.25
☐ 122 Bob Golic	3.00	1.35	.35
☐ 123 Jack Gotta	4.00	1.80	.50
☐ 124 Dave Grosz	2.00	.90	.25
☐ 125 Neil Habig	3.00	1.35	.35
☐ 126 Jack Hill	2.00	.90	.25
☐ 127 Len Legault	2.00	.90	.25
☐ 128 Bob Ptacek	2.00	.90	.25
☐ 129 Roy Smith	2.00	.90	.25
☐ 130 Saskatchewan Roughriders Team Card	8.00	3.60	1.00
☐ 131 Lynn Bottoms	3.00	1.35	.35
☐ 132 Dick Fouts	3.00	1.35	.35
☐ 133 Wes Gideon	2.00	.90	.25
☐ 134 Cookie Gilchrist	15.00	6.75	1.85
☐ 135 Art Johnson	2.00	.90	.25
☐ 136 Bobby Kuntz	3.00	1.35	.35
☐ 137 Dave Mann	3.00	1.35	.35

☐ 138 Marty Martinello	2.00	.90	.25
☐ 139 Doug McNichol	2.00	.90	.25
☐ 140 Bill Mitchell	2.00	.90	.25
☐ 141 Danny Nykoluk	2.00	.90	.25
☐ 142 Walt Radzick	2.00	.90	.25
☐ 143 Tobin Rote	10.00	4.50	1.25
☐ 144 Jim Rountree	3.00	1.35	.35
☐ 145 Dick Shatto	8.00	3.60	1.00
☐ 146 Billy Shipp	2.00	.90	.25
☐ 147 Norm Stoneburgh	2.00	.90	.25
☐ 148 Toronto Argonauts Team Card	10.00	4.50	1.25
☐ 149 Dave Burkholder	2.00	.90	.25
☐ 150 Jack Delveaux	2.00	.90	.25
☐ 151 George Druxman	2.00	.90	.25
☐ 152 Farrell Funston	3.00	1.35	.35
☐ 153 Herb Gray	5.00	2.20	.60
☐ 154 Roger Hagberg	3.00	1.35	.35
☐ 155 Gerry James	6.00	2.70	.75
☐ 156 Henry Janzen	3.00	1.35	.35
☐ 157 Ronnie Latourelle	2.00	.90	.25
☐ 158 Hal Ledyard	2.00	.90	.25
☐ 159 Leo Lewis	6.00	2.70	.75
☐ 160 Steve Patrick	2.00	.90	.25
☐ 161 Cornel Piper	2.00	.90	.25
☐ 162 Ernie Pitts	2.00	.90	.25
☐ 163 Kenny Ploen	8.00	3.60	1.00
☐ 164 Norm Rauhaus	3.00	1.35	.35
☐ 165 Frank Rigney	6.00	2.70	.75
☐ 166 Gord Rowland	3.00	1.35	.35
☐ 167 Roger Savoie	2.00	.90	.25
☐ 168 Charlie Shepard	3.00	1.35	.35
☐ 169 Winnipeg Blue Bombers Team Card	20.00	5.00	2.00

1963 Topps CFL

JOE KAPP

The 1963 Topps CFL set features cards ordered by teams (which are in alphabetical order) with players preceding their respective team cards. Although the T.C.G. trademark appears on the cards, they are printed in Canada by O-Pee-Chee.

	NRMT	VG-E	GOOD
COMPLETE SET (88)	350.00	160.00	45.00
COMMON CARD (1-88)	2.50	1.10	.30

☐ 1 Willie Fleming	12.00	3.00	1.20
☐ 2 Dick Fouts	3.50	1.55	.45
☐ 3 Joe Kapp	15.00	6.75	1.85
☐ 4 Nub Beamer	2.50	1.10	.30
☐ 5 By Bailey	6.00	2.70	.75
☐ 6 Tom Walker	2.50	1.10	.30
☐ 7 Sonny Homer	3.50	1.55	.45
☐ 8 Tom Hinton	5.00	2.20	.60
☐ 9 Lonnie Dennis	2.50	1.10	.30
☐ 10 British Columbia Lions Team Card	7.50	3.40	.95
☐ 11 Ed Buchanan	2.50	1.10	.30
☐ 12 Ernie Danjean	2.50	1.10	.30
☐ 13 Eagle Day	6.00	2.70	.75
☐ 14 Earl Lunsford	5.00	2.20	.60
☐ 15 Don Luzzi	5.00	2.20	.60
☐ 16 Tony Pajaczkowski	5.00	2.20	.60
☐ 17 Jerry Keeling	15.00	6.75	1.85
☐ 18 Pat Holmes	2.50	1.10	.30
☐ 19 Wayne Harris	15.00	6.75	1.85
☐ 20 Calgary Stampeders Team Card	7.50	3.40	.95
☐ 21 Tommy Joe Coffey	7.50	3.40	.95
☐ 22 Mike Lashuk	2.50	1.10	.30
☐ 23 Bobby Walden	3.50	1.55	.45
☐ 24 Don Getty	8.00	3.60	1.00
☐ 25 Len Vella	2.50	1.10	.30
☐ 26 Ted Frechette	2.50	1.10	.30
☐ 27 E.A. Sims	2.50	1.10	.30
☐ 28 Nat Dye	2.50	1.10	.30
☐ 29 Edmonton Eskimos Team Card	7.50	3.40	.95
☐ 30 Bernie Faloney	10.00	4.50	1.25
☐ 31 Hal Patterson	8.00	3.60	1.00
☐ 32 John Barrow	6.00	2.70	.75
☐ 33 Sam Fernandez	2.50	1.10	.30
☐ 34 Garney Henley	12.00	5.50	1.50
☐ 35 Joe Zuger	3.50	1.55	.45
☐ 36 Hardiman Cureton	2.50	1.10	.30
☐ 37 Zeno Karcz	3.50	1.55	.45
☐ 38 Bobby Kuntz	3.50	1.55	.45
☐ 39 Hamilton Tiger-Cats Team Card	7.50	3.40	.95
☐ 40 George Dixon	6.00	2.70	.75
☐ 41 Don Clark	3.50	1.55	.45
☐ 42 Marv Luster	6.00	2.70	.75

☐ 43 Bobby Jack Oliver	3.50	1.55	.45
☐ 44 Billy Ray Locklin	2.50	1.10	.30
☐ 45 Sandy Stephens	6.00	2.70	.75
☐ 46 Milt Crain	3.50	1.55	.45
☐ 47 Meco Poliziani	2.50	1.10	.30
☐ 48 Ted Elsby	2.50	1.10	.30
☐ 49 Montreal Alouettes Team Card	9.00	4.00	1.10
☐ 50 Russ Jackson	15.00	6.75	1.85
☐ 51 Ron Stewart	8.00	3.60	1.00
☐ 52 Dave Thelen	6.00	2.70	.75
☐ 53 Kaye Vaughan	5.00	2.20	.60
☐ 54 Joe Poirier	3.50	1.55	.45
☐ 55 Moe Racine	2.50	1.10	.30
☐ 56 Whit Tucker	10.00	4.50	1.25
☐ 57 Ernie White	2.50	1.10	.30
☐ 58 Ottawa Rough Riders Team Card	7.50	3.40	.95
☐ 59 Bob Ptacek	2.50	1.10	.30
☐ 60 Ray Purdin	2.50	1.10	.30
☐ 61 Dale West	3.50	1.55	.45
☐ 62 Neil Habig	2.50	1.10	.30
☐ 63 Jack Gotta	3.50	1.55	.45
☐ 64 Billy Gray	2.50	1.10	.30
☐ 65 Don Walsh	2.50	1.10	.30
☐ 66 Bill Clarke	2.50	1.10	.30
☐ 67 Saskatchewan Rough-riders Team Card	7.50	3.40	.95
☐ 68 Jackie Parker	15.00	6.75	1.85
☐ 69 Dave Mann	3.50	1.55	.45
☐ 70 Dick Shatto	6.00	2.70	.75
☐ 71 Norm Stoneburgh UER (Misspelled Stoneburg on card front)	2.50	1.10	.30
☐ 72 Clare Exelby	2.50	1.10	.30
☐ 73 Art Johnson	2.50	1.10	.30
☐ 74 Doug McNichol	2.50	1.10	.30
☐ 75 Danny Nykoluk	2.50	1.10	.30
☐ 76 Walt Radzick	2.50	1.10	.30
☐ 77 Toronto Argonauts Team Card	9.00	4.00	1.10
☐ 78 Leo Lewis	6.00	2.70	.75
☐ 79 Kenny Ploen	7.00	3.10	.85
☐ 80 Henry Janzen	3.50	1.55	.45
☐ 81 Charlie Shepard	3.50	1.55	.45
☐ 82 Roger Hagberg	3.50	1.55	.45
☐ 83 Herb Gray	6.00	2.70	.75
☐ 84 Frank Rigney	5.00	2.20	.60
☐ 85 Jack Delveaux	2.50	1.10	.30
☐ 86 Ronnie Latourelle	2.50	1.10	.30
☐ 87 Winnipeg Blue Bombers Team Card	7.50	3.40	.95
☐ 88 Checklist Card	50.00	12.50	5.00

1964 Topps CFL

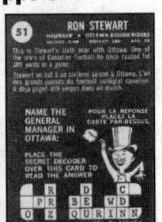

RON STEWART

The 1964 Topps CFL set features cards ordered by teams (which are in alphabetical order) with players preceding their respective team cards. Although the T.C.G. trademark appears on the cards, they were printed in Canada by O-Pee-Chee.

	NRMT	VG-E	GOOD
COMPLETE SET (88)	350.00	160.00	45.00
COMMON CARD (1-88)	2.50	1.10	.30

☐ 1 Willie Fleming	12.00	3.00	1.20
☐ 2 Dick Fouts	3.50	1.55	.45
☐ 3 Joe Kapp	15.00	6.75	1.85
☐ 4 Nub Beamer	2.50	1.10	.30
☐ 5 Tom Brown	5.00	2.20	.60
☐ 6 Tom Walker	2.50	1.10	.30
☐ 7 Sonny Homer	3.50	1.55	.45
☐ 8 Tom Hinton	5.00	2.20	.60
☐ 9 Lonnie Dennis	2.50	1.10	.30
☐ 10 B.C. Lions Team	7.50	3.40	.95
☐ 11 Lovell Coleman	3.50	1.55	.45
☐ 12 Ernie Danjean	2.50	1.10	.30
☐ 13 Eagle Day	5.00	2.20	.60
☐ 14 Jim Furlong	2.50	1.10	.30
☐ 15 Don Luzzi	5.00	2.20	.60
☐ 16 Tony Pajaczkowski	5.00	2.20	.60
☐ 17 Jerry Keeling	6.00	2.70	.75
☐ 18 Pat Holmes	2.50	1.10	.30
☐ 19 Wayne Harris	7.50	3.40	.95
☐ 20 Calgary Stampeders Team Card	7.50	3.40	.95
☐ 21 Tommy Joe Coffey	7.50	3.40	.95
☐ 22 Al Ecuyer	2.50	1.10	.30
☐ 23 Checklist Card	35.00	16.00	4.40
☐ 24 Don Getty	6.00	2.70	.75
☐ 25 Len Vella	2.50	1.10	.30
☐ 26 Ted Frechette	2.50	1.10	.30

☐ 27 E.A. Sims	2.50	1.10	.30
☐ 28 Nat Dye	2.50	1.10	.30
☐ 29 Edmonton Eskimos Team Card	7.50	3.40	.95
☐ 30 Bernie Faloney	15.00	6.75	1.85
☐ 31 Hal Patterson	8.00	3.60	1.00
☐ 32 John Barrow	6.00	2.70	.75
☐ 33 Tommy Grant	6.00	2.70	.75
☐ 34 Garney Henley	8.00	3.60	1.00
☐ 35 Joe Zuger	3.50	1.55	.45
☐ 36 Hardiman Cureton	2.50	1.10	.30
☐ 37 Zeno Karcz	3.50	1.55	.45
☐ 38 Bobby Kuntz	3.50	1.55	.45
☐ 39 Hamilton Tiger-Cats Team Card	7.50	3.40	.95
☐ 40 George Dixon	7.50	3.40	.95
☐ 41 Dave Hoppmann	2.50	1.10	.30
☐ 42 Dick Walton	2.50	1.10	.30
☐ 43 Jim Andreotti	3.50	1.55	.45
☐ 44 Billy Ray Locklin	2.50	1.10	.30
☐ 45 Fred Burket	2.50	1.10	.30
☐ 46 Milt Crain	3.50	1.55	.45
☐ 47 Meco Poliziani	2.50	1.10	.30
☐ 48 Ted Elsby	2.50	1.10	.30
☐ 49 Montreal Alouettes Team Card	10.00	4.50	1.25
☐ 50 Russ Jackson	15.00	6.75	1.85
☐ 51 Ron Stewart	8.00	3.60	1.00
☐ 52 Dave Thelen	5.00	2.20	.60
☐ 53 Kaye Vaughan	5.00	2.20	.60
☐ 54 Joe Poirier	3.50	1.55	.45
☐ 55 Moe Racine	2.50	1.10	.30
☐ 56 Whit Tucker	6.00	2.70	.75
☐ 57 Ernie White	2.50	1.10	.30
☐ 58 Ottawa Rough Riders Team Card	7.50	3.40	.95
☐ 59 Bob Ptacek	2.50	1.10	.30
☐ 60 Ray Purdin	2.50	1.10	.30
☐ 61 Dale West	3.50	1.55	.45
☐ 62 Neil Habig	2.50	1.10	.30
☐ 63 Jack Gotta	3.50	1.55	.45
☐ 64 Billy Gray	2.50	1.10	.30
☐ 65 Don Walsh	2.50	1.10	.30
☐ 66 Bill Clarke	2.50	1.10	.30
☐ 67 Saskatchewan Rough-riders Team Card	7.50	3.40	.95
☐ 68 Jackie Parker	15.00	6.75	1.85
☐ 69 Dave Mann	3.50	1.55	.45
☐ 70 Dick Shatto	6.00	2.70	.75
☐ 71 Norm Stoneburgh	2.50	1.10	.30
☐ 72 Clare Exelby	2.50	1.10	.30
☐ 73 Jim Christopherson	2.50	1.10	.30
☐ 74 Sherman Lewis	6.00	2.70	.75
☐ 75 Danny Nykoluk	2.50	1.10	.30
☐ 76 Walt Radzick	2.50	1.10	.30
☐ 77 Toronto Argonauts Team Card	10.00	4.50	1.25
☐ 78 Leo Lewis	6.00	2.70	.75
☐ 79 Kenny Ploen	6.00	2.70	.75
☐ 80 Henry Janzen	3.50	1.55	.45
☐ 81 Charlie Shepard	3.50	1.55	.45
☐ 82 Roger Hagberg	3.50	1.55	.45
☐ 83 Herb Gray	6.00	2.70	.75
☐ 84 Frank Rigney	5.00	2.20	.60
☐ 85 Jack Delveaux	2.50	1.10	.30
☐ 86 Ronnie Latourelle	2.50	1.10	.30
☐ 87 Winnipeg Blue Bombers Team Card	7.50	3.40	.95
☐ 88 Checklist Card	50.00	12.50	5.00

1965 Topps CFL

HALFBACK • TORONTO ARGONAUTS
DICK SHATTO

The 1965 Topps CFL set features 132 cards ordered by teams (which are in alphabetical order) with players also in alphabetical order. Card numbers 60 (1-60) and 132 (61-132) are checklist cards. Don Sutherlin, number 57, has number 51 on the back. Although the T.C.G. trademark appears on the cards, they were printed in Canada by O-Pee-Chee.

	NRMT	VG-E	GOOD
COMPLETE SET (132)	325.00	145.00	40.00
COMMON CARD (1-132)	2.00	.90	.25

☐ 1 Neil Beaumont	6.00	1.50	.60
☐ 2 Tom Brown	6.00	2.70	.75
☐ 3 Mike Cacic	2.00	.90	.25
☐ 4 Pat Claridge	2.00	.90	.25
☐ 5 Steve Cotter	2.00	.90	.25
☐ 6 Lonnie Dennis	2.00	.90	.25
☐ 7 Norm Fieldgate	4.00	1.80	.50
☐ 8 Willie Fleming	10.00	4.50	1.25
☐ 9 Dick Fouts	3.00	1.35	.35

☐ 10 Tom Hinton	4.00	1.80	.50
☐ 11 Sonny Homer	3.00	1.35	.35
☐ 12 Joe Kapp	12.00	5.50	1.50
☐ 13 Paul Seale	2.00	.90	.25
☐ 14 Steve Shafer	2.00	.90	.25
☐ 15 Bob Swift	2.00	.90	.25
☐ 16 Larry Anderson	2.00	.90	.25
☐ 17 Lu Bain	2.00	.90	.25
☐ 18 Lovell Coleman	3.00	1.35	.35
☐ 19 Eagle Day	4.00	1.80	.50
☐ 20 Jim Furlong	2.00	.90	.25
☐ 21 Wayne Harris	6.00	2.70	.75
☐ 22 Herman Harrison	12.00	5.50	1.50
☐ 23 Jerry Keeling	5.00	2.20	.60
☐ 24 Hal Krebs	2.00	.90	.25
☐ 25 Don Luzzi	4.00	1.80	.50
☐ 26 Tony Pajaczkowski	4.00	1.80	.50
☐ 27 Larry Robinson	4.00	1.80	.50
☐ 28 Bob Taylor	3.00	1.35	.35
☐ 29 Ted Woods	2.00	.90	.25
☐ 30 Jon Anabo	2.00	.90	.25
☐ 31 Jim Battle	2.00	.90	.25
☐ 32 Charlie Brown	2.00	.90	.25
☐ 33 Tommy Joe Coffey	8.00	3.60	1.00
☐ 34 Marcel Deleeuw	2.00	.90	.25
☐ 35 Al Ecuyer	2.00	.90	.25
☐ 36 Jim Higgins	2.00	.90	.25
☐ 37 Oscar Kruger	3.00	1.35	.35
☐ 38 Barry Mitchelson	2.00	.90	.25
☐ 39 Roger Nelson	4.00	1.80	.50
☐ 40 Bill Redell	2.00	.90	.25
☐ 41 E.A. Sims	2.00	.90	.25
☐ 42 Jim Thomas	2.00	.90	.25
☐ 43 Jim Thomas	2.00	.90	.25
☐ 44 Terry Wilson	2.00	.90	.25
☐ 45 Art Baker	2.00	.90	.25
☐ 46 John Barrow	6.00	2.70	.75
☐ 47 Dick Cohee	2.00	.90	.25
☐ 48 Frank Cosentino	4.00	1.80	.50
☐ 49 Johnny Counts	2.00	.90	.25
☐ 50 Tommy Grant	5.00	2.20	.60
☐ 51 Garney Henley (See also number 57)	8.00	3.60	1.00
☐ 52 Zeno Karcz	3.00	1.35	.35
☐ 53 Ellison Kelly	12.00	5.50	1.50
☐ 54 Bobby Kuntz	3.00	1.35	.35
☐ 55 Angelo Mosca	12.00	5.50	1.50
☐ 56 Bronko Nagurski	6.00	2.70	.75
☐ 57 Don Sutherin UER (number 51 on back)	12.00	5.50	1.50
☐ 58 Dave Viti	2.00	.90	.25
☐ 59 Joe Zuger	3.00	1.35	.35
☐ 60 Checklist 1-60	25.00	6.25	2.50
☐ 61 Jim Andreotti	3.00	1.35	.35
☐ 62 Harold Cooley	2.00	.90	.25
☐ 63 Nat Craddock	2.00	.90	.25
☐ 64 George Dixon	6.00	2.70	.75
☐ 65 Ted Elsby	2.00	.90	.25
☐ 66 Clare Exelby	2.00	.90	.25
☐ 67 Bernie Faloney	12.00	5.50	1.50
☐ 68 Al Irwin	2.00	.90	.25
☐ 69 Ed Learn	2.00	.90	.25
☐ 70 Moe Levesque	2.00	.90	.25
☐ 71 Bob Minihane	2.00	.90	.25
☐ 72 Jim Reynolds	2.00	.90	.25
☐ 73 Billy Roy	2.00	.90	.25
☐ 74 Billy Joe Booth	3.00	1.35	.35
☐ 75 Jim Cain	2.00	.90	.25
☐ 76 Larry DeGraw	2.00	.90	.25
☐ 77 Don Estes	2.00	.90	.25
☐ 78 Gene Gaines	5.00	2.20	.60
☐ 79 John Kennerson	2.00	.90	.25
☐ 80 Roger Kramer	3.00	1.35	.35
☐ 81 Ken Lehmann	3.00	1.35	.35
☐ 82 Bob O'Billovich	2.00	.90	.25
☐ 83 Joe Poirier	3.00	1.35	.35
☐ 84 Bill Quinter	2.00	.90	.25
☐ 85 Jerry Selinger	2.00	.90	.25
☐ 86 Bill Siekierski	2.00	.90	.25
☐ 87 Len Sparks	2.00	.90	.25
☐ 88 Whit Tucker	4.00	1.80	.50
☐ 89 Ron Atchison	4.00	1.80	.50
☐ 90 Ed Buchanan	2.00	.90	.25
☐ 91 Hugh Campbell	10.00	4.50	1.25
☐ 92 Henry Dorsch	2.00	.90	.25
☐ 93 Garner Ekstran	3.00	1.35	.35
☐ 94 Martin Fabi	2.00	.90	.25
☐ 95 Bob Good	2.00	.90	.25
☐ 96 Ron Lancaster	12.00	5.50	1.50
☐ 97 Bob Ptacek	2.00	.90	.25
☐ 98 George Reed	25.00	11.00	3.10
☐ 99 Wayne Shaw	2.00	.90	.25
☐ 100 Dale West	3.00	1.35	.35
☐ 101 Reg Whitehouse	2.00	.90	.25
☐ 102 Jim Worden	2.00	.90	.25
☐ 103 Ron Brewer	2.00	.90	.25
☐ 104 Don Fuell	2.00	.90	.25
☐ 105 Ed Harrington	3.00	1.35	.35
☐ 106 George Hughley	2.00	.90	.25
☐ 107 Dave Mann	3.00	1.35	.35
☐ 108 Marty Martinello	2.00	.90	.25
☐ 109 Danny Nykoluk	2.00	.90	.25
☐ 110 Jackie Parker	15.00	6.75	1.85
☐ 111 Dave Pivec	2.00	.90	.25
☐ 112 Walt Radzick	2.00	.90	.25

☐ 113 Lee Sampson	2.00	.90	.25
☐ 114 Dick Shatto	5.00	2.20	.60
☐ 115 Norm Stoneburgh	2.00	.90	.25
☐ 116 Jim Vollenweider	2.00	.90	.25
☐ 117 John Wydareny	3.00	1.35	.35
☐ 118 Billy Cooper	2.00	.90	.25
☐ 119 Farrell Funston	3.00	1.35	.35
☐ 120 Herb Gray	5.00	2.20	.60
☐ 121 Henry Janzen	3.00	1.35	.35
☐ 122 Leo Lewis	6.00	2.70	.75
☐ 123 Brian Palmer	2.00	.90	.25
☐ 124 Cornel Piper	2.00	.90	.25
☐ 125 Ernie Pitts	2.00	.90	.25
☐ 126 Kenny Ploen	6.00	2.70	.75
☐ 127 Norm Rauhaus	3.00	1.35	.35
☐ 128 Frank Rigney	4.00	1.80	.50
☐ 129 Roger Savoie	2.00	.90	.25
☐ 130 Dick Thornton	4.00	1.80	.50
☐ 131 Bill Whisler	2.00	.90	.25
☐ 132 Checklist 61-132	40.00	10.00	4.00

1965 Topps CFL Transfers

These four-color transfers were inserts in the 1965 Topps CFL packs. They measure approximately 2" by 3". These 1965 inserts are distinguished from the 1961 inserts by the notation "Printed in U.S.A." on the 1965 inserts.

	NRMT	VG-E	GOOD
COMPLETE SET (27)	500.00	220.00	60.00
COMMON CARD (1-27)	20.00	9.00	2.50
☐ 1 British Columbia Lions Crest	20.00	9.00	2.50
☐ 2 British Columbia Lions Pennant	20.00	9.00	2.50
☐ 3 Calgary Stampeders Crest	20.00	9.00	2.50
☐ 4 Calgary Stampeders Pennant	20.00	9.00	2.50
☐ 5 Edmonton Eskimos Crest	20.00	9.00	2.50
☐ 6 Edmonton Eskimos Pennant	20.00	9.00	2.50
☐ 7 Hamilton Tiger-Cats Crest	20.00	9.00	2.50
☐ 8 Hamilton Tiger-Cats Pennant	20.00	9.00	2.50
☐ 9 Montreal Alouettes Crest	20.00	9.00	2.50
☐ 10 Montreal Alouettes Pennant	20.00	9.00	2.50
☐ 11 Ottawa Rough Riders Crest	20.00	9.00	2.50
☐ 12 Ottawa Rough Riders Pennant	20.00	9.00	2.50
☐ 13 Saskatchewan Roughriders Crest	20.00	9.00	2.50
☐ 14 Saskatchewan Roughriders Pennant	20.00	9.00	2.50
☐ 15 Toronto Argonauts Crest	20.00	9.00	2.50
☐ 16 Toronto Argonauts Pennant	20.00	9.00	2.50
☐ 17 Winnipeg Blue Bombers Crest	20.00	9.00	2.50
☐ 18 Winnipeg Blue Bombers Pennant	20.00	9.00	2.50
☐ 19 Quebec Provincial Crest	20.00	9.00	2.50
☐ 20 Ontario Provincial Crest	20.00	9.00	2.50
☐ 21 Manitoba Provincial Crest	20.00	9.00	2.50
☐ 22 Saskatchewan Provincial Crest	20.00	9.00	2.50
☐ 23 Alberta Provincial Crest	20.00	9.00	2.50
☐ 24 British Columbia Provincial Crest	20.00	9.00	2.50
☐ 25 Northwest Territories Territorial Crest	20.00	9.00	2.50
☐ 26 Yukon Territory Territorial Crest	20.00	9.00	2.50
☐ 27 Canada	25.00	11.00	3.10

1981 Toronto Sun Argonauts

The television schedule portion of the Toronto Sun included one-sided large color portraits of Argonauts' players throughout the season. Each was designed to be cut from the publication, thus each includes a newsprint type back. The player's name and a brief write-up appear below the photo along with the team logo and "Meet the Argos" title line. The checklist below includes the known copies and is thought to be incomplete.

	MINT	NRMT	EXC
COMPLETE SET (11)	20.00	9.00	2.50
COMMON CARD (1-11)	2.00	.90	.25
☐ 7 Condredge Holloway	5.00	2.20	.60
☐ 14 Dan Manucci	2.00	.90	.25
☐ 19 Zenon Andrusyshyn	3.00	1.35	.35
☐ 25 Paul Pearson	2.00	.90	.25
☐ 30 Billy Hardee	2.00	.90	.25
☐ 32 Dave Newman	2.00	.90	.25
☐ 49 Danny Bass	3.00	1.35	.35
☐ 64 Leon Lyszkiewicz	2.00	.90	.25
☐ 69 Dan Ferrone	3.00	1.35	.35
☐ 72 Peter Muller	2.00	.90	.25
☐ 75 Gordon Judges	2.00	.90	.25

1988 Vachon CFL

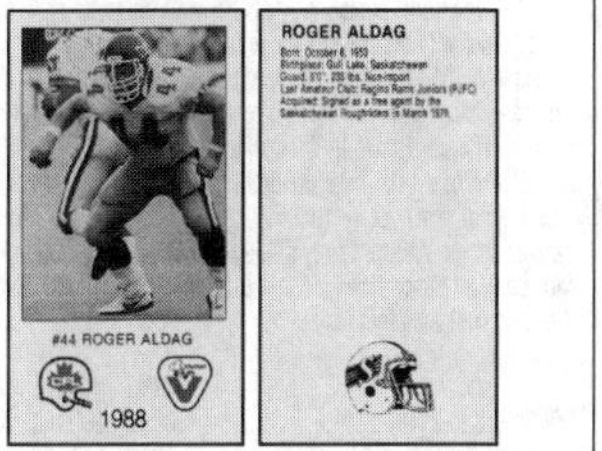

The 1988 Vachon CFL set contains 160 cards measuring 2" by 3 1/2", that is, standard business card size. The fronts have color action photos bordered in white; the vertically oriented backs have brief biographies and career highlights. These cards were printed on very thin stock. Since the cards are unnumbered, they have been ordered below alphabetically for reference. The card fronts contain the Vachon logo and the CFL logo.

	MINT	NRMT	EXC
COMPLETE SET (160)	135.00	60.00	17.00
COMMON CARD (1-160)	.75	.35	.09
☐ 1 David Albright	.75	.35	.09
☐ 2 Roger Aldag	1.00	.45	.12
☐ 3 Marv Allemang	.75	.35	.09
☐ 4 Damon Allen	5.00	2.20	.60
☐ 5 Gary Allen	1.00	.45	.12
☐ 6 Randy Ambrosie	.75	.35	.09
☐ 7 Mike Anderson	.75	.35	.09
☐ 8 Kent Austin	3.00	1.35	.35
☐ 9 Terry Baker	1.00	.45	.12
☐ 10 Danny Bass	3.00	1.35	.35
☐ 11 Nick Bastaja	.75	.35	.09
☐ 12 Greg Battle	2.50	1.10	.30
☐ 13 Lyle Bauer	.75	.35	.09
☐ 14 Jearld Baylis	2.00	.90	.25
☐ 15 Ian Beckstead	.75	.35	.09
☐ 16 Walter Bender	1.50	.70	.19
☐ 17 Nick Benjamin	1.00	.45	.12
☐ 18 David Black	.75	.35	.09
☐ 19 Leo Blanchard	.75	.35	.09
☐ 20 Trevor Bowles	1.00	.45	.12
☐ 21 Ken Braden	.75	.35	.09
☐ 22 Rod Brown	.75	.35	.09
☐ 23 Less Browne	1.00	.45	.12
☐ 24 Jamie Buis	.75	.35	.09
☐ 25 Tom Burgess	4.00	1.80	.50
☐ 26 Bob Cameron	1.25	.55	.16
☐ 27 Jan Carinci	.75	.35	.09
☐ 28 Tony Champion	2.50	1.10	.30
☐ 29 Jacques Chapdelaine	.75	.35	.09
☐ 30 Tony Cherry	2.50	1.10	.30
☐ 31 Lance Chomyc	1.00	.45	.12
☐ 32 John Congemi	2.00	.90	.25
☐ 33 Rod Connop	.75	.35	.09
☐ 34 David Conrad	.75	.35	.09
☐ 35 Grover Covington	2.00	.90	.25
☐ 36 Larry Crawford	1.25	.55	.16
☐ 37 James Curry	2.00	.90	.25
☐ 38 Marco Cyncar	1.00	.45	.12
☐ 39 Gabriel DeLaGarza	.75	.35	.09
☐ 40 Mike Derks	.75	.35	.09
☐ 41 Blake Dermott	1.00	.45	.12
☐ 42 Roy DeWalt SP	4.00	1.80	.50
☐ 43 Todd Dillon	1.25	.55	.16
☐ 44 Rocky DiPietro	2.00	.90	.25
☐ 45 Kevin Dixon SP	2.00	.90	.25
☐ 46 Tom Dixon	.75	.35	.09
☐ 47 Selwyn Drain	.75	.35	.09
☐ 48 Matt Dunigan	7.50	3.40	.95
☐ 49 Ray Elgaard	3.00	1.35	.35
☐ 50 Jerome Erdman	.75	.35	.09
☐ 51 Randy Fabi	.75	.35	.09
☐ 52 Gill Fenerty	2.50	1.10	.30
☐ 53 Denny Ferdinand	.75	.35	.09
☐ 54 Dan Ferrone	1.00	.45	.12
☐ 55 Howard Fields	.75	.35	.09
☐ 56 Matt Finlay	1.00	.45	.12
☐ 57 Rickey Foggie	2.00	.90	.25
☐ 58 Delbert Fowler	1.00	.45	.12
☐ 59 Ed Gataveckas	.75	.35	.09
☐ 60 Keith Gooch	.75	.35	.09
☐ 61 Miles Gorrell	.75	.35	.09
☐ 62 Mike Gray	.75	.35	.09
☐ 63 Leo Groenewegen	.75	.35	.09
☐ 64 Ken Hailey	.75	.35	.09
☐ 65 Harold Hallman	1.25	.55	.16
☐ 66 Tracey Ham	7.50	3.40	.95
☐ 67 Rodney Harding	2.00	.90	.25
☐ 68 Glenn Harper	.75	.35	.09
☐ 69 J.T. Hay	.75	.35	.09
☐ 70 Larry Hogue	.75	.35	.09
☐ 71 Ron Hopkins SP	2.00	.90	.25
☐ 72 Hank Ilesic	2.00	.90	.25
☐ 73 Bryan Illerbrun	.75	.35	.09
☐ 74 Lemont Jeffers	.75	.35	.09
☐ 75 James Jefferson	2.00	.90	.25
☐ 76 Rick Johnson	2.00	.90	.25
☐ 77 Chris Johnstone	.75	.35	.09
☐ 78 Johnnie Jones	.75	.35	.09
☐ 79 Milson Jones	1.50	.70	.19
☐ 80 Stephen Jones	2.00	.90	.25
☐ 81 Bobby Jurasin	2.50	1.10	.30
☐ 82 Jerry Kauric	1.00	.45	.12
☐ 83 Dan Kearns	.75	.35	.09
☐ 84 Trevor Kennerd	2.00	.90	.25
☐ 85 Mike Kerrigan	3.00	1.35	.35
☐ 86 Rick Klassen	2.00	.90	.25
☐ 87 Lee Knight	.75	.35	.09
☐ 88 Kevin Konar	1.00	.45	.12
☐ 89 Glenn Kulka	1.00	.45	.12
☐ 90 Doug(Tank) Landry	2.00	.90	.25
☐ 91 Scott Lecky	.75	.35	.09
☐ 92 Orville Lee	1.50	.70	.19
☐ 93 Marc Lewis	1.00	.45	.12
☐ 94 Eddie Lowe	1.00	.45	.12
☐ 95 Lynn Madsen	.75	.35	.09
☐ 96 Chris Major	3.00	1.35	.35
☐ 97 Doran Major	.75	.35	.09
☐ 98 Tony Martino	.75	.35	.09
☐ 99 Tim McCray	1.25	.55	.16
☐ 100 Mike McGruder	1.25	.55	.16
☐ 101 Sean McKeown SP	4.00	1.80	.50
☐ 102 Andy McVey	.75	.35	.09
☐ 103 Stan Mikawos	.75	.35	.09
☐ 104 James Mills	2.00	.90	.25
☐ 105 Larry Mohr	.75	.35	.09
☐ 106 Bernie Morrison	.75	.35	.09
☐ 107 James Murphy	2.00	.90	.25
☐ 108 Paul Osbaldiston	1.00	.45	.12
☐ 109 Anthony Parker	1.50	.70	.19
☐ 110 James Parker	2.00	.90	.25
☐ 111 Greg Peterson	.75	.35	.09
☐ 112 Tim Petros	1.25	.55	.16
☐ 113 Reggie Pleasant	1.25	.55	.16
☐ 114 Willie Pless	2.00	.90	.25
☐ 115 Bob Poley	.75	.35	.09
☐ 116 Tom Porras	1.50	.70	.19
☐ 117 Hector Pothier	.75	.35	.09
☐ 118 Jim Reid	1.25	.55	.16
☐ 119 Robert Reid	.75	.35	.09
☐ 120 Gilbert Renfroe	2.00	.90	.25
☐ 121 Tom Richards	1.25	.55	.16
☐ 122 Dave Ridgway	2.00	.90	.25
☐ 123 Rae Robirtis	.75	.35	.09
☐ 124 Gerald Roper	.75	.35	.09
☐ 125 Darryl Sampson	.75	.35	.09
☐ 126 Jim Sandusky	2.50	1.10	.30
☐ 127 David Sauve	.75	.35	.09
☐ 128 Art Schlichter	1.25	.55	.16
☐ 129 Ralph Scholz	.75	.35	.09
☐ 130 Mark Seale	.75	.35	.09
☐ 131 Dan Sellers	.75	.35	.09
☐ 132 Lance Shields	1.00	.45	.12
☐ 133 Ian Sinclair	1.25	.55	.16
☐ 134 Mike Siroishka	.75	.35	.09
☐ 135 Chris Skinner	1.00	.45	.12
☐ 136 Harry Skipper	1.00	.45	.12
☐ 137 Darrell Smith	3.00	1.35	.35
☐ 138 Tom Spoletini	.75	.35	.09
☐ 139 Steve Stapler	1.00	.45	.12
☐ 140 Bill Stevenson	.75	.35	.09
☐ 141 Gregg Stumon	1.25	.55	.16
☐ 142 Glen Suitor	1.00	.45	.12
☐ 143 Emanuel Tolbert	2.50	1.10	.30
☐ 144 Perry Tuttle SP	4.00	1.80	.50
☐ 145 Peter VandenBos	.75	.35	.09
☐ 146 Jake Vaughan	.75	.35	.09
☐ 147 Chris Walby	1.50	.70	.19
☐ 148 Mike Walker	1.50	.70	.19
☐ 149 Patrick Wayne	.75	.35	.09
☐ 150 James West	2.00	.90	.25
☐ 151 Brett Williams	1.50	.70	.19
☐ 152 David Williams	2.50	1.10	.30
☐ 153 Henry Williams	10.00	4.50	1.25
☐ 154 Tommie Williams	.75	.35	.09
☐ 155 Larry Willis	1.00	.45	.12
☐ 156 Don Wilson	.75	.35	.09
☐ 157 Earl Winfield	2.50	1.10	.30
☐ 158 Rick Worman	2.00	.90	.25
☐ 159 Larry Wruck	1.00	.45	.12
☐ 160 Kari Yli-Renko	.75	.35	.09

1989 Vachon CFL

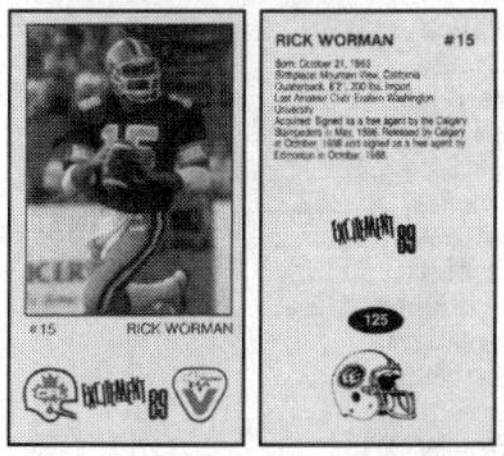

The 1989 Vachon CFL set consists of 160 cards. The cards were issued on 6" by 7" perforated panels, consisting of five player cards and one "Instant Prize Card" featuring instructions on how to play the contest. After perforation, the cards measure approximately 2" by 3 1/2". Starting in September 1989, these panels were inserted inside 6 million specially-marked packages of Vachon Cakes. (The collector could also send a self-addressed stamped envelope to receive an additional player card.) Prize cards carrying the following words were to be mailed in and made the holder eligible to receive the certain prizes: 1) Touchdown (one of ten V.I.P. trips for two to the 1989 Grey Cup game in the SkyDome in Toronto, with 250.00 spending money); 2) Field Goal (CFL game jersey); 3) Convert (ticket to the game of your choice); and 4) Single Point (.50 off your next purchase of Vachon family pack snack cakes). No prize was awarded for cards marked "Goal Line Stand." The fronts feature white-bordered color player photos; the CFL football helmet logo and Vachon's logo appear in the wider white border beneath the picture. The backs present biographical information, the card number, and the team helmet. The cards are checklisted below according to teams.

	MINT	NRMT	EXC
COMPLETE SET (160)	125.00	55.00	15.50
COMMON CARD (1-160)	.75	.35	.09
☐ 1 Tony Williams	1.00	.45	.12
☐ 2 Sean Foudy	.75	.35	.09
☐ 3 Tom Schimmer	.75	.35	.09
☐ 4 Ken Evraire	1.00	.45	.12
☐ 5 Gerald Wilcox	1.25	.55	.16
☐ 6 Damon Allen	4.00	1.80	.50
☐ 7 Tony Kimbrough	1.00	.45	.12
☐ 8 Dean Dorsey	1.00	.45	.12
☐ 9 Rocco Romano	.75	.35	.09
☐ 10 Ken Braden	.75	.35	.09
☐ 11 Kari Yli-Renko	.75	.35	.09
☐ 12 Darrel Hopper	.75	.35	.09
☐ 13 Irv Daymond	.75	.35	.09
☐ 14 Orville Lee	1.00	.45	.12
☐ 15 Steve Howlett	.75	.35	.09
☐ 16 Kyle Hall	.75	.35	.09
☐ 17 Reggie Ward	.75	.35	.09
☐ 18 Gerald Alphin	2.00	.90	.25
☐ 19 Troy Wilson	.75	.35	.09
☐ 20 Patrick Wayne	.75	.35	.09
☐ 21 Harold Hallman	1.25	.55	.16
☐ 22 John Congemi	1.50	.70	.19
☐ 23 Doran Major	.75	.35	.09
☐ 24 Hank Ilesic	1.50	.70	.19
☐ 25 Gilbert Renfroe	2.00	.90	.25
☐ 26 Rodney Harding	1.00	.45	.12
☐ 27 Todd Wiseman	.75	.35	.09
☐ 28 Chris Schultz	1.00	.45	.12
☐ 29 Carl Brazley	1.00	.45	.12
☐ 30 Darrell Smith	2.50	1.10	.30
☐ 31 Glenn Kulka	1.00	.45	.12
☐ 32 Bob Skemp	.75	.35	.09
☐ 33 Don Moen	1.00	.45	.12
☐ 34 Jearld Baylis	2.00	.90	.25
☐ 35 Lorenzo Graham	.75	.35	.09
☐ 36 Lance Chomyc	1.00	.45	.12
☐ 37 Warren Hudson	1.00	.45	.12
☐ 38 Gill Fenerty	2.00	.90	.25
☐ 39 Paul Masotti	1.00	.45	.12
☐ 40 Reggie Pleasant	1.25	.55	.16
☐ 41 Scott Flagel	1.00	.45	.12
☐ 42 Mike Kerrigan	2.00	.90	.25
☐ 43 Frank Robinson	1.00	.45	.12
☐ 44 Jacques Chapdelaine	.75	.35	.09
☐ 45 Miles Gorrell	.75	.35	.09
☐ 46 Mike Walker	1.50	.70	.19
☐ 47 Jason Riley	.75	.35	.09
☐ 48 Grover Covington	1.50	.70	.19
☐ 49 Ralph Scholz	.75	.35	.09
☐ 50 Mike Derks	.75	.35	.09
☐ 51 Derrick McAdoo	1.50	.70	.19
☐ 52 Rocky DiPietro	2.00	.90	.25
☐ 53 Lance Shields	1.00	.45	.12
☐ 54 Dale Sanderson	.75	.35	.09
☐ 55 Tim Lorenz	.75	.35	.09
☐ 56 Rod Skillman	1.00	.45	.12
☐ 57 Jed Tommy	.75	.35	.09
☐ 58 Paul Osbaldiston	1.00	.45	.12
☐ 59 Darrell Corbin	.75	.35	.09
☐ 60 Tony Champion	1.50	.70	.19
☐ 61 Romel Andrews	.75	.35	.09
☐ 62 Bob Cameron	1.25	.55	.16
☐ 63 Greg Battle	2.00	.90	.25
☐ 64 Rod Hill	1.00	.45	.12
☐ 65 Steve Rodehutskors	1.00	.45	.12
☐ 66 Trevor Kennerd	1.50	.70	.19

☐ 67 Moustafa Ali	1.00	.45	.12
☐ 68 Mike Gray	.75	.35	.09
☐ 69 Bob Molle	.75	.35	.09
☐ 70 Tim Jessie	1.00	.45	.12
☐ 71 Matt Pearce	.75	.35	.09
☐ 72 Will Lewis	1.00	.45	.12
☐ 73 Sean Salisbury	2.50	1.10	.30
☐ 74 Chris Walby	1.00	.45	.12
☐ 75 Jeff Croonen	.75	.35	.09
☐ 76 David Black	.75	.35	.09
☐ 77 Buster Rhymes	2.00	.90	.25
☐ 78 James Murphy	1.50	.70	.19
☐ 79 Stan Mikawos	.75	.35	.09
☐ 80 Lee Saltz	2.00	.90	.25
☐ 81 Bryan Illerbrun	.75	.35	.09
☐ 82 Donald Narcisse	3.00	1.35	.35
☐ 83 Milson Jones	1.00	.45	.12
☐ 84 Dave Ridgway	1.50	.70	.19
☐ 85 Glen Suitor	1.00	.45	.12
☐ 86 Terry Baker	1.00	.45	.12
☐ 87 James Curry	1.50	.70	.19
☐ 88 Harry Skipper	1.00	.45	.12
☐ 89 Bobby Jurasin	2.00	.90	.25
☐ 90 Gary Lewis	.75	.35	.09
☐ 91 Roger Aldag	1.00	.45	.12
☐ 92 Jeff Fairholm	2.00	.90	.25
☐ 93 David Albright	.75	.35	.09
☐ 94 Ray Elgaard	2.50	1.10	.30
☐ 95 Kent Austin	3.00	1.35	.35
☐ 96 Tom Burgess	3.00	1.35	.35
☐ 97 Richie Hall	.75	.35	.09
☐ 98 Eddie Lowe	1.00	.45	.12
☐ 99 Vince Goldsmith	1.00	.45	.12
☐ 100 Tim McCray	1.00	.45	.12
☐ 101 Leo Blanchard	.75	.35	.09
☐ 102 Tom Spoletini	.75	.35	.09
☐ 103 Dan Ferrone	1.00	.45	.12
☐ 104 Doug(Tank) Landry	1.50	.70	.19
☐ 105 Chris Major	1.50	.70	.19
☐ 106 Mike Palumbo	.75	.35	.09
☐ 107 Terrence Jones	2.00	.90	.25
☐ 108 Larry Willis	1.25	.55	.16
☐ 109 Kent Warnock	1.00	.45	.12
☐ 110 Tim Petros	1.00	.45	.12
☐ 111 Marshall Toner	.75	.35	.09
☐ 112 Ken Ford	.75	.35	.09
☐ 113 Ron Hopkins	1.00	.45	.12
☐ 114 Erik Kramer	7.50	3.40	.95
☐ 115 Stu Laird	1.00	.45	.12
☐ 116 Vernell Quinn	.75	.35	.09
☐ 117 Lemont Jeffers	.75	.35	.09
☐ 118 Derrick Taylor	.75	.35	.09
☐ 119 Jay Christensen	1.00	.45	.12
☐ 120 Mitchell Price	1.00	.45	.12
☐ 121 Rod Connop	.75	.35	.09
☐ 122 Mark Norman	.75	.35	.09
☐ 123 Andre Francis	1.00	.45	.12
☐ 124 Reggie Taylor	1.50	.70	.19
☐ 125 Rick Worman	1.00	.45	.12
☐ 126 Marco Cyncar	1.00	.45	.12
☐ 127 Blake Dermott	1.00	.45	.12
☐ 128 Jerry Kauric	1.00	.45	.12
☐ 129 Steve Taylor	2.00	.90	.25
☐ 130 Dave Richardson	.75	.35	.09
☐ 131 John Mandarich	1.00	.45	.12
☐ 132 Gregg Stumon	1.00	.45	.12
☐ 133 Tracey Ham	5.00	2.20	.60
☐ 134 Danny Bass	2.50	1.10	.30
☐ 135 Blake Marshall	1.50	.70	.19
☐ 136 Jeff Braswell	1.00	.45	.12
☐ 137 Larry Wruck	1.00	.45	.12
☐ 138 Warren Jones	1.00	.45	.12
☐ 139 Stephen Jones	1.50	.70	.19
☐ 140 Tom Richards	1.00	.45	.12
☐ 141 Tony Cherry	1.50	.70	.19
☐ 142 Anthony Parker	1.50	.70	.19
☐ 143 Gerald Roper	.75	.35	.09
☐ 144 Lui Passaglia	2.50	1.10	.30
☐ 145 Mack Moore	.75	.35	.09
☐ 146 Jamie Taras	.75	.35	.09
☐ 147 Rickey Foggie	1.50	.70	.19
☐ 148 Matt Dunigan	6.00	2.70	.75
☐ 149 Anthony Drawhorn	1.00	.45	.12
☐ 150 Eric Streater	1.25	.55	.16
☐ 151 Marcus Thomas	.75	.35	.09
☐ 152 Wes Cooper	.75	.35	.09
☐ 153 James Mills	1.00	.45	.12
☐ 154 Peter VandenBos	.75	.35	.09
☐ 155 Ian Sinclair	1.00	.45	.12
☐ 156 James Parker	1.50	.70	.19
☐ 157 Andrew Murray	.75	.35	.09
☐ 158 Larry Crawford	1.25	.55	.16
☐ 159 Kevin Konar	1.00	.45	.12
☐ 160 David Williams	1.50	.70	.19

1959 Wheaties CFL

 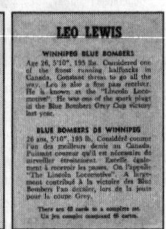

The 1959 Wheaties CFL set contains 48 cards, each measuring 2 1/2" by 3 1/2". The fronts contain a black and white photo on a one-colored striped field, with the player's name and team in black within a white rectangle at the lower portion. The back contains the player's name and team, his position, and brief biographical data in both English and French. The cards are quite similar in appearance to the 1956 Shredded Wheat set. These unnumbered cards are ordered below in alphabetical order. Every 1959 CFL game program contained a full-page ad for the Wheaties Grey Cup Game Contest. The ad detailed the card program which indicated that each specially marked package of Wheaties contained four cards.

	NRMT	VG-E	GOOD
COMPLETE SET (48)	4500.00	2000.00	550.00
COMMON CARD (1-48)	60.00	27.00	7.50
☐ 1 Ron Adam	60.00	27.00	7.50
☐ 2 Bill Bewley	75.00	34.00	9.50
☐ 3 Lynn Bottoms	75.00	34.00	9.50
☐ 4 Johnny Bright	150.00	70.00	19.00
☐ 5 Ken Carpenter	75.00	34.00	9.50
☐ 6 Tony Curcillo	60.00	27.00	7.50
☐ 7 Sam Etcheverry	250.00	110.00	31.00
☐ 8 Bernie Faloney	200.00	90.00	25.00
☐ 9 Cam Fraser	75.00	34.00	9.50
☐ 10 Don Getty	125.00	55.00	15.50
☐ 11 Jack Gotta	75.00	34.00	9.50
☐ 12 Milt Graham	60.00	27.00	7.50
☐ 13 Jack Hill	60.00	27.00	7.50
☐ 14 Ron Howell	75.00	34.00	9.50
☐ 15 Russ Jackson	200.00	90.00	25.00
☐ 16 Gerry James	125.00	55.00	15.50
☐ 17 Doug Kiloh	60.00	27.00	7.50
☐ 18 Ronnie Knox	75.00	34.00	9.50
☐ 19 Vic Kristopaitis	60.00	27.00	7.50
☐ 20 Oscar Kruger	60.00	27.00	7.50
☐ 21 Bobby Kuntz	75.00	34.00	9.50
☐ 22 Normie Kwong	175.00	80.00	22.00
☐ 23 Leo Lewis	150.00	70.00	19.00
☐ 24 Harry Lunn	60.00	27.00	7.50
☐ 25 Don Luzzi	100.00	45.00	12.50
☐ 26 Dave Mann	75.00	34.00	9.50
☐ 27 Bobby Marlow	90.00	40.00	11.00
☐ 28 Gerry McDougall	75.00	34.00	9.50
☐ 29 Doug McNichol	60.00	27.00	7.50
☐ 30 Rollie Miles	100.00	45.00	12.50
☐ 31 Red O'Quinn	90.00	40.00	11.00
☐ 32 Jackie Parker	250.00	110.00	31.00
☐ 33 Hal Patterson	150.00	70.00	19.00
☐ 34 Don Pinhey	60.00	27.00	7.50
☐ 35 Kenny Ploen	125.00	55.00	15.50
☐ 36 Gord Rowland	75.00	34.00	9.50
☐ 37 Vince Scott	90.00	40.00	11.00
☐ 38 Art Scullion	60.00	27.00	7.50
☐ 39 Dick Shatto	125.00	55.00	15.50
☐ 40 Bob Simpson	125.00	55.00	15.50
☐ 41 Jackie Simpson UER (Misspelled Jacki)	100.00	45.00	12.50
☐ 42 Bill Sowalski	60.00	27.00	7.50
☐ 43 Norm Stoneburgh	60.00	27.00	7.50
☐ 44 Buddy Tinsley	90.00	40.00	11.00
☐ 45 Frank Tripucka	100.00	45.00	12.50
☐ 46 Jim Van Pelt	60.00	27.00	7.50
☐ 47 Ernie Warlick	75.00	34.00	9.50
☐ 48 Nobby Wirkowski	100.00	45.00	12.50

1996 Headliners

This series of figures was produced by Corinthian Marketing. Each figures stands 3 1/4" tall. Also in the blister package the pieces comes in is a "Headliners Collector's Catalog." The figures were primarily sold through mass market retail outlets at a suggested retail price of $3.99. The values listed below refer to unopened packages. The figures are unnumbered and checklisted below in alphabetical order.

	MINT	NRMT	EXC
COMPLETE SET (40)	250.00	110.00	31.00
☐ Troy Aikman	10.00	4.50	1.25
☐ Marcus Allen	6.00	2.70	.75
☐ Drew Bledsoe	10.00	4.50	1.25
☐ Tim Brown	6.00	2.70	.75
☐ Cris Carter	6.00	2.70	.75
☐ Kerry Collins	10.00	4.50	1.25
☐ John Elway	6.00	2.70	.75
☐ Marshall Faulk	6.00	2.70	.75
☐ Brett Favre	12.00	5.50	1.50
☐ Jeff George	6.00	2.70	.75
☐ Kevin Greene	6.00	2.70	.75
☐ Charles Haley	6.00	2.70	.75
☐ Jim Harbaugh	6.00	2.70	.75
☐ Jeff Hostetler	6.00	2.70	.75
☐ Stan Humphries	6.00	2.70	.75
☐ Daryl Johnston	6.00	2.70	.75
☐ Jim Kelly	6.00	2.70	.75
☐ Leon Lett	6.00	2.70	.75
☐ Greg Lloyd	6.00	2.70	.75
☐ Dan Marino	12.00	5.50	1.50
☐ Steve McNair	10.00	4.50	1.25
☐ Natrone Means	6.00	2.70	.75
☐ Rick Mirer	6.00	2.70	.75
☐ Nate Newton	6.00	2.70	.75
☐ Jay Novacek	6.00	2.70	.75
☐ Neil O'Donnell	6.00	2.70	.75
☐ Jerry Rice	8.00	3.60	1.00
☐ Rashaan Salaam	6.00	2.70	.75
☐ Deion Sanders	6.00	2.70	.75
☐ Barry Sanders	6.00	2.70	.75
☐ Junior Seau	6.00	2.70	.75
☐ Heath Shuler	6.00	2.70	.75
☐ Bruce Smith	8.00	3.60	1.00
☐ Emmitt Smith	10.00	4.50	1.25
☐ Kordell Stewart	16.00	7.25	2.00
☐ Ricky Watters	6.00	2.70	.75
☐ Reggie White	6.00	2.70	.75
☐ Kevin Williams	6.00	2.70	.75
☐ Darren Woodson	6.00	2.70	.75
☐ Steve Young	8.00	3.60	1.00

1988 Kenner Starting Lineup

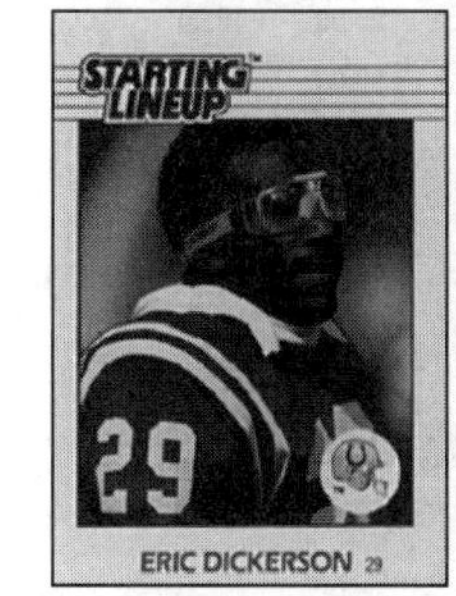

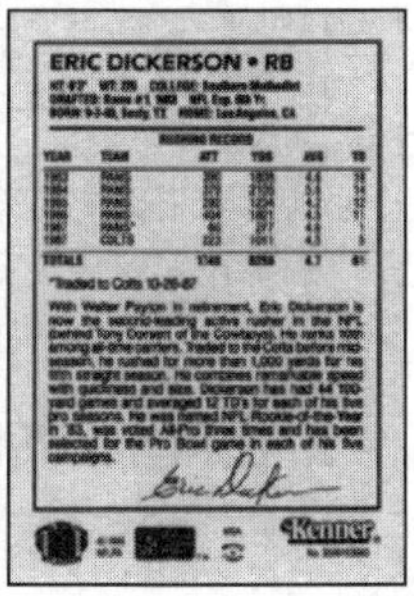

This set of 137 football figurines and collectors cards was issued by Cincinnati-based Kenner Toy Company. The statues feature top NFL stars in action poses and are accompanied by a standard-size card. The front of the card has either a posed or action color shot with a white border. The back has biographical and statistical information and a facsimile signature. The values listed below refer to unopened packages. The cards are unnumbered and checklisted below in alphabetical order. The four modes of distribution for the '88 Football set were team cases (24 pieces) issued in each teams respective region, All-Star cases (24 pieces) issued nationwide, retail catalogs and a 1-800 number. The individual player assortments within the team cases were not equal and caused certain pieces to be short prints. The Bills, Chargers, Cowboys and Raiders are the toughest teams to complete. The following players made up the All-Star case assortments: Marcus Allen (2 per case), Brian Bosworth (2), Eric Dickerson (2), John Elway (2), Dan Marino (3), Jim McMahon (3), Joe Montana (20, Phil Simms (2), Lawrence Taylor (3), Herschel Walker (2) and Reggie White (1). Three players, Tony Dorsett, Willie Gault and Marc Wilson were only made available through Sears and J.C. Penney's catalogs. Sears offered all three pieces while J.C. Penney's offered only the Willie Gault. Finally, in 1989, a company in conjunction with Kenner set up a 1-800 mail order business that sold all Kenner products made through 1989. The 1988 football sets were made available at approximately $7.00 per piece through this company.

	NRMT	EXC	DIS
COMPLETE SET (137)	7500.00	3800.00	1900.00
BLUE COLLECTOR SHOWCASE	30.00	15.00	7.50
GREEN DISPLAY STAND	40.00	20.00	10.00
☐ Marcus Allen	90.00	45.00	22.00
☐ Neal Anderson	35.00	17.50	8.75
☐ Chip Banks	90.00	45.00	22.00
☐ Mark Bavaro	45.00	22.00	11.00
☐ Cornelius Bennett	140.00	70.00	35.00
☐ Albert Bentley	35.00	17.50	8.75
☐ Duane Bickett	50.00	25.00	12.50
☐ Todd Blackledge	35.00	17.50	8.75
☐ Brian Bosworth	35.00	17.50	8.75
☐ Brian Brennan	45.00	22.00	11.00
☐ Bill Brooks	40.00	20.00	10.00
☐ James Brooks	50.00	25.00	12.50
☐ Eddie Brown	50.00	25.00	12.50
☐ Joey Browner	45.00	22.00	11.00
☐ Aundray Bruce	35.00	17.50	8.75
☐ Chris Burkett	130.00	65.00	32.00
☐ Keith Byars	40.00	20.00	10.00
☐ Scott Campbell	35.00	17.50	8.75
☐ Carlos Carson	35.00	17.50	8.75
☐ Harry Carson	35.00	17.50	8.75
☐ Anthony Carter	80.00	40.00	20.00
☐ Gerald Carter	45.00	22.00	11.00
☐ Michael Carter	75.00	38.00	19.00
☐ Tony Casillas	45.00	22.00	11.00
☐ Jeff Chadwick	35.00	17.50	8.75
☐ Deron Cherry	35.00	17.50	8.75
☐ Ray Childress	75.00	38.00	19.00
☐ Todd Christensen	80.00	40.00	20.00
☐ Gary Clark	60.00	30.00	15.00
☐ Mark Clayton	60.00	30.00	15.00
☐ Cris Collinsworth	90.00	45.00	22.00
☐ Doug Cosbie	90.00	45.00	22.00
☐ Roger Craig	45.00	22.00	11.00
☐ Randall Cunningham	45.00	22.00	11.00
☐ Jeff Davis	35.00	17.50	8.75
☐ Kenneth Davis	80.00	40.00	20.00
☐ Richard Dent	40.00	20.00	10.00
☐ Eric Dickerson	75.00	38.00	19.00
☐ Floyd Dixon	35.00	17.50	8.75
☐ Tony Dorsett	300.00	150.00	75.00
☐ Mark Duper	65.00	32.00	16.00
☐ Tony Eason	35.00	17.50	8.75
☐ Carl Ekern	45.00	22.00	11.00
☐ Henry Ellard	50.00	25.00	12.50
☐ John Elway	150.00	75.00	38.00
☐ Phillip Epps	35.00	17.50	8.75
☐ Boomer Esiason	75.00	38.00	19.00
☐ Jim Everett	40.00	20.00	10.00
☐ Brent Fullwood	45.00	22.00	11.00
☐ Mark Gastineau	35.00	17.50	8.75
☐ Willie Gault	125.00	60.00	31.00
☐ Bob Golic	35.00	17.50	8.75
☐ Jerry Gray	35.00	17.50	8.75
☐ Darrell Green	50.00	25.00	12.50
☐ Jacob Green	45.00	22.00	11.00
☐ Roy Green	45.00	22.00	11.00
☐ Steve Grogan	50.00	25.00	12.50
☐ Ronnie Harmon	120.00	60.00	30.00
☐ Bobby Hebert	40.00	20.00	10.00
☐ Alonzo Highsmith	35.00	17.50	8.75
☐ Drew Hill	35.00	17.50	8.75
☐ Earnest Jackson	35.00	17.50	8.75
☐ Rickey Jackson	45.00	22.00	11.00
☐ Vance Johnson	45.00	22.00	11.00
☐ Ed Jones	125.00	60.00	31.00
☐ James Jones	35.00	17.50	8.75
☐ Rod Jones	35.00	17.50	8.75
☐ Rulon Jones	40.00	20.00	10.00
☐ Steve Jordan	45.00	22.00	11.00
☐ E.J. Junior	35.00	17.50	8.75
☐ Jim Kelly	225.00	110.00	55.00
☐ Bill Kenney	35.00	17.50	8.75
☐ Bernie Kosar	35.00	17.50	8.75
☐ Tommy Kramer	40.00	20.00	10.00
☐ Dave Krieg	60.00	30.00	15.00
☐ Tim Krumrie	90.00	45.00	22.00
☐ Mark Lee	45.00	22.00	11.00
☐ Ronnie Lippett	35.00	17.50	8.75
☐ Louis Lipps	40.00	20.00	10.00
☐ Neil Lomax	35.00	17.50	8.75
☐ Chuck Long	35.00	17.50	8.75
☐ Howie Long	100.00	50.00	25.00
☐ Ronnie Lott	140.00	70.00	35.00
☐ Kevin Mack	35.00	17.50	8.75
☐ Mark Malone	80.00	40.00	20.00
☐ Dexter Manley	35.00	17.50	8.75
☐ Dan Marino	275.00	140.00	70.00
☐ Eric Martin	35.00	17.50	8.75
☐ Rueben Mayes	35.00	17.50	8.75
☐ Jim McMahon	35.00	17.50	8.75
☐ Freeman McNeil	35.00	17.50	8.75
☐ Karl Mecklenburg	40.00	20.00	10.00
☐ Mike Merriweather	35.00	17.50	8.75
☐ Stump Mitchell	35.00	17.50	8.75
☐ Art Monk	275.00	140.00	70.00
☐ Joe Montana	250.00	125.00	60.00
☐ Warren Moon	90.00	45.00	22.00
☐ Stanley Morgan	35.00	17.50	8.75
☐ Joe Morris	35.00	17.50	8.75
☐ Darrin Nelson	35.00	17.50	8.75
☐ Ozzie Newsome	50.00	25.00	12.50
☐ Ken O'Brien	35.00	17.50	8.75
☐ John Offerdahl	50.00	25.00	12.50
☐ Christian Okoye	45.00	22.00	11.00
☐ Mike Quick	35.00	17.50	8.75
☐ Jerry Rice	350.00	180.00	90.00
☐ Gerald Riggs	35.00	17.50	8.75
☐ Reggie Rogers	45.00	22.00	11.00
☐ Mike Rozier	35.00	17.50	8.75
☐ Jay Schroeder	45.00	22.00	11.00
☐ Mickey Shuler	45.00	22.00	11.00
☐ Phil Simms	35.00	17.50	8.75
☐ Mike Singletary	50.00	25.00	12.50
☐ Billy Ray Smith	130.00	65.00	32.00
☐ Bruce Smith	175.00	90.00	45.00
☐ J.T. Smith	35.00	17.50	8.75
☐ Troy Stradford	40.00	20.00	10.00
☐ Lawrence Taylor	70.00	35.00	17.50
☐ Vinny Testaverde	65.00	32.00	16.00
☐ Andre Tippett	35.00	17.50	8.75
☐ Anthony Toney	35.00	17.50	8.75
☐ Al Toon	35.00	17.50	8.75
☐ Jack Trudeau	35.00	17.50	8.75
☐ Herschel Walker	30.00	15.00	7.50
☐ Curt Warner	35.00	17.50	8.75
☐ Dave Waymer	35.00	17.50	8.75
☐ Charles White	35.00	17.50	8.75
☐ Danny White	80.00	40.00	20.00
☐ Randy White	175.00	90.00	45.00
☐ Reggie White	90.00	45.00	22.00
☐ James Wilder	35.00	17.50	8.75
☐ Doug Williams	35.00	17.50	8.75
☐ Marc Wilson	160.00	80.00	40.00
☐ Sammy Winder	35.00	17.50	8.75
☐ Kellen Winslow	300.00	150.00	75.00
☐ Rod Woodson	325.00	160.00	80.00
☐ Randy Wright	50.00	25.00	12.50

1989 Kenner Starting Lineup

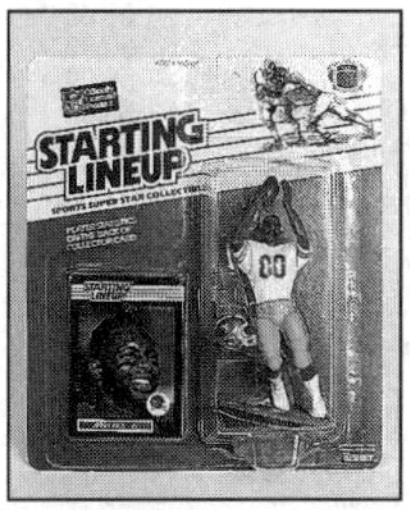

This set of 122 football figurines and collectors cards was issued by Cincinnati-based Kenner Toy Company. The statues feature top NFL stars in action poses and are accompanied by a standard-size card. The front has either a posed or action color shot with a black border. The back has biographical and statistical information and a facsimile signature of the player. The four modes of distribution for the '89 Football set were team cases issued in each teams respective region, All-Star cases issued nationwide, Superbowl Twenty-four, and a 1-800 number. Team cases consisted of 24 pieces and were issued in the regional area for that particular team. The individual player assortmetns within the team cases were not equal and caused certain pieces to be short prints. The Buffalo Bills and Philadelphia Eagles teams were the shortest printed teams. The Bill Bates, Jerome Brown, and Chris Spielman, are the three toughest figures in the set to currently find. This has also been the only time these three players have been issued. There were two nationwide All-Star case assortments, a AFC and a NFC. Each conferences' All-Star cases consisted of 15 different players making up the 24 piece assortments. The All-Star case players were, Marcus Allen, Neal Anderson, Cornelius Bennett, Bubby Brister, Eddie Brown, Tim Brown, Anthony Carter, Roger Craig, Randall Cunningham, John Elway, Boomer Esiason, Jim Everett, Keith Jackson, Neil Lomax, Howie Long, Dan Marino, Freeman McNeil, Joe Montana, Warren Moon, Jerry Rice, Phil Simms, Mike Singletary, John Stephens, Lawrence Taylor, Vinny Testaverde, Andre Tippett, Al Toon, Herschel Walker, Curt Warner, Reggie White. Also, approximately 25,000 of the Jerry Rice piece was given out at Superbowl XXIV. In 1989, a company in conjunction with Kenner set up a 1-800 mail order business that sold all Kenner products made through 1989. The 1989 football sets were made available at approximately $8.00 per piece through this company. Key first pieces of Bill Bates, Jerome Brown, Shane Conlan, Charles Haley, Michael Irvin, James Lofton, Anthony Munoz, Andre Reed, Chris Spielman, Thurman Thomas, and Steve Young combine to make this Kenner's best first piece class. There is one variation in the set. Ken O'Brien's name is misspelled (O'Brian) on the front of the collector card. This error came in team cases only and was corrected early in production. This misspelled name variation is considerably shorter than the corrected version. The error is not part of the complete set price. The values listed below refer to unopened packages. The cards are unnumbered and checklisted below in alphabetical order.

	NRMT	EXC	DIS
COMPLETE SET (122)	5000.00	2500.00	1250.00
☐ Marcus Allen	40.00	20.00	10.00
☐ Neal Anderson	30.00	15.00	7.50
☐ Carl Banks FP	30.00	15.00	7.50
☐ Bill Bates FP	225.00	110.00	55.00
☐ Mark Bavaro	30.00	15.00	7.50
☐ Cornelius Bennett	70.00	35.00	17.50
☐ Duane Bickett	50.00	25.00	12.50
☐ Bennie Blades FP	65.00	32.00	16.00
☐ Bubby Brister FP	30.00	15.00	7.50
☐ Bill Brooks FP	35.00	17.50	8.75
☐ James Brooks	30.00	15.00	7.50
☐ Eddie Brown	30.00	15.00	7.50
☐ Jerome Brown FP	250.00	125.00	60.00

☐ Tim Brown FP	70.00	35.00	17.50
☐ Joey Browner	30.00	15.00	7.50
☐ Kelvin Bryant FP	30.00	15.00	7.50
☐ Jim Burt FP	35.00	17.50	8.75
☐ Keith Byars	30.00	15.00	7.50
☐ Dave Cadigan FP	50.00	25.00	12.50
☐ Anthony Carter	35.00	17.50	8.75
☐ Michael Carter	40.00	20.00	10.00
☐ Chris Chandler FP	30.00	15.00	7.50
☐ Gary Clark	35.00	17.50	8.75
☐ Shane Conlan FP	100.00	50.00	25.00
☐ Jimbo Covert FP	50.00	25.00	12.50
☐ Roger Craig	30.00	15.00	7.50
☐ Randall Cunningham	30.00	15.00	7.50
☐ Richard Dent	30.00	15.00	7.50
☐ Hanford Dixon FP	30.00	15.00	7.50
☐ Chris Doleman FP	30.00	15.00	7.50
☐ Tony Dorsett	120.00	60.00	30.00
☐ Dave Duerson FP	30.00	15.00	7.50
☐ John Elway	90.00	45.00	22.00
☐ Boomer Esiason	35.00	17.50	8.75
☐ Jim Everett	30.00	15.00	7.50
☐ Thomas Everett FP	30.00	15.00	7.50
☐ Sean Farrell FP	30.00	15.00	7.50
☐ Bill Fralic FP	50.00	25.00	12.50
☐ Irving Fryar FP	90.00	45.00	22.00
☐ David Fulcher FP	30.00	15.00	7.50
☐ Ernest Givins FP	30.00	15.00	7.50
☐ Alex Gordon FP	30.00	15.00	7.50
☐ Charles Haley FP	175.00	90.00	45.00
☐ Bobby Hebert	35.00	17.50	8.75
☐ Johnny Hector FP	30.00	15.00	7.50
☐ Drew Hill	50.00	25.00	12.50
☐ Dalton Hilliard FP	30.00	15.00	7.50
☐ Bryan Hinkle FP	50.00	25.00	12.50
☐ Michael Irvin FP	125.00	60.00	31.00
☐ Keith Jackson FP	30.00	15.00	7.50
☐ Garry James FP	30.00	15.00	7.50
☐ Sean Jones FP	50.00	25.00	12.50
☐ Jim Kelly	200.00	100.00	50.00
☐ Joe Kelly FP	30.00	15.00	7.50
☐ Bernie Kosar	30.00	15.00	7.50
☐ Tim Krumrie	30.00	15.00	7.50
☐ Louis Lipps	50.00	25.00	12.50
☐ Eugene Lockhart FP	60.00	30.00	15.00
☐ James Lofton FP	80.00	40.00	20.00
☐ Neil Lomax	30.00	15.00	7.50
☐ Chuck Long	30.00	15.00	7.50
☐ Howie Long	50.00	25.00	12.50
☐ Ronnie Lott	100.00	50.00	25.00
☐ Kevin Mack	30.00	15.00	7.50
☐ Pete Mandley FP	30.00	15.00	7.50
☐ Dexter Manley	30.00	15.00	7.50
☐ Charles Mann FP	50.00	25.00	12.50
☐ Lionel Manuel FP	30.00	15.00	7.50
☐ Dan Marino	240.00	120.00	60.00
☐ Leonard Marshall FP	50.00	25.00	12.50
☐ Eric Martin	30.00	15.00	7.50
☐ Rueben Mayes	30.00	15.00	7.50
☐ Vann McElroy FP	35.00	17.50	8.75
☐ Dennis McKinnon FP	30.00	15.00	7.50
☐ Jim McMahon	30.00	15.00	7.50
☐ Steve McMichael FP	30.00	15.00	7.50
☐ Erik McMillan FP	30.00	15.00	7.50
☐ Freeman McNeil	30.00	15.00	7.50
☐ Keith Millard FP	50.00	25.00	12.50
☐ Chris Miller FP	35.00	17.50	8.75
☐ Frank Minnifield FP	50.00	25.00	12.50
☐ Art Monk	80.00	40.00	20.00
☐ Joe Montana	130.00	65.00	32.00
☐ Warren Moon	50.00	25.00	12.50
☐ Joe Morris	30.00	15.00	7.50
☐ Anthony Munoz FP	175.00	90.00	45.00
☐ Ricky Nattiel FP	30.00	15.00	7.50
☐ Darrin Nelson	30.00	15.00	7.50
☐ Danny Noonan FP	60.00	30.00	15.00
☐ Ken O'Brien Misspelled Name	75.00	38.00	19.00
☐ Ken O'Brien	30.00	15.00	7.50
☐ Steve Pelluer FP	60.00	30.00	15.00
☐ Mike Quick	30.00	15.00	7.50
☐ Andre Reed FP	130.00	65.00	32.00
☐ Jerry Rice	60.00	30.00	15.00
☐ Mike Rozier	30.00	15.00	7.50
☐ Jay Schroeder	30.00	15.00	7.50
☐ John Settle FP	30.00	15.00	7.50
☐ Mickey Shuler	30.00	15.00	7.50
☐ Phil Simms	30.00	15.00	7.50
☐ Mike Singletary	30.00	15.00	7.50
☐ Webster Slaughter FP	30.00	15.00	7.50
☐ Bruce Smith	150.00	75.00	38.00
☐ Chris Spielman FP	200.00	100.00	50.00
☐ John Stephens FP	30.00	15.00	7.50
☐ Kelly Stouffer FP	30.00	15.00	7.50
☐ Pat Swilling FP	50.00	25.00	12.50
☐ Lawrence Taylor	35.00	17.50	8.75
☐ Vinny Testaverde	40.00	20.00	10.00
☐ Thurman Thomas FP	160.00	80.00	40.00
☐ Andre Tippett	30.00	15.00	7.50
☐ Anthony Toney	30.00	15.00	7.50
☐ Al Toon	30.00	15.00	7.50
☐ Garin Veris FP	50.00	25.00	12.50
☐ Herschel Walker	30.00	15.00	7.50
☐ Curt Warner	30.00	15.00	7.50
☐ Reggie White	60.00	30.00	15.00
☐ Doug Williams	30.00	15.00	7.50
☐ John Williams FP	50.00	25.00	12.50
☐ Wade Wilson FP	30.00	15.00	7.50
☐ Ickey Woods FP	30.00	15.00	7.50
☐ Rod Woodson	250.00	125.00	60.00
☐ Steve Young FP	350.00	180.00	90.00

1989 Kenner Football Helmets

In 1989 Kenner was having a problem with many of its 1988 and 1989 Football pieces getting damaged or opened at retail outlets. People were after spare helmets for there collections and this lead to the production of the Football Helmets sets. There were helmets made for each of the AFC and NFC teams. There were four different packages AFC Offensive helmets, AFC Defensive helmets, NFC Offensive helmets and NFC Defensive helmets. The fask mask is different in the offensive and defensive versions. The original retail on this product was commonly $19.99. Many of these sets were later closed out at retail outlets for as little as $1.99. The packages are difficult to find in mint condition.

	NRMT	EXC	DIS
COMPLETE SET (4)	275.00	140.00	70.00
INDIVIDUAL PACKAGES	75.00	38.00	19.00

1990 Kenner Starting Lineup

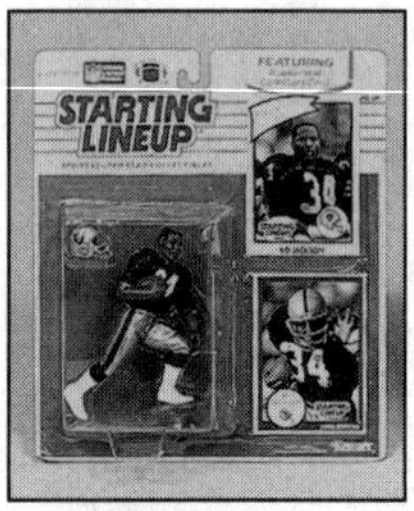

This set of 66 different football figurines and collectors cards was issued by Cincinnati-based Kenner Toy Company. The statues feature top NFL stars in action poses and are accompanied by two standard size cards. Each player has a posed and an action color shot card. The back has biographical and statistical information and a facsimile signature of the player. The values listed below refer to unopened packages. The cards are unnumbered and checklisted below in alphabetical order. Figures were issued in All-Star case assortments and team case (16 pieces) assortments. There were two nationwide All-Star case assortments, an AFC and an NFC. The AFC All-Star case assortment consisted of 10 players comprising of 16 pieces. The breakdown for the AFC case is John Elway (2 per case), Boomer Esiason, Bo Jackson (4), Jim Kelly (2), Bernie Kosar, Dan Marino, Warren Moon, Christian Okoye, Bruce Smith, and Ickey Woods (2). The Marino figure was the 1989 piece packaged in a 1990 box. The NFC All-Star case assortment consisted of 13 players making up the 16 piece case. The breakdown for the NFC case is Troy Aikman, Neal Anderson, Roger Craig, Randall Cunningham (2), Jim Everett, Don Majkowski, Keith Millard, Joe Montana (2), Barry Sanders, Deion Sanders, Mike Singletary, Herschel Walker (2) and Reggie White. The Jim Everett figure was the 1989 piece packaged in a 1990 box. There are eight jersey variations in this set. Neal Anderson, Roger Craig, John Elway, Boomer Esiason, Bernie Kosar, Joe Montana, Mike Singletary, and Reggie White all have a white jersey variation and a team color jersey variation. All the white jersey variations except the Boomer Esiason black jersey variation were distributed through All-Star cases. All the colored jersey variations except the Boomer Esiason white jersey variation were distributed through team cases. With these variations the set is 74 pieces. There is confirmation of a Randall Cunningham white jersey variation existing. The piece is the 1989 Cunningham figure in a 1990 package. Only a few of these have been reported. The set price only includes the road jersey variations.

	NRMT	EXC	DIS
COMPLETE SET (66)	1400.00	700.00	350.00
☐ Troy Aikman FP	50.00	25.00	12.50
☐ Neal Anderson Blue Uniform	14.00	7.00	3.50
☐ Neal Anderson White Uniform	14.00	7.00	3.50
☐ Mark Bavaro	18.00	9.00	4.50
☐ Steve Beuerlein FP	18.00	9.00	4.50
☐ Bubby Brister	14.00	7.00	3.50
☐ James Brooks	14.00	7.00	3.50
☐ Tim Brown	40.00	20.00	10.00
☐ Cris Carter FP	125.00	60.00	31.00
☐ Roger Craig Red Uniform	15.00	7.50	3.70
☐ Roger Craig White Uniform	18.00	9.00	4.50
☐ Randall Cunningham	15.00	7.50	3.70
☐ Hart Lee Dykes FP	14.00	7.00	3.50
☐ John Elway Orange Uniform	50.00	25.00	12.50
☐ John Elway White Uniform	40.00	20.00	10.00
☐ Boomer Esiason Black Uniform	20.00	10.00	5.00
☐ Boomer Esiason White Uniform	20.00	10.00	5.00
☐ Jim Everett	14.00	7.00	3.50
☐ Simon Fletcher FP	14.00	7.00	3.50
☐ Doug Flutie FP	140.00	70.00	35.00
☐ Dennis Gentry FP	14.00	7.00	3.50
☐ Dan Hampton FP	20.00	10.00	5.00
☐ Jim Harbaugh FP	65.00	32.00	16.00
☐ Rodney Holman FP	14.00	7.00	3.50
☐ Bobby Humphrey FP	14.00	7.00	3.50
☐ Michael Irvin	75.00	38.00	19.00
☐ Bo Jackson FP	14.00	7.00	3.50
☐ Keith Jackson	20.00	10.00	5.00
☐ Vance Johnson	14.00	7.00	3.50
☐ Jim Kelly	24.00	12.00	6.00
☐ Bernie Kosar Brown Uniform	18.00	9.00	4.50
☐ Bernie Kosar White Uniform	18.00	9.00	4.50
☐ Louis Lipps	14.00	7.00	3.50
☐ Don Majkowski FP	14.00	7.00	3.50
☐ Charles Mann	14.00	7.00	3.50
☐ Lionel Manuel	14.00	7.00	3.50
☐ Dan Marino	200.00	100.00	50.00
☐ Tim McGee FP	14.00	7.00	3.50
☐ Dave Meggett FP	14.00	7.00	3.50
☐ Mike Merriweather	14.00	7.00	3.50
☐ Eric Metcalf FP	20.00	10.00	5.00
☐ Keith Millard	14.00	7.00	3.50
☐ Joe Montana Red Uniform	50.00	25.00	12.50
☐ Joe Montana White Uniform	50.00	25.00	12.50
☐ Warren Moon	30.00	15.00	7.50
☐ Christian Okoye	14.00	7.00	3.50
☐ Tom Rathman FP	18.00	9.00	4.50
☐ Andre Reed	18.00	9.00	4.50
☐ Gerald Riggs	14.00	7.00	3.50
☐ Mark Rypien FP	15.00	7.50	3.70
☐ Barry Sanders FP	75.00	38.00	19.00
☐ Deion Sanders FP	40.00	20.00	10.00
☐ Ricky Sanders FP	14.00	7.00	3.50
☐ Clyde Simmons FP	18.00	9.00	4.50
☐ Phil Simms	14.00	7.00	3.50
☐ Mike Singletary Blue Uniform	14.00	7.00	3.50
☐ Mike Singletary White Uniform	14.00	7.00	3.50
☐ Webster Slaughter	14.00	7.00	3.50
☐ Bruce Smith	18.00	9.00	4.50
☐ John Stephens	14.00	7.00	3.50
☐ John Taylor FP	25.00	12.50	6.25
☐ Thurman Thomas	35.00	17.50	8.75
☐ Mike Tomczak FP	14.00	7.00	3.50
☐ Greg Townsend FP	15.00	7.50	3.70
☐ Odessa Turner FP	14.00	7.00	3.50
☐ Herschel Walker	14.00	7.00	3.50
☐ Steve Walsh FP	18.00	9.00	4.50
☐ Reggie White Green Uniform	30.00	15.00	7.50
☐ Reggie White White Uniform	30.00	15.00	7.50
☐ Wade Wilson	15.00	7.50	3.70
☐ Ickey Woods	14.00	7.00	3.50
☐ Donnell Woolford FP	15.00	7.50	3.70
☐ Tim Worley FP	14.00	7.00	3.50
☐ Felix Wright FP	14.00	7.00	3.50

1991 Kenner Starting Lineup

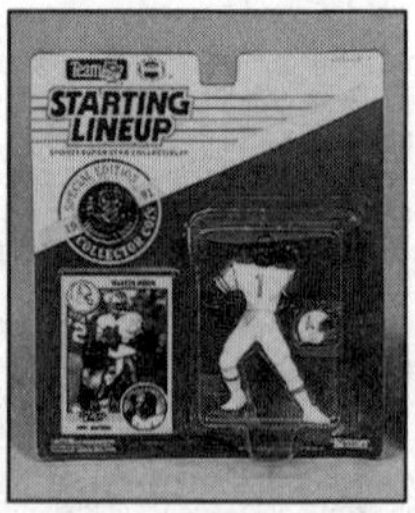

This set of 26 football figurines and collectors cards was issued by Cincinnati-based Kenner Toy Company. The statues feature top NFL stars in action poses and are accompanied by a standard-size card and a coin. The front of the card has either a posed or action color shot. The back has biographical and statistical information and a facsimile signature of the player. The values listed below refer to unopened packages. The cards are unnumbered and checklisted below in alphabetical order. Kenner cut the size of this set considerably compared to previous years. There were only three teams, the Bears, Bengals and Giants to have team cases in 1991. Everything else was released through a twenty-four piece All-Star case assortment. Steel and aluminum versions of the coin that comes with the figures also exists.

	MINT	NRMT	EXC
COMPLETE SET (26)	550.00	400.00	250.00
☐ Troy Aikman	80.00	60.00	36.00
☐ Flipper Anderson FP	14.00	10.50	6.25
☐ Neal Anderson	14.00	10.50	6.25
☐ James Brooks	14.00	10.50	6.25
☐ Eddie Brown	14.00	10.50	6.25
☐ Mark Carrier FP	14.00	10.50	6.25
☐ Boomer Esiason	14.00	10.50	6.25
☐ James Francis FP	18.00	13.50	8.00
☐ Jeff George FP	20.00	15.00	9.00
☐ Rodney Hampton FP	18.00	13.50	8.00
☐ Jim Harbaugh	35.00	26.00	16.00
☐ Jeff Hostetler FP	25.00	19.00	11.00
☐ Bobby Humphrey	14.00	10.50	6.25
☐ Don Majkowski	14.00	10.50	6.25
☐ Dan Marino	110.00	80.00	50.00
☐ Dave Meggett	14.00	10.50	6.25
☐ Joe Montana	35.00	26.00	16.00
☐ Warren Moon	20.00	15.00	9.00
☐ Christian Okoye	14.00	10.50	6.25
☐ Jerry Rice	30.00	22.00	13.50
☐ Andre Rison FP	20.00	15.00	9.00
☐ Barry Sanders	15.00	11.00	6.75
☐ Phil Simms	14.00	10.50	6.25
☐ Emmitt Smith FP	250.00	190.00	110.00
☐ Thurman Thomas	25.00	19.00	11.00
☐ Herschel Walker	14.00	10.50	6.25

1991 Kenner Headline Collection

This set of six football figurines and collectors cards was issued by Cincinnati-based Kenner Toy Company. The statues feature top NFL stars in action poses and are accompanied by a authentic newspaper article and a high gloss, black base used to insert the figurine and article into. The article is framed and describes a memorable moment from the previous season. The pieces came in a 12 piece case assortment. The case breakdown is John Elway (1), Boomer Esiason (2), Dan Marino (1), Joe Montana (4), Jerry Rice (1), and Barry Sanders (3). The values listed below refer to unopened packages. They are unnumbered and checklisted below in alphabetical order.

	MINT	NRMT	EXC
COMPLETE SET (6)	200.00	150.00	90.00
☐ John Elway	40.00	30.00	18.00
☐ Boomer Esiason	20.00	15.00	9.00
☐ Dan Marino	75.00	55.00	34.00
☐ Joe Montana	40.00	30.00	18.00
☐ Jerry Rice	30.00	22.00	13.50
☐ Barry Sanders	30.00	22.00	13.50

1992 Kenner Starting Lineup

This set of 26 football figurines and collectors cards was issued by Cincinnati-based Kenner Toy Company. The statues feature top NFL stars in action poses and are accompanied by a standard size card and a poster. The front of the card has either a posed or action color shot. The back has biographical and statistical information and a facsimile signature of the player. The poster folds out to be 11" X 14". The pieces came in two 16-piece case assortments. The values listed below refer to unopened packages. They are unnumbered and checklisted below in alphabetical order.

	MINT	NRMT	EXC
COMPLETE SET (26)	400.00	300.00	180.00
☐ Troy Aikman	30.00	22.00	13.50
☐ Earnest Byner FP	10.00	7.50	4.50
☐ Randall Cunningham	12.00	9.00	5.50
☐ Rodney Hampton	12.00	9.00	5.50
☐ Bobby Hebert	10.00	7.50	4.50
☐ Jeff Hostetler	12.00	9.00	5.50
☐ Michael Irvin	25.00	19.00	11.00
☐ Bo Jackson	12.00	9.00	5.50
☐ Haywood Jeffires FP	12.00	9.00	5.50
☐ Seth Joyner FP	12.00	9.00	5.50
☐ Jim Kelly	15.00	11.00	6.75
☐ Ronnie Lott	25.00	19.00	11.00
☐ Dan Marino	110.00	80.00	50.00
☐ Joe Montana	40.00	30.00	18.00
☐ Warren Moon	14.00	10.50	6.25
☐ Rob Moore FP	10.00	7.50	4.50

	MINT	NRMT	EXC
☐ Jerry Rice	35.00	26.00	16.00
☐ Andre Rison	12.00	9.00	5.50
☐ Mark Rypien	10.00	7.50	4.50
☐ Barry Sanders	18.00	13.50	8.00
☐ Deion Sanders	18.00	13.50	8.00
☐ Emmitt Smith	50.00	38.00	22.00
☐ Pat Swilling	12.00	9.00	5.50
☐ Derrick Thomas FP	25.00	19.00	11.00
☐ Thurman Thomas	12.00	9.00	5.50
☐ Steve Young	55.00	40.00	25.00

1992 Kenner Headline Collection

his set of six football figurines and collectors cards was issued by Cincinnati-based Kenner Toy Company. The statues feature top NFL stars in action poses and are accompanied by a authentic newspaper article and a high gloss, black base used to insert the figurine and article into. The article is framed and describes a memorable moment from the previous season. The pieces came in a 12-count case assortment. The values listed below refer to unopened packages. They are unnumbered and listed below in alphabetical order.

	MINT	NRMT	EXC
COMPLETE SET (6)	120.00	90.00	55.00
☐ Joe Montana	25.00	19.00	11.00
☐ Warren Moon	16.00	12.00	7.25
☐ Mark Rypien	14.00	10.50	6.25
☐ Barry Sanders	16.00	12.00	7.25
☐ Emmitt Smith	40.00	30.00	18.00
☐ Thurman Thomas	18.00	13.50	8.00

1993 Kenner Starting Lineup

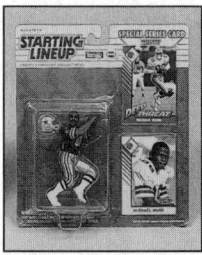

This set of 27 football figurines and collectors cards was issued by Cincinnati-based Kenner Toy Company. The statues feature top NFL stars in action poses and are accompanied by two standard size cards. Each player has a posed and an action color shot card. The back has biographical and statistical information and a facsimile signature of the player. The pieces came in two different 24-count case assortments. The values listed below refer to unopened packages. Since the pieces are unnumbered, we have listed this set in alphabetical order.

	MINT	NRMT	EXC
COMPLETE SET (27)	325.00	240.00	145.00
☐ Troy Aikman	20.00	15.00	9.00
☐ Cornelius Bennett	10.00	7.50	4.50
☐ Randall Cunningham	10.00	7.50	4.50
☐ Chris Doleman	10.00	7.50	4.50
☐ John Elway	25.00	19.00	11.00
☐ Barry Foster FP	10.00	7.50	4.50
☐ Michael Irvin	15.00	11.00	6.75
☐ Rickey Jackson	10.00	7.50	4.50
☐ Cortez Kennedy FP	12.00	9.00	5.50
☐ David Klingler FP	12.00	9.00	5.50
☐ Chip Lohmiller FP	14.00	10.50	6.25
☐ Russell Maryland FP	14.00	10.50	6.25
☐ Anthony Miller FP	14.00	10.50	6.25
☐ Chris Miller	10.00	7.50	4.50
☐ Joe Montana	45.00	34.00	20.00
☐ Warren Moon	20.00	15.00	9.00
Blue Uniform			
☐ Warren Moon	18.00	13.50	8.00
White Uniform			
☐ Andre Reed	10.00	7.50	4.50
☐ Barry Sanders	14.00	10.50	6.25
☐ Deion Sanders	14.00	10.50	6.25
☐ Junior Seau FP	12.00	9.00	5.50
☐ Sterling Sharpe FP	20.00	15.00	9.00
☐ Emmitt Smith	25.00	19.00	11.00
☐ Neil Smith FP	10.00	7.50	4.50
☐ Pete Stoyanovich FP	14.00	10.50	6.25
☐ Ricky Watters FP	20.00	15.00	9.00
☐ Rod Woodson	15.00	11.00	6.75
☐ Steve Young	30.00	22.00	13.50

1994 Kenner Starting Lineup

This set of 32 football figurines and collectors cards was issued by Cincinnati-based Kenner Toy Company. The statues feature top

NFL stars in action poses and are accompanied by a standard-size card. The front of the card has either a posed or action color shot. The back has biographical and statistical information and a facsimile signature of the player. The pieces came in two different 24-count case assortments. The values listed below refer to unopened packages. They are unnumbered and checklisted below in alphabetical order.

	MINT	NRMT	EXC
COMPLETE SET (32)	500.00	375.00	220.00
☐ Troy Aikman	18.00	13.50	8.00
☐ Jerome Bettis FP	25.00	19.00	11.00
☐ Drew Bledsoe FP	75.00	55.00	34.00
☐ Randall Cunningham	10.00	7.50	4.50
☐ Boomer Esiason	10.00	7.50	4.50
☐ Brett Favre FP	125.00	95.00	55.00
☐ Barry Foster	10.00	7.50	4.50
☐ Rodney Hampton	10.00	7.50	4.50
☐ Ronnie Harmon	10.00	7.50	4.50
☐ Garrison Hearst FP	15.00	11.00	6.75
☐ Rocket Ismail FP	15.00	11.00	6.75
☐ Brent Jones FP	14.00	10.50	6.25
☐ Cortez Kennedy	10.00	7.50	4.50
☐ Nick Lowery FP	14.00	10.50	6.25
☐ Dan Marino	35.00	26.00	16.00
☐ Eric Metcalf	14.00	10.50	6.25
☐ Rick Mirer FP	25.00	19.00	11.00
☐ Joe Montana	35.00	26.00	16.00
☐ Ken Norton FP	14.00	10.50	6.25
☐ Jerry Rice	20.00	15.00	9.00
☐ Andre Rison	10.00	7.50	4.50
☐ Barry Sanders	15.00	11.00	6.75
☐ Deion Sanders	14.00	10.50	6.25
☐ Junior Seau	10.00	7.50	4.50
☐ Phil Simms	10.00	7.50	4.50
☐ Emmitt Smith	25.00	19.00	11.00
☐ Lawrence Taylor	14.00	10.50	6.25
☐ Chris Warren	14.00	10.50	6.25
☐ Lorenzo White FP	10.00	7.50	4.50
☐ Reggie White	20.00	15.00	9.00
☐ Rod Woodson	10.00	7.50	4.50
☐ Steve Young	25.00	19.00	11.00

1995 Kenner Starting Lineup

This set of 33 football figurines and collectors cards was issued by Cincinnati-based Kenner Toy Company. The statues feature top NFL stars in action poses and are accompanied by a standard-size card. The front of the card has either a posed or action color shot. The back has biographical and statistical information and a facsimile signature of the player. The pieces came in three different 16-count case assortments. The set is highlighted by the Joe Montana retirement piece. The values listed below refer to unopened packages. They are unnumbered and checklisted below in alphabetical order.

	MINT	NRMT	EXC
COMPLETE SET (33)	400.00	300.00	180.00
☐ Troy Aikman	18.00	13.50	8.00
☐ Jerome Bettis	14.00	10.50	6.25
☐ Drew Bledsoe	25.00	19.00	11.00
☐ Steve Christie FP	12.00	9.00	5.50
☐ Ben Coates FP	18.00	13.50	8.00
☐ Randall Cunningham	10.00	7.50	4.50
☐ Willie Davis FP	10.00	7.50	4.50
☐ Jim Everett	10.00	7.50	4.50
☐ Marshall Faulk FP	25.00	19.00	11.00
☐ Brett Favre	45.00	34.00	20.00
☐ Irving Fryar	15.00	11.00	6.75
☐ Jeff George	10.00	7.50	4.50

	MINT	NRMT	EXC
☐ Stan Humphries FP	10.00	7.50	4.50
☐ Michael Irvin	15.00	11.00	6.75
☐ Johnny Johnson FP	10.00	7.50	4.50
☐ Seth Joyner	10.00	7.50	4.50
☐ Greg Lloyd FP	12.00	9.00	5.50
☐ Dan Marino	35.00	26.00	16.00
☐ Terry McDaniel FP	12.00	9.00	5.50
☐ Natrone Means	25.00	19.00	11.00
☐ Scott Mitchell FP	14.00	10.50	6.25
☐ Joe Montana	60.00	45.00	27.00
☐ Warren Moon	12.00	9.00	5.50
☐ Hardy Nickerson FP	10.00	7.50	4.50
☐ Michael Dean Perry FP	10.00	7.50	4.50
☐ Jerry Rice	18.00	13.50	8.00
☐ Barry Sanders	14.00	10.50	6.25
☐ Deion Sanders	15.00	11.00	6.75
☐ Shannon Sharpe FP	14.00	10.50	6.25
☐ Emmitt Smith	20.00	15.00	9.00
☐ Dan Wilkinson FP	12.00	9.00	5.50
☐ Steve Young	15.00	11.00	6.75
☐ Chris Zorich FP	12.00	9.00	5.50

1996 Kenner Starting Lineup

This set of 38 football figurines and collectors cards was issued by Cincinnati-based Kenner Toy Company. The statues feature top NFL stars in action poses and are accompanied by a standard-size card. The front of the card has either a posed or action color shot. The back has biographical and statistical information and a facsimile signature of the player. The set is highlighted by the first pieces of Mark Brunell, Kerry Collins, Steve McNair and Kordell Stewart. The set is considered complete without the Troy Aikman White Chest Double Star variation, the Troy Aikman Nations Mark and the Brett Favre Shopko. The values listed below refer to unopened packages. They are unnumbered and checklisted below in alphabetical order.

	MINT	NRMT	EXC
COMPLETE SET (38)	400.00	180.00	50.00
☐ Troy Aikman	15.00	6.75	1.85
☐ Troy Aikman	250.00	110.00	31.00
White Chest Double Star			
☐ Troy Aikman	25.00	11.00	3.10
Nations Mark			
☐ Terry Allen FP	18.00	8.00	2.20
☐ Steve Beuerlein	15.00	6.75	1.85
☐ Jeff Blake FP	15.00	6.75	1.85
☐ Drew Bledsoe	18.00	8.00	2.20
☐ Steve Bono FP	10.00	4.50	1.25
☐ Kyle Brady FP	10.00	4.50	1.25
☐ Robert Brooks FP	18.00	8.00	2.20
☐ Dave Brown FP	10.00	4.50	1.25
☐ Issac Bruce FP	14.00	6.25	1.75
☐ Mark Brunell FP	35.00	16.00	4.40

	MINT	NRMT	EXC
☐ Mark Carrier FP	10.00	4.50	1.25
☐ Cris Carter	12.00	5.50	1.50
☐ Kerry Collins FP	40.00	18.00	5.00
☐ John Elway	20.00	9.00	2.50
☐ Marshall Faulk	15.00	6.75	1.85
☐ Brett Favre	40.00	18.00	5.00
Shopko			
☐ Joey Galloway FP	15.00	6.75	1.85
☐ Kevin Greene FP	12.00	5.50	1.50
☐ Dan Marino	20.00	9.00	2.50
☐ Steve McNair FP	20.00	9.00	2.50
☐ Eric Metcalf	12.00	5.50	1.50
☐ Jay Novacek FP	12.00	5.50	1.50
☐ Bryce Paup FP	12.00	5.50	1.50
☐ Carl Pickens FP	12.00	5.50	1.50
☐ Frank Reich FP	12.00	5.50	1.50
☐ Errict Rhett FP	12.00	5.50	1.50
☐ Jerry Rice	15.00	6.75	1.85
☐ Rashaan Salaam FP	15.00	6.75	1.85
☐ Barry Sanders	15.00	6.75	1.85
☐ Deion Sanders	14.00	6.25	1.75
☐ Junior Seau	12.00	5.50	1.50
☐ Emmitt Smith	35.00	16.00	4.40
☐ Chris Spielman	12.00	5.50	1.50
☐ Kordell Stewart FP	50.00	22.00	6.25
☐ Ricky Watters	14.00	6.25	1.75
☐ Reggie White	18.00	8.00	2.20
☐ Harvey Williams FP	12.00	5.50	1.50
☐ Steve Young	14.00	6.25	1.75

VINTAGE AUTOGRAPH PRICE GUIDE

( ) H.O.F. Induction Year
d. Deceased
Campanella- Pre-Accident

FOOTBALL

Adderley, Herb-(1980)
3 X 5 — 5.00
8 X 10 Photo — 15.00
Single Signed Ball — 75.00

Alworth, Lance-(1978)
3 X 5 — 8.00
8 X 10 Photo — 20.00
Single Signed Ball — 100.00

Atkins, Doug-(1982)
3 X 5 — 5.00
8 X 10 Photo — 15.00
Single Signed Ball — 125.00

Morris "Red" Badgro [signature]

Badgro, Red-(1981)
3 X 5 — 5.00
8 X 10 Photo — 15.00
Single Signed Ball — 75.00

Barney, Lem-(1992)
3 X 5 — 5.00
8 X 10 Photo — 15.00
Single Signed Ball — 75.00

Battles, Cliff-(1968) d. 1981
3 X 5 — 50.00
8 X 10 Photo — 200.00
Single Signed Ball — 350.00

Baugh, Sammy-(1963)
3 X 5 — 25.00
8 X 10 Photo — 75.00
Single Signed Ball — 300.00

Bednarik, Chuck-(1967)
3 X 5 — 10.00
8 X 10 Photo — 20.00
Single Signed Ball — 125.00

Bell, Bobby-(1983)
3 X 5 — 5.00
8 X 10 Photo — 15.00
Single Signed Ball — 75.00

Berry, Raymond-(1973)
3 X 5 — 5.00
8 X 10 Photo — 15.00
Single Signed Ball — 100.00

Biletnikoff, Fred-(1988)
3 X 5 — 5.00
8 X 10 Photo — 15.00
Single Signed Ball — 100.00

Blanda, George-(1981)
3 X 5 — 5.00
8 X 10 Photo — 15.00
Single Signed Ball — 125.00

Blount, Mel-(1989)
3 X 5 — 5.00
8 X 10 Photo — 15.00
Single Signed Ball — 75.00

Bradshaw, Terry-(1989)
3 X 5 — 10.00
8 X 10 Photo — 30.00
Single Signed Ball — 150.00

Brown, Jim-(1971)
3 X 5 — 10.00
8 X 10 Photo — 30.00
Single Signed Ball — 150.00

Brown, Paul-(1967) d. 1991
3 X 5 — 15.00
8 X 10 Photo — 30.00
Single Signed Ball — 350.00

Brown, Roosevelt-(1975)
3 X 5 — 5.00
8 X 10 Photo — 15.00
Single Signed Ball — 100.00

Brown, Willie-(1984)
3 X 5 — 5.00
8 X 10 Photo — 15.00
Single Signed Ball — 75.00

Buchanan, Buck-(1990) d. 1992
3 X 5 — 15.00
8 X 10 Photo — 50.00
Single Signed Ball — 250.00

Dick Butkus [signature]

Butkus, Dick-(1979)
3 X 5 — 10.00
8 X 10 Photo — 20.00
Single Signed Ball — 125.00

Campbell, Earl-(1991)
3 X 5 — 5.00
8 X 10 Photo — 15.00
Single Signed Ball — 125.00

Christiansen, Jack-(1970) d. 1986
3 X 5 — 50.00
8 X 10 Photo — 150.00

Clark, Dutch-(1963) d. 1978
3 X 5 — 50.00
8 X 10 Photo — 175.00

Connor, George-(1975)
3 X 5 — 5.00
8 X 10 Photo — 15.00
Single Signed Ball — 75.00

Creekmur, Lou-(1996)
3 X 5 — 5.00
8 X 10 Photo — 15.00
Single Signed Ball — 75.00

Csonka, Larry-(1987)
3 X 5 — 8.00
8 X 10 Photo — 20.00
Single Signed Ball — 125.00

Davis, Al-(1992)
3 X 5 — 10.00
8 X 10 Photo — 20.00
Single Signed Ball — 100.00

Davis, Willie-(1981)
3 X 5 — 5.00
8 X 10 Photo — 15.00
Single Signed Ball — 75.00

Dawson, Len-(1987)
3 X 5 — 8.00
8 X 10 Photo — 20.00
Single Signed Ball — 125.00

Dierdorf, Dan-(1996)
3 X 5 — 5.00
8 X 10 Photo — 15.00
Single Signed Ball — 75.00

Ditka, Mike-(1988)
3 X 5 — 8.00
8 X 10 Photo — 20.00
Single Signed Ball — 125.00

Donovan, Art-(1968)
3 X 5 — 8.00
8 X 10 Photo — 15.00
Single Signed Ball — 125.00

Dorsett, Tony-(1994)
3 X 5 — 8.00
8 X 10 Photo — 20.00
Single Signed Ball — 100.00

Dudley, Bill-(1966)
3 X 5 — 5.00
8 X 10 Photo — 15.00
Single Signed Ball — 75.00

Edwards, Turk-(1969) d. 1973
3 X 5 — 125.00
8 X 10 Photo — 300.00

Fears, Tom-(1970)
3 X 5 — 5.00
8 X 10 Photo — 15.00
Single Signed Ball — 100.00

Flaherty, Ray-(1976) d. 1995
3 X 5 — 20.00
8 X 10 Photo — 50.00
Single Signed Ball — 200.00

Ford, Len-(1976) d. 1972
3 X 5 — 200.00
8 X 10 Photo — 500.00

Fortmann, Dan-(1965) d. 1995
3 X 5 — 30.00
8 X 10 Photo — 60.00
Single Signed Ball — 200.00

Fouts, Dan-(1993)
3 X 5 — 8.00
8 X 10 Photo — 20.00
Single Signed Ball — 100.00

Gatski, Frank-(1985)
3 X 5 — 5.00
8 X 10 Photo — 15.00
Single Signed Ball — 75.00

George, Bill-(1974) d. 1982
3 X 5 — 75.00
8 X 10 Photo — 150.00

Gibbs, Joe-(1996)
3 X 5 — 5.00
8 X 10 Photo — 15.00
Single Signed Ball — 75.00

Gifford, Frank-(1977)
3 X 5 — 8.00
8 X 10 Photo — 20.00
Single Signed Ball — 125.00

Gillman, Sid-(1983)
3 X 5 — 5.00
8 X 10 Photo — 15.00
Single Signed Ball — 75.00

Graham, Otto-(1965)
3 X 5 — 8.00
8 X 10 Photo — 20.00
Single Signed Ball — 150.00

Grange, Red-(1963) d. 1991
3 X 5 — 60.00
8 X 10 Photo — 150.00
Single Signed Ball — 750.00

Greene, Joe-(1987)
3 X 5 — 10.00
8 X 10 Photo — 25.00
Single Signed Ball — 125.00

Gregg, Forrest-(1977)
3 X 5 — 5.00
8 X 10 Photo — 15.00
Single Signed Ball — 75.00

Griese, Bob-(1990)
3 X 5 — 10.00
8 X 10 Photo — 25.00
Single Signed Ball — 125.00

Groza, Lou-(1974)
3 X 5 — 8.00
8 X 10 Photo — 20.00
Single Signed Ball — 100.00

Halas, George-(1963) d. 1983
3 X 5 — 60.00
8 X 10 Photo — 125.00
Single Signed Ball — 750.00

Ham, Jack-(1988)
3 X 5 — 5.00
8 X 10 Photo — 15.00
Single Signed Ball — 75.00

Hannah, John-(1991)
3 X 5 — 5.00
8 X 10 Photo — 15.00
Single Signed Ball — 75.00

Harris, Franco-(1990)
3 X 5 — 8.00
8 X 10 Photo — 20.00
Single Signed Ball — 125.00

Hein, Mel-(1963) d. 1992
3 X 5 — 20.00
8 X 10 Photo — 75.00
Single Signed Ball — 200.00

Hendricks, Ted-(1990)
3 X 5 — 5.00
8 X 10 Photo — 15.00
Single Signed Ball — 75.00

Hirsch, Elroy "Crazylegs"-(1968)
3 X 5 — 8.00
8 X 10 Photo — 20.00
Single Signed Ball — 125.00

Hornung, Paul-(1986)
3 X 5 — 10.00
8 X 10 Photo — 25.00
Single Signed Ball — 100.00

Houston, Ken-(1986)
3 X 5 — 5.00
8 X 10 Photo — 15.00
Single Signed Ball — 75.00

Hubbard, Cal-(1963) d. 1977
3 X 5 — 50.00
8 X 10 Photo — 200.00

Huff, Sam-(1982)
3 X 5 — 8.00
8 X 10 Photo — 20.00
Single Signed Ball — 100.00

Hutson, Don-(1963) d. 1997
3 X 5 — 12.00
8 X 10 Photo — 50.00
Single Signed Ball — 150.00

Johnson, Jimmy (DB)-(1994)
3 X 5 — 5.00
8 X 10 Photo — 15.00
Single Signed Ball — 75.00

Johnson, John Henry-(1987)
3 X 5 — 5.00
8 X 10 Photo — 15.00
Single Signed Ball — 75.00

Joiner, Charlie-(1996)
3 X 5 — 5.00
8 X 10 Photo — 15.00
Single Signed Ball — 75.00

Jones, Deacon-(1980)
3 X 5 — 5.00
8 X 10 Photo — 15.00
Single Signed Ball — 100.00

Jones, Stan-(1991)
3 X 5 — 5.00
8 X 10 Photo — 15.00
Single Signed Ball — 75.00

Jordan, Henry-(1995) d. 1977
3 X 5 — 200.00
8 X 10 Photo — 400.00

Jurgensen, Sonny-(1983)
3 X 5 — 8.00
8 X 10 Photo — 20.00
Single Signed Ball — 100.00

Kelly, Leroy-(1994)
3 X 5 — 5.00
8 X 10 Photo — 15.00
Single Signed Ball — 75.00

Lambert, Jack-(1990)
3 X 5 — 10.00
8 X 10 Photo — 25.00
Single Signed Ball — 125.00

Landry, Tom-(1990)
3 X 5 — 5.00
8 X 10 Photo — 15.00
Single Signed Ball — 100.00

Lane, Dick "Night Train"-(1974)
3 X 5 — 8.00
8 X 10 Photo — 20.00
Single Signed Ball — 100.00

Langer, Jim-(1987)
3 X 5 — 5.00
8 X 10 Photo — 15.00
Single Signed Ball — 75.00

Willie Lanier [signature]

Lanier, Willie-(1986)
3 X 5 — 5.00
8 X 10 Photo — 15.00
Single Signed Ball — 75.00

Largent, Steve-(1995)
3 X 5 — 8.00
8 X 10 Photo — 20.00
Single Signed Ball — 125.00

Lary, Yale-(1979)
3 X 5 — 5.00
8 X 10 Photo — 15.00
Single Signed Ball — 75.00

Lavelli, Dante-(1975)
3 X 5 — 5.00
8 X 10 Photo — 15.00
Single Signed Ball — 75.00

Layne, Bobby-(1967) d. 1986
3 X 5 — 60.00
8 X 10 Photo — 150.00
Single Signed Ball — 750.00

Lilly, Bob-(1980)
3 X 5 — 8.00
8 X 10 Photo — 20.00
Single Signed Ball — 100.00

Little, Larry-(1993)
3 X 5 — 5.00
8 X 10 Photo — 15.00
Single Signed Ball — 75.00

Lombardi, Vince-(1971) d. 1970
3 X 5 — 175.00
8 X 10 Photo — 400.00

Sid Luckman [signature]

Luckman, Sid-(1965)
3 X 5 — 8.00
8 X 10 Photo — 20.00
Single Signed Ball — 125.00

Mackey, John-(1992)
3 X 5 — 5.00
8 X 10 Photo — 15.00
Single Signed Ball — 75.00

Marchetti, Gino-(1972)
3 X 5 — 5.00
8 X 10 Photo — 15.00
Single Signed Ball — 75.00

Matson, Ollie-(1972)
3 X 5 — 8.00
8 X 10 Photo — 20.00
Single Signed Ball — 125.00

Maynard, Don-(1987)
3 X 5 — 5.00
8 X 10 Photo — 15.00
Single Signed Ball — 75.00

McAfee, George-(1966)
3 X 5 — 5.00
8 X 10 Photo — 15.00
Single Signed Ball — 75.00

McCormack, Mike-(1984)
3 X 5 — 5.00
8 X 10 Photo — 15.00
Single Signed Ball — 75.00

McElhenny, Hugh-(1970)
3 X 5 — 8.00
8 X 10 Photo — 20.00
Single Signed Ball — 125.00

Mitchell, Bobby-(1983)
3 X 5 — 5.00
8 X 10 Photo — 15.00
Single Signed Ball — 75.00

Mix, Ron-(1979)
3 X 5 — 5.00
8 X 10 Photo — 15.00
Single Signed Ball — 75.00

Moore, Lenny-(1975)
3 X 5 — 8.00
8 X 10 Photo — 20.00
Single Signed Ball — 100.00

Motley, Marion-(1968)
3 X 5 — 8.00
8 X 10 Photo — 20.00
Single Signed Ball — 100.00

Musso, George-(1982)
3 X 5 — 8.00
8 X 10 Photo — 20.00
Single Signed Ball — 100.00

Bronko Nagurski [signature]

Nagurski, Bronko-(1963) d. 1990
3 X 5 — 50.00
8 X 10 Photo — 150.00
Single Signed Ball — 400.00

Namath, Joe-(1985)
3 X 5 — 20.00
8 X 10 Photo — 50.00
Single Signed Ball — 175.00

Ernie Nevers [signature]

Nevers, Ernie-(1963) d. 1976
3 X 5 — 60.00
8 X 10 Photo — 150.00
Single Signed Ball — 500.00

Nitschke, Ray-(1978)
3 X 5 — 5.00
8 X 10 Photo — 15.00
Single Signed Ball — 75.00

Noll, Chuck-(1993)
3 X 5 — 5.00
8 X 10 Photo — 15.00
Single Signed Ball — 100.00

Nomellini, Leo-(1969)
3 X 5 — 5.00
8 X 10 Photo — 15.00
Single Signed Ball — 100.00

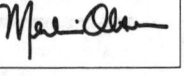
Merlin Olsen [signature]

Olsen, Merlin-(1982)
3 X 5 — 8.00
8 X 10 Photo — 20.00
Single Signed Ball — 100.00

Otto, Jim-(1980)
3 X 5 — 5.00
8 X 10 Photo — 15.00
Single Signed Ball — 100.00

Page, Alan-(1988)
3 X 5 — 5.00
8 X 10 Photo — 15.00
Single Signed Ball — 100.00

Parker, Clarence "Ace"-(1972)
3 X 5 — 5.00
8 X 10 Photo — 15.00
Single Signed Ball — 150.00

Parker, Jim-(1973)
3 X 5 — 5.00
8 X 10 Photo — 15.00
Single Signed Ball — 75.00

Payton, Walter-(1993)
3 X 5 — 10.00
8 X 10 Photo — 30.00
Single Signed Ball — 150.00

Perry, Joe-(1969)
3 X 5 — 5.00
8 X 10 Photo — 15.00
Single Signed Ball — 75.00

Pihos, Pete-(1970)
3 X 5 — 5.00
8 X 10 Photo — 15.00
Single Signed Ball — 75.00

Renfro, Mel-(1996)
3 X 5 — 5.00
8 X 10 Photo — 15.00
Single Signed Ball — 75.00

Riggins, John-(1992)
3 X 5 — 15.00
8 X 10 Photo — 40.00
Single Signed Ball — 125.00

Ringo, Jim-(1981)
3 X 5 — 5.00
8 X 10 Photo — 15.00
Single Signed Ball — 100.00

Robustelli, Andy-(1971)
3 X 5 — 5.00
8 X 10 Photo — 15.00
Single Signed Ball — 75.00

Rockne, Knute- d. 1931
3 X 5 — 400.00
8 X 10 Photo — 1500.00

Rooney, Art-(1964) d. 1988
3 X 5 — 25.00
8 X 10 Photo — 75.00

Rozelle, Pete-(1985) d. 1996
3 X 5 — 10.00
8 X 10 Photo — 20.00
Single Signed Ball — 175.00

Sayers, Gale-(1977)
3 X 5 — 8.00
8 X 10 Photo — 20.00
Single Signed Ball — 125.00

Schmidt, Joe-(1973)
3 X 5 — 5.00
8 X 10 Photo — 15.00
Single Signed Ball — 75.00

Selmon, Lee Roy-(1995)

3 X 5	5.00
8 X 10 Photo	15.00
Single Signed Ball	75.00

Shell, Art-(1989)

3 X 5	8.00
8 X 10 Photo	20.00
Single Signed Ball	100.00

Simpson, O.J.-(1985)

3 X 5	15.00
8 X 10 Photo	40.00
Single Signed Ball	175.00

Smith, Jackie-(1994)

3 X 5	5.00
8 X 10 Photo	15.00
Single Signed Ball	75.00

St. Clair, Bob-(1990)

3 X 5	5.00
8 X 10 Photo	15.00
Single Signed Ball	75.00

(Bart Starr signature)

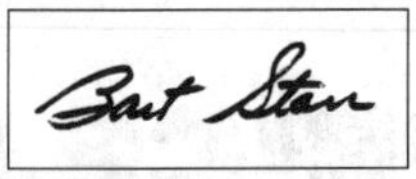

Starr, Bart-(1977)

3 X 5	8.00
8 X 10 Photo	20.00
Single Signed Ball	125.00

Staubach, Roger-(1985)

3 X 5	8.00
8 X 10 Photo	20.00
Single Signed Ball	125.00

Stautner, Ernie-(1969)

3 X 5	8.00
8 X 10 Photo	20.00
Single Signed Ball	100.00

Stenerud, Jan-(1991)

3 X 5	5.00
8 X 10 Photo	15.00
Single Signed Ball	75.00

Strong, Ken-(1967) d. 1979

3 X 5	50.00
8 X 10 Photo	150.00

Tarkenton, Fran-(1986)

3 X 5	8.00
8 X 10 Photo	20.00
Single Signed Ball	125.00

Taylor, Charley-(1984)

3 X 5	8.00
8 X 10 Photo	20.00
Single Signed Ball	100.00

Taylor, Jim-(1976)

3 X 5	8.00
8 X 10 Photo	20.00
Single Signed Ball	100.00

Thorpe, Jim-(1963) d. 1953

3 X 5	400.00
8 X 10 Photo	1250.00

Tittle, Y.A.-(1971)

3 X 5	8.00
8 X 10 Photo	20.00
Single Signed Ball	125.00

Trafton, George-(1964) d. 1971

3 X 5	75.00
8 X 10 Photo	300.00

Trippi, Charley-(1968)

3 X 5	8.00
8 X 10 Photo	20.00
Single Signed Ball	100.00

Tunnell, Emlen-(1967) d. 1975

3 X 5	50.00
8 X 10 Photo	150.00

Turner, Clyde "Bulldog"-(1966)

3 X 5	8.00
8 X 10 Photo	20.00

Unitas, Johnny-(1979)

3 X 5	10.00
8 X 10 Photo	25.00
Single Signed Ball	125.00

Upshaw, Gene-(1987)

3 X 5	5.00
8 X 10 Photo	15.00
Single Signed Ball	75.00

Van Brocklin, Norm-(1971) d. 1983

3 X 5	50.00
8 X 10 Photo	125.00
Single Signed Ball	400.00

Van Buren, Steve-(1965)

3 X 5	8.00
8 X 10 Photo	20.00
Single Signed Ball	125.00

Walker, Doak-(1986)

3 X 5	8.00
8 X 10 Photo	20.00
Single Signed Ball	100.00

Walsh, Bill-(1993)

3 X 5	5.00
8 X 10 Photo	15.00
Single Signed Ball	75.00

Warfield, Paul-(1983)

3 X 5	5.00
8 X 10 Photo	15.00
Single Signed Ball	75.00

Waterfield, Bob-(1965) d. 1983

3 X 5	50.00
8 X 10 Photo	125.00
Single Signed Ball	350.00

Weinmeister, Arnie-(1984)

3 X 5	5.00
8 X 10 Photo	15.00
Single Signed Ball	75.00

White, Randy-(1994)

3 X 5	5.00
8 X 10 Photo	15.00
Single Signed Ball	75.00

Willis, Bill-(1977)

3 X 5	5.00
8 X 10 Photo	15.00
Single Signed Ball	75.00

Wilson, Larry-(1978)

3 X 5	8.00
8 X 10 Photo	15.00
Single Signed Ball	100.00

Winslow, Kellen-(1995)

3 X 5	5.00
8 X 10 Photo	15.00
Single Signed Ball	75.00

Wojciechowicz, Alex-(1968) d. 1992

3 X 5	15.00
8 X 10 Photo	40.00

Wood, Willie-(1989)

3 X 5	5.00
8 X 10 Photo	15.00
Single Signed Ball	75.00

Modern Autograph Price Guide

Daryl Johnston replica mini

Jerry Rice authentic jersey

Junior Seau authentic mini

Player	FB Card	8X10 Photo	Game Ball	Replica Mini	Authen. Mini	Replica Jersey	Authen. Jersey
Karim Abdul-Jabbar	8.00	18.00	100.00	60.00	75.00	85.00	150.00
Troy Aikman	25.00	40.00	200.00	125.00	150.00	175.00	280.00
Marcus Allen	12.00	22.00	120.00	70.00	85.00	100.00	170.00
Terry Allen	7.00	16.00	90.00	55.00	70.00	80.00	140.00
Edgar Bennett	8.00	18.00	100.00	60.00	75.00	85.00	150.00
Jerome Bettis	10.00	20.00	110.00	65.00	80.00	90.00	160.00
Jeff Blake	10.00	20.00	110.00	65.00	80.00	90.00	160.00
Drew Bledsoe	18.00	30.00	165.00	100.00	120.00	140.00	230.00
Robert Brooks	7.00	16.00	90.00	55.00	70.00	80.00	140.00
Tim Brown	10.00	20.00	110.00	65.00	80.00	90.00	160.00
Isaac Bruce	8.00	18.00	100.00	60.00	75.00	85.00	150.00
Mark Brunell	10.00	20.00	110.00	65.00	80.00	90.00	160.00
Cris Carter	10.00	20.00	110.00	65.00	80.00	90.00	160.00
Ben Coates	7.00	16.00	90.00	55.00	70.00	80.00	140.00
Kerry Collins	12.00	22.00	120.00	70.00	85.00	100.00	170.00
Roger Craig	7.00	16.00	90.00	55.00	70.00	80.00	140.00
Randall Cunningham	7.00	16.00	90.00	55.00	70.00	80.00	140.00
Terrell Davis	10.00	20.00	110.00	65.00	80.00	90.00	160.00
Eric Dickerson	8.00	18.00	100.00	60.00	75.00	85.00	150.00
John Elway	18.00	30.00	165.00	100.00	120.00	140.00	230.00
Marshall Faulk	10.00	20.00	110.00	65.00	80.00	90.00	160.00
Brett Favre	25.00	40.00	200.00	125.00	150.00	175.00	280.00
Antonio Freeman	7.00	16.00	90.00	55.00	70.00	80.00	140.00
Gus Frerotte	7.00	16.00	90.00	55.00	70.00	80.00	140.00
Joey Galloway	8.00	18.00	100.00	60.00	75.00	85.00	150.00
Eddie George	10.00	20.00	110.00	65.00	80.00	90.00	160.00
Terry Glenn	8.00	18.00	100.00	60.00	75.00	85.00	150.00
Darrell Green	7.00	16.00	90.00	55.00	70.00	80.00	140.00
Kevin Greene	7.00	16.00	90.00	55.00	70.00	80.00	140.00
Rodney Hampton	7.00	16.00	90.00	55.00	70.00	80.00	140.00
Jim Harbaugh	8.00	18.00	100.00	60.00	75.00	85.00	150.00
Marvin Harrison	7.00	16.00	90.00	55.00	70.00	80.00	140.00
Jeff Hostetler	7.00	16.00	90.00	55.00	70.00	80.00	140.00
Stan Humphries	8.00	18.00	100.00	60.00	75.00	85.00	150.00
Michael Irvin	8.00	18.00	100.00	60.00	75.00	85.00	150.00
Rocket Ismail	7.00	16.00	90.00	55.00	70.00	80.00	140.00
Bo Jackson	10.00	20.00	110.00	65.00	80.00	90.00	160.00
Keyshawn Johnson	10.00	20.00	110.00	65.00	80.00	90.00	160.00
Daryl Johnston	8.00	18.00	100.00	60.00	75.00	85.00	150.00
Jim Kelly	12.00	22.00	120.00	70.00	85.00	100.00	170.00
Eddie Kennison	7.00	16.00	90.00	55.00	70.00	80.00	140.00
Bernie Kosar	8.00	18.00	100.00	60.00	75.00	85.00	150.00

Player	FB Card	8X10 Photo	Game Ball	Replica Mini	Authen. Mini	Replica Jersey	Authen. Jersey
Greg Lloyd	8.00	18.00	100.00	60.00	75.00	85.00	150.00
Howie Long	10.00	20.00	110.00	65.00	80.00	90.00	160.00
Ronnie Lott	10.00	20.00	110.00	65.00	80.00	90.00	160.00
Dan Marino	25.00	40.00	200.00	125.00	150.00	175.00	280.00
Curtis Martin	8.00	18.00	100.00	60.00	75.00	85.00	150.00
Steve McNair	8.00	18.00	100.00	60.00	75.00	85.00	150.00
Natrone Means	10.00	20.00	110.00	65.00	80.00	90.00	160.00
Art Monk	12.00	22.00	120.00	70.00	85.00	100.00	170.00
Joe Montana	20.00	32.00	180.00	110.00	130.00	150.00	250.00
Warren Moon	12.00	22.00	120.00	70.00	85.00	100.00	170.00
Herman Moore	10.00	20.00	110.00	65.00	80.00	90.00	160.00
Ken Norton Jr.	7.00	16.00	90.00	55.00	70.00	80.00	140.00
Neil O'Donnell	7.00	16.00	90.00	55.00	70.00	80.00	140.00
Terrell Owens	7.00	16.00	90.00	55.00	70.00	80.00	140.00
Carl Pickens	8.00	18.00	100.00	60.00	75.00	85.00	150.00
Andre Reed	7.00	16.00	90.00	55.00	70.00	80.00	140.00
Errict Rhett	7.00	16.00	90.00	55.00	70.00	80.00	140.00
Jerry Rice	20.00	32.00	180.00	110.00	130.00	150.00	250.00
Rashaan Salaam	7.00	16.00	90.00	55.00	70.00	80.00	140.00
Barry Sanders	18.00	30.00	165.00	100.00	120.00	140.00	230.00
Deion Sanders	16.00	28.00	150.00	90.00	110.00	125.00	200.00
Darnay Scott	7.00	16.00	90.00	55.00	70.00	80.00	140.00
Junior Seau	10.00	20.00	110.00	65.00	80.00	90.00	160.00
Shannon Sharpe	8.00	18.00	100.00	60.00	75.00	85.00	150.00
Sterling Sharpe	12.00	22.00	120.00	70.00	85.00	100.00	170.00
Phil Simms	12.00	22.00	120.00	70.00	85.00	100.00	170.00
Mike Singletary	8.00	18.00	100.00	60.00	75.00	85.00	150.00
Bruce Smith	10.00	20.00	110.00	65.00	80.00	90.00	160.00
Emmitt Smith	25.00	40.00	200.00	125.00	150.00	175.00	280.00
Neil Smith	7.00	16.00	90.00	55.00	70.00	80.00	140.00
Kordell Stewart	10.00	20.00	110.00	65.00	80.00	90.00	160.00
Lawrence Taylor	12.00	22.00	120.00	70.00	85.00	100.00	170.00
Vinny Testaverde	7.00	16.00	90.00	55.00	70.00	80.00	140.00
Derrick Thomas	7.00	16.00	90.00	55.00	70.00	80.00	140.00
Thurman Thomas	10.00	20.00	110.00	65.00	80.00	90.00	160.00
Herschel Walker	7.00	16.00	90.00	55.00	70.00	80.00	140.00
Chris Warren	8.00	18.00	100.00	60.00	75.00	85.00	150.00
Ricky Watters	10.00	20.00	110.00	65.00	80.00	90.00	160.00
Michael Westbrook	7.00	16.00	90.00	55.00	70.00	80.00	140.00
Reggie White	16.00	28.00	150.00	90.00	110.00	125.00	200.00
Rod Woodson	12.00	22.00	120.00	70.00	85.00	100.00	170.00
Steve Young	18.00	30.00	165.00	100.00	120.00	140.00	230.00

UDA PRICE GUIDE

UDA Troy Aikman

Jersey swatch w/SB patches/308	400.00
Cowboys Mini Helmet (authentic)	200.00
Official Super Bowl 27 Game Football/500	275.00
SI Cover 'Ride 'Em Cowboy' 2/8/93 Framed	120.00
8x10 Photo with Personalized Letter/500	120.00
8x10 Photo Charging w/letter/1997	110.00
Official NFL Game Football	250.00
16x20 Action Photo Framed/308	250.00
8x10 Photo SB 27/250	90.00
8x10 Photo 3X SB Champ/250	90.00
Mini Football	130.00
Cowboys Mini Helmet (replica)	150.00

UDA Michael Irvin

'95 SP All Pro #AP18 Double Die-Cut/500	50.00
Official NFL Game Football	150.00
Cowboys Mini Helmet (authentic)	120.00
8x10 Photo TD Celebration Unframed	50.00
Leather F1145 Football	110.00
Cowboys Mini Helmet (replica)	95.00
Mini Football	65.00

UDA Dan Marino Footballs

Official NFL Game Football	300.00
'343' Official NFL Game Football/343	350.00
Dan the Man Record Breaker Football/343	325.00
Dan the Man Record Breaker Mini Football/343	150.00
Leather F1145 Football	200.00
Mini Football	140.00

UDA Dan Marino Helmets

Official Dolphins Helmet	550.00
Dolphins Mini Helmet (authentic)	200.00
Dan the Man Mini Helmet (authentic)/343	225.00
Dan the Man Proline Helmet/343	550.00
Shadow box w/mini helmet and 5x7/500	350.00
Full Size Replica Dolphins Helmet	275.00
Dolphins Mini Helmet (replica)	150.00

UDA Dan Marino Other

1995 UD 2-Card set #103/250	100.00
Dolphins Aqua Jersey Unframed	325.00

Football Heroes 10-card set framed/2800	200.00
Dolphins White Jersey Unframed	325.00
16x20 Photo 40M Framed	275.00
16x20 Photo 40M Unframed	175.00
SI Cover 'Rookie on the Rise' Framed	130.00
SI Cover 'Dan the Man' Framed (NC)	130.00
1994 UD 2-Card set #136/1000	100.00
Most 3,000 Yard Seasons 3 1/2'x5' card/500	100.00
Official Baseball	100.00
Total Passing Yards Silver 3 1/2'x5' card/500	100.00
Dan the Man White Jersey Unframed/343	500.00
Dan the Man Photo Collection/343	700.00
Dan the Man Aqua Jersey Framed/343	650.00
8x10 Photo 300 TD-Mud Bowl	100.00
8x10 Photo 343 TD Game w/Banner	100.00

UDA Dan Marino/Joe Montana

8x10 Photo SB XIX Unframed (NC)	175.00
3 1/2 x 5 Commemorative Card (NC)	250.00
SI Cover 'SB Shootout' 1/21/85 Framed	175.00
8x10 Photo Taxi Unframed	150.00

UDA Joe Montana Footballs

Official NFL Game Football	275.00
Super Joe 4-Time SB Champ Mini FB/416	130.00
Super Joe 4-Time SB Champ Football/416	300.00
Leather F1145 Football	200.00
Notre Dame Career Stats Wilson F1145 FB	225.00
Notre Dame '77 Nat'l Champs White Panel FB	200.00

UDA Joe Montana Helmets

Official SF Helmet	500.00
Official Kansas City Helmet	350.00
Notre Dame Mini Helmet (authentic)	175.00
San Francisco Mini Helmet (authentic)	200.00
Super Joe Mini Helmet (authentic)/416	200.00
Super Joe Proline Helmet/416	500.00
Shadow box w/mini helmet and 8x10/500	300.00
Notre Dame full size helmet w/display	500.00
Kansas City Mini Helmet (replica)	130.00
San Francisco Mini Helmet (replica)	160.00
Full Size Kansas City Replica Helmet	200.00
Full Size SF Replica Helmet	275.00
Notre Dame Mini Helmet (replica)	150.00

UDA Joe Montana Jerseys

San Francisco Red Jersey Unframed	325.00
Kansas City Red Jersey Unframed	200.00
Kansas City White Jersey Unframed	200.00
Notre Dame Jersey Unframed (Blue)	450.00
Super Joe Red Jersey Unframed w/Patch/416	350.00
Super Joe White Jersey Framed w/Patch/416	550.00

UDA Joe Montana Other

SI 'Sportsman of the Year' 12/20/90 Framed	120.00
16x20 Photo Dropping Back Framed/500*	225.00
16x20 Photo Dropping Back Unframed/500*	150.00
SI Cover 'Joltin' Joe' 10/2/89 Framed	120.00
8x10 Photo 'Super Bowl Hero' Unframed	80.00
'94 UD #133 2-card set/1000	80.00
'94 UD #133 Card Blowup/500	80.00
8 1/2x11 Montana's Magic Sheet/1000	90.00
'95 UD Promo Card #19 2-card set/2500	80.00
Official Baseball/1995	90.00
'95 SP Die-Cut Tribute 3 1/2"x5" card/2500	80.00
'95 UD #19 Card Blowup/500	75.00

'Montana' Coffee Table Book w/sleeve/273	325.00
Notre Dame Nat'l Champ 8 1/2x11 Blowup/500	100.00
8x10 Photo ND Taking Snap Unframed	90.00
Notre Dame Golden Trad. 3 1/2'x5' card/1000	100.00
SI 'Joe Knows Super Bowl' 2/5/90 Framed	120.00
Super Joe Photo Collection w/Letter/416	650.00
Jersey swatch w/SB patches framed/416	400.00
8x10 Photo w/letter/250	100.00
'95 Comeback career 2-card set/500	75.00
MVP 2-card set/500	75.00
Notre Dame 8x10 photo w/letter/116	100.00
8x10 Photo Unframed	75.00
8x10 Tunnel Walk Photo Unframed	80.00

UDA Misc Football

Walter Payton Heroes 10-card set/2800 (NC)	200.00
Blanda Photo 'Splits the Uprights' Framed	65.00
Blanda Photo 'Stands in the Pocket' Framed	65.00
Hornung Photo 'Evades a Viking Framed	65.00
Blanda Photo 'Splits the Uprights' Unframed	50.00
Blanda Photo 'Stands in the Pocket' Unframed	50.00
Hornung Photo 'Evades a Viking Unframed	50.00
Gino Cappeletti 8x10 Photo Unframed	30.00
Steve Grogan 8x10 Photo Unframed	25.00
Walter Payton 'Heroes' 2-card set/2800	70.00
Bob Griese 8x10 Photo Unframed/500	35.00

Cereal Box Price Guide

1993 Minn.Vikings Div. Champs R	35.00
1994 Jerry Rice R	25.00
1994 Dallas Cowboys SB Champs R	18.00
1994 NFL 75th Ann. (Silver)	15.00
1995 Dan Marino	12.00
1995 San Francisco 49ers R	18.00
1995 Jacksonville Jaguars R	15.00
1995 Carolina Panthers R	15.00
1995 Oakland Raiders R	20.00
1995 SB 30 Ann. Aikm/Brads/Starr (18/34)	15.00
1995 St. Louis Rams R	15.00
1995 Neb.Cornhuskers Nat'l Champs R	25.00
1996 Deion Sanders (HF)	7.00
1996 Steve Young (CW)	12.00
1996 QBs: Aikman/Elway/Marino	15.00
1996 RBs: Allen/Sanders/Thomas	12.00

1996 WRs: Brown/Reed/Rice	10.00
1996 San Francisco 49ers 50th Ann. R	15.00
1996 Dallas Cowboys SB Champs R	15.00
1996 Baltimore Ravens R	15.00
1996 Pittsburgh Steelers AFC Champs R	15.00
1996 SB XXX (three-pack .75 oz)	35.00
1996 Neb.Cornhuskers Nat'l Champs R	15.00
1996 Northwestern Wildcats Big 10 Champs R	15.00
1997 SB 3D Troy Aikman (HF)	7.00
1997 SB 3D Marcus Allen ERR SB28	8.00
1997 SB 3D Marcus Allen COR SB18	7.00
1997 SB 3D Joe Namath	7.00
1997 SB 3D Roger Staubach	7.00
1997 SB 3D Steve Young (CW)	7.00
1997 G.B.Packers SB Champs R	15.00
1997 N.E.Patriots AFC Champs R	12.00

Kellogg's Corn Flakes Football

1983 Danny White	40.00

Wheaties Football

1986 Walter Payton Commem. (12)	50.00
1986 Walter Payton pointing FB (8)	65.00
1986 Walter Payton pointing FB (12/18/24)	45.00
1986 Chris Spielman (AAU) R	80.00

1988 Steve Largent	50.00
1988 Denver Broncos phantom R	30.00
1988 Washington Redskins SB Champs R	25.00
1990 B.Esiason/J.Kelly ProSet (12/18)	25.00
1991 Joe Montana R	50.00
1991 NY Giants SB Champs R	25.00
1991 SEC Football R	80.00
1992 Barry Sanders R	25.00
1992 Washington Redskins SB Champs R	30.00
1993 John Elway	30.00
1993 Jim Kelly	25.00
1993 Warren Moon	20.00
1993 Steve Young	20.00
1993 Buffalo Bills AFC Champs R	25.00
1993 Dallas Cowboys SB Champs R	25.00
1993 Pittsburgh Steelers Div. Champs R	35.00

Highland Mint Price Guide

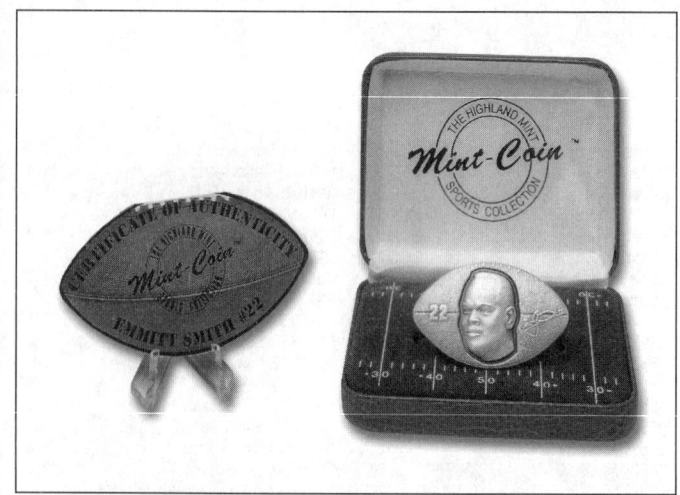

Football Mint-Cards
Topps

COMMON BRONZE CARD	35.00	50.00
COMMON SILVER CARD	150.00	200.00
Troy Aikman 89/G/375	450.00	600.00
Troy Aikman 89/S/500	240.00	300.00
Troy Aikman 89/B/2500	75.00	100.00
Marcus Allen 83/S/88	200.00	250.00
Marcus Allen 83/B/549	35.00	50.00
Jerome Bettis 93/S/301	175.00	225.00
Jerome Bettis 93/B/1566	35.00	50.00
Drew Bledsoe 93/G/375	550.00	700.00
Drew Bledsoe 93/S/500	240.00	300.00
Drew Bledsoe 93/B/2500	65.00	90.00
John Elway 84/S/500	175.00	225.00
John Elway 84/B/2020	35.00	50.00
Marshall Faulk 94/S/530	150.00	200.00
Marshall Faulk 94/B/2500	35.00	50.00
Brett Favre 92/S/110	240.00	300.00
Brett Favre 92/B/714	75.00	100.00
Michael Irvin 89/S/509	150.00	200.00
Michael Irvin 89/B/1633	35.00	50.00
Jim Kelly 87/S/419	175.00	225.00
Jim Kelly 87/B/1165	35.00	50.00
Dan Marino 84/G/375	550.00	700.00
Dan Marino 84/S/500	375.00	500.00
Dan Marino 84/B/2500	100.00	140.00
Natrone Means 93/S/136	175.00	225.00
Natrone Means 93/B/1026	35.00	50.00
Rick Mirer 93/S/384	175.00	225.00
Rick Mirer 93/B/1982	35.00	50.00
Jerry Rice 86/G/375	375.00	500.00
Jerry Rice 86/S/750	240.00	300.00
Jerry Rice 86/B/2500	55.00	75.00
Barry Sanders 89/G/375	375.00	500.00
Barry Sanders 89/S/750	175.00	225.00
Barry Sanders 89/B/2500	35.00	50.00
Deion Sanders 89/S/191	175.00	225.00
Deion Sanders 89/B/1033	35.00	50.00
Sterling Sharpe 89/S/171	175.00	225.00
Sterling Sharpe 89/B/901	35.00	50.00
Emmitt Smith 90/G/375	600.00	800.00
Emmitt Smith 90/S/750	375.00	500.00
Emmitt Smith 90/B/2500	90.00	125.00
Lawrence Taylor 84/S/585	150.00	200.00
Lawrence Taylor 84/B/1630	35.00	50.00
Steve Young 86/G/375	350.00	450.00
Steve Young 86/S/500	200.00	250.00
Steve Young 86/B/2500	45.00	60.00

Football Mint-Cards
Pinnacle/Score/UD

COMMON BRONZE MINT-CARD	35.00	50.00
COMMON SILVER MINT-CARD	150.00	200.00
Troy Aikman 89/S/1000	175.00	225.00
Troy Aikman 89/B/5000	35.00	50.00
Drew Bledsoe 94/S/1000	175.00	225.00
Drew Bledsoe 94/B/5000	35.00	50.00
Brett Favre 93/S/250	175.00	225.00
Brett Favre 93/B/1500	65.00	90.00
Dan Marino 94/G/500	375.00	500.00
Dan Marino 94/S/1000	200.00	250.00
Dan Marino 94/B/5000	75.00	100.00
Joe Montana 92/G/500	375.00	500.00
Joe Montana 92/S/1000	200.00	250.00
Joe Montana 92/B/5000	55.00	75.00
Errict Rhett 94/S/500	150.00	200.00
Errict Rhett 94/B/2500	35.00	50.00
Jerry Rice 95/S/500	200.00	250.00
Jerry Rice 95/B/2500	45.00	60.00
Rashaan Salaam 95/S/500	150.00	200.00
Rashaan Salaam 95/B/2500	35.00	50.00
Barry Sanders 89/S/250	175.00	225.00
Barry Sanders 89/B/1500	35.00	50.00
Heath Shuler 94/S/500	150.00	200.00
Heath Shuler 94/B/2500	35.00	50.00
Emmitt Smith 90/S/1000	200.00	250.00
Emmitt Smith 90/B/5000	90.00	125.00
Kordell Stewart 95/S/500	175.00	225.00
Kordell Stewart 95/B/2500	35.00	50.00

Football Legends
Mint-Cards

Joe Namath S/1000	175.00	225.00
Joe Namath B/5000	35.00	50.00

Roger Staubach S/500	175.00	225.00
Roger Staubach B/2500	35.00	50.00
Johnny Unitas S/500	175.00	225.00
Johnny Unitas B/2500	35.00	50.00

Football Sandblast
Mint-Cards

Dan Marino 96/S/500	200.00	250.00
Dan Marino 96/B/2500	55.00	75.00
Dan Marino 96/G/250	375.00	500.00

Football Mint-Coins

COMMON BRONZE MINT-COIN	8.00	12.00
COMMON SILVER MINT-COIN	14.00	20.00
Troy Aikman Gold Sig./1500	50.00	65.00
Troy Aikman S/7500	24.00	30.00
Troy Aikman B/25000	9.00	12.00
Jerome Bettis Rams S/2100	20.00	25.00
Jerome Bettis Steelers S/5400	11.00	14.00
Drew Bledsoe S/7500	20.00	25.00
Drew Bledsoe B/25000	9.00	12.00
John Elway S/7500	20.00	25.00
Marshall Faulk S/7500	15.00	20.00
Brett Favre S/7500	24.00	30.00
Brett Favre B/25000	11.00	14.00
Michael Irvin S/7500	15.00	20.00
Jim Kelly S/7500	15.00	20.00
Dan Marino G/100	1100.00	1350.00
Dan Marino Gold Sig./1500	75.00	100.00
Dan Marino S/7500	30.00	40.00
Dan Marino B/25000	12.00	15.00
Natrone Means S/7500	15.00	20.00
Rick Mirer S/7500	15.00	20.00

Joe Montana G/100	1100.00	1350.00
Joe Montana S/7500	24.00	30.00
Joe Montana B/25000	9.00	12.00
Jerry Rice Gold Sig./1500	35.00	50.00
Jerry Rice S/7500	20.00	25.00
Jerry Rice B/25000	9.00	12.00
Barry Sanders S/7500	20.00	25.00
Deion Sanders 49ers S/2690	20.00	25.00
Deion Sanders Cowboys S/4810	20.00	25.00
Deion Sanders B/25000	9.00	12.00
Junior Seau S/7500	15.00	20.00
Heath Shuler S/7500	15.00	20.00
Emmitt Smith G/100	1100.00	1350.00
Emmitt Smith Gold Sig./1500	65.00	90.00
Emmitt Smith S/7500	30.00	40.00
Emmitt Smith B/25000	11.00	14.00
Steve Young S/7500	20.00	25.00
Steve Young B/25000	9.00	12.00
Ki-Jana Carter S/7500	15.00	20.00
Kerry Collins S/7500	20.00	25.00
Trent Dilfer S/7500	15.00	20.00
John Elway Gold Sig./1500	35.00	50.00
Eddie George S/5000	20.00	25.00
Curtis Martin S/7500	20.00	25.00
Joe Namath S/7500	20.00	25.00
Rashaan Salaam S/7500	15.00	20.00
Kordell Stewart S/7500	20.00	25.00
Cowboys Set B/2500		
49ers B/2500		

Football Shaped
Medallions

COMMON SILVER MEDALLION	30.00	40.00
Dan Marino S/7500	30.00	40.00
Troy Aikman S/5000	30.00	40.00
Troy Aikman diamond/500	100.00	140.00
Brett Favre S/5000	30.00	40.00
Brett Favre diamond/500	100.00	140.00
Jerry Rice S/7500	30.00	40.00
Jerry Rice diamond/500	100.00	140.00
Emmitt Smith S/7500	30.00	40.00
Emmitt Smith diamond/500	100.00	140.00

Sports Illustrated Football

How to Use

The majority of Sports Illustrateds on the market are subscription copies that were distributed with mailing labels or inkjetted addresses. SI switched from labeling to inkjetting in the early '90s; the exact date varied by region.

The Price Guide refers to magazine in ExMt condition. ExMt magazines may have mailing labels or inkjetted addresses if they are otherwise flawless. Magazines without mailing labels or inkjetted addresses can still be considered ExMt if they have minor flaws such as dinged/frayed corners, light creases, fingerprints, scratches or scuffing.

Magazines with labels or addresses and minor flaws are valued at 50-75% the listed prices depending on severity. Flawless magazines without labels or addresses are considered Mint and are valued at 150% the listed prices. Magazines with major flaws such as heavy creases, stains, tears or writing are valued at 10-25% the listed prices depending on severity.

Cover Subjects and First Covers

Magazines are listed by main cover subject(s). In cases of covers with multiple subjects, only the most famous and/or prominent may be listed depending on space limitations.

For popular athletes with multiple cover appearances, a First Cover (FC) may be designated. This is generally applied to the first issue that the player was intentionally featured on the cover; he/she may have appeared in a small photo or in the background of an earlier cover. For instance, the "Baseball Salaries" issue (4/20/87) features mugshots of 43 players, but these are not considered FCs.

Issue Dates and Special Issues

Magazines are listed in order of issue date, which normally appears on the cover. However, special issues may list the date inside, or list only a season or year rather than a specific date. For the latter, the magazine is listed by the approximate date of release.

SI usually combines two weeks into one with a double issue at the end of the year; for these issues, the date is followed by an asterisk. Other designations used are SOY for SI's annual Sportsman of the Year issue, and PV for various event or season preview issues.

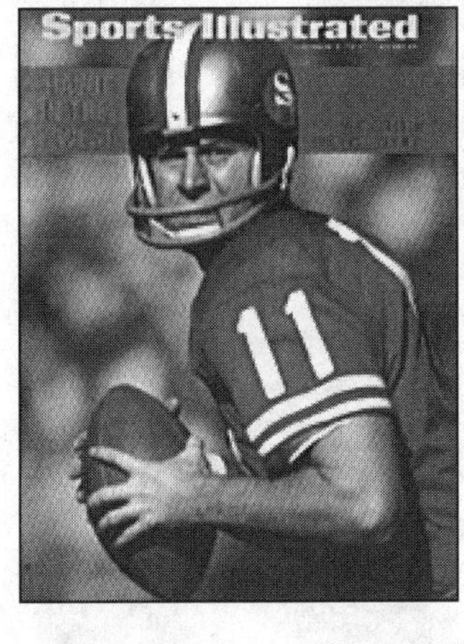

	EXMT	VGEX	G-VG
☐ 9/28/54 Calvin Jones	20.00	9.00	2.50
☐ 10/11/54 Oklahoma Band	8.00	3.60	1.00
☐ 11/1/54 College Football Issue	20.00	9.00	2.50
☐ 11/22/54 Y.A. Tittle (FC)	35.00	16.00	4.40
☐ 9/12/55 Bud Wilkinson	20.00	9.00	2.50
☐ 10/3/55 Doak Walker	35.00	16.00	4.40
☐ 10/17/55 Princeton Band	8.00	3.60	1.00
☐ 10/24/55 Hopalong Cassady	30.00	13.50	3.70
☐ 11/7/55 Bob Pelegrini	10.00	4.50	1.25
☐ 11/28/55 Don Holleder	20.00	9.00	2.50
☐ 12/26/55 Jim Swink	10.00	4.50	1.25
☐ 9/24/56 College Football Issue	15.00	6.75	1.85
☐ 10/8/56 Paul Brown	20.00	9.00	2.50
☐ 10/29/56 Paul Hornung (FC)	35.00	16.00	4.40
☐ 11/5/56 Yale Bulldog	6.00	2.70	.75
☐ 11/12/56 Michigan FB	10.00	4.50	1.25
☐ 11/26/56 USC vs. UCLA	10.00	4.50	1.25
☐ 12/3/56 Charley Conerly	15.00	6.75	1.85
☐ 12/24/56 Bowl Games Issue	10.00	4.50	1.25
☐ 9/23/57 College Football Issue	15.00	6.75	1.85
☐ 10/7/57 Ollie Matson	15.00	6.75	1.85
☐ 11/4/57 Bob Cox	8.00	3.60	1.00
☐ 11/18/57 Oklahoma Football	8.00	3.60	1.00
☐ 9/22/58 College Football Issue	12.00	5.50	1.50
☐ 10/6/58 Pro Football Issue	15.00	6.75	1.85
☐ 10/13/58 Ohio State Band	8.00	3.60	1.00
☐ 10/27/58 Chuck Zimmerman	8.00	3.60	1.00
☐ 11/24/58 Army Football	8.00	3.60	1.00
☐ 12/22/58 Bowl Games Issue	10.00	4.50	1.25
☐ 9/21/59 College Football Issue	15.00	6.75	1.85
☐ 10/5/59 Johnny Unitas (FC)	45.00	20.00	5.50
☐ 10/26/59 George Izo	10.00	4.50	1.25
☐ 11/9/59 Texas Football	10.00	4.50	1.25
☐ 9/19/60 College Football Issue	10.00	4.50	1.25
☐ 9/26/60 Pro FB PV: Jim Brown (FC)	35.00	16.00	4.40
☐ 12/19/60 Norm Van Brocklin	20.00	9.00	2.50
☐ 9/18/61 College Football Issue	15.00	6.75	1.85
☐ 9/25/61 Pro FB PV: Bart Starr (FC)	35.00	16.00	4.40
☐ 10/16/61 Terry Baker	15.00	6.75	1.85
☐ 10/23/61 Jon Arnett	15.00	6.75	1.85
☐ 11/20/61 Y.A. Tittle	20.00	9.00	2.50
☐ 11/27/61 Jim Saxton	8.00	3.60	1.00
☐ 12/18/61 Dan Currie	8.00	3.60	1.00
☐ 9/10/62 Pro FB PV: Jim Taylor (FC)	30.00	13.50	3.70
☐ 9/24/62 College Football Issue	15.00	6.75	1.85
☐ 10/8/62 Tommy McDonald	10.00	4.50	1.25
☐ 10/15/62 John Gibbs	8.00	3.60	1.00
☐ 10/29/62 Fran Tarkenton (FC)	30.00	13.50	3.70
☐ 11/19/62 Nick Pietrosante	8.00	3.60	1.00
☐ 11/26/62 Paul Dietzel	8.00	3.60	1.00
☐ 12/17/62 Frank Gifford	30.00	13.50	3.70
☐ 9/9/63 Pro Football: Cowboys	18.00	8.00	2.20
☐ 9/23/63 College Football Issue	15.00	6.75	1.85
☐ 10/14/63 Ronnie Bull	8.00	3.60	1.00
☐ 10/21/63 Duke Carlisle	8.00	3.60	1.00
☐ 11/4/63 Jack Cvercko	8.00	3.60	1.00
☐ 11/11/63 Referee	8.00	3.60	1.00
☐ 11/25/63 Willie Galimore	10.00	4.50	1.25
☐ 12/2/63 Roger Staubach (FC)	35.00	16.00	4.40
☐ 12/16/63 Tobin Rote	8.00	3.60	1.00
☐ 7/27/64 Tommy McDonald	10.00	4.50	1.25
☐ 8/17/64 Don Trull	8.00	3.60	1.00
☐ 9/7/64 Pro Football: Y.A.Tittle	15.00	6.75	1.85
☐ 9/21/64 College Football Issue	15.00	6.75	1.85
☐ 9/28/64 Tommy Mason	8.00	3.60	1.00
☐ 10/12/64 Dick Butkus (FC)	35.00	16.00	4.40
☐ 11/2/64 John Huarte	10.00	4.50	1.25
☐ 11/9/64 John David Crow	8.00	3.60	1.00
☐ 11/30/64 Alex Karras	12.00	5.50	1.50
☐ 12/14/64 Charley Johnson	10.00	4.50	1.25
☐ 1/4/65 Frank Ryan	7.00	3.10	.85
☐ 1/11/65 Ernie Koy	7.00	3.10	.85
☐ 7/19/65 Joe Namath (FC)	45.00	20.00	5.50
☐ 8/16/65 Y.A. Tittle	15.00	6.75	1.85
☐ 9/13/65 Pro FB PV: F.Tarkenton	20.00	9.00	2.50
☐ 9/20/65 College Football Issue	15.00	6.75	1.85
☐ 9/27/65 Frank Ryan	10.00	4.50	1.25
☐ 10/11/65 Ken Willard	7.00	3.10	.85
☐ 10/18/65 Tommy Nobis	10.00	4.50	1.25
☐ 11/1/65 S. Randle/C. Johnson	7.00	3.10	.85
☐ 11/8/65 Harry Jones	10.00	4.50	1.25
☐ 11/29/65 Dennis Gaubatz	7.00	3.10	.85
☐ 12/13/65 Lance Alworth	30.00	13.50	3.70
☐ 1/3/66 Bowl Games Issue	7.00	3.10	.85
☐ 1/10/66 Jim Taylor	20.00	9.00	2.50
☐ 7/25/66 Otto Graham	10.00	4.50	1.25
☐ 8/8/66 Frank Emanuel	8.00	3.60	1.00
☐ 8/15/66 Bear Bryant (FC)	18.00	8.00	2.20
☐ 8/22/66 P. Hornung/J.Taylor	20.00	9.00	2.50
☐ 9/12/66 Pro FB PV: Gale Sayers	30.00	13.50	3.70
☐ 9/19/66 Coll.FB PV: Gary Beban	15.00	6.75	1.85
☐ 10/3/66 Roman Gabriel	8.00	3.60	1.00
☐ 10/17/66 Joe Namath	35.00	16.00	4.40
☐ 10/31/66 Bart Starr	30.00	13.50	3.70
☐ 11/7/66 Terry Hanratty	20.00	9.00	2.50
☐ 11/21/66 Ross Fichtner	7.00	3.10	.85

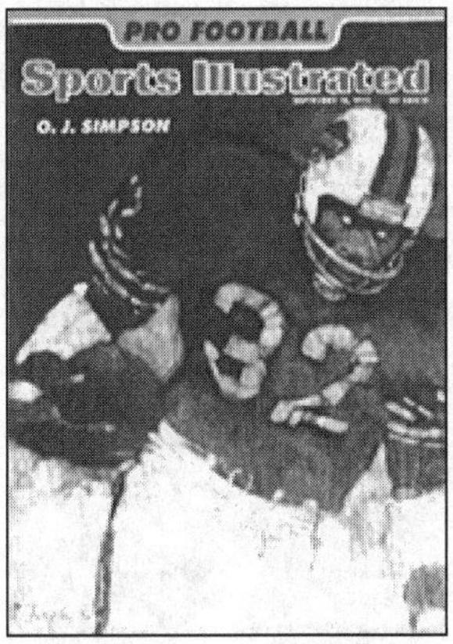

	EXMT	VGEX	G-VG
☐ 11/28/66 N.D. vs Mich. St. FB	8.00	3.60	1.00
☐ 12/12/66 Jim Nance	10.00	4.50	1.25
☐ 1/2/67 Bowl Games Issue	7.00	3.10	.85
☐ 1/9/67 Bart Starr	30.00	13.50	3.70
☐ 1/23/67 Super Bowl: Max McGee	35.00	16.00	4.40
☐ 8/14/67 Jim Taylor	12.00	5.50	1.50
☐ 9/11/67 Coll.FB PV: T.Hanratty	15.00	6.75	1.85
☐ 9/18/67 Pro Football Issue	15.00	6.75	1.85
☐ 10/1/67 John McKay	7.00	3.10	.85
☐ 10/8/67 Mike Phipps	7.00	3.10	.85
☐ 10/29/67 Tenn. vs Alabama FB	7.00	3.10	.85
☐ 11/6/67 Dan Reeves	8.00	3.60	1.00
☐ 11/20/67 O.J.Simpson (FC)/Beban	15.00	6.75	1.85
☐ 11/27/67 Jim Hart	8.00	3.60	1.00
☐ 12/18/67 Roman Gabriel	8.00	3.60	1.00
☐ 1/8/68 Super Bowl Issue	12.00	5.50	1.50
☐ 1/22/68 Vince Lombardi (FC)	30.00	13.50	3.70
☐ 7/15/68 Ray Nitschke	10.00	4.50	1.25
☐ 8/12/68 Paul Brown	8.00	3.60	1.00
☐ 9/9/68 College Football Issue	15.00	6.75	1.85
☐ 9/16/68 Pro FB PV: D.Meredith	15.00	6.75	1.85
☐ 10/14/68 O.J. Simpson	18.00	8.00	2.20
☐ 10/28/68 Forrest Gregg	8.00	3.60	1.00
☐ 11/11/68 Bruce Jankowski	7.00	3.10	.85
☐ 11/25/68 Earl Morrall	10.00	4.50	1.25
☐ 12/9/68 Joe Namath	25.00	11.00	3.10
☐ 12/16/68 Colts vs Packers	8.00	3.60	1.00
☐ 1/6/69 Tom Matte	8.00	3.60	1.00
☐ 1/20/69 Joe Namath	35.00	16.00	4.40
☐ 3/3/69 Vince Lombardi	12.00	5.50	1.50
☐ 6/16/69 Joe Namath	18.00	8.00	2.20
☐ 7/14/69 O.J. Simpson	12.00	5.50	1.50
☐ 7/28/69 Jurgensen/Lombardi	10.00	4.50	1.25
☐ 8/11/69 Joe Namath	18.00	8.00	2.20
☐ 8/25/69 O.J. Simpson	12.00	5.50	1.50
☐ 9/15/69 Coll.FB PV: Woody Hayes	12.00	5.50	1.50
☐ 9/22/69 Pro Football: Jim Turner	10.00	4.50	1.25
☐ 9/29/69 Jimmy Jones	7.00	3.10	.85
☐ 10/13/69 Bruce Kemp	7.00	3.10	.85
☐ 11/3/69 Minnesota Vikings	8.00	3.60	1.00
☐ 11/10/69 Steve Owens	8.00	3.60	1.00
☐ 11/24/69 Len Dawson (FC)	15.00	6.75	1.85
☐ 12/15/69 James Street	7.00	3.10	.85
☐ 1/5/70 Dave Osborn/Deacon Jones	8.00	3.60	1.00
☐ 1/19/70 Super Bowl: Len Dawson	25.00	11.00	3.10
☐ 2/9/70 Terry Bradshaw (FC)	25.00	11.00	3.10
☐ 8/10/70 Mike Garrett	8.00	3.60	1.00
☐ 8/17/70 Joe Namath	12.00	5.50	1.50
☐ 8/31/70 Les Shy	7.00	3.10	.85
☐ 9/14/70 Coll.FB PV: Archie Manning	15.00	6.75	1.85
☐ 9/21/70 NFL PV: Dick Butkus	20.00	9.00	2.50
☐ 10/5/70 Colorado vs Penn State	7.00	3.10	.85
☐ 10/12/70 Alex Karras	10.00	4.50	1.25
☐ 11/2/70 Monday Night Football	7.00	3.10	.85
☐ 11/9/70 Joe Theismann (FC)	10.00	4.50	1.25
☐ 11/23/70 George Blanda (FC)	12.00	5.50	1.50
☐ 12/7/70 Roman Gabriel	8.00	3.60	1.00

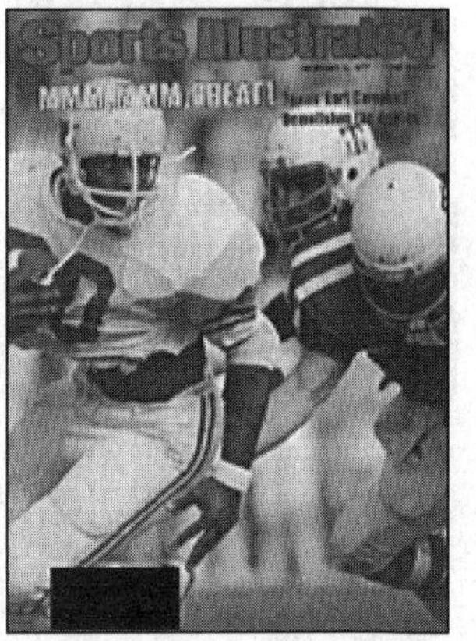

	EXMT	VGEX	G-VG
☐ 12/14/70 Steve Worsten	6.00	2.70	.75
☐ 1/11/71 Joe Theismann	10.00	4.50	1.25
☐ 1/18/71 Super Bowl PV: C.Morton	8.00	3.60	1.00
☐ 1/25/71 Super Bowl: Morrall/O'Brien	15.00	6.75	1.85
☐ 2/15/71 Jim Plunkett	8.00	3.60	1.00
☐ 5/17/71 James McAlister	6.00	2.70	.75
☐ 7/19/71 George Blanda	8.00	3.60	1.00
☐ 8/16/71 Calvin Hill	8.00	3.60	1.00
☐ 9/13/71 Coll.FB PV: T.Casanova	10.00	4.50	1.25
☐ 9/20/71 NFL PV: John Brodie	12.00	5.50	1.50
☐ 10/4/71 Sonny Sixkiller	7.00	3.10	.85
☐ 10/11/71 Joe Greene (FC)	12.00	5.50	1.50
☐ 11/1/71 Ed Marinaro	8.00	3.60	1.00
☐ 11/8/71 Norm Bulaich	7.00	3.10	.85
☐ 11/22/71 Okla. vs Nebraska FB	7.00	3.10	.85
☐ 1/3/72 Garo Yepremian	10.00	4.50	1.25
☐ 1/10/72 Orange Bowl: Nebraska	7.00	3.10	.85
☐ 1/24/72 Super Bowl: Duane Thomas	15.00	6.75	1.85
☐ 7/10/72 Johnny Unitas	12.00	5.50	1.50
☐ 7/24/72 Tommy Prothro	5.00	2.20	.60
☐ 8/7/72 Larry Csonka (FC)	12.00	5.50	1.50
☐ 9/11/72 Coll.FB PV: Bob Devaney	12.00	5.50	1.50
☐ 9/18/72 NFL PV: Walt Garrison	12.00	5.50	1.50
☐ 10/2/72 Greg Pruitt	6.00	2.70	.75
☐ 10/9/72 Joe Namath	15.00	6.75	1.85
☐ 10/30/72 Dave/Don Buckey	5.00	2.20	.60
☐ 11/20/72 Terry Davis	5.00	2.20	.60
☐ 12/4/72 Steve Spurrier (FC)	12.00	5.50	1.50
☐ 12/18/72 Lee Roy Jordan	10.00	4.50	1.25
☐ 1/8/73 Mercury Morris	8.00	3.60	1.00
☐ 1/22/73 Super Bowl: Bob Griese (FC)	15.00	6.75	1.85
☐ 8/6/73 John Matuszak	8.00	3.60	1.00
☐ 8/27/73 Duane Thomas	8.00	3.60	1.00
☐ 9/10/73 College Football Issue	15.00	6.75	1.85
☐ 9/17/73 NFL PV: Csonka/B.Griese	15.00	6.75	1.85
☐ 10/1/73 Anthony Davis	7.00	3.10	.85
☐ 10/8/73 Fran Tarkenton	10.00	4.50	1.25
☐ 10/29/73 O.J. Simpson	12.00	5.50	1.50
☐ 11/5/73 Anthony Davis	7.00	3.10	.85
☐ 12/3/73 Bear Bryant	10.00	4.50	1.25
☐ 12/17/73 Marv Hubbard	7.00	3.10	.85
☐ 1/7/74 Fran Tarkenton	10.00	4.50	1.25
☐ 1/21/74 Super Bowl: Larry Csonka	15.00	6.75	1.85
☐ 4/29/74 Bruce Hardy	5.00	2.20	.60
☐ 7/29/74 Terry Bradshaw	10.00	4.50	1.25
☐ 8/5/74 NFL Strike	5.00	2.20	.60
☐ 9/9/74 Coll.FB PV: Archie Griffin	12.00	5.50	1.50
☐ 9/16/74 NFL PV: O.J.Simpson	15.00	6.75	1.85
☐ 9/23/74 Joe Gilliam	8.00	3.60	1.00
☐ 9/30/74 Tom Clements	5.00	2.20	.60
☐ 11/4/74 Joe Washington	5.00	2.20	.60
☐ 11/18/74 Woody Green	5.00	2.20	.60
☐ 12/9/74 Anthony Davis	7.00	3.10	.85
☐ 1/6/75 Franco Harris (FC)	10.00	4.50	1.25
☐ 1/13/75 Super Bowl Issue	4.00	1.80	.50
☐ 1/20/75 Terry Bradshaw	10.00	4.50	1.25
☐ 6/9/75 Rocky Bleier	6.00	2.70	.75
☐ 7/28/75 Warfield/Csonka/Kiick	6.00	2.70	.75
☐ 8/25/75 Bart Starr	10.00	4.50	1.25
☐ 9/8/75 Col.FB PV: Switzer	4.00	1.80	.50
☐ 9/22/75 NFL PV: Joe Greene	10.00	4.50	1.25

☐ 9/29/75 Notre Dame FB	4.00	1.80	.50
☐ 11/10/75 Fran Tarkenton	10.00	4.50	1.25
☐ 11/24/75 Chuck Muncie	3.00	1.35	.35
☐ 12/8/75 Bubba Bean	3.00	1.35	.35
☐ 1/5/76 Preston Pearson	5.00	2.20	.60
☐ 1/12/76 Franco Harris	8.00	3.60	1.00
☐ 1/26/76 Lynn Swann	10.00	4.50	1.25
☐ 8/16/76 Calvin Hill	5.00	2.20	.60
☐ 8/23/76 Steve Spurrier	8.00	3.60	1.00

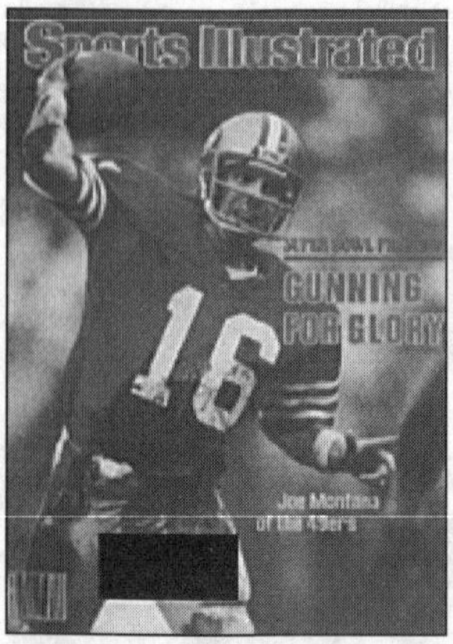

☐ 9/6/76 Rick Leach	4.00	1.80	.50
☐ 9/13/76 Bert Jones	5.00	2.20	.60
☐ 10/4/76 Mark Manges	3.00	1.35	.35
☐ 10/18/76 Chuck Foreman	4.00	1.80	.50
☐ 11/8/76 Tony Dorsett (FC)	12.00	5.50	1.50
☐ 11/22/76 Walter Payton (FC)	18.00	8.00	2.20
☐ 12/6/76 Rocky Bleier	5.00	2.20	.60
☐ 1/3/77 Raiders vs. Steelers	3.00	1.35	.35
☐ 1/10/77 Tony Dorsett	10.00	4.50	1.25
☐ 1/17/77 Ken Stabler (FC)	8.00	3.60	1.00
☐ 7/25/77 Conrad Dobler	4.00	1.80	.50
☐ 9/5/77 Ross Browner	3.00	1.35	.35
☐ 9/19/77 Ken Stabler	6.00	2.70	.75
☐ 10/3/77 Billy Sims	5.00	2.20	.60
☐ 10/17/77 Rubin Carter	3.00	1.35	.35
☐ 11/21/77 Dave Casper	5.00	2.20	.60
☐ 12/5/77 Earl Campbell (FC)	10.00	4.50	1.25
☐ 1/2/78 Mark Van Eeghan	4.00	1.80	.50
☐ 1/23/78 R.White/H.Martin	6.00	2.70	.75
☐ 8/14/78 Football brutality	3.00	1.35	.35
☐ 9/4/78 Roger Staubach	10.00	4.50	1.25
☐ 9/11/78 Lou Holtz	5.00	2.20	.60
☐ 10/2/78 Charles White	5.00	2.20	.60
☐ 10/9/78 Terry Bradshaw	8.00	3.60	1.00
☐ 11/13/78 Chuck Fusina	4.00	1.80	.50
☐ 11/20/78 Rick Berns	3.00	1.35	.35
☐ 12/4/78 Earl Campbell	6.00	2.70	.75
☐ 1/8/79 Alabama/Penn St. FB	3.00	1.35	.35
☐ 1/15/79 Terry Bradshaw	8.00	3.60	1.00
☐ 1/29/79 Rocky Bleier	6.00	2.70	.75
☐ 8/6/79 Kenny Stabler	6.00	2.70	.75
☐ 8/20/79 John Jefferson	3.00	1.35	.35
☐ 9/3/79 Earl Campbell	6.00	2.70	.75
☐ 9/10/79 Charles White/B.Sims	5.00	2.20	.60
☐ 9/24/79 Vagas Ferguson	3.00	1.35	.35
☐ 10/1/79 Dewey Selmon	3.00	1.35	.35
☐ 11/5/79 Franco Harris	6.00	2.70	.75
☐ 11/12/79 Jarvis Redwine	3.00	1.35	.35
☐ 11/26/79 Art Schlichter	3.00	1.35	.35
☐ 12/24/79* Stargell/Bradshaw SOY	10.00	4.50	1.25
☐ 1/7/80 Ricky Bell	3.00	1.35	.35
☐ 1/14/80 LC Greenwood/Pastorini	5.00	2.20	.60
☐ 1/28/80 John Stallworth	6.00	2.70	.75
☐ 9/1/80 Hugh Green	4.00	1.80	.50
☐ 9/8/80 NFL PV: Dave Logan	3.00	1.35	.35
☐ 9/22/80 Billy Sims	4.00	1.80	.50
☐ 11/10/80 LC Greenwood	5.00	2.20	.60
☐ 11/17/80 Herschel Walker (FC)	8.00	3.60	1.00
☐ 12/8/80 Vince Ferragamo	4.00	1.80	.50
☐ 1/12/81 Chuck Muncie	3.00	1.35	.35
☐ 1/19/81 Mark Van Eeghan	4.00	1.80	.50
☐ 2/2/81 Rod Martin	5.00	2.20	.60
☐ 7/20/81 Vince Ferragamo	4.00	1.80	.50
☐ 8/3/81 John Hannah	4.00	1.80	.50
☐ 8/24/81 Wendell Tyler	3.00	1.35	.35
☐ 8/31/81 Herschel Walker	6.00	2.70	.75
☐ 9/7/81 Jim Plunkett	4.00	1.80	.50
☐ 10/5/81 Marcus Allen (FC)	10.00	4.50	1.25
☐ 10/19/81 Texas vs Okla FB	3.00	1.35	.35
☐ 11/23/81 Bear Bryant	5.00	2.20	.60
☐ 12/7/81 Tony Dorsett	6.00	2.70	.75
☐ 12/14/81 Cris Collinsworth	5.00	2.20	.60
☐ 12/21/81 Earl Cooper	3.00	1.35	.35
☐ 1/11/82 Perry Tuttle	3.00	1.35	.35
☐ 1/18/82 Dwight Clark 'The Catch'	10.00	4.50	1.25
☐ 1/25/82 Joe Montana (FC)	15.00	6.75	1.85
☐ 2/1/82 Earl Cooper	5.00	2.20	.60
☐ 3/1/82 Herschel Walker	6.00	2.70	.75
☐ 4/26/82 Renaldo Nehemiah	4.00	1.80	.50
☐ 5/10/82 G.Frontiere/B.Jones	4.00	1.80	.50
☐ 6/14/82 Cocaine report/D.Reese	2.00	.90	.25
☐ 8/16/82 Walter Payton	8.00	3.60	1.00
☐ 8/23/82 Franco Harris	5.00	2.20	.60
☐ 8/30/82 Tom Cousineau	3.00	1.35	.35
☐ 9/1/82 Football Spectacular	3.00	1.35	.35
☐ 9/13/82 Wayne Peace	3.00	1.35	.35
☐ 9/27/82 NFL strike	2.00	.90	.25
☐ 10/4/82 Todd Blackledge	4.00	1.80	.50
☐ 11/8/82 John Elway (FC)	12.00	5.50	1.50
☐ 12/6/82 Redskins vs. Eagles	3.00	1.35	.35
☐ 12/13/82 Marcus Allen	6.00	2.70	.75
☐ 1/10/83 Greg Garrity	3.00	1.35	.35
☐ 1/17/83 Chuck Muncie	3.00	1.35	.35
☐ 1/24/83 Andra Franklin	3.00	1.35	.35
☐ 1/31/83 Redskins beat Dallas	3.00	1.35	.35
☐ 2/7/83 John Riggins	5.00	2.20	.60
☐ 3/7/83 Herschel Walker	5.00	2.20	.60
☐ 6/20/83 Marcus Dupree	3.00	1.35	.35
☐ 8/1/83 Richard Todd	3.00	1.35	.35
☐ 8/15/83 John Elway	10.00	4.50	1.25
☐ 8/29/83 Tony Dorsett	6.00	2.70	.75
☐ 9/1/83 College/Pro FB PV	3.00	1.35	.35
☐ 9/5/83 Mike Rozier	4.00	1.80	.50
☐ 9/26/83 Doug Flutie (FC)	5.00	2.20	.60
☐ 10/10/83 Joe Washington	4.00	1.80	.50
☐ 10/17/83 Eric Dickerson (FC)	5.00	2.20	.60
☐ 11/14/83 Dan Marino (FC)	15.00	6.75	1.85
☐ 12/12/83 Jim Brown	6.00	2.70	.75
☐ 12/19/83 John Riggins	4.00	1.80	.50
☐ 1/9/84 Keith Griffith	3.00	1.35	.35
☐ 1/16/84 Joe Theismann	4.00	1.80	.50
☐ 1/30/84 Jack Squirek	4.00	1.80	.50
☐ 7/30/84 Jack Lambert	4.00	1.80	.50
☐ 9/3/84 Joe Theismann	4.00	1.80	.50
☐ 9/5/84 Marino/Kosar FB PV	12.00	5.50	1.50
☐ 9/10/84 M.Clayton/D.Green	4.00	1.80	.50
☐ 10/1/84 Jeff Smith	3.00	1.35	.35
☐ 10/8/84 Sammy Winder	3.00	1.35	.35
☐ 10/15/84 Walter Payton	6.00	2.70	.75
☐ 11/5/84 Gerry Faust	3.00	1.35	.35
☐ 11/12/84 NFL Issue/Trouble	2.00	.90	.25
☐ 11/19/84 Mark Duper	3.00	1.35	.35
☐ 12/3/84 Doug Flutie	5.00	2.20	.60

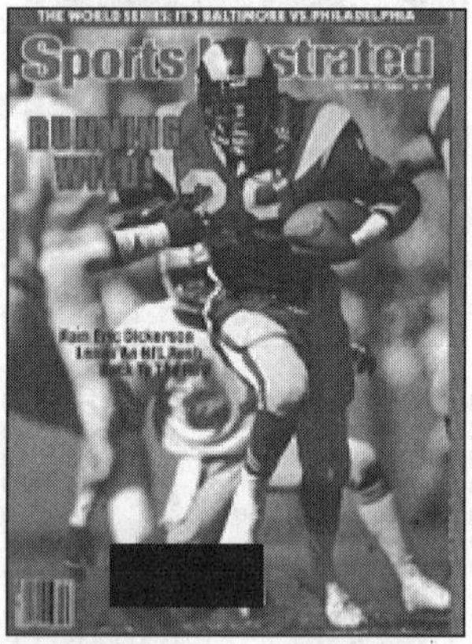

☐ 12/17/84 Eric Dickerson	4.00	1.80	.50
☐ 1/7/85 Walter Abercrombie	3.00	1.35	.35
☐ 1/14/85 Dan Marino	10.00	4.50	1.25
☐ 1/21/85 Marino/Montana	12.00	5.50	1.50
☐ 1/28/85 Roger Craig	5.00	2.20	.60
☐ 2/25/85 Doug Flutie	4.00	1.80	.50
☐ 5/27/85 Herschel Walker	4.00	1.80	.50
☐ 7/22/85 Howie Long	4.00	1.80	.50
☐ 8/12/85 Tony Dorsett	5.00	2.20	.60
☐ 8/26/85 Bernie Kosar	4.00	1.80	.50
☐ 9/4/85 Dickerson/McCallum FB PV	4.00	1.80	.50
☐ 10/7/85 Tony Robinson	3.00	1.35	.35
☐ 10/14/85 Eddie Robinson	4.00	1.80	.50
☐ 10/21/85 Jim McMahon (FC)	5.00	2.20	.60
☐ 11/11/85 D.J.Dozier/R.McDonald	3.00	1.35	.35
☐ 11/25/85 Danny White	4.00	1.80	.50
☐ 12/2/85 B.Jackson (FC)/Long/Dudek	6.00	2.70	.75
☐ 12/17/85 Marcus Allen	5.00	2.20	.60
☐ 1/13/86 Craig James	3.00	1.35	.35
☐ 1/20/86 Jim McMahon	4.00	1.80	.50
☐ 1/27/86 Mike Singletary	4.00	1.80	.50
☐ 2/3/86 D.Hampton/W.Marshall	5.00	2.20	.60
☐ 7/14/86 Bo Jackson BB	6.00	2.70	.75
☐ 7/21/86 Jim Kelly	5.00	2.20	.60
☐ 8/11/86 W.Perry/Too Tall Jones	4.00	1.80	.50
☐ 8/18/86 Herschel Walker	4.00	1.80	.50
☐ 9/3/86 McMahon/Bosworth FB PV	4.00	1.80	.50
☐ 9/22/86 Mich.vs Notre Dame FB	3.00	1.35	.35
☐ 9/29/86 M.Gastineau/L.Taylor	4.00	1.80	.50
☐ 10/13/86 John Elway	6.00	2.70	.75
☐ 11/24/86 Vinny Testaverde	3.00	1.35	.35
☐ 12/8/86 Walter Payton	6.00	2.70	.75
☐ 12/15/86 Mark Bavaro	3.00	1.35	.35
☐ 12/22/86* Joe Paterno SOY	5.00	2.20	.60
☐ 1/5/87 Brian Bosworth	3.00	1.35	.35
☐ 1/12/87 Ozzie Newsome	4.00	1.80	.50
☐ 1/19/87 Rich Karlis	2.00	.90	.25
☐ 1/26/87 Lawrence Taylor	4.00	1.80	.50
☐ 2/2/87 Phil Simms	5.00	2.20	.60
☐ 8/3/87 Vinny Testaverde	3.00	1.35	.35
☐ 8/24/87 Jim McMahon	3.00	1.35	.35
☐ 8/31/87 Col.FB PV:Tim Brown	5.00	2.20	.60
☐ 9/9/87 Pro FB PV: M.Bavaro	3.00	1.35	.35
☐ 9/21/87 John Elway	6.00	2.70	.75
☐ 10/12/87 Steve Walsh	3.00	1.35	.35
☐ 11/9/87 Eric Dickerson	3.00	1.35	.35
☐ 11/16/87 Rotnei Anderson	2.00	.90	.25
☐ 11/23/87 Dexter Manley	3.00	1.35	.35
☐ 11/30/87 Okla. vs. Neb. FB	3.00	1.35	.35
☐ 12/14/87 Bo Jackson BB/FB	6.00	2.70	.75
☐ 1/11/88 U of Miami Team	2.00	.90	.25
☐ 1/18/88 Anthony Carter	3.00	1.35	.35
☐ 1/25/88 John Elway	6.00	2.70	.75
☐ 2/8/88 Doug Williams	3.00	1.35	.35
☐ 8/1/88 Tony Dorsett	3.00	1.35	.35
☐ 8/29/88 Bernie Kosar	3.00	1.35	.35

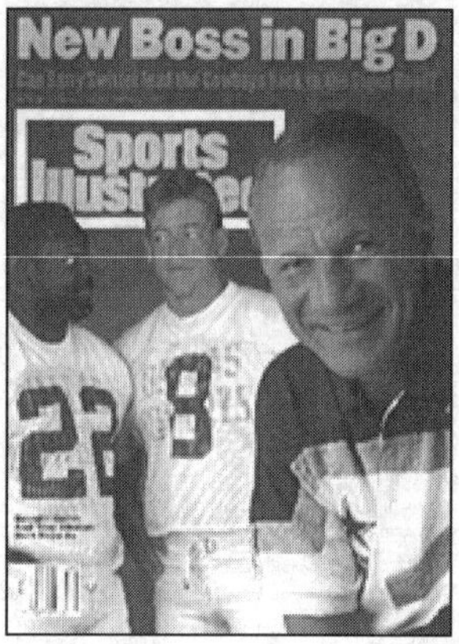

☐ 9/12/88 Jim McMahon	3.00	1.35	.35
☐ 10/24/88 Tony Rice/R.Maryland	3.00	1.35	.35
☐ 11/14/88 T.Landry/C.Noll	3.00	1.35	.35
☐ 11/21/88 Greg Bell	2.00	.90	.25
☐ 11/28/88 Rodney Peete	3.00	1.35	.35
☐ 12/5/88 Tony Rice	3.00	1.35	.35
☐ 1/9/89 Tony Rice	3.00	1.35	.35
☐ 1/16/89 Ickey Woods	2.00	.90	.25
☐ 1/30/89 Jerry Rice (FC)	10.00	4.50	1.25
☐ 2/27/89 C.Thompson/Switzer	2.00	.90	.25
☐ 3/20/89 Jimmy Johnson	5.00	2.20	.60
☐ 4/24/89 Tony Mandarich	2.00	.90	.25
☐ 6/12/89 Bo Jackson BB	4.00	1.80	.50
☐ 8/7/89 Boomer Esiason	3.00	1.35	.35
☐ 8/21/89 Troy Aikman (FC)	10.00	4.50	1.25
☐ 9/4/89 Col.FB PV: Lou Holtz	3.00	1.35	.35
☐ 9/11/89 Randall Cunningham	3.00	1.35	.35
☐ 9/25/89 Rocket Ismail	4.00	1.80	.50
☐ 10/2/89 Joe Montana	6.00	2.70	.75
☐ 10/23/89 Herschel Walker	3.00	1.35	.35
☐ 11/13/89 Deion Sanders (FC)	6.00	2.70	.75
☐ 11/27/89 Heisman race Emmitt etc	5.00	2.20	.60
☐ 12/4/89 Steve McGuire	2.00	.90	.25
☐ 1/8/90 Craig Erickson	3.00	1.35	.35
☐ 1/15/90 Jerry Rice	5.00	2.20	.60
☐ 1/22/90 John Elway	5.00	2.20	.60
☐ 2/5/90 J.Montana/G.McIntyre	6.00	2.70	.75
☐ 4/30/90 Jeff George	4.00	1.80	.50
☐ 8/6/90 Joe Montana	6.00	2.70	.75
☐ 8/27/90 Troy Aikman	5.00	2.20	.60
☐ 9/3/90 Todd Marinovich	2.00	.90	.25
☐ 9/10/90 Barry Sanders (FC)	6.00	2.70	.75
☐ 9/24/90 Rick Mirer	4.00	1.80	.50
☐ 10/8/90 O.J.Simpson	4.00	1.80	.50
☐ 10/15/90 Burt Grossman	3.00	1.35	.35
☐ 11/12/90 William Bell	2.00	.90	.25
☐ 11/26/90 Derek Brown	2.00	.90	.25
☐ 12/10/90 Ty Detmer	4.00	1.80	.50
☐ 12/24/90 Joe Montana SOY	6.00	2.70	.75
☐ 12/31/90* Pictures '90: S.Paige	4.00	1.80	.50
☐ 1/14/91 Dan Marino	6.00	2.70	.75
☐ 1/28/91 Ottis Anderson	3.00	1.35	.35
☐ 2/4/91 Everson Walls	4.00	1.80	.50
☐ 2/25/91 Rocket Ismail	3.00	1.35	.35
☐ 7/8/91 Lyle Alzado	3.00	1.35	.35
☐ 8/12/91 Eric Dickerson	3.00	1.35	.35
☐ 8/26/91 Col.FB PV: D.Klingler	2.00	.90	.25
☐ Fall '91 Classic SI: Red Grange	6.00	2.70	.75
☐ 9/2/91 Bruce Smith	4.00	1.80	.50
☐ 9/23/91 Desmond Howard	4.00	1.80	.50
☐ 10/7/91 Bobby Hebert	3.00	1.35	.35
☐ 10/14/91 G.Clark/L.Stinson	3.00	1.35	.35
☐ 12/2/91 Jim McMahon	3.00	1.35	.35
☐ 12/9/91 Desmond Howard	4.00	1.80	.50
☐ 12/16/91 Marinovich/S.Conlan	2.00	.90	.25
☐ 1/20/92 Thurman Thomas	4.00	1.80	.50
☐ 2/3/92 Mark Rypien	3.00	1.35	.35
☐ 4/27/92 Deion Sanders BB	4.00	1.80	.50
☐ 7/27/92 Joe Montana	5.00	2.20	.60
☐ 8/24/92 Deion Sanders BB/FB	4.00	1.80	.50
☐ 8/31/92 Col. FB PV: U of Miami	2.00	.90	.25
☐ 9/7/92 Jerry Rice	5.00	2.20	.60
☐ 9/14/92 Jim Harbaugh	3.00	1.35	.35
☐ 9/28/92 Tony Mandarich	2.00	.90	.25
☐ 10/12/92 Randall Cunningham	3.00	1.35	.35
☐ 12/7/92 FB injuries: J.Campen	2.00	.90	.25
☐ 1/11/93 Derric Lassic (Ala.only)	6.00	2.70	.75
☐ 1/18/93 Steve Young (FC)	6.00	2.70	.75
☐ 1/25/93 Emmitt Smith (FC)	8.00	3.60	1.00
☐ 2/1/93 Dr. Z Super Bowl pick	2.00	.90	.25
☐ 2/8/93 Troy Aikman	6.00	2.70	.75
☐ 3/15/93 Reggie White	4.00	1.80	.50
☐ 4/26/93 Joe Montana	5.00	2.20	.60
☐ 8/2/93 J.Elway/D.Reeves	3.00	1.35	.35
☐ 8/30/93 Col.FB PV: Bentley/Kanell	3.00	1.35	.35
☐ 9/6/93 Junior Seau	4.00	1.80	.50
☐ 9/13/93 Joe Montana	5.00	2.20	.60
☐ 10/4/93 Boomer/Gunnar Esiason	3.00	1.35	.35
☐ 10/11/93 Chuck Cecil	3.00	1.35	.35
☐ 10/25/93 Michael Irvin	4.00	1.80	.50
☐ 11/22/93 Jim Flanigan	2.00	.90	.25
☐ 11/29/93 BC vs. Notre Dame FB	2.00	.90	.25
☐ 12/6/93 Can NFL Be Saved?	2.00	.90	.25
☐ 12/20/93 Don Shula SOY	4.00	1.80	.50

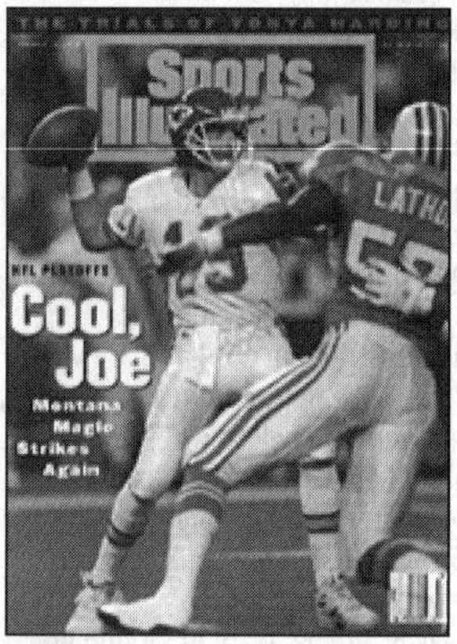

☐ 12/31/93 '93 Yr in Pictures: Aikman	10.00	4.50	1.25
☐ 1/10/94 Fla.St. FB: Matt Frier	3.00	1.35	.35
☐ 1/24/94 Joe Montana	4.00	1.80	.50
☐ 1/31/94 Emmitt Smith	6.00	2.70	.75
☐ 2/7/94 Emmitt Smith	5.00	2.20	.60
☐ 4/25/94 Dan Wilkinson	3.00	1.35	.35
☐ 5/16/94 Fla. St. FB scandal	2.00	.90	.25
☐ 6/27/94 O.J.Simpson	5.00	2.20	.60
☐ 8/1/94 E.Smith/Aikman/Switzer	6.00	2.70	.75
☐ 8/29/94 Col.FB PV: Arizona defense	3.00	1.35	.35
☐ 9/5/94 Will Wolford	3.00	1.35	.35
☐ 9/12/94 Dan Marino	5.00	2.20	.60
☐ 9/26/94 Steve McNair	4.00	1.80	.50
☐ 10/3/94 Michael Westbrook	4.00	1.80	.50
☐ 10/17/94 Natrone Means	3.00	1.35	.35
☐ 10/24/94 Freddie Scott	2.00	.90	.25
☐ 11/21/94 Ricky Watters	4.00	1.80	.50
☐ 12/5/94 Steelers vs. Raiders	3.00	1.35	.35
☐ 12/12/94 Cowboys: Emmitt etc	5.00	2.20	.60
☐ 12/26/94* Jerry Rice	5.00	2.20	.60
☐ 1/9/95 Tom Osborne	3.00	1.35	.35
☐ 1/16/95 S.Young/T.Aikman	6.00	2.70	.75
☐ 1/23/95 Steve Young	5.00	2.20	.60
☐ 2/6/95 Steve Young	5.00	2.20	.60
☐ 4/24/95 Joe Montana & family	4.00	1.80	.50
☐ 5/15/95 Erickson/Moeller/Cox	2.00	.90	.25
☐ 6/12/95 Should Miami Drop FB?	2.00	.90	.25
☐ 8/14/95 Gene Stallings (Ala.only)	6.00	2.70	.75
☐ 8/28/95 Col.FB PV: Keys.Johnson	3.00	1.35	.35
☐ Fall '95 Classic SI: Bobby Layne	5.00	2.20	.60
☐ 9/4/95 NFL PV: Dan Marino	5.00	2.20	.60
☐ 9/18/95 Emmitt Smith	5.00	2.20	.60
☐ 9/25/95 Danny Wuerffel	4.00	1.80	.50
☐ 10/9/95 Deion Sanders FB	4.00	1.80	.50
☐ 10/30/95 Bo Jackson	3.00	1.35	.35
☐ 11/13/95 Darnell Autry	3.00	1.35	.35
☐ 11/20/95 E.Grbac/R.Maryland	3.00	1.35	.35
☐ 12/4/95 Art Modell	2.00	.90	.25
☐ 12/11/95 Pat Riley/Don Shula	3.00	1.35	.35
☐ 12/25/95* Tommie Frazier (SW)	6.00	2.70	.75
☐ 12/25/95* Barry Sanders (MW)	6.00	2.70	.75
☐ 12/25/95* Steve Spurrier (SE)	6.00	2.70	.75
☐ 12/25/95* Steve Tasker (NE)	4.00	1.80	.50
☐ 1/15/96 Brett Favre (FC)	6.00	2.70	.75
☐ 1/22/96 Emmitt Smith	5.00	2.20	.60
☐ 2/1/96 '95-96 FB Yr in Pictures: Favre	10.00	4.50	1.25
☐ 2/5/96 Emmitt Smith	5.00	2.20	.60
☐ 5/13/96 D.Marino/J.Johnson	5.00	2.20	.60
☐ 7/1/96 Emmitt Smith	5.00	2.20	.60
☐ 8/26/96 Col.FB PV: PeytonManning	4.00	1.80	.50
☐ 9/2/96 NFL PV: Favre/Brooks/White	5.00	2.20	.60
☐ 9/9/96 Dolphins D: Steve Emtman	3.00	1.35	.35
☐ 9/16/96 Ahman Green	3.00	1.35	.35
☐ 9/23/96 Ron Powlus	3.00	1.35	.35
☐ 12/9/96 Warrick Dunn	4.00	1.80	.50
☐ 12/16/96 Brett Favre	5.00	2.20	.60
☐ 12/30/96* John Elway	4.00	1.80	.50

VINTAGE MEMORABILIA PRICE GUIDE

AAFC Championship Programs

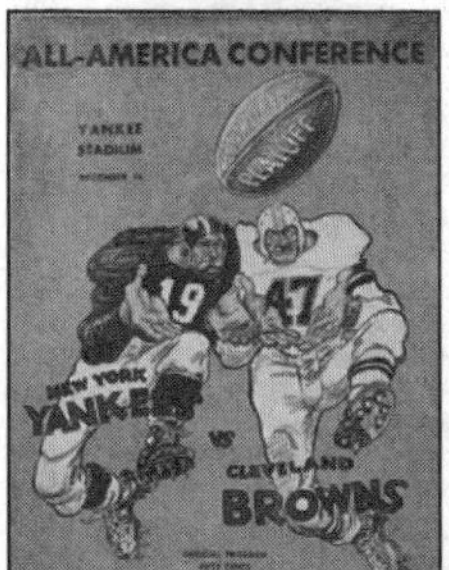

The All-America Football Conference began play in 1946 and folded after the 1949 season. The AAFC was the brainchild of Chicago sportswriter and sports promoter, Arch Ward. The AAFC was comprised of eight teams representing the cities of: Cleveland (Browns), San Francisco (49ers), Los Angeles (Dons), Chicago (Rockets, Hornets), New York (Yankees), Brooklyn (Dodgers), Buffalo (Bills) and Miami. The Miami Seahawks folded after the 1946 season, and were replaced by the Baltimore Colts. The Cleveland Browns, with a combined record of 47-4-3, won the AAFC title game in each of the league's four seasons. Three AAFC franchises, the San Francisco 49ers, Baltimore Colts and Cleveland Browns merged with the NFL for the 1950 season.

	Nr-Mt	Ex--Mt
1946 Browns vs Yankees	500.00	300.00
1947 Browns vs Yankees	400.00	250.00
1948 Browns vs Bills	450.00	300.00
1949 Browns vs 49'ers	450.00	300.00

AAFC Championship Ticket Stubs

	Nr-Mt	Ex-Mt
1946 Browns vs Yankees	350.00	250.00
1947 Browns vs Yankees	300.00	200.00
1948 Browns vs Bills	325.00	225.00
1949 Browns vs 49'ers	325.00	225.00

NFL Championship Programs

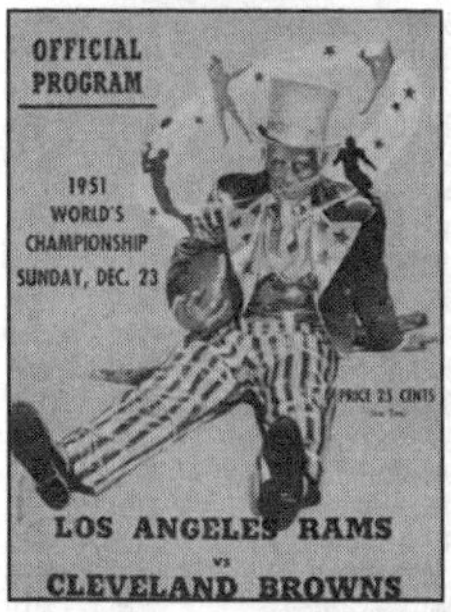

Pre-war programs are difficult to obtain in top condition and are graded Vg-Ex and Ex-Mt below.

	Nr-Mt	Ex-Mt
1933 Giants vs Bears	1500.00	1000.00
1934 Bears vs Giants	1400.00	900.00
1935 Giants vs Lions	1000.00	700.00
1936 Packers vs Redskins	800.00	500.00
1937 Redskins vs Bears	800.00	500.00
1938 Giants vs Packers	700.00	400.00
1939 Packers vs Giants	700.00	400.00
1940 Bears vs Redskins	800.00	500.00
1941 Bears vs Giants	700.00	450.00
1942 Redskins vs Bears	600.00	400.00
1943 Bears vs Redskins	600.00	400.00
1944 Packers vs Giants	600.00	400.00
1945 Rams vs Redskins	500.00	300.00
1946 Bears vs Giants	450.00	300.00
1947 Cardinals vs Eagles	350.00	200.00
1948 Eagles vs Cardinals	325.00	175.00
1949 Eagles vs Rams	400.00	250.00
1950 Browns vs Rams	400.00	250.00
1951 Rams vs Browns	300.00	150.00
1952 Lions vs Browns	300.00	150.00
1953 Browns vs Lions	250.00	125.00
1954 Lions vs Browns	250.00	125.00
1955 Browns vs Rams	200.00	100.00
1956 Bears vs Giants	200.00	100.00
1957 Browns vs Lions	200.00	100.00
1958 Colts vs Giants	200.00	100.00
1959 Giants vs Colts	200.00	100.00

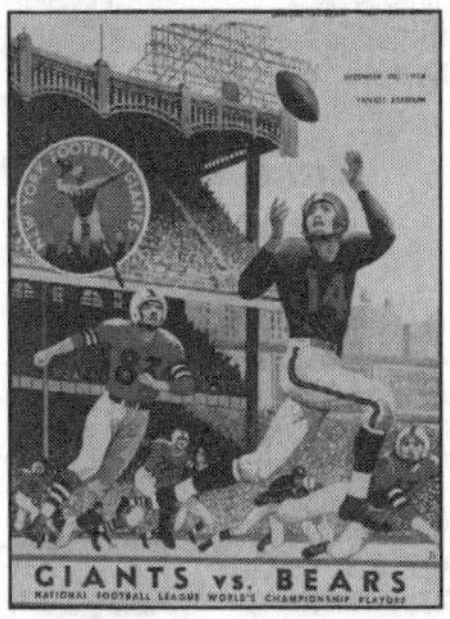

1960 Packers vs Eagles	150.00	75.00
1961 Giants vs Packers	200.00	100.00
1962 Giants vs Packers	150.00	75.00
1963 Giants vs Bears	150.00	75.00
1964 Colts vs Browns	150.00	75.00
1965 Browns vs Packers	175.00	80.00
1966 Packers vs Cowboys	125.00	65.00
1967 Cowboys at Packers	200.00	100.00
1968 Colts vs Cleveland	125.00	65.00
1969 Cleveland vs Vikings	125.00	65.00

NFL Championship Ticket Stubs

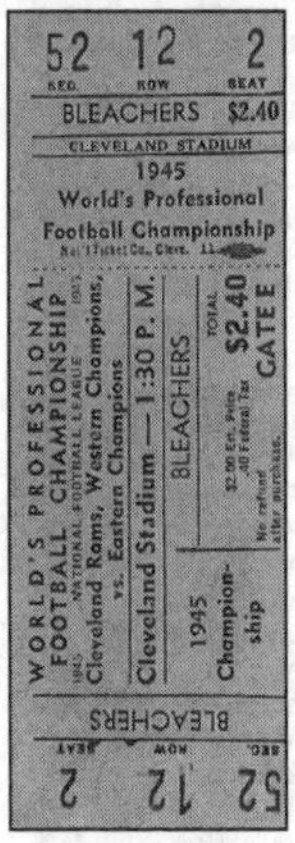

Pre-war ticket stubs are difficult to obtain in top condition and are graded Vg-Ex and Ex-Mt below. Complete tickets are valued 3 to 6 times that of a stub.

	Nr-Mt	Ex-Mt
1933 Giants vs Bears	450.00	300.00
1934 Bears vs Giants	400.00	250.00
1935 Giants vs Lions	400.00	250.00
1936 Packers vs Redskins	300.00	200.00
1937 Redskins vs Bears	250.00	150.00
1938 Giants vs Packers	225.00	125.00
1939 Packers vs Giants	225.00	125.00
1940 Bears vs Redskins	300.00	200.00
1941 Bears vs Giants	250.00	150.00
1942 Redskins vs Bears	200.00	125.00
1943 Bears vs Redskins	200.00	125.00
1944 Packers vs Giants	200.00	125.00
1945 Rams vs Redskins	175.00	100.00
1946 Bears vs Giants	175.00	100.00
1947 Cardinals vs Eagles	150.00	90.00
1948 Eagles vs Cardinals	125.00	75.00
1949 Eagles vs Rams	125.00	75.00
1950 Browns vs Rams	100.00	60.00
1951 Rams vs Browns	100.00	60.00
1952 Lions vs Browns	100.00	60.00
1953 Browns vs Lions	100.00	60.00
1954 Lions vs Browns	100.00	60.00
1955 Browns vs Rams	100.00	60.00
1956 Bears vs Giants	75.00	40.00
1957 Browns vs Lions	75.00	40.00
1958 Colts vs Giants	75.00	40.00
1959 Giants vs Colts	60.00	35.00
1960 Packers vs Eagles	60.00	35.00
1961 Giants vs Packers	125.00	75.00
1962 Giants vs Packers	60.00	35.00
1963 Giants vs Bears	60.00	35.00
1964 Colts vs Browns	75.00	40.00
1965 Browns vs Packers	50.00	30.00
1966 Packers vs Cowboys	125.00	75.00
1967 Cowboys at Packers	50.00	30.00
1968 Colts vs Cleveland	40.00	25.00
1969 Cleveland vs Vikings	40.00	25.00

AFL Championship Programs

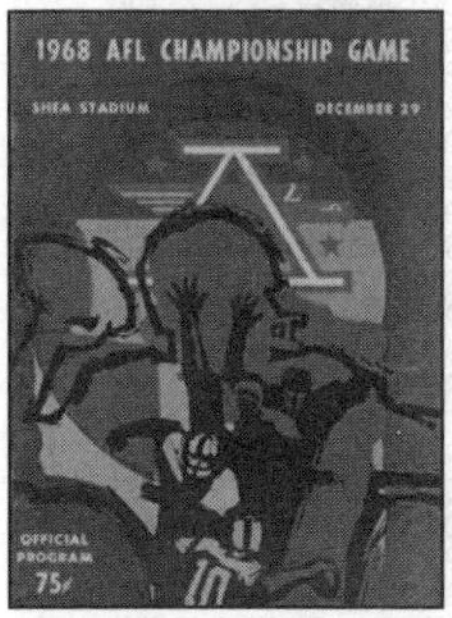

	Nr-Mt	Ex-Mt
1960 Chargers vs Oilers	350.00	250.00
1961 Oilers vs Chargers	325.00	225.00
1962 Texans vs Oilers	325.00	225.00
1963 Patriots vs Chargers	300.00	175.00
1964 Chargers vs Bills	250.00	150.00
1965 Bills vs Chargers	250.00	150.00
1966 Chiefs vs Bills	225.00	125.00
1967 Oilers vs Raiders	150.00	90.00
1968 Raiders vs Jets	250.00	150.00
1969 Chiefs vs Raiders	200.00	125.00

AFL Championship Ticket Stubs

	Nr-Mt	Ex-Mt
1960 Chargers vs Oilers	150.00	90.00
1961 Oilers vs Chargers	125.00	75.00
1962 Texans vs Oilers	125.00	75.00
1963 Patriots vs Chargers	100.00	60.00
1964 Chargers vs Bills	75.00	40.00
1965 Bills vs Chargers	75.00	40.00
1966 Chiefs vs Bills	50.00	30.00
1967 Oilers vs Raiders	50.00	30.00
1968 Raiders vs Jets	40.00	25.00
1969 Chiefs vs Raiders	40.00	25.00

Super Bowl Patches

Super Bowl patches were intended to be sold at each Super Bowl venue as a souvenir. In recent years several patches have been reprinted. It's difficult to differentiate original Super Bowl patches from reprints. However, original patches prior to Super Bowl XIV do not have the plastic coating applied to the backside like the current patches do.

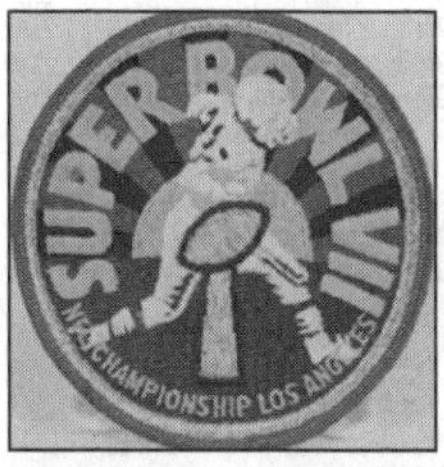

	Nr-Mt	Ex-Mt
1967 (I) Packers vs Chiefs	75.00	50.00
1968 (II) Packers vs Raiders	75.00	50.00
1969 (III) Jets vs Colts	75.00	50.00
1970 (IV) Chiefs vs Vikings	75.00	50.00
1971 (V) Colts vs Cowboys	60.00	40.00
1972 (VI) Cowboys vs Dolphins	60.00	40.00
1973 (VII) Dolphins vs Redskins	60.00	40.00
1974 (VIII) Dolphins vs Vikings	60.00	40.00
1975 (IX) Steelers vs Vikings	50.00	30.00
1976 (X) Steelers vs Cowboys	50.00	30.00
1977 (XI) Raiders vs Vikings	50.00	30.00
1978 (XII) Broncos vs Cowboys	50.00	30.00
1979 (XIII) Steelers vs Cowboys	50.00	30.00
1980 (XIV) Steelers vs Rams	25.00	15.00
1981 (XV) Eagles vs Raiders	25.00	15.00
1982 (XVI) 49ers vs Bengals	25.00	15.00
1983 (XVII) Redskins vs Dolph	25.00	15.00
1984 (XVIII) Raiders vs Redsk	25.00	15.00
1985 (XIX) 49ers vs Dolphins	25.00	15.00
1986 (XX) Bears vs Patriots	25.00	15.00
1987 (XXI) Giants vs Broncos	25.00	15.00
1988 (XXII) Redsk vs Broncos	25.00	15.00
1989 (XXIII) 49ers vs Bengals	20.00	12.00
1990 (XXIV) 49ers vs Broncos	20.00	12.00
1991 (XXV) Giants vs Bills	20.00	12.00
1992 (XXVI) Redskins vs Bills	20.00	12.00
1993 (XXVII) Bills vs Cowboys	20.00	12.00
1994 (XXVIII) Bills vs Cowboys	20.00	12.00
1995 (XXIX) 49ers vs Chargers	20.00	12.00
1996 (XXX) Steelers vs Cowboys	20.00	12.00
1997(XXXI) Packers vs Patriots	20.00	12.00

Super Bowl Press Pins

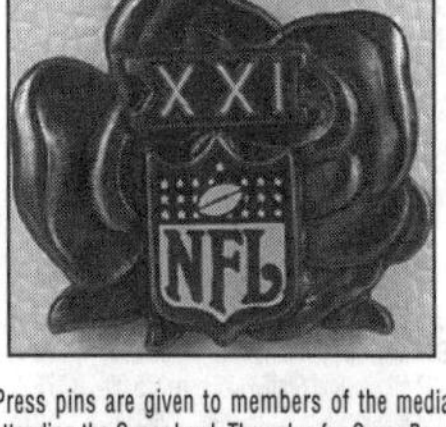

Press pins are given to members of the media attending the Super bowl. The value for Super Bowl I pin includes the tie-bar and cuff links. The value of the Super Bowl I pin by itself would be $900. There was no pin issued for Super Bowl II. The media recieved a charm. Also, the media attending Super Bowl III were given a tie-clasp rather than the traditional press pin. There were no press pins issued for either Super Bowl IV or V.

	Nr-Mt	Ex-Mt
1967 (I) Packers vs Chiefs	1500.00	900.00
1968 (II) Packers vs Raiders	1200.00	700.00
1969 (III) Jets vs Colts	1000.00	600.00
1970 (IV) Chiefs vs Vikings		
1971 (V) Colts vs Cowboys		
1972 (VI) Cowboys vs Dolphins	400.00	250.00
1973 (VII) Dolphins vs Redskins	350.00	200.00
1974 (VIII) Dolphins vs Vikings	250.00	150.00
1975 (IX) Steelers vs Vikings	250.00	150.00
1976 (X) Steelers vs Cowboys	250.00	150.00
1977 (XI) Raiders vs Vikings	250.00	150.00
1978 (XII) Broncos vs Cowboys	250.00	150.00
1979 (XIII) Steelers vs Cowboys	200.00	125.00
1980 (XIV) Steelers vs Rams	225.00	150.00
1981 (XV) Eagles vs Raiders	200.00	125.00
1982 (XVI) 49ers vs Bengals	350.00	250.00
1983 (XVII) Redskins vs Dolph	175.00	100.00
1984 (XVIII) Raiders vs Redsk	150.00	90.00
1985 (XIX) 49ers vs Dolphins	100.00	60.00
1986 (XX) Bears vs Patriots	100.00	60.00
1987 (XXI) Giants vs Broncos	125.00	75.00
1988 (XXII) Redsk vs Broncos	100.00	60.00
1989 (XXIII) 49ers vs Bengals	100.00	60.00
1990 (XXIV) 49ers vs Broncos	100.00	60.00
1991 (XXV) Giants vs Bills	100.00	60.00
1992 (XXVI) Redskins vs Bills	100.00	60.00
1993 (XXVII) Bills vs Cowboys	100.00	60.00
1994 (XXVIII) Bills vs Cowboys	100.00	60.00
1995 (XXIX) 49ers vs Chargers	125.00	75.00
1996(XXX) Steelers vs Cowboys	100.00	60.00
1997(XXXI) Packers vs Patriots	100.00	60.00

Super Bowl Programs

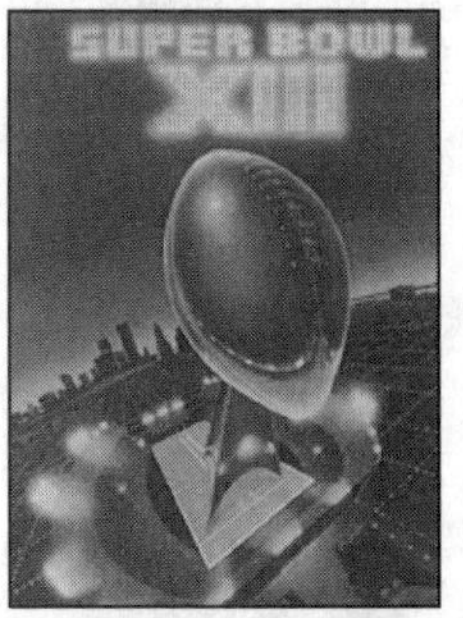

The program for Super Bowl V is sold at a premium due to a limited number being available on game day. Reportedly, a semi-truck carrying a quantity of programs crashed and overturned in route to the stadium. These programs were later destroyed. Beginning with Super Bowl X, game programs were available through the mail, thus the dropoff in values.

	Nr-Mt	Ex-Mt
1967 (I) Packers vs Chiefs	300.00	200.00
1968 (II) Packers vs Raiders	350.00	250.00
1969 (III) Jets vs Colts	300.00	200.00
1970 (IV) Chiefs vs Vikings	200.00	125.00
1971 (V) Colts vs Cowboys	400.00	300.00
1972 (VI) Cowboys vs Dolphins	150.00	90.00
1973 (VII) Dolphins vs Redskins	150.00	90.00
1974 (VIII) Dolphins vs Vikings	150.00	90.00
1975 (IX) Steelers vs Vikings	125.00	80.00
1976 (X) Steelers vs Cowboys	150.00	90.00
1977 (XI) Raiders vs Vikings	75.00	40.00
1978 (XII) Broncos vs Cowboys	75.00	40.00
1979 (XIII) Steelers vs Cowboys	60.00	35.00
1980 (XIV) Steelers vs Rams	60.00	35.00
1981 (XV) Eagles vs Raiders	30.00	18.00
1982 (XVI) 49ers vs Bengals	35.00	20.00
1983 (XVII) Redskins vs Dolp.	30.00	18.00
1984 (XVIII) Raiders vs Redsk	30.00	18.00
1985 (XIX) 49ers vs Dolphins	30.00	18.00
1986 (XX) Bears vs Patriots	30.00	18.00
1987 (XXI) Giants vs Broncos	20.00	12.00
1988 (XXII) Redskins vs Broncos	20.00	12.00
1989 (XXIII) 49ers vs Bengals	20.00	12.00
1990 (XXIV) 49ers vs Broncos	20.00	12.00
1991 (XXV) Giants vs Bills	15.00	8.00
1992 (XXVI) Redskins vs Bills	15.00	8.00
1993 (XXVII) Bills vs Cowboys	15.00	8.00
1994 (XXVIII) Bills vs Cowboys	15.00	8.00
1995 (XXIX) 49ers vs Chargers	15.00	8.00
1996(XXX) Steelers vs Cowboys	15.00	8.00
1997(XXXI) Packers vs Patriots	15.00	8.00

Super Bowl Ticket Stubs

Prices below are for game stubs. Complete unused tickets are valued 2 to 5 times that of the stub. The stub for Super Bowl IV is sold at a premium because many of Tulane Stadiums ticket takers tore the tickets in half instead of ripping them at the performation.

	Nr-Mt	Ex-Mt
1967 (I) Packers vs Chiefs	450.00	350.00
1968 (II) Packers vs Raiders	400.00	300.00
1969 (III) Jets vs Colts	350.00	250.00

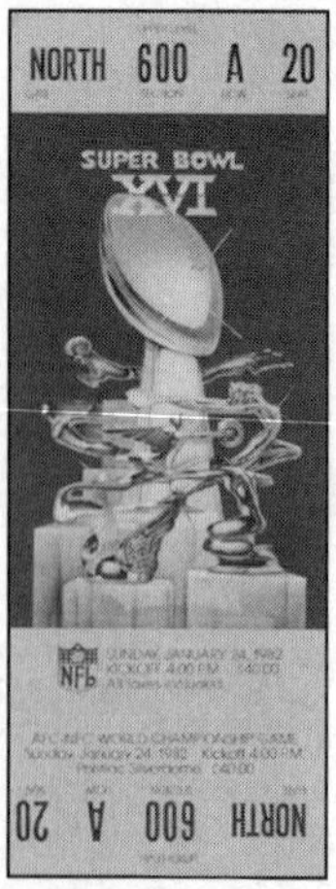

1970 (IV) Chiefs vs Vikings	450.00	350.00
1971 (V) Colts vs Cowboys	250.00	150.00
1972 (VI) Cowboys vs Dolphins	200.00	125.00
1973 (VII) Dolphins vs Redskins	175.00	100.00
1974 (VIII) Dolphins vs Vikings	200.00	125.00
1975 (IX) Steelers vs Vikings	150.00	90.00
1976 (X) Steelers vs Cowboys	175.00	100.00
1977 (XI) Raiders vs Vikings	150.00	90.00
1978 (XII) Broncos vs Cowboys	150.00	90.00
1979 (XIII) Steelers vs Cowboys	150.00	90.00
1980 (XIV) Steelers vs Rams	150.00	90.00

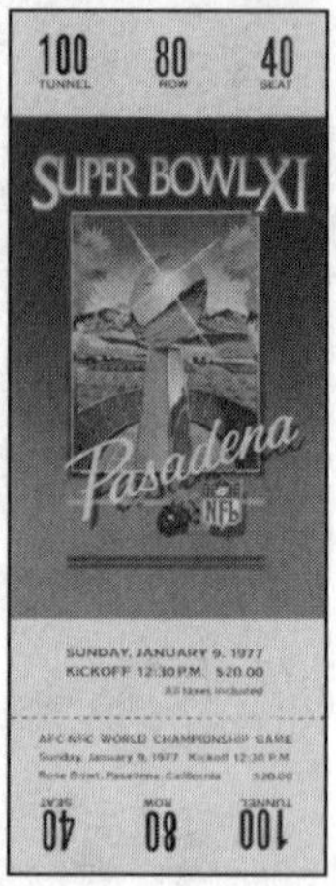

1981 (XV) Eagles vs Raiders	125.00	75.00
1982 (XVI) 49ers vs Bengals	125.00	75.00
1983 (XVII) Redskins vs Dolph	125.00	75.00
1984 (XVIII) Raiders vs Redsk	125.00	75.00
1985 (XIX) 49ers vs Dolphins	125.00	75.00
1986 (XX) Bears vs Patriots	100.00	60.00
1987 (XXI) Giants vs Broncos	100.00	60.00
1988 (XXII) Redsk vs Broncos	100.00	60.00
1989 (XXIII) 49ers vs Bengals	100.00	60.00
1990 (XXIV) 49ers vs Broncos	75.00	40.00
1991 (XXV) Giants vs Bills	100.00	60.00
1992 (XXVI) Redskins vs Bills	75.00	40.00
1993 (XXVII) Bills vs Cowboys	75.00	40.00
1994 (XXVIII) Bills vs Cowboys	75.00	40.00
1995 (XXIX) 49ers vs Chargers	75.00	40.00
1995(XXX) Steelers vs Cowboys	75.00	40.00
1997(XXXI) Packers vs Patriots	75.00	40.00

Cotton Bowl Programs

	Nr-Mt	Ex-Mt
1937 TCU/Marquette	400.00	250.00
1938 Rice/Colorado	300.00	200.00
1939 Texas Tech/St. Mary's (Cal)	300.00	175.00
1940 Clemson/Boston College	300.00	175.00
1941 Texas A & M/Fordham	325.00	175.00
1942 Texas A & M/Alabama	300.00	175.00
1943 Texas/Georgia Tech	300.00	175.00
1944 Texas/Randolph Field	250.00	150.00
1945 Oklahoma State/TCU	250.00	150.00
1946 Texas/Missouri	225.00	125.00
1947 Arkansas/LSU	225.00	125.00
1948 SMU/Penn State	200.00	100.00
1949 SMU/Oregon	175.00	90.00
1950 Rice/North Carolina	150.00	90.00
1951 Texas/Tennessee	150.00	80.00
1952 TCU/Kentucky	125.00	75.00
1953 Texas/Tennessee	125.00	75.00
1954 Rice/Alabama	125.00	75.00
1955 Arkansas/Georgia Tech	100.00	60.00
1956 TCU/Mississippi	100.00	60.00
1957 TCU/Rice	100.00	60.00
1958 Rice/Navy	90.00	50.00
1959 TCU/Air Force	75.00	50.00
1960 Texas/Syracuse	100.00	60.00
1961 Arkansas/Duke	75.00	40.00
1962 Texas/Mississippi	75.00	40.00
1963 Texas/LSU	75.00	40.00
1964 Texas/Navy	75.00	40.00
1965 Arkansas/Nebraska	60.00	35.00
1966 Arkansas/LSU	60.00	35.00
1967 Georgia/Wyoming	60.00	35.00
1968 Texas A & M/Alabama	50.00	25.00
1969 Texas/Tennessee	40.00	35.00
1970 Texas/Notre Dame	75.00	40.00
1971 Texas/Notre Dame	75.00	40.00
1972 Texas/Penn State	50.00	25.00
1973 Texas/Alabama	40.00	20.00
1974 Texas/Nebraska	40.00	20.00
1975 Baylor/Penn State	40.00	20.00
1976 Arkansas/Georgia	30.00	15.00
1977 Houston/Notre Dame	30.00	15.00
1978 Texas/Notre Dame	40.00	20.00
1979 Houston/Notre Dame	40.00	20.00
1980 Houston/Nebraska	25.00	15.00
1981- present	15.00	8.00

Cotton Bowl Ticket Stubs

	Nr-Mt	Ex-Mt
1937 TCU/Marquette	200.00	125.00
1938 Rice/Colorado	125.00	90.00
1939 Texas Tech/St. Mary's (Cal)	125.00	75.00
1940 Clemson/Boston College	125.00	75.00
1941 Texas A & M/Fordham	125.00	75.00
1942 Texas A & M/Alabama	100.00	60.00
1943 Texas/Georgia Tech	100.00	60.00
1944 Texas/Randolph Field	100.00	60.00
1945 Oklahoma State/TCU	100.00	60.00
1946 Texas/Missouri	75.00	40.00
1947 Arkansas/LSU	100.00	60.00
1948 SMU/Penn State	75.00	40.00
1949 SMU/Oregon	75.00	40.00
1950 Rice/North Carolina	60.00	30.00
1951 Texas/Tennessee	60.00	30.00
1952 TCU/Kentucky	60.00	30.00
1953 Texas/Tennessee	60.00	30.00
1954 Rice/Alabama	60.00	30.00
1955 Arkansas/Georgia Tech	50.00	30.00
1956 TCU/Mississippi	60.00	30.00
1957 TCU/Rice	60.00	40.00
1958 Rice/Navy	75.00	50.00
1959 TCU/Air Force	50.00	30.00
1960 Texas/Syracuse	75.00	45.00
1961 Arkansas/Duke	50.00	30.00
1962 Texas/Mississippi	50.00	30.00
1963 Texas/LSU	50.00	30.00
1964 Texas/Navy	50.00	30.00
1965 Arkansas/Nebraska	40.00	25.00
1966 Arkansas/LSU	50.00	30.00
1967 Georgia/Wyoming	50.00	25.00
1968 Texas A & M/Alabama	40.00	25.00
1969 Texas/Tennessee	35.00	20.00
1970 Texas/Notre Dame	80.00	50.00
1971 Texas/Notre Dame	80.00	50.00
1972 Texas/Penn State	35.00	20.00
1973 Texas/Alabama	35.00	20.00
1974 Texas/Nebraska	30.00	18.00
1975 Baylor/Penn State	30.00	18.00
1976 Arkansas/Georgia	25.00	15.00
1977 Houston/Notre Dame	25.00	15.00
1978 Texas/Notre Dame	30.00	18.00
1979 Houston/Notre Dame	30.00	18.00
1980 Houston/Nebraska	30.00	18.00
1981- present	20.00	10.00

Orange Bowl Programs

	Nr-Mt	Ex-Mt
1935 Bucknell/Miami	500.00	300.00
1936 Mississippi/Catholic U.	300.00	200.00
1937 Mississippi State/Duquesne	275.00	175.00
1938 Auburn/Michigan State	250.00	150.00
1939 Tennessee/Oklahoma	300.00	200.00
1940 Georgia Tech/Missouri	275.00	175.00
1941 Mississippi St./Georgetown	250.00	150.00
1942 Georgia/TCU	250.00	150.00
1943 Alabama/Boston College	250.00	150.00
1944 LSU/Texas A & M	225.00	125.00
1945 Georgia Tech./Tulsa	200.00	100.00
1946 Miami/Holy Cross	175.00	100.00
1947 Tennessee/Rice	150.00	80.00
1948 Georgia Tech/Kansas	125.00	70.00
1949 Georgia/Texas	100.00	60.00
1950 Kentucky/Santa Clara	100.00	60.00
1951 Miami/Clemson	125.00	75.00
1952 Georgia Tech/Baylor	100.00	60.00
1953 Alabama/Syracuse	100.00	60.00
1954 Maryland/Oklahoma	100.00	60.00
1955 Duke/Nebraska	150.00	80.00
1956 Maryland/Oklahoma	100.00	60.00
1957 Clemson/Colorado	90.00	50.00
1958 Duke/Oklahoma	100.00	60.00
1959 Syracuse/Oklahoma	100.00	60.00
1960 Georgia/Missouri	75.00	40.00
1961 Navy/Missouri	75.00	40.00
1962 LSU/Colorado	60.00	35.00
1963 Alabama/Oklahoma	60.00	35.00
1964 Auburn/Nebraska	60.00	35.00
1965 Alabama/Texas	100.00	60.00
1966 Alabama/Nebraska	60.00	30.00
1967 Flordia/Georgia Tech	50.00	25.00
1968 Tennessee/Oklahoma	50.00	25.00
1969 Penn State/Kansas	40.00	20.00
1970 Penn State/Missouri	40.00	20.00
1971 LSU/Nebraska	35.00	20.00
1972 Alabama/Nebraska	35.00	20.00
1973 Notre Dame/Nebraska	35.00	20.00
1974 LSU/Penn State	30.00	18.00
1975 Alabama/Notre Dame	30.00	18.00
1976 Oklahoma/Michigan	25.00	15.00
1977 Ohio State/Colorado	20.00	15.00
1978 Arkansas/Oklahoma	25.00	15.00
1979 Oklahoma/Nebraska	20.00	10.00
1980 Oklahoma/Flordia State	20.00	10.00
1981-present	15.00	8.00

Orange Bowl Ticket Stubs

	Nr-Mt	Ex-Mt
1935 Bucknell/Miami	300.00	200.00
1936 Mississippi/Catholic U.	150.00	90.00
1937 Mississippi State/Duquesne	150.00	90.00
1938 Auburn/Michigan State	125.00	75.00
1939 Tennessee/Oklahoma	125.00	75.00
1940 Georgia Tech/Missouri	125.00	75.00
1941 Mississippi St./Georgetown	100.00	60.00
1942 Georgia/TCU	125.00	75.00
1943 Alabama/Boston College	100.00	60.00
1944 LSU/Texas A & M	100.00	60.00
1945 Georgia Tech./Tulsa	75.00	45.00
1946 Miami/Holy Cross	75.00	40.00
1947 Tennessee/Rice	75.00	40.00
1948 Georgia Tech/Kansas	75.00	40.00
1949 Georgia/Texas	60.00	30.00
1950 Kentucky/Santa Clara	60.00	30.00
1951 Miami/Clemson	60.00	30.00
1952 Georgia Tech/Baylor	60.00	30.00
1953 Alabama/Syracuse	60.00	30.00
1954 Maryland/Oklahoma	60.00	30.00
1955 Duke/Nebraska	75.00	40.00
1956 Maryland/Oklahoma	60.00	30.00
1957 Clemson/Colorado	60.00	40.00
1958 Duke/Oklahoma	60.00	40.00
1959 Syracuse/Oklahoma	75.00	50.00
1960 Georgia/Missouri	50.00	30.00
1961 Navy/Missouri	50.00	30.00
1962 LSU/Colorado	40.00	25.00
1963 Alabama/Oklahoma	40.00	25.00
1964 Auburn/Nebraska	50.00	30.00
1965 Alabama/Texas	75.00	50.00
1966 Alabama/Nebraska	50.00	30.00
1967 Flordia/Georgia Tech	40.00	25.00
1968 Tennessee/Oklahoma	40.00	25.00
1969 Penn State/Kansas	35.00	20.00
1970 Penn State/Missouri	30.00	18.00
1971 LSU/Nebraska	30.00	18.00
1972 Alabama/Nebraska	30.00	18.00
1973 Notre Dame/Nebraska	40.00	25.00
1974 LSU/Penn State	25.00	15.00
1975 Alabama/Notre Dame	35.00	20.00
1976 Oklahoma/Michigan	25.00	15.00
1977 Ohio State/Colorado	25.00	15.00
1978 Arkansas/Oklahoma	30.00	18.00
1979 Oklahoma/Nebraska	25.00	15.00
1980 Oklahoma/Flordia State	25.00	15.00
1981-present	20.00	10.00

Rose Bowl Programs

Pre-war bowl programs and ticket stubs, are rarely found in Nr-Mt condition. These programs and ticket stubs are graded at Ex-Mt and Ex condition.

	Nr-Mt	Ex-Mt
1902 Stanford/Michigan	5000.00	3000.00
1916 Wash. State/Brown	2500.00	1500.00
1917 Oregon/Penn.	1500.00	800.00
1918 Mare Isle./Camp Lewis	1200.00	700.00
1919 Mare Isle./Great Lakes	1200.00	700.00
1920 Oregon/Harvard	1000.00	600.00
1921 California/Ohio State	1200.00	700.00
1922 Cal./ Wash. & Jeff.	1000.00	600.00
1923 USC/Penn State	1500.00	900.00
1924 Washington/Navy	1000.00	600.00
1925 Stan./Notre Dame	1800.00	1000.00
1926 Washington/Alabama	1200.00	600.00
1927 Stanford/Alabama	900.00	600.00
1928 Stanford/Pittsburgh	700.00	400.00
1929 Cal./Georgia Tech	1000.00	600.00
1930 USC/Pittsburgh	700.00	400.00
1931 Wash. St./Alabama	1200.00	700.00
1932 USC/Tulane	500.00	300.00
1933 USC/Pittsburgh	500.00	300.00
1934 Stanford/Columbia	600.00	350.00
1935 Stanford/Alabama	400.00	250.00
1936 Stanford/LSU	400.00	250.00
1937 Wash/Pittsburgh	350.00	200.00
1938 California/Alabama	350.00	200.00
1939 USC/Duke	300.00	150.00
1940 USC/Tennessee	300.00	150.00
1941 Stanford/ Nebraska	250.00	125.00
1942 Oregon State/Duke	500.00	300.00
1943 UCLA/Georgia	900.00	600.00
1944 USC/Washington	200.00	100.00
1945 USC/Tennessee	175.00	125.00
1946 USC/Alabama	150.00	125.00
1947 UCLA/Illinois	150.00	125.00
1948 USC/Michigan	150.00	125.00
1949 Cal./Northwestern	125.00	75.00
1950 California/Ohio State	125.00	75.00
1951 California/Michigan	125.00	75.00
1952 Stanford/Illinois	100.00	60.00
1953 UCLA/Wisconsin	100.00	60.00
1954 UCLA/Michigan State	100.00	60.00
1955 USC/Ohio State	100.00	60.00
1956 UCLA/Michigan State	75.00	40.00
1957 Oregon State/Iowa	45.00	20.00
1958 Oregon/Ohio State	75.00	40.00
1959 California/Iowa	60.00	30.00
1960 Washington/Wisconsin	60.00	30.00
1961 Washington/Minnesota	50.00	25.00
1962 UCLA/Minnesota	50.00	25.00
1963 USC/Wisconsin	75.00	40.00
1964 Washington/Illinois	50.00	25.00
1965 Oregon State/Michigan	50.00	25.00
1966 UCLA/Michigan State	40.00	20.00
1967 USC/Purdue	40.00	20.00
1968 USC/Indiana	50.00	25.00
1969 USC/Ohio State	50.00	25.00
1970 USC/Michigan	35.00	20.00
1971 Stanford/Ohio State	35.00	20.00
1972 Stanford/Michigan	35.00	20.00
1973 USC/Ohio State	35.00	20.00
1974 USC/Ohio State	25.00	15.00
1975 USC/Ohio State	25.00	15.00
1976 UCLA/Ohio State	25.00	15.00
1977 USC/Michigan	20.00	10.00
1978 Washington/Michigan	20.00	10.00
1979 USC/Michigan	20.00	10.00
1980 USC/Ohio State	20.00	10.00
1981-present	15.00	8.00

Rose Bowl Ticket Stubs

	Nr-Mt	Ex-Mt
1902 Stanford/Michigan	3000.00	1800.00
1916 Washington State/Brown	1200.00	700.00
1917 Oregon/Pennsylvania	750.00	400.00
1918 Mare Island/Camp Lewis	600.00	400.00
1919 Mare Island/Great Lakes	600.00	400.00
1920 Oregon/Harvard	500.00	300.00
1921 California/Ohio State	600.00	400.00
1922 California/ Wash. & Jeff.	500.00	300.00
1923 USC/Penn State	750.00	500.00
1924 Washington/Navy	500.00	300.00
1925 Stanford/Notre Dame	750.00	500.00
1926 Washington/Alabama	500.00	300.00
1927 Stanford/Alabama	350.00	200.00
1928 Stanford/Pittsburgh	300.00	175.00
1929 California/Georgia Tech	300.00	200.00
1930 USC/Pittsburgh	300.00	200.00
1931 Washington State/Alabama	500.00	300.00
1932 USC/Tulane	250.00	150.00
1933 USC/Pittsburgh	250.00	150.00
1934 Stanford/Columbia	250.00	150.00
1935 Stanford/Alabama	200.00	125.00
1936 Stanford/LSU	150.00	90.00
1937 Washington/Pittsburgh	100.00	60.00
1938 California/Alabama	125.00	75.00
1939 USC/Duke	125.00	75.00
1940 USC/Tennessee	100.00	60.00
1941 Stanford/ Nebraska	100.00	60.00
1942 Oregon State/Duke	300.00	200.00
1943 UCLA/Georgia	350.00	250.00
1944 USC/Washington	75.00	40.00
1945 USC/Tennessee	75.00	40.00
1946 USC/Alabama	75.00	40.00
1947 UCLA/Illinois	75.00	40.00
1948 USC/Michigan	60.00	30.00
1949 California/Northwestern	60.00	30.00
1950 California/Ohio State	75.00	40.00
1951 California/Michigan	75.00	40.00
1952 Stanford/Illinois	60.00	30.00
1953 UCLA/Wisconsin	60.00	30.00
1954 UCLA/Michigan State	60.00	30.00
1955 USC/Ohio State	60.00	40.00
1956 UCLA/Michigan State	50.00	30.00
1957 Oregon State/Iowa	40.00	25.00
1958 Oregon/Ohio State	50.00	30.00
1959 California/Iowa	50.00	30.00
1960 Washington/Wisconsin	50.00	30.00
1961 Washington/Minnesota	40.00	25.00
1962 UCLA/Minnesota	40.00	25.00
1963 USC/Wisconsin	50.00	30.00
1964 Washington/Illinois	40.00	25.00
1965 Oregon State/Michigan	40.00	25.00
1966 UCLA/Michigan State	40.00	25.00
1967 USC/Purdue	30.00	20.00
1968 USC/Indiana	60.00	35.00
1969 USC/Ohio State	60.00	35.00
1970 USC/Michigan	30.00	18.00
1971 Stanford/Ohio State	30.00	18.00
1972 Stanford/Michigan	30.00	18.00
1973 USC/Ohio State	30.00	18.00
1974 USC/Ohio State	25.00	15.00
1975 USC/Ohio State	25.00	15.00
1976 UCLA/Ohio State	25.00	15.00
1977 USC/Michigan	25.00	15.00
1978 Washington/Michigan	25.00	15.00
1979 USC/Michigan	25.00	15.00
1980 USC/Ohio State	25.00	15.00
1981-present	20.00	10.00

Sugar Bowl Programs

	Nr-Mt	Ex-Mt
1935 Tulane/Temple	900.00	600.00
1936 LSU/TCU	700.00	400.00
1937 LSU/Santa Clara	700.00	400.00
1938 LSU/Santa Clara	500.00	300.00
1939 TCU/Carnegie Tech.	350.00	200.00
1940 Texas A & M/Tulane	300.00	175.00
1941 Tennessee/Boston College	250.00	150.00
1942 Missouri/Fordham	175.00	100.00
1943 Tennessee/Tulsa	175.00	100.00
1944 Georgia Tech/Tulsa	150.00	80.00
1945 Alabama/Duke	200.00	125.00
1946 Okla. A & M/St. Mary's	150.00	80.00
1947 Georgia/North Carolina	150.00	80.00
1948 Alabama/Texas	175.00	90.00
1949 Oklahoma/North Carolina	150.00	80.00
1950 Oklahoma/LSU	125.00	75.00
1951 Oklahoma/Kentucky	125.00	75.00
1952 Tennessee/Maryland	100.00	60.00
1953 Mississippi/Georgia Tech	100.00	60.00
1954 Georgia Tech/W. Virginia	100.00	60.00
1955 Mississippi/Navy	75.00	40.00
1956 Georgia Tech/Pittsburgh	75.00	40.00
1957 Tennessee/Baylor	75.00	40.00
1958 Mississippi/LSU	75.00	40.00
1959 LSU/Clemson	75.00	40.00
1960 Mississippi/LSU	60.00	30.00
1961 Mississippi/Rice	60.00	30.00
1962 Alabama/Arkansas	60.00	30.00
1963 Mississippi/Arkansas	50.00	25.00
1964 Mississippi/Alabama	60.00	30.00
1965 LSU/Syracuse	50.00	25.00
1966 Florida/Missouri	50.00	25.00
1967 Alabama/Nebraska	50.00	25.00
1968 LSU/Wyoming	40.00	20.00
1969 Georgia/Arkansas	40.00	20.00
1970 Mississippi/Arkansas	40.00	20.00
1971 Tennessee/Air Force	35.00	20.00
1972 Auburn/Oklahoma	35.00	20.00
1973 Oklahoma/Penn State	35.00	20.00
1974 Alabama/Notre Dame	40.00	20.00
1975 Flordia/Nebraska	30.00	15.00
1976 Alabama/Penn State	30.00	15.00
1977 Georgia/Pittsburgh	30.00	15.00
1978 Alabama/Ohio State	20.00	10.00
1979 Alabama/Penn State	20.00	10.00
1980 Alabama/Arkansas	20.00	10.00
1981-present	15.00	8.00

Sugar Bowl Ticket Stubs

	Nr-Mt	Ex-Mt
1935 Tulane/Temple	500.00	300.00
1936 LSU/TCU	300.00	175.00
1937 LSU/Santa Clara	250.00	150.00
1938 LSU/Santa Clara	150.00	90.00
1939 TCU/Carnegie Tech.	150.00	90.00
1940 Texas A & M/Tulane	100.00	60.00
1941 Tennessee/Boston College	100.00	60.00
1942 Missouri/Fordham	125.00	75.00
1943 Tennessee/Tulsa	100.00	60.00
1944 Georgia Tech/Tulsa	75.00	40.00
1945 Alabama/Duke	75.00	45.00
1946 Okla. A & M/St. Mary's	75.00	40.00
1947 Georgia/North Carolina	75.00	40.00
1948 Alabama/Texas	75.00	40.00
1949 Oklahoma/North Carolina	60.00	30.00
1950 Oklahoma/LSU	75.00	40.00
1951 Oklahoma/Kentucky	60.00	30.00
1952 Tennessee/Maryland	60.00	30.00
1953 Mississippi/Georgia Tech	60.00	30.00
1954 Georgia Tech/W. Virginia	60.00	30.00
1955 Mississippi/Navy	50.00	30.00
1956 Georgia Tech/Pittsburgh	50.00	30.00
1957 Tennessee/Baylor	50.00	30.00
1958 Mississippi/LSU	50.00	30.00
1959 LSU/Clemson	50.00	30.00
1960 Mississippi/LSU	50.00	30.00
1961 Mississippi/Rice	40.00	25.00
1962 Alabama/Arkansas	50.00	30.00
1963 Mississippi/Arkansas	40.00	25.00
1964 Mississippi/Alabama	50.00	30.00
1965 LSU/Syracuse	40.00	25.00
1966 Florida/Missouri	40.00	25.00
1967 Alabama/Nebraska	40.00	25.00
1968 LSU/Wyoming	30.00	20.00
1969 Georgia/Arkansas	35.00	20.00
1970 Mississippi/Arkansas	30.00	18.00
1971 Tennessee/Air Force	30.00	18.00
1972 Auburn/Oklahoma	30.00	18.00
1973 Oklahoma/Penn State	30.00	18.00
1974 Alabama/Notre Dame	40.00	25.00
1975 Flordia/Nebraska	35.00	20.00
1976 Alabama/Penn State	25.00	15.00
1977 Georgia/Pittsburgh	25.00	15.00
1978 Alabama/Ohio State	25.00	15.00
1979 Alabama/Penn State	25.00	15.00
1980 Alabama/Arkansas	25.00	15.00
1981-present	20.00	10.00

Acknowledgments

A great deal of diligence, hard work, and dedicated effort went into this year's volume. The high standards to which we hold ourselves, however, could not have been met without the expert input and generous amount of time contributed by many people. Our sincere thanks are extended to each and every one of you.

Each year we refine the process of developing the most accurate and up-to-date information for this book. I believe this year's Price Guide is our best yet. Thanks again to all of the contributors nationwide (listed below) as well as our staff here in Dallas.

Those who have worked closely with us on this and many other books have again proven themselves invaluable — Action Sports Cards, Mike Aronstein, Jerry Bell, Bubba Bennett, Chuck Bennett (Clubhouse), Mike Blaisdell, Bill Bossert (Mid-Atlantic Sports Cards), John Bradley (JOGO), Ralph Ciarlo, Mike Caffey, Don Chubey, Classic (Ken Goldin), Joe Colabella, Collector's Edge (Alan Lewis), Alan Custer, Robert Der, Bill and Diane Dodge, Rick Donohoo, John Douglas, John Durkos, Fleer/SkyBox (Rich Bradley, Doug Drotman, and Ted Taylor), Gervise Ford, Steve Freedman, Larry and Jeff Fritsch, Mike Gallella, Steven Galletta, Dick Gilkeson, Steve Gold (AU Sports), Mike and Howard Gordon, George Grauer, Wayne Grove, Jerry and Etta Hersh, Michael Hattley, Mike Hersh, Gary Hlady, Ed Kabala, Wayne Kleman, Lew Lipset, Chris Martin (Chris Martin Enterprises), Michael McDonald (The Sports Page), Pat Mills, Michael Moretto, Mike Mosier, Playoff, NFL Properties (Bill Barron and Don Renzulli), Don Niemi, Lawrence Nyeste, Mike O'Brien, Richard Ochoa, Oldies and Goodies (Nigel Spill), Pacific Trading Cards, Michael Perrotta (Gridiron Collectibles), Pinnacle Jack Pollard, Gavin Riley, Greg Rosen, Rotman Productions, John Rumierz, San Diego Sport Collectibles, Barry Sanders, Kevin Savage, Mike Schechter (MSA), Rick Smith, Gerry Sobie (Foots), John Spalding, (Pat Quinn), Frank Steele, Murvin Sterling (Reno Sports Cards), Paul S. Taylor, Lee Temanson, Topps (Marty Appel and Sy Berger), Upper Deck, U-Trading Cards (Mike Livingston), Rob Veres (Burbank Sportscards), Brian Wentz, Dale Wesolewski (AbD. Cards), Bill Wesslund, Kit Young, Robert Zanze, Steve Zeller, Dean Zindler, and Tim Zwick. Finally we give a special acknowledgment to Dennis W. Eckes, "Mr. Sport Americana," whose untimely passing in 1991 was a real loss to the hobby and to me personally. The success of the Beckett Price Guides has always been the result of a team effort.

Many people have provided price input, illustrative material, checklist verifications, errata, and/or background information. At the risk of inadvertently overlooking or omitting these many contributors, we would like to individually thank A & J Cards, Jerry Adamic, Aliso Hills Stamp and Coin, Rich Altman, Neil Armstrong (World Series Cards), Athleticards (Richard Tattoli), Tom Barborich, Red Barnes, Bob Bawiel, Dean Bedell, Patrick Benes, Carl Berg, Eric Berger, Kevin Bergson, Skip Bertman, Beulah Sports(Jeff Blatt), Brian L. Bigelow, David Bitar, Virgil Burns, Danny Cariseo, Dale Carlson, Bud Carter, Sally Carves, Dwight Chapin, Howard Churchill, Ralph H. Ciarlo, Orr Cihlar, Craig Coddling, Jon Cohen, Matt Collett, Taylor Crane, Jim Curie, Paul Czuchna, Samuel Davis, Tony

Wayne Davis,Cliff Dolgins, Joseph Drelich, E and R Galleries, Ed Emmitt, The End Zone, Darrell Ereth, Doak Ewing, Bob Farmer, Terry Faulkner, Fleischman and Walsh, Craig Frank, Mark Franke, Richard Freiburghouse, Brian Froehlich, Gallagher Archives, Tony Galovich, Tom Giacchino, Michael R. Gionet, David Giove, Todd Goldenberg, Jeff Goldstein, Gregg Gornes, Joseph Griffin, Robert G. Gross, Hall's Nostalgia, Steve Hart,, Rod Heffern, Kevin Heffner, Dennis Heitland, Clay Hill, Russ Hoover, Nelson Hu, Don Hurry, Jeff Issler, Bob Ivanjack, Robert R. Jackson, Dan Jaskula, Terry Johnson, Craig Jones, Stewart Jones, Larry Jordon, Chuck Juliana, Loyd Jungling, Jay and Mary Kasper, Frank Katen, Jack Kemps (Triple Play), Rick Keplinger, John Kilian, Ron Klassnik, Don Knutsen, Bob and Bryan Kornfield, Terry Kreider, George Kruk, Thomas Kunnecke, Dan Lavin, Walter Ledzki, Marc Lefkowitz (Baseball Card Baron), Tom Leon (Unisource Collectibles), Irv Lerner, Ed Lim, Frank Lopez, Neil Lopez, Frank Lucito, Kevin Lynch, Bud Lyle, Jim Macie, Gary Madrack, Paul Marchant, Adam Martin, Alex McCollum, Bob McDonald, Steve McHenry, Carlos Medina, Fernando Mercado, Joseph A. Merkel (Chicago Sportscards), Chris Merrill, Blake Meyer, Lee Milazzo, Dick Millerd, Ron Moermond, John Morales, Brian Morris, Rusty Morse, Dick Mueller, Bob Nappe, Roger Neufeldt, Raymond Ng, John O'Hara, Glenn Olsen, Mike Orth, Andrew Pak, Clay Pasternack, Paul and Judy's, John Peavy, Mark Perna, Steve Peters, Ira Petsrillo, Tom Pfirrmann, Chris Pomerleau, Jeff Porter, Jeff Prillaman, Jonathan Pullano, Loran Pulver, Phil Regli, Tom Reid, Owen Ricker, Evelyn Roberts, Jim Roberts, Mark Rose, Chip Rosenberg, Blake and Sheldon Rudman, George Rusnak, Terry Ryan, Terry Sack, Joe Sak, Nathan Schank, R.J. Schulhof, Perry Schwartzberg, Dan Scolman, Rick Scruggs, Charlie Seaver, Burns Searfoss, Eric Shillito, Shinder's Cards, Bob Singer, John Smith, Keith Smith, Carl Specht, Don Spagnolo, Sportcards Etc., Vic Stanley, Bill Steinberg, Cary Stephenson, Dan Stickney, Jack Stowe, Del Stracke, Richard Strobino, Kevin Struss, Bob Swick, George Tahinos, D. Tisdale, Bud Tompkins, Greg Tranter, John Tumazos, Eric Valkys, Wayne Varner, Kevin M. VanderKelen, Bill Vizas, Tom Wall, Mike Wasserman, Keith Watson, Mark Watson, Rick Wilson, Jay Wolt (Cavalcade of Sports), Paul Wright, Darryl Yee, Sheraton Yee, and Eugene Zalewski.

Every year we make active solicitations for expert input. We are particularly appreciative of help (however extensive or cursory) provided for this volume. We receive many inquiries, comments and questions regarding material within this book. In fact, each and every one is read and digested. Time constraints, however, prevent us from personally replying. But keep sharing your knowledge. Your letters and input are part of the "big picture" of hobby information we can pass along to readers in our books and magazines. Even though we cannot respond to each letter, you are making significant contributions to the hobby through your interest and comments.

The effort to continually refine and improve this book also involves a growing number of people and types of expertise on our home team. Our company boasts a substantial Sports Data Publishing team, which strengthens our ability to provide comprehensive analysis of the marketplace. SDP capably handled numerous technical details and provided able assistance in the preparation of this edition.

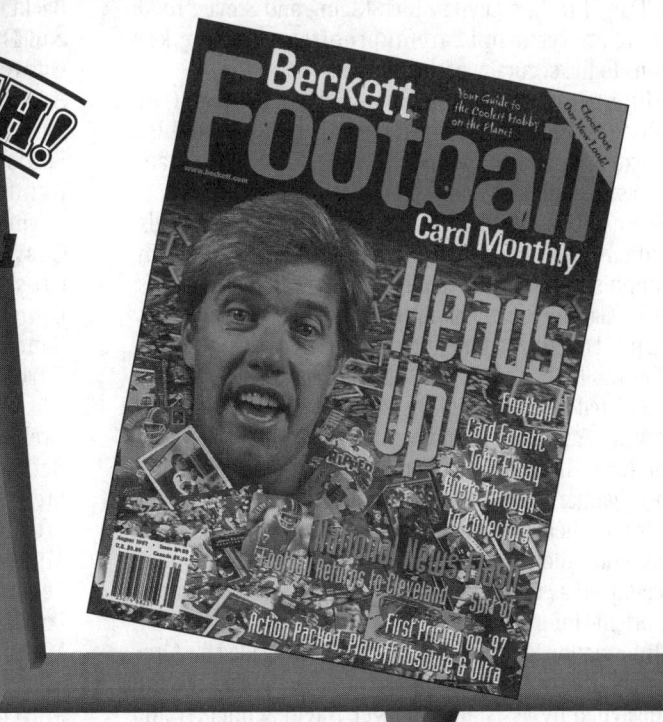

Our football analysts played a major part in compiling this year's book, travelling thousands of miles during the past year to attend sports card shows and visit card shops around the United States and Canada. The Beckett football specialists are Pat Blandford, Dan Hitt, Lon Levitan Rich Klein, and Steven Judd. Their pricing analysis and careful proofreading were key contributions to the accuracy of this annual.

Dan Hitt's coordination of input as Beckett Football Card Monthly Price Guide Editor helped immeasurably, as did Pat Blandford's extensive knowledge and pricing work. Steven Judd and Lon Levitan also contributed many hours of painstaking analysis.

They were ably assisted by Jeany Finch and Beverly Mills, who helped enter new sets and pricing information, and ably handled administration of our contributor Price Guide surveys. Card librarian Gabriel Rangel handled the ever-growing quantity of cards we need organized for efforts such as this.

The effort was led by SDP Senior Manager Pepper Hastings. They were ably assisted by the rest of the Price Guide analysts: Mike Jaspersen, Mark Anderson, Grant Sandground, Theo Chen, Ben Ecklar, Eddie Kelly, Allan Muir, Rob Springs and William Sutherland.

The price gathering and analytical talents of this fine group of hobbyists have helped make our Beckett team stronger, while making this guide and its companion monthly Price Guide more widely recognized as the hobby's most reliable and relied upon sources of pricing information.

The IS (Information Services) department, ably headed by Airey Baringer, played a critical role in technology. Working with software designed by assistant manager David Schneider and Yvonne Yeung, they spent countless hours programming, testing, and implementing it to simplify the handling of thousands of prices that must be checked and updated for each edition.

In the Production Department, Paul Kerutis, Marlon DePaula and Belinda Cross were responsible for the typesetting and for the card photos you see throughout the book.

Loretta Gibbs and Don Pendergraft spent tireless hours on the phone attending to the wishes of our dealer advertisers. Once the ad specifications were delivered to our offices, Phaedra Strecher used her computer skills to turn raw copy into attractive display advertisements.

In the years since this guide debuted, Beckett Publications has grown beyond any rational expectation. A great many talented and hard working individuals have been instrumental in this growth and success. Our whole team is to be congratulated for what we together have accomplished. Our Beckett Publications team is led by President Jeff Amano, Vice Presidents Claire Backus and Joe Galindo, Directors Mark Harwell, Reed Poole and Dave Stock, and Senior Managers Jeff Anthony, Beth Harwell and Pepper Hastings. They are ably assisted by Pete Adauto, Dana Alecknavage, Kaye Ball, Airey Baringer, Rob Barry, Therese Bellar, Andrea Bergeron, Eric Best, Julie Binion, Louise Bird, Amy Brougher, Bob Brown, Angie Calandro, Randall Calvert, Emily Camp, Mary Campana, Cara Carmichael, Eric Cash, Susan Catka, Jud Chappell, Albert Chavez, Marty Click, C.R. Conant, Andy Costilla, Belinda Cross, Randy Cummings, Von Daniel, Aaron Derr, Gary Doughty, Lauren Drews, Ryan Duckworth, Amy Durrett, Kandace Elmore, Eric Evans, Craig Ferris, Gean Paul Figari, Carol Fowler, Mary Gonzalez-Davis, Rosanna Gonzalez-Oleachea, Jeff Greer, Mary Gregory, Robert Gregory, Jenifer Grellhesl, Julie Grove, Tracy Hackler, Patti Harris, Steve Harris, Becky Hart, Mark Hartley, Joanna Hayden, Chris Hellem, Melissa Herzog, Yexin Huang, Tim Jaska, Julia Jernigan, Wendy Kizer, Gayle Klancnik, Rudy J. Klancnik, Brian Kosley, Michael Lallemont, Tom Layberger, Jane Ann Layton, Sara Leeman, Benedito Leme, Lori Lindsey, Stanley Lira, Kirk Lockhart, Sara Maneval, Louis Marroquin, John Marshall, Mike McAllister, Teri McGahey, Matt McGuire, Omar Mediano, Sherry Monday, Mila Morante, Terrence Morawski, Daniel Moscoso Jr., Mike Moss, Randy Mosty, Allan Muir, Hugh Murphy, Shawn Murphy, Bridget Norris, Mike Obert, Stacy Olivieri, Lisa O'Neill, Clark Palomino, Mike Pagel, Clark Palomino, Wendy Pallugna, Laura Patterson, Missy Patton, Mike Payne, Susan Plonka, Tim Polzer, John Randall, Bob Richardson, Tina Riojas, Lisa Runyon, Susan Sainz, David Schneider, Christine Seibert, Brett Setter (Special thanks for his Ryan information), Len Shelton, Dave Sliepka, Judi Smalling, Sheri Smith, Jeff Stanton, Margaret Steele, Marcia Stoesz, Mark Stokes, Dawn Sturgeon, Doree Tate, Jim Tereschuk, Roz Theesfeld, Doug Williams, Steve Wilson, Ed Wornson, Bryan Winstead, David Yandry, Mark Zeske and Jay Zwerner. The whole Beckett Publications team has my thanks for jobs well done. Thank you, everyone.

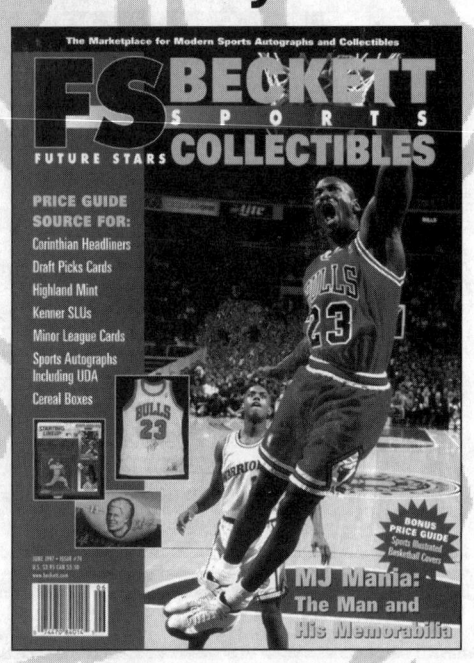